RANDOM HOUSE

Webster's Dictionary of American English

Advisory Board

Clifford Hill
Professor of Language and Education
Teachers College, Columbia University
New York

Tom McArthur
Editor of *English Today*
Cambridge, England

Elizabeth Rorschach
Professor of ESL
City College, City University of New York

Ladislav Zgusta
Professor of Linguistics
University of Illinois, Urbana

Staff

Carol G. Braham, *Project Editor*
Sol Steinmetz, *Editorial Director*

Enid Pearsons, *Senior Editor, Pronunciation and Style*
Robert Costello, *Review Editor*

Contributing Editors:
Robert Cohen
Barbara Colmer
Eric Larsen
Cathy McClure
William McGeveran
Rima McKinzey, *Pronunciation*
Trudy Nelson
Joyce O'Connor
Joe Patwell

Constance Baboukis, *Database Manager*
Jennifer Dowling, *Managing Editor*
Patricia Ehresmann, *Production Director*
Charles M. Levine, *Publisher*

RANDOM HOUSE

Webster's Dictionary of American English

Edited by
Gerard M. Dalgish, Ph.D.

Professor and ESL Director

Baruch College,

City University of New York

RANDOM HOUSE

New York

ABBREVIATIONS USED IN THIS DICTIONARY

adj.	adjective	N	north, northern
adv.	adverb	n.	noun
Brit.	British	nom.	nominative
cm	centimeter(s)	obj	object
conj.	conjunction	obj.	objective
def.	definition	part.	participle
defs.	definitions	pl.	plural
E	east, eastern	poss.	possessive
Eng.	English	pp.	past participle
esp.	especially	prep.	preposition
Fr.	French	pres.	present
ft.	foot, feet	pron.	pronoun
Ger.	German	pt.	preterit (past tense)
in.	inch(es)	S	south, southern
interj.	interjection	sing.	singular
It.	Italian	Sp.	Spanish
km	kilometer(s)	Syn.	Synonym (Study)
m	meter(s)	v.	verb
mi.	mile(s)	W	west, western
mm	millimeter(s)	yd.	yard(s)

Library of Congress Cataloging-in-Publication Data

Random House Webster's dictionary of American English / edited by
Gerard M. Dalgish.—1st ed.
p. cm.

ISBN 0-679-76425-9 (pbk.)

1. English language—Dictionaries. 2. English language—United States—Dictionaries. 3. Americanisms—Dictionaries. I. Dalgish, Gerard M.
PE1628.R2943 1997
423—dc20 96-31085
CIP

Random House Web address http://www.randomhouse.com/

Typeset and printed in the United States of America

Relaunched Edition 0-679-78007-6

9 8 7 6 5 4 3

New York Toronto London Sydney Auckland

Contents

Pronunciation Symbols for the Sounds of English inside front cover

Grammar Codes inside back cover

Advisory Board ii

Staff ii

Abbreviations Used in This Dictionary iv

Sample Page vi

Guide to the Dictionary viii

British and American Pronunciations and the International Phonetic Alphabet xiv

How to Use This Dictionary to Learn American English

- Spanish translation xvi
- Japanese translation xx
- Chinese translation xxiii

New Words in American English xxvi

The Dictionary A–Z 1

Illustrations

- apartment 31
- appliances and devices 34
- bank 56
- clothing 144
- hospital 359
- hotel 361
- house 363
- landscape 421
- office 513
- restaurant 631
- school 658
- city street 734
- supermarket 747
- bus and train terminal 768

Irregular Verbs 861

Nouns With Irregular or Alternate Plurals 865

Sample Page

- main entry
- syllable dots
- compound word
- standard pronunciation symbols
- International (IPA) pronunciation symbols
- variant pronunciation
- parts of speech
- numbered definitions
- noun plural
- grammatical information about noun
- verb inflected forms
- grammatical information about verb
- comparative and superlative of adjective
- grammatical information about adjective
- usage label
- idioms
- homograph number
- abbreviation

ea•sel (ē′zəl) /ˈiyzəl/ *n.* [*count*] a stand or frame for supporting or displaying at an angle an artist's canvas, a blackboard, etc.

eas•i•ly (ē′zə lē, ēz′lē) /ˈiyzəliy, ˈiyzliy/ *adv.* **1.** in an easy manner; without trouble: *She easily swam across the river.* **2.** without doubt: *This drawing is easily the best and wins first prize.* **3.** likely: *He may easily change his mind.*

eas′y chair′, *n.* [*count*] a usually large, upholstered armchair.

eb•on•y (eb′ə nē) /ˈɛbəniy/ *n., pl.* **-on•ies,** *adj.* **—***n.* **1.** [*noncount*] a hard, heavy, strong, dark wood from tropical Africa and Asia. **2.** [*count*] any tree providing such wood. **3.** [*noncount*] a deep, lustrous black. **—***adj.* **4.** made of ebony. **5.** of a deep, lustrous black.

e•bul•lient (i bul′yənt, i bo͝ol′-) /ɪˈbʌlyənt, ɪˈbʊl-/ *adj.* **1.** overflowing with enthusiasm, excitement, or liveliness: *They were in an ebullient mood as they tackled the new project.* **2.** bubbling up like a boiling liquid. **—e•bul′lience,** *n.* [*noncount*] **—e•bul′lient•ly,** *adv.*

ech•o (ek′ō) /ˈɛkow/ *n., pl.* **ech•oes,** *v.,* **ech•oed, ech•o•ing.** **—***n.* [*count*] **1.** a repetition of sound produced by the reflection of sound waves. **2.** a lingering trace or effect of something long past: *The estate is a mere echo of its former splendor.* **—***v.* **3.** [*no obj*] (of a place) to give out the sound of an echo; resound with an echo: *The hall echoed with cheers.* **4.** to repeat or be repeated by or as if by an echo: [*no obj*]: *Cheers echoed in the hall.* [~ + *obj*]: *The hall echoes the faintest sounds.* **5.** [~ + *obj*] to repeat, copy, or imitate the words, sentiments, etc., of (a person): *The candidate echoed his opponent in calling for lower taxes.* **6.** [~ + *obj*] to repeat, copy, or imitate (words, sentiments, etc.): *He echoed my call for vigilance.*

e•con•o•my (i kon′ə mē) /ɪˈkɑnəmiy/ *n., pl.* **-mies.** **1.** [*noncount*] thrifty management; wise care in the saving, spending, or using of money, materials, etc. **2.** [*count*] an act or means of such care: *Walking to work is one of my economies.* **3.** [*count*] the management of the resources of a community, country, etc., esp. with a view to its productivity. See -NOM-[1]. **—Related Words.** ECONOMY is a noun, ECONOMICS is a noun, ECONOMICAL is an adjective, ECONOMIZE is a verb: *The economy is improving. Economics is a hard subject. They bought an economical car. They need to economize on fuel.*

edge (ej) /ɛdʒ/ *n., v.,* **edged, edg•ing.** **—***n.* [*count*] **1.** a line or border at which a surface ends: *Grass grew along the edge of the road.* **2.** a brink; a verge: *at the edge of disaster.* **3.** the thin, sharp side of the blade of a cutting instrument or weapon. **4.** a quality of sharpness or keenness, often showing anger: *Her voice had an edge to it.* **5.** an improved position; advantage: *an edge on our competitors.* **—***v.* **6.** [~ + *obj*] to provide with an edge or border. **7.** to make or force (one's way) gradually, esp. by moving sideways or cautiously: [*no obj*]: *They edged slowly toward the door.* [~ + *obj*]: *She edged the car up to the curb.* **—*Idiom.*** **8. on edge,** in a state of irritability; tense; nervous. **9. set one's teeth on edge,** to cause extreme discomfort or unpleasantness.

edg•y (ej′ē) /ˈɛdʒiy/ *adj.,* **edg•i•er, edg•i•est.** nervously irritable; anxious; on edge: *edgy before a deadline.* **—edg•i•ly** (ej′ə lē) /ˈɛdʒəliy/ *adv.* **—edg′i•ness,** *n.* [*noncount*]

ed•i•to•ri•al (ed′i tôr′ē əl, -tōr′-) /ˌɛdɪˈtɔriyəl, -ˈtowr-/ *n.* [*count*] **1.** an article in a newspaper, magazine, etc., that presents the opinion of the publishers or editors. **—***adj.* [*before a noun*] **2.** of or relating to an editor or editing: *an editorial staff.* **—ed′i•to′ri•al•ly,** *adv.*

egg[1] (eg) /ɛg/ *n.* [*count*] **1.** the roundish reproductive body produced by female birds and most reptiles. **2.** Also called **egg′ cell′.** the cell that is produced by the female and that joins with a male cell to form a baby; the female gamete; ovum. **3.** *Informal.* a person: *He's a good egg.* **—*Idiom.*** **4. egg on one's face,** obvious embarrassment caused by one's own mistake: *After that dumb remark he had egg on his face.* **5. lay an egg,** *Informal.* to fail badly, esp. while trying to entertain: *With that last joke he really laid an egg.*

egg[2] (eg) /ɛg/ *v.* [~ + *obj* + *on*] to urge or encourage; incite: *He egged his opponent on to make the tennis match more exciting.*

EKG, an abbreviation of: **1.** electrocardiogram. **2.** electrocardiograph.

easel to **eyeglass**

e•lec′tor•al col′lege (e lek′tər əl) /ɛ'lɛktərəl/ *n.* [*proper noun; often: the + ~; often: Electoral College*] a group of people who are chosen by the voters in each state to elect the president and vice-president of the U.S.

en•rich (en rich′) /ɛn'rɪtʃ/ *v.* [~ + *obj*] **1.** to supply with riches or wealth: *The development of oil fields enriched that country.* **2.** to supply with a large amount of anything desirable: *new words that have enriched the language.* **3.** to add greater value or significance to: *Art can enrich life.* **4.** to improve in quality, as by adding desirable or useful ingredients: *to enrich soil. The breakfast cereal is enriched with vitamins.* —**en•rich′ment,** *n.* [*noncount*]: *programs of educational enrichment for gifted students.*

en•thu•si•as•tic (en tho͞o′zē as′tik) /ɛn,θuwziy'æstɪk/ *adj.* greatly interested in or deeply involved: *an enthusiastic hockey fan.* —**en•thu′si•as′tic•al•ly,** *adv.*: *She participated enthusiastically in the festivities.* —**Related Words.** ENTHUSIASTIC is an adjective, ENTHUSIASM and ENTHUSIAST are nouns: *They gave us an enthusiastic welcome. We were welcomed with enthusiasm. There were some water-polo enthusiasts in the group.*

ep•au•let or **ep•au•lette** (ep′ə let′, ep′ə let′) /'ɛpə,lɛt, ,ɛpə'lɛt/ *n.* [*count*] an ornamental shoulder piece, esp. on a uniform.

-equa- or **-equi-,** *root.* *-equa-, -equi-* comes from Latin, where it has the meaning "equal; the same." This meaning is found in such words as: EQUABLE, EQUAL, EQUALIZE, EQUILIBRIUM, EQUINOX, EQUITY, EQUIVOCAL, INEQUALITY, INEQUITY.

e•qui•nox (ē′kwə noks′, ek′wə-) /'iykwə,nɒks, 'ɛkwə-/ *n.* [*count*] one of the times when the sun crosses the earth's equator, making night and day of approximately equal length all over the earth and occurring about March 21 and September 22. See -EQUA-, -NOC-.

es•ca•la•tor (es′kə lā′tər) /'ɛskə,leytər/ *n.* [*count*] a continuously moving stairway on an endless loop for carrying passengers up or down. See illustration at STORE.

-ess, *suffix.* *-ess* is used to form a feminine noun: *count + -ess → countess; god + -ess → goddess; lion + -ess → lioness.* —**Usage.** The use of words ending in -ESS has declined sharply in the latter half of the 20th century, but some are still current: *actress* (but some women prefer *actor*); *adventuress; enchantress; governess; heiress* (largely in journalistic writing); *hostess* (but women who conduct radio and television programs are *hosts*); *seamstress; seductress; temptress;* and *waitress.*

e•ter•nal (i tûr′nl) /ɪ'tɜrnl̩/ *adj.* **1.** having no beginning or end; lasting forever: *the eternal movement of the planets.* **2.** perpetual; constant: *This eternal chatter is driving me crazy.* **3.** enduring; long-lasting: *eternal principles of truth.* —**e•ter′nal•ly,** *adv.* —**Syn.** ETERNAL, ENDLESS, EVERLASTING, PERPETUAL imply lasting or going on without ceasing. That which is ETERNAL is, by its nature, without beginning or end: *God, the eternal Being.* That which is ENDLESS never stops but goes on continuously as if in a circle: *an endless succession of years.* That which is EVERLASTING will last through all future time: *a promise of everlasting life.* PERPETUAL implies continuous renewal, a starting again and again, far into the future: *perpetual strife between nations.*

eu•tha•na•sia (yo͞o′thə nā′zhə) /,yuwθə'neyʒə/ *n.* [*noncount*] painless killing of a person, usually when the person is suffering from an incurable, esp. a painful, disease or condition. Also called **mercy killing.**

ex-, *prefix.* **1.** *ex-* comes from Latin, where it has the meaning "out, out of, away, forth." It is found in such words as: EXCLUDE, EXHALE, EXIT, EXPORT, EXTRACT. **2.** *ex-* is also used to mean "former; formerly having been": *ex-member (= former member).*

ex•plain (ik splān′) /ɪk'spleyn/ *v.* **1.** to make clear or understandable: [~ + *obj*]: *Please explain your plan.* [~ + *(that) clause*]: *I explained that the mistakes were my own.* **2.** to give the cause or reason of; account for: [~ + *obj*]: *How do you explain such rude behavior?* [*no obj*]: *I asked her to explain.* **3. explain away,** [~ + *away* + *obj*] to lessen the importance or significance of through explanation; justify: *She explained away her rude behaviour as a joke..*

eye•glass (ī′glas′) /'ay,glæs/ *n.* [*count*] **1. eyeglasses,** [*plural*] GLASS (def. 4). **2.** a single lens worn to aid vision; monocle.

guide words

capitalization

example phrases and sentences

run-on (derived) entry

word family

variant spelling

English root

cross reference to English roots

cross reference to illustration

suffix

usage note

synonym study

variant form

prefix

phrasal (two-word) verb

cross reference to another entry

Guide to the Dictionary

Random House Webster's Dictionary of American English is designed for anyone who is learning or studying English as a second or foreign language. Its primary focus is current American English, but information on British English is also provided. It is based on the Random House family of dictionaries, known and used widely for the clarity of their definitions. This dictionary has been specially designed to enable students and learners of English to unlock some of the more difficult features of English meaning, grammar, spelling, pronunciation, idiom, and usage. Studying and using this book is a good way to further one's knowledge of English, as well as to provide a bridge to more advanced reference books used by native speakers of English.

The Main Entry

The main entry is printed in large boldface type and extends to the left of the rest of the text. Main entries are listed in strict alphabetical order, regardless of whether they are single words, compounds, abbreviations, prefixes, or suffixes.

es•say•ist (es′ā ist) /ˈɛseyɪst/ *n.* [*count*] a writer of essays.

ESL, an abbreviation of: English as a second language.

Variant forms and variant spellings of the main entry are also printed in boldface type. Variants are placed to show whether they apply to all definitions of an entry or only to specific meanings. A variant that applies to only one definition will be placed after the definition number. Variants are introduced by the words "or," "also," or "Also called".

go•fer or **go-fer** (gō′fər) /ˈgowfər/ *n.* [*count*] *Slang.* an employee whose chief duty is running errands.

goose′ flesh′ or **goose′flesh′,** *n.* [*noncount*] a bristling of the hair on the skin, as from cold or fear. Also called **goose′ pim′ples, goose′ bumps′.** [*count; plural*]

Single-word entries have centered dots to show where the word can be divided into syllables. This is a guide to where to add a hyphen at the end of a line. Detailed rules for appropriate end-of-line hyphenation can be found in most English style manuals. In multiple-word or hyphenated main entries, individual words are not usually syllabified if they are also entered at their own alphabetical places.

ea•gle (ē′gəl) /ˈiygəl/ *n.* [*count*] a large, powerful, broad-winged bird having a large bill and claws to catch its prey.

exchange′ rate′, *n.* [*count*] the ratio at which a unit of the currency of one country can be exchanged for that of another country.

Pronunciation

This dictionary provides the pronunciation for any main entry that is not a combination of two or more other main entries. A pronunciation key representing the two systems of symbols used to represent sounds in this book appears on the inside front cover.

It is important to note the differences between these two systems—one a diacritical system, much like those that are standard in most American monolingual dictionaries, and the other a version of the well-known International Phonetic Alphabet

(IPA). A primary distinction between the two systems rests in their origins. IPA is based on the sound-spelling correspondences of the European languages that are derived from Latin. This is particularly evident in the system of vowels. A diacritical system, on the other hand, is based on English spellings, which is why it is sometimes referred to as "orthographically motivated." In other words, it is designed to focus learners on *English* sound-spelling correspondences, including those that reveal sound patterns among related words in English—patterns that would be hidden in IPA. For example, the stressed vowels in the words **divine** and **divinity** are both pronunciations for the letter *i*; in the diacritical system, the sounds are written as (ī) and (i), and the learner of English can clearly see that both of these sounds are ways of pronouncing the letter *i*. These same vowels would be rendered in IPA as /ay/ and /ɪ/.

However, since many learners are already familiar with the IPA pronunciation system, and can use knowledge of their own native languages to fix upon the sound each IPA symbol represents, a modified version of this system is also used with each pronounced entry. The two systems together, each supplementing and supporting the other, can provide a learning aid. As one becomes more and more familiar with the target language, English, the diacritical system will become an increasingly valuable guide to the relationships among English sounds and their common spellings.

DIACRITICAL SYSTEM

The pronunciation appears immediately after the entry and is surrounded by parentheses. If more than one pronunciation is possible, the more common one is listed first.

In words of two or more syllables, a primary stress mark (**ʹ**) follows the syllable having the primary (or greatest) stress. A secondary stress mark (ʹ) follows a syllable that has secondary stress (or stress that is not as strong as primary stress). Syllables are separated either by a stress mark or a space.

IPA

The pronunciation, enclosed in slash marks, immediately follows the standard dictionary pronunciation. The symbols shown reflect the same pronunciations, in the same order, as those shown in parentheses.

In words of two or more syllables, a primary stress mark /ˈ/ precedes the syllable having the primary (or greatest) stress. A secondary stress mark /ˌ/ precedes a syllable that has secondary stress (or stress that is not as strong as primary stress). No spaces separate syllables.

Parts of Speech

Part-of-speech labels refer to a word's grammatical category, or how the word may function in a sentence. The abbreviations used for parts of speech are explained in the chart on page xxviii.

If a main entry has more than one grammatical category, a part-of-speech label appears before each group of definitions given for that part of speech.

au•thor (ôʹthər) /ˈɔθər/ *n.* [*count*] **1.** someone who creates a book, article, etc.; writer. **2.** the maker of anything; creator: *the author of the new tax plan.* —*v.* [~ + *obj*] **3.** to be the author of: *to author a novel.*

Inflected Forms

Inflected forms are the changed forms, like plurals of nouns or past tenses of verbs, that a word may have depending on how it is used in a sentence. Inflected forms appear in boldface type after a part-of-speech label or after a grammar code that applies to the entire entry. This dictionary shows inflected forms for all nouns and verbs that have irregular forms. Also, the dictionary shows inflected forms for regular nouns and verbs whenever there might be confusion about spelling.

For nouns, the inflected plural forms are indicated by the abbreviation *pl.* before them.

de•i•ty (dē′i tē) /ˈdiyıtiy/ *n., pl.* **-ties.** [*count*] a god or goddess.

For verbs, inflected forms are listed in the following order: the past-tense form, the *-ed/-en* form or past participle (if it is different from the past tense), and the *-ing* form or present participle.

for•give (fər giv′) /fərˈgıv/ *v.*, **-gave** (-gāv′) /-ˈgeyv/ **-giv•en, -giv•ing.** to grant pardon for (an offense); absolve: [~ + *obj*]: *He has forgiven our sins.* [*no obj*]: *Forgive and go forward.*

halve (hav) /hæv/ *v.* [~ + *obj*], **halved, halv•ing.** to divide into two equal parts; share equally.

For adjectives and adverbs, inflected forms are shown for those that form the comparative and superlative with an internal change in form or by adding *-er* and *-est.*

hap•py (hap′ē) /ˈhæpiy/ *adj.*, **-pi•er, -pi•est.** delighted; pleased; glad.

good (go͝od) /gud/ *adj.*, **bet•ter** (bet′ər) /ˈbɛtər/ **best** (best) /bɛst/. satisfactory or excellent in quality, quantity, or degree: *She was a good teacher.*

Grammatical Information

This dictionary can tell the learner a great deal about the grammatical behavior of a word. Grammatical information is contained within "grammar codes" that have brackets [ ] around them. In general, a swung dash (~) within a bracketed grammar code stands for the main entry. For idioms, the swung dash usually stands for the entire idiom. Grammar codes are placed to show whether they apply to all definitions of an entry or only to specific meanings. If the grammar code applies to only one definition, it is placed after the definition number. If it applies to the entire entry or part of speech, it is placed after the part-of-speech label.

GRAMMAR CODE	EXPLANATION	EXAMPLE
	NOUN GRAMMAR CODES	
[*count*]	This is a count noun; it can be counted and has a plural. It can be used with the word *a* or *an* before it.	**as•sign•ment** (ə sin′mənt) /əˈsaynmənt/ *n.* [*count*] **1.** something assigned: *the homework assignments.* **2.** a position to which one is appointed: *an assignment as ambassador to France.*
[*noncount*]	This noun does not have a plural. It can be used with the word *much* or the phrase *a lot of,* but cannot be used with the word *a* or *an.* Mass nouns or abstract nouns belong in this group.	**laugh•ter** (laf′tər) /ˈlæftər/ *n.* [*noncount*] the action or sound of laughing: *much laughter in the classroom.*
[*count*]... [*noncount*]	Some English nouns are both countable and uncountable, depending on their use. If one definition covers both count and noncount senses, the count grammar code appears before the count example, and the noncount grammar code appears before the noncount example.	**en•mi•ty** (en′mi tē) /ˈɛnmıtiy/ *n., pl.* **-ties.** a feeling of bitter hostility or hatred; ill will: [*noncount*]: *Despite the truce, enmity remains between the two countries.* [*count*]: *tribal enmities that go back hundreds of years.*
[*plural*]	This noun is only used in the plural with a plural verb.	**en•trails** (en′trālz, -trəlz) /ˈɛntreylz, -trəlz/ *n.* [*plural*] the inner organs of a body, esp. the intestines: *The entrails of the chicken are removed before cooking.*
[*singular*]	This noun is only used in the singular with a singular verb. It can be used with *a* or *an* before it.	**free′ hand′,** *n.* [*count; singular*] unrestricted freedom or authority: *They gave the director a free hand to cut the budget wherever she wanted.*

[*the* + ~]	This noun is used with the word *the* before it. When adjectives are used as nouns they generally take *the* before them.	**lime•light** (līm′līt′) /'laym,layt/ *n.* [*noncount; the* + ~] a position at the center of public attention: *always trying to steal the limelight.* **lat•est** (lā′tist) /'leytɪst/ *n.* [*noncount; the* + ~] the most recent news, development, etc.: *Here's the latest from our news bureau.*

VERB GRAMMAR CODES

[~ + *obj*]	This is a transitive verb. It is followed by an object, usually a noun or pronoun. The example sentence or phrase will sometimes have a passive construction, in which the subject receives the action expressed by the verb.	**earn** (ûrn) /ɜrn/ *v.* [~ + *obj*] to receive in return for one's labor or service: *to earn a living as a waiter.* **en•cum•ber** (en kum′bər) /ɛn'kʌmbər/ *v.* [~ + *obj*] to weigh down; burden: *The hiker was encumbered by a heavy backpack.*
[~ + *obj* + *obj*]	This verb is followed by an indirect object and then a direct object.	**buy** (bī) /bay/ *v.,* **bought** (bôt) /bɔt/ **buy•ing.** to get possession of (something), esp. by paying money; purchase: [~ + *obj*]: *She bought a new computer.* [~ + *obj* + *obj*]: *She bought him a new computer.*
[*no obj*]	This is an intransitive verb. It is not followed by an object.	**e•vap•o•rate** (i vap′ə rāt′) /ɪ'væpə,reyt/ *v.,* **-rat•ed, -rat•ing.** [*no obj*] to disappear; vanish: *His hopes evaporated.*
[~ + *prep.* + *obj*]	This verb is followed by a prepositional phrase consisting of a preposition and its object. The grammar code will specify the correct or appropriate preposition. If there are parentheses around the preposition and its object, the prepositional phrase may be left out.	**em•bark** (em bärk′) /ɛm'bɑrk/ *v.* **1.** [*no obj; (~ + on + obj)*] to board a ship, aircraft, or other vehicle: *The passengers embarked on the ship at noon.* **2.** [~ + *on* + *obj*] to start or participate in an enterprise: *to embark on a business venture.*
[~ + *to* + *verb*]	This verb is followed by the word *to* and then by another verb in its infinitive form.	**choose** (cho͞oz) /tʃuwz/ *v.,* **chose** (chōz) /tʃowz/ **cho•sen** (chō′zən) /'tʃowzən/ **choos•ing.** [~ + *to* + *verb*] to prefer or decide (to do something): *to choose to speak.*
[~ + *obj* + *to* + *verb*]	This verb is followed by a noun or pronoun, then by the word *to,* and then by another verb. The last verb is in its infinitive form.	**in•struct** (in strukt′) /ɪn'strʌkt/ *v.* [~ + *obj* + *to* + *verb*] to give (someone) orders or directions; direct; order; command: *She instructed us to leave one by one.*
[~ + *clause*]	This verb is followed by a clause. In clauses beginning with the word *that,* this word can be left out if it is shown in parentheses.	**con•ceive** (kən sēv′) /kən'siyv/ *v.,* **-ceived, -ceiv•ing.** [~ + *that clause*] to hold as an opinion; think; believe: *I can't conceive that it would be of any use.*
[~ + *obj* + *prep.*] OR [~ + *prep.* + *obj*]	For some phrasal verbs that take an object, the object can either follow the verb or follow the preposition or adverb. For other phrasal verbs, the object must follow the preposition or adverb. A pronoun object must follow the verb. The grammar code will specify the correct or appropriate preposition.	**look** (lo͝ok) /lʊk/ *v.* **1.** [*no obj*] to turn one's eyes toward something or in some direction in order to see: *I'm looking at this book.* **2. look after,** [~ + *after* + *obj*] to take care of: *a babysitter to look after the kids.* **3. look over,** to examine, esp. briefly: [~ + *over* + *obj*]: *I looked over your term paper.* [~ + *obj* + *over*]: *I looked it over.*

[*not: be* + ~*-ing*] This verb is not used in the progressive tense; that is, it cannot appear in the *-ing* form following a form of the verb *be.*

ab•hor (ab hôr′) /æb'hɔr/ *v.* {*not: be* + ~*-ing;* ~ + *obj*}, **-horred, -hor•ring.** to hate very much; detest: *Gandhi abhorred violence all his life.*

[~ + *verb-ing*] This verb is followed by another verb in the *-ing* form.

hate (hāt) /heyt/ *v.,* **hat•ed, hat•ing.** [~ + *verb-ing*] to be unwilling; dislike: *I hate getting up early.*

ADJECTIVE GRAMMAR CODES

[*before a noun*] This adjective (or noun used like an adjective) must come before the noun it refers to; it cannot appear after a form of the verb *be.*

e•mol•lient (i mol′yənt) /ɪ'mɒlyənt/ *adj.* [*before a noun*] having the power to soften or soothe: *an emollient lotion for the skin.*

im•i•ta•tion (im′i tā′shən) /ˌɪmɪ'teyʃən/ *adj.* [*before a noun*] designed to imitate a genuine or superior article or thing: *imitation leather.*

[*be* + ~] This adjective must follow a form of the verb *be* and cannot appear before the noun it refers to.

li•a•ble (lī′ə bəl) /'layəbəl/ *adj.* [*be* + ~] **1.** legally responsible: *You are liable for the damage.* **2.** exposed or subject to something generally negative: *If you jump, you're liable to hurt yourself.*

Definitions

A single sequence of numbered definitions includes all parts of speech, phrasal verbs, and idioms. Usually, the most common or frequently occurring meanings appear first among the definitions.

Definitions that serve as cross references to another part of the alphabet, where the entry with the full definition is shown, are displayed in small capital letters.

mer′cy kill′ing, *n.* EUTHANASIA.

es•thet•ics (es thet′iks) /ɛs'θɛtɪks/ *n.* AESTHETICS.

When transitive and intransitive meanings of a word are similar, often one definition will cover both uses. The grammar codes and examples will clarify the differences.

e•lon•gate (i lông′gāt, i long′-) /ɪ'lɔŋgeyt, ɪ'lɒŋ- / *v.,* **-gat•ed, -gat•ing.** to (cause to) lengthen or extend: [~ + *obj*]: *Intense heat elongated the metal bar.* [*no obj*]: *The metal bar elongated under the intense heat.*

Examples

Example sentences or phrases inform the reader about the meaning of the word, how the word behaves grammatically in a sentence, and the attitudes that speakers have toward the word.

Examples clarify the grammar codes and definitions. However, they are most useful in showing which kinds of words regularly combine with the word being defined.

fruit (fro͞ot) /fruwt/ *n., pl.* **fruits,** (*esp. when thought of as a group*) **fruit.** the part of a plant that is developed from a flower, esp. when used as food: [*noncount*]: *Fruit provides vitamins.* [*count*]: *Apples and oranges are fruits.*

el•i•gi•ble (el′i jə bəl) /'ɛlɪdʒəbəl/ *adj.* being a proper or worthy choice; suitable: *an eligible mate.*

Phrasal Verbs

Phrasal verbs (sometimes known as two-word verbs) combine a verb and one or more prepositions or adverbs. Phrasal verbs are listed in boldface type in a single alphabetical group after all other verb definitions.

The bracketed grammar code following a phrasal verb or its definition will show whether it is transitive or intransitive. A swung dash (~) in the grammar code stands for the main entry.

break (brāk) /breyk/ *v.*, **broke** (brōk) /browk/ **bro•ken** (brō′kən) /'browkən/ **break•ing. 1.** to smash, split, or divide into parts violently: [~ + *obj*]: *He took the vase and broke it open.* [*no obj*]: *The vase broke.* **2. break down, a.** [*no obj*] to stop working; fail: *The car broke down on the highway.* **b.** to cause to collapse or stop working: [~ + *down* + *obj*]: *to break down resistance.* [~ + *obj* + *down*]: *to break it down.*

Idioms

Idioms are expressions whose meanings cannot be predicted from the usual meanings of their component words. Idioms are listed alphabetically in boldface type as the final numbered definitions in an entry. They are preceded by the label ***—Idiom.***

A swung dash (~) in the bracketed grammar code following an idiom usually stands for the entire idiom.

end (end) /ɛnd/ *n.* [*count*] **1.** the last part; extremity: *the two ends of a rope; the west end of town.* ***—Idiom.* 2. put an end to,** [~ + *obj*] to terminate; finish: *Let's put an end to this constant arguing.*

Run-on Words

Run-on words (sometimes called derivatives) are words that are closely related to the main entry. They are created or formed from the main entry without great differences in meaning or spelling. Run-on words are typically formed by adding a suffix. The meaning of a run-on word can be understood by combining the senses of its root word and suffix, taking into account the part of speech. The suffix will be listed in the dictionary as a main entry, where its meaning will be explained.

Run-on words appear in boldface type at the end of an entry, following the last definition but before usage or other supplementary notes.

en•light•en (en lit′n) /ɛn'laytn̩/ *v.* [~ + *obj*] to give intellectual understanding or knowledge to; instruct: *to enlighten students.* **—en•light′en•ment,** *n.* [*noncount*]

-ment, *suffix.* *-ment* is attached to verbs to form nouns that refer to a state or condition resulting from the action of a verb: *enlighten* + *-ment* → *enlightenment.*

English Roots

This dictionary includes as main entries several hundred common English roots, primarily from Latin and Greek, that form the base of many words in English. These roots have a boldface dash (**-**) before and after them so the reader understands that they are not words, just parts of words. A knowledge about the meaning of roots may help the learner to understand the meaning of an otherwise unfamiliar word.

Each root entry lists several English words that are built from the root. The dictionary entries for these words will have cross references to the root entry.

-fac-, *root.* *-fac-* comes from Latin, where it has the meaning "do; make." This meaning is found in such words as: BENEFACTOR, DE FACTO, FACSIMILE, FACT, FACTION, FACULTY, MANUFACTURE. See -FEC-, -FIC-.

fac•tion (fak′shən) /'fækʃən/ *n.* [*count*] a group within a larger group: *several factions of the Liberal Party.* See -FAC-.

Word Families

Word families are related words formed from the same root but having meanings that might be confused. They have different parts of speech.

Word families are discussed in notes at the end of selected entries in the dictionary. These notes are preceded by the label **—Related Words.** Words discussed in these notes may be separate main entries or run-on words.

en•thu•si•as•tic (en thōō′zē as′tik) /ɛn,θuwziy'æstɪk/ *adj.* greatly interested in or deeply involved: *an enthusiastic hockey fan.* **—en•thu′si•as′tic•al•ly,** *adv.* **—Related Words.** ENTHUSIASTIC is an adjective, ENTHUSIASM and ENTHUSIAST are nouns: *They gave us an enthusiastic welcome. We were welcomed with enthusiasm. There were some water-polo enthusiasts in the group.*

British and American Pronunciations and the International Phonetic Alphabet

English, like other languages, exists in a variety of forms called *dialects*. Dialects differ in vocabulary, grammar, and pronunciation. They usually indicate a speaker's geographic origins and—because individuals can, to some extent, change the way they speak—dialects can also indicate one's level of education.

Despite the ocean that separates England from America, the standard British and American dialects—the two dialects reflected in most dictionaries—have remained surprisingly similar since British settlers first brought their language to America nearly 400 years ago. There are differences in vocabulary (for example, the British say *lift* when Americans say *elevator*), but the major feature distinguishing British English from American English is the difference in the way they sound.

However, the differences in pronunciation are *not* as great as British and American learning materials seem to suggest. British and American pronunciations appear to be more unlike than they actually are because some of the International Phonetic Alphabet (IPA) symbols customarily used by British linguists and educators differ from those used for the same purpose by their American counterparts. Nevertheless, many of these symbols—British and American—represent substantially the same sounds.

Below we describe (1.) some of the real differences between British and American pronunciation. We then show (2.) how some IPA symbols traditionally differ in British and American dictionaries. The accompanying chart reveals that many words in the two countries are actually said in much the same way, in spite of the differing symbol systems.

1. Differences in Pronunciation

There are many dialects of English in both Great Britain and the United States. In dictionaries intended for general use, dictionary makers do not try to show how words are pronounced in all these dialects. Instead, British dictionaries show the usual pronunciations of England's educated upper class (referred to as *Received Pronunciation*, or *RP*). American dictionaries reflect the pronunciations used by most national radio and television broadcasters (a dialect often referred to as *Broadcast Network Standard*, or *BNS*).

Certain categories of sounds are consistently different in these two dialects. Most noticeable is the *r*. In British RP, the *r* is silent after a vowel, except when followed immediately by another vowel in the same word or the next word. Although some dialects of American English similarly omit the sound of *r* after a vowel, in American BNS the *r* is normally pronounced in all positions. Thus *bird, star,* and *port* are shown as /bɜːd/, /stɑː/, and /pɔːt/ in British materials, but as /bɜrd/, /stɑr/, and /pɔrt/ in American materials that use IPA.

Another letter pronounced differently is *a*. British speakers tend to use a "broad a" /ɑ/ in a group of words that includes *half, dance, plant,* and *rather*. Most Americans use a "flat a" /æ/ in these words.

Yet another general difference is the tendency of Americans to pronounce the "long u" sound of such words as *tune, due,* and *new* without the initial *y* sound (represented in British IPA by /j/) usually heard in British pronunciation.

In addition to general differences like these, there are individual words that have come to be pronounced differently in Britain and America. For example, the initial *sch-* of *schedule* is pronounced /sk/ in America but /ʃ/ in Britain (although *school* is pronounced the same—with an initial /sk/—in both countries). Some other words that sound strikingly different in Britain and America are:

ate (past tense of *eat*)	Br./et/	Am./eyt/	*laboratory*	Br./lə'bɒrətrɪ/	Am./'læbrəˌtɔriy/
			lieutenant	Br./lef'tenənt/	Am./luw'tɛnənt/
charade	Br./ʃə'rɑːd/	Am./ʃə'reyd/	*missile*	Br./'mɪsaɪl/	Am./'mɪsəl/
clerk	Br./klɑːk/	Am./klɜrk/	*privacy*	Br./'prɪvəsɪ/	Am./'prayvəsiy/
leisure	Br./'leʒə/	Am./liyʒər/			

2. Differences in Use of Symbols from the International Phonetic Alphabet

In any dialect, no two people pronounce words in exactly the same way. IPA symbols can therefore only approximate the sounds that an individual speaker might make in pronouncing a word. Linguists who study phonetics—the sounds of languages—sometimes reach different conclusions about what symbol (or combination of symbols) best represents the usual sound of a particular word in a particular dialect. Thus even among scholars in the same country, different representations are used for the same sound. This is true, in both England and the United States, especially for vowel sounds, which are difficult to describe precisely.

In the United States, more traditional sets of IPA symbols have been joined by a number of additional variations. The American scholars and educators who prefer these symbols reason that they better represent extremely subtle differences in sound. They have found them especially useful in helping students to understand how English vowels differ from those in other languages. The following chart shows some common IPA symbols used in dictionaries and other English-language learning materials.

While some of the symbol choices differ in British and American materials, they represent sounds that are the same or very similar in standard British and American dialects. The symbols in **bold print** are the ones used in this dictionary.

The initial sound in	**British IPA**	**American IPA**
*y*es	/j/	/j/ or **/y/**
*sh*eep	/ʃ/	**/ʃ/** or /š/
*ch*eap	/tʃ/	**/tʃ/** or /č/
*J*eep	/dʒ/	**/dʒ/** or /dž/
The indicated vowel sound in	**British IPA**	**American IPA**
f*a*ther	/ɑː/	**/ɑ/** or /a/
cit*y*	/ɪ/ or /i/	/ɪ/ or /i/ or **/iy/**
s*ee*	/iː	/i/ or **/iy/**
s*e*t	/e/or /ɛ/	/e/ or **/ɛ/**
s*aw*	/ɔː/	/ɔ/
t*oo*	/uː/	/u/ or **/uw/**
b*ir*d	/ɜː/	**/ɜ/**

The indicated vowel sound in	**British IPA**	**American IPA**
t*a*ke	/eɪ/ or /ei/	/eɪ/ or /e/ or /ei/ or **/ey/**
t*i*me	/aɪ/ or /ai/	/aɪ/ or /ai/ or **/ay/**
t*ow*n	/aʊ/ or /au/	/aʊ/ or /au/ or **/aw/**
t*oy*	/ɔɪ/ or /ɔi/	/ɔɪ/ or /ɔi/ or **/ɔy/**
t*o*p	/ɒ/	/ɑ/ or **/ɒ/**
t*oe*[1]	/ɛʊ/ or /ɛu/ or /əʊ/ or /əu/	/oʊ/ or /o/ or /ou/ or **/ow/**

1. Unlike the other sounds in this list, the "long o" sound in words like *toe* and *boat* is noticeably different in RP from BNS, as indicated by the initial /ə/ or /ɛ/ symbol and the absence of the /o/ symbol from all of the representations for that sound in British IPA. This entry is included in the chart, however, for the convenience of the reader in comparing the British and American materials.

Cómo utilizar este diccionario para aprender el inglés norteamericano

Este diccionario le ayudará a aprender el inglés norteamericano de varias formas. Primero, el diccionario mismo y las actividades sugeridas aqui le asistirán a mejorar su vocabulario y aprender nuevos vocablos, además de descubrir nuevas definiciones para muchas de las palabras que ya conoce. Segundo, al utilizar el diccionario irá perfeccionando su comprensión lectora. Y porque incluye prefijos, sufijos y radicales, podrá usarlo para ensanchar su vocabulario y hacer conjeturas educadas cuando se encuentre con palabras desconocidas. Tercero, puesto que este libro contiene claves gramaticales, listas de verbos y sustantivos irregulares, calificativos de uso y estilo y familias de vocablos, podrá evitar algunos de los errores más comunes cometidos por estudiantes del inglés. Cuarto, este diccionario le ayudará a usar el idioma con más fluidez a medida que va practicando el uso correcto de modismos y frases verbales, dos componentes muy importantes en el aprendizaje del inglés. Quinto, este libro le ayudará a familiarizarse con la pronunciación del inglés norteamericano y con la relación de ésta con la ortografía. Contiene dos sistemas de pronounciación: uno basado en el alfabeto fonético internacional y el otro en el método utilizado por los diccionarios preparados para hablantes nativos del inglés. Todas estas habilidades que irá desarrollando al usar este diccionario le ayudarán a mejor leer, escribir y hablar el inglés norteamericano.

Cómo mejorar su vocabulario y aprender palabras nuevas

Puesto que este diccionario fue preparado para el estudiante, no contiene demasiados términos técnicos y científicos, los cuales podrían resultarle poco familiares al usuario. Pero sí existen muchos vocablos de uso común que un estudiante del inglés puede no conocer, y este libro le ayudará a aprenderlos. Por ejemplo, aunque palabras como *coxcomb, voluntarism* y *wreak* son difíciles, no son términos técnicos ni científicos, y las podrá encontrar en este diccionario. Cuando se encuentre con palabras difíciles como éstas, le sugerimos que las apunte en una libreta o en tarjetas.

También debe tener en cuenta que los significados de algunas palabras se extienden mas allá del significado más básico, y algunos de estos significados ahora forman parte integrante del inglés norteamericano de hoy. Por ejemplo, los significados más simples de la palabra *woolly* son *"of or resembling wool"* y *"covered with wool"*; pero *woolly* también posée un significado figurado muy común: *"unclear; disorganized"*. Cuanta más atención le preste a <u>todas</u> las definiciones de cada palabra que estudia más podrá perfeccionar su vocabulario y su conocimiento del inglés norteamericano.

Otra manera de mejorar su vocabulario es el ir aprendiendo los nuevos significados que han ido adquiriendo ciertas palabras "viejas". Este diccionario contiene definiciones adicionales que incluyen estos significados nuevos para muchas palabras. Por ejemplo, a la palabra *input* durante un tiempo se la consideraba un sustantivo que significaba *"something that is put in"* y *"contribution of information or ideas"*. Pero este vocablo ha adquirido un nuevo significado en el inglés norteamericano: *"information or data to be stored in a computer"*; y más recientemente se viene utilizando como un verbo que significa *"to put data into a computer for storage"*. En este diccionario encontrará significados nuevos para muchos términos, puesto que el inglés crece constantemente. Así que asegúrese de leer todas las definiciones de cada palabra que busque; le sorprenderá cuántos significados diferentes tiene.

También podrá ensanchar su vocabulario al ir observando que muchas de las definiciones contienen los sinónimos de las palabras. Por ejemplo, la definición de la palabra *popular* termina con un punto y coma, y a éste le siguen dos sinónimos: *"looked on or thought of with approval or affection by people in general; well-liked; admired"*. Una de las definiciones de la palabra *maneuver* también contiene sinónimos: *"a clever movement, action, or trick; crafty tactic; a ploy"*. El estudio de los grupos de sinónimos le ayudará mucho a perfeccionar su vocabulario.

Cómo mejorar su comprensión lectora por medio de conjeturas educadas acerca de los significados de palabras desconocidas

Porque este diccionario incluye prefijos, sufijos y raices, podrá utilizarlo para aumentar su vocabulario y conjeturar inteligentemente sobre el significado de vocablos que no conoce. El catálogo de palabras regulares incluye muchas raices comunes de palabras inglesas. Un ejemplo es la raíz *-port-*, cuyo significado básico es *"carry"*. Podrá descubrir los significados de muchas palabras cuya construcción se basa en *-port-* examinando sus prefijos y sufijos y teniendo en cuenta que cada vocablo basado en esta raíz está de alguna forma asociado con el significado *"carry"*: *deport (de- + -port-), export (ex- + -port-), importance (im- + -port- + -ance), passport (pass + -port-), porter (-port- + -er), report (re- + -port-), support (sup- + -port-)* y *transport (trans- + -port-)*. Asimismo, si sabe que la raíz *-jud-* significa *"judge; law"*, podrá descubrir el significado de palabras como *adjudicate, injudicious* y *prejudice*. Le sugerimos que cuando se encuentre con una raíz, o una referencia a alguna raíz, apunte el significado de ésta, así como el significado de las palabras construidas con ella, e intente descubrir cómo la combinación de raices, prefijos y sufijos le pueden ayudar a averiguar el significado de las palabras.

Cómo evitar los errores más comunes cometidos por el estudiante de inglés

Podrá eludir algunos de los errores más comunes cometidos por el estudiante de inglés si utiliza este diccionario concienzudamente. Una forma de hacer esto es prestarle atención a las notas tituladas *Related Words* que aparecen al final de muchos de los artículos. Estas notas le darán una idea de cómo palabras relacionadas se utilizan de distintas maneras, de acuerdo con la parte de la oración que representen (sustantivo, adjetivo, adverbio, etc.). Por ejemplo, el artículo *angry* contiene una nota que le explica que *angry* es un adjetivo, mientras que la palabra relacionada *anger* es un sustantivo, y *angrily* es un adverbio. La nota le proporciona ejemplos del uso de cada uno de estos vocablos: *"They were very* angry *with you. He keeps his* anger *locked up inside. He stalked* angrily *out of the room"*. Otra palabra que suele confundir al estudiante es *annoy*. La nota que contiene el diccionario es la siguiente:

> ANNOY is a verb, ANNOYING is an adjective, ANNOYANCE is a noun: *That music annoys me. It is annoying music. Another annoyance was when the rain was late.*

Otra forma de evitar cometer los errores más comunes es estudiar las notas tituladas *Usage* que aparecen al final de muchos articulos. Por ejemplo, en el artículo *travel* hay una nota que explica la diferencia entre la palabra *travel* y su palabra relacionada, *trip: Compare TRIP and TRAVEL. For a particular amount of traveling, the noun* trip *is usually used: "I hope you had a pleasant trip. The trip took ten hours." The word* travel *is more often used as a noncount noun to refer to the general idea of traveling: "She is interested in travel and tourism." When* travels *is used, it refers to a journey or trip that has many stops or involves many places: "In all my travels I've never met so many helpful people."*

También aprenderá mucho consultando las listas que se encuentran en la parte posterior del diccionario. Una de las listas, *Irregular Verbs,* contiene verbos irregulares (*come-came-come, make-made-made, grow-grew-grown,* y muchos más), el uso de los cuales suele ser problemático no sólo para el estudiante de inglés, sino también para el hablante nativo. *Nouns with Irregular or Alternate Plurals* (algunos de los cuales llevan la palabra *the*) es otro catálogo incluido en este libro. El uso de estos catálogos le ayudará a corregir sus propios errores.

Este diccionario también incluye códigos gramaticales en casi todos los artículos. Por ejemplo, el código gramatical de uno de los significados de la palabra *reverse* es *{the + ~}*. Esto indica al estudiante que la palabra *the* debe preceder a la palabra *reverse: reverse, .. {noncount; the + ~} the opposite or contrary of something: His answer was the reverse of what we expected.* Los códigos gramaticales también explican qué preposiciones se usan con qué verbos. De esta forma, el código *{~ + to/toward + obj}* que aparece después del verbo *gravitate* significa que este verbo a veces es seguido por la preposición *to* o *toward.*

Ciertos de los calificativos utilizados en este diccionario le asistirán a escoger la palabra más apropiada para cada situación. Calificativos de posición o estilo como *"Informal"* o *"Disparaging"* le harán más consciente de las diferencias que existen entre vocablos con significados similares. Por ejemplo, le podría ser muy útil saber que el vocablo *police officer*, el cual denota respeto, se utiliza en ciertas situaciones, mientras que su sinónimo, *cop,* se usa en contextos más informales. Así pues, si pone atención a toda la información presentada en los artículos, podrá evitar errores embarazosos.

Modismos y frases verbales

Este diccionario también incluye muchos modismos y frases verbales, cada uno de los cuales debe ser aprendido entero, puesto que sus partes independientemente no suelen tener el mismo significado que el modismo completo. Busque la palabra raíz en cualquier artículo y encontrará el modismo o la frase verbal en negrita. Este diccionario no sólo le ofrece el significado del modismo o frase verbal, sino que también suele presentar importante información gramatical, así como ejemplos del uso de cada modismo o frase verbal.

Crack up es un ejemplo de una de las muchas frases verbales que este diccionario le ayudará a dominar. Busque la palabra *crack;* al terminar todos los significados de este verbo, hallará la frase *crack up* en negrita. El significado de esta frase es *"to (cause to) laugh hard without being able to stop".* Además encontrará información gramatical y ejemplos del uso de la frase para que pueda aprender a utilizarla correctamente. Los ejemplos para *crack up* son: *"{no obj}: He cracked up at the sight of her in those frumpy pajamas. {~ + up + obj}: That joke cracked up the audience. {~ + obj + up}: That joke cracked him up."*

El procedimiento es igual para estudiar la frase idiomática *off the cuff,* la cual se encuentra en negrita bajo el artículo *cuff. Off the cuff* es seguido por el calificativo *"Informal",* al cual le sigue el significado *"without preparing; extemporaneously; on the spur of the moment".* En este caso también hallará un ejemplo del uso de este modismo en forma de oración: *"The speaker made a few remarks off the cuff and then began his prepared speech."*

Podrá aumentar significativamente su conocimiento de modismos y frases verbales si considera cuidadosamente la palabra raíz, estudia el artículo que le corresponde en su totalidad hasta hallar el modismo o la frase, lee el significado de éste (considerando la información gramatical) y, por supuesto, examina detenidamente los ejemplos del uso del modismo o de la frase hasta llegar a tener una buena idea de cómo utiliarlo.

La pronunciación del inglés norteamericano y su relación con la ortografía

Este diccionario le ofrece dos métodos de pronunciación para cada vocablo. La primera pronunciación en cada artículo está basada en el sistema utilizado por la familia de diccionarios de Random House, el cual fue diseñado para hablantes nativos del inglés. Este sistema refleja las conexiones entre el sonido y la ortografía, y fue preparado para hablantes nativos que ya han aprendido el sistema de ortografía y de sonido del inglés norteamericano. Pero somos conscientes de que en muchos paises los estudiantes del inglés como idioma extranjero tienen más familiarización con el alfabeto fonético internacional (AFI). Además, el sistema de escritura (romanizado) de muchos idiomas corresponde, o es muy similar, al sistema del AFI. Estos estudiantes no nativos podrán sacar provecho a este libro porque también contiene una segunda pronunciación para cada vocablo, la cual se basa en el sistema del AFI. Si al principio el sistema de pronunciación para el hablante nativo le resulta demasiado difícil, puede utilizar el más familiar sistema del AFI.

Podrá fácilmente ir aprendiendo la correspondencia entre los dos sistemas de pronunciación al comparar los símbolos de ambos. Por ejemplo, la pronunciación de la palabra *grate* está representada por el sistema de Random House como *(grāt)* y en el del AFI como *(greyt)*. Puede verse que el *(ā)* de Random House es equivalente al *(ey)* del AFI. Al ir familiarizándose con el inglés, verá que la letra *a* seguida por una consonante mas la letra final *-e* casi siempre se pronuncia como el *(ā)* de Random House y el *(ey)* del AFI. El sonido vocálico en las palabras *came, cake, cane, cave, cage, cape,* etc. es un ejemplo. Así es que los hablantes nativos aprenden a asociar la ortografía del inglés con su sistema de sonidos. Una vez haya dominado este sistema, ya no necesitará el del AFI y podrá más fácilmente leer, comprender y pronunciar palabras nuevas.

Use este diccionario para aprender a leer, escribir y hablar el inglés norteamericano, y llegará el día en que podrá servirse con facilidad de los más avanzados diccionarios para hablantes nativos.

本書を用いたアメリカ英語の学習法

本書は，アメリカ英語を学習しようとする人のために作られた辞書である。

この辞書の第一の特長は，以下に述べるアドバイスを実践するだけで学習者は語彙を増やすことができ，新しい英語の表現を身につけられるという点である。学習者は，自分がすでに知っている単語にも別の語義があることを発見するであろう。

第二の特長は，英文読解力を向上させることができることである。本書に示された接頭辞，接尾辞，語根は学習者の語彙を増やし，それによって未知の語の意味を類推する力が養われるのである。

第三に，本書の文法コード（文型・用法），不規則変化の名詞・動詞，文体，スピーチラベル，類語などを学習することによって，英語を母国語とはしない学習者がしがちな誤りを防ぐことができる。

第四に，英語学習において特に重要なイディオム，動詞句の使い方を本書でマスターすることによって，より流暢な英語が使えるようになる。

第五の特長は，アメリカ英語の発音方法，発音とスペルとの関わりを理解できるような構成になっている点である。本書では国際音標文字（IPA）方式以外に，ネイティブ・スピーカー用の英語発音表記も併記している。

これら５つの特長から得られる知識が一体となって，アメリカ英語の読解力，文章力，会話力を学習者はさらに向上させることができるのである。

●語彙を増やし，新しく語の意味を知る

この辞書は英語を母国語としない外国人学習者向けに編集されているため，あまり耳慣れない高度に専門的な科学技術用語は取り上げていない。しかし，学習者が気づかないだけで一般にはよく使われている語も意外に多い。例えば，coxcomb, voluntarism, wreak などの単語は日常会話でよく使われるわけではないが，特に専門的な科学技術用語でもない。本書ではこのような語は見出し語にあげている。そこで，学習者は意味の難解な語に出会ったときは，ノートかカードに書き取っておくとよい。

語によっては基本的な意味から派生し，まったく別の意味を持つようになったものもあり，その派生的な意味のほうがアメリカ英語では一般的になっている場合もある。例えば，woolly の基本的な意味は of or resembling wool や covered with wool であるが，アメリカ英語では比喩的な unclear; disorganized の意味で使われる場合が一般的である。したがって，見出し語に付けられた語の定義にすべて目を通すようにすれば，学習者の語彙は飛躍的に増え，アメリカ英語を理解する力がさらに向上するはずである。

学習者がすでに知っていると思っている語にも別の新しい意味があり，それを学ぶことによっても語彙は増えてゆく。本書では，語の一般的な定義の他に新しい意味もつけ加えた。例えば，input はかつて something that is put in や contribution of information or ideas を意味する名詞であったが，アメリカ英語では information or data to be stored in a computer という新しい意味で使われるようになり，最近では to enter (data) into a computer for processing の意味の動詞としても使われている。

このように英語は絶えず変化しているのである。本書を読めば語の新しい意味を数多く知ることができるので，調べようとする語の定義部分にはすべて目を通してほしい。１つの語がいかに多くの意味を持っているかがわかるはずである。

また，語の定義の説明部分に出てくる同義語に目を向けるだけでも，さらに語彙力は増えてゆく。例えば，popular では，looked on or thought of with approval or affection by people in general; well-liked; admired のように，定義の説明の後のセミコロンに続けて同義語が 2 つあげられている。maneuver の定義でも a clever...movement，action，or trick;a crafty tactic; a ploy のように同義語が示されている。このような同義語グループを学習するだけでも語彙の数を大幅に増やすことができる。

●語意を類推することにより読解力を高める

本書には接頭辞，接尾辞，語根が示されているので，これらを活用して語彙を広げれば，知らない語の意味を的確に類推することができるようになる。

まず，本書は，英語でよく使われる語根，例えば -port- などを数多く見出し語にしている。-port- は carry という基本的意味を持った語根であるが，語根の前後の接頭辞・接尾辞をよく見て，その単語がなんらかの形で carry の意味を持っていることがわかれば，-port- を語根とする多くの単語の意味が類推できるようになる。deport（de- ＋ -port-），export（ex- ＋ -port-），importance（im- ＋ -port- ＋ -ance），passport（pass- ＋ -port-），porter（-port- ＋ -er），report（re- ＋ -port-），support（sup- ＋ -port-），transport（trans- ＋ -port-）などがその好例である。同様に，-jud- が judge; law の意味を持っていることさえ知っていれば，adjudicate, injudicious, prejudice といった未知の語の意味も類推することができる。

本書で語根あるいは語根参照の記述を見つけたら，語根の意味，同一語根の語を書き出し，どのような語根，接頭辞，接尾辞の組み合わせによって語義が成り立っているかを知るようにしてほしい。

●学習者にありがちな誤りをしないために

この辞書にくまなく目を通すようにしていれば，英語を母国語としない学習者がしがちな英語表現上の誤りを防ぐことができる。特に，語義の説明の後にある **—Related Words.** の注記をしっかり読んでおくこと。この注記では，関連語が会話の中でどのような品詞（名詞，形容詞，動詞，副詞など）として使われるかを示している。

例えば，見出し語 angry の項では，angry は形容詞，関連語の anger は名詞，angrily は副詞であることがわかるようになっている。この項には，*They were very angry with you. He keeps his anger locked up inside. He stalked angrily out of the room.* のように各品詞ごとの用例も付けられている。また，annoy もやっかいな語であるが，この語の説明は以下の通りである。

—Related Words. **ANNOY** is a verb, **ANNOYING** is an adjective, **ANNOYANCE** is a noun: *That music annoys me. It is annoying music. Another annoyance was when the train was late.*

さらに，学習者にありがちな誤りを防ぐためには，語義の説明の後に **—Usage.** と書かれた注記も大いに役に立つ。この注記は学習者が犯しやすい誤りについて説明している。例えば，見出し語 travel の項には，travel と類義語 trip との違いについて次のような説明がある。

—Usage. Compare **TRIP** and **TRAVEL**. For a particular amount of traveling, the noun **TRIP** is usually used: *I hope you had a pleasant trip. The trip took ten hours.* The word **TRAVEL** is more often used as a noncount noun to refer to the general idea of traveling: *She's interested in travel and tourism.* When **TRAVELS** is used, it refers to a journey or trip that has many stops or involves many places: *In all my travels I've never met so many helpful people.*

また，本書の巻末に付けられたリストを参照すると学習効果が大きくなる。その１つは，ときとして学習者ばかりでなくネイティブ・スピーカーにとってもやっかいな Irregular Verbs（come-came-come，make-made-made，grow-grew-grown など）のリストで，もう１つは，Nouns with Irregular or Alternate Plurals のリストである。これらのリストを参照することでもミスを発見することができる。

本書では，ほとんどの見出し語に文法コード（文型・用法）が付けられているが，文法コードは語に特有の用法があることを学習者に気づかせてくれる。例えば，reverse という語の定義の１つに付けられた文法コードは，[*noncount; the* ＋〜] the opposite or contrary of something: *His answer was the reverse of what we expected.* として，この語の前に the をつけなければならないことを示している。また，文法コードはある動詞がどんな前置詞をとるかも示している。見出し語 gravitate の後にある文法コード［～＋*to/toward* ＋ *obj*］は，gravitate に前置詞 to か toward がくることを表している。文法コードには必ず目を通しておくこと。

本書で使われているスピーチ・ラベルなどの表示は，場面や状況に合った的確なことば遣いをするための指標である。本文中に *Informal* や *Disparaging* のように示されたラベルで状況または文体を示し，それによって類義語の使い方の違いがわかるようになっている。つまり，ある状況のもとではていねいで尊敬の念を込めた police officer という語が使われる一方で，別の状況ではその同義語でより口語的な cop を使うほうが適切であるということが，このラベルによって示されている。

繰り返すが，このような注記のすべてに目を通して知っておくことが誤りを避ける最上の方法なのである。

●イディオム，動詞句の使い方を知る

本書に多数掲載されているイディオム，動詞句は，それらを形成する単語個々別々では意味をなさないので，単語のまとまりとして覚えなければならない。主な見出し語を引いてみればわかるように，イディオム，動詞句は太字で印刷されている。本書ではイディオム，動詞句の意味の定義だけでなく，重要な文法事項，用例もあげている。

動詞句 crack up を例にして，その使い方をマスターしてみよう。crack を引くと，定義などの説明の後に太字で印刷された **crack up** が出てくる。この動詞句の意味の 1 つに，to (cause to) laugh hard without being able to stop がある。本書ではさらに［*no obj*］: *He cracked up at the sight of her in those old frumpy pajamas.*［～＋ *up* ＋ *obj*］: That joke cracked up the audience.［～＋ *obj* ＋ *up*］: *That joke cracked him up.* のようにこの動詞句の使い方を文法的に説明し，用例もあげている。

同様にして，イディオム off the cuff の使い方を知ることができる。見出し語 cuff の説明の後に太字で印刷されたイディオム **off the cuff**，その後に口語ラベルの *Informal*，続いて without preparing; extemporaneously; on the spur of the moment の定義，次に用例として *The speaker made a few remarks off the cuff and then began his prepared speech.* があげられている。

まず単語のまとまりの中心となる語を引き，イディオムあるいは句の説明をすべて読み，その意味内容を理解し，文法的説明をノートにとり，用例を吟味してイディオムや動詞句の使い方を感じ取ることによって，それらの用法をより深く知ることができるようになるはずである。

●アメリカ英語の発音とつづり字との関係がわかる

本書では，すべての見出し語について発音表記を 2 種類示している。最初に記載されているのは Random House 系辞書で使われているネイティブ・スピーカー向けの発音表記である。これは英語のつづり字と発音との間の関連性を重視しており，アメリカ英語のつづり字を利用した発音表記に慣れているネイティブ・スピーカーにとっては発音しやすい表記法である。

しかし，英語を外国語として学ぶ世界各国の英語学習者たちが英語発音を国際音標文字 (IPA) で学んできたことも事実であり，多くの言語のローマ字表記法は IPA 方式によく似ている。そこで，本書ではこうした外国人学習者の便宜のために IPA 方式の発音表記も併記している。「ネイティブ・スピーカー用」の発音表記を難しいと感じる学習者は，2 つめのなじみやすい IPA 方式で発音すればよい。

Random House と IPA の発音表記を比較すると 2 つの表記法の類似点がわかってくる。例えば，grate の発音は Random House 方式では **(grāt)**，IPA 方式では /greyt/ のように表記される。これを見れば、Random House 方式の(ā)と IPA 方式の /ey/ が同じ発音であることがすぐにわかる。こうした対応関係が常に成り立っているのである。

英語に慣れるにしたがって，a のつづり字の後が「子音字＋e」で終わる語の a の発音は Random House 方式の(ā)，IPA 方式の /ey/ と同じ「二重母音の a」であることもわかるだろう。came, cake, cane, cave, cage, cape などの母音部分の発音はすべて同じである。ネイティブ・スピーカーが英語のつづり字と発音表記を関連づけるようになったのはこうした理由からである。この発音表記をマスターしてしまえば，IPA 方式は不要となり，新しい語に出くわしても簡単に読み，理解し，発音できるようになる。

本書を有効に利用して，アメリカ英語を読み，書き，話せるようになってほしい。やがてはネイティブ・スピーカーが使うようなより高度な辞書を読めるようになるはずである。

怎樣利用本辭典學習美國英語

使用本辭典可以幫助你學習地道的美國英語。首先，辭典正文和這裡提出的學習方法可幫助你擴增詞彙量和學習新的單詞。同時也可幫助你了解過去會的單詞的其他涵義。其次，使用本辭典也可提高你的閱讀理解能力。因爲本辭典包含了單詞的前綴、後綴和詞根，這些都有助於擴大你的詞彙，讓你能夠據以推測不認識的單詞。第三，本辭典包含了語法規則，可數與不可數名詞和動詞變化，文體或層次的標識，同類詞彙或相關詞彙。如此一來，你可以避免學習英語的人常犯的一些毛病。第四，美國英語中兩個重要的組成部分是慣用語和動詞短語，本辭典幫助你熟悉它們的用法，使你的英語更加流利。第五，本辭典可以幫助你了解美國發音與拼寫之間的關係。本書使用以國際音標 (IPA) 爲基礎的發音系統，但同時也包括了一般美國英語辭典常用的看字辨音系統。同時掌握這兩種系統，可提高你美國英語的讀、寫和説的能力。

學習新詞，增加詞彙

由於本辭典是爲學英語的人而設計，所以沒有收入一般人不熟悉的專業或科學名詞。但有許多常用的詞彙許多學英語的人仍然不太了解，本辭典可幫助他們熟悉這些詞彙。例如 coxcomb, voluntarism, 和 wreak 這樣的詞並非日常用語，也不是技術或科技詞彙，但你都可在本辭典中找到。我們建議你在遇到這種難詞時，把它們寫在筆記簿上或單詞卡上。

此外，我們應注意到某些詞的涵義除了最簡單或最基本的意義之外會不斷引申，而某些引申義在美國英語中已經變得非常普遍。舉例來説，wooly 一詞的最基本意思是 "of or resembling wool" 和 "covered with wool"；但它還有一個抽象的涵義則是 "unclear; disorganized"。特別留意單詞的各種不同涵義可大大提高你的詞彙量，增強你對美國英語的了解。

學習"舊詞"衍生的新義也會增加你的詞彙量。本辭典增列了常見詞彙產生的新義，如 input 一詞過去只用作名詞，意思是 "something that is put in" 和 "contribution of information or ideas"。 但目前在美國英語中產生了一個新的涵義: "information or data to be stored in a computer"，而且近來還被用作動詞，涵義爲 "to put data into a computer for storage" 。在本辭典中，你可以找到許多詞彙的新義，因爲英語不斷在發展變化。所以，在查找詞彙時，必須閱讀該詞所有的涵義，一個詞有這麼多的意思或許會讓你大吃一驚。

通過學習該詞各種涵義的同義詞也可擴大你的詞彙量。例如 popular 一詞，先解釋詞條的定義，緊接著分號之後的是兩個同義詞: "looked on or thought of with approval or affection by people in general; well-liked; admired"。 單詞 maneuver 詞條下的一個定義也提供了同義詞組: "a clever movement, action, or trick; a crafty tactic; a ploy"。學習這樣的同義詞組會大大增加你的詞彙量。

推測詞義，提高閱讀理解能力

由於本辭典包含了單詞的前綴、後綴和詞根，你可用來擴大你的詞彙並依此類推，推測你不認識的字的涵義。本書中的一般詞條都列舉了它們的詞根，例如詞根 -port- 的基本涵義是 "carry"。如果你知道詞根的涵義，再去查構成該詞的前綴和後綴，你就可以猜出許多從 -port- 這個詞根發展出來的詞的涵義，因爲這些詞都帶有 "carry" 的意思，如 deport (de- + -port-), export (ex- + -port-), importance (im- + -port- + -ance), passport (pass- + -port-), porter (-port- + -er),report (re- + -port-)， 和 transport (trans- + -port-)。 同樣地，如果你知道詞根 -jud- 的意思是 "judge; law"， 那麼你就可能猜出 adjudicate, injudicious 和 prejudice 這些你可能沒學過的新詞的意思。只要遇到詞根，或與詞根有關的，我們建議你記下詞根的涵義和從該詞根延伸出來的字彙，嘗試研究詞根、詞頭和詞尾如何組合構成一個單詞的意義。

避免英語中常犯的錯誤

好好利用本辭典，你就可以避免英文學習者常犯的錯誤。首先，你可以特別注意出現在各詞條後面的相關詞 ，即 [Related Words]。 這些注解可以讓你立刻明白相關詞彙在不同詞性

（名詞、形容詞、動詞、副詞）時的不同用法。 舉例來說，angry 詞條下面的注解提醒你 angry 是形容詞，相關詞 anger 是名詞， angrily 則是副詞。注解還舉例說明其用法: "They were very angry with you. He keeps his anger locked inside. He stalked angrily out of the room." 另一個較難的詞是 annoy; 下面是這個詞的注解:

ANNOY is a verb, ANNOYING is an adjective, ANNOYANCE is a noun: That music annoys me. It is annoying music. Another annoyance was when the train was late.

避免常犯錯誤的另一個方法是學習各詞條後面的用法注解 ，即〔Usage Note〕， 這類注解多數都解釋了學英語的人常犯的錯誤。以 travel 爲例，該詞條下的注解說明了 travel 和相關詞 trip 不同之處:

Compare TRIP and TRAVEL. For a particular amount of traveling, the noun TRIP is usually used: I hope you had a pleasant trip. The trip took ten hours. The word TRAVEL is more often used as a noncount noun to refer to the general idea of traveling: She's interested in travel and tourism. When TRAVELS is used, it refers to a journey or trip that has many stops or involves many places: In my travels I've never met so many helpful people.

參考辭典後面的附表，你也可從中學到很多。附表一列舉各種不規則動詞〔Irregular Verb〕（如： come-came-come, make-made-made, grow-grew-grown 等），這些最令學英語的人、甚至是以英語爲母語的人感到困擾。附表二還有名詞複數形的不規則變化表〔Nouns with Irregular or Alternate Plurals〕。參照以上附表可以幫助你找出自己的毛病。

本辭典中幾乎每個詞條都附有語法規則，可提醒你這個詞較特別的使用規則。比如 reverse 一詞，{the + ~} 表示該詞前面應加上冠詞 the。該詞條的說明爲：{noncount; the + ~} the opposite or contrary of something: "His answer was the reverse of what we expected." 語法規則還告訴你某些動詞必需搭配一定的介詞。如動詞 gravitate 後加上 {~ + to/toward + obj.} 表明這個動詞後面常使用介詞 to 或 toward。多留意這些語法規則是很重要的。

本辭典使用的某些標示可讓你根據不同的情境選擇正確的詞彙。像 informal 或 disparaging 這類點出用法情境或風格的詞可幫助你區別意義相近的詞；比方說，有些場合要使用較有禮貌、有敬意的 "police officer" ，但是在其他場合則可以使用比較不正式的 "cop" ，了解這種區別是很有用的。再者，多留意這些提示可以使你避免令人難堪的錯誤。

慣用語與動詞短語

本辭典收錄大量的慣用語和動詞短語，在英語中它們必須被當做整體來記憶，因爲短語本身與拆開的字面意義不同。 在查尋詞條時，你會注意到慣用語和動詞短語都用粗體字印出。本辭典不止有慣用語和動詞短語的定義，還提供重要的語法講解和例句。

例如，本辭典可以幫助讀者掌握 crack up 這個動詞短語的意義。在 crack 一詞的定義結束後，你會看到用粗體字印出的 **crack up**，此短語的定義是 "to (cause to) laugh hard without being able to stop." 此外，本辭典還提供語法結構，並舉例說明其使用方法: {no obj}: He cracked up at the sight of her in those frumpy pajamas.{~ + up + obj}: That joke cracked up the audience. {~ + obj + up}: That joke cracked him up.

習慣用語也是同樣處理，以 off the cuff 爲例，這一短語收在 cuff 詞條下，用粗體字印出 **off the cuff**，其後是 INFORMAL 標誌和釋義: "without preparing; extemporaneously; on the spur of the moment." 然後是例句: "The speaker made a few remarks off the cuff and then began his prepared speech." 藉著查尋生詞、學習與其相關的慣用語和短語、理解它們的涵義、銘記語法規則、研習例句、善用例句學習這些慣用語和動詞短語的用法，可以大大提升你在這方面的知識。

美國英語的發音及其與拼寫的關係

本辭典收錄的單詞以兩種發音系統標示。首先是適合一般美國讀者使用的 Random House 辭典發音系統。這一系統力圖反映英語發音與拼寫的關係，方便以英語為母語的讀者使用，因為他們很熟悉美式英語發音及拼音系統。但我們發覺，世界各地許多以英語為第二外語的人常使用的是改良過的國際音標 (IPA)。此外，許多語言使用的拼音系統(羅馬拼音)與國際音標對應或類似。由於本辭典同時為每個單詞提供國際音標之外的拼音系統，學習英語的人將受益非淺。如果無法馬上習慣 Random House 的拼音系統，初學者可用比較熟悉的國際音標系統作為後援。

仔細比較Random House 和國際音標的拼音符號，你可以很快掌握兩者的對應關係。舉例來說，grate 一詞的發音用 Random House 系統標注為〔grāt〕而國際音標系統則標為〔greyt〕。顯而易見地，Random House 的〔ā〕就等同於國際音標的〔ey〕，而且這樣的對應相當規則。經過一段時間的學習，你將發覺到字母 a 後面加上子音和不發音的 -e 常常是這個長音的"a"，也就是 Random House 的〔ā〕和國際音標的〔ey〕。came, cake, cane, cave, cage, cape 等詞中的母音都是發這個音。 這也正是一般美國人對應拼字與發音的方式。一旦你學會了這種識字辨音系統，就不再需要國際音標，日後遇到新詞時閱讀、理解與發音就容易的多了。

利用本辭典學習美國英語的讀、寫和發音，日後需要用到一般美國人所使用的高級辭典時，你就能夠駕輕就熟了，

New Words in American English

The vocabulary of English, especially American English, is growing at a remarkable rate. Among all the varieties of English around the world, including British English, it is American English that changes the fastest, adding more new words each year. New terms have entered the language mostly as a result of re-cent inventions or knowledge in the fields of science and technology. Social and cultural trends and fashions have also contributed to the great expansion of the English vocabulary. These new terms represent a variety of subject categories, both general and specialized.

Many new terms are borrowed from other languages, such as *pita* (from modern Greek) and *karaoke* (from Japanese). Other terms are formed by combining or blending two or more existing words, such as *camcorder* (from *camera* and *recorder*) and *alternative medicine.* The creation of abbreviations is another common method of word formation in English. The abbreviation *ATM* is certainly more convenient to use than the full phrase "automated-teller machine"; the shortened form *AIDS* is easier to pronounce and remember than the full form "acquired immune deficiency syndrome." New words are commonly derived from existing words by the addition of a prefix or suffix: *superstore* (prefix *super-*) and *cyberspace* (prefix *cyber-*). The coinage of new words that are not based on existing words is quite uncommon. Nevertheless individuals have invented terms that are both clever and descriptive. A large number of coinages are names of people or places.

Not only does the language add new vocabulary, but existing words change, broaden, or narrow their meanings over time. The new sense of *rocket scientist* (highly intelligent person) extends the original meaning (specialist in rocket design).

New terms are popularized and given life in our newspapers, magazines, books, and electronic documents, not to mention radio and television shows, motion pictures, and plays. Some new terms last only for the moment, as a passing fad, and are forgotten soon after their introduction. Other new terms are controversial because of their slang status, or because they are perceived to be offensive. It is not possible to foretell the future of a particular word. As for the future of English, the language is certain to continue its expansion in the course of the 21st cntury.

It is a difficult enough task to master the basic vocabulary of English, but a command of the language is not complete unless the learner is familiar with the terms that have entered English in recent years. A careful study of the following selection of words will reveal a great deal about our changing world.

---

abs (abz) /æbz/ *n.* [*plural; used with a plural verb*] *Informal.* the muscles of the stomach; abdominal muscles.

alter′native med′icine, *n.* [*noncount*] health care and treatments, including traditional Chinese medicine and folk medicine, that try to avoid the use of surgery and drugs.

an′swering machine′, *n.* [*count*] an electronic device that answers telephone calls with a recorded message and records the callers' messages on a tape.

a•ro•ma•ther•a•py (ə rō′mə ther′ə pē) /əˌrowmə-ˈθɛrəpiy/ *n.* [*noncount*] **1.** the use of pleasant fragrances to affect or change a person's mood or behavior. **2.** treatment of the skin by the application of fragrant oils from flowers or herbs.

as•par•tame (ə spär′tām, a spär′-, as′pər tām′) /əˈspɑrteym, æˈspɑr-, ˈæspərˌteym/ *n.* [*noncount*] an artificially made white powder that is much sweeter than sucrose and is used as a low-calorie sugar substitute.

assist′ed su′icide, *n.* [*count*] suicide in which a physician helps the person to commit suicide, as by supplying a poison.

au′dio book′ or **au′di•o•book′,** *n.* [*count*] a recording on cassette in which a book is read aloud, usually by the author or a professional actor.

bod′y pierc′ing, *n.* [*count*] the piercing of a part of the body, such as the navel or the nose, in order to insert a metal ring or other ornament.

boom′ box′ or **boom′box′,** *n.* [*count*] a large, powerful radio or combination radio and cassette player that can be carried around.

brew•pub (bro͞o′pub′) /ˈbruwˌpʌb/ *n.* [*count*] a bar or small restaurant serving beer that is brewed at a microbrewery located in the same building.

bu•lim•i•a (byo͞o lim′ē ə, -lē′mē ə, bo͞o-) /byuwˈlɪmiyə, -ˈliymiyə, buw-/ *n.* [*noncount*] a disturbance in eating habits marked by repeated instances of overeating followed by intentional vomiting or fasting.

car•jack•ing (kär′jak′ing) /ˈkɑrˌdʒækɪŋ/ *n.* [*count; noncount*] the crime of stealing a vehicle from its driver by using force or threats. —**car′jack′er,** *n.* [*count*]

chal•lenged (chal′injd) /ˈtʃælɪndʒd/ *adj.* (a polite word used to avoid offending someone) disabled or handicapped: *Several children in the school are physically or mentally challenged.*

choc•o•hol•ic (chô′kə hô′lik, -hol′ik, chok′ə-) /ˌtʃɔkəˈhɔlɪk, -ˈhɒlɪk, ˌtʃɒkə-/ *n.* [*count*] a person who craves chocolate and eats a lot of it.

chron′ic fatigue′ syn′drome, *n.* [*noncount*] a disease in which the person is always tired and has flu-like symptoms.

co•de•pend•ent (kō′di pen′dənt) /ˌkowdɪˈpɛndənt/ *adj.* **1.** of or relating to a relationship in which one person is addicted to alcohol or drugs and trys to manipulate or control the other person. —*n.* [*count*] **2.** a person who is in a codependent relationship. —**co′de•pend′en•cy, co′de•pend′ence,** *n.* [*count*]

contin′uing educa′tion, *n.* [*noncount*] a program of courses for adults offered by a high school, college, or other institution.

control′ freak′, *n.* [*count*] a person having a strong need to control or manipulate situations, events, and other people.

co•pay (kō′pā′) /ˈkowˌpey/ *n.* [*noncount*] a fixed sum, or a percentage of the customary fee, required by an health-insurance company to be paid by a patient to a health-care provider: *My copay is $10 for an office visit to my doctor.*

cy•ber•punk (sī′bər pungk′) /ˈsaybərˌpʌŋk/ *n.* **1.** [*noncount*] a type of science fiction featuring human interaction with supercomputers, usually in a large city. **2.** [*count*] *Slang.* a computer hacker.

cy•ber•space /ˈsaybərˌspeys/ *n.* [*noncount*] **1.** the worldwide system of linked computer networks, thought of as being a limitless environment for exchange of information and electronic communication. **2.** VIRTUAL REALITY (in this section).

defin′ing mo′ment, *n.* [*count*] a point at which the basic nature or character of a person, group, etc., is revealed or identified.

dig•e•ra•ti (dij′ə rä′tē, -rā′-) /ˌdɪdʒəˈrɑtiy, -ˈrey-/ *n.* [*plural; used with a plural verb*] people who are skilled with or knowledgeable about computers.

dis (dis) /dɪs/ *v.*, **dissed, dis•sing,** *n. Slang.* —*v.* [~ + *obj*] **1.** to show a lack of respect for (someone). **2.** to make (someone) feel unimportant; disparage. —*n.* [*count*] **3.** disrespect or criticism.

domes′tic vi′olence, *n.* [*noncount*] acts of violence

or abuse against a member of one's family, esp. in the home.

drive-by (drīv′bī′) /'drayv,bay/ *adj., n., pl.* **-bys.** —*adj.* [*before a noun*] **1.** accomplished while driving past the victim in a moving vehicle: *The gang member was killed in a drive-by shooting.* **2.** casual; superficial: *a drive-by news report.* **3.** involving a brief stay in a hospital: *drive-by surgery.* —*n.* [*count*] **4.** a drive-by shooting.

dweeb (dwēb) /dwiyb/ *n.* [*count*] *Slang.* a person who is considered to be unfashionable, socially awkward, or unpopular.

eat′ing disor′der, *n.* [*count*] any of various medical conditions, such as anorexia or bulimia, marked by severe disturbances in eating habits.

ed•u•tain•ment (ej′o͞o tān′mənt) /,ɛdʒʊ'teynmənt/ *n.* [*noncount*] television programs, books, computer software, etc., that are both educational and entertaining, esp. those intended for school-age children.

emp′ty nest′ syn′drome, *n.* [*noncount*] a depressed state felt by some parents after their children have grown up and left home.

er•go•nom•ics (ûr′gə nom′iks) /,ɜrgə'nɒmɪks/ *n.* [*used with a singular verb*] a science that coordinates the design and arrangement of equipment and office spaces with the abilities, limitations, and requirements of workers. —**er′go•nom′ic,** *adj.* —**er′go•nom′i•cal•ly,** *adv.*: *an ergonomically designed computer keyboard to increase comfort.*

fac•toid (fak′toid) /'fæktɔyd/ *n.* [*count*] **1.** something that is untrue or unproven but is presented as fact and believed to be true because of constant repetition. **2.** an insignificant or unimportant fact.

fa•ji•tas (fä hē′təz, fə-) /fɑ'hiytəz, fə-/ *n.* [*count; used with a singular or plural verb*] a Mexican dish consisting of thin strips of grilled beef or chicken with sliced peppers and onions, usually wrapped in tortillas.

fo′cus group′, *n.* [*count*] a representative group of people brought together and questioned about their opinions on political issues, new products, etc.: *The company formed a focus group of young women to discuss marketing plans for a new perfume.*

food′ court′, *n.* [*count*] a space, usually in a shopping mall, with a variety of fast-food stalls and a common eating area.

food•ie (fo͞o′dē) /'fuwdiy/ *n.* [*count*] *Slang.* a person who is very interested in food, esp. a gourmet.

401(k) (fôr′ō′wun′kā′, fōr′-) /'fɔr,ow'wʌn'key, 'fowr-/ *n.* [*count*] a savings plan that allows employees to contribute part of their income to an account whose funds are invested and usually withdrawn after retirement.

fre′quent fli′er, *n.* [*count*] an airline passenger participating in a program that provides bonuses based on distance traveled. —**fre′quent-fli′er,** *adj.*

GED, an abbreviation of: general equivalency diploma, a diploma that can be earned by people who have left high school before graduating.

geek (gēk) /giyk/ *n.* [*count*] *Slang.* a person who is considered to be different from others, esp. a teenager who is socially awkward or spends too much time studying.

genera′tion gap′, *n.* [*noncount*] a lack of communication between one generation and another, esp. between young people and their parents.

Generation X (eks) /ɛks/ *n.* [*noncount*] *Informal.* the generation born in the United States after 1965. —**Generation X'er,** *n.* [*count*]: *a new sitcom for Generation X'ers.*

gene′ ther′apy, *n.* [*noncount*] the treatment of a disease by replacing abnormal genes with normal ones, esp. through the use of viruses to carry the desired genes into the blood cells.

ge•nome (jē′nōm) /' dʒiynowm/ *n.* [*count*] a full set of chromosomes with all its genes; the total genetic make-up of a cell or organism. —**ge•no′mic,** *adj.*

glo′bal warm′ing, *n.* [*noncount*] an increase in the average temperature of the earth's atmosphere, causing changes in climate.

grunge (grunj) /grʌndʒ/ *n. Slang.* **1.** [*noncount*] dirt; filth; rubbish. **2.** [*count*] something of inferior quality. **3.** [*noncount*] a style or fashion of the early 1990's derived from a movement in rock music: in fashion characterized by untidy clothing and in music by aggressive, antisocial songs.

HDTV, an abbreviation of: high-definition television.

health′ care′ or **health′care′,** *n.* **1.** [*noncount*] the field or industry concerned with supplying services, equipment, and information related to maintaining and restoring physical and mental health. —*adj.* Also, **health′-care′. 2.** of, relating to, or involved in health care: *a health-care center; health-care workers.*

health′ club′, [*count*] a usually private club that offers its members various facilities for physical exercise, such as weightlifting machines and a swimming pool.

health′ food′, *n.* [*count*] a food that is believed to promote good health, as by being nutritious or by containing only natural ingredients.

high′-defini′tion tel′evision, *n.* [*noncount*] a television system that produces a sharper image and greater picture detail. *Abbr.:* HDTV

high′ top′, *n.* [*count*] a sneaker that covers the ankle.

home′ of′fice, *n.* [*count*] a room or space in one's home that is equipped and used as an office.

home′ page′, *n.* [*count*] the main page of a site on the World Wide Web, usually containing an index or table of contents to the documents stored at the site.

home•school•ing (hōm′sko͞o′ling) /'howm,skuwlɪŋ/ *n.* [*noncount*] the practice of teaching one's own children at home instead of sending them to school.

hot′-but′ton, *adj.* arousing strong feelings; very emotional: *abortion and other hot-button issues.*

HOV lane, *n.* [*count*] a highway or street lane reserved for high-occupancy vehicles with two or more passengers, usually marked with diamond shapes on the road.

hy•per•text (hī′pər tekst′) /'haypər,tɛkst/ *n.* [*noncount*] text, pictures, or other data stored in a computer and linked so that a user can move from an item in one electronic document to a related item in another document.

in•fo•mer•cial (in′fō mûr′shəl) /,ɪnfow'mɜrʃəl/ *n.* [*count*] a television commercial similar in length and format to a regular program, disguising the fact that it is an advertisement.

in′forma′tion su′perhighway, *n.* [*noncount*] the worldwide network of computers, providing access to electronic databases, e-mail, video materials, and a variety of other services. Also called **in′forma′tion high′way.**

in′-line′ skate′, *n.* [*count*] a roller skate with four hard-rubber wheels in a straight line. —**in′-line skat′ing,** *n.* [*noncount*]

In•ter•net (in′tər net′) /'ɪntər,nɛt/ *n.* [*noncount; usually: the + ~*] a large computer network linking smaller computer networks worldwide.

in′-your′-face′, *adj. Informal.* marked by or being bold and aggressive; provocative: *in-your-face journalism.*

Jet′ Ski′, *n.* [*count*] *Trademark.* a brand of PERSONAL WATERCRAFT (in this section).

ka•ra•o•ke (kar′ē ō′kē) /,kæriy'owkiy/ *n.* [*count*] a device that allows a person to sing along to the music of a song and record his or her voice, the original singing having been electronically eliminated.

Kwan•zaa or **Kwan•za** (kwän′zə) /'kwɑnzə/ *n.* [*count; noncount*], *pl.* **-zaas** or **-zas.** a harvest festival celebrated from December 26 until January 1 in some African-American communities.

lat•te (lä′tā) /'lɑtey/ *n.* [*count*] hot espresso served mixed with hot milk.

lev′el play′ing field′, *n.* a state of equality; an equal opportunity: *Our business needs a level playing field when competing with foreign companies.*

lite (līt) /layt/ *adj.* an informal, simplified spelling of LIGHT (in the sense "having fewer calories or less of a certain ingredient than the standard product"), used esp. in labeling, naming, or advertising products: *lite beer.*

low-fat, *adj.* of or being a food or style of cooking that contains or uses very little butter, oil, or other fat.

mad′ cow′ disease′, *n.* [*noncount*] a fatal brain disease of cattle, thought to be caused by an abnormal, proteinlike particle.

man′aged care′, *n.* [*noncount*] comprehensive health care provided by a health maintenance organization or similar system.

Mc- or **M^c^-,** *suffix.* a suffix derived from "McDonald's" (a fast-food restaurant chain), used to mean "of the same mediocre quality or kind; uniform": *McSchools that offer no individual attention; reading McNews instead of a serious newspaper.*

mi•cro•brew•er•y (mī′krō bro͞o′ə rē, -bro͝or′ē) /'maykrow,bruwəriy, -,brʊriy/ *n.* [*count*], *pl.* **-er•ies.** a small brewery usually producing unique or high quality beer.

mi•cro•fi•ber (mī′krō fī′bər) /'maykrow,faybər/ *n.* [*count*] a very fine lightweight polyester fiber, used esp. for clothing.

mi•cro•man•age (mī′krō man′ij) /'maykrow,mænɪdʒ/ *v.* [~ + *obj*], **-aged, -ag•ing.** to manage or control with great or too much attention to minor details: *The executive had no time to micromanage every part of his business.* **—mi′cro•man′age•ment,** *n.* [*noncount*]

mind′-bod′y, *adj.* taking into account the mental, physical, psychic, and spiritual connections between the state of the body and that of the mind: *mind-body medicine.*

mind′ games′, *n.* [*plural; used with a plural verb*] psychological manipulation or strategy, used esp. to gain an advantage or to force someone to do something.

min•i•van (min′ē van′) /'mɪniy,væn/ *n.* [*count*] a small passenger van, usually seating six or more people.

morph•ing (môr′fing) /'mɔrfɪŋ/ *n.* [*noncount*] a technique in which one image is gradually and smoothly changed into another by means of a computer, as in a motion picture or video: *My favorite part of the cartoon was the morphing of the hero into a wild animal.*

moun′tain bike′, *n.* [*count*] a bicycle designed for use on unpaved or hilly roads, having a sturdy frame and wider tires than a standard bicycle. **—moun′tain bik′er,** *n.* [*count*] **—moun′tain bik′ing,** *n.* [*noncount*]

mouse′ pad′, *n.* [*count*] a small foam rubber sheet used to provide a stable surface on which a computer mouse can be moved.

MRI, an abbreviation of: magnetic resonance imaging, a technique that produces images of tissues and organs of the body by means of a strong magnetic field and low-energy radio waves.

nail-bit•er (nāl′bī′tər) /'neyl,baytər/ *n.* [*count*] a situation that is marked by anxiety or tension.

new•bie (no͞o′bē, nyo͞o′-) /'nuwbiy, 'nyuw-/ *n.* [*count*] a beginner, esp. an inexperienced user of the Internet or of computers in general.

no-brain•er /'now'breynər/ *n.* [*count*] *Informal.* anything requiring little thought or effort; something easy or simple to understand or do.

out•sourc•ing (out′sôr′sing, -sōr′-) /,awt'sɔrsɪŋ, -'sowr-/ *n.* [*noncount*] the business practice of purchasing supplies, parts, or finished products from another company, or of using outside workers in the manufacturing process: *the outsourcing of foreign auto parts to reduce costs.*

pa•pa•raz•zo (pä′pə rät′sō) /,pɑpə'rɑtsow/ *n.* [*count*], *pl.* **-raz•zi** (-rät′sē) /-'rɑtsiy/. a freelance photographer, esp. one who takes candid photographs of celebrities for publication in magazines and newspapers.

pay′ tel′evision, *n.* [*noncount*] **1.** a service that broadcasts television programs to viewers who pay a monthly charge or a fee for each program. **2.** the programming provided by this service. Also called **pay-TV.**

per′sonal train′er, *n.* [*count*] a person who works with a individual client to plan or carry out an exercise or fitness program: *She hired a personal trainer to come to her home.*

per′sonal wa′tercraft, *n.* **1.** [*count*] a jet-propelled boat that is ridden by one or two persons like a motorcycle: *That shop rents out personal watercrafts, canoes, and rowboats.* **2.** [*plural; used with a plural verb*] such boats when thought of as a group: *Personal watercraft are not allowed in this bay.*

polit′ically correct′, *adj.* conforming to language, behavior, or attitudes that do not offend minority groups, disabled people, homosexuals, etc.

poop•er-scoop•er (po͞o′pər sko͞o′pər) /'puwpər,skuwpər/ *n.* [*count*] a scoop and a bag used to pick up the solid wastes of a dog or other pet from a street.

pri′mary care′, *n.* [*noncount*] medical care by a physician who is the patient's first contact with the health-care system and who may recommend a specialist if necessary. **—pri′mary-care′,** *adj.*: *primary-care physicians.*

repet′itive strain′ in′jury, *n.* [*noncount*] any of a group of medical conditions caused by the stress of repeated movements, marked by pain, numbness, or tingling in the hand or arm. *Abbr.:* RSI

right•size (rīt′sīz′) /'rayt,sayz/ *v.* [~ + *obj*], **-sized, -siz•ing.** to adjust to an appropriate size: *We will have to fire about 50 workers in order to rightsize our staff.*

road′ kill′, *n.* [*count*] the body of an animal killed on a road by a motor vehicle.

rock′et sci′ence, *n.* [*noncount*] **1.** the science of rocket design and flight; rocketry. **2.** something requiring great intelligence, esp. mathematical ability.

rock′et sci′entist, *n.* [*count*] **1.** a specialist in rocket design. **2.** a highly intelligent person, esp. one with mathematical ability.

Roll•er•blade (rō′lər blād′) /'rowlər,bleyd/ **1.** [*count*] *Trademark.* a brand of in-line skates. **—***v.* [~ + *obj*], **-blad•ed, -blad•ing. 2.** (*often: rollerblade*) to skate on in-line skates. **—roll′er•blad′er,** *n.* [*count*]

same′-sex′, *adj.* **1.** of or relating to two or more persons of the same gender: *same-sex friendships.* **2.** of or involving a sexual relationship between two men or between two women: *same-sex marriage.*

scrunch•y or **scrunch•ie** (skrun′chē) /'skrʌntʃiy/ *n.* [*count*], *pl.* **scrunch•ies.** an elastic fabric band, used to fasten the hair.

sec′ondhand smoke′, *n.* [*noncount*] tobacco smoke that is involuntarily inhaled when one is near or in the same room as a smoker.

shock′ jock′, *n.* [*count*] a radio disc jockey who features offensive or controversial material.

snail′ mail′, *n.* [*noncount*] standard postal service, as contrasted with electronic mail. Also called **s-mail.**

snow•board (snō′bôrd′, -bōrd′) /'snow,bɔrd, -,bowrd/ *n.* [*count*] a board that resembles a wide ski, used for gliding on snow while in a standing position. **—snow′board′er,** *n.* [*count*] **—snow′board′ing,** *n.* [*noncount*]

sound′ bite′, *n.* [*count*] a brief, striking statement taken from an interview or speech for use in a broadcast news story.

spell′ check′er, *n.* [*count*] a computer program for checking the spelling of words in an electronic document.

sport′-util′ity ve′hicle, *n.* [*count*] a sturdy passenger vehicle with a trucklike frame, designed for occasional use on hilly or unpaved roads.

sta′tionary bi′cycle, *n.* [*count*] an indoor exercise machine that is pedaled like a bicycle.

strang′er rape′, *n.* [*count*] sexual intercourse forced by a man upon a woman he does not know.

sun′block′ *n.* [*count; noncount*] a lotion that protects the skin against sunburn, often preventing tanning.

su•per•store (so͞o′pər stôr′, -stōr′) /'suwpər,stɔr, -,stowr/ *n.* [*count*] a very large store, esp. one selling a wide variety of goods.

SUV, *pl.* **SUVs.** an abbreviation of: sport-utility vehicle.

take′-no′-pris′oners, *adj.* very enthusiastic; aggressive: *a businessman with a take-no-prisoners style.*

tel•e•com•mut•ing (tel′i kə myo͞o′ting) /'tɛlɪkə-,myuwtɪŋ/ *n.* [*noncount*] the act or practice of working at home using a computer terminal that is electronically linked to one's office. **—tel′e•com•mut′er,** *n.* [*count*]

theme′ park′, *n.* [*count*] an amusement park whose attractions and rides are based on various themes, such as fairy tales or the American West.

track•ball (trak′bôl′) /'træk,bɔl/ *n.* [*count*] a computer device for controlling the pointer on a display screen by rotating a ball set inside a case.

tro′phy wife′, *n.* [*count*] the young, often second, wife of a rich middle-aged man.

V-chip (vē′chip′) /'viy,tʃɪp/ *n.* [*count*] a computer chip or other electronic device that blocks television reception of programs with violent or sexual content.

vir′tual real′ity, *n.* [*noncount*] the computer simulation of a realistic, three-dimensional environment, allowing the user to become an active participant through the use of special gloves, headphones, and goggles.

voice′ mail′, *n.* [*noncount*] a computerized system that answers telephone calls and records phone messages for later playback, used esp. in offices.

Web′ site′, *n.* [*count*] a connected group of pages on the World Wide Web, usually maintained by one person or organization and devoted to a single topic or several closely related topics.

wedg•ie (wej′ē) /'wɛdʒiy/ *n.* [*count*] *Informal.* the condition of having one's underpants or other clothing uncomfortably stuck between the buttocks.

World′ Wide′ Web′, *n.* [*noncount*] a system of extensively interlinked hypertext documents: a branch of the Internet. *Abbr.:* WWW

WWW, an abbreviation of: World Wide Web.

A, a (ā) /ey/ *n.* [*count*], *pl.* **A's** or **As, a's** or **as. 1.** the first letter of the English alphabet. **2.** a school grade or mark indicating excellence: *received an A in English.* **—*Idiom.* 3. from A to Z,** completely; thoroughly: *He knew the rules of the game from A to Z.*

a (ə; *when stressed* ā) /ə; *when stressed* ey/ *indefinite article.* [*usually before count nouns*] **1.** one: *a friend of mine; a month ago.* **2.** (used to refer to the class of things the noun belongs to): *A dog has four legs.* **3.** (used to refer to a rate or measurement with the noun) per; each: *My dentist charges $50 a filling.* **4.** (used before words like *little, lot, few*): *a little time; a few stars.* **5.** (used before noncount nouns to indicate a single portion, container, unit, type, or instance of that noun): *I'll have a coffee (= a cup of coffee) with sugar.* **6.** (used before a proper name): **a.** a certain; a particular: *A Mr. Johnson called and wants you to call back.* **b.** a work of art by: *The investor paid $5 million for a Van Gogh.*

A, *Symbol.* **1.** in music, the sixth tone of the C major scale. **2.** a major blood group.

a-[1], *prefix.* **1.** *a-* is used before some nouns to make them into adverbs showing "place where": *a- + shore → ashore = on (or into) the shore.* **2.** *a* is also used before some verbs to make them into words showing a state or process: *a- + sleep → asleep (= sleeping); a- + blaze → ablaze (= blazing).*

a-[2], *prefix.* *a-* is used before some adjectives to mean "not": *a- + moral → amoral (= without morals); a- + tonal → atonal (= without tone).*

A., an abbreviation of: **1.** America. **2.** American.

a., an abbreviation of: **1.** acre. **2.** active. **3.** adjective. **4.** alto. **5.** ampere. **6.** answer.

A-1 or **A 1** (ā′wun′) /'ey'wʌn/ *adj.* A ONE.

AA, an abbreviation of: **1.** Alcoholics Anonymous (a group helping its members to overcome problems caused by alcohol.) **2.** antiaircraft.

A.A., an abbreviation of: Associate of Arts (a degree from a two-year college).

AAA, an abbreviation of: **1.** Amateur Athletic Association. **2.** American Automobile Association.

aard•vark (ärd′värk′) /'ɑrd,vɑrk/ *n.* [*count*] a large African mammal having a piglike snout and long sticky tongue for feeding on ants and termites.

AB (ā′bē′) /'ey'biy/ *Symbol.* a major blood group.

ab-, *prefix.* *ab-* is used before some words and roots to mean "off, away": *abnormal (= away from what is normal).* Compare A-[2].

A.B., an abbreviation of: Bachelor of Arts.

a•back (ə bak′) /ə'bæk/ *adv.* **—*Idiom.* be taken aback,** to be surprised: *The tourist was taken aback by the garbage on the streets.*

ab•a•cus (ab′ə kəs) /'æbəkəs/ *n.* [*count*], *pl.* **ab•a•cus•es, ab•a•ci** (ab′ə sī′, -kī′) /'æbə,say, -,kay/. a device for calculating, made of a frame with rods on which balls or beads are moved.

ab•a•lo•ne (ab′ə lō′nē) /,æbə'lowniy/ *n.* [*count*], *pl.* **-nes.** a kind of mollusk or shellfish with a flat, oval shell.

a•ban•don (ə ban′dən) /ə 'bændən/ *v.* **1.** [~ + *obj*] to leave completely and finally; desert: *like rats abandoning a sinking ship.* **2.** [~ + *obj*] to give up; withdraw from: *to abandon hope.* **3.** [~ + *obj* + *to* + *obj*] to give up the control of: *The army abandoned the city to the enemy.* **4.** [~ + *oneself* + *to* + *obj*] to feel an emotion strongly and without restraint or moderation (usually of grief or sadness or joy). **—*n.*** [*noncount*] **5.** [*usually: with* + ~] the feeling of an emotion in a strong and in a carefree way. **—a•ban′don•ment,** *n.* [*noncount*]

a•ban•doned (ə ban′dənd) /ə 'bændənd/ *adj.* left behind or deserted: *an abandoned building; an abandoned kitten.*

a•base (ə bās′) /ə'beys/ *v.* [~ + *oneself*], **a•based, a•bas•ing.** to lower (oneself) in rank, dignity, or honor; humble: *had to abase himself before his boss to keep his job.* **—a•base′ment,** *n.* [*noncount*]

a•bashed (ə basht′) /ə'bæʃt/ *adj.* [*usually: be* + ~] feeling embarrassed or ashamed: *I am abashed to confess it was my fault.* **—a•bash•ed•ly** (ə bash′id lē) /ə'bæʃıdliy/ *adv.* **—a•bash′ment,** *n.* [*noncount*]

a•bate (ə bāt′) /ə'beyt/ *v.,* **a•bat•ed, a•bat•ing. 1.** [~ + *obj*] to reduce in amount, degree, intensity, etc.; lessen; diminish: *to abate a tax.* **2.** [*no obj*] to diminish in amount, degree, or intensity: *The hurricane has abated. Her fears have abated somewhat.* **—a•bate′ment,** *n.* [*noncount*]

ab•at•toir (ab′ə twär′) /'æbə,twɑr/ *n.* [*count*] a slaughterhouse.

ab•bé (a bā′) /æ'bey/ *n.* [*count*], *pl.* **-bés.** (esp. in France) (a title of respect for) a clergyman.

ab•bess (ab′is) /'æbıs/ *n.* [*count*] a woman who is the head of a convent of nuns.

ab•bey (ab′ē) /'æbiy/ *n.* [*count*], *pl.* **-beys. 1.** a monastery under an abbot or a convent under an abbess. **2.** the church of such a monastery or convent: *Westminster is a famous abbey.*

ab•bot (ab′ət) /'æbət/ *n.* [*count*] a man who is the head or superior of a monastery.

abbr. or **abbrev.,** an abbreviation of: abbreviation.

ab•bre•vi•ate (ə brē′vē āt′) /ə'briyviy,eyt/ *v.* [~ + *obj*], **-at•ed, -at•ing. 1.** [*usually: be* + ~*-ed* + *to*] to shorten (a word or phrase) by omitting letters so that the shortened form stands for the whole word or phrase: *United Nations is frequently abbreviated to UN.* **2.** to make briefer: *He abbreviated his speech.* See -BREV-.

ab•bre•vi•a•tion (ə brē′vē ā′shən) /ə,briyviy'eyʃən/ *n.* [*count*] a shortened form of a word or phrase used to represent the whole, as *Dr.* for *Doctor.* In American English, many abbreviations are written with periods: the U. S.A. In British English, abbreviations are not written with periods: the USA. The stress in an abbreviation is often on the last letter: I.B.M. (ī bē em′) /ay biy 'ɛm/. Compare ACRONYM, CONTRACTION.

ABC's or **ABCs** (ā′bē′sēz′) /'ey,biy'siyz/ *n. pl.* **1.** the alphabet: *Children learn their ABC's in kindergarten.* **2.** the basic skills of any subject.

ab•di•cate (ab′di kāt′) /'æbdı,keyt/ *v.,* **-cat•ed, -cat•ing.** to give up (an important position, responsibility, authority, duties, a high office, etc.): [~ + *obj*]: *He abdicated the throne of England.* [*no obj*]: *He decided to abdicate.* **—ab•di•ca•tion** (ab′di kā′shən) /,æbdı'keyʃən/ *n.* [*noncount*]

ab•do•men (ab′də mən) /'æbdəmən/ *n.* [*count*] the part of the body between the chest and the legs; belly.

ab•dom•i•nal (ab dom′ə nl) /æb 'dɒmə nl/ *adj.* of, relating to, or located in the abdomen: *abdominal pains.*

ab•duct (ab dukt′) /æb'dʌkt/ *v.* [~ + *obj*] to carry off (a person) illegally and by force; kidnap. **—ab•duc•tion** (ab-duk′shən) /æb'dʌkʃən/ *n.* [*count*] **—ab•duc′tor,** *n.* [*count*] See -DUC-.

a•bed (ə bed′) /ə'bɛd/ *adv.* in bed: *He was abed with the flu.*

ab•er•ra•tion (ab′ə rā′shən) /,æbə'reyʃən/ *n.* [*count*] a way of behaving or acting that deviates from the usual or normal way: *A warm spell is an aberration in winter.* **—ab•er•rant** (ə ber′ənt, ab′ər-) /ə'bɛrənt, 'æbər-/ *adj.* **—ab′er•ra′tion•al,** *adj.*

a•bet (ə bet′) /ə'bɛt/ *v.* [~ + *obj*], **a•bet•ted, a•bet•ting.** to help, usually in doing something wrong: *a charge of abetting the enemy.* **—a•bet′ment,** *n.* [*noncount*] **—a•bet′tor, a•bet′ter,** *n.* [*count*]

a•bey•ance (ə bā′əns) /ə'beyəns/ *n.* [*noncount*] in a state of temporary inactivity: *to hold a question in abeyance.*

ab•hor (ab hôr′) /æb'hɔr/ *v.* [*not: be* + ~*-ing;* ~ + *obj*], **-horred, -hor•ring.** to hate very much; detest: *Gandhi abhorred violence all his life.* **—ab•hor•rence** (ab hôr′-əns, -hor′-) /æb'hɔrəns, -'hɒr-/ *n.* [*noncount*] See -HORR-.

ab•hor•rent (ab hôr′ənt, -hor′-) /æb'hɔrənt, -'hɒr-/ *adj.* **1.** causing hatred; detestable; loathsome: *an abhorrent murder.* **2.** [*be* + ~ + *to*] completely opposed to: *That theory was abhorrent to civilized thinking.* **—ab•hor′rent•ly,** *adv.* See -HORR-.

a•bide (ə bīd′) /ə'bayd/ *v.,* **a•bode** (ə bōd′) /ə'bowd/ or **a•bid•ed, a•bid•ing. 1.** [*no obj*] to remain; continue; stay: *Abide with me.* **2.** [*no obj*] to dwell; reside; have one's abode. **3.** [~ + *obj; often with a negative word or phrase*] to tolerate; *can't abide dishonesty.* **4. abide by,** [~ + *by* + *obj*] **a.** to comply with; agree to go along with: *to abide by the court's decision.* **b.** to remain faithful to; keep: *to abide by a promise.* **—a•bid′ance,** *n.* [*noncount*]

a•bid•ing (ə bī′ding) /ə'baydıŋ/ *adj.* continuing without change: *an abiding faith in people.* **—a•bid′ing•ly,** *adv.*

a•bil•i•ty (ə bil′i tē) /ə'bılıtiy/ *n., pl.* **-ties.** power or skill to do, make, or think; talent: [*noncount*]: *has the ability to do well.* [*count*]: *His abilities are many.* See -HABIL-.

-ability, *suffix.* *-ability,* a combination of -ABLE and -ITY, is used to form nouns from adjectives that end in *-able*: *capable (adjective)* → *capability (noun); reliable (adjective)* → *reliability (noun).*

ab•ject (ab′jekt, ab jekt′) /ˈæbdʒɛkt, æbˈdʒɛkt/ *adj.* **1.** [*before a noun*] hopeless or wretched: *abject poverty.* **2.** showing no courage; contemptible: *an abject coward.* —**ab•ject′ly,** *adv.* —**ab•ject′ness,** *n.* [*noncount*] See -JEC-.

ab•jure (ab jŏŏr′) /æbˈdʒʊr/ *v.* [~ + *obj*], **-jured, -jur•ing.** to give up (a belief) formally or under oath; renounce: *abjured allegiance to her homeland.* See -JUR-.

ab•la•tive (ab′lə tiv) /ˈæblətɪv/ *adj.* **1.** of or concerning a case in grammar used to mark the starting point of an action and, in Latin, to indicate how something is done, or by whom or what it was done: *In the Latin translation of "from Tusculum," the Latin word "Tusculo" is in the ablative case.* —*n.* [*count*] **2.** the ablative case. **3.** a word or other form in this case. See -lat-[1].

a•blaze (ə blāz′) /əˈbleyz/ *adj.* [*be* + ~] **1.** on fire: *the forest was ablaze.* **2.** gleaming with or as if with light: *The sky was ablaze with stars.*

a•ble (ā′bəl) /ˈeybəl/ *adj.* (for def. 2) **a•bler, a•blest. 1.** [*be* + ~ + *to* + *verb*] having the necessary power, skill, knowledge, or resources to do something: *able to read music after just a few lessons.* **2.** having or showing unusual talent, intelligence, skill, or knowledge: *an able leader.* —**a•bly,** *adv.* —**Related Words.** ABLE is an adjective that usually comes after some form of BE, ABLY is an adverb, ABILITY is a noun: *John is able to run fast. He did the work ably and efficiently. John has the ability to run fast.* See -HABIL-.

-able, *suffix. -able* is used to form adjectives from verbs, with the meaning "capable of, fit for, tending to": *teach + -able* → *teachable (= capable of being taught); photograph + -able* → *photographable = (fit for photographing).* Compare -IBLE.

a′ble-bod′ied, *adj.* having a strong, healthy body; physically fit: *able-bodied soldiers.*

a•bloom (ə blōōm′) /əˈbluwm/ *adj.* [*be* + ~ + *with*] in bloom; blossoming; flowering: *The meadow was abloom with wildflowers.*

ab•lu•tion (ə blōō′shən) /əˈbluwʃən/ *n.* [*count*] a cleansing with water or other liquid, esp. as a religious ritual.

ABM, an abbreviation of: antiballistic missile.

ab•ne•gate (ab′ni gāt′) /ˈæbnɪˌgeyt/ *v.* [~ + *obj*], **-gat•ed, -gat•ing.** to refuse or deny (rights, comforts, etc.) to oneself; renounce; give up. —**ab•ne•ga•tion** (ab′ni gā′shən) /ˌæbnɪˈgeyʃən/ *n.* [*noncount*]: *the abnegation of worldly possessions and pleasures.* See -NEG-.

ab•nor•mal (ab nôr′məl) /æbˈnɔrməl/ *adj.* not normal or usual: *His wild behavior that day was clearly abnormal.* —**ab•nor•mal•i•ty** (ab′nôr mal′i tē) /ˌæbnɔrˈmælɪtiy/ *n.* [*count*], *pl.* **-ties.** —**ab•nor′mal•ly,** *adv.* See -NORM-.

a•board (ə bôrd′, ə bōrd′) /əˈbɔrd, əˈbowrd/ *adv., prep.* on, in, or into (a ship, train, airplane, etc.): *The ship sank, drowning all who were aboard. They went aboard the ship.*

a•bode[1] (ə bōd′) /əˈbowd/ *n.* [*count*] a place in which a person resides; residence; home.

a•bode[2] (ə bōd′) /əˈbowd/ *v.* a pt. and pp. of ABIDE.

a•bol•ish (ə bol′ish) /əˈbɒlɪʃ/ *v.* [~ + *obj*] to do away with completely: *to abolish slavery; abolish a law.*

ab•o•li•tion (ab′ə lish′ən) /ˌæbəˈlɪʃən/ *n.* [*noncount*] the act of abolishing or the state of being abolished, esp. the legal termination of slavery in the U.S. —**ab′o•li′tion•ism,** *n.* [*noncount*] —**ab′o•li′tion•ist,** *n.* [*count*], *adj.*

A-bomb (ā′bom′) /ˈeyˌbɒm/ *n.* ATOMIC BOMB.

a•bom•i•na•ble (ə bom′ə nə bəl) /əˈbɒmənəbəl/ *adj.* **1.** very hateful; detestable: *an abominable murder.* **2.** very unpleasant: *abominable weather.* **3.** very bad; deplorable: *abominable taste in clothes.* —**a•bom′i•na•bly,** *adv.*

a•bom•i•nate (ə bom′ə nāt′) /əˈbɒməˌneyt/ *v.* [~ + *obj*], **-nat•ed, -nat•ing.** to feel great dislike for; hate.

a•bom•i•na•tion (ə bom′ə nā′shən) /əˌbɒməˈneyʃən/ *n.* **1.** [*count*] something abominable. **2.** [*noncount*] great dislike: *She looked at him with abomination.*

ab•o•rig•i•nal (ab′ə rij′ə nl) /ˌæbəˈrɪdʒənl̩/ *adj.* **1.** [*usually before a noun*] original or earliest known: *the aboriginal people of the region.* —*n.* [*count*] **2.** ABORIGINE. —**ab′o•rig′i•nal•ly,** *adv.* See -ORI-.

ab•o•rig•i•ne (ab′ə rij′ə nē) /ˌæbəˈrɪdʒəniy/ *n.* [*count*] one of the original or earliest known inhabitants of a country or region, esp. of Australia. See -ORI-.

a•born•ing (ə bôr′ning) /əˈbɔrnɪŋ/ *adv.* in birth; before being carried out: *The scheme died aborning.*

a•bort (ə bôrt′) /əˈbɔrt/ *v.* **1.** [*no obj*] (of a female) to bring forth a fetus before it is able to live. **2.** [~ + *obj*] to cause to bring forth (a fetus) before it is able to live. **3.** [~ + *obj*] to cause (a pregnancy) to terminate. **4.** to (cause to) fail or stop too early; to come to an end: [*no obj*]: *The missile flight aborted.* [~ + *obj*]: *They aborted the space flight.* —*n.* [*count*] **5.** the ending of a missile flight, mission, etc., before completion: *Mission control, that's an abort.* See -ORI-.

a•bor•tion (ə bôr′shən) /əˈbɔrʃən/ *n.* **1.** [*noncount*] the ending of a pregnancy before term. **2.** [*count*] a procedure for ending a pregnancy before term. —**a•bor′tion•ist,** *n.* [*count*] See -ORI-.

a•bor•tive (ə bôr′tiv) /əˈbɔrtɪv/ *adj.* failing to succeed; unsuccessful: *an abortive rebellion.*

a•bound (ə bound′) /əˈbawnd/ *v.* **1.** [*no obj*] to occur or exist in great amount or numbers: *a stream in which trout abound.* **2.** [~ + *in* + *obj*] to be rich or well supplied: *The region abounds in coal.*

a•bout (ə bout′) /əˈbawt/ *prep.* **1.** concerning; on the subject of: *a novel about the Civil War.* Compare ON. **2.** connected or associated with: *an air of mystery about him.* **3.** near; close to; approximately: *She's about my height.* **4.** within the confines of: *somewhere about the house.* **5.** so as to be of use to: *Keep your wits about you.* **6.** here or there; in or on: *wandered about the neighborhood.* **7.** engaged in or occupied with: *While you're about it, please get me a soda.* **8.** having as a main concern or central purpose: *Fame was what his career was about.* —*adv.* **9.** nearly; almost: *Dinner is about ready.* **10.** nearby; not far off: *My papers are somewhere about.* **11.** in the opposite direction: *She swung the car about.* **12.** here and there: *to move furniture about; papers strewn about.* —*adj.* [*be* + ~] **13.** moving around; astir: *was up and about at dawn.* **14.** in existence; prevalent: *The flu is about.* —***Idiom.*** **15. be about to,** [~ + *verb*] be ready or likely to do something: *We're about to eat dinner.* Compare BE GOING TO under GO. **16. not about to,** not intending or likely to: *not about to lend you money.* **17. what about,** what plans or ideas do you have concerning (the person or thing mentioned)? *What about the money you hid away? (= What plans do you have for the money you hid away?)* **18. how about,** (used to make an offer or suggestion): *How about a cup of tea?* **19. It's about time,** the time has arrived to do (something): *It's about time to leave.* —**Usage.** Both ON and ABOUT mean "concerning"; ABOUT is used when the information given is of a more general nature and not too technical: *a romantic novel* ABOUT *the Civil War.* ON is used when the information is more particular, as by being scholarly or serious: *an important article* ON *the Civil War.*

a•bout-face (*n.* ə bout′fās′, ə bout′fās′; *v.* ə bout′fās′) /*n.* əˈbawtˌfeys, əˈbawtˈfeys; *v.* əˌbawtˈfeys/ *n., v.,* **-faced, -fac•ing.** —*n.* [*count*] **1.** (in military or similar marching) a 180° turn from the position of attention. **2.** a complete change in position, direction, principle, or thinking. —*v.* [*no obj*] **3.** to perform an about-face.

a•bove (ə buv′) /əˈbʌv/ *adv.* **1.** in, at, or to a higher place, position, or rank: *saw the rain clouds above.* **2.** higher in quantity or number; over: *persons age 18 and above.* **3.** mentioned or described before or earlier, esp. in a book or other piece of writing: *the remark quoted above.* **4.** higher than zero on the Fahrenheit scale: *In winter it's often only five above (= five degrees above zero).* —*prep.* **5.** in or to a higher place than; over: *to fly above the clouds.* **6.** more in quantity or number than; in excess of; over: *persons above 18 years of age.* **7.** superior in rank, authority, or standing to: *A major is above a captain.* **8.** not subject to: *above suspicion.* **9.** of too fine a character for: *She's above such trickery.* **10.** beyond, esp. north of: *six miles above Baltimore.* —*adj.* **11.** said, mentioned, or written above: *the above explanation.* —*n.* [*noncount*] **12.** [*the* + ~] things discussed or written about earlier: *All the above just proves what I've been saying.* **13.** heaven: *a gift from above.* **14.** a higher authority: *an order from above.* —***Idiom.*** **15. above all,** most importantly; principally. —**Usage.** Both ABOVE and OVER can mean "higher than". In expressions with numbers, esp. in measurements, it is more common to use OVER to mean "more than": *Over 600 students are enrolled here.* But for numbers that are thought of as on a vertical scale of measurement, such as the temperature on a thermometer, ABOVE is used: *Her temperature was almost three degrees above normal. Her SAT scores were well above average.*

a•bove•board (ə buv′bôrd′, -bōrd′) /əˈbʌvˌbɔrd, -ˌbowrd/ *adj.* without tricks or disguise; in the open.

ab•ra•ca•dab•ra (ab′rə kə dab′rə) /ˌæbrəkəˈdæbrə/ *n.*

[*noncount*] **1.** meaningless talk; gibberish; nonsense. **2.** a word used in magic tricks.

a•brade (ə brād′) /ə'breyd/ *v.* [~ + *obj*], **a•brad•ed, a•brad•ing.** to wear off (skin) by scraping or rubbing: *The harsh leather abraded his skin.*

a•bra•sion (ə brā′zhən) /ə'breyʒən/ *n.* **1.** [*noncount*] the act or process of abrading. **2.** [*count*] a scraped spot or area: *They found many abrasions on his leg.* See -RASE-.

a•bra•sive (ə brā′siv, -ziv) /ə'breysɪv, -zɪv/ *adj.* **1.** tending to abrade. **2.** annoyingly harsh: *an abrasive personality.* **—*n.*** [*count*] **3.** any material or substance used for grinding, polishing, smoothing, etc., as sandpaper. **—a•bra′sive•ly,** *adv.* **—a•bra′sive•ness,** *n.* [*noncount*]

a•breast (ə brest′) /ə'brɛst/ *adv., adj.* **1.** side by side; beside each other in a line: *They walked two abreast.* **—*Idiom.* 2. be** or **keep abreast of,** be informed about; be aware of; be up-to-date: *kept abreast of the new developments.*

a•bridge (ə brij′) /ə'brɪdʒ/ *v.* [~ + *obj*], **a•bridged, a•bridg•ing.** to shorten the length of: *to abridge a speech from an hour to ten minutes.* **—a•bridg′ment, a•bridge′ment,** *n.* [*count*] See -BREV-.

a•broad (ə brôd′) /ə'brɒd/ *adv.* **1.** in or to a foreign country or countries: *famous at home and abroad.* **2.** spread around; in circulation: *Rumors were abroad.*

ab•ro•gate (ab′rə gāt′) /'æbrə,geyt/ *v.* [~ + *obj*], **-gat•ed, -gat•ing.** to abolish by official means: *The dictator abrogated the treaty.* **—ab•ro•ga•tion** (ab′rə gā′shən) /,æbrə'geyʃən/ *n.* [*count*] See -ROGA-.

ab•rupt (ə brupt′) /ə'brʌpt/ *adj.* **1.** sudden or unexpected: *an abrupt departure.* **2.** so short as to be unfriendly or impolite: *an abrupt reply.* **3.** changing suddenly; sharp: *an abrupt turn in a road.* **—ab•rupt′ly,** *adv.* **—ab•rupt′ness,** *n.* [*noncount*] See -RUPT-.

ab•scess (ab′ses) /'æbsɛs/ *n.* [*count*] a swelling in the body caused by a gathering of pus: *She had a painful abscess in her gums.* **—ab′scessed,** *adj.*

ab•scond (ab skond′) /æb'skɒnd/ *v.* [*no obj; (~ + with + obj)*] to leave in a sudden and secret manner, esp. to avoid capture and legal prosecution: *The cashier absconded with the money.*

ab•sence (ab′səns) /'æbsəns/ *n.* **1.** [*noncount*] the state of being away or not being present: *Absence makes the heart grow fonder.* **2.** [*count*] a period of time of being away: *an absence of several weeks.* **3.** [*noncount*] lack; deficiency: *the absence of proof.*

ab•sent (*adj.* ab′sənt; *v.* ab sent′, ab′sənt) /*adj.* ˈæbsənt; *v.* æbˈsɛnt, ˈæbsənt/ *adj.* **1.** not in a certain place at a given time; not present: *He was absent from class again.* **2.** lacking; nonexistent: *Revenge was absent from his mind.* **3.** [*before a noun*] not attentive; preoccupied; absent-minded: *an absent stare.* **—*v.*** [~ + *oneself* (+ *from* + *obj*)] **4.** to take or keep (oneself) away: *to absent oneself from a meeting.* **—ab′sent•ly,** *adv.* **—Related Words.** ABSENT is an adjective, ABSENCE is a noun: *John was absent from school. Any more absences and John will be dropped from the course.*

ab•sen•tee (ab′sən tē′) /,æbsən'tiy/ *n.* [*count*] a person who is absent. **—ab′sen•tee′ism,** *n.* [*noncount*]: *a high rate of absenteeism from work.*

ab′sent-mind′ed or **ab′sent•mind′ed,** *adj.* preoccupied with one's thoughts so as to be unaware or forgetful of other matters. **—ab′sent-mind′ed•ly,** *adv.* **—ab′sent-mind′ed•ness,** *n.* [*noncount*]

ab•sinthe or **ab•sinth** (ab′sinth) /'æbsɪnθ/ *n.* [*noncount*] a strong green liqueur having a bitter licorice flavor.

ab•so•lute (ab′sə lo͞ot′, ab′sə lo͞ot′) /'æbsə,luwt, ,æbsə'luwt/ *adj.* **1.** [*before a noun*] total and complete; perfect: *That's an absolute lie!* **2.** not limited by laws or a constitution: *an absolute monarch.* **3.** [*before a noun*] not depending on comparison with other things: *absolute knowledge.* **—ab′so•lute′ness,** *n.* [*noncount*]

ab•so•lute•ly (ab′sə lo͞ot′lē) /,æbsə'luwtliy/ *adv.* **1.** completely; totally: *It is absolutely necessary to finish on time.* **2.** (used as an interjection) certainly: *Aren't you tired after studying all night? — Absolutely!*

ab′solute ze′ro, *n.* [*noncount*] the temperature of −273.16°C (−459.69°F), the point at which all molecules stop moving.

ab•so•lu•tion (ab′sə lo͞o′shən) /,æbsə'luwʃən/ *n.* [*noncount*] an act or instance of absolving, esp. the remission of sin given by a priest in the sacrament of reconciliation. See -SOLV-.

ab•solve (ab zolv′, -solv′) /æb'zɒlv, -'sɒlv/ *v.* [~ + *obj* + *of/from* + *obj; often: be ~ed of/from*], **-solved, -solv•ing. 1.** to free from guilt or blame: *The accused captain was absolved of any wrongdoing.* **2.** to release from a duty, obligation, or responsibility: *to be absolved from one's oath.* **3.** to grant remission of sins to. See -SOLV-.

ab•sorb (ab sôrb′, -zôrb′) /æb'sɔrb, -'zɔrb/ *v.* [~ + *obj*] **1.** to suck up or drink in (a liquid); soak up: *A sponge absorbs water.* **2.** to take (a company, organization, etc.) in and make it part of a larger group; assimilate; incorporate: *The empire absorbed many nations.* **3.** to get the full attention of: *This book will absorb the serious reader.* **4.** to take in without echo or bouncing: *walls that absorb sound.* **5.** to take in and utilize: *to absorb information.* **6.** to pay for (costs, taxes, etc.): *The big company absorbed the losses of the small company it took over.*

ab•sorb•ed (ab sôrbd′, -zôrbd′) /æb'sɔrbd, -'zɔrbd/ *adj.* [*usually:* ~ + *in/by* + *obj*] fully occupied: *She was absorbed in reading her book.*

ab•sorb•ent (ab sôr′bənt, -zôr′-) /æb'sɔrbənt, -'zɔr-/ *adj.* **1.** capable of absorbing: *absorbent bandages.* **—*n.*** [*count*] **2.** a substance that absorbs. **—ab•sorb′en•cy,** *n.* [*noncount*]

ab•sorb•ing (ab sôr′bing, -zôr′-) /æb 'sɔrbɪŋ, -'zɔr-/ *adj.* keeping someone's full attention: *an absorbing book.*

ab•sorp•tion (ab sôrp′shən, -zôrp′-) /æb'sɔrpʃən, -'zɔrp-/ *n.* [*noncount*] **1.** the process of absorbing or being absorbed. **2.** complete involvement: *She read her book with total absorption.*

ab•stain (ab stān′) /æb'steyn/ *v.* [*no obj*] **1.** [~ + *from* + *obj*] to keep oneself from doing, esp. from something regarded as improper or unhealthy; refrain: *to abstain from eating meat; She abstained from smoking and drinking for a month.* **2.** to keep oneself from casting one's vote: *a referendum in which two delegates abstained.* **—ab•stain′er,** *n.* [*count*] See -TAIN-.

ab•ste•mi•ous (ab stē′mē əs) /æb'stiymiyəs/ *adj.* sparing and moderate in eating and drinking; temperate: *He was abstemious in his habits.*

ab•sten•tion (ab sten′shən) /æb 'stɛnʃən/ *n.* [*noncount*] the practice or act of abstaining.

ab•sti•nence (ab′stə nəns) /'æbstənəns/ *n.* [*noncount*] the keeping of oneself from enjoyment of something: *abstinence from alcohol.* **—ab′sti•nent,** *adj.* See -TEN-.

ab•stract (*adj.* ab strakt′, ab′strakt; *n.* ab′strakt; *v.* abstrakt′) /*adj.* æbˈstrækt, ˈæbstrækt; *n.* ˈæbstrækt; *v.* æbˈstrækt/ *adj.* **1.** thought of apart from concrete realities or specific objects: *an abstract idea.* **2.** (of a word) describing a quality or idea apart from any specific object or instance: *an abstract word like* justice. **3.** difficult to understand; abstruse: *an abstract theory.* **4.** (of art) emphasizing line, color, and shape rather than specific objects or forms. **—*n.*** [*count*] **5.** a summary of a text, technical article, speech, etc: *Please include a 250-word abstract of the paper.* **—*v.*** [~ + *obj* (+ *from*)] **6.** to make a summary of or from (a piece of writing, a speech, etc.); summarize: *abstracted the main points from the essay.* **—*Idiom.* 7. in the abstract,** without reference to a specific object or instance; in theory: *He understood the idea in the abstract.* **—ab•stract′ly,** *adv.* **—ab′stract•ness,** *n.* [*noncount*] See -TRAC-.

ab•stract•ed (ab strak′tid) /æb'stræktɪd/ *adj.* lost in thought; preoccupied: *an abstracted scientist.*

ab•strac•tion (ab strak′shən) /æb'strækʃən/ *n.* **1.** [*count*] an abstract or general idea or term: *The idea of injustice was just an abstraction to her.* **2.** [*noncount*] absent-mindedness; inattention.

ab•struse (ab stro͞os′) /æb'struws/ *adj.* hard to understand: *abstruse theories of time and space.* **—ab•struse′ly,** *adv.* **—ab•struse′ness,** *n.* [*noncount*]

ab•surd (ab sûrd′, -zûrd′) /æb'sɜrd, -'zɜrd/ *adj.* without sense or logic; contrary to all reason or common sense: *Buying outdated computers now is clearly absurd.* **—ab•surd′i•ty,** *n., pl.* **-ties.** [*noncount*]: *the absurdity of paying taxes twice.* [*count*]: *full of jokes and other absurdities.* **—ab•surd′ly,** *adv.* **—ab•surd′ness,** *n.* [*noncount*]

a•bun•dance (ə bun′dəns) /ə'bʌndəns/ *n.* a great amount or quantity of: [*count; usually singular*]: *has an abundance of natural resources.* [*noncount*]: *has resources in abundance.*

a•bun•dant (ə bun′dənt) /ə'bʌndənt/ *adj.* **1.** present in great quantity; more than adequate: *an abundant supply of water.* **2.** [*after a noun*] well supplied; abounding: *a river abundant in salmon.* **—a•bun′dant•ly,** *adv.*

a•buse (*v.* ə byo͞oz′; *n.* ə byo͞os′) /*v.* ə'byuwz; *n.* ə'byuws/ *v.,* **a•bused, a•bus•ing,** *n.* **—*v.*** [~ + *obj*] **1.** to use wrongly or improperly; misuse: *to abuse authority.* **2.** to treat in a harmful or injurious way: *to abuse a horse by making it run too far.* **3.** to speak insultingly or harshly to or about: *to abuse someone over the tele-*

phone. **4.** to mistreat physically or sexually. **—*n.* 5.** wrong, improper, or excessive use; misuse: [*noncount*]: *drug abuse.* [*count*]: *That act was an abuse of power.* **6.** [*noncount*] harsh, coarse, insulting language. **7.** [*noncount*] harsh treatment: *The hostages suffered abuse during their captivity.* **8.** [*noncount*] physical or sexual mistreatment. **—a•bu•sive** (ə byōō′siv) /ə'byuwsɪv/ *adj.* **—a•bu•sive•ly,** *adv.*

a•but (ə but′) /ə'bʌt/ *v.,* **a•but•ted, a•but•ting.** to be adjacent; touch or join at the edge or border: [~ + *on/upon/against* + *obj*]: *The garden abuts on the next yard.* [~ + *obj*]: *The garden abuts the next yard.*

a•but•ment (ə but′mənt) /ə'bʌtmənt/ *n.* [*count*] a place where projecting parts meet, as in an arch.

a•buzz (ə buz′) /ə'bʌz/ *adj.* [*be* + ~ + *with*] alive with activity or talk: *The place was abuzz with rumors.*

a•bys•mal (ə biz′məl) /ə'bɪzməl/ *adj.* **1.** of or like an abyss: *abysmal depths.* **2.** extremely bad or severe: *abysmal weather.* **—a•bys′mal•ly,** *adv.*

a•byss (ə bis′) /ə'bɪs/ *n.* [*count*] **1.** a deep space, hole, or cavity too vast to be measured. **2.** the lowest or most hopeless depths; hell.

a•byss•al (ə bis′əl) /ə'bɪsəl/ *adj.* **1.** of or like an abyss; too great to be measured or understood. **2.** of or concerning the deepest areas of the ocean.

AC, an abbreviation of: **1.** air conditioning. **2.** Also, **ac, a.c., A.C.** alternating current.

A/C or **a/c,** an abbreviation of: **1.** account. **2.** air conditioning.

a•ca•cia (ə kā′shə) /ə'keyʃə/ *n.* [*count*], *pl.* **-cias.** a small tree or shrub with clusters of small yellow flowers.

ac•a•dem•ic (ak′ə dem′ik) /,ækə'dɛmɪk/ *adj.* **1.** [*before a noun*] of or relating to a school, esp. one for higher education: *an academic institution.* **2.** of or relating to school subjects that teach general intellectual skills rather than specific job skills: *academic subjects like English and mathematics.* **3.** not practical or directly useful: *Whether she wanted to come or not is an academic question because she's here now.* **—*n.*** [*count*] **4.** a student or teacher at a college or university. **—ac′a•dem′i•cal•ly,** *adv.*

ac•a•de•mi•cian (ak′ə də mish′ən, ə kad′ə-) /,ækədə'mɪʃən, ə,kædə-/ *n.* [*count*] a member of an association or institution for the advancement of arts, sciences, or letters.

a•cad•e•my (ə kad′ə mē) /ə'kædəmiy/ *n.* [*count*], *pl.* **-mies. 1.** a secondary or high school, esp. a private one. **2.** an association or institution for the advancement of art, literature, or science. **3.** a school or college for special training: *a military academy.*

a•can•thus (ə kan′thəs) /ə'kænθəs/ *n., pl.* **-thus•es, -thi** (-thī) /-θay/. a plant having spiny or toothed leaves and showy white or purplish flowers.

a cap•pel•la (ä′ kə pel′ə) /,ɑ kə'pɛlə/ *adv., adj. Music.* without instrumental accompaniment.

ac•cede (ak sēd′) /æk'siyd/ *v.* [~ + *to* + *obj*], **-ced•ed, -ced•ing. 1.** to agree; assent: *to accede to a request.* **2.** to attain or assume an office: *to accede to the throne.* See -CEDE-.

ac•cel•er•ate (ak sel′ə rāt′) /æk'sɛlə,reyt/ *v.,* **-at•ed, -at•ing. 1.** to (cause to) develop, progress, or advance faster: [*no obj*]: *The unemployment rate accelerated.* [~ + *obj*]: *Those policies accelerated unemployment.* **2.** to increase the speed (of): [~ + *obj*]: *The driver accelerated the car.* [*no obj*]: *The car accelerated.* **3.** [~ + *obj*] to hasten the occurrence of: *The economic policies accelerated the recession.* **—ac•cel•er•a•tion** (ak sel′ə rā′shən) /æk,sɛlə'reyʃən/ *n.* [*noncount*] See -CELER-.

ac•cel•er•a•tor (ak sel′ə rā′tər) /æk'sɛlə,reytər/ *n.* [*count*] a device, esp. a pedal, for controlling the speed of a motor vehicle engine. See -CELER-.

ac•cent (*n.* ak′sent; *v. also* ak sent′) /*n.* 'æksɛnt; *v. also* æk'sɛnt/ *n.* [*count*] **1.** the amount of prominence of a spoken sound, in terms of pronunciation, pitch, or a combination of these: *The accent in the word "absorb" is on the second syllable, "-sorb".* **2.** a mark indicating stress (as ′, ′ or ', ,), vowel quality (as French grave \`, acute ´, circumflex ^), pitch, etc. Also called **accent mark**. **3.** a way of pronouncing sounds, words, etc., that is usually found in the speech of a particular person, group, or locality: *a southern accent.* **4.** a way of pronouncing words that is recognized as being of foreign origin: *still speaks with an accent after ten years.* **5.** special attention or emphasis: *Our supervisor puts an accent on reliability.* **6.** a symbol used to indicate a particular unit of measure, such as feet (′) or inches (″), minutes (′) or seconds (″). **—*v.*** [~ + *obj*] **7.** to pronounce (a sound) with extra loudness, extra length, or higher pitch: *Accent the second syllable in the word "absorb".* **8.** to mark with a written accent or accents. **9.** to emphasize; accentuate. **—ac•cen′tu•al** (-sen′chōō əl) /-'sɛntʃuwəl/ *adj.*

ac•cen•tu•ate (ak sen′chōō āt′) /æk'sɛntʃuw,eyt/ *v.* [~ + *obj*], **-at•ed, -at•ing.** to give emphasis, importance, or prominence to: *Try to accentuate the positive aspects.* **—ac•cen•tu•a•tion** (ak sen′chōō ā′shən) /æk,sɛntʃuw'eyʃən/ *n.* [*noncount*]

ac•cept (ak sept′) /æk'sɛpt/ *v.* [~ + *obj*] **1.** to take or receive (something offered) willingly: *She accepted my apology.* **2.** to respond or answer affirmatively to: *to accept an invitation.* **3.** to undertake the responsibilities of: *to accept a job.* **4.** to admit formally, such as to a college or club. **5.** to include in a group: *Her classmates finally accepted the new girl.* **6.** to accommodate or reconcile oneself to: *to accept a painful situation.* **7.** to regard as true or sound; believe: *can't accept such a wild excuse.* **8.** to receive (a transplanted organ or tissue) without a bad reaction. Compare REJECT (def. 7). See -CEP-.

ac•cept•a•ble (ak sep′tə bəl) /æk'sɛptəbəl/ *adj.* **1.** worthy or capable of being accepted or received. **2.** meeting only minimum requirements: *barely acceptable school grades.* **3.** capable of being endured; tolerable: *acceptable risks.* **—ac•cept•a•bil•i•ty** (ak sep′tə bil′i tē) /æk,sɛptə'bɪlɪtiy/ **ac•cept′a•ble•ness,** *n.* [*noncount*] **—ac•cept′a•bly,** *adv.* See -CEP-.

ac•cept•ance (ak sep′təns) /æk'sɛptəns/ *n.* **1.** [*noncount*] the process or act of accepting. **2.** favorable reception; approval; favor: [*noncount*]: *I got a letter of acceptance.* [*count*]: *Acceptances to my invitations kept pouring in.* **3.** [*noncount*] the act of assenting or believing: *general acceptance of her theory.* See -CEP-.

ac•cept•ed (ak sep′tid) /æk'sɛptɪd/ *adj.* [*before a noun*] generally approved: *accepted principles of civilized behavior.*

ac•cept•ing (ak sep′ting) /æk'sɛptɪŋ/ *adj.* [*be* + ~ + *of*] willing to look upon or regard people or situations in a tolerant way: *Those people are accepting of hardship.* See -CEP-.

ac•cess (ak′ses) /'æksɛs/ *n.* [*noncount*] **1.** the ability or right to enter, approach, or use: *Who has access to a computer?* **2.** a way or means of approach or entrance: *The dead-end street was the only access to their house.* **—*v.*** [~ + *obj*] **3. a.** to enter the system of (a computer). **b.** to obtain (information) from a computer: *He accessed the data from his laptop.* See -CESS-.

ac•ces•si•ble (ak ses′ə bəl) /æk'sɛsəbəl/ *adj.* **1.** easy to approach, enter, or use: *The house was easily accessible.* **2.** available: *money easily accessible from a cash machine.* **—ac•ces•si•bil•i•ty** (ak ses′ə bil′i tē) /æk,sɛsə'bɪlɪtiy/ *n.* [*noncount*] **—ac•ces′si•bly,** *adv.* See -CESS-.

ac•ces•sion (ak sesh′ən) /æk'sɛʃən/ *n.* [*noncount*] the act of taking up a high office or position: *her accession to the throne of Russia.* See -CESS-.

ac•ces•so•ry (ak ses′ə rē) /æk'sɛsəriy/ *n.* [*count*], *pl.* **-ries. 1.** an extra part that improves or completes the basic part: *The car's accessories included a CD player.* **2.** *Law.* a person who, although absent, assists in committing a felony. See -CESS-.

ac•ci•dent (ak′si dənt) /'æksɪdənt/ *n.* [*count*] **1.** an unfortunate happening that occurs unintentionally: *An accident occurred on the icy road.* **2.** any event that happens unexpectedly: *Finding her was a happy accident.* **3. by accident,** unexpectedly: *I met her quite by accident.* See -CIDE-.

ac•ci•den•tal (ak′si den′tl) /,æksɪ'dɛntḷ/ *adj.* happening by accident and not by plan: *an accidental death.* **—ac′ci•den′tal•ly,** *adv.*

ac•claim (ə klām′) /ə'kleym/ *v.* [~ + *obj*] **1.** to praise or greet with loud or enthusiastic approval: *The critics acclaimed her book.* **—*n.*** [*noncount*] **2.** loud or enthusiastic approval or praise; acclamation. See -CLAIM-.

ac•cla•ma•tion (ak′lə mā′shən) /,æklə'meyʃən/ *n.* [*noncount*] **1.** a loud demonstration of welcome or approval: *The speech was greeted with acclamation.* **2.** an affirmative vote by shouts or applause instead of by ballot: *was elected by acclamation.*

ac•cli•mate (ak′lə māt′, ə klī′mit) /'æklə,meyt, ə'klaymɪt/ *v.* [~ *(+ obj)* + *to* + *obj*], **-mat•ed, -mat•ing.** to accustom or become accustomed to a new climate or environment: *The foreigners acclimated (themselves) to the tropical weather after a few months.* **—ac•cli•ma•tion** (ak′lə mā′shən) /,æklə'meyʃən/ *n.* [*noncount*]

ac•cli•ma•tize (ə klī′mə tīz′) /ə'klaymə,tayz/ *v.* [~ *(+ obj)* + *to* + *obj*], **-tized, -tiz•ing.** to acclimate. **—ac•cli•**

ma•ti•za•tion (ə klī′mə tə zā′shən) /əˌklaymətə'zeyʃən/ *n.* [*noncount*]

ac•cliv•i•ty (ə kliv′i tē) /ə'klɪvɪtiy/ *n.* [*count*], *pl.* **-ties.** an upward slope, as of a hill.

ac•co•lade (ak′ə lād′, -läd′) /'ækəˌleyd, -ˌlad/ *n.* [*count*] any award, honor, or notice of praise.

ac•com•mo•date (ə kom′ə dāt′) /ə'kɒməˌdeyt/ *v.* [~ + *obj*], **-dat•ed, -dat•ing. 1.** to do a favor to or for; provide for suitably: *accommodated both new and old customers.* **2.** [*not: be* + ~*ing*] to have enough room or lodging for; to make room for: *The convention center can accommodate over 400 guests.* **3.** to adjust: *She accommodated herself to the new rules.* See -MOD-. **—Syn.** See CONTAIN.

ac•com•mo•dat•ing (ə kom′ə dā′ting) /ə'kɒməˌdeytɪŋ/ *adj.* eager to help or please; obliging: *The guide was very accommodating when we asked to see the old ruins.*

ac•com•mo•da•tion (ə kom′ə dā′shən) /əˌkɒmə'deyʃən/ *n.* **1.** [*count*] Usually, **accommodations.** [*plural*] lodging: *The accommodations at that hotel were quite luxurious.* **2.** adjustment or reconciliation: [*noncount*]: *seeking accommodation from both sides in the dispute.* [*count*]: *made a small accommodation to their request.* **3.** [*count*] (in business) a loan.

ac•com•pa•ni•ment (ə kum′pə ni mənt, ə kump′ni-) /ə'kʌmpənɪmənt, ə'kʌmpnɪ-/ *n.* [*count*] something that accompanies, esp. a musical part supporting the principal part: *a piano accompaniment.*

ac•com•pa•nist (ə kum′pə nist, ə kump′nist) /ə'kʌmpənɪst, ə'kʌmpnɪst/ *n.* [*count*] a performer of musical accompaniments.

ac•com•pa•ny (ə kum′pə nē) /ə'kʌmpəniy/ *v.* [~ + *obj*], **-nied, -ny•ing. 1.** to go with: *She accompanied me on that journey* **2.** to be in association with: *Rain accompanied the thunder.* **3.** to play or sing an accompaniment to: *I accompanied her on guitar.*

ac•com•plice (ə kom′plis) /ə'kɒmplɪs/ *n.* [*count*] a person who knowingly helps another in a crime. See -PLIC-.

ac•com•plish (ə kom′plish) /ə'kɒmplɪʃ/ *v.* [~ + *obj*] to bring to a successful conclusion or end; achieve: *The pilot accomplished his mission.*

ac•com•plished (ə kom′plisht) /ə'kɒmplɪʃt/ *adj.* skilled; expert: *His daughter is an accomplished pilot.*

ac•com•plish•ment (ə kom′plish mənt) /ə'kɒmplɪʃmənt/ *n.* **1.** [*noncount*] the act of accomplishing. **2.** [*count*] anything accomplished, esp. an achievement done with skill.

ac•cord (ə kôrd′) /ə'kɔrd/ *v.* **1.** [~ + *with* + *obj*] to agree: *Refunding money without a receipt doesn't accord with company policy.* **2.** [~ + *obj* + *obj*] to grant; bestow: *They accorded the president great honor.* **—*n.*** [*count*] **3.** an agreement, esp. an international agreement: *an accord banning nuclear weapons in space.* **—*Idiom.* 4. in accord with,** [~ + *obj*] in agreement or harmony with: *That promotion was in accord with the manager's wishes.* **5. of one's own accord,** voluntarily or willingly: *She did the extra work of her own accord.* **6. with one accord,** with everyone in agreement: *They stood and with one accord sang the old hymn.* See -CORD-.

ac•cord•ance (ə kôr′dns) /ə'kɔrdns/ *n.* **—*Idiom.* in accordance with,** in conformity with: *in accordance with the law.*

ac•cord•ing•ly (ə kôr′ding lē) /ə'kɔrdɪŋliy/ *adv.* **1.** therefore; so: *Dinner was at eight o'clock; accordingly we arrived at 7:45.* **2.** in a manner that fits: *If you are rude to others, expected to be treated accordingly.*

accord′ing to′, *prep.* **1.** in accord with or in a way that fits: *They were rewarded according to how hard they worked.* **2.** as stated by: *According to my dictionary, there are several meanings for that word.*

ac•cor•di•on (ə kôr′dē ən) /ə'kɔrdiyən/ *n.* [*count*] a portable musical instrument with a keyboard and a pair of bellows for forcing air through small reeds. **—ac•cor′-di•on•ist,** *n.* [*count*]

ac•cost (ə kôst′, ə kost′) /ə'kɔst, ə'kɒst/ *v.* [~ + *obj*] to approach and speak to (someone), esp. in an aggressive manner.

ac•count (ə kount′) /ə'kawnt/ *n.* **1.** [*count*] a description of events or situations: *an eyewitness account.* **2.** [*count*] an amount of money deposited with a bank: *a savings account.* **3.** [*count*] a statement or record of financial transactions: *The accounts show us to be in trouble.* **4.** [*count*] a formal record of how much is owed to a particular person, business, etc: *He hasn't settled his account yet.* **5.** [*noncount*] a business relation in which credit is used: *He bought the clothes on account.* **—*v.*** [~ + *for* + *obj*] **6.** to give an explanation for: *Can you account for your fingerprints on the gun?* **7.** to be the cause or source of: *The New York market accounts for a lot of our sales.* **—*Idiom.* 8. call to account,** [*call* + *obj* + *to* + ~] **a.** to hold accountable; blame. **b.** to ask for an explanation of. **9. hold to account,** [*hold* + *obj* + *to* + ~] to consider responsible and answerable: *held the treasurer to account for the loss.* **10. on account of,** because of: *The game was postponed on account of rain.* **11. on no account,** absolutely not: *On no account should you hesitate to call on us.* **12. on someone's account,** for the sake of someone: *Don't do it on my account.* **13. take account of,** [~ + *obj*] to consider; make allowance for: *took account of the chance of rain.* **14. take into account,** to take into consideration: [*take* + *into* + ~ + *obj*]: *didn't take into account the cost of the project.* [*take* + *obj* + *into* + ~]: *took it into account.*

ac•count•a•ble (ə koun′tə bəl) /ə'kawntəbəl/ *adj.* **1.** [*be* + ~ + *to/for* + *obj*] answerable (to); responsible (for): *I am accountable to my supervisor. I am accountable for my own work.* **2.** [*be* + ~] able to be explained: *His actions were not believably accountable.* **—ac•count•a•bil•i•ty** (ə koun′tə bil′i tē) /əˌkawntə'bɪlɪtiy/ *n.* [*noncount*] **—ac•count′a•bly,** *adv.*

ac•count•an•cy (ə koun′tn sē) /ə 'kawntn̩ siy/ *n.* [*noncount*] accounting: *a degree in accountancy.*

ac•count•ant (ə koun′tnt) /ə'kawntnt/ *n.* [*count*] a person whose profession is accounting.

ac•count•ing (ə koun′ting) /ə'kawntɪŋ/ *n.* [*noncount*] the business or work of organizing, maintaining, and checking financial records.

ac•cou•ter•ments or **ac•cou•tre•ments** (ə ko͞o′trə-mənts, -tər-) /ə'kuwtrəmənts, -tər-/ *n.* [*plural*] clothing and equipment: *all the accoutrements of a big game hunter.*

ac•cred•it (ə kred′it) /ə'krɛdɪt/ *v.* [~ + *obj*] **1.** to certify as meeting official requirements. **2.** to provide with credentials: *to accredit a diplomatic envoy.* **—ac•cred′i•ta′tion,** *n.* [*noncount*]: *accreditation of the college.*

ac•cre•tion (ə krē′shən) /ə'kriyʃən/ *n.* an increase by growth or addition: [*noncount*]: *gradual accretion of coral in the sea.* [*count*]: *an accretion of wealth.*

ac•crue (ə kro͞o′) /ə'kruw/ *v.,* **-crued, -cru•ing. 1.** [*no obj*] to grow or increase over time, esp. by adding gradually: *The interest accrued at 6% a year.* **2.** [~ + *obj*] to collect and allow to accumulate: *She accrued some fine paintings.*

acct., an abbreviation of: **1.** account. **2.** accountant.

ac•cul•tur•a•tion (ə kul′chə rā′shən) /əˌkʌltʃə'reyʃən/ *n.* [*noncount*] the adoption of characteristics of a culture not one's own.

ac•cu•mu•late (ə kyo͞o′myə lāt′) /ə'kyuwmyəˌleyt/ *v.,* **-lat•ed, -lat•ing.** to gather or collect, esp. by degrees; heap up: [~ + *obj*]: *had accumulated a large collection of papers and books.* [*no obj*]: *Dust accumulated on the desktop.* **—ac•cu•mu•la•tion** (ə kyo͞o′myə lā′shən) /əˌkyuwmyə'leyʃən/ *n.* [*noncount; count*] **—ac•cu•mu•la•tive** (ə kyo͞o′myə lā′tiv, -lə tiv) /ə'kyuwmyəˌleytɪv, -lə tɪv/ *adj.*

ac•cu•ra•cy (ak′yər ə sē) /'ækyər ə siy/ *n.* [*noncount*] exactness; correctness; precision.

ac•cu•rate (ak′yər it) /'ækyərɪt/ *adj.* free from error; carefully precise: *accurate calculations.* **—ac′cu•rate•ly,** *adv.* **—ac′cu•rate•ness,** *n.* [*noncount*] See -CURA-.

ac•curs•ed (ə kûr′sid, ə kûrst′) /ə'kɜrsɪd, ə'kɜrst/ also **ac•curst** (ə kûrst′) /ə'kɜrst/ *adj.* **1.** [*before a noun*] damnable; terrible: *told an accursed lie.* **2.** being under a curse. **—ac•curs′ed•ly,** *adv.*

ac•cu•sa•tion (ak′yo͞o zā′shən) /ˌækyu'zeyʃən/ *n.* **1.** [*count*] a charge of guilt or blame: *false accusations.* **2.** [*noncount*] the act of accusing: *protested the accusation of the young man.* **—ac•cu•sa•to•ry** (ə kyo͞o′zə tôr′ē, -tōr′ē) /ə'kyuwzəˌtɔriy, -ˌtowriy/ *adj.*

ac•cu•sa•tive (ə kyo͞o′zə tiv) /ə'kyuwzətɪv/ *adj.* **1.** of or naming a grammatical case that indicates the object of a verb or sometimes a preposition: *In Latin the word* puel-lam *is the accusative form for "girl" when it is used as a direct object.* **—*n.*** [*count*] **2.** the accusative case, or a word in the accusative case: *Use the accusative in the next sentence.*

ac•cuse (ə kyo͞oz′) /ə'kyuwz/ *v.* [~ + *obj* (+ *of* + *obj*)], **-cused, -cus•ing.** to charge with a fault, offense, or crime: *They accused him (of murder).* **—ac•cus′er,** *n.* [*count*]

ac•cus•tom (ə kus′təm) /ə'kʌstəm/ *v.* [~ + *obj* + *to* + *obj*] to make (something) become familiar by use or habit; habituate: *had to accustom themselves to the climate.*

ac•cus•tomed (ə kus′təmd) /ə'kʌstəmd/ *adj.* **1.** [*before a noun*] customary: *took her accustomed place in line.* **2.** [*be* + ~ + *to*] used to: *was accustomed to getting his own way.*

AC/DC (ā′sē dē′sē) /ˌeysiy'diysiy/ **1.** an abbreviation of: alternating current or direct current. **—*adj.*** **2.** *Slang.* bisexual.

ace (ās) /eys/ *n., v.,* **aced, ac•ing,** *adj.* **—*n.*** [*count*] **1.** a playing card with a single spot: *an ace of hearts.* **2.** (in tennis, etc.) a point made on an untouched serve. **3.** a fighter pilot who downs at least five enemy aircraft. **4.** an expert: *the ace of the pitching staff.* **—*v.*** [~ + *obj*] **5.** to win a point against (an opponent) with an ace: *aced his opponent ten times in the match.* **6.** *Slang.* to defeat, esp. easily: [~ (+ *out*) + *obj*]: *She aced (out) her opponent.* [~ + *obj* + *out*]: *aced him out.* **7.** *Slang.* to receive a grade of A in or on: *aced the course.* **—*adj.*** **8.** [*before a noun*] excellent: *an ace player.* **—*Idiom.*** **9.** **ace in the hole,** [*count*] an advantage held in reserve: *His ace in the hole was the secret report he had on their finances.* Also, **ace up one's sleeve.**

a•cer•bic (ə sûr′bik) /ə'sɜrbɪk/ *adj.* **1.** sour or bitter in taste. **2.** sharply or bitterly severe: *acerbic criticism.* **—a•cer′bi•cal•ly,** *adv.* **—a•cer′bi•ty,** *n.* [*noncount*] See -ACR-.

a•ce•ta•min•o•phen (ə sē′tə min′ə fən) /əˌsiytə'mɪnəfən/ *n.* [*noncount*] a crystal-like substance used to reduce pain or fever.

ac•e•tate (as′i tāt′) /'æsɪˌteyt/ *n.* [*noncount*] a synthetic material used to make cloth.

a•ce•tic (ə sē′tik, ə set′ik) /ə'siytɪk, ə'sɛtɪk/ *adj.* of or producing vinegar or acetic acid.

ace′tic ac′id, *n.* [*noncount*] a strong-smelling liquid, the essential substance of vinegar.

ac•e•tone (as′i tōn′) /'æsɪˌtown/ *n.* [*noncount*] a flammable liquid used in paints and varnishes, as a solvent, etc. **—ac•e•ton•ic** (as′i ton′ik) /ˌæsɪ'tɒnɪk/ *adj.*

a•cet•y•lene (ə set′l ēn′, -in) /ə'sɛtl̩ˌiyn, -ɪn/ *n.* [*noncount*] a colorless gas, used esp. in metal cutting and welding.

ache (āk) /eyk/ *v.,* **ached** (ākt) /eykt/ **ach•ing,** *n.* **—*v.*** [*no obj*] **1.** to have a continuous dull pain: *His back ached from lifting.* **2.** to want (something) very much; yearn; long: [~ + *for* + *obj*]: *was aching for a hot shower.* [~ + *to* + *verb*]: *ached to have a drink.* **—*n.*** [*count*] **3.** a continuous dull pain. **—ach′ing•ly,** *adv.* **—ach′y,** *adj.,* **-i•er, -i•est.**

a•chieve (ə chēv′) /ə'tʃiyv/ *v.,* **a•chieved, a•chiev•ing.** **1.** [~ + *obj*] to bring to a successful end; to get by effort: *achieved her goal of becoming vice-president.* **2.** [*no obj*] to perform successfully: *Some smart children still do not achieve in school.* **—a•chiev′a•ble,** *adj.* **—a•chiev′er,** *n.* [*count*]

a•chieve•ment (ə chēv′ mnt) /ə 'tʃiyv mnt/ *n.* **1.** [*noncount*] successful accomplishment: *a sense of achievement.* **2.** [*count*] something successfully accomplished or performed: *50 home runs was quite an achievement.*

Achil′les heel′ (ə kil′ēz) /ə'kɪliyz/ *n.* [*count*] a weak or vulnerable spot: *His generous nature was his Achilles heel in business dealings.*

ac•id (as′id) /'æsɪd/ *n.* **1.** a chemical substance capable of turning blue litmus paper red; a substance with a sour taste: [*noncount*]: *How much acid is in the soil?* [*count*]: *An acid will dissolve the grease.* **2.** [*noncount*] *Slang.* the drug LSD. **—*adj.*** **3.** belonging or relating to acids. **4.** sharp or biting to the taste; sour: *the acid flavor of lime.* **5.** sharp, biting, or sarcastic: *acid criticism.* **—a•cid•ic** (ə-sid′ik) /ə'sɪdɪk/ *adj.* **—a•cid′i•ty,** *n.* [*noncount*] **—ac′id•ly,** *adv.* **—ac′id•ness,** *n.* [*noncount*] See -ACR-.

ac′id rain′, *n.* [*noncount*] rain containing acid-forming chemicals, resulting from the release into the atmosphere of industrial pollutants: *Acid rain has damaged trees and lakes in the environment.*

ac′id test′, *n.* [*count*] a difficult test that proves whether something is true, good, etc: *The ability to convince a reader is the acid test of writing skill.*

a•cid•u•lous (ə sij′ə ləs) /ə'sɪdʒələs/ *adj.* harsh; biting: *The prosecutor's acidulous remarks offended the jury.*

-acious, *suffix. -acious* is attached to some roots to form adjectives, with the meaning "tending to; abounding in:" *tenacious (*from *ten-* "hold on" + *-acious) = tending to hold on; loquacious (*from *loq(u)-* "talk" + *-acious) = tending to talk.* Compare -OUS.

-acity, *suffix. -acity* is attached to some roots to form nouns, with the meaning "tendency toward; abundance in:" *tenacity (*from *ten-* "hold on" + *-acity) = tendency toward holding on.*

ac•knowl•edge (ak nol′ij) /æk'nɒlɪdʒ/ *v.,* **-edged, -edg•ing.** **1.** to admit to be real or true: [~ + *obj*]: *The loser acknowledged defeat.* [~ + *that clause*]: *acknowledged that he had been defeated.* **2.** [~ + *obj (+ with + obj)*] to show or express recognition of: *The teacher acknowledged my presence with a smile.* **3.** [~ + *obj*] to recognize the authority or validity of: *acknowledged the truth of the accusations against him.* **4.** [~ + *obj*] to show or express appreciation for: *She acknowledged the applause.* **5.** [~ + *obj*] to make known the receipt of: *He wrote a thank-you note to acknowledge the gift.*

ac•knowl•edg•ment (ak nol′ij mnt) /æk 'nɒlɪdʒ mnt/ *n.* **1.** [*noncount; often: in* + ~ *(+ of)*] the act of acknowledging. **2.** [*count*] a message testifying to the receipt of something: *sent an acknowledgment that the gift had arrived.* **3.** [*count; often plural*] a piece of writing in a book thanking the people who have helped the author. Also, *esp. Brit.,* **ac•knowl′edge•ment.**

ACLU or **A.C.L.U.,** an abbreviation of: American Civil Liberties Union.

ac•me (ak′mē) /'ækmiy/ *n.* [*count; usually singular*] the highest point or stage; peak: *reached the acme of success.*

ac•ne (ak′nē) /'ækniy/ *n.* [*noncount*] a disorder of certain glands on the skin, characterized by pimples on the face, neck, and upper back.

ac•o•lyte (ak′ə līt′) /'ækəˌlayt/ *n.* [*count*] **1.** an attendant to a clergyman in a religious service. **2.** any attendant or follower.

a•corn (ā′kôrn, ā′kərn) /'eykɔrn, 'eykərn/ *n.* [*count*] the nut of an oak tree.

a•cous•tic (ə ko͞o′stik) /ə'kuwstɪk/ also **a•cous′ti•cal,** *adj.* [*before a noun*] **1.** concerning hearing, sound, or the science of sound: *the acoustic abilities of dolphins.* **2.** designed for controlling sound: *acoustic tile.* **3.** sounded without electric or electronic enhancement: *an acoustic guitar.* **—a•cous′ti•cal•ly,** *adv.*

a•cous•tics (ə ko͞o′stiks) /ə'kuwstɪks/ *n.* **1.** [*noncount; used with a singular verb*] the branch of physics that deals with sound and sound waves. **2.** [*plural; used with a plural verb*] the qualities of an enclosed space that determine how sounds are carried to a listener: *The acoustics of the concert hall were good.*

ac•quaint (ə kwānt′) /ə'kweynt/ *v.* [~ + *obj* + *with* + *obj*] to make familiar or conversant; inform: *I acquainted them with living conditions abroad.*

ac•quaint•ance (ə kwān′tns) /ə'kweyntns/ *n.* **1.** [*count*] a person whom one knows casually: *only a business acquaintance.* **2.** personal knowledge or information: [*noncount*]: *his acquaintance with African literature.* [*count*]: *I have some acquaintance with the Swedish language.*

acquaint′ance rape′, *n.* [*noncount*] forced sexual intercourse with a person known to the victim.

ac•qui•esce (ak′wē es′) /ˌækwiy'ɛs/ *v.* [*no obj; (~ + in/to + obj)*], **-esced, -esc•ing.** to agree or accept to do (something) without protest; comply: *The president acquiesced in the budget cutting plan.* **—ac′qui•es′cence,** *n.* [*noncount*] **—ac′qui•es′cent,** *adj.* See -QUIE-.

ac•quire (ə kwīᵊr′) /ə'kwayᵊr/ *v.* [~ + *obj*], **-quired, -quir•ing.** to get possession of, or gain through one's efforts: *acquired two new paintings; acquired new skills.* **—ac•quir′a•ble,** *adj.* **—ac•quire′ment,** *n.* [*noncount*]

ac•qui•si•tion (ak′wi zish′ən) /ˌækwɪ'zɪʃən/ *n.* **1.** [*noncount*] the act of acquiring. **2.** [*count*] something acquired: *His latest acquisition was a new car.* See -QUIS-.

ac•quis•i•tive (ə kwiz′i tiv) /ə'kwɪzɪtɪv/ *adj.* tending or seeking to acquire, often greedily: *was particularly acquisitive when it came to buying luxuries.* **—ac•quis′i•tive•ly,** *adv.* **—ac•quis′i•tive•ness,** *n.* [*noncount*]

ac•quit (ə kwit′) /ə'kwɪt/ *v.,* **-quit•ted, -quit•ting.** **1.** [~ + *obj (+ of + obj)*] to declare not guilty of a crime or offense: *The jury acquitted her of all charges.* **2.** [~ + *oneself*] to conduct (oneself); behave: *acquitted himself well in his first game.* See -QUIT-.

ac•quit•tal (ə kwit′l) /ə 'kwɪtl̩/ *n.* the act of declaring someone not guilty: [*noncount*]: *The jury voted for acquittal.* [*count*]: *How many acquittals were there?*

-acr-, *root. -acr-* comes from Latin, where it has the meaning "sharp". This meaning is found in such words as: ACERBIC, ACRID, ACRIMONIOUS, EXACERBATE.

a•cre (ā′kər) /'eykər/ *n.* [*count*] a unit of land measure, equal to 43,560 square feet.

a•cre•age (ā′kər ij) /'eykərɪdʒ/ *n.* [*noncount; count*] extent or area in acres; total number of acres.

ac•rid (ak′rid) /'ækrɪd/ *adj.* **1.** strong in taste or smell: *acrid fumes.* **2.** stinging; bitter: *acrid remarks.* **—ac′rid•ly,** *adv.* **—ac′rid•ness,** *n.* [*noncount*] See -ACR-.

ac•ri•mo•ni•ous (ak′ri mō nē əs) /ˌækrɪ mow niy əs/ *adj.* marked by bitterness: *an acrimonious argument.* See -ACR-.

ac•ri•mo•ny (ak′rə mō′nē) /ˈækrəˌmowniy/ *n.* [*noncount*] bitterness of manner, speech, etc: *The dispute was filled with acrimony.* See -ACR-.

-acro-, *root.* *-acro-* comes from Greek, where it has the meaning "high." This meaning is found in such words as: ACROBAT, ACRONYM, ACROPHOBIA.

ac•ro•bat (ak′rə bat′) /ˈækrəˌbæt/ *n.* [*count*] a performer of gymnastic feats. **—ac′ro•bat′ic,** *adj.* See -ACRO-.

ac•ro•bat•ics (ak′rə bat′iks) /ˌækrəˈbætɪks/ *n.* **1.** [*noncount; used with a singular verb*] the art or practice of acrobatic feats. **2.** [*plural; used with a plural verb*] feats of an acrobat; gymnastics: *The acrobatics of the high-wire performers were thrilling.* **3.** [*plural; used with a plural verb*] something marked by agility: *verbal acrobatics.* See -ACRO-.

ac•ro•nym (ak′rə nim) /ˈækrənɪm/ *n.* [*count*] a word formed from the initial letters or groups of letters of the words in a name or phrase, as *WAC* from *Women's Army Corps,* or *AIDS* from *acquired immune deficiency syndrome.* Compare ABBREVIATION. See -ACRO-, -ONYM-.

ac•ro•pho•bi•a (ak′rə fō′bē ə) /ˌækrəˈfowbiyə/ *n.* [*noncount*] fear of being at high places. **—ac′ro•pho′bic,** *adj., n.* [*count*] See -ACRO-.

a•cross (ə krôs′, ə kros′) /əˈkrɔs, əˈkrɒs/ *prep.* **1.** from one side to the other of: *a bridge across a river.* **2.** on or to the other side of; beyond: *across the sea.* **3.** so as to cross: *The path cut across the meadow.* **—*adv.* 4.** from one side to another; wide: *The crater was a mile across.* **5.** on the other side: *We'll soon be across.*

across′-the-board′, *adj.* applying to all inclusively; general: *an across-the-board pay increase.*

a•cryl•ic (ə kril′ik) /əˈkrɪlɪk/ *adj.* **1.** of or derived from acrylic acid. **—*n.* 2.** [*noncount*] a paint with acrylic in it. **3.** [*count*] a picture done with acrylic paint.

acryl′ic ac′id, *n.* [*noncount*] a strong-smelling liquid used in the manufacture of plastics.

-act-, *root.* *-act-* comes from Latin, where it has the meaning "to do, move". It is related to the root -AG-. This meaning is found in such words as: ACT, ACTION, EXACT, INEXACT, TRANSACT.

act (akt) /ækt/ *n.* [*count*] **1.** anything done or to be done; deed: *an act of mercy.* **2.** the process of doing: *caught in the act.* **3.** [*sometimes: Act*] a formal decision, law, or the like; a decree or edict: *an act of Congress.* **4.** one of the main divisions of a play or opera: *a drama in three acts.* **5.** a short performance by one or more entertainers, usually part of a variety show, circus, etc.: *an acrobatic act.* **6.** [*usually singular*] a display of insincere behavior assumed for effect; pretense: *Her apology was all an act.* **—*v.* 7.** [*no obj*] to do something; carry out an action. **8.** [*no obj; (~ + on + obj)*] to reach or issue a decision on some matter: *Congress failed to act (on the tax bill).* **9.** [*no obj*] to operate or function in a particular way: *acted as manager.* **10.** to produce an effect: *The medicine failed to act.* **11.** to conduct oneself in a particular fashion: [*no obj*]: *acted foolishly.* [*~ + obj*]: *to act one's age.* **12.** [*no obj*] to pretend; feign: *was just acting and wasn't really sorry.* **13.** to perform as an actor: [*no obj*]: *has acted on Broadway.* [*~ + obj*]: *to act Macbeth.* **14. act on** or **upon,** [*~ + on/upon + obj*] **a.** to act in accordance with; follow: *will act on (upon) your wishes immediately.* **b.** to have an effect on; affect: *The aspirin acted on the pain.* **15. act out, a.** [*~ + out + obj*] to show or express by gestures or actions: *He acted out his frustrations by throwing things.* **b.** to perform: [*~ + out + obj*]: *The students acted out the roles in the play.* [*~ + obj + out*]: *to act the roles out.* **16. act up,** [*no obj*] **a.** to fail to function properly: *The car's transmission is acting up.* **b.** to behave willfully: *The tired, cranky child acted up during the wedding.* **c.** (of a recurring ailment) to become troublesome: *His rheumatism is acting up.* **—*Idiom.* 17. clean up one's act,** to begin to behave in a more socially acceptable way. **18. get** or **have one's act together,** to behave or function responsibly and efficiently. **19. in the act of,** in the process of: *was caught in the act of climbing out the window.* See -ACT-.

act•ing (ak′ting) /ˈæktɪŋ/ *adj.* **1.** [*before a noun*] serving temporarily, esp. as a substitute during another's absence: *an acting mayor.* **—*n.* [*noncount*] 2.** the occupation or performance of an actor or actress.

ac•tion (ak′shən) /ˈækʃən/ *n.* **1.** [*noncount*] the process or state of acting or functioning; the state of being active: *We saw the team in action.* **2.** [*count*] something done or performed; act; deed: *His heroic actions on the battlefield.* **3.** [*noncount*] energetic, decisive activity: *a man of action.* **4.** [*noncount*] effect or influence: *the action of morphine on pain.* **5.** [*noncount*] the mechanism by which something is operated, as that of a gun or a piano. **6.** [*noncount*] military combat: *saw action in the war.* **7.** [*count; usually singular*] the story line of a literary or dramatic work: *The movie's action takes place in Mexico.* **8.** legal proceeding instituted by one party against another: [*count*]: *instituted an action against the thief.* [*noncount*]: *to bring action against a felon.* **9.** [*noncount*] *Slang.* interesting or exciting activity: *to go where the action is.* **—*Idiom.* 10. piece of the action,** *Informal.* a share in financial gain: *The investor wanted to get a piece of the action.* See -ACT-.

ac•tion•a•ble (ak′shən ə bl) /ˈækʃən ɔ bl/ *adj.* [*often: be + ~*] giving cause or reason for legal action: *actionable accusations.*

ac•ti•vate (ak′tə vāt′) /ˈæktəˌveyt/ *v.* [*~ + obj*], **-vat•ed, -vat•ing. 1.** to make active; cause to function or act: *Pushing the switch activates the car alarm.* **2.** to place (a military unit) on an active status: *activated the national guard unit.* **—ac•ti•va•tion** (ak′tə vā′shən) /ˌæktəˈveyʃən/ *n.* [*noncount*] **—ac′ti•va′tor,** *n.* [*count*] See -ACT-.

ac•tive (ak′tiv) /ˈæktɪv/ *adj.* **1.** engaged in action or activity: *an active life.* **2.** being in existence, progress, or motion: *active hostilities.* **3.** marked by energetic involvement: *active support.* **4.** involving physical exertion: *active sports.* **5.** characterized by current activity, participation, or use: *an active club member; an active bank account.* **6.** having a great deal of vigorous activity: *an active stock market.* **7.** (of a chemical) effective; capable of producing an effect: *Active ingredients in that toothpaste prevent cavities.* **8.** of or relating to a voice in grammar, a verb form, or construction in which the subject is usually the person or thing that performs or causes the action of the verb. In the verb form *write* in *I write letters every day,* the verb *write* is active (opposed to *passive*). **9.** (of a volcano) currently in eruption or likely to erupt. **10.** (of military personnel) currently on duty and prepared for military action. **—*n.* [*count*] 11.** the active voice, or a form in this voice: *Put that verb into the active.* **—ac′tive•ly,** *adv.* **—ac′tive•ness,** *n.* [*noncount*] See -ACT-.

ac•tiv•ism (ak′tə viz′əm) /ˈæktəˌvɪzəm/ *n.* [*noncount*] the belief in or practice of vigorous action or involvement to achieve political or other goals. **—ac′tiv•ist,** *n.* [*count*], *adj.*

ac•tiv•i•ty (ak tiv′i tē) /ækˈtɪvɪtiy/ *n., pl.* **-ties. 1.** [*noncount*] the state or quality of being active or lively. **2.** [*count*] a specific deed, action, or function: *social activities.*

ac•tor (ak′tər) /ˈæktər/ *n.* [*count*] **1.** a person who acts in stage plays, motion pictures, etc. **2.** a participant: *actors in history's great events.*

ac•tress (ak′tris) /ˈæktrɪs/ *n.* [*count*] a woman who acts in stage plays, motion pictures, etc.

ac•tu•al (ak′cho͞o əl) /ˈæktʃuwəlˈ *adj.* [*before a noun*] existing in act, fact, or reality; real: *the actual cost.* **—ac′tu•al•ly,** *adv.* **—Related Words.** ACTUAL is an adjective, ACTUALITY is a noun, ACTUALLY is an adverb, ACTUALIZE is a verb: *The actual facts are these. In actuality, the quarter didn't disappear; it was in the magician's hand. Actually I wanted to stay home. He wanted to actualize his potential.*

ac•tu•al•i•ty (ak′cho͞o al′i tē) /ˌæktʃuw ˈælɪ tiy/ *n., pl.* **-ties. 1.** [*noncount*] reality: *in actuality.* **2.** [*count; usually plural*] real conditions or facts: *the actualities of the case.*

ac•tu•al•ize (ak′cho͞o ə līz′) /ˈæktʃuwəˌlayz/ *v.* [*~ + obj*], **-ized, -iz•ing.** to make actual or real; turn into action or fact. **—ac•tu•al•i•za•tion** (ak′cho͞o ə lə zā′shən) /ˌæktʃuwələˈzeyʃən/ *n.* [*noncount*]

ac•tu•ary (ak′cho͞o er′ē) /ˈæktʃuwˌɛriy/ *n.* [*count*], *pl.* **-ar•ies.** a person who computes insurance premium rates, dividends, risks, etc., based on statistical data. **—ac•tu•ar•i•al** (ak′cho͞o âr′ē əl) /ˌæktʃuwˈɛəriyəl/ *adj.*

ac•tu•ate (ak′cho͞o āt′) /ˈæktʃuwˌeyt/ *v.* [*~ + obj*], **-at•ed, -at•ing. 1.** to move to action: *He was actuated by selfish motives.* **2.** to put into action: *to actuate a machine.* **—ac•tu•a•tion** (ak′cho͞o ā′shən) /ˌæktʃuwˈeyʃən/ *n.* [*noncount*] **—ac′tu•a′tor,** *n.* [*count*]

a•cu•i•ty (ə kyo͞o′i tē) /əˈkyuwɪtiy/ *n.* [*noncount*] sharpness; acuteness: *visual acuity; mental acuity.* See -ACR-.

a•cu•men (ə kyo͞o′mən, ak′yə-) /əˈkyuwmən, ˈækyə-/ *n.* [*noncount*] sharp or keen insight; shrewdness: *business acumen.* See -ACR-.

ac•u•punc•ture (ak′yo͝o pungk′chər) /ˈækyʊˌpʌŋktʃər/ *n.*

[*noncount*] a Chinese medical practice that treats illness or provides local pain relief by inserting needles at specified places in the body. —**ac′u•punc′tur•ist,** *n.* [*count*] See -ACR-, -PUNCT-.

a•cute (ə kyo͞ot′) /ə'kyuwt/ *adj.* **1.** sharp or severe in effect; intense: *acute pain.* **2.** extremely great or serious; critical: *an acute shortage of oil.* **3.** (of disease) of sudden onset and severe (disting. from *chronic*): *acute bronchitis.* **4.** very sharp in intellect, insight, or perception. **5.** extremely sensitive: *acute hearing.* **6. a.** (of an angle) less than 90°. **b.** (of a triangle) containing only acute angles. —**a•cute′ly,** *adv.* —**a•cute′ness,** *n.* [*noncount*] See -ACR-.

acute′ ac′cent, *n.* [*count*] a mark (′) placed over a vowel, esp. to show that the vowel is close or tense, as in French *é*, or long, as in Hungarian, or that the vowel or the syllable it is in bears the word stress, as in Spanish, or is pronounced with raised pitch, as in Classical Greek.

ad (ad) /æd/ *n.* [*count*] **1.** an advertisement. —*adj.* [*before a noun*] **2.** advertising: *an ad agency.*

A.D. or **AD,** an abbreviation of Latin *anno Domini*: in the year of the Lord; since Christ was born (used with dates): *Charlemagne was born in* A.D. *742.*

ad•age (ad′ij) /'ædɪdʒ/ *n.* [*count*] a traditional saying expressing a common experience or observation; proverb: *the old adage "a stitch in time saves nine".*

a•da•gio (ə dä′jō, -zhē ō′) /ə'dɑdʒow, -ʒiy,ow/ *Music.* —*adv.* **1.** slowly. —*adj.* **2.** slow.

ad•a•mant (ad′ə mənt, -mant′) /'ædəmənt, -,mænt/ *adj.* unyielding; inflexible: *an adamant refusal.* [*be* + ~ *(+ that clause)*]: *He was adamant that he was in the right.* —**ad′a•mant•ly,** *adv.*

Ad′am's ap′ple (ad′əmz) /'ædəmz/ *n.* [*count*] a lump of cartilage at the front of the throat that, esp. in men, sticks out.

a•dapt (ə dapt′) /ə'dæpt/ *v.* **1.** [~ + *obj*] to make suitable to new or different requirements or conditions; adjust or modify appropriately: *They adapted the movie for a TV miniseries.* **2.** [~ *(+ oneself)* + *to* + *obj)*] to adjust oneself to different conditions, environment, etc.: *My children adapted (themselves) to life abroad quite smoothly.* —**a•dapt•a•bil•i•ty** (ə dap′tə bil′i tē) /ə,dæptə'bɪlɪtiy/ *n.* [*noncount*] —**a•dapt′a•ble,** *adj.* See -APT-.

ad•ap•ta•tion (ad′əp tā′shən) /,ædəp'teyʃən/ *n.* **1.** [*noncount*] the act or process of adapting or the state of being adapted. **2.** [*count*] a change of a book, story, or other writing to a new form: *The movie was an adaptation of a novel.*

a•dapt•er or **a•dap•tor** (ə dap′tər) /ə'dæptər/ *n.* [*count*] **1.** one that adapts. **2.** a connector for joining parts or devices having different sizes, designs, etc.

add (ad) /æd/ *v.* **1.** [~ + *obj* + *to* + *obj*] to unite or join so as to bring about an increase: *We added a few more students to the class.* **2.** [~ + *obj*] to find the sum of: *We added the four numbers together.* **3.** [*no obj*] to perform arithmetic addition: *She could add almost as fast as a calculator.* **4.** [~ + *(that) clause*] to say or write further: *I'd like to add that I'm pleased to be here tonight.* **5.** [~ + *to* + *obj*] to be an addition: *His illness added to the family's troubles.* **6. add up, a.** to amount to the correct total: [*no obj*]: *These figures don't add up right.* [~ + *up* + *obj*]: *Add up the numbers.* [~ + *obj* + *up*]: *Add the numbers up.* **b.** [*no obj*] to seem reasonable or consistent: *The facts in that mystery just didn't add up.* **7. add up to,** [~ + *up* + *to* + *obj*] to amount to: *His ideas didn't add up to anything important.* —**add′a•ble, add′i•ble,** *adj.*

ad•den•dum (ə den′dəm) /ə'dendəm/ *n.* [*count*], *pl.* **-da** (-də). something added; esp., a section added to a book.

ad•der (ad′ər) /'ædər/ *n.* [*count*] **1.** the common European viper. **2.** a snake resembling the viper.

ad•dict (*n.* ad′ikt; *v.* ə dikt′) /*n.* 'ædɪkt; *v.* ə'dɪkt/ *n.* [*count*] **1.** one who is addicted to a substance, activity, or habit: *a drug addict; a sports addict.* —*v.* [~ + *obj; usually: be* + *addicted* + *to* + *obj*] **2.** to cause to become physiologically or psychologically dependent on an addictive substance: *was addicted to cocaine.* **3.** to devote (oneself) compulsively or obsessively: *was addicted to jogging.* —**ad•dic′tive,** *adj.*

ad•dic•tion (ə dik′shən) /ə 'dɪkʃən/ *n.* **1.** [*noncount*] the state of being addicted to something. **2.** [*count*] an example or case of this: *had addictions to nicotine and alcohol.*

ad•di•tion (ə dish′ən) /ə'dɪʃən/ *n.* **1.** [*noncount*] the act or process of adding or uniting: *Figure out your answer by addition.* **2.** [*count*] anything added, such as a room added to a building: *They built an addition to their house.* —***Idiom.*** **3. in addition,** besides; also: *She can sing, and, in addition, she can dance.* **4. in addition to,** as well as; besides: *In addition to being a singer, she's a dancer.* —**ad•di′tion•al,** *adj.* —**ad•di′tion•al•ly,** *adv.*

ad•di•tive (ad′i tiv) /'ædɪtɪv/ *n.* [*count*] something added to alter or improve the quality: *food additives.*

ad•dle (ad′l) /'ædl̩/ *v.,* **-dled, -dling. 1.** [~ + *obj*] to make confused: *a brain addled by drugs.* **2.** [*no obj*] to become rotten, as eggs.

add′-on′, *n.* [*count*] anything added on: *Air-conditioning was an add-on to the price of the car.*

ad•dress (*n.* ə dres′, ad′res; *v.* ə dres′) /*n.* ə'drɛs, 'ædrɛs; *v.* ə'drɛs/ *n.* **1.** [*count*] **a.** the place or name of the place where a person, organization, or the like is located or may be reached. **b.** the directions for delivery written on the outside of something to be mailed, as a letter. **2.** [*count*] a usually formal speech or written statement: *The senator delivered a passionate address.* **3.** [*noncount*] the proper name or title for use in speaking or writing to a person: *forms of address.* **4.** [*count*] a code that designates the location of information stored in computer memory. —*v.* [~ + *obj*] **5.** to direct a speech or statement to: *The president addressed the nation.* **6.** [~ + *obj* + *to* + *obj*] to communicate: *She addressed her remarks to the group.* **7.** [~ + *obj* + *as* + *obj*] to use a specified form or title in speaking or writing to: *Address him as "Sir."* **8.** to deal with or discuss: *The new laws don't address the issue of ownership.* **9.** to put the directions for delivery on: *to address a letter.* **10.** [~ + *oneself* + *to* + *obj*] to direct the energy or efforts of: *to address oneself to a task.*

ad•dress•ee (ad′re sē′, ə dre sē′) /,ædrɛ'siy, ədrɛ'siy/ *n.* [*count*] one to whom a piece of mail is addressed.

ad•duce (ə do͞os′, ə dyo͞os′) /ə'duws, ə'dyuws/ *v.* [~ + *obj*], **-duced, -duc•ing.** to bring forward, as in evidence: *Can you adduce any proof of her bad intentions?* See -DUC-.

ad•e•noid (ad′n oid′) /'ædn̩,ɔyd/ *n.* [*count*] Usually, **adenoids.** [*plural*] growths of soft tissue in the nasal passage above the throat. —**ad′e•noi′dal,** *adj.*

a•dept (*adj.* ə dept′; *n.* ad′ept, ə dept′) /*adj.* ə'dɛpt; *n.* 'ædɛpt, ə'dɛpt/ *adj.* **1.** very skilled; proficient; expert: *adept at juggling.* —*n.* **ad•ept** [*count*] **2.** an expert. —**a•dept′ly,** *adv.* —**a•dept′ness,** *n.* [*noncount*]

ad•e•quate (ad′i kwit) /'ædɪkwɪt/ *adj.* **1.** as much or as good as necessary for some requirement or purpose: *adequate rainfall for farming.* **2.** barely sufficient: *His work was adequate, nothing more.* —**ad•e•qua•cy** (ad′i-kwə sē) /'ædɪkwəsiy/ *n.* [*noncount*] —**ad′e•quate•ly,** *adv.* —**ad′e•quate•ness,** *n.* [*noncount*]

ad•here (ad hēr′) /æd'hɪər/ *v.,* **-hered, -her•ing. 1.** to stay attached; stick fast; cling: [*no obj*]: *The glued areas adhered.* [~ + *to* + *obj*]: *Mud adhered to my boots.* **2.** [~ + *to* + *obj*] to stay with; be faithful to: *to adhere to a plan.* —**ad•her•ence** (ad hēr′əns, -her′-) /æd'hɪərəns, -'hɛr-/ *n.* [*noncount*] See -HERE-.

ad•her•ent (ad hēr′ənt, -her′-) /æd'hɪərənt, -'hɛr-/ *n.* [*count*] **1.** one who stays attached to a belief, party, etc.: *a strong adherent of justice.* —*adj.* **2.** adhesive. See -HERE-.

ad•he•sion (ad hē′zhən) /æd'hiyʒən/ *n.* [*noncount*] the act, state, or quality of adhering.

ad•he•sive (ad hē′siv, -ziv) /æd'hiysɪv, -zɪv/ *adj.* **1.** coated with a sticky substance: *adhesive bandages.* **2.** tending to stick fast; clinging. —*n.* [*noncount*] **3.** a substance that causes something to adhere, as glue. **4.** ADHESIVE TAPE. See -HES-.

adhe′sive tape′, *n.* [*noncount*] tape coated with an adhesive substance, as for holding a bandage in place.

ad hoc (ad hok′, hōk′) /'æd hɒk, 'howk/ *adj.* concerned or dealing with a specific subject, purpose, or end.

ad ho•mi•nem (ad hom′ə nəm, -nem′) /'æd hɒmənəm, -,nɛm/ *adj.* attacking an opponent's character rather than answering an argument.

a•dieu (ə do͞o′, ə dyo͞o′) /ə'duw, ə'dyuw/ *interj., n.* [*count*], *pl.* **a•dieus, a•dieux.** good-bye; farewell.

ad in•fi•ni•tum (ad in′fə ni′təm, ad′ in-) /,æd ɪnfə'naytəm, ,æd ɪn-/ *adv.* to infinity; endlessly; without limit.

adj., an abbreviation of: **1.** adjective. **2.** adjunct. **3.** adjustment.

ad•ja•cent (ə jā′sənt) /ə'dʒeysənt/ *adj.* lying near, or close; touching; facing; adjoining: *an adjacent page; Their yards were adjacent.* [*be* + ~ + *to*]: *a field adjacent to the canal.* —**ad•ja′cen•cy,** *n.* [*noncount*] —**ad•ja′cent•ly,** *adv.* See -JEC-.

ad•jec•ti•val (aj′ik tī′vəl) /,ædʒɪk 'tayvəl/ *adj.* of or relating to adjectives. —**ad′jec•ti′val•ly,** *adv.*

ad•jec•tive (aj′ik tiv) /'ædʒɪktɪv/ *n.* [*count*] **1.** a member of a class of words that describe nouns, as *nice* in *a nice day,* or *beautiful* in *She is very beautiful. Abbr.:* adj. *—adj.* **2.** of, relating to, or functioning as an adjective; adjectival: *an adjective phrase.* See -JEC-.

ad•join (ə join′) /ə'dʒɔyn/ *v.* to be close to or in contact (with); abut: [*no obj*]: *Our rooms in the hotel adjoined.* [~ + *obj*]: *The lobby adjoined the dining room.* —**ad•join′ing,** *adj.: Our rooms were adjoining. Please book us into adjoining rooms.* See -JUNC-.

ad•journ (ə jûrn′) /ə'dʒɜrn/ *v.* **1.** [~ + *obj*] to suspend the meeting of (a legislature, court, etc.) to a future time, another place, or indefinitely: *adjourned the court until the next morning.* **2.** [*no obj; (~ + to + obj)*] to go to another place: *Let's adjourn to the living room.* —**ad•journ′ment,** *n.* [*count*] See -JOUR-.

ad•judge (ə juj′) /ə'dʒʌdʒ/ *v.* [~ + *obj* + *noun/adjective*], **-judged, -judg•ing. 1.** to declare formally; decree: *The will was adjudged void.* **2.** to consider; deem: *They adjudged her (to be) a liar.* See -JUD-.

ad•ju•di•cate (ə jo͞o′di kāt′) /ə'dʒuwdɪˌkeyt/ *v.,* **-cat•ed, -cat•ing. 1.** [~ + *obj*] to settle or determine (an issue or dispute) judicially: *The court adjudicated the case.* **2.** [*no obj; (~ + on/upon + obj)*] to act as judge: *The parole board adjudicates on the cases.* —**ad•ju•di•ca•tion** (ə-jo͞o′di kā′shən) /əˌdʒuwdɪ'keyʃən/ *n.* [*noncount*] —**ad•ju•di•ca•tive** (ə jo͞o′di kā′tiv, -kə tiv) /ə'dʒuwdɪˌkeytɪv, -kətɪv/ **ad•ju•di•ca•to•ry** (ə jo͞o′di kə tôr′ē, -tōr′ē) /ə'dʒuwdɪkəˌtɔriy, -ˌtowriy/ *adj.* —**ad•ju′di•ca′tor,** *n.* [*count*] See -JUD-.

ad•junct (aj′ungkt) /'ædʒʌŋkt/ *n.* [*count*] **1.** something added to another thing but that is not essential to it. **2.** a person who is an associate or assistant of another. *—adj.* **3.** associated in a temporary or subordinate relationship: *an adjunct professor.* See -JUNC-.

ad•just (ə just′) /ə'dʒʌst/ *v.* **1.** [~ + *obj*] to change (something) so that it fits, corresponds, looks, or works better: *to adjust the picture on a TV set.* **2.** [~ + *obj*] to decide on the amount to be paid in settlement of (an insurance claim). **3.** to adapt oneself; become adapted: [~ + *to* + *obj*]: *to adjust to new demands.* [~ + *oneself* + *to* + *obj*]: *They adjusted themselves to life in the tropics.* —**ad•just′a•ble,** *adj.* —**ad•just′er, ad•jus′tor,** *n.* [*count*] See -JUS-.

ad•just•ed (ə jus′tid) /ə 'dʒʌstɪd/ *adj.* having a balanced relationship with the world: *The adjusted child makes friends easily.*

ad•just•ment (ə just′mnt) /ə 'dʒʌstmnt/ *n.* **1.** [*count*] a change or correction made to something so that it fits, looks, or works better. **2.** [*noncount*] the state of being adjusted: *Adjustment to the new city took a month.*

ad•ju•tant (aj′ə tənt) /'ædʒətənt/ *n.* [*count*] a military staff officer who assists the commanding officer.

ad lib (ad lib′, ad′) /'æd lɪb, 'æd/ *adv.* freely and without prior planning: *added a few remarks ad lib.*

ad-lib (ad lib′, ad′-) /'æd lɪb, 'æd-/ *v.,* **-libbed, -lib•bing,** *adj.* *—v.* **1.** to improvise all or part of (a speech, a piece of music, etc.): [~ + *obj*]: *He ad-libbed his speech.* [*no obj*]: *He ad-libbed for an hour.* *—adj.* **2.** unrehearsed; impromptu: *ad-lib remarks.* —**ad-lib′ber,** *n.* [*count*]

Adm. or **ADM,** an abbreviation of: admiral.

adm., an abbreviation of: **1.** administration. **2.** administrative. **3.** administrator. **4.** admission.

ad•man (ad′man′, -mən) /'ædˌmæn, -mən/ *n.* [*count*], *pl.* **-men.** a person who works in advertising.

ad•min•is•ter (ad min′ə stər) /æd'mɪnəstər/ *v.* **1.** [~ + *obj*] to have executive charge of; manage: *He administered the department.* **2.** [~ + *obj*] to dispense; mete out: *to administer justice fairly.* **3.** [~ + *obj*] to give ritually or formally: *to administer the sacraments.* **4.** [~ + *obj (+ to + obj)*] to apply as a remedy: *administered a painkilling drug to the patient.* **5.** [~ + *obj (+ to + obj)*] to supervise the formal taking of: *administered the oath of office to the new President.* **6.** [~ + *to* + *obj*] to aid; minister: *administered to the poor.*

ad•min•is•trate (ad min′ə strāt′) /æd'mɪnəˌstreyt/ *v.,* **-trat•ed, -trat•ing.** to administer. —**ad•min′is•tra′tor,** *n.* [*count*]

ad•min•is•tra•tion (ad min′ə strā′shən) /ædˌmɪnə-'streyʃən/ *n.* **1.** [*noncount*] the management and control of a government or the like; the duties of an administrator. **2.** [*count*] a body of administrators or executive officials, esp. (*often cap.*) the officials of the executive branch of a government. **3.** [*count*] the period during which an administrator or body of administrators serves. **4.** [*noncount*] the act or process of administering. —**ad•min•is•tra•tive** (ad min′ə strā′tiv, -strə tiv) /æd'mɪnəˌstreytɪv, -strətɪv/ *adj.*

ad•mi•ra•ble (ad′mər ə bəl) /'ædmərəbəl/ *adj.* excellent; praiseworthy: *an admirable attempt at peacemaking.* —**ad′mi•ra•bly,** *adv.* See -MIR-.

ad•mi•ral (ad′mər əl) /'ædmərəl/ *n.* [*count*] the commander in chief of a naval fleet. —**ad′mi•ral•ship′,** *n.* [*noncount*]

ad•mi•ra•tion (ad′mə rā′shən) /ˌædmə'reyʃən/ *n.* [*noncount*] **1.** a feeling of pleasure, approval, and often respect or wonder: *had admiration for her skills.* **2.** an object of such feelings: *She was the admiration of all her friends.* See -MIR-.

ad•mire (ad mīᵊr′) /æd'mayᵊr/ *v.* [~ + *obj*], **-mired, -mir•ing. 1.** to regard with pleasure or approval, often mixed with wonder: *She admired the scenery.* **2.** to regard highly; respect; appreciate greatly: *The boy admired his father.* —**ad•mir′er,** *n.* [*count*] —**Related Words.** ADMIRE is a verb, ADMIRABLE is an adjective, ADMIRATION is a noun: *I admire your courage. Your courage is admirable. I have great admiration for your courage.* See -MIR-.

ad•mir•ing (ad mīᵊr′ing) /æd 'mayᵊrɪŋ/ *adj.* full of high regard: *an admiring glance.* —**ad•mir′ing•ly,** *adv.*

ad•mis•si•ble (ad mis′ə bəl) /æd'mɪsəbəl/ *adj.* able to be allowed or conceded; allowable: *admissible in court; an admissible excuse.* —**ad•mis•si•bil•i•ty** (ad mis′ə bil′i tē) /ædˌmɪsə'bɪlɪtiy/ *n.* [*noncount*] —**ad•mis′si•bly,** *adv.*

ad•mis•sion (ad mish′ən) /æd'mɪʃən/ *n.* **1.** the act of allowing; entrance: [*noncount*]: *Admission to the country was drastically reduced during the war.* [*count*]: *Admissions were down for new students.* **2.** [*noncount*] right or permission to enter: *A ticket will gain you admission.* **3.** [*noncount*] the price paid for entrance: *Admission is $6.00 on weekdays.* **4.** [*count*] acknowledgment of the truth of something: *an admission of guilt.* See -MIS-, -MIT-.

ad•mit (ad mit′) /æd'mɪt/ *v.,* **-mit•ted, -mit•ting. 1.** [~ + *obj*] to allow to enter; let in: *The theater admits adults only.* **2.** [~ + *obj*] to allow (someone) to join an organization: *to admit someone to a club.* **3.** [~ + *obj*] to allow or concede as valid: *to admit the force of an argument.* **4.** to acknowledge; confess: [~ + *obj*]: *He admitted his guilt.* [~ + *(that) clause*]: *He admitted that he was guilty.* [~ + *verb-ing*]: *He admitted robbing the bank.* [~ + *to* + *obj*]: *She admitted to the crime.* **5.** [~ + *obj*] to allow passage of: *This window admits lots of light.* **6.** [~ + *to* + *obj*] to permit entrance; give access: *This door admits to the garden.* **7.** [~ + *of* + *obj*] to allow; permit: *The facts admit of no other interpretation.* —**ad•mit′ted•ly,** *adv.: Admittedly, this isn't the world's greatest view.* See -MIT-. —**Related Words.** ADMIT is a verb, ADMISSIBLE is an adjective, ADMISSION is a noun: *The criminal admitted his guilt. The evidence was not admissible in a court of law. His statement was an admission of guilt.*

ad•mit•tance (ad mit′ns) /æd 'mɪtns/ *n.* [*noncount*] permission to enter: *couldn't gain admittance to the embassy.*

ad•mix (ad miks′) /æd'mɪks/ *v.* [~ + *obj*], **-mixed** or **-mixt** (-mikst′) /-'mɪkst/ **-mix•ing.** to mix together. —**ad•mix•ture** (ad miks′chər) /æd'mɪkstʃər/ *n.* [*noncount*]

ad•mon•ish (ad mon′ish) /æd'mɒnɪʃ/ *v.* **1.** [~ + *obj* + *to* + *verb*] to caution or advise about something; warn: *The judge admonished the jury to disregard the outburst.* **2.** [~ + *obj*] to correct or scold in a gentle manner: *admonished the children to be home on time.* —**ad•mon′ish•ment,** *n.* [*noncount*] See -MON-.

ad•mo•ni•tion (ad′mə nish′ən) /ˌædmə'nɪʃən/ *n.* **1.** [*count*] a gentle warning: *an admonition against lazy habits.* **2.** [*noncount*] mild criticism or counsel. —**ad•mon•i•to•ry** (ad mon′i tôr′ē, -tōr′ē) /æd'mɒnɪˌtɔriy, -ˌtowriy/ *adj.* See -MON-.

ad nau•se•am (ad nô′zē əm) /'æd nɔziyəm/ *adv.* to a sickening or extreme degree: *described the gruesome details ad nauseam.*

a•do (ə do͞o′) /ə'duw/ *n.* [*noncount*] **1.** delaying activity: *Without further ado, I now present our guest.* **2.** fuss; bustle; to-do: *much ado about party plans.*

a•do•be (ə dō′bē) /ə'dowbiy/ *n., pl.* **-bes** for 3. **1.** [*noncount*] sun-dried brick made of clay and straw. **2.** [*noncount*] the clay used to make such bricks. **3.** [*count*] a building made with adobe.

ad•o•les•cence (ad′l es′əns) /ˌædḷ'ɛsəns/ *n.* [*noncount*] the period in human development between puberty and adulthood. See -ALESC-.

ad•o•les•cent (ad′l es′ənt) /ˌædḷ'ɛsənt/ *adj.* **1.** relating to or being in adolescence: *an adolescent child.* **2.** immature; juvenile: *Adolescent behavior is not acceptable in an adult.* **—***n.* [*count*] **3.** a person in the period of adolescence; teenager. See -ALESC-.

a•dopt (ə dopt′) /ə'dɒpt/ *v.* [~ + *obj*] **1.** to take up and use or practice: *to adopt a nickname; adopt a wait-and-see attitude.* **2.** to take and rear (the child of others) as one's own child, esp. by a formal legal act: *to adopt a baby.* **3.** to accept formally: *The committee adopted the report.* **—a•dopt′a•bil′i•ty,** *n.* [*noncount*] **—a•dopt′a•ble,** *adj.* **—a•dopt′er,** *n.* [*count*] See -OPT-.

a•dop•tion (ə dop′shən) /ə 'dɒpʃən/ *n.* **1.** the act or process of adopting a child: [*noncount*]: *Adoption can be a long process.* [*count*]: *The rate of adoptions has risen.* **2.** [*noncount*] taking and carrying out a particular plan: *the adoption of the candidate's platform.*

a•dop•tive (ə dop′tiv) /ə 'dɒptɪv/ *adj.* [*before a noun*] having adopted a child: *adoptive parents.*

a•dor•a•ble (ə dôr′ə bəl, ə dōr′-) /ə'dɔrəbəl, ə'dowr-/ *adj.* **1.** worthy of adoration. **2.** very attractive or charming: *an adorable child.* **—a•dor′a•bly,** *adv.*

a•dore (ə dôr′, ə dōr′) /ə'dɔr, ə'dowr/ *v.* [~ + *obj*]; [*not: be* + ~*-ing*], **a•dored, a•dor•ing. 1.** to feel love for: *He adored his wife.* **2.** to worship as divine: *to adore God.* **3.** to like or admire very much: *I adore your new shoes.* [~ + *verb-ing*]: *They adored shopping.* **—ad•o•ra•tion** (ad′ə rā′shən) /ˌædə'reyʃən/ *n.* [*noncount*] **—a•dor′ing,** *adj.* **—a•dor′ing•ly,** *adv.*

a•dorn (ə dôrn′) /ə'dɔrn/ *v.* [~ + *obj*] **1.** to decorate or add beauty to, as by ornaments: *Garlands of flowers adorned their hair.* **2.** to make more glamorous: *Celebrities adorned the play's audience.* **—a•dorn′ment,** *n.* [*count; noncount*]

a•dren•a•line (ə dren′l in) /ə'drɛnl̩ɪn/ *n.* [*noncount*] a hormone that increases the heart rate and blood pressure in response to fear, anger, stress, etc.

a•drift (ə drift′) /ə'drɪft/ *adj.* [*be* + ~] **1.** floating without control; drifting: *The boats were adrift in the sea.* **2.** without aim, direction, or stability: *After he lost his job, he felt adrift.*

a•droit (ə droit′) /ə'drɔyt/ *adj.* **1.** expert in using the hands or body; nimble: *very adroit at carving figurines.* **2.** cleverly skillful, resourceful, or ingenious: *adroit at always getting his way.* **—a•droit′ly,** *adv.* **—a•droit′ness,** *n.* [*noncount*]

ad•u•late (aj′ə lāt′) /'ædʒəˌleyt/ *v.* [~ + *obj*], **-lat•ed, -lat•ing.** to admire or flatter too much: *fans adulating a rock star.* **—ad•u•la•tion** (aj′ə lā′shən) /ˌædʒə'leyʃən/ *n.* [*noncount*] **—ad′u•la′tor,** *n.* [*count*] **—ad•u•la•to•ry** (aj′ə lə tôr′ē, -tōr′ē) /'ædʒələˌtɔriy, -ˌtowriy/ *adj.*

a•dult (ə dult′, ad′ult) /ə'dʌlt, 'ædʌlt/ *n.* [*count*] **1.** a person who is fully grown, developed, or of age: *Only adults may purchase alcohol.* **—***adj.* [*usually: before a noun*] **2.** having attained full size and strength; mature: *adult plants.* **3.** intended only for adults; not suitable for children: *adult movies.* **4.** of or like a fully grown, mature person: *The teenager had a very adult expression on her face.* **—a•dult′hood,** *n.* [*noncount*]

a•dul•ter•ant (ə dul′tər ənt) /ə'dʌltərənt/ *n.* [*count*] a substance that adulterates.

a•dul•ter•ate (ə dul′tə rāt′) /ə'dʌltəˌreyt/ *v.*, **-at•ed, -at•ing.** [~ + *obj*] to make (a substance) impure by adding inferior or less desirable materials or elements: *The whiskey was adulterated with inferior alcohol.* **—a•dul′ter•ated,** *adj.* **—a•dul•ter•a•tion** (ə dul′tə rā′shən) /əˌdʌltə'reyʃən/ *n.* [*noncount*] **—a•dul′ter•a′tor,** *n.* [*count*]

a•dul•ter•y (ə dul′tə rē) /ə'dʌltəriy/ *n., pl.* **-ies.** (an act of) voluntary sexual intercourse between a married person and someone other than his or her lawful spouse: [*noncount*]: *Adultery in ancient times was often severely punished.* [*count*]: *committed many adulteries.* **—a•dul′ter•er,** *n.* [*count*] **—a•dul′ter•ess,** *n.* [*count*]: *An adulteress is a woman who commits adultery.* **—a•dul′ter•ous,** *adj.*

adv., an abbreviation of: **1.** adverb. **2.** advertisement.

ad•vance (ad vans′) /æd'væns/ *v.*, **-vanced, -vanc•ing,** *n., adj.* **—***v.* **1.** to move, send, or bring forward: [~ + *obj*]: *to advance a deadline; The general advanced his armies to the border.* [*no obj*]: *The army advanced to the border.* [*no obj;* (~ + *on* + *obj*)]: *He advanced on the city.* **2.** [~ + *obj*] to bring into consideration; suggest; propose: *advanced a proposal for a tax cut.* **3.** [~ + *obj*] to further the development, progress, or prospects of: *to advance one's interests.* **4.** to raise in rank; promote: [~ + *obj*]: *advanced the soldier from private to corporal.* [*no obj*]: *The soldier advanced rapidly through the ranks.* **5.** to increase in rate or amount: [~ + *obj*]: *The central bank quietly advanced interest rates.* [*no obj*]: *Prices advanced in the last quarter.* **6.** [~ + *obj* + *obj*] to furnish or supply on credit: *We advanced her money to buy a new car.* **7.** [*no obj*] to improve or make progress: *The economy advanced last year.* **—***n.* **8.** [*count*] a forward movement: *the advance of the troops.* **9.** [*count*] a development showing progress; a step forward; improvement; advancement: *The prize is awarded for advances in science.* **10.** Usually, **advances.** [*plural*] **a.** initial steps in forming an acquaintanceship, reaching an agreement, etc.: *made a few discreet advances toward a corporate merger.* **b.** sexually suggestive overtones: *She resisted his advances.* **11.** [*count*] a rise in price, value, etc: *Advances outnumbered declines on the stock market.* **12.** [*count*] a furnishing of something before an equivalent is received, esp. money or a payment: *an advance on one's salary.* **—***adj.* [*before a noun*] **13.** going or placed before: *an advance guard.* **14.** made, given, or issued ahead of time: *an advance payment.* **—*Idiom.*** **15. in advance, a.** beforehand: *Get your tickets in advance.* **b.** [*be* + ~ + *of* + *obj*] better developed: *These computers are far in advance of the old ones.*

ad•vanced (ad vanst′) /æd'vænst/ *adj.* **1.** highly developed: *an advanced country.* **2.** beyond the beginning, elementary, or intermediate: *advanced mathematics.* **3.** containing progressive ideas: *advanced theories of child care.* **4.** far along in time; old: *a person of advanced age.*

ad•vance•ment (ad vans′mənt) /æd 'vænsmənt/ *n.* development, growth, or improvement of a situation: [*noncount*]: *sought advancement at work.* [*count*]: *advancements in medicine.*

ad•van•tage (ad van′tij) /æd'væntɪdʒ/ *n., v.,* **-taged, -taging. —***n.* **1.** [*count*] circumstance, opportunity, etc., that is very favorable to success: *the advantages of a good education.* **2.** [*noncount*] benefit; gain; profit: *It will be to your advantage to study Chinese.* **3.** [*count*] a position of superiority or ascendancy: *Knowledge of foreign policy gave the candidate an advantage.* **—***v.* [~ + *obj*] **4.** to benefit: *How will this advantage you at work?* **—*Idiom.*** **5. take advantage of,** [~ + *obj*] **a.** to make use of for gain: *to take advantage of an opportunity.* **b.** to impose upon, esp. unfairly, as by exploiting a weakness: *You took unfair advantage of our friendship.* **6. to advantage,** in such a way as to have beneficial effects: *The lighting showed off the room to advantage.* **—ad•van•ta•geous** (ad′vən tā′jəs) /ˌædvən'teydʒəs/ *adj.* **—ad′van•ta′geous•ly,** *adv.*

ad•vent (ad′vent) /'ædvɛnt/ *n.* **1.** [*count*] an arrival; appearance; commencement: *the advent of the holiday season.* **2.** [*proper noun; usually: Advent*] **a.** the coming of Christ into the world. **b.** the period beginning four Sundays before Christmas commemorating the Advent of Christ. See -VEN-.

ad•ven•ture (ad ven′chər) /æd'vɛntʃər/ *n.* **1.** [*count*] an exciting or very unusual experience: *the adventures of Robin Hood.* **2.** [*noncount*] participation in exciting undertakings or enterprises: *a spirit of adventure.* **—ad•ven′tur•ous, ad•ven′ture•some,** *adj.* **—ad•ven′tur•ous•ly,** *adv.* See -VEN-.

ad•ven•tur•er (ad ven′chər ər) /æd'vɛntʃərər/ *n.* [*count*] **1.** a person who seeks adventure. **2.** a person who takes on commercial risk. **3.** a person who seeks power, wealth, or social rank by unscrupulous means.

ad•ven•tur•ess (ad ven′chər is) /æd'vɛntʃərɪs/ *n.* [*count*] **1.** a woman who seeks adventure. **2.** a woman who seeks power, wealth, or social rank by unscrupulous means.

ad•verb (ad′vûrb) /'ædvɜrb/ *n.* [*count*] a member of a class of words that modify or describe something about verbs, adjectives, other adverbs, or clauses. Adverbs usually express some relation of place *(here, there),* time *(now, then),* manner *(well, quickly),* degree (*very, extremely),* means, cause, result, etc. In English many adverbs have the ending *-ly. Abbr.:* adv. **—ad•ver′bi•al,** *adj.* See -VERB-.

ad•ver•sar•y (ad′vər ser′ē) /'ædvərˌsɛriy/ *n., pl.* **-ies.** [*count*] a person, group, etc., that opposes or attacks; opponent; enemy: *She was a dangerous political adversary.* **—ad•ver•sar•i•al** (ad′vər sâr′ē əl) /ˌædvər'sɛəriyəl/ *adj.* See -VERT-.

ad•verse (ad vûrs′, ad′vûrs) /æd'vɜrs, 'ædvɜrs/ *adj.* [*before a noun*] **1.** unfavorable or antagonistic: *adverse criticism.* **2.** opposing one's interests or wishes: *adverse circumstances.* **3.** being in an opposite direction: *adverse winds.* **—ad•verse′ly,** *adv.* **—ad•verse′ness,** *n.* [*noncount*] See -VERT-.

ad•ver•si•ty (ad vûr′si tē) /æd'vɜrsɪtiy/ *n., pl.* **-ties** for

2. **1.** [*noncount*] unfavorable fortune or fate; misfortune; trouble: *in times of adversity.* **2.** [*count*] an unfavorable or unfortunate event or circumstance: *to cope with life's many adversities.*

ad•vert[1] (ad vûrt′) /æd'vɜrt/ *v.* [~ + *to* + *obj*] to refer to: *adverted to the day's news.*

ad•vert[2] (ad′vərt) /'ædvərt/ *n. Brit.* ADVERTISEMENT.

ad•ver•tise (ad′vər tīz′, ad′vər tīz′) /'ædvərˌtayz, ˌædvər'tayz/ *v.*, **-tised, -tis•ing. 1.** to announce or praise (a product, service, etc.) in newspapers, radio, or television, in order to sell it: [~ + *obj*]: *to advertise a new brand of toothpaste.* [*no obj*]: *They advertised in the paper.* **2.** [~ + *obj*] to give information to the public about (an event, happening, etc.), esp. in a newspaper or on radio or television: *They advertised the rock star's upcoming appearances.* **3.** [~ + *for* + *obj*] to request something, esp. by placing a notice in a newspaper: *to advertise for a house to rent.* **—ad′ver•tis′er,** *n.* [*count*] See -VERT-.

ad•ver•tise•ment (ad′vər tīz′mənt, ad vûr′tis mənt, -tiz-) /ˌædvər'tayzmənt, æd'vɜrtɪsmənt, -tɪz-/ *n.* **1.** [*count*] a paid notice or announcement, as of goods for sale, in newspapers or magazines, on radio or television, etc. **2.** [*noncount*] the action of making public: *This news will receive wide advertisement.* See -VERT-.

ad•ver•tis•ing (ad′vər tīz′ing) /'ædvər ˌtayzɪŋ/ *n.* [*noncount*] the business or activity of making advertisements.

ad•ver•to•ri•al (ad′vər tôr′ē əl, -tōr′-) /ˌædvər'tɔriyəl, -'towr-/ *n.* [*count*] a newspaper or magazine advertisement that has the appearance of editorial matter.

ad•vice (ad vīs′) /æd'vays/ *n.* [*noncount*] an opinion or recommendation offered as a guide to action. See -VIS-.

ad•vis•a•ble (ad vī′zə bəl) /æd'vayzəbəl/ *adj.* recommended, wise, sensible, as a course of action: [*be* + ~]: *Preparing for an interview is advisable.* [*it* + *be* + ~ + *to* + *verb*]: *It's advisable to get a professional opinion.* **—ad•vis•a•bil•i•ty** (ad vī′zə bil′i tē) /ædˌvayzə'bɪlɪtiy/ *n.* [*noncount*] **—ad•vis′a•bly,** *adv.* See -VIS-.

ad•vise (ad vīz′) /æd'vayz/ *v.*, **-vised, -vis•ing. 1.** to give counsel or advice (to), esp. to recommend as wise or sensible: [~ + *obj*]: *I advised secrecy.* [*no obj*]: *We did as she advised.* [~ + *obj* + *to* + *verb*]: *I advised the new student to take a music course.* [~ + *verb-ing*]: *I advised taking a music course.* [~ + *against* + *obj*]: *I advised against taking too many courses.* **2.** to give (a person, group, etc.) information or notice; tell or inform: [~ + *obj* + *of* + *obj*]: *The police advised the suspect of his rights.* [~ + *obj* + *that clause*]: *They advised him that he might face imprisonment.* **—Related Words.** ADVISE is a verb, ADVICE is a noun, ADVISABLE is an adjective: *I advise you to study harder. My advice to you is that you should study harder. It is advisable that you study harder.*

ad•vis•ed•ly (ad vī′zid lē) /æd'vayzɪdliy/ *adv.* after careful consideration; deliberately: *to speak advisedly.*

ad•vise•ment (ad vīz′mənt) /æd'vayzmənt/ *n.* [*noncount; often: under* + ~] careful deliberation or consideration: *The petition was taken under advisement.*

ad•vis•er or **ad•vis•or** (ad vī′zər) /æd 'vayzər/ *n.* [*count*] a person who gives advice; counselor: *My adviser suggested I take your course.*

ad•vi•so•ry (ad vī′zə rē) /æd'vayzəriy/ *adj.*, *n.*, *pl.* **-ries. —*adj.* 1.** giving or containing advice: *an advisory letter to shareholders.* **2.** having the power or duty to advise: *an advisory council.* **—*n.*** [*count*] **3.** a report on existing or predicted conditions, often with advice for dealing with them: *an investor's advisory.* **4.** an announcement or bulletin that serves to advise and usually warn the public, such as of some potential hazard: *a storm advisory.*

ad•vo•ca•cy (ad′və kə sē) /'ædvə kə siy/ *n.* [*noncount*] the act of supporting something publicly. See -VOC-.

ad•vo•cate (*v.* ad′və kāt′; *n.* -kit, -kāt′) /*v.* 'ædvəˌkeyt; *n.* -kɪt, -ˌkeyt/ *v.*, **-cat•ed, -cat•ing,** *n.* **—*v.*** [~ + *obj*] **1.** to support or urge by argument: *advocates higher salaries for teachers.* **—*n.*** [*count*] **2.** a person who speaks or writes in support of a cause, person, etc.: *a strong advocate of military intervention.* **3.** a person or lawyer who pleads the cause of another in a court of law: *a judge advocate.* See -VOC-.

advt., an abbreviation of: advertisement.

adz or **adze** (adz) /ædz/ *n.* [*count*] a tool like an ax for cutting timber, with a curved blade mounted at a right angle to the handle.

ae•gis (ē′jis) /'iydʒɪs/ *n.* [*noncount*] ***—Idiom.* under the aegis of,** sponsored or supported by: *a concert under the aegis of the student government.*

ae•on (ē′ən, ē′on) /'iyən, 'iyɒn/ *n.* EON.

aer•ate (âr′āt) /'ɛəreyt/ *v.* [~ + *obj*], **-at•ed, -at•ing.** to expose to the action of air or to cause air to circulate through: *to aerate the lungs.* **—aer•a•tion** (â rā′shən) /ɛə'reyʃən/ *n.* [*noncount*] **—aer′a•tor,** *n.* [*count*]

aer•i•al (âr′ē əl) /'ɛəriyəl/ *adj.* **1.** of, in, produced by, or done in the air: *aerial photography.* **2.** inhabiting the air: *aerial creatures.* **3.** of or relating to aircraft: *aerial combat.* **—*n.*** [*count*] **4.** a radio or television antenna: *Put up the car's aerial.* **—aer′i•al•ly,** *adv.*

aer•i•al•ist (âr′ē ə list) /'ɛəriyəlɪst/ *n.* [*count*] an acrobat who performs on a trapeze.

aer•ie or **aer•y** or **ey•rie** (âr′ē, ēr′ē) /'ɛəriy, 'ɪəriy/ *n.* [*count*], *pl.* **-ies** or **-ries.** the nest of a bird of prey (such as an eagle or a hawk) located high on a hill or mountain.

aero-, a combining form meaning "air": *aerodynamics.* Also, *esp. before a vowel,* **aer-.**

aer•o•bat•ics (âr′ə bat′iks) /ˌɛərə'bætɪks/ *n.* [*plural: used with a plural verb*] stunts performed in flight by an aircraft. **—aer′o•bat′ic,** *adj.*: *aerobatic maneuvers.*

aer•o•bic (â rō′bik) /ɛə'rowbɪk/ *adj.* [*before a noun*] **1.** (of an organism or tissue) requiring the presence of air or free oxygen to sustain life: *aerobic organisms.* **2.** of or relating to aerobics: *aerobic dancing.* **—aer•o′bi•cal•ly,** *adv.*

aer•o•bics (â rō′biks) /ɛə'rowbɪks/ *n.* any of various exercises, as jogging and calisthenics, that stimulate and strengthen the heart: [*noncount; used with a singular verb*]: *Aerobics is a good way to lose weight.* [*plural; used with a plural verb*]: *The aerobics were fairly strenuous.* **—*adj.*** [*before a noun*] of or relating to aerobics: *aerobics classes.*

aer•o•dy•nam•ic (âr′ō dī nam′ik) /ˌɛərowday'næmɪk/ *adj.* **1.** [*before a noun*] of or relating to the study of the motion of air and other gases: *aerodynamic principles.* **2.** able to flow smoothly and easily through air: *an aerodynamic design.* **—aer′o•dy•nam′i•cal•ly,** *adv.*

aer•o•dy•nam•ics (âr′ō dī nam′iks) /ˌɛərowday'næmɪks/ *n.* **1.** [*noncount; used with a singular verb*] the study of the motion of air and other gases and of the effects of such motion on objects moving through air: *He had a course in aerodynamics. Aerodynamics is important in aircraft design.* **2.** [*plural; used with a plural verb*] the effects caused by an object in motion through air: *How good are the aerodynamics of that car?*

aer•o•nau•tics (âr′ə nô′tiks, -not′iks) /ˌɛərə'nɔtɪks, -'nɒtɪks/ *n.* [*noncount; used with a singular verb*] the science or art of flight. **—aer′o•nau′ti•cal,** *adj.*

aer•o•plane (âr′ə plān′) /'ɛərəˌpleyn/ *n. Brit.* AIRPLANE.

aer•o•sol (âr′ə sôl′, -sol′) /'ɛərəˌsɔl, -ˌsɒl/ *n.* [*count*] **1.** a metal can containing a liquid substance under pressure that can be released as a spray or foam. **—*adj.* 2.** being or containing a substance under pressure for dispensing as a spray or foam: *aerosol sprays.*

aer•o•space (âr′ō spās′) /'ɛərowˌspeys/ *n.* [*noncount*] **1.** the earth's atmosphere and the space beyond. **—*adj.*** [*before a noun*] **2.** of or relating to aerospace, or to the industry concerned with the design and building of spacecraft: *the aerospace industry.*

aes•thete or **es•thete** (es′thēt) /'ɛsθiyt/ *n.* [*count*] a person who has or claims to have great sensitivity toward the beauties of art.

aes•thet•ic or **es•thet•ic** (es thet′ik) /ɛs'θɛtɪk/ *adj.* of or relating to a sense of beauty or an appreciation of the arts: *a keen aesthetic sense.* **—aes•thet′i•cal,** *adj.* **—aes•thet′i•cal•ly,** *adv.*

aes•thet•ics or **es•thet•ics** (es thet′iks) /ɛs'θɛtɪks/ *n.* [*noncount; used with a singular verb*] the branch of philosophy dealing with the nature of art and beauty.

AF, an abbreviation of: **1.** Air Force. **2.** Anglo-French.

Af., an abbreviation of: African.

a•far (ə fär′) /ə'fɑr/ *adv.* ***—Idiom.* from afar,** from a long way off: *The princess saw him riding toward her from afar.*

af•fa•ble (af′ə bəl) /'æfəbəl/ *adj.* **1.** easy to approach and to talk to; friendly: *courteous and affable neighbors.* **2.** showing warmth and friendliness; pleasant: *an affable smile.* **—af•fa•bil•i•ty** (af′ə bil′i tē) /ˌæfə'bɪlɪtiy/ *n.* [*noncount*] **—af′fa•bly,** *adv.*

af•fair (ə fâr′) /ə'fɛər/ *n.* [*count*] **1.** anything requiring action or effort; business: *resolved the affair with your lawyer.* **2. affairs,** [*plural*] matters of commercial or public interest or concern: *affairs of state.* **3.** thing; matter: *Our new computer is a complex affair.* **4.** [*singular*] a private or personal concern: *That's none of your affair.* **5.** an often brief sexual relationship between two people not married to each other. **6.** an incident that causes argument, talk, and often public scandal. **7.** a social gathering or other organized festive occasion.

af•fect[1] (ə fekt′) /ə'fɛkt/ *v.* [~ + *obj*] **1.** to produce an effect or change in: *Cold weather affected the crops.* **2.** to impress the mind or move the feelings of: *The tragedy affected him deeply.* —**Related Words.** AFFECT is a verb, AFFECTED and AFFECTIONATE are adjectives, AFFECTION is a noun: *Nothing seems to affect him. The way he speaks is affected and phony. The cat is friendly and affectionate. She shows a lot of affection for everyone.*

af•fect[2] (ə fekt′) /ə'fɛkt/ *v.* **1.** to pretend; feign: [~ + *obj*]: *to affect concern for others.* [~ + *to* + *verb*]: *He affected to know a lot about ancient history.* **2.** [~ + *obj*] to assume pretentiously or for effect: *He affected an English accent.* **3.** [~ + *obj*] to use, wear, or adopt by choice: *to affect outrageous clothes.*

af•fec•ta•tion (af′ek tā′shən) /ˌæfɛk'teyʃən/ *n.* **1.** [*noncount*] the pretense of having a knowledge, standing, etc., that is not actually possessed; pose; airs: *the affectation of great wealth.* **2.** [*count*] an artificial way of behaving or talking.

af•fect•ed (ə fek′tid) /ə'fɛktɪd/ *adj.* characterized by artificiality or pretension: *an affected gesture.*

af•fect•ing (ə fek′ting) /ə'fɛktɪŋ/ *adj.* stirring the emotions; touching: *an affecting scene.* —**af•fect′ing•ly,** *adv.*

af•fec•tion (ə fek′shən) /ə'fɛkʃən/ *n.* fond attachment, devotion, or love: [*noncount*]: *a look of pure affection.* [*count*]: *You are ever in my affections.*

af•fec•tion•ate (ə fek′shə nit) /ə 'fɛkʃə nɪt/ *adj.* showing fondness or love: *an affectionate glance.* —**af•fec′tion•ate•ly,** *adv.*

af•fi•da•vit (af′i dā′vit) /ˌæfɪ'deyvɪt/ *n.* [*count*] a written declaration that is sworn to be true and that can be used in a court of law: *Sign the affidavit and send it back to your lawyer.*

af•fil•i•ate (*v.* ə fil′ē āt′; *n.* -it, -āt′) /*v.* ə'fɪliyˌeyt; *n.* -ɪt, -ˌeyt/ *v.*, **-at•ed, -at•ing,** *n.* —*v.* **1.** to attach or bring into close association or connection: [*no obj*]: *The two groups affiliated.* [~ + *obj; often: be + affiliated + with + obj*]: *The research center is affiliated with the university.* [~ + *oneself + with*]: *affiliated themselves with a political party.* —*n.* [*count*] **2.** a branch organization; a business organization owned or controlled by another concern: *a TV network's affiliates.* —**af•fil•i•a•tion** (ə fil′ē ā′shən) /əˌfɪliy'eyʃən/ *n.* [*count; noncount*]

af•fin•i•ty (ə fin′i tē) /ə'fɪnɪtiy/ *n., pl.* **-ties.** [~ + *for/with/to/between*] **1.** a natural liking for or attraction to a person, thing, idea, etc: [*noncount*]: *felt a sense of affinity with his new colleague.* [*count*]: *I felt a natural affinity for the group.* **2.** close resemblance, agreement, or connection due to a common ancestry: [*count*]: *The Scandinavian languages have many affinities with German.* [*noncount*]: *Latin has affinity with Greek.*

af•firm (ə fûrm′) /ə'fɜrm/ *v.* [~ + *obj*] **1.** to assert positively; say (something) is true: *to affirm one's loyalty.* [~ + *that clause*]: *He affirmed that he would not reveal my secret.* **2.** to confirm or ratify, esp. of a court decision: *The judgment was affirmed.* **3.** to express agreement with; support; uphold: *I affirmed my client's claim.* —**af•firm′a•ble,** *adj.*

af•fir•ma•tion (af′ər mā′shən) /ˌæfər'meyʃən/ *n.* **1.** [*noncount*] the action of stating or asserting that something is true: *an affirmation of faith.* **2.** [*noncount*] expressing agreement with or support of: *an affirmation of the citizens' rights.* **3.** [*count*] (in law) a solemn and formal statement not made under oath.

af•firm•a•tive (ə fûr′mə tiv) /ə'fɜrmətɪv/ *adj.* **1.** expressing affirmation or consent: *an affirmative reply.* —*n.* [*count*] **2.** a reply indicating affirmation: *had received a clear affirmative on that idea.* **3.** [*in the* + ~] a manner or mode that indicates assent: *a reply in the affirmative.* **4.** the side, as in a debate, that defends a proposition. —*interj.* **5.** (used to indicate agreement, assent, etc.): *"Tower to Flight 340, do you read?"—"Affirmative."* —**af•firm′a•tive•ly,** *adv.*

affirm′ative ac′tion, *n.* [*noncount*] a policy to increase opportunities for women and minorities, esp. in employment and education.

af•fix (*v.* ə fiks′; *n.* af′iks) /*v.* ə'fɪks; *n.* ˈæfɪks/ *v.* [~ + *obj (+ to + obj)*] **1.** to fasten, join, or attach: *to affix stamps to a letter.* **2.** to add on; append: *to affix a signature to a contract.* —*n.* [*count*] **3.** (in grammar) an element such as a prefix or suffix, added to a base or stem of a word to form another word. Examples are the past tense suffix *-ed* added to *want* to form *wanted,* or the negative prefix *im-* added to *possible* to form *impossible.* See -FIX-.

af•flict (ə flikt′) /ə'flɪkt/ *v.* [~ + *obj; often: be + afflicted + with*] to cause distress or great trouble with mental or bodily pain: *to be afflicted with arthritis.* —**af•flic•tion** (ə flik′shən) /ə'flɪkʃən/ *n.* [*count*]

af•flu•ence (af′lo͞o əns) /'æfluw əns/ *n.* [*noncount*] the state of having an abundance of money and material goods. See -FLU-.

af•flu•ent (af′lo͞o ənt) /'æfluwənt/ *adj.* having an abundance of money and material goods; wealthy: *an affluent society.* —**af′flu•ent•ly,** *adv.* —**Related Words.** AFFLUENT is an adjective, AFFLUENCE is a noun: *They have an affluent lifestyle. Don't make a show of your affluence.* See -FLU-.

af•ford (ə fôrd′, ə fōrd′) /ə'fɔrd, ə'fowrd/ *v.* **1.** [*not: be + ~-ing*]: to be able to undergo without serious consequence: [~ + *obj*]: *The country can't afford another drought.* [~ + *to* + *verb*]: *We can't afford to take the chance.* **2.** [*not: be + ~-ing; ~ + obj*] to be able to meet the expense of or pay for: *Can I afford a new car?* **3.** to furnish; supply; give: [~ + *obj* + *obj*]: *The sale afforded the stockholders a profit.* [~ + *obj + to + obj*]: *It afforded a substantial profit to the stockholders.* —**af•ford′a•ble,** *adj.*

af•front (ə frunt′) /ə'frʌnt/ *n.* [*count*] **1.** a deliberate act or display of disrespect; insult: *That false accusation was an affront to my integrity.* —*v.* [~ + *obj; usually: be + ~ed*] **2.** to cause offense to; insult: *was deeply affronted by the accusation.*

Af•ghan (af′gan, -gən) /'æfgæn, -gən/ *n.* [*count*] **1.** a person born or living in Afghanistan. **2.** one of the principal languages of Afghanistan. **3.** [*afghan*] a soft knitted or crocheted blanket, often in a geometric pattern. **4.** a hunting dog with long, silky hair.

a•fi•cio•na•do or **af•fi•cio•na•do** (ə fish′yə nä′dō, ə fē′ sē ə-) /əˌfɪʃyə'nɑdow, əˌfiy siy ə-/ *n.* [*count*], *pl.* **-dos.** an enthusiastic fan; devotee: *an aficionado of the opera.*

a•field (ə fēld′) /ə'fiyld/ *adv.* Usually: **far afield 1.** abroad; away from home: *The tourists came from far afield.* **2.** away from the subject: *Your essay has wandered far afield from the topic at hand.*

a•fire (ə fīᵊr′) /ə'fayᵊr/ *adj.* **1.** on fire: [*after a noun*]: *to set a house afire.* [*be* + ~]: *The house was afire.* **2.** [*be* + ~] very eager and excited: *was all afire with the thought of the trip.*

a•flame (ə flām′) /ə'fleym/ *adj.* **1.** on fire; ablaze; in flames: [*after a noun*]: *She set the curtains aflame.* [*be* + ~]: *The barn was aflame.* **2.** [*be* + ~] very eager and excited: *was aflame with desire.*

a•float (ə flōt′) /ə'flowt/ *adv., adj.* **1.** floating or staying on the surface of the water: *The ship was still afloat. We kept the raft afloat.* **2.** financially solvent: *The company was barely afloat after the recession wiped out its profits. He has succeeded in keeping the company afloat.* **3.** in circulation; passing from person to person: *A rumor was afloat.*

a•flut•ter (ə flut′ər) /ə'flʌtər/ *adj.* in a flutter; agitated or excited: [*be* + ~]: *She was all aflutter, thinking of the party.* [*after a noun*]: *hearts aflutter with delight.*

a•foot (ə fo͝ot′) /ə'fʊt/ *adj.* being made ready; in progress: [*after a noun*]: *There is a plan afoot.* [*be* + ~]: *The plans are afoot.*

a•fore•men•tioned (ə fôr′men′shənd ə fōr′-) /ə'fɔrˌmɛnʃənd, ə'fowr-/ *adj.* [*before a noun*] mentioned earlier: *the aforementioned papers.*

a•fore•said (ə fôr′sed′, ə fōr′-) /ə'fɔrˌsɛd, ə'fowr-/ *adj.* [*before a noun*] said or mentioned earlier or previously.

a•fore•thought (ə fôr′thôt′, ə fōr′-) /ə'fɔrˌθɔt, ə'fowr-/ *adj.* [*after a noun*] thought of previously; planned ahead of time; premeditated: *with malice aforethought.*

a•foul (ə foul′) /ə'fawl/ *adj.* [*after a noun*] **1.** in collision or entanglement: *a ship with its shrouds afoul.* —***Idiom.*** **2. run** or **fall afoul of,** [*run/fall* + ~ + *of* + *obj*] **a.** to become entangled with: *The boat ran afoul of the seaweed.* **b.** to come into conflict with: *He ran afoul of the law.*

a•fraid (ə frād′) /ə'freyd/ *adj.* [*be* + ~] **1.** feeling fear; filled with apprehension: *suddenly became afraid.* [~ + *of*]: *afraid of heights.* [~ + *to* + *verb*]: *was afraid to go outside.* **2.** [~ + *(that) clause*] feeling regret or unhappiness: *I'm afraid we can't go.* **3.** feeling reluctance or unwillingness: [~ + *of*]: *was afraid of asking questions.* [~ + *to* + *verb*]: *was afraid to ask questions.* [~ + *(that) clause*]: *Can't I stay overnight at her house?—I'm afraid you can't = (I'm sorry, but you can't).* —**Related Words.** AFRAID and FEARFUL are adjectives, FEAR is both a noun and a verb: *I was afraid of monsters. They are fear-*

ful of retaliation from the gang. He was paralyzed by fear. He fears that he may have to tell her what he did.

a•fresh (ə fresh′) /əˈfrɛʃ/ *adv.* anew; once more: *to start afresh.*

Af•ri•can (af′ri kən) /ˈæfrɪkən/ *adj.* **1.** of or relating to Africa. *—n.* [*count*] **2.** a person born or living in Africa.

Af′rican-Amer′ican also **Afro-American,** *n.* [*count*] **1.** a black American of African descent. *—adj.* **2.** of or relating to African-Americans.

Af•ri•kaans (af′ri käns′, -känz′) /ˌæfrɪˈkɑns, -ˈkɑnz/ *n.* [*noncount*] **1.** one of the official languages of the Republic of South Africa, developed from the language of 17th-century Dutch settlers. *—adj.* **2.** of or relating to Afrikaans or Afrikaners.

Af•ri•ka•ner (af′ri kä′nər, -kan′ər) /ˌæfrɪˈkɑnər, -ˈkænər/ *n.* [*count*] a white person born or living in South Africa who is a descendant of 17th-century Dutch settlers.

Af•ro (af′rō) /ˈæfrow/ *adj., n., pl.* **-ros.** *—adj.* [*before a noun*] **1.** of or relating to African-Americans or to black traditions, culture, etc.: *Afro societies. —n.* [*count*] **2.** a hairstyle of very curly or frizzy hair grown or cut into a full, bushy shape.

Afro-, a combining form of AFRICA: *Afro-Cuban.* Also, *esp. before a vowel,* **Afr-.**

Af•ro-A•mer•i•can (af′rō ə mer′i kən) /ˌæfrowəˈmɛrɪkən/ *n., adj.* AFRICAN-AMERICAN.

Af•ro•cen•tric (af′rō sen′trik) /ˌæfrowˈsɛntrɪk/ *adj.* centered on Africa or on African-derived cultures, such as those of Brazil, Cuba, and Haiti. —**Af′ro•cen′trism,** *n.* [*noncount*] —**Af′ro•cen′trist,** *n.* [*count*]

aft (aft) /æft/ *adv.* **1.** at, close to, or toward the stern of a ship or the tail of an aircraft: *Take a seat aft, please. —adj.* **2.** situated toward or at the stern or tail: *The seat was aft of the exit door.*

af•ter (af′tər) /ˈæftər/ *prep.* **1.** behind in place or position; following behind: *We marched one after the other.* **2.** following the completion of; in succession to: *Tell me after supper.* **3.** in consequence of: *After what has happened, I can never return.* **4.** below in rank or estimation: *placed after Shakespeare among English poets.* **5.** in imitation of: *a painting after the artist Raphael.* **6.** in pursuit or search of: *I'm after a better paying job.* **7.** concerning; about: *to inquire after a person.* **8.** in agreement or conformity with: *a man after my own heart.* **9.** in spite of: *After all her troubles, she's still optimistic.* **10.** with the same name as: *They named her after my grandmother. —adv.* **11.** behind; in the rear: *The marchers came first and the floats came after.* **12.** later in time; afterward: *They lived happily ever after. —adj.* **13.** [*only before a noun*] later; subsequent: *In after years we never heard from him. —conj.* **14.** subsequent to the time that: *After the boys left, we cleaned up the house.* —***Idiom.*** **15. after all, a.** nevertheless: *We were angry with her, but, after all, she was our child and we had to forgive her.* **b.** (used to remind the reader or listener that there is a strong basis for what is said): *Of course he's exhausted. After all, he's been driving for ten straight hours.*

af•ter•birth (af′tər bûrth′) /ˈæftərˌbɜrθ/ *n.* [*count*] the material expelled from the uterus after childbirth.

af•ter•burn•er (af′tər bûr′nər) /ˈæftərˌbɜrnər/ *n.* [*count*] a device for increasing the power of a jet engine by burning extra fuel in the exhaust gases.

af•ter•care (af′tər kâr′) /ˈæftərˌkɛər/ *n.* [*noncount*] the care and treatment of a patient recovering from an operation or trauma.

af•ter•ef•fect (af′tər i fekt′) /ˈæftərɪˌfɛkt/ *n.* [*count*] a delayed effect, as one that follows the stimulus that produced it: *the aftereffects of the drug.*

af•ter•glow (af′tər glō′) /ˈæftərˌglow/ *n.* [*count*] **1.** the glow frequently seen in the sky after sunset. **2.** the pleasant remembrance of a past experience, glory, etc.

af•ter•im•age (af′tər im′ij) /ˈæftərˌɪmɪdʒ/ *n.* [*count*] a visual image that stays in one's vision even after one looks away, closes one's eyes, etc.

af•ter•life (af′tər līf′) /ˈæftərˌlayf/ *n., pl.* **-lives.** life after death: [*noncount*]: *belief in the afterlife.* [*count*]: *Do you believe in an afterlife?*

af•ter•math (af′tər math′) /ˈæftərˌmæθ/ *n.* [*count; usually singular*] something that follows from an event: *in the aftermath of the war.*

af•ter•noon (af′tər no͞on′) /ˌæftərˈnuwn/ *n.* **1.** the time from noon until evening: [*count*]: *every afternoon.* [*noncount; by +* ~]: *I'll get it done by afternoon. —adj.* **2.** of, relating to, or occurring during the afternoon: *an afternoon nap.*

af•ter•taste (af′tər tāst′) /ˈæftərˌteyst/ *n.* [*count; usually singular*] **1.** a taste remaining after the substance causing it is no longer in the mouth. **2.** a feeling left after an unpleasant experience: *The performance left them with a bad aftertaste.*

af•ter•thought (af′tər thôt′) /ˈæftərˌθɔt/ *n.* **1.** [*noncount*] a later or second thinking; reconsideration: *On afterthought, you're right.* **2.** [*count*] something added later, such as a part or feature.

af•ter•ward (af′tər wərd) /ˈæftərwərd/ also **af′ter•wards,** *adv.* at a later time; subsequently.

af•ter•word (af′tər wûrd′) /ˈæftərˌwɜrd/ *n.* [*count*] a concluding section of a book; closing statement.

-ag-, *root.* *-ag-* comes from Latin and Greek, where it has the meaning "to move, go, do". This meaning is found in such words as: AGENDA, AGENT, AGILE, AGITATE, AGOG, EXAGGERATE.

a•gain (ə gen′) /əˈgɛn/ *adv.* **1.** once more; another time: *Spell your name again, please.* **2.** on the other hand: *It might happen, and again it might not.* See *then again* below. **3.** back to a condition, state, or place that existed before: *She was better for a while but now she is sick again.* —***Idiom.*** **4. again and again,** with many repetitions; often. **5. as much again,** twice as much. **6. then again,** on the other hand; however: *It might rain, but then again it might not.*

a•gainst (ə genst′) /əˈgɛnst/ *prep.* **1.** in opposition to; contrary to: *twenty votes against ten.* **2.** in resistance to or defense from: *protection against mosquitoes.* **3.** in an opposite direction to: *walking against the wind.* **4.** in or into contact with; upon: *Don't lean against the door.* **5.** in preparation for: *saving money against a rainy day.* **6.** having as background: *a design of flowers against a dark wall.* **7.** to be deducted from: *The loan was an advance against salary.* **8.** in competition with: *a race against time.* **9.** in contrast with: *Use reason as against emotion.* —***Idiom.*** **10. have something against,** [~ + *obj*] to be in opposition to; be opposed to: *She has something against my attending the class.*

a•gape (ə gāp′, ə gap′) /əˈgeyp, əˈgæp/ *adv.* **1.** with the mouth wide open, as in wonder: *stood there agape at the news. —adj.* [*after a noun*] **2.** wide open: *stood with his mouth agape.*

a•gar (ä′gär, ag′ər) /ˈɑgɑr, ˈægər/ *n.* [*noncount*] Also, **a′gar-a′gar.** a gel made from red algae, used in laboratories as a base to allow substances to grow and as a thickener in food.

ag•ate (ag′it) /ˈægɪt/ *n.* **1.** a stone used in jewelry, with curved, colored bands or other markings: [*noncount*]: *The pendant was made of beautiful agate.* [*count*]: *polished agates.* **2.** [*count*] a playing marble made of agate.

a•ga•ve (ə gä′vē, ə gā′-) /əˈgɑviy, əˈgey-/ *n.* [*noncount; count*] a desert plant having a single tall flower stalk and thick leaves, used for its fibers.

age (āj) /eydʒ/ *n., v.,* **aged, ag•ing** or **age•ing.** *—n.* **1.** the length of time during which a being or thing has existed; length of life or existence: [*noncount*]: *Trees of unknown age.* [*count*]: *Their ages are 10 and 13.* **2.** [*noncount*] a period of human life, measured by years from birth, when a person is regarded as having certain powers or being qualified for certain privileges or responsibilities: *has reached the age of reason; is under the legal drinking age; was over the age of military service.* **3.** [*noncount*] one of the periods or stages of human life: *a person of middle age.* **4.** [*noncount*] advanced years; old age: *His eyes were dim with age.* **5.** [*count*] a generation or a series of generations: *the ages not yet born.* **6.** [*count; often singular*] the period of history in which an individual lives:*the most famous architect of the age.* **7.** [*count; often: Age*] a particular period of history; a historical epoch: *the Bronze Age.* **8.** [*count; often plural*] a long period of time: *I haven't seen you for ages.* **9.** [*count*] average life expectancy: *The ages of different species of horses vary from 25 to 30 years. —v.* **10.** to (cause to) grow old: [*no obj*]: *She is aging gracefully.* [~ + *obj*]: *Worry aged him overnight.* **11.** to (cause to) come to maturity: [*no obj*]: *The wine aged in great wooden barrels.* [~ + *obj*]: *cheese aged for at least three years.* —***Idiom.*** **12. be** or **come of age,** to reach an age at which one may vote, etc., as specified by law: *had to be of age to drink beer legally.* —**Related Words.** AGE is both a noun and a verb, AGED and AGING are adjectives but they can also be used as plural nouns: *His age is twenty-one. He aged dramatically during the crisis. The aged have rights, too. The aging generation needs a variety of social services.*

-age, *suffix.* *-age* is used to form noncount mass or abstract nouns: **1.** It is used to form nouns from other nouns, with meanings such as "collection" (*coinage = a collection or group of coins*) and "quantity or measure" (*footage = quantity of feet in measurement*). **2.** It is also used to form nouns from verbs, with meanings such as "process" (*coverage = the act or process of covering*), "the outcome of, the fact of" or "the physical effect or remains of" (*spoilage = the result of spoiling; wreckage = the remains of wrecking*), and "amount charged" (*towage = charge for towing; postage = amount charged for posting, that is, sending through the mail*).

a•ged (ā′jid *for 1;* ājd *for 2, 3*) /ˈeydʒɪd *for 1;* eydʒd *for 2, 3* / *adj.* **1.** of advanced age; old: *my aged aunt.* **2.** of the age of: [*after a noun*]: *a man aged 40 years.* [*be* + ~]: *My daughter is aged 13.* **3.** brought to maturity or mellowness, as wine or cheese.

age•ism (ā′jiz əm) /ˈeydʒɪzəm/ *n.* [*noncount*] discrimination against older persons. **—age′ist,** *adj., n.* [*count*]

age•less (āj′lis) /ˈeydʒlɪs/ *adj.* **1.** not aging or appearing to grow old: *The actor seemed ageless.* **2.** lasting forever; eternal: *ageless beauty.* **—age′less•ly,** *adv.* **—age′less•ness,** *n.* [*noncount*]

a•gen•cy (ā′jən sē) /ˈeydʒənsiy/ *n., pl.* **-cies. 1.** [*count*] an organization, company, or bureau that provides a particular service: *a welfare agency; an employment agency.* **2.** [*count*] the place of business of an agent: *independent insurance agency.* **3.** [*noncount*] a means or method of exercising power or influence; a way something is accomplished: *awarded the contract through the agency of friends.* See -AG-.

a•gen•da (ə jen′də) /əˈdʒɛndə/ *n.* [*count*], *pl.* **-das** *or* **-da.** a list, plan, outline of things to be done or voted upon, etc.: *Make up an agenda for the meeting.* **—Usage.** Originally *agenda* was the plural of a now older *agendum*, but today it is thought of as a singular noun. See -AG-.

a•gent (ā′jənt) /ˈeydʒənt/ *n.* [*count*] **1.** a person or thing that acts. **2.** a person or business authorized to act on another's behalf: *The ballplayer's agent got him a higher salary.* **3.** a natural force or object producing or used for obtaining specific results: *Many insects are agents of fertilization.* **4.** a person who works for or manages an agency: *a travel agent.* **5.** a person who acts in an official capacity for a government agency: *an FBI agent.* **6.** (in grammar) a word or phrase, usually a noun or noun phrase, that performs or causes the action expressed by the verb. **7.** a drug, chemical, or substance that causes a chemical or biological reaction. **—a•gen•tial** (ā jen′shəl) /eyˈdʒɛnʃəl/ *adj.* **—Usage.** In an active sentence, the agent is usually the subject, such as *The police* in *The police caught the thief.* But in a PASSIVE sentence, the agent may appear after *by*, as in *The thief was caught by the police,* where the agent is still *the police.* In other passive sentences, the agent may not appear at all; *Your wallet was stolen* has no noun phrase that is the agent. See -AG-.

A′gent Or′ange, *n.* [*noncount*] a powerful herbicide containing small amounts of dioxin, used heavily during the Vietnam War.

age′-old′, *adj.* [*before a noun*] ancient; from a time long ago: *age-old traditions.*

ag•glom•er•a•tion (ə glom′ə rā′shən) /əˌglɒməˈreyʃən/ *n.* **1.** [*noncount*] the action of collecting or gathering into a cluster or mass. **2.** [*count*] a heap, cluster, or mass, usually untidy or messy: *a huge agglomeration of rubbish.*

ag•glu•ti•nate (ə glo͞ot′n āt′) /əˈgluwtn̩ˌeyt/ *v.* [*no obj*], **-nat•ed, -nat•ing.** to adhere, stick, or clump together: *In minutes the mixture agglutinated, forming a sticky mass.*

ag•glu•ti•na•tion (ə glo͞ot′n ā′shən) /ə ˌgluwtn̩ˈeyʃən/ *n.* **1.** [*noncount*] the act or process of agglutinating. **2.** [*count*] the mass or cluster formed by agglutinating.

ag•gran•dize (ə gran′dīz, ag′rən dīz′) /əˈgrændayz, ˈægrənˌdayz/ *v.* [~ + *obj*], **-dized, -diz•ing. 1.** to widen in scope; enlarge; extend: *The company aggrandized its operations overseas.* **2.** to make great or greater in power, wealth, rank, or honor: *They worked hard to aggrandize the family name.* **—ag•gran′dize•ment** (ə gran′diz mənt) /əˈgrændɪzmənt/ *n.* [*noncount*]

ag•gra•vate (ag′rə vāt′) /ˈægrəˌveyt/ *v.* [~ + *obj*], **-vat•ed, -vat•ing. 1.** to make worse or more severe; intensify: *remarks that only aggravated an already tense situation.* **2.** to annoy; irritate; exasperate: *The constant noise aggravated the readers.* **—ag•gra•va•tion** (ag′rə-vā′shən) /ˌægrəˈveyʃən/ *n.* [*noncount; count*] **—Usage.** Informally, the verb *aggravate* is used in both senses. However, the sense "to annoy" is sometimes objected to, and is used less often than the sense "to make worse" in formal speech and writing.

ag•gra•vat•ed (ag′rə vā′tid) /ˈægrəˌveytɪd/ *adj.* **1.** very annoyed; exasperated: *aggravated, weary commuters.* **2.** [*before a noun*] *Law.* characterized by some feature that makes a crime more serious: *aggravated assault.*

ag•gre•gate (*adjective, noun* ag′ri git, -gāt′; *verb* -gāt′) /*adjective, noun* ˈægrɪgɪt, -ˌgeyt; *verb* -ˌgeyt/ *adj., n., v.,* **-gat•ed, -gat•ing. —***adj.* [*before a noun*] **1.** formed by joining or collecting into a whole mass or sum; combined: *the aggregate amount.* **—***n.* [*count*] **2.** a sum, mass, or collection of individual items: *an aggregate of some 500 points earned over 5 years.* **—***v.* **3.** to (cause to) come together into one mass or whole: [~ + *obj*]: *Sociologists aggregated the data for several groups.* [*no obj*]: *The white blood cells aggregated in the wound to fight infection.* **—*Idiom.* 4. in the aggregate,** considered as a whole: *Savings in the aggregate are on the upswing.* See -GREG-.

ag•gres•sion (ə gresh′ən) /əˈgrɛʃən/ *n.* [*noncount*] **1.** the action of making unprovoked assaults or attacks against another, esp. so as to dominate. **2.** hostility toward or attack upon another, whether in words or in gestures or other acts: *The panhandler's aggression frightened the passersby.* **—ag•gres•sor** (ə gres′ər) /əˈgrɛsər/ *n.* [*count*] See -GRESS-.

ag•gres•sive (ə gres′iv) /əˈgrɛsɪv/ *adj.* **1.** characterized by or tending toward aggression; warlike; hostile: *the aggressive nature of the dictator's actions.* **2.** vigorously energetic: *an aggressive approach to solving problems.* **—ag•gres′sive•ly,** *adv.* **—ag•gres′sive•ness,** *n.* [*noncount*]

ag•grieved (ə grēvd′) /əˈgriyvd/ *adj.* injured or hurt because of injustice: *felt aggrieved by the criticism.*

a•ghast (ə gast′) /əˈgæst/ *adj.* [*be* + ~] filled with sudden fear, horror, or amazement: *was aghast after witnessing the accident.*

ag•ile (aj′əl, -il) /ˈædʒəl, -ayl/ *adj.* **1.** quick and well-coordinated in movement; nimble: *agile athletes.* **2.** mentally resourceful: *an agile mind.* **—ag′ile•ly,** *adv.* **—a•gil•i•ty** (ə jil′i tē) /əˈdʒɪlɪtiy/ *n.* [*noncount*] See -AG-.

ag•i•tate (aj′i tāt′) /ˈædʒɪˌteyt/ *v.,* **-tat•ed, -tat•ing. 1.** [~ + *obj*] to move or force into violent, irregular action: *The strong winds agitated the plane.* **2.** [~ + *obj*] to disturb or excite emotionally; upset; perturb: *Please don't agitate the patients.* **3.** [~ + *for/against* + *obj*] to arouse public interest and support for or against (a political or social cause): *to agitate for repeal of a tax.* **—ag•i•ta•tion** (aj′i tā′shən) /ˌædʒɪˈteyʃən/ *n.* [*noncount*] **—ag′i•ta′tor,** *n.* [*count*] See -AG-.

a•gleam (ə glēm′) /əˈgliym/ *adj.* gleaming; bright: *eyes agleam with pleasure.*

a•glit•ter (ə glit′ər) /əˈglɪtər/ *adj.* glittering; sparkling: *houses aglitter with lights.*

a•glow (ə glō) /əglow/ *adj.* [*be* + ~ (+ *with*)] glowing: *The room was aglow with firelight.*

ag•nos•tic (ag nos′tik) /ægˈnɒstɪk/ *n.* [*count*] **1.** a person who believes that no one can know for certain about the existence of God. **—***adj.* **2.** of or relating to agnostics. **—ag•nos•ti•cism** (ag nos′tə siz′əm) /ægˈnɒstəˌsɪzəm/ *n.* [*noncount*] See -GNOS-.

a•go (ə gō′) /əˈgow/ *adj.* [*after a noun*] **1.** gone by; past: *She got here five days ago.* **—***adv.* **2.** in the past: *It happened long ago.*

a•gog (ə gog′) /əˈgɒg/ *adj.* [*be* + ~] highly excited by eagerness, curiosity, anticipation, etc.: *was all agog with excitement when she heard the news.* See -AG-.

-agon-, *root.* *-agon-* comes from Greek, where it has the meaning "struggle, fight". This meaning is found in such words as: AGONIZE, AGONY, ANTAGONIST, PROTAGONIST.

ag•o•nize (ag′ə nīz′) /ˈægəˌnayz/ *v.* [~ + *over* + *obj*], **-nized, -niz•ing.** to suffer great pain, anguish, or anxiety, as by thinking about something continuously: *They agonized every night over their decision.* **—ag′o•nized,** *adj.*: *agonized cries of pain.* **—ag′o•niz•ing,** *adj.*: *an agonizing decision.* **—ag′o•niz′ing•ly,** *adv.* See -AGON-.

ag•o•ny (ag′ə nē) /ˈægəniy/ *n., pl.* **-nies.** extreme mental or physical pain or suffering: [*noncount*]: *to cry out in agony.* [*count*]: *suffered many agonies.* See -AGON-.

ag•o•ra•pho•bi•a (ag′ər ə fō′bē ə) /ˌægərəˈfowbiyə/ *n.* [*noncount*] fear of being in public places or open areas. **—ag′o•ra•pho′bic,** *adj., n.* [*count*]

-agr-, *root.* *-agr-* comes from Latin, where it has the meaning "farming; field". This meaning is found in such words as: AGRICULTURE, AGRONOMY.

a•grar•i•an (ə grâr′ē ən) /əˈgrɛəriyən/ *adj.* **1.** relating to land, land ownership, or the division of agricultural property. **2.** rural; agricultural: *an agrarian nation.* **—*n.*** [*count*] **3.** a person who favors the equal division of land. **—a•grar′i•an•ism,** *n.* [*noncount*] See -AGR-.

a•gree (ə grē′) /ə'griy/ *v.,* **a•greed, a•gree•ing. 1.** [~ + *with* + *obj*] to be of one mind: *I agree completely with you.* **2.** to have the same opinion: [~ + *on* + *obj*]: *We don't agree on politics.* [~ + *(that) clause*]: *We all agree that you need a vacation.* **3.** to give consent; assent; accept; approve: [~ + *to* + *obj*]: *Do you agree to those conditions?* [~ + *to* + *verb*]: *Do you agree to accept those conditions?* [~ + *that clause*]: *I agree that I will help your cause.* **4.** [~ + *on/upon* + *obj*] to arrive at a settlement or understanding: *The buyer and seller have agreed on/upon the price.* **5.** to be consistent; be the same as or similar to; correspond; harmonize: [*no obj*]: *His story and my story agree.* [~ + *with* + *obj*]: *Her story agrees with mine.* **6.** [~ + *with* + *obj*] to be healthful or pleasing: *Humid air doesn't agree with me.* **7.** (of a subject and a verb in English, or of a pronoun and the word it stands for) to correspond by having the correct forms: [~ + *with* + *obj*]: *The subject agrees with the verb.* [*no obj*]: *The subject and verb agree.* **—Related Words.** AGREE is a verb, AGREEABLE is an adjective, AGREEMENT is a noun: *I agree with what you say. I agreed that we would have to finish. The weather was very agreeable. We had an agreement about who takes care of the dog.* **—Usage.** In English, a subject agrees with its verb in certain tenses or for certain forms. In *he runs,* the third person singular verb *runs* agrees with the third person singular subject *he.* Also, certain possessive adjectives and pronouns must correspond to the nouns they modify or stand for in English. In the sentence *Steve or John should raise his hand,* the pronoun *his* agrees with the noun *Steve* or the noun *John.* It is usually considered incorrect to write *Steve or John should raise their hand,* because *their* would agree with a plural noun.

a•gree•a•ble (ə grē′ə bəl) /ə'griyəbəl/ *adj.* **1.** to one's liking; pleasing; pleasant: *agreeable manners; an agreeable voice.* **2.** willing to agree: *Are you agreeable to my plans?* **3.** suitable: *Are my plans agreeable to you?*

a•gree•ment (ə grē′mənt) /ə'griymənt/ *n.* **1.** [*noncount*] the act of agreeing or of coming to a mutual arrangement. **2.** [*count*] an arrangement accepted by all parties to a transaction: *At long last we had an agreement.* **3.** [*count*] a contract or other document giving details of such an arrangement: *Sign the agreement here.* **4.** [*noncount*] in English, the correspondence in form between the subject and verb in certain tenses, or between a noun and a possessive pronoun: *Subject verb agreement was her biggest grammar problem.*

ag•ri•busi•ness (ag′rə biz′nis) /'ægrə,bɪznɪs/ *n.* [*noncount*] the businesses associated with producing, processing, and distributing agricultural products. See -AGR-.

ag•ri•cul•ture (ag′ri kul′chər) /'ægrɪ,kʌltʃər/ *n.* [*noncount*] the science, art, or work concerned with cultivating land, raising crops, and feeding and raising livestock; farming. **—ag′ri•cul′tur•al,** *adj.* **—ag′ri•cul′tur•al•ist,** *n.* [*count*] **—ag′ri•cul′tur•al•ly,** *adv.* See -AGR-.

a•gron•o•my (ə gron′ə mē) /ə'grɒnəmiy/ *n.* [*noncount*] the science of farm management and of the production of crops. **—ag•ro•nom•ic** (ag′rə nom′ik) /,ægrə'nɒmɪk/ *adj.* **—a•gron′o•mist,** *n.* [*count*] See -NOM-[1], -AGR-.

a•ground (ə ground′) /ə'grawnd/ *adv.* onto the ground beneath a body of water: *The ship ran aground.*

a•gue (ā′gyo͞o) /'eygyuw/ *n.* [*noncount*] chills and fever, esp. when associated with malaria.

ah (ä) /ɑ/ *interj.* **1.** (used to express pain, surprise, pity, pleasure, and other emotions). **2.** (used to express hesitation in stating something): *I'm buying this for, ah, my colleague.*

a•ha (ä hä′) /ɑ'hɑ/ *interj.* (used to express triumph, agreement, discovery, or other emotions or feelings).

a•head (ə hed′) /ə'hɛd/ *adv.* **1.** in or to the front; before: *Can you see ahead without headlights?* **2.** in a forward direction; onward: *The train jerked ahead a few feet.* **3.** into or for the future: *It's wise to plan ahead.* **4.** so as to register a later time: *In spring we set the clock ahead one hour.* **—*adj.*** [*be* + ~] **5.** having the highest score so far, as in a competition; presently winning: *Our team was ahead at halftime.* **—*Idiom.* 6. ahead of,** [~ + *obj*] before or further than: *I always arrived ahead of the others.* **7. get ahead,** move onward to success: *to get ahead in the world.*

a•hem (*pronounced as a nasalized scraping sound, as if clearing the throat; spelling pron.* ə hem′, hem) /*pronounced as a nasalized scraping sound, as if clearing the throat; spelling pron.* ə'hɛm, hɛm/ *interj.* (used to attract attention or express a mild warning).

-aholic, *suffix. -aholic* (originally taken from the word ALCOHOLIC)) is used to form new words with the general meaning "a person who is addicted to or strongly desires (some object or activity)," the activity being shown by the initial part of the word. Thus, a *chargeaholic* is someone who uses a charge card a lot; a *foodaholic* is someone who always wants food. Compare -HOLIC.

a•hoy (ə hoi′) /ə'hɔy/ *interj.* (used at sea to call to another ship, attract attention, etc.): *Ahoy, there!*

aid (ād) /eyd/ *v.* **1.** to provide support (for) or relief (to); help: [~ + *obj*]: *accused of aiding the enemy.* [~ + *in* + *obj*]: *They aided in the development of the country.* **2.** [~ + *obj*] to promote the progress of; facilitate: *The sleeping pill will aid your sleep.* **—*n.*** **3.** [*noncount*] help or support; assistance: *financial aid to the country.* **4.** [*count*] a person or thing that aids or furnishes assistance: *an aid to digestion.*

aide (ād) /eyd/ *n.* [*count*] **1.** an assistant or helper, esp. a confidential one: *an administrative aide.* **2.** AIDE-DE-CAMP.

aide-de-camp (ād′də kamp′) /'eyddə'kæmp/ *n.* [*count*], *pl.* **aides-de-camp** (ādz-′) /eydz-'/. a military officer who assists a higher-ranking general or admiral.

AIDS (ādz) /eydz/ *n.* [*noncount*] an acronym from *acquired immune deficiency syndrome,* a disease of the immune system that makes the victim less able to resist infection, cancer, and neurological disorders.

ail (āl) /eyl/ *v.* **1.** [~ + *obj*] to cause pain, uneasiness, or trouble to: *What ails you, child?* **2.** [*no obj*] to be unwell; feel pain; be ill: *She's been ailing ever since she was bitten by that deer tick.*

ai•ler•on (ā′lə ron′) /'eylə,rɒn/ *n.* [*count*] a flap on the back surface of an aircraft wing, used to control the plane's roll and to perform banks.

ail•ment (āl′mənt) /'eylmənt/ *n.* [*count*] a physical disorder or illness.

aim (ām) /eym/ *v.* **1.** to point (a firearm, ball, etc.) so that the thing discharged or thrown will hit a target: [~ + *obj*]: *The police officer aimed the pistol and fired.* [*no obj*]: *He turned, aimed, and fired all in one motion.* [~ + *at* + *obj*]: *She aimed at the target.* [~ + *obj* + *at* + *obj*]: *She aimed a kick at him.* **2.** [~ + *obj* + *at* + *obj*] to direct toward a particular goal: *The lawyer aimed his remarks at the jury.* **3.** to strive; try: [~ + *at* + *verb-ing*]: *We aim at pleasing everyone.* [~ + *to* + *verb*]: *We aim to please.* **4.** [~ + *to* + *verb*] to intend: *She aims to go tomorrow.* **—*n.*** **5.** [*noncount*] the act of directing anything at or toward a target: *How good is your aim?* **6.** [*noncount*] the direction in which a weapon or missile is pointed: *His aim was a little off.* **7.** [*noncount*] the point to be hit: *to miss one's aim.* **8.** [*count*] purpose; intention: *It is my aim to reform the program.* **—*Idiom.* 9. take aim (at),** [*take* + ~ (+ *at* + *obj*)] to point a weapon or one's efforts at: *took aim at the target; took aim at reforming the bureaucrats.* **—aim′er,** *n.* [*count*]

aim•less (ām′lis) /'eymlɪs/ *adj.* purposeless; random: *aimless violence.* **—aim′less•ly,** *adv.* **—aim′less•ness,** *n.* [*noncount*]

ain't (ānt) /eynt/ *v.* **1.** *Nonstandard except in some dialects.* am not; are not; is not: *Well, it just ain't right.* **2.** *Nonstandard.* have not; has not; do not; does not; did not: *I ain't got nobody.*

air (âr) /ɛər/ *n.* **1.** [*noncount; often: the* + ~] the mixture of nitrogen, oxygen, and other gases that surrounds the earth and forms its atmosphere. **2.** [*noncount*] a light breeze: *The air stirred.* **3.** [*noncount; often: the* + ~] overhead space; sky: *The kite rose high in the air.* **4.** [*count; singular*] general character or appearance; aura: *had an air of mystery about him.* **5. airs,** [*plural*] an affected or haughty manner: *Stop putting on airs.* **6.** [*count*] a tune; melody: *humming a simple air.* **7.** [*noncount*] aircraft as a means of transportation: *to ship by air.* **8.** [*noncount*] *Informal.* an air-conditioning system: *a car equipped with air and a cassette player.* **—*v.*** **9.** to expose to the air; ventilate: [~ (+ *out*) + *obj*]: *to air (out) a room.* [~ + *obj* (+ *out*)]: *Let's air the room (out).* [*no obj; (~ + out)*]: *Let the room air (out).* **10.** [~ + *obj*] to bring to public notice; display: *to air one's opinions.* **11.** to broadcast or televise; to be broadcast or televised: [~ + *obj*]: *aired the program during prime time.* [*no obj*]: *The program airs in prime time.* **—*adj.*** **12.** operating by air pressure or by acting upon air: *an air pump.* **13.** of or relating to aircraft or to aviation: *air traffic control.* **—*Idiom.* 14. clear the air,** to get rid of or eliminate misunderstandings: *decided to discuss their differences* *and clear the air.* **15. in the air,** being talked about: *An interesting rumor is in the air.* **16. off the air,** not broadcasting or being broadcast: *Suddenly the station went off the air.* **17. on the air,** broadcasting or being broadcast: *The President is on the air tonight.* **18. up in the air,** not decided; unsettled: *Their plans are still up in the air.* **19. walk on air,** to feel very happy or elated. —**air′less,** *adj.* —**air′less•ness,** *n.* [*noncount*]

air′ bag′, *n.* [*count*] a plastic bag mounted in the passenger compartment of a motor vehicle that cushions the driver and passengers by inflating in the event of a collision.

air′ base′, *n.* [*count*] a military airport.

air•borne (âr′bôrn′, -bōrn′) /ˈɛərˌbɔrn, -ˌbowrn/ *adj.* **1.** carried by the air: *airborne pollution.* **2.** [*be* + ~] in flight; aloft: *The plane was soon airborne.*

air′ brake′, *n.* [*count*] a brake operated by compressed air: *a large truck with air brakes.*

air•brush (âr′brush′) /ˈɛərˌbrʌʃ/ *n.* [*count*] **1.** a device that turns paint to a fine mist and sprays it. —*v.* [~ + *obj*] **2.** to paint or decorate by using an airbrush. **3.** to remove or alter by or as if by means of an airbrush: *airbrushed the blemishes from the picture.*

air′-condi′tion, *v.* [~ + *obj*] to furnish with air conditioning. —**air′ condi′tioner,** *n.* [*count*]

air′ condi′tioning, *n.* [*noncount*] a system for reducing the temperature and humidity of the air in an enclosed space. —**air′-condi′tioning,** *adj.* [*before a noun*]: *a new air-conditioning system.*

air•craft (âr′kraft′) /ˈɛərˌkræft/ *n.* [*count*], *pl.* **-craft.** any machine that can fly, esp. airplanes, gliders, and helicopters.

air′craft car′rier, *n.* [*count*] a warship equipped with a large open deck for the taking off and landing of warplanes.

air•drop (âr′drop′) /ˈɛərˌdrɒp/ *v.*, **-dropped, -drop•ping,** *n.* —*v.* [~ + *obj*] **1.** to drop (persons, equipment, etc.) by parachute from an aircraft in flight. —*n.* [*count*] **2.** the act or process of airdropping.

air•field (âr′fēld′) /ˈɛərˌfiyld/ *n.* [*count*] a level area on which airplanes take off and land.

Air′ Force′, *n.* **1.** [*proper noun*] the U.S. department in charge of the nation's military air power. **2.** [*count; air force*] the military unit of any nation that carries out air operations.

air′ gun′, *n.* [*count*] a gun that fires by compressed air.

air•head (âr′hed′) /ˈɛərˌhɛd/ *n.* [*count*] *Slang.* a scatterbrained or simple-minded person. —**air′head′ed,** *adj.*

air′ kiss′, *n.* [*count*] a pursing of the lips in a pretended kiss.

air′ lane′, *n.* [*count*] a route regularly used by airplanes; airway.

air′ letter′, *n.* [*count*] a letter sent by air.

air•lift (âr′lift′) /ˈɛərˌlɪft/ *n.* [*count*] Also, **air′ lift′. 1.** the act, process, or system for transporting persons or cargo by aircraft, esp. in an emergency. —*v.* [~ + *obj*] **2.** to transport (persons or cargo) by airlift: *to airlift supplies.*

air•line (âr′līn′) /ˈɛərˌlayn/ *n.* [*count*] **1.** a company that owns or operates a system furnishing air transportation between specified points. —*adj.* [*before a noun*] **2.** of, for, or on an airline: *an airline pilot.*

air•lin•er (âr′lī′nər) /ˈɛərˌlaynər/ *n.* [*count*] a passenger aircraft operated by an airline.

air′ lock′, *n.* [*count*] an airtight chamber permitting passage to or from a space in which the air is kept under pressure.

air•mail or **air-mail** (âr′māl′) /ˈɛərˌmeyl/ *n.* [*noncount*] Also, **air′ mail′. 1.** a system of sending mail by airplane. **2.** the mail sent by this system: *The only deliveries were airmail.* —*adj.* [*before a noun*] **3.** of or relating to airmail: *airmail delivery.* —*adv.* **4.** by airmail: *to send letters airmail.* —*v.* **5.** to send by airmail: [~ + *obj*]: *airmailed the letters.* [~ + *obj* + *to* + *obj*]: *airmailed the letters to us.* [~ + *obj* + *obj*]: *airmailed us the letters.*

air•man (âr′mən) /ˈɛərmən/ *n.* [*count*], *pl.* **-men. 1.** a flyer, pilot, or member of an air force. **2.** *U.S. Air Force.* an enlisted person of one of the three lowest ranks **(air′man ba′sic, airman, air′man first′ class′).**

air′ mass′, *n.* [*count*] a body of air covering a wide area and having almost the same properties or characteristics throughout.

air•plane (âr′plān′) /ˈɛərˌpleyn/ *n.* [*count*] a heavier-than-air craft that has wings and is driven in flight by propellers or jet propulsion. Also, *esp. Brit.,* **aeroplane.**

air′ pock′et, *n.* [*count*] a downward current causing an aircraft to lose altitude suddenly.

air•port (âr′pôrt′, -pōrt′) /ˈɛərˌpɔrt, -ˌpowrt/ *n.* [*count*] a place that has facilities for the landing, takeoff, shelter, supply, and repair of aircraft.

air′ raid′, *n.* [*count*] a raid by aircraft, esp. for bombing a particular area.

air′ ri′fle, *n.* [*count*] a rifle fired by compressed air.

air•ship (âr′ship′) /ˈɛərˌʃɪp/ *n.* [*count*] a self-propelled, lighter-than-air craft in which the direction of flight can be controlled; dirigible. Compare BLIMP.

air•sick (âr′sik′) /ˈɛərˌsɪk/ *adj.* [*often: be* + ~] ill or sick from the motion of an aircraft. —**air′sick′ness,** *n.* [*noncount*]

air•space (âr′spās′) /ˈɛərˌspeys/ *n.* [*noncount*] the air or sky above a nation, considered to belong to that nation.

air′ strike′ or **air′strike′,** *n.* [*count*] an attack on a target by military aircraft.

air•strip (âr′strip′) /ˈɛərˌstrɪp/ *n.* [*count*] an aircraft runway without airport facilities.

air•tight (âr′tīt′) /ˈɛərˌtayt/ *adj.* **1.** sealed so as to prevent the entrance or escape of air or gas: *The food stayed fresh in the airtight container.* **2.** having no weak points that an opponent could use to get an advantage: *His alibi was airtight.*

air′-to-air′, *adj.* [*before a noun*] operating between airborne objects: *air-to-air missiles.*

air•waves (âr′wāvz′) /ˈɛərˌweyvz/ *n.* [*plural*] the radio waves used for radio and television broadcasting.

air•way (âr′wā′) /ˈɛərˌwey/ *n.* [*count*] **1.** AIR LANE. **2.** the passageway by which air passes from the nose or mouth to the air sacs of the lungs.

air•wor•thy (âr′wûr′thē) /ˈɛərˌwɜrðiy/ *adj.*, **-thi•er, -thi•est.** (of an aircraft) equipped and maintained in condition to fly. —**air′wor′thi•ness,** *n.* [*noncount*]

air•y (âr′ē) /ˈɛəriy/ *adj.*, **-i•er, -i•est. 1.** open to a free flow of fresh air; breezy: *airy rooms.* **2.** made up of or having the character of air; immaterial: *airy phantoms.* **3.** light in appearance; thin: *airy, almost see-through garments.* **4.** light in manner; sprightly; lively: *airy songs.* **5.** not solid; not substantial; unreal; imaginary: *airy responses to difficult questions.* **6.** snobbish; haughty: *a look of airy superiority.* —**air•i•ly** (âr′ə lē) /ˈɛərəliy/ *adv.* —**air′i•ness,** *n.* [*noncount*]

aisle (īl) /ayl/ *n.* [*count*] **1.** a walkway between or along sections of seats, shelves, counters, etc., as in a theater, church, or department store. See illustration at SUPERMARKET. —***Idiom.* 2. (rolling) in the aisles,** (of an audience) convulsed with laughter.

a•jar (ə jär′) /əˈdʒɑr/ *adj., adv.* partly open: *The door was ajar. She had left the door ajar.*

AK, an abbreviation of: Alaska.

a.k.a. or **aka,** an abbreviation of: also known as (used when identifying an alias): *Clark Kent, a.k.a. Superman.*

a•kim•bo (ə kim′bō) /əˈkɪmbow/ *adv.* with hand on hip and elbow bent outward: *to stand with arms akimbo.*

a•kin (ə kin′) /əˈkɪn/ *adj.* [*be* + ~ + *to*] having similar properties, qualities, preferences, etc.: *Her thoughts on the subject were akin to mine.*

-al[1], *suffix.* *-al* is used to form adjectives from nouns, with the meaning "relating to, of the kind of, having the form or character of:" *autumn* + *-al* → *autumnal (= relating to the season autumn); nature* + *-al* → *natural (= having the character of nature).*

-al[2], *suffix.* *-al* is used to form nouns from verbs, with the meaning "the act of:" *deny* + *-al* → *denial (= the act of denying); refuse* + *-al* → *refusal (= the act of refusing).*

AL, an abbreviation of: Alabama.

à la or **a la** (ä′ lä, al′ə) /ˈɑ lɑ, ˈælə/ *prep.* in the manner or style of: *a poem à la Byron.*

Ala., an abbreviation of: Alabama.

al•a•bas•ter (al′ə bas′tər) /ˈæləˌbæstər/ *n.* [*noncount*] **1.** a kind of white, chalklike gypsum substance used for ornaments and statues. —*adj.* Also, **al•a•bas•trine** (al′ə-bas′trin) /ˌæləˈbæstrɪn/. **2.** made of, or resembling, alabaster; smooth and white.

à la carte or **a la carte** (ä′lä kärt′, al′ə) /ˌɑˈlɑ kɑrt, ˌælə/ *adv., adj.* from or according to a menu having a separate price for each item: *We ordered à la carte. Everything is à la carte.*

a•lac•ri•ty (ə lak′ri tē) /əˈlækrɪtiy/ *n.* [*noncount*] cheerful readiness and quickness: *responded with alacrity.*

à la mode or **a la mode** or **a•la•mode** (ä′lä mōd′, al′ə-) /ˌɑˈlɑ mowd, ˌælə-/ *adj.* **1.** [*only: be* + ~] fashionable; up-to-date: *Her clothing was à la mode.* —*adv.* **2.** served with ice cream: *apple pie à la mode.*

a•larm (ə lärm′) /əˈlɑrm/ *n.* **1.** [*noncount*] a sudden fear or feeling of anxiety due to the awareness of danger;

fright: *jumped up in alarm.* **2.** [*count*] any sound, outcry, or information intended to warn of approaching danger: *The townspeople raised the alarm.* **3.** [*count*] an automatic device that serves to arouse or warn of danger: *The smoke alarm went off at 4 a.m.* **—***v.* [~ + *obj*] **4.** to make fearful or apprehensive; frighten: *The news of the invasion alarmed the neighboring countries.* **5.** to warn of danger. **6.** to equip with an alarm or alarms, as in case of fire or robbery.

a•larm•ing (ə lär′ming) /ə 'lɑrmɪŋ/ *adj.* frightening; worrisome: *an alarming rise in crime.* —**a•larm′ing•ly,** *adv.*

a•larm•ist (ə lär′mist) /ə'lɑrmɪst/ *n.* [*count*] **1.** a person who is easily alarmed and tends to raise alarms without sufficient reason. **—***adj.* **2.** of or like an alarmist.

Alas., an abbreviation of: Alaska.

a•las (ə las′) /ə'læs/ *interj.* (used to express regret or concern): *There was, alas, nothing we could do.*

al•ba•core (al′bə kôr′, -kōr′) /'ælbəˌkɔr, -ˌkowr/ *n.* [*count*], *pl.* **-cores,** (*or when thought of as a group*) **-core.** a long-finned fish of the tuna family.

Al•ba•ni•an (al bā′nē ən) /æl'beyniyən/ *adj.* **1.** of or relating to Albania. **2.** of or relating to the language spoken in Albania. **—***n.* **3.** [*count*] a person born or living in Albania. **4.** [*noncount*] the language spoken in Albania.

al•ba•tross (al′bə trôs′, -tros′) /'ælbəˌtrɔs, -ˌtrɒs/ *n.* [*count*], *pl.* **-tross•es,** (*esp. when thought of as a group*) **-tross** for 1. **1.** a large, web-footed, mostly white bird of southern tropical oceanic waters, having a large wingspread and able to remain aloft for long periods. **2.** something burdensome that gets in the way of action or progress: *This huge debt is the company's albatross.*

al•be•it (ôl bē′it) /ɔl'biyɪt/ *conj.* although; even if; even though: *a peaceful, albeit brief retirement.*

al•bi•no (al bī′nō) /æl'baynow/ *n.* [*count*], *pl.* **-nos. 1.** a person with pale skin, white hair, pinkish eyes, and vision problems due to the inability to produce the pigment melanin. **2.** an animal or plant with an abnormal lack of coloring. **—***adj.* [*before a noun*] **3.** of or like an albino: *albino rats.*

al•bum (al′bəm) /'ælbəm/ *n.* [*count*] **1.** a bound or loose-leaf book made up of blank pages for storing or displaying photographs or for collecting autographs. **2.** a recording containing musical selections, a complete play or opera, etc.: *The album sold several million copies.*

al•bu•men (al byo͞o′mən) /æl'byuwmən/ *n.* [*noncount*] **1.** the white of an egg. **2.** ALBUMIN.

al•bu•min or **al•bu•men** (al byo͞o′mən) /æl'byuwmən/ *n.* [*noncount*] a protein found in egg white, milk, blood, and other animal and vegetable tissues.

al•che•my (al′kə mē) /'ælkəmiy/ *n.* [*noncount*] **1.** a form of chemistry of the Middle Ages that tried to discover an elixir of life and a method for changing ordinary metals into gold. **2.** any seemingly magical process of changing something ordinary into something superior. —**al′che•mist,** *n.* [*count*]

al•co•hol (al′kə hôl′, -hol′) /'ælkəˌhɔl, -ˌhɒl/ *n.* [*noncount*] **1.** a colorless liquid produced by yeast fermentation and found in wine, beer, and liquor. **2.** whiskey, gin, vodka, or any other intoxicating liquor containing this liquid.

al•co•hol•ic (al′kə hô′lik, -hol′ik) /ˌælkə'hɔlɪk, -'hɒlɪk/ *adj.* **1.** of or relating to alcohol; containing or using alcohol: *alcoholic beverages.* **2.** caused by alcohol: *in an alcoholic daze.* **—***n.* [*count*] **3.** a person suffering from alcoholism.

al•co•hol•ism (al′kə hô liz′əm, -ho-) /'ælkəhɔˌlɪzəm, -hɒ-/ *n.* [*noncount*] a chronic disorder marked by acute dependence on alcohol, physical degeneration, and difficulty in functioning in society.

al•cove (al′kōv) /'ælkowv/ *n.* [*count*] a recessed space in a room: *a dining alcove.*

al•der (ôl′dər) /'ɔldər/ *n.* [*count*], *pl.* **alders** or **alder.** a shrub or tree of the birch family, growing in moist places in cool regions.

al•der•man (ôl′dər mən) /'ɔldərmən/ *n.* [*count*], *pl.* **-men.** a member of a legislative or governing body of a city.

ale (āl) /eyl/ *n.* [*noncount; count*] an alcoholic beverage that is made from malt and is darker and more bitter than beer.

a•lert (ə lûrt′) /ə'lɜrt/ *adj.* **1.** paying complete attention; wide-awake: *The children were alert, following the teacher's instructions.* **2.** watchful and ready to act; vigilant: *The prison guard was alert at his post.* [~ + *to*]: *remained alert to the danger.* **—***n.* [*count*] **3.** a warning or alarm of an impending military attack, a storm, etc.: *a tornado alert.* **4.** the period in which such a warning or alarm is in effect. **—***v.* [~ + *obj (+ to + obj)*] **5.** to warn (troops, ships, etc.) to prepare for a coming attack: *alerted the air squadron.* **6.** to make aware of; warn: *alerting the townspeople to the danger.* **—*Idiom.* 7. on the alert,** prepared for danger or opportunity. —**a•lert′ly,** *adv.* —**a•lert′ness,** *n.* [*noncount*]

-alesc-, *root.* *-alesc-* comes from Latin, where it has the meaning "grow, develop." This meaning is found in such words as: ADOLESCENCE, ADOLESCENT, COALESCE.

al•fal•fa (al fal′fə) /æl'fælfə/ *n.* [*noncount*] a plant of the legume family used esp. to feed animals.

al•fres•co or **al fres•co** (al fres′kō) /æl'frɛskow/ *adv.* **1.** out-of-doors: *to dine alfresco.* **—***adj.* [*before a noun*] **2.** outdoor: *an alfresco picnic.*

-alg-, *root.* *-alg-* comes from Greek, where it has the meaning "pain." This meaning is found in such words as: ANALGESIC, NEURALGIA, NOSTALGIA.

al•gae (al′jē) /'ældʒiy/ *n.pl.; sing.:* **-ga** (-gə). any of many groups of one-celled organisms containing chlorophyll and usually living in watery or damp environments. —**al•gal** (al′gəl) /'ælgəl/ *adj.*

al•ge•bra (al′jə brə) /'ældʒəbrə/ *n.* [*noncount*] the branch of mathematics that deals with general statements of relations, and uses letters and other symbols to represent numbers or values. —**al•ge•bra•ic** (al′jə brā′ik) /ˌældʒə'breyɪk/ *adj.* —**al′ge•bra′i•cal•ly,** *adv.*

Al•ge•ri•an (al jēr′ē ən) /æl'dʒɪəriyən/ *adj.* **1.** of or relating to Algeria. **—***n.* [*count*] **2.** a person born or living in Algeria.

al•go•rithm (al′gə rith′əm) /'ælgəˌrɪðəm/ *n.* [*count*] **1.** a set of rules to follow in a fixed order for solving a problem: *an algorithm to find the greatest common divisor of a group of numbers.* **2.** a sequence of steps designed for programming a computer to solve a specific problem. —**al•go•rith•mic** (al′gə rith′mik) /ˌælgə'rɪðmɪk/ *adj.*

-ali-, *root.* *-ali-* comes from Latin, where it has the meaning "other, different." This meaning is found in such words as: ALIAS, ALIBI, ALIEN, ALIENATE.

a•li•as (ā′lē əs) /'eyliyəs/ *n., pl.* **-as•es,** *adv.* **—***n.* [*count*] **1.** an additional or assumed name: *The novelist wrote under an alias.* **—***adv.* **2.** otherwise called: *"Smithers alias Smith" means that Smithers in other circumstances has called himself Smith.* See -ALI-.

al•i•bi (al′ə bī′) /'æləˌbay/ *n.* [*count*], *pl.* **-bis. 1.** the claim by an accused person of having been elsewhere when an offense was committed: *He has a good alibi for the night of the murder.* **2.** an excuse, esp. to avoid blame: *The boss doesn't want alibis.* **3.** a person used as one's excuse: *Her lover turned out to be her alibi.* See -ALI-.

al•ien (āl′yən, ā′lē ən) /'eylyən, 'eyliyən/ *n.* [*count*] **1.** a foreign-born person who is living in a country and has not been legally naturalized or been granted citizenship. **2.** a person who has been estranged or excluded; outsider. **3.** a being or creature from outer space; an extraterrestrial. **—***adj.* **4.** [*before a noun*] owing allegiance to another country; not naturalized; of or relating to aliens. **5.** [*only before a noun*] foreign: *a people accustomed to alien rulers.* **6.** unlike one's own; strange: *frightened by the alien environment; alien ideas.* See -ALI-.

al•ien•a•ble (āl′yə nə bəl, ā′lē ə-) /'eylyənəbəl, 'eyliyə-/ *adj. Law.* capable of being sold or transferred: *Certain rights are not alienable.* Compare INALIENABLE.

al•ien•ate (āl′yə nāt′, ā′lē ə-) /'eylyəˌneyt, 'eyliyə-/ *v.* [~ + *obj*], **-at•ed, -at•ing. 1.** to cause (someone) to be hostile or indifferent: *He has alienated most of his friends.* **2.** *Law.* to convey (title, property, etc.) to another: *to alienate lands.* See -ALI-.

al•ien•at•ed (āl′yə nā tid, ā′lē ə-) /'eylyə ney tɪd, 'eyliyə-/ *adj.* feeling separated or isolated: *felt alienated from other teenagers.*

al•ien•a•tion (āl′yə nā′shən, ā′lē ə-) /ˌeylyə 'neyʃən, ˌeyliyə-/ *n.* [*noncount*] a feeling of isolation or separation from one's surroundings.

a•light[1] (ə līt′) /ə'layt/ *v.* [*no obj*], **a•light•ed** or **a•lit** (ə-lit′) /ə'lɪt/ **a•light•ing. 1.** to climb down from a horse, descend from a vehicle to the ground, etc.: *She alighted gracefully from the limousine.* **2.** to descend and come to rest: *The bird alighted on the branch.*

a•light[2] (ə līt′) /ə'layt/ *adj.* having light; provided with light; lighted up: [*be* + ~]: *The room was alight.* [*after a noun*]: *eyes alight.*

a•lign (ə līn′) /ə'layn/ *v.* [~ + *obj*] **1.** to arrange in a straight line: *to align the beams in the ceiling.* **2.** to bring into alignment: *to align the wheels on a car.* **3.** to bring into agreement with a particular group, cause, etc.:

aligned himself with the minority party. [*be* + *aligned* + *with*]: *was aligned with the minority party.*

a•lign•ment (ə līn′mənt) /ə 'laynmənt/ *n.* **1.** [*noncount*] arrangement in a straight line; adjustment so that parts function properly. **2.** [*count*] a state of agreement or cooperation among groups, nations, etc.; alliance.

a•like (ə līk′) /ə'layk/ *adv.* **1.** in the same manner; equally: *to treat all customers alike.* **2.** similar or comparable: *Not all people are alike.*

al•i•men•ta•ry (al ə men′tə rē) /æl ə 'mɛntə riy/ *adj.* [*before a noun*] of or relating to food, nutrition, or digestion.

al•i•mo•ny (al′ə mō′nē) /'ælə,mowniy/ *n.* [*noncount*] an allowance paid to a spouse or former spouse for maintenance following a divorce or legal separation.

a•live (ə līv′) /ə'layv/ *adj.* **1.** [*be* + ~] living; existing; not dead or lifeless: *He was still alive after being buried in the snow for five days.* **2.** [*after a noun*] (used for emphasis) living: *the proudest person alive.* **3.** in force or operation; active: [*after a noun*]: *to keep hope alive.* [*be* + ~]: *Their hopes were still alive.* **4.** [*be* + ~] full of energy and spirit; lively: *alive and kicking.* —***Idiom.*** **5. alive to,** aware of: *keenly alive to the emotions of others.* **6. alive with,** filled with; swarming with: *The pond was alive with fish.* —**a•live′ness,** *n.* [*noncount*]

al•ka•li (al′kə lī′) /'ælkə,lay/ *n., pl.* **-lis, -lies,** *adj.* —*n.* **1.** any of various chemical substances that neutralize acids to form salts: [*noncount*]: *Alkali turns red litmus paper blue.* [*count*]: *Some alkalis are harmful to the growth of crops.* —*adj.* **2.** ALKALINE. —**al•ka•lin•i•ty** (al′kə lin′i tē) /,ælkə'lınıtiy/ *n.* [*noncount*]

al•ka•line (al′kə līn, -lin) /'ælkə layn, -lın/ *adj.* of, containing, or like an alkali: *Use alkaline batteries in this toy.*

al•ka•loid (al′kə loid′) /'ælkə,lɔyd/ *n.* [*count*] **1.** a bitter-tasting chemical compound common in plants, as caffeine, morphine, and nicotine. —*adj.* **2.** resembling an alkali; alkaline.

all (ôl) /ɔl/ *adj.* [*usually before a noun; but see definition 1*] **1.** the whole or full amount of or number of: [~ + *the* + *noncount noun*]: *She ate all the cake.* [~ + *some nouns of time*]: *I waited for her call all afternoon.* [~ (+ *the*) + *plural noun*]: *all (the) students.* [*after the subject of a sentence*]: *The girls all enjoy camping.* [*after a pronoun object of a sentence*]: *I've seen them all.* **2.** the greatest possible: *with all speed.* **3.** any; any whatever: *beyond all doubt.* **4.** entirely; purely: *The coat is all wool.* **5.** dominated by a particular feature: *I'm all thumbs (= very clumsy) when it comes to auto repairs.* —*pron.* **6.** the whole quantity, number, or entire amount: *Did you eat all of the peanuts?* —*n.* **7.** [*noncount*] one's whole interest, energy, or property: *Give it your all.* **8.** [*noncount*] the entire area, place, environment, or the like: *All is calm, all is bright.* **9.** [*plural; used with a plural verb*] every one; everybody (a formal use): *All rise, the court is in session.* **10.** [*noncount*] everything: *Is that all you've got to say?* —*adv.* **11.** wholly; entirely; completely: *all alone.* **12.** each; apiece: *The score was tied at one all.* —***Idiom.*** **13. all but,** [*be* + ~] almost; very nearly: *These batteries are all but dead.* **14. all in all,** everything considered; in general: *All in all, we're better off now than we were ten years ago.* **15. all out,** with one's best effort: *The team went all out to win the game.* **16. all the better,** so much the better: *If my opponent loses, all the better for me.* **17. all there,** [*usually with a negative word or phrase, or in questions*] mentally competent: *She doesn't seem all there.* **18. all told,** all together; all included: *All told, some sixty-five people came to the party.* **19. and all,** and so forth: *What with the late hour and all, we must leave.* **20. at all,** (used to give emphasis to a word or phrase, esp. a word or phrase with "any" in it): **a.** in the slightest degree or amount: *Aren't there any doughnuts left at all?* **b.** for any reason: *Why bother at all?* **c.** in any way: *didn't cause me any trouble at all.* **d.** (used in other phrases for emphasis): *Look, I'll take a job anywhere at all.* **21. for all (that),** in spite of (that); notwithstanding: *It was a difficult time living abroad, but for all that, it was a good year.* **22. in all,** all included; all together: *There were forty in all.* **23. of all,** (used to give emphasis after a word like "first", "last", "best"): *First of all, welcome to our college.*

Al•lah (al′ə, ä′lə) /'ælə, 'ɑlə/ *n.* [*proper noun*] the Muslim name for the Supreme Being; God.

all′-Amer′ican, *adj.* **1.** selected as the best in the United States (as in a sport): *an all-American college football team.* **2.** representing the entire United States: *the all-American games.* **3.** composed exclusively of American members or elements: *The all-American team played the German team.* —*n.* [*count*] **4.** an all-American player or team: *She was an all-American two years in a row.*

all′-around′ or **all-round,** *adj.* [*before a noun*] **1.** able to do many things; versatile: *an all-around athlete.* **2.** broadly applicable: *an all-around education.* **3.** being so in all matters: *an all-around good guy.*

al•lay (ə lā′) /ə'ley/ *v.* [~ + *obj*] **1.** to reduce (fear, etc.); calm: *allayed the child's fears.* **2.** to lessen or relieve; make better; alleviate: *Take this pill to allay the pain.*

all′ clear′, *n.* [*count*] **1.** a signal that a danger has passed. **2.** a signal to proceed: *got the all clear to start the campaign.*

al•le•ga•tion (al′i gā′shən) /,ælı'geyʃən/ *n.* [*count*] **1.** the act of alleging: *The court heard very serious allegations about his misconduct.* **2.** a statement or claim made with little or no proof: *upset about the allegations about their marriage.*

al•lege (ə lej′) /ə'lɛdʒ/ *v.* [~ + *obj*], **-leged, -leg•ing.** to state or claim (something) without proof: [~ + *that clause*]: *You allege that my client was at the scene.* [*be* + *alleged* + *to* + *verb*]: *My client was only alleged to have been there.*

al•leged (ə lejd′, ə lej′id) /ə'lɛdʒd, ə'lɛdʒıd/ *adj.* [*before a noun*] **1.** stated or claimed to be so: *an alleged murderer.* **2.** doubtful; suspect: *an alleged cure.* —**al•leg•ed•ly** (ə lej′id lē) /ə'lɛdʒıdliy/ *adv.*

al•le•giance (ə lē′jəns) /ə'liydʒəns/ *n.* loyalty or devotion to some person, group, cause, or the like, esp. loyalty of citizens to their government: [*count*]: *found out where his allegiances lie.* [*noncount*]: *He pledged allegiance to his new country.*

al•le•go•ry (al′ə gôr′ē, -gōr′ē) /'ælə,gɔriy, -,gowriy/ *n., pl.* **-ries. 1.** [*count*] a story or poem in which moral lessons are conveyed through the actions of fictional characters that serve as symbols: *the allegory of the Pied Piper.* **2.** [*noncount*] the use of allegory in literature. —**al•le•gor•i•cal** (al′ə gôr′i kəl, -gor′-) /,ælə'gɔrıkəl, -'gɒr-/ **al′le•gor′ic,** *adj.* —**al′le•gor′i•cal•ly,** *adv.* —**al′le•gor′ist,** *n.* [*count*]

al•le•gro (ə lā′grō, ə leg′rō) /ə'leygrow, ə'lɛgrow/ *adv., adj. Music.* rapid in tempo; rather fast.

al•le•lu•ia (al′ə lo͞o′yə) /,ælə'luwyə/ *interj., n., pl.* **-ias.** —*interj.* **1.** HALLELUJAH. —*n.* [*count*] **2.** a song of praise to God.

al•ler•gen (al′ər jən, -jen′) /'ælərdʒən, -,dʒɛn/ *n.* [*count*] a substance that brings about an allergic reaction. —**al′ler•gen′ic,** *adj.*

al•ler•gic (ə lûr′jik) /ə'lɜrdʒık/ *adj.* **1.** [*before a noun*] of or relating to allergy: *an allergic reaction to wool.* **2.** [*be* + ~ (+ *to*)] having an allergy: *She's allergic to dust.* **3.** [*be* + ~ + *to*] having a strong dislike: *was allergic to hard work.*

al•ler•gist (al′ər jist) /'ælərdʒıst/ *n.* [*count*] a physician who specializes in the treatment of allergies.

al•ler•gy (al′ər jē) /'ælərdʒiy/ *n.* [*count*], *pl.* **-gies. 1.** a reaction of the body to an otherwise harmless substance, typically marked by skin rash, swelling of tissues of the nose or throat, sneezing, or wheezing. **2.** a strong dislike: *an allergy to rude people.*

al•le•vi•ate (ə lē′vē āt′) /ə'liyviy,eyt/ *v.* [~ + *obj*], **-at•ed, -at•ing.** to make easier to endure: *to alleviate pain.* —**al•le•vi•a•tion** (ə lē′vē ā′shən) /ə,liyviy'eyʃən/ *n.* [*noncount*] See -LEV-.

al•ley (al′ē) /'æliy/ *n.* [*count*], *pl.* **-leys. 1.** a passage, such as behind a row of houses. **2.** a narrow back street. —***Idiom.*** **3. (right) up** or **down one's alley,** highly suited to one's interests or abilities.

al′ley cat′, *n.* [*count*] a stray cat.

al•ley•way (al′ē wā′) /'æliy,wey/ *n.* [*count*] an alley.

al•li•ance (ə lī′əns) /ə'layəns/ *n.* **1.** [*noncount*] the act of allying or the state of being allied. **2.** [*count*] a formal agreement or treaty between two or more nations to cooperate for specific purposes. **3.** [*count*] a merging of efforts or interests: *an alliance between church and state; an alliance between business and education.* **4.** [*noncount*] close relationship or correspondence; affinity: *the alliance between logic and metaphysics.*

al•lied (ə līd′, al′īd) /ə'layd, 'ælayd/ *adj.* **1.** joined by treaty or common cause: *allied nations.* **2.** [*before a noun*] related; kindred: *allied species.* **3.** [*before a noun; Allied*] of or relating to the Allies: *the Allied forces.*

Al•lies (al′īz, ə līz′) /'ælayz, ə 'layz/ *n.* [*plural*] **1.** the alliance of nations that fought in World War I against the Central Powers: France, Great Britain, Russia, and the U.S. **2.** the alliance of nations that fought in World War II against the Axis: Great Britain, Russia, the U.S., and others. **3.** the alliance of nations that fought in the Persian Gulf war against Iraq: Great Britain, France, Saudi Arabia, Egypt, the U.S., and others.

al•li•ga•tor (al′i gā′tər) /'ælɪˌgeytər/ *n.* [*count*] either of two crocodile-like reptiles of the southeastern U.S. and E China, having a broad snout.

al•lit•er•a•tion (ə lit′ə rā′shən) /əˌlɪtə'reyʃən/ *n.* [*noncount*] repetition of the same initial sound or sounds of two or more word groups, as in *from stem to stern.* **—al•lit•er•a•tive** (ə lit′ə rā′tiv, -ər ə tiv) /ə'lɪtəˌreytɪv, -ərətɪv/ *adj.* See -LIT-.

al•lo•cate (al′ə kāt′) /'æləˌkeyt/ *v.* [~ + *obj*], **-cat•ed, -cat•ing.** to set apart for a particular purpose; assign: *to allocate space.* [~ + *obj* + *for* + *obj*]: *They allocated the money for purchasing computers.* [~ + *obj* + *obj*]: *They allocated him a small room.* **—al•lo•ca•tion** (al′ə-kā′shən) /ˌælə'keyʃən/ *n.* [*noncount; count*] See -LOC-.

al•lot (ə lot′) /ə'lɒt/ *v.* [~ + *obj*], **-lot•ted, -lot•ting. 1.** to set apart for a purpose: *to allot money for a park.* **2.** to divide or give out by shares or portions: *to allot the farmland among the heirs.*

al•lot•ment (ə lot′mənt) /ə 'lɒtmənt/ *n.* **1.** [*noncount*] the assigning or giving out of portions: *limited allotment.* **2.** [*count*] a portion so assigned or distributed.

all′-out′, *adj.* [*before a noun*] using all one's resources; complete; total: *an all-out effort.*

al•low (ə lou′) /ə'law/ *v.* **1.** [*not: be* + *~-ing*] to give permission to or for; permit: [~ + *obj*]: *I won't allow it.* [~ + *obj* + *to* + *verb*]: *How often does she allow a student to miss class?* [~ + *verb-ing*]: *The school does not allow smoking on campus.* **2.** [*not: be* + *~ing;* ~ + *obj* + *obj*] to let have; give as one's share: *The school allowed each person $100 for expenses.* **3.** [*not: be* + *~-ing;* ~ + *obj* + *to* + *verb*] to permit by neglect: *How could you allow that to happen?* **4.** [*not: be* + *~-ing;* ~ + *(that) clause*] to admit; acknowledge: *I had to allow that he was right.* **5.** [~ + *obj*] to approve, as for payment: *The insurance adjustor allowed my claim for a new windshield.* **6.** [~ + *obj* (+ *for* + *obj*)] to assign or allocate (time to do something); set apart in reserve: *Allow an hour for changing planes.* **7.** [*not: be* + *~-ing;* ~ + *of*] to make possible; admit: *Your premise allows of only one conclusion.* **8. allow for,** [~ + *for* + *obj*] to make provision for: *to allow for breakage.*

al•low•a•ble (ə lou′ə bəl) /ə 'lawə bəl/ *adj.* that may be permitted: *allowable tax deductions.*

al•low•ance (ə lou′əns) /ə'lawəns/ *n.* [*count*] **1.** an amount or share set aside for a purpose: *a dietary allowance of 900 calories a day.* **2.** a sum of money set aside for a particular purpose: *an allowance of $200 for travel.* **3.** a sum of money given on a regular basis: *Each child got a weekly allowance.* **—Idiom. 4. make allowance(s) for,** [~ + *obj*] **a.** to overlook the existence or nature of: *We have to make allowances for her faults.* **b.** to allow for, as by reserving time, money, etc., for: *We have to make allowances for the traffic.*

al•loy (*n.* al′oi, ə loi′; *v.* ə loi′) /*n.* 'ælɔy, ə'lɔy; *v.* ə'lɔy/ *n.* [*count*] **1.** a substance made up of two or more metals. **2.** anything added that serves to reduce quality or purity. **3.** any mixture of things: *an alloy of good and evil.* **—*v.*** [~ + *obj*] **4.** to mix (metals or metal with nonmetal) so as to form an alloy. See UNALLOYED.

all′ right′, *adv.* **1.** yes; very well: *All right, you can go.* **2.** (used in a question) do you agree?: *We'll meet tomorrow, all right?* **3.** satisfactorily; acceptably: *Her work is coming along all right.* **4.** without fail; certainly: *You'll hear about this, all right!* **—*adj.*** [*be* + ~] **5.** safe; healthy; uninjured: *Are you sure you're all right?* **6.** acceptable; passable: *His performance was barely all right.* **7.** reliable; good: *That fellow is really all right.*

all′-round′, *adj.* ALL-AROUND.

all•spice (ôl′spis′) /'ɔlˌspays/ *n.* [*noncount*] a powder made of berries of an aromatic tropical American tree and used as a spice.

all′-star′, *adj.* [*before a noun*] **1.** made up of athletes chosen as the best at their positions from all teams in a league or region: *an all-star team.* **2.** consisting entirely of star performers: *an all-star cast.* **—*n.*** [*count*] **3.** a player selected for an all-star team.

all′-time′, *adj.* [*before a noun*] **1.** never equaled or surpassed: *Production will reach an all-time high.* **2.** regarded as such in its entire history: *an all-time favorite song.*

al•lude (ə lo͞od′) /ə'luwd/ *v.* [~ + *to*], **-lud•ed, -lud•ing.** to make an allusion; refer: *Who are you alluding to?* See -LUD-.

al•lure (ə lo͝or′) /ə'lʊr/ *v.,* **-lured, -lur•ing,** *n.* **—*v.*** [~ + *obj*] **1.** to attract or tempt by something flattering or desirable: *Her beauty allured him.* **—*n.*** [*noncount*] **2.** fascination; charm; appeal: *the allure of money.* **—al•lure′-ment,** *n.* [*noncount; count*]

al•lur•ing (ə lo͝or′ing) /ə 'lʊrɪŋ/ *adj.* exerting allure: *alluring eyes.* **—al•lur′ing•ly,** *adv.*

al•lu•sion (ə lo͞o′zhən) /ə'luwʒən/ *n.* **1.** [*count*] a passing or casual reference to something, either directly or implied: *an allusion to Shakespeare.* **2.** [*noncount*] the act of alluding: *No allusion to his criminal record was allowed in the trial.* **—al•lu•sive** (ə lo͞o′siv) /ə'luwsɪv/ *adj.* **—al•lu′sive•ly,** *adv.* **—al•lu′sive•ness,** *n.* [*noncount*] See -LUD-.

al•ly (*n.* al′ī, ə lī′; *v.* ə lī′) /*n.* 'ælay, ə'lay; *v.* ə'lay/ *n., pl.* **-lies,** *v.,* **-lied, -ly•ing. —*n.*** [*count*] **1.** a nation, group, or person associated with another or others for some common cause or purpose. See ALLIES. **—*v.* 2.** to unite formally, such as by treaty, league, or marriage; enter into an alliance: [~ + *oneself* + *to/with* + *obj*]: *Russia allied itself with France.* [*no obj*]: *They allied against the common enemy.* **3.** [~ + *oneself* + *to/with* + *obj*] to associate or connect by some mutual relationship: *They allied themselves with the stockholders to gain control of the company.*

-ally, *suffix. -ally* is used to form adverbs from certain adjectives ending in -IC: *terrific (adj.)* + *-ally* → *terrifically (adv.).*

al•ma ma•ter (äl′mə mä′tər, al′-; al′mə mā′tər) /'ɑlmə mɑtər, 'æl-; 'ælmə meytər/ *n.* [*count*] a school, college, or university at which one has studied.

al•ma•nac (ôl′mə nak′) /'ɔlməˌnæk/ *n.* [*count*] an annual publication containing a calendar for the coming year, important dates, and the times of such phenomena as sunrises and sunsets.

al•might•y (ôl mī′tē) /ɔl'maytiy/ *adj.* **1.** having unlimited power; omnipotent, as God: *a concept of an almighty being.* **2.** having very great power, influence, etc.: *the almighty dollar.* **3.** [*before a noun*] *Informal.* extreme; terrible: *in an almighty rage.* **—*adv.* 4.** *Informal.* extremely: *It's almighty hot.* **—*n.* 5. the Almighty,** [*proper noun*] God.

al•mond (ä′mənd, am′ənd) /'ɑmənd, 'æmənd/ *n.* **1.** [*count*] the nutlike kernel of the fruit of a tree of the rose family. **2.** [*count*] the tree itself. **3.** [*noncount*] a pale tan color. **—*adj.*** [*only before a noun*] **4.** of the color, taste, or shape of an almond. **5.** made or flavored with almonds. **—al′mond•like′, al′mond•y,** *adj.*

al•most (ôl′mōst, ôl mōst′) /'ɔlmowst, ɔl'mowst/ *adv.* very nearly; all but: *to pay almost nothing for a car.*

alms (ämz) /ɑmz/ *n.* [*plural*] money, food, or other donations given to the needy.

al•oe (al′ō) /'ælow/ *n.* [*count*], *pl.* **-oes. 1.** a chiefly African shrub of the lily family. **2.** a type of aloe that yields a juice used in skin lotion.

a•loft (ə lôft′, ə loft′) /ə'lɔft, ə'lɒft/ *adv.* **1.** in or into the air; far above the ground: *were aloft seconds after takeoff.* **—*prep.* 2.** on or at the top of: *flags flying aloft the castle.*

a•lo•ha (ə lō′ə, ä lō′hä) /ə'lowə, ɑ'lowhɑ/ *n.* [*count*], *pl.* **-has,** *interj.* **1.** hello; greetings. **2.** farewell.

a•lone (ə lōn′) /ə'lown/ *adj.* **1.** [*be* + ~] separate, apart; by oneself: *alone in the wilderness.* **2.** [*after a noun or pronoun*] to the exclusion of all others or all else: *You can't live by bread alone.* **3.** [*be* + ~] unequaled; unexcelled. **4.** [*after a noun*] only; nothing else being necessary: *Her name alone was enough to draw a crowd.* **—*adv.* 5.** by oneself: *She lives alone.* **6.** solely; exclusively: *This glassware is sold by us alone.* **7.** without aid or help: *The baby can stand alone.* **—Idiom. 8. leave** or **let alone,** [*leave/let* + *obj* + ~] to refrain from bothering or interfering with: *left him alone with his thoughts.* **9. leave** or **let well enough alone,** to leave things as they are: *Let's leave well enough alone and stop tinkering.* **10. let alone,** not to mention: *too tired to walk, let alone run.* **—a•lone′ness,** *n.* [*noncount*]

a•long (ə lông′, ə long′) /ə'lɔŋ, ə'lɒŋ/ *prep.* **1.** over the length or direction of; in a line with: *walking along the highway at night.* **2.** in the course of: *I lost my hat along the way.* **3.** in conformity or accordance with: *Let's keep going along the lines we proposed earlier.* **—*adv.* 4.** parallel: *He ran along beside me.* **5.** so as to go forward or progress; onward: *Move along.* **6.** as a companion; with one: *She took her brother along.* **7.** from one person or place to another: *The order was passed along.* **8.** toward a goal or completion: *The work is coming along quite nicely.* **9.** as an accompanying item: *Bring along your umbrella.* **—Idiom. 10. all along,** from the start: *has* *been hiding something all along.* **11. along with, a.** together with; at the same time as: *They escaped along with a few other prisoners.* **b.** in cooperation or company with: *He planned the project along with his associates.* **12. be along,** [*no obj*] *Informal.* to arrive at a place: *They should be along soon.*

a•long•side (ə lông′sīd′, ə long′-) /ə'lɔŋ'sayd, ə'lɒŋ-/ *adv.* **1.** along or at the side of something: *We brought the boat alongside.* **—***prep.* **2.** by the side of: *We brought the boat alongside the dock.* **3. alongside of,** beside; alongside: *parked alongside of the house.*

a•loof (ə lo͞of′) /ə'luwf/ *adj.* **1.** reserved; not showing interest: *a reputation of being aloof.* **—***adv.* **2.** at a distance in feeling or manner: *remained aloof from his classmates.* **—a•loof′ness,** *n.* [*noncount*]

a•loud (ə loud′) /ə'lawd/ *adv.* **1.** in the normal tone and loudness of the speaking voice: *They could not speak aloud at the movies.* **2.** with the speaking voice: *read the story aloud to the children.* **3.** loudly: *to cry aloud in grief.*

al•pac•a (al pak′ə) /æl'pækə/ *n., pl.* **-as. 1.** [*count*] a South American hoofed mammal having long, soft, silky fleece, related to the llama. **2.** [*noncount*] the fleece of this animal; yarn or fabric made of this fleece.

al•pha (al′fə) /'ælfə/ *n.* [*count*], *pl.* **-phas. 1.** the first letter of the Greek alphabet (A, α). **2.** the first of any series; beginning: *from alpha to omega (= from beginning to end).*

al•pha•bet (al′fə bet′, -bit) /'ælfə,bɛt, -bɪt/ *n.* [*count*] **1.** the letters of a language in their customary order. **2.** basic facts; rudiments; ABC's: *the alphabet of biology.*

al•pha•bet•i•cal (al′fə bet′i kəl) /,ælfə 'bɛtɪ kəl/ *adj.* arranged according to the order of the letters in the alphabet. **—al′pha•bet′i•cal•ly,** *adv.*

al•pha•bet•ize (al′fə bi tīz′) /'ælfəbɪ,tayz/ *v.* [~ + *obj*], **-ized, -iz•ing.** to put or arrange in alphabetical order: *In no time the computer alphabetized the mailing list for us.* **—al•pha•bet•i•za•tion** (al′fə bet′ə zā′shən, -bi tə-) /,ælfə,bɛtə'zeyʃən, -bɪ tə-/ *n.* [*noncount*] **—al′pha•bet•iz′er,** *n.* [*count*]

al•pha•nu•mer•ic (al′fə no͞o mer′ik, -nyo͞o-) /,ælfənuw'mɛrɪk, -nyuw-/ also **al′pha•nu•mer′i•cal,** *adj.* using letters, numbers, and often special characters or symbols: *an alphanumeric code.* **—al′pha•nu•mer′i•cal•ly,** *adv.*

al•pine (al′pīn, -pin) /'ælpayn, -pɪn/ *adj.* **1.** of or relating to any high mountains: *alpine slopes.* **2.** [*before a noun; Alpine*] of or relating to the Alps. **3.** growing in or living in the heights above the timberline: *alpine plants.* **4.** [*often: Alpine*] of or relating to downhill or slalom skiing: *an Alpine event.*

al•read•y (ôl red′ē) /ɔl'rɛdiy/ *adv.* **1.** [*often with a perfect tense like present perfect or past perfect*] previously; before some specified or implied time: *I'm sorry, she has already left for the day. She had already arrived and was waiting for you.* **2.** so soon; so early; sooner than expected: *I can't believe she is already here.* **3.** *Informal.* (used to express exasperation or impatience): *Let's go already!* **—Usage.** See STILL.

al•right (ôl rīt′) /ɔl'rayt/ *adv., adj.* ALL RIGHT. **—Usage.** ALRIGHT is used in informal writing, but ALL RIGHT is preferred in formal, edited writing.

al•so (ôl′sō) /'ɔlsow/ *adv.* **1.** in addition; additionally; too; besides: *He was thin, and he was also tall.* **2.** likewise; in the same manner: *They have a dog and we have one also.*

al′so-ran′, *n.* [*count*] **1.** a contestant who fails to win a competition. **2.** one who always has little or no success; a failure.

al•tar (ôl′tər) /'ɔltər/ *n.* [*count*] a raised place or structure, as a platform, where religious rites are performed.

-alte-, *root.* *-alte-* comes from Latin, where it has the meaning "other, different." This meaning is found in such words as: ALTER, ALTERNATE, ALTERNATIVE, ALTERNATOR, ALTRUISM, ALTRUIST.

al•ter (ôl′tər) /'ɔltər/ *v.* **1.** to change; (to cause to) be different or modified in some way, as size, style, course, or the like: [~ + *obj*]: *to alter a coat.* [*no obj*]: *Her schedule has altered drastically.* **2.** [~ + *obj*] to castrate or spay: *The cat had been altered.* See -ALTE-.

al•ter•a•tion (ôl′tə rā′shən) /,ɔltə 'reyʃən/ *n.* **1.** [*noncount*] the changing or modifying of something: *The jacket needs alteration.* **2.** [*count*] a change, modification, or adjustment: *Can we make alterations to the contract?*

al•ter•ca•tion (ôl′tər kā′shən) /,ɔltər'keyʃən/ *n.* [*count*] a heated or angry dispute; noisy argument or conflict.

al′ter e′go, *n.* [*count*] **1.** an inseparable friend. **2.** a substitute; counterpart. **3.** the opposite side of one's personality. See -ALTE-.

al•ter•nate (*verb* ôl′tər nāt′, al′-; *adjective, noun* -nit) /*verb* 'ɔltər,neyt, 'æl-; *adjective, noun* -nɪt/ *v.,* **-nat•ed, -nat•ing,** *adj., n.* **—***v.* **1.** to interchange regularly with one another in time or place: [~ + *with* + *obj*]: *Day alternates with night.* [~ + *obj*]: *They alternated hot and cold compresses on the injury.* **2.** [~ + *between* + *obj*] to change back and forth between states, actions, etc.: *He alternates between hope and despair.* **3.** to take turns: [~ + *in* + *obj*]: *The children alternate in doing chores.* [~ + *obj*]: *The children alternate chores.* **—***adj.* [*before a noun*] **4.** interchanged repeatedly one for another: *alternate periods of clouds and sun.* **5.** every second one of a series: *Read only the alternate lines.* **6.** ALTERNATIVE (def. 4): *Do you have an alternate plan?* **—***n.* [*count*] **7.** a person authorized to take the place of another: *I sent my alternate to the meeting.* **—al•ter•nate•ly** (ôl′tər nit lē, al′-) /'ɔltərnɪtliy, 'æl-/ *adv.* **—al•ter•na•tion** (ôl′tər nā′shən, al′-) /,ɔltər'neyʃən, ,æl-/ *n.* [*count; noncount*] See -ALTE-.

al′ternating cur′rent, *n.* [*noncount*] an electric current that reverses direction at regular periods of time. *Abbr.:* AC Compare DIRECT CURRENT.

al•ter•na•tive (ôl tûr′nə tiv, al-) /ɔl'tɜrnətɪv, æl-/ *n.* [*count*] **1.** a choice limited to one option among two or more possibilities: *You have the alternative of riding, walking, or biking.* **2.** a choice among only two possibilities such that if one is chosen, the other cannot be chosen: *Here are the alternatives: surrender or die.* **3.** one of these choices: *The alternative to riding is walking.* **—***adj.* [*before a noun*] **4.** allowing for a choice between two or more things: *an alternative plan.* **5.** being different from the usual: *alternative lifestyles; alternative energy sources.* **—al•ter′na•tive•ly,** *adv.* See -ALTE-. **—Syn.** See CHOICE.

al•ter•na•tor (ôl′tər nā′tər, al′-) /'ɔltər,neytər, 'æl-/ *n.* [*count*] a generator of alternating current, used in motor vehicles, etc. See -ALTE-.

al•though (ôl *th*ō′) /ɔl'ðow/ *conj.* in spite of the fact that; even though; though: *Although we miss you, we will not ask you to return.* **—Usage.** See BUT.

-alti-, *root.* *-alti-* comes from Latin, where it has the meaning "high; height." This meaning is found in such words as: ALTIMETER, ALTITUDE, ALTO, EXALT.

al•tim•e•ter (al tim′i tər, al′tə mē′tər) /æl'tɪmɪtər, 'æltə,miytər/ *n.* [*count*] a device used in aircraft to determine altitude during flight. See -ALTI-.

al•ti•tude (al′ti to͞od′, -tyo͞od′) /'æltɪ,tuwd, -,tyuwd/ *n.* **1.** the height of a thing above a certain point, esp. the height above sea level on earth: [*noncount*]: *Maintain your altitude at 30,000 feet.* [*count*]: *descended to a lower altitude.* **2.** Usually, **altitudes.** [*plural*] a high place or region: *had difficulty breathing at mountain altitudes.* See -ALTI-.

al•to (al′tō) /'æltow/ *n., pl.* **-tos,** *adj.* **—***n.* [*count*] **1.** CONTRALTO. **2.** COUNTERTENOR. **3.** the second highest part of a four-part chorus. **4.** the second highest instrument in a family of musical instruments. **—***adj.* [*before a noun*] **5.** of, relating to, or having the tonal range of an alto. See -ALTI-.

al•to•geth•er (ôl′tə ge*th*′ər, ôl′tə ge*th*′ər) /,ɔltə'gɛðər,' ɔltə,gɛðər/ *adv.* **1.** wholly; entirely; completely: *an altogether fitting memorial.* **2.** with all or everything included: *The debt amounted altogether to twenty dollars.* **3.** with everything considered: *Altogether, it was worth the expense.* **—*Idiom.* 4. in the altogether,** *Informal.* nude; naked.

al•tru•ism (al′tro͞o iz′əm) /'æltruw,ɪzəm/ *n.* [*noncount*] concern for the welfare, happiness, and well-being of others; selflessness. **—al′tru•ist,** *n.* [*count*] **—al′tru•is′tic,** *adj.* **—al′tru•is′ti•cal•ly,** *adv.* See -ALTE-.

al•um[1] (al′əm) /'æləm/ *n.* [*noncount*] a white, crystal-like salt used in medicine, dyeing, and tanning.

a•lum[2] (ə lum′) /ə'lʌm/ *n.* [*count*] *Informal.* an alumna or alumnus.

al•u•min•i•um (al′yə min′ē əm) /,ælyə'mɪniyəm/ *n.* [*noncount*] *Chiefly Brit.* ALUMINUM.

a•lu•mi•num (ə lo͞o′mə nəm) /ə'luwmənəm/ *n.* [*noncount*] a silver-white metallic element, light in weight and not easily corroded or tarnished, used in alloys and for lightweight products.

a•lum•na (ə lum′nə) /ə'lʌmnə/ *n.* [*count*], *pl.* **-nae** (-nē, -nī). a woman who is a graduate or former student of a specific school, college, or university.

a•lum•nus (ə lum′nəs) /ə'lʌmnəs/ *n.* [*count*], *pl.* **-ni** (-nī,

-nē). a graduate or former student of a specific school, college, or university.

al•ways (ôl′wāz, -wēz) /'ɔlweyz, -wiyz/ *adv.* **1.** every time; on every occasion; without exception: *We always sleep late on Saturday.* **2.** all the time; continuously; uninterruptedly: *The light is always burning.* **3.** forever: *Will you always love me?* **4.** in any event; if necessary: *If it rains I can always stay home.*

Alz′hei•mer's disease′ (alz′hī mərz, älts′-, ôlz′-, ôlts′-) /'ælzhay mərz, 'ɑlts-, 'ɔlz-, 'ɔlts-/ *n.* [*noncount*] a disease usually beginning in late middle age, characterized by progressive memory loss and mental deterioration.

am (am; *unstressed* əm, m) /æm; *unstressed* əm, m/ *v.* 1st pers. sing. pres. indic. of BE.

AM, an abbreviation of: **1.** amplitude modulation, a method of sending a signal on a radio wave. **2.** a system of broadcasting using this method. Compare FM.

-am-,[1] *root.* *-am-* comes from Latin, where it has the meaning "love, like." This meaning is found in such words as: AMIABLE, AMOROUS, AMOUR, PARAMOUR.

-am-,[2] *root.* *-am-* comes from Latin, where it has the meaning "take out; come out". This meaning is found in such words as: EXAMPLE, SAMPLE.

Am., an abbreviation of: **1.** America. **2.** American.

A.M., an abbreviation of Latin *Artium Magister*: Master of Arts.

a.m. or **A.M.,** an abbreviation of Latin *ante meridiem*: **1.** before noon (used with hours of a day). **2.** the period from midnight to noon, esp. the period of daylight prior to noon. Compare P.M.

a•mal•gam (ə mal′gəm) /ə'mælgəm/ *n.* **1.** [*noncount*] an alloy of mercury with another metal or metals. **2.** [*noncount*] an alloy chiefly of silver mixed with mercury and variable amounts of other metals, used as a dental filling. **3.** [*count*] a mixture or combination: *an amalgam of facts and myths.*

a•mal•ga•mate (ə mal′gə māt′) /ə'mælgə,meyt/ *v.,* **-mat•ed, -mat•ing. 1.** to mix or merge so as to make a combination; blend: [~ + *obj*]: *They planned to amalgamate the two companies.* [*no obj*]: *The three schools decided to amalgamate.* **2.** [~ + *obj*] to mix or alloy (a metal) with mercury. —**a•mal•ga•ma•tion** (ə mal′gə-mā′shən) /ə,mælgə'meyʃən/ *n.* [*count; noncount*]

a•man•u•en•sis (ə man′yo͞o en′sis) /ə,mænyuw'ɛnsɪs/ *n.* [*count*], *pl.* **-ses** (-sēz). a person employed to write what another dictates; secretary. See -MAN-[1].

am•a•ranth (am′ə ranth′) /'æmə,rænθ/ *n.* [*count*] **1.** a plant cultivated esp. for its showy flower clusters. **2.** an imaginary flower that never dies.

am•a•ret•to (am′ə ret′ō, ä′mə-) /,æmə'rɛtow, ,ɑmə-/ *n.* [*noncount*] an almond-flavored liqueur.

am•a•ryl•lis (am′ə ril′is) /,æmə'rɪlɪs/ *n.* [*count*] a plant with large red or pink flowers, popular as a houseplant.

a•mass (ə mas′) /ə'mæs/ *v.* [~ + *obj*] **1.** to gather so as to keep for oneself: *worked hard to amass a fortune.* **2.** to collect into a mass; accumulate: *amassing sufficient evidence to convict the felon.*

am•a•teur (am′ə cho͝or′, -chər, -tər) /'æmə,tʃʊr, -tʃər, -tər/ *n.* [*count*] **1.** a person who engages in an activity for pleasure rather than for money. **2.** an athlete who has not competed for payment or for a monetary prize (contrasted with *professional*). **3.** a person inexperienced or unskilled in a particular activity. —*adj.* [*usually: before a noun*] **4.** relating to, characteristic of, or engaged in by an amateur: *amateur tennis.* **5.** amateurish: *amateur efforts at ballet dancing.* —**am′a•teur•ism,** *n.* [*noncount*]

am•a•teur•ish (am′ə cho͝or′ish, -chûr′-, -tûr′-) /,æmə 'tʃʊrɪʃ, -'tʃɜr-, -'tɜr-/ *adj.* unskillful; unprofessional; inexperienced: *amateurish paintings.* —**am′a•teur•ishly,** *adv.*

am•a•to•ry (am′ə tôr′ē, -tōr′ē) /'æmə,tɔriy, -,towriy/ *adj.* of or relating to lovers or lovemaking: *amatory poetry.* See -AM-.

a•maze (ə māz′) /ə'meyz/ *v.,* **a•mazed, a•maz•ing.** to overwhelm with surprise or sudden wonder; astonish greatly: [~ + *obj*]: *The magician's tricks amazed the children.* [*It* + ~ + *obj* + *(that) clause*]: *It amazed me that you would believe those lies.*

a•maze•ment (ə māz′mənt) /ə 'meyzmənt/ *n.* [*noncount*] surprise; astonishment; wonder: *looked around in amazement.*

a•maz•ing (ə mā′zing) /ə'meyzɪŋ/ *adj.* causing astonishment, wonder, or admiration: *What an amazing view!* —**a•maz′ing•ly,** *adv.*

Am•a•zon (am′ə zon′) /'æmə,zɒn/ *n.* [*count*] **1.** (in legends of the ancient Greeks) a member of a nation of female warriors. **2.** [*often: amazon*] a tall, powerful, forceful woman. —**Am•a•zo•ni•an** (am′ə zō′nē ən) /,æmə'zowniyən/ *adj.*

am•bas•sa•dor (am bas′ə dər, -dôr′) /æm'bæsədər, -,dɔr/ *n.* [*count*] **1.** a diplomatic official of the highest rank, sent by one country to live in another as its representative. **2.** an unofficial representative: *a good-will ambassador.* —**am•bas•sa•do•ri•al** (am bas′ə dôr′ē əl, -dōr′-) /æm,bæsə'dɔriyəl, -'dowr-/ *adj.*

am•ber (am′bər) /'æmbər/ *n.* [*noncount*] **1.** a yellow, red, or brown translucent fossil resin used in jewelry. **2.** the yellowish brown color of resin. —*adj.* **3.** of the color of amber; yellowish brown. **4.** made of amber.

ambi-, *prefix.* *ambi-* comes from Latin, where it has the meanings "both" and "around." These meanings are found in such words as: AMBIANCE, AMBIGUOUS, AMBIVALENCE.

am•bi•ance or **am•bi•ence** (am′bē əns) /'æmbiyəns/ *n.* the mood or atmosphere of a place; environment: [*count*]: *The restaurant had a delightful ambiance.* [*noncount*]: *That place lacks ambiance.* —**Syn.** See ENVIRONMENT.

am•bi•dex•trous (am′bi dek′strəs) /,æmbɪ'dɛkstrəs/ *adj.* able to use both hands equally well. —**am•bi•dex•ter•i•ty** (am′bi dek ster′i tē) /,æmbɪdɛk'stɛrɪtiy/ *n.* [*noncount*] —**am′bi•dex′trous•ly,** *adv.* —**am′bi•dex′trous•ness,** *n.* [*noncount*] See AMBI-.

am•bi•ent (am′bē ənt) /'æmbiyənt/ *adj.* present on all sides: *the ambient air.* See AMBI-.

am•bi•gu•i•ty (am′bi gyo͞o′i tē) /,æmbɪ'gyuwɪtiy/ *n., pl.* **-ties. 1.** [*noncount*] doubtfulness or uncertainty of meaning or intention: *a comment full of ambiguity.* **2.** [*noncount*] doubt; uncertainty: *the ambiguity of the victory.* **3.** [*count*] a word, expression, etc., that can have more than one meaning. See AMBI-.

am•big•u•ous (am big′yo͞o əs) /æm'bɪgyuwəs/ *adj.* **1.** open to or having several possible meanings or interpretations: *He gave an ambiguous answer to that question.* **2.** doubtful; uncertain: *in an ambiguous position.* —**am•big′u•ous•ly,** *adv.*

am•bi•tion (am bish′ən) /æm'bɪʃən/ *n.* **1.** [*noncount*] a strong desire for achievement or distinction. **2.** [*count*] the object or state desired or sought after: *A career on the stage is just one of her ambitions.* See AMBI-.

am•bi•tious (am bish′əs) /æm'bɪʃəs/ *adj.* **1.** characterized by ambition: *an ambitious lawyer.* **2.** requiring a great deal of effort, cost, ability, etc.: *an ambitious program for fighting crime.* —**am•bi′tious•ly,** *adv.* —**am•bi′tious•ness,** *n.* [*noncount*]

am•biv•a•lence (am biv′ə ləns) /æm'bɪvələns/ also **am•biv′a•len•cy,** *n.* [*noncount*] uncertainty or indecision, esp. when caused by the inability to make a choice or by a desire to say or do two opposite things at the same time. —**am•biv′a•lent,** *adj.* —**am•biv′a•lent•ly,** *adv.*

-ambl-, *root.* *-ambl-* comes from Latin, where it has the meaning "walk." This meaning is found in such words as: AMBLE, AMBULANCE, AMBULATE, CIRCUMAMBULATE, PERAMBULATOR.

am•ble (am′bəl) /'æmbəl/ *v.,* **-bled, -bling,** *n.* —*v.* [*no obj*] **1.** to go at a slow, easy pace; stroll; saunter: *She ambled along the seashore.* —*n.* [*count*] **2.** an ambling pace or slow, easy walk. —**am′bler,** *n.* [*count*] See -AMBL-.

am•bro•sia (am brō′zhə) /æm'browʒə/ *n.* [*noncount*] **1.** the food of the ancient Greek and Roman gods. **2.** something delightful to the taste or smell. —**am•bro′•sial,** *adj.*

am•bu•lance (am′byə ləns) /'æmbyələns/ *n.* [*count*] a specially equipped vehicle for carrying sick or injured people to a hospital. See -AMBL-.

am•bu•la•to•ry (am′byə lə tôr′ē, -tōr′ē) /'æmbyələ,tɔriy, -,towriy/ *adj.* capable of walking or moving about from place to place: *The patient was ambulatory after bed rest.* See -AMBL-.

am•bush (am′bo͝osh) /'æmbʊʃ/ *n.* **1.** [*noncount*] an act or instance of lying hidden so as to attack by surprise: *The highwaymen waited in ambush near the road.* **2.** [*count*] an act or instance of attacking unexpectedly from a concealed position. **3.** [*noncount*] the concealed position itself: *They fired from ambush.* —*v.* [~ + *obj*] **4.** to attack from ambush.

a•me•ba or **a•moe•ba** (ə mē′bə) /ə'miybə/ *n.* [*count*], *pl.* **-bas, -bae** (-bē). a one-celled organism found in streams, ponds, and soil.

a•mel•io•rate (ə mēl′yə rāt′) /ə'miylyə,reyt/ *v.,* **-rat•ed, -rat•ing.** to make or become better or more satisfactory; improve: [~ + *obj*]: *Her apology ameliorated the situa-*

tion. [*no obj*]: *The situation ameliorated when both sides shook hands.* —**a•mel•io•ra•tion** (ə mēl′yə rā′shən) /əˌmiylyə'reyʃən/ *n.* [*noncount*]

a•men (ā′men′, ä′men′) /'ey'mɛn, 'ɑ'mɛn/ *interj.* **1.** (used after a prayer to express solemn agreement) it is so; so be it. **2.** (used to express agreement or approval) certainly; yes.

a•me•na•ble (ə mē′nə bəl, ə men′ə-) /ə'miynəbəl, ə'mɛnə-/ *adj.* [*usually: be + ~ + to*] **1.** ready or willing to answer, act, agree, or yield: *The author was amenable to making a few changes.* **2.** liable to be called to account; answerable; responsible: *All citizens are amenable to the law.*

a•mend (ə mend′) /ə'mɛnd/ *v.* [*~ + obj*] **1.** to modify, rephrase, or change (a bill, constitution, etc.) by formal procedure: *Congress may amend the proposed tax bill.* **2.** to change for the better; improve: *She needs to amend her ways.*

a•mend•ment (ə mend′mənt) /ə'mɛndmənt/ *n.* **1.** [*noncount*] the act of amending. **2.** [*count*] an alteration of or addition to a bill, constitution, etc. **3.** [*count*] a change made by amending.

a•mends (ə mendz′) /ə'mɛndz/ *n.* [*count*] —***Idiom.*** **make amends,** to pay back or compensate, as for an injury, loss, or insult: [*no obj*]: *promised to make amends.* [*~ + to + obj + for*]: *How can I make amends to you for the oversight?*

a•men•i•ty (ə men′i tē) /ə'mɛnɪtiy/ *n.* [*count*], *pl.* **-ties. 1.** an agreeable way or manner; courtesy; civility: *She observed the social amenities.* **2.** any feature that provides comfort, convenience, or pleasure: *The hotel has a swimming pool and other amenities.*

Am•er•a•sian (am′ə rā′zhən) /ˌæmə'reyʒən/ *n.* [*count*] a person of mixed American and Asian descent.

A•mer•i•can (ə mer′i kən) /ə'mɛrɪkən/ *adj.* **1.** of or relating to the United States of America. **2.** of or relating to North or South America; of or relating to the Western Hemisphere. —*n.* [*count*] **3.** a person born or living in the United States of America, esp. a citizen. **4.** a person born or living in the Western Hemisphere. **5.** a Native American, or an American Indian.

A•mer•i•ca•na (ə mer′i kan′ə, -kä′nə) /əˌmɛrɪ'kænə, -'kɑnə/ *n.* [*plural or noncount*] materials, as books, papers, and maps, relating to the history, culture, and geography of the United States.

Amer′ican In′dian, *n.* [*count*] a member of any of the original peoples of the Western Hemisphere, usually excluding the Aleuts and Eskimos.

A•mer•i•can•ism (ə mer′i kə niz′əm) /ə'mɛrɪkəˌnɪzəm/ *n.* **1.** [*count*] a custom, trait, or linguistic feature special or peculiar to the United States: *The word "you-all" meaning "you (plural)" is an Americanism.* **2.** [*noncount*] devotion to or preference for the U.S. and its institutions.

A•mer•i•can•ize (ə mer′i kə nīz′) /ə'mɛrɪkəˌnayz/ *v.,* **-ized, -iz•ing.** to make or become American in character; assimilate to U.S. customs and institutions: [*~ + obj*]: *Public school Americanized the immigrant children.* [*no obj*]: *The immigrant family wished to Americanize.* —**A•mer•i•can•i•za•tion** (ə mer′i kə nə zā′shən) /ə'mɛrɪkənə'zeyʃən/ *n.* [*noncount*]

Amer′ican plan′, *n.* [*count*] (in hotels) a system of paying a fixed rate that covers room, service, and all meals.

Amer′ican Sign′ Lan′guage, *n.* [*proper noun*] a visual-gesture sign language used by deaf people in the U.S. and English-speaking parts of Canada. *Abbr.:* ASL

Am•er•ind (am′ə rind) /'æmərɪnd/ *n.* [*count*] AMERICAN INDIAN. Also called **Am•er•in•di•an** (am′ə rin′dē ən) /ˌæmə'rɪndiyən/.

am•e•thyst (am′ə thist) /'æməθɪst/ *n.* **1.** [*count*] a purple or violet quartz, used as a gem. **2.** [*noncount*] a purplish tint. —*adj.* **3.** having the color of amethyst.

a•mi•a•bil•i•ty (ā′mē i bil′ə tē) /ˌeymiy ɪ 'bɪlə tiy/ *n.* [*noncount*] the quality of being friendly, agreeable, or pleasant. See -AM-.

a•mi•a•ble (ā′mē ə bəl) /'eymiyəbəl/ *adj.* **1.** having or showing agreeable qualities; friendly; sociable: *an amiable gathering.* **2.** pleasant: *an amiable little resort.* —**a′mi•a•bly,** *adv.* See -AM-.

am•i•ca•ble (am′i kə bəl) /'æmɪkəbəl/ *adj.* marked by goodwill; friendly: *The divorce was amicable.* —**am•i•ca•bil•i•ty** (am′i kə bil′i tē) /ˌæmɪkə'bɪlɪtiy/ *n.* [*noncount*] —**am′i•ca•bly,** *adv.*

a•mid (ə mid′) /ə'mɪd/ also **a•midst** (ə midst′) /ə 'mɪdst/ *prep.* in the middle of; surrounded by; among: *Amid all the bushes stood a lonely tree.*

a•mid•ships (ə mid′ships′) /ə'mɪdˌʃɪps/ also **a•mid′ship′,** *adv.* in or toward the middle of a ship or aircraft.

a•mi•go (ə mē′gō, ä mē′-) /ə'miygow, ɑ'miy-/ *n.* [*count*], *pl.* **-gos.** a male friend.

a•mi′no ac′id (ə mē′nō) /ə'miynow/ *n.* [*count*] a compound that is one of the building blocks from which proteins are constructed.

a•miss (ə mis′) /ə'mɪs/ *adv.* **1.** out of the right or proper course, order, or condition: *Things went amiss.* —*adj.* [*be + ~*] **2.** improper; wrong; faulty: *Something is amiss.*

am•i•ty (am′i tē) /'æmɪtiy/ *n.* [*noncount*] a peaceful relationship, such as between nations: *complete amity with our neighbors to the north.*

am•mo (am′ō) /'æmow/ *n.* [*noncount*] *Informal.* ammunition.

am•mo•nia (ə mōn′yə) /ə'mownyə/ *n.* [*noncount*] a colorless, strong-smelling gas or liquid, used chiefly for cleaning, refrigeration, and explosives.

am•mu•ni•tion (am′yə nish′ən) /ˌæmyə'nɪʃən/ *n.* [*noncount*] **1.** fired or detonated material used in combat, esp. bullets or shells fired by guns. **2.** any material used to defend or attack a viewpoint, claim, etc.: *These statistics will be my ammunition when I present my proposal.*

am•ne•sia (am nē′zhə) /æm'niyʒə/ *n.* [*noncount*] loss of memory caused by brain injury, shock, etc. —**am•ne•si•ac** (am nē′zhē ak′, -zē-) /æm'niyʒiyˌæk, -ziy-/ **am•ne•sic** (am nē′sik, -zik) /æm'niysɪk, -zɪk/ *n.* [*count*], adj. See -MNE-.

am•nes•ty (am′nə stē) /'æmnəstiy/ *n., pl.* **-ties. 1.** a general pardon for offenses, esp. political offenses, against a government: [*noncount*]: *The new regime promised amnesty for all former prisoners.* [*count*]: *The rebel soldiers were able to return under a general amnesty.* **2.** a forgetting or overlooking of any past offense: [*noncount*]: *The Parking Bureau promises amnesty for all unpaid tickets if you pay the last few.* [*count*]: *an amnesty mediated by the student government.* See -MNE-.

am•ni•o•cen•te•sis (am′nē ō sen tē′sis) /ˌæmniyowsɛn'tiysɪs/ *n.* [*count*], *pl.* **-ses** (-sēz). the insertion of a hollow needle through the abdomen of a pregnant woman into the uterus for withdrawing a sample of fluid to determine the sex and genetic condition of the fetus.

a•moe•ba (ə mē′bə) /ə'miybə/ *n., pl.* **-bas, -bae** (-bē). AMEBA.

a•mok (ə muk′, ə mok′) /ə'mʌk, ə'mɒk/ *adj., adv.* AMUCK.

a•mong (ə mung′) /ə'mʌŋ/ *prep.* **1.** in, into, or through the midst or middle of: *She was among friends.* **2.** in the midst of, so as to influence: *He did missionary work among the local people.* **3.** with a share for each of: *Divide the fruit among you.* **4.** in the class or group of; one of: *That is among the things we must do. New York is among the most exciting cities in the world.* **5.** with most or many of: *He was a candidate popular among the people.* **6.** by the joint or reciprocal action of: *They quarreled among themselves.* **7.** familiar to or characteristic of: *a proverb among the Spanish people.* —**Usage.** See BETWEEN.

a•mongst (ə mungst′) /ə'mʌŋst/ *prep.* AMONG.

a•mor•al (ā môr′əl, ā mor′-) /ey'mɔrəl, ey'mɒr-/ *adj.* neither moral nor immoral. —**a•mo•ral•i•ty** (ā′mə ral′i-tē) /ˌeymə'rælɪtiy/ *n.* [*noncount*] —**a•mor′al•ly,** *adv.* See -MOR-.

am•o•rous (am′ər əs) /'æmərəs/ *adj.* relating to or expressing love, esp. sexual love: *amorous glances.* —**am′o•rous•ly,** *adv.* —**am′o•rous•ness,** *n.* [*noncount*] See -AM-.

a•mor•phous (ə môr′fəs) /ə'mɔrfəs/ *adj.* **1.** lacking definite form; shapeless: *amorphous clouds.* **2.** of no particular kind or character; unstructured; unorganized: *his amorphous style of writing.* —**a•mor′phous•ly,** *adv.* —**a•mor′phous•ness,** *n.* [*noncount*] See -MORPH-.

am•or•tize (am′ər tīz′, ə môr′tīz) /'æmərˌtayz, ə'mɔrtayz/ *v.* [*~ + obj*], **-tized, -tiz•ing. 1.** to complete the payment of (a debt) by periodic payments to the creditor: *amortized the loan.* **2.** to write off the cost of (an asset) gradually: *to amortize an expense over five years.* —**am•or•ti•za•tion** (am′ər tə zā′shən) /'æmərtə'zeyʃən/ *n.* [*noncount*] See -MORT-.

a•mount (ə mount′) /ə'mawnt/ *n.* [*count*] **1.** the sum total of two or more quantities or sums; whole: *the final amount that we actually pay for this car.* **2.** quantity; measure: [*~ + of + noncount noun*]: *We met a great amount of resistance to the plan.* [*~ + of + plural noun*]: *Huge amounts of crops lay unharvested.* —*v.* [*~ + to + obj; not: be + ~-ing*] **3.** to total; add up to: *The bill amounts to $300.* **4.** to be equal in value, effect, or extent; be worth; mean: *All those fine words amount to nothing.* **5.** to turn into; become: *a bright student who should amount to something one day.*

a•mour (ə mŏŏr′) /ə'mʊr/ *n.* [*count*] a love affair, esp. a secret one. See -AM-.

a•mour-pro•pre (A MŎŎR PRÔ ′PRᵊ) /amuwrprɔ 'prᵊ/ *n.* [*noncount*] *French.* self-esteem; self-respect.

amp[1] (amp) /æmp/ *n.* [*count*] ampere.

amp[2] (amp) /æmp/ *n.* [*count*] an amplifier.

amp., an abbreviation of: **1.** amperage. **2.** ampere.

am•per•age (am′pər ij, am pēr′-) /'æmpərɪdʒ, æm'pɪər-/ *n.* [*noncount*] the strength of an electric current measured in amperes. *Abbr.:* amp.

am•pere (am′pēr, am pēr′) /'æmpɪər, æm'pɪər/ *n.* [*count*] a unit of electrical current. *Abbr.:* A, amp.

am•per•sand (am′pər sand′) /'æmpər,sænd/ *n.* [*count*] a character or symbol (& or &) used to mean "and", as in *Smith & Wesson, Inc.*

am•phet•a•mine (am fet′ə mēn′, -min) /æm'fɛtə,miyn, -mɪn/ *n.* [*count*] a drug that stimulates the central nervous system, used in medicine to counteract depression and often abused as a stimulant.

amphi-, *prefix. amphi-* comes from Greek, where it has the meaning "both; on two sides". This meaning is found in such words as: AMPHIBIAN, AMPHIBIOUS, AMPHITHEATER.

am•phib•i•an (am fib′ē ən) /æm'fɪbiyən/ *n.* [*count*] **1.** any cold-blooded animal including frogs and salamanders that has gills to breathe in the water and later develops lungs for breathing on land. **2.** an airplane designed for taking off from and landing on both land and water. **3.** a military vehicle capable of traveling on land or in water. **—*adj.* 4.** belonging or relating to amphibians. **5.** AMPHIBIOUS.

am•phib•i•ous (am fib′ē əs) /æm'fɪbiyəs/ *adj.* **1.** living on land and in water. **2.** (capable of) operating on both land and water. **—am•phib′i•ous•ly,** *adv.*

am•phi•the•a•ter (am′fə thē′ə tər) /'æmfə,θiyətər/ *n.* [*count*] an oval or round area, building, or room with rows of seats that slope up around a central open area. Often, **am′phi•the′a•tre.**

-ampl-, *root. -ampl-* comes from Latin, where it has the meaning "enough; enlarge." This meaning is found in such words as: AMPLE, AMPLIFY, AMPLITUDE.

am•ple (am′pəl) /'æmpəl/ *adj.* **1.** fully sufficient for the purpose; plentiful: *an ample reward.* **2.** large; roomy: *The apartment comes with ample storage space.* **—am′ply,** *adv.* See -AMPL-.

am•pli•fi•er (am′plə fī′ər) /'æmplə,fayər/ *n.* [*count*] an electronic device that amplifies sound, current, voltage, etc. See -AMPL-.

am•pli•fy (am′plə fī′) /'æmplə,fay/ *v.,* **-fied, -fy•ing. 1.** [~ + *obj*] to make (sound) louder by mechanical or electronic means: *The sounds of the guitar are then amplified and sent through the speakers.* **2.** [~ + (*on* +) *obj*] to add to or expand by giving further details: *They asked the president to amplify (on) his earlier remarks.* **—am•pli•fi•ca•tion** (am′plə fi kā′shən) /,æmpləfɪ'keyʃən/ *n.* [*noncount; count*] See -AMPL-.

am•pli•tude (am′pli tōōd′, -tyōōd′) /'æmplɪ,tuwd, -,tyuwd/ *n.* [*noncount*] **1.** the state or quality of being ample; fullness; largeness. **2.** large or full measure; abundance. See -AMPL-.

am•pule or **am•pul** or **am•poule** (am′pyōōl, -pōōl) /'æmpyuwl, -puwl/ *n.* [*count*] a sealed glass or plastic bulb containing solutions or drugs for injection.

am•pu•tate (am′pyŏŏ tāt′) /'æmpyʊ,teyt/ *v.* [~ + *obj*], **-tat•ed, -tat•ing.** to cut off surgically (all or part of a limb or digit of the body): *forced to amputate her leg.* **—am•pu•ta•tion** (am′pyŏŏ tā′shən) /,æmpyʊ'teyʃən/ *n.* [*noncount; count*] See -PUTE-.

am•pu•tee (am′pyŏŏ tē′) /,æmpyʊ'tiy/ *n.* [*count*] a person who has lost all or part of an arm, hand, leg, etc., by amputation.

amt., an abbreviation of: amount.

a•muck or **amok** (ə muk′) /ə'mʌk/ *adj.* **1.** [*be* + ~] mad with a wild frenzy: *was amuck with rage.* **—*adv.,* *Idiom.* 2. run** or **go amuck** or **amok,** [*no obj*] to go or rush about wildly; be out of control: *The mob had run amuck.*

am•u•let (am′yə lit) /'æmyəlɪt/ *n.* [*count*] a charm worn to keep evil away or to bring good fortune.

a•muse (ə myōōz′) /ə'myuwz/ *v.* [~ + *obj*], **a•mused, a•mus•ing. 1.** to hold the attention of (someone); entertain or keep occupied: *The video games amused the children for hours.* **2.** to cause (someone) to laugh, smile, or the like: *The comedian's jokes amused everyone.*

a•muse•ment (ə myōōz′mənt) /ə 'myuwzmənt/ *n.* **1.** [*noncount*] the state or condition of being amused; enjoyment; entertainment. **2.** [*count*] an activity to pass time enjoyably: *The city offers many amusements.*

amuse′ment park′, *n.* [*count*] a park with recreational devices such as a Ferris wheel, roller coaster, etc., and usually having booths for games and refreshments.

a•mus•ing (ə myōōz′ing) /ə 'myuwzɪŋ/ *adj.* causing (someone) to laugh or providing amusement: *an amusing story.*

an (ən; *when stressed* an) /ən; *when stressed* æn/ *indefinite article.* the form of A used before an initial vowel sound: *an arch, an honor, an hourly wage.* **—Usage.** Sometimes, esp. in British English, *an* is used before an initial *h* if the *h* is silent or weakly pronounced and the syllable is unstressed: "an histor′ian"; "an histor′ic event".

an-, *prefix. an-* is attached to roots or stems beginning with a vowel or *h*, and means "not; without; lacking": *anaerobic (= without oxygen); anonymous (= without name).* Compare A-[2].

-an, *suffix. -an* has the general meaning "of, pertaining to, having qualities of". **1.** It is used to form adjectives and nouns from names of places or people, with the meanings: **a.** being connected with a place: *Chicago + -an → Chicagoan;* **b.** having membership in a group of: *Episcopal + -(i)an → Episcopalian;* **2.** It is used to form adjectives with the meaning "of or like (someone); supporter or believer of": *Christ + -(i)an → Christian; Freud + -(i)an → Freudian (= supporter of or believer in the theories of Sigmund Freud).* **3.** It is used to form nouns from words ending in *-ic* or *-y*, with the meaning "one who works with ": *electric + -(i)an → electrician; comedy + -an → comedian.*

an′a•bol′ic ster′oid (an′ə bol′ik) /,ænə'bɒlɪk/ *n.* [*count*] a class of hormones that help cause muscle tissue to grow.

a•nach•ro•nism (ə nak′rə niz′əm) /ə'nækrə,nɪzəm/ *n.* [*count*] **1.** an error made in which a person, object, happening, etc., is assigned a date or period other than the correct one: *It is an anachronism to write that atomic bombs were used in the Civil War.* **2.** a thing or person that belongs to an earlier time and is out of place in the present. See -CHRON-.

a•nach•ro•nis•tic (ə nak′rə nis′tik) /ə ,nækrə 'nɪstɪk/ *adj.* being or characteristic of an anachronism: *A biplane is an anachronistic sight in the age of the Space Shuttle.* **—a•nach′ro•nis′ti•cal•ly,** *adv.*

an•a•con•da (an′ə kon′də) /,ænə'kɒndə/ *n.* [*count*], *pl.* **-das.** a very large South American snake that constricts its prey in its coils.

an•aes•the•sia (an′əs thē′zhə) /,ænəs'θiyʒə/ *n.* ANESTHESIA. **—an•aes•thet•ic** (an′əs thet′ik) /,ænəs'θɛtɪk/ *n.* [*count*], *adj.* **—an•aes•the•tist** (ə nes′thi tist) /ə'nɛsθɪtɪst/ *n.* [*count*]

an•a•gram (an′ə gram′) /'ænə,græm/ *n.* [*count*] a word, phrase, or sentence formed from another by rearranging its letters: *"Angel" is an anagram of "glean."*

a•nal (ān′l) /'eynl̩/ *adj.* **1.** [*before a noun*] of, relating to, or near the anus. **2.** of or relating to a type of adult behavior that includes being meticulous, rigid, and ungenerous. **—a′nal•ly,** *adv.*

an•al•ge•sic (an′l jē′zik, -sik) /,ænl̩ 'dʒiyzɪk, -sɪk/ *adj.* [*before a noun*] **1.** causing a reduction or elimination of pain: *an analgesic drug.* **—*n.*** [*count*] **2.** a drug that reduces or eliminates pain. See -ALG-.

an•a•log (an′l ôg′, -og′) /'ænl̩ ,ɔg, -,ɒg/ *n.* **1.** ANALOGUE **—*adj.*** [*before a noun*] **2.** representing data by measuring voltage or some continuous variable quantity. **3.** being a method of sound recording in which sound waves are converted into electrical signals. **4.** displaying a readout of information by a pointer or by hands on a dial, rather than by numerical digits (opposed to *digital*): *an analog wristwatch.* See -LOG-.

a•nal•o•gous (ə nal′ə gəs) /ə'næləgəs/ *adj.* having similar characteristics: *The human brain is analogous to a computer.* **—a•nal′o•gous•ly,** *adv.* **—a•nal′o•gous•ness,** *n.* [*noncount*]

an•a•logue or **an•a•log** (an′l ôg′, -og′) /'ænl̩,ɔg, -,ɒg/ *n.* [*count*] something having a strong similarity in form or function to something else: *An insect's wings and a bird's wings are analogues.*

a•nal•o•gy (ə nal′ə jē) /ə'nælədʒiy/ *n.* [*count*], *pl.* **-gies. 1.** a similarity between like features of two things, on which a comparison may be based: *an analogy between* *the heart and a pump.* **2.** any similarity or comparability: *I see no analogy between our situations.* **3. by analogy,** by way of comparison: *By analogy, the heart is a pump and the brain is a computer.* **—an•a•log•i•cal** (an′l oj′i-kəl) /ˌænḷ'ɒdʒɪkəl/ *adj.*

a•nal•y•sand (ə nal′ə sand′, -zand′) /ə'nælәˌsænd, -ˌzænd/ *n.* [*count*] a person undergoing psychoanalysis.

a•nal•y•sis (ə nal′ə sis) /ə'næləsɪs/ *n., pl.* **-ses** (-sēz′) /-ˌsiyz/. **1.** the process of analyzing: [*noncount*]: *analysis of a problem.* [*count*]: *chemical analyses.* **2.** [*count*] a presentation of the results of this process: *The newspaper article was a good analysis of the problem.* **3.** [*noncount*] PSYCHOANALYSIS. See -LYS-.

an•a•lyst (an′l ist) /'ænḷɪst/ *n.* [*count*] **1.** a person who analyzes or who is skilled in analysis. **2.** a psychoanalyst. See -LYS-.

an•a•lyt•ic (an′l it′ik) /ˌænḷ 'ɪtɪk/ or **an′a•lyt′i•cal,** *adj.* of or relating to analysis: *analytic reasoning.* **—an′a•lyt′i•cal•ly,** *adv.* See -LYS-.

an•a•lyze (an′l īz′) /'ænḷˌayz/ *v.* [~ + *obj*], **-lyzed, -lyz•ing. 1.** to examine or study something so as to separate it into the pieces that make it up, and to figure out its essential features: *to analyze the blood on the murder weapon.* **2.** to examine carefully and in detail so as to identify causes, key factors, possible results, etc.: *They analyzed the political situation.* **3.** to psychoanalyze. See -LYS-. **—Related Words.** ANALYZE is a verb, ANALYSIS is a noun, ANALYTICAL is an adjective: *The computer analyzed the data. The computer produced an analysis in seconds. She has an analytical mind.*

an•a•pest or **an•a•paest** (an′ə pest′) /'ænəˌpɛst/ *n.* [*count*] a three-syllable foot in poetry having two unaccented syllables (short beats) followed by one accented syllable (long beat).

an•ar•chism (an′ər kiz′əm) /'ænərˌkɪzəm/ *n.* [*noncount*] a political doctrine calling for the ending of law and government restraint on society. **—an′ar•chist,** *n.* [*count*] **—an′ar•chis′tic,** *adj.* See -ARCH-.

an•ar•chy (an′ər kē) /'ænərkiy/ *n.* [*noncount*] **1.** a state of society without government or law: *They favored anarchy over tyranny.* **2.** confusion; chaos; disorder: *Their household was in a state of anarchy.* **—an•ar•chic** (an-är′kik) /æn'ɑrkɪk/ **an•ar′chi•cal,** *adj.* **—an•ar′chi•cal•ly,** *adv.* See -ARCH-.

a•nath•e•ma (ə nath′ə mə) /ə'næθəmə/ *n., pl.* **-mas.** a person or thing detested or loathed: [*noncount*]: *The idea of extravagance is anathema to them.* [*count*]: *It was an anathema to her way of thinking.*

an•a•tom•i•cal (an′ə tom′i kəl) /ˌænə 'tɒmɪ kəl/ also **an′a•tom′ic,** *adj.* [*before a noun*] of or relating to the structure of the bodies of animals and plants: *anatomical studies.* **—an′a•tom′i•cal•ly,** *adv.*

a•nat•o•my (ə nat′ə mē) /ə'nætəmiy/ *n., pl.* **-mies. 1.** [*noncount*] the science dealing with the structure of animals and plants. **2.** [*count*] the structure of an animal or plant, or of any of its parts. See -TOM-.

-ance, *suffix.* **1.** *-ance* is attached to some adjectives ending in -ANT to form nouns with the meaning "quality or state of": *brilliant + -ance → brilliance.* **2.** *-ance* is also attached to some verb roots to form nouns: *appear + -ance → appearance; resemble + -ance → resemblance.* See -ANT, -ENCE.

an•ces•tor (an′ses tər) /'ænsɛstər/ *n.* [*count*] **1.** a person from whom someone is descended; forebear: *Their ancestors were early pioneers.* **2.** one that serves as an earlier prototype; forerunner: *The horse and buggy was an ancestor to the automobile.* **—an′ces•tress,** *n.* [*count*] **—Related Words.** ANCESTOR and ANCESTRY are nouns, ANCESTRAL is an adjective: *One of her ancestors was a king. She is of noble ancestry. They returned to the ancestral home.*

an•ces•tral (an ses′trəl) /æn 'sɛstrəl/ *adj.* [*before a noun*] of or inherited from ancestors: *an ancestral home.*

an•ces•try (an′ses trē) /'ænsɛstriy/ *n., pl.* **-tries. 1.** [*count, usually singular*] the group of people from whom someone descended: *had an ancestry of Puritan settlers.* **2.** [*noncount*] line of descent; lineage: *of Chinese ancestry.*

an•chor (ang′kər) /'æŋkər/ *n.* [*count*] **1.** a heavy device attached by a cable to a vessel and cast overboard to keep the vessel from drifting by becoming secured to the bottom. **2.** a person or thing that can be relied on for support or security: *In times of distress she was our anchor.* **3.** the main broadcaster on a program of news, sports, etc. **4.** a person in a relay race who competes last. **—*v.* 5.** [~ + *obj*] to hold fast by or as if by an anchor: *anchored the ship in the harbor.* **6.** [*no obj*] to cast anchor: *The ship anchored in the harbor.* **7.** to act or serve as a radio or television anchor (for): [~ + *obj*]: *She anchored the evening news.* [*no obj*]: *She anchored for seven years.* **—*Idiom.* 8. at anchor,** kept in place by an anchor: *a ship at anchor.*

an•chor•age (ang′kər ij) /'æŋkərɪdʒ/ *n.* [*count*] a place for anchoring ships.

an•chor•man or **-wom•an** or **-per•son** (ang′kər mən) /'æŋkərmən/ or (-wo͝om′ən) /-ˌwʊmən/ or (-pûr′sən) /-ˌpɜrsən/ *n.* [*count*], *pl.* **-men** or **-wom•en** or **-per•sons. 1.** ANCHOR (def. 4). **2.** ANCHOR (def. 3).

an•cho•vy (an′chō vē, -chə-, an chō′vē) /'æntʃowviy, -tʃə-, æn'tʃowviy/ *n.* [*count*], *pl.* **-vies.** a small fish often salted and dried, canned, or made into a paste and used in cooking.

an•cient (ān′shənt) /'eynʃənt/ *adj.* **1.** of, dating from, or in a time long past, esp. before the end of the Western Roman Empire A.D. 476: *ancient civilizations of Greece and Egypt.* **2.** very old; aged: *an ancient wise man.* **—*n.*** [*count*] **3. the ancients,** the civilized people of a long time ago, esp. the Greeks, Romans, Hebrews, and Egyptians: *the writings and culture of the ancients.* **4.** a very old person. **—an′cient•ness,** *n.* [*noncount*]

an•cient•ly (ān′shənt lē) /'eynʃəntliy/ *adv.* in ancient times.

an•cil•lar•y (an′sə ler′ē) /'ænsəˌlɛriy/ *adj., n., pl.* **-ies. —*adj.* 1.** subordinate; subsidiary: *working in an ancillary position.* [*be* + ~ + *to* + *obj*]: *Buying a new car is ancillary to my goal of buying a house.* **2.** [*before a noun*] serving as a supplement: *ancillary teaching materials.* **—*n.*** [*count*] **3.** something that is an ancillary.

-ancy, a combination of -ANCE and -Y, used to form nouns denoting state or quality: *brilliant + -ancy → brilliancy.* See -ANCE.

and (and; *unstressed* ənd, ən, *or, esp. after t, n, or d,* n), *conj.* **1.** (used to connect words, phrases, or clauses) with, as well as, or in addition to: *pens and pencils.* **2.** added to; plus: *2 and 2 are 4.* **3.** then; afterwards; after that: *He finished and went to bed.* **4.** also; at the same time: *to sleep and dream.* **5.** *Informal.* (used instead of *to* between two verbs) to: *Try and do it (= Try to do it).* **6.** (used to introduce a result of what comes before it) then; as a result: *Study hard and you will pass this test (= If you study hard, then you will pass this test).* **7.** but; on the contrary: *He tried to run five miles and couldn't.* **8.** (used to suggest or imply that there are differences in things that have the same name): *There are bargains and bargains, so watch out. (= Some things are truly bargains, but other things, that seem like bargains, are not really so.)* **—*n.*** [*count*] **9.** [*usually plural*] an added or extra condition, rule, or item: *She clearly succeeded, no ifs, ands, or buts about it.* **—*Idiom.* 10. and so forth** or **so on,** and more of the same or similar kind: *first, second, third, and so forth.*

an•dan•te (än dän′tā, an dan′tē) /ɑn'dɑntey, æn'dæntiy/ *adv., adj. Music.* moderately slow.

and•i•ron (and′ī′ərn) /'ændˌayərn/ *n.* [*count*] one of a pair of metal stands for holding logs in a fireplace.

and/or (and′ôr′) /'ænd'ɔr/ *conj.* Use *and/or* to imply that either or both of the things mentioned may be affected or involved: *You can get contact lenses and/or regular glasses at half price (= You can get either contact lenses or glasses, or you can get both at half price).*

-andro-, *root. -andro-* comes from Greek, where it has the meaning "male; man." This meaning is found in such words as: ANDROGYNOUS, ANDROID, POLYANDRY.

an•drog•y•nous (an droj′ə nəs) /æn'drɒdʒənəs/ *adj.* having both masculine and feminine characteristics: *androgynous plants or animals.* **—an•drog•y•ny** (an droj′ə-nē) /æn'drɒdʒəniy/ *n.* [*noncount*] See -ANDRO-, -GYN-.

an•droid (an′droid) /'ændrɔyd/ *n.* [*count*] a robot in the human form. See -ANDRO-.

an•ec•dote (an′ik dōt′) /'ænɪkˌdowt/ *n.* [*count*] a short story about an interesting or amusing incident or event, often biographical. **—an′ec•do′tal,** *adj.*

a•ne•mi•a (ə nē′mē ə) /ə'niymiyə/ *n.* [*noncount*] **1.** a condition of the body in which the hemoglobin of red blood cells has been reduced, leading to weakness and paleness. **2.** a lack of power, vigor, or vitality: *the anemia of the economy.*

a•ne•mic (ə nē′mik) /ə 'niymɪk/ *adj.* **1.** having or suffering from anemia: *an anemic child.* **2.** lacking power, vigor, or substance: *anemic profits.* **—a•ne′mi•cal•ly,** *adv.*

an•e•mom•e•ter (an′ə mom′i tər) /ˌænə'mɒmɪtər/ *n.* [*count*] any instrument for measuring the speed of wind. See -METER-.

a•nem•o•ne (ə nem′ə nē′) /ə'nɛmə,niy/ *n.* [*count*] **1.** a plant of the buttercup family, having petallike sepals in red, white, or purple, or a variety of colors. **2.** SEA ANEMONE.

an•es•the•sia or **an•aes•the•sia** (an′əs thē′zhə) /,ænəs'θiyʒə/ *n.* [*noncount*] loss of sensation in the whole body or in certain areas: *drugs that induce anesthesia in surgical patients.*

an•es•the•si•ol•o•gy (an′əs thē′zē ol′ə jē) /,ænəs,θiyziy'ɒlədʒiy/ *n.* [*noncount*] the science of administering anesthetics. —**an′es•the′si•ol′o•gist,** *n.* [*count*]

an•es•thet•ic (an′əs thet′ik) /,ænəs'θɛtɪk/ *n.* [*count*] **1.** a substance that produces anesthesia. —*adj.* **2.** of, relating to, or causing anesthesia: *an anesthetic drug.*

an•es•the•tist (ə nes′thi tist) /ə'nɛsθɪtɪst/ *n.* [*count*] a person who administers anesthetics.

an•es•the•tize (ə nes′thi tīz′) /ə'nɛsθɪ,tayz/ *v.* [~ + *obj*], **-tized, -tiz•ing.** to cause (a person, animal, etc.) to feel no pain by administering an anesthetic. —**an•es•the•ti•za•tion** (ə nes′thi tə zā′shən) /ə,nɛsθɪtə'zeyʃən/ *n.* [*noncount*]

an•eu•rysm or **an•eu•rism** (an′yə riz′əm) /'ænyə,rɪzəm/ *n.* [*count*] an abnormal widening of the walls of a blood vessel caused when the vessel grows weak.

a•new (ə nōō′, ə nyōō′) /ə'nuw, ə'nyuw/ *adv.* over again; once more (often in a new way): *to start anew.*

an•gel (ān′jəl) /'eyndʒəl/ *n.* [*count*] **1.** a spiritual creature that is an attendant of God, often represented as having the form of a human being with wings. **2.** a person resembling an angel, as in beauty, purity, or kindliness: *You're an angel to help with the children.* **3.** one who provides financial backing for some undertaking, as a theatrical work. —**an•gel•ic** (an jel′ik) /æn'dʒɛlɪk/ *adj.* —**an•gel′i•cal•ly,** *adv.*

an•gel•fish (ān′jəl fish′) /'eyndʒəl,fɪʃ/ *n.* [*count*], *pl.* (*esp. when thought of as a group*) **-fish,** (*esp. for different kinds or species*) **-fish•es.** a brightly colored South American freshwater fish.

an′gel food′ cake′, *n.* [*noncount; count*] a light, delicate white cake made with stiffly beaten egg whites and no shortening or egg yolks.

an•ger (ang′gər) /'æŋgər/ *n.* [*noncount*] **1.** a strong feeling of displeasure or rage; wrath: *His anger rose at the insult.* —*v.* [~ + *obj*] **2.** to make (someone) angry: *His inconsiderateness angered me.*

an•gi•na (an ji′nə) /æn'dʒaynə/ *n.* [*noncount*] **1.** any attack of painful spasms or crushing pressure accompanied by a sensation of suffocating. **2.** ANGINA PECTORIS.

angi′na pec′to•ris (pek′tə ris) /'pɛktərɪs/ *n.* [*noncount*] a sensation of crushing pressure in the chest, sometimes spreading to the back or arm.

an•gi•o•plas•ty (an′jē ə plas′tē) /'ændʒiyə,plæstiy/ *n.* [*count*], *pl.* **-ties.** the surgical repair of a blood vessel.

an•gi•o•sperm (an′jē ə spûrm′) /'ændʒiyə,spɜrm/ *n.* [*count*] any plant that has its seeds enclosed in a fruit, grain, pod, or capsule: *All flowering plants are angiosperms.* —**an′gi•o•sper′mous,** *adj.*

an•gle[1] (ang′gəl) /'æŋgəl/ *n., v.,* **-gled, -gling.** —*n.* [*count*] **1. a.** the space within two lines or three or more surfaces that meet at a common point: *placed a chair in the angle of the wall.* **b.** the figure so formed: *a right angle.* **2.** a viewpoint; standpoint: *She looked at the problem from a fresh angle.* **3.** *Informal.* a secret motive: *He's been too friendly lately—what's his angle?* **4. at an angle,** not straight; obliquely: *The branch juts out at an angle.* —*v.* **5.** to move in or at an angle: [~ + *obj*]: *He angled the car into the narrow driveway.* [*no obj*]: *The road angles sharply to the right.* **6.** [~ + *obj*] to set, direct, aim, or adjust at an angle: *to angle a spotlight.* **7.** [~ + *obj*] to slant (a piece of reporting) toward a point of view: *The newspaper angled the story to make the mayor look good.*

an•gle[2] (ang′gəl) /'æŋgəl/ *v.* [*no obj*], **-gled, -gling. 1.** to fish with hook and line: *He was angling all morning.* **2.** [~ + *for* + *obj*] to use sly means to attain: *was angling for compliments.* —**an′gler,** *n.* [*count*]

an•gle•worm (ang′gəl wûrm′) /'æŋgəl,wɜrm/ *n.* [*count*] an earthworm, as used for bait in angling.

An•gli•can (ang′gli kən) /'æŋglɪkən/ *adj.* **1.** of or relating to the Church of England. **2.** of or relating to England or its inhabitants. —*n.* [*count*] **3.** a member of the Church of England or of a church connected to it. —**An′gli•can•ism,** *n.* [*noncount*]

An•gli•cize (ang′glə sīz′) /'æŋglə,sayz/ *v.* [~ + *obj; sometimes: anglicize*], **-cized, -ciz•ing.** to make English in form or character: *The French word "adieu" is Anglicized to make it sound like (ə dōō′).*

An•glo (ang′glō) /'æŋglow/ *n., pl.* **-glos,** *adj.* —*n.* [*count*] **1.** a white American of non-Hispanic descent. **2.** a Canadian whose first language is English, as distinguished from French-speaking Canadians. —*adj.* **3.** of or relating to Anglos.

Anglo-, a prefix, used as a combining form of ENGLISH: *Anglo-Norman; Anglo-Catholic.*

An•glo•phile (ang′glə fīl′) /'æŋglə,fayl/ also **An•glo•phil** (-fil) /-fɪl/ *n.* [*count*] a person who is friendly to or admires England or English customs, institutions, etc.

An•glo•phobe (ang′glə fōb′) /'æŋglə,fowb/ *n.* [*count*] a person who hates or fears England or anything English. —**An′glo•pho′bi•a,** *n.* [*noncount*]

An•glo-Sax•on (ang′glō sak′sən) /'æŋglow'sæksən/ *n.* **1.** [*count*] a person who lived in any of the kingdoms formed by the West Germanic people who invaded and occupied Britain in the 5th and 6th centuries A.D. **2.** [*noncount*] the language of the Anglo-Saxons, also called Old English. —*adj.* **3.** of or relating to the Anglo-Saxons, or to the period of Anglo-Saxon rule in Britain.

An•go•lan (ang gō′lən) /æŋ'gowlən/ *n.* [*count*] **1.** a person born or living in Angola. —*adj.* **2.** of or relating to Angola.

An•go•ra (ang gôr′ə, -gōr′ə, an-) /æŋ'gɔrə, -'gowrə, æn-/ *n., pl.* **-ras,** *adj.* —*n.* **1.** [*count*] one of a breed of long-haired cats, goats, or rabbits. **2.** [*noncount; often: angora*] the long hair of the Angora goat or of the Angora rabbit. **3.** [*count; usually: angora*] a garment made from this. —*adj.* **4.** [*usually: angora*] made from angora: *an angora hat.*

an•gry (ang′grē) /'æŋgriy/ *adj.,* **-gri•er, -gri•est. 1.** feeling anger or strong resentment: *an angry parent.* [*be* + ~ + *at/with*]: *She was angry at the dean. I was angry with the children that night.* [*be* + ~ + *about*]: *I was angry about the insult.* **2.** [*usually before a noun*] showing, expressing, caused by, or characterized by anger; wrathful: *angry words.* **3.** *Chiefly New England and Midland U.S.* [*before a noun*] inflamed; red: *an angry sore.* **4.** [*usually: before a noun*] showing characteristics associated with anger: *an angry sea; angry clouds.* —**an′gri•ly,** *adv.* —**Related Words.** ANGRY is an adjective, ANGER is a noun, ANGRILY is an adverb: *They were very angry with you. He keeps his anger locked up inside. He stalked angrily out of the room.*

angst (ängkst) /ɑŋkst/ *n.* [*noncount*] a feeling of dread, anxiety, or anguish.

an•guish (ang′gwish) /'æŋgwɪʃ/ *n.* [*noncount*] great suffering or pain: *the anguish of grief.* —**an′guished,** *adj.*

an•gu•lar (ang′gyə lər) /'æŋgyələr/ *adj.* **1.** forming an angle; marked by angles. **2.** bony, lean, or skinny; gaunt: *a tall, angular man.* **3.** acting or moving stiffly: *an awkward, angular dancer.* —**an′gu•lar•ly,** *adv.*

an•gu•lar•i•ty (ang′gyə lar′i tē) /,æŋgyə 'lærɪ tiy/ *n., pl.* **-ties. 1.** [*noncount*] the quality of being angular. **2.** [*count*] an angular outline; sharp corner: *the angularities of the city skyline.*

-anima-, *root. -anima-* comes from Latin, where it has the meaning "spirit, soul." This meaning is found in such words as: ANIMATE, ANIMATED, ANIMOSITY, ANIMUS, INANIMATE.

an•i•mal (an′ə məl) /'ænəməl/ *n.* [*count*] **1.** a living creature that can move on its own and actively acquire food and digest it and has senses and nervous systems to respond rapidly to the surroundings. **2.** a creature other than a human being: *We believe we are higher than the animals.* **3.** a mammal: *There are plenty of birds, fish, and wild animals in the park.* **4.** the physical, sensual, or sexual nature of human beings: [*usually: the* + ~]: *a scene that brought out the animal in the viewer.* **5.** an inhuman person; brute: *You're acting like an animal.* **6.** thing: *A perfect job? Is there any such animal?* —*adj.* **7.** of, relating to, or derived from animals: *animal fats.* **8.** relating to the physical, sensual, or sexual nature of humans: *animal needs.*

an•i•mal•cule (an′ə mal′kyōōl) /,ænə'mælkyuwl/ *n.* [*count*] a microscopically small organism.

an′imal rights′, *n.* [*plural*] the rights of animals to decent treatment and protection from abuse.

an•i•mate (*verb* an′ə māt′; *adjective* -mit) /*verb* 'ænə,meyt; *adjective* -mɪt/ *v.,* **-mat•ed, -mat•ing,** *adj.* —*v.* [~ + *obj*] **1.** to give life to; make alive: *Her presence animated the party.* **2.** to move or stir to action; motivate; inspire; encourage: *The move to a new office animated the staff.* **3.** to give motion to: *We saw leaves animated by the breeze.* **4.** to produce in the form of an animated cartoon. —*adj.* **5.** alive; possessing life: *animate beings.* **6.** (of a noun) having, or seeming to have, the ability to move, think, and act under one's own power (opposed to *inanimate*): *In the sentence "John blew the candle out", John is an animate noun.* —**an′i•ma′tor,** *n.* [*count*] See -ANIMA-.

an•i•mat•ed (an′i māt id) /ˈænɪ meyt ɪd/ *adj.* lively; full of vigor: *an animated conversation.* See -ANIMA-.

an′imated cartoon′, *n.* [*count*] a motion picture made up of a sequence of drawings, each slightly different, so that when filmed and run through a projector the figures seem to move.

an•i•ma•tion (an′ə mā′shən) /ˌænəˈmeyʃən/ *n.* **1.** [*noncount*] animated quality; liveliness; enthusiasm: *the animation on her face.* **2.** [*noncount*] the process of preparing animated cartoons. **3.** [*count*] an animated cartoon. See -ANIMA-.

an•i•mism (an′ə miz′əm) /ˈænəˌmɪzəm/ *n.* [*noncount*] the belief that natural objects, natural phenomena, and the universe itself possess souls. —**an′i•mist,** *n.* [*count*], *adj.* —**an′i•mis′tic,** *adj.*

an•i•mos•i•ty (an′ə mos′i tē) /ˌænəˈmɒsɪtiy/ *n., pl.* **-ties.** strong hostility or antagonism: [*noncount*]: *felt great animosity toward their tormentor.* [*count*]: *The old animosities surfaced again.* See -ANIMA-.

an•i•mus (an′ə məs) /ˈænəməs/ *n.* [*noncount*] strong dislike or enmity; animosity. See -ANIMA-.

an•ise (an′is) /ˈænɪs/ *n.* **1.** [*count*] a Mediterranean plant of the parsley family, having seeds that yield aniseed. **2.** [*noncount*] aniseed.

an•i•seed (an′ə sēd′, an′is sēd′) /ˈænəˌsiyd, ˈænɪsˌsiyd/ *n.* [*noncount*] the strong-smelling seed of anise, used in cooking and liqueurs for its licoricelike flavor.

an•i•sette (an′ə set′, -zet′) /ˌænəˈsɛt, -ˈzɛt/ *n.* [*noncount*] a liqueur flavored with aniseed.

ankh (angk) /æŋk/ *n.* [*count*] a cross with a loop at the top, used esp. in ancient Egypt as a symbol of life.

an•kle (ang′kəl) /ˈæŋkəl/ *n.* [*count*] **1.** the joint between the foot and leg. **2.** the slender part of the leg above the foot.

an•klet (ang′klit) /ˈæŋklɪt/ *n.* [*count*] **1.** a sock that reaches just above the ankle. **2.** an ornamental circlet worn around the ankle.

-ann-, *root.* *-ann-* comes from Latin, where it has the meaning "year." This meaning is found in such words as: ANNALS, ANNIVERSARY, ANNUAL, ANNUITY, BIANNUAL, SEMIANNUAL, SUPERANNUATED.

an•nals (an′lz) /ˈænlz/ *n.* [*plural*] **1.** historical records; chronicles; stories of events: *the annals of war.* **2.** a journal containing the formal reports of an organization: *looking up the reference in the medical annals.* —**an•nal•ist** (an′l ist) /ˈænl̩ɪst/ *n.* [*count*] See -ANN-.

an•ne•lid (an′l id) /ˈænl̩ɪd/ *n.* [*count*] a worm that has parts of the body loosely connected in a row, as an earthworm.

an•nex (*v.* ə neks′, an′eks; *n.* an′eks, -iks) /*v.* əˈnɛks, ˈænɛks; *n.* ˈænɛks, -ɪks/ *v.* [~ + *obj*] **1.** to attach or add, esp. to something larger or more important: *annexed a building to their headquarters.* **2.** to take control of (territory) from another country, often by force: *Germany annexed Czechoslovakia.* —*n.* [*count*] Also, *esp. Brit.,* **an′nexe. 3.** something annexed: *an annex to a treaty.* **4.** a building or an addition to a building, added to a larger one. —**an•nex•a•tion** (an′ek sā′shən) /ˌænɛkˈseyʃən/ *n.* [*noncount*] See -NEC-.

an•ni•hi•late (ə ni′ə lāt′) /əˈnayəˌleyt/ *v.* [~ + *obj*], **-lat•ed, -lat•ing. 1.** to reduce to complete ruin or nonexistence; destroy completely: *The mad scientist planned to annihilate the world.* **2.** to destroy the main part or body of: *In the first days the fighters annihilated the enemy air force.* **3.** to defeat; vanquish: *Our team was annihilated in the playoffs.* —**an•ni•hi•la•tion** (ə ni′ə lā′shən) /əˌnayəˈleyʃən/ *n.* [*noncount*] —**an•ni′hi•la′tor,** *n.* [*count*]

an•ni•ver•sa•ry (an′ə vûr′sə rē) /ˌænəˈvɜrsəriy/ *n., pl.* **-ries,** *adj.* —*n.* [*count*] **1.** the date of an important past event that is celebrated or remembered every year: *That date was the anniversary of the invasion.* **2.** the celebration of an anniversary, esp. of a wedding: *had 200 guests at their anniversary.* —*adj.* [*before a noun*] **3.** of or relating to an anniversary: *an anniversary party.* See -ANN-.

an•no•tate (an′ə tāt′) /ˈænəˌteyt/ *v.* [~ + *obj*], **-tat•ed, -tat•ing.** to supply (a text) with critical or explanatory notes. —**an′no•ta′tive,** *adj.* —**an′no•ta′tor,** *n.* [*count*] See -NOTA-.

an•no•ta•tion (an′ə tā shən) /ˌænə tey ʃən/ *n.* **1.** [*noncount*] the act of annotating. **2.** [*count*] a mark or note added to text or pictures. See -NOTA-.

an•nounce (ə nouns′) /əˈnawns/ *v.,* **-nounced, -nounc•ing. 1.** to make known publicly or officially; proclaim: [~ + *obj*]: *announced her candidacy for the presidency.* [~ + (*that*) *clause*]: *announced that she would run for president.* **2.** [~ + *obj*] to state the approach or presence of: *to announce a guest.* **3.** to serve as an announcer (of): [~ + *obj*]: *He announced the program during the wedding reception.* [*no obj*]: *He announced for the radio station.* **4.** [*used with quotations*] to state; declare: *"My bags are packed and I'm leaving," she announced.* **5.** [~ + *for* + *obj*] to declare one's candidacy: *is expected to announce for governor.* See -NOUNCE-.

an•nounce•ment (ə nouns′mənt) /ə ˈnawnsmənt/ *n.* [*count*] **1.** a public notice or statement about something. **2.** a short advertisement in the newspaper: *announcements about apartments to share.* **3.** a brief spoken message (on the radio or TV), esp. a commercial: *We'll be back right after these announcements.* **4.** a card that announces a wedding or other important event.

an•nounc•er (ə noun′sər) /əˈnawnsər/ *n.* [*count*] a person who announces, esp. one who introduces programs, reads advertisements, etc., on radio or television.

an•noy (ə noi′) /əˈnɔy/ *v.* [~ + *obj*] to disturb or bother in a way that displeases, troubles, or irritates: [~ + *obj*]: *My neighbor's loud television annoys me.* [*It* + ~ + *obj* + *that clause*]: *It annoyed me that my neighbors played their TV late at night.* —**Related Words.** ANNOY is a verb, ANNOYING is an adjective, ANNOYANCE is a noun: *That music annoys me. It is annoying music. Another annoyance was when the train was late.*

an•noy•ance (ə noi′əns) /əˈnɔyəns/ *n.* **1.** [*count*] a person or thing that annoys: *That brat is a real annoyance.* **2.** [*noncount*] the feeling of being annoyed: *felt annoyance at being forced to wait.*

an•noy•ing (ə noi′ing) /ə ˈnɔyɪŋ/ *adj.* causing annoyance; bothersome; irritating: *an annoying cough.* —**an•noy′ing•ly,** *adv.*

an•nu•al (an′yo͞o əl) /ˈænyuwəl/ *adj.* [*before a noun*] **1.** of or for a year; yearly: *my annual salary.* **2.** occurring or returning once a year: *an annual celebration.* **3.** (of a plant) living for only one growing season: *an annual plant.* —*n.* [*count*] **4.** a plant that lives for one growing season. **5.** a publication issued once a year. —**an′nu•al•ly,** *adv.* See -ANN-.

an′nual ring′, *n.* [*count*] a yearly formation of new wood in woody plants that can be seen as a ring on the cross section of a tree trunk.

an•nu•i•tant (ə no͞o′i tnt, ə nyo͞o′-) /əˈnuwɪtnt, əˈnyuw-/ *n.* [*count*] a person who receives an annuity.

an•nu•i•ty (ə no͞o′i tē, ə nyo͞o′-) /əˈnuwɪtiy, əˈnyuw-/ *n.* [*count*], *pl.* **-ties. 1.** a certain income paid yearly for a fixed period, often for the person's lifetime. **2.** the policy or form of insurance that provides such an income. See -ANN-.

an•nul (ə nul′) /əˈnʌl/ *v.* [~ + *obj*], **-nulled, -nul•ling.** to make or declare (something to be) no longer valid; invalidate: *to annul a marriage; to annul an agreement.* See -NULL-.

an•nu•lar (an′yə lər) /ˈænyələr/ *adj.* having the form of a ring.

an•nul•ment (ə nul′mənt) /ə ˈnʌlmənt/ *n.* **1.** [*noncount*] a declaring that a contract, marriage, or agreement is invalid. **2.** [*count*] a statement or declaration that a contract, marriage, or agreement is invalid.

an•nun•ci•a•tion (ə nun′sē ā′shən) /əˌnʌnsiyˈeyʃən/ *n.* [*count*] an act or instance of announcing; proclamation. See -NUNC-.

an•ode (an′ōd) /ˈænowd/ *n.* [*count*] **1.** the electrode or terminal by which current enters a cell, such as a battery, etc. **2.** the negative terminal of a cell or battery. **3.** the positive terminal, electrode, or element of an electron tube.

an•o•dyne (an′ə dīn′) /ˈænəˌdayn/ *n.* [*count*] **1.** anything that relieves pain or distress: *Work on the book was the anodyne that took his mind off his grief.* —*adj.* **2.** relieving pain or discomfort; soothing: *the anodyne effect of watching ocean waves.*

a•noint (ə noint′) /əˈnɔynt/ *v.* **1.** [~ + *obj* (+ *with* + *obj*)] to rub oil or ointment on the body so as to make sacred or holy in a ceremony. **2.** [~ + *obj*] to choose formally: *The president anointed his vice-president as his successor.* —**a•noint′ment,** *n.* [*noncount*]

a•nom•a•lous (ə nom′ə ləs) /ə ˈnɒmə ləs/ *adj.* differing from the expected or usual; irregular; abnormal. —**a•nom′a•lous′ly,** *adv.* See -NOM-[1].

a•nom•a•ly (ə nom′ə lē) /əˈnɒməliy/ *n., pl.* **-lies. 1.** [*noncount*] a difference or change from the common type, rule, arrangement, or form; irregularity; abnormality **2.** [*count*] someone or something that differs from the expected or usual: *A dog with two tails is an anomaly.* **3.** [*count*] an unexpected, unusual, or strange condition, situation, or quality: *It was an anomaly for the weather to be warm in winter.* See -NOM-[1].

a•non (ə non′) /ə'nɒn/ *adv. Older Use.* in a short time; soon: *"I'll see you anon," she said, laughingly.*

anon., an abbreviation of: **1.** anonymous. **2.** anonymously.

a•no•nym•i•ty (an′ə nim′i tē) /ˌænə 'nɪmɪ tiy/ *n.* [*noncount*] the state or condition of being anonymous. See -ONYM-.

a•non•y•mous (ə non′ə məs) /ə'nɒnəməs/ *adj.* **1.** lacking the name of the author, writer, etc.: *an anonymous poem.* **2.** not giving a name; not identifying oneself: *an anonymous donor.* **3.** lacking or not showing individuality, unique character, or any special or unusual quality: *drab, anonymous houses.* **—a•non′y•mous•ly,** *adv.* See -ONYM-.

a•noph•e•les (ə nof′ə lēz′) /ə'nɒfəˌliyz/ *n.* [*count*], *pl.* **-les.** a mosquito some species of which transmit malaria to humans.

an•o•rex•i•a (an′ə rek′sē ə) /ˌænə'rɛksiyə/ *n.* [*noncount*] an eating disorder in which the victim suffers from a fear of being fat and so diets too much to become unhealthily thin.

an•o•rex•ic (an′ə rek′sik) /ˌænə 'rɛksɪk/ *adj.* Also, **an•o•rec•tic** (an′ə rek′tik) /ˌænə 'rɛktɪk/. **1.** having the disorder of anorexia. **—***n.* [*count*] **2.** a person who suffers from anorexia.

an•oth•er (ə nuth′ər) /ə'nʌðər/ *adj.* [*before a noun*] **1.** being one more; being more of the same; further; additional: *Have another piece of cake.* [~ + *number word* + *plural count noun*]: *Come in for an appointment in another three weeks.* **2.** different; distinct; of a different kind: *to visit another country and see how different life is there.* **3.** very similar to; of the same kind or category as: *would like to be another Shakespeare.* **—***pron.* **4.** one more; an additional one: *There is one book and here is another.* **5.** a different one; something different: *She kept going from one thing to another.*

an•swer (an′sər) /'ænsər/ *n.* [*count*] **1.** a spoken or written reply or response to a question, request, letter, etc.: *My answer was "yes".* **2.** a correct response to a question: *When was the Declaration of Independence signed? The answer is 1776.* **3.** counterpart: *the French answer to the Beatles.* **4.** an action that serves as a reply or response: *Her answer to my proposal was a shrug of the shoulders.* **5.** a solution to a problem: *never claimed to have all the answers.* **6. in answer (to),** by way of responding or replying: *I offer these arguments in answer to your criticism.* **—***v.* **7.** to speak or write in response (to); make answer (to); reply (to): [*no obj*]: *She answered quietly.* [~ + *obj*]: *The nominee answered the questions with humor.* **8.** to respond by an act or motion: [*no obj*]: *When the phone rang, she was afraid to answer.* [~ + *obj*]: *They answered the doorbell.* [~ + *with* + *obj*]: *He answered with a laugh.* [~ + *obj* + *with* + *obj*]: *They answered the attack with a full-scale assault of their own.* **9.** [*not: be* + ~*-ing*] to conform; correspond (to): [~ + *to* + *obj*]: *She answered to the description.* [~ + *obj*]: *The suspect answers the police description.* **10.** [~ + *obj* (+ *with* + *obj*)] to solve: *answered the unemployment crisis with prompt actions.* **11. answer back,** to reply impolitely or rudely (to): [*no obj*]: *Don't answer back.* [~ + *obj* + *back*]: *Don't answer your teacher back like that.* **12. answer for,** [~ + *for* + *obj*] **a.** to act or suffer in consequence: *He must answer for his criminal acts.* **b.** to be or to declare oneself responsible or accountable: *to answer for the President's safety.*

an•swer•a•ble (an′sər ə bəl) /'ænsər ə bəl/ *adj.* **1.** [*be* + ~ + *to*] accountable (to someone higher in authority): *I am answerable only to the chairman.* **2.** [*be* + ~ + *for*] responsible: *You are answerable for your own actions.* **3.** able to be answered: *an answerable question.*

ant (ant) /ænt/ *n.* [*count*] **1.** a small insect that lives in highly organized colonies. **—*Idiom.*** **2. have ants in one's pants,** *Slang.* to be impatient or eager to act.

-ant, *suffix.* **1.** *-ant* is attached to some verbs to form adjectives with the meaning "doing or performing (the action of the verb)": *please* + *-ant* → *pleasant* (= *doing the pleasing*). **2.** *-ant* is also attached to some verbs to form nouns with the meaning "one who does or performs (the action of the verb, often a formal action)": *serve* + *-ant* → *servant* (= *one who serves*); *apply* (+ *ic*) + *-ant* → *applicant* (= *one who formally applies, as for a job*). **3.** *-ant* is attached to some verbs to form nouns with the meaning: "substance that does or performs (the action of the verb)": *cool* (*verb* = *"to make cool"*) + *-ant* → *coolant* (= *substance to keep engines cool*). See -ENT.

ant•ac•id (ant as′id) /ænt'æsɪd/ *adj.* **1.** counteracting or neutralizing acidity, esp. of the stomach. **—***n.* [*count*] **2.** an antacid medicine. See -ACR-.

an•tag•o•nism (an tag′ə niz′əm) /æn'tægəˌnɪzəm/ *n.* active hostility or opposition: [*noncount*]: *The proposal provoked antagonism among committee members.* [*count*]: *Antagonisms rose sharply.* See -AGON-.

an•tag•o•nist (an tag′ə nist) /æn'tægənɪst/ *n.* [*count*] **1.** opponent; adversary: *considered his opponent a dangerous antagonist.* **2.** (in drama or literature) the opponent of the hero or protagonist. **—an•tag′o•nis′tic,** *adj.* **—an•tag′o•nis′ti•cal•ly,** *adv.* See -AGON-.

an•tag•o•nize (an tag′ə nīz′) /æn'tægəˌnayz/ *v.* [~ + *obj*], **-nized, -niz•ing.** to cause to become hostile; make an enemy or opponent of: *His speech antagonized many voters.* See -AGON-. **—Related Words.** ANTAGONIZE is a verb, ANTAGONISTIC is an adjective, ANTAGONIST and ANTAGONISM are nouns: *He antagonizes people too easily. He is very antagonistic toward his fellow workers. His antagonist confronted him again. There was great antagonism between the two nations.*

ant•arc•tic (ant ärk′tik, -är′tik) /ænt'ɑrktɪk, -'ɑrtɪk/ *adj.* of, at, or near the South Pole.

ant′ bear′, *n.* AARDVARK.

an•te (an′tē) /'æntiy/ *n., v.,* **-ted** or **-teed, -te•ing.** **—***n.* [*count*] **1.** a sum of money in the card game of poker, put into the pot by each player before the deal. **2.** cost; price: *tried to raise the ante.* **—***v.* **ante up, 3.** (in poker) to put (one's initial stake) into the pot: [~ + *up* + *obj*]: *Ante up your bets now.* [*no obj*]: *Ante up and let's play.* **4.** to produce or pay (one's share): [~ + *up* + *obj*]: *had to ante up a dollar to help pay the fine.* [*no obj*]: *All right, ante up.*

ante-, *prefix.* **1.** *ante-* is attached to roots and means "happening before": *antebellum* (= *before the war*). **2.** *ante-* also means "located in front of": *anteroom* (= *room located in front of another*).

ant•eat•er (ant′ē′tər) /'æntˌiytər/ *n.* [*count*] an animal having a long snout, a sticky tongue, and strong claws, that feeds on ants and termites.

an•te•bel•lum (an′tē bel′əm) /'æntiy'bɛləm/ *adj.* [*often: before a noun*] before or existing before a war, esp. the American Civil War: *the antebellum South.* See -BELL-.

an•te•ced•ent (an′tə sēd′nt) /ˌæntə'siydnt/ *adj.* **1.** preceding; prior; coming before: *an antecedent event.* **—***n.* [*count*] **2.** something that comes or happens before another: *Isolated skirmishes were antecedents of the war.* **3. antecedents,** [*plural*] ancestors: *Where did your antecedents come from?* **4.** a word, phrase, or clause, usually a noun, that is replaced, usually later, by a pronoun or other substitute. *Jane* is the antecedent (of the pronoun *she*) in the sentence: *Jane lost a glove and she is upset.* **—an′te•ced′ence,** *n.* [*noncount*] See -CEDE-.

an•te•cham•ber (an′tē chām′bər) /'æntiyˌtʃeymbər/ *n.* [*count*] an anteroom.

an•te•date (an′ti dāt′) /'æntɪˌdeyt/ *v.* [~ + *obj*], **-dat•ed, -dat•ing.** **1.** to precede in time: *The ruins in southern Africa antedated some of the medieval fortresses of Europe.* **2.** to put a date on (a letter, check, document) that is earlier than the true date.

an•te•di•lu•vi•an (an′tē di lo͞o′vē ən) /ˌæntiydɪ'luwviyən/ *adj.* **1.** [*often: before a noun*] of or belonging to the period before the Flood in the Bible. **2.** old-fashioned; antiquated: *Antediluvian ideas kept the company from going forward.*

an•te•lope (an′tl ōp′) /'æntḷˌowp/ *n.* [*count*], *pl.* **-lopes,** (*esp. when thought of as a group*) **-lope.** a deerlike animal of Africa and Asia.

an•te me•rid•i•em (an′tē mə rid′ē əm, -em′) /'æntiy mə'rɪdiyəm, -ˌɛm/ *adj.* being the time after midnight and before noon. See A.M.

an•ten•na (an ten′ə) /æn'tɛnə/ *n.* [*count*], *pl.* **-ten•nas** for 1, **-ten•nae** (-ten′ē) /-'tɛniy/ for 2. **1.** an aerial; a wire or set of wires attached to metal rods by which radio or television signals are sent out or received. See illustration at HOUSE. **2.** one of the two long, thin, jointed, movable parts on the heads of insects, lobsters, and related animals that can feel or sense things in the surroundings.

an•te•ri•or (an tēr′ē ər) /æn'tɪəriyər/ *adj.* **1.** located before or at the front of (opposed to *posterior*): *the anterior fin of a fish.* **2.** occurring before or earlier in time; earlier. **—an•te′ri•or•ly,** *adv.*

an•te•room (an′tē ro͞om′, -ro͝om′) /'æntiyˌruwm, -ˌrʊm/ *n.* [*count*] a room that opens up to a larger room, esp. a waiting room.

an•them (an′thəm) /'ænθəm/ *n.* [*count*] **1.** a song, such as of praise, devotion, or patriotism. **2.** a hymn.

an•ther (an′thər) /'ænθər/ *n.* [*noncount*] the part of a flower that carries pollen.

ant•hill (ant′hil′) /'ænt,hɪl/ *n.* [*count*] a mound of earth formed by a colony of ants in building their nest.

an•thol•o•gy (an thol′ə jē) /æn'θɒlədʒiy/ *n.* [*count*], *pl.* **-gies.** a collection of selected writings: *an anthology of poetry.* —**an•thol′o•gist,** *n.* [*count*] —**an•thol•o•gize** (an thol′ə jīz′) /æn'θɒlə,dʒayz/ *v.* [~ + *obj*], **-gized, -giz•ing.**

an•thra•cite (an′thrə sīt′) /'ænθrə,sayt/ *n.* [*noncount*] a hard coal that burns slowly with little smoke or flame.

an•thrax (an′thraks) /'ænθræks/ *n.* [*noncount*], *pl.* **-thra•ces** (-thrə sēz′) /-θrə,siyz/. an infectious disease of cattle, sheep, and other mammals that can be transmitted to humans, as by handling infected wool, and that is marked by skin ulcers.

-anthro-, *root.* *-anthro-* comes from Greek, where it has the meaning "man, human." This meaning is found in such words as: ANTHROPOCENTRIC, ANTHROPOID, ANTHROPOLOGY, ANTHROPOMORPHISM, MISANTHROPE. See -ANDRO-.

an•thro•po•cen•tric (an′thrə pō sen′trik) /,ænθrəpow'sɛntrɪk/ *adj.* tending to believe that human beings are the central fact of the universe and to interpret everything in terms of human experience and values. —**an′thro•po•cen′tri•cal•ly,** *adv.* —**an′thro•po•cen′trism,** *n.* [*noncount*] See -ANTHRO-.

an•thro•poid (an′thrə poid′) /'ænθrə,pɔyd/ *adj.* **1.** resembling humans: *anthropoid apes.* —*n.* [*count*] **2.** APE (def. 1). See -ANTHRO-.

an•thro•pol•o•gy (an′thrə pol′ə jē) /,ænθrə'pɒlədʒiy/ *n.* [*noncount*] the science that deals with the origins, physical and cultural development, biological features, and social customs and beliefs of humankind. —**an•thro•po•log•i•cal** (an′thrə pə loj′i kəl) /,ænθrəpə'lɒdʒɪkəl/ *adj.* —**an′thro•po•log′i•cal•ly,** *adv.* —**an′thro•pol′o•gist,** *n.* [*count*] See -ANTHRO-.

an•thro•po•mor•phic (an′thrə pə môr′fik) /,ænθrəpə'mɔrfɪk/ also **an′thro•po•mor′phous,** *adj.* **1. a.** thought of as being human in form or attributes: *ancient anthropomorphic gods.* **b.** attributing human characteristics to nonhuman objects. **2.** resembling a human form: *an anthropomorphic carving.* —**an′thro•po•mor′phi•cal•ly,** *adv.* —**an′thro•po•mor′phism,** *n.* [*noncount*] See -ANTHRO-, -MORPH-.

an•ti (an′tī, an′tē) /'æntay, 'æntiy/ *n.* [*count*], *pl.* **-tis.** a person opposed: *We have many supporters and a few antis.*

anti-, *prefix.* *anti-* is attached to nouns and adjectives and means: **1.** against, opposed to: *anti-Semitic, antislavery.* **2.** preventing, counteracting, or working against: *anticoagulant, antifreeze.* **3.** destroying or disabling: *antiaircraft, antipersonnel.* **4.** identical to in form or function, but lacking in some important ways: *anticlimax, antihero, antiparticle.* **5.** an antagonist or rival of: *Antichrist, antipope.* **6.** situated opposite: *Anti-Lebanon.* Also, *before a vowel,* **ant-.**

an•ti•a•bor•tion (an′tē ə bôr′shən, an′tī-) /,æntiyə'bɔrʃən, ,æntay-/ *adj.* [*before a noun*] opposed to abortion. —**an′ti•a•bor′tion•ist,** *n.* [*count*]

an•ti•air•craft (an′tē âr′kraft′, an′tī-) /,æntiy'ɛər,kræft, ,æntay-/ *adj.* [*before a noun*] designed for or used in defense against enemy aircraft: *antiaircraft artillery.*

an•ti-A•mer•i•can (an′tē ə mer′i kən, an′tī-) /,æntiyə'mɛrɪkən, ,æntay-/ *adj.* opposed or hostile to the U.S. or to its people, principles, or policies. —**an′ti-A•mer′i•can•ism,** *n.* [*noncount*]

an•ti•bac•te•ri•al (an′tē bak tēr′ē əl, an′tī-) /,æntiybæk'tɪəriyəl, ,æntay-/ *adj.* [*before a noun*] destructive to or interfering with the growth of bacteria: *antibacterial soap.*

an•ti•bal•lis•tic (an′tē bə lis′tik, an′tī-) /,æntiybə'lɪstɪk, ,æntay-/ *adj.* [*before a noun*] designed to intercept and destroy ballistic missiles: *an antiballistic missile.*

an•ti•bi•ot•ic (an′ti bī ot′ik, -bē-) /,æntɪbay'ɒtɪk, -biy-/ *n.* [*count*] **1.** a chemical substance, as penicillin, that can inhibit or destroy the growth of bacteria and other microorganisms. —*adj.* [*before a noun*] **2.** of or involving antibiotics: *an antibiotic medicine.* —**an′ti•bi•ot′i•cal•ly,** *adv.*

an•ti•bod•y (an′ti bod′ē) /'æntɪ,bɒdiy/ *n.* [*count*], *pl.* **-bod•ies.** a protein produced by the body to fight substances like viruses that cause disease.

an•tic (an′tik) /'æntɪk/ *n.* [*count*] **1.** Usually, **antics.** [*plural*] a playful or silly trick: *Her antics in class got her into trouble.* —*adj.* **2.** foolishly playful; funny; amusing: *antic behavior.*

an•ti•can•cer (an′tē kan′sər, an′tī-) /,æntiy'kænsər, ,æntay-/ *adj.* [*before a noun*] used or effective in the prevention or treatment of cancer: *the promise of new anticancer drugs.*

An•ti•christ (an′ti krīst′) /'æntɪ,kraystʹ/ *n.* **1.** [*proper noun; usually: the* + ~] a personage or power expected to corrupt the world but be conquered by Christ's Second Coming. **2.** [*count; often: antichrist*] **a.** any opponent of or disbeliever in Christ. **b.** a false Christ.

an•tic•i•pate (an tis′ə pāt′) /æn'tɪsə,peyt/ *v.,* **-pat•ed, -pat•ing. 1.** to realize or feel beforehand; foresee: [~ + *obj*]: *We anticipate a sell-out crowd tonight.* [~ + *verb-ing*]: *We anticipate running into problems.* [~ + *that clause*]: *The government hadn't anticipated that the economy would fall so fast.* **2.** to look forward to, esp. confidently or with pleasure: [~ + *obj*]: *I was anticipating my promotion.* [~ + *verb-ing*]: *anticipates getting a promotion.* [~ + *that clause*]: *anticipates that you will get your promotion.* **3.** [~ + *obj*] to perform (an action) before another has had time to act: *We anticipated our rival's strategy and made the first move.* **4.** [~ + *obj*] to answer (a question), obey (a command), or satisfy (a request) before it is made: *anticipated the surgeon by handing her the scalpel before she asked for it.* **5.** [~ + *obj*] to make (some action) ineffective by countering it in advance: *We anticipated their attack by stationing our bombers to the south.* —**an•ti•ci•pa•tion** (an tis′ə pā′shən) /æn,tɪsə'peyʃən/ *n.* [*noncount*] See -CEP-.

an•tic•i•pa•to•ry (an tis′ə pə tôr ē, -tōr-) /æn 'tɪsə pə tɔr iy, -towr-/ *adj.* [*often: before a noun*] characterized by anticipation.

an•ti•cli•max (an′tē klī′maks, an′tī-) /,æntiy'klaymæks, ,æntay-/ *n.* **1.** [*count*] something that is far less important, powerful, or striking than expected; a letdown or disappointment: *After a great series, the final, losing game was an anticlimax.* **2.** [*noncount*] descent in power, quality, or dignity: *a weary sense of anticlimax.* —**an•ti•cli•mac•tic** (an′tē klī mak′tik, -klə-, an′tī-) /,æntiyklay'mæktɪk, -klə-, ,æntay-/ *adj.*

an•ti•clock•wise (an′ti klok′wīz) /,æntɪ'klɒkwayz/ *adj. Brit.* COUNTERCLOCKWISE.

an•ti•co•ag•u•lant (an′tē kō ag′yə lənt, an′tī-) /,æntiykow'ægyələnt, ,æntay-/ *adj.* [*before a noun*] **1.** Also, **an•ti•co•ag•u•la•tive** (an′tē kō ag′yə lā′tiv, -lə tiv, an′tī-) /,æntiykow'ægyə,leytɪv, -lətɪv, ,æntay-/. preventing coagulation, esp. of blood. —*n.* [*count*] **2.** an anticoagulant agent.

an•ti•com•mu•nism (an′tē kom′yə niz′əm, an′tī-) /,æntiy 'kɒmyə ,nɪzəm, ,æntay-/ *n.* [*noncount*] opposition to communism. —**an′ti•com′mu•nist,** *n.* [*count*], *adj.*

an•ti•de•pres•sant or **an•ti-de•pres•sant** (an′tē di-pres′ənt, an′tī-) /,æntiydɪ'prɛsənt, ,æntay-/ *adj.* **1.** used to relieve or treat mental depression: *antidepressant drugs.* —*n.* [*count*] **2.** a drug used to treat mental depression.

an•ti•dote (an′ti dōt′) /'æntɪ,dowt/ *n.* [*count*] **1.** a medicine or other remedy used against the effects of poison, disease, etc. **2.** something that prevents or works against injurious or unwanted effects: *One antidote for crime is more police on the street.*

an•ti•freeze (an′ti frēz′, an′tē-) /'æntɪ,friyz, 'æntiy-/ *n.* [*noncount*] a liquid added to the water in the cooling system of a vehicle to keep the water from freezing.

an•ti•gen (an′ti jən, -jen′) /'æntɪdʒən, -,dʒɛn/ *n.* [*count*] a protein that can cause the body to react by producing an antibody that fights infection or disease. —**an′ti•gen′ic,** *adj.* —**an′ti•gen′i•cal•ly,** *adv.* See -GEN-.

an•ti•he•ro (an′tē hēr′ō, an′tī-) /'æntiy,hɪərow, 'æntay-/ *n.* [*count*], *pl.* **-roes.** a main character (in a book, play, or movie) who lacks the qualities expected of a hero.

an•ti•his•ta•mine (an′tē his′tə mēn′, -min, an′tī-) /,æntiy'hɪstə,miyn, -mɪn, ,æntay-/ *n.* [*count*] a drug that can block the action of substances in the body that cause sneezing, sniffling, or other reactions of colds and allergies.

an•ti•in•tel•lec•tu•al (an′tē in′tl ek′cho͞o əl, an′tī-) /,æntiy,ɪntḷ'ɛktʃuwəl, ,æntay-/ *adj.* **1.** opposed to, hostile to, or distrustful of intellectuals or intellectual interests. —*n.* [*count*] **2.** an anti-intellectual person. —**an′ti-in′tel•lec′tu•al•ism,** *n.* [*noncount*]

an•ti•knock (an′tē nok′, an′tī-) /,æntiy'nɒk, ,æntay-/ *adj.* [*before a noun*] of, concerning, or being a material added to gasoline or other fuel for a car or truck engine to run smoothly by eliminating or minimizing knock.

an•ti•mat•ter (an′tē mat′ər, an′tī-) /ˈæntiyˌmætər, ˈæntay-/ *n.* [*noncount*] matter composed of antiparticles.

an•ti•mis•sile (an′tē mis′əl, an′tī-) /ˌæntiyˈmɪsəl, ˌæntay-/ *adj.* [*before a noun*] designed or used in defense against enemy guided missiles.

an•ti•mo•ny (an′tə mō′nē) /ˈæntəˌmowniy/ *n.* [*noncount*] a brittle white metallic element used chiefly in alloys and in compounds in medicine.

an•ti•par•ti•cle (an′tē pär′ti kəl, an′tī-) /ˈæntiyˌpɑrtɪkəl, ˈæntay-/ *n.* [*count*] an atomic particle whose properties are identical in size to those of a specific elementary particle but are of opposite sign.

an•ti•pas•to (an′ti pä′stō, -pas′tō, än′tē pä′-) /ˌæntɪˈpɑstow, -ˈpæstow, ˌɑntiyˈpɑ-/ *n., pl.* **-pas•tos, -pas•ti** (-pä′stē, -pas′tē) /-ˈpɑstiy, -ˈpæstiy/. an Italian appetizer, often an assortment of foods, such as olives, anchovies, salami, and peppers: [*noncount*]: *I'll have antipasto before the meal.* [*count*]: *will have an antipasto first.*

an•tip•a•thet•ic (an tip′ə thet′ik) /æn ˌtɪpə ˈθɛtɪk/ *adj.* [*be* + ~ *(+ to/toward)*] unsympathetic; hostile: *feels completely antipathetic toward his noisy neighbors.* See -PATH-.

an•tip•a•thy (an tip′ə thē) /ænˈtɪpəθiy/ *n., pl.* **-thies. 1.** [*noncount*] a deep, habitual dislike; aversion: *antipathy toward inhuman behavior.* **2.** [*count*] an object of antipathy. See -PATH-.

an•ti•per•son•nel (an′tē pûr′sə nel′, an′tī-) /ˌæntiyˌpɜrsəˈnɛl, ˌæntay-/ *adj.* [*before a noun*] designed to destroy or disable enemy troops: *antipersonnel land mines.*

an•ti•per•spi•rant (an′ti pûr′spər ənt) /ˌæntɪˈpɜrspərənt/ *n.* [*count*] **1.** a preparation for reducing perspiration. **—*adj.*** [*before a noun*] **2.** inhibiting perspiration: *antiperspirant sprays.*

an•ti•phon (an′tə fon′) /ˈæntəˌfɒn/ *n.* [*count*] a song to be chanted or sung responsively. **—an•tiph•o•nal** (an tif′ə nl) /ænˈtɪfənl/ *adj.* **—an•tiph′o•nal•ly,** *adv.* **—an•tiph•o•ny** (an tif′ə nē) /ænˈtɪfəniy/ *n.* [*count*], *pl.* **-nies**.

an•tip•o•des (an tip′ə dēz′) /ænˈtɪpəˌdiyz/ *n.* [*plural*] two places directly opposite each other on the globe. **—an•tip•o•dal** (an tip′ə dl) /ænˈtɪpədl/ *adj.*

an•ti•pol•lu•tion (an′tē pə lo͞o′shən, an′tī-) /ˌæntiypəˈluwʃən, ˌæntay-/ *adj.* [*before a noun*] designed to prevent or reduce environmental pollution: *antipollution laws.*

an•ti•quar•i•an (an′ti kwâr′ē ən) /ˌæntɪˈkwɛəriyən/ *adj.* **1.** concerned with or relating to antiquities, esp. books. **—*n.*** [*count*] **2.** an antiquary. **—an′ti•quar′i•an•ism,** *n.* [*noncount*]

an•ti•quar•y (an′ti kwer′ē) /ˈæntɪˌkwɛriy/ *n.* [*count*], *pl.* **-ies.** an expert on, student of, or collector of old or ancient objects.

an•ti•quated (an′ti kwā′tid) /ˈæntɪˌkweytɪd/ *adj.* obsolete or old-fashioned; outmoded: *replaced our antiquated computer system.*

an•tique (an tēk′) /ænˈtiyk/ *adj., n., v.,* **-tiqued, -ti•quing. —*adj.*** [*before a noun*] **1.** of or belonging to the past; not modern: *antique times.* **2.** of or belonging to ancient Rome or Greece. **3.** in the tradition or style of an earlier period: *antique carvings; antique cabinets.* **4.** concerned with selling or buying old objects such as furniture: *an antique dealer; an antique shop.* **—*n.*** [*count*] **5.** something produced in an earlier period, or, according to U.S. customs laws, 100 years before date of purchase: *beautiful and rare antiques.* **—*v.* 6.** [~ + *obj*] to treat so as to give an antique appearance: *to antique the old chest of drawers.* **7.** [*no obj*] to shop for or collect antiques: *went antiquing.*

an•tiq•ui•ty (an tik′wi tē) /ænˈtɪkwɪtiy/ *n., pl.* **-ties. 1.** [*noncount*] the quality of being ancient; ancientness: *a bowl of great antiquity.* **2.** [*noncount*] ancient times; former ages: *in the days of antiquity.* **3.** [*noncount*] the period of history before the Middle Ages. **4.** [*count; usually plural*] things belonging to or remaining from ancient times, as relics or customs.

an•ti-Sem•ite (an′tē sem′īt, an′tī-) /ˌæntiyˈsɛmayt, ˌæntay-/ *n.* [*count*] a person who discriminates against or is prejudiced or hostile toward Jews. **—an•ti-Se•mit•ic** (an′tē sə mit′ik, an′tī-) /ˌæntiysəˈmɪtɪk, ˌæntay-/ *adj.* **—an′ti-Se•mit′i•cal•ly,** *adv.* **—an•ti-Sem•i•tism** (an′tē-sem′i tiz′əm, an′tī-) /ˌæntiyˈsɛmɪˌtɪzəm, ˌæntay-/ *n.* [*noncount*]

an•ti•sep•sis (an′tə sep′sis) /ˌæntəˈsɛpsɪs/ *n.* [*noncount*] destruction of microorganisms that cause disease.

an•ti•sep•tic (an′tə sep′tik) /ˌæntəˈsɛptɪk/ *adj.* **1.** [*before a noun*] causing the destruction of microorganisms that cause disease: *an antiseptic solution.* **2.** free from microorganisms that cause disease: *The surgical instruments are antiseptic.* **3.** lacking in warmth or other humanizing qualities; cold: *an antiseptic waiting room.* **—*n.* 4.** a solution or substance that can destroy germs or harmful microorganisms: [*noncount*]: *The doctor put antiseptic on the wound.* [*count*]: *I bought an antiseptic at the drugstore.* **—an′ti•sep′ti•cal•ly,** *adv.*

an•ti•so•cial (an′tē sō′shəl, an′tī-) /ˌæntiyˈsowʃəl, ˌæntay-/ *adj.* **1.** unwilling or unable to associate in a normal or friendly way with other people: *an antisocial recluse.* **2.** (of behavior) marked by an unwillingness or inability to participate normally in society. **—an′ti•so′cial•ly,** *adv.*

an•tith•e•sis (an tith′ə sis) /ænˈtɪθəsɪs/ *n., pl.* **-ses** (-sēz′) /-ˌsiyz/. **1.** [*noncount*] opposition; contrast: *the antithesis of right and wrong.* **2.** [*count; often: the* + ~ + *of*] the direct opposite: *Her strength was the very antithesis of cowardice.* **—an•ti•thet•i•cal** (an′tə thet′i kəl) /ˌæntəˈθɛtɪkəl/ **an′ti•thet′ic,** *adj.* **—an′ti•thet′i•cal•ly,** *adv.* See -THES-.

an•ti•tox•in (an′ti tok′sin, an′tē-) /ˌæntɪˈtɒksɪn, ˌæntiy-/ *n.* [*count*] a substance that works against a specific toxin. See -TOX-.

an•ti•trust (an′tē trust′, an′tī-) /ˌæntiyˈtrʌst, ˌæntay-/ *adj.* [*before a noun*] opposing or designed to restrain trusts, monopolies, or other large combinations of business and capital: *antitrust laws.*

ant•ler (ant′lər) /ˈæntlər/ *n.* [*count*] one of the branched horns of an animal of the deer family. **—ant′lered,** *adj.*

an•to•nym (an′tə nim) /ˈæntənɪm/ *n.* [*count*] a word opposite in meaning to another: Fast *is an antonym of* slow. Compare SYNONYM (def. 1). **—an•ton•y•mous** (an-ton′ə məs) /ænˈtɒnəməs/ *adj.* See -ONYM-.

ants•y (ant′sē) /ˈæntsiy/ *adj.,* **-i•er, -i•est.** *Informal.* nervous; impatient.

a•nus (ā′nəs) /ˈeynəs/ *n.* [*count*], *pl.* **a•nus•es.** the opening at the lower end of the alimentary canal through which waste passes out of the body.

an•vil (an′vil) /ˈænvɪl/ *n.* [*count*] **1.** a heavy iron block on which heated metals are hammered into desired shapes. **2.** a small, similarly shaped bone that is part of the ear.

anx•i•e•ty (ang zī′i tē) /æŋˈzayɪtiy/ *n., pl.* **-ties. 1. a.** [*noncount*] distress or uneasiness caused by fear of danger or misfortune: *She was full of anxiety over the delay.* **b.** [*count*] an instance or cause of anxiety: *the anxieties of modern life.* **2.** [*noncount*] a sense of overwhelming fear or dread often with acute physical symptoms, as palpitations and sweating.

anx•ious (angk′shəs, ang′-) /ˈæŋkʃəs, ˈæŋ-/ *adj.* **1.** full of mental distress or of fear of danger or misfortune; troubled; worried: *felt anxious about her health.* **2.** [*before a noun*] causing mental distress or fear: *We had a few anxious moments when she leaned from the window.* **3.** [*be* + ~] earnestly desirous; eager: [~ + *for*]: *She's very anxious for promotion.* [~ + *to* + *verb*]: *I was anxious to meet you.* [~ + *for* + *obj* + *to* + *verb*]: *I was anxious for them to meet you.* [~ + *that clause*]: *We are very anxious that you come to see us.* **—anx′ious•ly,** *adv.* **—anx′ious•ness,** *n.* [*noncount*] **—Related Words.** ANXIOUS is an adjective, ANXIOUSLY is an adverb, ANXIETY is a noun: *I was anxious about the results. I anxiously awaited the results. We were filled with anxiety waiting for the results.*

an•y (en′ē) /ˈɛniy/ *adj.* [*before a noun*] **1.** one, a, an, or some; one or more without being specific or without identifying: [*in questions*]: *Do you have any cigarettes?* [*with negative words or phrases*]: *I wasn't in any danger.* [*in sentences with "if"*]: *If you have any witnesses, produce them.* **2.** whatever or whichever it may be; no matter which: *Buy that at any price.* **3.** [*in questions*] in whatever quantity or number, great or small; some: *Do you have any butter? Do you see any holes there?* **4.** every; all: *Any schoolchild would know that.* **5.** [*with negative words*] at all; none (of a particular thing): *She can't endure any criticism.* **—*pron.* 6.** an unspecified person or persons; anybody; anyone: *He did better than any before him.* **7.** a single one or ones; an unspecified thing or things; a quantity or number: [*with negative words*]: *We do not have any left.* [*in questions*]: *Don't you have any?* **—*adv.* 8.** in whatever degree; to some extent; at all: [*in questions*]: *Do you feel any better?* [*with negative words*]: *I can't go on any longer.* **—*Idiom.* 9. any which way,** in any manner whatever; carelessly. **—Usage.** See SOME.

an•y•bod•y (en′ē bod′ē, -bud′ē) /ˈɛniyˌbɒdiy, -ˌbʌdiy/ *pron., n., pl.* **-ies. —*pron.* 1.** somebody; someone: [*with negative words or phrases*]: *There wasn't anybody there* *who could help.* [*in questions*]: *Isn't there anybody who can help me?* **2.** everyone or everybody; no matter who: [*only in affirmative sentences*]: *Anybody there will know where the train station is.* **—*n.*** [*count*] **3.** a person of some importance: *Everybody who is anybody will be there.* **—Usage.** See SOMEBODY.

an•y•how (en′ē hou′) /'ɛniy,haw/ *adv.* **1.** in any way whatever: *We'll catch them anyhow we can.* **2.** in any case; at all events; in spite of that: *I told her not to go, but she did anyhow.* **3.** in a careless manner: *clothes strewn anyhow about the room.*

an•y•more (en′ē môr′, -mōr′) /,ɛniy'mɔr, -'mowr/ *adv.* **1.** any longer: [*with negative words or phrases*]: *couldn't see me anymore.* [*in questions*]: *Do you play tennis anymore?* **2.** *U.S. Dialect.* nowadays; presently: *Yogurt and nuts is all we eat anymore.*

an•y•one (en′ē wun′, -wən) /'ɛniy,wʌn, -wən/ *pron.* any person at all; anybody: [*in questions*]: *Did anyone see the accident?* [*with negative words or phrases*]: *I didn't see anyone there.* **—Usage.** See SOMEONE.

an•y•place (en′ē plās′) /'ɛniy,pleys/ *adv.* ANYWHERE: [*in questions*]: *Would you like to go anyplace tonight?* [*with negative words or phrases*]: *I don't want to go anyplace tonight.*

an•y•thing (en′ē thing′) /'ɛniy,θɪŋ/ *pron.* **1.** any thing whatever; something: [*in questions*]: *Do you have anything for a toothache?* [*with negative words or phrases*]: *I don't have anything for you today.* **2.** no matter what: *She'll do anything to get promoted.* **—*adv.*** **3.** in any way; at all: *Does it taste anything like chocolate?* **—*Idiom.*** **4. anything but,** in no degree or respect; not in the least: *He's anything but handsome.* **5. anything like,** [*with negative words or phrases*] at all like (something); at all: *The test isn't anything like as hard as last week's.* **6. for anything,** [*with negative words or phrases*] (used to give greater force or show greater feeling): *I wouldn't jump off that ledge for anything (= nothing could convice me to do it).* **7. like anything,** (used to give greater force or show greater feeling): *The thief ran away like anything (= ran very fast).* **8. or anything,** (used to refer to other things or possibilities similar to ones just mentioned): *If you want to see me or talk to me or anything, just stop in.* **—Usage.** See SOMETHING.

an•y•time (en′ē tīm′) /'ɛniy,taym/ *adv.* **1.** at any time; whenever: *Come and see me.—When can I come? —Anytime is fine.* **2.** without doubt or exception: *I can do better than that anytime.*

an•y•way (en′ē wā′) /'ɛniy,wey/ *adv.* **1.** in any case; anyhow; regardless; besides: *I don't need help, but thanks anyway.* **2.** (used to continue or resume telling a story, explaining something, finishing a conversation, etc.): *Anyway, after all that we finally found the document.*

an•y•where (en′ē hwâr′, -wâr′) /'ɛniy,hwɛər, -,wɛər/ *adv.* **1.** in, at, or to any place: [*with negative words or phrases*]: *She won't go anywhere without her doll.* [*in questions*]: *Is there a doctor anywhere?* **2.** to any extent or degree: [*with negative words or phrases*]: *I'm not anywhere near finished.* [*in questions*]: *Is the book anywhere near finished?* **3.** (in or at) any place, direction, or point on a scale: *The attack could come from anywhere.* **—*Idiom.*** **4. get** or **go anywhere,** [*no obj*] to make progress to achieve success: *You'll never get anywhere with that attitude.*

an•y•wise (en′ē wīz′) /'ɛniy,wayz/ *adv.* in any way or respect.

A-OK or **A-O•kay** (ā′ō kā′) /'eyow'key/ *adj., adv. Informal.* OK; perfect: [*adverb*]: *Everything's going A-OK.* [*adjective; be + ~*]: *The landing was A-OK.*

A one or **A 1** (ā′ wun′) /'ey' wʌn/ *adj.* [*before a noun*] first-class; excellent: *We ate at an A one restaurant.*

a•or•ta (ā ôr′tə) /ey'ɔrtə/ *n.* [*count*], *pl.* **-tas, -tae** (-tē). the main artery of mammals, carrying blood pumped from the left side of the heart to the rest of the body. **—a•or′tic,** *adj.*

AP, Associated Press.

Ap., an abbreviation of: April.

A/P or **a/p,** an abbreviation of: **1.** account paid. **2.** accounts payable. **3.** authority to pay or purchase.

a•pace (ə pās′) /ə'peys/ *adv.* quickly; rapidly: *Work on the building is proceeding apace.*

a•part (ə pärt′) /ə'pɑrt/ *adv.* **1.** into pieces or parts; to pieces: *to take a watch apart.* **2.** separated or away from in place, time, motion, or point of view: *cities thousands of miles apart.* **3.** to or at one side, with respect to place, purpose, or function: *kept apart from the group.* **4.** separately or individually in consideration: *to think about each factor apart from the others.* **5.** so as to distinguish one from another: *I can't tell the sisters apart.* **6.** [*after a noun*] aside: *Joking apart, what do you think?* **—*adj.*** **7.** [*be + ~ (+ from)*] separated and not living or being together: *hated being apart from each other.* **8.** [*after a noun*] having unique characteristics: *He's in a class apart.* **—*Idiom.*** **9. apart from,** aside from; except for: *had no money, apart from some loose change.* **—a•part′ness,** *n.* [*noncount*] See -PAR-.

a•part•heid (ə pärt′hāt, -hīt) /ə'pɑrtheyt, -hayt/ *n.* [*noncount*] **1.** in the Republic of South Africa, a former policy of keeping people of different races apart by law. **2.** any similar system of segregation. See -PAR-.

a•part•ment (ə pärt′mənt) /ə'pɑrtmənt/ *n.* [*count*] **1.** a room or a group of rooms used as a residence. **2.** an apartment house. SEE ILLUSTRATION.

apart′ment house′ or apart′ment build′ing, *n.* [*count*] a building containing a number of apartments.

ap•a•thet•ic (ap′ə thet′ik) /,æpə 'θɛtɪk/ *adj.* having or showing little emotion or excitement; indifferent: *felt too apathetic to enjoy anything.* See -PATH-.

ap•a•thy (ap′ə thē) /'æpəθiy/ *n.* [*noncount*] lack of interest in or concern for things; indifference. See -PATH-.

ape (āp) /eyp/ *n., v.,* **aped, ap•ing.** **—*n.*** [*count*] **1.** a manlike animal similar to monkeys, with long arms, a broad chest, and no tail. **2.** an imitator; mimic. **3.** a large, clumsy person. **—*v.*** [*~ + obj*] **4.** to imitate; mimic: *tried to ape the mannerisms of the hostess.* **—*Idiom.*** **5. go ape,** *Slang.* to become violently emotional or angry: *My parents will go ape if I stay out that late.* **6. go ape over,** [*~ + obj*] to be extremely enthusiastic about: *goes ape over rock stars.* **—ape′like′,** *adj.*

a•pé•ri•tif (ä per′i tēf′, ə per′-) /ɑ,pɛrɪ'tiyf, ɔ,pɛr-/ *n.* [*count*] an alcoholic drink taken to stimulate the appetite before a meal.

ap•er•ture (ap′ər chər) /'æpərtʃər/ *n.* [*count*] **1.** an opening, such as a hole, slit, or gap. **2.** Also called **ap′erture stop′.** an opening that limits the amount of light that can enter the lens of a camera or telescope.

a•pex (ā′peks) /'eypɛks/ *n.* [*count*], *pl.* **a•pex•es, a•pi•ces** (ā′pə sēz′, ap′ə-) /'eypə,siyz, 'æpə-/. **1.** the highest point; summit: *the apex of a mountain; the apex of a career.* **2.** the tip or point: *the apex of the tongue.*

a•pha•sia (ə fā′zhə) /ə'feyʒə/ *n.* [*noncount*] the loss of the ability to speak or understand a language one knows, due to disease or injury of the brain. **—a•pha•sic** (ə fā′zik) /ə'feyzɪk/ *adj., n.* [*count*]

a•phe•li•on (ə fē′lē ən) /ə'fiyliyən/ *n.* [*count*], *pl.* **a•phe•li•a** (ə fē′lē ə) /ə'fiyliyə/. the point in the orbit of a planet or a comet when it is farthest from the sun. Compare PERIHELION. See -HELIO-.

a•phid (ā′fid, af′id) /'eyfɪd, 'æfɪd/ *n.* [*count*] a tiny insect that sucks the sap from the stems and leaves of various plants.

aph•o•rism (af′ə riz′əm) /'æfə,rɪzəm/ *n.* [*count*] a short, clever saying which carries a general truth.

aph•ro•dis•i•ac (af′rə dē′ze ak′, -diz′ē ak′) /,æfrə'diyzɛ,æk, -'dɪziy,æk/ *adj.* **1.** Also, **aph•ro•di•si•a•cal** (af′rə də zī′ə kəl, -sī′-) /,æfrədə'zayəkəl, -'say-/. arousing or believed to arouse sexual desire. **—*n.*** [*count*] **2.** a food, drug, or other agent that arouses or is believed to arouse sexual desire.

a•pi•ar•y (ā′pē er′ē) /'eypiy,ɛriy/ *n.* [*count*], *pl.* **-ies.** a place where bees are kept to produce honey.

a•pi•cal (ā′pi kəl, ap′i-) /'eypɪkəl, 'æpɪ-/ *adj.* **1.** of, at, or forming the apex. **2.** (of a speech sound) articulated principally with the tip of the tongue: *"t" and "d" in English are apical sounds.* **—a′pi•cal•ly,** *adv.*

a•pi•ces (ā′pə sēz) /'eypə siyz/ *n.* [*plural*] a pl. of APEX.

a•piece (ə pēs′) /ə'piys/ *adv.* [*after a noun*] for each one; each: *The muffins cost a dollar apiece.*

ap•ish (āp′ish) /'eypɪʃ/ *adj.* **1.** resembling an ape. **2.** foolish; silly: *his apish grin.* **—ap′ish•ly,** *adv.*

a•plen•ty (ə plen′tē) /ə'plɛntiy/ *adj.* [*after a noun*] **1.** of sufficient or generous amount: *He had troubles aplenty.* **—*adv.*** **2.** sufficiently; enough: *practiced aplenty for the game.*

a•plomb (ə plom′, ə plum′) /ə'plɒm, ə'plʌm/ *n.* [*noncount*] self-confidence; self-assurance; poise: *He handled the difficult questions with his customary aplomb.*

APO or **A.P.O.,** an abbreviation of: Army Post Office.

a•poc•a•lypse (ə pok′ə lips) /ə'pɒkəlɪps/ *n.* **1.** [*proper noun: the Apocalypse*] a prophecy about a final struggle in which the forces of good triumph over the forces of evil. **2.** [*count*] any great disaster.

a•poc•a•lyp•tic (ə pok′ə lip′tik) /ə ,pɒkə 'lɪptɪk/ *adj.* of, relating to, or predicting future total destruction: *an*

apartment

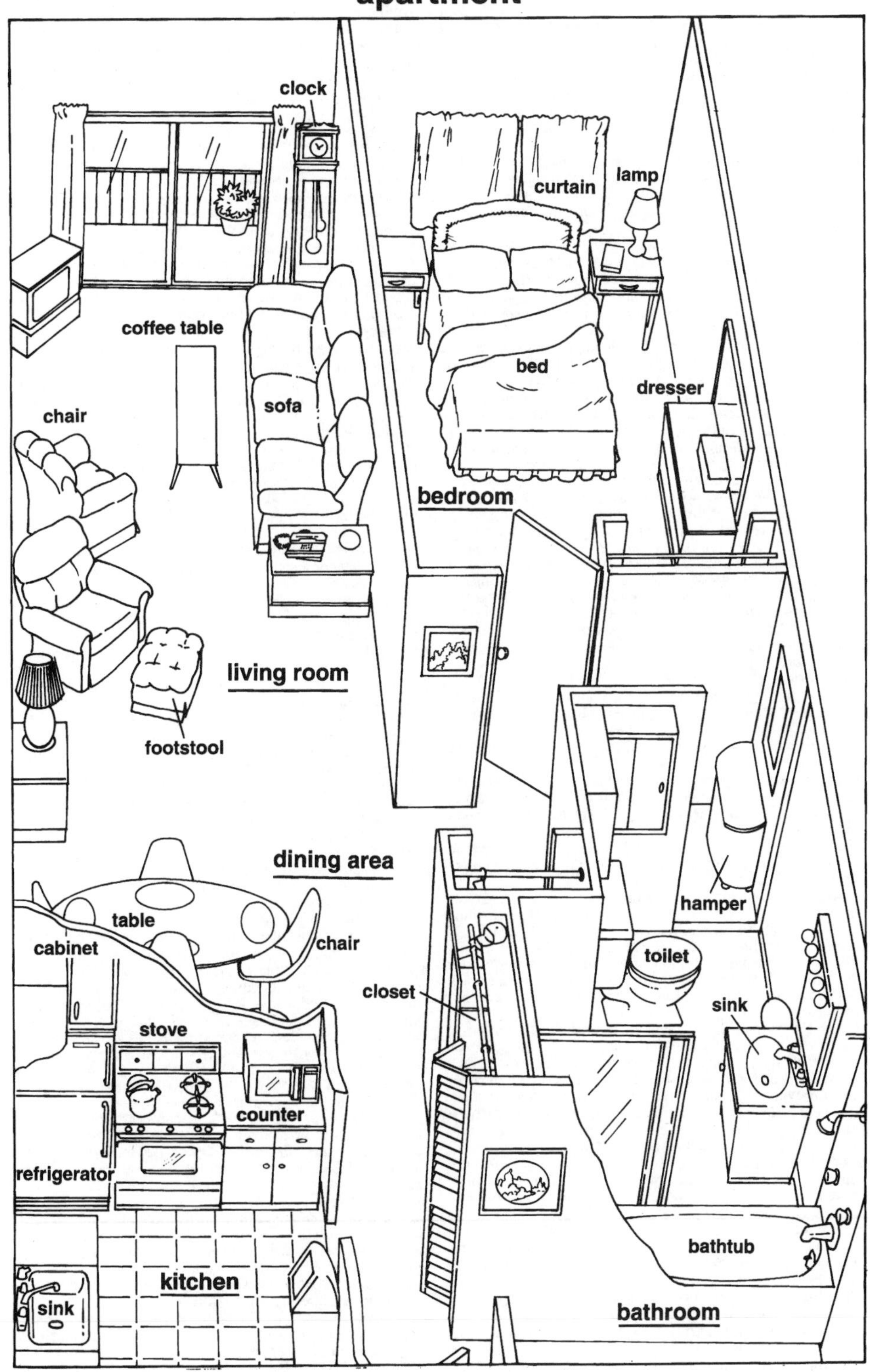
clock
curtain
lamp
coffee table
bed
dresser
sofa
chair
bedroom
living room
footstool
dining area
hamper
table
cabinet
chair
toilet
closet
sink
stove
counter
refrigerator
bathtub
sink
kitchen
bathroom

apocalyptic war; apocalyptic writings. —**a•poc′a•lyp′ti•cal•ly,** *adv.*

a•poc•ry•pha (ə pok′rə fə) /ə'pɒkrəfə/ *n.* **1.** [*usually: the Apocrypha; proper noun; used with a singular verb*] a group of books not found in the Jewish Bible or Protestant Old Testament but that are included in the Septuagint and Vulgate. **2.** [*plural; used with a plural verb*] writings or statements of uncertain origin.

a•poc•ry•phal (ə pok′rə fəl) /ə'pɒkrəfəl/ *adj.* **1.** (*cap.*) of or relating to the Apocrypha. **2.** of doubtful authenticity: *an apocryphal account of his relationship with the president.* —**a•poc′ry•phal•ly,** *adv.*

ap•o•gee (ap′ə jē′) /'æpə,dʒiy/ *n.* [*count*] **1.** the point in the orbit of the moon or of an artificial satellite at which it is farthest from the earth. Compare PERIGEE. **2.** the most exalted point: *the apogee of artistic development.* See -GEO-.

a•po•lit•i•cal (ā′pə lit′i kəl) /,eypə'lɪtɪkəl/ *adj.* not involved or interested in politics. —**a′po•lit′i•cal•ly,** *adv.*

a•pol•o•get•ic (ə pol′ə jet′ik) /ə,pɒlə'dʒɛtɪk/ *adj.* **1.** containing an apology: *an apologetic letter.* **2.** presented in defense: *apologetic arguments.* —**a•pol′o•get′i•cal•ly,** *adv.*

ap•o•lo•gi•a (ap′ə lō′jē ə) /,æpə'lowdʒiyə/ *n.* [*count*], *pl.* **-as.** a defense of strongly held beliefs, attitudes, or actions: *The speech was an apologia for slavery.*

a•pol•o•gist (ə pol′ə jist) /ə'pɒlədʒɪst/ *n.* [*count*] a person who defends an idea, faith, cause, or institution.

a•pol•o•gize (ə pol′ə jīz′) /ə'pɒlə,dʒayz/ *v.*, **-gized, -giz•ing.** to make an apology: [*no obj*]: *He apologized when he spilled coffee.* [~ + *to* + *obj*]: *I apologized to her.* [~ + *for* + *obj*]: *I apologized for my rudeness.*

a•pol•o•gy (ə pol′ə jē) /ə'pɒlədʒiy/ *n.*, *pl.* **-gies. 1.** an expression of regret for having committed an error or for being rude: [*count*]: *I sent an apology to her right away.* [*noncount*]: *a gesture of apology.* **2.** [*count*] a defense or justification of a cause or doctrine: *His treatise was supposed to be an apology for war.* **3.** [*count*] an inferior substitute; excuse: *was a poor apology for a parent.* —**Related Words.** APOLOGY is a noun, APOLOGIZE is a verb, APOLOGETIC is an adjective: *You owe her an apology. You should apologize to her. He was very apologetic about spilling the ink.* See -LOG-.

ap•o•plec•tic (ap ə plek′tik) /æp ə 'plɛktɪk/ *adj.* **1.** of, relating to, or showing symptoms of stroke: *an apoplectic condition.* **2.** so intensely angry as to appear to suffer from apoplexy: *apoplectic with rage.*

ap•o•plex•y (ap′ə plek′sē) /'æpə,plɛksiy/ *n.* STROKE[1] (def. 5).

a•pos•ta•sy (ə pos′tə sē) /ə'pɒstəsiy/ *n.* [*noncount; count*], *pl.* **-sies.** abandonment of one's religious faith or of something that one was once loyal to, as a political party.

a•pos•tate (ə pos′tāt, -tit) /ə'pɒsteyt, -tɪt/ *n.* [*count*] **1.** a person who commits apostasy. —*adj.* **2.** of or characterized by apostasy.

a pos•te•ri•o•ri (ā′ po stēr′ē ôr′ī, -ōr′ī, -ôr′ē, -ōr′ē) /,ey pɒ,stɪəriy'ɔray, -'owray, -'ɔriy, -'owriy/ *adj.* **1.** reasoning from particular examples to a general principle or law: *An example of a posteriori reasoning is: "The car is running, there must be gas in it."* **2.** not existing in the mind prior to or apart from experience; only testable by experience: *The statement "pigs can't fly" must be checked a posteriori.*

a•pos•tle (ə pos′əl) /ə'pɒsəl/ *n.* [*count*] **1.** [*sometimes: Apostle*] any of the original 12 disciples called by Jesus to preach the gospel. **2.** any of the first or best-known Christian missionaries in a region. **3.** a pioneer of a reform movement; proponent: *an apostle of social change.*

ap•os•tol•ic (ap′ə stol′ik) /,æpə'stɒlɪk/ also **ap′os•tol′i•cal,** *adj.* **1.** of or characteristic of an apostle. **2.** of or relating to the pope; papal: *an apostolic delegate.*

a•pos•tro•phe[1] (ə pos′trə fē) /ə'pɒstrəfiy/ *n.* [*count*] the sign ('), used to indicate the omission of one or more letters in a word, as in *we'll* for *we will,* or *gov't* for *government.*

a•pos•tro•phe[2] (ə pos′trə fē) /ə'pɒstrəfiy/ *n.* [*count*] a turning away while speaking in order to talk to someone not present, or to an object or idea that represents a person. See -STROPH-.

a•poth•e•car•y (ə poth′ə ker′ē) /ə'pɒθə,kɛriy/ *n.* [*count*], *pl.* **-ies. 1.** a pharmacist. **2.** a pharmacy.

ap•o•thegm (ap′ə them′) /'æpə,θɛm/ *n.* [*count*] a short saying; aphorism.

a•poth•e•o•sis (ə poth′ē ō′sis, ap′ə thē′ə sis) /ə,pɒθiy'owsɪs, ,æpə'θiyəsɪs/ *n.* [*count*], *pl.* **-ses** (-sēz, -sēz′) /-siyz, -,siyz/. **1.** the elevation of a person to the rank of a god. **2.** [~ + *of*] the ideal or best example (of something); epitome.

ap•pall or **ap•pal** (ə pôl′) /ə'pɔl/ *v.* [~ + *obj*], **-palled, -pall•ing.** to fill or overcome with horror, shock, or fear; dismay greatly: *The terrible fire appalled the neighbors.*

ap•palled (ə pôld′) /ə'pɔld/ *adj.* **1.** shocked; horrified; feeling disgust or dismay: *were appalled when they heard the awful news.* [*be* +~+ *at/with/by*]: *She was appalled at the low grade she got.* [*be* +~+ *to* + *verb*]: *was appalled to see his enemy again.* **2.** [*before a noun*] showing shock or horror: *appalled expressions on their faces.*

ap•pall•ing (ə pôl′ing) /ə 'pɔlɪŋ/ *adj.* **1.** shocking; horrifying: *an appalling accident.* **2.** awful; terrible: *The food was appalling.* —**ap•pall′ing•ly,** *adv.*

ap•pa•rat•us (ap′ə rat′əs, -rā′təs) /,æpə'rætəs, -'reytəs/ *n.*, *pl.* **-tus, -tus•es. 1.** [*noncount*] a group of instruments, machinery, or materials having a particular function: *firefighting apparatus.* **2.** [*count*] any complex instrument or mechanism for a particular purpose: *made an apparatus from wires and tubes to signal the ship.* **3.** [*count*] the means by which a system functions: *the apparatus of government.* See -PARE-[1].

ap•par•el (ə par′əl) /ə'pærəl/ *n.* [*noncount*] clothing, esp. outerwear; garments; attire: *winter apparel.*

ap•par•ent (ə par′ənt, ə pâr′-) /ə'pærənt, ə'pɛər-/ *adj.* **1.** [*be* + ~] open to view: *The crack in the wall was apparent.* [~ + *to*]: *It was apparent to everyone.* **2.** [*be* + ~] capable of being easily understood; obvious: *The solution was apparent.* [~ + *to*]: *It was apparent to us all.* [*It* + *be* + ~ (+ *to* + *obj*) + (*that*) *clause*]: *It was apparent (to everyone) that they had cheated on the test.* **3.** [*before a noun*] according to appearances but not necessarily: *He was the apparent winner.* **4.** [*after a noun*] entitled by birth to inherit a title or estate: *the heir apparent.*

ap•par•ent•ly (ə par′ənt lē) /ə 'pærənt liy/ *adv.* it seems; it appears (that); seemingly: *Apparently, you won the prize.*

ap•pa•ri•tion (ap′ə rish′ən) /,æpə'rɪʃən/ *n.* [*count*] a ghostly appearance: *thought she saw the apparition of her late husband.*

ap•peal (ə pēl′) /ə'piyl/ *n.* **1.** [*count*] an earnest plea; request (for help); entreaty; plea: *an appeal for help.* **2.** [*count*] a request to higher authority for a decision: *He filed an appeal for a hearing.* **3.** an application or request for review by a higher court: [*count*]: *The lawyer filed an appeal for a retrial.* [*noncount*]: *found guilty on appeal.* **4.** [*noncount*] the power or ability to attract or stimulate the mind or emotions: *The game has lost its appeal.* —*v.* **5.** [*no obj*] to make an earnest plea: *appealed to the public for help.* **6.** to apply for review of a case or particular issue to a higher tribunal: [*no obj*]: *The lawyer will appeal to the Supreme Court.* [~ + *obj*]: *The lawyer appealed the case.* **7.** [~ + *to* + *obj*] to call upon for proof or corroboration or support: *He appealed to statistics to reinforce his case.* **8.** [~ + *to*] to exert an attraction: *The red hat appeals to me.*

ap•peal•ing (ə pē′ling) /ə 'piylɪŋ/ *adj.* **1.** having great appeal; attractive; pleasing: *an appealing smile.* **2.** begging; pleading: *gave an appealing glance for mercy.*

ap•pear (ə pēr′) /ə'pɪər/ *v.* [*no obj*] **1.** [*not: be* + ~*-ing*] to come into sight; become visible: *A man suddenly appeared in the doorway.* **2.** [*not: be* + ~*-ing*] to have the appearance of being; seem: [~ + *adjective*]: *to appear wise.* [~ + *to* + *verb*]: *She appears to be sleeping.* **3.** [*not: be* + ~*-ing*] to be obvious or easily known and understood: [*It* + ~ + (*that*) *clause*]: *It appears that you are right.* **4.** to perform: *She appeared in several movies.* **5.** to put in an appearance; show up; arrive: *She appeared briefly at the party.* **6.** to come before a tribunal, esp. as a party or counsel to a proceeding: *You'll appear before the court tomorrow.* **7.** [*not: be* + ~*-ing*] to come to be available for use; come out: *Your new book will appear next year.*

ap•pear•ance (ə pēr′əns) /ə'pɪərəns/ *n.* **1.** [*count*] the act or process of appearing. **2.** [*noncount*] outward look; looks: *a person of noble appearance.* **3.** [*count*] **appearances,** [*plural*] outward show, impressions, indications, or circumstances: *By all appearances, they enjoyed themselves.* —***Idiom.*** **4. put in an appearance,** to attend a gathering for a short time.

ap•pease (ə pēz′) /ə'piyz/ *v.* [~ + *obj*], **-peased, -peas•ing. 1.** to bring to a state of calm; pacify: *to appease an angry parent with apologies.* **2.** to satisfy; relieve: *The fruit appeased his hunger.* **3.** to give in to someone's demands so as to lessen anger or prevent fighting; placate. —**ap•peas′er,** *n.* [*count*]

ap•pease•ment (ə pēz mənt) /ə piyz mənt/ *n.* [*noncount*] the practice of giving in to demands so as to lessen anger or prevent fighting: *hoped that a policy of appeasement might keep the invaders away.*

ap•pel•late (ə pel′it) /ə'pɛlɪt/ *adj.* [*before a noun*] **1.** of or relating to appeals in court. **2.** (of a court) having the authority to review and decide appeals from a lower court.

ap•pel•la•tion (ap′ə lā′shən) /ˌæpə'leyʃən/ *n.* [*count*] an identifying name, title, or designation.

ap•pend (ə pend′) /ə'pɛnd/ *v.* [~ + *obj* (+ *to* + *obj*)] **1.** to add as a piece at the end of a writing: *to append a note to a letter.* **2.** to put on; to affix: *to append one's signature to a will.* See -PEND-.

ap•pend•age (ə pen′dij) /ə'pɛndɪdʒ/ *n.* [*count*] **1.** a smaller or less important part that joins a central structure. **2.** a person in a subordinate or dependent position. See -PEND-.

ap•pen•dec•to•my (ap′ən dek′tə mē) /ˌæpən'dɛktəmiy/ *n.* [*count*], *pl.* **-mies.** surgical removal of the human appendix. See -TOM-.

ap•pen•di•ci•tis (ə pen′də si′tis) /əˌpɛndə'saytɪs/ *n.* [*noncount*] infection and inflammation of the human appendix.

ap•pen•dix (ə pen′diks) /ə'pɛndɪks/ *n.* [*count*], *pl.* **-dix•es, -di•ces** (-də sēz′) /-dəˌsiyz/. **1.** additional or extra material at the end of a text: *An appendix to the grammar table lists all the place names that take "the" in English, like "United States".* **2.** any additional or extra part; appendage. **3.** an outgrowth on the large intestine, shaped like a worm. See -PEND-.

ap•per•tain (ap′ər tān′) /ˌæpər'teyn/ *v.* [~ + *to*] to belong to (someone) as a right; relate to: *privileges that appertain to royalty.*

ap•pe•tite (ap′i tīt′) /'æpɪˌtayt/ *n.* [*noncount*] **1.** a desire for food or drink: *Loss of appetite may signal illness.* **2.** [*count*] a strong desire or taste for something; passion: *an appetite for luxury.* See -PET-.

ap•pe•tiz•er (ap′i ti′zər) /'æpɪˌtayzər/ *n.* [*count*] a small portion of a food or drink served before or at the beginning of a meal to stimulate the appetite.

ap•pe•tiz•ing (ap′i ti′zing) /'æpɪˌtayzɪŋ/ *adj.* **1.** appealing to or stimulating the appetite: *the appetizing smells from the kitchen.* **2.** appealing; tempting: *Working overtime didn't sound appetizing to him.* —**ap′pe•tiz′ing•ly,** *adv.*

ap•plaud (ə plôd′) /ə'plɔd/ *v.* **1.** to clap the hands together in approval or appreciation (of): [*no obj*]: *The audience applauded wildly.* [~ + *obj*]: *They applauded her performance.* **2.** [~ + *obj*] to express approval of; praise: *We applauded their decision.* See -PLAUD-.

ap•plause (ə plôz′) /ə'plɔz/ *n.* [*noncount*] hand clapping as a demonstration of approval or appreciation.

ap•ple (ap′əl) /'æpəl/ *n.* [*count*] **1.** the usually round red, green, or yellow fruit of a small tree of the rose family. **2.** the tree itself. —***Idiom.*** **3. apple of one's eye,** one greatly loved or valued: *That child is the apple of her father's eye.*

ap•ple•jack (ap′əl jak′) /'æpəlˌdʒæk/ *n.* [*noncount*] a brandy made from cider.

ap′ple pie′, *n.* [*count*] **1.** a pie made of cooked apples. —***Idiom.*** **2. as American as apple pie,** fully American; American in every respect: *A picnic on the 4th of July is as American as apple pie.* **3. in apple-pie order,** in excellent condition: *The classroom is in apple-pie order.*

ap•ple•sauce (ap′əl sôs′) /'æpəlˌsɔs/ *n.* [*noncount*] a food made of apples stewed and ground to a soft mass and sometimes spiced with cinnamon.

ap•pli•ance (ə pli′əns) /ə'playəns/ *n.* [*count*] **1.** a device or machine used esp. in the home to carry out a specific function, as toasting bread or chilling food. SEE ILLUSTRATION. **2.** any instrument, apparatus, or device for a particular use: *The dentist calls the braces on her teeth appliances.*

ap•pli•ca•ble (ap′li kə bəl, ə plik′ə-) /'æplɪkəbəl, ə'plɪkə-/ *adj.* capable of being applied; relevant; suitable; appropriate: *a solution applicable to the problem; a rule applicable to everyone.* —**ap•pli•ca•bil•i•ty** (ap′li kə bil′i-tē, ə plik′ə-) /ˌæplɪkə'bɪlɪtiy, əˌplɪkə-/ *n.* [*noncount*]

ap•pli•cant (ap′li kənt) /'æplɪkənt/ *n.* [*count*] a person who applies for or requests something; a candidate: *an applicant for a job.*

ap•pli•ca•tion (ap′li kā′shən) /ˌæplɪ'keyʃən/ *n.* **1.** [*noncount*] the act of putting to a special use or purpose: *the application of common sense.* **2.** [*count*] the use to which something is put: *new applications of the technology.* **3.** [*noncount*] appropriateness; relevance: *I don't think your complaint has any application to this case.* **4.** [*noncount*] petition; request: *application for admission to college.* **5.** [*count*] a form to be filled out by an applicant: *Fill out and sign the application.* **6.** [*noncount*] hard work, attention, and concentration: *demonstrated great application to her studies.* **7.** [*count*] an act or instance of spreading or administering: *an application of varnish.* **8.** [*count*] a salve, ointment, or the like, spread on or applied as a soothing or healing agent: *an application for burned skin.* **9.** [*count*] a special use to which a computer is put: *spreadsheets and other applications.* See -PLIC-.

ap•pli•ca•tor (ap′li kā′tər) /'æplɪˌkeytər/ *n.* [*count*] a simple device for applying medication, cosmetics, or other substances.

ap•plied (ə plīd′) /ə'playd/ *adj.* [*before a noun*] having a practical purpose or use: *applied engineering.* Compare THEORETICAL.

ap•pli•qué (ap′li kā′) /ˌæplɪ'key/ *n., v.,* **-quéd, -qué•ing.** —*n.* [*count*] **1.** a cutout design applied to a piece of material: *an appliqué was ironed on to the t-shirt.* —*v.* [~ + *obj*] **2.** to apply (a cutout) as an appliqué to.

ap•ply (ə plī′) /ə'play/ *v.,* **-plied, -ply•ing. 1.** [~ + *obj* + *to* + *obj*] to make use of as relevant or suitable: *applied the theory to the problem.* **2.** [*no obj*] to be relevant; to pertain; to be suitable: *The theory doesn't apply in this case.* **3.** [~ + *obj*] to put to use; employ; put into effect: *to apply the brakes.* **4.** [~ + *obj* + *to* + *obj*] to designate as appropriate: *Don't apply any such term to me.* **5.** [~ + *obj* + *to* + *obj*] to assign to a specific purpose: *He applied part of his salary to savings.* **6.** [~ + *oneself* + *to* + *obj*] to devote (oneself) to: *I tried to apply myself to the job.* **7.** to lay or spread on: [~ + *obj* + *to* + *obj*]: *She applied the paint to the wall.* [*no obj*]: *This paint applied easily.* **8.** [~ + *obj* + *to* + *obj*] to bring into contact: *to apply a match to gunpowder.* **9.** to make an application or request: [~ + *to* + *obj*]: *She applied to several colleges.* [~ + *for* + *obj*]: *He applied for the job.* —**ap•pli′er,** *n.* [*count*]

ap•point (ə point′) /ə'pɔynt/ *v.* [~ + *obj*] **1.** to name or assign officially: [~ + *obj* + *obj*]: *appointed him chairman.* [~ + *obj* + *to* + *obj*]: *They appointed him to the position of chairman.* **2.** to fix; set: *to appoint a time for the meeting.* **3.** to equip; furnish: *They appointed the house luxuriously.* See -POINT-.

ap•point•ed (ə poin′tid) /ə 'pɔyntɪd/ *adj.* **1.** [*before a noun*] fixed; set; decided on: *arrived at the appointed hour.* **2.** equipped; furnished: *luxuriously appointed rooms.*

ap•point•ee (ə poin tē′, ap′oin tē′) /əpɔyn'tiy, ˌæpɔyn'tiy/ *n.* [*count*] a person who is appointed to an office, position, etc.

ap•poin•tive (ə poin′tiv) /ə'pɔyntɪv/ *adj.* [*often: before a noun*] (of a job or position) filled or staffed by appointment: *an appointive position.*

ap•point•ment (ə point′mənt) /ə'pɔyntmənt/ *n.* **1.** an agreement for a meeting arranged in advance: [*count*]: *We made an appointment to meet again.* [*noncount*]: *You can visit the museum by appointment.* **2.** [*noncount*] the act of appointing or choosing, as to an office or position: *the appointment of the chairman.* **3.** [*count*] an office to which a person is appointed: *an appointment as ambassador.* **4.** [*count*] Usually, **appointments.** [*plural*] equipment, furnishings, or furniture: *the handsome appointments of the castle.*

ap•por•tion (ə pôr′shən, ə pōr′-) /ə'pɔrʃən, ə'powr-/ *v.* [~ + *obj* (+*among/between* + *obj*)] to divide (parts or shares) and distribute by some rule: *to apportion expenses among the three men.* —**ap•por′tion•ment,** *n.* [*noncount*]

ap•po•site (ap′ə zit) /'æpəzɪt/ *adj.* [~ + (*to/for* + *obj*)] suitable; appropriate: *A smile is an apposite response to a friendly greeting.*

ap•po•si•tion (ap′ə zish′ən) /ˌæpə'zɪʃən/ *n.* [*noncount*] **in apposition,** (of two consecutive nouns in a sentence) referring to the same person or thing. In the sentence "Washington, our first president, was born in Virginia", the nouns *Washington* and *our first president* are in apposition. —**ap•pos•i•tive** (ə poz′i tiv) /ə'pɒzɪtɪv/ *adj.*

ap•prais•al (ə prā′zəl) /ə 'preyzəl/ *n.* an act of estimating or determining the worth of something: [*count*]: *We gave him an appraisal of the jewelry.* [*noncount*]: *received a look of careful appraisal.*

ap•praise (ə prāz′) /ə'preyz/ *v.* [~ + *obj*], **-praised, -prais•ing.** to determine or estimate the worth (of something), esp. its monetary value: *The art collector appraised the painting.* —**ap•prais′er,** *n.* [*count*]

appliances and devices

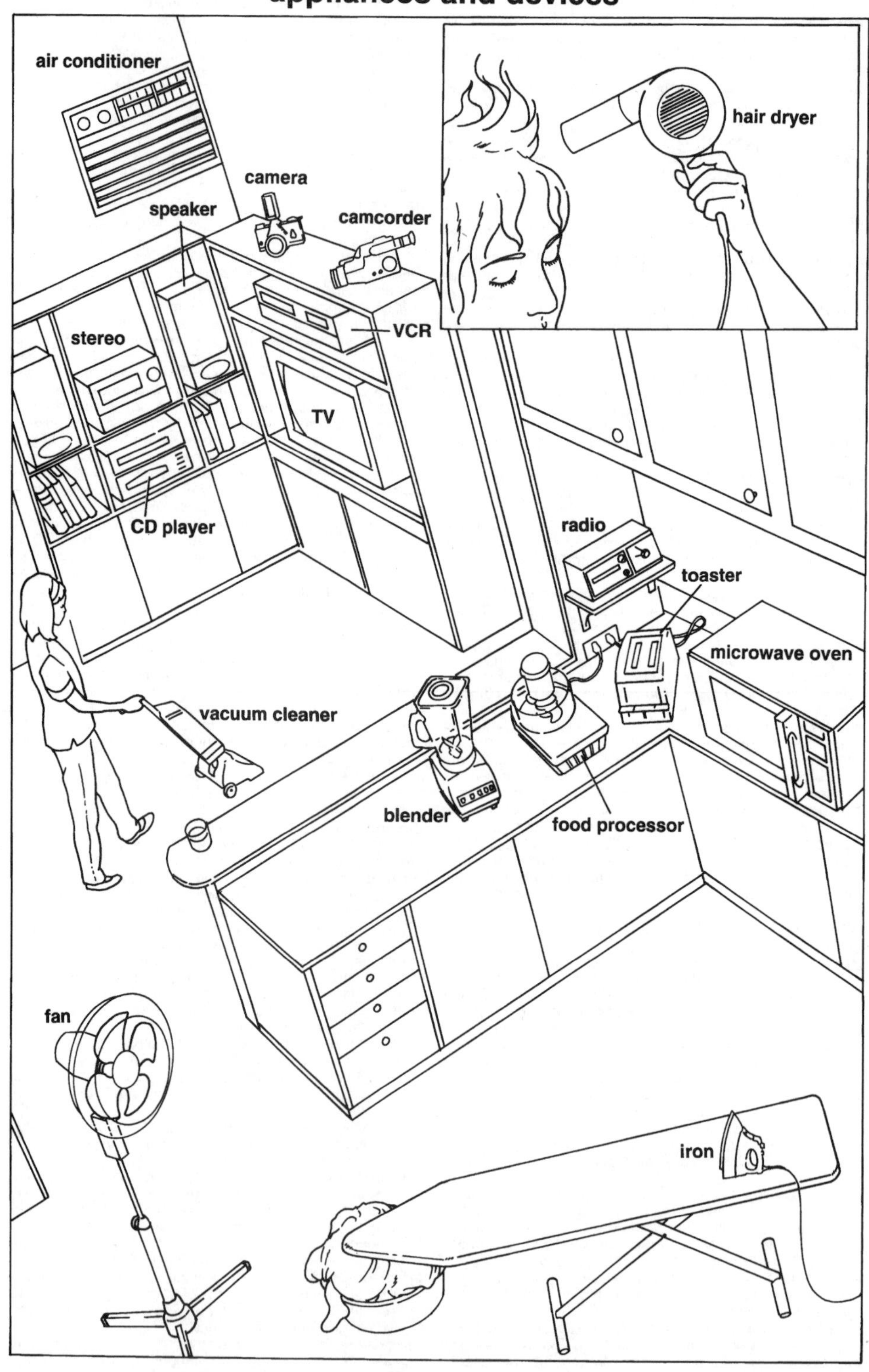

ap•pre•ci•a•ble (ə prē′shē ə bəl, -shə bəl) /ə'priyʃiyəbəl, -ʃəbəl/ *adj.* enough to be noticed; considerable: *an appreciable sum of money.* —**ap•pre•ci•a•bly** (ə prē′shē ə blē, -shə blē) /ə'priyʃiyəbliy, -ʃəbliy/ *adv.*

ap•pre•ci•ate (ə prē′shē āt′) /ə'priyʃiy,eyt/ *v.*, **-at•ed, -at•ing. 1.** [~ + *obj*] to be grateful or thankful for: *I appreciate your help.* **2.** [~ + *obj*] to value or regard highly: *They appreciate good food.* **3.** to be fully conscious of; be aware of; understand fully: [~ + *obj*]: *She appreciates the dangers of the situation.* [~ + *that clause*]: *I certainly can appreciate that the situation is difficult.* **4.** [*no obj*] to increase in value: *The property appreciated rapidly.* See -PRECI-.

ap•pre•ci•a•tion (ə prē′shē ā′shən) /ə,priyʃiy'eyʃən/ *n.* **1.** [*noncount*] gratitude; thankful recognition: *showed appreciation by applauding.* **2.** clear perception and understanding of something: [*noncount*]: *a course in art appreciation.* [*count; usually singular*]: *hasn't a clear appreciation of the difficulties.* **3.** [*noncount*] an increase or rise in the value of something: *Property appreciation led to higher taxes.*

ap•pre•cia•tive (ə prē′shə tiv, -shē ə-) /ə'priyʃətɪv, -ʃiyə-/ *adj.* feeling or showing appreciation: *the loud applause of an appreciative audience.* —**ap•pre′cia•tive•ly,** *adv.*

ap•pre•hend (ap′ri hend′) /,æprɪ'hɛnd/ *v.* [~ + *obj*] **1.** to take into custody; arrest: *The police apprehended the burglars.* **2.** to grasp the meaning of; perceive: *could apprehend the difference between the two words.* See -PREHEND-.

ap•pre•hen•sion (ap′ri hen′shən) /,æprɪ'hɛnʃən/ *n.* **1.** suspicion or fear of future trouble; foreboding: [*count*]: *had apprehensions about the upcoming meeting.* [*noncount*]: *I was filled with apprehension.* **2.** [*noncount*] ability to understand: *her apprehension of the dangerous situation.* **3.** [*noncount*] the act of arresting; seizure: *prompt apprehension of criminals.* See -PREHEND-.

ap•pre•hen•sive (ap′ri hen′siv) /,æprɪ'hɛnsɪv/ *adj.* uneasy or fearful about the future: *We were all apprehensive as we waited for the lab test results.* —**ap′pre•hen′sive•ly,** *adv.* —**ap′pre•hen′sive•ness,** *n.* [*noncount*] See -PREHEND-.

ap•pren•tice (ə pren′tis) /ə'prɛntɪs/ *n.*, *v.*, **-ticed, -tic•ing.** —*n.* [*count*] **1.** a person who works for another in order to learn a trade: *an apprentice to a plumber.* **2.** a learner; novice. —*v.* **3.** [~ + *obj*] to send (someone) to work for another to learn a trade: *We apprenticed him to a plumber.* **4.** [*no obj*] to serve as an apprentice: *He apprenticed for six years.* —**ap•pren′tice•ship′,** *n.* [*count*]: *an apprenticeship as an electrician.* [*noncount*]: *Apprenticeship lasts two years.*

ap•prise (ə prīz′) /ə'prayz/ *v.* [~ + *obj* + *of* + *obj*], **-prised, -pris•ing.** to give notice to; inform: *I apprised her of his intentions.* See -PRIS-.

ap•proach (ə prōch′) /ə'prowtʃ/ *v.* **1.** to come nearer (to): [~ + *obj*]: *The plane approached the runway.* [*no obj*]: *We watched as the plane approached.* **2.** [~ + *obj*] to come within range for comparison: *As a poet he can't approach Keats.* **3.** [~ + *obj*] to make contact with, usually in order to start negotiations with: *We approached the company with an offer.* **4.** [~ + *obj*] to begin work on; set about: *to approach the problem from a new angle.* —*n.* [*count*] **5.** an act or instance of approaching: *the approach of a train; the approach of winter.* **6.** a means of access or of coming to: *the major approaches to the city.* **7.** the method used or steps taken in setting about a task: *the problem needs a different approach.*

ap•proach•a•ble (ə prō′chə bəl) /ə 'prowtʃəbəl/ *adj.* **1.** [*be* + ~] that is accessible; that someone can easily arrive at: *The entrance is approachable from the park's south side.* **2.** friendly and easy to talk to: *His boss and his colleagues were very approachable.*

ap•pro•ba•tion (ap′rə bā′shən) /,æprə'beyʃən/ *n.* [*noncount*] approval; praise; commendation: *The film received the approbation of the critics.* See -PROB-.

ap•pro•pri•ate (*adjective:* ə prō′prē it; *verb:* -āt′) /*adjective:* ə'prowpriyɪt; *verb:* -,eyt/ *adj.*, *v.*, **-at•ed, -at•ing.** —*adj.* **1.** particularly suitable; fitting; correct: *appropriate behavior.* [*be* + ~ + *to*]: *remarks appropriate to the occasion.* —*v.* [~ + *obj*] **2.** to set apart for a specific purpose: *appropriated funds for an environmental study.* **3.** to take for oneself; steal: *They appropriated my ideas as their own.* —**ap•pro′pri•ate•ly,** *adv.* —**ap•pro′pri•ate•ness,** *n.* [*noncount*] See -PROPR-.

ap•pro•pri•a•tion (ə prō′prē ā′shən) /ə,prowpriy'eyʃən/ *n.* **1.** [*noncount*] the act of setting apart funds for a specific purpose. **2.** [*count*] the funds set apart. See -PROPR-.

ap•prov•al (ə pro͞o′vəl) /ə'pruwvəl/ *n.* **1.** [*noncount*] the act of approving or acceptance; approbation: *Her nomination was met with full approval.* **2.** permission; acceptance: [*noncount*]: *The new drug has government approval.* [*count*]: *an approval for a mortgage.* **3.** [*noncount*] a feeling of liking, admiring, or favoring: *The teacher smiled at the student with approval.* —***Idiom.*** **4. on approval,** that may be tried or tested and returned if found not to be satisfactory: *We bought the VCR on approval.* See -PROB-, -PROV-.

ap•prove (ə pro͞ov′) /ə'pruwv/ *v.*, **-proved, -prov•ing. 1.** to have a favorable view of: [~ + *obj*]: *I can't approve rude behavior.* [*no obj;* (~ + *of* + *obj*)]: *My parents didn't approve of my friends.* **2.** [~ + *obj*] to find to be acceptable: *Do you approve the plan?* **3.** [~ + *obj*] to confirm formally; ratify; pass: *The Senate voted to approve the bill.* See -PROB-, -PROV-.

ap•proved (ə pro͞ovd′) /ə 'pruwvd/ *adj.* generally accepted as correct or appropriate: *a list of approved books.*

ap•prov•ing (ə pro͞o′ving) /ə 'pruwvɪŋ/ *adj.* showing support, agreement, or appreciation of: *an approving smile.* —**ap•prov′ing•ly,** *adv.*

approx., an abbreviation of: **1.** approximate. **2.** approximately.

ap•prox•i•mate (*adjective:* ə prok′sə mit; *verb:* -māt′) /*adjective:* ə'prɒksəmɪt; *verb:* -,meyt/ *adj.*, *v.*, **-mat•ed, -mat•ing.** —*adj.* **1.** nearly exact; not perfectly accurate: *The approximate time was 10 o'clock.* —*v.* **2.** to approach closely to; to come close (to): [~ + *obj*]: *He approximated the ideal of a perfect leader.* [~ + *to* + *obj*]: *His notions didn't approximate to reality.* **3.** [~ + *obj* (+ *at* + *obj*)] to estimate: *She approximated the distance at a mile.* —**ap•prox′i•mate•ly,** *adv.* See -PROX-.

ap•prox•i•ma•tion (ə prok′sə mā′shən) /ə ,prɒksə 'meyʃən/ *n.* [*count*] **1.** an amount or estimate that is almost correct but not exact: *These numbers are just approximations.* **2.** the quality or state of being near or close: *only an approximation of rational behavior.* See -PROX-.

ap•pur•te•nance (ə pûr′tn əns) /ə'pɜrtn̩əns/ *n.* [*count*] **1.** something subordinate to another; adjunct. **2. appurtenances,** [*plural*] accessories: *has such appurtenances as a jacuzzi and air conditioning.*

Apr or **Apr.,** an abbreviation of: April.

ap•ri•cot (ap′ri kot′, ā′pri-) /'æprɪ,kɒt, 'eyprɪ-/ *n.* [*count*] **1.** the yellowish orange, peachlike fruit of a tree of the rose family. **2.** the tree itself.

A•pril (ā′prəl) /'eyprəl/ *n.* [*proper noun*] the fourth month of the year, containing 30 days. *Abbr.:* Apr.

a pri•o•ri (ā′ prī ôr′ī, -ōr′ī) /,ey pray'ɔray, -'owray/ *adj.* **1.** from a general law to a particular instance; reasoning from cause to effect: *a priori thinking.* **2.** existing in the mind independent of experience; valid independently of observation: *an a priori belief.* Compare A POSTERIORI.

a•pron (ā′prən) /'eyprən/ *n.* [*count*] **1.** a garment covering part of the front of the body worn to protect the clothing. **2.** a paved area near an airfield's buildings and hangars where planes are parked. **3.** the part of a stage floor in front of the curtain. —***Idiom.*** **4. tied to one's mother's apron strings,** (chiefly of a male person) controlled, influenced, or dominated too much by one's mother.

ap•ro•pos (ap′rə pō′) /,æprə'pow/ *adj.* **1.** being appropriate and timely; well-suited: *found his remarks on war to be very apropos.* —*adv.* **2.** by the way; incidentally: *Apropos, what is happening with your plans?* —***Idiom.*** **3. apropos of,** with reference to; concerning: *Apropos of the preceding statement, can you tell us anything further?* See -PROPR-.

apse (aps) /æps/ *n.* [*count*] a recess in a building, shaped in a half circle or with many sides, usually at the end of a church, with a domed roof.

apt (apt) /æpt/ *adj.* **1.** [*be* + ~ + *to* + *verb*] likely; having a tendency: *It's apt to be cold in the evenings.* **2.** being quick to learn; bright: *a very apt pupil.* **3.** suited to the purpose or occasion; suitable: *an apt metaphor.* —**apt′ly,** *adv.* —**apt′ness,** *n.* [*noncount*] See -APT-.

apt., an abbreviation of: apartment.

-apt-, *root.* *-apt-* comes from Latin, where it has the meaning "fit, proper." This meaning is found in such words as: ADAPT, APT, APTITUDE, INEPT.

ap•ti•tude (ap′ti to͞od′, -tyo͞od′) /'æptɪ,tuwd, -,tyuwd/ *n.* innate ability or skill; talent: [*count*]: *an aptitude for mathematics.* [*noncount*]: *musical aptitude.* See -APT-.

aq•ua (ak′wə, ä′kwə) /'ækwə, 'ɑkwə/ *n.* [*noncount*] a light greenish blue color.

aqua-, *prefix. aqua-* comes from Latin, where it has the meaning "water". This meaning is found in such words as: AQUACULTURE, AQUARIUM, AQUATIC, AQUEDUCT, AQUEOUS, AQUIFER.

aq•ua•cul•ture (ak′wə kul′chər, ä′kwə-) /ˈækwəˌkʌltʃər, ˈɑkwə-/ *n.* [*noncount*] the planned and controlled growing of underwater animals or plants, as fish, shellfish, and seaweed, in a natural or artificial environment.

aq•ua•ma•rine (ak′wə mə rēn′, ä′kwə-) /ˌækwəməˈriyn, ˌɑkwə-/ *n.* **1.** [*noncount; count*] a transparent, light blue or greenish blue beryl used as a gem. **2.** [*noncount*] a light blue-green or greenish blue color.

aq•ua•naut (ak′wə nôt′, -not′, ä′kwə-) /ˈækwəˌnɔt, -ˌnɒt, ˈɑkwə-/ *n.* [*count*] a scuba diver who works for an extended period of time in and around a submerged dwelling.

aq•ua•plane (ak′wə plān′, ä′kwə-) /ˈækwəˌpleyn, ˈɑkwə-/ *n., v.,* **-planed, -plan•ing.** —*n.* [*count*] **1.** a board that skims over water when it is towed at high speed by a motorboat, ridden for recreation. —*v.* [*no obj*] **2.** to ride an aquaplane.

a•quar•i•um (ə kwâr′ē əm) /əˈkwɛəriyəm/ *n.* [*count*], *pl.* **-i•ums, -i•a** (-ē ə) /-iyə/. **1.** a glass-sided, water-filled tank in which fish or other underwater animals or plants are kept. **2.** a building or institution in which fish or other underwater animals or plants are kept for exhibit and study.

a•quat•ic (ə kwat′ik, ə kwot′-) /əˈkwætɪk, əˈkwɒt-/ *adj.* **1.** living or growing in water: *aquatic plant life.* **2.** [*before a noun*] taking place or practiced on or in water: *Swimming is an aquatic sport.* —*n.* [*count*] **3.** an aquatic plant or animal. **4. aquatics,** [*plural*] sports practiced on or in water. —**a•quat′i•cal•ly,** *adv.*

aq•ua•vit (ä′kwə vēt′, ak′wə-) /ˈɑkwəˌviyt, ˈækwə-/ *n.* [*noncount*] a dry Scandinavian liquor flavored with caraway seeds.

aq•ue•duct (ak′wi dukt′) /ˈækwɪˌdʌkt/ *n.* [*count*] **1.** an artificial conduit or canal for conducting water from a distance. **2.** (in the body) a canal through which liquids pass. See -DUC-.

a•que•ous (ā′kwē əs, ak′wē-) /ˈeykwiyəs, ˈækwiy-/ *adj.* of, like, or containing water: *an aqueous solution.*

a′queous hu′mor, *n.* [*count*] the watery fluid between the cornea and the lens of the eye.

aq•ui•fer (ak′wə fər) /ˈækwəfər/ *n.* [*count*] a geological formation of rock, gravel, or sand that contains or conducts groundwater.

aq•ui•line (ak′wə līn′, -lin) /ˈækwəˌlayn, -lɪn/ *adj.* relating to or resembling an eagle, esp. curved or hooked like an eagle's beak: *an aquiline nose.* —**aq′ui•lin′i•ty** (-lin′i-tē) /-ˈlɪnɪtiy/ *n.* [*noncount*]

-ar, *suffix.* **1.** *-ar* is attached to some nouns (many of which have an *l* before the end) to form adjectives: *circle + -ar → circular; single + -ar → singular.* **2.** *-ar* is also attached to some verbs to form nouns with the meaning "one who does or performs an act of": *beg + -ar → beggar; lie + -ar → liar.*

AR, an abbreviation of: Arkansas.

A/R, an abbreviation of: accounts receivable.

Ar•ab (ar′əb) /ˈærəb/ *n.* [*count*] **1.** a person born or living in an Arabic-speaking nation. **2.** a member of a group of people who have lived since ancient times in the Arabian Peninsula. —*adj.* **3.** of or relating to Arabs.

ar•a•besque (ar′ə besk′) /ˌærəˈbɛsk/ *n.* [*count*] **1.** an ornamental style in which designs, as of flowers, are represented in complex patterns. **2.** a pose in ballet.

A•ra•bi•an (ə rā′bē ən) /əˈreybiyən/ *adj.* of or relating to Arabia or Saudi Arabia.

Ara′bian horse′, *n.* [*count*] a breed of horses raised originally in Arabia and noted for their intelligence, grace, and speed.

Ar•a•bic (ar′ə bik) /ˈærəbɪk/ *n.* [*noncount*] **1.** a language spoken in countries of the Arabian Peninsula, or in other countries in the Middle East and North Africa. *Abbr.:* Ar —*adj.* **2.** of or relating to Arabic.

Ar′abic nu′meral, *n.* [*count*] any of the number symbols 0, 1, 2, 3, 4, 5, 6, 7, 8, 9, in general European use since the 12th century.

Ar•ab•ist (ar′ə bist) /ˈærə bɪst/ *n.* [*count*] a student of or expert in Arab peoples, Arabic language, or Arab culture.

ar•a•ble (ar′ə bəl) /ˈærəbəl/ *adj.* capable of or suitable for producing crops: *arable acreage; Can the desert be made arable?* —**ar•a•bil•i•ty** (ar′ə bil′i tē) /ˌærəˈbɪlɪtiy/ *n.* [*noncount*]

a•rach•nid (ə rak′nid) /əˈræknɪd/ *n.* [*count*] a small animal of a group that includes spiders, scorpions, mites, and ticks, having a body in two parts with eight legs.

ar•bi•ter (är′bi tər) /ˈɑrbɪtər/ *n.* [*count*] a person given the power to decide matters at issue; judge; umpire.

ar•bi•trage (är′bi träzh′) /ˈɑrbɪˌtrɑʒ/ *n., v.,* **-traged, -trag•ing.** —*n.* [*noncount*] **1.** the simultaneous sale and purchase of a security or commodity in different markets to profit from unequal prices. —*v.* [*no obj*] **2.** to engage in arbitrage. —**ar′bi•trag′er,** *n.* [*count*]

ar•bi•trar•y (är′bi trer′ē) /ˈɑrbɪˌtrɛriy/ *adj.* **1.** decided on or done by personal discretion, rather than by reason: *an arbitrary decision.* **2.** having unlimited power; despotic: *an arbitrary government.* **3.** capricious; unreasonable; unsupported: *an arbitrary demand for obedience.* —**ar•bi•trar•i•ly** (är′bi trer′ə lē) /ˌɑrbɪˈtrɛrəliy/ *adv.* —**ar′bi•trar′i•ness,** *n.* [*noncount*]

ar•bi•trate (är′bi trāt′) /ˈɑrbɪˌtreyt/ *v.,* **-trat•ed, -trat•ing.** **1.** to act or decide as arbitrator or arbiter; decide between two sides; determine: [*no obj; (~ + between + obj)*]: *She has been asked to arbitrate between the two sides.* [*~ + obj*]: *She has been asked to arbitrate the issue.* **2.** to send or settle (a matter) to arbitration: [*no obj*]: *They were tired of lengthy negotiations, so they agreed to arbitrate.* [*~ + obj*]: *to arbitrate their dispute.* —**ar′bi•tra′tion,** *n.* [*noncount*]

ar•bi•tra•tor (är′bi trā′tər) /ˈɑrbɪˌtreytər/ *n.* [*count*] a person with the power to decide a dispute or settle differences.

ar•bor (är′bər) /ˈɑrbər/ *n.* [*count*] a leafy shelter formed by or covered with tree branches, shrubs, etc.

ar•bo•re•al (är bôr′ē əl, -bōr′-) /ɑrˈbɔriyəl, -ˈbowr-/ *adj.* **1.** of or relating to trees; treelike: *arboreal surroundings.* **2.** living in trees: *arboreal animals.*

ar•bo•re•tum (är′bə rē′təm) /ˌɑrbəˈriytəm/ *n.* [*count*], *pl.* **-tums, -ta** (-tə). a parklike area in which many different trees or shrubs are grown for study or display.

ar•bor•vi•tae (är′bər vī′tē) /ˌɑrbərˈvaytiy/ *n.* [*count*] an evergreen tree of the cypress family.

ar•bu•tus (är byōō′təs) /ɑrˈbyuwtəs/ *n.* [*count*], *pl.* **-tus•es.** **1.** an evergreen tree or shrub of the heath family. **2.** Also called **trailing arbutus.** a creeping plant with white or pink flower clusters.

arc (ärk) /ɑrk/ *n.* [*count*] **1.** any unbroken part of the circumference of a circle: *an arc of twenty degrees.* **2.** something curved or arched like a bow. **3.** the light formed in a gap between two electrodes when electricity flows through them: *the arc of the light bulb.* —*v.* [*no obj*] **4.** to form an electric arc: *The current arced across the electrodes.* **5.** to move in a curved line: *The ball arced through the air.*

ARC or **A.R.C.,** an abbreviation of: American Red Cross.

ar•cade (är kād′) /ɑrˈkeyd/ *n.* [*count*] **1.** an arched or covered passageway, usually with shops on each side. **2.** an establishment or area with coin-operated games.

ar•cane (är kān′) /ɑrˈkeyn/ *adj.* known or understood only by those with special knowledge; mysterious: *arcane rituals.*

arch[1] (ärch) /ɑrtʃ/ *n.* [*count*] **1.** a curved construction over an opening. **2.** a doorway, gateway, or opening having a curved head; archway. **3.** anything bowed or curved like an arch: *the arch of the foot.* —*v.* **4.** to form (into) an arch: [*no obj*]: *The elms arched over the road.* [*~ + obj*]: *The cat arched its back as a warning.*

arch[2] (ärch) /ɑrtʃ/ *adj.* **1.** crafty; sly; mischievous or cunning: *an arch little grin.* **2.** chief; main: *They were arch foes.* —**arch′ly,** *adv.* —**arch′ness,** *n.* [*noncount*]

-arch-, *root.* **1.** *-arch-* comes from Greek, where it has the meaning "chief; leader; ruler." This meaning is found in such words as: ANARCHY, ARCHBISHOP, ARCHDIOCESE, HIERARCHY, MATRIARCH, MONARCH, MONARCHY, PATRIARCH. **2.** *-arch-* is also used to form nouns that refer to persons who are the most important, most notable, or the most extreme examples of (the following noun): *archenemy (= the most important enemy); archconservative (= the most extreme example of a conservative).* **3.** *-arch-* also appears with the meaning "first, earliest, original, oldest in time." This meaning is found in such words as: ARCHAEOLOGY, ARCHAIC, ARCHAISM, ARCHETYPE.

arch., an abbreviation of: **1.** archaic. **2.** architect. **3.** architecture.

ar•chae•ol•o•gy or **ar•che•ol•o•gy** (är′kē ol′ə jē) /ˌɑrkiyˈɒlədʒiy/ *n.* [*noncount*] the scientific study of ancient peoples and their cultures by analyzing their remaining tools, utensils, and other objects. —**ar•chae•o•log•i•cal** (är′kē ə loj′i kəl) /ˌɑrkiyəˈlɒdʒɪkəl/ *adj.* —**ar′chae•ol′o•gist,** *n.* [*count*] See -ARCH-.

ar•cha•ic (är kā′ik) /ɑrˈkeyɪk/ *adj.* **1.** out-of-date or outmoded; antiquated: *archaic attitudes.* **2.** (of a word or phrase) commonly used in an earlier time but now rare: *archaic meanings.* —**ar•cha′i•cal•ly,** *adv.* See -ARCH-.

ar•cha•ism (är′kē iz′əm, -kā-) /'ɑrkiy,ɪzəm, -key-/ *n.* [*count*] an archaic word, phrase, or style. See -ARCH-.

arch•an•gel (ärk′ān′jəl) /'ɑrk,eyndʒəl/ *n.* [*count*] a chief angel.

arch•bish•op (ärch′bish′əp) /'ɑrtʃ'bɪʃəp/ *n.* [*count*] a bishop of the highest rank. See -ARCH-.

arch•bish′op•ric (ärch′bish′ə prik) /,ɑrtʃ'bɪʃəprɪk/ *n.* [*count*] the position of, rank of, or province of an archbishop.

arch•dea•con (ärch′dē′kən) /'ɑrtʃ'diykən/ *n.* [*count*] a clergyman who ranks next below a bishop.

arch•di•o•cese (ärch′dī′ə sēs′, -sis) /,ɑrtʃ'dayə,siys, -sɪs/ *n.* [*count*] the local area or region governed by an archbishop. —**arch′di•oc′e•san** (ärch′dī os′ə sən) /,ɑrtʃ-day'ɒsəsən/ *adj.* See -ARCH-.

arch•duke (ärch′do͞ok′, -dyo͞ok′) /'ɑrtʃ'duwk, -'dyuwk/ *n.* [*count*] a prince of the former ruling house of Austria.

arch•en•e•my (ärch′en′ə mē) /'ɑrtʃ'ɛnəmiy/ *n.* [*count*], *pl.* **-mies.** a chief enemy.

ar•che•ol•o•gy (är′kē ol′ə jē) /,ɑrkiy'ɒlədʒiy/ *n.* ARCHAEOLOGY.

arch•er (är′chər) /'ɑrtʃər/ *n.* [*count*] a person who shoots with a bow and arrow.

ar•cher•y (är′chə rē) /'ɑrtʃəriy/ *n.* [*noncount*] the practice of shooting with a bow and arrow at a target.

ar•che•typ•al (är′ki tī′pəl) /'ɑrkɪ ,taypəl/ or **ar•che•typ•i•cal** (är′ki tip′i kəl) /,ɑrkɪ 'tɪpɪ kəl/ *adj.* being an archetype. —**ar′che•typ′al•ly, ar′che•typ′i•cal•ly,** *adv.*

ar•che•type (är′ki tīp′) /'ɑrkɪ,tayp/ *n.* [*count*] **1.** the original model from which all things of the same kind are copied. **2.** the best or most complete example of something. See -ARCH-, -TYPE-.

arch•fiend (ärch′fēnd′) /'ɑrtʃ'fiynd/ *n.* [*count*] a chief fiend.

ar•chi•pel•a•go (är′kə pel′ə gō′) /,ɑrkə'pɛlə,gow/ *n.* [*count*], *pl.* **-gos, -goes. 1.** a large group or chain of islands. **2.** a large body of water with many islands.

ar•chi•tect (är′ki tekt′) /'ɑrkɪ,tɛkt/ *n.* [*count*] **1.** a person who designs buildings. **2.** the main person responsible for making something: *the architects of the plan.*

ar•chi•tec•ton•ics (ar′ki tek ton′iks) /,ærkɪtɛk'tɒnɪks/ *n.* [*noncount; used with a singular verb*] the science of planning and constructing buildings.

ar•chi•tec•tur•al (är′ki tek′chər əl) /,ɑrkɪ 'tɛktʃər əl/ *adj.* [*before a noun*] of or relating to the design and construction of buildings and other structures. —**ar′chi•tec′tur•al•ly,** *adv.*

ar•chi•tec•ture (är′ki tek′chər) /'ɑrkɪ,tɛktʃər/ *n.* [*noncount*] **1.** the profession of designing buildings. **2.** the character or style of building: *Romanesque architecture.* **3.** the structure or design of something: *the architecture of a novel.*

ar•chive (är′kīv) /'ɑrkayv/ *n.* [*count; usually plural*] **1. archives,** a place where public documents are preserved. **2.** Usually, **archives.** the documents and other materials preserved in such a place. —*v.* [~ + *obj*] **3.** to preserve in or as if in an archive: *They archived the papers.* —**ar•chi′val,** *adj.*

ar•chi•vist (är′kə vist, -kī-) /'ɑrkə vɪst, -kay-/ *n.* [*count*] a person who collects or is responsible for archives.

arch•way (ärch′wā′) /'ɑrtʃ,wey/ *n.* [*count*] **1.** an entrance or passage under an arch. **2.** an arch over a passage.

-archy, a combining form meaning "rule," "government," forming abstract nouns that correspond to personal nouns ending in -ARCH: *monarchy; oligarchy; patriarchy.*

arc•tic (ärk′tik, är′tik) /'ɑrktɪk, 'ɑrtɪk/ *adj.* **1.** (*often:* *Arctic*) of, relating to, or located at or near the North Pole: *the arctic region.* **2.** coming from the North Pole or the arctic region: *an arctic wind.* **3.** extremely cold; frigid: *an arctic winter.* **4.** extremely cold in character: *an arctic smile.* **5.** [*before a noun*] designed for use in extremely cold conditions: *arctic clothing.* —*n.* [*proper noun; the* + ~*; often: Arctic*] **6.** the region lying north of the Arctic Circle. —**arc′ti•cal•ly,** *adv.*

-ard or **-art,** *suffix.* *-ard* or *-art* is attached to some verbs and nouns to form nouns that refer to persons who regularly do an activity, or who are characterized in a certain way, as indicated by the stem: *dullard (= one who is dull); drunkard (= one who is drunk).*

ar•dent (är′dnt) /'ɑrdnt/ *adj.* **1.** [*before a noun*] showing strong or intense feeling; fervent: *an ardent prayer.* **2.** intensely devoted; avid; enthusiastic: *an ardent baseball fan.* —**ar′dent•ly,** *adv.*

ar•dor (är′dər) /'ɑrdər/ *n.* [*noncount*] **1.** great warmth of feeling; fervor: *revolutionary ardor.* **2.** zeal; enthusiasm: *approached the task with ardor.* Also, *esp. Brit.,* **ar′dour.**

ar•du•ous (är′jo͞o əs) /'ɑrdʒuwəs/ *adj.* **1.** requiring great energy or exertion: *arduous tasks.* **2.** full of hardship; severe: *an arduous winter.* —**ar′du•ous•ly,** *adv.* —**ar′du•ous•ness,** *n.* [*noncount*]

are[1] (är; *unstressed* ər) /ɑr; *unstressed* ər/ *v.* a form of the verb BE, used in the present tense when the subject is *you* or when the subject is a plural noun or pronoun: *You are all I have. The boys are all here. Are they coming in?*

are[2] (âr, är) /ɛər, ɑr/ *n.* [*count*] a surface measure equal to 100 square meters, equivalent to 119.6 sq. yds.; 1/100 of a hectare. *Abbr.:* a

ar•e•a (âr′ē ə) /'ɛəriyə/ *n.* [*count*], *pl.* **-as. 1.** a part of a space or a surface: *the dark areas in the painting.* **2.** a place or part of the world; geographical region: *the downtown area.* **3.** a section reserved for a specific function: *the dining area.* **4.** a particular subject of study or knowledge; field: *new areas of interest.* **5.** a measurement of a surface, equal to the length multiplied by the width. —**ar′e•al,** *adj.*

ar′ea code′, *n.* [*count*] a three-digit number that is used before a telephone number typically when dialing a long-distance call.

ar′ea rug′, *n.* [*count*] a rug that covers only part of a floor.

a•re•na (ə rē′nə) /ə'riynə/ *n.* [*count*], *pl.* **-nas. 1.** a central area used for sports or other forms of entertainment and surrounded by seats for spectators. **2.** a building that contains an arena. **3.** the oval space in the center of a Roman amphitheater. **4.** a field of competition or activity: *the arena of politics.*

are′na the′ater, *n.* [*count*] a theater with seats arranged on at least three sides around a central stage.

aren't (ärnt, är′ənt) /ɑrnt, 'ɑrənt/ *contraction.* **1.** a shortened form of *are not: You aren't really going to do that, are you?* **2.** (used in a question) a shortened form of *am not: Aren't I good enough for the job?*

Ar•gen•tine (är′jən tēn′, -tīn′) /'ɑrdʒən,tiyn, -,tayn/ *n.* **1.** [*count*] a person born or living in Argentina. **2.** [*proper noun; the* + ~] another name for Argentina: *vacationing in the Argentine.* —*adj.* **3.** of or relating to Argentina. Also, **Ar•gen•tin•e•an** (är′jən tin′ē ən) /,ɑrdʒən'tɪniyən/.

ar•gon (är′gon) /'ɑrgɒn/ *n.* [*noncount*] a colorless, odorless, inactive gas used in light bulbs.

ar•go•sy (är′gə sē) /'ɑrgəsiy/ *n.* [*count*], *pl.* **-sies. 1.** a large merchant ship. **2.** a fleet of such ships.

ar•got (är′gō, -gət) /'ɑrgow, -gət/ *n.* [*noncount*] a special vocabulary used by a particular group that is hard for outsiders to understand: *the argot of drug dealers.*

ar•gu•a•ble (är′gyo͞o ə bəl) /'ɑrgyuw ə bəl/ *adj.* [*often: it* + *be* + ~ + *that clause*] **1.** open to argument; debatable. **2.** likely to be proved correct by argument: *It's arguable that Einstein was the greatest scientist of his time.* —**ar′gu•a•bly,** *adv.*

ar•gue (är′gyo͞o) /'ɑrgyuw/ *v.,* **-gued, -gu•ing. 1.** to present or state reasons for or against a thing: [*no obj*]: *argued in favor of capital punishment.* [~ + *for/against* + *obj*]: *argued for capital punishment.* [~ + *obj*]: *to argue a case.* [~ + *that clause*]: *His essay argued that the death penalty should be abolished.* **2.** [*no obj*] to disagree or quarrel; dispute: *have been arguing all day.* **3.** [~ + *obj* + *out of* + *obj*] to persuade: *We tried to argue her out of the idea.* —**Related Words.** ARGUE is a verb, ARGUMENT is a noun, ARGUMENTATIVE is an adjective: *I argued with her about the money. We had an argument about money. He was in a very argumentative mood.*

ar•gu•ment (är′gyə mənt) /'ɑrgyəmənt/ *n.* **1.** [*count*] a disagreement or quarrel in words. **2.** [*count*] a discussion involving differing points of view; debate. **3.** [*count*] a statement, reason, or fact for or against a point: *an argument in favor of disarmament.* **4.** [*noncount*] discourse intended to persuade: *Argument proved useless.*

ar•gu•men•ta•tion (är′gyə men tā′shən) /,ɑrgyəmɛn'teyʃən/ *n.* [*noncount*] the process of developing or presenting an argument; reasoning; debate.

ar•gu•men•ta•tive (är′gyə men′tə tiv) /,ɑrgyə'mɛntətɪv/ *adj.* **1.** fond of arguing or disagreeing frequently. **2.** involving or using logical arguments or persuasion: *an argumentative essay.* —**ar′gu•men′ta•tive•ly,** *adv.* —**ar′gu•men′ta•tive•ness,** *n.* [*noncount*]

ar•gyle (är′gīl) /'ɑrgayl/ *n.* [*count; often: Argyle*] **1.** (in knitting) a diamond-shaped pattern using two or more colors. **2.** a piece of clothing knitted with this pattern: *argyle socks.*

a•ri•a (är′ē ə, âr′ē ə) /'ɑriyə, 'ɛəriyə/ *n.* [*count*], *pl.* **-as.** an elaborate melody sung solo, as in an opera.

-arian (-ā′rē ən) /-'eyriy ən/ *suffix.* **1.** *-arian* is attached to some nouns and adjectives that end in -ARY to form personal nouns: *library + -arian → librarian; seminary + -arian → seminarian; veterinary + -arian → veterinarian.* **2.** *-arian* is also attached to some roots to form nouns with the meaning "a person who supports, calls for, or practices the principles of (the root noun)": *authority + -arian → authoritarian (= one who believes in central authority); totality + -arian → totalitarian (= one who believes in total governmental rule).*

ar•id (ar′id) /'ærɪd/ *adj.* **1.** extremely dry: *the arid desert.* **2.** lacking vitality; uninteresting: *an arid imagination.* —**a•rid•i•ty** (ə rid′i tē) /ə'rɪdɪtiy/ *n.* [*noncount*] —**ar′id•ly,** *adv.*

a•right (ə rit′) /ə'rayt/ *adv.* correctly; to rights: *I want to set things aright.*

a•rise (ə rīz′) /ə'rayz/ *v.* [*no obj*], **a•rose** (ə rōz′) /ə'rowz/ **a•ris•en** (ə riz′ən) /ə'rɪzən/ **a•ris•ing. 1.** to get up from sitting, lying, or kneeling; rise: *He arose from his chair.* **2.** to awaken; wake up: *She arose at 6 a.m.* **3.** to move upward; ascend: *Smoke arose from the chimney.* **4.** to appear; spring up; result: *Problems arise daily.* [~ + *from* + *obj*]: *What consequences will arise from this?*

ar•is•toc•ra•cy (ar′ə stok′rə sē) /ˌærə'stɒkrəsiy/ *n., pl.* **-cies. 1.** [*noncount*] a class of persons holding high rank or special privileges, esp. nobility. **2.** a government or state ruled by such a class: [*noncount*]: *a belief in aristocracy.* [*count*]: *aristocracies of the old world.* **3.** [*count*] any class or group thought of as the best because of education, ability, or wealth: *an aristocracy of merit.*

a•ris•to•crat (ə ris′tə krat′) /ə'rɪstəˌkræt/ *n.* [*count*] a member of an aristocracy. —**a•ris′to•crat′ic,** *adj.* —**a•ris′to•crat′i•cal•ly,** *adv.*

a•rith•me•tic (*n.* ə rith′mə tik; *adj.* ar′ith met′ik) /*n.* ə'rɪθmətɪk; *adj.* ˌærɪθ'mɛtɪk/ *n.* [*noncount*] **1.** the method, process, or study of adding, subtracting, multiplying, and dividing numbers. —*adj.* **ar•ith•met•ic 2.** Also, **ar′ith•met′i•cal.** of or relating to the rules of arithmetic: *arithmetical computations.* —**ar′ith•met′i•cal•ly,** *adv.*

Ariz., an abbreviation of: Arizona.

ark (ärk) /ɑrk/ *n.* [*proper noun; often: the + ~*] **1.** [*sometimes: Ark*] (in the Bible) the vessel built by Noah for safety during the Flood. **2.** Also called **ark of the covenant.** a wooden chest containing two stone tablets inscribed with the Ten Commandments.

Ark., an abbreviation of: Arkansas.

arm[1] (ärm) /ɑrm/ *n.* [*count*] **1. a.** the upper limb of the human body. **b.** the upper limb from shoulder to elbow: *The doctor gave me an injection in the arm.* **2.** any part or attachment that resembles an arm, as a projecting support on a chair. **3.** a branch, section, or part of an organization: *an arm of the government.* —***Idiom.* 4. an arm and a leg,** a great deal of money: *That will cost an arm and a leg.* **5. arm in arm,** with arms linked together or intertwined: *walking along arm in arm.* **6. at arm's length,** at a distance that discourages intimacy: *kept her associates at arm's length.* **7. (long) arm of the law,** the power or authority of the law or law enforcement. **8. twist someone's arm,** to bring strong pressure to bear on someone. **9. with open arms,** cordially; hospitably: *welcomed her with open arms.*

arm[2] (ärm) /ɑrm/ *n.* [*count*] **1.** Usually, **arms.** [*plural*] weapons, esp. guns, rifles, or firearms. **2. arms,** [*plural*] the heraldic designs or symbols on a shield. —*v.* **3.** to (cause to) be equipped with weapons: [*no obj*]: *The country is arming for war.* [~ + *oneself*]: *The rebels armed themselves.* [~ + *obj*]: *They armed their troops.* **4.** [~ + *obj*] to activate, equip, or prepare (something) for specific purpose or effective use: *to arm the security system.* —***Idiom.* 5. bear arms, a.** to carry weapons: *claimed the right to bear arms.* **b.** to serve as a member of the armed forces: *He had to bear arms as a youth of only sixteen.* **6. take up arms,** to prepare for or go to war. **7. under arms,** (of troops) trained and equipped for battle. **8. up in arms,** indignant: *is up in arms about the effort to discredit him.*

-arm-, *root.* -arm- comes from Latin, where it has the meaning "weapon." This meaning is found in such words as: ARMADA, ARMAMENT, ARMS, DISARMAMENT.

ar•ma•da (är mä′də, -mā′-) /ɑr'mɑdə, -'mey-/ *n.* [*count*], *pl.* **-das.** [*Often: Armada*] a fleet of warships: *The Spanish Armada was defeated by the English navy.* See -ARM-.

ar•ma•dil•lo (är′mə dil′ō) /ˌɑrmə'dɪlow/ *n.* [*count*], *pl.* **-los.** an animal related to the anteater and covered with jointed plates of bone and horn.

Ar•ma•ged•don (är′mə ged′n) /ˌɑrmə'gɛdn̩/ *n.* [*count*] **1.** the place where the final battle between good and evil will be fought. **2.** [*armageddon*] any large-scale and decisive or final conflict.

ar•ma•ment (är′mə mənt) /'ɑrməmənt/ *n.* **1.** [*noncount*] the arms and equipment with which a military unit is supplied. **2.** [*count*] Usually, **armaments.** [*plural*] the armed forces of a country, or its military strength when thought of as a group. **3.** [*noncount*] the process of arming for war. See -ARM-.

ar•ma•ture (är′mə chər) /'ɑrmətʃər/ *n.* **1.** [*noncount*] the protective covering of an animal or plant. **2.** [*count*] **a.** the part of an electric generator in which the electricity is produced. **b.** the moving part in an electrical device, as a buzzer or relay, that is moved by a magnetic field.

arm•chair (ärm′châr′) /'ɑrmˌtʃɛər/ *n.* [*count*] **1.** a chair with sidepieces or arms to support a person's forearms or elbows. —*adj.* [*before a noun*] **2.** theorizing without the benefit of practical experience: *armchair generals.*

armed (ärmd) /ɑrmd/ *adj.* **1.** carrying a weapon: *an armed assailant.* **2.** [*before a noun*] involving or using people with weapons or guns: *an armed assault on the kidnapper's hideout.* **3.** [*be + ~ + with*] having in one's possession ready for use: *was armed with the facts.*

armed′ forc′es, *n.* [*plural*] the military, naval, and air forces of a nation or of a number of nations. Also called **armed′ serv′ices.**

Ar•me•ni•an (är mē′nē ən) /ɑr'miyniyən/ *adj.* **1.** of or relating to Armenia. **2.** of or relating to the language spoken by many of the people of Armenia. —*n.* **3.** [*count*] a person born or living in Armenia. **4.** [*noncount*] the language spoken by many of the people of Armenia.

arm•ful (ärm′fo͝ol′) /'ɑrmˌfʊl/ *n.* [*count*], *pl.* **-fuls.** the amount one or both arms can hold.

arm•hole (ärm′hōl′) /'ɑrmˌhowl/ *n.* [*count*] an opening for the arm in a garment.

ar•mi•stice (är′mə stis) /'ɑrməstɪs/ *n.* [*count*] an agreement to stop fighting and discuss peace; truce.

arm•let (ärm′lit) /'ɑrmlɪt/ *n.* [*count*] an ornamental band worn high on the arm.

ar•mor (är′mər) /'ɑrmər/ *n.* [*noncount*] **1.** any covering that serves as a defense or protection against weapons. **2.** motor-driven units of military forces. —*v.* [~ + *obj*] **3.** to cover or equip with armor. Also, *esp. Brit.,* **ar′mour.** See -ARM-.

ar•mored (är′mərd) /'ɑrmərd/ *adj.* **1.** covered with or protected by armor: *an armored car.* **2.** having vehicles, weapons, etc., protected by armor: *armored divisions.*

ar•mor•er (är′mər ər) /'ɑrmərər/ *n.* [*count*] **1.** a maker or repairer of arms or armor. **2.** a person who manufactures, repairs, or services firearms.

ar•mor•y (är′mə rē) /'ɑrməriy/ *n.* [*count*], *pl.* **-ies. 1.** a storage place for weapons. **2.** a factory where weapons are made. See -ARM-.

arm•pit (ärm′pit′) /'ɑrmˌpɪt/ *n.* [*count*] the hollow place under the arm at the shoulder.

arm•rest (ärm′rest′) /'ɑrmˌrɛst/ *n.* [*count*] a support for the forearm, such as at the side of a seat.

arms (ärmz) /ɑrmz/ *n.* [*plural*] See ARM.

ar•my (är′mē) /'ɑrmiy/ *n.* [*count*], *pl.* **-mies. 1.** the military forces of a nation, esp. the forces that fight on land. **2.** a body of people trained and armed for war: *an army of insurgents.* **3.** any organized or large group: *an army of census takers.*

a•ro•ma (ə rō′mə) /ə'rowmə/ *n.* [*count*], *pl.* **-mas.** a strong, noticeable, and pleasant odor; fragrance: *the aroma of freshly brewed coffee.* —**ar•o•mat•ic** (ar′ə-mat′ik) /ˌærə'mætɪk/ *adj.*: *aromatic oils.*

a•rose (ə rōz′) /ə'rowz/ *v.* pt. of ARISE.

a•round (ə round′) /ə'rawnd/ *adv.* **1.** in a circle or in a ring; on all sides: *The crowd gathered around and watched.* **2.** in all directions (when viewed from a point in the center of somewhere): *could see for miles around.* **3.** in the region about a place; here and there: *They travel around together.* **4.** when measured around the outside of a circle: *The tree was 40 inches around.* **5.** in a circular or rounded course; moving in a circle; with a spinning or rotating movement: *The car's wheels were spinning around in the snow.* **6.** through a sequence or series, as of places or persons: *We showed our visitors around.* **7.** through a repeating period of time: *Lunchtime rolled around again.* **8.** by an indirect way; not in a straight or direct course: *The lane goes around past the stables.* **9. a.** in or to another, opposite direction or course: *twisted her head around and saw him coming.* **b.** to another, usually opposite, opinion: *After our arguments, she finally came around.* **10.** back into consciousness: *The smelling salts brought her around.* **11.** somewhere near; somewhere about; nearby: *I'll be around for an hour or so.* **12.** present and available: *There aren't many jobs around now.* **13.** to a specific place (known to the speaker and hearer): *Come around to see me.* —*prep.* **14.** about; on all sides; circling; surrounding: *wrapped paper around the package.* **15.** on the edge, border, or outer part of: *a skirt with fringe around the bottom.* **16.** from place to place in; about: *to get around town.* **17.** in all or various directions from: *She looked around the room.* **18.** in the vicinity of; near to: *the countryside around Boston.* **19.** approximately; about: *How about meeting around five o'clock?* **20.** here and there in: *people around the city.* **21.** somewhere in or near: *had to stay around the house.* **22.** to all or various parts of: *We wandered around the park.* **23.** so as to make a circle surrounding: *The tour boat sails around the island.* **24.** reached by making a turn or partial turn about: *The church is just around the corner.* **25.** so as to revolve or rotate about a center: *the earth's motion around its axis.* **26.** personally close to: *All the advisers around him say he should retire.* **27.** so as to overcome: *got around the problem by raising prices.* —***Idiom.*** **28. been around,** [*no obj*] gone through much experience: *He looked as if he had been around and knew the score.*

a•rous•al (ə rou′zəl) /əˈrawzəl/ *n.* [*noncount*] the state or condition of being alert or stimulated.

a•rouse (ə rouz′) /əˈrawz/ *v.* [~ + *obj*], **a•roused, a•rous•ing. 1.** to stir up; excite: *The fiery speech aroused the crowd.* **2.** to stimulate sexually. **3.** to wake (somebody) up: *She aroused them at noon.* Compare ROUSE.

ar•peg•gi•o (är pej′ē ō′, -pej′ō) /ɑrˈpɛdʒiyˌow, -ˈpɛdʒow/ *n.* [*count*], *pl.* **-gi•os.** (in music) the sounding of the notes of a chord one after the other very quickly.

ar•raign (ə rān′) /əˈreyn/ *v.* [~ + *obj*] to call or bring (someone) before a court of law to answer a charge. —**ar•raign′ment,** *n.* [*count*]: *An arraignment takes place before a trial.* [*noncount*]: *to set a date for arraignment.*

ar•range (ə rānj′) /əˈreyndʒ/ *v.,* **-ranged, -rang•ing. 1.** [~ + *obj*] to place in proper, desired, or convenient order; organize: *arranged the flowers attractively.* **2.** to come to an understanding (about): [~ + *for* + *obj*]: *We arranged for delivery of the newspaper.* [~ + *for* + *obj* + *to* + *verb*]: *arranged for them to deliver the newspaper.* [~ + *to* + *verb*]: *arranged to have them met at the airport.* [~ + *it* + *that clause*]: *She arranged it that we would all meet them there.* **3.** to make plans or preparation (for): [~ + *for* + *obj*]: *Let's arrange for a conference.* [~ + *obj* (+ *for* + *obj*)]: *Please arrange a meeting for next week.* **4.** [~ + *obj*] to set (a musical work) in a different way: *a piano piece arranged for orchestra.* —**ar•rang′er,** *n.* [*count*]

ar•range•ment (ə rānj′mənt) /ə ˈreyndʒmənt/ *n.* **1.** [*noncount*] the act of putting things in proper order: *the arrangement of items on a table.* **2.** [*count*] something that has been put in proper order: *a beautiful floral arrangement.* **3.** [*count*] a plan: *made funeral arrangements.* **4.** agreement; settlement: [*count*]: *made an arrangement to pay off the debt.* [*noncount*]: *Can't we come to some sort of arrangement?* **5.** [*count*] a piece of music set in a format different from the original.

ar•rant (ar′ənt) /ˈærənt/ *adj.* [*before a noun*] (used to emphasize something negative) complete; thorough; absolute: *an arrant fool; arrant nonsense.*

ar•ray (ə rā′) /əˈrey/ *v.* [~ + *obj*] **1.** to place, position, or set out in proper or desired order: *to array troops for battle.* **2.** to dress with beautiful or ornamental clothing: *arrayed in their finest silks.* —*n.* **3.** [*noncount*] order or arrangement, as of troops drawn up for battle. **4.** [*count*] an impressive grouping: *presented them with an array of facts.* **5.** [*count*] a regular or systematic arrangement: *an array of figures showing revenues and expenses.* **6.** [*noncount*] clothing; dress: *in fine array.*

ar•rears (ə rērz′) /əˈrɪərz/ *n.* [*plural*] **1.** Usually, **(in) arrears.** the state of being late in repaying a debt: *were two months in arrears.* **2.** money owed: *arrears of unpaid wages.*

ar•rest (ə rest′) /əˈrɛst/ *v.* [~ + *obj*] **1.** to seize (a person) by legal authority: *The police arrested the burglar.* **2.** to catch and hold; attract: *A loud noise arrested our attention.* **3.** to stop (something) or to cause (something) to slow down: *The new drug seemed to arrest the progress of the disease.* —*n.* [*count*] **4.** the taking of a person into legal custody (as by the police): *made an arrest.* **5.** an act of stopping or the state of being stopped: *cardiac arrest.* —***Idiom.*** **6. under arrest,** in custody of the police.

ar•rest•ing (ə res′ting) /əˈrɛstɪŋ/ *adj.* **1.** attracting attention; striking: *a person of arresting good looks.* **2.** [*before a noun*] making or having made an arrest: *the arresting officer.* —**ar•rest′ing•ly,** *adv.*

ar•rhyth•mi•a (ə rith′mē ə, ā rith′-) /əˈrɪðmiyə, eyˈrɪð-/ *n.* [*noncount*] a disturbance in the rhythm of the heartbeat. —**ar•rhyth′mic, ar•rhyth′mi•cal,** *adj.*

ar•ri•val (ə rī′vəl) /əˈrayvəl/ *n.* **1.** an act of arriving; a coming: [*count*]: *Their arrival was delayed by traffic.* [*noncount*]: *She was welcomed on arrival.* **2.** [*noncount*] the attainment of any object or condition: *the arrival of jet-powered flight.* **3.** [*count*] a person or thing that arrives or has arrived: *a new arrival at the school.*

ar•rive (ə rīv′) /əˈrayv/ *v.* [*no obj*], **-rived, -riv•ing. 1.** to come to a place in a journey; reach one's destination: *They have just arrived in town.* **2.** to come to be present; happen: *The moment of truth has arrived.* **3.** to attain a position of success in the world: *She felt she had finally arrived in society.* **4.** to be born: *The baby arrived at noon.* **5. arrive at,** [~ + *at* + *obj*] to reach or attain; come to; decide: *arrived at an agreement.*

ar•ri•ve•der•ci (ə rē′və der′chē) /əˌriyvəˈdɛrtʃiy/ *interj. Italian.* until we see each other again.

ar•ro•gance (ar′ə gəns) /ˈærə gəns/ *n.* [*noncount*] a manner of behaving as if one were more important than others.

ar•ro•gant (ar′ə gənt) /ˈærəgənt/ *adj.* **1.** acting as if one were more important than others: *rude and arrogant officials.* **2.** characterized by arrogance: *arrogant behavior.* —**ar′ro•gant•ly,** *adv.* See -ROGA-.

ar•ro•gate (ar′ə gāt′) /ˈærəˌgeyt/ *v.* [~ (+ *to* + *oneself*) + *obj*], **-gat•ed, -gat•ing.** to claim to have or do (something) even though one has no right to do so: *She arrogated to herself the power to make changes.*

ar•row (ar′ō) /ˈærow/ *n.* [*count*] **1.** a slender, long stick with feathers at the back end and a point at the tip that is shot from a bow. **2.** anything resembling an arrow, as a drawing used to show direction or movement.

ar•row•head (ar′ō hed′) /ˈærowˌhɛd/ *n.* [*count*] a pointed tip on an arrow: *arrowheads of flint.*

ar•row•root (ar′ō ro͞ot′, -ro͝ot′) /ˈærowˌruwt, -ˌrʊt/ *n.* **1.** [*count*] a tropical American plant grown for the starch that can be made from it. **2.** [*noncount*] the easily digested starch of this plant, used as a thickener in cooking.

ar•roy•o (ə roi′ō) /əˈrɔyow/ *n.* [*count*], *pl.* **-os.** (chiefly in the southwestern U.S.) a small, narrow, steep-sided channel in the ground that is usually dry except after heavy rains.

ar•se•nal (är′sə nl) /ˈɑrsənl̩/ *n.* [*count*] **1.** a military establishment for producing and storing weapons, ammunition, etc. **2.** a collection or supply of weapons: *the nation's arsenal of nuclear weapons.* **3.** a supply of any useful item: *an arsenal of colorful phrases.*

ar•se•nic (är′sə nik) /ˈɑrsənɪk/ *n.* [*noncount*] **1.** a grayish white substance, one of the chemical elements, that can be made into a dangerous poison. **2.** the poison made from arsenic.

ar•son (är′sən) /ˈɑrsən/ *n.* [*noncount*] the crime of deliberately setting fire to property. —**ar′son•ist,** *n.* [*count*]

art[1] (ärt) /ɑrt/ *n.* **1.** [*noncount*] the making of things considered beautiful: *Art is her field of activity.* **2.** [*noncount*] the objects produced in this way: *a great collection of Japanese art.* **3.** [*noncount*] the activity, skill, or subject of study concerned with producing such objects: *majored in art in college.* **4.** [*count*] a field or category of art: *Dance is an art.* **5.** [*noncount*] any field using the skills or techniques of art: *industrial art.* **6.** [*noncount*] ARTWORK (def. 2). **7.** [*count; usually singular*] skill in conducting any human activity: *the art of conversation.* **8. arts,** [*plural*] a branch of study in a college or university, including history, languages, music, philosophy, or literature, as opposed to scientific subjects.

art[2] (ärt) /ɑrt/ *v. Archaic.* second person singular present indicative form of the verb BE used with "thou," an old form of "You": *Thou art.*

-art, *suffix. -art* is a variant form of -ARD. It is found in such words as: BRAGGART.

art., an abbreviation of: article.

art′ dec′o (dek′ō) /ˈdɛkow/ *n.* [*noncount; often: Art Deco*] a style of decorative art originating in the 1920's that uses geometric shapes and curved lines.

ar•te•ri•al (är tēr′ē əl) /ɑr ˈtɪəriy əl/ *adj.* [*usually: before* *a noun*] **1.** of or having to do with an artery: *arterial blood flow.* **2.** being a main or most important route or connection to a place: *an arterial highway.*

ar•te•ri•o•scle•ro•sis (är tēr′ē ō sklə rō′sis) /ɑr͵tɪər-iyowsklə'rowsɪs/ *n.* [*noncount*] abnormal thickening in the walls of arteries, and the loss of the ability of these walls to stretch easily.

ar•ter•y (är′tə rē) /'ɑrtəriy/ *n.* [*count*], *pl.* **-ies. 1.** a blood vessel that carries blood from the heart to any part of the body. **2.** a main route or highway.

ar•te′sian well′ (är tē′zhən) /ɑr'tiyʒən/ *n.* [*count*] a well in which water rises under pressure without being pumped.

art•ful (ärt′fəl) /'ɑrtfəl/ *adj.* **1.** slyly crafty or cunning; tricky; ingenious: *artful in twisting stories.* **2.** done with or characterized by art or skill: *the magician's artful performance.* **—art′ful•ly,** *adv.* **—art′ful•ness,** *n.* [*noncount*]

ar•thrit•ic (är thrit′ik) /ɑr 'θrɪtɪk/ *adj.* **1.** having stiff, swollen, or painful joints caused by arthritis: *After my leg injury I became arthritic.* **2.** [*before a noun*] characterized by the pains of arthritis: *arthritic pain.* **—*n.*** [*count*] **3.** a person suffering from the pains of arthritis.

ar•thri•tis (är thrī′tis) /ɑr'θraytɪs/ *n.* [*noncount*] a condition in which one or more joints are swollen, painful, or inflamed.

ar•thro•pod (är′thrə pod′) /'ɑrθrə͵pɒd/ *n.* [*count*] an animal without a backbone, having a body in segments, jointed limbs, and a shell covering, and including insects, spiders, and crustaceans. See -POD-.

ar•ti•choke (är′ti chōk′) /'ɑrtɪ͵tʃowk/ *n.* [*count*] **1.** Also called **globe artichoke.** a tall plant like a thistle, with a head and fleshy leaf-like scales eaten as a vegetable. **2.** JERUSALEM ARTICHOKE.

ar•ti•cle (är′ti kəl) /'ɑrtɪkəl/ *n.* [*count*] **1.** a piece of writing appearing in a newspaper, etc.: *She wrote a magazine article.* **2.** any individual or particular member taken from a class or group of things: *an article of clothing.* **3.** a clause or part of an agreement, contract, or treaty: *articles of confederation.* **4.** one of a small class of words in English, *a, an,* and *the,* that are linked to nouns and that show whether the noun is definite or indefinite. Compare DEFINITE ARTICLE, INDEFINITE ARTICLE.

ar•tic•u•late (*adjective:* är tik′yə lit; *verb:* -lāt′) /*adjective:* ɑr'tɪkyəlɪt; *verb:* -͵leyt/ *adj., v.,* **-lat•ed, -lat•ing. —*adj.*** **1.** (of speech or speech sounds) pronounced clearly and distinctly: *articulate pronunciation.* **2.** capable of, expressed with, or showing clarity: *the candidate's articulate speech.* **3.** [*before a noun*] having joints or parts that are joined: *articulate segments of a worm.* **—*v.*** **4.** to pronounce (speech sounds) clearly and distinctly: [*no obj*]: *She articulated so as to be understood.* [~ + *obj*]: *She articulated the vowels carefully.* **5.** [~ + *obj*] to put (an idea) clearly into speech: *articulated his philosophy clearly.* **6.** to unite by a joint or joints: [*no obj*]: *The shoulder and arm bones articulate.* [~ + *obj*]: *The bones are articulated.* **—ar•tic′u•late•ly,** *adv.* **—ar•tic′u•late•ness,** *n.* [*noncount*]

ar•tic•u•lat•ed (är tik′yə lā tid) /ɑr 'tɪkyə ley tɪd/ *adj.* [*before a noun*] hinged or linked between parts: *A train is an articulated vehicle.*

ar•tic•u•la•tion (är tik′yə lā′shən) /ɑr ͵tɪkyə 'leyʃən/ *n.* [*noncount*] **1.** the expressing of an idea in speech or in words: *Her articulation of the plan was convincing.* **2.** the act of pronouncing or producing speech sounds: *the proper articulation of "th" in English.* **3.** the act of joining or the state of being joined: *the articulation of skeletal bones.*

ar•ti•fact (är′tə fakt′) /'ɑrtə͵fækt/ *n.* [*count*] any object made by human beings, esp. a tool from an earlier time discovered at an archaeological site.

ar•ti•fice (är′tə fis) /'ɑrtəfɪs/ *n.* **1.** [*count*] a clever trick: *Makeup is an artifice used by actors.* **2.** [*noncount*] the use of a clever trick; trickery; craftiness.

ar•tif•i•cer (är tif′ə sər, är′tə fə-) /ɑr'tɪfəsər, 'ɑrtəfə-/ *n.* [*count*] a skillful or artistic worker; craftsman; artisan.

ar•ti•fi•cial (är′tə fish′əl) /͵ɑrtə'fɪʃəl/ *adj.* **1.** made by human skill; not natural: *an artificial satellite.* **2.** imitation; not real: *artificial vanilla flavoring.* **3.** lacking naturalness; false; forced: *an artificial smile.* **—ar•ti•fi•ci•al•i•ty** (är′tə fish′ē al′i tē) /͵ɑrtə͵fɪʃiy'ælɪtiy/ *n.* [*noncount*] **—ar′ti•fi′cial•ly,** *adv.*

artifi′cial intel′ligence, *n.* [*noncount*] the capability of computer programs and devices to perform functions similar to human abilities to learn and to make decisions.

artifi′cial respira′tion, *n.* [*noncount*] the forcing of air into and out of the lungs of a person whose breathing has stopped.

ar•til•ler•y (är til′ə rē) /ɑr'tɪləriy/ *n.* [*noncount*] **1.** large guns or missile launchers mounted on wheels. **2.** the troops or the branch of an army using and caring for artillery. **—ar•til′ler•y•man,** *n.* [*count*], *pl.* **-men.**

ar•ti•san (är′tə zən) /'ɑrtəzən/ *n.* [*count*] a person who practices a craft or trade requiring skilled use of the hands.

art•ist (är′tist) /'ɑrtɪst/ *n.* [*count*] **1.** a person who practices or is proficient in one of the arts. **2.** a person proficient in a performing art, as an actor or musician. **3.** a person who shows special skill: *That baseball pitcher is a real artist with a curveball.*

ar•tiste (är tēst′) /ɑr'tiyst/ *n.* [*count*] a professional actor, singer, dancer, or other public performer.

ar•tis•tic (är tis′tik) /ɑr'tɪstɪk/ *adj.* **1.** beautiful; attractive; like good art: *an artistic flower arrangement.* **2.** of or characteristic of art or artists: *fought for artistic freedom.* **3.** showing skill in how something is done. **—ar•tis′ti•cal•ly,** *adv.*

art•ist•ry (är′ti strē) /'ɑrtɪstriy/ *n.* [*noncount*] **1.** skill, ability, or workmanship of an artist. **2.** skill or outstanding ability to do anything, esp. in a creative manner: *artistry in the kitchen.*

art•less (ärt′lis) /'ɑrtlɪs/ *adj.* **1.** free from tricks, cunning, or craftiness; honest: *an artless manner.* **2.** not artificial; natural; simple: *artless beauty.* **—art′less•ly,** *adv.* **—art′less•ness,** *n.* [*noncount*]

art nou•veau (ärt′ no͞o vō′, är′) /͵ɑrt nuw'vow, ͵ɑr/ *n.* [*noncount; often: Art Nouveau*] a style of art in the late 19th century characterized by curved lines and shapes patterned on natural forms.

art•work (ärt′wûrk′) /'ɑrt͵wɜrk/ *n.* [*noncount*] **1.** an object or objects produced by artists: *the artwork on the ceiling of that old cathedral.* **2.** drawings, photographs, or illustrations to be included in a book or magazine.

art•y (är′tē) /'ɑrtiy/ also **art•sy** (ärt′sē) /'ɑrtsiy/ *adj.,* **-i•er, -i•est.** *Informal.* showing a pretentious interest in the arts: *arty people always dropping names of well-known painters and sculptors.* **—art′i•ness,** *n.* [*noncount*]

-ary, *suffix.* **1.** *-ary* is attached to some nouns to form adjectives with the meaning: "relating to, connected with": *element + -ary → elementary; honor + -ary → honorary.* **2.** *-ary* is attached to some roots to form personal nouns, or nouns that refer to objects that hold or contain things: *secretary; -libr- (= root meaning "book") + -ary → library (= place for holding books); glossary (= place containing specialized words and their meanings).* **3.** *-ary* is attached to some nouns to form adjectives with the meanings "contributing to; for the purpose of": *inflation + -ary → inflationary (= contributing to inflation); compliment + -ary → complimentary (= for the purpose of complimenting).*

as (az; *unstressed* əz) /æz; *unstressed* əz/ *adv.* **1.** to the same degree or amount; equally: *It costs three times as much.* **2.** for example: *a number of spring flowers, as the tulip.* **3.** thought or considered to be: *the square as distinct from the rectangle.* **4.** in the manner indicated: *She sang as promised.* **—*conj.*** **5.** to the same degree or extent that: *I like to do as I please.* **6.** in the degree or manner of; in the same degree or manner that: *Do as we do.* **7.** at the same time that; while; when: *Pay as you enter.* **8.** since; because: *As you are leaving last, lock the door.* **9.** though: *Strange as it seems, it is true.* **10.** [*so + adjective + ~ + to + verb*] that the result or effect was: *His voice was so loud as to make everyone stare.* **—*pron.*** **11.** [*the same + ~*] that; who; which: *I have the same trouble as you had.* **12.** a fact that: *She spoke the truth, as can be proved.* **—*prep.*** **13.** in the role, function, job, or status of: *to act as leader.* **14.** to the same degree or extent that: *Quick as a flash he was out the door.* **15.** by way of; for (a reason): *I bought you this toy as a special treat.* **—*Idiom.*** **16. as . . . as,** [~ + *adjective/adverb* + ~] (used to express similarity or equality between one person or thing and another): *She is as rich as Croesus (= She and Croesus are equally or similarly rich).* **17. as far as,** to the degree or extent that: *It is an excellent plan, as far as I can tell.* **18. as for** or **as to,** with respect to; about; concerning: *As for staying away, I wouldn't think of it.* **19. as good as, a.** equivalent to: *It now works as good as new.* **b.** true to; trustworthy as: *He has always been as good as his word.* **20. as if** or **as though,** as it would be if: *It was as if the world had come to an end.* **21. as is,** in whatever condition something is in when offered, esp. if damaged: *You must buy the car* *as is.* **22. as it were,** in a way; so to speak: *He became, as it were, a man without a country.* **23. as of,** beginning on; on and after; from: *This price is effective as of next Sunday.* **24. as such, a.** as being what is indicated; in that capacity; because of what someone or something is: *An officer of the law, as such, is entitled to respect (= An officer of the law, because he or she is an officer of the law, is entitled to respect).* **b.** in itself or in themselves: *The job, as such, does not appeal to me. (= The job, being the kind of job it is, does not appeal to me.)* **25. as yet,** up to the present time: *I don't, as yet, have a decent salary.*

A.S., an abbreviation of: Associate in Science.

ASAP or **A.S.A.P.** or **a.s.a.p.,** an abbreviation of: as soon as possible.

as•bes•tos (as bes′təs, az-) /æsˈbɛstəs, æz-/ *n.* [*noncount*] a soft gray mineral that occurs as a fiber-like substance, formerly used for making fireproof articles and in building insulation. Sometimes, **as•bes′tus.**

as•cend (ə send′) /əˈsɛnd/ *v.* **1.** to move, climb, or go upward (upon or along); mount: [*no obj*]: *The elevator ascended to the penthouse.* [~ + *obj*]: *She ascended the stairs gracefully.* **2.** [*no obj*] to rise to a higher point, rank, degree, etc.: *ascended rapidly in the company hierarchy.* **3. ascend the throne,** to become a king or queen. See -SCEND-.

as•cend•an•cy or **as•cend•en•cy** (ə sen′dən sē) /əˈsɛndənsiy/ also **as•cend′ance, as•cend′ence,** *n.* [*noncount*] the state of being in power, or of governing or controlling.

as•cend•ant or **as•cend•ent** (ə sen′dənt) /əˈsɛndənt/ *n.* [*count*] **1.** a position of dominance. *—adj.* [*before a noun*] **2.** rising: *an ascendant middle class.* **3.** superior; dominant.

as•cen•sion (ə sen′shən) /əˈsɛnʃən/ *n.* **1.** [*count*] the act of ascending; ascent. **2. the Ascension,** [*proper noun*] the bodily ascending of Christ from earth to heaven.

as•cent (ə sent′) /əˈsɛnt/ *n.* [*count*] **1.** the act of ascending. **2.** movement upward from a lower to a higher state, degree, grade, or status; advancement: *rapid ascent through the ranks.* **3.** the degree of tilting upward: *a steep ascent.*

as•cer•tain (as′ər tān′) /ˌæsərˈteyn/ *v.* to find out definitely; get to know: [~ + *obj*]: *We tried hard to ascertain all the facts in the case.* [~ + *(that) clause*]: *We ascertained that she told the truth.* See -CERT-.

as•cet•ic (ə set′ik) /əˈsɛtɪk/ *n.* [*count*] **1.** a person who practices self-denial and leads a simple, severe life without luxuries or pleasures, usually for religious reasons. *—adj.* Also, **as•cet′i•cal. 2.** practicing the life of an ascetic. **3.** showing the effects of an ascetic life: *a lean ascetic face.* —**as•cet′i•cal•ly,** *adv.* —**as•cet•i•cism** (ə set′i siz′əm) /əˈsɛtɪˌsɪzəm/ *n.* [*noncount*]

ASCII (as′kē) /ˈæskiy/ *n.* [*proper noun*] a code for computers in which characters are represented by the numbers 0 through 127: *ASCII is an abbreviation of "American Standard Code for Information Interchange."*

a•scor′bic ac′id (ə skôr′bik) /əˈskɔrbɪk/ *n.* [*noncount*] a vitamin occurring naturally esp. in citrus fruits and green vegetables, and that is essential for normal metabolism. Also called **vitamin C.**

as•cot (as′kət, -kot) /ˈæskət, -kɒt/ *n.* [*count*] a tie or scarf with broad ends looped to lie flat one upon the other, sometimes held with a pin.

as•cribe (ə skrīb′) /əˈskrayb/ *v.* [~ + *obj* + *to* + *obj*], **-cribed, -crib•ing. 1.** to believe or consider (something or someone) to be the cause or source of (something): *She ascribed her failures to bad luck.* **2.** to believe that (something) was made or done by (someone): *ascribed this painting to Picasso.* —**as•crip•tion** (ə skrip′shən) /əˈskrɪpʃən/ *n.* [*noncount*] See -SCRIB-.

a•sep•tic (ə sep′tik, ā sep′-) /əˈsɛptɪk, eyˈsɛp-/ *adj.* free from the germs that cause disease or infection: *aseptic surgical gloves.* —**a•sep′ti•cal•ly,** *adv.*

a•sex•u•al (ā sek′sho͞o əl) /eyˈsɛkʃuwəl/ *adj.* **1.** having no sex or sexual organs; not involving sexual processes of reproduction. **2.** free from or unaffected by sexuality: *an asexual friendship.* —**a•sex•u•al•i•ty** (ā sek′sho͞o al′i tē) /eyˌsɛkʃuwˈælɪtiy/ *n.* [*noncount*] —**a•sex′u•al•ly,** *adv.*

ash[1] (ash) /æʃ/ *n.* **1.** (pieces of) the gray or black powdery matter that remains after burning: [*noncount*]: *a volcano belching ash.* [*count*]: *cigarette ashes.* **2.** [*noncount*] finely pulverized lava thrown out by a volcano in eruption: *The city was covered with ash from the eruption.* **3.** [*noncount*] a light, silvery gray color. **4. ashes,** [*plural*] **a.** ruins, esp. the remains of something destroyed or lost forever: *left only with the ashes of former triumphs.* **b.** the remains of a disintegrated or cremated dead body.

ash[2] (ash) /æʃ/ *n.* **1.** [*count*] any of various trees of the olive family. **2.** [*noncount*] the tough wood of any of these trees.

a•shamed (ə shāmd′) /əˈʃeymd/ *adj.* feeling shame: [*be* + ~ + *of*]: *He was ashamed of himself.* [*be* + ~ + *to* + *verb*]: *She was ashamed to cry.* [*be* + ~ + *that clause*]: *She was ashamed that she had failed the test.* —**a•sham•ed•ly** (ə shā′mid lē) /əˈʃeymɪdliy/ *adv.* —**Usage.** See SHAME.

ash•en (ash′ən) /ˈæʃən/ *adj.* ash-colored; gray; extremely pale: *His face turned ashen with fear.*

a•shore (ə shôr′, ə shōr′) /əˈʃɔr, əˈʃowr/ *adv.* to or onto the shore: *She swam ashore from the raft.*

ash•ram (äsh′rəm) /ˈɑʃrəm/ *n.* [*count*] **1.** a quiet place away from populated areas, used for retreat or instruction in Hinduism. **2.** the community living there.

ash•tray (ash′trā′) /ˈæʃˌtrey/ *n.* [*count*] a bowl or small dish for tobacco ashes of smokers.

ash•y (ash′ē) /ˈæʃiy/ *adj.,* **-i•er, -i•est. 1.** pale: *her ashy face.* **2.** covered with ashes: *ashy ground.*

A•sian (ā′zhən) /ˈeyʒən/ *adj.* **1.** of or relating to Asia. *—n.* [*count*] **2.** a person born or living in Asia.

A•si•at•ic (ā′zhē at′ik) /ˌeyʒiyˈætɪk/ *adj., n.* [*count*] *Sometimes Offensive.* ASIAN.

a•side (ə sīd′) /əˈsayd/ *adv.* **1.** on or to one side; sideways: *She put her book aside and got up.* **2.** away from one's thoughts or consideration: *to put one's cares aside.* **3.** in reserve; in a separate place, as for safekeeping: *I put some money aside.* **4.** away from a group or area, esp. for privacy: *He took her aside to discuss the plan.* **5.** [*at the end of a phrase*] put apart; notwithstanding: *All kidding aside, let's talk seriously.* *—n.* [*count*] **6.** something spoken by an actor to or for the audience and supposedly not heard by others on stage. **7.** words spoken so as not to be heard by others present. **8.** a digression from a main topic. —***Idiom.*** **9. aside from, a.** in addition to; besides: *Aside from being too small, the jacket's color is ugly.* **b.** except for: *Aside from a few minor mistakes, this is a very good paper.*

as•i•nine (as′ə nīn′) /ˈæsəˌnayn/ *adj.* silly; stupid: *asinine remarks.* —**as′i•nine′ly,** *adv.* —**as•i•nin•i•ty** (as′ə nin′i tē) /ˌæsəˈnɪnɪtiy/ *n.* [*noncount; count*]

ask (ask, äsk) /æsk, ɑsk/ *v.* **1.** to put a question (to); inquire (of): [*no obj*]: *I asked but I never got an answer.* [~ + *obj*]: *I asked her but she didn't answer.* [~ + *obj* + *clause*]: *I asked him if they were going home.* **2.** to request information about: [~ + *obj*]: *He was ashamed to ask the question.* [~ + *after* + *obj*]: *He asked after you.* **3.** [~ + *obj*] to put into words so as to gain information, attention, etc.; utter: *You have to ask the right questions.* **4.** to request (of): [~ + *for* + *obj*]: *I asked for a little more time.* [~ + *obj*]: *I have to ask a favor of you.* [~ + *obj* + *obj*]: *Could I ask you a favor?* [~ + *to* + *verb*]: *I asked to leave early.* [~ + *obj* + *to* + *verb*]: *I asked her to leave early, but she wanted to stay.* **5.** [~ + *obj*] (of a price) **a.** to demand; expect: *What price are they asking?* **b.** to set a price of: *to ask $40 for the hat.* **6.** [~ + *obj* + *to* + *obj*] to invite: *to ask guests to dinner.* **7.** [~ + *for* + *obj*] to request to speak to (someone): *Your sister called and asked for you.* —***Idiom.*** **8. ask for it** or **ask for trouble,** to invite problems by continuing with risky or annoying behavior: *He's really asking for it, coming in late.*

a•skance (ə skans′) /əˈskæns/ *adv.* **1.** with a side glance; sidewise. **2.** [*look* + ~ + *at/on*] with disapproval or doubt: *My friends looked askance at my scheme.*

a•skew (ə skyo͞o′) /əˈskyuw/ *adv.* **1.** to one side; crookedly: *The picture was hanging askew.* *—adj.* [*be* + ~] **2.** crooked; not level or straight: *Your tie is askew.*

ask′ing price′, *n.* [*count*] the price at which something is offered by a seller.

a•sleep (ə slēp′) /əˈsliyp/ *adv.* **1.** in or into a state of sleep: *The baby was lying fast asleep in the crib.* *—adj.* [*be* + ~] **2.** sleeping: *He is asleep.* **3.** dormant; inactive: *The volcano has been asleep for years.* **4.** numb: *My foot is asleep.* **5.** inattentive; not paying attention: *He was asleep on the job.* —***Idiom.*** **6. fall asleep, a.** go into a state of sleep. **b.** (of a part of the body) become numb: *My foot fell asleep after a few hours of sitting still.*

a•so•cial (ā sō′shəl) /eyˈsowʃəl/ *adj.* not social; withdrawn from society; not caring about normal standards of behavior.

asp (asp) /æsp/ *n.* [*count*] a poisonous snake of Europe and Asia, esp. the horned viper.

as•par•a•gus (ə spar′ə gəs) /ə'spærəgəs/ *n.* [*noncount*] **1.** a plant of the lily family, grown for its edible shoots. **2.** the shoots themselves.

ASPCA, an abbreviation of: the American Society for the Prevention of Cruelty to Animals.

as•pect (as′pekt) /'æspɛkt/ *n.* **1.** [*count*] a particular part, feature, or phase of something: *There are many aspects to this problem.* **2.** [*count*] a particular way in which a thing may be looked at or considered; side: *Both aspects of the decision must be considered.* **3.** [*count*] appearance to the eye or mind: *The room took on the aspect of a prison cell.* **4.** expression (on one's face); attitude: [*count*]: *an aspect of quiet determination.* [*noncount*]: *was gloomy in aspect.* **5.** [*count*] the side or surface facing a given direction: *the northern aspect of the building.* **6.** [*noncount*] a grammatical category for verbs that indicates how long the action described is, whether it is repeating, if it is beginning, or if it has been completed: *The progressive aspect in English is indicated by a form of the verb "be" plus the -ing form of the main verb, as in "I am reading."* —**as•pec•tu•al** (a spek′chōō-əl) /æ'spɛktʃuwəl/ *adj.: the aspectual markers of English verb phrases.* See -SPEC-.

as•pen (as′pən) /'æspən/ *n.* [*count*] a kind of poplar tree of Europe and North America, having leaves that tremble in the slightest breeze.

as•per•i•ty (ə sper′i tē) /ə'spɛrɪtiy/ *n.* [*noncount*] **1.** harshness or sharpness of tone, temper, or manner; severity: *criticized them with some asperity.* **2.** hardship; difficulty; rigor: *a climate of great asperity.*

as•per•sion (ə spûr′zhən, -shən) /ə'spɜrʒən, -ʃən/ *n.* **1.** [*count; usually plural*] a damaging and usually false remark or criticism. —***Idiom.*** **2. cast aspersions on,** [~ + *obj*] to make false or misleading comments damaging to someone's reputation: *They cast aspersions on his qualities as a leader.*

as•phalt (as′fôlt) /'æsfɔlt/ *n.* [*noncount*] **1.** any of several kinds of dark-colored substances mixed with gravel, crushed rock, or the like used for paving: *They laid the asphalt for the driveway.* —*v.* [~ + *obj*] **2.** to pave with asphalt: *asphalted the driveway.*

as•phyx•i•a (as fik′sē ə) /æs'fɪksiyə/ *n.* [*noncount*] a dangerous condition involving loss of consciousness or death, caused by lack of oxygen in the blood, such as from suffocation.

as•phyx•i•ate (as fik′sē āt′) /æs'fɪksiy,eyt/ *v.,* **-at•ed, -at•ing. 1.** [~ + *obj*] to cause (someone) to lose consciousness or die by preventing normal breathing, as by gas or by smothering: *asphyxiated by carbon monoxide in the closed garage.* **2.** [*no obj*] to die or lose consciousness in this way: *The prisoners all asphyxiated in the sealed compartment.* —**as•phyx•i•a•tion** (as fik′sē-ā′shən) /æs,fɪksiy'eyʃən/ *n.* [*noncount*]

as•pic (as′pik) /'æspɪk/ *n.* [*noncount*] a jelly made with meat or fish juice, or tomato juice and gelatin, chilled and used in molded dishes or as a topping.

as•pir•ant (as′pər ənt, ə spīᵊr′ənt) /'æspərənt, ə'spayᵊrənt/ *n.* [*count*] a person who aspires: *numerous aspirants for the leader's affections.*

as•pi•rate (*v.* as′pə rāt′; *n., adj.* -pər it) /*v.* 'æspə,reyt; *n., adj.* -pərɪt/ *v.,* **-rat•ed, -rat•ing,** *n., adj.* —*v.* [~ + *obj*] **1. a.** to pronounce (a speech sound, esp. a sound like *p, t,* or *k*) so as to produce a puff of breath, as in the *t* of *top: In English the sounds of* p, t *and* k *at the beginning of most words are aspirated.* **b.** to pronounce (the beginning of a word or syllable) with an *h*-sound: *The* h *of the word* honor *is not aspirated, but the* h *of* habit *is aspirated.* **2. a.** to remove (a fluid) from a body cavity with a long hollow needle: *The doctor aspirated fluid from the cyst.* **b.** to inhale (fluid or a foreign body): *Small children sometimes aspirate foreign bodies such as peanuts.* —*n.* [*count*] **3.** a speech sound produced with a puff of breath, as initial *p, t,* or *k* in English or initial *h*-sounds: *The* p *in English* pot *is an aspirate, but the* p *in* spot *is not.* —*adj.* **4.** (of a speech sound) pronounced with aspiration; aspirated: *an aspirate* k *sound.*

as•pi•ra•tion (as′pə rā′shən) /,æspə'reyʃən/ *n.* **1.** [*count*] a strong desire; ambition; goal: *The presidency had been her aspiration since college.* **2.** [*noncount*] the pronouncing of a speech sound accompanied by a puff of breath: *English sounds like* p,t, *or* k *at the beginning of words have aspiration.* **3.** [*noncount*] the act of removing a fluid from the body with a hollow needle with suction.

as•pire (ə spīᵊr′) /ə'spayᵊr/ *v.* [*no obj*], **-pired, -pir•ing.** to long for, aim for, or try to get ambitiously: [~ + *to/after* + *obj*]: *He aspired to literary greatness.* [~ + *to* + *verb*]: *She aspired to become a professor.* —**as•pir′er,** *n.* [*count*] See -SPIR-.

as•pi•rin (as′pər in, -prin) /'æspərɪn, -prɪn/ *n., pl.* **-rin, -rins. 1.** [*noncount*] a white substance made from salicylic acid and used to relieve pain and fever; acetylsalicylic acid. **2.** [*count*] a tablet of aspirin: *Take an aspirin.*

as•pir•ing (ə spīᵊr′ing) /ə 'spayᵊrɪŋ/ *adj.* [*before a noun*] longing or aiming to be: *an aspiring actor.* —**as•pir′-ing•ly,** *adv.*

ass[1] (as) /æs/ *n.* [*count*] **1.** Also called **donkey.** a long-eared, slow, sure-footed mammal, related to the horse and used chiefly to carry things. **2.** a stupid, foolish, or stubborn person.

ass[2] (as) /æs/ *n.* [*count*] *Vulgar.* **1.** the buttocks. **2.** the rectum.

as•sail (ə sāl′) /ə'seyl/ *v.* [~ + *obj*] **1.** to attack vigorously or violently; assault: *The Marines assailed the enemy stronghold.* **2.** to attack verbally: *The press assailed the candidates.* **3.** to beset: *He was assailed by doubts.* —**as•sail′a•ble,** *adj.*

as•sail•ant (ə sā′lənt) /ə 'seylənt/ *n.* [*count*] an attacker: *Although she was blind she managed to beat off her assailant in the dark house.*

as•sas•sin (ə sas′in) /ə'sæsɪn/ *n.* [*count*] someone who murders for hire or from fanaticism.

as•sas•si•nate (ə sas′ə nāt′) /ə'sæsə,neyt/ *v.* [~ + *obj*], **-nat•ed, -nat•ing. 1.** to kill (someone) for hire or from fanaticism. **2.** to harm viciously: *to assassinate a person's character.* —**as•sas•si•na•tion** (ə sas′ə nā′shən) /ə,sæsə'neyʃən/ *n.* [*noncount; count*]

as•sault (ə sôlt′) /ə'sɔlt/ *n.* **1.** [*count*] a sudden violent attack; onslaught: *launched an assault on the enemy stronghold.* **2.** *Law.* an unlawful physical attack upon another, esp. an attempt or threat to do bodily harm: [*count*]: *Several assaults with deadly weapons.* [*noncount*]: *convicted of assault.* **3.** [*count*] RAPE[1] (defs. 1, 2). —*v.* [~ + *obj*] **4.** to make an assault upon: *The marines assaulted the hilltop.* **5.** to attack unlawfully; attempt to do bodily harm to another: *They assaulted the police officers.* **6.** RAPE[1] (def. 6).

assault′ ri′fle, *n.* [*count*] an automatic rifle that has features of a submachine gun.

as•say (*v.* a sā′; *n.* as′ā, a sā′) /*v.* æ'sey; *n.* 'æsey, æ'sey/ *v.* [~ + *obj*] **1.** to examine, analyze, or evaluate: *to assay a situation.* **2.** to examine and analyze (an ore, etc.) to determine how pure it is. —*n.* [*count*] **3.** an analysis of the parts of a substance, esp. to find out the amount of metal in an ore or alloy, or the amount of a drug in a substance.

as•sem•blage (ə sem′blij) /ə'sɛmblɪdʒ/ *n.* **1.** [*count*] a group of persons or things: *a great assemblage for the royal wedding.* **2.** [*noncount*] the act of assembling or the state of being assembled.

as•sem•ble (ə sem′bəl) /ə'sɛmbəl/ *v.,* **-bled, -bling. 1.** to come or bring together; gather into one place; meet: [*no obj*]: *The crowd assembled in the waiting room.* [~ + *obj*]: *The guides assembled the tourists together.* **2.** [~ + *obj*] to put together; put together the parts of: *assembled model airplanes.* See -SEMBLE-.

as•sem•bly (ə sem′blē) /ə'sɛmbliy/ *n., pl.* **-blies. 1.** a gathering or coming together of a number of persons: [*noncount*]: *an assembly of schoolchildren.* [*count; usually singular*]: *A great assembly of people appeared at the wedding.* **2.** [*count*] a group of persons gathered together in this way, as for educational purposes: *He addressed the assembly promptly at nine o'clock.* **3.** [*Usually: Assembly; proper noun*] a legislative body, esp. a lower house of the law-making body: *elected to the Assembly for a term of two years.* **4.** [*noncount*] a bugle call summoning troops to fall into ranks. **5.** [*noncount*] the putting together of parts, as of machinery, from parts of standard sizes: *assembly of the new bomber.* **6.** [*count*] a piece of such machinery so assembled: *airplane tail assemblies.* See -SEMBLE-.

assem′bly line′, *n.* [*count*] an arrangement of machines, tools, and workers in which a product is assembled in order as it is moved along a line by a conveyor belt.

as•sem•bly•man (ə sem′blē mən) /ə'sɛmbliymən/ *n.* [*count*], *pl.* **-men.** a member of a legislative assembly.

as•sent (ə sent′) /ə'sɛnt/ *v.* **1.** [*no obj; (~ + to + obj)*] to agree; give agreement: *They assented to that new proposal.* —*n.* [*noncount*] **2.** agreement, as to a proposal: *gave his assent to the plan.* See -SENT-.

as•sert (ə sûrt′) /ə'sɜrt/ *v.* [~ + *obj*] **1.** to state strongly or positively; declare strongly: *asserted his innocence.* [~ + *(that) clause*]: *asserted that he was innocent of the* *crime.* **2.** to make a claim to: *Minorities are now asserting their right to be heard.* —***Idiom.*** **3. assert oneself,** to claim one's rights or declare one's views firmly.

as•ser•tion (ə sûr′shən) /ə'sɜrʃən/ *n.* **1.** [*count*] a strong declaration, often without support or reason; allegation: *unfounded assertions.* **2.** an act of asserting: [*noncount*]: *the assertion of rights for minorities.* [*count*]: *an assertion of power.*

as•ser•tive (ə sûr′tiv) /ə'sɜrtɪv/ *adj.* confidently aggressive or self-assured; forceful: *an assertive personality.* —**as•ser′tive•ly,** *adv.* —**as•ser′tive•ness,** *n.* [*noncount*]

as•sess (ə ses′) /ə'sɛs/ *v.* [~ + *obj*] **1.** to estimate officially the value of (property) for tax purposes: *assessed the house at one million dollars.* **2.** to determine the amount of (damages, etc.): *The insurance adjustor assessed the damage at $1,000.* **3.** to impose a tax or other charge on: *to assess the club members for expenses.* **4.** to evaluate the importance or character of: *They met to assess the crisis.* See -SESS-.

as•sess•ment (ə ses′mənt) /ə 'sɛsmənt/ *n.* [*count*] **1.** the act or process of assessing: *a quick assessment of the situation.* **2.** the amount of money that a piece of property or some item is judged to be worth.

as•ses•sor (ə ses′ər) /ə 'sɛsər/ *n.* [*count*] a person who assesses the value of property, taxes, valuables, etc. See -SESS-.

as•set (as′et) /'æsɛt/ *n.* [*count*] **1.** a useful and desirable thing or quality: *math skill is an asset in business.* **2. assets,** [*plural*] **a.** the total resources of a person or business. **b.** the items listed on a balance sheet, esp. in relation to liabilities and capital. **c.** all property available to pay debts.

as•sid•u•ous (ə sij′o͞o əs) /ə'sɪdʒuwəs/ *adj.* **1.** diligent: *assiduous studying.* **2.** working diligently at a task; industrious: *an assiduous student.* —**as•sid′u•ous•ly,** *adv.* —**as•sid′u•ous•ness,** *n.* [*noncount*] See -SID-.

as•sign (ə sīn′) /ə'sayn/ *v.* **1.** to give out; allocate: [~ + *obj*]: *They assigned rooms at the hotel.* [~ + *obj* + *obj*]: *They assigned us a room.* [~ + *obj* + *to* + *obj*]: *They assigned a room to us.* **2.** to give out or announce as a task: [~ + *obj*]: *assigned his best man to the job.* [~ + *obj* (+ *to* + *obj*)]: *The teacher assigned a lot of homework (to the class).* [~ + *obj* + *obj*]: *The teacher assigned them a lot of homework.* [~ + *obj* + *to* + *verb*]: *They assigned a guard to watch.* **3.** [~ + *obj* + *to*] to appoint to a post or duty: *They assigned her to the day shift.* **4.** [~ + *obj*] to designate; name; specify: *Let's assign a day for a meeting.* **5.** [~ + *obj*] to give as a reason: *to assign a cause to certain unexplained events.* See -SIGN-.

as•sig•na•tion (as′ig nā′shən) /ˌæsɪg'neyʃən/ *n.* [*count*] an appointment for a meeting, esp. of lovers. See -SIGN-.

as•sign•ment (ə sīn′mənt) /ə'saynmənt/ *n.* [*count*] **1.** something assigned: *the homework assignments.* **2.** a position to which one is appointed: *an assignment as ambassador to France.*

as•sim•i•late (ə sim′ə lāt′) /ə'sɪməˌleyt/ *v.,* **-lat•ed, -lat•ing. 1.** [~ + *obj*] to take in and use as one's own; absorb; understand: *He tried to assimilate new ideas.* **2. a.** [*no obj*] (of a person from a different background) to adjust (oneself) to the dominant cultural group or national culture: *The immigrants assimilated rapidly.* **b.** [~ + *obj* (+ *into* + *obj*)] to bring (people from a different background) into a more dominant cultural group or national culture: *Guest workers need to be assimilated into that country.* **3.** [~ + *obj*] to convert to substances suitable for use: *to assimilate food.* —**as•sim•i•la•tion** (ə sim′ə-lā′shən) /əˌsɪmə'leyʃən/ *n.* [*noncount*] See -SIMIL-.

as•sist (ə sist′) /ə'sɪst/ *v.* **1.** to give support or aid (to); help: [~ + *obj*]: *She assisted me with my homework.* [*no obj;* (~ + *in/with* + *obj*)]: *He was asked to assist with the investigation.* —*n.* [*count*] **2.** (in sports) a play or pass helping a teammate to score or put out an opponent: *The basketball player had eight assists.* **3.** a helpful act: *He needed an assist when he was upset like that.* —**as•sis′tance,** *n.* [*noncount*] See -SIST-. —**Related Words.** ASSIST is a verb and a noun, ASSISTANT and ASSISTANCE are nouns, ASSISTANT can also be used as an adjective: *They ran forward to assist her. He needed an assist with the heavy packages. He is the doctor's assistant. She needed assistance getting out of bed. She is an assistant professor.*

as•sis•tant (ə sis′tənt) /ə'sɪstənt/ *n.* [*count*] **1.** a person who assists; helper: *was an assistant to the manager.* —*adj.* [*before a noun*] **2.** serving in a subordinate position: *an assistant secretary.*

as•sizes (ə sīz′əz) /ə'sayzəz/ *n.* [*plural*] (in England) trial sessions held regularly by a high court.

assn. or **Assn.,** an abbreviation of: association.

assoc., an abbreviation of: **1.** associate. **2.** associated. **3.** association.

as•so•ci•ate (*v.* ə sō′shē āt′, -sē-; *n., adj.,* -it, -āt′) /*v.* ə'sowʃiyˌeyt, -siy-; *n., adj.,* -ɪt, -ˌeyt/ *v.,* **-at•ed, -at•ing,** *n., adj.* —*v.* **1.** [~ + *obj* + *with* + *obj*] to connect or bring together in the mind: *I associate rainy days with spring.* **2.** [~ + *oneself* + *with* + *obj*] to connect or commit (oneself) as a colleague with another or with a group: *He refused to associate himself with cheats.* **3.** to unite; combine: [~ + *obj*]: *Coal was associated with shale.* [*no obj*]: *Coal and shale that associate in layers.* **4.** [~ + *with* + *obj*] to keep company as a friend, companion, or ally: *wouldn't allow her to associate with anyone who smoked or drank.* **5.** [*no obj*] to join together as partners or colleagues: *The two groups associated to form a political party.* —*n.* [*count*] **6.** a person who shares actively in an enterprise; co-worker. —*adj.* [*before a noun*] **7.** connected or related, esp. as a colleague: *an associate judge on the court.* **8.** having subordinate status: *an associate member of the staff.* See -SOC-. —**Related Words.** ASSOCIATE is a noun, a verb, and an adjective, ASSOCIATION is a noun: *She is an associate of mine. She associates with a nice group of people. She is an associate professor. We joined a neighborhood association to help fight crime.*

as•so•ci•a•tion (ə sō′sē ā′shən, -shē-) /əˌsowsiy'eyʃən, -ʃiy-/ *n.* **1.** [*count*] an organization of people with a common purpose: *an alumni association.* **2.** [*noncount*] the act of associating or the state of being associated: *I learned from my association with them.* **3.** [*count*] an idea suggested by or connected with something else: *Thinking of the small town I grew up in evokes many pleasant associations.* See -SOC-.

as•sort•ment (ə sôrt′mənt) /ə'sɔrtmənt/ *n.* [*count*] a collection of various kinds of things; mixed collection. —**as•sort′ed,** *adj.*

asst., an abbreviation of: assistant.

as•sume (ə so͞om′) /ə'suwm/ *v.* [~ + *obj*], **-sumed, -sum•ing. 1.** to take for granted without proof; suppose: *to assume that everyone wants peace.* **2.** to take upon oneself: *to assume responsibility.* **3.** to take over the duties or responsibilities of: *to assume the office of treasurer.* **4.** to pretend to have or be; feign: *to assume a humble manner.* —**as•sump•tion** (ə sump′shən) /ə'sʌmpʃən/ *n.* [*count; noncount*] See -SUM-.

as•sure (ə sho͝or′) /ə'ʃʊr/ *v.* [~ + *obj*], **-sured, -sur•ing. 1.** to declare positively or confidently to: *She assured us that everything would be all right.* **2.** to make (a future event) sure; guarantee: *This contract assures the company's profit this month.* **3.** to give confidence to; reassure. **4.** *Chiefly Brit.* to insure against loss. —**as•sur′ance,** *n.* [*count; noncount*]

as•ter (as′tər) /'æstər/ *n.* [*count*] a plant having rays of white, pink, or blue around a yellow disk. See -ASTRO-.

as•ter•isk (as′tə risk) /'æstərɪsk/ *n.* [*count*] a symbol (*), used as a reference mark or to indicate omission, doubtful matter, etc. See -ASTRO-.

a•stern (ə stûrn′) /ə'stɜrn/ *adv.* **1.** in a position behind a specified vessel: *The submarine was astern of its target.* **2.** at the back part of a ship: *The lookouts went astern.* **3.** in a backward direction: *The tug towed the barge astern to the shipyard.*

as•ter•oid (as′tə roid′) /'æstəˌrɔyd/ *n.* [*count*] any of the small, solid bodies that revolve about the sun in orbit chiefly between Mars and Jupiter. See -ASTRO-.

asth•ma (az′mə, as′-) /'æzmə, 'æs-/ *n.* [*noncount*] a breathing disorder often caused by an allergic reaction and characterized by spasms in the lungs, wheezing, and difficulty in breathing out.

asth•mat•ic (az mat′ik, as-) /æz 'mætɪk, æs-/ *n.* [*count*] **1.** a person who suffers from asthma. —*adj.* **2.** suffering from or caused by asthma.

a•stig•ma•tism (ə stig′mə tiz′əm) /ə'stɪgməˌtɪzəm/ *n.* a failure of the eye to see properly because parallel rays of light from the outside image do not line up and meet at a single point on the retina: [*noncount*]: *has astigmatism in one eye.* [*count; usually singular*]: *had a slight astigmatism.* —**as•tig•mat•ic** (as′tig mat′ik) /ˌæstɪg'mætɪk/ *adj.*

a•stir (ə stûr′) /ə'stɜr/ *adj.* [*be* + ~] **1.** being active; lively: *Suddenly the class was astir with interest.* **2.** out of bed: *awake and astir before dawn.*

as•ton•ish (ə ston′ish) /ə'stɒnɪʃ/ *v.* [~ + *obj*] to fill with sudden wonder; amaze: *The sudden victory astonished* *everybody.* —**Related Words.** ASTONISH is a verb, ASTONISHED and ASTONISHING are adjectives, ASTONISHMENT is a noun: *The tricks astonished the kids. The astonished onlookers gasped in amazement. The astonishing tricks entertained us for quite a while. You could see the look of astonishment on their faces.*

as•ton•ished (ə ston′isht) /əˈstɒnɪʃt/ *adj.* very surprised or amazed: *The astonished students couldn't believe they had all failed the physics test.*

as•ton•i•shing (ə ston′i shing) /əˈstɒnɪ ʃɪŋ/ *adj.* causing great surprise or amazement: *an astonishing victory.*

as•ton•ish•ment (ə ston′ish mənt) /əˈstɒnɪʃ mənt/ *n.* [*noncount*] a feeling of great surprise or amazement.

as•tound (ə stound′) /əˈstawnd/ *v.* [~ + *obj*] to overwhelm with amazement; astonish: *We were astounded by this amazing feat.*

as•tound•ing (ə stoun′ding) /əˈstawndɪŋ/ *adj.* causing great amazement or surprise; astonishing: *an astounding feat of strength.* —**as•tound′ing•ly,** *adv.*

as•tra•khan (as′trə kən, -kan′) /ˈæstrəkən, -ˌkæn/ *n.* [*noncount*] the tightly curled black or gray wool of lambs that come from Astrakhan, a Russian city, used for garments.

as•tral (as′trəl) /ˈæstrəl/ *adj.* of, concerning, or resembling stars: *astral bodies.* —**as′tral•ly,** *adv.*

a•stray (ə strā′) /əˈstrey/ *adv.* **1.** off the correct or known path or route; lost: *The letter must have gone astray.* **2.** away into error, confusion, or undesirable action or thought: *Wicked companions led her astray.* —*adj.* [*be* + ~] **3.** lost: *I was astray and couldn't find my way.* **4.** confused; in error: *was astray in those calculations.*

a•stride (ə strīd′) /əˈstrayd/ *prep.* **1.** with a leg on each side of; straddling: *rode astride the horse.* **2.** on both sides of: *Budapest lies astride a river.* —*adv.* **3.** in a posture of striding or straddling: *riding astride.*

as•trin•gent (ə strin′jənt) /əˈstrɪndʒənt/ *adj.* **1.** causing the skin to contract or tighten; styptic: *astringent lotion.* **2.** harshly biting; severe: *astringent criticism.* —*n.* [*count*] **3.** an astringent substance: *Apply an astringent to the cut.* —**as•trin′gen•cy,** *n.* [*noncount*] —**as•trin′gent•ly,** *adv.*

-astro-, *root.* *-astro-,* or *-aster-,* comes from Greek, where it has the meanings "star; heavenly body; outer space." These meanings are found in such words as: ASTER, ASTERISK, ASTEROID, ASTROLOGY, ASTRONOMY, ASTRONAUT, ASTRONAUTICS, DISASTER.

as•tro•labe (as′trə lāb′) /ˈæstrəˌleyb/ *n.* [*count*] an astronomical instrument used in ancient times to determine the position of the sun or stars. See -ASTRO-.

as•trol•o•gy (ə strol′ə jē) /əˈstrɒlədʒiy/ *n.* [*noncount*] the belief that heavenly bodies influence human affairs; the study of such influence. —**as•trol′o•ger, as•trol′o•gist,** *n.* [*count*] —**as•tro•log•i•cal** (as′trə loj′i kəl) /ˌæstrəˈlɒdʒɪkəl/ *adj.* See -ASTRO-.

as•tro•naut (as′trə nôt′, -not′) /ˈæstrəˌnɔt, -ˌnɒt/ *n.* [*count*] a person trained for space flight. See -ASTRO-, -NAUT-.

as•tro•nau•tics (as′trə nô′tiks, -not′iks) /ˌæstrəˈnɔtɪks, -ˈnɒtɪks/ *n.* [*noncount; used with a singular verb*] the science and technology of space flight. See -ASTRO-.

as•tron•o•mer (ə stron′ə mər) /əˈstrɒnəmər/ *n.* [*count*] a person who studies the moon, planets, stars, and the universe. See -ASTRO-.

as•tro•nom•i•cal (as′trə nom′i kəl) /ˌæstrəˈnɒmɪkəl/ also **as′tro•nom′ic,** *adj.* **1.** [*usually: before a noun*] of, relating to, or connected with astronomy. **2.** huge: *astronomical debts.* —**as′tro•nom′i•cal•ly,** *adv.*

astronom′ical u′nit, *n.* [*count*] a unit of length, equal to the distance of the earth from the sun: about 93 million miles (150 million km). *Abbr.:* AU

as•tron•o•my (ə stron′ə mē) /əˈstrɒnəmiy/ *n.* [*noncount*] the science that deals with the moon, planets, stars, and the universe beyond earth. See -NOM-[1], -ASTRO-.

as•tro•phys•ics (as′trō fiz′iks) /ˌæstrowˈfɪzɪks/ *n.* [*noncount; used with a singular verb*] the branch of astronomy that deals with the physical properties of celestial bodies and the interaction between matter and radiation. —**as•tro•phys•i•cist** (as′trō fiz′ə sist) /ˌæstrowˈfɪzəsɪst/ *n.* [*count*]

as•tute (ə sto͞ot′, ə styo͞ot′) /əˈstuwt, əˈstyuwt/ *adj.* **1.** very perceptive; wise: *an astute analysis of our problems.* **2.** crafty; quick to see an advantage: *an astute politician.* —**as•tute′ly,** *adv.* —**as•tute′ness,** *n.* [*noncount*]

a•sun•der (ə sun′dər) /əˈsʌndər/ *adv.* into separate parts; in or into pieces; apart: *The curtains were torn asunder.*

a•sy•lum (ə sī′ləm) /əˈsayləm/ *n.* **1.** [*count*] (esp. formerly) an institution for the care esp. of the mentally ill, orphans, or the poor. **2.** [*noncount*] protection given to a person or group, esp. political refugees. **3.** a place of safety or refuge: [*noncount*]: *He sought asylum far from his native land.* [*count*]: *countries that were asylums for refugees.*

a•sym•met•ric (ā′sə me′trik) /ˌeysəˈmɛtrɪk/ also **a′sym•met′ri•cal,** *adj.* having two sides or halves that are differently shaped: *an asymmetrical pattern.* —**a•sym•me•try** (ā sim′i trē) /eyˈsɪmɪtriy/ *n.* [*noncount*]

at (at; *unstressed* ət, it) /æt; *unstressed* ət, ɪt/ *prep.* **1.** (used to indicate a point, place, or location, as an address): *We met at the library.* **2.** (used to indicate a point of time): *It happened at midnight.* **3.** (used to indicate a location or position on a scale, or in order): *The temperature is at zero.* **4.** (used to indicate an occurrence or when something happens): *At low tide the waves aren't dangerous.* **5.** (used to indicate amount, degree, or rate): *went at great speed.* **6.** (used to indicate a direction, goal, or an attempt to do something or reach something): *Look at that; aimed at the target.* **7.** (used to indicate occupation or involvement): *watching the children at play.* **8.** (used to indicate a state or condition): *at peace with the world.* **9.** (used to indicate how something is done or accomplished): *They held me up at gunpoint.* **10.** (used to indicate a cause or source): *amazed at his skill.* **11.** (used to indicate relative quality or value): *I'll sell it to you at cost.*

at•a•vism (at′ə viz′əm) /ˈætəˌvɪzəm/ *n.* **1.** [*noncount*] the reappearance in an individual of characteristics, feelings, or behavior like those of some earlier ancestor. **2.** Also, **at•a•vist** (at′ə vist) /ˈætə vɪst/. [*count*] an individual who behaves this way; throwback. —**at′a•vis′tic,** *adj.*

ate (āt) /eyt/ *v.* the pt. of EAT.

-ate, *suffix.* **1.** *-ate* is used to form adjectives with the meaning "showing; full of": *passion + -ate → passionate (= showing passion); consider + -ate → considerate (= showing the action of considering); literate.* **2.** *-ate* is used to form verbs with the meaning "cause to become (like); act as": *regular + -ate → regulate (= make regular, act by rule); active + -ate → activate (= cause to become active); hyphenate; calibrate.* **3.** *-ate* is used to form nouns with the meanings: **a.** a group of people: *elector + -ate → electorate (= group who elect).* **b.** an area ruled by: *caliph (a kind of ruler) + -ate → caliphate (= area ruled by a caliph); protector + -ate → protectorate (= area ruled by a protecting nation).* **c.** the office, institution, or function of: *consul + -ate → consulate; magistrate; potentate.*

at•el•ier (at′l yā′) /ˌætlˈyey/ *n.* [*count*] a workshop or studio, esp. of an artist, artisan, or designer.

a•the•ism (ā′thē iz′əm) /ˈeyθiyˌɪzəm/ *n.* [*noncount*] the doctrine or belief that there is no God. —**a′the•ist,** *n.* [*count*] —**a′the•ist′ic,** *adj.* See -THEO-.

-athl-, *root.* *-athl-* comes from Greek, where it has the meaning "contest, prize." This meaning is found in such words as: ATHLETE, ATHLETICS, PENTATHLON.

ath•lete (ath′lēt) /ˈæθliyt/ *n.* [*count*] a person trained or skilled in athletics. See -ATHL-. —**Related Words.** ATHLETE is a noun, ATHLETIC is an adjective, ATHLETICS is a noun: *The Olympic athletes came from all over the world. She took part in an athletic competition. Athletics is an important part of the school's program.*

ath′lete's foot′, *n.* [*noncount*] ringworm of the feet.

ath•let•ic (ath let′ik) /æθˈlɛtɪk/ *adj.* **1.** physically active and strong; good at athletics or sports: *an athletic child.* **2.** [*before a noun*] of, like, or involving an athlete; for athletics: *an athletic field.* —**ath•let′i•cal•ly,** *adv.* See -ATHL-.

ath•let•ics (ath let′iks) /æθˈlɛtɪks/ *n.* **1.** [*plural; used with a plural verb*] athletic sports, such as running, rowing, or boxing. **2.** [*noncount; used with a singular verb*] the practice of athletic exercises or principles: *Athletics produces world-class competitors.* See -ATHL-.

-ation, *suffix.* *-ation* is attached to some verbs or adjectives (some of which end in -ATE) to form nouns, with the meaning "state or process of": *starve + -ation → starvation (= condition of starving); separate + -ation → separation (= state of being separate).*

-ative, *suffix.* *-ative* is attached to some verbs (some of which end in -ATE) and nouns to form adjectives: *regulate + -ative → regulative (= with the power to regulate); norm (= rule) + -ative → normative (= having rules).*

at•las (at′ləs) /ˈætləs/ *n.* [*count*] a book or bound collection of maps, charts, plates, or tables illustrating a subject: *a world atlas; a road atlas.*

ATM, an abbreviation of: automated-teller machine. See illustration at BANK.

at•mos•phere (at′məs fēr′) /ˈætməs,fɪər/ *n.* **1.** [*count*] **a.** [*usually singular; usually: the* + ~] the gases surrounding the earth; the air. **b.** the gases surrounding a planet, esp. the earth; air. **2.** [*count*] (in science) a unit of pressure, equal to the normal pressure of the air at sea level, about 14.7 pounds per square inch. **3.** [*count*] a surrounding mood that seems to fill a place, event, or situation: *an atmosphere of tension filled the classroom.* **4.** [*noncount*] a distinctive quality; character: *The room has a cozy atmosphere.* —**at•mos•pher•ic** (at′məs fer′ik, -fēr′-) /,ætməsˈfɛrɪk, -ˈfɪər-/ *adj.*

at•mos•pher•ics (at′məs fer′iks, -fēr′-) /,ætməsˈfɛrɪks, -ˈfɪər-/ *n.* **1.** [*plural; used with a plural verb*] radio noise caused by natural electromagnetic disturbances in the atmosphere. **2.** [*noncount; used with a singular verb*] the study of such phenomena: *Atmospherics is an important part of atmosphere studies.* **3.** [*plural; used with a plural verb*] the mood that a place or situation seems to have or to cause: *The atmospherics were electrifying at the boxing match.*

at. no., an abbreviation of: atomic number.

at•oll (at′ôl, -ol, -ōl) /ˈætɔl, -ɒl, -owl/ *n.* [*count*] a ring-shaped coral reef surrounding a lagoon.

at•om (at′əm) /ˈætəm/ *n.* [*count*] **1. a.** the smallest part of an element that still has the chemical properties of the element. **b.** this part of an element as the source of nuclear energy. **2.** a very small quantity: *There was not even an atom of truth in that remark.* See -TOM-.

a•tom•ic (ə tom′ik) /əˈtɒmɪk/ *adj.* [*before a noun*] **1.** of, relating to, resulting from, or using atoms, atomic energy, or atomic bombs. **2.** existing as free, uncombined atoms: *atomic hydrogen.* —**a•tom′i•cal•ly,** *adv.* See -TOM-.

atom′ic bomb′ or **at′om bomb′,** *n.* [*count*] a bomb whose power comes from splitting atoms of certain elements. Also called **A-bomb.**

atom′ic clock′, *n.* [*count*] an extremely accurate clock that uses the frequency of atoms of certain substances, as cesium, to regulate its speed.

atom′ic en′ergy, *n.* [*noncount*] the energy released by reactions in the atoms of certain elements; nuclear energy.

atom′ic mass′ or **atom′ic weight′,** *n.* [*count*] the mass of an atom that counts the number of protons and neutrons in its nucleus.

atom′ic num′ber, *n.* [*count*] the number of protons in the nucleus of an atom of an element.

at•om•ize (at′ə miz′) /ˈætə,mayz/ *v.* [~ + *obj*], **-ized, -iz•ing. 1.** to reduce (a liquid) to fine particles or spray: *to atomize a perfume.* **2.** to destroy (a target) with nuclear weapons. **3.** to split or divide (a group) into many sections, parts, or pieces. —**at•om•i•za•tion** (at′ə mi zā′shən) /,ætəmɪˈzeyʃən/ *n.* [*noncount*]

at•om•iz•er (at′ə mi′zər) /ˈætə,mayzər/ *n.* [*count*] a device that reduces liquids to a fine spray.

a•ton•al (ā tōn′l) /eyˈtownḷ/ *adj.* marked by atonality. See -TON-.

a•to•nal•i•ty (ā′tō nal′i tē) /,eytow ˈnælɪ tiy/ *n.* [*noncount*] music that does not rely on tonal centers or keys.

a•tone (ə tōn′) /əˈtown/ *v.* [~ + *for* + *obj*], **a•toned, a•ton•ing.** to make amends, as for an offense or sin.

a•tone•ment (ə tōn′mənt) /əˈtownmənt/ *n.* [*noncount*] **1.** an act or instance of atoning: *atonement for murder.* **2.** [*sometimes: the Atonement*] the Christian doctrine that God and humankind were reconciled by the suffering of Christ.

a•top (ə top′) /əˈtɒp/ *prep.* on the top of: *atop a hill.*

-ator, *suffix.* -*ator* is attached to verbs ending in -ATE to form nouns, with the meaning "person or thing that does or performs (the action of the verb)": *agitate* + *-ator* → *agitator* (= *person who agitates; machine that agitates); vibrate* + *-ator* → *vibrator* (= *thing that vibrates); narrator; generator; mediator; incubator.*

a•tri•um (ā′trē əm) /ˈeytriyəm/ *n.* [*count*], *pl.* **a•tri•a** (ā′trē ə) /ˈeytriyə/ **a•tri•ums. 1. a.** a central courtyard open to the sky, or a lobby with a skylight. **b.** the main or central room of an ancient Roman house, open to the sky at the center. **2.** a hollow space in the body, esp. one of the two upper chambers of the heart. —**a′tri•al,** *adj.*

a•tro•cious (ə trō′shəs) /əˈtrowʃəs/ *adj.* **1.** terribly wicked, cruel, or brutal: *an atrocious crime.* **2.** very bad or tasteless; abominable; appalling: *atrocious table manners.* —**a•tro′cious•ly,** *adv.* —**a•tro′cious•ness,** *n.* [*noncount*]

a•troc•i•ty (ə tros′i tē) /əˈtrɒsɪtiy/ *n., pl.* **-ties. 1.** [*noncount*] the quality or state of being atrocious; brutal behavior. **2.** [*count*] an atrocious act, thing, or circumstance.

at•ro•phy (a′trə fē) /ˈætrəfiy/ *n., v.,* **-phied, -phy•ing.** —*n.* [*noncount*] **1.** a wasting away of the body, as from poor nutrition, nerve damage, or disuse. —*v.* [*no obj*] **2.** to undergo atrophy; wither; degenerate: *His crippled leg began to atrophy with no exercise.* **3.** to become weakened; decline: *Industry atrophied in bad economic times.* —**at′ro•phied,** *adj.*

att., an abbreviation of: **1.** attached. **2.** attention. **3.** attorney.

at•tach (ə tach′) /əˈtætʃ/ *v.* **1.** to fasten or affix; join; connect: [~ + *obj*]: *to attach papers with a staple.* [~ + *obj* + *to* + *obj*]: *She attached the check to the tax form.* **2.** [~ + *obj* + *to* + *obj*] to join in action or function; make part of: *He attached himself to the gang.* **3.** [~ + *obj* + *to* + *obj*] to place on temporary duty with a military unit: *I was attached to the air division.* **4.** [~ + *obj* + *to* + *obj*] to include as a condition of something: *One proviso is attached to this agreement: you must tell no one about it.* **5.** [~ + *obj* + *to* + *obj*] to connect; attribute: *I wouldn't attach any significance to his remark.* **6.** [~ + *obj*] to take (persons or property) by legal authority: *attached part of his paycheck.* **7.** [~ + *to* + *obj*] to adhere; belong: *No blame attaches to him.*

at•ta•ché (a ta shā′, at′ə-) /ætæˈʃey, ,ætə-/ *n.* [*count*], *pl.* **-chés.** a diplomatic official or a military officer assigned to an embassy, esp. in a technical capacity.

attaché′ case′, *n.* [*count*] a flat, usually stiff briefcase for carrying business papers, documents, etc.

at•tached (ə tacht′) /ə ˈtætʃt/ *adj.* **1.** [*be* + ~ + *to*] fond of: *She is deeply attached to her family.* **2.** married or otherwise committed to another: *bachelors and others not yet attached.*

at•tach•ment (ə tach′mənt) /əˈtætʃmənt/ *n.* **1.** [*noncount*] the act of attaching or the state of being attached. **2.** [*noncount*] a feeling that binds one to a cause; strong belief in something; devotion: *strong attachment to religion.* **3.** [*count*] a feeling of fondness or devotion to someone or something: *began to feel an attachment to her new car.* **4.** [*count*] something that attaches to something else; something fastened or tied on. **5.** [*noncount*] the act of seizing property by legal authority.

at•tack (ə tak′) /əˈtæk/ *v.* **1.** to attempt to harm in an aggressive way; begin fighting with: [~ + *obj*]: *The dog attacked the prowler.* [*no obj*]: *The mugger attacked and ran away.* **2.** to begin hostilities against: [~ + *obj*]: *We attacked the enemy.* [*no obj*]: *The enemy may attack at dawn.* **3.** [~ + *obj*] to blame or criticize severely: *The politician attacked his opponent's ideas.* **4.** [~ + *obj*] to set about doing or working on vigorously: *The starving man attacked the meal.* **5.** [~ + *obj*] (of disease, poison, etc.) to begin to affect; harm: *That disease attacks the brain cells.* —*n.* **6.** the act of attacking; assault: [*count*]: *Several attacks took place at night.* [*noncount*]: *The village came under attack from the air.* **7.** [*count*] an episode of suffering from a disease or other condition: *a heart attack.* **8.** [*count*] an experiencing of some sensation or response: *an attack of remorse.* —**at•tack′er,** *n.* [*count*]

at•tain (ə tān′) /əˈteyn/ *v.* [~ + *obj*] to come to or arrive at; gain; achieve: *to attain one's goals.* —**at•tain•a•bil•i•ty** (ə tā′nə bil′i tē) /ə,teynəˈbɪlɪtiy/ *n.* [*noncount*] —**at•tain′a•ble,** *adj.* —**at•tain′er,** *n.* [*count*] See -TAIN-.

at•tain•ment (ə tān′mənt) /əˈteynmənt/ *n.* **1.** [*noncount*] the act or process of attaining: *the attainment of independence.* **2.** [*count*] something attained; achievement; accomplishment: *professional attainments.*

at•tar (at′ər) /ˈætər/ *n.* [*noncount*] a perfume or oil obtained from flowers or petals.

at•tempt (ə tempt′) /əˈtɛmpt/ *v.* **1.** to make an effort at; try; undertake: [~ + *obj*]: *They attempted a long hike.* [~ + *to* + *verb*]: *will attempt to finish the race.* [~ + *verb-ing*]: *She attempted walking across the tightrope.* —*n.* [*count*] **2.** an effort made to accomplish something: *The sketch was my first attempt.* **3.** an attack or assault: *An attempt was made on his life.*

at•tend (ə tend′) /əˈtɛnd/ *v.* **1.** [~ + *obj*] to be present at: *Children attend school each day.* **2.** to go with or happen as a result; accompany: [~ + *obj*]: *Fever may attend the flu.* [~ + *on/upon* + *obj*]: *The events that attended on the assassination were mysterious.* **3.** to take care (of); look after; deal with: [~ + *obj*]: *The nurse was at-*

tending her patient. [~ + *to* + *obj*]: *We were attending to the burn victims.* **4.** to wait upon; accompany or serve: [~ + *obj*]: *The retainers attended their lord.* [~ + *to* + *obj*]: *The salespeople couldn't attend to all the customers at once.* [~ + *upon* + *obj*]: *They had to attend upon the queen.* **5.** to pay attention; give care or thought to: [*no obj*]: *Attend closely while the teacher is speaking.* [~ + *to* + *obj*]: *Be sure to attend to your work.* See -TEND-.

at•tend•ance (ə ten′dəns) /ə'tɛndəns/ *n.* **1.** [*noncount*] the act of attending: *Regular attendance in class counts toward your grade.* **2.** [*count; singular*] the number of persons present: *a big attendance at last night's game.* **3. in attendance, a.** present: *How many people were in attendance?* **b.** able to look after or care for someone: *A doctor was in attendance.*

at•tend•ant (ə ten′dənt) /ə'tɛndənt/ *n.* [*count*] **1.** a person who waits on, cares for, or looks after someone or something. **—*adj.*** [*before a noun*] **2.** being present or in attendance; accompanying: *the champion with his attendant admirers.* **3.** associated; related: *poverty and its attendant hardships.*

at•ten•tion (*n.* ə ten′shən; *interj.* ə ten′shun′) /*n.* ə'tɛnʃən; *interj.* ə,tɛn'ʃʌn/ *n.* **1.** [*noncount*] the act of using the mind to concentrate on something: *listening with rapt attention to the speech.* **2.** [*noncount*] thoughtful consideration with a view to action: *I promise to give that matter my personal attention.* **3.** [*noncount*] kindness, courtesy, or high regard: *lavished attention on the guests.* **4. attentions,** [*plural*] acts of courtesy or devotion that show affection: *little attentions he bestowed on his wife.* **5.** [*noncount*] a position of standing with body erect, eyes forward, arms to the sides, and heels together. **—*interj.*** **6.** (used as a command to come to a position of attention). **7. pay attention (to),** give full thought, consideration, or notice to: [*no obj*]: *Pay attention while I show you what to do.* [*pay* + ~ + *to* + *obj*]: *Pay attention to your driving!*

atten′tion def′icit disor′der, *n.* [*noncount*] a disorder characterized by the inability to concentrate on tasks, by impulsiveness, and often overactivity.

at•ten•tive (ə ten′tiv) /ə 'tɛntɪv/ *adj.* **1.** showing attention: *attentive students.* **2.** thoughtful of others; polite: *was attentive to his aging mother.* **—at•ten′tive•ly,** *adv.* **—at•ten′tive•ness,** *n.* [*noncount*]

at•ten•u•ate (ə ten′yo͞o āt′) /ə'tɛnyuw,eyt/ *v.* [~ + *obj*], **-at•ed, -at•ing. 1.** to reduce in force, intensity, effect, or strength; weaken: *to attenuate desire.* **2.** to make thin. **—at•ten′u•a′tion,** *n.* [*noncount*]

at•test (ə test′) /ə'tɛst/ *v.* **1.** [~ + *obj*] to bear witness to, esp. officially: *I can attest the truth of her statement.* **2.** to give proof or evidence of: [~ + *to* + *obj*]: *I can attest to her reliability.* [~ + *obj*]: *This essay attests your writing ability.* See -TEST-.

at•tes•ta•tion (at′es tā′shən) /,ætɛs'teyʃən/ *n.* [*count*] a statement officially sworn to be true; testimony.

at•tic (at′ik) /'ætɪk/ *n.* [*count*] the part of a building, esp. of a house, directly under a roof.

at•tire (ə tiᵊr′) /ə'tayᵊr/ *v.,* **-tired, -tir•ing,** *n.* **—*v.*** [*usually: be attired*] **1.** to dress, array, or adorn, esp. for fancy occasions or ceremonies. **—*n.*** [*noncount*] **2.** clothes, esp. rich or splendid garments.

at•ti•tude (at′i to͞od′, -tyo͞od′) /'ætɪ,tuwd, -,tyuwd/ *n.* [*count*] **1.** manner or way one thinks about, behaves toward, or feels toward someone or something: *a cheerful attitude.* **2.** position or posture of the body: *knelt in a prayerful attitude.* **3.** the way in which an aircraft is lined up esp. with respect to the horizon. **4.** [*usually: an* + ~] *Slang.* a testy, uncooperative disposition: *has too much attitude and not enough ability.* **—at′ti•tu′di•nal** (at′i-to͞od′n l, -tyo͞od′-) /,ætɪ'tuwdn̩l, -'tyuwd-/ *adj.*

at•ti•tu•di•nize (at′i to͞od′n īz′, -tyo͞od′-) /,ætɪ'tuwdn̩,ayz, -'tyuwd-/ *v.* [*no obj*], **-nized, -niz•ing.** to assume a pretended mental attitude: *Stop attitudinizing and tell us what you really think.*

attn., an abbreviation of: attention.

at•tor•ney (ə tûr′nē) /ə'tɜrniy/ *n.* [*count*], *pl.* **-neys.** a lawyer.

attor′ney gen′eral, *n.* [*count*], *pl.* **attorneys general, attorney generals.** (*often caps.*) the chief law officer of a country or state and head of its legal department.

at•tract (ə trakt′) /ə'trækt/ *v.* [~ + *obj*] **1.** to cause to approach or come near; pull: *Magnets attract metal objects.* **2.** to draw by appealing to the emotions or senses: *The hearings attracted a lot of publicity.* **—at•trac′tor,** *n.* [*count*] See -TRAC-. **—Related Words.** ATTRACT is a verb, ATTRACTIVE is an adjective, ATTRACTION is a noun: *Magnets attract iron or steel. That actress is very attractive. A feeling of attraction came over her when she met him.*

at•tract•ant (ə trak′tənt) /ə'træktənt/ *n.* [*count*] a substance, usually a chemical, that attracts; lure.

at•trac•tion (ə trak′shən) /ə'trækʃən/ *n.* **1.** [*noncount*] the act, power, or property of attracting. **2.** [*noncount*] attractive quality; magnetic charm: *exerted a great attraction over the crowd.* **3.** [*count*] a characteristic or quality that provides pleasure; attractive feature: *tourist attractions.* **4.** [*noncount*] the electric or magnetic force that acts between oppositely charged bodies. See -TRAC-.

at•trac•tive (ə trak′tiv) /ə'træktɪv/ *adj.* **1.** providing pleasure or delight, esp. in appearance or manner; charming: *an attractive personality; an attractive face.* **2.** arousing interest; appealing: *an attractive idea.* **3.** having the quality of attracting: *the attractive power of gravity.* **—at•trac′tive•ly,** *adv.* **—at•trac′tive•ness,** *n.* [*noncount*] See -TRAC-.

at•trib•ut•able (ə trib′yə tə bəl) /ə 'trɪbyə tə bəl/ *adj.* [*be* + ~ + *to*] likely to have been caused by: *Some mistakes were attributable to fatigue and human error.*

at•trib•ute (*v.* ə trib′yo͞ot; *n.* a′trə byo͞ot′) /*v.* ə'trɪbyuwt; *n.* 'ætrə,byuwt/ *v.,* **-ut•ed, -ut•ing,** *n.* **—*v.*** [~ + *obj* + *to* + *obj*] **1.** to consider that something is the result of something else: *She attributes his bad temper to ill health.* **2.** to believe that a person or thing has a certain quality or characteristic: *It is a mistake to attribute too little intelligence to one's colleagues.* **3.** to reckon as created by an indicated source: *attributed the play to Shakespeare; attributed the remarks to me.* **—*n.*** [*count*] **4.** a quality or property believed to belong to a person or thing: *Sensitivity is one of his attributes.* **—at′tri•bu′tion,** *n.* [*noncount*]: *Those remarks are not for attribution, so you may not identify the speaker.*

at•trib•u•tive (ə trib′yə tiv) /ə'trɪbyətɪv/ *adj.* **1.** of or relating to an adjective or noun that comes directly before a noun it modifies. *The adjective* sunny *in the noun phrase* a sunny day *is attributive, and so is the noun* television *in the phrase* a television screen. **—*n.*** [*count*] **2.** an attributive word. **—at•trib′u•tive•ly,** *adv.*

at•tri•tion (ə trish′ən) /ə'trɪʃən/ *n.* [*noncount*] **1.** a reduction or decrease in numbers, size, or strength: *a gradual attrition in enrollment of foreign students.* **2.** a wearing down or weakening of resistance as a result of continuous pressure: *a war of attrition.* **3.** a gradual reduction in work force resulting usually from retirements, resignations, and deaths.

at•tuned (ə to͞ond′, ə tyo͞ond′) /ə'tuwnd, ə'tyuwnd/ *adj.* [*be* + ~ + *to*] **1.** being in harmony with; well-adjusted to: *She was attuned to country living. My ears were not attuned to the sound of gunfire.* **2.** keenly alert to: *attuned to any criticism.*

atty., an abbreviation of: attorney.

ATV, an abbreviation of: all-terrain vehicle, a vehicle, usually with three large wheels, designed to be used in areas where normal vehicles cannot be driven.

a•twit•ter (ə twit′ər) /ə'twɪtər/ *adj.* [*be* + ~] excited; alert: *The audience was all atwitter with anticipation.*

at. wt., an abbreviation of: atomic weight.

a•typ•i•cal (ā tip′i kəl) /ey'tɪpɪkəl/ also **a•typ′ic,** *adj.* not typical; unusual: *an atypical reaction for such a calm man.* **—a•typ′i•cal•ly,** *adv.* See -TYPE-.

au•burn (ô′bərn) /'ɔbərn/ *n.* [*noncount*] **1.** a reddish brown color. **—*adj.*** **2.** of this color: *auburn hair.*

au cou•rant (ō′ ko͞o rän′) /,ow ku'rɑ̃/ *adj.* **1.** [*be* + ~] up-to-date: *Those fashions are au courant.* **2.** [*be* + ~ + *with*] fully aware or familiar: *is au courant with the latest trends.*

auc•tion (ôk′shən) /'ɔkʃən/ *n.* [*count*] **1.** Also called **public sale.** a publicly held sale at which property or goods are sold to the highest bidder: [*count*]: *They held an auction to get rid of the equipment in the barn.* [*noncount*]: *They sold the house at auction.* **—*v.*** **2.** to sell by auction: [~ + *obj*]: *The bank auctioned the houses.* [~ + *off* + *obj*]: *auctioned off the old furniture.* [~ + *obj* + *off*]: *They auctioned the old furniture off.*

auc•tion•eer (ôk′shə nēr′) /,ɔkʃə'nɪər/ *n.* [*count*] a person who runs an auction.

-aud-, *root.* -*aud*- comes from Latin, where it has the meaning "hear." This meaning is found in such words as: AUDIBLE, AUDIENCE, AUDIO, AUDIT, AUDITION, AUDITORIUM, INAUDIBLE.

au•da•cious (ô dā′shəs) /ɔ'deyʃəs/ *adj.* **1.** extremely bold or daring: *an audacious plan to row a boat across the Atlantic.* **2.** extremely impolite; impudent: *audacious* behavior that would be punished. —**au•da′cious•ly,** *adv.* —**au•da′cious•ness,** *n.* [*noncount*]

au•dac•i•ty (ô das′i tē) /ɔ'dæsɪtiy/ *n.* [*noncount*] **1.** boldness or daring; nerve: *had the audacity to try something never tried before.* **2.** extreme impoliteness; impudence: *the audacity of his showing up three hours late!*

au•di•ble (ô′də bəl) /'ɔdəbəl/ *adj.* capable of being heard: *The student's answers were barely audible.* —**au•di•bil•i•ty** (ô′də bil′i tē) /ˌɔdə'bɪlɪtiy/ *n.* [*noncount*] —**au′di•bly,** *adv.* See -AUD-.

au•di•ence (ô′dē əns) /'ɔdiyəns/ *n.* [*count*] **1.** the group of people listening to or viewing a public event. **2.** the people reached by a radio or television show, by a book, etc.; the public: *a television audience of several million people.* **3.** a regular group of people that shows its interest for something; a following: *Politicians who promise to lower taxes have a large audience.* **4.** opportunity to be heard; chance to speak; a hearing: *He just wants a fair audience.* **5.** a formal meeting: *a private audience with the Pope.* See -AUD-.

au•di•o (ô′dē ō′) /'ɔdiyˌow/ *adj.* [*before a noun*] **1.** of, relating to, or used in the sending, receiving, or producing of sound: *audio equipment.* —*n.* [*noncount*] **2.** the elements of television that deal with sound: *The audio was OK but there was no picture.* **3.** the job or field of study concerned with sound recording, transmission, reception, and reproduction. See -AUD-.

au•di•o•phile (ô′dē ə fīl′) /'ɔdiyəˌfayl/ *n.* [*count*] a person who is strongly interested in high-quality sound reproduction.

au•di•o•tape (ô′dē ō tāp′) /'ɔdiyowˌteyp/ *n.* [*count*] magnetic tape on which sound is recorded; cassette. See illustration at SCHOOL.

au•di•o•vis•u•al or **au•di•o-vis•u•al** (ô′dē ō vizh′o͞o əl) /ˌɔdiyow'vɪʒuwəl/ *adj.* [*before a noun*] **1.** of, relating to, involving, or directed at both hearing and sight: *Audiovisual facilities included a VCR, a tape player, and a television monitor.* —*n.* **2. audiovisuals,** [*plural*] teaching aids using such facilities.

au•dit (ô′dit) /'ɔdɪt/ *n.* [*count*] **1.** an official examination and inspection of financial accounts and records: *an audit of the university's expenditures.* **2.** the inspection of something, as a building, to determine its safety, efficiency, or the like. —*v.* **3.** [~ + *obj*] to make an official examination of (accounts, records, etc.): *They audited our tax returns last year.* **4.** to attend (classes, lectures, etc.) as an auditor: [~ + *obj*]: *She audited the English class.* [*no obj*]: *She's not officially registered, so she's just auditing.* **5.** [~ + *obj*] to make an examination or inspection of (a building or other facility) to check safety or efficiency. See -AUD-.

au•di•tion (ô dish′ən) /ɔ'dɪʃən/ *n.* [*count*] **1.** a trial performance by an actor, singer, etc., to determine suitability for a part in a play, film, musical group, etc. —*v.* **2.** [~ + *obj*] to hear or view in an audition: *The director auditioned several hundred actors.* **3.** [*no obj;* (~ + *for* + *obj*)] to compete in an audition: *She auditioned for the part.* See -AUD-.

au•di•tor (ô′di tər) /'ɔdɪtər/ *n.* [*count*] **1.** a person who does financial audits. **2.** a student who attends a course to listen but not receive credit.

au•di•to•ri•um (ô′di tôr′ē əm, -tōr′-) /ˌɔdɪ'tɔriyəm, -'towr-/ *n.* [*count*], *pl.* **-to•ri•ums** or, sometimes, **-to•ri•a** (-tôr′ē ə, -tōr′-) /-'tɔriyə, -'towr-/. **1.** the space in a theater, school, or other public building for the audience: *The school band performed in the auditorium.* **2.** a building for public gatherings; hall. See -AUD-.

au•di•to•ry (ô′di tôr′ē, -tōr′ē-) /'ɔdɪˌtɔriy, -ˌtowriy-/ *adj.* relating to hearing or to the ear. See -AUD-.

Aug or **Aug.,** an abbreviation of: August.

au•ger (ô′gər) /'ɔgər/ *n.* [*count*] a tool for boring holes.

aught[1] (ôt) /ɔt/ *n.* [*noncount*] anything whatever; any part: *For aught I know, it may be true.*

aught[2] (ôt) /ɔt/ *n.* [*count*] zero (0).

aug•ment (ôg ment′) /ɔg'mɛnt/ *v.* [~ + *obj*] to make larger; enlarge in size, number, or strength; increase: *He taught English after work to augment his income.* —**aug′men•ta′tion,** *n.* [*count*] —**aug•ment′er,** *n.* [*count*]

au grat•in (ō grat′n, ō grät′n) /'ow grætn̩, 'ow grɑtn̩/ *adj.* [*after a noun*] topped with buttered breadcrumbs, grated cheese, or both and browned in an oven or broiler: *potatoes au gratin.*

au•gur (ô′gər) /'ɔgər/ *n.* [*count*] **1.** someone claiming to foretell future events; prophet. —*v.* **2.** [~ + *obj*] to divine or predict, as if from omens: *could not augur the future of the economy.* **3.** [~ + *for* + *obj*] to be a sign of good or bad things to come: *The movement of troops augurs poorly for peace. The decline in prices augurs well for the economy.*

au•gu•ry (ô′gyə rē) /'ɔgyəriy/ *n.* [*count*], *pl.* **-ries.** an indication of the future; omen; sign.

au•gust (ô gust′) /ɔ'gʌst/ *adj.* causing feelings of reverence: *an august personage.*

Au•gust (ô′gəst) /'ɔgəst/ *n.* [*proper noun*] the eighth month of the year, containing 31 days. *Abbr.:* Aug.

auk (ôk) /ɔk/ *n.* [*count*] a black and white diving bird of northern seas, having webbed feet and small wings.

aunt (ant, änt) /ænt, ɑnt/ *n.* [*count*] **1.** the sister of one's father or mother. **2.** the wife of one's uncle.

au pair (ō pâr′) /'ow pɛər/ *n.* [*count*] **1.** a person, esp. a young foreign visitor in a country, employed to take care of children, do housework, etc., in exchange for room and board. —*adj.* [*before a noun*] **2.** of, relating to, or employed under such an arrangement: *an au pair helper.*

au•ra (ôr′ə) /'ɔrə/ *n.* [*count*], *pl.* **-ras.** a quality or character surrounding something or someone: *He had an aura of respectability.*

au•ral (ôr′əl) /'ɔrəl/ *adj.* **1.** of or relating to the ear or to the sense of hearing: *aural stimulation.* **2.** [*before a noun*] of or relating to ability to understand spoken language: *aural comprehension of English.* —**au′ral•ly,** *adv.*

au•re•ole (ôr′ē ōl′) /'ɔriyˌowl/ also **au•re•o•la** (ô rē′ə-lə) /ɔ'riyələ/ *n.* [*count*], *pl.* **-oles** also **-o•las.** a ring of light or color that circles something; halo.

au re•voir (ō′ rə vwär′) /ˌow rə'vwɑr/ *interj. French.* until we see each other again; good-bye for now.

au•ri•cle (ôr′i kəl) /'ɔrɪkəl/ *n.* [*count*] **1.** the outer ear. **2.** one of the upper chambers of the heart; atrium.

au•ric•u•lar (ô rik′yə lər) /ɔ'rɪkyələr/ *adj.* **1.** of or relating to the ear or to hearing; aural. **2.** told in private: *an auricular confession.*

au•ro•ra (ə rôr′ə, ə rōr′ə) /ə'rɔrə, ə'rowrə/ *n.* [*count*], *pl.* **au•ro•ras, au•ro•rae** (ə rôr′ē, ə rōr′ē) /ə'rɔriy, ə'rowriy/. **1.** dawn. **2.** bands of colored light in the upper atmosphere, visible at night in polar areas.

auro′ra aus•tra′lis (ô strā′lis) /ɔ'streylɪs/ *n.* [*count; usually singular; the* + ~] the aurora of the Southern Hemisphere. Also called **southern lights.**

auro′ra bo•re•al′is (bôr′ē al′is, -ā′lis, bōr′-) /ˌbɔriy'ælɪs, -'eylɪs, ˌbowr-/ *n.* [*count; usually singular; the* + ~] the aurora of the Northern Hemisphere. Also called **northern lights.**

aus•pic•es (ô′spə siz) /'ɔspə sɪz/ *n.* [*plural*] Usually, **under the auspices of,** with the support and approval of; helped by: *under the auspices of the government.*

aus•pi•cious (ô spish′əs) /ɔ'spɪʃəs/ *adj.* **1.** promising success; favorable: *auspicious signs.* **2.** favored by fortune; prosperous: *an auspicious year.* —**aus•pi′cious•ly,** *adv.* —**aus•pi′cious•ness,** *n.* [*noncount*]

Aus•sie (ô′sē; *esp. Brit.* oz′ē, ô′zē) /'ɔsiy; *esp. Brit.* 'ɒziy, 'ɔziy/ *n.* [*count*], *adj.* [*before a noun*] *Informal.* (an) Australian.

aus•tere (ô stēr′) /ɔ'stɪər/ *adj.* **1.** severe in manner, appearance, or morals; strict; serious: *an austere man of the church.* **2.** without excess, luxury, or ease: *an austere life.* **3.** without decoration or ornament; severely simple: *an austere room.* —**aus•tere′ly,** *adv.* —**aus•tere′ness,** *n.* [*noncount*]

aus•ter•i•ty (ô ster′ə tē) /ɔ 'stɛrə tiy/ *n., pl.* **-ties. 1.** [*noncount*] a simple lifestyle; not using luxuries: *the austerity of life in the wilderness.* **2.** hardship caused by war, economic downturn, etc.: [*noncount*]: *in times of austerity.* [*count*]: *the austerities of wartime.*

Aus•tral•ian (ô strāl′yən) /ɔ'streylyən/ *n.* **1.** [*count*] a person born or living in Australia. **2.** [*noncount*] any of the languages spoken by the aboriginal inhabitants of Australia. —*adj.* **3.** of or relating to Australia.

Aus•tri•an (ô′strē ən) /'ɔstriyən/ *n.* [*count*] **1.** a person born or living in Austria. —*adj.* **2.** of or relating to Austria.

au•then•tic (ô then′tik) /ɔ'θɛntɪk/ *adj.* **1.** not false; genuine; real: *an authentic team jacket.* **2.** that can be believed; trustworthy; true: *an authentic report.* —**au•then′ti•cal•ly,** *adv.*

au•then•ti•cate (ô then′ti kāt′) /ɔ'θɛntɪˌkeyt/ *v.* [~ + *obj*], **-cat•ed, -cat•ing. 1.** to establish (something) as genuine, real, or true: *The signature was not authenticated.* **2.** to establish or prove conclusively the origin of (a painting, book, etc.): *to authenticate a painting.* —**au•then•ti•ca•tion** (ô then′ti kā′shən) /ɔˌθɛntɪ'keyʃən/ *n.* [*noncount*]: *The signature is subject to authentication.* [*count; usually singular*]: *I need an authentication on a credit card, please.*

au•then•tic•i•ty (ô′then tis′i tē, ô′thən-) /ˌɔθɛn'tɪsɪtiy, ˌɔθən-/ *n.* [*noncount*] the condition of being authentic, genuine, or true: *verified the authenticity of the signature.*

au•thor (ô′thər) /'ɔθər/ *n.* [*count*] **1.** someone who creates a book, article, etc.; writer. **2.** the writer of a software program. **3.** the maker of anything; creator: *the author of the new tax plan.* **—***v.* [~ + *obj*] **4.** to be the author of: *to author a novel.*

au•thor•i•tar•i•an (ə thôr′i târ′ē ən, ə thor′-) /əˌθɔrɪ'tɛəriyən, əˌθɒr-/ *adj.* **1.** of, favoring, or requiring complete obedience to authority: *an authoritarian military code.* **2.** of, relating to, or being a government in which authority is centered in one person or in a small group that has complete control over the people: *an authoritarian regime.* **—***n.* [*count*] **3.** a person who favors or acts according to authoritarian principles. —**au•thor′i•tar′i•an•ism,** *n.* [*noncount*]

au•thor•i•ta•tive (ə thôr′i tā′tiv, ə thor′-) /ə'θɔrɪˌteytɪv, ə'θɒr-/ *adj.* **1.** having or showing authority; official: *authoritative orders.* **2.** supported by evidence and accepted; able to be trusted: *the authoritative account of the story.* **3.** having an air or appearance of authority: *an authoritative manner.* —**au•thor′i•ta′tive•ly,** *adv.* —**au•thor′i•ta′tive•ness,** *n.* [*noncount*]

au•thor•i•ty (ə thôr′i tē, ə thor′-) /ə'θɔrɪtiy, ə'θɒr-/ *n., pl.* **-ties. 1.** [*noncount*] the right, power, or ability to control, command, or decide. **2.** [*noncount*] power or right officially given; authorization; permission. **3.** [*count*] a body of persons to whom the right to command or decide issues is given, as a government. **4.** [*count*] Usually, **authorities.** [*plural*] persons having the legal power to make and enforce the law; government: *surrendered to the authorities.* **5.** [*count*] an accepted source of information or advice: *That book is the authority on the subject.* **6.** [*count*] an expert on a subject: *Ask questions of a real authority on baseball.* **7.** [*noncount*] forcefulness; showing strong belief or conviction: *speaks with authority when he lectures.* **—*Idiom.* 8. have it on good authority,** [~ + *that clause*] to have information from a reliable source: *I have it on good authority that she is about to announce her candidacy.*

au•thor•i•za•tion (ô′thə rə zā′shən) /ˌɔθə rə 'zeyʃən/ *n.* the official permission or right given to do something: [*noncount*]: *had government authorization to conduct research.* [*count*]: *needs a written authorization.*

au•thor•ize (ô′thə rīz′) /'ɔθəˌrayz/ *v.,* **-ized, -iz•ing. 1.** [~ + *obj* + *to* + *verb*] to give authority to: *I am not authorized to pay you now.* **2.** [~ + *obj*] to give authority for: *He authorized increased spending on medical research.*

au•thor•ship (ô′thər ship′) /'ɔθərˌʃɪp/ *n.* [*noncount*] **1.** the source of a written, musical, or artistic work: *debated the authorship of that poem.* **2.** the career of writing.

au•tism (ô′tiz əm) /'ɔtɪzəm/ *n.* [*noncount*] a usually developmental disorder characterized by reduced ability to communicate, a withdrawal into oneself, and detachment from reality. —**au•tis•tic** (ô tis′tik) /ɔ'tɪstɪk/ *adj.* —**au•tis′ti•cal•ly,** *adv.*

au•to (ô′tō) /'ɔtow/ *n.* [*count*], *pl.* **-tos.** an automobile.

auto-, *prefix. auto-* comes from Greek, where it has the meaning "self." This meaning is found in such words as: AUTOCRAT, AUTOGRAPH, AUTONOMOUS, AUTONOMY, AUTOPSY. Also, *esp. before a vowel,* **aut-.**

au•to•bahn (ô′tə bon′) /'ɔtə ˌbɒn/ *n.* [*count*] a highway in Germany.

au•to•bi•o•graph•i•cal (ô′tə bī ə graf′i kəl) /ˌɔtə bay ə 'græfɪ kəl/ *adj.* of or relating to books or a history of a person's life as told or written by that person. See -GRAPH-.

au•to•bi•og•ra•phy (ô′tə bī og′rə fē) /ˌɔtəbay'ɒgrəfiy/ *n.* [*count*], *pl.* **-phies.** a history of a person's life written or told by that person. —**au′to•bi•og′ra•pher,** *n.* [*count*] See -GRAPH-.

au•toc•ra•cy (ô tok′rə sē) /ɔ'tɒkrəsiy/ *n., pl.* **-cies. 1.** [*noncount*] government in which one person has unlimited power or authority. **2.** [*count*] a nation, state, or community ruled by an autocrat.

au•to•crat (ô′tə krat′) /'ɔtəˌkræt/ *n.* [*count*] **1.** a ruler who has unlimited or complete power. **2.** a person who makes decisions or gives orders to others in an autocratic manner: *an office autocrat.*

au•to•crat•ic (ô′tə kra′tik) /ˌɔtə 'krætɪk/ *adj.* **1.** of or relating to the rule of an autocrat: *an autocratic government.* **2.** exercising power in a tyrannical way; despotic: *autocratic management style.* —**au′to•crat′i•cal•ly,** *adv.*

au•to•di•dact (ô′tō dī′dakt, -dī dakt′) /ˌɔtow'daydækt, -day'dækt/ *n.* [*count*] a self-taught person; a person who has learned a subject without formal instruction. —**au′to•di•dac′tic,** *adj.* —**au′to•di•dac′ti•cal•ly,** *adv.*

au•to•graph (ô′tə graf′) /'ɔtəˌgræf/ *n.* [*count*] **1.** a person's signature, esp. that of a famous person for keeping as a memento. **—***v.* [~ + *obj*] **2.** to write one's name on or in: *autographed the baseball for a fan.* See -GRAPH-.

au•to•im•mune (ô′tō i myōōn′) /ˌɔtowɪ'myuwn/ *adj.* [*before a noun*] of or relating to the part of the immune system of an organism that acts against its own components. —**au′to•im•mu′ni•ty,** *n.* [*noncount*]

au•to•mate (ô′tə māt′) /'ɔtəˌmeyt/ *v.,* **-mat•ed, -mat•ing.** to use machines instead of people to do the work of (a mechanical process, etc.); apply the principles of automation to: [~ + *obj*]: *We need to automate those procedures.* [*no obj*]: *The investors want us to automate.* —**au•to•ma•tion** (ô′tə mā′shən) /ˌɔtə'meyʃən/ *n.* [*noncount*]

au′tomated-tell′er machine′, *n.* [*count*] an electronic machine that provides banking services when it is activated by inserting a special plastic card. *Abbr.:* ATM

au•to•mat•ic (ô′tə mat′ik) /ˌɔtə'mætɪk/ *adj.* **1.** having the capability of operating independently without human aid: *an automatic sprinkler system.* **2.** occurring without conscious thought, as certain muscular actions; involuntary; reflex: *The blink of an eyelid is an automatic action.* **3.** done unconsciously or from force of habit; mechanical: *His smoking had become automatic.* **4.** always following some other event as its cause; certain to happen: *Driving drunk means an automatic fine.* **5.** (of a firearm) able to be fired repeatedly with one squeeze of the trigger: *automatic rifles.* **—***n.* [*count*] **6.** a machine or device that operates automatically: *Most washing machines are automatics.* **7.** an automatic pistol or rifle. **8.** an automobile equipped with automatic transmission. **—*Idiom.* 9. on automatic,** being operated or controlled by or as if by an automatic device. —**au′to•mat′i•cal•ly,** *adv.*

au′tomat′ic pi′lot, *n.* [*count*] **1.** an electronic control system that automatically keeps an aircraft, ship, spacecraft, etc., on course. Also called **autopilot. —*Idiom.* 2. on automatic pilot,** being operated or controlled by or as if by an automatic device; on automatic.

au•tom•a•ton (ô tom′ə ton′, -tn) /ɔ'tɒməˌtɒn, -tn̩/ *n.* [*count*], *pl.* **-tons, -ta** (-tə) /-tə/. **1.** a small mechanical figure built to act and move as if by its own power; robot. **2.** a person who acts mechanically.

au•to•mo•bile (ô′tə mə bēl′, ô′tə mə bēl′) /ˌɔtəmə'biyl, 'ɔtəməˌbiyl/ *n.* [*count*] **1.** a passenger vehicle usually having four wheels and a gasoline or diesel engine. **—***adj.* [*before a noun*] **2.** automotive: *the automobile industry.* See -MOT-.

au•to•mo•tive (ô′tə mō′tiv, ô′tə mō′tiv) /ˌɔtə'mowtɪv, 'ɔtəˌmowtɪv/ *adj.* [*before a noun*] **1.** of or relating to automobiles or other motor vehicles: *automotive parts.* **2.** propelled by a self-contained motor. See -MOT-.

au′to•nom′ic nerv′ous sys′tem (ô′tə nom′ik) /ˌɔtə'nɒmɪk/ *n.* [*count*] the system of nerves that controls the involuntary functions of the heart, blood vessels, certain muscles, glands, and other parts of the body. See -NOM-[1].

au•ton•o•mous (ô ton′ə məs) /ɔ'tɒnəməs/ *adj.* **1.** self-governing: *an autonomous republic.* **2.** able to act on one's own; independent: *With your own business you will be autonomous.* —**au•ton′o•mous•ly,** *adv.* See -NOM-[1].

au•ton•o•my (ô ton′ə mē) /ɔ'tɒnəmiy/ *n.* [*noncount*] **1.** (of a state or government) self-government; independence. **2.** freedom of action: *The corporation gives their agents a fair amount of autonomy.* See -NOM-[1].

au•to•pi•lot (ô′tō pī′lət) /'ɔtowˌpaylət/ *n.* [*count*] automatic pilot.

au•top•sy (ô′top sē) /'ɔtɒpsiy/ *n., pl.* **-sies,** *v.,* **-sied, -sy•ing. —***n.* [*count*] **1.** the examination or inspection of a dead body to determine the cause of death; postmortem. **2.** a critical analysis of something past: *After the game the coach conducted an autopsy of the team's performance.* **—***v.* [~ + *obj*] **3.** to perform an autopsy on: *autopsied the body.* See -OPTI-, -OPT-.

au•tumn (ô′təm) /'ɔtəm/ *n.* **1.** the season between summer and winter; fall: [*noncount*]: *In autumn the leaves fall.* [*count*]: *Autumns are fairly mild in that region.* **2.** [*noncount*] a time of late maturity: *the autumn of one's life.* —**au•tum•nal** (ô tum′nl) /ɔ'tʌmnl̩/ *adj.*

aux•il•ia•ry (ôg zil′yə rē, -zil′ə-) /ɔg'zɪlyəriy, -'zɪlə-/ *adj., n., pl.* **-ries. —***adj.* **1.** additional; secondary; used as a substitute or reserve when needed: *an auxiliary power station.* **2.** giving support; serving as an aid: *They served in an auxiliary capacity.* **—***n.* [*count*] **3.** a person or thing that gives aid; helper. **4.** an auxiliary organization: *The women's auxiliary raised money for the school.* **5.** AUXILIARY VERB.

auxil′iary verb′, *n.* [*count*] a verb used with a main verb, to express time, aspect, mood, etc. Examples of auxiliaries are: *Did* in *Did you go?; have* in *We have spoken;* and *can* in *They can see.*

av., an abbreviation of: **1.** avenue. **2.** average.

a•vail (ə vāl′) /ə'veyl/ *v.* **1.** to be of use or value to; profit: [~ + *obj*]: *All our efforts availed us little.* [*no obj*]: *Nothing you do will avail.* **2. avail oneself of,** [~ + *oneself* + *of* + *obj*] to make use or take advantage: *You should avail yourself of every opportunity for financial aid.* **—***n.* [*noncount*] **3. to no avail, to little avail,** without success: *I searched for a job, but to no avail.*

a•vail•a•bil•i•ty (ə vā′lə bil′i tē) /ə,veylə'bɪlɪtiy/ *n.* [*noncount*] the condition of being available.

a•vail•a•ble (ə vā′lə bəl) /ə'veyləbəl/ *adj.* **1.** suitable or ready for use; at hand: *I used whatever tools were available.* **2.** easily obtained; easy to use: *Plenty of information was available.* **3.** free or ready to be seen, spoken to, employed, etc.: *She is not available for comment.*

av•a•lanche (av′ə lanch′) /'ævə,læntʃ/ *n.* [*count*] **1.** a large mass of snow, ice, etc., that comes loose from a mountain slope and slides or falls suddenly downward. **2.** anything like an avalanche in suddenness and volume: *received an avalanche of fan mail.*

a•vant-garde (ä′vänt′gärd′, av′änt-) /,ɑvɑnt'gɑrd, ,ævɑnt-/ *n.* [*plural; used with a plural verb*] **1.** the group of artists, writers, musicians, filmmakers, etc., whose work is considered modern, advanced, or experimental. **—***adj.* **2.** characteristic of or belonging to the avant-garde: *The paintings were very avant-garde.*

av•a•rice (av′ər is) /'ævərɪs/ *n.* [*noncount*] extreme greed for wealth. **—av•a•ri•cious** (av′ə rish′əs) /,ævə'rɪʃəs/ *adj.* **—av′a•ri′cious•ly,** *adv.*

a•vast (ə vast′) /ə'væst/ *v.* (used as a nautical command) Stop!

av•a•tar (av′ə tär′) /'ævə,tɑr/ *n.* [*count*] an appearance of a Hindu god, esp. in human form.

avdp., an abbreviation of: avoirdupois.

ave., an abbreviation of: avenue.

a•venge (ə venj′) /ə'vɛndʒ/ *v.* [~ + *obj*], **a•venged, a•veng•ing. 1.** to take or get revenge for (something): *wanted to avenge the murder of his sister.* **2.** to take or get revenge for or on behalf of (someone): *avenged her by finding her murderers.* **—a•veng′er,** *n.* [*count*] See -VENGE-.

av•e•nue (av′ə nyo͞o′, -no͞o′) /'ævə,nyuw, -,nuw/ *n.* [*count*] **1.** a wide street or main road. **2.** a way or means of getting to or from something: *avenues of escape.* See -VEN-.

a•ver (ə vûr′) /ə'vɜr/ *v.* [~ + *obj*], **a•verred, a•ver•ring.** to declare in a very positive or strong manner; assert: *He averred his innocence.* [~ + *that clause*]: *She averred that her child would never cheat on a test.* See -VERT-.

av•er•age (av′ər ij, av′rij) /'ævərɪdʒ, 'ævrɪdʒ/ *n., adj., v.,* **-aged, -ag•ing. —***n.* **1.** [*count*] the number that results from adding several quantities together and then dividing that total by the number of quantities that were added; arithmetic mean: *Their high-school averages were very high, usually 97 or above.* **2.** a typical, usual, or normal amount, rate, degree, level, etc.: [*count; usually singular*]: *The people in that village lived for an average of seventy years.* [*noncount*]: *Her work is well above average.* **—***adj.* **3.** [*before a noun*] of, relating to, or forming an average: *The average rainfall is only six inches a year.* **4.** [*before a noun*] typical; common; ordinary: *the average person.* **5.** of middle quality; fair: *got only average grades in school.* **—***v.* **6.** [~ + *obj*] to find an average of: *She averaged the scores of her last three tests and came up with 93.* **7.** [~ + *obj*] to do, have, or get on the average: *to average seven hours of sleep a night.* **8. average out,** [+ *out* (+ *to* + *obj*)] to reach or show an average: *My taxes average out to a third of my income. I earn different amounts each month, but it usually averages out.* **—*Idiom.* 9. on the** or **an average,** usually; typically: *On the average I see about ten students a day.*

a•verse (ə vûrs′) /ə'vɜrs/ *adj.* [*be* + ~ + *to*] having a strong feeling of opposition to; unwilling: *not averse to spending the night here.* See -VERT-.

a•ver•sion (ə vûr′zhən, -shən) /ə'vɜrʒən, -ʃən/ *n.* [*count*] **1.** a strong feeling of dislike, disgust, or hatred toward something and a desire to avoid it: *She has an aversion to snakes.* **2.** a cause or object of such a feeling: *Snakes are an aversion of hers.* See -VERT-.

a•vert (ə vûrt′) /ə'vɜrt/ *v.* [~ + *obj*] **1.** to turn away or aside: *to avert one's eyes.* **2.** to ward off; prevent from happening; avoid: *to avert an accident.* See -VERT-.

avg., an abbreviation of: average.

a•vi•an (ā′vē ən) /'eyviyən/ *adj.* [*usually: before a noun*] of or relating to birds: *an avian species.*

a•vi•ar•y (ā′vē er′ē) /'eyviy,ɛriy/ *n.* [*count*], *pl.* **-ies.** a large enclosed area in which birds are kept.

a•vi•a•tion (ā′vē ā′shən) /,eyviy'eyʃən/ *n.* [*noncount*] **1.** the design, development, production, operation, or use of aircraft. **2.** military aircraft.

a•vi•a•tor (ā′vē ā′tər) /'eyviy,eytər/ *n.* [*count*] a pilot of an airplane or other heavier-than-air aircraft.

a•vi•a•trix (ā′vē ā′triks) /,eyviy'eytrɪks/ *n.* [*count*], *pl.* **-a•tri•ces** (-ā′trə sēz′) /-'eytrə,siyz/. a woman aviator.

av•id (av′id) /'ævɪd/ *adj.* **1.** [*before a noun*] enthusiastic; ardent: *an avid moviegoer.* **2.** [*be* + ~ + *for*] very desirous; eager: *was avid for movies.* **—av′id•ly,** *adv.*

a•vi•on•ics (ā′vē on′iks) /,eyviy'ɒnɪks/ *n.* [*noncount; used with a singular verb*] the science and development of electronic devices used in aerospace vehicles. **—a′vi•on′ic,** *adj.*

av•o•ca•do (av′ə kä′dō, ä′və-) /,ævə'kɑdow, ,ɑvə-/ *n.* [*count*], *pl.* **-dos. 1.** a large, pear-shaped fruit having green to blackish skin and a soft, light green inside that can be eaten. **2.** a tropical American tree that bears this fruit. **3.** a yellowish-green color.

av•o•ca•tion (av′ə kā′shən) /,ævə'keyʃən/ *n.* [*count*] a secondary occupation: *The surgeon's avocation is teaching the handicapped.* See -VOC-.

a•void (ə void′) /ə'vɔyd/ *v.* [~ + *obj*] **1.** to keep away from; stay or keep clear of: *A low-fat diet can help you avoid a heart attack.* **2.** [~ + *verb-ing*] to prevent from happening: *She wore those shoes to avoid slipping.*

a•void•a•ble (ə void′əbl) /ə 'vɔydəbl/ *adj.* that can be avoided or prevented: *Lung cancer may be avoidable if you quit smoking.* **—a•void′a•bly,** *adv.*

a•void•ance (ə void′ns) /ə 'vɔydns/ *n.* [*noncount*] the act of avoiding or preventing.

av•oir•du•pois (av′ər də poiz′) /,ævərdə'pɔyz/ *n.* [*noncount*] the system of weights, based on the pound of 16 ounces, used in Great Britain and the U.S.: *The ton of 2,000 pounds is an avoirdupois measurement.* [*used after a measurement*]: *16 ounces avoirdupois. Abbr.:* av.; avdp.; avoir.

a•vow (ə vou′) /ə'vaw/ *v.* [~ + *obj*] to declare openly; acknowledge: *He avowed an interest in the issue.* [~ + (*that*) *clause*]: *He avowed that he had indeed made those remarks.*

a•vow•al (ə vou′əl) /ə 'vawəl/ *n.* [*count*] the act or instance of avowing.

a•vowed (ə voud′) /ə 'vawd/ *adj.* [*before a noun*] openly acknowledged: *an avowed feminist.* **—a•vow•ed•ly** (ə vou′id lē) /ə'vawɪdliy/ *adv.*

a•vun•cu•lar (ə vung′kyə lər) /ə'vʌŋkyələr/ *adj.* of, relating to, or characteristic of an uncle: *avuncular affection.*

a•wait (ə wāt′) /ə'weyt/ *v.* [~ + *obj*] **1.** to wait for; expect; look for: *She was still awaiting an answer.* **2.** to be in store for; come soon after to (someone): *A pleasant surprise awaited her.*

a•wake (ə wāk′) /ə'weyk/ *v.,* **a•woke** (ə wōk′) /ə'wowk/ or **a•waked** (ə wākt′) /ə'weykt/ **a•woke** or **a•waked** or **a•wo•ken** (ə wō′kən) /ə'wowkən/ **a•wak•ing,** *adj.* **—***v.* **1.** to (cause to) come out of sleep: [*no obj*]: *She awoke at dawn.* [~ + *obj*]: *The noise awoke me.* **2.** to (cause to) become active or alert (to): [*no obj*]: *My interest awoke when I saw the chance for profit.* [~ + *obj*]: *The project awoke his interest.* **3.** [*no obj;* (~ + *to* + *obj*)] to become conscious of something: *I finally awoke to the facts.* **—***adj.* [*be* + ~] **4.** waking; not sleeping: *I was awake all night.* **5.** [~ + *to*] alert to (some danger, problem, etc.); aware of: *not awake to the danger.*

a•wak•en (ə wā′kən) /ə'weykən/ *v.* to waken: [*no obj*]: *She awakened at dawn.* [~ + *obj*]: *She awakened the children.*

a•wak•en•ing (ə wā′kə ning) /ə 'weykə nɪŋ/ *adj.* [*usually before a noun*] **1.** becoming active; quickening: *an awakening interest in music.* **—***n.* [*count*] **2.** the act of awaking from sleep: *an early awakening.* **3.** the beginning of some activity: *an awakening of interest in languages.* **4.** realization: *It was a rude awakening when the money ran out.*

a•ward (ə wôrd′) /ə'wɔrd/ *v.* **1.** to give because of merit; bestow: [~ + *obj*]: *The panel awards the prizes.* [~ + *obj* + *obj*]: *The Nobel Committee awarded him the prize money.* [~ + *obj* + *to* + *obj*]: *The Committee awarded the literature prize to her.* **2.** to give (someone a sum of money) as the result of a court decision: [~ + *obj*]: *The jury awarded damages.* [~ + *obj* + *obj*]: *The jury awarded the plaintiff damages.* [~ + *obj* + *to* + *obj*]: *The jury awarded damages to the plaintiff.* **—*n.*** [*count*] **3.** something awarded, as a payment, medal, or judgment: *received an award of a fellowship.*

a•ware (ə wâr′) /ə'wɛər/ *adj.* **1.** having knowledge or realization of; conscious of: [*be* + ~ + *of*]: *Be aware of the danger.* [*be* + ~ + *(that) clause*]: *I wasn't aware that it was dangerous.* **2.** informed; alert; knowledgeable: *politically aware.* —**a•ware′ness,** *n.* [*noncount*]

a•wash (ə wosh′, ə wôsh′) /ə'wɒʃ, ə'wɔʃ/ *adj., adv.* **1.** level with and washed by the waves: *The deck of the boat was awash.* **2.** covered with water: *The streets were awash with the floodwaters.* **3.** covered; filled: *a garden awash in colors.*

a•way (ə wā′) /ə'wey/ *adv.* **1.** from this or that place; from here or from there; off: *to go away.* **2.** aside; to another place; in another direction: *turned his eyes away.* **3.** far; apart; at a distance from: *Stand away back.* **4.** out of one's possession or use: *to give money away.* **5.** in or into a place for storage or safekeeping: *folded the clothes and put them away.* **6.** out of existence: *The image began to fade away.* **7.** so as to be removed or separated: *Don't take me away from her.* **8.** continuously; repeatedly: *She was typing away madly.* **9.** without hesitation: *Fire away.* **—*adj.*** **10.** [*be* + ~] absent; gone: *I hate to be away from home.* **11.** [*after a number or amount*] distant in place or time (from): *The town is six miles away.* **12.** [*be* + ~] on one's way: *The plane left; they're well away by now.*

awe (ô) /ɔ/ *n., v.,* **awed, aw•ing.** **—*n.*** [*noncount*] **1.** a powerful feeling of reverence, fear, or wonder produced by someone or something overwhelming. **2. in awe of,** feeling reverence, fear, or wonder: *I stood in awe of the huge monument.* **—*v.*** [~ + *obj*] **3.** to cause (someone) to feel awe: *The imposing statue of a huge lion awed the children into silence.*

awed (ôd) /ɔd/ *adj.* showing awe: *spoke in awed voices.*

a•weigh (ə wā′) /ə'wey/ *adj.* (of an anchor) just free of the bottom: *They shouted "Anchors aweigh!"*

awe•some (ô′səm) /'ɔsəm/ *adj.* **1.** causing or showing awe: *an awesome sight.* **2.** *Slang.* very impressive: *Those clothes are totally awesome!* —**awe′some•ly,** *adv.* —**awe′some•ness,** *n.* [*noncount*]

awe•struck (ô′struk′) /'ɔˌstrʌk/ also **awe•strick•en** (ô′strik′ən) /'ɔˌstrɪkən/ *adj.* filled with awe: *an awestruck crowd of admirers.*

aw•ful (ô′fəl) /'ɔfəl/ *adj.* **1.** extremely bad; unpleasant; disagreeable: *the awful smell of gas.* **2.** causing shock or fear; dreadful; terrible: *an awful accident.* **3.** [*before a noun*] *Informal.* very great: *knows an awful lot about art.* **—*adv.*** **4.** *Informal.* very; extremely; awfully: *It's awful hot in here.*

aw•ful•ly (ô′fə lē, ôf′lē) /'ɔfəliy, 'ɔfliy/ *adv.* **1.** very; extremely: *It's awfully hot in here.* **2.** in a very bad manner: *The chorus sang awfully.*

a•while (ə hwīl′, ə wīl′) /ə'hwayl, ə'wayl/ *adv.* for a short time: *Stay awhile.*

awk•ward (ôk′wərd) /'ɔkwərd/ *adj.* **1.** clumsy; not having much skill: *an awkward dancer.* **2.** lacking grace or ease, as in movement or posture: *took an awkward swing at the ball.* **3.** lacking social graces or manners: *always feels awkward at office parties.* **4.** difficult to use or handle: *an awkward tool.* **5.** requiring skill or tact; difficult: *an awkward situation.* —**awk′ward•ly,** *adv.* —**awk′ward•ness,** *n.* [*noncount*]

awl (ôl) /ɔl/ *n.* [*count*] a pointed instrument for piercing small holes in leather, wood, etc.

awn•ing (ô′ning) /'ɔnɪŋ/ *n.* [*count*] a piece of canvas or other material extending over a doorway, window, etc., for protection from the weather.

a•woke (ə wōk′) /ə'wowk/ *v.* a pt. and pp. of AWAKE.

AWOL (*pronounced as initials, or as* ā′wôl, ā′wol) /*pronounced as initials, or as* ˈeywɔl, ˈeywɒl/ *adj.* **1.** absent without leave; away from military duties without permission, but without the intention of deserting. **—*adv.*** **2.** into AWOL status: *He's gone AWOL.* **—*n.*** [*count*] **3.** a soldier who is AWOL.

a•wry (ə rī′) /ə'ray/ *adj.* **1.** [*be* + ~] turned or twisted aside; askew: *His jacket was awry.* **—*adv.*** **2.** away from the expected or proper direction: *Our plans went awry.*

ax or **axe** (aks) /æks/ *n., pl.* **ax•es** (ak′siz) /'æksɪz/ *v.,* **axed, ax•ing.** **—*n.*** [*count*] **1.** a tool with a blade on a handle, used for hewing, chopping, splitting, etc. **2. the ax, a.** a sudden dismissal from a job, task, etc.: *The new president gave her the ax.* **b.** any sudden removal or ending (of a project, etc.): *The new tax plan got the ax in Congress.* **—*v.*** [~ + *obj*] **3.** to shape or trim with an ax. **4.** to dismiss, restrict, or remove, esp. unfairly and suddenly. **—*Idiom.*** **5. have an ax to grind,** to have a personal or selfish motive: *I have no ax to grind, so I'm willing to listen to all sides.*

ax•i•al (ak′sē əl) /'æksiyəl/ *adj.* **1.** relating to or forming an axis. **2.** situated on an axis. —**ax′i•al•ly,** *adv.*

ax•i•om (ak′sē əm) /'æksiyəm/ *n.* [*count*] **1.** a statement that is believed to be the truth and that requires no proof or argument; a principle or rule universally accepted: *It is an old axiom of politics that the richest candidate always wins.* **2.** a statement or proposition assumed to be true without proof for the sake of studying what would happen if it were in fact true.

ax•i•o•mat•ic (ak′sē ə mat′ik) /ˌæksiy ə 'mætɪk/ *adj.* **1.** obviously true and needing no proof: *It's axiomatic that the sun will rise in the east tomorrow.* **2.** (of a statement in logic, mathematics, etc.) assumed to be true so that one could study what would happen if it should in fact be true. —**ax′i•o•mat′i•cal•ly,** *adv.*

ax•is (ak′sis) /'æksɪs/ *n.* [*count*], *pl.* **ax•es** (ak′sēz) /'æksiyz/. **1.** the line around which a rotating body, as the earth, turns. **2.** a line used as the starting point in a graph to figure the position of a point. **3. the Axis,** (in World War II) the nations that fought against the Allies. **4.** an alliance of two or more nations to coordinate policies: *a new European-African-Middle East axis.*

ax•le (ak′səl) /'æksəl/ *n.* [*count*] the pin, bar, rod, or shaft on which a pair of wheels rotates.

ax•on (ak′son) /'æksɒn/ *n.* [*count*] the part of a nerve cell that sends impulses away from the cell body.

a•ya•tol•lah (ä′yə tō′lə) /ˌɑyə'towlə/ *n.* [*count*] a title for a Shi'ite cleric with advanced knowledge of Islamic law.

aye or **ay** (ī) /ay/ *adv., interj.* **1.** yes: *Aye, sir.* **—*n.*** [*count*] **2.** an affirmative vote or voter: *"Sixteen ayes, 5 no's: the ayes have it."*

AZ, an abbreviation of: Arizona.

a•zal•ea (ə zāl′yə) /ə'zeylyə/ *n.* [*count*], *pl.* **-eas.** a shrub of the heath family, with funnel-shaped flower clusters.

az•i•muth (az′ə məth) /'æzəməθ/ *n.* [*count*] an angle or arc used to measure direction and distance in astronomy, navigation, surveying, gunnery, etc.

AZT, *Trademark.* azidothymidine: a drug used esp. in the treatment of AIDS.

az•ure (azh′ər) /'æʒər/ *n.* [*noncount*] **1.** the blue of a clear or unclouded sky; a light, purplish shade of blue. **—*adj.*** **2.** of or having the color azure.

B, b (bē) /biy/ *n.* [*count*], *pl.* **Bs** or **B's, bs** or **b's.** the second letter of the English alphabet, a consonant.

B, *Symbol.* **1.** the second in order or in a series. **2.** [*sometimes: b*] a grade or mark indicating that something is good but not of the highest quality: *You need two B's to pull up your average.* **3.** a major blood group.

b., an abbreviation of: **1.** bachelor. **2.** bass. **3.** born.

B.A., an abbreviation of: Bachelor of Arts.

baa (ba, bä) /bæ, bɑ/ *n.* [*count*] **1.** the sound that a sheep makes. **—***v.* [*no obj*] **2.** to make a baa.

bab•ble (bab′əl) /'bæbəl/ *v.,* **-bled, -bling,** *n.* **—***v.* **1.** to make meaningless sounds: [*no obj*]: *babbles in her sleep.* [~ + *obj*]: *The guest babbled her apologies.* **2.** to talk too much or foolishly; chatter: [*no obj*]: *The two friends babbled on for hours.* [~ + *obj*]: *The spy babbled state secrets.* [~ + *(that) clause*]: *He babbled that the enemy was invading.* **3.** [*no obj*] to make a continuous murmuring sound: *a babbling brook.* **—***n.* [*noncount*] **4.** poorly pronounced words; imperfect speech: *the babble of little babies.* **5.** foolish, meaningless, or too much talk; chatter: *the babble in the room before the class began.* **6.** a murmuring sound or sounds.

babe (bāb) /beyb/ *n.* [*count*] **1.** a baby or small child. **2.** *Slang (sometimes disparaging and offensive).* a girl or woman.

ba•bel (bā′bəl, bab′əl) /'beybəl, 'bæbəl/ *n.* [*count; usually singular*] a confused mixture of sounds or voices: *a babel of delegates' voices.*

ba′bies'-breath′, *n.* BABY'S-BREATH.

ba•boon (ba bo͞on′) /bæ'buwn/ *n.* [*count*] a large monkey of Africa and Arabia, that has a nose and mouth like a dog.

ba•bush•ka (bə bo͝osh′kə, -bo͞osh′-) /bə'bʊʃkə, -'buwʃ-/ *n.* [*count*], *pl.* **-kas.** a woman's head scarf, shaped or folded in a triangle and worn with two ends tied under the chin.

ba•by (bā′bē) /'beybiy/ *n., pl.* **-bies,** *adj., v.,* **-bied, -by•ing.** **—***n.* [*count*] **1.** an infant or very young child. **2.** the youngest member of a group, as of a family. **3.** an immature or childish person: *Don't be a baby: this shot won't hurt.* **4.** *Informal.* **a.** *(sometimes disparaging and offensive).* a girl or woman. **b.** something that requires one's special attention or of which one is esp. proud: *That proposal is her baby.* **—***adj.* [*before a noun*] **5.** of, for, or like a baby: *a baby blanket; baby talk.* **6.** smaller than the usual: *baby eggplants.* **—***v.* [~ + *obj*] **7.** to treat like a baby; pamper: *to baby a sick child.* **8.** to use with special care; treat gently: *He babied his new car.*

ba′by blue′, *n.* [*noncount*] a very light blue.

ba′by boom′, *n.* [*count*] [*sometimes: Baby Boom*] a period of sharp increase in the birthrate, as that following World War II. **—ba′by boom′er,** *n.* [*count*]

ba′by car′riage, *n.* [*count*] a carriage with four wheels, to be pushed by a person walking. Also called **ba′by bug′gy.**

ba′by grand′, *n.* [*count*] the smallest form of a grand piano.

ba•by•hood (bā′bē ho͝od′) /'beybiyˌhʊd/ *n.* [*noncount*] the time or period of life of a baby; infancy.

ba•by•ish (bā′bē ish) /'beybiyɪʃ/ *adj.* of, like, or characteristic of a baby: *babyish drawings.* **—ba′by•ish•ly,** *adv.* **—ba′by•ish•ness,** *n.* [*noncount*]

ba•by•proof or **ba•by-proof** (bā′bē pro͞of) /'beybiy pruwf/ *adj., v.* CHILDPROOF.

ba′by's-breath′ or **ba′bies'-breath′,** *n.* [*noncount*] a tall plant with numerous small white or pink flowers.

ba′by-sit′ or **ba′by•sit′,** *v.,* **-sat, -sit•ting.** **1.** to take care of (a child) while the parents are temporarily away: [*no obj*]: *I baby-sat while she went shopping.* [~ + *obj*]: *She baby-sat our children.* **2.** [~ + *obj*] to take responsibility for; tend: *You can baby-sit the car while I'm away.* **—ba′by-sit′ter, ba′by•sit′ter,** *n.* [*count*]

bac•ca•lau•re•ate (bak′ə lôr′ē it, -lor′-) /ˌbækə'lɔriyɪt, -'lɒr-/ *n.* BACHELOR'S DEGREE.

bac•cha•nal (bä′kə näl′, bak′ə nal′) /ˌbɑkə'nɑl, ˌbækə'næl/ *n.* [*count*] a wild party, often marked by heavy drinking. **—bac•cha•na•li•an** (bä′kə nā′lē ən, bak′ə-) /ˌbɑkə'neyliyən, ˌbækə-/ *adj.* [*before a noun*]: *a bacchanalian orgy.*

bach•e•lor (bach′ə lər, bach′lər) /'bætʃələr, 'bætʃlər/ *n.* [*count*] **1.** an unmarried man. **2.** a person who has earned a bachelor's degree.

bach′elor's degree′, *n.* [*count*] a degree awarded by a college to a person who has completed undergraduate studies. Also called **baccalaureate.**

ba•cil•lus (bə sil′əs) /bə'sɪləs/ *n.* [*count*], *pl.* **-cil•li** (-sil′ī) /-'sɪlay/. a rod-shaped or cylindrical type of bacterium.

back (bak) /bæk/ *n.* [*count*] **1.** the rear part of the human body from the neck to the end of the spine. **2.** the part of an animal's body corresponding to the human back: *stroked her dog on the back.* **3.** the part that forms the back or reverse of an object or structure: *I sat at the back of the room.* **4.** the spine; backbone: *broke his back.* **5.** a player, as in football, stationed to the rear of front-line play. **—***v.* **6.** [~ + *obj*] to support, as with money: *We'll back his plan if you do.* **7.** [~ + *obj*] to bet on: *to back a horse in a race.* **8.** to (cause to) move backward: [*no obj*]: *She backed slowly into the garage.* [~ + *obj*]: *He backed the truck to the platform.* **9.** [~ + *obj*] to furnish with or be a back for: *backed the picture with cardboard.* **10.** [~ + *onto* + *obj*] to lie at the back of something: *The house backs onto the river.* **11. back down or off,** [*no obj*] to give up an argument or position: *backed down from her stubborn refusal.* **12. back out,** [*no obj*] to fail to keep a promise; withdraw: *Don't try to back out of the deal.* **13. back up, a.** to bring or come to a complete stop or standstill: [~ + *up* + *obj; usually passive*]: *Traffic is backed up to the bridge.* [*no obj*]: *Traffic backed up quickly because of the accident.* **b.** to (cause to) become clogged due to a stoppage: [*no obj*]: *The sink backs up almost every week.* [~ + *up* + *obj*]: *That garbage will back up your septic tank.* **c.** [~ + *up* + *obj*] to copy (a computer file or program) as a precaution against failure. **—***adj.* **14.** [*before a noun*] situated at or in the rear: *the back door.* **15.** [*before a noun*] far away; remote: *The farmer didn't plant the back pasture.* **16.** [*before a noun*] of or belonging to the past: *the back issues of a magazine.* **17.** [*before a noun*] owed from an earlier time; overdue: *She was rehired and given back pay.* **—***adv.* **18.** at, to, or toward the rear; backward: *Please step back.* **19.** in, at, or toward an original starting place, time, or condition: *He went back to his home town. Put your coat back on.* **—*Idiom.* 20. back and forth,** backward and forward; to and fro: *pacing back and forth while I waited for the news.* **21. behind one's back,** without one's knowledge; *They talked about me behind my back.* **22. get one's back up,** [*no obj*] to become annoyed; take offense: *Don't get your back up; it was just a joke.* **23. go back on,** [~ + *obj*] **a.** to fail to keep: *Several times he went back on his word.* **b.** to be disloyal to; betray: *She went back on her friend.* **24. (in) back of,** at the rear of; behind: *There's a small garden in back of the house.* **—Usage.** Although some people object to the use of IN BACK OF with the meaning 'behind," it is fully established as standard in American English and appears in all types of speech and writing: *The car was parked in back of the house.*

back•ache (bak′āk′) /'bækˌeyk/ *n.* a pain or ache in the back: [*noncount*]: *suffering from backache.* [*count*]: *Backaches kept him off the team.*

back•bench•er (bak′ben′chər) /'bæk'bɛntʃər/ *n.* [*count*] a member of a law-making body, esp. the British Parliament, who is not a party leader.

back•bite (bak′bīt′) /'bækˌbayt/ *v.,* **-bit, -bit•ten** or (*Informal*) **-bit; -bit•ing.** to attack the character of (a person who is not present); slander: [~ + *obj*]: *always backbiting me to my friends.* [*no obj*]: *backbiting and gossiping.* **—back′bit′er,** *n.* [*count*]

back•board (bak′bôrd′) /'bækˌbɔrd/ *n.* [*count*] **1.** a board placed at or forming the back of something. **2.** the vertical board at the end of a basketball court to which the basket is attached.

back•bone (bak′bōn′) /'bækˌbown/ *n.* **1.** [*count*] the spinal column; spine. **2.** [*noncount*] strength of character. **3.** [*count*] the main strength or support of something: *The small farmer was the backbone of the republic.*

back•break•ing (bak′brā′king) /'bækˌbreykɪŋ/ *adj.* requiring great work, effort, or strength.

back′ burn′er, *n.* [*noncount*] **—*Idiom.* on the back burner,** set aside to be dealt with later: *The issue was put on the back burner until after the election.*

back•date (bak′dāt′) /'bækˌdeyt/ *v.* [~ + *obj*], **-dat•ed, -dat•ing.** to put a date earlier than the actual date on; predate.

back•drop (bak′drop′) /'bækˌdrɒp/ *n.* [*count*] **1.** the rear curtain of a stage setting. **2.** [*usually singular*] the setting of an event: *Paris is the backdrop for this movie.*

back•er (bak′ər) /ˈbækər/ *n.* [*count*] a person who supports or aids a cause or activity: *His backers in the crowd quickly shouted down the protesters.*

back•field (bak′fēld′) /ˈbækˌfiyld/ *n.* [*count*] **1.** the members of a football team stationed behind the linemen or the linebackers. **2.** the area in which the backfield plays.

back•fire (bak′fīᵊr′) /ˈbækˌfayᵊr/ *v.,* **-fired, -fir•ing,** *n.* —*v.* [*no obj*] **1.** (of a car engine) to have a loud explosion that occurs too soon for proper combustion. **2.** to have a result opposite to that expected; go wrong. —*n.* [*count*] **3.** (in a car engine) an explosive igniting of fuel that occurs too soon for proper combustion.

back•gam•mon (bak′gam′ən) /ˈbækˌgæmən/ *n.* [*noncount*] a game for two persons in which pieces are moved around a board according to throws of the dice.

back•ground (bak′ground′) /ˈbækˌgrawnd/ *n.* [*count*] **1.** [*usually singular*] the ground, parts, people, or things at the back or rear, as of a picture, a painting, or a place. **2.** a person's origin, education, and experience in relation to his or her status: *comes from a musical background.* **3.** the conditions or causes of an event or situation: *The book explores the background of the war.* —*adj.* [*before a noun*] **4.** of, relating to, or being a background: *background noise.*

back•hand (bak′hand′) /ˈbækˌhænd/ *n.* [*count*] **1.** a stroke, as with a racket, made with the back of the hand turned forward. **2.** [*usually singular*] handwriting that slopes toward the left: *I recognized her backhand on the envelope.* —*adj.* [*before a noun*] **3.** backhanded. —*adv.* **4.** in a backhanded way. —*v.* [~ + *obj*] **5.** to strike with a backhand. —**back′hand′er,** *n.* [*count*]

back•hand•ed (bak′han′did) /ˈbækˌhændɪd/ *adj.* **1.** performed with the back of the hand turned forward: *a backhanded tennis stroke.* **2.** sloping in a downward direction from left to right: *backhanded writing.* **3.** ambiguous and often the opposite in meaning: *a backhanded compliment.* —*adv.* **4.** with the hand across the body: *caught the ball backhanded.* —**back′hand′ed•ly,** *adv.*

back•ing (bak′ing) /ˈbækɪŋ/ *n.* **1.** [*noncount*] aid; support: *the backing of the president.* **2.** [*noncount*] supporters thought of as a group: *His backing includes civil-rights organizations.* **3.** [*count; usually singular*] something that forms a support: *Put a cardboard backing on the photo.*

back•lash (bak′lash′) /ˈbækˌlæʃ/ *n.* [*count*] a strong negative reaction, as to some social or political change: *a backlash by voters to rising property taxes.*

back•less (bak′lis) /ˈbæklɪs/ *adj.* (of clothing) not having a back.

back•log (bak′lôg′, -log′) /ˈbækˌlɔg, -ˌlɒg/ *n.* [*count*] a group of unfinished tasks.

back′ or′der, *n.* [*count*] an order for merchandise that is temporarily not in stock but will be delivered as soon as it is received.

back•pack (bak′pak′) /ˈbækˌpæk/ *n.* [*count*] **1.** a pack or knapsack carried on one's back. See illustration at SCHOOL. —*v.* [*no obj*] **2.** to hike using a backpack. —**back′pack′er,** *n.* [*count*]

back′-ped′al, *v.* [*no obj*], **-ped•aled, -ped•al•ing** or (*esp. Brit.*) **-ped•alled, -ped•al•ling. 1.** to slow down the forward motion of a bicycle by pressing backward on the pedals. **2.** to reverse one's previous stand on a matter: *When voters complained about the new tax, the senator backpedaled.*

back•rest (bak′rest′) /ˈbækˌrɛst/ *n.* [*count*] a support used to rest one's back.

back′seat driv′er (bak′sēt′) /ˈbækˌsiyt/ *n.* [*count*] an automobile passenger who offers the driver directions, instructions, advice, or criticism that are not asked for.

back•side (bak′sīd′) /ˈbækˌsayd/ *n.* [*count*] rump; buttocks.

back•slap•ping (bak′slap′ing) /ˈbækˌslæpɪŋ/ *n.* [*noncount*] a big, usually false display of friendliness. —**back′slap′per,** *n.* [*count*]

back•slash (bak′slash′) /ˈbækˌslæʃ/ *n.* [*count*] a short, oblique stroke (\).

back•slide (bak′slīd′) /ˈbækˌslayd/ *v.* [*no obj*], **-slid, -slid** or **-slid•den, -slid•ing.** to return to bad habits, or undesirable activities: *Addicts often backslide into drug use.* —**back′slid′er,** *n.* [*count*]

back•space (bak′spās′) /ˈbækˌspeys/ *v.,* **-spaced, -spac•ing,** *n.* —*v.* [*no obj*] **1.** to move the typing element of a typewriter or the cursor on a computer display one space backward. —*n.* [*count*] **2.** the key on a typewriter or computer keyboard used for backspacing.

back•stage (bak′stāj′) /ˈbækˈsteydʒ/ *adv.* **1.** behind the stage in a theater. —*adj.* [*before a noun*] **2.** located or occurring backstage. **3.** of or relating to the private lives of entertainers: *backstage gossip.* —*n.* [*noncount*] **4.** a backstage area of a theater.

back•stop (bak′stop′) /ˈbækˌstɒp/ *n.* [*count*] **1.** a barrier, as a wall, that prevents a ball from going beyond the normal playing area. **2.** *Baseball.* the catcher.

back•stretch (bak′strech′) /ˈbækˈstrɛtʃ/ *n.* [*count*] the straight part of a race track leading to the finish line.

back•stroke (bak′strōk′) /ˈbækˌstrowk/ *n.* **1.** [*count*] a backhanded stroke. **2.** [*noncount*] a swimming stroke performed lying on one's back.

back′ talk′, *n.* [*noncount*] an impolite, audacious answer; impudence.

back′ to back′ or **back′-to-back′,** *adj.* [*usually: before a noun*] following one immediately after the other; consecutive: *back-to-back defeats.*

back•track (bak′trak′) /ˈbækˌtræk/ *v.* [*no obj*] **1.** to return over the same course, path, or route. **2.** to withdraw from a position; reverse a policy: *Because of budget cuts they backtracked from their plans to expand.*

back•up (bak′up′) /ˈbækˌʌp/ *n.* **1.** [*count*] a person or thing that supports; backing. **2.** [*noncount*] an accumulation due to stoppage. **3.** an alternate or substitute kept in reserve: [*count*]: *She kept her original disks and her backups in a safe place.* [*noncount*]: *What backup do you have in case the power fails?*

back•ward (bak′wərd) /ˈbækwərd/ *adv.* Also, **back′-wards. 1.** toward the back or rear: *I leaned backward in my chair.* **2.** with the back moving first or facing forward: *The helicopter flew backward.* **3.** in the reverse of the usual or right way: *counting backward from 100.* **4.** toward the past: *Looking backward, I remember how I felt.* —*adj.* **5.** [*before a noun*] directed toward the back or past: *a backward look.* **6.** [*before a noun*] reversed; returning: *a backward movement.* **7.** behind in time, progress, or development: *send help to backward countries.* **8.** bashful or hesitant; shy: *a little backward giving his opinions.* —***Idiom.*** **9. backward(s) and forward(s),** in every detail; thoroughly. **10. bend, lean,** or **fall over backward,** [*no obj*] to make a serious effort: *He bent over backward to be polite.* —**back′ward•ly,** *adv.* —**back′ward•ness,** *n.* [*noncount*]

back•wa•ter (bak′wô′tər, -wot′ər) /ˈbækˌwɔtər, -ˌwɒtər/ *n.* **1.** [*noncount*] water held or forced back, as by a dam. **2.** [*count*] a place or condition of backwardness: *a cultural backwater.*

back•woods (bak′wo͝odz′) /ˈbækˈwʊdz/ *n.* [*noncount; used with a singular verb*] wooded or partly uncleared and unsettled districts.

back•yard (bak′yärd′) /ˈbækˈyɑrd/ *n.* [*count*] the yard behind a house.

ba•con (bā′kən) /ˈbeykən/ *n.* [*noncount*] **1.** the back and sides of a hog, salted and dried or smoked. —***Idiom.*** **2. bring home the bacon,** to support oneself and one's family.

bac•te•ri•a (bak tēr′ē ə) /bækˈtɪəriyə/ *n.* [*plural*], *sing.* **bac•te•ri•um** (bak tēr′ē əm) /bækˈtɪəriyəm/. a group of microscopic, one-celled organisms, some of which are involved in infectious diseases, fermentation, and decay. —**bac•te′ri•al,** *adj.*

bac•te•ri•ol•o•gy (bak tēr′ē ol′ə jē) /bækˌtɪəriyˈɒlədʒiy/ *n.* [*noncount*] a branch of microbiology dealing with bacteria. —**bac•te•ri•o•log•i•cal** (bak tēr′ē ə loj′i kəl) /bækˌtɪəriyəˈlɒdʒɪkəl/, **bac•te′ri•o•log′ic,** *adj.* —**bac•te′-ri•ol′o•gist,** *n.* [*count*]

bac•te•ri•um (bak tēr′ē əm) /bækˈtɪəriyəm/ *n.* [*count*] the singular form of BACTERIA.

bad (bad) /bæd/ *adj.,* **worse** (wûrs) /wɜrs/ **worst** (wûrst) /wɜrst/; (*Slang*) **bad•der, bad•dest** for 16; *n., adv.* —*adj.* **1.** not good in any manner or degree: *bad traffic.* **2.** wicked or evil in character: *the bad witch.* **3.** of low or inferior quality; deficient: *bad roads.* **4.** disobedient or naughty: *She was a very bad girl today.* **5.** inaccurate; incorrect: *a bad guess.* **6.** causing injury or harm: *Sugar is bad for the teeth.* **7.** suffering from sickness, pain, or injury: *He was so bad yesterday that he stayed in bed.* **8.** diseased, decayed, or weakened: *a bad heart.* **9.** spoiled or rotten: *The milk has gone bad.* **10.** disagreeable; unpleasant: *bad dreams.* **11.** severe; intense: *a bad flood.* **12.** regretful, sorry, sad, or upset: *He felt bad about leaving.* **13.** showing or having a lack of skill or ability: *What a bad actor!* [*be* + ~ + *at*]: *I was really bad at drawing.* **14.** unfortunate or unfavorable: *bad news.* **15.** [*before a* *noun*] (of a debt) unlikely to be paid and so treated as a loss: *bad loans.* **16.** *Slang.* outstandingly good; first-rate: *He is one bad drummer.* **—*n.*** [*noncount*] **17.** something that is bad: *to take the bad with the good.* **—*adv.*** **18.** *Informal.* badly: *She wanted it bad enough to steal it.* **—*Idiom.*** **19. badly** or **bad off,** poor; destitute: *They were badly off during the Depression.* **20. in a bad way,** in severe trouble or distress: *She's in a bad way now.* **21. not (half, so,** or **too) bad,** somewhat good; tolerable: *not half bad for a first effort.* **22. too bad, a.** (used to express regret or disappointment): *You didn't pass? Oh, that's too bad.* **b.** (used to express impatience or lack of concern): *You don't like it here? Too bad.* —**bad′ness,** *n.* [*noncount*] **—Usage.** You can use the adjective BAD, meaning "unpleasant, unattractive, unfavorable, spoiled, etc.," after such verbs as *sound, smell, look,* and *taste: The music sounds bad. The locker room smells bad. You look pretty bad; are you sick? After the rainstorm the water tasted bad.* After the verb *feel,* you can also use the adjective BADLY when describing physical or emotional states: *She was feeling badly that day.* That use is considered standard, although BAD is more common in formal writing. BAD as an adverb appears mainly in informal situations: *He wanted it pretty bad.* See also BADLY, GOOD.

bad•die or **bad•dy** (bad′ē) /ˈbædiy/ *n.* [*count*], *pl.* **-dies.** *Slang.* a villain or criminal.

bade (bad) /bæd/ *v.* a pt. of BID.

badge (baj) /bædʒ/ *n.* [*count*] **1.** a special mark, token, or device worn as a sign of membership, authority, or achievement. **2.** any distinctive mark.

badg•er (baj′ər) /ˈbædʒər/ *n.* [*count*] **1.** a burrowing, nocturnal mammal. **—*v.*** [~ + *obj*] **2.** to bother or annoy continuously; pester: *Reporters seemed to enjoy badgering the president.*

bad•lands (bad′landz′) /ˈbæd,lændz/ *n.* [*plural*] a barren area in which soft rock layers have eroded into unusual forms.

bad•ly (bad′lē) /ˈbædliy/ *adv.,* **worse** (wûrs) /wɜrs/ **worst** (wûrst) /wɜrst/ *adj.* **—*adv.*** **1.** in a bad way; incorrectly, inadequately, or unfavorably: *speaks French badly; a marriage that turned out badly.* **2.** in a wicked, evil, or morally wrong way. **3.** in a naughty or socially wrong way: *behaved badly in front of the guests.* **4.** to a great extent or degree; very much: *wants the job badly.* **5.** very unpleasantly; severely: *was injured badly during the shootout.* **6.** with great distress or emotional display: *took the news badly.* **—*adj.*** **7.** in ill health; sick: *He felt badly and had a high fever.* **8.** sorry; regretful: *I feel badly about your loss.* **—*Idiom.*** **9. badly off,** [*be* + ~] **a.** in need of: *We are quite badly off for money.* **b.** not having much money; poor.

bad•min•ton (bad′min tn, bad′mitn) /ˈbædmɪntn̩, ˈbædmɪtn̩/ *n.* [*noncount*] a game played on a rectangular court by players with light rackets used to hit a shuttlecock over a high net.

bad′-mouth′ or **bad′mouth′,** *v.* [~ + *obj*] to criticize, often disloyally: *disliked her boss, but never bad-mouthed him.*

baf•fle (baf′əl) /ˈbæfəl/ *v.,* **-fled, -fling,** *n.* **—*v.*** [~ + *obj*] **1.** to confuse or bewilder; mystify: *baffled by her odd behavior.* **—*n.*** [*count*] **2.** something that slows down, interferes with, or deflects a flow, as of light, etc. —**baf′fler,** *n.* [*count*]

baf•fle•ment (baf′əl mnt) /ˈbæfəl mnt/ *n.* [*noncount*] the state of being baffled: *His look of complete bafflement showed that he didn't understand English.*

bag (bag) /bæg/ *n., v.,* **bagged, bag•ging.** **—*n.*** [*count*] **1.** a container made of a soft material, as paper or plastic, that can be closed at the mouth. **2.** a piece of luggage: *The airline lost my bag.* **3.** a purse; handbag: *The thief snatched her bag.* **4.** the amount a bag can hold: *a bag of candy.* **5.** *Slang.* a small envelope containing narcotics. **6.** something, as skin, hanging loosely: *bags under his eyes.* **7.** a base in baseball. **8.** *Slang (offensive).* an ugly woman. **9.** [*usually singular*]*Slang.* a person's hobby; avocation: *Jazz isn't my bag.* **—*v.*** **10.** [*no obj*] to hang loosely; swell or bulge: *These slacks bag at the knees.* **11.** [~ + *obj*] to pack or put in a bag: *bagged my groceries.* **12.** [~ + *obj*] to kill or catch, as in hunting: *He bagged two geese.* **—*Idiom.*** **13. in the bag,** *Informal.* almost certain to be obtained or achieved: *I thought victory was in the bag.* **14. leave (someone) holding the bag,** *Informal.* to leave (someone) to take the consequences: *His accomplices flew to South America and left him holding the bag.*

ba•gel (bā′gəl) /ˈbeygəl/ *n.* [*count*] a chewy, doughnut-shaped roll of dough that is simmered in water and baked.

bag•gage (bag′ij) /ˈbægɪdʒ/ *n.* [*noncount*] **1.** trunks, suitcases, etc., used in traveling; luggage: *How much baggage are you taking on your trip?* **2.** something that limits one's freedom; impediments: *Emotional baggage from his first marriage prevented him from remarrying.*

bag•gy (bag′ē) /ˈbægiy/ *adj.,* **-gi•er, -gi•est.** hanging loosely: *baggy trousers.* —**bag′gi•ness,** *n.* [*noncount*]

bag′ la′dy, *n.* [*count*] a homeless woman who carries her belongings in shopping bags.

bag•pipe (bag′pīp′) /ˈbæg,payp/ *n.* [*count*] Often, **bagpipes.**[*plural*] a reed instrument made up of a melody pipe and other pipes sounded by air forced out of a leather bag. —**bag′pip′er,** *n.* [*count*]

bah (bä, ba) /bɑ, bæ/ *interj.* (used to express contempt or annoyance): *"Bah, humbug," said Scrooge.*

Ba•ha•mi•an (bə hā′mē ən) /bəˈheymiyən/ *n.* [*count*] **1.** a person born or living in the Bahamas. **—*adj.*** **2.** of or relating to the Bahamas: *Bahamian English.*

bail[1] (bāl) /beyl/ *n.* [*noncount*] **1.** money given to a court of law to guarantee that a person released from jail will return at an appointed time. **2.** the state of release after paying bail. **—*v.*** **3. bail out, a.** to pay the bail for: [~ + *obj* + *out*]: *Her father bailed her out.* [~ + *out* + *obj*]: *We bailed out the protesters.* **b.** to help (someone) to get out of a difficult situation: [~ + *obj* + *out*]: *I bailed her out with some money.* [~ + *out* + *obj*]: *I bailed out the child by explaining why he was late.* **—*Idiom.*** **4. jump bail,** to run away while free on bail.

bail[2] (bāl) /beyl/ *v.* **1.** [~ + *obj*] to remove (water) from a boat, as with a bucket: *They bailed gallons of water from the boat.* **2. bail out,** to make a parachute jump from an airplane: [*no obj*]: *The pilot told his crew to bail out.* [~ + *out* + *of* + *obj*]: *They bailed out of the fiery jet.* **—*n.*** [*count*] **3.** a container, such as a dipper, used for bailing.

bail•iff (bā′lif) /ˈbeylɪf/ *n.* [*count*] **1.** an officer who keeps order in the court, makes arrests, etc. **2.** (in Britain) the chief magistrate in a town. **3.** (esp. in Britain) an overseer of an estate.

bail•i•wick (bā′lə wik′) /ˈbeylə,wɪk/ *n.* [*count*] **1.** the district of a bailiff. **2.** a person's area of skill, knowledge, or authority: *Helping people get justice is his bailiwick.*

bail•out (bāl′out′) /ˈbeyl,awt/ *n.* [*count*] **1.** the act of parachuting from an aircraft. **2.** a rescue from financial distress.

bait (bāt) /beyt/ *n.* **1.** [*noncount*] something, esp. food, used as a lure in fishing or hunting. **2.** something that tempts or entices: [*noncount*]: *used a beautiful woman as bait to trap the spy.* [*count; usually singular*]: *used the low price as a bait to get me to sign a deal.* **—*v.*** [~ + *obj*] **3.** to prepare (a hook or trap) with bait: *baited the mouse trap with cheese.* **4.** to set dogs upon (an animal): *Baiting bears is cruel.* **5.** to torment, esp. with vicious remarks: *Hecklers baited the speaker.*

baize (bāz) /beyz/ *n.* [*noncount*] a soft, feltlike fabric used for the tops of game tables.

bake (bāk) /beyk/ *v.,* **baked, bak•ing,** *n.* **1.** to cook by dry heat in an oven: [~ + *obj*]: *My wife bakes delicious pies.* [*no obj*]: *Her husband likes to bake.* **2.** [*no obj*] to become baked: *It took the bread an hour to bake.* **3.** [~ + *obj*] to harden or dry by heating: *baked clay pots in a special oven.*

bak•er (bā′kər) /ˈbeykər/ *n.* [*count*] a person who bakes, esp. one who makes and sells bread, cake, etc.

bak′er's doz′en, *n.* [*count; usually singular*] a dozen plus one; 13.

bak•er•y (bā′kə rē, bāk′rē) /ˈbeykəriy, ˈbeykriy/ *n.* [*count*], *pl.* **-er•ies.** a place where baked goods are made or sold. Also called **bake•shop** (bāk′shop′) /ˈbeyk,ʃɒp/.

bak′ing pow′der, *n.* [*noncount*] powder used in baking to cause dough to rise.

bak′ing so′da, *n.* [*noncount*] sodium bicarbonate.

bak•sheesh (bak′shēsh, bak shēsh′) /ˈbækʃiyʃ, bækˈʃiyʃ/ *n.* [*noncount*] (esp. in the Near and Middle East) money given as a tip or a bribe; gratuity.

bal•a•lai•ka (bal′ə lī′kə) /,bæləˈlaykə/ *n.* [*count*], *pl.* **-kas.** a Russian stringed instrument with a triangular body, three strings, and a neck like a guitar.

bal•ance (bal′əns) /ˈbæləns/ *n., v.,* **-anced, -anc•ing.** **—*n.*** **1.** a state of being steady; equilibrium: [*noncount*]: *The two weights are in balance now.* [*count; usually singular*]: *trying to establish a new balance of nature's organisms.* **2.** [*count; usually singular*] something that produces a state of balance: *Her caution was the perfect balance to his impulsiveness.* **3.** [*noncount*] the ability to maintain the body in a state of equilibrium: *Gymnasts* *need superior balance.* **4.** [*count*] an instrument for weighing objects. **5.** [*count; usually singular*] something that remains; the rest: *I'll do the balance of the work after vacation.* **6.** [*count*] the amount of money in a bank account. **—***v.* **7.** to bring to or hold in a state of balance: [~ + *obj*]: *She can balance a book on her head.* [*no obj*]: *She balanced on one leg.* **8. a.** [~ + *obj*] to add up the two sides of (an account) and determine the difference or make them equal: *The accountant balanced the books.* **b.** [*no obj*] to be in a state in which debts are equal to credits: *The checkbook balances.* **9.** [~ + *obj* + *with/against* + *obj*] to compare the relative weight or importance of (two things): *You'll have to balance working longer hours against the opportunity to earn more money.* **10.** [~ + *obj*] to serve as a weight or influence on one side against another; offset: *Fatigue was balanced by excitement.* **—*Idiom.* 11. in the balance,** with the outcome in doubt or suspense: *The election hung in the balance.* **12. off balance, a.** not steady: *I was caught off balance and down I went.* **b.** confused or surprised: *The question threw me off balance.* **13. on balance,** with all things considered: *On balance living abroad was a good experience.*

bal′ance beam′, *n.* [*count*] **1.** a narrow wooden rail used for performing feats of balance in gymnastics. **2.** a gymnastic event for women in which a balance beam is used.

bal′ance of pow′er, *n.* [*noncount*] a condition in which no single nation is strong enough to dominate the others.

bal′ance sheet′, *n.* [*count*] a statement of the financial position of a business on a specified date.

bal•co•ny (bal′kə nē) /ˈbælkəniy/ *n.* [*count*], *pl.* **-nies. 1.** an elevated platform on the outside wall of a building. **2.** an upstairs seating area in a theater.

bald (bôld) /bɔld/ *adj.*, **-er, -est. 1.** having little or no hair on the head. **2.** [*before a noun*] without ornament; blunt: *a bald lie.* —**bald′ly,** *adv.* —**bald′ness,** *n.* [*noncount*]

bald′ ea′gle, *n.* [*count*] a large eagle of the U.S. and Canada having a white head.

bal•der•dash (bôl′dər dash′) /ˈbɔldərˌdæʃ/ *n.* [*noncount*] nonsense.

bald•ing (bôl′ding) /ˈbɔldɪŋ/ *adj.* becoming bald.

bale (bāl) /beyl/ *n., v.,* **baled, bal•ing. —***n.* [*count*] **1.** a large bundle, esp. one tied tightly: *loading a few bales of cotton.* **—***v.* [~ + *obj*] **2.** to make into bales.

bale•ful (bāl′fəl) /ˈbeylfəl/ *adj.* (of appearance or actions) threatening evil; menacing. —**bale′ful•ly,** *adv.*

balk (bôk) /bɔk/ *v.* to stop abruptly and refuse to go on: [*no obj*]: *The horse balked when the rider tried to force him over the wall.* [~ + *at* + *verb-ing*]: *He went along with the robbery but balked at committing murder.*

balk•y (bô′kē) /ˈbɔkiy/ *adj.*, **-i•er, -i•est.** likely to balk: *a balky car engine.* —**balk′i•ness,** *n.* [*noncount*]

ball[1] (bôl) /bɔl/ *n.* **1.** [*count*] a round body; sphere: *a ball of yarn.* **2.** [*count*] a round body for use in games, as baseball or golf. **3.** [*noncount*] a game played with a ball, esp. baseball or softball. **4.** [*count*] a bullet or a solid round object shot from a gun or cannon. **5.** [*count*] a part of the human body that is rounded: *the ball of the thumb.* **—***v.* **6.** to form into a ball: [~ + *obj*]: *balled her fists and glared at him.* [*no obj*]: *Snow balled on the dog's paws.* **7. ball up,** to make into a mess; confuse: [~ + *up* + *obj*]: *really balled up the assignment.* [~ + *obj* + *up*]: *balled it up badly.* **—*Idiom.* 8. on the ball, a.** [*be* + ~] paying attention; alert: *really on the ball when you spotted that mistake.* **b.** [*have* + *a lot* + ~] intelligence and ability: *Your daughter has a lot on the ball.* **9. play ball,** to work together; cooperate: *If I refuse to play ball, they'll get someone who will.*

ball[2] (bôl) /bɔl/ *n.* [*count*] **1.** a large, formal party featuring social dancing. **—*Idiom.* 2. have a ball,** *Informal.* to have a good time.

bal•lad (bal′əd) /ˈbæləd/ *n.* [*count*] **1.** a simple poem that tells a story and is adapted for singing. **2.** a slow sentimental popular song.

bal•last (bal′əst) /ˈbæləst/ *n.* [*noncount*] **1.** heavy material such as rock carried on ships to make them heavier and more controllable. **2.** gravel or broken stone placed under the ties of a railroad to keep the tracks steady.

ball′ bear′ing, *n.* [*count*] a small hard ball placed in a groove between two moving parts of a machine to allow the parts to move smoothly.

bal•le•ri•na (bal′ə rē′nə) /ˌbæləˈriynə/ *n.* [*count*], *pl.* **-nas.** a female ballet dancer.

bal•let (ba lā′, bal′ā) /bæˈley, ˈbæley/ *n.* **1.** [*noncount*] a form of theatrical dance that involves formalized movements. **2.** [*count*] a theatrical work with ballet dancing, music, and scenery. **3.** [*count*] a company of ballet dancers. —**bal•let•ic** (ba let′ik, bə-) /bæˈlɛtɪk, bə-/ *adj.*

bal•lis′tic mis′sile (bə lis′tik) /bəˈlɪstɪk/ *n.* [*count*] a missile that is powered and guided at the beginning of its launch and then falls freely.

bal•lis•tics (bə lis′tiks) /bəˈlɪstɪks/ *n.* [*noncount; usually used with a singular verb*] the science or study of the motion of missiles.

bal•loon (bə lo͞on′) /bəˈluwn/ *n.* [*count*] **1.** a rubber bag that can be inflated with gas, used as a toy. **2.** a bag of strong, light material filled with a gas lighter than air so as to rise through the air. **—***v.* [*no obj*] **3.** to ride in a balloon. **4.** to puff out like a balloon. **5.** to increase at a rapid rate: *His weight ballooned when he quit smoking.* **—***adj.* [*before a noun*] **6.** puffed out like a balloon: *balloon sleeves.* —**bal•loon′ist,** *n.* [*count*]

bal•lot (bal′ət) /ˈbælət/ *n.* **1.** [*count*] a sheet on which a vote is registered. **2.** the method or act of secret voting: [*count; usually singular*]: *elected her treasurer in a secret ballot.* [*noncount; by* + ~]: *chosen by ballot.* **3.** [*noncount*] the right to vote. **4.** [*noncount*] the whole number of votes cast or recorded. **—***v.* [*no obj*] **5.** to vote by ballot.

ball•park (bôl′pärk′) /ˈbɔlˌpɑrk/ *n.* [*count*] **1.** a park or stadium where ball games, esp. baseball, are played. **—***adj.* [*before a noun*] **2.** being a guess or estimate: *If you don't know exactly how much the repairs will cost, give us a ballpark figure.* **—*Idiom.* 3. in the ballpark,** close to the correct or expected amount: *Your price estimate wasn't exactly right, but it was in the ballpark.*

ball•point (bôl′point′) /ˈbɔlˌpɔynt/ *n.* [*count*] a pen in which the point is a small ball that rolls against a supply of ink. Also called **ball′point pen′.**

ball•room (bôl′ro͞om′, -ro͝om′) /ˈbɔlˌruwm, -ˌrʊm/ *n.* [*count*] a large room for dancing.

bal•ly•hoo (bal′ē ho͞o′) /ˈbæliyˌhuw/ *n.* [*noncount*] exaggerated claims or statements, as in advertising or publicity; much to-do.

balm (bäm) /bɑm/ *n.* [*noncount*] **1.** a sweet-smelling oil or ointment used for healing, soothing, or relieving pain. **2.** something that soothes or comforts: *Her friendship was a balm to his hurt feelings.*

balm•y (bä′mē) /ˈbɑmiy/ *adj.*, **-i•er, -i•est. 1.** mild and refreshing; soothing: *balmy weather.* **2.** *Informal.* crazy or eccentric. —**balm′i•ness,** *n.* [*noncount*]

ba•lo•ney or **bo•lo•ney** (bə lō′nē) /bəˈlowniy/ *n.* [*noncount*] **1.** *Slang.* foolishness; nonsense. **2.** BOLOGNA.

bal•sa (bôl′sə, bäl′-) /ˈbɔlsə, ˈbɑl-/ *n., pl.* **-sas. 1.** [*count*] a tropical American tree that yields a light, soft wood. **2.** [*noncount*] the wood of the balsa.

bal•us•ter (bal′ə stər) /ˈbæləstər/ *n.* [*count*] an upright support for a railing. —**bal′us•tered,** *adj.*

bal•us•trade (bal′ə strād′) /ˈbæləˌstreyd/ *n.* [*count*] a railing with its supporting balusters.

bam•boo (bam bo͞o′) /bæmˈbuw/ *n., pl.* **-boos. 1.** a tall tropical grass with woody, usually hollow stems and stalks of narrow leaves: [*noncount*]: *The panda feeds on bamboo.* [*count*]: *hacking through the bamboos.* **2.** [*noncount*] the stem of a bamboo.

bam•boo•zle (bam bo͞o′zəl) /bæmˈbuwzəl/ *v.* [~ + *obj*], **-zled, -zling.** to trick, deceive, or mislead (someone): *It's easy to bamboozle a gullible person.* [~ + *obj* + *into*]: *She bamboozled her boss into giving her the day off.* [~ + *obj* + *out of*]: *They bamboozled the alcoholic out of his wallet.*

ban (ban) /bæn/ *v.,* **banned, ban•ning,** *n.* **—***v.* **1.** to prohibit, forbid, or bar; interdict: [~ + *obj*]: *The two countries agreed to ban the testing of nuclear weapons.* [~ + *obj* + *from*]: *She was banned from competition.* **—***n.* [*count*] **2.** a prohibition by law: *a ban on smoking.*

ba•nal (bə nal′, -näl′, bān′l) /bəˈnæl, -ˈnɑl, ˈbeynl̩/ *adj.* lacking freshness or originality; trite: *a banal plot.* —**ba•nal′ly,** *adv.*

ba•nal•i•ty (bə nal′ə tē) /bə ˈnælə tiy/ *n., pl.* **-ties. 1.** [*noncount*] the state or quality of being banal. **2.** [*count*] an instance of banal writing, speaking, or thinking.

ba•nan•a (bə nan′ə) /bəˈnænə/ *n., pl.* **-nan•as. 1.** [*noncount*] a tropical plant grown for its nutritious fruit. **2.** the curved, yellow fruit of the banana: [*noncount*]: *two cups of mashed banana.* [*count*]: *Bananas are full of potassium.*

ba•nan•as (bə nan′əz) /bəˈnænəz/ *adj. Slang.* **1.** [*be* + ~] crazy: *You must be bananas if you think I believe you.* **2. go bananas, a.** to become excited. **b.** to become unbalanced, as with anger.

band[1] (band) /bænd/ *n.* [*count*] **1.** a group of persons, animals, or things acting or working together: *a band of protesters.* **2.** a group of musicians who play chiefly brass, woodwind, and percussion instruments: *a school band.* **3.** a musical group of a specialized type: *a rock band.* **—*v.* 4.** to unite in a troop, company, or group: [*no obj*]: *The men banded together to look for the lost child.* [~ + *obj*]: *The men were banded together to chase the outlaws out of town.*

band[2] (band) /bænd/ *n.* [*count*] **1.** a thin, flat strip of material, used esp. for fastening, binding, or as decoration: *The hat had a band of ribbon.* **2.** a stripe, as of color: *white paper with a red band.* **3.** a plain or simply styled ring: *a gold wedding band.* **4.** a specific range of frequencies, esp. a set of radio frequencies. **—*v.*** [~ + *obj*] **5.** to mark with or attach a band to: *The farmer banded the carrots in bunches.*

band•age (ban′dij) /ˈbændɪdʒ/ *n., v.,* **-aged, -ag•ing.** **—*n.*** [*count*] **1.** a strip of material, as cloth, used to cover a wound or sprain. See illustration at HOSPITAL. **—*v.*** [~ + *obj*] **2.** to tie, bind, or cover with a bandage.

Band′-Aid′, *n.* [*count*] **1.** *Trademark.* an adhesive bandage with a gauze pad in the center. **2.** [*often: band-aid*] a temporary solution to a problem: *small federal grants that are only band-aids.*

ban•dan•na (ban dan′ə) /bænˈdænə/ *n.* [*count*], *pl.* **-nas.** a large, usually brightly colored handkerchief often worn around the neck or head.

B and B or **B&B,** an abbreviation of: bed-and-breakfast.

ban•dit (ban′dit) /ˈbændɪt/ *n.* [*count*] a robber, esp. a member of a marauding band of thieves.

ban•do•leer or **ban•do•lier** (ban′dl ēr′) /ˌbændḷˈɪər/ *n.* [*count*] a wide belt with small loops or pockets for bullets, worn over the shoulder by soldiers.

band•stand (band′stand′) /ˈbændˌstænd/ *n.* [*count*] a raised platform for the players in a band.

b and w or **b&w,** an abbreviation of: black and white (a type of motion picture, photograph, TV show, etc.).

band•wag•on (band′wag′ən) /ˈbændˌwægən/ *n.* [*count*] **1.** a wagon for carrying a band of musicians, as in a circus. **—*Idiom.* 2. climb** or **jump on the bandwagon,** to join a party, cause, or movement that appears to be gaining popular support or becoming successful.

ban•dy (ban′dē) /ˈbændiy/ *v.,* **-died, -dy•ing,** *adj.* **—*v.*** [~ + *obj*] **1.** to pass from one to another freely; exchange: *Various ideas were bandied about.* **—*adj.* 2.** (of legs) curving outward; bowed: *a cowboy with bandy legs.* **—ban′di•ness,** *n.* [*noncount*]

ban′dy-leg′ged (-leg′id, -legd′) /-ˌlɛgɪd, -ˌlɛgd/ *adj.* bowlegged.

bane (bān) /beyn/ *n.* [*count; usually singular*] **1.** a person or thing that ruins: *Gambling was the bane of his life.* **2.** a poison (used in combination, as in the names of poisonous plants): *wolfsbane; henbane.*

bang[1] (bang) /bæŋ/ *n.* [*count*] **1.** a sudden loud, explosive noise, as the firing of a gun: *slammed the door with a bang.* **2.** a strong, violent blow: *a nasty bang on the head.* **3.** [*usually singular*] *Informal.* thrill; excitement: *gets the biggest bang out of mud wrestling.* **—*v.* 4.** to strike violently or noisily; pound: [*no obj*]: *The police banged on the door.* [~ + *obj*]: *She banged the table with her fists.* **5.** to bump painfully: [*no obj*]: *My head banged into the wall.* [~ + *obj*]: *I banged my knee.* **6.** [*no obj*] to make a loud, explosive noise: *The shutter banged against the wall.* **7. bang up,** to cause physical harm to: [~ + *up* + *obj*]: *badly banged up in the accident.* [~ + *obj* + *up*]: *banged the car up.* **—*adv.* 8.** precisely; exactly: *stood bang in the middle of the road.*

bang[2] (bang) /bæŋ/ *n.* [*count*] Often, **bangs.** [*plural*] a fringe of hair cut to fall over the forehead.

Ban•gla•desh•i (bäng′lə desh′ē) /ˌbɑŋləˈdɛʃiy/ *n., pl.* **-desh•is,** *adj.* **—*n.*** [*count*] **1.** a person born or living in Bangladesh. **—*adj.* 2.** of or relating to Bangladesh.

ban•gle (bang′gəl) /ˈbæŋgəl/ *n.* [*count*] a ring-shaped band or bracelet worn around the wrist or ankle.

bang′-up′, *adj.* [*before a noun*] *Informal.* excellent; extraordinary: *did a bang-up job.*

ban•ish (ban′ish) /ˈbænɪʃ/ *v.* [~ + *obj*] **1.** to send (someone) away, esp. to exile; expel: *Napoleon was banished to an island.* **2.** to send or drive out, esp. from the mind: *to banish sad thoughts.* **—ban•ish•ment,** *n.* [*noncount*]

ban•is•ter or **ban•nis•ter** (ban′ə stər) /ˈbænəstər/ *n.* [*count*] Sometimes, **banisters.** [*plural*] a handrail and its supporting posts, esp. on a staircase; balustrade.

ban•jo (ban′jō) /ˈbændʒow/ *n.* [*count*], *pl.* **-jos, -joes.** a stringed musical instrument with a neck, a round body, and a front of tightly stretched parchment. **—ban′jo•ist,** *n.* [*count*]

bank[1] (bangk) /bæŋk/ *n.* [*count*] **1.** a long pile or heap; mass: *a bank of clouds.* **2.** a slope; incline: *trees planted on the bank to the highway.* **3.** the slope of land that borders a stream, river, or lake: *The banks of the river had overflowed.* **—*v.* 4.** [~ + *obj*] to border with or like a bank: *a round area banked with seats.* **5.** to pile up or form into a bank: [~ + *obj*]: *The plow banked the snow into my driveway.* [*no obj*]: *The snow banked up about 30 feet during the blizzard.* **6.** [~ + *obj*] to cover (a fire) with ashes to make it burn more slowly. **7.** [*no obj*] to tip or incline to one side: *The plane banked to the left.* **8.** [*no obj*] (of a road) to slope upward from the inner edge to the outer edge at a curve: *The road banks at a sharp angle here.*

bank[2] (bangk) /bæŋk/ *n.* [*count*] **1.** a business institution for receiving, lending, and keeping money safe. SEE ILLUSTRATION. **2.** a small container for holding money, esp. coins. **3.** a special storage place: *a blood bank.* **4.** a reserve or collection: *data banks.* **—*v.* 5.** to keep or deposit (money) in a bank: [~ + *obj*]: *banked her salary.* [*no obj*]: *Where do you bank?* **6. bank on** or **upon,** [~ + *on/upon* + *obj*] to count on; depend on: *If she says she'll be there, you can bank on it.*

bank[3] (bangk) /bæŋk/ *n.* [*count*] **1.** a group of objects in a line or a row. **2.** a number of similar devices connected to act together: *a bank of computer terminals.*

bank′ card′, *n.* [*count*] a card issued by a bank for credit or identification purposes.

bank•er (bang′kər) /ˈbæŋkər/ *n.* [*count*] a person employed by a bank, esp. as an executive.

bank′ hol′iday, *n.* [*count*] a weekday on which banks are closed, as for a legal holiday.

bank•ing (bang′king) /ˈbæŋkɪŋ/ *n.* [*noncount*] the business carried on by or with a bank.

bank•roll (bangk′rōl′) /ˈbæŋkˌrowl/ *n.* [*count; usually singular*] **1.** money in one's possession. **—*v.*** [~ + *obj*] **2.** to provide funds for; to finance: *The government bankrolls the welfare system.*

bank•rupt (bangk′rupt, -rəpt) /ˈbæŋkrʌpt, -rəpt/ *n.* [*count*] **1.** a person found by a court to be unable to pay debts and whose property is divided among creditors. **—*adj.* 2.** not having enough money to pay debts. **—*v.*** [~ + *obj*] **3.** to make bankrupt.

bank•rupt•cy (bangk′rupt sē, -rəp sē) /ˈbæŋkrʌptsiy, -rəpsiy/ *n., pl.* **-cies. 1.** [*noncount*] the state of being bankrupt. **2.** [*count*] an instance of becoming bankrupt: *Many bankruptcies were filed during the recession.*

ban•ner (ban′ər) /ˈbænər/ *n.* [*count*] **1.** a flag, as of a country. **2.** a piece of material, such as cloth, carried in processions. **—*adj.*** [*before a noun*] **3.** leading; outstanding: *a banner year for soybeans.*

ban•nis•ter (ban′ə stər) /ˈbænəstər/ *n.* BANISTER.

ban•quet (bang′kwit) /ˈbæŋkwɪt/ *n.* [*count*] **1.** a large, splendid feast. **2.** a large public dinner, esp. one to honor a person. **—*v.* 3.** [~ + *obj*] to entertain with a banquet. **—ban′quet•er, ban•que•teer** (bang′kwi tēr′) /ˌbæŋkwɪˈtɪər/ *n.* [*count*]

ban•shee (ban′shē) /ˈbænʃiy/ *n.* [*count*], *pl.* **-shees.** (in Irish folklore) a spirit in the form of a wailing woman who appears to or is heard by members of a family as a sign that one of them is about to die.

ban•tam (ban′təm) /ˈbæntəm/ *n.* [*count*] a chicken of a very small size.

ban•tam•weight (ban′təm wāt′) /ˈbæntəmˌweyt/ *n.* [*count*] a boxer who weighs up to 118 pounds (53 kg).

ban•ter (ban′tər) /ˈbæntər/ *n.* [*noncount*] **1.** playful teasing. **—*v.*** [*no obj*] **2.** to tease playfully: *The president bantered with reporters.*

Ban•tu (ban′tōō) /ˈbæntuw/ *n., pl.* **-tus, -tu,** *adj.* **—*n.*** [*count*] **1.** a member of a group of black African people in southern and central Africa whose languages and cultures are interrelated. **2.** a grouping of languages spoken by the Bantu. **—*adj.* 3.** of or relating to the Bantu or to the group of languages spoken by them.

ban•yan (ban′yən) /ˈbænyən/ *n.* [*count*] an East Indian fig tree with branches that send out roots to the ground and sometimes cause the tree to spread over a wide area.

ba•o•bab (bā′ō bab′) /ˈbeyowˌbæb/ *n.* [*count*] a large tropical African tree that has an extremely thick trunk and a gourdlike fruit.

bap•tism (bap′tiz əm) /ˈbæptɪzəm/ *n.* **1.** [*noncount*] a ceremony in which a person is sprinkled or covered with water as a sign of acceptance into the Christian church.

bank

passbooks
2345
National
checks
PAY J. DOE
123
Ten Dollars + No cents
cash
video camera
safe-deposit boxes
teller
ATM
deposit and withdrawal slips
security guard

2. [*count*] an instance or occasion of baptism: *Babies sometimes cry during their baptisms.* —**bap•tis•mal** (bap tiz′məl) /bæp'tɪzməl/ *adj.*

Bap•tist (bap′tist) /'bæptɪst/ *n. [count]* **1.** a branch of the Christian church whose members baptize believers by covering them completely with water. *—adj.* **2.** of or relating to Baptists.

bap•tize (bap tīz′, bap′tīz) /bæp'tayz, 'bæptayz/ *v.* [~ + *obj (+ obj)*], **-tized, -tiz•ing. 1.** to sprinkle with or cover with water in baptism: *She was baptized a Roman Catholic.* **2.** to give a name to at baptism; christen: *She was baptized Barbara.* —**bap•tiz′er,** *n.* [*count*]

bar (bär) /bɑr/ *n., v.,* **barred, bar•ring,** *prep.* *—n.* [*count*] **1.** a long, evenly shaped piece of some solid substance, as metal or wood, used esp. as a safeguard or obstruction: *The prisoners looked through the bars of their cells.* **2.** a piece of solid material that is longer than it is wide: *a bar of soap.* **3.** a ridge or bank of material such as sand near the surface of a body of water. **4.** something that blocks one's path or progress: *His accent is a bar to his becoming a radio announcer.* **5.** a counter or place where beverages, esp. liquors, are served to customers: *had a drink at the bar.* See illustration at HOTEL. **6. a.** [*count; usually singular: the* + ~] the legal profession: *admitted to the bar.* **b.** the practicing members of the legal profession. **c.** a railing in a courtroom separating the public from the judges, etc. **7.** a line marking the division between two measures of music. *—v.* [~ + *obj*] **8.** to equip or fasten with a bar or bars: *barred the door.* **9.** to block by or as if by bars: *The police barred the exits.* **10.** to prevent; exclude: *a religion that bars divorce; barred from membership in a club.* *—prep.* **11.** except; excluding; omitting; but: *We were all invited bar none.*

barb (bärb) /bɑrb/ *n.* [*count*] **1.** a point curving backward from a hook or arrowhead. **2.** a deliberately unkind remark.

bar•bar•i•an (bär bâr′ē ən) /bɑr'bɛəriyən/ *n.* [*count*] a person regarded as wild, primitive, or uncivilized. —**bar•bar′i•an•ism,** *n.* [*noncount*]

bar•bar•ic (bär bar′ik) /bɑr'bærɪk/ *adj.* **1.** lacking civilization; primitive. **2.** cruel. —**bar•bar′i•cal•ly,** *adv.*

bar•ba•rism (bär′bə riz′əm) /'bɑrbə,rɪzəm/ *n.* **1.** [*noncount*] the state of being barbarous. **2.** [*count*] a barbarous act.

bar•bar•i•ty (bär bar′i tē) /bɑr'bærɪtiy/ *n., pl.* **-ties. 1.** [*noncount*] brutal behavior; cruelty. **2.** [*count*] an act or instance of barbarity.

bar•ba•rous (bär′bər əs) /'bɑrbərəs/ *adj.* **1.** not civilized; wild. **2.** savage; cruel. —**bar′ba•rous•ly,** *adv.*

bar•be•cue or **bar•be•que** (bär′bi kyo͞o′) /'bɑrbɪ,kyuw/ *n., v.,* **-cued** or **-qued, -cu•ing** or **-qu•ing.** *—n.* [*count*] **1.** a grill for cooking food over an open fire. **2.** a meal, usually outdoors, at which food is roasted over an open fire. *—v.* **3.** to broil or roast (food) over an open fire: [*no obj*]: *It's a pleasant evening; let's barbecue for a change.* [~ + *obj*]: *Let's barbecue steaks.*

barbed (bärbd) /bɑrbd/ *adj.* **1.** having a barb or barbs. **2.** intended to be unpleasant and unkind; cutting.

barbed′ wire′, *n.* [*noncount*] wire with sharply pointed barbs used esp. for fences. Also called **barbwire.**

bar•be•que (bär′bi kyo͞o′) /'bɑrbɪ,kyuw/ *n., v.,* **-qued, -qu•ing.** BARBECUE.

bar•ber (bär′bər) /'bɑrbər/ *n.* [*count*] a person whose job is to cut the hair of men or boys.

bar•bi•tu•rate (bär bich′ər it, -ə rāt′) /bɑr'bɪtʃərɪt, -ə,reyt/ *n.* [*count*] a chemical used in medicine to calm people.

barb•wire (bärb′wīᵊr′) /'bɑrb'wayᵊr/ *n.* [*noncount*] BARBED WIRE.

bar′ code′, *n.* [*count*] a series of lines printed on or applied to an item for identification by an optical scanner.

bard (bärd) /bɑrd/ *n.* [*count*] a poet.

bare (bâr) /bɛər/ *adj.,* **bar•er, bar•est,** *v.,* **bared, bar•ing.** *—adj.* **1.** without covering or clothing; naked: *bare legs.* **2.** without the usual furnishings, etc.: *bare walls without pictures.* **3.** [*before a noun*] not more than; only: *a bare three miles.* **4.** [*before a noun*] being scarcely enough; minimum: *the bare necessities.* *—v.* [~ + *obj*] **5.** to uncover; show: *The dog bared its teeth.* **6.** to let (something) be known; divulge: *bared damaging new facts.* —**bare′ness,** *n.* [*noncount*]

bare•back (bâr′bak′) /'bɛər,bæk/ also **bare′backed′,** *adj., adv.* on a horse with no saddle: *a bareback rider; rode bareback.*

bare′ bones′, *n.* [*plural*] the essential facts of something: *Reduce this report to its bare bones.*

bare•faced (bâr′fāst′) /'bɛər,feyst/ *adj.* [*usually: before a noun*] showing no shame; brazen: *a barefaced lie.* —**bare•fac•ed•ly** (bâr′fā′sid lē, -fāst′-) /'bɛər,feysɪdliy, -,feyst-/ *adv.* —**bare′fac′ed•ness,** *n.* [*noncount*]

bare•foot (bâr′fo͝ot′) /'bɛər,fʊt/ also **bare′foot′ed,** *adj., adv.* with bare feet: *a barefoot boy; ran barefoot down the hill.*

bare•hand•ed (bâr′han′did) /'bɛər'hændɪd/ *adj., adv.* with hands uncovered: *a barehanded grab at the ball; caught the baseball barehanded.*

bare•ly (bâr′lē) /'bɛərliy/ *adv.* **1.** no more than; scarcely: *barely enough money to pay the rent.* **2.** in a bare way; scantily; meagerly: *a barely furnished room.*

bar•gain (bär′gən) /'bɑrgən/ *n.* [*count*] **1.** a purchase to one's advantage, esp. at less than the usual cost. **2.** an agreement between parties: *made a bargain to take turns driving.* *—v.* **3.** to discuss the terms of a bargain; negotiate: [*no obj*]: *bargained skillfully.* [~ + *with* + *obj*]: *Management bargained with labor.* [~ + *for* + *obj*]: *She might bargain for custody of the children.* **4. bargain on** or **for** [~ + *on/for* + *obj*] to expect to get; anticipate receiving: *She got more than she bargained for when she married him.* —***Idiom.*** **5. drive a hard bargain,** to argue very hard to get a favorable agreement. **6. in** or **into the bargain,** in addition; besides.

barge (bärj) /bɑrdʒ/ *n., v.,* **barged, barg•ing.** *—n.* [*count*] **1.** a flat-bottomed boat, usually pushed or towed, for carrying heavy freight or passengers. *—v.* **2.** [*no obj*] to move aggressively and clumsily: *The police began to barge through the crowd.* **3. barge in,** [*no obj*] to intrude or interfere, esp. rudely: *There's no need to barge in.* **4. barge in on,** [~ + *in* + *on* + *obj*] to interrupt or interfere in, esp. rudely: *She barged in on our meeting.*

bar′ graph′, *n.* [*count*] a graph with parallel bars of differing lengths to illustrate differing amounts.

bar•i•tone (bar′i tōn′) /'bærɪ,town/ *n.* [*count*] **1.** a male singing part lower than a tenor and higher than a bass. **2.** a singer with such a voice. See -TON-.

bar•i•um (bâr′ē əm, bar′-) /'bɛəriyəm, 'bær-/ *n.* [*noncount*] a whitish, soft metallic element.

bark[1] (bärk) /bɑrk/ *n.* [*count*] **1.** the sharp cry of a dog, fox, or similar animal. **2.** a short, explosive sound, as of coughing: *the bark of machine guns.* *—v.* **3.** [*no obj*] (of a dog or other animal) to make a bark: *The dog barked all night.* **4.** [*no obj*] to make a sound similar to a bark: *The big guns barked.* **5.** to speak sharply or harshly: [~ + *obj*]: *a habit of barking orders.* [*no obj*]: *barked at his subordinate.* —***Idiom.*** **6. bark up the wrong tree,** to direct one's efforts in the wrong place.

bark[2] (bärk) /bɑrk/ *n.* [*noncount*] **1.** the outside covering of the woody stems of plants, esp. of trees. *—v.* [~ + *obj*] **2.** to scrape the skin of, as by rubbing: *barked his shins.*

bark[3] or **barque** (bärk) /bɑrk/ *n.* [*count*] a sailing vessel with three or more masts and square sails.

bark•er (bär′kər) /'bɑrkər/ *n.* [*count*] a person who stands at the entrance to a show and calls out its attractions to people walking by.

bar•ley (bär′lē) /'bɑrliy/ *n.* [*noncount*] **1.** a cereal plant of the grass family. **2.** the grain of barley, used as food and in making beer and whiskey.

bar•maid (bär′mād′) /'bɑr,meyd/ *n.* [*count*] a woman who serves drinks at a bar; bartender.

bar•man (bär′mən) /'bɑrmən/ *n.* [*count*], *pl.* **-men.** a man who serves drinks at a bar; bartender.

bar mitz•vah (bär mits′və) /'bɑr mɪtsvə/ *n.* [*count; often: Bar Mitzvah*] **1.** a ceremony for admitting a boy of 13 as an adult member of the Jewish community. **2.** a boy participating in a bar mitzvah.

barn (bärn) /bɑrn/ *n.* [*count*] a building for storing hay and grain, and often for keeping animals. See illustration at LANDSCAPE.

bar•na•cle (bär′nə kəl) /'bɑrnəkəl/ *n.* [*count*] a shellfish living in salt water and attaching itself to ship bottoms and floating timber. —**bar′na•cled,** *adj.*

barn•storm (bärn′stôrm′) /'bɑrn,stɔrm/ *v.* [*no obj*] to travel in rural areas conducting a political campaign, speaking in public, or giving dramatic shows.

barn•yard (bärn′yärd′) /'bɑrn,yɑrd/ *n.* [*count*] a yard that is next to or surrounds a barn.

ba•rom•e•ter (bə rom′i tər) /bə'rɒmɪtər/ *n.* [*count*] **1.** an instrument that measures atmospheric pressure. **2.** something that indicates changes: *The stock market is a barometer of the economy.* —**bar•o•met•ric** (bar′ə me′trik) /,bærə'mɛtrɪk/ *adj.* See -METER-.

bar•on (bar′ən) /ˈbærən/ *n.* [*count*] **1.** a member of the lowest grade of nobility. **2.** a powerful, wealthy person: *a railroad baron.*

bar•on•ess (bar′ə nis) /ˈbærənɪs/ *n.* [*count*] **1.** the wife of a baron. **2.** a woman holding the rank of baron. **—Usage.** See -ESS.

bar•on•et (bar′ə nit, bar′ə net′) /ˈbærənɪt, ˌbærəˈnɛt/ *n.* [*count*] a member of an order of honor, ranking below the barons.

ba•ro•ni•al (bə rō′nē əl) /bəˈrowniyəl/ *adj.* [*usually before a noun*] of, relating to, or suitable for a baron.

ba•roque (bə rōk′) /bəˈrowk/ *adj.* **1.** [*often: Baroque*] of or being a style of architecture and art of the early 17th to mid-18th century marked by lively decoration and dramatic effect. **2.** [*sometimes: Baroque*] of or relating to the musical period following the Renaissance, extending roughly from 1600 to 1750.

barque (bärk) /bɑrk/ *n.* BARK[3].

bar•rack (bar′ək) /ˈbærək/ *n.* [*count*] Usually, **barracks.** [*plural*] a building or group of buildings in which soldiers can live or work.

bar•ra•cu•da (bar′ə ko͞o′də) /ˌbærəˈkuwdə/ *n.* [*count*], (*esp. when thought of as a group*) **-da,** (*esp. for kinds or species*) **-das.** a long, slender fish of warm seas.

bar•rage (bə räzh′) /bəˈrɑʒ/ *n., v.,* **-raged, -rag•ing.** **—***n.* [*count*] **1.** heavy continuous gunfire to protect troops or to stop an enemy advance. **2.** an overwhelming amount, as of words: *a barrage of questions.* **—***v.* [~ + *obj*] **3.** to subject to a barrage: *barraged by questions from reporters.*

bar•rel (bar′əl) /ˈbærəl/ *n., v.,* **-reled, -rel•ing** or (*esp. Brit.*) **-relled, -rel•ling.** **—***n.* [*count*] **1.** a rounded container for liquids. **2.** the amount that a barrel can hold: *a barrel of crude oil.* **3.** the metal tubelike part of a gun from which the bullet comes out. **—***v.* **4.** [~ + *obj*] to put or pack in a barrel or barrels. **5.** [*no obj*] to drive or move at high speed: *They were barreling along at 95 miles an hour.* **—*Idiom.*** **6. over a barrel,** placed in a difficult situation.

bar•ren (bar′ən) /ˈbærən/ *adj.* **1.** not producing offspring; sterile. **2.** not able to grow crops: *barren fields.* **3.** [*before a noun*] not producing results; fruitless: *a barren effort.* **4.** unable to interest or attract: *a barren period in architecture.* **—bar′ren•ly,** *adv.* **—bar′ren•ness,** *n.* [*noncount*]

bar•rette (bə ret′) /bəˈrɛt/ *n.* [*count*] a clasp for holding a woman's or girl's hair in place.

bar•ri•cade (bar′i kād′) /ˈbærɪˌkeyd/ *n., v.,* **-cad•ed, -cad•ing.** **—***n.* [*count*] **1.** a barrier of large objects, intended to stop an enemy: *a barricade of overturned buses.* **—***v.* [~ + *obj*] **2.** to block with a barricade. **3.** to shut in with or as if with a barricade: *He barricaded himself behind a folding screen.*

bar•ri•er (bar′ē ər) /ˈbæriyər/ *n.* [*count*] **1.** something, such as a fence, that bars passage or progress. **2.** something that obstructs or limits: *trade barriers.*

bar•ring (bär′ing) /ˈbɑrɪŋ/ *prep.* except for; excepting: *Barring further delays, I'll be there.*

bar•ri•o (bär′ē ō′, bar′-) /ˈbɑriyˌow, ˈbær-/ *n.* [*count*], *pl.* **-ri•os.** a section of a U.S. city inhabited chiefly by Spanish-speaking people.

bar•ris•ter (bar′ə stər) /ˈbærəstər/ *n.* [*count*] (in England) a lawyer who may speak in the higher courts. Compare SOLICITOR (def. 3).

bar•room (bär′ro͞om′, -ro͝om′) /ˈbɑrˌruwm, -ˌrʊm/ *n.* [*count*] an establishment or room with a bar for the serving of alcoholic beverages.

bar•row (bar′ō) /ˈbærow/ *n.* **1.** HANDBARROW. **2.** WHEELBARROW. **3.** *Brit.* PUSHCART.

bar•tend•er (bär′ten′dər) /ˈbɑrˌtɛndər/ *n.* [*count*] a person who mixes and serves alcoholic drinks at a bar. See illustration at HOTEL. **—bar′tend′,** *v.* [*no obj*]

bar•ter (bär′tər) /ˈbɑrtər/ *v.* **1.** to trade by exchanging goods rather than by money: [*no obj*]: *When money was scarce they simply bartered.* [~ + *obj*]: *to barter wheat for machinery.* **—***n.* [*noncount*] **2.** the act or practice of bartering.

bar•y•on (bar′ē on′) /ˈbæriyˌɒn/ *n.* [*count*] a heavy subatomic particle. **—bar′y•on′ic,** *adj.* [*before a noun*]

ba•sal (bā′səl, -zəl) /ˈbeysəl, -zəl/ *adj.* **1.** of, at, or forming a base. **2.** being a basis. **—ba′sal•ly,** *adv.*

ba•salt (bə sôlt′, bas′ôlt, bā′sôlt) /bəˈsɔlt, ˈbæsɔlt, ˈbeysɔlt/ *n.* [*noncount*] the dark, dense rock produced from lava. **—ba•sal′tic, ba•sal•tine** (bə sôl′tin, -tīn) /bəˈsɔltɪn, -tayn/ *adj.*

base[1] (bās) /beys/ *n., adj., v.,* **based, bas•ing.** **—***n.* [*count*] **1.** the part on which something stands: *The base of the lamp was made of marble.* **2.** a fundamental principle; basis: *data to be used as a base for further research.* **3.** the principal element in a mixture: *A soup with a base of chicken broth.* **4.** a starting point from which something is begun. **5.** a place from which military operations proceed: *an army base.* **6. a.** any of the four corners of a baseball diamond. **b.** a square canvas sack marking such a corner. **7. a.** the lower side of a figure, such as a triangle, in geometry; the side to which an altitude can be drawn. **b.** the number that serves as a starting point for certain mathematical operations. **c.** the number of symbols used in a numerical system. **8.** a chemical compound that reacts with an acid to form a salt. **9.** the part of a word to which certain prefixes, suffixes, or other markers may be added. **—***adj.* [*before a noun*] **10.** serving as or forming a base: *the explorer's base camp.* **—***v.* **11.** [~ + *obj* + *on/upon* + *obj*] to make, form, or establish: *He based the book on his own life.* **12.** [~ + *obj* + *at/on* + *obj*] to station or place at a base: *an air squadron based on Guam.* **—*Idiom.*** **13. off base,** *Informal.* seriously wrong: *The president's advisers were off base when they predicted an easy victory.* **14. touch base,** [*no obj*] to get into contact; communicate: *Touch base with me before you leave.* **—Syn.** BASE, BASIS, and FOUNDATION all refer to anything upon which a structure is built and upon which it rests. BASE usually refers to a physical structure that supports something: *the base of a statue.* BASIS more often refers to a mental or figurative support: *the basis of a report.* FOUNDATION implies a strong, solid, secure structure underneath: *the foundation of a skyscraper; the foundation of a theory.*

base[2] (bās) /beys/ *adj.,* **bas•er, bas•est.** **1.** not honorable; morally low: *base motives of greed.* **2.** of little value; worthless: *base materials.* **—base′ly,** *adv.* **—base′ness,** *n.* [*noncount*]

base•ball (bās′bôl′) /ˈbeysˌbɔl/ *n.* **1.** [*noncount*] a game involving the batting of a hard ball, played by two teams of nine players each on a large field with four bases. **2.** [*count*] the ball used in baseball.

base•board (bās′bôrd′, -bōrd′) /ˈbeysˌbɔrd, -ˌbowrd/ *n.* [*count*] a line of boards forming the base of an interior wall.

-based, *suffix.* *-based* is attached to some nouns to form adjectives. **1.** It is attached to nouns of place to form adjectives meaning "operating or working from": *ground* + *-based* → *ground-based (= operating from the ground); New York* + *-based* → *New York-based (= working from New York).* **2.** It is attached to nouns to form adjectives meaning "making use of": *computer* + *based* → *computer-based (= making use of computers; as in "computer-based instruction"); logic* + *-based* → *logic-based (= making use of logic).*

base•less (bās′lis) /ˈbeyslɪs/ *adj.* having no base; groundless: *a baseless claim; baseless fears.*

base•line (bās′līn′) /ˈbeysˌlayn/ *n.* [*count*] **1.** the area on a baseball diamond within which a runner must stay when running from one base to another. **2.** the line at each end of a tennis court that marks the in-bounds limit of play. **3.** a basic standard; guideline: *These results formed a baseline for future studies.* Also, **base′ line′.** See -LIN-.

base•ment (bās′mənt) /ˈbeysmənt/ *n.* [*count*] a floor or story of a building that is partly or completely underground.

base′ on balls′, *n.* [*count*], *pl.* **bases on balls.** *Baseball.* the awarding of first base to a batter to whom four balls have been pitched.

ba•ses[1] (bā′sēz) /ˈbeysiyz/ *n.* pl. of BASIS.

bas•es[2] (bā′siz) /ˈbeysɪz/ *n.* pl. of BASE[1].

bash (bash) /bæʃ/ *v.* **1.** to strike with a blow; smash: [~ + *obj*]: *bashed her head against the shelf.* [*no obj*]: *The car bashed into a tree.* **—***n.* [*count*] **2.** a blow: *a bash on the nose.* **3.** a lively party.

bash•ful (bash′fəl) /ˈbæʃfəl/ *adj.* shy. **—bash′ful•ly,** *adv.* **—bash′ful•ness,** *n.* [*noncount*]

-bash•ing, *combining form.* Use *-bashing* joined after another word to form: **1.** nouns meaning "physical assaults against (the noun)": *gay* + *-bashing* → *gay-bashing (= physical assault against gay people).* **2.** nouns meaning "verbally attacking": *China* + *-bashing* → *China-bashing (= verbally attacking China).*

ba•sic (bā′sik) /ˈbeysɪk/ *adj.* **1.** [*before a noun*] of, relating to, or forming a base or basis; fundamental: *a basic principle.* **2. a.** of or relating to a chemical base. **b.** ALKALINE. **—***n.* [*count*] **3.** Often, **basics.** [*plural*] something that is basic; an essential.

BASIC (bā′sik) /ˈbeysɪk/ *n.* [*proper noun or count*] B(eginner's) A(ll-purpose) S(ymbolic) I(nstruction) C(ode): a high-level computer programming language that uses English words and punctuation marks.

ba•si•cal•ly (bā′sik lē) /ˈbeysɪkliy/ *adv.* fundamentally; primarily.

bas•il (baz′əl, bā′zəl) /ˈbæzəl, ˈbeyzəl/ *n.* [*noncount*] a sweet-smelling herb of the mint family whose leaves are used in cooking.

ba•sil•i•ca (bə sil′i kə) /bəˈsɪlɪkə/ *n.* [*count*], *pl.* **-cas.** an early Christian or medieval church with an oblong shape rounded at the end and two or four side aisles. —**ba•sil′i•can,** *adj.*

ba•sin (bā′sən) /ˈbeysən/ *n.* [*count*] **1.** a round container shaped like a bowl to hold liquid. **2.** the quantity that a basin can hold. **3.** a hollow place containing water. **4.** a sheltered area along a shore: *a yacht basin.* **5.** an area of land drained by a river: *the Amazon basin.*

ba•sis (bā′sis) /ˈbeysɪs/ *n.* [*count*], *pl.* **-ses** (-sēz). a bottom or base; foundation: *no basis for your opinion.* —**Syn.** See BASE[1].

bask (bask) /bæsk/ *v.* [*no obj*] **1.** to be exposed to pleasant warmth: *basking in the sun.* **2.** to take great pleasure: *The actor basked in appreciative applause.*

bas•ket (bas′kit) /ˈbæskɪt/ *n.* [*count*] **1.** a container made of flexible, woven material. **2.** anything like a basket in shape or use: *a wastepaper basket.* **3.** an open net hanging from a metal hoop in basketball.

bas•ket•ball (bas′kit bôl′) /ˈbæskɪtˌbɔl/ *n.* **1.** [*noncount*] a game played by two teams who attempt to score points by tossing a ball through a basket on the opponent's side of the court. **2.** [*count*] the round, inflated ball used in basketball.

bas-re•lief (bä′ri lēf′, bas′-) /ˌbɑrɪˈliyf, ˌbæs-/ *n.* [*noncount*] sculpture in which the figures stand out slightly from the background.

bass[1] (bās) /beys/ *adj.* **1.** of the lowest pitch or range: *a bass clarinet.* **2.** of, relating to, or being the lowest part in harmonic music. —*n.* [*count*] **3.** the bass part. **4.** a bass voice, singer, or instrument. **5.** DOUBLE BASS.

bass[2] (bas) /bæs/ *n., pl.* (*esp. when thought of as a group*) **bass,** (*esp. for kinds or species*) **bass•es.** an edible freshwater or saltwater fish.

bas•si•net (bas′ə net′) /ˌbæsəˈnɛt/ *n.* [*count*] a basket with a hood over one end, for use as a baby's cradle.

bas•so (bas′ō, bä′sō) /ˈbæsow, ˈbɑsow/ *n.* [*count*], *pl.* **-sos, -si** (-sē). a bass singer.

bas•soon (ba sōōn′, bə-) /bæˈsuwn, bə-/ *n.* [*count*] a large woodwind instrument of low range. —**bas•soon′ist,** *n.* [*count*]

bas•tard (bas′tərd) /ˈbæstərd/ *n.* [*count*] **1.** a person born of unmarried parents. **2. a.** *Offensive.* a mean, cruel, hateful person: *That bastard stole all my money.* **b.** *Slang.* a person, esp. a man: *That poor bastard, losing his kids in the plane crash.*

baste[1] (bāst) /beyst/ *v.* [~ + *obj*], **bast•ed, bast•ing.** to sew with long, loose temporary stitches. —**bast′er,** *n.* [*count*]

baste[2] (bāst) /beyst/ *v.* [~ + *obj*], **bast•ed, bast•ing.** to moisten (food) with drippings, etc., while cooking.

bas•tion (bas′chən) /ˈbæstʃən/ *n.* [*count*] **1.** a portion of a wall of a fortress that stands out from the main wall. **2.** a safeguard against harm: *a bastion of democracy.*

bat[1] (bat) /bæt/ *n., v.,* **bat•ted, bat•ting.** —*n.* [*count*] **1.** a club used in certain games, as baseball, to strike the ball. **2.** a heavy stick or cudgel. —*v.* **3.** [~ + *obj*] to strike or hit with or as if with a bat. **4.** [*no obj*] to take one's turn as a batter. —***Idiom.*** **5. go to bat for,** [~ + *obj*] *Informal.* to help by speaking or acting in favor of.

bat[2] (bat) /bæt/ *n.* [*count*] a flying nocturnal mammal, often the size of a mouse.

bat[3] (bat) /bæt/ *v.* [~ + *obj*], **bat•ted, bat•ting. 1.** to wink or flutter: *batted her eyelashes.* —***Idiom.*** **2. not bat an eye,** to show no emotion: *didn't bat an eye when I told her about the murder.*

-bat-, *root.* -*bat*- comes from Latin, where it means "beat, fight." This meaning is found in such words as: BATTALION, BATTEN, BATTLE, COMBAT.

batch (bach) /bætʃ/ *n.* [*count*] **1.** a quantity taken together; lot: *a batch of tickets.* **2.** a quantity made at one baking: *a batch of cookies.* **3.** a group of jobs, data, or commands treated as a unit for computer processing.

bat•ed (bā′tid) /ˈbeytɪd/ *adj.* —**Idiom. with bated breath,** holding one's breath because of strong emotion: *I waited by the phone with bated breath.*

bath (bath) /bæθ/ *n.* [*count*], *pl.* **baths** (ba*th*z, bä*th*z, baths, bäths). **1.** a washing of something, esp. the body, for cleansing or medical treatment: *a warm bath to relax your aching muscles.* **2.** a container for water or other cleansing liquid, as a bathtub. **3.** BATHROOM. **4.** Often, **baths.** [*plural*] a swimming pool. **5.** Usually, **baths.** [*plural*] a resort visited for medical treatment by bathing; spa. **6.** a preparation, as an acid solution, into which something is dipped. —***Idiom.*** **7. take a bath,** *Informal.* to suffer a large financial loss: *When interest rates suddenly went up, we took a bath on most of our deals.* —**Related Words.** BATH is a noun, BATHE is a verb: *The baby needed a bath. He bathed the baby in warm water.*

bathe (bā*th*) /beyð/ *v.,* **bathed, bath•ing,** *n.* —*v.* **1.** [~ + *obj*] to give a bath to; wash: *I carefully bathed the baby in warm water.* **2.** [*no obj*] to take a bath or sunbath: *I shaved, bathed, and got dressed for the evening.* **3.** [~ + *obj*] to apply water or other liquid to: *The nurse bathed the wound.* **4.** [~ + *obj*] to cover or surround: *Sunlight was bathing the room. The runner was bathed in sweat.* **5.** [*no obj*] to swim for pleasure: *They went bathing but the water was too cold.* —*n.* [*count*] **6.** *Brit.* an act of bathing; bath; swim. —**bath•er,** *n.* [*count*]

bath•ing (bā′*th*ing) /ˈbeyðɪŋ/ *n.* [*noncount*] going into water to bathe or swim: *Bathing in that area was getting a little dangerous.*

bath′ing suit′, *n.* [*count*] a garment worn for swimming. Also called **swimsuit.**

ba•thos (bā′thos, -thōs) /ˈbeyθɒs, -θows/ *n.* [*noncount*] (in writing) a sudden change in subject matter from a high and serious topic to a commonplace and ridiculous one.

bath•robe (bath′rōb′) /ˈbæθˌrowb/ *n.* [*count*] a loose, coatlike garment worn before and after a bath or swimming, over sleepwear, or as casual clothing at home. See illustration at CLOTHING.

bath•room (bath′rōōm′, -rŏŏm′) /ˈbæθˌruwm, -ˌrʊm/ *n.* [*count*] **1.** a room equipped with a bathtub or shower and usually a sink and toilet. See illustration at APARTMENT. **2.** TOILET (def. 2). —***Idiom.*** **3. go to** or **use the bathroom,** to urinate or defecate.

bath•tub (bath′tub′) /ˈbæθˌtʌb/ *n.* [*count*] a large, long container to sit in while bathing. See illustration at APARTMENT.

bath•y•sphere (bath′ə sfēr′) /ˈbæθəˌsfɪər/ *n.* [*count*] a large, hollow, ball-shaped machine that can be lowered into the ocean by a cable, used to study deep-sea life.

ba•tik (bə tēk′) /bəˈtiyk/ *n.* **1.** [*noncount*] a technique of coloring and designing on cloth, using wax to cover those parts of the cloth not to be colored. **2.** [*count*] the design or a fabric so decorated: *a beautiful batik of a Tanzanian woman carrying firewood on her head.*

bat mitz•vah (bät mits′və, bäs) /ˈbɑt mɪtsvə, bɑs/ also **bas mitzvah,** *n.* [*count; often: Bat Mitzvah*] **1.** a ceremony for a girl of 12 or 13, paralleling the bar mitzvah. **2.** a girl participating in a bat mitzvah.

ba•ton (bə ton′, ba-) /bəˈtɒn, bæ-/ *n.* [*count*] **1.** a light, thin wand with which a conductor directs an orchestra or band: *He indicated the beat with his baton.* **2.** a metal rod twirled by a leader of a marching band. **3.** a thin cylinder passed from one member of a relay team to the next. **4.** a short heavy stick carried by a police officer.

bats (bats) /bæts/ *adj. Slang.* insane; crazy.

bat•tal•ion (bə tal′yən) /bəˈtælyən/ *n.* [*count*] an army unit made up of a headquarters and two or more companies. See -BAT-.

bat•ten (bat′n) /ˈbætn̩/ *n.* [*count*] **1.** a strip of wood fastened on other boards to keep them in place. **2.** a length of material used on a ship to fasten down a cover over a hatch. —***Idiom.*** **3. batten down the hatches, a.** to secure the covers of a ship's hatches with battens. **b.** to prepare to meet an emergency: *The tornado is coming, so we had better batten down the hatches here and get to the cellar.* See -BAT-.

bat•ter[1] (bat′ər) /ˈbætər/ *v.* **1.** to beat continuously or hard; pound repeatedly: [~ + *at/against* + *obj*]: *The waves battered against the shoreline.* [~ + *obj*]: *finally battered the door down.* **2.** [~ + *obj*] to beat (a person) over and over again, or to abuse in some other way: *accused of battering his former wife and child.* —**bat′ter•er,** *n.* [*count*] —**bat′ter•ing,** *n.* [*noncount*]: *accused of baby battering.*

bat•ter[2] (bat′ər) /ˈbætər/ *n.* [*noncount*] a thin mixture of flour, eggs, and milk or water, beaten together and used in cooking: *Pour some batter carefully into the frying pan.*

bat•ter[3] (bat′ər) /ˈbætər/ *n.* [*count*] a player who swings a bat or whose turn it is to bat, as in baseball or cricket.

bat′tering ram′, *n.* [*count*] a device used to force entrance to a building, batter down walls, etc.

bat•ter•y (bat′ə rē) /ˈbætəriy/ *n., pl.* **-ter•ies. 1.** [*count*] a device that produces electricity, made up of a combination of two or more connected electric cells: *The car battery was dead.* **2.** [*count*] a group of guns or other weapons operated in one place: *huge batteries of anti-aircraft guns.* **3.** [*count*] any group or series of similar things, esp. used for a common purpose: *a battery of aptitude tests.* **4.** [*noncount*] *Law.* an unlawful attack upon another person, esp. by beating or wounding: *accused of aggravated battery.* **5.** [*count*] a baseball pitcher and catcher considered as a unit. See -BAT-.

bat•tle (bat′l) /ˈbætl̩/ *n., v.,* **-tled, -tling. —***n.* **1.** a fight between two opposing military forces: [*count*]: *Several important battles took place for control of this seaport.* [*noncount*]: *He got a medal for wounds received in battle.* **2.** [*count*] any conflict between two persons, groups, etc.: *the battle of the sexes.* **—***v.* **3.** to fight (with an opponent) in a conflict: [*no obj*]: *The two armies battled furiously.* [~ + *against/with* + *obj*]: *battling against inflation and unemployment; They battled with the Germans for control of the sea.* [~ + *obj*]: *battled the Germans for control of the sea.* [~ + *for* + *obj*]: *battling for his life.* **4.** to struggle; try to accomplish or achieve: [~ + *to* + *verb*]: *battling to reduce our taxes.* [~ + *obj* + *to* + *verb*]: *battling the big car companies to lower their prices.* See -BAT-.

bat′tle-ax′ or **bat′tle-axe′,** *n.* [*count*] **1.** a large ax formerly used as a weapon of war. **2.** *Slang.* a fierce, quarrelsome, aggressive older woman.

bat•tle•field (bat′l fēld′) /ˈbætl̩ˌfiyld/ *n.* [*count*] **1.** the field or ground on which a battle is fought. **2.** Also called **bat•tle•ground** (bat′l ground′) /ˈbætl̩ˌgrawnd/. an area or subject of conflict: *The classroom had become a battlefield over competing attitudes concerning Columbus.*

bat•tle•ment (bat′l mənt) /ˈbætl̩mənt/ *n.* [*count*] Often, **battlements.** [*plural*] a low wall on the top of a castle with spaces for shooting through.

bat•tle•ship (bat′l ship′) /ˈbætl̩ˌʃɪp/ *n.* [*count*] the most heavily armored kind of warship.

bat•ty (bat′ē) /ˈbætiy/ *adj.,* **-ti•er, -ti•est.** *Slang.* crazy: *a real batty idea.* —**bat′ti•ness,** *n.* [*noncount*]

bau•ble (bô′bəl) /ˈbɔbəl/ *n.* [*count*] a cheap, showy ornament; trinket.

baud (bôd) /bɔd/ *n.* [*noncount*] a unit used to measure the speed of signaling or data transfer, as on a computer or telephone system, equal to the number of pulses or bits per second.

baulk (bôk) /bɔk/ *v., n. Chiefly Brit.* BALK.

baux•ite (bôk′sīt, bō′zīt) /ˈbɔksayt, ˈbowzayt/ *n.* [*noncount*] a claylike rock from which aluminum is produced.

bawd (bôd) /bɔd/ *n.* [*count*] **1.** a woman who maintains a brothel; a madam. **2.** a prostitute.

bawd•y (bô′dē) /ˈbɔdiy/ *adj.,* **-i•er, -i•est.** indecent; lewd; obscene.

bawl (bôl) /bɔl/ *v.* **1.** [*no obj*] to cry or wail loudly and strongly: *The baby was bawling all night.* **2.** to cry out: [*no obj*]: *She bawled down the hallway at me.* [~ + *obj*]: *The drunk was bawling this song all night.* [~ + *out* + *obj*]: *The captain bawled out the orders.* [*used with quotations*]: *There was an old woman bawling, "Repent, ye sinners!"* **3. bawl out,** *Informal.* to scold vigorously: [~ + *obj* + *out*]: *The dean bawled the students out for cheating.* [~ + *out* + *obj*]: *The dean bawled out the students who had been caught cheating.* **—***n.* [*count*] **4.** a loud shout or outcry: *I heard a loud bawl and then silence.*

bay¹ (bā) /bey/ *n.* [*count*] a body of water enclosed by a curve of the coast around it.

bay² (bā) /bey/ *n.* [*count*] **1.** any of the parts a large building or room may be divided into and used for a purpose: *backed the truck into the loading bay.* **2.** any portion or compartment of an aircraft: *a cargo bay.*

bay³ (bā) /bey/ *n.* **1.** [*count*] a deep, long howl. **2.** [*noncount; often: at* + ~] the position of an animal that is forced to stop running away from hunters chasing it and to face and resist them. **—***v.* [*no obj*] **3.** to howl, esp. with a deep, long sound: *A hound was baying at the moon.*

bay⁴ (bā) /bey/ *n.* LAUREL (def. 1).

bay⁵ (bā) /bey/ *n.* **1.** [*count*] a horse having a reddish-brown body and black mane, tail, and lower legs. **2.** [*noncount*] a reddish-brown color. **—***adj.* [*usually before a noun*] **3.** (esp. of a horse) reddish-brown.

bay′ leaf′, *n.* the dried leaf of the laurel, used as a flavoring in cooking: [*noncount*]: *Use bay leaf for flavor.* [*count*]: *Grind the bay leaves.*

bay•o•net (bā′ə nit, -net′, bā′ə net′) /ˈbeyənɪt, -ˌnɛt, ˌbeyəˈnɛt/ *n., v.,* **-net•ed** or **-net•ted, -net•ing** or **-net•ting. —***n.* [*count*] **1.** a steel weapon like a knife or dagger attached to a rifle and used for hand-to-hand combat. **—***v.* [~ + *obj*] **2.** to stab, kill, or wound with a bayonet.

bay•ou (bī′o͞o, bī′ō) /ˈbayuw, ˈbayow/ *n.* [*count*], *pl.* **-ous.** (in the southern U.S.) a body of water, usually muddy and still or with a slow current.

bay′ win′dow, *n.* [*count*] a large window sticking out from an outside wall and forming an alcove of a room.

ba•zaar (bə zär′) /bəˈzɑr/ *n.* [*count*] **1.** a marketplace, esp. in the Middle East. **2.** a sale of various things (often homemade or secondhand) to benefit some charity, etc.: *The church held a bazaar to raise money.*

ba•zoo•ka (bə zo͞o′kə) /bəˈzuwkə/ *n.* [*count*], *pl.* **-kas.** a tube-shaped rocket launcher that can be carried by a soldier and fired from the shoulder.

BB (bē′bē′) /ˈbiyˌbiy/ *n.* [*count*] a small, round ball that may be fired from an air rifle: *One of the BBs hit the target with a clang.* Also called **BB shot.**

B.B.A., an abbreviation of: Bachelor of Business Administration: *She received her B.B.A. in five years.*

BBC, an abbreviation of: British Broadcasting Corporation.

bbl., an abbreviation of: barrel (the measurement of an amount of oil, etc.)

BBQ, an abbreviation of: barbecue.

BBS, an abbreviation of: bulletin board service: a computerized facility that a computer user reaches by a modem, for collecting and sending electronic messages and software programs.

B.C. or **BC,** an abbreviation of: before Christ; in the years before Christ was born (used with dates).

B.C.E., an abbreviation of: **1.** Bachelor of Chemical Engineering. **2.** Bachelor of Civil Engineering. **3.** before the Christian (or Common) Era (used with dates).

bdrm., bedroom.

be (bē; *unstressed* bē, bi) /biy; *unstressed* biy, bɪ/ *v.* and *auxiliary verb. Present forms: singular; 1st person form:* **am,** *2nd person form:* **are,** *3rd person form:* **is.** *Present plural form:* **are.** *Past forms: singular; 1st person form:* **was,** *2nd person form:* **were,** *3rd person form:* **was.** *Past plural form:* **were.** *Present subjunctive form:* **be.** *Past subjunctive form:* **were.** *Present participle form:* **be•ing.** *Past participle form:* **been. —***v.* [*usually: not: be* + ~*-ing*] **1.** to have (the quality, job, etc., mentioned); used to connect the subject with an adjective, or to another noun or a phrase in order to describe, identify, or say more about the subject: *Wilt is tall. I am Barbara. Indira Gandhi was the first woman prime minister of India.* **2.** to exist or live: *Shakespeare's famous line "To be or not to be" asks if life is worth living. There is a man with five cats on my street (= A man with five cats lives/exists on my street).* See definition 10 below. **3.** to take place; occur: *The wedding was last week.* **4.** to occupy a place or position: *The book is on the table. We will be in Oslo in a few minutes. Where were you?* **5.** to belong to a group: *Whales are mammals.* **6.** to continue or remain as before: *Let things be.* **7.** (used as a verb to introduce a question or in a command, request, or piece of advice): *Is that right? Be quiet! Don't be so mean. Be careful about what you say.* **8.** (used after *it* or *there* in order to delay talking about the real subject of a sentence, or as a way of introducing something new about the subject): *It was she who was late for the class (real subject = "she"). There was a fly in my soup (real subject = "fly").* Note: in sentences with *there*, the form of *be* agrees with the real subject that follows: *There was a fly in my soup ("was" agrees with "fly"); There were flies in my soup ("were" agrees with "flies").* See THERE, IT. **9.** (used in a short answer where it stands for a longer phrase that has *be* in the question): *Is he coming? Yes, he* **is** *(= Yes, he is coming.) Are you the new president of the Chinese club? No, I* **am** *not (= No, I am not the new president of the Chinese club).* **10.** (used in a short question, called a tag question, that comes after a subject and verb to ask for the listener's agreement): *She is not very pretty,* **is** *she? You are running pretty hard,* **aren't** *you?* **—***auxiliary verb.* **11.** (used with the *-ing* form (the present participle) of another, main verb to show continuous activity): *I am waiting. We were talking.* **12.** (used with *to* plus the root form (the infinitive) of another verb to express a command, or indicate future action): *He is to see me today (= He will see me today). You are not to leave before six*

(= You must not leave before six). I am to start my new job next week (= I will start my new job next week). **13.** (used with the past participle of another verb to form the passive voice, that is, to show the action of the verb has been done to the subject of the sentence): *The policeman was shot. Your passports have been sent on.* **—Usage.** The verb BE is special in English, first because it functions as an auxiliary, but also in the way it works as a main verb. It changes forms depending on its subject in the present and past tenses. Like the verbs DO and HAVE, the verb BE comes first in questions that can be answered with the words "yes" or "no": *Am I sure? Is she crazy? Are you there?* Finally, the verb BE can have the word NOT after it (again like *do* and *have*): *She is not crazy.* When BE is used as a main verb, it seldom is used in the progressive tenses; we indicate this in this book by the symbol [*not: be + ~-ing*]. When talking about people's activity or how they behave, sometimes BE as a main verb can take the *-ing* form of itself: *I'm being careful (= I am acting in a careful manner); You're being so patient (= You are acting in so patient a manner).* We do not use BE in the *-ing* form to talk about states of the mind, or of feeling: *I am happy now* (**not:** *I am being happy now*); *He is tired now* (**not:** *He is being tired now*).

be-, *prefix.* **1.** *be-* is attached to words to make verbs with the meaning "to make, become, treat as": *be- + cloud → becloud (= make like a cloud, hard to see); be- + friend → befriend (= treat someone as a friend).* **2.** *be-* is also attached to adjectives and verbs ending in *-ed* to mean "covered all over; completely; all around": *be- + decked → bedecked (= decked or covered all over); be- + jeweled → bejeweled (= covered with jewels).*

B.E., an abbreviation of: **1.** Bachelor of Education. **2.** Bachelor of Engineering.

beach (bēch) /biytʃ/ *n.* [*count*] **1.** an area of sand along a shore: *the beaches of the islands of Greece.* **—***v.* **2.** to run (a boat) onto a beach: [*~ + obj*]: *We beached the boat and headed inland.* [*no obj*]: *The boats beached and the soldiers got out.*

beach•ball or **beach ball** (bēch′bôl′) /ˈbiytʃˌbɔl/ *n.* [*count*] a large, light, inflated ball, used for games at the seashore, in swimming pools, etc.

beach′ bug′gy, *n.* DUNE BUGGY.

beach•comb•er (bēch′kō′mər) /ˈbiytʃˌkowmər/ *n.* [*count*] a person who gathers or collects for sale items from beaches, like driftwood, shells, etc.

beach•head (bēch′hed′) /ˈbiytʃˌhɛd/ *n.* [*count*] the area that a military force landing on an enemy shore attempts to control first before further advancing: *That unit established a beachhead before pushing inland.*

bea•con (bē′kən) /ˈbiykən/ *n.* [*count*] **1.** a guiding signal, as a light, esp. one in a high position. **2.** a tower used for such purposes. **3.** a lighthouse, signal buoy in the water, etc., to warn and guide vessels. **4. a.** RADIO BEACON. **b.** a radio device sending out a signal as an aid to navigation.

bead (bēd) /biyd/ *n.* [*count*] **1.** a small object of glass, wood, etc., with a hole through it, often put on a string with others of its kind in necklaces, etc. **2. beads,** [*plural*] **a.** a necklace of beads. **b.** a rosary. **3.** a small drop of liquid or a bubble in a liquid: *Beads of sweat popped out on his head.* **—***v.* **4.** to form beads or a bead on: [*~ + obj*]: *The perspiration beaded his face.* [*no obj*]: *The moisture beaded on the glass.* **—*Idiom.* 5. draw** or **get a bead on,** [*~ + obj*] to take careful aim at (a target): *The hit man got a bead on his victim.*

bead•y (bē′dē) /ˈbiydiy/ *adj.* [*often before a noun*], **-i•er, -i•est.** beadlike; small, round, and shining: *the mouse's beady eyes.* **—bead′i•ness,** *n.* [*noncount*]

bea•gle (bē′gəl) /ˈbiygəl/ *n.* [*count*] a kind of small, short-legged dog with drooping ears and usually a black, tan, and white coat.

beak (bēk) /biyk/ *n.* [*count*] **1.** the hard, curved, horny part of a bird's mouth; bill. **2.** any horny or stiff mouthpart of an animal that sticks out or is curved like a bird's. **3.** *Slang.* a person's nose: *His beak curved out and down.* **—beaked** (bēkt, bē′kid) /biykt, ˈbiykɪd/ *adj.*

beak•er (bē′kər) /ˈbiykər/ *n.* [*count*] **1.** a large drinking cup or glass with a wide mouth. **2.** a cuplike container, esp. one used in a laboratory. **3.** the contents of a beaker.

beam (bēm) /biym/ *n.* [*count*] **1.** a long piece or bar of metal, wood, etc., used to support a roof, building, or other structure: *The beams in the basement had rotted away.* **2.** the widest part of a ship (used in measurement): *a fifteen-foot beam.* **3.** a long piece of wood mounted horizontally off the ground, used in gymnastics by women: *Watch her dismount from the beam.* **4.** a ray or stream of light or other radiation, as subatomic particles: *Beams of light danced off the window. The scientists shot a beam of electrons.* **5.** a radio signal sent along a narrow course, used to guide pilots. **—***v.* **6.** [*~ + obj*] to send out in or as if in beams or rays: *They beamed the X-rays through the material.* **7.** [*no obj*] to emit beams, as of light or heat: *The sun beamed through the dreary clouds.* **8.** [*~ + obj*] to transmit (a signal) in a particular direction: *We beamed the signal to the satellite.* **9.** to smile radiantly or happily: [*no obj*]: *beamed with satisfaction.* [*~ + obj*]: *beamed a smile of pure happiness.*

bean (bēn) /biyn/ *n.* [*count*] **1.** the nutritious seed of various plants of the legume family, eaten as a vegetable: *a can of beans.* **2.** a plant producing such seeds. **3.** any of various other beanlike seeds or plants: *the smell of freshly ground coffee beans.* **4.** *Informal.* a person's head: *Now you're using your bean.* **5. beans,** [*plural*] *Informal.* (used with negative words or phrases) the slightest amount: *He doesn't know beans about navigation.* **—***v.* [*~ + obj*] **6.** *Informal.* to hit on the head, esp. with a baseball. **—*Idiom.* 7. spill the beans,** *Informal.* to disclose a secret: *So, now she knows about the surprise; I wonder who spilled the beans?*

bear[1] (bâr) /bɛər/ *v.,* **bore** (bôr, bōr) /bɔr, bowr/ **borne** or **born** (bôrn) /bɔrn/ **bear•ing. 1.** [*~ + obj*] to hold up or support: *The columns can bear the weight of the roof.* **2.** to give birth to: [*~ + obj*]: *She was able to bear a child.* [*~ + obj + obj*]: *She bore her husband a child (= She bore for her husband a child).* **3.** [*~ + obj*] to produce by natural growth: *That tree bears fruit every year.* **4.** [*~ + obj*] to hold up under; be capable of: *This claim doesn't bear close examination.* **5.** [*~ + obj*] to drive or push: *The crowd bore us along Fifth Avenue.* **6.** [*~ + oneself*] to carry or conduct (oneself, etc.): *She bore herself bravely after her son's death.* **7.** [*often: with a negative word or phrase, or in questions*] to suffer without complaining: [*~ + obj*]: *I can't bear it.* [*~ + to + verb*]: *How can he even bear to look at her?* [*~ + verb-ing*]: *I can't bear your nagging anymore.* **8.** to be worthy of; be fit for: [*~ + obj*]: *That silly story doesn't bear repetition.* [*~ + verb-ing*]: *What he said doesn't bear repeating.* **9.** [*~ + obj*] to carry; bring: *Beware of Greeks bearing gifts.* **10.** to carry in the mind or heart; feel toward: [*~ + obj + to/toward*]: *I no longer bear any malice toward her.* [*~ + obj + obj*]: *I no longer bear her any malice.* **11.** [*~ + obj*] to transmit or spread (gossip, etc.): *I'm sorry to be the one to bear the bad news.* **12.** [*~ + obj*] to give or offer: *to bear testimony.* **13.** [*~ + obj + to*] to exhibit; show: *My daughter bears a remarkable resemblance to me.* **14.** [*~ + obj*] to possess as a quality or characteristic: *"This letter bears your signature, does it not?" the lawyer asked.* **15.** [*no obj*] to move or go in a (certain) direction or course: *Bear left at the traffic light.* **16. bear down,** [*no obj*] to try or struggle harder: *to bear down and do better in your studies.* **17. bear down on,** [*~ + down + on + obj*] **a.** to press or push down on: *Bear down hard on the screw as you turn the screwdriver.* **b.** to approach or move toward rapidly and threateningly: *She bore down angrily on me as soon as I got in the office.* **18. bear on** or **upon,** [*~ + on/upon + obj*] to show or have a connection to: *I can't see how this evidence bears on the case.* **19. bear out,** [*~ + obj + out*] to support; confirm or uphold: *The figures will bear me out.* **20. bear up,** [*no obj*] to face hardship bravely; endure: *bearing up very well ever since the tragedy.* **21. bear with,** [*~ + with + obj*] to be patient with: *If you'll just bear with me for a few minutes, we'll have the movie running again.* **—Usage.** Be careful with the forms BORN and BORNE as past participles of the verb BEAR. BORNE is the past participle in all senses that do not refer to physical birth: *The wheat fields have borne abundantly this year. Judges have always borne a burden of responsibility.* BORNE is also the form when the sense is "to bring forth (young)" and the focus is on the mother rather than on the child. In such cases, BORNE is preceded by a form of *have* or followed by *by: She had borne a son the previous year.* When the focus is on the offspring or on something that is brought forth as if by birth, BORN is the standard spelling, and it occurs only in passive constructions: *My friend was born in Ohio. A strange desire was born of the tragic experience.*

bear[2] (bâr) /bɛər/ *n., pl.* **bears,** (*esp. when thought of as a group*) **bear,** *adj.* **—***n.* [*count*] **1.** a large, stocky mammal with thick, rough fur and a very short tail. **2.** a gruff, clumsy, or rude person. **3.** one who believes that stock prices will decline: *Bears dominated the market today as* *prices fell.* **—*adj.*** [*before a noun*] **4.** marked by declining prices and increased selling of stocks: *a bear market.* —**bear′like′,** *adj.*

bear•a•ble (bâr′ə bəl) /ˈbɛərəbəl/ *adj.* that can be borne: *The pain was bearable.*

beard (bērd) /bɪərd/ *n.* [*count*] **1.** hair growing on the lower part of the face: *I shaved my beard before the interview.* **2.** a similar growth on the chin of some animals: *the beard of a goat.* **—*v.*** [~ + *obj*] **3.** to oppose (someone) boldly; defy: *It took courage for him to beard the board of directors.*

beard•ed (bēr′did) /ˈbɪərdɪd/ *adj.* having or wearing a beard.

bear•er (bâr′ər) /ˈbɛərər/ *n.* [*count*] **1.** a person or thing that carries: *the bearer of bad news.* **2.** one who presents an order for money or goods: *Pay to the bearer of this note the sum of one hundred dollars.*

bear′ hug′, *n.* [*count*] a very forceful, tight hug: *He gave him a bear hug that took his breath away.*

bear•ing (bâr′ing) /ˈbɛərɪŋ/ *n.* **1.** the manner in which one behaves or carries oneself: [*noncount*]: *She was a person of very dignified bearing.* [*count; singular*]: *She had a very regal bearing.* **2.** [*noncount*] the act of enduring or the capacity to endure: *The grief she suffered was almost beyond bearing.* **3.** [*usually:* ~ + *on*] reference, relation, or connection: [*noncount*]: *That fact has no bearing on the problem.* [*count; usually singular*]: *Does what you discovered have a bearing on this case?* **4.** [*count*] the part of a machine that supports and guides a moving part: *A bearing will greatly reduce friction.* **5.** [*count*] Often, **bearings.** [*plural*] direction or relative position: *The pilot radioed the plane's bearings.* **6.** [*count*] Often, **bearings.** [*plural*] a sense of direction or purpose in one's job or life: *The new trainee just needs time to get his bearings.*

bear•ish (bâr′ish) /ˈbɛərɪʃ/ *adj.* **1.** like a bear; rough, burly, or clumsy. **2.** (of the stock market) declining in prices: *a bearish market.* —**bear′ish•ly,** *adv.* —**bear′ish•ness,** *n.* [*noncount*]

bear•skin (bâr′skin′) /ˈbɛərˌskɪn/ *n.* [*count*] **1.** the skin of a bear. **2.** a tall, black fur cap forming part of a dress uniform in some armies.

beast (bēst) /biyst/ *n.* [*count*] **1.** any nonhuman animal, esp. a large, four-footed mammal: *the sounds of the beasts in the barn.* **2.** the crude nature common to humans and animals, esp. greed, lust, or rage: *Seeing her with him just brought out the beast in me.* **3.** a cruel, coarse, or filthy person: *He's always been a beast to her.*

beast•ie (bē′stē) /ˈbiystiy/ *n.* [*count*] a small animal.

beast•ly (bēst′lē) /ˈbiystliy/ *adj.,* **-li•er, -li•est,** *adv.* **—*adj.*** **1.** of or like a beast; bestial: *the beastly sounds in the barnyard.* **2.** nasty; unpleasant; disagreeable; unkind: *beastly weather; beastly behavior.* **—*adv.*** **3.** *Chiefly Brit. Informal.* very; exceedingly: *It's beastly cold outside.* —**beast′li•ness,** *n.* [*noncount*]

beast′ of bur′den, *n.* [*count*] an animal used for work, as a donkey, mule, or ox.

beat (bēt) /biyt/ *v.,* **beat, beat•en** or **beat, beat•ing,** *n., adj.* **—*v.*** **1.** to strike forcefully and repeatedly: [~ + *obj*]: *to beat a door down.* [*no obj*]: *She beat on the door until he finally answered.* **2.** to hit (a person or animal) repeatedly so as to cause injury; thrash: *beat him and left him for dead.* **3.** to smash against: [~ + *obj*]: *listening to the rain beating the trees.* [*no obj*]: *We heard the rain beating on the trees.* **4.** to flutter or flap: [~ + *obj*]: *a bird beating its wings.* [*no obj*]: *The hummingbird's wings were beating at least 100 times a second.* **5.** to hit (a drum) so as to make a sound: [~ + *obj*]: *The bagpipers began to beat their drums to start the parade.* [*no obj*]: *We could hear the drum beating in the distance.* **6.** [~ + *obj*] to stir (ingredients for a mixture) vigorously: *Beat the egg whites well.* **7.** [~ + *obj*] to break, shape, or make by hitting: *to beat swords into plowshares.* **8.** [~ + *obj*] to make (a path) by repeated walking: *beat a path through the jungle.* **9.** [~ + *obj*] to mark or keep (time) by strokes, as with a metronome: *Can't you beat time to this music?* **10.** [~ + *obj*] to defeat in a contest; do better than: *finally beat him in that match.* **11.** [~ + *obj*] *Informal.* to be better than: *Making reservations on the phone sure beats waiting in line.* **12.** [~ + *obj*] *Informal.* to baffle: *It beats me how he got the job.* **13.** [~ + *obj*] *Informal.* to soften or overcome the bad effects of: *He tried to beat the system by helping people directly.* **14.** [~ + *obj*] *Slang.* to escape or avoid (blame): *beat the rap by pleading temporary insanity.* **15.** [*no obj*] to throb or pulsate: *My heart was beating wildly every time she looked at me.* **16. beat back,** [~ + *back* + *obj*] to force (an enemy) back; force to withdraw: *The troops beat back the first assault.* **17. beat down,** [~ + *down* + *obj*] to subdue: *He was able to beat down his opposition.* **18. beat off,** to ward off; push back: [~ + *off* + *obj*]: *Our army beat off their attacks.* [~ + *obj* + *off*]: *We beat them off easily.* **19. beat out,** to defeat; win: [~ + *out* + *obj*]: *to beat out the competition.* [~ + *obj* + *out*]: *to beat them out.* **20. beat up,** to strike repeatedly so as to cause painful injury; thrash: [~ + *obj* + *up*]: *The gang beat him up.* [~ + *up* + *obj*]: *The gang beat up anyone they could.* **—*n.*** **21.** [*count*] a stroke or blow, or the sound made from such a stroke: *Give us two beats on the drum, then start the guitars.* **22.** [*count*] a throb or pulsing: *a pulse of 60 beats per minute.* **23.** [*count; usually singular*] the major rhythm of a piece of music: *All her songs have a great beat.* **24.** [*count; usually singular*] one's assigned area of responsibility: *The police officer's beat was my neighborhood.* **—*adj.*** **25.** [*be* + ~] *Informal.* exhausted; worn out: *really beat after staying up all night.* **26.** [*before a noun; often:* *Beat*] of or characteristic of members of the Beat Generation: *beat poetry.* **—*Idiom.*** **27. beat it,** *Informal.* to go away: *I told you to beat it and leave me alone.*

beat•en (bēt′n) /ˈbiytn̩/ *adj.* [*usually: before a noun*] **1.** formed by blows; hammered: *a dish of beaten brass.* **2.** walked on a great deal; commonly used: *a well-beaten path.* **—*Idiom.*** **3. off the beaten track** or **path,** out of the ordinary; unusual: *We found a little restaurant off the beaten track.*

beat•er (bē′tər) /ˈbiytər/ *n.* [*count*] **1.** a person or thing that beats: *Wife-beaters do not receive light sentences from that judge.* **2.** a tool for beating something: *Use the beater to get those egg whites fluffy.*

Beat′ Genera′tion, *n.* [*count; usually singular; often: beat generation*] members of the generation that reached maturity in the 1950's, in favor of the relaxation of conventions and artistic norms.

be•a•tif•ic (bē′ə tif′ik) /ˌbiyəˈtɪfɪk/ *adj.* showing peaceful, calm happiness; saintly: *gave a beatific smile.* —**be′a•tif′i•cal•ly,** *adv.*

be•at•i•fy (bē at′ə fī′) /biyˈætəˌfay/ *v.* [~ + *obj*], **-fied, -fy•ing.** (in the Roman Catholic Church) to declare (a dead person) to be among the blessed and entitled to specific religious honor: *The Church beatified Joan of Orleans.* —**be•at•i•fi•ca•tion** (bē at′ə fi kā′shən) /biyˌætəfɪˈkeyʃən/ *n.* [*count*]: *A beatification takes some time.* [*noncount*]: *a candidate for beatification.*

beat•ing (bē′ting) /ˈbiytɪŋ/ *n.* **1.** [*count*] the receiving of strokes from someone who beats: *Beatings began to increase in the neighborhood.* **2.** [*count*] a defeat or reverse; loss; setback: *took several beatings before we bounced back.* **3.** [*noncount*] throbbing: *Can you feel the beating of my heart?*

beat•nik (bēt′nik) /ˈbiytnɪk/ *n.* [*count; sometimes: Beatnik*] one who rejects acceptable behavior; a member of the Beat Generation.

beat-up (bēt′up′) /ˈbiytˈʌp/ *adj. Informal.* dilapidated; broken-down: *my old, beat-up train set got restored.*

beau (bō) /bow/ *n.* [*count*], *pl.* **beaus, beaux** (bōz). a girl's or woman's sweetheart.

beaut (byo͞ot) /byuwt/ *n.* [*count*] *Informal.* (often used ironically) a beautiful or remarkable person or thing: *That black eye of yours is a real beaut.*

beau•te•ous (byo͞o′tē əs, -tyəs) /ˈbyuwtiyəs, -tyəs/ *adj.* beautiful. —**beau′te•ous•ly,** *adv.*

beau•ti•cian (byo͞o tish′ən) /byuwˈtɪʃən/ *n.* [*count*] one who styles and dresses the hair.

beau•ti•ful (byo͞o′tə fəl) /ˈbyuwtəfəl/ *adj.* **1.** having beauty: *a beautiful view of the mountains.* **2.** excellent; wonderful; remarkable: *a beautiful putt on the seventh hole.* **—*interj.*** **3.** (often used ironically) wonderful; excellent; remarkable: *"Failed again? Oh, beautiful," he mumbled to himself.* —**beau′ti•ful•ly,** *adv.*: *She dressed beautifully.*

beau•ti•fy (byo͞o′tə fī′) /ˈbyuwtəˌfay/ *v.* [~ + *obj*], **-fied, -fy•ing.** to make beautiful: *the campaign to beautify our highways by reducing litter.* —**beau•ti•fi•ca•tion** (byo͞o′tə fi kā′shən) /ˌbyuwtəfɪˈkeyʃən/ *n.* [*noncount*] —**beau′ti•fi′er,** *n.* [*count*]

beau•ty (byo͞o′tē) /ˈbyuwtiy/ *n., pl.* **-ties. 1.** [*noncount*] the quality that gives pleasure to the mind or the senses; the quality of being beautiful: *Beauty is only skin deep.* **2.** [*count*] a beautiful person, esp. a woman: *She's a real beauty.* **3.** [*count*] something beautiful, as an animal or a work of art. **4.** [*count*] Often, **beauties.** [*plural*] something beautiful in nature: *looking at the beauties of nature on an island in the Baltic.* **5.** [*count*] a particular advantage: *One of the beauties of this plan is its low cost.* **6.** [*count*] (often used ironically) something remarkable or excellent: *My old car was a beauty.*

beau′ty par′lor, *n.* [*count*] an establishment for women to have their hair cut or styled and for other beauty treatments. Also called **beau′ty salon′, beau′ty shop′.**

beaux (bōz) /bowz/ *n.* [*plural*] a pl. of BEAU.

beaux arts (bō zär′) /bow'zɑr/ *n.* [*plural*] the fine arts.

bea•ver (bē′vər) /'biyvər/ *n., pl.* **-vers,** (*esp. when thought of as a group*) **-ver** for 1. **1.** [*count*] a large rodent that lives in water, having webbed hind feet and a large flat tail. **2.** [*noncount*] the fur of this animal: *crazy enough to wear a beaver coat to the animal rights convention.* **3.** *Informal.* an active, hard-working person: *She was an eager beaver, working late every night.*

be•bop (bē′bop′) /'biy,bɒp/ *n.* BOP[1].

be•calm•ed (bi kämd′) /bɪ'kɑmd/ *adj.* (of a sailing ship) still, because of the absence of wind: *My stomach got worse when the ship was becalmed.*

be•came (bi kām′) /bɪ'keym/ *v.* a pt. of BECOME.

be•cause (bi kôz′, -kuz′) /bɪ'kɔz, -'kʌz/ *conj.* **1.** for the reason that; due to the fact that: *always late because it took so long to get dressed.* **—***prep.* **2. because of,** for the reason of; on account of; due to: *The train was late because of the bad weather.* **—Usage.** Use BECAUSE before the reason or cause for something when there are two clauses you are joining; use BECAUSE OF when a noun phrase, not a clause, describes the reason for something.

beck (bek) /bɛk/ *n.* [*noncount*] **—*Idiom.* at someone's beck and call,** ready and willing to do what someone wishes: *was always at the boss's beck and call.*

beck•on (bek′ən) /'bɛkən/ *v.* [~ *(+ to) + obj*] **1.** to signal, summon, or direct (someone) to come near, as by waving the hand or moving a finger: *He beckoned (to) me and I went into his office.* **2.** to call to; attract; lure; entice: *Fame and fortune beckoned (to) him.* **—beck′on•er,** *n.* [*count*]

be•cloud (bi kloud′) /bɪ'klawd/ *v.* [~ + *obj*] **1.** to obscure with clouds. **2.** to make confused: *Problems began to becloud the real issues.*

be•come (bi kum′) /bɪ'kʌm/ *v.,* **-came, -come, -com•ing. 1.** [~ + *adjective*] to come, change, or grow to be (as specified): *I became tired and went to bed.* **2.** [~ + *noun*] to come into being: *She became a ballerina.* **3.** [~ + *obj; not: be + ~-ing*] to be attractive on; suit: *That dress becomes you.* **4.** [~ + *obj; not: be + ~-ing*] to be suitable to the dignity or rank: *conduct that becomes an officer.* See BECOMING. **—*Idiom.* 5. become of,** [~ + *obj; used in questions*] to happen to (someone or something); to be the fate of (someone or something): *Whatever became of him?*

be•com•ing (bi kum′ing) /bɪ'kʌmɪŋ/ *adj.* **1.** giving a pleasing effect or attractive appearance: *wore a becoming hairdo.* **2.** [*usually: be +* ~] suitable; proper: *Such language during that speech was not becoming.*

bed (bed) /bɛd/ *n., v.,* **bed•ded, bed•ding. —***n.* **1.** [*count*] a piece of furniture on which one sleeps or rests: *The hotel room had two double beds.* See illustration at APARTMENT. **2.** [*noncount*] the act of or time for sleeping: *It's time for bed!* **3.** [*count*] an area of ground for growing plants: *a flower bed.* **4.** [*count*] the bottom of a body of water: *the sea bed.* **5.** [*count*] an area on the bottom of a body of water that has a supply of plant or animal life: *an oyster bed.* **—***v.* [~ + *obj*] **6.** to provide with or put to a bed: *We bedded them for a week.* **—*Idiom.* 7. get up on the wrong side of the bed,** to be cranky and fussy from the moment one awakes: *He's mean today; he must have gotten up on the wrong side of the bed.* **8. go to bed,** [*no obj*] to retire, esp. for the night: *They're really tired, let them go to bed.* **9. go to bed with,** [~ + *obj*] to have sexual relations with: *He just wants to go to bed with you.* **10. in bed, a.** beneath the covers of a bed: *still in bed at two in the afternoon.* **b.** having sexual intercourse: *found him in bed with his secretary.* **11. make a bed,** to fit a bed with sheets and blankets.

B.Ed., an abbreviation of: Bachelor of Education.

be•daub (bi dôb′) /bɪ'dɔb/ *v.* [~ + *obj*] to smear all over with something wet and sticky; soil: *Her face was bedaubed with mud.*

bed•bug or **bed bug** (bed′bug′) /'bɛd,bʌg/ *n.* [*count*] a wingless bug that sucks blood and lives in houses and beds.

bed•clothes (bed′klōz′, -klōt͟hz′) /'bɛd,klowz, -,klowðz/ *n.* [*plural*] coverings for a bed, as sheets and blankets; bedding: *He threw off the bedclothes and jumped out of bed.*

bed•ding (bed′ing) /'bɛdɪŋ/ *n.* [*noncount*] **1.** BEDCLOTHES. **2.** litter, straw, dried grass, etc., used as a bed for animals: *the bedding in a barn stall.*

be•deck (bi dek′) /bɪ'dɛk/ *v.* [~ + *obj* + *with*] to decorate; to hang ornaments or decorations on: *a veteran bedecked with medals.*

be•dev•il (bi dev′əl) /bɪ'dɛvəl/ *v.* [~ + *obj*], **-iled, -il•ing** or (*esp. Brit.*) **-illed, -il•ling. 1.** to trouble in a mean way. **2.** to cause confusion; complicate. **—be•dev′il•ment,** *n.* [*noncount*]

bed•fel•low (bed′fel′ō) /'bɛd,fɛlow/ *n.* [*count*] a person who joins with another for a short time because it is useful or profitable to do so: *Politics makes strange bedfellows.*

bed•lam (bed′ləm) /'bɛdləm/ *n.* [*noncount*] a place or condition of wild noise and confusion: *The classroom was total bedlam when I walked in.*

bed′ of ros′es, *n.* [*count; singular; a* + ~] a situation of ease and luxury; a very agreeable position: *Did you think marriage was going to be a bed of roses?*

Bed•ou•in (bed′o͞o in, bed′win) /'bɛduwɪn, 'bɛdwɪn/ *n.* [*count*], *pl.* **-ins,** (*esp. when thought of as a group*) **-in. 1.** a nomadic Arab of the deserts of SW Asia and N Africa. **2.** a wanderer; nomad.

bed•pan (bed′pan′) /'bɛd,pæn/ *n.* [*count*] a shallow pan shaped like the seat of a toilet, for use by the bedridden.

be•drag•gled (bi drag′əld) /bɪ'drægəld/ *adj.* limp, wet, or untidy, as with rain or dirt: *all cold and bedraggled after falling into the stream.*

bed•rid•den (bed′rid′n) /'bɛd,rɪdn̩/ *adj.* staying in bed because of illness, injury, etc.

bed•rock (bed′rok′) /'bɛd,rɒk/ *n.* **1.** [*noncount*] unbroken solid rock in the earth below the soil. **2.** [*count*] the bottom or lowest layer (of rock). **3.** [*count*] a firm foundation or basis: *claimed that democracy was the bedrock of our country.*

bed•room (bed′ro͞om′, -ro͝om′) /'bɛd,ruwm, -,rʊm/ *n.* [*count*] **1.** a room used for sleeping. See illustration at APARTMENT. **—***adj.* [*before a noun*] **2.** concerned mainly with love affairs: *a typical bedroom comedy.* **3.** inhabited largely by commuters: *bedroom suburbs.*

bed•side (bed′sīd′) /'bɛd,sayd/ *n.* [*count; usually singular*] **1.** the side of a bed, esp. the place of someone taking care of or visiting a sick person: *at my bedside when I got ill.* **—***adj.* **2.** at or for a bedside: *a bedside examination.*

bed•sore (bed′sôr′, -sōr′) /'bɛd,sɔr, -,sowr/ *n.* [*count*] a sore on the skin, caused by prolonged pressure on a bedridden patient.

bed•spread (bed′spred′) /'bɛd,sprɛd/ *n.* [*count*] an outer covering, usually decorated, for a bed.

bed•stead (bed′sted′, -stid) /'bɛd,stɛd, -stɪd/ *n.* [*count*] the framework of a bed, holding up the springs and a mattress.

bed•time (bed′tīm′) /'bɛd,taym/ *n.* the time a person goes to bed: [*noncount*]: *Come on kids, it's bedtime.* [*count*]: *earlier bedtimes.*

bee (bē) /biy/ *n.* [*count*] **1.** an insect known for its sting and for making honey. **2.** a social gathering to perform some task, etc.: *a quilting bee.* **—*Idiom.* 3. have a bee in one's bonnet,** to be continually thinking or talking about a single idea: *got something of a bee in his bonnet about deregulation.*

beech (bēch) /biytʃ/ *n.* **1.** [*count*] a tree having a smooth gray bark and small, triangular nuts. **2.** [*noncount*] the wood of such a tree.

beef (bēf) /biyf/ *n., pl.* **beefs** for 2, *v.* **—***n.* **1.** [*noncount*] the flesh of a cow, steer, or bull raised and killed for meat: *They roasted beef on the fire.* **2.** [*count*] *Slang.* a complaint: *"You got a beef, go see the manager."* **—***v.* **3.** [*no obj*] *Slang.* to complain; grumble: *Quit beefing and get back to work.* **4. beef up,** [~ + *up* + *obj*] to add strength, numbers, force, etc., to: *Beef up that report with some facts and figures.*

beef•steak (bēf′stāk′) /'biyf,steyk/ *n.* [*noncount*] a portion of beef for broiling, pan-frying, etc.

beef•y (bē′fē) /'biyfiy/ *adj.,* **-i•er, -i•est. 1.** of or like beef: *a beefy taste.* **2.** brawny; muscular: *a beefy cop.* **—beef′i•ness,** *n.* [*noncount*]

bee•hive (bē′hīv′) /'biy,hayv/ *n.* [*count*] **1.** a living place for bees: *The beehive had become as tall and wide as a person.* **2.** a crowded, busy place: *The office had become a beehive of activity.* **3.** something resembling the shape of a beehive, as a high hairdo.

been (bin) /bɪn/ *v.* pp. of BE.

beep (bēp) /biyp/ *n.* [*count*] **1.** a short, high-pitched tone produced by an automobile horn or other electronic device as a signal to call or warn: *The beep of the computer tells you that you have hit the wrong key.* **—v. 2.** to (cause to) make or emit such a sound: [*no obj*]: *The car beeped at me until I fastened my seatbelt.* [~ + *obj*]: *The driver beeped her horn.*

beep•er (bē′pər) /ˈbiypər/ *n.* [*count*] a pocket-size device that beeps when the person carrying it receives a telephone message: *left her beeper at home.*

beer (bēr) /bɪər/ *n.* **1.** [*noncount*] an alcoholic drink made by brewing and fermenting certain grains, having a slightly bitter taste. **2.** [*noncount*] any of various drinks made from roots, sugar, yeast, etc.: *root beer; ginger beer.* **3.** [*count*] a single serving (in a glass, or other container) of beer: *We'll have three beers.*

bees•wax (bēz′waks′) /ˈbiyzˌwæks/ *n.* WAX[1] (def. 1).

beet (bēt) /biyt/ *n.* **1.** [*noncount*] a plant having a fleshy red or white root. **2.** [*count*] the root of such a plant: *We had beets for dinner.*

bee•tle (bēt′l) /ˈbiytl̩/ *n.* [*count*] an insect having hard, horny front wings that cover and protect the wings used for flight.

be•fall (bi fôl′) /bɪˈfɔl/ *v.* [~ + *obj*], **-fell, -fall•en, -fall•ing.** to happen to (someone), esp. by chance: *What had befallen them?*

be•fit (bi fit′) /bɪˈfɪt/ *v.* [~ + *obj*], **-fit•ted, -fit•ting.** to be proper or appropriate for: *The food and service befitted a luxury hotel.*

be•fit•ting (bi fit′ing) /bɪˈfɪtɪŋ/ *adj.* suitable for; proper to; fitting: *accommodations befitting a queen.* **—be•fit′•ting•ly,** *adv.*

be•fog•ged (bi fogd′, -fôgd) /bɪ ˈfɒgd, -fɔgd/ *adj.* confused; dazed or puzzled.

be•fore (bi fôr′, -fōr′) /bɪˈfɔr, -ˈfowr/ *prep.* **1.** previous to; earlier than: *Call me before noon.* **2.** in front or ahead of: *She stood before the window.* **3.** in preference to; rather than: *They would die before surrendering.* **4.** in the presence or sight of: *hated to appear before a live audience.* **5.** under the consideration or jurisdiction of: *She was summoned before a magistrate.* **6.** viewed by; as seen and judged by: *a crime before God and humanity.* **7.** without figuring or deducting: *What is your gross income before deductions?* **—adv. 8.** in time preceding; previously: *Haven't we met somewhere before?* **9.** earlier or sooner: *I think I saw her the week before.* **—conj. 10.** previous to the time when: *See me before you go.* **11.** sooner than; rather than: *I will die before I give in.*

be•fore•hand (bi fôr′hand′, -fōr′-) /bɪˈfɔrˌhænd, -ˈfowr-/ *adv.* in advance; ahead of time; earlier: *Anticipate the problems beforehand.*

be•friend (bi frend′) /bɪˈfrɛnd/ *v.* [~ + *obj*] to act as a friend to; help: *She was one of the few people there willing to befriend a new freshman.*

be•fud•dle (bi fud′l) /bɪˈfʌdl̩/ *v.* [~ + *obj*], **-dled, -dling.** to confuse: *Those fancy arguments befuddled me.* **—be•fud′dle•ment,** *n.* [*noncount*]: *in a state of complete befuddlement.*

beg (beg) /bɛg/ *v.,* **begged, beg•ging. 1.** [~ + *obj*] to ask for something as a gift or as a favor: *to beg alms; to beg forgiveness.* **2.** [*no obj*] to ask someone for money or charity; live by doing this: *children and old women begging in the streets.* **3.** to ask (someone) to give or do something; implore: [~ + *obj* + *for* + *obj*]: *He begged me for help.* [~ + *obj* + *to* + *verb*]: *I begged him to drive slowly.* [~ + *of* + *obj*]: *I beg of you, stop this drinking!* **4.** [~ + *obj*] to avoid; evade: *a report that begs the whole problem.* **5.** [~ + *to* + *verb*] to take the liberty of (saying or doing something); to allow oneself: *He begged to differ with you on that topic.* **6. beg off,** to request permission not to do (something assigned): [~ + *off* + *obj*]: *I begged off that assignment.* [~ + *verb-ing*]: *I begged off serving on that committee.* **—*Idiom.* 7. beg the question,** to assume the truth of the point in dispute: *If you try to prove that the death penalty reduces crime by saying that crime is reduced by having the death penalty, you are begging the question.* **8. go begging,** [*no obj*] to remain open or available: *That job went begging for lack of qualified applicants.*

be•gan (bi gan′) /bɪˈgæn/ *v.* pt. of BEGIN.

be•gat (bi gat′) /bɪˈgæt/ *v. Archaic.* pt. of BEGET.

be•get (bi get′) /bɪˈgɛt/ *v.* [~ + *obj*], **-got, -got•ten** or **-got, -get•ting. 1.** (esp. of a male) to become the father of (offspring); procreate: *In the Bible, Isaac begat Jacob.* **2.** to cause; produce as an effect: *Power begets power.*

beg•gar (beg′ər) /ˈbɛgər/ *n.* [*count*] **1.** a person who begs: *Thousands of people became beggars in the streets after the war.* **2.** *Chiefly Brit.* a person; fellow: *You lucky beggar!* **—v.** [~ + *obj*] **3.** to cause to become a beggar; impoverish: *The tyrant beggared the country at the expense of the people.* **—*Idiom.* 4. beggar description,** to be impossible to describe because words would be inadequate: *The dirt, noise, and poverty of the place beggar description.*

beg•gar•ly (beg′ər lē) /ˈbɛgərliy/ *adj.* [*usually before a noun*] **1.** like or befitting a beggar. **2.** so little or low as to be very inadequate: *a beggarly salary.*

be•gin (bi gin′) /bɪˈgɪn/ *v.,* **-gan** (-gan′) /-ˈgæn/ **-gun** (-gun′) /-ˈgʌn/ **-gin•ning. 1.** to proceed to the first part of (an action); start: [*no obj*]: *The movie begins at 6 p.m.* [~ + *obj*]: *We'd like you to begin work tomorrow.* [~ + *to* + *verb*]: *I began to feel dizzy.* [~ + *verb-ing*]: *began crying after the movie started.* **2.** to come into existence; arise: [*no obj*]: *The custom of women wearing shorter skirts began during the war.* [~ + *as* + *obj*]: *The restaurant began as a small cafeteria.* [~ + *obj* + *as*]: *He began his political career as a state senator.* **3.** [~ + *with* + *obj*] to have a first part: *"Cicero" begins with a C.* **4.** [~ + *to* + *verb; used with a negative word or phrase, or in questions*] to succeed to the slightest extent or amount: *The financial aid won't begin to cover expenses.* **—*Idiom.* 5. to begin with,** in the first place; the first reason (is): *We need this book. To begin with, there isn't much written about the subject.* **—Usage.** In the first meaning of BEGIN, it is possible to use the *-ing* form or the *to* + *verb* (INFINITIVE) form after it: *She stood up and began* ***playing*** or ***to play*** *the trumpet.* Although both are possible, there is a slight difference in meaning. With the *-ing* form we expect the trumpet playing to go on for a while, and assume that in the past (perhaps) there has been some playing. With the *to* + *verb* form there is a possibility that her playing might soon be stopped, interrupted, or cut short; the playing may not continue for quite so long. **—Syn.** BEGIN, COMMENCE, INITIATE, START (when followed by a noun or verb in the *-ing* form) refers to setting into motion or progress something that continues for some time. BEGIN is the common term: *She began knitting a sweater in March.* COMMENCE is a more formal word, often suggesting a more prolonged or complicated beginning: *The lawyers commenced court proceedings against my client.* INITIATE implies an active and often clever or exciting first action in a new field: *The scientists initiated a new procedure for deriving more energy from the atom.* START means to make a first move or set out on a course of action: *The workers started paving the street.*

be•gin•ner (bi gin′ər) /bɪˈgɪnər/ *n.* [*count*] a person or thing that begins something and has just started to learn it; novice: *just a beginner at computer programming.*

be•gin•ning (bi gin′ing) /bɪˈgɪnɪŋ/ *n.* [*count*] **1.** an act of starting: *the beginning of hostilities.* **2.** [*usually singular*] the point at which anything starts: *Register for my course at the beginning of the term.* **3.** the first part: *the beginning of the book.* **4.** Often, **beginnings.** [*plural*] an initial or basic stage: *The beginnings of modern chemistry are found in the works of the alchemists.* **5.** [*usually singular*] origin; source: *A misunderstanding was the beginning of their quarrel.* **—adj.** [*before a noun*] **6.** basic or introductory: *beginning Spanish.*

be•gone (bi gôn′, -gon′) /bɪˈgɔn, -ˈgɒn/ *v.* (*used as a command*) Go away! Depart!

be•go•nia (bi gōn′yə, -gō′nē ə) /bɪˈgownyə, -ˈgowniyə/ *n.* [*count*], *pl.* **-nias.** a tropical plant grown for its ornamental leaves and flowers.

be•got (bi got′) /bɪˈgɒt/ *v.* a pt. and a pp. of BEGET.

be•got•ten (bi got′n) /bɪˈgɒtn̩/ *v.* a pp. of BEGET.

be•grudge (bi gruj′) /bɪˈgrʌdʒ/ *v.,* **-grudged, -grudg•ing. 1.** [~ + *obj* + *obj*] to envy or resent the good fortune of (someone else): *begrudged her friend the scholarship.* **2.** [~ + *obj*] to be reluctant to give, grant, or allow: *did not begrudge the money she spent on education.* **—be•grudg′ing•ly,** *adv.*: *He acted begrudgingly to those who had been promoted past him.*

be•guile (bi gīl′) /bɪˈgayl/ *v.,* **-guiled, -guil•ing. 1.** to cheat; mislead; deceive: [~ + *obj* + *into* + *obj*]: *He beguiled his students into thinking they would pass the test.* [~ + *obj* + *with*]: *beguiled her with a lot of promises.* **2.** [~ + *obj*] to charm: *There are numerous small shops to beguile the tourist.* **3.** [~ + *obj*] to pass (time) pleasantly: *They beguiled the hours away.* **—be•guile′ment,** *n.* [*noncount*] **—be•guil′er,** *n.* [*count*]

be•guil•ing (bi gī′ling) /bɪ ˈgaylɪŋ/ *adj.* charming; attractive: *her beguiling smile.* **—be•guil′ing•ly,** *adv.*: *looked up at her beguilingly.*

be•gun (bi gun′) /bɪˈgʌn/ *v.* pp. of BEGIN.

be•half (bi haf′) /bɪˈhæf/ *n.* [*noncount*] **—*Idiom.* in** or

on behalf of. Also, **in** or **on someone's behalf.** as a representative of (someone); (speaking) in place of or for: *On behalf of the president, who could not be with us tonight, I am happy to be speaking to you.*

be•have (bi hāv′) /bɪ'heyv/ *v.*, **-haved, -hav•ing. 1.** [*no obj*] to act or react in a particular way: *The car behaves well in traffic.* **2.** to act properly: [*no obj*]: *Did the child behave?* [~ + *oneself*]: *to behave oneself in public.*

be•hav•ior (bi hāv′yər) /bɪ'heyvyər/ *n.* [*noncount*] **1.** the manner of behaving: *Your behavior today in class was bad.* **2.** the activity of a human or animal that can be observed: *argued that all behavior is a reaction to something outside an individual.* **3.** the action of any material under given circumstances: *Describe the behavior of this metal when heated.* **—*Idiom.* 4. be on one's best behavior,** to act or behave as properly as one can: *The children were on their best behavior.* —**be•hav′ior•al,** *adj.*: *the behavioral sciences.* —**be•hav′ior•al•ly,** *adv.*

be•hav•ior•ism (bi hāv′yə riz′əm) /bɪ'heyvyə,rɪzəm/ *n.* [*noncount*] the theory that psychology can be studied only through the examination and analysis of behavioral events that can be observed, and not by trying to examine mental states. —**be•hav′ior•ist,** *n.* [*count*]: *the most famous of the behaviorists.* —**be•hav′ior•is′tic,** *adj.*: *Behavioristic analyses can't tell us much about language ability.* —**be•hav′ior•is′ti•cal•ly,** *adv.*

be•hav•iour (bi hāv′yər) /bɪ'heyvyər/ *n. Chiefly Brit.* BEHAVIOR.

be•head (bi hed′) /bɪ'hɛd/ *v.* [~ + *obj*] to cut off the head of; decapitate: *How many people were beheaded during the French Revolution?* —**be•head′al,** *n.* [*count*] —**be•head′er,** *n.* [*count*]

be•held (bi held′) /bɪ'hɛld/ *v.* pt. and pp. of BEHOLD.

be•he•moth (bi hē′məth) /bɪ'hiyməθ/ *n.* [*count*] any creature or thing of monstrous size or power: *The government had become a behemoth.*

be•hest (bi hest′) /bɪ'hɛst/ *n.* [*count; usually singular*] a command; directive: *at the king's behest; at the behest of the king.*

be•hind (bi hīnd′) /bɪ'haynd/ *prep.* **1.** at or toward the rear of: *Look behind the house.* **2.** later than; after: *already well behind schedule.* **3.** in the state of making less progress than: *fallen behind our opponents.* **4.** on the farther side of; beyond: *right there, behind the mountain ahead of us.* **5.** in a role of supporting: *Are you behind me in this?* **6.** hidden by: *a great deal of hatred behind that smile of hers.* **7.** responsible for starting or operating (something): *Who was behind all these rumors?* **8.** having had (experience, etc.) in a time already passed: *twenty years' experience behind him.* **—*adv.* 9.** at or toward the rear; rearward: *to lag behind.* **10.** in a place or stage already passed: *left our bad times behind.* **11.** slow; late: *several months behind in her rent.* **—*adj.*** [*be* + ~] **12.** late; not on schedule: *I'm way behind now; can I call you back later?* **—*n.*** [*count*] **13.** *Informal.* the backside; buttocks.

be•hold (bi hōld′) /bɪ'howld/ *v.*, **-held, -hold•ing,** *interj.* **—*v.*** [~ + *obj*] **1.** to observe; look at; see: *He beheld the splendor of the city before him.* **—*interj.* 2.** look; see: *And, behold, three sentries of the King did appear.* —**be•hold′er,** *n.* [*count*]: *Beauty is in the eye of the beholder.*

be•hold•en (bi hōl′dən) /bɪ'howldən/ *adj.* [*be* + ~ + *to* + *obj*] owing something to someone; obligated; indebted: *a man who was beholden to no one.*

be•hoove (bi ho͞ov′) /bɪ'huwv/ *v.* [*usually: it* + ~ + *obj* + *to* + *verb*], **-hooved, -hoov•ing.** to be necessary or proper for; be worthwhile to (do something): *It behooves us to reconsider.*

beige (bāzh) /beyʒ/ *n.* [*noncount*] **1.** a light grayish brown, as of undyed wool. **—*adj.* 2.** of the color beige.

be•ing (bē′ing) /'biyɪŋ/ *n.* **1.** [*noncount*] the fact of existing; existence: *brought this council into being to find new solutions.* **2.** [*noncount*] conscious, living existence; life: *How did we come into being?* **3.** [*count*] a living thing; creature: *Are there intelligent beings on other planets?* **4.** [*count*] a human being; person. **—*conj.* 5.** [~ + *how/that*] *Chiefly Dialect.* since; because; considering: *Being that we don't really know you, how can we vote for you?* **—*v.* 6.** (used in a phrase to explain something about the rest of the sentence): *I was scared and feeling pretty anxious, this being my first time in a new country.*

be•jew•eled (bi jo͞o′əld) /bɪ'dʒuwəld/ *adj.* adorned or decorated with or as if with jewels.

bel (bel) /bɛl/ *n.* [*count*] ten decibels (a measurement of sound intensity).

be•la•bor (bi lā′bər) /bɪ'leybər/ *v.* [~ + *obj*] **1.** to explain or worry about too much: *Why did he keep belaboring that obvious point?* **2.** to beat; pummel. Also, *esp. Brit.,* **be•la′bour.** See -LAB-.

be•lat•ed (bi lā′tid) /bɪ'leytɪd/ *adj.* coming or being after the expected time: *a belated birthday card.* —**be•lat′ed•ly,** *adv.*: *I was invited somewhat belatedly to the party.* —**be•lat′ed•ness,** *n.* [*noncount*]

belch (belch) /bɛltʃ/ *v.* **1.** [*no obj*] to send out gas noisily from the stomach through the mouth: *He took a swallow of beer and belched happily.* **2.** to gush forth; send forth violently: [*no obj;* (~ + *out*)]: *Smoke belched (out) from the chimney.* [~ (+ *out*) + *obj*]: *The tailpipe was belching (out) clouds of smoke.* **—*n.*** [*count*] **3.** an act or instance of belching: *let out a belch.* —**belch′er,** *n.* [*count*]

be•lea•guer (bi lē′gər) /bɪ'liygər/ *v.* [~ + *obj*] **1.** to surround and attack with military forces: *The city was beleaguered for days by the enemy.* **2.** to give trouble or difficulties to; harass: *the beleaguered taxpayers.*

bel•fry (bel′frē) /'bɛlfriy/ *n.* [*count*], *pl.* **-fries. 1.** a tower for a bell. **2.** the part of a steeple in which a bell is hung.

Bel•gian (bel′jən) /'bɛldʒən/ *n.* [*count*] **1.** a person born or living in Belgium. **—*adj.* 2.** of or relating to Belgium.

be•lie (bi lī′) /bɪ'lay/ *v.* [~ + *obj*], **-lied, -ly•ing. 1.** to contradict: *His trembling hands belied his calm voice.* **2.** to give a false impression of: *Her clear features and dark hair belied her age.*

be•lief (bi lēf′) /bɪ'liyf/ *n.* **1.** [*count*] something believed: *a deep belief in his ability to succeed.* **2.** [*noncount*] confidence in the truth or existence of something not immediately susceptible to rigorous proof: *My belief in God has nothing to do with my scientific inquiries.* **3.** [*noncount*] confidence; faith; trust: *children's belief in their parents.* **4.** [*count*] something believed as a part of faith: *religious beliefs.*

be•lieve (bi lēv′) /bɪ'liyv/ *v.* [*not: be* + ~*-ing*], **-lieved, -liev•ing. 1.** [~ + *obj*] to have faith in the truth of: *I can't believe that story.* [~ + *(that) clause*]: *I don't believe (that) the earth is flat.* **2.** [~ + *obj*] to have confidence in the statements of (a person): *If my daughter says she wasn't cheating, I believe her.* **3.** to hold as an opinion; suppose; think: [~ + *(that) clause*]: *I believe (that) they are out of town.* [*no obj*]: *Do you think they are coming? I believe so.* **4. believe in,** [~ + *in* + *obj*] **a.** to be sure of the truth or existence of: *to believe in God.* **b.** to have faith in the reliability or honesty of; trust: *I can help you only if you believe in me.* **c.** to accept that (something) is a good idea or is worthwhile: *I believe in getting to work early.* —**be•liev•a•bil•i•ty** (bi lē′və bil′i tē) /bɪ,liyvə'bɪlɪtiy/ **be•liev′a•ble•ness,** *n.* [*noncount*]: *the believability of your story.* —**be•liev′a•ble,** *adj.*: *Her story of rape is highly believable.* —**be•liev′a•bly,** *adv.* —**be•liev′er,** *n.* [*count*] —**be•liev′ing•ly,** *adv.* **—Related Words.** BELIEVE is a verb, BELIEF is a noun, BELIEVABLE is an adjective: *I don't believe you. Her religious beliefs guide her life. That story is not believable.*

be•lit•tle (bi lit′l) /bɪ'lɪtl̩/ *v.* [~ + *obj*], **-tled, -tling.** to think of, or cause others to think of (something) as less important than appearances indicate: *Don't belittle your accomplishments.*

bell (bel) /bɛl/ *n.* [*count*] **1.** a hollow metal instrument shaped like a cup that produces a ringing sound when struck: *The church bells ring at 7:00.* **2.** any device, as an electronic circuit, that produces a similar sound: *I rang the bell and waited for my first customer.* **3.** the stroke or sound of a bell: *There's the bell; someone is at the door.* **4.** something in the form of a bell, as the open end of a musical wind instrument. **—*v.* 5.** [~ + *obj*] to put a bell on: *belled the cat so birds would be able to hear it.* **6.** [*no obj*] to take or have the form of a bell: *The slacks belled out at the bottom.* **—*Idiom.* 7. ring a bell,** to call to mind, esp. a vague recollection: *His name rings a bell but I can't quite remember.* **8. saved by the bell, a.** (of a boxer) saved from a knockout by a gong signaling the end of a round. **b.** (of any person) spared from trouble by some outside event.

-bell-, *root.* -*bell*- comes from Latin, where it has the meaning "war." This meaning is found in such words as: ANTEBELLUM, BELLICOSE, BELLIGERENCE, BELLIGERENT.

bel•la•don•na (bel′ə don′ə) /,bɛlə'dɒnə/ *n.* **1.** [*count*] Also called **deadly nightshade.** a poisonous plant, of the nightshade family, having purplish red flowers and black berries. **2.** [*noncount*] a poisonous substance made from this.

bell′-bot′tom, *adj.* **1.** Also, **bell′-bot′tomed.** (of trousers) wide and curving open at the bottoms of the legs:

bell-bottom jeans. **—*n.* 2. bell-bottoms,** [*plural*] bell-bottom trousers: *bell-bottoms and army jacket.*

bell•boy (bel′boi′) /ˈbɛlˌbɔy/ *n.* BELLHOP.

belle (bel) /bɛl/ *n.* [*count*] a woman or girl admired for her beauty and charm: *the belle of the ball.*

belles-let•tres (bel let′rə) /bɛlˈlɛtrə/ *n.* [*noncount; used with a singular verb*] literature that is polished and elegant but often unimportant. —**bel•let•rist** (bel let′trist) /bɛlˈlɛttrɪst/ *n.* [*count*] —**bel•let•ris•tic** (bel′li tris′tik) /ˌbɛllɪˈtrɪstɪk/ *adj.*

bell•hop (bel′hop′) /ˈbɛlˌhɒp/ *n.* [*count*] a person employed by a hotel to carry luggage and run errands. See illustration at HOTEL.

bel•li•cose (bel′i kōs′) /ˈbɛlɪˌkows/ *adj.* eager or likely to fight; aggressive. —**bel′li•cose′ly,** *adv.* —**bel•li•cos•i•ty** (bel′i kos′i tē) /ˌbɛlɪˈkɒsɪtiy/ **bel′li•cose′ness,** *n.* [*noncount*] See -BELL-.

-bel•lied (bel′ēd) /ˈbɛliyd/ *combining form.* Use *-bellied* to form adjectives meaning "having a certain kind (size, shape, color, etc.) of belly": *big* + *-bellied* → *big-bellied (= having a big belly); yellow* + *-bellied* → *yellow-bellied (of a bird, having a yellow belly), etc.*

bel•lig•er•ence (bə lij′ər əns) /bəˈlɪdʒərəns/ *n.* [*noncount*] a belligerent condition or attitude. See -BELL-.

bel•lig•er•en•cy (bə lij′ər ən sē) /bəˈlɪdʒərənsiy/ *n.* [*noncount*] **1.** position or status of being at war. **2.** BELLIGERENCE.

bel•lig•er•ent (bə lij′ər ənt) /bəˈlɪdʒərənt/ *adj.* **1.** [*before a noun*] engaged in warfare: *set up embargoes against the belligerent nations.* **2.** showing readiness to fight: *a belligerent tone.* **—*n.*** [*count*] **3.** a state or nation at war. **4.** a person engaged in fighting. —**bel•lig′er•ent•ly,** *adv.* See -BELL-.

bel•low (bel′ō) /ˈbɛlow/ *v.* **1.** to shout or speak in a loud voice similar to the cry of a bull: [*no obj*]: *The gym teacher kept bellowing at us.* [~ + *obj*]: *He bellowed a warning at us.* [*used with quotations*]: *"Step back," he bellowed.* **2.** [*no obj*] (of an animal) to roar; bawl: *The cows bellowed in the distance.* **—*n.*** [*count*] **3.** an act or sound of bellowing: *He let out a loud bellow.* —**bel′low•er,** *n.* [*count*]

bel•lows (bel′ōz) /ˈbɛlowz/ *n.* [*count; used with a singular or plural verb*] **1.** a device for producing a strong current of air by drawing air in and pushing it out through a tube: *a bellows for increasing the draft to a fire.* **2.** something resembling a bellows, as lungs.

bell′ pep′per, *n.* SWEET PEPPER.

bell•weth•er (bel′weth′ər) /ˈbɛlˌwɛðər/ *n.* [*count*] a person or thing that leads or indicates a trend: *California is frequently a bellwether of political change in the country.*

bel•ly (bel′ē) /ˈbɛliy/ *n., pl.* **-lies,** *v.,* **-lied, -ly•ing. —*n.*** [*count*] **1.** the abdomen of an animal: *cheetahs resting on their bellies in the hot sun.* **2.** the stomach: *His huge belly hung out over his belt.* **3.** the interior of something: *a ship's belly.* **—*v.* 4.** to (cause to) fill out or swell: [~ + *obj*]: *Wind bellied the sails.* [*no obj*]: *sails bellying in the wind.* **5. belly up,** [*no obj*] *Informal.* to approach very closely: *He bellied up to the bar and shouted for a drink.* **—*Idiom.* 6. go** or **turn belly up,** *Informal.* to come to an end; die; fail: *When his business went belly up he refused to give up.*

bel•ly•ache (bel′ē āk′) /ˈbɛliyˌeyk/ *n., v.,* **-ached, -ach•ing. —*n.*** [*count*] **1.** a pain in the abdomen or bowels. **—*v.*** [*no obj*] **2.** *Informal.* to complain; grumble: *Quit bellyaching and get back to work.*

bel•ly•but•ton or **bel′ly but′ton** (bel′ē but′n) /ˈbɛliy bʌtn̩/ *n.* [*count*] *Informal.* NAVEL.

bel′ly dance′, *n.* [*count*] a dance performed by a woman with curving movements of the hips and abdomen. —**bel′ly danc′er,** *n.* [*count*] —**bel′ly danc′ing,** *n.* [*noncount*]

bel•ly•ful (bel′ē fo͝ol′) /ˈbɛliyˌfʊl/ *n.* [*count; usually singular*], *pl.* **-fuls.** too much of something: *I've had a bellyful of his complaints.*

bel′ly laugh′, *n.* [*count*] a loud, hearty laugh: *She let out a great belly laugh.*

be•long (bi lông′, -long′) /bɪˈlɔŋ, -ˈlɒŋ/ *v.* [*not: be + ~-ing*] **1.** [*no obj*] to be properly situated: *This book belongs on the shelf.* **2.** [*no obj*] to be appropriate or suitable: *That shirt doesn't belong with that jacket.* **3.** [*no obj*] to feel accepted as part of a group, etc.; fit in: *Many immigrants feel as though they don't belong here.* **4. belong to,** [~ + *to* + *obj*] **a.** to be the property of: *The scarf belongs to me.* **b.** to be a part of; to match or fit with: *That cover belongs to this jar.* **c.** to be a member of: *They belong to three clubs.*

be•long•ing (bi lông′ing, -long′-) /bɪˈlɔŋɪŋ, -ˈlɒŋ-/ *n.* **1. belongings,** [*plural*] possessions; personal effects: *Get all of your belongings put away.* **2.** [*noncount*] a feeling of being accepted or welcome: *had a sense of belonging.*

be•lov•ed (bi luv′id, -luvd′) /bɪˈlʌvɪd, -ˈlʌvd/ *adj.* **1.** greatly loved: [*before a noun*]: *my dear, beloved wife.* [*be* + ~ + *of*]: *She was beloved of readers everywhere.* **—*n.*** [*count; singular only*] **2.** a person beloved: *Her beloved had died.*

be•low (bi lō′) /bɪˈlow/ *adv.* **1.** in or toward a lower place: *Look out below!* **2.** on, in, or toward a lower deck or floor: *five flights below.* **3.** beneath the surface of the water: *The submarine quickly dived below.* **4.** at a later point (on a page or in a piece of writing): *See the illustration below.* **5.** in a lower rank or grade: *He was demoted to the class below.* **6.** under zero on the temperature scale: *It was twenty-six below, with a high wind.* **—*prep.* 7.** lower down than: *below the surface of the sea.* **8.** lower in rank, degree, rate, etc.: *It was sold below cost.*

belt (belt) /bɛlt/ *n.* [*count*] **1.** a band of flexible material that encircles the waist: *He had a belt that carried weapons.* See illustration at CLOTHING. **2.** any band, strip, or stripe that encircles: *The surface of Jupiter has a number of broadly colored belts.* **3.** an extended region (of the earth, etc.) having distinctive properties or characteristics: *the industrial areas called the Rust Belt because heavy industry like steel has long been gone from it.* **4.** an endless band passing around pulleys, used to transmit motion or to convey objects: *The fan belt in the car snapped. The assembly-line belt carries the bottles to boxes for shipping.* **5.** *Slang.* **a.** a hard blow; punch. **b.** a swallow of liquor. **—*v.*** [~ + *obj*] **6.** [~ *(+ on)* + *obj*] to fasten on by means of a belt: *He belted (on) his raincoat.* **7.** [~ + *out* + *obj*] to sing (a song) loudly and energetically: *belted out the song to tremendous applause.* **8.** *Slang.* **a.** [~ + *down* + *obj*] to swallow (a drink of liquor): *He belted down his drink.* **b.** to hit; strike: *used to belt his wife when he got drunk.* **—*Idiom.* 9. below the belt, a.** unfair: *a nasty lie that was really below the belt.* **b.** unfairly: *He hit below the belt with that lie about you.* **10. under one's belt, a.** in one's stomach: *Get some food under your belt.* **b.** as part of one's background: *Get some experience under your belt.* —**belt′less,** *adj.*

belt•way (belt′wā′) /ˈbɛltˌwey/ *n.* [*count*] a highway around the outer boundary of an urban area.

be•lu•ga (bə lo͞o′gə) /bəˈluwgə/ *n., pl.* **-gas,** *(esp. when thought of as a group)* **-ga. 1.** a large white sturgeon, valued as a source of caviar. **2.** Also called **white whale.** a small, white, toothed whale, having a rounded head.

be•moan (bi mōn′) /bɪˈmown/ *v.* [~ + *obj*] to express sadness or grief over; lament: *to bemoan one's fate.*

be•mused (bi myo͞ozd′) /bɪˈmyuwzd/ *adj.* bewildered; confused; puzzled: *a bemused expression on his face.* —**be•mus•ed•ly** (bi myo͞o′zid lē) /bɪˈmyuwzɪdliy/ *adv.* —**be•muse′ment,** *n.* [*noncount*]: *a look of bemusement on his face.*

bench (bench) /bɛntʃ/ *n.* [*count*] **1.** a long seat for several people: *a park bench.* See illustration at TERMINAL. **2.** a seat occupied by a judge: *The judge glared down at the prisoner from her bench.* **3.** [*singular; often: the* + ~] such a seat when it is thought of as a symbol of the office and dignity of a judge: *appointed to the bench last year.* **4.** the seat on which the players of a team sit during a game while not playing. **5.** a worktable or workbench: *a carpenter's bench.* **—*v.*** [~ + *obj*] **6.** to remove from or keep from participating in a game: *had to bench his star player when he didn't show up for practice.*

bench•mark or **bench mark** (bench′märk′) /ˈbɛntʃˌmɑrk/ *n.* [*count*] **1.** a mark made on a measuring device at a known height from which other heights may be calculated. *Abbr.:* BM **2.** a standard or reference by which others can be measured or judged: *He set as his benchmarks the achievements of others.*

bend (bend) /bɛnd/ *v.,* **bent** (bent) /bɛnt/ **bend•ing,** *n.* **—*v.* 1.** [~ + *obj*] to force (something) from a straight form into a curved form: *could bend steel in his bare hands.* **2.** [*no obj*] (of something) to become curved: *a bow that bends easily.* **3.** to (cause to) lean away from an upright position: [~ + *obj*]: *bent her head in prayer.* [*no obj*]: *She bent over my desk to take a look at the computer.* **4.** [~ + *obj* + *to* + *obj*] to guide (oneself) in a particular direction: *She bent her energies to the task. She bent herself to finishing her homework.* [*be bent on*]: *was bent on finishing the job.* **5.** [*no obj*] to turn or head in a particular direction: *The road bent south.* **6.** to (cause to) submit or give in: [~ + *to* + *obj*]: *I bent to his will.* [~ + *obj* + *to* + *obj*]: *He bent me to his will.* **7.** [~ + *obj*] to make less harsh; relax (restrictions): *We were* *willing to bend the rules to allow her to study English.* —*n.* [*count*] **8.** the act of bending: *The new plan represents a slight bend to the pressures of politics.* **9.** something that bends or is bent: *At the bend in the road you bear to the right.* **10. the bends,** [*plural; used with a plural verb*] a painful condition caused by bubbles of nitrogen gas in the blood: *The bends are sometimes a big problem for deep-sea divers.* —***Idiom.*** **11. around** or **round the bend,** *Informal.* insane; crazy: *She has driven me right around the bend with her constant phone calls.* **12. bend** or **lean** or **fall over backward,** [*no obj*] to exert oneself as much as possible: *The teacher bent over backward in giving you extra time.* **13. bend someone's ear,** to talk to someone at length: *The dean bent my ear for an hour with the same old ideas for new classes.*

bend•er (ben′dər) /'bɛndər/ *n.* [*count*] **1.** a person or thing that bends. **2.** *Slang.* a time of drinking a lot of alcoholic beverages; spree; binge.

-bene-, *root.* *-bene-* comes from Latin, where it has the meaning "well." This meaning is found in such words as: BENEDICTION, BENEFACTOR, BENEFICENT, BENEFICIAL, BENEFIT, BENEVOLENT.

be•neath (bi nēth′) /bɪ'niyθ/ *adv.* **1.** in or to a lower position; below: *From the mountain he looked down to the fjord beneath.* —*prep.* **2.** below; under: *They lived beneath the same roof.* **3.** farther down than: *the drawer beneath the top one.* **4.** lower down on a slope than: *beneath the crest of a hill.* **5.** less important than; inferior to: *A captain is beneath a major.* **6.** below the level or dignity of; not worthy of: *Your remarks are beneath contempt (= Your remarks are not even worthy of contempt, they are so bad).*

ben•e•dic•tion (ben′i dik′shən) /ˌbɛnɪ'dɪkʃən/ *n.* **1.** [*count*] an utterance of good wishes or a blessing: *concluded the service with a benediction.* **2.** [*noncount*] the act of blessing: *raised her hand in benediction.* —**ben•e•dic•to•ry** (ben′i dik′tə rē) /ˌbɛnɪ'dɪktəriy/ *adj.* See -BENE-, -DICT-.

ben•e•fac•tion (ben′ə fak′shən, ben′ə fak′-) /'bɛnəˌfækʃən, ˌbɛnə'fæk-/ *n.* [*count*] **1.** an act of doing good; a good deed: *known for his many benefactions.* **2.** a benefit given; a charitable donation: *His benefactions were numerous and private.* See -BENE-, -FAC-.

ben•e•fac•tor (ben′ə fak′tər) /'bɛnəˌfæktər/ *n.* [*count*] a person who does a good deed: *The benefactors of the college will have to give even more this year.* See -BENE-, -FAC-.

ben•e•fac•tress (ben′ə fak′tris) /'bɛnəˌfæktrɪs/ *n.* [*count*] a woman who does a good deed: *The college could call on many benefactresses over the year for donations.* See -BENE-, -FAC-.

be•nef•i•cence (bə nef′ə səns) /bə'nɛfəsəns/ *n.* [*noncount*] the quality or state of being beneficent: *He helped me because of his own beneficence.* See -BENE-, -FAC-.

be•nef•i•cent (bə nef′ə sənt) /bə'nɛfəsənt/ *adj.* **1.** doing good; charitable: *his beneficent work for charitable organizations.* **2.** beneficial: *The new drug was found to be beneficent in treating some cases.* —**be•nef′i•cent•ly,** *adv.* See -BENE-, -FAC-.

ben•e•fi•cial (ben′ə fish′əl) /ˌbɛnə'fɪʃəl/ *adj.* giving benefit; doing good: *the beneficial effect of sunshine.* —**ben′e•fi′cial•ly,** *adv.* —**ben′e•fi′cial•ness,** *n.* [*noncount*] See -BENE-, -FAC-, -FIC-.

ben•e•fi•ci•ar•y (ben′ə fish′ē er′ē, -fish′ə rē) /ˌbɛnə'fɪʃiyˌɛriy, -'fɪʃəriy/ *n.* [*count*], *pl.* **-ar•ies.** **1.** one that receives benefits: *The rich are the only beneficiaries of the new tax bill.* **2.** a person designated to receive property under a will or trust: *My daughters are the sole beneficiaries.* See -BENE-, -FAC-.

ben•e•fit (ben′ə fit) /'bɛnəfɪt/ *n.* **1.** [*noncount*] something advantageous or good: *Is it of benefit to you to help someone you detest?* **2.** [*count*] a payment made to help someone, given by an insurance company or public agency: *provided many health-care benefits.* **3.** [*count*] a social event held to raise money for an organization, cause, or person: *The rock group gave a benefit for victims of the drought in Africa.* —*v.* **4.** [~ + *obj*] to do good to; be of service to: *a health-care program that will benefit everyone.* **5.** to gain benefit from (something); profit: [*no obj*]: *When the blood drive was over, the Red Cross had clearly benefited.* [~ + *from* + *obj*]: *I learned to benefit from experience.* —***Idiom.*** **6. for (someone's) benefit,** so as to produce a desired effect (in another's mind): *The judge smiled for the benefit of the cameras.* **7. give someone the benefit of the doubt,** to believe that someone is telling the truth, or is innocent of wrongdoing, in the absence of any proof for or against the person: *We don't really know if Joe was cheating or not; I'd be inclined to give him the benefit of the doubt.* See -BENE-. —**Related Words.** BENEFIT is both a noun and a verb, BENEFICIAL is an adjective: *His insurance plan provides medical benefits. The new rules don't benefit me. Certain foods are beneficial to your health.*

be•nev•o•lence (bə nev′ə ləns) /bə'nɛvələns/ *n.* **1.** [*noncount*] desire to do good: *praised for her benevolence.* **2.** [*count*] an act of kindness; charitable gift: *His benevolences made it possible for many poor children to attend good schools.* See -BENE-, -VOL-.

be•nev•o•lent (bə nev′ə lənt) /bə'nɛvələnt/ *adj.* **1.** having or expressing benevolence: *a benevolent smile.* **2.** desiring to help others: *gifts from benevolent alumni.* —**be•nev′o•lent•ly,** *adv.* See -BENE-, -VOL-.

be•night•ed (bi nī′tid) /bɪ'naytɪd/ *adj.* [*before a noun*] ignorant; unenlightened: *the benighted masses.*

be•nign (bi nīn′) /bɪ'nayn/ *adj.* **1.** having or showing a gentle nature; gracious: *a benign smile.* **2.** mild; comfortable: *benign weather.* **3.** not malignant: *a benign tumor.* —**be•nign′ly,** *adv.*

ben•ny (ben′ē) /'bɛniy/ *n.* [*count*], *pl.* **-nies.** *Slang.* an amphetamine tablet: *He took some bennies so he could stay awake studying the night before the test.*

bent (bent) /bɛnt/ *adj.* **1.** curved; crooked: *a bent back.* **2.** [*be* + ~ + *on/upon*] determined; set: *is bent upon finding the truth.* **3.** *Chiefly Brit.* **a.** corrupt; dishonest: *They videotaped the bent clerk taking a bribe.* **b.** *Offensive.* homosexual. —*n.* [*count; singular*] **4.** a special talent or interest; flair: *She has a bent for painting.*

be•numbed (bi numd′) /bɪ'nʌmd/ *adj.* made numb: *fingers benumbed by cold.*

ben•zene (ben′zēn, ben zēn′) /'bɛnziyn, bɛn'ziyn/ *n.* [*noncount*] a colorless, strong-smelling liquid compound, C_6H_6, used in making chemicals and dyes and as a solvent.

ben•zine (ben′zēn, ben zēn′) /'bɛnziyn, bɛn'ziyn/ *n.* [*noncount*] a colorless liquid mixture obtained from hydrocarbons, used in cleaning and dyeing: *Maybe benzine will get that stain off your jacket.*

be•queath (bi kwēth′, -kwēth′) /bɪ'kwiyð, -'kwiyθ/ *v.* [~ + *obj* (+ *to*) + *obj*] **1.** to dispose of (property or money) by means of a will: *I bequeath all my worldly goods to my wife. She bequeathed her sister all her favorite toys.* **2.** to hand down; pass on: *What sort of environment will we bequeath to our children?*

be•quest (bi kwest′) /bɪ'kwɛst/ *n.* **1.** [*noncount*] the act of bequeathing. **2.** [*count*] an item bequeathed to another: *a substantial bequest to his favorite charity.*

be•rate (bi rāt′) /bɪ'reyt/ *v.* [~ + *obj*], **-rat•ed, -rat•ing.** to scold; yell at; rebuke: *The coach thought that if he berated his players, they might snap out of their lazy habits.*

be•reave (bi rēv′) /bɪ'riyv/ *v.* [~ + *obj* + *of*], **-reaved** or **-reft** (-reft′) /-'rɛft/ **-reav•ing.** **1.** to take away from and make sad, esp. by death: *Illness bereaved them of their mother. She was bereaved of her husband (= Death bereaved her of her husband)* **2.** to deprive cruelly: *War bereft us of our home.* —**be•reav′er,** *n.* [*count*]

be•reaved (bi rēvd′) /bɪ'riyvd/ *adj.* **1.** (of a person) saddened at having lost a loved one by death: *the bereaved widow in black.* —*n.* [*count; the* + ~] **2. the bereaved,** [*plural; used with a plural verb*] bereaved persons: *paid his respects to the bereaved.*

be•reave•ment (bi rēv′mənt) /bɪ 'riyvmənt/ *n.* **1.** [*noncount*] the condition of being bereaved: *wondered if bereavement would make him more bitter.* **2.** [*count*] an instance or occasion of such a loss: *Several recent deaths made them ponder their bereavements.*

be•reft (bi reft′) /bɪ'rɛft/ *v.* **1.** a pt. and pp. of BEREAVE: *bereft of her husband.* —*adj.* **2.** deprived: *Are they bereft of their senses?*

be•ret (bə rā′) /bə'rey/ *n.* [*count*] a soft cap without a brim, with a flat or rounded top.

berg (bûrg) /bɜrg/ *n.* [*count*] an iceberg.

be•rib•boned (bi rib′ənd) /bɪ'rɪbənd/ *adj.* adorned with ribbons: *beribboned war veterans.*

ber•i•ber•i (ber′ē ber′ē) /'bɛriy'bɛriy/ *n.* [*noncount*] a disease of the nerves caused by a deficiency of vitamin B_1.

berm (bûrm) /bɜrm/ *n.* [*count*] **1.** a level strip of ground at the top of a slope. **2.** the shoulder of a road. **3.** a mound of snow or dirt: *dug in inside their berms.*

Ber•mu′da shorts′ (bər myōō′də) /bər 'myuwdə/ *n.* [*plural*] short pants extending almost to the knee.

ber•ry (ber′ē) /'bɛriy/ *n.* [*count*], *pl.* **-ries.** any small, soft, round, usually juicy fruit growing on a bush or tree, as the strawberry, grape, or tomato.

ber•serk (bər sûrk′, -zûrk′) /bər'sɜrk, -'zɜrk/ *adj.* violently or destructively frenzied: *She went berserk at the idea, shouting, pulling books down off the wall, and throwing things into the fireplace.* —**ber•serk′ly,** *adv.*

berth (bûrth) /bɜrθ/ *n.* [*count*] **1.** a shelflike sleeping space, as on a ship: *We had adjoining sleeping berths.* **2.** a space assigned to a ship in which to dock or lie at anchor: *The tugboat eased the liner into its berth.* **3.** a job; place: *competing for berths on the Olympic team.* —*v.* **4.** to find, or provide with, a sleeping space: [~ + *obj*]: *They were berthed in the cabin bedrooms.* [*no obj*]: *They berthed in the lower deck of the ship.* **5.** (of a ship) to (cause it to) come to a dock: [~ + *obj*]: *The captain berthed the ship and went below.* [*no obj*]: *The ship berthed smoothly.* —***Idiom.*** **6. give a wide berth to,** [~ + *obj*] to keep a careful distance from: *I'd give a wide berth to that job applicant.*

ber•yl (ber′əl) /'bɛrəl/ *n.* [*noncount*] a mineral, found in the gems emerald and aquamarine.

be•ryl•li•um (bə ril′ē əm) /bə'rɪliyəm/ *n.* [*noncount*] a hard, light metallic element, used chiefly to reduce fatigue in springs and electrical contacts.

be•seech (bi sēch′) /bɪ'siytʃ/ *v.,* **-sought** (-sôt′) /-'sɔt/ or **-seeched, -seech•ing.** to beg or ask for strongly or urgently; implore; appeal: [~ + *obj*]: *I beseech you, let my people go!* [~ + *obj* + *to* + *verb*]: *They besought us to leave at once.* —**be•seech′er,** *n.* [*count*]

be•seech•ing (bi sēch′ing) /bɪ 'siytʃɪŋ/ *adj.* begging or asking for something urgently: *She gave me a beseeching look.* —**be•seech′ing•ly,** *adv.*: *She looked beseechingly at him.*

be•set (bi set′) /bɪ'sɛt/ *v.* [~ + *obj*], **-set, -set•ting. 1.** to attack on all sides: *beset by an angry mob of protesters.* **2.** to surround; hem in: *He was beset with a lot of problems all at once.* **3.** to set (something) in place; put in: *a gold crown beset with jewels.*

be•side (bi sīd′) /bɪ'sayd/ *prep.* **1.** by the side of; near: *Sit down beside me.* **2.** compared with: *Beside her, other writers seem amateurish.* **3.** not relevant to: *Your argument is beside the point.* **4.** BESIDES (defs. 4, 5). —*adv.* **5.** along the side of something: *We walked, and the dog ran along beside.* —***Idiom.*** **6. beside oneself,** [*be* + ~ + *with*] frantic; feeling strong emotion about: *She was beside herself with fury.* —**Usage.** To express the prepositional meanings "over and above," "in addition to," and "except," BESIDES is preferred to BESIDE, esp. in careful writing. However, BESIDE sometimes occurs with these meanings as well, even in formal writing.

be•sides (bi sīdz′) /bɪ'saydz/ *adv.* **1.** moreover; furthermore; also: *I'd really like to go and besides, I promised them I would come.* **2.** in addition: *There are three elm trees and two maples besides.* **3.** otherwise; else: *They had a roof over their heads but not much besides.* —*prep.* **4.** over and above; in addition to: *Besides his mother he has a sister to support.* **5.** other than; except: *There is no one here besides us.* —**Usage.** See BESIDE.

be•siege (bi sēj′) /bɪ'siydʒ/ *v.* [~ + *obj*], **-sieged, -sieg•ing. 1.** to surround and attack: *The city was besieged for months.* **2.** to crowd around; crowd in upon: *Vacationers besieged the travel office.*

be•smirch (bi smûrch′) /bɪ'smɜrtʃ/ *v.* [~ + *obj*] **1.** to make dirty; soil; sully. **2.** to ruin by taking away the honor of (someone's good name): *His campaign plan was simply to besmirch his opponent's reputation.*

be•sot•ted (bi sot′əd) /bɪ'sɒtəd/ *adj.* stupid or foolish because of alcoholic drink, love, etc.: *besotted with gin.* —**be•sot′ted•ness,** *n.* [*noncount*]

be•sought (bi sôt′) /bɪ'sɔt/ *v.* a pt. and pp. of BESEECH.

be•spat•tered (bi spat′ərd) /bɪ'spætərd/ *adj.* covered with: *clothes bespattered with mud.*

be•speak (bi spēk′) /bɪ'spiyk/ *v.* [~ + *obj*], **-spoke, -spo•ken** or **-spoke, -speak•ing. 1.** to ask for in advance; reserve beforehand: *to bespeak a seat in a theater.* **2.** to show; indicate: *This generous act bespeaks a kindly heart.*

be•spec•ta•cled (bi spek′tə kəld) /bɪ'spɛktəkəld/ *adj.* wearing eyeglasses.

best (best) /bɛst/ *adj., superlative form of* GOOD. **1.** of the highest quality; the most excellent: *Only the best students apply to our school.* **2.** most suitable or appropriate; of most benefit or of greatest advantage: *Is this the best way to handle the problem?* [*it* + *be* + ~ + *clause*]: *I thought it would be best if we discussed this first.* [*it* + *be* + ~ + *to* + *verb*]: *It would be best not to wake her up.* —*adv., superlative form of* WELL. **3.** most excellently or suitably; most well: *They gave her an opera role that best suits her voice.* **4.** in or to the highest degree; most: *She is the best-known actress of our time.* —*n.* [*count*] **5.** [*the* + ~] someone or something that is best: *Even the best of us makes mistakes.* **6.** [*one's* + ~] a person's finest clothing: *Promise me you'll wear your best to the wedding next week.* **7.** [*one's* + ~] a person's highest degree of ability, effort, or health: *We're all trying ways to do our best.* **8.** [*one's* + ~] salutations: *Give them my best.* (= *Convey to them my good wishes*). —*v.* [~ + *obj*] **9.** to get the better of; beat: *That team bested us in the finals.* —***Idiom.*** **10. (all) for the best,** producing good as the final result: *It turned out to be all for the best when I didn't get that job.* **11. as best one can,** in the best way possible: *As best I can tell, we're the first ones here.* **12. at best,** even under the most favorable circumstances possible: *The job won't be finished for a month at best.* **13. get** or **have the best of,** [~ + *obj*] **a.** to gain the advantage over. **b.** to defeat; subdue: *The pain got the best of him.* **14. had best,** [~ + *root form of a verb*] ought to: *You had best phone your mother.* **15. make the best of,** [~ + *obj*] to cope with; accept: *We're only going to be living here for a year; let's make the best of it.* See BETTER.

bes•tial (bes′chəl, bēs′-) /'bɛstʃəl, 'biys-/ *adj.* **1.** of or like a beast. **2.** savage; revolting: *bestial behavior.* —**bes′tial•ly,** *adv.*

bes•ti•al•i•ty (bes′chē al′i tē, bēs′-) /ˌbɛstʃiy'ælɪtiy, ˌbiys-/ *n.* [*noncount*] **1.** brutish, revolting, or savage behavior. **2.** sexual relations between a person and an animal.

be•stir (bi stûr′) /bɪ'stɜr/ *v.* [~ + *obj*], **-stirred, -stir•ring.** to rouse (someone) to action; stir up: *The army bestirred themselves when they saw the enemy.*

best′ man′, *n.* [*count*] the chief attendant of the bridegroom at a wedding: *The best man fumbled nervously in his pockets and finally produced the ring.*

be•stow (bi stō′) /bɪ'stow/ *v.* [~ + *obj* + *on/upon* + *obj*] to present as a gift; give; confer: *The committee bestowed a great honor on him.* —**be•stow′al,** *n.* [*count; singular*]: *the bestowal of such a great honor.*

be•stride (bi strīd′) /bɪ'strayd/ *v.* [~ + *obj*], **-strode** or **-strid, -strid•den** or **-strid, -strid•ing. 1.** to stand or sit with one leg on each side of (something): *She bestrode her horse.* **2.** to tower over; dominate: *The colossal monument bestrode the ancient harbor.*

best•sell•er (best′sel′ər) /'bɛst'sɛlər/ *n.* [*count*] a product, as a book, that sells very well at a given time. —**best′-sell′ing,** *adj.*: *a best-selling novel.*

bet (bet) /bɛt/ *v.,* **bet** or **bet•ted, bet•ting,** *n.* —*v.* **1. a.** to risk (something of value) on the result of some unknown event; wager: [~ + *obj*]: *How much did she bet?* [~ + *obj* + *on* + *obj*]: *She bet $5.00 on that horse.* [~ + *obj* + *(that) clause*]: *She bet $5.00 that her horse would win.* [*no obj*]: *Do you want to bet?* **b.** to enter into an agreement with (someone) on such a risk: [~ + *obj* + *obj*]: *She bet me $5.00.* [~ + *obj* + *obj* + *(that) clause*]: *She bet me $5.00 that her horse would come in first.* [~ + *with* + *obj*]: *She likes to bet with me.* **2.** [*usually: I* + ~ + *(that) clause*] to claim as if in a bet; to be certain of: *I bet you forgot it.* **3.** [*you* + ~] *Informal.* (used to show agreement in a forceful way with what has been said or will be said): *Do you want a little more time to finish the homework? —You bet!* (= *Yes, I/we want more time*). *You bet we care about it!* (= *Yes! We care about it!*) **4.** [*I* + ~] (used to express sarcasm, or to show disagreement): *"And so I promise lower taxes and a better world for everybody," the candidate said. "I bet," muttered John.* —*n.* [*count*] **5.** an agreement to risk something of value on an uncertain future event; wager: *I made a bet with my wife.* **6.** a thing risked: *a two-dollar bet.* **7.** something that is bet on: *That looks like a good bet.* **8.** [*usually: singular*] a person or thing considered a good choice: *a sure bet to get the job.*

be•ta (bā′tə) /'beytə/ *n.* [*count*], *pl.* **-tas.** the second letter of the Greek alphabet (Β, β).

bête noire (bāt′ nwär′, bet′) /ˌbeyt' nwɑr, ˌbɛt/ *n.* [*count*], *pl.* **bêtes noires** (bāt′ nwärz′, bet′) /ˌbeyt' nwɑrz, ˌbɛt/. a person or thing that is very disliked or feared: *The special writing test was the bête noire of students.*

be•to•ken (bi tō′kən) /bɪ'towkən/ *v.* [~ + *obj*] to be a sign of; indicate: *Her deep frown betokened her feelings of sadness.*

be•tray (bi trā′) /bɪ'trey/ *v.* [~ + *obj*] **1.** [~ + *obj* (+ *to* + *obj*)] to deliver or expose to an enemy by treachery: *Benedict Arnold tried to betray his country to the enemy.* **2.** to be unfaithful or disloyal to: *to betray one's friends.* **3.** to reveal or make known (a secret given in confidence): *to betray a plan.* **4.** to reveal unconsciously (something a person would prefer to hide): *The nervousness on her face betrays her insecurity.* **5.** to be unfaithful to (someone) by having sexual relations with someone else: *He vowed never to betray his wife again.* —**be•tray′er,** *n.* [*count*]

be•tray•al (bi trā′əl) /bɪ 'treyəl/ *n.* **1.** [*noncount*] betraying or being betrayed: *At that point we feared betrayal more than anything else.* **2.** [*count*] an act of betraying or being betrayed: *When he failed to support her, she took it as a betrayal.*

be•troth•al (bi trō′thəl, -trô′thəl) /bɪ'trowðəl, -'trɔθəl/ *n.* [*count*] the act or state of being engaged to be married: *The mayor had not announced a betrothal in that village for some time.*

be•trothed (bi trōthd′, -trôtht′) /bɪ'trowðd, -'trɔθt/ *adj.* [*be* + ~] **1.** engaged to be married: *She was betrothed to the richest man in the village.* —*n.* [*count; singular and plural*] **2.** the person to whom one is betrothed: *escorted the betrothed to the church.*

bet•ted (bet′id) /'bɛtɪd/ *v.* a pt. and pp. of BET[1].

bet•ter (bet′ər) /'bɛtər/ *adj. comparative form of* GOOD. **1.** of higher or superior quality or excellence: *We got a better view of the city from the top of the Empire State Building.* **2.** morally superior: *Those politicians are no better than thieves.* **3.** of superior suitability; preferable: *There could not be a better time for action.* [*it* + *be* + ~ + *verb-ing*]: *It's better having short lines with more bank tellers.* [*it* + *be* + ~ + *to* + *verb*]: *It is better to have loved and lost than never to have loved at all.* [*it* + *be* + ~ + *that clause*]: *It's better that we stop meeting like this.* **4.** larger; greater: *This homework assignment will take the better part of a day to finish.* **5.** improved in health; healthier than before: *Well, are you feeling any better today?* —*adv., comparative form of* WELL. **6.** in a more appropriate manner: *Behave better when your grandparents come over.* **7.** to a greater degree; more completely: *She knows the way better than I do.* —*v.* **8.** to (cause to) improve: [~ + *obj*]: *She worked hard to better the lot of the needy.* [*no obj*]: *Economic conditions have not bettered.* **9.** [~ + *obj*] to improve upon: *We have bettered last year's production.* —*n.* [*count*] **10.** [*usually singular*] something that is preferable: *the better of two choices.* **11.** Usually, **betters.** [*plural*] those superior to oneself: *Stop thinking of them as your betters.* —*Idiom.* **12. better off,** [*be* + ~] **a.** in better circumstances: *Are we better off than we were four years ago?* **b.** [*be* + ~] more fortunate; happier: *You are better off without him.* **13. for the better,** in a way that is an improvement: *His health changed for the better.* **14. get** or **have the better of,** [~ + *obj*] **a.** to have or get an advantage over: *They have the better of me in the opening part of the race.* **b.** to prevail against; win over: *Her curiosity got the better of her.* **15. go (someone) one better,** to exceed someone else's efforts; surpass: *She did her rival one better by coming to the meeting better prepared.* **16. had better,** [~ + *root form of a verb*] ought to: *We had better renegotiate this contract.* **17. think better of,** [~ + *obj*] **a.** to reconsider or think (something) over again: *I was tempted to make a wisecrack, but thought better of it and kept quiet.* **b.** to form a higher opinion of: *I'm sure she thinks better of you now that she knows how kind you are.*

bet•ter•ment (bet′ər mənt) /'bɛtərmənt/ *n.* [*noncount*] the act or process of bettering; improvement: *We are working for the betterment of all mankind.*

bet•tor or **bet•ter** (bet′ər) /'bɛtər/ *n.* [*count*] a person who bets: *the bettors lining up at the window.*

be•tween (bi twēn′) /bɪ'twiyn/ *prep.* **1.** in the space separating: *We traveled between New York and Chicago by railroad.* **2.** intermediate to in time, quantity, or degree: *I'll meet you sometime between twelve and one o'clock.* **3.** linking; connecting; to and from: *The ship sails between Stockholm and Copenhagen.* **4.** in equal portions for each of: *The couple split the profits between them.* **5.** among: *a treaty between five countries.* See Usage Note below. **6.** by (means of) the common participation of: *Between us, we can finish the job.* **7.** in the choice or contrast of: *the difference between good and bad.* **8.** by the combined effect of: *They were both married before, so they have seven children between them.* **9.** existing as a secret with: *We'll keep this between ourselves (= This will be a secret with you and me). Between you and me, I think he's a fool.* **10.** involving; concerning: *war between nations.* **11.** in the way of; blocking: *Something came between us, and we didn't care for each other anymore.* —*adv.* **12.** in the intervening space or time: *two windows with a door between.* —*Idiom.* **13. few and far between,** rare; seldom; infrequent: *The visits became few and far between as we grew apart.* **14. in between,** in an intermediate position: *Our house is in between a playground and an alley.* —**be•tween′ness,** *n.* [*noncount*]: *a feeling of betweenness, of not being completely here in America or there in Hong Kong.* —**Usage.** By strict or traditional usage rules, AMONG expresses relationship when more than two are involved, and BETWEEN is used for only two: *to decide among coffee, tea, juice, or milk; to decide between tea and coffee.* BETWEEN, however, continues to be used to express relationship of persons or things considered individually, no matter how many: *Between holding public office, teaching, and raising a family, she has little free time.* And BETWEEN is always used to express location or position in the middle of any number of things that are limits or boundaries around the point: *This city is located at a point between New York, Chicago, and Pittsburgh.* Although not usually accepted as good usage, BETWEEN YOU AND I is heard occasionally in the speech of educated persons. By the strict rules of grammar, any and all pronouns that are the object of a preposition must be in the objective case: *between you and me; between her and them.*

be•twixt (bi twikst′) /bɪ'twɪkst/ *prep., adv.* **1.** between. —*Idiom.* **2. betwixt and between,** neither the one nor the other; in a middle position.

bev•eled (bev′əld) /'bɛvəld/ *adj.* oblique; slanted; sloping: *beveled edges.* Also, *esp. Brit.,* **bevelled.**

bev•er•age (bev′ər ij, bev′rij) /'bɛvərɪdʒ, 'bɛvrɪdʒ/ *n.* [*count*] any liquid that can be drunk, esp. a liquid other than water.

bev•y (bev′ē) /'bɛviy/ *n.* [*count*], *pl.* **bev•ies.** a large group or collection: *a bevy of sailors.*

be•wail (bi wāl′) /bɪ'weyl/ *v.* [~ + *obj*] to express deep sorrow for; lament: *a child bewailing the loss of her dog.*

be•ware (bi wâr′) /bɪ'wɛər/ *v.* [*usually in a command*] to be wary (of); be cautious or careful (about): [~ + *obj*]: *Beware his wit.* [~ + *of* + *obj*]: *Beware of the dog!*

be•wil•der (bi wil′dər) /bɪ'wɪldər/ *v.* [~ + *obj*] to confuse or puzzle: *Her sudden decision not to see me anymore bewildered me.*

be•wil•dered (bi wil′dərd) /bɪ 'wɪldərd/ *adj.* confused; puzzled: *The bewildered child looked for his mother.*

be•wil•der•ing (bi wil′dər ing) /bɪ 'wɪldər ɪŋ/ *adj.* confusing; puzzling: *bewildering instructions.* —**be•wil′der•ing•ly,** *adv.*: *bewilderingly complex directions.*

be•wil•der•ment (bi wil′dər mənt) /bɪ'wɪldərmənt/ *n.* [*noncount*] the state of being bewildered: *I looked around in bewilderment at the unnamed streets.*

be•witch (bi wich′) /bɪ'wɪtʃ/ *v.* [~ + *obj*] **1.** to affect by witchcraft or magic: *Morgaine bewitched Arthur.* **2.** to charm; fascinate: *She bewitched me with her smile.* —**be•witched′,** *adj.*: *bewitched by her singing.* —**be•witch′ing,** *adj.*: *a bewitching smile.* —**be•witch′ing•ly,** *adv.*: *sang bewitchingly.*

be•yond (bē ond′, bi yond′) /biy'ɒnd, bɪ'yɒnd/ *prep.* **1.** on, at, or to the farther side of: *beyond the fence.* **2.** more distant than: *beyond the horizon.* **3.** outside the limits or reach of: *pain beyond endurance.* **4.** outside the limits of one's ability (to understand, etc.): *It's beyond me why she stole the money.* **5.** superior to; surpassing: *wise beyond her peers.* **6.** more than; in excess of; over and above: *to stay beyond one's welcome.* —*adv.* **7.** farther on or away: *Go as far as the house and beyond.* —*Idiom.* **8. the beyond, a.** that which is at a great distance. **b.** Also, **the great beyond.** the afterlife; life after death.

bf or **b.f.,** an abbreviation of: boldface.

B.F.A., an abbreviation of: Bachelor of Fine Arts.

bi (bī) /bay/ *adj., n.* [*count*], *pl.* **bis, bi's.** *Slang.* bisexual.

bi-, *prefix.* *bi-* comes from Latin, where it has the meaning "twice, two." This meaning is found in such words as: BICENTENNIAL, BIENNIAL, BIGAMY, BILATERAL, BINOCULARS, BIPARTISAN, BIPED, BISECT, BIWEEKLY. —**Usage.** In some words, esp. words referring to time periods, the prefix *bi-* has two meanings: "twice a + ~" and "every two + ~-s". Thus, *biannual* means both "twice a year" and "every two years." Be careful; check many of these words.

bi•an•nu•al (bī an′yoo əl) /bay'ænyuwəl/ *adj.* **1.** occurring twice in one year. **2.** occurring once every two years. —**bi•an′nu•al•ly,** *adv.* See -ANN-. —**Usage.** See BI-.

bi•as (bī′əs) /'bayəs/ *n., adj., v.,* **-ased, -as•ing** or (*esp. Brit.*) **-assed, -as•sing.** —*n.* [*count*] **1.** a tendency toward judging something without full knowledge of it; prejudice: *He has a bias against anyone who is black.* **2.** a particular tendency toward something: *She has a natural bias* *for handwork and athletics.* **3.** a slanting or diagonal line of direction, esp. across a woven fabric. **—*adj.*** [*usually: before a noun*] **4.** (of the cut of a fabric) diagonal; slanted. **—*v.*** [~ + *obj*] **5.** to influence unfairly: *The lawyer made a tearful plea to bias the jury.* **—*Idiom.* 6. on the bias, a.** in the diagonal direction of the cloth. **b.** out of line; slanting. **—Syn.** BIAS and PREJUDICE both mean a strong and unfairly formed inclination of the mind or opinion about something or someone. A BIAS may be favorable or unfavorable: *bias in favor of or against an idea.* PREJUDICE implies a judgment already formed and even more unreasoning than BIAS, and usually implies an unfavorable opinion: *prejudice against a race.*

bi•ased (bī′əst) /ˈbayəst/ *adj.* having or showing bias: *handed in a biased report.* Also, *esp. Brit.,* **bi′assed.**

bi•ath•lon (bī ath′lon) /bayˈæθlɒn/ *n.* [*count*] a contest of cross-country skiing and shooting.

bib (bib) /bɪb/ *n.* [*count*] **1.** a shield of cloth tied under the chin to protect the clothing. **2.** the front part of an apron or the like above the waist.

Bib., an abbreviation of: **1.** Bible. **2.** biblical.

Bi•ble (bī′bəl) /ˈbaybəl/ *n.* [*count*] **1.** [*the* + ~] the collection of sacred writings of the Christian religion, consisting of the Hebrew Scriptures and the New Testament. **2.** Also called **Hebrew Scriptures.** [*the* + ~] the collection of sacred writings of the Jewish religion: consisting of the Five Books of Moses (the Torah), the books of the Prophets, and various other sacred writings, including the Psalms, and collectively known to Christians as the Old Testament. **3.** [*often: bible*] a book that is a copy of these writings: *always carried a small bible with him.* **4.** [*usually: bible*] any book esteemed for its usefulness and authority: *a bird-watchers' bible.* See -BIBLIO-.

Bib•li•cal (bib′li kəl) /ˈbɪblɪkəl/ *adj.* [*often: biblical*] **1.** of or in the Bible: *a Biblical name.* **2.** in accord with the Bible: *Biblical justification.* —**Bib′li•cal•ly,** *adv.*

-biblio-, *root.* *-biblio-* comes from Greek, where it has the meaning "book." This meaning is found in such words as: BIBLE, BIBLIOGRAPHER, BIBLIOGRAPHY, BIBLIOPHILE.

bib•li•og•ra•pher (bib′lē og′rə fər) /ˌbɪbliyˈɒgrəfər/ *n.* [*count*] an expert in bibliography. See -BIBLIO-, -GRAPH-.

bib•li•og•ra•phy (bib′lē og′rə fē) /ˌbɪbliyˈɒgrəfiy/ *n.* [*count*], *pl.* **-phies.** a list of works, esp. a list of source materials used in preparing a work or referred to in the text: *a bibliography on the topic of abortion.* —**bib•li•o•graph•ic** (bib′lē ə graf′ik) /ˌbɪbliyəˈgræfɪk/ **bib′li•o•graph′i•cal,** *adj.* —**bib′li•o•graph′i•cal•ly,** *adv.* See -BIBLIO-, -GRAPH-.

bib•li•o•phile (bib′lē ə fīl′, -fil) /ˈbɪbliyəˌfayl, -fɪl/ *n.* [*count*] one who loves or collects books. See -BIBLIO-, -PHIL-.

bi•cam•er•al (bī kam′ər əl) /bayˈkæmərəl/ *adj.* having two chambers, as a legislative body: *a bicameral legislature.* —**bi•cam′er•al•ism,** *n.* [*noncount*] See BI-.

bi•carb (bī kärb′) /bayˈkɑrb/ *n.* *Informal.* SODIUM BICARBONATE.

bi•car•bo•nate (bī kär′bə nit, -nāt′) /bayˈkɑrbənɪt, -ˌneyt/ *n.* [*noncount*] a chemical, specifically a salt of carbonic acid.

bicar′bonate of so′da, *n.* SODIUM BICARBONATE.

bi•cen•ten•ar•y (bī′ sen ten′ə rē, bī sen′tn er′ē) /ˌbaysɛnˈtɛnəriy, bayˈsɛntn̩ˌɛriy/ *adj., n., pl.* **-ar•ies.** BICENTENNIAL.

bi•cen•ten•ni•al (bī′sen ten′ē əl) /ˌbaysɛnˈtɛniyəl/ *adj.* [*before a noun*] **1.** relating to or in honor of a 200th anniversary. **2.** lasting 200 years. **3.** occurring every 200 years. **—*n.*** [*count*] **4.** a 200th anniversary. See -ENN-.

bi•ceps (bī′seps) /ˈbaysɛps/ *n.* [*count*], *pl.* **-ceps, -ceps•es** (-sep siz) /-sɛpsɪz/. a muscle with two points of origin, as the muscle on the front of the upper arm.

bick•er (bik′ər) /ˈbɪkər/ *v.* [*no obj*] to argue about something unimportant: *bickering over shoelaces.*

bi•coast•al (bī kōs′tl) /bayˈkowstl̩/ *adj.* occurring or existing on two coasts, esp. on both the E and W coasts of the U.S.

bi•cul•tur•al•ism (bī kul′chər ə liz′əm) /bayˈkʌltʃərəˌlɪzəm/ *n.* [*noncount*] the presence of two different cultures in the same country or region: *the biculturalism of a region like Harlem.* —**bi•cul′tur•al,** *adj.*

bi•cus•pid (bī kus′pid) /bayˈkʌspɪd/ *adj.* **1.** Also, **bi•cus•pi•date** (bī kus′pi dāt′) /bayˈkʌsˌpɪˈdeyt/. having or ending in two points, as certain teeth. **—*n.*** [*count*] **2.** one of eight teeth located in pairs on each side of the upper and lower jaws in front of the molars.

bi•cy•cle (bī′si kəl, -sik′əl, -sī′kəl) /ˈbaysɪkəl, -ˌsɪkəl, -ˌsaykəl/ *n., v.,* **-cled, -cling.** **—*n.*** [*count*] **1.** a vehicle with two wheels, pedals connected to the rear wheel by a chain, handlebars for steering, and a seat like a saddle. **—*v.*** [*no obj*] **2.** to ride a bicycle: *They bicycled down to the store.* —**bi•cy•clist** (bī′si klist) /ˈbaysɪklɪst/ **bi′cy•cler,** *n.* [*count*] See -CYCLE-.

bid (bid) /bɪd/ *v.,* **bade** (bad) /bæd/ or **bid, bid•den** or **bid, bid•ding,** *n.* **—*v.*** **1.** to command (someone to do something): [~ + *obj* (+ *to*) + *verb*]: *The king bade them (to) rise and speak freely.* [~ + *obj*]: *Do as I bid you.* [*no obj*]: *Do as I bid.* **2.** to say as a greeting, wish, etc.: [~ + *obj* + *obj*]: *She bid him goodnight.* [~ + *obj* + *to* + *obj*]: *We bid a warm welcome to our distinguished visitors.* **3.** to offer (a certain sum) as the price one will charge or pay: [~ + *obj* (+ *for* + *obj*)]: *They bid $25,000 (for the job) and got the contract.* [*no obj;* (~ + *for* + *obj*)]: *I can't bid (for that vase); I don't have enough money.* **4.** [~ + *obj*] to enter a bid of (a given quantity or suit at cards): *When my bridge partner bid six diamonds my heart nearly stopped beating.* **—*n.*** [*count*] **5.** an act or instance of bidding. **6. a.** an offer to make a specified number of points or to take a specified number of card tricks: *My bid was for five hearts.* **b.** the turn of a person to bid: *Wait; it's my bid.* **7.** an invitation: *a bid to join a club.* **8.** an attempt to attain some purpose: *made a bid for the nomination.* —**bid′der,** *n.* [*count*]

bid•den (bid′n) /ˈbɪdn̩/ *v.* a pp. of BID.

bid•ding (bid′ing) /ˈbɪdɪŋ/ *n.* [*noncount*] **1.** command; summons: *at his bidding.* **2.** bids thought of as a group, or a period during which bids are made or received: *The bidding was fast and furious.* **—*Idiom.* 3. do someone's bidding,** to give in to someone's orders or wishes: *I was willing to do her bidding.*

bid•dy (bid′ē) /ˈbɪdiy/ *n.* [*count*], *pl.* **-dies.** a fussy old woman.

bide (bīd) /bayd/ *v.* [*no obj*], **bid•ed** or **bode** (bōd) /bowd/ **bid•ed, bid•ing.** **1.** to wait; remain: *We bided at home during the winter.* **—*Idiom.* 2. bide one's time,** to wait for a favorable opportunity: *bided his time, planning revenge.*

bi•det (bē dā′) /biyˈdey/ *n.* [*count*] a low basin in a bathroom, used for bathing the genital area.

bi•di•rec•tion•al (bī′di rek′shə nl, -dī-) /ˌbaydɪˈrɛkʃənl̩, -day-/ *adj.* capable of reacting or functioning in two directions: *a bidirectional antenna.* —**bi•di•rec•tion•al•i•ty** (bī′di rek′shə nal′i tē, -dī-) /ˌbaydɪˌrɛkʃəˈnælɪtiy, -day-/ *n.* [*noncount*] —**bi′di•rec′tion•al•ly,** *adv.*

bi•en•ni•al (bī en′ē əl) /bayˈɛniyəl/ *adj.* **1.** happening once every two years: *biennial games.* **2.** lasting or enduring for two years: *a biennial life cycle.* **3.** (of a plant) blooming and forming seeds in the second year of life. **—*n.*** [*count*] **4.** an event occurring once in two years. **5.** a biennial plant. Also, **biyearly** (for defs. 1, 2). —**bi•en′ni•al•ly,** *adv.* See -ENN-.

bi•en•ni•um (bī en′ē əm) /bayˈɛniyəm/ *n.* [*count*], *pl.* **-en•ni•ums, -en•ni•a** (-en′ē ə) /-ˈɛniyə/. a period of two years. See -ENN-.

bier (bēr) /bɪər/ *n.* [*count*] a stand on which a coffin is placed before burial: *gathered round the bier.*

bi•fo•cal (bī fō′kəl, bī′fō′-) /bayˈfowkəl, ˈbayˌfow-/ *adj.* **1.** having two points of focus. **2.** (of an eyeglass or contact lens) having two portions, one for near and one for far vision: *wasn't ready for bifocal lenses just yet.* **—*n.*** [*plural*] **3. bifocals,** bifocal eyeglasses or contact lenses: *With my bifocals I can read and see things at a distance.*

bi•fur•cate (*v., adj.* bī′fər kāt′, bī fûr′kāt; *adj. also* -kit) /*v., adj.* ˈbayfərˌkeyt, bayˈfɜrkeyt; *adj. also* -kɪt/ *v.,* **-cat•ed, -cat•ing,** *adj.* **—*v.*** **1.** to fork into two branches: [*no obj*]: *The road bifurcates up ahead.* [~ + *obj*]: *If you bifurcate your computer program at this point, you'll have two choices, each of which should lead you to the desired result.* **—*adj.*** **2.** divided into two branches. —**bi′fur•ca′tion,** *n.* [*count*]: *a bifurcation in the road.* [*noncount*]: *trying to avoid unnecessary bifurcation in program design.*

big (big) /bɪg/ *adj.,* **big•ger, big•gest,** *adv.* **—*adj.*** **1.** large in size, height, width, or amount: *a big house.* **2.** [*before a noun*] of major concern or importance; outstanding; influential: *a big problem.* **3.** grown-up; mature: *You are big enough to know better.* **4.** [*before a noun*] elder: *my big sister.* **5.** [*before a noun*] large-scale and powerful: *big government.* **6.** [*be* + ~] known or used widely; popular: *Jazz became big in the 1920's.* **7.** generous; magnanimous: *She was big enough to forgive him.* **8.** boastful; pompous: *a big talker.* **9.** loud: *a big voice.* **—*adv.*** **10.** successfully: *The new plans went over big.* **—*Idiom.* 11. be big on,** [~ + *obj*] *Informal.* to have a special liking or enthusiasm for: *That teacher is big on neatness.* —**big′gish,** *adj.* —**big′ness,** *n.* [*noncount*]

big•a•mist (big′ə mist) /ˈbɪgəmɪst/ *n.* [*count*] a person who commits bigamy. See -GAM-.

big•a•mous (big′ə məs) /ˈbɪgəməs/ *adj.* **1.** having two spouses at the same time: *He was bigamous at the time, but no one knew it.* **2.** involving bigamy: *a bigamous marriage.*

big•a•my (big′ə mē) /ˈbɪgəmiy/ *n.* [*noncount*] the act of marrying one person while being legally married to another: *Bigamy is acceptable in that culture.* See -GAM-.

big′ bang′ the′ory, *n.* [*noncount*] a theory that the universe began with an explosion of matter and is still expanding from the force of that explosion.

big′ deal′, *n.* [*count*] *Informal.* **1.** something or someone important or impressive: *I'm only a few minutes late; what's the big deal?* **—*interj.*** **2.** (used to show that one considers something to be unimportant or not impressive): *So you're the mayor's cousin — big deal!*

big•gie or **big•gy** (big′ē) /ˈbɪgiy/ *n.* [*count*], *pl.* **-gies.** *Informal.* **1.** an important or influential person: *visited the biggies in the mayor's office.* **2.** something very large, important, or successful: *That test was a biggy.*

big•heart•ed (big′här′tid) /ˈbɪgˈhɑrtɪd/ *adj.* generous; kind: *She was always bighearted.* —**big′heart′ed•ness,** *n.* [*noncount*]

bight (bīt) /bayt/ *n.* [*count*] **1.** a loop or slack part in a rope. **2. a.** a bend or curve in the shore of a sea. **b.** a body of water bounded by such a bend.

big•mouth (big′mouth′) /ˈbɪgˌmawθ/ *n.* [*count*] a loud, talkative, boastful person.

big•ot (big′ət) /ˈbɪgət/ *n.* [*count*] a person affected by bigotry: *kept talking like a bigot.*

big•ot•ed (big′ə tid) /ˈbɪgətɪd/ *adj.* of, relating to, or marked by bigotry: *The whole town was bigoted.*

big•ot•ry (big′ə trē) /ˈbɪgətriy/ *n.* [*noncount*] **1.** extreme unwillingness to accept the possibility that an idea differing from one's own may be correct: *We must fight bigotry with patience.* **2.** the actions, prejudices, etc., of a bigot: *encountered bigotry wherever she went.*

big′ shot′, *n.* [*count*] *Informal.* an important or influential person: *He was a big shot in the film industry.*

big′-tick′et, *adj.* [*before a noun*] costly; expensive: *big-ticket items like refrigerators or cars.*

big•wig (big′wig′) /ˈbɪgˌwɪg/ *n.* [*count*] *Informal.* an important person, esp. a high-ranking official: *political bigwigs.*

bike (bīk) /bayk/ *n., v.,* **biked, bik•ing.** **—*n.*** [*count*] **1.** a bicycle, motorbike, or motorcycle. **—*v.*** [*no obj*] **2.** to ride a bike: *We biked up and down Holland.*

bik•er (bī′kər) /ˈbaykər/ *n.* [*count*] **1.** a person who rides a bike. **2.** *Informal.* a member of a motorcycle gang.

bi•ki•ni (bi kē′nē) /bɪˈkiyniy/ *n.* [*count*], *pl.* **-nis.** **1.** a very small two-piece bathing suit for women or a one-piece bathing suit for men. **2.** Often, **bikinis.** [*plural*] underpants fitted low on the hip.

bi•la•bi•al (bī lā′bē əl) /bayˈleybiyəl/ *adj.* **1.** (of a speech sound) produced with the lips close together or touching, as the sounds (p), (b), (m), and (w). **—*n.*** [*count*] **2.** a bilabial speech sound.

bi•lat•er•al (bī lat′ər əl) /bayˈlætərəl/ *adj.* of, relating to, or involving two sides: *signed a bilateral agreement.* —**bi•lat′er•al•ly,** *adv.* See -LAT-[2].

bile (bīl) /bayl/ *n.* [*noncount*] **1.** a bitter yellow or greenish liquid produced by the liver, that aids in digestion of fats. **2.** bad temper; peevishness.

bilge (bilj) /bɪldʒ/ *n.* **1.** [*count*] Also, **bilges.** an area at the bottom of a ship where dirty water collects. **2.** [*noncount*] Also called **bilge water.** water collected there. **3.** [*noncount*] *Slang.* foolish or worthless talk: *Your excuse sounds like a lot of bilge.*

bi•lin•gual (bī ling′gwəl) /bayˈlɪŋgwəl/ *adj.* **1.** able to speak two languages, esp. with native ability: *bilingual in French and Italian.* **2.** expressed in, involving, or using two languages: *a bilingual dictionary.* **—*n.*** [*count*] **3.** a bilingual person: *A true bilingual would have no trouble translating this paragraph.* —**bi•lin′gual•ly,** *adv.* See BI-, -LING-.

bi•lin•gual•ism (bī ling′gwə liz′əm) /bayˈlɪŋgwəˌlɪzəm/ *n.* [*noncount*] **1.** the ability to speak two languages fluently: *worked hard to achieve bilingualism.* **2.** the habitual use of two languages: *a policy encouraging bilingualism in government.*

bil•ious (bil′yəs) /ˈbɪlyəs/ *adj.* **1.** of or relating to bile. **2.** sick; ill; upset in the stomach: *feeling bilious after drinking all night.* **3.** peevish; irritable; cranky: *the bilious old man next door.* —**bil′ious•ness,** *n.* [*noncount*]: *His biliousness always depressed his staff.*

bilk (bilk) /bɪlk/ *v.* [~ + *obj* + *of* + *obj*] to defraud; cheat: *That smooth-talking guy bilked her of her life savings.* —**bilk′er,** *n.* [*count*]

bill[1] (bil) /bɪl/ *n.* [*count*] **1.** a statement of the money owed for goods or services: *I'd like to discuss the amount of this bill for car repairs.* **2.** a piece of paper money worth a specified amount: *a ten-dollar bill.* **3.** a proposal for a new law: *a gun-control bill.* **4.** [*usually singular*] entertainment scheduled for presentation: *a twin bill for the price of one movie.* **—*v.*** **5.** to send a list of charges to: [~ + *obj*]: *We'll bill you later for the amount.* [~ + *obj* + *obj*]: *billed me one hundred dollars to tow the car.* **6.** [~ + *obj*] to advertise (something) or otherwise make (it) known by public notice: *She was billed to play the part of Ophelia.* **7.** [~ + *obj* (+ *as*) + *obj*] to advertise or claim (something) as having (some qualities): *The economic summit meeting was billed as a historic moment in time.* **—*Idiom.*** **8. fill the bill,** to fit a particular purpose; be suitable: *Yes, that costume fills the bill; I'll take it.*

bill[2] (bil) /bɪl/ *n.* [*count*] **1.** the parts of a bird's jaws that have a horny covering; beak. **2.** the visor of a cap. **—*v.*** [*no obj*] **3.** to join bills: *two birds billing.* **—*Idiom.*** **4. bill and coo,** [*no obj*] to kiss or hold someone closely and whisper in an intimate way.

bill•a•ble (bil′ə bəl) /ˈbɪləbəl/ *adj.* chargeable.

bill•board (bil′bôrd′, -bōrd′) /ˈbɪlˌbɔrd, -ˌbowrd/ *n.* [*count*] a flat surface on which large advertisements or notices are posted: *Billboards were banned from most of that highway.*

-billed, *combining form.* Use *-billed* after adjectives to mean "having a bill or beak of a (specified kind, shape, or color)": *yellow + -billed → yellow-billed (= having a yellow bill).*

bil•let (bil′it) /ˈbɪlɪt/ *n.* [*count*] **1.** lodging for a soldier, etc., as in a private home: *His billet was a drafty old home in a valley of the Loire.* **2.** an official order directing the addressee to provide such lodging. **—*v.*** **3.** [~ + *obj*] to direct (a soldier) to a place to live and stay: *The general billeted his men in the finest old castles.* **4.** [~ + *obj*] to provide a place to stay for; quarter: *Many citizens were happy to billet the soldiers in their homes.* **5.** [*no obj*] to be quartered; stay: *They billeted in some fancy older homes.*

bil•let-doux (bil′ā do͞o′, bil′ē-) /ˈbɪleyˈduw, ˈbɪliy-/ *n.* [*count*], *pl.* **bil•lets-doux** (bil′ā do͞oz′, -do͞o′, bil′ē-) /ˈbɪleyˈduwz, -ˈduw, ˈbɪliy-/. a love letter.

bill•fold (bil′fōld′) /ˈbɪlˌfowld/ *n.* [*count*] a thin, flat, folding case for carrying paper money.

bil•liard (bil′yərd) /ˈbɪlyərd/ *adj.* [*before a noun*] of, for, or used in billiards: *a billiard parlor.*

bil•liards (bil′yərdz) /ˈbɪlyərdz/ *n.* [*noncount; used with a singular verb*] any of several games played with hard balls driven with a long, smooth wooden cue into pockets on a cloth-covered table: *Billiards was an easy game for him.*

bill•ing (bil′ing) /ˈbɪlɪŋ/ *n.* **1.** [*noncount*] the listing of the name of a performer, act, etc., on a sign outside a theater, or on a poster, etc.: *She always received top billing.* **2.** [*noncount*] advertising; publicity: *Advance billing made the show a sellout.* **3.** [*noncount*] the preparing or sending out of bills or requests for payment: *the billing and filing operations.* **4.** [*count*] the amount of business done by a firm within a certain time: *billings of $10 million a year.* **5.** [*noncount*] the cost of goods or services billed to a customer within a period.

bil•lion (bil′yən) /ˈbɪlyən/ *n.* [*count*], *pl.* **-lions,** [*or, after a number*] **-lion,** *adj.* **—*n.*** **1.** a cardinal number represented in the U.S. by 1 followed by 9 zeros, and in Great Britain by 1 followed by 12 zeros: *the sum of two billion dollars* **2.** any vaguely large number: *I've told you a billion times.* **—*adj.*** [*before a noun*] **3.** equal in number to a billion: *a billion-dollar industry.* —**bil′lionth,** *adj., n.* [*count*] **—Usage.** See HUNDRED.

bil•lion•aire (bil′yə nâr′, bil′yə nâr′) /ˌbɪlyəˈnɛər, ˈbɪlyəˌnɛər/ *n.* [*count*] a person with money, property, or other things of value worth a billion or more dollars, francs, pounds, etc.

bill′ of fare′, *n.* [*count*] **1.** a list of food available at a restaurant. **2.** a program of entertainment: *What is the bill of fare for the evening?*

bill′ of goods′, *n.* [*count; usually singular*] **1.** a quantity of items for sale, as an order or shipment. **2.** a falsely advertised or defective article: *sold me a bill of goods.*

bill′ of sale′, *n.* [*count*] a document transferring the right of ownership of personal property from seller to buyer.

bil•low (bil′ō) /'bɪlow/ *n.* [*count*] **1.** a great wave of the sea. **2.** any large mass that sweeps along or rises like waves of the sea: *billows of smoke.* —*v.* [*no obj*] **3.** to rise or roll in billows; surge: *The waves billowed in the storm.* **4.** to swell out, puff up, etc.: *skirts billowing out as the women danced.*

bil•ly (bil′ē) /'bɪliy/ *n.* [*count*], *pl.* **-lies.** a heavy wooden stick used by the police: *Swinging their billy clubs, the police waded into the crowd.* Also called **bil′ly club′.**

bil′ly goat′, *n.* [*count*] a male goat.

bim•bo (bim′bō) /'bɪmbow/ *n.* [*count*], *pl.* **-bos, -boes.** *Slang.* **1.** a foolish, stupid, or inept person. **2.** a woman of loose morals.

bi•month•ly (bī munth′lē) /bay'mʌnθliy/ *adj., n., pl.* **-lies,** *adv.* —*adj.* **1.** occurring once every two months: *Bimonthly reports are due on the first of February, April, etc., throughout the year.* **2.** occurring twice a month; semimonthly. —*n.* [*count*] **3.** a bimonthly publication. —*adv.* **4.** every two months: *See your doctor bimonthly.* **5.** twice a month; semimonthly. —**Usage.** See BI-.

bin (bin) /bɪn/ *n., v.,* **binned, bin•ning.** —*n.* [*count*] **1.** a box or enclosed place for storing grain, coal, or the like. —*v.* [~ + *obj*] **2.** to store in a bin.

bi•na•ry (bī′nə rē, -ner ē) /'baynəriy, -nɛriy/ *adj., n., pl.* **-ries.** —*adj.* **1.** consisting of or involving two parts or things. **2.** of or relating to a system of numbers called base 2, in which the only numbers that can be used are 0 and 1. **3.** referring to a chemical compound containing only two elements or groups, as sodium chloride.

bind (bīnd) /baynd/ *v.,* **bound** (bound) /bawnd/ **bind•ing,** *n.* —*v.* **1.** [~ + *obj*] to fasten or tie (something) with a string, rope, etc.: *She bound her hair with a ribbon.* **2.** to bandage: [~ + *obj (+ up)*]: *to bind one's wounds (up).* [~ + *(+ up) + obj*]: *to bind (up) his wounds.* **3.** [~ + *obj*] to cause to cohere: *Ice bound the soil.* **4.** [~ + *obj*] to unite or join by any tie: *to be bound by a contract.* **5.** [~ + *obj; usually: be + bound + to*] to place under obligation: *She was bound to secrecy by the oath she took.* **6.** [~ + *obj*] to fasten or secure (sheets of paper) within a cover: *to bind a book in leather.* —*n.* [*count; usually singular*] **7.** a difficult situation or predicament: *This tight schedule has us in a bind.* —**bind′a•ble,** *adj.*

bind•er (bīn′dər) /'bayndər/ *n.* [*count*] **1.** a fastener; a person or thing that binds: *The book was at the binder's when I was looking for it.* **2.** a hard cover with clasps or rings for holding loose papers together: *She has a three-ring binder for her notes and essays.*

bind•er•y (bīn′də rē, -drē) /'bayndəriy, -driy/ *n.* [*count*], *pl.* **-er•ies.** a place where books are bound.

bind•ing (bīn′ding) /'bayndɪŋ/ *n.* **1.** [*noncount*] the act of fastening, securing, or the like: *the binding of our lives together in marriage.* **2.** [*noncount*] anything that binds, as a strip of material that protects or decorates the edge of a tablecloth, etc. **3.** [*count*] the covering within which the pages of a book are bound: *This book had a leather binding.* **4.** [*count*] a fastening to lock a boot onto a ski: *My bindings came loose and my skis went flying off.* —*adj.* **5.** likely to bind or restrict the movements (of someone): *a shirt too binding to wear.* **6.** having power to bind; that must be obeyed; obligatory: *a binding contract that he couldn't get out of.*

binge (binj) /bɪndʒ/ *n., v.,* **binged, bing•ing.** —*n.* [*count*] **1.** a time in which one eats or drinks a great deal: *on a binge for several days.* **2.** a period of time in which an activity is done a great deal or too much: *a shopping binge before Christmas.* —*v.* [*no obj*] **3.** to go on a binge: *out binging after exams.*

bin•go (bing′gō) /'bɪŋgow/ *n.* [*noncount; sometimes: Bingo*] **1.** a game of chance in which each player has a card with rows of numbers, a caller announces numbers drawn at random, and a game is won when a player can match and cover five numbers in a row: *We went to play bingo at the church last Friday night.* —*interj.* **2.** (used to call a win in bingo): *Bingo! I won!* **3.** (used to indicate surprise at something unexpected): *We're driving along and bingo—the tire explodes!*

bin•oc•u•lar (bə nok′yə lər, bī-) /bə'nɒkyələr, bay-/ *n.* **1. binoculars** [*plural*] an instrument for viewing distant objects, consisting of two small telescopes fitted together side by side. —*adj.* **2.** involving both eyes: *binocular vision.* —**bin•oc•u•lar•i•ty** (bə nok′yə lar′i tē, bī-) /bə,nɒkyə'lærɪtiy, bay-/ *n.* [*noncount*] See -OCUL-.

bi•no•mi•al (bī nō′mē əl) /bay'nowmiyəl/ *n.* [*count*] **1.** an algebraic expression that is a sum or difference of two terms, as $3x + 2y$ and $x^2 - 4x$. —*adj.* [*usually before a noun*] **2.** of or relating to a term that has two parts: *a binomial equation.* See -NOM-[2].

bi•o (bī′ō) /'bayow/ *n., pl.* **bi•os. 1.** [*count*] biography: *a bio on the first president of the country.* **2.** [*noncount*] biology: *I had a rough course in bio last term.*

bio-, *prefix. bio-* comes from Greek, where it has the meaning "life." This meaning is found in such words as: BIODEGRADABLE, BIOLOGY, BIOSPHERE.

bi•o•chem•is•try (bī′ō kem′ə strē) /,bayow'kɛməstriy/ *n.* [*noncount*] the scientific study of the chemical substances and processes of living matter. —**bi•o•chem•i•cal** (bī′ō kem′i kəl) /,bayow'kɛmɪkəl/ *adj.* —**bi′o•chem′•ist,** *n.* [*count*]

bi•o•de•grad•a•ble (bī′ō di grā′də bəl) /,bayowdɪ'greydəbəl/ *adj.* capable of decaying through the action of living organisms: *biodegradable paper.* —**bi•o•de•grad•a•bil•i•ty** (bī′ō di grā′də bil′i tē) /,bayowdɪ,greydə'bɪlɪtiy/ *n.* [*noncount*]: *the biodegradability of nonplastic containers.* See -GRAD-.

bi•o•eth•ics (bī′ō eth′iks) /,bayow'ɛθɪks/ *n.* [*noncount; used with a singular verb*] a field of study concerned with the social and ethical issues of certain special medical procedures such as organ transplants: *Bioethics asks questions about what we should do or not do for terminally ill patients.*

bi•o•feed•back (bī′ō fēd′bak′) /,bayow'fiyd,bæk/ *n.* [*noncount*] a method of learning to adjust a particular body function, such as temperature or muscle tension, by keeping track of it with the aid of an electronic device.

bi•og•ra•pher (bī og′rə fər, bē-) /bay'ɒgrəfər, biy-/ *n.* [*count*] a writer of biography.

bi•o•graph•i•cal (bī′ə graf′i kəl) /,bayə'græfɪkəl/ also **bi′o•graph′ic,** *adj.* **1.** of or relating to a person's life: *Please include a few biographical notes in your application.* **2.** of, relating to, or containing biography: *a biographical dictionary.* —**bi′o•graph′i•cal•ly,** *adv.*

bi•og•ra•phy (bī og′rə fē, bē-) /bay'ɒgrəfiy, biy-/ *n., pl.* **-phies. 1.** [*count*] a written account of another person's life: *Boswell wrote a famous biography of Samuel Johnson.* **2.** [*noncount*] such writings thought of as a group. See -GRAPH-.

bi•o•log•i•cal (bī′ə loj′i kəl) /,bayə'lɒdʒɪkəl/ also **bi′o•log′ic,** *adj.* **1.** of or relating to biology: *biological sciences.* **2.** [*before a noun*] using chemical or living organisms (such as viruses, etc.) to harm an enemy: *biological weapons.* **3.** [*before a noun*] related by blood rather than by adoption: *biological parents.* —**bi′o•log′i•cal•ly,** *adv.*

biolog′ical clock′, *n.* [*count*] **1.** an inborn mechanism of the body that controls its cycles, such as those of sleeping and waking. **2.** such a mechanism when it is seen as marking the passing of one's youth and esp. of a woman's ability to bear children: *wanted to have a baby because she heard her biological clock ticking.*

bi•ol•o•gy (bī ol′ə jē) /bay'ɒlədʒiy/ *n.* [*noncount*] **1.** the scientific study of life or living matter in all its forms and processes: *always had an interest in biology.* **2.** the features, aspects, structure, or behavior characteristic of a living thing or group of living things: *studying the biology of worms.* —**bi•ol′o•gist,** *n.* [*count*]

bi•on•ic (bī on′ik) /bay'ɒnɪk/ *adj.* **1.** having normal bodily functions strengthened or improved by electronic devices: *a bionic hand.* **2.** *Informal.* having superhuman capacity: *a bionic salesman.* —**bi•on′i•cal•ly,** *adv.*

bi•on•ics (bī on′iks) /bay'ɒnɪks/ *n.* [*noncount; used with a singular verb*] the study of the means by which humans perform tasks and of the application of the findings to the design of electronic devices and mechanical parts: *using bionics to improve robotic equipment.*

bi•o•phys•ics (bī′ō fiz′iks) /,bayow'fɪzɪks/ *n.* [*noncount; used with a singular verb*] the branch of biology that applies physics to the study of biological structures. —**bi′o•phys′i•cal,** *adj.* —**bi•o•phys•i•cist** (bī′ō fiz′ə sist) /,bayow 'fɪzəsɪst/ *n.* [*count*]

bi•op•sy (bī′op sē) /'bayɒpsiy/ *n., pl.* **-sies,** *v.,* **-sied, -sy•ing.** —*n.* [*count*] **1.** the removal of a piece of tissue from a living body in order to find out if it is diseased: *performed a biopsy on the lump in her breast.* **2.** a piece of tissue obtained in this way: *the biopsy from her breast had no cancer.* —*v.* [~ + *obj*] **3.** to remove (living tissue) for diagnosis: *biopsied the tissue from his liver.* See -OPT-, -OPTI-.

bi•o•rhythm (bī′ō rith′əm) /'bayow,rɪðəm/ *n.* [*count*] an inborn cycle in an organism, such as sleep and wake cycles: *biorhythms all confused after our traveling.*

BIOS (bī′ōs) /'bayows/ *n.* [*count*] the part of a computer that directs many basic functions of the system, such as booting and keyboard control.

bi•o•sphere (bī′ə sfēr′) /ˈbayəˌsfɪər/ *n.* [*count*] **1.** [*usually: singular; the* + ~] the part of the earth's crust, waters, and atmosphere that supports life: *harming the biosphere with chemicals.* **2.** the biological system containing the entire earth and its living organisms: *When there is an imbalance in one part of the biosphere, it affects all the other parts as well.* See -SPHERE-.

bi•o•tech•nol•o•gy (bī′ō tek nol′ə jē) /ˌbayowtɛkˈnɒlədʒiy/ *n.* [*noncount*] the use of living organisms in the manufacture of drugs for environmental management. —**bi•o•tech•ni•cal** (bī′ō tek′ni kəl) /ˌbayowˈtɛknɪkəl/ **bi•o•tech•no•log•i•cal** (bī′ō tek′nl oj′i kəl) /ˌbayowˌtɛknl̩ˈɒdʒɪkəl/ *adj.* —**bi′o•tech•nol′o•gist,** *n.* [*count*]

bi•par•ti•san (bī pär′tə zən) /bayˈpɑrtəzən/ *adj.* representing or including members from two factions: *bipartisan support from both Democrats and Republicans.* —**bi•par′ti•san•ism,** *n.* [*noncount*] —**bi•par′ti•san•ship′,** *n.* [*noncount*]: *We need bipartisanship in the law-making process.* See -PAR-.

bi•par•tite (bī pär′tīt) /bayˈpɑrtayt/ *adj.* divided into or of two parts or involving two parties: *a bipartite treaty.*

bi•ped (bī′ped) /ˈbaypɛd/ *n.* [*count*] **1.** a two-footed animal: *Humans and some monkeys are bipeds.* —*adj.* **2.** Also, **bi•ped′al.** having two feet. See -PED-[1].

bi•plane (bī′plān′) /ˈbayˌpleyn/ *n.* [*count*] an airplane with two sets of wings, one above the other: *The old biplanes performed for the airshow.*

bi•ra•cial (bī rā′shəl) /bayˈreyʃəl/ *adj.* consisting of, representing, or combining members of two separate races: *biracial marriages.* —**bi•ra′cial•ism,** *n.* [*noncount*]

birch (bûrch) /bɜrtʃ/ *n.* **1.** [*count*] a tree having a smooth, peeling outer bark and close-grained wood. **2.** [*noncount*] the wood itself. **3.** [*count*] a birch rod used esp. for whipping. —*adj.* **4.** of, relating to, or made of birch: *birch beer.*

bird (bûrd) /bɜrd/ *n.* **1.** [*count*] any warm-blooded, egg-laying animal having feathers: *watched the birds soaring overhead.* **2.** [*count*] *Slang.* a person, esp. one having some special or unusual feature: *a strange bird.* **3.** [*count*] *Informal.* an aircraft, spacecraft, or guided missile: *We're tracking the birds on radar at about five miles out and approaching fast.* **4.** [*count*] *Chiefly Brit. Slang.* a girl or young woman: *a really smashing pair of birds.* —***Idiom.*** **5. bird in the hand,** [*count*] a thing that is actually possessed, as opposed to a thing that one wishes one had: *A bird in the hand is worth two in the bush.* Also, **bird in hand. 6. birds of a feather,** [*plural*] people with similar attitudes, interests, or experience: *Birds of a feather flock together (= People with the same interests often stay together).* **7. eat like a bird,** to eat just a little. **8. for the birds,** [*be* + ~]. *Informal.* worthless; silly: *I think that plan is for the birds; don't even suggest it to the boss.* **9. kill two birds with one stone,** to achieve two purposes with a single effort: *She killed two birds with one stone by shopping and visiting the museum on the same trip.*

bird•brain (bûrd′brān′) /ˈbɜrdˌbreyn/ *n.* [*count*] *Slang.* a stupid or scatterbrained person. —**bird′brained′, bird′-brained′,** *adj.*

bird•ie (bûr′dē) /ˈbɜrdiy/ *n., v.,* **-ied, -ie•ing.** —*n.* [*count*] **1.** a small bird: *Mommy, look at the birdie!* **2.** a score of one stroke less than par on a golf hole: *shot a birdie on that par 5.* —*v.* [~ + *obj*] **3.** to make a birdie on (a golf hole): *birdied the last three holes.*

bird′ of par′adise, *n., pl.* **birds of paradise** [*count*] a songbird of New Guinea, the males of which have elegant, brightly colored feathers.

bird's′-eye′, *adj.* [*before a noun*] seen from far above; panoramic: *a bird's-eye view of the city from the Empire State Building.*

birth (bûrth) /bɜrθ/ *n.* **1.** [*noncount*] an act or instance of being born: *What was the date of your birth?* **2.** [*count*] the act or process of bringing forth young; childbirth: *a long and difficult birth.* **3.** [*noncount*] descent; nationality (because one was born in a particular place): *Greek by birth.* **4.** [*count; usually singular*] any coming into existence; origin: *the birth of an idea.* —***Idiom.*** **5. give birth to,** [~ + *obj*] **a.** to bear (a child): *She gave birth to a boy.* **b.** to initiate; originate: *Einstein gave birth to a whole new way of looking at matter and energy.*

birth′ control′, *n.* [*noncount*] methods of restricting the number of children born, usually through control or prevention of conception; contraception.

birth•day (bûrth′dā′) /ˈbɜrθˌdey/ *n.* [*count*] **1.** the anniversary of a birth: *We had a birthday party for her.* **2.** the day of a person's birth: *My birthday is December 28.* **3.** a day commemorating the founding or beginning of something: *celebrating the birthday of our church.*

birth′day suit′, *n.* [*count; usually singular; one's* + ~] *Informal.* bare skin; nakedness.

birth•ing (bûr′thing) /ˈbɜrθɪŋ/ *n.* [*count*] an act or instance of giving birth, esp. by natural childbirth.

birth•mark (bûrth′märk′) /ˈbɜrθˌmɑrk/ *n.* [*count*] a minor spot on a person's skin at birth.

birth•place (bûrth′plās′) /ˈbɜrθˌpleys/ *n.* [*count*] place of birth or origin: *We visited the birthplace of Greta Garbo.*

birth•rate (bûrth′rāt′) /ˈbɜrθˌreyt/ *n.* [*count*] the number of births for every 1,000 people in a given place in a given time: *Birthrates are rising in some poorer countries.*

birth•right (bûrth′rīt′) /ˈbɜrθˌrayt/ *n.* any right or privilege which a person should have because of being born: [*count*]: *Some see basic necessities, housing, and health care as a birthright.* [*noncount*]: *By birthright you are entitled to respect.*

birth•stone (bûrth′stōn′) /ˈbɜrθˌstown/ *n.* [*count*] a gemstone traditionally associated with the month or sign of the zodiac of one's birth: *Her birthstone was a garnet.*

bis•cuit (bis′kit) /ˈbɪskɪt/ *n.* [*count*] **1.** a small, soft, raised bread, leavened with baking soda: *biscuits and gravy for dinner.* **2.** *Chiefly Brit.* **a.** a crisp flat bread made without leavening; cracker: *a plain biscuit to calm your stomach.* **b.** a cookie: *biscuits and tea.*

bi•sect (bī sekt′, bī′sekt) /bayˈsɛkt, ˈbaysɛkt/ *v.* **1.** [~ + *obj*] to cut or divide into two approximately equal parts: *Use your compass to bisect an angle.* **2.** [~ + *obj*] to intersect or cross: *The highway bisects the road at this point.* **3.** [*no obj*] to split into two, as a road; fork: *The road bisects here.* —**bi•sec•tion** (bī sek′shən) /bayˈsɛkʃən/ *n.* [*count*]: *a bisection of the two angles.* [*noncount*]: *learning bisection of angles in geometry.* —**bi•sec′tor, bi′sec•tor,** *n.* [*count*] See -SECT-.

bi•sex•u•al (bī sek′sho͞o əl) /bayˈsɛkʃuwəl/ *adj.* **1.** of both sexes. **2.** combining male and female organs in one individual; hermaphroditic. **3.** sexually responsive to and interested in both males and females. —*n.* [*count*] **4.** an animal or plant that has the reproductive organs of both sexes. **5.** a person sexually responsive to both males and females. —**bi•sex•u•al•i•ty** (bī sek′sho͞o al′i tē) /bayˌsɛkʃuwˈælɪtiy/ *n.* [*noncount*]: *concerned about her husband's bisexuality.*

bish•op (bish′əp) /ˈbɪʃəp/ *n.* [*count*] **1.** a person who supervises a diocese and is a member of the highest order of the ministry. **2.** one of two chess pieces that may be moved any distance diagonally.

bish•op•ric (bish′əp rik) /ˈbɪʃəprɪk/ *n.* [*count*] the area of responsibility of a bishop, or the office of a bishop.

bis•muth (biz′məth) /ˈbɪzməθ/ *n.* [*noncount*] an easily broken, grayish white metallic element used in the manufacture of alloys and in medicine.

bi•son (bī′sən, -zən) /ˈbaysən, -zən/ *n.* [*count*], *pl.* **-son.** a North American buffalo having a large head and high, humped shoulders.

bisque (bisk) /bɪsk/ *n.* [*noncount*] a thick cream soup, esp. of finely chopped and mixed shellfish.

bis•tro (bis′trō, bē′strō) /ˈbɪstrow, ˈbiystrow/ *n.* [*count*], *pl.* **-tros. 1.** a small, modest, European-style restaurant or café. **2.** a small nightclub or bar.

bit[1] (bit) /bɪt/ *n.* [*count*] **1.** the mouthpiece of a horse's bridle. **2.** a small thin shaft that can be used in a drill or tool for boring into something by twisting: *needed a smaller bit for his drill.* —***Idiom.*** **3. chafe** or **champ at the bit,** to become impatient and restless because of delay: *champing at the bit to get started on the test.*

bit[2] (bit) /bɪt/ *n.* **1.** [*count*] a small piece of something: *bits and pieces of wood.* **2.** [*a* + ~ + *of* + *noncount noun*] a small quantity of something: *I'd like a bit of wine to go with this.* **3.** [*a* + ~] a short time: *Wait a bit.* **4.** [*count; singular; the* + ~] behavior or actions associated with a particular situation, etc.: *doing the Honest Abe bit.* **5.** [*count*] Also called **bit part.** a very small role in a play, movie, or show, containing few or no lines. —***Idiom.*** **6. a bit,** somewhat; a little: *a bit late to be up watching TV.* **7. a bit much,** more than can be tolerated: *When he started making fun of the boss, it became just a bit much.* **8. bit by bit,** by degrees; gradually: *"Bit by bit, the bird builds its nest" is a French proverb.* **9. do one's bit,** to contribute one's share to an effort: *I'd like to do my bit for the orphan's fund.* **10. every bit,** quite; just: *every bit as good as you said it would be.*

bit[3] (bit) /bɪt/ *n.* [*count*] a single, basic unit of computer information, valued at either 0 or 1.

bit[4] (bit) /bɪt/ *v.* pt. and a pp. of BITE.

bitch (bich) /bɪtʃ/ *n.* [*count*] **1.** a female dog, wolf, or fox. **2.** *Slang.* an unpleasant, nasty, spiteful, or selfish woman: *She's a real bitch today.* **3.** *Slang.* anything very difficult or unpleasant: *Man, that test was a bitch.* **—*v.* 4.** [*no obj*] *Slang.* to complain; gripe: *bitches about how everyone hates her.* **—bitch′i•ness,** *n.* [*noncount*]: *Your bitchiness affects everyone here at work.* **—bitch•y,** *adj.*, **-i•er, -i•est:** *He was really bitchy yesterday after he was fired.*

bite (bīt) /bayt/ *v.*, **bit** (bit) /bɪt/ **bit•ten** (bit′n) /ˈbɪtn̩/ or **bit, bit•ing,** *n.* **—*v.* 1.** to cut or tear with the teeth:[~ + *obj*]: *The cat bit me.* [~ + *into* + *obj*]: *The cat bit into my arm.* **2.** to cut (something) off with the teeth; sever: [~ + *off* + *obj*]: *bit off a piece of meat.* [~ + *obj* + *off*]: *bit a piece off.* **3.** [~ + *obj*] to grip with the teeth: *Our hero bit the rope and hung off the cliff by his teeth.* **4.** (of an insect) to sting: [~ + *obj*]: *bitten by a mosquito.* [*no obj*]: *The flies are biting today.* **5.** [~ + *obj*] to cause to sting: *faces bitten by the icy wind.* **6.** to take firm hold (of): [~ + *obj*]: *studded tires that bite the road.* [*no obj*]: *When you feel the gears beginning to bite, let up on the clutch.* **7.** [*no obj*] **a.** (of fish) to take bait (and hence get caught): *Are the fish biting today?* **b.** to respond to an offer or suggestion: *It was a pretty good offer, but she didn't bite.* **—*n.*** [*count*] **8.** an act of biting. **9.** a wound made by biting: *The doctors treated several dog bites.* **10.** a cutting, stinging, or nipping effect: *That wine had quite a bite to it.* **11.** a piece bitten off: *Chew each bite carefully.* **12.** [*usually singular*] a small meal: *Let's go out for a bite.* **13.** a morsel of food: *I'll have a little bite of your salmon.* **14.** a portion demanded or taken: *a big bite of my paycheck.* **15.** the way the upper and lower teeth come together: *The orthodontist said I needed work to correct my bite.* **—*Idiom.* 16. bite off more than one can chew,** to attempt something that exceeds one's ability: *Writing a novel was biting off more than he could chew.* **17. bite one's tongue,** to suppress one's anger: *I thought I might lose my temper so I bit my tongue instead.* **18. bite someone's head off,** to respond with anger to someone's question or comment: *When the students asked for more time to write their papers, the teacher nearly bit their heads off.* **19. bite the bullet.** See BULLET (def. 6). **20. bite the dust.** See DUST (def. 14). **21. bite the hand that feeds one,** to repay kindness with malice or injury: *I had helped him throughout his career, but when he got into trouble he turned and bit the hand that fed him.* **22. put the bite on,** [~ + *obj*] *Slang.* to try to borrow or get money from: *Let's put the bite on auntie, she's got plenty of dough.*

bit•ing (bī′ting) /ˈbaytɪŋ/ *adj.* **1.** [*before a noun*] sharp; painful: *biting cold.* **2.** cutting; sarcastic: *a biting remark.* **—bit′ing•ly,** *adv.*

bit′ part′, *n.* BIT[2] (def. 5).

bit•ten (bit′n) /ˈbɪtn̩/ *v.* a pp. of BITE.

bit•ter (bit′ər) /ˈbɪtər/ *adj.* **1.** having a harsh taste; not sour, sweet, or salty: *bitter herbs.* **2.** [*before a noun*] hard to bear: *a bitter sorrow.* **3.** [*before a noun*] causing pain: *a bitter chill.* **4.** characterized by hostility: *bitter enemies.* **5.** [*before a noun*] experienced at great cost: *a bitter lesson.* **—*n.*** [*noncount*] **6.** *Brit.* an ale that tastes bitter because it is made with hops: *two pints of your best bitter.* **—bit′ter•ly,** *adv.*: *a bitterly cold night.* **—bit′ter•ness,** *n.* [*noncount*]

bit′ter end′, *n.* [*count; usually singular*] the conclusion of a difficult situation: *stayed with him until the bitter end.*

bit•tern (bit′ərn) /ˈbɪtərn/ *n.* [*count*] a brown and whitish wading bird of the heron family.

bit•ter•sweet (bit′ər swēt′) /ˈbɪtərˌswiyt/ *adj.* **1.** both bitter and sweet to the taste: *bittersweet chocolate.* **2.** both pleasant and painful: *a bittersweet memory.* **—*n.*** [*count*] **3.** a climbing or trailing plant of the nightshade family. **4.** a climbing plant having orange capsules. **—bit′ter•sweet′ly,** *adv.* **—bit′ter•sweet′ness,** *n.* [*noncount*]

bit•ty (bit′ē) /ˈbɪtiy/ *adj.*, **-ti•er, -ti•est. 1.** tiny; itty-bitty: *just a bitty little thing.* **2.** *Chiefly Brit.* containing or consisting of small bits.

bi•tu•men (bī to͞o′mən, -tyo͞o′-, bi-) /bayˈtuwmən, -ˈtyuw-, bɪ-/ *n.* [*noncount*] a black, sticky substance, such as asphalt.

bi•tu•mi•nize (bī to͞o′mə nīz′, -tyo͞o′-, bi-) /bayˈtuwməˌnayz, -ˈtyuw-, bɪ-/ *v.* [~ + *obj*], **-nized, -niz•ing.** to convert into or treat with bitumen: *a project of bituminizing the roads.*

bi•tu•mi•nous (bī to͞o′mə nəs, -tyo͞o′-, bi-) /bayˈtuwmənəs, -ˈtyuw-, bɪ-/ *adj.* **1.** resembling or containing bitumen. **2.** of or relating to bituminous coal.

bitu′minous coal′, *n.* [*noncount*] a soft coal that can be readily burned.

bi•valve (bī′valv′) /ˈbayˌvælv/ *n.* [*count*] **1.** a mollusk, such as the oyster, having side shells joined on a hinge. **—*adj.* 2.** having two shells united by a hinge.

biv•ou•ac (biv′o͞o ak′, biv′wak) /ˈbɪvuwˌæk, ˈbɪvwæk/ *n.*, *v.*, **-acked, -ack•ing. —*n.*** [*count*] **1.** a temporary military camp. **—*v.*** [*no obj*] **2.** to come together in such a place: *They bivouacked for the evening in that area.*

bi•week•ly (bī wēk′lē) /bayˈwiykliy/ *adj.*, *n.*, *pl.* **-lies,** *adv.* **—*adj.* 1.** occurring once every two weeks: *a biweekly magazine.* **2.** occurring twice in one week; semiweekly. **—*n.*** [*count*] **3.** a magazine, newspaper, etc., issued every other week. **—*adv.* 4.** every two weeks: *The class meets biweekly, every other Monday.* **5.** twice in one week. **—Usage.** See BI-.

bi•year•ly (bī yēr′lē) /bayˈyɪərliy/ *adj.* **1.** happening once every two years; biennial. **2.** happening twice in one year; biannual. **—*adv.* 3.** every two years. **4.** twice yearly. **—Usage.** See BI-.

bi•zarre (bi zär′) /bɪˈzɑr/ *adj.* unusual in appearance, style, or character: *a bizarre coincidence.* **—bi•zarre′ly,** *adv.* **—bi•zarre′ness,** *n.* [*noncount*]

bks., an abbreviation of: books.

blab (blab) /blæb/ also **blab•ber** (blab′ər) /ˈblæbər/ *v.*, **blabbed** also **blab•bered, blab•bing** also **blab•ber•ing.** to talk (about something) without thought; to reveal by talking this way: [~ + *obj*]: *You know he'll just blab all the secrets.* [*no obj*]: *It's time to stop blabbing.*

blab•ber•mouth (blab′ər mouth′) /ˈblæbərˌmawθ/ *n.* [*count*] a person who talks too much, esp. one who reveals secrets.

black (blak) /blæk/ *adj.*, **-er, -est,** *n.*, *v.* **—*adj.* 1.** lacking hue and brightness; absorbing light without reflecting any of its rays: *black ink.* **2.** characterized by absence of light; enveloped in darkness: *a black night.* **3.** [*sometimes: Black*] **a.** of, relating to, or belonging to any of the various populations having dark skin coloring, specifically the dark-skinned peoples of Africa, Oceania, and Australia. **b.** AFRICAN-AMERICAN (def. 2): *black Americans.* **4.** soiled or stained with dirt. **5.** gloomy; pessimistic; dismal: *a black future.* **6.** (of a play or writing) dealing with grim topics, esp. in a morbidly satirical way: *black comedy.* **7.** sullen or hostile: *a black look.* **8.** harmful, evil, or wicked: *a black heart.* **9.** (of coffee) served without milk or cream: *black coffee.* **10.** indicating disgrace or dishonor: *a black mark.* **—*n.*** [*noncount*] **11.** the color at one end of the gray scale, opposite to white. **12.** black clothing, esp. as a sign of mourning: *She was dressed in black.* **—*v.*** [~ + *obj*] **13.** to make black; put black on; blacken: *She blacked his eye with that one punch.* **14. black out, a.** [*no obj*] to temporarily lose consciousness or memory: *blacked out after they hit me on the head.* **b.** [~ + *out* + *obj*] to hide or obscure (a city) by concealing all light in defense against air raids: *blacked out the city by switching off all lights.* **c.** [~ + *out* + *obj*] to impose a broadcast blackout on (an area): *The network blacked out the New York City area.* **—*Idiom.* 15. in the black,** operating at a profit: *The company was operating in the black again.* **—black′ish,** *adj.* **—Usage.** BLACK, COLORED, and NEGRO have all been used to describe or name dark-skinned African peoples or their descendants. COLORED, now somewhat old-fashioned, is often considered offensive. In the late 1950's BLACK began to replace NEGRO, and it is still the most widely used and accepted term. Common as both an adjective and a noun, BLACK is usually not capitalized except in proper names or titles (*Black Muslim; Black English*). By the close of the 1980's AFRICAN-AMERICAN, urged by leaders in the American black community, had begun to replace BLACK in both print and speech, esp. when used by American blacks to refer to themselves.

black′-and-blue′, *adj.* discolored, as by bruising: *a black-and-blue mark on my knee.*

black′-and-white′, *adj.* **1.** showing or displaying only black and white or gray tones; lacking color: *black-and-white photos.* **2.** (of an issue, problem, or situation) having only two possible sides or only two possible values: *those who think in black-and-white terms.* **—*Idiom.* 3. in black and white,** written down: *I'd like to see your plans in black and white.*

black•ball (blak′bôl′) /ˈblækˌbɔl/ *v.* [~ + *obj*] to vote against (an applicant, etc.): *blackballed him when he applied to the country club.* **—black′ball′er,** *n.* [*count*]

black′ belt′, *n.* [*count*] **1.** a black cloth waistband awarded to a participant in judo, etc., to indicate the highest level: *got his black belt after years of training.* **2.** a person at this level: *Three black belts were on his bodyguard staff.*

black•ber•ry (blak′ber′ē, -bə rē) /'blæk,bɛriy, -bəriy/ *n.* [*count*], *pl.* **-ries. 1.** the black or dark purple fruit of certain plants of the rose family. **2.** a plant bearing blackberries.

black•bird (blak′bûrd′) /'blæk,bɜrd/ *n.* [*count*] **1.** a bird having shiny black or mostly black coloring, as the red-winged blackbird. **2.** a common European thrush, the male of which is black with a yellow bill.

black•board (blak′bôrd′, -bōrd′) /'blæk,bɔrd, -,bowrd/ *n.* [*count*] a sheet of smooth material, esp. dark slate, used for writing with chalk: *The students went up to the blackboard and wrote their examination sentences.* See illustration at SCHOOL.

black•en (blak′ən) /'blækən/ *v.* **1.** to (cause to) grow or become black: [~ + *obj*]: *The commandos blackened their faces.* [*no obj*]: *The sky blackened.* **2.** [~ + *obj*] to speak evil of; defame; slander: *They blackened their opponent's good name.*

Black′ (or **black′**) **Eng′lish,** *n.* [*proper noun*] a dialect of American English spoken by some members of black communities in North America: *His students pointed out that there were many varieties of Black English even in small areas of New York.*

black′ eye′, *n.* [*count*] a blackening of the skin around the eye, resulting from a blow, etc.: *had a black eye and a swollen lip.*

black′-eyed pea′ (blak′īd′) /'blæk,ayd/ *n.* a plant of the legume family, extensively cultivated in the southern U.S.

black•guard (blag′ärd, -ərd) /'blægɑrd, -ərd/ *n.* [*count*] a scoundrel; a wicked or dishonorable person.

black•head (blak′hed′) /'blæk,hɛd/ *n.* [*count*] a small, black-tipped spot on the skin, esp. on the face.

black′ hole′, *n.* [*count*] a large object in an area of space that has gravity so strong that no light or other radiation can escape from it: *Black holes may have been formed at the beginning of the universe.*

black•jack (blak′jak′) /'blæk,dʒæk/ *n.* **1.** [*count*] a short, leather-covered club, made of a heavy head on a flexible handle and used as a weapon. **2.** [*noncount*] **a.** Also called **twenty-one.** a gambling game of cards, in which a player needs to get more points than the dealer to win, but not more than 21: *They played blackjack at the casino.* **b.** an ace together with a ten or a face card drawn as the first two cards dealt in a hand of this game: *got blackjack three times in a row!*

black•list (blak′list′) /'blæk,lɪst/ *n.* [*count*] **1.** a list of persons who are under suspicion, disfavor, or censure: *on the organization's blacklist for years after his one mistake in the company.* **—***v.* [~ + *obj*] **2.** to put on a blacklist: *For years he was blacklisted from working in Hollywood.*

black′ mag′ic, *n.* [*noncount*] magic used for evil purposes; sorcery.

black•mail (blak′māl′) /'blæk,meyl/ *n.* [*noncount*] **1.** an act of frightening someone into making a payment of money, as by revealing secrets: *accused of blackmail based on the threatening letters he wrote.* **2.** the payment made: *The blackmail was $25,000.* **3.** any similar act of threatening someone into doing something undesirable: *The spoiled brat used emotional blackmail on his parents.* **—***v.* [~ + *obj*] **4.** to force (someone) into paying blackmail: *For years his partner blackmailed him with those pictures he had taken.* —**black′mail′er,** *n.* [*count*]

black′ mark′, *n.* [*count*] an indication of failure or a record of having done something wrong.

black′ mar′ket, *n.* [*noncount*] **1.** the illegal buying and selling of goods or changing of currency: *the black market for American blue jeans in Russia.* **2.** a place where such activity is carried on: *You could get all kinds of liquor in the black market.* —**black′ marketeer′, black′ mar′keter,** *n.* [*count*]: *The black marketeers had a thriving business.*

Black′ Mus′lim, *n.* [*count*] a member of the Nation of Islam, an African-American sect of the Islamic religion.

black•ness (blak′nis) /'blæknɪs/ *n.* [*noncount*] **1.** the quality or state of being black. **2.** the quality or state of being a black person.

black•out (blak′out′) /'blæk,awt/ *n.* [*count*] **1.** the turning off or covering over of all visible lights, usually as a precaution against air raids. **2.** a period of failure of all electrical power: *A blackout is sometimes caused by an unusually heavy demand for electricity.* **3.** a temporary loss of consciousness: *After he fell he suffered a temporary blackout.* **4.** complete stoppage of a television or radio broadcast, as by an electrical storm.

black′ sheep′, *n.* [*count*], *pl.* **black sheep.** one who causes embarrassment to his or her group or family because of bad behavior.

black•smith (blak′smith′) /'blæk,smɪθ/ *n.* [*count*] one who makes objects from iron, esp. horseshoes.

black′ tie′, *n.* **1.** [*count*] a black bow tie, worn with semiformal evening dress. **2.** [*noncount*] semiformal evening dress for men (distinguished from *white tie*): *Most of the male guests were in black tie.* —**black′-tie′,** *adj.*: *a black-tie reception.*

black•top (blak′top′) /'blæk,tɒp/ *n., v.,* **-topped, -top•ping. —***n.* **1.** [*noncount*] a paving substance, such as asphalt, having bitumen in it: *They've been spreading blacktop on the potholes.* **2.** [*count*] a road covered with blacktop: *When you turn off the blacktop, you'll be on a dirt road.* **—***v.* [~ + *obj*] **3.** to pave with blacktop: *They've just finished blacktopping the driveway.*

black′ wid′ow, *n.* [*count*] a poisonous black spider of warm regions.

blad•der (blad′ər) /'blædər/ *n.* [*count*] **1.** a hollow organ in the body that is shaped like a bag and may hold gases or liquids, esp. urine. **2.** something resembling a bladder, such as the inside lining of a football inflated with air.

blade (blād) /bleyd/ *n.* [*count*] **1.** the flat cutting part of an implement, as a knife: *The blade on this knife is dull.* **2.** SWORD. **3.** a similar part, as of a mechanism, used for clearing, etc: *windshield wiper blades.* **4.** the leaf of a plant, esp. of a grass: *a few blades of grass; The blades of this leaf have three sharp points.* **5.** the metal part of an ice skate that comes into contact with the ice; runner: *the edge of her blade.* **6.** a thin, flat part of something: *the blade of an oar.* **7.** a dashing, swaggering, or jaunty young man: *a gay blade.*

-bladed, *combining form.* The combining form *-bladed* is used after words to mean "having a blade or blades": *a single-bladed leaf (= a leaf having a single blade).*

blah (blä) /blɑ/ *Slang.* **—***n.* **1.** [*noncount*] meaningless, unimportant talk; nonsense: *He just kept talking and saying nothing, just blah, blah.* **2. the blahs,** [*plural*] a feeling of fatigue, discomfort, or mild depression: *Cloudy weather often gives me the blahs.*

blame (blām) /bleym/ *v.,* **blamed, blam•ing,** *n.* **—***v.* [~ + *obj*] **1.** to hold (someone) responsible: *Don't blame me for the delay.* **2.** to find fault with; criticize: [*used with a negative word or phrase, or in questions*]: *I don't blame you for leaving.* **3.** [~ + *obj* + *on* + *obj*] to place the responsibility for (a fault, etc.) on: *always blames his mistakes on me.* **—***n.* [*noncount*] **4.** an act of finding fault; disapproval; criticism: *I received most of the blame for the collapse.* **5.** responsibility for anything deserving of criticism: *took the blame for our error.* **—*Idiom.* 6. to blame,** responsible; at fault: *The explosion was accidental; no one was to blame.* —**blame′less,** *adj.*: *a blameless life.* —**blame′less•ly,** *adv.* —**blame′less•ness,** *n.* [*noncount*] —**blam′er,** *n.* [*count*]

blame•wor•thy (blām′wûr′thē) /'bleym,wɜrðiy/ *adj.* deserving blame; at fault. —**blame′wor′thi•ness,** *n.* [*noncount*]

blanch (blanch) /blæntʃ/ *v.* **1.** [~ + *obj*] to boil (food) briefly, as to prepare for freezing: *Blanch the vegetables in boiling water for no more than fifteen seconds.* **2.** to make or turn pale, as with sickness or fear: [~ + *obj*]: *A long illness had blanched her cheeks of their natural color.* [*no obj*]: *He blanched at the news.*

bland (bland) /blænd/ *adj.,* **-er, -est. 1.** pleasantly gentle or agreeable: *a bland, affable manner.* **2.** not highly flavored or spicy; nonirritating: *That sauce is too bland.* **3.** lacking in special interest or liveliness; dull: *bland elevator music.* —**bland′ly,** *adv.* —**bland′ness,** *n.* [*noncount*]: *the blandness of English food.*

blan•dish•ment (blan′dish mənt) /'blændɪʃmənt/ *n.* [*count*] Often, **blandishments.** [*plural*] something, as an action, that tends to flatter or coax: *the offer of a new office and other blandishments.*

blank (blangk) /blæŋk/ *adj.,* **-er, -est,** *n., v.* **—***adj.* **1.** having no marks: *blank paper.* **2.** not filled in: *a blank check.* **3.** with no ornaments or openings: *a blank wall.* **4.** containing no recorded sound or images: *a blank videotape.* **5.** expressionless: *a blank look on her face.* **6.** confused, puzzled, or without understanding: *He looked blank when I asked for his ticket.* **7.** without thoughts or ideas: *My mind went blank.* **8.** complete; utter: *blank stupidity.* **—***n.* [*count*] **9.** a place where something is lacking; an empty space: *Her mind is a blank whenever it comes to that episode.* **10.** a space in a printed form, etc., to be filled in: *Fill in the blanks with your answers.* **11.** a printed form containing such spaces: *Take the blank to that table, fill it in, and bring it back to me.* **12.** a dash put in place of an omitted letter or letters, esp. to avoid writing a word considered profane or obscene. **13.** a cartridge for a gun that has explosive powder inside but no bullet: *fired blanks into the air.* **—*v.*** [~ + *obj*] **14.** to keep (an opponent) from scoring in a game: *managed to blank the Giants for six innings.* **—*Idiom.*** **15. draw a blank, a.** to be unsuccessful: *The detective drew a blank in the investigation.* **b.** to fail to remember: *I drew a blank when she asked me for their phone number.* **—blank′ly,** *adv.*: *She stared blankly at me when I asked her for directions.* **—blank′ness,** *n.* [*noncount*]

blank′ check′, *n.* **1.** [*count*] a bank check with a signature but without the amount written in: *She signed a blank check and told me to fill in the amount.* **2.** [*count; usually: a* + ~] permission or authority to do something without restrictions: *gave him a blank check to reorganize the department.*

blan•ket (blang′kit) /ˈblæŋkɪt/ *n.* [*count*] **1.** a large rectangular piece of soft fabric, used as a bed covering: *just groaned and pulled the blanket over her head.* **2.** any covering or layer that extends over something: *a blanket of snow.* **—*v.*** [~ + *obj* (+ *with* + *obj*)] **3.** to cover with or as if with a blanket: *blanketed the neighborhood with pictures of our candidate.* **—*adj.*** [*before a noun*] **4.** covering or intended to cover a large class of things: *a blanket proposal covering every aspect of trade negotiations.*

blank′ verse′, *n.* [*noncount*] poetry lacking rhyme, esp. verses having five stressed syllables: *blank verse of Shakespeare's plays.*

blare (blâr) /blɛər/ *v.*, **blared, blar•ing,** *n.* **—*v.*** **1.** to emit a loud, unpleasant sound: [*no obj*]: *No one could sleep with his radio blaring all night.* [~ + *obj*]: *Her radio was blaring rock music.* **—*n.*** [*count; singular*] **2.** a loud, unpleasant noise; clamor: *the blare of the trombones right in front of the microphone.*

blar•ney (blär′nē) /ˈblɑrniy/ *n.* [*noncount*] **1.** flattery: *feeding her blarney to convince her he likes her.* **2.** misleading lies or nonsense: *a lot of blarney about why he was late.*

bla•sé (blä zā′, blä′zā) /blɑˈzey, ˈblɑzey/ *adj.* indifferent to or bored with life: *a blasé teenager.*

blas•pheme (blas fēm′, blas′fēm) /blæsˈfiym, ˈblæsfiym/ *v.*, **-phemed, -phem•ing.** to speak blasphemy: [*no obj*]: *accused him of blaspheming.* [~ + *obj*]: *blaspheming the name of God.* **—blas•phem•er** (blas fē′mər, blas′fē-, -fə-) /blæsˈfiymər, ˈblæsfiy-, -fə-/ *n.* [*count*]

blas•phe•mous (blas′fə məs) /ˈblæsfəməs/ *adj.* saying or committing blasphemy: *blasphemous preachings.* **—blas′phe•mous•ly,** *adv.* **—blas′phe•mous•ness,** *n.* [*noncount*]

blas•phe•my (blas′fə mē) /ˈblæsfəmiy/ *n., pl.* **-mies.** (an act of) speaking or acting irreverently or disrespectfully concerning God or sacred things: [*noncount*]: *shouted that what she had just said was blasphemy.* [*count*]: *to be punished for many blasphemies.*

blast (blast) /blæst/ *n.* [*count*] **1.** a sudden and violent gust of wind: *a chill blast from the north.* **2.** the blowing of a trumpet, whistle, etc.: *several blasts of the trumpet.* **3.** a loud, sudden sound or noise: *a harsh blast from the radio.* **4.** a forceful throw, hit, etc.: *hit a blast down third base.* **5.** the act of exploding; explosion: *a nuclear blast.* **6.** [*usually: a* + ~] *Slang.* something that gives great pleasure, esp. a wild party: *had a blast at their parties.* **7.** a vigorous outburst of criticism; attack: *a blast of negative media attention.* **—*v.*** **8.** to produce a loud, blaring noise by or as if by blowing: [~ + *obj*]: *to blast a horn.* [*no obj*]: *The drivers were blasting on their horns.* **9.** [~ + *obj*] to shatter by or as if by an explosion; ruin or destroy: *blasted the enemy communications center.* **10.** to make, form, or open up by using explosions, etc.: [~ + *obj*]: *to blast a tunnel.* [*no obj*]: *They were instructed not to blast in that area.* **11.** [~ + *obj*] to criticize vigorously; denounce: *The judge blasted his critics.* **12.** [~ + *obj*] to hit or propel with great force: *blasted that serve right past his opponent.* **13. blast off,** [*no obj*] (of a rocket) to leave a launch pad: *The missile blasted off.* **—*interj.*** **14.** (used as a mild curse or swear expression): *Blast it, why does the phone ring whenever I'm in the shower?* **—*Idiom.*** **15. (at) full blast,** at maximum capacity or ability: *The radio was on at full blast.*

blast′ fur′nace, *n.* [*count*] a large vertical furnace for melting iron ore.

blast•off (blast′ôf′, -of′) /ˈblæstˌɔf, -ˌɒf/ *n.* [*count*] the launching of a rocket, guided missile, or spacecraft.

bla•tant (blāt′nt) /ˈbleytnt/ *adj.* very obvious and noticeable in a bad way: *a blatant error; a blatant crime.* **—bla′tant•ly,** *adv.*

blath•er (blath′ər) /ˈblæðər/ *n.* [*noncount*] **1.** foolish, excess talk: *His boasts were just a lot of blather.* **—*v.*** [*no obj*] **2.** to talk foolishly: *an idiot who blathers on.* **—blath′er•er,** *n.* [*count*]

blaze[1] (blāz) /bleyz/ *n., v.*, **blazed, blaz•ing.** **—*n.*** [*count*] **1.** a bright flame or fire: *A small blaze started in the kitchen.* **2.** a very bright glow of color or light: *a blaze of jewels.* **3.** [*usually singular: a* + ~] a sudden, intense outburst, as of passion or excitement: *a blaze of anger.* **—*v.*** [*no obj*] **4.** to burn brightly: *The bonfire blazed for hours.* **5.** to shine brightly, like a flame: *The car headlights blazed ahead.* **6.** to flare suddenly (as with intense emotion): *Her eyes blazed when she saw us cheating.* **7. blaze away,** [*no obj*] to shoot steadily: *blazed away with their machine guns.*

blaze[2] (blāz) /bleyz/ *n., v.*, **blazed, blaz•ing.** **—*n.*** [*count*] **1.** a mark made on a tree, as with paint, to indicate a trail or boundary. **2.** a white area down the center of the face of a horse, cow, etc. **—*v.*** [~ + *obj*] **3.** to indicate or mark with blazes: *to blaze a trail.* **4.** to lead the way in forming or finding: *blazed the way for space travel.*

blaz•er (blā′zər) /ˈbleyzər/ *n.* [*count*] **1.** something that blazes or shines brightly. **2.** a sports jacket with metal buttons: *wearing our gray school blazers.*

blaz•ing (blā′zing) /ˈbleyzɪŋ/ *adj.* of tremendous intensity, heat, color, or force: *blazing temperatures.*

bla•zon (blā′zən) /ˈbleyzən/ *v.* [~ + *obj*] to set forth publicly and very obviously; proclaim: *The actor's name was blazoned across the tabloids.*

bldg., an abbreviation of: building.

bleach (blēch) /bliytʃ/ *v.* **1.** to make whiter or lighter in color, as by a chemical agent: [~ + *obj*]: *Don't bleach this red sweater when you do the laundry.* [*no obj*]: *A few old bones had bleached in the sun.* **—*n.*** [*noncount*] **2.** a chemical, usually liquid substance that makes (clothes) whiter in color: *Add bleach during the wash cycle.* **—bleach′a•ble,** *adj.*

bleach•er (blē′chər) /ˈbliytʃər/ *n.* [*count*] **1.** Usually, **bleachers.** a section of low-priced seating at a stadium, made of boards and not covered by a roof: *That ball was hit into the bleachers.* **—*adj.*** [*before a noun*] **2.** of or relating to this section at a stadium: *bleacher seats.*

bleak (blēk) /bliyk/ *adj.*, **-er, -est.** **1.** bare, cold, and uninviting: *the bleak winter landscape.* **2.** without hope or encouragement; dreary: *looking at a bleak future.* **—bleak′ly,** *adv.*: *stared bleakly out the window.* **—bleak′ness,** *n.* [*noncount*]: *the bleakness of a long, cold winter.*

blear•y (blēr′ē) /ˈblɪəriy/ *adj.*, **-i•er, -i•est.** **1.** (of the eyes) blurred or dimmed, as from tiredness: *His eyes were bleary after staying up all night studying.* **2.** indistinct; unclear: *a bleary view of the morning until after his coffee.* **—blear•i•ly** (blēr′ə lē) /ˈblɪərəliy/ *adv.*: *looked over at me blearily.* **—blear′i•ness,** *n.* [*noncount*]

blear•y-eyed (blēr′ē īd′) /ˈblɪərˌiy ayd/ also **blear-eyed** (blēr′īd′) /ˈblɪərˌayd/ *adj.* having inflamed or teary eyes: *bleary-eyed from studying.*

bleat (blēt) /bliyt/ *v.* **1.** to utter the cry of a sheep or goat: [*no obj*]: *The sheep were bleating in the field.* [~ + *obj*]: *The goats bleated a warning.* **2.** to talk in a whining, complaining tone: [*no obj*]: *always bleating about her problems.* [~ + (*that*) *clause*]: *bleated that he had always worked hard.* **—*n.*** [*count*] **3.** the cry of a sheep or goat. **4.** any similar sound: *the bleat of distant horns.* **5.** foolish or complaining talk; babble. **—bleat′er,** *n.* [*count*] **—bleat′ing•ly,** *adv.*

bleed (blēd) /bliyd/ *v.*, **bled** (bled), **bleed•ing.** **1.** to lose or discharge blood: [*no obj*]: *almost bled to death.* [~ + *obj*]: *He bled at least five pints of blood.* **2.** [~ + *obj*] to take or draw blood from: *In the old days, people were bled to cure them of disease.* **3.** to drain or draw sap, water, etc., from: [~ (+ *off*) + *obj*]: *We bled (off) the car radiator by opening a valve.* [~ + *obj* (+ *off*)]: *We bled the car radiator (off).* **4.** [*no obj*] to run together, as colors or dyes: *The colors bled when the dress was washed in hot water.* **5.** [~ + *obj*] to remove trapped air from, as by opening a valve: *to bleed the brakes.* **6.** [*no obj*] to feel pity or anguish: *My heart bleeds for you.* **7.** [~ + *obj*] to take too much money from (as if by blackmail): *Those car repair dealers were bleeding us with* *their high prices.* —***Idiom.*** **8. bleed dry,** [~ + *obj* + *dry*] to use up or take away all money, resources, etc., as through excessive demands: *bled us dry with all her demands.*

bleed•er (blē′dər) /ˈbliydər/ *n.* [*count*] **1.** a person whose bleeding does not stop normally, such as a hemophiliac. **2.** *Brit. Slang.* chap; fellow.

bleed•ing (blē′ding) /ˈbliydɪŋ/ *n.* [*noncount*] **1.** the act or process of losing blood: *Has the bleeding stopped from his cut yet?* **2.** the act or process of drawing blood from a person, esp. surgically. —*adj., adv.* **3.** *Brit. Slang.* (used before nouns or adjectives to show an attitude of strong emotion or feeling about the noun or adjective) great; very; extremely: [*before a noun*]: *a bleeding fool (= a very great fool).* [*before an adjective*]: *a bleeding silly idea (= a very silly idea).*

bleed′ing heart′, *n.* [*count*] a person who makes a great show of pity or concern for others: *advised not to listen to the bleeding hearts.*

bleep (blēp) /bliyp/ *n.* [*count*] **1.** a brief beeping sound made by an electronic device: *The answering machine emitted a bleep.* **2.** such a sound used to replace objectionable material, as in a broadcast. **3.** (used to replace an obscene or objectionable word): *"What the bleep do you think you're doing?" he shouted.* —*v.* **4.** (of an electronic device) to give off or emit a series of bleeps as a signal (to): [*no obj*]: *The answering machine bleeped and I left my message.* [~ + *obj*]: *We bleeped the doctor on her electronic pager.* **5.** [~ + *obj*] to delete or block (sound) from a recording or broadcast to prevent an objectionable word from being broadcast: *They bleeped the comedian's obscene lines.* —**bleep′er,** *n.* [*count*]

bleep•ing (blē′ping) /ˈbliypɪŋ/ *adj.* [*before a noun*] (used to replace an obscene word): *Get that bleeping cat out of here!*

blem•ish (blem′ish) /ˈblɛmɪʃ/ *v.* [~ + *obj*] **1.** to destroy the perfection of; mar; sully: *His reputation was blemished by scandal in his second term.* —*n.* [*count*] **2.** a mark that spoils the appearance, such as a pimple or scar: *a blemish on her nose.* **3.** a defect or flaw; stain: *the one blemish on his otherwise perfect academic record.*

blench (blench) /blɛntʃ/ *v.* [*no obj*] to make a sudden movement away from something because of fear; shrink; flinch; quail.

blend (blend) /blɛnd/ *v.* **1.** to mix smoothly together: [~ + *obj* + *and* + *obj*]: *Blend the flour and eggs together.* [~ + *obj* + *with* + *obj*]: *Blend the eggs with the flour.* [*no obj*]: *Oil and water do not blend.* **2.** [~ + *obj*] to prepare by mixing various types or varieties: *I blend this tea by mixing chamomile with pekoe.* **3.** to fit or combine in a pleasing way: [*no obj*]: *Their voices blend beautifully.* [~ + *with* + *obj*]: *The houses were designed to blend with the foliage.* [~ + *in*]: *She blends right in with her new department.* **4.** to have no visible separation into parts: [*no obj*]: *The blue sea and the blue sky seemed to blend.* [~ + *into* + *obj*]: *The turtle's shell blended into the mud, making it almost invisible.* —*n.* [*count*] **5.** a mixture produced by blending: *a blend of coffee.* **6.** a word made or formed by putting together parts of other words, as *motel,* made from *motor* and *hotel,* or *guesstimate,* from *guess* and *estimate.*

blend•er (blen′dər) /ˈblɛndər/ *n.* [*count*] **1.** a person or thing that blends. **2.** an electric machine used to chop, liquefy, or mix foods: *She dumped a banana and orange juice into the blender and in a few moments we had a delicious drink.* See illustration at APPLIANCE.

bless (bles) /blɛs/ *v.* [~ + *obj*], **blessed** or **blest** (blest) /blɛst/ **bless•ing. 1.** to make (something) holy or sacred by a religious rite: *The priest blessed the offering.* **2.** to ask for God's divine favor upon or for: *Bless this house.* **3.** [~ + *obj* + *with* + *obj*] to give some benefit to; endow: *Nature blessed me with strong teeth.* **4.** to praise as holy; glorify: *Bless the Lord.* **5. Bless you! a.** (used to convey thanks, affection, or best wishes to someone): *"Bless you," she said when I dropped a few coins in her basket.* **b.** (used to express polite concern after someone has sneezed): *"Ahchoo!" she sneezed. "Bless you," he responded.*

bless•ed (bles′id; *esp. for 2* blest) /ˈblɛsɪd; *esp. for 2* blɛst/ *adj.* **1.** sacred; holy; worthy of worship: *the Blessed Virgin.* **2.** favored (as by God); fortunate: *blessed with common sense.* **3.** wonderful; glorious: *the blessed assurance of a steady income.* **4.** (used before a noun to show strong emotion): *He took every blessed cent we had (= We are upset that he took all our money).* —**bless′ed•ly,** *adv.* —**bless′ed•ness,** *n.* [*noncount*]

bless•ing (bles′ing) /ˈblɛsɪŋ/ *n.* [*count*] **1.** the act or words of a person who blesses: *The priest gave his blessing to the soldiers.* **2.** a favor or gift (as bestowed by God), thereby bringing happiness: *the blessings of liberty.* **3.** praise, esp. grace said before or after a meal: *Who will say a blessing?* **4.** [*usually: the/one's* + ~] approval or good wishes: *The law has the governor's blessing.* —***Idiom.*** **5. a blessing in disguise,** something that seems bad at first but later turns out well: *Being turned down for that job was a blessing in disguise, because in just a year the company went bankrupt and I would have been fired first.* **6. count one's blessings,** to be thankful for something: *You should count your blessings that you have your health.*

blest (blest) /blɛst/ *v.* **1.** a pt. and pp. of BLESS. —*adj.* **2.** BLESSED.

blew (blo͞o) /bluw/ *v.* **1.** the pt. of BLOW[2]. **2.** the pt. of BLOW[3].

blight (blīt) /blayt/ *n.* **1.** [*noncount*] a disease of plants, in which there is loss of color and wilting: *All my houseplants suffered from blight.* **2.** the state or result of ruin, difficulty, or damage: [*noncount*]: *Crime and corruption are the beginnings of urban blight.* [*count*]: *pollution and war as blights on the planet.* —*v.* [~ + *obj*] **3.** to cause to wither: *The disease blighted all the elms and oaks.* **4.** to destroy; ruin; frustrate: *Illness blighted her hopes.*

bli•mey or **bli•my** (blī′mē) /ˈblaymiy/ *interj. Brit. Informal.* (used to express surprise or excitement): *"Blimey!" she exclaimed, "Was all the money taken?"*

blimp (blimp) /blɪmp/ *n.* [*count*] a nonrigid airship or dirigible, with a motor enabling forward motion: *The blimp circled the stadium slowly.*

blind (blīnd) /blaynd/ *adj.,* **-er, -est,** *v., n., adv.* —*adj.* **1.** unable to see; lacking sight: *blind from birth.* **2.** [*be* + ~ + *to*] unwilling or unable to take note of or understand: *blind to the faults of their children.* **3.** [*before a noun*] not characterized or determined by or based on reason or control: *blind, random chance.* **4.** hidden from view, esp. from oncoming motorists: *There were numerous accidents at that blind corner.* **5.** performed without necessary knowledge beforehand: *a blind purchase.* **6.** of or relating to a method of designing and conducting experiments that prevents investigators or the people being tested from knowing the theories or conditions being tested: *blind experiments.* —*v.* [~ + *obj*] **7.** to make sightless, as by injuring, dazzling, or bandaging the eyes: *The sudden bright lights in his eyes blinded him.* **8.** to keep (someone) from reasoning, judging, or deciding in one's normal way: *blinded by the promises the salesman made.* [~ + *obj* + *to* + *obj*]: *Her charm blinded me to her faults.* —*n.* [*count*] **9.** Also, **blinds.** a covering for a window made of thin, long slats of wood, etc., attached to a string so as to enable raising or lowering it, thereby adjusting the amount of light coming in; venetian blind. **10.** cloth or other material on a roller pulled down to cover a window; window shade. **11.** an action or organization for concealing a true purpose; deception: *just a blind to throw us off the track.* **12. the blind,** [*plural; used with a plural verb*] people lacking the sense of sight: *built special facilities for the blind.* —*adv.* **13.** to the point of losing consciousness: *to drink oneself blind.* **14.** without the ability to see clearly; blindly: *to drive blind through a storm.* **15.** without guidance, relevant information, etc.: *to work blind.* **16.** to an extreme degree; completely: *to cheat someone blind.* **17.** not using eyesight but relying instead only on instruments for navigation: *They had to fly blind and land in the driving snow.* —**blind′ly,** *adv.: walked blindly right into the trap.* —**blind′ness,** *n.* [*noncount*]

blind′ al′ley, *n.* [*count*] **1.** a roadway open at only one end. **2.** a situation offering no help, opportunity, or reward: *Searching in our old files is a blind alley.*

blind′ date′, *n.* [*count*] **1.** a social meeting arranged by a third person between two people who have not met before: *met her on a blind date.* **2.** either of the two people in such an arrangement: *I was her blind date for the evening.*

blind•er (blīn′dər) /ˈblayndər/ *n.* [*count*] **1.** one of a pair of leather flaps attached to a horse's bridle to prevent it from seeing sideways; a blinker. **2.** Usually, **blinders.** [*plural*] something that gets in the way of seeing or understanding something: *She has blinders on when it comes to grasping why people get angry at her.*

blind•fold (blīnd′fōld′) /ˈblaynd,fowld/ *v.* [~ + *obj*] **1.** to prevent (a person's) sight by covering the eyes with a cloth: *blindfolded the hostage.* —*n.* [*count*] **2.** a cloth or bandage for covering the eyes: *The blindfold slipped a* *little.* **—***adj.* **3.** done with or as if with the eyes covered: *a blindfold test.*

blind•ing (blīn′ding) /ˈblaɪndɪŋ/ *adj.* **1.** bright enough to dazzle: *a blinding light.* **2.** very clear to see: *saw at once the blinding truth of her accusations.* —**blind′ing•ly,** *adv.: It was blindingly clear what her true intentions were.*

blind′ spot′, *n.* [*count*] **1.** a small area of the inside of the eye, where it continues to the optic nerve, that is not sensitive to light. **2.** [*usually singular; the/one's* + ~] an area behind a driver's field of vision not reflected in the rearview mirror: *I didn't see the car behind; he was in my blind spot.* **3.** a subject one does not know much about or is not appreciative of: *a blind spot when it came to chemistry.*

blin•i (blin′ē, blē′nē) /ˈblɪniy, ˈbliyniy/ *n.* [*count*], *pl.* **blin•i, blin•is.** a small pancake, usually made with buckwheat flour and often served with caviar and sour cream.

blink (blingk) /blɪŋk/ *v.* **1.** to open and close (the eye): [*no obj*]: *He blinked when I opened the curtains.* [~ + *obj*]: *She blinked her eyes rapidly.* **2.** to shine (something) unsteadily or rapidly on or off: [*no obj*]: *The lights blinked in the darkness.* [~ + *obj*]: *He blinked his lights as a warning to other motorists.* **—***n.* [*count*] **3.** an act of blinking: *a quick blink of the eyes.* **—*Idiom.*** **4. a** or **the blink of the eye,** a very short period of time: *In a blink of the eye the mouse had disappeared through a hole in the wall.* **5. on the blink,** [*be* + ~] not working properly; in need of repair: *Oh no, the computer is on the blink again.*

blink•er (bling′kər) /ˈblɪŋkər/ *n.* [*count*] **1.** a device for flashing light signals: *He put on his blinkers and coasted to the side of the road.* **2.** a flashing light, as for regulating traffic.

blink•ered (bling′kərd) /ˈblɪŋkərd/ *adj.* narrow-minded; not considering other people's opinions: *They had a blinkered view of the world from their small island.*

blintze (blints, blint′sə) /blɪnts, ˈblɪntsə/ also **blintz** (blints) /blɪnts/ *n.* [*count*] a thin pancake folded around a filling of cheese or fruit and fried or baked.

blip (blip) /blɪp/ *n., v.,* **blipped, blip•ping.** **—***n.* [*count*] **1.** a spot of light on a display screen, esp. one on a radar screen indicating the position of an aircraft: *The radar operators lost the blip they were tracking.* **2.** a brief interruption in a sound recording or video film: *kept hearing little blips as our voices and pictures were distorted.*

bliss (blis) /blɪs/ *n.* [*noncount*] great or perfect happiness: *a feeling of bliss whenever he was with her.*

bliss•ful (blis′fəl) /ˈblɪsfəl/ *adj.* full of, enjoying, or producing bliss: *I fell into a blissful sleep.* —**bliss′ful•ly,** *adv.: The young child was blissfully unaware of the danger.* —**bliss′ful•ness,** *n.* [*noncount*]

blis•ter (blis′tər) /ˈblɪstər/ *n.* [*count*] **1.** a thin swelling on the skin containing watery matter, as from a burn or friction: *had a blister on my heel.* **2.** any similar swelling, as an air bubble in a coat of paint: *This brush will prevent paint blisters from forming.* **—***v.* **3.** to (cause to) become swollen; to (cause to) get a blister on: [~ + *obj*]: *The shoes blistered my toes.* [*no obj*]: *The paint blistered in the sun.* **4.** [~ + *obj*] to subject to intense heat: *The tropical heat blistered the coast.* **5.** [~ + *obj*] to criticize or rebuke severely: *He blistered his aides.*

blis•ter•ing (blis′tər ing) /ˈblɪstərɪŋ/ *adj.* **1.** causing blisters. **2.** (of sunlight, heat, etc.) very severe or intense: *the blistering heat of the tropical island.* **3.** very fast or rapid: *The runner kept up a blistering pace.* **4.** reflecting great anger or hostility: *The candidate released a blistering attack.* —**blis′ter•ing•ly,** *adv.: a blisteringly fast pace.*

blithe (blīth, blīth) /blayð, blayθ/ *adj.* **blith•er, blith•est.** **1.** carefree; heedless: *a blithe disregard for her feelings.* **2.** lighthearted in disposition; cheerful. —**blithe′ly,** *adv.: I blithely assumed everything was fine.*

blith•er•ing (blith′ər ing) /ˈblɪðər ɪŋ/ *adj.* [*before a noun*] full of foolish talk; stupid: *a blithering idiot.*

blitz (blits) /blɪts/ *n.* [*count*] **1.** a sudden, swift, and overwhelming military attack. **2.** any swift, vigorous attack or defeat. **—***v.* [~ + *obj*] **3.** to attack, defeat, or destroy with or as if with a blitz: *blitzed all our proposals.*

blitz•krieg (blits′krēg′) /ˈblɪtsˌkriyg/ *n.* BLITZ (def. 1).

bliz•zard (bliz′ərd) /ˈblɪzərd/ *n.* [*count*] **1.** a storm with dry, driving snow, strong winds, and intense cold. **2.** an extremely large amount of something all at one time; avalanche: *received a blizzard of hate mail.*

blk., an abbreviation of: **1.** black. **2.** block.

bloat•ed (blō′tid) /ˈblowtɪd/ *adj.* **1.** puffed up; swollen: *a bloated corpse.* **2.** too full, as from eating too much: *bloated after that dinner.*

blob (blob) /blɒb/ *n.* [*count*] **1.** a lump of a thick, liquid substance: *a blob of glue.* **2.** an object having no distinct shape or definition: *Can you see that blob in the snow?*

bloc (blok) /blɒk/ *n.* [*count*] **1.** a group of people, etc., united for a particular purpose: *the farm bloc composed of members of Congress from the Plains states.* **2.** a group of nations that share common interests and usually act together.

block (blok) /blɒk/ *n.* [*count*] **1.** a large, solid piece of wood, stone, etc.: *A concrete cinder block supported the car.* **2.** one of a set of cube-shaped pieces used as a child's toy: *playing happily with their blocks.* **3.** a piece of wood or metal with designs that have been engraved on it, used for printing. **4.** anything that stops or prevents movement: *The sink has a block in it.* **5.** a stoppage in thinking, speech, or writing: *writer's block.* **6.** *Sports.* a hindering of an opponent or an opponent's play: *his block on the tackler allowed me to score.* **7.** an amount, quantity, or portion taken as a unit: *a block of theater tickets.* **8.** a small section of a city, town, etc., surrounded by streets: *They lived on my block when I was growing up.* **9.** *Slang.* a person's head: *threatened to knock his block off.* **—***v.* **10.** [~ + *obj*] to get in the way of; hinder: *to block one's exit.* **11. block up,** to (cause to) have a block in: [*no obj*]: *The toilet blocked up all the time.* [~ + *up* + *obj*]: *Try to block up those holes in the wall.* [~ + *obj* + *up*]: *to block them up.* **12.** [~ + *obj*] mount on a block: *They blocked the car on the ramp.* **13.** [~ + *obj*] to shape or prepare on or as if on a block: *to block a sweater.* **14.** [~ + *obj*] (in word processing or computer use) to mark off (text or data) for moving, printing, etc.: *Hit the F12 key and block the text you want to delete.* **15.** *Sports.* to get in the way of or obstruct (an opposing player) by physical contact: [~ + *obj*]: *Bart blocked Dexter, allowing Gerry to run for the touchdown.* [*no obj*]: *Harry didn't block well on that last play.* **16.** [*no obj*] to suffer a stoppage in thinking, speaking, or writing: *I just seemed to block when it came to taking a test.* **17. block in** or **out,** to outline roughly without details: [~ + *in/out* + *obj*]: *blocked out our ideas for the room arrangement.* [~ + *obj* + *in/out*]: *to block them out.* **—*Idiom.*** **18. on the block,** for sale at an auction.

block•ade (blo kād′) /blɒˈkeyd/ *n., v.,* **-ad•ed, -ad•ing.** **—***n.* [*count*] **1.** the closing off of a port, city, etc., by an enemy to prevent anyone from coming in or going out. **—***v.* [~ + *obj*] **2.** to close off (a port, etc.): *They blockaded the port for weeks.* —**block•ad′er,** *n.* [*count*]

block•age (blok′ij) /ˈblɒkɪdʒ/ *n.* **1.** [*noncount*] an act of blocking, or the state of being blocked: *Hair in the shower drain results in blockage of the pipes.* **2.** [*count*] something that blocks or prevents things from going through: *a blockage in the pipes.*

block′ and tack′le, *n.* [*count*] the ropes or chains passed around blocks containing pulleys that are used to hoist heavy things.

block•bust•er (blok′bus′tər) /ˈblɒkˌbʌstər/ *n.* [*count*] a very popular, profitable motion picture, etc.

block•head (blok′hed′) /ˈblɒkˌhɛd/ *n.* [*count*] a stupid person; dunce. —**block′head′ed,** *adj.*

block•house (blok′hous′) /ˈblɒkˌhaws/ *n.* [*count*] **1.** a building or small fort of wood. **2.** a concrete structure to protect people who control rocket launchings.

bloke (blōk) /blowk/ *n.* [*count*] *Chiefly Brit.* man; fellow; guy.

blond (blond) /blɒnd/ *adj.,* **-er, -est,** *n.* **—***adj.* **1.** (of a person) having light-colored hair: *a blond young man.* **2.** light colored: *blond wood.* **—***n.* [*count*] **3.** a blond person: *A blond met us at the door.* —**blond′ish,** *adj.* —**blond′ness,** *n.* [*noncount*] **—Usage.** See BLONDE.

blonde (blond) /blɒnd/ *adj.* **1.** (of a woman or girl) having light-colored hair. **—***n.* [*count*] **2.** a woman or girl having this coloration. —**blonde′ness,** *n.* [*noncount*] **—Usage.** BLONDE is still widely used for the noun specifying a woman or girl with fair hair. Some people think this is insulting to women (or *sexist*), preferring BLOND for all persons. BLOND is the usual spelling for the adjective referring to either sex (*an energetic blond girl; two blond sons*) or describing hair, complexion, etc. BLONDE is still occasionally applied to a female (*the blonde model and her escort*) and in British English is the preferred spelling for all senses of the adjective.

blood (blud) /blʌd/ *n.* **1.** [*noncount*] the red fluid that flows through the heart throughout the body. **2.** [*noncount*] a similar fluid in other animals. **3.** [*noncount*] something regarded as a source of energy or new life: *The company needs new blood.* **4.** [*noncount*] bloodshed; slaughter: *the blood of the battlefield.* **5.** [*noncount*] temperament; passion; emotion: *a person of hot* blood. **6.** [*noncount*] relationship by family: *They are related by blood.* ***—Idiom.*** **7. bad blood,** deep, long-lasting hatred: *bad blood between the two families for decades.* **8. get** or **have one's blood up,** to become or be enraged, emotional, etc.: *Injustice of any sort always gets my blood up.* **9. in cold blood,** with complete lack of feeling or mercy: *shot the two young children in cold blood.* **10. make one's blood boil,** to cause feelings of resentment, anger, or indignation: *Such carelessness makes my blood boil.* **11. make one's blood run cold,** to fill with great fear or terror: *The dark, deserted street made her blood run cold.*

blood′ bank′, *n.* [*count*] a place where blood or blood plasma is collected and distributed.

blood•bath (blud′bath′) /ˈblʌd,bæθ/ *n.* [*count*] a cruel slaughter; massacre: *A bloodbath followed the overthrow of that dictator.*

blood′ count′, *n.* [*count*] the count of the number of red and white blood cells and platelets in a certain amount of blood: *A high blood count may indicate leukemia.*

blood•cur•dling (blud′kûrd′ling, -kûr′dl ing) /ˈblʌd,kɜrdlɪŋ, -,kɜrdlɪŋ/ *adj.* [*usually before a noun*] causing fear or terror: *a blood curdling scream.*

-blood•ed (blud′id) /ˈblʌdɪd/ *combining form.* The combining form *-blooded* is used after words to make adjectives that mean "having the blood of a (specified) kind": *warm-blooded animals (= animals that have warm blood, blood that does not change temperature).*

blood′ group′, *n.* [*count*] any of the classes or types into which human blood can be divided. Also called **blood type.**

blood•hound (blud′hound′) /ˈblʌd,hawnd/ *n.* [*count*] one of a breed of hound, often used in tracking people.

blood•less (blud′lis) /ˈblʌdlɪs/ *adj.* **1.** without blood: *a bloodless procedure in the doctor's office.* **2.** very pale: *a bloodless face.* **3.** accomplished without violence or killing: *a bloodless coup.* **4.** without spirit or vigor: *a cold, bloodless smile on his face.*

blood•let•ting (blud′let′ing) /ˈblʌd,lɛtɪŋ/ *n.* [*noncount*] **1.** the act of letting blood out by cutting open a vein: *Bloodletting was once performed by barbers.* **2.** BLOODSHED.

blood•mo•bile (blud′mə bēl′) /ˈblʌdmə,biyl/ *n.* [*count*] a truck with equipment for receiving blood donations.

blood′ mon′ey, *n.* [*noncount*] **1.** a fee paid to a hired murderer. **2.** payment made to the next of kin of a murdered person, paid by the murderer or his relatives. **3.** money obtained through the suffering of others.

blood′ poi′soning, *n.* [*noncount*] a condition caused by the invasion of the blood by posion or germs, in which the victim has chills and fever.

blood′ pres′sure, *n.* a measure of the pressure of the blood pushing against the inner walls of the blood vessels as the heart beats: [*noncount*]: *Eating salty foods raises one's blood pressure.* [*count; usually singular*]: *a blood pressure of 120 over 80.*

blood•shed (blud′shed′) /ˈblʌd,ʃɛd/ *n.* [*noncount*] killing, as in war or murder; slaughter: *The bloodshed during the Civil War was the worst this country has ever known.*

blood•shot (blud′shot′) /ˈblʌd,ʃɒt/ *adj.* (of the white part of the eyes) red because of widened blood vessels.

blood•stained (blud′stānd′) /ˈblʌd,steynd/ *adj.* **1.** stained with blood. **2.** guilty of murder or bloodshed: *a warlike people known for their bloodstained history.*

blood•stream (blud′strēm′) /ˈblʌd,striym/ *n.* [*count; singular; the* + ~] the blood flowing through the body's system of veins and arteries: *a drug coursing through the bloodstream.*

blood•suck•er (blud′suk′ər) /ˈblʌd,sʌkər/ *n.* [*count*] **1.** any animal that sucks blood, esp. a leech. **2.** a person who takes as much from others as possible. **—blood′suck′ing,** *adj.* [*usually before a noun*]: *that bloodsucking young nephew of mine.*

blood•thirst•y (blud′thûr′stē) /ˈblʌd,θɜrstiy/ *adj.* eager to shed blood: *a bloodthirsty criminal.* **—blood′thirst′i•ness,** *n.* [*noncount*]

blood′ type′, *n.* [*count*] BLOOD GROUP: *There are four blood types: A, B, AB, and O.*

blood′ ves′sel, *n.* [*count*] any tube of the body through which the blood flows.

blood•y (blud′ē) /ˈblʌdiy/ *adj.,* **-i•er, -i•est,** *v.,* **-ied, -y•ing,** *adv.* **—***adj.* **1.** stained or covered with or containing blood: *a bloody shirt.* **2.** bleeding: *a bloody nose.* **3.** characterized by or inclined to bloodshed: *bloody battles.* **4.** *Chiefly Brit. Slang.* (used before a noun or other word to convey intensity or strong feeling) [*before a noun*]: *That was a bloody shame (= a very great shame).* [*before an adjective*]: *It was a bloody great commotion (= a very nasty disturbance). That was bloody awful (= very awful).* **—***v.* [~ + *obj*] **5.** to stain or smear with blood: *hands bloodied from the stabbing.* **6.** to cause to bleed: *His nose had been bloodied by the bully.* **—blood′i•ness,** *n.* [*noncount*]: *The violence and bloodiness in that movie made him sick.*

bloom (blo͞om) /bluwm/ *n.* **1.** [*count*] the flower of a plant. **2.** [*noncount*] the state of flowering: *lilacs in bloom.* **3.** [*noncount*] the time of greatest beauty, life, strength, or freshness: *the bloom of youth.* **4.** [*count*] a glow that signals or indicates such a state: *a bloom of health on her face.* **—***v.* [*no obj*] **5.** to produce or yield flowers or blossoms: *The roses bloom every few days.* **6.** to grow well or thrive; flourish; blossom: *His talent for languages bloomed.* [~ + *into* + *obj*]: *bloomed into a promising trombone player in high school.* **7.** to be in or achieve a state of beauty and vigor: *began to bloom with good health.*

bloo•mer (blo͞o′mər) /ˈbluwmər/ *n.* [*count*] **1.** a plant that blooms: *a night bloomer.* **2.** a person who develops skills to the fullest capacity: *She was a late bloomer.*

bloo•mers (blo͞o′mərz) /ˈbluwmərz/ *n.* [*plural*] **1.** loose trousers gathered at the knee, formerly worn by women for gymnastics or sports. **2.** women's underpants of similar, but less bulky, design.

bloom•ing (blo͞o′ming) /ˈbluwmɪŋ/ *adj.* **1.** in bloom; flowering; blossoming: *blooming flowers.* **2.** glowing, as with youthful vigor and freshness: *blooming with good health.* **3.** [*before a noun*] *Chiefly Brit.* (used to intensify or convey emotion about the next word): *a blooming idiot.*

bloop (blo͞op) /bluwp/ *v.* [~ + *obj*] **1.** *Baseball.* to hit (a pitched ball) as a blooper: *blooped a single to left.* **—***n.* [*count*] **2.** BLOOPER (def. 2).

bloop•er (blo͞o′pər) /ˈbluwpər/ *n.* [*count*] **1.** an embarrassing mistake, such as misspoken words on a broadcast. **2.** *Baseball.* a fly ball that carries just beyond the infield.

blos•som (blos′əm) /ˈblɒsəm/ *n.* **1.** the flower of a plant: [*count*]: *apple blossoms.* [*noncount*]: *The tree was covered in blossom.* **2.** [*noncount*] the state of flowering: *The cherry trees are in blossom.* **—***v.* [*no obj*] **3.** (of a tree or bush) to produce or yield blossoms: *The tree blossomed quickly.* **4.** (of a flower) to open up; bloom: *The roses blossomed last week.* **5.** to develop successfully; grow; flourish: *His talent blossomed at the university.* [~ + *into* + *obj*]: *blossomed into a beautiful young woman.*

blot (blot) /blɒt/ *n., v.,* **blot•ted, blot•ting.** **—***n.* [*count*] **1.** a spot or stain: *blots of ink.* **2.** a blemish on a person's reputation: *She'll try to erase this blot on her past.* **—***v.* [~ + *obj*] **3.** to make a blot: *blotted the paper with a spot of ink.* **4.** to spot, stain, or soil; ruin: *blotted her reputation for fairness.* **5. blot out,** [~ + *out* + *obj*] **a.** to hide; prevent (something) from being seen: *Clouds blotted out the sun.* **b.** to destroy completely; obliterate; wipe out: *tried to blot out any memory of that horrible night.*

blotch (bloch) /blɒtʃ/ *n.* [*count*] **1.** a large, irregular spot or blot: *blotches on her neck.* **—***v.* [~ + *obj*] **2.** to mark with blotches: *the clothes blotched with dark red stains.* **—blotch•i•ly** (bloch′ə lē) /ˈblɒtʃəliy/ *adv.* **—blotch•y,** *adj.,* **-i•er, -i•est:** *blotchy marks on her forehead.*

blot•ter (blot′ər) /ˈblɒtər/ *n.* [*count*] **1.** a piece of special paper that absorbs ink. **2.** a book in which events are recorded as they occur: *a police blotter.*

blot′ting pa′per, *n.* [*noncount*] soft, absorbent paper, used esp. to dry the ink on a piece of writing.

blot•to (blot′ō) /ˈblɒtow/ *adj.* [*be* + ~] *Slang.* very drunk: *He was blotto after that all-night party.*

blouse (blous, blouz) /blaws, blawz/ *n.* [*count*] a garment, usually for women and children, covering the body from the neck or shoulders to the waistline. See illustration at CLOTHING.

blow[1] (blō) /blow/ *n.* [*count*] **1.** a sudden, hard stroke with a hand, fist, or weapon: *a quick blow to the back of the neck.* **2.** a sudden shock or terrible event: *Her being fired was a terrible blow.* **3.** a sudden attack or drastic action: *The army struck a blow to the south.* ***—Idiom.*** **4. at one blow,** with a single act: *became wealthy and famous at one blow.* Also, **at a blow. 5. come to blows,** to begin to fight, esp. physically: *came to blows at the meeting.* **6. strike a blow for,** [~ + *obj*] to further or advance the cause of: *to strike a blow for civil rights.*

blow² (blō) /blow/ *v.,* **blew** (blo͞o) /bluw/ **blown, blow•ing,** *n.* **—***v.* **1.** (of the wind or air) **a.** [*no obj*] to be in motion: *The wind blew all night.* **b.** [~ + *obj*] to move something along with a current of air: *The wind blew dust in my eyes.* **c.** to (cause to) fall or collapse by a current of air: [~ + *down/over* + *obj*]: *A windstorm blew down the tent.* [~ + *obj* + *down/over*]: *A windstorm blew the tent over.* **2.** [*no obj*] to move along, carried by or as if by the wind: *The dust blew into my eyes.* **3.** [~ + *obj*] to shape (glass, smoke, etc.) with a current of air: *blew a smoke ring.* **4.** to produce or give off a current of air, as with the mouth or a bellows: [*no obj*]: *blew into the microphone.* [~ + *obj*]: *He blew smoke into my eyes.* **5.** (of a horn, etc.) to (cause to) give out sound: [*no obj*]: *As the trumpets were blowing the queen approached.* [~ + *obj*]: *drivers blowing their horns.* **6.** to (cause to) make a blowing sound: [*no obj*]: *The sirens blew at noon.* [~ + *obj*]: *The town blows its whistle at noon.* **7. a.** (of a fuse, etc.) to (cause to) stop functioning, as by bursting or melting [*no obj; (~ + out)*]: *The fuse blew. The tire blew (out).* **b.** [~ *(+ out)* + *obj*]: *The surge of electricity blew the fuse. That nail blew (out) the tire.* **8.** *Slang.* to leave (from); depart (from): [*no obj*]: *Here come the cops! Let's blow!* [~ + *obj*]: *Let's blow this town!* **9.** to (cause to) explode: [~ + *obj*]: *A mine blew the ship to bits.* [*no obj*]: *When that bomb blows, it'll take everyone with it!* **10.** *Informal.* [~ + *obj*] to waste (money); squander: *I blew $100 on dinner.* **11.** [~ + *obj*] *Informal.* **a.** to mishandle, ruin, or bungle: *It was your last chance and you blew it!; blew his lines in the play.* **b.** to waste or lose: *The team blew a large lead in the third quarter.* **12. blow away, a.** to kill, esp. by gunfire: [~ + *obj* + *away*]: *blew the bad guys away.* [~ + *away* + *obj*]: *blew away all the bad guys.* **b.** to defeat decisively; trounce: [~ + *away* + *obj*]: *The Chargers blew away the Jets by a score of 60 to 0.* [~ + *obj* + *away*]: *The Chargers blew the Jets away.* **c.** [~ + *obj* + *away*] to overwhelm with emotion, etc.: *I was blown away when they told me he was killed.* **13. blow out, a.** to (cause to) go out; (cause to) become extinguished: [~ + *out* + *obj*]: *She blew out all the candles.* [~ + *obj* + *out*]: *She blew them out.* [*no obj*]: *The fire finally blew out.* **b.** [~ + *oneself/itself* + *out*] to (cause to) lose force; to cease: *The storm has blown itself out.* **14. blow over,** [*no obj*] **a.** to pass away; subside: *The storm blew over in minutes.* **b.** to be forgotten: *The scandal will blow over eventually.* **15. blow up, a.** to (cause to) explode: [*no obj*]: *The bridge blew up in a roar of flames and light.* [~ + *up* + *obj*]: *The bombs blew up the embassy.* [~ + *obj* + *up*]: *They blew the depot up.* **b.** [~ + *obj* + *up*] to exaggerate; enlarge: *You're blowing this whole thing up out of proportion.* **c.** [*no obj*] to lose one's temper: *blew up at her secretary but apologized after lunch.* **d.** to fill with air or gas; inflate: [~ + *up* + *obj*]: *to blow up a balloon.* [~ + *obj* + *up*]: *to blow it up.* **—***n.* [*count*] **16.** a blast of air or wind. **—*Idiom.*** **17. blow off steam,** to release tension, as by activity, etc.: *blowing off steam before the big match tomorrow.* **18. blow one's cool,** to lose one's composure; to become nervous, etc.: *When it's your turn to speak, don't blow your cool.* **19. blow one's mind,** to overwhelm (someone), as with excitement, pleasure, or dismay: *The thought of becoming a multimillionaire blows my mind.* **20. blow one's stack** or **top,** to become very angry: *When she came home late her father blew his stack.* **21. blow the lid off,** [~ + *obj*] to expose (scandal or illegal actions) to public view: *This story will blow the lid off the conspiracy.*

blow′-by′-blow′, *adj.* [*before a noun*] describing every detail and step: *a blow-by-blow account of a tennis match.*

blow′-dry′, *v.,* **-dried, -dry•ing,** *n., pl.* **-drys.** **—***v.* [~ + *obj*] **1.** to dry or style (hair) with a blow-dryer: *Her hair was perfectly blow-dried.* **—***n.* [*count*] **2.** an act or instance of blow-drying.

blow′-dry′er, *n.* [*count*] a small, usually hand-held electrical appliance that sends out a flow of heated air, used to dry and often style the hair.

blow•er (blō′ər) /ˈblowər/ *n.* [*count*] **1.** a person or thing that blows. **2.** a machine for pushing or sending air through something. **3.** *Chiefly Brit. Slang.* a telephone.

blow′-hard′, *n.* [*count*] a boastful and talkative person: *Was that blow-hard still talking about himself?*

blown (blōn) /blown/ *v.* **1.** pp. of BLOW². **—***adj.* **2.** formed by blowing: *blown glass.*

blow•out (blō′out′) /ˈblowˌawt/ *n.* [*count*] **1.** a sudden bursting of an automobile tire: *A sudden blowout left us stranded on the highway.* **2.** a big, expensive party: *a big blowout for her graduation.*

blow•torch (blō′tôrch′) /ˈblowˌtɔrtʃ/ *n.* [*count*] **1.** a small device that shoots out an extremely hot flame, used esp. in metalworking. **—***v.* [~ + *obj*] **2.** to burn with or as if with a blowtorch.

blow•up (blō′up′) /ˈblowˌʌp/ *n.* [*count*] **1.** an explosion: *The blowups occurred one after the other.* **2.** a violent argument or outburst of temper: *a big blowup over their daughter's husband.* **3.** Also, **blow′-up′.** an enlargement of a photograph: *looked at the blowup of the original and saw that his hand had a small scar.*

blow•y (blō′ē) /ˈblowiy/ *adj.,* **-i•er, -i•est.** **1.** windy: *a chill, blowy day.* **2.** easily blown about: *thin, blowy hair.*

blowz•y or **blows•y** (blou′zē) /ˈblawziy/ *adj.,* **-i•er, -i•est.** **1.** having a rough, red complexion. **2.** poorly dressed; dirty in appearance. **—blowz•i•ly** (blou′zə lē) /ˈblawzəliy/ *adv.*

BLT, *n.,* [*count*] *pl.* **BLTs, BLT's.** a bacon, lettuce, and tomato sandwich.

blub•ber (blub′ər) /ˈblʌbər/ *n.* [*noncount*] **1.** the layer of fat below the skin of a whale. **2.** excess body fat: *With all that blubber, you should go on a diet.* **—***v.* **3.** to weep or cry noisily and without restraint: [*no obj*]: *blubbering about how I never cared about her.* [~ + *that clause*]: *blubbering that I never cared about her.*

blub•ber•y (blub′ə rē) /ˈblʌbəriy/ *adj.* **1.** having a lot of blubber; fat: *a blubbery fellow in sweatpants.* **2.** puffy; swollen: *blubbery lips.*

bludg•eon (bluj′ən) /ˈblʌdʒən/ *n.* [*count*] **1.** a short, heavy club with one end thicker and heavier than the other. **—***v.* [~ + *obj*] **2.** to strike or knock down with a bludgeon: *bludgeoned the victim to death.* **3.** to force (someone) into doing something by threats: *bludgeoned me into testifying against my best friend.* **—bludg′-eon•er,** *n.* [*count*]

blue (blo͞o), *n., adj.,* **blu•er, blu•est,** *v.,* **blued, blu•ing** or **blue•ing.** **—***n.* **1.** [*noncount*] the pure color of a clear sky; the primary color between green and violet. **2.** [*count*] something having a blue color. **3. the blue,** [*noncount*] **a.** the sky: *The plane shot off into the blue.* **b.** the sea: *The boat sank into the deep blue.* **—***adj.* **4.** of the color blue: *a beautiful blue sky.* **5.** sad or depressed in spirits: *I'm feeling a little blue today, thinking about old friends.* **6.** [*before a noun*] holding or offering little hope; dismal; bleak: *a blue outlook.* **7.** [*usually before a noun*] deriving from strict moral or religious observance; puritanical: *Blue laws kept stores closed on Sundays.* **8.** indecent; off-color; obscene: *a blue movie.* **—***v.* [~ + *obj*] **9.** to make (something) blue; dye (something) a blue color. **—*Idiom.*** **10. blue in the face,** at an extreme point of frustration, irritation, etc.: *to argue till one is blue in the face.* **11. out of the blue,** suddenly and unexpectedly: *Out of the blue, she inherited a fortune.* **—blue′ness,** *n.* [*noncount*] See BLUES.

blue•bell (blo͞o′bel′) /ˈbluwˌbɛl/ *n.* [*count*] a plant having blue, bell-shaped flowers.

blue•ber•ry (blo͞o′ber′ē, -bə rē) /ˈbluwˌbɛriy, -bəriy/ *n.* [*count*], *pl.* **-ries.** **1.** a bluish berry that can be eaten, growing on shrubs of the heath family. **2.** any of these shrubs.

blue•bird (blo͞o′bûrd′) /ˈbluwˌbɜrd/ *n.* [*count*] a North American songbird of the thrush family, the male of which is mostly or entirely blue.

blue blood (blo͞o′ blud′ *for 1;* blo͞o′ blud′ *for 2*) /ˈbluwˌ blʌd *for 1;* ˈbluwˈ blʌd *for 2*/ *n.* **1.** [*count*] an aristocrat or member of a socially important family: *a resort for all the blue bloods.* **2.** [*noncount*] aristocratic background: *the blue blood of royalty.* **—blue′-blood′ed,** *adj.*: *an important blue-blooded family.*

blue′ chip′, *n.* [*count*] a common stock issued by a company with a reputation for secure financial strength: *Blue chips are low-risk investments.* **—blue′-chip′,** *adj.*

blue′-col′lar, *adj.* [*often: before a noun*] of or relating to factory workers, manual laborers, etc., who usually do physical work, wear work clothes, and earn weekly wages: *employed in a blue-collar job.* Compare WHITE-COLLAR.

blue•fish (blo͞o′fish′) /ˈbluwˌfɪʃ/ *n.* [*count*], *pl. (esp. when thought of as a group)* **-fish,** *(esp. for kinds or species)* **-fish•es.** **1.** a blue fish that travels in schools and can be eaten. **2.** any of various other fishes, usually of a bluish color.

blue•grass (blo͞o′gras′) /ˈbluwˌgræs/ *n.* [*noncount*] **1.** a grass having dense clumps of bluish green blades. **2.** a kind of country music played on the banjo, fiddle, guitar, and bass.

blue•jack•et (blo͞o′jak′it) /ˈbluwˌdʒækɪt/ *n.* [*count*] a sailor, esp. in the U.S. or British navy.

blue′ jay′, *n.* [*count*] a bird of E North America, having a crested head, a bright blue back, and a gray breast.

blue′ jeans′, *n.* [*plural*] close-fitting trousers made of blue denim: *Blue jeans were originally work pants.*

blue′ law′, *n.* [*count*] any law that forbids certain practices, as doing business or dancing, on Sunday: *No stores were open because of blue laws.*

blue•nose (blo͞o′nōz′) /ˈbluwˌnowz/ *n.* [*count*] a person who observes overly strict principles, esp. regarding pleasure; prude: *The town bluenoses wouldn't talk to her.*

blue′-pen′cil, *v.* [~ + *obj*], **-ciled, -cil•ing** or *(esp. Brit.)* **-cilled, -cil•ling.** to change or edit (a piece of writing, etc.) to improve it: *blue-penciled the report before it went.*

blue•print (blo͞o′print′) /ˈbluwˌprɪnt/ *n.* [*count*] **1.** a photographic print made by a process that produces white lines on a blue background, used chiefly for plans: *the architect's blueprints.* **2.** a detailed outline or plan of action: *a blueprint for success.*

blue′ rib′bon, *n.* [*count*] the highest award or distinction, as a blue ribbon given as the first prize in a contest.

blues (blo͞oz) /bluwz/ *n.* **1. the blues,** [*noncount; used with a plural verb*] depressed spirits; sadness: *I usually get the blues after the holidays.* **2.** [*noncount; used with a singular or plural verb*] a type of slow, sad, black folk music, characterized by three-line stanzas in which the second line usually repeats the first. **3.** [*plural*] *Informal.* police. —**blues′y,** *adj.: bluesy music.*

blue•stock•ing (blo͞o′stok′ing) /ˈbluwˌstɒkɪŋ/ *n.* [*count*] *Often Disparaging.* a woman interested in literature or other areas but not in traditionally feminine areas.

blue′ streak′, *n.* [*noncount*] —***Idiom.*** **talk a blue streak,** [*no obj*] to talk rapidly and without stopping: *They stayed up all night talking a blue streak till morning.*

bluff[1] (bluf) /blʌf/ *adj.,* **-er, -est,** *n.* —*adj.* **1.** good-naturedly direct, blunt, or frank: *a bluff way of speaking that is refreshing.* **2.** presenting a bold, broad, and very steep front: *a bluff cliff.* —*n.* [*count*] **3.** a cliff, headland, or hill with a broad, steep face: *leaning carefully out over the bluffs.* —**bluff′ness,** *n.* [*noncount*]: *His bluffness is just an act; he's really very sneaky.*

bluff[2] (bluf) /blʌf/ *v.* **1.** to mislead or deceive (someone) by putting on a bold front: [~ + *obj*]: *Don't try to bluff me; I know all your tricks.* [*no obj*]: *He's bluffing; I'm sure he can't overrule you.* **2.** [~ + *obj*] to achieve by bluffing: *I tried to bluff my way into the job.* **3.** to deceive (an opponent in poker) by betting heavily on a weak hand: [*no obj*]: *I think you're bluffing, so I'll meet your bet.* [~ + *obj*]: *He tried to bluff me with a pair of two's.* —*n.* **4.** an act or instance of bluffing: [*count*]: *It's just a bluff to get me to show what I know.* [*noncount*]: *I think his scare tactics are just bluff.* **5.** [*count*] a person who bluffs; bluffer: *He's just a bluff.* —***Idiom.*** **6. call someone's bluff,** to challenge someone to carry out a threat: *If she thinks she can threaten us with firing us all, I think it's time we called her bluff.* —**bluff′er,** *n.* [*count*]

blu•ing or **blue•ing** (blo͞o′ing) /ˈbluwɪŋ/ *n.* [*noncount*] a substance, such as indigo, used to whiten clothes or give them a bluish tinge.

blu•ish or **blue•ish** (blo͞o′ish) /ˈbluwɪʃ/ *adj.* rather or slightly blue. —**blu′ish•ness,** *n.* [*noncount*]

blun•der (blun′dər) /ˈblʌndər/ *n.* [*count*] **1.** a stupid mistake: *One of his first blunders was to make fun of the teacher's name.* —*v.* [*no obj*] **2.** to move or act clumsily or stupidly: [~ + *into*]: *We blundered into the wrong room.* [~ + *along*]: *We blundered along down the road.* **3.** to make a mistake, esp. through carelessness or confusion: *We blundered when we tried to take a shortcut.* —**blun′der•er,** *n.* [*count*]

blun•der•buss (blun′dər bus′) /ˈblʌndərˌbʌs/ *n.* [*count*] **1.** a short gun having a wide mouth so as to scatter shot. **2.** an insensitive, blundering person.

blun•der•ing (blun′dər ing) /ˈblʌndər ɪŋ/ *adj.* [*before a noun*] clumsy; careless: *What a blundering fool!* —**blun′der•ing•ly,** *adv.*

blunt (blunt) /blʌnt/ *adj.,* **-er, -est,** *v.* —*adj.* **1.** having a thick or dull edge or point: *a blunt pencil.* **2.** abrupt in manner, without politeness: *asked blunt questions about my finances.* —*v.* **3.** to (cause to) become blunt; dull: [~ + *obj*]: *You'll blunt the scissors on that cardboard.* [*no obj*]: *The scissors will blunt on that cardboard.* **4.** [~ + *obj*] to weaken the strength of: *Wine can blunt the senses.* —**blunt′ly,** *adv.: To put it bluntly, you're simply no good.* —**blunt′ness,** *n.* [*noncount*]: *I found his bluntness and directness refreshing.* —**Syn.** BLUNT, BRUSQUE, and CURT describe people's manners and speech. BLUNT suggests too much frankness and a lack of consideration or regard for the feelings of others: *blunt and tactless remarks.* BRUSQUE suggests a sharpness and abruptness that are almost rude: *a brusque denial; a brusque word or two.* CURT applies esp. to short, quick language that takes us by surprise because we are expecting more: *a curt reply.*

blur (blûr) /blɜr/ *v.,* **blurred, blur•ring,** *n.* —*v.* **1.** to (cause to) become hard to see or hear: [*no obj*]: *Her eyes blurred with tears. His speech blurred the more he drank.* [~ + *obj*]: *The fog blurred the outline of the car.* **2.** [~ + *obj*] to make a dirty mark or smear on (something): *She blurred the ink on the letter with her tears.* **3.** [~ + *obj*] to dull or weaken (a distinction between things that should be separate): *blurred the distinction between true reform and total destruction.* —*n.* [*count; usually singular*] **4.** a smudge or smear that obscures: *a blur of smoke.* **5.** something seen or remembered indistinctly: *The ship was a blur on the horizon. Parts of the trip were just a blur.* —**blurred,** *adj.: old and blurred photos.*

blurb (blûrb) /blɜrb/ *n.* [*count*] a brief notice that describes a book, play, etc., esp. one full of praise: *The blurb on the book jacket promised "action, thrills, adventure, and romance."*

blur•ry (blûr′ē) /ˈblɜriy/ *adj.,* **-ri•er, -ri•est.** blurred; indistinct. —**blur′ri•ness,** *n.* [*noncount*]: *suffered from blurriness of vision.*

blurt (blûrt) /blɜrt/ *v.* to say or tell (something) suddenly, accidentally, or thoughtlessly: [~ *(+ out)* + *obj*]: *He blurted (out) the secret.* [~ + *obj* (+ *out*)]: *He blurted the secret (out) before we could stop him.*

blush (blush) /blʌʃ/ *v.* [*no obj*] **1.** to redden, as from embarrassment: *blushed when they praised her.* **2.** to feel shame or embarrassment: *blushed at those critical remarks.* —*n.* **3.** [*count; usually singular*] a reddening, as of the face: *A quick blush rose on her face.* **4.** [*noncount*] BLUSHER (def. 2): *She put some blush on her face to cover her paleness.* —***Idiom.*** **5. at first blush,** at first glance: *At first blush we might think the problem is very simple.* —**blush′ing,** *adj.: the blushing bride.*

blush•er (blush′ər) /ˈblʌʃər/ *n.* **1.** [*count*] a person who blushes, esp. readily. **2.** [*noncount*] a cosmetic, similar to rouge, used to add color to the cheeks: *applying some blusher to a pale face.* Also, **blush′-on.**

blus•ter (blus′tər) /ˈblʌstər/ *v.* [*no obj*] **1.** (of wind) to roar or blow roughly: *the blustering wind.* **2.** to make loud but empty threats: *blustered about how they would beat us all up.* —*n.* [*noncount*] **3.** boisterous noise and violence: *the bluster of a storm at sea.* **4.** noisy, empty threats or protests: *That's just bluster; he has no real intention of firing you.* —**blus′ter•er,** *n.* [*count*] —**blus′ter•ing•ly,** *adv.* —**blus′ter•ous,** *adj.*

blus•ter•y (blus′tər ē) /ˈblʌstər iy/ *adj.* rough; windy, cold, and wild: *a raw, blustery winter day.*

blvd., an abbreviation of: boulevard.

B.O., an abbreviation of: **1.** *Informal.* body odor. **2.** box office.

b.o., an abbreviation of: **1.** back order. **2.** box office.

bo•a (bō′ə) /ˈbowə/ *n.* [*count*], *pl.* **bo•as. 1.** a nonpoisonous, chiefly tropical snake that constricts its prey. **2.** a scarf or snake-shaped garment usually of feathers.

boar (bôr, bōr) /bɔr, bowr/ *n.* [*count*] **1.** a male pig kept for breeding. **2.** a wild Old World swine.

board (bôrd, bōrd) /bɔrd, bowrd/ *n.* **1.** [*count*] a long rectangular piece of wood sawed thin: *Please nail a couple of boards over the hole for now.* **2.** [*count*] a flat piece of wood or other hard material used for a purpose: *Write your sentence up on the board (= a blackboard).* **3.** [*count*] a sheet of wood, cardboard, etc., on which a game is played: *a chess board.* **4.** [*noncount*] material made in large sheets, as plasterboard. **5.** [*count*] an official group or committee that directs an activity: *a board of directors.* **6.** [*noncount*] daily meals, esp. as provided for pay: *How much is room and board in that hotel?* **7.** [*count*] **a.** a piece of fiberglass or other material upon which computer chips are mounted. **b.** CIRCUIT BOARD (def. 1). **8.** a switchboard. —*v.* **9.** to cover or close with boards: [~ + *up/over* + *obj*]: *boarded up the old house.* [~ + *obj* + *up/over*]: *boarded the fence over.* **10.** [~ + *obj*] to provide (someone) with meals, esp. for pay: *The retired couple boarded several college students.* **11.** [~ + *with/at* + *obj*] to take one's meals and lodging at a fixed price: *Several college students boarded with the couple.* **12.** to go on board (of a ship, etc.): [*no obj*]: *Passengers should board through the door on my left.* [~ + *obj*]: *Passengers were just beginning to board the ship.* **13.** [~ + *obj*] to allow on board: *Flight 678 will* *board passengers.* —***Idiom.*** **14. across the board,** so as to apply to all equally: *to raise salaries across the board.* **15. on board, a.** on or in a ship, or other vehicle: *a hundred passengers on board.* **b.** *Baseball.* on base: *Two men were out but two were on board.* **c.** present and functioning as a member of a team or organization: *The new trainee was welcomed on board by the chairman.*

board•er (bôr′dər, bōr′-) /'bɔrdər, 'bowr-/ *n.* [*count*] **1.** a person, esp. a lodger, who is supplied with regular meals at someone's house. **2.** a pupil at a boarding school.

board′ game′, *n.* [*count*] any game played on a board, esp. one in which pieces are moved, such as chess or checkers.

board•ing•house or **board•ing house** (bôr′ding hous′, bōr′-) /'bɔr,dɪŋ haws, 'bowr-/ *n.* [*count*], *pl.* **hous•es** a private house at which meals and lodging may be obtained.

board′ing school′, *n.* [*count*] a school at which the pupils receive meals and lodging as well as an education (distinguished from *day school*).

board•room or **board room** (bôrd′ro͞om′, -ro͝om′, bōrd′-) /'bɔrd,ruwm, -,rʊm, 'bowrd-/ *n.* [*count*] a room set aside for meetings of a board, esp. of a corporation: *dark dealings in the boardroom.*

board•walk (bôrd′wôk′, bōrd′-) /'bɔrd,wɔk, 'bowrd-/ *n.* [*count*] a footpath made of wooden boards.

boast (bōst) /bowst/ *v.* **1.** to speak (of someone or something) with exaggeration and too much pride, esp. about oneself: [*no obj*]: *He was always boasting.* [~ + *of/about* + *obj*]: *boasting about his law school.* [~ + *that clause*]: *boasted that he had won every track award in school.* **2.** [~ + *obj*] to be proud to own or have; be lucky to possess: *The town boasts two new schools.* —*n.* [*count*] **3.** a thing boasted of; a cause for pride: *It was my boast that I never missed a day of work.* **4.** instances of exaggerated speech or bragging: *empty boasts.* —**boast′er,** *n.* [*count*] —**boast′ful,** *adj.* —**boast′ful•ly,** *adv.* —**boast′ful•ness,** *n.* [*noncount*] —**boast′ing•ly,** *adv.*

boat (bōt) /bowt/ *n.* [*count*] **1.** a vessel for transport by water. **2.** a small ship, generally for specialized use: *a fishing boat.* **3.** a boat-shaped serving dish: *a gravy boat.* —***Idiom.*** **4. in the same boat,** in similar difficult circumstances: *We're all in the same boat, so we should work together.* **5. miss the boat,** *Informal.* **a.** to fail to take advantage of an opportunity: *He missed the boat when he applied too late.* **b.** to miss the point of; fail to understand: *I missed the boat on that explanation.* **6. rock the boat.** See ROCK[2] (def. 12).

boat•er (bō′tər) /'bowtər/ *n.* [*count*] **1.** a stiff straw hat with a shallow, flat top or crown, a ribbon band, and a straight brim. **2.** one who travels in a boat.

boat′ peo′ple, *n.* [*plural*] refugees who have fled a country by boat, usually without enough food or water.

boat•swain or **bo's'n** or **bo•sun** (bō′sən) /'bowsən/ *n.* [*count*] a petty officer on a warship or on a merchant vessel who is in charge of rigging, anchors, cables, and other equipment.

bob[1] (bob) /bɒb/ *n., v.,* **bobbed, bob•bing.** —*n.* [*count*] **1.** a short, jerky motion: *A bob of her head told me she had noticed me.* —*v.* **2.** to move (something) quickly down and up: [~ + *obj*]: *She bobbed her head.* [*no obj*]: *bobbed up and down in the water, waving for help.* **3.** [~ + *obj*] to indicate with such a motion: *She bobbed a greeting without looking up from her work.* **4. bob up,** [*no obj*] to appear unexpectedly.

bob[2] (bob) /bɒb/ *n., v.,* **bobbed, bob•bing.** —*n.* [*count*] **1.** a short, caplike haircut that is even on all sides. **2.** a float for a fishing line: *She put her string through the bob and watched it float on the lake.* —*v.* **3.** [~ + *obj*] to cut (hair, etc.) short: *to bob one's hair.* **4.** [~ + *for* + *obj*] to try to snatch floating or dangling objects with the teeth: *bobbing for apples.*

bob[3] (bob) /bɒb/ *n., pl.* **bob.** *Brit.* SHILLING.

bob•bin (bob′in) /'bɒbɪn/ *n.* [*count*] a round object upon which yarn or thread is wound.

bob•ble (bob′əl) /'bɒbəl/ *n., v.,* **-bled, -bling.** —*n.* [*count*] **1.** a momentary fumbling of a baseball. **2.** an error; mistake. —*v.* [~ + *obj*] **3.** to fumble (a baseball) momentarily: *hardly ever bobbles a ball.*

bob•by (bob′ē) /'bɒbiy/ *n.* [*count*], *pl.* **-bies.** *Brit.* a policeman.

bob′by pin′, *n.* [*count*] a flat metal pin used for holding hair tightly in place.

bob•cat (bob′kat′) /'bɒb,kæt/ *n.* [*count*], *pl.* **-cats,** (*esp. when thought of as a group*) **-cat.** a North American lynx.

bob•o•link (bob′ə lingk′) /'bɒbə,lɪŋk/ *n.* [*count*] a North American songbird.

bob•sled (bob′sled′) /'bɒb,slɛd/ *n., v.,* **-sled•ded, -sled•ding.** —*n.* [*count*] **1.** a long sled for two or four riders, having a brake and a steering wheel to direct the sled down a fast path with sharp curves. —*v.* [*no obj*] **2.** to ride on a bobsled. —**bob′sled′der,** *n.* [*count*]: *He trained to be an Olympic bobsledder.*

bob•white (bob′hwīt′, -wīt′) /'bɒb'hwayt, -'wayt/ *n.* [*count*] a small New World quail having spotty feathers and coloring.

boc•cie or **boc•ci** or **boc•ce** (boch′ē) /'bɒtʃiy/ *n.* [*noncount*] a type of lawn bowling played usually on a long, narrow dirt court: *The old Italian men were playing their fiftieth game of boccie.*

bod (bod) /bɒd/ *n.* [*count*] *Informal.* **1.** body: *We thought they all had fabulous bods.* **2.** *Brit.* a person: *She's a very nice bod indeed.*

bo•da•cious (bō dā′shəs) /bow'deyʃəs/ *adj. Chiefly Dialect.* **1.** [*before a noun*] complete; unmitigated: *She was a bodacious flirt.* **2.** remarkable; outstanding: *That is one bodacious story.* —**bo•da′cious•ly,** *adv.*

bode[1] (bōd) /bowd/ *v.* [~ + *well/ill/evil* + *for*] **bod•ed, bod•ing.** to be a sign or omen of; signal; portend: *The promotion bodes well for his future.*

bode[2] (bōd) /bowd/ *v.* a pt. of BIDE.

bo•de•ga (bō dā′gə) /bow'deygə/ *n.* [*count*], *pl.* **-gas.** (esp. among Spanish-speaking Americans) a grocery store.

bod•ice (bod′is) /'bɒdɪs/ *n.* [*count*] the part of a woman's dress covering the body above the waistline.

-bod•ied (bod′ēd) /'bɒdiyd/ *combining form.* Use *-bodied* after another adjective to mean "having a body of a (certain) kind": *a flat-bodied fish (= a fish having a flat body); a wide-bodied car.*

bod•i•ly (bod′l ē) /'bɒdḷiy/ *adj.* [*before a noun*] **1.** of or relating to the body: *accused of bodily assault.* —*adv.* **2.** involving the whole body, or the whole mass of something: *The tornado picked the car up bodily.*

bod•kin (bod′kin) /'bɒdkɪn/ *n.* [*count*] a small needle.

bod•y (bod′ē) /'bɒdiy/ *n., pl.* **bod•ies,** *adj.* —*n.* **1.** [*count*] **a.** the complete structure of a person, animal, plant, or other organism. **b.** the main portion of a person or animal, comprising the trunk but not the head, arms, and legs. **c.** a corpse: *The body was cremated.* **2.** [*count*] the main mass of a thing, as the hull of a ship or the section of a car in which passengers are carried. **3.** [*count*] *Physics.* a mass, esp. one considered as a whole: *Bodies in motion tend to stay in motion.* **4.** [*count*] the principal part of a speech or document: *You need an introduction and conclusion around the body of your essay.* **5.** [*count*] an object in space, as a planet or star. **6.** [*count*] a group or organization: *the student body.* **7.** [*count*] a separate and distinct piece of matter: *a foreign body in one's eye.* **8.** [*noncount*] substance; consistency or richness: *a wine with good body.* **9.** [*count*] an amount or quantity of: *several large bodies of water in that area.* —*adj.* [*before a noun*] **10.** of or relating to the body; bodily: *body parts.*

bod′y o′dor, *n.* [*noncount*] the smell of a person's body, esp. caused by sweat: *overpowering body odor in the locker room.* Also, **B.O.**

bod′y bag′, *n.* [*count*] a zippered bag used to transport a dead body.

bod•y•build•ing or **bod•y-build•ing** (bod′ē bil′ding) /'bɒd,iy bɪldɪŋ/ *n.* [*noncount*] the developing of muscles through weight training, etc.: *bodybuilding competitions.* —**bod′y•build′er, bod′y-build′er,** *n.* [*count*]

bod′y count′, *n.* [*count*] the number of persons in the military killed in an action or during a specified period.

bod′y Eng′lish, *n.* [*noncount*] a twisting of the body by a player to help a ball that has already been hit, etc., to travel in the desired direction: *gave the ball some body English.*

bod•y•guard (bod′ē gärd′) /'bɒdiy,gɑrd/ *n.* [*count*] a person or group of persons hired to guard an individual.

bod′y lan′guage, *n.* [*noncount*] communication through gestures, facial expressions, etc., often accomplished without the person being aware of its effect: *friendly words but hostile body language.*

bod′y pol′itic, *n.* [*count; usually singular*] a people thought of as a political community.

bof•fo (bof′ō) /'bɒfow/ *n., pl.* **-fos,** *adj. Slang.* —*n.* [*count*] **1.** something very successful, as a play in the theater, etc. —*adj.* **2.** highly successful.

bog[1] (bog, bôg) /bɒg, bɔg/ *n., v.,* **bogged, bog•ging.** —*n.* [*count*] **1.** an area of wet, spongy ground. —*v.* **2. bog down,** to sink in or as if in a bog: [*no obj*]: *The truck bogged down in the snow.* [~ + *obj* + *down*]: *The slow computer bogged us down.* —**bog′gy,** *adj.,* **-gi•er, -gi•est.**

bog[2] (bog, bôg) /bɒg, bɔg/ *n.* [*count*] Usually, **bogs.** [*plural*] *Brit. Slang.* a lavatory; bathroom.

bo•gey (bō′gē; *for 2 also* bŏŏg′ē) /ˈbowgiy; *for 2 also* ˈbʊgiy/ *n., pl.* **-geys,** *v.* **-gied, -gey•ing.** —*n.* [*count*] **1.** a golf score of one stroke over par on a hole: *scored a bogey.* **2.** BOGY. —*v.* **3.** (in golf) to make a bogey (on a golf hole): [*no obj*]: *He bogied twice in the last six holes.* [~ + *obj*]: *He bogied the last two holes.*

bo•gey•man (bŏŏg′ē man′, bō′gē-) /ˈbʊgiyˌmæn, ˈbowgiy-/ also **boogeyman,** *n.* [*count*], *pl.* **-men.** an evil spirit supposed to carry off naughty children: *The bogeyman will get you if you don't watch out!*

bog•gle (bog′əl) /ˈbɒgəl/ *v.,* **-gled, -gling. 1.** to (cause the mind to) be overwhelmed: [~ + *at* + *obj*]: *The mind boggles at the thought (idea) of such distances as light years.* [~ + *obj*]: *Vast distances boggle the mind.* **2.** [*no obj*] to hesitate because of fear or a scruple: *We shouldn't boggle at this opportunity to make a profit.* —**bog′gler,** *n.* [*count*]

bo•gie (bō′gē, bŏŏg′ē) /ˈbowgiy, ˈbʊgiy/ *n.* BOGY.

bo•gus (bō′gəs) /ˈbowgəs/ *adj.* false; counterfeit; phony: *The thief gave a bogus address.*

bo•gy or **bo•gey** or **bo•gie** (bō′gē, bŏŏg′ē) /ˈbowgiy, ˈbʊgiy/ *n.* [*count*], *pl.* **-gies** or **-geys. 1.** an evil spirit. **2.** anything that haunts or frightens (someone); a barrier or block that keeps someone from doing something: *Fear is the major bogy of novice mountain climbers.*

bo•he•mi•an (bō hē′mē ən) /bowˈhiymiyən/ *n.* [*count*] **1.** one who lives in a casual way and acts differently from most of society. —*adj.* **2.** of, relating to, or characteristic of this way of living: *developed a bohemian lifestyle her father did not approve of.* —**bo•he′mi•an•ism,** *n.* [*noncount*]

boil[1] (boil) /bɔyl/ *v.* **1.** to (cause to) change from a liquid to a gas as a result of heat: [*no obj*]: *When the water boils, turn off the heat.* [~ + *obj*]: *Boil some water for tea.* **2.** to cook (something) in boiling water: [*no obj*]: *The eggs boiled for three minutes.* [~ + *obj*]: *Boil the eggs for three minutes.* **3.** [*no obj*] to contain or hold a liquid that boils: *The kettle is boiling (= The kettle contains water that is boiling).* **4.** [*no obj*] to be in an agitated state: *The sea boiled in the storm.* **5.** [*no obj*] to be deeply upset: *boiling with anger.* **6. boil down,** [~ + *down* + *obj*] **a.** to reduce or lessen by boiling: *Boil down the liquid to about half.* **b.** to shorten; abridge; condense: *Boil down all that research into a summary.* **7. boil down to,** [~ + *down* + *to* + *obj*] to amount to: *His statement boils down to a failure to support you.* **8. boil over,** [*no obj*] **a.** to overflow while or as if while boiling: *That pot is boiling over.* **b.** to be unable to hold back anger, excitement, etc.: *felt all her anger boiling over.* —*n.* [*count; singular*] **9.** the act or state of boiling: *Bring the water to a boil.*

boil[2] (boil) /bɔyl/ *n.* [*count*] a painful swelling on the skin having pus inside, usually caused by an infection.

boiled (boild) /bɔyld/ *adj.* heated to a point where liquid begins to turn to gas; cooked by being heated this way: *boiled potatoes.*

boil•er (boi′lər) /ˈbɔylər/ *n.* [*count*] **1.** a large, closed container in which water is heated to make steam: *Call the landlord; the boiler is out again.* **2.** a vessel, such as a kettle, for boiling or heating.

boil•er•plate or **boil•er plate** (boi′lər plāt′) /ˈbɔyˌlər pleyt/ *n.* [*noncount*] **1.** plating of iron or steel for the shells of boilers, or for covering the sides of ships, etc.: *three-inch boilerplate on that ship.* **2.** the same phrasing used again and again to different audiences.

boil•ing (boi′ling) /ˈbɔylɪŋ/ *adj.* **1.** having reached the temperature when a liquid turns into a gas: *boiling water.* **2.** fiercely churning: *the boiling seas.* **3.** uncomfortably warm: *Could you lower the heat; we're boiling in here.* **4.** (of anger, etc.) intense; fierce: *boiling anger.* —*adv.* **5.** to an extreme degree; very: *I was boiling mad. It was boiling hot.*

boil′ing point′, *n.* [*count*] **1.** the temperature at which a boiling liquid begins to turn into a gas. **2.** [*usually singular*] the point beyond which one becomes visibly angry, outraged, or the like: *I had reached my boiling point with those nasty kids.* **3.** [*usually singular*] the point at which matters reach a crisis: *The situation had reached the boiling point between the two countries.*

bois•ter•ous (boi′stər əs, -strəs) /ˈbɔystərəs, -strəs/ *adj.* rough and noisy; clamorous: *boisterous laughter.* —**bois′ter•ous•ly,** *adv.*: *schoolchildren laughing boisterously.* —**bois′ter•ous•ness,** *n.* [*noncount*]

bold (bōld) /bowld/ *adj.,* **-er, -est. 1.** unafraid in the face of danger; courageous: *bold and daring pilots.* **2.** ignoring good manners by not showing respect; impudent: *a bold child who always talks back to her parents.* **3.** finding new solutions; inventive or imaginative: *a bold solution to a perplexing problem.* **4.** very bright or very dark; striking to the eye; flashy; showy: *a shirt with a bold pattern.* —**bold′ly,** *adv.*: *They boldly went where no one had gone before.* —**bold′ness,** *n.* [*noncount*]: *Enough of your boldness; go to your room!*

bold•face (bōld′fās′) /ˈbowldˌfeys/ *n.* [*noncount*] **1.** type or print that has thick, heavy lines, used for emphasis, headings, etc.: **This is boldface.** —*adj.* [*often: before a noun*] **2.** typeset or printed in boldface.

bold′-faced′, *adj.* [*before a noun*] **1.** very daring in being impolite; impudent; brazen: *What she told us turned out to be a bold-faced lie.* **2.** (of type) having thick, heavy lines.

bo•le•ro (bə lâr′ō, bō-) /bəˈlɛərow, bow-/ *n.* [*count*], *pl.* **-ros. 1.** a Spanish dance; the music for this dance. **2.** a waist-length jacket worn open in front.

Bo•liv•i•an (bə liv′ē ən, bō-) /bəˈlɪviyən, bow-/ *n.* [*count*] **1.** a person born or living in Bolivia. —*adj.* **2.** of or relating to Bolivia.

boll (bōl) /bowl/ *n.* [*count*] a pod of a plant, such as of flax or cotton.

bol•lix (bol′iks) /ˈbɒlɪks/ *Informal.* —*v.* **1.** to do something clumsily; bungle: [~ + *obj*]: *The job was bollixed completely.* [~ + *up* + *obj*]: *He bollixed up the job.* [~ + *obj* + *up*]: *He bollixed it up.* —*n.* [*count*] **2.** a job badly or clumsily done; a bungle.

boll′ wee′vil, *n.* [*count*] a beetle that attacks bolls of cotton.

bo•lo•gna (bə lō′nē, -nə) /bəˈlowniy, -nə/ *n.* [*noncount*] a sausage made of beef and pork: *a bologna sandwich.*

bo•lo•ney (bə lō′nē) /bəˈlowniy/ *n.* BALONEY.

Bol•she•vik (bōl′shə vik, -vēk′, bol′-) /ˈbowlʃəvɪk, -ˌviyk, ˈbɒl-/ *n.* [*count*], *pl.* **-viks, -vik•i** (-vik′ē, -vē′kē) /-ˌvɪkiy, -ˌviykiy/. **1. a.** a member of the radical part of the Russian Social-Democratic Workers' Party, 1903–17. **b.** (after 1918) a member of the Russian Communist Party. **2.** a member of any Communist Party. **3.** [*often: bolshevik*] *Disparaging.* any person with radical or revolutionary political ideas. —**Bol•she•vism** (bōl′shə viz′əm, bol′) /ˈbowlʃəˌvɪzəm, ˈbɒl/ *n.* [*noncount*] —**Bol′she•vist,** *n.* [*count*], *adj.*

bol•ster (bōl′stər) /ˈbowlstər/ *n.* [*count*] **1.** a long, tube-shaped pillow or cushion for a bed, etc. —*v.* [~ + *obj*] **2.** to add to, support, or uphold: *They bolstered their claim with new evidence.* —**bol′ster•er,** *n.* [*count*]

bolt (bōlt) /bowlt/ *n.* [*count*] **1.** any of several types of strong screws threaded to receive a nut and used to hold things together: *Tighten the bolts with a good wrench.* **2.** a movable bar slid into a socket to fasten a door, etc.: *The jailer threw back the bolt on the old, rusty prison door.* **3.** the part of a lock drawn back by the action of the key. **4.** a sudden dash, flight, or escape: *The mouse made a quick bolt to get away.* **5.** a length of fabric, woven goods, etc., esp. as it comes on a roll from the loom. **6.** (on a rifle) a sliding bar that pushes a cartridge into the firing chamber. **7.** a thunderbolt: *Jupiter hurling his bolts to earth.* —*v.* **8.** [~ + *obj*] to fasten with or as if with a bolt: *He bolted the muffler back onto the car.* **9.** [*no obj*] to make a sudden run or escape: *He bolted from the room.* **10.** to discontinue support (of) or participation (in); break with: [~ + *obj*]: *She decided to bolt the Republican party and vote Democratic.* [*no obj*]: *Twenty Democrats bolted on that vote.* **11.** to swallow (one's food or drink) quickly: [~ + *obj*]: *He bolted his breakfast and ran to catch his train.* [~ + *down* + *obj*]: *He bolted down his breakfast.* [~ + *obj* + *down*]: *He bolted his breakfast down.* —***Idiom.*** **12. bolt out of** or **from the blue,** a sudden and entirely unforeseen event: *The news that she would not be rehired came as a bolt from the blue.* **13. bolt upright,** stiffly or rigidly straight: *He sat bolt upright when the teacher caught him napping.*

bomb (bom) /bɒm/ *n.* [*count*] **1.** a case filled with an explosive and used as a weapon. **2.** an aerosol can and its contents: *A bug bomb contains spray that kills bugs.* **3.** *Slang.* **a.** an absolute failure: *That show was a complete bomb and closed in a few days.* **b.** *Brit.* a success; hit: *That show was a complete bomb and sold hundreds of* *tickets every night.* **4. the bomb,** [*count; singular*] **a.** ATOMIC BOMB. **b.** nuclear weapons thought of as a group. —*v.* **5.** [~ + *obj*] to hurl bombs at or drop bombs upon: *the day they bombed Pearl Harbor.* **6.** [~ + *obj*] *Slang.* to defeat decisively; trounce: *We played against our teachers and bombed them fifty-five to nothing.* **7.** [*no obj*] *Slang.* to fail completely; flop: *The play bombed in Boston.*

bom•bard (bom bärd′, bəm-) /bɒm'bɑrd, bəm-/ *v.* [~ + *obj*] **1.** to subject to bombardment: *began to bombard the coastline defenses twenty miles away.* **2.** to hit or attack with force: *The hurricane bombarded the coastline.* **3.** to attack verbally: *bombarded the candidate with questions.*

bom•bar•dier (bom′bər dēr′, -bə-) /ˌbɒmbər'dɪər, -bə-/ *n.* [*count*] the crew member of a bombing plane who operates the bombsight and releases the bombs.

bom•bard•ment (bom bärd′mənt, bəm-) /bɒm 'bɑrdmənt, bəm-/ *n.* **1.** [*count; noncount*] strong and steady attack by cannons or bombs: *The bombardment from the air continued all night.* **2.** an outpouring of complaints or questions, often experienced as harassment: [*count*]: *a bombardment of questions from reporters.* [*noncount*]: *the bombardment of cartoons and commercials on children.*

bom•bast (bom′bast) /'bɒmbæst/ *n.* [*noncount*] important-sounding, pompous words; rhetoric: *After all the bombast we couldn't figure out what he was trying to say.* —**bom•bas′tic,** *adj.*

bombed (bomd) /bɒmd/ *adj. Slang.* completely drunk or drugged: *so bombed he couldn't walk.*

bomb•er (bom′ər) /'bɒmər/ *n.* [*count*] **1.** an airplane equipped to carry and drop bombs. **2.** a person who drops or sets bombs, esp. as an illegal act: *a bunch of mad bombers and revolutionaries.*

bomb•proof (bom′pro͞of′) /'bɒmˌpruwf/ *adj.* **1.** strong enough to resist the explosive force of bombs: *a bombproof shelter.* —*v.* [~ + *obj*] **2.** to make bombproof: *bombproofed the shelter.*

bomb•shell (bom′shel′) /'bɒmˌʃɛl/ *n.* [*count*] something or someone having a sensational effect: *His resignation came as a bombshell.*

bo•na fide or **bo•na-fide** (bō′nə fīd′) /'bownəˌfayd/ *adj.* **1.** made, done, etc., in good faith; without fraud: *a bona fide statement of intent to sell.* **2.** authentic; genuine; real: *a bona fide sample of Lincoln's handwriting.*

bo•nan•za (bə nan′zə, bō-) /bə'nænzə, bow-/ *n.* [*count*], *pl.* **-zas.** a source or period of great and sudden wealth or luck: *a bonanza for lottery players.*

bon ap•pé•tit (bôn′ ap′ə tē′) /'bɔnˌ æpə'tiy/ *interj. French.* (used to wish someone a hearty appetite).

bon•bon (bon′bon′) /'bɒnˌbɒn/ *n.* [*count*] **1.** a small chocolate-coated candy. **2.** any candy.

bond (bond) /bɒnd/ *n.* **1.** [*count*] something that binds or holds together: *This superglue creates a bond strong enough to hold five hundred pounds.* **2.** [*count*] an agreement or feeling that unites one person to another, or to a way of behaving: *a baby's bond to its mother; the bonds of marriage.* **3.** [*count; usually singular*] firm assurance or promise: *My word is my bond.* **4.** [*count*] an agreement in which one guarantees to pay a sum of money on or before a specified day: *bought war bonds to support the war effort.* **5.** [*noncount*] money paid as a promise to appear in court; bail: *He met bond and was released.* **6.** [*count*] the attraction between atoms in a molecule: *a covalent bond.* —*v.* **7.** to connect, or bind, or join (two materials): [*no obj*]: *The two materials will bond if you heat them.* [~ + *obj*]: *Use this glue to bond the two materials.* **8.** [*no obj*] to establish a bond, as between a parent and offspring: *Immediately after birth the baby and its mother bond.* —**bond′ing,** *n.* [*noncount*]

bond•age (bon′dij) /'bɒndɪdʒ/ *n.* [*noncount*] slavery; the state of being bound by another: *a country held in bondage by the oppressor.*

bonds (bondz) /bɒndz/ *n.* [*plural*] chains or ropes used to tie up a prisoner.

bone (bōn) /bown/ *n., v.,* **boned, bon•ing.** —*n.* **1. a.** [*count*] one of the parts of the skeleton of an animal's body: *broke a bone in his arm.* **b.** [*noncount*] the hard, strong white tissue forming these parts: *This area is surrounded by bone.* **2.** [*count*] such a part from an animal that can be eaten: *some soup bones.* **3. bones,** [*plural*] **a.** the skeleton. **b.** a body: *to rest one's weary bones.* **4.** [*noncount*] the color of bone; ivory or off-white. —*v.* **5.** [~ + *obj*] to remove the bones from: *to bone a turkey.* **6. bone up,** [*no obj*] *Informal.* to study hard for; cram: *to bone up for an exam.* —***Idiom.*** **7. feel in one's bones,** [*feel* + *obj* + *in* + *one's* + *bones*] to be sure or certain of something without knowing why: *There's going to be a problem with her; I can feel it in my bones.* **8. have a bone to pick with someone,** to have a reason for arguing with someone: *I have a bone to pick with you: Why were all your workers taking two-hour lunches?* **9. make no bones about,** [~ + *obj*] to act or speak openly, without fear and without hesitating: *made no bones about her contempt for her boss.* **10. to the bone, a.** to the bare minimum: *Social services have been cut to the bone.* **b.** to an extreme degree; completely: *I'm chilled to the bone.*

bone′ chi′na, *n.* [*noncount*] fine, naturally white china made with powdered bone.

bone′-dry′, *adj.* [*usually: be* + ~] **1.** very dry. **2.** very thirsty.

bone•head (bōn′hed′) /'bownˌhɛd/ *Slang.* —*n.* [*count*] **1.** a stupid person; blockhead: *That bonehead even misspelled his name.* —*adj.* **2.** Also, **bone′head′ed.** characteristic of or done by such a person: *a real bonehead comment.* —**bone′head′ed•ness,** *n.* [*noncount*]

bone′ meal′ or **bone′meal′,** *n.* [*noncount*] bones ground to a powder, used as fertilizer or food.

bone′ of conten′tion, *n.* [*count*] *Informal.* a subject that is argued about; a point of dispute: *That type of test has been a bone of contention for years.*

bon•er (bō′nər) /'bownər/ *n.* [*count*] a stupid mistake; blunder.

bon•fire (bon′fīᵊr′) /'bɒnˌfayᵊr/ *n.* [*count*] a large fire built in the open air: *a big bonfire to celebrate the Fourth of July.*

bon•go (bong′gō, bông′-) /'bɒŋgow, 'bɔŋ-/ *n.* [*count*], *pl.* **-gos, -goes.** one of a pair of small drums, played by beating with the fingers: *musicians playing bongos.*

bon•kers (bong′kərz) /'bɒŋkərz/ *adj.* [*be/go* + ~] *Slang.* silly; mad; crazy: *He's completely bonkers over her.*

bon mot (bôɴ mō′) /'bɔ̃ mow/ *n.* [*count*], *pl.* **bons mots** (bôɴ mōz′) /'bɔ̃ mowz/. a clever remark or comment.

bon•net (bon′it) /'bɒnɪt/ *n.* [*count*] **1.** a hat tying under the chin and framing the face. **2.** *Brit.* an automobile hood: *Pop open the bonnet and let's see what's wrong.*

bon•ny (bon′ē) /'bɒniy/ *adj.,* **-ni•er, -ni•est.** *Chiefly Brit.* **1.** attractive; handsome; pretty: *a bonny lass and laddie (= a pretty girl and handsome boy).* **2.** pleasing; agreeable: *a bonny idea.*

bon•sai (bon sī′, bon′sī) /bɒn'say, 'bɒnsay/ *n., pl.* **-sai. 1.** [*count*] a tree or shrub made very small by cutting back the roots and pinching the branches: *a number of bonsai in the botanical gardens.* **2.** [*noncount*] the art of growing such a plant: *courses in bonsai.*

bo•nus (bō′nəs) /'bownəs/ *n.* [*count*], *pl.* **-nus•es.** something given over and above the normal or expected, esp. a sum of money: *received a handsome bonus for clinching the deal.*

bon vo•yage (bon′voi äzh′, bôɴ′) /'bɒnvɔy'ɑʒ, 'bɔ̃/ *interj.* (used to wish someone a pleasant trip): *Bon voyage! See you when you get back.*

bon•y (bō′nē) /'bowniy/ *adj.,* **-i•er, -i•est. 1.** of or like bone. **2.** full of bones: *This fish is very bony.* **3.** having bones that stick out; big-boned: *bony knees.* **4.** skinny; gaunt; emaciated: *a tall, bony fellow in old clothes.* —**bon′i•ness,** *n.* [*noncount*]

boo (bo͞o) /buw/ *interj., n., pl.* **boos,** *v.* —*interj.* **1.** (used to express contempt or disapproval or to startle or frighten): *"Boo! Did I scare you?" she asked.* —*n.* [*count*] **2.** an exclamation of contempt or disapproval: *a boo from the bleachers.* —*v.* **3.** to cry "boo" (at someone): [*no obj*]: *The fans booed when it became clear that their team would lose again.* [~ + *obj*]: *The fans booed the pitcher.*

boob[1] (bo͞ob) /buwb/ *Slang.* —*n.* [*count*] **1.** a fool or stupid person. —*v.* [*no obj*] **2.** *Brit.* to blunder: *He boobed again and failed that test.*

boob[2] (bo͞ob) /buwb/ *n.* [*count*] *Slang (sometimes vulgar).* a female breast.

boo-boo (bo͞o′bo͞o′) /'buwˌbuw/ *n.* [*count*], *pl.* **-boos.** *Slang.* **1.** a stupid mistake; blunder. **2.** a minor injury.

boob′ tube′, *n. Slang.* **1.** [*noncount; usually: the* + ~] television: *What's on the boob tube tonight?* **2.** [*count; usually singular*] a television set: *sat in front of the boob tube for hours.*

boo•by[1] (bo͞o′bē) /'buwbiy/ *n.* [*count*], *pl.* **-bies. 1.** a stupid person; dunce. **2.** a black- or brown-and-white, goose-sized bird living near the sea.

boob•y[2] (bo͞o′bē) /'buwbiy/ *n.* [*count*], *pl.* **boob•ies.** *Slang (sometimes vulgar).* a female breast.

boo′by prize′, *n.* [*count*] a prize given as a joke to the one that comes in last in a game: *The booby prize was actually a pair of tickets to a play.*

boo′by trap′, *n.* [*count*] **1.** a hidden bomb set off when a person who does not know it is there steps on it, touches a wire, or the like: *used a metal detector to search for booby traps.* **2.** any hidden trap set for a person who does not expect it: *The booby trap—a bucket of cold water over the partly open door—caught the next person who came in.* —**boo′by-trap′, -trapped, -trap•ping,** *v.* [~ + *obj*]: *to booby-trap a jungle path.*

boo•dle (bo͞od′l) /ˈbuwdl̩/ *n.* [*count; usually singular*] **1.** collection; bunch: *Send the whole boodle back to the factory.* **2.** a large quantity of something, esp. money.

boog•ey•man (bo͝og′ē man′) /ˈbʊgiyˌmæn/ *n., pl.* **-men.** BOGEYMAN.

boog•ie (bo͝og′ē) /ˈbʊgiy/ *n., v.,* **-ied, -ie•ing.** —*n.* [*noncount*] **1.** BOOGIE-WOOGIE. **2.** a lively form of rock, based on the blues. —*v.* [*no obj*] **3.** to dance to rock music: *They boogied all night long.* **4.** *Slang.* to go: *Let's boogie on down to the corner.*

boog•ie-woog•ie (bo͝og′ē wo͝og′ē) /ˈbʊgiyˈwʊgiy/ *n.* [*noncount*] a style of jazz piano blues that constantly repeats a bass line while the higher music parts freely improvise on the melody.

boo•hoo (bo͞o′ho͞o′) /ˌbuwˈhuw/ *v.,* **-hooed, -hoo•ing,** *n., pl.* **-hoos.** *Informal.* —*v.* [*no obj*] **1.** to cry or sob noisily; blubber: *always boohooing about all his troubles.* —*n.* [*count*] **2.** the sound of noisy weeping: *Boohoos echoed from the children's bedroom.*

book (bo͝ok) /bʊk/ *n.* [*count*] **1.** a work printed on sheets of paper bound together within covers: *a book of poems.* See illustration at SCHOOL. **2.** a number of sheets of paper bound together, for writing, etc.: *a spiral book for notes.* **3.** a set or packet of tickets, checks, etc., bound together like a book: *a book of matches.* **4.** a division of a literary work, esp. one of the larger divisions: *the books of the Bible.* **5. the Book,** the Bible. **6. the book,** a set of rules, standards, or actions to be followed: *He knows every trick in the book by now.* **7.** the words or text of a musical piece; the script or story of a play. **8. books,** [*plural*] the financial records of a business, etc.: *adjusting the books to hide the fact that money was being taken.* —*v.* **9.** [~ + *obj*] to register, esp. after being arrested: *booked him for manslaughter.* **10.** [~ + *obj*] to make a reservation for (a hotel room, plane trip, etc.): *We booked several flights just to be sure.* **11.** [~ + *obj*] to register or list (a person) for a hotel room, passage on a ship, an appointment, etc.: *booked us on the next cruise.* **12.** [~ + *obj*] to engage for one or more performances: *We booked that new rock group.* **13. book in** (or **out**), [*no obj*] to sign in (or out), as at a hotel, etc.: *We booked in at the Savoy.* **14. book up,** [~ + *obj*] to sell or buy out, fill up, or the like: *booked up the hotel for the World Series.* —*adj.* [*before a noun*] **15.** of, relating to, or dealing with books: *a book salesman.* **16.** derived or learned entirely from books: *book knowledge.* —***Idiom.*** **17. by the book,** according to the established form: *Do it by the book for now; later we can try shortcuts or new tricks.* **18. in one's book,** according to one's personal judgment: *In my book, she was simply the greatest actress of all time.* **19. know** or **read like a book,** to know or understand (someone or something) completely: *knew the city like a book.* **20. off the books,** done or performed (esp. for cash) without records, to avoid income tax: *working for him off the books.* **21. one for the book(s),** something extraordinary: *That triple play in the first inning was one for the books.*

book•bind•ing (bo͝ok′bīn′ding) /ˈbʊkˌbayndɪŋ/ *n.* [*noncount*] **1.** the process or art of binding books. **2.** the binding on a book. —**book′bind′er,** *n.* [*count*] —**book′-bind′er•y,** *n.* [*count*], *pl.* **-er•ies.**

book•case (bo͝ok′kās′) /ˈbʊkˌkeys/ *n.* [*count*] a set of shelves for books: *bookcases overflowing with books.* See illustration at OFFICE.

book′ club′, *n.* [*count*] a company that sells books to its members through the mail and often at a discount.

book•end (bo͝ok′end′) /ˈbʊkˌɛnd/ *n.* [*count*] a support placed at each end of a row of books to hold them upright.

book•ie (bo͝ok′ē) /ˈbʊkiy/ *n.* BOOKMAKER (def. 1).

book•ing (bo͝ok′ing) /ˈbʊkɪŋ/ *n.* [*count*] **1.** a contract or scheduled performance of a professional entertainer: *His booking at the nightclub was in doubt after his arrest.* **2.** RESERVATION (def. 4): *Please confirm the booking we made last week for flight 270.*

book•ish (bo͝ok′ish) /ˈbʊkɪʃ/ *adj.* **1.** greatly enjoying reading or studying: *our bookish young daughter.* **2.** more acquainted with books than with real life: *the bookish life of a university professor.* **3.** very stiff and overly formal: *a bookish way of speaking.*

book•keep•ing (bo͝ok′kē′ping) /ˈbʊkˌkiypɪŋ/ *n.* [*noncount*] the system or occupation of keeping detailed records of a company's business dealings. —**book′keep′-er,** *n.* [*count*]

book•let (bo͝ok′lit) /ˈbʊklɪt/ *n.* [*count*] a little book, esp. one with paper covers; pamphlet: *The booklet on Prague told us which sights to see during the winter.*

book•mak•er (bo͝ok′mā′kər) /ˈbʊkˌmeykər/ *n.* [*count*] **1.** a person who makes a business of accepting the bets of others on sports contests, esp. illegally: *The bookmakers are not doing good business on this fight; everyone expects the champ to lose, so no one is betting.* **2.** a person who designs, prints, or manufactures books. —**book′mak′ing,** *n.* [*noncount*], *adj.*

book•mark (bo͝ok′märk′) /ˈbʊkˌmɑrk/ *n.* [*count*] a marker between the pages of a book to mark one's place.

book•mo•bile (bo͝ok′mə bēl′, -mō-) /ˈbʊkməˌbiyl, -mow-/ *n.* [*count*] a motor vehicle for carrying books as a traveling library.

book•sell•er (bo͝ok′sel′ər) /ˈbʊkˌsɛlər/ *n.* [*count*] one who sells books, esp. the proprietor of a bookstore.

book•shelf (bo͝ok′shelf′) /ˈbʊkˌʃɛlf/ *n.* [*count*], *pl.* **-shelves.** a shelf for holding books, esp. one of the shelves in a bookcase.

book•store (bo͝ok′stôr′, -stōr′) /ˈbʊkˌstɔr, -ˌstowr/ *n.* [*count*] a store where books are sold. Also called **book•shop** (bo͝ok′shop′) /ˈbʊkˌʃɒp/.

book′ val′ue, *n.* [*count*] the value of a business, property, etc., as shown on a financial statement or established list: *a car with a low book value.*

book•worm (bo͝ok′wûrm′) /ˈbʊkˌwɜrm/ *n.* [*count*] **1.** one who greatly enjoys reading or studying. **2.** any of various insects that feed on books.

boom[1] (bo͞om) /buwm/ *v.* **1.** to make a deep, echoing sound: [*no obj*]: *The cannons boomed.* [~ + *obj*]: *The cannons boomed a deafening roar.* **2.** to announce or say with a booming sound or voice: [*used with quotations*]: *"Back inside!" he boomed as the tornado struck.* [~ + *out* + *obj*]: *The guns boomed out an answer to the attack.* [*no obj;* ~ + (*out*)]: *His voice boomed (out) from his office.* **3.** [*no obj*] to progress or increase quickly and strongly: *Business is booming.* —*n.* [*count*] **4.** a deep, long, echoing sound: *the booms from the battleship's guns.* **5.** a rapid increase in sales, worth, etc.: *a housing boom.* **6.** a period of rapid economic growth: *the boom years of prosperity.* —**boom′ing,** *adj.*: *a deep, booming voice.*

boom[2] (bo͞om) /buwm/ *n.* [*count*] **1.** a pole sticking out from a ship's mast and used to extend sails, handle cargo, etc. **2.** a chain, cable, or anything that serves to block the passage of ships. **3.** (on a motion-picture or television stage) a long pole for holding and moving a microphone or camera. —***Idiom.*** **4. lower the boom,** to act strongly to punish wrongdoing: *finally lowered the boom on the drug dealers.*

boo•mer•ang (bo͞o′mə rang′) /ˈbuwməˌræŋ/ *n.* [*count*] **1.** a curved piece of wood used by the Australian Aborigines as a throwing club that can be thrown so as to return to the thrower. **2.** something, as a scheme, that does injury to the person who started it: *His call for greater efficiency turned out to be a boomerang when his own department was shown to be the least efficient.* —*v.* **3.** to cause harm to the person who starts an action; backfire: [*no obj*]: *The plan boomeranged when we were trapped instead of our victim.* [~ + *on* + *obj*]: *The plan boomeranged on us.*

boon (bo͞on) /buwn/ *n.* [*count; usually singular*] **1.** something to be thankful for; a blessing; benefit: *The lower fares are a boon to senior citizens.* **2.** something that is asked for; a favor.

boon•docks (bo͞on′doks′) /ˈbuwnˌdɒks/ *n.* [*the* + ~] a remote area: *Instead of promoting him, they sent him off to the boondocks.*

boon•dog•gle (bo͞on′dog′əl, -dô′gəl) /ˈbuwnˌdɒgəl, -ˌdɔgəl/ *n., v.,* **-gled, -gling.** —*n.* [*count*] **1.** work of no real value done to look busy, esp. a government project. —*v.* **2.** [~ + *obj*] to deceive or attempt to deceive: *We were all boondoggled by his fast talk.* **3.** [*no obj*] to do work of little value merely to keep or look busy. —**boon′dog′gler,** *n.* [*count*]

boon•ies (bo͞o′nēz) /ˈbuwniyz/ *n.* [*the* + ~] *Informal.* a remote area; the boondocks: *transferred him to the boonies.*

boor (bŏŏr) /bʊr/ *n.* [*count*] a rude, impolite, or unmannerly person. —**boor′ish,** *adj.* —**boor′ish•ly,** *adv.* —**boor′ish•ness,** *n.* [*count*]

boost (bo͞ost) /buwst/ *v.* [~ + *obj*] **1.** to lift by pushing from below: *I boosted the youngster into the top of her bunk bed.* **2.** to help (someone) by speaking well of: *boosted his friend as likely to win the election.* **3.** to increase; raise: *to boost prices.* —*n.* [*count*] **4.** an upward shove or raise; lift: *gave him a little boost into his highchair.* **5.** an increase; rise: *a boost in prices.* **6.** an act or remark that helps one's morale, efforts, etc.: *After praise from the coach, the whole team felt a boost in morale.*

boost•er (bo͞o′stər) /ˈbuwstər/ *n.* [*count*] **1.** a person or thing that boosts, esp. an energetic supporter: *The president's biggest booster was the senator from his home state.* **2.** the first stage of a rocket and the principal source of thrust. **3.** Also called **boost′er shot′.** a dose of a medicine given to maintain a previous one: *a booster shot for tetanus.*

boot¹ (bo͞ot) /buwt/ *n.* [*count*] **1.** a strong, heavy shoe for the foot and all or part of the leg: *hiking boots; winter boots.* See illustration at CLOTHING. **2.** a shoe, esp. one of rubber worn over another shoe for protection against wetness, etc. **3.** *Brit.* the trunk of an automobile. **4.** a metal device used on an illegally parked car that, when attached to a wheel, keeps it from moving. **5.** a U.S. Navy or Marine recruit. **6.** a kick: *a quick boot to the ball.* **7. the boot,** *Slang.* a dismissal or discharge: *to give someone the boot for always being late.* —*v.* [~ + *obj*] **8.** to kick; drive by kicking: *booted the ball all the way to the goal line.* **9.** to fumble or fail to catch (a baseball): *booted several easy ground balls.* **10.** to put boots on; equip or provide with boots. **11.** Also, **bootstrap.** to start (a computer) by loading the operating system: *Put in your starting disk and boot the computer by pressing Control.* **12.** *Slang.* to dismiss; discharge: *He was booted from his third job in a month.* —***Idiom.*** **13. die with one's boots on,** to die while active in one's work; esp., in battle. **14. get the boot,** *Informal.* to be fired from a job: *He got the boot after only five months.* **15. lick someone's boots,** to flatter (someone) too much; toady: *always licking the manager's boots.*

boot² (bo͞ot) /buwt/ *n.* [*noncount*] —***Idiom.*** **to boot,** in addition; besides: *My best friend is charming, witty, and a doctor to boot.*

boot′ camp′, *n.* a camp for training U.S. Navy or Marine recruits: [*no article*]: *He went to boot camp for six weeks.* [*count*]: *He went to several boot camps as part of his fact-finding mission.*

boot•ee (bo͞o′tē) /ˈbuwtiy/ *n.* [*count*], *pl.* **-tees.** Also, **bootie.** a baby's socklike shoe, usually knitted or crocheted.

booth (bo͞oth) /buwθ/ *n.* [*count*], *pl.* **booths** (bo͞o*th*z, bo͞oths). **1.** a stall or small tent for the sale or display of goods: *booths at the flea market.* **2.** a small compartment or boxlike room intended for a specific use by one occupant: *a telephone booth; a voting booth.* **3.** a partly enclosed compartment, as in a restaurant: *Do you want to sit in a booth or at the counter?*

boot•leg (bo͞ot′leg′) /ˈbuwt,lɛg/ *n., v.,* **-legged, -leg•ging,** *adj.* —*n.* [*noncount*] **1.** alcoholic liquor unlawfully made, sold, or transported. **2.** something, such as a CD, made, reproduced, or sold unlawfully. —*v.* **3.** to make, transport, sell, or deal in (goods) unlawfully: [~ + *obj*]: *They bootlegged the tapes for huge profits.* [*no obj*]: *bootlegging for years before anyone noticed.* —*adj.* [*before a noun*] **4.** made, sold, or transported unlawfully: *bootleg whiskey.* —**boot′leg′ger,** *n.* [*count*]

boot•strap (bo͞ot′strap′) /ˈbuwt,stræp/ *n., adj., v.,* **-strapped, -strap•ping.** —*n.* [*count*] **1.** a loop sewn at the top or on each side of a boot to make it easier to pull the boot on. —*adj.* [*before a noun*] **2.** relying on one's own efforts: *mounted a bootstrap operation running for office.* —*v.* [~ + *obj*] **3.** *Computers.* BOOT¹ (def. 12). —***Idiom.*** **4. pull oneself up by one's (own) bootstraps,** to become a success through one's own efforts: *The congressman claimed that he had pulled himself up by his own bootstraps.*

boo•ty (bo͞o′tē) /ˈbuwtiy/ *n.* [*noncount*] valuable things or goods taken by thieves or from an enemy in war; plunder; pillage: *slaves and gold taken as booty.*

booze (bo͞oz) /buwz/ *n., v.,* **boozed, booz•ing.** *Informal.* —*n.* **1.** [*noncount*] any alcoholic drink, as whiskey: *"Too much booze," she mumbled.* **2.** [*count*] time spent drinking alcoholic drinks: *in a foggy booze of partying.* —*v.* [*no obj*] **3.** to drink alcoholic liquor to excess: *went out boozing late last night.* —***Idiom.*** **4. booze it up,** [*no obj*] to drink excessively: *were boozing it up all night long.* —**booz′er,** *n.* [*count*]

bop¹ (bop) /bɒp/ *n., v.,* **bopped, bop•ping.** —*n.* [*noncount*] **1.** Also called **bebop.** jazz music characterized by dissonant harmonies, fast speeds, and complex rhythms and melodies. —*v.* [*no obj*] **2.** to dance to bop music. **3.** *Slang.* to move, go, or proceed: *They bopped down the street.*

bop² (bop) /bɒp/ *v.,* **bopped, bop•ping,** *n. Slang.* —*v.* [~ + *obj*] **1.** to strike, as with the fist or a stick; hit: *cartoon characters bopping each other on the head.* —*n.* [*count*] **2.** a blow: *a few bops on the head.*

bop•per (bop′ər) /ˈbɒpər/ *n.* TEENYBOPPER.

bo•rax (bôr′aks, -əks, bōr′-) /ˈbɔræks, -əks, ˈbowr-/ *n.* [*noncount*] white powder used as a cleansing agent.

bor•del•lo (bôr del′ō) /bɔrˈdɛlow/ *n.* [*count*], *pl.* **-los.** a brothel.

bor•der (bôr′dər) /ˈbɔrdər/ *n.* [*count*] **1.** the part or edge of a surface that forms its outer boundary: *a book with a red cover and a black border; a border of flowers across their front lawn.* **2.** the line that separates one country, province, etc., from another: *The border between the two countries cuts across this mountain range.* **3.** the land that lies along the boundary line: *The pilots were able to flee across the border into Switzerland.* —*v.* **4.** [~ + *obj*] to form a border along: *Tall trees bordered the road.* **5.** to lie on the border (of); share a border (with): [~ + *obj*]: *Sweden borders Norway and Finland.* [~ + *on* + *obj*]: *Sweden borders on Norway and Finland.* **6. border on,** [~ + *on* + *obj*] to approach (something) closely in character; be almost the same as: *This ridiculous situation borders on comedy.* —**Syn.** See BOUNDARY.

bor•der•line (bôr′dər līn′) /ˈbɔrdər,layn/ *n.* [*count*] **1.** Also, **bor′der line′.** a boundary line; something marking a division. **2.** [*usually singular*] an uncertain condition between one situation and another: *at the borderline of sleep and wakefulness.* —*adj.* [*before a noun*] **3.** on or near a border or boundary. **4.** not quite meeting accepted standards: *borderline alcoholism (= in between alcoholism and its absence). I had several borderline applications to decide on; should we interview them or not?*

bore¹ (bôr, bōr) /bɔr, bowr/ *v.,* **bored, bor•ing,** *n.* —*v.* **1.** to pierce (a solid substance) with a drill: [~ + *obj*]: *bored a hole into the wall.* [*no obj*]: *bored through the walls.* **2.** [~ + *obj*] to make (a tunnel, etc.) by cutting through a core of material: *bored a tunnel under the English Channel.* **3.** [~ + *through* + *obj*] to move forward slowly and steadily: *bored through the crowd of people.* **4.** [~ + *into* + *obj*] to look or stare deeply at: *Her eyes bored straight into mine.* —*n.* **5.** [*count*] a hole made by boring. **6.** [*after a number*] the inside diameter of a hole or hollow round object, such as a gun barrel: *a 12-bore shotgun (= a shotgun in which the gun barrel is 12 gauge in diameter).*

bore² (bôr, bōr) /bɔr, bowr/ *v.,* **bored, bor•ing,** *n.* —*v.* [~ + *obj*] **1.** to make (someone) weary by dullness, etc.: *The long speech bored me.* —*n.* [*count*] **2.** a dull, tiresome, or uninteresting person: *She's such a bore.* **3.** something that causes boredom or annoyance: *The play was a bore.* —**Related Words.** BORE is a noun and a verb, BORING and BORED are adjectives, BOREDOM is a noun: *He's a terrible bore. The movie bored him. The movie was boring. The bored students fell asleep during his lecture. The kids were dying of boredom, cooped up in the house all day.*

bore³ (bôr, bōr) /bɔr, bowr/ *v.* a pt. of BEAR¹.

bored (bôrd, bōrd) /bɔrd, bowrd/ *adj.* made tired by dullness: *bored kids at home watching TV.* [*be* + ~ + *with*]: *students bored with the substitute teacher.*

bore•dom (bôr′dəm, bōr′-) /ˈbɔrdəm, ˈbowr-/ *n.* [*noncount*] the state of being bored: *the boredom of staying home every day.*

bor•er (bôr′ər, bōr′-) /ˈbɔrər, ˈbowr-/ *n.* [*count*] **1.** a person or thing that pierces. **2.** a tool used for boring; auger.

bo′ric ac′id (bôr′ik, bōr′-) /ˈbɔrɪk, ˈbowr-/ *n.* [*noncount*] a white, crystalline acid, H_3BO_3, used chiefly in making ceramics.

bor•ing (bôr′ing, bōr′-) /ˈbɔrɪŋ, ˈbowr-/ *adj.* causing boredom: *a boring speech; a boring teacher.* —**bor′ing•ly,** *adv.: a boringly useless speech.*

born (bôrn) /bɔrn/ *adj.* **1.** [*be* + ~] brought forth by birth: *was born on October 27.* **2.** [*be* + ~] brought into existence: *That's when the idea was born.* **3.** possessing from birth the quality or character stated: [*before a noun*]: *a born musician; a born loser.* [*be* + ~ + *to* + *verb*]: *I was born to love her.* **4.** (used after a place name and before a noun to describe where the noun that follows was born): *a German-born scientist (= a scientist who was born in Germany).* —*v.* **5.** a pp. of BEAR[1]. —***Idiom.*** **6. be born of,** [~ + *obj*] to exist as a result of: *He finished the task with a speed that was born of experience.* **7. be born yesterday,** to be naive or inexperienced: *Don't tell me your dog ate your homework; I wasn't born yesterday.* —**Usage.** See BEAR[1].

born′-again′, *adj.* [*often: before a noun*] **1.** pledging oneself to (Christian) faith through an intensely religious experience: *became a born-again Christian after the ordeal.* **2.** characterized by newly adopted enthusiasm: *became a born-again conservative.*

borne (bôrn, bōrn) /bɔrn, bowrn/ *v.* a pp. of BEAR[1]. —**Usage.** See BEAR[1].

bo•ron (bôr′on, bōr′-) /ˈbɔrɒn, ˈbowr-/ *n.* [*noncount*] a nonmetallic element occurring in nature only in combination, as in borax or boric acid, and used in alloys and nuclear reactors.

bor•ough (bûr′ō, bur′ō) /ˈbɜrow, ˈbʌrow/ *n.* [*count*] **1.** (in certain U.S. states) a self-governing town or village. **2.** one of the five counties of New York City: *The Bronx is one of the boroughs of New York City.* **3.** (in Great Britain) **a.** a self-governing, incorporated urban community. **b.** a town or constituency represented by a Member of Parliament.

bor•row (bor′ō, bôr′ō) /ˈbɒrow, ˈbɔrow/ *v.* **1.** to obtain (something) with a promise to return it: [~ + *obj*]: *Can I borrow a pencil?* [*no obj*]: *Consumers should avoid borrowing.* **2.** [~ + *obj*] to take or adopt as one's own: *English borrowed many words from French.* **3.** (in subtraction) to take from one column (such as the tens column) and add to the next lower column (such as the ones or units column): [~ + *obj*]: *24 minus 9. Let's see. Borrow one ten and add it to the four to get fourteen, then subtract nine from fourteen, that's five.* [*no obj*]: *Did you learn how to borrow yet in school?* —**bor′row•er,** *n.* [*count*]: *Big borrowers won't get a tax break.* —**Usage.** Compare BORROW and LEND. One way to keep the meanings distinct is to think of BORROW as "take," while LEND is "give." So you can *borrow* something you don't have, and you can *lend* something you do have.

bor•row•ing (bor′ō ing, bôr′-) /ˈbɒrowɪŋ, ˈbɔr-/ *n.* **1.** [*noncount*] the act of borrowing money: *Government does too much borrowing and spending.* **2.** [*count*] something borrowed, as a foreign word or phrase: *In Swahili some days of the week are borrowings from Arabic.*

borscht (bôrsht) /bɔrʃt/ also **borsch** (bôrsh) /bɔrʃ/ **borshch** (bôrsh, bôrshch) /bɔrʃ, bɔrʃtʃ/ *n.* [*noncount*] any of various E European soups made with beets.

bosh (bosh) /bɒʃ/ *n.* [*noncount*] nonsense: *No one believes that; it's just bosh.*

bo's'n (bō′sən) /ˈbowsən/ *n.* BOATSWAIN.

bos•om (bo͝oz′əm, bo͞o′zəm) /ˈbʊzəm, ˈbuwzəm/ *n.* [*count*] **1.** the breast of a human being: *The father held the baby to his bosom.* **2.** the breasts of a woman: *She had a large bosom and wide hips.* **3.** the part of a garment that covers the breast. **4.** the breast thought of as the center of feelings or emotions; the soul; the heart: *Anger lay in her bosom.* **5.** a state of enclosing warmth or closeness: *taken into the bosom of the family.* —*adj.* **6.** [*before a noun*] intimate or confidential: *a bosom friend.*

bos•om•y (bo͝oz′ə mē, bo͞o′zə-) /ˈbʊzəmiy, ˈbuwzə-/ *adj.* having a large bosom: *a bosomy woman.*

boss (bôs, bos) /bɔs, bɒs/ *n.* [*count*] **1.** a person who employs or superintends workers: *He was my boss for four years.* **2.** a politician who controls a party organization: *the boss of the South Side.* **3.** a person who is in charge: *Who's the boss in this house?* —*v.* **4.** [~ + *obj*] to be master of or over; control: *likes to boss the show.* **5.** to order around in an unfriendly and arrogant way: [~ + *obj* + *around*]: *She likes to boss her kids around.* [~ + *around* + *obj*]: *to boss around the kids.*

bos•sa no•va (bos′ə nō′və, bô′sə) /ˈbɒsˈə nowvə, ˈbɔsə/ *n., pl.* **bossa no•vas. 1.** [*noncount*] jazz-influenced music from Brazil, related in rhythm to the samba. **2.** [*count*] a dance performed to this music.

boss•y (bô′sē, bos′ē) /ˈbɔsiy, ˈbɒsiy/ *adj.,* **-i•er, -i•est.** given to ordering people about; domineering. —**boss•i•ly** (bô′sə lē, bos′ə-) /ˈbɔsəliy, ˈbɒsə-/ *adv.* —**boss′i•ness,** *n.* [*noncount*]

bo•sun (bō′sən) /ˈbowsən/ *n.* BOATSWAIN.

bot., an abbreviation of: **1.** botanical. **2.** botanist.

-botan-, *root.* *-botan-* comes from Greek, where it has the meaning "plant, herb." This meaning is found in such words as: BOTANICAL, BOTANIST, BOTANY.

bo•tan•i•cal (bə tan′i kəl) /bəˈtænɪkəl/ *adj.* [*usually: before a noun*] Also, **bo•tan′ic. 1.** of, relating to, or derived from plants: *beautiful botanical gardens.* **2.** of or relating to botany: *botanical research.* See -BOTAN-.

bot•a•nist (bot′n ist) /ˈbɒtn̩ɪst/ *n.* [*count*] a specialist in botany. See -BOTAN-.

bot•a•ny (bot′n ē) /ˈbɒtn̩iy/ *n.* [*noncount*] the biological science of plant life. See -BOTAN-.

botch (boch) /bɒtʃ/ *v.* **1.** to spoil by poor or clumsy work; bungle: [~ + *obj*]: *He botched the throw to first base.* [~ + *up* + *obj*]: *He botched up every job we gave him.* [~ + *obj* + *up*]: *He botched it up; I can tell.* [*no obj;* ~ + *up*]: *He always botches up.* —*n.* [*count*] **2.** a poor piece of work; mess; bungle: *He's made a real botch of that paint job.*

both (bōth) /bowθ/ *adj.* [*before a noun*] **1.** [~ + *(the +) plural noun*] one and the other; two together: *I met both sisters. I met both the sisters.* —*pron.* **2.** the one as well as the other: *Both were ill. I'll work or play but I can't do both.* [~ + *of*]: *Both of us were ill. I want to see both of you now.* —*conj.* **3.** alike; equally: *I am both ready and willing. I can speak both English and Russian.*

both•er (bo*th*′ər) /ˈbɒðər/ *v.* **1.** [~ + *obj*] to give trouble to: *Noise bothers me.* **2.** [~ + *obj*] to bewilder; confuse: *His inability to get the joke bothered him.* **3.** to worry; distress: [*It* + ~ + *obj* + *that clause*]: *It bothers me that no one told us the bus wouldn't show up.* **4.** [*used with a negative word or phrase, or in questions*] to take the trouble; trouble or inconvenience oneself: [~ + *about/with* + *obj*]: *Don't bother with her; she's just a kid.* [~ + *to* + *verb*]: *Don't bother to call.* [~ + *verb-ing*]: *Should I bother finishing this book?* —*n.* **5.** [*noncount*] something or someone troublesome: *some bother with our neighbor that required us to call the police.* **6.** [*noncount*] effort, work, or worry: *Gardening takes more bother than it's worth.* **7.** [*count; usually singular*] a worried or perplexed state: *Don't get into such a bother!* —*interj.* **8.** *Chiefly Brit.* (used to express mild irritation): *Oh bother! I've dropped my pen.* —***Idiom.*** **9. can't be bothered,** (used to emphasize that the action that follows is unnecessary): *She can't be bothered drying all those dishes.*

both•er•some (bo*th*′ər səm) /ˈbɒðərsəm/ *adj.* causing worry; troublesome: *a bothersome problem.*

bot•tle (bot′l) /ˈbɒtl̩/ *n., v.,* **-tled, -tling.** —*n.* [*count*] **1.** a container for holding liquids, having a neck and mouth and made of glass or plastic: *Bring your empty bottles back to the store.* **2.** the contents or capacity of such a container: *to drink a whole bottle of wine.* **3.** bottled milk formulas or substitutes given to infants instead of mother's milk: *raised on the bottle.* —*v.* **4.** [~ + *obj*] to put into or seal in a bottle: *to bottle grape juice.* **5. bottle up,** [~ + *up* + *obj*] to hold in, control, or keep back: *Don't bottle up your anger; let it out.* [~ + *obj* + *up*]: *to bottle it up inside.* —***Idiom.*** **6. hit the bottle,** *Slang.* to drink alcohol to excess: *He's hitting the bottle again; you can tell from the way he walks.*

bot•tle•neck (bot′l nek′) /ˈbɒtl̩ˌnɛk/ *n.* [*count*] **1.** a narrow passageway, such as on a highway where lanes merge, causing traffic to slow or stop: *the bottleneck on the bridge where tolls are collected.* **2.** a place or stage at which progress is slowed: *hit a bottleneck in the production of that new drug.*

bot•tom (bot′əm) /ˈbɒtəm/ *n.* [*count; usually: the* + ~] **1.** the lowest or deepest part of anything: *the bottom of a page.* **2.** the under or lower side; underside: *the bottom of a keyboard.* **3.** [*singular; the* + ~] the ground under a body of water: *found the gangster's body at the bottom of the river.* **4.** the end farthest from an entrance; the far end: *the house at the bottom of the road.* **5.** the seat of a chair: *a piece of gum on the bottom of the chair.* **6.** *Informal.* the buttocks; rump. **7. bottoms,** [*plural; used with a plural verb*] the trousers or pants of a pair of pajamas: *The pajama bottoms have a drawstring around the waist.* **8.** the second half of an inning in baseball: *the bottom of the sixth.* **9.** the lowest level of dignity or status: *The workers at the bottom do all the work.* —*v.* **10. bottom out,** [*no obj*] to reach the lowest state or level: *The sagging economy has finally bottomed out.* —*adj.* [*before a noun*] **11.** of or relating to the bottom; on or at the bottom: *the bottom floor.* **12.** lowest: *the bottom button on a shirt.* —***Idiom.*** **13. at bottom,** in reality; basically: *a nice guy at bottom.* **14. at the bottom of,** really causing; responsible for: *Who is at the bottom of all these leaks to the media?* **15. bet one's bottom dollar, a.** to bet the last of one's money or resources. **b.** to be positive or assured: *You can bet your bottom dollar I'll* *be on time to receive the money!* **16. bottoms up.** This expression is used before swallowing a drink: *"Bottoms up," he said and downed his drink.* **17. from the bottom of one's heart,** very sincerely: *I want to thank you from the bottom of my heart.* **18. get to the bottom of,** [~ + *obj*] to determine the cause of: *wanted to get to the bottom of this mystery.*

bot•tom•less (bot′əm lis) /'bɒtəmlɪs/ *adj.* **1.** lacking a bottom. **2.** very deep: *the bottomless ocean.* **3.** seemingly unlimited: *a bottomless supply of money.* **4. a.** nude or nearly nude below the waist: *a bottomless dancer.* **b.** featuring bottomless entertainers: *a bottomless bar.*

bot′tom line′, *n.* [*count*] **1.** the last line of a financial statement, used for showing net profit or loss. **2.** the deciding or crucial factor: *The bottom line is the president doesn't want to hire you.* **3.** the result or outcome: *The bottom line was the same: The Jets lost again.* —**bot′-tom-line′,** *adj.* [*usually before a noun*]: *a bottom-line mentality, interested only in profits or losses.*

bot•u•lism (boch′ə liz′əm) /'bɒtʃəˌlɪzəm/ *n.* [*noncount*] a sometimes fatal disease caused by eating preserved foods that have been spoiled.

bou•doir (bo͞o′dwär, -dwôr) /'buwdwɑr, -dwɔr/ *n.* [*count*] a woman's bedroom or private sitting room.

bouf•fant (bo͞o fänt′) /buw'fɑnt/ *adj.* [*usually before a noun*] **1.** puffed out; full: *a bouffant hairstyle.* —*n.* [*count*] **2.** a woman's hairstyle in which the hair has an overall puffed-out appearance.

bough (bou) /baw/ *n.* [*count*] a branch of a tree, esp. one of the larger branches.

bought (bôt) /bɔt/ *v.* a pt. and pp. of BUY.

bouil•la•baisse (bo͞o′yə bās′, bo͞ol′-) /ˌbuwyə'beys, ˌbuwl-/ *n.* a stew containing several kinds of fish and shellfish: [*noncount*]: *Some bouillabaisse would be nice.* [*count*]: *She prepared a magnificent bouillabaisse for her guests.*

bouil•lon (bo͝ol′yon, bo͞o′-) /'bʊlyɒn, 'buw-/ *n.* [*noncount*] a clear broth made by straining the liquid in which beef, chicken, fish, etc., has been cooked.

boul•der (bōl′dər) /'bowldər/ *n.* [*count*] a large rounded or worn rock.

boul•e•vard (bo͝ol′ə värd′) /'bʊləˌvɑrd/ *n.* [*count*] a broad avenue in a city, usually having areas at the sides or center for trees, grass, or flowers.

bounce (bouns) /bawns/ *v.,* **bounced, bounc•ing,** *n.* —*v.* **1.** to (cause to) strike a surface and rebound: [*no obj*]: *The box bounced down the stairs.* [~ + *off* + *obj*]: *The ball bounced off the wall and I caught it.* [~ + *obj*]: *He bounced the ball, took aim, and shot.* **2.** [*no obj*] to move or walk in a lively manner: *She bounced out of the room, overjoyed that we would be getting a dog.* **3.** [*no obj*] (of a check) to be refused payment by a bank because there is not enough money in one's account: *Your last check bounced and we won't accept another.* **4.** [~ + *obj*] to refuse or be unable to pay money on (a check) because there is not enough money in one's account: *He's bounced a few checks.* **5.** [~ + *obj*] *Slang.* to eject, expel, or dismiss (someone) quickly or with force: *They bounced him from the club for making trouble.* **6. bounce back,** [*no obj*] to recover quickly: *She was pretty ill with the flu, but she bounced back nicely.* —*n.* **7.** [*count*] a bound or rebound: *He caught the ball and threw it on two bounces to second base.* **8.** [*noncount*] ability to rebound: *This ball has more bounce when it is inflated properly.* **9.** [*noncount*] vitality; energy; liveliness: *a bounce in his step after the good news.* **10. the bounce,** [*noncount*] *Slang.* a dismissal, rejection, or expulsion.

bounc•er (boun′sər) /'bawnsər/ *n.* [*count*] one who is employed at a bar, etc., to remove or eject disorderly persons.

bounc•ing (boun′sing) /'bawnsɪŋ/ *adj.* [*before a noun*] stout, strong, or active: *gave birth to a bouncing baby boy.*

bounc•y (boun′sē) /'bawnsiy/ *adj.,* **-i•er, -i•est. 1.** tending to bounce or bounce well. **2.** resilient: *a carpet that is bouncy underfoot.* **3.** animated; lively: *a bouncy, bubbly personality.*

bound[1] (bound) /bawnd/ *v.* **1.** a pt. and pp. of BIND. —*adj.* **2.** tied; in bonds: *a bound prisoner.* **3.** made fast as if by a band or bond. **4.** secured within a cover, as a book: *a bound book.* **5.** [*usually: be* + ~] under an obligation: *Even the police are bound by laws.* [~ + *to* + *verb*]: *I felt bound to tell you what they say about you.* **6.** [*be* + ~ + *to* + *verb*] certain; sure: *He's so fast he's bound to win the race.* [*It* + *be* + ~ + *to* + *verb*]: *It is bound to happen.* —***Idiom.*** **7. bound up with** or **in,** [*be* + ~ + *obj*] **a.** very closely connected with: *Her future is too bound up with his career.* **b.** devoted or attached to: *I've been bound up in this project for years.*

bound[2] (bound) /bawnd/ *v.* [*no obj*] **1.** to move by leaps; jump: *He bounded out the door.* **2.** to rebound; bounce: *He started to fall, but then bounded off the wall as he went down.* —*n.* [*count*] **3.** a leap onward or upward; jump: *With a great bound, the dog flew out the window.* **4.** a rebound; bounce.

bound[3] (bound) /bawnd/ *n.* [*count*] **1.** Usually, **bounds.** [*plural*] limit or boundary: *within the bounds of reason.* —*v.* [*usually: be* + *bounded by*] **2.** to limit by or as if by bounds: *Spain is bounded on the east by Portugal.* —***Idiom.*** **3. in bounds,** within official boundaries: *They ruled that the player was in bounds.* **4. out of bounds, a.** beyond or past official boundaries: *threw the ball out of bounds.* **b.** forbidden; prohibited: *Drinking alcoholic beverages is out of bounds for her.*

bound[4] (bound) /bawnd/ *adj.* [*be* + ~ + *for*] going or intending to go; destined; heading for: *The train is bound for Denver.*

-bound[1], *combining form.* Use *-bound* after certain nouns to mean "stuck or surrounded by (something)": *snow* + *-bound* → *snowbound* (= *stuck in and surrounded by snow*).

-bound[2], *combining form.* Use *-bound* after words of direction to indicate "going to; heading toward": *east* + *-bound* → *eastbound* (= *going to the east; heading toward the east*).

bound•a•ry (boun′də rē, -drē) /'bawndəriy, -driy/ *n.* [*count*], *pl.* **-ries.** something that indicates bounds or limits, as a line: *A mountain range forms a natural boundary between the two countries.* —**Syn.** BOUNDARY, BORDER, FRONTIER refer to something that divides one territory, state, country, etc., from another. BOUNDARY most often refers to a line on a map; it may be a physical feature, such as a river: *Boundaries on this map are shown in red.* BORDER refers to a political or geographic dividing line; it may also refer to the region next to the actual line: *crossing the Mexican border.* FRONTIER refers specifically to a border between two countries or the region adjoining this border: *Soldiers guarded the frontier between Russia and China.*

bound•er (boun′dər) /'bawndər/ *n.* [*count*] an unprincipled man; cad.

bound•less (bound′lis) /'bawndlɪs/ *adj.* having no bounds; unlimited: *her boundless energy and enthusiasm.*

boun•te•ous (boun′tē əs) /'bawntiyəs/ *adj.* **1.** giving freely; generous: *a bounteous patron of the arts.* **2.** freely given; plentiful; abundant: *a bounteous crop.* —**boun′te•ous•ly,** *adv.* —**boun′te•ous•ness,** *n.* [*noncount*]: *overwhelmed by the bounteousness of this great country.*

boun•ti•ful (boun′tə fəl) /'bawntəfəl/ *adj.* **1.** generous in giving gifts or favors. **2.** abundant; ample; plentiful: *a bountiful supply; a bountiful harvest.* —**boun′ti•ful•ly,** *adv.* —**boun′ti•ful•ness,** *n.* [*noncount*]: *overwhelmed by the bountifulness of the people.*

boun•ty (boun′tē) /'bawntiy/ *n., pl.* **-ties. 1.** [*count*] a payment offered by a government for doing something: *The bounty for a captured snake would be about $50.00.* **2.** [*noncount*] generosity: *noted for her bounty to the arts.*

bou•quet (bō kā′, bo͞o- *for 1;* bo͞o kā′ *for 2*) /bow'key, buw- *for 1;* buw'key *for 2*/ *n.* [*count*] **1.** a bunch of arranged flowers: *The bride carried a bouquet of pink roses.* **2.** the characteristic aroma of a wine, etc.: *This newly arrived wine has a distinctive bouquet.*

bour•bon (bûr′bən) /'bɜrbən/ *n.* [*noncount*] Also called **bour′bon whis′key.** a straight whiskey distilled from corn: *Bourbon was originally the corn whiskey from Bourbon County, Kentucky.*

bour•geois (bo͝or zhwä′) /bʊr'ʒwɑ/ *n., pl.* **-geois,** *adj.* —*n.* [*count*] **1.** a member of the bourgeoisie. **2.** a person interested in material things and concerned with respectability. —*adj.* **3.** belonging to or characteristic of the middle class: *typically bourgeois values.* **4.** characterized by or concerned with material things and respectability.

bour•geoi•sie (bo͝or′zhwä zē′) /ˌbʊrʒwɑ'ziy/ *n.* [*noncount; usually: the* + ~] **1.** the middle class. **2.** (in Marxist theory) the property-owning capitalist class, who by definition are in conflict with the working class.

bout (bout) /bawt/ *n.* [*count*] **1.** a contest, as of boxing; match. **2.** a period or spell: *a bout of illness.*

bou•tique (bo͞o tēk′) /buw'tiyk/ *n.* [*count*] a small shop, esp. one that sells fashionable items.

bou•zou•ki (bŏŏ zōō′kē) /bʊ'zuwkiy/ *n.* [*count*], *pl.* **-kis.** a long-necked, guitarlike musical instrument of Greece.

bo•vine (bō′vin, -vēn) /'bowvayn, -viyn/ *adj.* **1.** [*before a noun*] of or relating to the subfamily of animals that includes cattle and buffalo. **2.** oxlike; cowlike; dull.

bow[1] (bou) /baw/ *v.* **1.** to bend the knee or body, or to incline the head, so as to show respect or greeting: [*no obj*]: *bowing as the king and queen walked in.* [~ + *down*]: *bowed down almost to the ground.* [~ + *obj*]: *bowed his head in prayer.* **2.** to bend or curve downward: [*no obj*]: *The pines bowed low in the storm.* [~ + *obj*]: *The heavy snow bowed the trees down low.* **3.** to (cause to) give in or yield; to (cause to) submit: [~ + *to* + *obj*]: *You'll have to bow to the inevitable.* [~ + *obj; usually: be + bowed*]: *They were bloody but not bowed (= not defeated completely).* **4. bow out,** [*no obj*] to withdraw by choice; retire: *He didn't want to campaign anymore, so he decided to bow out.* **—*n.*** [*count*] **5.** a downward movement of the head or body in greeting, thanks, etc.: *She made a short bow after the play.* **—*Idiom.*** **6. bow and scrape,** [*no obj*] to be overly polite: *He was always bowing and scraping to the boss.* **7. take a bow,** to step forward or stand up to receive recognition, applause, etc.: *Stand up, Helen, and take a bow.*

bow[2] (bō) /bow/ *n.* [*count*] **1.** a strong, flexible strip of wood or other material, bent by a string stretched between its ends and used for shooting arrows: *hunting with a bow and arrow.* **2.** a bend or curve: *She tied the ribbon in a bow.* **3.** a readily loosened knot for joining the ends of a ribbon or string, having two loops: *a pretty bright bow in her hair.* **4.** a flexible rod having horsehairs that stretch from end to end, used for playing a musical instrument like a violin: *The musicians all raised their bows.* **—*adj.*** [*before a noun*] **5.** curved outward at the center; bent: *bow legs.* See BOWLEGGED. **—*v.*** **6.** to perform with a bow on a stringed instrument: [*no obj*]: *She hadn't learned to bow smoothly yet.* [~ + *obj*]: *She tried to bow her fiddle but always missed.*

bow[3] (bou) /baw/ *n.* [*count*] **1.** the front or forward end of a ship or airplane: *After the torpedo hit, the bow was crushed in.* **—*adj.*** [*usually: before a noun*] **2.** of or relating to the bow of a ship: *bow riggings.*

bowd•ler•ize (bōd′lə rīz′, boud′-) /'bowdlə,rayz, 'bawd-/ *v.* [~ + *obj*], **-ized, -iz•ing.** to change (a play, novel, or other artistic work) by removing or changing the parts considered rude or vulgar: *The town council tried to bowdlerize that controversial book.* **—bowd•ler•i•za•tion** (bōd′lə ri zā′shən, boud′-) /ˌbowdlərɪ'zeyʃən, ˌbawd-/ *n.* [*count*] **—bowd′ler•iz′er,** *n.* [*count*]

bow•el (bou′əl, boul) /'bawəl, bawl/ *n.* [*count*] **1.** Usually, **bowels.** [*plural*] the intestine: *The baby's bowels are out of control.* **2. bowels,** [*plural*] the inward or interior parts: *The silver mine was deep in the bowels of the earth.* **—*Idiom.*** **3. move one's bowels,** to send waste matter out through the bowels: *The doctor wanted to know how often the baby moved her bowels.*

bow′el move′ment, *n.* [*count*] the sending of waste matter out through the bowels.

bow•er (bou′ər) /'bawər/ *n.* [*count*] **1.** a leafy shelter, as in a garden; an arbor. **2.** a summer cottage in the woods.

bow′ie knife′ (bō′ē, bōō′ē) /'bowiy, 'buwiy/ *n.* [*count*] a heavy knife having a long, single-edged blade.

bowl[1] (bōl) /bowl/ *n.* [*count*] **1.** a deep, round dish or basin, used chiefly for holding liquids, etc.: *Mix the vegetables in the bowl.* **2.** the contents of a bowl: *a bowl of cherries.* **3.** a rounded, cuplike, hollow part: *the bowl of a pipe.* **4.** a stadium: *At the Hollywood Bowl we watched the football game.*

bowl[2] (bōl) /bowl/ *n.* **1.** [*count*] a heavy ball used in lawn bowling. **2. bowls,** [*noncount; used with a singular verb*] LAWN BOWLING: *He tried to play bowls but he wasn't any good.* **3.** [*count*] a delivery of the ball in bowling or lawn bowling. **—*v.*** **4.** [*no obj*] to play at bowling or lawn bowling: *He likes to bowl (or go bowling) on Saturday night.* **5.** [~ + *obj*] to roll the ball in bowling, or attain by bowling: *He bowled the ball smoothly down the lane. She bowls a good game.* **6. bowl over, a.** to surprise greatly: [~ + *obj* + *over*]: *That news really bowled us over.* [~ + *over* + *obj*]: *The news really bowled over her friends.* **b.** to knock down by crashing into: [~ + *obj* + *over*]: *He nearly bowled us over on his way past.* [~ + *over* + *obj*]: *He bowled over the fence and flowers.*

bow•leg•ged (bō′leg′id, -legd′) /'bowˌlɛgɪd, -ˌlɛgd/ *adj.* having the legs curved outward from the knees: *had become bowlegged after riding a horse all day.* **—bow′-leg′ged•ness,** *n.* [*noncount*]

bowl•er[1] (bō′lər) /'bowlər/ *n.* [*count*] **1.** a person who bowls. **2.** *Cricket.* the player who throws the ball to be played by the batsman.

bowl•er[2] (bō′lər) /'bowlər/ *n.* DERBY (def. 3). Also, **bowl′-er hat′.**

bowl•ing (bō′ling) /'bowlɪŋ/ *n.* [*noncount*] any of several games in which players roll balls at standing objects: *Bowling was their favorite pastime on Saturday nights.*

bowl′ing green′, *n.* [*count*] a level, smooth area where the grass has been mowed short for lawn bowling.

bow•man (bō′mən) /'bowmən/ *n.* [*count*], *pl.* **-men.** someone who shoots arrows with a bow; an archer.

bow•string (bō′string′) /'bowˌstrɪŋ/ *n.* [*count*] **1.** the string of an archer's bow. **2.** a string on the bow of a musical instrument, made of horsehair.

bow′ tie′ (bō) /bow/ *n.* [*count*] a small necktie tied in a bow at the collar.

bow•wow (bou′wou′, -wou′) /'bawˌwaw, -'waw/ *n.* [*count*] **1.** the bark of a dog. **2.** an imitation of this.

box[1] (boks) /bɒks/ *n.* **1.** [*count*] a container with stiff sides and often with a lid or cover: *They put all their books in boxes.* **2.** [*count*] the items in a box; the amount contained in a box: *a box of candy.* **3.** POST-OFFICE BOX. **4.** [*count*] a small, partly enclosed area in a theater, etc., in which a few people can sit and watch a performance, etc. **5.** [*count*] a small partly enclosed area in a courtroom for witnesses or the jury: *the witness box.* **6.** [*count*] a small enclosed area or shelter: *a sentry's box.* **7.** [*count*] a part of a printed page with a square or rectangular border, which contains material to read, or a space to be filled in: *See the box below for more information.* **8.** [*count*] any enclosing, protective case: *a fire-alarm box.* **9.** [*count*] any of various spaces on a baseball field marking the playing positions of the pitcher, catcher, etc.: *stepped into the batter's box.* **—*v.*** [~ + *obj*] **10.** to put into a box: *The apples were boxed and shipped.* **11.** to keep in or as if in a box; to block or prevent (someone): [~ + *obj* + *in*]: *They boxed her in.* [~ + *in* + *obj*]: *The company has a policy of boxing in anyone who is female.*

box[2] (boks) /bɒks/ *v.* **1.** [~ + *obj*] to strike with the hand or fist, esp. on the ear. **2.** to fight against (someone) in a boxing match: [~ + *obj*]: *The champ boxed that contender twice.* [*no obj*]: *enjoys boxing.*

box[3] (boks) /bɒks/ *n.* [*count*] an evergreen shrub or small tree having shiny, dark green leaves, used for hedges.

box•car (boks′kär′) /'bɒksˌkɑr/ *n.* [*count*] a completely enclosed railroad freight car.

box•er (bok′sər) /'bɒksər/ *n.* [*count*] **1.** a person who fights as a sport; prizefighter. **2.** a German breed of medium-sized, shorthaired dogs with a short, square nose. **3. boxers,** [*plural*] BOXER SHORTS.

box′er shorts′, *n.* [*plural*] men's loose-fitting undershorts with an elastic waistband.

box•ing (bok′sing) /'bɒksɪŋ/ *n.* [*noncount*] the act, technique, or profession of fighting with the fists.

box′ing glove′, *n.* [*count*] one of a pair of heavily padded leather mittens worn by boxers.

box′ num′ber, *n.* [*count*] a number used as a mailing address and to which mail is sent, usually to a corresponding small box in a post office: *Put the box number in the corner of the envelope.*

box′ of′fice, *n.* **1.** [*count*] the office of a theater, etc., at which tickets are sold: *Tickets are available from the box office.* **2.** [*noncount*] the amount of money from tickets purchased for a play, etc.: *a good box office last night.* **—box′-of′fice,** *adj.* [*usually: before a noun*]: *box-office receipts.*

box′ spring′, *n.* [*count*] a set of springs used under a mattress to form a bed.

box•y (bok′sē) /'bɒksiy/ *adj.*, **-i•er, -i•est.** like or resembling a box, esp. in shape: *The old boxy shape for cars gave way to a streamlined look.*

boy (boi) /bɔy/ *n.* [*count*] **1.** a male child, from birth to full growth. **2.** a young man who lacks maturity, judgment, etc.: *He's just a boy; he doesn't know how to act around girls.* **3.** *Informal.* a grown man, esp. when referred to familiarly: *I think the boys in the lab need to work on this a little longer.* **4.** a son: *We have two boys and two girls.* **5.** a male who is from or native to a given place: *He's a country boy.* **6.** *Disparaging and Offensive.* a man considered to be inferior in race, nationality, etc.: *I made a terrible mistake when I called the waiter over by saying, in Greek, "My boy, please come here."* **—*interj.*** **7.** (used to show wonder or approval or worry, displeasure, or contempt): *Boy! Just look at that!*

boy•cott (boi′kot) /ˈbɔykɒt/ *v.* [~ + *obj*] **1.** to join together in preventing dealings with (a company, etc.), as a means of protest: *The neighborhood boycotted the overpriced supermarket.* **2.** to refrain from buying or using (something) as a means of protest: *urging the public to boycott imported goods.* **—***n.* [*count*] **3.** an instance of boycotting: *a lettuce boycott.* —**boy′cott•er,** *n.* [*count*]

boy•friend (boi′frend′) /ˈbɔyˌfrɛnd/ *n.* [*count*] a male with whom someone is having a romantic affair.

boy•hood (boi′ho͝od) /ˈbɔyhʊd/ *n.* the state of being a boy; the period of time of being a boy: [*noncount*]: *I remember my boyhood as a fun-filled time.* [*count; singular*]: *a troubled boyhood in difficult times.*

boy•ish (boi′ish) /ˈbɔyɪʃ/ *adj.* of or like a boy; youthful: *a cute, boyish smile.* —**boy′ish•ly,** *adv.*: *He was boyishly polite and yet shy.* —**boy′ish•ness,** *n.* [*noncount*]

boy′ scout′, *n.* [*count*] [*sometimes: Boy Scout*] a member of an organization of boys **(Boy′ Scouts′),** having as its goals the development of character, self-reliance, and usefulness to others.

boy•sen•ber•ry (boi′zən ber′ē, -sən-) /ˈbɔyzənˌbɛriy, -sən-/ *n.* [*count*], *pl.* **-ries.** a fruit like a blackberry with a flavor similar to that of a raspberry: *boysenberry jam.*

bo•zo (bō′zō) /ˈbowzow/ *n.* [*count*], *pl.* **-zos.** *Slang.* a stupid, rude person: *He was a complete bozo during that meeting, clowning and interrupting.*

BPD or **B.P.D.,** an abbreviation of: barrels per day.

bps or **BPS,** an abbreviation of: bits per second.

bra (brä) /brɑ/ *n.* [*count*] a woman's undergarment, worn to support the breasts; brassiere. See illustration at CLOTHING.

brace (brās) /breys/ *n.*, *v.*, **braced, brac•ing. —***n.* [*count*] **1.** something that holds parts in place, such as a clamp; something that helps make something rigid: *He nailed in a brace to support the beams.* **2.** Usually, **braces.** [*plural*] a set of wires or bands attached to the teeth, used to straighten crooked teeth: *got braces when she was twelve.* **3.** a device on part of a person's body for supporting a weak joint or joints. **4.** a pair; couple: *a brace of birds killed in that hunting trip.* **5.** one of two characters, {or}, used to enclose words or lines to be considered together. **—***v.* [~ + *obj*] **6.** to furnish, fasten, or strengthen with or as if with a brace: *He braced the sagging wall with a piece of wood.* **7.** [~ + *oneself*] to prepare (oneself) for something unpleasant: *couldn't brake in time and braced herself for the crash.*

brace•let (brās′lit) /ˈbreyslɪt/ *n.* [*count*] an ornamental band for the wrist or arm or, sometimes, for the ankle. —**brace′let•ed,** *adj.*

brac•er (brā′sər) /ˈbreysər/ *n.* [*count*] a stimulating drink, esp. one of liquor.

brac•ing (brā′sing) /ˈbreysɪŋ/ *adj.* stimulating; invigorating: *the bracing cold.* —**brac′ing•ly,** *adv.*: *a bracingly cold day.*

brack•en (brak′ən) /ˈbrækən/ *n.* [*noncount*] a large fern that grows in woods and on hills.

brack•et (brak′it) /ˈbrækɪt/ *n.* [*count*] **1.** a supporting piece sticking out from a wall to support the weight of a shelf, etc., or to reinforce the angle between two pieces. **2.** a wall fixture for holding a lamp, clock, etc. **3.** Also called **square bracket.** one of two marks, [or], used in writing or printing to enclose information added as extra but not essential: *I put my comments on the side in brackets.* **4.** a grouping, as of persons in relation to their income or age: *travels in a different social bracket.* **—***v.* [~ + *obj*] **5.** to furnish with or support by a bracket or brackets: *He bracketed the fittings with braces.* **6.** to place (words, etc.) within brackets. **7.** to group in a class together: *The problems of the inner city were bracketed together in that article.*

brack•ish (brak′ish) /ˈbrækɪʃ/ *adj.* slightly salty or briny: *brackish water.* —**brack′ish•ness,** *n.* [*noncount*]

bract (brakt) /brækt/ *n.* [*count*] a leaflike plant part, usually at the base of a flower.

brad (brad) /bræd/ *n.* [*count*] a small, thin nail having either a small, deep head or a projection to one side of the head end.

brag (brag) /bræg/ *v.*, **bragged, brag•ging.** to boast; to say or declare something in a proud way: [*no obj; (~ + about + obj)*]: *always bragging about her wonderful children.* [~ + *that clause*]: *He bragged that he had shot a lion.* —**brag′ger,** *n.* [*count*]

brag•ga•do•ci•o (brag′ə dō′shē ō′) /ˌbrægəˈdowʃiyˌow/ *n.*, *pl.* **-ci•os. 1.** [*noncount*] empty boasting; bragging: *full of braggadocio.* **2.** [*count*] a boasting person; braggart: *He was both a braggadocio and a liar.*

brag•gart (brag′ərt) /ˈbrægərt/ *n.* [*count*] one who brags: *Don't believe everything that braggart tells you about his accomplishments.*

Brah•man (brä′mən) /ˈbrɑmən/ *n.*, *pl.* **-mans. 1.** [*count*] Also, **Brahmin.** a member of the highest class among the Hindus. **2.** [*proper noun*] Also, **Brahma.** (in Hinduism) the supreme being, the first source and ultimate goal of all beings. **3.** [*count*] a breed of cattle developed from Indian stock, esp. a grayish American breed. —**Brah•man•ism, Brah•min•ism,** *n.* [*noncount*]

Brah•ma•ni or **Brah•ma•nee** (brä′mə nē) /ˈbrɑməniy/ *n.* [*count*], *pl.* **-nis** or **-nees.** a woman of the Brahman class.

Brah•min (brä′min) /ˈbrɑmɪn/ *n.* [*count*] **1.** BRAHMAN (def. 1). **2.** (esp. in New England) a person from an old, upper-class family. **3.** someone who considers himself or herself above others: *acted like a Brahmin, but deep down he was just like everyone else.*

braid (brād) /breyd/ *v.* [~ + *obj*] **1.** to weave together three or more strips or strands of (hair, etc.); plait: *She braided her hair by herself.* **2.** to form by such weaving: *They were able to braid a rope.* **—***n.* [*count*] **3.** a braided length or plait, esp. of hair: *She had fastened her hair into a braid.* **4.** a ropelike band formed by plaiting strands of silk or other material, used as trimming.

braid•ed (brā′did) /ˈbreydɪd/ *adj.* decorated with bands of braids.

braid•ing (brā′ding) /ˈbreydɪŋ/ *n.* [*noncount*] braided material or work.

Braille (brāl) /breyl/ *n.* [*noncount; often: braille*] a system of writing, devised by L. Braille for use by the blind, in which combinations of raised dots stand for letters, numbers, punctuation marks, etc., that are read by touch.

brain (brān) /breyn/ *n.* [*count*] **1.** the mass of nerve tissue in the head of humans and animals that is the center of the nervous system. **2.** Sometimes, **brains.** understanding; intellectual power; intelligence: *He has a good brain for math. She sometimes acts as if she has no brains.* **3. brains,** *Slang.* [*the* + ~; *used with a singular verb*] a member of a group who is regarded as having the intelligence necessary to lead: *Who was the brains behind this evil plot?* **4.** *Informal.* an extremely intelligent person: *She's a real brain in chemistry.* **—***v.* [~ + *obj*] **5.** *Slang.* to hit or bang on the head: *What are you doing, braining your little brother?* **—*Idiom.* 6. beat** or **rack one's brains (out),** [*no obj*] *Informal.* to try very hard to work out a problem, remember something, etc.: *beat her brains out trying to come up with a fair solution.* **7. beat someone's brains out,** [*no obj*] to injure by hitting or beating very hard, as by hitting on the head: *She leaped on top of him and beat his brains out.* **8. pick someone's brains,** to obtain information by questioning another person: *didn't prepare for the exam but counted on picking his roommate's brains.*

brain•child (brān′chīld′) /ˈbreynˌtʃayld/ *n.* [*count*], *pl.* **-chil•dren.** a product of one's thinking or planning: *The school play was his brainchild, not mine.*

brain′-dead′ or **brain′ dead′,** *adj.* having undergone brain death: *She was brain-dead on arrival at the hospital.*

brain′ death′, *n.* [*noncount*] complete stopping of brain function: *Brain death is sometimes used as a legal definition of death.*

brain′ drain′, *n.* [*count*] a loss of trained professionals to another company, etc., that offers greater opportunity, etc.: *the brain drain from poor countries to rich ones.*

brain•less (brān′lis) /ˈbreynlɪs/ *adj.* lacking intelligence or good sense; stupid; foolish.

brain•storm (brān′stôrm′) /ˈbreynˌstɔrm/ *n.* [*count*] **1.** a sudden inspiration or idea: *She suddenly got a brainstorm: pin the crime on her lover and escape with the money.* **—***v.* **2.** [*no obj*] to engage in brainstorming: *They brainstormed for most of the morning.* **3.** [~ + *obj*] to subject (a problem) to brainstorming: *The research team brainstormed the problem all day.*

brain•storm•ing (brān′stôr′ming) /ˈbreynˌstɔrmɪŋ/ *n.* [*noncount*] a group technique for solving problems, coming up with new ideas, etc., by meeting together and allowing almost any idea to be brought up.

brain•teas•er (brān′tē′zər) /ˈbreynˌtiyzər/ *n.* [*count*] a puzzle whose solution requires thought.

brain′ trust′, *n.* [*count; usually singular*] a group of experts from different fields who act as unofficial consultants on matters of policy and strategy: *The candidate gathered her brain trust around her.*

brain•wash (brān′wosh′, -wôsh′) /ˈbreynˌwɒʃ, -ˌwɔʃ/ *v.* to force (someone) to go through brainwashing; to put (someone) through brainwashing: [~ + *obj*]: *The enemy brainwashed all its prisoners in special cells.* [~ + *obj* + *into*]: *They brainwashed the captured pilot into believing he was a CIA agent.*

brain•wash•ing (brān′wosh′ing, -wô′shing) /ˈbreyn-ˌwɒʃɪŋ, -ˌwɔʃɪŋ/ *n.* [*noncount*] **1.** a method of forcing someone to change attitudes or beliefs, esp. through psychological techniques: *endured cruel brainwashing for years.* **2.** any method of controlling someone's attitudes or beliefs, esp. one based on mindless repetition or induced confusion: *protested that the cult had subjected their daughter to brainwashing.*

brain′ wave′, *n.* [*count*] **1.** Usually, **brain waves.** [*plural*] electrical currents or force given off by the brain when it is active: *a special device to record the activity of brain waves during dreaming.* **2.** BRAINSTORM (def. 1).

brain•y (brā′nē) /ˈbreyniy/ *adj.*, **-i•er, -i•est.** *Informal.* intelligent; clever; intellectual: *I liked her: she was brainy, beautiful, and kind.* —**brain′i•ness,** *n.* [*noncount*]

braise (brāz) /breyz/ *v.* [~ + *obj*], **braised, brais•ing.** to cook (food) by frying quickly in fat and then simmering in liquid in a covered pot.

brake (brāk) /breyk/ *n., v.,* **braked, brak•ing.** —*n.* [*count*] **1.** a device for slowing or stopping a vehicle or other moving mechanism, usually by friction. **2. brakes,** [*plural*] the drums, shoes, etc., making up such a device on a vehicle: *The brakes need adjusting.* **3.** anything that has a slowing or stopping effect: *He seemed to act like a brake on our momentum.* —*v.* **4.** to slow or stop by or as if by a brake: [~ + *obj*]: *He braked the car with a lurch.* [*no obj*]: *She braked carefully in the snow.*

bram•ble (bram′bəl) /ˈbræmbəl/ *n.* [*count*] **1.** a prickly shrub of the rose family. **2.** any rough, prickly shrub.

bran (bran) /bræn/ *n.* [*noncount*] the flakes that are left when grain is ground up.

branch (branch) /bræntʃ/ *n.* [*count*] **1.** an armlike division of the stem of a tree or shrub: *The branches of oak trees form a V-shape.* **2.** a limb, section, or division of a main system: *the branches of a deer's antlers; the branches of the armed forces.* **3.** a local division of a business, library, or other organization: *The bank has several branches in your neighborhood.* —*v.* [*no obj*] **4.** to put forth branches; spread in branches: *These trees branch at heights of fifteen feet.* **5.** [~ + *off*] to divide into separate parts; diverge: *The road branches off to the left.* **6. branch out,** [*no obj*] to expand or extend in new directions: *The company branched out into electronics and computers.*

brand (brand) /brænd/ *n.* [*count*] **1.** make or version of a product, as indicated by a trademark or the like: *the best brand of coffee.* **2.** a mark made to indicate kind, grade, etc.: *They put the T-Bar brand on that cow.* **3.** BRANDING IRON. **4.** a distinctive kind or variety: *an unfunny brand of humor.* **5.** a burning or partly burned piece of wood. —*v.* **6.** [~ + *obj*] to label or mark with or as if with a brand: *The cowboys roped the calf and branded it.* **7.** [~ + *obj* + *obj*] to label (someone) as being or having done something shameful.

brand′ing i′ron, *n.* [*count*] a long-handled metal rod with a stamp at one end, used for branding cattle with a symbol.

bran•dish (bran′dish) /ˈbrændɪʃ/ *v.* [~ + *obj*] to shake, wave, or display (something), esp. in a threatening way: *the gunman brandishing his weapon.*

brand′ name′, *n.* [*count*] a name, etc., used by a company to identify its products or services in a special way; trademark: *"Kleenex" is a brand name.* —**brand′-name′,** *adj.* [*usually: before a noun*]: *brand-name products.*

brand-new (bran′no͞o′, -nyo͞o′, brand′-), /ˈbrænˈnuw, -ˈnyuw, ˈbrænd-/, *adj.* entirely new: *Her brand-new car was stolen the first day she drove it.*

bran•dy (bran′dē) /ˈbrændiy/ *n., pl.* **-dies.** an alcoholic drink made from wine or fermented fruit juice: [*noncount*]: *Brandy certainly has a distinctive aroma.* [*count*]: *Bartender, we'd like three brandies, please.*

brash (brash) /bræʃ/ *adj.*, **-er, -est. 1.** impolite or rude; tactless: *a brash young man.* **2.** hastily or rashly undertaken: *a brash decision.* **3.** energetic or spirited, esp. in an irreverent way: *a brash new musical.* —**brash′ly,** *adv.* —**brash′ness,** *n.* [*noncount*]

brass (bras) /bræs/ *n.* [*noncount*] **1.** a metal alloy of copper and zinc: *candlesticks made of brass.* **2. the brass,** [*used with a plural verb*] ornaments, utensils, etc., made of brass: *We asked the butler to clean the silver and the brass.* **3. the brass,** [*used with a plural verb*] musical instruments made of brass, usually in a band or orchestra: *The brass sounded particularly good during that piece.* **4. the brass,** [*used with a plural verb*] high-ranking military officers: *You'd better ask the brass about that first.* **5.** too much self-assurance; impudence: *He had the brass to claim we had cheated him, whereas he had cheated us.* —*adj.* **6.** of, made of, or relating to brass.

bras•se•rie (bras′ə rē′) /ˌbræsəˈriy/ *n.* [*count*] a restaurant or tavern that serves drinks, esp. beer, and simple food.

brass′ hat′, *n.* [*count*] *Informal.* a top-ranking army or navy officer: *The soldiers all dreaded the arrival of the brass hats.*

bras•siere or **bras•sière** (brə zēr′) /brəˈzɪər/ *n.* [*count*] a woman's undergarment for supporting the breasts. Also called **bra.**

brass′ tacks′, *n.* [*plural*] —***Idiom.* get down to brass tacks,** to discuss the most important facts; to come to the real business: *Let's get down to brass tacks here; what must I do to pass this course?*

brass•y (bras′ē) /ˈbræsiy/ *adj.*, **-i•er, -i•est. 1.** made of, covered with, or looking like the color of brass. **2.** harsh-sounding and too loud: *brassy notes.* **3.** loud, too bold, or harsh in manners; brazen: *his brassy manner at the interview.*

brat (brat) /bræt/ *n.* [*count*] a child who is annoying, spoiled, or impolite. —**brat′ty,** *adj.*, **-ti•er, -ti•est.**

brat•wurst (brat′wûrst, brät′-) /ˈbrætwɜrst, ˈbrɑt-/ *n.* a sausage made of pork, spices, and herbs: [*noncount*]: *They were cooking bratwurst on the grill.* [*count*]: *I'll take two bratwursts with mustard.*

bra•va•do (brə vä′dō) /brəˈvɑdow/ *n.* [*noncount*] an overly showy and often false display of courage or boldness: *He tried to answer his accusers with a show of bravado.*

brave (brāv) /breyv/ *adj.*, **brav•er, brav•est,** *n., v.,* **braved, brav•ing.** —*adj.* **1.** having or showing courage; unafraid of dangerous things: *The brave soldier ran forward and rescued his wounded comrade.* —*n.* **2. the brave,** [*used with a plural verb*] brave people: *Only the brave risk charging at a machine gun.* **3.** [*count*] a warrior, esp. among North American Indians: *The chief consulted with his braves and decided to attack at dawn.* —*v.* [~ + *obj*] **4.** to meet or face with courage: *He was unafraid to brave the dangers of spying.* **5. brave it out,** [*no obj*] to defy a dangerous or difficult situation: *After he was caught cheating, he met with the dean and tried to brave it out.* —**brave′ly,** *adv.: acted bravely in the face of danger.* —**Syn.** BRAVE, COURAGEOUS, VALIANT, FEARLESS refer to facing danger or difficulties with moral strength and the willingness to continue or keep on fighting. BRAVE is a general word that suggests daring and a desire to keep going: *a brave pioneer.* COURAGEOUS implies a higher or nobler kind of bravery, esp. the bravery that results from an inborn quality of mind or spirit: *Courageous leaders choose to do what is right, not what is easiest.* VALIANT implies an inner strength that people can see in one's brave deeds, often in battle: *a valiant knight.* FEARLESS implies coolness and a willingness not to back down or give up in the face of danger: *a fearless firefighter.*

brav•er•y (brā′və rē) /ˈbreyvəriy/ *n.* [*noncount*] brave spirit or conduct; courage; valor.

bra•vo (brä′vō, brä vō′) /ˈbrɑvow, brɑˈvow/ *interj., n., pl.* **-vos.** —*interj.* **1.** (used to praise a performer). —*n.* [*count*] **2.** a shout of "bravo!": *The bravos rang from the whole auditorium after the school play.*

bra•vu•ra (brə vyo͝or′ə, -vo͝or′ə, brä-) /brəˈvyʊrə, -ˈvʊrə, brɑ-/ *n.* [*count*], *pl.* **-ras.** a display of daring; brilliant performance.

brawl (brôl) /brɔl/ *n.* [*count*] **1.** a noisy fight in a public place: *The barroom brawl spilled out into the street.* —*v.* [*no obj*] **2.** to fight angrily and noisily: *groups of demonstrators brawling in the street.* —**brawl′er,** *n.* [*count*]

brawn (brôn) /brɔn/ *n.* [*noncount*] **1.** strong, well-developed muscles: *In those sexy soap operas he gets a chance to display his brawn.* **2.** muscular strength: *It was a case of brains winning out over brawn.*

brawn•y (brô′nē) /ˈbrɔniy/ *adj.*, **-i•er, -i•est.** muscular; strong: *his brawny arms.* —**brawn′i•ness,** *n.* [*noncount*]

bray (brā) /brey/ *n.* [*count*] **1.** the loud cry of a donkey. **2.** any similar sound. —*v.* **3.** to utter a bray: [*no obj*]: *The donkey brayed.* [~ + *obj*]: *He brayed a warning.*

bra•zen (brā′zən) /ˈbreyzən/ *adj.* **1.** bold and shameless or impudent: *brazen disrespect.* —***Idiom.* 2. brazen it out** or **through,** [*no obj*] to face something shamelessly: *Even though she was wrong, she went into the meeting* *determined to brazen it out and get her job back.* **—bra′zen•ly,** *adv.* **—bra′zen•ness,** *n.* [*noncount*]

bra•zier (brā′zhər) /ˈbreyʒər/ *n.* [*count*] a metal container for holding coals or other fuel, used for cooking or for heating a room.

Bra•zil•ian (brə zil′yən) /brəˈzɪlyən/ *n.* [*count*] **1.** a person born or living in Brazil. **—***adj.* **2.** of or relating to Brazil.

breach (brēch) /briytʃ/ *n.* **1.** an act of disobeying or violating a law or promise: [*count*]: *a breach of promise.* [*noncount*]: *You are in breach of contract if you do not leave the house that you sold.* **2.** [*count*] a gap or hole made in a wall, fortification, or line of soldiers: *found a breach in our defenses.* **3.** [*count*] a bringing to an end of friendly relations: *the breach caused during that war, when each country supported different sides.* **—***v.* [~ + *obj*] **4.** to make an opening or hole in (defenses, etc.): *In minutes the commandos breached our defenses.*

breach′ of the peace′, *n.* [*count*] a riot, disturbance, or fighting in public.

bread (bred) /brɛd/ *n.* [*noncount*] **1.** a food made of baked dough and containing flour, water or milk, and yeast: *Buy two loaves of bread at the store.* See illustration at SUPERMARKET. **2.** food as a requirement of staying alive; livelihood: *to earn one's bread.* **3.** *Slang.* money: *I had no bread and no way of getting a job.* **—***v.* [~ + *obj*] **4.** to coat (meat, etc.) with breadcrumbs for cooking: *Bread the veal thoroughly.* **—*Idiom.* 5. break bread,** to eat a meal, esp. with others: *They sat down and broke bread.*

bread′ and but′ter, *n.* [*noncount*] a basic means of income; sustenance: *Teaching was his bread and butter.* **—bread′-and-but′ter,** *adj.* [*before a noun*]: *housing and other bread-and-butter issues.*

bread•bas•ket (bred′bas′kit) /ˈbrɛdˌbæskɪt/ *n.* [*count*] an area of a country that produces large amounts of grain: *The Midwest of the United States is the breadbasket of the country.*

bread•box (bred′boks′) /ˈbrɛdˌbɒks/ *n.* [*count*] a container for storing baked goods to keep them fresh.

bread•crumb (bred′krum′) /ˈbrɛdˌkrʌm/ *n.* [*count; usually plural*] a crumb of bread, used esp. for stuffing and for coating food before cooking.

bread•fruit (bred′fro͞ot′) /ˈbrɛdˌfruwt/ *n.* **1.** a large round fruit from a tree of the mulberry family: [*noncount*]: *Baked breadfruit tastes a lot like bread.* [*count*]: *Chop off a few breadfruits.* **2.** [*count*] this tree itself.

breadth (bredth, bretth) /brɛdθ, brɛtθ/ *n.* **1.** the measure of the distance from side to side of a solid object; width: [*noncount*]: *The table was ten feet in breadth.* [*count*]: *The breadths of the columns varied too much.* **2.** [*noncount*] the extent, scope, or range of something: *We hired her because of the breadth of her knowledge.*

bread•win•ner (bred′win′ər) /ˈbrɛdˌwɪnər/ *n.* [*count*] a person who earns enough money to support someone: *Who is the breadwinner in that household?*

break (brāk) /breyk/ *v.,* **broke** (brōk) /browk/ **bro•ken** (brō′kən) /ˈbrowkən/ **break•ing,** *n.* **—***v.* **1.** to smash, split, or divide into parts violently: [~ + *obj*]: *He took the vase and broke it open.* [*no obj*]: *The vase broke.* **2.** to (cause to) stop working, as through wear or damage: [~ + *obj*]: *I broke my watch.* [*no obj*]: *My watch broke.* **3.** [~ + *obj*] to disobey or disregard (a law, promise, etc.): *She broke her promise not to drink.* **4.** to fracture a bone of: [~ + *obj*]: *He broke his arm.* [*no obj*]: *His arm broke when he fell on it.* **5.** to burst through (the surface of); rupture: [~ + *obj*]: *When you fell you just broke the skin, so there's only a little blood.* [*no obj*]: *The blood vessel broke and blood poured out.* **6.** to interrupt (quiet, peace, or some continuing process or activity): [~ + *obj*]: *A scream broke the silence.* [*no obj*]: *Let's break for lunch and come back later.* **7.** to (cause to) come to an end; stop: [~ + *obj*]: *He broke radio contact when he realized he was being intercepted.* [*no obj*]: *Radio contact broke after just a few moments.* **8.** [~ + *obj*] to discover the system, etc., for figuring out (a code): *During World War II the United States had broken the Japanese war codes.* **9.** [~ + *obj*] to exchange for, or divide into, smaller units: *Can you break a ten-dollar bill?* **10.** [~ + *obj*] to make a way through; penetrate: *The stone broke the surface of the water.* **11.** [~ + *obj*] to escape from, esp. by force: *to break jail.* **12.** [~ + *obj*] to better (a record): *When he jumped over eight feet he broke the old record of 7 feet 10 inches.* **13.** [~ + *obj*] to tell or reveal: *They broke the news to us gently.* **14.** [~ + *obj*] to solve: *to break a murder case.* **15.** [~ + *obj*] to ruin financially; bankrupt: *had made many enemies who worked together to break him.* **16.** to (cause to) be overcome or worn down; (cause to) give in to pressure: [~ + *obj*]: *The police broke the spy in just a few hours.* [*no obj*]: *The captured spy broke quickly.* **17.** [~ + *obj*] to lessen the power or intensity of: *In order to break your fall, slap your arm against the floor as you go down.* **18.** [~ + *obj*] to train to obedience; tame: *to break a horse.* **19.** [~ + *obj* + *of* + *obj*] to train away from a habit or practice: *tried to break him of his habit of biting his fingernails.* **20.** [~ + *obj*] to stop the flow of (a current): *He broke the circuit by disconnecting the wires.* **21.** to become detached or disassociated: [~ + *from/with* + *obj*]: *decided to break from the past and leave her small town for good.* **22.** to (cause a news item to) be released, published, or aired: [*no obj*]: *The story broke the next day in most newspapers.* [~ + *obj*]: *The reporter promised not to break the story.* **23.** [*no obj*] to free oneself or escape suddenly, as from restraint: *She broke free and dashed away.* **24.** to run or dash toward something suddenly; force one's way: [~ + *for*]: *He broke for the goal line.* [*no obj*]: *The hunters broke through the underbrush.* **25.** [*no obj*] (of the day or dawn) to grow light: *Day was breaking.* **26.** [*no obj*] to appear or begin violently and suddenly: *After some rumbling in the distance, the storm suddenly broke.* **27.** [*no obj*] to give way or fail, as health or spirit: *Her spirit broke when her two daughters died so young.* **28.** (to cause the heart) to be overwhelmed with sorrow: [*no obj*]: *His heart broke when she married another.* [~ + *obj*]: *He broke her heart when he married another.* **29.** [*no obj*] (of the voice) to waver or change tone abruptly, as from emotion or the beginning of maturity: *When she started to talk about the attack, her voice broke. When he turned fourteen his voice began to break.* **30.** to drop, turn, or change direction down sharply and considerably: [*no obj*]: *Stock prices broke quickly at the New York exchange.* [~ + *obj*]: *The pitcher broke his curveball over the plate and the batter swung at it.* **31.** [*no obj*] to fall or collapse by colliding with something: *The waves broke on the shore.* **32.** [*no obj*] to make the opening play in pool by scattering the racked balls with the cue ball: *She won the toss to break and the game began.* **33.** [*no obj*] to leave the starting point in a race: *The horses broke from the gate.* **34. break away,** [*no obj;* ~ + *away* (+ *from* + *obj*)] **a.** to leave, esp. suddenly: *One of the suspects broke away and dashed into the subway station.* **b.** to cut off connections with (a group or tradition): *decided to break away from the Democratic party and form his own.* **35. break down, a.** [*no obj*] to stop working; fail: *The car broke down on the highway.* **b.** to cause to collapse or stop working: [~ + *down* + *obj*]: *to break down resistance.* [~ + *obj* + *down*]: *to break it down.* **c.** to separate into component parts: [*no obj*]: *These proteins will break down in your stomach.* [~ + *down* + *obj*]: *Enzymes in your stomach break down proteins.* [~ + *obj* + *down*]: *Let me break it down (= analyze the situation) for you.* **d.** [*no obj*] to lose control over one's emotions, esp. to cry: *just broke down and began sobbing.* **e.** [*no obj*] to have a complete physical or mental collapse. **36. break even,** [*no obj*] to finish something with no loss and no gain: *lucky just to break even this year.* **37. break in, a.** [*no obj*] to enter a house or property by force or unlawfully: *The thief broke in yesterday.* **b.** to train to a new situation: [~ + *in* + *obj*]: *He managed to break in a new assistant.* [~ + *obj* + *in*]: *He managed to break her in in just a few days.* **c.** to wear or use (something new) and thereby ease stiffness, tightness, etc.: [~ + *in* + *obj*]: *to break in his new shoes.* [~ + *obj* + *in*]: *to break them in.* **d.** [*no obj*] to interrupt: *He broke in with an objection.* **38. break in on** or **upon,** [~ + *in* + *on* + *obj*] to intrude upon: *I'm sorry to break in on you like this.* **39. break into,** [~ + *into* + *obj*] **a.** to interrupt: *broke into the conversation and began shouting.* **b.** to express (an emotion, etc.) suddenly: *broke into a huge smile when she saw me.* **c.** to begin making a sound: *broke into a song.* **d.** to enter (a profession): *She broke into journalism when she was eighteen.* **e.** to enter (property) by force: *broke into the storage room and grabbed the safe.* **40. break off, a.** to cut off or remove (a part of) by breaking: [~ + *off* + *obj*]: *I broke off a piece of meat.* [~ + *obj* + *off*]: *to break a piece off.* **b.** to stop suddenly; discontinue: [~ + *off* + *obj*]: *The two nations decided to break off relations.* [~ + *obj* + *off*]: *to break them off.* **41. break out, a.** [*no obj*] to begin suddenly; arise: *An epidemic broke out.* **b.** [*no obj;* (~ + *out* + *in*)] (of a person's appearance) to have a mark or spots on the skin appear suddenly: *Her face broke out in red blotches.* **c.** [~ + *out* + *obj*] to take out or prepare for use: *to break out the parachutes.* **d.** [*no obj*] to escape; flee: *The prisoner broke out at about noon.* **42. break up, a.** [*no obj*] to separate; scatter: *The crowd broke up and people went on their way.* **b.** to (cause to) come to an end; discontinue: [~ + *up* + *obj*]: *The cops broke up the fight.* [~ + *obj* + *up*]: *All right, break it up!* [*no obj*]: *The meeting broke up.* **c.** to (cause a personal relationship to) end: [*no obj*]: *decided to break up after five years.* [~ + *up* + *obj*]: *Their children didn't break up their marriage.* [~ + *obj* + *up*]: *to break it up.* **d.** to (cause someone to) laugh a great deal: [*no obj*]: *When she heard that joke she just broke up.* [~ + *obj* + *up*]: *That joke just broke her up.* **43. break with,** [~ + *with* + *obj*] to separate from: *to break with one's family.* —*n.* [*count*] **44.** an opening made by or as if by breaking: *a break in the window.* **45.** an act or instance of breaking; rupture: *heard a sharp crack and knew that she had suffered a clean break of her leg.* **46.** [*usually singular*] an interruption or stopping of something: *a break with tradition.* **47.** a brief rest, as from work: *Let's take a break; I'm tired of all this homework.* **48.** a sudden and obvious change: *waited for a break in the weather.* **49.** an attempt to escape: *Let's make a break for it!* **50.** a case or piece of luck, esp. good luck: *What a lucky break!* **51. the breaks,** [*plural*] *Informal.* the way things happen; fate: *Those are the breaks.* **52.** the opening play in a game of pool, in which the white ball is shot to scatter the balls. —***Idiom.*** **53. break camp,** to pack up tents and equipment and start again on a journey or march. **54. break (new) ground, a.** to begin construction, esp. of a building: *to break ground for a new housing development.* **b.** to start something new or from the beginning: *The latest study linking heart attacks with smoking cigarettes doesn't really break any new ground.*

break•a•ble (brā′kə bəl) /ˈbreykə bəl/ *adj.* easy to break: *breakable glass ornaments.*

break•age (brā′kij) /ˈbreykɪdʒ/ *n.* **1.** [*noncount*] the act of breaking or the state of being broken: *breakage in the water pipes.* **2.** [*count*] the amount or quantity of things broken: *the breakages due to the hurricane.* **3.** [*noncount*] an allowance for things that are broken, such as items shipped: *Breakage to be paid will not be more than original cost.*

break•a•way (brāk′ə wā′) /ˈbreykəˌwey/ *n.* [*count*] **1.** an act or instance of breaking away (as in basketball from defensive players); separation from a group: *made a breakaway from the Democratic party.* —*adj.* [*before a noun*] **2.** of or pointing to something that separates or comes away from the main body: *the breakaway faction of the Republican party.*

break•down (brāk′doun′) /ˈbreykˌdawn/ *n.* [*count*] **1.** an act or instance of breaking down, such as a loss of ability to function effectively: *The car had yet another breakdown.* **2.** a loss of mental or physical health: *had a bad breakdown when her husband left her.* **3.** a division into parts, etc.; classification; analysis: *gave us a breakdown of the prospects for the new product.*

break•er (brā′kər) /ˈbreykər/ *n.* [*count*] **1.** a person or thing that breaks. **2.** a wave that breaks or dashes into foam: *We watched the breakers on the beach as the sun set behind us.*

break′-e′ven or **break′e′ven,** *adj.* [*usually: before a noun*] of or relating to the point at which income is equal to expenses: *Businesses are now looking for the break-even point.*

break•fast (brek′fəst) /ˈbrɛkfəst/ *n.* **1.** the first meal of the day; morning meal: [*noncount*]: *What did you have for breakfast?* [*count*]: *He had a big breakfast that day.* —*v.* **2.** to eat breakfast: [*no obj; (~ + on + obj)*]: *They breakfasted and left early. They breakfasted on fish and tea.*

break′-in′, *n.* [*count*] an illegal act of entering a home, office, etc., by force.

break•neck (brāk′nek′) /ˈbreykˌnɛk/ *adj.* [*before a noun*] fast enough to be dangerous: *running at breakneck speed down the slope.*

break•out (brāk′out′) /ˈbreykˌawt/ *n.* [*count*] **1.** an escape, often by force, as from a prison: *Several convicted murderers planned the prison breakout.* **2.** a sudden, widespread appearance of something, as of a disease. **3.** a list of items or details; breakdown.

break•through (brāk′thro͞o′) /ˈbreykˌθruw/ *n.* [*count*] **1.** an important and sudden advance, etc., as in science, that removes a barrier to progress: *Pasteur's discovery about the nature of germs was an important breakthrough in the treatment of diseases.* **2.** an act or instance of removing or getting past a barrier: *The army made its breakthrough at dawn.*

break•up (brāk′up′) /ˈbreykˌʌp/ *n.* [*count*] **1.** a dividing into smaller parts; dispersal: *the breakup of large businesses into small, private firms.* **2.** the ending of a personal relationship: *Everyone expected the breakup of their marriage.*

break•wa•ter (brāk′wô′tər, -wot′ər) /ˈbreykˌwɔtər, -ˌwɒtər/ *n.* [*count*] a barrier in a harbor to break the force of waves.

breast (brest) /brɛst/ *n.* **1.** [*count*] either of the two parts on the chest of a woman that produce milk: *The baby cried softly at its mother's breast.* **2.** [*count*] the outer, front part of the body from the neck to the waist; chest: *a bullet through the breast.* **3.** [*count*] the part of the body as the center of emotion or where feelings are located: *The father's breast swelled with pride.* **4.** (a piece of) meat cut from the front part of a bird or animal: [*noncount*]: *We ordered breast of chicken.* [*count*]: *The butcher chopped three chicken breasts and weighed them.* —***Idiom.*** **5. beat one's breast,** to display grief, sorrow, etc., loudly and with a great show: *He wailed and beat his breast, claiming he was innocent.* **6. make a clean breast of,** [~ + *obj*] to tell the truth about (one's wrongdoing); confess: *It would be better to just make a clean breast of the matter.*

breast•bone (brest′bōn′) /ˈbrɛstˌbown/ *n.* [*count*] the long bone in the center of the chest; sternum.

breast′-feed′, *v.* [~ + *obj*], **-fed, -feed•ing.** to feed (a baby) with milk from the breast: *Babies who are breast-fed are often healthier than babies who are fed from a bottle.* —**breast′-feed′ing,** *n.* [*noncount*]: *The number of mothers practicing breast-feeding has increased in recent years.*

breast•plate (brest′plāt′) /ˈbrɛstˌpleyt/ *n.* [*count*] a piece of armor for protecting the chest.

breast•stroke (brest′strōk′, bres′-) /ˈbrɛstˌstrowk, ˈbrɛs-/ *n.* [*count*] a swimming stroke done face down in the water, in which the two hands are moved forward, outward, and backward starting from in front of the chest, while the legs move in a frog kick.

breath (breth) /brɛθ/ *n.* **1.** [*noncount; usually: one's* + ~] the air taken into and sent out of the lungs while breathing: *It's cold enough to see your breath today.* **2.** [*count*] a single act of taking in air and sending it out of the lungs: *Take a deep breath.* **3.** [*noncount; usually: one's* + ~] the ability to breathe easily and normally: *I stopped to catch my breath.* **4.** [*count*] a slight suggestion or hint: *had never been touched by even a breath of scandal.* **5.** [*count*] a light current of air: *A breath of wind filtered into the room.* —***Idiom.*** **6. below** or **under one's breath,** in a low voice or whisper: *"So glad to see you," she said. "I can't say the same," he muttered under his breath.* **7. hold one's breath,** to stop breathing for a short period of time: *She held her breath and dove into the water.* **8. in the same** (or **next**) **breath,** almost at the same time: *She promised to pay us for the work and then in the next breath suggested we should do it voluntarily.* **9. out of breath,** breathless from exertion: *I was completely out of breath after five flights of stairs.* **10. save one's breath,** to avoid futile talk or discussion: *We were told to save our breath.* **11. take one's breath away,** to make one as if breathless with astonishment: *The beauty of the sea took my breath away.* —**Related Words.** BREATH is a noun, BREATHE is a verb, and BREATHLESS and BREATHTAKING are adjectives: *His breath smelled of whiskey. He couldn't breathe. She was breathless from excitement. The view is breathtaking.*

breath•a•ble (brē′thə bəl) /ˈbriyðəbəl/ *adj.* **1.** fresh and fit to be breathed: *The air was hardly breathable in the garage.* **2.** allowing air and moisture to pass through; porous: *breathable fabrics.* —**breath•a•bil•i•ty** (brē′thə-bil′i tē) /ˌbriyðəˈbɪlɪtiy/ *n.* [*noncount*]

Breath•a•lyz•er (breth′ə lī′zər) /ˈbrɛθəˌlayzər/ *Trademark.* [*count*] a breath analyzer that tests the breath for the presence of alcohol.

breathe (brēth) /briyð/ *v.,* **breathed** (brēthd), **breath•ing. 1.** to take (air, etc.) into the lungs and send (it) out; inhale and exhale: [*no obj*]: *The patient began to breathe normally. She began to breathe in and out normally.* [~ + *obj*]: *Just breathe that pure mountain air!* **2.** [*no obj*] to live; exist: *The ruined economy is barely breathing.* **3.** [*no obj*] (of a material) to allow air and moisture to pass through easily: *That polyester shirt doesn't breathe.* **4.** [*no obj*] (of a wine) to be open to the air after being uncorked, in order to develop flavor and bouquet: *We opened the bottle and let the wine breathe.* **5.** [~ + *obj*

+ *into* + *obj*] to put in as if by breathing; infuse: *tried to breathe life into the party.* **6.** [~ + *obj*] to speak; whisper; murmur: *Don't breathe a word of it to anyone.* —***Idiom.*** **7. breathe down someone's neck,** to watch or follow someone closely, in order to control or chase after: *I hate working here because the boss is always breathing down my neck.* **8. breathe easily** or **breathe easy** or **breathe freely,** [*no obj*] to have relief from worry, fear, tension, or pressure: *You can all breathe easy now: the operation was a success.* **9. breathe one's last,** to die.

breath•er (brē′t͟hər) /ˈbriyðər/ *n.* [*count*] a pause, as for breath; a break: *"I need a breather," he puffed.*

breath′ing space′, *n.* [*noncount*] **1.** Also called **breath′ing spell′.** a chance to rest or think: *Give me a little breathing space to figure this out.* **2.** sufficient space in which to move, etc.: *I need a little breathing space; I feel so crowded in that tiny room.* Also called **breath′ing room′.**

breath•less (breth′lis) /ˈbrɛθlɪs/ *adj.* **1.** without breath, or breathing with difficulty: *breathless after running up five flights of stairs.* **2.** causing loss of breath, as from excitement, fear, etc.: *a breathless ride.* —**breath′less•ly,** *adv.: ran up and introduced herself breathlessly.* —**breath′less•ness,** *n.* [*noncount*]

breath•tak•ing (breth′tā′king) /ˈbrɛθˌteykɪŋ/ *adj.* amazing; remarkable; astonishing: *The trapeze artist performed a few breathtaking flips.* —**breath′tak′ing•ly,** *adv.: a breathtakingly beautiful view.*

bred (bred) /brɛd/ *v.* a pt. and pp. of BREED.

breech (brēch) /briytʃ/ *n.* [*count*] the rear part of the barrel of a gun, where the bullet is loaded.

breech•es (brich′iz) /ˈbrɪtʃɪz/ *n.* [*plural*] **1.** knee-length trousers. **2.** *Informal.* TROUSERS: *Tom pulled down his breeches and jumped into the river.* —***Idiom.*** **3. too big for one's breeches,** too proud; conceited: *too big for her breeches, always bragging about what she can accomplish.*

breed (brēd) /briyd/ *v.,* **bred** (bred) /brɛd/ **breed•ing,** *n.* —*v.* **1.** [*no obj*] to produce young; reproduce; procreate: *Mosquitoes breed in still ponds.* **2.** [~ + *obj*] to cause (plants or animals) to produce offspring and to be improved by selection: *They breed livestock.* **3.** [~ + *obj*] to give rise to; cause; produce: *Dirt breeds disease.* **4.** [~ + *obj*] to develop by training or education: *born and bred in Oxford.* —*n.* [*count*] **5.** a certain type or group of animals within a species, developed and maintained by humans: *What breed are your cattle?*

breed•er (brē′dər) /ˈbriydər/ *n.* [*count*] **1.** an animal, plant, or person that produces young. **2.** a person who raises animals or plants for breeding. **3.** Also called **breed′er reac′tor.** a nuclear reactor in which more material is produced than is used up.

breed•ing (brē′ding) /ˈbriydɪŋ/ *n.* [*noncount*] **1.** the producing of young: *When is the breeding season for these sheep?* **2.** the improvement as by careful mating: *the careful breeding of Arabian stallions.* **3.** the result of one's upbringing as shown in good manners: *a woman of good breeding and excellent taste.*

breed′ing ground′, *n.* [*count*] **1.** a place where animals breed. **2.** a place suitable for developing something: *That drug-infested neighborhood is a breeding ground for violence.*

breeze (brēz) /briyz/ *n., v.,* **breezed, breez•ing.** —*n.* [*count*] **1.** a wind or current of air, esp. a light one: *A gentle breeze blew through the curtains.* **2.** [*usually singular*] an easy task: *That quiz was a breeze.* —*v.* **3.** [~ + *into/in* + *obj*] to move in a carefree and confident manner: *He breezed into the classroom and sat down.* **4. breeze through,** [~ + *through* + *obj*] to complete (work, etc.) quickly and easily: *We breezed through the test and were out of there an hour early.* —***Idiom.*** **5. shoot** or **bat the breeze,** *Slang.* to talk aimlessly; chat: *two old men sitting on the porch and shooting the breeze.*

breez•y (brē′zē) /ˈbriyziy/ *adj.,* **-i•er, -i•est. 1.** having many breezes: *a breezy day at the beach.* **2.** light; carefree; free and easy: *a breezy style of writing.* —**breez•i•ly** (brē′zə lē) /ˈbriyzəliy/ *adv.* —**breez′i•ness,** *n.* [*noncount*]

breth•ren (bret͟h′rin) /ˈbrɛðrɪn/ *n.* [*plural*] **1.** male members, as of a congregation; brothers. **2.** fellow members (of a church or organization).

-brev-, *root. -brev-* comes from Latin, where it has the meaning "short." This meaning is found in such words as: ABBREVIATE, ABRIDGE, BREVITY, BRIEF.

brev•i•ty (brev′i tē) /ˈbrɛvɪtiy/ *n.* [*noncount*] shortness (of speech, etc.); briefness: *the brevity of life.* See -BREV-.

brew (bro͞o) /bruw/ *v.* **1.** to make (beer, etc.) by boiling and fermenting the ingredients: [~ + *obj*]: *Beer is brewed from malt and hops.* [*no obj*]: *The beer is brewing in these vats.* **2.** to prepare (tea, etc.) with boiling water: [~ + *obj*]: *She brewed a pot of tea for us.* [*no obj*]: *Let the tea brew for five minutes.* **3.** [~ + *obj*] to plan or think up: *They just want to brew mischief.* **4.** [*no obj; usually: be* + ~*-ing*] to start to develop; begin: *A storm is brewing in the Atlantic.* —*n.* **5.** [*noncount*] an amount of a beverage brewed in a single process: *this year's brew.* **6.** a liquid mixture, esp. a liquid produced from a mixture of unusual ingredients: [*count*]: *a witches' brew of lemon juice, honey, and whiskey.* [*noncount*]: *Make some witches' brew for your cold.* **7.** *Informal.* **a.** [*noncount*] beer or ale: *a party with plenty of brew.* **b.** [*count*] a serving of beer or ale: *Ask for a couple of brews.*

brew•er (bro͞o′ər) /ˈbruwər/ *n.* [*count*] a person who prepares ale, beer, or another brewed beverage.

brew•er•y (bro͞o′ə rē, bro͝or′ē) /ˈbruwəriy, ˈbrʊriy/ *n.* [*count*], *pl.* **-er•ies.** a building or company for brewing beer.

bri•ar (brī′ər) /ˈbrayər/ *n.* BRIER.

bribe (brīb) /brayb/ *n., v.,* **bribed, brib•ing.** —*n.* [*count*] **1.** money given to persuade someone to do something illegal: *The customs official agreed to take a bribe.* **2.** anything given in order to influence: *The babysitter had to give the child a bribe of an extra piece of cake.* —*v.* **3.** to give or promise a bribe to: [~ + *obj*]: *We tried to bribe the customs official.* [~ + *obj* + *to* + *verb*]: *We bribed him to let us go through.*

brib•er•y (brī′bə rē) /ˈbraybəriy/ *n.* [*noncount*] the act or practice of giving or accepting a bribe: *In that country bribery was a way of doing business.*

bric-a-brac or **bric-à-brac** (brik′ə brak′) /ˈbrɪkəˌbræk/ *n.* small articles collected for decoration; knickknacks; trinkets: [*noncount; used with a singular verb*]: *She had bric-a-brac that was scattered all over the room.* [*count; used as a plural with a plural verb*]: *The bric-a-brac were lined up on shelves.*

brick (brik) /brɪk/ *n.* **1.** (a block of) clay hardened by being burnt in a furnace and used for building, paving, etc.: [*count*]: *He replaced the broken bricks in the fireplace.* [*noncount*]: *Our apartment building is brick on the outside.* **2.** [*count*] a block having a similar size and shape: *a brick of ice cream.* **3.** *Informal.* a helpful, friendly person. —*v.* **4. brick up,** [~ + *up* + *obj*] to build, fill in, or pave with bricks: *They bricked up the hole in the wall.* —*adj.* **5.** made of or constructed with bricks: *a brick wall.* —***Idiom.*** **6. like a ton of bricks,** with sudden or powerful weight or force: *The news hit him like a ton of bricks.*

brick•bat (brik′bat′) /ˈbrɪkˌbæt/ *n.* [*count*] **1.** a piece of broken brick or rock, esp. one used for throwing. **2.** an unkind remark; criticism: *had to suffer through the brickbats of her political enemies.*

brick•lay•ing (brik′lā′ing) /ˈbrɪkˌleyɪŋ/ *n.* [*noncount*] the act or occupation of building by laying bricks in construction. —**brick′lay′er,** *n.* [*count*]

brick•work (brik′wûrk′) /ˈbrɪkˌwɜrk/ *n.* [*noncount*] construction using brick: *inferior brickwork on the chimney.*

brid•al (brīd′l) /ˈbraydl̩/ *adj.* [*before a noun*] of or for a bride or a wedding: *a bridal gown.*

bride (brīd) /brayd/ *n.* [*count*] a newly married woman or one about to be married.

bride•groom (brīd′gro͞om′, -gro͝om′) /ˈbraydˌgruwm, -ˌgrʊm/ *n.* [*count*] a newly married man or one about to be married.

brides•maid (brīdz′mād′) /ˈbraydzˌmeyd/ *n.* [*count*] a woman who attends the bride at a wedding ceremony.

bridge[1] (brij) /brɪdʒ/ *n., v.,* **bridged, bridg•ing.** —*n.* [*count*] **1.** a structure that reaches across a river, road, etc., and provides a way of crossing. **2.** a raised platform on a ship from which the captain directs the course: *The helmsman came onto the bridge and reported to the captain.* **3.** the upper line of the nose between the eyes: *a lump on the bridge of his nose.* **4.** the part of a pair of eyeglasses that joins the two lenses across the nose. **5.** an artificial replacement of missing teeth: *She had a bridge inserted where her teeth had broken.* **6.** a thin wedge that raises the strings of a musical instrument above the part that provides sound. **7.** a part of a musical arrangement, piece of writing, etc., that connects or links two other sections: *The songs usually have two verses, then a bridge, then a third verse.* **8.** a link or connection between two related items, etc.: *a bridge of friendship and trust.* —*v.* [~ + *obj*] **9.** to make a bridge or passage over: *A wooden plank bridged the stream.*

10. to join by or as if by a bridge: *The mediators tried to bridge the gap.* —***Idiom.*** **11. burn one's bridges (behind one),** to eliminate all possibilities of turning back: *She burned her bridges (behind her) when she called us liars and angrily walked out.*

bridge[2] (brij) /brɪdʒ/ *n.* [*noncount*] a card game for two teams of two players each in which one team tries to accomplish a certain number of plays declared in advance: *The four of them played bridge all night.*

bridge•head (brij′hed′) /ˈbrɪdʒˌhɛd/ *n.* [*count*] a position taken by an army on the enemy side of a river to protect the crossing of friendly troops: *established a bridgehead and began moving up troops.*

bridge•work (brij′wûrk′) /ˈbrɪdʒˌwɜrk/ *n.* [*noncount*] **1.** dental bridges thought of as a group: *The insurance policy does not cover bridgework.* **2.** the art or process of building bridges.

bri•dle (brīd′l) /ˈbraydl̩/ *n., v.,* **-dled, -dling.** —*n.* [*count*] **1.** part of the harness of a horse, made up of a leather band around the head, bit, and reins: *They led their horses around by the bridles.* **2.** anything that holds back or restrains: *Put a bridle on your temper.* —*v.* **3.** [~ + *obj*] to put a bridle on: *They bridled the horses.* **4.** [~ + *obj*] to control or hold back; curb: *You've got to bridle your temper.* **5.** to draw up the head and draw in the chin, so as to show contempt or resentment: [~ + *at* + *obj*]: *He bridled at the suggestion that he should work like a common person.* [*used with quotations*]: *She bridled, "I refuse to go along with such an outrageous scheme."*

bri′dle path′, *n.* [*count*] a wide path for riding horses.

brie (brē) /briy/ *n.* [*noncount*] a soft, disk-shaped cheese with a creamy center and a whitish crust.

brief (brēf) /briyf/ *adj.,* **-er, -est,** *n., v.* —*adj.* **1.** lasting or taking a short time: *We took a brief pause from the meeting.* **2.** using few words; short; concise: *Write a brief outline.* **3.** very short or small in fit; scanty: *a brief bathing suit.* —*n.* [*count*] **4.** a short statement or a written item using few words: *Please prepare a brief for the president.* **5.** a written statement given to a court by a lawyer presenting the most important facts, points of law, and arguments. **6. briefs,** [*plural*] close-fitting legless underpants with an elastic waistband: *a pair of briefs.* See illustration at CLOTHING. —*v.* [~ + *obj*] **7.** to instruct (someone) or give relevant information to: *I briefed the new teacher.* —***Idiom.*** **8. in brief,** in a few words; in short: *What you are saying, in brief, is that we're broke.* —**brief′er,** *n.* [*count*]: *The president's briefers and press secretaries met ahead of time.* See -BREV-.

brief•case (brēf′kās′) /ˈbriyfˌkeys/ *n.* [*count*] a flat case with a handle, often of leather, for carrying books, papers, etc.

brief•ing (brē′fing) /ˈbriyfɪŋ/ *n.* [*count*] **1.** a summary of relevant information or instructions: *The captain prepared a briefing on the plans for the attack.* **2.** a meeting at which such information is given.

brief•ly (brēf′lī) /ˈbriyflay/ *adv.* **1.** happening or done in a short period of time: *She smiled briefly at him.* **2.** using few words: *He spoke briefly and then returned to his room.*

bri•er[1] or **bri•ar** (brī′ər) /ˈbrayər/ *n.* **1.** [*count*] a plant or shrub that is prickly and has thorny stems. **2.** [*noncount*] a tangled mass of prickly plants: *We heard the animals crashing through the brier.*

bri•er[2] or **bri•ar** (brī′ər) /ˈbrayər/ *n.* [*count*] **1.** a type of plant, the white heath, with a woody root which is used for making tobacco pipes. **2.** a pipe made of this.

brig (brig) /brɪg/ *n.* [*count*] **1. a.** a ship with two masts and square sails. **b.** [*often: the* + ~] the room or part of a ship where prisoners are kept: *Take them to the brig and keep them there till we get to shore.* **2.** a prison; guardhouse.

bri•gade (bri gād′) /brɪˈgeyd/ *n.* [*count*] **1.** a military unit: *A brigade consists of a headquarters and two or more regiments, squadrons, groups, or battalions.* **2.** a large body of troops. **3.** a group of individuals organized for a purpose: *the rescue brigade.*

brig•a•dier (brig′ə dēr′) /ˌbrɪgəˈdɪər/ *n.* [*count*] a military officer of the rank between colonel and major general.

brig•and (brig′ənd) /ˈbrɪgənd/ *n.* [*count*] an armed robber or bandit, esp. in mountain or forest regions: *The brigands of the cowboy days are gone forever.* —**brig•and•age** (brig′ən dij) /ˈbrɪgəndɪdʒ/ *n.* [*noncount*]

bright (brīt) /brayt/ *adj.,* **-er, -est,** *n.* —*adj.* **1.** giving off or reflecting light: *a bright, sunny room.* **2.** (of colors) strong; clear; brilliant: *bright red.* **3.** quick to learn; intelligent; smart: *a bright student.* **4.** (of a remark or an idea) clever, smart, or original: *That was a bright idea to line up the recycling bins near the photocopying machines.* **5.** cheerful; happy; lively: *a bright smile.* **6.** favorable; promising; showing signs of success: *a bright future.* —*n.* **7. brights,** [*plural*] bright motor vehicle headlights used for driving, esp. under conditions when it is hard to see: *Put on your brights in these country lanes.* —**bright′ly,** *adv.* —**bright′ness,** *n.* [*noncount*]: *As the sun went down, the brightness of the room gave way to darkness.*

bright•en (brīt′n) /ˈbraytn̩/ *v.* [*no obj;* ~ + *obj*] **1.** to become or make bright or brighter. **2.** to become or make more cheerful. —**bright′en•er,** *n.* [*count*]

bright-eyed (brīt′īd′) /ˈbraytˌayd/ *adj.* **1.** having bright eyes. **2.** alertly eager: *a bright-eyed young teacher.* —***Idiom.*** **3. bright-eyed and bushy-tailed,** full of energy and enthusiasm: *Get a good night's sleep so you'll be bright-eyed and bushy-tailed in the morning.*

bril•liance (bril′yəns) /ˈbrɪlyəns/ *n.* [*noncount*] the state or quality of being brilliant: *The huge diamond glowed with brilliance.*

bril•lian•cy (bril′yən sē) /ˈbrɪlyənsiy/ *n.* [*noncount*] brilliance.

bril•liant (bril′yənt) /ˈbrɪlyənt/ *adj.* **1.** shining brightly; sparkling; glittering: *brilliant jewels.* **2.** distinguished; outstanding: *a brilliant performance.* **3.** having or showing great intelligence, talent, etc.: *I taught several brilliant students that year.* **4.** [*before a noun*] strong and clear in tone or color: *The African sky was a brilliant blue that day.* —**bril′liant•ly,** *adv.*: *performed brilliantly.*

brim (brim) /brɪm/ *n., v.,* **brimmed, brim•ming.** —*n.* [*count*] **1.** the upper edge of anything hollow, such as a glass, cup, or bowl. **2.** an edge that sticks out: *the brim of a hat.* —*v.* **3.** [~ + *(over* +*) with* + *obj*] to be full to the brim or to the top edge: *Her eyes brimmed (over) with tears when I told her we were moving.* —***Idiom.*** **4. to the brim,** to the top: *Fill the cup to the brim, but don't let it spill.*

brim•ful or **brim•full** (brim′fŏŏl′) /ˈbrɪmˈfʊl/ *adj.* full or filled to the top or brim: [*after a noun*]: *She gave him a mug brimful of beer.* [*be* + ~ + *of*]: *He was just brimful of good ideas that day.*

brim•ming (brim′ing) /ˈbrɪmɪŋ/ *adj.* **1.** full or filled to the top: *a brimming cup of hot tea.* **2.** [~ + *with*] holding or containing: *brimming with new plans.*

brim•stone (brim′stōn′) /ˈbrɪmˌstown/ *n.* [*noncount*] **1.** SULFUR. —***Idiom.*** **2. fire and brimstone,** (warnings about) hell for sinners: *a sermon full of fire and brimstone.*

brine (brīn) /brayn/ *n.* [*noncount*] **1.** water containing salt, as for pickling food: *pickles in brine.* **2.** the water of the sea.

bring (bring) /brɪŋ/ *v.* [~ + *obj*], **brought** (brôt) /brɔt/ **bring•ing. 1.** to carry or cause (someone or something) to come toward the speaker; convey: [~ + *obj* + *to* + *obj*]: *Can you bring the children to our party? Bring the clock to me.* [~ + *obj* + *obj*]: *Bring me that broken part.* **2.** [~ + *obj*] to cause to come toward oneself; attract: *The screams brought the police to the scene of the crime.* **3.** to cause to occur or exist; produce: [~ + *obj*]: *The medicine brought rapid relief.* [~ + *obj* + *obj*]: *All his money couldn't bring him happiness.* **4.** [~ + *obj* + *to* + *obj*] to cause to come into a particular position, state, or condition: *The jokes and funny scenes brought laughter to the audience.* **5.** [~ + *oneself* + *to* + *verb*] to persuade or force oneself to do something: *I couldn't bring myself to sell those family heirlooms.* **6.** [~ + *obj*] to sell for: *These lamps will bring a good price.* **7.** [~ + *obj* + *to* + *obj*] to lead to (a place, point, or direction): *This brings me to my next point: how dreams are measured by scientific means.* **8. bring about,** [~ + *about* + *obj*] to accomplish; cause: *The recession will bring about higher unemployment.* **9. bring around** or **round,** [~ + *obj* + *around*] **a.** to convince (someone) of a belief or opinion: *brought her around to our point of view.* **b.** to restore to consciousness, as after a faint: *The batter fell unconscious, but the doctor brought him around.* **10. bring down, a.** to injure, capture, or kill: [~ + *down* + *obj*]: *The hunters brought down six quail.* [~ + *obj* + *down*]: *They brought the ducks down easily.* **b.** to cause to fall: [~ + *down* + *obj*]: *The enemy brought down only six aircraft.* [~ + *obj* + *down*]: *Enemy fire brought six aircraft down.* **c.** [~ + *obj* + *down*] to cause to be unhappy or in low spirits: *Gloomy weather really brings me down.* **11. bring forth,** [~ + *forth* + *obj*] **a.** to give birth to; bear: *to bring forth young.* **b.** to give rise to; introduce: *His study brought forth new findings.* **12. bring forward,** to introduce; suggest: [~ + *obj* + *forward*]: *He brought his plan forward.* [~ + *forward* + *obj*]: *He brought forward the plan.* **13. bring in, a.** to make money; produce as profit or income: [~ + *in* + *obj*]: *This new car will bring in profits.* [~ + *obj* + *in*]: *This will bring lots of money in.* **b.** to present officially; submit: [~ + *in* + *obj*]: *The jury is ready to bring in a verdict.* [~ + *obj* + *in*]: *The jury is ready to bring a verdict in.* **c.** to arrest and take to jail: [~ + *in* + *obj*]: *The police brought in the mob leader for questioning.* [~ + *obj* + *in*]: *brought him in for questioning.* **d.** to introduce; cause to be part of (a job, work, or a process): [~ + *in* + *obj*]: *She brought in a new secretary.* [~ + *obj* + *in*]: *wanted to bring outsiders in.* **14. bring off,** to accomplish, carry out, or achieve: [~ + *off* + *obj*]: *The generals couldn't bring off a coup.* [~ + *obj* + *off*]: *They couldn't bring it off.* **15. bring on,** to cause to happen or exist: [~ + *on* + *obj*]: *The bright lights brought on a crushing headache.* [~ + *obj* + *on*]: *What brought the flu on?* **16. bring out, a.** to reveal or cause to appear or be seen: [~ + *out* + *obj*]: *That difficult job brought out the bad side of her nature.* [~ + *obj* + *out*]: *She has a bad temper, and working at that difficult job brought it out.* **b.** [~ + *out* + *obj*] to make noticeable; emphasize: *That blue sweater brings out the color of your eyes.* **c.** to publish or produce: [~ + *out* + *obj*]: *The company brought out a new product.* [~ + *obj* + *out*]: *The company brought the new car out with a lot of publicity.* **17. bring to,** [~ + *obj* + *to*] to bring back to consciousness: *tried to bring the accident victim to.* **18. bring up, a.** to care for and educate during childhood; rear: [~ + *up* + *obj*]: *They brought up their children with sound values.* [~ + *obj* + *up*]: *My father brought us up alone.* **b.** to introduce or mention for attention or consideration: [~ + *obj* + *up*]: *Why don't you bring that idea up at the next club meeting?* [~ + *up* + *obj*]: *We weren't allowed to bring up your new idea.* **c.** to vomit: [~ + *up* + *obj*]: *bringing up her baby food again.* [~ + *obj* + *up*]: *The baby food must not agree with her because she's bringing it up again.*

brink (bringk) /brɪŋk/ *n.* [*count; usually singular*] **1.** the edge of any steep place or of land bordering water: *the brink of the cliff.* **2.** any extreme edge; verge. **3.** a critical point beyond which something will occur: verge: *on the brink of disaster.*

brink•man•ship (bringk′mən ship′) /ˈbrɪŋkmənˌʃɪp/ also **brinks•man•ship** (bringks′-) /ˈbrɪŋks-/ *n.* [*noncount*] the policy of creating a dangerous situation and risking a great deal in order to achieve the greatest advantage: *wound up playing a dangerous game of international and military brinksmanship.*

brin•y (brī′nē) /ˈbrayniy/ *adj.*, **-i•er, -i•est.** of or like brine; salty. —**brin′i•ness,** *n.* [*noncount*]

bri•quette or **bri•quet** (bri ket′) /brɪˈkɛt/ *n.* [*count*] a small block of charcoal used for fuel, esp. in barbecuing: *The briquettes were glowing red.*

brisk (brisk) /brɪsk/ *adj.*, **-er, -est. 1.** quick and active; lively: *brisk trading in the market.* **2.** sharp and stimulating; fresh: *brisk weather.* **3.** abrupt; somewhat too quick: *a brisk tone of voice.* —**brisk′ly,** *adv.*: *The wind blew briskly down the street.* —**brisk′ness,** *n.* [*noncount*]: *Her briskness bothered me at first.*

bris•ket (bris′kit) /ˈbrɪskɪt/ *n.* [*noncount*] a cut of meat, esp. beef, from the breast, or from the part of the breast lying next to the ribs.

bris•tle (bris′əl) /ˈbrɪsəl/ *n.*, *v.*, **-tled, -tling.** —*n.* **1.** (a) short, stiff, rough hair: [*count*]: *Hogs' bristles are used to make brushes.* [*noncount*]: *That brush felt like it was made of bristle.* —*v.* [*no obj*] **2.** (of hair) to stand or rise stiffly: *I could feel the hairs on the back of my neck bristle.* **3.** to become stiff and straight because of anger: *He bristled when I asked him to move his feet out of the aisle.* **4. bristle with,** [~ + *with* + *obj*] to have or be filled with a great number or amount of (something): *The building was bristling with security guards.* —**bris′tly,** *adj.*, **-tli•er, -tli•est.**

Brit (brit) /brɪt/ *n.* [*count*] *Informal.* a person from the United Kingdom; Briton (def. 1).

Brit., an abbreviation of: **1.** Britain. **2.** British.

britch•es (brich′iz) /ˈbrɪtʃɪz/ *n.* BREECHES.

Brit•ish (brit′ish) /ˈbrɪtɪʃ/ *adj.* **1.** of or relating to Great Britain. **2.** used esp. by the people living in Great Britain: *The word "lift" meaning "elevator" is a British expression.* —*n.* **3.** [*plural; the + ~; used with a plural verb*] the people born or living in Great Britain.

Brit•ish•er (brit′i shər) /ˈbrɪtɪʃər/ *n.* BRITON.

Brit′ish ther′mal u′nit, *n.* [*count*] the amount of heat needed to raise the temperature of 1 lb. (0.4 kg) of water 1°F. *Abbr.:* Btu, BTU

Brit•on (brit′n) /ˈbrɪtn̩/ *n.* [*count*] a person born or living in Great Britain.

brit•tle (brit′l) /ˈbrɪtl̩/ *adj.*, **-tler, -tlest,** *n.* —*adj.* **1.** having hardness and stiffness but breaking easily; easily damaged; frail: *brittle icicles.* **2.** having a sharp, tense quality; lacking friendliness; cold: *a brittle tone of voice.* —*n.* [*noncount*] **3.** a kind of candy made of melted sugar, usually with nuts, brittle when cooled: *She made peanut brittle.* —**brit′tle•ness,** *n.* [*noncount*]

broach (brōch) /browtʃ/ *n.* **1.** BROOCH. —*v.* **2.** [~ + *obj*] to mention or suggest for the first time: *I waited until he was in a good mood before I broached the subject of my raise.* **3.** [~ + *obj*] to draw (beer, etc.), as by tapping: *to broach beer from a keg.* **4.** [*no obj*] to break the surface of water from below: *After the depth charge exploded the submarine broached, then quickly sank.*

broad (brôd) /brɔd/ *adj.*, **-er, -est,** *n.* —*adj.* **1.** wide; of great breadth: *The Mississippi River is its broadest at this point.* **2.** [*after a noun of measurement*] measured from side to side: *three feet broad.* **3.** [*before a noun*] open; full; clear: *robbed in broad daylight.* **4.** not limited or narrow; extensive: *Our teacher has a broad range of interests.* **5.** [*before a noun*] general: *in the broad sense of the term.* **6.** plain or clear; obvious: *a broad hint about the job layoffs.* —*n.* [*count*] **7.** [*usually singular*] the broad part of anything: *the broad of his back.* **8.** *Slang (offensive).* a woman: *Bring in the broads.* —**broad′ly,** *adv.*: *Broadly speaking, I think it's safe to say he's dangerous to society.* —**broad′ness,** *n.* [*noncount*]

broad•band (brôd′band′) /ˈbrɔdˌbænd/ *adj.* [*before a noun*] of, relating to, or able to receive a continuous, wide range or band of electromagnetic frequencies: *a broadband receiver.*

broad•cast (brôd′kast′) /ˈbrɔdˌkæst/ *v.*, **-cast** or **-cast•ed, -cast•ing,** *n.*, *adj.* —*v.* **1.** to transmit (programs) from a radio or television station: [~ + *obj*]: *We broadcast our English-language programs on this channel at six o'clock.* [*no obj*]: *We were broadcasting on all the major channels.* **2.** [~ + *obj*] to speak or present on a radio or television program: *The president will broadcast his appeal for help.* **3.** [~ + *obj*] to spread (news, etc.) widely; tell many people: *broadcast lies all over town.* —*n.* [*count*] **4.** something broadcast, such as a single radio or television program: *We interrupt this broadcast to bring you a special warning.* —*adj.* [*before a noun*] **5.** (of programs) transmitted from a radio or television station. **6.** of or relating to broadcasting: *courses in broadcast journalism.* —**broad′cast′er,** *n.* [*count*]

broad•cast•ing (brôd′kas′ting) /ˈbrɔdˌkæstɪŋ/ *n.* [*noncount*] **1.** the act of transmitting speech, music, etc., by radio, television, etc. **2.** radio or television as a business or profession: *Broadcasting is a multimillion-dollar industry.*

broad•en (brôd′n) /ˈbrɔdn̩/ *v.* to become or make broad or broader: [*no obj*]: *Our children's interests broadened after trips to museums.* [~ + *obj*]: *We have always tried to broaden our minds.*

broad′ jump′, *n.* LONG JUMP.

broad′-mind′ed, *adj.* free from narrowness; respecting the views or opinions of others: *Back then it was very broad-minded to allow your daughter to go out with someone from another town.* —**broad′-mind′ed•ness,** *n.* [*noncount*]

broad•side (brôd′sīd′) /ˈbrɔdˌsayd/ *n.*, *adv.*, *v.*, **-sid•ed, -sid•ing.** —*n.* [*count*] **1.** a firing of all the guns on one side of a warship at the same time: *A few broadsides at the unprotected sailboat persuaded its crew to surrender.* **2.** any strong or complete attack on someone, as by criticism: *The candidate was hit with several political broadsides from the media.* —*adv.* **3.** with the broader side facing toward a certain point or object: *The truck hit the fence broadside.* **4.** in a wide-ranging manner; at random: *to attack the policies broadside.* —*v.* [~ + *obj*] **5.** to collide with or run into the side of: *The truck swung off the road and broadsided the house.* **6.** to make strong verbal attacks on: *His political opponents broadsided the candidate.*

bro•cade (brō kād′) /browˈkeyd/ *n.* [*noncount*] a heavy fabric woven with an elaborate raised design.

broc•co•li (brok′ə lē) /ˈbrɒkəliy/ *n.* [*noncount*] a plant whose leafy stalks and clusters of usually green flower buds are eaten as a vegetable.

bro•chure (brō sho͝or′) /browˈʃʊr/ *n.* [*count*] a short booklet; a pamphlet or leaflet: *The brochure described the hotel.*

bro•gan (brō′gən) /ˈbrowgən/ *n.* [*count*] a heavy, sturdy shoe, esp. an ankle-high work shoe.

brogue[1] (brōg) /browg/ *n.* [*count*] **1.** an Irish accent in the pronunciation of English: *O'Malley answered in that rich brogue of his.* **2.** any strong regional accent.

brogue[2] (brōg) /browg/ *n.* [*count*] **1.** a shoe, esp. a rough shoe of untanned leather formerly worn in Ireland and Scotland. **2.** BROGAN.

broil (broil) /brɔyl/ *v.* **1.** to (cause to) be cooked by direct heat; grill: [~ + *obj*]: *Let's broil a couple of steaks.* [*no obj*]: *The meat's broiling; take it off when the outside is dark.* **2.** to (cause to) be very hot; scorch: [*no obj*]: *The oven is broiling.* [*no obj; it + be + ~*]: *It's broiling out there; stay inside in the air-conditioned room.* [~ + *obj*]: *Don't stay out too long in this August sun; it'll broil you.* —*n.* **3.** (a piece of) meat for broiling: [*noncount*]: *She bought London broil and tenderized it.* [*count*]: *She brought home a London broil for dinner.*

broil•er (broi′lər) /ˈbrɔylər/ *n.* [*count*] **1.** a small oven in which food is broiled by heat from above: *Set the broiler to 475 degrees.* **2.** a grate or pan used to broil food: *Take the drippings from the broiler and add it to make your gravy.* **3.** a young chicken suitable for broiling.

broke (brōk) /browk/ *v.* **1.** pt. of BREAK. —*adj.* [*be + ~*] **2.** without money: *I was broke that week, so I borrowed some money to pay the rent.* —***Idiom.*** **3. go broke,** [*no obj*] to go bankrupt; be without funds to conduct business: *In that business people are forever going broke.* **4. go for broke,** [*no obj*] *Slang.* to use one's abilities or one's means to the fullest in taking a dangerous risk: *He decided to go for broke and put all his money into the new business.*

bro•ken (brō′kən) /ˈbrowkən/ *v.* **1.** pp. of BREAK. —*adj.* **2.** reduced to small pieces: *cut himself on the broken glass.* **3.** ruptured; torn; fractured: *His arm was broken in three places.* **4.** not working or functioning; damaged: *I think my watch is broken again.* **5.** not kept; violated: *a broken promise.* **6.** interrupted or disconnected: *a broken line.* **7.** weakened in strength, etc.; crushed by bad experiences: *a broken heart.* **8.** [*before a noun*] (of language) imperfectly spoken: *couldn't understand his broken English.* **9.** spoken in a halting or hesitant manner, as under emotional strain: *In a broken voice he begged for forgiveness.* **10.** [*before a noun*] divided or disrupted, as by divorce: *broken families.* **11.** [*before a noun*] not smooth; rough or irregular: *broken ground.*

bro′ken-down′, *adj.* **1.** dilapidated or ruined: *Those nice apartments had become broken-down shells.* **2.** out of working order, as from use or age: *The broken-down car was towed off the highway.*

bro•ken•heart•ed (brō′kən här′tid) /ˈbrowkənˈhɑrtɪd/ *adj.* suffering from great sorrow; heartbroken. —**bro′ken•heart′ed•ly,** *adv.* —**bro′ken•heart′ed•ness,** *n.* [*noncount*]

bro•ker (brō′kər) /ˈbrowkər/ *n.* [*count*] **1.** an agent in business who buys or sells for another: *an insurance broker.* **2.** one who acts as an intermediary in arranging marriages, negotiating agreements, etc.: *a marriage broker.* **3.** STOCKBROKER. —*v.* [~ + *obj*] **4.** to act as a broker for: *to broker the sale of a house.* **5.** to negotiate or arrange as a broker: *Party officials brokered the deal between the president and his vice-presidential candidate.*

bro•mide (brō′mīd) /ˈbrowmayd/ *n.* [*count*] **1.** a drug formerly used to calm patients. **2.** a meaningless saying or expression; platitude: *He gave us the same old bromides.*

bro•mine (brō′mēn, -min) /ˈbrowmiyn, -mɪn/ *n.* [*noncount*] a dark reddish liquid element obtained from ocean water and used chiefly in gasoline antiknock compounds.

bron•chi (brong′kē, -kī) /ˈbrɒŋkiy, -kay/ *n.* [*plural*] pl. of BRONCHUS.

bron•chi•al (brong′kē əl) /ˈbrɒŋkiyəl/ *adj.* of or relating to the bronchi: *a bronchial infection.*

bron′chial tube′, *n.* [*count*] a bronchus or any of its branches.

bron•chi•tis (brong kī′tis) /brɒŋˈkaytɪs/ *n.* [*noncount*] an illness of the lining of the bronchial tubes, caused by infection or by breathing in irritating substances.

bron•chus (brong′kəs) /ˈbrɒŋkəs/ *n.* [*count*], *pl.* **-chi** (-kē, -kī). either of the two branches of the windpipe that extend into the lungs to carry air.

bron•co (brong′kō) /ˈbrɒŋkow/ also **bronc** (brongk) /brɒŋk/ *n.* [*count*], *pl.* **bron•cos** also **broncs.** a pony or mustang of the western U.S., esp. one that is not tamed or is imperfectly tamed: *trying to ride a bucking bronco.*

bron•to•saur (bron′tə sôr′) /ˈbrɒntəˌsɔr/ *n.* [*count*] a huge, four-footed, plant-eating dinosaur.

Bronx′ cheer′ (brongks) /brɒŋks/ *n.* RASPBERRY (def. 4): *The candidate got a Bronx cheer.*

bronze (bronz) /brɒnz/ *n., v.,* **bronzed, bronz•ing,** *adj.* —*n.* **1.** [*noncount*] a yellowish brown metal that is an alloy of copper and tin: *Many of the weapons and utensils of those ancient people were made of bronze.* **2.** [*noncount*] a metallic brownish color: *the handsome bronze of his tan.* **3.** [*count*] a sculpture, medal, or artistic object made of bronze: *a beautiful bronze on exhibit.* —*v.* [~ + *obj*] **4.** to give the appearance or color of bronze or brown to, as a tan which comes from exposure to the sun: *The sun bronzed the lifeguard's skin.* —*adj.* **5.** of the color bronze. **6.** made of or coated with bronze.

brooch (brōch, brōōch) /browtʃ, bruwtʃ/ also **broach,** *n.* [*count*] a clasp or piece of jewelry having a pin at the back for passing through the clothing and a catch for fastening and holding the point of the pin: *She wore a Christmas tree brooch.*

brood (brōōd) /bruwd/ *n.* [*count*] **1.** a number of young produced at one time: *The mother duck watched over her brood.* **2.** a family or group in a household: *How is the Jones brood?* —*v.* [*no obj*] **3.** to sit upon eggs that will be hatched, as a bird. **4.** to keep thinking about a subject for a long time, often with anger or resentment: *We found him in his room, brooding on/over his failure to get a job after two years of trying.* —*adj.* [*before a noun*] **5.** kept for breeding: *a brood hen.*

brood•ing (brōō′ding) /ˈbruwdɪŋ/ *adj.* **1.** causing a feeling of fear; threatening: *a dark, brooding scene.* —*n.* [*noncount*] **2.** continual thinking about something for a long time, often with anger or resentment: *Her brooding over her problems had gone on too long.*

brook[1] (brŏŏk) /brʊk/ *n.* [*count*] a small natural stream of fresh water.

brook[2] (brŏŏk) /brʊk/ *v.* [~ + *obj*] [*used with a negative word or phrase, or in questions*] to bear; suffer; tolerate: *I will brook no interference.*

broom (brōōm, brŏŏm) /bruwm, brʊm/ *n.* **1.** [*count*] a tool for sweeping, made up of a brush on a long handle: *He took the broom and began sweeping the broken glass out of the way.* **2.** [*noncount*] a shrub or small tree with yellow flowers on long branches.

broom•stick (brōōm′stik′, brŏŏm′-) /ˈbruwmˌstɪk, ˈbrʊm-/ *n.* [*count*] the long, slender handle of a broom: *In the movie the witch rides away on her broomstick.*

bros. or **Bros.,** an abbreviation of: brothers.

broth (brôth, broth) /brɔθ, brɒθ/ *n.* **1.** a thin soup in which meat, fish, or vegetables have been cooked in water: [*count*]: *a delicious broth of onion and fish.* [*noncount*]: *Make some broth by boiling the turkey bones and keeping the liquid.* **2.** [*count*] a liquid that contains ingredients suitable for growing small organisms: *Scientists prepared a broth and managed to get the fungus to reproduce in the laboratory.*

broth•el (broth′əl, broth′-, brô′thəl, -thəl) /ˈbrɒθəl, ˈbrɒð-, ˈbrɔθəl, -ðəl/ *n.* [*count*] a house of prostitution.

broth•er (bruth′ər) /ˈbrʌðər/ *n., pl.* **broth•ers,** (*Archaic*) **breth•ren;** (breth′rən) /ˈbrɛðrən/; *interj.* —*n.* [*count*] **1.** a male relative who has the same parents as another: *She had only one brother.* **2.** a man or person in the same group, nationality, etc., as another: *We should remember that all these people are our brothers.* **3.** [*often: Brother*] a man who devotes himself to the duties of a religious order without taking holy orders. **4.** *Slang.* fellow; buddy: *Brother, can you spare a dime?* —*interj.* **5.** (used to show disappointment, disgust, or surprise): *Oh, brother! I forgot my tickets.*

broth•er•hood (bruth′ər hŏŏd′) /ˈbrʌðərˌhʊd/ *n.* **1.** [*noncount*] the quality of feeling a bond of friendship, affection, warmth, or loyalty toward another: *a strong sense of brotherhood.* **2.** [*count*] an organization of people working in a certain trade or profession: *the brotherhood of firefighters.*

broth′er-in-law′, *n.* [*count*], *pl.* **broth•ers-in-law. 1.** the brother of one's husband or wife. **2.** the husband of one's sister. **3.** the husband of one's wife's or husband's sister.

broth•er•ly (bruth′ər lē) /ˈbrʌðərliy/ *adj.* [*before a noun*] of or like a brother; affectionate and loyal: *in the city of brotherly love.* —**broth′er•li•ness,** *n.* [*noncount*]

brought (brôt) /brɔt/ *v.* pt. and pp. of BRING.

brou•ha•ha (brōō′hä hä′, brōō′hä hä′, brōō hä′hä) /ˈbruwhɑˌhɑ, ˌbruwhɑˈhɑ, bruwˈhɑhɑ/ *n.* [*count*], *pl.* **-has.**

a small, unimportant event involving too much uproar: *The department had a little brouhaha last week when the copying machine broke.*

brow (brou) /braw/ *n.* [*count*] **1.** the forehead; the area or ridge over the eye: *Her brow was wrinkled as she concentrated on the problem.* See *knit one's brows* under KNIT. **2.** the hair growing on the ridge; eyebrow. **3.** the edge of a steep place: *the brow of a hill.*

brow•beat (brou′bēt′) /ˈbrawˌbiyt/ *v.* [~ + *obj*], **-beat, -beat•en, -beat•ing.** to frighten with threats and cause (someone) to do something; bully: *She browbeat me into taking on all this extra work.* —**brow′beat′er,** *n.* [*count*]

brown (broun) /brawn/ *n., adj.,* **-er, -est,** *v.* **1.** [*noncount*] the dark color of wood, with a slight yellowish or reddish hue: *It was a beautiful brown, soft and yet strong.* —*adj.* **2.** of the color brown: *The brown gravy looked great on the potatoes.* **3.** having skin of this color: *invited all people, white, yellow, brown and black, to join him.* **4.** sunburned or tanned: *Her legs and back get brown in the summer.* —*v.* **5.** to make or become brown: [*no obj*]: *His skin browned through the summer.* [~ + *obj*]: *The sun browned his skin in the summer.* **6.** to fry, sauté, roast, etc., to a brown color: [*no obj*]: *The chicken is browning nicely.* [~ + *obj*]: *Brown the pieces of chicken.* **7. brown out,** [~ + *obj*] to subject to a brownout: *The power failure browned out half of the state.* —**brown′ish,** *adj.* —**brown′ness,** *n.* [*noncount*]

brown′-bag′, *v.* [~ + *obj*], **-bagged, -bag•ging.** to bring (one's lunch) to work, often in a small brown paper bag: *He always brown-bagged his lunch, unlike other executives.* —**brown′-bag′ger,** *n.* [*count*]

brown′ belt′, *n.* [*count*] **1.** a brown cloth waistband given to one who studies a martial art, to indicate a middle level of expertise. **2.** a person at this level.

brown′ bet′ty (bet′ē) /ˈbɛtiy/ *n.* [*count*], *pl.* **brown bet•ties.** a baked dessert made of apples or other fruit, breadcrumbs, sugar, butter, and spices.

brown•ie (brou′nē) /ˈbrawniy/ *n.* [*count*] **1.** a good-natured fairy or elf who secretly helps at night with household chores. **2.** a square piece of dense, chewy cake, usually chocolate: *She baked a dozen brownies.* **3.** [*sometimes: Brownie*] a member of the division of the Girl Scouts or the Girl Guides for girls 6–8 years old: *She was a Brownie for three years.*

Brown′ie point′, *n.* [*count*] *Informal.* credit for having done something as a favor, in order to gain recognition or advancement: *How many Brownie points did you get for carrying the teacher's books?*

brown′-nose′, *v.,* **-nosed, -nos•ing,** *n. Slang.* —*v.* **1.** to try to get favors from (someone) by behaving in an overly friendly way: [*no obj*]: *He was surprised to learn that brown-nosing wouldn't work with her.* [~ + *obj*]: *He tried to brown-nose the French teacher by staying after school and helping her clean the room.* —*n.* [*count*] **2.** Also, **brown′-nos′er.** someone who behaves in this way; toady; sycophant.

brown•out (broun′out′) /ˈbrawnˌawt/ *n.* [*count*] a deliberate reduction of the electric power sent out by a region's electrical generating company, esp. a reduction in voltage to prevent a blackout: *The brownout occurred on a hot afternoon.*

brown′ rice′, *n.* [*noncount*] rice from which the outer bran layers have not been removed by polishing.

brown•stone (broun′stōn′) /ˈbrawnˌstown/ *n.* **1.** [*noncount*] a reddish brown sandstone, used as a building material: *houses of beautiful old brownstone.* **2.** [*count*] a building, or house attached to others in a row, which is made with this stone on the front: *The party was at a fashionable brownstone.*

brown′ sug′ar, *n.* [*noncount*] sugar that retains some molasses or to which molasses has been added.

browse (brouz) /brawz/ *v.,* **browsed, brows•ing,** *n.* —*v.* [*no obj*] **1.** to eat or feed on bushes, leaves, etc.; graze: *The deer were browsing in the meadows.* **2.** to glance at or read parts of a book, magazine, etc., casually: *browsed through the Sunday newspaper.* **3.** to look in an unhurried way at goods displayed for sale, as in a store: *We browsed through the first floor of the department store, waiting for a gift idea to come to us.* —*n.* [*count*] **4.** an act or instance of browsing: *a quick browse through the hardware section.* —**brows′er,** *n.* [*count*]

brr (bûr) /bɜr/ *interj.* (used to express feelings of cold): *"Brr, it's cold," she said. "Please turn up the heat."*

bru•in (bro͞o′in) /ˈbruwɪn/ *n.* [*count*] a bear, esp. a European brown bear.

bruise (bro͞oz) /bruwz/ *v.,* **bruised, bruis•ing,** *n.* —*v.* **1.** to injure by striking or pressing, without breaking the skin but causing a discolored spot to develop: [~ + *obj*]: *bruised her knee against the chair.* [*no obj*]: *With that disease the patient bruises easily.* **2.** to injure or hurt slightly, as with an insult or unkind remark; offend: [~ + *obj*]: *Those sharp insults bruised her feelings.* [*no obj*]: *We both bruise too easily.* —*n.* [*count*] **3.** an injury due to bruising: *black-and-blue bruises on her arms and legs.* —**bruised,** *adj.*: *The bruised fruit had so many spots on it that we had to throw it out.* —**bruis′ing,** *adj.*: *He won the election only after a bruising campaign.*

bruis•er (bro͞o′zər) /ˈbruwzər/ *n.* [*count*] *Informal.* a strong, tough man: *A couple of bruisers blocked our way.*

brunch (brunch) /brʌntʃ/ *n.* **1.** a meal that serves as both breakfast and lunch: [*noncount*]: *We'll go out for brunch on Sunday about eleven o'clock.* [*count*]: *What can you eat at these brunches?* —*v.* [*no obj*] **2.** to eat brunch: *We'll brunch at eleven o'clock.*

bru•net (bro͞o net′) /bruwˈnɛt/ *adj.* **1.** (esp. of a white male) having dark hair; brunette. —*n.* [*count*] **2.** a person with dark hair and, often, dark eyes and darkish or olive skin.

bru•nette (bro͞o net′) /bruwˈnɛt/ *adj.* **1.** (of the hair, eyes, skin, etc., of a white person) of a dark color or tone: *brunette hair.* **2.** (of a white person) having dark hair and, often, dark eyes and darkish or olive skin: *I was met by a striking brunette tour guide at the airport.* —*n.* [*count*] **3.** a person, esp. a female, with such coloring: *Several brunettes walked by.*

brunt (brunt) /brʌnt/ *n.* [*noncount*] —***Idiom.*** **bear** or **take the brunt of,** [~ + *obj*] to suffer or absorb the main force or impact of (an attack or blow): *Our town bore the brunt of the storm.*

brush[1] (brush) /brʌʃ/ *n.* [*count*] **1.** a hand-held instrument of bristles and a handle, used for painting, cleaning, grooming, etc.: *The painter took a thin brush and began painting the wall.* **2.** an act of brushing; application of a brush: *a few quick brushes of her hair.* **3.** a close approach, esp. to something undesirable or harmful; skirmish: *a brush with disaster.* **4. the brush,** [*singular*] a rejection or rebuff: *to get the brush from one's lover.* Compare BRUSH-OFF. —*v.* [~ + *obj*] **5.** to sweep, paint, groom, etc., with a brush. **6.** to touch lightly in passing; pass lightly over: *The plane just brushed the surface of the water.* **7. brush aside** or **away,** to disregard; ignore: [~ + *obj* + *aside/away*]: *He brushed our objections aside.* [~ + *aside/away* + *obj*]: *He brushed aside our objections.* **8. brush off,** [~ + *obj* + *off*] to send (someone) away; to refuse to listen to: *He tried to start a conversation with her, but she brushed him off.* **9. brush up (on),** [~ + *up* (+ *on*) + *obj*] to revive or review (studies, a skill, etc.): *had to brush up on his mathematics.* —**brush′er,** *n.* [*count*]

brush[2] (brush) /brʌʃ/ *n.* [*noncount*] **1.** a thick, heavy, dense growth of bushes, shrubs, etc.: *The fox disappeared into the brush.* **2.** BRUSHWOOD (defs. 1, 2).

brushed (brusht) /brʌʃt/ *adj.* [*before a noun*] (of a fabric) having been treated by a brushing process in order to soften: *brushed cotton.*

brush′-off′, *n.* [*count*] an act of suddenly sending someone away, or of refusing to speak with him or her: *He tried to introduce himself to the beautiful actress, but she gave him the brush-off.*

brush•wood (brush′wo͝od′) /ˈbrʌʃˌwʊd/ *n.* [*noncount*] **1.** the wood of branches that have been cut or broken off. **2.** a pile of such branches. **3.** land where such branches are piled.

brusque (brusk) /brʌsk/ *adj.* abrupt in manner; curt: *He was quite brusque with the students who came to him for help.* —**brusque′ly,** *adv.*: *She brusquely showed me the door.* —**brusque′ness,** *n.* [*noncount*] —**Syn.** See BLUNT.

Brus′sels sprout′ (brus′əlz) /ˈbrʌsəlz/ *n.* [*count*] **1.** Usually, **Brussels sprouts.** a plant having small heads or buds along the stalk that look like tiny cabbages. **2.** **Brussels sprouts,** the heads or buds, eaten as a vegetable.

bru•tal (bro͞ot′l) /ˈbruwtl/ *adj.* **1.** cruel; savage; inhuman: *The gang led a brutal attack on their enemies.* **2.** harsh; severe; difficult to put up with: *a brutal storm.* **3.** accurate, direct, and clear, but displeasing: *You must face the brutal fact that you cannot walk again.* —**bru′tal•ly,** *adv.*: *I found her remarks brutally honest.*

bru•tal•i•ty (bro͞o tal′i tē) /bruwˈtælɪtiy/ *n., pl.* **-ties.** **1.** [*noncount*] the quality of being brutal: *a suspect claiming police brutality.* **2.** [*count*] a brutal act or practice: *a serial killer who committed atrocities and brutalities.*

bru•tal•ize (bro͞ot′l īz′) /ˈbruwtlˌayz/ *v.* [~ + *obj*], **-ized,**

-**iz•ing.** **1.** to make brutal or cruel: *His upbringing in that slum brutalized him.* **2.** to treat (someone) with brutality: *The dictator brutalized his people.* —**bru•tal•i•za•tion** (bro͞ot′l i zā′shən) /ˌbruwtḷɪ'zeyʃən/ *n.* [*noncount*]

brute (bro͞ot) /bruwt/ *n.* [*count*] **1.** an animal; beast: *It has been said that we humans are somewhere between angels and brutes.* **2.** a savage, insensitive, or crude person: *She thought he was just a big brute.* **3.** [*singular*] the animal qualities, desires, etc., of humans: *to bring out the brute in someone.* —*adj.* [*before a noun*] **4.** like an animal, as in strength or cruelty: *brute force.*

brut•ish (bro͞o′tish) /'bruwtɪʃ/ *adj.* **1.** brutal; gross; uncivilized: *his brutish behavior at the party.* **2.** bestial; like an animal: *his brutish attempts to force sex with her.* —**brut′ish•ly,** *adv.* —**brut′ish•ness,** *n.* [*noncount*]

B.S., an abbreviation of: Bachelor of Science.

b/s, an abbreviation of: bill of sale.

B.S.A., an abbreviation of: Boy Scouts of America.

B.Sc., an abbreviation of: Bachelor of Science.

bsh., an abbreviation of: bushel.

bsmt, an abbreviation of: basement.

bth, an abbreviation of: bathroom.

btl., an abbreviation of: bottle.

btry., an abbreviation of: battery.

Btu or **BTU,** an abbreviation of: British thermal unit.

bu., an abbreviation of: **1.** bureau. **2.** bushel.

bub (bub) /bʌb/ *n.* [*count; usually singular*] *Slang.* (used as an often very impolite term of address): *"Hey, bub, move it out of here," he yelled at the slow-moving car.*

bub•ble (bub′əl) /'bʌbəl/ *n., v.,* **-bled, -bling.** —*n.* [*count*] **1.** a round body of gas in a liquid: *The bubbles rose to the top of the kettle as the water boiled.* **2.** anything that seems to be solid but is not; a delusion or false hope: *One day her bubble burst.* **3.** a canopy, shelter, or structure in the shape of a ball; dome: *The huge bubble enclosed the stadium.* —*v.* [*no obj*] **4.** to form, produce, or release bubbles: *The boiling water was bubbling.* **5.** to flow or spout with a gurgling noise: *A fountain bubbled in the hotel lobby.* **6.** to proceed or go along in a lively, sparkling manner: *The play bubbled with fun.* **7. bubble over,** [*no obj*] to overflow with liveliness or happiness: *bubbling over with joy at the prospect of moving to a new house.*

bub′ble bath′, *n.* **1.** [*noncount*] a powder or liquid that makes foam in bath water, often giving it a pleasant smell: *Pour one capful of bubble bath in the water.* **2.** [*count*] a bath with such a substance added to the water: *The kids liked to play in a bubble bath.*

bub•ble•gum (bub′əl gum′) /'bʌbəlˌgʌm/ *n.* [*noncount*] chewing gum that can be blown into bubbles.

bub•bly (bub′lē) /'bʌbliy/ *adj.,* **-bli•er, -bli•est,** *n., pl.* **-blies.** —*adj.* **1.** full of or producing bubbles: *bubbly champagne.* **2.** lively; enthusiastic; cheerful; bouncy: *a bubbly personality.* —*n.* [*noncount*] **3.** *Informal.* CHAMPAGNE: *We shared a small bottle of bubbly on New Year's Eve.* —**bub′bli•ness,** *n.* [*count*]

buc•ca•neer (buk′ə nēr′) /ˌbʌkə'nɪər/ *n.* [*count*] a pirate, esp. one who attacked Spanish colonies and ships along the American coast in the second half of the 17th century.

buck[1] (buk) /bʌk/ *n.* [*count*] **1.** the male of the deer, antelope, rabbit, and other animals. **2.** BUCKSKIN (def. 1). **3.** a casual shoe made of buckskin: *used to wear white bucks.* **4.** a daring, dashing, or spirited man or youth. —*adj.* [*before a noun*] **5.** of the lowest rank within a military designation: *a buck private.*

buck[2] (buk) /bʌk/ *v.* **1.** [*no obj*] (of an animal wearing a saddle or carrying a pack) to leap with the back arched and land with head low and forelegs stiff: *The donkey bucked when it saw the snake.* **2.** [~ + *obj*] to throw or attempt to throw (a rider) by leaping this way: *That wild bronco bucked its rider in just five seconds.* **3.** [*no obj*] (of a vehicle, etc.) to operate unevenly: *When he put the car in gear it began to buck wildly.* **4.** to resist or oppose stubbornly: [~ + *obj*]: *She bucked the system.* [~ + *at* + *obj*]: *He bucked at the suggestion to reduce his staff.* **5.** [~ + *obj*] to force a way through (an obstacle): *bucked the odds against him and succeeded anyway.* **6. buck up,** to make or become cheerful: [*no obj*]: *Don't feel so bad about losing; buck up and try again.* [~ + *obj* + *up*]: *Let's try to buck the losers up.*

buck[3] (buk) /bʌk/ *n.* [*noncount*] **1.** final responsibility: *The buck stops here.* —*v.* [~ + *obj*] **2.** to pass (something) along to another, esp. to avoid responsibility: *He didn't know what to do, so he bucked the issue to his superior.* —***Idiom.*** **3. pass the buck,** to shift responsibility or blame to another person: *Quit passing the buck all the time!*

buck[4] (buk) /bʌk/ *adv. Informal.* completely; stark: *buck naked.*

buck[5] (buk) /bʌk/ *n.* [*count*] *Slang.* a dollar: *Can't you lend me a few bucks till Saturday?*

buck•a•roo (buk′ə ro͞o′, buk′ə ro͞o′) /'bʌkəˌruw, ˌbʌkə'ruw/ *n.* [*count*], *pl.* **-roos.** *Western U.S.* a cowboy.

buck•et, (buk′it) /'bʌkɪt/ *n.* [*count*] **1.** a deep, round container with a flat bottom, an open top, and a handle; pail: *He put the mop in the bucket of water.* **2.** something, as a scoop, shaped like this: *the bucket on a steam shovel.* **3.** an amount (of something) carried in a bucket; bucketful: *a bucket of sand.* **4.** [*plural*] a large amount: *It's raining buckets out there.* —***Idiom.*** **5. a drop in the bucket,** a small, inadequate amount: *That donation of fifty cents was just a drop in the bucket.* **6. kick the bucket,** *Slang.* to die: *Too bad old Charrington kicked the bucket last week.*

buck•et•ful (buk′it fo͝ol′) /'bʌkɪtˌfʊl/ *n.* [*count*], *pl.* **-fuls.** the amount that a bucket can hold.

buck′et seat′, *n.* [*count*] an individual seat with a back partly enclosing the body, as in some automobiles: *This model's bucket seats fold forward.*

buck•le (buk′əl) /'bʌkəl/ *n., v.,* **-led, -ling.** —*n.* [*count*] **1.** a piece of metal attached to one end of a belt or strap, used for fastening to the other end of the same strap or to another strap: *His brass belt buckle flashed in the light.* —*v.* **2.** to fasten with a buckle or buckles: [~ + *obj*]: *Buckle your seat belt.* [~ + *on* + *obj*]: *The officer buckled on his pistol.* [~ + *obj* + *on*]: *He buckled his pistol on.* **3.** [*no obj*] to bend because of fatigue: *Suddenly my knees buckled.* **4.** to bend, curl, or collapse suddenly because of heat or pressure: [*no obj*]: *When the earthquake hit, several highways buckled.* [~ + *obj*]: *The intense heat buckled the road.* **5. buckle down,** [*no obj*] to set to work with strength and determination: *Just buckle down and practice.* **6. buckle under,** [*no obj*] to surrender, give way, or yield to another: *The stubborn worker finally began to buckle under.* **7. buckle up,** [*no obj*] to fasten one's belt, seat belt, or buckles: *Please buckle up now; we're about to land.*

buck•shot (buk′shot′) /'bʌkˌʃɒt/ *n.* [*noncount*] a large size of lead shot or pellets used in shotgun shells for hunting pheasants, ducks, etc.

buck•skin (buk′skin′) /'bʌkˌskɪn/ *n.* **1.** [*noncount*] a strong, soft, yellowish or grayish leather, originally prepared from the skin of a buck or deer. **2. buckskins,** [*plural*] breeches or shoes made of buckskin.

buck•tooth (buk′to͞oth′) /'bʌk'tuwθ/ *n.* [*count*], *pl.* **-teeth** (-tēth′) /-'tiyθ/. a tooth that sticks forward or out, esp. an upper front tooth: *The child needs braces because of his buckteeth.* —**buck•toothed** (buk′to͞otht′) /'bʌkˌtuwθt/ *adj.*

buck•wheat (buk′hwēt′, -wēt′) /'bʌkˌhwiyt, -ˌwiyt/ *n.* [*noncount*] **1.** a plant grown for its edible triangular seeds. **2.** the seeds of this plant, made into flour or a cereal. **3.** Also called **buck′wheat flour′.** flour made from buckwheat seeds. —*adj.* [*usually before a noun*] **4.** made with buckwheat flour: *buckwheat pancakes.*

bu•col•ic (byo͞o kol′ik) /byuw'kɒlɪk/ *adj.* of or relating to country living, esp. to ideal country living; pastoral: *the bucolic setting of the old farms in the background.* —**bu•col′i•cal•ly,** *adv.*

bud[1] (bud) /bʌd/ *n., v.,* **bud•ded, bud•ding.** —*n.* **1.** [*count*] any of the small parts on the end of a plant stem, from which leaves or flowers develop: *The plants were showing a few buds by late April.* **2.** [*noncount*] a state of putting forth buds: *roses in bud.* —*v.* [*no obj*] **3.** to produce buds: *The plants began to bud in early April.* **4.** to begin to develop: *His genius began to bud at an early age.* —***Idiom.*** **5. in the bud,** not developed but showing promise: *a playwright in the bud.* **6. nip in the bud,** [*nip* + *obj* + *in the* + ~] to stop (something) in the earliest stages: *to nip a mutiny in the bud.*

bud[2] (bud) /bʌd/ *n.* (used as a term of address to a man or boy) buddy; friend: *"Hey bud, can you help me out, please," he called.*

Bud•dhism (bo͞o′diz əm, bo͝od′iz-) /'buwdɪzəm, 'bʊdɪz-/ *n.* [*noncount*] an Asian religion, originated in India by Buddha (Gautama), holding that life is full of suffering caused by desire and that the way to end this suffering is through overcoming these desires. —**Bud′dhist,** *n.* [*count*], *adj.*

bud•ding (bud′ing) /'bʌdɪŋ/ *adj.* [*before a noun*] in an early stage of development: *a budding artist.*

bud•dy (bud′ē) /'bʌdiy/ *n.* [*count*], *pl.* **-dies.** **1.** a friend:

All his buddies showed up for the surprise party. **2.** BUD[2]: *Buddy, can you spare a dime?*

bud′dy sys′tem, *n.* [*count*] an arrangement or system in which two persons, such as swimmers, watch out for each other's safety.

budge (buj) /bʌdʒ/ *v.* [*often used with a negative*], **budged, budg•ing. 1.** to (cause to) move slightly: [*no obj*]: *The car wouldn't budge.* [~ + *obj*]: *couldn't budge the car out of the snowbank.* **2.** to (cause to) change one's opinion or stated position; (cause to) give in: [*no obj*]: *refused to budge on the question.* [~ + *obj*]: *We couldn't budge her on the issue.*

budg•er•i•gar (buj′ə rē gär′) /ˈbʌdʒəriy,gɑr/ *n.* [*count*] an Australian parakeet, green with black and yellow marks. Also, **budgie.**

budg•et (buj′it) /ˈbʌdʒɪt/ *n.* [*count*] **1.** an estimate of expected income and expenses: *drew up a budget and asked everyone to stick to it.* **2.** a list showing item by item how funds will be or have been used, etc., for a given period: *showed him our budget of expenses.* **3.** a sum of money set aside for a particular purpose: *The school construction budget won't be enough.* **—*adj.*** [*before a noun*] **4.** reasonably or cheaply priced: *budget seats.* **—*v.* 5.** to plan or deal with an amount of (funds, time, etc.): [~ + *obj*]: *We budgeted our time carefully.* [~ + *for* + *obj*]: *We couldn't budget for every emergency.*

budg•et•ar•y (buj′i ter′ē) /ˈbʌdʒɪ ˌtɛriy/ *adj.* [*before a noun*] of or relating to a budget: *a budgetary deficit.*

budg•ie (buj′ē) /ˈbʌdʒiy/ *n.* BUDGERIGAR.

buff (buf) /bʌf/ *n.* **1.** [*noncount*] light-yellow leather originally made from buffalo skin. **2.** [*noncount*] a brownish yellow color; tan. **3.** [*count*] one who knows a lot about a certain subject: *World War II buffs.* **4.** [*noncount; the* + ~] *Informal.* bare skin: *streaked across the room in the buff.* **—*adj.* 5.** of the color buff. **—*v.*** [~ + *obj*] **6.** to clean, polish, or shine with a piece of some soft material: *buffed my shoes to a bright shine.*

buf•fa•lo (buf′ə lō′) /ˈbʌfə,low/ *n., pl.* **-loes, -los,** (*esp. when thought of as a group*) **-lo,** *v.,* **-loed, -lo•ing. —*n.*** [*count*] **1.** a large wild ox, such as the bison. **—*v.*** [~ + *obj*] *Informal.* **2.** to puzzle or confuse; baffle: *Those test questions really buffaloed him.* **3.** [~ + *obj* + *into* + *obj*] to intimidate by a display of power, etc.: *buffaloed me into doing that job.*

buff•er[1] (buf′ər) /ˈbʌfər/ *n.* [*count*] **1.** an apparatus at the end of a railroad car, etc., for absorbing shock during coupling, etc. **2.** one that shields and protects against harm, or lessens the impact of a shock or other misfortune: *That small country was created as a buffer against the two warring states around it.* **3.** a temporary storage area that holds data until a computer is ready to process it. **—*v.*** [~ + *obj*] **4.** to cushion, shield, or protect.

buff•er[2] (buf′ər) /ˈbʌfər/ *n.* [*count*] a device for polishing or buffing.

buff•er[3] (buf′ər) /ˈbʌfər/ *n.* [*count*] *Brit. Slang.* a foolish person.

buf•fet[1] (buf′it) /ˈbʌfɪt/ *n.* [*count*] **1.** a blow delivered with the hand or fist. **—*v.*** [~ + *obj*] **2.** to strike against or push repeatedly: *The wind buffeted the house.* **3.** to struggle against; battle: *buffeted by a series of financial disasters.*

buf•fet[2] (bə fā′, bo͞o-) /bəˈfey, bʊ-/ *n.* [*count*] **1.** a meal laid out so that guests may serve themselves: *a buffet of cold cuts, salads, and desserts.* **2.** a counter, bar, or table for food or refreshments. **3.** a restaurant with such a counter or table. **—*adj.*** [*before a noun*] **4.** served from or as a buffet: *a buffet supper.*

buf•foon (bə fo͞on′) /bəˈfuwn/ *n.* [*count*] one who amuses others by jokes, pranks, etc. **—buf•foon′er•y,** *n.* [*noncount*]: *"What buffoonery is this?" he thundered.*

bug (bug) /bʌg/ *n., v.,* **bugged, bug•ging. —*n.*** [*count*] **1.** Also called **true bug.** an insect having sucking mouthparts and thickened, leathery wings in front. **2.** (loosely) any insect. **3.** *Informal.* a disease, or the microorganism causing the disease: *I've got the flu bug.* **4.** a defect, error, or imperfection, as in computer software: *Work out the bugs in that program.* **5.** [*usually singular*] *Informal.* **a.** a short-lived interest in or enthusiasm for something: *He's got the sports-car bug.* **b.** someone very enthusiastic about a certain subject; fan: *Someone who is interested in photography is called a camera bug or a shutter bug.* **6.** a hidden microphone or other device used to hear or record information, etc.: *planted the bug in his suspect's room.* **—*v.* 7.** [~ + *obj*] to install a secret listening device in or on: *The phone was bugged.* **8.** [~ + *obj*] *Informal.* to annoy or pester: *Quit bugging me!* **9.** [*no obj*] (of the eyes) to bulge: *His eyes bugged out of his head.* **10. bug off,** [*no obj*] *Slang.* to leave or depart (often used as a command): *"Come here often?" he asked from the next barstool. "Bug off!" she answered.* **—*Idiom.* 11. put a bug in someone's ear,** to give someone a subtle suggestion: *put a bug in his ear to start counting up everyone's vacation days.*

bug•a•boo (bug′ə bo͞o′) /ˈbʌgə,buw/ *n.* [*count*], *pl.* **-boos.** something that causes fear or worry but may not be real; bugbear; bogy.

bug•bear (bug′bâr′) /ˈbʌg,bɛər/ *n.* [*count*] **1.** a persistent problem or source of annoyance. **2.** any source, real or imaginary, of fright or fear.

bug-eyed (bug′īd′) /ˈbʌg,ayd/ *adj.* with bulging eyes, as from surprise or wonderment.

bug•ger[1] (bug′ər, bo͝og′-) /ˈbʌgər, ˈbʊg-/ *n.* [*count*] **1.** *Informal.* (used to express affection, or to show anger or contempt) a fellow or lad: *He's a cute little bugger.* **2.** *Informal.* any object or thing: *See if this little bugger fits in the slot.* **3.** *Chiefly Brit. Slang.* **a.** a despicable person, esp. a man. **b.** an annoying thing. **—*v.* 4.** [~ + *obj*] *Chiefly Brit. Slang.* to cause problems for, esp. by deceiving: *This little gadget is buggering the works.* **5. bugger off,** [*no obj*] *Chiefly Brit. Slang.* BUG (def. 10): *told me to bugger off.*

bug•ger[2] (bug′ər) /ˈbʌgər/ *n.* [*count*] a person who installs electronic eavesdropping devices.

bug•gered (bug′ərd, bo͝og′-) /ˈbʌgərd, ˈbʊg-/ *adj. Chiefly Brit. (vulgar).* **1.** [*be* + ~ + *if*] damned: *I'll be buggered if I'll help you.* **2.** ruined; spoiled: *The motor's all buggered.* **3.** [*I'll* + *be* + *buggered*] (used to express amazement or great surprise): *It's really you, then? Well, I'll be buggered; I never expected to see you again.*

bug•gy[1] (bug′ē) /ˈbʌgiy/ *n.* [*count*], *pl.* **-gies. 1.** a light, four-wheeled, horse-drawn carriage with a single seat. **2.** BABY CARRIAGE.

bug•gy[2] (bug′ē) /ˈbʌgiy/ *adj.,* **-gi•er, -gi•est. 1.** infested with bugs. **2.** *Slang.* crazy; insane: *She's gone buggy.* **3.** (of a computer program or software) not working well because of mistakes in programming: *The program is still too buggy for everyday users.* **—bug′gi•ness,** *n.* [*noncount*]

bu•gle (byo͞o′gəl) /ˈbyuwgəl/ *n., v.,* **-gled, -gling. —*n.*** [*count*] **1.** a brass wind instrument resembling a horn but usually without keys or valves. **—*v.*** [*no obj*] **2.** to sound a bugle. **—bu′gler,** *n.* [*count*]

build (bild) /bɪld/ *v.,* **built** (bilt) /bɪlt/ **build•ing,** *n.* **—*v.* 1.** to make (a house, etc.) by putting together parts: [~ + *obj*]: *How many years did it take to build the Empire State Building?* [*no obj*]: *The town wants to build in that area.* **2.** to start, increase, or strengthen; grow intense: [~ *(+ up)* + *obj*]: *He came to this country and built (up) the family business.* [~ + *obj (+ up)*]: *to build it (up).* [*no obj; (~ + up)*]: *The tension in that story builds (up) toward a climax.* See BUILD UP below. **3.** [~ + *obj (+ into)*] to form, shape, or create: *The military school builds boys into men.* **4. build in** or **into,** [~ + *in/into* + *obj*] to make something a part of something else: *An allowance for travel was built into the budget.* **5. build on** or **upon,** [~ + *on/upon* + *obj*] **a.** to have as a basis: *a relationship built on trust.* **b.** to form or construct a plan, system of thought, etc.: *to build on the philosophies of the past.* **6. build up,** [~ + *up* + *obj*] **a.** to develop, strengthen, or increase: *She built up my confidence.* **b.** to improve the strength or health of: *weightlifting to build up his body.* **c.** to fill up with houses or other buildings: *My old neighborhood has really been built up.* **—*n.*** [*count; singular*] **7.** the shape or structure of a person's body or muscles; physique: *She had a strong build.*

build•er (bil′dər) /ˈbɪldər/ *n.* [*count*] a person who builds buildings or houses as a job.

build•ing (bil′ding) /ˈbɪldɪŋ/ *n.* **1.** [*count*] anything (such as a house, etc.) built on an area of land, having a roof and walls and usually intended to be kept in one place: *Many of the old buildings were being fixed.* **2.** [*noncount*] the act or business of constructing houses, etc.

build•up or **build-up** (bild′up′) /ˈbɪld,ʌp/ *n.* [*count; usually singular*] **1.** an increase, as in amount, strength, or intensity: *a buildup of suspense.* **2.** praise or publicity to make something or someone well-known, popular, etc.: *The speaker gave our visitor quite a buildup before her speech.*

built (bilt) /bɪlt/ *v.* **1.** the pt. and pp. of BUILD. **—*adj.*** [*be* + ~] *Informal.* **2.** having a good physique or figure: *The lifeguard was really built.*

built′-in′, *adj.* [*usually: before a noun*] **1.** built so as to be a part of a larger construction: *built-in bookcases.* **2.**

existing as a natural part; inherent: *built-in safety mechanisms.*

built′-up′, *adj.* [*usually: before a noun*] **1.** built by the fastening together of several parts: *a shoe with a built-up heel.* **2.** (of an area) filled in with houses: *In built-up areas the speed limit is 50 m.p.h.*

bulb (bulb) /bʌlb/ *n.* [*count*] **1.** a rounded root or underground stem of a plant, such as the onion or tulip. **2.** any round, enlarged part, esp. at the end of a long object: *the bulb of a thermometer.* **3.** the part of an incandescent lamp made of glass, through which electricity passes, producing light.

bul•bous (bul′bəs) /ˈbʌlbəs/ *adj.* **1.** shaped like a bulb; rounded: *a red, bulbous nose.* **2.** having or growing from bulbs.

Bul•gar•i•an (bul gâr′ē ən, bo͝ol-) /bʌlˈgɛəriyən, bʊl-/ *n.* **1.** [*count*] a person born or living in Bulgaria. **2.** [*noncount*] the language spoken by many of the people of Bulgaria. *—adj.* **3.** of or relating to Bulgaria. **4.** of or relating to the language spoken by many of the people of Bulgaria.

bulge (bulj) /bʌldʒ/ *n., v.,* **bulged, bulg•ing.** *—n.* [*count*] **1.** a rounded part that sticks out of something: *She started to exercise to reduce the bulge at her waistline.* **2.** a sudden increase, as in volume: *The graphs show the bulge in unemployment for that month.* *—v.* [*no obj*] **3.** to swell or bend outward; stick out: *His stomach bulged out over his belt.* **4.** [~ + *with*] to be filled completely: *The briefcase bulged with papers.*

bulk (bulk) /bʌlk/ *n.* **1.** [*noncount*] great weight, size, or mass: *the great bulk of the aircraft carrier.* **2.** [*count; usually singular*] the body of a living creature, esp. when large or heavy: *swung his considerable bulk off the chair.* **3.** [*count; singular: the* + ~ + *of*] the greater part or amount: *The bulk of the debt was paid.* **4.** FIBER (def. 5). *—adj.* [*before a noun*] **5.** being or involving material in bulk: *The newsletters were sent by bulk mail.* *—v.* [*no obj*] **6.** to increase in size; expand; swell. **7.** to be of great weight, size, or importance: *The problem bulks large in his mind.* ***—Idiom.*** **8. in bulk,** in large quantities or amounts: *rice sold in bulk.*

bulk•head (bulk′hed′) /ˈbʌlk,hɛd/ *n.* [*count*] a wall-like construction inside a ship, etc., that forms separate sections: *watertight bulkheads.*

bulk•y (bul′kē) /ˈbʌlkiy/ *adj.,* **-i•er, -i•est. 1.** of large bulk: *bulky packages.* **2.** large or big: *The fashion was for bulky sweaters.* —**bulk′i•ness,** *n.* [*noncount*]

bull[1] (bo͝ol) /bʊl/ *n.* [*count*] **1.** the male of the cow family: *The bull charged the matador in the arena.* **2.** the male of certain other animals, as the elephant: *the bull elephants.* **3.** a person who believes that stock prices will increase: *The bulls went on a spree today, and the stock market soared.* Compare BEAR. *—adj.* [*before a noun*] **4.** marked by rising prices, esp. of stocks: *a bull market.* ***—Idiom.*** **5. bull in a china shop,** an awkward or clumsy person: *He was like a bull in a china shop at that party, tripping over guests and getting in the way.* **6. take the bull by the horns,** to attack a difficult or risky problem boldly: *He decided to take the bull by the horns and confront his boss.*

bull[2] (bo͝ol) /bʊl/ *n.* [*count*] a formal document issued by a pope: *the papal bull.*

bull[3] (bo͝ol) /bʊl/ *Slang.* *—n.* [*noncount*] **1.** exaggerations; lies; nonsense: *That story about his rescuing those flyers was complete bull.* *—v.* [~ + *obj*] **2.** to try to fool or impress by lies or exaggeration: *Don't bull me; just tell me what's going on.* ***—Idiom.*** **3. shoot the bull,** to engage in friendly, easygoing conversation: *We sat around all night shooting the bull.*

bull•dog (bo͝ol′dôg′, -dog′) /ˈbʊl,dɔg, -,dɒg/ *n.* [*count*] **1.** an English breed of short, wide, muscular dogs with short hair. **2.** a stubborn person; one who does not give up easily.

bull•doze (bo͝ol′dōz′) /ˈbʊl,dowz/ *v.* [~ + *obj*], **-dozed, -doz•ing. 1.** to clear, move, or reshape (the land) with or as if with a bulldozer: *They bulldozed the area and started construction.* **2.** to knock down or clear away by or as if by using a bulldozer: *to bulldoze trees from a site.* **3.** [~ + *obj* + *into* + *verb-ing*] to force (someone) to do (something) by bullying; coerce: *We bulldozed him into buying the computer.* **4.** [~ + *obj*] to force (something) in the manner of a bulldozer: *bulldozed his plan through Congress.*

bull•doz•er (bo͝ol′dō′zər) /ˈbʊl,dowzər/ *n.* [*count*] a large, powerful tractor having a large blade at the front end.

bul•let (bo͝ol′it) /ˈbʊlɪt/ *n.* [*count*] **1.** a small piece of metal fired from a gun: *One bullet struck an innocent bystander.* ***—Idiom.*** **2. bite the bullet,** to force oneself to perform a painful task, or to endure an unpleasant situation: *bit the bullet and went in to see the boss, expecting to be fired.*

bul•le•tin (bo͝ol′i tn, -tin) /ˈbʊlɪtn̩, -tɪn/ *n.* [*count*] **1.** a brief, official statement issued publicly: *We interrupt this program to bring you an important bulletin.* **2.** a publication regularly issued by an organization, etc.: *read in the church bulletin that our friend's baby would be baptized.* **3.** a catalog describing the courses taught at a college.

bul′letin board′, *n.* [*count*] a board for putting up bulletins, notices, etc. See illustration at OFFICE.

bul•let•proof (bo͝ol′it pro͞of′) /ˈbʊlɪt,pruwf/ *adj.* (of vehicles, clothing, etc.) capable of absorbing or reducing the impact of a bullet: *a bulletproof vest.*

bul′let train′, *n.* [*count*] a high-speed passenger train, esp. in Japan: *The bullet train travels at more than 150 m.p.h.*

bull•fight (bo͝ol′fīt′) /ˈbʊl,fayt/ *n.* [*count*] a traditional Spanish entertainment in which a bull is fought in a certain way and killed with a sword. —**bull′fight′er,** *n.* [*count*] —**bull′fight′ing,** *n.* [*noncount*]

bull•finch (bo͝ol′finch′) /ˈbʊl,fɪntʃ/ *n.* [*count*] a finch of Europe and Asia, the male of which has a black, white, and bluish-gray back with a rosy breast.

bull•frog (bo͝ol′frog′, -frôg′) /ˈbʊl,frɒg, -,frɔg/ *n.* [*count*] a large North American frog having a deep voice: *the constant croaking of the bullfrogs.*

bull•head•ed (bo͝ol′hed′id) /ˈbʊl,hɛdɪd/ *adj.* unreasonably or stupidly stubborn; obstinate: *a bullheaded person who wouldn't listen to new ideas.* —**bull′head′ed•ly,** *adv.* —**bull′head′ed•ness,** *n.* [*noncount*]

bull•horn or **bull horn** (bo͝ol′hôrn′) /ˈbʊl,hɔrn/ *n.* [*count*] a high-powered, electrical loudspeaker: *Talking through the bullhorn, the detective persuaded the gunman to surrender.*

bul•lion (bo͝ol′yən) /ˈbʊlyən/ *n.* [*noncount*] gold or silver in the form of bars or ingots.

bull•ish (bo͝ol′ish) /ˈbʊlɪʃ/ *adj.* **1.** like a bull; stupid or stubborn. **2. a.** (of the stock market) characterized by or causing a trend toward rising prices: *a bullish market after the economic forecast.* **b.** optimistic, esp. about general business conditions: *We're bullish on those bonds.* —**bull′ish•ly,** *adv.* —**bull′ish•ness,** *n.* [*noncount*]

bul•lock (bo͝ol′ək) /ˈbʊlək/ *n.* [*count*] a bull that has had its sexual organs removed; steer.

bull′ pen′ or **bull′pen′,** *n.* [*count*] **1. a.** a place where relief pitchers warm up during a baseball game. **b.** the relief pitchers on a team, considered as a whole: *The bullpen is a little tired.* **2.** *Informal.* a large cell for holding prisoners temporarily.

bull•ring (bo͝ol′ring′) /ˈbʊl,rɪŋ/ *n.* [*count*] an arena where a bullfight is held.

bull′ ses′sion, *n.* [*count*] an informal group discussion in which people speak freely without a specific goal or focus.

bull's′-eye′, *n.* [*count*], *pl.* **-eyes. 1.** the circular spot at the center of a target. **2.** a shot that hits this. **3.** any statement or act that achieves a desired result directly.

bull′ ter′rier, *n.* [*count*] an English breed of strong medium-sized dogs with an oval head.

bul•ly (bo͝ol′ē) /ˈbʊliy/ *n., pl.* **-lies,** *v.,* **-lied, -ly•ing,** *adj., interj.* *—n.* [*count*] **1.** one who bothers and hurts smaller people: *The class bully cornered him at his locker and demanded money.* *—v.* **2.** to use one's strength to bother (smaller people) in this way: [~ + *obj*]: *She was bullied constantly at school.* [~ + *obj* + *into* + *verb-ing*]: *bullied into going along with the plan.* *—adj.* **3.** *Informal.* fine; excellent: *Teddy Roosevelt called the presidency his "bully pulpit," because it was an excellent position from which to speak directly to the American people.* *—interj.* **4.** (used to express approval, or sarcastic approval): *"I did it!" "Bully for you," he mumbled.*

bul•ly•boy (bo͝ol′ē boi′) /ˈbʊliy,bɔy/ *n.* [*count*] a rough man, or one hired to injure or kill another; hoodlum.

bul•rush (bo͝ol′rush′) /ˈbʊl,rʌʃ/ *n.* [*count; usually plural*] any of various rushes of the sedge cattail families.

bul•wark (bo͝ol′wərk, -wôrk, bul′-) /ˈbʊlwərk, -wɔrk, ˈbʌl-/ *n.* [*count*] **1.** a wall of earth or other material built for defense; rampart. **2.** any protection against danger, injury, or annoyance. **3.** a person or thing that gives strong support or encouragement.

bum[1] (bum) /bʌm/ *n., v.,* **bummed, bum•ming,** *adj.,* **bum•mer, bum•mest.** *—n.* [*count*] **1.** a person who avoids work and lives off others. **2.** *Informal.* a person who is very interested in something; enthusiast: *a ski* *bum; a beach bum.* **3.** *Informal.* an incompetent or worthless person: *"Get another job, you bums," he yelled.* **—v. 4.** [~ + *obj* (+ *off* + *obj*)] *Informal.* to borrow (something) without a promise to return: *Can I bum a cigarette (off you)?* **5. bum around,** [*no obj*] *Informal.* to spend time or wander aimlessly: *All vacation long we just bummed around.* **—adj.** [*before a noun*] *Slang.* **6.** of poor or miserable quality; worthless: *a bum deal on that useless car.* **7.** false or misleading: *A bum rap is when you are falsely accused of something.* **8.** lame: *a bum leg.* **—*Idiom.* 9. bum (someone) out,** [~ + *obj* + *out*] *Slang.* to disappoint, upset, or annoy: *That test really bummed me out.*

bum[2] (bum) /bʌm/ *n.* [*count*] *Brit. Slang.* the buttocks; rump: *falling on his bum.*

bum•ble[1] (bum′bəl) /ˈbʌmbəl/ *v.* [*no obj*], **-bled, -bling. 1.** to do a poor job; bungle; muddle. **2.** to stumble awkwardly or clumsily: *He bumbled into the room.* —**bum′bler,** *n.* [*count*]

bum•ble[2] (bum′bəl) /ˈbʌmbəl/ *v.* [*no obj*], **-bled, -bling.** to make a buzzing, humming sound, as a bee.

bum•ble•bee or **bum•ble bee** (bum′bəl bē′) /ˈbʌmbəl,biy/ *n.* [*count*] any of several large, hairy bees.

bum•bling (bum′bling) /ˈbʌmblɪŋ/ *adj.* [*before a noun*] tending to make awkward mistakes or blunders; inept.

bum•mer (bum′ər) /ˈbʌmər/ *n.* [*count*] *Slang.* any unpleasant experience: *Getting into an accident the first time that I had the car was a bummer.*

bump (bump) /bʌmp/ *v.* **1.** to come into contact with; collide with: [~ + *obj*]: *The car bumped a truck.* [~ + *against* + *obj*]: *The car bumped against a tree.* [~ + *into* + *obj*]: *She bumped into me.* **2.** [~ + *obj*] to cause to strike or collide: *I bumped my arm.* **3.** [~ + *obj*] *Informal.* to remove or dismiss: *The airline bumped me from the flight.* **4.** [*no obj*] to proceed in a series of jolts or rough, uncomfortable shaking: *The old car bumped down the road.* **5. bump into,** [~ + *into* + *obj*] to meet by chance: *I bumped into her on the way home.* **6. bump off,** *Slang.* to murder: [~ + *off* + *obj*]: *planned to bump off the mobster.* [~ + *obj* + *off*]: *planned to bump him off.* **—n.** [*count*] **7.** a collision; blow: *The ship came into the dock with a slight bump.* **8.** a swelling or raised bruise from a blow: *He got a bump on the head.* **9.** a small, uneven area raised above the level of the surrounding surface: *many bumps on the road.*

bump•er (bum′pər) /ˈbʌmpər/ *n.* [*count*] **1.** a metal band or bar, usually horizontal, for protecting the front or rear of a vehicle, etc.: *flashy chrome bumpers.* **2.** any protective guard, pad, or disk for absorbing shock and preventing damage from bumping: *railroad bumpers.* **—adj.** [*before a noun*] **3.** unusually large; abundant: *a bumper crop.*

bump′er stick′er, *n.* [*count*] a strip of paper for sticking onto the rear bumper of an automobile, having an advertisement, political slogan, etc., printed on it: *bumper stickers for all sorts of causes.*

bump′er-to-bump′er, *adj.* slow-moving because of lines of cars one behind the other: *bumper-to-bumper traffic.*

bump•kin (bump′kin) /ˈbʌmpkɪn/ *n.* [*count*] an awkward, simple person from the country; yokel.

bump•tious (bump′shəs) /ˈbʌmpʃəs/ *adj.* conceited; self-important. —**bump′tious•ly,** *adv.* —**bump′tious•ness,** *n.* [*noncount*]

bump•y (bum′pē) /ˈbʌmpiy/ *adj.,* **-i•er, -i•est. 1.** full of bumps: *a bumpy road.* **2.** full of bounces or jolts: *a bumpy ride.* —**bump′i•ness,** *n.* [*noncount*]

bum's′ rush′, *n.* [*count; singular*] *Slang.* a rude or sudden dismissal: *gave me the bum's rush right after dinner.*

bun (bun) /bʌn/ *n.* [*count*] **1.** a round bread roll, plain or sweetened: *I'll have a sweet bun with my coffee.* **2.** hair tied into a round knot; this hairstyle: *hair tied into a severe bun.* **3. buns,** [*plural*] *Slang.* buttocks.

bunch (bunch) /bʌntʃ/ *n.* [*count*] **1.** a cluster held together: *a bunch of grapes.* **2.** [*singular; a* + ~ + *of*] a group of people or things: *a bunch of papers.* **3.** [*singular; a* + ~ (+ *of*)] a large quantity; lots: *Thanks a bunch.* [*a* + ~ + *of* + *noncount noun*]: *That's a bunch of garbage.* [*a* + ~ + *of* + *plural noun*]: *a bunch of students.* **—v. 4.** [~ + *obj*] to group together: *all bunched together in the crowded elevator.* **5. bunch up, a.** [*no obj*] to stay in a group: *The sheriff told his men not to bunch up but to spread out.* **b.** (of fabric or clothing) to gather into folds: [~ + *up* + *obj*]: *My clothes were all bunched up after being in suitcases for so long.* [*no obj*]: *Your clothes will bunch up if you keep them in the suitcase.*

bun•dle (bun′dl) /ˈbʌndl̩/ *n., v.,* **-dled, -dling. —n.** [*count*] **1.** an item wrapped for carrying; package: *He brought in a few bundles from the car.* **2.** several objects or a quantity of material gathered or bound together: *a bundle of hay; a bundle of wood.* **3.** [*singular; a* + ~ + *of*] a number of things considered together. **4.** a large amount of something; a lot of: *He's a bundle of nerves (= He is very nervous).* **5.** *Slang.* a great deal of money: *made a bundle in that last deal.* **—v. 6.** [~ + *obj*] to wrap in a bundle: *She bundled the packages together.* **7.** [~ + *obj* (+ *off/into/out*)] to send or push away (off, etc.) hurriedly: *They bundled her off to the country. The police bundled him into the car.* **8.** [~ + *obj*] to supply or include (products or services) in one sale for one price: *The computer comes bundled with software and diskettes.* **9. bundle up,** to dress warmly or snugly: [*no obj*]: *Bundle up; it's cold outside.* [~ + *obj* + *up*]: *We bundled the kids up in layers of clothes.*

bung[1] (bung) /bʌŋ/ *n.* [*count*] a small piece of wood, used as a stopper for an opening of a barrel.

bung[2] (bung) /bʌŋ/ *v.* [~ + *obj*] **1.** to beat. **2.** *Brit. Slang.* to throw or shove carelessly, quickly, or violently: *Just bung it in the machine and see what happens.*

bun•ga•low (bung′gə lō′) /ˈbʌŋgə,low/ *n.* [*count*] a small house or summer cottage.

bun•gee (bun′jē) /ˈbʌndʒiy/ *n.* [*count*] **1.** an elasticized cord, typically with a hook at each end, used to bind a suitcase to a wheeled carrier, etc. **2.** a similar cord attached to the edge of a high place at one end and to the leg of a jumper at the other, used in a sport of jumping off high places and bouncing. Also called **bun′gee cord′.**

bun•gle (bung′gəl) /ˈbʌŋgəl/ *v.,* **-gled, -gling,** *n.* **—v. 1.** to do clumsily, awkwardly, or badly; botch: [~ + *obj*]: *The electrician bungled the wiring job.* [*no obj*]: *If she keeps bungling, she'll lose the job.* **—n.** [*count*] **2.** a job or work that has been done clumsily: *a complete bungle.* —**bun′gled,** *adj.: the bungled assassination attempt.* —**bun′gler,** *n.* [*count*] —**bun′gling,** *n.* [*noncount*]: *equal amounts of bungling and stupidity.*

bun•ion (bun′yən) /ˈbʌnyən/ *n.* [*count*] a painful swelling or lump on the big toe.

bunk[1] (bungk) /bʌŋk/ *n.* [*count*] **1.** a bed built into the wall, as on a ship, with one on top of another. **—v. 2.** [*no obj*] to occupy a bunk or bed: *bunked together in the Navy.* **3.** [~ + *obj*] to provide with a place to sleep: *They bunked us in cots.*

bunk[2] (bungk) /bʌŋk/ *n.* [*noncount*] *Informal.* nonsense: *I can't believe your story; it sounds like a lot of bunk.*

bunk′ bed′, *n.* [*count*] either of two single beds connected one above the other.

bun•ker (bung′kər) /ˈbʌŋkər/ *n.* [*count*] **1.** a large bin or receptacle. **2.** a partially underground chamber, built as a bomb shelter: *stayed in his bunker during the shelling.* **3.** *Golf.* any obstacle, such as a sand trap, constituting a hazard: *His first shot went into the bunker.*

bunk•house (bungk′hous′) /ˈbʌŋk,haws/ *n.* [*count*] a rough building with bunk beds, used for sleeping by ranch workers or campers.

bun•ko or **bun•co** (bung′kō) /ˈbʌŋkow/ *n.* [*count*], *pl.* **-kos** or **-cos.** *Informal.* a scheme or swindle to take a person's money.

bun•kum or **bun•combe** (bung′kəm) /ˈbʌŋkəm/ *n.* [*noncount*] insincere talk; nonsense; claptrap; humbug.

bun•ny (bun′ē) /ˈbʌniy/ *n., pl.* **-nies,** *adj.* **—n.** [*count*] **1.** a rabbit, esp. a young one. **2.** *Slang* (*sometimes disparaging and offensive*). an attractive young woman, often engaged in a sport: *a beach bunny (= a young woman hanging around the beach).* **—adj.** [*before a noun*] **3.** designed for or used by beginners in skiing: *a bunny slope.*

Bun′sen burn′er (bun′sən) /ˈbʌnsən/ *n.* [*count*] a gas burner with a hot flame, commonly used in chemical laboratories.

bunt (bunt) /bʌnt/ *v.* **1.** to tap (a pitched baseball) a short distance from home plate: [*no obj*]: *He bunted at the first pitch.* [~ + *obj*]: *He managed to bunt the fastball.* **—n.** [*count*] **2. a.** the act of bunting a baseball: *a perfect bunt.* **b.** a bunted baseball: *His bunt rolled a bit.* —**bunt′er,** *n.* [*count*]

bun•ting[1] (bun′ting) /ˈbʌntɪŋ/ *n.* [*noncount*] patriotic and brightly colored decorations made from cloth or paper, usually in the form of draperies, wide streamers, etc.

bun•ting[2] (bun′ting) /ˈbʌntɪŋ/ *n.* [*count*] a small, chiefly seed-eating songbird.

bun•ting[3] (bun′ting) /ˈbʌntɪŋ/ *n.* [*count*] a hooded sleeping garment for infants.

bu•oy (bo͞o′ē, boi) /ˈbuwiy, bɔy/ *n.* [*count*] **1.** an anchored float used as a marker for ships. **2.** a ringlike life preserver. —*v.* [~ + *obj*] **3. a.** to keep afloat. **b.** to encourage; cheer up: *Her courage was buoyed by the doctor's assurances.* **4.** to mark with buoys.

buoy•an•cy (boi′ən sē, bo͞o′yən sē) /'bɔyənsiy, 'buwyənsiy/ also **buoy′ance,** *n.* [*noncount*] **1.** the power to float or rise in a fluid: *That piece of light wood has a lot of buoyancy.* **2.** the power of a liquid to support an object so that it floats: *Buoyancy is the pressure of a liquid pushing upward on an object that is in that liquid.* **3.** lightness of spirit; cheerfulness.

buoy•ant (boi′ənt, bo͞o′yənt) /'bɔyənt, 'buwyənt/ *adj.* of or relating to buoyancy. —**buoy′ant•ly,** *adv.*

bur (bûr) /bɜr/ *n.* [*count*] **1.** a prickly case around the seeds of certain plants, as the chestnut. **2.** any bur-bearing plant. **3.** BURR[1] (defs. 1, 3). **4.** a rotary cutting tool like a drill.

bur., an abbreviation of: bureau.

burb (bûrb) /bɜrb/ *n.* [*count*] *Slang.* Usually, **burbs.** [*plural*] suburbs: *Many families flocked to the burbs.*

bur•ble (bûr′bəl) /'bɜrbəl/ *v.,* **-bled, -bling,** *n.* —*v.* [*no obj*] **1.** to make a bubbling sound; gurgle: *The baby sat in his highchair, burbling happily.* **2.** to speak in an excited manner; babble: *burbling about her new job.* —*n.* [*count*] **3.** a bubbling sound: *The baby let out a little burble of joy.*

bur•den (bûr′dn) /'bɜrdn̩/ *n.* [*count*] **1.** that which is carried; load: *a burden of five hundred pounds.* **2.** that which is difficult to bear; onus: *weighed down by the burden of leadership.* —*v.* [~ + *obj*] **3.** to load heavily: *burdened with all the packages.* **4.** to trouble; cause worry: *I don't mean to burden you with all my problems.* —**bur′dened,** *adj.* [*be* + ~]: *He was burdened with worries.*

bur′den of proof′, *n.* [*noncount; the* + ~] the obligation to offer enough evidence in a court of law to support an accusation: *In a criminal case in the U.S., the burden of proof rests on the prosecution.*

bur•den•some (bûr′dn səm) /'bɜrdn̩səm/ *adj.* causing worry; tiresome: *becoming burdensome with his complaints.*

bu•reau (byo͝or′ō) /'byʊrow/ *n.* [*count*], *pl.* **bu•reaus, bu•reaux** (byo͝or′ōz) /'byʊrowz/. **1.** a chest of drawers: *The keys are right on top of the bureau.* **2.** a division of a government department: *the weather bureau.* **3.** an office that collects and distributes information; agency; branch: *The personnel bureau handles that.* **4.** *Chiefly Brit.* a writing desk with drawers for papers.

bu•reauc•ra•cy (byo͝o rok′rə sē) /byʊ'rɒkrəsiy/ *n., pl.* **-cies. 1.** [*noncount*] government by a rigid, complex, and usually large number of bureaus, administrators, and self-important officials: *No one wants more bureaucracy.* **2.** [*count*] a body of officials and administrators in this system: *worked hard to make the bureaucracy more effective.* **3.** [*noncount*] rules, routines, and procedures of such a system: *bogged down with the bureaucracy of trying to leave the country.*

bu•reau•crat (byo͝or′ə krat′) /'byʊrəˌkræt/ *n.* [*count*] a member of a bureaucracy. —**bu′reau•crat′ic,** *adj.*: *bureaucratic foul-ups.* —**bu′reau•crat′i•cal•ly,** *adv.*

burg (bûrg) /bɜrg/ *n.* [*count*] *Informal.* a small town: *The swindlers got out of this burg before they got caught.*

bur•geon (bûr′jən) /'bɜrdʒən/ *v.* [*no obj*] to grow or develop quickly; flourish: *The town was burgeoning into a city.*

burg•er (bûr′gər) /'bɜrgər/ *n.* [*count*] a hamburger: *two burgers, one with catsup and pickles.*

-burger, *suffix.* *-burger* (originally taken from the word HAMBURGER) is attached to roots and some words to form nouns that mean "the food added to, or substituted for, a basic hamburger": *cheese* + *-burger* → *cheeseburger* (= *a hamburger with cheese added on top*); *fish* + *-burger* → *fishburger* (= *fish substituted for the meat of a hamburger*).

burgh•er (bûr′gər) /'bɜrgər/ *n.* [*count*] one who lives in a town or borough, esp. a wealthy or rich member of the middle class.

bur•glar (bûr′glər) /'bɜrglər/ *n.* [*count*] one who commits burglary.

bur•glar•ize (bûr′glə rīz′) /'bɜrgləˌrayz/ *v.* [~ + *obj*], **-ized, -iz•ing.** to commit burglary.

bur•glar•proof (bûr′glər pro͞of′) /'bɜrglərˌpruwf/ *adj.* **1.** safeguarded or made safe from or secure against burglary: *a burglarproof home.* —*v.* [~ + *obj*] **2.** to make burglarproof: *a simple way to burglarproof your home.*

bur•gla•ry (bûr′glə rē) /'bɜrgləriy/ *n., pl.* **-ries.** the crime of breaking into and entering the house, office, etc., of another to steal: [*noncount*]: *was found guilty of burglary.* [*count*]: *over fifty burglaries in three months.*

bur•gle (bûr′gəl) /'bɜrgəl/ *v.* [~ + *obj*], **-gled, -gling.** *Informal.* to burglarize: *They'd burgled the office.*

bur•gun•dy (bûr′gən dē) /'bɜrgəndiy/ *n., pl.* **-dies** for 1. **1.** a red or white wine, esp. one from central France: [*noncount*]: *barrels of burgundy.* [*count*]: *a wonderfully clear burgundy.* **2.** [*noncount*] a grayish red-brown to blackish-purple color.

bur•i•al (ber′ē əl) /'bɛriyəl/ *n.* the act or ceremony of burying a dead body: [*noncount*]: *Burial for those sailors was at sea.* [*count*]: *Burials are not permitted on Friday evenings there.*

bur•lap (bûr′lap) /'bɜrlæp/ *n.* [*noncount*] a plain, coarse fabric of jute or hemp used for bags, etc.

bur•lesque (bər lesk′) /bər'lɛsk/ *n.* **1.** a comic piece that imitates or makes fun of a subject, as of fancy literary or dramatic pieces, etc.: [*count*]: *a burlesque of odes to nature.* [*noncount*]: *Some of the best criticisms of that society come from burlesque.* **2.** a stage show featuring vulgar comic and striptease acts: [*noncount*]: *Burlesque in the early 1900's in America was not hard to break into.* [*count*]: *We went to several burlesques.* —*adj.* [*usually before a noun*] **3.** of, relating to, or like stage-show burlesque: *burlesque shows.* —**Syn.** BURLESQUE, CARICATURE, PARODY, TRAVESTY refer to pieces of writing or plays in a theater that imitate works or subjects in order to achieve a humorous purpose. The device of BURLESQUE is making fun of serious or light subjects through comparison with their opposites: *a burlesque of high and low life.* CARICATURE, usually associated with drawings, cartoons, or other visual effects in literary works, uses exaggeration of the details that everyone knows about a character or thing: *The caricature emphasized his large nose.* PARODY achieves its humor through applying the style or technique of writing (words, phrases, sentences, conversations) of a well-known work or author to some other, unexpected subjects: *a parody of Hemingway.* TRAVESTY takes a serious subject and uses a style or language that seems absurd: *a travesty of a senator making a speech.*

bur•ly (bûr′lē) /'bɜrliy/ *adj.,* **-li•er, -li•est.** large in size; stout; sturdy: *a couple of burly cops.* —**bur′li•ness,** *n.* [*noncount*]

Bur•mese (bər mēz′, -mēs′) /bər'miyz, -'miys/ *n., pl.* **-mese. 1.** [*count*] a person born or living in Burma. **2.** [*noncount*] the language spoken by many of the people in Burma. —*adj.* **3.** of or relating to Burma. **4.** of or relating to the language spoken by many of the people in Burma.

burn (bûrn) /bɜrn/ *v.,* **burned** or **burnt** (bûrnt) /bɜrnt/ **burn•ing,** *n.* —*v.* **1.** to (cause to) be on fire: [*no obj*]: *The house is burning.* [~ + *obj*]: *The fire burned the house down.* **2.** to (cause to) use up or consume fuel and give off energy: [*no obj*]: *The lights were burning all night.* [~ + *obj*]: *That plane burns a lot of fuel in a short time.* **3.** to (cause to) be hot: [*no obj*]: *She was burning with a high fever.* [~ + *obj*]: *The hot pavement burned my feet through my shoes.* **4.** to (cause to) produce or feel sharp pain: [*no obj*]: *The whiskey burned in his throat.* [~ + *obj*]: *The iodine burned his cut.* **5.** to (cause to) be damaged or destroyed by fire, heat, or acid: [*no obj*]: *Turn off the heat; the steak is burning.* [~ + *obj*]: *The acid burned his face and left a scar.* **6.** [*no obj; usually: be* + *~-ing*] to feel strong emotion: *He was burning with rage.* **7.** to sunburn: [*no obj*]: *Better get out of the sun; your shoulders are burning.* [~ + *obj*]: *I was badly burned at the beach.* **8.** [*no obj*] *Slang.* to die in an electric chair: *The prosecutor promised him he'd burn for that crime.* **9.** [~ + *obj*] to kill or execute by burning: *Joan of Arc was burned at the stake.* **10.** [~ + *obj*] *Slang.* to cheat, deceive, or swindle: *burned in a phony stock deal.* **11.** [*be* + *~-ing* + *to* + *verb*] to be very eager (to do something specified): *I was burning to tell you what happened.* **12. burn down,** to burn completely; to burn to the ground: [*no obj*]: *All the houses on that block burned down.* [~ + *down* + *obj*]: *They burned down the house.* [~ + *obj* + *down*]: *They burned the house down.* **13. burn off,** (of morning mist) to (cause to) disappear by the warmth of the rising sun: [~ + *off* + *obj*]: *The morning sun burned off the fog.* [*no obj*]: *The fog had burned off.* **14. burn out, a.** [~ *(+ itself)* + *out)*] to cease or stop functioning because something has been burned up or worn out: *The rocket engine burned out. The firemen let the fire burn (itself) out.* **b.** [~ *(+ oneself)* + *out*] to become exhausted or uninterested through overwork: *After twenty years at the same job, he had burned himself out and wanted a change.* **15. burn up, a.** to burn completely: [*no obj*]: *The missile pieces began to burn up as they entered the earth's atmosphere.* [~ + *up* + *obj*]: *She burned up all his old love letters.* [~ + *obj* + *up*]:

She burned the letters up. **b.** *Informal.* to (cause to) become angry: [*no obj*]: *He's sitting in his office, burning up, every minute that you're late.* [~ + *obj* + *up*]: *That kind of whining really burns me up!* —*n.* [*count*] **16.** an injury caused by heat, etc., characterized by a painful reddening of the skin. —***Idiom.*** **17. burn a hole in one's pocket,** (of money that is handy) to cause a desire to spend quickly: *The money from his first paycheck was burning a hole in his pocket.* **18. burn the candle at both ends,** to use up one's strength or energy by too much activity. **19. burn the midnight oil,** to work, study, etc., until late at night: *burning the midnight oil before that test.*

burn•er (bûr′nər) /'bɜrnər/ *n.* [*count*] **1.** a person or thing that burns: *an oil burner.* **2.** the part of a gas or electric fixture or appliance, as a stove, from which flame or heat comes out.

burn•ing (bûr′ning) /'bɜrnɪŋ/ *adj.* [*usually before a noun*] **1.** very hot; simmering: *the burning summer sidewalks.* **2.** intense; passionate: *a burning desire to kiss her.* **3.** urgent or crucial; important: *a burning question.*

bur•nish (bûr′nish) /'bɜrnɪʃ/ *v.* [~ + *obj*] to polish (a surface) by rubbing: *The silver was burnished to a beautiful finish.* —**bur′nished,** *adj.*: *burnished silver bracelets.*

burn•out (bûrn′out′) /'bɜrn,awt/ *n.* [*noncount*] **1.** the ending of effective combustion in a rocket engine due to lack of fuel. **2.** fatigue and frustration resulting from prolonged stress and overwork.

burnt (bûrnt) /bɜrnt/ *v.* a pt. and pp. of BURN.

burp (bûrp) /bɜrp/ *Informal.* —*n.* [*count*] **1.** a belch: *let out a long burp.* —*v.* **2.** to (cause to) belch: [*no obj*]: *In his culture it is polite to burp after a meal to express appreciation and thanks to the cook.* [~ + *obj*]: *She burped the baby.*

burr[1] (bûr) /bɜr/ *n.* [*count*] **1.** a ragged edge formed on metal while during drilling, shearing, or engraving. **2.** a rough lump that sticks out on any object, as on a tree. **3.** a hand-held rotary power tool used to cut small holes. —*v.* [~ + *obj*] **4.** to form a rough point or edge on. **5.** to remove burrs from. Also, **bur** (for defs. 1, 3).

burr[2] (bûr) /bɜr/ *n.* [*count*] **1.** a special pronunciation of (r) in some Northern English dialects or as in Scottish English. **2.** a whirring noise. —*v.* [*no obj*] **3.** to make a whirring sound: *The phones in Europe don't seem to ring; they burr.*

bur•ri•to (bə rē′tō) /bə'riytow/ *n.* [*count*], *pl.* **-tos.** a kind of Mexican food, a flour tortilla folded over a filling, as of beef, cheese, or refried beans.

bur•ro (bûr′ō, bŏŏr′ō) /'bɜrow, 'bʊrow/ *n.* [*count*], *pl.* **-ros.** a donkey, esp. a small one used to carry things.

bur•row (bûr′ō, bur′ō) /'bɜrow, 'bʌrow/ *n.* [*count*] **1.** a hole or tunnel in the ground made by an animal: *The rabbit reached its burrow.* —*v.* **2.** to dig a burrow (into): [*no obj*]: *He burrowed into the ground.* [~ + *obj*]: *The rabbit burrowed its way down through the ground.* **3.** [*no obj*] to move or proceed by or as if by digging: *She burrowed under the covers.* —**bur′row•er,** *n.* [*count*]

bur•sar (bûr′sər, -sär) /'bɜrsər, -sɑr/ *n.* [*count*] a treasurer or business officer, esp. of a college or university: *Go to the bursar's office and pick up your check.*

bur•sa•ry (bûr′sə rē) /'bɜrsəriy/ *n.* [*count*], *pl.* **-ries.** *Brit.* a college scholarship.

bur•si•tis (bər sī′tis) /bər'saytɪs/ *n.* [*noncount*] inflammation of a small sac near a bone that is used in moving, such as a shoulder.

burst (bûrst) /bɜrst/ *v.*, **burst** or, often, **burst•ed, burst•ing,** *n.* —*v.* **1.** to (cause to) break, or fly apart suddenly: [*no obj*]: *The balloon burst.* [~ + *obj*]: *The cold weather burst the pipes.* **2.** [*no obj*] to come forth suddenly and with force or impact: *The police burst into the room.* **3.** to give sudden expression to a feeling: [~ + *into* + *obj*]: *burst into tears.* [~ + *out*]: *He burst out laughing.* [~ + *with* + *obj*]: *We nearly burst with pride.* **4.** [*no obj*] to appear suddenly: *The sun burst through the clouds.* —*n.* [*count*] **5.** an act or instance of bursting: *several bursts of machine gun fire.* **6.** a sudden, intense display, as of effort: *She put on a burst of speed.* **7.** a sudden expression, as of emotion: *a burst of rage.*

bur•y (ber′ē) /'bɛriy/ *v.* [~ + *obj*], **-ied, -y•ing.** **1.** to put (a dead body) in the ground or a vault, or into the sea, often with ceremony: *buried next to his wife of fifty years.* **2.** to put in the ground and cover with earth: *The treasure was buried in six feet of earth.* **3.** to cover with something: *He was buried in the rubble of the building.* **4.** [*often:* ~ + *oneself/itself*] plunge into; sink into: *The bullet had buried itself in the tree.* **5.** to conceal from sight; hide: *to bury a card in the deck.* **6.** [~ + *oneself*] to be occupied in: *He buried himself in his work.* —***Idiom.*** **7. bury one's head in the sand,** to ignore the facts of a situation: *You have to take a stand on this issue and stop burying your head in the sand.* **8. bury the hatchet,** to stop fighting: *decided to bury the hatchet and see if we could work together once more.*

bus[1] (bus) /bʌs/ *n.*, *pl.* **bus•es, bus•ses,** *v.*, **bused** or **bussed, bus•ing** or **bus•sing.** —*n.* [*count*] **1.** a large, long motor vehicle equipped with seating for passengers: *The children waited for the school bus.* See illustration at STREET. —*v.* **2.** to travel by bus; to carry, convey, or transport by bus: [*no obj*]: *Let's see if we can bus back to the hotel.* [~ + *obj*]: *People were bused in to take part in the demonstration.* **3.** [~ + *obj*] to transport (pupils) to school by bus, esp. as a means of achieving racial integration: *claimed that children are bused to schools in trips that take an hour or more.*

bus[2] (bus) /bʌs/ *v.*, **bused** or **bussed** (bust) /bʌst/ **bus•ing** or **bus•sing.** to work as a busboy or busgirl: [*no obj*]: *He bused most school nights and weekends.* [~ + *obj*]: *See if he'll bus that table now.*

bus., an abbreviation of: business.

bus•boy or **bus boy** (bus′boi′) /'bʌs,bɔy/ *n.* [*count*] a waiter's helper in a restaurant or other public dining room.

bus•by (buz′bē) /'bʌzbiy/ *n.* [*count*], *pl.* **-bies.** a tall military hat of fur or feathers.

bus•girl or **bus girl** (bus′gûrl′) /'bʌs,gɜrl/ *n.* [*count*] a girl or woman who works as a waiter's helper.

bush (bŏŏsh) /bʊʃ/ *n.* **1.** [*count*] a low plant with many branches that arise from near the ground. **2.** [*count*] something resembling or suggesting this: *a large bush of hair.* **3.** [*noncount; usually: the* + ~] **a.** a large uncleared area covered with plant growth: *Our cat disappeared into the bush that night.* **b.** a large, mostly uncleared area with few people. —***Idiom.*** **4. beat around** or **about the bush,** to avoid talking about a subject directly: *beat around the bush for a while before asking for permission to marry their daughter.*

bush., an abbreviation of: bushel.

bush′ ba′by, *n.* [*count*] an animal like a monkey, with large eyes and ears and woolly fur.

bushed (bŏŏsht) /bʊʃt/ *adj.* [*usually: be* + ~] *Informal.* exhausted; tired out: *completely bushed after that walk.*

bush•el (bŏŏsh′əl) /'bʊʃəl/ *n.* [*count*] **1.** a unit of dry measure containing 4 pecks, equivalent in the U.S. to 2150.42 cubic inches or 35.24 liters, and in Great Britain to 2219.36 cubic inches or 36.38 liters **(imperial bushel).** *Abbr.:* bu., bush. **2.** a container of this capacity. **3.** a large, unspecified amount: *a bushel of kisses.*

bush′ league′, *n.* [*count*] a secondary baseball league.

bush•man (bŏŏsh′mən) /'bʊʃmən/ *n.* [*count*], *pl.* **-men.** **1.** a woodsman. **2.** *Australian.* a dweller in the bush.

bush•whack (bŏŏsh′hwak′, -wak′) /'bʊʃ,hwæk, -,wæk/ *v.* **1.** [*no obj*] to make one's way through woods by cutting at undergrowth. **2.** [~ + *obj*] to ambush; hide in the woods and surprise and attack (someone): *The gang bushwhacked the campers.* —**bush′whack′er,** *n.* [*count*]

bush•y (bŏŏsh′ē) /'bʊʃiy/ *adj.*, **-i•er, -i•est.** resembling a bush; thick and shaggy: *bushy whiskers.* —**bush′i•ness,** *n.* [*noncount*]

busi•ness (biz′nis) /'bɪznɪs/ *n.* **1.** [*noncount*] the buying and selling of goods for profit; trade; commerce: *majored in business at her university.* **2.** [*count*] a person or corporation that buys and sells goods: *started a business from the ground up.* **3.** [*count*] a store, office, etc., where trade is carried on: *a small business on Main Street.* **4.** [*noncount*] amount or volume of trade: *Business is up (= The amount of trade is increasing).* **5.** [*noncount*] something with which a person is rightfully concerned: *Words are a writer's business.* **6.** [*noncount*] affair; project; activity: *I'm fed up with the whole business.* **7. the business,** [*noncount*] harsh or rough treatment, such as a scolding: *gave him the business for missing such an easy catch.* —*adj.* [*before a noun*] **8.** of or relating to business: *studying business journalism.* —***Idiom.*** **9. get down to business,** to apply oneself to serious matters: *That's enough small talk; let's get down to business.* **10. have no business,** [~ + *verb-ing*] to have no right: *You had no business breaking into my office.* **11. (to) mean business,** to be completely serious: *I think the gunman means business.* **12. mind one's own business,** to keep from meddling in the affairs of others: *kept telling her to mind her own business.*

busi•ness•like (biz′nis līk′) /'bɪznɪs,layk/ *adj.* **1.** showing qualities that are good in business. **2.** efficient but not warm or personal: *a quick, businesslike nod.*

busi•ness•man (biz′nis man′) /ˈbɪznɪsˌmæn/ *n.* [*count*], *pl.* **-men.** a man employed in business.

busi•ness•per•son (biz′nis pûr′sən) /ˈbɪznɪsˌpɜrsən/ *n.* [*count*] a person employed in business.

busi•ness•wom•an (biz′nis wo͝om′ən) /ˈbɪznɪsˌwʊmən/ *n.* [*count*], *pl.* **-wom•en.** a woman employed in business.

bus•ing or **bus•sing** (bus′ing) /ˈbʌsɪŋ/ *n.* [*noncount*] the transporting of students by bus to public schools outside their neighborhoods, esp. in an effort to achieve racial balance.

bus′man's hol′iday (bus′mənz) /ˈbʌsmənz/ *n.* [*count*] a vacation from work spent in an activity similar to one's work.

buss (bus) /bʌs/ *n., v.,* **bussed, buss•ing.** KISS.

bus•ses (bus′iz) /ˈbʌsɪz/ *n.* [*plural*] a pl. of BUS[1].

bust[1] (bust) /bʌst/ *n.* [*count*] **1.** a statue or painting of the upper part of the human body: *a bronze bust in the hallway.* **2.** the breasts of a woman; bosom.

bust[2] (bust) /bʌst/ *v. Informal.* **1.** to burst: [~ + *obj*]: *Why did you bust those balloons?* [*no obj*]: *Did they all bust open?* **2.** [~ + *obj*] *Informal.* **a.** to hit: *She busted him in the face.* **b.** to break: *I fell and busted my arm.* **3.** to damage or destroy: [~ + *up* + *obj*]: *He busted up the place.* [~ + *obj* + *up*]: *Get Bugsy to bust the place up.* **4.** [~ + *up*] to break up; separate; split up: *He and his wife busted up a month ago.* **5.** [~ + *out of* + *obj*] to escape or flee from jail: *They busted out of prison.* **6.** [~ + *obj*] *Slang.* **a.** to place under arrest: *"Freeze! You're busted!" shouted the cop.* **b.** to enter (a house) in a police raid: *The police busted her house.* **—***n.* [*count*] **7.** *Informal.* something unsuccessful; a failure: *The play turned out to be a real bust.* **8.** a sudden economic decline; depression: *a bust in the economy.* **9.** *Slang.* **a.** an arrest: *The rookie got credit for the bust of the Mafia boss.* **b.** a police raid. **—***adj.* [*go* + ~] **10.** *Informal.* bankrupt; broke: *Our business went bust after the war.*

bust•er (bus′tər) /ˈbʌstər/ *n.* [*count*] *Informal.* **1.** a person who destroys something: *crime busters.* **2.** [*often: Buster*] (used as a familiar but mildly impolite term of address to a man or boy): *Watch it, Buster!*

bus•tle[1] (bus′əl) /ˈbʌsəl/ *v.,* **-tled, -tling,** *n.* **—***v.* **1.** [~ + *about*] to move or act with great energy: *the chef bustling about in the kitchen.* **2.** [~ + *with* + *obj*] (of a place) to have a lot of (something) in, at, or near: *The office bustled with activity.* **3.** [~ + *obj*] to hustle: *She bustled me out of the cold room.* **—***n.* [*noncount*] **4.** excited, noisy activity: *much hustle and bustle.*

bus•tle[2] (bus′əl) /ˈbʌsəl/ *n.* [*count*] a framework or pad formerly worn under the back of a woman's skirt to support and display the fabric.

bus•tling (bus′ling) /ˈbʌslɪŋ/ *adj.* **1.** (of a place) full of people; busy; lively: *a bustling little department store.* [*be* + ~ + *with*]: *The office was bustling with activity.* **2.** busy; full of energy: *bustling porters at a train station.*

bust•y (bus′tē) /ˈbʌstiy/ *adj.,* **-i•er, -i•est.** (of a woman) having a large bust; bosomy.

bus•y (biz′ē) /ˈbɪziy/ *adj.,* **bus•i•er, bus•i•est,** *v.,* **bus•ied, bus•y•ing. —***adj.* **1.** actively working on something: *busy on a new project.* **2.** not at leisure: *I'm afraid he'll be busy all day and can't see you.* **3.** full of work: *You certainly lead a busy life.* **4.** (of a telephone line) in use: *Your phone was busy all night.* **5.** cluttered with fussy details: *a busy painting to distract visitors.* **—***v.* [~ + *oneself* (+ *with* + *obj*)] **6.** to make or keep busy: *busied himself with the drinks.* **—bus′i•ly,** *adv.: busily at work on their test papers.* **—bus′y•ness,** *n.* [*noncount*] **—Related Words.** BUSY is an adjective and a verb, BUSILY is an adverb: *He is too busy to see you now. They busied themselves preparing dinner. He went busily about the house, cleaning and tidying up.*

bus•y•bod•y (biz′ē bod′ē) /ˈbɪziyˌbɒdiy/ *n.* [*count*], *pl.* **-bod•ies.** one who meddles with the affairs of others: *all those busybodies telling me what to do.*

bus•y•work (biz′ē wûrk′) /ˈbɪziyˌwɜrk/ *n.* [*noncount*] work of no value assigned so that a person will look busy.

but (but; *unstressed* bət) /bʌt; *unstressed* bət/ *conj.* **1.** on the contrary: *My brother went, but I did not.* **2.** and yet; nevertheless: *The story is strange but true (= The story is strange and yet it is true).* **3.** except: *She did nothing but complain (= She did nothing except that she complained).* **4.** otherwise than: *There is no hope but through prayer (= There is no hope other than the hope of prayer).* **5.** without the (additional) circumstance that: *It never rains but it pours (= It never rains without also pouring). No leaders ever existed but they were optimists (= No leaders existed who were not optimists; All leaders who ever existed were optimists).* **6.** that (used esp. after words like *doubt, deny,* etc., with a negative word like *not*): *I don't doubt but you'll do it.* **7.** (used to show a feeling of happiness, shock, or surprise about something): *But that's wonderful! But that's amazing!* **8.** *Informal.* than: *It no sooner started raining but it stopped.* **9.** with the exception of: *No one replied but me. Everyone but John was there.* **10.** other than: *She is nothing but trouble (= She is nothing other than trouble; she is a lot of trouble).* **—***adv.* **11.** only; just: *There is but one answer.* **—***n.* **12. buts,** [*plural*] objections: *You'll do as you're told, no buts about it.* **—*Idiom.* 13. but for,** except for; were it not for; if something had not happened or existed: *We would still be prisoners there but for the daring rescue by the commandos (= We would still be prisoners if the daring rescue had not happened).*

bu•tane (byo͞o′tān, byo͞o tān′) /ˈbyuwteyn, byuwˈteyn/ *n.* [*noncount*] a colorless gas, used chiefly as fuel.

butch (bo͝och) /bʊtʃ/ *Slang.* **—***adj.* **1. a.** (of a woman) having behavior, etc., associated with males. **b.** (of a male) exaggeratedly masculine in appearance or manner. **2.** of or relating to a haircut in which the hair is closely cropped: *a butch hairdo.* **—***n.* [*count*] **3.** a butch person.

butch•er (bo͝och′ər) /ˈbʊtʃər/ *n.* [*count*] **1.** one who kills animals and prepares the meat for food or for market; one who sells meat in a shop: *He worked as a butcher in the stockyards.* **2.** a person guilty of brutal murder: *The prison commander was known as the "butcher" because of all the executions he ordered.* **—***v.* [~ + *obj*] **3.** to slaughter (animals) and prepare the meat for market: *He butchered the calf.* **4.** to kill brutally or excessively: *He butchered thousands of civilians.*

butch•er•y (bo͝och′ə rē) /ˈbʊtʃəriy/ *n., pl.* **-er•ies. 1.** [*noncount*] brutal or excessive slaughter of animals or humans: *His untamed soldiers were well trained in butchery.* **2.** [*noncount*] the trade or business of a butcher. **3.** [*count*] *Brit.* a slaughterhouse.

but•ler (but′lər) /ˈbʌtlər/ *n.* [*count*] the chief male servant of a household: *The butler met us at the door.*

butt[1] (but) /bʌt/ *n.* [*count*] **1.** the end of anything, esp. thought of as a base, support, or handle: *He swung up the butt of his rifle.* **2.** an end that is not used up: *a cigar butt.* **3.** *Slang.* a cigarette: *passing around a few butts.* **4.** *Slang.* the buttocks: *a quick kick in the butt.*

butt[2] (but) /bʌt/ *n.* [*count; usually singular*] an object of jokes, etc.: *The kid was the butt of all our pranks.*

butt[3] (but) /bʌt/ *v.* **1.** to strike or push (something) with the head or horns: [*no obj*]: *The rams were butting and pushing.* [~ + *obj*]: *The rams were butting each other.* **2. butt in** (or **out**), [*no obj*] to interfere (or stop interfering) in the affairs of others: *wished his mother-in-law would stop butting in; When he tried to help them, one of them snapped, "Butt out, jerk, and leave us alone!"* **—***n.* [*count*] **3.** a push or blow with the head or horns.

butt[4] (but) /bʌt/ *n.* [*count*] a large barrel or cask for wine, beer, ale, etc.

butte (byo͞ot) /byuwt/ *n.* [*count*] a single hill or mountain rising sharply above the surrounding flatter land, esp. in the western U.S. and Canada.

but•ter (but′ər) /ˈbʌtər/ *n.* [*noncount*] **1.** a soft whitish or yellowish fat that is separated from milk or cream when it is churned, used as a spread and in cooking. **2.** any of various other soft spreads for bread or for baking: *apple butter.* **—***v.* [~ + *obj*] **3.** to put butter on or in: *He buttered the toast.* **4. butter up,** to flatter or praise (someone) too much: [~ + *obj* + *up*]: *buttered her up by telling her what a great boss she was.* [~ + *up* + *obj*]: *He liked to butter up every new boss he had.*

but•ter•ball (but′ər bôl′) /ˈbʌtərˌbɔl/ *n.* [*count*] a chubby person.

but•ter•cup (but′ər kup′) /ˈbʌtərˌkʌp/ *n.* [*count*] a plant having yellow flowers and deeply cut leaves.

but•ter•fin•gers (but′ər fing′gərz) /ˈbʌtərˌfɪŋgərz/ *n.* [*count; used with a singular verb*], *pl.* **-gers.** a person who frequently drops things; a clumsy person: *"You're a real butterfingers today," she remarked.* **—but′ter•fin′•gered,** *adj.*

but•ter•fly (but′ər flī′) /ˈbʌtərˌflay/ *n.* [*count*], *pl.* **-flies. 1.** a flying insect that has a slender body and broad wings. **2.** one who wanders aimlessly from one interest to another: *a social butterfly.* **3. butterflies,** [*plural*] *Informal.* a nervous feeling, as from anxiety: *The butterflies vanish once I start my talk.* **4.** a racing breaststroke in which the swimmer brings both arms out of the water in forward, circular motions and kicks the legs up and down together.

but•ter•milk (but′ər milk′) /ˈbʌtərˌmɪlk/ *n.* [*noncount*] the liquid remaining after butter has been separated from milk or cream.

but•ter•scotch (but′ər skoch′) /ˈbʌtərˌskɒtʃ/ *n.* [*noncount*] **1.** a hard, brittle substance or candy made with butter, brown sugar, etc. **2.** the flavor of this candy, used in puddings, pastries, etc. **3.** a golden brown color.

but•ter•y[1] (but′ə rē) /ˈbʌtəriy/ *adj.* like, containing, or spread with butter: *a very buttery cake.*

but•ter•y[2] (but′ə rē, bu′trē) /ˈbʌtəriy, ˈbʌtriy/ *n.* [*count*], *pl.* **-ter•ies.** *Brit.* a room in a college or university where students may buy food and drink.

but•tock (but′ək) /ˈbʌtək/ *n.* [*count*] Usually, **buttocks.** [*plural*] (in humans) either of the two fleshy parts of the body forming the lower and back part of the trunk: *In informal English the buttocks are also called the fanny or behind.*

but•ton (but′n) /ˈbʌtn̩/ *n.* [*count*] **1.** a small disk or similar hard object attached to clothing and serving as a fastener when passed through a hole or loop: *He couldn't fasten the top button near his collar.* **2.** a badge or emblem with a name or slogan, for wearing on a jacket, etc.: *campaign buttons.* **3.** a small knob or disk pressed to start a machine, open a door, etc.: *He pushed the button and the elevator door closed.* **—*v.*** **4.** to fasten or attach with or as if with a button or buttons: [~ + *obj* (+ *up*)]: *Button your coat (up).* [~ (+ *up*) + *obj*]: *Button (up) your coat.* **5.** [*no obj*] to be capable of being buttoned: *This coat buttons in the front.* **—*Idiom.*** **6. button up,** [*no obj*] Also, **button (up) one's lip.** to keep silent, as to keep a secret: *Better button up until the deal goes through.* **7. (right) on the button,** exactly at the desired time, goal, etc.: *She came at ten o'clock, right on the button.*

but′ton-down′, *adj.* **1.** (of a collar) having holes at the ends with which it can be buttoned to the front of the garment. **2.** (of a garment) having a button-down collar: *a button-down shirt.* **3.** Also, **but′toned down′.** too conventional or conservative: *the button-down mentality of that company.*

but•ton•hole (but′n hōl′) /ˈbʌtn̩ˌhowl/ *n., v.,* **-holed, -hol•ing.** **—*n.*** [*count*] **1.** the hole through which a button is passed and by which it is fastened. **—*v.*** [~ + *obj*] **2.** to stop (someone) and keep in conversation: *The reporters buttonholed the witness outside the courtroom.*

but•tress (bu′tris) /ˈbʌtrɪs/ *n.* [*count*] **1.** a support that sticks out from the wall of a building to keep it steady: *the buttresses of the old cathedrals in England.* **2.** any prop or support: *the buttresses of civilized society.* **—*v.*** [~ + *obj*] **3.** to support by means of a buttress; prop up: *The builders buttressed this wall with stone structures that are marvels of engineering.* **4.** to give support or encouragement to: *Try to buttress the points you make in these chapters with some details.*

bux•om (buk′səm) /ˈbʌksəm/ *adj.* **1.** (of a woman) large in the bosom. **2.** (of a woman) plump and cheerful. **—bux′om•ness,** *n.* [*noncount*]

buy (bī) /bay/ *v.,* **bought** (bôt) /bɔt/ **buy•ing,** *n.* **—*v.*** **1.** to get possession of (something), esp. by paying money; purchase: [~ + *obj*]: *She bought a new computer.* [~ + *obj* + *obj*]: *She bought him a new computer.* [~ + *obj* + *for* + *a noun showing an amount*]: *She bought the computer for only $499.* [*no obj*]: *He buys at low prices.* **2.** to obtain by exchange or sacrifice: [~ + *obj*]: *to buy favor with flattery; Victory can only be bought with bloodshed.* [~ + *obj* + *obj*]: *Buy me some happiness.* **3.** [~ + *obj*] to bribe: *The senator claimed he couldn't be bought.* **4.** [~ + *obj; not: be* + ~*-ing*] to equal (some amount of) purchasing power: *A dollar doesn't buy much these days.* **5.** [~ + *obj*] *Informal.* to accept or believe: *I don't buy that explanation.* **6. buy into,** [~ + *into* + *obj*] to purchase a share in: *He bought into the syndicate deal for the construction of new downtown housing.* **7. buy off,** to get rid of (a claim, etc.) by payment; to bribe: [~ + *obj* + *off*]: *See if you can buy him off.* [~ + *off* + *obj*]: *Buy off as many politicians as you can.* **8. buy out, a.** [~ + *out* + *obj*] to purchase (shares in a company) so as to gain control of: *He bought out the company and tried to resell it.* **b.** to purchase all the business shares belonging to (another): [~ + *obj* + *out*]: *When the businessman retired, his partner bought him out.* [~ + *out* + *obj*]: *They bought out all the other partners.* **9. buy up,** to buy as much of (something) as is available: [~ + *up* + *obj*]: *bought up all the oil on the market.* [~ + *obj* + *up*]: *They tried to buy it all up.* **—*n.*** [*count*] **10.** a bargain: *The couch and the stereo are good buys.* **—*Idiom.*** **11. buy time,** *Informal.* to put off some action or decision: [*no obj*]: *tried to buy time by making conversation while he tried to remember her name.* [*buy* + *obj* + *time*]: *Buy me some time while I figure out what to say.*

buy•er (bī′ər) /ˈbayər/ *n.* [*count*] a person who buys; a purchaser, esp. for a store.

buy′ers' mar′ket, *n.* [*count*] a market in which goods and services are plentiful and prices are relatively low. Compare SELLERS' MARKET.

buy•out (bī′out′) /ˈbayˌawt/ *n.* [*count*] an act or instance of buying out.

buzz (buz) /bʌz/ *n.* [*count*] **1.** a low, humming sound, as of bees or machinery: *The buzz of the machinery stopped suddenly.* **2.** lively or excited activity: *the buzz in the room before class.* **3.** *Informal.* a phone call: *I'll give you a buzz tonight.* **4.** *Slang.* a feeling of happiness caused by slight drinking; pleasant intoxication: *a slight buzz from the beer.* **—*v.*** **5.** to (cause to) make a low, vibrating, humming sound: [*no obj*]: *The flies buzzed in the barnyard.* [~ + *obj*]: *The fly buzzed its wings.* **6.** [*no obj*] to be filled with such a sound, as a room: *The dining hall buzzed with excitement.* **7.** [*no obj*] to whisper; gossip: *The town is buzzing about the scandal.* **8.** [*no obj*] to move busily from place to place: *He buzzed around town.* **9.** to signal or summon with a buzzer: *She buzzed her secretary.* **10.** [~ + *obj*] *Informal.* to make a phone call to: *Is it OK if I buzz you tonight?* **11.** [~ + *obj*] to fly a plane very low over: *to buzz a stadium.* **12. buzz off,** [*no obj*] *Slang.* to go; leave: *told him to buzz off.*

buz•zard (buz′ərd) /ˈbʌzərd/ *n.* [*count*] **1.** a broad-winged hawk of Europe and Asia. **2.** a vulture of the Americas, esp. the turkey vulture. **3.** a grouchy or greedy person.

buzz•er (buz′ər) /ˈbʌzər/ *n.* [*count*] a person or thing that buzzes.

buzz′ saw′, *n.* [*count*] a power-operated circular saw.

buzz•word (buz′wûrd′) /ˈbʌzˌwɜrd/ *n.* [*count*] a word or phrase that has come into fashion and is overused: *The latest buzzword, multiculturalism, meant different things to different people.*

BW, an abbreviation of: black-and-white.

bx., *pl.* **bxs.** an abbreviation of: box.

by (bī) /bay/ *prep., adv., n., pl.* **byes.** **—*prep.*** **1.** near to or next to: *a home by a lake.* **2.** over the surface of, or using as a route or way of travel: *She came by air.* **3.** to and beyond a place; past: *We drove by the church.* **4.** to, into, or at: *Come by my office.* **5.** during: *We drove by night.* **6.** with the accompaniment of: *by the light of the silvery moon.* **7.** not later than; before: *I'll be done by five o'clock.* **8.** to the extent or amount of: *He was taller by three inches.* **9.** (of a part of the body) holding onto: *grabbed me by the arm.* **10.** from the evidence of: *By his own account he was there.* **11.** according to: *a bad movie by any standards.* **12.** through the work or action of: **a.** [*after a verb that is passive, and before the noun that caused the action of the verb*]: *The booklet was issued by the government. This book was written by a team of experts.* **b.** [*after a noun that refers to an action, and before the next noun that performs or does that action*]: *a shooting by a police officer.* **13.** through the means of: *Do you want to pay by cash, check, or credit card?* **14.** existing as a result of the creative power or invention of: *a poem by Emily Dickinson.* **15.** as a result of; on the basis of: *we met by chance.* **16.** in support of; for: *to do well by one's children.* **17.** (of things that come after each other) after; next after: *put the puzzle together piece by piece.* **18.** used before the second of two numbers to express the operations of multiplication or division, or to convey dimensions: **a.** (in multiplication): *Multiply 18 by 57 (= 18 x 57).* **b.** (in division): *Divide 99 by 33 (= 99÷33)* **c.** (in measuring spaces): *a room 10 feet by 12 feet (= a room 10 feet in one direction and 12 feet in another direction).* **19.** in terms, groups, or amounts of: *Apples are sold by the bushel.* **20.** born of: *She had a son by her first husband.* **—*adv.*** **21.** at hand; near: *The school is close by.* **22.** to and beyond a point; past: *The car drove by.* **23.** to or at someone's home, office, etc.: *Won't you stop by later?* **24.** past; over: *in times gone by.* **—*n.*** **25.** BYE[1]. **—*Idiom.*** **26. by and by,** before long; soon, or eventually; in time: *We'll understand it all, by and by.* **27. by and large,** in general; on the whole: *We have a good school, by and large.* **28. (all) by oneself,** alone: *She changed the flat tire all by herself.* **—Usage.** Compare BY and WITH when referring to how an action is done. We use BY to refer to a description of an action, often with the *-ing* form of the verb: *I took the wheel off by jacking up the car and loosening the nuts.* We use WITH before the tool we use to do the action: *I took the wheel* *off with the jack handle and loosened the nuts with a wrench.*

bye[1] (bī) /bay/ *n.* [*count*] Also, **by. 1.** a secondary matter. ***—Idiom.* 2. by the bye,** by the way; incidentally.

bye[2] or **by** (bī) /bay/ *interj.* GOOD-BYE.

bye-bye (*interj.* bī′bī′; *n., adv.* bī′bī′) /*interj.* ˈbayˈbay; *n., adv.* ˈbayˌbay/ *interj.* **1.** GOOD-BYE. *—n.* [*noncount*] **2.** *Baby Talk.* sleep. *—adv.,* ***Idiom.* 3. go bye-bye,** *Baby Talk.* to leave; depart; go out: *Let's put on our jackets; it's time to go bye-bye.*

by′-elec′tion or **bye′-elec′tion,** *n.* [*count*] a special election held between general elections to fill a vacancy, esp. in the British Parliament.

by•gone (bī′gôn′, -gon′) /ˈbayˌgɔn, -ˌgɒn/ *adj.* [*before a noun*] **1.** earlier; former; past: *bygone days.* ***—Idiom.*** **2. let bygones be bygones,** to put aside past disagreements: *willing to let bygones be bygones.*

by•law or **bye•law** (bī′lô′) /ˈbayˌlɔ/ *n.* [*count*] a rule governing the internal affairs of a corporation, organization, etc.: *The by-laws say you can't be fired without a hearing first.*

by•line or **by-line** (bī′līn′) /ˈbayˌlayn/ *n.* [*count*] a printed line in a newspaper or magazine, usually below the title or heading of a story, giving the author's name: *Her name appeared in the bylines of major newspapers.*

by•pass or **by-pass** (bī′pas′) /ˈbayˌpæs/ *n., v.,* **-passed, -passed** or **-past, -pass•ing.** *—n.* [*count*] **1.** a road allowing motorists to avoid heavy traffic points or to drive around an obstruction. **2.** a surgical operation in which the flow of blood through a diseased organ is redirected around the blockage: *a coronary bypass operation. —v.* [~ + *obj*] **3.** to avoid by following a bypass: *We bypassed the city.* **4.** to neglect to consult or to ignore the opinion or decision of: *I bypassed the manager and went straight to the owner.* See -PASS-[1].

by•play or **by-play** (bī′plā′) /ˈbayˌpley/ *n.* [*noncount*] an action or speech carried on to the side while the main action proceeds, esp. on the stage: *I couldn't focus on the byplay because the main action was so exciting.*

by′-prod′uct, *n.* [*count*] **1.** a secondary or incidental product: *This acid is produced as a by-product of fermentation.* **2.** the result of another action, often not foreseen or intended: *An unfortunate by-product of democracy could be more ethnic hatred.*

by•stand•er (bī′stan′dər) /ˈbayˌstændər/ *n.* [*count*] a person present but not involved; onlooker: *He claimed to be an innocent bystander.*

byte (bīt) /bayt/ *n.* [*count*] a group of bits, usually eight, processed by a computer as a unit: *The file started was as big as 23,000 bytes.*

by•way (bī′wā′) /ˈbayˌwey/ *n.* [*count*] a seldom-used road: *He knew all the little byways and shortcuts in the town.*

by•word (bī′wûrd′) /ˈbayˌwɜrd/ *n.* [*count*] **1.** a common saying; proverb: *"A penny saved is a penny earned" is their byword.* **2.** a person or thing thought of as characteristic of a particular quality: *Eichmann had become the byword for genocide.*

byz•an•tine (biz′ən tēn′, -tīn′) /ˈbɪzənˌtiyn, -ˌtayn/ *adj.* characterized by complicated scheming or intrigue: *a byzantine plot for retaining his power.*

C, c (sē) /siy/ *n.* [*count*], *pl.* **Cs** or **C's, cs** or **c's.** the third letter of the English alphabet, a consonant.

C, *Symbol.* **1.** [*sometimes: c*] (in some grading systems) a grade or mark indicating fair or average quality. **2. a.** the tonic note of the C major scale. **b.** a written or printed note representing this tone. **3.** [*sometimes: c*] the Roman numeral for 100. **4.** Celsius: *The temperature is 10℃ (said as "10 degrees Celsius").* **5.** centigrade. **6.** carbon. **7.** Also, **C-note.** *Slang.* a hundred-dollar bill.

c, an abbreviation of: circa (used with a year): *c1775.*

c, *Symbol.* **1.** the velocity of light in a vacuum: approximately 186,000 miles per second or 299,793 kilometers per second. **2.** the velocity of sound.

C., an abbreviation of: **1.** Calorie. **2.** College. **3.** Conservative.

c., an abbreviation of: **1.** calorie. **2.** carat. **3.** centigrade. **4.** centimeter. **5.** chapter. **6.** circa (used with a year): *c. 1775.* **7.** copyright. **8.** cubic.

CA, an abbreviation of: California.

ca or **ca.,** an abbreviation of: circa (used with a year): *ca 476* B.C.

cab (kab) /kæb/ *n.* **1.** a taxicab: [*count*]: *It's hard to get a cab in this rain.* [*noncount; by + ~*]: *We went home by cab.* **2.** [*count*] the covered or enclosed part of a truck, crane, etc., where the operator sits.

ca•bal (kə bal′) /kə'bæl/ *n.* [*count*] a small group of secret plotters: *The cabal met to plan an attack upon the government.*

ca•ban•a (kə ban′ə, -ban′yə) /kə'bænə, -'bænyə/ *n.* [*count*], *pl.* **-as.** a small cabin or tent for changing one's clothes esp. on a beach or by a swimming pool.

cab•a•ret (kab′ə rā′) /ˌkæbə'rey/ *n.* **1.** [*count*] a restaurant providing food, drink, and often a floor show. **2.** [*noncount*] the entertainment at a cabaret.

cab•bage (kab′ij) /'kæbɪdʒ/ *n.* **1.** [*count*] a plant, of the mustard family, having a short stem and leaves that form into a rounded head. **2.** [*noncount*] the head or leaves of this plant, eaten cooked or raw: *I ate corned beef and cabbage.* **3.** [*noncount*] *Slang.* money, esp. paper money.

cab•by or **cab•bie** (kab′ē) /'kæbiy/ *n.* [*count*], *pl.* **-bies.** *Informal.* a person who drives a taxicab.

cab•in (kab′in) /'kæbɪn/ *n.* [*count*] **1.** a small cottage, usually simply designed and built: *a log cabin.* **2.** the enclosed space for the pilot, cargo, or passengers in an airplane or space vehicle. **3.** an apartment or room in a ship, as for passengers.

cab′in cruis′er, *n.* [*count*] a power-driven pleasure boat having a cabin equipped for living or sleeping.

cab•i•net (kab′ə nit) /'kæbənɪt/ *n.* [*count*] **1.** a piece of furniture with shelves, etc., for holding or displaying items: *a kitchen cabinet for pots and pans.* See illustration at APARTMENT. **2.** the case enclosing a radio, television, etc. **3.** [*often: Cabinet; the + ~*] a group of persons who officially advises a sovereign or a chief executive. —*adj.* [*before a noun*] **4.** of or relating to a political cabinet: *a cabinet meeting.*

ca•ble (kā′bəl) /'keybəl/ *n., v.,* **-bled, -bling.** —*n.* **1.** a strong rope made of strands of metal wire, used to support bridges, etc.: [*noncount*]: *The material is reinforced cable.* [*count*]: *the cables holding up a suspension bridge.* **2.** a cord of metal wire used to carry electrical power, etc.: [*noncount*]: *miles of electrical cable.* [*count*]: *The cables cut across the town lines.* **3.** [*count*] a cablegram. **4.** [*noncount*] cable television: *That hotel has cable.* —*v.* **5.** to send (a message) by cable: [*no obj*]: *He cabled from Europe asking for money.* [*~ + obj*]: *He cabled the message.* [*~ + (that) clause*]: *He cabled that he needed money.* **6.** [*~ + obj*] to send a cablegram to: *We cabled him last week.* **7.** to send (money) by sending an instruction to a bank: [*~ + obj*]: *She cabled fifty dollars to him.* [*~ + obj + obj*]: *She cabled him fifty dollars.*

ca′ble car′ or **ca′ble-car′,** *n.* [*count*] a vehicle pulled along a track by a cable, as up a steep hill: [*count*]: *The cable car climbed up to the fortress.* [*noncount; by + ~*]: *traveled by cable car through San Francisco.*

ca•ble•cast (kā′bəl kast′) /'keybəlˌkæst/ *n., v.,* **-cast** or **-cast•ed, -cast•ing.** —*n.* [*count*] **1.** a television broadcast made on cable television. —*v.* [*~ + obj*] **2.** to broadcast on cable television: *They cablecasted old movies.* —**ca′ble•cast′er,** *n.* [*count*]

ca•ble•gram (kā′bəl gram′) /'keybəlˌgræm/ *n.* [*count*] a telegram sent by underwater cable.

ca′ble-read′y, *adj.* (of a television set) allowing a direct connection with a cable television hookup.

ca′ble tel′evision, *n.* [*noncount*] a system of televising programs to private subscribers by means of special cable. Also called **cable TV.**

ca•boo•dle (kə bo͞od′l) /kə'buwdl̩/ *n.* [*noncount; the + whole + ~*] *Informal.* the entire amount of; the lot, pack, or crowd: *Get rid of the whole caboodle.*

ca•boose (kə bo͞os′) /kə'buws/ *n.* [*count*] a car on a freight train, used as a place for the crew to eat and sleep and usually attached to the rear of the train.

ca•ca•o (kə kä′ō, -kā′ō) /kə'kɑow, -'keyow/ *n.* [*count*], *pl.* **-os. 1.** a small tropical American evergreen tree grown for its seeds, the source of cocoa and chocolate. **2.** Also, **cocoa.** the fruit or seeds of this tree.

cache (kash) /kæʃ/ *n., v.,* **cached, cach•ing.** —*n.* [*count*] **1.** a hiding place, as for food, supplies, or valuables. **2.** anything hidden in a cache: *a cache of rifles.* —*v.* [*~ + obj*] **3.** to hide or store in a cache: *They cached their weapons.*

ca•chet (ka shā′) /kæ'ʃey/ *n.* **1.** [*noncount*] superior status; prestige: *a job with cachet.* **2.** [*count; usually singular*] a distinguishing feature: *has the cachet of a noble name.*

cack•le (kak′əl) /'kækəl/ *v.,* **-led, -ling,** *n.* —*v.* **1.** [*no obj*] to utter a high, broken cry, as a hen does: *The hens cackled excitedly.* **2.** [*no obj*] to laugh in this way: *The mad scientist cackled with glee.* **3.** [*~ + obj*] to express with a cackling sound: *They cackled their disapproval.* —*n.* **4.** [*count*] the act or sound of cackling: *high-pitched cackle.* **5.** [*noncount*] chatter; foolish talk. —**cack′ler,** *n.* [*count*]

ca•coph•o•ny (kə kof′ə nē) /kə'kɒfəniy/ *n.* [*count; usually singular*], *pl.* **-nies.** a harsh sound or mixture of sounds: *a cacophony of many voices.* —**cac•o•phon•ic** (kak′ə fon′ik) /ˌkækə'fɒnɪk/ *adj.* See -PHON-.

cac•tus (kak′təs) /'kæktəs/ *n.* [*count*], *pl.* **-ti** (-tī), **-tus•es, -tus.** a flowering plant of hot, dry regions, with large, rounded, leafless stems usually with spines.

cad (kad) /kæd/ *n.* [*count*] a man who behaves badly or unfairly, esp. toward women.

CAD (kad) /kæd/ *n.* [*noncount*] computer-aided design.

-cad-, *root.* -*cad-* comes from Latin, where it has the meaning "fall". This meaning is found in such words as: CADENCE, CADENZA, DECADENT. See -CIDE-[2].

ca•dav•er (kə dav′ər) /kə'dævər/ *n.* [*count*] a dead body, esp. a human body to be examined medically; corpse.

ca•dav•er•ous (kə dav′ər əs) /kə'dævərəs/ *adj.* pale and gaunt; ghastly: *a cadaverous face.* —**ca•dav′er•ous•ness,** *n.* [*noncount*]

cad•die (kad′ē) /'kædiy/ *n., pl.* **-dies,** *v.,* **-died, -dy•ing.** —*n.* [*count*] **1.** a person hired to carry a golf player's clubs, etc. **2.** a device with wheels used for moving heavy objects: *a luggage caddie.* —*v.* [*no obj*] **3.** to work as a caddie: *She caddied for several summers.*

cad•dy (kad′ē) /'kædiy/ *n.* [*count*], *pl.* **-dies.** a small container for holding tea leaves.

ca•dence (kād′ns) /'keydns/ *n.* [*count*] **1.** rhythm in the flow of sounds or words: *the cadence of the drummers.* **2.** the flow or rhythm of events: *the cadences of modern life.* **3.** a slight falling or rising in pitch of the voice in speaking: *Listen to the cadence in English questions and statements.* See -CAD-.

ca•den•za (kə den′zə) /kə'dɛnzə/ *n.* [*count*], *pl.* **-zas.** a musical passage, introduced near the end of a concerto, and played by one musician: *a complex cadenza.* See -CAD-.

ca•det (kə det′) /kə'dɛt/ *n.* [*count*] a student in a service school who is training to be an officer.

cadge (kaj) /kædʒ/ *v.,* **cadged, cadg•ing.** to obtain (money, etc.) by begging or depending on another's generosity; sponge: [*no obj; (~ + from + obj)*]: *always cadging from his friends.* [*~ + obj*]: *He cadged a meal.* —**cadg′er,** *n.* [*count*]

ca•dre (kad′rē, kä′drā) /'kædriy, 'kɑdrey/ *n.* [*count*] a small group of people, as soldiers, able to train and lead a larger group.

Cae•sar•e•an or **Cae•sar•i•an** (si zâr′ē ən) /sɪ'zɛəriyən/ *adj., n.* [*sometimes: caesarean, caesarian*] CESAREAN.

cae•su•ra or **ce•su•ra** (si zho͝or′ə, -zo͝or′ə, siz yo͝or′ə)

/sɪ'ʒʊrə, -'zʊrə, sɪz'yʊrə/ *n.* [*count*], *pl.* **cae•su•ras** or **ce•su•ras, cae•su•rae** or **ce•su•rae** (si zhŏŏr′ē, -zŏŏr′ē, siz-yŏŏr′ē) /sɪ'ʒʊriy, -'zʊriy, sɪz'yʊriy/. a break or pause in a line of poetry.

ca•fé or **ca•fe** (ka fā′, kə-) /kæ'fey, kə-/ *n.* [*count*], *pl.* **-fés** or **-fes. 1.** a small restaurant, often with a section extending onto the sidewalk. **2.** a barroom, cabaret, or nightclub.

caf•e•te•ri•a (kaf′i tēr′ē ə) /ˌkæfɪ'tɪəriyə/ *n.* [*count*], *pl.* **-as. 1.** a restaurant in which diners select food at a counter and carry it to tables. **2.** a lunchroom, as for employees or students.

caf•feine (ka fēn′, kaf′ēn) /kæ'fiyn, 'kæfiyn/ *n.* [*noncount*] a white, bitter chemical, obtained from coffee or tea, used in medicine as a stimulant.

caf•tan or **kaf•tan** (kaf′tan, kaf tan′) /'kæftæn, kæf'tæn/ *n.* [*count*] a long garment with long sleeves, sometimes with a sash at the waist, worn chiefly in the Middle East. **—caf′taned,** *adj.*

cage (kāj) /keydʒ/ *n., v.,* **caged, cag•ing. —***n.* [*count*] **1.** a boxlike enclosure with wires or bars forming the sides, for keeping birds or animals: *a bird cage.* **2.** a prison. **3.** a similar enclosure used like an elevator for workers at a construction site, etc. **4.** a frame with a net attached to it, forming the goal in ice hockey and field hockey. **—***v.* [~ + *obj*] **5.** to put or keep in or as if in a cage: *They caged the escaped tiger.* **—caged,** *adj.*

cag•ey or **cag•y** (kā′jē) /'keydʒiy/ *adj.,* **-i•er, -i•est.** cautious, careful, wary, or shrewd: *a cagey reply to his question.* **—cag•i•ly** (kā′jə lē) /'keydʒəliy/ *adv.: The candidate replied cagily that he would need to study that question.* **—cag•i•ness** (kā′jē nis) /'keydʒiynɪs/ *n.* [*noncount*]

ca•hoot (kə hŏŏt′) /kə'huwt/ *n. Informal.* **—*Idiom.*** **in cahoots,** [*often:* ~ + *with* + *obj*] working together secretly, usually to do something illegal: *a policeman in cahoots with the drug dealers.*

cairn (kârn) /kɛərn/ *n.* [*count*] a heap of stones set up as a landmark, boundary, monument, etc.

cais•son (kā′son, -sən) /'keysɒn, -sən/ *n.* [*count*] **1.** a structure built to protect workers, esp. a chamber for use in underwater construction. **2.** a two-wheeled wagon used for carrying ammunition for cannons.

ca•jole (kə jōl′) /kə'dʒowl/ *v.* [~ + *obj* (+ *into*)], **-joled, -jol•ing.** to persuade by promises, false praise, or humor: *We cajoled the ticket taker into letting us in free.* **—ca•jole′ment,** *n.* [*noncount*] **—ca•jol′er,** *n.* [*count*] **—ca•jol′er•y,** *n.* [*noncount*]: *They tried cajolery instead of threats.* **—ca•jol′ing•ly,** *adv.*

cake (kāk) /keyk/ *n., v.,* **caked, cak•ing. —***n.* **1.** a sweet, baked, breadlike food: [*count*]: *She made birthday cakes for the children's party.* [*noncount*]: *a few pieces of cake.* **2.** [*count*] a shaped or molded mass of other food: *a fish cake.* **3.** [*count*] a shaped block of something: *a cake of soap.* **—***v.* **4.** to form into a dry layer or crust on the outside; to coat: [~ + *obj*]: *The windshield was caked with dirt.* [*no obj*]: *The mud caked on his shoes.* **—*Idiom.*** **5. a piece of cake,** something that can be done easily, often with enjoyment: *said the test was a piece of cake.* **6. have one's cake and eat it too,** to have the advantages of something without its disadvantages. **7. take the cake,** to be an outstanding example; rank first: *That crazy stunt really took the cake.*

cake•walk (kāk′wôk′) /'keykˌwɔk/ *n.* [*count*] **1.** a dance with a special strutting step. **2.** something easy or certain: *Winning the prize will be a real cakewalk.*

Cal., an abbreviation of: California.

cal., an abbreviation of: **1.** caliber. **2.** calorie.

cal•a•bash (kal′ə bash′) /'kæləˌbæʃ/ *n.* **1.** [*count*] a tree that has large, rounded gourdlike fruit. **2.** [*count*] the fruit of any of these plants. **3.** [*noncount*] the dried, hollowed-out shell of any of these fruits, used to make the bowl of a tobacco pipe.

cal•a•boose (kal′ə bŏŏs′) /'kæləˌbuws/ *n.* [*count*] *Slang.* jail; prison.

cal•a•mine (kal′ə mīn′, -min) /'kæləˌmayn, -mɪn/ *n.* [*noncount*] a pink powder of zinc oxide, used in lotions for the treatment of minor skin irritations, as insect bites and poison ivy.

ca•lam•i•ty (kə lam′i tē) /kə'læmɪtiy/ *n.* [*count*], *pl.* **-ties.** a great misfortune or disaster: *suffered from one calamity after another: disease, war, famine, and drought.* **—ca•lam′i•tous,** *adj.*

cal•ci•fy (kal′sə fī′) /'kælsəˌfay/ *v.,* **-fied, -fy•ing.** to make or become hard or bony from calcium deposits: [*no obj*]: *The bones calcified.* [~ + *obj*]: *The calcium salts work to calcify the bones.*

cal•ci•um (kal′sē əm) /'kælsiyəm/ *n.* [*noncount*] a silver-white metallic element found in limestone and chalk and that also occurs in animals in bone and shell.

cal•cu•late (kal′kyə lāt′) /'kælkyəˌleyt/ *v.,* **-lat•ed, -lat•ing. 1.** to determine (something) by using mathematical methods; compute: [*no obj*]: *She calculated in her head a moment.* [~ + *obj*]: *The students tried to calculate the speed of the train.* [~ + (*that*) *clause*]: *They calculated that fifty-two shelves would fill the room.* **2.** to arrive at an opinion by reasoning or practical experience; estimate: [~ + *obj*]: *First, calculate the effects of firing your workers.* [~ + *clause*]: *We can't begin to calculate what he will do next.* **3.** [*be* + ~*-ed* + *to* + *verb*] to be made suitable for a purpose: *racist remarks calculated to get a lot of coverage from the media.*

cal•cu•lat•ed (kal′kyə lā′tid) /'kælkyəˌleytɪd/ *adj.* **1.** carefully thought out or planned: *a calculated threat to get us to agree to his demands.* **2.** [*before a noun*] deliberate; intentional: *a calculated risk.* **—cal′cu•lat′ed•ly,** *adv.* **—cal′cu•lat′ed•ness,** *n.* [*noncount*]

cal•cu•lat•ing (kal′kyə lā′ting) /'kælkyəˌleytɪŋ/ *adj.* thinking about one's own benefit without emotion; selfishly scheming: *She gave him a calculating look.* **—cal′cu•lat′ing•ly,** *adv.*

cal•cu•la•tion (kal′kyə lā′shən) /ˌkælkyə'leyʃən/ *n.* **1.** the act or process of calculating; computation: [*noncount*]: *I did some rapid calculation in my head.* [*count*]: *The machine's calculations took only seconds.* **2.** [*count*] the result or product of calculating: *My calculations weren't correct.* **3.** [*count*] an estimate based on the known facts; forecast: *My calculation is that she won't want to continue the lawsuit.* **4.** [*noncount*] forethought; prior or careful planning: *They put a lot of calculation into this.* **5.** [*noncount*] scheming selfishness: *a look of cold calculation.* **—cal′cu•la′tive** (kal′kyə lā′tiv, -lə tiv) /'kælkyə ˌleytɪv, -lətɪv/ **cal′cu•la′tion•al,** *adj.*

cal•cu•la•tor (kal′kyə lā′tər) /'kælkyəˌleytər/ *n.* [*count*] a small electronic device that performs mathematical calculations.

cal•cu•lus (kal′kyə ləs) /'kælkyələs/ *n.* [*noncount*] **1.** a branch of mathematics that calculates amounts that change constantly: *Calculus can help you figure out how fast an object falls.* **2.** a hard, yellowish substance on teeth formed from dental plaque; tartar.

cal•dron (kôl′drən) /'kɔldrən/ *n.* CAULDRON.

cal•en•dar (kal′ən dər) /'kæləndər/ *n.* [*count*] **1.** a chart or list displaying the days of each month and week in a year. See illustration at OFFICE. **2.** any of various systems of reckoning time, esp. with reference to the beginning, length, and divisions of the year: *the Gregorian calendar.* **3.** a list or register, esp. one arranged by hours, days, or weeks, as of appointments, etc.: *The court calendar was fully booked.* **—***adj.* [*before a noun*] **4.** divided into days or months: *A calendar year is usually 365 days.*

calf[1] (kaf) /kæf/ *n., pl.* **calves** (kavz). **1.** [*count*] the young of the domestic cow or other cowlike animal. **2.** [*count*] the young of certain other mammals, such as the elephant, seal, and whale. **3.** [*noncount*] calfskin.

calf[2] (kaf) /kæf/ *n.* [*count*], *pl.* **calves** (kavz). the fleshy part of the back of the human leg below the knee.

calf•skin (kaf′skin′) /'kæfˌskɪn/ *n.* [*noncount*] leather made from the skin or the hide of a calf: *a wallet of calfskin.*

cal•i•ber (kal′ə bər) /'kæləbər/ *n.* **1.** [*count*] the measurement of the inside width of the barrel of a gun: *a .50-caliber machine gun.* **2.** [*noncount*] the degree of how good something is: *work of the highest caliber.* Also, *esp. Brit.,* **cal′i•bre.**

cal•i•brate (kal′ə brāt′) /'kæləˌbreyt/ *v.* [~ + *obj*], **-brat•ed, -brat•ing. 1.** to mark (a measuring instrument) with dividing points of degree or quantity: *This thermometer is calibrated with Celsius and Fahrenheit markings.* **2.** to set, check, or correct the measuring points of (an instrument that measures things). **—cal′i•brated,** *adj.* **—cal•i•bra•tion** (kal′ə brā′shən) /ˌkælə'breyʃən/ *n.* [*count*]: *the calibrations on a thermometer.* [*noncount*]: *How exact is that calibration?* **—cal′i•bra′tor, cal′i•brat′er,** *n.* [*count*]

cal•i•co (kal′i kō′) /'kælɪˌkow/ *n., pl.* **-coes, -cos. 1.** [*noncount*] a plain-woven, cotton cloth printed with a pattern, usually on one side. **2.** [*noncount*] *Brit.* plain white cotton cloth. **3.** [*count*] an animal having a spotted or multicolored coat, esp. a cat.

ca•lif (kā′lif, kal′if) /'keylɪf, 'kælɪf/ *n.* CALIPH.

Calif., an abbreviation of: California.

cal•i•per or **cal•li•per** (kal′ə pər) /'kæləpər/ *n.* [*count*] Usually, **calipers.** [*plural*] an instrument for measuring thicknesses and diameters, usually made up of a pair of adjustable legs.

ca•liph or **ca•lif** (kā′lif, kal′if) /ˈkeylɪf, ˈkælɪf/ *n.* [*count*] a former title for a religious and civil ruler of the Islamic world: *Caliphs claimed to be the successors of Muhammad.* —**cal•iph•ate** (kal′ə fāt, kā′lə fāt) /ˈkæləfət, ˈkeylə fət/ *n.* [*count*]: *A caliph ruled over an area called a caliphate.*

cal•is•then•ics or **cal•lis•then•ics** (kal′əs then′iks) /ˌkæləsˈθɛnɪks/ *n.* **1.** [*plural; used with a plural verb*] exercises designed to develop physical health and vigor: *The calisthenics were not too hard for her.* **2.** [*noncount; used with a singular verb*] the art, practice, or a session of such exercises: *Calisthenics is a good way to keep fit.*

calk (kôk) /kɔk/ *v., n.* (chiefly in technical use) CAULK.

call (kôl) /kɔl/ *v.* **1.** to cry out in a loud voice; shout: [~ + *obj*]: *to call someone's name.* [~ + *for* + *obj*]: *She called for someone to help her.* [~ + *to* + *obj*]: *He called to his children out on the field.* **2.** [~ + *obj*] to ask or invite to come; summon: *Call a doctor, quick!* **3.** to communicate or try to communicate with (someone) by telephone: [~ + *obj*]: *She called her boyfriend twice.* [*no obj*]: *I called, but no one was home.* **4.** [~ + *obj*] to read over (a list) in a loud voice, as to see whether certain people are there: *The instructor called the roll.* **5.** [~ + *obj*] to announce (a meeting, etc.) and invite people to attend; convoke; convene: *He called a meeting for next week.* **6.** [~ + *obj*] to announce as an authority; proclaim: *The union leader called a strike.* **7.** [~ + *obj*] to direct or attract (attention): *Let me call your attention to this painting.* **8.** to name or address (someone) as (someone or something): [~ + *obj* + *obj*]: *My friends call me Ray.* [~ + *obj* + *by* + *obj*]: *We always called James by his nickname, Jim.* **9.** to designate or describe (someone or something) as (someone or something): [~ + *obj* + *noun*]: *She called me a liar.* [~ + *obj* + *adjective*]: *I'd call it crazy.* **10.** [~ + *obj*] to forecast or predict correctly: *Last year an economist said a recession was already on the way; well, she called it perfectly.* **11.** [~ + *obj*] (of a sports official) **a.** to pronounce a judgment on (a shot, etc.): *The batter was called out on strikes.* **b.** to put an end to (a contest) because of bad weather, etc.: *The officials called the game because of darkness.* **12.** to declare as a bet (the side of a coin that will turn up): [~ + *obj*]: *He called heads but it landed tails.* [*no obj*]: *Call while the coin is in the air.* **13.** [~ + *obj*] **a.** to demand payment or fulfillment of (a loan or debt): *They called his debt of $100,000.* **b.** (in poker) to bet the same amount as (another bettor): *I called that fifty-cent bet.* **14.** [*no obj*] (of a bird or animal) to utter its characteristic cry: *We listened to the birds calling in the meadow.* **15. call back, a.** to request or demand to return; recall: [~ + *back* + *obj*]: *The automobile company called back those defective minivans.* [~ + *obj* + *back*]: *They called the minivans back.* **b.** to return a telephone call or the telephone call of (someone): [*no obj*]: *I'll call back in an hour.* [~ + *obj* + *back*]: *I called the salesman back.* **16. call down, a.** to request or pray for: [~ + *down* + *obj*]: *called down the Lord's mercy on all sinners.* [~ + *obj* + *down*]: *He called the Lord's mercy down on his people.* **b.** [~ + *obj* + *down*] to reprimand; scold: *He was called down for his poor work.* **17. call for,** [~ + *for* + *obj*] **a.** to go or come to get; pick up; fetch: *I'll call for you at seven o'clock.* **b.** to demand; request strongly; urge to happen: *The students called for an end to tuition increases.* **c.** to require; need: *This emergency calls for prompt action.* **18. call off, a.** to summon or take away: [~ + *off* + *obj*]: *Call off your dog!* [~ + *obj* + *off*]: *Call him off!* **b.** to cancel (something planned): [~ + *off* + *obj*]: *The teacher called off the test.* [~ + *obj* + *off*]: *to call it off because of the snow.* **19. call on** or **upon,** [~ + *on/upon* + *obj*] **a.** to ask; appeal to: *We call on your generosity.* [~ + *on/upon* + *obj* + *to* + *verb*]: *We called upon the President to do something for them.* **b.** to visit for a short time: *He wanted to call on his girlfriend.* **20. call out, a.** to speak in a loud voice; shout: [~ + *obj* + *out*]: *She called my name out and I stood up.* [~ + *out* + *obj*]: *She called out my name.* **b.** [~ + *out* + *obj*] to summon into service or action: *Call out the militia!* **21. call up, a.** to bring forward for consideration or action: [~ + *up* + *obj*]: *He called up the information from the computer.* [~ + *obj* + *up*]: *Can you call the student's name up and see what his status is?* **b.** [~ + *up* + *obj*] to cause to remember; recall; evoke: *The trip called up happy memories of my youth.* **c.** to make a telephone call to: [~ + *obj* + *up*]: *When I call you up, your line's busy.* [~ + *up* + *obj*]: *Call up every John Smith until you find the right one.* **d.** to summon for action, esp. military service: [~ + *up* + *obj*]: *The Pentagon called up most of the National Guard units.* [~ + *obj* + *up*]: *The Pentagon will call them up for duty.* —*n.* **22.** [*count*] a cry or shout: *I heard a call for help.* **23.** [*count*] the typical sound or cry of a bird or other animal: *the call of the blue jay.* **24.** [*count*] an act or instance of telephoning: *Give me a call when you're ready.* **25.** [*count*] a short visit: *Let's pay a call on our favorite aunt.* **26.** [*count*] a signal made by a bugle, alarm, etc.: *The firefighters responded to twenty calls during that snowstorm.* **27.** [*count*] a summons, invitation, or bidding: *The emergency squad went out on a call.* **28.** [*noncount*] fascination or appeal: *the call of the wild.* **29.** [*noncount*] a need or occasion: *no call for panic.* **30.** [*count*] a demand or claim: *a call on one's time.* **31.** [*count*] a judgment by an umpire or other official of a contest: *a bad call by the referee.* —***Idiom.*** **32. on call,** readily available for summoning upon short notice: *stayed at the hospital on call from 11 to 6.*

call•er (kô′lər) /ˈkɔlər/ *n.* [*count*] **1.** a person who pays a short visit: *The patient had several callers.* **2.** a person who calls, as one who makes a telephone call.

call′ girl′, *n.* [*count*] a female prostitute who makes appointments by telephone.

cal•lig•ra•phy (kə lig′rə fē) /kəˈlɪgrəfiy/ *n.* [*noncount*] beautiful handwriting. —**cal•lig′ra•pher, cal•lig′ra•phist,** *n.* [*count*] See -GRAPH-.

call•ing (kô′ling) /ˈkɔlɪŋ/ *n.* [*count; usually singular*] **1.** a profession or trade: *Her calling was medicine.* **2.** a strong impulse: *a calling to the priesthood.*

cal•li•o•pe (kə lī′ə pē) /kəˈlayəpiy/ *n.* [*count*] a musical instrument made up of steam whistles played from a keyboard.

cal•lous (kal′əs) /ˈkæləs/ *adj.* **1.** (of the skin) made hard; hardened by or as if by callus: *His hands were callous after years of hard work.* **2.** insensitive; uncaring; unsympathetic: *had a callous attitude toward the homeless.* —**cal′loused,** *adj.*: *rough, calloused hands.* —**cal′lous•ly,** *adv.*: *treated him callously.* —**cal′lous•ness,** *n.* [*noncount*]

cal•low (kal′ō) /ˈkælow/ *adj.* immature or inexperienced: *a callow youth of no experience.* —**cal′low•ness,** *n.* [*noncount*]

call′-up′, *n.* [*count*] an order to report for active military service.

cal•lus (kal′əs) /ˈkæləs/ *n.* [*count*], *pl.* **-lus•es.** a hardened or thickened part of the skin, caused by rubbing.

calm (käm) /kɑm/ *adj.,* **-er, -est,** *n., v.* —*adj.* **1.** without rough motion; still: *a calm sea.* **2.** not windy: *a calm day.* **3.** free from excitement; tranquil: *a calm manner.* —*n.* [*noncount*] **4.** stillness of weather: *the calm before a storm.* **5.** freedom from excitement; peacefulness; tranquillity: *Calm returned once more to our little village.* —*v.* **6.** to (cause to) become quiet, peaceful, or free from worry: [*no obj;* (~ + *down*)]: *The sky and sea calmed (down) and the sun came out.* [~ + *obj*]: *The Gospels claim that Jesus calmed the sea.* [~ + *down* + *obj*]: *Can't you calm down those children?* [~ + *obj* + *down*]: *Maybe this drink will calm you down.* —**calm′ly,** *adv.* —**calm′ness,** *n.* [*noncount*] —**Syn.** CALM, COLLECTED, COMPOSED, COOL all carry a meaning of "free from being overly excited." CALM implies staying steady in the midst of disturbance all around: *He remained calm throughout the crisis.* COLLECTED implies having complete command of one's thoughts, feelings, and behavior, usually as a result of effort: *The witness was remarkably collected during questioning.* COMPOSED implies having inner peace with dignity and some self-confidence: *He was pale but composed during the interview.* COOL suggests having clear judgment without strong feelings: *He was cool in the face of danger.*

ca•lor•ic (kə lôr′ik, -lor′-) /kəˈlɔrɪk, -ˈlɒr-/ *adj.* **1.** of or relating to calories. **2.** of or relating to heat.

cal•o•rie (kal′ə rē) /ˈkæləriy/ *n.* [*count*], *pl.* **-ries. 1.** Also called **gram calorie, small calorie.** an amount of heat necessary to raise the temperature of one gram of water by one degree celsius. **2.** a unit of measure of the amount of heat or energy that a certain food produces: *a diet of 2,000 calories a day.*

cal•o•rif•ic (kal′ə rif′ik) /ˌkæləˈrɪfɪk/ *adj.* of or relating to calories or conversion into heat; producing heat.

ca•lum•ni•ate (kə lum′nē āt′) /kəˈlʌmniyˌeyt/ *v.* [~ + *obj*], **-at•ed, -at•ing.** to make false and hurtful statements about (someone); slander. —**ca•lum•ni•a•tion** (kə lum′nē ā′shən) /kəˌlʌmniyˈeyʃən/ *n.* [*noncount*] —**ca•lum′ni•a′tor,** *n.* [*count*]

cal•um•ny (kal′əm nē) /ˈkæləmniy/ *n., pl.* **-nies. 1.**

[*count*] a lie designed to injure a reputation: *She was spreading calumnies about her opponent.* **2.** [*noncount*] the practice of making lying, hurtful statements: *She was the target of vicious calumny.*

calve (kav) /kæv/ *v.*, **calved, calv•ing.** to give birth to (a calf): [*no obj*]: *Our cow calved in the spring.* [~ + *obj*]: *She calved two offspring.*

calves (kavz) /kævz/ *n. pl.* of CALF.

ca•lyp•so (kə lip′sō) /kə'lɪpsow/ *n., pl.* **-sos.** a musical style, or a song, of West Indian origin, influenced by jazz: [*noncount*]: *In calypso the singers often make up the words.* [*count*]: *She sang a lively calypso.*

ca•ma•ra•de•rie (kä′mə rä′də rē, -rad′ə-, kam′ə-) /ˌkɑmə'rɑdəriy, -'rædə-, ˌkæmə-/ *n.* [*noncount*] a feeling of good-fellowship: *an easy camaraderie among friends.*

cam•ber (kam′bər) /'kæmbər/ *v.* **1.** to curve upward in the middle: [*no obj*]: *The road cambers enough here so the water drains off.* [~ + *obj*]: *The engineers didn't camber the road enough.* **—*n.*** [*count*] **2.** a slight arching or upward curve, such as the curve of a plane's wing.

cam•bi•um (kam′bē əm) /'kæmbiyəm/ *n.* [*count*], *pl.* **-bi•ums, -bi•a** (-bē ə) /-biyə/. a layer of plant tissue between the inner bark and wood: *The cambium forms the annual rings in trees.*

Cam•bo•di•an (kam bō′dē ən) /kæm'bowdiyən/ *adj.* **1.** of or relating to Cambodia. **—*n.*** [*count*] **2.** a person born or living in Cambodia.

cam•bric (kām′brik) /'keymbrɪk/ *n.* [*noncount*] a thin, plain, usually white cotton or linen fabric: *a shirt of cambric.*

cam•cord•er (kam′kôrd′ər) /'kæmˌkɔrdər/ *n.* [*count*] a small portable or hand-held video recorder. See illustration at APPLIANCE.

came (kām) /keym/ *v.* pt. of COME.

cam•el (kam′əl) /'kæməl/ *n.* **1.** [*count*] either of two large, long-necked animals with one or two humps on the back. **2.** [*noncount*] a color ranging from yellowish tan to yellowish brown.

ca•mel•lia (kə mēl′yə, -mē′lē ə) /kə'miylyə, -'miyliyə/ *n.* [*count*], *pl.* **-lias.** a shrub of the tea family, having shiny evergreen leaves and flowers that resemble roses.

cam′el's hair′ also **cam′el•hair′,** *n.* [*noncount*] **1.** the hair of the camel, used esp. for cloth. **2.** a soft cloth made of this hair, usually tan in color. **—cam′el's-hair′, cam′el-hair′,** *adj.*

Cam•em•bert (kam′əm bâr′) /'kæməmˌbɛər/ *n.* [*noncount*] a soft cheese made from cow's milk.

cam•e•o (kam′ē ō′) /'kæmiyˌow/ *n., pl.* **-os,** *adj.* **—*n.*** [*count*] **1.** a piece of jewelry with a design or figure that is slightly raised from the background: *The cameo had a woman's head in profile.* **2.** Also called **cam′eo role′.** a small but notable part, as in a film, played esp. by a well-known performer. **—*adj.*** [*before a noun*] **3.** of or relating to a cameo role: *a cameo appearance.*

cam•er•a (kam′ər ə) /'kæmərə/ *n.* [*count*], *pl.* **-as. 1.** a usually hand-held device for taking pictures or films: *a still camera; a movie camera.* See illustration at APPLIANCE. **2.** (in a television transmitting apparatus) the device in which the picture to be televised is formed before it is changed into electric impulses. **—*Idiom.* 3. in camera, a.** in the privacy of a judge's chambers: *The lawyers and the judge discussed the problem in camera.* **b.** privately; not in public. **4. off camera,** out of the range of a camera: *made a gesture off camera.* **5. on camera,** being filmed or televised by a live camera.

cam•er•a•man (kam′ər ə man′, -mən) /'kæmərəˌmæn, -mən/ *n.* [*count*], *pl.* **-men.** a person who operates a camera, esp. a motion-picture or television camera.

cam•o•mile (kam′ə mīl′, -mēl′) /'kæməˌmayl, -ˌmiyl/ *n.* CHAMOMILE.

cam•ou•flage (kam′ə fläzh′) /'kæməˌflɑʒ/ *n., v.,* **-flaged, -flag•ing. —*n.*** [*noncount*] **1.** the act of hiding parts of a military installation so that they cannot be easily seen by the enemy. **2.** concealment by some means that alters or hides the appearance: *The lizard changes color as camouflage.* **3.** an act intended to hide one's true actions or wishes: *His friendliness is just camouflage to make us feel safe.* **—*v.*** [~ + *obj*] **4.** to disguise, hide, or deceive by means of camouflage: *We camouflaged our tanks and guns.*

camp[1] (kamp) /kæmp/ *n.* **1. a.** [*count*] a place where a group of people sleeps in tents or other temporary shelters: *an army camp; a prison camp.* **b.** [*noncount*] such tents or shelters when thought of as a group: *He wrote us several letters from camp.* **c.** [*noncount*] the persons in this place or shelter: *The whole camp was up and running.* **2.** [*noncount*] army life: *Training camp was very tough.* **3.** a recreation area in the country, with many facilities for sports: [*count*]: *an expensive camp upstate.* [*noncount*]: *The kids are in camp this summer.* **4.** [*count*] a group of people favoring the same ideals, etc.: *Last year, Senator, you were in a camp calling for increased taxes.* **—*v.*** [*no obj*] **5.** to establish or put together a camp: *The army camped by the river.* **6. camp out,** [*no obj*] to live or sleep in a tent or shelter temporarily: *They camped out by the stream.*

camp[2] (kamp) /kæmp/ *n.* [*noncount*] **1.** something that amuses because it is exaggerated or tasteless: *a lot of camp in that performance.* **—*v.*** [*no obj*] **2.** Also, **camp it up.** to speak or behave in a teasing or too theatrical manner: *camped it up during their show.* **—*adj.* 3.** campy: *camp Hollywood musicals.*

cam•paign (kam pān′) /kæm'peyn/ *n.* [*count*] **1.** a series of military operations for a specific goal, esp. as part of a war: *the European campaign.* **2.** a course of planned activities designed for some specific purpose: *a sales campaign.* **—*v.* 3.** to serve in or go on a campaign: [*no obj*]: *She campaigned all year long.* [~ + *for* + *obj*]: *He was campaigning for governor.* [~ + *to* + *verb*]: *They campaigned to get tougher laws.* —**cam•paign′er,** *n.* [*count*]

camp•er (kam′pər) /'kæmpər/ *n.* [*count*] **1.** a person who camps outdoors for recreation, esp. in the wilderness. **2.** a person who attends a summer camp or day camp. **3.** a trucklike vehicle, van, or trailer equipped for camping.

camp•fire (kamp′fīᵊr′) /'kæmpˌfayᵊr/ *n.* [*count*] an outdoor fire for warmth or cooking.

camp′ fol′lower, *n.* [*count*] **1.** a person not officially connected with a military unit but who follows an army camp, esp. a prostitute. **2.** a person who supports a group without belonging officially to it.

camp•ground (kamp′ground′) /'kæmpˌgrawnd/ *n.* [*count*] a place for a camp in a tent or in the open air.

cam•phor (kam′fər) /'kæmfər/ *n.* [*noncount*] a strong-smelling substance used chiefly to repel moths.

camp•site or **camp-site** (kamp′sīt′) /'kæmpˌsayt/ *n.* [*count*] a place used or suitable for camping.

cam•pus (kam′pəs) /'kæmpəs/ *n., pl.* **-pus•es.** the grounds, often including the buildings, of a college or other school: [*count*]: *one of the most beautiful campuses.* [*noncount*]: *In those days you had to be back on campus by midnight.*

camp•y (kam′pē) /'kæmpiy/ *adj.*, **-i•er, -i•est.** of, relating to, or characterized by theatrical camp: *a campy spoof of the operetta.* **—camp•i•ly** (kam′pə lē) /'kæmpəliy/ *adv.* **—camp′i•ness,** *n.* [*noncount*]

can[1] (kan; *unstressed* kən) /kæn; *unstressed* kən/ *auxiliary (modal) verb. All present tense forms:* **can,** *past:* **could. —*auxiliary verb*** [~ + *root form of a verb*] **1.** to be able to; have the ability to: *She can solve the problem easily.* **2.** to know how to: *I can play chess, but not very well.* **3.** to have the right or qualifications to: *He can change whatever he wants to in the script.* **4.** may; have permission to: *Can I speak to you for a moment?* **5.** to have the possibility to: *A coin can land on either side.* **6.** (used in questions) **a.** (used to ask if something is possible): *Can that be the chairman on the phone? (= Is it possible that the chairman is on the phone?)* **b.** (used to urge or request someone to do something; often: ~ + *not*): *Can't we just sit down and discuss this instead of fighting? (= I request that we sit down and discuss this.)* **7.** (used in negative statements) must not: *They're getting married? It can't be true!* **—*Idiom.* 8. can but,** to be able to do nothing else except; can only: *We can but try.* **—Usage.** CAN and MAY are both often used in the sense of possibility: *A power failure can* (or *may*) *occur at any time.* Traditional grammar books insist that only MAY conveys "permission," but both words are now regularly used with this meaning: *Can* (or *May*) *I borrow your tape recorder?* CAN occurs this way chiefly in spoken English; MAY occurs more frequently in formal speech and writing. In negative constructions, CAN'T or CANNOT is more common than MAY NOT; the contraction MAYN'T is rare: *You can't park in the driveway.* CAN BUT and CANNOT BUT are formal and old-fashioned expressions suggesting that there is no other way to do something.

can[2] (kan) /kæn/ *n., v.,* **canned, can•ning. —*n.*** [*count*] **1.** a sealed container for food, etc., such as of aluminum: *He opened several cans of beer.* **2.** the contents of, or the quantity or amount of things inside: *a can of mushroom soup.* **3.** a usually large bucket or container for garbage, etc.: *Throw that away in the trash can.* **4.** [*usually singular: the* + ~] *Slang* (*usually vulgar*). toilet; bathroom. **5.** [*usually singular: the + ~*] *Slang.* jail: *sent to the can for twenty years.* **6.** [*usually singular: the + ~*] *Slang* (*sometimes vulgar*). buttocks. **—*v.*** [*~ + obj*] **7.** to preserve (food) by sealing in a can, jar, etc.: *She canned the strawberries in summer.* **8.** *Slang.* to dismiss (someone) from a job; fire: *They canned him after nearly twenty years on the job.* **9.** *Slang.* to put a stop to: *Can that noise!* **—*Idiom.*** **10. in the can,** (of a task, etc.) completed; finished.

can., an abbreviation of: **1.** canceled. **2.** canon.

Ca•na•di•an (kə nā′dē ən) /kəˈneydiyən/ *adj.* **1.** of or relating to Canada. **—*n.*** [*count*] **2.** a person born or living in Canada.

Cana′dian ba′con, *n.* [*noncount*] bacon made from the back or sides of a pig.

ca•nal (kə nal′) /kəˈnæl/ *n.* **1.** an artificial waterway dug through land, for navigation, etc.: [*count*]: *the Panama Canal.* [*noncount*]: *They traveled down by canal.* **2.** [*count*] a tube or tube-shaped passage in the body for food, etc.; duct: *the alimentary canal in humans.*

can•a•pé (kan′ə pē, -pā′) /ˈkænəpiy, -ˌpey/ *n.* [*count*], *pl.* **-pés.** a cracker or small piece of bread topped with cheese or other savory food.

ca•nard (kə närd′, -när′) /kəˈnɑrd, -ˈnɑr/ *n.* [*count*] a false, usually harmful or misleading report.

ca•nar•y (kə nâr′ē) /kəˈnɛəriy/ *n., pl.* **-ies. 1.** [*count*] a small, greenish yellow finch of the Canary Islands. **2.** [*noncount*] a light, clear yellow color: *painted in canary and blue.* **3.** *Slang.* INFORMER (def. 1).

canc., an abbreviation of: **1.** cancel. **2.** canceled. **3.** cancellation.

can•can (kan′kan′) /ˈkænˌkæn/ *n.* [*count*] a lively, high-kicking dance popular about 1830 in Paris.

can•cel (kan′səl) /ˈkænsəl/ *v.,* **-celed, -cel•ing** or *(esp. Brit.)* **-celled, -cel•ling. 1.** [*~ + obj*] to make no longer valid, etc.; remove or call back: *The general canceled all military leaves.* **2.** [*~ + obj*] to decide or announce that (a planned event) will not take place; call off: *She canceled the picnic.* **3.** [*~ + obj; often: be + ~-ed*] to mark with lines or to put holes in (a check, postage stamp, etc.) so as to prevent reuse: *The check had been canceled.* **4.** [*~ + obj*] to balance; make up for: *His sincere apology canceled his sarcastic remark.* **5.** [*~ + obj*] (in mathematics) to eliminate (a number or variable) by drawing a line through a factor that is common to both the denominator and numerator of a fraction or to equivalent terms on opposite sides of an equation: *To reduce a fraction you cancel the factors that are common in the top and the bottom.* **6.** [*~ + obj*] to cross out (words, etc.) by drawing a line through the item. **7. cancel out,** to (cause to) balance or compensate for one another: [*no obj*]: *The two opposing forces cancel out.* [*~ + obj + out*]: *The two armies cancel each other out.* [*~ + out + obj*]: *One effect of the force cancels out the other.* **—can′cel•er;** *esp. Brit.,* **can′cel•ler,** *n.* [*count*]

can•cel•la•tion (kan′sə lā′shən) /ˌkænsə ˈleyʃən/ *n.* **1.** [*noncount*] the act of canceling or calling off: *cancellation of new orders for cars.* **2.** [*count*] an instance of canceling or calling off; something called off: *The hotel reported hundreds of cancellations.*

can•cer (kan′sər) /ˈkænsər/ *n.* **1. a.** [*count*] a harmful growth in the body, caused when cells increase without control: *Many cancers spread throughout the body.* **b.** [*noncount*] any disease characterized by such growths: *cancer of the liver.* **2.** [*count*] an evil that spreads and brings destruction: *Racial hatred is a cancer in our society.* **—can′cer•ous,** *adj.*

can•de•la•bra (kan′dl ä′brə, -ab′rə) /ˌkændlˈɑbrə, -ˈæbrə/ *n.* [*count*], *pl.* **-bras** for 2. **1.** a pl. of CANDELABRUM: *Those candelabra were not destroyed in the fire.* **2.** a candelabrum: *The candelabra was not destroyed in the fire.*

can•de•la•brum (kan′dl ä′brəm) /ˌkændlˈɑbrəm/ *n.* [*count*], *pl.* **-bra** (-brə), **-brums.** an ornamental holder with several branching candlesticks.

can•did (kan′did) /ˈkændɪd/ *adj.* **1.** open and sincere; honest: *a candid critic.* **2.** not posed; informal: *a candid photo.* **—can′did•ly,** *adv.* **—can′did•ness,** *n.* [*noncount*]

can•di•da•cy (kan′di də sē) /ˈkændɪ də siy/ *n.* [*noncount*] the condition of being a candidate: *announced her candidacy for mayor.*

can•di•date (kan′di dāt′, -dit) /ˈkændɪˌdeyt, -dɪt/ *n.* [*count*] **1.** a person who seeks a political office, etc.: *the seven presidential candidates.* **2.** a person deserving of a certain fate: *a candidate for the poorhouse.* **3.** a student studying for a degree: *a bachelor of arts candidate.*

can•died (kan′dēd) /ˈkændiyd/ *adj.* [*before a noun*] cooked or covered in sugar or syrup: *candied yams.*

can•dle (kan′dl) /ˈkændl/ *n., v.,* **-dled, -dling. —*n.*** [*count*] **1.** a long, usually slender piece of wax with a wick in the middle, burned to give light. See illustration at RESTAURANT. **—*Idiom.*** **2. hold a candle to,** [*~ + obj; used with a negative word or phrase, or in questions*] to compare favorably with: *No one can hold a candle to her for fine artistic work.*

can•dle•stick (kan′dl stik′) /ˈkændlˌstɪk/ *n.* [*count*] a device having a hole, a cuplike opening, or a spike for holding a candle: *the heavy brass candlesticks.*

can•dor (kan′dər) /ˈkændər/ *n.* [*noncount*] the state or quality of being candid: *She spoke with total candor and even bluntness.* Also, *esp. Brit.,* **can′dour.**

can•dy (kan′dē) /ˈkændiy/ *n., pl.* **-dies. 1.** [*noncount*] a sweet food made mostly of sugar or syrup and usually cooked or baked: *homemade candy.* **2.** [*count*] a single piece of such a food: *a few small candies.*

cane (kān) /keyn/ *n., v.,* **caned, can•ing. —*n.* 1.** [*count*] a short staff used to assist one in walking. **2.** [*count*] a long, hollow woody stem with joints, such as that of the bamboo plant. **3.** [*noncount*] the material of this stem, esp. split rattan, woven or used to make chair seats, etc.: *a chair of bamboo cane.* **4.** SUGARCANE. **—*v.*** [*~ + obj*] **5.** to hit or beat with a cane. **6.** to furnish or make with cane: *to cane chairs.*

cane′ sug′ar, *n.* [*noncount*] sugar obtained from sugarcane: *Use white cane sugar for this cake.*

ca•nine (kā′nīn) /ˈkeynayn/ *adj.* [*before a noun*] **1.** of or like a dog: *The canine patrol is a group of dogs used in police work.* **2.** of or relating to any of the four pointed teeth found next to the incisors: *canine teeth.* **—*n.*** [*count*] **3.** a dog. **4.** one of the four pointed teeth of the jaws.

can•is•ter (kan′ə stər) /ˈkænəstər/ *n.* [*count*] **1.** a small box or jar for holding tea, coffee, etc. **2.** a sealed container holding a substance kept under pressure: *The canisters of tear gas exploded in the crowd.*

can•ker (kang′kər) /ˈkæŋkər/ *n.* **1.** [*count*] an inflamed or sore area, esp. in the mouth. **2.** [*count*] an area of diseased tissue, esp. in woody stems. **3.** [*noncount*] the disease that causes these sores or infected areas: *The lilacs were destroyed by canker.* **4.** [*count*] something evil that spreads like disease and destroys; blight: *the canker of poverty and violence.* Also called **can′ker sore′** (for defs. 1, 2). **—can′ker•ous,** *adj.*

can•na•bis (kan′ə bis) /ˈkænəbɪs/ *n.* **1.** [*count*] the hemp plant. **2.** [*noncount*] any of the various parts of the plant from which hashish, marijuana, bhang, and similar drugs are prepared. **3.** MARIJUANA.

canned (kand) /kænd/ *adj.* **1.** preserved in a can or jar: *canned peaches.* **2.** [*before a noun*] recorded or prerecorded: *canned music.* **3.** prepared in advance for repeated use: *He gave his canned campaign speech.*

can•ner•y (kan′ə rē) /ˈkænəriy/ *n.* [*count*], *pl.* **-ies.** a factory where foods are canned.

can•ni•bal (kan′ə bəl) /ˈkænəbəl/ *n.* [*count*] a person or animal that practices cannibalism.

can•ni•bal•ism (kan′ə bə liz′əm) /ˈkænə bə ˌlɪzəm/ *n.* [*noncount*] the act or practice by a human being of eating human flesh, or the act or practice by an animal of eating its own kind. **—can•ni•bal•is•tic** (kan′ə bə lis′tik) /ˌkænəbəˈlɪstɪk/ *adj.*

can•ni•bal•ize (kan′ə bə līz′) /ˈkænəbəˌlayz/ *v.* [*~ + obj*], **-ized, -iz•ing.** to remove parts from (a machine, etc.) to repair or make a similar unit: *cannibalized the backup generator to get the main one going again.* **—can•ni•bal•i•za•tion** (kan′ə bə lə zā′shən) /ˌkænəbələˈzeyʃən/ *n.* [*noncount*]

can•non (kan′ən) /ˈkænən/ *n.* [*count*], *pl.* **-nons,** (*esp. when thought of as a group*) **-non.** a mounted gun for firing heavy projectiles: *The general moved his cannons into the left flank. Thirty cannon were used.*

can•non•ade (kan′ə nād′) /ˌkænəˈneyd/ *n.* [*count*] a continued firing of cannons, esp. during an attack.

can•non•ball (kan′ən bôl′) /ˈkænənˌbɔl/ *n.* [*count*] a heavy round ball made of iron or steel, designed to be fired from a cannon.

can•not (kan′ot, ka not′, kə-) /ˈkænɒt, kæˈnɒt, kə-/ *auxiliary (modal) verb phrase.* [*~ + root form of a verb*] **1.** a form of *can not.* **—*Idiom.*** **2. cannot but,** [*~ + root form of verb*] to have no alternative but to; cannot help but: *We cannot but choose otherwise.* **—Usage.** CANNOT is sometimes spelled CAN NOT. The one-word spelling is preferred. Its contraction, *can't,* is found chiefly in speech and informal writing. See also CAN[1], HELP.

can•ny (kan′ē) /ˈkæniy/ *adj.,* **-ni•er, -ni•est. 1.** clever; astute; shrewd: *He's a canny tennis player.* **2.** careful and clever with money: *a canny old bookkeeper.* **—can•ni•ly** (kan′l ē) /ˈkænl̩iy/ *adv.* **—can′ni•ness,** *n.* [*noncount*]: *Behind his country-boy manner is very high-powered political canniness.*

ca•noe (kə no͞o′) /kəˈnuw/ *n., v.,* **-noed, -noe•ing. —***n.* [*count*] **1.** a slender boat pointed at both ends. **—***v.* [*no obj*] **2.** to go in a canoe: *She canoed down the river.* **—ca•noe′ist,** *n.* [*count*]

can′ of worms′, *n.* [*count*] a source of many problems: *a controversial subject that could become a can of worms.*

can•on[1] (kan′ən) /ˈkænən/ *n.* [*count*] **1.** a rule or law of a church established by authority. **2.** a principle or standard of behavior: *You have gone past the canons of good behavior.* **3.** an officially recognized set of sacred or authentic writings in a field.

can•on[2] (kan′ən) /ˈkænən/ *n.* [*count*] a member of a church assigned to a cathedral.

ca•ñon (kan′yən) /ˈkænyən/ *n.* CANYON.

ca•non•i•cal (kə non′i kəl) /kəˈnɒnɪkəl/ *adj.* [*usually: before a noun*] Also, **ca•non′ic. 1.** relating to, established by, or allowed by a canon: *a canonical law.* **2.** authorized; recognized: *canonical books.* **—ca•non′i•cal•ly,** *adv.*

can•on•ize (kan′ə nīz′) /ˈkænəˌnayz/ *v.* [~ + *obj*], **-ized, -iz•ing.** to declare (someone) officially as a saint: *When was she canonized?* **—can•on•i•za•tion** (kan′ə nə zā′shən) /ˌkænənəˈzeyʃən/ *n.* [*noncount*]: *The canonization of Joan of Arc took place in 1920.*

can•o•py (kan′ə pē) /ˈkænəpiy/ *n.* [*count*], *pl.* **-pies. 1.** a covering held up on poles or hung above a bed, throne, etc. **2.** a similar covering or awning stretching from the doorway of a building to a curb. **3.** the cover formed by the leafy upper branches of the trees in a forest: *The monkeys climbed high into the canopy and couldn't be seen.* **—can′o•pied,** *adj.*: *canopied terraces.*

cant[1] (kant) /kænt/ *n.* [*noncount*] insincere, false, or hypocritical statements: *a lot of pretentious cant.*

cant[2] (kant) /kænt/ *n.* [*count*] **1.** a sudden movement that tilts or overturns a thing. **2.** a slanting or tilted position. **—***v.* [*no obj*] **3.** to tilt or turn with a sudden jerk: *The boat canted violently.*

can't (kant) /kænt/ contraction of *cannot.* **—Usage.** See CAN[1], CANNOT.

can•ta•loupe or **can•ta•loup** (kan′tl ōp′) /ˈkæntl̩ˌowp/ *n.* a melon with a hard green or yellow skin and pale orange or reddish yellow flesh: [*count*]: *We bought two cantaloupes at the grocery store.* [*noncount*]: *There was no cantaloupe at the market today.*

can•tan•ker•ous (kan tang′kər əs) /kænˈtæŋkərəs/ *adj.* bad-tempered; quarrelsome; grouchy: *The coach is especially cantankerous today.* **—can•tan′ker•ous•ly,** *adv.* **—can•tan′ker•ous•ness,** *n.* [*noncount*]

can•ta•ta (kən tä′tə) /kənˈtɑtə/ *n.* [*count*], *pl.* **-tas.** a musical work for church or the stage, not meant to be acted.

can•teen (kan tēn′) /kænˈtiyn/ *n.* [*count*] **1.** a small container used for carrying water or other liquids. **2.** a store and cafeteria at a military base. **3.** a small restaurant where simple foods or snacks are sold, as in a factory or school.

can•ter (kan′tər) /ˈkæntər/ *n.* [*count*] **1.** an easy gallop: *The horses set off at a canter.* **—***v.* **2.** to (cause to) ride at a canter: [*no obj*]: *The horses cantered around the palace.* [~ + *obj*]: *The ceremonial guards cantered their horses.*

can•ti•cle (kan′ti kəl) /ˈkæntɪkəl/ *n.* [*count*] a hymn or chant chiefly from the Bible, used in church services.

can•ti•le•ver (kan′tl ē′vər, -ev′ər) /ˈkæntl̩ˌiyvər, -ˌɛvər/ *n.* [*count*] a long, rigid beam or bracket that supports a larger construction, such as a balcony. See -LEV-.

can•to (kan′tō) /ˈkæntow/ *n.* [*count*], *pl.* **-tos.** one of the main or larger divisions of a long poem.

can•ton (kan′tn, -ton) /ˈkæntn̩, -tɒn/ *n.* [*count*] a small district of a territory or country, esp. one of the states of the Swiss confederation. **—can′ton•al,** *adj.*

can•tor (kan′tər) /ˈkæntər/ *n.* [*count*] the religious official of a synagogue who sings or chants the prayers.

can•vas (kan′vəs) /ˈkænvəs/ *n.* **1.** [*noncount*] a closely woven, heavy cloth of cotton used esp. for tents, etc. **2.** [*noncount*] a piece of this or similar material on which a painting is made: *some beautiful paintings on canvas.* **3.** [*count*] a painting on canvas: *Those canvases sold for two million each.* **4.** [*count; usually singular: the* + ~] the floor of a boxing ring, traditionally covered with canvas: *He was knocked to the canvas in the first round.*

can•vas•back (kan′vəs bak′) /ˈkænvəsˌbæk/ *n.* [*count*], *pl.* **-backs,** *(esp. when thought of as a group)* **-back.** a North American duck, the male of which has a whitish back and a reddish brown head and neck.

can•vass (kan′vəs) /ˈkænvəs/ *v.* **1.** to ask for votes, etc., from (a district): [~ + *obj*]: *She canvassed her friends and the people on her block.* [*no obj; sometimes:* ~ + *for* + *obj*]: *She was canvassing for votes most of the week.* **—***n.* [*count*] **2.** an act of asking for votes, views, etc.: *a quick canvass of voters leaving the polls.* **—can′vass•er,** *n.* [*count*]

can•yon (kan′yən) /ˈkænyən/ *n.* [*count*] a deep valley with steep sides.

cap[1] (kap) /kæp/ *n., v.,* **capped, cap•ping. —***n.* [*count*] **1.** a close-fitting covering for the head, usually having no brim: *a woolen cap.* **2.** a hat that signals one's rank, occupation, or the like: *a nurse's cap.* **3.** a top, lid, or cover of a container or bottle: *a bottle cap.* **4.** summit; top: *the cap of a hill.* **5.** an upper limit, as one set by law on prices, wages, etc.; ceiling: *urged a cap on wage increases of only 2%.* **6.** a noise-making device for toy pistols, made of a small quantity of explosive wrapped in paper. **—***v.* [~ + *obj*] **7.** to provide or cover with or as if with a cap: *Clouds capped the mountaintop.* **8.** [~ + *obj* + *with* + *obj*] to complete: *She capped her career with a victory.* **9.** [~ + *obj* + *with* + *obj*] to follow with something better; outdo: *to cap one joke with one even funnier.* **10.** to put a maximum limit on: *They promised to cap wages but not prices.*

cap[2] (kap) /kæp/ *n.* [*count*] a capsule, esp. of a narcotic drug.

ca•pa•bil•i•ty (kā′pə bil′i tē) /ˌkeypəˈbɪlɪtiy/ *n.* **1.** power; ability; the quality of being capable: [*noncount*]: *She is an actress of great capability.* [*count*]: *We admire her capabilities as an instructor.* **2.** the power or ability to wage a war: [*noncount*]: *the nuclear capability of that country.* [*count*]: *nuclear and weapons research capabilities.*

ca•pa•ble (kā′pə bəl) /ˈkeypəbəl/ *adj.* **1.** having power and ability; competent: *a capable instructor.* **2. be capable of,** to have the ability for; have the skill, motivation, etc., necessary for: *He doesn't seem to be capable of murder. I'm sure she is capable of performing well.* **—ca′pa•ble•ness,** *n.* [*noncount*] **—ca′pa•bly,** *adv.*

ca•pa•cious (kə pā′shəs) /kəˈpeyʃəs/ *adj.* able to hold much: *her capacious leather handbag.* **—ca•pa′cious•ly,** *adv.* **—ca•pa′cious•ness,** *n.* [*noncount*]

ca•pac•i•ty (kə pas′i tē) /kəˈpæsɪtiy/ *n., pl.* **-ties,** *adj.* **—***n.* **1.** the maximum amount or number that can be contained; volume: [*count; usually singular*]: *a jug with a capacity of two quarts.* [*noncount*]: *The stadium was filled to capacity.* **2.** the power or ability of the mind; mental ability: [*noncount*]: *Those calculus problems were beyond my capacity.* [*count*]: *People bring different capacities to the language learning process.* **3.** [*count; usually singular*] ability to perform, yield, or withstand: *a high capacity to withstand pressure.* **4.** [*count*] position; function; role: *asked to serve in an advisory capacity.* **—***adj.* [*before a noun*] **5.** reaching the maximum number: *a capacity crowd.*

cape[1] (kāp) /keyp/ *n.* [*count*] a piece of clothing without sleeves, fastened at the neck and falling loosely from the shoulders: *The magician swept his cape forward.* **—caped,** *adj.*

cape[2] (kāp) /keyp/ *n.* [*count*] a piece of land extending out into the sea.

ca•per[1] (kā′pər) /ˈkeypər/ *v.* [*no obj*] **1.** to skip about in a happy, light manner: *lambs capering in the meadows.* **—***n.* [*count*] **2.** a playful leap or skip. **3.** a prank or trick; silly act: *a student caper.* **4.** *Slang.* a criminal act, as a robbery.

ca•per[2] (kā′pər) /ˈkeypər/ *n.* [*count*] **1.** a spiny bush of Mediterranean regions, having single white flowers. **2.** its flower bud, pickled and used as a seasoning.

cap•il•lar•y (kap′ə ler′ē) /ˈkæpəˌlɛriy/ *n., pl.* **-ies,** *adj.* **—***n.* [*count*] **1.** one of the tiny, hairlike blood vessels between the arteries and the veins. **—***adj.* [*before a noun*] **2.** of or relating to the attraction or the pushing away between a liquid and a solid: *Capillary action causes oil to rise in the wick of a lantern.*

cap•i•tal (kap′i tl) /ˈkæpɪtl̩/ *n.* **1.** [*count*] the city that is the official center of government of a country, etc.: *Sacramento, not Los Angeles, is the capital of California.* **2.** [*count*] a city thought of as being of special importance in some field of activity: *Hollywood, the entertainment* *capital.* **3.** CAPITAL LETTER. **4.** [*noncount*] the wealth owned or used in business by an individual, etc.: *The companies needed capital for investment.* —*adj.* [*before a noun*] **5.** of or relating to financial capital: *capital investment.* **6.** principal; primary: *a subject of capital concern.* **7.** chief, esp. as being the center of government: *a capital city.* **8.** excellent; first-rate: *a capital hotel.* **9.** of or indicating a capital letter; uppercase: *Your name begins with capital B.* **10.** involving the loss of life: *capital punishment (= punishment by death).* **11.** to be punished by death: *a capital crime (= a crime for which the punishment is death).*

cap′ital gain′, *n.* [*count*] profit from the sale of assets, as bonds or real estate.

cap′ital goods′, *n.pl.* machines and tools used in the production of other goods.

cap•i•tal•ism (kap′i tl iz′əm) /ˈkæpɪtlˌɪzəm/ *n.* [*noncount*] an economic system in which investment in and ownership of the means of production and distribution are privately or corporately owned.

cap•i•tal•ist (kap′i tl ist) /ˈkæpɪtlɪst/ *n.* [*count*] **1.** a person who invests capital in business enterprises. **2.** a person who favors capitalism. **3.** a very wealthy person.

cap•i•tal•i•za•tion (kap′i tl ə zā′shən) /ˌkæpɪtləˈzeyʃən/ *n.* [*noncount*] **1.** the act or process of capitalizing. **2.** the total investment of the owner or owners in a business enterprise.

cap•i•tal•ize (kap′i tl īz′) /ˈkæpɪtlˌayz/ *v.* [~ + *obj*], **-ized, -iz•ing.** **1.** to write or print in capital letters or with an initial capital. **2.** to authorize a certain amount of stocks and bonds in the corporate charter of: *to capitalize a corporation.* **3.** to supply with capital. **4. capitalize on,** [~ + *on* + *obj*] to take advantage of; turn to one's advantage: *to capitalize on one's opportunities.*

cap′ital let′ter, *n.* [*count*] a letter of the alphabet that differs from its corresponding lowercase letter in form and height.

ca•pit•u•late (kə pich′ə lāt′) /kəˈpɪtʃəˌleyt/ *v.* [*no obj*], **-lat•ed, -lat•ing.** **1.** to surrender usually after agreeing to certain terms. **2.** [*sometimes:* ~ + *to* + *obj*] to give up resistance; yield: *to capitulate to someone's pleas.* —**ca•pit•u•lant** (kə pich′ə lənt) /kəˈpɪtʃələnt/ *n.* [*count*] —**ca•pit′u•la′tor,** *n.* [*count*]

cap•let (kap′lit) /ˈkæplɪt/ *n.* [*count*] an oval-shaped tablet with a smooth surface that eases swallowing.

ca•pon (kā′pon, -pən) /ˈkeypɒn, -pən/ *n.* [*count*] a young castrated male chicken used as food.

cap•puc•ci•no (kap′ə chē′nō, kä′pə-) /ˌkæpəˈtʃiynow, ˌkɑpə-/ *n.* hot espresso coffee with foaming steamed milk added: [*noncount*]: *a cup of cappuccino.* [*count*]: *ordered two cappuccinos.*

ca•price (kə prēs′) /kəˈpriys/ *n.* **1.** [*count*] a sudden, unpredictable change. **2.** [*noncount*] a tendency to change one's mind without motive. —**ca•pri•cious** (kə-prish′əs) /kəˈprɪʃəs/ *adj.* —**ca•pri′cious•ly,** *adv.* —**ca•pri′cious•ness,** *n.* [*noncount*]

caps., an abbreviation of: capital letters.

cap•size (kap′siz) /ˈkæpsayz/ *v.,* **-sized, -siz•ing.** to turn bottom up; overturn: [*no obj*]: *The boat capsized.* [~ + *obj*]: *The wind capsized their boat.* —**cap′siz•a•ble,** *adj.*

cap•stan (kap′stən, -stan) /ˈkæpstən, -stæn/ *n.* [*count*] a windlass rotated in a horizontal plane for winding in ropes, etc.

cap•stone (kap′stōn′) /ˈkæpˌstown/ *n.* [*count*] **1.** a finishing stone of a structure. **2.** the most glorious and usually final achievement: *The Nobel prize was the capstone of his long career.*

cap•sule (kap′səl, -so͞ol) /ˈkæpsəl, -suwl/ *n.* [*count*] **1.** a very small, usually tube-shaped casing with a dose of medicine inside, designed to be swallowed. **2.** a similar structure in a plant, esp. a case containing a seed or seeds. **3.** Also called **space capsule.** a sealed cabin in which a person or animal can ride in flight in space. —*adj.* [*before a noun*] **4.** short and concise; briefly described: *a capsule report; a capsule summary.*

capt., an abbreviation of: captain.

cap•tain (kap′tən) /ˈkæptən/ *n.* [*count*] **1.** a person in authority over others: *She was the captain of the field hockey team.* **2.** an officer in the army above a first lieutenant or in the navy above a commander: *the first female captain in the army.* **3.** an officer of any rank who commands a military vessel or pilots an airplane: *Captain, should we set a new course?* **4.** a person of great power and influence, esp. based on wealth: *captains of industry.* —*v.* [~ + *obj*] **5.** to lead as a captain: *He captained the team victories.* —**cap•tain•cy** (kap′tən sē) /ˈkæptənsiy/ *n.* [*noncount*]

cap•tion (kap′shən) /ˈkæpʃən/ *n.* [*count*] **1.** a title or explanation for a picture: *The caption under the photo read, "Winter in the Alps."* **2.** a subtitle for a movie or a television program. —*v.* [~ + *obj*] **3.** to supply a caption or captions for: *a French film captioned in English.*

cap•ti•vate (kap′tə vāt′) /ˈkæptəˌveyt/ *v.* [~ + *obj*], **-vat•ed, -vat•ing.** to charm or attract strongly; enchant; fascinate: *She had completely captivated him with her wit.* —**cap′ti•vat′ing,** *adj.*: *She was a captivating movie star.* —**cap′ti•vat′ing•ly,** *adv.* —**cap•ti•va•tion** (kap′tə-vā′shən) /ˌkæptəˈveyʃən/ *n.* [*noncount*] —**cap′ti•va′tor,** *n.* [*count*]

cap•tive (kap′tiv) /ˈkæptɪv/ *n.* [*count*] **1.** a prisoner: *They freed their captives before surrendering.* —*adj.* [*before a noun*] **2.** kept or held in confinement: *captive animals.* **3.** unable to avoid listening to something: *Her dinner guests were always a captive audience for her stories.* —***Idiom.*** **4. take** or **hold (someone) captive,** to take or keep (someone) as a prisoner, esp. in war: *We took them captive.*

cap•tiv•i•ty (kap tiv′i tē) /kæpˈtɪvɪtiy/ *n.* [*count; noncount*], *pl.* **-ties.** the state or period of being held, imprisoned, enslaved, or confined; servitude or bondage; imprisonment.

cap•tor (kap′tər) /ˈkæptər/ *n.* [*count*] a person who has captured a person or thing.

cap•ture (kap′chər) /ˈkæptʃər/ *v.,* **-tured, -tur•ing,** *n.* —*v.* [~ + *obj*] **1.** to take by force; take prisoner: *The patrol captured a few dozen soldiers.* **2.** to gain control of; hold: *She captured my attention immediately.* **3.** to take possession of, as in a contest: *to capture a pawn in chess.* **4.** to represent or record (a feeling, etc.): *a movie that captures life in Berlin in the 1930's.* —*n.* **5.** [*noncount*] the act of capturing; seizure: *On the day of the capture we were out on a patrol.* **6.** [*count*] the person or thing captured.

car (kär) /kɑr/ *n.* **1.** an automobile: [*count*]: *We needed to buy a new car.* [*noncount; by* + ~]: *She has to get to work by car.* See illustration at LANDSCAPE. **2.** [*count*] a vehicle running on rails or tracks: *The train had eight cars, including the dining car.* **3.** [*count*] the part of an elevator, etc., that carries the passengers, etc.

car., an abbreviation of: carat.

ca•rafe (kə raf′, -räf′) /kəˈræf, -ˈrɑf/ *n.* [*count*] **1.** a wide-mouthed bottle with a lip, for holding and serving beverages. **2.** the amount held in such a bottle: *We drank a carafe of wine.*

car•a•mel (kar′ə məl, -mel′, kär′məl) /ˈkærəməl, -ˌmɛl, ˈkɑrməl/ *n.* **1.** [*noncount*] a liquid made by cooking sugar until it darkens, used for flavoring food: *The candy apple had caramel baked onto it.* **2.** [*count*] a chewy candy made from sugar, butter, milk, etc.

car•a•pace (kar′ə pās′) /ˈkærəˌpeys/ *n.* [*count*] a shield or shell of hard material covering some of an animal, such as a turtle.

car•at (kar′ət) /ˈkærət/ *n.* **1.** a unit of weight in gemstones, 200 milligrams (about 3 grains of troy or avoirdupois weight): [*count*]: *How many carats did it weigh?* [*singular; before a noun*]: *an eighteen–carat diamond.* **2.** KARAT.

car•a•van (kar′ə van′) /ˈkærəˌvæn/ *n., v.,* **-vaned** or **-vanned, -van•ing** or **-van•ning.** —*n.* [*count*] **1.** a group of travelers journeying together for safety in passing through deserts, etc. **2.** a large covered vehicle for conveying passengers, goods, etc.; van. **3.** *Chiefly Brit.* HOUSE TRAILER.

car•a•van•sa•ry (kar′ə van′sə rē) /ˌkærəˈvænsəriy/ also **car•a•van•se•rai** (kar′ə van′sə rī′, -rā′) /ˌkærəˈvænsəˌray, -ˌrey/ *n.* [*count*], *pl.* **-sa•ries** also **-se•rais.** (in the Near East) an inn for people in caravans.

car•a•way (kar′ə wā′) /ˈkærəˌwey/ *n.* [*noncount*] **1.** a plant of the parsley family. **2.** the sweet-smelling seedlike fruits of this plant, used in cooking and medicine.

car•bine (kär′bēn, -bīn) /ˈkɑrbiyn, -bayn/ *n.* [*count*] a light, gas-operated rifle.

car•bo•hy•drate (kär′bō hi′drāt, -bə-) /ˌkɑrbowˈhaydreyt, -bə-/ *n.* **1.** any of a class of substances made of carbon, hydrogen, and oxygen, including starches and sugars: [*count*]: *Carbohydrates are produced in green plants by photosynthesis.* [*noncount*]: *Change the amount of carbohydrate in your diet.* **2.** [*count*] a food containing a large amount of starch or sugar, esp. refined sugar: *eating too many carbohydrates as snacks.* See -HYDR-.

car•bol′ic ac′id (kär bol′ik) /kɑrˈbɒlɪk/ *n.* [*noncount*] a chemical substance used in cleaning and to kill germs.

car•bon (kär′bən) /ˈkɑrbən/ *n.* **1.** [*noncount*] an element combined with other elements in all organic matter, and found in a pure form as diamond and graphite. **2.** [*count*] a sheet of paper with writing or other marks copied onto it by the use of carbon paper. **3.** [*count*] a sheet of carbon paper.

car•bon•at•ed (kär′bə nā′təd) /'kɑrbə,neytəd/ *adj.* containing carbon dioxide so as to produce bubbles: *carbonated drinks.* —**car•bon•a•tion** (kär′bə nā′shən) /,kɑrbə'neyʃən/ *n.* [*noncount*]: *This soda has lost its carbonation.*

car′bon-date′, *v.* [~ + *obj*], **-dat•ed, -dat•ing.** to estimate the age of (something organic) by measuring how much radioactive carbon is in the object: *carbon-dated the seeds to the time of Christ.* —**car′bon dat′ing,** *n.* [*noncount*]

car′bon di•ox′ide (dī ok′sīd) /day'ɒksayd/ *n.* [*noncount*] a colorless, odorless gas formed during respiration: *When we breathe out we give off carbon dioxide.*

car′bon mon•ox′ide (mon ok′sid, mə nok′-) /mɒn'ɒksayd, mə'nɒk-/ *n.* [*noncount*] a colorless, odorless, poisonous gas produced when carbon burns with insufficient air.

car′bon pa′per, *n.* [*noncount*] paper with a preparation of carbon or other material on one side, placed between two sheets of plain paper in order to reproduce on the lower sheet whatever is being written or typed on the upper.

car•bun•cle (kär′bung kəl) /'kɑrbʌŋkəl/ *n.* [*count*] a very painful swelling of the skin caused by a group of deep, interconnected boils. —**car′bun•cled,** *adj.* —**car•bun′cu•lar,** *adj.*

car•bu•re•tor or **car•bu•ret•er** (kär′bə rā′tər, -byə-) /'kɑrbə,reytər, -byə-/ *n.* [*count*] a device in a car engine for mixing fuel and air to produce a mixture that can be exploded to provide power: *tried adjusting the carburetor.* Also, *esp. Brit.,* **car•bu•ret•tor, car•bu•ret•ter** (kär′byə ret′ər) /'kɑrbyə,rɛtər/.

car•cass (kär′kəs) /'kɑrkəs/ *n.* [*count*] **1.** the dead body of an animal, esp. of a slaughtered animal. **2.** *Slang.* the body of a human being: *Get your carcass off my desk!*

car•cin•o•gen (kär sin′ə jən) /kɑr'sɪnədʒən/ *n.* [*count*] any substance that tends to produce a cancer. See -GEN-.

car•cin•o•gen•ic (kär′sin ə jen′ik) /,kɑrsɪn ə 'dʒɛnɪk/ *adj.* **1.** causing cancer: *carcinogenic substances.* —*n.* [*count*] **2.** a carcinogen.

card[1] (kärd) /kɑrd/ *n.* **1.** [*count*] a usually rectangular piece of stiff paper used to record information, etc: *She showed her identification card and was let in.* **2.** [*count*] one of a set of cards with spots, etc., used in playing various games. **3. cards,** (*noncount; used with a singular verb*) a game or games played with such a set. **4.** [*count*] something useful in attaining an objective, likened to a high card in a game: *I had one more card to play: my friendship with the president.* **5.** [*count*] a folded piece of thin cardboard printed with a message of holiday greeting, etc. **6.** POSTCARD. **7.** an amusing or prankish person. —***Idiom.*** **8. in the cards,** destined or certain to occur. **9. put** or **lay one's cards on the table,** to be completely straightforward; conceal nothing.

card[2] (kärd) /kɑrd/ *n.* [*count*] Also called **carding machine. 1.** a machine for combing fibers, as of cotton or wool, before spinning. —*v.* [~ + *obj*] **2.** to comb (fibers) with this machine. —**card′er,** *n.* [*count*]

Card., an abbreviation of: Cardinal.

card•board (kärd′bôrd′, -bōrd′) /'kɑrd,bɔrd, -,bowrd/ *n.* [*noncount*] **1.** thin, stiff pasteboard, used for boxes, etc. —*adj.* **2.** resembling cardboard, esp. in thinness or cheapness: *an apartment with cardboard walls.* **3.** not fully lifelike: *a movie with a cardboard hero.*

card′-car′rying, *adj.* [*before a noun*] **1.** admittedly belonging to a group or party: *a card-carrying Communist.* **2.** identified with or dedicated to an ideal, profession, or interest: *a card-carrying humanist.*

card′ cat′alog, *n.* [*count*] a file of cards arranged in some definite order and listing the items in the collection of a library. See illustration at SCHOOL.

car•di•ac (kär′dē ak′) /'kɑrdiy,æk/ *adj.* [*before a noun*] of or relating to the heart, or to treatment of the heart: *cardiac disease.*

car•di•gan (kär′di gən) /'kɑrdɪgən/ *n.* [*count*] a knitted sweater or jacket usually without a collar, that opens down the front.

car•di•nal (kär′dn l) /'kɑrdn̩l/ *adj.* [*before a noun*] **1.** of the greatest significance: *a matter of cardinal importance; a cardinal sin.* —*n.* [*count*] **2.** a high church official appointed by the pope. **3.** a common crested songbird of North America, the male of which is bright red.

car′dinal num′ber, *n.* [*count*] any of the numbers that express amount, as *one, two, three.*

car•di•o•gram (kär′dē ə gram′) /'kɑrdiyə,græm/ *n.* ELECTROCARDIOGRAM.

car•di•ol•o•gy (kär′dē ol′ə jē) /,kɑrdiy'ɒlədʒiy/ *n.* [*noncount*] the study of the heart and its functions. —**car′di•ol′o•gist,** *n.* [*count*]

car•di•o•vas•cu•lar (kär′dē ō vas′kyə lər) /,kɑrdiyow'væskyələr/ *adj.* of, relating to, or affecting the heart and blood vessels: *the cardiovascular system; cardiovascular diseases.*

card•sharp (kärd′shärp′) /'kɑrd,ʃɑrp/ also **card•sharp•er** (kärd′shär′pər) /'kɑrd,ʃɑrpər/ *n.* [*count*] a person, esp. a professional gambler, who cheats at card games. Also called **card′ shark′.** —**card′sharp′ing,** *n.* [*noncount*]

care (kâr) /kɛər/ *n., v.,* **cared, car•ing.** —*n.* **1.** [*noncount*] a troubled state of mind: *I felt burdened with care at the time.* **2.** [*count*] a cause or object of worry or concern: *lots of cares.* **3.** [*noncount*] serious attention; precision; caution: *to devote care to one's work.* **4.** [*noncount*] protection; charge: *We left our cat in the care of friends.* —*v.* **5.** to be concerned (about); have regard (about): [*no obj; often:* ~ + *about* + *obj*]: *Does the president really care about education?* [~ + *clause*]: *He cares what other people think.* **6.** [~ + *clause; used with a negative word or phrase, or in questions*] to object or mind: *I don't care if you come late.* **7.** [~ + *for* + *obj*] to look after; provide assistance for someone: *Will you care for the children while I am away?* **8.** [*with a negative word or phrase, or in questions*] to desire; like: [~ + *to* + *verb*]: *Would you care to dance?* [~ + *for* + *obj*]: *Would you care for dessert?* —***Idiom.*** **9. could(n't) care less,** to be completely unconcerned or not worried: *I could(n't) care less if it rains or not.* **10. take care, a.** to be certain (to do something): [~ + *to* + *verb*]: *Take care not to burn yourself.* [~ + *that clause*]: *He took care that everyone was paid on time.* **b.** (no obj; used as an expression of farewell or good-bye): *I'll see you tomorrow; take care!* **11. take care of,** [~ + *obj*] **a.** to watch over; be responsible for: *Who will take care of the children?* **b.** to deal with; attend to: *My wife takes care of all the bills.* —**Related Words.** CARE is a noun and a verb; CAREFUL is an adjective: *He handled the bomb with great care. He cared about what happened to his children. He was very careful handling the bomb.* —**Usage.** COULD CARE LESS, the apparent opposite of COULDN'T CARE LESS, is actually used interchangeably with it to express indifference. Both versions are common mainly in informal speech.

ca•reen (kə rēn′) /kə'riyn/ *v.* to (cause to) lean or tip to one side while in motion; sway: [*no obj*]: *The car careened around the corner.* [~ + *obj*]: *He careened the car around the corner and roared off.*

ca•reer (kə rēr′) /kə'rɪər/ *n.* **1.** [*count*] a profession that is one's most important work in life: *Women should have the same opportunity for the career of their choice as men do.* **2.** [*count*] a person's general course of action through some or all of life: *a short career as a soldier.* **3.** [*noncount*] speed, esp. full speed. —*v.* [*no obj*] **4.** to go at full speed: *The car went careering down the highway.* —*adj.* [*before a noun*] **5.** having as a career; professional: *He was a career diplomat.*

ca•reer•ist (kə rēr′ist) /kə 'rɪərɪst/ *n.* [*count*] a person who makes a career the most important or meaningful part of life.

care•free (kâr′frē′) /'kɛər,friy/ *adj.* being without worry.

care•ful (kâr′fəl) /,kɛərfəl/ *adj.* **1.** cautious in one's actions: *a careful driver.* [*be* + ~ + *to* + *verb*]: *He was careful not to get her mad.* **2.** (used as a command) watch out; be cautious: *Careful! It's going to break!* **3.** done or performed with accuracy or caution; taking pains in one's work: *He was a careful typist.* —**care′ful•ly,** *adv.* —**care′ful•ness,** *n.* [*noncount*]

care•giv•er (kâr′giv′ər) /'kɛər,gɪvər/ *n.* [*count*] **1.** a person who cares for someone sick or disabled. **2.** an adult who cares for a child: *In many cases it is no longer the parent who is the primary caregiver.*

care•less (kâr′lis) /'kɛərlɪs/ *adj.* **1.** not paying enough attention to what one does: *He made a few careless mistakes on that exam.* **2.** not exact or accurate: *careless work.* **3.** [*sometimes:* ~ + *of*] without thinking of results; heedless or indifferent: *careless of other people's feelings.* **4.** not caring or troubling; unconcerned: *a careless little laugh.* —**care′less•ly,** *adv.* —**care′less•ness,** *n.* [*noncount*]

ca•ress (kə res′) /kə'rɛs/ *n.* [*count*] **1.** a light stroking gesture expressing affection or care. —*v.* [~ + *obj*] **2.** to touch or stroke lightly in or as if in affection: *She caressed the child's hot forehead.*

car•et (kar′it) /'kærɪt/ *n.* [*count*] a mark (^) made in written or printed matter to show the place where something is to be inserted.

care•tak•er (kâr′tā′kər) /'kɛər,teykər/ *n.* [*count*] **1.** a person in charge of the maintenance or upkeep of a building, etc. **2.** CAREGIVER. —*adj.* [*before a noun*] **3.** temporarily performing the duties of an office: *a caretaker government.*

care•worn (kâr′wôrn′, -wōrn′) /'kɛər,wɔrn, -,wowrn/ *adj.* showing signs of care or worry: *the exhausted, careworn look on his face.*

car•fare (kär′fâr′) /'kɑr,fɛər/ *n.* [*noncount*] the amount charged for a ride on a subway or bus.

car•go (kär′gō) /'kɑrgow/ *n., pl.* **-goes, -gos.** the load of goods carried by a ship, airplane, etc.: [*noncount*]: *The plane was loaded with cargo.* [*count*]: *It was a cargo of natural gas.*

car•i•bou (kar′ə bōō′) /'kærə,buw/ *n.* [*count*], *pl.* **-bous,** (*esp. when thought of as a group*) **-bou.** the reindeer of North America.

car•i•ca•ture (kar′i kə chər, -chŏŏr′) /'kærɪkətʃər, -,tʃʊr/ *n., v.,* **-tured, -tur•ing.** —*n.* **1.** [*count*] a picture exaggerating the special features of a person or thing: *The magazine with the caricature of the dictator was banned.* **2.** [*noncount*] the art or process of producing such pictures: *a master at caricature.* **3.** [*count*] any imitation so distorted that it is unfair or misleadingly false: *The essay was a caricature of real scholarship.* —*v.* [~ + *obj*] **4.** to make a caricature of: *caricatured politicians on both the left and the right.* —**Syn.** See BURLESQUE.

car•ies (kâr′ēz) /'kɛəriyz/ *n.* [*noncount; used with a singular verb*] decay of the teeth or the bones: *dental caries.* —**car′i•ous,** *adj.*

car•il•lon (kar′ə lon′, -lən) /'kærə,lɒn, -lən/ *n.* [*count*] a set of bells hung in a tower and rung by hand, pedal action, or machinery.

car•ing (kâr′ing) /'kɛərɪŋ/ *adj.* **1.** showing concern for others; compassionate: *grew up to be a caring adult.* —*n.* [*noncount*] **2.** concern; compassion.

car•mine (kär′min, -min) /'kɑrmɪn, -mayn/ *n.* [*noncount*] **1.** crimson or purplish red color. —*adj.* **2.** crimson; purplish red.

car•nage (kär′nij) /'kɑrnɪdʒ/ *n.* [*noncount*] the slaughter or killing of a great number of people, as in battle: *horrifying carnage in the city after the bombing.*

car•nal (kär′nl) /'kɑrnl̩/ *adj.* relating to or characterized by the passions of the body; sexual: *carnal desire.* —**car′nal•ly,** *adv.*

car•na•tion (kär nā′shən) /kɑr'neyʃən/ *n.* [*count*] a plant having long-stalked, fragrant flowers in a variety of colors.

car•ni•val (kär′nə vəl) /'kɑrnəvəl/ *n.* **1.** [*count*] a traveling amusement show having games, rides, etc. **2.** [*count*] a festival: *a winter carnival.* **3.** [*noncount*] the season preceding Lent: *We went to Brazil for carnival.*

car•ni•vore (kär′nə vôr′, -vōr′) /'kɑrnə,vɔr, -,vowr/ *n.* [*count*] an animal that eats flesh. See -VOR-.

car•niv•o•rous (kär niv′ər əs) /kɑr'nɪvərəs/ *adj.* flesh-eating: *Tigers are carnivorous animals.* See -VOR-.

car•ol (kar′əl) /'kærəl/ *n., v.,* **-oled, -ol•ing** or (*esp. Brit.*) **-olled, -ol•ling.** —*n.* [*count*] **1.** a song, esp. of joy. **2.** a Christmas song or hymn. —*v.* [*no obj; often: go + (out) + ~-ing*] **3.** to sing Christmas songs, esp. in a group outdoors: *They went out caroling on Christmas Eve.* —**car′ol•er;** *esp. Brit.,* **car′ol•ler,** *n.* [*count*]

car•om (kar′əm) /'kærəm/ *n.* [*count*] **1.** a shot (in billiards, etc.) that hits and rebounds off something: *The carom went in the side pocket.* —*v.* [*no obj; often: ~ + off + obj*] **2.** to hit and rebound (off something): *The ball caromed off the wall.*

ca•rot•id (kə rot′id) /kə'rɒtɪd/ *n.* [*count*] Also called **carot′id ar′tery.** either of two large arteries on each side of the neck that carry blood from the heart to the head.

ca•rouse (kə rouz′) /kə'rawz/ *v.* [*no obj*], **-roused, -rous•ing.** to behave drunkenly: *out all night carousing.* —**ca•rous′er,** *n.* [*count*]

car•ou•sel (kar′ə sel′, kar′ə sel′) /,kærə'sɛl, 'kærə,sɛl/ *n.* [*count*] **1.** MERRY-GO-ROUND (def. 1). **2.** a revolving conveyor belt on which items are placed: *a baggage carousel at an airport.*

carp[1] (kärp) /kɑrp/ *v.* to find fault; complain without a good reason: [*no obj; often: ~ + at + obj*]: *He's always carping at his employees.* [~ + *that clause*]: *forever carping that we waste paper clips.*

carp[2] (kärp) /kɑrp/ *n.* [*count*], *pl.* (*esp. when thought of as a group*) **carp,** (*esp. for kinds or species*) **carps.** a large freshwater fish widely used as a food fish.

car•pal (kär′pəl) /'kɑrpəl/ *adj.* [*before a noun*] **1.** of or relating to the bones of the wrist: *the carpal joint.* —*n.* [*count*] **2.** any of the bones of the wrist.

car•pe di•em (kär′pā dē′əm, kär′pē) /'kɑr'pey diyəm, 'kɑrpiy / *Latin.* seize the day; enjoy the present.

car•pen•ter (kär′pən tər) /'kɑrpəntər/ *n.* [*count*] a person who practices carpentry.

car•pen•try (kär′pən trē) /'kɑrpəntriy/ *n.* [*noncount*] the work or skill of making or building things of wood: *The house needs some carpentry.*

car•pet (kär′pit) /'kɑrpɪt/ *n.* [*count*] **1.** a heavy, thick, woven fabric for covering floors. **2.** any surface or covering resembling a carpet; layer: *a carpet of wildflowers in the meadow.* —*v.* [~ + *obj*] **3.** to cover with or as if with a carpet: *They decided to carpet the hallway.* —***Idiom.*** **4. on the carpet,** summoned for a scolding; in trouble: *His boss called him on the carpet after his last mistake.*

car•pet•bag•ger (kär′pit bag′ər) /'kɑrpɪt,bægər/ *n.* [*count*] **1.** a Northerner who went to the South after the Civil War to exploit the confused conditions: *Carpetbaggers got their name from the little bags made of carpet material that they carried their belongings in.* **2.** any person, esp. a politician, who moves to a new place to live only to advance a political career.

car•pet•ing (kär′pi ting) /'kɑrpɪtɪŋ/ *n.* [*noncount*] carpets, or material for carpets: *wall-to-wall carpeting.*

car•pool (kär′pōōl′) /'kɑr,puwl/ *n.* [*count*] Also, **car′ pool′.** **1.** an arrangement among automobile owners by which each in turn drives the others to and from a designated place: *The drivers formed a carpool to save money.* —*v.* [*no obj*] **2.** Also, **car′-pool′.** to form or participate in a carpool: *They carpooled to work.* —**car′-pool′er,** *n.* [*count*]

car•port (kär′pôrt′, -pōrt′) /'kɑr,pɔrt, -,powrt/ *n.* [*count*] a roof projecting from a building for sheltering an automobile.

car•rel or **car•rell** (kar′əl) /'kærəl/ *n.* [*count*] a desk or small work area reserved for private study in a library.

car•riage (kar′ij) /'kærɪdʒ/ *n.* **1.** [*count*] a wheeled vehicle for carrying persons, such as one pulled by horses: *The princess stepped down gracefully from the carriage.* **2.** [*count*] a baby carriage. **3.** [*count*] *Brit.* a railway passenger coach. **4.** [*count*] a movable part, as of a machine, designed for carrying something: *The carriage on a dot-matrix printer holds paper.* **5.** [*noncount*] the manner in which a person's head and body are held when standing, etc.; posture: *a woman of graceful carriage.*

car•ri•er (kar′ē ər) /'kæriyər/ *n.* [*count*] **1.** a person or thing that carries: *A newspaper carrier delivers the local paper on weekdays.* **2.** an individual or company engaged in transporting passengers or goods for profit. **3.** an insurance company. **4.** AIRCRAFT CARRIER. **5.** an individual carrying a disease who may be immune to the disease but transmits it to others.

car′rier pig′eon, *n.* [*count*] a pigeon trained to fly from a certain destination to another carrying messages; a homing pigeon.

car•ri•on (kar′ē ən) /'kæriyən/ *n.* [*noncount*] decaying, rotting flesh from a dead animal: *Vultures feed on carrion.*

car•rot (kar′ət) /'kærət/ *n.* **1.** [*count*] a plant of the parsley family, having fernlike leaves and small white flowers. **2.** the long, orange to yellow root of this plant, eaten raw or cooked: [*count*]: *Chop the five carrots into pieces.* [*noncount*]: *Take the boiled carrot and strain it.* **3.** [*count*] something offered as an incentive to encourage someone to do something: *Can you give the union leaders a carrot to bring their members to reason?* —**car′rot•y,** *adj.*: *bright orange, carroty hair.*

car•rou•sel (kar′ə sel′, kar′ə sel′) /,kærə'sɛl, 'kærə,sɛl/ *n.* CAROUSEL.

car•ry (kar′ē) /'kæriy/ *v.,* **-ried, -ry•ing.** **1.** [~ + *obj*] to move (something) while holding or supporting; transport: *I'll carry the groceries home.* **2.** [~ + *obj*] to wear, hold, or have around one: *I always carry my driver's license.* **3.** [~ + *obj; usually not: be + ~-ing*] to contain or be capable of containing; hold: *The minivan carries seven people.* **4.** [~ + *obj*] to serve as a way of sending or transmitting (something); communicate: *The networks carried her speech live.* **5.** [*no obj*] to be able to reach some distance; be transmitted or sent: *Sounds carry well over water.* **6.** [~ + *obj*] to be the means of moving (something) by force; drive: *The flood carried cars and houses downriver.* **7.** [~ + *obj*] to be pregnant with: *She may be carrying twins.* **8.** [~ + *obj*] to sing (a melody) on pitch: *He could barely carry a tune.* **9.** [~ + *oneself*] to hold (oneself) in a certain manner; behave in a certain way: *carries herself with dignity.* **10. a.** [*no obj*] (of a bill) to pass through a process of voting: *The motion carried by a vote of fifty to thirty-one.* **b.** [~ + *obj*] to obtain the passage of (a bill): *The committee carried the bill.* **11.** [~ + *obj; not: be* + ~*-ed*] to gain a majority of votes in (a state, etc.): *The president is not sure he can carry his own state in the election.* **12.** [~ + *obj*] to support or bear the weight or burden of (something not performing well): *The star carried the whole play.* **13.** [~ + *obj; not: be* + ~*-ing*] (of an action) to have as a consequence: *Failing to pay your fine carries an additional penalty of fifty dollars.* **14.** [~ + *obj*] to keep on hand or in a store for sale: *We don't carry that brand in this store.* **15. carry away,** [~ + *away* + *obj; usually: be* + ~*-ed* + *away*] to stir strong emotions in; cause to lose control: *Don't get carried away—it's only a movie.* **16. carry forward,** to make progress with: [~ + *forward* + *obj*]: *They'll want to carry forward his plans.* [~ + *obj* + *forward*]: *Let's carry the plans forward.* **17. carry off, a.** to win (a prize or honor): [~ + *off* + *obj*]: *She carried off all the prizes in mathematics.* [~ + *obj* + *off*]: *She carried the prizes off last year.* **b.** to deal with successfully: [~ + *off* + *obj*]: *The disorganized junta couldn't carry off the coup.* [~ + *obj* + *off*]: *I thought we carried it off pretty smoothly.* **18. carry on, a.** [~ + *on* + *obj*] to manage; conduct: *I don't know if we can carry on a conversation here.* **b.** [*no obj; often:* ~ + *on* + *with* + *obj*] to continue without stopping; persevere: *I carried on with my work while the kids were howling.* **c.** to be noisy, loud, or excited; be disruptive; act up: *"Stop carrying on like that or you'll get detention," she yelled.* **d.** [~ + *on* + *with* + *obj*] to have a sexual relationship with: *Who was he carrying on with this time?* **19. carry out, a.** to put into operation; execute: [~ + *obj* + *out*]: *expected the troops to carry his orders out.* [~ + *out* + *obj*]: *Can you carry out this plan?* **b.** to accomplish; complete: [~ + *out* + *obj*]: *He carried out his plan to return to college.* [~ + *obj* + *out*]: *He was determined to carry it out.* **20. carry through, a.** to accomplish; complete: [~ + *through* + *obj*]: *She carried through her plan to invest in the stock market.* [~ + *obj* + *through*]: *She carried the plan through.* **b.** [~ + *obj* + *through* + *obj*] to support or help through a difficult situation: *Her support carried him through the crisis.* **c.** [*no obj; often:* ~ + *through* + *to* + *obj*] to continue to be present: *Violence done to children will carry through to the next generation.* —***Idiom.*** **21. carry the day,** to succeed in a situation by persuading others: *I'm sure he'll carry the day.* **22. carry (something) too far,** [~ + *obj* + *too far*] to do (something) too much; overdo: *Don't you think you're carrying this argument a little too far?*

car•ry•all (kar′ē ôl′) /ˈkæriyˌɔl/ *n.* [*count*] a large bag or lightweight piece of luggage.

car′ry-on′, *adj.* [*before a noun*] **1.** of a size suitable for being carried by a passenger onto an airplane: *carry-on luggage.* —*n.* [*count*] **2.** a piece of carry-on luggage.

car•ry•o•ver (kar′ē ō′vər) /ˈkæriyˌowvər/ *n.* [*count*] something extended or postponed from one time to another.

car′ seat′, *n.* [*count*] a removable seat for holding a small child safely in an automobile.

car•sick (kär′sik′) /ˈkarˌsɪk/ *adj.* ill with motion sickness during automobile travel. —**car′sick′ness,** *n.* [*noncount*]

cart (kärt) /kart/ *n.* [*count*] **1.** a two-wheeled vehicle pulled by horses, oxen, etc., and used to carry goods, for farming, etc. **2.** any small vehicle pushed or pulled by hand: *a shopping cart.* See illustration at SUPERMARKET. —*v.* [~ + *obj*] **3.** to haul, as in a cart or truck: *They carted the old furniture to the dump.* **4. cart off** or **away,** to take away (someone unwilling to go): [~ + *obj* + *off/away*]: *The police carted them off to jail.* [~ + *off/away* + *obj*]: *carted away all seven of them to jail.* —***Idiom.*** **5. put the cart before the horse,** to do or place things in wrong order; do things backward.

carte blanche (kärt′ blänch′, blänsh′) /ˈkartˈ blantʃ, ˈblɑ̃ʃ/ *n.* [*noncount*] full freedom or power to act: *gave his chief of staff carte blanche to fire anyone he chose.*

car•tel (kär tel′) /karˈtɛl/ *n.* [*count*] a group formed to act as a unit, esp. to control prices in some business: *The oil cartel sent oil prices skyrocketing.*

car•ti•lage (kär′tl ij) /ˈkartl̩ɪdʒ/ *n.* **1.** [*noncount*] a firm, elastic tissue in the body: *He tore some cartilage in his knee.* **2.** [*count*] a part or structure made of cartilage: *injured an ankle cartilage.*

car•tog•ra•phy (kär tog′rə fē) /karˈtɒgrəfiy/ *n.* [*noncount*] the production of maps. —**car•tog′ra•pher,** *n.* [*count*] See -GRAPH-.

car•ton (kär′tn) /ˈkartn̩/ *n.* [*count*] **1.** a cardboard or plastic box used for storage or shipping. **2.** a smaller box or container used for holding unit amounts of food, etc.: *Bring back two cartons of milk.* **3.** the amount a carton can hold; the contents of a carton: *drank a carton of juice.*

car•toon (kär to͞on′) /karˈtuwn/ *n.* [*count*] **1.** a drawing in a newspaper, magazine, etc., that comments amusingly on someone or some situation or carries some message: *political cartoons.* **2.** COMIC STRIP. **3.** a television or motion-picture film in which the characters and background are pictures that are drawn: *animated cartoons.* —**car•toon′ist,** *n.* [*count*]

car•tridge (kär′trij) /ˈkartrɪdʒ/ *n.* [*count*] **1.** a rounded tube or case that holds an explosive powder and a bullet for shooting from a gun or rifle. **2.** a case containing an explosive substance, as for blasting. **3.** a small container or tube filled with material to be inserted into a mechanism: *a film cartridge.*

cart•wheel (kärt′hwēl′, -wēl′) /ˈkartˌhwiyl, -ˌwiyl/ *n.* [*count*] **1.** an acrobatic movement in which a standing person turns and throws the body down and sideways, landing first on the hands and then on the feet. —*v.* [*no obj*] **2.** to perform cartwheels: *She cartwheeled down the hill.* **3.** to roll forward end over end: *The flaming plane cartwheeled into the sea.*

carve (kärv) /karv/ *v.,* **carved, carv•ing. 1.** to cut (a solid material) so as to form something: [~ + *obj*]: *to carve a piece of ebony.* [*no obj*]: *They have been carving for years.* **2.** [~ + *obj*] to form from a solid material by cutting: *carved unusual statues out of wood and ivory.* **3.** to cut (meat) into pieces or slices: [~ + *obj*]: *She carved the turkey expertly.* [*no obj*]: *Let him carve this year.* **4.** [~ + *obj*] to decorate with designs or figures cut on the surface: *The craftsman carved the top and sides of the chest.* **5.** [~ + *obj*] to cut (a design) into solid material: *She carved her initials on the tree.* **6.** [~ + *out* + *obj*] to make or create for oneself: *He carved out a successful career in business.* —**carv′er,** *n.* [*count*]

cas•cade (kas kād′) /kæsˈkeyd/ *n., v.,* **-cad•ed, -cad•ing.** —*n.* [*count*] **1.** a waterfall descending over a steep, rocky surface. **2.** anything that resembles a waterfall; torrent: *a cascade of hair falling down her shoulders.* **3.** an arrangement of a lightweight fabric in folds falling one over another: *a cascade of lace.* —*v.* [*no obj*] **4.** to fall in or like a cascade: *water cascading down the mountain.*

case[1] (kās) /keys/ *n.* [*count*] **1.** one instance or an example of the occurrence of something: *a case of poor judgment.* **2.** [*usually: be* + *the* + ~] the actual state of things: *If that's the case, you'd better get here sooner.* **3.** situation; circumstance: *a hopeless case.* **4.** a patient or client, as of a physician or social worker. **5.** an instance of disease, injury, etc., requiring attention: *a very bad case of arthritis.* **6.** a specific occurrence requiring discussion or investigation: *We now come to the case of the professor turned down for reappointment.* **7.** a statement of facts, reasons, etc., used to support an argument: *We presented a strong case against the proposed law.* **8.** a suit or action before a judge: *The murder case came before the new judge.* **9.** in grammar, the form of a word, usually of a noun, pronoun, or adjective, that serves to show the relation of the word to other words in a sentence: *The case of the pronoun "he" shows that it is the subject of the sentence "He is ready." The case of the pronoun "me" shows that it is the object of the sentence "John saw me."* —***Idiom.*** **10. get off someone's case,** *Slang.* to stop nagging or criticizing someone. **11. in any case,** regardless of circumstances; whatever happens: *We were ready, in any case, for war.* **12. in case,** if it should happen that; if: *Please walk the dog in case I don't come back on time.* **13. in case of,** in the event of; if there should be: *In case of fire, exit quietly down the stairs.* **14. in no case,** under no condition; never: *In no case should you run down those stairs.* **15. on someone's case,** [*be* + ~ (+ *about* + *obj*)] *Informal.* nagging or criticizing someone: *She's always on my case about my finances.*

case[2] (kās) /keys/ *n., v.,* **cased, cas•ing.** —*n.* [*count*] **1.** a container for enclosing something, such as for carrying or safekeeping: *She put the jewels back in their case.* **2.** an outer covering: *a knife case.* **3.** a box with its contents: *a case of soda.* **4.** the amount contained in a box or other container: *drank a case of beer.* **5.** the particular form of a written letter, either capital (uppercase) or small (lowercase). —*v.* [~ + *obj*] **6.** to put or enclose in a case. **7.** *Slang.* to examine carefully (a house, etc.) esp. in planning a crime: *We cased the joint last night; we can get in, no problem.*

ca•sein (kā′sēn, -sē in) /ˈkeysiyn, -siyɪn/ *n.* [*noncount*] a protein from milk, forming the basis of cheese.

case•load or **case load** (kās′lōd′) /ˈkeysˌlowd/ *n.* [*count; usually singular*] the number of cases handled by a court, agency, etc., over a period: *a caseload of ten clients a day.*

case•ment (kās′mənt) /ˈkeysmənt/ *n.* [*count*]. Also called **case′ment win′dow.** a window that has hinges on the sides.

case•work (kās′wûrk′) /ˈkeysˌwɜrk/ *n.* [*noncount*] social work involving contact between the social worker and the client. —**case′work′er,** *n.* [*count*]

cash (kash) /kæʃ/ *n.* [*noncount*] **1.** money in the form of coins or banknotes: *$5,000 in cash and the rest in traveler's checks.* **2.** money or an equivalent, as a check, paid at the time of making a purchase. **3.** money: *We're completely out of cash.* See illustration at BANK. —*v.* **4.** [~ + *obj*] to give or obtain cash for (a check, etc.): *Can you cash this check here?* **5. cash in,** [~ + *in* + *obj*] to turn in and get cash for (one's chips), as in a gambling casino. **6. cash in on,** [~ + *in* + *on* + *obj*] to profit from; use to one's advantage: *He cashed in on the deal his partner made.* —**cash′less,** *adj.*

cash′ crop′, *n.* [*count*] a crop intended to be sold: *such cash crops as tobacco.*

cash•ew (kash′o͞o, kə sho͞o′) /ˈkæʃuw, kəˈʃuw/ *n.* [*count*] **1.** a tropical American tree with yellowish pink flowers in open clusters. **2.** Also called **cash′ew nut′.** the small, edible nut of this tree.

cash•ier[1] (ka shēr′) /kæˈʃɪər/ *n.* [*count*] **1.** an employee who totals purchases and collects payment from customers, or who dispenses money in a bank. **2.** an executive who oversees the finances of a company.

cash•ier[2] (ka shēr′) /kæˈʃɪər/ *v.* [~ + *obj*] to dismiss from a position esp. with disgrace: *He was cashiered from the navy.*

cashier's′ check′, *n.* [*count*] a check drawn by a bank on its own funds and signed by its cashier.

cash′ machine′, *n.* AUTOMATED-TELLER MACHINE.

cash•mere or **kash•mir** (kazh′mēr, kash′-) /ˈkæʒmɪər, ˈkæʃ-/ *n.* [*noncount*] the fine, soft wool of the Kashmir goat, or yarn made from this wool.

cash′ reg′ister, *n.* [*count*] a machine in a business that indicates the amounts of individual sales and has a money drawer for making change. See illustration at SUPERMARKET.

cas•ing (kā′sing) /ˈkeysɪŋ/ *n.* [*count*] **1.** a case or covering; housing: *shell casings.* **2.** the framework around a door or window. **3.** the tube-shaped case for making the outside of sausage, etc.

ca•si•no (kə sē′nō) /kəˈsiynow/ *n.* [*count*], *pl.* **-nos.** a building used for professional gambling, for meetings, or for dancing.

cask (kask) /kæsk/ *n.* [*count*] **1.** a container like a barrel, for holding alcoholic drinks. **2.** the quantity such a container holds.

cas•ket (kas′kit) /ˈkæskɪt/ *n.* [*count*] **1.** a coffin. **2.** a small chest or box, such as for jewels.

cas•sa•va (kə sä′və) /kəˈsɑvə/ *n., pl.* **-vas. 1.** [*count*] a tropical American plant having thick roots. **2.** [*noncount*] flour or the starch from the roots of this plant, the source of tapioca.

cas•se•role (kas′ə rōl′) /ˈkæsəˌrowl/ *n.* [*count*] **1.** a usually large, covered baking dish, as of glass or pottery. **2.** any food baked in such a dish: *tuna casseroles.*

cas•sette (kə set′, ka-) /kəˈsɛt, kæ-/ *n.* [*count*] **1.** a plastic case in which audiotape or videotape runs between two reels for recording or playing back. **2.** a container for a roll of photographic film.

cas•sock (kas′ək) /ˈkæsək/ *n.* [*count*] a long, close-fitting garment like a robe, worn by members of the clergy.

cast (kast) /kæst/ *v.,* **cast, cast•ing,** *n.* —*v.* **1.** [~ + *obj*] to throw or hurl; fling: *to cast dice.* **2.** [~ + *obj*] to direct (the eye, etc.): *She kept casting glances at me across the room.* **3.** [~ + *obj*] to cause to fall; put or send forth: *This special lightbulb casts a soft light.* **4.** [~ + *obj*] to draw (lots), as in telling fortunes: *The soldiers cast lots to see who would draw guard duty.* **5.** [~ + *obj*] to throw out (a fishing line, etc.): *I was casting my line from the shore when it got tangled with hers.* **6.** [~ + *obj*] to shed or drop: *The snake cast its skin.* **7.** [~ + *obj*] to put or place, esp. by force: *The villain was cast into prison.* **8.** [~ + *obj*] to deposit or give (a ballot): *cast his ballot for president.* **9.** [~ + *obj*] to form or arrange; plan out: *He cast his speech in more military terms.* **10. a.** [~ + *obj*] to select actors for (a play, etc.): *The directors and producers were casting the part of Hamlet.* **b.** to assign a role to (an actor): [~ + *obj*]: *They cast him in the role of Caesar.* [~ + *obj* + *as* + *obj*]: *They cast him as Hamlet in their production.* **11.** [~ + *obj*] to form (an object) by pouring metal, etc., into a mold and letting it harden: *The statue was cast from bronze.* **12. cast about** or **around, a.** [~ + *about/around* + *obj*] to search; look: *I cast about the room to find a container.* **b.** [~ + *for* + *obj*] to seek: *always casting around for some way to make more money.* **c.** [*no obj*] to devise a plan; scheme: *She was casting about to get the boss's attention.* **13. cast away** or **aside,** to reject; discard: [~ + *away/aside* + *obj*]: *They cast aside our objections.* [~ + *obj* + *away/aside*]: *Don't cast it away.* **14. cast back,** [~ + *obj* + *back*] to refer to something past; go back to something past: *I cast my mind back to the days of my childhood.* **15. cast off, a.** [~ + *off* + *obj*] to discard; throw away; reject: *We cast off our doubts and signed the contract.* **b.** to let go or let loose, as a ship from a mooring: [~ + *off* + *obj*]: *The sailors cast off the ropes and set sail.* [~ + *obj* + *off*]: *They cast the ropes off and set sail.* **c.** [~ + *off* + *obj*] to complete a knitted fabric by looping over or removing (the final stitches): *began to cast off the last row of stitches.* **16. cast out,** [~ + *out* + *obj*] to force to leave; expel; banish: *They said he could cast out demons and heal the sick.* —*n.* [*count*] **17.** the act of throwing. **18.** a throw of dice: *After each cast, the player may bid or take a card.* **19.** the act of throwing a fishing line or net onto the water: *My first cast went out about fifteen feet.* **20.** [*usually singular*] the group of performers in a play, etc.; players: *The cast threw a party after the last performance.* **21.** something made by pouring liquid metal, etc., into a mold and letting it harden. **22.** a rigid, hard covering used to protect and hold in place a broken bone: *They put my arm in a cast.* **23.** sort; kind; style; quality: *minds of a philosophical cast.* **24.** a turning of the eye to the side.

cas•ta•net (kas′tə net′) /ˌkæstəˈnɛt/ *n.* [*count*] Usually, **castanets.** [*plural*] a small musical instrument made up of two shells of wood held in the palm of the hand and clicked together to accompany dancing.

cast•a•way (kast′ə wā′) /ˈkæstəˌwey/ *n.* [*count*] **1.** a person whose ship has been wrecked and who has landed on a deserted island. **2.** anything cast adrift or thrown away. **3.** an outcast.

caste (kast) /kæst/ *n.* **1.** [*count*] any of the social divisions of Hindu society. **2.** [*count*] a social division limited to people of the same rank, occupation, etc., by birth: *castes of rich and poor.* **3.** [*noncount*] the rigid system of dividing or distinguishing among people in social groups in these ways. **4.** [*noncount*] social position conferred upon one by a caste system: *to lose caste.*

cast•er (kas′tər) /ˈkæstər/ *n.* [*count*] **1.** a person or thing that casts. **2.** a small wheel on a swivel, set under a piece of furniture, etc., to make it easier to move.

cas•ti•gate (kas′ti gāt′) /ˈkæstɪˌgeyt/ *v.* [~ + *obj*], **-gat•ed, -gat•ing.** to reprimand or criticize severely: *The principal castigated the pupils for vandalizing the school.* —**cas•ti•ga•tion** (kas′ti gā′shən) /ˌkæstɪˈgeyʃən/ *n.* [*noncount*] —**cas′ti•ga′tor,** *n.* [*count*]

cast•ing (kas′ting) /ˈkæstɪŋ/ *n.* **1.** [*count*] something cast in a mold. **2.** [*noncount*] the process of choosing actors for a play, etc.

cast′ i′ron, *n.* [*noncount*] an alloy of iron, carbon, and other elements, cast as a soft and strong, or as a hard and brittle, iron.

cast′-i′ron, *adj.* [*before a noun*] **1.** made of cast iron. **2.** not subject to change or exception: *a cast-iron rule.* **3.** strong; hardy: *a cast-iron stomach.*

cas•tle (kas′əl) /ˈkæsəl/ *n., v.,* **-tled, -tling.** —*n.* [*count*] **1.** a fortified, protected building, usually with a wall around it, owned by a prince or noble esp. in former times. **2.** a large and stately residence, esp. one that imitates the forms of a medieval castle. **3.** any place providing security and privacy: *the old saying, a man's home is his castle.* **4.** *Chess.* the rook; one of the two corner pieces in the first row. —*v.* **5.** *Chess.* to move (the king) two squares to the side and bring the rook to the square the king has passed over: [~ + *obj*]: *He castled his king as a final defense.* [*no obj*]: *He tried castling to protect his king.*

cast•off (kast′ôf′, -of′) /ˈkæstˌɔf, -ˌɒf/ *adj.* [*before a noun*] **1.** thrown away; rejected; discarded: *He was wear-*

ing castoff clothes. **—*n.*** [*count*] **2.** a person or thing that has been cast off: *I was wearing my older brother's cast-offs for years.*

cas′tor oil′ (kas′tər) /'kæstər/ *n.* [*noncount*] a pale oil squeezed out of the bean of the castor plant, used as a lubricant and to stimulate the bowels.

cas•trate (kas′trāt) /'kæstreyt/ *v.* [~ + *obj*], **-trat•ed, -trat•ing. 1.** to remove the testes of; emasculate: *The veterinarian castrated the two bulls.* **2.** to weaken; remove the strength of: *The budget cuts only serve to castrate any future projects.* **—cas•tra•tion** (ka strā′shən) /kæ'streyʃən/ *n.* [*noncount*]: *punishes rapists with castration.* [*count*]: *The doctor had finished the castrations on the herd by midday.*

cas•u•al (kazh′o͞o əl) /'kæʒuwəl/ *adj.* **1.** happening by chance: *a casual meeting on the corner.* **2.** [*usually: before a noun*] without serious intention; not thorough: *He made a casual remark about her glasses.* **3.** seeming or pretending not to care; apathetic: *He had a casual air.* **4.** [*usually: before a noun*] (of clothes, etc.) able to be worn on informal occasions; not dressy: *casual slacks.* **5.** [*before a noun*] irregular; occasional: *She was just a casual visitor.* **—*n.*** [*plural*] **6.** clothes worn or used on informal occasions: *a set of smart casuals.* **—cas′u•al•ly,** *adv.* **—cas′u•al•ness,** *n.* [*noncount*]

cas•u•al•ty (kazh′o͞o əl tē) /'kæʒuwəltiy/ *n.* [*count*], *pl.* **-ties. 1.** *Military.* a member of the armed forces removed from service by death, wounds, sickness, etc.: *Casualties were heavy in that last battle.* **2.** one who is injured or killed in an accident. **3.** any person or thing harmed or destroyed as a result of some act or event: *Their house was one of the casualties of the earthquake.*

cas•u•is•try (kazh′o͞o is trē) /'kæʒuwɪs triy/ *n.* [*noncount*] reasoning that is deliberately too clever. **—cas′u•ist,** *n.* [*count*]

cat (kat) /kæt/ *n.* [*count*] **1.** a small, furry, carnivorous animal often kept as a pet: *Our cats like to play with string.* **2.** a grouping of similar animals, as the lion, tiger, leopard, or jaguar, and including numerous small wild cats: *The cats were kept next to the bears at the zoo.* **3.** *Slang.* a person, esp. a man: *a cool cat.* **—*Idiom.* 4. let the cat out of the bag,** to reveal, tell, or make known a secret.

cat., an abbreviation of: catalog; catalogue.

cat•a•clysm (kat′ə kliz′əm) /'kætəˌklɪzəm/ *n.* [*count*] **1.** a violent and sudden event that produces great social changes; upheaval: *The revolution was a cataclysm of major importance in that century.* **2.** a sudden and violent action producing changes in the earth's surface, as a flood or earthquake; catastrophe. **—cat′a•clys′mic, cat′a•clys′mal,** *adj.* **—cat′a•clys′mi•cal•ly,** *adv.*

cat•a•comb (kat′ə kōm′) /'kætəˌkowm/ *n.* [*count; usually plural*] an underground burial place made up of tunnels and rooms: *the famous catacombs near Rome, Italy.*

cat•a•log (kat′l ôg′, -og′) /'kætḷˌɔg, -ˌɒg/ *n.* [*count*] **1.** a pamphlet that contains a list or record of information, such as of items for sale, arranged in an orderly way and often including descriptions or illustrations: *We looked through the catalog for courses in English.* **2.** a list of the books or other materials in a library arranged according to any of various systems. **3.** a long list or record of any sort: *a catalog of complaints.* **—*v.*** [~ + *obj*] **4.** to enter (items) in a catalog: *cataloged the books alphabetically by author's last name.* **5.** to make a list of: *The prosecution cataloged a long series of crimes.*

cat•a•logue (kat′l ôg′, -og′) /'kætḷˌɔg, -ˌɒg/ *n., v.,* **-logued, -logu•ing.** CATALOG.

ca•tal•pa (kə tal′pə) /kə'tælpə/ *n.* [*count*], *pl.* **-pas.** a tree from North America and E Asia, having white flower clusters and long, beanlike seed pods.

ca•tal•y•sis (kə tal′ə sis) /kə'tæləsɪs/ *n.* [*noncount*] the causing or speeding up of a chemical change by the addition of a catalyst.

cat•a•lyst (kat′l ist) /'kætḷɪst/ *n.* [*count*] **1.** a substance that causes or speeds up a chemical reaction without itself being affected: *The enzyme was a catalyst in that reaction.* **2.** a person or thing that brings about change. See -LYS-.

cat•a•ma•ran (kat′ə mə ran′) /ˌkætəmə'ræn/ *n.* [*count*] a sailboat with a frame set on two parallel hulls.

cat•a•pult (kat′ə pult′, -po͝olt′) /'kætəˌpʌlt, -ˌpʊlt/ *n.* [*count*] **1.** an ancient military engine for hurling heavy stones, etc. **2.** *Brit.* SLINGSHOT. **3.** a device for launching an airplane from the deck of a ship. **—*v.* 4.** to hurl or be hurled from or as if from a catapult: [~ + *obj*]: *The crash catapulted her right through the windshield.* [*no obj*]: *The plane catapulted off the deck and into the air.* **5.** to move quickly, suddenly, or forcibly: [~ + *obj*]: *His first album catapulted him to fame.* [*no obj*]: *She catapulted into first place in figure skating.*

cat•a•ract (kat′ə rakt′) /'kætəˌrækt/ *n.* [*count*] **1.** a descent of water over a steep surface. **2.** an abnormal growth on the lens of the eye: *to remove cataracts by laser surgery.*

ca•tarrh (kə tär′) /kə'tɑr/ *n.* [*noncount*] irritation in the nose and throat causing an excessive flow of liquids or mucus.

ca•tas•tro•phe (kə tas′trə fē) /kə'tæstrəfiy/ *n.* [*count*] **1.** a sudden and widespread disaster: *The flood was a major catastrophe that killed thousands.* **2.** a great misfortune or failure; fiasco: *Losing his job was a catastrophe to him.* **3.** the point in a drama following the climax and introducing the conclusion. See -STROPH-.

cat•a•stroph•ic (kat′ə strof′ik) /ˌkætə'strɒfɪk/ *adj.* **1.** of or relating to a catastrophe: *the catastrophic consequences of nuclear war.* **2.** having serious and harmful effects: *the high cost of treatments for her catastrophic illness.* **3.** extremely bad.

cat•bird (kat′bûrd′) /'kætˌbɜrd/ *n.* [*count*] a songbird with a catlike call.

cat•boat (kat′bōt′) /'kætˌbowt/ *n.* [*count*] a boat having one mast set well forward with a single large sail.

cat•call (kat′kôl′) /'kætˌkɔl/ *n.* [*count*] a high-pitched, shrill, loud shout of disapproval at a theater, etc.: *whistles and catcalls as the politician climbed onto the stage.*

catch (kach) /kætʃ/ *v.,* **caught** (kôt) /kɔt/ **catch•ing,** *n.* **—*v.* 1.** [~ + *obj*] to seize or capture, esp. after chasing: *The police tried for weeks to catch the thief.* **2.** [~ + *obj*] to trap or ensnare: *I was caught in a dead-end job.* **3.** [~ + *obj*] to take and hold (something thrown, etc.): *She caught the ball.* **4.** [~ + *obj*] to surprise or notice, as in some action: [~ + *obj* + *verb-ing*]: *I caught them cheating.* [~ + *obj*]: *She caught me in the act of cheating on my test.* **5.** [~ + *obj*] to find (someone) in a particular condition, usually missing something: *He was caught with his guard down (= He was not prepared).* **6.** [~ + *obj*] to receive, incur, or contract (a disease): *He caught a cold at the overnight party.* **7.** [~ + *obj*] to be in time to get aboard: *We caught the train at Trondheim.* **8.** [~ + *obj*] to take hold of; clasp: *He caught her in an embrace.* **9.** to (cause to or allow to) become gripped, stuck, or entangled: [~ + *obj*]: *I caught my coat on that nail and it ripped.* [*no obj*]: *My sleeve caught on that nail.* **10.** [~ + *obj*] to attract; charm; attract the attention of: *She was caught by his winning smile.* **11.** [~ + *oneself*] to hold (oneself) back or restrain (oneself) suddenly: *He had to catch himself so that he wouldn't overreact.* **12.** [~ + *obj*] to see or attend (a show, etc.): *Did you catch that new musical?* **13.** [~ + *obj*] to strike; hit: *The blow caught him on the head.* **14.** to fasten with or as if with a catch; to (cause to) take hold: [*no obj*]: *The lock won't catch.* [~ + *obj*]: *See if you can catch the lock on the chain.* **15.** [~ + *obj*] to grasp with the intellect; comprehend: *I caught the meaning of that joke but didn't dare laugh.* **16.** [~ + *obj*] to hear clearly: *I couldn't catch what you said; could you repeat that?* **17.** [~ + *obj*] to be aware of (a smell, etc.): *I caught a whiff of her perfume.* **18.** [~ + *obj*] to record or represent successfully: *This photo caught her expression perfectly.* **19.** [*no obj*] to become lighted; ignite: *The green logs just won't catch.* **20. catch at,** [~ + *at* + *obj*] to grasp at eagerly: *The children caught at the teacher's skirt.* **21. catch on,** [*no obj*] **a.** to become popular: *For a long while her songs just didn't catch on.* **b.** to grasp the meaning; understand: *I'm a little slow but eventually I catch on.* [~ + *on* + *to* + *obj*]: *She didn't catch on to my explanation.* **22. catch out,** [~ + *obj* + *out*] to catch or discover in lies or an error: *They caught him out in a lie.* **23. catch up, a.** [~ + *up* + *with/to* + *obj*] to overtake someone or something moving: *I caught up with her and pulled her arm.* **b.** [~ + *up* + *with* + *obj*] to overwhelm suddenly: *The truth caught up with him and he realized what he had done.* **c.** [~ + *up* + *on* + *obj*] to do enough so that one is no longer behind: *He was catching up on his work on weekends.* **d.** [*usually: be* + *caught* + *up*] to be involved or interested very strongly: *He was caught up in his work and neglected his family.* **—*n.* 24.** [*count*] the act of catching. **25.** [*count*] anything that catches, esp. a device for slowing motion, as a handle on a window. **26.** [*count*] any tricky or concealed problem or drawback: *There must be a catch somewhere.* **27.** [*count; usually singular*] a slight, momentary break or crack in the voice: *She answered with a catch in her voice and started to cry.* **28.** [*count*] something caught, as a quantity of fish: *We brought home quite a catch.* **29.** [*count*] a person or thing worth getting, esp. as a desirable partner in marriage: *What a catch she would be.* **30.** [*noncount*] a game in which a ball is thrown from one person to another: *We went out in the yard to play catch.* **—*Idiom.*** **31. catch it,** *Informal.* to receive a reprimand or punishment: *You'll really catch it if you don't finish your homework.* —**catch′a•ble,** *adj.*

catch•er (kach′ər) /'kætʃər/ *n.* [*count*] **1.** a person or thing that catches. **2.** the baseball player stationed behind home plate to catch pitches not hit by the batter.

catch•ing (kach′ing) /'kætʃɪŋ/ *adj.* [*be* + ~] **1.** (of a disease) easily passed on to another; contagious or infectious: *The flu is catching.* **2.** spreading rapidly to or easily affecting others: *At the office her enthusiasm is catching.* **3.** attractive; alluring.

Catch-22 (kach′twen′tē to͞o′) /'kætʃ,twɛntiy'tuw/ *n., pl.* **Catch-22's, Catch-22s.** a frustrating situation in which one is trapped by contradictory rules or conditions: [*count*]: *You can't get a credit card unless you have a good credit rating. But to get a good credit rating, you need a credit card; it's a Catch-22.* [*noncount*]: *Any way you look at it, it's Catch-22.*

catch′-up′, *adj.* [*before a noun*] **1.** intended to keep up with or surpass a standard or a competitor: *catch-up pay raises.* **—*Idiom.*** **2. play catch-up,** to attempt to overtake a competitor by using desperate methods: *We were forced to play catch-up and take chances.*

catch•up (kach′əp, kech′-) /'kætʃəp, 'kɛtʃ-/ *n.* KETCHUP.

catch•word (kach′wûrd′) /'kætʃ,wɜrd/ *n.* [*count*] a well-known and effective word or phrase repeated so often that it becomes a slogan. Also called **catch•phrase** (kach′frāz′) /'kætʃ,freyz/.

catch•y (kach′ē) /'kætʃiy/ *adj.,* **-i•er, -i•est. 1.** pleasing and easily remembered; likely to attract interest or attention: *a catchy tune.* **2.** tricky; deceptive: *a catchy question.* —**catch′i•ness,** *n.* [*noncount*]

cat•e•chism (kat′i kiz′əm) /'kætɪ,kɪzəm/ *n.* [*count*] a book containing a summary of the principles of a subject in the form of questions and answers.

cat•e•gor•i•cal (kat′i gôr′i kəl, -gor′-) /,kætɪ'gɔrɪkəl, -'gɒr-/ also **cat′e•gor′ic,** *adj.* being without exceptions or conditions; absolute: *a categorical denial.* —**cat′e•gor′i•cal•ly,** *adv.*: *I can state categorically that I have never seen her before.*

cat•e•go•rize (kat′i gə riz′) /'kætɪgə,rayz/ *v.* [~ + *obj*], **-rized, -riz•ing. 1.** to arrange in categories or classes; classify: *We categorized the snowflakes into several shapes.* **2.** to describe by labeling or giving a name to; characterize: *He was categorized as a slow reader.* —**cat•e•go•ri•za•tion** (kat′i gər ə zā′shən) /,kætɪgərə'zeyʃən/ *n.* [*noncount*]: *strict categorization of types.* [*count*]: *My categorizations of the writings were not always accepted.*

cat•e•go•ry (kat′i gôr′ē, -gōr′ē) /'kætɪ,gɔriy, -,gowriy/ *n.* [*count*], *pl.* **-ries.** any group or division in a system of classification: *several categories of students: part-time, full-time, degree, and nondegree.*

ca•ter (kā′tər) /'keytər/ *v.* **1.** to provide food, etc., such as for a party or wedding: [*no obj*]: *a new company, catering for private parties.* [~ + *obj*]: *The company agreed to cater the reception.* **2.** [~ + *to* + *obj*] to provide or supply what is needed or gives pleasure, etc.: *She caters to her children.* —**ca′ter•er,** *n.* [*count*]

cat′er-cor′nered (kat′i-, kat′ē-, kat′ər-) /'kætɪ-, 'kætiy-, 'kætər-/ *adj.* **1.** diagonal. **—*adv.*** **2.** diagonally.

cat•er•pil•lar (kat′ə pil′ər, kat′ər-) /'kætə,pɪlər, 'kætər-/ *n.* [*count*] a small wormlike animal with a long body separated in parts, several pairs of legs, and biting mouthparts, eventually becoming a butterfly or moth.

cat•er•waul (kat′ər wôl′) /'kætər,wɔl/ *v.* [*no obj*] **1.** to utter long wailing cries, such as cats make. **—*n.*** [*count*] Also, **cat′er•waul′ing. 2.** a long, wailing cry. —**cat′er•waul′er,** *n.* [*count*]

cat•fish (kat′fish′) /'kæt,fɪʃ/ *n., pl. (esp. when thought of as a group)* **-fish,** *(esp. for kinds or species)* **-fish•es.** a fish lacking scales and having spines around the mouth that resemble a cat's whiskers.

cat•gut (kat′gut′) /'kæt,gʌt/ *n.* [*noncount*] a strong cord made from the dried intestines of animals, used as string for musical instruments, as surgical sutures, etc.

ca•thar•sis (kə thär′sis) /kə'θarsɪs/ *n., pl.* **-ses** (-sēz) /-siyz/. the relieving of emotional tensions, esp. through a work of art, as of tragedy: [*noncount*]: *Catharsis results from pity and fear as one watches drama.* [*count*]: *Writing a journal was a catharsis for him as he tried to overcome his anxiety.*

ca•thar•tic (kə thär′tik) /kə'θartɪk/ *adj.* **1.** of or relating to catharsis: *After the death of his children he returned to his work and found it cathartic.* **2.** causing the bowels to relax and to empty: *cathartic medicine.* **—*n.*** [*count*] **3.** a strongly laxative medicine.

ca•the•dral (kə thē′drəl) /kə'θiydrəl/ *n.* [*count*] the principal church of a diocese, or any important church.

cath•e•ter (kath′i tər) /'kæθɪtər/ *n.* [*count*] a thin flexible tube inserted into a blood vessel or other opening in the body, to allow fluids to pass into or out of it, or to carry examining instruments: *inserted a catheter through the patient's artery to see where the blockage was.*

cath•ode (kath′ōd) /'kæθowd/ *n.* [*count*] the electrode by which current leaves a battery, etc., or the negative terminal of such a cell.

cath′ode-ray′ tube′, *n.* [*count*] a device to display images on a television receiver or computer monitor.

cath•o•lic (kath′ə lik, kath′lik) /'kæθəlɪk, 'kæθlɪk/ *adj.* having a wide range; including most or all: *catholic interests.*

Cath•o•lic (kath′ə lik, kath′lik) /'kæθəlɪk, 'kæθlɪk/ *adj.* **1.** of, relating to, or belonging to the Roman Catholic Church. **—*n.*** [*count*] **2.** a member of the Roman Catholic Church. —**Ca•thol•i•cism** (kə thol′ ə siz′əm) /kə'θɒlə,sɪzəm/ *n.* [*noncount*]

cat•kin (kat′kin) /'kætkɪn/ *n.* [*count*] a spike of flowers with no petals, as on the willow.

cat•nap (kat′nap′) /'kæt,næp/ *n., v.,* **-napped** (-napt′) /-,næpt/ **-nap•ping. —*n.*** [*count*] **1.** a short, light nap: *a quick catnap on the sofa.* **—*v.*** [*no obj*] **2.** to sleep briefly; doze.

cat•nip (kat′nip) /'kætnɪp/ *n.* [*noncount*] a plant of the mint family, containing oils attractive to cats.

cat-o'-nine-tails (kat′ə nīn′tālz′) /,kætə'nayn,teylz/ *n.* [*count*], *pl.* **-tails.** a whip, usually having nine cords fastened to a handle, used for flogging someone as punishment.

CAT′ scan′ (kat) /kæt/ *n.* [*count*] **1.** an examination performed with a CAT scanner: *The doctors performed two CAT scans on her last week.* **2.** an x-ray image obtained by examination with a CAT scanner: *The CAT scans show some blockage here in the aorta.* Also called **CT scan.**

CAT′ scan′ner, *n.* [*count*] a device using narrow beams of x-rays at various angles to produce computerized images of a cross-section of the body: *The CAT scanner gives images of the body's soft tissues too, not just the bones.* Also called **CT scanner.**

cat•sup (kat′səp, kech′əp, kach′-) /'kætsəp, 'kɛtʃəp, 'kætʃ-/ *n.* KETCHUP.

cat•tail (kat′tāl′) /'kæt,teyl/ *n.* [*count*] a tall marsh plant resembling a reed.

cat•tle (kat′l) /'kætl̩/ *n.* [*plural; used with a plural verb*] large farm animals, as cows and steers, raised for their meat or milk.

cat•ty (kat′ē) /'kætiy/ *adj.,* **-ti•er, -ti•est. 1.** mean in a sly way; malicious; spiteful: *catty remarks.* **2.** catlike; feline. —**cat•ti•ly** (kat′lē) /'kætliy/ *adv.* —**cat′ti•ness,** *n.* [*noncount*]

CATV, an abbreviation of: community antenna television, a cable television service for areas where reception is ordinarily poor or impossible.

cat•walk (kat′wôk′) /'kæt,wɔk/ *n.* [*count*] a narrow walkway, esp. one high above the surrounding area.

cau•cus (kô′kəs) /'kɔkəs/ *n.* [*count*] **1. a.** a meeting of the members of a political party to select candidates, determine policy, etc. **b.** a group or faction within a lawmaking body that pursues its interests through the legislative process. **2.** any group or meeting organized to further a special interest or cause: *the civil-rights caucus.* **—*v.*** [*no obj*] **3.** to hold or meet in a caucus: *The women's rights group caucused and decided not to back the candidate.*

cau•dal (kôd′l) /'kɔdl̩/ *adj.* of, at, or near the tail end of the body.

caught (kôt) /kɔt/ *v.* pt. and pp. of CATCH.

caul•dron or **cal•dron** (kôl′drən) /'kɔldrən/ *n.* [*count*] a large kettle or boiler.

cau•li•flow•er (kô′lə flou′ər, -lē-, kol′ə-, kol′ē-) /'kɔlə,flawər, -liy-, 'kɒlə-, 'kɒliy-/ *n.* **1.** [*count*] a form of a cultivated plant of the mustard family, with a compact, usually whitish head. **2.** [*noncount*] the head of this plant, used as a vegetable.

caulk or **calk** (kôk) /kɔk/ *v.* [~ + *obj*] **1.** to fill or seal with a material the seams in (a window, ship's hull, etc.) to keep water or air out: *He caulked the windows.* **2.** to fill or seal (a joint, etc.) with this material: *She caulked the cracks in the tiles.* **—*n.*** [*noncount*] **3.** Also, **caulk•ing.** a material used to caulk.

caus•al (kô′zəl) /ˈkɔzəl/ *adj.* **1.** of or relating to a cause: *tried to establish a causal relationship between depression and suicide.* **2.** expressing a cause, as the conjunctions *because* and *since.* —**cau•sal•i•ty** (kô zal′i tē) /kɔˈzælɪtiy/ *n.* [*noncount; count*], *pl.* **-ties.** —**caus′al•ly,** *adv.*

cau•sa•tion (kô zā′shən) /kɔˈzeyʃən/ *n.* [*noncount*] the relation of cause to effect; causality; the concept that everything that happens must have a cause. —**cau•sa′tion•al,** *adj.*

cause (kôz) /kɔz/ *n., v.,* **caused, caus•ing.** —*n.* **1.** [*count*] a person that acts or a thing that occurs so as to produce a specific result: *What was the cause of the accident?* **2.** [*noncount*] the reason or motive for some action: *to complain without cause.* **3.** [*count*] a principle, ideal, goal, or movement to which a person or group is dedicated: *the Socialist cause.* —*v.* **4.** to be the cause of; bring about: [~ + *obj*]: *What caused the accident?* [~ + *obj* + *obj*]: *My error caused me a lot of trouble.* [~ + *obj* + *to* + *verb*]: *What caused him to get so excited?*

′cause (kôz, kuz, *unstressed* kəz) /kɔz, kʌz, *unstressed* kəz/ *conj. Informal.* because: *Don't leave, 'cause we'll be sad if you go.*

cause cé•lè•bre (kôz′ sə leb′) /ˈkɔz səˈlɛb/ *n.* [*count*], *pl.* **causes cé•lè•bres** (kôz′ sə leb′) /ˈkɔz səˈlɛb/. a controversial person, issue, etc., that attracts great public attention.

cause•way (kôz′wā′) /ˈkɔzˌwey/ *n.* [*count*] a raised road, as over a body of water.

caus•tic (kô′stik) /ˈkɔstɪk/ *adj.* **1.** capable of burning, corroding, or destroying living tissue: *Acid is caustic.* **2.** severely critical or sarcastic: *caustic remarks.* —**caus′ti•cal•ly,** *adv.*

-caut-, *root.* -*caut*- comes from Latin, where it has the meaning "care; careful." This meaning is found in such words as: CAUTION, CAUTIOUS, CAVEAT, PRECAUTION, PRECAUTIONARY.

cau•ter•ize (kô′tə rīz′) /ˈkɔtəˌrayz/ *v.* [~ + *obj*], **-ized, -iz•ing.** to burn (a wound) with a hot iron, an electric current, or a caustic substance, esp. to close, stop bleeding, or prevent infection. —**cau•ter•i•za•tion** (kô tə rə zā′shən) /kɔtərəˈzeyʃən / *n.* [*noncount*]

cau•tion (kô′shən) /ˈkɔʃən/ *n.* **1.** [*noncount*] alertness in a dangerous situation; care: *Proceed with caution.* **2.** [*count*] a warning against danger or evil: *The referee issued several cautions to the boxer during the match.* —*v.* **3.** to give advice (to); to give a warning (to): [*no obj*]: *I would caution against optimism.* [~ + *obj*]: *The referee cautioned him about his penalties.* [~ + *obj* + *to* + *verb*]: *I caution you not to over-exercise.* [~ + *obj* + *that clause*]: *They cautioned her that she would lose her driver's license.* See -CAUT-.

cau•tion•ar•y (kô′shə ner′ē) /ˈkɔʃə ˌnɛriy/ *adj.* [*before a noun*] serving as a warning: *a cautionary tale.*

cau•tious (kô′shəs) /ˈkɔʃəs/ *adj.* showing or using caution: *a cautious approach.* —**cau′tious•ly,** *adv.* —**cau′tious•ness,** *n.* [*noncount*] See -CAUT-.

cav•al•cade (kav′əl kād′) /ˌkævəlˈkeyd/ *n.* [*count*] **1.** a procession of people riding on horses, in cars, etc.; parade: *The circus cavalcade marched around the ring.* **2.** any noteworthy series: *a cavalcade of sports events.*

cav•a•lier (kav′ə lēr′) /ˌkævəˈlɪər/ *n.* [*count*] **1.** a mounted soldier; knight. —*adj.* **2.** casually indifferent or disdainful: *his cavalier treatment of others' property.* **3.** nonchalant; carefree; lighthearted: *A cavalier approach to your studies will get you into trouble.* —**cav′a•lier′ly,** *adv.*

cav•al•ry (kav′əl rē) /ˈkævəlriy/ *n.* [*count*], *pl.* **-ries. 1.** a unit of troops on horseback. **2.** soldiers in motorized units: *The fifth cavalry drove across the desert.*

cave (kāv) /keyv/ *n., v.,* **caved, cav•ing.** —*n.* [*count*] **1.** a hollow place in the earth, esp. one into a hill, mountain, etc., or underground. —*v.* **2. cave in, a.** to (cause to) fall in; to (cause to) collapse: [*no obj*]: *The roof is caving in.* [~ + *in* + *obj*]: *Someone caved in his skull with a rock.* [~ + *obj* + *in*]: *to cave it in with a rock.* **b.** [*no obj*] to yield; surrender; give in: *At last I caved in and bought a new car.*

ca•ve•at (kav′ē ät′, -at′) /ˈkæviyˌɑt, -ˌæt/ *n.* [*count*] a warning or caution; admonition: *A quick caveat: be sure of the reliability of your data.*

cave′-in′, *n.* [*count*] **1.** a collapse, as of anything hollow: *A cave-in trapped the miners in the tunnel.* **2.** an act of yielding to the demands, etc., of another: *A cave-in to her demands brings more demands.*

cave′ man′, *n.* [*count*] **1.** a person who lived in a cave, esp. in the Stone Age. **2.** a man who behaves in a rough, primitive manner.

cav•ern (kav′ərn) /ˈkævərn/ *n.* [*count*] a cave, esp. one that is large and mostly underground.

cav•i•ar (kav′ē är′) /ˈkæviyˌɑr/ *n.* [*noncount*] the eggs of sturgeon, salmon, etc., salted and eaten esp. as an appetizer.

cav•il (kav′əl) /ˈkævəl/ *v.,* **-iled, -il•ing** or (*esp. Brit.*) **-illed, -il•ling,** *n.* —*v.* [*no obj;* (~ + *at/about* + *obj*)] **1.** to raise unimportant objections: *Let's not cavil at details now; we are in agreement.* —*n.* [*count*] **2.** an unimportant objection: *She raised a few cavils just to show resistance.*

cav•i•ty (kav′i tē) /ˈkævɪtiy/ *n.* [*count*], *pl.* **-ties. 1.** any hollow place in a solid object. **2.** a hollow space within the body: *in the chest cavity.* **3.** a pit in a tooth, produced by decay.

ca•vort (kə vôrt′) /kəˈvɔrt/ *v.* [*no obj*] **1.** to jump, prance, or caper about: *The children were cavorting on the playground.* **2.** to make merry: *cavorting at a party on New Year's Eve.*

caw (kô) /kɔ/ *n.* [*count*] **1.** the loud, harsh call of the crow. —*v.* [*no obj*] **2.** to make this cry.

cay•enne (kī en′, kā-) /kayˈɛn, key-/ *n.* [*noncount*] **1.** a sharp-tasting powder used to flavor foods, made of the pods and seeds of a pepper plant. **2.** the long, wrinkled, twisted fruit of this plant. Also called **cayenne′ pep′per.**

CB, an abbreviation of: citizens band.

cc, an abbreviation of: **1.** carbon copy. **2.** copies. **3.** cubic centimeter.

cc. or **c.c.,** an abbreviation of: **1.** carbon copy. **2.** copies. **3.** cubic centimeter.

CD, an abbreviation of: **1.** certificate of deposit. **2.** compact disc.

CD player, *n.* [*count*] a device for playing compact discs. See illustration at APPLIANCE.

cease (sēs) /siys/ *v.,* **ceased, ceas•ing,** *n.* —*v.* **1.** to (cause to) stop or discontinue: [*no obj*]: *Hostilities must cease.* [~ + *obj*]: *We agree to cease hostilities.* [~ + *verb-ing*]: *They ceased fighting temporarily.* [~ + *to* + *verb*]: *Her good fortune never ceases to amaze me.* —*n.* [*noncount*] **2.** stopping; cessation: *The noise went on for hours without cease.*

cease′-fire′, *n.* [*count*] a stopping of hostilities; truce: *The UN cease-fire broke down yesterday.*

cease•less (sēs′lis) /ˈsiyslɪs/ *adj.* without stop; unending: *ceaseless rain.* —**cease′less•ly,** *adv.: Our neighbor's dog barked ceaselessly.* —**cease′less•ness,** *n.* [*noncount*]

ce•dar (sē′dər) /ˈsiydər/ *n.* **1.** [*count*] an evergreen, cone-bearing tree having wide, spreading branches and red wood: *tall cedars growing by the water.* **2.** [*noncount*] the sweet-smelling wood of this tree, used in furniture and to keep moths away.

-cede-, *root.* -*cede*- comes from Latin, where it has the meaning "go away from; withdraw; yield." This meaning is found in such words as: ACCEDE, ANTECEDENT, CEDE, CONCEDE, PRECEDE, PRECEDENT, RECEDE, SECEDE. See -CEED-, -CESS-.

cede (sēd) /siyd/ *v.* [~ + *obj*], **ced•ed, ced•ing.** to yield or formally surrender to another: *Mexico ceded territory to the United States.* See -CEDE-.

ce•dil•la (si dil′ə) /sɪˈdɪlə/ *n.* [*count*], *pl.* **-las.** a mark (¸) placed under a letter to indicate its pronunciation, as under *c* in French or Portuguese to indicate that it is pronounced (s) rather than (k), as in *façade.*

-ceed-, *root.* -*ceed*- comes from Latin, where it has the meaning "go; move; yield." It is related to -CEDE-. This meaning is found in such words as: PROCEED, SUCCEED.

ceil•ing (sē′ling) /ˈsiylɪŋ/ *n.* [*count*] **1.** the overhead inside surface of a room. **2.** an upper limit on an amount, as the amount of money that can be spent, etc.: *proposed putting a ceiling on government spending.* **3.** the height above ground level of the lowest layer of clouds that cover more than half of the sky: *The ceiling was low and visibility poor.*

-ceive-, *root.* -*ceive*- comes from Latin, where it has the meaning "get, receive." This meaning is found in such words as: CONCEIVE, DECEIVE, PERCEIVE, RECEIVE, TRANSCEIVER.

cel•e•brant (sel′ə brənt) /ˈsɛləbrənt/ *n.* [*count*] **1.** a participant in any celebration. **2.** the priest performing a religious ceremony, esp. of the Eucharist.

cel•e•brate (sel′ə brāt′) /ˈsɛləˌbreyt/ *v.,* **-brat•ed, -brat•ing. 1.** to show that (a day) is special by having ceremonies, parties, or other festivities: [~ + *obj*]: *to celebrate Christmas.* [*no obj*]: *We decided not to celebrate too* *much this year.* **2.** [~ + *obj*] to make known publicly; praise widely; proclaim: *His book celebrates the joys of growing up in Connecticut.* **3.** [~ + *obj*] to perform (a religious ceremony) with appropriate prayers, actions, gestures, and ceremonies; make holy or blessed: *The Pope celebrated Communion on Easter.* —**cel′e•bra′tive,** *adj.* —**cel′e•bra′tor, cel′e•brat′er,** *n.* [*count*]

cel•e•brat•ed (sel′ə brā′tid) /ˈsɛlə͵breytɪd/ *adj.* [*usually: before a noun*] famous; well-known; renowned: *a celebrated author and critic.*

cel•e•bra•tion (sel′ə brā′shən) /͵sɛlə ˈbreyʃən/ *n.* **1.** an event or occasion of celebrating: [*count*]: *The postwar celebrations went on for days.* [*noncount*]: *a period of quiet celebration.* **2.** [*noncount*] praise: *Celebration for this fine author came only after her death.*

cel•e•bra•to•ry (sel′ə brə tôr′ē, -tōr′ē) /ˈsɛlə brə͵tɔriy, -͵towriy/ *adj.* [*before a noun*] planned in order to celebrate: *a celebratory birthday dinner.*

ce•leb•ri•ty (sə leb′ri tē) /səˈlɛbrɪtiy/ *n., pl.* **-ties. 1.** [*count*] a famous or well-known person: *Numerous television celebrities attended the ceremony.* **2.** [*noncount*] fame; renown: *had gained celebrity for heroism.*

-celer-, *root.* *-celer-* comes from Latin, where it has the meaning "swift, quick." This meaning is found in such words as: ACCELERATE, CELERITY, DECELERATE.

ce•ler•i•ty (sə ler′i tē) /səˈlɛrɪtiy/ *n.* [*noncount*] swiftness; quickness; speed: *carried out the orders with celerity.* See -CELER-.

cel•er•y (sel′ə rē) /ˈsɛləriy/ *n.* [*noncount*] a plant of the parsley family, eaten raw or cooked.

ce•les•tial (sə les′chəl) /səˈlɛstʃəl/ *adj.* [*before a noun*] **1.** of, relating to, or guided by the visible heaven: *celestial navigation.* **2.** of or relating to the spiritual heaven; heavenly; divine: *celestial peace.*

cel•i•ba•cy (sel′ə bə sē) /ˈsɛləbəsiy/ *n.* [*noncount*] **1.** a state or condition of abstaining from sexual relations. **2.** a state or condition of being unmarried: *Roman Catholic priests take a vow of celibacy.*

cel•i•bate (sel′ə bit) /ˈsɛləbɪt/ *n.* [*count*] **1.** a person who abstains from sexual relations. **2.** a person who remains unmarried, esp. for religious reasons. —*adj.* **3.** observing a religious vow not to marry: *Their religion does not require ministers to be celibate.* **4.** not married: *She had remained celibate because her elderly parents needed her.* **5.** not having sexual relations: *remained celibate for fear of AIDS.*

cell (sel) /sɛl/ *n.* [*count*] **1.** a small room, such as in a convent or a prison. **2.** any of various small compartments forming part of a whole: *The worker bees deposit their food in the cells of the honeycomb.* **3.** the most basic unit of structure of an organism: *The cell contains a nucleus, a membrane, and a cell wall.* **4.** a small group within a larger organization: *a local cell of the socialist party.* **5.** a device that converts chemical, heat, or light energy into electricity: *a dry cell.* **6.** one of the separate areas covered by a radio transmitter in a cellular phone system: *Calls within the cell are cheaper than those outside the cell.*

cel•lar (sel′ər) /ˈsɛlər/ *n.* [*count*] **1.** a room or set of rooms underground and usually beneath a building: *The furnace is down in the cellar.* **2.** [*usually singular: the* + ~] the last or lowest place in a ranking: *The ball club went from the cellar to first place in just one year.*

cel•list (chel′ist) /ˈtʃɛlɪst/ *n.* [*count*] one who plays the cello.

cel•lo (chel′ō) /ˈtʃɛlow/ *n.* [*count*], *pl.* **-los.** a musical instrument that is the second largest member of the violin family; violoncello.

cel•lo•phane (sel′ə fān′) /ˈsɛlə͵feyn/ *n.* [*noncount*] a transparent, thin, flexible material like plastic or paper, used for wrapping.

cel•lu•lar (sel′yə lər) /ˈsɛlyələr/ *adj.* relating to, characterized by, or shaped like cells: *the transport of cellular products to the rest of the body.*

cel′lular phone′, *n.* [*count*] a mobile telephone using a system of radio transmitters, each covering separate areas. Also called **cel′lular tel′ephone.**

cel•lu•lite (sel′yə lit′, -lēt′) /ˈsɛlyə͵layt, -͵liyt/ *n.* [*noncount*] lumpy fat deposits under the skin, esp. in the thighs and buttocks.

cel•lu•loid (sel′yə loid′) /ˈsɛlyə͵lɔyd/ *n.* [*noncount*] **1.** a tough plastic formerly used as a base for motion-picture film. **2.** motion-picture film: *captured the drama on celluloid.*

cel•lu•lose (sel′yə lōs′) /ˈsɛlyə͵lows/ *n.* [*noncount*] a carbohydrate that is the chief substance of the cell walls of plants and is found in wood, cotton, hemp, paper, etc.

Cel•si•us (sel′sē əs) /ˈsɛlsiyəs/ *adj.* of, relating to, or measured according to a temperature scale **(Cel′sius scale′)** in which 0° represents the point at which ice forms, and 100° represents the point at which steam forms; Centigrade: [*after a noun or number*]: *It was 10 degrees Celsius, not bad for a winter's day.* [*before a noun*]: *Our teacher told us to give the results in Celsius numbers.* Compare FAHRENHEIT.

Celt•ic (kel′tik, sel′-) /ˈkɛltɪk, ˈsɛl-/ *n.* **1.** a family of languages spoken by the Celts, an ancient W European people, and including the modern languages Irish, Scottish Gaelic, Welsh, and Breton. —*adj.* **2.** of or relating to the Celts or their languages.

ce•ment (si ment′) /sɪˈmɛnt/ *n.* **1.** [*noncount*] a mixture of clay and limestone, usually mixed with water and sand, etc., to form concrete, used as a building material: *a floor made of cement.* **2.** [*noncount*] any soft, sticky substance that dries hard and is used for mending broken objects: *a jar of paper cement.* **3.** [*count; usually singular*] anything that binds or unites: *Their children were the cement of their family.* —*v.* [~ + *obj*] **4.** to unite or join by or as if by cement: *Cement part 65a to part 65b; set aside to dry.* **5.** to coat or cover with cement: *The workers cemented the floors of the apartment building.*

ce•ment′ mix′er, *n.* [*count*] **1.** a machine with a revolving container in which the ingredients of concrete are mixed. **2.** a truck equipped with such a machine.

cem•e•ter•y (sem′i ter′ē) /ˈsɛmɪ͵tɛriy/ *n.* [*count*], *pl.* **-ies.** a burial ground for dead people: *We visited her grave in the town cemetery.*

cen•o•taph (sen′ə taf′) /ˈsɛnə͵tæf/ *n.* [*count*] a monument built in memory of a deceased person whose body is buried elsewhere.

cen•ser (sen′sər) /ˈsɛnsər/ *n.* [*count*] a container in which incense is burned.

cen•sor (sen′sər) /ˈsɛnsər/ *n.* [*count*] **1.** an official who examines books, television programs, etc., for the purpose of removing or changing parts judged to be immoral, undesirable, or for other reasons: *The military censors kept us from reporting where these missiles hit.* —*v.* [~ + *obj*] **2.** to examine and change or remove (parts of a book, etc.) as a censor does: *censored our reports from Saudi Arabia.* —**cen•so′ri•al** (sen sôr′ē əl, -sōr′-) /sɛnˈsɔriyəl, -ˈsowr-/ *adj.*

cen•so•ri•ous (sen sôr′ē əs, -sōr′-) /sɛnˈsɔriyəs, -ˈsowr-/ *adj.* [*sometimes, after a noun* or *be:* ~ + *of*]: severely critical; disapproving strongly; finding fault: *The letters were censorious of the president and the media alike.* —**cen•so′ri•ous•ly,** *adv.* —**cen•so′ri•ous•ness,** *n.* [*noncount*]

cen•sor•ship (sen′sər ship′) /ˈsɛnsər͵ʃɪp/ *n.* [*noncount*] the act or practice of censoring: *military censorship on outgoing news reports.*

cen•sure (sen′shər) /ˈsɛnʃər/ *n., v.,* **-sured, -sur•ing.** —*n.* **1.** [*noncount*] strong expression of disapproval: *received a great deal of censure for falsifying those results.* **2.** an official reprimand, as by a legislative body: [*noncount*]: *The senator got only a vote of censure from Congress, even though he was guilty of theft.* [*count*]: *This soldier received two censures for sleeping on guard duty.* —*v.* [~ + *obj*] **3.** to criticize in a harsh manner; show strong disapproval of: *Congress censured him for stealing money.*

cen•sus (sen′səs) /ˈsɛnsəs/ *n.* [*count*], *pl.* **-sus•es.** an official count of the population of a country, state, etc., with details as to age, sex, occupation, etc.: *The United States has a census every ten years.*

cent (sent) /sɛnt/ *n.* [*count*] **1.** a coin that is the smallest unit of money of the U.S., equal to 1/100 of a dollar: *A penny is a coin that is worth one cent.* **2.** a unit of money of various other nations equal to 1/100 of the basic currency. See -CENT-.

cent., an abbreviation of: **1.** centigrade. **2.** central.

-cent-, *root.* *-cent-* comes from Latin, where it has the meaning "one hundred." This meaning is found in such words as: CENT, CENTENNIAL, CENTIGRADE, CENTIMETER, CENTIPEDE, CENTURY, PERCENT.

cen•taur (sen′tôr) /ˈsɛntɔr/ *n.* [*count*] a race of creatures in Greek myth having the head, chest, and arms of a man, and the body and legs of a horse.

cen•te•nar•i•an (sen′tn âr′ē ən) /͵sɛntn̩ˈɛəriyən/ *adj.* [*usually before a noun*] **1.** of, relating to, or having existed 100 years. —*n.* [*count*] **2.** a person who has reached the age of 100. See -CENT-.

cen•ten•ar•y (sen ten′ə rē, sen′tn er′ē) /sɛnˈtɛnəriy, ˈsɛntn̩͵ɛriy/ *adj., n., pl.* **-ies.** —*adj.* **1.** of or marking a period of 100 years. **2.** occurring once in every 100 years. *—n.* [*count*] **3.** a centennial. **4.** a century. See -CENT-.

cen•ten•ni•al (sen ten′ē əl) /sɛn'tɛniyəl/ *adj.* **1.** of, relating to, or marking a 100th anniversary. **2.** lasting 100 years. *—n.* [*count*] **3.** a 100th anniversary or its celebration. —**cen•ten′ni•al•ly,** *adv.* See -CENT-.

cen•ter (sen′tər) /'sɛntər/ *n.* [*count*] **1.** the middle part or point of something; core: *the center of town; the center of the earth.* **2.** the point equally distant from all sides of an object; a point around which a circle may be drawn; a point around which something revolves or turns: *Measure the circle from the center to any point on the edge to get the radius.* **3.** [*usually singular; usually: the* + ~] the source of an influence, action, or force: *the center of a problem.* **4.** a focus, as of interest or concern: *For a few moments she was the center of attention.* **5.** a principal point, place, or object: *a shipping center.* **6.** a building or part of a building that is used as a meeting place, or that deals with a particular subject, emergency, etc.: *A crisis center was set up during the flood emergency.* **7.** SHOPPING CENTER. **8.** [*usually: Center*] (esp. in Europe) the members of a parliament who hold views between those of the Right and Left and who sit in the center of the chamber. *—v.* **9.** [~ + *obj*] to place in or on a center; move, or adjust to or on a center: *centered the subject in the camera's viewfinder.* **10.** to collect to or around a center; focus; concentrate: [~ + *obj* + *on* + *obj*]: *He centered his novel on the Civil War.* [~ + *on/around* + *obj*]: *His novel centers on the Civil War.* *—adj.* **11.** (of a political party or position) considered moderate or in between the left and right positions: *a center party.* Also, *esp. Brit.,* **centre.**

cen•tered (sen′tərd) /'sɛntərd/ *adj.* [*sometimes: after a noun or verb*] **1.** having (a certain thing) as a central focus or base: *a family-centered activity.* **2.** [*noun* + ~ + *on* + *obj*] focused; fixed: *an obsession centered on germs.* **3.** at the same distance from all areas; situated in the center: *pages with centered text.* **4.** [*often: verb* + ~] inwardly calm and steady: *Stay centered and you'll do fine on the test.*

cen′ter of grav′ity, *n.* [*count*], *pl.* **centers of gravity. 1.** a point on an object where the object balances perfectly because the weight is evenly balanced. **2.** the focus or main point of importance or stability: *The monarchy was England's center of gravity.*

cen•ter•piece (sen′tər pēs′) /'sɛntər,piys/ *n.* [*count*] **1.** an object used on the center of a dining table, esp. as an ornament. **2.** the central or outstanding point or feature of something: *The centerpiece of the new plan was a reduction in the capital gains tax.*

centi-, *prefix. centi-* is attached to roots to mean "hundredth" or "hundred": *centiliter (= one hundredth of a liter); centipede (= (creature having) one hundred feet).*

cen•ti•grade (sen′ti grād′) /'sɛntɪ,greyd/ *adj.* **1.** divided into 100 degrees: *a centigrade scale.* **2.** [*after a noun or number*] [*Centigrade*] CELSIUS: *It was only 5 degrees Centigrade, about 41 degrees Fahrenheit.* See -CENT-.

cen•ti•gram (sen′ti gram′) /'sɛntɪ,græm/ *n.* [*count*] 1/100 of a gram. Also, *esp. Brit.,* **cen′ti•gramme′.**

cen•ti•li•ter (sen′tl ē′tər) /'sɛntḷ,iytər/ *n.* [*count*] 1/100 of a liter, equivalent to 0.6102 cubic inch, or 0.338 U.S. fluid ounce. *Abbr.:* cl Also, *esp. Brit.,* **cen′ti•li′tre.**

cen•ti•me•ter (sen′tə mē′tər) /'sɛntə,miytər/ *n.* [*count*] 1/100 of a meter, equivalent to 0.3937 inch. Also, *esp. Brit.,* **cen′ti•me′tre.** See -CENT-, -METER-.

cen•ti•pede (sen′tə pēd′) /'sɛntə,piyd/ *n.* [*count*] a small wormlike animal with a pair of legs on each of its segments, the first pair being modified into poison fangs. See -CENT-, -PED-[1].

cen•tral (sen′trəl) /'sɛntrəl/ *adj.* **1.** [*usually: before a noun*] of, in, at, or near the center: *Our home is in a central region of town.* **2.** [*before a noun*] being or making up something from which all other related things proceed: *He reported to the central administration.* **3.** most important; principal; main; chief: [*before a noun*]: *He had a central position in the department.* [*be* + ~ + *to* + *obj*]: *Einstein's discoveries were central to modern physics for decades.* —**cen′tral•ly,** *adv.: The apartment is centrally located.*

cen•tral•i•ty (sen tral′i tē) /sɛn'trælɪtiy/ *n.* [*noncount*] a central position or condition: *cultural and political centrality.*

cen•tral•ize (sen′trə līz′) /'sɛntrə,layz/ *v.,* **-ized, -iz•ing.** to (cause to) come under one central control, esp. in government: [~ + *obj*]: *to centralize the power of the military.* [*no obj; often:* ~ + *in* + *obj*]: *Power tends to centralize in the hands of those who use it.* —**cen•tral•i•za•tion** (sen′trə lə zā′shən) /,sɛntrələ'zeyʃən/ *n.* [*noncount*]

cen•tre (sen′tər) /'sɛntər/ *n., v.,* **-tred, -tring.** *Chiefly Brit.* CENTER.

cen•trif•u•gal (sen trif′yə gəl, -ə gəl) /sɛn'trɪfyəgəl, -əgəl/ *adj.* moving outward from the center (opposed to *centripetal*): *Centrifugal force causes a stone at the end of a rope to pull away from you when you twirl the rope.* —**cen•trif′u•gal•ly,** *adv.* See -FUG-.

cen•tri•fuge (sen′trə fyo͞oj′) /'sɛntrə,fyuwdʒ/ *n., v.,* **-fuged, -fug•ing.** *—n.* [*count*] **1.** a machine that spins at high speed and separates substances of different densities. *—v.* [~ + *obj*] **2.** to put (something) through the action of a centrifuge: *They centrifuged the blood samples and analyzed them.* See -FUG-.

cen•trip•e•tal (sen trip′i tl) /sɛn'trɪpɪtḷ/ *adj.* moving or directed toward the center (opposed to *centrifugal*): *When you twirl a string with a rock at the end of it, the string provides centripetal force.* —**cen•trip′e•tal•ly,** *adv.* See -PET-.

cen•trist (sen′trist) /'sɛntrɪst/ *n.* [*count*] **1.** [*sometimes: Centrist*] a person with moderate political views: *This political party no longer has room for centrists.* *—adj.* [*usually: before a noun*] **2.** having moderate political views: *The party was looking for a centrist candidate.*

cen•tu•ri•on (sen to͝or′ē ən, -tyo͝or′-) /sɛn'tʊriyən, -'tyʊr-/ *n.* [*count*] (in the Roman army) the commander of a group of one hundred soldiers. See -CENT-.

cen•tu•ry (sen′chə rē) /'sɛntʃəriy/ *n.* [*count*], *pl.* **-ries. 1.** a period of 100 years: *the amazing changes of the past century.* **2.** one of the periods of 100 years counted from a recognized date, esp. from the assumed date of the birth of Jesus: *The twentieth century began in 1901 and ends in the year 2000.* See -CENT-.

CEO or **C.E.O.,** an abbreviation of: chief executive officer.

-cep-, *root. -cep-* comes from Latin, where it has the meaning "get, receive, take." This meaning is found in such words as: ACCEPT, ANTICIPATE, PERCEPTION, RECEPTION. See -CEIVE-.

ce•ram•ic (sə ram′ik) /sə'ræmɪk/ *adj.* **1.** of or relating to products made from clay, pottery, and brick, or to their manufacture: *ceramic tiles for the bathroom.* *—n.* [*noncount*] **2.** hard material made from clay or from a ceramic process.

ce•ram•ics (sə ram′iks) /sə'ræmɪks/ *n.* **1.** [*noncount; used with a singular verb*] the art of making objects of clay and heating them to make them hard: *a course in ceramics.* **2.** [*plural; used with a plural verb*] articles or objects made from clay, earthenware, etc.: *Beautiful ceramics were smashed and left on the floor.*

ce•re•al (sēr′ē əl) /'sɪəriyəl/ *n.* **1.** [*count*] a plant of the grass family, such as wheat, that gives grain that can be eaten: *wild cereals growing on the plains.* **2.** [*noncount*] the grain itself: *harvesting the cereal.* **3.** some preparation of this grain that can be eaten, esp. a breakfast food: [*noncount*]: *has two bowls of cereal every morning.* [*count*]: *cereals with too much sugar in them.*

ce•re•bral (sə rē′brəl, ser′ə-) /sə'riybrəl, 'sɛrə-/ *adj.* **1.** [*before a noun*] of or relating to the cerebrum: *The cerebral cortex is involved with higher thinking processes.* **2.** characterized by the use of the intellect and not by the feelings or intuition: *Chess is a cerebral game.*

cere′bral pal′sy, *n.* [*noncount*] muscular weakness and difficulty in coordinating movement because of damage to the brain at birth.

ce•re•brum (sə rē′brəm, ser′ə-) /sə'riybrəm, 'sɛrə-/ *n.* [*count*], *pl.* **-brums, -bra** (-brə). the forward and upper part of the brain, involved with movement and thinking.

cer•e•mo•ni•al (ser′ə mō′nē əl) /,sɛrə'mowniyəl/ *adj.* **1.** of, relating to, or characterized by ceremony; formal: *a ceremonial occasion.* *—n.* **2. a.** [*count*] a ceremonial act or the order in which acts are done: *The ceremonials include hymns.* **b.** [*noncount*] a system of formal acts performed in a ceremony: *A prince is crowned by strict ceremonial.* —**cer′e•mo′ni•al•ly,** *adv.*

cer•e•mo•ni•ous (ser′ə mō′nē əs) /,sɛrə'mowniyəs/ *adj.* carefully observant or fond of ceremony: *ceremonious farewells on the last day of the pope's visit.* —**cer′e•mo′ni•ous•ly,** *adv.: He went ceremoniously from room to room.* —**cer′e•mo′ni•ous•ness,** *n.* [*noncount*]

cer•e•mo•ny (ser′ə mō′nē) /'sɛrə,mowniy/ *n., pl.* **-nies. 1.** [*count*] the formal activities conducted on some solemn or important occasion: *the marriage ceremony.* **2.** [*noncount*] all the actions, words, or formal behavior on such an occasion: *We wanted a simple wedding, without a lot of ceremony.* **3.** [*noncount*] any formal act, esp. a meaningless one: *His bow was mere ceremony.* **4.** [*noncount*] a gesture or act of politeness or civility: *the ceremony of a handshake.* **—*Idiom.*** **5. stand on ceremony,** to behave in a formal or ceremonious manner: *We're friends, so there's no need to stand on ceremony.* **6. without ceremony,** [*noncount*] quickly and informally; without fuss: *accepted the honor without ceremony.*

-cern-, *root. -cern-* comes from Latin, where it has the meanings "separate; decide." These meanings are found in such words as: CONCERN, DISCERN.

-cert-, *root. -cert-* comes from Latin, where it has the meaning "certain; sure; true." This meaning is found in such words as: ASCERTAIN, CERTAIN, CERTIFICATE, CERTIFY, CONCERT, DISCONCERTED.

cert., an abbreviation of: **1.** certificate. **2.** certified. **3.** certify.

cer•tain (sûr′tn) /ˈsɜrtn̩/ *adj.* **1.** free from doubt or reservation; confident: [*be* + ~ + *(that) clause*]: *I'm certain that I passed the test.* [*be* + ~ + *of* + *verb-ing*]: *She is certain of winning.* **2.** destined; sure to happen: [*be* + ~ + *to* + *verb*]: *She is certain to be at the party (= It is sure to happen that she will be at the party).* **3.** bound to come; that will surely follow and cannot be avoided: *War was certain after Germany invaded Poland.* **4.** established as true or sure; that cannot be argued about: [*it* + *be* + ~ + *(that) clause*]: *It is certain that you tried.* **5.** trustworthy; unfailing; reliable: *His aim was certain.* **6.** [*before a noun*] fixed; agreed upon; settled: *For a certain amount I can get you across the border.* **7.** [*before a noun*] (used before a person or thing that is known in the mind of the speaker or writer, but that is being introduced to the listener): *A certain Mr. Smith has been trying to meet you.* **8.** [*before a noun; a* + ~] some though not much; a kind of: *There was a certain reluctance on his part.* **—*pron.*** **9.** [~ + *of* + *the* + *plural noun*] some; particular ones: *Certain of the school board members abstained from voting.* **—*Idiom.*** **10. for certain,** certainly; for sure: *I didn't know for certain whether I would be hired.* See -CERT-.

cer•tain•ly (sûr′tn lē) /ˈsɜrtn̩ liy/ *adv.* **1.** surely; without doubt; undoubtedly: *You certainly have done a fine job.* **2.** (used to show strong feeling or enthusiasm about something, to show agreement with what has been said, or to answer "yes" to a question): *This is certainly a fine party, isn't it? Can I have my pen back, please? —Certainly, sir.* See -CERT-.

cer•tain•ty (sûr′tn tē) /ˈsɜrtn̩tiy/ *n., pl.* **-ties. 1.** [*noncount*] the state of being certain: *This philosopher claims that we can't know anything with certainty.* **2.** [*count*] something certain; an assured fact: *a mathematical certainty that we would finish in first place.* See -CERT-.

cer•ti•fi•a•ble (sûr′ti fī′ə bl) /ˌsɜrtɪˈfayə bl/ *adj.* **1.** that can be certified: *certifiable evidence.* **2.** insane: *This weird behavior shows that she's certifiable.* **—cer′ti•fi′a•bly,** *adv.* See -CERT-.

cer•tif•i•cate (sər tif′i kit) /sərˈtɪfɪkɪt/ *n.* [*count*] a written document that gives proof that something is true: *She received a certificate from the London School of Economics.* See -CERT-, -FIC-.

certif′icate of depos′it, *n.* [*count*], *pl.* **certificates of deposit.** a written statement from a bank, showing the interest given for money deposited. *Abbr.:* CD

cer•ti•fi•ca•tion (sûr′tə fi kā′shən) /ˌsɜrtəfɪˈkeyʃən/ *n.* [*noncount*] the act of certifying or the state of being certified.

cer′tified check′, *n.* [*count*] a check drawn by a bank against funds made available by the writer of the check: *paid for the car with a certified check.*

cer′tified pub′lic account′ant, *n.* [*count*] an accountant who is certified by a state examining board as having completed the requirements of state law to be a public accountant.

cer•ti•fy (sûr′tə fī′) /ˈsɜrtəˌfay/ *v.,* **-fied, -fy•ing. 1.** to declare that something is certain or true; confirm: [~ + *obj*]: *As an expert witness he was able to certify the truth of her claim.* [~ + *(that) clause*]: *was able to certify that this was the murder weapon.* **2.** [~ + *obj*] to give a license to (someone), often by providing a certificate: *All the teachers in our program are certified.* **3.** [~ + *obj*] to guarantee (a check): *The bank certified our check and I brought it back to the car dealer.* **4.** [~ + *obj*] to declare (a person) legally insane. **5.** [~ + *(that) clause*] to tell or inform someone with certainty; assure someone: *I can certify that she is one of the best teachers I have seen.* See -CERT-.

cer•ti•tude (sûr′ti to͞od′, -tyo͞od′) /ˈsɜrtɪˌtuwd, -ˌtyuwd/ *n.* [*noncount*] freedom from doubt, esp. in matters of faith or opinion; certainty. See -CERT-.

cer•vi•cal (sûr′vik əl) /ˈsɜrvɪk əl/ *adj.* [*before a noun*] **1.** of, relating to, or for the neck: *A cervical support was fitted around the accident victim's neck.* **2.** of or relating to the cervix: *cervical cancer.*

cer•vix (sûr′viks) /ˈsɜrvɪks/ *n.* [*count*], *pl.* **cer•vix•es, cer•vi•ces** (sûr′və sēz′) /ˈsɜrvəˌsiyz/. **1.** the neck, esp. the back part. **2.** any necklike part, esp. the lower, opening part of the uterus or womb.

Ce•sar•e•an (si zâr′ē ən) /sɪˈzɛəriyən/ *n.* [*count*] [*sometimes: cesarean*] **1.** Also called **Cesar′ean sec′tion, C-section.** surgical removal of an unborn baby from the uterus. **—*adj.*** **2.** [*sometimes: cesarean*] of or relating to a Cesarean. Also, **Caesarean, Caesarian, Ce•sar′i•an.**

-cess-, *root. -cess-* comes from Latin, where it has the meaning "move, yield." It is related to -CEDE-. This meaning is found in such words as: ACCESS, ACCESSIBLE, ACCESSORY, CESSION, PROCESS, PROCESSION, RECESS, RECESSION, SUCCESS, SUCCESSION.

ces•sa•tion (se sā′shən) /sɛˈseyʃən/ *n.* [*count; usually singular*] a stopping; ceasing: *a cessation of hostilities.*

ces•sion (sesh′ən) /ˈsɛʃən/ *n.* **1.** [*noncount*] the act of giving up or ceding, as by treaty. **2.** [*count*] something given up or ceded, such as territory. See -CESS-.

cess•pool (ses′po͞ol′) /ˈsɛsˌpuwl/ *n.* [*count*] **1.** an underground container for receiving the waste from a house. **2.** a place of filth or immorality.

cf., an abbreviation of Latin *confer*: compare.

Ch., an abbreviation of: **1.** channel. **2.** chapter.

ch., an abbreviation of: chapter.

cha-cha (chä′chä′) /ˈtʃɑˌtʃɑ/ *n., pl.* **-chas,** *v.,* **-chaed, -cha•ing. —*n.*** [*count*] **1.** a Latin-American ballroom dance based upon a quick three-step movement. **—*v.*** [*no obj*] **2.** to dance the cha-cha.

chafe (chāf) /tʃeyf/ *v.,* **chafed, chaf•ing. 1.** to (cause to) become sore by rubbing: [~ + *obj*]: *The clothes chafed the baby badly.* [*no obj*]: *Those tight diapers are chafing.* **2.** to (cause to) be irritated or annoyed: [~ + *at/under* + *obj*]: *He chafed at their unkind remarks.* [~ + *obj*]: *Those unkind remarks really chafed him.* **3.** [~ + *obj*] to warm by rubbing: *to chafe cold hands.*

chaff[1] (chaf) /tʃæf/ *n.* [*noncount*] **1.** the outer coverings of seeds of grains separated during beating or threshing: *to separate the wheat from the chaff.* **2.** something worthless; refuse: *Your paper has some good ideas but it's hard to find them in all the chaff.*

chaff[2] (chaf) /tʃæf/ *v.* **1.** to tease; ridicule slightly; kid: [~ + *obj*]: *The schoolkids liked to chaff him about his ears.* [*no obj*]: *just chaffing around.* **—*n.*** [*noncount*] **2.** good-natured teasing.

chaf•finch (chaf′inch) /ˈtʃæfɪntʃ/ *n.* [*count*] a common finch of Europe and Asia, often kept as a pet.

cha•grin (shə grin′) /ʃəˈgrɪn/ *n., v.,* **-grined** or **-grinned, -grin•ing** or **-grin•ning. —*n.*** [*noncount*] **1.** a feeling of annoyance or humiliation: *To my complete chagrin I realized I didn't have enough money to pay for dinner.* **—*v.*** [~ + *obj; usually: be* + ~*-ed*] **2.** to annoy by disappointment or humiliation.

chain (chān) /tʃeyn/ *n.* **1.** a series of metal rings passing through one another, used for hauling, for supporting, or as decoration: [*count*]: *Fixing the bicycle chain was a greasy, dirty job.* [*noncount*]: *Buy a long length of chain for the motor.* **2. chains, a.** [*count; used with a plural verb*] strong, usually metal rings attached to a prisoner's hands or feet. **b.** [*noncount; usually, in* + ~] bondage; servitude: *to live one's life in chains.* **3.** [*count*] a series of things connected one after the other: *See if you can reconstruct the chain of events leading up to the murder.* **4.** [*count*] a range of mountains one after the other. **5.** [*count*] a number of businesses under one ownership or management: *a hotel chain.* **6.** [*count*] a unit of length equal to 100 feet (30 m) or 66 feet (20 m), used by surveyors. **—*v.*** [~ + *obj*] **7.** to fasten, tie up, or confine with or as if with a chain: *They chained the prisoners together.* [~ + *obj* + *up*]: *They chained the prisoners up.* [~ + *up* + *obj*]: *She chained up her dogs at night.*

chain′ mail′, *n.* MAIL[2] (def. 1).

chain′ reac′tion, *n.* [*count*] **1.** a reaction in which the substance produced in one reaction causes additional reactions: *a nuclear chain reaction.* **2.** a series of events in which each event is the result of the one coming before it, and the cause of the one following it.

chain′ saw′, *n.* [*count*] a portable power saw having teeth on a chain that rotates continuously. **—chain′-saw′,** *v.* [~ + *obj*]

chain′-smoke′, *v.,* **-smoked, -smok•ing.** to smoke

continually, esp. by lighting one cigarette, etc., from the preceding one: [*no obj*]: *He waited nervously, chain-smoking.* [~ + *obj*]: *She chain-smoked three packs a day.* —**chain′ smok′er, chain′-smok′er,** *n.* [*count*]

chair (châr) /tʃɛər/ *n.* [*count*] **1.** a seat, esp. for one person, usually having four legs for support and a rest for the back: *I pulled my chair up to the table.* See illustration at APARTMENT. **2.** a position of authority, such as of a judge; a seat of office or authority: *a chair in the department of business.* **3.** the person occupying such a seat of office, esp. one with the authority to run a meeting: *Address your remarks to the chair, please.* **4. the chair,** [*usually singular*] *Informal.* ELECTRIC CHAIR: *sentenced the prisoner to the chair.* —*v.* [~ + *obj*] **5.** to direct the running of (a meeting, etc.); act as chairperson of: *She chaired the meeting on the sales campaign.* —***Idiom.*** **6. take** (or **be in**) **the chair,** to open or preside at a meeting; act as chairperson. —**Usage.** In many cases the word *chair* has become the simplest term to use for both *chairman* and *chairperson.* Many speakers do not wish to offend women by using the word *chairman,* while others feel it is unnatural to use *chairperson.* The result is that *chair* has become the preferred word for the meaning "person who occupies a seat or position of authority, or who directs the running of a meeting, department, etc."

chair•lift (châr′lift′) /ˈtʃɛərˌlɪft/ *n.* [*count*] a series of chairs hanging from a cable driven by motors, for carrying skiers up the side of a slope.

chair•man (châr′mən) /ˈtʃɛərmən/ *n.* [*count*], *pl.* **-men.** the officer in charge of running a meeting, etc., or the head of a board or department. —**chair′man•ship′,** *n.* [*noncount*] —**Usage.** See CHAIR.

chair•per•son (châr′pûr′sən) /ˈtʃɛərˌpɜrsən/ *n.* [*count*] a person in charge of running a meeting, etc., or the head of a board or department. —**chair′per′son•ship′,** *n.* [*noncount*] —**Usage.** See CHAIR.

chaise (shāz) /ʃeyz/ *n.* [*count*] **1.** a light, open carriage for two persons, usually with a hood and two wheels, pulled by a horse. **2.** CHAISE LONGUE.

chaise longue (shāz′ lông′) /ˈʃeyzˈ lɔŋ/ *n.* [*count*], *pl.* **chaise longues, chaises longues** (shāz′) /ˈʃeyz/. a chair for reclining, having a seat lengthened to form a complete leg rest. Also called **chaise lounge** (shāz′ lounj′, chās′) /ˈʃeyzˈ lawndʒ, ˈtʃeys/.

cha•let (sha lā′, shal′ā) /ʃæˈley, ˈʃæley/ *n.* [*count*] **1.** a Swiss wooden house common in the Alps, having a very steeply slanting roof and often decorative carving. **2.** a cottage, house, ski lodge, etc., built in this style.

chal•ice (chal′is) /ˈtʃælɪs/ *n.* [*count*] **1.** a cup for the wine of the Eucharist in the Christian church. **2.** a drinking cup or goblet.

chalk (chôk) /tʃɔk/ *n.* [*noncount*] **1.** a soft, white, powdery substance made of limestone. **2.** a solid piece of chalk or chalklike substance for marking or writing on a blackboard. —*v.* [~ + *obj*] **3.** to apply with chalk: *He chalked a few numbers on the blackboard.* **4. chalk up, a.** [~ + *up* + *obj*] to score or earn, such as points in a game: gain: *chalked up several victories in a row pitching for the Tigers.* **b.** [~ + *up* + *obj* + *to* + *obj*] to give as a reason; attribute: *Chalk up that bad episode to lack of experience.* [~ + *obj* + *up* + *to* + *obj*]: *Chalk it up to lack of experience.*

chalk•board (chôk′bôrd′, -bōrd′) /ˈtʃɔkˌbɔrd, -ˌbowrd/ *n.* [*count*] a blackboard.

chalk•y (chô′kē) /ˈtʃɔkiy/ *adj.,* **-i•er, -i•est.** of, covered with, or like chalk: *a white, chalky face; a chalky taste.*

chal•lenge (chal′inj) /ˈtʃælɪndʒ/ *n., v.,* **-lenged, -leng•ing.** —*n.* **1.** a call to compete in a contest or in a fight: [*count*]: *I accept your challenge to a duel.* [*noncount*]: *A hint of challenge appeared on his face.* **2.** something that by its nature is a test or a difficult thing to accomplish: [*count*]: *Space exploration offers a challenge to humankind.* [*noncount*]: *I'd like work with a bit more challenge than this useless drudgery.* **3.** [*count;* ~ + *to*] a demand, request, or question to explain or justify something: *His criticism was a challenge to every proposal we had made.* —*v.* [~ + *obj*] **4.** [~ + *obj* + *to* + *obj*] to summon (someone) to a contest or fight: *He challenged his foe to a duel.* **5.** to test (someone) because of its difficulty: *This obstacle course will really challenge him.* **6.** to demand or question whether (something or someone) is correct, proper, or qualified: *The leaders of the revolt challenged the dictator's authority.* **7.** to halt and demand identification from: *The guard challenged the reporter when she tried to enter the army base.* —**chal′leng•er,** *n.* [*count*]

chal•leng•ing (chal′in jing) /ˈtʃælɪn dʒɪŋ/ *adj.* **1.** testing someone's skill or ability because of its difficulty: *The exam was a challenging test.* **2.** questioning or demanding; defiant: *His daughter gave him a challenging glare.*

cham•ber (chām′bər) /ˈtʃeymbər/ *n.* [*count*] **1.** a private room in a house or apartment, esp. a bedroom. **2.** a room in a palace or an official home: *We saw the queen's meeting chambers.* **3. a.** a law-making group or a branch of such a group: *the upper and lower chambers of a legislature.* **b.** a room housing such an assembly. **4. chambers,** [*plural*] a place where a judge listens to matters not needing action in the open courtroom. **5.** an enclosed space; cavity: *a chamber of the heart.* —*adj.* [*before a noun*] **6.** of, relating to, or performing chamber music: *chamber players.*

cham•ber•lain (chām′bər lin) /ˈtʃeymbərlɪn/ *n.* [*count*] **1.** an official who manages the living quarters of a noble family. **2.** a high official of a royal court.

cham•ber•maid (chām′bər mād′) /ˈtʃeymbərˌmeyd/ *n.* [*count*] a maid who cleans bedrooms and bathrooms.

cham′ber mu′sic, *n.* [*noncount*] music for performing in a room and played by a small group of instruments.

cham′ber of com′merce, *n.* [*count*], *pl.* **chambers of commerce.** an association made up mostly of people in business, to promote the commercial interests of an area.

cham′ber pot′, *n.* [*count*] a pot-shaped container used as a bedroom toilet.

cha•me•le•on (kə mē′lē ən, -mēl′yən) /kəˈmiyliyən, -ˈmiylyən/ *n.* [*count*] **1.** a slow-moving lizard having the ability to change color to match its surroundings. **2.** a person who changes his or her mind too easily or who is fickle. —**cha•me′le•on•like′,** *adj.*: *their chameleonlike ability to shift opinion.*

cham•ois (sham′ē; *for 1 also* sham wä′) /ˈʃæmiy; *for 1 also* ʃæmˈwɑ/ *n., pl.* **cham•ois, cham•oix** (sham′ēz; *for 1 also* sham wä′) /ˈʃæmiyz; *for 1 also* ʃæmˈwɑ/ **1.** [*count*] a small antelope much like a goat, of the high mountains of Europe. **2.** [*noncount*] a soft, pliable leather from various animal skins dressed with oil. **3.** [*count*] a piece of this leather. Also, **shammy** (for defs. 2, 3).

cham•o•mile or **cam•o•mile** (kam′ə mīl′, -mēl′) /ˈkæməˌmayl, -ˌmiyl/ *n.* [*count*] a plant having strong-smelling leaves, used in medicine and to make tea.

champ[1] (champ, chomp) /tʃæmp, tʃɒmp/ also **chomp,** *v.* to bite upon or grind (something), esp. impatiently: [~ + *obj*]: *The horses champed the oats.* [*no obj*]: *The kids were champing noisily at the dinner table.*

champ[2] (champ) /tʃæmp/ *n.* [*count*] *Informal.* a champion: *The champ knocked out five of his opponents.*

cham•pagne (sham pān′) /ʃæmˈpeyn/ *n.* a sparkling dry white wine from the region of Champagne in France, or a similar wine produced elsewhere: [*noncount*]: *Champagne has a lot of bubbles in it.* [*count*]: *domestic and imported champagnes.*

cham•pi•on (cham′pē ən) /ˈtʃæmpiyən/ *n.* [*count*] **1.** a person or thing defeating all opponents: *He was the spelling champion last year.* [*as a title; no article*]: *became champion of the world.* **2.** a person who fights for or defends any person or cause: *became a champion of the poor.* —*v.* [~ + *obj*] **3.** to act as champion of (a cause); defend; support: *He championed the cause of liberty.*

cham•pi•on•ship (cham′pē ən ship′) /ˈtʃæmpiyənˌʃɪp/ *n.* **1.** [*count*] the distinction or condition of being a champion. **2.** [*noncount*] advocacy or defense: *championship of human rights.* **3.** [*count*] a contest to determine a champion.

chance (chans) /tʃæns/ *n., v.,* **chanced, chanc•ing,** *adj.* —*n.* **1.** [*noncount*] the part of an event that seems unpredictable; luck or fortune: *Chance seems to have a lot to do with getting a job these days.* **2.** a possibility or probability of anything happening; likelihood: [*count*]: *Your chances of success improve the harder you work.* [*noncount*]: *not much chance of his changing his mind.* **3. chances,** [*plural*] probability: *The chances are that the train hasn't left yet.* **4.** [*count*] an opportunity: *Now is your chance.* **5.** [*count*] a risk or hazard: *He took an awfully big chance investing all that money.* **6.** [*count*] a ticket in a lottery or prize drawing: *I bought five chances for a dollar each.* —*v.* **7.** [*It* + ~ + *(that) clause*] to happen accidentally or in an unplanned way: *It chanced that our arrivals coincided.* **8.** [~ + *to* + *verb*] to do something accidentally: *I chanced to overhear their conversations.* **9.** [~ + *obj; often:* ~ + *it*] to take the chances or risks of; risk: *I'll have to chance it, whatever the outcome.*

10. chance on or **upon,** [~ + *on/upon* + *obj*] to meet unexpectedly and accidentally: *I chanced upon her at the party last night.* **—*adj.*** [*before a noun*] **11.** not planned or expected; accidental: *a chance occurrence.* **—*Idiom.* 12. by any chance,** possibly: *Do you think that by any chance you'd be free for dinner?* **13. by chance,** unintentionally; accidentally: *I met her by chance.* **14. on the (off) chance,** counting on the (slight) possibility: *On the off chance that the painters are finished by tonight, you can sand the floors tomorrow.*

chan•cel (chan′səl) /ˈtʃænsəl/ *n.* [*count*] the space around the altar of a church.

chan•cel•lor (chan′sə lər, -slər) /ˈtʃænsələr, -slər/ *n.* [*count*] **1.** the chief minister of state in some governments, as in Germany. **2.** the chief administrative officer in some American universities. **3.** *Brit.* the honorary head of a university. **—chan′cel•lor•ship′,** *n.* [*noncount*]

chanc•y (chan′sē) /ˈtʃænsiy/ *adj.,* **-i•er, -i•est.** hazardous or risky; uncertain: *The invasion turned out to be pretty chancy.* **—chanc′i•ness,** *n.* [*noncount*]

chan•de•lier (shan′dl ēr′) /ˌʃændḷˈɪər/ *n.* [*count*] a branched holder for lights that is hung from a ceiling.

change (chānj) /tʃeyndʒ/ *v.,* **changed, chang•ing,** *n.* **—*v.* 1.** to (cause to) become different: [~ + *obj*]: *She decided to change her name.* [~ + *obj* (+ *from* + *obj*) + *to* + *obj*]: *She changed her name (from Smetana) to Smithers.* [*no obj*]: *Things change.* [~ + *from* + *obj* + *to* + *obj*]: *The mood changed from happiness to gloom.* **2.** to (cause to) become something different; transform: [~ + *obj* + *into* + *obj*]: *The witch changed the prince into a toad.* [~ + *into* + *obj*]: *His kids thought he changed into a grouchy old man.* **3.** to exchange for another or others: [~ + *obj*]: *I changed the lightbulb in the hall.* **4.** to transfer from one (bus, etc.) to another: [~ + *obj*]: *I changed buses and went on to Sixth Street.* [*no obj*]: *You have to change at 42nd Street for the shuttle.* **5.** [~ + *obj* (+ *for* + *obj*)] to give or get smaller money in exchange for: *Can you change this twenty for two fives and a ten?* **6.** [~ + *obj* + *to/for* + *obj*] to give or get foreign money in exchange for: *I need to change these American dollars to Tanzanian shillings.* **7.** to remove and replace the coverings or clothes of: [~ + *obj*]: *to change a baby.* [*no obj; often:~ + out of/into*]: *Let me change out of these work clothes into something more comfortable.* **—*n.* 8.** the act of changing or the result of being changed: [*count*]: *a change in her routine.* [*noncount*]: *no change in the patient's condition.* **9.** [*count*] a replacement or substitution: *The car needs an oil change every 5,000 miles.* **10.** [*count; usually singular*] a fresh set of clothes: *Be sure to pack a change of clothes for the trip.* **11.** [*noncount*] new and different things, actions, experiences; novelty: *We need to hire a person who adjusts easily to change.* **12.** [*noncount*] the passing from one state, condition, etc., to another: *social change.* **13.** [*noncount*] the money returned when the amount offered in payment is larger than the amount owed: *Your change from a dollar is sixteen cents.* **14.** [*noncount*] coins: *rattling the change in his pocket.* **—*Idiom.* 15. for a change,** in order to do something differently from the usual way: *The busy executive began to stay home for a change.* **—chang′er,** *n.* [*count*]

change•able (chān′jə bəl) /ˈtʃeyndʒəbəl/ *adj.* likely to change often; unpredictable: *He has a changeable nature.*

change•ling (chānj′ling) /ˈtʃeyndʒlɪŋ/ *n.* [*count*] an infant exchanged for another child usually secretly.

change′ of life′, *n.* MENOPAUSE.

change•o•ver (chānj′ō′vər) /ˈtʃeyndʒˌowvər/ *n.* [*count*] a conversion from one condition, system, machine, etc., to another: *a changeover from oil heat to gas.*

chan•nel (chan′l) /ˈtʃænḷ/ *n., v.,* **-neled, -nel•ing** or *(esp. Brit.)* **-nelled, -nel•ling. —*n.*** [*count*] **1.** the bottom or deeper part of a waterway: *The twenty-foot channel in the harbor was marked by buoys.* **2.** a route for boats between two bodies of water. **3.** a narrow body of water between a continent and an island: *the English Channel.* **4.** a course into which something may be moved or directed: *channels of trade.* **5. channels,** [*plural*] the official course of communicating or of getting things done: *You'll have to go through channels to reach the governor.* **6.** a frequency band or wavelength on which radio and television signals are broadcast: *Switch to another channel; I don't like this program.* **—*v.* 7.** [~ + *obj* (+ *to/into* + *obj*)] to direct toward or into a course of action: *You need to channel your energy to more constructive uses.*

chant (chant) /tʃænt/ *n.* [*count*] **1.** a short, simple melody or song, such as a religious song. **2.** a phrase, slogan, or the like that is repeated, as by a crowd: *The chant went up, "Four more years! Four more years!"* **—*v.* 3.** to sing to a chant, esp. in a church service: [~ + *obj*]: *chanting psalms.* [*no obj*]: *chanting softly in church.* **4.** to repeat (a phrase, etc.), often insistently: [~ + *obj*]: *The workers were chanting slogans.* [*used with quotations*]: *"Down with the great Satan!" they chanted.* [*no obj*]: *chanting in rhythm.*

Cha•nu•kah (ᴋʜä′nə kə, hä′-) /ˈxɑnəkə, ˌhɑ-/ *n.* HANUKKAH.

cha•os (kā′os) /ˈkeyɒs/ *n.* [*noncount*] a state of confusion or disorder: *Economic chaos resulted from his policies.*

cha•ot•ic (kā ot′ik) /keyˈɒtɪk/ *adj.* marked by chaos. **—cha•ot′i•cal•ly,** *adv.*

chap[1] (chap) /tʃæp/ *v.,* **chapped, chap•ping.** to (cause to) become cracked, roughened, and reddened: [~ + *obj*]: *The wind chapped her face and lips.* [*no obj*]: *Her lips chapped in the cold.* **—chapped,** *adj.*: *Heal those dry, chapped lips with this special cream.*

chap[2] (chap) /tʃæp/ *n.* [*count*] *Chiefly Brit.* fellow; guy: *I like that chap, don't you?*

chap. or **Chap.,** an abbreviation of: chapter.

chap•ar•ral (shap′ə ral′, chap′-) /ˌʃæpəˈræl, ˌtʃæp-/ *n.* [*count*] a thick, dense growth of shrubs or small trees: *the high chaparral at the top of the canyon.*

chap•el (chap′əl) /ˈtʃæpəl/ *n.* [*count*] **1.** a separate part of a church, or a small structure like a church, used for special religious services. **2.** a room or building for worship that is in or is part of another institution, such as a hospital: *We waited in the hospital chapel.*

chap•er•on or **chap•er•one** (shap′ə rōn′) /ˈʃæpəˌrown/ *n., v.,* **-oned, -on•ing. —*n.*** [*count*] **1.** a person, usually an older woman, who accompanies a young unmarried woman in public. **2.** a person who attends a party or dance for young people to supervise their behavior. **—*v.* 3.** [~ + *obj*] to attend or accompany as chaperon: *The high school teachers chaperoned the dance.* **4.** [*no obj*] to act as a chaperon: *asked the teachers if they would chaperon.*

chap•lain (chap′lin) /ˈtʃæplɪn/ *n.* [*count*] a member of the clergy who serves with a military unit, or who works with the chapel of a college or hospital. **—chap′lain•cy,** *n.* [*noncount*]

chaps (chaps, shaps) /tʃæps, ʃæps/ *n.* [*plural*] sturdy leather leggings like wide-legged trousers, worn over work pants, typically by cowboys.

chap•ter (chap′tər) /ˈtʃæptər/ *n.* **1.** a main division of a book or the like, usually having a number or title: [*count*]: *The author finished one chapter of his book every six weeks.* [~ + *number*]: *Chapter 6 was all about the solar system.* **2.** [*count*] an important part or division of anything: *He began a new chapter in his life at the new university.*

char[1] (chär) /tʃɑr/ *v.,* **charred, char•ring. 1.** to burn or (cause to) become reduced to charcoal: [~ + *obj*]: *The flames had charred the corpses beyond recognition.* [*no obj*]: *The corpses charred in the fire.* **2.** [~ + *obj*] to burn slightly; scorch: *The flame charred the steak.*

char[2] (chär) /tʃɑr/ *n., v.,* **charred, char•ring.** *Chiefly Brit.* **—*n.*** [*count*] **1.** CHARWOMAN. **—*v.*** [*no obj*] **2.** to work at cleaning offices or houses.

char., an abbreviation of: character.

char•a•banc (shar′ə bang′, -bangk′) /ˈʃærəˌbæŋ, -ˌbæŋk/ *n.* [*count*] *Brit.* a large bus used on sightseeing tours.

char•ac•ter (kar′ik tər) /ˈkærɪktər/ *n.* **1.** [*noncount*] the collection of qualities that form the individual nature of a person or thing, and that make it different from others: *The chief flaw in her character was impatience.* **2.** [*noncount*] one such feature or characteristic: *His note was mostly positive in character.* **3.** [*noncount*] moral or ethical strength; honesty: *a woman of strong character.* **4.** [*noncount*] reputation: *a stain on one's character.* **5.** [*noncount*] special, often interesting qualities: *an old pub with a lot of character.* **6.** [*count*] a person, esp. with reference to behavior: *A suspicious character was standing in the hallway.* **7.** [*count*] an odd or unusual person: *She's quite a character, isn't she?* **8.** [*count*] a person represented in a drama, story, etc.: *One of the characters is Hamlet.* **9.** [*count*] a symbol used in a system of writing: *Chinese characters.* **—*adj.*** [*before a noun*] **10.** (of a role in a play, film, etc.) having or requiring unusual qualities: *played some character parts, mostly as a villain.* **11.** (of an actor) acting or specializing in such roles: *became a character actor, playing the bad guy in Westerns.* **—*Idiom.* 12. in** (or **out of**) **character,** like (or not like) the way that is usual for someone: *She seems so cranky today; that's very out of character.*

char•ac•ter•is•tic (kar′ik tə ris′tik) /ˌkærɪktə'rɪstɪk/ *adj.* **1.** showing the character of a person or thing; typical: *It was characteristic of her not to take all the credit.* **—*n.*** [*count*] **2.** a quality (of someone or something) that is typical or special: *She had the high forehead that is a characteristic of that family.* **—char′ac•ter•is′ti•cal•ly,** *adv.*

char•ac•ter•ize (kar′ik tə rīz′) /'kærɪktəˌrayz/ *v.,* **-ized, -iz•ing. 1.** [~ + *obj*] to be a characteristic of: *Brutality characterizes that horrible dictator.* **2.** [~ + *obj* + *as*] to describe the character of: [~ + *obj* + *as* + *noun*]: *The president characterized that dictator as a scoundrel.* [~ + *obj* + *as* + *adjective*]: *I'd characterize him as crazy.* **—char•ac•ter•i•za•tion** (kar′ik tər ə zā′shən) /ˌkærɪktərə'zeyʃən/ *n.* [*count*]: *an actor's skillful characterizations.* [*noncount*]: *unfair characterization of librarians as old maids.*

cha•rade (shə rād′) /ʃə'reyd/ *n.* **1. charades,** [*noncount; used with a singular verb*] a game in which players act out, without speaking, a word, phrase, title, etc., often syllable by syllable, for members of their team to guess. **2.** [*count*] a word or phrase acted out in this game. **3.** [*count*] an obvious lie, pretense, or deception; travesty: *The whole job interview was just a charade.*

char•broil (chär′broil′) /'tʃɑrˌbrɔyl/ *v.* [~ + *obj*] to broil on a grill over a charcoal fire: *The burgers were charbroiled perfectly.*

char•coal (chär′kōl′) /'tʃɑrˌkowl/ *n.* **1.** [*noncount*] the black, carbon material made by heating a substance, such as wood, in very little air: *the summer smells of charcoal on the barbecue.* **2.** [*noncount*] a pencil of charcoal used for drawing. **3.** [*count*] a drawing made with charcoal: *a fine charcoal of the old town hall.*

charge (chärj) /tʃɑrdʒ/ *v.,* **charged, charg•ing,** *n.* **—*v.*** **1.** to ask (money) for payment: [*no obj*]: *Does the hotel charge for television?* [~ + *obj* (+ *for* + *obj*)]: *The hotel charges ten dollars extra a night for television.* **2.** to ask a price or fee of (someone): [~ + *obj* (+ *for*)]: *Did the hotel charge you for the cable television?* [~ + *obj* + *obj*]: *They charged us money for using the cable TV.* **3.** [~ + *obj*] to make a record of (a purchase) so that it can be paid for at some future time: *He charged the coat on his credit card.* **4. a.** [~ + *obj*] to attack; rush forward against: *The cavalry charged the enemy.* **b.** [*no obj*] to rush suddenly or violently: *They charged up the hill after her.* **5.** [~ + *obj* + *with* + *obj*] to accuse formally or in law: *They charged her with theft.* **6.** to command or give an order or instruction to: [~ + *obj* + *with* + *obj*]: *The vice-president charged his assistant with management of the budget.* [~ + *obj* + *to* + *verb*]: *The judge charged the jury to ignore the testimony.* **7.** [~ + *obj*] to fill or refill so as to make ready for use: *to charge a musket.* **8.** [~ + *obj*] to put electrical energy into: *They charged the dead battery and started the car.* **9.** [~ + *obj; usually: be* + ~*-ed* + *with* + *obj*] to fill, as with emotion; create a feeling in: *The air was charged with excitement.* **—*n.*** **10.** [*count*] a fee or price asked or imposed: *a charge of six dollars for admission.* **11.** [*noncount*] expense or cost: *We'll repair the damage at no charge.* **12.** [*count*] an attack, as of soldiers; onrush: *the Charge of the Light Brigade.* **13.** [*count*] someone or something given to one's care: *The young thieves were Fagin's charges.* **14.** [*count*] a command or instruction: *The judge issued a charge to the jury not to talk about the case.* **15.** [*count*] an accusation: *The state dropped the main charge of theft.* **16.** [*count*] a quantity of explosive to be set off at one time. **17.** [*count*] an amount of electricity put into a battery; electric charge. **18.** [*count; usually singular*] *Informal.* a thrill that causes pleasure or laughter; kick: *I got quite a charge out of watching her.* **—*Idiom.*** **19. in charge,** in command; having the care or responsibility: *Who's in charge here?* **20. take charge,** [~ + *of* + *obj*] to assume control or responsibility: *expected her to take charge of the situation.*

char•gé (shär zhā′, shär′zhā) /ʃɑr'ʒey, 'ʃɑrʒey/ *n.* [*count*], *pl.* **-gés** (-zhāz′; -zhāz) /-'ʒeyz; -ʒeyz/. a chargé d'affaires.

charge′ account′, *n.* [*count*] an account, esp. in a store, that permits a customer to buy goods and be billed at a later date: *to open a charge account.*

charge′ card′, *n.* [*count*] an identification card used to make purchases on a charge account.

chargé′ d'af•faires′ (də fâr′) /də'fɛər/ *n.* [*count*], *pl.* **chargés d'af•faires** (də fâr′) /də'fɛər/. an official placed in charge of diplomatic business when an ambassador or minister is absent.

charg•er (chär′jər) /'tʃɑrdʒər/ *n.* [*count*] **1.** a person or thing that charges or makes charges. **2.** WARHORSE (def. 1).

char•i•ot (char′ē ət) /'tʃæriyət/ *n.* [*count*] a light, horse-drawn vehicle, usually two-wheeled and having room for two standing riders, used in battle, races, etc.

cha•ris•ma (kə riz′mə) /kə'rɪzmə/ *n.* [*noncount*] a quality of an individual to attract people, lead them, etc.; personal magnetism: *a leader with great charisma.*

char•is•mat•ic (kar′iz mat′ik) /ˌkærɪz'mætɪk/ *adj.* **1.** of, having, or characteristic of charisma: *a charismatic leader.* **2.** [*usually: before a noun*] of or relating to Christians who seek a special religious experience, including speaking in tongues. **—*n.*** [*count*] **3.** a Christian who emphasizes such a religious experience.

char•i•ta•ble (char′i tə bəl) /'tʃærɪtəbəl/ *adj.* **1. a.** generous in gifts to aid the poor, etc.: *They were charitable people who always helped others.* **b.** of, concerned with, or organized for charity: *a charitable institution.* **2.** kindly or tolerant in judging people: *His charitable remarks were welcome after that nasty speech.* **—char′i•ta•ble•ness,** *n.* [*noncount*] **—char′i•ta•bly,** *adv.*

char•i•ty (char′i tē) /'tʃærɪtiy/ *n., pl.* **-ties. 1.** [*noncount*] gifts of money or things to aid the poor, ill, or helpless: *She was too proud to accept charity.* **2.** a charitable fund, organization, foundation, or institution: [*noncount*]: *He gave a lot to charity but no one ever knew it.* [*count*]: *Various charities provided food for the homeless.* **3.** [*noncount*] a generous feeling, esp. toward those in need: *to do something out of charity.* **4.** [*noncount*] tolerance in judging others: *He had the charity to forgive those hateful remarks.*

char•la•tan (shär′lə tn) /'ʃɑrlətn̩/ *n.* [*count*] a person who pretends to have knowledge or skill; fraud. **—char′la•tan•ism, char′la•tan•ry,** *n.* [*noncount*]

Charles•ton (chärlz′tən, chärl′stən) /'tʃɑrlztən, 'tʃɑrlstən/ *n.* [*count*] **1.** a vigorous, rhythmic ballroom dance popular in the 1920's. **—*v.*** [*no obj*] **2.** to dance the Charleston.

char′ley horse′ (chär′lē) /'tʃɑrliy/ *n.* [*count*] a cramp or a sore muscle, esp. in the leg, resulting from strain.

charm (chärm) /tʃɑrm/ *n.* **1.** a power of pleasing, as through beauty: [*noncount*]: *The child actress displayed a lot of charm.* [*count*]: *She used all her charms on him.* **2.** [*count*] a small ornament or trinket to be worn on a bracelet, necklace, etc.: *Many charms dangled from her bracelet.* **3.** [*count*] **a.** something worn or carried on one's person to bring good luck; amulet. **b.** words or chants that are said or sung to do this. **4.** [*noncount*] *Physics.* one of the properties of a quark. **—*v.*** [~ + *obj*] **5.** to delight or please greatly by attractiveness: *He charmed teachers and students alike. I was charmed to be asked to serve as president.* **—charm′er,** *n.* [*count*] **—charm′ing,** *adj.* **—charm′ing•ly,** *adv.* **—Related Words.** CHARM is a noun and a verb, CHARMING is an adjective: *He is a man of great charm. He charmed them into letting him stay. She is a charming young lady.*

charmed (chärmd) /tʃɑrmd/ *adj.* fortunate; lucky: *She led a charmed life.*

chart (chärt) /tʃɑrt/ *n.* [*count*] **1.** a sheet giving information in diagrams, such as graphs: *Check the chart to see which income bracket you are in.* See illustration at HOSPITAL. **2.** a map, esp. a map of the sea: *The captain took out the charts for the Southern Hemisphere.* **3.** an outline map showing special conditions or facts: *a weather chart.* **4. the charts,** [*plural*] the rankings of popular musical recordings, usually based on sales for the week: *was number one on the charts for ten weeks.* **—*v.*** [~ + *obj*] **5.** to make a chart of; make a record of: *to chart our economic development.* **6.** to plan: *to chart a course of action.*

char•ter (chär′tər) /'tʃɑrtər/ *n.* [*count*] **1.** a document issued by a state describing the conditions under which a body is organized: *The royal charter established that city almost 900 years ago.* **2.** a document defining the formal organization of an institution; constitution: *the Charter of the United Nations.* **3.** an arrangement by which a ship, airplane, etc., is hired for use at a particular time for a particular group: *organizing a charter for a trip to London.* **4.** a tour, vacation, or trip using such an arrangement: *a charter to London.* **—*v.*** [~ + *obj*] **5.** to issue a charter to: *to charter a bank.* **6.** to hire for use for a specified time: *The company chartered a bus for the picnic.* **—*adj.*** [*before a noun*] **7.** of or involving transportation specially hired or leased and not part of a regularly scheduled service: *a charter boat for fishing.*

char′ter mem′ber, *n.* [*count*] an original or founding member of a club, organization, etc.

char•wom•an (chär′wŏŏm′ən) /'tʃɑr,wʊmən/ *n.* [*count*], *pl.* **-wom•en.** a woman hired to do general cleaning.

char•y (châr′ē) /'tʃɛəriy/ *adj.* [*usually: be* + ~ + *of*], **-i•er, -i•est.** cautious or careful; wary: *chary of walking on icy sidewalks.* —**char•i•ly** (châr′ə lē) /'tʃɛərəliy/ *adv.* —**char′i•ness,** *n.* [*noncount*]

chase (chās) /tʃeys/ *v.,* **chased, chas•ing,** *n.* —*v.* **1.** to follow rapidly or intently in order to overtake, etc.; pursue: [~ + *obj*]: *The police chased the thief down the street.* [~ + *after* + *obj*]: *They chased after the thief.* **2.** to follow or devote one's attention to with the hope of attracting, etc.: [~ + *obj*]: *He's been chasing that job for years.* [~ + *after* + *obj*]: *He's been chasing after my job.* **3.** [~ + *obj*] to drive or send out by force: *The dog chased the cat out of the room.* **4.** [*no obj; often:* ~ + *around (+ verb-ing)*] to rush; hasten: *She was chasing around all afternoon looking for a gift.* —*n.* [*count*] **5.** the act of chasing; pursuit: *I gave up the chase and went home.* —***Idiom.*** **6. give chase,** to go in pursuit: *In a few minutes other police patrols gave chase.*

chas•er (chā′sər) /'tʃeysər/ *n.* [*count*] **1.** a person or thing that chases or pursues. **2.** a milder beverage taken after a strong drink of liquor: *whiskey with a beer chaser.*

chasm (kaz′əm) /'kæzəm/ *n.* [*count*] **1.** a wide, deep crack in the earth's surface. **2.** a wide split in opinions, etc., esp. one producing a break in relations: *to overcome the great chasm between our two nations.* —**chasmed,** *adj.*

chas•sis (chas′ē, shas′ē) /'tʃæsiy, 'ʃæsiy/ *n.* [*count*], *pl.* **chas•sis** (chas′ēz, shas′-) /'tʃæsiyz, 'ʃæs-/. **1.** the frame, wheels, and machinery of a motor vehicle. **2.** a frame for mounting the circuits of a radio or television set.

chaste (chāst) /tʃeyst/ *adj.,* **chast•er, chast•est. 1.** not engaging in sexual relations. **2.** decent and modest: *a chaste little kiss on the cheek.* —**chaste′ly,** *adv.: dressed chastely in a long bathrobe.* —**chaste′ness,** *n.* [*noncount*]

chas•ten (chā′sən) /'tʃeysən/ *v.* [~ + *obj*] **1.** to inflict punishment or suffering upon (someone) in order to correct: *The huge defeat chastened the overconfident team.* **2.** to make humble or restrained: *We were chastened by the knowledge of how little we really knew.* —**chas′ten•ing•ly,** *adv.*

chas•tise (chas tīz′, chas′tīz) /tʃæs'tayz, 'tʃæstayz/ *v.* [~ + *obj*], **-tised, -tis•ing. 1.** to punish severely, such as by beating. **2.** to criticize or scold severely: *The president chastised the press for its false reports.* —**chas•tise•ment** (chas′tiz mənt, chas tīz′-) /'tʃæstɪzmənt, tʃæs'tayz-/ *n.* [*noncount; count*] —**chas•tis′er,** *n.* [*count*]

chas•ti•ty (chas′ti tē) /'tʃæstɪtiy/ *n.* [*noncount*] the state or quality of being chaste: *Nuns take vows of chastity.*

chat (chat) /tʃæt/ *v.,* **chat•ted, chat•ting,** *n.* —*v.* **1.** [*no obj*] to talk in an informal way: *We chatted for a while in the café.* **2. chat up,** *Brit.* to talk to in a friendly way in order to try to flirt with (someone): [~ + *up* + *obj*]: *He was chatting up every girl who walked into the pub.* [~ + *obj* + *up*]: *chatting him up shamelessly.* —*n.* [*count*] **3.** an informal conversation: *a nice long chat about my future.*

châ•teau or **cha•teau** (sha tō′) /ʃæ'tow/ *n.* [*count*], *pl.* **-teaus** (-tōz′) /-'towz/ **-teaux** (-tōz′, -tō′) /-'towz, -'tow/. a castle or large country house or estate, esp. in France.

chat•tel (chat′l) /'tʃætl̩/ *n.* [*count*] an article of personal property that can be moved.

chat•ter (chat′ər) /'tʃætər/ *v.* [*no obj*] **1.** to talk rapidly and without purpose or direction; jabber: *The children were chattering about their weekend adventures.* **2.** to make rapid, speechlike sounds, such as a monkey or bird: *The monkeys were chattering in the forest.* **3.** to make a rapid noise caused by the striking together of separate parts: *teeth chattering from the cold.* —*n.* [*noncount*] **4.** rapid talk without a purpose: *Cut the chatter and let's get back to work.* **5.** the act or sound of chattering: *the chatter of printers.* —**chat′ter•er,** *n.* [*count*]

chat•ter•box (chat′ər boks′) /'tʃæt,ər bɒks/ *n.* [*count*] an overly talkative person.

chat•ty (chat′ē) /'tʃætiy/ *adj.,* **-ti•er, -ti•est. 1.** having or characterized by a friendly, informal style: *a long, chatty letter.* **2.** fond of chatting; eager to chat: *She sneaked out the side door to avoid her chatty neighbor.* —**chat•ti•ly** (chat′l ē) /'tʃætliy/ *adv.* —**chat′ti•ness,** *n.* [*noncount*]

chauf•feur (shō′fər, shō fûr′) /'ʃowfər, ʃow'fɜr/ *n.* [*count*] **1.** a person hired to drive an automobile for the owner. **2.** a person hired to drive a car or limousine for paying passengers. —*v.* [~ + *obj*] **3.** to drive (a vehicle) as a chauffeur: *chauffeured a limousine.* **4.** to transport by car: *to chauffeur the kids to school.*

chau•vin•ism (shō′və niz′əm) /'ʃowvə,nɪzəm/ *n.* [*noncount*] strong, unthinking devotion to one's country, a group, or one's sex, or to a cause.

chau•vin•ist (shō′və nist) /'ʃowvənɪst/ *n.* [*count*] **1.** someone who is characterized by chauvinism. —*adj.* **2.** having or showing the quality of chauvinism: *a chauvinist attitude.* —**chau′vin•is′tic,** *adj.*

cheap (chēp) /tʃiyp/ *adj.,* **-er, -est,** *adv., n.* —*adj.* **1.** costing very little; inexpensive: *We sat in the cheap seats at the circus.* **2.** [*usually; before a noun*] charging low prices: *a cheap store.* **3.** poorly made; inferior; shoddy: *Those cheap sneakers fell apart after only a few weeks.* **4.** costing little work or trouble: *Talk is cheap.* **5.** mean; cruel and deserving contempt: *a cheap joke.* **6.** [*be* + ~] of little account or value: *Life was cheap in that frontier town.* **7.** embarrassed: *I felt cheap after I had left her all alone.* **8.** stingy; miserly: *That was cheap of her, not to share any of her candy.* **9.** (of money) able to be borrowed at low interest: *Money is cheap and that should make housing starts rise.* —*adv.* **10.** at a low price or small cost: *I got that tape cheap.* —***Idiom.*** **11. on the cheap,** inexpensively; economically: *He did everything on the cheap.* —**cheap′ly,** *adv.* —**cheap′ness,** *n.* [*noncount*] —**Syn.** CHEAP, INEXPENSIVE both suggest low cost. CHEAP now often suggests that the item is poorly made or a showy imitation of something better: *a cheap fabric.* INEXPENSIVE emphasizes a low price (although more expensive than CHEAP) and suggests that the value is equal to the cost: *I didn't pay much for this inexpensive dress.* INEXPENSIVE is sometimes used to avoid the more insulting CHEAP.

cheap•en (chē′pən) /'tʃiypən/ *v.* [~ + *obj*] **1.** to make cheap or cheaper. **2.** to cause to seem less honorable: *cheapened herself by appearing in a sleazy film.* **3.** to decrease the quality of; make inferior.

cheap•skate (chēp′skāt′) /'tʃiyp,skeyt/ *n.* [*count*] *Informal.* a stingy person; one unwilling to spend money: *I felt like a cheapskate, tipping him only a quarter.*

cheat (chēt) /tʃiyt/ *v.* **1.** to lie (to) or behave dishonestly (with): [*no obj*]: *She had a bad experience in Italy with a street merchant who cheated.* [~ + *obj*]: *She cheated me.* [~ + *obj* + *out of* + *obj*]: *She cheated me out of my inheritance.* **2.** to violate rules or agreements: [*no obj*]: *They were afraid the enemy would cheat during any weapons inspection.* [~ + *at* + *obj*]: *to cheat at cards.* **3.** [*no obj*] to take an examination in a dishonest way, such as by having improper means of getting answers: *I'm sure she was cheating on that test.* **4. cheat on,** [~ + *on* + *obj*] to be sexually unfaithful to (someone). **5.** [~ + *obj*] to get away from; escape from: *to cheat death.* —*n.* [*count*] **6.** a person who cheats; an impostor: *She's a cheat and a crook.* **7.** an act that cheats or deceives; swindle.

check (chek) /tʃɛk/ *v.* **1.** [~ + *obj*] to stop the motion of suddenly or with force; restrain: *The pilot checked his speed and landed quickly.* **2.** [~ + *obj*] to examine or test the correctness of, such as by comparison: *I checked the answers on the exam.* **3.** [*no obj*] to prove to be right: *Well, everything checks; the butler committed the murder.* **4.** [~ + *obj*] to inspect or test the condition, safety, etc., of: *We had our mechanic check the car for any damage.* **5.** to mark so as to indicate choice, completion, etc.: [~ + *obj*]: *Check the box next to the item you think is right.* [~ + *off* + *obj*]: *I checked off the items on the shopping list.* [~ + *obj* + *off*]: *I checked them off as I went down the list.* **6.** to search through to find (something); make an inquiry (into): [~ + *obj*]: *You'll have to check the files for the letter.* [~ + *into* + *obj*]: *You'll have to check into those missing files, too.* **7.** [~ + *obj*] to leave (personal belongings) to be kept temporarily: *Check your coats at the door.* **8.** [~ + *obj*] to leave (baggage) to be sent on, as at an airport: *We checked our suitcases and walked to the gate for our flight.* **9.** [~ + *obj*] to mark with or in a pattern of squares: *The fabric was checked.* **10. check in,** [*no obj*] to register or report one's arrival: *Check in at the counter and pick up your boarding passes there.* **11. check (up) on,** [~ (+ *up*) + *on* + *obj*] to investigate or inspect: *wondered why they were checking (up) on him.* **12. check out, a.** [*no obj*] to leave a hotel, etc., officially, esp. after settling one's account: *Let's check out early and get on the road by 6:30.* **b.** [*no obj*] to prove to be right or true: *Well, his story checks out; there were witnesses who saw him.* **c.** to find out if something is right or true: [~ + *out* + *obj*]:

Check out his story with the people in the bar. [~ + *obj* + *out*]: *You'd better check him out again; I'm not sure he's innocent.* **d.** to prove to be in working condition or safe: [*no obj*]: *This engine checks out; let's see if the problem occurs in the next one.* [~ + *out* + *obj*]: *Check out boiler number 10 and see if there's an overload.* [~ + *obj* + *out*]: *We'd better check it out.* **e.** to lend or borrow (an item) officially, as from a library: [~ + *out* + *obj*]: *You can check out six books at a time.* [~ + *obj* + *out*]: *You can check six books out.* **f.** [*no obj*] *Informal.* to leave suddenly: *He checked out of there fast.* **g.** *Slang.* to examine carefully: [~ + *out* + *obj*]: *Hey, check out this car.* [~ + *obj* + *out*]: *I've got quality watches for sale; check them out.* **—*n.*** **13.** Also, *Brit.*, **cheque.** a written order directing a bank to pay money: [*count*]: *He wrote her a check for fifty-five dollars.* [*noncount; by* + ~]: *I'll pay for this by check.* See illustration at BANK. **14.** [*count*] a slip showing an amount owed, esp. at a restaurant: *The waitress wrote out our check.* **15.** [*count*] a ticket given for items left in a checkroom, to customers waiting to be served, etc.: *I lost my claim check for the luggage.* **16.** [*count*] a mark, often indicated by (✓), to indicate that something has been noted, etc.: *I put a check next to the items that you need to revise.* **17.** [*count*] a search or examination: *a quick check of the company records.* **18.** [*count*] a test or inspection, such as to find out quality or performance: *The mechanic ran a check on the engine.* **19.** [*count*] a means of, or an act of, stopping or restraining: *a check on his speed in the race.* **20.** [*count*] a pattern formed of squares: *pants with checks.* **21.** [*noncount*] (in chess) the exposure of the king to direct attack: *Your king is in check; you must move it or eliminate the attacker.* **—*adj.*** [*usually: before a noun*] **22.** serving to stop, control, etc.: *a check valve.* **23.** ornamented with a checkered pattern; checkered: *check pants.* **—*interj.*** **24.** (used as a call in chess to warn that an opponent's king is in check). **25.** *Informal.* all right! agreed!: *"We'll be back for our cut, OK?" "Check!"* **—*Idiom.*** **26. in check,** kept controlled; under restraint: *to hold one's anger in check.*

check•book (chek′bo͝ok′) /ˈtʃɛkˌbʊk/ *n.* [*count*] a pad of blank checks for paying money from an account.

checked (chekt) /tʃɛkt/ *adj.* having a pattern of colored squares or checks: *checked pants and jacket.*

check•er[1] (chek′ər) /ˈtʃɛkər/ *n.* **1.** [*count*] a small, usually red or black disk of plastic or wood used in playing checkers. **2. checkers,** Also called, *Brit.*, **draughts.** [*noncount; used with a singular verb*] a game played by two persons, each with 12 playing pieces, on a checkerboard: *Checkers is a good introduction to chess.* Also, *Brit.*, **chequer.**

check•er[2] (chek′ər) /ˈtʃɛkər/ *n.* [*count*] **1.** a person or thing that checks. **2.** a cashier, as in a supermarket. **3.** an employee of a checkroom.

check•er•board (chek′ər bôrd′, -bōrd′) /ˈtʃɛkərˌbɔrd, -ˌbowrd/ *n.* [*count*] **1.** a board marked into 64 squares of two colors, in eight vertical and eight horizontal rows, on which checkers or chess is played. **2.** a design resembling this.

check•ered (chek′ərd) /ˈtʃɛkərd/ *adj.* showing changes in different directions: *a checkered past.*

check′ing account′, *n.* [*count*] a bank account against which checks can be written by the depositor.

check•list or **check list** (chek′list′) /ˈtʃɛkˌlɪst/ *n.* [*count*] Also, **check′ list′.** a list of items for comparing, checking correctness, or for other checking purposes.

check•mate (chek′māt′) /ˈtʃɛkˌmeyt/ *n.*, *v.*, **-mat•ed, -mat•ing,** *interj.* **—*n.*** [*noncount*] **1.** an act in chess of arranging pieces so that the opponent's king is placed into a check from which it cannot escape: *The game ended in checkmate.* **2.** a thwarting or defeat: *It was checkmate for that dictator once the UN agreed on action.* **—*v.*** [~ + *obj*] **3.** to maneuver (someone) so that no escape is possible; mate: *He checkmated his opponent in twenty moves.* **4.** to check completely; defeat: *The dictator found himself checkmated between the embargo and the coup attempts.* **—*interj.*** **5.** (used by a chess player when placing the opponent's king in checkmate and ending the game).

check•out or **check-out** (chek′out′) /ˈtʃɛkˌawt/ *n.* **1.** [*noncount*] the procedure of leaving and paying for one's quarters at a hotel: *Checkout is at the front desk.* **2.** [*noncount*] the time by which a guest at a hotel must leave a room: *Checkout is at noon.* **3.** [*count*] Also called **check′out count′er.** a counter where customers pay for purchases, as in a supermarket.

check•point (chek′point′) /ˈtʃɛkˌpɔynt/ *n.* [*count*] a place along a border, etc., where travelers are stopped for inspection.

check•room (chek′ro͞om′, -ro͝om′) /ˈtʃɛkˌruwm, -ˌrʊm/ *n.* [*count*] a room where hats, coats, parcels, etc., may be checked.

check•up (chek′up′) /ˈtʃɛkˌʌp/ *n.* [*count*] a physical examination by a physician.

ched•dar (ched′ər) /ˈtʃɛdər/ *n.* [*noncount*] a hard smooth cheese that varies in flavor from mild to sharp.

cheek (chēk) /tʃiyk/ *n.* **1.** [*count*] either side of the face below the eye and above the jaw: *She kissed me on the cheek.* **2.** [*noncount*] rude or disrespectful behavior; impudence: *He's got a lot of cheek, talking back to his parents.* **—*Idiom.*** **3. cheek by jowl,** [*noncount; often:* ~ + *with*] very close in intentions, ideas, etc.; side by side: *The vice-president is cheek by jowl with the boss on this deal.*

cheek•bone (chēk′bōn′) /ˈtʃiykˌbown/ *n.* [*count*] the bone that forms the top part of the cheek below the eye: *a fashion model with high cheekbones.*

cheek•y (chē′kē) /ˈtʃiykiy/ *adj.*, **-i•er, -i•est.** rude or disrespectful; insolent. **—cheek•i•ly** (chē′kə lē) /ˈtʃiykəliy/ *adv.*: *She answered cheekily that she'd do it when she was good and ready.* **—cheek′i•ness,** *n.* [*noncount*]

cheep (chēp) /tʃiyp/ *v.* [*no obj*] **1.** to chirp; peep. **—*n.*** [*count*] **2.** a chirp.

cheer (chēr) /tʃɪər/ *n.* **1.** [*count*] a shout of encouragement, etc.: *Cheers went up as the champion entered the ring.* **2.** [*count*] a special shout or words to chant, used by spectators to encourage an athletic team, contestant, etc. **3.** [*noncount*] gladness, gaiety, or animation: *The news of her recovery filled us with cheer.* **4.** [*noncount*] something that gives comfort or joy: *words of cheer.* **5.** [*noncount*] feeling or spirits: *Be of good cheer.* **6.** [*noncount*] food and drink: *to invite friends for Christmas cheer.* **—*interj.*** **7. cheers,** (used as a greeting or toast): *They raised their glasses and said "Cheers!"* **—*v.*** **8.** to give shouts of approval, etc., to (someone or something): [~ + *obj*]: *They cheered his remarks about tax cuts.* [*no obj*]: *When the champ entered the ring, the crowd cheered.* **9.** [~ + *obj*] to gladden; raise the spirits of: *The good news cheered her.* **10. cheer on,** to encourage or urge on or forward: [~ + *on* + *obj*]: *The crowd cheered on their hometown heroes.* [~ + *obj* + *on*]: *My fans cheered me on just when I was getting tired.* **11. cheer up,** to become or make happier or more cheerful: [*no obj*]: *Cheer up, you'll be out of here in no time.* [~ + *obj* + *up*]: *Let's cheer him up.* [~ + *up* + *obj*]: *We have to work harder at cheering up the patients.* **—cheer′ing•ly,** *adv.*

cheer•ful (chēr′fəl) /ˈtʃɪərfəl/ *adj.* **1.** full of cheer; happy; in good spirits: *She was especially cheerful that morning.* **2.** pleasant; bright; causing a feeling of cheer: *the cheerful surroundings of her room.* **3.** showing good spirits: *a cheerful song.* **4.** [*before a noun*] wholehearted; willing: *a cheerful giver.* **—cheer′ful•ly,** *adv.* **—cheer′ful•ness,** *n.* [*noncount*]

cheer•i•o (chēr′ē ō′, chēr′ē ō′) /ˈtʃɪəriyˌow, ˌtʃɪəriyˈow/ *interj.* *Chiefly Brit.* **1.** good-bye; farewell. **2.** (used to express good wishes).

cheer•lead•er (chēr′lē′dər) /ˈtʃɪərˌliydər/ *n.* [*count*] one who leads spectators in cheering, esp. at an athletic event.

cheer•less (chēr′lis) /ˈtʃɪərlɪs/ *adj.* gloomy; dreary: *a cheerless hotel room.* **—cheer′less•ly,** *adv.* **—cheer′less•ness,** *n.* [*noncount*]

cheer•y (chēr′ē) /ˈtʃɪəriy/ *adj.*, **-i•er, -i•est.** **1.** being in good spirits; cheerful; happy: *She looked quite cheery that morning.* **2.** showing cheer; enlivening: *a cheery letter; a cheery smile.* **—cheer•i•ly** (chēr′ə lē) /ˈtʃɪərəliy/ *adv.* **—cheer′i•ness,** *n.* [*noncount*]

cheese[1] (chēz) /tʃiyz/ *n.* **1.** a food prepared from the curds of milk separated from the whey: [*noncount*]: *Cheese sometimes has a strong smell.* [*count*]: *several good cheeses from France.* **2.** [*count*] a mass of this substance: *a huge cheese in the shop.*

cheese[2] (chēz) /tʃiyz/ *n.* [*count; usually: big* + ~] *Slang.* an important or powerful person: *He's the big cheese of the operation in South America.*

cheese•burg•er (chēz′bûr′gər) /ˈtʃiyzˌbɜrgər/ *n.* [*count*] a hamburger topped with a melted slice of cheese.

cheese•cake (chēz′kāk′) /ˈtʃiyzˌkeyk/ *n.* **1.** a cake with a firm texture made with sweetened cream cheese: [*noncount*]: *a slice of cheesecake.* [*count*]: *She helped to make a cheesecake with cherry filling.* **2.** [*noncount*] *Informal.* photographs of attractive women with few or no clothes on.

cheese•cloth (chēz′klôth′, -kloth′) /ˈtʃiyzˌklɔθ, -ˌklɒθ/ *n.* [*noncount*] a lightweight cotton cloth of loose, open plain weave.

chees•y (chē′zē) /ˈtʃiyziy/ *adj.,* **-i•er, -i•est. 1.** of or like cheese: *a cheesy taste.* **2.** *Slang.* inferior or cheap; shoddy. —**chees′i•ness,** *n.* [*noncount*]

chee•tah (chē′tə) /ˈtʃiytə/ *n.* [*count*] a swift, long-legged, black-spotted cat of SW Asia and Africa.

chef (shef) /ʃɛf/ *n.* [*count*] **1.** the chief cook, esp. in a restaurant, responsible for the menu and in charge of food preparation. **2.** any cook.

chef-d'oeu•vre (*Fr.* she dœ′vʀᵊ) /*Fr.* ʃɛˈdœvrᵊ/ *n.* [*count*], *pl.* **chefs-d'oeu•vre** (she dœ′vʀᵊ) /ʃɛˈdœvrᵊ/. a masterpiece.

chem., an abbreviation of: **1.** chemical. **2.** chemist. **3.** chemistry.

chem•i•cal (kem′i kəl) /ˈkɛmɪkəl/ *n.* [*count*] **1.** a substance produced by or used in chemistry: *poisonous chemicals.* **2. chemicals,** [*plural*] *Slang.* narcotic or mind-altering drugs: *a dependency on chemicals.* —*adj.* [*before a noun*] **3.** of, used in, or produced by chemistry or chemicals: *chemical agents.* —**chem′i•cal•ly,** *adv.*

chem•ist (kem′ist) /ˈkɛmɪst/ *n.* [*count*] **1.** a specialist in chemistry. **2.** *Chiefly Brit.* DRUGGIST.

chem•is•try (kem′ə strē) /ˈkɛməstriy/ *n.* [*noncount*] **1.** the science that studies the composition, properties, and activity of substances and various elementary forms of matter: *She studied chemistry at college.* **2.** chemical properties, reactions, etc., taken as a group: *She is studying the chemistry of carbon.* **3. a.** relationship between people in which there is mutual understanding; rapport: *Their chemistry was good and they worked together well.* **b.** sexual attraction: *The romantic leads have great chemistry.*

che•mo•ther•a•py (kē′mō ther′ə pē, kem′ō-) /ˌkiymowˈθɛrəpiy, ˌkɛmow-/ *n.* [*noncount*] Also, **che•mo** (kē′mō) /ˈkiymow/. the treatment of disease using chemicals that kill organisms that produce disease, or chemicals that destroy cancerous tissue.

che•nille (shə nēl′) /ʃəˈniyl/ *n.* [*noncount*] a fabric made with yarn that is thick and velvety, used esp. in bedspreads.

cheque (chek) /tʃɛk/ *n. Brit.* CHECK (def. 13).

cher•ish (cher′ish) /ˈtʃɛrɪʃ/ *v.* [~ + *obj*] **1.** to regard as valuable or precious: *The early settlers cherished freedom.* **2.** to care for tenderly and with love; nurture: *cherished his children.* **3.** to cling fondly to: *to cherish a memory.*

che•root (shə ro͞ot′) /ʃəˈruwt/ *n.* [*count*] a cigar having open, flat ends.

cher•ry (cher′ē) /ˈtʃɛriy/ *n., pl.* **-ries,** *adj.* —*n.* **1.** [*count*] the soft, red, pulpy fruit of any of various trees of the rose family: *a bowl of cherries.* **2.** [*count*] the tree bearing such a fruit. **3.** [*noncount*] the reddish wood of the cherry tree, used in making furniture. **4.** [*noncount*] a bright red color. —*adj.* **5.** bright red. **6.** containing cherries or cherrylike flavoring: *cherry cough drops.* **7.** [*usually: before a noun*] made of cherry wood.

cher•ub (cher′əb) /ˈtʃɛrəb/ *n.* [*count*], *pl.* **cher•u•bim** (cher′ə bim, -yo͞o bim) /ˈtʃɛrəbɪm, -yʊbɪm/ for 1; **cher•ubs** for 2. **1.** a kind of angel, often represented as a winged child. **2.** a person, esp. a child, with a sweet, chubby, innocent face. —**che•ru•bic** (chə ro͞o′bik) /tʃəˈruwbɪk/ *adj.*

cher•vil (chûr′vəl) /ˈtʃɜrvəl/ *n.* [*noncount*] an herb of the parsley family, having strong-smelling leaves.

chess (ches) /tʃɛs/ *n.* [*noncount*] a game played on a chessboard by two people who each move 16 pieces of six kinds to bring the opponent's king into checkmate.

chess•board (ches′bôrd′, -bōrd′) /ˈtʃɛsˌbɔrd, -ˌbowrd/ *n.* [*count*] a checkerboard used for playing chess.

chess•man (ches′man′, -mən) /ˈtʃɛsˌmæn, -mən/ *n.* [*count*], *pl.* **-men.** any piece used in the game of chess.

chest (chest) /tʃɛst/ *n.* [*count*] **1.** the front portion of the body enclosed by the ribs; thorax: *The policeman had been shot in the chest.* **2.** a box, usually with a lid, for storage, safekeeping of valuables, shipping, etc. **3.** CHEST OF DRAWERS. **4.** a small cabinet, esp. one hung on a wall, for storage, as for medicines, etc.: *the top shelf of the medicine chest.* —***Idiom.*** **5. get something off one's chest,** [*get + obj + off + one's +* ~] to discuss a problem that one has kept to oneself: *I've got to get this worry off my chest.* —**chest′ful** (-fo͝ol) /-fʊl/ *n.* [*count*], *pl.* **-fuls:** *was wearing a chestful of medals.*

chest•nut (ches′nut′, -nət) /ˈtʃɛsˌnʌt, -nət/ *n.* **1.** [*count*] any of several tall trees of the beech family, having nuts that can be eaten. **2.** [*count*] the nut of such a tree. **3.** [*noncount*] the wood of any of these trees. **4.** [*noncount*] a reddish brown color. **5.** [*count*] an old joke, etc., that is no longer funny. **6.** [*count*] a horse having a reddish brown or brown body with mane and tail of the same or a lighter color. —*adj.* **7.** reddish brown. —**chest′nut′ty,** *adj.*

chest′ of drawers′, *n.* [*count*], *pl.* **chests of drawers.** a piece of furniture, a set of drawers in a frame, often mounted on short legs, for holding clothing, household linens, etc.

chest•y (ches′tē) /ˈtʃɛstiy/ *adj.,* **-i•er, -i•est. 1.** (of the voice) sounding deep or as if filled with liquid. **2.** having a well-developed chest or bosom.

chev•ron (shev′rən) /ˈʃɛvrən/ *n.* [*count*] **1.** a badge of one or more V-shaped stripes worn on the sleeve by noncommissioned officers to indicate rank. **2.** any V-shaped ornament, marker, or object. —**chev′roned,** *adj.*

chew (cho͞o) /tʃuw/ *v.* **1.** to crush or grind (something) with the teeth: [~ + *obj*]: *She was chewing gum.* [*no obj*]: *Don't chew with your mouth open.* **2.** to tear or mangle, as if by chewing: [~ + *up* + *obj*]: *The sorting machine chewed up the letters.* [~ + *obj* + *up*]: *The machine just chewed them up.* **3.** [~ + *obj*] to make by or as if by chewing: *The puppy chewed a hole in the rug.* **4.** to think about; meditate on; consider at length: [~ + *obj (+ over)*]: *to chew a problem over in one's mind.* [~ *(+ over)* + *obj*]: *The more you chew over this problem, the worse it will seem.* [~ + *on* + *obj*]: *He chewed on it briefly, then spoke up.* **5. chew out,** *Slang.* to scold harshly: [~ + *out* + *obj*]: *The boss chewed out the sales manager.* [~ + *obj* + *out*]: *She really chewed him out for that.* —*n.* [*count*] **6.** an act or instance of chewing. **7.** something chewed or intended for chewing: *a little chew of candy.* —***Idiom.*** **8. chew the fat** or **rag,** *Informal.* to converse in a relaxed or aimless manner; chat. —**chew′er,** *n.* [*count*]

chew′ing gum′ (cho͞o′ing) /ˈtʃuwɪŋ/ *n.* [*noncount*] a sweetened substance for chewing, usually made of chicle: *a stick of chewing gum.*

chew•y (cho͞o′ē) /ˈtʃuwiy/ *adj.,* **-i•er, -i•est.** (of food) not easily chewed, esp. because of toughness or stickiness: *a chewy candy.* —**chew′i•ness,** *n.* [*noncount*]

chg. or **chge.,** an abbreviation of: **1.** change. **2.** charge.

chic (shēk) /ʃiyk/ *adj.,* **-er, -est,** *n.* —*adj.* **1.** attractive and fashionable; stylish: *the chic look from Paris.* —*n.* [*noncount*] **2.** elegance, esp. in dress design. —**chic′ly,** *adv.* —**chic′ness,** *n.* [*noncount*]

Chi•ca•na (chi kä′nə) /tʃɪˈkɑnə/ *n.* [*count*], *pl.* **-nas.** a Mexican-American woman or girl.

chi•can•er•y (shi kā′nə rē, chi-) /ʃɪˈkeynəriy, tʃɪ-/ *n., pl.* **-ies.** the use of sly or evasive language to trick or deceive: [*noncount*]: *What political chicanery is he up to now?* [*count*]: *the chicaneries we endured last time.*

Chi•ca•no (chi kä′nō) /tʃɪˈkɑnow/ *n.* [*count*], *pl.* **-nos.** a Mexican-American, esp. a male.

chi•chi (shē′shē′) /ˈʃiyˌʃiy/ *adj.* overly showy; trendy; ostentatious: *an expensive, chichi restaurant.*

chick (chik) /tʃɪk/ *n.* [*count*] **1.** a young chicken or other bird. **2.** *Slang (often offensive).* a young woman.

chick•a•dee (chik′ə dē′) /ˈtʃɪkəˌdiy/ *n.* [*count*] a small North American bird of the titmouse family, with white cheeks and a dark-colored throat and cap.

chick•en (chik′ən) /ˈtʃɪkən/ *n.* **1.** [*count*] a domesticated bird developed in a number of breeds for its flesh, eggs, and feathers: *A hen is a female chicken.* **2.** [*noncount*] the flesh of the chicken used as food. **3.** [*count*] *Slang.* a cowardly or fearful person: *Come on, don't be such a chicken.* **4.** [*noncount*] a contest that may result in very serious, sometimes fatal consequences if one of the participants makes an error or does not yield. —*adj.* [*be* + ~] **5.** *Informal.* cowardly; frightened: *He won't do it; he's chicken.* —*v.* **6. chicken out,** [*no obj*] to withdraw from or back out of a promise, esp. because of fear.

chick′en feed′, *n.* [*noncount*] *Slang.* a small, insignificant sum of money.

chick′en-heart′ed, *adj.* fearful; cowardly. —**chick′en-heart′ed•ly,** *adv.*

chick•en•pox or **chick•en pox** (chik′ən poks′) /ˈtʃɪkˌən pɒks/ *n.* [*noncount*] a disease, commonly of children, marked by fever and the eruption of red spots or blisters on the skin.

chick•pea (chik′pē′) /ˈtʃɪkˌpiy/ *n.* **1.** [*noncount*] a widely cultivated plant of the legume family, having pods that contain pealike seeds. **2.** [*count*] the seeds of this plant, used as a food. Also called **garbanzo.**

chick•weed (chik′wēd′) /ˈtʃɪkˌwiyd/ *n.* [*noncount*] a common weed with white flowers.

chic•le (chik′əl) /ˈtʃɪkəl/ *n.* [*noncount*] a gumlike substance obtained from tropical American trees, used chiefly in chewing gum. Also called **chic′le gum′.**

chic•o•ry (chik′ə rē) /ˈtʃɪkəriy/ *n., pl.* **-ries. 1.** a plant having blue flowers and oblong leaves with toothlike edges, cultivated as a salad plant and for its root: [*count*]: *a garden of chicories.* [*noncount*]: *a bundle of chicory.* **2.** [*noncount*] the root of this plant used as a substitute for or additive to coffee.

chide (chīd) /tʃayd/ *v.* [~ + *obj*], **chid•ed** or **chid** (chid) /tʃɪd/ **chid•ed** or **chid** or **chid•den** (chid′n) /ˈtʃɪdn̩/ **chid•ing.** to scold or reproach: *She chided me for not speaking up to the boss when I had the chance.* **—chid′ing•ly,** *adv.*

chief (chēf) /tʃiyf/ *n.* [*count*] **1.** the head or leader of an organized body: *the chief of police.* **2.** the ruler of a tribe or clan: *an Indian chief.* **3.** *Informal.* BOSS[1]: *You're the workers and she's the chief.* **—*adj.*** [*before a noun*] **4.** highest in rank or authority: *the chief magistrate.* **5.** most important; principal: *the chief difficulty.* **—*Idiom.* 6. in chief,** [*after a noun*] highest in rank: *commander in chief (= commander who is highest in rank).* **—chief′dom,** *n.* [*noncount*]

chief•ly (chēf′lē) /ˈtʃiyfliy/ *adv.* **1.** most importantly; principally: *He proposed a tax cut chiefly to get reelected.* **2.** for the most part; mainly: *The car is made chiefly in the United States.*

chief•tain (chēf′tən) /ˈtʃiyftən/ *n.* [*count*] **1.** the chief of a clan or a tribe. **2.** a leader of a group, band, etc.: *the robbers' chieftain.*

chif•fon (shi fon′) /ʃɪˈfɒn/ *n.* [*noncount*] a soft, thin fabric of silk, nylon, or rayon.

chig•ger (chig′ər) /ˈtʃɪgər/ *n.* [*count*] the six-legged, bloodsucking larva of a mite that lives on humans and other mammals. Also called **harvest mite.**

chi•gnon (shēn′yon) /ˈʃiynyɒn/ *n.* [*count*] a large, smooth twist, roll, or knot of hair worn by women at the back of the neck or head. **—chi′gnoned,** *adj.*

chi•hua•hua (chi wä′wä) /tʃɪˈwɑwɑ/ *n.* [*count*] one of a Mexican breed of very small dogs with a rounded head.

chil•blain (chil′blān) /ˈtʃɪlbleyn/ *n.* [*count*] Usually, **chilblains.** [*plural*] a swollen, painful area on the hands and feet caused by exposure to cold and moisture. **—chil′blained,** *adj.*

child (chīld) /tʃayld/ *n.* [*count*], *pl.* **chil•dren** (chil′drən) /ˈtʃɪldrən/. **1.** a young boy or girl: *A young child doesn't usually want to share his or her toys.* **2.** a son or daughter: *He has two children, a boy and a girl.* **3.** a baby or infant: *the rights of the unborn child are to be balanced by the right to privacy of the mother.* **4.** a person who behaves in a childish manner. **5.** any person or thing regarded as the product of particular circumstances or influences: *Abstract art is a child of the 20th century.* **—*Idiom.* 6. with child,** (of a human female) pregnant. **—child′less,** *adj.* **—child′less•ness,** *n.* [*noncount*]

child•bear•ing (chīld′bâr′ing) /ˈtʃayldˌbɛərɪŋ/ *n.* [*noncount*] **1.** the act of bringing forth children. **—*adj.*** [*before a noun*] **2.** capable of, suitable for, or relating to the bearing of children: *not yet of childbearing age.*

child•birth (chīld′bûrth′) /ˈtʃayldˌbɜrθ/ *n.* an act or instance of bringing forth a child: [*noncount*]: *Childbirth in those days was risky.* [*count*]: *That day the doctor supervised childbirths that went normally.*

child•hood (chīld′ho͝od) /ˈtʃayldhʊd/ *n.* the state or period of being a child: [*noncount*]: *those happy days of childhood.* [*count; usually singular*]: *He had a difficult childhood.*

child•ish (chīl′dish) /ˈtʃayldɪʃ/ *adj.* **1.** immature; babyish: *Don't be so childish; stop pouting and whining.* **2.** of or relating to a child or children: *a childish face.* **—child′ish•ly,** *adv.: Stop behaving so childishly; grow up!* **—child′ish•ness,** *n.* [*noncount*]: *Stop your childishness at once.*

child•proof or **child-proof** (chīld′pro͞of′) /ˈtʃayldˌpruwf/ *adj.* **1.** incapable of being opened, tampered with, or operated by a child: *medicine containers with childproof caps.* **2.** made free of hazard for a child: *a childproof home.* **—*v.*** [~ + *obj*] **3.** to make childproof: *They spent weeks childproofing their home.*

chil•dren (chil′drən) /ˈtʃɪldrən/ *n.* pl. of CHILD.

child's′ play′, *n.* [*noncount*] something very easily done.

chil•e (chil′ē) /ˈtʃɪliy/ *n., pl.* **chil•es.** CHILI.

Chil•e•an (chil′ē ən) /ˈtʃɪliyən/ *adj.* **1.** of or relating to Chile. **—*n.*** [*count*] **2.** a person born or living in Chile.

chil•i or **chil•e** (chil′ē) /ˈtʃɪliy/ *n., pl.* **chil•ies** or **chil•es. 1.** [*count*] Also called **chili pepper.** the harsh-smelling pod of any of several species of pepper, used in cooking. **2.** CHILI CON CARNE. **3.** [*noncount*] a dish similar to chili con carne but containing no meat.

chil′i (or **chil′e**) **con car′ne** (kon kär′nē) /ˈkɒn kɑrniy/ *n.* [*noncount*] a spicy dish made with beef, chilies or chili powder, tomatoes, and beans.

chill (chil) /tʃɪl/ *n.* [*count*] **1.** a piercing coldness: *The chill of winter had penetrated the little cabin.* **2.** a feeling or sensation of cold: *I had chills and a fever.* **3.** a sudden feeling of fear or alarm: *A chill went down her spine when she heard the word "unemployment."* **4.** a depressing influence or feeling: *His presence cast a chill over everyone.* **5.** unfriendliness; coolness: *I could feel a definite chill as I was introduced to the committee.* **—*adj.*** **6.** moderately cold; chilly: *a chill evening.* **7.** *Slang.* COOL (def. 8). **—*v.* 8.** to (cause to) become cold: [*no obj*]: *Let the wine chill for a while.* [~ + *obj*]: *The cold wind chilled me to the bone.* **9. chill out,** [*no obj*] *Slang.* to calm down; relax. **—chill′ness,** *n.* [*noncount*]

chill•er (chil′ər) /ˈtʃɪlər/ *n.* [*count*] **1.** one that chills. **2.** a frightening or suspenseful story or film. **3.** a device for cooling.

chill•ing (chil′ing) /ˈtʃɪlɪŋ/ *adj.* **1.** causing a feeling of cold: *a chilling wind.* **2.** frightening; causing fear; terrifying: *a chilling scream.* **3.** discouraging; depressing; causing a feeling of gloom: *The threat of war had a chilling effect.* **—chill′ing•ly,** *adv.*

chill•y (chil′ē) /ˈtʃɪliy/ *adj.,* **-i•er, -i•est. 1.** noticeably cold; nippy: *a chilly breeze.* **2.** without warmth of feeling: *The president gave only a chilly reply to that journalist.* **—chill′i•ly,** *adv.* **—chill′i•ness,** *n.* [*noncount*]

chime (chīm) /tʃaym/ *n., v.,* **chimed, chim•ing. —*n.* 1.** Often, **chimes.** [*plural*] **a.** a set of bells producing musical tones when struck. **b.** a musical instrument consisting of such a set, esp. a glockenspiel. **c.** the musical tone thus produced: *the soft chimes of the grandfather clock.* **—*v.* 2.** [*no obj*] to sound harmoniously or in chimes, such as a set of bells: *The church bells chimed at noon.* **3.** [*no obj*] to produce a musical sound by striking a bell, etc.; ring chimes: *The doorbell chimed.* **4.** [~ + *obj*] to indicate, announce, etc., by chiming: *Bells chimed the hour.* **5. chime in, a.** to enter a conversation, esp. to interrupt: [*no obj*]: *I was all set to chime in when the boss began to speak.* [*used with quotations*]: *They chimed in, "Let's try it."* **b.** [~ + *in* + *with* + *obj*] to be compatible; agree: *This chimes in with what he said before about foreign students.* **c.** [~ + *in* + *with* + *obj*] to say or speak by chiming in: *He chimed in with a warning about higher costs.* **—chim′er,** *n.* [*count*]

chi•me•ra or **chi•mae•ra** (ki mēr′ə, kī-) /kɪˈmɪərə, kay-/ *n.* [*count*], *pl.* **-ras. 1.** [*often: Chimera*] a monster of Greek myth, represented with a lion's head, a goat's body, and a serpent's tail. **2.** an unlikely dream; an unrealistic hope.

chi•mer•i•cal (ki mer′i kəl, -mēr′-, kī-) /kɪˈmɛrɪkəl, -ˈmɪər-, kay-/ also **chi•mer′ic,** *adj.* **1.** unreal; imaginary. **2.** wildly fanciful; highly unrealistic.

chim•ney (chim′nē) /ˈtʃɪmniy/ *n.* [*count*], *pl.* **-neys. 1.** a structure containing a passage by which the smoke, etc., of a fire or furnace are carried off. See illustration at HOUSE. **2.** a tube surrounding the flame of a lamp.

chimp (chimp) /tʃɪmp/ *n.* [*count*] a chimpanzee.

chim•pan•zee (chim′pan zē′, chim pan′zē) /ˌtʃɪmpænˈziy, tʃɪmˈpænziy/ *n.* [*count*] a large manlike ape of Africa, having a dark coat and a relatively bare face.

chin (chin) /tʃɪn/ *n., v.,* **chinned, chin•ning. —*n.*** [*count*] **1.** the lowest part of the face, below the mouth: *He cut his chin shaving.* **—*v.* 2.** [~ + *oneself (+ up)*] to grasp an overhead bar and pull (oneself) upward until the chin is above or level with the bar. **—*Idiom.* 3. keep one's chin up,** to maintain one's courage.

chi•na (chī′nə) /ˈtʃaynə/ *n.* [*noncount*] **1.** a material made from baked clay originally imported from China and used for making plates, etc.; porcelain: *China is very delicate.* **2.** any plates or tableware made of porcelain or ceramic: *She brought out her best china.*

Chi•na•town (chī′nə toun′) /ˈtʃaynəˌtawn/ *n.* [*proper noun*] the main Chinese district in any city outside China.

chin•chil•la (chin chil′ə) /tʃɪnˈtʃɪlə/ *n., pl.* **-las. 1.** [*count*] a small South American rodent raised for its silvery gray fur. **2.** [*noncount*] the fur itself.

Chi•nese (chī nēz′, -nēs′) /tʃayˈniyz, -ˈniys/ *n., pl.* **-nese. 1.** [*noncount*] the standard language of China: *Chinese, or Mandarin, is based on the speech of Beijing.* **2.** [*noncount*] any of the other related languages spoken in China. **3.** [*count*] a person born or living in China.

—*adj.* **4.** of or relating to China. **5.** of or relating to the languages spoken in China.

chink[1] (chingk) /tʃɪŋk/ *n.* [*count*] **1.** a crack: *a chink in a wall.* **2.** a narrow opening: *a chink between two buildings.*

chink[2] (chingk) /tʃɪŋk/ *v.* **1.** to (cause to) make a short, sharp, ringing sound, such as of glasses striking together: [*no obj*]: *The glasses chinked together.* [~ + *obj*]: *They chinked their glasses together.* —*n.* [*count*] **2.** a chinking sound.

chi•no (chē′nō) /ˈtʃiynow/ *n., pl.* **-nos. 1.** [*noncount*] a cotton cloth used for sportswear, etc. **2.** Usually, **chinos.** [*plural*] trousers of this cloth.

chintz (chints) /tʃɪnts/ *n.* [*noncount*] a cotton fabric often printed in patterns, used for slipcovers, etc.

chintz•y (chint′sē) /ˈtʃɪntsiy/ *adj.,* **-i•er, -i•est. 1.** of, like, or decorated with chintz. **2.** cheap, inferior, or gaudy: *That chintzy nightstand fell apart.* **3.** stingy; miserly: *That was a pretty chintzy party the boss threw.*

chin′-up′, *n.* [*count*] an act or instance of chinning a horizontal bar or the like.

chip (chip) /tʃɪp/ *n., v.,* **chipped, chip•ping.** —*n.* [*count*] **1.** a small, slender piece, such as of wood, separated by chopping or breaking: *Wood chips flew everywhere.* **2.** a very thin slice or small piece of food, candy, etc.: *potato chips; chocolate chips* **3.** a mark or flaw made by the breaking off of a small piece: *This glass has a chip.* **4.** a small round disk, used as a token for money in roulette, poker, etc.; counter: *He put all his chips on number fifteen.* **5.** Also called **microchip.** a tiny slice of semiconducting material on which a transistor or an integrated circuit is formed: *memory chips for computers.* **6. chips,** [*plural*] *Chiefly Brit.* FRENCH FRIES. —*v.* **7.** [~ + *obj*] to break off or gouge out (a bit): *He chipped the paint off the wall.* **8.** to cut or break a bit or fragment (from): [~ + *obj*]: *to chip a tooth.* [*no obj*]: *My tooth chipped when I fell.* **9.** [~ + *obj*] to shape or produce by cutting or flaking away pieces: *to chip a figure out of wood.* **10. chip in, a.** [~ + *in* + *obj*] to give as one's share; contribute: *We each chipped in five dollars.* **b.** [*no obj*] to share a cost or burden by giving money, aid, or the like: *Let's chip in on a birthday cake.* **c.** [*no obj*] to interrupt a conversation and add one's own remarks: *Right in the middle of my talk someone chipped in.* —***Idiom.* 11. chip off the old block,** a person who strongly resembles a parent: *His son is a chip off the old block.* **12. have a chip on one's shoulder,** to be constantly angry or ready to quarrel or fight. **13. when the chips are down,** when the need for support is greatest: *This is one guy who'll help you when the chips are down.*

chip•munk (chip′mungk) /ˈtʃɪpmʌŋk/ *n.* [*count*] a small, striped ground squirrel.

chipped′ beef′, *n.* [*noncount*] thin slices of dried beef, often served in a cream sauce.

chip•per (chip′ər) /ˈtʃɪpər/ *adj.* marked by or being in light, good humor; vivacious; jaunty; cheerful: *I was feeling chipper after a brisk walk.*

chip′ shot′, *n.* [*count*] a shot in golf on approaching a green that is intentionally hit high into the air: *His chip shot landed on the green and stayed there.*

chiro-, *prefix. chiro-* comes from Greek, where it has the meaning "hand." This meaning is found in such words as: CHIROPODIST, CHIROPRACTOR.

chi•rop•o•dist (ki rop′ə dist, kī-) /kɪˈrɒpədɪst, kay-/ *n.* [*count*] PODIATRIST. —**chi•rop′o•dy,** *n.* [*noncount*] See -POD-.

chi•ro•prac•tor (kī′rə prak′tər) /ˌkayrəˈpræktər/ *n.* [*count*] a person trained in a system of medicine for treatment of the back, based upon the interactions of the spine and nervous system: *Chiropractors treat patients by adjusting parts of the spinal column.*

chirp (chûrp) /tʃɜrp/ *n.* [*count*] **1.** the short, sharp sound made by small birds. **2.** any similar sound, esp. of a cheerful, excited tone: *She let out a chirp of delight.* —*v.* **3.** [*no obj*] to make the sound of a chirp: *Birds chirped outside my window.* **4.** [*used with quotations*] to say or express with such a sound: *"Good morning!" she chirped happily.* —**chirp′er,** *n.* [*count*]

chis•el (chiz′əl) /ˈtʃɪzəl/ *n., v.,* **-eled, -el•ing** or *(esp. Brit.)* **-elled, -el•ling.** —*n.* [*count*] **1.** a metal tool like a wedge with a cutting edge at the end of the blade, used for cutting or shaping wood, stone, etc. —*v.* **2.** [~ + *obj*] to shape or fashion by or as if by a chisel: *He chiseled a hole in the wood.* **3.** *Slang.* [~ + *obj* + *out of* + *obj*] **a.** to cheat or swindle (someone): *He chiseled her out of her money.* **b.** to get (money) by cheating or trickery: *He chiseled the money out of her.* —**chis′el•er;** *esp. Brit.,* **chis′el•ler,** *n.* [*count*]

chit[1] (chit) /tʃɪt/ *n.* [*count*] **1.** a signed note for money owed for food, drink, etc. **2.** any receipt or similar document, esp. of an informal nature.

chit[2] (chit) /tʃɪt/ *n.* [*count*] **1.** a child. **2.** a lively young woman.

chit•chat (chit′chat′) /ˈtʃɪtˌtʃæt/ *n., v.,* **-chat•ted, -chat•ting.** —*n.* [*noncount*] **1.** light conversation; gossip: *some chitchat about the new boss.* —*v.* [*no obj*] **2.** to talk easily or casually.

chit•ter•lings or **chit•lings** or **chit•lins** (chit′linz, -lingz) /ˈtʃɪtlɪnz, -lɪŋz/ *n.* the small intestine of swine, esp. prepared as food: [*count; used with a singular or plural verb*]: *The chitlings were thrown into the pot.* [*noncount; used with a singular verb*]: *Chitlings cooked southern style is their favorite dish.*

chiv•al•rous (shiv′əl rəs) /ˈʃɪvəlrəs/ *adj.* **1.** having the qualities of chivalry. **2.** considerate and courteous to women; gallant: *chivalrous men.* —**chiv′al•rous•ly,** *adv.* —**chiv′al•rous•ness,** *n.* [*noncount*]

chiv•al•ry (shiv′əl rē) /ˈʃɪvəlriy/ *n.* [*noncount*] **1.** the qualities expected of a knight, including courage, generosity, and courtesy. **2.** the institution of knighthood in the Middle Ages.

chive (chīv) /tʃayv/ *n.* [*count*] Usually, **chives.** [*plural*] a small bulb-shaped plant, related to the onion.

chlo•ride (klôr′īd, klōr′-) /ˈklɔrayd, ˈklowr-/ *n.* [*noncount*] a compound containing chlorine, as methyl chloride.

chlo•ri•nate (klôr′ə nāt′, klōr′-) /ˈklɔrəˌneyt, ˈklowr-/ *v.* [~ + *obj*], **-nat•ed, -nat•ing.** to treat (something, such as water) with chlorine, esp. for disinfecting: *They chlorinated the swimming pool to disinfect it.* —**chlo•ri•na•tion** (klôr′ə nā′shən, klōr′-) /ˌklɔrəˈneyʃən, ˌklowr-/ *n.* [*noncount*]

chlo•rine (klôr′ēn, klōr′-) /ˈklɔriyn, ˈklowr-/ *n.* [*noncount*] an element, a heavy, greenish yellow poisonous gas, used to purify water and to make bleaching powder.

chlo•ro•form (klôr′ə fôrm′, klōr′-) /ˈklɔrəˌfɔrm, ˈklowr-/ *n.* [*noncount*] **1.** a colorless liquid used chiefly in medicine to dissolve other substances, and once used as an anesthetic. —*v.* [~ + *obj*] **2.** to administer chloroform to, esp. in order to make unconscious or kill.

chlo•ro•phyll or **chlo•ro•phyl** (klôr′ə fil, klōr′-) /ˈklɔrəfɪl, ˈklowr-/ *n.* [*noncount*] the green substance in plant leaves that produces food by photosynthesis.

chm. or **chmn.,** an abbreviation of: chairman.

chock (chok) /tʃɒk/ *n.* [*count*] **1.** a wedge or block holding an object steady: *Place a chock behind one wheel before you jack up the car.* —*v.* [~ + *obj*] **2.** to provide with or hold in place with a chock or chocks: *She chocked the car and began to change the tires.*

chock•a•block or **chock-a-block** (chok′ə blok′) /ˈtʃɒkəˈblɒk/ *adj.* [*be* + ~ + *with*] **1.** extremely full; jammed: *The room was chock-a-block with celebrities.* —*adv.* **2.** in a crowded way; closely; tightly: *The room was jammed chock-a-block with people.*

chock-full (chok′fo͝ol′, chuk′-) /ˈtʃɒkˈfʊl, ˈtʃʌk-/ *adj.* [*be* + ~] full to the limit; crammed: *This food is chock-full of cholesterol.*

choc•o•late (chô′kə lit, chok′ə-, chôk′lit, chok′-) /ˈtʃɔkəlɪt, ˈtʃɒkə-, ˈtʃɔklɪt, ˈtʃɒk-/ *n.* **1.** [*noncount*] a food made from cacao, often sweetened and flavored. **2.** [*count*] a piece of candy made from such a preparation: *a box of chocolates for Valentine's Day.* **3.** [*noncount*] a syrup or flavoring made from such a preparation: *an ice-cream sundae with chocolate on top.* **4.** [*noncount*] a beverage made by dissolving such a preparation in milk or water: *a mug of hot chocolate.* —*adj.* **5.** [*before a noun*] made or flavored with chocolate: *a chocolate cake.* **6.** having the color of chocolate; dark-brown. —**choc′o•lat•y, choc′o•lat•ey,** *adj.*

choice (chois) /tʃɔys/ *n., adj.,* **choic•er, choic•est.** —*n.* **1.** [*count*] an act or instance of choosing; selection: *a wise choice of friends.* **2.** [*noncount*] the right, power, or opportunity to choose: *no choice but to go along.* **3.** [*count*] the person or thing chosen: *Blue is my choice for the rug.* **4.** [*count*] an abundance or variety from which to choose: *a wide choice of styles.* —*adj.* [*before a noun*] **5.** worthy of being chosen: *choice cuts of meat.* **6.** carefully selected: *a few choice words for his enemies.* —***Idiom.* 7. of choice,** that is generally preferred: *Surgery might be the treatment of choice for the problem.* —**choice′ly,** *adv.* —**choice′ness,** *n.* [*noncount*] —**Syn.** CHOICE, ALTERNATIVE, OPTION suggest the power of choosing between things. CHOICE implies the opportunity to choose freely: *Her choice for dessert was ice cream.* ALTERNATIVE suggests a chance to choose only one of a few possibilities: *I had the alternative of going to the party or staying home alone.* OPTION emphasizes the right or privilege of choosing: *He had the option of taking the prize money or a gift.*

choir (kwīᵊr) /kwayᵊr/ *n.* [*count*] **1.** a group of singers, esp. performing in a church service. **2.** a group of instruments of the same kind: *a brass choir.* See -CHOR-.

choke (chōk) /tʃowk/ *v.*, **choked, chok•ing,** *n.* —*v.* **1.** to stop the breath of (someone) by squeezing or blocking the windpipe; strangle: [~ + *obj*]: *Let go of my neck; you're choking me.* [*no obj*]: *He's choking; quick, get a doctor.* [~ + *on* + *obj*]: *The baby is choking on that hard candy!* **2.** [~ + *obj*] to stop by filling; obstruct; clog: *Grease choked the drain.* **3.** [~ + *obj*] to fill to the limit; pack: *The closet was choked with toys.* **4.** to keep back, hold back, or suppress (a feeling, etc.): [~ + *back/down* + *obj*]: *She choked back her sobs.* [~ + *obj* + *back/down*]: *to choke them down.* **5.** [*no obj;* ~ *(+ up)*] to become too tense to perform well: *I don't know why I forgot my speech; I just choked (up) and couldn't go on.* **6.** **choke off,** to stop or obstruct by or as if by choking: [~ + *off* + *obj*]: *to choke off the fuel supply.* [~ + *obj* + *off*]: *to choke it off.* **7.** **choke up,** to (cause to) become speechless, as from emotion: [*no obj*]: *I just choked up and couldn't say a thing.* [~ + *obj* + *up*]: *This award chokes me up; I don't know what to say.* —*n.* [*count*] **8.** the act or sound of choking. **9.** any mechanism that regulates the flow of elements by blocking a passage.

choke•point (chōk′point′) /ˈtʃowkˌpɔynt/ *n.* [*count*] a place of greatest congestion; bottleneck: *The tolls at that bridge were the biggest chokepoint on the highway.*

chok•er (chō′kər) /ˈtʃowkər/ *n.* [*count*] **1.** one that chokes. **2.** something fitting snugly around the neck, such as a necklace or high collar.

chol•er•a (kol′ər ə) /ˈkɒlərə/ *n.* [*noncount*] a contagious infection of the small intestine caused by bacteria and transmitted through drinking water. —**chol•e•ra•ic** (kol′ə rā′ik) /ˌkɒləˈreyɪk/ *adj.*

cho•les•ter•ol (kə les′tə rōl′, -rôl′) /kəˈlɛstəˌrowl, -ˌrɔl/ *n.* [*noncount*] a substance found in animal fats: *high levels of cholesterol in the blood.*

chomp (chomp) /tʃɒmp/ *v.*, *n.* CHAMP¹.

choose (cho͞oz) /tʃuwz/ *v.*, **chose** (chōz) /tʃowz/ **cho•sen** (chō′zən) /ˈtʃowzən/ **choos•ing.** —*v.* **1.** to select from a number of possibilities; pick by preference: [~ + *obj*]: *She chose July for her wedding.* [*no obj*]: *Choose carefully.* **2.** [~ + *to* + *verb*] to prefer or decide (to do something): *to choose to speak.* **3.** **choose up, a.** [~ + *up* + *obj*] to select the team members of: *chose up sides before the game.* **b.** [*no obj*] to pick players for opposing teams. —**Related Words.** CHOOSE is a verb, CHOICE is a noun and an adjective, CHOOSY is an adjective: *He chose Susan as a dance partner. His choice was Susan. That was a choice piece of meat. He is a choosy shopper.*

choos•y (cho͞o′zē) /ˈtʃuwziy/ *adj.*, **-i•er, -i•est.** hard to please; very particular, esp. in making a selection. —**choos′i•ness,** *n.* [*noncount*]

chop¹ (chop) /tʃɒp/ *v.*, **chopped, chop•ping,** *n.* —*v.* **1.** to cut or separate (something) with quick, heavy blows, using a sharp tool like an ax: [~ + *down/off* + *obj*]: *to chop down a tree. She chopped off a branch.* [*no obj*]: *He chopped at the tree but couldn't make a dent in it.* **2.** [~ *(+ up)* + *obj*] to cut into smaller pieces; mince: *to chop (up) celery.* **3.** [~ + *obj*] to hit with a sharp, downward stroke: *He chopped the guard on the neck.* —*n.* [*count*] **4.** an act or instance of chopping: *One chop and the wood was split.* **5.** an individual cut or portion of lamb, mutton, pork, or veal, usually containing a rib: *barbecued pork chops.* **6.** an area of choppy water: *sailing in a rough chop.*

chop² (chop) /tʃɒp/ *n.* [*count*] Usually, **chops.** [*plural*] **1.** the jaw. **2.** the lower part of the cheek; the flesh over the lower jaw.

chop³ (chop) /tʃɒp/ *n.* [*count*] a stamp or seal used as an identification mark, esp. in the Far East: *He put his chop on the bank form and let us go.*

chop•per (chop′ər) /ˈtʃɒpər/ *n.* [*count*] **1.** a person or thing that chops. **2.** a short ax with a large blade, used for cutting up meat. **3.** a helicopter: *Choppers with wounded were landing.* **4.** a motorcycle. —*v.* [*no obj*] **5.** to travel by helicopter or motorcycle: *They choppered over to the landing zone.*

chop•py (chop′ē) /ˈtʃɒpiy/ *adj.*, **-pi•er, -pi•est.** **1.** (of the sea, a lake, etc.) forming short, irregular, broken waves. **2.** uneven in style: *short, choppy sentences.* —**chop•pi•ly** (chop′ə lē) /ˈtʃɒpəliy/ *adv.* —**chop′pi•ness,** *n.* [*noncount*]

chop•stick (chop′stik′) /ˈtʃɒpˌstɪk/ *n.* [*count*] one of a pair of thin sticks held between the thumb and fingers and used as an eating utensil.

chop′ su′ey (chop′so͞o′ē) /ˈtʃɒpˈsuwiy/ *n.* [*noncount*] a Chinese-style dish of meat and vegetables, usually served with rice.

-chor-, *root.* -*chor*- comes from Greek, where it has the meaning "sing, dance." This meaning is found in such words as: CHOIR, CHORAL, CHORD, CHOREOGRAPH, CHOREOGRAPHY, CHORISTER, CHORUS.

cho•ral (kôr′əl, kōr′-) /ˈkɔrəl, ˈkowr-/ *adj.* [*before a noun*] of a chorus or a choir: *a choral hymn.* See -CHOR-.

chord¹ (kôrd) /kɔrd/ *n.* [*count*] **1.** a feeling or emotion: *Your story struck a sympathetic chord in me.* **2.** the straight line between two points on a given curve.

chord² (kôrd) /kɔrd/ *n.* [*count*] a combination of three or more musical tones sounded at the same time. See -CHOR-.

chore (chôr, chōr) /tʃɔr, tʃowr/ *n.* [*count*] **1.** a small or routine job to do. **2.** **chores,** [*plural*] the everyday work around a house or farm: *Finish your chores and then you can go out.* **3.** a hard or unpleasant task: *a real chore to stand on line to buy food every day.*

cho•re•o•graph (kôr′ē ə graf′, kōr′-) /ˈkɔriyəˌgræf, ˈkowr-/ *v.* [~ + *obj*] **1.** to provide the choreography for: *to choreograph a ballet.* **2.** to manage or direct: *choreographing all aspects of a political career.* See -CHOR-.

cho•re•og•ra•phy (kôr′ē og′rə fē, kōr′-) /ˌkɔriyˈɒgrəfiy, ˌkowr-/ *n.* [*noncount*] **1.** the art of composing ballets and other dances and planning the movements and patterns of dancers: *She studied choreography with a famous dance coach.* **2.** the movements and patterns composed for a dance: *spellbinding choreography.* —**cho′re•og′ra•pher,** *n.* [*count*] —**cho•re•o•graph•ic** (kôr′ē ə graf′ik, kōr′-) /ˌkɔriyəˈgræfɪk, ˌkowr-/ *adj.* —**cho′re•o•graph′i•cal•ly,** *adv.* See -CHOR-, -GRAPH-.

chor•is•ter (kôr′ə stər, kor′-) /ˈkɔrəstər, ˈkɒr-/ *n.* [*count*] a singer in a choir. See -CHOR-.

chor•tle (chôr′tl) /ˈtʃɔrtl/ *v.*, **-tled, -tling,** *n.* —*v.* **1.** to chuckle gleefully: [*no obj*]: *She chortled quietly to herself.* [~ + *obj*]: *to chortle one's joy.* —*n.* [*count*] **2.** a gleeful chuckle. —**chor′tler,** *n.* [*count*]

cho•rus (kôr′əs, kōr′-) /ˈkɔrəs, ˈkowr-/ *n.*, *pl.* **-rus•es,** *v.*, **-rused, -rus•ing.** —*n.* [*count*] **1. a.** a group of persons singing together: *She sang in her school chorus.* **b.** (in an opera) such a group singing choral parts with individual singers: *a Greek chorus.* **c.** a piece of music for singing in unison. **d.** a part of a song played or sung at repeated parts in a song; refrain: *The song had a catchy chorus.* **2.** singing, speaking, or expressing something at the same time or with the same message: *a chorus of jeers.* **3.** (in a musical show) those performers who sing or dance as a group and do not play starring roles. —*v.* **4.** to sing or speak simultaneously: [~ + *obj*]: *They all chorused their praise.* [*used with quotations*]: *"Oh, not us!" they chorused.* —***Idiom.*** **5.** **in chorus,** at the same time; in unison: *The class answered the question in chorus.* See -CHOR-.

chose (chōz) /tʃowz/ *v.* pt. of CHOOSE.

cho•sen (chō′zən) /ˈtʃowzən/ *v.* **1.** pp. of CHOOSE. —*adj.* [*before a noun*] **2.** selected from several; preferred: *my chosen profession.* **3.** ELECT (def. 8). —*n.* **4.** **the chosen,** [*plural; used with a plural verb*] ELECT (def. 9): *Only the chosen are allowed past these doors.*

chow (chou) /tʃaw/ *n.* [*noncount*] *Slang.* **1.** food, esp. a meal: *thought Army chow was pretty awful.* —*v.* [*no obj*] **2.** **chow down,** to eat, esp. heartily.

chow•der (chou′dər) /ˈtʃawdər/ *n.* [*noncount*] a thick soup usually made with seafood or vegetables, potatoes, milk, and various seasonings: *clam chowder; corn chowder.*

chow′ mein′ (mān) /meyn/ *n.* [*noncount*] a Chinese-style dish of vegetables, shredded meat, and fried noodles.

Chr., an abbreviation of: **1.** Christ. **2.** Christian.

Christ (krīst) /krayst/ *n.* **1.** [*proper noun*] Jesus of Nazareth, held by Christians to be the son of God and the Messiah. **2.** [*often: the* + ~] (in the New Testament) the Messiah prophesied in the Old Testament. **3.** [*count*] someone regarded as similar to Jesus of Nazareth: *Several false Christs proclaimed themselves.* —**Christ′like′,** *adj.*

chris•ten (kris′ən) /ˈkrɪsən/ *v.* [~ + *obj*], **1.** to receive into the Christian church by baptism; baptize: *The minis-*

ter christened our daughter. **2.** [~ + *obj* + *proper noun*] to give a name to at baptism: *She was christened Anne.* **3.** to name and dedicate: *christened the ship by breaking a bottle of champagne against it.* **4.** to make use of for the first time: *Let's christen the new silverware.* —**chris′ten•er,** *n.* [*count*] —**chris′ten•ing,** *n.* [*count*]: *attended a christening.*

Chris•ten•dom (kris′ən dəm) /ˈkrɪsəndəm/ *n.* [*noncount*] **1.** Christians thought of as a group: *in the name of all Christendom.* **2.** the Christian world, ideas, etc.: *the spread of Christendom through the empire.*

Chris•tian (kris′chən) /ˈkrɪstʃən/ *adj.* **1.** of, relating to, or derived from Jesus Christ or His teachings: *Christian ideals.* **2.** of, relating to, or belonging to the religion based on the teachings of Jesus Christ: *a southern Christian church.* **3.** exhibiting a spirit proper to a follower of Jesus Christ: *a Christian attitude toward her enemies.* —*n.* [*count*] **4.** a person who professes belief in Jesus Christ; an adherent of Christianity. **5.** a person who exemplifies the teachings of Christ: *a real Christian to us in our time of need.*

Chris•ti•an•i•ty (kris′chē an′i tē) /ˌkrɪstʃiyˈænɪtiy/ *n.* [*noncount*] **1.** the Christian religion, including the Catholic, Protestant, Eastern, and Orthodox churches. **2.** Christian beliefs or practices. **3.** CHRISTENDOM.

Chris′tian name′, *n.* [*count*] the name given to one at baptism, as distinguished from the family name; given name.

Christ•mas (kris′məs) /ˈkrɪsməs/ *n.* [*noncount; count*] the annual festival of the Christian church commemorating Jesus' birth, celebrated in the Western Church on December 25.

Christ′mas tree′, *n.* [*count*] an evergreen tree, or an artificial tree that resembles one, decorated at Christmas with ornaments and lights.

-chrom-, *root.* *-chrom-* comes from Greek, where it has the meaning "color." This meaning is found in such words as: CHROMATIC, CHROMOSOME, MONOCHROME.

chro•ma•tic (krō mat′ik, krə-) /krowˈmætɪk, krə-/ *adj.* **1.** of or relating to color. **2.** of or naming a musical scale in which the notes progress by half tones. See -CHROM-.

chrome (krōm) /krowm/ *n.* [*noncount*] **1.** (not in technical use) CHROMIUM (def. 1). **2.** chromium-plated or other bright metallic trim, as on an automobile.

chro•mi•um (krō′mē əm) /ˈkrowmiyəm/ *n.* [*noncount*] **1.** a bright, shiny metal element used in making alloy steels. **2.** (not in technical use) CHROME (def. 2).

chro•mo•some (krō′mə sōm′) /ˈkrowməˌsowm/ *n.* [*count*] one of a set of threadlike structures in a cell that carry the genes determining an individual's inherited traits: *There are 23 pairs of chromosomes in the human body.* —**chro′mo•so′mal,** *adj.* See -CHROM-, -SOM-.

-chron-, *root.* *-chron-* comes from Greek, where it has the meaning "time." This meaning is found in such words as: ANACHRONISM, CHRONIC, CHRONICLE, CHRONOLOGY, SYNCHRONIZE.

chron., an abbreviation of: **1.** chronicle. **2.** chronological. **3.** chronology.

chron•ic (kron′ik) /ˈkrɒnɪk/ *adj.* **1.** [*usually: before a noun*] being such habitually or for a long time: *a chronic liar.* **2.** (of a disease) lasting a long time; coming back again frequently: *chronic bronchitis.* Compare ACUTE. **3.** [*before a noun*] (of a person) having long had a disease or the like: *a chronic drug abuser.* —**chron′i•cal•ly,** *adv.: They are chronically late for work.* See -CHRON-.

chron•i•cle (kron′i kəl) /ˈkrɒnɪkəl/ *n., v.,* **-cled, -cling.** —*n.* [*count*] **1.** a record of events in the order in which they occurred: *the Anglo-Saxon Chronicles of King Alfred's reign.* —*v.* [~ + *obj*] **2.** to record in or as if in a chronicle; set down: *The novel chronicles the general's rise to power and his subsequent fall.* —**chron′i•cler,** *n.* [*count*] See -CHRON-.

chron•o•log•i•cal (kron′l oj′i kəl) /ˌkrɒnḷˈɒdʒɪ kəl/ *adj.* of or relating to chronology: *the chronological order of events.* —**chron′o•log′i•cal•ly,** *adv.* See -CHRON-.

chro•nol•o•gy (krə nol′ə jē) /krəˈnɒlədʒiy/ *n., pl.* **-gies.** **1.** [*count*] a table or list of the order in which things occur; the order in which things occur: *Give us a chronology of the events.* **2.** [*noncount*] the science of arranging time in periods and figuring the dates and historical order of past events. —**chro•nol′o•gist, chro•nol′o•ger,** *n.* [*count*] See -CHRON-.

chrys•a•lis (kris′ə lis) /ˈkrɪsəlɪs/ *n.* [*count*], *pl.* **chrys•a•lis•es, chry•sal•i•des** (kri sal′i dēz′) /krɪˈsælɪˌdiyz/. a moth or butterfly in the stage between a larva and an adult.

chry•san•the•mum (kri san′thə məm) /krɪˈsænθəməm/ *n.* [*count*] **1.** a garden plant having autumn flowers in many different colors and sizes. **2.** the flower of any such plant.

chub•by (chub′ē) /ˈtʃʌbiy/ *adj.,* **-bi•er, -bi•est.** round and plump: *a chubby face.* —**chub′bi•ness,** *n.* [*noncount*]

chuck[1] (chuk) /tʃʌk/ *v.* [~ + *obj*] **1.** to toss; throw: *Chuck the ball over here!* **2.** to throw away; throw out: *Can't we chuck all these old boxes?* **3.** to resign from: *He's chucked his job and gone to live in the mountains.* **4.** to pat or tap lightly, as under the chin: *I chucked my niece under her chin.* —*n.* [*count*] **5.** a light pat or tap: *a little chuck under the chin.* **6.** a toss; pitch.

chuck[2] (chuk) /tʃʌk/ *n.* **1.** [*noncount*] the cut of beef between the neck and the shoulder blade: *ground chuck for hamburgers.* **2.** [*count*] a block or log used as a chock.

chuck[3] (chuk) /tʃʌk/ *n.* [*noncount*] food; provisions: *A chuck wagon was a wagon that carried the cowboys' food.*

chuck•hole (chuk′hōl′) /ˈtʃʌkˌhowl/ *n.* [*count*] a hole in a road; pothole.

chuck•le (chuk′əl) /ˈtʃʌkəl/ *v.,* **-led, -ling,** *n.* —*v.* [*no obj*] **1.** to laugh in a soft, quiet manner: *chuckling at his odd ideas.* —*n.* [*count*] **2.** a soft, quiet laugh: *a little chuckle.*

chug[1] (chug) /tʃʌg/ *n., v.,* **chugged, chug•ging.** —*n.* [*count*] **1.** a short, dull, explosive sound: *the steady chug of an engine.* —*v.* [*no obj*] **2.** to make this sound: *The motor chugged.* **3.** to move while making this sound: *The train chugged up the side of the mountain.*

chug[2] (chug) /tʃʌg/ *v.,* **chugged, chug•ging.** to chug-a-lug.

chug-a-lug (chug′ə lug′) /ˈtʃʌgə ˌlʌg/ *v.,* **-lugged, -lug•ging.** *Slang.* to drink (a large amount of beer) all at once: [~ + *obj*]: *chug-a-lugging pitchers of beer.* [*no obj*]: *sick from a night of chug-a-lugging.*

chum (chum) /tʃʌm/ *n., v.,* **chummed, chum•ming.** —*n.* [*count*] **1.** a close companion or friend; pal: *college chums.* —*v.* **2. chum around with,** [~ + *around* + *with* + *obj*] to associate with (someone) closely: *chumming around with bad people.*

chum•my (chum′ē) /ˈtʃʌmiy/ *adj.,* **-mi•er, -mi•est.** friendly; close; sociable: *He was chummy with the boss.* —**chum•mi•ly** (chum′ə lē) /ˈtʃʌməliy/ *adv.: put his arm chummily around his friend's shoulder.* —**chum′mi•ness,** *n.* [*noncount*]

chump (chump) /tʃʌmp/ *n.* [*count*] **1.** *Informal.* a person easily fooled; a fool: *He was such a chump to believe her lies.* —***Idiom.*** **2. off one's chump,** *Brit.* crazy.

chunk (chungk) /tʃʌŋk/ *n.* [*count*] **1.** a thick mass, lump, or piece of anything; hunk: *a chunk of meat.* **2.** a large or significant amount of something: *A large chunk of the budget went for defense spending.*

chunk•y (chung′kē) /ˈtʃʌŋkiy/ *adj.,* **-i•er, -i•est.** **1.** (of people) thick or stout; stocky: *The coach put the chunky guy on the line where his weight was an advantage.* **2.** in chunks; full of chunks: *chunky soup.* —**chunk•i•ly** (chung′kə lē) /ˈtʃʌŋkəliy/ *adv.* —**chunk′i•ness,** *n.* [*noncount*]

church (chûrch) /tʃɜrtʃ/ *n.* **1.** [*count*] a building for public Christian worship. **2.** [*noncount*] a religious service in such a building: *late for church again.* **3.** [*sometimes: Church*] **a.** [*the* + ~; *count; usually singular*] the whole body of Christian believers; Christendom: *The Church faces a crisis in leadership.* **b.** [*count*] any major division of this body; a Christian denomination: *Several churches took positions against the amendment.* **c.** [*noncount*] the clergy or church officials who have authority in decisions: *What is the church's position on this issue?* **4.** [*noncount*] organized religion as distinguished from the state: *the separation of church and state.*

church•go•er (chûrch′gō′ər) /ˈtʃɜrtʃˌgowər/ *n.* [*count*] a person who goes to church, esp. regularly. —**church′go′ing,** *n.* [*noncount*]

church•man (chûrch′mən) /ˈtʃɜrtʃmən/ *n., pl.* **-men.** CLERGYMAN.

Church′ of Eng′land, *n.* [*proper noun*] the established church in England.

church•yard (chûrch′yärd′) /ˈtʃɜrtʃˌyard/ *n.* [*count*] the ground near a church, used as a graveyard.

churl•ish (chûr′lish) /ˈtʃɜrlɪʃ/ *adj.* grouchy; bad-tempered; rude and impolite: *was spoken to roughly by a churlish clerk.* —**churl′ish•ly,** *adv.* —**churl′ish•ness,** *n.* [*noncount*]

churn (chûrn) /tʃɜrn/ *n.* [*count*] **1.** a machine in which cream is beaten to make butter. —*v.* **2.** [~ + *obj*] to shake, beat, or stir vigorously to make into butter: *to* *churn cream.* **3.** to shake or move about vigorously or violently: [~ (+ up) + obj]: *The storm churned (up) the sea.* [~ + obj + up]: *The storm churned it up.* [no obj]: *The sea was churning and the boat rocked back and forth.* **4.** [no obj] to have a feeling or sensation as if moving or shaking: *His stomach was churning from anxiety.* **5. churn out,** to produce quickly as if by machine and in large numbers or great quantity: [~ + out + obj]: *She was churning out numerous articles and book reviews.* [~ + obj + out]: *She was churning them out rapidly.* —**churn′er,** *n.* [count]

chute[1] (sho͞ot) /ʃuwt/ *n.* [count] **1.** a sloping trough or shaft for sending water, grain, etc., to a lower level: *a mail chute; a laundry chute.* **2.** a waterfall or steep descent, as in a river. **3.** a water slide, as at an amusement park.

chute[2] (sho͞ot) /ʃuwt/ *n.* [count] a parachute. —**chut′ist,** *n.* [count]

chut•ney (chut′nē) /ˈtʃʌtniy/ *n.* [noncount] a strong-tasting relish of Indian origin combining fruit, vinegar, sugar, and spices.

chutz•pa or **chutz•pah** (kho͝ot′spə, ho͝ot′-) /ˈkhʊtspə, ˈhʊt-/ *n.* [noncount] *Slang.* boldness; impudence: *You have a lot of chutzpah asking for still more money.*

CIA or **C.I.A.,** an abbreviation of: Central Intelligence Agency.

ciao (chou) /tʃaw/ *interj.* (used in greeting or parting): *"Ciao," she answered with a little wave of her hand.*

ci•ca•da (si kā′də, -kä′-) /sɪˈkeydə, -ˈkɑ-/ *n.* [count], *pl.* **-das, -dae** (-dē). a large insect, maturing in cycles of 5 to 17 years, the adult male of which produces a prolonged high-pitched, shrill sound.

-cide-[1], *root.* *-cide-* comes from Latin, where it has the meaning "kill; cut down". This meaning is found in such words as: GENOCIDE, GERMICIDE, HERBICIDE, HOMICIDE, INSECTICIDE, MATRICIDE, PATRICIDE, SUICIDE.

-cide-[2], *root.* *-cide-* comes from Latin, where it has the meaning "fall, happen." It is related to -CAD-. This meaning is found in such words as: ACCIDENT, INCIDENT.

ci•der (sī′dər) /ˈsaydər/ *n.* [noncount] the juice pressed from apples.

ci•gar (si gär′) /sɪˈgɑr/ *n.* [count] **1.** a cylinder of tobacco prepared for smoking: *some fine Havana cigars.* —***Idiom.*** **2. no cigar,** (used to indicate that an effort was not good enough to achieve or accomplish something): *a nice try, but no cigar.*

cig•a•rette or **cig•a•ret** (sig′ə ret′) /ˌsɪgəˈrɛt/ *n.* [count] a narrow, short roll of finely cut tobacco wrapped in thin paper.

cig•a•ril•lo (sig′ə ril′ō) /ˌsɪgəˈrɪlow/ *n.* [count], *pl.* **-los.** a small, thin cigar.

ci•lan•tro (si län′trō, -lan′-) /sɪˈlɑntrow, -ˈlæn-/ *n.* [noncount] CORIANDER (def. 1).

cinch (sinch) /sɪntʃ/ *n.* [count] **1.** a strong rope for holding a pack or saddle: *tightening the cinches.* **2.** [a + ~] *Informal.* **a.** something sure or easy: *Fixing this leak was a cinch.* **b.** a person or thing certain to fulfill an expectation: *She's a cinch to win the contest. It's a cinch that she'll win the contest.* —*v.* [~ + obj] **3.** to tie on or fasten with a cinch: *They cinched the packs to the horse.* **4.** *Informal.* to make sure of; guarantee: *Your support will cinch the deal.*

cin•der (sin′dər) /ˈsɪndər/ *n.* [count] **1.** a burned piece of coal, wood, etc.: *a smoldering cinder.* **2. cinders,** [plural] anything left over after burning; ashes: *Cinders from the volcano fell on the car.* **3. to a cinder,** completely black: *The cookies she had left in the oven had burned to a cinder.*

cin•e•ma (sin′ə mə) /ˈsɪnəmə/ *n., pl.* **-mas. 1.** [noncount] motion pictures, as an art or industry: *The cinema was her life.* **2.** [count] a motion-picture theater: *Which cinema has the new horror movie?* —**cin•e•mat•ic** (sin′ə mat′ik) /ˌsɪnəˈmætɪk/ *adj.*

cin•e•ma•tog•ra•phy (sin′ə mə tog′rə fē) /ˌsɪnəməˈtɒgrəfiy/ *n.* [noncount] the art or technique of motion-picture photography. —**cin′e•ma•tog′ra•pher,** *n.* [count] See -GRAPH-.

cin′é•ma vé•ri•té′ (ver′i tā′) /ˌvɛrɪˈtey/ *n.* [noncount] a technique of filmmaking in which the camera records actual persons and events without the director intervening or interfering.

cin•na•mon (sin′ə mən) /ˈsɪnəmən/ *n.* [noncount] a sweet-smelling spice made from the inner bark of various Asian trees of the laurel family.

ci•pher (sī′fər) /ˈsayfər/ *n.* [count] **1.** ZERO. **2.** any of the Arabic numerals or figures. **3.** a person or thing of little or no value; nothing: *was a mere cipher in that department.* **4. a.** a secret method of writing, as by code: *developed a cipher to use in communicating.* **b.** writing done by such a method; a coded message: *We couldn't read the cipher.* **5.** the key to a secret method of writing: *She uncovered the cipher after days of analysis.* —*v.* [~ + obj] **6.** to write in or as in cipher: *ciphered messages.* Also, *esp. Brit.,* **cypher.**

cir., an abbreviation of: **1.** about; circa (used with years): *cir. 1800.* **2.** circular.

circ., an abbreviation of: **1.** about; circa (used with years): *circ. 1800.* **2.** circuit. **3.** circular. **4.** circulation.

cir•ca (sûr′kə) /ˈsɜrkə/ *prep., adv.* (used before a date) about; approximately: *landed in North America circa 1000.*

cir•cle (sûr′kəl) /ˈsɜrkəl/ *n., v.,* **-cled, -cling.** —*n.* [count] **1.** a closed curve consisting of all the points at a given distance from the center: *She drew a circle.* **2.** the flat surface or plane made up by such a curve: *"Somewhere in this circle is our missing submarine," said the general.* **3.** any ringlike object or arrangement: *a circle of dancers.* **4.** the area within which something acts, exerts influence, etc.; realm; sphere: *a wide circle of influence.* **5.** a number of persons joined by something in common: *a circle of friends.* —*v.* **6.** [~ + obj] to enclose in a circle: *Circle the correct answer.* **7.** to move in a circle around: [~ + obj]: *The police circled the house cautiously.* [no obj]: *The squadron circled at 20,000 feet.* **8.** [~ + obj]to bypass; go around; evade: *The ship circled the iceberg.* —***Idiom.*** **9. come full circle,** to find oneself back where one started: *We'd come full circle in our tour of the city.* —**cir′cler,** *n.* [count]

cir•clet (sûr′klit) /ˈsɜrklɪt/ *n.* [count] **1.** a small circle. **2.** a ring or ring-shaped ornament.

cir•cuit (sûr′kit) /ˈsɜrkɪt/ *n.* [count] **1.** a circular journey: *the earth's circuit around the sun.* **2.** a regular journey from place to place, as by salespeople covering a route: *the campus lecture circuit.* **3.** the line around any area or object; the distance around an area or object: *a complete circuit of the whole town.* **4.** the complete path of an electric current: *This diagram shows all the circuits and where they connect.* **5.** a means of transmitting signals, usually two channels: *Our circuits have been broken; can we re-establish communication?* **6.** a number of theaters or the like controlled by one management.

cir′cuit break′er, *n.* [count] a device for stopping the flow of electricity through an electric circuit: *old fuses replaced with circuit breakers.*

cir′cuit court′, *n.* [count] a court that holds sessions at various intervals in different sections of a judicial district.

cir•cu•i•tous (sər kyo͞o′i təs) /sərˈkyuwɪtəs/ *adj.* going around instead of in a straight line; roundabout; not direct: *The agent took a circuitous route back to her hotel.* —**cir•cu′i•tous•ly,** *adv.* —**cir•cu′i•tous•ness,** *n.* [noncount]

cir•cuit•ry (sûr′ki trē) /ˈsɜrkɪtriy/ *n.* [noncount] **1.** the parts or pieces of an electric circuit: *the circuitry in these old houses.* **2.** the plan or system of such a circuit.

cir•cu•lar (sûr′kyə lər) /ˈsɜrkyələr/ *adj.* **1.** having the form of a circle; round: *A bright, circular object suddenly appeared in the sky.* **2.** [usually: before a noun] of or relating to a circle: *the circular diameter.* **3.** moving in or forming a circle or a circuit: *a circular path.* **4.** attempting to prove a conclusion by using a statement that depends on the conclusion: *a circular argument.* **5.** [before a noun](of a letter, etc.) intended for general circulation. —*n.* [count] **6.** a letter or notice intended for the public or for anyone to see: *She posted the circular on the bulletin board.* —**cir•cu•lar•i•ty** (sûr′kyə lar′i tē) /ˌsɜrkyəˈlærɪtiy/ *n.* [noncount] —**cir′cu•lar•ly,** *adv.*

cir•cu•late (sûr′kyə lāt′) /ˈsɜrkyəˌleyt/ *v.,* **-lat•ed, -lat•ing. 1.** to move in a circle or circuit, such as blood in the body: [no obj]: *Fresh air circulated down to our cabin in the ship.* [~ + obj]: *That system circulates blood to all parts of the body.* **2.** [no obj] to pass from place to place, from person to person, etc.: *I circulated among the guests during the party.* **3.** (of materials in a library) to (cause to) be available on loan outside the library: [no obj]: *This book doesn't circulate because it's a reference book.* [~ + obj]: *We don't circulate reference books.* **4.** to (cause to) pass or be sold from place to place, etc.; disseminate; distribute: [~ + obj]: *She promised to circulate a report.* [no obj]: *The report of his death was circulating quickly through the town.*

cir•cu•la•tion (sûr′kyə lā′shən) /ˌsɜrkyəˈleyʃən/ *n.* **1.** [noncount] an act or instance of circulating or being circulated. **2.** [noncount] the continuous movement of blood through the heart and blood vessels, pumped by the heart: *His poor circulation was keeping him weak.* **3.** [*noncount*] any similar circuit, such as of the sap in plants or air currents in a room: *Turn on the fan; maybe that will help the circulation in this room.* **4.** the number of items distributed over a given period, such as copies of a newspaper sold by a publisher, or books lent by a library: [*noncount*]: *The newspaper increased circulation to 30,000 copies a day.* [*count; usually singular*]: *a circulation of over 500,000 in just one year.* **5.** [*noncount*] the total of coins, bills, etc., in use as money.

cir•cu•la•to•ry (sûr′kyə lə tôr′ē, -tōr′ē) /ˈsɜrkyə lə ˌtɔriy, -ˌtowriy/ *adj.* [*before a noun*] of or relating to the system of organs and tissues involved in circulating blood and lymph through the body.

circum-, *prefix. circum-* comes from Latin, where it has the meaning "round, around." This meaning is found in such words as: CIRCUIT, CIRCUITOUS, CIRCUMCISE, CIRCUMFERENCE, CIRCUMLOCUTION, CIRCUMNAVIGATE, CIRCUMSTANCE, CIRCUMVENT, CIRCUS.

cir•cum•cise (sûr′kəm siz′) /ˈsɜrkəmˌsayz/ *v.* [~ + *obj*], **-cised, -cis•ing. 1.** to remove the foreskin of (a male). **2.** to remove the clitoris of (a female). **—cir•cum•cis•ion** (sûr′kəm sizh′ən) /ˌsɜrkəmˈsɪʒən/ *n.* [*count*]: *performed two circumcisions.* [*noncount*]: *Circumcision is a rite among some peoples.* See -CISE-.

cir•cum•fer•ence (sər kum′fər əns) /sərˈkʌmfərəns/ *n.* [*count*] **1.** the outer boundary, esp. of a circular area; perimeter: *We walked around the circumference of the lake.* **2.** the length of such a boundary: *The circumference of a circle is equal to π times the diameter.* See -FER-.

cir•cum•flex (sûr′kəm fleks′) /ˈsɜrkəmˌflɛks/ *n.* [*count*] a mark (^, ˇ, or ˜) placed over a vowel in some languages or phonetic systems to indicate that the vowel is pronounced with a particular quality or quantity. See -FLECT-, -FLEX-.

cir•cum•lo•cu•tion (sûr′kəm lō kyōō′shən) /ˌsɜrkəmlowˈkyuwʃən/ *n.* a roundabout or indirect way of speaking: [*count*]: *a long-winded circumlocution to the effect that I was fired.* [*noncount*]: *Enough circumlocution; just get to the point.* See -LOC-, -LOQ-.

cir•cum•nav•i•gate (sûr′kəm nav′i gāt′) /ˌsɜrkəmˈnævɪˌgeyt/ *v.* [~ + *obj*], **-gat•ed, -gat•ing.** to sail or fly completely around: *The explorer circumnavigated the globe.* See -NAV-.

cir•cum•scribe (sûr′kəm skrīb′) /ˈsɜrkəmˌskrayb/ *v.* [~ + *obj*], **-scribed, -scrib•ing. 1.** to draw a line around; encircle. **2.** to keep or enclose (something) within bounds; restrict: *His powers were carefully circumscribed.* See -SCRIB-.

cir•cum•spect (sûr′kəm spekt′) /ˈsɜrkəmˌspɛkt/ *adj.* watchful and careful; avoiding risks: *circumspect behavior.* **—cir•cum•spec•tion** (sûr′kəm spek′shən) /ˌsɜrkəmˈspɛkʃən/ *n.* [*noncount*] **—cir′cum•spect′ly,** *adv.* See -SPEC-.

cir•cum•stance (sûr′kəm stans′) /ˈsɜrkəmˌstæns/ *n.* **1.** Usually, **circumstances.** [*plural*] the conditions surrounding or affecting something: *What were the circumstances of his death?* **2. circumstances,** [*plural*] the condition or state of a person with respect to income: *a family in reduced circumstances.* **3.** [*count*] an incident, occurrence, or fact: *a fortunate circumstance.* **4.** [*noncount*] events or actions that cannot be controlled or planned; fate: *simply a victim of circumstance.* **5.** [*noncount*] ceremonious display: *too much pomp and circumstance at the graduation.* ***—Idiom.*** **6. under no circumstances,** never, regardless of events or conditions: *Under no circumstances will you be given a second chance.* **7. under the circumstances,** because of conditions that exist at the moment: *Under the circumstances we can't let you register for your courses.* See -STAN-.

cir•cum•stan•tial (sûr′kəm stan′shəl) /ˌsɜrkəmˈstænʃəl/ *adj.* **1.** based on details that imply but do not prove: *There is strong circumstantial evidence against your client.* **2.** dealing with circumstances; particular; full of descriptions. **—cir′cum•stan′tial•ly,** *adv.*

cir•cum•vent (sûr′kəm vent′) /ˌsɜrkəmˈvɛnt/ *v.* [~ + *obj*] **1.** to go around or bypass: *to circumvent a traffic jam by taking another route.* **2.** to avoid (a problem, etc.) by tricks: *She circumvented the rule against bribes by demanding and receiving high "consultant fees."* **—cir′cum•vent′er, cir′cum•ven′tor,** *n.* [*count*] **—cir′cum•ven′tion,** *n.* [*noncount*] See -VEN-.

cir•cus (sûr′kəs) /ˈsɜrkəs/ *n.* [*count*], *pl.* **-cus•es. 1.** a large public show featuring performing animals, clowns, etc.: *tickets to the circus.* **2.** (in ancient Rome) a large, usually U-shaped or oval open-air enclosure surrounded by rising rows of seats, for chariot races, etc. **3.** *Brit.* an open circle or plaza where several streets come together: *Piccadilly Circus.* **4.** a display of uncontrolled or wild activity: *The meeting soon turned into a circus.* **—*adj.*** [*before a noun*] **5.** noisy, wild, or uncontrolled: *The quiet class had degenerated into a circus atmosphere.* **—cir′cus•y,** *adj.*

cir•rho•sis (si rō′sis) /sɪˈrowsɪs/ *n.* [*noncount*] a chronic disease of the liver in which fibrous tissue replaces normal tissue. **—cir•rhosed′,** *adj.* **—cir•rhot•ic** (si rot′ik) /sɪˈrɒtɪk/ *adj.*

cir•rus (sir′əs) /ˈsɪrəs/ *n.* [*noncount*] a high-altitude cloud having thin white threads or narrow bands.

-cise-, *root. -cise-* comes from Latin, where it has the meaning "cut (down). " It is related to -CIDE-[2]. This meaning is found in such words as: CIRCUMCISE, DECISIVE, INCISION, INCISIVE, INCISOR, PRECISE, SCISSORS.

cis•tern (sis′tərn) /ˈsɪstərn/ *n.* [*count*] a reservoir, tank, or container for storing or holding water or other liquid: *a cistern on the roof of a building.*

cit., an abbreviation of: **1.** citation. **2.** cited. **3.** citizen.

cit•a•del (sit′ə dl, -ə del′) /ˈsɪtədḷ, -əˌdɛl/ *n.* [*count*] **1.** a fortress for defending a city. **2.** any strongly fortified place; stronghold: *a citadel of right-wing economists.*

ci•ta•tion (sī tā′shən) /sayˈteyʃən/ *n.* [*count*] **1.** a quotation from a passage in writing, used in support of a claim: *His citations include the most up-to-date scholars in the subject.* **2.** a speech or letter given to praise someone for heroic deeds: *given five citations for bravery in Korea.* **3.** a summons to appear in a court of law: *gave me a citation for speeding.*

cite[1] (sīt) /sayt/ *v.* [~ + *obj*], **cit•ed, cit•ing. 1.** to quote (a book, author, etc.), esp. as an authority: *He cited Einstein's work as proof of this theory.* **2.** to mention in support or argument; refer to as an example: *He cited instances of abuse in the nursing home.* **3.** to summon to appear in court: *He was cited for contempt of court.* **4.** to mention (a soldier, etc.) in official dispatches, as for gallantry: *He was cited for bravery in Korea.* **5.** to praise, as for outstanding service or devotion to duty: *He was cited for his aid to the flood victims.*

cite[2] (sīt) /sayt/ *n.* CITATION (def. 1).

cit•i•zen (sit′ə zən, -sən) /ˈsɪtəzən, -sən/ *n.* [*count*] a member of a state who owes allegiance to its government and is entitled to its protection: *She became a citizen after living here for ten years.*

cit•i•zen•ry (sit′ə zən rē, -sən-) /ˈsɪtəzənriy, -sən-/ *n.* [*noncount*] citizens thought of as a group: *the American citizenry.*

cit′izens band′, *n.* [*count*] [*often: Citizens Band; often used before another noun*] a band of radio frequencies used for short-distance private communications: *had citizens band radios and communicated with each other along the highway. Abbr.:* CB

cit•i•zen•ship (sit′ə zən ship′, -sən-) /ˈsɪtə zənˌʃɪp, -sən-/ *n.* [*noncount*] the state or condition of being a citizen: *His citizenship is American because he was born in the U.S.*

cit′ric ac′id (si′trik) /ˈsɪtrɪk/ *n.* [*noncount*] a kind of acid occurring esp. in citrus fruits, used chiefly as a flavoring.

cit•ron (si′trən) /ˈsɪtrən/ *n.* **1.** [*count*] a pale yellow fruit resembling the lemon. **2.** [*count*] the tree itself. **3.** [*noncount*] the skin or rind of the fruit candied and preserved.

cit•rus (si′trəs) /ˈsɪtrəs/ *n., pl.* **-rus•es,** *adj.* **—*n.*** **1.** [*count*] a small tree or shrub of the family that includes the lemon, lime, orange, tangerine, and grapefruit. **2.** [*noncount*] the fruit of any of these trees or shrubs, having a shiny skin and tart-to-sweet juicy pulp: *Most citrus is a good source of vitamin C.* **—*adj.*** [*usually: before a noun*]. **3.** Also, **cit′rous.** of or relating to such trees or shrubs, or their fruit.

cit•y (sit′ē) /ˈsɪtiy/ *n.* [*count*], *pl.* **cit•ies. 1.** a large or important town: *She hated life in the city.* **2.** [*usually singular*] the people who live in a city thought of as a group: *The entire city is celebrating the arrival of the astronauts.*

cit′y hall′, *n.* **1.** the administration building of a city government: [*count*]: *In city halls throughout the state mayors are awaiting news of state budget cuts.* [*proper noun*]: *a march on City Hall.* **2.** [*noncount*] a city government: *City hall wants to fight the new fare increase because this is an election year.* **3.** [*noncount*] *Informal.* bureaucratic rules and regulations, esp. of a city government: *You can't fight city hall.*

Civ., an abbreviation of: **1.** civil. **2.** civilian.

civ•ic (siv′ik) /ˈsɪvɪk/ *adj.* [*before a noun*] **1.** of or relating to a city; municipal: *a new civic center.* **2.** of or relating to citizenship; civil: *civic pride.* —**civ′i•cal•ly,** *adv.*

civ•ics (siv′iks) /ˈsɪvɪks/ *n.* [*noncount; used with a singular verb*] the study of the privileges and obligations of citizens: *Civics was a course I had in eighth grade.*

civ•il (siv′əl) /ˈsɪvəl/ *adj.* **1.** [*usually: before a noun*] of, relating to, or consisting of citizens: *civil life; civil society.* **2.** [*before a noun*] of the ordinary life and affairs of citizens: *They had a civil wedding ceremony at City Hall and then a religious one in a church.* **3.** coolly polite; correct but not friendly: *You could at least give me a civil greeting in the morning.* —**civ′il•ly,** *adv.*: *He answered the question civilly enough.* —**civ′il•ness,** *n.* [*noncount*] —**Related Words.** CIVIL is an adjective, CIVILIZATION is a noun, CIVILIZE is a verb, CIVILIZED is an adjective: *He spoke with a civil tongue. They study ancient civilizations. They tried to civilize the ragtag children they found. They weren't very civilized in their behavior.*

civ′il engineer′ing, *n.* [*noncount*] the science of the design of public works, such as roads, bridges, dams, harbors, etc., and the application of this science to the supervision of their construction or maintenance. —**civ′il engineer′,** *n.* [*count*]

ci•vil•ian (si vil′yən) /sɪˈvɪlyən/ *n.* [*count*] **1.** a person who is not on active duty with a military, naval, police, or firefighting organization: *Thousands of civilians had been killed or injured in the war.* —*adj.* [*before a noun*] **2.** of or relating to civilians: *civilian casualties.*

ci•vil•i•ty (si vil′i tē) /sɪˈvɪlɪtiy/ *n., pl.* **-ties.** **1.** [*noncount*] courtesy; politeness: *There is an absence of the most basic civility in that city.* **2.** [*count*] a polite action or expression: *the civilities of diplomacy.*

civ•i•li•za•tion (siv′ə lə zā′shən) /ˌsɪvələˈzeyʃən/ *n.* **1.** [*noncount*] an advanced state of human society, in which a high level of culture has been reached: *Civilization is hard to measure, but ancient societies had achieved it.* **2.** those people that reached such a state: [*noncount*]: *the contributions of ancient Greek civilization.* [*count*]: *great African civilizations of the past.* **3.** [*noncount*] cities or populated areas in general: *The first thing they did when they returned to civilization was to have a decent meal.*

civ•i•lize (siv′ə līz′) /ˈsɪvəˌlayz/ *v.* [~ + *obj*], **-lized, -liz•ing.** to bring out of a backward or uneducated state; make enlightened or refined: *Rome civilized the barbarians.*

civ′il law′, *n.* [*noncount*] the body of laws dealing with private matters or rights of citizens: *Marriage is a matter of civil law.*

civ′il lib′erty, *n.* **1.** [*count*] a basic or fundamental right guaranteed to an individual by the laws of a country: *He claimed his civil liberties were being infringed.* **2.** [*noncount*] the liberty of an individual to act on such a right without interference: *the notion of civil liberty in a fundamentalist religious society.* —**civ′il libertar′ian,** *n.* [*count*]

civ′il rights′, *n.* [*plural; often: Civil Rights*] rights to personal liberty, esp. as established by the 13th and 14th Amendments to the U.S. Constitution: *the struggle for civil rights for blacks.* —**civ′il-rights′,** *adj.* [*before a noun*]: *a civil-rights bill.*

civ′il serv′ant, *n.* [*count*] a civil-service employee.

civ′il serv′ice, *n.* [*noncount*] those branches of public service concerned with civil government functions: *a lifetime job in the civil service.*

civ′il war′, *n.* **1.** a war between political groups or regions within the same country: [*noncount*]: *disagreements escalating into civil war.* [*count*]: *The country had endured many civil wars in its history.* **2.** [*usually: the Civil War*] the war in the U.S. between the North and the South, 1861–65.

civ•vies or **civ•ies** (siv′ēz) /ˈsɪviyz/ *n.* [*plural*] *Informal.* civilian clothes: *She got out of her uniform and changed into her civvies.*

ck., an abbreviation of: check.

clack (klak) /klæk/ *v.* **1.** to make a quick sharp sound, as by striking or cracking: [*no obj*]: *I could hear her high heels clacking on the marble floor.* [~ + *obj*]: *She clacked the pieces of the toy together.* —*n.* [*count*] **2.** a clacking sound.

clad (klad) /klæd/ *v.* **1.** a pt. and pp. of CLOTHE. —*adj.* [*usually used with a noun or adverb*] **2.** dressed: *poorly-clad vagrants.* **3.** covered: *vine-clad cottages.*

claim (klām) /kleym/ *v.* **1.** [~ + *obj*] to demand by or as if by a right: *to claim an estate by inheritance.* **2.** to state (something) as true or as a fact: [~ + *(that) clause*]: *claimed that she was telling the truth.* [~ + *to* + *verb*]: *She claimed to be telling the truth.* **3.** [~ + *obj*] to require (something) as proper: *to claim respect.* **4.** [~ + *obj*] to take or expect to receive (credit, etc.): *The terrorists claimed responsibility for the attack.* **5.** [~ + *obj*] to call for; collect (something missing or held for another): *Has anyone claimed the lost wallet?* **6.** [~ + *obj*] to take (lives, casualties): *The war claimed the lives of thousands of civilians.* —*n.* [*count*] **7.** a demand for something due: *to make unreasonable claims on a doctor's time.* **8.** an assertion of something as a fact: *I make no claims to originality.* **9.** a right to claim or demand: *His claim to the heavyweight title is disputed.* **10.** something that is claimed: *The settler put in a claim for the land across the river.* **11.** a request or demand for payment in accordance with an insurance policy, law, etc.: *I submitted my insurance claim.* —***Idiom.*** **12. lay claim to,** [~ + obj] to declare oneself entitled to: *Both sides laid claim to the territory.* See -CLAIM-.

-claim-, *root.* -*claim*- comes from Latin, where it has the meaning "call out; talk; shout." This meaning is found in such words as: ACCLAIM, CLAIM, CLAMOR, EXCLAIM, PROCLAIM.

claim•ant (klā′mənt) /ˈkleymənt/ *n.* [*count*] a person who makes a claim.

clair•voy•ance (klâr voi′əns) /klɛər ˈvɔyəns/ *n.* [*noncount*] a special ability to see the future, or sense things beyond normal perception.

clair•voy•ant (klâr voi′ənt) /klɛərˈvɔyənt/ *adj.* **1.** of, relating to, having, or claiming to have clairvoyance. —*n.* [*count*] **2.** a clairvoyant person. —**clair•voy′ant•ly,** *adv.*

clam (klam) /klæm/ *n., v.,* **clammed, clam•ming.** —*n.* [*count*] **1.** a soft-bodied shellfish with two shells that close tight around it. **2.** *Informal.* a secretive or silent person. **3.** *Slang.* a dollar. —*v.* [*no obj*] **4.** to dig clams: *They went clamming on the beaches.* **5. clam up,** *Informal.* to refuse to talk or reply: *He's so shy that he clams up in public.*

clam•bake (klam′bāk′) /ˈklæmˌbeyk/ *n.* [*count*] **1.** a seaside picnic at which clams and other seafood are baked. **2.** *Informal.* any social gathering, esp. a noisy one.

clam•ber (klam′bər) /ˈklæmbər/ *v.* [*no obj*] **1.** to climb, using both feet and hands: *We clambered onto the bus.* —*n.* [*count*] **2.** an act or instance of clambering. —**clam′ber•er,** *n.* [*count*]

clam•my (klam′ē) /ˈklæmiy/ *adj.,* **-mi•er, -mi•est.** covered with a cold, sticky moisture: *clammy hands.* —**clam•mi•ly** (klam′ə lē) /ˈklæməliy/ *adv.* —**clam′mi•ness,** *n.* [*noncount*]

clam•or (klam′ər) /ˈklæmər/ *n.* [*count*] **1.** a loud and continued noise: *the clamor of traffic.* **2.** a loud uproar, such as from a crowd of people: *The clamor in the shop spilled out into the street.* **3.** an angry or strong expression of desire or of dissatisfaction: *raised a clamor against higher taxation.* —*v.* **4.** to make a clamor: [*no obj; (~ + for + obj)*]: *They clamored for a voice in the decision-making process.* [~ + *that clause*]: *They clamored that their demands were not being listened to.* [~ + *to* + *verb*]: *We clamored to be heard.* Also, *esp. Brit.,* **clam′our.** See -CLAIM-.

clamp (klamp) /klæmp/ *n.* [*count*] **1.** a device for fastening two things together: *Adjust the clamp to hold this piece of wood while I drill a hole here.* —*v.* **2.** [~ + *obj*] to fasten with a clamp or as if in a clamp: *He clamped the glued pieces together for a stronger bond. I clamped my mouth shut and said no more.* **3. clamp down,** [~ + *down (+ on + obj)*] to impose stricter control: *to clamp down on crime.*

clan (klan) /klæn/ *n.* [*count*] **1.** a group of families claiming descent from a common ancestor: *Scottish clans.* **2.** any family group or large family: *Our whole clan gathers for Thanksgiving.*

clan•des•tine (klan des′tin) /klænˈdɛstɪn/ *adj.* done in secrecy: *a clandestine meeting of conspirators.* —**clan•des′tine•ly,** *adv.* —**clan•des′tine•ness, clan•des•tin•i•ty** (klan′des tin′i tē) /ˌklændɛsˈtɪnɪtiy/ *n.* [*noncount*]

clang (klang) /klæŋ/ *v.* **1.** to give out a loud, ringing sound, such as that of a large bell: [*no obj*]: *The fire bells clanged in the distance.* [~ + *obj*]: *They clanged the bells on the firetruck.* **2.** [*no obj*] to move with such sounds: *The trolley clanged down the street.* —*n.* [*count*] **3.** a clanging sound: *A loud clang and the prizefight began.*

clang•or (klang′ər, klang′gər) /ˈklæŋər, ˈklæŋgər/ *n.* [*noncount*] loud, echoing, clanging noise. Also, *esp. Brit.,* **clang′our.** —**clang′or•ous,** *adj.* —**clang′or•ous•ly,** *adv.*

clank (klangk) /klæŋk/ *n.* [*count*] **1.** a sharp, short, hard sound, like that produced by two pieces of metal striking: *the clank of chains.* —*v.* **2.** to (cause to) make such a sound: [*no obj*]: *The prisoner's chains clanked as he walked.* [~ + *obj*]: *He clanked the chains.* **3.** [*no obj*] to move with such sounds: *The huge tank clanked down the streets.*

clap[1] (klap) /klæp/ *v.,* **clapped, clap•ping,** *n.* —*v.* **1.** to strike the palms of (one's hands) together: [*no obj*]: *They clapped as the president entered the room.* [~ + *obj*]: *We clapped our hands until they ached.* **2.** [~ + *obj*] to strike (someone) with a light slap, as in friendly greeting: *He clapped his friend on the back.* **3.** [~ + *obj*] to strike (an object) against something quickly and forcefully, producing a sharp sound: *She clapped the book shut.* **4.** [*no obj*] to make an abrupt, sharp sound, as of flat surfaces striking against each other: *The window shutters clapped in the wind.* **5.** to put or place quickly or forcefully: [~ + *on* + *obj*] *He clapped on his hat and dashed outside.* [~ + *obj* + *on*]: *He clapped handcuffs on the gunman and brought him outside.* —*n.* [*count*] **6.** an act of clapping: *A few claps turned into thunderous applause.* **7.** a slap or tap: *There was the mayor, giving out his usual claps on the back.* **8.** a loud and quick or explosive noise, such as of thunder: *Claps of thunder woke her up during the storm.*

clap[2] (klap) /klæp/ *n.* [*noncount; often: the* + ~] *Slang* (*vulgar*). gonorrhea.

clap•board (klab′ərd, klap′bôrd′, -bōrd′) /ˈklæbərd, ˈklæpˌbɔrd, -ˌbowrd/ *n.* [*count*] **1.** a long, thin board used in covering the outer walls of buildings. —*adj.* [*usually: before a noun*] **2.** of or made of clapboard.

clap•per (klap′ər) /ˈklæpər/ *n.* [*count*] **1.** a person who applauds. **2.** the tongue of a bell.

clap•trap (klap′trap′) /ˈklæpˌtræp/ *n.* [*noncount*] nonsense; insincere or empty language; foolish, unbelievable talk.

clar•et (klar′it) /ˈklærɪt/ *n.* dry red table wine, esp. from the Bordeaux region of France: [*noncount*]: *a glass of claret.* [*count*]: *several good clarets.*

clar•i•fy (klar′ə fī′) /ˈklærəˌfay/ *v.* [~ + *obj*], **-fied, -fy•ing. 1.** to make (an idea, etc.) clear or understandable: *You need a couple of examples here to clarify your main point.* **2.** to free (the mind, etc.) from confusion: *to clarify one's thoughts.* **3.** to make into a clear liquid: *to clarify butter.* —**clar•i•fi•ca•tion** (klar′ə fə kā′shən) /ˌklærəfəˈkeyʃən/ *n.* [*noncount*]: *The lawyers asked for clarification on the legal issue of insanity.* [*count*]: *After your clarifications I understand the situation better.* —**clar′i•fi′er,** *n.* [*count*]

clar•i•net (klar′ə net′) /ˌklærəˈnɛt/ *n.* [*count*] a woodwind instrument in the form of a long tube with a single reed attached to its mouthpiece. —**clar′i•net′ist, clar′i•net′tist,** *n.* [*count*]

clar•i•ty (klar′i tē) /ˈklærɪtiy/ *n.* [*noncount*] the state or quality of being clear; lucidity: *the clarity of pure water; clarity of thought.*

clash (klash) /klæʃ/ *v.* **1.** to strike with a loud, harsh noise: [*no obj*]: *The cymbals clashed.* [~ + *obj*]: *The tower bell clashed its mournful note.* **2.** to conflict; disagree: [*no obj; (~ + on + obj)*]: *The two opponents frequently clashed on this issue.* [~ + *with* + *obj*]: *Your ideas often clash with mine.* **3.** to engage in a physical conflict or contest: [*no obj; (~ + on + obj)*]: *The police and the rioters clashed on the streets.* [~ + *with* + *obj*]: *The police clashed with the demonstrators.* **4.** [*no obj*] (of colors or patterns) to be incompatible: *The red and purple really clash.* —*n.* [*count*] **5.** a loud, harsh noise, as of a collision: *The clash of cymbals woke him up during the concert.* **6.** a conflict, esp. of views or interests: *another clash between liberals and conservatives.* **7.** a battle, fight, or skirmish: *a bloody clash on the streets.*

clasp (klasp) /klæsp/ *n.* [*count*] **1.** a device for fastening together two or more things or parts: *He'd broken the small clasp on the necklace.* **2.** a firm grasp or grip of the hand. —*v.* [~ + *obj*] **3.** to fasten with or as if with a clasp. **4.** to grasp or grip with the hand: *He clasped me by the arm.* **5.** to hold in a tight embrace; hug: *He clasped the child to him.*

class (klas) /klæs/ *n.* **1.** [*count*] a number of persons or things thought of as belonging together; kind; sort: *the class of living things.* **2.** [*count*] **a.** a group of students meeting regularly: *My writing class had 28 students.* **b.** the period in which they meet: *The class is on Mondays and Wednesdays.* **c.** a meeting of such a group: *During our last class we talked about verb tenses in English.* **3.** [*count*] a group of students graduated in the same year: *the class of '92.* **4.** a level of society sharing the same characteristics; social rank: [*count*]: *the blue-collar class.* [*noncount*]: *socialists fighting against the concept of class.* **5.** [*noncount*] a division of people or things according to rank, quality, etc.: *a hotel of the highest class.* **6.** [*noncount*] *Informal.* grace or dignity, as in behavior: *She showed a lot of class during that interview.* —*adj.* **7.** [*before a noun*] *Informal.* of high quality: *She was a class act—never lost her temper and always treated people kindly.* —*v.* **8.** to place or arrange in a class; classify: [~ + *obj*]: *to class doctors with lawyers.* [~ + *obj* + *as* + *obj*]: *We classed them as believers in the same God as ourselves.* —***Idiom.*** **9. in a class by itself** or **oneself,** having no equal; unequaled: *a car in a class by itself; was in a class by himself when it came to scoring goals.*

class., an abbreviation of: **1.** classic. **2.** classical. **3.** classification. **4.** classified.

class′ ac′tion, *n.* [*noncount*] a legal process representing the interests of a group of people. —**class′-ac′tion,** *adj.*: *a class-action suit.*

class′ con′sciousness, *n.* [*noncount*] **1.** awareness of one's social or economic rank in society. **2.** a feeling of identification and togetherness with those of the same class as oneself. —**class′-con′scious,** *adj.*: *class-conscious people.*

clas•sic (klas′ik) /ˈklæsɪk/ *adj.* [*usually: before a noun*] **1.** of the first or highest quality or rank: *a classic work.* **2.** serving as a standard; definitive: *a classic method of teaching.* **3.** CLASSICAL (defs. 1, 2). **4.** of or obeying an established set of standards or methods; traditional or typical of its kind: *a classic example of fine writing.* **5.** of long-lasting interest, quality, or style: *a classic movie.* —*n.* [*count*] **6.** an author, artist, literary work, or artistic production of long-lasting quality: *Students had to read the classics in college.* **7.** an author or literary work of ancient Greece or Rome. **8. the classics,** [*plural*] the literature and languages of ancient Greece and Rome. **9.** something noteworthy of its kind and worth remembering: *Your funny reply was a classic.*

clas•si•cal (klas′i kəl) /ˈklæsɪkəl/ *adj.* [*before a noun*] **1.** of or relating to ancient Greece and Rome, or of ancient Greek and Roman literature or art: *classical architecture; classical literature; classical languages.* **2.** of, relating to, or being music of the European tradition, including opera, symphonies, chamber music, and works for solo instrument. **3.** [*often: Classical*] of or relating to a style of literature or art that follows established treatments and standards and emphasizes simplicity and balance in form. **4.** accepted as having authority, as distinguished from experimental and unproven: *Classical physics held that there were only three dimensions.* **5.** having simplicity in style: *classical elegance.* —*n.* [*noncount*] **6.** classical music. —**clas′si•cal•ly,** *adv.*

clas•si•cism (klas′ə siz′əm) /ˈklæsəˌsɪzəm/ also **clas•si•cal•ism** (klas′i kə liz′əm) /ˈklæsɪkəˌlɪzəm/ *n.* [*noncount*] **1.** the principles or styles characteristic of the literature and art of ancient Greece and Rome. **2.** the classical style in literature and art: *Classicism kept much emotion out of its art and music.*

clas•si•fi•ca•tion (klas′ə fi kā′shən) /ˌklæsəfɪˈkeyʃən/ *n.* **1.** [*noncount*] the act or state of classifying. **2.** [*count*] a group or class into which something is classified: *Your classifications don't take into account some important differences.*

clas•si•fied (klas′ə fīd) /ˈklæsəfayd/ *adj.* **1.** divided or listed by classes or categories. **2.** officially secret; kept from the knowledge of the general public: *busy shredding classified documents.* —*n.* [*count*] **3.** a classified ad: *looked in the classifieds for an apartment.*

clas′sified ad′, *n.* [*count*] a brief advertisement in a newspaper or magazine, dealing with offers of or requests for jobs, houses, etc. Also called **clas′sified advertise′ment, want ad.** —**clas′sified ad′vertising,** *n.* [*noncount*]

clas•si•fy (klas′ə fī′) /ˈklæsəˌfay/ *v.* [~ + *obj*], **-fied, -fy•ing. 1.** to arrange or organize by classes: *She classified her students into three groups: low, average, and high.* **2.** to limit the availability of (information, etc.) to certain persons only: *The government classified those documents until the year 2010.* —**clas′si•fi′a•ble,** *adj.*

class•mate (klas′māt′) /ˈklæsˌmeyt/ *n.* [*count*] a member of the same class at a school or college.

class•room (klas′ro͞om′, -ro͝om′) /ˈklæsˌruwm, -ˌrʊm/ *n.* [*count*] a room, as in a school, in which classes are held. See illustration at SCHOOL.

class•y (klas′ē) /ˈklæsiy/ *adj.,* **-i•er, -i•est.** *Informal.* of high quality, rank, or grade; elegant: *We went to a classy nightclub.* —**class′i•ness,** *n.* [*noncount*]

clat•ter (klat′ər) /ˈklætər/ *v.* **1.** to (cause to) make a loud, rattling sound, such as that produced by hard objects striking one another: [*no obj*]: *The dishes were clattering in the dishwasher.* [~ + *obj*]: *Stop clattering the pots and pans.* **2.** [*no obj*] to move rapidly with such a sound: *The train clattered down the track.* —*n.* [*count; usually singular*] **3.** a rattling noise; racket; din: *the clatter of machinery.* —**clat′ter•er,** *n.* [*count*] —**clat′ter•y,** *adj.*

clause (klôz) /klɔz/ *n.* [*count*] **1.** (in grammar) a group of words containing a subject and predicate and forming either a part of a sentence or a whole simple sentence: *The clause* John went home *could stand on its own in its own sentence, or it could be a clause as part of a longer sentence:* John went home because Mary walked in. **2.** a separate and particular section or provision in a contract or other legal document: *Which clause in the agreement refers to payments?* —**claus′al,** *adj.*

claus•tro•pho•bi•a (klô′strə fō′bē ə) /ˌklɔstrəˈfowbiyə/ *n.* [*noncount*] an abnormal fear of being in enclosed or narrow places: *couldn't stay in the cave because of his claustrophobia.* —**claus′tro•phobe′,** *n.* [*count*] See -CLOS-.

claus•tro•pho•bic (klô′strə fō′bik) /ˌklɔstrəˈfowbɪk/ *adj.* **1.** suffering from or as if from claustrophobia. **2.** causing a feeling of claustrophobia: *a claustrophobic little apartment in the city.* See -CLOS-.

clav•i•chord (klav′i kôrd′) /ˈklævɪˌkɔrd/ *n.* [*count*] an early keyboard instrument, similar to a piano.

claw (klô) /klɔ/ *n.* [*count*] **1.** a sharp, curved nail on the foot of an animal, such as on a cat. **2.** a similar curved limb of an insect. **3.** any part or thing resembling a claw, as the end of the head of a hammer. —*v.* **4.** to tear, scratch, etc., with or as if with claws: [~ + *obj*]: *The cat clawed a hole in the couch.* [~ + *at* + *obj*]: *My little niece clawed at my legs to climb back up.* **5.** [~ + *obj*] to proceed by or as if by using the hands or claws: *They clawed their way through the jungle.* **6.** [~ + *obj*] to struggle against difficult odds: *She clawed her way to the top.*

clay (klā) /kley/ *n.* [*noncount*] **1.** a natural earthy material that is stiff and sticky when wet, used for making bricks, pottery, etc.: *They baked the clay in the sun into bricks.* **2.** earth; mud.

clean (klēn) /kliyn/ *adj.* and *adv.*, **-er, -est,** *v.* —*adj.* **1.** free from dirt; unsoiled; unstained: *a clean dress.* **2.** free from foreign or extra matter; pure: *clean sound.* **3.** free from pollution: *clean air; clean energy.* **4.** free from roughness or irregularity: *a clean cut with a scalpel.* **5.** gracefully beautiful; trim: *the clean lines of a ship.* **6.** morally pure; innocent; honorable: *to lead a clean life.* **7.** not cheating; showing good sportsmanship: *a clean fighter.* **8.** inoffensive in language or content: *clean books.* **9.** innocent of crime: *He had a clean record.* **10.** free from defects or flaws: *a clean diamond.* **11.** made without any difficulty; quickly and smoothly done: *a clean getaway.* **12.** smoothly and skillfully performed; adroit: *a clean swing of the bat.* **13.** [*before a noun*] complete; total: *a clean break with tradition.* **14.** empty; bare: *a clean sheet of paper.* —*adv.* **15.** in a clean manner; cleanly: *ran up the stairs and got clean away.* **16.** so as to be clean: *This shirt will never wash clean.* **17.** *Informal.* completely; quite: *The bullet passed clean through the wall.* —*v.* **18.** to perform or undergo a process of cleaning: [*no obj*]: *This new countertop cleans easily.* [~ + *obj*]: *I cleaned the room.* **19.** [~ + *obj*] to dry-clean: *Clean and press the pants.* **20.** [~ + *obj*] to remove the insides and other parts from (poultry, etc.) that cannot be eaten; dress: *She cleaned the turkey.* **21. clean out, a.** to empty in order to straighten or clean: [~ + *out* + *obj*]: *I had to clean out my desk to find what I was looking for.* [~ + *obj* + *out*]: *I cleaned it out before dinner.* **b.** to take all the money from (someone); steal or take everything from (a store, etc.): [~ + *obj* + *out*]: *They managed to clean him out at poker.* [~ + *out* + *obj*]: *They cleaned out the gangster and his men with a perfect scam.* **22. clean up, a.** to wash or tidy up: [*no obj*]: *Let me clean up and I'll be right in.* [~ + *up* + *obj*]: *Please clean up your room.* [~ + *obj* + *up*]: *Would you clean the room up?* **b.** to get rid of undesirable persons, features, mistakes, etc., in: [~ + *up* + *obj*]: *to clean up the errors in an essay.* [~ + *obj* + *up*]: *Can you clean them up now?* **c.** to put an end to; finish: [~ + *up* + *obj*]: *to clean up yesterday's chores.* [~ + *obj* + *up*]: *to clean them up.* **d.** [*no obj*] to make a large profit or a lot of money: *Buy now while the prices are low and later you'll really clean up.* —***Idiom.*** **23. come clean,** [*no obj*] *Slang.* to tell the truth, esp. to admit one's guilt: *finally came clean and admitted she had been the one.* —**clean′a•ble,** *adj.* —**clean′ness,** *n.* [*noncount*] —**Related Words.** CLEAN is a verb and an adjective, CLEANLINESS is a noun: *We cleaned the house. Take a clean plate. Cleanliness is essential in a hospital.*

clean′-cut′, *adj.* **1.** having a distinct, regular shape. **2.** clearly outlined: *a clean-cut design.* **3.** neat and wholesome-looking: *At least her boyfriend is smart and clean-cut.* **4.** definitely clear; clear-cut; easy to understand or see: *clean-cut decisions.*

clean•er (klē′nər) /ˈkliynər/ *n.* [*count*] **1.** a person who cleans, esp. as an occupation. **2.** an apparatus for cleaning: *a vacuum cleaner.* **3.** a preparation for use in cleaning: *harsh detergent cleaners.* **4.** the owner or operator of a dry-cleaning establishment. **5.** Usually, **cleaners.** [*plural*] a dry-cleaning establishment: *I took the clothes to the cleaners yesterday.* —***Idiom.*** **6. take (someone) to the cleaners,** [*take* + *obj* + *to* + *the* + ~*-s*]*Slang.* to take the money or property of, esp. by cheating: *discovered they'd been taken to the cleaners by a swindler.*

clean•ly (*adj.* klen′lē; *adv.* klēn′lē) /*adj.* ˈklɛnliy; *adv.* ˈkliynliy/ *adj.*, **-li•er, -li•est,** *adv.* —*adj.* **1.** personally neat; careful to keep or make clean: *a cleanly appearance.* —*adv.* **2.** in a clean manner: *slid cleanly down the chute.* —**clean•li•ness** (klen′lē nis) /ˈklɛnliynɪs/ *n.* [*noncount*]: *Cleanliness is next to godliness.*

cleanse (klenz) /klɛnz/ *v.*, **cleansed, cleans•ing. 1.** [~ + *obj*] to make clean: *She cleansed the wound with alcohol.* **2.** to remove (something) from (something) by or as if by cleaning: [~ + *obj* + *from* + *obj*]: *to cleanse sin from the soul.* [~ + *obj* + *of* + *obj*]: *to cleanse our souls of sin.*

cleans•er (klenz′ər) /ˈklɛnzər/ *n.* a substance that cleanses: [*noncount*]: *Pour soap cleanser directly on the stain.* [*count*]: *All these kitchen cleansers work the same.*

clean•up (klēn′up′) /ˈkliynˌʌp/ *n.* [*count*] the act or process of cleaning up: *the cleanup after that oil spill.*

clear (klēr) /klɪər/ *adj.* and *adv.*, **-er, -est,** *v.* —*adj.* **1.** free from darkness or cloudiness: *a clear day.* **2.** transparent: *The water was clear when we went snorkeling.* **3.** without stains, defect, or blemish: *She had very clear skin.* **4.** of a pure, even color: *a clear yellow.* **5.** easily seen; sharply defined: *a clear outline.* **6.** easily heard: *the clear sound of the church bells.* **7.** free from hoarse, harsh, or rasping qualities: *She spoke in a loud, clear voice.* **8.** easily understood; without ambiguity: *The alternatives are clear: fight or lose.* **9.** entirely understandable; completely understood: *Let's get this clear: you want to leave and never come back?* **10.** distinct; evident; plain; obvious: *a clear case of cheating.* **11.** free from confusion, uncertainty, or doubt: *Her clear thinking got us out of danger.* **12.** free from blame or guilt: *I have a clear conscience.* **13.** calm; untroubled: *Her clear eyes looked back at me steadily.* **14.** free from obstructions or obstacles; open: *a clear path; The road was clear after that slowdown.* **15.** [*be* + ~] free from contact with; not tangled up with: *He kept clear of her after the argument.* **16.** complete; absolute; undoubted: *a clear victory for our side.* **17.** free from obligation, liability, or debt: *a return of 4 percent, clear of taxes.* **18.** without deduction; net: *a clear profit of $1,000.* —*adv.* **19.** in a clear or distinct manner; clearly: *He could hear me loud and clear.* **20.** so as not to be in contact with or near; away: *Stand clear of the closing doors.* **21.** entirely; completely; clean: *to cut a piece clear off.* —*v.* **22.** [~ + *obj (+ of + obj)*] to remove people or objects from (something): *to clear the table of dishes.* **23.** [~ + *obj*] to remove (people or objects): *Clear the dishes off the table.* **24.** to (cause to) become clear, clean, transparent: [*no obj*]: *The sky cleared.* [~ + *obj*]: *This lotion will clear the blemishes from your skin.* **25.** to (cause to) become free of confusion, doubt, or uncertainty: [~ + *obj*]: *to clear the mind.* [*no obj*]: *Her mind cleared and she knew what she had to do.* **26.** to (cause to) make (something) understandable; to (cause to) be free from misunderstanding: [~ + *obj*]: *Her reply cleared the confusion.* [*no obj*]: *The confusion cleared and we knew what we had to do.* **27.** [~ + *obj*] to make or construct (a path, etc.) by removing obstacles: *The huge snowplows cleared the road.* **28.** [~ + *obj*] to remove trees or other obstructions from (land), such as for farming: *The settlers cleared the land for farming.* **29.** [~ + *obj*] to eat all the food on: *to clear one's plate.* **30.** [~ + *obj*] to make a dry, scraping noise in (the throat) by forcing air through, often to express disapproval or to attract attention: *He coughed but he couldn't clear his throat.* **31.** [~ + *obj*] to free of anything suggesting disgrace: *She fought to clear her name.*

32. [~ + *obj* + *of* + *obj*] to free (a person accused of something) from suspicion or guilt: *The jury cleared the defendant of the charge.* **33.** [~ + *obj*] to pass by or over without contact: *The ship cleared the reef.* **34.** [~ + *obj*] to pass through or away from: *The bill cleared the Senate.* **35.** (of a check) to (cause to) go through the banking system and be accepted for payment: [*no obj*]: *took five days for our check to clear.* [~ + *obj*]: *Can't they clear this check any faster?* **36.** [~ + *obj*] (of mail, etc.) to process, etc.: *We clear over ten thousand such requests a day.* **37.** [~ + *obj*] to gain as clear profit: *to clear $1,000 in a transaction.* **38.** [~ + *obj*] to receive official permission before taking action on (a plan): *had to clear the plan with headquarters.* **39.** [~ + *obj*] to give clearance to; give official permission to: *The tower cleared the plane for takeoff.* **40.** [~ + *obj*] to free (a ship, etc.) by satisfying customs: *Customs cleared the ship and allowed it to unload.* **41.** [~ + *obj*] to jump (a specific height or distance): *He cleared six feet in the high jump.* **42.** [*no obj*] to disappear; vanish: *These problems will clear shortly.* **43. clear away** or **off, a.** to (cause to) leave, vanish, or disappear: [*no obj*]: *The storm clouds cleared away.* [~ + *obj* + *away*]: *The sun cleared the clouds away.* [~ + *away* + *obj*]: *The sun cleared away the clouds.* **b.** to remove (something) from an area to make clean: [~ + *away/off* + *obj*]: *She cleared off the books from her desk.* [~ + *obj* + *away/off*]: *She cleared them away.* **44. clear out, a.** to remove the contents of: [~ + *out* + *obj*]: *Clear out the closet.* [~ + *obj* + *out*]: *to clear it out.* **b.** to remove; take away: [~ + *out* + *obj*]: *Clear out the mess in your room.* [~ + *obj* + *out*]: *Clear it out, now!* **c.** [*no obj*] to go away, esp. quickly: *Clear out, and don't come back!* **d.** to drive or force out: [~ + *out* + *obj*]: *First we'll have to clear out the enemy from the territory.* [~ + *obj* + *out*]: *We'll have to clear them out first.* **45. clear up, a.** to make clear; explain: [~ + *up* + *obj*]: *Let me see if I can clear up this misunderstanding.* [~ + *obj* + *up*]: *Let's see if we can clear this mystery up.* **b.** to put in order; tidy up: [~ + *up* + *obj*]: *Can you clear up this mess?* [~ + *obj* + *up*]: *Can you clear it up?* **—*Idiom.* 46. clear the air,** to get rid of feelings of anger or distrust by discussing them openly: *The two decided to meet and clear the air before their dispute got worse.* **47. in the clear,** free from danger, blame, or guilt: *I was finally in the clear after I proved I was right.* **—clear′er,** *n.* [*count*] **—clear′ness,** *n.* [*noncount*]

clear•ance (klēr′əns) /ˈklɪərəns/ *n.* **1.** the act of clearing: [*noncount*]: *The plane waited for clearance to take off.* [*count*]: *A clearance for working under that sort of visa takes time.* **2.** the distance between two objects; an amount of clear space: [*noncount*]: *There isn't much clearance between the roof of this van and the garage opening.* [*count; usually singular*]: *a clearance of only a few inches under that bridge.* **3.** [*noncount*] a formal authorization permitting access to classified information, etc.: *I applied for clearance to read those sealed documents.* **4.** [*count*] Also called **clear′ance sale′.** the selling of merchandise at reduced prices to make room for new goods: *a holiday clearance.*

clear-cut (klēr′kut′) /ˈklɪərˈkʌt/ *adj.* **1.** formed with or having clear outlines. **2.** completely clear; completely evident: *a clear-cut case of treason.*

clear•head•ed (klēr′hed′id) /ˈklɪərˈhɛdɪd/ *adj.* having or showing an alert mind: *clear-headed thinking in this situation.* **—clear′head′ed•ly,** *adv.*: *He didn't think clearheadedly.* **—clear′head′ed•ness,** *n.* [*noncount*]

clear•ing (klēr′ing) /ˈklɪərɪŋ/ *n.* **1.** [*noncount*] the act of a person or thing that clears; the process of becoming clear. **2.** [*count*] a piece of land that contains no trees or bushes: *a clearing in the woods.*

clear•ing•house or **clear′ing house′** (klēr′ing hous′) /ˈklɪərˌɪŋ haws/ *n.* [*count*] **1.** a place where bank accounts are settled. **2.** a central office for the collection and distribution of materials, etc.: *Contact the clearinghouse on consumer complaints first.*

clear•ly (klēr′lē) /ˈklɪərliy/ *adv.* **1.** in a clear manner; distinctly: *I could see clearly once I cleaned my glasses.* **2.** obviously; without a doubt: *Clearly, you've antagonized him.*

cleat (klēt) /kliyt/ *n.* [*count*] **1.** a wedge-shaped block fastened to a surface to serve as a support or to provide sure footing. **2.** a piece of hard rubber attached to the sole of a shoe to provide traction: *players wearing cleats in the muddy field.* **3.** a shoe fitted with such pieces: *putting on their cleats.*

cleav•age (klē′vij) /ˈkliyvɪdʒ/ *n.* **1.** [*noncount*] the act of cleaving or splitting. **2.** [*count*] the state of being cleft: *a cleavage between the lower and upper classes.* **3.** [*noncount*] the area between a woman's breasts, esp. when revealed by a low-cut neckline.

cleave[1] (klēv) /kliyv/ *v.* [~ + *to* + *obj*], **cleaved, cleav•ing. 1.** to stick closely to; cling: *His tongue cleaved to the roof of his mouth.* **2.** to remain faithful: *to cleave to one's principles.*

cleave[2] (klēv) /kliyv/ *v.*, **cleft** (kleft) /klɛft/ or **cleaved** or **clove** (klōv) /klowv/ **cleft** or **cleaved** or **clo•ven** (klō′vən) /ˈklowvən/ **cleav•ing. 1.** to (cause to) split or divide by or as if by a cutting blow: [*no obj*]: *The wood cleaved in two clean pieces.* [~ + *obj*]: *He cleaved the wood in two neat pieces.* **2.** [~ + *obj*] to make by or as if by cutting: *to cleave a path through the wilderness.* **3.** [~ (+ *through*) + *obj*] to penetrate or pass through (water, etc.): *The bow of the boat cleaved (through) the water cleanly.*

cleav•er (klē′vər) /ˈkliyvər/ *n.* [*count*] a heavy knife or long-bladed hatchet, esp. one used by butchers.

clef (klef) /klɛf/ *n.* [*count*] a sign at the beginning of a musical staff to show the pitch of the notes.

cleft[1] (kleft) /klɛft/ *n.* [*count*] **1.** a space or opening made by cleavage; a split: *a cleft in the rock formations.* **2.** a hollow area or indentation: *a cleft in her chin.*

cleft[2] (kleft) /klɛft/ *v.* **1.** a pt. and pp. of CLEAVE[2]. **—*adj.* 2.** cloven; split; divided.

cleft′ pal′ate, *n.* [*count*] a narrow opening in the roof of the mouth existing at birth.

clem•a•tis (klem′ə tis, kli mat′is) /ˈklɛmətɪs, klɪˈmætɪs/ *n.* [*noncount*] a plant or woody vine of the buttercup family.

clem•en•cy (klem′ən sē) /ˈklɛmən siy/ *n.* [*noncount*] **1.** mercy or kind treatment; leniency: *The judge explained why she was granting him clemency.* **2.** mildness; moderation: *the clemency of California weather.*

clem•ent (klem′ənt) /ˈklɛmənt/ *adj.* of or relating to clemency: *a clement judge; clement weather.* **—clem′ent•ly,** *adv.*

clench (klench) /klɛntʃ/ *v.* [~ + *obj*] **1.** to close (the hands, etc.) tightly: *clenched his fists in frustration.* **2.** to grasp firmly; grip: *I clenched the cigar in my teeth.*

cler•gy (klûr′jē) /ˈklɜrdʒiy/ *n.* [*plural; used with a plural verb*] the group of appointed or ordained leaders in a religion, as distinguished from the laity.

cler•gy•man (klûr′jē mən) /ˈklɜrdʒiymən/ *n.* [*count*], *pl.* **-men.** a member of the clergy.

cler•ic (kler′ik) /ˈklɛrɪk/ *n.* [*count*] a member of the clergy.

cler•i•cal (kler′i kəl) /ˈklɛrɪkəl/ *adj.* **1.** of, relating to, appropriate for, or assigned to an office clerk: *made a clerical error in the report.* **2.** doing the work of a clerk: *an increase in our clerical staff.* **3.** of, relating to, or characteristic of the clergy or a cleric: *clerical clothes.* **—cler′i•cal•ly,** *adv.*

clerk (klûrk) /klɜrk/ *n.* [*count*] **1.** a person employed to keep records or perform general tasks in an office, etc.: *worked as a law clerk for a judge.* **2.** a salesclerk: *Ask another clerk about finding your size.*

clev•er (klev′ər) /ˈklɛvər/ *adj.*, **-er, -est. 1.** mentally bright; having quick intelligence; able: *a clever student in his class.* **2.** skillful with the hands or body; dexterous or nimble: *She was very clever with her hands, especially at woodworking.* **3.** skillful in a dishonest way; cunning: *a clever scheme to get around the regulations.* **4.** showing inventiveness or originality; ingenious: *a clever idea.* **—clev′er•ly,** *adv.*: *was cleverly led into a trap.* **—clev′er•ness,** *n.* [*noncount*]

cli•ché or **cli•che** (klē shā′, kli-) /kliyˈʃey, klɪ-/ *n.* [*count*] **1.** an overused or trite expression, plot, style, etc.: *The phrases* sadder but wiser, *or* strong as an ox *are clichés.* **2.** anything that has become trite through overuse. **—cli•chéd′,** *adj.*: *a clichéd remark.*

click (klik) /klɪk/ *n.* [*count*] **1.** a slight, sharp sound: *the click of the key in a latch.* **—*v.* 2.** to (cause to) give off or make such a sound: [*no obj*]: *The lock clicked softly.* [~ + *obj*]: *He clicked the light switch on.* **3.** [*no obj*] *Informal.* **a.** to succeed; make a hit: *His career finally clicked with that hit record.* **b.** to fit together; function well together: *Their personalities don't click.* **c.** to become suddenly clear or understood: *His mind clicked and he figured a way out.* **4.** [~ + *on* + *obj*] *Computers.* to press and release a mouse button rapidly, as to select an icon: *Click on the trash icon to erase the file.* **5.** [~ + *obj*] to strike together with a click: *He clicked his heels and saluted.* **—click′er,** *n.* [*count*]

cli•ent (klī′ənt) /ˈklayənt/ *n.* [*count*] **1.** a person or group that uses the professional advice or services of a lawyer, etc.: *argued that his client was innocent of the charges.* **2.** a person who is receiving the benefits, etc., of a social welfare agency, etc.: *I see hundreds of clients a week.* **3.** a customer. **—cli′ent•less,** *adj.*

cli•en•tele (klī′ən tel′) /ˌklayən'tɛl/ *n.* [*count; usually singular*] clients or customers thought of as a group: *a loyal clientele.*

cliff (klif) /klɪf/ *n.* [*count*] a high, steep rock face; precipice: *The car drove off the cliff onto the rocks below.* See illustration at LANDSCAPE.

cliff′-hang′er or **cliff′hang′er,** *n.* [*count*] a situation in which the outcome is uncertain up to the very last moment.

cli•mac•tic (klī mak′tik) /klay'mæktɪk/ *adj.* of, relating to, or being a climax: *the climactic scene of the movie.*

cli•mate (klī′mit) /'klaymɪt/ *n.* [*count*] **1.** the general weather conditions of a region, averaged over a series of years: *The climate in that country was cloudy, cool, or cold.* **2.** a region or area that has a given climate: *Dad retired to live in a warm climate.* **3.** the general attitudes or conditions of a group, period, or place: *a climate of political unrest.*

cli•mat•ic (klī mat′ik) /klay'mætɪk/ *adj.* [*before a noun*] of or relating to climate: *undergoing gradual climatic changes.* **—cli•mat′ic•al•ly,** *adv.*

cli•max (klī′maks) /'klaymæks/ *n.* [*count*] **1.** the most intense point in the development of something; culmination: *Being elected president was the climax of his career.* **2.** (in a literary work) the decisive moment in a plot: *The climax of the play is the murder of the hero.* **3.** an orgasm. **—***v.* **4.** to bring to or reach a climax: [*no obj*]: *The play climaxes early.* [~ + *obj*]: *The election victory climaxed a long career in politics.*

climb (klīm) /klaym/ *v.* **1.** to go up or ascend: [*no obj*]: *The sun climbed over the hill.* [~ + *obj*]: *to climb the stairs.* **2.** [*no obj*] to slope upward: *The road climbs steeply.* **3.** to move on or proceed using the hands and feet, esp. on or from an elevated area: [~ + *into* + *obj*]: *The bodyguards climbed quickly into the car.* [~ + *out of* + *obj*]: *We climbed out of the car.* [~ + *over* + *obj*]: *shot while trying to climb over the fence.* [~ + *along* + *obj*]: *He climbed along the ledge.* [~ + *obj*]: *The prisoners climbed the wall and escaped.* **4.** [*no obj*] to ascend in fame or fortune: *You can climb fairly high if you have money.* **5.** [*no obj*] (of numbers, etc.) to rise or increase in value: *Prices climbed by as much as fifty cents a share today.* **—***n.* [*count*] **6.** a climbing; an ascent by climbing: *a climb to the top of the hill.* **7.** a place to be climbed: *That peak is quite a climb.* **—climb′er,** *n.* [*count*]

clime (klīm) /klaym/ *n.* CLIMATE.

clinch (klinch) /klɪntʃ/ *v.* **1.** [~ + *obj*] to settle (a matter) completely or decisively: *They clinched the deal in an hour.* **2.** (of boxers) to hold (another) about the arms or body to hinder the opponent's punches: [~ + *obj*]: *clinched his opponent.* [*no obj*]: *just trying to clinch and get a breather.* **3.** [*no obj*] *Slang.* to embrace, esp. passionately: *The lovers clinched.* **—***n.* [*count*] **4.** the act of clinching: *boxers in a clinch.* **—clinch′ing,** *adj.*: *a clinching argument.*

clinch•er (klin′chər) /'klɪntʃər/ *n.* [*count*] **1.** a person or thing that clinches. **2.** a statement, etc., that settles something decisively: *When we found he was lying, that was the clincher.*

cling (kling) /klɪŋ/ *v.,* **clung** (klung) /klʌŋ/ **cling•ing,** *n.* **—***v.* **1.** [~ + *to*] to adhere closely; stick to: *Wet paper clings to glass.* **2.** to hold tight, as by grasping or embracing; cleave: [~ + *to* + *obj*]: *The child clung to her mother.* [*no obj;* ~ + *together*]: *We clung together and wouldn't let go.* **3.** [~ + *to* + *obj*] to remain attached, as to a person, etc.: *She's clinging to the past; she has to go forward and forget him.* **—***n.* [*noncount*] **4.** a condition of clinging: *the cling of a garment.* **—cling′y,** *adj.,* **-i•er, -i•est.**

cling•ing (kling′ing) /'klɪŋɪŋ/ *adj.* **1.** sticking to, or fitting tightly to, the body: *a clinging, hot blouse.* **2.** overly attached or dependent on another: *has gotten over being a clinging child.*

clin•ic (klin′ik) /'klɪnɪk/ *n.* [*count*] **1.** a place for the medical treatment of patients who are not staying at a hospital. **2.** a group of physicians, etc., working together or sharing facilities: *a blood-disease clinic.* **3.** a group meeting for extra instruction: *a reading clinic.*

clin•i•cal (klin′i kəl) /'klɪnɪkəl/ *adj.* **1.** [*before a noun*] of or relating to a clinic or a hospital: *clinical buildings.* **2.** concerned with or based on actual observation and treatment of disease in patients, and not on theory or research: *need to conduct clinical studies on patients.* **3.** overly logical and factual; cold and uncaring: *his clinical detachment as he watched his life fall apart.* **—clin′i•cal•ly,** *adv.*: *described the disease clinically.*

cli•ni•cian (kli nish′ən) /klɪ'nɪʃən/ *n.* [*count*] a physician involved in the treatment and observation of patients, and not engaged in research.

clink[1] (klingk) /klɪŋk/ *v.* **1.** to (cause to) make a light, sharp, ringing sound: [*no obj*]: *The coins clinked together.* [~ + *obj*]: *We always clink our glasses together and say "Cheers!"* **—***n.* [*count*] **2.** a clinking sound.

clink[2] (klingk) /klɪŋk/ *n.* [*count; usually singular: the* + ~] *Slang.* a prison; jail; lockup: *Throw him in the clink!*

clink•er[1] (kling′kər) /'klɪŋkər/ *n.* [*noncount*] a mass of matter that cannot be burnt and is fused together, as by the burning of coal.

clink•er[2] (kling′kər) /'klɪŋkər/ *n.* [*count*] *Slang.* **1.** a wrong note in a musical performance. **2.** any mistake or error. **3.** a failure; a product of inferior quality: *The car turned out to be a clinker.*

clip[1] (klip) /klɪp/ *v.,* **clipped, clipped** or **clipt** (klipt) /klɪpt/ **clip•ping,** *n.* **—***v.* **1.** [~ + *obj*] to cut off or out, as with scissors; to trim or give shape to something: *to clip a rose from a bush; to clip a hedge.* **2.** [~ + *obj*] to cut short; curtail: *We clipped our visit by a week.* **3.** [~ + *obj*] *Informal.* to hit with a quick, sharp blow: *He clipped me on the jaw.* **4.** [*no obj*] to move swiftly: *The motorcycle clipped along the highway.* **—***n.* [*count*] **5.** the act of clipping; something clipped off. **6.** FILM CLIP. **7.** *Informal.* CLIPPING (def. 2). **8.** *Informal.* a quick, sharp blow: *a clip to the jaw.* **9.** [*usually: singular*] rate; pace: *moving at a rapid clip.*

clip[2] (klip) /klɪp/ *n., v.,* **clipped, clip•ping.** **—***n.* [*count*] **1.** a device that grips tightly, esp. a clasp for holding together papers, etc. **2.** a frame holding cartridges to be put into the magazine of a gun: *an ammunition clip.* **3.** an article of jewelry clipped onto clothing, etc.: *She wore a diamond clip on her blouse.* **—***v.* **4.** to fasten with or as if with a clip: [~ + *on*]: *This earring clips on to the ear.* [~ + *obj*]: *The secretary clipped the reports together.*

clip•board (klip′bôrd′, -bōrd′) /'klɪpˌbɔrd, -ˌbowrd/ *n.* [*count*] a small board used to write on, with a clip at the top for holding papers.

clip′ joint′, *n.* [*count*] *Slang.* a business, as a nightclub, that overcharges or cheats its customers.

clip•per (klip′ər) /'klɪpər/ *n.* [*count*] **1.** a person or thing that clips. **2.** Often, **clippers.** [*plural; often used with a plural verb*] a cutting tool, esp. shears: *hedge clippers.* **3.** Usually, **clippers.** [*plural; usually used with a plural verb*] a tool for cutting hair, toenails, etc. **4.** a swift sailing vessel, esp. a three-masted ship built in the U.S. around 1845–70.

clip•ping (klip′ing) /'klɪpɪŋ/ *n.* [*count*] **1.** the act of a person or thing that clips. **2.** a piece of something that has been clipped: *lawn clippings.* **3.** an article, etc., clipped from a newspaper or magazine: *clippings for apartments for rent.*

clique (klēk, klik) /kliyk, klɪk/ *n.* [*count*] a small group of people who keep others from joining them: *all the little cliques in school.* **—cli′quey, cli′quy,** *adj.*: *a cliquey group.* **—cli′quish,** *adj.* **—cli′quish•ly,** *adv.* **—cli′quish•ness,** *n.* [*noncount*]

clit•o•ris (klit′ər is, kli tôr′is, -tōr′-) /'klɪtərɪs, klɪ'tɔrɪs, -'towr-/ *n.* [*count*], *pl.* **clit•o•ris•es, cli•to•ri•des** (kli tôr′i dēz′, -tōr′-) /klɪ'tɔrɪˌdiyz, -'towr-/. the small organ at the front part of the female genitals. **—clit′o•ral,** *adj.*

cloak (klōk) /klowk/ *n.* [*count*] **1.** a loose outer garment, such as a cape: *a beautiful cloak of ermine.* **2.** something that covers or conceals; disguise: *They negotiated under a cloak of secrecy.* **—***v.* [~ + *obj*] **3.** to cover with or as if with a cloak: *The magician was cloaked in black silk.* **4.** to hide; conceal: *They cloaked their fear with jokes.*

cloak′-and-dag′ger, *adj.* [*before a noun*] of or relating to spying or mystery: *a cloak-and-dagger tale of international espionage.*

cloak•room (klōk′rōōm′, -rŏŏm′) /'klowkˌruwm, -ˌrʊm/ *n.* [*count*] **1.** a room in which outer garments may be left for a while. **2.** *Brit.* a baggage room, as at a railway station.

clob•ber[1] (klob′ər) /'klɒbər/ *v.* [~ + *obj*] *Informal.* **1.** to hit, beat, or batter severely: *We clobbered the thief with a baseball bat.* **2.** to defeat decisively or completely: *We clobbered them, 56-0!*

clob•ber[2] (klob′ər) /'klɒbər/ *n.* [*noncount*] *Brit. Informal.* clothes or other personal articles.

clock (klok) /klɒk/ *n.* [*count*] **1.** a relatively large instrument for telling time. See illustration at OFFICE. **2.** TIME

CLOCK. **3.** a meter for measuring and recording speed, etc.: *The skier is racing against the clock.* **4.** BIOLOGICAL CLOCK. **—*v.*** **5.** [~ + *obj*] to time, test, or determine by means of a clock or watch: *The racehorse was clocked at two minutes thirty seconds.* **6. clock in** (or **out**), [*no obj*] to begin (or end) the day's work, esp. by punching a time clock: *What time did you clock in today?* **—*Idiom.*** **7. around the clock,** [*noncount*] **a.** for the entire 24-hour day without pause: *The factory shifts worked around the clock.* **b.** without stopping for rest; tirelessly: *working at this project around the clock.*

clock′ ra′dio, *n.* [*count*], *pl.* **clock radios.** a radio combined with an alarm clock serving as a timer to turn the radio on or off at a set time.

clock•wise (klok′wīz′) /ˈklɒkˌwayz/ *adv.* **1.** in the same direction as the movement of the hands of a clock when viewed from the front or from above: *The handle turns clockwise.* **—*adj.*** **2.** directed clockwise: *a clockwise movement.*

clock•work (klok′wûrk′) /ˈklɒkˌwɜrk/ *n.* **1.** [*noncount*] the mechanism of a clock. **2.** [*count*] any mechanism similar to that of a clock: *toys run by a winding clockwork.* **—*Idiom.*** **3. like clockwork,** [*noncount*] with regularity or precision: *Here she comes, home at 6:30, like clockwork.*

clod (klod) /klɒd/ *n.* [*count*] **1.** a lump or mass, esp. of earth or clay. **2.** a stupid or very clumsy person. **—clod′dish,** *adj.* **—clod′dish•ly,** *adv.* **—clod′dish•ness,** *n.* [*noncount*]

clod•hop•per (klod′hop′ər) /ˈklɒdˌhɒpər/ *n.* [*count*] **1.** a clumsy person; bumpkin. **2. clodhoppers,** [*plural*] strong, heavy shoes.

clog (klog, klôg) /klɒg, klɔg/ *v.,* **clogged, clog•ging,** *n.* **—*v.*** **1.** to (cause to) become blocked or choked up: [~ + *obj*]: *All that hair has clogged the drain.* [~ + *obj* + *up*]: *Hair has clogged the drain up again.* [~ + *up* + *obj*]: *That slime has clogged up the drainpipe.* [*no obj;* (~ + *up*)]: *The drain has clogged (up) again.* **2.** [~ + *obj*] to fill too much; overfill; jam: *Cars clogged the highway.* **—*n.*** [*count*] **3.** anything that restricts movement: *a clog in the drain.* **4.** a shoe or sandal with a thick sole of wood, cork, etc.

clogged (klogd, klôgd) /klɒgd, klɔgd/ *adj.* [~ (+ *up*)] (of the nose or throat) blocked up so that breathing is difficult: *a badly clogged nose.*

clois•ter (kloi′stər) /ˈklɔystər/ *n.* [*count*] **1.** a covered walk, esp. in a church or other religious building, opening onto a courtyard. **2.** a courtyard bordered with such walks. **3.** a place for religious people to live, such as a monastery. **—*v.*** [~ + *oneself*] **4.** to keep away from the world in a monastery: *She cloistered herself in the convent.* **5.** to shut away from the world and live apart: *cloistered himself in his library with his books.* See -CLOS-.

clomp (klomp) /klɒmp/ *v.* CLUMP (def. 5).

clone (klōn) /klown/ *n., v.,* **cloned, clon•ing.** **—*n.*** [*count*] **1. a.** a living thing that is identical in its genes to the unit or individual from which it was obtained. **b.** a group of identical individuals that come from the same original individual. **2.** a person or thing that duplicates another in appearance, etc.: *The new computers are clones of the original model.* **—*v.*** [~ + *obj*] **3.** to produce a copy of: *cloned the new machines by using the same microchip.* **4.** to cause to grow as a clone: *They cloned some remarkable organisms in their laboratory.* **—clon′al,** *adj.* **—clon′er,** *n.* [*count*]

clop (klop) /klɒp/ *n., v.,* **clopped, clop•ping.** **—*n.*** [*count*] **1.** a sound made by a horse's hoof striking the ground. **—*v.*** [*no obj*] **2.** to make or move with such a sound.

-clos-, *root.* *-clos-* comes from Latin, where it has the meaning "close." This meaning is found in such words as: CLOISTER, CLOSE, CLOSET, DISCLOSE, ENCLOSE.

close (*v., n.* klōz; *adj., adv.* klōs) /*v., n.* klowz; *adj., adv.* klows/ *v.,* **closed, clos•ing,** *adj.,* **clos•er, clos•est,** *adv., n.* **—*v.*** **1.** to (cause to) become shut: [*no obj*]: *The door closed with a bang.* [~ + *obj*]: *closed her eyes and slept.* **2.** to stop or obstruct (a gap, etc.): [~ (+ *up*) + *obj*]: *to close (up) a hole in the wall.* [~ + *obj* (+ *up*)]: *to close it (up).* **3.** [~ + *obj*] to restrict passage across; prevent access to: *The country closed its border to tourists.* **4. a.** [~ + *obj*] to bring together the parts of: *She closed her lips.* **b.** [*no obj*]: *Her lips closed.* **5.** to (cause to) come to an end: [~ + *obj*]: *The chair moved to close debate.* [*no obj*]: *The sermon closed with a warning not to forget God's poor.* **6.** to end or conclude (a business deal) successfully: [~ + *obj*]: *We closed a deal that was good for both our companies.* [*no obj*]: *They managed to close on the house they wanted.* **7.** to stop giving the usual services (of): [*no obj*]: *School closed for the summer.* [~ + *obj*]: *The owners closed the store for the night.* **8.** [~ + *obj*] to shut down; suspend the operation of: *The police closed the bar for selling liquor to minors.* **9.** [*no obj*] (of a stock) to be priced at the end of a day or when stocks are traded: *The American Exchange closed up at an average 50 cents a share.* **10. close down,** to end operation (of); discontinue; stop: [*no obj*]: *The radio station closed down at 3 a.m.* [~ + *down* + *obj*]: *The owners closed down the steel mills.* [~ + *obj* + *down*]: *The owners closed them down and left.* **11. close in on** or **upon,** [~ + *in* + *on/upon* + *obj*] **a.** to approach quietly and secretly, such as to capture or kill: *They closed in on the wounded animal.* **b.** to surround, as if to suffocate: *The fog closed in on us.* **12. close out, a.** to reduce the price of (merchandise) for quick sale: [~ + *out* + *obj*]: *They closed out mattresses.* [~ + *obj* + *out*]: *closed bedroom sets out.* **b.** [~ + *out* + *obj*] to dispose of completely; liquidate: *to close out a bank account.* **—*adj.*** **13.** [*be* + ~ (+ *to* + *obj*)] being near in space or time; nearby: *Our apartment is close to the train station. Winter must be close; it's gotten colder.* **14.** [*often: be* + ~ (+ *to* + *obj*)] marked by similarity in degree, etc.: *Dark pink is close to red.* **15.** [*before a noun*] near in a kind of family relationship: *He was a close relative.* **16.** [*before a noun*] based on a strong feeling of respect, honor, or love; intimate; dear: *She's a close friend.* **17.** [*be* + ~ + *to* + *obj*] not differing much from (the subject talked about): *Your remarks are close to treason!* **18.** fitting tightly: *a close sweater.* **19.** [*before a noun*] careful; strict; thorough; searching: *Close investigation revealed the accountant's error.* **20.** nearly even or equal: *a close contest.* **21.** having the parts near to each other; compact; dense: *cloth with a close weave.* **22.** confined; narrow; stuffy: *It's pretty close in here; can't we turn on the air-conditioner?* **23.** [*be* + ~] practicing secrecy; secretive: *They were very close about their home country.* **—*adv.*** **24.** [*often:* ~ + *to* + *obj*] near; close by; closely: *I live fairly close to the train station; stood close to her friend.* **—*n.*** [*count; usually singular*] **25.** the act of closing. **26.** the end or conclusion: *At the close of the century we expect worse global warming.* **—*Idiom.*** **27. close ranks,** to join forces in a show of loyalty, esp. to deal with difficulty: *It's time for us to close ranks and stay together.* **28. close up,** from close range; in a detailed manner: *When you examine this painting close up, you'll see it's not genuine.* **—close•ly** (klōs′lē) /ˈklowsliy/ *adv.* **—close•ness** (klōs′nis) /ˈklowsnɪs/ *n.* [*noncount*] **—clos•er** (klō′zər) /ˈklowzər/ *n.* [*count*] See -CLOS-.

close′ call′ (klōs) /klows/ *n.* [*count*] a narrow escape from danger or trouble.

closed (klōzd) /klowzd/ *adj.* **1.** not open for business: *The stores are closed on Sundays.* **2.** no longer operating: *All the closed shops in the mall reflect the decline of the economy.*

closed′-cap′tioned, *adj.* (of a television program) broadcast with captions visible with a special device, for people who cannot hear well.

closed′-cir′cuit tel′evision, *n.* [*noncount*] a system of televising by cable to designated viewing sets.

closed′ shop′, *n.* [*count*] a business in which union membership is a condition of employment.

close•fist•ed (klōs′fis′tid) /ˈklowsˈfɪstɪd/ *adj.* not generous in spending; stingy; miserly.

close′-fit′ting (klōs′-) /ˈklows-/ *adj.* (of a garment) fitting tightly or snugly to the body: *a close-fitting jacket.*

close′-knit′ (klōs-) /klows-/ *adj.* tightly united or connected socially, religiously, politically, etc.: *a close-knit family.*

close•mouthed (klōs′mouthd′, -moutht′) /ˈklowsˈmawðd, -ˈmawθt/ *adj.* [*often: be* + ~] giving no information; uncommunicative: *very close-mouthed about the reasons she was fired.*

close•out (klōz′out′) /ˈklowzˌawt/ *n.* [*count*] **1.** a sale on all goods before the business itself is sold. **2.** a sale on merchandise that will no longer be carried by the store.

clos•et (kloz′it) /ˈklɒzɪt/ *n.* [*count*] **1.** a small room or cabinet for storing clothing, food, etc. See illustration at APARTMENT. **2.** WATER CLOSET. **—*adj.*** [*before a noun*] **3.** secret, hidden, or private: *a closet homosexual.* **—*v.*** [~ + *obj*] **4.** to shut up in a room for a conference, etc.: *The President was closeted with the senators for three hours.* **—*Idiom.*** **5. come out of the closet,** to reveal a fact about oneself previously kept hidden or unmentioned, as one's homosexuality. See -CLOS-.

close•up (klōs′up′) /ˈklowsˌʌp/ *n.* [*count*] **1.** a photograph taken at close range. **2.** an intimate view or presentation.

clos•ing (klō′zing) /ˈklowzɪŋ/ *adj.* **1.** [*before a noun*] ending; final: *the closing days of the election primary.* **—***n.* [*count*] **2.** the conclusion of a business deal, esp. the buying and selling of a house: *signed the papers at the closing.*

clo•sure (klō′zhər) /ˈklowʒər/ *n.* **1.** the act of closing or the state of being closed: [*count*]: *the closures of several companies.* [*noncount*]: *forcing closure of the border.* **2.** [*noncount*] a bringing to an end; conclusion: *His writing needs better closure; he doesn't know how to end an essay.* See -CLOS-.

clot (klot) /klɒt/ *n., v.,* **clot•ted, clot•ting.** **—***n.* [*count*] **1.** a semisolid mass, such as of blood: *Blood clots had blocked his arteries.* **2.** *Brit.* BLOCKHEAD. **—***v.* **3.** to (cause to) form into clots; coagulate: [*no obj*]: *That substance helps blood to clot faster.* [~ + *obj*]: *That substance clots blood.*

cloth (klôth, kloth) /klɔθ, klɒθ/ *n., pl.* **cloths** (klôthz, klothz, klôths, kloths), *adj.* **—***n.* **1.** [*noncount*] fabric made by weaving or knitting from wool, silk, polyester, etc., used for clothing, upholstery, etc. **2.** [*count*] a piece of such a fabric for a particular purpose: *a cloth for dusting.* **3. the cloth,** [*noncount*] the clergy: *a man of the cloth.* **—***adj.* [*before a noun*] **4.** of or made of cloth: *a cloth cap.* **5.** clothbound: *cloth-cover books.* **—cloth′like′,** *adj.*

clothe (klōth) /klowð/ *v.* [~ + *obj*], **clothed** or **clad** (klad) /klæd/ **cloth•ing.** **1.** to dress; attire: *clothed in elegant finery.* **2.** to provide (someone) with clothing: *The church needs money to clothe the poor.* **3.** to cover with or as if with clothing: *The mountains were clothed in clouds.*

clothes (klōz, klōthz) /klowz, klowðz/ *n.* [*plural*] garments for the body; articles of dress. **—Usage.** The "th" sounds in CLOTH "fabric" and its plural CLOTHS "pieces of fabric" are pronounced quite differently from CLOTHES "garments for the body and things you wear." Notice too that the meanings are different, and that one's CLOTHES may or may not be made of CLOTH. The noncount noun CLOTHING (the "th" sound here is like that of CLOTHES) is a more formal word for CLOTHES, and it must be used when we want to refer to just one thing we wear: *one article of clothing.*

clothes•horse (klōz′hôrs′, klōthz′-) /ˈklowzˌhɔrs, ˈklowðz-/ *n.* [*count*] **1.** a person too fond of clothes. **2.** a frame on which to hang wet laundry.

clothes•line (klōz′līn′, klōthz′-) /ˈklowzˌlayn, ˈklowðz-/ *n.* [*count*] a line for hanging clothes to dry, usually outdoors.

clothes•pin (klōz′pin′, klōthz′-, klōs′-) /ˈklowzˌpɪn, ˈklowðz-, ˈklows-/ *n.* [*count*] a device made like a clip for fastening articles to a clothesline.

cloth•ing (klō′thing) /ˈklowðɪŋ/ *n.* [*noncount*] clothes considered as a group; apparel: *We need to provide warm clothing to the homeless.* SEE ILLUSTRATION. **—Usage.** See CLOTHES.

cloud (kloud) /klawd/ *n.* [*count*] **1.** a white or gray mass of particles of water or ice in the air: *The clouds blocked the sun.* **2.** any similar mass, esp. of smoke or dust: *clouds of smoke.* **3.** a great number of insects, etc., flying in a group that resembles such a mass. **4.** anything that causes fear, suspicion, etc.: *Everyone could see the clouds of war beginning to gather.* **—***v.* **5.** to cover with or as if with clouds: [~ + *obj*]: *Steam had clouded the mirror.* [*no obj*]: *The mirror clouded with steam.* **6.** [~ + *obj*] to make sad or gloomy: *The death of her father clouded the publication of her book.* **7.** [~ + *obj*] to confuse; make hard to understand: *Don't try to cloud the issue with unnecessary details.* **8.** to reveal distress, anxiety, etc., in (a part of one's face): [~ + *obj*]: *Worry clouded his brow.* [*no obj;* ~ *(+ over)*]: *Her brow clouded (over) with anger.* **—*Idiom.*** **9. have one's head in the clouds, a.** to be lost in thought; be daydreaming. **b.** to be impractical. **10. on a cloud** or **on cloud nine,** [*be* + ~] very happy; in high spirits: *I was on cloud nine when she said she would marry me.* **11. under a cloud,** in disgrace; under suspicion: *He's still under a cloud from his earlier conviction for robbery.* **—cloud′less,** *adj.*

cloud•burst (kloud′bûrst′) /ˈklawdˌbɜrst/ *n.* [*count*] a sudden and very heavy rainfall.

cloud•y (klou′dē) /ˈklawdiy/ *adj.,* **-i•er, -i•est.** **1.** full of clouds; covered with clouds: *cloudy skies.* **2.** hard to see through; not clear: *cloudy old windows.* **3.** unclear; confused: *cloudy thinking.* **—cloud′i•ness,** *n.* [*noncount*]

clout (klout) /klawt/ *n.* **1.** [*count*] a blow or hit, esp. with the hand; cuff: *got a clout on the head.* **2.** [*noncount*] *Informal.* influence upon people who make decisions: *still had a lot of clout in the sales department.* **—***v.* [~ + *obj*] **3.** to hit or cuff: *She clouted the intruder on the head.* **—clout′er,** *n.* [*count*]

clove[1] (klōv) /klowv/ *n.* [*count*] **1.** the dried flower bud of a tropical tree of the myrtle family, used as a spice: *The cloves came from Zanzibar.* **2.** the tree itself.

clove[2] (klōv) /klowv/ *n.* [*count*] one of the small bulbs formed in certain plants, as garlic.

clove[3] (klōv) /klowv/ *v.* a pt. of CLEAVE[2].

clo•ven (klō′vən) /ˈklowvən/ *v.* **1.** a pp. of CLEAVE[2]. **—***adj.* **2.** cleft; split; divided in two parts: *the cloven hoof of a goat.*

clo•ver (klō′vər) /ˈklowvər/ *n., pl.* **-vers,** (*esp. when thought of as a group*) **-ver.** **1.** a plant of the legume family, having three leaves joined together: [*count*]: *looking for a rare four-leaf clover to bring good luck.* [*noncount*]: *cattle eating clover in the pasture.* **—*Idiom.*** **2. in clover,** [*noncount*] living a life of prosperity and comfort. **—clo′vered,** *adj.*

clo•ver•leaf (klō′vər lēf′) /ˈklowvərˌliyf/ *n., pl.* **-leafs, -leaves,** *adj.* **—***n.* [*count*] **1.** a road arrangement resembling a four-leaf clover in form, for permitting traffic between two intersecting highways: *We got onto the cloverleaf and entered the highway going south.* **—***adj.* [*before a noun*] **2.** shaped like a leaf of clover: *a cloverleaf arrangement of roads.*

clown (kloun) /klawn/ *n.* [*count*] **1.** a performer, esp. in a circus, who wears a funny costume and makeup, and acts to make people laugh. **2.** one who does pranks to make people laugh; a joker: *He was a clown who had his classmates laughing.* **3.** *Slang.* a fool. **—***v.* [*no obj;* ~ *(+ around)*] **4.** to act like a clown; act silly or playfully: *The girls were clowning (around) most of the night.* **—clown′ish,** *adj.* **—clown′ish•ly,** *adv.* **—clown′ish•ness,** *n.* [*noncount*]

cloy•ing (kloi′ing) /ˈklɔyɪŋ/ *adj.* unpleasant because of excess: *cloying perfume.*

clr., an abbreviation of: clear.

club (klub) /klʌb/ *n., v.,* **clubbed, club•bing.** **—***n.* **1.** [*count*] a heavy stick that can be used as a weapon; cudgel: *The police swung their clubs at the demonstrators.* **2.** [*count*] a stick used to hit a ball in various games, such as golf: *a set of golf clubs.* **3.** [*count*] a group of people organized for a social purpose: *an athletic club.* **4.** [*count*] the building or rooms used or occupied by such a group: *a game of tennis at the club.* **5.** [*count*] an organization that offers its members certain benefits: *a book club.* **6.** [*count*] a nightclub or cabaret. **7. a.** [*count*] a black figure on a playing card that resembles a three-leafed clover. **b.** [*count*] a card bearing such figures: *My last card was a club.* **c. clubs,** the suit of cards so marked: [*noncount; used with a singular verb*]: *Clubs has the lowest value in bridge.* [*count; used with a plural verb*]: *Clubs were bid first.* **—***v.* **8.** [~ + *obj*] to beat with or as if with a club: *The riot police clubbed the demonstrators and hauled them away.* **9.** [*no obj;* ~ *(+ together)*] to combine or join (together): *They clubbed (together) to buy their teacher a going-away present.*

club•foot (klub′fo͝ot′) /ˈklʌbˌfʊt/ *n., pl.* **-feet.** **1.** [*count*] a badly formed twisted foot, present at birth. **2.** [*noncount*] the condition of having such a foot: *afflicted with clubfoot.* **—club′foot′ed,** *adj.*

club•house (klub′hous′) /ˈklʌbˌhaws/ *n.* [*count*] **1.** a building or room occupied by a club. **2.** the dressing room of an athletic team.

club′ sand′wich, *n.* [*count*] a sandwich typically consisting of three slices of toast or bread with two layers of meat, lettuce, tomato, and mayonnaise.

club′ so′da, *n.* SODA WATER (def. 1).

cluck (kluk) /klʌk/ *v.* [*no obj*] **1.** to utter the cry of a hen brooding or calling her chicks. **—***n.* [*count*] **2.** a clucking sound.

clue (klo͞o) /kluw/ *n., v.,* **clued, clu•ing.** **—***n.* [*count*] **1.** anything that guides or directs in the solving of a problem, game, puzzle, etc.: *I don't have a clue why he's so upset.* **—***v.* **2. clue in,** [~ + *obj* + *in*] to provide with necessary information: *Can you clue us in on the arrangements?*

clump (klump) /klʌmp/ *n.* [*count*] **1.** a small group or cluster, esp. of trees or plants. **2.** a lump or mass: *a clump of muddy fur.* **3.** a heavy, thumping sound, etc.: *the clump of feet on the stairs.* **—***v.* **4.** [*no obj*] Also, **clomp.** to walk heavily and clumsily: *His heavy boots clumped on the stairs.* **5.** to (cause to) be gathered into

clothing

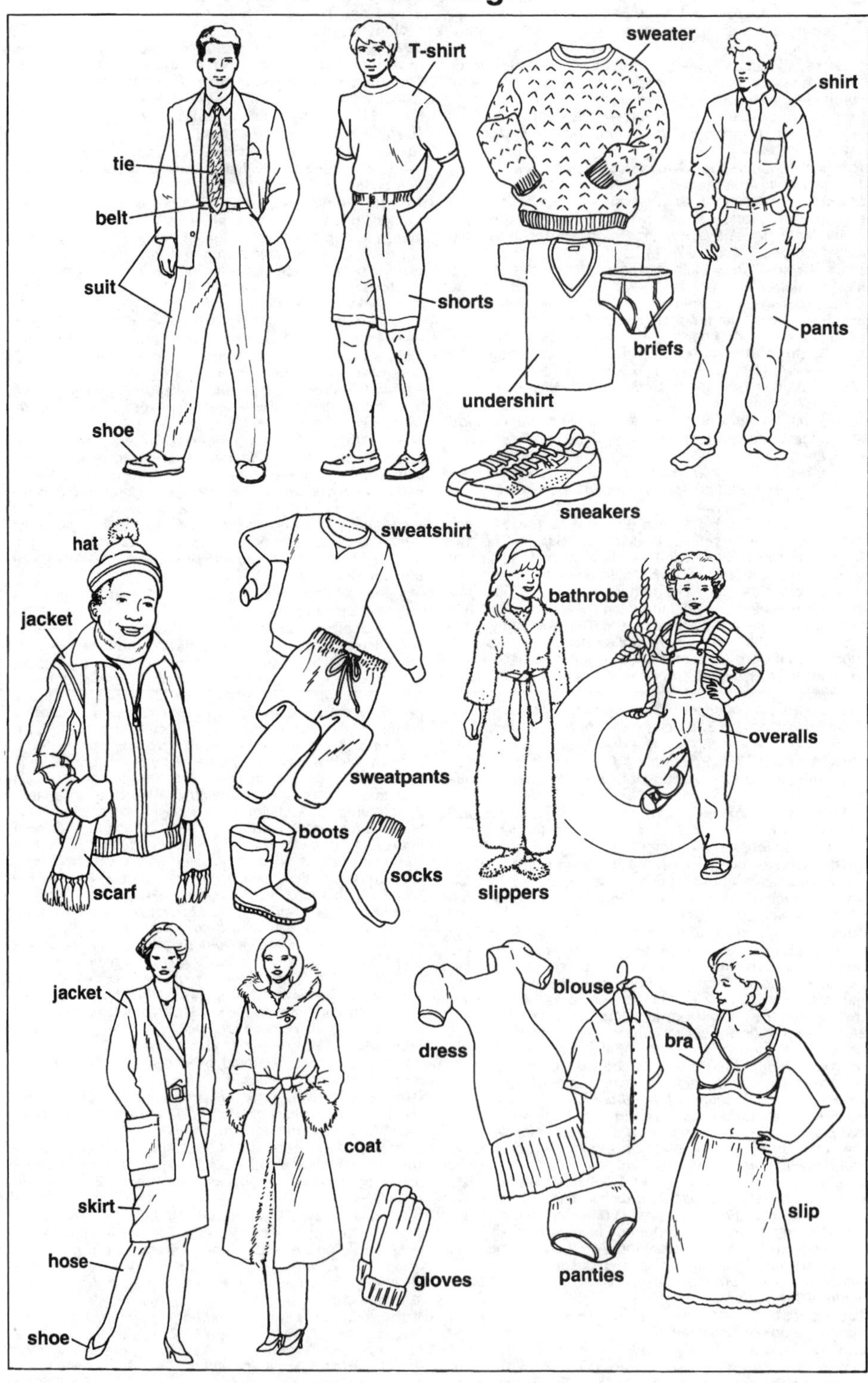

T-shirt
sweater
shirt
tie
belt
suit
shorts
pants
briefs
undershirt
shoe
sneakers
hat
sweatshirt
jacket
bathrobe
overalls
sweatpants
boots
socks
scarf
slippers
jacket
blouse
dress
bra
coat
skirt
slip
hose
gloves
panties
shoe

clumps; to (cause to) form into a clump: [*no obj; (~ + together)*]: *The settlers clumped (together) into little villages.* [*~ + obj (+ together)*]: *The towns were clumped (together) in little pockets.*

clum•sy (klum′zē) /'klʌmziy/ *adj.,* **-si•er, -si•est. 1.** awkward in movement or use; lacking skill: *a clumsy dancer.* **2.** awkwardly or poorly done: *a clumsy apology.* **3.** awkward or difficult to control or handle: *The heavy motorcycle was clumsy on the road.* —**clum′si•ly,** *adv.* —**clum′si•ness,** *n.* [*noncount*]

clung (klung) /klʌŋ/ *v.* pt. and pp. of CLING.

clunk (klungk) /klʌŋk/ *n.* [*count*] a heavy, dull sound: *We heard a clunk on the roof.*

clunk•er (klung′kər) /'klʌŋkər/ *n.* [*count*] *Informal.* **1.** something worthless or inferior. **2.** an old, worn-out machine, esp. a car.

clunk•y (klung′kē) /'klʌŋkiy/ *adj.,* **-i•er, -i•est.** *Informal.* awkwardly heavy; clumsy: *big clunky shoes.*

clus•ter (klus′tər) /'klʌstər/ *n.* [*count*] **1.** a number of things of the same kind, growing or held together; bunch: *a cluster of flowers.* **2.** a group of persons or things close together: *That cluster of stars is held together by gravitation.* —*v.* **3.** to form or gather in a cluster: [*no obj*]: *The students clustered around the professor.* [*~ + obj*]: *The students were clustered around the professor.*

clutch[1] (kluch) /klʌtʃ/ *v.* **1.** [*~ + obj*] to seize with or as if with the hands; hold tightly: *The little girl clutched her doll tightly.* **2. clutch at,** [*~ + obj*] **a.** to try to grasp or hold: *She clutched at my hand as I turned away.* **b.** to try to use, esp. in a desperate way and when all else fails: *I clutched at any excuse I could think of.* **3.** [*no obj*] to operate the clutch in a vehicle: *He clutched carefully and pulled out smoothly.* —*n.* [*count*] **4.** Often, **clutches.** [*plural*] power or control, esp. when escape is impossible: *fell into the clutches of the enemy.* **5.** a tight grip or hold: *Her clutch was strong on my arm.* **6. a.** a mechanism for connecting or disconnecting a shaft that drives a mechanism, such as in a car to shift gears: *The clutch isn't working properly.* **b.** a pedal or other control for operating this: *He pushed in the clutch and released it.* —*adj.* [*before a noun*] **7.** done in a critical situation: *a clutch shot that won the game.* **8.** dependable in crucial situations: *a clutch player.*

clutch[2] (kluch) /klʌtʃ/ *n.* [*count*] **1.** the number of eggs produced at one time: *a clutch of only three eggs.* **2.** a number of similar things.

clut•ter (klut′ər) /'klʌtər/ *v.* **1.** to fill with things in a disorderly manner: [*~ + (+ up) + obj*]: *Newspapers cluttered (up) the living room.* [*~ + obj (+ up)*]: *Don't clutter it (up).* —*n.* [*noncount*] **2.** a disorderly heap; litter: *a room full of clutter.*

cm or **cm.,** an abbreviation of: centimeter.

cmdg., an abbreviation of: commanding.

Cmdr., an abbreviation of: Commander.

cml., an abbreviation of: commercial.

CO, an abbreviation of: **1.** Colorado. **2.** Commanding Officer. **3.** conscientious objector.

co-, *prefix.* **1.** *co-* comes from Latin, where it has the meaning "joint, jointly, together." This meaning is found in such words as: COSTAR, COWORKER. **2.** A similar meaning for this prefix is "auxiliary, helping." This meaning is found in such words as: COPILOT.

Co. or **co.,** an abbreviation of: **1.** Company. **2.** County.

C/o or **c/o,** an abbreviation of: care of.

c.o., an abbreviation of: **1.** care of. **2.** carried over.

coach (kōch) /kowtʃ/ *n.* **1.** a large, horse-drawn, four-wheeled carriage, usually enclosed: [*count*]: *The coach pulled up and President Lincoln got aboard.* [*noncount; by/on + ~*]: *They traveled by coach to Fort Courage.* **2.** a bus; public motorbus: [*count*]: *Take the airport coach to the center of the city.* [*noncount; by/on + ~*]: *We traveled by coach to the center of the city.* **3.** [*count*]an ordinary railroad car. **4.** [*noncount*] a class of airline travel less expensive than first class: *His seat was in coach.* **5.** [*count*] a person who trains an athlete or team: *a football coach.* **6.** [*count*] a private instructor for a singer, actor, etc.: *a drama coach.* —*v.* **7.** to instruct or work as a coach: [*~ + obj*]: *to coach golfers.* [*no obj*]: *He wanted to coach but never got the chance.* —*adv.* **8.** in coach-class seats: *to fly coach.*

coach•man (kōch′mən) /'kowtʃmən/ *n.* [*count*], *pl.* **-men.** a man employed to drive a coach or carriage.

co•ag•u•late (kō ag′yə lāt′) / kow'ægyə,leyt/ *v.,* **-lat•ed, -lat•ing.** to change from a fluid into a thickened mass, as blood does when it forms a clot; congeal: [*no obj*]: *The blood from the wound coagulated.* [*~ + obj*]: *This substance does not coagulate the blood.* —**co•ag•u•la•tion** (kō ag′yə lā′shən) /kow,ægyə'leyʃən/ *n.* [*noncount*]

coal (kōl) /kowl/ *n.* **1.** [*noncount*] a mineral substance made of carbon, used as a fuel: *Coal is formed from dead vegetative matter.* **2.** [*count*] a piece of glowing or burned wood or other combustible substance: *a few coals still burning in the fireplace.* **3.** [*noncount*] charcoal. —***Idiom.*** **4. rake** or **haul over the coals,** [*rake/haul + obj + over the + ~-s*] to scold or reprimand severely: *raked him over the coals for falling asleep on guard duty.*

co•a•lesce (kō′ə les′) /,kowə'lɛs/ *v.* [*no obj*], **-lesced, -lesc•ing. 1.** to unite; join together: *The various groups coalesced into one party.* **2.** to blend or come together: *Their ideas coalesced into a new theory.* —**co′a•les′cence,** *n.* [*noncount*] See -ALESC-.

co•a•li•tion (kō′ə lish′ən) /,kowə'lɪʃən/ *n.* [*count*] a combination, esp. a temporary one between different groups, etc.: *The coalition government was formed by liberals, radicals, and socialists.* —**co′a•li′tion•al,** *adj.* —**co′a•li′tion•ist,** *n.* [*count*]

coal′ tar′, *n.* [*noncount*] a thick black liquid obtained from coal, used in making dyes and drugs.

coarse (kôrs, kōrs) /kɔrs, kowrs/ *adj.,* **coars•er, coars•est. 1.** made up of relatively large parts or particles: *coarse sand.* **2.** lacking in delicacy of texture, etc.: *coarse fabric; coarse skin.* **3.** lacking refinement; unpolished: *coarse manners.* **4.** vulgar; obscene: *coarse language.* —**coarse′ly,** *adv.* —**coarse′ness,** *n.* [*noncount*]

coars•en (kôr′sən, kōr′-) /'kɔrsən, 'kowr-/ *v.* to (cause to) become coarse: [*no obj*]: *His skin coarsened after years of working in the sun.* [*~ + obj*]: *That harsh weather coarsened his skin.*

coast (kōst) /kowst/ *n.* [*count*] **1.** the land next to the sea; seashore: *We drove along the coast on Route 1.* **2.** the region next to this land: *Up and down the eastern coast the storm raged.* **3.** a slide down a hill or slope, as on a sled. —*v.* [*no obj*] **4.** to descend or go down, as in a car, on a bicycle, etc., without using power: *We cut off the motor and coasted into town.* **5.** to go forward or progress with little effort: *In senior year many students want to coast through to graduation.* —***Idiom.*** **6. the coast is clear,** nothing is present to interfere with one's progress: *The guard's gone and the coast is clear; forward, men!*

coast•al (kōs′tl) /'kowstl/ *adj.* [*before a noun*] of or relating to the coast; located near or on the coast: *coastal waters; coastal towns; a coastal highway.*

coast•er (kō′stər) /'kowstər/ *n.* [*count*] **1.** a person or thing that coasts. **2.** a small dish or mat, esp. for placing under a glass. **3.** ROLLER COASTER.

Coast′ Guard′, *n.* [*proper noun; usually: the + ~*] a U.S. military service whose duty is to enforce laws of the sea, save lives and property at sea, etc.

coast•line (kōst′līn′) /'kowst,layn/ *n.* [*count*] **1.** the outline of a coast; shoreline: *a rugged coastline.* **2.** the land and water lying next to a shoreline.

coat (kōt) /kowt/ *n.* [*count*] **1.** an outer garment covering at least the upper part of the body: *He put on his warm winter coat.* See illustration at CLOTHING. **2.** a natural covering, such as hair, the bark of a tree, or the skin of a fruit: *an animal's fur coat.* **3.** a layer of anything that covers a surface: *a coat of paint.* —*v.* [*~ + obj*] **4.** to cover with a layer or coating: *furniture coated with dust.*

coat•ing (kō′ting) /'kowtɪŋ/ *n.* [*count*] a layer that covers a surface: *a thick coating of dust.*

coat′ of arms′, *n.* [*count*], *pl.* **coats′ of arms′.** a full display of the special designs, in the form of a shield, that represent a noble family.

coat′ of mail′, *n.* [*count*], *pl.* **coats′ of mail′.** a piece of clothing made of chain mail or metal scales, worn by knights on the upper part of the body.

coat•tail (kōt′tāl′) /'kowt,teyl/ *n.* [*count*] **1.** one of the two tails on the back of a man's dress coat or jacket. —*adj.* [*before a noun*] **2.** gained by association with another: *one of the coattail benefits of joining the union.* —***Idiom.*** **3. on someone's coattails,** aided by association with another: *elected to office on the President's coattails.*

co•au•thor (kō ô′thər, kō′ô′-) /kow'ɔθər, 'kow,ɔ-/ *n.* [*count*] **1.** one of two or more joint authors: *the book's coauthors.* —*v.* [*~ + obj*] **2.** to be a coauthor of: *He coauthored several important texts.*

coax (kōks) /kowks/ *v.* **1.** to attempt to influence by gentle persuasion, etc.; persuade: [*~ + obj + to + verb*]: *Maybe you can coax her to sing.* [*~ + obj + into + verb-ing*]: *See if you can coax them into giving us the* recipe. [*used with quotations*]: *"Come on," he coaxed,"you can do it."* **2.** [~ + *obj* + *from* + *obj*] to obtain or get (something) by coaxing: *to coax a secret from someone.* **3.** [~ + *obj*] to maneuver into a desired position by careful handling: *He coaxed the large chair through the tiny door.* **—coax′er,** *n.* [*count*] **—coax′ing•ly,** *adv.*: *He spoke coaxingly to the cat.*

co•ax′ial ca′ble (kō ak′sē əl) /kow'æksiyəl/ *n.* [*count*] a cable used for transmitting high-frequency signals.

cob (kob) /kɒb/ *n.* [*count*] **1.** CORNCOB (def. 1): *We ate corn on the cob at the summer picnic.* **2.** a male swan.

co•balt (kō′bôlt) /'kowbɔlt/ *n.* [*noncount*] a hard whitish metal element used to produce a blue coloring.

cob•ble[1] (kob′əl) /'kɒbəl/ *v.* [~ + *obj*], **-bled, -bling. 1.** to mend (shoes, etc.); patch: *He cobbled shoes for a living.* **2.** [~ (+ *together*)] to put together roughly or clumsily: *They cobbled (together) a temporary agreement.*

cob•ble[2] (kob′əl) /'kɒbəl/ *n., v.,* **-bled, -bling.** —*n.* [*count*] **1.** a cobblestone. —*v.* [~ + *obj*] **2.** to pave with cobblestones: *The streets were cobbled with bricks.*

cob•bler (kob′lər) /'kɒblər/ *n.* [*count*] **1.** a person who cobbles. **2.** a deep fruit pie with a thick biscuit crust: *a peach cobbler.*

cob•ble•stone (kob′əl stōn′) /'kɒbəl,stown/ *n.* a stone used in paving: [*count*]: *a sidewalk paved with cobblestones.* [*noncount*]: *a road made of cobblestone.* **—cob′ble•stoned′,** *adj.*: *a cobblestoned street.*

co•bra (kō′brə) /'kowbrə/ *n.* [*count*], *pl.* **-bras.** a poisonous snake that can flatten its neck into the shape of a hood.

cob•web (kob′web′) /'kɒb,wɛb/ *n.* [*count*] **1.** a web of threads produced by a spider: *brushing the cobwebs off his arm.* **2. cobwebs,** [*plural*] confusion or indistinctness: *clearing the cobwebs out of one's brain.*

co•caine (kō kān′, kō′kān) /kow'keyn, 'kowkeyn/ *n.* [*noncount*] a crystallike substance made from coca leaves, used to kill pain and also used as an illegal drug: *addicted to cocaine.*

coc•cyx (kok′siks) /'kɒksɪks/ *n.* [*count*], *pl.* **coc•cy•ges** (kok sī′jēz, kok′si jēz′) /kɒk'saydʒiyz, 'kɒksɪ,dʒiyz/. a triangular bone at the lower end of the spinal column; tailbone.

coch•le•a (kok′lē ə, kō′klē ə) /'kɒkliyə, 'kowkliyə/ *n.* [*count*], *pl.* **-le•ae** (-lē ē′, -lē ī′) /-liy,iy, -liy,ay/ **-le•as.** the spiral-shaped part of the inner ear in mammals. **—coch′le•ar,** *adj.*

cock[1] (kok) /kɒk/ *n.* [*count*] **1.** a male chicken; rooster. **2.** the male of any bird. **3.** Also called **stopcock.** a hand-operated valve or faucet that controls the flow of liquid or gas. **4.** *Slang* (*vulgar*). PENIS. —*v.* [~ + *obj*] **5.** to draw back the hammer of (a firearm) before firing: *He cocked the gun, aimed, and fired.* **6.** to draw back (the fist) in preparation for throwing or hitting: *He cocked his arm as if to throw the ball.*

cock[2] (kok) /kɒk/ *v.* [~ + *obj*] to make (something) stand erect: *The puppy cocked its ear at the sound.*

cock•a•ma•mie or **cock•a•ma•my** (kok′ə mā′mē) /'kɒkə,meymiy/ *adj.* [*usually: before a noun*] *Slang.* ridiculous; nonsensical: *another of his cockamamie ideas.*

cock′-and-bull′ sto′ry, *n.* [*count*] an absurd story presented as an excuse: *a cock-and-bull story about how the dog ate her homework.*

cock•a•too (kok′ə to͞o′) /'kɒkə,tuw/ *n.* [*count*], *pl.* **-toos.** a large, usually white crested parrot of Australia and New Guinea.

cocked′ hat′ (kokt) /kɒkt/ *n.* [*count*] a man's hat having a wide, stiff brim turned up on two or three sides.

cock•er•el (kok′ər əl) /'kɒkərəl/ *n.* [*count*] a young rooster.

cock′er span′iel, *n.* [*count*] one of a breed of small spaniels.

cock•eyed (kok′īd′) /'kɒk,ayd/ *adj. Slang.* **1.** tilted or slanted to one side; off-center: *The wall map is cockeyed.* **2.** foolish; absurd; crazy: *a cockeyed scheme.*

cock•fight (kok′fīt′) /'kɒk,fayt/ *n.* [*count*] a fight set up between gamecocks usually fitted with spurs: *to bet on a cockfight.* **—cock′fight′ing,** *n.* [*noncount*]

cock•le (kok′əl) /'kɒkəl/ *n.* [*count*] **1.** a shellfish with two connected heart-shaped shells. **2.** COCKLESHELL (defs. 1, 2). **—*Idiom.* 3. cockles of one's heart,** the place of one's deepest feelings: *The happy story warmed the cockles of my heart.*

cock•le•shell (kok′əl shel′) /'kɒkəl,ʃɛl/ *n.* [*count*] **1.** the shell of a cockle. **2.** the shell of any other shellfish with two connected shells.

cock•ney (kok′nē) /'kɒkniy/ *n., pl.* **-neys. 1.** [*count; sometimes: Cockney*] an inhabitant of the East End district of London, England. **2.** [*noncount; sometimes: Cockney*] the speech of this population. **—cock′ney, cock•ney•ish,** *adj.*: *a cockney accent.*

cock•pit (kok′pit′) /'kɒk,pɪt/ *n.* [*count*] a space in the forward body of an airplane containing the flying controls and seat for the pilot.

cock•roach (kok′rōch′) /'kɒk,rowtʃ/ *n.* [*count*] an insect that has a flattened body and is a common household pest. Also called **roach.**

cocks•comb (koks′kōm′) /'kɒks,kowm/ *n.* [*count*] the red growth or comb that grows on the top of the head of a cock.

cock•sure (kok′sho͝or′) /'kɒk'ʃʊr/ *adj.* overly sure; overconfident: *a cocksure manner.* **—cock′sure′ly,** *adv.* **—cock′sure′ness,** *n.* [*noncount*]

cock•tail (kok′tāl′) /'kɒk,teyl/ *n.* **1.** [*count*] any of various chilled mixed drinks, made up typically of an alcoholic liquor mixed with flavorings. **2.** a cold mixture of small pieces of food served as an appetizer: [*noncount*]: *He ate shrimp cocktail every chance he had.* [*count*]: *He had only fruit cocktail for lunch.* **3.** [*count*] a mixture made up of many different ingredients: *a cocktail of jet fuel and kerosene, alcohol and ethanol.* **—*adj.*** [*before a noun*] **4.** styled for more formal or festive occasions: *a cocktail dress.* **5.** used in or suitable for cocktails: *a jar of cocktail onions.*

cock•y (kok′ē) /'kɒkiy/ *adj.,* **-i•er, -i•est.** arrogant; conceited; cocksure: *a brash, cocky manner.* **—cock•i•ly** (kok′ə lē) /'kɒkəliy/ *adv.* **—cock′i•ness,** *n.* [*noncount*]

co•coa (kō′kō) /'kowkow/ *n.* **1.** [*noncount*] a powder made from cacao seeds. **2.** CACAO (def. 2). **3.** [*noncount*] a beverage made by mixing cocoa powder with hot milk or water. **4.** [*count*] a serving of this beverage: *I'll have two hot cocoas, please.*

co•co•nut or **co•coa•nut** (kō′kə nut′) /'kowkə,nʌt/ *n.* **1.** [*count*] the large, hard-shelled seed of the coconut palm tree, lined with a white edible meat and containing a milky liquid. **2.** [*noncount*] the meat of the coconut, used in cooking: *This candy has coconut in it.*

co•coon (kə ko͞on′) /kə'kuwn/ *n.* [*count*] **1.** the silky envelope spun by caterpillars, serving as a protective covering while they are developing. **2.** anything that encloses like a cocoon: *A cocoon of blankets, sheets, and pillows kept her warm.*

cod (kod) /kɒd/ *n., pl. (esp. when thought of as a group)* **-cod,** *(esp. for kinds or species)* **-cods. 1.** [*count*] a fish found in cool, N Atlantic waters, caught for food: *caught a cod.* **2.** [*noncount*] its flesh, eaten as food: *a dish of baked cod.*

C.O.D. or **c.o.d.,** an abbreviation of: cash, or collect, on delivery.

co•da (kō′də) /'kowdə/ *n.* [*count*], *pl.* **-das. 1.** an ending passage of a piece of music. **2.** a conclusion, esp. a summary of preceding themes, such as in a drama.

cod•dle (kod′l) /'kɒdl̩/ *v.* [~ + *obj*], **-dled, -dling. 1.** to treat too tenderly or too carefully; pamper: *She coddled her son and never let him take care of himself.* **2.** to cook (eggs, etc.) in water just below the boiling point.

code (kōd) /kowd/ *n., v.,* **cod•ed, cod•ing.** —*n.* **1.** [*count*] a system for communication by telegraph, etc., in which the letters are represented by long and short sounds, etc.: *Morse code.* **2.** a system used to keep a message short or secret, with letters or symbols assigned meanings known only to the sender and receiver: [*count*]: *They tried to crack the code used by the enemy.* [*noncount*]: *a message written in code.* **3.** [*count*] letters, numbers, or other symbols used in a code system to represent or identify something: *The code for your English course is 4907.* **4.** [*count*] a collection of rules or regulations, such as for a business: *a local health code.* **5.** [*count*] the statements or instructions in a computer program: *We'll have to look at the code to see why this program crashed.* —*v.* [~ + *obj*] **6.** to translate (a message) into a code; encode: *He coded the message and sent it to London.* **—cod′er,** *n.* [*count*]

co•deine (kō′dēn) /'kowdiyn/ *n.* [*noncount*] a white substance obtained from opium and used chiefly to relieve pain and coughing.

code′ word′, *n.* [*count*] a word or phrase that has a different meaning from its apparent meaning, used to communicate something secretly.

co•dex (kō′deks) /'kowdɛks/ *n.* [*count*], *pl.* **co•di•ces** (kō′də sēz′, kod′ə-) /'kowdə,siyz, 'kɒdə-/. a book of writing written by hand, usually of a classic or the Scriptures.

cod•fish (kod′fish′) /'kɒd,fɪʃ/ *n., pl. (esp. when thought* *of as a group)* **-fish,** *(esp. for kinds or species)* **-fish•es.** COD.

codg•er (koj′ər) /ˈkɒdʒər/ *n.* [*count*] a man who behaves oddly or in an unusual way, esp. one who is elderly.

cod•i•cil (kod′ə səl) /ˈkɒdəsəl/ *n.* [*count*] a note to a will containing a change of something in the original.

cod•i•fy (kod′ə fī′, kō′də-) /ˈkɒdəˌfay, ˈkowdə-/ *v.* [∼ + *obj*], **-fied, -fy•ing.** to arrange or put (laws, etc.) into a code: *We want to codify the procedures.* —**cod′i•fi′er,** *n.* [*count*]

co•ed or **co-ed** (kō′ed′, -ed′) /ˈkowˈɛd, -ˌɛd/ *adj.* **1.** serving both men and women alike; coeducational: *co-ed classes.* **2.** of or relating to a coed: *Coed dress rules were different from those for males.* **—*n.*** [*count*] **3.** a female student in a coeducational institution.

co•ed•u•ca•tion (kō′ej o͝o kā′shən) /ˌkowɛdʒʊˈkeyʃən/ *n.* [*noncount*] the education of both sexes in the same institution and in the same classes. —**co′ed•u•ca′tion•al,** *adj.*: *coeducational schooling.*

co•erce (kō ûrs′) /kowˈɜrs/ *v.,* **-erced, -erc•ing. 1.** [∼ + *obj* + *into* + *verb-ing*] to compel by force or violence: *She coerced him into signing that document.* **2.** [∼ + *obj*] to bring about through force: *to coerce obedience.* —**co•erc′er,** *n.* [*count*] —**co•er•cive** (kō ûr′siv) /kowˈɜrsɪv/ *adj.*

co•er•cion (kō ûr′shən) /kow ˈɜrʃən/ *n.* [*noncount*] the act of coercing: *a lot of coercion to make her cooperate.*

co•ex•ist (kō′ig zist′) /ˌkowɪgˈzɪst/ *v.* [*no obj*] **1.** to exist at the same time: *The two empires coexisted on opposite sides of the globe.* **2.** (esp. of nations) to exist together peacefully: *We coexisted for years with our enemies.* —**co′ex•ist′ence,** *n.* [*noncount*]

cof•fee (kô′fē, kof′ē) /ˈkɔfiy, ˈkɒfiy/ *n.* **1.** [*noncount*] a beverage made from hot water poured over the roasted ground or crushed seeds **(cof′fee beans′)** of the fruit of certain coffee trees. **2.** [*noncount*] the seeds or fruits themselves, or a powder similar to the ground seeds, used to make the beverage. **3.** [*noncount*] a tropical tree that produces coffee beans. **4.** [*count*] a cup of coffee: *I'll have two coffees, one with sugar and one without.* **5.** [*noncount*] medium to dark brown. **—*adj.*** [*usually before a noun*] **6.** of a coffee color. **7.** flavored with coffee.

cof′fee break′, *n.* [*count*] a break from work for coffee, a snack, etc.

cof•fee•house (kô′fē hous′, kof′ē-) /ˈkɔfiyˌhaws, ˈkɒfiy-/ *n.* [*count*] an establishment that serves coffee and other refreshments.

cof′fee klatsch′ (or **klatch′**), *n.* KAFFEEKLATSCH.

cof•fee•pot (kô′fē pot′, kof′ē-) /ˈkɔfiyˌpɒt, ˈkɒfiy-/ *n.* [*count*] a container, usually with a handle and a spout or lip, in which coffee is made or served, or both.

cof′fee shop′, *n.* [*count*] a small restaurant serving light meals.

cof′fee ta′ble, *n.* [*count*] a low table, usually placed in front of a sofa. See illustration at APARTMENT.

cof•fer (kô′fər, kof′ər) /ˈkɔfər, ˈkɒfər/ *n.* [*count*] **1.** a box or chest, esp. one for valuables. **2. coffers,** [*plural*] the treasury of an organization; its funds: *Our coffers are empty.*

cof•fin (kô′fin, kof′in) /ˈkɔfɪn, ˈkɒfɪn/ *n.* [*count*] the box in which the body of a dead person is buried; casket.

cog (kog, kôg) /kɒg, kɔg/ *n.* [*count*] **1.** a gear tooth that fits into the slot on a wheel with similar teeth, to transfer motion or power **2.** a cogwheel. **3.** a person who plays a minor part in an organization, etc.: *He's just a small cog in this business.*

co•gent (kō′jənt) /ˈkowdʒənt/ *adj.* convincing; believable: *some cogent arguments in favor of hiring her.* —**co′gen•cy,** *n.* [*noncount*]: *an argument with force and cogency.* —**co′gent•ly,** *adv.*: *argued cogently.*

cog•i•tate (koj′i tāt′) /ˈkɒdʒɪˌteyt/ *v.* [*no obj*], **-tat•ed, -tat•ing.** to ponder; think about something; meditate: *cogitating about how he had gotten himself into this mess.* —**cog•i•ta•tion** (koj′i tā′shən) /ˌkɒdʒɪˈteyʃən/ *n.* [*noncount*]: *Even after long cogitation there was no solution.* —**cog′i•ta′tor,** *n.* [*count*]

co•gnac (kōn′yak, kon′-) /ˈkownyæk, ˈkɒn-/ *n.* [*often: Cognac*] brandy produced near the town of Cognac, in W central France: [*noncount*]: *He swirled the glass of cognac.* [*count*]: *a very good cognac.*

cog•nate (kog′nāt) /ˈkɒgneyt/ *adj.* descended from the same language or form: *cognate words.* See -NAT-.

cog•ni•tion (kog nish′ən) /kɒgˈnɪʃən/ *n.* [*noncount*] the mental act of learning; understanding; perception: *Scientists were watching the subject's brain waves during cognition.* —**cog•ni′tion•al,** *adj.* —**cog•ni•tive** (kog′ni tiv) /ˈkɒgnɪtɪv/ *adj.*: *the cognitive processes of language learning.* See -GNOS-.

cog•ni•zance (kog′nə zəns) /ˈkɒgnəzəns/ *n.* [*noncount*] **1.** awareness or realization; notice: *to take cognizance of a slighting remark.* **2.** the range or scope of a person's knowledge, etc.: *perceptions beyond my cognizance.*

cog•ni•zant (kog′nə zənt) /ˈkɒgnə zənt/ *adj.* [*be* + ∼ + *of*] aware; mindful: *is cognizant of the problem.* See -GNOS-.

co•gno•scen•ti (kon′yə shen′tē, kog′nə-) /ˌkɒnyəˈʃɛntiy, ˌkɒgnə-/ *n., pl.* **-te** (-tā, -tē) /-tey, -tiy/. [*count*] well-informed persons, esp. those with expert knowledge of a particular field: *The cognoscenti were aware of the play on words in that song, but most listeners didn't catch it.*

cog•wheel (kog′hwēl′, -wēl′) /ˈkɒgˌhwiyl, -ˌwiyl/ *n.* [*count*] a gearwheel, esp. one having teeth inserted into slots.

co•hab•it (kō hab′it) /kowˈhæbɪt/ *v.* **1.** [*no obj*] to live together as husband and wife without being married. **2.** [∼ + *obj*] to dwell with another or share the same place, as different species of animals: *Can man cohabit the earth with the rest of nature?* —**co•hab•it•ant** (kō hab′it-nt) /kowˈhæbɪtnt/ **co•hab′it•er,** *n.* [*count*] —**co•hab•i•ta•tion** (kō hab′i tā′shən) /kowˌhæbɪˈteyʃən/ *n.* [*noncount*] See -HAB-.

co•here (kō hēr′) /kowˈhɪər/ *v.* [*no obj*], **-hered, -her•ing. 1.** to stick together; be united: *The plastic and wood can't cohere without special glue.* **2.** to be logically connected; be consistent: *The arguments cohere nicely.* See -HERE-.

co•her•ence (kō hēr′əns, -her′-) /kow ˈhɪərəns, -ˈhɛr-/ *n.* [*noncount*] a quality, state, or condition that is coherent: *Your paper needs more coherence to be believable.* See -HERE-.

co•her•ent (kō hēr′ənt, -her′-) /kowˈhɪərənt, -ˈhɛr-/ *adj.* **1.** logically connected; consistent: *a coherent speech.* **2.** speaking, talking, or thinking lucidly: *The patient is coherent now.* **3.** having a natural agreement of parts; harmonious: *a coherent design.* —**co•her′ent•ly,** *adv.* See -HERE-.

co•he•sion (kō hē′zhən) /kowˈhiyʒən/ *n.* [*noncount*] the act or state of cohering: *social cohesion.*

co•he•sive (kō hē′səv) /kow ˈhiysəv/ *adj.* fitting well together; working or relating well together: *We tried to make the group more cohesive.* —**co•he′sive•ly,** *adv.* —**co•he′sive•ness,** *n.* [*noncount*] See -HES-.

coif (kwäf) /kwɑf/ *n., v.* COIFFURE.

coif•fure (kwä fyo͝or′) /kwɑˈfyʊr/ *n., pl.* **-fures,** *v.,* **-fured, -fur•ing. —*n.*** [*count*] **1.** a style of arranging the hair. **—*v.*** [∼ + *obj*] **2.** to arrange (the hair) in a coiffure: *They coiffured her hair.* —**coif•fur′ist,** *n.* [*count*]

coil (koil) /kɔyl/ *v.* **1.** to wind (something) into rings one above the other or one around the other: [*no obj*]: *Smoke coiled up the chimney.* [∼ + *obj*]: *She coiled her scarf around her neck.* **2.** [∼ + *obj*] to gather (rope, etc.) into loops: *Coil the garden hose and hang it in the garage.* **—*n.*** [*count*] **3.** a series of spirals or rings into which something is wound: *a coil of rope.* **4.** a single such ring: *hair tied into a tight coil.* **5.** an arrangement of pipes, as in a radiator.

coin (koin) /kɔyn/ *n.* **1.** [*count*] a piece of metal stamped and issued by a government as money: *How many coins do you have in your pocket?* **2.** [*noncount*] a number of such pieces: *She paid him in coin.* **3.** [*noncount*] *Informal.* money; cash: *You have any coin, man?* **—*adj.*** [*before a noun*] **4.** [*sometimes:* ∼*-operated*] operated by the insertion of a coin or coins: *a coin-operated laundry.* **—*v.*** [∼ + *obj*] **5.** to make (coins) by stamping metal: *They coined nickels and dimes at the mint.* **6.** to invent; fabricate: *to coin an expression.* **—*Idiom.* 7. pay someone back in his** or **her own coin,** to strike back against someone by using the person's own methods. —**coin′a•ble,** *adj.* —**coin′er,** *n.* [*count*]: *a coiner of new words.*

coin•age (koi′nij) /ˈkɔynɪdʒ/ *n.* **1.** [*noncount*] the act or process of making coins: *When did coinage begin?* **2.** [*noncount*] the types of coins issued by a nation: *a museum displaying Greek coinage.* **3.** [*count*] an invented word: *"Ecdysiast" is a coinage of H. L. Mencken.*

co•in•cide (kō′in sīd′) /ˌkowɪnˈsayd/ *v.,* **-cid•ed, -cid•ing. 1.** to occupy the same place or time: [*no obj*]: *Our vacations coincided this year.* [∼ + *with* + *obj*]: *My vacation didn't coincide with my children's.* **2.** (of two objects) to correspond exactly: [*no obj*]: *The two triangles I cut out coincide.* [∼ + *with* + *obj*]: *This one coincides with the other.* **3.** to agree; concur: [*no obj*]: *Our opinions coin-*

cide more often than not. [~ + *with* + *obj*]: *My opinion didn't coincide with hers this time.* See -CIDE-.

co•in•ci•dence (kō in′si dəns) /kow'ɪnsɪdəns/ *n.* a surprising chance occurrence of two or more events at once: [*noncount*]: *Our meeting was pure coincidence.* [*count*]: *What a coincidence, meeting you here!*

co•in•ci•den•tal (kō′in sə den′tl) /ˌkowɪnsə'dɛntl̩/ *adj.* happening by coincidence: *Our meeting was coincidental; no one planned it.*

co•i•tus (kō′i təs) /'kowɪtəs/ *n.* [*noncount*] sexual intercourse, esp. between a man and a woman. —**co•i•tal** (kō′i tl) /'kowɪtl̩/ *adj.*

coke[1] (kōk) /kowk/ *n.* [*noncount*] the solid carbon product obtained from coal and used chiefly as a fuel.

coke[2] (kōk) /kowk/ *n., v.,* **coked, cok•ing.** *Slang.* —*n.* [*noncount*] **1.** cocaine. —*v.* [~ + *obj* (+ *up*)] **2.** to affect with cocaine: *completely coked (up) when we found him.*

col-, *prefix. col-* is another form of COM- that is used before roots beginning with *l*: *collateral.*

Col., an abbreviation of: **1.** Colonel. **2.** Colorado.

col., an abbreviation of: **1.** college. **2.** colonial. **3.** colony. **4.** color. **5.** colored. **6.** column.

co•la (kō′lə) /'kowlə/ *n., pl.* **-las.** a carbonated soft drink containing an extract made from kola nuts: [*noncount*]: *They drink too much cola.* [*count*]: *Of all the colas on the market, which one do you like best?*

COLA (kō′lə) /'kowlə/ *n.* [*count*], *pl.* **COLAs** or **COLA's.** cost-of-living adjustment: an automatic adjustment in wages or social-security payments to take into account rises in the cost of living.

col•an•der (kul′ən dər, kol′-) /'kʌləndər, 'kɒl-/ *n.* [*count*] a container with many small holes in the bottom and sides, used for draining and straining foods.

cold (kōld) /kowld/ *adj.,* **-er, -est,** *n., adv.* —*adj.* **1.** having a relatively low temperature: *The water is cold.* **2.** [*be* + ~] feeling an uncomfortable lack of warmth; chilled: *I'm really cold today; where's my sweater?* **3.** having a temperature lower than what is normal, expected, or usual: *cold hands.* **4.** [*before a noun*] (of food) cooked, then cooled before eaten: *cold chicken for a sandwich.* **5.** lacking in passion, enthusiasm, etc.: *cold reason.* **6.** not affectionate or friendly: *a cold reply.* **7.** lacking sensual desire; frigid: *Her touch was cold.* **8.** [*be* + ~] unconscious because of a severe blow, shock, etc.: *He was knocked cold.* See *out cold* below. **9.** no longer fresh; faint: *By the time they figure out who robbed the store, the trail will be cold.* **10.** [*be* + ~] (in games) distant from the object of search or the correct answer: *What was your guess? "Hawaii?" No, you're cold, the right answer was "Fiji."* —*n.* **11.** [*noncount*] the absence of heat or warmth: *the cold of deep space.* **12.** [*noncount*] the sensation produced by loss of heat from the body: *The cold of the steel floor on his face woke the prisoner.* **13.** [*noncount; the* + ~] cold weather: *Don't stay out in the cold too long.* **14.** [*count*] Also called **common cold.** an illness of the lungs, throat, and nose, with sneezing, coughing, etc., caused by viruses: *Some people think vitamin C helps prevent colds.* —*adv.* **15.** with complete knowledge and ability; thoroughly: *He knew his speech cold.* **16.** without preparation or prior notice: *He walked into the interview cold.* —***Idiom.*** **17. catch** or **take (a) cold,** [*no obj*] to become afflicted with a cold. **18. have** or **get cold feet,** [*no obj*] to be afraid or unwilling to do something; to lack courage: *We got cold feet and didn't go through with our plan.* **19. leave (someone) cold,** to fail to excite or interest (someone): *The thought of him as governor leaves me cold.* **20. out cold,** unconscious because of a severe blow: *The guard was out cold when we found him.* **21. (out) in the cold,** neglected; ignored; forgotten: *He was left out in the cold when he lost the election.* **22. throw cold water on,** to dampen someone's enthusiasm about: *The boss threw cold water on our plans for expansion.* —**cold′ly,** *adv.*: *He denied me coldly when I asked for a raise.* —**cold′ness,** *n.* [*noncount*]

cold′-blood′ed or **cold′blood′ed,** *adj.* **1.** of or referring to animals, as fishes and reptiles, whose blood temperature changes with the temperature of the air or water surrounding them: *cold-blooded crocodiles.* **2.** done or acting without emotion: *a cold-blooded killer.* **3.** sensitive to cold: *I'm cold-blooded and need very warm clothes in winter.* —**cold′-blood′ed•ly,** *adv.*: *He was cold-bloodedly left behind to die.* —**cold′-blood′ed•ness,** *n.* [*noncount*]

cold′ cream′, *n.* [*noncount*] a cream used as a cosmetic for cleansing or soothing the face and neck.

cold′ cuts′, *n.* [*plural*] slices of various prepared meats and sometimes cheeses served cold: *a table loaded with cold cuts.*

cold′ front′, *n.* [*count*] the zone separating two air masses, in which the cooler mass replaces the warmer: *a cold front pushing down from Canada.*

cold′ shoul′der, *n.* [*count*] deliberate indifference or other unfriendly treatment: *We gave her the cold shoulder whenever we saw her.* —**cold′-shoul′der,** *v.* [~ + *obj*]: *We cold-shouldered him after he reported to the boss about us.*

cold′ sore′, *n.* [*count*] a cluster of blisters appearing in or around the mouth or sometimes the nostril, caused by a virus. Also called **fever blister.**

cold′ tur′key, *n.* [*noncount*] **1.** sudden and complete withdrawal from the use of an addictive substance: *went cold turkey to stop smoking.* —*adv.* **2.** abruptly and completely: *to withdraw cold turkey from a drug.* **3.** without preparation: *He gave the speech cold turkey.* —**cold′-tur′key,** *adj.*: *cold-turkey withdrawal.*

cold′ war′, *n.* [*count*] **1.** intense political or military rivalry between nations just short of armed fighting. **2.** [*Cold War; often: the* + ~] such rivalry after World War II between the Soviet Union and the U.S., and their allies: *With the breakup of Communism the two leaders declared that the Cold War was over.*

cole•slaw (kōl′slô′) /'kowlˌslɔ/ *n.* [*noncount*] a salad of chopped raw cabbage and seasoned mayonnaise.

col•ic (kol′ik) /'kɒlɪk/ *n.* [*noncount*] **1.** sharp, sudden pain in the abdomen or bowels. **2.** a condition in infants characterized by colic: *That baby must have colic; she's been screaming for hours.* —**col′ick•y,** *adj.*: *She was a colicky baby.*

col•i•se•um (kol′i sē′əm) /ˌkɒlɪ'siyəm/ *n.* [*count*] a stadium or large theater for sporting events, exhibitions, etc.

co•li•tis (kə lī′tis, kō-) /kə'laytɪs, kow-/ *n.* [*noncount*] inflammation of the colon.

coll., an abbreviation of: **1.** college. **2.** collegiate. **3.** colloquial.

col•lab•o•rate (kə lab′ə rāt′) /kə'læbəˌreyt/ *v.,* **-rat•ed, -rat•ing. 1.** to work together; cooperate, as on writing a book, etc.: [*no obj;* (~ + *on* + *obj*)]: *The two writers collaborated on the script.* [~ + *with*]: *He collaborated with Ira Gershwin.* **2.** [*no obj;* (~ + *with* + *obj*)] to cooperate with an enemy nation, esp. with an enemy occupying one's country: *guilty of collaborating; found guilty of collaborating with the enemy.* —**col•lab•o•ra•tion** (kə lab′ə rā′shən) /kəˌlæbə'reyʃən/ *n.* [*noncount*] —**col•lab•o•ra•tive** (kə lab′ə rā′tiv, -ə rə tiv) /kə'læbəˌreytɪv, -ərətɪv/ *adj.* —**col•lab′o•ra′tor,** *n.* [*count*] See -LAB-.

col•lage (kə läzh′) /kə'lɑʒ/ *n.* **1.** [*noncount*] a technique of making a work of art by pasting on a surface various materials such as newspaper clippings or parts of photographs around a common theme. **2.** [*count*] a work produced by this technique. **3.** [*count*] a film, book, story, play, or other work that shifts suddenly from one unrelated scene or image to another, or that combines different styles in one: *The book was a strange collage of history, sociology, science fiction, and war theory.* —**col•lag′ist,** *n.* [*count*]

col•lapse (kə laps′) /kə'læps/ *v.,* **-lapsed, -laps•ing,** *n.* —*v.* **1.** to fall or cave in; crumble suddenly: [*no obj*]: *The bridge collapsed in the earthquake.* [~ + *obj*]: *The weight of the snow collapsed the roof.* **2.** [*no obj*] to be made so that sections or parts can be folded up, as for storage: *The baby's playpen collapses easily.* **3.** [~ + *obj*] to fold up (sections) for storage: *We collapsed the playpen and stowed it in the car.* **4.** [*no obj*] to break down; fail utterly: *The peace talks have collapsed once again.* **5.** [*no obj*] to fall unconscious or fall down, such as from a heart attack or exhaustion. **6.** [*no obj*] to fall or decline suddenly, as in value: *The market collapsed and investors lost money.* —*n.* **7.** [*noncount*] a falling in, down, or together: *trapped by the collapse of a tunnel.* **8.** a sudden, complete failure; breakdown: [*count*]: *a mental collapse.* [*noncount*]: *a system facing collapse at any moment.* —**col•laps′i•ble,** *adj.*: *Collapsible chairs can easily be stored.* —**col•laps•i•bil•i•ty** (kə lap′sə bil′i tē) /kəˌlæpsə'bɪlɪtiy/ *n.* [*noncount*] See -LAPS-.

col•lar (kol′ər) /'kɒlər/ *n.* [*count*] **1.** the part of a shirt, blouse, etc., that goes around the neckline of the garment. **2.** anything worn or placed around the neck. **3.** a leather or metal band fastened around the neck of an animal: *We put the collar on the puppy and took her out for a walk.* **4.** *Informal.* an arrest; capture: *The police made the collar only minutes after the mugging.* —*v.* [~ + *obj*] **5.** to seize by the collar or neck. **6.** to stop and keep (someone) in conversation: *She collared me in the* *hallway and asked when I would have the report finished.* **7.** *Informal.* to place under arrest: *The police managed to collar him just a few blocks away.* **—col′lar•less,** *adj.*

col•lar•bone (kol′ər bōn′) /ˈkɒlərˌbown/ *n.* [*count*] one of the two bones that extend from the shoulder at the front of the body and are attached to the breastbone.

col•late (kə lāt′, kō′lāt, kol′āt) /kəˈleyt, ˈkowleyt, ˈkɒleyt/ *v.* [~ + *obj*], **-lat•ed, -lat•ing. 1.** to arrange (pages) in their proper order: *Please collate these copies and staple them.* **2.** to compare (texts, etc.) critically: *Collate our findings and see what similarities there are.* **—col•la′tor,** *n.* [*count*] See -LAT-[1].

col•lat•er•al (kə lat′ər əl) /kəˈlætərəl/ *n.* [*noncount*] **1.** security, pledged or promised to a bank or other lender if payment of a loan cannot be made: *Their house was their collateral for the college loan.* **—*adj.* 2.** accompanying; auxiliary: *Collateral damage during the war meant the damage inflicted on nonmilitary targets.* **3.** additional and proving or confirming: *We found this collateral evidence at the scene of the crime.* **4.** made secure by collateral: *collateral property.* **5.** [*before a noun*](of a relative) descended from the same stock, but in a different line: *collateral relatives descended through different sons or daughters.* **—col•lat′er•al•ly,** *adv.* See -LAT-[2].

col•la•tion (kə lā′shən, kō-, ko-) /kəˈleyʃən, kow-, kɒ-/ *n.* **1.** the act of collating; fact or result of being collated: [*noncount*]: *With this machine, collation takes only seconds.* [*count*]: *A collation of all the data will take years.* **2.** [*count*] a light meal, esp. one on a day of fasting.

col•league (kol′ēg) /ˈkɒliyg/ *n.* [*count*] a fellow member of a profession; an associate: *a business colleague.*

col•lect (kə lekt′) /kəˈlɛkt/ *v.* **1.** to gather together; assemble: [*no obj*]: *The youth group collected in the parking lot.* [~ + *obj*]: *We collected the kids and hustled them onto the bus.* **2.** [~ + *obj*] to obtain many examples of (something), or make a collection of (something), as a hobby: *She likes to collect stamps.* **3.** to ask for or demand and receive payment: [*no obj*]: *The newspaper carrier collects on Mondays.* [~ + *obj*]: *He collected debts from poor people.* **4.** [*no obj;* (~ + *on* + *obj*)] to receive payment that one is owed: *We finally collected from the insurance company on the damage to our house.* **5.** [~ + *obj*] to regain control of (oneself or one's thoughts or emotions): *He took a moment to collect himself.* **6.** [~ + *obj*] to call for and take with one: *Did you collect your mail?* **7.** [*no obj*] to accumulate; gather in a layer: *A lot of dust collected on the computer screen.* **—*adj., adv.* 8.** requiring payment by the recipient: [*adjective; often before a noun*]: *a collect telephone call.* [*adverb*]: *to call collect.* See -LEC-.

col•lect•ed (kə lek′tid) /kəˈlɛktɪd/ *adj.* **1.** [*usually: be* + ~] having control of one's feelings; calm; self-possessed: *During the trial he was very calm and collected.* **2.** [*usually: before a noun*] brought together, as many different works: *her collected essays.* **—col•lect′ed•ly,** *adv.* **—Syn.** See CALM.

col•lec•tion (kə lek′shən) /kə ˈlɛkʃən/ *n.* **1.** [*count*] a group of objects, etc., gathered together: *a collection of old records.* **2.** the act of collecting: [*noncount*]: *Garbage collection is on Fridays.* [*count*]: *Collections are suspended on holidays.* **3.** [*count*] **a.** an activity intended to raise money, such as for some charitable cause: *We organized a collection for the homeless.* **b.** the money obtained in such an activity: *We took in a collection of $1,000 for new books.*

col•lec•tive (kə lek′tiv) /kəˈlɛktɪv/ *adj.* **1.** formed by collection. **2.** forming a whole; combined: *our collective assets.* **3.** [*before a noun*] characteristic of a group: *their collective will.* **4.** [*before a noun*] organized according to the principles of collectivism: *a collective farm.* **—*n.*** [*count*] **5.** an organization in a collectivist system, esp. a collective farm. **—col•lec′tive•ly,** *adv.*: *They acted collectively in turning down the offer.*

collec′tive bar′gaining, *n.* [*noncount*] the process by which wages, working conditions, etc., are discussed and agreed upon for all employees in the union.

collec′tive noun′, *n.* [*count*] a noun, such as *herd, jury,* or *clergy,* that appears singular in formal shape but names a group of individuals or objects. **—Usage.** A COLLECTIVE NOUN will sometimes be used with a singular verb and sometimes with a plural verb. This depends on whether the word is being used to refer to the group as a unit or to its members as individuals. In American English a noun naming an organization that is thought of as a unit is usually treated as singular: *The corporation is holding its annual meeting. The government has taken action.* In British English, such nouns are commonly treated as plurals: *The corporation are holding their annual meeting. The government are in agreement.* In formal speech and writing COLLECTIVE NOUNS are usually not treated as both singular and plural in the same sentence; if the verb is singular, the pronoun referring to it should also be singular: *The enemy is fortifying its position.* If the verb is plural, the pronoun should be plural: *The enemy are bringing up their heavy artillery.* When the nouns *couple* and *pair* refer to people, they are usually treated as plurals: *The newly married couple have bought a house. The pair are busy furnishing their new home.* The COLLECTIVE NOUN *number,* when preceded by *a,* is treated as a plural: *A number of solutions were suggested.* When *number* is preceded by *the,* it is usually treated as a singular: *The number of solutions offered was astounding.* Other common COLLECTIVE NOUNS are *audience, class, committee, crew, crowd, family, flock, group, panel,* and *staff.*

col•lec•tiv•ism (kə lek′tə viz′əm) /kəˈlɛktəˌvɪzəm/ *n.* [*noncount*] the socialist principle or system of control by which the people collectively, or the state, are in charge of all means of production or economic activity. **—col•lec′tiv•ist,** *n.* [*count*], *adj.* **—col•lec′tiv•is′tic,** *adj.*

col•lec•ti•vize (kə lek′tə vīz′) /kəˈlɛktəˌvayz/ *v.* [~ + *obj*], **-vized, -viz•ing.** to organize (a people, etc.) according to collectivism: *The state had collectivized the heavy industry.* **—col•lec•ti•vi•za•tion** (kə lek′tə və zā′shən) /kəˌlɛktəvəˈzeyʃən/ *n.* [*noncount*]

col•lec•tor (kə lek′tər) /kə ˈlɛktər/ *n.* [*count*] **1.** a person who makes a collection of something, as a hobby or for interest: *He was an antiques collector.* **2.** a person who collects money, debts, etc: *a debt collector.*

col•lege (kol′ij) /ˈkɒlɪdʒ/ *n.* **1.** a school or institution of higher education that grants a bachelor's degree: [*count*]: *She chose a college that had a good business department.* [*noncount*]: *He was in college during the war.* **2.** [*count*] an organized group or union of people with common interests, duties, or powers: *the college of physicians.*

col•le•giate (kə lē′jit, -jē it) /kəˈliydʒɪt, -dʒiyɪt/ *adj.* [*before a noun*] **1.** of, relating to, or being a college: *the collegiate system of colleges and universities.* **2.** of, characteristic of, or intended for college students: *collegiate life.* **—col•le′giate•ly,** *adv.* **—col•le′giate•ness,** *n.* [*noncount*]

col•lide (kə līd′) /kəˈlayd/ *v.,* **-lid•ed, -lid•ing. 1.** to strike each other forcefully; crash: [*no obj*]: *The two trains collided at a speed of over 50 mph.* [~ + *with* + *obj*]: *The car collided with that tree.* **2.** to clash; conflict: [*no obj*]: *Our views often collided, but we respected each other.* [~ + *with* + *obj*]: *My opinions collide with my opponent's.*

col•lie (kol′ē) /ˈkɒliy/ *n.* [*count*], *pl.* **-lies.** one of a breed of large Scottish sheepherding dogs.

col•lier•y (kol′yə rē) /ˈkɒlyəriy/ *n.* [*count*], *pl.* **-lier•ies.** a coal mine.

col•li•sion (kə lizh′ən) /kə ˈlɪʒən/ *n.* **1.** [*noncount*] the act of colliding: *to reduce the chance of collision.* **2.** [*count*] an example or instance of this: *a midair collision.*

col•lo•cate (kol′ə kāt′) /ˈkɒləˌkeyt/ *v.,* **-cat•ed, -cat•ing. 1.** [~ + *obj*] to arrange in proper order, esp. side by side. **2.** (of a word) to be arranged with another word or phrase, esp. as a common occurrence: [~ + *with* + *obj*]: *The word* look *collocates with the word* at *in the phrase* look at. [*no obj*]: *The words* look *and* at *collocate.* **—col•lo•ca•tion** (kol′ə kā′shən) /ˌkɒləˈkeyʃən/ *n.* [*noncount*]: *the study of collocation.* [*count*]: *a dictionary with the most common collocations.*

colloq., an abbreviation of: **1.** colloquial. **2.** colloquialism. **3.** colloquially.

col•lo•qui•al (kə lō′kwē əl) /kəˈlowkwiyəl/ *adj.* characteristic of or suitable to familiar conversation, rather than formal writing; informal: *colloquial style; colloquial expressions.* **—col•lo′qui•al•ly,** *adv.* **—Syn.** COLLOQUIAL, CONVERSATIONAL, INFORMAL refer to types of speech or to usages that are not on a formal level. The word COLLOQUIAL is often mistakenly used as if it had the sense of disapproval, or as if it referred to "vulgar" or "bad" or "incorrect" usage, but it simply describes a casual or familiar style used in speaking and writing: *colloquial expressions.* CONVERSATIONAL refers to a style used in speech, in simple meetings between two speakers: *The newsletter was written in an easy conversational style.* INFORMAL means without formality, without strict attention to set forms, and it describes the ordinary, everyday language of cultivated speakers: *informal English.* See -LOQ-.

col•lo•qui•um (kə lō′kwē əm) /kəˈlowkwiyəm/ *n.*

[*count*], *pl.* **-qui•ums, -qui•a** (-kwē ə) /-kwiyə/. a conference of experts on a specific topic. See -LOQ-.

col•lo•quy (kol′ə kwē) /ˈkɒləkwiy/ *n.* [*count*], *pl.* **-quies. 1.** a conversation; dialogue. **2.** a conference; meeting. —**col•lo•quist** (kol′ə kwist) /ˈkɒləkwɪst/ *n.* [*count*] See -LOQ-.

col•lude (kə lo͞od′) /kəˈluwd/ *v.*, **-lud•ed, -lud•ing.** to work together secretly to commit fraud or an illegal act: [~ + *with* + *obj*]: *The union leaders were colluding with management.* [*no obj*]: *The union and management were colluding.* —**col•lud′er,** *n.* [*count*] See -LUD-.

col•lu•sion (kə lo͞o′zhən) /kəˈluwʒən/ *n.* [*noncount*] the practice or an instance of colluding: *The oil companies were accused of collusion to raise oil prices.* [*in* + ~]: *He acted in collusion with the gang leader.* —**col•lu•sive** (kə lo͞o′siv) /kəˈluwsɪv/ *adj.* See -LUD-.

Colo., an abbreviation of: Colorado.

co•logne (kə lōn′) /kəˈlown/ *n.* [*noncount*] mildly perfumed water; eau de Cologne. Also called **Cologne′ wa′-ter.**

Co•lom•bi•an (kə lum′bē ən) /kəˈlʌmbiyən/ *adj.* **1.** of or relating to Colombia. —*n.* [*count*] **2.** a person born or living in Colombia.

co•lon[1] (kō′lən) /ˈkowlən/ *n.* [*count*] **1.** the sign (:) used to mark a major division in a sentence, indicating that what follows is further explanation of what precedes. **2.** the sign (:) used to separate groups of numbers, as hours from minutes in *5:30,* or the elements of a ratio or proportion in *1: 2:: 3: 6.*

co•lon[2] (kō′lən) /ˈkowlən/ *n.* [*count*], *pl.* **-lons, -la** (-lə). the lower part of the large intestine extending to the rectum.

colo•nel (kûr′nl) /ˈkɜrnl̩/ *n.* [*count*] **1.** an officer in the U.S. Army, Air Force, or Marine Corps ranking above lieutenant colonel. **2.** an officer of similar rank in other nations. —**colo′nel•cy,** *n.* [*noncount*]

co•lo•ni•al (kə lō′nē əl) /kəˈlowniyəl/ *adj.* **1.** [*before a noun*] of or relating to a colony or colonies: *colonial expansion.* **2.** [*before a noun; often: Colonial*] of or relating to the 13 British colonies that became the United States of America, or to their period: *the Colonial legislatures.* —*n.* [*count*] **3.** an inhabitant of a colony: *colonials fighting for independence.* **4.** a house in the Colonial style: *a charming old Colonial.* —**co•lo′ni•al•ly,** *adv.*

co•lo•ni•al•ism (kə lō′nē ə liz′əm) /kəˈlowniyəˌlɪzəm/ *n.* [*noncount*] the policy by which a nation tries to extend its authority over other peoples or territories: *The former colonies protest loudest against colonialism.* —**co•lo′ni•al•ist,** *n.* [*count*], *adj.*

col•o•nist (kol′ə nist) /ˈkɒlənɪst/ *n.* [*count*] **1.** an inhabitant of a colony: *American colonists were loyal to England in the early days of settlement.* **2.** one who establishes a colony: *The colonists had run out of food.*

col•o•nize (kol′ə nīz′) /ˈkɒləˌnayz/ *v.* [~ + *obj*], **-nized, -niz•ing.** to establish a colony in; settle: *They colonized the region.* —**col′o•niz′a•ble,** *adj.* —**col•o•ni•za•tion** (kol′ə nə zā′shən) /ˌkɒlənəˈzeyʃən/ *n.* [*noncount*] —**col′o•niz′er,** *n.* [*count*]

col•on•nade (kol′ə nād′) /ˌkɒləˈneyd/ *n.* [*count*] **1.** a series of regularly spaced columns holding up arches. **2.** a row of trees, as on each side of a road. —**col′on•nad′ed,** *adj.*: *colonnaded boulevards.*

col•o•ny (kol′ə nē) /ˈkɒləniy/ *n.* [*count*], *pl.* **-nies. 1.** a group of people who leave their native country to form a settlement in a new land that is to be connected with the parent nation: *The colony was poor and suffered greatly.* **2.** the country or district so settled: *Virginia was one of the first of the English colonies.* **3. the Colonies,** the British colonies that formed the original 13 states of the United States. **4.** a group of individuals coming from the same country or having the same interests, living in a particular place: *the American colony in Paris.* **5.** a group of people forced to live apart from society, because of disease or criminal behavior: *a leper colony; a penal colony.* **6.** a group of organisms of the same kind in the same area.

col•or (kul′ər) /ˈkʌlər/ *n.* **1.** [*noncount*] the quality of an object that gives it a certain appearance when light is reflected by it; hue: *Surprisingly, color is not part of an object, because color only arises when light strikes the object and is reflected.* **2.** [*count*] the particular appearance an object seems to reflect when different wavelengths of light strike the eye: *the primary colors red, blue, and yellow.* **3.** [*noncount*] the natural hue of the skin, esp. of the face; complexion: *He was discriminated against on the basis of color.* **4.** [*noncount*] skin tone other than white, as an indicator of a person's racial or ethnic group: *persons of color.* **5.** [*noncount*] (in people with white skin) a pinkish complexion, usually indicating good health: *Her color doesn't look good; she's too pale.* **6.** [*noncount*] lively, vivid, of special quality, as in a piece of writing: *That article was written with color and flair.* **7.** [*count*] paint or something used for coloring, as dye: *oil colors.* **8.** [*noncount*] background information, such as statistics given by a sportscaster during a broadcast: *During the game he described the plays while she provided color about the players.* **9. colors,** [*plural*] **a.** a colored badge or uniform worn or displayed to signify allegiance, etc. **b.** viewpoint or attitude; character; personality: *He changes his colors depending on the person he's with.* **c.** a flag, ensign, etc., particularly a national flag. **10.** [*noncount*] outward appearance; false show; guise: *a lie that had the color of truth.* **11.** [*noncount*] *Physics.* a theoretical property of the special particles called quarks. —*adj.* [*before a noun*] **12.** involving, using, or possessing color: *a color TV.* —*v.* **13.** [~ + *obj*] to give or apply color to; dye: *She colored her hair blonde.* **14.** [~ + *obj*] to cause to appear different from what is real: *She colored her account of the incident.* **15.** [~ + *obj*] to give a special character to; affect: *My experiences in that country color my judgment about it.* **16.** [*no obj*] to take on or change color: *The leaves haven't begun to color yet.* **17.** [*no obj*] to flush; blush: *Their faces colored whenever we talked about sex.* —***Idiom.*** **18. change color,** [*no obj*] **a.** to blush. **b.** to turn pale. **19. see** or **show someone's true colors,** to see or show how someone truly is, without pretense or a false show. **20. with flying colors,** very successfully: *She passed the tests with flying colors.* Also, *esp. Brit.,* **colour.** —**col′or•er,** *n.* [*count*]

col•or•a•tion (kul′ə rā′shən) /ˌkʌləˈreyʃən/ *n.* [*noncount*] appearance with regard to color: *the bold coloration of some birds.*

col•o•ra•tu•ra (kul′ər ə to͝or′ə, -tyo͝or′ə, kōl′-) /ˌkʌlərəˈtʊrə, -ˈtyʊrə, ˌkowl-/ *n., pl.* **-ras. 1.** [*noncount*] fancy, complicated patterns in music for singing. **2.** [*count*] a soprano of high range who specializes in such music.

col′or-blind′, *adj.* **1. a.** unable to distinguish one or more colors, such as red and green. **b.** unable to distinguish all colors, seeing only shades of gray, black, and white. **2.** free from racial bias: *a color-blind attitude in hiring.* —**col′or blind′ness,** *n.* [*noncount*]

col•ored (kul′ərd) /ˈkʌlərd/ *adj.* **1.** having a certain color or colors: *He used colored chalk on the board.* **2.** *Often Offensive.* belonging completely or in part to a race other than the white, esp. to the black race. **3.** *Often Offensive.* relating to the black race. **4.** influenced, biased, or distorted: *colored opinions.* —*n.* **5.** *Often Offensive.* **a.** [*count*] a black person. **b.** [*plural; used with a plural verb*] black persons when they are thought of as a group. —**Usage.** See BLACK.

col•or•fast (kul′ər fast′) /ˈkʌlərˌfæst/ *adj.* keeping the original color without fading or running after washing: *colorfast yarn.* —**col′or•fast′ness,** *n.* [*noncount*]

col•or•ful (kul′ər fəl) /ˈkʌlərfəl/ *adj.* **1.** having many colors or a great deal of color: *colorful fabrics.* **2.** having lively, striking, or spirited parts: *a colorful narrative.* —**col′or•ful•ly,** *adv.* —**col′or•ful•ness,** *n.* [*noncount*]

col•or•ing (kul′ər ing) /ˈkʌlərɪŋ/ *n.* [*noncount*] **1.** the act or method of applying color. **2.** appearance as to color: *healthy coloring.* **3.** a substance used to color something: *food coloring.*

col•or•ize (kul′ə rīz′) /ˈkʌləˌrayz/ *v.* [~ + *obj*], **-ized, -iz•ing.** to cause to appear in color; enhance with color, esp. by computer: *They colorized a famous black-and-white movie for television.* —**col•or•i•za•tion** (kul′ə rə zā′shən) /ˌkʌlərəˈzeyʃən/ *n.* [*noncount*]

col•or•less (kul′ər lis) /ˈkʌlərlɪs/ *adj.* **1.** [*sometimes: after a noun*] without color: *socks colorless from too many washings.* **2.** pale; pallid; dull in color: *a colorless complexion.* **3.** lacking liveliness or excitement; dull; uninteresting: *He has a colorless personality.* —**col′or•less•ly,** *adv.* —**col′or•less•ness,** *n.* [*noncount*]

co•los•sal (kə los′əl) /kəˈlɒsəl/ *adj.* extremely great in size, extent, or degree; gigantic; huge: *colossal sums of money.* —**co•los′sal•ly,** *adv.*

co•los•sus (kə los′əs) /kəˈlɒsəs/ *n.* [*count*], *pl.* **-los•si** (-los′ī) /-ˈlɒsay/ **-los•sus•es. 1.** any statue of gigantic size. **2.** anyone or anything gigantic: *a superpower that once was the colossus of the modern world.*

col•our (kul′ər) /ˈkʌlər/ *n., adj., v. Chiefly Brit.* COLOR.

colt (kōlt) /kowlt/ *n.* [*count*] **1.** a young male animal of the horse family. **2.** a young or inexperienced person.

colt•ish (kōl′tish) /ˈkowltɪʃ/ *adj.* of or resembling a colt.

col•um•bine (kol′əm bīn′) /ˈkɒləmˌbayn/ *n.* [*count*] a plant of the buttercup family, having bright white and blue flowers.

col•umn (kol′əm) /ˈkɒləm/ *n.* [*count*] **1.** a tall, straight, slender upright support; a pillar used for support or standing alone as a monument: *The old post office building had several marble columns in front.* **2.** any object, mass, or formation shaped like this: *a column of smoke.* **3.** a vertical row or list: *Add this column of figures.* **4.** a vertical arrangement of print on a page of a book, etc.: *There are two columns on this page.* **5.** an article that is a regular feature of a newspaper or magazine: *a column on political affairs.* **6.** a long, narrow file of troops, ships, marchers, etc.: *columns of tanks.* —**col′umned, col•um•nat•ed** (kol′əm nā′tid) /ˈkɒləmˌneytɪd/ *adj.*

col•um•nist (kol′əm nist) /ˈkɒləmnɪst/ *n.* [*count*] a person who writes a newspaper column.

com-, *prefix. com-* comes from Latin, where it has the meaning "with, together with." This meaning is found in such words as: COMBINE, COMMUTE, COMPARE. For variants before other sounds, see CO-, COL-[1], CON-, COR-.

Com., an abbreviation of: **1.** Commander. **2.** Commission. **3.** Commissioner. **4.** Committee. **5.** Commodore.

com., an abbreviation of: **1.** comedy. **2.** commander. **3.** commerce. **4.** commercial. **5.** committee. **6.** common. **7.** commonly. **8.** communications.

co•ma (kō′mə) /ˈkowmə/ *n.* [*count*], *pl.* **-mas.** a state of deep unconsciousness, often caused by a serious head injury: *in a coma that lasted for months.*

com•a•tose (kom′ə tōs′, kō′mə-) /ˈkɒməˌtows, ˈkowmə-/ *adj.* **1.** affected with or suffering from a coma. **2.** lacking vitality or alertness; sleepy: *comatose from the wine.*

comb (kōm) /kowm/ *n.* [*count*] **1.** a toothed strip of some hard material used to arrange or hold the hair. **2.** the fleshy growth on the head of roosters. **3.** a honeycomb, or any similar group of cells. —*v.* [~ + *obj*] **4.** to arrange (the hair) with a comb: *He combed his hair back.* **5.** to search everywhere in: *to comb the files for a missing letter.*

comb., an abbreviation of: **1.** combination. **2.** combined. **3.** combining.

com•bat (*v.* kəm bat′, kom′bat; *n.* kom′bat) /*v.* kəmˈbæt, ˈkɒmbæt; *n.* ˈkɒmbæt/ *v.,* **-bat•ed, -bat•ing** or (*esp. Brit.*) **-bat•ted, -bat•ting,** *n.* —*v.* **1.** to fight or contend against; oppose vigorously: [~ + *obj*]: *to combat crime.* [~ + *obj* + *with* + *obj*]: *to combat disease with antibiotics.* —*n.* **2.** [*noncount*] armed fighting with enemy forces: *The day of combat had arrived for the men of Squadron 1.* **3.** [*count*] a struggle or contest, as between two persons, teams, or ideas: *in a combat for first place.* See -BAT-.

com•bat•ant (kəm bat′nt) /kəm ˈbætnt/ *n.* [*count*] a person fighting in a war, as opposed to civilians.

com•bi•na•tion (kom′bə nā′shən) /ˌkɒmbəˈneyʃən/ *n.* **1.** [*noncount*] the act of combining or the state of being combined. **2.** [*count*] a number of things combined: *a combination of ideas.* **3.** [*count*] something formed by combining: *A chord is a combination of notes.* **4.** [*count*] the set of numbers or letters used to open a lock or a safe: *He forgot the combination to his locker.*

com•bine (*v.* kəm bīn′; *n.* kom′bīn) /*v.* kəmˈbayn; *n.* ˈkɒmbayn/ *v.,* **-bined, -bin•ing,** *n.* —*v.* **1.** to join in a close union; unite to form one thing: [~ + *obj*]: *combined flour, sugar, eggs, and water to make a cake.* [*no obj*]: *The dirt and water combined to form mud.* **2.** to have or show (qualities, etc.) in union: [~ + *obj*] *His bold new plan combines practicality and originality.* [~ + *obj* + *with* + *obj*]: *combines practicality with originality.* **3.** to unite for a common purpose; join: [~ + *obj*]: *Two factions combined efforts.* [*no obj*]: *Two factions combined to defeat the proposal.* —*n.* [*count*] **4.** a combination, esp. a combination of persons or groups acting together for some goal, as a syndicate, cartel, or bloc. **5.** a harvesting machine for cutting and threshing grain in the field. —**com•bin′er,** *n.* [*count*]

com•bined (kəm bīnd′) /kəm ˈbaynd/ *adj.* **1.** [*be* + ~ *(*+ *with); sometimes: after a noun or pronoun (*+ *with)*] brought together; united as qualities or features: *She is a good teacher and that, combined with her great scholarship, makes her an ideal candidate.* **2.** [*before a noun*] being, acted on, done, or performed by two or more people or groups together: *the combined military forces.*

com•bo (kom′bō) /ˈkɒmbow/ *n.* [*count*], *pl.* **-bos.** *Informal.* **1.** a small jazz or dance band: *We listened to the new combo.* **2.** a combination: *ordered a steak and lobster combo.*

com•bus•ti•ble (kəm bus′tə bəl) /kəmˈbʌstəbəl/ *adj.* **1.** capable of catching fire and burning; flammable: *combustible materials.* **2.** easily excited: *a combustible temper.* —*n.* [*count*] **3.** a combustible substance. —**com•bus•ti•bil•i•ty** (kəm bus′tə bil′i tē) /kəmˌbʌstəˈbɪlɪtiy/ *n.* [*noncount*]

com•bus•tion (kəm bus′chən) /kəmˈbʌstʃən/ *n.* [*noncount*] the act or process of burning: *combustion of fuel and air in a chamber.* —**com•bus′tive,** *adj.*

Comdr. or **comdr.,** an abbreviation of: commander.

come (kum) /kʌm/ *v.,* **came** (kām) /keym/ **come, com•ing. 1.** to approach or move toward someone or something: [*no obj*]: *Come a little closer.* [~ + *to* + *verb*]: *Can't you come to see me more often?* [~ + *verb-ing*]: *The tide came rushing in.* **2.** [*no obj*] to arrive by movement or through time: *The train is coming; step back.* **3.** [*no obj*] to move into view; appear: *The light comes and goes.* **4.** [*not: be* + *~-ing;* ~ + *to* + *obj*] to extend; reach: *The dress comes to her knees.* **5.** to take place; occur; happen: [*no obj*]: *Her trumpet solo comes in the third act.* [~ + *to* + *verb*]: *How could such a thing come to exist?* **6.** [*not: be* + *~-ing; no obj*] to be available, be produced, be found, etc.: *Toothpaste comes in a tube.* **7.** [~ + *of* + *obj*] to arrive or appear as a result: *This comes of carelessness.* **8.** to enter, get into, or be brought into a specified state or condition: [~ + *into* + *obj*]: *The word multicultural has come into popular use.* [~ + *to* + *obj*]: *The war came to an abrupt halt.* **9.** [*no obj*] to do or manage; go along or progress; fare: *How are you coming with your term paper? How's it coming?* **10.** [*no obj*] to become or seem to become a specified way: *We came unglued (= overly nervous) at the thought of another exam that day.* **11.** (used as a command to call attention, or to express impatience, etc.): *Come, come, can't we agree on one little point here?* **12.** [*no obj*] *Slang.* to have an orgasm. **13. come about, a.** to come to pass; happen: [*no obj*]: *How did such a mess come about, anyway?* [*it* + ~ + *(that) clause*]: *It came about that he had to cancel his vacation.* **b.** [*no obj*] to turn a ship or boat at an angle in the wind. **14. come across** or **upon, a.** [~ + *across/upon* + *obj*] to find or encounter, esp. by chance: *Look at these photos that I came across.* **b.** [*no obj*] to do what one has promised or is expected to do: *He finally came across and did it.* See COME THROUGH below. **c.** [*no obj*] to be understandable or convincing: *The humor doesn't come across.* **d.** [~ + *across* + *as* + *noun/adjective*] to make a particular impression: *He comes across as a cold person. The teacher comes across as very cruel, but that is misleading.* **15. come again,** (used as a request to repeat a statement): *I didn't hear you; come again.* **16. come along,** [*no obj*] **a.** to accompany a person or group: *We're going to the mall; you can come along if you like.* **b.** to proceed or advance: *The project is coming along on schedule.* **c.** to appear: *An opportunity came along to invest in real estate.* **17. come around** or **round, a.** [*no obj*] Also, **come to.** to recover consciousness; revive: *The unconscious patient finally came around.* **b.** [~ + *around* + *to* + *obj*] to change one's opinion, etc., esp. to agree with another's: *She finally came around to our point of view.* **c.** [*no obj*] to stop being angry, etc.: *She's mad and upset now, but I'm sure she'll come around.* **d.** [*no obj*] to visit: *Why don't you come around and see me some time?* **18. come apart,** [*no obj*] to break or fall into pieces: *The doll just came apart when touched.* **19. come at,** [~ + *at* + *obj*] **a.** to arrive at; reach or attain: *How did he come at such a sum?* **b.** to rush at; attack: *came at me with a knife.* **20. come back, a.** [~ + *back (*+ *to* + *obj)*] to return, esp. to one's memory: *I remember now; it's all coming back to me.* **b.** [~ + *back (*+ *to* + *obj)*] to return to a former position, place, or state: *Do you have any idea when he'll come back?* **c.** [*no obj*] to become fashionable or popular again: *Short skirts are coming back again.* **21. come between,** [~ + *between* + *obj*] to separate; get in the way of; interrupt: *Nothing can come between us.* **22. come by,** [~ + *by* + *obj*] to obtain; find; acquire: *We never came by such good fortune again.* **23. come down,** [*no obj*] **a.** to fall down; collapse: *The entire building came down on them.* **b.** to lose wealth, rank, etc.: *The senator has really come down in the world.* **c.** [~ + *down (*+ *to* + *obj)*] to be handed down or passed on by tradition or inheritance: *This ancient song comes down to us from Norway.* **d.** [*no obj*] to be relayed or passed along from a higher authority: *Our orders will come down tomorrow.* **e.** to lead or point in a basic, important way, such as a choice or problem; be the deciding factor: [~ + *down* + *to* + *obj*]: *It all comes down to a sense of pride.* [~ + *down* + *to* + *verb-ing*]: *It all comes down to living or dying.* **24. come down on**

or **upon,** [~ + *down* + *on/upon* + *obj*] to scold or reprimand; punish: *Why did you come down on her so hard?* **25. come down with,** [~ + *down* + *with* + *obj*] to become sick from or afflicted with (an illness): *She came down with the flu.* **26. come from,** [~ + *from* + *obj*] **a.** [*not: be* + ~*-ing*] to have been born in (a place); be a resident of (a place): *He came from Greece.* **b.** [*not: be* + ~*-ing*] to have as a beginning or source: *Pearls come from oysters.* **c.** [*in negative expressions or in questions; usually: be* + ~*-ing* + *from*] be a starting point in thinking or reasoning: *I can't understand where he's coming from.* **27. come in,** [*no obj*] **a.** to enter: *The door's open; come in!* **b.** to arrive: *The train comes in at 6:00 p.m.* **c.** to come into use or fashion: *Long skirts have come in again.* **d.** to begin to produce or yield: *The oil well finally came in.* **e.** to finish in a race or competition: *Our team came in fifth.* **28. come in for,** [~ + *in* + *for* + *obj*] to receive; get; be subjected to: *He's going to come in for a lot of criticism.* **29. come into,** [~ + *into* + *obj*] **a.** to acquire; get: *I came into a bit of money winning a wager.* **b.** to inherit: *She came into a lot of money after her cousin died.* **c.** to get to be in (a state): *The president's car suddenly came into view and everyone cheered.* **30. come off,** [*no obj*] **a.** to happen; occur: *The invasion came off just before dawn.* **b.** to reach the end; conclude: *We want this project to come off without any delay.* **c.** to be effective or successful, esp. in the specified way: *She didn't come off well in that interview.* **31. Come off it,** (often used as a command) to stop: *Come off it; we know where you were.* **32. come on, a.** [~ + *on/upon* + *obj*] to meet or find unexpectedly or by accident: *I just happened to come on (upon) a book in the library that has the references you need.* **b.** [*no obj*] (of a disease) to begin to develop: *I can feel a cold coming on.* **c.** [*no obj*] to make progress; develop; flourish: *Just when the challenger was coming on in the primaries, another scandal broke.* **d.** [*no obj*] to appear on stage; make one's entrance: *He came on to thunderous applause.* **e.** [*no obj*] to begin to be shown, broadcast, etc.: *The game came on at one o'clock.* **f.** [*no obj*] (used as a command) to hurry; move along: *Come on, before it rains!* **g.** [*no obj*] (used to ask someone to do something): *Come on, have dinner with us.* **h.** [~ + *on (+ to + obj)*] *Slang.* to make sexual advances: *He was coming on (to her) and she didn't know how to respond.* **33. come out,** [*no obj*] **a.** to appear or be seen: *Suddenly the sun came out.* **b.** to be published or made known; appear: *The story came out in all the papers.* **c.** to make a debut in society, etc. **d.** to appear and be available to the public: *When will this new wonder drug come out?* **e.** to end; result; emerge: *The lawsuit came out badly for both sides.* **f.** to make public acknowledgment of being homosexual. **34. come out for** (or **against**), [~ + *out* + *for/against* + *obj*] to state or declare one's support for (or opposition to): *The president is expected to come out for the new tax bill.* **35. come out with,** [~ + *out* + *with* + *obj*] to reveal by stating; blurt out; say: *He came out with a ridiculous remark.* **36. come over,** [~ + *over* + *obj*] to happen to; affect: *What's come over him?* **37. come round,** [*no obj*] **a.** (of a sailing vessel) to head toward the wind; come to. **b.** to come around. **38. come through, a.** [~ + *through* + *obj*] to endure difficulty, illness, etc., successfully: *She came through the war safely.* **b.** [*no obj*] to fulfill needs or meet demands: *My friend will come through; he has never disappointed me before.* **39. come to, a.** [*no obj*] to recover consciousness: *Stand back, he's coming to.* **b.** [~ + *to* + *obj; not: be* + ~*-ing*] to amount to; total: *The expenses came to $5,000 after deductions.* **c.** [*usually: it* + ~ + *to* + *obj; not: be* + ~*-ing*] to concern: *When it comes to quality this is first-rate.* **d.** [~ + *to* + *obj; sometimes: it* + ~ + *to* + *obj*] to enter or be recalled in the mind; occur to the mind or memory: *Suddenly it came to me; I knew her from Paris.* **40. come under,** [~ + *under* + *obj*] **a.** to be the responsibility of: *This matter comes under the State Department.* **b.** to be subjected to; be forced to suffer: *came under a lot of criticism for hiring her.* **c.** [*not: be* + ~*-ing*] to be placed in a certain category of: *Copying your classmate's paper comes under the heading of cheating.* **41. come up,** [*no obj*] **a.** to be mentioned or be referred to; arise: *Your name came up in conversation.* **b.** to be presented for action or discussion: *The farm bill comes up on Monday.* **42. come up to,** [~ + *up* + *to* + *obj*] **a.** to approach; near: *She came up to the star and asked for his autograph.* **b.** to compare with as to quantity, excellence, etc.; equal: *Your work just doesn't come up to our high standards.* **43. come up with,** [~ + *up* + *with* + *obj*] to produce; supply: *What new plan did you come up with?* **44. to come,** in the future: *In years to come, we hope to solve these problems.*

come•back (kum′bak′) /ˈkʌmˌbæk/ *n.* [*count*] **1.** a return to the higher success of an earlier time: *I think he is staging a comeback.* **2.** a clever or effective answer; retort: *had a nasty comeback to his criticism of her plan.*

co•me•di•an (kə mē′dē ən) /kəˈmiydiyən/ *n.* [*count*] a professional entertainer who makes an audience laugh by telling jokes, doing impressions, etc.

co•me•di•enne (kə mē′dē en′) /kəˌmiydiyˈɛn/ *n.* [*count*] a woman who is a comic entertainer or actress.

come•down (kum′doun′) /ˈkʌmˌdawn/ *n.* [*count*] an embarrassing descent from previous importance: *quite a comedown for the physicist to have to sweep streets.*

com•e•dy (kom′i dē) /ˈkɒmɪdiy/ *n., pl.* **-dies. 1.** [*count*] a play, etc., of light and humorous character with a cheerful ending. **2.** [*noncount*] the branch of drama concerned with this.

come•ly (kum′lē, kom′-) /ˈkʌmliy, ˈkɒm-/ *adj.,* **-li•er, -li•est.** pleasing in appearance; attractive; good-looking; pleasant to look at. —**come′li•ness,** *n.* [*noncount*]

come′-on′, *n.* [*count*] something done or said in order to attract or lure customers: *Their advertisements were just come-ons; nothing was on sale.*

com•er (kum′ər) /ˈkʌmər/ *n.* [*count*] a person or thing that is progressing well or is very promising: *That writer is a real comer and has a great future.*

com•et (kom′it) /ˈkɒmɪt/ *n.* [*count*] a body in space made up of a bright, central solid mass and a tail of dust and gas and that orbits the sun: *Halley's comet.* —**com•et•ar•y** (kom′i ter′ē) /ˈkɒmɪˌtɛriy/ *adj.*

come•up•pance (kum′up′əns) /ˌkʌmˈʌpəns/ *n.* [*count; usually singular*] a scolding or punishment deserved: *got his comeuppance when he came to work late.*

com•fit (kum′fit, kom′-) /ˈkʌmfɪt, ˈkɒm-/ *n.* [*count*] a candy containing a nut or piece of fruit.

com•fort (kum′fərt) /ˈkʌmfərt/ *v.* [~ + *obj*] **1.** to soothe or reassure; bring cheer to; console: *to comfort someone after a loss.* **2.** to make physically comfortable: *Her job was to comfort the sick.* —*n.* **3.** [*noncount*] words or acts that show concern for someone suffering; consolation: *spoke a few words of comfort to the dying patient.* **4.** [*count*] a person or thing that gives consolation or relief: *a comfort to her parents in their old age.* **5.** [*noncount*] a state of ease and satisfaction of bodily wants: *a life of comfort.* **6.** [*count*] something that promotes such a state: *One of his comforts is the color TV in the bathroom.* —**com′fort•ing•ly,** *adv.* See -FORT-.

com•fort•a•ble (kumf′tə bəl, kum′fər tə bəl) /ˈkʌmftəbəl, ˈkʌmfərtəbəl/ *adj.* **1.** (of clothing, furniture, etc.) producing or giving physical comfort: *a comfortable old couch.* **2.** [*be* + ~] in a state of physical or mental comfort; contented and undisturbed: *I was comfortable sitting in the old chair.* **3.** adequate or sufficient: *a comfortable salary.* —**com′fort•a•ble•ness,** *n.* [*noncount*] —**com′fort•a•bly,** *adv.*

com•fort•er (kum′fər tər) /ˈkʌmfərtər/ *n.* [*count*] **1.** one that comforts. **2.** a thick quilted bedcover.

com′fort sta′tion, *n.* [*count*] a room or building with toilet and lavatory facilities for public use: *The next comfort station on the highway is fifty miles away.*

com•fy (kum′fē) /ˈkʌmfiy/ *adj.,* **-fi•er, -fi•est.** *Informal.* comfortable: *got comfy and watched some TV.* —**com′fi•ness,** *n.* [*noncount*]

com•ic (kom′ik) /ˈkɒmɪk/ *adj.* **1.** [*before a noun*] **a.** relating to or characterized by comedy: *a few comic scenes in a tragic play.* **b.** performing in or writing comedy: *He worked as a comic actor.* **2.** causing laughter; humorous; funny: *The baby began making comic noises.* —*n.* [*count*] **3.** a comedian: *a standup comic.* **4. comics,** [*plural; often: the* + ~] a section of a newspaper featuring comic strips. **5.** a comic book: *I still remember the first comic I bought; it cost 10 cents.*

com•i•cal (kom′i kəl) /ˈkɒmɪkəl/ *adj.* producing laughter; amusing; funny. —**com′i•cal•ly,** *adv.* —**com′i•cal•ness,** *n.* [*noncount*]

com′ic book′, *n.* [*count*] a magazine made up of comic strips: *bought a Superman comic book.*

com′ic strip′, *n.* [*count*] a sequence of drawings telling or showing a comic incident, an adventure, etc., often appearing in daily newspapers.

com•ing (kum′ing) /ˈkʌmɪŋ/ *n.* [*count*] **1.** approach; arrival; advent: *They awaited the coming of the king.* —*adj.* [*before a noun*] **2.** following or approaching; next: *the coming year.* **3.** promising future fame or success: *a coming actor.* —***Idiom.*** **4. comings and goings,** [*plu-*

ral] actions of arriving and departing: *all the comings and goings in the busy train station.*

comm., an abbreviation of: **1.** commander. **2.** commerce. **3.** commission. **4.** committee.

com•ma (kom′ə) /'kɒmə/ *n.* [*count*], *pl.* **-mas.** the sign (,), a mark of punctuation used to indicate a division in a sentence, as in setting off a word, phrase, or clause *(First, we take the milk, and then we beat the butter.)*, to separate items in a list *(eggs, milk, and butter)*, to mark off thousands in numerals *(5,000)*, and, in some parts of Europe, as a decimal point *(My German students wrote "A kilogram weighs 2,2 pounds.")*

com•mand (kə mand′) /kə'mænd/ *v.* **1.** to direct with authority; order: [*no obj*]: *We did as he commanded.* [~ + *obj* + *to* + *verb*]: *The general commanded his troops to march the rest of the way.* [~ + *that clause*]: *He commanded that they follow him.* [*used with quotations*]: *"Stand at attention, soldier!" he commanded.* **2.** [~ + *obj*] to demand: *to command silence.* **3.** [~ + *obj*] to deserve and receive (respect, attention, etc.): *Her words command respect.* **4.** [~ + *obj*] to dominate by reason of location (such as by being higher); overlook: *The hill commands the sea.* **5.** [~ + *obj*] to have authority or control over: *He commanded an army base of a thousand soldiers.* **—n. 6.** [*noncount*] the act of commanding or ordering with authority; control: *Admiral, you have lost command of your ship.* [*be* + *in* + ~]: *The lieutenant was in command of a platoon.* **7.** [*count*] an order given by one in authority: *He issued several commands.* **8.** [*count*] an order in prescribed words, such as one given at close-order drill: *The command was "Right shoulder arms!"* **9.** expertise; mastery; strong ability: [*count; usually singular*]: *has a working command of four languages.* [*noncount*]: *His spoken command of Russian was perfect.* **10.** [*count*] a signal, as a keystroke, instructing a computer to perform a specific task: *He issued several commands to clear the screen.* **—adj.** [*before a noun*] **11.** ordered or requested: *She gave a command performance before the queen.* See -MAND-.

com•man•dant (kom′ən dant′, -dänt′) /ˌkɒmən'dænt, -'dɑnt/ *n.* [*count*] the commanding officer of a place, group, etc., esp. the head of a military unit or school.

com•man•deer (kom′ən dēr′) /ˌkɒmən'dɪər/ *v.* [~ + *obj*] **1.** to seize (private property) for military or other public use: *The military commandeered all the jeeps.* **2.** to seize or take unfairly: *He commandeered the best office furniture for his own use.*

com•mand•er (kə man′dər) /kə'mændər/ *n.* [*count*] **1.** a person in authority; chief officer; leader. **2.** the officer in command of a military unit. **3.** an officer in the U.S. Navy or Coast Guard ranking below a captain and above a lieutenant commander.

command′er in chief′, *n.* [*count*], *pl.* **commanders in chief. 1.** Also, **Command′er in Chief′.** the supreme commander of the armed forces of a nation. **2.** an officer in command of a particular portion of an armed force.

com•mand•ment (kə mand′mənt) /kə'mændmənt/ *n.* [*count*] **1.** a command or mandate. **2.** [*sometimes: Commandment*] any of the Ten Commandments.

com•man•do (kə man′dō) /kə'mændow/ *n.* [*count*], *pl.* **-dos, -does. 1. a.** a military combat unit specially trained and organized for surprise raids. **b.** a member of such a unit. **2.** a member of an assault team against terrorist attacks: *The commandos surrounded the airport.*

com•mem•o•rate (kə mem′ə rāt′) /kə'mɛməˌreyt/ *v.* [~ + *obj*], **-rat•ed, -rat•ing. 1.** to serve as a memorial or reminder of: *The monument commemorates a naval victory.* **2.** to honor the memory of by some observance: *to commemorate Bastille Day.* **—com•mem•o•ra•ble** (kə-mem′ər ə bəl) /kə'mɛmərəbəl/ *adj.* **—com•mem′o•ra′tor,** *n.* [*count*] See -MEM-.

com•mem•o•ra•tion (kə mem′ə rā′shən) /kəˌmɛmə'reyʃən/ *n.* **1.** [*noncount*] an act of commemorating something: [*in* + ~]: *a ceremony in commemoration of war veterans.* **2.** [*count*] a ceremony or occasion to commemorate something: *a small commemoration on Memorial Day.*

com•mem•o•ra•tive (kə mem′ər ə tiv) /kə'mɛmərətɪv/ *adj.* [*before a noun*] commemorating something: *a commemorative stamp.*

com•mence (kə mens′) /kə'mɛns/ *v.*, **-menced, -menc•ing.** to begin; start: [*no obj*]: *Let the festivities commence.* [~ + *obj*]: *We can commence the meeting.* [~ + *verb-ing*]: *Commence firing!* [~ + *to* + *verb*]: *He commenced to speak.* **—com•menc′er,** *n.* [*count*] **—Syn.** See BEGIN.

com•mence•ment (kə mens′mənt) /kə'mɛnsmənt/ *n.* **1.** [*noncount*] an act of commencing: *commencement of hostilities.* **2.** the ceremony of awarding degrees at the end of the academic year: [*noncount*]: *Will I see you at commencement?* [*count*]: *The famous poet was asked to speak at several commencements this year.*

com•mend (kə mend′) /kə'mɛnd/ *v.* [~ + *obj*] **1.** to present or mention as worthy of confidence, attention, etc.; recommend: *to commend one friend to another.* **2.** to entrust; deliver with confidence: *I commend my child to your care.* **3.** to single out or choose (someone) for special praise: *to commend a soldier for bravery.* **—com•mend′a•ble,** *adj.*: *It was commendable that you admitted your mistake.* **—com•mend′a•ble•ness,** *n.* [*noncount*] **—com•mend′a•bly,** *adv.*: *performed the task commendably.*

com•men•da•tion (kom′ən dā′shən) /ˌkɒmən'deyʃən/ *n.* [*count*] **1.** the act of commending; recommendation; praise. **2.** something that commends, as a formal recommendation or an official citation.

com•men•su•rate (kə men′sər it, -shər-) /kə'mɛnsərɪt, -ʃər-/ *adj.* [*usually: be* + ~] corresponding in amount or degree; proportionate: *The salary will be commensurate with your experience.* **—com•men′su•rate•ly,** *adv.* **—com•men′su•rate•ness,** *n.* [*noncount*]

com•ment (kom′ent) /'kɒmɛnt/ *n.* **1.** [*count*] a remark, observation, or criticism: *a comment about the weather.* **2.** [*noncount*] gossip; talk: *His absence gave rise to comment.* **3.** [*count*] a criticism or interpretation about a state of affairs: *The play is a comment on modern society.* **—v. 4.** to make remarks, observations, or criticisms: [~ (+ *on* + *obj*)]: *The president refused to comment (on that issue).* [*used with quotations*]: *"I never dress like that," she commented.* **—*Idiom.* 5. no comment,** [*noncount*] (used when the speaker wishes to say nothing in response to a question). **—com′ment•er,** *n.* [*count*]

com•men•tar•y (kom′ən ter′ē) /'kɒmənˌtɛriy/ *n.*, *pl.* **-ies. 1.** a series of comments, explanations, or descriptions: [*noncount*]: *provided commentary on the players.* [*count*]: *a running commentary on the game.* **2.** [*count*] an essay or other long writing that gives an explanation or interpretation: *Write a commentary on one of Shakespeare's plays.* **3.** [*count*] anything serving to illustrate a point about a state of affairs: *The high dropout rate is a sad commentary on our school system.* See -MEN-.

com•men•ta•tor (kom′ən tā′tər) /'kɒmənˌteytər/ *n.* [*count*] a person who discusses news, sports events, or other topics on television or radio: *a TV sports commentator.*

com•merce (kom′ərs) /'kɒmərs/ *n.* [*noncount*] **1.** an exchange of goods or commodities between different countries or between areas of the same country; trade: *commerce with overseas countries.* **2.** social relations, esp. the exchange of views, attitudes, etc. See -MERC-.

com•mer•cial (kə mûr′shəl) /kə'mɜrʃəl/ *adj.* [*usually: before a noun*] **1.** of, relating to, or characteristic of commerce: *the commercial world.* **2.** engaged in, used for, or suitable to commerce or business: *Commercial vehicles include trucks and some vans.* **3.** made, produced, or marketed to be sold or to make a profit: *commercial theater.* **4.** paid for by advertisers: *commercial television.* **—n.** [*count*] **5.** a paid advertisement or announcement on radio or television: *The TV show was interrupted by too many commercials.* **—com•mer′cial•ly,** *adv.* See -MERC-.

com•mer•cial•ism (kə mûr′shə liz′əm) /kə'mɜrʃəˌlɪzəm/ *n.* [*noncount*] **1.** the principles, practices, and spirit of commerce. **2.** too much emphasis on making a profit: *The author bowed to the demands of commercialism and changed his play to have a happy ending.*

com•mer•cial•ize (kə mûr′shə līz′) /kə'mɜrʃəˌlayz/ *v.* [~ + *obj*], **-ized, -iz•ing. 1.** to make commercial in character, methods, etc.; make profitable or introduce profit into: *tried to commercialize her home baking.* **2.** to emphasize the money-making aspects of (something), by cheapening: *Christmas has become very commercialized.* **—com•mer•cial•i•za•tion** (kə mûr′shə lə zā′shən) /kəˌmɜrʃələ'zeyʃən/ *n.* [*noncount*]: *commercialization of the Olympics.*

com•mis•er•ate (kə miz′ə rāt′) /kə'mɪzəˌreyt/ *v.* [~ + *with* + *obj*], **-at•ed, -at•ing.** to feel, express, or share sorrow; sympathize: *I commiserated with him over the loss of his mother.* **—com•mis•er•a•tion** (kə miz′ə rā′shən) /kəˌmɪzə'reyʃən/ *n.* [*noncount*]: *sad feelings of commiseration.* [*count*]: *We offer commiserations to the losers of the contest.* **—com•mis′er•a′tor,** *n.* [*count*] See -MISER-.

com•mis•sar (kom′ə sär′) /ˈkɒmə,sɑr/ *n.* [*count*] **1.** the head of a major governmental division in the former U.S.S.R. **2.** an official in a communist government whose duties include political training and teaching. See -MIS-.

com•mis•sar•i•at (kom′ə sâr′ē ət) /,kɒməˈsɛəriyət/ *n.* [*count*] a major governmental division in the former U.S.S.R.

com•mis•sar•y (kom′ə ser′ē) /ˈkɒmə,sɛriy/ *n.* [*count*], *pl.* **-ies. 1.** a store that sells food and supplies in a military post, etc. **2.** a dining room or cafeteria. See -MIS-.

com•mis•sion (kə mish′ən) /kəˈmɪʃən/ *n.* **1.** [*count*] an order to perform a task, job, or duty: *I received this commission directly from the king.* **2.** [*count*] the authority, position, or rank of an officer in any of the armed forces: *She resigned her commission.* **3.** [*count*] a group of persons given authority, such as to investigate wrongdoing or discover the facts about something: *a special commission to investigate political corruption.* **4.** [*count*] a task or matter committed to one's charge; official assignment: *The architect received a commission to design an office building.* **5.** [*noncount*] the act of committing or perpetrating a crime, error, etc.: *The commission of a crime was not clearly established in court.* **6.** a sum or percentage of money allowed to agents, etc., for their services, usually based on the value or price of what gets sold: [*noncount; on/by* + ~]: *He works on commission, so in a slow week of sales he doesn't make much money.* [*count*]: *He gets a commission of 10% on all sales above $5,000.* **—*v.* 7.** to give a commission to: [~ + *obj* + *to* + *verb*]: *commissioned the panel to investigate the charges of bribery.* [~ + *obj*]: *He was commissioned in the Army in 1946.* **—*Idiom.* 8. in** (or **out of**) **commission,** [*noncount*] in (or not in) service or operating order: *We'll have to walk; the elevator is out of commission again.* See -MIS-, -MIT-.

commis′sioned of′ficer, *n.* [*count*] a military or naval officer holding rank by having been appointed.

com•mis•sion•er (kə mish′ə nər) /kəˈmɪʃənər/ *n.* [*count*] **1.** a person who is a member of a commission: *The commissioners voted 6 to 5 in favor of the plan.* **2.** a government official in charge of a department or district: *the police commissioner.* **3.** an official chosen by an athletic association and given broad authority: *the baseball commissioner.*

com•mit (kə mit′) /kəˈmɪt/ *v.* [~ + *obj*] **1.** [~ + *oneself*] to declare that one has a certain opinion or position: *The senator would not commit herself on the upcoming vote.* **2.** [~ + *oneself* + *to* + *obj*] to obligate (oneself), such as by a pledge: *He committed himself to helping the poor.* **3.** to entrust, esp. for safekeeping; commend: *to commit one's soul to God.* **4.** to put (something) in a place or state for keeping: *She decided to commit her ideas to writing.* **5.** [~ + *obj* + *to* + *obj*] to assign or send for a certain purpose; allocate: *The general committed his troops to battle.* **6.** to do; perform; perpetrate: *to commit murder.* **7.** to send (someone) to a prison or mental institution by legal authority: *He was committed to an institution for the criminally insane.* See -MIT-.

com•mit•ment (kə mit′mənt) /kəˈmɪtmənt/ *n.* **1.** [*count*] a firm promise or pledge: *He made a commitment to his wife.* **2.** [*noncount*] a strong or firm belief shown by one's actions; loyalty: *a lifetime of commitment to the poor.* **3.** [*count*] a responsibility that takes up or occupies one's time: *Because of his commitments at home his work began to suffer.*

com•mit•tal (kə mit′l) /kəˈmɪtl̩/ *n.* [*noncount*] the act of committing, esp. to a mental institution.

com•mit•ted (kə mit′id) /kəˈmɪtɪd/ *adj.* [*usually: before a noun*] dedicated; giving one's complete loyalty to something: *a committed teacher.*

com•mit•tee (kə mit′ē) /kəˈmɪtiy/ *n.* [*count*] a group of persons elected or appointed to perform some function, such as to investigate a particular matter. See -MIT-. **—Usage.** See COLLECTIVE NOUN.

com•mode (kə mōd′) /kəˈmowd/ *n.* [*count*] **1.** a low cabinet or similar piece of furniture containing drawers or shelves. **2.** TOILET (def. 1). **3.** a portable toilet, esp. one on a chairlike frame, as for an invalid.

com•mo•di•ous (kə mō′dē əs) /kəˈmowdiyəs/ *adj.* large; having space; ample; roomy: *a commodious apartment.* **—com•mo′di•ous•ly,** *adv.* **—com•mo′di•ous•ness,** *n.* [*noncount*] See -MOD-.

com•mod•i•ty (kə mod′i tē) /kəˈmɒdɪtiy/ *n.* [*count*], *pl.* **-ties.** an article of trade or commerce, esp. a product that can be bought or sold: *wheat, rice, automobiles, and other commodities.*

com•mo•dore (kom′ə dôr′, -dōr′) /ˈkɒmə,dɔr, -,dowr/ *n.* [*count*] **1.** (formerly) a commissioned officer in the U.S. Navy or Coast Guard ranking above a captain. **2.** an officer in the British navy in temporary command of a squadron.

com•mon (kom′ən) /ˈkɒmən/ *adj.,* **-er, -est,** *n.* **—*adj.* 1.** belonging equally to, or shared alike by: *We all have a common objective, to stop the mayor's reelection.* **2.** relating to or belonging to an entire community, nation, or culture: *They had a common language, English.* **3.** [*before a noun*] widespread; general; universal: *There was common understanding that he would be promoted.* **4.** of frequent occurrence; usual; familiar: *It was a common error.* **5.** of mediocre quality: *a rough, common fabric.* **6.** having or showing bad manners; socially unacceptable: *common manners.* **7.** [*before a noun*] lacking rank, station, etc.; ordinary; not special: *a common soldier; common table salt.* **8.** [*before a noun*] in keeping with accepted standards; fundamental: *common decency.* **—*n.*** [*count*] **9.** Often, **commons.** [*plural*] a piece of land owned or used by the people living in a community, as a park. **10. commons,** [*plural*] the common people. **—*Idiom.* 11. in common,** [*noncount*] in joint possession or use; shared equally: *We have much in common with people from other cultures.* **—com′mon•ly,** *adv.*: *It's commonly understood that people say thank you when they receive a gift.* **—com′mon•ness,** *n.* [*noncount*]

com′mon cold′, *n.* [*count; often: the* + ~] COLD (def. 14).

com′mon denom′inator, *n.* [*count*] **1.** a number that is a multiple of all the denominators of a set of fractions. **2.** a trait, characteristic, or attitude common to a group: *The common denominator of all these groups is their desire to keep the judge from getting the position.*

com•mon•er (kom′ə nər) /ˈkɒmənər/ *n.* [*count*] a member of the class of people without a title of nobility: *The king wouldn't let his daughter marry a commoner.*

com′mon law′, *n.* [*noncount*] the system of law coming first from England, based on custom or court decision. **—com′mon-law′,** *adj.* [*before a noun*]: *a common-law marriage.*

Com′mon Mar′ket, *n.* **1.** [*proper noun; noncount; usually: the* + ~] EUROPEAN ECONOMIC COMMUNITY. **2.** [*count; often: common market*] any economic association of nations.

com′mon noun′, *n.* [*count*] a noun that may be preceded by an article or other limiting modifier and that designates any or all of a class of things and not an individual, as *man, city, horse, music.* Also called **com′mon name′.**

com•mon•place (kom′ən plās′) /ˈkɒmən,pleys/ *adj.* **1.** ordinary; uninteresting; usual: *commonplace expressions in his writing.* **—*n.*** [*count*] **2.** a well-known or obvious remark or statement; platitude: *It is a commonplace that the world has grown more complex.* **3.** anything common or uninteresting.

com′mon sense′, *n.* [*noncount*] sound practical judgment: *It's just good common sense to look both ways before crossing a street.* **—com′mon-sense′,** *adj.* [*before a noun*]: *a commonsense attitude.* **—com′mon•sen′si•cal, com′mon•sen′si•ble,** *adj.* **—com′mon•sen′si•cal•ly, com′mon•sen′si•bly,** *adv.*

com•mon•wealth (kom′ən welth′) /ˈkɒmən,wɛlθ/ *n.* **1.** [*count*] the people of a nation or state, seen as a political unit. **2.** [*count; Commonwealth*] a group of self-governing nations associated by their own choice and linked with common objectives. **3. the Commonwealth,** [*proper noun*] COMMONWEALTH OF NATIONS.

Com′monwealth of Na′tions, *n.* [*proper noun; noncount*] a voluntary association of independent nations linked by history as parts of the former British Empire. Formerly, **British Commonwealth of Nations.**

com•mo•tion (kə mō′shən) /kəˈmowʃən/ *n.* violent, noisy action; disturbance; fuss; agitation: [*count; singular*]: *a sudden commotion at the back of the room.* [*noncount*]: *What is all the commotion about?* See -MOT-.

com•mu•nal (kə myo͞on′l) /kəˈmyuwnl̩/ *adj.* **1.** used or shared in common: *a communal stove.* **2.** of, by, or belonging to the people of a community: *communal land.* **3.** relating to a commune or a community: *communal life.* **—com•mu′nal•ly,** *adv.*

com•mune[1] (kə myo͞on′) /kəˈmyuwn/ *v.* [*no obj*], **-muned, -mun•ing. 1.** to converse or talk together. **2.** [~ + *with* + *obj*] to be in close communication: *to commune with nature.*

com•mune[2] (kom′yo͞on) /ˈkɒmyuwn/ *n.* [*count*] **1.** a small group of persons living together, sharing possessions, work, income, etc. **2.** a group of persons working together as a team, esp. to run a collective farm.

com•mu•ni•ca•ble (kə myo͞o′ni kə bəl) /kə'myuwnɪkəbəl/ *adj.* easily communicated or transmitted to another: *a communicable disease.* —**com•mu•ni•ca•bil•i•ty** (kə myo͞o′ni kə bil′i tē) /kə,myuwnɪkə'bɪlɪtiy/ **com•mu′ni•ca•ble•ness,** *n.* [*noncount*]

com•mu•ni•cant (kə myo͞o′ni kənt) /kə'myuwnɪkənt/ *n.* [*count*] a member of a church allowed to receive Communion.

com•mu•ni•cate (kə myo͞o′ni kāt′) /kə'myuwnɪ,keyt/ *v.,* **-cat•ed, -cat•ing. 1.** [~ + *obj*] to give to another; transmit: *to communicate a disease.* **2.** to give or exchange (thoughts, etc.) by writing, speaking, etc.: [*no obj*]: *They were trying to understand how dolphins communicate.* [~ + *with* + *obj*]: *We have to communicate with the chairman on this.* [~ + *obj*]: *You have to learn to communicate your ideas clearly.* **3.** [*no obj*] to express thoughts, feelings, or information easily: *She has trouble communicating and won't succeed in advertising.* —**com•mu′ni•ca′tor,** *n.* [*count*]

com•mu•ni•ca•tion (kə myo͞o′ni kā′shən) /kə,myuwnɪ'keyʃən/ *n.* **1.** [*noncount*] **a.** the act or process of communicating; fact of being communicated. **b.** the sending or exchanging of thoughts, opinions, or information by speech, writing, or signs: *We studied animal communication.* **2.** [*count*] some thought or information sent or transmitted, esp. a document or message giving news, instructions, etc.: *the latest communication from the front.* **3. communications, a.** [*plural; used with a plural verb*] means of sending messages, orders, etc., including telephone, telegraph, radio, and television: *With modern communications we can telephone anywhere in the world.* **b.** [*noncount; used with a singular verb*] the professions of journalism, broadcasting, etc. **c.** [*noncount; used with a singular verb*] the study of effective communication: *studying communications and communications skills.* —**com•mu′ni•ca′tion•al,** *adj.*

com•mu•ni•ca•tive (kə myo͞o′nə kə tiv) /kə'myuwnəkətɪv/ *adj.* **1.** of or relating to communication: *excellent communicative skills.* **2.** talkative; able or ready to talk with others: *The lost little boy was not communicative.*

com•mun•ion (kə myo͞on′yən) /kə'myuwnyən/ *n.* **1.** [*often: Communion*] Also called **Holy Communion. a.** [*noncount*] the act of receiving the bread and wine at a Christian eucharistic service. **b.** [*noncount*] the bread and wine so received. **2.** [*count*] a group of people having a common religious faith; denomination: *the Anglican communion.* **3.** [*noncount*] the exchanging or sharing of thoughts or emotions: *communion with nature.*

com•mu•ni•qué (kə myo͞o′ni kā′) /kə,myuwnɪ'key/ *n.* [*count*] an official bulletin or communication: *The leaders issued a joint communiqué.*

com•mu•nism (kom′yə niz′əm) /'kɒmyə,nɪzəm/ *n.* [*noncount*] **1.** a theory or system of social organization based on the holding of all property in common, with ownership by the state. **2.** [*often: Communism*] a political doctrine or movement based on Marxism seeking the overthrow of capitalism and the creation of a classless society.

com•mu•nist (kom′yə nist) /'kɒmyənɪst/ *n.* [*count*] **1.** [*Communist*] a member of a Communist Party: *The Communists couldn't get a majority.* **2.** a supporter or advocate of communism. **3.** a person regarded as supporting leftist causes. —*adj.* **4.** [*Communist*] of or relating to a Communist Party or to Communism. **5.** relating to communists or communism. —**com′mu•nis′tic,** *adj.*

com•mu•ni•ty (kə myo͞o′ni tē) /kə'myuwnɪtiy/ *n.* [*count*], *pl.* **-ties. 1.** a group of people who live in a specific location, share government, and often have a common cultural and historical heritage: *the Haitian community in the city.* **2.** a locality inhabited by such a group. **3.** a social, political, or other group sharing common characteristics or interests: *the business community.* **4.** [*usually; singular*] the public; society. **5.** a group of interacting plant and animal populations in a given area: *studying the desert community.* **6.** condition of sharing or having things in common.

commu′nity col′lege, *n.* [*count*] a junior college supported in part by local government funds.

commu′nity prop′erty, *n.* [*noncount*] property of a husband and wife, considered in some states to be jointly owned.

com•mu•ta•tion (kom′yə tā′shən) /,kɒmyə'teyʃən/ *n.* **1.** [*count*] the changing of a prison sentence or other penalty to one less severe. **2.** [*noncount*] the act of commuting, as to and from work: *I spend three hours a day in commutation.* See -MUT-.

com•mute (kə myo͞ot′) /kə'myuwt/ *v.,* **-mut•ed, -mut•ing,** *n.* —*v.* **1.** [~ + *obj*] to change (a penalty) to a less severe one: *commuted the death sentence to life imprisonment.* **2.** [~ + *obj*] to change (one kind of payment) into or for another, as by substitution: *The government commuted his pension to a lump sum.* **3.** [*no obj*] to travel regularly over some distance, as from a suburb into a city and back again: *She commutes from upstate to the city every day.* —*n.* [*count*] **4.** a trip made by commuting: *How long is your commute?* See -MUT-.

com•mut•er (kə myo͞o′tər) /kə'myuwtər/ *n.* [*count*] a person who travels regularly back and forth over some distance.

comp[1] (komp) /kɒmp/ *n.* [*noncount*] composition: *taking classes in comp and speech.*

comp[2] (komp) /kɒmp/ *n.* [*noncount*] compensation: *unemployment comp.*

comp., an abbreviation of: **1.** comparative. **2.** compare. **3.** compensation. **4.** complement. **5.** complete. **6.** composition. **7.** compositor. **8.** compound. **9.** comprehensive.

com•pact[1] (*adj.* kəm pakt′, kom′pakt; *v.* kəm pakt′; *n.* kom′pakt) /*adj.* kəm'pækt, 'kɒmpækt; *v.* kəm'pækt; *n.* 'kɒmpækt/ *adj.* **1.** joined or packed together; dense; solid: *compact soil.* **2.** designed to be small in size or economical in operation: *a compact kitchen.* **3.** expressed with few words: *a compact review of the news.* —*v.* [~ + *obj*] **4.** to join or pack closely together; condense: *Try to compact this report.* **5.** to crush or compress into a tight, solid form: *to compact rubbish.* —*n.* [*count*] **6.** a small case containing a mirror and face powder. **7.** an automobile larger than a subcompact but smaller than a midsize car. —**com•pact′ly,** *adv.* —**com•pact′ness,** *n.* [*noncount*] See -PACT-.

com•pact[2] (kom′pakt) /'kɒmpækt/ *n.* [*count*] a formal agreement between two or more parties, states, etc.; contract. See -PACT-.

com′pact disc′, *n.* [*count*] a small optical disc on which music, data, or images are digitally recorded for playback. *Abbr.:* CD

com•pac•tor (kəm pak′tər, kom′pak-) /kəm'pæktər, 'kɒmpæk-/ *n.* [*count*] an appliance that compresses trash into small bundles.

com•pan•ion (kəm pan′yən) /kəm'pænyən/ *n.* [*count*] **1.** a person who frequently accompanies another; comrade. **2.** a person in a long-term, intimate relationship with another; partner. **3.** a person employed to accompany, assist, or live with another: *working as a nurse and companion to an elderly lady.* **4.** a mate or match for something: *I was looking for the companion to the statuette.* —**com•pan′ion•less,** *adj.*

com•pan•ion•a•ble (kəm pan′yən ə bəl) /kəm'pænyənəbəl/ *adj.* friendly; making a good companion.

com•pan•ion•ship (kəm pan′yən ship′) /kəm'pænyən,ʃɪp/ *n.* [*noncount*] friendship; friendly relations or company.

com•pan•ion•way (kəm pan′yən wā′) /kəm'pænyən,wey/ *n.* [*count*] a stair or ladder within the hull of a vessel.

com•pa•ny (kum′pə nē) /'kʌmpəniy/ *n., pl.* **-nies. 1.** [*count*] a number of individuals associated together. **2.** [*noncount*] a guest or guests: *We're having company tonight.* **3.** [*noncount*] companionship; association: *We always enjoy her company.* **4.** [*count*] a number of persons united for joint action, esp. for business: *a publishing company; a dance company.* **5.** [*count*] a unit of troops. —***Idiom.* 6. keep company, a.** [*keep* + ~ + *with* + *obj*] to associate in courtship: *She keeps company with a teacher.* **b.** [*no obj*] (of a couple) to spend time together regularly; go out on dates. **7. keep someone company,** [*keep* + *obj* + ~] to be a companion to someone: *Keep the kids company until I get back.* **8. part company,** [*no obj*] **a.** to separate: *We parted company at the airport.* **b.** to cease association or friendship: *We parted company after many years.* **c.** to take an opposite view; differ: *That's where he and I part company: he wants to tax the poor, and I want to tax the rich.*

compar., an abbreviation of: comparative.

com•pa•ra•ble (kom′pər ə bəl) /'kɒmpərəbəl/ *adj.* **1.** capable of being compared; permitting comparison: *Are the Roman and British empires comparable?* **2.** worthy of comparison: *shops comparable to those on Fifth Avenue.* **3.** usable for comparison; similar: *We have no comparable data on Russian farming.* —**com•pa•ra•bil•i•ty** (kom′pər ə bil′i tē) /,kɒmpərə'bɪlɪtiy/ **com′pa•ra•ble•**

ness, *n.* [*noncount*] —**com′pa•ra•bly,** *adv.: Are those two cars comparably equipped?* See -PAR-.

com•par•a•tive (kəm par′ə tiv) /kəm'pærətɪv/ *adj.* **1.** [*before a noun*] using comparison as a method of study: *comparative anatomy.* **2.** [*before a noun*] measured, judged, or estimated by comparison: *He was a comparative stranger to the town.* **3.** of or naming a form of adjectives and adverbs used to show an increase in quality, quantity, or intensity: *The words* smaller, better, *and* more carefully *are the comparative forms of* small, good, *and* carefully. Compare POSITIVE (def. 22), SUPERLATIVE (def. 2). —*n.* [*count*] **4.** the comparative form of an adjective or adverb: *The comparative of* good *is the word* better. —**com•par′a•tive•ly,** *adv.: This book is comparatively easy to read.*

com•pare (kəm pâr′) /kəm'pɛər/ *v.,* **-pared, -par•ing,** *n.* —*v.* **1.** to examine (two or more things, etc.) to note similarities and differences: [~ + *obj*]: *to compare two restaurants.* [~ + *obj* + *with* + *obj*]: *The pictures were compared with those of known spies.* [~ + *obj* + *to/with* + *obj*]: *Compare the Chicago of today to that of the 1920's.* **2.** [~ + *obj* + *to/with* + *obj*] to consider or describe as similar; liken: *"Shall I compare thee to a summer's day?"* **3.** [~ + *with* + *obj*] to be worthy of comparison: *Whose plays can compare with Shakespeare's?* **4.** [~ + *with* + *obj*] to be in similar standing; be alike: *No one can compare with you; you're the best!* **5.** [~ + *with* + *obj*] to appear in quality, progress, etc., as specified: *Their development compares poorly with that of neighboring nations.* **6.** [~ + *obj*] to give the forms for the comparison of (an adjective or adverb): *Compare the adjectives* good *and* tall *to get the forms* better *and* taller. —*n.* [*noncount*] **7.** comparison: *a beauty beyond compare.* —***Idiom.*** **8. compared with** or **to,** [~ + *with/to* + *obj*] in comparison or contrast with; as opposed to: *Compared with the rest of the world, the standard of living there is very high. Compared to the rest of the class, your grades are high.* **9. compare notes,** to exchange views: *We compared notes on how our jobs were going.* See -PAR-. —**Related Words.** COMPARE is a verb, COMPARISON is a noun, COMPARABLE is an adjective: *Compare the two items to see which is cheaper. She made a comparison of the two items. The two items are of comparable price.*

com•par•i•son (kəm par′ə sən) /kəm'pærəsən/ *n.* **1.** the act of comparing: [*count*]: *A comparison between our two countries shows some important differences.* [*noncount; in/by* + ~]: *In comparison with some other countries, the cost of food in the U.S. is low.* **2.** [*noncount*] a likeness; similarity; capability of being compared: *There is simply no comparison between your work and hers.*

com•part•ment (kəm pärt′mənt) /kəm'pɑrtmənt/ *n.* [*count*] a separate room, section, part, etc. —**com•part•men•tal** (kəm pärt men′tl) /kəmpɑrt'mɛntl̩/ *adj.* See -PAR-.

com•part•men•tal•ize (kəm pärt men′tl īz′) /kəmpɑrt'mɛntl̩ˌayz/ *v.* [~ + *obj*], **-ized, -iz•ing.** to divide into categories or compartments: *Why do they keep trying to compartmentalize us into their narrow little images?* —**com•part•men•tal•i•za•tion** (kəm pärt men′tl i zā′shən) /kəmpɑrtˌmɛntl̩ɪ'zeyʃən/ *n.* [*noncount*]

com•pass (kum′pəs, kom′-) /'kʌmpəs, 'kɒm-/ *n.* [*count*] **1.** an instrument for determining directions. **2.** Often, **compasses.** [*plural*] a V-shaped instrument for drawing circles, measuring distances, etc. **3.** space within limits; area; extent; range; scope; limit: *the broad compass of the novel.* See -PASS-¹.

com•pas•sion (kəm pash′ən) /kəm'pæʃən/ *n.* [*noncount*] a feeling of sympathy for another's misfortune. —**com•pas′sion•ate** (-ə nit) /-ənɪt/ *adj.* —**com•pas′sion•ate•ly,** *adv.*

com•pat•i•ble (kəm pat′ə bəl) /kəm'pætəbəl/ *adj.* **1.** capable of living or existing together in peace and harmony: *The couple were obviously not compatible.* **2.** [*often: be* + ~ + *with* + *obj*] able to exist with something else: *My blood type is not compatible with yours.* **3.** [*often: be* + ~ + *with* + *obj*] consistent: *claims not compatible with the facts.* **4.** [*often: be* + ~ + *with* + *obj*] **a.** (of software) able to run on a specified computer. **b.** (of hardware) able to work with a specified device. —*n.* [*count*] **5.** a computer able to work with most of the software of another system. —**com•pat•i•bil•i•ty** (kəm pat′ə bil′i tē) /kəmˌpætə'bɪlɪtiy/ **com•pat′i•ble•ness,** *n.* [*noncount*] —**com•pat′i•bly,** *adv.* See -PAT-.

com•pa•tri•ot (kəm pā′trē ət) /kəm'peytriyət/ *n.* [*count*] a native or inhabitant of one's own country; fellow citizen. See -PATR-.

com•pel (kəm pel′) /kəm'pɛl/ *v.,* **-pelled, -pel•ling. 1.** [~ + *obj* + *to* + *verb*] to force or drive (someone) to do something; require: *compelled to work hard by the thought of being fired.* **2.** [~ + *obj*] to secure or bring about by force or power: *She managed to compel obedience from her staff.* See -PEL-.

com•pel•ling (kəm pel′ing) /kəm'pɛlɪŋ/ *adj.* **1.** convincing; forceful: *compelling reasons.* **2.** very interesting; demanding one's attention: *The spy thriller was a compelling story.* —**com•pel′ling•ly,** *adv.*

com•pen•di•um (kəm pen′dē əm) /kəm'pɛndiyəm/ *n.* [*count*], *pl.* **-di•ums, -di•a** (-dē ə) /-diyə/. a brief treatment of a subject: *a compendium of useful information.* See -PEND-.

com•pen•sate (kom′pən sāt′) /'kɒmpənˌseyt/ *v.,* **-sat•ed, -sat•ing. 1.** to pay (someone) for something lost, damaged, or missing so as to replace it; give (someone) an equivalent: [~ + *obj* + *for* + *obj*]: *Let me compensate you for your trouble.* [~ + *for* + *obj*]: *Your apologies will not compensate for this damage.* **2.** to make up for; offset; counterbalance: [~ + *obj*]: *He compensated his homeliness with charm.* [~ + *for* + *obj*]: *The good acting in the play compensated for its horrible musical score.* **3.** [~ (+ *for* + *obj*)] to counterbalance a force, as by adjusting a mechanism: *With every step he had to compensate for the weight he was carrying on his right side.* —**com•pen•sa•to•ry** (kəm pen′sə tôr′ē, -tōr′ē) /kəm'pɛnsəˌtɔriy, -ˌtowriy/ **com′pen•sa′tive,** *adj.*

com•pen•sa•tion (kom′pən sā′ shən) /ˌkɒmpən'seyʃən/ *n.* [*noncount*] **1.** money given to make up for a loss, damage, etc.; damages: *workers' compensation.* **2.** salary. **3.** an action, adjustment, or counterbalancing that makes up for something unfortunate.

com•pete (kəm pēt′) /kəm'piyt/ *v.* [*no obj*], **-pet•ed, -pet•ing.** to struggle to outdo another for acknowledgment, a prize, etc.; engage in a contest: *Birds compete for food with squirrels.* See -PET-. —**Related Words.** COMPETE is a verb, COMPETITION is a noun, COMPETITIVE is an adjective: *They like to compete against each other. Competition should help lower prices. Prices were not always competitive.*

com•pe•tence (kom′pi təns) /'kɒmpɪtəns/ *n.* [*noncount*] the quality of being competent; adequacy. See -PET-.

com•pe•tent (kom′pi tənt) /'kɒmpɪtənt/ *adj.* **1.** having suitable or sufficient skill, knowledge, experience, etc., for some purpose; properly qualified: *We hired a competent electrician.* **2.** adequate but not exceptional: *Your work is competent, but here we strive for excellence.* **3.** (esp. of a witness) qualified as to age or soundness of mind. —**com′pe•tent•ly,** *adv.: He handled the chores competently enough.* See -PET-.

com•pe•ti•tion (kom′pi tish′ən) /ˌkɒmpɪ'tɪʃən/ *n.* **1.** [*noncount*] the act of competing; rivalry for a prize, etc. **2.** [*count*] a contest for some prize, honor, or advantage: *an ice-skating competition.* **3.** [*noncount*] the rivalry offered by a competitor: *Small businesses are getting a lot of competition from the chain stores.* **4.** [*noncount*] a competitor or competitors: *Our coaches watched films of the competition.* **5.** [*noncount*] the struggle among living things, for food, space, etc.: *competition in the survival of the fittest.* See -PET-.

com•pet•i•tive (kəm pet′i tiv) /kəm'pɛtɪtɪv/ *adj.* **1.** of or relating to competition: *competitive sports.* **2.** overly interested in competing. **3.** having the ability to compete; able to match or exceed one's competitors: *Our prices are competitive, especially when compared with those of the leading manufacturer.* —**com•pet′i•tive•ly,** *adv.: We played competitively in the games.* —**com•pet′i•tive•ness,** *n.* [*noncount*]

com•pet•i•tor (kəm pet′i tər) /kəm'pɛtɪtər/ *n.* [*count*] a person, team, company, etc., that competes; rival.

com•pi•la•tion (kom′pə lā′shən) /ˌkɒmpə'leyʃən/ *n.* **1.** [*noncount*] the act of compiling or putting something together, such as documents, records, or reports: *careful compilation of the data.* **2.** [*count*] the result of such compiling: *a compilation of recent advances in the field.*

com•pile (kəm pīl′) /kəm'payl/ *v.* [~ + *obj*], **-piled, -pil•ing.** to put together (documents, selections, or other materials) in one book or work from materials taken from various sources: *to compile data.*

com•pla•cen•cy (kəm plā′sən sē) /kəm'pleysənsiy/ also **com•pla′cence,** *n.* [*noncount*] a feeling of security while unaware of unpleasant possibilities; self-satisfaction. See -PLAC-.

com•pla•cent (kəm plā′sənt) /kəm'pleysənt/ *adj.* feeling complacency: *After his raise in salary he became complacent and didn't work very hard.* See -PLAC-.

com•plain (kəm plān′) /kəm'pleyn/ *v.* **1.** to express dissatisfaction, resentment, pain, grief, etc.; find fault: [*no obj*]: *She's always whining and complaining.* [~ + *of/about* + *obj*]: *complained of head pains; complaining about the weather.* [~ + *(that) clause*]: *She complained that no one was treating her fairly.* **2.** [~ + *to* + *obj*] to make a formal protest, accusation, or complaint: *You must complain to the police.* —**com•plain′er,** *n.* [*count*] —**com•plain′ing•ly,** *adv.* —**Related Words.** COMPLAIN is a verb, COMPLAINT is a noun: *They always complain about the homework. They brought their complaints to their teacher.*

com•plain•ant (kəm plā′nənt) /kəm'pleynənt/ *n.* [*count*] a person or group that makes a complaint, as in a legal action.

com•plaint (kəm plānt′) /kəm'pleynt/ *n.* **1.** an expression of discontent, regret, pain, resentment, or grief: [*count*]: *The police did not listen to her complaints.* [*noncount*]: *I've written several letters of complaint.* **2.** a cause of such discontent; reason for complaining: [*count*]: *Her complaint was that no one listened to her.* [*noncount*]: *You don't have good grounds for complaint about noise.* **3.** [*count*] a cause of bodily pain or ailment; malady: *to suffer from a rare complaint.*

com•plai•sance (kəm plā′zəns) /kəm'pleyzəns/ *n.* [*noncount*] willingness, readiness, or inclination to please.

com•plai•sant (kəm plā′sənt, -zənt) /kəm'pleysənt, -zənt/ *adj.* of, relating to, or showing complaisance. —**com•plai′sant•ly,** *adv.*

com•ple•ment (*n.* kom′plə mənt; *v.* kom′plə ment′) /*n.* 'kɒmpləmənt; *v.* 'kɒmplə,mɛnt/ *n.* [*count*] **1.** something that completes or makes perfect. **2.** the quantity or amount that completes anything: *We now have a full complement of instructors.* **3.** (in grammar) a word or group of words that comes after the verb and that describes or is identified with the subject, as *small* in *The house is small,* or that describes or is identified with the object, as *president* in *They elected him president.* —*v.* [~ + *obj*] **4.** to complete, such as by adding good qualities to; form a complement to: *The excellent coffee complemented the brandy and dessert.*

com•ple•men•ta•ry (kom′plə men′tə rē) /,kɒmplə'mɛntəriy/ *adj.* complementing or completing.

com•plete (kəm plēt′) /kəm'pliyt/ *adj., v.,* **-plet•ed, -plet•ing.** —*adj.* **1.** having all parts or elements; lacking nothing: *a complete set of golf clubs.* **2.** finished; ended; concluded: *a complete orbit of the sun.* **3.** [*before a noun*] having all the required or expected qualities, characteristics, or skills: *a complete scholar.* **4.** [*before a noun*] thorough; total; undivided or absolute: *a complete stranger.* **5.** (of a subject or predicate) having all words or phrases that describe or modify included: *The complete subject of* The dappled pony gazed over the fence *is* The dappled pony. —*v.* [~ + *obj*] **6.** to make whole, entire, or perfect: *Hiking boots complete the outdoor look.* **7.** to bring to an end; finish: *She always completes her tasks.* —**com•plete′ness,** *n.* [*noncount*] See -PLET-. —**Syn.** COMPLETE, ENTIRE, INTACT suggest that there is no lack or defect, and that no part has been removed. COMPLETE implies that something has all its parts and is fully developed or perfected; it may also mean that a process or purpose has been carried to fulfillment: *a complete explanation; a complete assignment.* ENTIRE describes something having all its elements in an unbroken single unit: *an entire book.* INTACT implies that something has remained in its original condition, complete and without having been broken: *a package delivered intact.*

com•plete•ly (kəm plēt′lē) /kəm'pliytliy/ *adv.* thoroughly; totally; altogether: *The air force completely destroyed the enemy fighters.*

com•ple•tion (kəm plē′shən) /kəm'pliyʃən/ *n.* [*noncount*] the state of having been finished or completed.

com•plex (*adj.* kəm pleks′, kom′pleks; *n.* kom′pleks) /*adj.* kəm'plɛks, 'kɒmplɛks; *n.* 'kɒmplɛks/ *adj.* **1.** composed of many related parts: *a complex system.* **2.** having a complicated arrangement of parts or pieces, often so as to be hard to deal with or understand: *complex machinery.* —*n.* [*count*] **3.** a complicated group, system, or assembly of related things that form a whole: *an apartment complex; a business complex.* **4.** a group of related ideas, desires, and impulses that influence one's attitudes and behavior: *He had a complex about dark rooms. She had an inferiority complex.* —**com•plex′ly,** *adv.* —**com•plex′ness,** *n.* [*noncount*] See -PLEX-.

com•plex•ion (kəm plek′shən) /kəm'plɛkʃən/ *n.* [*count*] **1.** the natural color, texture, and appearance of the skin, esp. of the face. **2.** appearance; general or overall character: *This testimony puts a different complexion on things.* **3.** viewpoint, attitude, or belief: *one's political complexion.* —**com•plex′ion•al,** *adj.*

com•plex•ioned (kəm plek′shənd) /kəm'plɛkʃənd/ *adj.* (used after another adjective) having a certain complexion: *a light-complexioned person* (= *a person having a light complexion).*

com•plex•i•ty (kəm plek′si tē) /kəm'plɛksɪtiy/ *n., pl.* **-ties. 1.** [*noncount*] the state or condition of being complex: *the complexity of the human mind.* **2.** [*count*] something that is complex: *The complexities of modern life were too much for him.* See -PLEX-.

com′plex sen′tence, *n.* [*count*] a sentence containing one or more dependent clauses in addition to the main clause, such as the sentence *When the bell rings, we will all walk out,* which is made up of *When the bell rings* (a dependent clause), and *we will all walk out* (the main clause).

com•pli•ance (kəm plī′əns) /kəm'playəns/ *n.* [*noncount*] **1.** the act of complying. **2.** a tendency to comply. **3.** conformity; accordance: *He acted in strict compliance with orders.*

com•pli•ant (kəm plī′ənt) /kəm 'playənt/ *adj.* tending to comply.

com•pli•cate (kom′pli kāt′) /'kɒmplɪ,keyt/ *v.* [~ + *obj*], **-cat•ed, -cat•ing.** to make (something) complex, intricate, or difficult: *He didn't want to complicate his life with marriage.* See -PLIC-.

com•pli•cat•ed (kom′pli kā′tid) /'kɒmplɪ,keytɪd/ *adj.* **1.** made up of connected parts; complex; intricate: *a complicated apparatus that never worked correctly.* **2.** difficult to analyze, understand, or explain: *a complicated problem.* —**com′pli•cat′ed•ly,** *adv.* —**com′pli•cat′ed•ness,** *n.* [*noncount*]

com•pli•ca•tion (kom′pli kā′shən) /,kɒmplɪ'keyʃən/ *n.* [*count*] a problem or difficulty added to an already existing situation.

com•plic•i•ty (kəm plis′i tē) /kəm'plɪsɪtiy/ *n.* [*noncount*] the state of being an accomplice; partnership in wrongdoing. —**com•plic′i•tous, com•plic′it,** *adj.* See -PLIC-.

com•pli•ment (*n.* kom′plə mənt; *v.* kom′plə ment′) /*n.* 'kɒmpləmənt; *v.* 'kɒmplə,mɛnt/ *n.* [*count*] **1.** an expression of praise or admiration: *He paid her a nice compliment on her dress.* **2.** a formal act or gesture of respect or of high regard: *The mayor paid her the compliment of a police escort.* —*v.* [~ + *obj* (+ *on* + *obj*)] **3.** to pay a compliment to; praise: *He complimented the hostess on the dinner.* —**com′pli•ment′er,** *n.* [*count*]

com•pli•men•ta•ry (kom′plə men′tə rē, -trē) /,kɒmplə'mɛntəriy, -triy/ *adj* **1.** expressing a compliment: *a complimentary remark.* **2.** [*usually: before a noun*] given free as a gift or courtesy: *complimentary tickets to the game.* —**com′pli•men′ta•ri•ly,** *adv.* —**com′pli•men′ta•ri•ness,** *n.* [*noncount*]

com•ply (kəm plī′) /kəm'play/ *v.* [*no obj;* (~ + *with* + *obj*)], **-plied, -ply•ing.** to act or be in accordance with wishes, requirements, or conditions; obey: *We cannot comply with your demands for the files.* See -PLIC-.

com•po•nent (kəm pō′nənt) /kəm'pownənt/ *n.* [*count*] **1.** a basic or fundamental part from which something is made. **2.** a part of a mechanical or electrical system: *hi-fi components.* —*adj.* [*before a noun*] **3.** being or serving as an element in something larger; constituent: *component parts.* —**com•po•nen•tial** (kom′pə nen′shəl) /,kɒmpə'nɛnʃəl/ *adj.* See -PON-. —**Syn.** See ELEMENT.

com•port (kəm pôrt′, -pōrt′) /kəm'pɔrt, -'powrt/ *v.* **1.** [~ + *oneself*] to carry or conduct (oneself); behave: *to comport oneself with dignity.* **2.** [~ + *with* + *obj*] to be in agreement or harmony: *Your statement does not comport with the facts.* See -PORT-.

com•pose (kəm pōz′) /kəm'powz/ *v.* [~ + *obj*], **-posed, -pos•ing. 1.** to be or make up the parts of; form the basis of: [*be* + ~*-ed* + *of* + *obj*]: *His spaghetti sauce was composed of many ingredients.* **2.** to create (a musical, literary, or dance work): *He composed symphonies. Compose an essay of 500 words.* **3.** to arrange the elements of: *The sculptor composed his pieces with precision and beauty.* **4.** to bring to a condition of calmness; settle down: *He took a moment to compose himself, then walked out of the courtroom.* See -POS-.

com•posed (kəm pōzd′) /kəm'powzd/ *adj.* calm; tranquil; serene; self-controlled: *The defendant remained composed during the trial.* —**Syn.** See CALM.

com•pos•er (kəm pō′zər) /kəm'powzər/ *n.* [*count*] a person who composes music. See -POS-.

com•pos•ite (kəm poz′it) /kəm'pɒzɪt/ *adj.* **1.** made up of different elements; blended; compound: *The artist* *made a composite drawing of the two faces.* **—n.** [*count*] **2.** something made up of different or separate parts; a blend: *My job is a composite of teacher, boss, and administrator.* —**com•pos′ite•ly,** *adv.* See -POS-.

com•po•si•tion (kom′pə zish′ən) /ˌkɒmpə'zɪʃən/ *n.* **1.** [*noncount*] the elements of which something is composed; makeup. **2.** [*count*] a material formed from two or more substances: *various compositions of different toxic chemicals.* **3.** [*noncount*] the act or process of producing a piece of writing: *the art of composition.* **4.** [*count*] something composed, such as a short essay or a piece of music: *Write a composition on how you spent your summer vacation.* **5.** [*noncount*] the organization of the different parts of a work of art so as to achieve a whole: *The painting's composition is excellent but the color scheme is odd.* See -POS-.

com•pos•i•tor (kəm poz′i tər) /kəm'pɒzɪtər/ *n.* [*count*] a person who sets the type or text for printing. See -POS-.

com•post (kom′pōst) /'kɒmpowst/ *n.* [*noncount*] **1.** a mixture of decaying plant or animal matter used for fertilizing soil. **—v.** [~ + *obj*] **2.** to use in compost; make compost of: *They composted the dead branches and leaves to enrich the soil.* —**com′post•er,** *n.* [*count*] See -POS-.

com•po•sure (kəm pō′zhər) /kəm'powʒər/ *n.* [*noncount*] self-controlled manner or state of mind; calmness. See -POS-.

com•pote (kom′pōt) /'kɒmpowt/ *n.* **1.** [*noncount*] fruit stewed in a syrup. **2.** [*count*] a stemmed dish for serving fruit, nuts, candy, etc.

com•pound[1] (*adj., v.* kom′pound, kəm pound′; *n.* kom′pound) /*adj., v.* ˈkɒmpawnd, kəmˈpawnd; *n.* ˈkɒmpawnd/ *adj.* [*before a noun*] **1.** composed of two or more ingredients: *Bronze is a compound metal made of copper and tin.* **2.** having or involving two or more actions or functions: *The mouth is a compound organ.* **3.** (of a word) **a.** made up of two or more parts that are also words, as *housetop, many-sided, playact,* or *upon.* **b.** made up of two or more parts that are also bases, as *biochemistry* or *ethnography.* **4.** (of a verb tense) made up of an auxiliary verb and a main verb, as *are swimming, have spoken,* or *will write* (opposed to *simple*). **—n.** [*count*] **5.** something formed by compounding or combining parts, elements, etc.: *Water is a compound of hydrogen and oxygen.* **6.** a compound word, esp. one composed of two or more words, as *moonflower* or *rainstorm.* **—v.** [~ + *obj*] **7.** to put together into a whole; combine: *to compound drugs to form a new medicine.* **8.** to make or form by combining parts; construct: *The medicine was compounded from various drugs.* **9.** to increase or add to, esp. so as to worsen: *When he started arguing with the police officer it only compounded his problems.* **10.** to pay (interest) on the interest already earned as well as on the principal: *The bank compounds interest on a savings account.* —**com•pound′a•ble,** *adj.* —**com•pound′er,** *n.* [*count*] See -POUND-.

com•pound[2] (kom′pound) /'kɒmpawnd/ *n.* [*count*] a separate area, usually fenced or walled, containing barracks or other structures.

com′pound frac′ture, *n.* [*count*] a fracture in which the broken bone comes out through the skin.

com′pound in′terest, *n.* [*noncount*] interest paid on both the principal and on previously obtained interest.

com′pound sen′tence, *n.* [*count*] a sentence containing two or more coordinate clauses, usually joined by one or more coordinate conjunctions, such as the sentence *The lightning flashed and the rain fell,* which consists of *The lightning flashed* (an independent clause), *and* (a coordinate conjunction), and *the rain fell* (a second independent clause).

com•pre•hend (kom′pri hend′) /ˌkɒmprɪ'hɛnd/ *v.* [~ + *obj*] to understand the nature or meaning of; grasp with the mind; perceive: *I could hear what he was saying but I couldn't comprehend it.* —**com′pre•hend′i•ble,** *adj.* —**com′pre•hend′ing•ly,** *adv.* See -PREHEND-.

com•pre•hen•si•ble (kom′pri hen′sə bəl) /ˌkɒmprɪ'hɛnsəbəl/ *adj.* capable of being comprehended: *Scientists should make their findings comprehensible to the public.* —**com•pre•hen•si•bil•i•ty** (kom′pri hen′sə bil′i tē) /ˌkɒmprɪˌhɛnsə'bɪlɪtiy/ **com′pre•hen′si•ble•ness,** *n.* [*noncount*]: *They should try for better comprehensibility in their writing.* —**com′pre•hen′si•bly,** *adv.*

com•pre•hen•sion (kom′pri hen′shən) /ˌkɒmprɪ'hɛnʃən/ *n.* [*noncount*] **1.** the act or process of comprehending. **2.** capacity of the mind to perceive and understand; power to grasp ideas. See -PREHEND-.

com•pre•hen•sive (kom′pri hen′siv) /ˌkɒmprɪ'hɛnsɪv/ *adj.* wide in scope or in content: *a comprehensive knowledge of physics.* See -PREHEND-.

com•press (*v.* kəm pres′; *n.* kom′pres) /*v.* kəmˈprɛs; *n.* ˈkɒmprɛs/ *v.* [~ + *obj*] **1.** to press or squeeze together; force into less space: *The fuel mixture is compressed in the chamber by the piston.* **2.** to condense, shorten, or abbreviate: *She compressed a one-hour lecture into a twenty-minute talk.* **—n.** [*count*] **3.** a soft pad held on the body to provide pressure or to supply moisture, cold, heat, or medication. —**com•press•i•bil•i•ty** (kəm pres′ə bil′i tē) /kəmˌprɛsə'bɪlɪtiy/ *n.* [*noncount*] —**com•press′i•ble,** *adj.* See -PRESS-.

com•pres•sion (kəm presh′ən) /kəm'prɛʃən/ *n.* [*noncount*] the act of compressing or the state of being compressed. See -PRESS-.

com•pres•sor (kəm pres′ər) /kəm'prɛsər/ *n.* [*count*] a person or thing that compresses, esp. a pump for increasing pressure of gases.

com•prise (kəm prīz′) /kəm'prayz/ *v.* [~ + *obj; not: be* + ~*-ing*], **-prised, -pris•ing. 1.** to include or contain: *The Soviet Union comprised several republics.* **2.** to consist of; be composed of: *The advisory board comprises six members.* **3.** to form or constitute: *Seminars and lectures comprised the day's activities.* —***Idiom.*** **4. be comprised of,** [*be* + ~*-ed* + *of* + *obj*] to consist of; be composed of: *The United States is comprised of fifty states.* —**com•pris′al,** *n.* [*noncount*] See -PRIS-.

com•pro•mise (kom′prə mīz′) /'kɒmprəˌmayz/ *n., v.,* **-mised, -mis•ing.** **—n. 1.** [*noncount*] the settlement of differences between two parties in which both sides give up something. **2.** [*count*] the result of such a settlement. **3.** [*count*] something intermediate or midway between two different things. **—v. 4.** [*no obj*] to make a compromise or compromises: *Both sides managed to compromise in order to settle the strike.* **5.** [~ + *obj*] to expose to danger, suspicion, scandal, etc.; jeopardize: *Faulty building construction compromises our safety.* **6.** to adjust or surrender (one's principles) dishonorably: [*no obj;* (~ + *with* + *obj*)]: *How could he compromise with his principles like that?* [~ + *obj*]: *compromised his beliefs when he failed to support her.* —**com′pro•mis′er,** *n.* [*count*] —**com′pro•mis′ing,** *adj.: a compromising situation.* —**com′pro•mis′ing•ly,** *adv.* See -MIS-.

comp•trol•ler (kən trō′lər) /kən'trowlər/ *n.* CONTROLLER (def. 1). —**comp•trol′ler•ship′,** *n.* [*noncount*]

com•pul•sion (kəm pul′shən) /kəm'pʌlʃən/ *n.* **1.** [*noncount*] the act of compelling or the state of being compelled. **2.** [*count*] a strong, irresistible impulse to perform an act, esp. one that is irrational or contrary to one's will. See -PULS-.

com•pul•sive (kəm pul′siv) /kəm'pʌlsɪv/ *adj.* **1.** resulting from or caused by a compulsion: *compulsive overeating.* **2.** not able to be resisted; having the power to compel: *Cartoons are almost compulsive TV shows to young children.* —**com•pul′sive•ly,** *adv.: gambled compulsively.*

com•pul•so•ry (kəm pul′sə rē) /kəm'pʌlsəriy/ *adj., n., pl.* **-ries. —adj. 1.** put into force by law or rules; obligatory: *compulsory routines in the ice-skating competition.* **2.** using compulsion; compelling; forceful: *compulsory measures to control rioting.* **—n.** [*count*] **3.** something that must be done as part of a contest: *In the compulsories she scored the highest of all the ice skaters.* —**com•pul′so•ri•ly,** *adv.* —**com•pul′so•ri•ness,** *n.* [*noncount*] See -PULS-.

com•punc•tion (kəm pungk′shən) /kəm'pʌŋkʃən/ *n.* [*usually with negative words*] a feeling of uneasiness for doing wrong; remorse: [*noncount*]: *The victim felt no compunction in shooting the teens who had attacked him.* [*count*]: *The student had no compunctions about cheating.* See -PUNCT-.

com•pu•ta•tion (kom′pyŏŏ tā′shən) /ˌkɒmpyʊ'teyʃən/ *n.* **1.** [*noncount*] the act of computing or calculating: *How fast does the computer do computation?* **2.** [*count*] the result of computing: *My computations show that we made a profit.* —**com′pu•ta′tion•al,** *adj.* See -PUTE-.

com•pute (kəm pyōōt′) /kəm'pyuwt/ *v.,* **-put•ed, -put•ing. 1.** [~ + *obj*] to determine by calculation or by using a computer; calculate: *Compute the distance from the earth to the moon.* **2.** [*no obj*] to use a computer: *He had been computing since 1978.* —**com•put•a•bil•i•ty** (kəm pyōō′tə bil′i tē) /kəmˌpyuwtə'bɪlɪtiy/ *n.* [*noncount*] —**com•put′a•ble,** *adj.* —**com•put′ing,** *n.* [*noncount*] —**com•put•ist** (kəm pyōō′tist, kom′pyŏŏ-) /kəm'pyuwtɪst, 'kɒmpyʊ-/ *n.* [*count*] See -PUTE-. —**Related Words.** COMPUTE is a verb, COMPUTER is a noun, COMPUTATIONAL is an adjective: *Compute your average from the* *grades you have. The computer works too slowly. There were some difficult computational steps to follow in the experiment.*

com•put•er (kəm pyo͞o′tər) /kəm'pyuwtər/ *n.* an electronic device designed for performing operations on data at high speed: [*count*]: *Computers keep coming down in price.* [*noncount; by +* ~]: *I did the entire project by computer.* See illustration at OFFICE. See -PUTE-.

com•put•er•ize (kəm pyo͞o′tə riz′) /kəm'pyuwtə,rayz/ *v.*, **-ized, -iz•ing. 1.** [~ + *obj*] to control, process, or store (data) by a computer: *They computerized their Christmas mailing list.* **2.** to equip (a business, etc.) with computers: [~ + *obj*]: *to computerize a business.* [*no obj*]: *I wonder when our company will computerize?* —**com•put•er•iz•a•ble** (kəm pyo͞o′tə ri′zə bəl) /kəm,pyuwtə'rayzəbəl/ *adj.* —**com•put•er•i•za•tion** (kəm-pyo͞o′tər ə zā′shən) /kəm,pyuwtərə'zeyʃən/ *n.* [*noncount*] —**com•put′er•ized,** *adj.*: *Our writing center is fully computerized now.*

comput′erized ax′ial to•mog′ra•phy (tə mog′rə-fē) /tə'mɒgrəfiy/ *n.* [*noncount*] the process of producing a CAT scan. Compare CAT SCANNER.

comput′er vi′rus, *n.* VIRUS (def. 4).

Comr., an abbreviation of: Commissioner.

com•rade (kom′rad, -rəd) /'kɒmræd, -rəd/ *n.* **1.** [*count*] a person who shares in one's activities, etc.; companion; friend. **2.** a fellow member of a group, political party, etc., esp. of a Communist party: [*count*]: *meeting with their comrades and plotting revolution.* [*before a name*]: *Comrade Dolgikh will speak first.* —**com′rade•ly,** *adv.* —**com′rade•ship′,** *n.* [*noncount*]

con[1] (kon) /kɒn/ *adj.* **1.** against (a proposition, etc.): *pro and con arguments.* —*adv.* **2.** against: *They argued pro and con all night.* —*n.* [*count*] **3.** the argument, position, or person arguing against something: *The cons have it, 20 to 15.* Compare PRO[1].

con[2] (kon) /kɒn/ *adj., v.,* **conned, con•ning,** *n.* —*adj.* **1.** involving dishonesty and trickery; deceitful: *swindled by a con artist.* —*v.* **2.** to swindle; trick: [~ + *obj* + *out of* + *obj*]: *The crooks conned her out of her life savings.* [~ + *obj*]: *She was conned quite smoothly.* **3.** to persuade by deception, threats, exaggeration, etc.: [~ + *obj*]: *He conned her with a scary story about witches.* [~ + *obj* + *into* + *obj*]: *conned me into going out with her.* —*n.* [*count*] **4.** a swindle: *one of the oldest cons in the book.* **5.** a lie, exaggeration, or self-serving talk.

con[3] (kon) /kɒn/ *n.* [*count*] *Informal.* a convict.

con-, *prefix.* *con-* is a variant spelling of COM-. It comes from Latin, where it has the meaning "together, with." This meaning is found in such words as: CONDONE, CONNECTION, CONVENE.

conc., an abbreviation of: **1.** concentrate. **2.** concentrated. **3.** concentration. **4.** concerning. **5.** concrete.

con•cat•e•nate (kon kat′n āt′, kən-) /kɒn'kætn̩,eyt, kən-/ *v.,* **-nat•ed, -nat•ing,** *adj.* —*v.* [~ + *obj*] **1.** to link together as in a series or chain: *Individual sounds are concatenated quickly in normal speech.* —*adj.* **2.** linked together. —**con•cat•e•na•tion** (kon kat′n ā′shən, kən-) /kɒn,kætn̩'eyʃən, kən-/ *n.* [*count*]

con•cave (kon kāv′, kon′kāv) /kɒn'keyv, 'kɒnkeyv/ *adj.* curved inward like the inside of a sphere: *a concave lens.* Compare CONVEX. —**con•cave′ly,** *adv.* —**con•cave′-ness,** *n.* —**con•cav•i•ty** (kon kav′i tē) /kɒn'kævɪtiy/ *n.* [*noncount; count*], *pl.* **-ties.**

con•ceal (kən sēl′) /kən'siyl/ *v.* [~ + *obj*] **1.** to hide; cover or keep from sight: *A high wall concealed the house.* **2.** to keep secret; avoid disclosing: *to conceal one's true motives.* —**con•ceal′a•ble,** *adj.* —**con•ceal′er,** *n.* [*count*] —**con•ceal′ment,** *n.* [*noncount*]

con•cede (kən sēd′) /kən'siyd/ *v.,* **-ced•ed, -ced•ing. 1.** [~ + *(that) clause*] to acknowledge as true, just, or proper; admit: *He finally conceded (that) she was right.* **2.** to acknowledge (an opponent's score, etc.) before it is officially established: [~ + *obj*]: *to concede an election.* [*no obj*]: *When does the candidate intend to concede?* **3.** to give or grant as a right or privilege; yield: [~ + *obj* + *obj*]: *conceded the rebels the disputed territory.* [~ + *obj* + *to* + *obj*]: *conceded the territory to the rebels.* —**con•ced′er,** *n.* [*count*] See -CEDE-.

con•ceit (kən sēt′) /kən'siyt/ *n.* [*noncount*] an overly favorable opinion of one's own ability, importance, etc.; vanity: *conceit about her good looks.*

con•ceit•ed (kən sē′tid) /kən'siytɪd/ *adj.* of, relating to, or showing conceit.

con•ceive (kən sēv′) /kən'siyv/ *v.,* **-ceived, -ceiv•ing. 1.** [~ + *obj*] to form (a notion, etc.) in the mind; devise: *He conceived the project while on vacation.* **2.** [~ + *of* + *obj*] to form an idea; think; envision; imagine: *couldn't conceive of living without a television.* **3.** [~ + *that clause*] to hold as an opinion; think; believe: *I can't conceive that it would be of any use.* **4.** [~ *(+ of)* + *obj* + *as* + *obj*] to form a notion of (something) as (something else); consider; see: *We can conceive (of) the third dimension as a right angle to a flat two-dimensional surface.* **5.** to become pregnant (with): [*no obj*]: *After three years of treatment with fertility drugs she finally conceived.* [~ + *obj*]: *The child was conceived during their stay in Africa.* —**con•ceiv′er,** *n.* [*count*] See -CEIVE-.

con•cen•trate (kon′sən trāt′) /'kɒnsən,treyt/ *v.,* **-trat•ed, -trat•ing,** *n.* —*v.* **1.** to direct (one's attention or efforts) to a point of focus: [*no obj; sometimes:* ~ + *on* + *obj*]: *I couldn't concentrate because the girls were fighting again. I couldn't concentrate on my work.* [~ + *obj (+ on + obj)*]: *He concentrated his attention (on the problem of domestic violence).* **2.** [*no obj*] to come to or toward a point, place, group, etc.: *The population tended to concentrate in the cities.* **3.** [~ + *obj*] to put or bring into a common center or single point, place, group, etc.: *population concentrated in the industrial cities.* **4.** to (cause to) become more intense, as by removing or reducing the amount of liquid: [*no obj*]: *The gravy thickened and concentrated in the microwave.* [~ + *obj*]: *Concentrate the gravy by boiling it.* —*n.* [*count*] **5.** a concentrated form of something; product of concentration: *Mix water with the juice concentrate.*

con•cen•tra•ted (kon′sən trā′təd) /'kɒnsən,treytəd/ *adj.* **1.** made thicker or more intense, as by reducing the amount of liquid: *Mix three cans of water with the concentrated orange juice.* **2.** focused; intense: *a concentrated barrage on the command headquarters.*

con•cen•tra•tion (kon′sən trā′shən) /,kɒnsən'treyʃən/ *n.* **1.** [*noncount*] the directing of one's efforts to one point: *will need all her concentration to perform a triple toe jump.* **2.** the bringing to a single point: [*noncount*]: *The party worked for the concentration of power in the hands of the few.* [*count*]: *large concentrations of immigrants.*

concentra′tion camp′, *n.* [*count*] a guarded compound for the confinement of political prisoners, minorities, etc.

con•cen•tric (kən sen′trik) /kən'sɛntrɪk/ *adj.* (esp. of circles or spheres) having a common center. —**con•cen′tri•cal•ly,** *adv.* —**con•cen•tric•i•ty** (kon′sən tris′i-tē) /,kɒnsən'trɪsɪtiy/ *n.* [*noncount*]

con•cept (kon′sept) /'kɒnsɛpt/ *n.* [*count*] a general notion or idea; conception: *no concept of right or wrong.* See -CEP-.

con•cep•tion (kən sep′shən) /kən'sɛpʃən/ *n.* **1.** [*noncount*] fertilization; the process in which there is union of sperm and egg. **2.** [*count*] a notion; general idea; concept: *had no conception of the forces that would be used against him.* **3.** [*noncount*] the act or power of forming notions, ideas, or concepts in the mind: *The conception of the plan was fine; it was the implementation that never worked.* —**con•cep′tion•al,** *adj.* —**con•cep•tive** (kən-sep′tiv) /kən'sɛptɪv/ *adj.* See -CEP-.

con•cep•tu•al (kən sep′cho͞o əl) /kən'sɛptʃuwəl/ *adj.* [*usually: before a noun*] of or relating to concepts formed in the mind: *the conceptual skills of children.* —**con•cep′tu•al•ly,** *adv.*

con•cep•tu•al•ize (kən sep′cho͞o ə līz′) /kən'sɛpt-ʃuwə,layz/ *v.* [~ + *obj*], **-ized, -iz•ing.** to form into a concept; make a concept of: *He tried to conceptualize the book as a movie.* —**con•cep•tu•al•i•za•tion** (kən-sep′cho͞o ə lə zā′shən) /kən,sɛptʃuwələ'zeyʃən/ *n.* [*noncount*]

con•cern (kən sûrn′) /kən'sɜrn/ *v.* [~ + *obj*] **1.** [*not: be* + ~*-ing*] to be of interest or importance to; affect; involve: *Drug abuse concerns us all.* **2.** [*not: be* + ~*-ing*] to relate to; be connected with; be about: *This next episode concerns our hero trying to rescue the heroine.* **3.** [~ + *oneself* + *with* + *obj*] to interest or engage: *He concerned himself with every aspect of the business.* **4.** [~ + *obj*] to trouble, worry, or make unhappy; disturb: *Your headaches concern me.* —*n.* **5.** [*noncount*] something that relates to a person; one's business or affair; something important to a person: *That problem is of no concern to us.* **6.** [*noncount*] worry, solicitude, or anxiety: *to show concern for the homeless.* **7.** [*count*] a commercial or manufacturing company; firm: *business concerns in that region.* See -CERN-. —**Related Words.** CONCERN is a noun and a verb, CONCERNED is an adjective, CONCERNING is a preposition: *His low grades concern me. One of my concerns is his low grades. We are concerned par-*

ents. Concerning the payments, how should we arrange them?

con•cerned (kən sûrnd′) /kən'sɜrnd/ *adj.* **1.** interested or affected: *concerned citizens.* **2.** troubled or anxious: *a concerned look on her face.* **3.** [*often: after a noun; sometimes: be* + ~] having a connection or involvement; participating: *All persons concerned will meet in the dean's office.* —**con•cern•ed•ly** (kən sûr′nid lē) /kən'sɜrnɪdliy/ *adv.* —**con•cern′ed•ness,** *n.* [*noncount*]

con•cern•ing (kən sûr′ning) /kən'sɜrnɪŋ/ *prep.* relating to; regarding; about: *a dispute concerning health benefits.*

con•cert (kon′sûrt) /'kɒnsɜrt/ *n.* [*count*] **1.** a public performance of music or dancing. —***Idiom.*** **2. in concert,** [*noncount*] together; jointly: *to act in concert.* See -CERT-.

con•cert•ed (kən sûr′tid) /kən'sɜrtɪd/ *adj.* [*before a noun*] **1.** determined; serious; sincere: *made a concerted effort to get there on time.* **2.** performed, devised, or designed in cooperation: *a concerted attack on the bridges.* —**con•cert′ed•ly,** *adv.* —**con•cert′ed•ness,** *n.* [*noncount*]

con•cer•ti•na (kon′sər tē′nə) /ˌkɒnsər'tiynə/ *n., pl.* **-nas,** *v.,* **-naed** (-nəd) /-nəd/ **-na•ing** (-nə ing) /-nəɪŋ/. —*n.* [*count*] **1.** a musical instrument resembling an accordion. —*v.* [*no obj*] **2.** to fold or collapse in the manner of a concertina: *The front and back of the car concertinaed in the crash.* —**con′cer•ti′nist,** *n.* [*count*]

con•cert•mas•ter (kon′sərt mas′tər) /'kɒnsərtˌmæstər/ *n.* [*count*] the principal first violinist in a symphony orchestra.

con•cer•to (kən cher′tō) /kən'tʃɛrtow/ *n.* [*count*], *pl.* **-tos, -ti** (-tē) /-tiy/. a musical composition for one or more instruments and orchestra.

con•ces•sion (kən sesh′ən) /kən'sɛʃən/ *n.* [*count*] **1. a.** the act of conceding something, such as a point in an argument. **b.** the point conceded: *They made a few concessions to the protesters.* **2.** something given by a controlling authority, such as a grant of land or a privilege: *overseas trade concessions.* **3.** a space given for a business or service to use: *the refreshment concession at a theater.* —**con•ces′sion•al,** *adj.*

con•ces•sion•aire (kən sesh′ə nâr′) /kənˌsɛʃə'nɛər/ also **con•ces•sion•er** (kən sesh′ə nər) /kən'sɛʃənər/ *n.* [*count*] the owner, operator, or holder of a concession.

conch (kongk, konch) /kɒŋk, kɒntʃ/ *n.* [*count*], *pl.* **conchs** (kongks) /kɒŋks/ **con•ches** (kon′chiz) /'kɒntʃɪz/. **1.** a marine shellfish having a thick pointed spiral shell with a wide outer lip. **2.** the shell of a conch.

con•cierge (kon′sē ârzh′) /ˌkɒnsiy'ɛərʒ/ *n.* [*count*], *pl.* **-cierges** (-sē âr′zhiz, -sē ârzh′) /-siy'ɛərʒɪz, -siy'ɛərʒ/. **1.** (esp. in France) a person who has charge of the entrance of a building. **2.** a member of a hotel staff in charge of special services for guests.

con•cil•i•ate (kən sil′ē āt′) /kən'sɪliyˌeyt/ *v.* [~ + *obj*], **-at•ed, -at•ing.** to overcome the distrust or hostility of; placate; win the goodwill of: *tried to conciliate the angry union members.* —**con•cil′i•at′ing,** *adj.* —**con•cil′i•at′ing•ly,** *adv.* —**con•cil•i•a•tion** (kən sil′ē ā′shən) /kənˌsɪliy'eyʃən/ *n.* [*noncount*] —**con•cil′i•a′tor,** *n.* [*count*]

con•cil•i•a•to•ry (kən sil′ē ə tôr′ē, -tōr′ē) /kən'sɪliyəˌtɔriy, -ˌtowriy/ *adj.* of, relating to, or showing conciliation; peacemaking: *conciliatory union negotiators.*

con•cise (kən sīs′) /kən'says/ *adj.* expressing much in few words; succinct. —**con•cise′ly,** *adv.: wrote clearly and concisely about the problem.* —**con•cise′ness,** *n.* [*noncount*] See -CISE-. —**Syn.** CONCISE, SUCCINCT, TERSE refer to speech or writing that uses few words to say much. CONCISE implies that unnecessary details have been cut out: *a concise summary of the ambassador's speech.* SUCCINCT suggests clear expression as well as shortness: *was praised for her succinct statement of the problem.* TERSE suggests brevity combined with wit or polish, but it may also suggest impoliteness or brusqueness: *a terse prose style; offended by his terse reply.*

con•clave (kon′klāv, kong′-) /'kɒnkleyv, 'kɒŋ-/ *n.* [*count*] **1.** a private or secret meeting, esp. one that has special authority or influence. **2.** the assembly or meeting of the cardinals for the election of a pope.

con•clude (kən klōōd′) /kən'kluwd/ *v.,* **-clud•ed, -clud•ing. 1.** to (cause to) come to an end; finish: [~ + *obj*]: *concluded the service with a prayer.* [*no obj*]: *The party concluded at ten o'clock.* **2.** to say in conclusion: [*used with quotations*]: *"And so, my fellow Americans..." he concluded.* [*no obj*]: *concluded with a joke.* **3.** [~ + *obj*] to bring to a decision; settle: *to conclude a treaty.* **4.** to determine by reasoning; infer: [~ + *that clause*]: *By your smile I conclude that the news is good.* [~ + *obj* + *from* + *obj*]: *What can you conclude from your data?*

con•clu•sion (kən klōō′zhən) /kən'kluwʒən/ *n.* [*count*] **1.** the end or close; final part: *The conclusion of his essay contained a summary of the main points.* **2.** a belief or opinion resulting from deduction or inference: *The conclusion follows simply enough from the arguments.* **3.** a final decision or judgment: *It is the conclusion of this committee that the employee did in fact steal money.* **4.** a settlement or arrangement: *worked hard for the conclusion of a new contract.* —***Idiom.*** **5. in conclusion,** [*noncount*] lastly; to conclude: *The essay's last paragraph began "In conclusion..."* **6. jump to conclusions,** to arrive at or form a judgment too quickly.

con•clu•sive (kən klōō′siv) /kən'kluwsɪv/ *adj.* serving to settle a question; decisive: *The conclusive evidence was his fingerprint on the gun.* —**con•clu′sive•ly,** *adv.: The prosecutor proved her point conclusively.* —**con•clu′sive•ness,** *n.* [*noncount*]

con•coct (kən kokt′) /kən'kɒkt/ *v.* [~ + *obj*] **1.** to prepare by combining ingredients: *to concoct a meal from leftovers.* **2.** to make up; invent: *to concoct an excuse.* —**con•coct′er, con•coc′tor,** *n.* [*count*] —**con•coc•tion** (kən kok′shən) /kən'kɒkʃən/ *n.* [*count*]: *made up some weird concoction for me to drink.*

con•com•i•tant (kon kom′i tənt, kən-) /kɒn'kɒmɪtənt, kən-/ *adj.* existing or occurring together with something else; additional: *an event and its concomitant circumstances.* —**con•com′i•tant•ly,** *adv.*

con•cord (kon′kôrd, kong′-) /'kɒnkɔrd, 'kɒŋ-/ *n.* [*noncount*] **1.** [*often: in* + ~] agreement or harmony between persons, groups, etc.: *Canada and the United States have lived in concord for many years.* **2.** AGREEMENT (def. 4): *concord between subject and verb.* See -CORD-.

con•cord•ance (kən kôr′dns) /kən'kɔrdns/ *n.* **1.** [*noncount; often: in* + ~] agreement; concord; harmony: *a strike not in concordance with the desires of the membership.* **2.** [*count*] an alphabetical index of the principal words of a book, with a reference to the passage in which each occurs. See -CORD-.

con•course (kon′kôrs, -kōrs, kong′-) /'kɒnkɔrs, -kowrs, 'kɒŋ-/ *n.* [*count*] **1.** an assemblage; gathering: *a concourse of people.* **2.** a boulevard or other broad thoroughfare. **3.** a large open space for accommodating crowds, as at an airport: *Go to the lower concourse for Gate 65.* See -COUR-.

con•crete (kon′krēt, kong′-, kon krēt′, kong-), *adj.* **1.** [*often: before a noun*] being a real or actual thing; solid; substantial: *concrete proof.* **2.** [*often: before a noun*] relating to or concerned with real instances rather than abstractions; specific: *some concrete proposals.* **3.** referring to a real thing, as opposed to an abstract quality: *The words "cat," "water," and "teacher" refer to concrete things, whereas the words "truth," "excellence," and "adulthood" refer to abstract things.* **4.** [*often: before a noun*] made of concrete: *concrete blocks.* —*n.* [*noncount*] **5.** an artificial, stonelike building material made by mixing cement and sand with water and allowing the mixture to harden. —**con•crete′ly,** *adv.* —**con•crete′ness,** *n.* [*noncount*]

con•cu•bine (kong′kyə bīn′, kon′-) /'kɒŋkyəˌbayn, 'kɒn-/ *n.* [*count*] **1.** a woman who cohabits with a man to whom she is not legally married. **2.** (among peoples who allow more than one wife) a secondary wife, usually of inferior rank.

con•cur (kən kûr′) /kən'kɜr/ *v.,* **-curred, -cur•ring. 1.** to agree in opinion: [~ + *with* + *obj*]: *Do you concur with that statement?* [~ + *that clause*]: *The soldiers concurred that the casualties had been light.* **2.** [*no obj*] to cooperate; work or act together: *Both parties concurred in urging settlement of the dispute.* **3.** [*no obj*] to coincide; occur at the same time. See -CUR-.

con•cur•rence (kən kûr′əns, -kur′-) /kən'kɜrəns, -'kʌr-/ *n.* [*noncount*] **1.** agreement; mutual consent: *When the two parties reach concurrence they will sign a contract.* **2.** the fact of events occurring at the same time: *The concurrence of the two events made for an exciting time.* See -CUR-.

con•cur•rent (kən kûr′ənt, -kur′-) /kən'kɜrənt, -'kʌr-/ *adj.* **1.** occurring or existing at the same time or at the same place: *serving two concurrent prison sentences.* **2.** acting in conjunction; cooperating: *the concurrent efforts of medical researchers.* —**con•cur′rent•ly,** *adv.* See -CUR-.

con•cus•sion (kən kush′ən) /kən'kʌʃən/ *n.* [*count*] **1.** injury to the brain due to a blow or a fall: *He suffered a* *mild concussion in the football game.* **2.** the act or action of violently shaking or jarring: *concussions from the huge mortar shells.* —**con•cus•sive** (kən kus′iv) /kən'kʌsɪv/ *adj.*

con•demn (kən dem′) /kən'dɛm/ *v.* [~ + *obj*] **1.** to express an unfavorable judgment or opinion of; declare as unacceptable: *condemned the invasion but took no action.* **2.** to sentence to punishment, esp. a severe punishment: [~ + *obj* + *to* + *obj*]: *to condemn a murderer to death.* [~ + *obj* + *to* + *verb*]: *She was condemned to die.* **3.** [~ + *obj* + *to* + *obj*] to force into a specified, usually unhappy state: *His lack of education may condemn him to a life of poverty.* **4.** to give grounds for convicting: *His acts condemn him.* **5.** to judge or declare (a property, etc.) to be unfit for use or service: *The inspectors finally condemned that old building.* —**con•dem•na•tion** (kon′dem nā′shən) /ˌkɒndɛm'neyʃən/ *n.* [*noncount*]: *Condemnation of the invasion came swiftly.* [*count*]: *His condemnations of the terrorists were insincere.* —**con•dem•na•to•ry** (kən dem′nə tôr′ē, -tōr′ē) /kən'dɛmnəˌtɔriy, -ˌtowriy/ *adj.*: *a condemnatory speech.* —**con•demn•er** (kən dem′ər) /kən'dɛmər/ **con•dem•nor** (kən dem′ər, -dem nôr′) /kən'dɛmər, -dɛm'nɔr/ *n.* [*count*]

con•den•sa•tion (kən dən sā′shən) /kəndən'seyʃən/ *n.* **1.** [*noncount*] drops of liquid formed by condensing. **2.** the act or state of condensing or shortening: [*noncount*]: *The lengthy essay was reduced by condensation to just a few pages.* [*count*]: *The book is a condensation of five volumes.*

con•dense (kən dens′) /kən'dɛns/ *v.*, **-densed, -dens•ing. 1.** [~ + *obj*] to make more dense or compact; reduce (a speech, etc.) to a shorter form: *She condensed the half-hour speech to a five-minute version.* **2.** to (cause to) change to a denser form, as by cooling: [*no obj*]: *The water vapor condensed into droplets.* [~ + *obj*]: *The cold condensed the water vapor into droplets on the glass.*

condensed′ milk′, *n.* [*noncount*] whole milk made very thick by removing some water from it, with sugar added.

con•dens•er (kən den′sər) /kən'dɛnsər/ *n.* [*count*] **1.** a person or thing that condenses. **2.** an apparatus for condensing, esp. for reducing gases to liquid.

con•de•scend (kon′də send′) /ˌkɒndə'sɛnd/ *v.* **1.** to behave as if descending from a superior position to a lower position: [*no obj*]: *He wouldn't condescend, even though he clearly was my superior.* [~ + *to* + *verb*]: *The boss will condescend to see you now.* **2.** [~ + *to* + *verb*] to put aside one's dignity or higher rank voluntarily and take on equality with an inferior: *The royal party has graciously condescended to appear at the charity ball.* —**con•des•cend′ing,** *adj.* —**con•des•cen•sion** (kon′də-sen′shən) /ˌkɒndə'sɛnʃən/ *n.* [*noncount*]: *Lady Alice dealt with us without a hint of condescension.* See -SCEND-.

con•di•ment (kon′də mənt) /'kɒndəmənt/ *n.* [*count*] something used to flavor food, such as salt or spices.

con•di•tion (kən dish′ən) /kən'dɪʃən/ *n.* **1.** [*count*] a particular way of being; particular state of existing: *Your car is in poor condition.* **2.** [*noncount*] state of health: *He is in no condition to run in the marathon.* **3.** [*count*] an abnormal or diseased state of the body: *suffered from a hereditary heart condition.* **4.** [*count*] social position: *A person of your condition can't expect to marry a member of the nobility.* **5.** [*count*] Usually, **conditions.** [*plural*] existing circumstances: *poor living conditions.* **6.** [*count*] a circumstance that restricts or limits: *A tornado can happen only under certain conditions.* **7.** [*count; often: on* (+ *modifier*) + ~] something demanded as a necessary or essential part of an agreement; stipulation: *I'll go on the condition that you'll come too. The conditions and terms of this contract are confusing.* —*v.* [~ + *obj*] **8.** to put in a healthy, fit, or proper state; prepare, such as by training: *Constant exercise conditioned him for the race.* **9.** [~ + *oneself*] to accustom (oneself) to something: *He had conditioned himself to the cold.* **10.** [~ + *obj* + *to* + *verb*] to influence the opinions or actions of (another): *The hypnotist had conditioned him to twitch his hand whenever he had feelings of inadequacy.* **11.** to apply a conditioner to: *to condition one's hair.*

con•di•tion•al (kən dish′ə nl) /kən'dɪʃənl/ *adj.* **1.** depending on a condition; not absolute: *They agreed to a conditional and temporary truce.* [*be* + ~ + *on* + *obj*]: *His acceptance was conditional on a number of factors.* **2.** (of a sentence, clause, mood, or word) involving or expressing a condition, as the first clause in the sentence *If you provide me with a lawyer, I'll sign the contract.* —**con•di′tion•al•ly,** *adv.*

con•di•tioned (kən dish′ənd) /kən'dɪʃənd/ *adj.* **1.** existing under or subject to conditions. **2.** predictable or consistent in behavior or thought, due to being subjected to certain circumstances or conditions: *a conditioned response.* **3.** learned or acquired through conditioning: *conditioned behavior patterns.*

con•di•tion•er (kən dish′ən ər) /kən'dɪʃənər/ *n.* a thick liquid applied to the hair to make it easier to comb, etc.: [*noncount*]: *Apply conditioner after shampooing.* [*count*]: *conditioners for every type of hair.*

con•do (kon′dō) /'kɒndow/ *n.*, *pl.* **-dos.** CONDOMINIUM.

con•dole (kən dōl′) /kən'dowl/ *v.* [~ + *with* + *obj*], **-doled, -dol•ing.** to express sympathy with a person suffering sorrow, misfortune, or grief: *I condoled with her after she lost the race.* —**con•dol′ing•ly,** *adv.*

con•dol•ence (kən dōl′əns) /kən'dowləns/ *n.* **1.** [*noncount*] sympathy or sorrow: *I sent her an expression of condolence over the loss of her mother.* **2.** [*count; usually plural*] an expression of sympathy or sorrow: *We sent our condolences to our teacher on the death of her mother.*

con•dom (kon′dəm) /'kɒndəm/ *n.* [*count*] a thin sheath, worn over the penis during intercourse to prevent conception or disease.

con•do•min•i•um (kon′də min′ē əm) /ˌkɒndə'mɪniyəm/ *n.* [*count*] **1.** an apartment house or other complex in which the units are individually owned, with each owner receiving a deed to the unit purchased, including the right to sell or mortgage that unit, and sharing in joint ownership of any common grounds, passageways, etc. **2.** a unit in such a building: *They had a one-bedroom condominium in Florida.*

con•done (kən dōn′) /kən'down/ *v.* [~ + *obj*], **-doned, -don•ing.** to disregard, overlook, or approve of (something unacceptable, illegal, etc.): *We can't condone our children's violent acts.*

con•dor (kon′dôr) /'kɒndɔr/ *n.* [*count*] a large vulture of North and South America.

con•duc•ive (kən do͞o′siv, -dyo͞o′-) /kən'duwsɪv, -'dyuw-/ *adj.* [*be* + ~ + *to* + *obj/verb-ing*] leading, causing, or contributing to a result: *Exercise is conducive to good health.* See -DUC-.

con•duct (*n.* kon′dukt; *v.* kən dukt′) /*n.* ˈkɒndʌkt; *v.* kənˈdʌkt/ *n.* [*noncount*] **1.** personal behavior; deportment: *immature conduct during class.* **2.** the way something is organized or carried out; management: *the conduct of a business.* **3.** the act of leading; guidance; escort: *promised him safe conduct out of the country.* —*v.* **4.** [~ + *oneself*] to behave or manage (oneself): *conducted themselves well at the ceremonies.* **5.** [~ + *obj*] to direct in action or course; manage; carry on: *conducted the family business.* **6.** to direct (an orchestra, etc.) as leader: [*no obj*]: *A famous maestro is conducting in tonight's concert.* [~ + *obj*]: *conducted the school orchestra for years.* **7.** [~ + *obj*] to lead or guide; escort: *to conduct a tour.* **8.** [~ + *obj*] to serve as a channel for (heat, etc.); allow to pass through: *Copper conducts electricity.* —**con•duct•i•bil•i•ty** (kən duk′tə bil′i tē) /kənˌdʌktə'bɪlɪtiy/ *n.* [*noncount*] —**con•duct′i•ble,** *adj.* See -DUC-.

con•duc•tion (kən duk′shən) /kən'dʌkʃən/ *n.* [*noncount*] the ability of a substance to allow energy to pass through it. —**con•duc•tive** (kən duk′tiv) /kən'dʌktɪv/ *adj.* See -DUC-.

con•duc•tor (kən duk′tər) /kən'dʌktər/ *n.* [*count*] **1.** a person who conducts; director or manager: *a tour conductor.* **2.** an employee on a bus, train, or other public transportation who is in charge of its movement and its passengers. See illustration at TERMINAL. **3.** a person who directs an orchestra, band, or chorus. **4.** a substance that readily conducts heat, etc.: *a good conductor of electricity.*

con•duit (kon′dwit, -do͞o it, -dyo͞o it) /'kɒndwɪt, -duwɪt, -dyuwɪt/ *n.* [*count*] **1.** a channel for carrying water. **2.** a channel through which anything is carried: *a conduit for information.*

cone (kōn) /kown/ *n.* [*count*] **1.** a solid in which the bottom or base is a circle and the sides are smooth, curved lines narrowing to a point at the top. **2.** anything shaped like a cone: *the cone of a volcano.* **3.** the seed-bearing structure of certain trees, such as the pine.

co•ney (kō′nē, kun′ē) /'kowniy, 'kʌniy/ *n.*, *pl.* **-neys.** CONY.

con•fab (*n.* kon′fab; *v.* kən fab′, kon′fab) /*n.* ˈkɒnfæb; *v.* kənˈfæb, ˈkɒnfæb/ *n.*, *v.*, **-fabbed, -fab•bing.** *Informal.* —*n.* [*count*] **1.** a confabulation. —*v.* [*no obj*] **2.** to confabulate; chat.

con•fab•u•late (kən fab′yə lāt′) /kən'fæbyə,leyt/ *v.* [*no obj*], **-lat•ed, -lat•ing.** to have an informal or private conversation. —**con•fab•u•la•tion** (kən fab′yə lā′shən) /kən,fæbyə'leyʃən/ *n.* [*count*]

con•fec•tion (kən fek′shən) /kən'fɛkʃən/ *n.* **1.** [*count*] a sweet preparation, as a candy. **2.** [*noncount*] the process of confecting something. **3.** [*count*] something made up or confected; concoction. **4.** [*count*] something, as a garment, that is very delicate or elaborate.

con•fec•tion•er (kən fek′shə nər) /kən'fɛkʃənər/ *n.* [*count*] a person who makes or sells candies.

con•fec•tion•er•y (kən fek′shə ner′ē) /kən'fɛkʃə,nɛriy/ *n., pl.* **-er•ies. 1.** [*noncount*] confections or candies thought of as a group. **2.** [*noncount*] the work or business of a confectioner. **3.** [*count*] a confectioner's shop.

confed., an abbreviation of: **1.** confederate. **2.** confederation.

con•fed•er•a•cy (kən fed′ər ə sē) /kən'fɛdərəsiy/ *n.* [*count*], *pl.* **-cies. 1.** an alliance between persons, states, etc., to achieve some purpose. **2. the Confederacy,** [*noncount*] CONFEDERATE STATES OF AMERICA. See -FED-.

con•fed•er•ate (*adj., n.* kən fed′ər it; *v.* kən fed′ə rāt′) /*adj., n.* kən'fɛdərɪt; *v.* kən'fɛdə,reyt/ *adj., n., v.,* **-at•ed, -at•ing.** —*adj.* [*usually: before a noun*] **1.** united in an alliance or conspiracy. **2.** [*Confederate*] of or relating to the Confederate States of America. —*n.* [*count*] **3.** a person, nation, etc., united with others in a confederacy; an ally. **4.** someone working with another in an illegal or criminal act; an accomplice. **5.** [*Confederate*] a supporter of the Confederate States of America. —*v.* **6.** to unite in a league, alliance, or conspiracy: [*no obj*]: *If those independent states manage to confederate, their combined power could be a threat to us.* [~ + *obj*]: *He tried to confederate the various states into one power.* See -FED-.

Confed′erate States′ of Amer′ica, *n.* [*proper noun; the* + ~] the group of 11 Southern states that withdrew from the federal Union of the U.S. in 1860–61.

con•fed•er•a•tion (kən fed′ə rā′shən) /kən,fɛdə'reyʃən/ *n.* [*count*] **1.** a league or alliance, esp. of states united for common purposes: *The prime minister tried to pull those states into a confederation after the collapse of the central government.* **2. the Confederation,** the union of the 13 original U.S. states under the Articles of Confederation 1781–89. —**con•fed′er•a′tion•ism,** *n.* [*noncount*] —**con•fed′er•a′tion•ist,** *n.* [*count*] See -FED-.

con•fer (kən fûr′) /kən'fɜr/ *v.,* **-ferred, -fer•ring. 1.** [*no obj; sometimes:* ~ + *on* + *obj*] to discuss something together; compare ideas or opinions: *We conferred for a moment and returned to the discussion.* **2.** [~ + *obj* + *on* + *obj*] to give as a gift, honor, etc., to someone: *to confer a degree on a graduate.* —**con•fer′ra•ble,** *adj.* —**con•fer′ral, con•fer′ment,** *n.* [*noncount*] —**con•fer′rer,** *n.* [*count*] See -FER-. —**Syn.** See CONSULT.

con•fer•ence (kon′fər əns) /'kɒnfərəns/ *n.* [*count*] **1.** a meeting for consultation or discussion: *a conference between a student and her adviser.* **2.** an association of athletic teams; league: *the college football conferences.* —***Idiom.*** **3. in conference,** [*noncount*] having a meeting: *Tell them I'm in conference now and can't be disturbed.* —**con•fer•en•tial** (kon′fə ren′shəl) /,kɒnfə'rɛnʃəl/ *adj.* See -FER-.

con•fess (kən fes′) /kən'fɛs/ *v.* **1.** to acknowledge or admit (a fault, etc.): [~ + *obj*]: *confessed his guilt to the police.* [~ + *to* + *obj*]: *He confessed to the crime.* [~ + *(that) clause*]: *confessed (that) he was the killer.* **2.** [~ + *(that) clause*] to admit as true; concede: *I must confess (that) I haven't read the book.* **3.** to declare or acknowledge (one's sins), esp. to God or to a priest: [~ + *obj*]: *He confessed his sins to the priest.* [*no obj*]: *He confessed every day.* —**con•fess′a•ble,** *adj.* See -FESS-.

con•fessed (kən fest′) /kən'fɛst/ *adj.* [*before a noun*] admitted openly or declared: *a confessed rapist.* —**con•fes•sed•ly** (kən fes′id lē) /kən'fɛsɪdliy/ *adv.*: *was confessedly the culprit.*

con•fes•sion (kən fesh′ən) /kən'fɛʃən/ *n.* **1.** [*noncount*] an act of confessing: *Confession is good for the soul.* **2.** [*count*] something confessed: *the candidate's confessions of wrongdoing.* **3.** [*count*] a formal acknowledgment of guilt by a person accused of a crime: *He signed his confession and they took him off to the cell.* See -FESS-.

con•fes•sion•al (kən fesh′ə nl) /kən'fɛʃənl/ *adj.* **1.** of or characteristic of confession. —*n.* [*count*] **2.** a place for hearing confessions by a priest. See -FESS-.

con•fes•sor (kən fes′ər) /kən'fɛsər/ *n.* [*count*] **1.** a person who confesses. **2.** a priest who is authorized by the church to hear confessions.

con•fet•ti (kən fet′ē) /kən'fɛtiy/ *n.* [*noncount*] small bits of colored paper thrown or dropped from a height at festive events.

con•fi•dant (kon′fi dant′, -dänt′) /'kɒnfɪ,dænt, -,dɑnt/ *n.* [*count*] a person to whom another tells secrets: *Her secretary was her only confidant.*

con•fide (kən fīd′) /kən'fayd/ *v.,* **-fid•ed, -fid•ing.** to tell (secrets) to another in trust: [~ + *in* + *obj*]: *She wouldn't confide in me.* [~ + *obj*]: *She was afraid to confide her plans to me.* [~ + *that clause*]: *The paratrooper confided that he closed his eyes whenever he jumped out of planes.* —**con•fid′er,** *n.* [*count*] See -FID-.

con•fi•dence (kon′fi dəns) /'kɒnfɪdəns/ *n.* **1.** [*noncount*] belief in the reliability of a person or thing; reliance: *The bank manager had full confidence in his employees.* **2.** [*noncount*] belief in oneself and one's powers or abilities: *He would be a better speaker if he had more confidence.* **3.** [*noncount*] a feeling of being certain; assurance: *to speak with confidence of a fact.* **4.** [*count*] a piece of confidential communication: *to exchange confidences.* —***Idiom.*** **5. in confidence,** [*noncount*] as a secret or private matter: *I'm telling you this in strictest confidence.* See -FID-.

con′fidence game′, *n.* [*count*] a swindle in which the swindler, after gaining the victim's confidence, robs the victim by cheating at a gambling game, or the like. Also called, *Brit.,* **con′fidence trick′.**

con•fi•dent (kon′fi dənt) /'kɒnfɪdənt/ *adj.* **1.** [*be* + ~] having full assurance; sure; certain: [*be* + ~ + *of*]: *He was confident of success.* [~ + *(that) clause*]: *He was confident (that) they would succeed.* **2.** sure of oneself; self-confident: *a confident performer.* —**con′fi•dent•ly,** *adv.*: *I confidently expected him to do the job.* —**Related Words.** CONFIDENT is an adjective, CONFIDENTLY is an adverb, CONFIDENCE is a noun: *He was confident that he would get the job. He walked confidently into the room, prepared for the interview. He has a lot of confidence in his abilities.*

con•fi•den•tial (kon′fi den′shəl) /,kɒnfɪ'dɛnʃəl/ *adj.* **1.** spoken, written, or acted on in secret: *Your personal file is confidential.* **2.** indicating or showing private or secret matters: *spoke in confidential tones.* **3.** [*before a noun*] entrusted with secrets or private affairs: *He is my confidential secretary.* —**con•fi•den•ti•al•i•ty** (kon′fi den′shē al′i tē) /,kɒnfɪ,dɛnʃiy'ælɪtiy/ *n.* [*noncount*]: *The confidentiality of the client will be respected.* —**con′fi•den′tial•ly,** *adv.* See -FID-.

con•fid•ing (kən fīd′ing) /kən'faydɪŋ/ *adj.* trusting; willing to trust someone else with private or personal matters: *She became very confiding, and I found out the truth.*

con•fig•u•ra•tion (kən fig′yə rā′shən) /kən,fɪgyə'reyʃən/ *n.* [*count*] the arrangement of the parts or elements of a thing.

con•fine (*v.* kən fīn′; *n.* kon′fīn) /*v.* kən'fayn; *n.* 'kɒnfayn/ *v.,* **-fined, -fin•ing,** *n.* —*v.* [~ + *obj (+ to + obj)*] **1.** to enclose within bounds; limit or restrict: *confined himself to a few remarks.* **2.** to keep in; prevent from leaving because of imprisonment, illness, etc.: *confined to a mental institution.* —*n.* [*count*] **3.** Usually, **confines.** [*plural*] a boundary or bound; limit; border: *He stayed within the confines of the hotel.* **4.** Often, **confines.** [*plural*] region; territory. See -FIN-.

con•fine•ment (kən fīn′mənt) /kən'faynmənt/ *n.* [*noncount*] the state or condition of being confined: *His confinement after the heart attack didn't last long.*

con•firm (kən fûrm′) /kən'fɜrm/ *v.* [~ + *obj*] **1.** to establish the truth of (something); verify: *The secretary would not confirm the reports.* [~ + *that clause*]: *confirmed that my client was there at the time of the murder.* **2.** to acknowledge with assurance; make certain: *The hotel promised to confirm my reservation.* **3.** to make valid by formal or legal act; ratify: *In the end she was confirmed by the Senate and appointed to the court.* **4.** to administer the rite of confirmation to: *He was confirmed when he was thirteen.* —**con•firm′a•ble,** *adj.* —**con•firm•a•bil•i•ty** (kən fûr′mə bil′i tē) /kən,fɜrmə'bɪlɪtiy/ *n.* [*noncount*] —**con•firm′er,** *n.* [*count*]

con•fir•ma•tion (kon′fər mā′shən) /,kɒnfər'meyʃən/ *n.* [*noncount*] **1.** the act of confirming or the state of being confirmed: *Confirmation of the bombing came as the TV news actually was showing it on the air.* **2.** a rite administered to baptized persons in some Christian churches. **3.** a ceremony among some Jews in which a young person is formally admitted as an adult member of the Jewish community. —**con′fir•ma′tion•al,** *adj.*

con•firmed (kən fûrmd′) /kən'fɜrmd/ *adj.* [*before a*

noun] firmly established or settled in a habit or condition; unlikely to change: *a confirmed bachelor.*

con•fis•cate (kon′fə skāt′) /ˈkɒnfəˌskeyt/ *v.* [~ + *obj*], **-cat•ed, -cat•ing.** to seize (something) by legal authority: *I thought the soldiers would confiscate our camera, but they let us keep it.* —**con•fis•ca•tion** (kon′fə skā′shən) /ˌkɒnfəˈskeyʃən/ *n.* [*noncount*] —**con′fis•ca′tor,** *n.* [*count*]

con•fla•gra•tion (kon′flə grā′shən) /ˌkɒnfləˈgreyʃən/ *n.* [*count*] a destructive fire over a wide area: *Firefighters responded to the conflagration in the factory district.*

con•flict (*v.* kən flikt′; *n.* kon′flikt), *v.* **1.** to disagree; be in opposition; clash: [*no obj*]: *Our views conflict.* [~ + *with* + *obj*]: *My views on language learning conflict with yours.* —*n.* **2.** a fight, battle, or struggle: [*noncount*]: *Armed conflict is not the only way to solve disputes.* [*count*]: *conflicts that lasted for months.* **3.** disagreement; quarrel; argument: [*noncount; sometimes: in* + ~]: *The department was in conflict over the hiring of full professors.* [*count*]: *A conflict arose when the department tried to hire a famous professor.* —**con•flict′ing,** *adj.*: *conflicting points of view.*

con′flict of in′terest, *n.* [*count*], *pl.* **conflicts of interest.** the circumstance in which a public official, corporate officer, etc., might benefit personally from his or her official actions or influence.

con•flu•ence (kon′flo͞o əns) /ˈkɒnfluwəns/ *n.* [*count*] **1. a.** a flowing together of two or more streams. **b.** their place of joining: *the confluence of the Ohio and Mississippi rivers.* **2.** a coming together of people or things. See -FLU-.

con•form (kən fôrm′) /kənˈfɔrm/ *v.* **1.** [~ + *to* + *obj*] to act in accordance or agreement; comply: *to conform to rules.* **2.** [*no obj*] to act in accordance with the standards, etc., expected by a group: *You'll have to conform if you don't want to feel isolated from others.* **3.** [~ + *obj*] to bring (something) into agreement or correspondence: *The architect conformed the plans for the mall to the new specifications.* —**con•form′er,** *n.* [*count*] See -FORM-.

con•form•ist (kən fôr′mist) /kənˈfɔrmɪst/ *n.* [*count*] a person who conforms, esp. with the standards expected by society.

con•form•i•ty (kən fôr′mi tē) /kənˈfɔrmɪtiy/ *n.* [*noncount*] **1.** an act of conforming: *Too much emphasis on conformity can bring dullness to a group.* **2.** agreement; obedience: *conformity to one's beliefs.*

con•found (kən found′; *for 3 usually* kon′found′) /kənˈfawnd; *for 3 usually* ˈkɒnˈfawnd/ *v.* [~ + *obj*] **1.** to amaze; confuse; perplex: *The army's lightning attack confounded the enemy.* **2.** [~ + *obj* + *with* + *obj*] to mix up by mistake; *This analysis confounded truth with errors and lies.* —***Idiom.*** **3. Confound it!** (used as a mild oath to express one's irritation): *Confound it! Pick up those books now!* —**con•found′ing•ly,** *adv.*

con•found•ed (kon′foun′did) /ˌkɒnˈfawndɪd/ *adj.* [*before a noun*] (used to express irritation with the person or thing named): *The confounded plane is late.*

con•frere (kon′frâr) /ˈkɒnfrɛər/ *n.* [*count*] a fellow member, such as of a profession; a colleague.

con•front (kən frunt′) /kənˈfrʌnt/ *v.* [~ + *obj*] **1.** to face (someone) in hostility: *Two police officers confronted me and demanded identification.* **2.** [~ + *obj* + *with* + *obj*] to present or put facts or evidence to (someone): *They confronted him with the evidence.* **3.** to occur or arise as something to be dealt with: *the obstacles that confronted us.* —**con•front′er,** *n.* [*count*]

con•fron•ta•tion (kon′frən tā′shən) /ˌkɒnfrənˈteyʃən/ *n.* the act of confronting: [*count*]: *A confrontation with UN forces is the last thing he wants.* [*noncount*]: *The use of confrontation won't lead to peace.* —**con′fron•ta′tion•al,** *adj.*

Con•fu•cian•ism (kən fyo͞o′shə niz′əm) /kənˈfyuwʃəˌnɪzəm/ *n.* [*noncount*] the system of ethics, education, and political thinking taught by Confucius, a Chinese philosopher, stressing love for humanity, reverence for parents, and harmony in thought and conduct. —**Con•fu′cian,** *adj., n.* [*count*] —**Con•fu′cian•ist,** *n.* [*count*], *adj.*

con•fuse (kən fyo͞oz′) /kənˈfyuwz/ *v.* [~ + *obj*], **-fused, -fus•ing. 1.** to cause to make a mistake; mix up: *The flood of questions confused me.* **2.** to make hard to understand, unclear, or indistinct: *Let's not confuse matters.* **3.** to fail to distinguish between (two things): *I always confuse the twins.* [~ + *obj* + *with* + *obj*]: *I always confuse one twin with the other.* —**Related Words.** CONFUSE is a verb, CONFUSION is a noun, CONFUSED and CONFUSING are adjectives: *All those numbers just confused me. The airport was a scene of confusion. Confused students looked at one another nervously. It was a confusing homework problem.*

con•fused (kən fyo͞ozd′) /kənˈfyuwzd/ *adj.* **1.** hard to understand; mixed up; unclear: *Your writing seems confused.* **2.** (of a person) having difficulty understanding or doing something: *The two confused tourists got lost in the mall.* —**con•fus•ed•ly** (kən fyo͞o′zid lē) /kənˈfyuwzɪdliy/ *adv.* —**con•fus′ed•ness,** *n.* [*noncount*]

con•fus•ing (kən fyo͞o′zing) /kənˈfyuwzɪŋ/ *adj.* hard to understand; unclear: *a confusing answer to a question.* —**con•fus′ing•ly,** *adv.*

con•fu•sion (kən fyo͞o′zhən) /kənˈfyuwʒən/ *n.* [*noncount*] **1.** bewilderment; puzzlement: *Imagine our confusion when I started teaching in the wrong room.* **2.** [*often: in* + ~] disorder; chaos; upheaval: *The army retreated in confusion.* **3.** lack of clearness or distinctness: *Your writing suffers from too much confusion.*

Cong., an abbreviation of: **1.** Congress. **2.** Congressional.

con•ga (kong′gə) /ˈkɒŋgə/ *n., pl.* **-gas,** *v.,* **-gaed, -ga•ing.** —*n.* [*count*] **1.** a Cuban dance of three steps forward followed by a kick performed by a group in single file. **2.** a tall, cone-shaped Afro-Cuban drum, played with the hands. —*v.* [*no obj*] **3.** to dance a conga.

con•geal (kən jēl′) /kənˈdʒiyl/ *v.* to change from a soft or liquid state to a solid state, as by cooling; thicken: [*no obj*]: *The gelatin will congeal in the refrigerator.* [~ + *obj*]: *The cold has congealed the gelatin.* —**con•geal′er,** *n.* [*count*] —**con•geal′ment,** *n.* [*noncount*]

con•gen•ial (kən jēn′yəl) /kənˈdʒiynyəl/ *adj.* **1.** agreeable, suitable, or pleasing: *felt happy in the congenial surroundings.* **2.** suited to each other in tastes, thinking, temperament, etc.; compatible: *a congenial couple.* —**con•ge•ni•al•i•ty** (kən jē′nē al′i tē) /kənˌdʒiyniyˈælɪtiy/ **con•gen′ial•ness,** *n.* [*noncount*] —**con•gen′ial•ly,** *adv.*

con•gen•i•tal (kən jen′i tl) /kənˈdʒɛnɪtl̩/ *adj.* **1.** present or existing at the time of birth: *a congenital abnormality.* **2.** having by nature the character stated: *a congenital fool.* —**con•gen′i•tal•ly,** *adv.* —**con•gen′i•tal•ness,** *n.* [*noncount*] See -GEN-.

con•ges•ted (kən jest′id) /kənˈdʒɛstɪd/ *adj.* of, relating to, or marked by congestion. —**con•ges′tive,** *adj.*

con•ges•tion (kən jes′chən) /kənˈdʒɛstʃən/ *n.* [*noncount*] **1.** a condition of overcrowding: *Congestion on major roads is worse than usual.* **2.** a condition in the body in which there is an abnormal accumulation of fluid: *The congestion in his chest made it hard for him to breathe.* See -GEST-.

con•glom•er•ate (*n., adj.* kən glom′ər it, kəng-; *v.* kən glom′ə rāt′) /*n., adj.* kənˈglɒmərɪt, kəŋ-; *v.* kənˈglɒməˌreyt/ *n., adj., v.,* **-at•ed, -at•ing.** —*n.* [*count*] **1.** a thing composed of unrelated elements mixed together. **2.** a business corporation made up of divisions that specialize in unrelated industries. —*adj.* [*often: before a noun*] **3.** made up of unrelated elements. **4.** gathered into a rounded mass. **5.** of or relating to a corporate conglomerate. —*v.* [~ + *obj*] **6.** to bring together into a mass. **7.** to gather into a rounded mass or close grouping.

con•glom•er•a•tion (kən glom′ə rā′shən, kəng-) /kənˌglɒməˈreyʃən, kəŋ-/ *n.* [*count*] a group made up of unrelated things: *The stew was a conglomeration of fish, chicken, and beef.*

Con•go•lese (kong′gə lēz′, -lēs′) /ˌkɒŋgəˈliyz, -ˈliys/ *adj., n., pl.* **-lese.** —*adj.* **1.** of or relating to the People's Republic of the Congo. —*n.* [*count*] **2.** a person born or living in the People's Republic of the Congo.

con•grat•u•late (kən grach′ə lāt′) /kənˈgrætʃəˌleyt/ *v.* [~ + *obj* (+ *on* + *obj*)], **-lat•ed, -lat•ing. 1.** to express pleasure to (a person) on a happy occasion: *congratulated the newlyweds; congratulated her on her promotion.* **2.** [~ + *oneself*] to feel pride in (oneself) for an accomplishment or good fortune: *congratulated himself on his narrow escape.* —**con•grat′u•la′tor,** *n.* [*count*] —**con•grat•u•la•to•ry** (kən grach′ə lə tôr′ē, -tōr′ē) /kənˈgrætʃələˌtɔriy, -ˌtowriy/ *adj.*: *a congratulatory message.* See -GRAT-.

con•grat•u•la•tion (kən grach′ə lā′shən) /kənˌgrætʃəˈleyʃən/ *n.* **1.** [*noncount*] the act of congratulating. **2. congratulations,** [*plural*] an expression of pleasure in the good fortune of another: *We sent our congratulations to the happy couple.* —*interj.* **3. congratulations.** (used to express pleasure in the good fortune of another): *Congratulations! You graduated.*

con•gre•gate (kong′gri gāt′) /ˈkɒŋgrɪˌgeyt/ *v.* [*no obj*], **-gat•ed, -gat•ing.** to come together in a body; collect:

The crowd congregated around him as he began his speech. —**con′gre·ga′tor,** *n.* [*count*] See -GREG-.

con·gre·ga·tion (kong′gri gā′shən) /ˌkɒŋgrɪ'geyʃən/ *n.* [*count*] an assembly of people who meet for worship: *The congregation bowed heads and prayed silently.* —**con·gre·ga′tion·al,** *adj.* —**con′gre·ga′tion·al·ism,** *n.* [*noncount*] —**con′gre·ga′tion·al·ist,** *n.* [*count*], *adj.* See -GREG-.

con·gress (kong′gris) /'kɒŋgrɪs/ *n.* **1.** [*proper noun; Congress*] the national law-making body of the U.S.: [*no article*]: *Congress was not in session when we visited Washington.* [*the* + ~]: *The Congress won't agree to that plan.* **2.** [*count*] the national law-making body of a nation, esp. of a republic. **3.** [*count*] a formal meeting of representatives for discussing a matter of interest. See -GRESS-.

con·gres·sion·al (kən gresh′ə nl, kəng-) /kən'grɛʃənḷ, kəŋ-/ *adj.* [*before a noun; sometimes: Congressional*] of or relating to a congress or to the U.S. Congress: *called for Congressional hearings.*

con·gress·man (kong′gris mən) /'kɒŋgrɪsmən/ *n.* [*count*], *pl.* **-men.** [*often: Congressman*] a member of a congress: *Several congressmen were accused of bribery.* [*proper noun*]: *Congressman, what position do you take on this issue? Congressman Smith voted against us.*

con·gress·wom·an (kong′gris wo͝om′ən) /'kɒŋgrɪsˌwʊmən/ *n.* [*count*], *pl.* **-wom·en.** [*often: Congresswoman*] a female member of a congress: *There were only a few congresswomen at that time.* [*proper noun*]: *Congresswoman, what is your position on that issue? I voted for Congresswoman Jones.*

con·gru·ent (kong′gro͞o ənt, kən gro͞o′-, kəng-) /'kɒŋgruwənt, kən'gruw-, kəŋ-/ *adj.* **1.** agreeing; similar: *congruent opinions.* **2.** [*sometimes: (be +) ~ + with + obj*] fitting; appropriate: *Is the punishment congruent with the crime?* —**con′gru·ent·ly,** *adv.*

con·gru·i·ty (kən gro͞o′i tē, kəng-) /kən'gruwɪtiy, kəŋ-/ *n., pl.* **-ties. 1.** [*noncount*] the state or quality of being congruent. **2.** [*count*] a point of agreement.

con·ic (kon′ik) /'kɒnɪk/ also **con′i·cal,** *adj.* having the form of, resembling, or relating to a cone: *a conical hat.*

co·ni·fer (kō′nə fər, kon′ə-) /'kownəfər, 'kɒnə-/ *n.* [*count*] a class of chiefly evergreen trees and shrubs, such as the pine and cypress, that have seeds on dry scales arranged as a cone. See -FER-.

co·nif·er·ous (kō nif′ər əs, kə-) /kow'nɪfərəs, kə-/ *adj.* [*often: before a noun*] made up of conifer trees.

conj., an abbreviation of: conjunction.

con·jec·ture (kən jek′chər) /kən'dʒɛktʃər/ *n., v.,* **-tured, -tur·ing.** —*n.* **1.** [*noncount*] the forming or expressing of an opinion without sufficient proof: *Do you know that for a fact or is it only conjecture?* **2.** [*count*] an opinion or theory so formed or expressed: *Another conjecture was that the butler did it.* —*v.* **3.** to form or express an opinion without sufficient evidence; guess: [~ + *that clause*]: *I conjectured that he was about fifty.* [*no obj*]: *The situation turned out as he had conjectured.* —**con·jec′tur·al,** *adj.* —**con·jec′tur·er,** *n.* [*count*] See -JEC-.

con·join (kən join′) /kən'dʒɔyn/ *v.* [~ + *obj*] to link or join two clauses with a coordinate conjunction: *The two clauses were conjoined with the conjunction* and. —**con·join′er,** *n.* [*count*]

con·ju·gal (kon′jə gəl) /'kɒndʒəgəl/ *adj.* [*before a noun*] **1.** of, relating to, or characteristic of marriage: *conjugal bliss.* **2.** of or relating to the relation of husband and wife, esp. the sexual relationship: *conjugal rights.* —**con·ju·gal·i·ty** (kon′jə gal′i tē) /ˌkɒndʒə'gælɪtiy/ *n.* [*noncount*] —**con′ju·gal·ly,** *adv.*

con·ju·gate (kon′jə gāt′) /'kɒndʒəˌgeyt/ *v.* [~ + *obj*], **-gat·ed, -gat·ing.** to display the forms of (a verb), in a fixed order: *To conjugate the present tense of the verb* be *we gave the following:* am, is, are.

con·ju·ga·tion (kon′jə gā′shən) /ˌkɒndʒə'geyʃən/ *n.* [*count*] the set of forms of a verb or the display of these in order. —**con′ju·ga′tion·al,** *adj.*

con·junc·tion (kən jungk′shən) /kən'dʒʌŋkʃən/ *n.* **1.** [*count*] one of a small class of words that connect words, phrases, clauses, or sentences, such as *and, because, but,* and *unless.* **2.** [*noncount; sometimes: in* + ~] the act of joining or the state of being joined; association; combination: *The police worked in conjunction with the army.* **3.** [*count*] a combination of events or circumstances. —**con·junc′tion·al,** *adj.* See -JUNC-.

con·junc·tive (kən jungk′tiv) /kən'dʒʌŋktɪv/ *adj.* **1.** serving to connect; connective: *conjunctive tissue.* **2.** conjoined; joint. **3.** of, relating to, or functioning like a conjunction; serving to connect two clauses or sentences, as *however* and *furthermore.* See -JUNC-.

con·junc·ti·vi·tis (kən jungk′tə vī′tis) /kənˌdʒʌŋktə'vaytɪs/ *n.* [*noncount*] inflammation of the watery membrane surrounding the eye and the inside of the eyelids.

con·jure (kon′jər, kun′-) /'kɒndʒər, 'kʌn-/ *v.,* **-jured, -jur·ing. 1.** to make, produce, or cause to appear by or as if by magic: [~ + *(up)* + *obj*]: *to conjure (up) a miracle.* [~ + *obj (+ up)*]: *He conjured the right disk (up) from somewhere and put it into the computer.* **2.** [*no obj*] to practice magic or tricks. **3.** [~ + *up* + *obj*] to bring to mind; imagine; think about: *The island of Gotland conjures up images of yellow-flowered fields and churches.* See -JUR-.

conk[1] (kongk, kôngk) /kɒŋk, kɔŋk/ *Slang.* —*v.* [~ + *obj*] **1.** to strike on the head: *She conked him and ran out before the police came.* —*n.* [*count*] **2.** the head. **3.** a blow on the head.

conk[2] (kongk, kôngk) /kɒŋk, kɔŋk/ *v. Slang.* **1.** [~ + *out*] (of a machine or engine) to break down or fail; slow down or stop: *The engine just conked out and the plane nosed down quickly.* **2.** [~ + *out/off*] to go to sleep: *My wife usually conks out by ten-thirty.* **3.** [~ + *out*] to lose consciousness; faint: *He conked out after hitting his head.*

Conn., an abbreviation of: Connecticut.

con·nect (kə nekt′) /kə'nɛkt/ *v.* **1.** to (cause to) become linked together; join or unite: [*no obj*]: *These two wires can't connect because they're the wrong length.* [~ + *obj*]: *Connect these two wires carefully.* **2.** [~ + *obj*] to establish telephone communication with or for: *Hold on please, I'm trying to connect you now.* **3.** [~ + *obj*] to link to an electrical or telephone system; hook up: *I don't know when they'll come to connect your phones.* **4.** [~ + *obj* + *with* + *obj*] to associate in the mind: *A good doctor connects what the patient says with what she learns from the examination.* **5.** (of trains, etc.) to run so as to make connections: [*no obj*]: *These two buses don't connect; you'll have to walk a bit.* [~ + *with* + *obj*]: *The train from Washington connects with the train to Pittsburgh in New York.* **6.** [*no obj*] *Informal.* to meet or establish communication; make contact: *I'm sorry we didn't connect; maybe next time we will.* **7.** [*no obj*] to hit successfully or solidly: *The batter connected for a home run.* —**con·nect·i·bil·i·ty, con·nect·a·bil·i·ty** (kə nek′tə bil′i tē) /kəˌnɛktə'bɪlɪtiy/ *n.* [*noncount*] —**con·nect′i·ble, con·nect′a·ble,** *adj.* —**con·nec′tor, con·nect′er,** *n.* [*count*] See -NEC-.

con·nect·ed (kə nek′tid) /kə'nɛktɪd/ *adj.* **1.** joined; associated; related: *connected events.* **2.** related by birth or marriage, or having a relationship that helps one's career, etc.: *to be well connected.*

con·nec·tion (kə nek′shən) /kə'nɛkʃən/ *n.* **1.** [*noncount*] the act or state of connecting or the state of being connected: *We're waiting for connection to the town sewer system.* **2.** [*count*] anything that connects; link: *an electrical connection.* **3.** association; relationship: [*noncount*]: *There is no connection with any other firm.* [*count*]: *a connection between breathing polluted air and lung disease.* **4.** [*count*] logical association or development; mental association: *Discuss the connection between the two events in your assignment.* **5.** [*count*] Usually, **connections.** [*plural*] associates, relatives, or friends, esp. when they are thought of as having influence: *His connections helped him get that job.* **6.** [*count*] the meeting of planes, etc., for transfer of passengers: *Stockholm has good connections with the rest of Scandinavia.* **7.** [*count*] the plane, boat, etc., boarded in making a travel connection: *I got there just in time to watch my connection leaving the station* **8.** [*count*] a channel of communication: *can't hear because of a bad telephone connection.* **9.** [*count*] Often, **connections.** [*plural*] a source of supply, esp. for scarce or illegal materials or goods: *has connections in ports all over the world.* —***Idiom.*** **10. in connection with,** [*in* + ~ + *with* + *obj*] concerning; relating to; of or about (the next person or thing stated): *You are wanted in connection with the murder of the colonel.* Also, *Brit.,* **connexion.** See -NEC-.

con·nec·tive (kə nek′tiv) /kə'nɛktɪv/ *adj.* **1.** serving or tending to connect: *connective tissue.* —*n.* [*count*] **2.** something that connects. **3.** a word, such as a conjunction, used to connect words, phrases, clauses, and sentences. —**con·nec·tiv·i·ty** (kon′ek tiv′i tē) /ˌkɒnɛk'tɪvɪtiy/ *n.* [*noncount*]

con·nive (kə nīv′) /kə'nayv/ *v.,* **-nived, -niv·ing. 1. a.** to cooperate or work together secretly, esp. for something wrong or illegal: [~ *(+ with + obj)* + *to* + *verb (+ obj)*]: *He connived with his friends to get the job.* **b.** [~

+ *obj*] to make (one's way) by scheming or plotting: *She connived her way into power.* **2.** [~ + *at* + *obj*] to avoid noticing something one is expected to oppose or condemn. —**con•niv′er,** *n.* [*count*] —**con•niv′ing,** *adj.*

con•nois•seur (kon′ə sûr′, -so͝or′) /ˌkɒnəˈsɜr, -ˈsʊr/ *n.* [*count*] a person with good judgment, esp. in art or matters of taste: *a connoisseur of wines.* —**con′nois•seur′ship,** *n.* [*noncount*]

con•no•ta•tion (kon′ə tā′shən) /ˌkɒnəˈteyʃən/ *n.* [*count*] a secondary meaning of a word or expression that comes to mind or is suggested in addition to its primary meaning: *The word* home *often has the connotation "a place of warmth and affection."* Compare DENOTATION. —**con•no•ta•tive** (kon′ə tā′tiv, kə nō′tə-) /ˈkɒnəˌteytɪv, kəˈnowtə-/ **con•no•tive** (kə nō′tiv) /kəˈnowtɪv/ *adj.* See -NOTA-.

con•note (kə nōt′) /kəˈnowt/ *v.* [~ + *obj*], **-not•ed, -not•ing.** to carry or suggest a connotation: *A fireplace connotes comfort and hospitality.* See -NOTA-.

con•nu•bi•al (kə no͞o′bē əl, -nyo͞o′-) /kəˈnuwbiyəl, -ˈnyuw-/ *adj.* [*before a noun*] of or relating to marriage; matrimonial: *connubial bliss.* —**con•nu•bi•al•i•ty** (kə-no͞o′bē al′i tē, -nyo͞o′-) /kəˌnuwbiyˈælɪtiy, -ˌnyuw-/ *n.* [*noncount*] —**con•nu′bi•al•ly,** *adv.*

con•quer (kong′kər) /ˈkɒŋkər/ *v.* **1.** to take or acquire by force of arms; win in war: [~ + *obj*]: *to conquer a foreign land.* [*no obj*]: *Caesar wrote, "I came, I saw, I conquered."* **2.** [~ + *obj*] to overcome by force; defeat: *to conquer an enemy.* **3.** [~ + *obj*] to win by effort, personal appeal, etc.: *She conquered the hearts of the audience.* **4.** [~ + *obj*] to gain control over (fear, a bad habit, etc.); master. —**con′quer•a•ble,** *adj.* —**con′quer•or,** *n.* [*count*] See -QUER-.

con•quest (kon′kwest, kong′-) /ˈkɒnkwɛst, ˈkɒŋ-/ *n.* **1.** [*noncount*] the act or process of conquering: *wanted conquest for its own sake.* **2.** [*noncount*] the winning of favor, affection, love, etc.: *the conquest of someone's heart.* **3.** [*count*] a person whose favor or affection has been won: *My sister was one of his many conquests.* **4.** [*count*] anything taken or won by conquering, as a nation, a territory, or riches. See -QUES-.

con•quis•ta•dor (kong kwis′tə dôr′, -kēs′-) /kɒŋˈkwɪstəˌdɔr, -ˈkiys-/ *n.* [*count*], *pl.* **con•quis•ta•dors, con•quis•ta•do•res** (kong kēs′tə dôr′ēz, -āz) /kɒŋˌkiystəˈdɔriyz, -eyz/. one of the Spanish conquerors of the Americas, esp. of Mexico and Peru, in the 16th century.

Cons., an abbreviation of: Conservative.

cons., an abbreviation of: **1.** consonant. **2.** constable. **3.** construction.

con•science (kon′shəns) /ˈkɒnʃəns/ *n.* **1.** the sense of what is right or wrong in one's acts, thoughts, or motives: [*noncount*]: *a matter of conscience, not of opportunity.* [*count*]: *My conscience keeps getting in the way of easy decisions.* —***Idiom.*** **2. in (all** or **good) conscience,** [*noncount*] in all reason and fairness: *I can't do that in good conscience because I would be betraying my friends.* **3. on one's conscience,** (of a wrongdoing); burdening one with guilt: *The crime had been on his conscience for years.* See -SCI-.

con•sci•en•tious (kon′shē en′shəs) /ˌkɒnʃiyˈɛnʃəs/ *adj.* **1.** very careful; thorough; painstaking: *She was a conscientious student who always did her work.* **2.** acting according to conscience; fair: *a conscientious judge.* —**con′sci•en′tious•ly,** *adv.*: *conscientiously working on the book.* —**con′sci•en′tious•ness,** *n.* [*noncount*]

conscien′tious objec′tion, *n.* [*noncount*] refusal because of moral or religious beliefs to fight in a military conflict or to serve in the armed forces. —**conscien′tious objec′tor,** *n.* [*count*]

con•scious (kon′shəs) /ˈkɒnʃəs/ *adj.* **1.** [*be* + ~ (+ *of*)] aware of one's own existence, surroundings, etc.: *Is a mouse conscious in the same way a human is?* **2.** fully aware of something: [*be* + ~ + *of*]: *When he worked he was not conscious of the passage of time.* [*be* + ~ + *that clause*]: *When he worked he was not conscious that so much time had passed.* **3.** having the mind or mental processes fully active; awake: *He wanted to be conscious during the cornea operation.* **4.** known to oneself; felt: *his conscious guilt.* **5.** deliberate; intentional: *a conscious effort not to yawn.* **6.** deeply aware of or concerned about (This word is sometimes used after other words to form adjectives that refer to the thing concerned about): *money-conscious (= deeply aware of or concerned about money).* —*n.* **7. the conscious,** [*noncount*] the part of the mind that one is aware of. —**con′scious•ly,** *adv.* See -SCI-.

con•sci•ous•ness (kon′shəs nəs) /ˈkɒnʃəsnəs/ *n.* **1.** [*noncount*] the state of being awake: *I lost consciousness immediately.* **2.** [*count; usually singular*] the conscious mind; one's conscious thoughts: *a consciousness that something wasn't right.* **3.** [*noncount*] the ideas, beliefs, or opinions held by a group of people: *class consciousness.*

con•script (*v.* kən skript′; *n., adj.* kon′skript) /*v.* kənˈskrɪpt; *n., adj.* ˈkɒnskrɪpt/ *v.* [~ + *obj*] **1.** to call (someone) by law to enter military service: *The Army conscripted thousands from that city.* —*n.* [*count*] **2.** a person called this way; recruit. —*adj.* [*before a noun*] **3.** enrolled or formed by conscription; drafted: *a conscript soldier.* —**con•script′a•ble,** *adj.* See -SCRIB-.

con•se•crate (kon′si krāt′) /ˈkɒnsɪˌkreyt/ *v.* [~ + *obj*], **-crat•ed, -crat•ing. 1.** to make or declare (something) sacred; dedicate (something) to the service of a deity: *The church was consecrated in 1944. She consecrated her life to God.* **2.** to make (something) an object of honor; dedicate: *a day that was consecrated to the memory of Dr. Martin Luther King, Jr.* **3.** to admit or ordain (a bishop, etc.) to a sacred office. —**con•se•cra•tion** (kon′si krā′shən) /ˌkɒnsɪˈkreyʃən/ *n.* [*noncount*]: *a life of consecration to God.* [*count*]: *When did the consecration of the cathedral take place?* —**con′se•cra′tor,** *n.* [*count*] —**con•se•cra•to′ry** (kon′si krə tôr′ē, -tōr′ē) /ˈkɒnsɪkrəˌtɔriy, -ˌtowriy/ **con′se•cra′tive,** *adj.*

con•sec•u•tive (kən sek′yə tiv) /kənˈsɛkyətɪv/ *adj.* following one another in succession or order: *consecutive numbers such as 5, 6, 7, 8.* —**con•sec′u•tive•ly,** *adv.* —**con•sec′u•tive•ness,** *n.* [*noncount*] See -SEQ-.

con•sen•sus (kən sen′səs) /kənˈsɛnsəs/ *n., pl.* **-sus•es. 1.** [*count; often singular*] unanimous judgment or belief that a group comes to after discussion: *The consensus was that they should meet twice a month.* **2.** [*noncount*] general agreement; concord; harmony: *You won't find consensus among the doctors on the best procedure for you.* See -SENS-.

con•sent (kən sent′) /kənˈsɛnt/ *v.* **1.** to permit, approve, or agree (as to a wish): [*no obj*]: *We asked our parents for permission to use the boat, but they wouldn't consent.* [~ + *to* + *obj*]: *She consented to the plan.* [~ + *to* + *verb*]: *consented to marry him.* —*n.* [*noncount*] **2.** permission, approval, or agreement: *gave his consent to the marriage.* —**con•sent′er,** *n.* [*count*] See -SENS-.

con•se•quence (kon′si kwens′, -kwəns) /ˈkɒnsɪˌkwɛns, -kwəns/ *n.* **1.** [*count*] the effect, result, or outcome of something occurring earlier: *What will be the consequences of threatening him with military intervention?* **2.** [*noncount*] importance or significance: *a matter of no consequence.* —***Idiom.*** **3. in consequence,** [*noncount*] consequently; as a result; therefore: *In consequence, you'll have to be careful.* **4. take the consequences,** to suffer something unpleasant as a result of some other action, event, etc.: *If you don't pay your bills you'll have to take the consequences.* See -SEQ-.

con•se•quent (kon′si kwent′, -kwənt) /ˈkɒnsɪˌkwɛnt, -kwənt/ *adj.* [*before a noun*] following as an effect; resulting: *The recession has a consequent impact on jobs.* —**con′se•quent•ly,** *adv.* See -SEQ-.

con•se•quen•tial (kon′si kwen′shəl) /ˌkɒnsɪˈkwɛnʃəl/ *adj.* **1.** [*before a noun*] following as an effect or outcome: *the war and the consequential collapse of his dictatorship.* **2.** of importance: *a consequential sum of money.* —**con′se•quen′tial•ly,** *adv.* See -SEQ-.

con•ser•va•tion (kon′sər vā′shən) /ˌkɒnsərˈveyʃən/ *n.* [*noncount*] **1.** the controlled use of natural resources to preserve or protect them or to prevent waste: *fought for the conservation of our natural resources.* **2.** the protection, restoration, and preservation of works of art. —**con′ser•va′tion•al,** *adj.* See -SERV-².

con•ser•va•tion•ist (kon′sər vā′shə nist) /ˌkɒnsərˈveyʃənɪst/ *n.* [*count*] a person who calls for or promotes conservation, esp. of natural resources. See -SERV-².

con•serv•a•tism (kən sûr′və tiz′əm) /kənˈsɜrvəˌtɪzəm/ *n.* [*noncount*] **1.** the desire to preserve or restore what is established and to limit change. **2.** the principles and practices of political conservatives. See -SERV-².

con•serv•a•tive (kən sûr′və tiv) /kənˈsɜrvətɪv/ *adj.* **1.** of or relating to conservatism: *a conservative outlook on any changes to the curriculum.* **2.** cautiously moderate; safe: *A conservative estimate shows an increase in inflation to 9%.* **3.** traditional in style or manner: *Wear a conservative suit to your interview.* **4.** [*Conservative*] of or relating to a conservative political party, esp. the Conservative Party of Great Britain. **5.** of or relating to the principles of political conservatism: *believed the incumbent was not conservative enough.* **—n.** [*count*] **6.** a person who is conservative in principles, habits, etc. **7.** a supporter of conservative political policies. **8.** [*Conservative*] a member of a conservative political party, esp. the Conservative Party of Great Britain. **—con•serv′a•tive•ly,** *adv.* **—con•serv′a•tive•ness,** *n.* [*noncount*] See -SERV-[2].

con•serv•a•to•ry (kən sûr′və tôr′ē, -tōr′ē) /kən'sɜrvəˌtɔriy, -ˌtowriy/ *n.* [*count*], *pl.* **-ries. 1.** a school giving training in art, drama, or music, esp. a school of music. **2.** a building with a glass roof, for growing and displaying plants; greenhouse. See -SERV-[2].

con•serve (*v.* kən sûrv′; *n.* kon′sûrv, kən sûrv′) /*v.* kənˈsɜrv; *n.* ˈkɒnsɜrv, kənˈsɜrv/ *v.*, **-served, -serv•ing,** *n.* **—v.** [~ + *obj*] **1.** to prevent injury, waste, or loss of: *Conserve your strength for the race.* **2.** to use or manage (natural resources) wisely: *Conserve the environment.* **—n.** [*noncount*] **3.** a mixture of fruits cooked with sugar to a jamlike thickness. **—con•serv′a•ble,** *adj.* **—con•serv′er,** *n.* [*count*] See -SERV-[2].

con•sid•er (kən sid′ər) /kən'sɪdər/ *v.* **1.** to think carefully or seriously about; contemplate; ponder: [~ + *obj*]: *The committee is considering its next move.* [*no obj*]: *The salesman gave us no time to consider.* [~ + *verb-ing* (+ *obj*)]: *He considered taking a new job.* **2.** [*not: be* + *~-ing*] to think of or believe (something) to be a certain way; have an opinion about: [~ + *obj* (+ *as*) + *adjective*]: *I consider the matter (as) settled.* [~ + *obj* + *noun*]: *I consider him a first-rate mechanic.* **3.** [~ + *obj*] to bear in mind; make allowance for: *Her behavior was justified if you consider her reasons.* **4.** [~ + *obj*] to treat with thoughtfulness; show consideration for: *to consider other people's feelings.* **—Related Words.** CONSIDER is a verb, CONSIDERATE and CONSIDERABLE are adjectives, CONSIDERATION is a noun: *I consider him a friend. He is a considerate gentleman. They have considerable wealth. After some consideration, I decided to quit my job.*

con•sid•er•a•ble (kən sid′ər ə bəl) /kən'sɪdərəbəl/ *adj.* rather large or great; substantial: *a considerable length of time; a considerable fortune.* **—con•sid′er•a•bly,** *adv.*

con•sid•er•ate (kən sid′ər it) /kən'sɪdərɪt/ *adj.* showing kind regard for the feelings of others; thoughtful: *She's such a considerate person, always asking how I'm feeling.* **—con•sid′er•ate•ly,** *adv.* **—con•sid′er•ate•ness,** *n.* [*noncount*]

con•sid•er•a•tion (kən sid′ə rā′shən) /kənˌsɪdə'reyʃən/ *n.* **1.** [*noncount*] the act of considering: *We will give your application the consideration it deserves.* **2.** [*count*] something kept in mind in making a decision: *Age could not be a consideration in the hiring process.* **3.** [*noncount*] sympathetic respect; thoughtfulness: *showed consideration for others' feelings.* **4.** [*count*] a recompense or payment, as for work done; compensation. ***—Idiom.*** **5. in consideration of,** [*in* + ~ + *of* + *obj*] **a.** in view of: *In consideration of her fine work, they decided to give her a raise.* **b.** as payment for: *In consideration of the work, the publisher agrees to give the author 50 free books.* **6. of little** or **no consideration,** [*noncount*] of little or no importance: *Money was of no consideration here.* **7. take into consideration,** to consider; take into account: [*take* + *into* + ~ + *obj*]: *The judge took into consideration her past history before making a decision.* [*take* + *obj* + *into* + ~]: *took it into consideration.*

con•sid•ered (kən sid′ərd) /kən'sɪdərd/ *adj.* **1.** [*before a noun*] resulting from careful thought: *In her considered opinion, the accused was guilty of all charges.* **2.** [*after an adverb*] thought of in the specified way; judged: *Her work is well considered in most academic circles.*

con•sid•er•ing (kən sid′ər ing) /kən'sɪdərɪŋ/ *prep.* **1.** taking into account; in view of: *The campaign was a success, considering the lack of money.* **—adv. 2.** *Informal.* (used after a statement) with all facts or circumstances being considered: *He paints very well, considering (= He paints well, if you consider all the facts).* **—conj. 3.** (used before a clause): If one takes into consideration the fact that: *Considering they are newcomers, they've accomplished a lot.*

con•sign (kən sīn′) /kən'sayn/ *v.* [~ + *obj*] **1.** to hand over or deliver, esp. for sale: *to consign goods to a warehouse.* **2.** to transfer to another's custody or charge; entrust: *He was consigned to the care of a foster home.* **3.** [~ + *obj* + *to* + *obj*] to set (something) apart and away from oneself; banish: *Marxism was consigned to the rubbish heap of history.* **—con•sign′a•ble,** *adj.* See -SIGN-.

con•sign•ment (kən sīn′mənt) /kən'saynmənt/ *n.* **1.** [*noncount*] the act of consigning. **2.** [*count*] something consigned. ***—Idiom.*** **3. on consignment,** [*noncount*] (of goods) sent to an agent for sale, with the sender keeping ownership until a sale is made.

con•sist (kən sist′) / kən'sɪst / *v.* [*not: be* + *~-ing*] **1.** [~ + *of* + *obj*] to be made up, formed, or composed: *This cake consists mainly of sugar, flour, and butter.* **2.** [~ + *in* + *obj*] to be contained; have as a main part: *The charm of Paris does not consist only in its beauty.* See -SIST-.

con•sist•en•cy (kən sis′tən sē) /kən'sɪstənsiy/ also **con•sist′ence,** *n., pl.* **-en•cies** also **-enc•es. 1.** degree of density, firmness, etc.: [*noncount*]: *a liquid with the consistency of cream.* [*count*]: *The milkshakes come in different consistencies.* **2.** [*noncount*] the state of staying constantly with the same principles, direction, etc.: *He shows no consistency in his behavior.* **3.** [*noncount*] agreement, harmony, or uniformity among the parts of a complex thing.

con•sist•ent (kən sis′tənt) /kən'sɪstənt/ *adj.* of, relating to, or showing consistency: *took actions that were consistent with their views.* **—con•sist′ent•ly,** *adv.*: *He consistently opposed the war.*

con•so•la•tion (kon′sə lā′shən) /ˌkɒnsə'leyʃən/ *n.* **1.** [*noncount*] the act of consoling; the state of being consoled: *Write a letter of consolation to the widow.* **2.** someone or something that consoles: [*noncount*]: *It won't be much consolation, but you did win the lawsuit.* [*count*]: *I had one consolation: we still had our family together.* See -SOLA-.

con•sole[1] (kən sōl′) /kən'sowl/ *v.* [~ + *obj*], **-soled, -sol•ing.** to lessen the grief, sorrow, or disappointment of; give comfort to: *Nothing could console her after the death of her children.* **—con•sol′a•ble,** *adj.* **—con•sol′er,** *n.* [*count*] **—con•sol′ing•ly,** *adv.* See -SOLA-.

con•sole[2] (kon′sōl) /'kɒnsowl/ *n.* [*count*] **1.** a television, phonograph, or radio cabinet designed to stand on the floor. **2.** the control unit of a computer, including the keyboard and monitor. **3.** the control unit of a mechanical, electrical, or electronic system: *the console of a pipe organ.* **4.** a storage container mounted between bucket seats in an automobile.

con•sol•i•date (kən sol′i dāt′) /kən'sɒlɪˌdeyt/ *v.*, **-dat•ed, -dat•ing. 1.** to (cause to) unite; bring together (parts) into a single, larger form, organization, etc.: [*no obj*]: *The company consolidated.* [~ + *obj*]: *The company consolidated several divisions.* **2.** to (cause to) be made solid, firm, or secure: [~ + *obj*]: *The candidate moved to consolidate the gains he'd made in the primaries.* [*no obj*]: *The power had consolidated at the top of the party.* **—con•sol•i•da•tion** (kən sol′i dā′shən) /kənˌsɒlɪ'deyʃən/ *n.* [*noncount*]: *consolidation of political power in her hands.* **—con•sol′i•da′tor,** *n.* [*count*]

con•som•mé (kon′sə mā′) /ˌkɒnsə'mey/ *n.* a clear soup made from meat: [*count*]: *a beef consommé.* [*noncount*]: *Prepare consommé from leftover bones and meat.*

con•so•nance (kon′sə nəns) /'kɒnsənəns/ *n.* [*noncount*] **1.** accord or agreement. **2.** correspondence of sounds; harmony of sounds. **3.** a repetition of consonants, esp. those after a stressed vowel, as in *march, lurch,* but often of all the consonants, as in *stick, stuck.* Compare ALLITERATION (def. 1). See -SON-.

con•so•nant (kon′sə nənt) /'kɒnsənənt/ *n.* **1.** a speech sound produced by stopping or changing the flow of air from the lungs (opposed to *vowel*). **2.** a letter or other symbol representing a consonant sound. **—adj.** [*be* + ~ + *with*] **3.** in accord or agreement: *behavior that was consonant with his character.* See -SON-.

con•sort (*n.* kon′sôrt, *v.* kən sôrt′) /*n.* ˈkɒnsɔrt, *v.* kənˈsɔrt/ *n.* [*count*] **1.** a husband or wife, esp. of a king or queen. **—v.** [~ + *with* + *obj*] **2.** to associate; keep company: *to consort with criminals.* **—con•sort′er,** *n.* [*count*] See -SORT-.

con•sor•ti•um (kən sôr′shē əm, -tē-) /kən'sɔrʃiyəm, -tiy-/ *n.* [*count*], *pl.* **-ti•a** (-shē ə, -tē ə) /-ʃiyə, -tiyə/. **1.** a combination, as of corporations, for carrying out a business venture: *a consortium of banks.* **2.** an association; partnership: *a consortium of diverse interests.* See -SORT-.

con•spic•u•ous (kən spik′yo͞o əs) /kən'spɪkyuwəs/ *adj.* easily seen or noticed; striking: *an award for conspicuous bravery.* **—con•spic′u•ous•ly,** *adv.* **—con•spic′u•ous•ness, con•spi•cu•i•ty** (kon′spi kyo͞o′i tē) /ˌkɒnspɪ'kyuwɪtiy/ *n.* [*noncount*]

con•spir•a•cy (kən spir′ə sē) /kən'spɪrəsiy/ *n., pl.* **-cies. 1.** [*noncount*] the act of conspiring: *accused of conspiracy in the murder.* **2.** [*count*] a plan made in secret by two or more persons to commit an unlawful or treacherous act: *The conspiracy was to kill the president.* **3.** [*count*] a group of conspirators. —**con•spir′a•tive,** *adj.*

con•spir•a•tor (kən spir′ə tər) /kən'spayrətər/ *n.* [*count*] a person involved in a conspiracy. —**con•spir•a•to•ry** (kən spir′ə tôr′ē, -tōr′ē) /kən'spırə,tɔriy, -,towriy/ *adj.*

con•spir•a•to•ri•al (kən spir′ə tôr′ē əl, -tōr′-) /kən 'spayrə'tɔriyəl, -'towr-/ *adj.* **1.** of or relating to a conspiracy: *a conspiratorial plot.* **2.** acting or behaving as if involved in a conspiracy: *a conspiratorial wink.* —**con•spir′a•to′ri•al•ly,** *adv.*

con•spire (kən spīər′) /kən'spayər/ *v.,* **-spired, -spir•ing. 1.** to agree together, esp. secretly, to do something wrong, evil, or illegal: [*no obj; (~ + against + obj)*]: *They were conspiring against me.* [*~ + to + verb (+ obj)*]: *conspiring to overthrow the government.* **2.** to act or work together toward the same goal: [*~ + to + verb*]: *A number of events conspired to keep me from finishing the assignment.* [*~ + against + obj*]: *These events conspired against my finishing on time.* —**con•spir′er,** *n.* [*count*] —**con•spir′ing•ly,** *adv.* See -SPIR-.

const., an abbreviation of: **1.** constable. **2.** constant. **3.** construction.

con•sta•ble (kon′stə bəl) /'kɒnstəbəl/ *n.* [*count*] **1.** an officer of the peace in a town or township, having minor police and judicial functions. **2.** *Chiefly Brit.* POLICE OFFICER.

con•stab•u•lar•y (kən stab′yə ler′ē) /kən'stæbyə,lɛriy/ *n.* [*count*], *pl.* **-lar•ies.** the group of constables of a district.

con•stan•cy (kon′stən sē) /'kɒnstənsiy/ *n.* [*noncount*] **1.** the quality of staying constant. **2.** regularity; stability.

con•stant (kon′stənt) /'kɒnstənt/ *adj.* **1.** not changing; staying the same: *Driving at a constant speed saves gas.* **2.** continuing without pause; not stopping: *constant noise.* **3.** faithful, as in love, devotion, or loyalty: *a constant friend during all the turmoil.* —*n.* [*count*] **4.** something that does not change or vary: *The speed of light was postulated as a constant.* —**con′stant•ly,** *adv.* See -STAN-.

con•stel•la•tion (kon′stə lā′shən) /,kɒnstə'leyʃən/ *n.* [*count*] **1.** any of various groups of stars that have been named, such as the Big Dipper. **2.** a group of ideas, objects, etc., related in some way: *an illness with a constellation of symptoms.*

con•ster•na•tion (kon′stər nā′shən) /,kɒnstər'neyʃən/ *n.* [*noncount*] a sudden, alarming shock or fear that results in great confusion: *The crook had a look of complete consternation on her face when the police surrounded her.*

con•sti•pate (kon′stə pāt′) /'kɒnstə,peyt/ *v.* [*~ + obj*], **-pat•ed, -pat•ing.** to cause constipation in: *That food constipates the baby.* —**con′sti•pat′ed,** *adj.*: *The poor baby is badly constipated.*

con•sti•pa•tion (kon′stə pā′shən) /,kɒnstə'peyʃən/ *n.* [*noncount*] a condition of the bowels in which the feces are hardened and defecation is difficult.

con•stit•u•en•cy (kən stich′o͞o ən sē) /kən'stɪtʃuwənsiy/ *n.* [*count*], *pl.* **-cies. 1.** a body of constituents; the voters in an area who are represented by an elected official. **2.** the area itself. **3.** any body of supporters, customers, etc.; clientele: *That theory has its own constituency, made up mostly of young scientists.* See -STIT-.

con•stit•u•ent (kən stich′o͞o ənt) /kən'stɪtʃuwənt/ *adj.* [*before a noun*] **1.** serving to make up or form the basis of a thing: *the constituent parts of a motor.* —*n.* [*count*] **2.** an element, material, etc., that makes up a whole; component: *the constituents of an atom.* **3.** a person who authorizes another to act in his or her behalf, such as a voter in a district represented by an elected official: *The constituents of the district voted the councilwoman out of office.* —**con•stit′u•ent•ly,** *adv.* —**Syn.** See ELEMENT.

con•sti•tute (kon′sti to͞ot′, -tyo͞ot′) /'kɒnstɪ,tuwt, -,tyuwt/ *v.* [*~ + obj*], **-tut•ed, -tut•ing. 1.** [*not: be + ~-ing*] to form (something) from parts: *Carbohydrates and fats do not constitute a balanced diet.* **2.** [*not: be + ~-ing*] to be the same as: *Her behavior constitutes a direct threat to his power.* **3.** to appoint to an office or position: *He was constituted treasurer.* —**con′sti•tut′er, con′sti•tu′tor,** *n.* [*count*] See -STIT-.

con•sti•tu•tion (kon′sti to͞o′shən, -tyo͞o′-) /,kɒnstɪ'tuwʃən, -'tyuw-/ *n.* **1.** [*count; usually singular*] the way in which a thing is formed or arranged; makeup or composition of a thing: *the constitution of the members of the department.* **2.** [*count; usually singular*] the physical character of the body with regard to health, etc.: *He had a strong constitution and seldom caught a cold.* **3.** [*proper noun; the + Constitution*] the fundamental law of the U.S., put into effect in 1789. **4.** [*count*] the system of fundamental principles according to which something is governed: *the club's constitution and by-laws.* **5.** [*count*] the document in which these principles are written. See -STIT-.

con•sti•tu•tion•al (kon′sti to͞o′shə nl, -tyo͞o′-) /,kɒnstɪ'tuwʃənl, -'tyuw-/ *adj.* **1.** of, relating to, or concerned with the constitution of a state, organization, etc.: *a constitutional scholar.* **2.** [*before a noun*] provided by or in agreement with such a constitution: *a constitutional law.* **3.** belonging to or part of the character of a person: *They have a constitutional dislike for anyone who cannot speak their language perfectly.* —*n.* [*count*] **4.** a walk or other mild exercise taken for the benefit of one's health: *out in the woods for an evening constitutional.*

constr., an abbreviation of: construction.

con•strain (kən strān′) /kən'streyn/ *v.* [*~ + obj*] **1.** to make (someone) do something; compel: *He was constrained to admit the offense.* **2.** to hold back; repress or restrain: *He constrained his impulse to tell her the secret.* —**con•strain′a•ble,** *adj.* —**con•strain′er,** *n.* [*count*] —**con•strain′ing•ly,** *adv.* See -STRAIN-.

con•strained (kən strānd′) /kən'streynd/ *adj.* **1.** forced; awkward; stiff: *greeted the job candidate with a constrained smile.* **2.** [*be/feel + ~ + to + verb*] forced to do something; compelled: *felt constrained to donate some money.*

con•straint (kən strānt′) /kən'streynt/ *n.* **1.** [*count*] a limitation; something that restricts one's actions or powers: *There were so many constraints in my new position that I had more responsibility and less authority.* **2.** [*noncount*] the holding back or tight controlling of natural feelings and desires: *He kept his voice quiet with constraint and subdued his anger.* See -STRAIN-.

con•strict (kən strikt′) /kən'strɪkt/ *v.* **1.** to (cause to) be tight, narrower, or smaller; compress: [*no obj*]: *The blood vessels constricted immediately.* [*~ + obj*]: *This medicine will constrict the blood vessels.* **2.** [*~ + obj*] **a.** to limit or restrain (the actions of) someone: *The new constitution constricts the powers of the chairman.* **b.** to limit or restrain the actions or powers of (someone): *The regulations constrict the chairman in his duties.* —**con•stric′tive,** *adj.* See -STRICT-.

con•stric•tion (kən strik′shən) /kən'strɪkʃən/ *n.* **1.** [*noncount*] an act of constricting: *Constriction of his powers had a bad effect on the whole company.* **2.** [*count*] something that constricts: *constrictions on his ability to get things done.* **3.** [*count; usually singular*] a feeling of tightness or squeezing: *He was suffering from a constriction of the chest.* **4.** [*noncount*] the act of squeezing something: *The boa kills its prey by constriction.* See -STRICT-.

con•stric•tor (kən strik′tər) /kən'strɪktər/ *n.* [*count*] a snake that kills by squeezing its prey.

con•struct (*v.* kən strukt′; *n.* kon′strukt) /*v.* kən'strʌkt; *n.* 'kɒnstrʌkt/ *v.* [*~ + obj*] **1.** to build or form by putting together parts: *to construct a house from prefabricated parts.* —*n.* [*count*] **2.** something constructed or built. **3.** a product of thought: *a theoretical construct.* —**con•struc′tor, con•struct′er,** *n.* [*count*] See -STRU-.

con•struc•tion (kən struk′shən) /kən'strʌkʃən/ *n.* **1.** [*noncount*] the act, process, or art of constructing: *a building of solid construction.* **2.** [*count*] something constructed; structure: *What a complicated construction that table of yours is.* **3.** [*noncount*] the occupation or industry of building: *Can you make money in construction?* **4.** [*count*] an arrangement of two or more words, phrases, or sentences in a grammatical unit: *the past perfect construction.* See -STRU-.

con•struc•tion•ist (kən struk′shə nist) /kən'strʌkʃənɪst/ *n.* [*count*] a person who interprets laws or a constitution in a stated manner. —**con•struc′tion•ism,** *n.* [*noncount*]

con•struc•tive (kən struk′tiv) /kən'strʌktɪv/ *adj.* causing or leading to development; helping to improve: *constructive criticism.* —**con•struc′tive•ly,** *adv.* —**con•struc′tive•ness,** *n.* [*noncount*] See -STRU-.

con•strue (kən stro͞o′) /kən'struw/ *v.* [*~ + obj + as + obj*], **-strued, -stru•ing.** to explain the meaning of; interpret: *My comments were incorrectly construed as criticism.* —**con•stru•a•bil•i•ty** (kən stro͞o′ə bil′i tē) /kən,struwə'bɪlɪtiy/ *n.* [*noncount*] —**con•stru′a•ble,** *adj.* —**con•stru′al,** *n.* [*noncount*] —**con•stru′er,** *n.* [*count*] See -STRU-.

con•sul (kon′səl) /'kɒnsəl/ *n.* [*count*] **1.** an official appointed by the government of a country to look after its interests and the welfare of its citizens in another country. **2.** either of the two chief magistrates of the Roman republic. **—con′su•lar,** *adj.* **—con′sul•ship′,** *n.* [*noncount*]

con•su•late (kon′sə lit) /ˈkɒnsəlɪt/ *n.* [*count*] **1.** the place officially occupied by a consul. **2.** the position, authority, or term of service of a consul.

con•sult (kən sult′) /kənˈsʌlt/ *v.* **1.** to seek guidance or information from: [~ + *obj*]: *Be sure to consult a lawyer.* [~ + *with* + *obj*]: *Be sure to consult with a lawyer before you do anything.* **2.** [~ + *obj*] to refer to (a book, etc.) for information: *to consult a dictionary.* **3.** [*no obj*] to give professional or expert advice; serve or work as a consultant. **—Syn.** CONSULT, CONFER imply talking over a situation or a subject with someone. To CONSULT is to seek advice, opinions, or guidance from a qualified person or source: *to consult with a financial analyst.* To CONFER is to exchange views, ideas, or information in a discussion: *The partners conferred about the decline in sales.*

con•sult•ant (kən sul′tnt) /kənˈsʌltnt/ *n.* [*count*] a person who gives professional or expert advice: *The company hired a board of consultants.* **—con•sult′an•cy,** *n.* [*noncount*]

con•sul•ta•tion (kon′səl tā′shən) /ˌkɒnsəlˈteyʃən/ *n.* **1.** the act of consulting or of being consulted; discussion: [*count*]: *After consultations with the carpenter, we redesigned the kitchen.* [*noncount*]: *The famous detective was called in for consultation on the case.* **2.** [*count*] a meeting, as between a doctor and patient, in which specific problems are discussed.

con•sul•ta•tive (kən sul′tə tiv) /kənˈsʌltətɪv/ *adj.* [*before a noun*] of or for consulting; advisory: *a consultative committee.*

con•sume (kən so͞om′) /kənˈsuwm/ *v.,* **-sumed, -sum•ing. 1.** [~ + *obj*] to use up; expend: *The minivan consumes a lot of gas.* **2.** [~ + *obj*] to eat or drink up; devour: *consumed several six-packs of beer.* **3.** [~ + *obj*] to destroy, as by burning: *Fire consumed the forest.* **4.** [~ + *obj*] to keep the interest of; engross: *I was consumed with curiosity.* **5.** [*no obj*] to use or use up consumer goods: *If consumers don't consume, then workers won't work.* See -SUM-.

con•sum•er (kən so͞o′mər) /kənˈsuwmər/ *n.* [*count*] **1.** a person or thing that consumes. **2.** (in economics) a person or organization that buys something or uses a service: *Have consumers lost confidence in the economy?* **—con•sum′er•ship′,** *n.* [*noncount*]

con•sum•er•ism (kən so͞o′mə riz′əm) /kənˈsuwməˌrɪzəm/ *n.* [*noncount*] **1.** a movement for the protection of the consumer against defective products, etc.: *The rise of consumerism has led to increased awareness of false advertising.* **2.** too much emphasis on the consumption of goods. **—con•sum′er•ist,** *n.* [*count*], *adj.*

con•sum•mate (*v.* kon′sə māt′; *adj.* kən sum′it, kon′sə mit) /*v.* ˈkɒnsəˌmeyt; *adj.* kənˈsʌmɪt, ˈkɒnsəmɪt/ *v.,* **-mat•ed, -mat•ing,** *adj.* **—***v.* [~ + *obj*] **1.** to bring to a state of perfection; fulfill: *Her joy was consummated by winning the gold medal in the Olympics.* **2.** to bring to a state of completion, such as a business agreement; complete: *At last we were able to consummate the deal.* **3.** to complete (the union of a marriage) by the first marital sexual intercourse. **—***adj.* [*before a noun*] **4.** complete or perfect; supremely skilled; superb: *She was a consummate master of the violin.* **5.** of the highest or most extreme degree; utter: *It was a work of consummate skill.* **—con•sum′mate•ly,** *adv.* **—con•sum•ma•tion** (kon′səmā′shən) /ˌkɒnsəˈmeyʃən/ *n.* [*noncount; count*] **—con′sum•ma′tor,** *n.* [*count*] **—con•sum•ma•to•ry** (kənsum′ə tôr′ē, -tōr′ē) /kənˈsʌməˌtɔriy, -ˌtowriy/ *adj.*

con•sump•tion (kən sump′shən) /kənˈsʌmpʃən/ *n.* [*noncount*] **1.** the act of consuming. **2.** the amount consumed: *the high consumption of gasoline.* **3.** the using up of goods and services: *Conspicuous consumption is the public display of the expensive goods that one can afford to buy.* **4.** *Older Use.* tuberculosis of the lungs. See -SUM-.

con•sump•tive (kən sump′tiv) /kənˈsʌmptɪv/ *adj.* **1.** suffering from or affected with consumption. **—***n.* [*count*] **2.** *Older Use.* a person suffering from tuberculosis. See -SUM-.

cont., an abbreviation of: **1.** containing. **2.** contents. **3.** continent. **4.** continental. **5.** continue. **6.** continued. **7.** contract. **8.** contraction.

con•tact (kon′takt) /ˈkɒntækt/ *n.* **1.** [*noncount*] the act or state of touching or of being near enough to touch: *The rear wheels lost contact with the road.* **2.** [*noncount*] the act or state of being in communication: *The pilot of the plane lost contact with the control tower.* [*in* + ~]: *still in contact with my high school friends.* **3.** [*count*] a person who can gain access to favors, influential people, etc.: *had a contact down at city hall.* **4.** [*count*] a part of an electric circuit that joins electric conductors, used for completing or interrupting a circuit: *The reason for the power failure was that some contacts were worn and failed to complete a circuit.* **5.** [*count*] contact lens: *She wears contacts.* **—***v.* [~ + *obj*] **6.** to communicate with; get in touch with; reach: *We'll contact you by phone.* **—con′tact•ee′,** *n.* [*count*] **—con•tac•tu•al** (kon tak′cho͞o əl) /kɒnˈtæktʃuwəl/ *adj.* See -TACT-.

con′tact lens′, *n.* [*count*] either of a pair of small plastic disks that stay in place on the eye by surface tension and are designed to correct vision defects.

con•ta•gion (kən tā′jən) /kənˈteydʒən/ *n.* **1.** [*noncount*] the spread of disease by contact: *In an effort to slow contagion the authorities isolated from the public anyone suspected of having the disease.* **2.** [*count*] a disease so communicated. **3.** [*noncount*] the quick spread of an idea, etc., among a group: *affected by the contagion of hysteria sweeping the country.* See -TACT-.

con•ta•gious (kən tā′jəs) /kənˈteydʒəs/ *adj.* **1.** (of a disease) able to be spread by bodily contact with an infected person or object: *contagious meningitis.* **2.** (of a person) carrying or spreading a contagious disease: *Don't come near me; I'm still contagious.* **3.** tending to spread from person to person: *contagious laughter.* **—con•ta′gious•ly,** *adv.* **—con•ta′gious•ness,** *n.* [*noncount*]

con•tain (kən tān′) /kənˈteyn/ *v.* [~ + *obj*] **1.** [*not: be* + ~*-ing*] to hold or include within its volume or area: *This glass contains water.* **2.** [*not: be* + ~*-ing*] to have as contents or parts; include: *That food contains some dangerous chemicals.* **3.** [*not: be* + ~*-ing*] to be capable of holding; have capacity for: *The bottle contained only a quart.* **4.** [*not: be* + ~*-ing*] to be equal to: *A quart contains two pints.* **5.** to keep under proper control; restrain: *He could not contain his amusement.* **6.** to prevent or hold back the advance, spread, or influence of: *worked night and day to contain the epidemic.* **—con•tain′a•ble,** *adj.* See -TAIN-. **—Syn.** CONTAIN, HOLD, and ACCOMMODATE express the idea that something is designed in such a way that something else can exist or be placed within it. CONTAIN refers to what is actually within a certain container. HOLD emphasizes the idea of keeping something within bounds; it refers also to the greatest amount or number that can be kept within a given container. ACCOMMODATE means to contain comfortably or conveniently, or to meet the needs of a certain number. A plane that ACCOMMODATES fifty passengers may be able to HOLD sixty, but at a given time may CONTAIN only thirty. See -TAIN-.

con•tain•er (kən tā′nər) /kənˈteynər/ *n.* [*count*] **1.** anything that contains or can contain something, as a carton. **2.** a large, reusable box for keeping together smaller crates or cartons in a single shipment: *The ships unloaded the containers and the dock workers removed the crates from inside them.*

con•tain•er•i•za•tion (kən tā′nər ə zā′shən) /kənˌteynərəˈzeyʃən/ *n.* [*noncount*] a method of shipping freight in similar, sealed, movable containers whose contents do not have to be unloaded at each point of transfer.

con•tain•er•ize (kən tā′nə rīz′) /kənˈteynəˌrayz/ *v.* [~ + *obj*], **-ized, -iz•ing. 1.** to package by containerization. **2.** to ship in containers.

con•tain•ment (kən tān′mənt) /kənˈteynmənt/ *n.* [*noncount*] the policy of holding back the spread of another country's power or influence.

con•tam•i•nant (kən tam′ə nənt) /kənˈtæmənənt/ *n.* [*count*] something that contaminates: *Somehow contaminants had gotten into the town's supply of drinking water.*

con•tam•i•nate (kən tam′ə nāt′) /kənˈtæməˌneyt/ *v.* [~ + *obj*], **-nat•ed, -nat•ing. 1.** to make impure, harmful, or unusable by contact or mixture with something unclean; pollute; taint: *The oil spill contaminated the sea.* **2.** to make (something) harmful by the addition of radioactive material: *After the nuclear power plant accident, crops were badly contaminated in the area.* **—con•tam•i•na•ble** (kən tam′ə nə bəl) /kənˈtæmənəbəl/ *adj.* **—con•tam′i•nat′ed,** *adj.: contaminated water supplies.* **—con•tam•i•na•tion** (kən tam′ə nā′shən) /kənˌtæməˈneyʃən/ *n.* [*noncount*]: *trying to prevent contamination of our water supplies.* **—con•tam′i•na′tor,** *n.* [*count*]

contd., an abbreviation of: continued.

con•tem•plate (kon′təm plāt′) /ˈkɒntəmˌpleyt/ *v.* [~ + *obj*], **-plat•ed, -plat•ing. 1.** to look at with continued attention; observe thoughtfully: *The new students contem-*

plated each other nervously. **2.** to consider thoroughly; think about fully or deeply: *contemplated the problem before he announced his decision.* **3.** to have in view as a purpose; intend: *to contemplate bribery.* [~ + *verb-ing*]: *We contemplated buying a new car next year.* **—con′tem•pla′tor,** *n.* [*count*]

con•tem•pla•tion (kon′təm plā′shən) /ˌkɒntəm'pleyʃən/ *n.* [*noncount*] **1.** the act of contemplating: *The child resumed her contemplation of the squirrels outside her window.* **2.** the act of thinking deeply or fully about something: *After a great deal of contemplation, he announced his decision.*

con•tem•pla•tive (kən tem′plə tiv, kon′təm plā′tiv) /kən'tɛmplətɪv, 'kɒntəmˌpleytɪv/ *adj.* thoughtful; thinking deeply or fully: *the contemplative tone of his speeches.*

con•tem•po•ra•ne•ous (kən tem′pə rā′nē əs) /kənˌtɛmpə'reyniyəs/ *adj.* living or occurring during the same period of time. **—con•tem′po•ra′ne•ous•ly,** *adv.* **—con•tem′po•ra′ne•ous•ness,** *n.* [*noncount*] See -TEMP-.

con•tem•po•rar•y (kən tem′pə rer′ē) /kən'tɛmpəˌrɛriy/ *adj., n., pl.* **-rar•ies.** **—***adj.* [*before a noun*] **1.** existing, occurring, or living at the same time: *Hitler was contemporary with Mussolini.* **2.** of the present time; modern: *contemporary architecture.* **—***n.* [*count*] **3.** a person or thing belonging to the same time or period with another: *Hemingway and Fitzgerald were contemporaries.* **4.** a person of the same age as another; *a teenager and her contemporaries.* **—con•tem•po•rar•i•ly** (kən tem′pə-rer′ə lē) /kənˌtɛmpə'rɛrəliy/ *adv.* **—con•tem′po•rar′i•ness,** *n.* [*noncount*] See -TEMP-.

con•tempt (kən tempt′) /kən'tɛmpt/ *n.* [*noncount*] **1.** a lack of respect; scorn; disregard: *She gave me a look of pure contempt.* [*in* + ~]: *He was held in contempt by his profession.* **2.** deliberate disobedience to, or open disrespect for, the rules or orders of a court or legislative body: *charged with contempt of court.* **—Syn.** CONTEMPT, DISDAIN, SCORN imply strong feelings of disapproval and dislike toward what seems worthless. CONTEMPT is disapproval with disgust: *to feel contempt for a weakling.* DISDAIN is a feeling that a person or thing is beneath one's dignity and unworthy of one's notice, respect, or concern: *a disdain for crooked dealing; a disdain for common people.* SCORN carries with it the meaning of open or undisguised contempt often combined with mocking or ridiculing: *He showed only scorn for those who were not as ambitious as himself.*

con•tempt•i•ble (kən temp′tə bəl) /kən'tɛmptəbəl/ *adj.* worthy of, or held in, contempt. **—con•tempt•i•bil•i•ty** (kən temp′tə bil′i tē) /kənˌtɛmptə'bɪlɪtiy/ **con•tempt′i•ble•ness,** *n.* [*noncount*] **—con•tempt′i•bly,** *adv.* **—Usage.** See CONTEMPTUOUS.

con•temp•tu•ous (kən temp′cho͞o əs) /kən'tɛmptʃuwəs/ *adj.* showing or expressing contempt; scornful: *contemptuous of those below him.* **—con•temp′tu•ous•ly,** *adv.* **—con•temp′tu•ous•ness,** *n.* [*noncount*] **—Usage.** CONTEMPTUOUS refers to a person or thing that *shows* contempt: *a contemptuous look (= the look on the face shows the person's contempt).* CONTEMPTIBLE refers to the act or deed that is bad and dishonorable and that deserves our contempt: *contemptible cowardice (= cowardice that deserves our contempt).*

con•tend (kən tend′) /kən'tɛnd/ *v.* **1.** to struggle in competition; compete: [~ + *for* + *obj*]: *to contend for first prize.* [~ + *against/with* + *obj*]: *She contended against the opposition.* **2.** [~ + *that clause*] to declare; assert or say earnestly; claim: *She contended that taxes were too high.* **—con•tend′er,** *n.* [*count*]: *He was a contender for the heavyweight crown.* See -TEND-.

con•tent[1] (kon′tent) /'kɒntɛnt/ *n.* **1.** [*count*] Usually, **contents.** [*plural*] **a.** something contained: *The contents of the box rattled after I dropped it.* **b.** the topics covered in a book or document. **c.** the chapters of a book or document: *a table of contents.* **2.** [*noncount*] something expressed; meaning; substance: *It's a clever play but it lacks content.* **3.** the amount of a substance contained: [*noncount*]: *high calcium content.* [*count; usually singular*]: *Those fruits have a high content of vitamin C.* See -TEN-.

con•tent[2] (kən tent′) /kən'tɛnt/ *adj.* [*be* + ~] **1.** satisfied with what one is or has; contented: *He was content and settled back to enjoy his life.* **2.** willing or resigned, as to do or accept something: *He was not content with my answer, so I added a few more remarks.* [~ + *to* + *verb*]: *was content to let the matter drop.* **—***v.* [~ + *obj*] **3.** to make content: *These pleasures did not content me any longer.* **—***n.* [*noncount*] **4.** the state or feeling of being contented: *To her great content, the kids had cleaned up their rooms.* **—con•tent′ly,** *adv.* **—con•tent′ness,** *n.* [*noncount*] See -TEN-.

con•tent•ed (kən ten′tid) /kən'tɛntɪd/ *adj.* satisfied; content. **—con•tent′ed•ly,** *adv.*: *Sighing contentedly, she lay down for a nap.* **—con•tent′ed•ness,** *n.* [*noncount*]

con•ten•tion (kən ten′shən) /kən'tɛnʃən/ *n.* **1.** [*noncount*] a struggling in opposition; conflict: *This is a bad time for contention, just before the wedding.* **2.** [*noncount; often: noun* + *of* + ~] disagreement in debate; dispute: *The main point of contention was the school budget.* **3.** [*count*] an argument one puts forward; opinion or belief: *It's my contention that we must consolidate our businesses.* **—*Idiom.*** **4. be in contention,** [*noncount*] to be competing, as for a job, etc.: *He's in contention for the position of manager.* **—con•ten′tious,** *adj.* See -TEN-.

con•tent•ment (kən tent′mənt) /kən'tɛntmənt/ *n.* [*noncount*] the state of being contented; satisfaction: *a smile of pure contentment.*

con•test (*n.* kon′test; *v.* kən test′) /*n.* 'kɒntɛst; *v.* kən'tɛst/ *n.* [*count*] **1. a.** a competition between rivals: *She won the beauty contest.* **b.** a struggle for victory: *a bitter contest of wills.* **—***v.* [~ + *obj*] **2.** to struggle or fight for, as in battle, etc.: *They were contesting the 10th district Congressional seat.* **3.** to argue against; dispute: *to contest a will.* **4.** to object to; challenge: *They contested his right to speak.* **—con•test′a•ble,** *adj.* **—con•test′a•ble•ness,** *n.* [*noncount*] **—con•test′a•bly,** *adv.* **—con•test′er,** *n.* [*count*] See -TEST-.

con•test•ant (kən tes′tənt) /kən'tɛstənt/ *n.* [*count*] a person who takes part in a contest or competition: *All the contestants are winners in the Olympics.*

con•text (kon′tekst) /'kɒntɛkst/ *n.* **1.** the parts of a statement that come before or follow a word or passage and influence its meaning or effect: [*count*]: *They tried to guess from the context what the message meant.* [*noncount*]: *What he said was taken out of context and was completely misunderstood.* **2.** [*count*] the facts that surround a particular event, etc.: *We need to understand the whole context of the struggle in the Middle East.* **—con•text•u•al** (kən teks′cho͞o əl) /kən'tɛkstʃuwəl/ *adj.*: *contextual circumstances.*

con•tig•u•ous (kən tig′yo͞o əs) /kən'tɪgyuwəs/ *adj.* **1. a.** touching; in contact. **b.** being close without touching; near. **2.** adjacent in time: *contiguous events.* **—con•tig′u•ous•ly,** *adv.* **—con•tig′u•ous•ness,** *n.* [*noncount*] See -TACT-.

con•ti•nent (kon′tn ənt) /'kɒntṇənt/ *n.* **1.** [*count*] one of the seven main masses of land on the earth: Europe, Asia, Africa, North America, South America, Australia, and Antarctica. **2. the Continent,** [*proper noun; the* + ~] the mainland of Europe, as distinguished from the British Isles. See -TEN-.

con•ti•nen•tal (kon′tn en′tl) /ˌkɒntṇ'ɛntḷ/ *adj.* **1.** [*before a noun*] of, coming from, or typical of a continent: *a continental climate.* **2.** [*often: before a noun; usually: Continental*] of or relating to the mainland of Europe, to Europeans, or to European customs and attitudes: *Continental Europe has seen too many modern wars.* **3.** [*often: before a noun; Continental*] of or relating to the 13 American colonies during and immediately after the American Revolution. **4.** [*before a noun*] of or relating to the continent of North America: *Postage is free within the continental U.S.* **—***n.* [*count*] **5.** [*Continental*] a soldier in the American army during the American Revolution. **6.** [*usually: Continental*] a person living in the mainland of Europe. **—con′ti•nen′tal•ly,** *adv.*

con′ti•nen′tal break′fast, *n.* a light breakfast served in hotels: [*count*]: *a continental breakfast of buttered toast and coffee.* [*noncount*]: *a room with continental breakfast included.*

con′tinen′tal drift′, *n.* [*noncount*] the sideways movement of continents resulting from the motion of the earth's crust.

con′tinen′tal shelf′, *n.* [*count*] the part of a continent that is under water in shallow seas.

con•tin•gen•cy (kən tin′jən sē) /kən'tɪndʒənsiy/ *n.* [*count*], *pl.* **-cies.** a chance or possibility that might occur: *They were prepared with a plan for every contingency.*

con•tin•gent (kən tin′jənt) /kən'tɪndʒənt/ *adj.* [*be* + ~ + *on*] **1.** dependent on something else; conditional: *The plans for an outdoor wedding were contingent on the weather.* **—***n.* [*count*] **2.** a group of soldiers, ships, etc., assembled to help a larger force: *His contingent was sent to Saudi Arabia.* **3.** any one of the groups that make up a larger group: *The gay and lesbian contingent of the parade was finally allowed to march.* —**con•tin′gent•ly,** *adv.*

con•tin•u•al (kən tin′yo͞o əl) /kən'tɪnyuwəl/ *adj.* **1.** happening regularly or frequently: *continual bus departures.* **2.** happening without much interruption: *the continual rain all through April and May.* —**con•tin′u•al•ly,** *adv.* —**Usage.** Use CONTINUAL for actions that are repeated frequently or occur over and over again (especially actions that are annoying): *The dog's continual barking was driving me nuts.* The word CONTINUOUS is used for actions that keep going and do not stop: *The world of that novel was one long continuous war, between Eastasia and Oceania, or Eurasia and Oceania, it never mattered which.*

con•tin•u•ance (kən tin′yo͞o əns) /kən'tɪnyuwəns/ *n.* **1.** [*noncount*] the fact of continuing. **2.** [*count*] adjournment of a legal proceeding to a future day: *The judge granted a continuance to give the lawyer time to prepare her defense.*

con•tin•u•a•tion (kən tin′yo͞o ā′shən) /kən,tɪnyuw'eyʃən/ *n.* **1.** [*noncount*] the act of continuing or the state of being continued: *continuation of the same tired old policies.* **2.** [*count*] something that continues a preceding thing by being of the same or a similar kind: *A continuation of the old series will be broadcast on Channel 13 next year.*

con•tin•ue (kən tin′yo͞o) /kən'tɪnyuw/ *v.,* **-ued, -u•ing. 1.** to (cause to) go on without interruption, as in some course or action: [*no obj*]: *The road continues for three miles.* [~ + *obj*]: *The army continued the battle for another three weeks.* **2.** to (cause to) go on after interrupting; resume: [*no obj*]: *He continued with his work after dinner.* [~ + *obj*]: *He continued his work after dinner.* **3.** to (cause to) last long or endure: [*no obj*]: *The strike continued for two months.* [~ + *obj*]: *The union voted to continue the strike for two months.* **4.** [*no obj;* ~ + *as* + *noun*] to remain in a particular state, position, etc.: *He agreed to continue as commander.* **5.** to keep on with; persist (in): [~ + *verb-ing*]: *She sat up and continued reading.* [~ + *to* + *verb*]: *She sat up and continued to read.* **6.** [*used with quotations*] to keep talking from the point of stopping or being interrupted: *"Pay no attention to the man behind the curtain," he continued.* —**Related Words.** CONTINUE is a verb, CONTINUOUS is an adjective, CONTINUITY is a noun: *I continued to try harder. There was a continuous line of cars on the road. There was no continuity at work because the rules were always changing.* —**Syn.** CONTINUE, ENDURE, PERSIST, LAST all have the meaning "existing without interruption for some lengthy period of time." CONTINUE implies going on or existing without a break or an interruption: *The rain continued for two days.* ENDURE, used of people or things, implies steady continuing despite influences that tend to weaken, get in the way, or destroy: *The temple has endured for centuries.* PERSIST implies an ability to go on longer than expected while facing opposition: *to persist in an unpopular belief.* LAST implies remaining in good condition or having an adequate supply: *I hope the liquor lasts until the end of the party.*

con•ti•nu•i•ty (kon′tn o͞o′i tē, - yo͞o′-) /,kɒntn̩'uwɪtiy, -'yuw-/ *n.* [*noncount*] **1.** the state or quality of being smoothly continuous and uninterrupted: *The U.S. has enjoyed political continuity since the Civil War.* **2.** the condition in a motion-picture scene in which all details of the action, speaking, effects, etc., follow one another smoothly: *The scene had fluidity and continuity.*

con•tin•u•ous (kən tin′yo͞o əs) /kən'tɪnyuwəs/ *adj.* **1.** [*before a noun*] uninterrupted in time; without stopping: *continuous noise during the movie.* **2.** [*before a noun*] being in immediate connection in space: *one continuous line of dancers.* **3.** PROGRESSIVE (def. 7).: *Some verbs, like* contain, *don't take the continuous tense for all meanings.* —**con•tin′u•ous•ly,** *adv.* —**con•tin′u•ous•ness,** *n.* [*noncount*] —**Usage.** See CONTINUAL.

con•tin•u•um (kən tin′yo͞o əm) /kən'tɪnyuwəm/ *n.* [*count*], *pl.* **-tin•u•a** (-tin′yo͞o ə) /-'tɪnyuwə/. a continuous extent, series, or number of things together as a whole, but with no noticeable division into parts: *the space-time continuum.*

con•tort (kən tôrt′) /kən'tɔrt/ *v.* to (cause to) become twisted, bent, or strained: [*no obj*]: *His face contorted with rage.* [~ + *obj*]: *Anger contorted his face.* See -TORT-.

con•tor•tion (kən tôr′shən) /kən'tɔrʃən/ *n.* **1.** [*noncount*] the act or process of contorting or the state of being contorted. **2.** [*count*] an example of twisting or contorting: *The contortions some people put their bodies through on those exercise machines, just to get in shape!*

con•tor•tion•ist (kən tôr′shə nist) /kən'tɔrʃənɪst/ *n.* [*count*] a person who performs gymnastic feats involving contorted positions. —**con•tor′tion•is′tic,** *adj.*

con•tour (kon′to͝or) /'kɒntʊr/ *n.* [*count*] **1.** the outline of a figure or body: *That chair is comfortable because it follows the contour of the body.* **2.** CONTOUR LINE. —*v.* [~ + *obj*] **3.** to mold or shape so as to fit a certain form: *The airplane seats were carefully contoured for maximum comfort.* —*adj.* [*before a noun*] **4.** shaped to fit a particular form: *contour sheets for a mattress.* **5.** of or relating to a system of plowing and cultivating hilly land along the natural contours of the slopes to prevent the runoff of water and soil erosion.

con′tour line′, *n.* [*count*] a line on a map that represents the location of points at the same elevation: *saw from the contour lines that we had several hundred more feet to climb.*

contr., an abbreviation of: **1.** contract. **2.** contraction. **3.** control. **4.** controller.

contra-, *prefix. contra-* comes from Latin, where it has the meaning "against, opposite, opposing." This meaning is found in such words as: CONTRABAND, CONTRACEPTION, CONTRADICT, CONTRARY.

con•tra•band (kon′trə band′) /'kɒntrə,bænd/ *n.* [*noncount*] **1.** anything prohibited by law from being imported or exported; goods imported or exported illegally. —*adj.* [*before a noun*] **2.** prohibited from export or import: *contraband furs.*

con•tra•cep•tion (kon′trə sep′shən) /,kɒntrə'sɛpʃən/ *n.* [*noncount*] the prevention of pregnancy by various drugs, techniques, or devices; birth control. See -CEP-.

con•tract (*n., adj., and usually for v. 8* kon′trakt; *otherwise v.* kən trakt′) /*n., adj., and usually for v. 8* 'kɒntrækt; *otherwise v.* kən'trækt/ *n.* **1.** an agreement between two or more parties for the doing or not doing of something specified, or the written form of such an agreement: [*count*]: *The ballplayer signed another multimillion-dollar contract.* [*noncount; often: under* + ~]: *I'm under contract to finish the work by June of next year.* **2.** [*count*] *Slang.* an arrangement for a hired assassin to kill a specific person: *They had a contract out on the rival mobster.* —*adj.* [*before a noun*] **3.** under contract; arranged by special contract: *a contract freight carrier.* —*v.* **4.** to draw together or (cause to) be smaller; draw the parts (of) together: [*no obj*]: *Her pupils contracted in the bright light.* [~ + *obj*]: *The nerves fire and contract the muscle.* **5.** [~ + *obj*] to shorten (a word, etc.) by combining or omitting some of its elements: *The word* will *is contracted to* 'll *in the word* she'll. **6.** [~ + *obj*] to get (an illness), as by exposure to something contagious: *Several children contracted Lyme disease.* **7.** [~ + *obj*] to get (a debt) as an obligation; incur: *to contract a debt.* **8.** to enter into an agreement with (someone), as to do work by formal contract: [~ + *obj*]: *We contracted outside workers who would do the job.* [~ + *with* + *obj*]: *We contracted with nonunion workers to do the job.* [~ + *to* + *verb*]: *We contracted to do the job.* [~ + *obj* + *to* + *verb*]: *We contracted a freelancer to do the work.* —**con′tract•ee′,** *n.* [*count*] —**con•tract′i•ble,** *adj.* —**con•trac•tile** (kən trak′tl) /kən'træktl̩/ *adj.* See -TRAC-.

con•trac•tion (kən trak′shən) /kən'trækʃən/ *n.* **1.** [*count*] an act or instance of contracting: *a contraction of about two inches in the cold weather.* **2.** [*noncount*] the quality or state of being contracted: *the problem of contraction in the cold.* **3.** [*count*] a shortened form of a word or group of words, with the letters that were left out often replaced in written English by an apostrophe, such as *isn't* for *is not, they're* for *they are,* or *e'er* for *ever.* **4.** [*noncount*] a decrease in economic and industrial activity (opposed to *expansion*): *Another six months of contraction and we'll have a real recession on our hands.* See -TRAC-. —**Usage.** Contractions *(isn't, couldn't, can't, he'll)* occur chiefly, although not exclusively, in informal speech and writing. They are common in personal letters, business letters, journalism, and fiction; rare in scientific and scholarly writing. See -TRAC-.

con•trac•tor (kon′trak tər, kən trak′tər) /'kɒntræktər, kən'træktər/ *n.* [*count*] **1.** a person who enters into a contract to provide supplies or perform work at a certain price, esp. in construction. **2.** something that contracts, esp. a muscle.

con•trac•tu•al (kən trak′cho͞o əl) /kən'træktʃuwəl/ *adj.* [*before a noun*] being, including, or in the form of a written or agreed contract: *They have a contractual agreement to sell the product.*

con•tra•dict (kon′trə dikt′) /ˌkɒntrə'dɪkt/ *v.* [∼ + *obj*] **1.** to say the opposite of: *She always contradicted me.* **2.** to imply that the opposite of (something) is true: *His despicable way of life contradicts his lofty stated principles.* —**con′tra•dict′a•ble,** *adj.* —**con′tra•dict′er, con′tra•dic′tor,** *n.* [*count*] See -DICT-.

con•tra•dic•tion (kon′trə dik′shən) /ˌkɒntrə'dɪkʃən/ *n.* **1.** [*noncount; often: in* + ∼ + *to* + *obj*] the act or fact of contradicting: *This is in complete contradiction to what you said before.* **2.** [*count*] something that contradicts: *Saying that someone is fat and also skinny seems to be a contradiction.* See -DICT-.

con•tra•dic•to•ry (kon′trə dik′tə rē) /ˌkɒntrə'dɪktə riy/ *adj.* involving contradiction; opposing or inconsistent: *contradictory opinions.*

con•tra•in•di•cate (kon′trə in′di kāt′) /ˌkɒntrə'ɪndɪˌkeyt/ *v.* [∼ + *obj*], **-cat•ed, -cat•ing.** to make (a medical procedure, etc.) something to be advised against: *That problem of congestion in the lungs contraindicates the use of anesthesia.* —**con•tra•in•di•ca•tion** (kon′trə in′di kā′shən) /ˌkɒntrəˌɪndɪ'keyʃən/ *n.* [*count*]

con•tral•to (kən tral′tō) /kən'træltow/ *n.* [*count*], *pl.* **-tos. 1.** the lowest female voice or voice part. **2.** a singer with a contralto voice.

con•trap•tion (kən trap′shən) /kən'træpʃən/ *n.* [*count*] an odd or strange-looking machine: *That contraption looks like a sewing machine hooked up to a bicycle.*

con•tra•pun•tal (kon′trə pun′tl) /ˌkɒntrə'pʌntl̩/ *adj.* [*before a noun*] **1.** of, relating to, or involving musical counterpoint. **2.** made up of two or more relatively independent melodies sounded together. —**con′tra•pun′tal•ly,** *adv.*

con•trar•i•wise (kon′trer ē wīz′) /'kɒntrɛriyˌwayz/ *adv.* **1.** in the opposite direction or way. **2.** on the contrary; in direct opposition.

con•trar•y (kon′trer ē; *for 3 also* kən trâr′ē) /'kɒntrɛriy; *for 3 also* kən'trɛəriy/ *adj., n., pl.* **-ies,** *prep.* —*adj.* **1.** opposite in nature or character; opposed: *Those opinions are contrary to fact.* **2.** [*sometimes: after a noun*] opposite in desired direction; unfavorable: *contrary winds.* **3.** unreasonable; constantly disagreeing; stubbornly opposed: *Many two-year-olds enjoy being contrary.* —*n.* [*count*] **4.** something contrary or opposite; either of two contrary things. —*prep.* **5. contrary to,** [∼ + *to* + *obj*] in opposition; in an opposite manner or way; counter: *to act contrary to one's principles.* —***Idiom.* 6. on the contrary,** [*noncount*] (used after some other statement) in opposition to what has been stated: *"You'll be home at five." "On the contrary, I'll be lucky to get home by ten."* **7. to the contrary,** [*noncount*] to the opposite effect: *I do care, whatever you may say to the contrary.* —**con•trar•i•ly** (kon′trer ə lē, kən trâr′-) /'kɒntrɛrəliy, kən'trɛər-/ *adv.* —**con′trar•i•ness,** *n.* [*noncount*]

con•trast (*v.* kən trast′, kon′trast; *n.* kon′trast) /*v.* kən'træst, 'kɒntræst; *n.* 'kɒntræst/ *v.* **1.** [∼ + *obj* + *and/with* + *obj*] to compare in order to show differences: *In the essay you have to contrast your hometown's transportation system with that of a big city system.* **2.** [∼ + *with* + *obj*] to form a contrast: *The singer's soothing voice contrasts with her wild appearance.* —*n.* **3.** [*noncount; often: in* + ∼ + *with*] the act of contrasting or the state of being contrasted: *In contrast with your views, the president believes just the opposite.* **4.** [*count*] a striking difference between two things: *a big contrast in views between the two opponents.* **5.** [*count*] a person or thing that is strikingly unlike another in comparison: *a great contrast between the first candidate and the second.* —**con•trast′ing•ly,** *adv.*

con•tra•vene (kon′trə vēn′) /ˌkɒntrə'viyn/ *v.* [∼ + *obj*], **-vened, -ven•ing. 1.** to come or be in conflict with; oppose: *to contravene a statement.* **2.** to act against; violate: *contravened the law of the tribe.* See -VEN-.

con•tre•temps (kon′trə tän′) /'kɒntrəˌtɑ̃/ *n.* [*count*], *pl.* **-temps** (-tänz′) /-ˌtɑ̃z/. an embarrassing accident or disagreement. See -TEMP-.

contrib., an abbreviation of: **1.** contribution. **2.** contributor.

con•trib•ute (kən trib′yo͞ot) /kən'trɪbyuwt/ *v.,* **-ut•ed, -ut•ing. 1.** to give (money, etc.) with others, as to a common fund: [*no obj*]: *Can you contribute toward the present we're getting him?* [∼ + *obj*]: *What can you contribute to help the poor?* **2.** to provide (an article, etc.) for publication: [*no obj*]: *Our editor contributes regularly to that magazine.* [∼ + *obj*]: *My wife contributes poetry to that journal.* —***Idiom.* 3. contribute to,** [∼ + *to* + *obj*] to be an important factor in; lead to: *asserted that smoking contributes to cancer.* —**con•trib′u•tive,** *adj.* —**con•trib′u•tive•ly,** *adv.* —**con•trib′u•tor,** *n.* [*count*] —**con•trib•u•to•ry** (kən trib′yə tôr′ē, -tōr′ē) /kən'trɪbyəˌtɔriy, -ˌtowriy/ *adj.* [*before a noun*]

con•tri•bu•tion (kon′trə byo͞o′shən) /ˌkɒntrə'byuwʃən/ *n.* **1.** [*noncount*] the act of contributing. **2.** [*count*] something contributed: *made several contributions to the meeting.* **3.** [*count*] a piece of writing or a drawing provided for publication: *This issue features contributions from two of the most respected scientists in the world.*

con•trite (kən trīt′, kon′trīt) /kən'trayt, 'kɒntrayt/ *adj.* filled with, or showing, a sense of guilt and the desire to make up for some wrongdoing: *a contrite sinner.* —**con•trite′ly,** *adv.* —**con•trite′ness,** *n.* [*noncount*]

con•triv•ance (kən trī′vəns) /kən'trayvəns/ *n.* **1.** [*count*] something contrived, esp. a mechanical device: *The strange contrivance actually worked and people began to trust it.* **2.** [*noncount*] the act or manner of contriving: *His life of contrivance finally caught up with him when he tried to trick the same person twice.* **3.** [*count*] a plan or scheme: *The challenger's pledge was just a contrivance to get elected.*

con•trive (kən trīv′) /kən'trayv/ *v.,* **-trived, -triv•ing. 1.** [∼ + *obj*] to plan with great cleverness; figure out; invent: *They managed to contrive a means of escape.* **2.** [∼ + *to* + *verb*] to bring about by a plan, scheme, etc.; find a way to do something, esp. by scheming: *He contrived to gain their votes.* —**con•triv′er,** *n.* [*count*]

con•trived (kən trīvd′) /kən'trayvd/ *adj.* **1.** planned: *Her supposedly chance and accidental meeting with me was actually a contrived one.* **2.** awkward, unnatural, and forced: *The way you ended your essay was a bit contrived.*

con•trol (kən trōl′) /kən'trowl/ *v.,* **-trolled, -trol•ling,** *n.* —*v.* [∼ + *obj*] **1.** to regulate, govern, or command; manage: *The pilot controlled the plane from the cockpit.* **2.** to hold (something) in check; hold (something) back: *to control one's emotions.* **3.** to prevent the spread of: *The firefighters worked to control the forest fire.* —*n.* **4.** [*noncount*] the act or power of controlling: *Who has control over the newspaper now?* **5.** [*noncount*] check or restraint: *My anger was under control.* **6.** [*count*] a person who acts as a check; controller. **7. controls,** [*plural*] an arrangement of devices, such as switches, for regulating or directing the operation of a machine: *The controls are easy to understand and within easy reach of the driver.* —***Idiom.* 8. at the controls,** in charge of; managing; directing: *Is anyone at the controls at headquarters?* —**con•trol′la•ble,** *adj.*: *At this point the problem is still controllable.* —**con•trol′la•bly,** *adv.* —**con•trol′ling,** *adj.* [*before a noun*]: *has a controlling interest in the company.*

con•trol•ler (kən trō′lər) /kən'trowlər/ *n.* [*count*] **1.** a government official or an officer of a business firm in charge of financial accounts and transactions; comptroller: *The state controller decided that contributions to the pension fund would stop.* **2.** a person who regulates or restrains. **3.** a regulating mechanism; governor. —**con•trol′ler•ship′,** *n.* [*noncount*]

con•tro•ver•sial (kon′trə vûr′shəl, -sē əl) /ˌkɒntrə'vɜrʃəl, -siyəl/ *adj.* **1.** of, characterized by, or subject to controversy: *a controversial decision to give the rapist probation and not a jail term.* **2.** enjoying controversy; eager to engage in controversy: *a controversial figure in politics.* —**con′tro•ver′sial•ly,** *adv.* See -VERT-.

con•tro•ver•sy (kon′trə vûr′sē) /'kɒntrəˌvɜrsiy/ *n., pl.* **-sies.** a fierce and long public dispute concerning a matter of opinion; argument: [*count*]: *A new controversy arose regarding the politician's finances.* [*noncount*]: *Everywhere he went, in everything he did, he created controversy.* See -VERT-.

con•tuse (kən to͞oz′, -tyo͞oz′) /kən'tuwz, -'tyuwz/ *v.* [∼ + *obj*], **-tused, -tus•ing.** to injure (tissue), esp. without breaking the skin; bruise. —**con•tu•sive** (kən -to͞o′siv, -tyo͞o′-) /kən-'tuwsɪv, -'tyuw-/ *adj.*

con•tu•sion (kən to͞o′zhən, -tyo͞o′-) /kən'tuwʒən, -'tyuw-/ *n.* [*count*] an injury to the skin but without breaking the skin; bruise: *escaped from the accident with only a few contusions.*

co•nun•drum (kə nun′drəm) /kə'nʌndrəm/ *n.* [*count*] **1.** a riddle whose answer involves a pun. **2.** anything that puzzles.

con•ur•ba•tion (kon′ər bā′shən) /ˌkɒnər'beyʃən/ *n.* [*count*] a large urban area, resulting from the expansion of several cities into each other: *The different towns in the conurbation maintained their separate identities.* See -URB-.

con•va•lesce (kon′və les′) /ˌkɒnvə'lɛs/ *v.* [*no obj*],

-lesced, -lesc•ing. to recover health and strength after illness: *He needed a few weeks to convalesce at home.*

con•va•les•cence (kon′və les′əns) /ˌkɒnvəˈlɛsəns/ *n.* **1.** [*noncount*] an act or instance of convalescing: *Get plenty of rest during convalescence.* **2.** [*count*] the amount of time needed for convalescing: *a convalescence of only a couple of weeks.*

con•va•les•cent (kon′və les′ənt) /ˌkɒnvəˈlɛsənt/ *n.* [*count*] **1.** a person who is convalescing. *—adj.* [*before a noun*] **2.** of or relating to convalescence: *convalescent leave.*

con•vec•tion (kən vek′shən) /kənˈvɛkʃən/ *n.* [*noncount*] the transfer of heat by the circulation of heated liquid or gas: *Does a room's radiator get its heat by convection?* —**con•vec′tion•al,** *adj.*

con•vene (kən vēn′) /kənˈviyn/ *v.,* **-vened, -ven•ing.** to (cause to) assemble or come together for a meeting: [*no obj*]: *The meeting convened at 3:00 p.m.* [~ + *obj*]: *The chair convened the meeting at 3:00 p.m.* —**con•ven′a•ble,** *adj.* —**con•ven′er, con•ve′nor,** *n.* [*count*] See -VEN-.

con•ven•ience (kən vēn′yəns) /kənˈviynyəns/ *n.* **1.** [*noncount*] the quality of being convenient: *For convenience, let's refer to this book as "the dictionary" instead of using its full name.* **2.** [*count*] anything, such as an appliance, that saves or simplifies work: *Your apartment will have all the modern conveniences.* **3.** [*noncount*] a convenient situation or time: *Please schedule a meeting at your earliest convenience (= as soon as possible).* **4.** [*noncount*] advantage or accommodation; comfort: *Shopping bags are for the customers' convenience.* **5.** [*count*] *Chiefly Brit.* lavatory. *—adj.* [*before a noun*] **6.** [*sometimes used before other words to form adjectives that refer to easy use of the thing named*] easy to obtain, use, or reach; made for convenience: *convenience-size packages of food; convenience foods.* See -VEN-.

con•ven•ient (kən vēn′yənt) /kənˈviynyənt/ *adj.* **1.** suitable or agreeable to the purpose; useful; helpful: *Public transportation is very convenient.* **2.** near or at hand; easily reached; accessible: *The new homes are convenient to all transportation.* **3.** [*before a noun*] happening to be near and useful at a particular moment: *They sat down on a convenient ledge and looked out over the sea.* —**con•ven′ient•ly,** *adv.: conveniently located only minutes from the train station.* See -VEN-. —**Related Words.** CONVENIENT is an adjective, CONVENIENTLY is an adverb, CONVENIENCE is a noun: *The store is very convenient because it is right down the street. The store is conveniently located right down the street. Modern conveniences like running water and electricity were like magic to them.*

con•vent (kon′vent, -vənt) /ˈkɒnvɛnt, -vənt/ *n.* [*count*] **1.** a community of people, esp. nuns, devoted to religious life under a superior. **2.** the building or buildings occupied by such a community. See -VEN-.

con•ven•tion (kən ven′shən) /kənˈvɛnʃən/ *n.* **1.** [*count*] a formal meeting to discuss matters of concern: *a convention of lawyers.* **2.** [*count*] an assembly of delegates of a political party to nominate candidates and adopt party rules and decisions: *the Democratic convention.* **3.** [*count*] a practice established by usage; custom: *It is a mapmaker's convention to show north at the top of a map.* **4.** [*noncount*] general agreement; accepted usage, esp. of procedure: *The youth of the sixties were fighting against convention.* See -VEN-.

con•ven•tion•al (kən ven′shə nl) /kənˈvɛnʃənl̩/ *adj.* **1.** conforming to or following accepted standards: *conventional behavior.* **2.** [*usually: before a noun*] of or relating to accepted usage; traditional: *conventional symbols in physics for various quantities, like "c" for the speed of light.* **3.** ordinary rather than original: *conventional and boring writing.* **4.** [*before a noun*] not using nuclear weapons or energy; nonnuclear: *conventional warfare.* —**con•ven′tion•al•ly,** *adv.* See -VEN-.

con•ven•tion•eer (kən ven′shə nēr′) /kənˌvɛnʃəˈnɪər/ *n.* [*count*] a person who participates in a convention.

con•verge (kən vûrj′) /kənˈvɜrdʒ/ *v.,* **-verged, -verg•ing.** **1.** to tend to meet at a point: [*no obj*]: *The train lines converge in this one small area.* [~ + *obj*]: *The lens converges the light rays to this one point.* **2.** [~ + *on* + *obj*] to rush together in one place; gather all at once: *The reporters converged on the star as she stepped out of the limousine.* **3.** [*no obj*] to develop toward a common result: *Our political views, at first widely different, later began to converge.* —**con•ver′gence,** *n.* [*count*]: *a convergence of opinions.* [*noncount*]: *societies facing cultural convergence as worldwide communication expands.* —**con•ver′gent,** *adj.*: *convergent views.* See -VERG-.

con•ver•sant (kən vûr′sənt, kon′vər-) /kənˈvɜrsənt, ˈkɒnvər-/ *adj.* [*be* + ~ + *with* + *obj*] familiar with something by use or study; knowledgeable: *conversant with Spanish history.* —**con•ver′sance, con•ver′san•cy,** *n.* [*noncount*] See -VERT-.

con•ver•sa•tion (kon′vər sā′shən) /ˌkɒnvərˈseyʃən/ *n.* **1.** [*noncount*] informal talk; oral communication between people: *hadn't mastered the art of conversation at cocktail parties.* **2.** [*count*] an instance of this: *long conversations on the phone.* See -VERT-.

con•ver•sa•tion•al (kon′vər sā′shən əl) /ˌkɒnvərˈseyʃənəl/ *adj.* [*before a noun*] of or relating to conversation or a conversation: *It's a conversational convention not to interrupt someone telling a joke.* —**con′ver•sa′tion•al•ly,** *adv.* See -VERT-. —**Syn.** See COLLOQUIAL.

con•ver•sa•tion•al•ist (kon′vər sā′shə nl ist) /ˌkɒnvərˈseyʃənl̩ɪst/ *n.* [*count*] a person who enjoys and contributes to good conversation.

conversa′tion piece′, *n.* [*count*] any object that arouses comment because of some striking quality.

con•verse[1] (kən vûrs′) /kənˈvɜrs/ *v.* [*no obj; often:* ~ + *with* + *obj*], **-versed, -vers•ing.** to engage in conversation: *They were seen conversing for a few minutes and then leaving together.* See -VERT-.

con•verse[2] (*adj.* kən vûrs′, kon′vûrs; *n.* kon′vûrs) /*adj.* kənˈvɜrs, ˈkɒnvɜrs; *n.* ˈkɒnvɜrs/ *adj.* [*before a noun*] **1.** opposite or contrary in direction, action, sequence, etc.; turned around: *They hold converse views on the matter of abortion.* *—n.* [*count; singular; often: the* + ~] **2.** something opposite or contrary: *You say we'll win but I believe the converse is true.* —**con•verse′ly,** *adv.* See -VERT-.

con•ver•sion (kən vûr′zhən, -shən) /kənˈvɜrʒən, -ʃən/ *n.* **1.** [*noncount*] the act or process of converting or the state of being converted: *chemical conversion.* **2.** change from one belief, etc., to another: [*count*]: *a political conversion from one party to another.* [*noncount*]: *People doubt the sincerity of his conversion to supply-side economics.* **3.** [*noncount*] a change of one kind of component for another: *conversion from oil heat to gas heat.* **4.** [*count*] the making of an additional score in football or basketball. See -VERT-.

con•vert (*v.* kən vûrt′; *n.* kon′vûrt) /*v.* kənˈvɜrt; *n.* ˈkɒnvɜrt/ *v.* **1.** to change into something of different form or properties; transform: [~ + *obj*]: *Electricity is converted into heat to warm the room.* [*no obj*]: *The agent's pen converts to a radio receiver and transmitter.* **2.** to (cause to) adopt a different belief, etc.: [*no obj*]: *My Methodist father converted when he married my Catholic mother.* [~ + *to* + *obj*]: *He converted to Judaism.* [~ + *obj (+ to + obj)*]: *St. Patrick converted Ireland to Christianity.* **3.** [~ + *obj* + *(in)to* + *obj*] to turn to another use or purpose: *They wanted to convert the study into a nursery.* **4.** [~ + *obj* + *(in)to* + *obj*] to obtain an equivalent value for in an exchange or calculation, such as money or units of measurement: *to convert yards into meters; to convert French francs to American dollars.* **5.** [~ + *obj* + *(in)to* + *obj*] to cause (a substance) to undergo a chemical change: *to convert sugar into alcohol.* **6.** [*no obj*] to make a conversion in football or basketball. *—n.* [*count*] **7.** a person who has been converted. See -VERT-.

con•ver•ter (kən vûr′tər) /kənˈvɜrtər/ *n.* [*count*] a device for converting something to another form: *We needed a converter in Europe to run our American tape recorder because the electric current is different there.*

con•vert•i•ble (kən vûr′tə bəl) /kənˈvɜrtəbəl/ *adj.* **1.** capable of being converted: *This piece is convertible to a lawn chair or a chaise longue.* **2.** having a folding top, such as an automobile. **3.** exchangeable for something of equal value: *a convertible currency.* **4.** having a seat that folds out for use as a bed: *a convertible sofa.* *—n.* [*count*] **5.** an automobile or boat with a folding top. **6.** a convertible sofa. —**con•vert•i•bil•i•ty** (kən vûr′tə bil′i tē) /kənˌvɜrtəˈbɪlɪtiy/ *n.* [*noncount*]

con•vex (kon veks′) /kɒnˈvɛks/ *adj.* curved or rounded outward like the outside of a circle or sphere. Compare CONCAVE. —**con•vex′ly,** *adv.*

con•vey (kən vā′) /kənˈvey/ *v.* [~ + *obj*] **1.** to take from one place to another; transport: *They conveyed the cargo to the battlefront.* **2.** to communicate; tell; make known: *to convey a message.* **3.** to lead or conduct, such as a channel or medium; transmit: *to convey electric power from a generating station.* —**con•vey′a•ble,** *adj.* —**con•vey′or, con•vey′er,** *n.* [*count*]

con•vey•ance (kən vā′əns) /kən'veyəns/ *n.* **1.** [*noncount*] the act of conveying: *the conveyance of a message.* **2.** [*count*] a means of transporting, esp. a vehicle.

convey′or belt′, *n.* [*count*] a continuous belt or chain for carrying materials or objects short distances.

con•vict (*v.* kən vikt′; *n.* kon′vikt) /*v.* kən'vɪkt; *n.* 'kɒnvɪkt/ *v.* **1.** to prove or declare (someone) guilty of an offense, esp. after a legal trial: [~ + *obj*]: *The defendant was convicted and sent to jail.* [~ + *obj* + *of* + *obj*]: *The jury convicted him of murder.* **—***n.* [*count*] **2.** a person found guilty of a crime and serving a sentence in prison. See -VICT-.

con•vic•tion (kən vik′shən) /kən'vɪkʃən/ *n.* **1. a.** [*noncount*] firm belief: *He spoke with conviction and sincerity.* **b.** [*count*] a fixed or firm belief: *He has no convictions, so he'll do anything for money.* **2. a.** [*count*] the declaration, as by a jury, that someone is guilty of breaking the law or committing a crime. **b.** [*noncount*] the sentence one must serve for being declared guilty: *conviction was for five years.*

con•vince (kən vins′) /kən'vɪns/ *v.*, **-vinced, -vinc•ing. 1.** to cause (someone) to believe in, or agree to, something by using argument: [~ + *obj* + *of* + *obj*]: *The prosecutor could not convince the jurors of the defendant's guilt.* [~ + *obj* + *(that) clause*]: *could not convince the jurors that the defendant was guilty.* **2.** [~ + *obj* + *to* + *verb*] to persuade; coax: *We finally convinced them to stay.* **—con•vinc′er,** *n.* [*count*] **—con•vinc•i•bil•i•ty** (kən vin′sə bil′i tē) /kən,vɪnsə'bɪlɪtiy/ *n.* [*noncount*] **—con•vin′ci•ble,** *adj.* See -VINC-.

con•vinced (kən vinst′) /kən'vɪnst/ *adj.* **1.** [*be* + ~ + *of* + *obj*] made certain by persuasion: *She was convinced of my innocence.* **2.** [*before a noun*] believing in something fully or completely: *a convinced atheist.* **—con•vinc•ed•ly** (kən vin′sid lē) /kən'vɪnsɪdliy/ *adv.*

con•vin•cing (kən vin′sing) /kən'vɪnsɪŋ/ *adj.* [*sometimes: after a noun*] causing belief in or acceptance of something: *a convincing performance as Lady Macbeth.* **—con•vin′cing•ly,** *adv.: She argued convincingly for money for education.*

con•viv•i•al (kən viv′ē əl) /kən'vɪviyəl/ *adj.* **1.** friendly; agreeable: *a convivial atmosphere.* **2.** fond of feasting and company; jovial: *convivial guests.* **—con•viv•i•al•i•ty** (kən viv′ē al′i tē) /kən,vɪviy'ælɪtiy/ *n.* [*noncount*] **—con•viv′i•al•ly,** *adv.* See -VIV-.

con•vo•ca•tion (kon′və kā′shən) /,kɒnvə'keyʃən/ *n.* **1.** [*noncount*] the act of convoking. **2.** [*count*] a group of people called together: *The school year began with a general convocation in the auditorium.* **—con′vo•ca′tion•al,** *adj.* See -VOC-.

con•voke (kən vōk′) /kən'vowk/ *v.* [~ + *obj*], **-voked, -vok•ing.** to call together; summon to meet or assemble: *The Vice-President can convoke the full Senate.* **—con•vok′er,** *n.* [*count*] See -VOC-.

con•vo•lut•ed (kon′və lo͞o′tid) /'kɒnvə,luwtɪd/ *adj.* **1.** of or marked by convolutions: *a convoluted pattern of leaves and flowers.* **2.** very involved; difficult to understand: *convoluted answers to simple questions.* **—con′vo•lut′ed•ness,** *n.* [*noncount*]

con•vo•lu•tion (kon′və lo͞o′shən) /,kɒnvə'luwʃən/ *n.* [*count*] **1.** a single turn of anything that coils or is coiled; whorl. **2.** the act of rolling or coiling together. **—con′vo•lu′tion•al, con•vo•lu•tion•ar•y** (kon′və lo͞o′shə ner′ē) /,kɒnvə'luwʃə,nɛriy/ *adj.*

con•voy (kon′voi; *v. also* kən voi′) /'kɒnvɔy; *v. also* kən'vɔy/ *n.* [*count*] **1.** a fleet of ships traveling with an escort. **2.** a group of vehicles traveling together, esp. for protection. **—***v.* [~ + *obj*] **3.** to accompany or escort (ships, etc.), for protection: *The Navy convoyed the merchant ships across the Atlantic.*

con•vulse (kən vuls′) /kən'vʌls/ *v.*, **-vulsed, -vuls•ing. 1.** [~ + *obj*] to shake violently; agitate: *The civil war convulsed the country.* **2.** [~ + *obj*] to cause to shake violently with emotion: *convulsed with laughter.* **3.** to (cause to) suffer violent, sudden movements of the muscles: [*no obj*]: *He fell to the subway floor and began to convulse.* [~ + *obj*]: *The cold convulsed the patient's muscles.* **—con•vul′sive,** *adj.*

con•vul•sion (kən vul′shən) /kən'vʌlʃən/ *n.* **1.** [*count*] an act or instance of convulsing: *Her disease caused her to suffer convulsions.* **2.** [*noncount*] violent agitation or disturbance: *The country was thrown into a state of convulsion.* **3.** [*count*] an outburst of laughter.

co•ny or **co•ney** (kō′nē, kun′ē) /'kowniy, 'kʌniy/ *n.* [*count*], *pl.* **-nies.** a rabbit.

coo (ko͞o) /kuw/ *v.*, **cooed, coo•ing,** *n.* **—***v.* **1.** to make or imitate the soft, murmuring sound of doves: [*no obj*]: *the baby cooing quietly in the bassinet.* [~ + *obj*]: *cooing a quiet tune.* **—***n.* [*count*] **2.** a cooing sound.

cook (ko͝ok) /kʊk/ *v.* **1.** to prepare (food) by heat: [~ + *obj*]: *Who's going to cook dinner tonight?* [*no obj*]: *I don't feel like cooking.* **2.** [*no obj*] (of food) to undergo cooking: *The rice is cooking.* **3.** [~ + *obj*] *Informal.* to make (accounts) false by changing in a dishonest way: *The accountant tried to cook the books.* **4.** [*no obj*] *Informal.* to take place or develop: *What's cooking around here—anything happening?* **5.** [*no obj*] *Slang.* to perform or do something extremely well or with energy and style: *The band is really cooking tonight.* **6. cook up,** [~ + *up* + *obj*] *Informal.* to make up (an excuse, etc.) in order to deceive: *What new scheme are you cooking up this time?* **—***n.* [*count*] **7.** a person who cooks.

cook•book (ko͝ok′bo͝ok′) /'kʊk,bʊk/ *n.* [*count*] a book containing recipes for cooking food.

cook•er•y (ko͝ok′ə rē) /'kʊkəriy/ *n.*, *pl.* **-ies. 1.** [*noncount*]the art of cooking. **2.** [*count*] a kitchen.

cook•ie or **cook•y** (ko͝ok′ē) /'kʊkiy/ *n.* [*count*], *pl.* **-ies. 1.** a small, flat, sweetened cake made from dough and baked on a pan: *a plate of chocolate chip cookies.* **2.** *Slang.* **a.** a person: *He's a smart cookie; he won't get caught by the cops.* **b.** *Sometimes Offensive.* an alluring woman. ***—Idiom.* 3. that's the way the cookie crumbles,** (used after a description of an event to imply that things normally occur this way and nothing more can be done): *"The train was late again." "Well, that's the way the cookie crumbles."* **4. toss** or **spill one's cookies,** *Slang.* to vomit.

cook•ing (ko͝ok′ing) /'kʊkɪŋ/ *n.* [*noncount*] **1.** the act or practice of preparing food: *She took a class in cooking.* **2.** the food so prepared: *She loves Japanese cooking.* **—***adj.* [*before a noun*] **3.** specially made for cooking: *two tablespoons of cooking sherry.*

cook•out (ko͝ok′out′) /'kʊk,awt/ *n.* [*count*] **1.** an outdoor party at which food is cooked and eaten. **2.** a meal cooked and eaten in the open.

cool (ko͞ol) /kuwl/ *adj.*, **-er, -est,** *adv.*, *n.*, *v.* **—***adj.* **1.** somewhat cold; neither warm nor cold: *a cool room.* **2.** giving a feeling of coolness: *a cool breeze.* **3.** providing relief from heat: *a cool dress; a cool drink.* **4.** not excited; calm: *cool in the face of disaster.* **5.** not hasty; deliberate: *a cool and calculated action.* **6.** lacking in interest, friendliness, or enthusiasm: *a cool reply to an invitation.* **7.** [*before a noun or number*] *Informal.* not exaggerated; exactly so: *demanding a cool million dollars to release the hostages.* **8.** *Slang.* **a.** great; excellent: *What a cool play that was!* **b.** socially acceptable, right, or proper: *It's not cool to arrive at a party too early.* **—***adv.* **9.** *Informal.* in a cool manner; coolly: *Play it cool.* **—***n.* [*noncount*] **10.** a cool part, place, or time: *in the cool of the evening.* **11.** [*often: one's* +~] calmness; composure; poise: *Keep your cool and don't get angry.* **—***v.* **12.** to (cause to) become cool: [*no obj*]: *The cake cooled on the plate.* [~ + *off*]: *We cooled off with a quick swim.* [~ + *obj*]: *The air conditioner cooled the room adequately.* [~ + *obj* + *off*]: *The swim in the river cooled us off.* [~ + *off* + *obj*]: *They cooled off the horse by pouring water on its back.* **13.** to (cause to) become less excited, friendly, interested, or cordial: [*no obj*]: *She cooled visibly when I invited her to my house.* [~ + *obj*]: *Disappointment cooled whatever enthusiasm she might have had.* ***—Idiom.* 14. cool down, a.** to (cause to) become cooler: [*no obj*]: *The feverish child just wouldn't cool down.* [~ + *obj* + *down*]: *They tried cold washcloths to cool her down.* [~ + *down* + *obj*]: *to cool down the patients.* **b.** to (cause to) become less angry or excited; (cause to) become calm: [*no obj*]: *She finally cooled down enough to talk about the fight.* [~ + *obj* + *down*]: *I took him aside and cooled him down before he did anything crazy.* **15. cool it,** [*no obj*] *Slang.* calm down: *Cool it before you say something you'll be sorry for.* **—cool′ly,** *adv.* **—cool′ness,** *n.* [*noncount*] **—Syn.** See CALM.

cool•ant (ko͞o′lənt) /'kuwlənt/ *n.* a substance used to reduce the temperature of a system below a certain value: [*count*]: *coolants made from alcohol mixtures.* [*noncount*]: *Coolant had spilled over the engine.*

cool•er (ko͞o′lər) /'kuwlər/ *n.* [*count*] **1.** a container for keeping something cool: *The cooler was loaded with soda.* **2.** water cooler: *People stood around the cooler chatting.* **3.** [*usually: the* + ~] *Slang.* jail.

coo•lie (ko͞o′lē) /'kuwliy/ *n.* [*count*], *pl.* **-lies.** a worker or laborer hired at very low wages for unskilled work, esp. formerly in the Far East.

coon (ko͞on) /kuwn/ *n.* [*count*] **1.** raccoon. **2.** *Slang* (*disparaging and offensive*). a black person.

co-op (kō′op) /ˈkowɒp/ *n.* [*count*] a cooperative business, building, or apartment: *The apartment building is now a co-op.*

coop (ko͞op, ko͝op) /kuwp, kʊp/ *n.* [*count*] **1.** a cage in which poultry are penned. **2.** *Slang.* prison. **—***v.* [~ + *obj*] **3.** to place in or as if in a coop: *The parents had cooped the children in the attic all day.* [~ + *up* + *obj*]: *They cooped up the chickens in the barn.* [~ + *obj* + *up*]: *They cooped me up in this tiny cell.* **—*Idiom.* 4. fly the coop,** to leave or depart abruptly: *The police were too late; the crooks had flown the coop.*

co•op•er•ate or **co-op•er•ate** (kō op′ə rāt′) /kowˈɒpəˌreyt/ *v.*, **-at•ed, -at•ing.** [*no obj; sometimes:* ~ + *with* + *obj*] to work together for a common purpose: *The New York City police cooperated with the force in Boston in catching the crook.* **—co•op•er•a•tion** (kō op′ə rā′shən), /kowˌɒpəˈreyʃən/, *n.* [*noncount*]: *Cooperation between Scotland Yard and the FBI couldn't have been better.* **—co•op′er•a′tor,** *n.* [*count*] See -OPER-. **—Related Words.** COOPERATE is a verb, COOPERATIVE is an adjective, COOPERATION is a noun: *He cooperates with his fellow workers. She is very cooperative at work. There wasn't much cooperation between the two departments.*

co•op•er•a•tive or **co-op•er•a•tive** (kō op′ər ə tiv, -op′rə tiv, -op′ə rā′tiv) /kowˈɒpərətɪv, -ˈɒprətɪv, -ˈɒpəˌreytɪv/ *adj.* **1.** [*often: before a noun*] of, relating to, or showing cooperation: *joint, cooperative military exercises.* **2.** relating to economic cooperation: *a cooperative business.* **—***n.* [*count*] **3.** a jointly owned business operated by its members for their own benefit: *an agricultural cooperative.* **4.** Also called **co-op, coop′erative apart′ment. a.** a building owned and managed by a corporation in which shares are sold that entitle the shareholders to occupy individual units in the building. **b.** an apartment in such a building. Compare CONDOMINIUM. **—co•op′er•a•tive•ly,** *adv.* **—co•op′er•a′tive•ness,** *n.* [*noncount*]

co-opt (kō opt′) /kowˈɒpt/ *v.* [~ + *obj*] **1.** to elect as a member: *They co-opted him for the board.* **2.** to take as one's own; preempt: *The party co-opted the small group as part of its larger organization.* See -OPT-.

co•or•di•nate or **co-or•di•nate** (*adj.*, *n.* kō ôr′dn it, -āt′; *v.* kō ôr′dn āt′) /*adj.*, *n.* kowˈɔrdn̩ɪt, -ˌeyt; *v.* kowˈɔrdn̩ˌeyt/ *adj.*, *n.*, *v.*, **-nat•ed, -nat•ing. —***adj.* **1.** of the same degree; equal in importance. **2.** of the same grammatical rank in a construction, as *Jack* and *Jill* in the phrase *Jack and Jill,* or *got up* and *shook hands* in the sentence *He got up and shook hands.* See COORDINATING CONJUNCTION. **—***n.* [*count*] **3.** *Math.* any of the numbers, or pairs of numbers, that point to the position of a point or line by reference to a fixed figure, system of lines, etc.: *You feed the coordinates of the target into the computer and it fires the torpedo.* **4. coordinates,** [*plural*] articles, as of clothing, that harmonize in color, material, or style. **—***v.* [~ + *obj*] **5.** to arrange the parts of (an organization, activity, etc.) in proper position or sequence; manage the elements of: *She coordinated the relief efforts in the Sudan.* **6.** to make the parts of (the body) work together correctly or smoothly: *The children suffering from that brain disease could not coordinate their movements.* **—co•or′di•nate•ly,** *adv.* **—co•or′di•na′tor,** *n.* [*count*] See -ORD-.

coor′dinating conjunc′tion, *n.* [*count*] a conjunction connecting grammatical elements of equal rank, as *and* in *Sue and Tom* or *or* in *I can't decide if I should stay or go.*

co•or•di•na•tion or **co-or•di•na•tion** (kō ôr′dn ā′shən) /kowˌɔrdn̩ˈeyʃən/ *n.* [*noncount*] **1.** the act or state of coordinating or of being coordinated. **2.** proper order or relationship: *Without coordination among the departments, students will be confused about the courses they have to take.* **3.** correct interaction of functions or parts: *The drug causes you to lose your coordination.*

coot (ko͞ot) /kuwt/ *n.* [*count*] **1.** a small gray or black and white swimming and diving water bird. **2.** *Informal.* a foolish or irritating person, esp. one who is elderly.

cop[1] (kop) /kɒp/ *v.*, **copped, cop•ping.** *Informal.* **1.** to seize or steal: *She copped first prize in the contest.* **2. cop out,** [*no obj*] to avoid a responsibility: *He was going to help us but at the last minute he copped out.* [~ + *out* + *on* + *obj*]: *Don't cop out on us again.* **—*Idiom.* 3. cop a plea,** to plea-bargain.

cop[2] (kop) /kɒp/ *n.* [*count*] *Informal.* a police officer.

cop., an abbreviation of: copyright; copyrighted.

cope (kōp) /kowp/ *v.*, **coped, cop•ing. 1.** [~ + *with* + *obj*] to struggle on fairly even terms or with some success: *I will try to cope with his rudeness.* **2.** [*no obj*] to deal with responsibilities calmly: *After his breakdown he couldn't cope any longer.*

cop•i•er (kop′ē ər) /ˈkɒpiyər/ *n.* [*count*] **1.** a person or thing that copies. **2.** a machine that makes copies of original documents, esp. by xerography. See illustration at OFFICE.

co•pi•lot (kō′pī′lət) /ˈkowˌpaylət/ *n.* [*count*] a pilot who is second in command of an aircraft.

co•pi•ous (kō′pē əs) /ˈkowpiyəs/ *adj.* **1.** large in quantity or number: *She always takes copious notes in class.* **2.** producing an abundant supply: *a copious harvest.* **—co′pi•ous•ly,** *adv.* **—co′pi•ous•ness,** *n.* [*noncount*]

cop′-out′, *n.* [*count*] an act or instance of failing to keep a promise or of avoiding a responsibility: *His usual cop-out for not visiting his children is that he has to work on weekends.*

cop•per[1] (kop′ər) /ˈkɒpər/ *n.* **1.** [*noncount*] a metal element having a reddish brown color, used as an electrical conductor and to make alloys, as brass and bronze. **2.** [*noncount*] a reddish brown. **3.** [*count*] a coin of copper or bronze. **4.** [*count*] *Brit.* a large kettle for cooking or for boiling laundry. **—cop′per•y,** *adj.*

cop•per[2] (kop′ər) /ˈkɒpər/ *n.* [*count*] *Slang.* a police officer.

cop•per•head (kop′ər hed′) /ˈkɒpərˌhɛd/ *n.* [*count*] **1.** a North American snake, a pit viper having a copper-colored head. **2.** [*Copperhead*] a Northerner who supported the South during the Civil War.

cop•ra (kop′rə, kō′prə) /ˈkɒprə, ˈkowprə/ *n.* [*noncount*] the dried meat of the coconut, from which coconut oil is squeezed out.

copse (kops) /kɒps/ also **cop•pice** (kop′is) /ˈkɒpɪs/ *n.* [*count*] a group of small trees or bushes; small woods.

cop•ter (kop′tər) /ˈkɒptər/ *n.* [*count*] a helicopter.

cop•u•la (kop′yə lə) /ˈkɒpyələ/ *n.* [*count*], *pl.* **-las, -lae** (-lē′) /-ˌliy/. a verb, such as *be, seem,* or *look,* that serves as a connecting link or establishes an identity between a subject and a complement (a noun or adjective that comes next): *In the sentence* John is a student, *the word* is *functions as a copula because it establishes an identity between* John *and* student. Also called **linking verb. —cop′u•lar,** *adj.*

cop•u•late (kop′yə lāt′) /ˈkɒpyəˌleyt/ *v.* [*no obj*], **-lat•ed, -lat•ing.** to engage in sexual intercourse. **—cop•u•la•tion** (kop′yə lā′shən) /ˌkɒpyəˈleyʃən/ *n.* [*noncount*]

cop•y (kop′ē) /ˈkɒpiy/ *n.*, *pl.* **cop•ies,** for 1, 2, *v.*, **cop•ied, cop•y•ing. —***n.* **1.** [*count*] an imitation or reproduction of an original: *They brought in a copy of a famous painting. I made three copies of the contract and mailed back two of them.* **2.** [*count*] one single example of a book, newspaper, etc.: *I'll mail you a copy of my book.* **3.** [*noncount*] matter to be reproduced in printed form: *The editor thought the author's copy was acceptable.* **4.** [*noncount*] the text of a news story, advertisement, or the like: *The ad agency wrote the copy for the commercial.* **5.** [*noncount*] something interesting enough to be printed in a newspaper: *Political gossip is always good copy.* **—***v.* **6.** [~ + *obj*] **a.** to make a copy of; reproduce: *I copied the article and gave it to the class to read.* **b.** to undergo copying; be able to be copied: *Certain colors don't copy well on these older machines.* **7.** [*no obj*] to make a copy or copies; reproduce: *That old machine copies poorly.* **8.** [~ + *obj*] to follow as a pattern; imitate: *He was always copying his brother.*

cop•y•cat (kop′ē kat′) /ˈkɒpiyˌkæt/ *n.*, *adj.*, *v.*, **-cat•ted, -cat•ting. —***n.* [*count*] Also, **cop′y cat′. 1.** a person or thing that imitates another exactly. **—***adj.* [*before a noun*] **2.** imitating a well-known event: *a copycat crime.* **—***v.* [~ + *obj*] **3.** to imitate; mimic.

cop•y•right (kop′ē rīt′) /ˈkɒpiyˌrayt/ *n.* **1.** the legal ownership and control of a literary, musical, artistic, or other work: [*noncount*]: *There is no copyright for this book in certain countries.* [*count*]: *I have a copyright on that software.* **—***adj.* **2.** of or relating to copyrights: *copyright laws.* **3.** Also, **cop′y•right′ed.** protected by copyright. **—***v.* [~ + *obj*] **4.** to secure a copyright on: *The book was copyrighted in 1982.* **—cop′y•right′a•ble,** *adj.* **—cop′y•right′er,** *n.* [*count*]

cop•y•writ•er (kop′ē rī′tər) /ˈkɒpiyˌraytər/ *n.* [*count*] a writer of information, esp. for advertisements or publicity releases. **—cop′y•writ′ing,** *n.* [*noncount*]

co•quette (kō ket′) /kowˈkɛt/ *n.* [*count*] a woman who behaves in a playful but insincere way to attract men; a flirt. **—co•quet′tish,** *adj.* **—co•quet′tish•ly,** *adv.* **—co•quet′tish•ness,** *n.* [*noncount*]

cor-, *prefix. cor-* is another form of COM- that is used before roots beginning with *r*: *correlate.*

cor., an abbreviation of: **1.** corner. **2.** correct. **3.** corrected. **4.** correction.

cor•al (kôr′əl, kor′-) /ˈkɔrəl, ˈkɒr-/ *n.* **1.** [*count*] the hard, often brightly colored skeleton of certain small sea animals called polyps, or any of the animals themselves. **2.** [*noncount*] such skeletons when thought of as a mass: *We dived down and examined the beautiful coral.* **3.** [*noncount*] a color ranging from reddish to pinkish yellow. *—adj.* **4.** made of coral. **5.** making coral: *a coral polyp.* **6.** resembling coral, esp. in color. **—cor′al•like′,** *adj.*

cor′al snake′, *n.* [*count*] a poisonous snake with bands of red, yellow, and black.

cord (kôrd) /kɔrd/ *n.* **1.** a string made of several strands braided, twisted, or woven together: [*count*]: *The cords were wrapped tightly around the trunk.* [*noncount*]: *He found some cord and tied up the packages.* **2.** a small, flexible, electrical cable covered with rubber for protection: [*count*]: *I kept getting tangled up in the electric cord while vacuuming.* [*noncount*]: *How many yards of cord will we need?* **3. cords,** [*plural*] clothing, as trousers, made of fabric with cordlike strips, esp. corduroy. **4.** [*count*] a cordlike structure of the body: *the spinal cord.* **5.** [*count*] a unit of volume used chiefly for fuel wood, measuring 8 ft. long, 4 ft. wide, and 4 ft. high (2.4 m × 1.2 m × 1.2 m).

-cord-, *root. -cord-* comes from Latin, where it has the meaning "heart." This meaning is found in such words as: ACCORD, CONCORD, CONCORDANCE, CORDIAL, DISCORD.

cor•dial (kôr′jəl) /ˈkɔrdʒəl/ *adj.* **1.** courteous and gracious; warm: *a cordial reception.* **2.** [*before a noun*] sincere; strongly felt: *They had a cordial dislike for each other.* *—n.* **3.** a strong, sweetened liqueur: [*noncount*]: *a bottle of cherry cordial.* [*count*]: *He drank several peppermint cordials.* **—cor′dial•ly,** *adv.* **—cor′dial•ness,** *n.* [*noncount*] See -CORD-.

cord•ite (kôr′dīt) /ˈkɔrdayt/ *n.* [*noncount*] a slow-burning explosive powder that looks like cord.

cord•less (kôrd′lis) /ˈkɔrdlɪs/ *adj.* **1.** lacking a cord. **2.** (of an electrical appliance) requiring no wire leading to an external electricity source: *a cordless telephone.*

cor•don (kôr′dn) /ˈkɔrdn̩/ *n.* [*count*] **1.** a line of police, soldiers, etc., guarding an area or preventing people from passing through it. **2.** a cord, braid, or ribbon worn as an ornament or badge. *—v.* **3.** to surround or blockade with or as if with a cordon: [~ + *off* + *obj*]: *Police cordoned off the street.* [~ + *obj* + *off*]: *Police cordoned the area off.*

cor•du•roy (kôr′də roi′, kôr′də roi′) /ˈkɔrdəˌrɔy, ˌkɔrdəˈrɔy/ *n.* **1.** [*noncount*] a cotton fabric with raised ridges like cords running lengthwise on the surface: *The pants were of gray corduroy.* **2. corduroys,** [*plural*] trousers made of this fabric: *On Saturdays he always wore a sweater and an old pair of corduroys.* *—adj.* **3.** of, relating to, or resembling corduroy: *a corduroy jacket.*

core (kôr, kōr) /kɔr, kowr/ *n., v.,* **cored, cor•ing.** *—n.* [*count*] **1.** the central part of a fleshy fruit, containing the seeds: *Remove the cores from the apples.* **2.** [*singular*] the central part of the earth: *the pressure at the earth's core.* **3.** the most important or essential part of anything: *the core of the new curriculum for business majors.* **4.** the region in a nuclear reactor that contains the radioactive material used to produce energy. *—v.* [~ + *obj*] **5.** to remove the core of (fruit): *Core the apples.* ***—Idiom.*** **6. to the core,** [*noncount*] completely; thoroughly: *The villain was rotten to the core.* **—core′less,** *adj.*

co•ri•an•der (kôr′ē an′dər, kōr′-) /ˈkɔriyˌændər, ˈkowr-/ *n.* [*noncount*] **1.** Also called **cilantro.** an herb of the parsley family, used in cooking. **2.** the seeds of this herb, used whole or ground as a flavoring.

cork (kôrk) /kɔrk/ *n.* **1.** [*noncount*] **a.** a layer of dead tissue below the bark in woody plants. **b.** the thick, lightweight layer of wood of a Mediterranean oak used for making floats, stoppers for bottles, etc. **2.** [*count*] a piece of cork, rubber, or the like used as a stopper. *—v.* **3.** [~ *(+ up)* + *obj*] to close or stop up (something with an opening, such as a bottle) with or as if with a cork: *She corked (up) the bottle.* **4.** [~ + *up* + *obj*] to control (one's emotions) tightly: *He's corked up all his feelings of rage.* ***—Idiom.*** **5. blow** or **pop one's cork,** *Informal.* to lose one's temper: *blew his cork when he saw the expense accounts.*

cork•er (kôr′kər) /ˈkɔrkər/ *n.* [*count*] *Informal.* someone or something astonishing or excellent.

cork•ing (kôr′king) /ˈkɔrkɪŋ/ *Informal.* *—adj.* **1.** excellent; fine: *a corking adventure movie.* *—adv.* **2.** very; extremely: *a corking good time.*

cork•screw (kôrk′skrōō′) /ˈkɔrkˌskruw/ *n.* [*count*] **1.** a tool with a metal piece in the shape of a spiral with a point at one end and a handle at the other, used for pulling corks from bottles. *—adj.* [*before a noun*] **2.** resembling a corkscrew; spiral: *a corkscrew curl.* *—v.* [*no obj*] **3.** to move in a spiral or zigzag course: *The plane lost control and corkscrewed down.*

cor•mo•rant (kôr′mər ənt) /ˈkɔrmərənt/ *n.* [*count*] a dark-colored diving seabird having a long neck and a throat pouch for holding fish.

corn[1] (kôrn) /kɔrn/ *n.* **1.** [*noncount*] Also called **Indian corn;** *esp. technical and Brit.,* **maize. a.** a tall cereal plant having a solid stem and kernels growing on large ears. **b.** the kernels of this plant, used for food. **c.** the ears of this plant. **2.** [*noncount*] **a.** the edible seed of certain other cereal plants, esp. wheat in England and oats in Scotland. **b.** the plants themselves. **3.** SWEET CORN. **4.** [*count*] a single grain of certain plants, as pepper, wheat, etc.: *She ground up a few corns of pepper for flavoring.* **5.** [*noncount*] *Informal.* old-fashioned, boring, or overly sentimental material, as a joke, story, or piece of music. *—v.* [~ + *obj*] **6.** to preserve, season, or cook (food) with salty water: *Dad corned his own beef.* **—corned,** *adj.: corned beef and cabbage.*

corn[2] (kôrn) /kɔrn/ *n.* [*count*] a hard, horny growth of skin tissue formed over a bone, esp. on the toes, as a result of pressure or friction.

corn•ball (kôrn′bôl′) /ˈkɔrnˌbɔl/ *Informal.* *—n.* [*count*] **1.** a person who likes overly sentimental jokes, stories, music, etc. **2.** a country bumpkin; HICK. *—adj.* **3.** CORNY: *more cornball jokes and gags.*

corn′ bread′ or **corn′bread′,** *n.* [*noncount*] a bread, esp. a quick bread, made with cornmeal.

corn•cob (kôrn′kob′) /ˈkɔrnˌkɒb/ *n.* [*count*] **1.** the long woody core on which the grains of an ear of corn grow. **2.** Also called **corn′cob pipe′.** a tobacco pipe with a bowl made from a corncob.

cor•ne•a (kôr′nē ə) /ˈkɔrniyə/ *n.* [*count*], *pl.* **-ne•as.** the clear, front, curved part of the outer coat of the eye. **—cor′ne•al,** *adj.: a corneal transplant.*

cor•ner (kôr′nər) /ˈkɔrnər/ *n.* [*count*] **1.** the place at which two lines, sides, edges, or surfaces meet; angle: *a chair in the corner of the room.* **2.** an angle, end, side, or edge: *a coffee table with sharp corners.* **3.** the point where two streets meet, or where one street bends sharply: *I drove around the corner too fast and the car skidded.* **4.** [*usually: singular*] an awkward or embarrassing position, esp. one from which escape is impossible; predicament: *I was backed into a corner by the evidence.* **5.** a region or part, esp. a distant part: *The pilgrims came from every corner of the empire.* **6.** [*usually: singular*] a situation in which only one person, business, etc., controls the available supply of something, such as a product or service: *a corner on the oil market.* *—adj.* [*before a noun*] **7.** situated on or at a corner where two streets meet: *the corner drugstore.* *—v.* **8.** [~ + *obj*] to force into an awkward situation in which escape, refusal, etc., is difficult or impossible: *The policeman cornered the crook in a back alley.* [*often:* ~ + *obj* + *into* + *verb-ing*]: *She cornered me into serving on the finance committee.* **9.** [~ + *obj*] to gain control of (a stock, etc.): *That country had cornered the market on oil.* **10.** [*no obj*] (of an automobile) to turn, esp. at a speed relatively high for the angle of the turn. ***—Idiom.*** **11. cut corners,** to reduce costs, time, or effort in carrying something out by leaving out certain steps: *looking for a way to cut corners.* **12. just around the corner,** [*noncount*] near in time or place; close by or close to happening: *predicted that an improvement in the economy was just around the corner.* **13. turn the corner,** to begin to make improvement; start to recover: *The day after the operation he turned the corner and was soon sent home.*

cor•ner•stone (kôr′nər stōn′) /ˈkɔrnərˌstown/ *n.* [*count*] **1.** a stone representing the starting place in the construction of a building. **2.** the foundation on which something is developed: *The speed of light as a constant is the cornerstone of Einstein's theories.*

cor•net (kôr net′; *esp. Brit.* kôr′nit) /kɔrˈnɛt; *esp. Brit.* ˈkɔrnɪt/ *n.* [*count*] **1.** a wind instrument with valves, of the trumpet family. **2.** *Brit.* an ice-cream cone.

corn•flakes (kôrn′flāks′) /ˈkɔrnˌfleyks/ *n.* [*plural*] a breakfast cereal consisting of small flakes made with corn.

cor•nice (kôr′nis) /ˈkɔrnɪs/ *n.* [*count*] any prominent molded piece, such as a strip of plaster that sticks out on the top of a wall or doorway.

corn•meal (kôrn′mēl′) /ˈkɔrnˌmiyl/ *n.* [*noncount*] meal made of corn.

corn′ pone′, *n.* [*noncount*] *Southern U.S.* corn bread, esp. of a plain or simple kind.

corn•row (kôrn′rō′) /ˈkɔrnˌrow/ *n.* [*count*] **1.** a narrow braid of hair plaited tightly against the scalp. **—*v.*** [~ + *obj*] **2.** to arrange (hair) in cornrows.

corn•stalk (kôrn′stôk′) /ˈkɔrnˌstɔk/ *n.* [*count*] the stalk or stem of corn, esp. Indian corn.

corn•starch (kôrn′stärch′) /ˈkɔrnˌstɑrtʃ/ *n.* [*noncount*] a starch or a starchy flour made from corn and used for thickening gravies or sauces, making puddings, etc.

cor•nu•co•pi•a (kôr′nə kō′pē ə, -nyə-) /ˌkɔrnəˈkowpiyə, -nyə-/ *n.* [*count*], *pl.* **-pi•as. 1.** an object shaped like a curved horn, containing a rich supply of food and drink and used as a symbol of abundance: *a Thanksgiving cornucopia.* **2.** an abundant, overflowing supply: *a cornucopia of new ideas for software development.*

corn•y (kôr′nē) /ˈkɔrniy/ *adj.,* **-i•er, -i•est.** *Informal.* old-fashioned or overly sentimental: *corny jokes; a pair of corny comedians.* **—corn′i•ness,** *n.* [*noncount*]

cor•ol•lar•y (kôr′ə ler′ē, kor′-) /ˈkɔrəˌlɛriy, ˈkɒr-/ *n.* [*count*], *pl.* **-ies.** an immediate consequence; a conclusion that follows naturally: *An unfortunate corollary to his economic plan is high unemployment.*

co•ro•na (kə rō′nə) /kəˈrownə/ *n.* [*count*], *pl.* **-nas, -nae** (-nē). **1.** a circle of light seen around the sun or moon, esp. during an eclipse. **2.** a long, straight cigar, rounded at the closed end.

cor•o•nal (*n.* kôr′ə nl, kor′-; *adj. usually* kə rōn′l) /*n.* ˈkɔrənl̩, ˈkɒr-; *adj. usually* kəˈrownl̩/ *n.* [*count*] **1.** a crown; coronet. **2.** a garland. **—*adj.* 3.** of or relating to a coronal or corona.

cor•o•nar•y (kôr′ə ner′ē, kor′-) /ˈkɔrəˌnɛriy, ˈkɒr-/ *adj., n., pl.* **-ies. —*adj.*** [*before a noun*] **1.** of or relating to the heart, or to the arteries near the heart: *a coronary artery.* **—*n.*** [*count*] **2.** a heart attack, esp. a coronary thrombosis.

cor′onary thrombo′sis, *n.* a condition in which an artery leading to the heart is blocked by a blood clot: [*count*]: *suffered from a massive coronary thrombosis.* [*noncount*]: *the increase in coronary thrombosis.*

cor•o•na•tion (kôr′ə nā′shən, kor′-) /ˌkɔrəˈneyʃən, ˌkɒr-/ *n.* [*count*] the act or ceremony of crowning a sovereign.

cor•o•ner (kôr′ə nər, kor′-) /ˈkɔrənər, ˈkɒr-/ *n.* [*count*] an officer in a county whose function is to investigate any death not clearly resulting from natural causes.

cor•o•net (kôr′ə net′, kor′-) /ˌkɔrəˈnɛt, ˌkɒr-/ *n.* [*count*] **1.** a small crown worn by nobles or peers. **2.** a crownlike ornament for the head, such as of flowers, gold, or jewels.

corp. or **Corp.,** an abbreviation of: **1.** corporal. **2.** corporation.

-corp-, *root.* *-corp-* comes from Latin, where it has the meaning "body." This meaning is found in such words as: CORPORA, CORPORAL, CORPORATION, CORPS, CORPSE, CORPUS, CORPUSCLE, INCORPORATE.

cor•po•ra (kôr′pər ə) /ˈkɔrpərə/ *n.* [*plural*] a pl. of CORPUS. See -CORP-.

cor•po•ral[1] (kôr′pər əl, -prəl) /ˈkɔrpərəl, -prəl/ *adj.* bodily; physical: *corporal punishment.* **—cor′po•ral•ly,** *adv.* See -CORP-.

cor•po•ral[2] (kôr′pər əl, -prəl) /ˈkɔrpərəl, -prəl/ *n.* [*count*] **1.** a U.S. Army enlisted man or woman ranking above a private first class. **2.** an enlisted man or woman in the U.S. Marine Corps ranking above a lance corporal. **3.** an enlisted man or woman of similar rank in the armed services of other countries. See -CORP-.

cor•po•rate (kôr′pər it, -prit) /ˈkɔrpərɪt, -prɪt/ *adj.* [*before a noun*] **1.** of, for, or belonging to a corporation or corporations: *a corporate executive.* **2.** of or relating to a united group; united; combined: *corporate action.* **—cor′po•rate•ly,** *adv.* **—cor′po•rate•ness,** *n.* [*noncount*] See -CORP-.

cor′porate raid′er, *n.* [*count*] a person who seizes control of a company, as by secretly buying its stock.

cor•po•ra•tion (kôr′pə rā′shən) /ˌkɔrpəˈreyʃən/ *n.* [*count*] **1.** an association of individuals, created by law and having an existence apart from that of its members. **2.** a large business organization formed this way: *working for a large, faceless, multinational corporation.* **3.** [*often: Corporation*] the principal officials of a city or town. See -CORP-. **—Usage.** See COLLECTIVE NOUN.

cor•po•re•al (kôr pôr′ē əl, -pōr′-) /kɔrˈpɔriyəl, -ˈpowr-/ *adj.* **1.** of the nature of the physical body; bodily. **2.** able to be touched or felt; material: *corporeal property.* **—cor•po•re•al•i•ty** (kôr pôr′ē al′i tē, -pōr′-) /kɔrˌpɔriyˈælɪtiy, -ˌpowr-/ **cor•po′re•al•ness,** *n.* [*noncount*] **—cor•po′re•al•ly,** *adv.* See -CORP-.

corps (kôr, kōr) /kɔr, kowr/ *n.* [*count*], *pl.* **corps** (kôrz, kōrz). **1.** a part of the army or armed forces, such as a group assigned special duties: *the Marine Corps.* **2.** a group of persons associated or who act together: *the Moscow press corps.* See -CORP-.

corpse (kôrps) /kɔrps/ *n.* [*count*] a dead body, esp. of a human being. See -CORP-.

corps•man (kôr′mən, kōr′-) /ˈkɔrmən, ˈkowr-/ *n.* [*count*], *pl.* **-men. 1.** a person in the U.S. Navy working as a pharmacist or hospital assistant. **2.** a person in the Medical Corps of the U.S. Army who gives first aid to the wounded on the battlefield.

cor•pu•lence (kôr′pyə ləns) /ˈkɔrpyələns/ *n.* [*noncount*] fatness; largeness of body. **—cor′pu•lent,** *adj.*: *a corpulent man who loved to eat.* See -CORP-.

cor•pus (kôr′pəs) /ˈkɔrpəs/ *n.* [*count*], *pl.* **-po•ra** (-pər ə) /-pərə/ for 1, 3, **-pus•es** for 2. **1.** a large or complete collection of writings: *the entire corpus of Old English poetry.* **2.** a collection of utterances, taken as a sample of a given language or dialect and used for linguistic analysis: *Working with the corpus on the computer you will find many interesting facts about English.* **3.** the body of a person or animal, esp. when dead. See -CORP-.

cor•pus•cle (kôr′pə səl, -pus əl) /ˈkɔrpəsəl, -pʌsəl/ *n.* [*count*] an unattached cell, esp. a blood or lymph cell. **—cor•pus•cu•lar** (kôr pus′kyə lər) /kɔrˈpʌskyələr/ *adj.* See -CORP-.

corr., an abbreviation of: **1.** corrected. **2.** correction. **3.** correspondence. **4.** correspondent. **5.** corresponding.

cor•ral (kə ral′) /kəˈræl/ *n., v.,* **-ralled, -ral•ling. —*n.*** [*count*] **1.** an enclosed area or pen for horses, etc. **2.** an arrangement of wagons in a closed circle, formed for defense. **—*v.*** [~ + *obj*] **3.** to confine in or as if in a corral: *She corralled me at the party and I couldn't get away.* **4.** *Informal.* **a.** to seize; capture: *The police corralled the fleeing suspects.* **b.** to collect or win: *to corral votes.*

cor•rect (kə rekt′) /kəˈrɛkt/ *v.* [~ + *obj*] **1.** to set or make right; remove the errors or faults from: *The mechanic corrected the timing of the engine.* **2.** to point out or mark the errors in: *to correct examination papers.* **3.** [*used with quotations*] to make (a reply) so as to set something right: *"Mr. Holmes, come in please." "It's Castle, sir," I corrected.* **4.** to scold or punish in order to improve: *Don't correct your child in public.* **5.** to work against the effect of (something undesirable): *Her contact lenses correct her poor eyesight.* **—*adj.* 6.** conforming to fact or truth; accurate; without mistakes: *Your answer was correct.* **7.** in accordance with an accepted standard; proper: *correct behavior.* **—cor•rect′a•ble, cor•rect′i•ble,** *adj.* **—cor•rect′ly,** *adv.* **—cor•rect′ness,** *n.* [*noncount*] **—cor•rec′tor,** *n.* [*count*] See -RECT-.

cor•rec•tion (kə rek′shən) /kəˈrɛkʃən/ *n.* **1.** [*count*] something done to take the place of something wrong or inaccurate: *The corrections were in red ink.* **2.** [*noncount*] the act of correcting: *the correction of bad habits.* **3.** [*noncount*] punishment or chastisement. **4.** [*count*] Usually, **corrections.** [*plural*] the various methods, such as jail sentences, parole, and probation, by which society deals with convicted criminals: *the department of corrections.* **—cor•rec′tion•al,** *adj.*

cor•re•late (*v., adj.* kôr′ə lāt′, kor′-; *n.* kôr′ə lit, -lāt′, kor′-) /*v., adj.* ˈkɔrəˌleyt, ˈkɒr-; *n.* ˈkɔrəlɪt, -ˌleyt, ˈkɒr-/ *v.,* **-lat•ed, -lat•ing,** *adj., n.* **—*v.* 1.** to show or establish a connection between: [~ + *obj*]: *to correlate expenses and income.* [~ + *obj* + *with* + *obj*]: *to correlate expenses with income.* **2.** [*no obj*] to have a relation or connection: *A person's height and his eating of certain foods don't correlate.* [~ + *with* + *obj*]: *A person's weight usually correlates with his eating habits.* **—*adj.* 3.** (of two things) related. **—*n.*** [*count*] **4.** either of two related things, esp. when one implies the other: *a correlate of income with tax savings.* **—cor′re•lat′a•ble,** *adj.* **—cor•rel•a•tive** (kə rel′ə tiv) /kəˈrɛlətɪv/ *adj.* See -LAT-[1].

cor•re•la•tion (kôr′ə lā′shən, kor′-) /ˌkɔrəˈleyʃən, ˌkɒr-/ *n.* relation of, or connection between, two or more things: [*count*]: *a strong correlation between smoking and lung cancer.* [*noncount*]: *There is little correlation between cramming for the test and passing it.* **—cor′re•la′tion•al,** *adj.* See -LAT-[1].

cor•re•spond (kôr′ə spond′, kor′-) /ˌkɔrəˈspɒnd, ˌkɒr-/ *v.* **1.** to be in agreement or conformity; match: [*no obj*]: *His actions and his words don't always correspond.* [~ +

with/to + obj]: *His actions don't correspond with his words.* **2.** [~ + *to* + *obj*] to be similar: *The U.S. Congress corresponds to the British Parliament.* **3.** to communicate by exchange of letters: [*no obj*]: *corresponded for years before they finally met.* [~ + *with* + *obj*]: *My daughter corresponded with several classmates for years after graduation.* —**cor′re•spond′ing•ly,** *adv.* See -SPOND-.

cor•re•spond•ence (kôr′ə spon′dəns, kor′-) /ˌkɔrəˈspɒndəns, ˌkɒr-/ *n.* **1.** [*noncount*] communication by exchange of letters: *Our parents cut off all correspondence between us.* **2.** a letter or letters that pass between correspondents: [*count*]: *I have here a correspondence between you and the defendant.* [*noncount*]: *She kept all the correspondence between her and her lawyers in a safe-deposit box.* **3.** agreement; similarity; conformity: [*count*]: *There is a one-to-one correspondence between each sound and each written letter in Finnish, but not in Swedish.* [*noncount*]: *There is some correspondence between the sound of a word and its meaning, or else we couldn't communicate.* See -SPOND-.

cor•re•spond•ent (kôr′ə spon′dənt, kor′-) /ˌkɔrəˈspɒndənt, ˌkɒr-/ *n.* [*count*] **1.** a person who communicates by letters. **2.** a person who works for a newspaper, television network, etc., to gather and report news from a distant place: *in touch with the paper's correspondent in Moscow.* See -SPOND-.

cor•re•spond•ing (kôr′ə spon′ding, kor′-) /ˌkɔrə ˈspɒndɪŋ, ˌkɒr-/ *adj.* equivalent; matching; related: *Enrollment is down compared to the corresponding semesters last year.* —**cor′re•spond′ing•ly,** *adv.*

cor•ri•dor (kôr′i dər, kor′-) /ˈkɔrɪdər, ˈkɒr-/ *n.* [*count*] **1.** a passageway connecting rooms, apartments, etc.; hallway. **2.** a thickly populated part of a country with major land and air transportation routes: *Storms crippled air traffic along the Northeast corridor today.*

cor•rob•o•rate (kə rob′ə rāt′) /kəˈrɒbəˌreyt/ *v.* [~ + *obj*], **-rat•ed, -rat•ing.** to support by giving proof; confirm: *corroborated my account of the accident.* —**cor•rob•o•ra•tion** (kə rob′ə rā′shən) /kəˌrɒbəˈreyʃən/ *n.* [*noncount*]: *The police are looking for corroboration of your statement.* —**cor•rob•o•ra•tive** (kə rob′ə rā′tiv, -ər ə tiv) /kəˈrɒbəˌreytɪv, -ərətɪv/ **cor•rob•o•ra•to•ry** (kə rob′ər ə tôr′ē, -tōr′ē) /kəˈrɒbərəˌtɔriy, -ˌtowriy/ *adj.: corroborative testimony.*

cor•rode (kə rōd′) /kəˈrowd/ *v.,* **-rod•ed, -rod•ing.** to (cause to) become worn away gradually, esp. by chemical action: [*no obj*]: *The battery had corroded.* [~ + *obj*]: *The acid corroded the battery.*

cor•ro•sion (kə rō′zhən) /kəˈrowʒən/ *n.* [*noncount*] **1.** the act or process of corroding or of being corroded. **2.** the substance resulting from corroding: *Use a rag to wipe away the corrosion from the fender.*

cor•ro•sive (kə rō′siv) /kəˈrowsɪv/ *adj.* causing corrosion: *The salt water has a corrosive effect on cars.*

cor•ru•gated (kôr′ə gāt′id, kor′-) /ˈkɔrəˌgeytɪd, ˈkɒr-/ *adj.* bent into folds and ridges; wrinkled: *hovels with corrugated tin roofs.*

cor•rupt (kə rupt′) /kəˈrʌpt/ *adj.* **1.** guilty of dishonest practices: *a corrupt judge.* **2.** immoral; depraved: *corrupt sexual practices; a corrupt society.* **3.** made inferior or unusable by errors or damage, such as a text: *The electronic file was corrupt.* —*v.* [~ + *obj*] **4.** to cause to be ruined; pervert: *to corrupt youth.* **5.** to infect; taint: *Columbus was accused of corrupting Indian cultures.* —**cor•rupt′er, cor•rup′tor,** *n.* [*count*] —**cor•rupt′i•ble,** *adj.* —**cor•rupt′ly,** *adv.* —**cor•rupt′ness,** *n.* [*noncount*] See -RUPT-.

cor•rup•tion (kə rup′shən) /kəˈrʌpʃən/ *n.* [*noncount*] **1.** an act or instance of corrupting: *a police department free of corruption.* **2.** forcing young people to behave immorally: *charged with corruption of a minor.* **3.** decay: *the corruption of the body after death.*

cor•sage (kôr säzh′) /kɔrˈsɑʒ/ *n.* [*count*] a small decorative bouquet of flowers worn by a woman.

cor•set (kôr′sit) /ˈkɔrsɪt/ *n.* [*count*] **1.** a close-fitting, stiff undergarment, worn esp. to support the hips and waist. —*v.* [~ + *obj*] **2.** to dress with or as if with a corset. —**cor′set•less,** *adj.*

cor•tege or **cor•tège** (kôr tezh′) /kɔrˈtɛʒ/ *n.* [*count*] a procession, esp. for a funeral.

cor•tex (kôr′teks) /ˈkɔrtɛks/ *n.* [*count*], *pl.* **-ti•ces** (-tə sēz′) /-təˌsiyz/. **1.** the outer layer of a body organ or structure, as of the cerebrum. **2.** the bark of a plant stem or tree trunk.

cor•ti•sone (kôr′tə zōn′, -sōn′) /ˈkɔrtəˌzown, -ˌsown/ *n.* [*noncount*] a hormone used chiefly in the treatment of autoimmune and inflammatory diseases.

cor•us•cate (kôr′ə skāt′, kor′-) /ˈkɔrəˌskeyt, ˈkɒr-/ *v.* [*no obj*], **-cat•ed, -cat•ing.** to give off bright, vivid flashes of light; sparkle; gleam.

cor•vette (kôr vet′) /kɔrˈvɛt/ *n.* [*count*] **1.** a wooden warship having one level of guns. **2.** a lightly armed ship, used esp. as a convoy escort, in size between a destroyer and a gunboat.

cos (kos, kôs) /kɒs, kɔs/ *n.* ROMAINE.

cos, an abbreviation of: cosine.

cos., an abbreviation of: **1.** companies. **2.** counties.

co•sign (kō′sīn′, kō sīn′) /ˈkowˌsayn, kowˈsayn/ *v.* to sign as a cosigner: [*no obj*]: *Cosign here, please.* [~ + *obj*]: *Cosign the document here, please.* See -SIGN-.

co•sig•na•to•ry (kō sig′nə tôr′ē, -tōr′ē) /kowˈsɪgnəˌtɔriy, -ˌtowriy/ *adj., n., pl.* **-ries.** —*adj.* **1.** signing jointly with another or others. —*n.* [*count*] **2.** a person who signs a document jointly with another or others; cosigner.

co•sign•er (kō′sī′nər, kō sī′-) /ˈkowˌsaynər, kowˈsay-/ *n.* [*count*] a cosignatory: *Her husband is a cosigner on the mortgage.*

-cosm-, *root.* -*cosm*- comes from Greek, where it has the meaning "world, universe; order, arrangement." This meaning is found in such words as: COSMETIC, COSMIC, COSMOPOLITAN, COSMOS, MICROCOSM.

cos•met•ic (koz met′ik) /kɒzˈmɛtɪk/ *n.* [*count*] **1.** a powder, lotion, or other preparation to make the face, skin, etc., more beautiful. See illustration at STORE. **2. cosmetics,** [*plural*] measures taken to make something seem better but without being better: *Hiring a few minority employees was just cosmetics to stave off criticism.* —*adj.* **3.** done or performed to improve beauty, esp. of the face: *cosmetic surgery after the accident.* **4.** done to improve the appearance of something without improving it: *made a few cosmetic attempts to hire more people from minorities.* —**cos•met′i•cal•ly,** *adv.* See -COSM-.

cos•me•tol•o•gy (koz′mi tol′ə jē) /ˌkɒzmɪˈtɒlədʒiy/ *n.* [*noncount*] the art or profession of cosmetically treating the skin, hair, and nails. —**cos′me•tol′o•gist,** *n.* [*count*]

cos•mic (koz′mik) /ˈkɒzmɪk/ *adj.* **1.** [*before a noun*] of, relating to, or characteristic of the cosmos: *cosmic events when the universe was born.* **2.** [*before a noun*] vast: *cosmic distances.* **3.** of great impact; enormous: *a matter of cosmic importance.* —**cos′mi•cal•ly,** *adv.* See -COSM-.

cos′mic ray′, *n.* [*count*] a radiation of high penetrating power coming from outer space.

cos•mog•o•ny (koz mog′ə nē) /kɒzˈmɒgəniy/ *n.* [*count*], *pl.* **-nies.** a theory or story of the origin of the universe. —**cos•mo•gon•ic** (koz′mə gon′ik) /ˌkɒzməˈgɒnɪk/ *adj.* —**cos•mog′o•nist,** *n.* [*count*]

cos•mol•o•gy (koz mol′ə jē) /kɒzˈmɒlədʒiy/ *n.* **1.** [*noncount*] the study of the structure of the universe, esp. of space, time, etc.: *Astronomers and philosophers alike are interested in cosmology.* **2.** a theory of the origin and structure of the universe. —**cos•mo•log•i•cal** (koz′mə loj′i kəl) /ˌkɒzməˈlɒdʒɪkəl/ **cos′mo•log′ic,** *adj.* —**cos′mo•log′i•cal•ly,** *adv.* —**cos•mol•o•gist** (koz mol′ə jist) /kɒzˈmɒlədʒɪst/ *n.* [*count*]

cos•mo•naut (koz′mə nôt′, -not′) /ˈkɒzməˌnɔt, -ˌnɒt/ *n.* [*count*] a Russian or Soviet astronaut. See -COSM-, -NAUT-.

cos•mop•o•lis (koz mop′ə lis) /kɒzˈmɒpəlɪs/ *n.* [*count*] an internationally important city. See -COSM-, -POLIS-.

cos•mo•pol•i•tan (koz′mə pol′i tn) /ˌkɒzməˈpɒlɪtn/ *adj.* **1.** of or relating to the whole world, or to a great part of it: *the cosmopolitan nature of international agreements.* **2. a.** belonging to all the world; not limited to one part of the world: *a cosmopolitan world view.* **b.** worldly; sophisticated: *the cosmopolitan customer who demands the very best.* —*n.* [*count*] **3.** a person free from local or national bias: *a cosmopolitan who had lived in several countries.* —**cos′mo•pol′i•tan•ism,** *n.* [*noncount*] See -COSM-, -POLIS-.

cos•mos (koz′məs, -mōs) /ˈkɒzməs, -mows/ *n.* [*count; usually singular; the* + ~], *pl.* **-mos, -mos•es.** the universe when it is thought of as an orderly, structured system: *intelligent life in the cosmos.* See -COSM-.

cos•set (kos′ət) /ˈkɒsət/ *v.* [~ + *obj*] to treat (someone) as a favorite; pamper.

cost (kôst, kost) /kɔst, kɒst/ *n., v.,* **cost** or, for 4, 9, **cost•ed, cost•ing.** —*n.* **1.** [*count; usually singular*] the price paid to buy, produce, or maintain anything: *The cost of a new home in that area is about $500,000.* **2.** [*count*] an outlay or expenditure of money, time, etc.:

Production costs are too high. **3.** [*count; usually singular*] a sacrifice or penalty to endure: *The battle was won, but at a heavy cost in casualties.* **4.** [*noncount*] the price that the seller of merchandise paid to buy it: *We are selling these chairs at cost, so hurry in today.* **5. costs,** [*plural*] money awarded to a person who wins a court action, to pay for legal expenses. **—*v.* 6.** [*not: be + ~-ing*] to require the payment of (money) in an exchange; have (a sum of money) as the price of: [~ + *obj*]: *That camera costs $200.* [~ + *obj* + *obj*]: *That camera cost us $200.* **7.** to result in the loss or injury of: [~ + *obj*]: *Carelessness costs lives.* [~ + *obj* + *obj*]: *Drugs can cost you your life.* **8.** [~ + *obj* + *obj*] to cause to pay: *Worrying cost me many sleepless nights.* **9.** [~ + *obj*] to estimate the cost of (manufactured articles, etc.): *We spent weeks trying to cost the new computer lab.* **—*Idiom.* 10. at all costs,** by any means necessary: *You've got to keep that programmer working for us at all costs.* **—Related Words.** COST is a noun and a verb, COSTLY is an adjective: *The costs are high. How much does it cost? Those are costly diamonds.*

co•star or **co-star** (*n.* kō′stär′; *v.* kō′stär′) /*n.* ˈkowˌstɑr; *v.* ˌkowˈstɑr/ *n., v.,* **-starred, -star•ring.** **—*n.*** [*count*] **1.** a performer who is as important as another in a movie, etc. **—*v.* 2.** to be a costar: [*no obj*]: *Fred Astaire and Ginger Rogers costarred in many movies together.* [~ + *with* + *obj*]: *Ginger costarred in many movies with Fred.* **3.** [~ + *obj*] (of a movie) to present as a costar or costars: *The movie costarred Ginger Rogers and Fred Astaire.*

Cos•ta Ri•can (kos′tə rē′kən, kô′stə, kō′-) /ˈkɒstəˈriykən, ˈkɔstə, ˈkow-/ *adj.* **1.** of or relating to Costa Rica. **—*n.*** [*count*] **2.** a person born or living in Costa Rica.

cost•ly (kôst′lē, kost′-) /ˈkɔstliy, ˈkɒst-/ *adj.,* **-li•er, -li•est. 1.** costing much; high in price: *a costly mink coat.* **2.** resulting in great loss: *a costly mistake.* **—cost′li•ness,** *n.* [*noncount*]

cost′ of liv′ing, *n.* [*count; usually singular: the* + ~] the average that one pays for necessary goods and services, as food, clothing, and rent: *The cost of living has risen faster than the average working family's income.*

cos•tume (kos′to͞om, -tyo͞om) /ˈkɒstuwm, -tyuwm/ *n., v.,* **-tumed, -tum•ing,** *adj.* **—*n.* 1.** style of dress typical of a particular nation, group, or historical period: [*count*]: *peasants in their native costumes.* [*noncount*]: *the costume of the Revolutionary War days.* **2.** [*count*] clothing of period, place, etc., or for a particular occasion such as a party: *The circus clown put on his costume.* **3.** [*count*] a set of garments selected for wear at a single time; outfit; ensemble. **—*v.*** [~ + *obj*] **4.** to provide with a costume; dress. **—*adj.*** [*before a noun*] **5.** of or characterized by the wearing of costumes: *a costume party.*

cos′tume jew′elry, *n.* [*noncount*] inexpensive jewelry made of nonprecious metals and stones.

co•sy (kō′zē) /ˈkowziy/ *adj.,* **-si•er, -si•est,** *n., pl.* **-sies,** *v.,* **-sied, -sy•ing.** COZY.

cot (kot) /kɒt/ *n.* [*count*] **1.** a light portable bed, esp. one of canvas on a folding frame. **2.** *Brit.* a child's crib.

cot, an abbreviation of: cotangent.

co•te•rie (kō′tə rē) /ˈkowtəriy/ *n.* [*count*] a group of people who associate closely, esp. an exclusive group; clique: *a tight coterie of film buffs and critics.*

co•til•lion (kə til′yən, kō-) /kəˈtɪlyən, kow-/ *n.* [*count*] **1.** a formal ball for young society women. **2.** any of various dances in which a head couple leads the other dancers through elegant steps or patterns.

cot•tage (kot′ij) /ˈkɒtɪdʒ/ *n.* [*count*] a small house or a modest vacation house, as at a lake or mountain resort.

cot′tage cheese′, *n.* [*noncount*] a soft, loose, white, mild-flavored, unripened cheese made from skim milk.

cot•ter (kot′ər) /ˈkɒtər/ *n.* [*count*] **1.** a pin or wedge inserted into an opening to secure something. **2.** Also, **cotter pin.** a pin having a split end that is spread after being pushed through a hole to prevent it from working loose.

cot•ton (kot′n) /ˈkɒtn̩/ *n.* **1.** [*noncount*] a soft, white substance made up of the fibers of the seeds of plants of the mallow family, used in making fabrics. **2.** [*noncount*] the plant itself, having spreading branches and broad, lobed leaves. **3.** [*noncount*] such plants as a group and as a cultivated crop. **4.** [*noncount*] cloth, thread, etc., made of cotton: *The sheets were 100% cotton.* **5.** [*count; usually plural*] clothes made of cotton: *Wash the cottons separately.* **—*v.* 6. cotton to** or **on to,** [~ + *to/on to* + *obj*] *Informal.* **a.** to become fond of; begin to like: *The baby cottoned on to me immediately.* **b.** to approve of; agree with: *to cotton to a suggestion.*

cot′ton gin′, *n.* [*count*] a machine for separating the fibers of cotton from the seeds. Also called **gin.**

cot•ton•mouth (kot′n mouth′) /ˈkɒtn̩ˌmawθ/ *n.* [*count*] a poisonous snake, a pit viper, of southeastern U.S. swamps. Also called **water moccasin.**

cot•ton•tail (kot′n tāl′) /ˈkɒtn̩ˌteyl/ *n.* [*count*] a North American rabbit of the genus having a white tail.

cot•ton•wood (kot′n wo͝od′) /ˈkɒtn̩ˌwʊd/ *n.* [*count*] an American poplar tree with cottony tufts on the seeds.

cot•y•le•don (kot′l ēd′n) /ˌkɒtlˈiydn̩/ *n.* [*count*] the primary leaf of the embryo of seed plants.

couch (kouch) /kawtʃ/ *n.* [*count*] **1.** a long piece of furniture for seating, typically having a back and an armrest; sofa. **2.** a long, upholstered seat with a headrest at one end, on which a person lies down during psychoanalysis. **—*v.* 3.** [~ + *obj*] to arrange or frame (words, etc.) in a certain way; express indirectly: *couching a threat in pleasant words.*

couch′ pota′to, *n.* [*count*], *pl.* **couch potatoes.** *Informal.* a person whose leisure time is spent watching television.

cou•gar (ko͞o′gər) /ˈkuwgər/ *n.* [*count*], *pl.* **-gars,** (*esp. when thought of as a group*) **-gar.** a large, brownish-gray cat of North and South America. Also called MOUNTAIN LION, PANTHER, PUMA.

cough (kôf, kof) /kɔf, kɒf/ *v.* **1.** [*no obj*] **a.** to expel air from the lungs suddenly with a harsh noise: *The baby was coughing most of the night.* **b.** to expel (matter) from the lungs while coughing: [~ (+ *up*) + *obj*]: *He coughed (up) blood.* [~ + *obj* + *up*]: *to cough blood up.* **2.** [*no obj*] to make a noise like coughing: *The plane's engine coughed and died.* **3. cough up,** *Informal.* to produce reluctantly; hand over unwillingly: [~ + *up* + *obj*]: *Come on, cough up the money.* [~ + *obj* + *up*]: *Just cough it up.* **—*n.*** [*count*] **4.** the act or sound of coughing: *let out a little cough.* **5.** [*usually singular*]an illness characterized by coughing: *The baby's cough has gotten worse.* **6.** a sound similar to a cough, as of an engine firing improperly: *The gun gave out a soft cough.* **—cough′er,** *n.* [*count*]

could (ko͝od; *unstressed* kəd) /kʊd; *unstressed* kəd/ *auxiliary (modal) verb.* [~ + *root form of a verb*] **1.** the past tense of CAN[1]: *Once I could run five miles a day.* **2.** (used to express possibility): *That could never be true.* **3.** (used to express a possible condition): *You could do it if you tried.* **4.** (used to make polite requests): *Could you open the door for me, please?* **5.** (used to ask permission): *Could I borrow your pen?* **6.** (used to offer suggestions or give advice): *You could go back and ask for more information.*

could•n't (ko͝od′nt) /ˈkʊdnt/ contraction of *could not: Couldn't we get together next week?*

could•'ve (ko͝od′əv) /ˈkʊdəv/ contraction of *could have,* when *have* is used as an auxiliary verb and appears before another verb: *I wish I could've been there.*

cou•lee (ko͞o′lē) /ˈkuwliy/ *n.* [*count*] **1.** *Chiefly Western U.S. and Western Canada.* a deep ravine formed by running water. **2.** a small valley.

coun•cil (koun′səl) /ˈkawnsəl/ *n.* [*count*] **1.** a meeting for consultation, discussion, or advice: *a church council.* **2.** a body appointed or elected to give advice, to make rules, or to administer an organization: *the governor's council on housing.* **—Usage.** COUNCIL and COUNSEL are not the same but are pronounced similarly. COUNCIL is a noun. Its most common sense is "an assembly of persons brought together for discussion or the like." COUNSEL is both a noun and a verb. Its most common meaning as a noun is "advice given to another." In law, COUNSEL means "legal adviser or advisers." As a verb, COUNSEL means "to advise."

coun•cil•man (koun′səl mən) /ˈkawnsəlmən/ *n.* [*count*], *pl.* **-men.** a member of a council, esp. the legislative body of a city or town.

coun•ci•lor or **coun•cil•lor** (koun′sə lər, -slər) /ˈkawnsələr, -slər/ *n.* [*count*] a member of a council. **—coun′ci•lor•ship′,** *n.* [*noncount*]

coun•sel (koun′səl) /ˈkawnsəl/ *n., pl.* **-sel** for 2, *v.,* **-seled, -sel•ing** or (*esp. Brit.*) **-selled, -sel•ling.** **—*n.* 1.** [*noncount*] advice: *I sought his counsel before applying for promotion.* **2.** the lawyer or lawyers representing one party or the other in court: [*count*]: *"Does counsel have an objection?" the judge asked.* [*noncount*]: *On the advice of counsel, I refuse to answer.* **—*v.* 3.** to give advice to or about; advise: [~ + *obj*]: *He counseled the committee to proceed slowly.* [~ + *against* + *verb-ing*]: *She* *counseled against leaving the country.* [~ + *obj* + *to* + *verb*]: *We counseled him to accept the deal.* [*used with quotations*]: *"I would go straight for promotion," he counseled.* —***Idiom.*** **4. keep one's own counsel,** to remain silent: *She kept her own counsel on the issue.* —**Usage.** See COUNCIL.

coun•se•lor (koun′sə lər, -slər) /ˈkawnsələr, -slər/ *n.* [*count*] **1.** a person who counsels; adviser: *Please see a counselor to help you with these forms.* **2.** a supervisor at a children's camp: *The counselors weren't watching the children.* **3.** a lawyer, esp. a trial lawyer: *Counselor, please approach the bench.* Also, *esp. Brit.,* **coun′sel•lor.** —**coun′se•lor•ship′,** *n.* [*noncount*]

count[1] (kount) /kawnt/ *v.* **1.** [~ + *obj*] to check over (objects) one by one to determine the total number: *We counted all the towels in the rooms.* **2.** to list or name the numerals up to: [~ (+ *up*) + *to* + *a number*]: *Close your eyes and count (up) to ten.* [~ + *obj* (+ *up*) + *to* + *a number*]: *He counted the numbers (up) to fifty in Swahili.* **3.** [*not: be* + ~*-ing;* ~ + *obj*] to include; take into account: *Count her among the chosen.* **4.** [*not: be* + ~*-ing; no obj*] to be worth something; have value; matter: *Every bit of help counts.* [~ + *as* + *obj*]: *The computer doesn't count as office furniture.* [~ + *for* + *obj*]: *His twenty years of service should count for something.* **5.** to consider or regard: [~ + *obj* + *adjective*]: *counted himself lucky.* [~ + *obj* + *among* + *obj*]: *counted among the greatest minds of the century.* **6. count against,** [~ + *against* + *obj*] to cause trouble for; work against: *If I revealed my true feelings, it would count against me.* **7. count down,** [*no obj*] to count backward from a number to zero: *At the launch pad they counted down from ten to zero, ignition, and lift-off.* **8. count in,** [~ + *obj* + *in*] to include: *Free tickets? Count me in!* **9. count on** or **upon,** [~ + *on/upon* + *obj*] to depend or rely on: *We're counting on you to be there.* **10. count out, a.** to declare (a boxer) the loser in a bout because of inability to stand up before the referee has counted to 10: [~ + *obj* + *out*]: *They counted the champion out.* [~ + *out* + *obj*]: *The referee counted out the champion.* **b.** [~ + *obj* + *out*] to exclude; leave (something) out; keep (someone) out or not involved: *Swimming in the Moscow River on New Year's Day? Count me out!* **c.** to count and apportion or give out: [~ + *out* + *obj*]: *The girls counted out their money in little piles.* [~ + *obj* + *out*]: *We counted the money out.* **11. count up,** to add up; figure a total of by counting: [~ + *up* + *obj*]: *I counted up the hours I had already spent and groaned.* [~ + *obj* + *up*]: *Count today's hours up and add them to the total.* —*n.* **12.** [*count*] the act of counting; reckoning; calculation: *They did a few counts to check the number of votes.* **13.** the number obtained by counting; the total: [*count*]: *The count was fifty to nothing.* [*noncount*]: *I lost count of the number of hours I spent.* **14.** [*count*] a separate charge in a legal proceeding against a defendant: *two counts of embezzlement.*

count[2] (kount) /kawnt/ *n.* [*count*] (in some European countries) a nobleman equivalent in rank to an English earl.

count[3] (kount) /kawnt/ This book uses the symbol [*count*] to stand for COUNTABLE noun. A countable noun is one that has a particular meaning or use in which we can imagine more than one item. So, a noun like *boy* has the meaning "a young male person," and for that meaning we can imagine more than one such person, so *boy* is a countable noun. The noun *sugar,* on the other hand, normally is a noun that cannot be counted, and so this book calls it NONCOUNT, with the symbol [*noncount*]. But this example demonstrates how difficult this notion can be, because even the normally noncount noun *sugar* can have a countable use or meaning, namely, "a spoonful of sugar." That meaning of *sugar* is [*count*], and so we can say "Give me two sugars, please," meaning "two spoonfuls (or packets, etc.) of sugar." The noun itself is not [*count*] or [*noncount*]; the particular use of the noun is.

count•a•ble (koun′tə bəl) /ˈkawntəbəl/ *adj.* (esp. of a noun, or a meaning of a noun) able to be counted: *countable nouns like* boy, desk, *and* ring. —**count′a•bly,** *adv.: The noun* sugar *is used countably in the sentence "Give me two sugars, please."* See COUNT[3] above.

count•down (kount′doun′) /ˈkawnt,dawn/ *n.* [*count*] the backward counting from the starting point of a rocket launching with the moment of firing given as zero: *The countdown of the launching was halted just before zero because of a faulty coupling.*

coun•te•nance (koun′tn əns) /ˈkawntṇəns/ *n., v.,* **-nanced, -nanc•ing.** —*n.* [*count*] **1.** appearance, esp. the expression of the face: *a sad countenance.* **2.** the face itself: *I was happy to see your countenance.* —*v.* [~ + *obj*] **3.** to permit or tolerate; approve; allow: *I won't countenance that kind of language in the house.* —**coun′te•nanc′er,** *n.* [*count*] See -TENT-.

count•er[1] (koun′tər) /ˈkawntər/ *n.* [*count*] **1.** a table or surface on which goods can be shown, etc.: *Bring your goods to the checkout counter.* **2.** (in restaurants, etc.) a long, narrow table with stools for the customers, behind which meals are prepared and served: *The waitress tossed our food down on the counter.* **3.** a long, flat surface for the preparation of food in a kitchen: *Just put the dishes on the counter for now.* See illustration at APARTMENT. **4.** anything used to keep account, esp. a disk or other small object used in a game, as checkers. —***Idiom.*** **5. over the counter,** [*noncount*] **a.** (of the sale of stock) through a broker's office rather than through the stock exchange. **b.** (of the sale of medicinal drugs) without requiring a prescription: *You can buy that drug over the counter in any shop.* **6. under the counter,** [*noncount*] illegally: *If we buy the tickets under the counter using dollars, we'll get a much better price and exchange rate.*

count•er[2] (koun′tər) /ˈkawntər/ *n.* [*count*] **1.** a person or thing that counts. **2.** an instrument for detecting and registering radiation.

coun•ter[3] (koun′tər) /ˈkawntər/ *adv.* **1.** [~ + *to* + *obj*] in the reverse direction; contrary: *This ran counter to what we expected.* —*adj.* [*be* + ~ + *to* + *obj*] **2.** opposite; opposed; contrary: *The attack was counter to our expectations.* —*n.* [*count*] **3.** something opposite or contrary to something else, such as a statement or action made to oppose another: *He made a quick counter to the guard's remark about ignorant tourists.* —*v.* [~ + *obj*] **4.** to oppose, esp. so as to weaken: *I countered her arguments by pointing out the advantages of my plan.*

counter-, *prefix.* counter- has the meaning "against, counter to, opposed to." This meaning is found in such words as: COUNTERATTACK, COUNTERCLOCKWISE.

coun•ter•act (koun′tər akt′) /,kawntərˈækt/ *v.* [~ + *obj*] to act in opposition to; frustrate by contrary action: *This medicine will counteract the effects of the disease.* —**coun′ter•ac′tant,** *adj.* —**coun•ter•ac•tion** (koun′tər-ak′shən) /,kawntərˈækʃən/ *n.* [*count*] —**coun′ter•ac′tive,** *adj.* —**coun′ter•ac′tive•ly,** *adv.*

coun•ter•at•tack (koun′tər ə tak′) /ˈkawntərə,tæk/ *n.* **1.** an attack made to reply to or oppose another attack: [*count*]: *The army launched a counterattack across the river.* [*noncount*]: *the concept of counterattack in modern warfare.* —*v.* [*no obj*] **2.** to make a counterattack: *to counterattack at dawn.*

coun•ter•bal•ance (*n.* koun′tər bal′əns; *v.* koun′tər-bal′əns) /*n.* ˈkawntər,bæləns; *v.* ,kawntərˈbæləns/ *n., v.,* **-anced, -anc•ing.** —*n.* [*count*] **1.** a weight balancing another weight; an equal power or influence acting against another. —*v.* [~ + *obj*] **2.** to oppose with an equal weight, force, or influence: *to counterbalance a load.*

coun•ter•clock•wise (koun′tər klok′wīz′) /,kawntərˈklɒk,wayz/ *adj., adv.* in a direction opposite to that of the normal turning of the hands of a clock.

coun•ter•cul•ture (koun′tər kul′chər) /ˈkawntər-,kʌltʃər/ *n.* [*noncount*] the culture and lifestyle of those people who reject the generally accepted values and behavior of society: *members of the counterculture of the 1960's.*

coun•ter•es•pi•o•nage (koun′tər es′pē ə näzh′, -nij) /,kawntərˈɛspiyə,nɑʒ, -nɪdʒ/ *n.* [*noncount*] the detection of, and steps or measures taken against, enemy spying.

coun•ter•feit (koun′tər fit′) /ˈkawntər,fɪt/ *adj.* **1.** made in imitation of something genuine with the intention of deceiving; forged: *a plot to make counterfeit money.* **2.** pretended; unreal: *counterfeit grief.* —*n.* [*count*] **3.** an imitation intended to be used as genuine; forgery: *The expert held up the $20 bill and exclaimed, "It's an obvious counterfeit."* —*v.* **4.** to make a counterfeit (of); forge: [*no obj*]: *guilty of counterfeiting.* [~ + *obj*]: *The crooks counterfeited five-dollar bills.* **5.** [~ + *obj*] to pretend to have (an emotion, etc.): *counterfeiting his grief for the benefit of the observers.* —**coun′ter•feit′er,** *n.* [*count*]

coun•ter•in•sur•gen•cy (koun′tər in sûr′jən sē) /,kawntərɪnˈsɜrdʒənsiy/ *n., pl.* **-cies.** a program of combating guerrilla warfare: [*noncount*]: *a policy of counterinsurgency against the guerrillas.* [*count*]: *a number of counterinsurgencies against the guerrillas.* —**coun′ter•in•sur′gent,** *n.* [*count*], *adj.*

coun•ter•in•tel•li•gence (koun′tər in tel′i jəns) /,kawntərɪnˈtɛlɪdʒəns/ *n.* [*noncount*] the activity of an intelligence service against the intelligence-gathering of a foreign power.

count•er•man (koun′tər man′) /ˈkawntərˌmæn/ *n.* [*count*], *pl.* **-men.** a person who waits on customers from behind a counter, as in a cafeteria.

coun•ter•mand (*v.* koun′tər mand′, koun′tər mand′; *n.* koun′tər mand′) /*v.* ˌkawntərˈmænd, ˈkawntərˌmænd; *n.* ˈkawntərˌmænd/ *v.* [~ + *obj*] **1.** to give a second command that cancels (a command already given): *The general countermanded his first order to attack.* **—***n.* [*count*] **2.** a command, order, etc., canceling one already given. See -MAND-.

coun•ter•meas•ure (koun′tər mezh′ər) /ˈkawntər-ˌmɛʒər/ *n.* [*count*] an opposing action; an action or measure taken against another: *the plane's electronic countermeasures to avoid detection by radar.*

coun•ter•pane (koun′tər pān′) /ˈkawntərˌpeyn/ *n.* [*count*] a quilt or covering for a bed; bedspread.

coun•ter•part (koun′tər pärt′) /ˈkawntərˌpɑrt/ *n.* [*count*] a person or thing closely resembling another, esp. in function: *The new Russian president came to Washington to meet his counterpart.* See -PAR-.

coun•ter•point (koun′tər point′) /ˈkawntərˌpɔynt/ *n.* **1.** POLYPHONY (def. 1). **2.** [*count*] any element contrasted with another.

coun•ter•pro•duc•tive (koun′tər prə duk′tiv) /ˌkawntə-rprəˈdʌktɪv/ *adj.* producing the opposite effect from what was intended: *Your apology was counterproductive because no one believes you meant it sincerely.* **—coun′-ter•pro•duc′tive•ly,** *adv.*

coun•ter•rev•o•lu•tion (koun′tər rev′ə lo͞o′shən) /ˈkawntərˌrɛvəˈluwʃən/ *n.* a revolution against a government recently established by a revolution: [*noncount*]: *An attempt at counterrevolution failed.* [*count*]: *They staged a counterrevolution.* **—coun′ter•rev′o•lu′tion•ar•y,** *n.* [*count*], *pl.* **-ar•ies**: *a city full of counterrevolutionaries.* **—***adj.*: *counterrevolutionary strategy.*

coun•ter•sign (koun′tər sīn′) /ˈkawntərˌsayn/ *n.* [*count*] **1.** a sign used in reply to another sign. **2.** a signature added to another signature, esp. to show that the first one is genuine. **—***v.* [~ + *obj*] **3.** to sign (a document that has been signed by someone else), esp. in order to provide identification: *Countersign the document where I've marked the lines with x's.*

coun•ter•ten•or (koun′tər ten′ər) /ˈkawntərˌtɛnər/ *n.* [*count*] **1.** a tenor who can approximate the vocal range of a female alto. **2.** a voice part for a countertenor.

count•ess (koun′tis) /ˈkawntɪs/ *n.* [*count*] **1.** the wife or widow of a count in the nobility of continental Europe or of an earl in the British peerage. **2.** a woman having the rank of a count or earl in her own right.

count•less (kount′lis) /ˈkawntlɪs/ *adj.* [*usually: before a noun*] so vast a number as to be beyond counting; innumerable: *countless stars in the sky.*

count′ noun′, *n.* [*count*] a noun that is countable. See COUNT[3].

coun•tri•fied (kun′trə fīd′) /ˈkʌntrəˌfayd/ *adj.* made to be like the country in appearance, conduct, etc.; rural: *those charmingly simple countrified ways of hers.*

coun•try (kun′trē) /ˈkʌntriy/ *n., pl.* **-tries,** *adj.* **—***n.* **1.** [*count*] a state or nation: *European countries.* **2.** [*count*] the territory or land of a nation: *the country of France.* **3.** [*count*] the people of a district, state, or nation: *That whole country hates foreigners.* **4.** [*count*] the land of one's birth or citizenship. **5.** [*count; singular: the* + ~] rural districts, as opposed to cities or towns: *We both grew up in the country.* **6.** [*noncount*] an area marked by certain characteristics, etc.: *Pennsylvania Dutch country.* **7.** COUNTRY MUSIC. **—***adj.* [*before a noun*] **8.** of, from, or characteristic of the country: *a country boy.* **9.** of or relating to country music: *a country singer.*

coun′try-and-west′ern, *n.* COUNTRY MUSIC.

coun′try club′, *n.* [*count*] a club outside a city or town, usually in the country, with facilities for sports.

coun′try danc′ing, *n.* [*noncount*] dancing originally from rural England, esp. dancing in which the dancers face each other in two rows.

coun•try•man (kun′trē mən) /ˈkʌntriymən/ *n.* [*count*], *pl.* **-men.** a native or inhabitant of one's own country.

coun′try mu′sic, *n.* [*noncount*] music originally from the folk music of the Southeast and the cowboy music of the West.

coun•try•side (kun′trē sīd′) /ˈkʌntriyˌsayd/ *n.* [*noncount*] a particular section of a country, esp. a rural section: *beautiful countryside three hours north of the city.*

coun•ty (koun′tē) /ˈkawntiy/ *n.* [*count*], *pl.* **-ties. 1.** the largest local division of government in most states of the U.S.. **2.** a unit of local government in Great Britain, Canada, etc. **3.** the people of a county: *Last year the county voted for the first time.*

coup (ko͞o) /kuw/ *n.* [*count*], *pl.* **coups** (ko͞oz). **1.** a highly successful, unexpected act or move: *It was quite a coup to get the Russian hockey star to come and play in New York.* **2.** (among the Plains Indians of North America) a daring deed performed in battle by a warrior. **3.** COUP D'ÉTAT.

coup de grâce (ko͞o′ də gräs′) /ˌkuwˈ də grɑs/ *n.* [*count*], *pl.* **coups de grâce** (ko͞o′də gräs′) /ˌkuwˈdə grɑs/. **1.** a death blow, esp. one to end suffering: *The veterinarian applied the coup de grâce to the badly injured horse.* **2.** any finishing or decisive act, move, or stroke: *The coup de grâce was the winning goal in the last minute of play.*

coup d'é•tat (ko͞o′ dā tä′) /ˌkuw deyˈtɑ/ *n.* [*count*], *pl.* **coups d'é•tat** (ko͞o′ dā täz′, -tä′) /ˌkuw deyˈtɑz, -ˈtɑ/. a sudden and decisive action that results in a forceful change of government: *The generals staged a coup d'état.*

coupe (ko͞op) /kuwp/ *n.* [*count*] a closed, two-door car shorter than a sedan of the same model.

cou•ple (kup′əl) /ˈkʌpəl/ *n., v.,* **-pled, -pling. —***n.* [*count*] **1.** a combination of two of a kind; pair: *Arrange the chairs in couples.* **2.** a grouping of two persons, such as a married pair, or dance partners: *What a lovely couple they make.* **3. a couple of,** [~ + *of* + *a plural noun*] a few; several; more than one but not many: *It's a couple of miles farther on.* **—***v.* **4.** [~ + *obj*] to fasten or associate together in a pair or pairs: *The trainmen coupled the cars together.* **5.** [~ + *obj* + *with* + *obj*] to join; connect: *The economic demands were coupled with cries for political freedom.* **6.** [*no obj*] to have sex; copulate. **—Usage.** Compare PAIR and COUPLE, which both take *a* before and *of* after, and have the meaning "a group of two." PAIR is used when the two items mentioned next come as a set, with one not usually used without the other: *a pair of socks, a pair of gloves,* or when there is one item that has two parts, as in *a pair of shorts, a pair of scissors.* COUPLE is used for things of the same kind that happen to be two in number: *a couple of books, a couple of chairs.* Only COUPLE has the sense of "a few, several," as in *a couple of miles away.* COUPLE therefore can mean "two (or more)"; PAIR will almost always mean "two (or less)."

cou•plet (kup′lit) /ˈkʌplɪt/ *n.* [*count*] a pair of lines of poetry or verse, esp. a pair of the same length that rhyme and come one after the other.

cou•pling (kup′ling) /ˈkʌplɪŋ/ *n.* **1.** [*noncount*] the act of a person or thing that couples. **2.** [*count*] a connection between two railroad cars.

cou•pon (ko͞o′pon, kyo͞o′-) /ˈkuwpɒn, ˈkyuw-/ *n.* [*count*] **1.** a portion of a ticket, label, or the like, entitling the holder to something, or for use as an order blank, etc.: *clipped a few discount coupons from the paper.* **2.** a separate piece of paper, ticket, etc., for the same purpose.

-cour-, *root.* *-cour-* comes ultimately from Latin, where it has the meaning "run, happen." It is related to *-cur-*. This meaning is found in such words as: CONCOURSE, COURIER, COURSE, DISCOURSE, RECOURSE.

cour•age (kûr′ij, kur′-) /ˈkɜrɪdʒ, ˈkʌr-/ *n.* [*noncount*] the quality of mind that enables a person to face difficulty, danger, etc., without fear; bravery. **—cou•ra•geous** (kə-rā′jəs) /kəˈreydʒəs/ *adj.* **—cou•ra′geous•ly,** *adv.*

cour•i•er (kûr′ē ər, ko͝or′-) /ˈkɜriyər, ˈkʊr-/ *n.* **1.** a messenger: [*count*]: *A special courier brought us the overnight package.* [*noncount*]: *It was brought by courier.* **2.** [*count*] a tour guide for a travel agency. See -COUR-.

course (kôrs, kōrs) /kɔrs, kowrs/ *n., v.,* **coursed** (kôrst, kōrst) /kɔrst, kowrst/ **cours•ing. —***n.* **1.** a direction or route to be taken: [*count*]: *Our course took us over the Grand Canyon.* [*noncount*]: *The flight was well off course.* **2.** [*count*] the path along which anything moves: *the course of a stream.* **3.** [*count; usually: singular*] the continuous passage through time or a succession of stages: *in the course of a year.* **4.** [*count*] area, etc., on which a game is played, a race is run or sailed, etc.: *the downhill ski course.* **5.** [*count; usually: singular*] a particular manner of proceeding: *planned a course of action.* **6.** [*count*] a normal manner of procedure: *The disease ran its course.* **7.** [*count*] a planned or prescribed series: *suggested a course of medical treatment for my painful back.* **8.** [*count*] a program of instruction, such as in a college; class or number of classes: *I took three courses: reading, writing, and mathematics.* **9.** [*count*] a part of a meal served at one time: *Dad's main course was always roast beef.* **—v.** [*no obj*] **10.** to run, race, or move swiftly: *blood coursing through his veins.* **—*Idiom.* 11. in due course,** [*noncount*] in the proper order of events: *You'll get your promotion in due course.* **12. of course,** [*noncount*] **a.** certainly; definitely: *"I don't know if I can do this on time." "Of course you can!"* **b.** in the usual order of things: *The world would be a better place without him, but of course that's not possible.* See -COUR-.

court (kôrt, kōrt) /kɔrt, kowrt/ *n.* **1. a.** a place where legal justice is administered: [*count*]: *There will be order in this court.* [*noncount*]: *They tried to settle the case out of court.* **b.** [*count*] a group of people, such as judges, lawyers, and a jury, authorized to hear and decide legal cases: *The court gasped in astonishment at the testimony.* **2.** [*count*] an open area surrounded by buildings, walls, etc.: *Flowers and trees grew in the court of our building.* **3.** [*count*]a short street. **4.** [*count*] a smooth, level, four-sided area marked with lines, on which to play tennis, etc.: *The court was slippery in the rain.* **5.** [*count*] the residence of a king, queen, or other high-ranking person; palace: *at the king's court.* **6.** [*count*] the people accompanying a king, queen, or other high-ranking person: *Some of his plays were performed before the court of the queen.* **7.** [*noncount*] devotion; attention in order to win favor; homage: *The knight wanted to pay court to his fair maiden.* **—v. 8.** [~ + *obj*] to try to win the favor or goodwill of: *the president's tax plan to court the rich.* **9.** to seek the affections of; try to attract; woo: [~ + *obj*]: *He was courting a young lady when I met him.* [*no obj*]: *They were courting but couldn't marry for a few years.* **10.** (of animals) to attempt to attract (a mate) by engaging in certain specific behavior: [~ + *obj*]: *The male courts a female by wrapping his neck around her.* [*no obj*]: *The males court to attract a mate but don't always succeed.* **11.** [~ + *obj*] to act so as to cause, lead to, or get (something bad); risk: *courting disaster by talking to your boss that way.* **—*Idiom.* 12. hold court,** to act as the center of attention for one's admirers: *She held court out on the veranda.*

cour•te•ous (kûr′tē əs) /ˈkɜrtiyəs/ *adj.* of, relating to, or showing courtesy: *a courteous note of thanks.* **—cour′te•ous•ly,** *adv.*: *I always try to treat my students courteously.* **—cour′te•ous•ness,** *n.* [*noncount*]

cour•te•san (kôr′tə zən, kōr′-) /ˈkɔrtəzən, ˈkowr-/ *n.* [*count*] (esp. formerly) a woman who is looked after by noblemen or men of wealth and kept for a sexual relationship.

cour•te•sy (kûr′tə sē) /ˈkɜrtəsiy/ *n., pl.* **-sies. 1.** [*noncount*] good manners or social conduct; polite behavior: *Treat everyone with courtesy.* **2.** [*count; usually plural*] a courteous, respectful act or expression: *exchanging a few courtesies.* **3.** [*noncount*] favor, help, or generosity: *The actors appeared through the courtesy of their union.* **—*prep.* 4. courtesy of,** [~ + *of* + *obj*] thanks to; by the generosity of: *The show comes live from Hollywood, courtesy of the Public Broadcasting System.*

court•house (kôrt′hous′, kōrt′-) /ˈkɔrtˌhaws, ˈkowrt-/ *n.* [*count*] a building in which courts of law are held.

cour•ti•er (kôr′tē ər, kōr′-) /ˈkɔrtiyər, ˈkowr-/ *n.* [*count*] **1.** a person who is often at the court of a king; attendant. **2.** a person who flatters.

court•ly (kôrt′lē, kōrt′-) /ˈkɔrtliy, ˈkowrt-/ *adj.,* **-li•er, -li•est.** refined; elegant: *courtly manners.* **—court′li•ness,** *n.* [*noncount*]

court′-mar′tial, *n., pl.* **courts-mar•tial, court-mar•tials,** *v.,* **-tialed, -tial•ing** or (*esp. Brit.*) **-tialled, -tial•ling. —*n.*** [*count*] **1.** a military court that hears cases against members of the armed forces. **2.** a trial by such a court. **—*v.*** [~ + *obj*] **3.** to try (military personnel) by court-martial: *The major was court-martialed for mutiny.*

court•room (kôrt′ro͞om′, -ro͝om′, kōrt′-) /ˈkɔrtˌruwm, -ˌrʊm, ˈkowrt-/ *n.* [*count*] a room in which the sessions of a law court are held: *If there isn't silence the judge will clear the courtroom.*

court•ship (kôrt′ship, kōrt′-) /ˈkɔrtʃɪp, ˈkowrt-/ *n.* **1.** [*noncount*] the act by one person of trying to win the favorable attention of another, esp. by a man toward a woman: *When it came to courtship he was clumsy and inexperienced.* **2.** [*count*] the period during which such courting takes place: *a brief courtship of only a few months.* **3.** [*noncount*] behavior in animals before and during mating, often including elaborate displays: *courtship displays.*

court•yard (kôrt′yärd′, kōrt′-) /ˈkɔrtˌyɑrd, ˈkowrt-/ *n.* [*count*] a court open to the sky, esp. one enclosed on all four sides.

cous•cous (ko͞os′ko͞os) /ˈkuwskuws/ *n.* [*noncount*] **1.** a North African dish of steamed semolina, served usually with a spicy stew. **2.** the grainy semolina used in this dish.

cous•in (kuz′ən) /ˈkʌzən/ *n.* [*count*] **1.** the son or daughter of an uncle or aunt: *cousins on my father's side.* **2.** a person or thing related to another by similar natures, languages, etc.: *the Americans and all their English-speaking cousins.*

cou•ture (ko͞o to͝or′) /kuwˈtʊr/ *n.* [*noncount*] **1.** fashion design, or the business of such design. **2.** fashion designers when thought of as a group. **3.** the apparel created by such designers. **—*adj.*** [*usually: before a noun*] **4.** created by a fashion designer or relating to or suggesting such creation: *the couture look.*

cou•tu•ri•er (ko͞o to͝or′ē ər, -ē ā′) /kuwˈtʊriyər, -iyˌey/ *n.* [*count*] a person who works in couture: *high-priced Hollywood couturiers.*

cove (kōv) /kowv/ *n.* [*count*] a small opening or recess in the shoreline of a sea, lake, or river; a small, sheltered bay.

cov•en (kuv′ən, kō′vən) /ˈkʌvən, ˈkowvən/ *n.* [*count*] an assembly of witches, esp. a group of thirteen.

cov•e•nant (kuv′ə nənt) /ˈkʌvənənt/ *n.* [*count*] **1.** a formal agreement between two or more persons to do or not do something. **2.** a formal agreement of legal validity, esp. one under seal. See -VEN-.

cov•er (kuv′ər) /ˈkʌvər/ *v.* **1.** [~ + *obj*] to be or serve as a covering for; extend over: *Snow covered the fields.* **2.** [~ + *obj*] to place something upon, as for protection, concealment, or warmth: *She covered the baby with a blanket.* **3.** [~ + *obj*] to protect or conceal (the head, body, etc.) with clothes, etc.; wrap: *She covered her shoulders with a shawl.* **4.** [~ + *obj*] to bring upon (oneself): *covered himself with honors.* **5.** [~ + *obj*] to spread on or over; put over the surface of; coat: *to cover bread with honey.* **6.** [~ + *obj*] to deal with; apply to: *The new rules cover working conditions.* **7.** [~ + *obj*] to deal with (a subject); have (something) as the subject matter: *The book covers 18th-century English history.* **8.** [~ + *obj*] to be enough to meet or to be able to pay for (a charge, etc.): *The loan is to cover my losses.* **9.** [~ + *obj*] to act as a reporter of (an event, etc.): *The news team covered the hostage crisis for that magazine.* **10.** [~ + *obj*] to insure against risk or loss: *This policy covers you against everything.* **11.** [~ + *obj*] to protect or guard (a fellow soldier, etc.) during combat by taking a position from which the enemy can be fired upon: *His fighter squadron covered the bombers on their run over enemy territory.* **12.** [~ + *obj*] to aim at, as with a pistol: *Don't move; you're covered.* **13.** to take temporary charge of or responsibility for in place of another: [~ + *for* + *obj*]: *Cover for me at the office while I go to the dentist.* [~ + *obj*]: *I'll cover her classes while she's sick.* **14.** [~ + *for* + *obj*] to hide the action of another by providing an alibi or by acting in the other's place: *I covered for her by telling the police she was with me.* **15.** [~ + *obj*] to achieve or accomplish (a distance) traveled over; pass or travel over: *We covered about ten miles hiking.* **16.** [*not: be* + ~*-ing;* ~ + *obj*] to spread over; occupy; take up: *The territory covers an area the size of North Dakota.* **17. cover up, a.** to cover completely; enfold: [~ + *up* + *obj*]: *She covered up the sleeping children with a blanket.* [~ + *obj* + *up*]: *She covered them up with warm blankets.* **b.** to keep (something) secret: [*no obj*]: *One of the conspirators didn't want to cover up.* [~ + *up* + *for* + *obj*]: *Another one may have tried to cover up for his superior.* [~ + *up* + *obj*]: *The general couldn't cover up everything that had happened..* [~ + *obj* + *up*]: *His mistress tried to cover everything up but had to tell the truth.* **—*n.* 18.** [*count*] something that covers, such as the lid of a container or the casing of a book: *a book cover.* **19.** [*plural; the* + ~] a blanket, quilt, or the like: *He threw off the covers.* **20.** [*noncount*] protection; shelter: *The soldiers searched frantically for cover.* **21.** [*noncount*] anything that hides; concealment: *under cover of darkness.* **22.** [*count*] a false or assumed identity or occupation that masks the real one: *My cover was trade negotiator, but in fact I was a spy.* **23.** COVER CHARGE. **—*Idiom.* 24. cover all (the) bases,** to anticipate all the possible results: *Before he met with them he covered all the bases by preparing in his mind answers to everything that they might ask.* **25. take cover,** to seek shelter or safety: *When it rained we took cover under the trees.* **—cov′er•er,** *n.* [*count*]

cov•er•age (kuv′ər ij) /ˈkʌvərɪdʒ/ *n.* [*noncount*] **1.** protection against a risk as listed in an insurance policy: *coverage against fire, theft, flood, and earthquakes.* **2.** the reporting or broadcasting of news: *coverage of the Olympics.*

cov•er•all (kuv′ər ôl′) /ˈkʌvərˌɔl/ *n.* Often, **coveralls.** [*plural*] a one-piece work garment worn over other clothing as protection: *My coveralls are torn.*

cov′er charge′, *n.* [*count*] an additional charge made by a restaurant for providing entertainment: *a cover charge of twenty dollars.*

cov′ered wag′on, *n.* [*count*] a large wagon with a high canvas top, esp. such a wagon used by pioneers to cross the North American plains in the 19th century.

cov•er•ing (kuv′ər ing) /ˈkʌvərɪŋ/ *n.* [*count*] **1.** something laid over or wrapped around a thing, esp. for hiding or protection: *We used the burlap bags as a covering in the cold.* **—***adj.* [*before a noun*] **2.** providing explanation: *a covering memo to accompany the charts.*

cov•er•let (kuv′ər lit) /ˈkʌvərlɪt/ *n.* [*count*] a bed quilt that does not cover the pillow; bedspread.

cov′er sto′ry, *n.* [*count*] **1.** a magazine article highlighted by an illustration on the cover. **2.** a false story made up to conceal a true purpose; alibi: *His cover story was that he was a visiting reporter, but in truth he was an industrial spy.*

co•vert (*adj.* kō′vərt, kuv′ərt; *n.* kuv′ərt, kō′vərt) /*adj.* ˈkowvərt, ˈkʌvərt; *n.* ˈkʌvərt, ˈkowvərt/ *adj.* **1.** concealed; secret; disguised: *covert operations behind enemy lines.* **—***n.* [*count*] **2.** an area of trees or bushes giving shelter to game; thicket. **—co′vert•ly,** *adv.*: *I glanced covertly at them while they argued.* **—co′vert•ness,** *n.* [*noncount*]

cov′er-up′, *n.* [*count*] means of concealing or preventing exposure or wrongdoing: *planned the cover-up to keep people from finding out about the burglary.*

cov•et (kuv′it) /ˈkʌvɪt/ *v.* [~ + *obj*] **1.** to desire improperly: *to covet another's property.* **2.** to wish for strongly or eagerly; desire greatly: *coveted a position in the main office.* **—cov′et•er,** *n.* [*count*]

cov•et•ous (kuv′ə təs) /ˈkʌvətəs/ *adj.* showing or involving an improper desire or wish for something: *looking with covetous eyes at his neighbor's beautiful wife.* **—cov′et•ous•ly,** *adv.* **—cov′et•ous•ness,** *n.* [*noncount*]

cow[1] (kou) /kaw/ *n.* [*count*] **1.** the mature female of cattle: *The cows were kept for their milk.* **2.** *Informal.* a domestic bovine of either sex and any age: *Look at all the cows in the field.* **3.** the female of various other large animals, such as the elephant. **—*Idiom.* 4. have a cow,** *Slang.* to become very excited or angry; have a fit: *told his teacher not to have a cow just because he forgot his homework.* **—cow′like′,** *adj.*

cow[2] (kou) /kaw/ *v.* [~ + *obj*] to frighten with threats; intimidate: *I was cowed into agreeing with the boss.*

cow•ard (kou′ərd) /ˈkawərd/ *n.* [*count*] a person who shows a shameful lack of courage: *That coward always ran away from a fight.*

cow•ard•ice (kou′ər dis) /ˈkawərdɪs/ *n.* [*noncount*] lack of courage.

cow•ard•ly (kou′ərd lē) /ˈkawərdliy/ *adj.* lacking courage; of or like a coward: *cowardly actions.*

cow•bird (kou′bûrd′) /ˈkawˌbɜrd/ *n.* [*count*] a blackbird of North America often found near cattle.

cow•boy (kou′boi′) /ˈkawˌbɔy/ *n.* [*count*] **1.** a man on horseback who tends cattle: *The cowboys branded the calves.* **2.** a reckless vehicle driver: *The police never catch the cowboys on the interstate.*

cow•er (kou′ər) /ˈkawər/ *v.* [*no obj*] to pull back and away from, as in fear; cringe: *The children cowered before the storm.* **—cow′er•ing•ly,** *adv.*

cow•girl (kou′gûrl′) /ˈkawˌgɜrl/ *n.* [*count*] a woman or girl on horseback who herds and tends cattle.

cow•hand (kou′hand′) /ˈkawˌhænd/ *n.* [*count*] a person employed on a cattle ranch; cowboy or cowgirl.

cow•hide (kou′hīd′) /ˈkawˌhayd/ *n.* **1.** [*count*] the skin or hide of a cow. **2.** [*noncount*] the leather made from it.

cowl (koul) /kawl/ *n.* [*count*] **1.** a hooded garment worn by monks. **2.** the hood itself. **3.** the forward part of the body of a motor vehicle supporting the rear of the hood and the windshield.

cow•lick (kou′lik′) /ˈkawˌlɪk/ *n.* [*count*] a small bit of hair on the head that grows in a direction different from that of the rest of the hair.

cow•man (kou′mən) /ˈkawmən/ *n.* [*count*], *pl.* **-men. 1.** a rancher. **2.** a cowboy.

co•work•er (kō′wûr′kər, kō wûr′-) /ˈkowˌwɜrkər, kowˈwɜr-/ *n.* [*count*] a fellow worker: *His coworkers get along with him just fine.*

cow•poke (kou′pōk′) /ˈkawˌpowk/ *n.* [*count*] a cowboy or cowgirl.

cow•punch•er (kou′pun′chər) /ˈkawˌpʌntʃər/ *n.* [*count*] a cowboy or cowgirl.

cow•rie or **cow•ry** (kou′rē) /ˈkawriy/ *n.* [*count*], *pl.* **-ries. 1.** a shellfish of the sea having a glossy oval shell with a narrow, toothed opening. **2.** the shell of this shellfish, sometimes used as currency in Asia and Africa.

cow•slip (kou′slip) /ˈkawslɪp/ *n.* [*count*] a flower, an English primrose having sweet-smelling yellow blossoms.

cox•comb (koks′kōm′) /ˈkɒksˌkowm/ *n.* [*count*] a conceited, foolish, or pretentious man; fop.

coy (koi) /kɔy/ *adj.* **1.** shy or reserved; coquettish: *She gave the prince a coy little smile.* **2.** shy; modest. **3.** reluctant to reveal one's plans: *We won't be coy; you're the one we want to hire.* **—coy′ish•ness,** *n.* [*noncount*] **—coy′ly,** *adv.* **—coy′ness,** *n.* [*noncount*]

coy•o•te (kī ō′tē, kī′ōt) /kayˈowtiy, ˈkayowt/ *n.* [*count*], *pl.* **-tes,** (*esp. when thought of as a group*) **-te.** a medium-sized North American animal resembling a wolf.

co•zy (kō′zē) /ˈkowziy/ *adj.*, **-zi•er, -zi•est,** *n.*, *pl.* **-zies,** *v.*, **-zied, -zy•ing. —***adj.* **1.** snugly warm and comfortable: *a cozy little house.* **2.** convenient, beneficial, or helpful as a result of some dishonest, deceitful, or illegal activity: *a cozy little agreement among the competing firms.* **—***n.* [*count*] **3.** a padded covering for a teapot, etc., to retain the heat. **—***v.* **4. cozy up, a.** to (cause to) become more cozy: [*no obj*]: *They cozied up by the fire.* [~ + *up* + *obj*]: *New curtains cozied up the room.* [~ + *obj* + *up*]: *New curtains will cozy it up.* **b.** [~ + *up* + *to* + *obj*] to try to become friendly with someone in power to gain some benefit for oneself: *cozied up to the boss to get a promotion.* Sometimes, **cosy. —co•zi•ly** (kō′zə lē) /ˈkowzəliy/ *adv.* **—co′zi•ness,** *n.* [*noncount*]

CPA or **C.P.A.,** an abbreviation of: certified public accountant.

cpd., an abbreviation of: compound.

CPI, an abbreviation of: consumer price index.

cpl., an abbreviation of: corporal.

CPR, an abbreviation of: cardiopulmonary resuscitation, an emergency procedure using medical techniques intended to restore breathing or heartbeat to an injured person.

cps, an abbreviation of: **1.** characters per second. **2.** cycles per second.

CPU, an abbreviation of: central processing unit: the most important and basic part of a computer system, containing the circuitry to execute program instructions. Compare MICROPROCESSOR.

cr., an abbreviation of: **1.** credit. **2.** creditor. **3.** crown.

crab[1] (krab) /kræb/ *n.*, *v.*, **crabbed, crab•bing. —***n.* **1.** [*count*] a sea animal, a crustacean having a wide, flattened body and five pairs of legs, the front legs being the largest and having claws. **2.** [*noncount*] the flesh of the crab. **—***v.* **3.** [*no obj*] to fish for crabs. **4.** to move (something) sideways; scuttle: [*no obj*]: *The soldiers crabbed forward quickly and dug in.* [~ + *obj*]: *They crabbed their tanks forward, shooting quickly, reloading, and then moving again.* **—crab′ber,** *n.* [*count*] **—crab′like′,** *adj.*

crab[2] (krab) /kræb/ *n.*, *v.*, **crabbed, crab•bing. —***n.* [*count*] **1.** a bad-tempered, unpleasant person: *The English teacher was an old crab to the kids.* **—***v.* [*no obj*] **2.** to find fault; complain: *You were always crabbing; didn't you like it there?*

crab′ ap′ple, *n.* [*count*] **1.** a small hard, sour apple, used for making jelly. **2.** a tree bearing such fruit.

crab•bed (krab′id) /ˈkræbɪd/ *adj.* **1.** difficult to read: *crabbed handwriting.* **2.** hard to understand; intricate and obscure: *crabbed short stories and poetry.* **3.** bad-tempered; unpleasant in attitude: *the crabbed old English teacher.*

crab•by (krab′ē) /ˈkræbiy/ *adj.*, **-bi•er, -bi•est.** bad-tempered; unpleasant: *a crabby old banker.* **—crab•bi•ly** (krab′ə lē) /ˈkræbəliy/ *adv.* **—crab′bi•ness,** *n.* [*noncount*]

crab′ grass′, *n.* [*noncount*] a weed grass that grows in thick patches on lawns.

crack (krak) /kræk/ *v.* **1.** to break without separation of parts; (cause to) become marked by lines that indicate a break: [*no obj*]: *The window cracked when a rock hit it.* [~ + *obj*]: *The rock cracked the glass.* **2.** to break open or into many parts: [~ + *obj*]: *cracked an egg into the bowl.* [*no obj*]: *The egg cracked when it hit the floor.* **3.** to break with a sudden, sharp sound: [*no obj*]: *The wood in the fireplace cracked suddenly.* [~ + *obj*]: *I cracked a few pieces of wood and added them to the fire.* **4.** to (cause to) make a sudden, sharp sound; snap: [*no obj*]:

The whip cracked and the lions roared. [~ + *obj*]: *I cracked my knuckles nervously.* **5.** [*no obj*] (of the voice) to break abruptly; change to the wrong pitch: *The tenor's voice cracked on that high note.* **6.** [*no obj*] to break down, esp. under severe psychological pressure: *He finally cracked from all the stress.* **7.** to strike forcefully: [*no obj*]: *His head cracked against the mantelpiece.* [~ + *obj*]: *She cracked his head with the vase.* **8.** [~ + *obj*] to solve or reveal, esp. after much effort: *to crack a murder case.* **9.** [~ + *obj*] *Informal.* to break into (a safe, etc.): *tried to crack the safe but couldn't.* **10.** [~ + *obj*] *Informal.* **a.** to open slightly, such as a door or window: *Crack the windows and let's get some fresh air.* **b.** to open (a book) in order to study or read: *It was a little late to be cracking the books.* **11. crack down,** to take severe measures, esp. in enforcing regulations: [*no obj*]: *tried to crack down, but by then things had gotten out of control.* [~ + *down* + *on* + *obj*]: *a campaign to crack down on drug pushers.* **12. crack up,** *Informal.* **a.** [*no obj*] to suffer a mental breakdown: *He cracked up when his wife left him.* **b.** to (cause to) crash (an automobile or airplane): [*no obj*]: *The car spun out of control and cracked up.* [~ + *up* + *obj*]: *cracked up his father's brand-new car.* [~ + *obj* + *up*]: *He cracked the car up the first time he drove it.* **c.** to (cause to) laugh hard without being able to stop: [*no obj*]: *He cracked up at the sight of her in those old frumpy pajamas.* [~ + *up* + *obj*]: *That joke cracked up the audience.* [~ + *obj* + *up*]: *That joke cracked him up.* —*n.* **13.** [*count*] a break without separation of parts: *a few cracks on the windshield.* **14.** [*count*] a slight opening, as between boards in a floor: *We plastered the cracks in the wall.* **15.** [*count*] a sudden, sharp noise: *The crack of a rifle shot rang out.* **16.** [*count*] the snap of or as of a whip. **17.** [*count*] a heavy or strong blow: *a crack to the jaw.* **18.** [*count*] a sharp or funny remark: *"Another crack like that and you'll be out of here," the umpire yelled.* **19.** [*count*] a break in the tone of the voice: *answered with a small crack in her voice.* **20.** [*count*] a chance; try: *I'd like a crack at that.* **21.** [*noncount*] highly addictive, purified cocaine in the form of pellets for smoking. —*adj.* [*before a noun*] **22.** skillful; excellent; of high quality: *a crack shot.* —***Idiom.*** **23. crack a smile,** *Informal.* to smile, esp. hesitantly. **24. get cracking,** [*no obj*] to get moving; hurry up: *We're late—let's get cracking.*

crack•down (krak′doun′) /ˈkræk,dawn/ *n.* [*count*] the severe enforcing of regulations, esp. to punish opponents, serious lawbreakers, etc., strongly or harshly: *The police commissioner promised a crackdown on street crime.*

cracked (krakt) /krækt/ *adj.* **1.** broken without separation of parts: *cracked walls.* **2.** damaged; injured: *cracked ribs.* **3.** *Informal.* eccentric; mad: *The captain is cracked; we may have to mutiny.* **4.** broken in tone, as the voice: *answering in a cracked voice.* —***Idiom.*** **5. cracked up to be,** [*after a negative word or phrase*] *Informal.* expected by reputation to be: *I hear the play is not what it's cracked up to be.*

crack•er (krak′ər) /ˈkrækər/ *n.* [*count*] **1.** a thin, crisp biscuit. **2.** a firecracker. —*adj.* [*be/go* + ~] **3. crackers,** *Informal.* wild; crazy: *to go crackers from too much work.*

crack•er•jack (krak′ər jak′) /ˈkrækər,dʒæk/ *n.* [*count*] **1.** a person or thing that shows outstanding ability or excellence. —*adj.* **2.** exceptionally fine: *a crackerjack worker.*

crack•head (krak′hed′) /ˈkræk,hɛd/ *n.* [*count*] *Slang.* a habitual user of cocaine in the form of crack.

crack•house or **crack house** (krak′hous′) /ˈkræk,haws/ *n.* [*count*] a place where cocaine in the form of crack is bought, sold, and smoked.

crack•le (krak′əl) /ˈkrækəl/ *v.,* **-led, -ling,** *n.* —*v.* [*no obj*] **1.** to make slight, sudden, sharp noises: *The campfire crackled in the night.* **2.** to exhibit liveliness, excitement, or the like; sparkle: *The play crackled with wit.* —*n.* [*count*] **3.** the act or sound of crackling: *the crackle of the breakfast cereal.*

crack•pot (krak′pot′) /ˈkræk,pɒt/ *n.* [*count*] **1.** a person who is eccentric, foolish, odd, or irrational: *I had to deal with lots of crackpots at the Motor Vehicles office.* —*adj.* [*before a noun*] **2.** strange; eccentric; foolish; irrational: *another crackpot scheme to make money.*

crack•up (krak′up′) /ˈkræk,ʌp/ *n.* [*count*] **1.** a crash; collision: *a two-car crackup on the highway.* **2.** a mental breakdown: *She's heading for a crackup if she keeps worrying like that.*

-cracy, *suffix.* *-cracy* comes ultimately from Greek, where it has the meaning "power; rule; government", and is attached to roots to form nouns that mean "rule; government": *auto-* + *-cracy* → *autocracy (= government by one ruler); theo- ("God")* + *-cracy* → *theocracy (= a country governed by the rule of God or a god).* Compare **-CRAT.**

cra•dle (krād′l) /ˈkreydḷ/ *n., v.,* **-dled, -dling.** —*n.* [*count*] **1.** a small bed for an infant: *She rocked the baby gently in the cradle.* **2.** the place where something develops or grows in its early years: *Boston is the cradle of the American Revolution.* **3.** a support for objects placed horizontally, such as the support for the receiver of a telephone. —*v.* [~ + *obj*] **4.** to hold gently or protectively: *cradled the little puppy in her arms.*

craft (kraft) /kræft/ *n., pl.* **crafts** or, for 4, 6, **craft,** *v.* —*n.* **1.** [*count*] an art or trade requiring special skill, esp. of the hands: *an arts and crafts festival.* **2.** [*noncount*] skill; ability to use the hands well or to do a job well: *He flew the plane with craft that comes from years of experience.* **3.** [*noncount*] cunning; deceit. **4.** [*count*] a ship or other vessel: *He took his small craft out to sea.* **5.** [*plural; used with a plural verb*] a number of ships or other vessels when thought of as a group: *Small craft are warned to stay clear.* **6.** [*count*] an aircraft. **7.** [*plural; used with a plural verb*] aircraft when thought of as a group. —*v.* [~ + *obj*] **8.** to make (an object, product, etc.) with great skill and care: *The carver crafted the miniature wooden horses with great skill; a carefully crafted novel.*

crafts•man (krafts′mən) /ˈkræftsmən/ *n.* [*count*], *pl.* **-men. 1.** a person who is skilled in a craft; artisan: *Fine craftsmen made this boat.* **2.** an artist. —**crafts′man•ship′,** *n.* [*noncount*]: *the fine craftsmanship of the carvings.*

craft•y (kraf′tē) /ˈkræftiy/ *adj.,* **-i•er, -i•est.** skillful in dishonest schemes; deceitful: *a crafty old spy.* —**craft•i•ly** (kraf′tə lē) /ˈkræftəliy/ *adv.*: *He craftily persuaded her that we were the villains.* —**craft′i•ness,** *n.* [*noncount*]

crag (krag) /kræg/ *n.* [*count*] a steep, rugged rock, or part of a rock that sticks out: *looking out over the edge of the crag to the sea.*

crag•gy (krag′ē) /ˈkrægiy/ *adj.,* **-gi•er, -gi•est. 1.** full of crags. **2.** rugged; rough-hewn: *a craggy, weather-beaten face.*

cram (kram) /kræm/ *v.,* **crammed, cram•ming. 1.** [~ + *obj*] to fill (something) by force with more than it can easily hold: *crammed his mouth full of food.* **2.** [~ + *obj* + *down/into* + *obj*] to force or stuff (something): *crammed all his belongings into the tiny car.* **3.** [~ + *into* + *obj*] to crowd; jam: *A mob crammed into the hall.* **4.** [*no obj*] to study for an examination by memorizing facts at the last minute: *stayed up all night cramming for the exam.*

cramp[1] (kramp) /kræmp/ *n.* **1.** Often, **cramps.** [*plural*] a sudden and uncontrolled spasm of a muscle, as in a limb or bodily organ: *had cramps in his stomach.* —*v.* **2.** to (cause to) feel a cramp: [*no obj*]: *My muscles cramp at the slightest bit of cold.* [~ + — *obj*]: *The cold cramped my leg muscles.*

cramp[2] (kramp) /kræmp/ *v.* [~ + *obj*] **1.** to restrict or hamper: *I was cramped in the tiny room with a small desk and computer.* —***Idiom.*** **2. cramp one's style,** to prevent one from showing one's best abilities: *She cramped my style with her constant interruptions.*

cramped (krampt) /kræmpt/ *adj.* **1.** severely limited in space; small and crowded: *cramped closets.* **2. a.** (of handwriting) small and with the letters and words crowded together. **b.** (of a style of writing) hard to understand; crabbed.

cran•ber•ry (kran′ber′ē, -bə rē) /ˈkræn,bɛriy, -bəriy/ *n.* [*count*], *pl.* **-ries. 1.** the sour red berry of certain plants of the heath family, used esp. to make a sauce or juice: *cranberry sauce.* **2.** the plant itself, growing wild in bogs or cultivated in acid soils.

crane (krān) /kreyn/ *n., v.,* **craned, cran•ing.** —*n.* [*count*] **1.** a large wading bird with long legs, bill, and neck. **2.** a large device for lifting and moving very heavy objects. —*v.* **3.** to stretch (the neck) as a crane does, esp. to see better: [*no obj*]: *She craned to see what had stopped the cars ahead.* [~ + *obj*]: *He craned his neck to see who was ahead of him.*

cra•ni•al (krā′nē əl) /ˈkreyniyəl/ *adj.* [*before a noun*] of or relating to the cranium: *a cranial hemorrhage.*

cra•ni•um (krā′nē əm) /ˈkreyniyəm/ *n.* [*count*], *pl.* **-ni•ums, -ni•a** (-nē ə) /-niyə/. **1.** the skull of any animal with a backbone. **2.** the part of the skull that encloses the brain.

crank (krangk) /kræŋk/ *n.* [*count*] **1.** an arm or lever for imparting motion to a rotating shaft. **2.** *Informal.* a bad-tempered, grouchy person: *an old crank.* **3.** a person who has strange ideas or who supports bizarre causes: *had to deal with all sorts of cranks among the public.* **—***v.* **4.** [~ + *obj*] to rotate or move (something) by means of a crank: *cranked the window open.* **5.** to start (an engine) by turning the crankshaft: [~ + *obj*]: *I tried cranking the engine but it wouldn't start.* [*no obj*]: *The engine cranked until the battery wore down, but it still wouldn't start.* **6. crank out,** to produce a large number of (something) in a mechanical way: [~ + *out* + *obj*]: *managed to crank out two bestsellers within a few months.* [~ + *obj* + *out*]: *She could really crank them out in a hurry.* **7. crank up, a.** [*no obj*] to get started: *The new theater season is cranking up with a gala benefit.* **b.** [~ + *up* + *obj*] to stimulate or produce: *to crank up enthusiasm for a new product.* **—***adj.* [*usually: before a noun*] **8.** of, relating to, or done by an unbalanced person: *a crank phone call.*

crank•shaft (krangk′shaft′) /ˈkræŋkˌʃæft/ *n.* [*count*] (in an internal-combustion engine) a shaft having one or more cranks.

crank•y (krang′kē) /ˈkræŋkiy/ *adj.,* **-i•er, -i•est. 1.** ill-tempered; grouchy: *She's cranky when she doesn't sleep enough.* **2.** eccentric; erratic. **3.** malfunctioning: *a cranky, balky car.* **—crank•i•ly** (krang′kə lē) /ˈkræŋkəliy/ *adv.: She complained crankily.* **—crank′i•ness,** *n.* [*noncount*]

cran•ny (kran′ē) /ˈkræniy/ *n.* [*count*], *pl.* **-nies. 1.** a small, narrow opening in a wall, rock, etc.; crevice. **2.** a place or corner out of view; nook: *She'd found a little cranny to sit and read in.*

crap (krap) /kræp/ *n., v.,* **crapped, crap•ping. —***n.* **1.** *Vulgar.* **a.** [*noncount*] EXCREMENT. **b.** [*count*] an act of defecation. **2.** [*noncount*] *Slang.* (*sometimes vulgar*). nonsense; false statements; exaggeration. **3.** [*noncount*] junk; litter: *Get rid of all this crap in your room.* **—***v.* [*no obj*] **4.** *Vulgar.* to defecate.

craps (kraps) /kræps/ *n.* [*noncount; used with a singular verb*] a game of dice.

crash (krash) /kræʃ/ *v.* **1.** to make a loud, clattering noise:[*no obj*]: *The windows crashed from the explosion.* [~ + *obj*]: *The explosion crashed the windows.* **2.** to (cause to) break or fall to pieces with noise: [*no obj*]: *The glass crashed to the floor.* [~ + *obj*]: *He crashed his glass to the floor angrily.* **3.** (of moving objects) to collide violently and noisily: [*no obj*]: *The two cars left the road and crashed.* [~ + *into* + *obj*]: *The cars crashed into a wall.* **4.** to cause (a moving vehicle) to collide with another object violently: [~ + *obj*]: *He crashed his car on the highway.* [~ + *obj* + *into/through* + *obj*]: *He crashed his car into the wall.* **5.** to move, force, or drive with violence and noise: [~ + *into/through* + *obj*]: *The truck crashed through the gate.* [~ + *obj* + *into/through* + *obj*]: *The driver crashed the truck into the gate.* **6.** [*no obj*] (of an aircraft) to land in such a way that damage or destruction cannot be avoided: *The pilot tried to land but the plane crashed.* **7.** [~ + *obj*] to cause (an aircraft) to suffer severe damage or destruction in landing: *The pilot crashed the plane into the mountain.* **8.** [*no obj*] to collapse or fail suddenly, such as a financial enterprise: *The stock market crashed.* **9.** [*no obj*] *Slang.* **a.** to sleep: *I've got to crash; can I use that bed?* **b.** to fall asleep: *I'm crashing; see you tomorrow.* **c.** to stay temporarily without payment: *I crashed with my brother for a week.* **10.** [*no obj*] *Slang.* to experience unpleasant sensations when a stimulant drug wears off. **11.** [*no obj*] (of a computer) to shut down because of something wrong with the hardware or software: *The computer crashed and I lost all my data.* **12.** [~ + *obj*] to enter or force one's way into (an event) without an invitation: *tried to crash the party.* **—***n.* [*count*] **13.** an act or instance of crashing: *several bad early-morning crashes on the interstate highway.* **14.** the emergency landing of an aircraft, etc., usually causing severe damage. **15.** a sudden general collapse of a business, the stock market, etc.: *the famous stock market crash of 1929.* **—***adj.* [*before a noun*] **16.** involving a strong, intensive effort, esp. to deal with an emergency, meet a deadline, etc.: *went on a crash diet.*

crash′-land′, *v.* to land (an aircraft) in an emergency so that damage or destruction is unavoidable: [*no obj*]: *The plane crash-landed in the field.* [~ + *obj*]: *The pilot crash-landed the plane on the carrier deck.* **—crash′-land′ing,** *n.* [*count*]

crash′ pad′, *n.* [*count*] *Slang.* a place to sleep or live temporarily and at no cost.

crass (kras) /kræs/ *adj.,* **-er, -est.** without refinement; gross: *crass manners.* **—crass′ly,** *adv.* **—crass′ness,** *n.* [*noncount*]

-crat, *suffix.* -*crat* comes ultimately from Greek, where it has the meaning "ruler; person having power", and is attached to roots to form nouns that mean "ruler; member of a ruling body": *auto-* + *-crat* → *autocrat (= a ruler governing alone).* Compare -CRACY.

crate (krāt) /kreyt/ *n., v.,* **crat•ed, crat•ing. —***n.* [*count*] **1.** a wooden box made of slats, for packing, shipping, or storing: *A few crates of fruit fell from the truck.* **2.** the quantity, esp. of fruit, that is packed in a crate. **3.** *Informal.* something old or worn-out, esp. an automobile. **—***v.* [~ + *obj*] **4.** to pack in a crate: *They crated the bananas.*

cra•ter (krā′tər) /ˈkreytər/ *n.* [*count*] **1.** a bowl-shaped hole in the ground formed by volcanic action, a meteoroid, or the like: *the craters of the moon.* **2.** the hole in the ground where a bomb or shell has exploded. **—***v.* [~ + *obj*] **3.** to make a crater or craters in: *The runway had been cratered by bombs.*

cra•vat (krə vat′) /krəˈvæt/ *n.* [*count*] **1.** NECKTIE (def. 1). **2.** a scarf worn about the neck and folded at the front with the ends tucked into the neckline of one's shirt.

crave (krāv) /kreyv/ *v.,* **craved, crav•ing. 1.** [~ + *obj*] to long for; desire eagerly: *craves honor and fame more than money.* **2.** [~ + *for/after* + *obj*] to have strong need or desire: *craved for the safety and security of home.* **3.** [~ + *obj*] to require; need: *a problem craving your prompt attention.*

cra•ven (krā′vən) /ˈkreyvən/ *adj.* showing a shameful lack of courage; cowardly. **—cra′ven•ly,** *adv.: He gave in cravenly to whatever the boss asked for.* **—cra′ven•ness,** *n.* [*noncount*]

crav•ing (krā′ving) /ˈkreyvɪŋ/ *n.* [*count*] a strong or eager desire; yearning: *He felt a great craving for a cigarette.*

craw•fish (krô′fish′) /ˈkrɔˌfɪʃ/ *n., pl.* (*esp. when thought of as a group*) **-fish,** (*esp. for kinds or species*) **-fish•es.** CRAYFISH.

crawl (krôl) /krɔl/ *v.* **1.** [*no obj*] to move with the head or face downward and the body close to the ground, or on the hands and knees. **2.** [*no obj*] to move or progress slowly: *a line of cars crawling toward the beach.* **3.** [*no obj*] to behave in a way that indicates deep fear or that is an attempt to win favor: *He came crawling to the boss to ask for his job back.* **4.** [*often: be* + ~*-ing;* ~ + *with* + *obj*] to be full of: *The hut was crawling with insects.* **5.** [~ + *obj*] to visit or go to (pubs, restaurants, etc.) one after the other: *a night of crawling the pubs.* **—***n.* [*count*] **6.** the act of crawling; a slow, crawling motion. **7.** a slow rate of progress: *moving at a crawl through the toll gates.* **8.** a swimming stroke performed with the front of the body facing downward and one arm then the other rotating over the head, combined with flutter kicks of the legs. **—*Idiom.* 9. make one's skin crawl,** [] to give a feeling of disgust or horror: *Watching the snakes made my skin crawl.*

crawl•space or **crawl space** (krôl′spās′) /ˈkrɔlˌspeys/ *n.* [*count*] (in a building) an area that can be reached only by crawling, for access to plumbing, storage, etc.: *Raccoons had gotten into the crawlspaces.*

crawl•y (krô′lē) /ˈkrɔliy/ *adj.,* **-i•er, -i•est,** *n., pl.* **crawl•ies. —***adj.* **1.** characterized by crawling, such as worms or insects, and causing a feeling of disgust or horror. **—***n.* [*count*] **2.** a crawling insect, small reptile, etc.

cray•fish (krā′fish′) /ˈkreyˌfɪʃ/ also **crawfish,** *n.* [*count*], *pl.* (*esp. when thought of as a group*) **-fish,** (*esp. for kinds or species*) **-fish•es.** Also called **craw•dad** (krô′dad′) /ˈkrɔˌdæd/ **craw•dad•dy** (-dad′ē) /-ˌdædiy/. a freshwater shellfish with five pairs of legs, resembling a small lobster.

cray•on (krā′on, -ən) /ˈkreyɒn, -ən/ *n.* **1.** a pointed stick of colored wax or chalk, used for drawing or coloring: [*count*]: *a brand new box of crayons.* [*noncount*]: *a drawing done in crayon.* **—***v.* **2.** to draw or color with a crayon or crayons: [*no obj*]: *The children have been crayoning all day.* [~ + *obj*]: *crayoned their pictures.*

craze (krāz) /kreyz/ *v.,* **crazed, craz•ing,** *n.* **—***v.* [~ + *obj*] **1.** to make insane or wildly excited; derange: *crazed with the desire for revenge.* **—***n.* [*count*] **2.** a popular fad; mania; person or object of great popular interest: *That singing star was a big craze in Japan for years.*

cra•zy (krā′zē) /ˈkreyziy/ *adj.,* **-zi•er, -zi•est,** *n., pl.* **-zies. —***adj.* **1.** mentally unbalanced; insane. **2.** impractical; foolish; stupid: *a crazy scheme.* [*be* + ~ + *to* + *verb*]: *I thought she was crazy to get married.* [*it* + *be* + ~ + *to* + *verb*]: *It was crazy to get married so young.* **3.**

[*be* + ~ + *about* + *obj*] very eager, excited, or enthusiastic: *He's crazy about computers.* **4.** [*be* + ~ + *about* + *obj*] very fond of; attracted to; infatuated by: *She's crazy about him.* **5.** unusual; very odd; bizarre: *What a crazy hat he was wearing.* **6. drive someone crazy,** [*drive* + *obj* + ~] to annoy or bother someone greatly: *The kids were driving him crazy.* —*n.* [*count*] **7.** *Slang.* an unpredictable person; one who behaves in an odd, bizarre, or foolish way. —***Idiom.*** **8. like crazy,** *Slang.* with great enthusiasm or energy; wildly: *We worked like crazy all morning.* —**cra′zi•ly,** *adv.: We drove crazily to get there on time.* —**cra′zi•ness,** *n.* [*noncount*]

creak (krēk) /kriyk/ *v.* **1.** to (cause to) make a sharp, scraping, or squeaking sound: [*no obj*]: *The rusty old gate creaked.* [~ + *obj*]: *He creaked the door when he opened it.* **2.** [*no obj*] to move slowly with or as if with such a sound: *The broken-down car creaked along slowly.* —*n.* [*count*] **3.** a creaking sound: *I heard a few creaks from the old floorboards.* —**creak′y,** *adj.,* **-i•er, -i•est.**

cream (krēm) /kriym/ *n.* **1.** [*noncount*] the fatty, smooth, thick part of milk: *I'll take cream and sugar in my coffee, please.* **2.** [*noncount*] a substance like this, containing medicine or other ingredients, applied to the skin: *some first-aid cream for a rash.* **3.** [*noncount*] any of various foods made with cream or milk or that are thick and smooth like cream: *cream of mushroom soup; Bavarian cream.* **4.** [*count*] the best part of anything: *the cream of society.* **5.** [*noncount*] a yellowish white color. —*v.* [~ + *obj*] **6.** to mix (butter and sugar, etc.) to a smooth, creamy mass: *Cream the mixture thoroughly.* **7.** [~ (+ *off*) + *obj*] to take the best part of: *The defense ministry creamed (off) the brightest engineers.* **8.** *Slang.* **a.** to beat up; hit or strike badly: *The gang creamed a few victims.* **b.** to win decisively over: *We creamed the Giants by a score of 50-0.* —*adj.* **9.** of the color cream; cream-colored.

cream′ cheese′, *n.* [*noncount*] a soft, white, unripened cheese that is easily spread, made of sweet milk and sometimes cream.

cream•er (krē′mər) /'kriymər/ *n.* **1.** [*count*] a small jug or pitcher for serving cream. **2.** [*count*] an apparatus for separating cream from milk. **3.** [*noncount*] a product made chiefly from corn syrup, used esp. in coffee as a substitute for cream or milk.

cream•er•y (krē′mə rē) /'kriyməriy/ *n.* [*count*], *pl.* **-ies.** **1.** a place where milk and cream are processed or where butter and cheese are produced. **2.** a place for the sale of milk and milk products.

cream′ of tar′tar, *n.* [*noncount*] a white salt, used chiefly in baking powder.

cream′ puff′, *n.* [*count*] **1.** a light, hollow pastry filled with custard or whipped cream. **2.** a weak or timid person. **3.** a vehicle or machine that has been kept in unusually good condition.

cream•y (krē′mē) /'kriymiy/ *adj.,* **-i•er, -i•est.** thick and smooth like cream; of or like cream: *soft, creamy butter.*

crease (krēs) /kriys/ *n., v.,* **creased, creas•ing.** —*n.* [*count*] **1.** a line or furrow on paper, cloth, etc., produced by folding, striking, etc.: *a single crease on slacks.* **2.** a wrinkle, esp. one on the face: *creases caused by age and worry.* —*v.* **3.** to (cause to) become creased; wrinkle: [*no obj*]: *his forehead creased with worry.* [~ + *obj*]: *Years of worry had creased his forehead.* **4.** [~ + *obj*] to wound or injure slightly by a shot: *The bullet just creased his shoulder.*

cre•ate (krē āt′) /kriy'eyt/ *v.* [~ + *obj*], **-at•ed, -at•ing.** **1.** to cause to come into being: *The belief is that God created the universe.* **2.** to bring into being from one's imagination: *He created a new theory of the universe.* **3.** to arrange, bring about, or produce (a feeling, emotion, etc.): *This proposal is bound to create more confusion.* **4.** to establish; set up: *The government created several new agencies.*

cre•a•tion (krē ā′shən) /kriy'eyʃən/ *n.* **1.** [*noncount*] the act of creating, or the fact of being created: *Scholars no longer try to investigate the creation of language.* **2. the Creation,** [*noncount*] the original bringing into existence of the universe by God. **3.** [*noncount*] the world; universe: *In all of creation there is not another one quite like this.* **4.** [*count*] something created: *Disney's creations brought joy to children everywhere.*

cre•a•tion•ism (krē ā′shə niz′əm) /kriy'eyʃə,nɪzəm/ *n.* [*noncount*] **1.** the doctrine or belief that the creation of the universe occurred in exactly the same way as told in the Bible. **2.** the doctrine that God creates out of nothing a new human soul for each individual born. —**cre•a′tion•ist,** *n.* [*count*], *adj.*

cre•a•tive (krē ā′tiv) /kriy'eytɪv/ *adj.* **1.** having the quality or power of creating: *a very creative writer.* **2.** resulting from original thought; imaginative: *gave us some creative suggestions.* **3.** producing intentionally false information, etc.: *Creative bookkeeping made his losses profits.* —**cre•a′tive•ly,** *adv.* —**cre•a′tive•ness,** *n.* [*noncount*]

cre•a•tiv•i•ty (krē′ā tiv′i tē) /,kriyey'tɪvɪtiy/ *n.* [*noncount*] the ability to produce original, imaginative ideas, solutions, or the like: *uses creativity in problem solving.*

cre•a•tor (krē ā′tər) /kriy'eytər/ *n.* **1.** [*count*] a person or thing that creates. **2. the Creator,** [*proper noun*] God.

crea•ture (krē′chər) /'kriytʃər/ *n.* [*count*] **1.** an animal, esp. a nonhuman: *all creatures of the planet.* **2.** any being: *creatures of the imagination.* **3.** person; human being: *She's a lovely creature.* **4.** a person under the control or influence of another person or thing: *a creature of habit.*

crèche (kresh) /krɛʃ/ *n.* [*count*] **1.** a representation of Mary, Joseph, and others around the crib of Jesus in the stable at Bethlehem. **2.** a home for foundlings. **3.** *Brit.* DAY NURSERY.

-cred-, *root.* *-cred-* comes from Latin, where it has the meaning "believe." This meaning is found in such words as: CREDENCE, CREDENTIAL, CREDIBLE, CREDIT, CREDO, CREDULOUS, CREED, INCREDIBLE.

cre•dence (krēd′ns) /'kriydns/ *n.* [*noncount*] **1.** belief as to the truth of something: *to give credence to an advertiser's claims.* **2.** something that establishes a claim to belief or confidence. See -CRED-.

cre•den•tial (kri den′shəl) /krɪ'dɛnʃəl/ *n.* [*count*] Usually, **credentials.** [*plural*] **1.** evidence of a person's identity, position, etc., usually in written form: *No one is admitted without credentials.* **2.** anything that provides the basis for confidence, as in one's qualifications: *His credentials for the new job are impressive.* See -CRED-.

cre•den•za (kri den′zə) /krɪ'dɛnzə/ *n.* [*count*], *pl.* **-zas.** a low, closed cabinet for papers, supplies, etc., in an office.

cred•i•bil•i•ty (kred′ə bil′i tē) /,krɛdə'bɪlɪtiy/ *n.* [*noncount*] the state or quality of being believed or trusted.

credibil′ity gap′, *n.* [*count; usually singular*] the difference between what is said (as by politicians) and what is true or is believed to be true: *The senator's credibility gap is widening.*

cred•i•ble (kred′ə bəl) /'krɛdəbəl/ *adj.* **1.** capable of being believed; trustworthy: *The jury considered her testimony credible.* **2.** effective or reliable: *credible new defense weapons.* —**cred′i•bly,** *adv.: We have to respond credibly to their attacks or they won't believe we are serious.* See -CRED-.

cred•it (kred′it) /'krɛdɪt/ *n.* **1.** [*noncount*] public praise or commendation given for some action, etc.: *He was happy to take all the credit, and none of the blame.* **2.** [*count; usually singular*] a source of pride or honor: *Those Olympic athletes were a credit to our nation.* **3.** [*noncount*] trust; credibility; belief: *The story of his illness gained credit when he failed to show up at the meeting.* **4.** [*noncount*] **a.** permission for a customer to have goods or use services that will be paid for at a later date: *We have credit with that company.* **b.** one's reputation for paying bills or debts on time: *My credit is good.* **5. a.** [*noncount*] official acceptance of the work of a student in a course of study: *received credit for that course.* **b.** [*count*] one official unit of such work usually representing attendance at one class per week throughout a semester, quarter, or term: *He took fifteen credits in English.* **6.** [*count*] a sum of money due to a person: *Your account shows a credit of $50.* **7.** [*count*] a deposit or sum of money against which a person may draw money: *a credit of $5,000 in savings.* **8.** [*count*] **a.** an entry in a business account showing value received: *several questionable entries among the credits.* **b.** the right-hand side of an account on which such entries are made (opposed to *debit*). **c.** an entry, or the total shown, on the credit side. **9. credits,** [*plural*] the names of all who contributed to a motion-picture or a television program, usually listed at the end. —*v.* **10. a.** [~ + *obj* + *with/to* + *obj*] to give responsibility for; ascribe; attribute: *Those herbs were credited with almost supernatural healing powers.* **b.** [~ + *obj* + *with* + *obj*] to believe to be or have: *I credited him with more intelligence than that.* **11.** [~ + *obj*] to believe or trust: *Can you credit the governor's press releases?* **12.** [~ + *obj* + *to/with* + *obj*] to enter on the credit side of an account; give credit for or to: *He credited $50 to my account.* —***Idiom.*** **13. do someone credit,** to be a source of honor for someone. [*do + obj + ~*]: *Your passing the test under such difficult circumstances does you credit.* Also, **do credit to someone.** [*do + ~ + to + obj*]: *The hard work and training do credit to your team, win or lose.* **14. on credit,** [*noncount*] by future payment: *to buy a sofa on credit with 10% down payment.* **15. to one's credit,** [*noncount*] **a.** deserving of praise: *To his credit he did admit his mistake.* **b.** belonging to one; having as one's accomplishments: *He had thirty published articles to his credit.* See -CRED-.

cred•it•a•ble (kred′i tə bəl) /ˈkrɛdɪtəbəl/ *adj.* bringing or deserving credit, honor, or praise: *The candidate made a creditable showing in the primary.* —**cred′it•a•ble•ness, cred•it•a•bil•i•ty** (kred′i tə bil′i tē) /ˌkrɛdɪtəˈbɪlɪtiy/ *n.* [*noncount*] —**cred′it•a•bly,** *adv.*

cred′it card′, *n.* [*count*] a card that entitles a person to make purchases on credit.

cred•i•tor (kred′i tər) /ˈkrɛdɪtər/ *n.* [*count*] one to whom money is owed.

cre•do (krē′dō, krā′-) /ˈkriydow, ˈkrey-/ *n.* [*count*], *pl.* **-dos.** a set of principles of belief; any creed or formula of belief: *the credo of the Roman Catholic Church.* See -CRED-.

cred•u•lous (krej′ə ləs) /ˈkrɛdʒələs/ *adj.* willing to believe or trust too readily; gullible: *He's so credulous that he will believe anything you say.* —**cre•du•li•ty** (kri do͞o′li tē, -dyo͞o′-) /krɪˈduwlɪtiy, -ˈdyuw-/ *n.* [*noncount*] —**cred′u•lous•ly,** *adv.* —**cred′u•lous•ness,** *n.* [*noncount*] See -CRED-.

creed (krēd) /kriyd/ *n.* [*count*] **1.** a formal, ritual statement of the chief principles of Christian belief. **2.** an accepted system of religious or other belief: *His creed was simply this: be true to yourself.* See -CRED-.

creek (krēk, krik) /kriyk, krɪk/ *n.* [*count*] **1.** a stream smaller than a river. —***Idiom.*** **2. up the creek,** [*noncount*] *Slang.* in a difficult or hopeless situation: *No job, no money, no food —we're really up the creek now.*

creel (krēl) /kriyl/ *n.* [*count*] **1.** a wickerwork basket, used esp. for carrying fish. **2.** a wicker trap for fish, etc.

creep (krēp) /kriyp/ *v.,* **crept** (krept) /krɛpt/ or, sometimes, **creeped; creep•ing,** *n.* —*v.* **1.** [*no obj*] to move slowly with the body close to the ground, on hands and knees: *The baby crept along on the carpet.* **2.** [*~ + up*] to approach slowly and without being noticed: *He crept up to the door.* **3.** [*no obj*] to go forward slowly and often with difficulty: *The car crept up the hill.* **4.** [*~ + up + on + obj*] to sneak up behind someone: *The prisoner crept up on the guard.* **5.** [*~ + in/into + obj*] to become noticed slowly over time: *The writer's bias creeps into the story.* **6.** [*no obj*] (of a plant) to grow along the ground, a wall, etc. —*n.* [*count*] **7.** *Slang.* a peculiar or disgusting person. **8. the creeps,** a sensation of fear, disgust, or the like, as of something crawling over the skin: *That movie gave me the creeps.* —***Idiom.*** **9. make one's flesh creep,** to cause one to be frightened or disgusted: *That horror movie will make your flesh creep.* See CRAWL.

creep•er (krē′pər) /ˈkriypər/ *n.* [*count*] **1.** a person or thing that creeps. **2.** a plant that grows upon or just beneath the surface of the ground, sending out small roots from the stem: *Ivy is a creeper.*

creep•y (krē′pē) /ˈkriypiy/ *adj.,* **-i•er, -i•est. 1.** causing a creeping feeling of the skin, as from horror or fear: *a creepy ghost story.* **2.** *Slang.* (of a person) odd; bizarre; weird: *Her blind date turned out to be really creepy.* —**creep•i•ly** (krē′pə lē) /ˈkriypəliy/ *adv.* —**creep′i•ness,** *n.* [*noncount*]

cre•mate (krē′māt) /ˈkriymeyt/ *v.* [*~ + obj*], **-mat•ed, -mat•ing.** to burn (a dead body) to ashes: *He was cremated and his ashes were scattered over Lake Michigan.* —**cre•ma•tion** (kri mā′shən) /krɪˈmeyʃən/ *n.* [*noncount*]: *For some time cremation was not permitted here.* [*count*]: *presiding over several cremations in one day.*

cre•ma•to•ri•um (krē′mə tôr′ē əm, -tōr′-, krem′ə-) /ˌkriyməˈtɔriyəm, -ˈtowr-, ˌkrɛmə-/ *n., pl.* **-tor•i•a** (-tôr′ē-ə, -tōr′-) /-ˈtɔriyə, -ˈtowr-/ **-tor•i•ums.** CREMATORY.

cre•ma•to•ry (krē′mə tôr′ē, -tōr′ē, krem′ə-) /ˈkriyməˌtɔriy, -ˌtowriy, ˈkrɛmə-/ *n.* [*count*], *pl.* **-ries. 1.** a funeral establishment or the like where cremation is done. **2.** a furnace for cremating.

crème or **creme** (krem, krēm) /krɛm, kriym/ *n., pl.* **crèmes** (kremz, krēmz, krem). cream: [*noncount*]: *Apply some first-aid crème.* [*count*]: *different crèmes for your tasting pleasure.*

Cre•ole (krē′ōl) /ˈkriyowl/ *n.* **1.** [*count*] **a.** a French-speaking person of Louisiana descended from the earliest French and Spanish settlers. **b.** a French-speaking person of Louisiana of mixed black and French or Spanish ancestry. **2.** [*count; usually: creole*] a pidgin language that has become the native language of a speech community. Compare PIDGIN. —*adj.* **3.** [*sometimes: creole*] of, relating to, or characteristic of a Creole or Creoles. **4.** [*usually: creole; often: after a noun*] made with tomatoes, peppers, onions, and spices and served with rice: *shrimp creole.*

cre•o•sote (krē′ə sōt′) /ˈkriyəˌsowt/ *n., v.,* **-sot•ed, -sot•ing.** —*n.* [*noncount*] **1.** a strong-smelling, oily liquid made from coal and wood tar and used to preserve wood. —*v.* [*~ + obj*] **2.** to treat with creosote.

crepe (krāp; *for 2 also* krep) /kreyp; *for 2 also* krɛp/ *n., pl.* **crepes** (krāps; *for 2 also* kreps *or* krep) /kreyps; *for 2 also* krɛps *or* krɛp/. —*n.* **1.** [*noncount*] a lightweight fabric of silk, cotton, or other fiber, with a finely wrinkled or bumpy surface. **2.** [*count*] a thin, light, delicate pancake. **3.** [*noncount*] Also called **crepe paper.** paper with a wrinkled or bumpy surface: *The high school kids decorated the gym with crepe paper for the dance.* **4.** [*noncount*] Also called **crepe rubber.** pressed, crinkled rubber, often used to make the soles of shoes. Also, **crêpe** (for defs. 1, 2).

crept (krept) /krɛpt/ *v.* pt. and pp. of CREEP.

cre•scen•do (kri shen′dō, -sen′dō) /krɪˈʃɛndow, -ˈsɛndow/ *n., pl.* **-dos, -di** (-dē), *adj., adv.* —*n.* [*count*] **1.** a steady increase in loudness, force, or intensity: *a growing crescendo of protest.* **2.** a climax; peak: *Calls for his resignation were reaching a crescendo.* —*adj.* **3.** increasing in force, volume, or loudness: *a crescendo passage in music.* —*adv.* **4.** in the manner of a crescendo: *The passage is played crescendo.*

cres•cent (kres′ənt) /ˈkrɛsənt/ *n.* [*count*] **1.** a shape resembling a half circle or part of a ring, tapering to points at the ends. **2.** something, such as a roll or cookie, having this shape. **3.** the figure of the moon in its first or last quarter, resembling such a shape. —*adj.* **4.** shaped like a crescent: *a crescent roll.*

cress (kres) /krɛs/ *n.* [*noncount*] a plant of the mustard family, esp. the watercress, having strong-tasting leaves often used for salad.

crest (krest) /krɛst/ *n.* [*count*] **1.** the highest part of a hill or mountain range; summit. **2.** the highest point or level: *The president was riding the crest of his popularity.* **3.** the point of highest flood, as of a river: *The water level is high, but it hasn't reached the crest yet.* **4.** the foamy top of a wave. **5.** a tuft or other natural growth on the top of the head of an animal. **6.** COAT OF ARMS (def. 2). —*v.* [*no obj*] **7.** to form or reach a crest, as a wave or river: *The river hasn't crested yet.* **8.** to reach the highest point: *The general's popularity crested after the great victory.* —**crest′ed,** *adj.* [*before a noun*]: *a crested finch.* —**crest′less,** *adj.*

crest•fall•en (krest′fô′lən) /ˈkrɛstˌfɔlən/ *adj.* [*often: be + ~*] dejected; discouraged: *He was crestfallen when he found out his visa would not be renewed.*

cre•tin (krēt′n) /ˈkriytn̩/ *n.* [*count*] **1.** a person affected with cretinism. **2.** a stupid or boorish person; idiot. —**cre•ti•noid** (krēt′n oid′) /ˈkriytn̩ˌɔyd/ *adj.* —**cre′tin•ous,** *adj.*

cre•tin•ism (krēt′n iz′əm) /ˈkriytn̩ˌɪzəm/ *n.* [*noncount*] a condition existing at birth in which a lack of thyroid secretion results in bodily deformity and mental retardation.

cre•vasse (krə vas′) /krəˈvæs/ *n.* [*count*] a deep crack in the earth's surface, the ice of a glacier, etc.

crev•ice (krev′is) /ˈkrɛvɪs/ *n.* [*count*] a crack forming an opening; cleft; rift; fissure. —**crev′iced,** *adj.*

crew (kro͞o) /kruw/ *n.* [*count*] **1.** a group of people working together: *a demolition crew.* **2. a.** the people who operate a ship, aircraft, or spacecraft: *the pilot and her crew.* **b.** the sailors, but not the officers, of a ship's company. **3.** the team that rows a racing shell. —*v.* [*no obj*] **4.** to serve as a member of a crew, as for a racing shell or on a ship: *He crewed for twelve years.* —**Usage.** See COLLECTIVE NOUN.

crew′ cut′, *n.* [*count*] a haircut in which all the hair is cut very close to the head.

crib (krib) /krɪb/ *n., v.,* **cribbed, crib•bing.** —*n.* [*count*] **1.** a child's bed with enclosed sides. **2.** a box or bin for holding food for animals. **3.** a bin for storing grain, salt, etc. **4.** *Informal.* a translation or list of correct answers, used dishonestly by students while taking exams: *The teacher caught me with a crib for the Latin test.* —*v.* **5.** *Informal.* **a.** [*no obj*] to use a crib, as in an examination.

b. to steal; plagiarize: [~ *(+ off/from + obj)*]: *I'm sure he was cribbing (from my paper), so I changed the answers just before handing them in.* [~ + *obj (+ off/from + obj)*]: *He cribbed the answers (off me).* —**crib′ber,** *n.* [*count*]

crib•bage (krib′ij) /ˈkrɪbɪdʒ/ *n.* [*noncount*] a card game, basically for two players, in which points for certain combinations of cards are scored on a small pegboard (**crib′bage board′**).

crib′ death′, *n.* SUDDEN INFANT DEATH SYNDROME.

crick (krik) /krɪk/ *n.* [*count*] **1.** a sharp, painful spasm or stiffening of the muscles, as of the neck or back: *a bad crick in my neck.* —*v.* [~ + *obj*] **2.** to give a crick or painful feeling of stiffening to (the back, etc.): *I cricked my back when I picked her up.*

crick•et[1] (krik′it) /ˈkrɪkɪt/ *n.* [*count*] **1.** a jumping insect that produces loud noises by rubbing its wings together. **2.** a small, hand-held metal toy that makes a clicking noise when pressed.

crick•et[2] (krik′it) /ˈkrɪkɪt/ *n.* [*noncount*] **1.** a game, popular esp. in England, for two teams of 11 members each. **2.** [*usually with a negative word or phrase or in questions*] fair play; honorable conduct: *It's not cricket to ask such questions.* —**crick′et•er,** *n.* [*count*]

cried (krīd) /krayd/ *v.* pt. and pp. of CRY.

cri•er (krī′ər) /ˈkrayər/ *n.* [*count*] **1.** a person who cries. **2.** an official who makes public announcements.

crime (krīm) /kraym/ *n.* **1.** [*count*] an action considered harmful to the public good and legally prohibited: *He had committed several crimes: murder, burglary, and rape.* **2.** [*noncount*] the activity of such wrongdoing, or those performing it: *a new program to fight crime in the city; the head of organized crime.* **3.** [*count*] any serious wrongdoing: *crimes against humanity.* **4.** [*count*] a foolish act or practice: *It's a crime to let that beautiful garden go to ruin.* —**Syn.** CRIME, OFFENSE, SIN agree in referring to a breaking of law. CRIME usually refers to any serious breaking of a public law: *the crime of treason.* OFFENSE is used of a less serious violation of a public law, or of a violation of a social or moral rule: *a traffic offense; an offense against propriety.* SIN means a breaking of a moral or divine law: *the sin of envy.*

crim•i•nal (krim′ə nl) /ˈkrɪmənl̩/ *adj.* **1.** of the nature of or involving crime: *a criminal organization.* **2.** [*often: before a noun*] dealing with crime or its punishment: *a criminal lawyer.* **3.** senseless; foolish: *a criminal waste of food.* —*n.* [*count*] **4.** a person who is convicted of, or who commits, a crime: *The criminals won't get away with what they've been doing.* —**crim′i•nal•ly,** *adv.*: *a home for the criminally insane.*

crim•i•nol•o•gy (krim′ə nol′ə jē) /ˌkrɪməˈnɒlədʒiy/ *n.* [*noncount*] the study of crime and criminals and their effects on society. —**crim•i•no•log•i•cal** (krim′ə nl oj′i kəl) /ˌkrɪmənl̩ˈɒdʒɪkəl/ *adj.* —**crim′i•no•log′i•cal•ly,** *adv.* —**crim′i•nol′o•gist,** *n.* [*count*]

crimp (krimp) /krɪmp/ *v.* [~ + *obj*] **1.** to press into small regular folds; make wavy. **2.** to curl (hair), esp. with a curling iron: *enjoyed crimping her hair.* **3.** to restrain, hinder, or interfere with; hold back: *You crimp his progress when you keep interrupting him.* —*n.* [*count*] **4.** Usually, **crimps.** [*plural*] waves or curls, esp. in crimped hair. —***Idiom.*** **5. put a crimp in,** [~ + *obj*] to interfere with; hinder: *This bad weather puts a crimp in our plans for a picnic.* —**crimp′er,** *n.* [*count*]

crim•son (krim′zən, -sən) /ˈkrɪmzən, -sən/ *adj.* **1.** deep purplish red. —*n.* [*noncount*] **2.** a crimson color, pigment, or dye.

cringe (krinj) /krɪndʒ/ *v.* [*no obj*], **cringed, cring•ing. 1.** to move down and away, esp. in fear; cower: *cringed when he saw the policeman with the nightstick.* **2.** to react toward something or someone with embarrassment, slight disgust, or reluctance; wince: *I cringed at the thought of having to confront her again.*

crin•kle (kring′kəl) /ˈkrɪŋkəl/ *v.*, **-kled, -kling,** *n.* —*v.* **1.** [*no obj*] to wrinkle; ripple: *This fabric crinkles easily, so try not to sit on it for long.* **2.** [~ + *obj*] to bend or twist: *He crinkled the paper while he spoke.* **3.** [*no obj*] to make the small sounds of wrinkling or bending; rustle: *The paper crinkled in the fireplace.* —*n.* [*count*] **4.** a wrinkle: *little crinkles around the eyes.* —**crin′kled,** *adj.* —**crin′kly,** *adj.*, **-kli•er, -kli•est:** *crinkly scraps of paper.*

crin•o•line (krin′l in) /ˈkrɪnl̩ɪn/ *n.* **1.** [*noncount*] a stiff, rough fabric used as lining or for support in garments, hats, etc. **2.** [*count*] a petticoat made of crinoline and worn to make a skirt flare out. See -LIN-.

crip•ple (krip′əl) /ˈkrɪpəl/ *n.*, *v.*, **-pled, -pling.** —*n.* [*count*] **1.** *Sometimes Offensive.* **a.** a lame or disabled person or animal. **b.** a person disabled in any way: *a mental cripple.* —*v.* [~ + *obj*] **2.** to make a cripple of; lame: *The bullet in his spine had crippled him permanently.* **3.** to damage; keep from working well; impair: *The snowstorm crippled the railway system.* —**crip′pled,** *adj.* —**crip′pler,** *n.* [*count*]

crip•pling (krip′ling) /ˈkrɪplɪŋ/ *adj.* **1.** [*before a noun*] damaging to one's health: *a crippling disease.* **2.** damaging; harmful: *crippling taxes.*

cri•sis (krī′sis) /ˈkraysɪs/ *n.*, *pl.* **-ses** (-sēz). **1.** a turning point in a situation: [*count*]: *a crisis in their marriage.* [*noncount*]: *It was a time of great crisis for him.* **2.** [*count*] a condition of instability, as in international relations, that leads to an important change: *the Middle East crisis.*

crisp (krisp) /krɪsp/ *adj.*, **-er, -est,** *n.* —*adj.* Also, **crisp•y, -i•er, -i•est. 1.** hard but brittle: *crisp crackers.* **2.** firm and fresh: *crisp lettuce.* **3.** clear; quick; precise: *a crisp reply.* **4.** brisk; unfriendly or cool: *His tone was crisp and formal.* **5.** bracing; cold but giving a feeling of vigor: *crisp weather.* **6.** lively; pithy: *a crisp tempo.* —*n.* [*count*] **7.** *Brit.* POTATO CHIP. **8.** a dessert of apples or other fruit baked with a crunchy topping of crumbs, sugar, etc.: *an apple crisp.* —**crisp′er,** *n.* [*count*] —**crisp′ly,** *adv.*: *answered crisply that it was none of my business.* —**crisp′ness,** *n.* [*noncount*]

criss•cross (kris′krôs′, -kros′) /ˈkrɪsˌkrɔs, -ˌkrɒs/ *v.* **1.** [~ + *obj*] to pass back and forth over: *The traveling salesman crisscrossed the country.* **2.** [*no obj*] to be arranged in a crisscross pattern: *The lines of the highways on the map crisscrossed in front of me.* —*adj.* [*before a noun*] **3.** Also, **criss′crossed′.** having many crossing lines, paths, or the like: *peasant skirts with beautiful crisscross designs.* —*n.* [*count*] **4.** a crisscross mark, pattern, etc. —*adv.* **5.** in a crisscross manner; crosswise.

crit., an abbreviation of: **1.** critic. **2.** criticism. **3.** criticized.

cri•te•ri•on (krī tēr′ē ən) /krayˈtɪəriyən/ *n.* [*count*], *pl.* **-te•ri•a** (-tēr′ē ə) /-ˈtɪəriyə/ **-te•ri•ons.** a standard by which to judge or criticize: *Which criterion is the most important when you grade essays?*

crit•ic (krit′ik) /ˈkrɪtɪk/ *n.* [*count*] **1.** a person who judges or criticizes: *critics of the political scene.* **2.** a person who evaluates written or artistic works, dramatic performances, etc., as for a newspaper: *a film critic.* **3.** a person who tends to find fault or make harsh judgments: *Your critics will always find a reason to blame you.* —**Related Words.** CRITIC is a noun, CRITICAL is an adjective, CRITICISM is a noun, CRITICIZE is a verb: *He is a harsh critic of the president. He is very critical of the president. His criticism of the president was very strong. He enjoys criticizing the president.*

crit•i•cal (krit′i kəl) /ˈkrɪtɪkəl/ *adj.* **1.** inclined to find fault or to judge severely: *remarks far too critical of the queen.* **2.** [*before a noun*] of or relating to critics or criticism: *a critical edition of Chaucer.* **3.** [*before a noun*] very careful; involving or requiring skillful judgment as to truth, merit, etc.: *Critical readers will find much of interest.* **4.** of decisive importance; crucial: *a critical moment in American politics.* **5.** of great or necessary importance; essential; indispensable: *A critical ingredient in the bomb is the primer that sets off the larger explosive.* **6.** caused by or constituting a crisis: *a critical shortage of food.* **7.** (of a patient's condition) having unstable and abnormal heartbeat, blood pressure, etc.: *The gunshot victim is listed in critical condition.* —**crit′i•cal•ly,** *adv.*: *The book was critically acclaimed.*

crit•i•cism (krit′ə siz′əm) /ˈkrɪtəˌsɪzəm/ *n.* **1.** [*noncount*] an act of criticizing: *Criticism of the paper was constructive.* **2.** [*noncount*] an act of passing severe judgment; censure: *leveled their harshest criticism at the judge.* **3.** [*count*] an unfavorable judgment: *Her criticisms of the proposal were that it was impractical and unfair.* **4.** the act or occupation of evaluating a literary or artistic work, musical or dramatic performance, etc.: [*noncount*]: *a piece of literary criticism.* [*count*]: *She wrote her criticism of the new play for the newspaper.*

crit•i•cize (krit′ə sīz′) /ˈkrɪtəˌsayz/ *v.*, **-cized, -ciz•ing. 1.** to find fault (with); judge unfavorably or harshly: [~ + *obj*]: *criticizes her students instead of encouraging them.* [~ + *obj* + *for* + *obj*]: *criticized me for not caring about my work.* [*no obj*]: *always criticizing and never has anything good to say.* **2.** [~ + *obj*] to judge or discuss the merits or faults of; evaluate: *The students present their work and criticize it together.*

cri•tique (kri tēk′) /krɪˈtiyk/ *n.*, *v.*, **-tiqued, -ti•quing.** —*n.* [*count*] **1.** an article or essay judging a piece of writing or other work; review: *He wrote a critique of the new art show.* **2.** a critical comment on some subject, problem, etc.: *a thoughtful critique of the economic problems.* **—v.** [~ + *obj*] **3.** to review or analyze critically: *The commentator critiqued the new play.*

crit•ter (krit′ər) /ˈkrɪtər/ *n.* [*count*] *Informal.* any creature: *A fence will keep those critters from roaming.*

croak (krōk) /krowk/ *v.* **1.** [*no obj*] to utter a low, harsh cry, such as the sound of a frog: *frogs croaking in the evening.* **2.** to speak with a low, hoarse, scratchy voice: [*no obj*]: *Because of her sore throat she was croaking all day.* [~ + *obj*]: *He croaked his answer from bed.* [*used with quotations*]: *"I feel like I'm gonna die," he croaked after his tonsillectomy.* **3.** [*no obj*] *Slang.* to die: *He almost croaked right there, but we rescued him.* **—n.** [*count*] **4.** the act or sound of croaking: *the croaks of the bullfrogs.* **—croak′y,** *adj.,* **-i•er, -i•est.**

cro•chet (krō shā′) /krowˈʃey/ *n., v.,* **-cheted** (-shād′) /-ˈʃeyd/ **-chet•ing** (-shā′ing) /-ˈʃeyɪŋ/. **—n.** [*noncount*] **1.** Also, **crocheting.** needlework done with a hooked needle **(crochet′ hook′** or **crochet′ nee′dle)** for pulling the thread or yarn through interconnected loops: *showed us the beautiful crocheting that she'd worked.* **—v. 2.** [*no obj*] to do this needlework: *She spent the afternoon crocheting.* **3.** [~ + *obj*] to form or make by crocheting: *crocheted a sweater and a vest.* **—cro•chet′er,** *n.* [*count*]

crock (krok) /krɒk/ *n.* [*count*] **1.** a clay or earthenware pot, jar, or other container. **2.** a fragment of earthenware.

crocked (krokt) /krɒkt/ *adj. Slang.* drunk.

crock•er•y (krok′ə rē) /ˈkrɒkəriy/ *n.* [*noncount*] cups, saucers, plates, etc., made of baked clay or earth; earthenware.

croc•o•dile (krok′ə dīl′) /ˈkrɒkəˌdayl/ *n.* **1.** [*count*] a meat-eating reptile of warm waters, with a large jaw, a long, narrow snout, a large tail, and very sharp teeth. **2.** [*noncount*] the tanned skin or hide of this reptile: *a handbag of crocodile.* **3.** [*count*] *Brit.* a long line of people, esp. schoolchildren walking by twos.

croc′odile tears′, *n.* [*plural*] expression of sorrow or grief that is false and insincere: *shedding crocodile tears over the misfortunes of the people he had helped to ruin.*

cro•cus (krō′kəs) /ˈkrowkəs/ *n.* [*count*], *pl.* **-cus•es.** a small bulb-shaped plant of the iris family, cultivated for its showy flowers that bloom in spring. **—cro′cused,** *adj.*

crois•sant (krə sänt′, kwä-) /krəˈsɑnt, kwɑ-/ *n.* [*count*], *pl.* **-sants** (-sänts′) /-ˈsɑnts/. a crescent-shaped roll of rich, flaky pastry.

crone (krōn) /krown/ *n.* [*count*] a withered, witchlike old woman. **—cron′ish,** *adj.*

cro•ny (krō′nē) /ˈkrowniy/ *n.* [*count*], *pl.* **-nies.** a close friend; companion; chum; associate: *always managed to find jobs for his cronies.*

crook (kro͝ok) /krʊk/ *n.* [*count*] **1.** an instrument having a bent or curved part, such as a shepherd's staff hooked at one end; hook. **2.** the curved part of the inside of the arm when the elbow is bent: *I held the baby in the crook of my left arm.* **3.** a bend or curve: *Turn left at the crook in the road ahead.* **4.** a dishonest person, esp. a swindler or thief. **—v. 5.** to bend; curve: [~ + *obj*]: *The manager crooked his finger and invited us in.* [*no obj*]: *The road crooked to the left.*

crook•ed (kro͝ok′id) /ˈkrʊkɪd/ *adj.* **1.** not straight; bent; uneven: *a crooked line.* **2.** off balance; to one side: *a crooked little smile.* **3.** dishonest or illegal: *a crooked deal.* **—crook′ed•ly,** *adv.* **—crook′ed•ness,** *n.* [*noncount*]

croon (kro͞on) /kruwn/ *v.* **1.** to sing or hum softly: [*no obj*]: *The baby was crooning softly to herself.* [~ + *obj*]: *I crooned a little song to her.* **2.** to sing in a smooth, slightly exaggerated manner: [~ + *obj*]: *The star crooned his songs and the audience loved it.* [*no obj*]: *He would croon for a bit while sitting on a high stool.* **3.** [*used with quotations*] to say (something) in a crooning manner: *"Honey, you know you're the only one I love," he crooned.* **—croon′er,** *n.* [*count*]

crop (krop) /krɒp/ *n., v.,* **cropped, crop•ping. —n.** [*count*] **1.** the plant, or the product of a plant, produced while growing or when gathered: *the wheat crop.* **2.** the yield of such produce grown in one season; harvest: *The winter wheat crop was the largest in years.* **3.** the yield of any product in a season: *the maple syrup crop.* **4.** a group of persons or things appearing or occurring together: *the new crop of freshmen.* **5.** Also called **craw.** a pouch in the food passage of many birds, in which food is held for later digestion. **6.** a close cutting of something, such as the hair: *a short crop of hair.* **—v. 7.** [~ + *obj*] to cut or bite off the top of (a plant, etc.): *sheep cropping the grass.* **8.** [~ + *obj*] to cut off the ends or a part of: *to crop the ears of a dog.* **9.** [~ + *obj*] to cut short: *to crop the hair.* **10.** [~ + *obj*] to trim (a photographic print or negative). **11. crop up,** [*no obj*] to appear, esp. suddenly: *As soon as we deal with one emergency, another crops up.*

crop′-dust′ing, *n.* [*noncount*] the spraying of pesticides on crops, usually from an airplane.

crop•land (krop′land′) /ˈkrɒpˌlænd/ *n.* [*noncount*] land used for cultivating crops.

cro•quet (krō kā′) /krowˈkey/ *n.* [*noncount*] a lawn game played by knocking wooden balls through metal wickets with mallets.

cro•quette (krō ket′) /krowˈkɛt/ *n.* [*count*] a small cake or ball of finely ground meat, fish, vegetables, or other food coated with egg and breadcrumbs and fried in oil.

cross (krôs, kros) /krɔs, krɒs/ *n., v., adj.,* **-er, -est. —n.** [*count*] **1.** a figure made up of two lines drawn across each other usually at right angles. **2.** a mark, usually an X, used as a signature or to indicate location, an error, etc.: *The crosses mark the places where you must sign your name.* **3.** a wooden structure made up of a piece standing upright and another attached across it, upon which people were formerly put to death. **4. the Cross,** [*proper noun*] the cross upon which Jesus died. **5.** a figure of a cross, or of the Cross as a Christian emblem: *rows and rows of crosses in the cemetery.* **6.** a sign made with the hand outlining the figure of a cross upon the upper part of the body, done as an act of religious devotion. **7.** a cause of trouble, suffering, or misfortune: *He had to bear the cross of his children's attempted suicides.* **8.** a crossing of animals or plants, or an animal or plant produced this way; crossbreed: *The mule is a cross between a female horse and a male donkey.* **9.** a person or thing intermediate in character between two others: *The school seemed to be a cross between a train station and a cathedral: noisy and crowded one second, then quiet and serene the next.* **—v. 10.** to move from one side to the other side of (a street, etc.): [~ + *obj*]: *Cross the street at the corner.* [*no obj*]: *She crossed to the other side of the room.* **11.** [~ + *obj*] to assist (a person) across a street or intersection: *The crossing guard is at the corner to cross the children in the morning.* **12.** to cancel by marking with a cross or drawing a line through or across: [~ + *off* + *obj*]: *I crossed off the items on the shopping list.* [~ + *out* + *obj*]: *She had crossed out my name on the list.* [~ + *obj* + *off/out*]: *to cross names off.* **13.** to intersect; meet: [*no obj*]: *The paths of our lives crossed again.* [~ + *obj*]: *Highway 50 crosses highway 80 right here.* **14. a.** [~ + *obj*] to go over and beyond: *We crossed the border at exactly 5:35 a.m.* **b.** [*no obj*] to meet and then pass: *I think our two letters must have crossed in the mail.* **15.** to cause (members of two different species, etc.) to breed with each other: [~ + *obj* + *with* + *obj*]: *Mendel crossed green peas with yellow peas.* [~ + *obj*]: *Mendel crossed green and yellow peas to see what would result.* **16.** [~ + *obj*] to oppose openly; get in the way of: *She can be nice and even charming as long as you don't cross her.* **17.** [~ + *obj*] to place across each other, on top of each other, or crosswise: *He crossed his legs.* **18.** [~ + *oneself*] to make the sign of the cross upon or over: *He crossed himself in front of the casket.* **19. cross over,** [*no obj*] **a.** to switch loyalty or allegiance: *Many Republicans have crossed over and voted Democrat.* **b.** to change successfully from one field to another: *She was able to cross over from jazz to pop music.* **20. cross up, a.** to deceive; double-cross: [~ + *obj* + *up*]: *If you try to cross us up, you'll regret it.* [~ + *up* + *obj*]: *No one crosses up the Duke and lives to tell about it.* **b.** to confuse: [~ + *up* + *obj*]: *Our team tried to cross up the opposition by switching our plays.* [~ + *obj* + *up*]: *We nearly succeeded in crossing them up.* **—adj. 21.** angry and annoyed; ill-humored: *I felt cross because I hadn't slept well.* **—*Idiom.* 22. cross one's mind,** to occur to one: *The idea never crossed my mind.* **—cross′ly,** *adv.*: *"I'm too tired to get up," she answered crossly.* **—cross′ness,** *n.* [*noncount*]

cross•bar (krôs′bär′, kros′-) /ˈkrɔsˌbɑr, ˈkrɒs-/ *n.* [*count*] **1.** a horizontal bar, line, or stripe. **2. a.** [*usually: singular*] the horizontal bar forming part of the goalposts, as in football and soccer. **b.** a horizontal bar used for gymnastics. **c.** a horizontal bar that must be cleared in performing the pole vault or high jump.

cross•beam (krôs′bēm′, kros′-) /ˈkrɔsˌbiym, ˈkrɒs-/ *n.*

[*count*] a horizontal beam in a structure serving as a support.

cross•bones (krôs′bōnz′, kros′-) /ˈkrɔsˌbownz, ˈkrɒs-/ *n.* [*plural*] a representation of two bones placed crosswise, usually below a skull, to symbolize death.

cross•bow (krôs′bō′, kros′-) /ˈkrɔsˌbow, ˈkrɒs-/ *n.* [*count*] a medieval weapon made up of a bow attached across a piece of wood, having a trigger mechanism to release the bowstring and fire a projectile with great force. —**cross′bow′man,** *n.* [*count*], *pl.* **-men.**

cross•breed (krôs′brēd′, kros′-) /ˈkrɔsˌbriyd, ˈkrɒs-/ *v.*, **-bred, -breed•ing,** *n.* —*v.* [~ + *obj*] **1.** to breed (two different varieties of the same species) or mate or breed (one variety) with another variety of the same species: *They tried to crossbreed the two varieties of orange to produce a sweeter, juicier fruit.* —*n.* [*count*] **2.** an animal or plant that is a cross or mixture of breeds.

cross-coun•try (*adj.* krôs′kun′trē, kros′-; *n.* -kun′trē, -kun′-) /*adj.* ˈkrɔsˌkʌntriy, ˈkrɒs-; *n.* -ˈkʌntriy, -ˌkʌn-/ *adj.* [*before a noun*] **1.** directed or proceeding over fields, through woods, etc., rather than on a road or track: *a cross-country race.* **2.** from one end of the country to the other: *a cross-country flight.* —*n.* [*noncount*] **3.** a cross-country sport or race: *a gold medal in cross-country.*

cross•cur•rent (krôs′kûr′ənt, -kur′-, kros′-) /ˈkrɔsˌkɜrənt, -ˌkʌr-, ˈkrɒs-/ *n.* [*count*] **1.** a current, as in a stream, moving across the main current. **2.** Often, **crosscurrents.** [*plural*] a tendency or movement that fights or goes against another.

cross′-exam′ine, *v.* [~ + *obj*], **-ined, -in•ing. 1.** (in a court of law) to examine (a witness called and examined by the opposing side), esp. for the purpose of checking, clarifying, or showing to be false that witness's testimony. **2.** to question closely or minutely: *My parents cross-examined me when I got home late from the party.* —**cross′-examina′tion,** *n.* [*noncount*]: *On cross-examination, the witness blurted out the truth.* [*count*]: *conducted a cross-examination.* —**cross′-exam′iner,** *n.* [*count*]

cross′-eyed′, *adj.* having or showing a condition of the eyes in which one or both eyes turn inward: *a cross-eyed look.*

cross′ fire′ or **cross′fire′,** *n.* **1.** gunfire coming from two or more positions so that the lines of fire cross one another: [*count; usually singular*]: *If the troops attack, they'll be in a vicious crossfire.* [*noncount*]: *They tried to avoid the crossfire and focused their attack carefully.* **2.** [*noncount*] a situation involving conflicting claims, forces, arguments, etc.: *She was caught in the crossfire, attacked from one side for being too careful and from the other for not forging ahead.*

cross•ing (krô′sing, kros′ing) /ˈkrɔsɪŋ, ˈkrɒsɪŋ/ *n.* [*count*] **1.** the act of a person or thing that crosses: *endured a very rough and stormy crossing over the Atlantic.* **2.** a place where two or more lines, streets, tracks, etc., cross each other. **3.** a place at which a road, railroad track, river, etc., may be crossed: *The truck has to come to a full stop at each railroad crossing.*

cross-leg•ged (krôs′leg′id, -legd′) /ˈkrɔsˌlɛgɪd, -ˌlɛgd/ *adj., adv.* **1.** having the knees wide apart and the ankles crossed. **2.** having one leg placed across the other.

cross•o•ver (krôs′ō′vər, kros′-) /ˈkrɔsˌowvər, ˈkrɒs-/ *n.* **1.** [*count*] a bridge or other structure for crossing over a river, highway, etc.: *Take the exit just past the crossover.* **2. a.** [*noncount*] music that crosses over in style and often appeals to a broader audience: *crossover from country-and-western to pop.* **b.** [*count*] a performer of crossover. **3.** [*count*] a member of one political party who votes in the primary of another party: *We received a lot of votes from crossovers in the primary.*

cross•patch (krôs′pach′, kros′-) /ˈkrɔsˌpætʃ, ˈkrɒs-/ *n.* [*count*] a bad-tempered person.

cross•piece (krôs′pēs′, kros′-) /ˈkrɔsˌpiys, ˈkrɒs-/ *n.* [*count*] a piece placed across something; horizontal piece: *The crosspiece will support the ceiling.*

cross′-pur′pose, *n.* [*count*] **1.** an opposing or contrary purpose. —***Idiom.* 2. at cross-purposes,** in a way that involves misunderstanding or produces frustrations on both sides, usually unintentionally: *We were working at cross-purposes but couldn't see that we were getting in each other's way.*

cross′-refer′, *v.* [~ + *obj*], **-ferred, -fer•ring.** to refer to (some information) by a cross reference: *The book cross-refers the word* gallon *to* quart *and* quart *back to* gallon.

cross′ ref′erence, *n.* [*count*] a reference from one part of a book, index, etc., to related material in another part.

cross′-ref′erence, *v.* [~ + *obj*], **-enced, -enc•ing. 1.** to provide with cross references. **2.** to cross-refer.

cross•road (krôs′rōd′, kros′-) /ˈkrɔsˌrowd, ˈkrɒs-/ *n.* [*count*] **1.** a road that crosses another road or a main road. **2.** Often, **crossroads. a.** a place where roads meet or intersect: *The first crossroads was a checkpoint where they asked to see our passports.* **b.** a point at which a vital important decision must be made: *My life was at a crossroads.*

cross′ sec′tion, *n.* [*count*] **1.** a slice of something made by cutting across it, esp. at right angles to the longest part: *This photo is a cross section of the brain.* **2.** a representative sample or example showing all characteristic parts, etc., of the whole: *tried to determine what would appeal to a large cross section of voters.*

cross•town (krôs′toun′, kros′-) /ˈkrɔsˌtawn, ˈkrɒs-/ *adj.* [*usually: before a noun*] **1.** extending or traveling across to the opposite side of a town or city: *You can take a crosstown bus if it's raining.* —*adv.* **2.** across a town or city: *to hurry crosstown to the opera house.*

cross-train (krôs′trān′, kros′-) /ˈkrɔsˈtreyn, ˈkrɒs-/ *v.* [~ + *obj*] to train (a worker, athlete, etc.) to be skilled and efficient at different work, tasks, etc.: *That company will benefit in the future by cross-training its workers now.*

cross•walk (krôs′wôk′, kros′-) /ˈkrɔsˌwɔk, ˈkrɒs-/ *n.* [*count*] a lane marked off for pedestrians to use when crossing a street. See illustration at STREET.

cross•wise (krôs′wīz′, kros′-) /ˈkrɔsˌwayz, ˈkrɒs-/ also **cross•ways** (krôs′wāz′,kros′-) /ˈkrɔsˌweyz,ˈkrɒs-/ *adv.* across; diagonally; transversely; from one corner to the other.

cross′word puz′zle (krôs′wûrd′, kros′-) /ˈkrɔsˌwɜrd, ˈkrɒs-/ *n.* [*count*] a puzzle in which words corresponding to numbered clues or definitions are fitted into a pattern of horizontal and vertical squares, one letter per square, so that most letters form parts of two words. Also called **cross′word′.**

crotch (kroch) /krɒtʃ/ *n.* [*count*] **1.** a place where something divides, such as the human body between the legs: *The pants were measured from his crotch down to the tops of his shoes.* **2.** the part of trousers, panties, etc., where the two legs or panels join.

crotch•et (kroch′it) /ˈkrɒtʃɪt/ *n.* [*count*] an odd idea; strange notion.

crotch•et•y (kroch′i tē) /ˈkrɒtʃɪtiy/ *adj.* grouchy and ill-tempered: *a crotchety old neighbor.*

crouch (krouch) /krawtʃ/ *v.* [*no obj*] **1.** to stoop low with the knees bent: *He crouched down and began to whisper in his little boy's ear.* **2.** to bend close to the ground preparing to spring, as a cat does. —*n.* [*count*] **3.** the act of crouching: *The boxer went into a crouch.*

croup (kro͞op) /kruwp/ *n.* a disease of the throat and windpipe, characterized by a hoarse cough and difficult breathing: [*noncount*]: *The little girl had croup most of the week.* [*count; singular*]: *suffering from a bad croup.* —**croup′y,** *adj.*, **-i•er, -i•est.:** *She was pretty croupy most of the night.*

crou•pi•er (kro͞o′pē ər, -pē ā′) /ˈkruwpiyər, -piyˌey/ *n.* [*count*] the attendant at a gambling table.

crou•ton (kro͞o′ton, kro͞o ton′) /ˈkruwtɒn, kruwˈtɒn/ *n.* [*count*] a small cube of fried or toasted bread, used in salads, soups, etc.

crow[1] (krō) /krow/ *n.* [*count*] **1.** a large, strong-billed songbird typically black and found nearly worldwide: *crows in the trees, cawing unceasingly.* —***Idiom.* 2. as the crow flies,** in a straight line; by the most direct route: *It's only a few miles as the crow flies, but more like twenty through the mountain roads.* **3. eat crow,** to be forced to admit one's mistake; suffer humiliation.

crow[2] (krō) /krow/ *v.*, **crowed** or, for 1, (*esp. Brit.*), **crew** (kro͞o) /kruw/; **crowed; crow•ing;** *n.* —*v.* **1.** [*no obj*] to utter the characteristic cry of a rooster. **2.** [~ + *over/about* + *obj*] to gloat over a triumph or victory; boast or brag: *They were crowing over their victory in the tournament.* **3.** [*no obj*] to utter a cry of pleasure. —*n.* [*count*] **4.** the cry of a rooster. **5.** a cry of pleasure. —**crow′er,** *n.* [*count*]

crow•bar (krō′bär′) /ˈkrowˌbɑr/ *n.* [*count*] a steel bar used as a lever.

crowd (kroud) /krawd/ *n.* [*count*] **1.** a large number of people gathered together; throng: *The crowd broke up and people went on their way.* **2.** any group having something in common, or sharing the same interests: *the theater crowd.* **3.** a group of spectators; audience: *the opening night crowd.* —*v.* **4.** [*no obj*] to gather in large numbers; throng: *They crowded around to watch the police give first aid.* **5.** to press closely together; squeeze into a small space; cram: [*no obj*]: *The reporters crowded close to the president.* [~ + *obj*]: *The police crowded us back into the street.* **6.** [~ + *obj*] to fill, such as by pressing or thronging into: *The partygoers crowded the streets.* **7.** [~ + *obj*] to put or place under constant pressure: *They were crowding me, asking for a decision I wasn't ready to give.* **—Syn.** CROWD, MULTITUDE, SWARM, THRONG refer to large numbers of people. CROWD suggests a moving, pushing, uncomfortable, and possibly disorderly company: *A crowd gathered to listen to the speech.* MULTITUDE emphasizes the great number of persons or things but suggests that there is space enough for all: *a multitude of people at the market on Saturdays.* SWARM, when it is used of people, is usually contemptuous, suggesting a moving, restless, often noisy, crowd: *A swarm of dirty children played in the street.* THRONG suggests a company that presses together or forward, often with some common aim: *The throng pushed forward to see the cause of the excitement.* **—Usage.** See COLLECTIVE NOUN.

crowd•ed (krou′did) /ˈkrawdɪd/ *adj.* **1.** filled with people; having too many people: *just another face in the crowded lecture hall.* **2.** uncomfortable because of overcrowding: *I felt crowded in the jammed subway car.*

crown (kroun) /krawn/ *n.* [*count*] **1.** an ornament worn on the head, esp. a circular piece of gold set with gems and worn by a monarch as a symbol of power. **2.** [*singular; the + ~; often: Crown*] the power or rule of a sovereign: *a representative of the Crown.* **3.** an ornamental wreath or circlet for the head, given as an award or a mark of victory or distinction: *a crown of laurel leaves.* **4.** a championship title: *He won the batting crown for two years in a row.* **5.** the top or highest part of anything, such as of a hat or the head: *a little bald spot on the crown of his head.* **6. a.** the part of a tooth covered by enamel. **b.** an artificial substitute, as of gold or porcelain, for the crown of a tooth. **7.** a former British silver coin, equal to five shillings. **8.** any of various monetary units or coins with a name meaning "crown," as the koruna, króna, or krone: *Seven Norwegian crowns used to equal one American dollar.* **—***v.* [~ + *obj*] **9.** to invest with a regal crown, or with regal dignity and power: *The Emperor was crowned in Paris.* **10.** to honor or reward. **11.** to be at the top or highest part of: *The fog crowned the top of the mountain.* **12.** to bring to a successful or triumphant conclusion: *He crowned his great career with the Nobel prize.* **13.** *Informal.* to hit on the top of the head: *threatened to crown him with the baseball bat.* **14.** to cap (a tooth) with a false crown. **15.** [*in the game of checkers*] to change (a checker) into a king after having safely reached the last row. **—crown′er,** *n.* [*count*]

crown•ing (krou′ning) /ˈkrawnɪŋ/ *adj.* making complete or perfect: *a crowning achievement.*

crown′ prince′, *n.* [*count*] a prince who will become king when the present ruler dies.

crow's′-foot′, *n.* [*count*], *pl.* **-feet.** Usually, **crow's-feet.** [*plural*] tiny wrinkles at the outer corners of the eyes resulting from age or constant squinting.

crow's′-nest′ or **crow's′ nest′,** *n.* [*count*] a platform or shelter for a lookout high on a ship's mast.

CRT, an abbreviation of: **1.** cathode-ray tube. **2.** a computer terminal or monitor that includes a cathode-ray tube.

cru•cial (kro͞o′shəl) /ˈkruwʃəl/ *adj.* of highest, greatest, or most critical importance: *a crucial experiment.* **—cru′cial•ly,** *adv.: The weather crucially affected the decision to proceed.*

cru•ci•ble (kro͞o′sə bəl) /ˈkruwsəbəl/ *n.* [*count*] **1.** a container or pot of metal used for heating substances to high temperatures. **2.** a severe test or trial, esp. one that causes a lasting change or influence.

cru•ci•fix (kro͞o′sə fiks) /ˈkruwsəfɪks/ *n.* [*count*] **1.** a cross with the figure of Jesus mounted upon it. **2.** any cross.

cru•ci•fix•ion (kro͞o′sə fik′shən) /ˌkruwsəˈfɪkʃən/ *n.* **1.** the act of crucifying or the state of being crucified: [*noncount*]: *Crucifixion was a particularly barbaric way to be killed.* [*count*]: *Crucifixions were attended by great crowds of people.* **2.** [*proper noun; Crucifixion; the + ~*] the death of Jesus upon the Cross. **3.** [*count*] a picture or other representation of this.

cru•ci•form (kro͞o′sə fôrm′) /ˈkruwsəˌfɔrm/ *adj.* **1.** cross-shaped. **—***n.* [*count*] **2.** a cross.

cru•ci•fy (kro͞o′sə fī′) /ˈkruwsəˌfay/ *v.* [~ + *obj*], **-fied, -fy•ing.** **1.** to put to death by nailing or binding the hands and feet to a cross: *He was crucified and left to die.* **2.** to punish or criticize severely or cruelly; torment: *The media will crucify you for that opinion.*

crude (kro͞od) /kruwd/ *adj.,* **crud•er, crud•est,** *n.* **—***adj.* **1.** in a raw or unrefined state: *crude sugar; crude oil.* **2.** showing a lack of polish or skill; rough; undeveloped: *a crude shelter; a crude drawing.* **3.** lacking culture, refinement, etc.; vulgar: *crude behavior.* **—***n.* [*noncount*] **4.** CRUDE OIL. **—crude′ly,** *adv.* **—crude′ness,** *n.* [*noncount*]

crude′ oil′, *n.* [*noncount*] petroleum as it comes from the ground, before refining. Also called **crude′ petro′leum.**

cru•di•tés (kro͞o′di tā′) /ˌkruwdɪˈtey/ *n.* [*plural*] raw vegetables cut up and served as appetizers.

cru•el (kro͞o′əl) /ˈkruwəl/ *adj.,* **-er, -est.** **1.** willfully causing pain to others: *people who are cruel to animals.* **2.** enjoying the pain or distress of others: *a cruel and selfish tyrant.* **3.** causing or marked by great pain or distress: *a cruel war.* **4.** severe; merciless; brutal: *a cruel winter.* **—cru′el•ly,** *adv.* **—cru′el•ness,** *n.* [*noncount*]

cru•el•ty (kro͞o′əl tē) /ˈkruwəltiy/ *n., pl.* **-ties.** behavior or action that causes pain to others: [*noncount*]: *cruelty to animals.* [*count*]: *His little cruelties toward her showed how jealous he was of her great success.*

cru•et (kro͞o′it) /ˈkruwɪt/ *n.* [*count*] a glass bottle, esp. one for holding vinegar, oil, etc., for the table.

cruise (kro͞oz) /kruwz/ *v.,* **cruised, cruis•ing,** *n.* **—***v.* **1.** [*no obj*] to sail about on a pleasure trip: *We cruised to the Bahamas.* **2.** to patrol (a body of water), as a warship does: [*no obj*]: *The Coast Guard cutter cruised along the coast.* [~ + *obj*]: *The destroyer cruised the area of the wreckage.* **3.** [*no obj*] to travel at a constant speed that permits maximum efficiency: *announced that our plane would cruise at 37,000 feet.* **4.** to travel about (some place) slowly, as to look for customers or to maintain order: [*no obj*]: *Taxis and police cars were cruising in the downtown area.* [~ + *obj*]: *The police were cruising the red-light district.* **5.** *Informal.* to go or look about (the streets, public areas or places, etc.) in search of a sexual partner: [*no obj*]: *cruising on the streets.* [~ + *obj*]: *cruising the bars.* **—***n.* [*count*] **6.** a pleasure voyage on a ship: *We went on a cruise to see the Arctic Circle.*

cruise′ mis′sile, *n.* [*count*] a guided missile designed to fly at low altitudes to avoid radar detection.

cruis•er (kro͞o′zər) /ˈkruwzər/ *n.* [*count*] **1.** a person or thing that cruises. **2.** one of a class of warships of medium size, designed for high speed and long cruising radius. **3.** SQUAD CAR. **4.** CABIN CRUISER.

crul•ler (krul′ər) /ˈkrʌlər/ *n.* [*count*] **1.** a twisted, oblong doughnut. **2.** a light raised doughnut, usually having a ridged surface and topped with white icing.

crumb (krum) /krʌm/ *n.* [*count*] **1.** a small particle of bread, cake, etc.: *dusted the crumbs off the table.* **2.** a fragment of anything; bit: *They listened to the speaker with complete attention, waiting for a few crumbs of insight.* **3.** *Slang.* a hateful person: *That crumb had the nerve to come back here and demand more money.*

crum•ble (krum′bəl) /ˈkrʌmbəl/ *v.,* **-bled, -bling.** **1.** to (cause to) break into small fragments: [*no obj*]: *The ancient paper crumbled in his hands.* [~ + *obj*]: *I crumbled the dried leaves in my fingers.* **2.** [*no obj*] to disintegrate gradually; collapse; lose strength: *The ancient empire was crumbling from within.* **—crum′bly,** *adj.,* **-bli•er, -bli•est.**

crum•my (krum′ē) /ˈkrʌmiy/ *adj.,* **-mi•er, -mi•est.** *Informal.* **1.** dirty and run-down; shabby: *a crummy little hotel.* **2.** of little value; worthless: *a crummy old toy.* **3.** wretched; miserable: *I had a really crummy evening.* **—crum′mi•ness,** *n.* [*noncount*]

crum•pet (krum′pit) /ˈkrʌmpɪt/ *n.* [*count*] a small, round, soft bread toasted on a griddle.

crum•ple (krum′pəl) /ˈkrʌmpəl/ *v.,* **-pled, -pling.** **1.** to (cause to) shrivel into small wrinkles or into a small, compact mass: [~ + *obj*]: *I crumpled the note in my hand.* [~ + *up* + *obj*]: *She crumpled up the note.* [~ + *obj* + *up*]: *She crumpled it up.* [*no obj*]: *The front of the car had crumpled from the impact.* **2.** to (cause to) give way suddenly; (cause to) collapse: [*no obj*]: *The stairway crumpled under his weight.* [~ + *obj*]: *The explosion crumpled the building in seconds.* **—crum′ply,** *adj.*

crunch (krunch) /krʌntʃ/ *v.* **1.** [~ + *obj*] to chew with a sharp crushing noise: *crunching his breakfast cereal.* [~ + *on* + *obj*]: *crunching on his breakfast cereal.* **2.** to crush or grind noisily: [~ + *obj*]: *Our boots crunched the snow as we walked over it.* [*no obj*]: *The gravel in the road crunched under the car.* **3.** [*no obj*] to proceed with a crushing noise: *cars crunching along the gravel road.*

4. [~ + *obj*] to work with or process (data) in large amounts, esp. by computer: *Crunch the data and bring me an analysis of it by tomorrow.* **—*n.*** [*count*] **5.** an act or sound of crunching: *I heard a loud crunch and looked out the window.* **6.** a shortage or reduction: *the energy crunch.* **7.** distress or hard times due to such a shortage or reduction: *in a budget crunch for nearly three years.* **—crunch′y,** *adj.*, **-i•er, -i•est.**

cru•sade (kro͞o sād′) /kruw'seyd/ *n., v.,* **-sad•ed, -sad•ing.** **—*n.*** [*count*] **1.** [*often: Crusade*] any of the military campaigns or wars undertaken by the Christians of Europe in the 11th, 12th, and 13th centuries to recapture the Holy Land from the Muslims. **2.** a strong movement, campaign, or activity on behalf of a cause: *a literacy crusade.* **—*v.*** [*no obj*] **3.** to go on or take part in a crusade: *She was crusading for more aid to the unemployed.* **—cru•sad′er,** *n.* [*count*]

crush (krush) /krʌʃ/ *v.* **1.** [~ + *obj*] to press or squeeze with a force that destroys or changes the shape of: *The women crushed the grapes to make wine.* **2.** [~ + *obj*] to pound into small particles: *I crushed some ice and added it to her drink.* **3.** to (cause to) wrinkle, crease, or collapse into tiny folds: [~ + *obj*]: *She crushed the paper and threw it away.* [*no obj*]: *This material crushes too easily to be of any use.* **4.** [~ + *obj*] to force out by pressing or squeezing: *He crushed the juice from the grapes.* **5.** [~ + *obj*] to hug or embrace tightly: *He crushed the princess in his arms.* **6.** [~ + *obj*] to overwhelm; destroy completely: *The Rangers crushed the Islanders 10-1 last night at the arena.* **7.** [~ + *obj*] to shock or upset; affect grievously: *The news of his death crushed me.* **8.** to (cause to) move forward with force: [*no obj*]: *The reporters tried to crush into the courtroom.* [~ + *obj*]: *The surging crowd crushed us against the wall.* **—*n.*** **9.** [*noncount*]the act of crushing or the state of being crushed; pressure; force. **10.** [*count; usually singular*] a great crowd; throng: *a crush of people.* **11.** [*count*] *Informal.* an intense, brief feeling of love or attraction for someone: *had a crush on you in high school.* **—crush′a•ble,** *adj.* **—crush′er,** *n.* [*count*] **—crush′ing,** *adj.*: *a crushing defeat at the polls.*

crust (krust) /krʌst/ *n.* [*count*] **1.** the brown, hard outer surface of a loaf of bread. **2.** a slice of bread from the end of the loaf. **3.** the pastry containing the filling of a pie or other dish. **4. a.** any hard outer covering or coating, as of ice or snow. **b.** [*usually singular*] the outer layer of the earth: *The earth's crust is about 22 mi. (35 km) deep under the continents and 6 mi. (10 km) deep under the oceans.* **—*v.*** [~ + *obj*] **5.** to cover with a crust: *The road was crusted with snow and ice.* **—crust′al,** *adj.*: *the earth's crustal plates.*

crus•ta•cean (kru stā′shən) /krʌ'steyʃən/ *n.* [*count*] a chiefly water-dwelling shellfish, an arthropod, typically having the body covered with a hard shell, as lobsters, shrimps, and crabs.

crust•y (krus′tē) /'krʌstiy/ *adj.,* **-i•er, -i•est.** **1.** having a hard crust: *crusty bread.* **2.** bad-tempered; grouchy; impatient: *a crusty old neighbor.*

crutch (kruch) /krʌtʃ/ *n.* [*count*] **1.** a staff or support to assist a person in walking, usually having a crosspiece at one end to fit under the armpit: *I had to use crutches after I sprained my knee.* See illustration at HOSPITAL. **2.** anything that serves as a temporary support or aid; prop: *the use of liquor as a psychological crutch.*

crux (kruks) /krʌks/ *n.* [*count*], *pl.* **crux•es, cru•ces** (kro͞o′sēz) /'kruwsiyz/. the central or most important point; essence: *The crux of the matter is that he's going to resign unless we do something about it.*

cry (krī) /kray/ *v.,* **cried, cry•ing,** *n., pl.* **cries.** **—*v.*** **1.** [*no obj*] to utter sounds, esp. of grief or suffering, usually with tears: *She cried with pain.* **2.** [*no obj*] to shed tears, with or without sound; weep: *He cried all night the day his mother died.* **3.** [~ + *oneself*] to bring (oneself) to a certain state or condition by weeping: *The baby cried himself to sleep.* **4.** to call loudly; shout: [*no obj; (~ + out)*]: *She cried out with pain when she tripped and fell.* [*~ (+ out) + obj*]: *He cried a warning as the wolf sprang at them.* [*used with quotations; ~ (+ out)*]: *"Help!" she cried (out).* **5.** [*no obj*] (of an animal) to give forth a characteristic call: *The seagulls cried.* **6.** [~ + *for* + *obj*] to beg or plead for something: *to cry for mercy.* **7.** [~ + *obj*] to announce publicly: *to cry one's wares to sell.* **8. cry out against,** [~ + *out against* + *obj*] to speak out against: *His book cries out against bigotry and hatred.* **9. cry out for,** [~ + *out* + *for* + *obj*] to show or demonstrate an urgent need for attention to: *These decaying streets cry out for repair.* **—*n.*** [*count*] **10.** the act or sound of crying: *cries of outrage.* **11.** a period or fit of weeping: *had a good cry.* **12.** the characteristic call of an animal: *the cries of the seagulls.* **13.** an urgent request; appeal: *a cry for help.* **14.** a shout of encouragement, such as a political or party slogan, or words to troops in battle: *a battle cry.* **—*Idiom.*** **15. a far cry,** [*noncount*] altogether or completely different: *The small town was a far cry from the inner city he lived in.* **16. cry over spilled milk,** [*used with a negative word or phrase*] to regret what cannot be changed or undone: *There is no use crying over spilled milk.*

cry•ba•by (krī′bā′bē) /'kray,beybiy/ *n.* [*count*], *pl.* **-bies.** a person who cries or complains with little cause.

cry•ing (krī′ing) /'krayɪŋ/ *adj.* [*before a noun*] **1.** demanding attention, repair, etc.: *a crying need for more money for schools.* **2.** terribly and obviously bad; abominable; flagrant: *It's a crying shame that we don't spend more on education.* **—cry′ing•ly,** *adv.*

cry•o•gen•ics (krī′ə jen′iks) /,krayə'dʒɛnɪks/ *n.* [*noncount; used with a singular verb*] the scientific study of extremely low temperatures.

crypt (kript) /krɪpt/ *n.* [*count*] an underground chamber or vault, used as a burial place.

cryp•tic (krip′tik) /'krɪptɪk/ *adj.* **1.** mysterious; puzzling: *cryptic remarks about her work.* **2.** secret; occult: *cryptic writing.* **—cryp′ti•cal•ly,** *adv.*

crys•tal (kris′tl) /'krɪstļ/ *n.* **1.** [*noncount*] a clear, transparent mineral or glass resembling ice, like quartz. **2.** [*count*] a piece of such mineral, cut and used as decoration: *glimmering crystals on her necklace.* **3.** [*count*] a single grain of a crystallike substance: *A few crystals of sugar fell to the floor.* **4.** [*noncount*] glass of fine quality and a high degree of brilliance: *a goblet of Orrefors crystal.* **5.** [*noncount*] glassware, esp. for the table and ornamental objects, made of such glass: *Put out the china and the crystal.* **6.** [*count*] the glass or plastic cover over the face of a watch: *The blow to his wrist had shattered the crystal on his watch.* **7.** [*count*] a quartz crystal shaped to vibrate at a particular frequency, used to control the timing of a watch. **—*adj.*** **8.** made of crystal. **9.** [*before a noun*] resembling crystal; clear; transparent: *the crystal waters of the Aegean Sea.*

crys•tal•line (kris′tl in) /'krɪstļɪn/ *adj.* **1.** of, like, containing, or in the form of crystals. **2.** clear, bright, or glittering like crystal: *the crystalline Aegean Sea.*

crys•tal•lize (kris′tl iz′) /'krɪstļ,ayz/ *v.,* **-lized, -liz•ing.** **1.** to (cause to) form into crystals; (cause to) assume crystallike form: [*no obj*]: *The minerals crystallized in the heat.* [~ + *obj*]: *Great heat crystallized these minerals long ago.* **2.** to (cause to) become definite or concrete in form: [~ + *obj*]: *to crystallize an idea.* [*no obj*]: *His ideas hadn't yet crystallized.* **3.** [~ + *obj*] to coat with sugar. **—crys′tal•liz′a•ble,** *adj.* **—crys•tal•li•za•tion** (kris′tl ə-zā′shən) /,krɪstļə'zeyʃən/ *n.* [*noncount*] **—crys′tal•liz′-er,** *n.* [*count*]

C/S, an abbreviation of: cycles per second.

C-sec•tion (sē′sek′shən) /'siy,sɛkʃən/ *n. Informal.* CESAREAN.

CST or **C.S.T.** or **c.s.t.,** an abbreviation of: Central Standard Time.

CT, an abbreviation of: **1.** Also **C.T.** Central Time. **2.** Connecticut.

Ct., an abbreviation of: **1.** Connecticut. **2.** Count.

ct., an abbreviation of: **1.** carat. **2.** cent. **3.** county. **4.** court.

ctn, an abbreviation of: cotangent.

ctn., *pl.* **ctns.** an abbreviation of: carton.

ctr., an abbreviation of: center.

cts., an abbreviation of: cents.

CT scan, *n.* CAT SCAN.

cu or **cu.,** an abbreviation of: cubic.

cub (kub) /kʌb/ *n.* [*count*] **1.** the young of certain animals, esp. the bear, wolf, or lion. **2.** a young and inexperienced person, esp. a young man. **3.** CUB SCOUT.

Cu•ban (kyo͞o′bən) /'kyuwbən/ *adj.* **1.** of or relating to Cuba. **—*n.*** [*count*] **2.** a person born or living in Cuba.

cub•by•hole (kub′ē hōl′) /'kʌbiy,howl/ *n.* [*count*] **1.** a small hole, usually one of several in a row, to store letters, papers, etc. **2.** a small, snug place: *My office there was a cubbyhole of only six feet by six feet.*

cube (kyo͞ob) /kyuwb/ *n., v.,* **cubed, cub•ing.** **—*n.*** [*count*] **1.** a solid object with sides that are six equal squares, or an object similar to this: *a sugar cube.* **2.** the number resulting from multiplying a number by itself twice; the third power of a quantity. **3.** *Slang.* one of a pair of dice; a die. **—*v.*** [~ + *obj*] **4.** to make into a cube or cubes, as by cutting: *He cubed the carrots and potatoes.* **5.** to multiply (a number) by itself twice; raise (a number) to the third power: *If you cube the number 4, you get 64.* —**cub′er,** *n.* [*count*]

cube′ root′, *n.* [*count*] a quantity of which a given quantity is the cube: *The cube root of 64 is 4.*

cu•bic (kyōō′bik) /ˈkyuwbɪk/ *adj.* [*before a noun*] **1.** of or relating to the measurement of volume: *the cubic contents.* **2.** relating to a unit of linear measure that is multiplied by itself twice to form a unit of measure for volume: *A cubic foot is one foot in length, one foot in width, and one foot in height.*

cu•bi•cle (kyōō′bi kəl) /ˈkyuwbɪkəl/ *n.* [*count*] a small space or compartment in a large room or area set off by a divider: *There was a computer in each cubicle.*

cub•ism (kyōō′biz əm) /ˈkyuwbɪzəm/ *n.* [*noncount; sometimes: Cubism*] a style of painting and sculpture in which natural forms are made to look like geometrical figures or lines. —**cub′ist,** *n.* [*count*]

cu•bit (kyōō′bit) /ˈkyuwbɪt/ *n.* [*count*] an ancient unit of measurement based on the length of the forearm from the elbow to the tip of the middle finger, usually from 17 to 21 inches (43 to 53 cm).

cub′ scout′, *n.* [*count; sometimes: Cub Scout*] a member of the junior division (ages 8–10) of the Boy Scouts.

cuck•old (kuk′əld) /ˈkʌkəld/ *n.* [*count*] **1.** the husband of an unfaithful wife. —*v.* [~ + *obj*] **2.** to make a cuckold of (a husband): *Queen Guinevere cuckolded her husband, King Arthur.*

cuck•oo (kōō′kōō, kŏŏk′ōō) /ˈkuwkuw, ˈkʊkuw/ *n., pl.* **-oos,** *v.,* **-ooed, -oo•ing,** *adj.* —*n.* [*count*] **1.** a slim, stout-billed, long-tailed bird. **2.** a common Eurasian cuckoo with a monotonous, repeated call. **3.** the call of this cuckoo, or an imitation of it. **4.** *Informal.* a crazy, silly, or foolish person. —*adj.* **5.** *Informal.* crazy; silly; foolish: *a cuckoo idea.*

cu•cum•ber (kyōō′kum bər) /ˈkyuwkʌmbər/ *n.* **1.** [*count*] a creeping plant of the gourd family, occurring in many cultivated forms. **2.** the edible fleshy green-skinned fruit of this plant: [*count*]: *I cut up two cucumbers and added them to the salad.* [*noncount*]: *Do you think this salad will taste better with cucumber?*

cud (kud) /kʌd/ *n.* [*noncount*] **1.** the coarse food that a cow, goat, etc., brings back up from its first stomach to its mouth for further chewing. —***Idiom.*** **2. chew one's** or **the cud,** *Informal.* to think about something deeply; meditate or ponder.

cud•dle (kud′l) /ˈkʌdl/ *v.,* **-dled, -dling,** *n.* —*v.* **1.** to hold close in an affectionate manner; hug tenderly; lie close (to): [~ + *obj*]: *We cuddled the baby until she calmed down.* [*no obj*]: *We were cuddling in the back seat of the car.* [~ + *up*]: *We cuddled up by the fire and got warm.* —*n.* [*count*] **2.** an act of cuddling; hug; embrace.

cudg•el (kuj′əl) /ˈkʌdʒəl/ *n., v.,* **-eled, -el•ing,** or (*esp. Brit.*) **-elled, -el•ling.** —*n.* [*count*] **1.** a short, thick stick used as a weapon; club. —*v.* [~ + *obj*] **2.** to strike with a cudgel; beat. —***Idiom.*** **3. cudgel one's brains,** to try hard to understand or remember: *I was cudgeling my brains to recall her name.*

cue[1] (kyōō) /kyuw/ *n., v.,* **cued, cu•ing.** —*n.* [*count*] **1.** anything said or done, on or off stage, followed by a specified speech or action: *The gunshot is your cue to enter.* **2.** anything that serves as a signal about what to do or say: *When he started to talk about the finances, that was our cue to get up quietly and leave.* —*v.* **3.** to give a cue to; prompt: [~ + *obj* + *to* + *verb*]: *The announcer cued the audience to applaud.* [~ + *obj*]: *She cued me with a wink and we quietly left the lecture.* **4.** [~ + *obj*] to search for and reach (a track on a recording): *The disc jockey cued the next song and waited to play it.* **5. cue in,** [~ + *obj* + *in*] *Informal.* to give information, news, etc., to; inform: *We cued him in on the plans.* —***Idiom.*** **6. on cue,** [*noncount*] occurring or happening when or as if expected: *We were talking about lateness when, right on cue, my assistant walked in fifteen minutes late.*

cue[2] (kyōō) /kyuw/ *n., v.,* **cued, cu•ing.** —*n.* [*count*] **1.** a long, narrow wooden rod, tipped with leather, used to strike the ball in pool, billiards, etc. **2.** a stick used to propel the disks in shuffleboard. **3.** QUEUE (defs. 1, 2). —*v.* [~ + *obj*] **4.** to strike with a cue.

cue′ ball′, *n.* [*count*] (in billiards or pool) the usually white ball a player strikes with the cue, as distinguished from the object balls.

cuff[1] (kuf) /kʌf/ *n.* [*count*] **1.** a fold or band at the end of a sleeve, serving as a trim: *a coffee stain on the right cuff of my shirt.* **2.** the turned-up fold at the bottom of a trouser leg: *Something had caught on the cuffs of his slacks.* **3.** Usually, **cuffs.** [*plural*] handcuffs: *The prisoner rubbed his wrists where the cuffs had been.* **4.** an inflatable wrap placed around the upper arm and used with a device for recording blood pressure. —*v.* [~ + *obj*] **5.** to make a cuff on. **6.** to handcuff: *The police cuffed the suspects.* —***Idiom.*** **7. off the cuff,** *Informal.* without preparing; extemporaneously; on the spur of the moment: *The speaker made a few remarks off the cuff and then began his prepared speech.* **8. on the cuff,** *Slang.* on credit.

cuff[2] (kuf) /kʌf/ *v.* [~ + *obj*] **1.** to strike, esp. with the open hand. —*n.* [*count*] **2.** a blow with the open hand.

cuff′ link′ or **cuff′link′,** *n.* [*count*] one of a pair of linked ornamental buttons or buttonlike devices for fastening a shirt cuff.

cui•sine (kwi zēn′) /kwɪˈziyn/ *n.* [*noncount*] **1.** a style or manner of cooking: *French cuisine.* **2.** the food prepared, as by a restaurant: *The cuisine there is excellent.*

cul-de-sac (kul′də sak′, kŏŏl′-) /ˈkʌldəˌsæk, ˈkʊl-/ *n.* [*count*], *pl.* **culs-de-sac. 1.** a street, lane, etc., closed at one end; dead-end street: *a house at the end of the cul-de-sac.* **2.** any situation in which further progress is impossible: *That line of investigation is a cul-de-sac.*

cu•li•nar•y (kyōō′lə ner′ē, kul′ə-) /ˈkyuwləˌnɛriy, ˈkʌlə-/ *adj.* [*before a noun*] of, relating to, or used in cooking or the kitchen: *the culinary arts.*

cull (kul) /kʌl/ *v.* [~ + *obj*] to choose; select; pick: *I culled some of the best ideas from that journal.* —**cull′er,** *n.* [*count*]

cul•len•der (kul′ən dər) /ˈkʌləndər/ *n.* COLANDER.

cul•mi•nate (kul′mə nāt′) /ˈkʌlməˌneyt/ *v.* [~ + *in* + *obj*], **-nat•ed, -nat•ing. 1.** to reach the highest development: *His career culminated in the winning of the Nobel prize.* **2.** to arrive at a final stage after a long development: *Their disagreement culminated in a quarrel.* —**cul•mi•na•tion** (kul′mə nā′shən) /ˌkʌlməˈneyʃən/ *n.* [*count*]

cu•lottes (kōō lots′, kyōō-) /kuwˈlɒts, kyuw-/ also **cu•lotte′,** *n.* [*plural*] women's trousers, usually knee-length or calf-length, cut full to resemble a skirt: *Her culottes were cool in the summer.*

-culp-, *root.* *-culp-* comes from Latin, where it has the meaning "blame." This meaning is found in such words as: CULPABLE, CULPRIT.

cul•pa•ble (kul′pə bəl) /ˈkʌlpəbəl/ *adj.* [*be* + ~] deserving blame; guilty: *He was culpable, but whether he could be charged legally was another story.* —**cul•pa•bil•i•ty** (kul′pə bil′i tē) /ˌkʌlpəˈbɪlɪtiy/ **cul′pa•ble•ness,** *n.* [*noncount*]: *The question of culpability is the heart of the matter.* —**cul′pa•bly,** *adv.* See -CULP-.

cul•prit (kul′prit) /ˈkʌlprɪt/ *n.* [*count*] **1.** a person guilty of an offense or fault, or one accused: *led in the culprits to stand before the judge.* **2.** a thing responsible for some bad effect: *The doctors found the culprit: the tick responsible for Lyme disease.* See -CULP-.

cult (kult) /kʌlt/ *n.* [*count*] **1.** a system of worship, esp. with reference to its rites and ceremonies: *the cult of devil worship.* **2.** a system of devotion to a person, ideal, fad, etc.: *the cult of the Beatles in the 1960's.* **3.** the members of such a system: *The cult promised revenge for putting its leader in jail.* —*adj.* [*before a noun*] **4.** of or relating to a cult: *a cult movie; She was a cult figure (= A cult was devoted to her).* —**cult′ism,** *n.* [*noncount*] —**cult′ist,** *n.* [*count*]

cul•ti•vate (kul′tə vāt′) /ˈkʌltəˌveyt/ *v.* [~ + *obj*], **-vat•ed, -vat•ing. 1.** to prepare and work on (land) in order to raise crops: *The soil was carefully cultivated.* **2.** to promote or improve the growth of (a crop): *They cultivated wheat and corn there.* **3.** to produce (an organism) in a culture: *to cultivate a strain of bacteria.* **4.** to develop or improve by education or training: *to cultivate a talent.* **5.** to promote or take action to advance the growth or development of (an art, etc.); foster: *to cultivate the arts.* **6.** to seek to foster (friendship, etc.): *cultivated an easy-going attitude in dealing with others.* **7.** to seek the acquaintance or friendship of (a person): *began to cultivate the student who sat behind him.* —**cul•ti•va•tion** (kul′tə-vā′shən) /ˌkʌltəˈveyʃən/ *n.* [*noncount*] —**cul′ti•va•tor,** *n.* [*count*]

cul•ti•vated (kul′ti vā′tid) /ˈkʌltɪˌveytɪd/ *adj.* **1.** [*before a noun*] (of plants, crops, etc.) grown or developed through preparation and work; not growing wild: *cultivated crops.* **2.** showing or having good taste, manners, or education; refined.

cul•tur•al (kul′chər əl) /ˈkʌltʃərəl/ *adj.* **1.** of or relating to culture: *cultural traditions.* **2.** [*before a noun*] of or relating to music, art, and literature: *I had missed much of the cultural world.*

cul•ture (kul′chər) /ˈkʌltʃər/ *n., v.,* **-tured, -tur•ing.** **—***n.* **1.** [*noncount*] artistic and intellectual activities and products: *a city of great culture.* **2.** [*noncount*] enlightenment or refinement coming from a knowledge of what is excellent in the arts: *The queen was a woman of culture.* **3.** [*noncount*] development or improvement of the mind or body by education or training: *physical and mental culture.* **4.** [*noncount*] the sum total of ways of living built up by a group of human beings and handed down from one generation to another: *We pass on to our children our culture, beliefs, and customs.* **5.** a particular form or stage of civilization, such as that of a nation or period: [*noncount*]: *ancient Greek culture.* [*count*]: *Early cultures of the period had no notion of the world to the west.* **6.** [*count*] the behaviors and beliefs characteristic of a particular group: *the youth culture.* **7. a.** [*noncount*] the growing or cultivation of microorganisms, or of tissues, for scientific study, medicinal use, etc. **b.** [*count*] the cells, tissue, or other products resulting from such cultivation: *a bacteria culture.* **8.** [*noncount*] the raising of plants or animals, esp. with a view to their improvement. **—***v.* [~ + *obj*] **9.** to grow (microorganisms, etc.) in or on a specially designed medium. **—Related Words.** CULTURE is a noun, CULTURAL is an adjective: *They found evidence of ancient cultures. There is a need for more cultural awareness.*

cul•tured (kul′chərd) /ˈkʌltʃərd/ *adj.* **1.** enlightened; refined. **2.** artificially nurtured or grown: *cultured bacteria.* **3.** cultivated; tilled.

cul′ture shock′, *n.* [*noncount*] a feeling of confusion and distress experienced by a person who is exposed to a foreign culture: *The company wants to hire someone experienced in overseas living who won't be affected by culture shock.*

cul•vert (kul′vərt) /ˈkʌlvərt/ *n.* [*count*] a drain or channel crossing under a road, sidewalk, etc.; sewer.

-cum-, *root.* *-cum-* comes from Latin, where it has the meaning "with." It is used between two words to mean "with; combined with; along with": *a garage-cum-workshop (= a garage that is combined with a workshop).*

cum., an abbreviation of: cumulative.

cu. m., an abbreviation of: cubic meter.

cum•ber•some (kum′bər səm) /ˈkʌmbərsəm/ *adj.* **1.** burdensome; heavy or bulky to carry, wear, etc.: *The desk was too cumbersome to pick up and move.* **2.** slow and inefficient; clumsy: *the cumbersome process of renewing a driver's license.* **—cum′ber•some•ness,** *n.* [*noncount*]

cum•in (kum′ən, ko͝om′- *or, often,* ko͞o′mən, kyo͞o′-) /ˈkʌmən, ˈkʊm- *or, often,* ˈkuwmən, ˈkyuw-/ *n.* [*noncount*] **1.** a small plant of the parsley family, with sweet-smelling, seedlike fruit used as a spice. **2.** the fruit or seeds of this plant, used as a spice.

cum•mer•bund (kum′ər bund′) /ˈkʌmərˌbʌnd/ *n.* [*count*] a wide sash worn at the waist, esp. one worn with a tuxedo.

cu•mu•la•tive (kyo͞o′myə lə tiv, -lā′tiv) /ˈkyuwmyələtɪv, -ˌleytɪv/ *adj.* increasing steadily by successive additions: *the cumulative, damaging effect of all the punches on the boxer's brain.* **—cu′mu•la•tive•ly,** *adv.*

cu•mu•lo•nim•bus (kyo͞o′myə lō nim′bəs) /ˌkyuwmyəlowˈnɪmbəs/ *n.* [*count*], *pl.* **-bi** (-bī) /-bay/ **-bus•es.** a cloud indicating thunderstorm conditions, having the shape of a tall anvil.

cu•mu•lus (kyo͞o′myə ləs) /ˈkyuwmyələs/ *n.* [*count*], *pl.* **-li** (-lī′) /-ˌlay/. a cloud having dense individual elements in the form of puffs, mounds, or towers, with flat bases and tops

cu•ne•i•form (kyo͞o nē′ə fôrm′, kyo͞o′nē ə-) /kyuwˈniyəˌfɔrm, ˈkyuwniyə-/ *adj.* **1.** having slim wedge-shaped elements, such as the characters used in writing by the ancient Akkadians and others. **—***n.* [*noncount*] **2.** cuneiform characters or writing.

cun•ning (kun′ing) /ˈkʌnɪŋ/ *n.* [*noncount*] **1.** skill used in a shrewd or sly manner to deceive; guile: *In some fables it is the fox that has a lot of cunning.* **—***adj.* **2.** shrewd; crafty; sly; deceptive: *that cunning old politician.* **—cun′ning•ly,** *adv.* **—cun′ning•ness,** *n.* [*noncount*]

cup (kup) /kʌp/ *n., v.,* **cupped, cup•ping.** **—***n.* [*count*] **1.** a small, open container of china, metal, etc., usually with a handle, used as a drinking vessel for hot beverages: *We put out the cups and saucers for coffee and tea.* **2.** a cup with its contents: *had a cup of hot coffee for breakfast.* **3.** the quantity contained in a cup: *poured out a cup of coffee.* **4.** a unit of capacity equal to 8 fluid ounces (237 milliliters) or 16 tablespoons; half pint: *two cups of flour.* **5.** an ornamental bowl, vase, etc., offered as a prize for a contest: *When she won the tennis tournament, she held up the silver cup for everyone to see.* **6.** any cuplike part, utensil, etc.: *the cup of a flower.* **7.** either of the two forms that cover the breasts in a brassiere. **8.** an athletic supporter reinforced with rigid plastic or metal. **—***v.* [~ + *obj*] **9.** to take, place, or hold in or as if in a cup: *He cupped the baby's face in his hands.* **10.** to form into a cuplike shape: *He cupped his hands and caught the ball.* **—*Idiom.*** **11. in one's cups,** [*be* + ~] intoxicated; drunk. **12. one's cup of tea,** [*noncount; used esp. in a negative phrase*] something suited or attractive to one.

cup•board (kub′ərd) /ˈkʌbərd/ *n.* [*count*] a closet with shelves for dishes, cups, food, etc.

cup•cake (kup′kāk′) /ˈkʌpˌkeyk/ *n.* [*count*] a small cake, baked in a cup-shaped mold.

cup•ful (kup′fo͝ol) /ˈkʌpfʊl/ *n.* [*count*], *pl.* **-fuls.** **1.** the amount a cup can hold. **2.** a measure equal to 8 fluid ounces (237 milliliters); cup: *one cupful of milk.*

Cu•pid (kyo͞o′pid) /ˈkyuwpɪd/ *n.* **1.** [*proper noun*] the Roman god of sensual love, the son of Venus, commonly represented as a winged, naked infant boy with a bow and arrows. **2.** [*count; cupid*] a similar winged being, or a representation of one, esp. as a symbol of love.

cu•pid•i•ty (kyo͞o pid′i tē) /kyuwˈpɪdɪtiy/ *n.* [*noncount*] eager or overwhelming desire, esp. to possess something, such as money or property; greed; avarice.

cu•po•la (kyo͞o′pə lə) /ˈkyuwpələ/ *n.* [*count*], *pl.* **-las.** a part of a roof shaped like an inverted bowl. **—cu′po•laed,** *adj.*

cur (kûr) /kɜr/ *n.* [*count*] **1.** a dog of mixed breed, esp. a worthless or unfriendly one. **2.** a mean, cowardly person: *Only a cur would treat a child like that!*

-cur-, *root.* *-cur-* comes from Latin, where it has the meanings "run; happen." These meanings are found in such words as: CONCUR, CONCURRENT, CURRENCY, CURRENT, CURRICULUM, CURSIVE, CURSOR, CURSORY, OCCUR, OCCURRENCE, RECUR, RECURRENCE. See -COUR-.

cur., an abbreviation of: **1.** currency. **2.** current.

-cura-, *root.* *-cura-* comes from Latin, where it has the meaning "help; care." This meaning is found in such words as: ACCURATE, CURABLE, CURATE, CURATIVE, CURATOR, CURE, MANICURE, PEDICURE, SECURE, SINECURE.

cur•able (kyo͝or′ə bəl) /ˈkyʊrəbəl/ *adj.* able to be cured: *a curable disease.* See -CURA-.

cu•ra•re or **cu•ra•ri** (kyo͝o rär′ē, ko͝o-) /kyʊˈrɑriy, kʊ-/ *n.* [*noncount*] a blackish substance made chiefly from tropical plants, used as an arrow poison.

cu•rate (kyo͝or′it) /ˈkyʊrɪt/ *n.* [*count*] a member of the clergy who assists a rector or vicar. See -CURA-.

cur•a•tive (kyo͝or′ə tiv) /ˈkyʊrətɪv/ *adj.* [*before a noun*] **1.** serving to cure or heal: *the curative effects of careful diet and exercise.* **—***n.* [*count*] **2.** a curative medicine, diet, or course of exercise; remedy. See -CURA-.

cu•ra•tor (kyo͝o rā′tər, kyo͝or′ā-) /kyʊˈreytər, ˈkyʊrey-/ *n.* [*count*] the person in charge of a museum, zoo, etc.: *the curator of the Metropolitan Museum of Art.* **—cu•ra•to•ri•al** (kyo͝or′ə tôr′ē əl, -tōr′-) /ˌkyʊrəˈtɔriyəl, -ˈtowr-/ *adj.* **—cu•ra′tor•ship′,** *n.* [*noncount*] See -CURA-.

curb (kûrb) /kɜrb/ *n.* [*count*] **1.** a rim, esp. of joined stones or concrete, along a street, forming an edge for a sidewalk: *I tripped on the curb crossing the street.* **2.** anything that restrains or controls; restraint; check: *a curb on spending.* **—***v.* [~ + *obj*] **3.** to control with or as if with a curb; restrain; check: *We'll have to curb spending this year.* **4.** to cause (a dog) to keep in the gutter near the curb when defecating: *The sign read, "Curb your dog."*

curd (kûrd) /kɜrd/ *n.* a thick substance obtained from milk when it sours, used as food or made into cheese: [*noncount*]: *small curd cottage cheese.* [*count*]: *eating her curds and whey.*

cur•dle (kûr′dl) /ˈkɜrdl̩/ *v.,* **-dled, -dling.** **1.** to change into curd; turn sour: [*no obj*]: *After a week the cream will begin to curdle.* [~ + *obj*]: *The acid in that coffee will curdle the milk you put in.* **—*Idiom.*** **2. curdle one's blood** or **make one's blood curdle,** to fill one with horror or fear: *Those terrifying screams made my blood curdle.* **—cur′dler,** *n.* [*count*]

cure (kyo͝or) /kyʊr/ *n., v.,* **cured, cur•ing.** **—***n.* [*count*] **1.** a medicine or treatment to heal or restore health; remedy: *a cure for cancer.* **2.** successful treatment that restores health: *a complete cure.* **3.** a means of correcting or relieving anything troublesome or harmful: *a cure for inflation.* **—***v.* **4.** [~ + *obj*] to restore (someone) to health; heal: *Those little pills cured me completely.* **5.** [~ + *obj*] to relieve or rid of (an illness, problem, etc.): *We* *need to take drastic steps to cure unemployment.* **6.** [~ + *obj*] to prepare (meat, etc.) for preservation by smoking, salting, aging, etc.: *They cure the ham in a smokehouse.* **7.** [*no obj*] (of meat, etc.) to undergo a process of preservation by smoking, salting, etc.: *The meat cures for several months in the warehouse.* —**cur′er,** *n.* [*count*] See -CURA-.

cu•ré (kyŏŏ rā′, kyŏŏr′ā) /kyʊ'rey, 'kyʊrey/ *n.* [*count*], *pl.* **-rés.** (in France) a parish priest.

cure′-all′, *n.* [*count*] a cure for all ills or for everything wrong: *He thinks cutting taxes is a cure-all for the economy.*

cur•few (kûr′fyōō) /'kɜrfyuw/ *n.* [*count*] **1.** an order establishing a time after which certain regulations apply, esp. that no unauthorized persons may be outdoors or that places of public assembly must be closed: *The army imposed a curfew on certain days and all evenings.* **2.** a regulation requiring a person to be home at a stated time, such as one imposed by a parent on a child: *Parents should establish a curfew and make sure it is obeyed.* **3.** the time at which a curfew starts: *must get home before my curfew.* **4.** the period during which a curfew is in effect: *I was out during the curfew.*

cu•rie (kyŏŏr′ē, kyŏŏ rē′) /'kyʊriy, kyʊ'riy/ *n.* [*count*], *pl.* **-ries.** a unit of activity of radioactive substances.

cu•ri•o (kyŏŏr′ē ō′) /'kyʊriy,ow/ *n.* [*count*], *pl.* **-ri•os.** a usually small article, object of art, etc., valued as a curiosity.

cu•ri•os•i•ty (kyŏŏr′ē os′i tē) /,kyʊriy'ɒsɪtiy/ *n.*, *pl.* **-ties.** **1.** [*noncount*] the desire to learn or know about anything; inquisitiveness: *Just out of curiosity, what are you doing tomorrow night?* **2.** [*count*] a curious or rare thing: *several old curiosities in the museum shop.*

cu•ri•ous (kyŏŏr′ē əs) /'kyʊriyəs/ *adj.* **1.** eager to learn or know; inquisitive: *Most children are born naturally curious.* **2.** taking an impolite or too great interest in others' affairs; prying: *curious neighbors, always peeking out the windows.* **3.** arousing attention or interest through being unusual; strange; novel: *That was a curious sight, even for New York.* [*it* + *be* + ~ + *that clause*]: *It is curious that not one city office knows where I can get my refund.* —**cu′ri•ous•ly,** *adv.* —**cu′ri•ous•ness,** *n.* [*noncount*]

curl (kûrl) /kɜrl/ *v.* **1.** to (cause to) grow in or form small rings; (cause to) become curved or wavy: [*no obj*]: *When she was young, her hair curled naturally.* [~ + *obj*]: *She spent a lot of time curling her hair.* **2.** to (cause to) curve, twist, or coil: [*no obj*]: *The sleeping cat's tail curled around its body.* [~ + *obj*]: *The cat curled its tail around itself.* **3.** [*no obj*] to move in a curving direction: *The road curls a little to the left.* **4. curl up,** [*no obj*] **a.** to sit or lie down cozily: *to curl up with a good book.* **b.** to become twisted up on the edges: *All his old papers had curled up.* —*n.* [*count*] **5.** a coil or small ring of hair: *blond curls.* **6.** anything of a spiral or curved shape: *curls of wood on the workshop floor.* —***Idiom.*** **7. curl one's** or **the hair,** to fill one with horror: *That new horror movie will really curl your hair.* **8. curl one's lip,** to raise a corner of one's lip, as in an expression of disdain or scorn.

curl•er (kûr′lər) /'kɜrlər/ *n.* [*count*] a small device used to curl the hair.

cur•lew (kûr′lōō) /'kɜrluw/ *n.* [*count*] a large shorebird having a long, slender bill that curves down.

curl•i•cue or **cur•ly•cue** (kûr′li kyōō′) /'kɜrlɪ,kyuw/ *n.* [*count*] a fancy curl or twist.

curl•y (kûr′lē) /'kɜrliy/ *adj.*, **-i•er, -i•est.** having curls; arranged in the shape of curls: *curly blond hair.*

cur•mudg•eon (kər muj′ən) /kər'mʌdʒən/ *n.* [*count*] a bad-tempered person: *That old curmudgeon never smiles at anyone.* —**cur•mudg′eon•ly,** *adj.*

cur•rant (kûr′ənt, kur′-) /'kɜrənt, 'kʌr-/ *n.* [*count*] **1.** a small seedless raisin used in cooking. **2.** the small, round, sour berry of certain shrubs. **3.** the shrub itself.

cur•ren•cy (kûr′ən sē, kur′-) /'kɜrənsiy, 'kʌr-/ *n.*, *pl.* **-cies.** **1.** money in circulation as a medium of exchange in a country: [*noncount*]: *Where can I exchange my foreign currency?* [*count*]: *At that time the Japanese yen was a very strong currency compared to the American dollar.* **2.** [*noncount*] general acceptance; prevalence; vogue: *That story gained greater currency as time went on.* See -CUR-.

cur•rent (kûr′ənt, kur′-) /'kɜrənt, 'kʌr-/ *adj.* **1.** [*before a noun*] belonging to the time passing; present: *the current rate of inflation.* **2.** generally or commonly used or accepted; prevalent: *current usage in English.* **3.** most recent; new; most up-to-date: *current events.* **4.** publicly or commonly reported or known: *a rumor current among insiders.* —*n.* [*count*] **5.** a portion of a large body of water or mass of air that moves in a certain direction: *The raft was swept into the current and carried out to sea.* **6.** the movement or flow of electric charge, measured in amperes: *The current was switched off so that the train crews could walk safely on the tracks.* **7.** a general tendency, course, or trend, as of thinking or ideas: *a current of unrest among the students.* —**cur′rent•ly,** *adv.*: *This style is currently in fashion.* See -CUR-.

cur•ric•u•lum (kə rik′yə ləm) /kə'rɪkyələm/ *n.* [*count*], *pl.* **-la** (-lə), **-lums.** **1.** all the courses of study given in a school, etc.: *The college offers a wide curriculum in many disciplines.* **2.** the regular course of study in a school, etc.: *the social studies curriculum.* —**cur•ric′u•lar,** *adj.*: *the office of curricular guidance.* See -CUR-.

curric′ulum vi′tae (vi′tē) /'vaytiy/ *n.* [*count*], pl. **curricula vitae.** a brief biographical résumé of one's career and training, as prepared by a person applying for a job.

cur•ry[1] (kûr′ē, kur′ē) /'kɜriy, 'kʌriy/ *n.*, *pl.* **-ries,** *v.*, **-ried, -ry•ing.** —*n.* **1.** a strong-smelling and strong-tasting food cooked in a sauce with curry powder: [*count*]: *The restaurant offered several good curries.* [*noncount*]: *Hot curry can be injurious to your palate.* **2.** [*noncount*] curry powder. **3.** [*noncount*] a sauce containing curry powder. —*v.* [~ + *obj*] **4.** to cook or flavor (food) with curry powder.

cur•ry[2] (kûr′ē, kur′ē) /'kɜriy, 'kʌriy/ *v.* [~ + *obj*], **-ried, -ry•ing.** **1.** to rub, clean, and brush (a horse) with a special comb. —***Idiom.*** **2. curry favor,** [~ + *with* + *obj*] to seek to advance oneself through falsely praising another: *She tried to curry favor with the boss by telling her how smart she was.*

cur′ry pow′der, *n.* [*noncount*] a strong-smelling mixture of ground spices, such as turmeric, coriander, cumin, and pepper, used esp. in Indian food.

curse (kûrs) /kɜrs/ *n.*, *v.*, **cursed** or **curst** (kûrst) /kɜrst/ **curs•ing.** —*n.* [*count*] **1.** the expression of a wish that misfortune happen to someone: *The witch put a curse on the young princess.* **2.** a swearword, esp. one used in anger or for emphasis: *All I got for my trouble was a shower of curses.* **3.** an evil, misfortune, trouble, or difficult time in one's life: *The drought was a curse to the people of Ethiopia.* **4.** [*the* + ~] *Slang.* the menstrual period; menstruation. —*v.* **5.** [~ + *obj*] to wish evil upon (someone or something): *He cursed me and all I stood for.* **6.** to swear (at); say or utter swearwords (to): [*no obj*]: *I hit my finger with the hammer and cursed silently to myself.* [~ + *at* + *obj*]: *They cursed loudly at the outfielder for dropping the easy fly ball.* [~ + *obj*]: *She cursed him and walked away.* **7.** [~ + *obj*] to complain against (something) often with swearwords: *I cursed the bad luck that had ever brought me to that place.* —**curs′er,** *n.* [*count*]

curs•ed (kûr′sid, kûrst) /'kɜrsɪd, kɜrst/ *adj.* **1.** under a curse; damned: *cursed for their sins.* **2.** deserving a curse; hateful; terrible: *this cursed job.* **3.** [*be* + ~ + *with* + *obj*] suffering because of some circumstance: *I was cursed with a violent temper.* —**curs′ed•ly,** *adv.*

cur•sive (kûr′siv) /'kɜrsɪv/ *adj.* **1.** (of handwriting) in flowing strokes with the letters joined together. **2.** (of typeset material) resembling handwriting: *a cursive font.* —**cur′sive•ly,** *adv.* —**cur′sive•ness,** *n.* [*noncount*] See -CUR-.

cur•sor (kûr′sər) /'kɜrsər/ *n.* [*count*] **1.** a movable, usually blinking, symbol on a computer screen, used to indicate where data such as text or commands may be typed. **2.** a sliding object, as the lined glass on a slide rule, that can be set at any point on a scale. See -CUR-.

cur•so•ry (kûr′sə rē) /'kɜrsəriy/ *adj.* going rapidly over something; hasty; superficial: *a cursory glance.* —**cur•so•ri•ly** (kûr′sər ə lē) /'kɜrsərəliy/ *adv.* —**cur′so•ri•ness,** *n.* [*noncount*] See -CUR-.

curt (kûrt) /kɜrt/ *adj.*, **-er, -est.** rudely brief in speech, or too quick in manner: *a curt reply to my friendly greeting.* —**curt′ly,** *adv.*: *answered curtly that he was too busy to talk.* —**curt′ness,** *n.* [*noncount*] —**Syn.** See BLUNT.

cur•tail (kər tāl′) /kər'teyl/ *v.* [~ + *obj*] to cut short; reduce: *The trip was curtailed because of bad weather.* —**cur•tail′er,** *n.* [*count*] —**cur•tail′ment,** *n.* [*noncount*]: *curtailment of foreign aid.* See -TAIL-.

cur•tain (kûr′tn) /'kɜrtn̩/ *n.* [*count*] **1.** a hanging piece of fabric used to shut out the light from a window, decorate a room, etc. See illustration at APARTMENT. **2. a.** a movable drapery that hangs in front of a stage and conceals it from the audience. **b.** the start or end of a performance, scene, act, or play, esp. the time at which a performance begins: *The curtain is at seven o'clock.* **3.** anything that shuts off, covers, or conceals: *a curtain of artillery fire; a curtain of darkness.* **4. curtains,** [*it* + *be* + ~] *Slang.* the end; death, esp. by violence: *As the gunmen surrounded him, he knew it was curtains.*

cur′tain call′, *n.* [*count*] the appearance of a performer or group of performers at the conclusion of a play, etc., to receive the applause of the audience.

curt•sy (kûrt′sē) /'kɜrtsiy/ *n., pl.* **-sies,** *v.,* **-sied, -sy•ing.** —*n.* [*count*] **1.** a respectful bow made by women and girls, consisting of bending the knees and lowering the body. —*v.* [*no obj*] **2.** to make a curtsy: *I was surprised when the housekeeper curtsied to us.*

cur•va•ceous (kûr vā′shəs) /kɜr'veyʃəs/ *adj.* (of a woman) having a well-shaped figure with attractive curves. —**cur•va′ceous•ly,** *adv.* —**cur•va′ceous•ness,** *n.* [*noncount*]

cur•va•ture (kûr′və chər, -cho͝or′) /'kɜrvətʃər, -ˌtʃʊr/ *n.* **1.** [*noncount*] the act of curving or the state of being curved. **2.** [*noncount*] a curved shape or condition, often abnormal: *curvature of the spine.* **3.** [*count*] the degree of curving of a line or surface: *a curvature of 20 degrees.*

curve (kûrv) /kɜrv/ *n., v.,* **curved, curv•ing,** *adj.* —*n.* [*count*] **1.** a continuously bending line, without angles: *a curve in the road.* **2.** Also called **curve′ ball′.** a baseball pitch thrown with a spin that causes the ball to turn from a normal straight path. **3.** a misleading or deceptive trick: *That was a mean curve from the professor.* **4.** an academic grading system based on the scale of performance of the group, so that those performing better, regardless of their actual knowledge, receive higher grades: *to mark on a curve.* —*v.* **5.** to (cause to) bend in a curve; take the course of a curve: [*no obj*]: *The road curved sharply to the left.* [~ + *obj*]: *The bowler curved the ball to the right.* —***Idiom.*** **6. throw someone a curve,** to take someone by surprise: *The economy threw all the investors a curve by refusing to regain strength when expected.*

curv•y (kûr′vē) /'kɜrviy/ *adj.,* **-i•er, -i•est. 1.** shaped like a curve: *some curvy lines on the TV screen.* **2.** curvaceous: *curvy chorus girls.*

cush•ion (ko͝osh′ən) /'kʊʃən/ *n.* [*count*] **1.** a soft pad or bag filled with feathers, air, etc., and used to sit, lie, or lean on: *dozing off on the nice soft cushions.* **2.** anything similar in form or function, such as a pad to prevent excessive pressure. **3.** something that lessens the effects of hardship or distress: *They intended their savings account to be their cushion if times got bad.* —*v.* [~ + *obj*] **4.** to supply or furnish with a cushion or cushions. **5.** to lessen or soften the effects of: *to cushion a blow.* —**cush′ion•y,** *adj.*

cush•y (ko͝osh′ē) /'kʊʃiy/ *adj.,* **-i•er, -i•est.** *Informal.* **1.** involving little effort and providing much profit: *a cushy job, teaching only two hours a week.* **2.** soft and comfortable: *a cushy pillow.* —**cush′i•ness,** *n.* [*noncount*]

cusp (kusp) /kʌsp/ *n.* [*count*] **1.** a point or pointed end, as on the crown of a tooth. **2.** a point that marks the beginning of a change: *on the cusp of a new era.*

cus•pid (kus′pid) /'kʌspɪd/ *n.* [*count*] any of the four canine teeth in humans. Also called **cuspid tooth.**

cuss (kus) /kʌs/ *Informal.* —*v.* **1.** to use profanity (to); curse (at): [*no obj*]: *He was cussing as they took him off to jail.* [~ + *at* + *obj*]: *cussing at his captors* [~ + *obj*]: *He cussed me under his breath.* —*n.* [*count*] **2.** an obscene word; curse. **3.** a person or animal: *a strange old cuss.*

cus•tard (kus′tərd) /'kʌstərd/ *n.* [*noncount*] a food, esp. a dessert, made with eggs, milk, and usually sugar, baked or boiled until thickened.

cus•to•di•an (ku stō′dē ən) /kʌ'stowdiyən/ *n.* [*count*] **1.** a person who has custody: *Who will be your children's custodian?* **2.** a person entrusted with guarding or maintaining a property; caretaker: *The custodian locked the museum.* —**cus•to′di•an•ship′,** *n.* [*noncount*]

cus•to•dy (kus′tə dē) /'kʌstədiy/ *n.* [*noncount*] **1. a.** keeping; guardianship; care. **b.** (in a legal separation or divorce) the right of deciding where and how a child or children will live, be schooled, etc. **2.** [*often: in/into* + ~] the state of being kept or guarded by officers of the law: *The suspect was taken into custody.*

cus•tom (kus′təm) /'kʌstəm/ *n.* **1.** [*count*] a habitual practice; the usual way of acting: *It was a custom of mine to get coffee every morning.* **2.** [*noncount*] such ways of acting when thought of as a group; convention; tradition: *a slave to custom.* **3. customs, a.** duties or fees imposed by law on imported or exported goods: [*noncount; used with a singular verb*]: *Customs isn't too much on that new car, is it?* [*plural; used with a plural verb*]: *The customs on that product are very high in my country.* **b.** [*noncount; used with a singular verb*] the government department that collects these duties: *Customs is very particular about that brand of car as an import here.* **c.** [*noncount; used with a singular verb*] the section of an airport, etc., where baggage is checked for illegally imported goods and for goods subject to the payment of duty: *Which way is customs?* —*adj.* [*before a noun*] **4.** made specially for individual customers: *custom shoes.* **5.** dealing in things so made, or doing work to order: *a custom tailor.* —**Syn.** CUSTOM, HABIT, PRACTICE mean an established way of doing things. CUSTOM, applied to a community or to an individual, implies a more or less permanent way of acting, seen over and over again in tradition and social attitudes: *the custom of giving gifts at Christmas.* HABIT, applied particularly to an individual, implies repetition of the same action resulting from a natural or deep tendency or inclination to perform it: *He has an annoying habit of interrupting the speaker.* PRACTICE applies to a regularly followed procedure or pattern in doing things: *It is his practice to verify all statements.*

cus•tom•ar•y (kus′tə mer′ē) /'kʌstəˌmɛriy/ *adj.* **1.** according to or depending on custom; expected by custom: *the customary, once-a-month meeting.* [*it* + *be* + ~ + *for* + *obj*]: *It is customary for many Americans to send greeting cards around Christmas.* **2.** [*before a noun*] (of behavior, etc.) habitual; usual: *his customary cup of coffee.* —**cus•tom•ar•i•ly** (kus′tə mer′ə lē; *for emphasis,* kus′tə mâr′ə lē) /'kʌstəˌmɛrəliy; *for emphasis,* ˌkʌstə'mɛərəliy/ *adv.*: *She is customarily late for meetings.*

cus′tom-built′, *adj.* built to individual order: *a custom-built guitar.*

cus•tom•er (kus′tə mər) /'kʌstəmər/ *n.* [*count*] **1.** a person who purchases goods or services from another; buyer: *I was one of their most loyal customers.* See illustration at STORE. **2.** *Informal.* a person one has dealings with: *a tough customer.*

cus•tom•ize (kus′tə mīz′) /'kʌstəˌmayz/ *v.* [~ + *obj*], **-ized, -iz•ing.** to modify or build (something) according to an individual's request: *They'll customize your car to give you bucket seats.* —**cus•tom•i•za•tion** (kus′tə mə zā′shən) /ˌkʌstəmə'zeyʃən/ *n.* [*noncount*] —**cus′tom•iz′er,** *n.* [*count*]

cus′tom-made′, *adj.* made to individual order: *custom-made shoes.*

cut (kut) /kʌt/ *v.,* **cut, cut•ting,** *adj., n.* —*v.* **1.** to penetrate with or as if with a sharp-edged instrument or object: [~ + *obj*]: *I cut my face while shaving yesterday.* [*no obj*]: *The axe won't cut anymore.* **2.** [~ + *obj*] to divide with or as if with a sharp-edged instrument; sever: *I cut the birthday cake.* **3.** to detach or remove with or as if with a sharp-edged instrument; slice off: [~ + *obj*]: *to cut a slice of bread.* [~ + *out* + *obj*]: *Cut out a short article from the paper.* [~ + *obj* + *out*]: *Cut a short article out and hand it in.* [~ + *obj* + *out* + *of* + *obj*]: *Cut a short article out of the newspaper.* [~ + *off* + *obj*]: *The queen yelled, "Cut off her head!"* [~ + *obj* + *off*]: *Cut her head off!* See CUT OFF below. **4.** [*no obj*] to become detached or removed by or as if by a sharp-edged instrument: *The meat is so tender it cuts easily with a fork.* **5.** [~ + *obj*] to set (someone or something) free or loose by severing rope, chains, etc.: *I cut the prisoner free with my knife.* **6.** to saw down; fell: [~ + *obj*]: *to cut timber.* [~ + *down* + *obj*]: *to cut down a tree.* [~ + *obj* + *down*]: *to cut a tree down.* See CUT DOWN below. **7.** [~ + *obj*] to trim by clipping, shearing, or pruning: *to cut hair.* **8.** [~ + *obj*] to mow; reap; harvest: *to cut grain.* **9.** [~ + *obj*] to reduce the length of; shorten: *to cut a speech short.* **10.** [~ + *obj*] to lower, reduce, or curtail: *to cut prices.* **11.** [~ + *obj*] to dissolve: *a detergent that cuts grease.* **12.** [~ + *obj*] to intersect; cross: *The top lines are cut at 90-degree angles by other lines.* **13.** [~ + *across/through* + *obj*] to move or cross, esp. in the most direct way: *to cut across an empty lot.* **14.** [~ + *obj*] *Informal.* to cease; stop; discontinue: *Cut the kidding.* **15.** [~ + *obj*] to halt the running of, such as an engine; stop: *When I give you the signal, cut the engine.* See CUT OFF below. **16.** [~ + *obj*] to grow (a tooth) through the gum: *cutting her baby teeth.* **17.** [~ + *obj*] **a.** to produce a pattern in (glass) by grinding and polishing: *The craftsmen cut some fine crystal.* **b.** to make or fashion by cutting, such as a garment. **18.** [~ + *obj*] to fail to attend; make oneself absent from: *began to cut classes and skip homework.* **19.** to wound the feelings (of): [~ + *obj*]: The way you treated me cut me badly. [*no obj*]: *His criticisms cut deep.* **20.** to divide (a pack of cards) at random parts, as by removing cards from the top: [~ + *obj*]: *He cut the deck and fanned the cards on the table.* [*no obj*]: *Whose turn is it to cut?* **21.** [~ + *obj*] **a.** to record a selection on (magnetic tape): *cut a new record last week.* **b.** to make a recording of (a song, etc.): *cut two songs in one session.* **22.** [*no obj*] to make a sudden or sharp change in direction; swerve: *The runner cut to the left and moved upfield quickly.* **23. cut across,** [~ + *across* + *obj*] to go beyond considerations of; transcend: *The new tax program cuts across party lines.* **24. cut back, a.** to shorten (something growing) by cutting off the end: [~ + *back* + *obj*]: *You'll need to cut back the roses.* [~ + *obj* + *back*]: *Cut the roses back.* **b.** to reduce or discontinue: [~ + *back* + *obj*]: *to cut back steel production.* [~ + *obj* + *back*]: *to cut steel production back to lower levels.* [~ + *back* + *on* + *obj*]: *We'll have to cut back on those expensive meals.* **25. cut down, a.** Also, **cut down on.** [~ *(+ down)* + *on* + *obj*] to lessen or curtail; decrease: *to cut down on snacks.* **b.** to destroy, kill, or disable: [~ + *down* + *obj*]: *The hurricane cut down everything in its path.* [~ + *obj* + *down*]: *The machine guns cut the enemy down.* **26. cut in, a.** [*no obj*] to move or thrust a vehicle, etc., suddenly between others: *His car cut in suddenly in front of mine.* **b.** [*no obj*] to interpose; interrupt: *She would always cut in with some remark.* **c.** [*no obj*] to interrupt a dancing couple in order to dance with one of them: *May I cut in, please?* **d.** [~ + *obj* + *in*] to include, such as in a business deal or card game: *We'll cut you in for 50% of the profits.* **27. cut off, a.** to intercept: [~ + *off* + *obj*]: *His brigade cut off the enemy.* [~ + *obj* + *off*]: *The cavalry cut them off.* **b.** to interrupt: [~ + *off* + *obj*]: *The shouting cut off the speaker before she could finish.* [~ + *obj* + *off*]: *They cut her off before she was finished.* **c.** to disconnect a phone connection with (someone) suddenly: [~ + *off* + *obj*]: *I cut off that salesman and returned to dinner.* [~ + *obj* + *off*]: *I cut the salesman off.* **d.** to stop suddenly; discontinue: [~ + *off* + *obj*]: *They cut off funding for the project.* [~ + *obj* + *off*]: *They cut funding off for next year.* **e.** to halt the operation of; turn off: [~ + *off* + *obj*]: *They cut off the power.* [~ + *obj* + *off*]: *They cut the power off.* **f.** [~ + *obj* + *off*] to take away the right (of someone) to inherit; disinherit: *His family cut him off without a cent.* **g.** [~ + *obj*] to separate; sever. See CUT above, (def. 3). **28. cut out, a.** to omit, delete, or remove; excise: [~ + *out* + *obj*]: *Cut out a few extra paragraphs here.* [~ + *obj* + *out*]: *Cut a few paragraphs out.* **b.** to form by or as if by cutting: [~ + *out* + *obj*]: *She cut out heart-shaped pieces from the red paper.* [~ + *obj* + *out*]: *She cut a few pages out.* **c.** to discontinue; stop: [~ + *out* + *obj verb-ing*]: *promised to cut out smoking.* [~ + *obj* + *out*]: *Now cut that out; you're disturbing me.* **d.** [~ + *obj; usually: be* + ~ + *out* + *for* + *obj*] to plan; arrange: *Your work is cut out for you.* **e.** [*no obj*] *Slang.* to leave suddenly: *Let's cut out and go home early.* **f.** [*no obj*] (of an engine, etc.) to stop running: *Suddenly the engine of the plane just cut out.* **29. cut up, a.** to cut into pieces or sections: [~ + *up* + *obj*]: *He cut up a few pieces of cheese.* [~ + *obj* + *up*]: *He cut the cake up and passed it around.* **b.** to use a sharp instrument, such as a knife, to injure with wounds: [~ + *up* + *obj*]: *Her attacker began to cut up her face.* [~ + *obj* + *up*]: *began to cut her face up.* **c.** [*no obj*] *Informal.* to play pranks; misbehave: *As a kid he was always cutting up in class.* **—*adj.*** **30.** separated or shaped by cutting: *cut flowers; a cut diamond.* **31.** reduced by or as if by cutting: *cut prices.* **—*n.*** [*count*] **32.** the result of cutting, as an incision, passage, or channel: *a deep cut in the wood.* **33.** the act of cutting, as with a knife or whip: *a quick cut at the rope.* **34.** an amount or piece cut off: *a cut of meat.* **35.** a share, esp. of earnings or profits: *an agent's cut of 5% on the deal.* **36.** a reduction in price, salary, etc.: *a cut of 25% on our best merchandise.* **37.** the manner or fashion in which anything is cut: *the cut of a dress.* **38.** style; manner; kind: *a man of his cut.* See A CUT ABOVE below. **39.** a passage or course straight across or through: *a cut through the woods.* **40.** an act, speech, etc., that wounds the feelings of another: *That insult was a deep cut.* **41.** an absence, as from a class at which attendance is required: *You have four cuts already.* **42.** the change from one shot or scene of a film to another: *a quick cut to the musician in his happier days.* **43.** an individual song, etc., on a record or tape: *added that cut as an afterthought.* **—*Idiom.*** **44. a cut above,** somewhat superior to: *Your work was a cut above the rest.* **45. cut a figure,** to give a certain impression of oneself: *That elderly statesman still manages to cut a distinguished figure.* **46. cut both ways,** to have or result in advantages as well as disadvantages: *The deal cuts both ways; you might benefit greatly or suffer tremendous losses.* **47. cut it,** [~ + *obj; usually: with negative words or phrases, or in questions*] *Informal.* to perform effectively or successfully: *He can't seem to cut it in the financial world.* **48. cut it fine,** to calculate precisely, without allowing for error: *Our connecting train will leave at 3:35, but we won't get there until 3:31; isn't that cutting it just a bit fine?* **49. cut one's teeth on,** [~ + *one's teeth* + *on* + *obj*] to do at an early stage or age: *He cut his teeth on reporting, working for his town newspaper at the early age of eight.* **50. cut out for,** [~ + *obj; usually: with negative words and phrases, or in questions*] fitted for; capable of: *He's just not cut out for the military.* **51. cut short,** to end abruptly before completion; interrupt: [~ + *obj* + *short*]: *cut the performance short and left early.* [~ + *short* + *obj*]: *They cut short the concert and everyone went home early.*

cut′-and-dried′ also **cut′-and-dry′,** *adj.* **1.** settled in advance; not needing much discussion; clear-cut: *This issue seems fairly cut-and-dried; let's vote on it now.* **2.** routine: *cut-and-dried operations.*

cut•back (kut′bak′) /ˈkʌtˌbæk/ *n.* [*count*] **1.** a reduction in rate, quantity, etc.: *a cutback in production.* **2.** a return in the course of a story, film, etc., to earlier events.

cute (kyo͞ot) /kyuwt/ *adj.,* **cut•er, cut•est. 1.** charmingly attractive, esp. in a pert or dainty way: *a cute baby.* **2.** mentally keen; clever; shrewd: *That was a cute move, getting the boss to back you.* **—cute′ly,** *adv.* **—cute′ness,** *n.* [*noncount*]

cute•sy or **cute•sie** (kyo͞ot′sē) /ˈkyuwtsiy/ *adj.,* **-si•er, -si•est.** *Informal.* cute in a deliberate or forced way; coy. **—cute′si•ness,** *n.* [*noncount*]

cu•ti•cle (kyo͞o′ti kəl) /ˈkyuwtɪkəl/ *n.* [*count*] the hardened skin that surrounds the edges of a fingernail or toenail.

cut•ie (kyo͞o′tē) /ˈkyuwtiy/ *n.* [*count*] *Informal.* a charmingly attractive person: *My niece is a real cutie.*

cut•lass or **cut•las** (kut′ləs) /ˈkʌtləs/ *n.* [*count*] a short, heavy, slightly curved sword with a single cutting edge.

cut•ler•y (kut′lə rē) /ˈkʌtləriy/ *n.* [*noncount*] cutting instruments when thought of as a group, esp. utensils used at the table for cutting and eating food.

cut•let (kut′lit) /ˈkʌtlɪt/ *n.* [*count*] **1.** a slice of meat for broiling or frying. **2.** a flat croquette of minced food.

cut•off (kut′ôf′, -of′) /ˈkʌtˌɔf, -ˌɒf/ *n.* [*count*] **1.** an act or instance of cutting off. **2.** a point serving as the limit beyond which something is no longer possible: *We'll start the bargaining at 50%, but 35% is the cutoff; we won't go lower than that.* **3.** a road, passage, etc., that leaves another, usually providing a shortcut: *a cutoff from the main highway.* **4. cutoffs,** [*plural*] shorts made by cutting the legs off a pair of trousers, esp. jeans: *wanted my old jeans to use for making cutoffs.* **—*adj.*** [*before a noun*] **5.** being a limit or ending: *the cutoff date for applications.*

cut•out (kut′out′) /ˈkʌtˌawt/ *n.* [*count*] **1.** something cut out from something else, such as a pattern cut from paper: *The girls were playing with paper-doll cutouts.* **2.** a device that automatically interrupts an electric current, etc.: *He hit the cutout and the machinery stopped.*

cut′-rate′, *adj.* [*before a noun*] **1.** offered at a reduced rate or price: *cut-rate prices.* **2.** offering goods or services at reduced prices: *a cut-rate store.*

cut•ter (kut′ər) /ˈkʌtər/ *n.* [*count*] **1.** a person who cuts, as one who cuts film for editing. **2.** a machine, tool, or other device for cutting: *a wire cutter.* **3.** a lightly armed government boat.

cut•throat (kut′thrōt′) /ˈkʌtˌθrowt/ *n.* [*count*] **1.** a person who cuts throats; murderer. **—*adj.*** **2.** murderous. **3.** ruthless: *cutthroat competition.*

cut•ting (kut′ing) /ˈkʌtɪŋ/ *n.* [*count*] **1.** the act of a person or thing that cuts, or something cut, cut off, or cut out. **2.** a piece, such as a root or leaf, cut from a plant and used to start a new plant: *gave us cuttings from his coleus plants.* **3.** a clipping from a newspaper, etc.: *She kept all the cuttings from the newspapers.* **—*adj.*** **4.** [*before a noun*] designed or used for cutting: *a cutting tool.* **5.** piercing, such as a wind: *the cutting north wind.* **6.** sarcastic: *a vicious, cutting remark.* **—cut′ting•ly,** *adv.*

cut•tle•fish (kut′l fish′) /ˈkʌtḷˌfɪʃ/ *n., pl.* (*esp. when thought of as a group*) **-fish,** (*esp. for kinds or species*) **-fish•es.** any flattened shellfish with a hard internal shell.

cut•up (kut′up′) /ˈkʌtˌʌp/ *n.* [*count*] *Informal.* a clown or show-off; prankster.

CW, an abbreviation of: chemical warfare.

cw, an abbreviation of: clockwise.

-cy, *suffix. -cy* is used to form nouns. **1.** It is attached to adjectives that have stems that end in *-t, -te, -tic,* and esp. *-nt* **a.** to form abstract nouns: *democrat + -cy → democracy; accurate + -cy → accuracy; expedient + -cy → expediency; lunatic + -cy → lunacy.* **b.** to form action nouns: *vacant + -cy → vacancy; occupant + -cy → occupancy.* **2.** *-cy* is attached to nouns with the meaning "rank or office of": *captain + -cy → captaincy (= rank or office of a captain); magistra(te) + -cy → magistracy (= office of a magistrate).*

Cy., an abbreviation of: county.

cy•a•nide (sī′ə nid′, -nid) /ˈsayəˌnayd, -nɪd/ *n.* [*noncount*] a strong poison, potassium cyanide.

cy•ber•na•tion (sī′bər nā′shən) /ˌsaybərˈneyʃən/ *n.* [*noncount*] the use of computers to control automatic processes, esp. in manufacturing.

cy•ber•net•ics (sī′bər net′iks) /ˌsaybərˈnɛtɪks/ *n.* [*noncount; used with a singular verb*] a field of study that compares the control and communication systems of the body with mechanical or electronic systems of control and communication. **—cy′ber•net′ic, cy′ber•net′i•cal,** *adj.* **—cy•ber•net•i•cist** (sī′bər net′ə sist) /ˌsaybərˈnɛtəsɪst/ **cy•ber•ne•ti•cian** (sī′bər ni tish′ən) /ˌsaybərnɪˈtɪʃən/ *n.* [*count*]

cy•cla•men (sī′klə mən, -men′, sik′lə-) /ˈsaykləmən, -ˌmɛn, ˈsɪklə-/ *n.* [*count*] a plant of the primrose family, having white, purple, or red flowers.

cy•cle (sī′kəl) /ˈsaykəl/ *n., v.,* **-cled, -cling.** **—*n.*** [*count*] **1.** any complete round or repeating series of events: *the cycle of the four seasons.* **2.** a recurring period of time, esp. one in which certain events repeat themselves: *a cycle of no more than 50 seconds.* **3.** a bicycle, motorcycle, tricycle, or the like. **4.** a group of poems, songs, etc., about a central theme or figure: *the Arthurian cycle.* **—*v.*** [*no obj*] **5.** to ride or travel by bicycle, motorcycle, or the like: *They cycled into town for groceries.* See -CYCLE-.

-cycle-, *root. -cycle-* comes from Greek, where it has the meaning "cycle; circle; wheel." This meaning is found in such words as: BICYCLE, CYCLE, CYCLO, CYCLONE, CYCLOTRON, RECYCLE, TRICYCLE.

cy•clic (sī′klik, sik′lik) /ˈsayklɪk, ˈsɪklɪk/ also **cy′clic•al,** *adj.* happening or occurring in cycles: *cyclic events.* See -CYCLE-.

cy•clist (sī′klist) /ˈsayklɪst/ also **cy•cler** (sī′klər) /ˈsayklər/ *n.* [*count*] a person who rides or travels by bicycle, motorcycle, or the like. See -CYCLE-.

cy•clo (sē′klō, sī-) /ˈsiyklow, say-/ *n.* [*count*], *pl.* **-clos.** a three-wheeled pedaled or motorized taxi in SE Asia. See -CYCLE-.

cy•clone (sī′klōn) /ˈsayklown/ *n.* [*count*] **1.** a violent storm with circular wind motion: *The cyclone struck the islands with devastating force.* **2.** (not in technical use) a tornado. **—cy•clon•ic** (sī klon′ik) /sayˈklɒnɪk/ *adj.: cyclonic winds.* See -CYCLE-.

cy•clo•tron (sī′klə tron′, sik′lə-) /ˈsaykləˌtrɒn, ˈsɪklə-/ *n.* [*count*] an accelerator in which atomic or subatomic particles move in spiral paths in a constant magnetic field. See -CYCLE-.

cyg•net (sig′nit) /ˈsɪgnɪt/ *n.* [*count*] a young swan.

cyl•in•der (sil′in dər) /ˈsɪlɪndər/ *n.* [*count*] **1.** a surface shape or solid having long straight sides and two flat round ends; a shape resembling a tube with a top and bottom. **2.** any object or part shaped like a cylinder, as the part of a revolver holding the bullets, or a part of an engine where a piston compresses the air and fuel mixture. **—cyl′in•dered,** *adj.*

cy•lin•dri•cal (sə lin′dri kəl) /səˈlɪndrɪkəl/ *adj.* having the shape or form of a cylinder.

cym•bal (sim′bəl) /ˈsɪmbəl/ *n.* [*count*] a plate of brass or bronze that produces a sharp, ringing sound when struck. **—cym′bal•ist,** *n.* [*count*]

cyn•ic (sin′ik) /ˈsɪnɪk/ *n.* [*count*] **1.** a person who believes that only selfishness is the cause of all human actions: *a cynic who never understood anyone's charity toward another.* **2.** a person who shows or expresses a bitterly negative attitude, as by making hateful remarks about others. **—cyn′i•cal,** *adj.* **—cyn•i•cism** (sin′i siz′-əm) /ˈsɪnɪˌsɪzəm/ *n.* [*noncount*]

cy•pher (sī′fər) /ˈsayfər/ *n., v. Chiefly Brit.* CIPHER.

cy•press (sī′prəs) /ˈsayprəs/ *n.* **1.** [*count*] an evergreen, cone-bearing tree having dark-green, scalelike, overlapping leaves. **2.** [*noncount*] the wood of this tree.

Cyp•ri•ot (sip′rē ət) /ˈsɪpriyət/ *n.* [*count*] **1.** a person born or living in Cyprus. **—*adj.*** **2.** of or relating to Cyprus.

cyst (sist) /sɪst/ *n.* [*count*] an abnormal saclike growth of the body in which liquid or matter is contained. **—cys′tic,** *adj.*

cys′tic fi•bro′sis (fī brō′sis) /fayˈbrowsɪs/ *n.* [*noncount*] a disease in which certain glands of the body produce thickened mucus that clogs the lungs and leads to breathing difficulties.

czar or **tsar** or **tzar** (zär, tsär) /zɑr, tsɑr/ *n.* [*count*] **1.** an emperor or king. **2.** [*often: Czar*] the former emperor of Russia. **3.** any person exercising great authority or power: *a czar of industry.*

cza•ri•na (zä rē′nə, tsä-) /zɑˈriynə, tsɑ-/ *n.* [*count*], *pl.* **-nas.** the wife of a czar; a Russian empress.

Czech (chek) /tʃɛk/ *adj.* **1.** of or relating to the Czech Republic. **2.** or or relating to the language spoken by many of the people in the Czech Republic. **—*n.*** **3.** [*count*] a person born or living in the Czech Republic. **4.** [*noncount*] the language spoken by many of the people in the Czech Republic.

D, d (dē) /diy/ *n.* [*count*], *pl.* **Ds** or **D's, ds** or **d's. 1.** the fourth letter of the English alphabet, a consonant. **2.** [*sometimes: d*] (in some grading systems) a grade or mark indicating poor or barely acceptable quality.

d', *Pron. Spelling.* do (esp. before *you*): *How d'you like them?*

'd, 1. contraction of *had: They'd already left.* **2.** contraction of *would: I'd like to see it.* **3.** contraction of *did: Where'd you go?* **4.** contraction of *-ed: She OK'd the plan.*

D, *Symbol.* [*sometimes: d*] the Roman numeral for 500.

D., an abbreviation of: **1.** day. **2.** December. **3.** Democrat. **4.** Democratic. **5.** Doctor.

d., an abbreviation of: **1.** date. **2.** daughter. **3.** day. **4.** deceased. **5.** diameter. **6.** died.

DA or **D.A.,** an abbreviation of: District Attorney.

dab (dab) /dæb/ *v.,* **dabbed, dab•bing,** *n.* **—***v.* **1.** to pat or tap gently: [~ + *obj*]: *I dabbed my eyes with a handkerchief.* [~ + *at* + *obj*]: *She dabbed at the stain on her dress.* **2.** [~ + *obj*] to apply (a substance) by light strokes: *He dabbed some paint on the wall.* **3.** [~ + *obj*] to apply a moist substance onto: *He dabbed the burn with some ointment.* **—***n.* [*count*] **4.** a quick or light pat, as with something soft: *applied her makeup with a few quick dabs.* **5.** a small lump or quantity: *a dab of rouge.*

dab•ble (dab′əl) /'dæbəl/ *v.,* **-bled, -bling. 1.** to play and splash in or as if in water, esp. with the hands or feet: [*no obj*]: *dabbling in the water.* [~ + *obj*]: *dabbling her toes in the bath water.* **2.** [*no obj*] to work without serious thought or action: *to dabble in literature.* **—dab•bler** (dab′lər) /'dæblər/ *n.* [*count*]

da•cha (dä′chə) /'dɑtʃə/ *n.* [*count*] a Russian country house or villa.

dachs•hund (däks′ho͝ont′, -ho͝ond′) /'dɑks,hʊnt, -,hʊnd/ *n.* [*count*] one of a German breed of dogs having very short legs and a long body and ears.

Da•cron (dā′kron, dak′ron) /'deykrɒn, 'dækrɒn/ *Trademark.* a brand of polyester fiber.

dad (dad) /dæd/ *n.* [*count*] *Informal.* father.

dad•dy (dad′ē) /'dædiy/ *n.* [*count*], *pl.* **-dies.** *Informal.* father.

dad′dy-long′legs or **dad′dy long′legs** (lông′ legz′, long′-) /'lɔŋ, lɛgz, 'lɒŋ-/ *n.* [*count*], *pl.* **-long•legs.** a spiderlike insect having a compact, rounded body and usually extremely long, slender legs. Also called **harvestman.**

da•do (dā′dō) /'deydow/ *n.* [*count*], *pl.* **-does, -dos.** the lower broad part of an interior wall when specially finished with wallpaper, paneling, paint, etc., so as to differ from the upper part.

daf•fo•dil (daf′ə dil) /'dæfədɪl/ *n.* [*count*] **1.** a plant of the amaryllis family, esp. one having a yellow flower with a trumpetlike crown or top. **2.** the flower itself.

daf•fy (daf′ē) /'dæfiy/ *adj.,* **-fi•er, -fi•est.** *Informal.* silly; crazy; foolish: *a daffy movie.* **—daf′fi•ness,** *n.* [*noncount*]

daft (daft) /dæft/ *adj.,* **-er, -est. 1.** [*often: be* + ~] senseless, stupid, or foolish: *He was daft to do that.* **2.** insane; crazy; mad: *a daft idea.*

dag•ger (dag′ər) /'dægər/ *n.* [*count*] **1.** a short, swordlike weapon with a pointed blade and a handle. **2.** Also called **obelisk.** a printer's mark (†) used esp. for references. **—*Idiom.* 3. look daggers at,** [~ + *obj*] to look at (someone) with anger: *She looked daggers at me when I said it was fine for our guests to stay late.*

dahl•ia (dal′yə, däl′-) /'dælyə, 'dɑl-/ *n.* [*count*], *pl.* **-ias.** a garden plant of Mexico and Central America, having thick, bulging roots and showy flowers.

dai•ly (dā′lē) /'deyliy/ *adj., adv., n., pl.* **-lies. —***adj.* [*before a noun*] **1.** of, done, occurring, or coming out each day: *daily attendance.* **2.** computed by the day: *a daily quota.* **—***adv.* **3.** every day; day by day: *The plane arrived daily from Dar es Salaam.* **—***n.* [*count*] **4.** a newspaper appearing each day or each weekday: *For a while the two dailies competed evenly in St. Louis, but eventually only one survived.*

dain•ty (dān′tē) /'deyntiy/ *adj.,* **-ti•er, -ti•est,** *n., pl.* **-ties. —***adj.* **1.** of delicate beauty; pretty; neat: *a dainty lace handkerchief.* **2.** pleasing to the taste and, often, temptingly served: *dainty pastries.* **3.** fussy; choosy; fastidious: *a dainty eater.* **—***n.* [*count*] **4.** something delicious to the taste; a delicacy. **—dain•ti•ly** (dān′tl ē) /'deyntḷiy/ *adv.* **—dain′ti•ness,** *n.* [*noncount*]

dai•qui•ri (dī′kə rē, dak′ə-) /'daykəriy, 'dækə-/ *n.* [*count*], *pl.* **-ris.** a cocktail of rum, lemon or lime juice, and sugar, sometimes with fruit added.

dair•y (dâr′ē) /'dɛəriy/ *n., pl.* **dair•ies,** *adj.* **—***n.* [*count*] **1.** a place where milk and cream are kept and butter and cheese are made. **2.** a company that processes or distributes such products, or a store that sells them. **—***adj.* [*before a noun*] **3.** of or relating to a dairy or a dairy farm: *the dairy industry.* **4.** of or relating to milk, cream, butter, cheese, etc.: *dairy products.*

dair•y•ing (dâr′ē ing) /'dɛəriyɪŋ/ *n.* [*noncount*] the business of a dairy.

dair•y•maid (dâr′ē mād′) /'dɛəriy,meyd/ *n.* [*count*] a girl or woman who is employed in a dairy.

dair•y•man or **-wom•an** (dâr′ē mən, -man′) /'dɛəriymən, -,mæn/ or (-wo͝om′ən) /-'wʊmən/ *n.* [*count*], *pl.* **-men** or **-wom•en.** an owner, manager, or employee of a dairy.

da•is (dā′is, dī′-) /'deyɪs, 'day-/ *n.* [*count*] a raised platform for a lectern, throne, seats of honor, etc.: *The speaker climbed to the dais and began his speech.*

dai•sy (dā′zē) /'deyziy/ *n.* [*count*], *pl.* **-sies. 1.** a plant that has a flower head of a yellow disk and white rays. **—*Idiom.* 2. push up daisies,** *Informal.* to be dead and buried: *Why, he's been pushing up daisies these past twenty years!*

dale (dāl) /deyl/ *n.* [*count*] a valley, esp. a broad valley.

dal•ly (dal′ē) /'dæliy/ *v.* [*no obj*], **-lied, -ly•ing. 1.** to waste time; delay: *Come straight home and don't dally.* **2.** to act playfully coy with; flirt: *dallied with every handsome man.* **—dal•li•ance** (dal′ē əns) /'dæliyəns/ *n.* [*noncount*] **—dal′li•er,** *n.* [*count*]

Dal•ma•tian (dal mā′shən) /dæl'meyʃən/ *n.* [*count*] one of a breed of medium-sized shorthaired dogs having a white coat marked with black or brown spots.

dam[1] (dam) /dæm/ *n., v.,* **dammed, dam•ming. —***n.* [*count*] **1.** a barrier to obstruct or control the flow of water, built across a stream or river: *When the dam broke, the flood spread to the village.* **2.** a body of water held back by a dam: *You can go fishing and canoeing in the dam.* **—***v.* [~ *(+ up)* + *obj*] **3.** to furnish with a dam; obstruct or confine with or as if with a dam: *to dam (up) a river; had dammed up his feelings.*

dam[2] (dam) /dæm/ *n.* [*count*] a female parent of a domestic animal, such as a horse, goat, or sheep.

dam•age (dam′ij) /'dæmɪdʒ/ *n., v.,* **-aged, -ag•ing. —***n.* **1.** [*noncount*] injury, harm, or destruction that reduces value, usefulness, etc.; harmful effect: *The earthquake caused great damage to the city.* **2. damages,** [*plural*] the money estimated to be equal to the loss or injury sustained: *to pay $10,000 in damages.* **—***v.* [~ + *obj*] **3.** to cause harm, injury, or destruction to; have a harmful effect on: *The fire damaged our house.* **—dam•age•a•ble** (dam′i jə bəl) /'dæmɪdʒəbəl/ *adj.*

dam′age control′, *n.* [*noncount*] efforts to counter the effects of unfavorable publicity, to reduce losses, or the like.

dam•ask (dam′əsk) /'dæməsk/ *n.* [*noncount*] **1.** a decoratively patterned, usually reversible fabric, used for tablecloths, curtains, etc. **—***adj.* [*before a noun*] **2.** made of or resembling damask: *a damask cloth.*

dame (dām) /deym/ *n.* [*count*] **1.** [*Dame*] (in Britain) the official title of a woman who holds a rank equivalent to that of a knight: *Dame Anne Hathaway.* **2.** a matronly woman of advanced age; matron. **3.** *Slang (sometimes offensive).* a woman; female.

damn (dam) /dæm/ *v.* [~ + *obj*] **1.** to condemn as a failure: *The critics damned the new play.* **2.** to ruin: *damned by his gambling habit.* **3.** to condemn to eternal punishment or to hell; doom. **—***interj.* **4.** (used to express anger, annoyance, disgust, etc.): *"Damn!" he swore as he stumbled into the coffee table.* **—***n.* [*count; singular; used with negative words or phrases, or in questions*] **5.** something worthless or of little or no value: *His promise is not worth a damn.* **—***adj.* [*before a noun*] **6.** DAMNED (defs. 2, 3).: *I think you're a damn fool.* **—***adv.* **7.** DAMNED: *You know damn well I wasn't there.* **—*Idiom.* 8. damn with faint praise,** to praise in such a way that the result is to condemn: *The letter of recommendation said, "She does her work as well as can be expected," thus damning her with faint praise.*

dam•na•ble (dam′nə bəl) /'dæmnəbəl/ *adj.* **1.** worthy of being damned; deserving condemnation. **2.** very bad;

detestable, abominable, or outrageous: *a damnable lie.* —**dam′na•bly,** *adv.*

dam•na•tion (dam nā′shən) /dæm'neyʃən/ *n.* [*noncount*] **1.** the act of damning or the state of being damned. —*interj.* **2.** (used to express anger, upset, etc.)

damned (damd) /dæmd/ *adj., superlative* **damned•est, damnd•est** (dam′dist) /'dæmdɪst/ *adv.* —*adj.* **1.** condemned or doomed, esp. to eternal punishment: *damned souls.* **2.** [*before a noun*] detestable; awful: *Get that damned dog out of here!* **3.** [*before a noun*] complete; absolute: *a damned nuisance.* —*adv.* **4.** extremely; very; absolutely: *a damned good singer; too damned lazy.* —*n.* [*plural; used with a plural verb*] **5. the damned,** souls that have been condemned to hell or eternal punishment.

damp (damp) /dæmp/ *adj.,* **-er, -est,** *n., v.* —*adj.* **1.** slightly wet; moist: *The towels were still damp.* —*n.* [*noncount*] **2.** moisture; humidity; moist air: *the damp of the morning.* —*v.* **3.** [~ + *obj*] to make damp; moisten. **4.** [~ (+ *down*) + *obj*] to reduce, check, or slow down the energy, action, etc., of: *His loss didn't damp (down) his enjoyment of living.* **5.** [~ (+ *down*) + *obj*] to extinguish: *to damp (down) a furnace.* —**damp′ly,** *adv.* —**damp′ness,** *n.* [*noncount*]

damp•en (dam′pən) /'dæmpən/ *v.* **1.** to (cause to) become damp or moistened: [*no obj*]: *The clothes dampened in the humidity.* [~ + *obj*]: *He dampened the cloth.* **2.** to (cause to) become dull or depressed: [*no obj*]: *His spirits dampened at the thought.* [~ + *obj*]: *to dampen one's spirits.* —**damp′en•er,** *n.* [*count*]

damp•er (dam′pər) /'dæmpər/ *n.* [*count*] **1.** a movable plate for controlling the amount of air in a stove, furnace, etc. **2.** a device in a musical instrument to reduce the volume of sound.

dam•sel (dam′zəl) /'dæmzəl/ *n.* [*count*] a maiden, originally one of noble birth: *rescuing a damsel in distress.*

dam•son (dam′zən, -sən) /'dæmzən, -sən/ *n.* [*count*] **1.** a small, dark blue or purple plum. **2.** the tree on which it grows.

dance (dans) /dæns/ *v.,* **danced, danc•ing,** *n.* —*v.* **1.** to move following a rhythm and in a pattern of steps, esp. to the accompaniment of music: [*no obj*]: *She danced in the best Broadway shows.* [~ + *obj*]: *She danced every dance with him.* **2.** [*no obj*] to leap, skip, etc., as from excitement or emotion; move nimbly or quickly: *We danced for joy.* **3.** [*no obj*] to bob up and down; move lightly and quickly: *The toy sailboats danced on the pond.* —*n.* **4.** [*count*] a series of steps or bodily motions following a rhythm and usually done to music. **5.** [*count*] a round of dancing; set: *May I have this dance?* **6.** [*noncount*] the art of dancing: *to study dance.* **7.** [*count*] a social gathering or party for dancing; ball: *I met her at a high-school dance.* —***Idiom.*** **8. dance attendance on,** [~ + *obj*] to pay a great deal of attention to (someone) with a great show of doing so: *dancing attendance on her boss.* —**danc′er,** *n.* [*count*]

dan•de•li•on (dan′dl ī′ən) /'dændḷˌayən/ *n.* [*count*] a weedy plant having edible, toothed leaves, golden-yellow flowers, and clusters of white, hairy seeds.

dan•der (dan′dər) /'dændər/ *n.* [*noncount*] *Informal.* anger; temper: *Don't get your dander up.*

dan•dle (dan′dl) /'dændḷ/ *v.* [~ + *obj*], **-dled, -dling.** to move (a child) lightly up and down, on one's knee or in one's arms.

dan•druff (dan′drəf) /'dændrəf/ *n.* [*noncount*] small scales that form on and are shed from the scalp.

dan•dy (dan′dē) /'dændiy/ *n., pl.* **-dies,** *adj.,* **-di•er, -di•est.** —*n.* [*count*] **1.** a man overly concerned about his appearance; fop. **2.** something or someone of exceptional or excellent quality: *Look at this new car; isn't it a dandy?* —*adj.* **3.** fine; excellent; first-rate; very good: *a dandy idea.*

Dane (dān) /deyn/ *n.* [*count*] a person born or living in Denmark.

dan•ger (dān′jər) /'deyndʒər/ *n.* **1.** [*noncount*] exposure to the chance of harm or injury; risk; peril: *a life full of danger.* **2.** [*count*] an instance or cause of harm, injury, or peril; risk: *One of the dangers is risk of lightning.*

dan•ger•ous (dān′jər əs) /'deyndʒərəs/ *adj.* **1.** full of danger or risk: *a dangerous intersection.* **2.** able or likely to cause physical injury: *Smoking may be dangerous to your health.* —**dan′ger•ous•ly,** *adv.*

dan•gle (dang′gəl) /'dæŋgəl/ *v.,* **-gled, -gling.** **1.** to (cause to) hang or swing loosely: [*no obj*]: *The rope dangled out the window.* [~ + *obj*]: *She dangled the rope out the window.* **2.** [~ + *obj* + *before* + *obj*] to offer as a means of persuading: *He dangled a salary increase before me.* —**dan′gler,** *n.* [*count*]

Dan•ish (dā′nish) /'deynɪʃ/ *adj.* **1.** of or relating to the Danes, the people living in Denmark. **2.** of or relating to Denmark. **3.** of or relating to the language spoken in Denmark. —*n.* **4.** [*noncount*] the language spoken in Denmark. **5.** [*sometimes: danish*] a type of flaky, rich pastry, often filled with cheese or fruit: [*noncount*]: *That store sells great Danish.* [*count*]: *A cheese danish and a coffee to go, please.*

dank (dangk) /dæŋk/ *adj.,* **-er, -est.** unpleasantly moist or humid; damp and, often, chilly: *a dank cellar.* —**dank′ly,** *adv.* —**dank′ness,** *n.* [*noncount*]

dap•per (dap′ər) /'dæpər/ *adj.* **1.** neat, trim, or smart in dress or appearance: *You look dapper in that new suit.* **2.** lively and brisk: *to walk with a dapper step.*

dap•pled (dap′əld) /'dæpəld/ *adj.* marked with spots of a different shade or color from the background; having patches of shade and light: *the dappled sea.*

dare (dâr) /dɛər/ *v.,* **dared, dar•ing;** *pres. sing. 3rd pers.* **dares** or **dare,** *n.* —*v.* **1.** [~ + *obj* + *to* + *verb*] to challenge or persuade (a person) into a demonstration of courage or to do something: *I dare you to climb that.* **2.** [~ + *obj*] to face; risk: *He will dare any test to prove his manhood.* —*auxiliary or modal v.* [*not: be* + ~ *-ing*] **3.** As a verb that is like an AUXILIARY verb and like a MODAL verb, *dare* has the meaning "to have the courage or boldness to" (do something). It occurs with negative words or phrases, and in questions, as in the examples below: **a.** Like a modal verb, it is followed by the root form of the next verb: *He dared not speak to me like that. How dare you speak to me like that?* **b.** Like an auxiliary verb, it agrees with the subject in the present tense in sentences with negative words or phrases: *The girl dares not take another step.* **c.** Like a modal verb, in questions in the present tense, it has only one form, *dare,* even when the subject is *he, she,* or *it,* or a singular noun: *Dare he mention the subject again?* **d.** Like both modal and auxiliary verbs, in questions *dare* goes before the subject: *Dare I say it?* —*n.* [*count*] **4.** an act of daring or defiance; challenge: *I took that stupid dare.* —***Idiom.*** **5. I daresay.** Use this phrase to mean "I suppose (that)", or "perhaps," as in: *I daresay he's right (= I suppose he's right).* —**dar′er,** *n.* [*count*]

dare•dev•il (dâr′dev′əl) /'dɛərˌdɛvəl/ *n.* [*count*] **1.** a reckless and daring person. —*adj.* [*before a noun*] **2.** recklessly daring: *daredevil feats.* —**dare′dev′il•ry, dare•dev•il•try** (dâr′dev′əl trē) /'dɛərˌdɛvəltriy/ *n.* [*noncount*]

dare•say (dâr′sā′) /'dɛər'sey/ *v.* DARE (def. 5).

dar•ing (dâr′ing) /'dɛərɪŋ/ *n.* [*noncount*] **1.** adventurous courage; boldness; bravery: *a pilot of great daring.* —*adj.* **2.** bold or courageous; fearless: *a daring new economic plan.* —**dar′ing•ly,** *adv.*

dark (därk) /dɑrk/ *adj.,* **-er, -est,** *n.* —*adj.* **1.** having very little or no light: *a dark room.* **2.** giving off or reflecting little light: *a dark color.* **3.** [*before a noun or adjective indicating color*] close to black in color: *a dark brown.* **4.** not pale or fair: *She's dark but her children are blond.* **5.** gloomy; cheerless; dismal: *the dark days of the war.* **6.** considered to be or thought of as being without knowledge or culture, or unenlightened: *the Dark Ages.* **7.** [*before a noun*] hidden; concealed: *a deep, dark secret.* —*n.* [*noncount*] **8.** the absence of light; darkness: *the dark and gloom of the forest.* **9.** night; nightfall: *to come home before dark.* —***Idiom.*** **10. in the dark,** in ignorance; uninformed: *We were completely in the dark about his intentions.* —**dark′ly,** *adv.* —**dark′ness,** *n.* [*noncount*]

dark•en (där′kən) /'dɑrkən/ *v.* **1.** to (cause to) become dark or darker: [*no obj*]: *The sky darkened and a huge storm rolled in.* [~ + *obj*]: *We darkened the house by blocking all the windows.* **2.** to (cause to) become gloomy; sadden; dampen: [*no obj*]: *Her mood steadily darkened.* [~ + *obj*]: *Those setbacks darkened his mood.* —**dark′en•er,** *n.* [*count*]

dark′ horse′, *n.* [*count*] a racehorse, competitor, etc., that is somewhat unknown or that wins unexpectedly.

dark•room (därk′rōōm′, -rŏŏm′) /'dɑrkˌruwm, -ˌrʊm/ *n.* [*count*] a totally darkened room in which film, photographic paper, etc., is handled or developed.

dar•ling (där′ling) /'dɑrlɪŋ/ *n.* [*count*] **1.** a person who is very dear to another; one who is dearly loved: *My daughter is a little darling.* —*adj.* **2.** [*before a noun*] very dear; dearly loved; cherished: *my darling child.* **3.** charming; cute; lovable: *What a darling baby!*

darn[1] (därn) /dɑrn/ *v.* [~ + *obj*] **1.** to sew and mend with rows of stitches, sometimes by crossing and weaving rows in and out. —*n.* [*count*] **2.** a place or area that has been darned. —**darn′er,** *n.* [*count*]

darn[2] (därn) /dɑrn/ *adj.* **1.** Also, **darned.** damned [*before a noun*]: *It's a darn shame.* —*adv.* **2.** damned: *You're darn right I'm angry.* —*v.* [~ + *obj*] **3.** to curse; damn: *Darn that pesky fly!*

dart (därt) /dɑrt/ *n.* **1.** [*count*] a small, slender object pointed at one end and usually feathered at the other: *A poisoned dart hit him in the neck.* **2. darts,** [*noncount; used with a singular verb*] a game in which darts are thrown at a target having a bull's-eye in the center: *Darts is harder than it looks.* **3.** [*count*] a sudden swift movement: *The squirrel made a quick dart across the street.* **4.** [*count*] a tapered seam of fabric for adjusting the fit of clothing: *He adjusted the darts on the skirt.* —*v.* **5.** [*no obj*] to move swiftly; spring suddenly; dash: *The mice darted around the room.* **6.** [~ + *obj*] to move suddenly or rapidly: *She darted a quick glance at me.*

dart•er (där′tər) /ˈdɑrtər/ *n.* [*count*] **1.** a person or thing that darts. **2.** a small, darting, colorful fish, a North American perch.

dash (dash) /dæʃ/ *v.* **1.** to (cause to) strike or smash violently, esp. so as to break to pieces: [~ + *obj*]: *The waves dashed the boat to pieces.* [*no obj*]: *The waves dashed against the shore.* **2.** [~ + *obj*] to throw violently or suddenly: *dashed a plate against a wall in a fit of rage.* **3.** [~ + *obj*] to apply roughly, as by splashing; splatter: *to dash paint on a wall.* **4.** [~ + *obj*] to ruin, destroy, or frustrate: *The rain dashed our hopes for a picnic.* **5.** [*no obj*] to move with great speed; rush: *to dash around the corner.* **6. dash off, a.** [*no obj*] to hurry away; leave: *She dashed off before I could talk to her.* **b.** Also, **dash down.** to write, make, accomplish, etc., too quickly or hastily: [~ + *off* + *obj*]: *to dash off a letter.* [~ + *obj* + *off*]: *to dash it off in a hurry.* —*n.* [*count*] **7.** a small quantity of anything mixed with something else: *a dash of salt.* **8.** a hasty or sudden movement; a rush: *to make a mad dash for the door.* **9.** a short race: *the 100-yard dash.* **10.** a mark or sign (—), used variously in printed or written matter, esp. to note a break, pause, or hesitation, and to separate elements of a sentence or series of sentences, such as a question from its answer. —**dash′er,** *n.* [*count*]

dash•board (dash′bôrd′, -bōrd′) /ˈdæʃˌbɔrd, -ˌbowrd/ *n.* [*count*] the instrument panel of an automotive vehicle.

da•shi•ki (də shē′kē, dä-) /dəˈʃiykiy, dɑ-/ *n.* [*count*], *pl.* **-kis.** a loose, often colorfully patterned garment of African origin.

dash•ing (dash′ing) /ˈdæʃɪŋ/ *adj.* **1.** energetic and spirited; lively: *a dashing hero.* **2.** elegant, handsome, and gallant: *a dashing young cavalry officer.* —**dash′ing•ly,** *adv.*

das•tard (das′tərd) /ˈdæstərd/ *n.* [*count*] a sneaking coward. —**das′tard•ly,** *adj.*

DAT, an abbreviation of: digital audiotape.

da•ta (dā′tə, dat′ə) /ˈdeytə, ˈdætə/ *n.* **1.** [*plural; used with a plural verb*] a pl. of DATUM. **2.** [*plural; used with a plural verb*] individual facts, statistics, or items of information: *Do your data support your conclusions?* **3.** [*noncount; used with a singular verb*] a body or collection of facts; information: *The data is inconclusive.*

da′ta bank′ or **da′ta•bank′,** *n.* DATABASE.

da′ta•base′ or **da′ta base′,** *n.* [*count*] a collection of organized, related data, esp. one in electronic form that can be gathered, analyzed, or retrieved by a computer: *He made a database of the students in his class.*

da′ta proc′essing, *n.* [*noncount*] the automated processing of information, esp. by computers. —**da′ta proc′essor,** *n.* [*count*]: *worked as a data processor.*

date[1] (dāt) /deyt/ *n., v.,* **dat•ed, dat•ing.** —*n.* [*count*] **1.** time in terms of the month, day, and year at which some event happened or will happen: *an important date in American history.* **2.** the particular day of the month: *Is today's date the 7th or the 8th?* **3.** the time shown on a letter, document, coin, etc.: *a letter bearing the date January 16.* **4.** the time or period to which something belongs: *can meet again at a later date.* **5.** an appointment for a particular time, esp. a social meeting: *I took her out on a date. We made a date for next week.* **6.** a person with whom one has such an appointment: *Can I bring a date to the party?* **7.** an engagement (of a band, acting group, etc.) to perform; booking: *the group's next date in Tennessee.* —*v.* **8.** to belong to a particular period; start or exist from: [*no obj*]: *The architecture dates as far back as 1830.* [~ + *from* + *obj*]: *The letter dates from 1873.* [~ + *back* + *to* + *obj*]: *The custom dates back to the Victorian era.* **9.** to go out socially on dates (with): [*no obj*]: *She's not old enough to be dating.* [~ + *obj*]: *He's dating his best friend's sister.* **10.** [~ + *obj*] to mark or furnish with a date: *The word processor dates your document automatically.* **11.** [~ + *obj*] to estimate the period or time of: *a new method to date archaeological ruins.* **12.** [~ + *obj*] to show the age of: *Singing those tunes from the 1950's really dates me.* —***Idiom.*** **13. to date,** up to the present time; until now: *We've seen nothing to date that would change our minds.* **14. up to date,** in accord with the latest styles, information, or technology: *fashion that is always up to date; Our new computers are up to date; the up-to-date office communication systems.* —**dat′a•ble, date′a•ble,** *adj.* —**dat′er,** *n.* [*count*]

date[2] (dāt) /deyt/ *n.* [*count*] the oblong, brown, sweet, fleshy fruit of a palm tree growing in hot climates.

dat•ed (dā′tid) /ˈdeytɪd/ *adj.* **1.** having or showing a date: *a dated engraving by Rembrandt.* **2.** out-of-date; old-fashioned; no longer up to date: *Some slang terms become dated quickly.* —**dat′ed•ness,** *n.* [*noncount*]

date′ rape′, *n.* [*noncount*] sexual intercourse forced upon the person with whom one has a date.

da•tive (dā′tiv) /ˈdeytɪv/ *adj.* **1.** of or referring to a grammatical case that indicates the indirect object of a verb or the object of certain prepositions: *In the Latin sentence* pecuniam mihi dedit *which means "He or she gave me money," the word* mihi *which means "to me," is in the dative case.* —*n.* [*count*] **2.** the dative case. **3.** a word or other form in the dative case.

da•tum (dā′təm, dat′əm) /ˈdeytəm, ˈdætəm/ *n.* [*count*], *pl.* **da•ta** (dā′tə, dat′ə) /ˈdeytə, ˈdætə/. a single piece of information, as a fact, statistic, or code; an item of data.

daub (dôb) /dɔb/ *v.* **1.** to cover or coat with soft, sticky matter: [~ + *obj* + *with* + *obj*]: *Daub the surface with plaster.* [~ + *obj* + *on* + *obj*]: *Daub plaster on the surface.* **2.** [~ + *obj*] to smear, smudge, make dirty: *walls daubed with fingerprints.* **3.** to apply unskillfully, as paint or colors: [~ + *obj* + *with* + *obj*]: *He daubed his canvas with paint.* [~ + *obj* + *on* + *obj*]: *He daubed paint on his canvas.* —**daub′er,** *n.* [*count*]

daugh•ter (dô′tər) /ˈdɔtər/ *n.* [*count*] **1.** the female child of a parent. **2.** a person related as if by the ties of daughter to parent: *a true daughter of the revolution.* **3.** anything personified as female and considered with respect to its origin: *Latin and its daughter languages, Spanish, French, and Italian.*

daugh′ter-in-law′, *n.* [*count*], *pl.* **daugh•ters-in-law.** the wife of one's son: *Do all their daughters-in-law live nearby?*

daunt (dônt, dänt) /dɔnt, dɑnt/ *v.* [~ + *obj*] to lessen the courage of; dismay; dishearten: *Don't be daunted by the remaining work.* —**daunt′ing•ly,** *adv.*

daunt•less (dônt′lis, dänt′-) /ˈdɔntlɪs, ˈdɑnt-/ *adj.* not intimidated; fearless; brave; bold: *a dauntless hero.* —**daunt′less•ly,** *adv.* —**daunt′less•ness,** *n.* [*noncount*]

dav•en•port (dav′ən pôrt′, -pōrt′) /ˈdævənˌpɔrt, -ˌpowrt/ *n.* [*count*] **1.** a large sofa, often one that can be converted into a bed. **2.** a small writing desk.

daw•dle (dôd′l) /ˈdɔdl̩/ *v.,* **-dled, -dling.** to move or act too slowly; idle; loiter: [*no obj*]: *Quit dawdling and get to work.* [~ + *away* + *obj*]: *dawdled away the morning.* [~ + *obj* + *away*]: *to dawdle the time away.* —**daw′dler,** *n.* [*count*]

dawn (dôn) /dɔn/ *n.* **1.** the first appearance of daylight in the morning; daybreak; sunrise: [*noncount*]: *We got up at dawn.* [*count*]: *What a beautiful dawn!* **2.** [*count; usually singular*] the beginning or rise of anything; advent: *the dawn of civilization.* —*v.* [*no obj*] **3.** to begin to grow light in the morning: *The day dawned without a cloud.* **4.** to begin to open or develop: *A new era of peace is dawning.* **5.** to begin to be known, realized, seen, or understood: [~ + *on/upon* + *obj*]: *The idea suddenly dawned upon her.* [*It* + ~ + *on/upon* + *obj*]: *It suddenly dawned on me that I was late.*

day (dā) /dey/ *n.* [*count*] **1.** the time between sunrise and sunset: *I work most of the day at the office and most of the night at home.* **2.** the light of day; daylight: *In Tanzania the days are as long as the nights.* **3.** a division of time equal to 24 hours, from one midnight to the next: *seven days in one week.* **4.** a similar division of time for another planet: *the Martian day.* **5.** the portion of a day in which one works: *put in an eight-hour day.* **6.** a particular date, period, or time: *in olden days; What day is her birthday?* **7.** a time thought to provide benefit or opportunity: *His day will come.* **8.** Usually, **days.** period of life: *His days are numbered.* **9.** a particular period of time: *In my day we called them motorcars.* **10.** [*often: the* + ~]

the contest or battle going on at the moment: *to win the day.* **—*Idiom.* 11. call it a day,** to stop working for the rest of the day: *Let's call it a day; we've worked eighteen hours.* **12. day in, day out,** every day without fail; regularly. Also, **day in and day out**: *Her constant nagging, day in and day out, is driving me crazy.* **13. make someone's day,** to make someone very happy or pleased: *Seeing my kids smile just makes my day.*

day•bed (dā′bed′) /ˈdeyˌbɛd/ *n.* [*count*] a couch that can be used as a sofa by day and a bed by night.

day•break (dā′brāk′) /ˈdeyˌbreyk/ *n.* [*noncount*] the first appearance of daylight in the morning; dawn.

day′ care′, *n.* [*noncount*] daytime care for children who are too young to go to school, for the elderly, or for those with health problems. **—day′-care′,** *adj.* [*before a noun*]: *a day-care center.*

day•dream (dā′drēm′) /ˈdeyˌdriym/ *n.* [*count*] **1.** a pleasant series of thoughts imagined while awake; reverie: *in a daydream about life in the country.* **2.** a plan or dream unlikely to happen: *His daydream is to retire to a tropical island.* **—*v.* 3.** to have daydreams: [*no obj*]: *daydreaming about the future.* [~ + *(that) clause*]: *daydreamed that she had won the lottery.* **—day′dream′er,** *n.* [*count*]

day•light (dā′līt′) /ˈdeyˌlayt/ *n.* [*noncount*] **1.** the period of light during a day: *In December in Sweden there is hardly any daylight.* **2.** daybreak; dawn: *Attack at daylight.* **3.** public knowledge or awareness; openness: *When this information is brought to daylight, the mayor will have a lot of explaining to do.* **4. daylights,** wits: *You scared the daylights out of me.* **—*adj.*** [*before a noun*] **5.** done, used, or taking place in daylight: *a daring, daylight robbery at the bank.*

day′light-sav′ing (or **day′light sav′ing**) **time′,** *n.* [*noncount*] time in which clocks are set one hour ahead of standard time.

day•time (dā′tīm′) /ˈdeyˌtaym/ *n.* [*noncount*] **1.** the time between sunrise and sunset: *The sky grew dark even in the daytime.* **—*adj.*** [*before a noun*] **2.** of, occurring, or done during the day: *daytime classes.*

day′-to-day′, *adj.* [*before a noun*] **1.** occurring each day; daily: *day-to-day troubles.* **2.** concerned only with immediate needs without regard for the future: *a day-to-day existence, from paycheck to paycheck.*

daze (dāz) /deyz/ *v.,* **dazed, daz•ing,** *n.* **—*v.*** [~ + *obj*] **1.** to cause (someone) to be unable to think clearly because of a blow; stun: *The fall on his head dazed him.* **2.** to overwhelm; dazzle: *The beauty of the Grand Canyon dazed us.* **—*n.*** [*count; singular*] **3.** a dazed condition: *still in a daze after the accident.*

daz•zle (daz′əl) /ˈdæzəl/ *v.,* **-zled, -zling,** *n.* **—*v.*** [~ + *obj*] **1.** to blind temporarily with bright light: *The headlights dazzled the deer.* **2.** to impress deeply; astonish with delight: *The star dazzled his audience.* **—*n.*** [*noncount*] **3.** brightness of light that interferes with seeing properly: *the dazzle of the blue sea on a sunny day at the beach.* **4.** impressive, exciting, or delightful quality: *lured to the city by the dazzle of an acting career.* **—daz′zler,** *n.* [*count*] **—daz′zling,** *adj.*: *a dazzling smile.*

dB or **db,** an abbreviation of: decibel.

DC or **D.C.,** an abbreviation of: District of Columbia.

D-day or **D-Day** (dē′dā′) /ˈdiyˌdey/ *n.* [*noncount*] a day set for beginning something, esp. June 6, 1944, the day of the invasion of W Europe by Allied forces in World War II.

DDT, *n.* [*noncount*] a poisonous chemical that was formerly widely used as an insecticide.

de-, *prefix. de-* comes from Latin, and is used to form verbs and some adjectives with the following meanings: **1.** motion or being carried down from, away, or off: *deplane (= move down or off a plane); descend (= move or go down);* **2.** reversing or undoing the effects of an action: *deflate (= reverse the flow of air out of something); dehumanize (= reverse the positive, humanizing effects of something);* **3.** taking out or removal of a thing: *decaffeinate (= take out the caffeine from something); declaw (= remove the claws of an animal);* **4.** finishing or completeness of an action: *defunct (= completely non-functioning); despoil (= completely spoil).*

DE, an abbreviation of: Delaware.

dea•con (dē′kən) /ˈdiykən/ *n.* [*count*] a member of the Christian clergy below the rank of a priest, or a nonclerical officer having various duties.

de•ac•ti•vate (dē ak′tə vāt′) /diyˈæktəˌveyt/ *v.* [~ + *obj*], **-vat•ed, -vat•ing. 1.** to make inactive: *to deactivate a chemical.* **2.** to disband or break up (a military unit). **—de•ac•ti•va•tion** (dē ak′tə vā′shən) /diyˌæktəˈveyʃən/ *n.* [*noncount*]

dead (ded) /dɛd/ *adj.,* **-er, -est,** *n., adv.* **—*adj.* 1.** no longer living: *The victim was dead on arrival at the hospital.* **2.** not endowed with life; inanimate: *a dead planet, like Mercury.* **3.** [*before a noun*] resembling death; deathlike: *a dead faint.* **4.** having no sensation or feeling; numb: *My arm felt dead after I fell asleep on it.* **5.** (of an emotion) no longer felt; extinguished: *a dead passion.* **6.** not working; inoperative: *a dead battery.* **7.** stagnant or stale: *dead air.* **8.** utterly tired; exhausted: *I was dead after that twenty-hour day.* **9.** (of a language) no longer in use as a means of oral communication among a people. **10.** dull or inactive: *a dead business day.* **11.** [*before a noun*] total; complete; absolute: *The car squealed to a dead stop.* **12.** [*before a noun*] exact; precise: *the dead center of a target.* **13.** *Sports.* out of play: *a dead ball.* **—*n.* 14.** [*noncount; often: the* + ~ + *of*] the period of greatest darkness, coldness, etc.: *the dead of night.* **15. the dead,** [*plural; used with a plural verb*] dead people; those who have died: *the souls of the dead.* **—*adv.* 16.** absolutely; completely; very much: *dead tired.* **17.** directly; straight: *The target is dead ahead.* **—*Idiom.* 18. dead to rights,** in the very act of committing a crime or doing wrong: *I had them dead to rights when they submitted identical term papers.* **—Related Words.** DEAD is an adjective and a noun, DEADLY is an adjective, DEATH is a noun, DIE is a verb, DEATHLY is an adjective: *The police found the dead body. The dead cannot rise from their graves. It was a deadly mistake. He is afraid of death. He is afraid to die. He is deathly pale.*

dead•beat (ded′bēt′) /ˈdɛdˌbiyt/ *n.* [*count*] **1.** a person who avoids paying debts. **2.** a person who lives off money from others.

dead•bolt (ded′bōlt′) /ˈdɛdˌbowlt/ *n.* [*count*] a lock bolt that is moved into position by the turning of a knob or key rather than by spring action.

dead•en (ded′n) /ˈdɛdn̩/ *v.* [~ + *obj*] **1.** to make less sensitive, intense, strong, or effective: *pills to deaden pain.* **2.** to make dull or lifeless: *The criticism deadened my enthusiasm.* **—dead′en•ing,** *adj.*

dead′ end′, *n.* [*count*] **1.** an end of a street, corridor, etc., that has no exit: *Our apartment building stands on a dead end.* **2.** a position with no hope of progress; blind alley: *That job was a dead end.* **—dead′-end′,** *adj.* [*before a noun*]

dead′ heat′, *n.* [*count*] a race in which two or more competitors finish in a tie.

dead•line (ded′līn′) /ˈdɛdˌlayn/ *n.* [*count*] the time by which something must be finished: *Our deadline was only two hours away.*

dead•lock (ded′lok′) /ˈdɛdˌlɒk/ *n.* [*count*] **1.** a state, as in negotiations, in which no agreement can be reached, due esp. to unwillingness to compromise; stalemate: *Negotiations soon reached a deadlock.* **2.** (in sports) a tied score: *a 5-5 deadlock after six innings.* **—*v.* 3.** to (cause to) come to a deadlock: [*no obj*]: *Negotiations deadlocked after two hours.* [~ + *obj*]: *A few stubborn people deadlocked the negotiations.*

dead•ly (ded′lē) /ˈdɛdliy/ *adj.,* **-li•er, -li•est,** *adv.* **—*adj.* 1.** causing or tending to cause death; lethal: *a deadly disease.* **2.** aiming to kill or destroy: *convicted of using a deadly weapon.* **3.** like death; deathly: *a deadly appearance.* **4.** extremely boring: *another deadly lecture.* **5.** excessive; extreme; very great: *a deadly silence.* **6.** extremely accurate: *a deadly shot.* **—*adv.* 7.** in a manner suggesting death: *deadly pale.* **8.** excessively; completely: *deadly dull.* **—dead′li•ness,** *n.* [*noncount*]

dead•pan (ded′pan′) /ˈdɛdˌpæn/ *adj., adv., v.,* **-panned, -pan•ning. —*adj.* 1.** marked by a careful pretense of seriousness; straight-faced: *deadpan humor.* **—*adv.* 2.** in a deadpan manner: *told the joke utterly deadpan.* **—*v.* 3.** to perform in a deadpan manner: [*no obj*]: *an actor deadpanning.* [~ + *obj*]: *deadpanned her lines perfectly.*

dead′ weight′ or **dead′weight′,** *n.* [*count; usually singular*] the heavy weight of anything not moving.

dead•wood (ded′wŏŏd′) /ˈdɛdˌwʊd/ *n.* [*noncount*] **1.** dead branches or trees. **2.** useless or unprofitable persons or things: *The company wanted to get rid of its deadwood.*

deaf (def) /dɛf/ *adj.,* **-er, -est,** *n.* **—*adj.* 1.** partly or completely without the sense of hearing: *deaf from birth.* **2.** [*be* + ~ + *to*] refusing to listen to advice, to be persuaded, or to pay attention to: *was deaf to all the advice I gave him.* **—*n.* 3. the deaf,** [*plural; used with a plural verb*] deaf people as a group: *The TV show is broadcast* *with special captions for the deaf.* —**deaf′ness,** *n.* [*noncount*]

deaf•en (def′ən) /ˈdɛfən/ *v.* [~ + *obj*] **1.** to make deaf. **2.** to overwhelm or stun with noise: *The sirens deafened me.* —**deaf′en•ing,** *adj.*

deaf′-mute′, *Often Offensive.* —*adj.* **1.** unable to hear and speak. —*n.* [*count*] **2.** a person who is unable to hear and speak.

deal (dēl) /diyl/ *v.,* **dealt** (delt) /dɛlt/ **deal•ing,** *n.* —*v.* **1.** [*not: be + ~-ing; ~ + with + obj*] to be about; to be concerned with; to have to do with: *Botany deals with the study of plants.* **2.** [~ + *with* + *obj*] to take necessary action with respect to a thing or person; to handle or see to: *Law courts deal with criminals.* **3.** [~ + *with* + *obj*] to act, behave, or conduct oneself toward persons: *You have to learn how to deal with all sorts of people.* **4.** [~ + *in/with* + *obj*] to trade or do business: *to deal in used cars.* **5.** to deliver; administer: [~ + *obj* + *to* + *obj*]: *to deal a heavy blow to his opponent.* [~ + *obj* + *obj*]: *He dealt his opponent a heavy blow.* **6.** to give out or distribute something, such as playing cards, among a number of people: [*no obj*]: *Whose turn is it to deal?* [~ + *obj*]: *The person on the left deals the cards.* [~ + *obj* + *to* + *obj*]: *I dealt two cards to each player.* [~ + *obj* + *obj*]: *I dealt each player two cards.* [~ + *out* + *obj*]: *I dealt out the children's allowances one by one.* **7.** *Slang.* to buy and sell (drugs) illegally: [*no obj*]: *He was dealing when we arrested him.* [~ + *obj*]: *dealing all sorts of drugs.* —*n.* [*count*] **8.** a business transaction or arrangement: *The company will make a deal with a Japanese firm.* **9.** an arrangement in which both sides benefit: *the best deal in town.* **10.** a secret or underhand agreement or bargain: *made some deals to get the bill passed.* **11.** *Informal.* treatment received in dealing with another: *He got a raw deal when he was fired.* **12.** the set of playing cards in one's hand. —***Idiom.*** **13. a great** or **good deal (of),** an unknown but large quantity or amount (of); a lot (of): *has a great deal of money to spend; feels a good deal better.* **14. deal someone in,** [~ + *obj* + *in*] *Slang.* to include someone: *If this is a plot to get revenge on him, then deal me in.* —**deal′er,** *n.* [*count*]

deal•er•ship (dē′lər ship′) /ˈdiylər,ʃɪp/ *n.* [*count*] a sales agency having permission to sell a product.

deal•ing (dē′ling) /ˈdiylɪŋ/ *n.* **1.** Usually, **dealings.** [*plural*] interaction; business activity: *commercial dealings.* **2.** [*noncount*] method or manner of conduct in relation to others: *a reputation for honest dealing.*

dean (dēn) /diyn/ *n.* [*count*] **1.** an official in a college, esp. the head of faculty, or one in charge of students, etc. **2.** an official in charge of a church or a diocese. **3.** the senior member, in length of service, of a profession, etc.: *the dean of American composers.*

dear (dēr) /dɪər/ *adj.,* **-er, -est,** *n., adv., interj.* —*adj.* **1.** (used as a conventional greeting or in the salutation of a letter as an expression of respect, friendship, etc.): *Dear Sir or Madam. My dear friends.* **2.** beloved; much loved; precious: *The burglars had taken our dearest possessions.* **3.** heartfelt; earnest: *He had no dearer wish.* **4.** expensive: *Tomatoes were dear in the winter.* —*n.* [*count*] **5.** a kind or generous person: *You're a dear to look after the children.* **6.** a beloved one: *Come here, my dears, and give your granddaddy a big hug.* **7.** an affectionate or familiar term of address (sometimes considered offensive when used to a stranger, subordinate, etc.) —*interj.* **8.** (used as an exclamation of surprise, distress, etc.): *Oh dear, I've lost the phone number.* —**dear′ness,** *n.* [*noncount*]

Dear′ John′, *n.* [*count*] a letter, esp. to a soldier, from a woman informing him that she is ending their relationship or wants a divorce: *a Dear John from home.*

dear•ly (dēr′lē) /ˈdɪərliy/ *adv.* **1.** greatly; deeply; with much feeling or emotion: *He loves his daughter dearly.* **2.** at a high or terrible cost; with much suffering: *paid dearly for that victory.*

dearth (dûrth) /dɜrθ/ *n.* [*count; usually singular*] a scarcity or lack: *a dearth of good writers of computer manuals.*

death (deth) /dɛθ/ *n.* **1.** the act of dying; the end of life. [*noncount*]: *jogging right up to the day of his death.* [*count*]: *all those deaths due to drunk driving.* **2.** [*noncount*] the state of being dead: *hands as cold as death.* **3.** [*count; usually singular*] end; destruction; extinction: *Democracy for that country meant the death of civilization as they knew it.* **4.** [*usually: Death; proper noun*] the agent of death represented as a person, usually pictured as a robed figure or skeleton carrying a scythe. **5.** [*count; usually singular; the* + ~] a cause of death: *You'll be the death of me yet!* —***Idiom.*** **6. at death's door,** in serious danger of dying; gravely ill: *at death's door several times from heart attacks.* **7. do to death,** [*do* + *obj* + *to* + ~] to do so often that boredom sets in: *a comic plot that's been done to death.* **8. put to death,** to kill; execute: [*put* + *obj* + *to* + ~]: *They put him to death immediately.* [*put* + *to* + ~ + *obj*]: *That government put to death over 1,000 dissidents.* **9. to death,** to a degree that cannot be endured any longer: *sick to death of your bickering.* —**death′like′,** *adj.*

death•bed (deth′bed′) /ˈdɛθ,bɛd/ *n.* [*count*] **1.** the bed on which a person dies; the last hours before death: *confessed the crime on his deathbed.* —*adj.* [*before a noun*] **2.** of, relating to, or occurring at such a time: *a deathbed confession.*

death•blow (deth′blō′) /ˈdɛθ,blow/ *n.* [*count*] anything that ends or destroys hope or expectation: *Those losses were the deathblow to his attempts to modernize the plant.*

death•less (deth′lis) /ˈdɛθlɪs/ *adj.* not subject to death; immortal: *deathless glory.* —**death′less•ly,** *adv.*

death•ly (deth′lē) /ˈdɛθliy/ *adj.* [*before a noun*] **1.** extreme; intense: *He had a deathly fear of snakes.* **2.** resembling death: *a deathly paleness.* —*adv.* **3.** in the manner of death: *deathly pale.* **4.** completely; utterly: *She's deathly afraid of me.*

death′ row′, *n.* [*noncount*] prison cells for prisoners awaiting execution.

death•trap (deth′trap′) /ˈdɛθ,træp/ *n.* [*count*] a structure, place, or situation where there is risk of death.

deb (deb) /dɛb/ *n.* DEBUTANTE.

de•ba•cle (də bä′kəl, -bak′əl) /dəˈbɑkəl, -ˈbækəl/ *n.* [*count*] a complete and total disaster, failure, or fiasco: *The last meeting was a debacle and nothing was accomplished.*

de•bar (di bär′) /dɪˈbɑr/ *v.* [~ + *obj* (+ *from*)], **-barred, -bar•ring.** to shut out or exclude; prohibit: *He will be debarred from the college if he fails again.* —**de•bar′ment,** *n.* [*noncount*]

de•bark (di bärk′) /dɪˈbɑrk/ *v.* DISEMBARK. —**de•bar•ka•tion** (dē′bär kā′shən) /,diybɑrˈkeyʃən/ *n.* [*noncount*]

de•base (di bās′) /dɪˈbeys/ *v.* [~ + *obj*], **-based, -bas•ing. 1.** to lower in quality or value: *Inflation has debased the country's currency.* **2.** [~ + *oneself*] to disgrace (oneself): *You will debase yourself by accepting a bribe.* —**de•base′ment,** *n.* [*noncount*]

de•bat•a•ble (di bā′tə bl) /dɪˈbeytəbl/ *adj.* **1.** that may be debated: *I haven't made up my mind yet; the issue is still debatable.* **2.** doubtful; questionable; uncertain: *Many of his arguments are highly debatable; I wouldn't believe them if I were you.*

de•bate (di bāt′) /dɪˈbeyt/ *n., v.,* **-bat•ed, -bat•ing.** —*n.* **1.** [*count*] a discussion involving opposing viewpoints: *a lively debate over the issue of raising taxes.* **2.** [*count*] a formal contest in which the affirmative and negative sides of an issue are argued for by opposing speakers. **3.** [*noncount*] deliberation; consideration: *After some debate they made their decision.* —*v.* **4.** [~ (+ *about*) + *clause*] to deliberate; consider: *We debated (about) whether we should go or stay here.* **5.** [~ (+ *about*) + *obj*] to argue or discuss (a question), as in a group: *We debated (about) the issue most of the night.* **6.** to have a formal debate (with): [*no obj*]: *When we left, the teams were still debating.* [~ + *obj*]: *I had to debate the best speaker in the district.* —**de•bat′er,** *n.* [*count*] —**de•bat′ing,** *n.* [*noncount*]

de•bauch (di bôch′) /dɪˈbɔtʃ/ *v.* [~ + *obj*] to cause (someone) to become corrupt in virtue, esp. with regard to drinking or sexual behavior. —**de•bauched′,** *adj.* —**de•bauch′er•y,** *n.* [*noncount; count*], *pl.* **er•ies.**

de•bil•i•tate (di bil′i tāt′) /dɪˈbɪlɪ,teyt/ *v.* [~ + *obj*], **-tat•ed, -tat•ing.** to make (someone) weak; deprive (someone) of strength: *The hepatitis he suffered overseas debilitated him.* —**de•bil′i•ta•ting,** *adj.* —**de•bil′i•ta′tion,** *n.* [*noncount*]

de•bil•i•ty (di bil′i tē) /dɪˈbɪlɪtiy/ *n., pl.* **-ties. 1.** [*noncount*] a weakened state; weakness. **2.** [*count*] a handicap or disability: *a painful debility.*

deb•it (deb′it) /ˈdɛbɪt/ *n.* [*count*] **1.** the record kept of money owed or spent. **2. a.** a recorded item of debt. **b.** any entry or the total shown on the debit side of an account. **c.** the left-hand, or debit, side of an account. **3.** a failing or shortcoming: *one of the debits in that plan.* —*v.* [~ + *obj*] **4.** to charge with or as a debt: *They debited my account for the amount I owed.*

deb′it card′, *n.* [*count*] a card through which payments are made electronically from the bank account of the card holder.

deb•o•nair (deb′ə nâr′) /ˌdɛbəˈnɛər/ *adj.* **1.** suave; worldly; sophisticated: *looked very debonair in a tuxedo.* **2.** carefree; jaunty: *a debonair manner.* —**deb′o•nair′ly,** *adv.*

de•brief (dē brēf′) /diyˈbriyf/ *v.* [~ + *obj*] to ask (someone) questions in order to obtain useful information or intelligence: *The pilots were debriefed after the last bombing run.*

de•bris or **dé•bris** (də brē′, dā′brē) /dəˈbriy, ˈdeybriy/ *n.* [*noncount*] the remains of something destroyed; ruins: *searched in the debris of the bombed building for survivors.*

debt (det) /dɛt/ *n.* **1.** [*count*] something that is owed or that one should pay to another: *We owe him a great debt of gratitude for his help.* **2.** [*noncount*] an obligation to pay or perform something: *He was in debt to the amount of $200,000.* —**debt′or,** *n.* [*count*]

de•bug (dē bug′) /diyˈbʌg/ *v.* [~ + *obj*], **-bugged, -bug•ging. 1.** to find and remove defects or errors from: *to debug a computer program.* **2.** to remove electronic bugs from (a room or building): *The CIA finally managed to debug the building.* **3.** to rid of insect pests. —**de•bug′ger,** *n.* [*count*]

de•bunk (di bungk′) /dɪˈbʌŋk/ *v.* [~ + *obj*] to show (something) to be false or exaggerated; expose: *to debunk a theory.*

de•but or **dé•but** (dā byōō′, dā′byōō) /deyˈbyuw, ˈdeybyuw/ *n.* [*count*] **1.** a first public appearance or presentation, as of a performer: *The hit TV show made its debut back in 1990.* —*v.* [*no obj*] **2.** to perform for the first time before an audience: *He debuted in a nightclub in 1989.* —*adj.* [*before a noun*] **3.** of or being a first appearance: *a debut recital.*

deb•u•tante or **déb•u•tante** (deb′yŏŏ tänt′) /ˈdɛbyʊˌtɑnt/ *n.* [*count*] a young woman receiving her first formal introduction into society.

-dec-, *root.* *-dec-* comes from Latin and Greek, where it has the meaning "ten." This meaning is found in such words as: DECADE, DECALOGUE, DECATHLON, DECENNIAL, DECIMAL, DECIMATE.

Dec or **Dec.,** an abbreviation of: December.

dec•ade (dek′ād) /ˈdɛkeyd/ *n.* [*count*] **1.** a period of ten years: *He's been on the movie scene for decades.* **2.** a period of ten years beginning with a year whose last digit is zero: *the decade of the 1990's.* See -DEC-.

dec•a•dence (dek′ə dəns) /ˈdɛkədəns/ also **dec′a•den•cy,** *n.* [*noncount*] the act or process of falling into decay; deterioration or decline: *A long period of decadence came at the end of the empire.* See -CAD-.

dec•a•dent (dek′ə dənt) /ˈdɛkədənt/ *adj.* relating to or marked by decadence. See -CAD-.

de•caf•fein•ate (dē kaf′ə nāt′) /diyˈkæfəˌneyt/ *v.* [~ + *obj*], **-at•ed, -at•ing.** to remove caffeine from: *They use plain water to decaffeinate the coffee beans.* —**de•caf′-fein•at′ed,** *adj.*: *a cup of decaffeinated coffee.*

de•cal (dē′kal) /ˈdiykæl/ *n.* [*count*] a design on specially prepared paper for transfer to wood, metal, or glass.

de•camp (di kamp′) /dɪˈkæmp/ *v.* [*no obj*] **1.** to pack up equipment and leave a camping ground: *The army decamped and moved south.* **2.** to depart hastily and often secretly: *The treasurer decamped with all the money.* —**de•camp′ment,** *n.* [*noncount*]

de•cant (di kant′) /dɪˈkænt/ *v.* [~ + *obj*] to pour (a liquid) from one container to another, often slowly and carefully.

de•cant•er (di kan′tər) /dɪˈkæntər/ *n.* [*count*] a decorative vessel for holding and serving wine or the like.

de•cap•i•tate (di kap′i tāt′) /dɪˈkæpɪˌteyt/ *v.* [~ + *obj*], **-tat•ed, -tat•ing.** to cut off the head of. —**de•cap•i•ta•tion** (di kap′i tā′shən) /dɪˌkæpɪˈteyʃən/ *n.* [*noncount*]: *death by decapitation.* —**de•cap′i•ta′tor,** *n.* [*count*]

de•cath•lon (di kath′lon) /dɪˈkæθlɒn/ *n.* [*count*] an athletic contest having ten different track-and-field events. See -DEC-.

de•cay (di kā′) /dɪˈkey/ *v.* **1.** to (cause to) become decomposed; rot: [*no obj*]: *The tree began to decay soon after it was cut down.* [~ + *obj*]: *Candy can decay your teeth.* **2.** [*no obj*] to decline in health or prosperity; deteriorate: *The transit system is rapidly decaying.* —*n.* [*noncount*] **3.** decomposition; rot: *The house is in a state of decay.* **4.** a gradual and continuing decline: *the decay of standards.* —**de•cayed′,** *adj.*: *decayed timber.* —**de•cay′ing,** *adj.*: *the smell of decaying vegetation.*

-dece-, *root.* *-dece-* comes from Latin, where it has the meaning "correct, proper." This meaning is found in such words as: DECENT, INDECENT.

de•cease (di sēs′) /dɪˈsiys/ *n.* [*count; usually singular*] the act of dying; death: *at his decease.*

de•ceased (di sēst′) /dɪˈsiyst/ *adj.* **1.** dead: *All the members of his family were deceased.* —*n.* [*noncount; the* + ~*; used with a singular or plural verb*] **2.** a dead person or persons: *The deceased was in his forties. All the deceased were family members.*

de•ce•dent (di sēd′nt) /dɪˈsiydnt/ *n.* [*count; often: the* + ~] *Law.* a deceased person. See -CAD-.

de•ceit (di sēt′) /dɪˈsiyt/ *n.* **1.** [*noncount*] the quality of being dishonest or deceitful; cheating; duplicity: *too much deceit practiced against consumers.* **2.** [*count*] an act or instance of such quality: *numerous deceits against consumers.* See -CEIVE-.

de•ceit•ful (di sēt′fəl) /dɪˈsiytfəl/ *adj.* **1.** given to deceiving: *Her saying one thing and doing another shows how deceitful she is.* **2.** intended to deceive; misleading: *a deceitful action.* —**de•ceit′ful•ly,** *adv.* —**de•ceit′ful•ness,** *n.* [*noncount*]: *We found evidence of his deceitfulness.*

de•ceive (di sēv′) /dɪˈsiyv/ *v.,* **-ceived, -ceiv•ing.** to mislead by a false appearance or statement; delude: [~ + *obj*]: *I never thought she would deceive me.* [~ + *obj* + *into* + *verb-ing*]: *They deceived her into thinking she would be promoted.* —**de•ceiv′er,** *n.* [*count*] —**de•ceiv′ing•ly,** *adv.* See -CEIVE-.

de•cel•er•ate (dē sel′ə rāt′) /diyˈsɛləˌreyt/ *v.,* **-at•ed, -at•ing. 1.** to (cause to) slow down or decrease the speed of: [*no obj*]: *The car decelerated to a stop.* [~ + *obj*]: *He decelerated the truck.* **2.** to slow the rate of increase of: [*no obj*]: *with inflation finally decelerating.* [~ + *obj*]: *efforts to decelerate inflation.* —**de•cel•er•a•tion** (dē sel′ə rā′shən) /diyˌsɛləˈreyʃən/ *n.* [*noncount*]: *the slow deceleration down to subsonic speed.* —**de•cel′er•a′tor,** *n.* [*count*]: *a decelerator to inflation.* See -CELER-.

De•cem•ber (di sem′bər) /dɪˈsɛmbər/ *n.* the 12th month of the year, containing 31 days. [*proper noun*]: *See you in December.* [*count*]: *It was two Decembers ago when she visited us. Abbr.:* Dec.

de•cen•cy (dē′sən sē) /ˈdiysənsiy/ *n., pl.* **-cies. 1.** [*noncount*] the state or quality of being decent: *At least have the decency to apologize.* **2. decencies,** [*plural*] standards of proper and acceptable behavior; proprieties: *has the decencies expected in modern society.*

de•cen•ni•al (di sen′ē əl) /dɪˈsɛniyəl/ *adj.* **1.** of or for ten years; occurring every ten years. —*n.* [*count*] **2.** a decennial anniversary or its celebration. —**de•cen′ni•al•ly,** *adv.* See -DEC-.

de•cent (dē′sənt) /ˈdiysənt/ *adj.* **1.** acting or being in agreement with recognized and accepted standards of proper behavior or speech; not obscene: *Please use decent language in front of the children.* **2.** morally upright: *Although they may be hungry, decent people won't steal.* **3.** [*be* + ~] properly dressed: *I'm not decent yet; I'll be right down when I am.* **4.** adequate; passable; acceptable: *a decent room and dinner for a low price.* **5.** [*be* + ~ + *of*] kind; courteous: *was very decent of him to defend me.* —**de′cent•ly,** *adv.*: *He always acted decently toward me.* See -DECE-.

de•cen•tral•ize (dē sen′trə līz′) /diyˈsɛntrəˌlayz/ *v.* [~ + *obj*], **-ized, -iz•ing. 1.** to distribute the administrative powers of (a central authority) throughout local or regional divisions: *The board decentralized the administration of the local schools.* **2.** to move (things) away from a concentrated center: *decentralizing their subsidiaries.* —**de•cen′tral•i•za′tion,** *n.* [*noncount*]: *the new plan for decentralization.*

de•cep•tion (di sep′shən) /dɪˈsɛpʃən/ *n.* **1.** [*noncount*] the act of deceiving or the state of being deceived: *We pointed out the deception in the salesperson's claims.* **2.** [*count*] something that deceives or is intended to deceive; a trick; ruse: *another obvious deception.*

de•cep•tive (di sep′tiv) /dɪˈsɛptɪv/ *adj.* relating to or marked by deceit: *deceptive advertising, until you read the fine print.* —**de•cep′tive•ly,** *adv.*

deci-, *prefix.* *deci-* comes from Latin, where it has the meaning "ten." This meaning now appears in the names of units of measurement that are one-tenth the size of the unit named by the second element of the compound: *decibel (= one-tenth of a bel); deciliter (= one-tenth of a liter).* See -DEC-.

dec•i•bel (des′ə bel′, -bəl) /ˈdɛsəˌbɛl, -bəl/ *n.* [*count*] a unit that is used to express differences in power, esp. in measuring the loudness of sound. *Abbr.:* dB

de•cide (di sīd′) /dɪˈsayd/ *v.,* **-cid•ed, -cid•ing. 1.** to conclude (a dispute) by awarding victory to one side; settle: [~ + *obj*]: *to decide an argument.* [~ + *for/against/in favor of* + *obj*]: *decided in favor of the plaintiff.* **2.** [~ + *to* + *verb*] to choose; make up one's mind: *decided to learn how to type faster.* [~ + *(that) clause*]: *She decided that she would stay.* **3.** [~ + *obj* + *to* + *verb*] to bring (a person) to a decision; persuade or convince: *What decided you to take the job?* See -CIDE-[1]. —**Related Words.** DECIDE is a verb, DECISIVE is an adjective, DECISION is a noun: *He can't decide what to eat for breakfast. He's not very decisive when he needs to take action. He made a decision about what to eat for breakfast.*

de•cid•ed (di sī′did) /dɪ'saydɪd/ *adj.* **1.** [*before a noun*] clear and obvious; not ambiguous: *a decided improvement.* **2.** free from hesitation; determined: *dealing with her problems in a decided way.* —**de•cid′ed•ly,** *adv.*: *The economy has become decidedly worse.*

de•cid•u•ous (di sij′o͞o əs) /dɪ'sɪdʒuwəs/ *adj.* **1.** losing the leaves every year: *deciduous trees.* **2.** shed at a particular season or stage of growth: *deciduous teeth.* See -CIDE-[2].

dec•i•mal (des′ə məl, des′məl) /'dɛsəməl, 'dɛsməl/ *adj.* [*before a noun*] **1.** of or relating to tenths or to the number 10. **2.** proceeding by tens: *a decimal system.* —*n.* [*count*] **3.** DECIMAL FRACTION. See -DEC-.

dec′imal frac′tion, *n.* [*count*] a fraction whose denominator is a power of 10, usually indicated by a dot **(dec′imal point′)** before the numerator: as 0.4 = 4/10; 0.126 = 126/1000. See -DEC-.

dec•i•mate (des′ə māt′) /'dɛsə,meyt/ *v.* [~ + *obj*], **-mat•ed, -mat•ing. 1.** to destroy a great number or part of: *Cholera decimated the population.* **2.** (esp. in ancient Rome) to select by lot and kill every tenth person of. —**dec•i•ma•tion** (des′ə mā′shən) /,dɛsə'meyʃən/ *n.* [*noncount*] See -DEC-.

de•ci•pher (di sī′fər) /dɪ'sayfər/ *v.* [~ + *obj*] **1.** to make out the meaning of (something difficult to read): *I couldn't decipher his handwriting.* **2.** to decode: *to decipher a secret message.* —**de•ci′pher•a•ble,** *adj.*: *handwriting just barely decipherable.*

de•ci•sion (di sizh′ən) /dɪ'sɪʒən/ *n.* **1.** [*noncount*] the act or process of deciding: *I kept postponing the moment of decision.* **2.** [*count*] the act of making up one's mind: *a difficult decision.* **3.** [*count*] something decided; resolution: *My decision is to go ahead with the plan.* **4.** [*count*] a judgment, such as pronounced by a court: *The jury's decision was that he was guilty on all counts.* **5.** [*noncount*] the quality of being able to make a firm judgment: *spoke with decision.* **6.** the awarding of a victory in a boxing match when there is no knockout, based on scoring by the referee and judges: [*noncount*]: *He won by decision.* [*count*]: *won in a split decision.*

de•ci•sive (di sī′siv) /dɪ'saysɪv/ *adj.* **1.** having the power to decide: *The decisive argument was the savings his plan would bring.* **2.** displaying firmness; resolute: *a decisive manner.* **3.** unquestionable; definite: *a decisive lead of 30-0 by halftime.* —**de•ci′sive•ly,** *adv.* —**de•ci′sive•ness,** *n.* [*noncount*] See -CISE-.

deck (dek) /dɛk/ *n.* [*count*] **1.** a floorlike surface taking up one level of a hull of a vessel: *Our cabin was on the fifth deck down.* **2.** a surface suggesting the deck of a ship: *the upper deck of the sightseeing bus.* **3.** an open, unroofed porch extending from a house: *We relaxed outside on the wooden deck.* **4.** a pack of playing cards: *He shuffled the deck and cut it.* **5.** a cassette deck or tape deck. —*v.* **6.** [~ + *obj* + *out*] to dress in something fancy: *decked herself out in her jewels.* **7.** [~ + *out* + *obj*] to decorate so as to look fancy or festive: *We decked out the room with streamers.* **8.** [~ + *obj*] *Informal.* to knock (someone) down; to floor: *His opponent decked him.* —***Idiom.* 9. clear the decks,** to prepare for work by removing all previous work: *Let's clear the decks and get started on this new project.* **10. hit the deck,** to fall or drop to the floor or ground. **11. on deck, a.** present and ready to act or work. **b.** *Baseball.* next at bat.

de•claim (di klām′) /dɪ'kleym/ *v.* to speak aloud while, or as if, making a formal speech: [*no obj*]: *Marc Antony declaimed over the body of Caesar.* [~ + *obj*]: *He declaimed a speech.* —**de•claim′er,** *n.* [*count*] —**dec•la•ma•tion** (dek′lə mā′shən) /,dɛklə'meyʃən/ *n.* [*noncount*]: *much declamation.* [*count*]: *a very lengthy declamation.* —**de•clam•a•to•ry** (di klam′ə tôr′ē, -tōr′ē) /dɪ'klæmə,tɔriy, -,towriy/ *adj.*: *a declamatory way of speaking.* See -CLAIM-.

dec•la•ra•tion (dek′lə rā′shən) /,dɛklə'reyʃən/ *n.* [*count*] **1.** a firm statement; an assertion: *The witness's declaration convicted the killer.* **2.** an official announcement, notification, or proclamation: *a declaration of war.* **3.** a signed document that indicates some amount, as of taxes or the value of goods imported.

de•clar•a•tive (di klar′ə tiv) /dɪ'klærətɪv/ *adj.* of, relating to, or having the form of a sentence used in making a statement: *A declarative sentence is:* John is at home; *an interrogative sentence is:* Is John at home?

de•clare (di klâr′) /dɪ'klɛər/ *v.,* **-clared, -clar•ing. 1.** to make known; state clearly: [~ + *obj*]: *He declared his innocence to everyone who would listen.* [~ + *(that) clause*]: *declared that the city was unsafe.* [*used with quotations*]: *"I saw the defendant at the scene of the crime," he declared.* **2.** to announce or state officially; proclaim: [~ + *obj*]: *to declare a state of emergency.* [~ + *obj* + *obj*]: *The officials declared her the winner of the high jump.* [~ + *obj* + *adj*]: *My client was declared innocent.* [*used with quotations*]: *He declared, "I'm innocent!"* **3.** [~ + *obj*] to reveal; indicate: *Their appearance at the meeting declares their willingness to participate in the talks.* **4.** [~ + *obj*] to make a statement of (goods being brought into a country, income for taxation, etc.): *You have to declare your earnings for the whole year.* —**de•clar′a•ble,** *adj.*

de•clas•si•fy (dē klas′ə fī′) /diy'klæsə,fay/ *v.* [~ + *obj*], **-fied, -fy•ing.** to remove the security classification from (information, a document, etc.): *Now that the files are declassified you can read for yourself.*

de•clen•sion (di klen′shən) /dɪ'klɛnʃən/ *n.* [*count*] **1. a.** the changing of the forms of nouns, pronouns, and adjectives depending on their use in a sentence or their number. **b.** the whole set of inflected forms of such a word. **c.** a class of such words having similar sets of inflected forms: *the Latin second declension.* **2.** a bending, sloping, or moving downward.

de•cline (di klīn′) /dɪ'klayn/ *v.,* **-clined, -clin•ing,** *n.* —*v.* **1.** to deny consent (to do); refuse: [*no obj*]: *I asked her over, but she declined.* [~ + *obj*]: *He declined our invitation.* [~ + *to* + *verb*]: *He declined to say how he would vote.* **2.** [*no obj*] to slope or incline downward: *The hill declines sharply at this point.* **3.** [*no obj*] to fail in strength or health; deteriorate: *His health is declining.* **4.** [*no obj*] to become less; diminish: *to decline in popularity.* —*n.* **5.** [*count*] a downward slope; drop; downgrade: *There's a sharp decline in the road up ahead.* **6.** [*count*] a downward movement, such as of prices or population: *a decline in the stock market.* **7.** [*count*] a deterioration, such as in strength: *a sudden decline in his health.* **8.** [*noncount*] progress downward or toward the close or end of something: *Prices are in decline.* —**de•clin′er,** *n.* [*count*] —**de•clin′ing,** *adj.* [*before a noun*]: *declining stock market prices.*

de•code (dē kōd′) /diy'kowd/ *v.* [~ + *obj*], **-cod•ed, -cod•ing.** to translate (data or a message) from a code or cipher into the original language or form.

dé•col•le•tage or **de•col•le•tage** (dā′kol ə täzh′, dek′ə lə-) /,deykɒlə'tɑʒ, ,dɛkələ-/ *n.* [*count; usually singular*] the neckline of a dress cut low in the front.

dé•col•le•té or **de•col•le•te** (dā′kol ə tā′, dek′ə lə-) /,deykɒlə'tey, ,dɛkələ-/ *adj.* **1.** (of a garment) low-necked. **2.** wearing a low-necked garment.

de•col•o•nize (dē kol′ə nīz′) /diy'kɒlə,nayz/ *v.* [~ + *obj*], **-nized, -niz•ing.** to allow to become self-governing or independent: *The government decolonized its former possessions.* —**de•col′o•ni•za′tion,** *n.* [*noncount*]

de•com•mis•sion (dē′kə mish′ən) /,diykə'mɪʃən/ *v.* [~ + *obj*] to retire (a ship or airplane) from active service.

de•com•pose (dē′kəm pōz′) /,diykəm'powz/ *v.* [*no obj*], **-posed, -pos•ing. 1.** to separate into the essential parts: *Salt decomposes into sodium and chlorine.* **2.** to rot; become decayed: *the smell of decomposing vegetation.* —**de•com•po•si•tion** (dē′kom pə zish′ən) /,diykɒmpə'zɪʃən/ *n.* [*noncount*]: *decomposition of leaves.*

de•con•ges•tant (dē′kən jes′tənt) /,diykən'dʒɛstənt/ *adj.* [*before a noun*] **1.** relieving or clearing congestion of the nose and throat: *a decongestant cough syrup.* —*n.* [*count*] **2.** decongestant medicine.

de•con•tam•i•nate (dē′kən tam′ə nāt′) /,diykən'tæmə,neyt/ *v.* [~ + *obj*], **-nat•ed, -nat•ing.** to make (something) safe by removing dangerous substances: *to decontaminate the nuclear power plant where the leak took place.* —**de•con•tam•i•na•tion** (dē′kən tam′ə nā′shən) /,diykən,tæmə'neyʃən/ *n.* [*noncount*]

dé•cor or **de•cor** (dā kôr′, dā′kôr) /dey'kɔr, 'deykɔr/ *n.* [*count; usually singular*] style or manner of decoration, such as of a room: *a modern décor in the living room.*

dec•o•rate (dek′ə rāt′) /'dɛkə,reyt/ *v.* [~ + *obj*],

-rat•ed, -rat•ing. 1. to adorn with something ornamental or beautiful: *They decorate the streets with Christmas tree lights.* **2.** to honor (someone) with an award: *to decorate a soldier for bravery.* **—dec′o•ra′tor,** *n.* [*count*]: *an interior decorator.*

dec•o•ra•tion (dek′ə rā′shən) /ˌdɛkə'reyʃən/ *n.* **1.** [*count*] something used for decorating. **2.** [*noncount*] the act of decorating: *specializing in the decoration of private mansions.* **3.** [*count*] an award given and worn as a mark of honor: *Decorations covered the hero's chest.*

dec•o•ra•tive (dek′ər ə tiv) /'dɛkərətɪv/ *adj.* providing beauty; ornamenting: *some decorative woodwork and carvings.*

dec•o•rous (dek′ər əs) /'dɛkərəs/ *adj.* showing respect for social customs and manners; proper and suitable: *decorous behavior during the solemn occasion.* **—dec′o•rous•ly,** *adv.: He behaved as decorously as he could.*

de•co•rum (di kôr′əm, -kōr′-) /dɪ'kɔrəm, -'kowr-/ *n.* [*noncount*] dignified, proper conduct, manners, or appearance expected in polite society: *Act with decorum when you attend the funeral.*

de•cou•page or **dé•cou•page** (dā′ko͞o päzh′) /ˌdeykuw'pɑʒ/ *n., v.,* **-paged, -pag•ing. —*n.* 1.** [*noncount*] the art of decorating something with cutouts over which varnish or lacquer is applied. **2.** [*count*] the cutout itself: *a few decoupages on the classroom walls.* **—*v.*** [~ + *obj*] **3.** to decorate by decoupage.

de•coy (*n.* dē′koi; *v.* di koi′, dē′koi) / *n.* 'diykɔy; *v.* dɪ'kɔy, 'diykɔy/ *n.* [*count*] **1.** a person, thing, or action that lures another into danger or a trap: *The car the police were chasing was a decoy.* **2.** an artificial bird used to lure game into a trap or within gunshot: *a duck decoy.* **—*v.*** [~ + *obj* (+ *into* + *verb-ing*)] **3.** to lure, trick, or trap by or as if by a decoy: *The fighter pilots were decoyed by the enemy into shooting at unarmed missiles.*

de•crease (*v.* di krēs′; *n.* dē′krēs, di krēs′) / *v.* dɪ'kriys; *n.* 'diykriys, dɪ'kriys/ *v.,* **-creased, -creas•ing,** *n.* **—*v.* 1.** to lessen, esp. by degrees; (cause to) diminish: [*no obj*]: *Water consumption had to decrease to avoid a drought.* [~ + *obj*]: *They told us to decrease spending.* **—*n.*** [*count*] **2.** the act or process of decreasing. **3.** the amount by which a thing is lessened: *a decrease of only 15%.* **—de•creas′ing,** *adj.* [*before a noun*]: *decreasing interest rates.* **—de•creas′ing•ly,** *adv.*

de•cree (di krē′) /dɪ'kriy/ *n., v.,* **-creed, -cree•ing. —*n.*** [*count*] **1.** a formal order usually having the force of law: *a presidential decree.* **2.** a judicial decision or order: *The judge issued a decree forbidding him to leave the state.* **—*v.* 3.** to command, order, or decide by or as if by decree: [~ + *obj*]: *The king decreed an amnesty.* [~ + (*that*) *clause*]: *The judge decreed that the parent could visit the children five times a year.*

de•crep•it (di krep′it) /dɪ'krɛpɪt/ *adj.* **1.** (of a person) weakened by old age; feeble; infirm. **2.** worn out or broken down by long use; dilapidated: *a decrepit old apartment building.* **—de•crep′i•tude′,** *n.* [*noncount*]: *old buildings in various stages of decrepitude.*

de•cre•scen•do (dē′kri shen′dō, dā′-) /ˌdiykrɪ'ʃɛndow, ˌdey-/ *adv., adj., n., pl.* **-dos, -di** (-dē). *Music.* **—*adv.* 1.** gradually decreasing in loudness: *Play the piece decrescendo.* **—*adj.* 2.** gradually decreasing in loudness: *a decrescendo passage of five bars of music.* **—*n.*** [*count*] **3.** a gradual decrease in loudness.

de•crim•i•nal•ize (dē krim′ə nl īz′) /diy'krɪmənlˌayz/ *v.* [~ + *obj*], **-ized, -iz•ing.** to eliminate criminal penalties for: *to decriminalize the possession of marijuana.*

de•cry (di krī′) /dɪ'kray/ *v.* [~ + *obj*], **-cried, -cry•ing.** to condemn openly; denounce: *decried the regime's ruthlessness.*

ded•i•cate (ded′i kāt′) /'dɛdɪˌkeyt/ *v.,* **-cat•ed, -cat•ing. 1.** [~ + *obj* + *to* + *obj*] to devote or commit (something or someone) to some cause: *He dedicated himself to the clean-up of the river.* **2.** [~ + *obj* + *to* + *obj*] to offer (something) formally to a person or cause as a sign of respect: *I'd like to dedicate our first song to my mother.* **3.** [~ + *obj*] to mark the official opening of (a public building or highway), by formal ceremonies: *The school dedicated the new building on Sunday.* **4.** [~ + *obj*] to set aside for a specific purpose: *dedicated the money to charity.*

ded•i•cat•ed (ded′i kā′tid) /'dɛdɪˌkeytɪd/ *adj.* **1.** relating to or marked by dedication: *completely dedicated to the team.* **2.** [*often: before a noun*] set apart for a specific use, as a computer for a specific application: *a dedicated word processor.*

ded•i•ca•tion (ded′i kā′shən) /ˌdɛdɪ'keyʃən/ *n.* **1.** [*noncount*] commitment, interest, or work in achieving a goal: *complete dedication to her students.* **2.** [*count*] an inscription at the beginning of a book, offered as a sign of respect or thanks: *The dedication read simply "To my husband."* **3.** [*count*] a ceremony of formally opening something for a particular use: *the dedication of the new cathedral.*

de•duce (di do͞os′, -dyo͞os′) /dɪ'duws, -'dyuws/ *v.,* **-duced, -duc•ing.** to figure out (something) as a conclusion from something else; infer: [~ + *obj*]: *to deduce the path of the hurricane.* [~ + (*that*) *clause*]: *From her conversation I deduced that she had a large family.* **—de•duc′i•ble,** *adj.* See -DUC-.

de•duct (di dukt′) /dɪ'dʌkt/ *v.* [~ + *obj* (+ *from* + *obj*)] to take away from a total: *How much of this expense can you deduct from your taxes?* **—de•duct′i•ble,** *adj.: Is this income deductible?* See -DUC-.

de•duc•tion (di duk′shən) /dɪ'dʌkʃən/ *n.* **1. a.** [*noncount*] the act or process of deducting. **b.** [*count*] something that is or may be deducted: *a deduction of 10%.* **2. a.** [*noncount*] the act or process of inferring from known facts to a conclusion; the act or process of deducing: *remarkable powers of deduction.* **b.** [*count*] something deduced from known facts: *It was the detective's deduction that the robbery was an inside job.* **3. a.** [*noncount*] a process of reasoning in which a conclusion must follow from the premises presented; reasoning or concluding from the general to the particular or specific. **b.** [*count*] a conclusion reached by this process. **—de•duc•tive** (di-duk′tiv) /dɪ'dʌktɪv/ *adj.* See -DUC-.

deed (dēd) /diyd/ *n.* [*count*] **1.** something that is done; an act: *a good deed.* **2.** an achievement; feat: *deeds of daring.* **3.** an official record of a sale or a transfer of ownership, such as of a house: *Do you have the deed to the house in a safe place?* **—*v.*** [~ + *obj*] **4.** to transfer by deed: *deeded the property to his sons.*

dee•jay (dē′jā′) /'diyˌdʒey/ *n.* DISC JOCKEY.

deem (dēm) /diym/ *v.* [*not: be* + ~*-ing*] to have as an opinion; believe: [~ + *obj* + (*to be*) + *noun*]: *The council deemed him to be a traitor.*

de-em•pha•size (dē em′fə sīz′) /diy'ɛmfəˌsayz/ *v.* [~ + *obj*], **-sized, -siz•ing.** to place less emphasis upon; reduce the importance of: *to de-emphasize sports.* **—de-em•pha•sis** (dē em′fə sis) /diy'ɛmfəsɪs/ *n.* [*count*]

deep (dēp) /diyp/ *adj.* and *adv.,* **-er, -est,** *n.* **—*adj.* 1.** extending far down from the top or surface: *a deep well.* **2.** extending far in or back from the front: *a deep shelf.* **3.** extending far in width; broad: *a deep border.* **4.** [*after a noun indicating measurement*] having a certain specified dimension or amount in depth: *a tank 10 feet deep.* **5.** [~ + in] immersed or submerged: *The road was deep in snow.* **6.** [*before a noun*] coming from far down: *Now, take a deep breath.* **7.** made with the body bent or lowered to a considerable degree: *a deep curtsy.* **8.** difficult to understand; abstruse; *a book too deep for young children.* **9.** not superficial; serious; profound: *deep thoughts.* **10.** [*before a noun*] sincere; intense; great: *deep affections.* **11.** [*before a noun*] sound and heavy; undisturbed: *deep sleep.* **12.** strong, dark, and vivid in color: *a deep red.* **13.** low in pitch, such as sound: *a deep, rich voice.* **14.** mysterious; hidden: *deep secrets.* **15.** [~ + *in*] involved to a great extent: *to be deep in debt.* **16.** [*be* + ~ + *in*] giving one's full attention; absorbed; engrossed: *He was deep in thought.* **—*adv.* 17.** to or at a considerable or great depth: *We were about ten feet deep when our ears popped.* **18.** [*after a number, noun, or adjective indicating measurement*] to a depth or breadth of (the number, noun, or adjective mentioned): *The fans were lined up three deep around the block.* **19.** far on in time; late: *They worked deep into the night.* **20.** within; far down: *I still feel love for her deep in my heart.* **—*n.*** [*noncount*] **21.** [*often: the* + ~ + *of*] the midpoint or the part of greatest intensity: *the deep of winter; in the deep of the night.* **22. the deep,** *Literary.* the sea or ocean: *The deep was the drowned sailor's final resting place.* **—*Idiom.* 23. go off the deep end, a.** to become emotionally overwrought: *She went off the deep end when she was turned down for promotion.* **b.** to act without enough thought of the consequences: *The committee went off the deep end with the Christmas decorations.* **24. in deep,** involved: *He was in too deep with her and had to break off their relationship.* **25. in deep water,** in serious trouble: *The company is in deep water and can barely make ends meet.* **—deep′ly,** *adv.* **—deep′ness,** *n.* [*noncount*]

deep•en (dē′pən) /'diypən/ *v.* to (cause to) become deep or deeper: [*no obj*]: *Our troubles are deepening the more we get into debt.* [~ + *obj*]: *a silence that only deepened the mystery.*

deep′ freeze′, *n.* [*noncount*] the storage of food, furs, etc., in a place kept artificially cold.

deep′-freeze′, *v.* [~ + *obj*], **-freezed** or **-froze, -freezed** or **-fro•zen, -freez•ing. 1.** to quick-freeze (food): *They had deep-frozen the fish well ahead of time.* **2.** to store in a frozen state.

deep′-fry′, *v.* [~ + *obj*], **-fried, -fry•ing.** to fry in an amount of hot oil or fat that is enough to cover the food being cooked.

deep′-root′ed, *adj.* firmly implanted, fixed, or established: *a deep-rooted fear of strangers.*

deep′-sea′, *adj.* [*before a noun*] of or relating to the deeper parts of the sea: *deep-sea fishing.*

deep′-seat′ed, *adj.* firmly implanted, fixed, or established; unchanging: *a deep-seated loyalty.*

deep′ space′, *n.* [*noncount*] space beyond the solar system. Also called **outer space.**

deer (dēr) /dɪər/ *n.* [*count*], *pl.* **deer.** any of several cud-chewing animals, the males of which usually have antlers.

de-es•ca•late or **de•es•ca•late** (dē es′kə lāt′) /diy'ɛskə,leyt/ *v.*, **-lat•ed, -lat•ing.** to decrease in intensity, danger, or amount: [*no obj*]: *The war began to de-escalate.* [~ + *obj*]: *began to de-escalate the war.* —**de-es•ca•la•tion** (dē es′kə lā′shən) /diy,ɛskə'leyʃən/ *n.* [*noncount*]

def (def) /dɛf/ *adj. Slang.* excellent: *That hip-hop record is def!*

de•face (di fās′) /dɪ'feys/ *v.* [~ + *obj*], **-faced, -fac•ing.** to mar the surface or appearance of, such as by marking; disfigure: *defacing all the posters.* —**de•face′ment,** *n.* [*noncount*] See -FACE-.

de fac•to (dē fak′tō, dā) /diy 'fæktow, dey/ *adv.* **1.** in fact; in reality: *The army occupied the city de facto.* —*adj.* [*before a noun*] **2.** actually existing, esp. without lawful authority: *a situation of de facto segregation in most cities of the country.* See -FAC-.

def•a•ma•tion (def′ə mā′shən) /,dɛfə'meyʃən/ *n.* [*noncount*] the act of defaming: *He sued the newspaper for defamation of character.*

de•fam•a•to•ry (di fam′ə tôr′ē, -tōr′ē) /dɪ'fæmə,tɔriy, -,towriy/ *adj.* relating to or marked by defamation: *made defamatory statements about his opponent.*

de•fame (di fām′) /dɪ'feym/ *v.* [~ + *obj*], **-famed, -fam•ing.** to attack the good name or reputation of; slander or libel: *The candidates seem to enjoy defaming each other.*

de•fault (di fôlt′) /dɪ'fɔlt/ *n.* [*noncount*] **1.** failure to act, esp. failure to pay one's debts: *to face financial default.* **2.** failure to appear for or complete a match: *progressed into the finals because of his opponent's default.* **3.** a preset value that a computer system assumes or an action that it takes unless it is otherwise instructed: *When you start your computer from the A drive, then that is the default for later disk operations.* —*v.* **4.** [*no obj*] to fail to pay, perform a duty, etc.: *The bank had defaulted on that loan.* **5.** *Sports.* to fail to compete in (a contest); to lose by default: [*no obj*]: *He defaulted and left the tournament.* [~ + *obj*]: *He defaulted the match and left in disgust.* —***Idiom.*** **6. in default of,** for lack of; in the absence of: *In default of a workable plan they decided to proceed on a day-to-day basis.* —**de•fault′er,** *n.* [*count*]

de•feat (di fēt′) /dɪ'fiyt/ *v.* [~ + *obj*] **1.** to overcome in a contest; beat: *He was defeated in the last election.* **2.** to frustrate; thwart: *This kind of problem always defeats me.* —*n.* **3.** [*noncount*] the act of overcoming in a contest: *didn't accept defeat well.* **4.** [*count*] an instance of defeat; setback: *He suffered several defeats in close elections.* —**de•feat′er,** *n.* [*count*]

de•feat•ism (di fē′tiz əm) /dɪ'fiytɪzəm/ *n.* [*noncount*] the attitude of a person who expects defeat and thinks that further struggle is useless and hopeless: *defeatism in the face of likely losses.* —**de•feat′ist,** *n.* [*count*], *adj.*

def•e•cate (def′i kāt′) /'dɛfɪ,keyt/ *v.* [*no obj*], **-cat•ed, -cat•ing.** to pass waste matter from the bowels through the anus out of the body. —**def•e•ca•tion** (def′i kā′shən) /,dɛfɪ'keyʃən/ *n.* [*noncount*] See -FEC-.

de•fect (*n.* dē′fekt, di fekt′; *v.* di fekt′) / *n.* 'diyfɛkt, dɪ'fɛkt; *v.* dɪ'fɛkt/ *n.* [*count*] **1.** a fault or shortcoming; imperfection: *What defect in his character made him lie?* —*v.* [*no obj*] **2.** to desert a cause, country, etc., and go over to the opponent's side: *Would the spies want to defect to the West?* —**de•fec′tion,** *n.* [*noncount*]: *the defection of several members of the ambassador's staff.* [*count*]: *Defections increased during the crisis.* See -FEC-.

de•fec•tive (di fek′tiv) /dɪ'fɛktɪv/ *adj.* faulty; imperfect; not working properly or effectively: *One of the tires was defective.* See -FEC-.

de•fend (di fend′) /dɪ'fɛnd/ *v.* [~ + *obj*] **1.** ward off attack from; protect: *The armed forces defend our country.* **2.** to support or maintain by argument, evidence, etc.; uphold: *He defended the principle of freedom of the press.* **3.** to serve as attorney for (a defendant) in a trial: *defended her clients against the charge of conspiracy.* **4.** to attempt to retain (a championship title) in competition against a challenger. —**de•fend′er,** *n.* [*count*] —**Related Words.** DEFEND is a verb, DEFENSE is a noun, DEFENSIVE is an adjective: *The lawyer agreed to defend the murder suspect. The team's defense kept a lot of points from being scored. He seems defensive when you ask him what's wrong.* See -FEND-.

de•fend•ant (di fen′dənt) /dɪ'fɛndənt/ *n.* [*count*] one against whom a legal action is brought in a court: *The defendant had been accused by the manager of stealing from the company.*

de•fense (di fens′ *or, esp. for 8,* dē′fens) /dɪ'fɛns *or, esp. for 8,* 'diyfɛns/ *n.*, *v.*, **-fensed, -fens•ing.** —*n.* **1.** [*noncount*] a means of defending: *a weapon of defense.* **2.** [*count*] something that defends or protects: *We'll have to strengthen our border defenses.* **3.** [*noncount*] the arms production of a nation: *spending billions on defense.* **4.** [*noncount*] the defending of a cause by argument: *to speak in defense of anti-pollution laws.* **5.** [*count*] an argument defending some cause: *The speech was a brilliant defense of the notion of civil rights for all.* **6.** [*count; usually singular; often: the* + ~] the strategy adopted by a defendant for defending against the plaintiff's charge: *We'll base our defense on the testimony of the two witnesses.* **7.** DEFENSE MECHANISM. **8.** [*count*] **a.** the tactics or strategy of defending against attack. **b.** the players or team attempting to resist the attack of a team having the ball, puck, etc. —*v.* [~ + *obj*] **9.** to defend against (an opponent, play, etc.). —**de•fense′less,** *adj.* See -FEND-.

defense′ mech′anism, *n.* [*count*] an unconscious process, such as denial, that protects an individual from unacceptable or painful ideas or impulses.

de•fen•sible (di fen′sə bəl) /dɪ'fɛnsəbəl/ *adj.* that can be defended: *His client's conduct was defensible.*

de•fen•sive (di fen′siv) /dɪ'fɛnsɪv/ *adj.* **1.** [*before a noun*] of or relating to defense: *defensive weapons.* **2.** sensitive to criticism: *There's no need to be so defensive.* —*n.* [*noncount*] **3. on the defensive,** to be in a position or attitude of defense; to be sensitive to criticism. See -FEND-.

de•fer[1] (di fûr′) /dɪ'fɜr/ *v.* [~ + *obj*], **-ferred, -fer•ring. 1.** to postpone; delay; put off action on: *The pension is deferred until after age 65.* **2.** to exempt temporarily from being drafted into military service: *He was deferred because he was in college.* —**de•fer′ment,** *n.* [*count*]: *He tried to get a deferment from military service.* See -FER-.

de•fer[2] (di fûr′) /dɪ'fɜr/ *v.* [~ + *to* + *obj*], **-ferred, -fer•ring.** to yield respectfully in judgment or opinion: *I deferred to my father's authority.* See -FER-.

def•er•ence (def′ər əns) /'dɛfərəns/ *n.* [*noncount*] **1.** respectful yielding to the will of another: *In deference to her superior knowledge, I decided to follow her advice.* **2.** respectful or courteous behavior or attitude toward: *treated her with deference.* See -FER-. —**def•er•en•tial** (def′ə ren′shəl) /,dɛfə'rɛnʃəl/ *adj.* —**def′er•en′tial•ly,** *adv.*

de•fi•ance (di fī′əns) /dɪ'fayəns/ *n.* [*noncount*] **1.** a bold resistance to authority; open disregard or contempt: *The strike was an act of open defiance.* —***Idiom.*** **2. in defiance of,** despite; notwithstanding: *In defiance of all the rules, demonstrators marched in front of the presidential mansion.*

de•fi•ant (di fī′ənt) /dɪ'fayənt/ *adj.* relating to or marked by defiance: *a defiant attitude.* —**de•fi′ant•ly,** *adv.*

de•fi•cien•cy (di fish′ən sē) /dɪ'fɪʃənsiy/ *n.*, *pl.* **-cies. 1.** [*noncount*] the state or condition of lacking something: *suffering from vitamin deficiency.* **2.** [*count*] something lacking: *a patient with a calcium deficiency.* **3.** [*count*] something imperfect; flaw; defect: *In spite of its deficiencies, this is basically a very good paper.*

de•fi•cient (di fish′ənt) /dɪ'fɪʃənt/ *adj.* relating to or marked by deficiency: *deficient in math skills.*

def•i•cit (def′ə sit) /'dɛfəsɪt/ *n.* [*count*] **1.** the amount by which a sum of money falls short of the required amount. **2.** a loss, such as in the operation of a business. **3.** the amount by which spending exceeds income: *the staggering amount of the Federal deficit.*

de•file[1] (di fīl′) /dɪˈfayl/ *v.* [~ + *obj*], **-filed, -fil•ing. 1.** to make foul, dirty, or unclean. **2.** to desecrate: *The infidels had defiled the shrine.* **3.** to dishonor or spoil: *Insults alone will not defile his honor.* —**de•file′ment,** *n.* [*noncount*] —**de•fil′er,** *n.* [*count*]

de•file[2] (di fīl′, dē′fīl) /dɪˈfayl, ˈdiyfayl/ *n.* [*count*] a narrow passage, esp. between mountains.

de•fine (di fīn′) /dɪˈfayn/ *v.* [~ + *obj*], **-fined, -fin•ing. 1.** to set forth the meaning of: *His job was to define new words that were not yet in the dictionaries.* **2.** to explain or identify the nature of; describe: *We had to define what our problems were before we could solve them.* **3.** to determine or fix the boundaries of; specify clearly: *to define responsibilities.* **4.** to make clear the outline or form of; delineate: *The black tree was clearly defined against a yellow background.* —**de•fin′er,** *n.* [*count*] See **-FIN-.**

def•i•nite (def′ə nit) /ˈdɛfənɪt/ *adj.* **1.** clearly defined; precise: *a definite period of time.* **2.** positive; certain; sure: *He was definite about his feelings.* **3.** clear; with no uncertainty: *I want a definite answer.* —**def′i•nite•ness,** *n.* [*noncount*] See **-FIN-.**

def′inite ar′ticle, *n.* [*count*] an article, such as English *the,* that modifies a noun which is already known to the speaker and hearer.

def•i•nite•ly (def′ə nit lē) /ˈdɛfənɪtliy/ *adv.* certainly; surely; doubtlessly: *She will definitely have a place on the team next year.*

def•i•ni•tion (def′ə nish′ən) /ˌdɛfəˈnɪʃən/ *n.* **1.** [*count*] the formal statement of the meaning of something: *She wrote definitions for "quark" and "atom."* **2.** [*noncount*] the condition of being definite: *The photograph has fine definition.* **3.** [*noncount*] sharpness of the image formed by an optical system: *Adjust the definition on the TV monitor.* See **-FIN-.**

de•fin•i•tive (di fin′i tiv) /dɪˈfɪnɪtɪv/ *adj.* **1.** serving to define, set, or specify definitely: *gave a definitive statement on the crisis.* **2.** most reliable or complete: *the definitive text on disorders of the circulatory system.* —**de•fin′i•tive•ly,** *adv.*

de•flate (di flāt′) /dɪˈfleyt/ *v.,* **-flat•ed, -flat•ing. 1.** [~ + *obj*] to release the air or gas from (something inflated): *They deflated the tire tubes and changed the outer walls.* **2.** [*no obj*] (of something inflated) to have the air or gas be released from: *The tire quickly deflated when it was punctured by the nail.* **3.** [~ + *obj*] to lessen or reduce (one's hopes); dash: *The bad news really deflated our hopes for improvement.* **4.** [~ + *obj*] to reduce (currency or prices) from an inflated condition: *The economy was badly deflated.* See **-FLAT-.**

de•fla•tion (di flā′shən) /dɪˈfleyʃən/ *n.* [*noncount*] **1.** the act of deflating or the state of being deflated: *a feeling of deflation after all that bad news.* **2.** a fall in the general price level or a contraction of credit and available money in the economy.

de•flect (di flekt′) /dɪˈflɛkt/ *v.* **1.** to bend or turn aside: [*no obj*]: *The shot deflected into the net past the goalie.* [~ + *obj*]: *He deflected the shot past the goalie.* **2.** [~ + *obj*] to divert; turn aside and reduce the harm of: *He managed to deflect criticism onto someone else.* —**de•flec•tion** (di flek′shən) /dɪˈflɛkʃən/ *n.* [*noncount*]: *deflection of any criticism that came his way.* [*count*]: *scored on several deflections past the goalie.* —**de•flec′tor,** *n.* [*count*] See **-FLECT-.**

de•fog (dē fog′, -fôg′) /diyˈfɒg, -ˈfɔg/ *v.* [~ + *obj*], **-fogged, -fog•ging.** to remove the fog or moisture from (a car window). —**de•fog′ger,** *n.* [*count*]: *An automatic defogger is standard for that car.*

de•fo•li•ant (dē fō′lē ənt) /diyˈfowliyənt/ *n.* [*count*] a chemical preparation for defoliating plants. See **-FOLI-.**

de•fo•li•ate (dē fō′lē āt′) /diyˈfowliyˌeyt/ *v.* [~ + *obj*], **-at•ed, -at•ing. 1.** to strip the leaves off. **2.** to destroy or cause widespread loss of leaves in (an area of jungle). —**de•fo′li•a′tion,** *n.* [*noncount*] —**de•fo′li•a′tor,** *n.* [*count*] See **-FOLI-.**

de•for•est (dē fôr′ist, -for′-) /diyˈfɔrɪst, -ˈfɒr-/ *v.* [~ + *obj*] to remove the trees and forests of: *environmentalists working to prevent the pharmaceutical companies from deforesting that land.* —**de•for•est•a•tion** (dē fôr′i stā′shən, -for′-) /diyˌfɔrɪˈsteyʃən, -ˌfɒr-/ *n.* [*noncount*]: *against deforestation of the Amazon.*

de•form (di fôrm′) /dɪˈfɔrm/ *v.* [~ + *obj*] **1.** to mar the natural form of; disfigure: *a body badly deformed by a birth defect.* **2.** to mar the beauty of; spoil: *How could they deform such a beautiful landscape?* —**de•for•ma•tion** (dē′fôr mā′shən) /ˌdiyfɔrˈmeyʃən/ *n.* [*noncount; count*] See **-FORM-.**

de•formed (di fôrmd′) /dɪˈfɔrmd/ *adj.* misshapen; disfigured: *deformed as the result of an injury.*

de•form•i•ty (di fôr′mi tē) /dɪˈfɔrmɪtiy/ *n., pl.* **-ties. 1.** [*noncount*] the quality or state of being deformed: *the causes of birth deformity.* **2.** [*count*] an improperly formed part of the body: *a deformity that makes walking difficult.* See **-FORM-.**

de•fraud (di frôd′) /dɪˈfrɔd/ *v.* [~ + *obj* + *of* + *obj*] to deprive of a right, money, or property by fraud: *He defrauded them of their life savings.* —**de•fraud′er,** *n.* [*count*]

de•fray (di frā′) /dɪˈfrey/ *v.* [~ + *obj*], to pay all or part of: *to help defray some of the costs.*

de•frost (di frôst′, -frost′) /dɪˈfrɔst, -ˈfrɒst/ *v.* **1.** to (cause to) become free of ice or frost: [~ + *obj*]: *We defrosted the refrigerator again.* [*no obj*]: *The refrigerator is defrosting.* **2.** to thaw (frozen food): [~ + *obj*]: *Defrost the meat in the microwave.* [*no obj*]: *The meat is on the counter defrosting.* —**de•frost′er,** *n.* [*count*]

deft (deft) /dɛft/ *adj.,* **-er, -est.** skillful; nimble; quick: *She returned the serve with a deft backhand.* —**deft′ly,** *adv.*

de•funct (di fungkt′) /dɪˈfʌŋkt/ *adj.* **1.** no longer in effect or use: *a defunct law.* **2.** no longer in existence; dead. See **-FUNCT-.**

de•fuse (dē fyōōz′) /diyˈfyuwz/ *v.* [~ + *obj*], **-fused, -fus•ing. 1.** to remove the fuse from (a bomb). **2.** to make less dangerous or tense: *defused a tense situation.* See **-FUS-.**

de•fy (di fī′) /dɪˈfay/ *v.,* **-fied, -fy•ing. 1.** [~ + *obj*] to challenge the power of; resist boldly or openly: *They seemed to enjoy defying my authority.* **2.** [~ + *obj* + *to* + *verb*] to challenge (a person) to do something thought of as impossible: *I defy you to tell the difference between these two brands.* **3.** to offer resistance to; withstand: [~ + *obj*]: *The plane seems to defy gravity.* [~ + *obj* + *to* + *verb*]: *The problem defies all attempts to solve it.*

de•gen•er•ate (*v.* di jen′ə rāt′; *adj., n.* -ər it) / *v.* dɪˈdʒɛnəˌreyt; *adj., n.* -ərɪt/ *v.,* **-at•ed, -at•ing,** *adj., n.* —*v.* [*no obj*] **1.** to decline or get worse in personal qualities; deteriorate: *Idleness caused his character to degenerate.* **2.** [~ (+ *into* + *obj*)] to lower or become lower in quality; fall from a high or normal standard. —*adj.* **3.** having declined in personal qualities; deteriorated; degraded; depraved: *a degenerate ruler.* —*n.* [*count*] **4.** a person who has declined, esp. in morals, from a standard: *a drunken degenerate.* —**de•gen•er•a•cy** (di jen′ər ə sē) /dɪˈdʒɛnərəsiy/ *n.* [*noncount*] —**de•gen•er•a•tion** (di jen′ə rā′shən) /dɪˌdʒɛnəˈreyʃən/ *n.* [*noncount*]: *physical degeneration.* —**de•gen′er•a•tive** (-ər ə tiv, -ə rā′tiv) /-ərətɪv, -əˌreytɪv/ *adj.* See **-GEN-.**

de•grade (di grād′) /dɪˈgreyd/ *v.,* **-grad•ed, -grad•ing. 1.** [~ + *obj*] to lower in dignity or in respect; debase: *She wouldn't degrade herself by cheating.* **2.** [*no obj*] (esp. of an organic compound) to break down or decompose: *plastics that degrade for a thousand years.* —**deg•ra•da•tion** (deg′rə dā′shən) /ˌdɛgrəˈdeyʃən/ *n.* [*noncount*]: *facing the degradation of their liberty.* —**de•gra′ding,** *adj.*: *a degrading task.* See **-GRAD-.**

de•gree (di grē′) /dɪˈgriy/ *n.* [*count*] **1.** any of a series of steps or stages; a point in any scale; level; grade: *improved by degrees.* **2.** extent or scope of an action or state: *I go along with them to a certain degree.* **3.** a stage in a scale of rank or station: *a lord of high degree.* **4.** an academic title given upon the completion of studies, or as an honorary recognition of achievement: *a Master's degree.* **5.** a unit of measure, esp. of temperature, marked on the scale of a measuring instrument: *The thermometer said it was 26 degrees outside.* **6.** the 360th part of the circumference of a circle, often represented by the sign °: *an angle of 45°.* **7.** the classification of a crime according to its seriousness: *murder in the first degree.* **8.** one of the set of forms of adjectives and adverbs used to express differences in quality, quantity, or intensity. —***Idiom.*** **9. by degrees,** by easy stages; gradually.

de•hu•man•ize (dē hyōō′mə nīz′) /diyˈhyuwməˌnayz/ *v.* [~ + *obj*], **-ized, -iz•ing.** to deprive of human qualities: *Brutal treatment dehumanized the prisoners.* —**de•hu•man•i•za•tion** (dē hyōō′mə nə zā′shən) /diyˌhyuwmənəˈzeyʃən/ *n.* [*noncount*] —**de•hu′ma•niz′ing,** *adj.*

de•hu•mid•i•fi•er (dē′hyōō mid′ə fī′ər) /ˌdiyhyuwˈmɪdəˌfayər/ *n.* [*count*] a device for removing moisture from indoor air. —**de′hu•mid′i•fy,** *v.* [~ + *obj*], **-fied, -fy•ing.**

de•hy•drate (dē hī′drāt) /diyˈhaydreyt/ *v.* [~ + *obj*], **-drat•ed, -drat•ing.** to remove water from, esp. to free (fruit, vegetables, etc.) from moisture in order to preserve; dry: *The vegetables were dehydrated and sealed in packages.* —**de•hy•dra•tion** (dē′hī drā′shən) /ˌdiyhay'dreyʃən/ *n.* [*noncount*]

de•ice or **de-ice** (dē īs′) /diy'ays/ *v.* [~ + *obj*], **-iced, -ic•ing.** to free (something, such as a windshield) of ice; prevent or remove ice. —**de•ic′er, de-ic′er,** *n.* [*count*]

de•i•fy (dē′ə fī′) /'diyəˌfay/ *v.* [~ + *obj*], **-fied, -fy•ing.** to make a god of; worship as a god: *to deify wealth.* —**de•i•fi•ca•tion** (dē′ə fi kā′shən) /ˌdiyəfɪ'keyʃən/ *n.* [*noncount*]: *deification of the Roman emperors.*

deign (dān) /deyn/ *v.* [~ + *to* + *verb*] to consider to be fit, proper, or in accordance with one's dignity: *She would not deign to visit us.*

de•i•ty (dē′i tē) /'diyɪtiy/ *n., pl.* **-ties. 1.** [*count*] a god or goddess. **2. the Deity,** [*proper noun; the* + ~] God.

dé•jà vu (dā′zhä vo͞o′, vyo͞o′) /ˌdeyʒɑ 'vuw, 'vyuw/ *n.* [*noncount*] the illusion of having experienced something that is actually being encountered for the first time.

de•ject•ed (di jek′tid) /dɪ'dʒɛktɪd/ *adj.* depressed in spirits; disheartened; low-spirited: *He was dejected when she turned down his proposal.* —**de•jec′ted•ly,** *adv.*: *She answered dejectedly that she had failed.* —**de•jec•tion** (di jek′shən) /dɪ'dʒɛkʃən/ *n.* [*noncount*]: *feelings of dejection.*

Del., an abbreviation of: Delaware.

de•lay (di lā′) /dɪ'ley/ *v.* **1.** to put off to a later time; postpone: [~ + *verb-ing*]: *The principal delayed opening the school.* [~ + *obj*]: *The committee delayed action on the matter.* **2.** [~ + *obj*] to interfere with the progress of; slow down; hold back: *The fog delayed the plane's landing.* **3.** [*no obj*] to put off action; linger; loiter: *If you delay now, you'll just have to do more later.* —*n.* **4.** [*noncount*] the act of delaying; procrastination; loitering: *Please finish your work without delay.* **5.** [*count*] a postponement: *a delay of forty-eight hours.* **6.** [*count*] an act or instance of being delayed; stoppage: *The delay was caused by a three-car accident.* —**de•lay′er,** *n.* [*count*] —**de•lay′ing,** *adj.* [*before a noun*]: *delaying tactics designed to wear us out.*

de•lec•ta•ble (di lek′tə bəl) /dɪ'lɛktəbəl/ *adj.* delightful; highly pleasing; attractive: *a delectable meal.*

del•e•gate (*n.* del′i git; *v.* -gāt′) / *n.* 'dɛlɪgɪt; *v.* -ˌgeyt/ *n., v.,* **-gat•ed, -gat•ing.** —*n.* [*count*] **1.** a person authorized to act for another; agent; representative: *delegates from a union.* —*v.* **2.** [~ + *obj* (+ *to* + *verb*)] to send or appoint (someone) as a representative: *We have delegated her to represent our city.* **3.** [~ + *obj* (+ *to* + *obj*)] to commit (powers) to another as agent: *He delegated his authority to me.* See -LEG-.

del•e•ga•tion (del′i gā′shən) /ˌdɛlɪ'geyʃən/ *n.* **1.** [*count*] a group or body of delegates: *We sent a delegation in to see the boss.* **2.** [*noncount*] the act of delegating: *delegation of authority.* See -LEG-.

de•lete (di lēt′) /dɪ'liyt/ *v.* [~ + *obj*], **-let•ed, -let•ing.** to strike out or remove (something written or printed); cancel; erase. —**de•le•tion** (di lē′shən) /dɪ'liyʃən/ *n.* [*noncount*]: *Mark those paragraphs for deletion.* [*count*]: *deletions from the list.*

del•e•te•ri•ous (del′i tēr′ē əs) /ˌdɛlɪ'tɪəriyəs/ *adj.* injurious to health; harmful: *the deleterious effects of the drug.*

del•i (del′ē) /'dɛliy/ *n.* [*count*], *pl.* **del•is** (del′ēz) /'dɛliyz/. delicatessen: *She missed the deli when she moved away.*

de•lib•er•ate (*adj.* di lib′ər it; *v.* -ə rāt′) / *adj.* dɪ'lɪbərɪt; *v.* -əˌreyt/ *adj., v.,* **-at•ed, -at•ing.** —*adj.* **1.** relating to or marked by deliberation: *a deliberate lie.* **2.** careful, slow, even, or unhurried: *a deliberate decision; deliberate speech.* —*v.* **3.** to weigh in the mind; consider: [~ + *obj*]: *to deliberate a question.* [~ + *clause*]: *They deliberated whether to hire him or not.* [*no obj*]: *The jury deliberated for three hours.* —**de•lib•er•ate•ly** (di lib′ər it-lē) /dɪ'lɪbərɪtliy/ *adv.*: *They lied deliberately.* See -LIBRA-.

de•lib•er•a•tion (di lib′ə rā′shən) /dɪˌlɪbə'reyʃən/ *n.* **1.** [*noncount*] careful, unhurried consideration before decision: *planned with great deliberation.* **2.** [*count*] a formal consultation or discussion: *Their deliberations went on for hours.* **3.** [*noncount*] deliberate quality; leisureliness of action: *examined the painting with great deliberation.*

del•i•ca•cy (del′i kə sē) /'dɛlɪkəsiy/ *n., pl.* **-cies. 1.** [*noncount*] fineness of texture or quality: softness; daintiness: *the delicacy of lace.* **2.** [*count*] something delightful or pleasing, esp. a food: *delicacies that aroused the appetite.* **3.** [*noncount*] the quality of being easily broken; fragility: *the delicacy of his health.* **4.** [*noncount*] the quality of requiring or involving great care or consideration of others: *negotiations of great delicacy.*

del•i•cate (del′i kit) /'dɛlɪkɪt/ *adj.* **1.** relating to or marked by delicacy. **2.** so fine as to be scarcely felt or sensed: *a light, delicate flavor.* **3.** soft or faint, as in color: *Paint the walls a delicate blue.* **4.** requiring great care, caution, or tact: *delicate negotiations; a delicate topic.* **5.** capable of noticing or distinguishing subtle differences; sensitive: *That instrument is so delicate it can detect earthquakes thousands of miles away.* **6.** easily disgusted; squeamish: *a violent movie not for the delicate viewer.* —**del′i•cate•ly,** *adv.* —**del′i•cate•ness,** *n.* [*noncount*]

del•i•ca•tes•sen (del′i kə tes′ən) /ˌdɛlɪkə'tɛsən/ *n.* [*count*] a store selling ready-to-eat foods.

de•li•cious (di lish′əs) /dɪ'lɪʃəs/ *adj.* **1.** pleasing to the senses, esp. taste or smell: *delicious chocolate cake.* **2.** very amusing; delightful: *delicious gossip.* —**de•li′cious•ly,** *adv.*: *deliciously prepared foods.* —**de•li′cious•ness,** *n.* [*noncount*]

de•light (di līt′) /dɪ'layt/ *n.* **1.** [*noncount*] great enjoyment; joy; happiness: *I get a great deal of delight from watching my children read their books.* **2.** [*count*] something that gives great pleasure: *The zoo is a delight to visit.* —*v.* **3.** [~ + *obj*] to give delight to: *The circus will delight young and old alike.* **4.** [~ + *in* + *verb-ing*] to have or take great pleasure: *She delights in walking.* —**de•light′ed,** *adj.*: [*be* + ~ + *to* + *verb*] *I was delighted to see you.*

de•light•ful (di līt′fəl) /dɪ'laytfəl/ *adj.* giving delight; highly pleasing: *a delightful surprise.* —**de•light′ful•ly,** *adv.*

de•lim•it (di lim′it) /dɪ'lɪmɪt/ *v.* [~ + *obj*] to mark or establish the limits or boundaries of: *to delimit the powers of the special UN task force in the region.*

de•lin•e•ate (di lin′ē āt′) /dɪ'lɪniyˌeyt/ *v.* [~ + *obj*], **-at•ed, -at•ing. 1.** to trace the outline of. **2.** to portray or describe in words: *He delineated a few of his proposals for the budget.* —**de•lin•e•a•tion** (di lin′ē ā′shən) /dɪˌlɪniy'eyʃən/ *n.* [*count*]: *delineations of new proposals.* [*noncount*]: *precise, careful delineation.* See -LIN-.

de•lin•quent (di ling′kwənt) /dɪ'lɪŋkwənt/ *adj.* **1.** guilty of a misdeed or offense. **2.** past due: *a delinquent account.* —*n.* [*count*] **3.** a person who is delinquent, esp. a juvenile delinquent. —**de•lin′quen•cy,** *n.* [*noncount; count*] *pl.* **-cies.** —**de•lin′quent•ly,** *adv.*

de•lir•i•ous (di lēr′ē əs) /dɪ'lɪəriyəs/ *adj.* **1.** relating to or marked by delirium: *delirious with fever.* **2.** wild with excitement, enthusiasm, etc.: *The crowd at the concert became delirious.* —**de•lir′i•ous•ly,** *adv.*: *moaning deliriously through the night.* —**de•lir′i•ous•ness,** *n.* [*noncount*]

de•lir•i•um (di lēr′ē əm) /dɪ'lɪəriyəm/ *n.* [*count*], *pl.* **-i•ums, -i•a** (-ē ə) /-iyə/. **1.** a temporary mental disturbance marked by restlessness, excitement, and delusions. **2.** a state of violent or great excitement or emotion: *The crowd went into a delirium.*

de•liv•er (di liv′ər) /dɪ'lɪvər/ *v.* **1.** [~ + *obj*] to carry and turn over to the person receiving: *delivered the letter last week.* **2.** [*no obj*] to provide a service for carrying and turning over letters, goods, and products: *That pizza place delivers at no extra charge.* **3.** [~ + *obj*] to give into another's possession or keeping; hand over; surrender: *to deliver a prisoner to the police.* **4.** [~ + *obj*] to give forth in words; utter or pronounce: *to deliver a speech.* **5.** [~ + *obj*] to strike or throw: *to deliver a blow.* **6.** [~ + *obj* + *from* + *obj*] to set free or liberate; save: *Moses delivered his people from bondage.* **7.** [~ + *obj*] to help or assist at the birth of: *The doctor delivered the baby.* **8.** to do or carry out (something) as promised: [~ + *obj*]: *In this job you have to deliver results.* [*no obj*]: *I expect you to deliver on your promises soon.* See -LIBER-.

de•liv•er•ance (di liv′ər əns) /dɪ'lɪvərəns/ *n.* [*noncount*] **1.** an act or instance of delivering. **2.** the act of being set free; salvation; liberation; rescue.

de•liv•er•y (di liv′ə rē) /dɪ'lɪvəriy/ *n., pl.* **-ies. 1.** the act of delivering: [*count*]: *A delivery on weekends would be nice.* [*noncount*]: *Mail delivery was never regular.* **2.** [*count*] something delivered: *Bring the deliveries to the back door.* **3.** [*noncount*] manner of giving a speech, such as the pronunciation or choice of words: *the speaker's fine delivery.* **4.** [*noncount*] the act or manner of giving or sending forth: *the pitcher's delivery of the ball.* **5.** [*count*] the act of giving birth to a child: *an easy delivery.*

dell (del) /dɛl/ *n.* [*count*] a small, usually wooded valley; vale.

del•ta (del′tə) /'dɛltə/ *n.* [*count*], *pl.* **-tas. 1.** the fourth letter of the Greek alphabet (Δ, δ). **2.** anything triangular, like the Greek capital delta (Δ). **3.** a flat, triangular area of land with rich soil lying between branches of the mouth of a river.

de•lude (di lo͞od′) /dɪ'luwd/ *v.* [~ + *obj*], **-lud•ed, -lud•ing.** to mislead the mind or judgment of; deceive; fool; trick: *He deluded himself into thinking he'd lost weight.* See -LUD-.

del•uge (del′yo͞oj) /'dɛlyuwdʒ/ *n., v.,* **-uged, -ug•ing.** —*n.* [*count*] **1.** a great flood of water. **2. the Deluge,** FLOOD (def. 3). **3.** a drenching rain; downpour: *a deluge from the skies.* —*v.* [~ + *obj*] **4.** to flood; inundate: *The flooding river deluged the town.* **5.** to overwhelm: *We deluged our representatives with requests.*

de•lu•sion (di lo͞o′zhən) /dɪ'luwʒən/ *n.* **1.** [*noncount*] the state of being deluded: *suffering from delusion.* **2.** [*count*] a false belief or opinion: *delusions of grandeur.* —**de•lu•sive** (di lo͞o′siv) /dɪ'luwsɪv/ *adj.* See -LUD-. —**Usage.** See ILLUSION.

de•luxe or **de luxe** (də luks′, -lo͝oks′) /də'lʌks, -'lʊks/ *adj.* [*before a noun*] splendid; luxurious: *a deluxe hotel.*

delve (delv) /dɛlv/ *v.,* **delved, delv•ing.** to dig into; make a deep and thorough search: [~ + *into* + *obj*]: *We delved into the files to find out when the event happened.* [~ + *among* + *obj*]: *delving among old shelves.* —**delv′er,** *n.* [*count*]

dem-, *prefix. dem-* comes from Greek, where it has the meaning "people." This meaning is found in such words as: DEMAGOGUE, DEMOCRACY, DEMOGRAPHY.

de•mag•net•ize (dē mag′ni tīz′) /diy'mægnɪ,tayz/ *v.* [~ + *obj*], **-ized, -iz•ing.** to remove magnetization from. —**de•mag•net•i•za•tion** (dē mag′ni tə zā′shən) /diy,mægnɪtə'zeyʃən/ *n.* [*noncount*]

dem•a•gogue or **dem•a•gog** (dem′ə gog′, -gôg′) /'dɛmə,gɒg, -,gɔg/ *n.* [*count*] a political leader who gains power by arousing people's emotions and prejudices. —**dem•a•gog•ic** (dem′ə gog′ik, -goj′-) /,dɛmə'gɒgɪk, -'gɒdʒ-/ *adj.* —**dem′a•gogu′er•y, dem•a•go•gy** (dem′ə-gō′jē, -goj′ē) /'dɛmə,gowdʒiy, -,gɒdʒiy/ *n.* [*noncount*]

de•mand (di mand′) /dɪ'mænd/ *v.* **1.** to ask for with authority; claim as a right: [~ + *obj*]: *We demanded justice.* [~ + *to* + *verb*]: *I demanded to know what we had done wrong.* [~ + *(that) clause*]: *She demanded that we resign.* **2.** [~ + *obj*] to call for, need, or require as right, proper, or necessary: *This task demands patience.* —*n.* **3.** [*count*] the act of demanding. **4.** [*count*] something demanded: *There were demands for immediate pay raises.* **5.** [*count*] a necessary thing; an urgent requirement: *the conflicting demands of family and job.* **6.** [*noncount*] the desire and means to purchase goods: *Economics studies the amount of consumer demand.* **7.** [*noncount*] the state of being wanted or sought for purchase or use: *an article in great demand.* —***Idiom.*** **8. on demand, a.** upon request or presentation for payment: *The bill is payable on demand.* **b.** when requested: *abortion on demand.* See -MAND-.

de•mand•ing (di man′ding) /dɪ'mændɪŋ/ *adj.* **1.** requiring or asking for more than is generally felt by others to be due: *a demanding teacher.* **2.** calling for great, intensive effort or attention: *He had a demanding job.* —**de•mand′ing•ly,** *adv.*

de•mar•cate (di mär′kāt, dē′mär kāt′) /dɪ'mɑrkeyt, 'diymɑr,keyt/ *v.* [~ + *obj*], **-cat•ed, -cat•ing.** to determine or mark off the boundaries of: *to demarcate a boundary.* —**de•mar•ca•tion** (dē′mär kā′shən) /,diymɑr'keyʃən/ *n.* [*noncount*]: *Lines of demarcation were drawn between the two sides.*

de•mean (di mēn′) /dɪ'miyn/ *v.* [~ + *obj*] to lower in dignity or standing; debase; degrade: *You demean the presidency by such conduct.* —**de•mean′ing,** *adj.*: *said manual labor was demeaning.*

de•mean•or (di mē′nər) /dɪ'miynər/ *n.* [*noncount*] conduct; behavior; manner: *His calm demeanor hides his tension.* Also, *esp. Brit.,* **de•mean′our.**

de•ment•ed (di men′tid) /dɪ'mɛntɪd/ *adj.* crazy; insane; mad.

de•men•tia (di men′shə) /dɪ'mɛnʃə/ *n.* [*noncount*] **1.** severely impaired memory and reasoning ability, associated with damaged brain tissue. **2.** insanity; madness.

de•mer•it (di mer′it) /dɪ'mɛrɪt/ *n.* [*count*] **1.** a mark against a person for misconduct or failure to finish a job, etc.: *a few demerits for his sloppy work.* **2.** fault; bad aspect of something: *the demerits of working for that company.*

demi-, *prefix. demi-* comes from French, where it has the meaning "half." This meaning is found in such words as: DEMIGOD, DEMITASSE.

dem•i•god (dem′ē god′) /'dɛmiy,gɒd/ *n.* [*count*] a being in mythology who is partly divine and partly human.

dem•i•john (dem′i jon′) /'dɛmɪ,dʒɒn/ *n.* [*count*] a large bottle with a short, narrow neck.

de•mil•i•ta•rize (dē mil′i tə rīz′) /diy'mɪlɪtə,rayz/ *v.* [~ + *obj*], **-rized, -riz•ing.** to deprive of military character; remove the military from: *The UN forces stood in the demilitarized zone and prevented the enemies from meeting.*

de•mise (di mīz′) /dɪ'mayz/ *n.* [*count; usually singular*] **1.** death: *the demise of former great stars.* **2.** the ending of something, such as by failure or ruin; fall; collapse: *the demise of the Roman Empire.* See -MIS-.

dem•i•tasse (dem′i tas′, -täs′, dem′ē-) /'dɛmɪ,tæs, -,tɑs, 'dɛmiy-/ *n.* [*count*] a small cup for serving strong black coffee.

dem•o (dem′ō) /'dɛmow/ *n.* [*count*], *pl.* **dem•os. 1.** a tape recording of a new song or unknown performer, distributed for demonstration purposes. **2.** a car used for demonstration: *The demo we drove handled poorly.*

demo-, *prefix. demo-,* like DEM-, comes from Greek, where it has the meaning "people, population." This meaning is found in such words as: DEMOCRACY, DEMOGRAPHY.

de•mo•bi•lize (dē mō′bə līz′) /diy'mowbə,layz/ *v.* [~ + *obj*], **-lized, -liz•ing.** to disband (troops); to discharge (a person) from military service: *The soldiers waited to be demobilized.* —**de•mo•bi•li•za•tion** (dē mō′bə lə zā′shən) /diy,mowbələ'zeyʃən/ *n.* [*noncount*] See -MOB-.

de•moc•ra•cy (di mok′rə sē) /dɪ'mɒkrəsiy/ *n., pl.* **-cies. 1.** [*noncount*] government by the people; a form of government in which the supreme power rests with the people and is used directly by them or by their elected agents under a free electoral system. **2.** [*count*] a state, country, or nation having such a form of government. **3.** [*noncount*] a state or condition of society in which there is formal equality of rights and privileges: *democracy in the workplace.*

dem•o•crat (dem′ə krat′) /'dɛmə,kræt/ *n.* [*count*] **1.** an advocate of democracy. **2.** a person who believes in political or social equality. **3.** [*Democrat*] a member of the Democratic Party.

dem•o•crat•ic (dem′ə krat′ik) /,dɛmə'krætɪk/ also **dem′o•crat′i•cal,** *adj.* **1.** relating to, or of the nature of, democracy or a democracy: *a democratic government.* **2.** relating to or characterized by political or social equality: *democratic principles of electing delegates.* **3.** calling for or supporting democracy: *democratic rallies in support of the overthrow of communism.* **4.** [*before a noun; Democratic*] of, relating to, or characteristic of the Democratic Party. —**dem′o•crat′i•cal•ly,** *adv.*

Dem′ocrat′ic Par′ty, *n.* [*proper noun; the* + ~] one of the two major political parties in the U.S.

de•moc•ra•tize (di mok′rə tīz′) /dɪ'mɒkrə,tayz/ *v.* [~ + *obj*], **-tized, -tiz•ing.** to make democratic: *The union decided to democratize its voting procedures.* —**de•moc•ra•ti•za•tion** (di mok′rə tə zā′shən) /dɪ,mɒkrətə'zeyʃən/ *n.* [*noncount*]: *calling for the democratization of the labor unions.*

de•mog•ra•phy (di mog′rə fē) /dɪ'mɒgrəfiy/ *n.* [*noncount*] the science of vital and social statistics of populations. —**de•mog′ra•pher,** *n.* [*count*]: *Demographers were studying the census data carefully.* —**dem•o•graph•ic** (dem′ə graf′ik) /,dɛmə'græfɪk/ *adj.*: *demographic trends in the U.S.* —**dem′o•graph′i•cal•ly,** *adv.* —**dem′o•graph′ics,** *n.* [*plural*]: *the demographics of the immigrant population.* See -GRAPH-.

de•mol•ish (di mol′ish) /dɪ'mɒlɪʃ/ *v.* [~ + *obj*] **1.** to destroy or tear down (a building): *They are going to demolish the old apartment building where I grew up.* **2.** to put an end to; destroy: *Those arguments will demolish anything his lawyer has to say.*

dem•o•li•tion (dem′ə lish′ən) /,dɛmə'lɪʃən/ *n.* **1.** the act of knocking down or demolishing: [*noncount*]: *the army expert in demolition.* [*count*]: *demolitions in the downtown area.* **2.** [*noncount*] the act of putting an end to: *the demolition of my arguments by her rebuttal.*

de•mon (dē′mən) /'diymən/ *n.* [*count*] **1.** an evil spirit; fiend: *a ceremony to exorcise demons from the haunted house.* **2.** a wicked or cruel person. **3.** one with great energy: *a demon for work.* —**de•mon•ic** (di mon′ik) /dɪ'mɒnɪk/ *adj.*

de•mo•ni•ac (di mō′nē ak′) /dɪ'mowniy,æk/ *adj.* Also, **de•mo•ni•a•cal** (dē′mə nī′ə kəl) /,diymə'nayəkəl/. **1.** of, relating to, or like a demon; demonic. **2.** possessed by or as if by a demon; raging; wild. —**de′mo•ni′a•cal•ly,** *adv.*

de•mon•stra•ble (di mon′strə bəl) /dɪ'mɒnstrəbəl/ *adj.* capable of being demonstrated: *a demonstrable lie.*

—**de•mon′stra•bly,** *adv.*: *a demonstrably false argument.*

dem•on•strate (dem′ən strāt′) /ˈdɛmənˌstreyt/ *v.,* **-strat•ed, -strat•ing. 1.** to describe, explain, or illustrate by examples; teach; show: [~ + *obj*]: *demonstrated the proper method of fastening the parachute.* [~ + *clause*]: *demonstrated how to fire the rifle.* **2.** to make evident or establish by reasoning; prove: [~ + *obj*]: *This demonstrates my point.* [~ + *(that) clause*]: *demonstrated that time had to be the fourth dimension.* **3.** [~ + *obj*] to display openly or publicly: *The firefighters demonstrated great courage.* **4.** [~ + *obj*] to exhibit the operation or use of (a product), esp. to a prospective customer: *going door to door, demonstrating vacuum cleaners.* **5.** [*no obj*] to make, give, or take part in a demonstration: *demonstrating against the new quotas.* See -MONSTR-. —**Related Words.** DEMONSTRATE is a verb, DEMONSTRATIVE is an adjective, DEMONSTRATION is a noun: *Let me demonstrate how this works. He's very demonstrative; he always hugs his children. There was a demonstration against the war.*

dem•on•stra•tion (dem′ən strā′shən) /ˌdɛmənˈstreyʃən/ *n.* [*count*] **1.** exhibition, display, or illustration that shows how something works: *a demonstration of the new manufacturing process.* **2.** an example or series of examples that provides proof of something, as of a theory: *a convincing demonstration.* **3.** a showing or expressing of emotion: *demonstrations of affection.* **4.** a march or public show of strong opinion: *a huge demonstration in the city's main square.*

de•mon•stra•tive (də mon′strə tiv) /dəˈmɒnstrətɪv/ *adj.* **1.** showing openly one's emotions: *a demonstrative parent.* **2.** indicating or singling out the thing referred to: *The word* this *is a demonstrative pronoun and adjective.* —*n.* [*count*] **3.** a demonstrative word, as *this* or *there.*

dem•on•stra•tor (dem′ən strā′tər) /ˈdɛmənˌstreytər/ *n.* [*count*] **1.** a person or thing that demonstrates. **2.** a person who takes part in a public demonstration, as by marching or picketing.

de•mor•al•ize (di môr′ə līz′, -mor′-) /dɪˈmɔrəˌlayz, -ˈmɒr-/ *v.* [~ + *obj*], **-ized, -iz•ing.** to deprive (someone) of spirit, courage, or discipline; destroy the morale of: *The terrible defeat demoralized the army.* —**de•mor•al•i•za•tion** (di môr′ə lə zā′shən, -mor′-) /dɪˌmɔrələˈzeyʃən, -ˌmɒr-/ *n.* [*noncount*]: *nationwide demoralization.* —**de•mor′al•ized,** *adj.*: *The demoralized army trudged home after the defeat.* —**de•mor′al•iz•ing,** *adj.*: *suffered a demoralizing defeat.* See -MOR-.

de•mote (di mōt′) /dɪˈmowt/ *v.* [~ + *obj*], **-mot•ed, -mot•ing.** to reduce to a lower grade or rank: *demoted to the rank of private.* —**de•mo•tion** (di mō′shən) /dɪˈmowʃən/ *n.* [*noncount*]: *Anyone breaking this rule is threatened with demotion.* [*count*]: *I'd suffered several demotions.* See -MOT-.

de•mur (di mûr′) /dɪˈmɜr/ *v.,* **-murred, -mur•ring,** *n.* —*v.* **1.** to object; take exception: [*no obj*]: *The majority were in favor, but a few demurred.* [~ + *at* + *obj*]: *They demurred at the thought of murder.* —*n.* [*noncount*] **2.** hesitation: *following any order without demur.* —**de•mur′ral,** *n.* [*count*]

de•mure (di myŏŏr′) /dɪˈmyʊr/ *adj.,* **-mur•er, -mur•est.** characterized by shyness and modesty: *a demure smile.* —**de•mure′ly,** *adv.*

den (den) /dɛn/ *n.* [*count*] **1.** the home or shelter of a wild animal: *the lion's den.* **2.** a room in a home providing an informal atmosphere for conversation, reading, etc.

den•drite (den′drīt) /ˈdɛndrayt/ *n.* [*count*] a branching part of a nerve cell that carries impulses toward the cell body.

de•ni•al (di nī′əl) /dɪˈnayəl/ *n.* **1.** [*count*] an assertion that another statement is false: *issued a denial of the story.* **2.** [*noncount*] a refusal to believe in the existence of a thing: *He's in denial; he refuses to recognize that his brother is a liar.* **3.** [*noncount*] the refusal to accept a claim or request: *denial of the most basic civil liberties.*

den•i•grate (den′i grāt′) /ˈdɛnɪˌgreyt/ *v.* [~ + *obj*], **-grat•ed, -grat•ing.** to speak damagingly of; degrade the character of: *to denigrate someone's character.* —**den•i•gra•tion** (den′i grā′shən) /ˌdɛnɪˈgreyʃən/ *n.* [*noncount*]: *the continual denigration of their political opponents.*

den•im (den′əm) /ˈdɛnəm/ *n.* **1.** [*noncount*] a heavy fabric of cotton woven with white and blue threads, used esp. for jeans. **2. denims,** [*plural; used with a plural verb*] trousers made of denim; jeans: *The denims were hung on the line after they were washed.*

den•i•zen (den′ə zən) /ˈdɛnəzən/ *n.* [*count*] an inhabitant; resident: *the denizens of the inner cities.*

de•nom•i•na•tion (di nom′ə nā′shən) /dɪˌnɒməˈneyʃən/ *n.* [*count*] **1.** a religious group: *To what denomination does he belong?* **2.** a grade or degree in a series of standards: *had a few bills of various denominations in his wallet: singles, fives, and twenties.* **3.** a name or designation, esp. one for a class of things. —**de•nom′i•na′tion•al,** *adj.* See -NOM-[2].

de•nom•i•na•tor (di nom′ə nā′tər) /dɪˈnɒməˌneytər/ *n.* [*count*] the term of a fraction, usually written under or after the line, that indicates the number of equal parts into which the unit is divided; divisor. Compare NUMERATOR.

de•no•ta•tion (dē′nō tā′shən) /ˌdiynowˈteyʃən/ *n.* [*count*] the specific meaning of a word or expression. Compare CONNOTATION. See -NOTA-.

de•note (di nōt′) /dɪˈnowt/ *v.* [*not: be* + *~-ing;* ~ + *obj*], **-not•ed, -not•ing.** to indicate clearly: *A fever often denotes an infection.* See -NOTA-.

de•noue•ment (dā′nōō män′) /ˌdeynuwˈmɑ̃/ *n.* [*count*] **1.** the final resolution of a plot, such as of a drama or novel. **2.** the outcome or resolution of a series of occurrences.

de•nounce (di nouns′) /dɪˈnawns/ *v.* [~ + *obj (+ as + obj)*], **-nounced, -nounc•ing. 1.** to condemn strongly, openly, or publicly: *denounced the plan as a waste of money.* **2.** to make a formal accusation against (someone), such as to the police or in a court: *They denounced him (as a criminal) to the police.* See -NOUNCE-.

dense (dens) /dɛns/ *adj.,* **dens•er, dens•est. 1.** having parts closely packed together; crowded: *a dense forest.* **2.** stupid; slow-witted. **3.** thick; intense; difficult to see through: *a very dense fog.* **4.** difficult to understand: *dense writing.* —**dense′ly,** *adv.* —**dense′ness,** *n.* [*noncount*]

den•si•ty (den′si tē) /ˈdɛnsɪtiy/ *n., pl.* **-ties. 1.** [*noncount*] the state or quality of being dense: *the density of the prose.* **2.** [*count*] the average number of inhabitants per unit of area: *a population density of 100 persons per square mile.* **3.** [*count*] *Physics.* the relation of mass to volume; mass per unit volume: *a density of 15 cubic centimeters per gram.* **4.** [*noncount*] a measure of how much data can be stored in a given amount of space on a disk, tape, or other computer storage medium: *a high-density disk.* **5.** [*noncount*] great stupidity or dullness.

dent (dent) /dɛnt/ *n.* [*count*] **1.** a depression in a surface, such as from a blow: *a few dents on the fender.* **2.** a noticeable effect, esp. of reduction: *a dent in one's pride.* **3.** slight progress: *I haven't made a dent in this pile of work.* —*v.* **4.** [~ + *obj*] to make a dent in or on: *dented the front end of the car.* **5.** [*no obj*] to become dented: *The car dents much too easily.* **6.** [~ + *obj*] to have the effect of reducing or slightly injuring: *The sarcastic remark dented my ego.*

-dent-, *root.* *-dent-* comes from Latin, where it has the meaning "tooth." This meaning is found in such words as: DENTAL, DENTIFRICE, DENTIST, DENTISTRY, DENTURE.

den•tal (den′tl) /ˈdɛntl̩/ *adj.* [*before a noun*] **1.** of or relating to the teeth: *dental care.* **2.** of or relating to dentistry or a dentist: *a dental surgeon.* See -DENT-.

den•ti•frice (den′tə fris) /ˈdɛntəfrɪs/ *n.* [*noncount*] a paste or other preparation for cleaning the teeth. See -DENT-.

den•tist (den′tist) /ˈdɛntɪst/ *n.* [*count*] a person whose profession is the care and treatment of teeth. —**den•tist•ry** (den′tis trē) /ˈdɛntɪstriy/ *n.* [*noncount*] See -DENT-.

den•ture (den′chər) /ˈdɛntʃər/ *n.* [*count*] **1.** an artificial replacement of one or more teeth. **2.** Often **dentures.** [*plural*] a replacement set of all the teeth of one or both jaws: *He takes out his dentures at night.* See -DENT-.

de•nude (di nōōd′, -nyōōd′) /dɪˈnuwd, -ˈnyuwd/ *v.* [~ + *obj*], **-nud•ed, -nud•ing.** to make naked or bare; remove the covering of; strip: *The storm denuded many trees.*

de•nun•ci•a•tion (di nun′sē ā′shən, -shē-) /dɪˌnʌnsiyˈeyʃən, -ʃiy-/ *n.* an act or instance of denouncing: [*count*]: *a denunciation of dishonest government.* [*noncount*]: *a lot of lies and denunciation.* See -NOUNCE-, -NUNC-.

de•ny (di nī′) /dɪˈnay/ *v.,* **-nied, -ny•ing. 1.** to state that (something) is not true: [~ + *obj*]: *ready to deny any accusation.* [~ + *verb-ing*]: *He denied making such a statement.* [~ + *(that) clause*]: *He denied that he had ever made such a statement.* **2.** [~ + *obj*] to refuse to agree to or go along with: *The union decided to deny my petition.* **3.** to withhold something from someone; refuse to grant a request of; refuse to give: [~ + *obj*]: *to deny access to information.* [~ + *obj* + *obj*]: *I could never* *deny her anything.* **—de•ni′a•ble,** *adj.* **—de•ni•a•bil•i•ty** (di nī′ə bil′i tē) /dɪˌnayəˈbɪlɪtiy/ *n.* [*noncount*]

de•o•dor•ant (dē ō′dər ənt) /diyˈowdərənt/ *n.* **1.** a substance for reducing odors: [*noncount*]: *He wore deodorant but it wasn't effective in that heat.* [*count*]: *a totally new deodorant.* **—***adj.* [*before a noun*] **2.** capable of destroying odors: *a deodorant spray.*

de•o•dor•ize (dē ō′də rīz′) /diyˈowdəˌrayz/ *v.* [~ + *obj*], **-ized, -iz•ing.** to rid of unpleasant odor: *a chemical that cleans and deodorizes rooms.* **—de•o′dor•iz′er,** *n.* [*count*]: *a room deodorizer.*

de•ox′y•ri′bo•nu•cle′ic ac′id (dē ok′si rī′bō no͞o-klē′ik, -klā′-, -nyo͞o-) /diyˈɒksɪˈraybownuwˈkliyɪk, -ˈkley-, -nyuw-/ *n.* See DNA.

de•part (di pärt′) /dɪˈpɑrt/ *v.* **1.** to go away; leave: [*no obj*]: *The train never departs on time.* [~ + *from* + *obj*]: *This train departs from Grand Central Station.* [~ + *obj*]: *Your train departs Stockholm at 0600 and arrives at Oslo at 16:30.* **2.** [~ + *from* + *obj*] to be different; differ; diverge: *Our method departs from theirs in several respects.* **3.** [~ + *from* + *obj*] to pass away; die: *He departed from this life at an early age.* See -PAR-.

de•part•ed (di pär′tid) /dɪˈpɑrtɪd/ *adj.* **1.** [*before a noun*] dead: *our departed brother.* **—***n.* **2. the departed,** [*count; the* + ~*; used with a singular or plural verb*] a dead person: *The departed led a good life.*

de•part•ment (di pärt′mənt) /dɪˈpɑrtmənt/ *n.* [*count*] **1.** a part of a larger structure; a division or branch, as of business: *assigned to a new department.* **2.** [*usually singular*] one's special area of activity, expertise, or responsibility: *Tax questions are just not my department.* **—de•part•men•tal** (di pärt men′tl, dē′pärt-) /dɪpɑrtˈmɛntl̩, ˌdiypɑrt-/ *adj.* See -PAR-.

de•part•men•tal•ize (di pärt men′tl īz′, dē′pärt-) /dɪpɑrtˈmɛntl̩ˌayz, ˌdiypɑrt-/ *v.* [~ + *obj*], **-ized, -iz•ing.** to divide into departments: *They departmentalized the business to achieve greater efficiency.* **—de•part•men•tal•i•za•tion** (di pärt men′tl ə zā′shən, dē′pärt-) /dɪpɑrtˌmɛntl̩əˈzeyʃən, ˌdiypɑrt-/ *n.* [*noncount*]

depart′ment store′, *n.* [*count*] a large store that sells a variety of goods organized by departments.

de•par•ture (di pär′chər) /dɪˈpɑrtʃər/ *n.* an act or instance of departing: [*count*]: *There are ten departures daily.* [*noncount*]: *Our departure is at seven a.m.* See -PAR-.

de•pend (di pend′) /dɪˈpɛnd/ *v.* **1.** [~ + *on/upon* + *obj*] to rely on; place trust in: *You may depend on our tact.* **2.** [~ + *on/upon*] to rely on for support or help: *Farmers depend upon the rain and the weather forecast.* **3.** [*not: be* + ~*-ing;* ~ + *on/upon*] to be determined by; to be conditioned by: *Our plans depend on the weather.* **4.** [*not: be* + ~*-ing; no obj; it* + ~] to be undecided; to be undetermined; to be pending: *Are you going to the party? —It depends; I may not. That all depends; are you going?* See -PEND-. **—Related Words.** DEPEND is a verb, DEPENDABLE is an adjective, DEPENDENT is an adjective and a noun, DEPENDENCE is a noun: *I knew I could depend on you to help me. You are very dependable. His children are dependent on him for support. He listed his children as dependents on his tax form. The teenagers still showed great dependence on their parents.*

de•pend•a•ble (di pen′də bəl) /dɪˈpɛndəbəl/ *adj.* worthy of trust; reliable: *a dependable employee.* **—de•pend•a•bil•i•ty** (di pen′də bil′i tē) /dɪˌpɛndəˈbɪlɪtiy/ *n.* [*noncount*] **—de•pend′a•bly,** *adv.* See -PEND-.

de•pend•ence (di pen′dəns) /dɪˈpɛndəns/ *n.* [*noncount*] **1.** the state of relying on someone or something for aid or support: *the dependence on the West for luxury items.* **2.** reliance; trust: *dependence on religion.* **3.** the state of being a condition for something to follow: *the dependence of an effect upon a cause.* **4.** the state of being psychologically or physiologically dependent on a drug: *the frightening dependence on drugs.* Sometimes, **de•pend′ance.** See -PEND-.

de•pend•en•cy (di pen′dən sē) /dɪˈpɛndənsiy/ *n., pl.* **-cies. 1.** [*noncount*] the state of being dependent: *drug dependency.* **2.** [*count*] a subject territory that is not an essential part of the ruling country. Sometimes, **de•pend′an•cy.** See -PEND-.

de•pend•ent (di pen′dənt) /dɪˈpɛndənt/ *adj.* **1.** relying on someone or something else for aid or support: *dependent on her parents until she got a job.* **2.** [*be* + ~ + *on* + *obj*] conditioned or determined by something else; contingent: *Our trip is dependent on the weather.* **3.** used only in connection with other forms, not in isolation; subordinate. In the sentence *I walked out when the bell rang,* the clause *when the bell rang* is a dependent clause. Compare INDEPENDENT (def. 8). **—***n.* [*count*] **4.** a person, such as a child, who depends on someone for aid or support: *Our children are no longer listed as dependents on our tax forms.* Often, *esp. for def. 4,* **de•pend′ant. —de•pend′ent•ly,** *adv.*

de•per•son•al•ize (dē pûr′sə nl īz′) /diyˈpɜrsənl̩ˌayz/ *v.* [~ + *obj*], **-ized, -iz•ing.** to make impersonal; to take away the personality of: *a registration system that depersonalizes students by referring to them by numbers.*

de•pict (di pikt′) /dɪˈpɪkt/ *v.* **1.** [~ + *obj*] to represent by or as if by painting or drawing: *depicted Napoleon with his hand inside his shirt.* **2.** [~ + *obj* + *as* + *noun/adjective*] to represent or characterize in words; describe: *The story depicts the hero as an evil opportunist.*

de•pic•tion (di pik′shən) /dɪˈpɪkʃən/ *n.* [*count*] a description, either written or by drawing or painting.

de•pil•a•to•ry (di pil′ə tôr′ē, -tōr′ē) /dɪˈpɪləˌtɔriy, -ˌtowriy/ *adj., n., pl.* **-ries. —***adj.* [*before a noun*] **1.** capable of removing hair: *depilatory cream for the legs.* **—***n.* [*count*] **2.** a liquid or cream for temporarily removing unwanted hair from the body.

de•plane (dē plān′) /diyˈpleyn/ *v.* [*no obj*], **-planed, -plan•ing.** to disembark from an airplane.

de•plete (di plēt′) /dɪˈpliyt/ *v.* [~ + *obj*], **-plet•ed, -plet•ing.** to decrease badly; use up the supply of: *The drought has seriously depleted our water supply.* **—de•ple•tion** (di plē′shən) /dɪˈpliyʃən/ *n.* [*noncount*]: *We were faced with the depletion of our supplies just before the battle.* See -PLET-.

de•plor•a•ble (di plôr′ə bəl, -plōr′-) /dɪˈplɔrəbəl, -ˈplowr-/ *adj.* causing or being a subject for grief or regret; lamentable: *deplorable living conditions.*

de•plore (di plôr′, -plōr′) /dɪˈplɔr, -ˈplowr/ *v.* [~ + *obj*], **-plored, -plor•ing. 1.** to regret deeply or strongly; lament: *We deplore what our own soldiers have done.* **2.** to express strong disapproval of; condemn; censure: *deplored the action taken against his country.*

de•ploy (di ploi′) /dɪˈplɔy/ *v.* [~ + *obj*] to arrange or move into position esp. for battle: *to deploy missiles.* **—de•ploy′ment,** *n.* [*noncount*]: *Troop deployment was efficiently accomplished.* [*count*]: *a deployment that exposes his right flank.* See -PLOY-.

de•pop•u•late (dē pop′yə lāt′) /diyˈpɒpyəˌleyt/ *v.* [~ + *obj*], **-lat•ed, -lat•ing.** to remove or reduce the population of: *cities depopulated by plagues.* **—de•pop•u•la•tion** (dē pop′yə lā′shən) /diyˌpɒpyəˈleyʃən/ *n.* [*noncount*]: *widespread depopulation of the agricultural region.* See -POP-.

de•port (di pôrt′, -pōrt′) /dɪˈpɔrt, -ˈpowrt/ *v.* **1.** [~ + *obj*] to expel (an alien) from a country; banish: *The federal authorities deported him for illegal entry.* **2.** [~ + *oneself*] to behave in a particular manner; to carry oneself in a certain way: *The young children deported themselves perfectly.* **—de•por•ta•tion** (dē′pôr tā′shən, -pōr-) /ˌdiypɔrˈteyʃən, -powr-/ *n.* [*noncount*]: *faced with immediate deportation.* [*count*]: *increases in the number of deportations.* See -PORT-.

de•port•ment (di pôrt′mənt, -pōrt′-) /dɪˈpɔrtmənt, -ˈpowrt-/ *n.* [*noncount*] conduct; behavior. See -PORT-.

de•pose (di pōz′) /dɪˈpowz/ *v.* [~ + *obj*], **-posed, -pos•ing.** to remove from office or position, esp. high office: *The nobles deposed the king.* See -POS-.

de•pos•it (di poz′it) /dɪˈpɒzɪt/ *v.* [~ + *obj*] **1.** to put or place (something) for safekeeping, esp. in a bank account: *He deposited the fifty dollars in his savings account.* **2.** to deliver and leave (an item): *He deposited his suitcases in the locker.* **3.** to insert (a coin) in a coin-operated device: *Deposit exact change.* **4.** to put or set down, esp. carefully: *She deposited the baby in the crib.* **5.** to lay or throw down by a natural process: *The river deposited soil at its mouth.* **6.** to give as security (for): *We deposited $500 on the new car.* **—***n.* [*count*] **7. a.** an instance of placing money in a bank account: *You can make a deposit at any branch office.* **b.** the money placed there: *a deposit of over $1,000.* **8.** anything given as security or in partial payment: *a bottle deposit of five cents.* **9.** something left or thrown down, such as by a natural process: *a deposit of rich soil left by the flood.* **10.** a naturally occurring accumulation or pile, esp. of oil or ore: *gold deposits in the river.* **—de•pos′i•tor,** *n.* [*count*]: *Bank depositors will use the new branch office.* See -POS-.

dep•o•si•tion (dep′ə zish′ən) /ˌdɛpəˈzɪʃən/ *n.* **1.** [*noncount*] removal from an office or position: *the deposition of the dictator.* **2.** [*noncount*] something deposited, such as soil or minerals, by a natural process; the act or process of this: *soil deposition over the centuries.* **3.** [*count*] a statement under oath, taken down in writing, to be used in court. See -POS-.

de•pos•i•to•ry (di poz′i tôr′ē, -tōr′ē) /dɪ'pɒzɪˌtɔriy, -ˌtowriy/ *n.* [*count*], *pl.* **-ries.** a place where something is deposited, as for safekeeping: *the night depository of a bank.* See -POS-.

de•pot (dē′pō) /'diypow/ *n.* [*count*] **1.** a railroad or bus station. **2. a.** a place in which supplies are stored. **b.** a place where recruits are received, classified, and sent out as replacements.

de•prave (di prāv′) /dɪ'preyv/ *v.* [~ + *obj*], **-praved, -prav•ing.** to make evil; corrupt. **—de•praved′,** *adj.* **—de•prav•i•ty** (di prav′i tē) /dɪ'prævɪtiy/ *n.* [*noncount; count*] *pl.* **-ties.**

dep•re•cate (dep′ri kāt′) /'dɛprɪˌkeyt/ *v.* [~ + *obj*], **-cat•ed, -cat•ing. 1.** to express disapproval of; urge reasons against. **2.** to speak of as having little value; belittle. **—dep′re•ca′ting,** *adj.* **—dep•re•ca•tion** (dep′ri kā′shən) /ˌdɛprɪ'keyʃən/ *n.* [*noncount*] **—dep•re•ca•to•ry** (dep′ri kə tôr′ē, -tōr′ē) /'dɛprɪkəˌtɔriy, -ˌtowriy/ *adj.*

de•pre•ci•ate (di prē′shē āt′) /dɪ'priyʃiyˌeyt/ *v.,* **-at•ed, -at•ing. 1.** [*no obj*] (of money, etc.) to decline or fall in value: *The car depreciated in value.* **2.** [~ + *obj*] to reduce or lower the value of: *Inflation has depreciated the country's currency.* **—de•pre•ci•a•tion** (di prē′shē ā′shən) /dɪˌpriyʃiy'eyʃən/ *n.* [*noncount*] See -PRECI-.

de•press (di pres′) /dɪ'prɛs/ *v.* [~ + *obj*] **1.** to make sad or gloomy; sadden: *Her sad news depressed me.* **2.** to lower in amount or value; lessen; weaken: *to depress the economy.* **3.** to put into a lower position; press down: *Depress the brake pedal.* **—de•press′ive,** *adj.* See -PRESS-. **—Related Words.** DEPRESS is a verb, DEPRESSED and DEPRESSING are adjectives, DEPRESSION is a noun: *Crime stories depress me. I'm very depressed. Those stories are depressing. She is suffering from depression.*

de•pres•sant (di pres′ənt) /dɪ'prɛsənt/ *adj.* [*before a noun*] **1.** tending to slow the activity of one or more bodily systems: *depressant drugs.* **—*n.*** [*count*] **2.** a drug or other agent that reduces extremes of emotion like irritability or excitement; a sedative: *They treated him with depressants.* See -PRESS-.

de•pressed (di prest′) /dɪ'prɛst/ *adj.* sad or gloomy; lowered in spirits: *felt depressed after failing the test.*

de•press•ing (di pres′ing) /dɪ'prɛsɪŋ/ *adj.* causing gloominess or a lowering of spirits: *depressing news about the economy.*

de•pres•sion (di presh′ən) /dɪ'prɛʃən/ *n.* **1.** [*count*] a depressed or sunken place or part; an area lower than the surrounding surface: *a depression in the carpet where the lamp had stood.* **2.** [*noncount*] sadness; dejection, esp. sadness greater and longer than considered normal: *suffered from long periods of depression.* **3.** [*count*] a period during which business, employment, and stock-market values fall; a decline in the economy: *In the 1930's the world experienced a severe depression.* **4.** [*count*] an area of low air pressure in the atmosphere: *a tropical depression in Bermuda.* See -PRESS-.

de•prive (di prīv′) /dɪ'prayv/ *v.* [~ + *obj* + *of* + *obj*], **-prived, -priv•ing.** to keep (someone) from having or enjoying something; keep or prevent (someone) from having or using: *to deprive a child of affection.* **—dep•ri•va•tion** (dep′rə vā′shən) /ˌdɛprə'veyʃən/ *n.* [*noncount*]: *a life of terrible hardship and deprivation.* [*count*]: *suffering terrible deprivations during the war.* See -PRIV-.

de•prived (di prīvd′) /dɪ'prayvd/ *adj.* lacking food, shelter, or money: *They gave money to help deprived children.*

de•pro•gram (dē prō′gram) /diy'prowgræm/ *v.* [~ + *obj*], **-grammed** or **-gramed, -gram•ming** or **-gram•ing.** to free (a person) from the influence of a cult, sect, etc., as by intensive retraining.

dept., an abbreviation of: **1.** department. **2.** deputy.

depth (depth) /dɛpθ/ *n.* **1.** a distance measured from the surface of something downward, or from the front backward or inward: [*noncount*]: *The lake was 300 feet in depth.* [*count*]: *The submarine dove to a depth of 300 feet. At depths below thirty feet my ears begin to pop.* **2.** [*noncount*] the quality of being complex or difficult to understand: *a question of great depth.* **3.** [*noncount*] gravity; seriousness: *explained the depth of the crisis facing the state.* **4.** [*noncount*] intensity, such as of silence or color: *a drawing with depth and richness of color.* **5.** [*noncount*] lowness of tonal pitch: *the depth of a voice.* **6.** the amount of a person's intelligence, insight, or emotion: [*count*]: *showed a remarkable depth of understanding for one so young.* [*noncount*]: *the depth of one's feelings.* **7. depths,** [*plural*] the deepest, farthest, or innermost part: *the depths of the forest.* **8.** Usually, **depths.** [*plural*] a low intellectual or moral condition: *How could he sink to such depths?* **9.** [*noncount*] the strength of a team's lineup of substitute players: *It's the depth of the bench that wins championships.* **—*Idiom.*** **10. in depth,** extensively; thoroughly: *The committee studied the problem in depth.* **11. out of** or **beyond one's depth,** beyond one's knowledge or capability: *He's out of his depth on that assignment.*

depth′ charge′, *n.* [*count*] an explosive device used underwater, esp. against submarines, and set to go off at a certain depth. Also called **depth′ bomb′.**

dep•u•ta•tion (dep′yə tā′shən) /ˌdɛpyə'teyʃən/ *n.* [*count*] a body of persons appointed to represent another: *The president met the deputation at the door.* See -PUTE-.

dep•u•tize (dep′yə tīz′) /'dɛpyəˌtayz/ *v.,* **-tized, -tiz•ing. 1.** [~ + *obj*] to appoint as deputy: *The boss deputized me to speak for her in her absence.* **2.** [*no obj*] to substitute for someone: *Can you deputize for me tomorrow?*

dep•u•ty (dep′yə tē) /'dɛpyətiy/ *n.* [*count*], *pl.* **-ties. 1.** a person appointed to act as a substitute for another: *the boss's deputy.* **2.** a person appointed or elected as assistant to a public official, serving as successor in the event of a vacancy: *The ambassador sent his deputy to see us.* **3.** a person representing a group of voters in certain lawmaking bodies. **—*adj.*** [*before a noun*] **4.** appointed, elected, or serving as an assistant: *the deputy secretary of foreign affairs.* See -PUTE-.

de•rail (dē rāl′) /diy'reyl/ *v.* **1.** (of a train, etc.) to (cause to) run off the rails of a track: [*no obj*]: *When the train derailed it was going at 100 mph.* [~ + *obj*]: *The train was derailed when it sped off the curve.* **2.** [~ + *obj*] to cause to be deflected or moved away from a purpose or course of direction: *A skiing accident derailed her dancing career.* **—de•rail′ment,** *n.* [*count*]

de•rail•leur (di rā′lər) /dɪ'reylər/ *n.* [*count*] a gear-shifting mechanism on a bicycle that shifts the chain from one gear wheel to another.

de•ranged (di rānjd′) /dɪ'reyndʒd/ *adj.* made insane; demented. **—de•range′ment,** *n.* [*noncount*]

Der•by (dûr′bē) /'dɜrbiy/ *n.* [*count*], *pl.* **-bies. 1.** any of certain important horse races, esp. the Kentucky Derby, that are held every year. **2.** [*derby*] a race or contest, usually one open to all who wish to enter. **3.** [*derby*] a man's stiff felt hat with rounded crown and narrow brim; bowler.

de•reg•u•late (dē reg′yə lāt′) /diy'rɛgyəˌleyt/ *v.* [~ + *obj*], **-lat•ed, -lat•ing.** to halt or reduce government regulation of: *to deregulate the airline industry.* **—de•reg•u•la•tion** (dē reg′yə lā′shən) /diyˌrɛgyə'leyʃən/ *n.* [*noncount*] See -REG-.

der•e•lict (der′ə likt) /'dɛrəlɪkt/ *adj.* **1.** [*often before a noun*] left or deserted; abandoned: *a derelict ship.* **2.** neglecting duty; delinquent: *fired for being derelict in his duties.* **—*n.*** [*count*] **3.** a person who has no home or means of support; vagrant. **4.** any abandoned possession, as a vessel left in open water.

der•e•lic•tion (der′ə lik′shən) /ˌdɛrə'lɪkʃən/ *n.* [*noncount*] deliberate neglect; delinquency: *dereliction of duty.*

de•ride (di rīd′) /dɪ'rayd/ *v.* [~ + *obj*], **-rid•ed, -rid•ing.** to laugh at in contempt; mock: *They derided his plan for saving money.*

de•ri•sion (di rizh′ən) /dɪ'rɪʒən/ *n.* [*noncount*] the act of deriding; contempt: *an object of derision.* **—de•ri•sive** (di rī′siv) /dɪ'raysɪv/ *adj.*: *derisive laughter.* **—de•ri′sive•ly,** *adv.*

der•i•va•tion (der′ə vā′shən) /ˌdɛrə'veyʃən/ *n.* [*noncount*] **1.** the act of deriving or the state of being derived: *the derivation of new plastics from chemicals.* **2.** source; origin: *a dance of German derivation.* **3.** the process of adding a prefix or suffix to the base form of a word, thereby forming a new word: *The process of derivation forms the word assignment, a noun, from assign, a verb.* Compare INFLECTION.

de•riv•a•tive (di riv′ə tiv) /dɪ'rɪvətɪv/ *adj.* **1.** not original; coming from something earlier: *His music was derivative and not innovative enough.* **—*n.*** [*count*] **2.** something derived or developed from something else, such as a word that has come from another.

de•rive (di rīv′) /dɪ'rayv/ *v.,* **-rived, -riv•ing. 1.** [~ + *obj* + *from* + *obj*] to receive from another source; gain; glean: *derives great satisfaction from her children.* **2.** to come from or trace from a source or origin: [~ + *obj* + *from* + *obj*]: *We can derive the word* deduct *from Latin.* [~ + *from* + *obj*]: *The word* deduct *derives from Latin.*

-derm-, *root.* *-derm-* comes from Greek, where it has the meaning "skin." This meaning is found in such words as: DERMATITIS, DERMATOLOGY, DERMIS, HYPODERMIC, PACHYDERM, TAXIDERMY.

der•ma•ti•tis (dûr′mə ti′tis) /ˌdɜrmə'taytɪs/ *n.* [*noncount*] a rash or inflammation of the skin. See -DERM-.

der•ma•tol•o•gy (dûr′mə tol′ə jē) /ˌdɜrmə'tɒlədʒiy/ *n.* [*noncount*] the branch of medicine dealing with the skin and its diseases. **—der•ma•to•log•i•cal** (dûr′mə tl oj′i-kəl) /ˌdɜrmət̩l'ɒdʒɪkəl/ *adj.* **—der•ma•tol•o•gist** (dûr′mə-tol′ə jist) /ˌdɜrmə'tɒlədʒɪst/ *n.* [*count*] See -DERM-.

der•mis (dûr′mis) /'dɜrmɪs/ *n.* [*noncount*] the thick layer of skin beneath the epidermis. See -DERM-.

de•rog•a•to•ry (di rog′ə tôr′ē, -tōr′ē) /dɪ'rɒgəˌtɔriy, -ˌtowriy/ *adj.* unfavorable; unflattering; belittling: *a derogatory remark.* See -ROGA-.

der•rick (der′ik) /'dɛrɪk/ *n.* [*count*] **1.** a crane for lifting cargo, such as on a ship. **2.** a framework like a tower over an oil well.

der•ri•ère or **der•ri•ere** (der′ē âr′) /ˌdɛriy'ɛər/ *n.* [*count*] the buttocks; rump.

der•rin•ger (der′in jər) /'dɛrɪndʒər/ *n.* [*count*] an old, short-barreled pocket pistol.

de•sal•i•nate (dē sal′ə nāt′) /diy'sæləˌneyt/ *v.*, **-nat•ed, -nat•ing.** DESALT. **—de•sal•i•na•tion** (dē sal′ə nā′shən) /diyˌsælə'neyʃən/ *n.* [*noncount*]

de•salt (dē sôlt′) /diy'sɔlt/ *v.* [~ + *obj*] to remove the salt from (esp. sea water), usually to make it drinkable.

de•scend (di send′) /dɪ'sɛnd/ *v.* **1.** to go from a higher to a lower place, level, or series: [*no obj*]: *The elevator descended rapidly to the bottom floor.* [~ + *obj*]: *She slowly descended the stairs.* **2.** [*no obj*] to slope, tend, or lead downward: *The path descends to the pond.* **3.** [~ + *from* + *obj*] to be derived from something in the past: *This festival descends from a rite of my ancestors.* **4.** [~ + *on/upon* + *obj*] to attack or approach as if attacking: *Thrill-seekers descended upon the scene of the crime.* **5.** [~ + *on* + *obj*] to fall or settle down on people, as or as if a cloud: *Silence descended on the audience.* **6.** [~ + *to* + *obj*] to come down from a certain standard or level of behavior; stoop: *You must never descend to such bickering.* See -SCEND-.

de•scend•ant (di sen′dənt) /dɪ'sɛndənt/ *n.* [*count*] one descended from a certain ancestor; an offspring: *a descendant of the kings of Ireland.* Compare ANCESTOR.

de•scend•ed (di sen′did) /dɪ'sɛndɪd/ *adj.* [*be* + ~ + *from*] having a certain ancestor or ancestry: *We are descended from the kings of Ireland.*

de•scent (di sent′) /dɪ'sɛnt/ *n.* **1.** [*count*] the act, process, or fact of descending: *The spectators watched the descent of the balloon.* **2.** [*count*] a downward inclination or slope: *a gradual descent to the lake.* **3.** [*noncount*] ancestry; the line tracing births to an ancestor: *He traces his descent to a small village in Thrace.* See -SCEND-.

de•scribe (di skrīb′) /dɪ'skrayb/ *v.*, **-scribed, -scrib•ing.** **1.** to tell in words what something is like: [~ + *obj*]: *to describe an accident in detail.* [~ + *clause*]: *Can you describe what he did next?* **2.** to pronounce or represent; characterize by adding a word or phrase: [~ + *obj* + *as* + *noun*]: *I would describe him as a tyrant.* [~ + *obj* + *as* + *adjective*]: *I'd describe the house as run-down.* **3.** [~ + *obj*] to draw or trace the outline of: *to describe an arc with a pencil.* See -SCRIB-.

de•scrip•tion (di skrip′shən) /dɪ'skrɪpʃən/ *n.* **1.** [*count*] a statement or an account that describes: *provided the police with a description of the killer.* **2.** [*noncount*] the act or method of describing: *A police officer develops good powers of observation and description.* **3.** [*count; usually singular*] sort; kind; variety: *She liked dogs of every description.* **—de•scrip•tive** (di skrip′tiv) /dɪ'skrɪptɪv/ *adj.*: *She wrote a descriptive essay of her favorite place.* **—de•scrip′tive•ly,** *adv.* See -SCRIB-.

des•e•crate (des′i krāt′) /'dɛsɪˌkreyt/ *v.* [~ + *obj*], **-crat•ed, -crat•ing.** to violate by treating with disrespect; defile: *desecrated the building by painting swastikas on the walls.* **—des•e•cra•tion** (des′i krā′shən) /ˌdɛsɪ'kreyʃən/ *n.* [*noncount*]

de•seg•re•gate (dē seg′ri gāt′) /diy'sɛgrɪˌgeyt/ *v.*, **-gat•ed, -gat•ing.** to eliminate racial or other segregation in: [~ + *obj*]: *to desegregate schools.* [*no obj*]: *The governor had promised never to desegregate.* **—de•seg•re•ga•tion** (dē seg′ri gā′shən) /diyˌsɛgrɪ'geyʃən/ *n.* [*noncount*]: *fighting for desegregation of schools.* See -GREG-.

de•sen•si•tize (dē sen′si tīz′) /diy'sɛnsɪˌtayz/ *v.* [~ + *obj*], **-tized, -tiz•ing.** **1.** to lessen the sensitivity of: *Constant noise can desensitize one's hearing.* **2.** to make unfeeling or callous: *citizens desensitized to the plight of the homeless.* **—de•sen•si•ti•za•tion** (dē sen′si tə zā′shən) /diyˌsɛnsɪtə'zeyʃən/ *n.* [*noncount*]

des•ert[1] (dez′ərt) /'dɛzərt/ *n.* [*count*] **1.** a hot, dry, sandy region with little or no rain or little water: *Some animals can survive in the desert on very little water.* **2.** any place lacking in something desirable: *The town was a cultural desert.* **—adj.** [*before a noun*] **3.** of, relating to, or like a desert: *desert wilderness.* **4.** occurring or living in the desert: *a desert palm.* **5.** designed or suitable for use in the desert.

de•sert[2] (di zûrt′) /dɪ'zɜrt/ *v.* **1.** [~ + *obj*] to leave (a person, etc.) without intending to return, esp. when done against the law or in breaking a promise: *He deserted his wife and children.* **2.** (of military personnel) to run away from (service, etc.) with the intention of never returning: [~ + *obj*]: *He deserted his platoon and went over to the enemy.* [*no obj*]: *He deserted in the midst of battle.* **3.** [~ + *obj*] to fail (someone) at a time of need: *None of his friends had deserted him.* **—de•sert′er,** *n.* [*count*]

de•sert[3] (di zûrt′) /dɪ'zɜrt/ *n.* [*count*] Often, **deserts.** [*plural*] reward or punishment that is deserved: *He got his just deserts when they discovered he'd lied to everyone.*

de•serve (di zûrv′) /dɪ'zɜrv/ *v.* [*not: be* + ~*-ing*], **-served, -serv•ing.** to merit, be worthy of, or have a claim to (reward, etc.) because of actions, qualities, or circumstances: [~ + *obj*]: *The teachers deserve a pay raise.* [~ + *to* + *verb*]: *A hard worker deserves to succeed.* See -SERV-[1].

de•served (di zûrvd′) /dɪ'zɜrvd/ *adj.* being worthy of reward, punishment, etc.: *It was a well-deserved victory.* **—de•serv•ed•ly** (dē zûr′vid lē) /diy'zɜrvɪdliy/ *adv.*: *They won the race, and deservedly so.*

de•serv•ing (di zûrv′ing) /dɪ'zɜrvɪŋ/ *adj.* **1.** worthy: *He gave the prize money to a deserving charity.* **2. deserving of,** being worthy of, or qualified for, reward, punishment, etc.: *behavior deserving of praise.*

des•ic•cate (des′i kāt′) /'dɛsɪˌkeyt/ *v.*, **-cat•ed, -cat•ing.** **1.** to (cause to) become thoroughly dry or to dry up: [*no obj*]: *The plants desiccated during the drought.* [~ + *obj*]: *The hot sun desiccated the plants.* **2.** to preserve (food) by removing moisture; dehydrate: *desiccated foods.* **—des•ic•ca•tion** (des′i kā′shən) /ˌdɛsɪ'keyʃən/ *n.* [*noncount*]

de•sid•er•a•tum (di sid′ə rā′təm, -rä′-) /dɪˌsɪdə'reytəm, -'rɑ-/ *n.* [*count*], *pl.* **-ta** (-tə) /-tə/. something wanted or needed.

de•sign (di zīn′) /dɪ'zayn/ *v.* **1.** [~ + *obj*] to prepare the preliminary plans for (work): *The engineer designed a new bridge.* **2.** to plan and fashion (clothing, etc.) in an artistic or skillful way: [~ + *obj*]: *He designed a new dress for the fashion show.* [*no obj*]: *She designed for many wealthy clients.* **3.** [*usually: be* + ~*-ed*] to develop, set up, and plan for a purpose: [~ + *obj*]: *That scholarship is designed for foreign students.* [~ + *obj* + *to* + *verb*]: *She designed the scholarship to help foreign students.* **4.** [~ + *obj*] to form or make up in the mind; plan: *The prisoner designed an intricate escape.* **—n. 5.** [*count*] an outline, sketch, or drawing of something to be done or constructed: *submitted designs for the new mall.* **6.** the way in which something is composed, shaped, or made: [*count*]: *I like the colors but not the overall design.* [*noncount*]: *to study art and design.* **7.** [*count*] a pattern; a pattern of decorations: *a little heart-shaped design on the bracelet.* **8. designs,** [*plural*] a hostile or aggressive project, plot, or scheme: *He seems to have designs on my wife.* See -SIGN-.

des•ig•nate (*v.* dez′ig nāt′; *adj.* -nit, -nāt′) / *v.* 'dɛzɪgˌneyt; *adj.* -nɪt, -ˌneyt/ *v.*, **-nat•ed, -nat•ing,** *adj.* **—v. 1.** [~ + *obj*] to mark or point out; specify: *He designated the points where we would meet.* **2.** [~ + *obj* + (*as* +) *obj*] to give a name or title to: *The neighborhood was designated (as) a historic landmark area.* **3.** to nominate or select; assign: [~ + *obj* + (*as* +) *obj*]: *She was designated (as) the chairperson.* [~ + *obj* + *to* + *verb*]: *She designated me to do the work.* **—adj. 4.** [*after a noun*] named or selected for an office or position, but not yet installed: *named ambassador-designate until her formal nomination procedure was finished.* **—des•ig•na•tion** (dez′ig nā′shən) /ˌdɛzɪg'neyʃən/ *n.* [*count*]: *nicknamed "pretty boy," a designation he didn't like but endured.* See -SIGN-.

des′ignated driv′er, *n.* [*count*] a person who abstains from alcoholic beverages at a gathering in order to be fit to drive companions home safely.

de•sign•er (di zī′nər) /dɪ'zaynər/ *n.* [*count*] **1.** a person who plans or creates designs, such as for works of art: *a* *fashion designer.* **—adj.** [*before a noun*] **2.** created by or as if by an eminent designer: *designer jeans.* See -SIGN-.

de•sign•ing (di zī′ning) /dɪ'zaynɪŋ/ *adj.* [*usually before a noun*] scheming; crafty. See -SIGN-.

de•sir•a•ble (di zīᵊr′ə bəl) /dɪ'zayᵊrəbəl/ *adj.* **1.** pleasing; suitable; attractive: *a desirable apartment.* **2.** arousing desire, esp. sexual desire: *She looked very desirable in that dress.* **3.** advisable; beneficial: *a desirable law.* **—de•sir•a•bil•i•ty** (di zīᵊr′ə bil′i tē) /dɪˌzayᵊrə'bɪlɪtiy/ *n.* [*noncount*] **—de•sir′a•bly,** *adv.*

de•sire (di zīᵊr′) /dɪ'zayᵊr/ *v.,* **-sired, -sir•ing,** *n.* **—v.** [*not: be + ~-ing*] **1.** to wish for; want or long for: [~ + *obj*]: *What he really desires is a raise.* [~ + *to* + *verb*]: *She desired to be a veterinarian.* [~ + *obj* + *to* + *verb*]: *What do you desire them to do?* **2.** [~ + *obj*] to want sexually. **3.** [~ + *obj*] to ask for; request: *The mayor desires your presence at the meeting.* **—n. 4.** [*count*] a longing or craving: *an uncontrollable desire for chocolate.* **5.** [*noncount*] a strong wish to have sexual relations. **—Related Words.** DESIRE is a noun and a verb, DESIRABLE is an adjective: *His desires cannot be met. He desires to see you. That is a desirable job.*

de•sir•ous (di zīᵊr′əs) /dɪ'zayᵊrəs/ *adj.* [*be* + ~ + *of*] having or characterized by desire: *desirous of fame.*

de•sist (di zist′, -sist′) /dɪ'zɪst, -'sɪst/ *v.* [~ (+ *from* + *obj*)] to cease, such as from some action; stop: *The company agreed to desist from false advertising.* See -SIST-.

desk (desk) /dɛsk/ *n.* [*count*] **1.** an article of furniture having a broad writing surface and drawers or compartments for papers, etc. See illustration at OFFICE. **2.** the section of a large organization, such as a newspaper, having responsibility for particular operations: *worked at the city desk.* **3.** a table or counter at which a specific job is performed or a service offered: *Go to the information desk and see if they can help you.* **—adj.** [*before a noun*] **4.** of a size or form suitable for use on a desk: *a desk lamp.* **5.** done at or based on a desk: *He had a boring desk job with no chance for exercise.*

desk•top (desk′top′) /'dɛskˌtɒp/ *adj.* [*before a noun*] made to fit or be used on a desk or table: *a desktop computer.*

desk′top pub′lishing, *n.* [*noncount*] the design and production of publications with a computer and a printer to generate text and graphics.

des•o•late (*adj.* des′ə lit; *v.* -lāt′) / *adj.* 'dɛsəlɪt; *v.* -ˌleyt/ *adj., v.,* **-lat•ed, -lat•ing.** **—adj. 1.** barren; empty of people; deserted: *a treeless, desolate landscape.* **2.** feeling lonely or hopeless; forlorn: *desolate over the loss of her job.* **—v.** [~ + *obj*] **3.** to destroy, demolish, or devastate: *coastal towns desolated by the storm.* **4.** to make sad or distressed: *desolated by the death of their good friend.* **—des′o•late•ly,** *adv.* **—des′o•late•ness,** *n.* [*noncount*] See -SOLE-.

des•o•la•tion (des′ə lā′shən) /ˌdɛsə'leyʃən/ *n.* [*noncount*] **1.** an act of desolating or the state of being desolated. **2.** devastation; ruin: *The desolation of the town was caused by one bomb.* **3.** loneliness: *feelings of desolation now that their friends have moved away.* **4.** sorrow; grief; woe: *their desolation at the death of their dog.* See -SOLE-.

de•spair (di spâr′) /dɪ'spɛər/ *n.* **1.** [*noncount*] loss of hope; hopelessness: *He sank into despair when his business failed.* **2.** [*count; usually singular*] a source of hopelessness: *He's the despair of his teachers.* **—v. 3.** to lose, give up, or be without hope: [*no obj*]: *Don't despair.* [~ + *of* + *obj*]: *to despair of humanity.*

des•patch (di spach′) /dɪ'spætʃ/ *v., n.* DISPATCH.

des•per•a•do (des′pə rä′dō, -rā′-) /ˌdɛspə'rɑdow, -'rey-/ *n.* [*count*], *pl.* **-does, -dos.** a bold, reckless outlaw, esp. in the early days of the American West: *desperadoes wanted in seven states.* See -SPER-.

des•per•ate (des′pər it) /'dɛspərɪt/ *adj.* **1.** wild, reckless, or dangerous because of despair: *a desperate killer.* **2.** having an urgent need, desire, etc.: [*be* + ~ + *for*]: *desperate for attention.* [*be* + ~ + *to* + *verb*]: *desperate to succeed.* **3.** leaving little or no hope; very serious or dangerous: *a desperate illness.* **4.** making a final effort; giving all: *a desperate attempt to save a life.* **5.** extreme or excessive: *desperate need.* **—des′per•ate•ly,** *adv.* See -SPER-.

des•per•a•tion (des′pə rā′shən) /ˌdɛspə'reyʃən/ *n.* [*noncount*] the state of being desperate: *In desperation they broke down the door and rescued the child.*

des•pi•ca•ble (des′pi kə bəl, di spik′ə-) /'dɛspɪkəbəl, dɪ'spɪkə-/ *adj.* deserving to be despised: *a despicable lie.*

de•spise (di spīz′) /dɪ'spayz/ *v.* [~ + *obj*], **-spised, -spis•ing.** to look on with contempt or disdain: *I despised their actions.*

de•spite (di spīt′) /dɪ'spayt/ *prep.* in spite of; notwithstanding: *I failed the test despite studying all night.*

de•spoil (di spoil′) /dɪ'spɔyl/ *v.* [~ + *obj*] to rob or take away another's possessions, things of value, etc.; plunder: *Barbarians despoiled the northern towns.* **—de•spoil′ment,** *n.* [*noncount*]

de•spond•en•cy (di spon′dən sē) /dɪ'spɒndənsiy/ also **de•spond′ence,** *n.* [*noncount*] the state of being despondent. See -SPOND-.

de•spond•ent (di spon′dənt) /dɪ'spɒndənt/ *adj.* greatly saddened and depressed: *It's easy to get despondent when your plans go wrong.* **—de•spond′ent•ly,** *adv.* See -SPOND-.

des•pot (des′pət, -pot) /'dɛspət, -pɒt/ *n.* [*count*] a ruler with absolute power; autocrat. **—des•pot•ic** (di spot′ik) /dɪ'spɒtɪk/ *adj.*: *a despotic tyrant.* **—des•pot′i•cal•ly,** *adv.* **—des•pot•ism** (des′pə tiz′əm) /'dɛspəˌtɪzəm/ *n.* [*noncount*]: *Fifty years of despotism ruined the country.*

des•sert (di zûrt′) /dɪ'zɜrt/ *n.* a sweet food, such as cake, served as the final course of a meal: [*noncount*]: *Would you like dessert?* [*count*]: *Cut back on your desserts.*

des•ti•na•tion (des′tə nā′shən) /ˌdɛstə'neyʃən/ *n.* [*count*] the place to which a person or thing travels or is sent: *The train's final destination is North White Plains.*

des•tined (des′tind) /'dɛstɪnd/ *adj.* [*be* + ~] **1.** intended or set apart for a purpose decided in advance: [~ + *for*]: *He was destined for greatness by the way he played saxophone as a kid.* [~ + *to* + *verb*]: *impractical ideas destined to fail.* **2.** [~ + *for*] set or headed in the direction of: *a plane destined for Los Angeles.*

des•ti•ny (des′tə nē) /'dɛstəniy/ *n., pl.* **-nies. 1.** [*count; often singular*] something that is to happen or that has happened; one's future or fortune: *Her destiny was to be a surgeon.* **2.** [*noncount*] the course of events thought of as being unavoidable, impossible to resist, and decided in advance; fate: *It's pure destiny that we met!*

des•ti•tute (des′ti to͞ot′, -tyo͞ot′) /'dɛstɪˌtuwt, -ˌtyuwt/ *adj.* **1.** without means to live: *money for destitute families.* **2.** [*be* + ~ + *of*] deprived of or lacking: *At that point I was destitute of feeling.* **—des•ti•tu•tion** (des′ti to͞o′shən, -tyo͞o′-) /ˌdɛstɪ'tuwʃən, -'tyuw-/ *n.* [*noncount*] See -STIT-.

de•stroy (di stroi′) /dɪ'strɔy/ *v.* [~ + *obj*] **1.** to ruin (a thing) by demolishing; injure beyond repair: *Fire destroyed several stores in the area.* **2.** to put an end to: *They destroyed communism from within.* **3.** to kill; slay: *had to destroy the injured animal.* **4.** to defeat completely; ruin; wreck: *I felt destroyed by the thought that she no longer needed me.* See -STRU-. **—Related Words.** DESTROY is a verb, DESTRUCTIVE is an adjective, DESTRUCTION is a noun: *The bombs destroyed the factory. The bombs were very destructive. The destruction caused by the bombs was tremendous.*

de•stroy•er (di stroi′ər) /dɪ'strɔyər/ *n.* [*count*] **1.** a person or thing that destroys. **2.** a fast, small warship: *Destroyers were good at hunting for submarines.* See -STRU-.

de•struct (di strukt′) /dɪ'strʌkt/ *adj.* [*before a noun*] **1.** serving or designed to destroy: *a destruct mechanism.* **—n.** [*noncount*] **2.** the act or process of intentional destruction: *He signaled for the automatic destruct as the missile veered off course.* **—v. 3.** to destroy or cause to be destroyed: [*no obj*]: *The missile will destruct when this button is pushed.* [~ + *obj*]: *They'll destruct the missile if it goes off course.* See -STRU-.

de•struc•tion (di struk′shən) /dɪ'strʌkʃən/ *n.* [*noncount*] the act of destroying or the condition of being destroyed: *The fire caused the destruction of two famous landmarks in the area.* **—de•struc′tive,** *adj.*: *the destructive power of one nuclear bomb.* **—de•struc′tive•ly,** *adv.* **—de•struc′tive•ness,** *n.* [*noncount*] See -STRU-.

des•ul•to•ry (des′əl tôr′ē, -tōr′ē) /'dɛsəlˌtɔriy, -ˌtowriy/ *adj.* lacking in purpose or method: *a desultory conversation.*

de•tach (di tach′) /dɪ'tætʃ/ *v.* [~ + *obj*] **1.** to unfasten and separate; disconnect: *Detach the trailer from the car.* **2.** to send (a regiment, vehicle, etc.) on a special mission: *A plane was detached to search for survivors.* **—de•tach′a•ble,** *adj.*

de•tached (di tacht′) /dɪ'tætʃt/ *adj.* **1.** not attached; separated: *a detached ticket stub.* **2.** having no wall in common with another building: *a detached house.* **3.** impartial or objective; neutral: *a detached judgment.* **4.** not involved or concerned; aloof: *felt detached from the problem.*

de•tach•ment (di tach′mənt) /dɪˈtætʃmənt/ *n.* **1.** [*noncount*] the act of detaching or the condition of being detached. **2.** [*noncount*] aloofness or indifference: *His air of detachment caused him to lose a lot of friends.* **3.** [*noncount*] freedom from bias; objectivity: *The judge needs detachment to arrive at a fair verdict.* **4.** [*count*] a unit of troops or ships detached for a special mission: *a special detachment to rescue the prisoners.*

de•tail (di tāl′, dē′tāl) /dɪˈteyl, ˈdiyteyl/ *n.* **1.** [*count*] a piece or item of a whole: *The picture he drew was perfect in every detail.* **2.** [*noncount*] particular or individual parts, taken as a group: *his attention to detail.* **3.** [*noncount*] complicated decoration created with great care and attention: *the careful detail in those tiny statues.* **4.** [*count*] a small section of a larger whole, esp. of a photograph magnified to show what the eye would not otherwise be able to see: *A close-up detail of the rocket launcher showed where the faulty hose was connected.* **5.** [*count*] an individual or group selected for a special task, or the task itself: *the kitchen detail.* **—***v.* [~ + *obj*] **6.** to mention one by one; list fully: *The employees were asked to detail their complaints.* **7.** to appoint or assign (soldiers) for duty: *A squad was detailed to find the deserters and bring them to the captain.* **—*Idiom.* 8. in detail,** item by item: *We went into each complaint in detail.* **—de•tailed′,** *adj.: a detailed explanation.* See -TAIL-.

de•tain (di tān′) /dɪˈteyn/ *v.* [~ + *obj*] **1.** to keep from proceeding; delay: *I was detained at a meeting and missed the bus.* **2.** to keep under restraint: *The police detained them for several hours.* **—de•tain′ment,** *n.* [*noncount*] See -TAIN-.

de•tect (di tekt′) /dɪˈtɛkt/ *v.* [~ + *obj*] **1.** to discover or notice the existence of; find or find out: *to detect the odor of gas.* **2.** to discover (a person) in an act: *to detect someone cheating.* **3.** to discover the true nature of: *I detected a note of pity in her voice.* **—de•tect′a•ble, de•tect′i•ble,** *adj.* **—de•tec•tion** (di tek′shən) /dɪˈtɛkʃən/ *n.* [*noncount*] **—de•tec′tor,** *n.* [*count*]

de•tec•tive (di tek′tiv) /dɪˈtɛktɪv/ *n.* **1.** a police officer or a private investigator whose job is to get information and evidence about crime: *detectives assigned to the case.* **—***adj.* [*before a noun*] **2.** of or relating to detection or detectives: *enjoyed detective novels.*

dé•tente or **de•tente** (dā tänt′) /deyˈtɑnt/ *n.* [*noncount*] a relaxing of tension, esp. between nations.

de•ten•tion (di ten′shən) /dɪˈtɛnʃən/ *n.* **1.** [*noncount*] the act of detaining or the state of being detained. **2.** [*noncount*] the keeping of a person in custody or confinement. **3.** the keeping of a student after school hours as a punishment: [*noncount*]: *got detention for two days in a row.* [*count*]: *giving out detentions to everyone in the French class.*

de•ter (di tûr′) /dɪˈtɜr/ *v.* [~ + *obj* (+ *from* + *verb-ing*)], **-terred, -ter•ring.** to discourage or prevent (someone) from acting: *The large dog deterred trespassers from entering.*

de•ter•gent (di tûr′jənt) /dɪˈtɜrdʒənt/ *n.* a cleansing agent that dissolves easily in water: [*noncount*]: *laundry detergent; dish detergent.* [*count*]: *strong detergents for greasy dishes.*

de•te•ri•o•rate (di tēr′ē ə rāt′) /dɪˈtɪəriyəˌreyt/ *v.* [*no obj*], **-rat•ed, -rat•ing.** to become worse or inferior in character: *The patient's condition has deteriorated over the last few hours.* **—de•ter•i•o•ra•tion** (di tēr′ē ə rā′shən) /dɪˌtɪəriyəˈreyʃən/ *n.* [*noncount*]: *The incident triggered the rapid deterioration of peaceful relations.*

de•ter•mi•na•tion (di tûr′mə nā′shən) /dɪˌtɜrməˈneyʃən/ *n.* **1.** [*count*] the act of determining: *a determination of the money owed to you.* **2.** [*count*] the settlement or decision of a dispute, question, etc., such as by a judge: *The judge made a determination that everyone found satisfactory.* **3.** [*noncount*] the quality of being resolute; firmness of purpose: *He showed great determination in finishing this book.*

de•ter•mine (di tûr′min) /dɪˈtɜrmɪn/ *v.,* **-mined, -min•ing. 1.** to settle, resolve, or decide (a dispute, etc.): [~ + *obj*]: *The date of the election has yet to be determined.* [~ + *to* + *verb*]: *They determined to leave the school at once.* [~ + (*that*) *clause*]: *They determined that they would travel to Texas this summer.* **2.** [~ + *obj*] to conclude or figure out, such as after thinking over, or observing: *I tried to determine the reasons for her actions.* **3.** [~ + *obj*] to cause, affect, or control: *Demand usually determines supply.* **—de•ter′mi•na•ble,** *adj.* **—Related Words.** DETERMINE is a verb, DETERMINED is an adjective, DETERMINATION is a noun: *Scientists were able to determine the curvature of space. He is determined to succeed. She has a lot of determination to succeed.* See -TERM-.

de•ter•mined (di tûr′mind) /dɪˈtɜrmɪnd/ *adj.* resolute; firm; unwilling to change; staunch; stubborn: *The kids made determined efforts to drive the babysitter crazy.* [*be* + ~ + *to* + *verb*]: *She is determined to finish her book on time.*

de•ter•min•er (di tûr′mən ər) /dɪˈtɜrmənər/ *n.* [*count*] a word that comes before a noun or a noun phrase including the ARTICLES (*a, an,* and *the*), DEMONSTRATIVES (*this, that, these,* and *those*), POSSESSIVES (*my, your, his, her, our, their*), as well as the following: *all, both, half, several, some, any, no, each, every, enough, either, neither, much, many, more, most, little, less, least, few, what, whatever, which, whichever.* **—Usage.** Two determiners do not usually come together before a noun; only one is normally used at a time: *the people, these people, my people, some people, several people;* **not** *the my people, etc.* Exceptions to this rule are the determiners *all, both,* and *half,* which can occur with some determiners: *all my children, both these days, half the amount.* Some determiners can be used as PRONOUNS. As pronouns, they may stand alone: *Many are called, but few are chosen. Enough is enough.* If they are followed by the preposition *of,* then another determiner almost always comes next before the noun: *Many of the people he met agreed with him. Most of my clients are honest.*

de•ter•rence (di tûr′əns, -tur′-, -ter′-) /dɪˈtɜrəns, -ˈtʌr-, -ˈtɛr-/ *n.* [*noncount*] the act of deterring.

de•ter•rent (di tûr′ənt) /dɪˈtɜrənt/ *adj.* **1.** serving or tending to deter. **—***n.* [*count*] **2.** something that deters: *Is capital punishment a deterrent to crime?* **3.** military strength to retaliate so strongly as to deter an enemy from attacking: *People began to wonder if a nuclear deterrent was necessary anymore.*

de•test (di test′) /dɪˈtɛst/ *v.* to feel great hatred for; hate: [~ + *obj*]: *They detest war.* [~ + *verb-ing*]: *I detest jogging.* **—de•test′a•ble,** *adj.: Selfishness is a detestable quality.* **—de•tes•ta•tion** (dē′te stā′shən) /ˌdiytɛˈsteyʃən/ *n.* [*noncount*] See -TEST-.

de•throne (dē thrōn′) /diyˈθrown/ *v.* [~ + *obj*], **-throned, -thron•ing.** to remove from a throne or position of power; depose: *The champion was dethroned in the second round of the match.*

det•o•nate (det′n āt′) /ˈdɛtn̩ˌeyt/ *v.,* **-nat•ed, -nat•ing.** to (cause to) explode: [*no obj*]: *The warhead detonated against the hull of the submarine.* [~ + *obj*]: *The soldiers detonated the explosives by remote control.* **—det′o•na′tor,** *n.* [*count*]: *Someone had removed the detonator, so the bomb wouldn't explode.* See -TON-.

det•o•na•tion (det′n ā′shən) /ˌdɛtn̩ˈeyʃən/ *n.* **1.** [*count*] a loud explosion: *Detonations echoed through the town all night during the bombardment.* **2.** [*noncount*] the work or action of causing a bomb to explode: *Detonation of mines was a high priority after the war.*

de•tour (dē′tŏŏr, di tŏŏr′) /ˈdiytʊr, dɪˈtʊr/ *n.* [*count*] **1.** a roundabout way to travel, esp. one used temporarily when the main route is closed: *We took a detour around the scene of the accident.* **—***v.* **2.** to (cause to) make a detour; (cause to) go by way of a detour: [*no obj*]: *We detoured around the traffic jam by heading east.* [~ + *obj*]: *The police detoured us around the scene of the accident.*

de•tox (*n.* dē′toks; *v.* dē toks′) / *n.* ˈdiytɒks; *v.* diyˈtɒks/ *n.* [*noncount*] *Informal.* **1.** detoxification: *alcohol detox.* **—***v.* **2.** to detoxify: [~ + *obj*]: *The clinic detoxes addicts.* [*no obj*]: *She detoxed at a clinic.*

de•tox•i•fi•ca•tion (dē tok′sə fi kā′shən) /diyˌtɒksəfɪˈkeyʃən/ *n.* [*noncount*] the process of helping a person to withdraw from alcohol or an addicting drug: *an expensive clinic for detoxification.*

de•tox•i•fy (dē tok′sə fī) /diyˈtɒksəfay/ *v.,* **-fied, -fy•ing. 1.** [~ + *obj*] to rid of poison. **2.** to (cause to) undergo detoxification: [~ + *obj*]: *Counselors worked to detoxify him.* [*no obj*]: *at a clinic detoxifying after years of cocaine use.* See -TOX-.

de•tract (di trakt′) /dɪˈtrækt/ *v.* **1.** [~ + *from* + *obj*] to take away a part, as from value or reputation; lessen: *That wild hairdo detracts from your appearance.* **2.** [~ + *obj* (+ *from* + *obj*)] to divert; distract: *trying to detract attention from the real problem.* **—de•trac•tion** (di trak′shən) /dɪˈtrækʃən/ *n.* [*noncount*] **—de•trac′tor,** *n.* [*count*] See -TRAC-.

det•ri•ment (de′trə mənt) /ˈdɛtrəmənt/ *n.* loss, damage, or disadvantage: [*count*]: *Lack of education is often a* *detriment to a good career.* [*noncount*]: *He worked too hard, to the detriment of his health.*

det•ri•ment•al (de′trə men′tl) /ˌdɛtrəˈmɛntl/ *adj.* harmful or damaging: *That mistake was detrimental to her career.*

de•tri•tus (di trī′təs) /dɪˈtraytəs/ *n.* [*noncount*] disintegrated material; debris.

deuce (do͞os, dyo͞os) /duws, dyuws/ *n.* **1.** [*count*] a card having two marks or the number two; a die having two dots on it: *a pair of deuces.* **2.** [*noncount*] a situation, such as a tied score in a tennis match, in which a player must score two successive points or games to win.

de•val•u•a•tion (di val′yo͞o ā′shən) /dɪˌvælyuwˈeyʃən/ *n.* the reducing of a currency's value: [*noncount*]: *The dollar was facing devaluation.* [*count*]: *news of another devaluation of the ruble.* See -VAL-.

de•val•ue (dē val′yo͞o) /diyˈvælyuw/ *v.* [~ + *obj*], **-val•ued, -val•u•ing. 1.** to set a lower exchange value on (a currency): *The shillings were devalued.* **2.** to treat or cause to be treated as not valuable; to lower the value of: *His work was devalued at his old job.* See -VAL-.

dev•as•tate (dev′ə stāt′) /ˈdɛvəˌsteyt/ *v.* [~ + *obj*], **-tat•ed, -tat•ing. 1.** to destroy terribly; ruin: *The fire devastated the city.* **2.** to overwhelm; crush: *This latest piece of bad news devastated us.* —**dev•as•ta•tion** (dev′ə stā′shən) /ˌdɛvəˈsteyʃən/ *n.* [*noncount*]: *devastation caused by the earthquake.* —**dev′as•ta′tor,** *n.* [*count*]

dev•as•tat•ed (dev′ə stā′tid) /ˈdɛvəˌsteytɪd/ *adj.* [*be* + ~] crushed, shocked, and overwhelmed: *She was devastated at the loss of her two sons in the war.*

dev•as•tat•ing (dev′ə stā′ting) /ˈdɛvəˌsteytɪŋ/ *adj.* **1.** destroying terribly; ruining: *a devastating fire.* **2.** crushing, shocking, and overwhelming: *the devastating loss of his sons.* **3.** cutting; cleverly or intelligently said or done: *devastating arguments against every proposal I made.*

de•vel•op (di vel′əp) /dɪˈvɛləp/ *v.* **1.** to bring out the possibilities (of); come or bring to a more advanced state: [*no obj*]: *Her reading skills were developing at a rapid pace.* [~ + *obj*]: *new plans to develop natural resources.* **2.** to (cause to) grow or expand: [*no obj*]: *Your biceps will develop quickly with that exercise.* [~ + *obj*]: *exercises to develop your biceps.* **3.** [~ + *obj*] to bring into being or activity; produce: *to develop new techniques.* **4.** to (cause to) come into an active state, such as by natural growth or internal processes: [*no obj*]: *Cancer developed rapidly in the lab mice.* [~ + *obj*]: *He had begun to develop an allergy.* **5.** [~ + *obj*] to elaborate or expand in detail; show in detail: *began to gather facts to develop his theory.* **6.** [~ + *obj*] to build on or improve (a piece of land), esp. so as to make more profitable: *The builders are developing that part of town.* **7.** to be made visible, clear, or easy to see; become manifest: [*no obj*]: *The plot develops slowly.* [*It* + ~ + *that clause*]: *It developed that my client had an alibi for that night.* **8.** to immerse (film) in chemicals so that an image becomes visible: [*no obj*]: *With this instant film, the picture develops in only one minute.* [~ + *obj*]: *How long will it take to develop these pictures?* —**de•vel′op•ment,** *n.* [*count*]: *Developments were proceeding so fast he could no longer keep up.* [*noncount*]: *the development of nuclear weapons.* —**Related Words.** DEVELOP is a verb, DEVELOPMENT is a noun, DEVELOPING and DEVELOPED are adjectives: *Learners want to develop good language skills. Their development was very slow. Developing countries are poor; developed countries are rich.*

de•vel•oped (di vel′əpt) /dɪˈvɛləpt/ *adj.* [*often: before a noun*] considered to be wealthy, industrialized, and modern: *the developed countries of the West.*

de•vel•op•er (di vel′ə pər) /dɪˈvɛləpər/ *n.* **1.** [*count*] a person or group of persons intending to build on or improve land so as to make a profit on it: *greedy land developers.* **2.** [*count*] a person whose skills are expanding: *an early developer in reading.* **3.** [*count*] a person bringing new products or techniques into being: *Developers of the theory must now look elsewhere for data to confirm it.* **4.** a chemical used for developing photographic film: [*noncount*]: *Pour more developer into the tank.* [*count*]: *Maybe we can buy a developer that doesn't smell so bad.*

de•vel•op•ing (di vel′əp ing) /dɪˈvɛləpɪŋ/ *adj.* [*often: before a noun*] considered to be lacking wealth or industry; poor: *The developing nations of the world were hit hardest by the rise in oil prices.*

de•vi•ant (dē′vē ənt) /ˈdiyviyənt/ *adj.* **1.** relating to or marked by deviation: *deviant behavior in public.* —*n.* [*count*] **2.** a person or thing that deviates: *a sexual deviant.* —**de′vi•ance,** *n.* [*noncount*] See -VIA-.

de•vi•ate (*v.* dē′vē āt′; *adj., n.* -it) / *v.* ˈdiyviyˌeyt; *adj., n.* -ɪt/ *v.*, **-at•ed, -at•ing,** *adj., n.* —*v.* [*no obj;* (~ + *from* + *obj*)] **1.** to practice deviation: *The witness deviated from the truth.* —*adj.* **2.** characterized by, or showing such behavior: *criminally deviate behavior.* —*n.* [*count*] **3.** a person or thing that deviates, esp. with regard to sexual behavior. See -VIA-.

de•vi•a•tion (dē′vē ā′shən) /ˌdiyviyˈeyʃən/ *n.* **1.** [*noncount*] behavior that differs or departs from what is considered and accepted as normal or standard esp. with regard to sexual behavior. **2.** [*count*] an example of differing from what is expected; a change: *Some deviations from the regular readings on the compass were due to the presence of metal objects.* See -VIA-.

de•vice (di vīs′) /dɪˈvays/ *n.* [*count*] **1.** a thing made for a particular purpose, esp. a mechanical or electric invention: *She invented a device that automatically closes windows when it rains.* **2.** a plan, scheme, or procedure, esp. a crafty one: *full of devices for arousing sympathy.* —***Idiom.*** **3. leave (one) to one's own devices,** to allow (a person) to act freely, without being watched: *We left the children to their own devices.*

dev•il (dev′əl) /ˈdɛvəl/ *n.* [*count*] **1. a.** [*proper noun; the* + ~*; sometimes: Devil*] the supreme spirit of evil; Satan: *The preacher warned that the Devil would take their souls.* **b.** an evil spirit that is an enemy of God. **2.** a wicked, cruel person: *The dictator was a devil to his people.* **3.** a clever or mischievous person: *Those little devils poured a bucket of water on my head.* **4.** an unlucky person: *That poor devil never knew what hit him.* **5. the devil,** (used to show mild anger, amazement, or emotion in questions): *What the devil do you mean?* —***Idiom.*** **6. a** or **the devil of a,** [*before a noun*] extremely bad, terrible, difficult, etc.: *We had the devil of a time changing the spark plugs.* **7. the devil to pay,** trouble to be faced later; repercussions: *There'll be the devil to pay for your misbehavior.*

dev•il•ish (dev′əl ish) /ˈdɛvəlɪʃ/ *adj.* **1.** of, like, or befitting the devil: *a devilish grin.* **2.** difficult; bad; terrible: *had a devilish time bathing the dog.* —**dev′il•ish•ly,** *adv.*

dev′il-may-care′, *adj.* reckless; careless: *a devil-may-care attitude.*

dev•il•ment (dev′əl mənt) /ˈdɛvəlmənt/ *n.* [*noncount*] mischief; deviltry.

dev′il's ad′vocate, *n.* [*count*] one who proposes or advocates an opposing view: *Let me play (the) devil's advocate and suggest what our opponent might think.*

dev•il•try (dev′əl trē) /ˈdɛvəltriy/ *n., pl.* **-tries. 1.** [*noncount*] reckless mischief. **2.** [*count*] a diabolic act or action.

de•vi•ous (dē′vē əs) /ˈdiyviyəs/ *adj.* **1.** departing or turning away from the most direct way; roundabout: *a devious course.* **2.** not straightforward; shifty; dishonest: *His devious business methods landed him in trouble.* —**de′vi•ous•ly,** *adv.* —**de′vi•ous•ness,** *n.* [*noncount*]: *the necessary deviousness to be a thief.* See -VIA-.

de•vise (di vīz′) /dɪˈvayz/ *v.* [~ + *obj*], **-vised, -vis•ing.** to plan; invent, or create from existing principles or ideas: *to devise a method.*

de•void (di void′) /dɪˈvɔyd/ *adj.* [*be* + ~ + *of*] not possessing; totally lacking; empty of: *The judge was devoid of any sympathy when I explained my case.*

de•volve (di volv′) /dɪˈvɒlv/ *v.*, **-volved, -volv•ing. 1.** [~ + *obj*] to transfer or delegate (a duty, etc.) to another; pass on: *The company president has devolved decision-making to the department managers.* **2.** [*no obj*] to be transferred or passed on from one to another: *The responsibility devolved on me.*

de•vote (di vōt′) /dɪˈvowt/ *v.* [~ + *obj* + *to* + *obj*], **-vot•ed, -vot•ing.** to apply (something) to a particular purpose; set apart or dedicate to: *to devote more of his time to study.* See -VOT-.

de•vot•ed (di vō′tid) /dɪˈvowtɪd/ *adj.* **1.** relating to or marked by devotion: *a devoted friend.* **2.** [*before a noun*] involving great care or attention: *decades of devoted research.* —**de•vot′ed•ly,** *adv.*

dev•o•tee (dev′ə tē′, -tā′) /ˌdɛvəˈtiy, -ˈtey/ *n.* [*count*] one who is enthusiastic about something; a fan: *gun devotees and their lobbies.* See -VOT-.

de•vo•tion (di vō′shən) /dɪˈvowʃən/ *n.* **1.** [*noncount*] earnest attachment to a cause, person, etc.: *His devotion to his children is plain to see.* **2.** [*noncount*] deep dedication, esp. to religion; consecration: *a life of devotion to God.* **3.** [*noncount*] the act of devoting: *demanding devotion to the Party.* **4.** Often, **devotions.** [*plural*] religious observance or prayers. —**de•vo′tion•al,** *adj.* [*before a noun*]: *devotional candles.*

de•vour (di vour′) /dɪˈvawr/ *v.* [~ + *obj*] **1.** to swallow or eat up hungrily: *He devoured several helpings of stew.* **2.** to consume destructively; demolish; destroy: *Fire devoured the museum.* **3.** to take in eagerly with the senses or intellect: *devoured one book after another.* **4.** [*usually: be + ~-ed + by*] to absorb completely; engross: *His mind was devoured by hatred.* See -VOR-.

de•vout (di vout′) /dɪ'vawt/ *adj.*, **-er, -est. 1.** devoted to divine worship or service; religious: *a devout Hindu.* **2.** [*before a noun*] serious; earnest; sincere: *a devout admirer of French painting.* —**de•vout•ly,** *adv.* —**de•vout′•ness,** *n.* [*noncount*] See -VOT-.

dew (do͞o, dyo͞o) /duw, dyuw/ *n.* [*noncount*] moisture from the atmosphere, esp. at night, and deposited in small drops upon a cool surface: *beads of dew.* —**dew′y,** *adj.*, **-i•er, -i•est.**

dew•drop (do͞o′drop′, dyo͞o′-) /'duw,drɒp, 'dyuw-/ *n.* [*count*] a drop of dew.

dew•lap (do͞o′lap′, dyo͞o′-) /'duw,læp, 'dyuw-/ *n.* [*count*] a loose, hanging fold of skin under the throat of an animal.

dew′ point′, *n.* [*count*] temperature at which dew begins to form.

dex•ter•i•ty (dek ster′i tē) /dɛk'stɛrɪtiy/ *n.* [*noncount*] skill in using the body or mind, esp. the hands: *manual dexterity.*

dex•ter•ous (dek′strəs, -stər əs) /'dɛkstrəs, -stərəs/ *adj.* skillful or nimble in the use of the hands, body, or mind.

dex•trose (dek′strōs) /'dɛkstrows/ *n.* [*noncount*] a form of glucose or sugar occurring in fruits and in animal tissues.

dho•ti (dō′tē) /'dowtiy/ *n.* [*count*], *pl.* **-tis.** a long loincloth worn by many Hindu men in India.

di-, *prefix. di-* comes from Greek, where it has the meaning "two, double". This meaning is found in such words as: DIODE, DIOXIN, DIPTYCH.

dia-, *prefix. dia-* comes from Greek, where it has the meanings "through, across, from point to point; completely." These meanings are found in such words as: DIAGNOSIS, DIALOGUE, DIALYSIS, DIAMETER, DIAPHANOUS, DIARRHEA.

di•a•be•tes (dī′ə bē′tis, -tēz) /,dayə'biytɪs, -tiyz/ *n.* [*noncount; used with a singular verb*] a disorder in which there are high levels of glucose in the blood and increased urine production.

di•a•bet•ic (dī′ə bet′ik) /,dayə'bɛtɪk/ *n.* [*count*] **1.** a person suffering from diabetes. —*adj.* [*before a noun*] **2.** of or relating to diabetics or diabetes: *diabetic medicine.*

di•a•bol•ic (dī′ə bol′ik) /,dayə'bɒlɪk/ also **di′a•bol′i•cal,** *adj.* **1.** devilish; fiendish; extremely wicked: *a diabolic plot to kill the president.* **2.** relating to or caused by a devil. —**di′a•bol′i•cal•ly,** *adv.* —**di′a•bol′i•cal•ness,** *n.* [*noncount*]

di•a•crit•ic (dī′ə krit′ik) /,dayə'krɪtɪk/ *n.* [*count*] Also called **diacrit′ical mark′.** a mark, as a cedilla (¸), tilde (˜), circumflex (ˆ), or macron (¯), added to a letter, used to indicate a sound different from that of the same letter without the mark, or to indicate stress.

di•a•dem (dī′ə dem′) /'dayə,dɛm/ *n.* [*count*] **1.** CROWN (def. 1). **2.** a headband worn as a symbol of royalty.

di•ag•nose (dī′əg nōs′, -nōz′) /'dayəg,nows, -,nowz/ *v.*, **-nosed, -nos•ing. 1.** to determine the identity of (a disease, etc.) by an examination: [*~ + obj*]: *He diagnosed cancer after the examination of the tissues.* [*~ + obj + as + obj*]: *She diagnosed the illness as cancer.* **2.** to determine the cause or nature of (a problem) from the visible signs: [*~ + obj*]: *The car mechanic diagnosed the problem.* [*~ + obj + as + obj*]: *The car mechanic diagnosed the problem as worn brake linings.* See -GNOS-.

di•ag•no•sis (dī′əg nō′sis) /,dayəg'nowsɪs/ *n.*, *pl.* **-ses** (-sēz) /-siyz/. **1. a.** the act or process of diagnosing: [*noncount*]: *Dad was in for diagnosis.* [*count*]: *A diagnosis would require a full-day examination.* **b.** [*count*] the decision reached from diagnosing: *The doctor announced her diagnosis: cancer.* **2.** an analysis of the cause or nature of a problem: [*count*]: *a careful diagnosis of our problems in the sales department.* [*noncount*]: *careful diagnosis of the problems in our schools.* —**di•ag•nos•tic** (dī′ag nos′tik) /,dayæg'nɒstɪk/ *adj.* —**di•ag•nos•ti•cian** (dī′ag no stish′ən) /,dayægnɒ'stɪʃən/ *n.* [*count*] See -GNOS-.

di•ag•o•nal (dī ag′ə nl) /day'ægənl/ *adj.* **1.** connecting two angles that are not next to each other, such as at opposite corners of a square: *a diagonal line.* **2.** having an oblique or slanting direction: *diagonal stripes.* —*n.* [*count*] **3.** a diagonal line or plane. —**di•ag′o•nal•ly,** *adv.*

di•a•gram (dī′ə gram′) /'dayə,græm/ *n.*, *v.*, **-gramed** or **-grammed, -gram•ing** or **-gram•ming.** —*n.* [*count*] **1.** a drawing that outlines and explains the parts or operation of something: *a diagram of an engine.* **2.** a chart or plan: *The first diagram is a pie chart showing spending.* —*v.* [*~ + obj*] **3.** to represent by a diagram; make a diagram of.

di•al (dī′əl, dīl) /'dayəl, dayl/ *n.*, *v.*, **di•aled** or **di•alled, di•al•ing** or **di•al•ling.** —*n.* [*count*] **1.** a plate or disk on a clock or watch, containing markings upon which the time of day is indicated by hands or pointers: *The second hand swept across the dial.* **2.** a plate with markings for indicating a measurement or number, usually by means of a pointer: *All the dials showed zero as the power went off.* **3.** a knob that can be rotated, used for regulating a mechanism, esp. one that tunes a radio or television. **4. a.** a rotating disk on a telephone that is used in making calls. **b.** a set of pushbuttons on a telephone that perform the same function. —*v.* **5.** [*~ + obj*] to register on or as if on a dial: *He dialed the numbers on the safe.* **6.** [*~ + (in +) obj*] to select by means of a dial: *I dialed in a country-and-western station on the radio.* **7.** [*~ + obj*] to make a telephone call to: *I dialed your number but got a busy signal.* **8.** [*no obj*] to dial a telephone: *I started to dial but then hung up.*

di•a•lect (dī′ə lekt′) /'dayə,lɛkt/ *n.* a variety of a language different from other varieties of the same language in that it has special features of sound, word arrangement, and vocabulary, and is used by a group of speakers set off from others either geographically or socially: [*count*]: *Cockney is the colorful dialect spoken in the East End of London.* [*noncount*]: *He lapsed into dialect.* —**di•a•lect•al** (dī′ə lek′tl) /,dayə'lɛktl/ *adj.*: *dialectal differences.*

di•a•logue or **di•a•log** (dī′ə lôg′, -log′) /'dayə,lɔg, -,lɒg/ *n.* **1.** conversation between two or more persons, or between two or more characters in a novel, drama, etc.: [*count*]: *A dialogue with him was more like a monologue; he spoke and I listened.* [*noncount*]: *The weakest part of the new play is dialogue; the characters don't sound believable.* **2.** [*count*] an exchange of ideas or opinions with a view to reaching an amicable agreement: *A dialogue was opened between the two leaders.* See -LOG-.

di•al•y•sis (dī al′ə sis) /day'æləsɪs/ *n.*, *pl.* **-ses** (-sēz′) /-,siyz/. a process, used in treating kidney disease, in which wastes are removed from the blood by a special machine: [*count*]: *Her dialysis lasts for an hour every two days.* [*noncount*]: *She's in for dialysis again this week.* See -LYS-.

di•am•e•ter (dī am′i tər) /day'æmɪtər/ *n.* **1.** [*count*] a straight line passing through the center of a figure, esp. one passing through the center of a circle or sphere. **2.** the length of such a line: [*count*]: *What is the diameter of the earth?* [*noncount; often: in + ~*]: *It is 25,000 miles in diameter.* See -METER-.

di•a•met•ri•cal•ly (dī′ə me′trik lē) /,dayə'mɛtrɪkliy/ *adv.* in direct opposition; at opposite extremes: *diametrically opposed opinions.* See -METER-.

dia•mond (dī′mənd, dī′ə-) /'daymənd, 'dayə-/ *n.* **1.** [*count*] a stone of pure and extremely hard crystallized carbon that when cut and polished is transparent, bright, and valued as a precious gem: *Coal and diamonds are both made of carbon.* **2.** [*plural*] a piece of jewelry containing diamonds: *She wore her diamonds.* **3.** [*count*] a four-sided figure with sides of equal length but with no right angles. **4. a.** [*count*] a red figure shaped that way on a playing card. **b.** [*count*] a card bearing such figures: *I had five diamonds.* **c. diamonds,** [*noncount; plural; used with a singular or plural verb*] the suit of playing cards marked this way: *Diamonds is the suit that is bid.* **5.** [*count*] the infield or the entire playing field in baseball. —*adj.* [*before a noun*] **6.** made of or set with diamonds: *a diamond ring.* **7.** having the shape of a diamond. **8.** indicating the 60th or 75th event of a series, such as a wedding anniversary. —***Idiom.* 9. a diamond in the rough,** [*count*] a person or thing of great worth but unpolished or uncultivated.

dia′mond lane′, *n.* [*count*] a highway lane reserved for buses and passenger vans and not for private cars, marked with a large diamond shape on the pavement.

di•a•per (dī′pər, dī′ə pər) /'daypər, 'dayəpər/ *n.* [*count*] **1.** a piece of folded cloth or other absorbent material worn as underpants by a baby: *throwaway paper diapers.* —*v.* [*~ + obj*] **2.** to put a diaper on: *diapered the baby.*

di•aph•a•nous (dī af′ə nəs) /day'æfənəs/ *adj.* very sheer and light; nearly transparent: *as diaphanous as a spider's web.*

di•a•phragm (dī′ə fram′) /'dayə,fræm/ *n.* [*count*] **1.** a wall of muscle separating two cavities, esp. separating the chest and lungs from the stomach and abdomen: *When the diaphragm contracts uncontrollably, you get hiccups.* **2.** a thin disk that vibrates when receiving or producing sound waves, such as in a telephone. **3.** a thin, dome-shaped contraceptive device usually of rubber, that covers the cervix. **4.** a device in a camera that controls the amount of light entering the instrument.

di•ar•rhe•a or **di•ar•rhoe•a** (dī′ə rē′ə) /ˌdayə'riyə/ *n.* [*noncount*] an intestinal disorder characterized by frequent and loose bowel movements: *a bad case of diarrhea.*

di•a•ry (dī′ə rē) /'dayəriy/ *n.* [*count*], *pl.* **-ries. 1.** a daily written record of one's observations and feelings: *Keep a diary of everyday happenings.* **2.** a book for keeping such a record: *She wrote in her diary.* **3.** a book for noting daily appointments: *I've checked my diary and I'm free next week.* **—di•a•rist** (dī′ə rist) /'dayərɪst/ *n.* [*count*]

Di•as•po•ra (dī as′pər ə) /day'æspərə/ *n.* **1.** [*proper noun; usually: the* + ~] the scattering of the Jews to countries outside of Palestine after the Babylonian captivity. **2.** [*count; diaspora*] a scattering by a group from a country; dispersion.

di•a•tribe (dī′ə trīb′) /'dayəˌtrayb/ *n.* [*count*] a bitter criticism or act of denouncing; tirade: *In her diatribe, she gave full vent to all her resentments.*

dib•ble (dib′əl) /'dɪbəl/ *n., v.,* **-bled, -bling. —***n.* [*count*] **1.** Also, **dib•ber** (dib′ər) /'dɪbər/. a small, hand-held, pointed tool for making holes in soil, such as for planting seedlings and bulbs. **—***v.* [~ + *obj*] **2.** to make holes (in soil) with a dibble: *Dibble the soil before planting.* **3.** to plant with a dibble.

dice (dīs) /days/ *n.pl., sing.* **die,** *v.,* **diced, dic•ing. —***n.* **1.** [*plural*] small cubes, marked on each side with one to six spots, used in games or gambling: *We rolled the dice and I had a ten.* **2.** [*noncount*] any of various games, esp. gambling games, played by shaking and throwing such cubes: *a game of dice.* **—***v.* [~ + *obj*] **3.** to cut into small cubes: *Dice the vegetables.* **—*Idiom.* 4. no dice, a.** of no use; ineffective: *We tried to reach you, but it was no dice.* **b.** (used to answer "no" to a request): *"Could you lend me $500?" —"Sorry, no dice!"*

di•chot•o•my (dī kot′ə mē) /day'kɒtəmiy/ *n.* [*count*], *pl.* **-mies.** division into two parts, esp. into two parts that are opposed: *a dichotomy between thought and action.* See -TOM-.

dick (dik) /dɪk/ *n.* [*count*] *Slang.* **1.** detective. **2.** *Vulgar.* PENIS.

dick•er (dik′ər) /'dɪkər/ *v.* [*no obj*] to bargain; haggle: *We dickered over the price.*

dick•ey or **dick•y** (dik′ē) /'dɪkiy/ *n.* [*count*], *pl.* **-eys** or **-ies. 1.** a garment that resembles the front or collar of a shirt, worn under a jacket or dress. **2.** a small bird.

-dict-, *root. -dict-* comes from Latin, where it has the meaning "say, speak." This meaning is found in such words as: BENEDICTION, CONTRADICT, DICTATE, DICTATOR, DICTION, DICTIONARY, DICTUM, EDICT, PREDICT.

dic•tate (*v.* dik′tāt, dik tāt′; *n.* dik′tāt) / *v.* 'dɪkteyt, dɪk'teyt; *n.* 'dɪkteyt/ *v.,* **-tat•ed, -tat•ing,** *n.* **—***v.* [~ + *obj*] **1.** to say or read out loud for another person or a machine to record: *She dictated a memo to her secretary.* **2.** to command with great authority; order forcefully: *The victorious nations were able to dictate peace terms.* **—***n.* [*count*] **3.** an order or command: *Usually their dictates are to be obeyed.* **4.** a guiding principle: *the dictates of conscience.* See -DICT-.

dic•ta•tion (dik tā′shən) /dɪk'teyʃən/ *n.* **1.** the act of dictating: [*noncount*]: *had a test in French dictation.* [*count*]: *Madame is always giving us dictations.* **2.** [*noncount*] the act of commanding: *There's no need for dictation from above.* See -DICT-.

dic•ta•tor (dik′tā tər, dik tā′tər) /'dɪkteytər, dɪk'teytər/ *n.* [*count*] **1.** a ruler who has absolute power without the consent of the people. **2.** a person who commands with forcefulness: *The secretary had become the dictator of the office.* **3.** a person who dictates, as to a secretary or a machine. See -DICT-.

dic•ta•to•ri•al (dik′tə tôr′ē əl, -tōr′-) /ˌdɪktə'tɔriyəl, -'towr-/ *adj.* **1.** of or relating to a dictator: *a president with no dictatorial powers.* **2.** overly demanding; domineering: *I resented his dictatorial manner.* See -DICT-.

dic•ta•tor•ship (dik tā′tər ship) /dɪk'teytərʃɪp/ *n.* **1.** government by a dictator: [*noncount*]: *rule by dictatorship.* [*count*]: *Would we see a dictatorship?* **2.** [*count*] a country ruled by a dictator or in a dictatorial manner: *Should the nation be doing business with dictatorships?* See -DICT-.

dic•tion (dik′shən) /'dɪkʃən/ *n.* [*noncount*] **1.** style of speaking or writing: *The student's poor diction prevented the professor from understanding her paper.* **2.** the accent, inflection, and tone that a speaker or singer has; enunciation: *the actress's clear diction.* See -DICT-.

dic•tion•ar•y (dik′shə ner′ē) /'dɪkʃəˌnɛriy/ *n.* [*count*], *pl.* **-ies. 1.** a book containing the words of a language, usually in alphabetical order, with information about their meanings, pronunciations, special forms, etc.; such a book having the words of one language expressed in another language: *a learner's dictionary of English; a Norwegian-English dictionary.* **2.** a book giving information on particular subjects or on a particular class of names, facts, etc., usually arranged alphabetically: *a biographical dictionary.* **3.** a list of words used by a word-processing program to check spellings in text. See -DICT-.

dic•tum (dik′təm) /'dɪktəm/ *n.* [*count*], *pl.* **-ta** (-tə) /-tə/ **-tums. 1.** an authoritative pronouncement; decree; order: *We'll have to go along with the boss's dictum.* **2.** a familiar saying; proverb; maxim: *the old dictum that blood is thicker than water.* See -DICT-.

did (did) /dɪd/ *v.* pt. of DO[1].

di•dac•tic (dī dak′tik) /day'dæktɪk/ also **di•dac′ti•cal,** *adj.* **1.** intended for instruction; instructive: *didactic poetry.* **2.** too eager or inclined to teach or lecture others: *He was a boring, didactic speaker.*

did•dle (did′l) /'dɪdl̩/ *v.* [~ + *obj*], **-dled, -dling.** *Informal.* to cheat; take money from unlawfully or dishonestly; swindle. **—did′dler,** *n.* [*count*]

didn't (did′nt) /'dɪdnt/ contraction of *did not*: *didn't go home until midnight.*

die[1] (dī) /day/ *v.* [*no obj*], **died, dy•ing. 1.** to cease to live; perish: *How many people died in the war?* [~ + *of* + *obj*]: *He died of thirst or starvation.* [~ + *from* + *obj*]: *He died from a gunshot wound.* **2.** [*often: be* + ~*-ing*] to lose force, strength, or vital qualities: *I think he's dying; you'd better come to the hospital now.* **3.** to cease to exist; vanish: *The happy look died on her face.* **4.** to cease to function; lose power; fade gradually: *The engine died.* **5.** [*often: be* + ~*-ing;* ~ + *of* + *obj*] to suffer as if fatally: *I'm dying of boredom!* **6.** [*often: be* + ~*-ing*] to desire strongly or wish for keenly: [~ + *for* + *obj*]: *I'm dying for a cup of coffee.* [~ + *to* + *verb*]: *I'm dying to go back to the mountains.* **7. die away,** (of a sound) to become fainter and then cease altogether: *The laughter died away.* **8. die down,** to become calm or quiet; subside: *The storm died down quickly.* **9. die off,** to die one after another until the number is greatly reduced: *Those languages are in danger of dying off and no one is there to record them.* **10. die out, a.** to cease to exist; become extinct: *Little mom-and-pop corner stores are in danger of dying out.* **b.** to die away; fade; subside: *Gradually the roar died out and the night became quiet.* **—*Idiom.* 11. die hard,** [*no obj*] to give way after a hard, bitter struggle: *Childhood beliefs die hard.*

die[2] (dī) /day/ *n.* [*count*], *pl.* **dies** for 1, **dice** for 2. **1.** any of various devices for cutting or forming material in a press or a stamping or forging machine. **2.** the singular form of DICE: *One die rolled right off the table.* **—*Idiom.* 3. the die is cast,** a decision has been made and cannot be changed: *When Caesar led his army across the Rubicon to take over Rome, he said the die was cast.*

die′-hard′ or **die′hard′,** *n.* [*count*] **1.** a person who vigorously resists change: *Some of the die-hards refused to accept the new government.* **—***adj.* [*usually: before a noun*] **2.** resistant to change.

di•er•e•sis (dī er′ə sis) /day'ɛrəsɪs/ *n.* [*count*], *pl.* **-ses** (-sēz′) /-ˌsiyz/. a sign (¨) placed over the second of two adjacent vowels to indicate that it is to be pronounced separately, as in the spellings *naïve* and *coöperate.* **—di•e•ret•ic** (dī′ə ret′ik) /ˌdayə'rɛtɪk/ *adj.*

die•sel (dē′zəl, -səl) /'diyzəl, -səl/ *adj.* [*often: before a noun*] **1.** being or referring to a machine or vehicle powered by a diesel engine: *a diesel locomotive.* **2.** of or used by a diesel engine: *diesel fuel.* **—***n.* **3.** [*count*] Also, **diesel engine.** an engine powered by heated oil, used by buses, trucks, and some cars. **4.** [*count*] a vehicle powered by a diesel engine: *Some diesels have trouble starting on cold days.* **5.** [*noncount*] Also, **diesel oil.** a type of heavy fuel oil used in a diesel engine.

di•et[1] (dī′it) /'dayɪt/ *n.* **1.** food and drink in relation to health: [*noncount*]: *the effect of diet on health.* [*count*]: *He'll have to watch his diet.* **2.** [*count*] a particular selection of food, esp. for improving a person's physical condition: *a low-fat diet.* **3.** [*count*] such a selection or a limitation on the amount a person eats for reducing weight: *to go on a diet.* **4.** [*count*] the foods habitually eaten by a person, animal, or group: *They live on a diet of roots,* *honey, and berries.* **5.** [*count*] anything done by habit or used over and over again: *watched a steady diet of talk shows.* **—***v.* [*no obj*] **6.** [*often: be* + *~-ing*] to select or limit the food one eats, esp. to lose weight: *No dessert for me, thanks, I'm dieting.* **—***adj.* [*before a noun*] **7.** suitable for consumption with a weight-reduction diet: *diet soft drinks.* **—di′et•er,** *n.* [*count*]

di•et[2] (dī′it) /ˈdayɪt/ *n.* [*count; often: the* + *~*] the legislative body of certain countries.

di•e•tar•y (dī′i ter′ē) /ˈdayɪˌtɛriy/ *adj.* [*before a noun*] of or relating to diet or the food one eats or is allowed to eat: *dietary restrictions.*

di•e•tet•ic (dī′i tet′ik) /ˌdayɪˈtɛtɪk/ *adj.* Also, **di′e•tet′i•cal. 1.** of or relating to diet; prepared or suitable for special diets. **—***n.* **2. dietetics,** [*noncount; used with a singular verb*] the science of nutrition and food preparation.

di•e•ti•tian or **di•e•ti•cian** (dī′i tish′ən) /ˌdayɪˈtɪʃən/ *n.* [*count*] a person who is an expert in nutrition or dietetics.

dif•fer (dif′ər) /ˈdɪfər/ *v.* [*no obj*] **1.** [*not: be* + *~-ing*] to be unlike, dissimilar, or distinct in nature or qualities: *The two candidates differ in style and substance.* [*~* + *from* + *obj*]: *This candidate differed from the others.* **2.** to disagree in opinion, belief, etc.; disagree: *differed sharply in their approach to tax credits.* [*~* + *with* + *obj*]: *I differ with my partner sometimes, but we usually agree.* **—Related Words.** DIFFER is a verb, DIFFERENT is an adjective, DIFFERENCE is a noun: *The two theories differ from each other. He is different from all the rest. There is no difference between them.* See -FER-.

dif•fer•ence (dif′ər əns, dif′rəns) /ˈdɪfərəns, ˈdɪfrəns/ *n.* **1.** [*noncount*] the state or relation of being different; dissimilarity. **2.** [*count*] an instance or point of unlikeness or dissimilarity: *the differences in their behavior.* **3.** [*noncount*] a significant change in a situation: *It made no difference what I said.* **4.** [*count*] a distinguishing characteristic; distinctive quality, feature, etc.: *There was a difference in her face after the ordeal.* **5.** the degree to which one person or thing differs from another: [*count; usually singular*]: *The difference in their ages is about six months.* [*noncount*]: *There isn't much difference between one politician and another.* **6.** [*count*] a disagreement in opinion; dispute; quarrel: *a strong difference of opinion.*

dif•fer•ent (dif′ər ənt, dif′rənt) /ˈdɪfərənt, ˈdɪfrənt/ *adj.* **1.** [*~* + *from*] not alike in character or quality; dissimilar: *Her hat is different from yours.* **2.** not identical; separate or distinct: *three different answers.* **3.** [*before a plural noun*] various; several: *Different people told me the same story.* **4.** not ordinary; unusual; original: *That hairdo you're wearing certainly is different!* **—dif′fer•ent•ly,** *adv.: They behaved differently when alone.*

dif•fer•en•tial (dif′ə ren′shəl) /ˌdɪfəˈrɛnʃəl/ *adj.* **1.** of or relating to difference. **—***n.* [*count*] **2.** a difference or the amount of difference between comparable things: *a wage differential between police and firefighters.*

dif•fer•en•ti•ate (dif′ə ren′shē āt′) /ˌdɪfəˈrɛnʃiyˌeyt/ *v.,* **-at•ed, -at•ing. 1.** [*~* + *obj* + *from* + *obj*] to form or mark differently from other such things; distinguish: *The chrome trim and tinted glass differentiate the high-price model from the standard one.* **2.** to see, understand, recognize, or perceive the difference in or between: [*~* + *between*]: *learned to differentiate between French and German wines.* [*~* + *obj* + *from* + *obj*]: *learned to differentiate a French wine from a German wine.* **—dif•fer•en•ti•a•tion** (dif′ə ren′shē ā′shən) /ˌdɪfəˌrɛnʃiyˈeyʃən/ *n.* [*noncount*]

dif•fi•cult (dif′i kult′, -kəlt) /ˈdɪfɪˌkʌlt, -kəlt/ *adj.* **1.** requiring special effort, skill, or planning: *a difficult job.* [*it* + *be* + *~* + *(for* + *obj* +*) to* + *verb*]: *It was difficult (for her) to get a good job.* **2.** hard to understand or solve: *a difficult problem.* **3.** hard to deal with or get along with: *a difficult pupil.* **4.** disadvantageous; trying; hampering: *under difficult conditions.* **5.** full of hardship, esp. financial hardship: *in these difficult times.* **—dif′fi•cult′ly,** *adv.*

dif•fi•cul•ty (dif′i kul′tē) /ˈdɪfɪˌkʌltiy/ *n., pl.* **-ties. 1.** [*noncount*] the fact or condition of being difficult: *The difficulty of the courses was too much for some students.* **2.** [*count*] Often, **difficulties.** [*plural*] an embarrassing situation, esp. of financial affairs: *had difficulties paying our bills each month.* **3.** [*count*] a disagreement or dispute: *Because of some difficulties with scheduling, the new course was cancelled.*

dif•fi•dent (dif′i dənt) /ˈdɪfɪdənt/ *adj.* lacking confidence in one's own ability; hesitant; reserved: *diffident in saying what he thinks.* **—dif′fi•dence,** *n.* [*noncount*]: *Their diffidence keeps them from making new friends.*

dif•fuse (*v.* di fyo͞oz′; *adj.* -fyo͞os′) / *v.* dɪˈfyuwz; *adj.* -ˈfyuws/ *v.,* **-fused, -fusing,** *adj.* **—***v.* **1.** to (cause to) spread or scatter widely: [*no obj*]: *The light diffused into the room.* [*~* + *obj*]: *Diffuse the light in your room to avoid glare.* **2.** [*~* + *obj*] to spread out freely without restriction; disseminate: *The printing press helped diffuse knowledge.* **—***adj.* **3.** widely spread or scattered; dispersed: *The room was bathed in soft, diffuse light.* **4.** characterized by wordiness in speech or writing; disjointed: *I got lost in your rather diffuse essay.* **—dif•fuse•ly** (di fyo͞os′lē) /dɪˈfyuwsliy/ *adv.* **—dif•fuse′ness,** *n.* [*noncount*] **—dif•fu•sion** (di fyo͞o′zhən) /dɪˈfyuwʒən/ *n.* [*noncount*]: *diffusion of gases into the atmosphere.* **—dif•fu•sive** (di fyo͞o′siv) /dɪˈfyuwsɪv/ *adj.* See -FUS-.

dig[1] (dig) /dɪg/ *v.,* **dug** (dug) /dʌg/ **dig•ging,** *n.* **—***v.* **1.** to break up and turn over earth, sand, etc., as with a shovel or spade: [*no obj*]: *We were digging in the tunnel most of the day.* [*~* + *obj*]: *The little gopher digs a maze of tunnels underground.* **2.** [*no obj*] to work by or as if by removing or turning over material: *I'll have to dig through the old files.* **3.** [*~* + *obj* + *in(to)*] to poke, thrust, or force: *He dug his heels into the ground.* **4. dig in,** [*no obj*] **a.** to keep or maintain one's opinion or position: *The negotiators dug in and refused to budge.* **b.** *Informal.* to start eating: *We dug in as soon as the food came out of the kitchen.* **5. dig out, a.** to hollow out by digging; free (something) by digging around: [*~* + *obj* + *out*]: *We dug the car out of the snow.* [*~* + *out* + *obj*]: *We dug out his car and got it going.* **b.** to find or discover by searching: [*~* + *out* + *obj*]: *I dug out an old pair of shoes and a jacket from the 60's.* [*~* + *obj* + *out* + *of* + *obj*]: *Can you dig the material out of the archives?* **6. dig up, a.** to discover in the course of digging and remove from the ground: [*~* + *up* + *obj*]: *The rescue workers dug up nearly fifty bodies in the rubble.* [*~* + *obj* + *up*]: *The coroner dug the body up and performed another autopsy.* **b.** [*~* + *up* + *obj*] to find or bring to light; discover: *The press dug up another scandal this week.* **—***n.* [*count*] **7.** a thrust; poke: *a quick dig in the ribs.* **8.** a cutting, sarcastic remark: *Someone had to get in a dig about my freckles.* **9.** an archaeological site undergoing excavation: *We visited the dig and saw the tools they had discovered.* **10. digs,** [*plural*] *Informal.* living quarters; lodgings: *Hey, these digs are great!* **—dig′ger,** *n.* [*count*]

dig[2] (dig) /dɪg/ *v.,* **dug** (dug) /dʌg/ **dig•ging.** *Slang.* **—***v.* **1.** to understand: [*~* + *obj*]: *Can you dig that?* [*no obj*]: *I'll be there, you dig?* **2.** [*~* + *obj*] to take notice of; look at carefully: *Dig those shoes he's wearing.* **3.** [*~* + *obj*] to like or enjoy: *I really dig those styles they wear.*

di•gest (*v.* di jest′, dī-; *n.* dī′jest) / *v.* dɪˈdʒɛst, day-; *n.* ˈdaydʒɛst/ *v.* **1.** (of food) to (cause to) change or be changed into a form that the body can use: [*no obj*]: *Some foods don't digest easily.* [*~* + *obj*]: *The baby had a hard time digesting such rich food.* **2.** [*~* + *obj*] to obtain ideas or meaning from; think over; take into the mind: *I tried to digest this article on nuclear energy.* **—***n.* [*count*] **3.** a collection of writing or of scientific matter, esp. when it is classified or condensed; summary: *a thirty-page digest of the news.* **—di•gest′i•ble,** *adj.*: *The food was easily digestible.* See -GEST-.

di•ges•tion (di jes′chən, dī-) /dɪˈdʒɛstʃən, day-/ *n.* **1.** [*noncount*] the process of digesting foods: *Digestion is hindered by running immediately after eating.* **2.** [*count; usually singular*] the function, power, or ability of digesting food: *My digestion got worse after surgery.* **—di•ges•tive** (di jes′tiv, dī-) /dɪˈdʒɛstɪv, day-/ *adj.*

dig•it (dij′it) /ˈdɪdʒɪt/ *n.* [*count*] **1.** any of the Arabic numerals of 1 through 9 and 0. **2.** any symbol of other number systems, as 0 or 1 in the binary: *There are only two digits in the binary system, 0 and 1.* **3.** a finger or toe: *He lost a digit in the war.*

dig•it•al (dij′i tl) /ˈdɪdʒɪtl̩/ *adj.* **1.** of, relating to, or resembling a digit or finger. **2.** performed or manipulated with a finger: *a digital switch.* **3.** of, relating to, or using data in the form of numerical digits: *a digital recording.* **4.** displaying a readout in numerical digits: *a digital clock.* Compare ANALOG. **—dig′it•al•ly,** *adv.*

dig′ital au′diotape, *n.* [*count*] magnetic tape on which sound is digitally recorded with high fidelity for playback.

dig•ni•fied (dig′nə fīd′) /ˈdɪgnəˌfayd/ *adj.* having or showing dignity.

dig•ni•fy (dig′nə fī′) /ˈdɪgnəˌfay/ *v.* [*~* + *obj*], **-fied, -fy•ing. 1.** to confer honor or dignity upon; honor. **2.** to give undeserved distinction or honor to: *Don't dignify his silly scratchings by calling it scholarship.*

dig•ni•tar•y (dig′ni ter′ē) /ˈdɪgnɪˌtɛriy/ *n.* [*count*], *pl.* **-tar•ies.** a person who holds a high rank or office.

dig•ni•ty (dig′ni tē) /ˈdɪgnɪtiy/ *n., pl.* **-ties. 1.** [*count; usually singular*] appearance and conduct that indicate self-respect and formality: *maintained her dignity throughout the trial.* **2.** [*noncount*] elevated rank, office, station, etc.: *the dignity of the high court.* **3.** [*noncount*] a sign or token of respect: *a question unworthy of the dignity of a reply.*

di•graph (dī′graf) /ˈdaygræf/ *n.* [*count*] a pair of letters representing a single speech sound, as *ea* in *meat* or *th* in *path.* See -GRAPH-.

di•gress (di gres′, dī-) /dɪˈgrɛs, day-/ *v.* [*no obj*] to wander away from the main topic: *Let me digress for a moment and tell you a short story.* **—di•gres•sion** (di-gresh′ən, dī-) /dɪˈgrɛʃən, day-/ *n.* [*noncount*]: *There's too much digression in your essay.* [*count*]: *a short digression from the topic.* **—di•gres′sive,** *adj.* See -GRESS-.

dike[1] or **dyke** (dīk) /dayk/ *n.*

dike[2] (dīk) /dayk/ *n.* DYKE[2].

di•lap•i•dat•ed (di lap′i dā′tid) /dɪˈlæpɪˌdeytɪd/ *adj.* fallen into partial ruin or decay, such as from age, misuse, wear, or neglect: *We bought a dilapidated old house.* **—di•lap•i•da•tion** (di lap′i dā′shən) /dɪˌlæpɪˈdeyʃən/ *n.* [*noncount*]: *a state of dilapidation.*

di•late (dī lāt′, dī′lāt) /dayˈleyt, ˈdayleyt/ *v.,* **-lat•ed, -lat•ing.** to (cause to) become wider, larger, or expanded: [*no obj*]: *The cat's eyes dilated in the darkness.* [~ + *obj*]: *The medicine will dilate the blood vessels.* **—di•la•tion** (dī lā′shən) /dayˈleyʃən/ *n.* [*noncount*] See -LAT-[2].

dil•a•to•ry (dil′ə tôr′ē, -tōr′ē) /ˈdɪləˌtɔriy, -ˌtowriy/ *adj.* tending to delay; intending to gain time: *a dilatory strategy.* See -LAT-[1].

di•lem•ma (di lem′ə) /dɪˈlɛmə/ *n.* [*count*], *pl.* **-mas.** a situation requiring a choice between equally undesirable alternatives: *I was in a dilemma: should I continue to work or go back to school?*

dil•et•tante (dil′i tänt′, dil′i tänt′) /ˈdɪlɪˌtɑnt, ˌdɪlɪˈtɑnt/ *n.* [*count*], *pl.* **-tantes, -tan•ti** (-tän′tē) /-ˈtɑntiy/. a person who is only superficially interested in an art, activity, or subject of study. **—dil′et•tan′tish,** *adj.* **—dil′et•tant′ism,** *n.* [*noncount*]

dil•i•gence (dil′i jəns) /ˈdɪlɪdʒəns/ *n.* [*noncount*] carefulness in work: *examined our accounting procedures with diligence.*

dil•i•gent (dil′i jənt) /ˈdɪlɪdʒənt/ *adj.* **1.** constant, careful, and earnest in effort and work: *a diligent student.* **2.** done or pursued with careful attention: *a diligent search.* **—dil′i•gent•ly,** *adv.*

dill (dil) /dɪl/ *n.* **1.** [*noncount*] a plant of the parsley family having sweet-smelling seeds and finely divided leaves used as a flavoring. **2.** [*noncount*] the seeds or leaves of this plant. **3.** [*count*] Also, **dill pickle.** a kind of pickle prepared with vinegar and spices, esp. with dill.

dil•ly•dal•ly (dil′ē dal′ē) /ˈdɪliyˌdæliy/ *v.* [*no obj*], **-lied, -ly•ing.** to waste time, esp. by indecision: *Quit dillydallying; are you going or not?*

di•lute (di lo͞ot′, dī-; *adj.* also dī′lo͞ot) /dɪˈluwt, day-; *adj.* ælsn ˈdayluwt/ *v.,* **-lut•ed, -lut•ing,** *adj.* **—v.** [~ + *obj*] **1.** to make (a liquid) thinner or weaker by the addition of water or other liquid: *Dilute the ammonia with water before you use it.* **2.** to reduce the strength of, as by adding or mixing something: *The professor's proposals were diluted by the lack of support from his department.* **—adj.** [*before a noun*] **3.** reduced in strength; weak: *serving dilute whiskey.* **—di•lu•tion** (di lo͞o′shən, dī-) /dɪˈluwʃən, day-/ *n.* [*noncount*]

dim (dim) /dɪm/ *adj.,* **dim•mer, dim•mest,** *v.,* **dimmed, dim•ming. —adj. 1.** not bright; lacking light or strength of light: *a dim room.* **2.** not seen clearly, distinctly, or in detail; indistinct; faint: *a dim outline.* **3.** not seeing clearly: *My eyes were dim with tears.* **4.** not likely to happen, succeed, or be favorable: *a dim chance of winning.* **5.** not clear to the mind; vague: *I had a dim suspicion he was trying to take my job.* **6.** slow to understand; stupid: *trying to help the dimmer students.* **—v. 7.** to (cause to) become or grow dim or dimmer: [*no obj*]: *The lights dimmed and the show started.* [~ + *obj*]: *Would someone please dim the lights?* **8.** [~ + *obj*] to switch (the headlights of a vehicle) from the high to the low beam. **9.** to (cause to) become less intense, strong, or favorable: [*no obj*]: *My hopes of getting any support for my project dimmed.* [~ + *obj*]: *The budget crisis really dimmed my hopes of staying on.* **—*Idiom.* 10. take a dim view of,** [~ + *obj*] to regard with disapproval or mild unbelief: *She takes a dim view of my attempts to make changes.* **—dim′ly,** *adv.* **—dim′ness,** *n.* [*noncount*]

dim., an abbreviation of: **1.** dimension. **2.** diminish. **3.** diminuendo.

dime (dīm) /daym/ *n.* [*count*] **1.** a coin of the U.S. and Canada worth 10 cents. **2.** *Slang.* **a.** ten dollars. **b.** a 10-year prison sentence. **c.** an amount of illegal drugs worth ten dollars. **—*Idiom.* 3. a dime a dozen,** common, abundant, and thus of little value: *Such proposals are a dime a dozen.*

di•men•sion (di men′shən) /dɪˈmɛnʃən/ *n.* [*count*] **1.** a property of space; extension of a line in a given direction: *A straight line has one dimension, a square has two dimensions, and a cube has three dimensions.* **2.** Usually, **dimensions.** [*plural*] measurement in length, width, and thickness; size: *Let's figure out the dimensions of the room to see how much paint we will need.* **3.** an aspect or factor (of a situation) to be considered; side: *The kiss they shared under the bridge added a new dimension to their relationship.* **4.** Usually, **dimensions.** [*plural*] the scope or importance (of a problem or situation); magnitude; size: *No one understood the dimensions of the problem.* **—di•men′sion•al,** *adj.*

di•min•ish (di min′ish) /dɪˈmɪnɪʃ/ *v.* **1.** to (cause to) seem smaller, decrease, or be reduced: [*no obj*]: *Suddenly the wind diminished and the seas grew calm again.* [~ + *obj*]: *Time will not diminish our friendship.* **2.** [~ + *obj*] to belittle; disparage: *It's not fair to diminish his efforts; he's worked extremely hard.* **—di•min′ished,** *adj.: the diminished supply of firewood.* **—di•min′ish•ing,** *adj.: We now face the problem of diminishing returns.* **—dim•i•nu•tion** (dim′ə no͞o′shən, -nyo͞o′-) /ˌdɪməˈnuwʃən, -ˈnyuw-/ *n.* [*count*]: *facing a constant diminution of financial aid.* [*noncount*]: *plans for diminution of the budget deficit.* See -MIN-.

di•min•u•en•do (di min′yo͞o en′dō) /dɪˌmɪnyuwˈɛndow/ *adj., adv., n., pl.* **-does.** *Music.* **—adj. 1.** gradually reducing in force or loudness: *a diminuendo passage on page three.* **—adv. 2.** done in this way: *playing the passage diminuendo.* **—n.** [*count*] **3.** a gradual reduction of force or loudness.

di•min•u•tive (di min′yə tiv) /dɪˈmɪnyətɪv/ *adj.* **1.** smaller than the average; tiny: *The Pygmies are a diminutive people.* **2.** relating to a form that indicates smallness, familiarity, affection, or triviality: *The diminutive suffix* -let *appears in the word* droplet, *which means "a small drop."* **—n.** [*count*] **3.** a diminutive prefix, suffix, etc., or the word formed by using it: *The suffix* -let *is a diminutive. The word* droplet *is a diminutive.* See -MIN-.

dim•mer (dim′ər) /ˈdɪmər/ *n.* [*count*] **1.** a person or thing that dims. **2.** a device by which the intensity of an electric light may be varied. **3.** a low-beam headlight.

dim•ple (dim′pəl) /ˈdɪmpəl/ *n., v.,* **-pled, -pling. —n.** [*count*] **1.** a small natural hollow on the surface of the human body, esp. one formed in the cheek in smiling. **—v.** [~ + *obj*] **2.** to mark with or as if with dimples; produce dimples in: *A smile dimpled her face.* **3.** to dent (a metal sheet) so as to permit use of special bolts or rivets. **—dim′ply,** *adj.*

dim sum (dim′ sum′) /ˈdɪm ˈsʌm/ *n.* [*noncount*] (in Chinese cooking) assorted small, usually steamed dumplings filled with meat, seafood, etc.

dim•wit (dim′wit′) /ˈdɪmˌwɪt/ *n.* [*count*] *Slang.* a stupid person. **—dim′wit′ted,** *adj.*

din (din) /dɪn/ *n., v.,* **dinned, din•ning. —n.** [*count; usually singular*] **1.** a loud, confused, continued noise: *the din from the neighbor's party.* **—v.** [~ + *obj* + *into* + *obj*] **2.** to say, utter, or teach continually: *The protesters were dinning their chants into our ears.*

dine (dīn) /dayn/ *v.,* **dined, din•ing. 1.** [*no obj*] to eat a meal, esp. the principal meal of the day; have dinner: *We'll dine with our friends tonight at about eight.* **2.** [~ + *obj*] to entertain at or provide with dinner: *After we wine and dine them, I'm sure they'll join our company.* **3. dine on,** [~ + *on* + *obj*] to eat (food) for a meal: *They were dining on roast duck.* **4. dine out,** [*no obj*] to eat a meal, esp. dinner, away from home: *We dined out with our friends.*

din•er (dī′nər) /ˈdaynər/ *n.* [*count*] **1.** a person who dines, esp. in a restaurant. **2.** a railroad car in which food is served. **3.** an inexpensive restaurant.

di•nette (dī net′) /dayˈnɛt/ *n.* [*count*] **1.** a small space or part of a room, often in or near the kitchen, serving as an informal dining area. **2.** Also called **dinette′ set′.** a table and set of chairs for such a space.

ding[1] (ding) /dɪŋ/ *v.* **1.** to (cause to) make a ringing sound: [*no obj*]: *The bell dinged.* [~ + *obj*]: *She dinged* *the bell.* —*n.* [*count*] **2.** a ringing sound: *the ding of a bell.*

ding² (ding) /dɪŋ/ *v. Informal.* [~ + *obj*] **1.** to cause surface damage to: *to ding a fender.* **2.** to strike with force; hit: *The batter dinged the ball into left.* —*n.* [*count*] **3.** a dent or scratch; nick: *a couple of dings on the hood.*

ding-a-ling (ding′ə ling′) /ˈdɪŋəˌlɪŋ/ *n.* [*count*] *Informal.* a stupid, foolish, or eccentric person.

din•ghy (ding′gē) /ˈdɪŋgiy/ *n.* [*count*], *pl.* **-ghies.** any small boat rowed, sailed, or driven by a motor.

din•go (ding′gō) /ˈdɪŋgow/ *n.* [*count*], *pl.* **-goes.** an Australian wild dog having a reddish-brown coat.

ding•us (ding′əs) /ˈdɪŋəs/ *n.* [*count*], *pl.* **-us•es.** *Informal.* a gadget, device, or object whose name is unknown or forgotten: *This dingus starts the motor.*

din•gy (din′jē) /ˈdɪndʒiy/ *adj.,* **-gi•er, -gi•est. 1.** of a dark, dull, or dirty color: *The clothes were dingy and needed bleaching.* **2.** shabby; dismal; dark: *a dingy little hotel room.* —**din′gi•ness,** *n.* [*noncount*]: *The darkness couldn't hide the dinginess of the room.*

din′ing room′, *n.* [*count*] a room in which meals are eaten.

dink•y (ding′kē) /ˈdɪŋkiy/ *adj.,* **-i•er, -i•est.** *Informal.* small and unimpressive: *a dinky apartment.*

din•ner (din′ər) /ˈdɪnər/ *n.* **1.** the main meal of the day: [*noncount*]: *We usually have dinner around six or six-thirty.* [*count*]: *We ate our dinners outside.* **2.** [*count*] a formal meal in honor of some person or occasion: *We gave him a going-away dinner.* —**Usage.** Many people use the words DINNER and SUPPER to mean the same thing, "a meal in the evening," but DINNER is usually more formal. For some people, LUNCH is the preferred word for "meal at midday," unless the meal is unusually large, formal, or special, in which case it may also be called DINNER.

din′ner jack′et, *n.* TUXEDO (def. 1).

di•no•saur (dī′nə sôr′) /ˈdaynəˌsɔr/ *n.* [*count*] **1.** any of various plant- or flesh-eating reptiles of prehistoric times, most of which had long tails and were very large. **2.** something that is too clumsy, out of date, or unable to adapt to change: *That old computer is a dinosaur; get a new one.*

dint (dint) /dɪnt/ *n.* [*noncount*] —***Idiom.*** **by dint of,** by the force of; through the power of: *to achieve success by dint of hard work.*

di•o•cese (dī′ə sis, -sēz′, -sēs′) /ˈdayəsɪs, -ˌsiyz, -ˌsiys/ *n.* [*count*] a district under the rule or authority of a bishop: *He was transferred from the Worcester diocese.* —**di•oc•e•san** (dī os′ə sən) /dayˈɒsəsən/ *adj.* [*before a noun*]: *the diocesan newsletter.*

di•ode (dī′ōd) /ˈdayowd/ *n.* [*count*] a device through which current can pass freely in only one direction.

di•o•ram•a (dī′ə ram′ə, -rä′mə) /ˌdayəˈræmə, -ˈrɑmə/ *n.* [*count*], *pl.* **-ram•as.** a scene or display produced in three dimensions by placing figures before a painted background.

di•ox•in (dī ok′sin) /dayˈɒksɪn/ *n.* [*noncount*] a general name for a family of chemicals called chlorinated hydrocarbons, esp. the poisonous, harmful by-product resulting from the manufacture of certain pesticides.

dip¹ (dip) /dɪp/ *v.,* **dipped, dip•ping,** *n.* —*v.* **1.** [~ + *obj*] to plunge quickly into a liquid, so as to moisten, dye, or take up some of the liquid: *She dipped the blouse into the hot water.* **2.** [~ + *obj*] to take up, such as by using a bucket or scoop: *to dip water out of a boat.* **3.** [~ + *obj*] to put (animals) in a solution containing pesticide: *to dip the sheep.* **4.** [~ + *obj*] to make (a candle) by repeatedly plunging a wick into melted tallow or wax: *At the craft fair the children were shown how to dip candles.* **5. dip into,** [~ + *into* + *obj*] **a.** to reach down into so as to remove something: *They dipped into the pot and pulled out some lobsters.* **b.** to withdraw or remove something in small amounts: *to dip into one's savings.* **c.** to become interested slightly in a subject, as by reading here and there: *to dip into astronomy.* **6.** [~ + *obj*] to lower and then raise: *to dip a flag in salute.* **7.** [*no obj*] to sink; go downward: *The sun dipped below the horizon.* **8.** [*no obj*] to decrease slightly or temporarily: *Stock-market prices often dip on Fridays.* —*n.* **9.** [*count*] the act of dipping. **10.** [*count*] something taken up by dipping, such as a scoop of ice cream: *two dips of ice cream.* **11.** a substance into which something is dipped, served as an appetizer: [*noncount*]: *two bowls of onion dip near the crackers.* [*count*]: *a dip made of yogurt.* **12.** [*noncount*] a solution containing pesticide for use in dipping animals: *sheep dip.* **13.** [*count*] a moderate or temporary decrease, such as in money, prices, etc.: *a dip in prices on Wall Street today.* **14.** [*count*] a downward slope, road, course, or movement: *a dip in the road.* **15.** [*count*] a brief swim: *a quick dip before lunch.*

dip² (dip) /dɪp/ *n.* [*count*] *Slang.* a naive, foolish, or obnoxious person.

diph•the•ri•a (dif thēr′ē ə, dip-) /dɪfˈθɪəriyə, dɪp-/ *n.* [*noncount*] a serious infectious disease affecting the nose and throat which makes swallowing and breathing difficult.

diph•thong (dif′thông, -thong, dip′-) /ˈdɪfθɔŋ, -θɒŋ, ˈdɪp-/ *n.* [*count*] **1.** a vowel sound that glides slightly from one sound to another but is considered to be a single sound, as the (oi) sound of *toy* or *boil.* **2.** (not in technical use) **a.** a digraph, as the *ea* of *meat.* **b.** a ligature, as æ.

di•plo•ma (di plō′mə) /dɪˈplowmə/ *n.* [*count*], *pl.* **-mas,** *Lat.* **-ma•ta** (-mə tə) /-mətə/. a document given by an educational institution granting a degree.

di•plo•ma•cy (di plō′mə sē) /dɪˈplowməsiy/ *n.* [*noncount*] **1.** the conduct by government officials of relations between nations: *international diplomacy.* **2.** the art or science of conducting such negotiations. **3.** skill in managing negotiations; tact: *We'll need a lot of diplomacy to tell him he's fired.*

dip•lo•mat (dip′lə mat′) /ˈdɪpləˌmæt/ *n.* [*count*] **1.** a person appointed by a national government to conduct official negotiations with other countries: *meetings with diplomats and ambassadors.* **2.** a tactful person: *We need a real diplomat to deal with the factions in the office.*

dip•lo•mat•ic (dip′lə mat′ik) /ˌdɪpləˈmætɪk/ *adj.* **1.** [*before a noun*] of, relating to, or engaged in diplomacy: *a diplomatic post; the diplomatic corps.* **2.** skilled in dealing with sensitive matters or people; tactful: *He's diplomatic enough not to bring up such a delicate issue.* —**dip′lo•mat′i•cal•ly,** *adv.*: *She handled the controversy very diplomatically.*

dip•per (dip′ər) /ˈdɪpər/ *n.* [*count*] **1.** a person or thing that dips. **2.** a cuplike container with a long handle, used for dipping.

dip•py (dip′ē) /ˈdɪpiy/ *adj.,* **-pi•er, -pi•est.** *Slang.* foolish or somewhat crazy.

dip•so•ma•ni•a (dip′sə mā′nē ə, -sō-) /ˌdɪpsəˈmeyniyə, -sow-/ *n.* [*noncount*] an irresistible or uncontrollable desire for alcoholic drink. —**dip′so•ma′ni•ac′,** *n.* [*count*]

dip•stick (dip′stik′) /ˈdɪpˌstɪk/ *n.* [*count*] a rod for measuring the depth of a liquid, as the level of oil in an engine.

dip•ter•ous (dip′tər əs) /ˈdɪptərəs/ *adj.* having two wings, such as a fly, or two winglike parts, such as certain seeds. See -PTER-.

dip•tych (dip′tik) /ˈdɪptɪk/ *n.* [*count*] a pair of pictures on two panels, usually hinged together. Compare TRIPTYCH.

dire (dīᵊr) /dayᵊr/ *adj.,* **dir•er, dir•est. 1.** causing or involving great fear or suffering; terrible: *dire consequences.* **2.** [*before a noun*] indicating trouble, disaster, or the like: *dire predictions of famine.* **3.** urgent; desperate: *in dire need of help.*

di•rect (di rekt′, dī-) /dɪˈrɛkt, day-/ *v.* **1.** [~ + *obj*] to manage or guide by advice, instruction, etc.; supervise: *She directs the affairs of the estate.* **2.** [~ + *obj* + *to* + *verb*] to give instructions to; order: *I directed him to leave the room.* **3.** to serve as a director in the production or performance of (a play, etc.): [~ + *obj*]: *He directed five movies.* [*no obj*]: *He directs with an even hand and a fine touch.* **4.** [~ + *obj* (+ *to* + *obj*)] to tell or show (a person) the way to a place; guide: *Can you direct me to the center of town?* **5.** [~ + *obj (+ toward + obj)*] to send toward a place; to channel or focus toward a given object or end: *to direct his aim; She directed her energies toward her work.* **6.** [~ + *obj* + *to* + *obj*] to address (words, a speech, etc.) to a person or persons: *She directed her remarks to the chairman.* **7.** [~ + *obj* + *to* + *obj*] to address (a letter, etc.) to someone: *to direct a package to their home.* —*adj.* **8.** proceeding in a straight line or by the shortest course; straight: *a direct route.* **9.** [*before a noun*] proceeding in an unbroken line of descent: *a direct descendant.* **10.** [*before a noun*] without intermediary agents; immediate: *insisted on direct contact with the negotiating team.* **11.** straightforward; frank; candid: *I want you to be as direct as possible.* **12.** [*before a noun*] absolute; exact: *the direct opposite.* —*adv.* **13.** in a direct manner; directly; straight: *We flew direct to Moscow.* —**di•rect′ness,** *n.* [*noncount*]: *The directness of her answers startled me.* See -RECT-. —**Related Words.** DIRECT is an adjective and a verb, DIRECTLY is an adverb, DIRECTION is a noun: *He is a direct person and always tells you what he's thinking. She directs movies. He answered the questions directly. In which direction is the wind blowing?*

direct′ cur′rent, *n.* [*noncount*] an electric current of constant and only one direction. *Abbr.*: DC Compare ALTERNATING CURRENT.

di•rec•tion (di rek′shən, dī-) /dɪ'rɛkʃən, day-/ *n.* **1.** [*noncount*] an act or instance of directing: *working with a minimum of direction.* **2.** the line along which anything lies, faces, or moves, with reference to the point or region toward which it is directed: [*count*]: *We wandered off in the wrong direction. The direction is north. We headed out in several directions at once.* [*noncount*]: *I have a bad sense of direction.* **3.** [*count*] a line of thought or action or a tendency or inclination: *the direction of contemporary thought.* **4.** Usually, **directions.** [*plural*] instructions or guidance: *confusing directions for assembling the furniture.* **5.** [*noncount*] management; control; supervision: *Under his direction the company's profits soared.* **6.** [*noncount*] the technique, art, or business of a stage or film director or of a musical conductor giving instructions: *Under her direction the orchestra played several pieces beautifully.* **7.** [*noncount*] a purpose or guiding orientation; focus: *He seems to lack direction in his life.* **—di•rec′tion•al,** *adj.* [*before a noun*]: *I turned on the car's right directional signal.* See -RECT-.

di•rec•tive (di rek′tiv, dī-) /dɪ'rɛktɪv, day-/ *adj.* **1.** serving to direct; directing. **—*n.*** [*count*] **2.** an instruction or direction; an order: *He received a directive from headquarters.*

di•rect•ly (di rekt′lē, dī-) /dɪ'rɛktliy, day-/ *adv.* **1.** in a direct line; straight: *She drove directly to school.* **2.** at once; without delay: *He left directly and didn't come back till later.* **3.** shortly; soon: *The guests will be arriving directly.* **4.** frankly; truthfully; candidly: *Don't be afraid to speak directly.* **—*conj.*** **5.** *Chiefly Brit.* as soon as: *Directly he arrived, he sat down.*

direct′ ob′ject, *n.* [*count*] a word or group of words representing the person or thing on which the action of a verb is performed, or toward which it is directed: *The pronoun* it *in* I saw it *is the direct object.*

di•rec•tor (di rek′tər, dī-) /dɪ'rɛktər, day-/ *n.* [*count*] **1.** a person or thing that directs. **2.** one of a group of persons chosen to govern the affairs of a company: *She was elected to the board of directors.* **3.** one who interprets the script and supervises the development of a theater, film, television, or radio production: *The director told the cameraman to give him a close-up.* **4.** CONDUCTOR (def. 3). **—di•rec′tor•ship′,** *n.* [*noncount*]

di•rec•to•rate (di rek′tər it, dī-) /dɪ'rɛktərɪt, day-/ *n.* [*count*] **1.** the office of a director. **2.** a body of directors.

di•rec•to•ry (di rek′tə rē, dī-) /dɪ'rɛktəriy, day-/ *n.* [*count*], *pl.* **-ries. 1.** a book containing an alphabetical index of the names and addresses of persons in an area or organization: *the telephone directory.* **2.** a board or tablet on a wall of a building listing the location of the occupants. **3. a.** a division in a structure that organizes the storage of computer files on a disk: *You can create a new directory by typing "md."* **b.** a listing of such stored files: *Bad news: your file is not listed in the directory.*

dirge (dûrj) /dɜrdʒ/ *n.* [*count*] **1.** a funeral song to mourn and honor the dead: *a slow, sad, ancient Irish dirge.* **2.** anything that resembles such a song, such as a poem of sorrow for the dead.

dir•i•gi•ble (dir′i jə bəl, di rij′ə-) /'dɪrɪdʒəbəl, dɪ'rɪdʒə-/ *n.* AIRSHIP.

dirt (dûrt) /dɜrt/ *n.* [*noncount*] **1.** any foul or filthy substance, such as mud: *I couldn't get the dirt off my clothes.* **2.** earth or soil, esp. when loose: *good dirt for growing vegetables.* **3.** something or someone vile or worthless: *She treated me like dirt.* **4.** moral filth; vileness. **5.** gossip, esp. of a malicious nature: *listening to the latest dirt.* **—*Idiom.*** **6. do someone dirt,** [*do + obj + ~*] to cause someone harm: *I would never do her dirt.*

dirt′-cheap′, *adj.* **1.** very cheap: *dirt-cheap prices.* **—*adv.*** **2.** very cheaply: *bought it dirt-cheap.*

dirt•y (dûr′tē) /'dɜrtiy/ *adj.*, **-i•er, -i•est,** *v.*, **-ied, -y•ing,** *adv.* **—*adj.*** **1.** soiled with dirt: *had to wash his dirty hands.* **2.** spreading dirt; soiling: *dirty smoke.* **3.** vile; mean; deserving contempt: *a dirty scoundrel.* **4.** obscene; pornographic; lewd: *a dirty joke; dirty pictures.* **5.** undesirable or unpleasant; disagreeable: *You left the dirty work for me.* **6.** very unfortunate or regrettable: *a dirty shame!* **7.** not fair or sportsmanlike; dishonest; dishonorable: *a dirty fighter.* **8.** hostile or resentful: *to give someone a dirty look.* **9.** not bright or clear; somewhat dull: *dirty blond hair.* **10.** received through illegal means: *dirty money from organized crime.* **—*v.*** **11.** to make or become dirty: [*~ + obj*]: *Try not to dirty your new white shoes.* [*no obj*]: *Those white socks dirty easily.* **—*adv.*** **12.** *Informal.* in a mean or underhand way: *The other high school football team played dirty.* **13.** *Informal.* in a lewd manner: *to talk dirty.* **—dirt•i•ly** (dûr′tl ē) /'dɜrtḷiy/ *adv.* **—dirt′i•ness,** *n.* [*noncount*]

dis-, *prefix. dis-* comes from Latin, where it has the literal meaning "apart." It now has the following meanings: **1.** opposite of: *disagreement (= opposite of agreement).* **2.** not: *disapprove (= not to approve); dishonest (= not honest); disobey (= not obey).* **3.** reverse; remove: *disconnect (= to remove the connection of); discontinue (= to stop continuing); dissolve (= remove the solidness of; make liquid).*

dis•a•bil•i•ty (dis′ə bil′i tē) /ˌdɪsə'bɪlɪtiy/ *n., pl.* **-ties. 1.** [*noncount*] lack of adequate strength or ability; incapacity: *a life of disability.* **2.** [*count*] a physical or mental handicap: *His disabilities were not going to stand in his way.* **3.** [*count*] anything that disables or puts one at a disadvantage.

dis•a•ble (dis ā′bəl) /dɪs'eybəl/ *v.* [*~ + obj*], **-bled, -bling.** to make unable or unfit; weaken or destroy the capability of; cripple: *That illness disabled him and left him unable to work.*

dis•a•buse (dis′ə byōōz′) /ˌdɪsə'byuwz/ *v.* [*~ + obj + of + obj*], **-bused, -bus•ing.** to free (someone) from deception or error: *Let me disabuse you of that foolish idea.*

dis•ad•van•tage (dis′əd van′tij) /ˌdɪsəd'væntɪdʒ/ *n.* [*count; usually singular*] **1.** absence of advantage or equality: *My years of experience at that old job actually put me at a disadvantage in this new one.* **2.** something that puts one in an unfavorable position or condition: *A bad temper is a disadvantage.* **—dis•ad•van•ta•geous** (dis ad′vən tā′jəs) /dɪsˌædvən'teydʒəs/ *adj.*

dis•ad•van•taged (dis′əd van′tijd) /ˌdɪsəd'væntɪdʒd/ *adj.* **1.** lacking the necessities and comforts of life: *disadvantaged families.* **—*n.*** **the disadvantaged,** [*plural; used with a plural verb*] **2.** people who lack such necessities and comforts.

dis•af•fect (dis′ə fekt′) /ˌdɪsə 'fɛkt/ *v.* [*~ + obj*] to lose or undo the affection of; make discontented: *That politician managed to disaffect every major voting bloc.* **—dis′af•fect′ed,** *adj.*: *the millions of disaffected voters.* **—dis•af•fec•tion** (dis′ə fek′shən) /ˌdɪsə'fɛkʃən/ *n.* [*noncount*]: *widespread voter disaffection.*

dis•a•gree (dis′ə grē′) /ˌdɪsə'griy/ *v.* **1.** [*usually: not: be + ~-ing*] to fail to agree; differ: [*no obj*]: *I'm afraid our conclusions disagree.* [*~ + with + obj*]: *The conclusions disagree with the facts.* **2.** [*~ + with + obj*] to differ in opinion; dissent: *Three of the judges disagreed with the verdict.* **3.** [*~ + with + obj*] (of the weather, food, etc.) to cause physical discomfort; have ill effects on: *Oysters disagree with me.* **—dis′a•gree′ment,** *n.* [*noncount*]: *The two sides are in disagreement.* [*count*]: *We had a violent disagreement.* **—Usage.** Compare AGREE and DISAGREE when they are followed by a clause, for example, *that the earth is round.* With AGREE two structures are possible: [*~ + with + the statement/claim/etc. + (that) clause*]: *I agree with the statement (or claim, etc.) that the earth is round;* and: [*~ + (that) clause*]: *I agree that the earth is round.* With DISAGREE only one structure is possible: [*~ + with + the statement/claim/etc. + (that) clause*]: *I disagree with the statement (or claim, etc.) that the earth is round.* **—Related Words.** DISAGREE is a verb, DISAGREEABLE is an adjective, DISAGREEMENT is a noun: *I disagree with you. The weather is disagreeable. We had several disagreements but we finally reached a settlement.*

dis•a•gree•a•ble (dis′ə grē′ə bəl) /ˌdɪsə'griyəbəl/ *adj.* **1.** opposite to one's taste or liking; offensive: *The cold weather has been really disagreeable.* **2.** unpleasant in manner; surly; grouchy: *She's always so disagreeable in the morning.* **—dis′a•gree′a•bly,** *adv.*

dis•al•low (dis′ə lou′) /ˌdɪsə'law/ *v.* [*~ + obj*] to reject; refuse to allow or accept; refuse to admit the validity of: *The judge disallowed our claim.*

dis•ap•pear (dis′ə pēr′) /ˌdɪsə'pɪər/ *v.* [*no obj*] **1.** to cease to be seen; vanish from sight: *The sun disappeared beneath the horizon.* **2.** to cease to exist or be known; pass away: *Dinosaurs disappeared millions of years ago.* **—dis′ap•pear′ance,** *n.* [*count; noncount*]

dis•ap•point (dis′ə point′) /ˌdɪsə'pɔynt/ *v.* [*~ + obj*] **1.** to fail to reach the expectations, hopes, or wishes of: *That last job rejection disappointed me badly.* **2.** to defeat the fulfillment of: *to disappoint hopes.* **—dis′ap•point′ment,** *n.* [*noncount*]: *The actress learned to handle disappointment.* [*count*]: *That third novel was a big disappointment.* **—Related Words.** DISAPPOINT is a verb, DISAPPOINTMENT is a noun, DISAPPOINTED and DISAPPOINTING are adjectives: *She disappointed him when she told a lie. He faced one disappointment after another. The disappointed team headed home after their loss. It was a disappointing loss.* See -POINT-.

dis•ap•point•ed (dis′ə poin′tid) /ˌdɪsə'pɔyntɪd/ *adj.* related to or marked by disappointment: *I was greatly disappointed at not getting the job.*

dis•ap•point•ing (dis′ə poin′ting) /ˌdɪsə'pɔyntɪŋ/ *adj.* causing or bringing about disappointment: *It was a disappointing loss for the whole team.*

dis•ap•prove (dis′ə pro͞ov′) /ˌdɪsə'pruwv/ *v.,* **-proved, -prov•ing. 1.** [~ + *obj*] to withhold approval from; refuse to allow: *Her request to be rehired was disapproved by the committee.* **2.** to have an unfavorable opinion; express disapproval: [*no obj*]: *She wants to go away to college but her parents disapprove.* [~ + *of* + *obj*]: *Her parents disapprove of her plan to go away to college.* **—dis′ap•prov′al,** *n.* [*noncount*]: *gave me a frowning look of disapproval.* **—dis′ap•prov′ing•ly,** *adv.* See -PROV-.

dis•arm (dis ärm′) /dɪs'ɑrm/ *v.* **1.** [~ + *obj*] to take away weapons from (someone): *The police disarmed the remaining suspects.* **2.** [~ + *obj*] to remove the fuze or other activating device from: *to disarm a bomb.* **3.** [~ + *obj*] to deprive of the means of attack or defense: *He was disarmed by her logic.* **4.** [~ + *obj*] to take away or remove anger, suspicion, etc.; win the affection or approval of; charm: *She can always disarm me with one of her happy little smiles.* **5.** [*no obj*] (of a country) to reduce or limit armed forces: *The superpowers never agreed to disarm.* See -ARM-.

dis•ar•ma•ment (dis är′mə mənt) /dɪs'ɑrməmənt/ *n.* [*noncount*] the act or policy of reducing the armed forces of a country, esp. of its nuclear weapons: *advocating complete and unconditional disarmament.* See -ARM-.

dis•arm•ing (dis är′ming) /dɪs'ɑrmɪŋ/ *adj.* taking away anger or suspicion, etc., as by being charming: *a disarming smile.* **—dis•arm′ing•ly,** *adv.*: *She smiled disarmingly.*

dis•ar•range (dis′ə rānj′) /ˌdɪsə'reyndʒ/ *v.* [~ + *obj*], **-ranged, -rang•ing.** to disturb the arrangement of; unsettle: *The kids came in and disarranged the place.*

dis•ar•ray (dis′ə rā′) /ˌdɪsə'rey/ *v.* [~ + *obj*] **1.** to put out of array or order; throw into disorder. **—*n.*** [*noncount*] **2.** disorder; confusion: *The unsupervised class was in total disarray.*

dis•as•so•ci•ate (dis′ə sō′shē āt′, -sē-) /ˌdɪsə'sowʃiyˌeyt, -siy-/ *v.* [~ + *obj*], **-at•ed, -at•ing.** to dissociate. See -SOC-.

dis•as•ter (di zas′tər) /dɪ'zæstər/ *n.* an overwhelming calamity or catastrophe: [*count*]: *The earthquake was a terrible disaster for that town.* [*noncount*]: *Those actions will result in disaster for the economy.* See -ASTRO-.

dis•ast•rous (di zas′trəs) /dɪ'zæstrəs/ *adj.* **1.** of or relating to a disaster: *a disastrous earthquake.* **2.** performed or done very poorly; failing badly: *He gave a disastrous presentation of his proposal.* **—dis•as′trous•ly,** *adv.* See -ASTRO-.

dis•a•vow (dis′ə vou′) /ˌdɪsə'vaw/ *v.* [~ + *obj*] to claim no knowledge of, connection with, or responsibility for: *The director disavowed any knowledge of my actions.* **—dis′a•vow′al,** *n.* [*noncount*]: *disavowal of any knowledge.* [*count*]: *issuing a disavowal of that position.*

dis•band (dis band′) /dɪs'bænd/ *v.* to (cause to) break up or dissolve (an organization): [*no obj*]: *The organization disbanded when its leader was arrested.* [~ + *obj*]: *The government tried to disband his little organization.*

dis•bar (dis bär′) /dɪs'bɑr/ *v.* [~ + *obj*], **-barred, -bar•ring.** to expel from the legal profession: *The lawyer was disbarred from practicing again.* **—dis•bar′ment,** *n.* [*noncount*]: *She faced disbarment for perjury.*

dis•be•lief (dis′bi lēf′) /ˌdɪsbɪ'liyf/ *n.* [*noncount*] refusing to believe: *My disbelief in his alibi was obvious.*

dis•be•lieve (dis′bi lēv′) /ˌdɪsbɪ'liyv/ *v.,* **-lieved, -liev•ing.** to have no belief in; refuse or reject belief in: [~ + *obj*]: *I disbelieved him and his story.* [*no obj*; (~ + *in* + *obj*)]: *I disbelieved in magic.*

dis•burse (dis bûrs′) /dɪs'bɜrs/ *v.* [~ + *obj*], **-bursed, -burs•ing.** to pay out (money), esp. for expenses; expend: *Salaries are disbursed by the paymaster's office.* **—dis•burse′ment,** *n.* [*noncount*]

disc (disk) /dɪsk/ *n.* [*count*] **1.** a phonograph record. **2.** DISK.

dis•card (*v.* di skärd′; *n.* dis′kärd) / *v.* dɪ'skɑrd; *n.* 'dɪskɑrd/ *v.* [~ + *obj*] **1.** to dispose of; get rid of: *We discarded some old clothes.* **2.** to throw out (a playing card) from one's hand: *I discarded a couple of low cards.* **—*n.*** [*count*] **3.** a person or thing that is cast out, rejected, or thrown out.

dis•cern (di sûrn′) /dɪ'sɜrn/ *v.* [*not: be* + ~*-ing*] **1.** [~ + *obj*] to perceive by the sight or by the intellect; recognize: *She could discern a faint light ahead in the forest.* **2.** to distinguish in the mind: [~ + *obj*]: *to discern right from wrong.* [~ + *that clause*]: *Can he discern that his enemies are doing harm to him?* **—dis•cern′i•ble, dis•cern′a•ble,** *adj.*: *The light was barely discernible in the distance.* **—dis•cern′ment,** *n.* [*noncount*] See -CERN-.

dis•cern•ing (di sûr′ning) /dɪ'sɜrnɪŋ/ *adj.* able to distinguish (things) in the mind: *very discerning in his analysis of the problem.* See -CERN-.

dis•charge (*v.* dis chärj′; *n.* dis′chärj, dis chärj′) / *v.* dɪs'tʃɑrdʒ; *n.* 'dɪstʃɑrdʒ, dɪs'tʃɑrdʒ/ *v.,* **-charged, -charg•ing,** *n.* **—*v.* 1.** [~ + *obj* (+ *from* + *obj*)] to release or send away: *They discharged him from prison.* **2.** [~ + *obj*] to fulfill or do (a duty, etc.): *He was no longer able to discharge his duties faithfully.* **3.** [~ + *obj*] to take away the employment of; dismiss (someone) from service: *His boss discharged him because of his absences.* **4.** [~ + *obj*] to pay (a debt): *discharging all his debts.* **5.** to (cause to) fire, go off, or shoot (a gun): [~ + *obj*]: *In crowded places the police should not discharge their weapons.* [*no obj*]: *The weapon discharged when it hit the ground.* **6.** to pour forth: [*no obj*]: *The oil was discharging from the tanker at the rate of thousands of gallons an hour.* [~ + *obj*]: *The tanker was discharging thousands of gallons of oil.* **7.** to (cause to) lose or give up a charge of electricity: [*no obj*]: *The weakened battery was no longer discharging.* [~ + *obj*]: *It can't discharge electricity if it's not connected properly.* **8.** [~ + *obj*] to remove or send forth (from); unload: *to discharge a ship.* **—*n.* 9.** [*count*] the act of firing a weapon. **10.** a sending or coming forth: [*noncount*]: *to halt further discharge of waste into the river.* [*count*]: *a discharge of five million tons of crude oil.* **11.** [*noncount*] something sent forth or emitted: *a lot of discharge from the wound.* **12.** a release or dismissal: [*count*]: *an honorable discharge from the army.* [*noncount*]: *discharge of several employees.*

dis•ci•ple (di sī′pəl) /dɪ'saypəl/ *n.* [*count*] **1.** one of the 12 apostles of Christ. **2.** a pupil or follower of another: *a disciple of Freud.*

dis•ci•pli•nar•i•an (dis′ə plə nâr′ē ən) /ˌdɪsəplə'nɛəriyən/ *n.* [*count*] **1.** a person who enforces or favors the use of discipline: *a strict disciplinarian.* **—*adj.*** [*before a noun*] **2.** disciplinary.

dis•ci•pli•na•ry (dis′ə pli nâr′ē) /'dɪsəplɪˌnɛəriy/ *adj.* [*before a noun*] of or relating to discipline: *a disciplinary teacher.*

dis•ci•pline (dis′ə plin) /'dɪsəplɪn/ *n., v.,* **-plined, -plin•ing.** **—*n.* 1.** [*noncount*] training to act in accordance with rules; drill: *military discipline.* **2.** [*noncount*] exercise that develops a skill; training: *Working at the typewriter every day is good discipline for a writer.* **3.** [*noncount*] behavior in accord with rules of conduct: *keeping good discipline in an army.* **4.** [*noncount*] punishment given by way of correction and training: *Discipline consisted of demerits for incorrect answers.* **5.** [*noncount*] the training effect of experience, difficulty, etc.: *the harsh discipline of poverty.* **6.** [*count*] a branch of instruction or learning: *the disciplines of history and economics.* **—*v.*** [~ + *obj*] **7.** to train by instruction and exercise; drill: *His dog was disciplined by a professional trainer.* **8.** to punish or penalize; correct: *Those teachers weren't afraid to discipline their students.* **—dis′ci•plined,** *adj.*: *The strictly disciplined army continued to march.*

disc′ jock′ey, *n.* [*count*] one who selects and plays recordings on a radio program or at a discotheque. *Abbr.*: DJ

dis•claim (dis klām′) /dɪs'kleym/ *v.* [~ + *obj*] to deny connection with; disavow; disown: *He disclaimed responsibility for the accident.* **—dis•claim′er,** *n.* [*count*]: *The company printed a disclaimer on the product.* See -CLAIM-.

dis•close (di sklōz′) /dɪ'sklowz/ *v.,* **-closed, -clos•ing. 1.** to make known; reveal: [~ + *obj*]: *to disclose a secret.* [~ + (*that*) *clause*]: *The company disclosed that it had lost money on the deal.* **2.** [~ + *obj*] to lay open to view: *In spring the flowers disclose their colors.* See -CLOS-.

dis•clo•sure (di sklō′zhər) /dɪ'sklowʒər/ *n.* **1.** [*non-*

count] the act of disclosing: *calling for full disclosure of the facts of the case.* **2.** [*count*] something revealed: *a damaging disclosure about the candidate's past.* See -CLOS-.

dis•co (dis′kō) /'dɪskow/ *n., pl.* **-cos,** *v.* **—***n.* **1.** [*count*] a discotheque: *dancing at a disco all night.* **2.** [*noncount*] a style of popular dance music with electronic instrumentation and a heavy, rhythmic beat. **—***v.* [*no obj*] **3.** to dance to disco: *discoing all night.*

dis•col•or (dis kul′ər) /dɪs'kʌlər/ *v.* to (cause to) spoil the color (of); fade or stain: [*no obj*]: *The carpet had discolored over the years.* [~ + *obj*]: *Water discolored the carpet.* **—dis•col•or•a•tion** (dis kul′ə rā′shən) /dɪsˌkʌlə'reyʃən/ *n.* [*noncount*]: *The carpet showed discoloration due to age.* [*count*]: *an ugly discoloration on the fruit.*

dis•com•bob•u•late (dis′kəm bob′yə lāt′) /ˌdɪskəm'bɒbyəˌleyt/ *v.* [~ + *obj*], **-lat•ed, -lat•ing.** to confuse; upset; frustrate: *The speaker was completely discombobulated by the hecklers.* **—dis•com•bob•u•la•tion** (dis′kəm bob′yə lā′shən) /ˌdɪskəmˌbɒbyə'leyʃən/ *n.* [*noncount*]

dis•com•fit (dis kum′fit) /dɪs'kʌmfɪt/ *v.* [~ + *obj*] to confuse and deject; upset; disconcert: *The tricky question about his finances discomfited the mayor.*

dis•com•fit•ure (dis kum′fi chər) /dɪs'kʌmfɪtʃər/ *n.* [*noncount*] confusion; a feeling of being upset: *the candidate's obvious discomfiture at the questions about his past.*

dis•com•fort (dis kum′fərt) /dɪs'kʌmfərt/ *n.* [*count*] **1.** an absence of comfort or ease: *a life of discomfort in a wheelchair.* **2.** anything disturbing to comfort: *the discomforts of waiting in the airport.* **—***v.* [~ + *obj*] **3.** to make uneasy: *Those minor annoyances don't discomfort me.* See -FORT-.

dis•com•pos•ure (dis′kəm pō′zhər) /ˌdɪskəm'powʒər/ *n.* [*noncount*] a condition of disorder and disturbance: *showed obvious discomposure when questioned.*

dis•con•cert (dis′kən sûrt′) /ˌdɪskən'sɜrt/ *v.* [~ + *obj*] to disturb (a person's) self-possession, as by throwing into confusion: *His constant shuffling of papers disconcerted me.* **—dis•con•cert′ed,** *adj.* **—dis•con•cert′ing,** *adj.* See -CERT-.

dis•con•nect (dis′kə nekt′) /ˌdɪskə'nɛkt/ *v.* **1.** [~ + *obj*] to interrupt the connection of (something) or between (two things): *The electricity company disconnected his house. I was talking on the phone and suddenly got disconnected.* **2.** [~ + *obj* + *from* + *obj*] to detach; separate: *Disconnect the power source from the computer before opening the back.* **—dis•con•nec•tion** (dis′kə-nek′shən) /ˌdɪskə'nɛkʃən/ *n.* [*noncount*]: *disconnection from reality.* [*count*]: *another disconnection before I could talk.* [*noncount*] See -NEC-.

dis•con•nect•ed (dis′kə nek′tid) /ˌdɪskə'nɛktɪd/ *adj.* **1.** (of ideas) disjointed; not holding together well: *a very disconnected essay.* **2.** (of a person) not coherent; seeming to be irrational: *The boy has seemed disconnected and strange ever since the incident.* **—dis′con•nect′ed•ly,** *adv.* **—dis′con•nect′ed•ness,** *n.* [*noncount*] See -NEC-.

dis•con•so•late (dis kon′sə lit) /dɪs'kɒnsəlɪt/ *adj.* very depressed, downhearted, or unhappy: *She is disconsolate over the loss of her pet.* **—dis•con′so•late•ly,** *adv.*: *They sat disconsolately in the corner.* See -SOLA-.

dis•con•tent (dis′kən tent′) /ˌdɪskən'tɛnt/ *n.* [*noncount*] **1.** Also, **dis′con•tent′ment.** lack of contentment; dissatisfaction: *a vague feeling of discontent.* **2.** a restless desire for what one does not have; a longing for something better.

dis•con•tent•ed (dis′kən ten′tid) /ˌdɪskən'tɛntɪd/ *adj.* dissatisfied; restlessly unhappy: *discontented with her dull life.*

dis•con•tin•ue (dis′kən tin′yo͞o) /ˌdɪskən'tɪnyuw/ *v.,* **-tin•ued, -tin•u•ing. 1.** to (cause to) come to an end or stop; cease: [~ + *obj*]: *I had to discontinue my class when I sprained my ankle.* [~ + *verb-ing*]: *He discontinued running in the cold weather.* [*no obj*]: *The job will discontinue in the spring.* **2.** [~ + *obj*] to cease using, producing, subscribing to, etc.: *The auto manufacturer discontinued that car back in 1989.* **—dis•con•tin•u•a•tion** (dis′kən tin′yo͞o ā′shən) /ˌdɪskənˌtɪnyuw'eyʃən/ *n.* [*count*]: *a discontinuation of business as usual.*

dis•con•ti•nu•i•ty (dis′kon tn o͞o′i tē, -yo͞o′-) /ˌdɪskɒntn̩'uwɪtiy, -'yuw-/ *n., pl.* **-ties. 1.** [*noncount*] lack of continuity; irregular development or progress: *a time of discontinuity in the artist's life.* **2.** [*count*] a break or gap: *a discontinuity in the growth of her self-esteem.*

dis•cord (dis′kôrd) /'dɪskɔrd/ *n.* **1.** [*noncount*] lack of concord or harmony between persons or things: *The couple split up after years of discord.* **2.** [*count*] an inharmonious combination of musical tones sounded together: *the discords in his music.* **—dis•cord′ant,** *adj.* See -CORD-.

dis•co•theque or **dis•co•thèque** (dis′kə tek′, dis′kə-tek′) /'dɪskəˌtɛk, ˌdɪskə'tɛk/ *n.* [*count*] a nightclub for dancing to live or recorded music. Also called **disco.**

dis•count (*v.* dis′kount, dis kount′; *n., adj.* dis′kount) / *v.* 'dɪskawnt, dɪs'kawnt; *n., adj.* 'dɪskawnt/ *v.* [~ + *obj*] **1.** to deduct a certain amount from (a bill, etc.): *They promise to discount prices at 25%.* **2.** to sell, or offer (something) for sale, at a reduced price: *Automakers never seem to discount their overpriced cars, even when sales are down.* **3.** to disregard: *I guess we shouldn't discount the possibility completely.* **4.** to allow for exaggeration in (a statement, etc.); believe less than completely: *You have to discount a lot of what he says about her.* **—***n.* [*count*] **5.** an amount deducted from the usual list price; a reduction in price: *a discount of 25% on plane tickets.* **—***adj.* [*before a noun*] **6.** selling at less than the usual price: *discount items at rock-bottom prices.* **7.** selling goods at a discount: *discount stores and discount houses.*

dis•cour•age (di skûr′ij, -skur′-) /dɪ'skɜrɪdʒ, -'skʌr-/ *v.,* **-aged, -ag•ing. 1.** [~ + *obj*] to take away courage; dishearten; dispirit: *Every job rejection discouraged him more.* **2.** [~ + *obj* + *from* + *verb-ing*] to dissuade; make (someone) less willing: *The broker discouraged him from buying stock.* **—dis•cour′aged,** *adj.*: *The discouraged team endured their fifth loss in a row.* **—dis•cour′ag•ing,** *adj.*: *a discouraging loss.* **—dis•cour′ag•ing•ly,** *adv.* **—Related Words.** DISCOURAGE is a verb, DISCOURAGED and DISCOURAGING are adjectives, DISCOURAGEMENT is a noun: *Such negative comments will discourage kids who are just beginning to read. The discouraged players gathered in the locker room after their loss. It was a discouraging loss. He faced a lot of discouragement before he won his first medal.*

dis•cour•age•ment (di skûr′ij mənt, -skur′-) /dɪ'skɜrɪdʒmənt, -'skʌr-/ *n.* **1.** [*noncount*] the state of discouraging or being discouraged: *His discouragement over the divorce is damaging his health.* **2.** opposition; attempting to persuade someone not to do something: [*noncount*]: *She faced hostility and discouragement in her struggle to become a firefighter.* [*count*]: *put up numerous discouragements to keep her from succeeding.*

dis•course (*n.* dis′kôrs, -kōrs; *v.* dis kôrs′, -kōrs′) / *n.* 'dɪskɔrs, -kowrs; *v.* dɪs'kɔrs, -'kowrs/ *n., v.,* **-coursed, -cours•ing. —***n.* **1.** [*noncount*] communication of thought by words; talk; conversation: *The lawyers enjoyed the time spent on intelligent discourse.* **2.** [*count*] a formal discussion of a subject, such as an essay or sermon: *a long discourse on the evils of drugs.* **—***v.* [~ + *on* + *obj*] **3.** to treat a subject formally in speech or writing: *The paper discourses at length on how students from different language backgrounds make the same kinds of mistakes in the use of articles.* See -COUR-.

dis•cour•te•ous (dis kûr′tē əs) /dɪs'kɜrtiyəs/ *adj.* not courteous; impolite; rude: *hurt by the discourteous remarks.*

dis•cour•te•sy (dis kûr′tə sē) /dɪs'kɜrtəsiy/ *n., pl.* **-sies. 1.** [*noncount*] lack of courtesy; bad manners; rudeness: *They have to endure the discourtesy of the city every day.* **2.** [*count*] a discourteous or impolite act: *They did me a discourtesy by not telling me about the meeting.*

dis•cov•er (di skuv′ər) /dɪ'skʌvər/ *v.* **1.** to gain knowledge of (something unknown): [~ + *obj*]: *Radioactivity was discovered by Marie Curie.* [~ + (*that*) *clause*]: *He discovered that not all prehistoric apes were the same.* **2.** [~ + *obj*] to notice or realize; find out about: *discovered the treasure quite by accident.* **—dis•cov′er•er,** *n.* [*count*] **—Syn.** Compare DISCOVER and INVENT, two words that deal with something new. DISCOVER is used when the object is an idea or place that existed before, but few people or no one knew about it, and someone comes into the knowledge of it. In the sentence *Columbus discovered the New World,* the New World clearly existed, and was known to the people living there, but not to Columbus and the people of his time. INVENT is used when the object is a device or thing built. In the sentence *Edison invented the light bulb,* the light bulb did not exist before Edison invented it, nor was it known by anyone.

dis•cov•er•y (di skuv′ər ē) /dɪ'skʌvəriy/ *n.* [*count*], *pl.* **-er•ies. 1.** the act of discovering: *the discovery of electricity.* **2.** the act of finding something out: *new discoveries about the universe.*

dis•cred•it (dis kred′it) /dɪs'krɛdɪt/ *v.* [~ + *obj*] **1.** to injure the reputation of; defame: *discredited my good name with gossip.* **2.** to destroy confidence in the reliability of: *to discredit a witness.* **—*n.*** [*noncount*] **3.** loss or lack of belief or confidence; distrust. **—dis•cred′it•a•ble,** *adj.*

dis•creet (di skrēt′) /dɪ'skriyt/ *adj.* careful or tactful in one's conduct or speech; circumspect; diplomatic: *a few discreet inquiries about his credit rating.* **—dis•creet′ly,** *adv.*

dis•crep•an•cy (di skrep′ən sē) /dɪ'skrɛpənsiy/ *n., pl.* **-cies. 1.** [*noncount*] the state or quality of lacking agreement; inconsistency: *discrepancy in the eyewitness accounts of the accident.* **2.** [*count*] an instance of difference or inconsistency: *a few discrepancies in the account of the accident.*

dis•crete (di skrēt′) /dɪ'skriyt/ *adj.* apart or detached from others; separate; distinct: *The college was reorganized into six discrete departments.*

dis•cre•tion (di skresh′ən) /dɪ'skrɛʃən/ *n.* [*noncount*] **1.** the power to decide or act according to one's own judgment: *The judge has discretion in the matter of sentencing.* **2.** the quality of being discreet; tactfulness: *I can count on your discretion to keep quiet about his drinking.* **—*Idiom.* 3. at one's discretion, at the discretion of,** in accordance with (someone's) judgment or will: *They may withdraw the money at their discretion and use it to pay for college.* **—dis•cre′tion•ar′y,** *adj.*: *discretionary funds.*

dis•crim•i•nate (di skrim′ə nāt′) /dɪ'skrɪmə ˌneyt / *v.,* **-nat•ed, -nat•ing. 1.** to make a distinction for or against a person on the basis of the group or class to which the person belongs, rather than according to merit: [*no obj*]: *No company should expect to discriminate today and get away with it.* [~ + *against* + *obj*]: *Those employers discriminated against women for higher-paying jobs.* [~ + *in favor of*]: *Is it acceptable to discriminate in favor of certain groups?* **2.** [~ + *between/among*] to make, take note of, or observe a difference: *He has trouble discriminating between red and green.*

dis•crim•i•nat•ing (di skrim′ə nāt′ing) /dɪ'skrɪməˌneytɪŋ/ *adj.* having the ability to distinguish or judge among things: *commercials aimed at the so-called discriminating buyer.*

dis•crim•i•na•tion (di skrim′ə nā′shən) /dɪˌskrɪmə'neyʃən/ *n.* [*noncount*] **1.** the act or practice of discriminating: *job discrimination.* **2.** the ability to make or see differences; the ability to distinguish or judge among things: *fine discrimination in his choice of wine.*

dis•crim•i•na•to•ry (di skrim′ə nə tôr′ē, -tōr′ē) /dɪ'skrɪmənəˌtɔriy, -ˌtowriy/ *adj.* relating to or marked by discrimination: *carefully monitored the company's discriminatory hiring practices for a future lawsuit.*

dis•cur•sive (di skûr′siv) /dɪ'skɜrsɪv/ *adj.* passing from one subject to another; rambling: *a discursive writing style.* See -CUR-.

dis•cus (dis′kəs) /'dɪskəs/ *n.* **1.** [*count*] a circular disk for throwing in athletic competition: *He threw the discus in the Olympics.* **2.** [*noncount*] the sport of throwing this disk for distance: *He got the gold medal in the discus.*

dis•cuss (di skus′) /dɪ'skʌs/ *v.* [~ + *obj*] to consider or examine by argument; debate: *He was happy to discuss anything with her.*

dis•cus•sant (di skus′ənt) /dɪ'skʌsənt/ *n.* [*count*] a person who participates in a formal discussion or symposium.

dis•cus•sion (di sku′shən) /dɪ'skʌʃən/ *n.* **1.** [*noncount*] the act of discussing: *I don't think his proposals leave much room for discussion.* **2.** [*count*] an instance of discussing: *We had a long discussion on why I shouldn't appeal his decision.*

dis•dain (dis dān′, di stān′) /dɪs'deyn, dɪ'steyn/ *v.* [*not: be* + *~-ing*] **1.** [~ + *obj*] to look upon or treat with contempt; despise; scorn: *He disdained all my offers of help.* **2.** to think unworthy of notice; consider beneath oneself: [~ + *to* + *verb*]: *She disdained to answer.* [~ + *verb-ing*]: *She disdained replying to the insults.* **—*n.*** [*noncount*] **3.** a feeling of contempt for anything unworthy; scorn: *a look of disdain on her face.* **—dis•dain′ful,** *adj.* **—Syn.** See CONTEMPT.

dis•ease (di zēz′) /dɪ'ziyz/ *n.* **1.** illness; sickness: [*noncount*]: *Disease may result from infection, deficient nutrition, or environmental factors.* [*count*]: *Flu is a contagious disease.* **2.** [*count*] any harmful condition, as of society. **—dis•eased′,** *adj.*: *the product of a diseased mind.*

dis•em•bark (dis′em bärk′) /ˌdɪsɛm'bɑrk/ *v.* **1.** [*no obj*] to go ashore from a ship: *The troops disembarked on the beach just before dawn.* **2.** [*no obj*] to leave an aircraft: *Passengers should disembark from the rear of the plane.* **3.** [~ + *obj*] to remove or unload (cargo) from a vehicle. **—dis•em•bar•ka•tion** (dis em′bär kā′shən) /dɪsˌɛmbɑr'keyʃən/ **dis′em•bark′ment,** *n.* [*noncount*]

dis•em•bod•ied (dis′em bod′ēd) /ˌdɪsɛm'bɒdiyd/ *adj.* [*before a noun*] being without a body; existing as if without a body: *A disembodied voice came out of the loudspeaker.* **—dis′em•bod′i•ment,** *n.* [*noncount*]

dis•em•bow•el (dis′em bou′əl) /ˌdɪsɛm'bawəl/ *v.* [~ + *obj*], **-eled** or **-elled, -el•ing** or **-el•ling.** to remove the bowels or inner organs of.

dis•en•chant•ed (dis′en chant′id) /ˌdɪsɛn'tʃæntɪd/ *adj.* no longer pleased with; disillusioned: *I had become completely disenchanted with my job.* **—dis′en•chant′ment,** *n.* [*noncount*]

dis•en•fran•chise (dis′en fran′chīz) /ˌdɪsɛn'fræntʃayz/ *v.* [~ + *obj*], **-chised, -chis•ing.** to take away the right of (a citizen) to vote: *The new laws disenfranchised some citizens.*

dis•en•gage (dis′en gāj′) /ˌdɪsɛn'geydʒ/ *v.,* **-gaged, -gag•ing. 1.** [*no obj*] (of an army) to stop fighting and move back: *As the enemy retreated, we were ordered to disengage.* **2.** to (cause to) become released from connection: [*no obj*]: *Suddenly the clutch just disengaged.* [~ + *obj*]: *Disengage the clutch and let's see what happens.* **3.** [~ + *obj*] to free (oneself) from; separate from: *I tried to disengage myself from his grip.* **—dis′en•gage′ment,** *n.* [*noncount*]

dis•en•tan•gle (dis′en tang′gəl) /ˌdɪsɛn'tæŋgəl/ *v.,* **-gled, -gling.** to (cause to) become free from entanglement: [~ + *obj*]: *They disentangled the ropes and heaved them on the ship.* [*no obj*]: *The wires disentangled and came loose.* **—dis′en•tan′gle•ment,** *n.* [*noncount*]

dis•es•tab•lish (dis′i stab′lish) /ˌdɪsɪ'stæblɪʃ/ *v.* [~ + *obj*] to withdraw or end state recognition or support from (a church). **—dis′es•tab′lish•ment,** *n.* [*noncount*]

dis•fa•vor (dis fā′vər) /dɪs'feyvər/ *n.* **1.** [*noncount*] unfavorable regard; displeasure; dislike: *feared the king's disfavor.* **2.** [*noncount*] the state of being regarded unfavorably; disrepute: *Short skirts are in disfavor this year.* **3.** [*count*] an unhelpful act; disservice: *You've done yourself a terrible disfavor.* Also, *esp. Brit.,* **dis•fa′vour.**

dis•fig•ure (dis fig′yər) /dɪs'fɪgyər/ *v.* [~ + *obj*], **-ured, -ur•ing.** to mar the appearance of; deform; deface: *He was badly disfigured in the fire.* **—dis•fig′ure•ment,** *n.* [*count; noncount*]

dis•fran•chise (dis fran′chīz) /dɪs'fræntʃayz/ or **dis•en•fran•chise** (dis′en fran′chīz) /ˌdɪsɛn'fræntʃayz/ *v.* [~ + *obj*], **-chised, -chis•ing.** to take away or disallow the right of (a citizen) to vote. **—dis•fran•chise•ment** (dis-fran′chīz mənt, -chiz-) /dɪs'fræntʃayzmənt, -tʃɪz-/ *n.* [*noncount*]

dis•gorge (dis gôrj′) /dɪs'gɔrdʒ/ *v.* [~ + *obj*], **-gorged, -gorg•ing.** to eject or throw out; empty out: *disgorging radioactive waste into the atmosphere.*

dis•grace (dis grās′) /dɪs'greys/ *n., v.,* **-graced, -grac•ing. —*n.* 1.** [*noncount*] the loss of respect or honor; ignominy: *He had to resign in disgrace.* **2.** [*count; usually singular*] a person, act, or thing that causes shame. **—*v.*** [~ + *obj*] **3.** to bring or reflect shame or dishonor upon: *She disgraced herself by passing out at the party.* **4.** to dismiss with discredit: *to be disgraced at court.* **—dis•grace′ful,** *adj.*: *disgraceful manners.* **—dis•grace′ful•ly,** *adv.*

dis•grun•tled (dis grun′tld) /dɪs'grʌntld/ *adj.* in a state of sulky dissatisfaction; discontented; irritated: *My father always became disgruntled if dinner was late.*

dis•guise (dis gīz′, di skīz′) /dɪs'gayz, dɪ'skayz/ *v.,* **-guised, -guis•ing,** *n.* **—*v.* 1.** [~ + *obj* + *as* + *obj*] to change the appearance of so as to mislead: *The army disguised the soldiers as ordinary villagers.* **2.** [~ + *obj*] to conceal the truth of by a false form or appearance; misrepresent: *to disguise his true intentions.* **—*n.* 3.** [*count*] something that serves or is intended to conceal identity, character, or quality: *Dressing as palace guards was a clever disguise.* **4.** [*noncount*] the process of disguising: *The jewel thief was a master of disguise.*

dis•gust (dis gust′, di skust′) /dɪs'gʌst, dɪ'skʌst/ *v.* [~ + *obj*] **1.** to offend the sensibilities of: *His terrible manners at the dinner table disgusted us.* **2.** to cause a feeling of strong sickness or nausea in: *The awful food at the hotel disgusted her.* **—*n.*** [*noncount*] **3.** repugnance caused by something offensive; strong hatred or aversion: *He couldn't hide his disgust at the atrocity.* **4.** a strong distaste; nausea: *Feelings of disgust and trembling came over her.* **—Related Words.** DISGUST is a verb and a noun, DISGUSTING and DISGUSTED are adjectives: *Violence disgusts me. He was filled with disgust by all that violence. The movie was disgusting. The disgusted workers went home early.*

dis•gust•ed (dis gus′tid, di skus′-) /dɪs'gʌstɪd, dɪ'skʌs-/ *adj.* overwhelmed by a feeling of disgust: *They were disgusted by the violence in the movie.*

dis•gust•ing (dis gus′ting, di skus′-) /dɪs'gʌstɪŋ, dɪ'skʌs-/ *adj.* bringing or causing a feeling of disgust: *a disgusting smell of rotting cabbage.*

dish (dish) /dɪʃ/ *n.* [*count*] **1.** a plate used esp. for holding or serving food: *Put the dishes on the table.* **2.** a container used to bake or cook food: *a glass baking dish for bread.* **3.** all the plates, bowls, cups, and utensils used at a meal: *Who will wash the dishes tonight?* **4.** a particular type of food or preparation of food: *This is an easy dish to make.* **5.** Also called **dish′ anten′na.** a dish-shaped reflector, used esp. for receiving satellite and microwave signals. **—***v.* **6. dish out,** *Informal.* **a.** [~ + *out* + *obj*] to deal out; distribute: *He dished out some food to the waiting customers.* **b.** to give out; inflict: [~ + *out* + *obj*]: *Their jailers dished out their punishment.* [~ + *obj* + *out*]: *She can dish it out, but can she take it, too?* **7. dish up,** [~ + *up* + *obj*] to put (food) on plates; distribute: *He dished up meals for the homeless.*

dish•cloth (dish′klôth′, -kloth′) /'dɪʃˌklɔθ, -ˌklɒθ/ *n.* [*count*] a cloth for washing dishes; dishrag.

dis•heart•en (dis här′tn) /dɪs'hɑrtn̩/ *v.* [~ + *obj*] to lower or depress the hope, courage, or spirits of; discourage: *News of another job rejection disheartened him badly.* **—dis•heart′ened,** *adj.*: *disheartened job seekers.* **—dis•heart′en•ing,** *adj.*: *disheartening economic news.*

di•shev•el•ed (di shev′əld) /dɪ'ʃɛvəld/ *adj.* or (*esp. Brit.*) **-elled.** (of appearance) in disarray; in loose disorder: *their disheveled apartment; disheveled hair.* **—di•shev′el•ment,** *n.* [*noncount*]

dis•hon•est (dis on′ist) /dɪs'ɒnɪst/ *adj.* **1.** not honest; untrustworthy: *I wouldn't do business with such dishonest car dealers.* **2.** showing lack of honesty: *That commercial had a lot of dishonest claims.* **—dis•hon′est•ly,** *adv.*: *He got most of his money dishonestly.*

dis•hon•es•ty (dis on′is tē) /dɪs'ɒnɪstiy/ *n.* [*noncount*] a lack of honesty.

dis•hon•or (dis on′ər) /dɪs'ɒnər/ *n.* **1.** [*noncount*] lack or loss of honor; disgrace; shame: *They chanted "Death before dishonor."* **2.** [*count*] indignity; insult: *Refusing an offer of help was a dishonor.* **—***v.* [~ + *obj*] **3.** to deprive of honor; disgrace; bring shame on: *The senator's corruption dishonored both himself and his family.* **4.** to refuse to pay (a check, draft, etc.). **—dis•hon′or•a•ble,** *adj.*: *Treason is a dishonorable act.*

dish•pan (dish′pan′) /'dɪʃˌpæn/ *n.* [*count*] a large pan in which dishes, pots, etc., are washed.

dish•rag (dish′rag′) /'dɪʃˌræg/ *n.* DISHCLOTH.

dish•tow•el (dish′tou′əl) /'dɪʃˌtawəl/ *n.* [*count*] a towel for drying dishes.

dish•wash•er (dish′wosh′ər, -wô′shər) /'dɪʃˌwɒʃər, -ˌwɔʃər/ *n.* [*count*] **1.** a person who washes dishes. **2.** a machine for washing dishes.

dis•il•lu•sion (dis′i lo͞o′zhən) /ˌdɪsɪ'luwʒən/ *v.* [~ + *obj*] **1.** to change an illusion or false belief; disenchant: *I hate to disillusion you, but your chances of winning are practically zero.* **—***n.* [*noncount*] **2.** a freeing or a being freed from illusion or conviction; disenchantment. **—dis′il•lu′sioned,** *adj.*: *disillusioned voters fed up with politics.* **—dis′il•lu′sion•ment,** *n.* [*noncount*]

dis•in•clined (dis′in klīnd′) /ˌdɪsɪn'klaynd/ *adj.* [*be* + ~ + *to* + *verb*] unwilling; averse; reluctant: *They are disinclined to fire someone without very good reason.*

dis•in•fect (dis′in fekt′) /ˌdɪsɪn'fɛkt/ *v.* [~ + *obj*] to cleanse of infection; destroy disease germs in: *to disinfect a wound.*

dis•in•fect•ant (dis′in fek′tənt) /ˌdɪsɪn'fɛktənt/ *n.* **1.** a substance that disinfects: [*noncount*]: *Pour some disinfectant on the wound.* [*count*]: *The bathroom spray has a disinfectant in it.* **—***adj.* [*before a noun*] **2.** capable of killing germs: *a disinfectant cleaner.*

dis•in•gen•u•ous (dis′in jen′yo͞o əs) /ˌdɪsɪn'dʒɛnyuwəs/ *adj.* lacking in frankness, truth, or sincerity; insincere: *She gave me a disingenuous answer.*

dis•in•her•it (dis′in her′it) /ˌdɪsɪn'hɛrɪt/ *v.* [~ + *obj*] **1.** to exclude (an heir) from inheriting: *After the incident his father disinherited him.* **2.** [*usually: be* + ~*-ed*] to deprive (a people) of their culture or identity: *Many minority groups throughout history have been disinherited by the majority.*

dis•in•te•grate (dis in′tə grāt′) /dɪs'ɪntəˌgreyt/ *v.*, **-grat•ed, -grat•ing.** to (cause to) lose solidness or strength; (cause to) break up or fall apart: [*no obj*]: *At that speed the plane began to disintegrate.* [~ + *obj*]: *The bullets tearing into the house disintegrated the flimsy walls.* **—dis•in•te•gra•tion** (dis in′tə grā′shən) /dɪsˌɪntə'greyʃən/ *n.* [*noncount*]

dis•in•ter (dis′in tûr′) /ˌdɪsɪn'tɜr/ *v.* [~ + *obj*], **-terred, -ter•ring. 1.** to take up or dig out of the place of burial; exhume: *The corpse was disinterred and re-examined by the coroner.* **2.** to bring (something) once absent back into view: *The committee disinterred a few old studies done by their predecessors to prove their point.* **—dis′in•ter′ment,** *n.* [*noncount*]

dis•in•ter•est•ed (dis in′tə res′tid, -tri stid) /dɪs'ɪntəˌrɛstɪd, -trɪstɪd/ *adj.* **1.** able to act fairly because not influenced by personal interest or advantage; unbiased: *We need some disinterested mediators to settle the dispute.* **2.** not interested; indifferent: *becoming disinterested in his children.* **—Usage.** Compare DISINTERESTED and UNINTERESTED. The first meaning of DISINTERESTED, "able to act fairly; unbiased" is quite different from UNINTERESTED, "not taking an interest." But the second meaning of DISINTERESTED listed here is identical to the meaning of UNINTERESTED, and some users of English feel that this use of DISINTERESTED is incorrect.

dis•joint•ed (dis join′tid) /dɪs'dʒɔyntɪd/ *adj.* separated; disconnected; out of order; badly arranged: *The movie was too disjointed to make much sense.* **—dis•joint′ed•ly,** *adv.* **—dis•joint′ed•ness,** *n.* [*noncount*] See -JUNC-.

disk (disk) /dɪsk/ *n.* [*count*] **1.** any thin, flat, circular plate or object. **2.** any surface that is flat and round, or seemingly so: *the disk of the sun.* **3.** DISC (def. 1). **4.** any of several types of materials for storing electronic or computer data, consisting of thin round plates of plastic or metal. **5.** any of various roundish, flat anatomical structures, esp. between the bones of the backbone.

disk•ette (di sket′) /dɪ'skɛt/ *n.* FLOPPY DISK.

dis•like (dis līk′) /dɪs'layk/ *v.*, **-liked, -lik•ing,** *n.* **—***v.* **1.** to regard with displeasure; to have aversion for: [~ + *obj*]: *I dislike selfish people.* [~ + *verb-ing*]: *I dislike jogging early in the morning.* **—***n.* **2.** [*noncount*] a feeling of strong displeasure toward something; antipathy: *My feeling wasn't exactly one of hatred, but more of strong dislike.* **3.** [*count*] something or someone causing such a feeling: *one of his strong dislikes.* **—Usage.** Compare LIKE and DISLIKE and the form of the verbs that may follow each. As the example above for DISLIKE shows, that verb may be followed by another verb in the *-ing* form: *I dislike jogging.* The verb LIKE on the other hand may be followed by a verb in the *-ing* form, but unlike DISLIKE it may also be followed by the *to* + *verb* (or infinitive) form: *I like jogging; I like to jog.* DISLIKE therefore is unlike LIKE.

dis•lo•cate (dis′lō kāt′, dis lō′kāt) /'dɪslowˌkeyt, dɪs'lowkeyt/ *v.* [~ + *obj*], **-cat•ed, -cat•ing. 1.** to put out of joint or out of position: *His shoulder was dislocated.* **2.** to throw out of order; upset: *Frequent strikes dislocated the economy.* **—dis•lo•ca•tion** (dis′lō kā′shən) /ˌdɪslow'keyʃən/ *n.* [*noncount*] See -LOC-.

dis•lodge (dis loj′) /dɪs'lɒdʒ/ *v.* [~ + *obj*], **-lodged, -lodg•ing.** to remove or force out of a particular place: *We needed a bulldozer to dislodge the rock.*

dis•loy•al (dis loi′əl) /dɪs'lɔyəl/ *adj.* false to one's allegiances; faithless: *He was disloyal to his own department by snitching to the boss.* **—dis•loy′al•ty,** *n.* [*noncount*]

dis•mal (diz′məl) /'dɪzməl/ *adj.* **1.** causing gloom or dejection; cheerless: *a dismal little office.* **2.** lacking skill; inept; poorly done: *a dismal effort by the basketball team.* **—dis′mal•ly,** *adv.*: *a dismally dreary day.*

dis•man•tle (dis man′tl) /dɪs'mæntl̩/ *v.* [~ + *obj*], **-tled, -tling.** to take apart; remove parts or pieces of; reduce the power of: *They dismantled the car to find out what was wrong with it.*

dis•may (dis mā′) /dɪs'mey/ *v.* [~ + *obj*] **1.** to break down the courage of completely; surprise unpleasantly: *The child's failing grades dismayed his parents.* **—***n.* [*noncount*] **2.** sudden or complete loss of courage: *My heart sank with dismay as I realized what I had done.*

dis•mem•ber (dis mem′bər) /dɪs'mɛmbər/ *v.* [~ + *obj*] **1.** to remove limbs of; divide limb from limb: *dismembered corpses.* **2.** to divide into parts; cut up: *He wants to dismember the company.* **—dis•mem′ber•ment,** *n.* [*noncount*]

dis•miss (dis mis′) /dɪs'mɪs/ *v.* [~ + *obj*] **1.** to direct or allow to leave: *The teacher dismissed the class early.* **2.**

to fire; discharge from office or service: *to dismiss an employee.* **3.** to put aside from consideration: *At first the editor dismissed the story as a rumor.* See -MIS-.

dis•mis•sal (dis mis′əl) /dɪs'mɪsəl/ *n.* **1.** [*count*] the act of dismissing: *several dismissals because of budget cuts.* **2.** [*noncount*] the act of discarding or rejecting something as unworthy: *made a quick dismissal of the offer.*

dis•mount (*v.* dis mount′; *n. also* dis′mount′) / *v.* dɪs'mawnt; *n. also* 'dɪs,mawnt/ *v.* [*no obj*] **1.** to get down or climb down from a horse or bicycle: *She dismounted from the motorcycle.* **—*n.*** [*count*] **2.** an act of dismounting, such as in gymnastics: *a dismount from the balance beam.*

dis•o•be•di•ence (dis′ə bē′dē əns) /,dɪsə'biydiyəns/ *n.* [*noncount*] lack of obedience; failure to obey: *Disobedience was punished quickly.*

dis•o•be•di•ent (dis′ə bē′dē ənt) /,dɪsə'biydiyənt/ *adj.* relating to or marked by disobedience: *Their disobedient children were never punished.*

dis•o•bey (dis′ə bā′) /,dɪsə'bey/ *v.* to fail or refuse to obey: [*no obj*]: *If you disobey, you'll just go to bed earlier.* [~ + *obj*]: *He was always disobeying his parents.* —**Related Words.** DISOBEY is a verb, DISOBEDIENT is an adjective, DISOBEDIENCE is a noun: *The child disobeyed his parents. The child was disobedient to his parents. His disobedience was punished.*

dis•or•der (dis ôr′dər) /dɪs'ɔrdər/ *n.* **1.** [*noncount*] lack of order; confusion: *When the burglars left, the room was in complete disorder.* **2.** [*count*] an irregularity: *a disorder in legal proceedings.* **3.** public disturbance; rioting: [*noncount*]: *The police could not cope with all the disorder in the streets.* [*count*]: *Several disorders rocked the township yesterday.* **4.** [*count*] a disturbance in health: *a mild stomach disorder.* **—*v.*** [~ + *obj*] **5.** to destroy the order of; disarrange: *The room was disordered when we arrived at the scene of the burglary.* **6.** to derange the health or functions of: *a disordered mind.*

dis•or•der•ly (dis ôr′dər lē) /dɪs'ɔrdərliy/ *adj.* **1.** characterized by disorder; untidy: *a disorderly living room.* **2.** unruly; behaving in an uncontrolled way: *disorderly conduct.* —**dis•or′der•li•ness,** *n.* [*noncount*]

dis•or•gan•ize (dis ôr′gə nīz′) /dɪs'ɔrgə,nayz/ *v.* [~ + *obj*], **-ized, -iz•ing.** to destroy the organization or orderly arrangement of; throw into confusion: *The secretary's sudden departure disorganized the whole company.* —**dis•or•gan•i•za•tion** (dis ôr′gə nə zā′shən) /dɪs,ɔrgənə'zeyʃən/ *n.* [*noncount*] See -ORGA-.

dis•or•gan•ized (dis ôr′gə nīzd′) /dɪs'ɔrgə,nayzd/ *adj.* in a state or condition of disorganization: *My desk is so disorganized that I can't find anything.*

dis•o•ri•ent (dis ôr′ē ent′, -ōr′-) /dɪs'ɔriy,ɛnt, -'owr-/ *v.* [~ + *obj*] **1.** to cause to lose one's way: *When I came up out of the subway, I was momentarily disoriented.* **2.** to confuse, esp. so that one loses perception of time, place, or one's personal identity: *When she regained consciousness she was disoriented and not sure how she had gotten there.* Also, *esp. Brit.,* **dis•or•i•en•tate** (dis ôr′ē en tāt′, -ōr′-) /dɪs'ɔriyən,teyt, -'owr-/. —**dis•o•ri•en•ta•tion** (dis ôr′ē en tā′shən, -ōr′-) /dɪs,ɔriyɛn'teyʃən, -,owr-/ *n.* [*noncount*] See -ORI-.

dis•own (dis ōn′) /dɪs'own/ *v.* [~ + *obj*] to refuse to acknowledge responsibility for: *disowned their daughter after she eloped.*

dis•par•age (di spar′ij) /dɪ'spærɪdʒ/ *v.* [~ + *obj*], **-aged, -ag•ing.** to belittle, ridicule, or discredit: *Don't disparage his attempts to become a doctor.* —**dis•par′age•ment,** *n.* [*noncount*] —**dis•par′ag•ing,** *adj.*: *disparaging remarks.* See -PAR-.

dis•pa•rate (dis′pər it, di spar′-) /'dɪspərɪt, dɪ'spær-/ *adj.* relating to or marked by disparity: *It was surprising to hear such disparate views from members of the same family.* See -PARE-[1].

dis•par•i•ty (di spar′i tē) /dɪ'spærɪtiy/ *n.* great difference; clear and obvious difference or distinctness: [*noncount*]: *We were shocked by the disparity in pay scales.* [*count*]: *Too often there's a great disparity between campaign promises and what the candidate does when elected.*

dis•pas•sion•ate (dis pash′ə nit) /dɪs'pæʃənɪt/ *adj.* free from or unaffected by passion; without personal feeling or bias: *He described the accident in a dispassionate and objective way.* —**dis•pas′sion•ate•ly,** *adv.* See -PASS-[2].

dis•patch (*v.* di spach′; *n. also* dis′pach) /*v.* dɪ'spætʃ; *n. also* 'dɪspætʃ/ *v.* [~ + *obj*] **1.** to send off or away with speed: *He dispatched his best troops to the borders.* **2.** to put to death; kill: *The injured horse was dispatched painlessly by its owner.* **3.** to transact or dispose of (a matter) promptly: *The negotiations were dispatched almost as soon as the two sides sat down to talk.* **—*n.* 4.** [*count; usually singular*] the sending off of a messenger, letter, troops, etc.: *the dispatch of a special brigade to the troubled region.* **5.** [*noncount*] prompt or speedy action: *done with dispatch.* **6.** [*count*] an official communication sent with speed: *The general sent a dispatch to his field commander.* **7.** [*count*] a news story transmitted to a newspaper by a reporter: *a dispatch from Nairobi.* —**dis•patch′er,** *n.* [*count*]: *The police dispatcher sent several squad cars to the area.*

dis•pel (di spel′) /dɪ'spɛl/ *v.* [~ + *obj*], **-pelled, -pel•ling.** to drive off or cause to vanish: *That fine performance dispelled any doubts about her abilities.* See -PEL-.

dis•pen•sa•ble (di spen′sə bəl) /dɪ'spɛnsəbəl/ *adj.* capable of being dispensed with; not necessary or essential: *lots of dispensable items in the budget.*

dis•pen•sa•ry (di spen′sə rē) /dɪ'spɛnsəriy/ *n.* [*count*], *pl.* **-ries. 1.** a place, such as in a hospital, where something is dispensed, esp. medicines: *Go down to the dispensary on the first floor and give them this prescription.* **2.** a public facility where medical care and medicines are furnished.

dis•pen•sa•tion (dis′pən sā′shən, -pen-) /,dɪspən'seyʃən, -pɛn-/ *n.* **1.** [*noncount*] an act or instance of dispensing: *the fair dispensation of justice.* **2.** [*noncount*] a certain order, system, or arrangement. **3.** [*count*] doing away with a general rule or law in a particular instance: *needed a special dispensation to marry outside the parish.*

dis•pense (di spens′) /dɪ'spɛns/ *v.* [~ + *obj*], **-pensed, -pens•ing. 1.** to deal out; distribute: *dispensed the money to charity.* **2.** to administer: *to dispense the law without bias.* **3.** to make up and distribute (medicine), esp. on prescription: *a license to dispense drugs.* **4. dispense with,** [~ + *with* + *obj*] to do away with; get rid of: *Can we dispense with the formalities?*

dis•pens•er (di spen′sər) /dɪ'spɛnsər/ *n.* [*count*] a container from which something may be poured, etc: *They filled the soap dispensers in the bathroom.*

dis•pers•al (di spûr′səl) /dɪ'spɜrsəl/ *n.* [*noncount*] the act of dispersing or of being dispersed: *the dispersal of the troops into the surrounding villages.*

dis•perse (di spûrs′) /dɪ'spɜrs/ *v.,* **-persed, -pers•ing. 1.** to (cause to) separate and move in different directions; (cause to) become scattered: [*no obj*]: *The crowd dispersed when the police arrived.* [~ + *obj*]: *The riot police dispersed the crowd.* **2.** [~ + *obj*] to spread widely; disseminate: *The seeds were dispersed on the plowed land.* **3.** to (cause to) vanish: [*no obj*]: *When the sun came out, the fog dispersed.* [~ + *obj*]: *The wind dispersed the fog.*

dis•per•sion (di spûr′zhən, -shən) /dɪ'spɜrʒən, -ʃən/ *n.* [*noncount*] dispersal: *the dispersion of radioactive particles.*

dis•pir•it (di spir′it) /dɪ'spɪrɪt/ *v.* [~ + *obj*] to deprive of spirit or hope; discourage; dishearten. —**dis•pir′it•ed,** *adj.*: *a dispirited team.*

dis•place (dis plās′) /dɪs'pleys/ *v.* [~ + *obj*], **-placed, -plac•ing. 1.** to compel (someone) to leave home or country: *a faceless bureaucracy that displaces the people.* **2.** to move or put out of place: *to displace a joint.* **3.** to take the place of; replace: *trying to displace me in my job.*

displaced′ per′son, *n.* [*count*] a person driven or expelled from a homeland by war, famine, etc.

dis•place•ment (dis plās′mənt) /dɪs'pleysmənt/ *n.* **1.** [*noncount*] the act of displacing; the state of being displaced: *the displacement of different scientific theories by new ones.* **2.** [*count*] the volume of the space through which a piston travels during a single stroke in an engine, pump, or the like. **3.** [*count*] the weight or the volume of liquid displaced by a body, such as a ship: *The ship had a displacement of 50,000 tons.*

dis•play (di splā′) /dɪ'spley/ *v.* [~ + *obj*] **1.** to show or exhibit; make visible: *The vendors displayed their fruit.* **2.** to reveal; demonstrate: *to display fear.* **3.** to show ostentatiously; flaunt: *displaying his trophies.* **4.** to show (computer data) on a screen: *Let's display the figures and see what we have.* **—*n.* 5.** an act or instance of displaying; exhibition: [*count*]: *fireworks displays on the Fourth of July.* [*noncount*]: *There was a fair amount on display but nothing worth buying.* **6.** [*count*] the visual representation of the output of an electronic device, such as on a computer screen: *The display is pretty clear but could be sharper.* **7.** [*count*] a pattern of animal behavior designed to attract and arouse a mate: *the courtship displays of penguins.*

dis•please (dis plēz′) /dɪs'pliyz/ *v.* [~ + *obj*], **-pleased, -pleas•ing.** to annoy, cause dissatisfaction in, or make angry: *Rude behavior displeases her greatly.*

dis•pleas•ure (dis plezh′ər) /dɪs'plɛʒər/ *n.* [*noncount*] dissatisfaction; disapproval: *an empty feeling of displeasure.*

dis•pos•a•ble (di spō′zə bəl) /dɪ'spowzəbəl/ *adj.* **1.** designed for or capable of being thrown away after use: *disposable diapers.* **2.** [*often: before a noun*] free for use; available: *Your disposable income is what is left after paying taxes and other essentials.* **—*n.*** [*count*] **3.** something disposable after use, such as a paper cup. **—dis•pos•a•bil•i•ty** (di spō′zə bil′i tē) /dɪˌspowzə'bɪlɪtiy/ *n.* [*noncount*] See -POS-.

dis•pos•al[1] (di spō′zəl) /dɪ'spowzəl/ *n.* [*noncount*] **1.** an act or instance of putting things in order; arrangement: *the disposal of the troops.* **2.** a disposing of or getting rid of something: *disposal of hazardous wastes.* **3.** power or right to use or have use of a thing; control: *The car was left at my disposal.* See -POS-.

dis•pos•al[2] (di spō′zəl) /dɪ'spowzəl/ *n.* [*count*] an electrical device in the drain of a sink for grinding up garbage. See -POS-.

dis•pose (di spōz′) /dɪ'spowz/ *v.*, **-posed, -pos•ing. 1.** [~ + *obj*] to give a tendency or inclination to; incline: *His temperament disposed him to argue.* **2.** [~ + *obj*] to put in a particular order or arrangement: *disposed his troops along the southern border.* **3. dispose of,** [~ + *of* + *obj*] **a.** to deal with conclusively; settle: *Let's dispose of this matter once and for all.* **b.** to get rid of; discard or destroy: *Dispose of the waste papers in this bin.* **c.** to give away or sell: *His property holdings will be disposed of in his will.* See -POS-.

dis•posed (di spōzd′) /dɪ'spowzd/ *adj.* [*be* + ~] **1.** [~ + *to* + *verb*] inclined, willing, or motivated to (do something): *The committee was not disposed to hold another meeting.* **2.** [~ + *to/toward*] inclined (toward or against); willing to work (for or against): *The president is favorably disposed toward the treaty.* See -POS-.

dis•po•si•tion (dis′pə zish′ən) /ˌdɪspə'zɪʃən/ *n.* [*count*] **1.** the predominant or prevailing tendency of one's spirits; characteristic attitude: *a cheerful disposition.* **2.** [~ + *to* + *verb*] state of mind regarding something; inclination: *a dangerous disposition to gamble.* **3.** arrangement or placing, such as of troops: *the careful disposition of the remaining troops.* **4.** final settlement of a matter: *What was the disposition of the case?* **5.** [*usually singular*] power to dispose of a thing; control: *The foundation has funds at its disposition to aid colleges.* See -POS-.

dis•pos•sess (dis′pə zes′) /ˌdɪspə'zɛs/ *v.* [~ + *obj*] to put (a person) out of occupancy (of a dwelling place): *If you pay your rent, you can't be dispossessed.* See -SESS-.

dis•pro•por•tion (dis′prə pôr′shən, -pōr′-) /ˌdɪsprə'pɔrʃən, -'powr-/ *n.* **1.** [*noncount*] lack of proportion; lack of proper relationship. **2.** [*count*] something out of proportion.

dis•pro•por•tion•ate (dis′prə pôr′shə nit, -pōr′-) /ˌdɪsprə'pɔrʃənɪt, -'powr-/ *adj.* lacking proportion or balance; too much or too little: *spends a disproportionate amount of time watching TV.*

dis•prove (dis pro͞ov′) /dɪs'pruwv/ *v.* [~ + *obj*], **-proved, -prov•ing.** to prove (an assertion, etc.) to be false or wrong; refute: *The latest evidence disproves the theory.* **—dis•prov′a•ble,** *adj.* See -PROV-.

dis•pu•ta•tion (dis′pyo͝o tā′shən) /ˌdɪspyʊ'teyʃən/ *n.* the act of disputing: [*noncount*]: *arguing with careful disputation.* [*count*]: *long disputations about what to do.* See -PUTE-.

dis•pu•ta•tious (dis′pyo͝o tā′shəs) /ˌdɪspyʊ'teyʃəs/ also **dis•put•a•tive** (di spyo͞o′tə tiv) /dɪ'spyuwtətɪv/ *adj.* fond of or enjoying disputation: *disputatious members of the committee.* **—dis′pu•ta′tious•ly,** *adv.*

dis•pute (di spyo͞ot′) /dɪ'spyuwt/ *v.*, **-put•ed, -put•ing,** *n.* **—*v.* 1.** to be in an argument or debate; argue: [*no obj*]: *The school board members spend their time disputing and getting nothing done.* [~ + *with* + *obj*]: *We were disputing with the committee on how to proceed.* **2.** to argue or debate about; argue against; call (something) in question: [~ + *obj*]: *The accountant disputes the figures you gave her.* [~ + *that clause*]: *The administration does not dispute that the cuts in personnel will hurt good service.* **—*n.* 3.** debate, controversy, or difference of opinion: [*count*]: *The dispute concerns capital punishment.* [*noncount*]: *much dispute over how to inspect nuclear weapons-producing plants.* **4.** [*count*] a quarrel; a fight: *a loud dispute in the middle of the night.* **—dis•put′a•ble,** *adj.* See -PUTE-.

dis•qual•i•fy (dis kwol′ə fī′) /dɪs'kwɒləˌfay/ *v.* [~ + *obj* (+ *from*)], **-fied, -fy•ing. 1.** to take away the right to participate in a contest because of a violation of the rules: *She was disqualified from the election because she did not register on time.* **2.** to make unfit or unqualified: *The lack of a good education might disqualify you from some jobs.* **—dis•qual•i•fi•ca•tion** (dis kwol′ə fi kā′shən) /dɪsˌkwɒləfɪ'keyʃən/ *n.* [*noncount*]: *Faced with disqualification, she decided to withdraw.* [*count*]: *Several disqualifications were announced after the race.*

dis•qui•et (dis kwī′it) /dɪs'kwayɪt/ *n.* [*noncount*] **1.** lack of calm or peace; anxiety; uneasiness. **—*v.*** [~ + *obj*] **2.** to upset; to take away calm or peace: *The news about the layoffs disquieted a lot of workers.* **—dis•qui′et•ed,** *adj.* **—dis•qui′et•ing,** *adj.*: *disquieting news about the war.*

dis•re•gard (dis′ri gärd′) /ˌdɪsrɪ'gɑrd/ *v.* [~ + *obj*] **1.** to pay no attention to; ignore: *Please disregard the mess and sit right here.* **—*n.*** [*noncount*] **2.** lack of regard or attention; neglect: *his complete disregard of orders.*

dis•re•pair (dis′ri pâr′) /ˌdɪsrɪ'pɛər/ *n.* [*noncount*] the condition of needing repair; a neglected state: *The house had fallen into total disrepair.*

dis•rep•u•ta•ble (dis rep′yə tə bəl) /dɪs'rɛpyətəbəl/ *adj.* having a bad reputation: *a disreputable part of town.* See -PUTE-.

dis•re•pute (dis′ri pyo͞ot′) /ˌdɪsrɪ'pyuwt/ *n.* [*noncount*] disfavor; the state of having lost a good reputation: *The secret service had fallen into disrepute with one scandal after another.* See -PUTE-.

dis•re•spect (dis′ri spekt′) /ˌdɪsrɪ'spɛkt/ *n.* [*noncount*] **1.** lack of respect; rudeness: *The disrespect she shows her parents is shocking.* **—*v.*** [~ + *obj*] **2.** to regard or treat with rudeness; insult: *Some students disrespect teachers and all authority figures.* **—dis′re•spect′ful,** *adj.*: *a disrespectful student.* **—dis′re•spect′ful•ly,** *adv.*: *behaving disrespectfully.* See -SPEC-.

dis•robe (dis rōb′) /dɪs'rowb/ *v.*, **-robed, -rob•ing.** to undress: [~ + *obj*]: *The nurse disrobed the elderly patient expertly.* [*no obj*]: *He was asked to disrobe and wait for the doctor.*

dis•rupt (dis rupt′) /dɪs'rʌpt/ *v.* [~ + *obj*] **1.** to cause disorder or turmoil in: *The war disrupted the lives of millions.* **2.** to interrupt the normal operation of: *The tornado disrupted broadcasting along the entire coast.* See -RUPT-.

dis•rup•tion (dis rup′shən) /dɪs'rʌpʃən/ *n.* **1.** [*noncount*] the act of disrupting: *the cruel disruption of lives during the war.* **2.** temporary interruption of something: [*noncount*]: *disruption of the phone lines.* [*count*]: *a few more disruptions of the broadcasts during the hurricane.* See -RUPT-.

dis•rup•tive (dis rup′tiv) /dɪs'rʌptɪv/ *adj.* causing disorder: *disruptive behavior in class.* See -RUPT-.

dis•sat•is•fac•tion (dis′sat is fak′shən, dis sat′-) /ˌdɪssætɪs'fækʃən, dɪsˌsæt-/ *n.* [*noncount*] the state or attitude of not being satisfied: *a lot of dissatisfaction on the job.* See -SAT-.

dis•sat•is•fy (dis sat′is fī′) /dɪs'sætɪsˌfay/ *v.* [~ + *obj*], **-fied, -fy•ing.** to fail to satisfy; disappoint; displease: *This new plan dissatisfies everyone.* **—dis•sat′is•fied′,** *adj.*: *dissatisfied with her examination results.* See -SAT-.

dis•sect (di sekt′, dī-) /dɪ'sɛkt, day-/ *v.* [~ + *obj*] **1.** to cut apart (an animal body, a plant, etc.) to examine the structure and relation of parts: *In biology class we had to dissect a frog.* **2.** to examine in detail part by part; analyze: *Your assignment is to dissect the poem.* **—dis•sec•tion** (di sek′shən, dī-) /dɪ'sɛkʃən, day-/ *n.* [*count*]: *performed several frog dissections.* [*noncount*]: *to subject the frog to dissection.* See -SECT-.

dis•sem•ble (di sem′bəl) /dɪ'sɛmbəl/ *v.* [*no obj*], **-bled, -bling.** to hide or conceal one's true motives or thoughts; speak or act hypocritically: *You can always tell if he's dissembling; his voice trembles when he lies.* **—dis•sem′blance,** *n.* [*noncount*] **—dis•sem′bler,** *n.* [*count*] See -SEMBLE-.

dis•sem•i•nate (di sem′ə nāt′) /dɪ'sɛməˌneyt/ *v.* [~ + *obj*], **-nat•ed, -nat•ing.** to scatter or spread widely; distribute: *The embassy disseminated information about its new programs.* **—dis•sem•i•na•tion** (di sem′ə nā′shən) /dɪˌsɛmə'neyʃən/ *n.* [*noncount*]: *the dissemination of Plato's philosophy.*

dis•sen•sion (di sen′shən) /dɪ'sɛnʃən/ *n.* [*noncount*] strong disagreement; discord: *a lot of dissension in the ranks of the ordinary soldiers.* See -SENS-.

dis•sent (di sent′) /dɪ'sɛnt/ *v.* **1.** to differ in thinking or opinion, esp. from the majority: [*no obj*]: *If enough of us dissent, the new regulation won't be passed.* [~ + *from* + *obj*]: *He enjoys dissenting from us.* —*n.* [*noncount*] **2.** difference of thinking or opinion; disagreement: *Dissent about the matter kept us from reaching an agreement.* —**dis•sent′er,** *n.* [*count*] See -SENT-.

dis•ser•ta•tion (dis′ər tā′shən) /ˌdɪsər'teyʃən/ *n.* [*count*] **1.** a thesis, esp. one written by a candidate for a doctoral degree: *wrote a dissertation on economic policy.* **2.** any formal speech or writing: *a dissertation on natural childbirth.*

dis•serv•ice (dis sûr′vis) /dɪs'sɜrvɪs/ *n.* [*count; usually singular*] an instance of hurting; an injustice: *He did you a disservice by not helping.* See -SERV-[1].

dis•si•dent (dis′i dənt) /'dɪsɪdənt/ *n.* [*count*] **1.** a person who dissents: *The dissidents marched in protest against the ban.* —*adj.* [*before a noun*] **2.** disagreeing or dissenting, such as in opinion or attitude: *The dissident members kept the issue from coming to a vote.* —**dis′si•dence,** *n.* [*noncount*] See -SID-.

dis•sim•i•lar (di sim′ə lər) /dɪ'sɪmələr/ *adj.* not similar; unlike; different: *dissimilar ways of doing things.* —**dis•sim•i•lar•i•ty** (di sim′ə lar′i tē) /dɪˌsɪmə'lærɪtiy/ *n., pl.* **-ties.** [*noncount*]: *great dissimilarity in the way they conduct elections.* [*count*]: *Write about the similarities and dissimilarities in the ways both characters deal with their crises.* See -SIMIL-.

dis•sim•u•late (di sim′yə lāt′) /dɪ'sɪmyəˌleyt/ *v.,* **-lat•ed, -lat•ing.** to conceal under a false appearance; dissemble: [~ + *obj*]: *dissimulated their intentions right up to the moment of the attack.* [*no obj*]: *They were just dissimulating, pretending to be friendly.* —**dis•sim•u•la•tion** (di sim′yə lā′shən) /dɪˌsɪmyə'leyʃən/ *n.* [*noncount*] —**dis•sim′u•la′tor,** *n.* [*count*] See -SIMIL-.

dis•si•pate (dis′ə pāt′) /'dɪsəˌpeyt/ *v.,* **-pat•ed, -pat•ing.** **1.** to (cause to) become scattered in various directions; disperse: [*no obj*]: *The fog dissipated when the sun rose.* [~ + *obj*]: *The police managed to dissipate the mob in minutes.* **2.** [~ + *obj*] to spend wastefully; misspend: *He dissipated his large inheritance.*

dis•si•pated (dis′ə pā′tid) /'dɪsəˌpeytɪd/ *adj.* relating to or marked by dissipation: *a dissipated life full of drugs.*

dis•si•pa•tion (dis′ə pā′shən) /ˌdɪsə'peyʃən/ *n.* [*noncount*] **1.** the act of wasting one's life in foolish or harmful pleasure: *Decades of dissipation had a powerful impact on his health.* **2.** the act of scattering or of being scattered: *the dissipation of the fog.*

dis•so•ci•ate (di sō′shē āt′, -sē-) /dɪ'sowʃiyˌeyt, -siy-/ *v.* [~ + *obj* + *from* + *obj*], **-at•ed, -at•ing.** to cut off or separate the association of; disconnect: *He tried to dissociate himself from his past.* —**dis•so•ci•a•tion** (di sō′shē ā′shən, -sē-) /dɪˌsowʃiy'eyʃən, -siy-/ *n.* [*noncount*]

dis•so•lute (dis′ə lo͞ot′) /'dɪsəˌluwt/ *adj.* enjoying immoral conduct; corrupt; dissipated: *He led a dissolute life, thinking only of his own pleasure.* —**dis′so•lute′ly,** *adv.* —**dis′so•lute′ness,** *n.* [*noncount*] See -SOLV-.

dis•so•lu•tion (dis′ə lo͞o′shən) /ˌdɪsə'luwʃən/ *n.* [*noncount*] **1.** the breaking of a bond or partnership: *the dissolution of a marriage.* **2.** the breaking up of an assembly or organization; dismissal: *the dissolution of the council.* **3.** a bringing or coming to an end; termination. See -SOLV-.

dis•solve (di zolv′) /dɪ'zɒlv/ *v.,* **-solved, -solv•ing.** **1.** to (cause to) become a mixture or solution of: [*no obj*]: *The sugar will dissolve in your coffee.* [~ + *obj*]: *Dissolve the sugar in the coffee by stirring it.* **2.** to (cause to) become undone; (cause to) come to an end: [~ + *obj*]: *They dissolved their marriage.* [*no obj*]: *He helplessly watched his marriage dissolve.* **3.** [~ + *obj*] to break up (an assembly); dismiss: *The king dissolved parliament.* **4.** [*no obj*] to lose intensity or strength: *Most of these problems won't simply dissolve.* **5. dissolve into,** [~ + *into* + *obj*] to break down emotionally; collapse: *dissolved into a fit of laughter.* See -SOLV-.

dis•so•nance (dis′ə nəns) /'dɪsənəns/ *n.* [*noncount*] **1.** harsh sound; discord: *the dissonance of the untuned violins.* **2.** lack of harmony or agreement: *no way to reconcile such dissonance of opinion.* —**dis′so•nant,** *adj.*: *dissonant colors.* See -SON-.

dis•suade (di swād′) /dɪ'sweyd/ *v.,* **-suad•ed, -suad•ing.** to advise (someone) against doing something; discourage: [~ + *obj*]: *Nothing could dissuade him.* [~ + *obj* + *from* + *verb-ing*]: *My teacher dissuaded me from going into business.* See -SUADE-.

dis•tance (dis′təns) /'dɪstəns/ *n., v.,* **-tanced, -tanc•ing.** —*n.* **1.** the amount of space between two things: [*count*]: *The distance between my school and the house is only one half mile.* [*noncount*]: *The train I take to work is within walking distance of our apartment.* **2.** [*noncount*] the state or fact of being apart in space; remoteness: *Distance from the city isn't a factor in our search for a new home.* **3.** [*noncount*] remoteness or difference in any respect: *the insurmountable social distance between classes.* **4.** [*count*] an area; space: *to walk a distance.* **5.** [*count; usually singular*] an amount of progress: *We've come quite a distance on this project.* **6.** [*noncount; the* + ~] a distant place: *I could just see a tree in the distance.* **7.** absence of warmth; coolness: [*count; usually singular*]: *You have to maintain a certain distance toward your students.* [*noncount*]: *There was some distance between them at our last meeting.* —*v.* [~ + *obj*] **8.** to leave behind at a distance; surpass: *He distanced his nearest competitor by almost one hundred yards.* **9.** [~ + *oneself*] to cause to appear distant or reserved: *He distanced himself from his coworkers.* —***Idiom.*** **10. go the distance,** [*no obj*] to complete something that requires sustained effort: *I don't know if we can go the distance on this project.* **11. keep (someone) at a distance,** to treat (someone) with coolness, lack of warmth, or reserve: *careful to keep her students at a distance.* **12. keep one's distance,** to remain apart and reserved: *I kept my distance and never once told her about my love for her.* See -STAN-.

dis•tant (dis′tənt) /'dɪstənt/ *adj.* **1.** far off in space; remote: *enjoyed traveling to distant lands.* **2.** [*usually: before a noun*] apart or far off in time: *in the distant past.* **3.** [*before a noun*] not closely related: *a distant relative.* **4.** (of a trip) long: *a distant journey of several months.* **5.** reserved or aloof: *In a cold and distant voice he told me to pack and leave.* **6.** not focused on the present: *He gave me a distant look and I wondered if he even recognized me.* See -STAN-.

dis•tant•ly (dis′tənt lē) /'dɪstəntliy/ *adv.* **1.** in the distance: *He could distantly make out the person following him.* **2.** not closely: *We're distantly related.* **3.** lacking warmth; coolly: *She greeted me distantly.*

dis•taste (dis tāst′) /dɪs'teyst/ *n.* dislike; a desire to avoid: [*count; usually singular*]: *a distaste for household chores.* [*noncount*]: *a look of distaste on his face.*

dis•taste•ful (dis tāst′fəl) /dɪs'teystfəl/ *adj.* causing distaste or dislike: *The violence in the film was distasteful.*

dis•tem•per (dis tem′pər) /dɪs'tɛmpər/ *n.* [*noncount*] an infectious disease esp. of dogs, with fever and difficulty in breathing.

dis•tend (di stend′) /dɪ'stɛnd/ *v.* to expand by stretching: [~ + *obj*]: *Air distends a balloon.* [*no obj*]: *The balloon distended to about five inches in length.* —**dis•ten•tion** (di sten′shən) /dɪ'stɛnʃən/ *n.* [*noncount*]: *suffering from distention of the stomach.* [*count*]: *a distention of several inches.* See -TEND-.

dis•till (di stil′) /dɪ'stɪl/ *v.* **1.** to heat (a liquid) hot enough to evaporate, then allowing it to cool: [~ + *obj*]: *They distilled the salt water and made it into drinking water.* [*no obj*]: *The liquid distills when heated.* **2.** [~ + *obj*] to get essential elements of an experience; extract: *She has distilled a number of wonderful stories from her experiences as a crime lab technician.* **3.** [*no obj*] to fall in drops; trickle. —**dis•till′er,** *n.* [*count*]

dis•til•late (dis′tl it, -āt′, di stil′it) /'dɪstl̩ɪt, -ˌeyt, dɪ'stɪlɪt/ *n.* [*count*] the product obtained from distilling: *petroleum distillates.*

dis•til•la•tion (dis′tl ā′shən) /ˌdɪstl̩'eyʃən/ *n.* [*noncount*] the process of distilling.

dis•till•er•y (di stil′ə rē) /dɪ'stɪləriy/ *n.* [*count*], *pl.* **-er•ies.** a place or establishment where the distilling of alcoholic liquors is done.

dis•tinct (di stingkt′) /dɪ'stɪŋkt/ *adj.* **1.** distinguished as not being the same; separate; dissimilar: *The two books are clearly distinct and made for different audiences.* [*be* + ~ + *from*]: *Her business life is distinct from her social life.* **2.** clear to the senses or the mind; plain; unmistakable: *a distinct shape.* **3.** [*before a noun*] unquestionably exceptional or notable; great; important: *a distinct honor.* —**dis•tinct′ly,** *adv.*: *Hanging out on a beach is distinctly more fun than working.* See -STIN-.

dis•tinc•tion (di stingk′shən) /dɪ'stɪŋkʃən/ *n.* **1.** [*noncount*] the act of distinguishing as different. **2.** [*count*] the recognizing of differences between two things: *old enough to make a distinction between right and wrong.* **3.** [*noncount*] a discrimination or act of choosing between things: *Death comes to all without distinction.* **4.**

[*count*] the condition of being different; difference: *the distinction between talk and action.* **5.** [*count*] a distinguishing quality or characteristic: *It has the distinction of being the oldest house in town.* **6.** [*noncount*] the act of distinguishing or treating with special favor: *She has become a painter of great distinction.* **7.** [*noncount*] marked superiority; excellence: *He passed all his exams with distinction.*

dis•tinc•tive (di stingk′tiv) /dɪ'stɪŋktɪv/ *adj.* serving to distinguish: *the zebra's distinctive stripes.* **—dis•tinc′tive•ly,** *adv.: his distinctively New England accent.* **—dis•tinc′tive•ness,** *n.* [*noncount*]

dis•tin•guish (di sting′gwish) /dɪ'stɪŋgwɪʃ/ *v.* **1.** [~ + *obj* + *from* + *obj*] to mark off as different; show a difference: *His height distinguishes him from the other boys.* **2.** to recognize as distinct or different: [~ + *between* + *obj*]: *I couldn't distinguish between some of the French vowels.* [~ + *obj* + *from* + *obj*]: *Can you distinguish right from wrong?* **3.** [~ + *obj*] to perceive or sense clearly by the senses; recognize: *Without my glasses I can't distinguish certain signs on the road.* **4.** [~ + *obj*] to set apart as different; characterize: *Her Italian accent distinguishes her.* **5.** [~ + *oneself*] to make prominent or eminent: *He distinguished himself in the arts.* **—dis•tin′guish•a•ble,** *adj.* See -STIN-.

dis•tin•guished (di sting′gwisht) /dɪ'stɪŋgwɪʃt/ *adj.* **1.** made well-known by excellence or success: *a distinguished scientist in neurology.* **2.** having an air of distinction, nobility, or dignity: *The men looked distinguished in their formal tuxedos.*

dis•tort (di stôrt′) /dɪ'stɔrt/ *v.* [~ + *obj*] **1.** to twist out of shape: *Pain had distorted his face.* **2.** to give a false meaning to; misrepresent: *That journalist distorted the candidate's remarks.* **3.** to reproduce or amplify (an electronic signal) inaccurately: *His voice over the loudspeaker was distorted.* See -TORT-.

dis•tor•tion (di stôr′shən) /dɪ'stɔrʃən/ *n.* **1.** an act of distorting or the state of being distorted: [*noncount*]: *The candidates accused the media of deliberate distortion.* [*count*]: *That story as written contains nothing but lies and distortions.* **2.** badly reproduced electronic signals: [*count*]: *a number of distortions introduced into the recording.* [*noncount*]: *too much distortion of the image.* See -TORT-.

dis•tract (di strakt′) /dɪ'strækt/ *v.* **1.** to draw away or divert; to keep (one's mind) from concentrating: [~ + *obj*]: *One of the group distracted me by asking for help.* [~ + *obj* + *from* + *obj*]: *The music distracted us from our work.* **2.** [~ + *obj*] to provide a pleasant diversion for; amuse; entertain: *I was distracted for a while and forgot my troubles.* See -TRAC-.

dis•trac•ting (di strak′ting) /dɪ'stræktɪŋ/ *adj.* **1.** serving to distract: *distracting noises and laughter.* **2.** amusing: *She thinks those computer games are pleasantly distracting.* See -TRAC-.

dis•trac•tion (di strak′shən) /dɪ'strækʃən/ *n.* **1.** [*count*] the act of distracting or the state of being distracted: *just a distraction to keep us from thinking about the real problem.* **2.** [*noncount*] mental distress or derangement: *You are driving me to distraction with that music.* **3.** a person or thing that prevents concentration: [*count*]: *The talking in the hallway was a distraction for the students.* [*noncount*]: *There was too much distraction at the office.* See -TRAC-.

dis•traught (di strôt′) /dɪ'strɔt/ *adj.* bewildered; deeply agitated: *The distraught mother waited for news of her child.*

dis•tress (di stres′) /dɪ'strɛs/ *n.* [*noncount*] **1.** sharp or strong anxiety, pain, or sorrow: *obvious signs of distress showing up during the crisis.* **2.** a state of extreme necessity, trouble, or misfortune: *a time of poverty and distress.* **3.** the state of a ship or airplane requiring immediate help, such as when on fire: *The aircraft radioed it was in distress.* **—***v.* **4.** to afflict with pain, anxiety, or sorrow:[~ + *obj*]: *The tragic news distressed us all.* [*it* + ~ + *obj* + *to* + *verb*]: *It distressed me to hear about the violence in the schools.* [~ + *obj* + *that clause*]: *It distressed me that there was so much violence in the schools.*

dis•tress•ing (di stres′ing) /dɪ'strɛsɪŋ/ *adj.* causing distress: *the distressing news of his death.*

dis•trib•ute (di strib′yo͞ot) /dɪ'strɪbyuwt/ *v.* [~ + *obj* (+ *among/to* + *obj*)], **-ut•ed, -ut•ing. 1.** to divide and give out in shares: *The relief agency will distribute the food among several countries; distributing political pamphlets on the streets.* **2.** to spread over an area; scatter: *to distribute seeds.* **3.** to sell or supply (merchandise) in an area: *He distributes cars for the rental agency in that region.*

dis•tri•bu•tion (di′strə byo͞o′shən) /ˌdɪstrə'byuwʃən/ *n.* **1.** [*count; usually singular*] an act or instance of distributing: *a more equitable distribution of wealth among rich and poor nations.* **2.** [*noncount*] selling or supplying of merchandise in an area: *in charge of distribution of goods for the region.* **3.** [*noncount*] arrangement; grouping: *the distribution of schools in different neighborhoods.*

dis•trib•u•tor (di strib′yə tər) /dɪ'strɪbyətər/ *n.* [*count*] **1.** a person or thing that distributes. **2.** a firm or company that markets a line of merchandise generally or within a given territory: *the beer distributor for the county.* **3.** a device in an engine that distributes the electricity to the spark plugs.

dis•trict (dis′trikt) /'dɪstrɪkt/ *n.* [*count*] a division of territory marked off for administrative, electoral, or other purposes: *the Wall Street district.* See -STRICT-.

dis′trict attor′ney, *n.* [*count*] an attorney who acts for the people or government within a specified district.

dis•trust (dis trust′) /dɪs'trʌst/ *v.* [~ + *obj*] **1.** to look at or consider (someone) with suspicion; have no trust in: *I have distrusted him ever since he cheated me.* **—***n.* [*noncount*] **2.** lack of trust; doubt; suspicion: *Their feelings of distrust about him have affected me, too.* **—dis•trust′ful,** *adj.*

dis•turb (di stûrb′) /dɪ'stɜrb/ *v.* [~ + *obj*] **1.** to interrupt the quiet, rest, or peace of; bother: *She'll be angry if you disturb her while she's in conference.* **2.** to interfere with; interrupt; hinder: *Only bad weather can disturb our plans for the picnic.* **3.** to interfere with the arrangement or order of: disarrange: *to disturb the papers on a desk.* **4.** to perplex; trouble; cause worry: *The sudden increase in thefts in the school disturbed the parents.* See -TURB-.

dis•turb•ance (di stûr′bəns) /dɪ'stɜrbəns/ *n.* **1.** [*noncount*] an act of disturbing or the state of being disturbed: *You can work here without disturbance.* **2.** [*count*] a riot, outbreak of public disorder, or fighting: *There were disturbances in that region before full-scale fighting broke out.* See -TURB-.

dis•turbed (di stûrbd′) /dɪ'stɜrbd/ *adj.* mentally or emotionally unsettled or upset: *The emotionally disturbed child needs special care.*

dis•turb•ing (di stûr′bing) /dɪ'stɜrbɪŋ/ *adj.* causing disturbance: *a disturbing discovery.* **—dis•turb′ing•ly,** *adv.: disturbingly high unemployment figures.*

dis•u•nite (dis′yo͞o nit′) /ˌdɪsyuw'nayt/ *v.* [~ + *obj*], **-nit•ed, -nit•ing.** to separate; disjoin; alienate. **—dis•u•ni•ty** (dis yo͞o′ni tē) /dɪs'yuwnɪtiy/ *n.* [*noncount*]

dis•use (*n.* dis yo͞os′; *v.* -yo͞oz′) / *n.* dɪs'yuws; *v.* -'yuwz/ *n.* [*noncount*] a state of ceasing to be used or practiced: *Happily such weapons have fallen into disuse.* **—dis•used′,** *adj.: old disused factories that were rotting away.*

ditch (dich) /dɪtʃ/ *n.* [*count*] **1.** a long, narrow channel dug in the ground, such as for drainage or irrigation; trench. **—***v.* **2.** to crash-land on water and abandon (an aircraft): [~ + *obj*]: *The pilot ditched the plane and climbed out on his raft.* [*no obj*]: *"We'll have to ditch!" yelled the co-pilot.* **3.** [~ + *obj*] *Slang.* **a.** to get rid of; abandon: *The robbers ditched the getaway car.* **b.** to leave or stop seeing (someone): *He ditched her before he could get too involved.*

dith•er (dith′ər) /'dɪðər/ *n.* [*count; singular; a* + ~] **1.** a state of excitement or agitated fear: *in a dither about what to do.* **—***v.* [*no obj*] **2.** to act without will; be hesitant: *He was dithering and wouldn't make up his mind unless forced to.*

dit•to (dit′ō) /'dɪtow/ *n., pl.* **-tos,** *adv., v.* **—***n.* **1.** [*noncount*] what has just been said or mentioned earlier; the above; the same (used in lists, etc.): *We bought two books at $45.00 each, ditto at $65.* **2.** [*count*] *Informal.* a duplicate; copy: *Make a ditto of this and mail it.* **—***adv.* **3.** (used after another phrase or sentence) just as already stated; likewise: the same: *"I'll have a beer." — "Ditto." (= I'll have one, too.)* **—***v.* [~ + *obj*] **4.** to make a copy of on a duplicating machine: *He dittoed several copies of the document.*

dit′to mark′, *n.* [*count*] Often, **ditto marks.** two small marks (") indicating the repetition of something, usually placed beneath the thing repeated.

dit•ty (dit′ē) /'dɪtiy/ *n.* [*count*], *pl.* **-ties.** a simple song.

ditz (dits) /dɪts/ *n.* [*count*] *Slang.* a foolish, forgetful, or stupid person. **—ditz′y,** *adj.,* **-zi•er, -zi•est.**

di•ur•nal (dī ûr′nl) /day'ɜrnl/ *adj.* **1.** of or belonging to the daytime. **2.** occurring each day; daily. **—di•ur′nal•ly,** *adv.*

div., an abbreviation of: **1.** divine. **2.** divinity. **3.** division. **4.** divorced.

di•va (dē′və, -vä) /ˈdiyvə, -vɑ/ *n., pl.* **-vas, -ve** (-ve) /-vɛ/. PRIMA DONNA (def. 1).

di•van (di van′) /dɪˈvæn/ *n.* [*count*] a couch, usually without arms or back, often usable as a bed.

dive (dīv) /dayv/ *v.,* **dived** or **dove** (dōv) /dowv/ **dived, div•ing,** *n.* **—***v.* **1.** [*no obj*] to plunge into water, esp. headfirst: *He dove straight into the pool.* **2.** to go underwater; submerge: [*no obj*]: *The submarine dove quickly as the destroyer searched for it.* [~ + *obj*]: *The captain dived his submarine deep to escape from the destroyers.* **3.** [*no obj*] to plunge, fall, or descend through the air: *The acrobats dived into nets.* **4.** (of an airplane) to (cause to) descend rapidly: [*no obj*]: *The fighter plane dove straight at the target.* [~ + *obj*]: *dived his plane straight at the enemy tanks.* **5.** [*no obj*] to jump or move quickly; dart: *The spy dived quickly into a doorway.* **6.** [*no obj*] to enter deeply or plunge into a subject, activity, etc.: *She dove straight into the new book and read all night.* **—***n.* [*count*] **7.** an act or instance of diving. **8.** a jump or plunge into water, esp. in a special way or posture. **9.** the steep, rapid descent of an airplane. **10.** a submerging, such as of a submarine. **11.** a dash, plunge, or lunge, as if throwing oneself at or into something: *The police officer made a quick dive for the weapon.* **12.** *Informal.* a dirty, cheap, disreputable bar or nightclub.

div•er (dī′vər) /ˈdayvər/ *n.* [*count*] **1.** a person who dives, esp. one wearing special breathing equipment: *Divers searched the wreckage of the submerged plane for survivors.* **2.** a person who plunges into the water in a special posture: *an Olympic-class diver.*

di•verge (di vûrj′, dī-) /dɪˈvɜrdʒ, day-/ *v.* [*no obj*], **-verged, -verg•ing. 1.** to move, lie, or extend in different directions from a common point: *The path diverges just after the cabin.* **2.** to differ in opinion, character, or form: *Our views on that matter diverge.* [~ + *from* + *obj*]: *My position diverges from that of the department.* See -VERG-.

di•ver•gence (di vûr′jəns, dī-) /dɪˈvɜrdʒəns, day-/ *n.* difference of opinion, character, or form: [*noncount*]: *I think too much divergence keeps us from ever agreeing.* [*count*]: *a divergence of opinion.* See -VERG-.

di•ver•gent (di vûr′jənt, dī-) /dɪˈvɜrdʒənt, day-/ *adj.* **1.** differing; disagreeing; different; conflicting: *I tried to combine their divergent views.* **2.** splitting off; dividing; separating: *The two roads run parallel for a while, then become divergent.* See -VERG-.

di•vers (dī′vərz) /ˈdayvərz/ *adj.* [*before a noun*] several; various: *divers groups are competing.*

di•verse (di vûrs′, dī-) /dɪˈvɜrs, day-/ *adj.* **1.** of a different kind, form, or character: *diverse ideas on how to raise children.* **2.** of various kinds or forms: *She has diverse interests: dogs, music, reading, gymnastics.* **—di•verse′ly,** *adv.* See -VERT-.

di•ver•si•fy (di vûr′sə fī′, dī-) /dɪˈvɜrsəˌfay, day-/ *v.,* **-fied, -fy•ing. 1.** to give or increase variety or diversity to: [~ + *obj*]: *to diversify the campus by hiring people with unusual interests.* [*no obj*]: *The college had already diversified greatly by hiring people with wider interests.* **2.** to distribute (investments) among different types of securities or industries: [~ + *obj*]: *to diversify one's holdings.* [*no obj*]: *They urged us to diversify and not keep all our money in one investment type.* **3.** to expand (a business or product line) by manufacturing a larger variety of different products: [~ + *obj*]: *He diversified the company.* [*no obj*]: *The overseas companies were diversifying more rapidly.* **—di•ver•si•fi•ca•tion** (di vûr′sə fi-kā′shən, dī-) /dɪˌvɜrsəfɪˈkeyʃən, day-/ *n.* [*noncount*] See -VERT-.

di•ver•sion (di vûr′zhən, dī-) /dɪˈvɜrʒən, day-/ *n.* **1.** the act of diverting: [*count*]: *a diversion of industry into the war effort.* [*noncount*]: *urging diversion of resources toward the poor and middle classes.* **2.** [*count*] **a.** a distraction away from business, care, or what one is paying attention to: *I took advantage of the diversion to scribble a note.* **b.** a recreation or pastime: *His only diversion these days is golf.* **3.** [*count*] a false attack intended to draw off attention from the point of main attack. **4.** [*count*] a channel made to change the flow of water from one course to another. **5.** [*count*] *Brit.* a detour on a highway or road. See -VERT-.

di•ver•sion•ar•y (di vûr′zhə ner′ē, dī-) /dɪˈvɜrʒəˌnɛriy, day-/ *adj.* [*before a noun*] intending to draw off attention from the main attack or concern: *a diversionary skirmish; diversionary tactics.*

di•ver•si•ty (di vûr′si tē, dī-) /dɪˈvɜrsɪtiy, day-/ *n., pl.* **-ties. 1.** [*noncount*] the state or fact of being diverse: *Diversity of opinion makes for a more interesting discussion.* **2.** [*count; usually singular*] variety: *The city has a diversity of people from all over the world.* **3.** [*count*] a point of difference: *cultural diversities.* See -VERT-.

di•vert (di vûrt′, dī-) /dɪˈvɜrt, day-/ *v.* [~ + *obj*] **1.** to turn aside or from a path or course; draw off to a different course or use: *We diverted our funds to paying for college.* **2.** to distract (the attention): *My attention was diverted for a moment by the accident.* **3.** to distract from serious occupation; entertain or amuse: *The children were diverted by the clown.* See -VERT-.

di•vest (di vest′, dī-) /dɪˈvɛst, day-/ *v.* [~ + *obj* + *of* + *obj*] **1.** to remove or strip of clothing: *He divested himself of his coat and sat down.* **2.** to take away, deprive, or strip (someone or something), esp. of property or rights: *The family was divested of its home.* **3.** to rid of or free from: *We managed to divest ourselves of responsibility.* **4.** to sell off; to get rid of through sale: *The traders quickly divested themselves of that stock.* **—di•vest′i•ture,** *n.* [*noncount; count*]

di•vide (di vīd′) /dɪˈvayd/ *v.,* **-vid•ed, -vid•ing,** *n.* **—***v.* **1.** to (cause to) become separated into parts: [~ + *obj*]: *I divided the class and took one section to the library and left the other to write an essay.* [~ + *obj* + *into* + *obj*]: *I divided the class into groups and took one to the library.* [*no obj*]: *The group divided and headed off in different directions.* [~ + *into* + *obj*]: *The audience divided into groups.* **2.** [~ + *(up +) obj* + *among/between* + *obj*] to deal out in parts; distribute in shares: *We divided (up) the pie among the five of us.* **3.** [~ + *obj*] to separate and classify, arrange, or put in order: *She divided the pencils by color.* **4.** [~ + *obj*] to separate in opinion or feeling; cause to disagree: *The issue divided the senators.* **5.** to separate (a number) into equal parts by division: **a.** [~ + *number* + *into* + *number*] to discover how many times one number is contained evenly in the second: *Divide 5 into 50; you'll get 10.* **b.** [~ + *number* + *by* + *number*] to discover how many times the first number contains the second number evenly: *Divide 50 by 5; you'll get 10.* **6.** [~ + *obj*] to mark a uniform scale on (a ruler, etc.): *The ruler is divided into centimeters.* **—***n.* [*count*] **7.** a division: *a divide in the road.* **8.** the line or zone of higher ground between two adjacent streams or drainage areas: *At the continental divide, rivers flow east and west.* **—di•vid′a•ble,** *adj.*

div•i•dend (div′i dend′) /ˈdɪvɪˌdɛnd/ *n.* [*count*] **1.** a number to be divided by a divisor: *If you divide 50 by 5, 50 is the dividend and 5 is the divisor; the quotient, or answer, is 10.* **2.** money paid to someone, such as a sum paid to shareholders: *a dividend of $50.* **3.** anything received in addition to what is expected; bonus: *The research project will pay great dividends.*

di•vid•er (di vī′dər) /dɪˈvaydər/ *n.* [*count*] **1.** a person or thing that divides: *a room divider.* **2. dividers,** [*plural*] a pair of compasses, such as for dividing lines or measuring.

div•i•na•tion (div′ə nā′shən) /ˌdɪvəˈneyʃən/ *n.* [*noncount*] the practice of trying to foretell future events or discover hidden knowledge by supernatural means: *the high priest's powers of divination.*

di•vine (di vīn′) /dɪˈvayn/ *adj.,* **-vin•er, -vin•est,** *n., v.,* **-vined, -vin•ing. —***adj.* **1.** of, like, or from a god; addressed or devoted to God or a god: *The altar was a place of divine worship.* **2.** *Informal.* extremely good; unusually lovely: *divine chocolate cake.* **—***n.* **3.** [*count*] a theologian; scholar in religion. **4.** [*count*] a priest or cleric. **5. the Divine, a.** [*proper noun*] God. **b.** [*noncount*] the spiritual aspect in humans regarded as godly or godlike. **—***v.* **6.** to discover or declare (something) by divination, magic, or as if by magic; prophesy: [~ + *obj*]: *The oracles were expected to divine the future.* [~ + *(that) clause*]: *How could we have divined that she would wish to retire so soon?* **7.** [~ + *obj*] to seek (water, metal, etc.) by means of a divining rod. **—di•vine′ly,** *adv.* **—di•vin′er,** *n.* [*count*]

divin′ing rod′, *n.* [*count*] a rod, esp. a forked stick of hazel, supposedly useful in locating underground water or metal deposits.

di•vin•i•ty (di vin′i tē) /dɪˈvɪnɪtiy/ *n., pl.* **-ties. 1.** [*noncount*] the quality of being divine: *questions about the divinity of Christ.* **2.** [*count*] a divine being; God. **3.** [*noncount*] the study or science of divine things; theology: *She studied divinity.*

di•vis•i•ble (di viz′ə bəl) /dɪˈvɪzəbəl/ *adj.* [*be* + ~] capable of being divided: *Physicists were searching for a particle of matter that is not divisible into smaller ones.*

—**di•vis•i•bil•i•ty** (di viz′ə bil′i tē) /dɪˌvɪzəˈbɪlɪtiy/ *n.* [*noncount*]

di•vi•sion (di vizh′ən) /dɪˈvɪʒən/ *n.* **1.** [*noncount*] the act or process of dividing; state of being divided: *In tropical Africa the division of the day is into twelve hours of light and twelve hours of darkness.* **2.** [*noncount*] the arithmetic operation of discovering how many times one number or quantity is contained in another: *fifteen problems in division for homework.* **3.** [*count*] something that divides or separates; partition: *a new division in the living room to create a small den.* **4.** [*count*] something that marks a division; dividing line or mark: *We looked over the mountain range that is the division between our two countries.* **5.** [*count*] one of the parts into which a thing is divided; section: *the upper division of the university.* **6.** separation by difference of opinion or feeling; disagreement; dissension: [*count*]: *a sharp division among the school board on the question of keeping Latin.* [*noncount*]: *He tried to fight against the discord and division that threatened the department.* **7.** [*count*] a military unit: *In the army a division is larger than a brigade and smaller than a corps.* **8.** [*count*] a category or grouping of teams or competitors according to standing, skill, weight, age, or the like. —**di•vi′sion•al,** *adj.* [*before a noun*]

di•vi•sive (di vī′siv) /dɪˈvaysɪv/ *adj.* creating feelings of disagreement or discord: *His tactics were divisive, trying to make everyone mad at one another.* —**di•vi′sive•ly,** *adv.* —**di•vi′sive•ness,** *n.* [*noncount*]

di•vi•sor (di vī′zər) /dɪˈvayzər/ *n.* [*count*] a number by which another number, the dividend, is divided: *If you divide 50 by 5, the number 5 is the divisor.*

di•vorce (di vôrs′, -vōrs′) /dɪˈvɔrs, -ˈvowrs/ *n., v.,* **-vorced, -vorc•ing.** —*n.* **1.** [*count*] a formal declaration dissolving a marriage and releasing both spouses by law from all marriage obligations: *She told him she wanted a divorce.* **2.** [*noncount*] formal separation of husband and wife: *Is divorce allowed in that religion?* —*v.* **3.** [~ + *obj*] to separate by divorce: *The judge divorced the couple.* **4.** [~ + *obj*] to break the marriage contract between oneself and (one's spouse) by divorce: *She divorced him after twenty years of marriage.* **5.** [*no obj*] to get a divorce: *She divorced and remarried later.* **6.** to separate; cut off: [*no obj*]: *Life and art cannot be divorced.* [~ + *obj* + *from* + *obj*]: *Can you divorce life from art?* —**di•vorced′,** *adj.*: *divorced couples.*

di•vor•cée or **di•vor•cee** (di vôr sā′, -sē′, -vōr-, -vôr′sā, -vōr′-) /dɪvɔrˈsey, -ˈsiy, -vowr-, -ˈvɔrsey, -ˈvowr-/ *n.* [*count*], *pl.* **-cées** or **-cees.** a divorced woman.

div•ot (div′ət) /ˈdɪvət/ *n.* [*count*] a piece of dirt or grass torn out or removed by a golf club while making a stroke.

di•vulge (di vulj′, dī-) /dɪˈvʌldʒ, day-/ *v.,* **-vulged, -vulg•ing.** to disclose or reveal (something private): [~ + *obj*]: *He promised not to divulge the whereabouts of the hiding place.* [~ + *(that) clause*]: *wouldn't divulge that he knew the facts.*

div•vy (div′ē) /ˈdɪviy/ *v.* [~ + *(up* +*) obj*], **-vied, -vy•ing.** *Informal.* to divide; distribute: *The thieves decided to divvy (up) the money they'd stolen.*

Dix•ie (dik′sē) /ˈdɪksiy/ *n.* [*proper noun*] the southern states of the United States, esp. those that were part of the Confederacy.

diz•zy (diz′ē) /ˈdɪziy/ *adj.,* **-zi•er, -zi•est,** *v.,* **-zied, -zy•ing.** —*adj.* **1.** having a sensation of things going round and round; giddy: *I always feel dizzy after riding the merry-go-round.* **2.** bewildered; confused: *I came out of the lecture a little dizzy from all those facts and figures.* **3.** [*before a noun*] causing giddiness or confusion; very great: *a dizzy height.* **4.** *Informal.* foolish; silly: *He can be really dizzy around pretty girls.* —*v.* [~ + *obj*] **5.** to make dizzy: *We drove at speeds that dizzied me.* —**diz•zi•ly** (diz′ə lē) /ˈdɪzəliy/ *adv.*: *I staggered dizzily.* —**diz′zi•ness,** *n.* [*noncount*] —**diz′zy•ing,** *adj.*: *drove at dizzying speed.*

DJ, an abbreviation of: disc jockey.

djel•la•bah or **djel•la•ba** (jə lä′bə) /dʒəˈlɑbə/ *n.* [*count*], *pl.* **-bahs** or **-bas.** a loose-fitting hooded gown or robe worn by men in North Africa.

DMZ, an abbreviation of: demilitarized zone.

DNA, *n.* [*noncount*] deoxyribonucleic acid, a long, double-stranded molecule that is arranged as a double helix and is the main constituent of the chromosome, carrying genes along its strands.

do[1] (do͞o; *unstressed* do͝o, də) /duw; *unstressed* dʊ, də/ *v.* and *auxiliary v., pres. sing. 1st* and *2nd pers.* **do,** *3rd* **does** (duz) /dʌz/ *pres. pl.* **do;** *past sing.* and *pl.* **did** (did) /dɪd/; *past part.* **done** (dun) /dʌn/; *pres. part.* **do•ing;** *n., pl.* **dos, do's.** —*v.* **1.** [~ + *obj*] to perform (an act, duty, role, etc.): *He does a great comedy act.* **2.** to execute (a piece of work): [~ + *obj*]: *to do a hauling job.* [~ + *obj* + *obj*]: *You did me a big favor just then.* **3.** [~ + *obj*] to accomplish; finish: *He has already done it.* **4.** [~ + *obj*] to put forth; exert: *Do your best.* **5.** to be the cause of (good, credit, etc.); bring about; effect: [~ + *obj*]: *Drugs can do harm to you.* [~ + *obj* + *obj*]: *Drugs can do you a lot of harm.* **6.** [~ + *obj*] to deal with, fix, clean, arrange, etc., (anything) as the case may require: *I did the windows and the laundry.* **7.** [*not: be* + ~*-ing*] to serve; be enough (for); suffice for:[~ + *obj*]: *This will do us for the present.* [*no obj*]: *I'm sure this money will do just fine. Will this do?* **8.** [*not: be* + ~*-ing;* ~ + *obj*] to allow or approve, as by custom or practice: *We don't do that sort of thing in this college.* **9.** [~ + *obj*] to travel (a distance of); cover by traveling: *We did 30 miles today.* **10.** [~ + *obj*] to travel at the rate of (a certain speed): *But officer, I was only doing 65 miles an hour.* **11.** [~ + *obj*] to make or prepare: *I'll do the salad.* **12.** [~ + *obj*] to serve (a term) in prison: *He did five years in prison.* **13.** [~ + *obj*] to study or work at or in the field of: *I have to do my math tonight.* **14.** [~ + *obj*] to travel through as a sightseer: *They did Greece in 3 weeks.* **15.** [~ + *obj*] to use (drugs), esp. habitually: *He had been doing a lot of cocaine.* **16.** [*no obj*] to act or conduct oneself; behave: *Do as I say, not as I do.* **17.** [*no obj*] to get along; fare; manage: *How are you doing at work?* **18.** [*no obj*] to be in a specified state of health: *Mother and child are doing fine.* —*auxiliary v.* [~ + *root form of a verb*] **19. a.** (used in questions before the subject): *Do you like music? When did he leave?* **b.** (used in negative sentences before the word *not,* unless the main verb is *be*): *I do not like you. I don't care. I didn't see you last night.* **c.** (used in certain inverted constructions before the subject): *Seldom does one see such greed.* **d.** (used to emphasize the main verb): *Do come up and see me some time. But I did tell you about the test!* **e.** (used to stand for, or repeat, another verb already mentioned): *I think as you do (= I think as you think). I enjoy jogging and John does, too (= and John enjoys jogging, too). John enjoys jogging, doesn't he?* **20. do away with,** [~ + *away* + *with* + *obj*] **a.** to put an end to; abolish: *We did away with that old custom years ago.* **b.** to kill: *He did away with most of his rivals.* **21. do for,** [~ + *for* + *obj*] **a.** [*usually: be* + *done* + *for*] to cause the defeat, ruin, or death of: *I'll really be done for if I don't finish this work.* **b.** *Chiefly Brit.* to keep house for; manage or provide for. **22. do in,** [~ + *obj* + *in*] **a.** to kill; murder: *They did him in with a knife.* **b.** to tire out or exhaust: *All that hard work really did me in.* **23. do out of,** [~ + *obj* + *out* + *of* + *obj*] *Informal.* to swindle; cheat: *They did him out of his life savings.* **24. do over, a.** to redecorate: [~ + *obj* + *over*]: *They did the room over.* [~ + *over* + *obj*]: *You've done over the entire living room; it looks great.* **b.** to do again: [~ + *obj* + *over*]: *Do the work over; it's a mess.* [~ + *over* + *obj*]: *You'll have to do over the work; it's a mess.* **25. do up, a.** [~ + *up* + *obj*] to wrap and tie up: *They did up the package and mailed it for me.* **b.** to pin up or arrange (the hair): [~ + *up* + *obj*]: *She did up her hair in a bun.* [~ + *obj* + *up*]: *She did her hair up in a bun.* **c.** [~ + *up* + *obj*] to renovate or clean: *They did up the old apartment and rented it out.* **d.** [~ + *up* + *obj*] to fasten: *Do up your coat.* **e.** [~ + *up* + *obj*] to dress: *The children were all done up in costumes.* **26. do with,** [*can/could* + ~ + *with* + *obj*] to benefit from; use: *I could surely do with a cup of coffee right about now.* **27. do without,** to forgo; dispense with: [~ + *without* + *obj*]: *We'll just have to do without a car until they fix it.* [*no obj*]: *We'll just have to do without for a while.* —*n.* [*count*] **28.** *Informal.* a burst of frenzied activity; action; commotion. **29.** *Informal.* a hairdo. **30.** a festive social gathering; party. —***Idiom.*** **31. dos and don'ts,** [*plural*] customs, rules, or regulations. —**do′a•ble,** *adj.*: *He assured me my project was doable.*

do[2] (dō) /dow/ *n.* [*count*], *pl.* **dos.** the musical syllable used for the first note of a scale.

doc (dok) /dɒk/ *n.* [*count*] *Informal.* a doctor.

-doc-, *root.* -doc- comes from Latin, where it has the meaning "to teach." This meaning is found in such words as: DOCILE, DOCTOR, DOCTRINE, DOCUMENT.

doc•ile (dos′əl) /ˈdɒsəl/ *adj.* easily managed or handled; tame. —**do•cil′i•ty** (-sil′i tē) /-ˈsɪlɪtiy/ *n.* [*noncount*] See -DOC-.

dock[1] (dok) /dɒk/ *n.* [*count*] **1.** a landing pier. **2.** the space or waterway between two wharves, such as for receiving a ship while in port. **3.** such a waterway with the surrounding piers, wharves, etc. **4.** a platform for loading and unloading trucks, etc.: *a loading dock.* **—***v.* **5.** to (cause to) come or go into a dock: [*no obj*]: *The ship docked and the passengers filed off.* [~ + *obj*]: *The pilot docked the ship and cut all the engines.* **6.** (of two space vehicles) to join together while in orbit: [*no obj*]: *The two vehicles docked in space and exchanged astronauts.* [~ + *obj*]: *The astronauts docked their vehicles and began to exchange cargo.*

dock[2] (dok) /dɒk/ *n.* [*count*] **1.** the fleshy part of an animal's tail. **2.** the part of a tail left after cutting or clipping. **—***v.* [~ + *obj*] **3.** to cut off the end of; cut short: *to dock a tail.* **4.** to deduct a part from (wages): *Their employer docked their pay.* **5.** to take away from (someone) something regularly enjoyed: *The campers were docked for disobeying their counselor.*

dock[3] (dok) /dɒk/ *n.* [*count*] the place in a courtroom where a prisoner is placed during trial.

dock·et (dok′it) /ˈdɒkɪt/ *n.* [*count*] **1.** a list of cases in court for trial. **2.** *Brit.* a writing on a letter or document stating its contents.

doc·tor (dok′tər) /ˈdɒktər/ *n.* [*count*] **1.** a person licensed to practice medicine. See illustration at HOSPITAL. **2.** a person who has been awarded a doctor's degree, the highest degree that can be offered by a university. **—***v.* **3.** to give medical treatment (to); act as a physician (to): [~ + *obj*]: *She doctored him back to health.* [*no obj*]: *He'd been doctoring since before we were born.* **4.** [~ + *obj*] to change falsely; tamper with; falsify: *to doctor the birthdate on a passport.* **5.** [~ + *obj*] to change or tamper with the ingredients of (a food or drink): *to doctor his drink with sedatives.* **—doc′tor·al,** *adj.* [*before a noun*]: *She was the first doctoral candidate in linguistics from that school.* See -DOC-.

doc·tor·ate (dok′tər it) /ˈdɒktərɪt/ *n.* DOCTOR'S DEGREE (def. 1).

doc′tor's degree′, *n.* [*count*] **1.** any of several academic degrees of the highest rank awarded by universities. **2.** a degree awarded to a graduate of a school of medicine, dentistry, or veterinary science.

doc·tri·naire (dok′trə nâr′) /ˌdɒktrəˈnɛər/ *adj.* inflexible and rigid about one's ideas: *a doctrinaire preacher.*

doc·trine (dok′trin) /ˈdɒktrɪn/ *n.* a particular principle, position, or policy taught, such as of a religion or government: [*count*]: *The church teaches the doctrine of free will.* [*noncount*]: *knowledgeable about church doctrine.* **—doc′tri·nal,** *adj.* [*before a noun*]: *shifts in doctrinal policies.* See -DOC-.

doc·u·dra·ma (dok′yə drä′mə, -dram′ə) /ˈdɒkyəˌdrɑmə, -ˌdræmə/ *n.* [*count*] a television film depicting current or historical events: *a docudrama tracing the story of a serial killer.*

doc·u·ment (*n.* dok′yə mənt; *v.* -ment′) / *n.* ˈdɒkyəmənt; *v.* -ˌmɛnt/ *n.* [*count*] **1.** a written paper providing proof or evidence, such as a passport, etc.; a legal or official paper: *classified documents about the new missile system.* **—***v.* [~ + *obj*] **2.** to support by documentary evidence, such as by giving references: *The lawyers worked to document their case.* **3.** to report on, write about, or make a film about (some historical event): *She documented the destruction she observed during the Gulf War.* **—doc·u·men·ta·tion** (dok′yə mən tā′shən) /ˌdɒkyəmənˈteyʃən/ *n.* [*noncount*]: *Do you have documentation that proves you paid these bills?* See -DOC-.

doc·u·men·ta·ry (dok′yə men′tə rē, -trē) /ˌdɒkyəˈmɛntəriy, -triy/ *adj., n., pl.* **-ries.** **—***adj.* [*before a noun*] **1.** relating to, made up of, or taken from documents: *documentary evidence.* **2.** showing or describing an actual event accurately and without fictional elements: *a documentary film.* **—***n.* [*count*] **3.** a documentary film, television program, etc.: *We saw a documentary on the war.*

dod·der (dod′ər) /ˈdɒdər/ *v.* [*no obj*] to shake; tremble; walk in an unsteady or shaky way. **—dod′der·ing,** *adj.*: *a doddering old man.*

dodge (doj) /dɒdʒ/ *v.,* **dodged, dodg·ing,** *n.* **—***v.* **1.** to move aside suddenly; to get out of the way of suddenly: [*no obj*]: *She threw a chair at me but I dodged out of the way.* [~ + *obj*]: *He managed to dodge most of the rocks thrown at him.* **2.** [~ + *obj*] to avoid, evade, or elude, esp. by dishonest or unlawful means: *They accused him of dodging his taxes.* **—***n.* [*count*] **3.** a quick, evasive movement to avoid a blow or the like: *He managed a quick dodge behind the rocks.* **4.** a shrewdly clever scheme to escape from something or to deceive: *She found a new dodge to keep from paying taxes.* **—dodg′er,** *n.* [*count*]

do·do (dō′dō) /ˈdowdow/ *n.* [*count*], *pl.* **-dos, -does.** **1.** a large, extinct, flightless bird of the pigeon family. **2.** *Slang.* a dull-witted, slow-reacting person.

doe (dō) /dow/ *n.* [*count*], *pl.* **does,** (*esp. when thought of as a group*) **doe.** the female of the deer, antelope, goat, rabbit, and certain other animals.

do·er (do͞o′ər) /ˈduwər/ *n.* [*count*] a person or thing that does something, esp. one who gets things done with efficiency: *One of them is a talker, but the other is a doer.*

does (duz) /dʌz/ *v.* 3rd pers. sing. pres. indic. of DO[1]: *She does not want to go.* See DO.

does·n't (duz′ənt) /ˈdʌzənt/ *v.* contraction of *does not*: *She doesn't really want to go with you.* See DO.

doff (dof, dôf) /dɒf, dɔf/ *v.* [~ + *obj*] to remove or take off, such as a hat or clothing: *He doffed his hat as they went by.*

dog (dôg, dog) /dɔg, dɒg/ *n., v.,* **dogged, dog·ging.** **—***n.* [*count*] **1.** a common four-legged animal kept as a pet and bred in many varieties. **2.** a wild four-legged animal related to this, such as the wolf. **3.** a despicable man or youth: *What a dirty dog he is, leaving you like that!* **4.** a fellow: *He's a lucky dog.* **5. dogs,** [*plural*] *Slang.* feet: *My dogs are killing me.* **6.** *Slang.* something worthless or of extremely poor quality: *That movie was a dog.* **7.** *Slang.* a very unattractive person. **—***v.* [~ + *obj*] **8.** to follow closely like a dog; pursue: *The agency was dogged by complaints.* **—*Idiom.*** **9. go to the dogs,** to go to a worse state or condition; deteriorate; degenerate. **10. let sleeping dogs lie,** to leave an existing situation alone rather than risk doing something to make it worse.

dog′-ear′ or **dog′ear′,** *n.* [*count*] **1.** (in a book) a corner of a page folded over to mark a place. **—***v.* [~ + *obj*] **2.** to fold down the corner of (a page in a book). **—dog′eared′,** *adj.*

dog·fight (dôg′fīt′, dog′-) /ˈdɔgˌfayt, ˈdɒg-/ *n.* [*count*] **1.** a violent fight between dogs. **2.** combat between enemy aircraft.

dog·fish (dôg′fish′, dog′-) /ˈdɔgˌfɪʃ, ˈdɒg-/ *n., pl.* (*esp. when thought of as a group*) **-fish,** (*esp. for kinds or species*) **-fish·es.** any of several small sharks.

dog·ged (dô′gid, dog′id) /ˈdɔgɪd, ˈdɒgɪd/ *adj.* [*before a noun*] persistent in effort; refusing to give up; tenacious: *his dogged determination.* **—dog′ged·ly,** *adv.*: *He doggedly insisted he was innocent.*

dog·ger·el (dô′gər əl, dog′ər-) /ˈdɔgərəl, ˈdɒgər-/ *n.* [*noncount*] poetry or verse that is silly or poorly written.

dog·gone (dôg′gôn′, -gon′, dog′-) /ˈdɔgˈgɔn, -ˈgɒn, ˈdɒg-/ *v.,* **-goned, -gon·ing,** *adj., superlative* **-gon·est,** *adv. Informal.* **—***v.* [~ + *obj; used without a subject*] **1.** to damn; confound: *Doggone it! Late again.* **—***adj.* [*before a noun*] **2.** Also, **doggoned.** damned; confounded: *That doggone cat has knocked over the lamp again.* **—***adv.* **3.** Also, **doggoned.** damned: *a doggone poor sport.*

dog·gy or **dog·gie** (dô′gē, dog′ē) /ˈdɔgiy, ˈdɒgiy/ *n.* [*count*], *pl.* **-gies.** **1.** a small dog or a puppy. **2.** a name for any dog.

dog′gy bag′, *n.* [*count*] a small bag provided by a restaurant for a customer to take home uneaten food from a meal.

dog·house (dog′hous′, dog′-) /ˈdɒgˌhaws, ˈdɒg-/ *n.* [*count*] **1.** a small shelter for a dog. **—*Idiom.*** **2. in the doghouse,** in disfavor or disgrace.

do·gie or **do·gey** or **do·gy** (dō′gē) /ˈdowgiy/ *n.* [*count*], *pl.* **-gies** or **-geys.** *Western U.S.* a calf without a mother.

dog·leg (dôg′leg′, dog′-) /ˈdɔgˌlɛg, ˈdɒg-/ *n., adj., v.,* **-legged, -leg·ging.** **—***n.* [*count*] **1.** a route or course that turns at a sharp angle. **—***adj.* [*before a noun*] **2.** turned or curved at a sharp angle: *a dogleg skiing course.* **—***v.* [*no obj*] **3.** to proceed around a sharp angle or along a zigzag course.

dog·ma (dôg′mə, dog′-) /ˈdɔgmə, ˈdɒg-/ *n., pl.* **-mas, -ma·ta** (-mə tə) /-mətə/. **1.** [*noncount*] a system of principles or tenets; doctrine: *political dogma.* **2.** [*count*] a specific principle of a doctrine put forth, such as by a church: *various dogmas about the divinity of Christ.*

dog·mat·ic (dôg mat′ik, dog-) /dɔgˈmætɪk, dɒg-/ *adj.* **1.** of the nature of a dogma; doctrinal. **2.** putting forward opinions in an aggressive and dictatorial manner: *He was offensive and dogmatic in our meeting.* **—dog·mat′i·cal·ly,** *adv.*

dog·ma·tism (dôg′mə tiz′əm, dog′-) /ˈdɔgməˌtɪzəm, ˈdɒg-/ *n.* [*noncount*] dogmatic putting forward of opinions, without listening to the opinions of others. **—dog′ma·tist,** *n.* [*count*]

do-good·er (do͞o′go͝od′ər) /ˈduwˈgʊdər/ *n.* [*count*] a person who has good intentions but is too unknowing and whose help has no effect.

dog′-tired′, *adj.* [*usually: be* + ~] utterly exhausted: *He was dog-tired after all that work.*

dog•trot (dôg′trot′, dog′-) /ˈdɔgˌtrɒt, ˈdɒg-/ *n., v.,* **-trot•ted, -trot•ting.** —*n.* [*count*] **1.** a gentle trot, like that of a dog: *He jogged off at a dogtrot.* —*v.* [*no obj*] **2.** to go at the speed of a dogtrot.

dog•wood (dôg′wŏŏd′, dog′-) /ˈdɔgˌwʊd, ˈdɒg-/ *n.* **1.** [*count*] a tree or shrub of Europe and America with pink or white blossoms. **2.** [*noncount*] the wood of this tree. —*adj.* [*before a noun*] **3.** made of such wood.

doi•ly (doi′lē) /ˈdɔyliy/ *n.* [*count*], *pl.* **-lies.** any small, ornamental mat, esp. one of embroidery or lace: *She had crocheted some pretty little doilies.*

do•ing (dōō′ing) /ˈduwɪŋ/ *n.* **1.** [*noncount*] performance; execution; something done: *It must have taken a lot of doing to get this finished on time.* **2. doings,** [*plural*] deeds; proceedings; events: *There were big doings at the mall last week.*

do-it-your•self (dōō′i chər self′, -it yər-) /ˈduwɪtʃərˈsɛlf, -ɪtyər-/ *adj.* **1.** designed for use by unskilled amateurs: *a do-it-yourself computer assembly kit.* —*n.* [*noncount*] **2.** the building or repairing of things for oneself, usually in one's own home. —**do′-it-your•self′er,** *n.* [*count*]

dol•drums (dōl′drəmz, dol′-, dôl′-) /ˈdowldrəmz, ˈdɒl-, ˈdɔl-/ *n.* [*plural*] **1.** a state of inactivity. **2. in the doldrums,** in a dull, depressed mood; in low spirits: *has been in the doldrums ever since he heard the bad news.*

dole (dōl) /dowl/ *n., v.,* **doled, dol•ing.** —*n.* [*count; usually singular*] **1.** an amount of money, etc., esp. given at regular intervals by a charity: *A dole is given to them every two weeks or so.* —*v.* [~ + *out* + *obj*] **2.** to give out (something) in small quantities: *to dole out water during a drought.* —***Idiom.*** **3. on the dole,** *Chiefly Brit.* receiving relief payments from the government.

dole•ful (dōl′fəl) /ˈdowlfəl/ *adj.* sorrowful; mournful: *a doleful sigh.* —**dole′ful•ly,** *adv.*

doll (dol) /dɒl/ *n.* [*count*] **1.** a small figure representing a baby or other human being, used esp. as a child's toy. **2.** *Slang.* **a.** a girl or woman: *"Who's the new doll in the corner?" he whispered.* **b.** a physically attractive person. **c.** a generous or helpful person: *Be a doll and help me wash the dishes.* **d.** [*sometimes: Doll*] an affectionate or familiar term of address (sometimes considered offensive when used to a stranger, subordinate, etc.). —*v.* **3. doll up,** to dress in fancy clothing with a lot of makeup, etc.: [~ + *up* + *obj*]: *She was all dolled up for the party.* [~ + *obj* + *up*]: *She had dolled herself up for the party.*

dol•lar (dol′ər) /ˈdɒlər/ *n.* [*count*] the basic monetary unit of various countries, including the U.S. and Canada.

dol•lop (dol′əp) /ˈdɒləp/ *n.* [*count*] **1.** a lump of some substance, usually a small amount: *a dollop of whipped cream.* —*v.* [~ + *obj*] **2.** to dispense in dollops.

dol•ly (dol′ē) /ˈdɒliy/ *n.* [*count*], *pl.* **-lies. 1.** *Informal.* a doll. **2.** a low truck or cart with small wheels for moving heavy loads.

dol•phin (dol′fin, dôl′-) /ˈdɒlfɪn, ˈdɔl-/ *n.* [*count*] **1.** a small-toothed mammal of the sea having a beaklike nose and mouth. Compare PORPOISE. **2.** Also called **dolphin-fish mahimahi.** either of two large, slender fishes of warm and temperate seas.

dolt (dōlt) /dowlt/ *n.* [*count*] a foolish or stupid person; blockhead; dunce. —**dolt′ish,** *adj.*

-dom, *suffix. -dom* is attached to some nouns and adjectives to form nouns, with the meanings: **1.** domain or area ruled: *king* + *-dom* → *kingdom (= area a king rules).* **2.** collection of persons: *official* + *-dom* → *officialdom (= a collection of officials).* **3.** rank: *earl* + *-dom* → *earldom (= the rank or position of an earl).* **4.** general condition: *free* + *-dom* → *freedom (= general condition of being free).*

do•main (dō mān′) /dowˈmeyn/ *n.* [*count*] **1.** a field or area of thought, etc; subject; area of interest: *He works in the domain of public health.* **2.** the territory governed by a ruler or government: *The domains stretched for hundreds of miles in every direction.*

dome (dōm) /dowm/ *n.* [*count*] **1.** a roof or ceiling that is rounded or in the form of a part of a sphere. **2.** *Slang.* a person's head: *the painter's bald dome.* —**domed,** *adj.: the domed basilica of St. Peter's.*

do•mes•tic (də mes′tik) /dəˈmɛstɪk/ *adj.* **1.** [*before a noun*] of or relating to the home: *domestic as opposed to industrial uses of natural gas.* **2.** devoted to home life: *He's very domestic and loves to stay at home.* **3.** [*before a noun*] tame; domesticated: *Cats are domestic animals.* **4.** [*before a noun*] of or relating to one's own country as apart from other countries; produced in one's own country: *domestic trade.* —*n.* [*count*] **5.** a household servant. —**do•mes′ti•cal•ly,** *adv.*

do•mes•ti•cate (də mes′ti kāt′) /dəˈmɛstɪˌkeyt/ *v.* [~ + *obj*], **-cat•ed, -cat•ing. 1.** to tame (an animal): *If you domesticate that raccoon, it will have trouble living in the wild.* **2.** to change or adapt (a plant) so as to be cultivated by and beneficial to human beings. **3.** to make (someone) become accustomed to life in a household: *I was fully domesticated by then, taking out the garbage and washing the dishes.* —**do•mes•ti•ca•tion** (də mes′ti-kā′shən) /dəˌmɛstɪˈkeyʃən/ *n.* [*noncount*]

do•mes•tic•i•ty (dō′me stis′i tē) /ˌdowmɛˈstɪsɪtiy/ *n.* [*noncount*] the state of being domestic or of liking home life: *a blissful view of domesticity.*

dom•i•cile (dom′ə sīl′, -səl, dō′mə-) /ˈdɒməˌsayl, -səl, ˈdowmə-/ *n., v.,* **-ciled, -cil•ing.** —*n.* [*count*] **1.** a place of residence. **2.** a permanent legal residence: *His domicile was in a country that had no taxes.* —*v.* [~ + *obj*] **3.** to establish a domicile in: *He was domiciled abroad for tax purposes.*

dom•i•nance (dom′ə nəns) /ˈdɒmənəns/ *n.* [*noncount*] **1.** the act or state of dominating. **2.** power or authority: *the dominance of one nation over another.*

dom•i•nant (dom′ə nənt) /ˈdɒmənənt/ *adj.* **1.** ruling or controlling; exerting authority: *The dominant powers took control of the conference.* **2.** of or relating to one of a pair of hereditary traits that masks the other when both are present in an organism. **3.** predominant; chief or foremost: *What are the dominant factors in inflation management?* —**dom′i•nant•ly,** *adv.*

dom•i•nate (dom′ə nāt′) /ˈdɒməˌneyt/ *v.* [~ + *obj*], **-nat•ed, -nat•ing. 1.** to rule over; control: *She completely dominates the family.* **2.** to tower above; overlook: *The church dominates the entire village.* **3.** to be the major factor or influence in: *The issue of gun control will dominate the next election.* —**dom•i•na•tion** (dom′ə-nā′shən) /ˌdɒməˈneyʃən/ *n.* [*noncount*] —**Related Words.** DOMINATE is a verb, DOMINANT is an adjective, DOMINATION is a noun: *That country tried to dominate its neighbors. She was a dominant force in the music world. The weaker country faced domination by stronger neighbors.*

dom•i•neer•ing (dom′ə nēr′ing) /ˌdɒməˈnɪərɪŋ/ *adj.* using or having great dominance or control; ruling strongly: *a domineering personality.*

Do•min•i•can (də min′i kən *for 1, 3;* dom′ə nē′kən *for 2, 4*) /dəˈmɪnɪkən *for 1, 3;* ˌdɒməˈniykən *for 2, 4* / *adj.* **1.** of or relating to the Dominican Republic. **2.** of or relating to Dominica. —*n.* [*count*] **3.** a person born or living in the Dominican Republic. **4.** a person born or living in Dominica.

do•min•ion (də min′yən) /dəˈmɪnyən/ *n.* **1.** [*noncount*] the power to govern: *The king declared he had sole dominion over this land.* **2.** [*count*] the territory subject to the control of a ruler or government: *The law was put into effect throughout the dominion.* **3.** [*count; often: Dominion*] any of the self-governing countries outside the United Kingdom that belong to the Commonwealth of Nations.

dom•i•no (dom′ə nō′) /ˈdɒməˌnow/ *n., pl.* **-noes. 1.** [*count*] a small, flat block, the face of which has two squares, each either blank or painted with dots. **2. dominoes,** [*noncount; used with a singular verb*] a game in which the ends of such pieces are matched: *Dominoes is not too hard to play.*

don[1] (don; *Sp., It.* dôn) /dɒn; *Sp., It.* dɔn/ *n.* **1.** [*proper noun; Don*] Mr.; Sir: a Spanish title put before a man's given name: *Don Diego was his name.* **2.** [*count*] (in Spanish-speaking countries) a lord or gentleman. **3.** [*count*] (in the English universities) a head, fellow, or tutor of a college. **4.** [*count*] the head of a Mafia family.

don[2] (don) /dɒn/ *v.* [~ + *obj*], **donned, don•ning.** to put on or dress in: *to don one's gloves.*

do•ña (dô′nyä) /ˈdɔnyɑ/ *n., pl.* **-ñas. 1.** [*proper noun; Doña*] Madam; Lady: a Spanish title put before a woman's given name: *Doña Melendez was her name.* **2.** [*count*] (in Spanish-speaking countries) a lady or gentlewoman.

do•nate (dō′nāt, dō nāt′) /ˈdowneyt, dowˈneyt/ *v.,* **-nat•ed, -nat•ing.** to present (something) as a gift: [~ + *obj*]: *She donated a pint of blood last year.* [~ + *obj* + *to* + *obj*]: *The millionaire donated money to charity.* [*no obj*]: *I've already donated, please don't ask again.*

do•na•tion (dō nā′shən) /dowˈneyʃən/ *n.* **1.** [*noncount*] the giving or act of donating something: *donation of his* *time and energy.* **2.** [*count*] something given, presented, or donated as a gift: *My donation was for fifty dollars.*

done (dun) /dʌn/ *v.* **1.** pp. of DO[1]: *I've already done the dishes.* **2.** *Nonstandard.* a pt. of DO[1]: *What you done to him was bad.* —*auxiliary verb.* **3.** *Southern U.S. Nonstandard.* (used often with a main verb in the past tense to indicate completed action): *I done told you.* —*adj.* **4. a.** finished; completed; accomplished: *That mass firing was a done deal long before we knew about it.* **b.** [*be* + ~] at a point of completion; through: *When you are done, turn out the lights.* **5.** cooked enough or properly: *The pie isn't done until the crust is brown. Is the meat done yet?* **6.** [*be* + ~] in keeping with acceptable behavior or practice: *That sort of thing simply isn't done.* **7.** accepted; agreed (used as an answer to a question): *"Is it a deal, then?"— "Done!"* —***Idiom.*** **8. be** or **have done with,** [*be/have* + ~ + *with* + *obj*] to break off relations with. **9. done for,** [*no obj*] **a.** dead or dying: *"I'm done for, so save yourself and get out of here," the dying marine whispered.* **b.** certain to suffer failure, trouble, or misfortune: *You'd better finish that work or you'll be done for.* **10. done in,** [*no obj*] very tired; exhausted: *I'm all done in after that five-mile walk.*

Don Juan (don wän′) /dɒn 'wɑn/ *n.* [*count*] a man who seduces many women.

don•key (dong′kē, dông′-, dung′-) /'dɒŋkiy, 'dɔŋ-, 'dʌŋ-/ *n.* [*count*], *pl.* **-keys. 1.** a long-eared domesticated mammal related to the horse: *Donkeys are better than horses on mountain trails.* **2.** a stupid, silly, or obstinate person.

do•nor (dō′nər) /'downər/ *n.* [*count*] **1.** a person who gives or donates. **2.** a provider of blood or an organ for transfusion or transplantation: *She is waiting for a kidney donor.* —*adj.* [*before a noun*] **3.** of or relating to the biological tissue of a donor: *a donor organ.* **4.** relating to, or for a giver of a donation: *a donor card.*

don't (dōnt) /downt/ *v.* **1.** contraction of *do not*: *Don't come in.* **2.** *Nonstandard* (*except in some dialects*). contraction of *does not*: *He don't care where the road goes.* —*n.* [*count*] **3. don'ts,** [*plural*] a list of practices to be avoided. Compare DO[1] (def. 31): *a long list of dos and don'ts.*

do•nut (dō′nət, -nut′) /'downət, -ˌnʌt/ *n.* DOUGHNUT.

doo•dad (do͞o′dad′) /'duwˌdæd/ *n.* [*count*] *Informal.* **1.** a trinket or bauble: *a dress decorated with little silver doodads.* **2.** a gadget; device; small object whose name is unknown or has been forgotten.

doo•dle (do͞od′l) /'duwdl/ *v.,* **-dled, -dling,** *n.* **1.** to draw or scribble idly: [*no obj*]: *She was doodling on the paper when I called on her.* [~ + *obj*]: *doodling designs in the margin.* —*n.* [*count*] **2.** a drawing produced by doodling. —**doo′dler,** *n.* [*count*]

doom (do͞om) /duwm/ *n.* [*noncount*] **1.** fate or destiny, esp. bad or adverse fate. **2.** ruin or death: *facing doom and destruction.* —*v.* [~ + *obj; usually: be* + ~*-ed*] **3.** to make sure that something will happen, esp. a bad fate; cause to fail: *We are doomed to make the same mistakes in the future.*

dooms•day (do͞omz′dā′) /'duwmzˌdey/ *n.* **1.** [*proper noun*] the day of the Last Judgment, at the end of the world. **2.** [*noncount*] nuclear destruction of the world: *a story about doomsday in the near future.*

door (dôr, dōr) /dɔr, dowr/ *n.* [*count*] **1.** a movable barrier of wood, glass, or metal for opening and closing an entranceway, cupboard, cabinet, or the like, usually turning on hinges or sliding in grooves: *He knocked on the door.* See illustration at HOUSE. **2.** a doorway: *He stood at the door, but she wouldn't let him in.* **3.** a building, house, apartment, or the like as represented by its entrance: *He lived two doors up the street.* **4.** any means of gaining something, or a way of getting to something; access; key: *the door to learning.* —***Idiom.*** **5. answer the door,** to go to the main door of one's living place and ask to know who has knocked, or to open it. **6. at death's door,** near death; dying. **7. next door,** at the house, building, or apartment next to the one already known or spoken about: *He fell in love with the girl next door.* **8. show someone the door,** to order someone to leave: *The bodyguard politely but firmly showed me the door.*

door•bell (dôr′bel′, dōr′-) /'dɔrˌbɛl, 'dowr-/ *n.* [*count*] a bell, chime, or buzzer connected with a door and rung by persons seeking admittance, making a delivery, etc.

door•man (dôr′man′, -mən, dōr′-) /'dɔrˌmæn, -mən, 'dowr-/ *n.* [*count*], *pl.* **-men.** a person who stays by the main door of an apartment house, nightclub, etc., and assists those entering and departing.

door•mat (dôr′mat′, dōr′-) /'dɔrˌmæt, 'dowr-/ *n.* [*count*] **1.** a mat placed before a door for people to wipe their shoes on before entering. **2.** a person who allows others to take advantage of him or her.

door•step (dôr′step′, dōr′-) /'dɔrˌstɛp, 'dowr-/ *n.* [*count*] a step in front of an outside door.

door′-to-door′, *adj.* [*before a noun*] **1.** proceeding from one house, apartment, or room to another: *a door-to-door salesman.* —*adv.* **2.** moving or proceeding this way: *going door-to-door selling magazines.*

door•way (dôr′wā′, dōr′-) /'dɔrˌwey, 'dowr-/ *n.* [*count*] **1.** the way of entering a building, room, etc. **2.** a means of gaining something, or a way of getting to something; access: *the doorway to success.*

dope (dōp) /dowp/ *n., v.,* **doped, dop•ing,** *adj.* —*n.* **1.** [*noncount*] *Slang.* a narcotic or illegal drug: *He was on dope for years.* **2.** [*noncount*] *Slang.* a narcotic preparation given to a horse to improve or hold back its performance in a race. **3.** [*noncount*] *Slang.* information; news: *What's the latest dope?* **4.** [*count*] *Informal.* a stupid person: *Tell those dopes to give you a raise.* —*v.* **5.** [*often: be* + ~*-ed* (+ *up*)] *Slang.* to affect with dope or drugs: *He was obviously doped (up), shouting and weaving down the street.* **6.** to give dope to; treat with dope: [~ (+ *up*) + *obj*]: *They had doped (up) the patient heavily before the operation.* [~ + *obj* (+ *up*)]: *They doped the horse (up) and it easily won the race.* **7. dope out,** *Slang.* to figure out: [~ + *out* + *obj*]: *I doped out most of the questions on the test.* [~ + *obj* + *out*]: *I finally doped it out: we were a threat to him.* [~ + *out* +(*that*) *clause*]: *I finally doped out that I was being threatened.*

dope•y or **dop•y** (dō′pē) /'dowpiy/ *adj.,* **-i•er, -i•est.** *Informal.* **1.** stupid; foolish: *That was a dopey thing to do.* **2.** sluggish or sleepy, as if from the use of narcotics or alcohol: *She was still dopey from the medication.*

dorm (dôrm) /dɔrm/ *n.* [*count*] a dormitory.

dor•mant (dôr′mənt) /'dɔrmənt/ *adj.* **1.** inactive, such as in sleep: *dormant plants and animals.* **2.** (of a volcano) not erupting. **3.** undeveloped or inactive; held back: *She had talents that lay dormant.* —**dor•man•cy** (dôr′mən sē) /'dɔrmənsiy/ *n.* [*noncount*]

dor•mer (dôr′mər) /'dɔrmər/ *n.* [*count*] a vertical or upright window built out from a sloping roof, or the structure holding this window. Also called **dor′mer win′dow.**

dor•mi•to•ry (dôr′mi tôr′ē, -tōr′ē) /'dɔrmɪˌtɔriy, -ˌtowriy/ *n., pl.* **-ries,** *adj.* —*n.* [*count*] **1.** a building, such as at a college, containing rooms for students to live in. **2.** a large room containing a number of beds and serving as sleeping quarters for a group of people: *the barracks dormitory.* —*adj.* [*before a noun*] **3.** of or referring to a community inhabited mainly by commuters: *dormitory suburbs.*

dor•mouse (dôr′mous′) /'dɔrˌmaws/ *n.* [*count*], *pl.* **-mice.** a small, usually bushy-tailed climbing rodent.

dor•sal (dôr′səl) /'dɔrsəl/ *adj.* [*before a noun*] **1.** of, relating to, or situated at the back of a fish: *the dorsal fin of the shark.* **2.** situated on or toward the upper side of the body, equivalent to the back in humans.

do•ry (dôr′ē, dōr′ē) /'dɔriy, 'dowriy/ *n.* [*count*], *pl.* **-ries.** a small boat with a narrow, flat bottom and high bow.

DOS (dôs, dos) /dɔs, dɒs/ *n.* [*noncount*] an operating system for microcomputers: *DOS is an abbreviation for disk operating system.*

dos•age (dō′səj) /'dowsədʒ/ *n.* [*count; usually singular*] the amount of medicine to be taken at one time: *The dosage should not exceed two tablets every four hours.*

dose (dōs) /dows/ *n., v.,* **dosed, dos•ing.** —*n.* [*count*] **1.** an amount of medicine to be taken at one time: *an hourly dose of medicine.* **2.** an intense and often disagreeable experience: *a dose of bad luck.* **3.** the amount of radiation to which something has been exposed: *The doses of radioactivity were already well past the lethal level.* —*v.* [~ + *obj*] **4.** to give a dose of medicine to: *We dosed her with non-aspirin tablets to reduce the fever.*

dos•si•er (dos′ē ā′, dô′sē ā′) /'dɒsiyˌey, 'dɔsiyˌey/ *n.* [*count*] a file of documents containing information about a person or topic.

dot (dot) /dɒt/ *n., v.,* **dot•ted, dot•ting.** —*n.* [*count*] **1.** a small, roundish mark made with or as if with a pen: *She forgot the dot on the letter* i *and so it looked like an* l. **2.** a small spot; speck: *She bought a blue dress with white dots on it.* **3.** a small amount: *a dot of butter.* **4.** a signal of shorter length than a dash, used in groups along with groups of dashes and spaces to represent letters, as in Morse code. —*v.* [~ + *obj*] **5.** to mark with or as if with a dot or dots: *to dot the letter* i. **6.** to cover, scatter, or sprinkle with or as if with dots: *From above we could see* *the trees dotting the landscape.* **—*Idiom.* 7. dot one's i's and cross one's t's,** to be meticulous and precise. **8. on the dot,** precisely; exactly at the time said: *We arrived at 6:00 on the dot.*

dot•age (dō′tij) /ˈdowtɪdʒ/ *n.* [*noncount*] **1.** a decline or weakening of the mind esp. as associated with old age: *In his dotage he didn't recognize me when I came to see him.* **2.** foolish affection; too much affection: *his dotage on his grandchildren.*

dote (dōt) /dowt/ *v.* [~ + *on* + *obj*], **dot•ed, dot•ing.** to give or show too much fondness or love: *Grandparents just love to dote on their grandchildren.* **—dot′ing•ly,** *adv.*

dot′-ma′trix, *adj.* [*usually: before a noun*] of or relating to a computer printer that forms characters and pictures with dots from a matrix.

dot•ted (dot′id) /ˈdɒtɪd/ *adj.* **1.** [*usually: before a noun*] made up of or consisting of a line or row of dots: *Sign on the dotted line below.* **2.** made up of many dots: *a bright red dotted bowtie.*

dot•ty (dot′ē) /ˈdɒtiy/ *adj.,* **-ti•er, -ti•est.** *Chiefly Brit.* **1.** behaving strangely; eccentric: *She was a dotty old woman.* **2.** [*be* + ~ + *about*] eager about (something); enthusiastic: *was dotty about horse-racing.*

dou•ble (dub′əl) /ˈdʌbəl/ *adj., n., v.,* **-bled, -bling,** *adv.* **—*adj.* 1.** twice as large, heavy, strong, etc.; twice as many in size, amount, number, extent, etc.: *The workers receive double pay for working on Sundays. He ordered a double whiskey.* **2.** [*before a noun*] made up of two similar parts or members; paired: *a double sink.* **3.** [*usually: before a noun*] suitable for two persons: *We rented a double room.* **4.** having two meanings; ambiguous: *His comment had a double meaning.* **5.** [*usually: before a noun*] hiding something dishonestly; deceitful: *He led a double life, working by day and thieving by night.* **6.** folded in two layers. **—*n.* 7.** anything that is twice the usual size, amount, strength, etc.: [*noncount*]: *She offered me double for the computer.* [*count*]: *He ordered a double of scotch from the bar.* **8.** [*count*] a person who exactly or closely resembles another: *She is the double of her mother.* **9.** [*count*] a hotel room with two beds or a double bed, for two people. **10.** [*count*] a substitute who performs stunts in a movie or TV show that are too hazardous for a star: *a stunt double.* **11.** [*count*] Also called **two-base hit.** a hit in baseball that allows the batter to reach second base safely. **12. doubles,** [*noncount; used with a singular verb*] a game or match, as in tennis, in which there are two players on each side: *a doubles match.* **—*v.* 13.** to (cause to) become double or twice as great; add an equal amount (of): [*no obj*]: *Our taxes doubled over a one-year period.* [~ + *obj*]: *The landlord doubled our rent.* **14.** to fold or bend with one part over another: [~ + *obj*]: *The mother doubled the sheets and blankets to keep the baby warmer.* [~ + *up/over* + *obj*]: *She doubled over the sheets and blankets to make the baby warmer.* [~ + *obj* + *up/over*]: *She doubled them up to keep the baby warmer.* **15.** [~ + *obj*] to clench; hold tightly: *to double one's fists.* **16.** [~ + *obj*] to pair; couple: *We doubled partners and began the country dance.* **17.** [~ + *as* + *obj*] to do a second job in addition to one's primary job; to serve in an additional capacity: *The director doubles as an actor.* **18.** [*no obj*] to hit a double in baseball. **19.** [*no obj*] to double-date: *We doubled last week, but this week I want to go out with her alone.* **20. double back,** [*no obj*] to turn back on a course; reverse direction: *I doubled back to see if I could find the missing earring.* **21. double up, a.** [*no obj*] to share quarters planned for only one person or family: *You can stay with us; we'll all just double up.* **b.** Also, **double over.** to (cause to) bend over, as from pain: [*no obj*]: *As the next wave of pain hit, he doubled over.* [~ + *obj* + *up/over*]: *The pain doubled him up and left him gasping on the floor.* [~ + *over/up* + *obj*]: *A punch like that would double over anyone.* **—*adv.* 22.** to twice the amount, extent, etc.; twofold: *We paid double for that room.* **23.** two together: *to sleep double.* **—*Idiom.* 24. double or nothing,** a bet in which one either wins twice as much as one has bet or gets nothing. **25. on the double,** without delay; rapidly: *Get up there on the double and report to the commander.*

dou′ble a′gent, *n.* [*count*] a spy in the service of two rival countries.

dou′ble-bar′reled, *adj.* **1.** (esp. of a shotgun) having two barrels mounted side by side. **2.** serving a double purpose: *a double-barreled attack.*

dou′ble bass′ (bās) /beys/ *n.* [*count*] the largest instrument of the violin family.

dou′ble-blind′, *adj.* of or relating to an experiment in which neither the researchers nor the subjects know which subjects are receiving the real treatment, medication, etc.: *A double-blind experiment was done to remove the possibility of bias.*

dou′ble boil′er, *n.* [*count*] a utensil consisting of two pots, one of which fits partway into the other; water is boiled in the lower pot to cook or warm food in the upper.

dou′ble-breast′ed, *adj.* (of a coat, jacket, etc.) having a front closure with a wide overlap that is secured at both the right and the left sides and typically shows two vertical rows of buttons when fastened.

doub′le chin′, *n.* [*count*] an extra fold or flap of skin under the chin and above the throat.

dou′ble-cross′, *v.* [~ + *obj*] to betray, cheat, or deceive. **—dou′ble-cross′er,** *n.* [*count*]

dou′ble date′, *n.* [*count*] a date on which two couples go out together. **—dou′ble-date′,** *v.* [*no obj*], **-dat•ed, -dat•ing:** *We double-dated last night.*

dou′ble-deal′ing, *n.* [*noncount*] **1.** deception or treachery; duplicity. **—*adj.* [*before a noun*] 2.** using deception; treacherous: *a double-dealing scoundrel.*

dou′ble-deck′er, *n.* [*count*] **1.** something with two decks or levels: *The bus was a double-decker.* **—*adj.*** [*before a noun*] **2.** having two decks or levels.

dou•ble en•ten•dre (dub′əl än tän′drə) /ˈdʌbəl ɑnˈtɑndrə / *n.* [*count*], *pl.* **dou•ble en•ten•dres** (dub′əl än tän′drəz) /ˈdʌbəl ɑnˈtɑndrəz/. a word or expression used so that it can be understood in two ways, esp. when one meaning is indelicate.

dou•ble•head•er (dub′əl hed′ər) /ˈdʌbəlˈhɛdər/ *n.* [*count*] two games usually played on the same day one after the other.

dou′ble-joint′ed, *adj.* having especially flexible joints that can bend in unusual ways or to an unusually great extent.

doub′le-park′, *v.* to park (a car) alongside another car already parked parallel to the curb: [*no obj*]: *If you double-park here, you'll get a ticket.* [~ + *obj*]: *He double-parked his car and hurried into the store.*

dou′ble stand′ard, *n.* [*count*] a set of principles applied differently to one group of people than to another.

dou•blet (dub′lit) /ˈdʌblɪt/ *n.* [*count*] a close-fitting jacket once worn by men.

dou′ble take′, *n.* [*count*] a surprised delayed response, as by taking a second look, in reaction to a person not recognized the first time.

dou′ble-talk′ or **dou′ble•talk′,** *n.* [*noncount*] **1.** speech or language that has two or more meanings, or has no meaning at all, but is used deliberately to deceive: *When I asked about his work, all I got was double-talk about "efficiency engineering."* **—*v.* 2.** [*no obj*] to use double-talk: *He was just double-talking, full of generalities and promising nothing.* **3.** [~ + *obj* (+ *into* + *obj*)] to persuade (someone) by double-talk: *He double-talked us (into doing what he wanted).*

dou•bloon (du blo͞on′) /dʌˈbluwn/ *n.* [*count*] a former gold coin of Spain and Spanish America.

dou•bly (dub′lē) /ˈdʌbliy/ *adv.* **1.** to a double measure or degree: *to be doubly cautious.* **2.** in a double manner: *doubly handicapped.*

doubt (dout) /dawt/ *v.* [*not: be* + ~*-ing*] **1.** to be uncertain about; wonder: [~ + *obj*]: *I doubt his honesty when it comes to his job, don't you? I doubt it.* [~ + (*that*) *clause*]: *I wouldn't doubt that she'd want to help.* [~ + *whether* + *clause; only in positive phrases*]: *I doubt whether she'll change her mind.* **2.** [~ + *obj*] to distrust: *I never doubted you; I was sure you would bring us the money.* **—*n.* 3.** a feeling of uncertainty: [*noncount*]: *a great deal of doubt about whether he'll win the election.* [*count*]: *You think everything will turn out well, but I have my doubts.* **4.** [*count; usually plural*] distrust or suspicion: *We have grave doubts about his honesty.* **—*Idiom.* 5. beyond (a** or **the shadow of) a doubt,** with certainty; definitely: *guilty beyond a shadow of a doubt.* **6. in doubt,** in a state of uncertainty: *The outcome of the election was in doubt.* **7. no doubt, a.** probably: *No doubt you'll be back at school tomorrow.* **b.** certainly: *As you have been told, no doubt, we expect the budget cuts to affect us.* **8. without doubt,** unquestionably; certainly: *She is, without doubt, the finest teacher in the school.* **—doubt′er,** *n.* [*count*] **—doubt′ing•ly,** *adv.*

doubt•ful (dout′fəl) /ˈdawtfəl/ *adj.* **1.** of uncertain outcome: *a doubtful future.* **2.** undecided in opinion or belief; hesitant: *I'm doubtful about whether I made the right choice.* **3.** of character or value that may not be genuine or real: *The painting is of doubtful authenticity.* **4.** unlikely; not probable: *It's doubtful I'll finish the work on time.* **—doubt′ful•ly,** *adv.*: *We looked on doubtfully as he tried to lift the couch.*

doubt•less (dout′lis) /ˈdawtlɪs/ *adv.* Also, **doubt′less•ly. 1.** without doubt; surely; certainly: *Doubtless he'll be here on time.* **2.** very probably; presumably: *She'll doubtless(ly) accept the job.* **—*adj.* 3.** sure; free from doubt.

dough (dō) /dow/ *n.* [*noncount*] **1.** flour combined with water, milk, etc., in a thick mass for baking: *We made our own dough for apple pie.* **2.** any similar soft, pasty mass. **3.** *Slang.* money: *Can you lend me some dough until payday?* **—dough′y,** *adj.,* **-i•er, -i•est:** *The pizza crust was too doughy and unbaked.*

dough•nut or **do•nut** (dō′nət, -nut′) /ˈdownət, -ˌnʌt/ *n.* [*count*] **1.** a small, ring-shaped cake of fried sweetened dough. **2.** a raised ball of fried dough, filled with jelly, custard, etc.

dough•ty (dou′tē) /ˈdawtiy/ *adj.,* **-ti•er, -ti•est.** courageous and unwilling to give up; resolute; valiant.

dour (dŏŏr, douᵊr) /dʊr, dawᵊr/ *adj.* severe; stern; gloomy: *a dour facial expression.* **—dour′ness,** *n.* [*noncount*]

douse (dous) /daws/ *v.* [~ + *obj*], **doused, dous•ing. 1.** to throw water on: *We doused the children with the hose.* **2.** to extinguish; put out: *to douse a candle.*

dove[1] (duv) /dʌv/ *n.* [*count*] **1.** a bird of the pigeon family. **2.** a person who calls for peace or a more friendly national attitude toward enemies.

dove[2] (dōv) /dowv/ *v.* a pt. of DIVE.

dove•tail (duv′tāl′) /ˈdʌvˌteyl/ *n.* [*count*] **1.** a joint formed in the shape of a wedge that fits tightly into a corresponding gap in another piece of wood. **—*v.*** [~ + *with* + *obj*] **2.** (of ideas, figures, etc.) to join or fit together smoothly or neatly: *My figures dovetailed nicely with theirs.*

dow•a•ger (dou′ə jər) /ˈdawədʒər/ *n.* [*count*] **1.** a woman who holds some title or property from her deceased husband. **2.** an elderly woman of stately dignity. **—*adj.*** [*before a noun*] **3.** relating to or characteristic of a dowager: *a dowager princess.*

dow•dy (dou′dē) /ˈdawdiy/ *adj.,* **-di•er, -di•est.** not stylish; drab; out-of-date: *dowdy clothes.* **—dow′di•ness,** *n.* [*noncount*]

dow•el (dou′əl) /ˈdawəl/ *n.* [*count*] a small rod, usually round and wooden, fitting into holes in two adjacent pieces to line them up.

down[1] (doun) /dawn/ *adv.* **1.** from higher to lower; toward or into a lower position or level: *Tell him to come down.* **2.** on or to the ground, floor, or the like: *to fall down.* **3.** to or in a sitting or lying position: *Sit down next to her.* **4.** to an area or district considered lower from a geographical standpoint, esp. southward: *We drove down to San Diego from Los Angeles.* **5.** to a lower value, level, or rate: *Slow down.* **6.** to a lesser pitch or volume: *Turn down the radio.* **7.** in or to a calmer or less active state: *The wind died down.* **8.** from an earlier to a later time: *the history of the church from the Middle Ages down to the present.* **9.** from a greater to a lesser strength, amount, etc.: *to water down a drink.* **10.** earnestly: *to get down to work.* **11.** on paper: *Write this down.* **12.** in cash at the time of purchase: *$50 down and $20 a month thereafter.* **13.** to the point of defeat or submission: *shouted down the opposition.* **14.** to the source or actual position: *to track someone down.* **15.** into a condition of ill health: *He came down with the flu.* **16.** in or into a lower status or condition: *He was kept down by lack of education.* **—*prep.* 17.** in a descending direction on or along; in a place moved farther away than: *They ran off down the street.* **—*adj.* 18.** [*before a noun*] directed downward; going down: *Take the down escalator on the left.* **19.** [*be/seem* + ~] sad; gloomy; depressed: *You seem pretty down today.* **20.** [*be* + ~] sick and in bed: *He's down with a bad cold.* **21.** [*be* + ~] behind an opponent or opponents in points: *We're down by twenty points.* **22.** [*be* + ~] having lost the amount indicated, esp. at gambling: *After that last race I'm only down $10.* **23.** finished or taken care of: *Five down and one to go.* **24.** [*be* + ~] out of order: *The computer is down again.* **25.** *Slang.* admired: *a down dude.* **—*n.*** [*count*] **26.** a turn for the worse; reverse: *It was another down for the company already in debt.* **27.** [*count*] *Football.* one of a series of four plays during which a team must advance the ball at least 10 yd. (9 m) to keep possession of it: *On that last series of downs the team moved the ball well.* **—*v.*** [~ + *obj*] **28.** to knock, throw, or bring down: *He downed his opponent with a quick right to the jaw.* **29.** to drink down, esp. quickly: *I downed the vodka in one gulp.* **30.** to defeat in a game or contest: *The Rangers downed the Flyers 2-0 last night.* **—*interj.* 31.** (used as a command or warning) get down: *Down in front, please (= Please sit down in front, so people behind you can see).* **—*Idiom.* 32. down cold** or **pat,** learned perfectly: *He always has his facts down cold before he argues with anyone.* **33. down in the mouth,** discouraged; sad; depressed: *He looks down in the mouth today.* **34. down on,** [~ + *obj*] hostile to: *Most of the party's regular members are down on his candidacy.* **35. down with,** [~ + *obj*] (used in a command or a wish, without a subject) to remove from power or do away with: *Down with the king!*

down[2] (doun) /dawn/ *n.* [*noncount*] **1.** the short, soft feathers of some birds, used for filling in clothing for warmth. **2.** fine, soft, short hair, such as on plants. **—*adj.*** [*before a noun*] **3.** filled with down: *a down jacket.*

down•beat (doun′bēt′) /ˈdawnˌbiyt/ *n.* [*count*] **1.** the downward stroke of a conductor's baton indicating the first beat of a measure. **2.** the first beat of a measure. **—*adj.* 3.** *Slang.* gloomy or depressing: *a movie with a downbeat ending.*

down•cast (doun′kast′) /ˈdawnˌkæst/ *adj.* **1.** directed downward, such as the eyes. **2.** dejected; sad or depressed: *Don't be so downcast because you lost.*

down•er (dou′nər) /ˈdawnər/ *n.* [*count*] *Informal.* **1.** a depressing experience or person: *That loss was a real downer for the team.* **2.** a drug that makes people sleepy or less excited; a depressant.

down•fall (doun′fôl′) /ˈdawnˌfɔl/ *n.* **1.** [*noncount*] overthrow; ruin: *the downfall of the dictator.* **2.** [*noncount*] something causing this: *Drugs were his downfall.* **3.** [*count; usually singular*] a sudden fall of rain or snow: *caught in a bad downfall.*

down•grade (doun′grād′) /ˈdawnˌgreyd/ *v.,* **-grad•ed, -grad•ing,** *n.* [~ + *obj*] **1.** to reassign to a lower level: *They downgraded the military alert from emergency to standby.* **—*n.*** [*count*] **2.** a downward slope, esp. of a road: *The downgrade is very steep for a heavy truck like this.* **3.** a lowering in status or importance.

down•heart•ed (doun′här′tid) /ˈdawnˈhɑrtɪd/ *adj.* dejected; depressed: *downhearted because she failed again.*

down•hill (*adv.* doun′hil′; *adj., n.* -hil′) / *adv.* ˈdawnˈhɪl; *adj., n.* -ˌhɪl/ *adv.* **1.** down the slope of a hill; downward: *She skied downhill quickly.* **2.** into a worse condition: *Things have gone downhill again.* **—*adj.* 3.** going downward on or as if on a hill: *a downhill trail.* **4.** [*be* + ~] easy; free of things that prevent one from finishing: *We're halfway; things will be all downhill now.* **5.** [*before a noun*] of or relating to skiing downhill: *a downhill skier.* **—*n.*** [*count*] **6.** a timed ski race down a steep trail: *He won the gold medal in the men's downhill.* Compare SLALOM.

down′-home′, *adj.* [*before a noun*] characterized by the simple, informal qualities typical of rural people esp. of the southern U.S.: *down-home cooking; down-home hospitality.*

down′ pay′ment, *n.* [*count*] an initial amount given as partial payment at the time of purchase.

down•pour (doun′pôr′, -pōr′) /ˈdawnˌpɔr, -ˌpowr/ *n.* [*count*] a heavy, drenching rain: *I got caught in a bad downpour.*

down•right (doun′rīt′) /ˈdawnˌrayt/ *adv.* **1.** completely; thoroughly: *She's downright angry.* **—*adj.*** [*before a noun*] **2.** thorough; absolute: *She told a downright lie.* **3.** frank; straightforward: *He's a downright kind of guy.* **—down′right′ness,** *n.* [*noncount*]

down•scale (doun′skāl′) /ˈdawnˌskeyl/ *adj., v.,* **-scaled, -scal•ing. —*adj.*** [*usually: before a noun*] **1.** moving toward the lower end of a social or economic scale: *aims its products at downscale customers.* **2.** plain, practical, or inexpensive; not luxurious: *downscale clothing.* **—*v.*** [~ + *obj*] **3.** DOWNSIZE (def. 1). **4.** to make less luxurious or expensive: *They downscaled the store and its product line.*

down•size (doun′sīz′) /ˈdawnˌsayz/ *v.,* **-sized, siz•ing. 1.** [~ + *obj*] to manufacture a smaller type of (a car): *Car manufacturers began to downsize their cars.* **2.** to reduce the number of; cut back: [~ + *obj*]: *The plant downsized its staff.* [*no obj*]: *The company will have to downsize to cut costs.*

Down's′ syn′drome, *n.* [*noncount*] Also, **Down syndrome.** a condition from birth of mental retardation and the development of a flat forehead.

down•stairs (*adv., n.* doun′stârz′; *adj.* -stârz′) / *adv., n.* ˈdawnˈstɛərz; *adj.* -ˌstɛərz/ *adv.* **1.** down the stairs; to or on a lower floor: *Come on downstairs and let's go out.* **—*adj.*** **2.** Also, **down′stair′.** [*before a noun*] relating to or situated on a lower floor, esp. the ground floor: *my downstairs neighbor.* **—*n.*** [*noncount; used with a singular verb*] **3.** the lower floor or floors of a building or their furnishings: *Downstairs has been dusted.*

down•state (*n., adv.* doun′stāt′; *adj.* -stāt′) / *n., adv.* 'dawn'steyt; *adj.* -ˌsteyt/ *n.* [*noncount*] **1.** the southern part of a U.S. state. **—*adj.*** **2.** located in or characteristic of this part: *the downstate regions.* **—*adv.*** **3.** in or to the downstate area: *campaigning downstate.*

down•stream (doun′strēm′) /'dawn'striym/ *adv.* **1.** in the direction of the current of a stream. **—*adj.*** **2.** relating to the later part of a process: *attempting to secure downstream financing.*

down•swing (doun′swing′) /'dawnˌswɪŋ/ *n.* [*count*] **1.** a downward swing, such as of a golf club. **2.** a downward trend, such as of business.

down′-to-earth′, *adj.* practical and realistic: *a down-to-earth approach to life.*

down•town (doun′toun′) /'dawn'tawn/ *adv.* **1.** to or in the main business section of a city: *This train goes downtown.* **—*adj.*** [*before a noun*] **2.** situated in, or relating to, the downtown section of a city: *the downtown area.* **—*n.*** [*noncount*] **3.** the downtown section of a city: *trying to rebuild the downtown of the city.*

down•trod•den (doun′trod′n) /'dawnˌtrɒdn̩/ also **down′trod′,** *adj.* harshly ruled; oppressed: *tried to help the downtrodden masses.*

down•turn (doun′tûrn′) /'dawnˌtɜrn/ *n.* [*count*] **1.** an act or instance of turning down, or the state of being turned down: *the downturn of a lower lip.* **2.** a downward trend; decline: *another economic downturn.*

down′ un′der, *adv.* in or to Australia or New Zealand.

down•ward (doun′wərd) /'dawnwərd/ *adv.* **1.** Also, **down′wards.** from a higher to a lower level or condition: *The car sank downward in the muddy river.* **2.** facing down: *She was lying face downward in the sand.* **3.** from a past time to the present: *The estate was handed downward from generation to generation.* **—*adj.*** [*before a noun*] **4.** moving to a lower level or condition: *a downward trend in the economy.*

down•wind (doun′wind′) /'dawn'wɪnd/ *adv.* **1.** in the direction toward which the wind is blowing: *We coasted downwind.* **2.** on or toward the side past which the wind has blown: *The elephant stood downwind of us and caught our scent.* **—*adj.*** **3.** moving or situated downwind.

down•y (dou′nē) /'dawniy/ *adj.*, **-i•er, -i•est.** **1.** of or like down: *downy pillows.* **2.** covered with down.

dow•ry (dou′rē) /'dawriy/ *n.* [*count*], *pl.* **-ries.** the money, goods, etc., that a wife brings to her husband at marriage.

dowse[1] (dous) /daws/ *v.*, **dowsed, dows•ing.** DOUSE.

dowse[2] (douz) /dawz/ *v.* [*no obj*], **dowsed, dows•ing.** to search for underground sources of water, metal, etc., using a divining rod.

-dox-, *root.* -*dox*- comes from Greek, where it has the meaning "opinion, idea, belief." This meaning is found in such words as: DOXOLOGY, ORTHODOX.

dox•ol•o•gy (dok sol′ə jē) /dɒk'sɒlədʒiy/ *n.* [*count*], *pl.* **-gies.** a hymn or short formula expressing praise to God. See -DOX-, -LOG-.

doy•en (doi en′, doi′ən, dwä yen′) /dɔy'ɛn, 'dɔyən, dwɑ'yɛn/ *n.* [*count*], *pl.* **doy•ens** (doi enz′, doi′ənz, dwä-yen′) /dɔy'ɛnz, 'dɔyənz, dw'yɛn/. the senior man, as in age or experience, of a group or profession: *He was the doyen of the press corps in Moscow.*

doy•enne (doi en′, doi′ən, dwä yen′) /dɔy'ɛn, 'dɔyən, dwɑ'yɛn/ *n.* [*count*], *pl.* **doy•ennes** (doi enz′, dwä yen′) /dɔy'ɛnz, dwɑ'yɛn/. the senior woman, as in age or experience, of a group or profession: *She was the doyenne of the press corps covering the Pentagon.*

doz., an abbreviation of: dozen.

doze (dōz) /dowz/ *v.*, **dozed, doz•ing,** *n.* **—*v.*** **1.** [*no obj*] to sleep lightly and briefly; nap: *dozing in the hammock when I called.* **2.** [*no obj;* (~ + *off*)] to fall into a light sleep unintentionally: *The students couldn't help but doze off during my lecture.* **3.** to pass (time) in napping: [~ + *away* + *obj*]: *to doze away the afternoon.* [~ + *obj* + *away*]: *to doze the afternoon away.* **—*n.*** [*count*] **4.** a nap.

doz•en (duz′ən) /'dʌzən/ *n., pl.* **doz•ens,** (*as after a numeral*) **doz•en,** *adj.* **—*n.*** **1.** a group of 12: [*count*]: *I'll have a dozen eggs.* [*after a number or measurement word; no plural*]: *I'll have two dozen eggs.* **—*adj.*** **2.** containing 12 parts.

DPT or **DTP,** an abbreviation of: diphtheria, tetanus, pertussis: a vaccine against these diseases.

Dr., an abbreviation of: **1.** Doctor. **2.** Drive (used in street names).

drab (drab) /dræb/ *adj.*, **drab•ber, drab•best,** *n.* **—*adj.*** **1.** lacking in brightness; dull: *a drab, cheerless office.* **2.** of the color drab. **—*n.*** [*noncount*] **3.** a brownish gray. **4.** any of several fabrics of this color. **—drab′ness,** *n.* [*noncount*]

draft (draft) /dræft/ *n.* **1.** [*count*] a drawing, sketch, or design: *The architect showed us a draft of her design.* **2.** [*count*] an early version of a writing that may be revised: *The first draft of the paper had some mistakes.* **3.** [*count*] a current of air in any enclosed space, esp. in a room: *I shivered as I felt a draft on my neck.* **4.** [*count*] a device for regulating the current of air in a fireplace, etc. **5.** [*count*] the taking of supplies or money from a source: *He wrote a draft for $100 for his cousin.* **6.** [*count; usually singular*] a selection of persons, as by lot, for military service, an athletic team, etc. **7.** [*count*] beer or ale drawn from a keg: *a glass of draft.* **8.** [*count*] an act of drinking or inhaling. **9.** [*count*] something drunk; a drink. **—*v.*** [~ + *obj*] **10.** to sketch: *She drafted her plans for the park.* **11.** to compose: *I drafted my speech.* **12.** to select by draft, such as for military service: *He was drafted and sent off early in the war.* **—*adj.*** [*before a noun*] **13.** used for pulling loads: *a draft horse.* **14.** drawn from a keg: *draft beer.* **15.** being in the early stages: *It's only a draft proposal.* **—*Idiom.*** **16. on draft,** available to be drawn from a keg: *beer on draft.* Also, *esp. Brit.*, **draught** (for defs. 1, 3, 4, 7–11, 13–16).

draft•ee (draf tē′) /dræf'tiy/ *n.* [*count*], *pl.* **-ees.** a person who is drafted for military service.

drafts•man (drafts′mən) /'dræftsmən/ *n.* [*count*], *pl.* **-men.** **1.** a person employed in making mechanical drawings. **2.** an artist skilled in drawing: *Matisse was a superb draftsman.* **—drafts′man•ship′,** *n.* [*noncount*]

draft•y (draf′tē) /'dræftiy/ *adj.*, **-i•er, -i•est.** characterized by uncomfortable currents of air: *We had to work in a cold, drafty room.* Also, *esp. Brit.*, **draughty.** **—draft′i•ness,** *n.* [*noncount*]

drag (drag) /dræg/ *v.*, **dragged, drag•ging,** *n., adj.* **—*v.*** **1.** [~ + *obj*] to pull slowly and with effort; haul: *dragged his injured foot behind him.* **2.** [*no obj*] to be pulled along; to move heavily or slowly and with great effort: *The bride's long dress began to drag along the ground.* **3.** [~ + *obj*] to search (a lake, etc.) with a net or hook: *began to drag the lake for bodies.* **4.** [~ + *obj*] to introduce or put in: *He drags his war stories into every conversation.* **5.** to (cause to) go on for too long a time: [*no obj*]: *The discussion dragged on for hours.* [~ + *obj* + *out*]: *They dragged the discussion out for three hours.* [~ + *out* + *obj*]: *to drag out a discussion.* **6.** [*no obj*] to feel listless and exhausted; to move in such a manner: *This heat has everyone dragging around.* **7.** [~ + *obj*] to pull (a graphic image) from one place to another on a computer monitor: *Drag the icon and release it.* **8.** [*no obj*] to lag behind: *He's dragging behind in the race.* **9.** [~ + *on* + *obj*] to take a puff: *to drag on a cigarette.* **10.** to bring up (an issue) unfairly: [~ + *up* + *obj*]: *They keep dragging up my past.* [~ + *obj* + *up*]: *They dragged those old stories up again.* **—*n.*** **11.** [*count*] a device for dragging the bottom of a body of water to recover objects. **12.** [*count*] a heavy frame drawn over the ground to smooth it. **13.** [*count*] someone or something that keeps one from achieving some goal: *He felt his wife had been a drag on his career as an actor.* **14.** [*count; usually: a* + ~] *Slang.* someone or something boring or uninteresting: *This party's a drag.* **15.** [*noncount*] the force in the air on a wing in motion through the air that tends to reduce its forward motion; resistance. **16.** [*count*] a puff on a cigarette, pipe, etc.: *He took a drag on a cigarette.* **17.** [*noncount*] *Slang.* clothing usually worn by the opposite sex: *He went to the dance in drag, wearing a dress and high heel shoes.* **18.** [*noncount*] *Slang.* influence; clout. **—*adj.*** **19.** *Slang.* associated with the opposite sex; transvestite.

drag•gy (drag′ē) /'drægiy/ *adj.*, **-gi•er, -gi•est.** **1.** tending to drag; sluggish: *I feel draggy; maybe I've got a fever.* **2.** boring; dull: *a draggy meeting.*

drag•net (drag′net′) /'drægˌnɛt/ *n.* [*count*] **1.** a net to be drawn along the bottom of a stream to catch fish, or along the ground for small game. **2.** an interlinked or connected system for finding or catching someone: *an international dragnet to catch the terrorist.*

drag•on (drag′ən) /'drægən/ *n.* [*count*] **1.** an imaginary monster that was supposed to be a huge winged reptile, often spouting fire. **2.** a fierce, combative person.

drag•on•fly (dragʹən flīʹ) /ˈdrægən,flay/ *n.* [*count*], *pl.* **-flies.** a nonstinging insect having the wings open when at rest.

dra•goon (drə gōōnʹ) /drəˈguwn/ *n.* [*count*] **1.** a member of a unit of soldiers on horseback. **—***v.* [~ + *obj* + *into*] **2.** to force (someone); coerce: *I was dragooned into helping the students register.*

dragʹ raceʹ, *n.* [*count*] a race between two or more automobiles starting from a standstill.

drain (drān) /dreyn/ *v.* **1.** to empty by drawing off liquid: [~ + *obj*]: *to drain a swamp.* [~ + *obj* (+ *of* + *obj*)]: *Drain the wound (of blood) before you apply the bandage.* [*no obj*]: *The crankcase has to drain before you put on the new filter.* **2.** [~ + *obj*] to empty by drinking: *He drained his glass in one huge swallow.* **3.** [~ + *obj* (+ *of* + *obj*)] to use up the resources of: *He drained his parents of every cent they had.* **—***n.* [*count*] **4.** a pipe or other device that allows a liquid to drain: *The drains are probably clogged.* **5.** something that causes a large outflow or depletion: *These constant doctor bills are a drain on our finances.* **—*Idiom.* 6. go down the drain,** to become without profit; be wasted: *All my work went down the drain because I didn't have time to finish.* **—drainʹer,** *n.* [*count*]

drain•age (drāʹnij) /ˈdreynɪdʒ/ *n.* [*noncount*] **1.** the act or process of draining: *The drainage in this area is sluggish.* **2.** a system of drains: *The drainage in the house is too old.* **3.** something drained off: *the drainage from the wound.*

drain•pipe (drānʹpīpʹ) /ˈdreyn,payp/ *n.* [*count*] a large pipe that carries away what comes out of waste and soil pipes.

drake (drāk) /dreyk/ *n.* [*count*] a male duck. Compare DUCK[1] (def. 2).

dram (dram) /dræm/ *n.* [*count*] **1. a.** a unit of apothecaries' weight, equal to 60 grains, or ⅛ of an ounce (3.89 grams). **b.** 1/16 of an ounce in avoirdupois weight (27.34 grains; 1.77 grams). **2.** a small drink of liquor. **3.** a small amount of anything.

dra•ma (dräʹmə, dramʹə) /ˈdrɑmə, ˈdræmə/ *n., pl.* **-mas. 1.** [*count*] a presentation in dialogue and action of a story involving conflict of characters, to be performed on the stage; play: *historical dramas.* **2.** [*noncount*] dramatic art or literature in general: *Lovers of drama will hate this play.* **3.** [*noncount*] an event or series of events having conflicting elements: *the drama of the election year.*

dra•mat•ic (drə matʹik) /drəˈmætɪk/ *adj.* **1.** [*before a noun*] of or relating to the drama: *important dramatic elements in the play.* **2.** involving conflict or difference; vivid: *dramatic colors.* **3.** highly effective or compelling: *a dramatic silence.* **—dra•matʹi•cal•ly,** *adv.*

dra•mat•ics (drə matʹiks) /drəˈmætɪks/ *n.* **1.** [*noncount; used with a singular verb*] the art of producing or acting dramas: *Dramatics is challenging.* **2.** [*plural; used with a plural verb*] dramatic productions, esp. by amateurs: *Our dramatics are simple affairs.* **3.** [*plural; used with a plural verb*] overly emotional or insincere behavior: *Then the tears and the dramatics started.*

dram•a•tist (dramʹə tist, dräʹmə-) /ˈdræmətɪst, ˈdrɑmə-/ *n.* [*count*] a writer of dramas; playwright.

dram•a•tize (dramʹə tīzʹ, dräʹmə-) /ˈdræmə,tayz, ˈdrɑmə-/ *v.,* **-tized, -tiz•ing. 1.** [~ + *obj*] to put (a piece of writing) into a form suitable for acting: *They dramatized the biography of the baseball star.* **2.** to express (something) in a vivid manner; present in a dramatic way: [*no obj*]: *I think you're overly dramatizing: she merely brushed against you.* [~ + *obj*]: *The reporters are dramatizing the small disagreement we had.* **—dram•a•ti•za•tion** (dramʹə tə zāʹshən, dräʹmə-) /ˌdræmətəˈzeyʃən, ˌdrɑmə-/ *n.* [*count*]: *The book had undergone several dramatizations.*

drank (drangk) /dræŋk/ *v.* a pt. and pp. of DRINK.

drape (drāp) /dreyp/ *v.* [~ + *obj*], **draped, drap•ing,** *n.* **—***v.* **1.** to cover or hang with cloth, esp. in graceful folds: *pictures draped with ribbons.* **2.** to adjust (fabric, etc.) into graceful folds: *carefully draped the fabric over the lectern.* **3.** to arrange, hang, or let fall carelessly: *to drape a towel on a doorknob.* **—***n.* [*count*] **4.** a curtain, usually of heavy fabric and long length, esp. one of a pair drawn open and shut across or hung at the sides of a window.

dra•per•y (drāʹpə rē) /ˈdreypəriy/ *n., pl.* **-per•ies. 1.** [*noncount*] coverings of fabric, esp. as arranged in loose, graceful folds. **2.** Usually, **draperies.** [*plural*] long curtains, often of heavy fabric. **3.** [*noncount*] cloths or textile fabrics thought of as a group. **4.** [*noncount*] *Brit.* the stock, shop, or business of someone who sells drapes or drapery.

dras•tic (drasʹtik) /ˈdræstɪk/ *adj.* acting with force or violence; violent: *We keep facing drastic cuts in spending.* **—drasʹti•cal•ly,** *adv.*: *kept cutting the budget drastically.*

draught (draft) /dræft/ *n., v., adj. Chiefly Brit.* DRAFT.

draught•y (drafʹtē, dräfʹ-) /ˈdræftiy, ˈdrɑf-/ *adj.,* **draught•i•er, draught•i•est.** *Chiefly Brit.* DRAFTY.

draw (drô) /drɔ/ *v.,* **drew** (drōō) /druw/ **drawn, draw•ing,** *n.* **—***v.* **1.** to (cause to) move in a particular direction by or as if by pulling; drag: [~ + *obj* + *along*]: *The horses drew the cart along.* [~ + *along*]: *The car drew slowly along the street.* [~ + *obj* + *away*]: *I drew her away from the crowd.* [*no obj;* ~ + *away*]: *She drew away from me.* [*no obj;* ~ + *in*]: *The car drew in to the curb.* [~ + *obj* + *in*]: *He drew the car in to the side and stopped.* [*no obj;* ~ + *out*]: *The car drew out into the traffic.* [~ + *obj* + *out*]: *I drew the car out into the middle lane.* [*no obj;* ~ + *off*]: *The train drew off before I could signal the conductor.* **2.** [~ + *obj* (+ *from* + *obj*)] to bring, take, or pull out, such as from a source: *to draw water from a well.* **3.** [~ + *obj*] to cause to come toward oneself; attract: *The sale drew large crowds.* **4.** to compose or create (something) in words or pictures; depict: [~ + *obj*]: *to draw a lifelike portrait.* [*no obj*]: *I really can't draw.* **5.** [~ + *obj*] to frame or formulate; figure out: *to draw a distinction.* **6.** to suck in; take (a breath) in: [~ + *obj*]: *to draw liquid through a straw.* [~ + *in* + *obj*]: *I drew in a deep breath to calm down.* **7.** [~ + *obj*] to produce; bring in: *The deposits draw interest.* **8.** to bend (a bow) by pulling back the string to shoot an arrow: [~ + *obj*]: *The archers drew their bows all at once.* [*no obj*]: *The archers all drew at once.* **9. a.** [~ + *obj*] to choose by or as if by lottery: *He was unlucky enough to draw kitchen cleanup twice in one week.* **b.** [~ + *obj*] to pick at random, as from among marked slips of paper or numbered tickets: *to draw straws to see who wins.* **c.** [*no obj*] to hold a lottery or the like: *to draw for prizes.* **10.** [~ + *obj*] (of a vessel) to need (a specific depth of water) to float: *The boat draws six feet.* **11.** to finish (a contest) with neither side winning; tie: [~ + *obj*]: *They drew the game at 37-37.* [*no obj*]: *They drew at 37-37.* **12.** [~ + *obj*] to take or be given (a playing card) from the pack: *I drew two sevens.* **13.** [~ + *obj*] to steep (tea) in boiling water: *She drew a nice pot of tea for us.* **14.** [*no obj*] to move or pass, esp. slowly or continuously: *The day draws near.* **15.** to take out a weapon for action: [~ + *obj*]: *He drew his gun quickly and fired.* [*no obj*]: *She drew and fired in one smooth motion.* **16. draw away,** [*no obj*] to move farther ahead: *One runner drew away from the pack.* **17. draw in, a.** [~ + *obj* + *in*] to cause to take part: *This is your fight; don't draw me in.* **b.** to make a sketch or drawing of: [~ + *in* + *obj*]: *to draw in a human figure.* [~ + *obj* + *in*]: *Draw it in with charcoal.* **18. draw off,** to move back or away: [~ + *off* + *obj*]: *He drew off the enemy.* [~ + *obj* + *off*]: *He drew the enemy off.* **19. draw on, a.** [*no obj*] to come nearer; approach: *Winter was drawing on.* **b.** to clothe oneself in: [~ + *on* + *obj*]: *to draw on one's gloves.* [~ + *obj* + *on*]: *He drew his gloves on.* **c.** [~ + *on* + *obj*] to use esp. as a source: *The newspaper article draws heavily on gossip.* **20. draw out, a.** to pull out; remove: [~ + *out* + *obj*]: *The dentist drew out the tooth.* [~ + *obj* + *out*]: *The dentist drew the tooth out.* **b.** to stretch out the time of; lengthen: [~ + *out* + *obj*]: *They told me to draw out my speech for as long as possible.* [~ + *obj* + *out*]: *I drew it out for as long as I could.* **c.** [~ + *obj* + *out*] to persuade to speak: *The police carefully drew the child out and learned what had happened.* **d.** [~ + *out* + *obj*] to get (information) from someone: *We finally drew out the truth from her.* **e.** to take (money) from a place of deposit: [~ + *out* + *obj*]: *We drew out $5,000 as the down payment.* [~ + *obj* + *out*]: *We drew some money out of our savings.* **21. draw up, a.** to write in legal form: [~ + *up* + *obj*]: *to draw up a contract.* [~ + *obj* + *up*]: *We drew the agreement up quickly.* **b.** to put into position; arrange in order: [*no obj*]: *The army drew up into its positions and waited.* [~ + *obj* + *up*]: *The general drew them up to the front lines.* **c.** [~ + *oneself* + *up*] to make (oneself) stand as straight or as tall as one can: *He drew himself up to his full height.* **d.** to bring or come to a stop; halt: [*no obj*]: *The bus drew up to the curb.* [~ + *obj* + *up*]: *The driver drew the bus up to the curb.* **—***n.* [*count*] **22.** an act of drawing. **23.** something that attracts customers, etc.: *That famous movie star is a big Hollywood draw.* **24.** something chosen at random, as a lot or chance: *a lottery draw.* **25.** a contest that ends in a tie: *The game ended in a draw.* —***Idiom.*** **26. beat someone to the draw,** to react more quickly than (an opponent): *We beat them to the draw and got our proposal in first.* **27. be the luck of the draw,** to be the result of chance: *It was the luck of the draw that I went first.*

draw•back (drô′bak′) /ˈdrɔˌbæk/ *n.* [*count*] an undesirable feature; disadvantage: *The cost was one of the drawbacks.*

draw•bridge (drô′brij′) /ˈdrɔˌbrɪdʒ/ *n.* [*count*] a bridge in which a section may be raised, lowered, or drawn aside, to leave a passage open for boats, barges, etc.

draw•er (drôr *for 1, 2;* drô′ər *for 3*) /drɔr *for 1, 2;* ˈdrɔər *for 3* / *n.* [*count*] **1.** a sliding horizontal container, such as in a file cabinet, that may be drawn out or pushed back in: *He opened the drawer of his file cabinet and pulled out the papers he needed.* See illustration at OFFICE. **2. drawers,** [*plural*] a garment with legs that covers the lower half of the body, esp. an undergarment. **3.** a person or thing that draws.

draw•ing (drô′ing) /ˈdrɔɪŋ/ *n.* **1.** [*count*] the act of a person or thing that draws. **2.** [*count*] a graphic representation by lines of an object or idea; a sketch or design, esp. one made with pen, pencil, or crayon: *He had a drawing of the bank vault in his pocket.* **3.** [*noncount*] the art or technique of making these: *I'm terrible at drawing.* **4.** [*count*] the selection of the winning chance sold by lottery or raffle: *We'll have a drawing at the end of the party.*

draw′ing card′, *n.* [*count*] a person or thing that attracts patrons: *The main drawing card is the tenor.*

draw′ing room′, *n.* [*count*] a formal reception room, esp. in an apartment or private house.

drawl (drôl) /drɔl/ *v.* **1.** to speak in a slow manner: [*no obj*]: *She drawled in that slow, lazy style of hers.* [~ + *obj*]: *She drawled a greeting to me.* —*n.* [*count*] **2.** an act of, or example of, speaking by drawling: *She had that drawl of the deep South.*

drawn (drôn) /drɔn/ *v.* **1.** pp. of DRAW. —*adj.* **2.** tense; looking tired, thin, or unhappy; haggard: *He looked nervous and drawn at the thought of more conflict.*

draw•string or **draw string** (drô′string′) /ˈdrɔˌstrɪŋ/ *n.* [*count*] a cord that closes or gathers something, such as the opening of a bag or garment, when one or both of its ends are pulled.

dray (drā) /drey/ *n.* [*count*] a low strong cart without sides, used for carrying heavy loads.

dread (dred) /drɛd/ *v.* **1.** [~ + *obj*] to fear greatly: *to dread death.* **2.** to be very reluctant to experience: [~ + *obj*]: *I dread the thought of arriving late.* [~ + *verb-ing*]: *I dreaded coming in late to meetings.* [~ + *to* + *think*]: *I dread to think what will happen next.* —*n.* **3.** [*noncount*] terror or apprehension about the future: *filled with horror and dread.* **4.** [*noncount*] a person or thing dreaded: *the dread of being late for the exam.* **5. dreads,** [*plural*] DREADLOCKS. —*adj.* [*before a noun*] **6.** greatly feared; frightful; terrible: *a dread disease.* —**dread′ed,** *adj.*

dread•ful (dred′fəl) /ˈdrɛdfəl/ *adj.* **1.** causing great dread, fear, or terror: *a dreadful storm.* **2.** extremely bad, unpleasant, or offensive: *a dreadful scandal; a dreadful smell.*

dread•ful•ly (dred′fəl ē) /ˈdrɛdfəliy/ *adv.* **1.** very; extremely: *It was a dreadfully bad day.* **2.** in a dreadful manner or way: *He drove dreadfully.*

dread•locks (dred′loks′) /ˈdrɛdˌlɒks/ *n.* [*plural*] a hairstyle of many long, ropelike locks.

dream (drēm) /driym/ *n.*, *v.*, **dreamed** or **dreamt** (dremt) /drɛmt/ **dream•ing,** *adj.* —*n.* [*count*] **1.** a sequence of images passing through the mind during sleep: *I had another dream about living abroad.* **2.** [*usually: singular; a* + ~] a state of the mind in which one does not pay attention to one's surroundings: *He's walking around in a dream these days.* **3.** a reverie about the future; reverie: *her dream of riches and success.* **4.** a goal; aim; hope; aspiration: *It had always been our dream to take the children to Europe.* **5.** something of unreal or striking excellence: *The sports car is a dream to drive.* —*v.* **6.** [*no obj*] to have a dream. **7.** to see or imagine in sleep or in a vision: [~ + *obj*]: *We dream all sorts of dreams.* [~ + *(that) clause*]: *I dreamed that a monster was chasing me.* [~ + *of/about* + *obj*]: *I dreamed of you last night.* **8.** to be lost in thought; pass (time) in dreaming: [*no obj*]: *Stop dreaming and get back to work.* [~ + *away* + *obj*]: *He's dreaming away his days.* [~ + *obj* + *away*]: *He's dreaming his days away.* **9. dream of,** [~ + *of* + *obj*] to consider, think about, or give serious thought to: *I wouldn't dream of leaving this great job.* **10. dream up,** to create or form in the imagination; conceive: [~ + *up* + *obj*]: *He dreamed up a new plan to save money.* [~ + *obj* + *up*]: *He dreamed the whole thing up.* —*adj.* [*before a noun*] **11.** most desirable; ideal: *a dream vacation.* —**dream′er,** *n.* [*count*]: *He was too much of a dreamer for the business world.* —**dream′less,** *adj.* —**dream′like′,** *adj.*

dream•y (drē′mē) /ˈdriymiy/ *adj.*, **-i•er, -i•est. 1.** vague; dim: *a dreamy memory of what had happened.* **2.** inducing dreams or a dreamlike mood, esp. pleasantly: *dreamy music.* **3.** given to daydreaming: *a soft-hearted, dreamy romantic.* **4.** wonderful: *a dreamy new car.* —**dream•i•ly** (drē′mə lē) /ˈdriyməliy/ *adv.*

drear•y (drēr′ē) /ˈdrɪəriy/ *adj.*, **-i•er, -i•est.** gloomy; depressing; cheerless: *a cold, dreary winter day in the north.* —**drear•i•ly** (drēr′ə lē) /ˈdrɪərəliy/ *adv.* —**drear′i•ness,** *n.* [*noncount*]

dredge (drej) /drɛdʒ/ *n.*, *v.*, **dredged, dredg•ing.** —*n.* [*count*] **1.** a powerful machine for removing earth, as by a scoop. —*v.* [~ + *obj*] **2.** to clear out with a dredge: *to dredge a river.* **3.** to remove (sand, etc.) from the bottom of a body of water: *to dredge the sand from the river bottom.* **4. dredge up,** to discover and reveal; unearth: [~ + *up* + *obj*]: *The media dredged up yet another scandal.* [~ + *obj* + *up*]: *to dredge stories up.* —**dredg′er,** *n.* [*count*]

dreg (dreg) /drɛg/ *n.* [*count*] **1. dregs,** [*plural*] the last part of liquid left in a container; grounds: *drank the dregs of his coffee.* **2.** Usually, **dregs.** [*plural*] the least valuable part of anything: *the dregs of society.*

drench (drench) /drɛntʃ/ *v.* [~ + *obj*] **1.** to wet thoroughly; soak: *I was drenched after the walk in the rain.* **2.** to cover or fill completely; bathe: *sunlight drenching the trees.* —**drench′ing,** *adj.*: *a drenching rainfall.*

dress (dres) /drɛs/ *n.* **1.** [*count*] an outer garment for women and girls, made up of an upper part and a skirt: *a beautiful red dress.* See illustration at CLOTHING. **2.** [*noncount*] clothing; clothes; garb, esp. those representative of a group of people: *The folk dancers appeared in the national dress of their country.* **3.** [*noncount*] formal clothing: *evening dress.* —*adj.* [*before a noun*] **4.** of or for a dress or dresses: *dress material for the gown.* **5.** of or for a formal occasion: *a full dress uniform.* **6.** requiring formal dress: *a dress reception.* —*v.* **7.** to put clothing on or upon; clothe: [*no obj*]: *I was dressing when the phone rang.* [~ + *oneself*]: *She was dressing herself in her mother's old wedding gown.* [~ + *obj*]: *Let's dress the kids or we'll never be on time.* **8.** [*no obj*] to put on or wear clothes of a specified sort: *dressed in their best clothes and went down to dinner.* **9.** [~ + *obj*] to decorate; trim: *to dress a store window.* **10.** [~ + *obj*] to comb out and do up (hair). **11.** [~ + *obj*] to trim and remove the inedible parts of (fowl, game, etc.) in preparation for cooking. **12.** [~ + *obj*] to pour a dressing on: *to dress a salad with oil and vinegar.* **13.** [~ + *obj*] to apply medication or a dressing to (a wound): *The nurse dressed the wound expertly.* **14. dress down, a.** to scold; yell at; reprimand: [~ + *down* + *obj*]: *The general dressed down the troops.* [~ + *obj* + *down*]: *He dressed them down for the awful performance.* **b.** [*no obj*] to dress informally or less formally: *His habit is to dress down for parties.* **15. dress up, a.** [*no obj*] to put on one's best or fanciest clothing: *I'll go to church if I don't have to dress up.* **b.** to dress in costume: [~ + *oneself* + *up*]: *He dressed himself up as a pirate.* [~ + *obj* + *up*]: *We dressed him up as a ghost.* [*no obj*]: *likes to dress up in her mother's hat and heels.* **c.** [~ + *up* + *obj*] to make more appealing or acceptable: *He dressed up some of those facts and figures.* —**Usage.** As a verb, DRESS has two important meanings with respect to clothes. One meaning is "to put clothes on," as in *I can dress quickly in the mornings. I get dressed quickly in the mornings.* This is similar to the expression PUT ON: *I put on my clothes quickly in the morning.* Another meaning of DRESS is "to wear clothes," as in *They dressed simply and casually.* However, it is more natural to say *They were dressed simply and casually (in their comfortable clothes)*; see DRESSED below. Note that the phrase *be dressed in* is closer to the meaning of WEAR: *They were dressed in their comfortable clothes.* (= *They wore their comfortable clothes).*

dres•sage (drə säzh′) /drəˈsɑʒ/ *n.* [*noncount*] the art of training a horse in precision of movement.

dress′ cir′cle, *n.* [*count*] the first rows of raised seats in a theater set apart for spectators in evening dress.

dressed (drest) /drɛst/ *adj.* **1.** [*be* + ~] wearing clothes: *You can come in now; I'm dressed.* **2.** [*be* + ~ + *in*] wearing the clothes mentioned: *They were dressed in* *their Sunday best.* **3.** having put on clothes: *was dressed and ready to go.* **—Usage.** See DRESS.

dress•er[1] (dres′ər) /ˈdrɛsər/ *n.* [*count*] **1.** a person who dresses. **2.** a person who dresses in a particular manner: *a fancy dresser.*

dress•er[2] (dres′ər) /ˈdrɛsər/ *n.* [*count*] **1.** a chest of drawers; bureau. See illustration at APARTMENT. **2.** a sideboard for dishes and cooking utensils.

dress•ing (dres′ing) /ˈdrɛsɪŋ/ *n.* **1.** a sauce, esp. for salad or other cold foods: [*noncount*]: *Do you like dressing on your salad?* [*count*]: *I'd like a turkey, chicken, or other fowl: turkey dressing.* **2.** [*noncount*] stuffing for a turkey, chicken, or other fowl: *turkey dressing.* **3.** [*count*] material used to dress or cover a wound while it heals: *The doctor will change the dressing.*

dress′ing-down′, *n.* [*count*] a severe scolding or reprimand.

dress′ing gown′, *n.* [*count*] a robe worn over one's sleeping garments.

dress•mak•er (dres′mā′kər) /ˈdrɛsˌmeykər/ *n.* [*count*] **1.** a person whose occupation is the making or adjusting of dresses, coats, etc. *—adj.* [*before a noun*] **2.** (of women's clothing) having soft lines and fine detail. **—dress′mak′ing,** *n.* [*noncount*]

dress′ rehears′al, *n.* [*count*] a rehearsal of a play as if for a performance, often the final rehearsal.

dress•y (dres′ē) /ˈdrɛsiy/ *adj.,* **-i•er, -i•est. 1.** proper or appropriate to more formal or festive occasions: *This blouse is too dressy for the office.* **2.** fancy or stylish: *a dressy reception.* **—dress′i•ness,** *n.* [*noncount*]

drew (dro͞o) /druw/ *v.* pt. of DRAW.

drib•ble (drib′əl) /ˈdrɪbəl/ *v.,* **-bled, -bling,** *n.* *—v.* **1.** to (cause to) flow in drops; trickle: [*no obj*]: *A little milk dribbled onto the floor.* [~ + *obj*]: *He dribbled some milk onto the cereal.* **2.** [*no obj*] (of saliva) to trickle from the mouth; drivel; slaver: *The baby was dribbling over her new dress.* **3.** to (cause to) move along a ball, by bouncing it: [*no obj*]: *She dribbled down the court, then rushed to the basket and shot.* [~ + *obj*]: *He dribbled the ball down the court.* *—n.* **4.** [*count*] a small trickling stream or a drop: *a dribble of water.* **5.** [*count*] a small quantity of anything: *a dribble of revenue.* **6.** [*noncount*] saliva that has come out of the mouth: *He wiped away some dribble from the baby's mouth.* **7.** [*count*] an act or instance of dribbling a ball or puck. **—drib′bler,** *n.* [*count*]

dribs and drabs (dribz′ən drabz′) /ˈdrɪbzənˈdræbz/ *n.* [*plural*] small, irregular amounts or numbers at a time: *He repaid the loan in dribs and drabs over a period of years.*

dried (drīd) /drayd/ *v.* pt. and pp. of DRY.

dri•er[1] (drī′ər) /ˈdrayər/ *n.* **1.** one that dries. **2.** DRYER (def. 1).

dri•er[2] (drī′ər) /ˈdrayər/ *adj.* comparative of DRY.

dri•est (drī′ist) /ˈdrayɪst/ *adj.* superlative of DRY.

drift (drift) /drɪft/ *n.* **1.** [*count*] a driving movement, as of a current of water: *a drift of some 10 to 15 miles a day.* **2.** [*count*] the course along which something moves: *a drift toward the political right.* **3.** [*count; usually singular*] a meaning; intent: *I get your drift (= I understand your meaning or intent).* **4.** [*count*] a heap of matter driven together: *Huge drifts of snow had accumulated overnight.* **5.** [*noncount*] CONTINENTAL DRIFT. *—v.* **6.** to (cause to) be carried along, by or as if by currents of water: [*no obj*]: *The boat drifted out to sea.* [~ + *obj*]: *The current drifted the boat out to sea.* **7.** [*no obj*] to wander without aim: *Some people just drift through life.* **8.** to (cause to) be driven into heaps: [*no obj*]: *The snow drifted into huge mounds overnight.* [~ + *obj*]: *The wind drifted the snow into huge mounds.*

drift•er (drif′tər) /ˈdrɪftər/ *n.* [*count*] **1.** a person or thing that drifts. **2.** a person who goes from one place, job, etc., to another but stays in each only briefly: *The drifter didn't say much, and didn't stay long.*

drift•wood (drift′wo͝od′) /ˈdrɪftˌwʊd/ *n.* [*noncount*] **1.** wood floating in water or washed ashore. **2.** such wood used in interior decoration.

drill[1] (dril) /drɪl/ *n.* **1.** [*count*] a tool with a cutting edge for making holes in firm materials, esp. by rotation: *an electric drill.* **2.** [*noncount*] *Military.* training in marching or other movements. **3. a.** [*count*] any practice or exercise, esp. for emergencies: *During the fire drill we all marched outside.* **b.** any repetitive or mechanical training or exercise: [*count*]: *a spelling drill.* [*noncount*]: *Latin lessons should be less drill and more fun.* **4.** [*count*] the correct or customary manner of proceeding: *figuring out the family's drill for dinner.* *—v.* **5.** [~ + *obj*] to pierce or bore a hole in (something) with a drill: *The dentist drilled the cavity and filled it.* **6.** to make (a hole) by penetrating or boring: [~ + *obj*]: *The dentist drilled a hole in the tooth.* [~ + *into* + *obj*]: *The dentist drilled into my tooth and cleaned out the cavity.* **7.** [*no obj*] to penetrate deeply beneath the earth to search for deposits of a natural substance: *drilling offshore for oil.* **8.** to instruct and exercise (military trainees) in marching, etc.: [~ + *obj*]: *The sergeant had drilled the men in his company well.* [*no obj*]: *The men had drilled all day and wanted a rest.* **9.** [~ + *obj*] to teach by strict repetition: *The teacher drilled grammar and the multiplication tables every day.* **10.** [~ + *obj*] to train or rehearse (a person) in a discipline, etc., by guided repetition: *The teacher drilled her students in the multiplication tables.* **—drill′er,** *n.* [*count*]

drill[2] (dril) /drɪl/ *n.* [*count*] **1.** a machine for sowing in rows and for covering the seeds when sown. **2.** a row of seeds or plants sown this way.

drill[3] (dril) /drɪl/ *n.* [*noncount*] a strong twilled fabric.

drill•mas•ter (dril′mas′tər) /ˈdrɪlˌmæstər/ *n.* [*count*] **1.** a person who trains others in something, esp. mechanically: *Their teacher was a tough drillmaster.* **2.** a person who instructs in military marching.

dri•ly (drī′lē) /ˈdrayliy/ *adv.* dryly.

drink (dringk) /drɪŋk/ *v.,* **drank** (drangk) /dræŋk/ **drunk** (drungk) /drʌŋk/ or, often, **drank, drink•ing,** *n.* *—v.* **1.** to take liquid into the mouth and swallow it: [~ + *obj*]: *drank some wine with dinner.* [*no obj*]: *He wasn't drinking that night because he was the designated driver.* **2.** [~ + *obj*] to swallow the contents of (a cup, etc.): *She drank a few cans of soda.* **3.** to drink alcoholic drinks, esp. too much and by habit; tipple: [*no obj*]: *It was no secret that he drank.* [~ + *oneself* + *into* + *obj*]: *He drank himself into a stupor.* **4. a.** [~ + *to* + *obj*] to show one's good wishes by swallowing some wine or other drink: *Let's drink to the bride and groom.* **b.** [~ + *obj*] to propose or participate in a toast to (a person or thing); toast: *They drank each other's health.* **5.** to take in through the senses, esp. with eagerness and pleasure: [~ + *in* + *obj*]: *I drank in his every sentence.* [~ + *obj* + *in*]: *drinking the mountain scenery in.* *—n.* **6.** [*count*] a liquid that is swallowed; beverage: *Let me have a drink of soda.* **7.** [*count*] liquor; alcohol: *Let's have our drinks at the bar.* **8.** [*noncount*] too much alcohol: *Drink was his downfall.* **9.** [*count*] a swallow or portion of liquid: *He swallowed a drink of water.* **10. the drink,** [*noncount*] a large body of water, such as a lake or the ocean: *Her teammates threw her in the drink.* **—drink′a•ble,** *adj.* **—drink′er,** *n.* [*count*] **—Related Words.** DRINK is a verb and a noun, DRUNK is a noun and an adjective, and DRUNKEN is an adjective: *He wants to drink some water. He wants a drink of water. He's a drunk. He's drunk again. What do you do with a drunken sailor?*

drip (drip) /drɪp/ *v.,* **dripped, drip•ping,** *n.* *—v.* **1.** [*no obj*] to let drops fall: *This faucet drips.* **2.** to (cause to) fall in drops; dribble: [*no obj*]: *The milk dripped out of the bottle and down her shirt.* [~ + *obj*]: *He dripped some water on her face.* *—n.* **3.** [*noncount*] an act of dripping: *the drip of the rain.* **4.** [*noncount*] liquid that drips: *Wipe the drip of water from your nose.* **5.** [*count; usually singular*] the sound made by falling drops: *the irritating drip of a faucet.* **6.** [*count*] *Slang.* a boring or colorless person: *a blind date with a real drip.* **7.** [*noncount*] the continuous, slow introduction of a fluid into the body, usually into a vein.

drip-dry (drip′drī′; *v. usually* -drī′) /ˈdrɪpˌdray; *v. usually* -ˈdray/ *v.,* **-dried, -dry•ing,** *adj., n., pl.* **-dries.** *—v.* **1.** [*no obj*] (of a garment) to dry unwrinkled when hung dripping wet. **2.** [~ + *obj*] to hang so as to drip-dry: *to drip-dry a shirt.* *—adj.* [*usually: before a noun*] **3.** able to be drip-dried: *drip-dry shirts.* *—n.* **4.** [*count*] something that can be drip-dried.

drip•ping (drip′ing) /ˈdrɪpɪŋ/ *n.* **1.** [*count*] the act of something that drips. **2.** Often, **drippings.** [*plural*] fat and juice from meat in cooking, used for basting. *—adj.* **3.** soaking: *I came out of the shower dripping wet.*

drive (drīv) /drayv/ *v.,* **drove** (drōv) /drowv/ **driv•en** (driv′ən) /ˈdrɪvən/ **driv•ing,** *n.* *—v.* **1.** to send or cause to move by force: [~ + *away* + *obj*]: *to drive away the flies.* [~ + *obj* + *away*]: *to drive the flies away.* **2.** to cause and guide the movement of (a vehicle, etc.); to operate: [~ + *obj*]: *He learned to drive a car at the age of fifteen; drove cattle on the range.* [*no obj*]: *Where did you learn how to drive like that?* **3.** to (cause to) go or be carried in a vehicle: [~ + *obj*]: *Let me drive you home.* [*no obj*]: *We drive to the beach.* **4.** to force to work, do, or act; compel; urge: [~ + *obj*]: *He drove the workers until they* *collapsed.* [~ + *obj* + *to* + *verb*]: *Pride drove him to finish the work on time.* **5.** [~ + *obj*] to carry (business, etc.) vigorously through: *to drive a hard bargain.* **6.** [~ + *obj*] to keep (machinery) going: *The engine drives the propellers.* **7.** [~ + *obj*] to hit, propel, or kick (a ball, etc.) with much force: *The batter drove the next pitch over the fence.* **8.** [~ + *obj*] to move (something) forward, as by hitting or striking: *He drove the nail through the wood with a hammer.* **9.** [*no obj*] to strive vigorously toward a goal or objective: *He kept driving to the top.* **10.** [*no obj*] to go before an impelling force: *The ship drove before the wind.* **11.** [*no obj*] to rush or dash violently: *The rain was driving in our faces.* **12. drive at,** [~ + *at* + *obj*] to intend to convey (a meaning): *I don't understand you; just what are you driving at?* **13. drive off,** to push or send back; repel; stop an attack of: [~ + *off* + *obj*]: *We managed to drive off the next attack.* [~ + *obj* + *off*]: *Somehow we drove them off.* **—*n.*** **14.** [*count*] the act of driving. **15.** [*count*] a trip in a vehicle, esp. for pleasure: *Let's take a drive upstate.* **16.** [*count*] a road for vehicles, such as to a private house. **17.** [*count*] an act of forcing along, such as of cattle: *an old West cattle drive.* **18.** [*count*] an inner urge directed toward satisfying a basic, instinctive need: *one's hunger drive.* **19.** [*count*] a vigorous action or course that heads toward a goal or objective: *her drive for the presidency.* **20.** [*count*] a strong military offensive. **21.** [*count*] a united effort to accomplish some specific purpose, such as for a charity: *We're having a charity drive.* **22.** [*noncount*] energy and initiative; motivation: *That student had a lot of drive.* **23.** [*noncount*] the power or energy to push a car forward: *front-wheel drive.* **24.** [*count*] an act or instance of driving a ball, puck, shuttlecock, or the like: *hit a deep drive over the fence for a home run.* **—*Idiom.*** **25. drive home,** to make (something) understood: [~ + *home* + *obj*]: *I tried to drive home the importance of hard work.* [~ + *obj* + *home*]: *I tried to drive the point home that we could not afford college.* **—driv′ing,** *adj.*: *We plowed through the driving rain.*

drive′-in′, *adj.* **1.** relating to or using a facility designed to accommodate customers in their automobiles: *a drive-in restaurant.* **—*n.*** [*count*] **2.** such a facility or business.

driv•el (driv′əl) /ˈdrɪvəl/ *n., v.,* **-eled** or **-elled, -el•ing** or **-el•ling.** **—*n.*** [*noncount*] **1.** saliva flowing from the mouth; slaver. **2.** childish, silly, or meaningless thinking; twaddle: *I had to listen to his drivel for hours.* **—*v.*** [*no obj*] **3.** to talk childishly or foolishly: *driveling on about her friends at school.*

driv•er (drī′vər) /ˈdrayvər/ *n.* [*count*] **1.** a person or thing that drives. **2.** a person who drives a vehicle. **3.** a person who drives animals, such as a cowboy. **4.** a golf club with a wooden head. **5.** software that controls the connection between a computer and another device, such as a printer.

drive′ shaft′, *n.* [*count*] a shaft for carrying power from a source to machinery, as in a car.

drive•way (drīv′wā′) /ˈdrayvˌwey/ *n.* [*count*] a road leading from a street to a building or house. See illustration at HOUSE.

driz•zle (driz′əl) /ˈdrɪzəl/ *v.,* **-zled, -zling,** *n.* **—*v.*** [*no obj*] **1.** to rain gently and steadily; sprinkle: *It was drizzling all day.* **—*n.*** [*noncount*] **2.** a very light rain. **—driz′zly,** *adj.*: *drizzly weather.*

droll (drōl) /drowl/ *adj.,* **-er, -est.** amusing in an odd way: *a very droll sense of humor.* **—droll′ness,** *n.* [*noncount*] **—drol′ly,** *adv.*

-drom-, *root.* *-drom-* comes from Greek, where it has the meaning "run; a course for running." This meaning is found in such words as: DROMEDARY, PALINDROME, SYNDROME.

drom•e•dar•y (drom′i der′ē, drum′-) /ˈdrɒmɪˌdɛriy, ˈdrʌm-/ *n.* [*count*], *pl.* **-dar•ies.** the single-humped camel of Arabia and N Africa. See -DROM-.

drone[1] (drōn) /drown/ *n.* [*count*] **1.** the male of the honeybee and other bees. **2.** a craft operated by remote control: *They sent the drone over enemy territory.* **3.** a person who lives on the work of others; a loafer. **4.** a boring, uninteresting person.

drone[2] (drōn) /drown/ *v.,* **droned, dron•ing,** *n.* **—*v.*** [*no obj*] **1.** to make a continued, low, monotonous sound: *We listened to the plane engine drone on until we fell asleep.* **2.** [~ *(+ on)*] to speak in or proceed in a dull, monotonous manner: *The meeting droned on for hours.* **—*n.*** [*count*] **3.** a musical instrument or one of its parts producing a continuous low tone, esp. a bagpipe. **4.** a monotonous low tone: *the steady drone of the airplane.*

drool (dro͞ol) /druwl/ *v.* **1.** [*no obj*] to water at the mouth; salivate: *The baby was drooling with his thumb in his mouth.* **2.** to show anticipation of pleasure: [~ + *at* + *obj*]: *I was drooling at the thought of debating him.* [~ + *over* + *obj*]: *The staff was drooling over having a day off.* **—*n.*** [*noncount*] **3.** saliva running down from one's mouth; drivel: *blobs of drool at the baby's mouth.*

droop (dro͞op) /druwp/ *v.* **1.** to (cause to) sag, sink, or hang down, such as from exhaustion: [*no obj*]: *The flowers drooped in the heat.* [~ + *obj*]: *an eagle drooping its wings.* **2.** [*no obj*] to fall into a weakened or dispirited state; flag; fade: *Our spirits drooped.* **—*n.*** [*count*] **3.** a sagging, sinking, bending, or hanging down, as from lack of support: *The droop of her shoulders told me immediately how the test had gone.* **—droop′i•ness,** *n.* [*noncount*] **—droop′y,** *adj.,* **-i•er, -i•est:** *You look a little droopy; are you feeling OK?*

drop (drop) /drɒp/ *n., v.,* **dropped, drop•ping.** **—*n.*** [*count*] **1.** a small amount of liquid produced in a globule: *A few drops of blood fell from the cut on her hand.* **2.** a very small amount of liquid: *to have a drop of tea.* **3.** a very small quantity of anything: *not even a drop of mercy.* **4.** Usually, **drops.** [*plural*] liquid medicine given from a medicine dropper, such as a solution for the eyes. **5.** a limited amount of an alcoholic beverage: *He takes a drop after dinner.* **6.** an act or instance of dropping; fall; descent: *The sudden drop startled the airplane's passengers.* **7.** the distance or depth to which anything drops: *a drop of ten feet.* **8.** a steep slope: *It's a short drop to the lake.* **9.** a decline in amount: *The stock market saw a drop of about fifty points.* **10.** a small, ball-shaped piece of candy: *Share the lemon drops with your sister.* **11.** a central place where items are left or delivered: *She sent her manuscript to the mail drop.* **12.** an instance of dropping persons or supplies by parachute or the amount or number dropped. **—*v.*** **13.** to (cause to) fall in globules such as water: [*no obj*]: *Water dropped from the ceiling onto the floor.* [~ + *obj*]: *He dropped some cream into his coffee.* **14.** to (cause to) fall vertically; (cause to) have an abrupt descent: [*no obj*]: *The fruit dropped off the tree.* [~ + *obj*]: *He dropped a few coconuts down to us.* **15.** to (cause to) sink or fall to the ground, floor, or bottom: [*no obj*]: *He dropped to his knees and prayed.* [~ + *obj*]: *He dropped his opponent with one punch.* **16.** to (cause to) fall lower in condition; diminish or lessen; reduce: [*no obj*]: *Prices dropped in the spring.* [~ + *obj*]: *The store dropped its prices, but sales didn't increase.* **17.** to (cause to) come to an end; stop; cease; lapse: [*no obj*]: *There the matter dropped.* [~ + *obj*]: *We dropped the matter.* **18.** to fall or move to a position that is lower, farther back, inferior, etc.: [*no obj*]: *to drop back in line.* [~ + *obj*]: *That loss dropped the team from the playoffs.* **19.** to withdraw (from); quit: [~ + *obj*]: *He dropped history and English.* [~ + *out of* + *obj*]: *to drop out of a race.* See DROP OUT below. **20.** [~ + *into* + *obj*] to pass or enter without effort into an activity or the like: *to drop into a deep sleep.* **21.** [~ + *in/by/over*] to make an unexpected visit at a place: *We were in the neighborhood so we thought we'd just drop in to see you.* **22.** [*no obj*] to cease to appear or be seen; vanish: *to drop from sight.* **23.** [~ + *obj*] *Slang.* to swallow (an illegal drug): *They dropped some acid.* **24.** [~ + *obj*] to utter or express casually or incidentally: *to drop a hint.* **25.** to write and send: [~ + *obj* + *to* + *obj*]: *Why not drop a note to her?* [~ + *obj* + *obj*]: *Drop me a note.* **26.** to set down or unload, such as from a ship or car: [~ + *obj*]: *Drop us at the corner.* [~ + *obj* + *off*]: *Can you drop us off at the corner?* [~ + *off* + *obj*]: *We dropped off the family at the train station.* **27.** [~ + *obj*] to leave out or omit (a letter) in speaking: *You drop your final* r*'s.* **28.** to (cause to) lower (the voice) in pitch or loudness: [*no obj*]: *His voice dropped as he approached.* [~ + *obj*]: *He dropped his voice to a whisper.* **29.** [~ + *obj*] to abandon; forget: *to drop one's old friends.* **30.** [~ + *obj* + *from* + *obj*] to dismiss (an employee, etc.); remove: *to drop a consultant from the payroll.* **31.** [~ + *obj*] to lose (a game, etc.): *He dropped fifty dollars on that horse race.* **32.** [~ + *obj*] to parachute (persons, etc.). **33.** [~ + *obj*] to resew in a lower position: *to drop the hem of a skirt.* **34. drop behind,** [*no obj*] to fail to keep maintaining the necessary pace, etc.: *With all her other activities she was dropping behind at school.* **35. drop off,** [*no obj*] **a.** to fall asleep: *She drops off at about eleven each night.* **b.** to decrease; decline: *Prices began to drop off significantly.* **36. drop out,** [*no obj*] **a.** to stop attending school or college: *I haven't seen that student of mine; do you think she's dropped out?* **b.** to leave or reject the customs, etc., of society in favor of pursuing one's own lifestyle: *He just dropped out and went to Tahiti.* —***Idiom.*** **37. at the drop of a hat,** for the smallest reason and without delay: *to argue at the drop of a hat.* **38. drop in the bucket,** a very small, insignificant amount: *What's a few million dollars at this point? A drop in the bucket.*

drop•let (drop′lit) /ˈdrɒplɪt/ *n.* [*count*] a little drop.

drop′-off′, *n.* [*count*] **1.** a vertical or very steep descent: *a drop-off of about one hundred feet.* **2.** a decline; decrease: *an unusual drop-off in sales.* **3.** a place where a person or thing can be left, received, accepted, etc.: *the taxi drop-off at the airport.*

drop•out or **drop-out** (drop′out′) /ˈdrɒpˌawt/ *n.* [*count*] **1.** a student who withdraws before completing a course. **2.** a person who withdraws from established society. **3.** a person who withdraws from a competition, task, etc.

drop•per (drop′ər) /ˈdrɒpər/ *n.* [*count*] **1.** a person or thing that drops. **2.** a glass tube with rubber at one end and a small opening at the other for drawing in a liquid and letting it out in drops; eyedropper.

dross (drôs, dros) /drɔs, drɒs/ *n.* [*noncount*] waste matter; refuse.

drought (drout) /drawt/ *n.* **1.** [*count*] a long period of dry weather: *The drought lasted for months.* **2.** [*noncount*] an extended shortage of water: *Drought had struck East Africa.*

drove[1] (drōv) /drowv/ *v.* pt. of DRIVE.

drove[2] (drōv) /drowv/ *n.* [*count*] Usually, **droves.** [*plural*] a large crowd in motion: *came in droves to buy lottery tickets.*

drown (droun) /drawn/ *v.* **1.** to (cause to) die from being put under water: [*no obj*]: *Several hundred people drowned in the flood.* [~ + *obj*]: *The flood drowned several hundred people.* **2.** [~ + *obj*] to destroy by or as if by flooding: *She drowned her sorrow in drinking.* **3.** [~ + *obj*] to flood or cover over with liquid; soak: *Most of the soybean crop was drowned in the torrential floods.* **4.** to overwhelm (with sounds, etc.) so as to make (someone or something) impossible to hear: [~ + *out* + *obj*]: *The roar of the plane drowned out the pilot's announcements.* [~ + *obj* + *out*]: *They drowned me out during my talk.* **5. drown in,** [~ + *in* + *obj*] to be overwhelmed by: *I was drowning in work.*

drowse (drouz) /drawz/ *v.* [*no obj*], **drowsed, drows•ing.** to be sleepy or half-asleep: *I was drowsing in the garden.*

drow•sy (drou′zē) /ˈdrawziy/ *adj.*, **-si•er, -si•est. 1.** half-asleep; sleepy: *The medicine made me drowsy.* **2.** causing or bringing about sleepiness: *drowsy spring weather.* —**drow′si•ness,** *n.* [*noncount*]: *drowsiness caused by medication.*

drub (drub) /drʌb/ *v.* [~ + *obj*], **drubbed, drub•bing.** to defeat completely, such as in a game: *We drubbed our opponents, 50-0.*

drudge (druj) /drʌdʒ/ *n.* [*count*] **1.** a person who does dull work. **2.** a person who works in a routine way.

drudg•er•y (druj′ər ē) /ˈdrʌdʒəriy/ *n.* [*noncount*] dull work: *taking the drudgery out of some of those household tasks.*

drug (drug) /drʌg/ *n.*, *v.*, **drugged, drug•ging.** —*n.* [*count*] **1.** a chemical used in medicines for the treatment of disease, or to improve physical or mental well-being: *Some drugs are useful in preventing disease.* **2.** a habit-forming or illegal substance, esp. a narcotic: *He was dealing in drugs.* —*v.* [~ + *obj*] **3.** to administer a medicinal drug to: *The hospital staff drugged him with sedatives.* **4.** to make unconscious or poison (someone) with a drug: *They tied him up, drugged him, and smuggled him across the border.* **5.** to mix (food or drink) with a drug: *I drugged his drink while he wasn't looking.*

drug•gie or **drug•gy** (drug′ē) /ˈdrʌgiy/ *n.* [*count*], *pl.* **-gies.** *Slang.* a habitual user of illegal drugs.

drug•gist (drug′ist) /ˈdrʌgɪst/ *n.* [*count*] **1.** PHARMACIST. **2.** the owner or operator of a drugstore.

drug•store or **drug store** (drug′stôr′, -stōr′) /ˈdrʌgˌstɔr, -ˌstowr/ *n.* [*count*] the place of business of a druggist, where medicines are sold, usually also selling cosmetics, stationery, etc.

dru•id (drōō′id) /ˈdruwɪd/ *n.* [*count; often: Druid*] a member of a religious order among the ancient Celts. —**dru′id•ism,** *n.* [*noncount*]

drum (drum) /drʌm/ *n.*, *v.*, **drummed, drum•ming.** —*n.* [*count*] **1.** a musical instrument made of a hollow body covered at one or both ends with a tightly stretched skin which is struck to produce sound: *She played drums for the school band.* **2.** the sound produced by such an instrument. **3.** a booming sound: *the steady drum of rain on the roof.* **4.** EARDRUM. **5.** a rounded object with flat ends, such as part of a machine: *brake drums on a car.* **6.** a rounded box or container: *rolling the oil drums off the ramp.* —*v.* **7.** [*no obj*] to beat or play a drum: *He drums for the school band.* **8.** to beat on anything continuously or in a rhythm: [~ + *obj*]: *He drummed his fingers on the table.* [*no obj*]: *He was drumming with his fingers on the table.* **9.** [*no obj*] to make a sound like that of a drum: *The rain was drumming on the tin roof.* **10. drum into,** to drive or force by repeating; repeat persistently: [~ + *obj* + *into* + *obj*]: *He tried to drum the idea of success into her head.* [~ + *into* + *obj* + *that clause* + *obj*]: *He tried to drum into her that success was important at all costs.* **11. drum out,** [~ + *obj* + *out*] to dismiss in disgrace: *He was drummed out of the Corps after that incident.* **12. drum up,** [~ + *up* + *obj*] to obtain, create. or call for (trade, etc.) through strong effort: *He was trying to drum up new business.* —***Idiom.*** **13. beat the drum for,** [~ + *obj*] to publicize: *The car companies were beating the drum for their new product.*

drum′ ma′jor, *n.* [*count*] the leader of a marching band.

drum′ majorette′, *n.* MAJORETTE.

drum•mer (drum′ər) /ˈdrʌmər/ *n.* [*count*] a person who plays a drum.

drum•stick (drum′stik′) /ˈdrʌmˌstɪk/ *n.* [*count*] **1.** a stick for beating a drum. **2.** the meaty leg of a chicken or turkey.

drunk (drungk) /drʌŋk/ *adj.* **1.** [*often: be* + ~] being in a temporary state in which one's abilities are affected by alcohol; intoxicated. **2.** [*often: be* + ~ + *with*] overcome by a strong feeling: *was drunk with success and power.* **3.** [*before a noun*] relating to or caused by intoxication or intoxicated persons: *laws aimed at preventing drunk driving and arresting drunk drivers.* —*n.* [*count*] **4. a.** a person who is intoxicated. **b.** a person who is often drunk; drunkard. **5.** a period of drinking alcohol heavily: *a week-long drunk.* —*v.* **6.** pp. and nonstandard pt. of DRINK. —**Usage.** See DRUNKEN.

drunk•ard (drung′kərd) /ˈdrʌŋkərd/ *n.* [*count*] a person who is often or habitually drunk.

drunk•en (drung′kən) /ˈdrʌŋkən/ *adj.* [*before a noun*] **1.** intoxicated; drunk: *the drunken man's inability to walk a straight line.* **2.** often or frequently drunk. **3.** relating to, caused by, or showing the effects of intoxication: *a drunken quarrel.* —**drunk′en•ly,** *adv.* —**drunk′en•ness,** *n.* [*noncount*] —**Usage.** Compare the adjectives DRUNK and DRUNKEN. Both can be used with nouns that refer to persons: *The man is drunk. A drunken customer.* DRUNKEN is used with nouns that do not refer to persons: *a drunken party, a drunken quarrel.* Only DRUNK can be used after the verb *be*, as in: *He is really drunk;* we would not say: *He is really drunken.* Usually, DRUNK is not used before a noun, unless the noun is *driver, driving*: *a drunk driver;* we would not say: *a drunk girl.*

dry (drī) /dray/ *adj.*, **dri•er, dri•est,** *v.*, **dried, dry•ing.** —*adj.* **1.** free from moisture; not wet: *dry branches.* **2.** having or characterized by little or no rain: *This dry weather is bad for the crops.* **3.** [*before a noun*] not under, in, or on water: *to be on dry land.* **4.** not now containing liquid; empty: *a dry river.* **5.** not yielding milk: *a dry cow.* **6.** free from tears: *dry eyes.* **7.** [*be* + ~] desiring drink; thirsty: *I'm so dry; let's stop in the diner for a soda.* **8.** causing thirst: *dry work.* **9.** served or eaten without butter, jam, etc.: *dry toast.* **10.** (of bread, etc.) stale: *The bread was dry.* **11.** [*before a noun*] of or relating to nonliquid substances bought or sold: *A peck is a unit of dry measure.* **12.** (esp. of wines) not sweet: *a dry, white wine.* **13.** characterized by or prohibiting the manufacture and sale of alcoholic liquors: *At that time Iowa was a dry state.* **14.** free from the use of alcoholic drink; sober: *The alcoholic has been dry for several years now.* **15.** dull; uninteresting: *Is dictionary making a dry subject?* **16.** expressed in a straight-faced, matter-of-fact way: *dry humor.* **17.** unproductive: *Even the greatest artists sometimes have dry years.* —*v.* **18.** to (cause to) become dry or to lose moisture: [~ + *obj*]: *She dried her hair with a towel.* [*no obj*]: *The paint will dry in two hours. Leave the dishes to dry.* **19. dry out,** [*no obj*] to undergo treatment for drug or alcohol abuse. **20. dry up, a.** to cease to exist; evaporate: [*no obj*]: *The river bed dried up.* [~ + *up* + *obj*]: *The heat had dried up the lake.* [~ + *obj* + *up*]: *The heat had dried it up.* **b.** [*no obj*] *Informal.* to stop talking: *Oh, dry up and leave us alone!* —**dry′ly,** *adv.* —**dry′ness,** *n.* [*noncount*]

dry′ clean′ing, *n.* [*noncount*] **1.** the cleaning of garments, etc., with chemicals: *Dry cleaning is recom-*

mended for that sweater. **2.** garments and other items for such cleaning: *Don't forget to pick up the dry cleaning today.* **—dry′-clean′,** *v.* [~ + *obj*]: *You have to dry-clean that blouse.* **—dry′ clean′er,** *n.* [*count*]

dry′ dock′, *n.* a structure that can contain a ship, so that workers can repair all parts of the hull: [*count*]: *several dry docks on the eastern coast.* [*noncount; in* + ~]: *The ship is in dry dock.*

dry•er (drī′ər) /ˈdrayər/ *n.* [*count*] **1.** Also, **drier.** a machine or appliance for removing moisture, as by forced heat: *a clothes dryer; a hair dryer.* **2.** DRIER[1] (defs. 1, 2).

dry′-eyed′, *adj.* not crying or weeping.

dry′ goods′, *n.* [*plural*] textile fabrics as distinguished esp. from groceries and hardware.

dry′ ice′, *n.* [*noncount*] the solid form of carbon dioxide, used chiefly as a refrigerant: *used dry ice to keep the ice cream cold.*

dry′ meas′ure, *n.* [*noncount*] the system of units used in measuring the volume of certain goods, such as grain.

dry′ run′, *n.* [*count*] a rehearsal; a practice or exercise: *We staged a dry run to see if our plan would work.*

DST or **D.S.T.,** an abbreviation of: daylight-saving time.

-du-, *root.* *-du-* comes from Latin, where it has the meaning "two." This meaning is found in such words as: DUAL, DUEL, DUET, DUO, DUPLEX, DUPLICATE, DUPLICITY.

du•al (do͞o′əl, dyo͞o′-) /ˈduwəl, ˈdyuw-/ *adj.* [*before a noun*] of, relating to, or meaning two; made up of two people, items, parts, etc., together: *dual ownership.* **—du′al•ism,** *n.* [*noncount*]: *the dualism of good and evil.* **—du•al•i•ty** (do͞o al′i tē, dyo͞o-) /duwˈælɪtiy, dyuw-/ *n.* [*noncount*] See -DU-.

dub[1] (dub) /dʌb/ *v.* [~ + *obj* + *obj*], **dubbed, dub•bing. 1.** to give a name, nickname, or title: *He was dubbed a hero.* **2.** to make or designate (someone) a knight by lightly touching him on the shoulder with a sword: *I dub thee Sir Lancelot.* **—dub′ber,** *n.* [*count*]

dub[2] (dub) /dʌb/ *v.* [~ + *obj*], **dubbed, dub•bing. 1.** to furnish (a film or tape) with a new soundtrack: *The movie was poorly dubbed.* **2.** to add (music, etc.) to a recording: *dubbed in the music.* **—dub′ber,** *n.* [*count*]

du•bi•ous (do͞o′bē əs, dyo͞o′-) /ˈduwbiyəs, ˈdyuw-/ *adj.* **1.** of doubtful quality; questionable: *dubious friends.* **2.** unsure; uncertain in opinion; hesitant: *dubious about our chances of success.* **—du′bi•ous•ly,** *adv.*

-duc-, *root.* *-duc-* comes from Latin, where it has the meaning "to lead." This meaning is found in such words as: ABDUCT, ADDUCE, AQUEDUCT, CONDUCIVE, CONDUCT, DEDUCE, DEDUCT, DUCAL, DUCT, DUKE, EDUCATE, INDUCE, INDUCTION, INTRODUCE, OVIDUCT, PRODUCE, PRODUCTION, REDUCE, REDUCTION, SEDUCE, SEDUCTION, VIADUCT.

du•cal (do͞o′kəl, dyo͞o′-) /ˈduwkəl, ˈdyuw-/ *adj.* [*before a noun*] of or relating to a duke or a dukedom. See -DUC-.

duch•ess (duch′is) /ˈdʌtʃɪs/ *n.* [*count*] **1.** the wife or widow of a duke. **2.** a woman who holds the rank of a duke.

duch•y (duch′ē) /ˈdʌtʃiy/ *n.* [*count*], *pl.* **-duch•ies.** the territory ruled by a duke or duchess.

duck[1] (duk) /dʌk/ *n., pl.* **ducks,** (*esp. when thought of as a group* for 1, 2) **duck. 1.** [*count*] a small, short-necked, web-footed swimming bird. **2.** [*count*] the female of this bird. Compare DRAKE. **3.** [*noncount*] the flesh of this bird, eaten as food: *Peking duck in orange sauce.*

duck[2] (duk) /dʌk/ *v.* **1.** to (cause to) bend suddenly, esp. in order to avoid something: [*no obj*]: *When the shooting started, we ducked behind a car.* [~ + *obj*]: *He ducked his head down as the shots rang out.* **2.** to avoid, or try to escape from (an unpleasant task, etc.); dodge: [~ + *obj*]: *He's trying to duck responsibility for his actions.* [~ + *out* (+ *of*) + *obj*]: *She ducked out the back to avoid the reporters.* **3.** to plunge (the whole body or the head) momentarily under water: [*no obj*]: *I ducked under the hose and washed my face.* [~ + *obj*]: *She ducked her head under the hose and washed off.* **—n.** [*count*] **4.** an act or instance of ducking: *a quick duck to the left.*

duck•ling (duk′ling) /ˈdʌklɪŋ/ *n.* [*count*] a young duck.

duct (dukt) /dʌkt/ *n.* [*count*] **1.** a tube, canal, or pipe by which a substance is conducted or carried: *The hero escapes by climbing through the air ducts and out of the building.* **2.** a tube carrying bodily liquids: *tear ducts.* **3.** a single enclosed passage for electrical wires or cables. **—duct′less,** *adj.* See -DUC-.

duct′ tape′ (duk, dukt) /dʌk, dʌkt/ *n.* [*noncount*] a silver-gray cloth tape that sticks strongly to an object, used in plumbing, household repairs, etc.

dud (dud) /dʌd/ *n.* [*count*] **1.** a device, person, or business that proves to be a failure: *His new play was a dud.* **2.** a shell or missile that fails to explode after being fired.

dude (do͞od, dyo͞od) /duwd, dyuwd/ *n.* [*count*] **1.** a man overly concerned with his clothes, grooming, and manners. **2.** *Slang.* a fellow: *a cool dude.* **3.** *Western U.S.* a person from an Eastern city who vacations on a ranch.

dude′ ranch′, *n.* [*count*] a ranch operated as a vacation resort.

dudg•eon (duj′ən) /ˈdʌdʒən/ *n.* [*noncount*] a feeling of offense or resentment; anger: *We left in high dudgeon.*

due (do͞o, dyo͞o) /duw, dyuw/ *adj.* **1.** [*be* + ~] **a.** owing or owed: *This bill is due next month.* **b.** immediately owed: *This bill is due.* **2.** [*be* + ~ + *to*] owing or deserved as a moral or natural right: *She is entitled to all the respect due to a scholar.* **3.** [*before a noun*] rightful; proper; fitting: *With all due respect we did consider your request.* **4.** adequate; enough; sufficient: *Allow a due margin for delay.* **5.** [*be* + ~] expected to be ready, be present, or arrive: *The plane is due at noon.* [~ + *to* + *verb*]: *The committee is due to meet at twelve-thirty.* **—n. 6.** [*noncount; usually: one's* + ~] something owed to someone: *We received our due when we conquered the country.* **7.** Usually, **dues.** [*plural*] a regular fee to be paid esp. to a group or organization: *yearly membership dues.* **—adv. 8.** directly or exactly: *due east.* **—*Idiom.* 9. due to,** [~ + *obj*] **a.** caused by: *The delay was due to an accident.* **b.** because of; owing to: *absence from school due to illness.* **10. give someone his** or **her due,** [*give* + *obj* + *his or her* ~] **a.** to treat someone fairly: *We gave him his due; nothing more.* **b.** to acknowledge someone's unexpectedly positive behavior: *Give that nasty supervisor his due, he was just trying to do his job.* **11. in due course** or **time,** in the natural order of events; eventually: *In due course you'll get your refund.* **12. pay one's dues,** to earn respect by working hard.

du•el (do͞o′əl, dyo͞o′-) /ˈduwəl, ˈdyuw-/ *n., v.,* **-eled** or **-elled, -el•ing** or **-el•ling. —n.** [*count*] **1.** a fight between two persons with deadly weapons according to an accepted procedure. **2.** a contest between two persons or teams: *The game promises to be a real duel between quarterbacks.* **—v. 3.** to fight in a duel: [*no obj*]: *They had been dueling for hours and finally called a draw.* [~ + *obj*]: *He dueled his opponent for hours.* **—du′el•er, du′el•ist,** *n.* [*count*] See -DU-.

due′ proc′ess of law′, *n.* [*noncount*] the regular administration of a system of laws. Also called **due′ proc′ess.**

du•et (do͞o et′, dyo͞o-) /duwˈɛt, dyuw-/ *n.* [*count*] a piece of music for two voices or instruments. See -DU-.

duf′fel bag′, *n.* [*count*] a large, rounded bag, esp. of canvas, for personal belongings.

duff•er (duf′ər) /ˈdʌfər/ *n.* [*count*] **1.** *Informal.* a slow, clumsy, incompetent person. **2.** a person incompetent at a specific sport, such as golf.

dug (dug) /dʌg/ *v.* a pt. and pp. of DIG.

dug•out (dug′out′) /ˈdʌg,awt/ *n.* [*count*] **1.** a boat made by hollowing out a log. **2.** a roofed structure in which baseball players sit when not on the field.

du jour (də zho͝or′, do͞o) /də ˈʒʊr, duw/ *adj.* [*after a noun*] as prepared or served on the particular day: *soup du jour.*

duke (do͞ok, dyo͞ok) /duwk, dyuwk/ *n.* [*count*] **1.** (in Continental Europe) the male ruler of a duchy; the ruler of a small state. **2.** a British nobleman holding the highest hereditary title outside the royal family. **3.** a nobleman of corresponding rank in certain other countries. **4. dukes,** [*plural*] *Slang.* fists or hands: *"Put up your dukes!" he cried, urging him to a fight.* See -DUC-.

duke•dom (do͞ok′dəm, dyo͞ok′-) /ˈduwkdəm, ˈdyuwk-/ *n.* [*count*] **1.** the position, rank, or title of a duke. **2.** the land or area ruled by a duke. See -DUC-.

dul•cet (dul′sit) /ˈdʌlsɪt/ *adj.* pleasant to the ear; having a pleasing melody; gentle: *dulcet tones.*

dull (dul) /dʌl/ *adj.,* **-er, -est,** *v.* **—adj. 1.** not sharp; blunt: *a dull knife.* **2.** causing boredom: *She almost fell asleep during his dull sermon.* **3.** not lively or spirited; listless: *always feels dull in hot weather.* **4.** not bright, intense, or clear; dim: *a dull, cloudy day.* **5.** [*before a noun*] having little depth of color: *the dull grey of the clouds.* **6.** slow in motion or action; sluggish: *a dull day in the stock market.* **7.** mentally slow; somewhat stupid. **8.** [*before a noun*] lacking keenness in the senses or feelings: *He had a dull pain in his stomach.* **—v. 9.** to (cause to) become dull: [*no obj*]: *His senses dulled as the drug swept through his body.* [~ + *obj*]: *The smell from the garbage dulled his appetite.* **—dull′ness,** *n.* [*noncount*] **—dul′ly,** *adv.*: *He answered dully that he didn't really care.*

dull•ard (dul′ərd) /ˈdʌlərd/ *n.* [*count*] a stupid, insensitive person.

du•ly (do͞o′lē, dyo͞o′-) /ˈduwliy, ˈdyuw-/ *adv.* **1.** in a due manner; properly; fittingly: *The hostess was duly thanked for her hospitality.* **2.** in or at the correct time; punctually: *The software duly appeared by New Year's.*

dumb (dum) /dʌm/ *adj.*, **-er, -est. 1.** lacking intelligence or good judgment; stupid; dull-witted: *He was dumb to try a stunt like that.* **2.** stupid; silly; useless: *What a dumb idea!* **3.** lacking the power of speech (often considered offensive when applied to humans): *a dumb animal.* **4.** temporarily unable to speak: *We were all dumb with astonishment at his outrageous comments.* **5.** refraining from any or much speech; silent: *I kept dumb.* **6.** made, experienced, etc., without speech: *in a dumb, furious rage.* **7.** lacking electronic processing power of its own: *a dumb computer terminal.* **—dumb′ly,** *adv.* **—dumb′ness,** *n.* [*noncount*]

dumb•bell (dum′bel′) /ˈdʌmˌbɛl/ *n.* [*count*] **1.** a hand weight for exercising, made up of two heavy weights connected by a bar. **2.** *Slang.* a stupid person.

dumb•found (dum found′, dum′found′) /dʌmˈfawnd, ˈdʌmˌfawnd/ *v.* [~ + *obj*] to make speechless with amazement: *dumbfounded by all the damage done by the storm.*

dumb•wait•er (dum′wā′tər) /ˈdʌmˌweytər/ *n.* [*count*] a small elevator, used for moving food, etc., between floors, such as in a restaurant.

dum•dum (dum′dum′) /ˈdʌmˌdʌm/ *n.* [*count*] a bullet that is hollow or soft at the front end and expands on impact. Also called **dum′dum bul′let.**

dum•my (dum′ē) /ˈdʌmiy/ *n., pl.* **-mies,** *adj.* **—***n.* [*count*] **1.** an object resembling a human figure, such as for displaying clothes: *the dummy in the shop window.* **2.** an imitation or copy of something, such as for use in a display: *lipstick dummies made of colored plastic.* **3.** *Informal.* a stupid person; fool; dolt: *Some dummy mixed up our application.* **4.** a person who has nothing to say or who takes no active part in affairs. **5.** one put forward to act for others while pretending to act for himself or herself. **6.** *Slang.* **a.** *Offensive.* a person who lacks the power of speech. **b.** a person who is always silent. **7.** (in bridge) the hand which is exposed and played by the person who has won the bidding. **8.** a bomb that cannot explode, used for practice exercises. **—***adj.* [*before a noun*] **9.** noting or relating to an imitation or copy: *some dummy shells in the gun.* **10.** put forward to act for others while seeming to act for oneself: *a dummy corporation that was actually controlled by a conglomerate.*

dump (dump) /dʌmp/ *v.* **1.** [~ + *obj*] to drop or let fall in; fling down or drop heavily or suddenly: *Dump the topsoil here.* **2.** to throw away or discard (garbage, etc.): [~ + *obj*]: *The company dumped the toxic wastes into this canal.* [*no obj*]: *a sewage pipe that dumps into the ocean.* **3.** [~ + *obj*] to unload or empty out (a container), such as by tilting: *He dumped the garbage can and went back inside.* **4.** [~ + *obj*] to empty out, such as from a container: *He dumped the papers from the wastebasket.* **5.** [~ + *obj*] to dismiss from a job: *The company dumped him after all those years.* **6.** [~ + *obj*] to rid oneself of (someone or something) suddenly and rudely: *Don't dump your troubles on me! He dumped her after 20 years of marriage.* **7.** to sell (goods) into foreign markets below cost in an effort to destroy foreign competition: [~ + *obj*]: *accused of dumping cars in the American market.* [*no obj*]: *Many politicians accuse foreign countries of dumping as a reason for the trade imbalances.* **8.** [~ + *obj*] to send out or copy (computer data), esp. to find out the reason for a failure. **9. dump on,** [~ + *on* + *obj*] to criticize harshly; abuse; insult: *They were always dumping on him.* **—***n.* [*count*] **10.** a place where garbage, etc., is deposited. **11.** a collection of ammunition, etc., deposited at some point for distribution. **12.** *Informal.* a place, area, house, or town that is run-down, dirty, or a mess: *He lived in a dump, with no kitchen or bathroom.* **13.** a copy of dumped computer data.

dump•ling (dump′ling) /ˈdʌmplɪŋ/ *n.* [*count*] **1.** a rounded mass of steamed and seasoned dough. **2.** a wrapping of dough enclosing fruit or some tasty filling.

dumps (dumps) /dʌmps/ *n.* [*plural*] **—*Idiom.* (down) in the dumps,** in a depressed or sad state of mind: *She's really (down) in the dumps about leaving home.*

Dump•ster (dump′stər) /ˈdʌmpstər/ *Trademark.* [*count*] a brand of large metal bin for refuse, designed to be hoisted onto a truck for emptying or hauling away.

dump•y (dum′pē) /ˈdʌmpiy/ *adj.*, **-i•er, -i•est.** short and stout: *a dumpy figure.*

dun[1] (dun) /dʌn/ *v.* [~ + *obj*], **dunned, dun•ning.** to make repeated demands upon, esp. for the payment of a debt: *kept dunning us about the overdue bill.*

dun[2] (dun) /dʌn/ *adj.* dull grayish brown or grayish yellow.

dunce (duns) /dʌns/ *n.* [*count*] a dull-witted or ignorant person.

dune (do͞on, dyo͞on) /duwn, dyuwn/ *n.* [*count*] a sand hill ridge formed by the wind, usually in deserts or near oceans: *The dunes were eroding fast and would disappear.*

dune′ bug′gy, *n.* [*count*] a small, lightweight, open automotive vehicle equipped with oversize, low-pressure tires for traveling along sand beaches.

dung (dung) /dʌŋ/ *n.* [*noncount*] excrement, esp. of animals; manure.

dun•ga•rees (dung′gə rēz′) /ˌdʌŋgəˈriyz/ *n.* [*plural*] **1.** work clothes, overalls, etc., of blue denim. **2.** BLUE JEANS.

dun•geon (dun′jən) /ˈdʌndʒən/ *n.* [*count*] a strong, dark prison or cell, such as in a medieval castle.

dunk (dungk) /dʌŋk/ *v.* [~ + *obj*] **1.** to dip (a biscuit, etc.) into coffee or the like, before eating. **2.** to put (someone or something) briefly under the surface of a liquid: *She dunked the shirt in some detergent.* **3.** to thrust or slam (a basketball) downward through the basket: *He leaped and dunked the ball through for the final score of the game.* **—***n.* [*count*] **4.** an act or instance of dunking.

du•o (do͞o′ō, dyo͞o′ō) /ˈduwow, ˈdyuwow/ *n.* [*count*], *pl.* **du•os. 1.** DUET. **2.** two persons associated with each other; couple: *referred to the two heroes as "the dynamic duo."* **3.** two things ordinarily found together; a pair: *a duo of lovebirds.* See -DU-.

du•o•de•num (do͞o′ə dē′nəm, dyo͞o′-; do͞o od′n əm, dyo͞o-) /ˌduwəˈdiynəm, ˌdyuw-; duwˈɒdnəm, dyuw-/ *n.* [*count*], *pl.* **du•o•de•na** (do͞o′ə dē′nə, dyo͞o′-; do͞o od′n ə, dyo͞o-) /ˌduwəˈdiynə, ˌdyuw-; duwˈɒdnə, dyuw-/ **du•o•de•nums.** the first portion of the small intestine. **—du•o•de•nal** (do͞o′ə dē′nl, dyo͞o′-; do͞o od′n əl, dyo͞o-) /ˌduwəˈdiynl, ˌdyuw-; duwˈɒdnəl, dyuw-/ *adj.* [*before a noun*]: *a duodenal ulcer.*

dupe (do͞op, dyo͞op) /duwp, dyuwp/ *n., v.,* **duped, dup•ing. —***n.* [*count*] **1.** a person who is easily tricked: *He was the dupe of the racketeers.* **2.** a person who serves a cause without question: *The senator accused them of being dupes of a communist conspiracy.* **—***v.* **3.** to make a dupe of; deceive; delude; trick: [~ + *obj*]: *The agency duped her.* [~ + *obj* + *into* + *obj*]: *They had duped me into the sale.* **—dup′er,** *n.* [*count*]

du•plex (do͞o′pleks, dyo͞o′-) /ˈduwplɛks, ˈdyuw-/ *n.* [*count*] **1.** an apartment for one family but having two levels. Also called **duplex apartment. 2.** a house built for two families. Also called **duplex house. —***adj.* [*before a noun*] **3.** having two parts; double; twofold. **4.** relating to or being a communications system that permits sending two messages at the same time in opposite directions over one channel. See -DU-, -PLEX-.

du•pli•cate (*n., adj.* do͞o′pli kit, dyo͞o′-; *v.* -kāt′) / *n., adj.* ˈduwplɪkɪt, ˈdyuw-; *v.* -ˌkeyt/ *n., v.,* **-cat•ed, -cat•ing,** *adj.* **—***n.* [*count*] **1.** an exact copy: *He made a duplicate and handed me the original.* **—***v.* [~ + *obj*] **2.** to make an exact copy of: *She duplicated a few copies of my letter and handed me the original.* **3.** to do or perform again; repeat: *You'll just have to duplicate your performance.* **—***adj.* [*before a noun*] **4.** exactly like or corresponding to something else: *a duplicate key.* **—*Idiom.* 5. in duplicate,** in two identical copies: *I'll need your letter, in duplicate, on my desk by morning.* **—du•pli•ca•tion** (do͞o′pli kā′shən, dyo͞o′-) /ˌduwplɪˈkeyʃən, ˌdyuw-/ *n.* [*noncount*]: *illegal duplication of material.* See -DU-, -PLIC-.

du•pli•ca•tor (do͞o′pli kā′tər, dyo͞o′-) /ˈduwplɪˌkeytər, ˈdyuw-/ *n.* [*count*] a machine for making duplicates. Also called **du′plicating machine′.**

du•plic•i•ty (do͞o plis′i tē, dyo͞o-) /duwˈplɪsɪtiy, dyuw-/ *n.* [*noncount*] deceitfulness in speech or conduct; false behavior: *He had behaved with duplicity, falsifying reports and stealing the money.* See -DU-, -PLIC-.

-dur-, *root.* *-dur-* comes from Latin, where it has the meanings "hard; strong; lasting." These meanings are found in such words as: DURABLE, DURATION, DURESS, DURING, ENDURE.

du•ra•ble (do͝or′ə bəl, dyo͝or′-) /ˈdʊrəbəl, ˈdyʊr-/ *adj.* **1.** highly resistant to wear, etc.; capable of enduring: *The raincoat is made of durable material.* **—***n.* **2. durables,** [*plural*] goods, such as household appliances, that are not used up immediately, but can be used for several years. Also called **durable goods. —du•ra•bil•i•ty** (do͝or′-

ə bil′i tē, dyŏŏr′-) /ˌdʊrəˈbɪlɪtiy, ˌdyʊr-/ *n.* [*noncount*]: *That car is noted for its exceptional durability.* —**du′ra•bly,** *adv.* See -DUR-.

du•ra•tion (dŏŏ rā′shən, dyŏŏ-) /dʊˈreyʃən, dyʊ-/ *n.* [*noncount*] **1.** the length of time something exists: *Luckily these viruses are of short duration.* **2. for the duration,** for as long as (something) lasts or continues: *He was drafted for the duration plus six.* See -DUR-.

du•ress (dŏŏ res′, dyŏŏ-) /dʊˈrɛs, dyʊ-/ *n.* [*noncount*] compulsion by threat or force; coercion: *He had signed the confession under duress.* See -DUR-.

dur•ing (dŏŏr′ing, dyŏŏr′-) /ˈdʊrɪŋ, ˈdyʊr-/ *prep.* **1.** throughout the duration of: *He lived in Florida during the winter.* **2.** at some time or point in the course of: *They departed during the night.* See -DUR-.

dusk (dusk) /dʌsk/ *n.* [*noncount*] the state or period of partial darkness between day and night; twilight: *We met at dusk and traveled through the night.*

dusk•y (dus′kē) /ˈdʌskiy/ *adj.*, **-i•er, -i•est. 1.** somewhat dark; dim: *dusky evening.* **2.** having a dark color: *dusky complexions.*

dust (dust) /dʌst/ *n.* [*noncount*] **1.** matter in fine, powdery, dry particles: *a layer of dust on the books.* **2.** any finely powdered substance, such as sawdust: *gold dust.* —*v.* **3.** to wipe the dust from (furniture, etc.): [*no obj*]: *On Fridays we dust and vacuum.* [~ + *obj*]: *We dusted the bookshelves.* **4.** [~ + *obj*] to sprinkle (crops, etc.) with a powder or dust: *to dust crops with insecticide.* **5.** [~ + *obj*] to sprinkle (a powder or other fine particles): *to dust insecticide on a rosebush.* **6. dust off,** to prepare to use again: [~ + *off* + *obj*]: *I dusted off those old speeches and got them ready for a new tour.* [~ + *obj* + *off*]: *to dust a few old speeches off.* —***Idiom.* 7. bite the dust, a.** to die: *He bit the dust in the last episode.* **b.** to suffer defeat: *She bit the dust in the later primaries.* **c.** to become ruined or unusable: *The old refrigerator has bitten the dust.* **8. make the dust fly,** to work with vigor. —**dust′less,** *adj.*

dust′ bin′, *n.* [*count*] *Brit.* a garbage can.

dust•er (dus′tər) /ˈdʌstər/ *n.* [*count*] **1.** a cloth, etc., for removing dust. **2.** an apparatus for sprinkling dust, powder, or the like. **3.** a person employed in spreading insecticide on crops from a low-flying aircraft.

dust•pan (dust′pan′) /ˈdʌstˌpæn/ *n.* [*count*] a short-handled shovellike utensil into which dust is swept.

dust•y (dus′tē) /ˈdʌstiy/ *adj.*, **-i•er, -i•est.** filled or covered with or as if with dust: *a hot dusty day.* —**dust′i•ness,** *n.* [*noncount*]

Dutch (duch) /dʌtʃ/ *adj.* **1.** of or relating to the Netherlands. **2.** of or relating to the language spoken in the Netherlands. —*n.* **3.** [*plural; the* + ~*; takes a plural verb*] the people born or living in the Netherlands. **4.** [*noncount*] the language spoken in the Netherlands. —***Idiom.* 5. go Dutch,** to pay one's own expenses, as on a date: *You can't take me out, but let's go Dutch one night.*

Dutch•man (duch′mən) /ˈdʌtʃmən/ *n.* [*count*], *pl.* **-men.** a person born or living in the Netherlands.

Dutch′ ov′en, *n.* [*count*] **1.** a large heavy pot with a close-fitting lid, used for stews, etc. **2.** a metal utensil, open in front, for roasting before an open fire. **3.** a brick oven in which the walls are preheated for cooking.

Dutch′ treat′, *n.* [*count*] a meal or entertainment for which each person pays his or her own way.

Dutch•wom•an (duch′wŏŏm′ən) /ˈdʌtʃˌwʊmən/ *n.* [*count*], *pl.* **-wom•en.** a woman born or living in the Netherlands.

du•ti•ful (dōō′tə fəl, dyōō′-) /ˈduwtəfəl, ˈdyuw-/ *adj.* performing the duties required of one; obedient: *a dutiful child.* —**du′ti•ful•ly,** *adv.: He dutifully followed all your instructions.*

du•ty (dōō′tē, dyōō′-) /ˈduwtiy, ˈdyuw-/ *n.*, *pl.* **-ties. 1.** [*noncount*] something that one is expected to do by obligation: *He had a strong sense of duty.* **2.** an action or task required by a person's position: [*count*]: *The duties of a clergyman involve performing marriages and visiting the sick.* [*noncount*]: *I reported for duty at twelve o'clock sharp.* **3.** a tax imposed by law on the import or export of goods; tariff: [*noncount*]: *How much duty did you have to pay on the refrigerator?* [*count*]: *Where do they collect customs duties?* —***Idiom.* 4. off/on duty,** not/ at one's post or work: *I can't drink; I'm still on duty.*

du•vet (dōō vā′, dyōō-) /duwˈvey, dyuw-/ *n.* [*count*] a quilt, often with a removable cover; comforter.

dwarf (dwôrf) /dwɔrf/ *n.*, *pl.* **dwarfs, dwarves** (dwôrvz) /dwɔrvz/ *adj.*, *v.* —*n.* [*count*] **1.** a person of abnormally small size. **2.** an animal or plant much smaller than the average. **3.** a small, imaginary being, often represented as a tiny old man, who is skilled as a worker and has magical powers. —*adj.* [*before a noun*] **4.** of unusually small stature or size: *dwarf marigolds.* —*v.* [~ + *obj*] **5.** to cause to seem small in size, etc., as by being much larger: *This current budget crisis dwarfs all our previous troubles.* —**dwarf′ish,** *adj.* —**dwarf′ism,** *n.* [*noncount*]

dwell (dwel) /dwɛl/ *v.* [*no obj*], **dwelt** (dwelt) /dwɛlt/ or **dwelled, dwell•ing. 1.** to live or stay as a permanent resident; reside: *He dwells in the country for most of the year.* **2. dwell on** or **upon,** [~ + *on/upon* + *obj*] to think, speak, or write about for a long time or often: *She dwelt at length on the similarities between the two paintings.*

dwell•er (dwel′ər) /ˈdwɛlər/ *n.* [*count*] a person (or animal) that lives in (an area): *Most city dwellers would welcome peaceful mornings.*

dwell•ing (dwel′ing) /ˈdwɛlɪŋ/ *n.* [*count*] a building or other place to live in: *a comfortable two-story dwelling.*

DWI, an abbreviation of: driving while intoxicated.

dwin•dle (dwin′dl) /ˈdwɪndl/ *v.* [*no obj*], **-dled, -dling.** to become smaller; diminish: *Our food supply began to dwindle.*

dye (dī) /day/ *n.*, *v.*, **dyed, dye•ing.** —*n.* **1.** a coloring material or matter: [*noncount*]: *Try some red dye on that sweater.* [*count*]: *They had a few dyes to use on that sweater.* —*v.* [~ + *obj*] **2.** to color (cloth, etc.) with or as if with a dye: *to dye a dress green.* —**dy′er,** *n.* [*count*]

dyed′-in-the-wool′, *adj.* [*before a noun*] through and through; complete: *a dyed-in-the-wool feminist.*

dy•ing (dī′ing) /ˈdayɪŋ/ *adj.* [*before a noun*] **1.** about to die: *a dying patient.* **2.** of or associated with death: *his dying hour.* **3.** given, uttered, or appearing just before death: *her dying words.* **4.** drawing to a close: *the dying year.* —*n.* **5.** [*noncount*] the act or process of ceasing to live, exist, or function: *a book on how to face dying with dignity.* **6. the dying,** [*plural; used with a plural verb*] people who are approaching death: *How can we help the dying gain better control of their last weeks?*

dyke[1] (dīk) /dayk/ *n.* DIKE[1].

dyke[2] or **dike** (dīk) /dayk/ *n.* [*count*] *Slang (disparaging and offensive).* a female homosexual; lesbian.

-dyn-, *root.* -*dyn*- comes from Greek, where it has the meaning "power." This meaning is found in such words as: DYNAMIC, DYNAMISM, DYNAMITE, DYNAMO, DYNASTY.

dy•nam•ic (dī nam′ik) /dayˈnæmɪk/ *adj.* Also, **dy•nam′i•cal. 1.** vigorously active or forceful; energetic: *a dynamic person.* **2.** characterized by or producing change or progress: *It's a dynamic process, not a static one.* **3.** of or relating to force, power, or motion. **4.** of or relating to the science of dynamics. —**dy•nam′i•cal•ly,** *adv.* See -DYN-.

dy•nam•ics (dī nam′iks) /dayˈnæmɪks/ *n.* **1.** [*noncount; used with a singular verb*] the branch of mechanics that deals with the motion of systems that are acted on by forces from outside the system: *Dynamics tells us how underwater forces work on the movement of submarines.* **2.** [*plural; used with a plural verb*] the motivating forces in a system; the pattern of development in a field: *the dynamics of sound change in English.*

dy•na•mism (dī′nə miz′əm) /ˈdaynəˌmɪzəm/ *n.* [*noncount*] **1.** a theory that seeks to explain phenomena of nature by the action of force. **2.** great energy, force, or power: *The new chairman had great dynamism.* See -DYN-.

dy•na•mite (dī′nə mīt′) /ˈdaynəˌmayt/ *n.*, *v.*, **-mit•ed, -mit•ing,** *adj.* —*n.* [*noncount*] **1.** a powerful explosive made with ammonium nitrate. **2.** any person or thing having a spectacular explosive effect: *That story was political dynamite.* —*v.* [~ + *obj*] **3.** to blow up, shatter, or destroy with dynamite: *The commandos dynamited the bridge.* —*adj.* **4.** *Informal.* wonderful or exciting: *a dynamite idea.* See -DYN-.

dy•na•mo (dī′nə mō′) /ˈdaynəˌmow/ *n.* [*count*], *pl.* **-mos. 1.** an electric generator, esp. for direct current. **2.** an energetic, forceful person: *She's a real dynamo.* See -DYN-.

dy•nas•ty (dī′nə stē) /ˈdaynəstiy/ *n.* [*count*] *pl.* **-ties. 1.** a sequence of rulers from the same family: *the Ming dynasty.* **2.** the period in which such a family rules: *occurring in the Han dynasty.* **3.** any succession of members of a powerful family or group: *the dynasty of the oil companies.* —**dy•nas•tic** (dī nas′tik) /dayˈnæstɪk/ *adj.* See -DYN-.

dys-, *prefix. dys-* comes from Greek, where it has the meaning "ill, bad." This meaning is found in such words as: DYSENTERY, DYSLEXIA, DYSPEPSIA.

dys•en•ter•y (dis′ən ter′ē) /ˈdɪsənˌtɛriy/ *n.* [*noncount*] an infectious disease of the large intestines, with diarrhea containing mucus and often blood.

dys•lex•i•a (dis lek′sē ə) /dɪsˈlɛksiyə/ *n.* [*noncount*] a reading disorder in which the person has difficulty in interpreting relationships in space, distinguishing shapes, or in integrating information taken in by hearing and sight. —**dys•lex′ic,** *adj., n.* [*count*] See -LEG-.

dys•pep•sia (dis pep′shə, -sē ə) /dɪsˈpɛpʃə, -siyə/ *n.* [*noncount*] impaired digestion; indigestion. —**dys•pep•tic** (dis pep′tik) /dɪsˈpɛptɪk/ *adj., n.* [*count*]

dz., an abbreviation of: dozen.

E, e (ē) /iy/ *n.* [*count*], *pl.* **Es** or **E's, es** or **e's.** the fifth letter of the English alphabet, a vowel.

E., an abbreviation of: **1.** Earth. **2.** east. **3.** eastern. **4.** engineering.

ea., an abbreviation of: each.

each (ēch) /iytʃ/ *adj.* **1.** every one of a group of two or more members, considered individually or one by one: [*before a singular count noun*]: *Each student has a different solution to the problem.* [*after a plural noun or pronoun*]: *The students each have a different solution to the problem.* **—pron. 2.** every one individually; each one: *Each has a different solution to the problem.* [~ + *of* + *the/my/these/etc.* + *plural noun*]: *Each of these students has a different solution to the problem.* **—adv. 3.** to, from, or for each; apiece: *The pens cost a dollar each.* **—Syn.** The pronouns or adjectives EACH and EVERY contrast in meaning but are sometimes confused or misused because both may be followed by a singular count noun: *Each/Every student is a winner.* EACH separates a group into individuals, but EVERY emphasizes the similarity of all the members of a group: *Each pianist plays that piece a little differently. Every pianist plays that piece the same way.* **—Usage.** When the adjective EACH follows a plural subject, the verb agrees with the subject: *The houses each have central heating.* When EACH is used as a pronoun, it is singular; when it is followed by an *of* phrase containing a plural noun or pronoun, it requires a singular verb: *Each of the candidates has spoken on the issue.* However, plural verbs occur frequently even in edited writing. Usage guides also advise that when referring to EACH with a pronoun, the pronoun must be singular: *Each club member had his own project.* But the use of plural pronouns has been increasing in the U.S., as in *Each club member had their own project,* partially to avoid sexism (that is, the use of *his* when meaning *his or her).* These same patterns of pronoun agreement are followed in the use of *anyone, anybody, everyone, everybody, no one, someone,* and *somebody.* See also THEY.

each′ oth′er, *pron.* [*used as an object to refer to the subject*] each the other; one another: *Those two love each other.* **—Usage.** Some guides to usage advise that EACH OTHER should be used when the subject referred back to is two persons or things; ONE ANOTHER should be used to refer back to three or more or an indefinite number. In standard practice, however, these expressions are used interchangeably, without distinction as to number.

ea•ger (ē′gər) /ˈiygər/ *adj.* having or showing strong desire or interest; longing impatiently: *He is an eager student.* [*be* + ~ + *for*]: *He is eager for success.* [*be* + ~ + *to* + *verb*]: *He is eager to try it.* **—ea′ger•ly,** *adv.*: *We eagerly awaited their arrival.* **—ea′ger•ness,** *n.* [*noncount*]

ea•gle (ē′gəl) /ˈiygəl/ *n.* [*count*] a large, powerful, broad-winged bird having a large bill and claws to catch its prey.

ea′gle-eyed′, *adj.* having unusually sharp ability to watch or observe: *She is an eagle-eyed editor who catches my slightest mistakes.*

ear[1] (ēr) /ɪər/ *n.* **1.** [*count*] the organ of hearing, including the outer part on either side of the head. **2.** [*noncount*] the sense of hearing: *sounds that are pleasing to the ear.* **3.** [*count; usually singular*] keen or sensitive ability to notice the differences among sounds, esp. musical sounds: *a good ear for music.* **4.** [*noncount*] attention; heed: *always had the boss's ear.* **—Idiom. 5. be all ears,** to be extremely attentive; listen: *Tell me about it; I'm all ears.* **6. by ear,** without reference to written music: *could play any tune by ear.* **—ear′less,** *adj.*

ear[2] (ēr) /ɪər/ *n.* [*count*] the top part or spike of a cereal plant, containing the seed grains.

ear•ache (ēr′āk′) /ˈɪərˌeyk/ *n.* [*count*] a pain or ache in the ear.

ear•drum (ēr′drum′) /ˈɪərˌdrʌm/ *n.* [*count*] a thin piece of tissue in the inside of the ear that vibrates when sound waves hit it.

earl (ûrl) /ɜrl/ *n.* [*count*] a British nobleman of a rank that is below a marquis and above a viscount.

ear′lobe′ or **ear′ lobe′,** *n.* [*count*] the soft, hanging lower part of the outer ear.

ear•ly (ûr′lē) /ˈɜrliy/ *adv.* and *adj.*, **-li•er, -li•est.** **—adv. 1.** in or during the beginning: *early in the year.* **2.** in the early part of the morning: *to get up early.* **3.** before the usual or appointed time; ahead of time: *The train arrived early!* **—adj. 4.** [*before a noun*] occurring in the beginning: *an early hour of the day.* **5.** occurring before the usual or appointed time: *an early dinner.* **6.** [*before a noun*] occurring in the near future: *I look forward to an early reply.* **—Idiom. 7. early on,** not long after the beginning. **—ear′li•ness,** *n.* [*noncount*]

ear•mark (ēr′märk′) /ˈɪərˌmɑrk/ *n.* [*count*] **1.** any mark or characteristic that identifies something: *Those plans have all the earmarks of a conspiracy.* **—v.** [~ + *obj*] **2.** to set aside for a specific purpose: *The budget earmarked $1,000 for repairs.*

ear•muff (ēr′muf′) /ˈɪərˌmʌf/ *n.* [*count*] one of a pair of connected coverings for the ears in cold weather.

earn (ûrn) /ɜrn/ *v.* [~ + *obj*] **1.** to receive in return for one's labor or service: *to earn a living as a waiter.* **2.** to deserve; to merit (something) as a reward for service: *He had earned a reputation for honesty.*

ear•nest (ûr′nist) /ˈɜrnɪst/ *adj.* **1.** serious in intention, purpose, or action: *The earnest young man had no use for jokes.* **2.** seriously important; grave: *an earnest request for forgiveness.* **—Idiom. 3. in earnest,** in full seriousness: *Work began in earnest as the deadline approached.* **—ear′nest•ly,** *adv.* **—ear′nest•ness,** *n.* [*noncount*]

earn•ings (ûr′ningz) /ˈɜrnɪŋz/ *n.* [*plural*] money earned; wages; profits: *My earnings seem to fall as inflation rises.*

ear•phone (ēr′fōn′) /ˈɪərˌfown/ *n.* [*count*] **1.** a sound receiver, as of a radio or telephone, that fits in or over the ear. **2.** Usually, **earphones.** [*plural*] a headset.

ear•ring (ēr′ing) /ˈɪərɪŋ/ *n.* [*count*] an ornament worn on or hanging from the lobe of the ear. **—ear′ringed,** *adj.*

ear•shot (ēr′shot′) /ˈɪərˌʃɒt/ *n.* [*noncount*] the distance within which a sound, voice, etc., can be heard: *I was out of earshot but could see them waving.*

ear•split•ting (ēr′split′ing) /ˈɪərˌsplɪtɪŋ/ *adj.* extremely loud or shrill in sound: *an ear-splitting crash.*

earth (ûrth) /ɜrθ/ *n.* **1.** the planet on which human beings live, third in order from the sun: [*proper noun: Earth*]: *Earth is the place we call home.* [*proper noun; the* + ~]: *The earth is one of the few planets known to have a carbon dioxide and oxygen atmosphere.* **2.** [*noncount*] the surface of this planet: *to fall to earth.* **3.** [*noncount*] soil and dirt, as distinguished from rock and sand: *The farmer examined a handful of earth.* **—Idiom. 4. on earth,** (used to express emphasis, disbelief, or emotion): **a.** (after words beginning with *wh-* that ask a question, or the word *how*): *Where on earth have you been? What on earth do you mean?* **b.** (after a phrase that has an adjective and a noun, to emphasize the adjective): *This is the worst job on earth.*

earth•en (ûr′thən) /ˈɜrθən/ *adj.* [*before a noun*] **1.** made up of earth: *an earthen floor.* **2.** made of baked clay: *an earthen pot.*

earth•ling (ûrth′ling) /ˈɜrθlɪŋ/ *n.* [*count*] *Informal.* a person who lives on the earth.

earth•ly (ûrth′lē) /ˈɜrθliy/ *adj.*, **-li•er, -li•est.** of or relating to the earth, esp. as opposed to heaven; worldly: *We were warned about being too occupied by earthly pleasures.*

earth•quake (ûrth′kwāk′) /ˈɜrθˌkweyk/ *n.* [*count*] vibrations in the earth's crust causing the ground to shake: *a devastating earthquake.*

earth•shak•ing (ûrth′shā′king) /ˈɜrθˌʃeykɪŋ/ *adj.* challenging or affecting basic beliefs, attitudes, or relationships: *earthshaking changes in our culture.*

earth•worm (ûrth′wûrm′) /ˈɜrθˌwɜrm/ *n.* [*count*] a long worm that has segments or rings on its body and that burrows in soil.

earth•y (ûr′thē) /ˈɜrθiy/ *adj.*, **earth•i•er, earth•i•est. 1.** of, like, or consisting of earth or soil: *an earthy smell.* **2.** realistic; practical: *earthy advice.* **3.** blunt; direct; frank: *an earthy sense of humor.* **—earth′i•ness,** *n.* [*noncount*]

ease (ēz) /iyz/ *n.*, *v.*, **eased, eas•ing.** **—n.** [*noncount*] **1.** freedom from concern, anxiety, or worry: *Let me put your mind at ease.* **2.** freedom from difficulty; facility: *We won the game with ease.* **3.** freedom from financial need; plenty: *a life of ease.* **—v. 4.** [~ + *obj*] to free from anxiety or care: *The pilot's calm voice eased the passengers' fears.* **5.** to (cause to) become less painful: [~ + *obj*]: *The aspirin eased his headache.* [*no obj*]: *As the aspirin took effect, his headache eased.* **6.** to (cause to) become less difficult or severe: [*no obj*]: *Tensions eased as the UN team arrived and organized a truce.* [~ + *obj*]: *The two leaders have been trying to ease tension between* *their countries.* [~ + *up/off* + *on* + *obj*]: *The boss has eased up on him now that he's doing good work.* **7.** to (cause to) be moved or shifted with great care: [~ + *obj*]: *The pilot eased the plane down the runway.* [*no obj*]: *The plane eased down the runway, then gradually took off.*

ea•sel (ē′zəl) /ˈiyzəl/ *n.* [*count*] a stand or frame for supporting or displaying at an angle an artist's canvas, a blackboard, etc.

eas•i•ly (ē′zə lē, ēz′lē) /ˈiyzəliy, ˈiyzliy/ *adv.* **1.** in an easy manner; without trouble: *She easily swam across the river.* **2.** without doubt: *This drawing is easily the best and wins first prize.* **3.** likely: *He may easily change his mind.*

eas•i•ness (ē′zē nis) /ˈiyziynɪs/ *n.* [*noncount*] the quality or condition of being easy.

east (ēst) /iyst/ *n.* [*noncount; usually: the* + ~] **1.** one of the four points of the compass, 90° to the right of north. *Abbr:* E **2.** the direction in which this point lies. **3.** [*usually: East*] a region or territory situated in this direction. *—adj.* **4.** directed or proceeding toward the east: *an east window.* **5.** coming from the east. **6.** lying toward or situated in the east. *—adv.* **7.** to, toward, or in the east: *heading east.* —**east′er•ly,** *adj., adv.* —**east•ward** (ēst′wərd) /ˈiystwərd/ *adj., adv.* —**east′wards,** *adv.*

Eas•ter (ē′stər) /ˈiystər/ *n.* [*proper noun*] **1.** a yearly Christian festival to celebrate the resurrection of Jesus Christ, observed on the first Sunday after the first full moon that occurs on or after March 21. **2.** the day on which this festival is celebrated.

east•ern (ē′stərn) /ˈiystərn/ *adj.* **1.** lying toward or situated in the east. **2.** directed or proceeding toward the east. **3.** coming from the east.

eas•y (ē′zē) /ˈiyziy/ *adj.* and *adv.,* **eas•i•er, eas•i•est.** *—adj.* **1.** requiring no great labor or effort: *The teacher gave us an easy assignment.* [*be* + ~ + *to* + *verb*]: *The assignment was easy to do.* **2.** free from pain or care: *an easy mind.* **3.** providing ease or comfort: *With all that money, he's always had an easy life.* **4.** [*before a noun*] easygoing; relaxed: *an easy manner.* **5.** not harsh or strict; lenient: *an easy teacher.* **6.** not burdensome; not oppressive: *easy terms on a loan.* **—*Idiom.*** **7. easy does it,** (used as a command or suggestion) be careful: *Easy does it when you lift the refrigerator.* **8. take it easy** or **go easy, a.** to not work too hard: *The doctor advised me to take it easy.* **b.** to not go too fast, or not act with too much excitement: *Take it easy, the speed limit is only 30 mph here.* **—Related Words.** EASY is an adjective, EASE is a noun and a verb, EASILY is an adverb, EASINESS is a noun: *That was easy homework. He did the homework with ease. He eased into his chair. He easily finished the homework. He was surprised by the easiness of the assignment.*

eas′y chair′, *n.* [*count*] a usually large, upholstered armchair.

eas•y•go•ing (ē′zē gō′ing) /ˈiyziyˈgowɪŋ/ *adj.* relaxed and casual; calm.

eat (ēt) /iyt/ *v.,* **ate** (āt; *esp. Brit.* et) /eyt; *esp. Brit.* ɛt/ **eat•en** (ēt′n) /ˈiytn̩/ **eat•ing,** *n.* *—v.* **1.** to take into the mouth and swallow for nourishment: [~ + *obj*]: *We ate dinner early.* [*no obj*]: *We haven't eaten all day.* **2.** [~ + *up/away/into* + *obj*] to use up, esp. wastefully; consume gradually or slowly: *Unexpected expenses ate up their savings.* **3.** [~ + *obj*] to make (a hole, passage, etc.), as by wearing away, gnawing, or corroding: *The acid ate a hole right through the metal.* *—n.* **4. eats,** [*plural*] *Informal.* food: *The eats are good there and the prices are cheap.* —**eat′er,** *n.* [*count*]

eat•er•y (ē′tə rē) /ˈiytəriy/ *n.* [*count*], *pl.* **-er•ies.** *Informal.* a restaurant.

eave (ēv) /iyv/ *n.* [*count*] Usually, **eaves.** [*plural*] the overhanging lower edge of a roof.

eaves•drop (ēvz′drop′) /ˈiyvz,drɒp/ *v.* [*no obj*], **-dropped, -drop•ping.** to listen secretly: *I didn't intend to eavesdrop, but I could hear them arguing.* —**eaves′-drop′per,** *n.* [*count*]

ebb (eb) /ɛb/ *n.* **1.** [*noncount*] the flowing back of the tide to a lower level as the water returns to the sea. **2.** [*count; usually singular*] a flowing backward or away; decline or decay; a state of decline. *—v.* [*no obj*] **3.** to flow back or away, such as the water of a tide: *A crab was left stranded on the beach as the tide ebbed.* **4.** to decline or decay; fade away: *His strength began to ebb.*

eb•on•y (eb′ə nē) /ˈɛbəniy/ *n., pl.* **-on•ies,** *adj.* *—n.* **1.** [*noncount*] a hard, heavy, strong, dark wood from tropical Africa and Asia. **2.** [*count*] any tree providing such wood. **3.** [*noncount*] a deep, lustrous black. *—adj.* **4.** made of ebony. **5.** of a deep, lustrous black.

e•bul•lient (i bul′yənt, i bŏŏl′-) /ɪˈbʌlyənt, ɪˈbʊl-/ *adj.* **1.** overflowing with enthusiasm, excitement, or liveliness: *They were in an ebullient mood as they tackled the new project.* **2.** bubbling up like a boiling liquid. —**e•bul′-lience,** *n.* [*noncount*] —**e•bul′lient•ly,** *adv.*

EC, an abbreviation of: European Community.

ec•cen•tric (ik sen′trik) /ɪkˈsɛntrɪk/ *adj.* **1.** departing from accepted or customary character; unconventional; peculiar; odd; strange: *eccentric behavior.* *—n.* [*count*] **2.** an eccentric person. —**ec•cen′tri•cal•ly,** *adv.*

ec•cen•tric•i•ty (ek′sen tris′i tē) /,ɛksɛnˈtrɪsɪtiy/ *n.* **1.** [*noncount*] peculiar, odd, or strange behavior. **2.** [*count*] an action, habit, or attitude that is peculiar, odd, or strange.

eccl. or **eccles.,** an abbreviation of: **1.** ecclesiastic. **2.** ecclesiastical.

ec•cle•si•as•tic (i klē′zē as′tik) /ɪ,kliyziyˈæstɪk/ *n.* [*count*] a member of the clergy, especially in the Christian church.

ec•cle•si•as•ti•cal (i klē′zē as′ti kəl) /ɪ,kliyziyˈæstɪkəl/ *adj.* of or relating to the church or the clergy; clerical; not secular.

ECG, an abbreviation of: **1.** electrocardiogram. **2.** electrocardiograph.

ech•e•lon (esh′ə lon′) /ˈɛʃə,lɒn/ *n.* [*count*] **1.** a level of command, authority, or rank: *the upper echelons of the administration.* **2.** a steplike formation, as of troops, ships, or planes.

ech•o (ek′ō) /ˈɛkow/ *n., pl.* **ech•oes,** *v.,* **ech•oed, ech•o•ing.** *—n.* [*count*] **1.** a repetition of sound produced by the reflection of sound waves. **2.** a lingering trace or effect of something long past: *The estate is a mere echo of its former splendor.* *—v.* **3.** [*no obj*] (of a place) to give out the sound of an echo; resound with an echo: *The hall echoed with cheers.* **4.** to repeat or be repeated by or as if by an echo: [*no obj*]: *Cheers echoed in the hall.* [~ + *obj*]: *The hall echoes the faintest sounds.* **5.** [~ + *obj*] to repeat, copy, or imitate the words, sentiments, etc., of (a person): *The candidate echoed his opponent in calling for lower taxes.* **6.** [~ + *obj*] to repeat, copy, or imitate (words, sentiments, etc.): *He echoed my call for vigilance.*

é•clair (ā klâr′, i klâr′, ā′klâr) /eyˈklɛər, ɪˈklɛər, ˈeyklɛər/ *n.* [*count*] an elongated pastry filled with custard or whipped cream and usually covered with frosting.

ec•lec•tic (i klek′tik) /ɪˈklɛktɪk/ *adj.* selecting or made up of elements from various sources: *an eclectic philosophy.* —**ec•lec•ti•cism** (i klek′ti siz′əm) /ɪˈklɛktɪ,sɪzəm/ *n.* [*noncount*]

e•clipse (i klips′) /ɪˈklɪps/ *n., v.,* **e•clipsed** (i klipst′) /ɪˈklɪpst/ **e•clips•ing.** *—n.* **1.** [*count*] the covering or cutting off of the light of one heavenly body by another: *lunar eclipse; solar eclipse.* **2.** [*noncount*] a reduction or loss of power, status, fame, or reputation: *The actor's reputation went into eclipse after the scandal.* *—v.* [~ + *obj*] **3.** to cause to undergo eclipse: *The moon eclipsed the sun.* **4.** to make less outstanding or important by comparison; surpass: *This eclipses all his former achievements.*

e•col•o•gi•cal (ek′ə loj′i kəl, ē′kə-) /,ɛkəˈlɒdʒɪkəl, ,iykə-/ *adj.* [*before a noun*] **1.** of or relating to the study of relations between living things and their environment. **2.** calling for the protection of air, water, and other natural resources from pollution or its effects; environmental. —**ec′o•log′i•cal•ly,** *adv.*

e•col•o•gist (i kol′ə jist) /ɪˈkɒlədʒɪst/ *n.* [*count*] a person who studies ecology.

e•col•o•gy (i kol′ə jē) /ɪˈkɒlədʒiy/ *n.* [*noncount*] **1.** the branch of biology dealing with the relations between living things and their environment. **2.** the set of relationships between organisms and their environment. **3.** the act or policy of calling for protection of the air, water, and other natural resources from pollution or its effects; environmentalism: *active in ecology.* See -LOGY.

econ., an abbreviation of: **1.** economic. **2.** economics. **3.** economy.

ec•o•nom•ic (ek′ə nom′ik, ē′kə-) /,ɛkəˈnɒmɪk, ,iykə-/ *adj.* **1.** [*before a noun*] of or relating to the production, distribution, and use of income, wealth, and goods and services. **2.** [*before a noun*] of or relating to the science of economics. **3.** ECONOMICAL.

ec•o•nom•i•cal (ek′ə nom′i kəl, ē′kə-) /,ɛkəˈnɒmɪkəl, ,iykə-/ *adj.* avoiding waste; thrifty; producing or resulting in profit or savings: *an economical meal.* —**ec′o•nom′i•cal•ly,** *adv.* **—Syn.** ECONOMICAL, THRIFTY, FRUGAL imply careful and efficient use of money, supplies, or resources. ECONOMICAL implies careful and wise planning in the use of resources so as to avoid unnecessary waste or expense: *It is economical to buy in large quantities.* THRIFTY adds the idea of working hard to save and of managing successfully: *She is a thrifty shopper and always looks for bargains.* FRUGAL suggests saving by denying oneself luxuries: *He is so frugal that he never takes taxis but walks instead.*

ec•o•nom•ics (ek′ə nom′iks, ē′kə-) /ˌɛkə'nɒmɪks, ˌiykə-/ *n.* **1.** [*noncount; used with a singular verb*] the science that deals with the production, distribution, and use of goods and services, or human welfare. **2.** [*plural; used with a plural verb*] financial considerations; aspects (of a situation) that are economically significant. **—e•con•o•mist** (i kon′ə mist) /ɪ'kɒnəmɪst/ *n.* [*count*]

e•con•o•mize (i kon′ə mīz′) /ɪ'kɒnəˌmayz/ *v.* [*no obj;* (~ + *on* + *obj*)], **-mized, -miz•ing.** to practice economy; spend carefully.

e•con•o•my (i kon′ə mē) /ɪ'kɒnəmiy/ *n., pl.* **-mies. 1.** [*noncount*] thrifty management; wise care in the saving, spending, or using of money, materials, etc. **2.** [*count*] an act or means of such care: *Walking to work is one of my economies.* **3.** [*count*] the management of the resources of a community, country, etc., esp. with a view to its productivity. See -NOM-[1]. **—Related Words.** ECONOMY is a noun, ECONOMICS is a noun, ECONOMICAL is an adjective, ECONOMIZE is a verb: *The economy is improving. Economics is a hard subject. They bought an economical car. They need to economize on fuel.*

ec•o•sys•tem (ek′ō sis′təm, ē′kō-) /'ɛkowˌsɪstəm, 'iykow-/ *n.* [*count*] a system formed by a community of living things, their environment, and the relationship between them.

ec•sta•sy (ek′stə sē) /'ɛkstəsiy/ *n., pl.* **-sies. 1.** [*noncount*] extreme joyfulness or happiness; rapture. **2.** [*count*] any overpowering emotion; sudden, intense feeling or excitement. **—ec•stat•ic** (ek stat′ik) /ɛk'stætɪk/ *adj.* **—ec•stat′ic•al•ly,** *adv.*

Ec•ua•do•ran (ek′wə dôr′ən) /ˌɛkwə'dɔrən/ *adj.* Also, **Ec•ua•dor•e•an, Ec•ua•do•ri•an** (ek′wə dôr′ē ən) /ˌɛkwə'dɔriyən/. **1.** of or relating to Ecuador. **—***n.* [*count*] **2.** a person born or living in Ecuador.

ec•u•men•i•cal (ek′yŏŏ men′i kəl) /'ɛkyʊ'mɛnɪkəl/ *adj.* **1.** promoting Christian unity throughout the world. **2.** involving or containing a mixture of diverse, esp. international, elements. **—ec′u•men′i•cal•ly,** *adv.*

ec•ze•ma (ek′sə mə) /'ɛksəmə/ *n.* [*noncount*] a condition of the skin that is accompanied by itching and sores.

ed (ed) /ɛd/ *n.* [*noncount*] *Informal.* education: *driver's ed.*

-ed, *suffix.* **1.** *-ed* is attached to words with the following rules of form: **a.** For most regular verbs that end in a consonant, *-ed* is added directly afterwards: *cross + -ed → crossed.* When the verb ends in *-y*, the *-y* changes to *-i-* and *-ed* is added: *ready + -ed → readied.* If the word ends in *-e*, an *e* is dropped: *save + -ed → saved.* **b.** The pronunciation of the suffix *-ed* depends on the *sound* that appears before it. After the sounds (p, k, f, th, s, sh *and* ch) /p, k, f, θ, s, ʃ *and* tʃ/ the suffix is pronounced (t) /t/: *cross + -ed → crossed* (krôst) /krɔst/; after the sounds (t, d) it is pronounced (id) /ɪd/: *edit + -ed → edited* (ed′i tid) /'ɛdɪ tɪd/; after all other sounds it is pronounced (d) /d/: *budge + -ed → budged* (bujd) /bʌdʒd/. **2.** *-ed* carries a number of different meanings. It is used **a.** to form the past tense and past participle of regular verbs: *He crossed the river. He had crossed the river when we got there.* **b.** to form an adjective indicating a condition or quality due to action of the verb: *inflated balloons (= balloons that have been inflated).* **c.** after nouns to form adjectives with the meaning "possessing, having, or characterized by (whatever the noun base is)": *beard + -ed → bearded (= possessing or having a beard).*

ed., an abbreviation of: **1.** *pl.* **eds.** edition. **2.** *pl.* **eds.** editor. **3.** education.

ed•dy (ed′ē) /'ɛdiy/ *n.* [*count*], *pl.* **-dies.** a whirling current of liquid, gas, dust, etc.

edge (ej) /ɛdʒ/ *n., v.,* **edged, edg•ing. —***n.* [*count*] **1.** a line or border at which a surface ends: *Grass grew along the edge of the road.* **2.** a brink; a verge: *at the edge of disaster.* **3.** the thin, sharp side of the blade of a cutting instrument or weapon. **4.** a quality of sharpness or keenness, often showing anger: *Her voice had an edge to it.* **5.** an improved position; advantage: *an edge on our competitors.* **—***v.* **6.** [~ + *obj*] to provide with an edge or border. **7.** to make or force (one's way) gradually, esp. by moving sideways or cautiously: [*no obj*]: *They edged slowly toward the door.* [~ + *obj*]: *She edged the car up to the curb.* **—*Idiom.* 8. on edge,** in a state of irritability; tense; nervous. **9. set one's teeth on edge,** to cause extreme discomfort or unpleasantness.

edge•wise (ej′wīz′) /'ɛdʒˌwayz/ also **edge•ways** (ej′wāz′) /'ɛdʒˌweyz/ *adv.* **1.** in the direction of the edge; sideways: *squeezed the papers in edgewise between the books.* **—*Idiom.* 2. get a word in edgewise,** to succeed in participating in a conversation when someone else is very talkative: *I can't get a word in edgewise when he is talking.*

edg•y (ej′ē) /'ɛdʒiy/ *adj.,* **edg•i•er, edg•i•est.** nervously irritable; anxious; on edge: *edgy before a deadline.* **—edg•i•ly** (ej′ə lē) /'ɛdʒəliy/ *adv.* **—edg′i•ness,** *n.* [*noncount*]

ed•i•ble (ed′ə bəl) /'ɛdəbəl/ *adj.* **1.** fit to be eaten as food; safe; eatable. **—***n.* **2.** Usually, **edibles.** [*plural*] edible substances; food. **—ed•i•bil•i•ty** (ed′ə bil′i tē) /ˌɛdə'bɪlɪtiy/ **ed′i•ble•ness,** *n.* [*noncount*]

e•dict (ē′dikt) /'iydɪkt/ *n.* [*count*] **1.** a decree issued by a sovereign or other authority: *an edict from the king announcing higher taxes.* **2.** any proclamation or command given by an authority: *another edict from the supervisor demanding that the men wear jackets and ties every day.* See -DIC-.

ed•i•fice (ed′ə fis) /'ɛdəfɪs/ *n.* [*count*] a building, esp. one of large size or imposing appearance: *a 50-story edifice.*

ed•i•fy (ed′ə fī′) /'ɛdəˌfay/ *v.* [~ + *obj*], **-fied, -fy•ing.** to instruct or benefit, esp. morally or spiritually; uplift; enlighten: *They read bible stories to edify their young children.* **—ed′i•fy′ing,** *adj.: an edifying speech to improve morale among the counselors.* **—ed•i•fi•ca•tion** (ed′ə fi kā′shən) /ˌɛdəfɪ'keyʃən/ *n.* [*noncount*]

ed•it (ed′it) /'ɛdɪt/ *v.* [~ + *obj*] **1.** to supervise or direct the preparation of (a publication): *Who edits the school newspaper?* **2.** to collect, prepare, and arrange (materials) for publication: *She edited the president's speeches.* **3.** to prepare (film, tape, etc.) by deleting, arranging, and changing material: *He spent a week editing the film for television.* **4.** to change or modify (computer data or text): *I edited the document on screen.* **—***n.* [*count*] **5.** an instance or the process of editing, as of correcting something: *a few minor edits.* **—ed′i•tor,** *n.* [*count*]

edit., an abbreviation of: **1.** edited. **2.** edition. **3.** editor.

e•di•tion (i dish′ən) /ɪ'dɪʃən/ *n.* [*count*] **1.** one of a series of printings of a book, newspaper, etc., produced at one time and differing from another by changes, additions, etc.: *the afternoon edition of the paper.* **2.** the format in which a literary work is published: *a paperback edition.* **3.** the whole number of impressions or copies of a book, newspaper, etc. **4.** a version, esp. of something presented to the public: *a limited edition of a classic car.*

ed•i•to•ri•al (ed′i tôr′ē əl, -tōr′-) /ˌɛdɪ'tɔriyəl, -'towr-/ *n.* [*count*] **1.** an article in a newspaper, magazine, etc., that presents the opinion of the publishers or editors. **—***adj.* [*before a noun*] **2.** of or relating to an editor or editing: *an editorial staff.* **—ed′i•to′ri•al•ly,** *adv.*

EDP, an abbreviation of: electronic data processing.

EDT or **E.D.T.,** an abbreviation of: Eastern daylight-saving time.

educ., an abbreviation of: **1.** educated. **2.** education. **3.** educational.

ed•u•ca•ble (ej′ŏŏ kə bəl) /'ɛdʒʊkəbəl/ *adj.* capable of being educated.

ed•u•cate (ej′ŏŏ kāt′) /'ɛdʒʊˌkeyt/ *v.* [~ + *obj*], **-cat•ed, -cat•ing. 1.** to teach (a person) by instruction or schooling; train: *an economist educated at Harvard.* **2.** to provide education for; send to school: *They raised and educated their two daughters.* **—ed′u•cat′ed,** *adj.* **—ed′u•ca′tor,** *n.* [*count*] **—Related Words.** EDUCATE is a verb, EDUCATED and EDUCATIONAL are adjectives, EDUCATION and EDUCATOR are nouns: *Teachers educate their students. We need a well-educated work force. There are new educational methods in classes today. Education is important. Parents and educators got together to decide how to solve the problem.* See -DUC-.

ed•u•ca•tion (ej′ŏŏ kā′shən) /ˌɛdʒʊ'keyʃən/ *n.* **1.** [*noncount*] the act or process of educating. **2.** [*count; usually singular*] a degree, level, or kind of schooling: *a college education.* **3.** [*noncount*] the science or art of teaching; teaching methods and theory: *You need six more courses in education to get your teacher's certificate.* **—ed′u•ca′tion•al,** *adj.* See -DUC-.

-ee, *suffix.* **1.** *-ee* is attached to verbs that take an object to form nouns with the meaning "the person who is the object of the action of the verb": *address* + *-ee* → *addressee (= the person whom someone else addresses).* **2.** *-ee* is attached to verbs that do not take an object to form nouns with the meaning "the one doing or performing the act of the verb": *escape* + *-ee* → *escapee (= one performing the act of escaping).* **3.** *-ee* is attached to other words to form nouns with the meaning "the one who is or does": *absent* + *-ee* → *absentee (= one who is absent).*

E.E., an abbreviation of: **1.** electrical engineer. **2.** electrical engineering.

EEC, an abbreviation of: European Economic Community.

EEG, an abbreviation of: electroencephalogram.

eel (ēl) /iyl/ *n.* [*count*], *pl.* (*esp. when thought of as a group*) **eel,** (*esp. for kinds or species*) **eels.** a long-bodied, snakelike fish.

EEO, an abbreviation of: equal employment opportunity.

-eer, *suffix. -eer* is used to form nouns with the meaning "the person who produces, handles, or is associated with" the base word: *engine* + *-eer* → *engineer (= person handling an engine).*

ee•rie or **ee•ry** (ēr′ē) /ˈɪəriy/ *adj.,* **-ri•er, -ri•est.** strange and mysterious, so as to inspire awe: *an eerie feeling in the graveyard.* **—ee ri•ly** (ēr′ə lē) /ˈɪərəliy/ *adv.* **—ee′ri•ness,** *n.* [*noncount*]

ef-, *prefix. ef-* is a form of EX- attached to roots beginning with *f: efficient.*

ef•face (i fās′) /ɪˈfeys/ *v.* [~ + *obj*], **-faced, -fac•ing. 1.** to wipe out; do away with: *to efface unhappy memories.* **2.** to rub out or erase: *Time had effaced the ancient inscriptions.* **3.** [~ + *oneself*] to make (oneself) less noticeable and more humble; behave modestly or shyly: *effaced himself before the boss.* See -FACE-.

ef•fect (i fekt′) /ɪˈfɛkt/ *n.* **1.** [*count*] something produced; a result or consequence. **2.** [*noncount*] power to produce results; force: *The protest had no effect.* **3.** [*noncount*] the state of being effective or operative; operation or execution: *to bring a plan into effect.* **4.** [*count*] a mental or emotional impression produced: *He's trying to create a mottled effect with those odd colors.* **—***v.* [~ + *obj*] **5.** to produce as an effect; bring about; accomplish: *to effect a change.* **—*Idiom.* 6. in effect, a.** essentially; basically: *in effect, a whole new way of rewarding workers.* **b.** operating or functioning; in force: *The new law is in effect.* **7. take effect,** to go into operation; begin to function; start to produce a result: *I could feel the whisky begin to take effect.* See -FEC-.

ef•fec•tive (i fek′tiv) /ɪˈfɛktɪv/ *adj.* **1.** able to accomplish a purpose: *very effective teaching methods.* **2.** in operation or in force; functioning: *The law becomes effective at midnight.* **3.** [*before a noun*] real; actual; in fact but not in theory: *The militia was the effective government at the time.* **4.** producing a deep or strong impression; striking: *an effective photograph.* **—ef•fec′tive•ly,** *adv.* **—ef•fec′tive•ness,** *n.* [*noncount*]

ef•fects (i fekts′) /ɪˈfɛkts/ *n.* [*plural*] personal property: *You can put your personal effects in this closet.*

ef•fec•tu•al (i fek′cho͞o əl) /ɪˈfɛktʃuwəl/ *adj.* producing or capable of producing an intended effect; adequate: *a social worker who is not effectual in dealing with teenagers.*

ef•fem•i•nate (i fem′ə nit) /ɪˈfɛmənɪt/ *adj.* (of a man or boy) having traits, tastes, habits, etc., traditionally considered feminine, such as softness or delicacy. **—ef•fem•in•a•cy** (i fem′ə nə sē) /ɪˈfɛmənəsiy/ *n.* [*noncount*] **—ef•fem′i•nate•ly,** *adv.*

ef•fer•vesce (ef′ər ves′) /ˌɛfərˈvɛs/ *v.* [*no obj*], **-vesced, -vesc•ing. 1.** to give off bubbles of gas, such as a carbonated liquid. **2.** to show enthusiasm, excitement, or liveliness. **—ef′fer•ves′cence,** *n.* [*noncount*] **—ef′fer•ves′cent,** *adj.*

ef•fi•ca•cious (ef′i kā′shəs) /ˌɛfɪˈkeyʃəs/ *adj.* capable of having the desired result or effect; effective. See -FEC-.

ef•fi•cient (i fish′ənt) /ɪˈfɪʃənt/ *adj.* performing or functioning effectively with the least waste of time and effort; competent: *an efficient secretary.* **—ef•fi•cien•cy** (i fish′ən sē) /ɪˈfɪʃənsiy/ *n.* [*noncount*] **—ef•fi′cient•ly,** *adv.* See -FEC-.

ef•fi•gy (ef′i jē) /ˈɛfɪdʒiy/ *n.* [*count*], *pl.* **-gies.** a representation or image, esp. of someone who is disliked, used for ridicule: *The protesters burned effigies of the dictator during the riots.*

ef•fort (ef′ərt) /ˈɛfərt/ *n.* **1.** [*noncount*] the use of physical or mental power: *It will take great effort to achieve a victory.* **2.** [*count*] a try; an attempt. **3.** [*count*] something done by hard work. **—ef′fort•less,** *adj.* **—ef′fort•less•ly,** *adv.* See -FORT-.

ef•fron•ter•y (i frun′tə rē) /ɪˈfrʌntəriy/ *n.* [*noncount*] shameless boldness; too much daring.

ef•fu•sive (i fyo͞o′siv) /ɪˈfyuwsɪv/ *adj.* overly expressive of emotion or feeling; lacking reserve: *Her effusive greetings always embarrassed him.* **—ef•fu′sive•ly,** *adv.* **—ef•fu′sive•ness,** *n.* [*noncount*] See -FUS-.

EFL, an abbreviation of: English as a foreign language.

e.g., an abbreviation of Latin *exempli gratia*: for example; for the sake of example; such as.

e•gal•i•tar•i•an (i gal′i târ′ē ən) /ɪˌgælɪˈtɛəriyən/ *adj.* believing in the equality of all people, esp. in political, economic, or social life. **—e•gal′i•tar′i•an•ism,** *n.* [*noncount*]

egg[1] (eg) /ɛg/ *n.* [*count*] **1.** the roundish reproductive body produced by female birds and most reptiles. **2.** Also called **egg′ cell′.** the cell that is produced by the female and that joins with a male cell to form a baby; the female gamete; ovum. **3.** *Informal.* a person: *He's a good egg.* **—*Idiom.* 4. egg on one's face,** obvious embarrassment caused by one's own mistake: *After that dumb remark he had egg on his face.* **5. lay an egg,** *Informal.* to fail badly, esp. while trying to entertain: *With that last joke he really laid an egg.*

egg[2] (eg) /ɛg/ *v.* [~ + *obj* + *on*] to urge or encourage; incite: *He egged his opponent on to make the tennis match more exciting.*

egg•nog (eg′nog′) /ˈɛgˌnɒg/ *n.* [*noncount*] a thick drink made of eggs, cream, sugar, and often liquor.

egg•plant (eg′plant′) /ˈɛgˌplænt/ *n.* **1.** [*count*] a plant grown for its edible, usually dark-purple fruit. **2.** [*noncount*] the fruit of this plant used as a vegetable.

egg′ roll′, *n.* [*count*] a food made up of a thin egg dough rolled around a mixture of minced meat or shrimp and vegetables, and fried in deep fat.

egg•shell (eg′shel′) /ˈɛgˌʃɛl/ *n.* [*count*] the shell of a bird's egg.

e•go (ē′gō) /ˈiygow/ *n., pl.* **e•gos. 1.** [*count*] the "I" or self of a person that experiences and reacts to the outside world. **2.** [*noncount*] egotism; self-importance: *unbearable ego.* **3.** [*noncount*] self-esteem or self-image: *a blow to his ego.*

e•go•cen•tric (ē′gō sen′trik) /ˌiygowˈsɛntrɪk/ *adj.* having little or no thoughts about interests or feelings other than one's own; self-centered: *egocentric demands.* **—e′go•cen′tri•cal•ly,** *adv.* **—e•go•cen•tric•i•ty** (ē′gō-sen tris′i tē) /ˌiygowsɛnˈtrɪsɪtiy/ *n.* [*noncount*] **—e•go•cen•trism** (ē′gō sen′triz əm) /ˌiygowˈsɛntrɪzəm/ *n.* [*noncount*]

e•go•ism (ē′gō iz′əm) /ˈiygowˌɪzəm/ *n.* [*noncount*] excessive care of or concern with oneself; selfishness. **—e′go•ist,** *n.* [*count*]

e•go•tism (ē′gə tiz′əm) /ˈiygəˌtɪzəm/ *n.* [*noncount*] too much reference to oneself in conversation or writing; conceit; self-centeredness. **—e′go•tist,** *n.* [*count*]

e′go trip′, *n.* [*count*] *Informal.* something done primarily to satisfy oneself: *This project has been just one long ego trip for her.*

e•gre•gious (i grē′jəs, -jē əs) /ɪˈgriydʒəs, -dʒiyəs/ *adj.* very bad; flagrant: *an egregious liar.* See -GREG-.

e•gress (ē′gres) /ˈiygrɛs/ *n.* [*count*] a means or place of going out; exit. See -GRESS-.

e•gret (ē′grit) /ˈiygrɪt/ *n.* [*count*] a usually white heron having long, graceful feathers.

E•gyp•tian (i jip′shən) /ɪˈdʒɪpʃən/ *adj.* **1.** of or relating to Egypt. **—***n.* **2.** [*count*] a person born or living in Egypt.

eh (ā, e) /ey, ɛ/ *interj.* (used like a question to express surprise or doubt or to seek agreement): *"Eh, what did you say?" "Well, that was easy, eh?"*

eight (āt) /eyt/ *n.* [*count*] **1.** a number, equal to seven plus one. **2.** a symbol for this number, such as 8 or VIII. **—eighth** (ātth, āth) /eytθ, eyθ/ *adj.*

eight•een (ā′tēn′) /ˈeyˈtiyn/ *n.* [*count*] **1.** a number, ten plus eight. **2.** a symbol for this number, as 18 or XVIII. **—eight′eenth′,** *adj.*

eight•y (ā′tē) /ˈeytiy/ *n.* [*count*], *pl.* **eight•ies. 1.** a number, ten times eight. **2.** a symbol for this number, as 80 or LXXX. **3. eighties,** [*plural*] the numbers from 80 through 89, as in referring to the years of a lifetime or of a century or to degrees of temperature: [*one's* + ~]: *He's in his eighties (= He is between 80 and 89 years of age).* [*the* + ~]: *The temperature is in the eighties.* **—eight′i•eth,** *adj.*

ei•ther (ē′thər, ī′thər) /ˈiyðər, ˈayðər/ *adj.* [~ + *singular count noun*] **1.** one or the other of two: *You may sit at* *either end of the table.* **2.** each of two; the one and the other: *There are trees on either side of the river.* **—*pron.*** **3.** one or the other: *Either will do.* **—*conj.*** **4.** (used with *or* to indicate a series of choices): *Either call or write.* **—*adv.*** **5.** (used with a negative word, phrase, or clause) as well; likewise: *If you don't go, I won't either.* **—Usage.** When used as the subject, the pronoun EITHER takes a singular verb even when followed by a prepositional phrase with a plural object: *Either of the shrubs grows well in this soil.* As an adjective EITHER refers only to two of anything. As a conjunction, EITHER often introduces a series of more than two: *pizza topped with either onions, peppers, or mushrooms.*

Usage guides say that when subjects are joined by EITHER . . . OR (or NEITHER . . . NOR), the verb is singular or plural depending on the noun or pronoun nearer the verb: *Either the parents or the school determines the program. Either the school or the parents determine the program.* See also NEITHER.

e•jac•u•late (i jak′yə lāt′) /ɪ'dʒækyəˌleyt/ *v.*, **-lat•ed, -lat•ing. 1.** to eject or discharge, esp. semen, from the body: [~ + *obj*]: *to ejaculate sperm.* [*no obj*]: *problems in ejaculating because of blockage.* **2.** [~ + *obj*] to utter suddenly and briefly; exclaim. **—e•jac′u•la′tion,** *n.* [*count; noncount*] See -JEC-.

e•ject (i jekt′) /ɪ'dʒɛkt/ *v.* [~ + *obj*] to drive or force out; expel: *The police ejected the noisy demonstrators from the mayor's office.* **—e•jec•tion** (i jek′shən) /ɪ'dʒɛkʃən/ *n.* [*count; noncount*] See -JEC-.

eke (ēk) /iyk/ *v.* **eked, ek•ing. eke out,** [~ + *out* + *obj*], to get or maintain with great effort and difficulty: *to eke out an income with odd jobs.*

EKG, an abbreviation of: **1.** electrocardiogram. **2.** electrocardiograph.

e•lab•o•rate (*adj.* i lab′ər it; *v.* -ə rāt′) /*adj.* ɪ'læbərɪt; *v.* -əˌreyt/ *adj., v.,* **-rat•ed, -rat•ing. —*adj.*** **1.** having many parts; complex: *an elaborate lighting system.* **2.** [*often: before a noun*] worked out in great detail; painstaking. **—*v.*** [*no obj;* (~ + *on* + *obj*)] **3.** to work out in great detail: *Could you elaborate please, Mr. Smith? Please elaborate on your idea.* **—e•lab′o•rate•ly,** *adv.* **—e•lab′o•rate•ness,** *n.* [*noncount*] **—e•lab•o•ra•tion** (i lab′ə rā′shən) /ɪˌlæbə'reyʃən/ *n.* [*noncount*] See -LAB-.

e•lapse (i laps′) /ɪ'læps/ *v.* [*no obj*], **e•lapsed, e•laps•ing.** (of time) to slip or pass by: *Too much time has elapsed since I last heard from you.* See -LAP-.

e•las•tic (i las′tik) /ɪ'læstɪk/ *adj.* **1.** capable of returning to its original length or shape after being stretched: *elastic stockings.* **2.** flexible; adaptable: *elastic rules.* **3.** bouncy or springy: *an elastic step.* **—*n.*** **4.** [*noncount*] fabric or material that is made elastic, as with strips of rubber. **5.** [*count*] RUBBER BAND. **—e•las•tic•i•ty** (i las-tis′i tē, ē′las-) /ɪlæs'tɪsɪtiy, ˌiylæs-/ *n.* [*noncount*]

e•lated (i lā′tid) /ɪ'leytɪd/ *adj.* extremely happy; overjoyed. **—e•la•tion** (i lā′shən) /ɪ'leyʃən/ *n.* [*noncount*] See -LAT-[1].

el•bow (el′bō) /'ɛlbow/ *n.* [*count*] **1.** the bend or joint of the arm between the upper arm and forearm. **2.** something bent like an elbow, such as a piece of pipe bent at an angle. **—*v.*** [~ + *obj*] **3.** to push aside with or as if with the elbow; jostle: *She elbowed him aside and took the seat.*

el′bow grease′, *n.* [*noncount*] physical exertion; hard work: *A little elbow grease and we'll have this place cleaned up in no time.*

el•bow•room (el′bō ro͞om′, -ro͝om′) /'ɛlbowˌruwm, -ˌrʊm/ *n.* [*noncount*] space in which to move freely: *This car needs more elbowroom.*

eld•er[1] (el′dər) /'ɛldər/ *adj. a compar. of* **old** *with* **eldest** *as superl.* [*before a noun; used only of people*] **1.** of greater age; older: *my elder sister.* **—*n.*** [*count*] **2.** an older person: *a boy who respects his elders.* **3.** an older, influential member of a community. **4.** (in certain Protestant churches) a person who is not a member of the clergy and is a governing officer, often assisting in services. **—Related Words.** ELDER is both an adjective and a noun, and ELDERLY is both an adjective and a noun: *Listen to your elders. She is my elder sister. Elderly gentlemen met us at the door. These seats are all reserved for the elderly.*

el•der[2] (el′dər) /'ɛldər/ *n.* [*count*] a shrub or tree having divided leaves and clusters of small berries.

el•der•ber•ry (el′dər ber′ē, -bə rē) /'ɛldərˌbɛriy, -bəriy/ *n.* [*count*], *pl.* **-ries.** the berries of the elder, used in making wine and jelly.

eld•er•ly (el′dər lē) /'ɛldərliy/ *adj.* **1.** approaching old age. **—*n.*** **2. the elderly,** [*plural; used with a plural verb*] elderly persons when they are thought of as a group: *The elderly often need social services.*

eld•est (el′dist) /'ɛldɪst/ *adj. a superl. of* **old** *with* **elder** *as compar.* oldest; of greatest age.

e•lect (i lekt′) /ɪ'lɛkt/ *v.* **1.** to choose or select by vote: [~ + *obj*]: *The voters elect a new mayor tomorrow.* [~ + *obj* + *obj*]: *They elected her mayor.* **2.** to determine in favor of (a method, course of action, etc.); choose: [~ + *to* + *verb*]: *I elected not to take the job because it involved too much traveling.* **—*adj.*** **3.** [*after a noun*] selected for an office, but not yet at work or sworn in: *the governor-elect.* **—Related Words.** ELECT is a verb, ELECTION is a noun, ELECTIVE is an adjective and a noun: *They elected him president. His election was a surprise. He took elective courses. He took several electives.*

e•lec•tion (i lek′shən) /ɪ'lɛkʃən/ *n.* the selection by vote of a candidate for office: [*noncount*]: *the right of election.* [*count*]: *What new surprise awaits us before the November election?* See -LEC-.

e•lec•tive (i lek′tiv) /ɪ'lɛktɪv/ *adj.* **1.** obtained by election: *elective office.* **2.** chosen by election: *elective officials.* **3.** open to choice; optional: *elective surgery; an elective course in science.* **—*n.*** [*count*] **4.** a course that is not required: *Her major is biology, but she has room for two music electives.* See -LEC-.

e•lec•tor (i lek′tər) /ɪ'lɛktər/ *n.* [*count*] **1.** a qualified voter. **2.** a member of the electoral college. See -LEC-.

e•lec′tor•al col′lege (e lek′tər əl) /ɛ'lɛktərəl/ *n.* [*proper noun; often: the* + ~*; often: Electoral College*] a group of people who are chosen by the voters in each state to elect the president and vice-president of the U.S.

e•lec•tor•ate (i lek′tər it) /ɪ'lɛktərɪt/ *n.* [*count*] the people who are entitled to vote in an election.

e•lec•tric (i lek′trik) /ɪ'lɛktrɪk/ *adj.* **1.** [*before a noun*] produced by or operated by electricity: *an electric shock; an electric shave; electric light.* **2.** thrilling; exciting: *an electric atmosphere in the stadium.*

e•lec•tri•cal (i lek′tri kəl) /ɪ'lɛktrɪkəl/ *adj.* **1.** ELECTRIC. **2.** concerned with electricity: *an electrical engineer.* **—e•lec′tri•cal•ly,** *adv.*

elec′tric chair′, *n.* **1.** [*count*] a chair used to electrocute criminals who are sentenced to death. **2.** [*noncount; the* + ~] the penalty of legal electrocution: *sentenced him to the electric chair.*

e•lec•tri•cian (i lek trish′ən, ē′lek-) /ɪlɛk'trɪʃən, ˌiylɛk-/ *n.* [*count*] a person who installs or repairs electric devices or electrical wiring.

e•lec•tric•i•ty (i lek tris′i tē, ē′lek-) /ɪlɛk'trɪsɪtiy, ˌiylɛk-/ *n.* [*noncount*] **1.** current or power produced by the presence and motion of electrons, protons, or positrons; electric current or power: *Turn on the electricity from the main power source.* **2.** a feeling of excitement or anticipation.

e•lec•tri•fy (i lek′trə fī′) /ɪ'lɛktrəˌfay/ *v.* [~ + *obj*], **-fied, -fy•ing. 1.** to charge with electricity; apply electricity to: *A neon sign must be electrified to work.* **2.** to supply with or equip for the use of electric power, as an area or railroad. **3.** to thrill, excite, or astonish: *The rock star electrified the audience with her performance.* **—e•lec•tri•fi•ca•tion** (i lek′tri fi kā′shən) /ɪˌlɛktrɪfɪ'keyʃən/ *n.* [*noncount*]: *the electrification of a village in the mountains.*

electro-, *prefix. electro-* comes from New Latin, and means "electric" or "electricity": *electro-* + *magnetic* → *electromagnetic.*

e•lec•tro•car•di•o•gram (i lek′trō kär′dē ə gram′) /ɪˌlɛktrow'kɑrdiyəˌgræm/ *n.* [*count*] the printed, graphic record that is produced by an electrocardiograph. *Abbr.:* EKG, ECG Also called **cardiogram.**

e•lec•tro•car•di•o•graph (i lek′trō kär′dē ə graf′) /ɪˌlɛktrow'kɑrdiyəˌgræf/ *n.* [*count*] a device that detects electric changes in the part of the nervous system that triggers the heartbeat, used to evaluate the heart's health. *Abbr.:* EKG, ECG

e•lec•tro•cute (i lek′trə kyo͞ot′) /ɪ'lɛktrəˌkyuwt/ *v.* [~ + *obj*], **-cut•ed, -cut•ing. 1.** to kill by electricity: *The bird fell onto the railroad tracks and was electrocuted.* **2.** to execute (a criminal) in an electric chair. **—e•lec•tro•cu•tion** (i lek′trə kyo͞o′shən) /ɪˌlɛktrə'kyuwʃən/ *n.* [*noncount; count*]

e•lec•trode (i lek′trōd) /ɪ'lɛktrowd/ *n.* [*count*] a point, or terminal, through which an electric current enters or leaves a battery or other electrical device.

e•lec•trol•y•sis (i lek trol′ə sis) /ɪlɛk'trɒləsɪs/ *n.* [*noncount*] **1.** the passage of an electric current through a substance, in order to change it chemically. **2.** the destruction of hair roots, tumors, etc., by an electric current. See -LYS-.

e•lec•tro•lyte (i lek′trə līt′) /ɪˈlɛktrəˌlayt/ *n.* [*count*] a substance, usually a liquid, that allows electricity to pass or be passed through it. See -LYS-.

e•lec•tro•mag•net•ism (e lek′trō mag′ni tiz′əm) /ɛˌlɛktrowˈmægnɪˌtɪzəm/ *n.* [*noncount*] **1.** the actions associated with electric and magnetic fields, and with electric charges and currents. **2.** the science that studies these phenomena. **—e•lec•tro•mag•net•ic** (e lek′trō-mag net′ik) /ɛˌlɛktrowmægˈnɛtɪk/ *adj.*

e•lec•tron (i lek′tron) /ɪˈlɛktrɒn/ *n.* [*count*] a fundamental particle that has a negative charge and exists outside the nucleus of an atom.

e•lec•tron•ic (i lek tron′ik, ē′lek-) /ɪlɛkˈtrɒnɪk, ˌiylɛk-/ *adj.* **1.** [*usually: before a noun*] of or relating to electronics or devices and systems developed through electronics: *electronic banking; electronic music.* **2.** of or relating to electrons. **3.** of, relating to, or controlled by computers: *electronic mail.* **—e•lec•tron′i•cal•ly,** *adv.*

e•lec•tron•ics (i lik tron′iks, ē′lek-) /ɪlɪkˈtrɒnɪks, ˌiylɛk-/ *n.* **1.** [*noncount; used with a singular verb*] the science dealing with the development and uses of electrons and electronic devices and systems. **2.** [*plural; used with a plural verb*] electronic devices or systems.

el•e•gant (el′i gənt) /ˈɛlɪgənt/ *adj.* graceful, polished, or luxurious in style, design, or form: *an elegant lady in her seventies.* **—el•e•gance** (el′i gəns) /ˈɛlɪgəns/ *n.* [*noncount*] **—el′e•gant•ly,** *adv.*: *She was dressed elegantly for the ball.*

el•e•gy (el′i jē) /ˈɛlɪdʒiy/ *n.* [*count*], *pl.* **-gies.** a mournful, melancholy, or sad poem, esp. one written for the dead.

elem., an abbreviation of: elementary.

el•e•ment (el′ə mənt) /ˈɛləmənt/ *n.* [*count*] **1.** a component or part of a whole: *Cells are the basic elements of the human body.* **2.** [*usually singular*] a certain amount: *an element of surprise.* **3.** one of a class of substances that cannot be chemically separated into simpler substances. **4. elements,** [*plural*] **a.** atmospheric forces; weather, esp. bad weather. **b.** the rudiments of an art or science: *the elements of physics.* **—*Idiom.* 5. in** (or **out of**) **one's element,** in a situation that is (not) familiar, enjoyable, or suitable: *She was in her element on the stage.* **—el′e•men′tal,** *adj.* **—el′e•men′tal•ly,** *adv.*
—Syn. ELEMENT, COMPONENT, CONSTITUENT, INGREDIENT refer to units that are parts of whole substances, systems, compounds, or mixtures. ELEMENT means a basic, fundamental part, of which there is no smaller part: *the elements of matter.* COMPONENT refers to one of a number of separate parts: *Iron and carbon are components of steel.* CONSTITUENT refers to an active and necessary part: *The constituents of a molecule of water are two atoms of hydrogen and one of oxygen.* INGREDIENT is most frequently used in nonscientific contexts to refer to any part that is combined into a mixture: *the ingredients of a successful marriage.*

el•e•men•ta•ry (el′ə men′tə rē) /ˌɛləˈmɛntəriy/ *adj.* **1.** of or relating to the simplest principles; plain: *The nurse took elementary precautions like boiling the water.* **2.** of or relating to an elementary school: *elementary education.* **3.** of the nature of the most basic particles; that cannot be broken down.

elemen′tary school′, *n.* a school giving instructions in basic subjects, often starting with a kindergarten and continuing for six or eight grades: [*count*]: *a choice between two elementary schools.* [*noncount*]: *When will your child go to elementary school?*

el•e•phant (el′ə fənt) /ˈɛləfənt/ *n.* [*count*], *pl.* **-phants,** (*esp. when thought of as a group*) **-phant.** a very large five-toed mammal having a long trunk and large tusks esp. in the males, living in Africa and India.

elev., an abbreviation of: elevation.

el•e•vate (el′ə vāt′) /ˈɛləˌveyt/ *v.* [~ + *obj*], **-vat•ed, -vat•ing. 1.** to raise to a higher place or position: *We need to elevate the level of our thinking.* **2.** to raise to a higher state or rank; promote: *The vice president was elevated to president.* See -LEV-.

el•e•va•tion (el′ə vā′shən) /ˌɛləˈveyʃən/ *n.* [*count*] **1.** the act of elevating or the state of being elevated. **2.** the altitude of a place above sea level or ground level: *a cliff at an elevation of about two hundred feet.* **3.** an elevated place: *We picnicked on an elevation.*

el•e•va•tor (el′ə vā′tər) /ˈɛləˌveytər/ *n.* [*count*] **1.** a moving platform or cage for carrying passengers or freight from one level to another, as in a building. See illustration at HOTEL. **2.** a building in which grain is stored and handled by means of a mechanical elevator and conveyor devices. See -LEV-.

e•lev•en (i lev′ən) /ɪˈlɛvən/ *n.* [*count*] **1.** a cardinal number, ten plus one. **2.** a symbol for this number, as 11 or XI. **—*adj.* 3.** amounting to eleven in number. **—e•lev′enth,** *adj.*

elf (elf) /ɛlf/ *n., pl.* **elves** (elvz) /ɛlvz/. [*count*] a small imaginary being who enjoys interfering in human affairs.

e•lic•it (i lis′it) /ɪˈlɪsɪt/ *v.* [~ + *obj*], to draw or bring out or forth; evoke: *to elicit a response.* See -LIC-.

el•i•gi•ble (el′i jə bəl) /ˈɛlɪdʒəbəl/ *adj.* **1.** being a proper or worthy choice; suitable: *an eligible mate.* **2.** meeting the stipulated requirements; qualified: [*be* + ~ + *to* + *verb*]: *Anyone over 21 is eligible to play this game.* **—el•i•gi•bil•i•ty** (el′i jə bil′i tē) /ˌɛlɪdʒəˈbɪlɪtiy/ *n.* [*noncount*] **—el•i•gi•bly** (el′i jə blē) /ˈɛlɪdʒəbliy/ *adv.* See -LEC-.

e•lim•i•nate (i lim′ə nāt′) /ɪˈlɪməˌneyt/ *v.* [~ + *obj*], **-nat•ed, -nat•ing. 1.** to get rid of; remove: *to eliminate poverty.* **2.** to omit; leave out: *help eliminate errors.* **3.** to defeat in a contest: *Our team was eliminated early in the tournament.* **—e•lim•i•na•tion** (i lim′ə nā′shən) /ɪˌlɪməˈneyʃən/ *n.* [*noncount*] See -LIM-.

e•lite or **é•lite** (i lēt′) /ɪˈliyt/ *n.* **1.** [*count; often used with a plural verb*] the choice, best, or most powerful members of a group, class, etc. **2.** [*noncount*] a 10-point type widely used in typewriters and having 12 characters to the inch. Compare PICA[1]. **—*adj.*** [*before a noun*] **3.** of the best or most select: *Elite paratroops went in first.* See -LEC-.

e•lix•ir (i lik′sər) /ɪˈlɪksər/ *n.* [*count*] **1.** an imaginary preparation believed to be capable of prolonging life, or of changing ordinary metal into gold. **2.** something that can cure all ills.

elk (elk) /ɛlk/ *n.* [*count*], *pl.* **elks,** (*esp. when thought of as a group*) **elk. 1.** Also called **wapiti.** a large North American deer. **2.** a moose.

el•lipse (i lips′) /ɪˈlɪps/ *n.* [*count*] a plane curve figure shaped like a flattened circle or oval.

el•lip•ti•cal (i lip′ti kəl) /ɪˈlɪptɪkəl/ *adj.* **1.** relating to or having the form of an ellipse: *an elliptical path around the sun.* **2.** having so many words or phrases left out that meaning is difficult to grasp; obscure. **—el•lip′ti•cal•ly,** *adv.*

elm (elm) /ɛlm/ *n.* **1.** [*count*] a shade tree having gradually spreading columns of branches. **2.** [*noncount*] the wood of this tree.

el•o•cu•tion (el′ə kyōō′shən) /ˌɛləˈkyuwʃən/ *n.* [*noncount*] the study and practice of clear public speaking See -LOQ-.

e•lon•gate (i lông′gāt, i long′-) /ɪˈlɔŋgeyt, ɪˈlɒŋ- / *v.,* **-gat•ed, -gat•ing.** to (cause to) lengthen or extend: [~ + *obj*]: *Intense heat elongated the metal bar.* [*no obj*]: *The metal bar elongated under the intense heat.* **—e•lon•ga•tion** (ē′lông gā′shən, ē′long-) /ˌiylɔŋˈgeyʃən, ˌiylɒŋ-/ *n.* [*count; noncount*]

e•lope (i lōp′) /ɪˈlowp/ *v.,* **e•loped, e•lop•ing.** to run off secretly to be married: [*no obj*]: *The young couple eloped.* [~ + *with* + *obj*]: *She eloped with him.* **—e•lope′ment,** *n.* [*noncount; count*]

el•o•quent (el′ə kwənt) /ˈɛləkwənt/ *adj.* **1.** skilled in or showing fluent, forceful, and appropriate speech: *an eloquent teacher.* **2.** (of actions, gestures, etc.) forcefully showing feeling or emotion. **—el•o•quence** (el′ə kwəns) /ˈɛləkwəns/ *n.* [*noncount*] **—el′o•quent•ly,** *adv.* See -LOQ-.

else (els) /ɛls/ *adj.* [*after words like* who, what, when, how, *etc. in questions; after pronouns like* someone, anything, no one, much, *etc.*] **1.** other than those persons or things mentioned: *What else could I do? I would have eaten anything else.* **2.** in addition to persons or things mentioned: *Who else was there?* **3.** other (used in the possessive after a pronoun and before the noun that is possessed): *someone else's money.* **—*adv.* 4.** [*or* + ~] if not: *Watch your step, or else you'll slip.* **5.** otherwise: *How else could I have acted?* **—*Idiom.* 6. or else,** or suffer the consequences: *Do exactly what I say, or else.*

else•where (els′hwâr′, -wâr′) /ˈɛlsˌhwɛər, -ˌwɛər/ *adv.* somewhere else; in or to some other place: *You will have to look elsewhere for an answer.*

e•lu•ci•date (i lōō′si dāt′) /ɪˈluwsɪˌdeyt/ *v.* [~ + *obj*], **-dat•ed, -dat•ing.** to make clear or understandable, esp. by explaining: *The teacher elucidated the difficult passages in the novel.* **—e•lu•ci•da•tion** (i lū′si dā′shən) /ɪˌluwsɪˈdeyʃən/ *n.* [*noncount*]

e•lude (i lōōd′) /ɪˈluwd/ *v.* [~ + *obj*], **e•lud•ed, e•lud•ing. 1.** to avoid capture by; escape from; evade: *The thief eluded the police.* **2.** to escape the understanding or comprehension of: *His popularity eludes me.* See -LUD-. —**Syn.** See ESCAPE.

e•lu•sive (i lōō′siv) /ɪ'luwsɪv/ also **e•lu′so•ry** (-sə rē) /-səriy/ *adj.* **1.** eluding one's understanding; hard to express or define: *elusive concepts in that poetry.* **2.** skillful at keeping away from, escaping from, or evading: *an elusive criminal.* —**e•lu′sive•ly,** *adv.* —**e•lu′sive•ness,** *n.* [*noncount*] See -LUD-.

elves (elvz) /ɛlvz/ *n.* pl. of ELF.

EM, an abbreviation of: electromagnetic.

'em (əm) /əm/ *pron. Informal.* them: *Now you see 'em, now you don't.*

em-, *prefix. em-* is a form of EN- used before roots beginning with *b, p,* and sometimes *m: embalm.* Compare IM-[1].

e•ma•ci•at•ed (i mā′shē ā′tid) /ɪ'meyʃiy,eytɪd/ *adj.* abnormally thin, esp. because of starvation or illness.

e-mail or **E-mail** (ē′māl′) /'iy,meyl/ *n.* [*noncount*] electronic mail: a system of sending messages from one computer to another or others.

em•a•nate (em′ə nāt′) /'ɛmə,neyt/ *v.,* **-nat•ed, -nat•ing.** to (cause to) flow out, issue forth, or come from: [~ + *from* + *obj*]: *The brook emanates from an underground spring.* [~ + *obj*]: *His whole face emanates patience.* —**em′a•na′tion,** *n.* [*count; noncount*]

e•man•ci•pate (i man′sə pāt′) /ɪ'mænsə,peyt/ *v.* [~ + *obj*], **-pat•ed, -pat•ing.** to make (someone) free from social, political, or legal restraint; set free; liberate: *to emancipate slaves.* —**e•man•ci•pa•tion** (i man′sə pā′shən) /ɪ,mænsə'peyʃən/ *n.* [*noncount*] —**e•man′ci•pa′tor,** *n.* [*count*]

e•mas•cu•late (i mas′kyə lāt′) /ɪ'mæskyə,leyt/ *v.* [~ + *obj*], **-lat•ed, -lat•ing.** to deprive of strength or vigor; weaken: *The court emasculated the laws against speeding by fining offenders only five dollars.* —**e•mas•cu•la•tion** (e mas′kyə lā′shən) /ɛ,mæskyə'leyʃən/ *n.* [*noncount*]

em•balm (em bäm′) /ɛm'bɑm/ *v.* [~ + *obj*], to preserve (a dead body) with chemicals or drugs. —**em•balm′er,** *n.* [*count*]

em•bank•ment (em bangk′mənt) /ɛm'bæŋkmənt/ *n.* [*count*] a bank or mound, as of earth or stone, built up to hold back water, carry a roadway, etc.

em•bar•go (em bär′gō) /ɛm'bɑrgow/ *n., pl.* **-goes,** *v.,* **-goed, -go•ing.** —*n.* [*count*] **1.** a restriction on commerce, esp. a government order prohibiting the movement of ships into or out of its ports, or restricting certain freight for shipment. —*v.* [~ + *obj*] **2.** to impose an embargo on: *The U.S. embargoed that enemy country.*

em•bark (em bärk′) /ɛm'bɑrk/ *v.* **1.** [*no obj;* (~ + *on* + *obj*)] to board a ship, aircraft, or other vehicle: *The passengers embarked on the ship at noon.* **2.** [~ + *on* + *obj*] to start or participate in an enterprise: *to embark on a business venture.* —**em•bar•ka•tion** (em′bär kā′shən) /,ɛmbɑr'keyʃən/ *n.* [*noncount*]

em•bar•rass (em bar′əs) /ɛm'bærəs/ *v.* to (cause to) become ashamed, uncomfortable, or ill at ease: [*no obj*]: *She embarrasses so easily.* [~ + *obj*]: *The child's crying embarrassed her parents.* —**em•bar′rass•ing,** *adj.*

em•bar•rass•ment (em bar′əs mənt) /ɛm'bærəsmənt/ *n.* **1.** [*noncount*] a feeling of shame, self-consciousness, or uncomfortableness: *embarrassment at forgetting my wallet.* **2.** [*count*] someone or something that causes such a feeling: *His speeches were an embarrassment to his party.*

em•bas•sy (em′bə sē) /'ɛmbəsiy/ *n.* [*count*], *pl.* **-sies. 1.** the official headquarters of an ambassador. **2.** a mission or group of officials and workers who are headed by an ambassador.

em•bat•tled (em bat′ld) /ɛm'bætld/ *adj.* engaged in or facing conflict or struggle: *embattled troops.*

em•bed (em bed′) /ɛm'bɛd/ *v.* [~ + *obj*], **-bed•ded, -bed•ding. 1.** to fix or put (something) firmly into a surrounding mass: *to embed stones in cement.* **2.** to contain or implant as an essential part: *His love of children is deeply embedded in his personality.*

em•bel•lish (em bel′ish) /ɛm'bɛlɪʃ/ *v.* [~ + *obj*] **1.** to make more beautiful by decorating or ornamenting; adorn: *a dress embellished with pearls.* **2.** to include extra and elaborate additions: *He embellished his signature with a drawing.*

em•ber (em′bər) /'ɛmbər/ *n.* [*count*] **1.** a small, still burning piece of coal, wood, etc., as in a dying fire. **2. embers,** [*plural*] the glowing remains of a fire that is no longer burning.

em•bez•zle (em bez′əl) /ɛm'bɛzəl/ *v.* [~ + *obj*], **-zled, -zling.** to steal (money) entrusted to one's care: *He embezzled thousands of dollars from the insurance company.* —**em•bez′zle•ment,** *n.* [*noncount*]: *imprisoned for stock embezzlement.* —**em•bez•zler** (em bez′lər) /ɛm'bɛzlər/ *n.* [*count*]

em•bit•ter (em bit′ər) /ɛm'bɪtər/ *v.* [~ + *obj*] to make (someone) bitter and angry; cause (someone) to feel bitterness: *Being fired from his job without good reasons embittered him.*

em•bla•zon (em blā′zən) /ɛm'bleyzən/ *v.* [~ + *obj*] to decorate brilliantly; adorn: *The tapestries in the collection were emblazoned with gold thread.*

em•blem (em′bləm) /'ɛmbləm/ *n.* [*count*] an object that symbolizes a quality, state, etc.; a symbol: *The olive branch is an emblem of peace.*

em•bod•y (em bod′ē) /ɛm'bɒdiy/ *v.* [~ + *obj*], **-bod•ied, -bod•y•ing. 1.** to give a concrete form to; be an example of; personify: *Her paintings embodied the spirit of the age.* **2.** to include; contain; comprise: *The testimony is embodied in the court record.* —**em•bod′i•ment,** *n.* [*noncount*]

em•bold•en (em bōl′dən) /ɛm'bowldən/ *v.* [~ + *obj*] to make bold; encourage.

em•boss (em bôs′, -bos′) /ɛm'bɔs, -'bɒs/ *v.* [~ + *obj*] to decorate (a surface) with raised designs or decorations: *He embossed the sword with the design of a bull.*

em•brace (em brās′) /ɛm'breys/ *v.,* **-braced, -brac•ing,** *n.* —*v.* **1.** to clasp in the arms; hug: [~ + *obj*]: *He embraced her and told her how glad he was to see her again.* [*no obj*]: *They embraced and kissed.* **2.** [~ + *obj*] to accept or adopt willingly: *I don't know whether they'll embrace your idea.* **3.** [*not: be* + *~-ing;* ~ + *obj*] to include or contain: *The report embraced all aspects of the housing situation.* —*n.* [*count*] **4.** an encircling hug with the arms: *She gave me a warm embrace.*

em•broi•der (em broi′dər) /ɛm'brɔydər/ *v.* **1.** [~ + *obj*] to decorate with embroidery: *She embroidered her dress with flowers.* **2.** [~ + *obj*] to form by or with embroidery: *She embroidered flowers on her dress.* **3.** [*no obj*] to do embroidery: *She embroiders as a way of relaxing.* **4.** [~ + *obj*] to add extra or imaginary details; embellish with ornate language: *She embroidered her story to hold her listeners' interest.* —**em•broi′der•er,** *n.* [*count*]

em•broi•der•y (em broi′də rē, -drē) /ɛm'brɔydəriy, -driy/ *n.* [*noncount*] **1.** the sewing of decorative designs with a needle and thread. **2.** embroidered work or decoration.

em•broil (em broil′) /ɛm'brɔyl/ *v.* [~ + *obj*] to involve in conflict or difficulty: *They were embroiled in a passionate debate about the budget.*

em•bry•o (em′brē ō′) /'ɛmbriy,ow/ *n.* [*count*], *pl.* **-os.** an animal in the early stages of development in the womb or egg. —**em•bry•on•ic** (em′brē on′ik) /,ɛmbriy'ɒnɪk/ *adj.*

em•cee (em′sē′) /'ɛm'siy/ *n., v.,* **-ceed, -cee•ing.** —*n.* [*count*] **1.** master of ceremonies; a person who introduces the acts or parts of a show or presentation: *She was the emcee at the awards dinner.* —*v.* [~ + *obj*] **2.** to serve or direct as master of ceremonies: *He emceed the game show.*

e•mend (i mend′) /ɪ'mɛnd/ *v.* [~ + *obj*] to revise or correct (errors, writing, etc.): *She emended the errors in his letter.* —**e•men•da•tion** (ē′men dā′shən) /,iymɛn'deyʃən/ *n.* [*count*]

em•er•ald (em′ər əld) /'ɛmərəld/ *n.* **1.** [*count*] a green gem, a rare kind of beryl. —*adj.* **2.** having a clear, deep green color.

e•merge (i mûrj′) /ɪ'mɜrdʒ/ *v.* [*no obj;* (~ + *from* + *obj*)], **e•merged, e•merg•ing. 1.** to come forth into view, as from hiding: *Two rabbits emerged from the bushes.* **2.** to come into existence or notice: *New evidence emerged from her investigation.* —**e•mer′gence,** *n.* [*noncount*] —**e•mer′gent,** *adj.* See -MERG-.

e•mer•gen•cy (i mûr′jən sē) /ɪ'mɜrdʒənsiy/ *n.* [*count*], *pl.* **-cies.** a sudden, urgent, usually unexpected event or happening requiring immediate action: *In an emergency, call the doctor.* See -MERG-.

em•er•y (em′ə rē) /'ɛməriy/ *n.* [*noncount*] a hard, grainy mineral used for grinding and polishing.

e•met•ic (i met′ik) /ɪ'mɛtɪk/ *adj.* **1.** causing vomiting: *an emetic medicine.* —*n.* [*count*] **2.** a medicine or agent that causes vomiting.

em•i•grate (em′i grāt′) /'ɛmɪ,greyt/ *v.* [*no obj*], **-grat•ed, -grat•ing.** to leave one country or region to settle in another; migrate: *My grandmother emigrated from Russia in 1930.* —**em•i•grant** (em′i grənt) /'ɛmɪgrənt/ *n.* [*count*] —**em•i•gra•tion** (em′i grā′shən) /,ɛmɪ'greyʃən/ *n.* [*count; noncount*] See -MIGR-.

—**Related Words.** EMIGRATE is a verb, EMIGRANT and ÉMIGRÉ are nouns: *They emigrated from their home country. They were emigrants. They were émigrés from eastern Europe.* —**Usage.** See IMMIGRATE.

é•mi•gré (em′i grā′, em′i grā′) /'ɛmɪˌgrey, ˌɛmɪ'grey/ *n.* [*count*] an emigrant, esp. a person who flees a native land because of political conditions.

em•i•nence (em′ə nəns) /'ɛmənəns/ *n.* **1.** [*noncount*] high rank or reputation: *gained a great deal of eminence.* **2.** [*proper noun; His/Your + Eminence*] a title of honor, applied to cardinals: *They introduced His Eminence, John Cardinal Mancini.*

em•i•nent (em′ə nənt) /'ɛmənənt/ *adj.* **1.** high in rank or reputation; top; distinguished: *an eminent scholar.* **2.** [*usually: before a noun*] greatest; utmost; remarkable; outstanding: *I was treated with eminent fairness.* —**em′i•nent•ly,** *adv.*

e•mir (ə mēr′, ā mēr′) /ə'mɪər, ey'mɪər/ *n.* [*count*] a chief, prince, commander, or head of state in some Islamic countries.

em•is•sar•y (em′ə ser′ē) /'ɛməˌsɛriy/ *n.* [*count*], *pl.* **-sar•ies.** a representative who is sent on a mission; a delegate who is sent to another person, country, or group with a message. See -MIS-.

e•mit (i mit′) /ɪ'mɪt/ *v.* [~ + *obj*], **e•mit•ted, e•mit•ting. 1.** to send forth (liquid, light, particles, etc.); discharge: *The fireplace emitted a pleasant warmth.* **2.** to utter (a sound): *to emit a cry.* —**e•mis•sion** (i mish′ən) /ɪ'mɪʃən/ *n.* [*count; noncount*] See -MIT-.

e•mol•lient (i mol′yənt) /ɪ'mɒlyənt/ *adj.* [*before a noun*] **1.** having the power to soften or soothe: *an emollient lotion for the skin.* —*n.* [*noncount*] **2.** an emollient substance.

e•mote (i mōt′) /ɪ'mowt/ *v.* [*no obj*], **e•mot•ed, e•mot•ing.** to show or pretend emotion, as in acting: *The actor's attempts to emote seemed silly and unreal.* See -MOT-.

e•mo•tion (i mō′shən) /ɪ'mowʃən/ *n.* [*count*] any of the feelings of joy, sorrow, fear, hate, love, etc.: *War produces strong emotions.* —**e•mo′tion•al,** *adj.* —**e•mo′tion•al•ly,** *adv.* See -MOT-.

Emp., an abbreviation of: **1.** Emperor. **2.** Empress.

em•pa•thize (em′pə thīz′) /'ɛmpəˌθayz/ *v.* [~ + *with* + *obj*], **-thized, -thiz•ing.** to experience empathy: *to empathize with someone's grief.*

em•pa•thy (em′pə thē) /'ɛmpəθiy/ *n.* [*noncount*] the power or ability to identify with another's feelings, thoughts, etc., as if they were one's own. See -PATH-.

em•per•or (em′pər ər) /'ɛmpərər/ *n.* [*count*] the male supreme ruler of an empire.

em•pha•sis (em′fə sis) /'ɛmfəsɪs/ *n., pl.* **-ses** (-sēz′) /-ˌsiyz/. **1.** [*noncount*] special stress or importance attached to something: *That university puts a lot of emphasis on its small classes.* **2.** [*count*] something given special stress or importance: *The main emphases of his speech were the budget and taxes.*

em•pha•size (em′fə sīz′) /'ɛmfəˌsayz/ *v.* [~ + *obj*], **-sized, -siz•ing.** to give emphasis to; stress: *He emphasized the point I had already made.*

em•phat•ic (em fat′ik) /ɛm'fætɪk/ *adj.* said or done with emphasis; strongly expressive; forceful: *The defendant made an emphatic denial of the charges.* —**em•phat′i•cal•ly,** *adv.*

em•phy•se•ma (em′fə sē′mə, -zē′-) /ˌɛmfə'siymə, -'ziy-/ *n.* [*noncount*] a disease of the lungs in which there is difficulty in breathing due to abnormal swelling of the air spaces. —**em′phy•se′mic,** *adj.*

em•pire (em′pīᵊr) /'ɛmpayᵊr/ *n.* [*count*] **1.** a group of nations, states, or peoples ruled over by an emperor, empress, or other powerful sovereign. **2.** a large and powerful business, company, or enterprise controlled by one person, family, or group.

em•pir•i•cal (em pir′i kəl) /ɛm'pɪrɪkəl/ *adj.* derived from or depending upon experience or observation alone. —**em•pir′i•cal•ly,** *adv.* —**em•pir•i•cism** (em pir′i siz′əm) /ɛm'pɪrɪˌsɪzəm/ *n.* [*noncount*]

em•ploy (em ploi′) /ɛm'plɔy/ *v.* [~ + *obj*] **1.** to hire the services of (a person or persons): *The cotton mill employs over three thousand workers.* **2.** to make use of for a specific task: *They employed new computers to produce the catalog.* **3.** to devote (time, energies, etc.) to a particular activity: *She employs her spare time in reading.* —*n.* [*noncount*] **4.** employment; service. —**em•ploy′a•ble,** *adj.* —**em•ploy′er,** *n.* [*count*] See -PLOY-.

—**Related Words.** EMPLOY is a verb and a noun, EMPLOYMENT, EMPLOYER, and EMPLOYEE are nouns, EMPLOYABLE is an adjective: *He employs unskilled workers in his factory. Is she still in their employ? Employment is down. His employer fired him. The employees don't like the boss. You aren't employable without computer skills.*

em•ploy•ee (em ploi′ē, em ploi ē′, em′ploi ē′) /ɛm'plɔyiy, ɛmplɔy'iy, ˌɛmplɔy'iy/ *n.* [*count*] a person who has been hired to work for another. See -PLOY-.

em•ploy•ment (em ploi′mənt) /ɛm'plɔymənt/ *n.* [*noncount*] **1.** an act or instance of employing a person or thing: *The plan requires the employment of great ingenuity.* **2.** the state of being employed: *to begin employment.* **3.** work or business; occupation: *She no longer had regular employment.* See -PLOY-.

em•po•ri•um (em pôr′ē əm, -pōr′-) /ɛm'pɔriyəm, -'powr-/ *n.* [*count*], *pl.* **-po•ri•ums, -po•ri•a** (-pôr′ē ə, -pōr′-) /-'pɔriyə, -'powr-/. a usually large retail store selling a great variety of articles.

em•pow•er (em pou′ər) /ɛm'pawər/ *v.* **1.** [~ + *obj* + *to* + *verb*] to give official or legal power or authority to: *The police are empowered to arrest suspected criminals.* **2.** [~ + *obj*] to provide with an ability; enable: *Some teachers want to empower their students by giving them the skills they need.* —**em•pow′er•ment,** *n.* [*noncount*]

em•press (em′pris) /'ɛmprɪs/ *n.* [*count*] **1.** a female ruler of an empire. **2.** the wife of an emperor.

emp•ty (emp′tē) /'ɛmptiy/ *adj.,* **-ti•er, -ti•est,** *v.,* **-tied, -ty•ing,** *n., pl.* **-ties.** —*adj.* **1.** containing nothing; without contents: *an empty toy box.* **2.** vacant; unoccupied; without people: *a lonely, empty house.* **3.** lacking force, effect, or significance; meaningless: *empty promises.* —*v.* **4.** to (cause to) become empty: [*no obj*]: *The lecture hall emptied.* [~ + *obj*]: *She emptied her glass.* —*n.* [*count*] **5.** an empty container: *Glass empties can be recycled.* —**emp′ti•ness,** *n.* [*noncount*]

emp′ty-hand′ed, *adj.* **1.** having nothing in the hands. **2.** having achieved nothing: *I came back from the meeting empty-handed.* **3.** bringing no gift, donation, etc.: *Don't come empty-handed to the party.*

EMT, an abbreviation of: emergency medical technician.

em•u•late (em′yə lāt′) /'ɛmyəˌleyt/ *v.* [~ + *obj*], **-lat•ed, -lat•ing.** to imitate (someone or something) in an effort to equal or do better than; to try to do as well as or better than: *The struggling companies want to emulate the successful overseas competition.* —**em•u•la•tion** (em′yə-lā′shən) /ˌɛmyə'leyʃən/ *n.* [*noncount*] —**em′u•la′tor,** *n.* [*count*]

e•mul•sion (i mul′shən) /ɪ'mʌlʃən/ *n.* [*count*] **1.** a mixture containing liquids that do not usually stay mixed. **2.** a chemical substance that is thinly applied to one surface of a photographic film to make it sensitive to light.

en-, *prefix. en-* is attached to adjectives or nouns to form verbs meaning: **1.** to cause (a person or thing) to be in (the place, condition, or state mentioned); to keep in or place in: *en-* + *rich* → *enrich (= to cause to be rich); en-* + *tomb* → *entomb (= to cause to be in a tomb);* **2.** to restrict on all sides, completely: *en-* + *circle* → *encircle (= to restrict on all sides within a circle).*

-en, *suffix.* **1.** *-en* is used to form verbs and adjectives. **a.** It is attached to some adjectives to form verbs with the meaning "to be or make": *hard* + *-en* → *harden (= to be or make hard).* **b.** It is attached to some nouns to form verbs with the meaning "to add to, cause to be, or have": *length* + *-en* → *lengthen (= to add length to; make long).* **2.** It is attached to some nouns that are materials or sources of something to form adjectives that describe the source or material: *gold* + *-en* → *golden (= like gold).*

en•a•ble (en ā′bəl) /ɛn'eybəl/ *v.* [~ + *obj* + *to* + *verb*], **-bled, -bling.** to make able; authorize; give power or ability: *The money will enable us to hire more workers.*

en•act (en akt′) /ɛn'ækt/ *v.* [~ + *obj*], **1.** to make into an act or law: *to enact a new tax law.* **2.** to represent in or as if in a play; act the part of: *enacted the role of the villain.* —**en•act′ment,** *n.* [*count*]

e•nam•el (i nam′əl) /ɪ'næməl/ *n.* [*noncount*] **1.** a glassy substance that is applied by heat to the surface of metal, pottery, etc., as a decoration or for protection. **2.** a paint that dries to a hard, shiny finish. **3.** the hard, shiny covering of the crown of a tooth.

en•am•ored (i nam′ərd) /ɪ'næmərd/ *adj.* filled with admiration or love: [*be* + ~ + *of*]: *They are enamored of each other.* [*be* + ~ + *with*]: *enamored with electronic toys.* Also, *esp. Brit.,* **en•am′oured.**

enc., an abbreviation of: **1.** enclosed. **2.** enclosure.

en•case (en kās′) /ɛn'keys/ *v.* [~ + *obj*], **-cased, -cas•ing.** to enclose in or as if in a case: *a jewel encased in satin.* —**en•case′ment,** *n.* [*noncount*]

-ence, *suffix.* **1.** *-ence* is attached to some adjectives ending in -ENT to form nouns with the meaning "quality or state of": *abstin(ent)* + *-ence* → *abstinence.* **2.** *-ence* is also attached to some verb roots to form nouns: *depend* + *-ence* → *dependence.* See -ANCE, -ENT.

en•chant (en chant′) /ɛn'tʃænt/ *v.* [~ + *obj*] **1.** to place (someone) under a magical spell; bewitch. **2.** to delight completely; charm; captivate: *Her performance enchanted the audience.*

en•chanted (en chant′id) /ɛn'tʃæntɪd/ *adj.* having a feeling of delight or captivation; charmed; delighted: *The enchanted audience applauded the singer's performance.*

en•chant•ment (en chant′mənt) /ɛn'tʃæntmənt/ *n.* **1.** [*noncount*] a feeling of delight or captivation. **2.** [*count*] a charm or magic spell: *The sorcerer murmured an enchantment over the sleeping prince.*

en•chi•la•da (en′chə lä′də, -lad′ə) /ˌɛntʃə'lɑdə, -'lædə/ *n.* [*count*], *pl.* **-das.** a Mexican tortilla that is rolled around a meat or cheese filling, covered with a chili-flavored sauce, and baked.

en•cir•cle (en sûr′kəl) /ɛn'sɜrkəl/ *v.* [~ + *obj*], **-cled, -cling. 1.** to form a circle around; surround: *Trees encircled the park.* **2.** to make a circling movement around: *The spaceship encircled the moon.* **—en•cir′cle•ment,** *n.* [*noncount*]

encl., an abbreviation of: **1.** enclosed. **2.** enclosure.

en•clave (en′klāv, än′-) /'ɛnkleyv, 'ɑn-/ *n.* [*count*] **1.** a country or part of a country surrounded by foreign territory. **2.** any small, distinct area or group enclosed or isolated within a larger one: *His neighborhood was an enclave of Italian families and their businesses.*

en•close (en klōz′) /ɛn'klowz/ *v.* [~ + *obj*], **-closed, -clos•ing. 1.** to close in on all sides; surround: *A high stone wall enclosed the estate.* **2.** to put in the same envelope or package with something else: *I am enclosing a check with this letter.* See -CLOS-.

en•clo•sure (en klō′zhər) /ɛn'klowʒər/ *n.* [*count*] **1.** an enclosed area, esp. a piece of land surrounded by a fence. **2.** something enclosed or included in the same envelope or package: *The enclosure was a check for $100.* See -CLOS-.

en•code (en kōd′) /ɛn'kowd/ *v.* [~ + *obj*], **-cod•ed, -cod•ing.** to convert (information, a message, etc.) into code. **—en•cod′er,** *n.* [*count*]

en•com•pass (en kum′pəs) /ɛn'kʌmpəs/ *v.* [~ + *obj*] **1.** to encircle; surround: *High mountains encompass the lake.* **2.** to include completely: *The reorganization plan encompasses all employees.* **—en•com′pass•ment,** *n.* [*noncount*] See -PASS-[1].

en•core (äng′kôr, -kōr, än′-) /'ɑŋkɔr, -kowr, 'ɑn-/ *interj.* **1.** (used by an audience in demanding a repeated or an additional performance) again; once more. **—*n.*** [*count*] **2.** a performance given in response to such a demand.

en•coun•ter (en koun′tər) /ɛn'kawntər/ *v.* [~ + *obj*] **1.** to come upon or meet with: *She encountered an old friend on the street.* **2.** to meet in conflict: *The pilots soon encountered the enemy planes.* **—*n.*** [*count*] **3.** a meeting with a person or thing: *a brief encounter on the street.* **4.** a meeting of people or groups in conflict: *a fierce encounter with the enemy.*

en•cour•age (en kûr′ij, -kur′-) /ɛn'kɜrɪdʒ, -'kʌr-/ *v.*, **-aged, -ag•ing. 1.** to inspire with courage, spirit, or confidence to do something: [~ + *obj*]: *She encouraged him with kind words throughout the ordeal.* [~ + *obj* + *to* + *verb*]: *Letters of support encouraged the mayor to run again.* **2.** [~ + *obj*] to stimulate by guidance, approval, etc.: *Your faith encourages me.* **3.** [~ + *obj*] to foster; help bring about: *Such unkind remarks only encourage prejudice.* **—en•cour′age•ment,** *n.* [*noncount*]

en•croach (en krōch′) /ɛn'krowtʃ/ *v.* [~ + *on/upon* + *obj*] to intrude upon the property or rights of another, esp. gradually or secretly: *Wiretapping encroaches on our right to privacy.* **—en•croach′ment,** *n.* [*noncount; count*]

en•crust•ed (en krus′tid) /ɛn'krʌstɪd/ *adj.* covered with hard coating or crust: *an old car encrusted with dirt.*

en•cum•ber (en kum′bər) /ɛn'kʌmbər/ *v.* [~ + *obj*] to weigh down; burden: *The hiker was encumbered by a heavy backpack.*

en•cum•brance (en kum′brəns) /ɛn'kʌmbrəns/ *n.* [*count*] something that weighs down or burdens.

en•cyc•li•cal (en sik′li kəl, -si′kli-) /ɛn'sɪklɪkəl, -'sayklɪ-/ *n.* [*count*] a letter from the pope to the bishops of the church. See -CYCLE-.

en•cy•clo•pe•di•a or **en•cy•clo•pae•di•a** (en si′klə pē′dē ə) /ɛnˌsayklə'piydiyə/ *n.* [*count*], *pl.* **-dias.** a book or set of books containing articles on various topics, usually in alphabetical arrangement, covering all branches of knowledge or all aspects of one subject. **—en•cy•clo•pe′dic,** *adj.* See -CYCLE-, -PED-[2].

end (end) /ɛnd/ *n.* [*count*] **1.** the last part; extremity: *the two ends of a rope; the west end of town.* **2.** a point that indicates the full extent of something; limit: *walked from end to end of the city.* **3.** the concluding part; conclusion; last point: *We are finally at the end of winter.* **4.** an intention or aim: *using evil means to achieve their ends.* **5.** an outcome; a result: *What will be the end of all this arguing?* **6.** death, destruction, or ruin: *This means the end of our hopes.* **7.** a piece or part left over; remnant: *threw the end of his cigarette over the side.* **8.** a share or part: *She takes care of the business end, and I take care of the public relations.* **—*v.* 9.** to (cause to) come to an end; conclude; terminate: [*no obj*]: *The concert ended and the crowd went home. The book ends on page 364.* [~ + *obj*]: *The chairman ended the meeting at ten o'clock.* **10.** [~ + *obj*] to form the end of: *Those remarks ended her speech.* **11.** [~ + *obj*] to cause the death or destruction of: *The fire ended their lives.* **12.** [*noun* + *to* + ~ + *all*] to surpass or go beyond: *a storm to end all storms.* **13. end in,** [~ + *in* + *obj*] to result: *The battle ended in a victory.* **14. end up,** [*no obj*] to reach a final state or condition: *I ended up tired, hungry, and broke.* [~ + *up* + *verb-ing*]: *We ended up parking many blocks away.* **—*adj.*** [*before a noun*] **15.** final or ultimate: *The end result is the same.* **—*Idiom.* 16. at the end of one's rope** or **tether,** at the end of one's resources, patience, or strength. **17. end to end,** in a row with ends touching: *to line up the playing cards end to end.* **18. go off the deep end,** to lose emotional control; behave irrationally. **19. in the end,** finally; after all: *We kept coming back to that car and in the end we bought it.* **20. keep** or **hold one's end up,** [*no obj*] to perform one's part or share adequately: *If you can hold your end up we'll finish on time.* **21. make (both) ends meet,** to manage to live on one's income: *trying to make both ends meet with two jobs.* **22. no end,** very much or many: *We were pleased no end by the enthusiastic response.* **23. on end, a.** with one end down; upright: *to stand a box on end.* **b.** continuously: *to talk for hours on end.* **24. put an end to,** [~ + *obj*] to terminate; finish: *Let's put an end to this constant arguing.*

en•dan•ger (en dān′jər) /ɛn'deyndʒər/ *v.* [~ + *obj*] **1.** to expose to danger: *to endanger one's life.* **2.** to threaten (an animal or plant species) with extinction. **—en•dan′ger•ment,** *n.* [*noncount*]

endan′gered spe′cies, *n.* [*count*] a species of plant or animal at risk of extinction because of human activity, changes in climate, etc., esp. when it is officially designated as such by a governmental or international agency.

en•dear (en dēr′) /ɛn'dɪər/ *v.* [~ + *obj* + *to* + *obj*] to make beloved: *He endeared himself to us with his gentle ways.* **—en•dear′ing,** *adj.*: *an endearing smile on her lips.* **—en•dear′ing•ly,** *adv.*

en•deav•or (en dev′ər) /ɛn'dɛvər/ *v.* [~ + *to* + *verb*] **1.** to exert oneself to do or effect something; make an effort; strive; try: *He always endeavored to be on time.* **—*n.* 2.** a strong effort; attempt: [*noncount*]: *a new field of endeavor.* [*count*]: *The boy made an honest endeavor to do the right thing.* Also, *esp. Brit.,* **en•deav′our.**

en•dem•ic (en dem′ik) /ɛn'dɛmɪk/ *adj.* characteristic of or confined to a particular place or people: *an endemic disease; a species of bat endemic to Mexico.*

end•ing (en′ding) /'ɛndɪŋ/ *n.* [*count*] **1.** the final or concluding part; end: *The best part of the book is the ending.* **2.** a part at the end of a word, esp. a suffix, such as the *-s* in *cuts.*

en•dive (en′dīv, än dēv′) /'ɛndayv, ɑn'diyv/ *n.* a plant having often curly-edged leaves used in salads.

end•less (end′lis) /'ɛndlɪs/ *adj.* **1.** having or seeming to have no end; boundless: *an endless highway through the open desert.* **2.** not stopping or ceasing; incessant: *the endless noise of construction work.* **—end′less•ly,** *adv.* **—end′less•ness,** *n.* [*noncount*] **—Syn.** See ETERNAL.

en•dorse (en dôrs′) /ɛn'dɔrs/ *v.* [~ + *obj*], **-dorsed, -dors•ing. 1.** to express or give approval or support of, esp. publicly: *to endorse a political candidate.* **2.** to designate oneself as receiver of by signing: *Endorse the check on the other side.* **—en•dors′er,** *n.* [*count*]

en•dorse•ment (en dôrs′mənt) /ɛn'dɔrsmənt/ *n.* the act of expressing or giving public support to a candidate, an idea, etc.: [*count*]: *endorsements from party leaders.* [*noncount*]: *He promised full endorsement of the plan.*

en•dow (en dou′) /ɛn'daw/ *v.* [~ + *obj*] **1.** to provide with a permanent fund or source of income, as by a donation: *An alumna endowed her college with a million* *dollars.* **2.** to furnish, as with some talent, faculty, or quality; equip: *Nature endowed him with a beautiful voice.* —**en•dow′ment,** *n.* [*count; noncount*]

en•dur•ance (en do͝or′əns, -dyo͝or′-) /ɛn'dʊrəns, -'dyʊr-/ *n.* [*noncount*] the ability to continue or last, esp. despite fatigue, stress, etc.; stamina: *Sailing across the Atlantic Ocean by oneself requires great endurance.* See -DUR-.

en•dure (en do͝or′, -dyo͝or′) /ɛn'dʊr, -'dyʊr/ *v.,* **-dured, -dur•ing. 1.** [~ + *obj*] to hold out against; bear patiently or without complaint; undergo: *I could hardly endure the heat.* **2.** [*no obj*] to continue to exist; last: *The music of Bach has endured through the ages.* —**en•dur′ing,** *adj.*: *deep and enduring affection.* See -DUR-.

end•ways (end′wāz′) /'ɛnd,weyz/ also **end′wise′** (-wīz′) /-,wayz/ *adv.* **1.** on end. **2.** with the end upward or forward.

en•e•ma (en′ə mə) /'ɛnəmə/ *n., pl.* **-mas. 1.** [*count*] the injection of a fluid into the rectum to empty the bowels. **2.** [*noncount*] the fluid injected.

en•e•my (en′ə mē) /'ɛnəmiy/ *n., pl.* **-mies,** *adj.* —*n.* [*count*] **1.** a person who hates or wishes harm to another; a hostile opponent. **2.** one who opposes someone or something; opponent; adversary: *enemies of the state.* **3.** [*usually singular; the* + ~] an opposing military force: *To stop the advance of the enemy, they positioned several tank divisions near the river.* —*adj.* [*before a noun*] **4.** being or belonging to an enemy: *enemy aircraft.*

en•er•get•ic (en′ər jet′ik) /,ɛnər'dʒɛtɪk/ *adj.* possessing or showing energy; active: *energetic exercise; an energetic personality.* —**en′er•get′i•cal•ly,** *adv.*: *bustling energetically from room to room.*

en•er•gize (en′ər jīz′) /'ɛnər,dʒayz/ *v.* [~ + *obj*], **-gized, -giz•ing.** to give energy to. —**en′er•giz′er,** *n.* [*count*]

en•er•gy (en′ər jē) /'ɛnərdʒiy/ *n., pl.* **-gies. 1.** [*noncount*] the capacity or power for vigorous activity: *I felt such energy that I jogged three miles.* **2.** Often, **energies.** [*plural*] an exertion of such power; effort: *She threw all her energies into the job.* **3.** [*noncount*] *Physics.* the capacity to do work. *Symbol:* E **4.** [*noncount*] any source of usable power, as fossil fuel, nuclear fission, electricity, or solar radiation.

en•er•vate (en′ər vāt′) /'ɛnər,veyt/ *v.* [~ + *obj*], **-vat•ed, -vat•ing.** to deprive of force or strength; weaken.

en•fee•bled (en fē′bəld) /ɛn'fiybəld/ *adj.* made feeble: *enfeebled by hunger.* —**en•fee′ble•ment,** *n.* [*noncount*]

en•fold (en fōld′) /ɛn'fowld/ *v.* [~ + *obj*] **1.** to wrap up; envelop; surround: *enfolded in a blanket; events enfolded in mystery.* **2.** to hug or clasp; embrace: *She enfolded me in her arms.*

en•force (en fôrs′, -fōrs′) /ɛn'fɔrs, -'fowrs/ *v.* [~ + *obj*], **-forced** (-fôrst′, -fōrst′) /-'fɔrst, -'fowrst/ **-forc•ing. 1.** to put or keep in force; force obedience to: *The police tried to enforce the new law.* **2.** to obtain by force; compel: *to enforce obedience.* —**en•forced′,** *adj.*: *an enforced curfew.* —**en•force′ment,** *n.* [*noncount*]

en•fran•chise (en fran′chīz) /ɛn'fræntʃayz/ *v.* [~ + *obj*], **-chised, -chis•ing.** to admit to citizenship, esp. to the right of voting. —**en•fran′chise•ment,** *n.* [*noncount*] —**en•fran′chis•er,** *n.* [*count*]

en•gage (en gāj′) /ɛn'geydʒ/ *v.,* **-gaged, -gag•ing. 1.** to occupy the attention or efforts of; involve: [~ + *obj* + *in* + *obj*]: *He engaged his daughter in conversation.* [~ + *in* + *obj*]: *He engaged in politics for many years.* **2.** [~ + *obj*] to hire; arrange for (someone) to provide a special service: *to engage a lifeguard for the beach.* **3.** [~ + *obj*] to attract and hold fast: *The book engaged my attention.* **4.** [~ + *obj*] to enter into conflict with: *The army engaged the enemy.* **5.** (of gears or the like) to interlock or cause to become interlocked: [~ + *obj*]: *He engaged the clutch and sped off.* [*no obj*]: *The clutch engaged and the car sped off.*

en•gaged (en gājd′) /ɛn'geydʒd/ *adj.* pledged to be married: *an engaged couple.*

en•gage•ment (en gāj′mənt) /ɛn'geydʒmənt/ *n.* [*count*] **1.** the act of engaging or the state of being engaged. **2.** an appointment or arrangement to be somewhere or do something at a particular time: *a dinner engagement. He was late for his business engagement.* **3.** an agreement to marry: *They announced their engagement in the newspaper.* **4.** a period or post of employment: *The singer had a two-week engagement at a nightclub.*

en•gen•der (en jen′dər) /ɛn'dʒɛndər/ *v.* [~ + *obj*] to produce, cause, or give rise to: *Heavy rains engender floods.* See -GEN-.

en•gine (en′jən) /'ɛndʒən/ *n.* [*count*] **1.** a machine for converting heat energy into mechanical energy or power in order to produce force and motion. **2.** a railroad locomotive.

en•gi•neer (en′jə nēr′) /,ɛndʒə'nɪər/ *n.* [*count*] **1.** a person who is trained in any of various branches of engineering: *a civil engineer; an electrical engineer.* **2.** a person who operates or is in charge of a railroad locomotive. —*v.* [~ + *obj*] **3.** to plan, build, construct, or manage as an engineer: *This bridge is engineered for heavy traffic.* **4.** to arrange, manage, or carry through by skillful or clever means: *He engineered the election of his friend.*

en•gi•neer•ing (en′jə nēr′ing) /,ɛndʒə'nɪərɪŋ/ *n.* [*noncount*] **1.** the practical application of science and mathematics, as in the design and construction of machines, vehicles, structures, roads, and systems. **2.** the work or profession of an engineer.

Eng•lish (ing′glish, -lish) /'ɪŋglɪʃ, -lɪʃ/ *adj.* **1.** of or relating to England. **2.** of or relating to the language spoken in England, the United States, Canada, Australia, and other countries. —*n.* **3.** [*plural; the* + ~*; used with a plural verb*] the people born or living in England. **4.** [*noncount*] the language spoken in England, the United States, Canada, Australia, and other countries.

Eng•lish•man (ing′glish mən, -lish-) /'ɪŋglɪʃmən, -lɪʃ-/ *n.* [*count*], *pl.* **-men.** a person born or living in England, esp. a man.

Eng•lish•wom•an (ing′glish wo͝om′ən, -lish-) /'ɪŋglɪʃ,wʊmən, -lɪʃ-/ *n.* [*count*], *pl.* **-wom•en.** a woman born or living in England.

en•grave (en grāv′) /ɛn'greyv/ *v.* [~ + *obj*], **-graved, -grav•ing. 1.** to cut or etch (letters, designs, etc.) into a hard surface, as of metal, stone, or wood: *The jeweler engraved a beautiful design on the ring.* **2.** to mark or ornament with cut or etched letters, designs, etc.: *She engraved the ring with his name.* **3.** to print from a surface that has been cut or etched. **4.** to impress deeply: *The beautiful image is engraved in my memory.* —**en•grav′a•ble,** *adj.* —**en•grav′er,** *n.* [*count*]

en•grav•ing (en grā′ving) /ɛn'greyvɪŋ/ *n.* **1.** [*noncount*] the act or art of a person who engraves. **2.** [*count*] an engraved design, impression, or print.

en•gross (en grōs′) /ɛn'grows/ *v.* [~ + *obj*] to occupy the mind or one's attention completely; absorb: *Crossword puzzles engrossed him for hours.*

en•gulf (en gulf′) /ɛn'gʌlf/ *v.* [~ + *obj*] **1.** to swallow up; cover up: *The stormy sea engulfed the ship.* **2.** to overwhelm or envelop completely: *The orchestra engulfed him in glorious sound.* —**en•gulf′ment,** *n.* [*noncount*]

en•hance (en hans′) /ɛn'hæns/ *v.* [~ + *obj*], **-hanced, -hanc•ing.** to increase the value, attractiveness, or quality of; improve: *A fine wine will enhance a delicious meal.* —**en•hance′ment,** *n.* [*noncount; count*]

e•nig•ma (ə nig′mə) /ə'nɪgmə/ *n.* [*count*], *pl.* **-mas. 1.** a puzzling event, situation, or person. **2.** a riddle.

en•joy (en joi′) /ɛn'dʒɔy/ *v.* **1.** to take pleasure in; experience with joy: [~ + *obj*]: *The audience enjoyed the new opera.* [~ + *verb-ing*]: *I enjoy walking from the train to school.* **2.** [~ + *obj*] to have the benefit of; have and use with satisfaction: *They enjoy one of the world's highest standards of living.* **3.** [*no obj; often in a suggestion*] *Informal.* to enjoy oneself: *Here's your dinner; enjoy!* —***Idiom.* 4. enjoy oneself,** to experience pleasure; have a good time; have fun: *Did you enjoy yourself at the party?* —**Related Words.** ENJOY is a verb, ENJOYABLE is an adjective, ENJOYMENT is a noun: *I enjoy old movies. Those days at the beach were enjoyable times. We shared a lot of enjoyment back then.* —**Usage.** The verb ENJOY usually takes an object, except for the very informal use of definition 3, where it is often used as a request or suggestion; for this meaning, *enjoy yourself* is still more usual. Note also that ENJOY may be followed by the *-ing* form of a verb: *I enjoy hiking/running/walking,* but not by the infinitive, or *to* + *verb* form. It differs therefore from LIKE, a verb with similar meaning, which may take either the *-ing* form or the *to* + *verb* form.

en•joy•a•ble (en joi′ə bəl) /ɛn'dʒɔyəbəl/ *adj.* giving joy or pleasure; pleasant: *an enjoyable day at the beach.*

en•joy•ment (en joi′mənt) /ɛn'dʒɔymənt/ *n.* **1.** [*noncount*] a feeling of joy or pleasure. **2.** [*count*] an activity that gives joy or pleasure: *life's little enjoyments.*

en•large (en lärj′) /ɛn'lardʒ/ *v.,* **-larged, -larg•ing. 1.** to (cause to) become larger; add (to): [*no obj*]: *That photograph will not enlarge well.* [~ + *obj*]: *to enlarge images 50 times the original size.* **2.** [~ + *on/upon* + *obj*] to add more information: *The lecturer enlarged upon her topic.* —**en•large′a•ble,** *adj.* —**en•larg′er,** *n.* [*count*]

en•large•ment (en lärj′mənt) /ɛn'lɑrdʒmənt/ *n.* **1.** [*noncount*] the state or condition of having increased. **2.** [*count*] something that is added on: *built an enlargement to the house.* **3.** [*count*] a photographic print that has been made larger than the original.

en•light•en (en līt′n) /ɛn'laytn̩/ *v.* [~ + *obj*] to give intellectual understanding or knowledge to; instruct: *to enlighten students.* **—en•light′en•ment,** *n.* [*noncount*]

en•list (en list′) /ɛn'lɪst/ *v.* **1.** [*no obj*] to join the armed forces: *As soon as war broke out he enlisted.* **2.** [~ + *obj*] to persuade (someone) to sign up for military service: *The Army recruiter enlists new soldiers.* **3.** [~ + *obj*] to obtain (a person, services, aid, etc.) for a cause or enterprise: *They enlisted our support.* **—en•list′er,** *n.* [*count*]

en•list•ment (en list′mənt) /ɛn'lɪstmənt/ *n.* **1.** [*noncount*] the act of enlisting or the state of being enlisted. **2.** [*count*] the period of time for which a person enlists.

en•liv•en (en lī′vən) /ɛn'layvən/ *v.* [~ + *obj*] to make active or lively; give life to; brighten; animate: *His jokes enlivened the party.* **—en•liv′en•ment,** *n.* [*noncount*]

en•mesh (en mesh′) /ɛn'mɛʃ/ *v.* [~ + *obj*] to catch in or as if in a net; entangle: *He was enmeshed in financial difficulties.* **—en•mesh′ment,** *n.* [*noncount*]

en•mi•ty (en′mi tē) /'ɛnmɪtiy/ *n., pl.* **-ties.** a feeling of bitter hostility or hatred; ill will: [*noncount*]: *Despite the truce, enmity remains between the two countries.* [*count*]: *tribal enmities that go back hundreds of years.*

en•nui (än wē′) /ɑn'wiy/ *n.* [*noncount*] a feeling of weariness and boredom.

e•nor•mi•ty (i nôr′mi tē) /ɪ'nɔrmɪtiy/ *n., pl.* **-ties. 1.** [*noncount*] outrageous or evil character: *We couldn't believe the enormity of the crime.* **2.** [*count*] something outrageous or evil, as an offense. **3.** [*noncount*] greatness of size or extent; hugeness; immensity: *The enormity of the task was overwhelming.* See -NORM-.

e•nor•mous (i nôr′məs) /ɪ'nɔrməs/ *adj.* much greater or larger than the usual: *an enormous mansion.* **—e•nor′-mous•ly,** *adv.*: *We are enormously proud of you.* **—e•nor′mous•ness,** *n.* [*noncount*] See -NORM-.

e•nough (i nuf′) /ɪ'nʌf/ *adj.* [*before a noun;* ~ + *for;* ~ + *to* + *verb*] **1.** adequate or sufficient for the purpose: [*before a noncount noun*]: *Do we have enough water for the trip? I think we have enough money to buy that car.* [*before a plural noun*]: *There are enough seats for everyone here.* **—*pron.*** **2.** an adequate or sufficient quantity, amount, or number: *Do you think 60% is enough?* [~ + *of*]: *We still have enough of the wine to last for a week or two. Enough of us are here to begin the meeting.* **—*adv.*** [*after a verb, adverb, or adjective*] **3.** in a quantity or degree that is sufficient for a purpose or necessary to satisfy a need; sufficiently: *You've worked enough; rest for a bit.* [~ + *to* + *verb*]: *She studied hard enough to pass the test.* **4.** fully or quite: *We're ready enough.* **5.** not very, but tolerably or passably; acceptably: *He sings well enough.* **—*interj.*** **6.** (used to express impatience or annoyance): *Enough! Stop fighting!*

en•quire (en kwīər′) /ɛn'kwayər/ *v.,* **-quired, -quir•ing.** INQUIRE.

en•quir•y (en kwīər′ē, en′kwə rē) /ɛn'kwayəriy, 'ɛnkwəriy/ *n., pl.* **-quir•ies.** INQUIRY. See -QUIR-.

en•rage (en rāj′) /ɛn'reydʒ/ *v.* [~ + *obj*], **-raged, -rag•ing.** to make extremely angry.

en•rap•ture (en rap′chər) /ɛn'ræptʃər/ *v.* [~ + *obj*] **-tured, -tur•ing.** to delight beyond measure; enchant: *Her beautiful songs enraptured audiences everywhere.*

en•rich (en rich′) /ɛn'rɪtʃ/ *v.* [~ + *obj*] **1.** to supply with riches or wealth: *The development of oil fields enriched that country.* **2.** to supply with a large amount of anything desirable: *new words that have enriched the language.* **3.** to add greater value or significance to: *Art can enrich life.* **4.** to improve in quality, as by adding desirable or useful ingredients: *to enrich soil. The breakfast cereal is enriched with vitamins.* **—en•rich′ment,** *n.* [*noncount*]: *programs of educational enrichment for gifted students.*

en•roll or **en•rol** (en rōl′) /ɛn'rowl/ *v.,* **-rolled, -roll•ing** or **-rol•ling.** to (cause to) become a member of a group, school, or course: [*no obj;* (~ + *in* + *obj*)]: *She enrolled in business school.* [~ + *obj* + *in* + *obj*]: *They enrolled me in the club when I paid the fee.*

en•roll•ment or **en•rol•ment** (en rōl′mənt) /ɛn'rowlmənt/ *n.* **1.** [*noncount*] the act or state of enrolling or being enrolled. **2.** [*count*] the number of people who are registered or enrolled.

en route (än ro͞ot′, en, äɴ) /'ɑn ruwt, ɛn, ɑ̃/ *adv.* on or along the way: *We met them en route to the party.*

en•sconce (en skons′) /ɛn'skɒns/ *v.* [~ + *oneself*], **-sconced, -sconc•ing.** to settle securely or snugly: *The kitten was ensconced in an armchair. He ensconced himself in the study to escape from the noise in the living room.*

en•sem•ble (än säm′bəl, -sämb′, äɴ-) /ɑn'sɑmbəl, -'sɑmb, ɑ̃-/ *n.* [*count*] **1.** all the parts of a thing taken together, so that each part is considered in relation to the whole: *The living room furniture is a striking ensemble.* **2.** the entire costume of an individual, esp. when the parts are in harmony: *She wore a beautiful ensemble from Paris.* **3.** a group of singers, musicians, etc., performing together: *a string ensemble.* See -SEMBLE-.

en•shrine (en shrīn′) /ɛn'ʃrayn/ *v.* [~ + *obj*] **-shrined, -shrin•ing.** to keep, hold, and protect as sacred: *Those basic rights are enshrined in the Constitution of the United States.* **—en•shrine′ment,** *n.* [*noncount*]

en•shroud (en shroud′) /ɛn'ʃrawd/ *v.* [~ + *obj*] to cover completely; conceal: *enshrouded in mystery.*

en•sign (en′sən) /'ɛnsən / *n.* [*count*] **1.** a flag or banner, such as a naval flag used to indicate nationality. **2.** the lowest commissioned officer in the navy or coast guard.

en•slave (en slāv′) /ɛn'sleyv/ *v.* [~ + *obj*], **-slaved, -slav•ing.** to put into slavery: *a lord who enslaved the peasants; enslaved by drugs.* **—en•slave′ment,** *n.* [*noncount*] **—en•slav′er,** *n.* [*count*]

en•snare (en snâr′) /ɛn'snɛər/ *v.* [~ + *obj*], **-snared, -snar•ing.** to capture or involve in a trap; entrap. **—en•snare′ment,** *n.* [*noncount*]

en•sue (en so͞o′) /ɛn'suw/ *v.* [*no obj*], **-sued, -su•ing.** to follow in order; come directly afterward: *An argument ensued after the meeting.* **—en•su′ing,** *adj.* [*before a noun*]: *In the ensuing year business improved.*

en•sure (en sho͝or′, -shûr′) /ɛn'ʃʊr, -'ʃɜr/ *v.* [~ + *obj*], **-sured, -sur•ing. 1.** to guarantee; make sure: *taking measures to ensure success.* [~ + *obj* + *obj*]: *This letter will ensure you an interview.* [~ + *(that) clause*]: *Come early to ensure that you get a seat.* **2.** to make secure or safe: *How can a good luck charm ensure your safety?*

-ent, *suffix.* **1.** *-ent* is attached to some verbs to form adjectives with the meaning "doing or performing (the action of the verb)": *differ* + *-ent* → *different.* **2.** *-ent* is also attached to some verbs to form nouns with the meaning "one who does or performs (the action)": *stud(y)* + *-ent* → *student (= one who studies).* See -ANT, -ENCE.

en•tail (en tāl′) /ɛn'teyl / *v.* [~ + *obj*] to cause or involve by necessity or as a consequence: *This project will entail a lot of work.* **—en•tail′ment,** *n.* [*noncount*] See -TAIL-.

en•tan•gle (en tang′gəl) /ɛn'tæŋgəl/ *v.* [~ + *obj*], **-gled, -gling. 1.** to make tangled; intertwine: *Dolphins were entangled in the nets.* **2.** to involve in difficulties; ensnare: *to be entangled in problems.* **—en•tan′gle•ment,** *n.* [*noncount; count*]

en•tente (än tänt′) /ɑn'tɑnt/ *n.* an understanding or agreement between nations to follow a particular policy.

en•ter (en′tər) /'ɛntər/ *v.* **1.** to come or go into: [~ + *obj*]: *to enter a room. The thought never entered my mind.* [*no obj*]: *Please knock before you enter.* **2.** [~ + *obj*] to become a member of; join; become involved in: *to enter the diplomatic corps.* **3.** [~ + *obj*] to cause to be admitted to or participate in: *to enter a horse in a race.* **4.** [~ *(+ into)* + *obj*] to share in; have an understanding of: *He is able to enter (into) the spirit of the competition.* **5.** [~ + *obj*] to put forward, submit, or register formally: *to enter a bid. The attorney entered an objection to the proceedings.* **6.** [~ *(+ on/upon/into)* + *obj*] to make a beginning in: *We are entering on a new phase in the relationship.* **7. enter into,** [~ + *into* + *obj*] **a.** to participate in: *entered into negotiations.* **b.** to form a basic or important part or ingredient of; concern: *Money doesn't enter into the decision.*

en•ter•prise (en′tər prīz′) /'ɛntər,prayz/ *n.* **1.** [*count*] an important, complicated, or difficult undertaking: *Attempts to reach the South Pole were daring enterprises.* **2.** [*noncount*] adventurous spirit or ingenuity: *showing enterprise in solving the puzzle.* **3.** [*count*] a business firm; company. **4.** [*noncount*] a system of doing or organizing business: *private enterprise.* See -PRIS-.

en•ter•pris•ing (en′tər prī′zing) /'ɛntər,prayzɪŋ/ *adj.* having or showing imagination and initiative: *an enterprising plan.*

en•ter•tain (en′tər tān′) /,ɛntər'teyn/ *v.* **1.** to hold the attention of (someone) pleasantly or agreeably; amuse; divert: [~ + *obj*]: *The film entertained us most of the afternoon.* [*no obj*]: *computer games that entertain as well* as educate. **2.** to show hospitality to: [~ + *obj*]: *entertaining my parents for the weekend.* [*no obj*]: *We entertain on weekends.* **3.** [~ + *obj*] to admit into or hold in the mind; consider: *to entertain an idea.* See -TAIN-.

en•ter•tain•er (en′tər tā′nər) /ˌɛntər'teynər/ *n.* [*count*] a singer, comedian, dancer, or other performer, esp. a professional one. See -TAIN-.

en•ter•tain•ment (en′tər tān′mənt) /ˌɛntər'teynmənt/ *n.* **1.** [*noncount*] the act of entertaining, as by providing food and hospitality to guests. **2.** [*noncount*] amusement; distraction from one's regular thoughts: *What do you do for entertainment?* **3.** [*count*] something affording pleasure or amusement: *plays, concerts, and other entertainments.* See -TAIN-.

en•thrall or **en•thral** (en thrôl′) /ɛn'θrɔl/ *v.* [~ + *obj*], **-thralled, -thrall•ing** or **-thral•ling.** to capture one's interest; captivate: *The circus acrobats enthralled the audience with daring feats.* —**en•thrall′ing,** *adj.*: *an enthralling adventure story.* —**en•thrall′ment,** *n.* [*noncount*]

en•throne (en thrōn′) /ɛn'θrown/ *v.* [~ + *obj*], **-throned, -thron•ing.** to place on or as if on a throne. —**en•throne′ment,** *n.* [*count*]

en•thuse (en thōōz′) /ɛn'θuwz/ *v.* [~ + *over* + *obj*], **-thused, -thus•ing.** to show enthusiasm: *enthusing over an exciting new plan.*

en•thu•si•asm (en thōō′zē az′əm) /ɛn'θuwziyˌæzəm/ *n.* **1.** [*noncount*] lively, absorbing interest; eager involvement: *We are looking forward to your visit with enthusiasm. Her enthusiasm for the plan was infectious.* **2.** [*count*] something in which lively, absorbing interest is shown; passion: *Rock climbing is one of his latest enthusiasms.* —**en•thu•si•ast** (en thōō′zē ast′, -ist) /ɛn'θuwziyˌæst, -ɪst/ *n.* [*count*]

en•thu•si•as•tic (en thōō′zē as′tik) /ɛnˌθuwziy'æstɪk/ *adj.* greatly interested in or deeply involved: *an enthusiastic hockey fan.* —**en•thu′si•as′tic•al•ly,** *adv.*: *She participated enthusiastically in the festivities.* —**Related Words.** ENTHUSIASTIC is an adjective, ENTHUSIASM and ENTHUSIAST are nouns: *They gave us an enthusiastic welcome. We were welcomed with enthusiasm. There were some water-polo enthusiasts in the group.*

en•tice (en tīs′) /ɛn'tays/ *v.*, **-ticed, -tic•ing.** to tempt or persuade (someone); lure: [~ + *obj*]: *Can we entice him to the party?* [~ + *obj* + *to* + *verb*]: *There is a way we can entice him to come.* [~ + *obj* + *into* + *obj*]: *We managed to entice him into coming.* —**en•tice′ment,** *n.* [*count; noncount*] —**en•tic′ing,** *adj.*: *It was a very enticing offer.*

en•tire (en tīᵊr′) /ɛn'tayᵊr/ *adj.* [*before a noun*] having all the parts or elements; whole; complete: *The entire class turned out for the game. His entire career was spent in the army.* —**en•tire′ly,** *adv.* —**en•tire′ness,** *n.* [*noncount*] —**Syn.** See COMPLETE.

en•tire•ty (en tīᵊr′tē -tī′ri-) /ɛn'tayᵊrtiy -'tayrɪ-/ *n.* [*noncount*] completeness; the whole: *You have to take into account the entirety of the situation. I copied the paper over in its entirety.*

en•ti•tle (en tīt′l) /ɛn'taytḷ/ *v.*, **-tled, -tling. 1.** [~ + *obj* + *to* + *obj*] to give a right or claim; qualify: *The position of vice president entitles her to a large office.* **2.** [~ + *obj* + *obj*] to call by a particular title or name: *Her book was entitled "The Early Operas of Mozart."*

en•ti•tle•ment (en tīt′l mənt) /ɛn'taytḷmənt/ *n.* **1.** [*noncount*] the right to guaranteed benefits under a government program: *She has obtained entitlement under the program for aid to dependent mothers.* **2.** [*count*] a benefit from such a program: *all the entitlements permitted under the law.*

en•ti•ty (en′ti tē) /'ɛntɪtiy/ *n.* [*count*], *pl.* **-ties.** something that exists as a distinct, separate, independent, or self-contained unit: *Germany was a single entity before World War II, became two entities after the war, and now is one entity again.*

en•to•mol•o•gy (en′tə mol′ə jē) /ˌɛntə'mɒlədʒiy/ *n.* [*noncount*] the branch of science dealing with insects. —**en′to•mol′o•gist,** *n.* [*count*]

en•tou•rage (än′tōō räzh′) /ˌɑntʊ'rɑʒ/ *n.* [*count*] a group of associates or assistants, as people traveling with an important person: *an opera star and her entourage.*

en•trails (en′trālz, -trəlz) /'ɛntreylz, -trəlz/ *n.* [*plural*] the inner organs of a body, esp. the intestines.

en•trance[1] (en′trəns) /'ɛntrəns/ *n.* **1.** [*count*] the act of entering: *She made a dramatic entrance into the hall.* **2.** [*count*] a point or place of entering, as a doorway: *The store posted a guard at each of the main entrances.* **3.** [*noncount*] the right, privilege, or permission to enter; admission: *exams for entrance into college.*

en•trance[2] (en trans′) /ɛn'træns/ *v.* [~ + *obj*], **-tranced, -tranc•ing.** to fill with delight or wonder; enthrall: *It was a gift that would entrance any child.*

en•trant (en′trənt) /'ɛntrənt/ *n.* [*count*] a person who takes part in a competition or contest.

en•trap (en trap′) /ɛn'træp/ *v.* [~ + *obj*], **-trapped, -trap•ping. 1.** to catch in or as if in a trap; ensnare. **2.** to lure into doing something illegal. —**en•trap′ment,** *n.* [*noncount*]

en•treat (en trēt′) /ɛn'triyt/ *v.* [~ + *obj* + *to* + *verb*] to ask (a person) with deep feeling; beg; implore; beseech: *to entreat the judge to show mercy.* —**en•treat′ing•ly,** *adv.*

en•treat•y (en trē′tē) /ɛn'triytiy/ *n.* [*count*], *pl.* **-treat•ies.** an act of entreating; plea: *an entreaty for mercy.*

en•trée or **en•tree** (än′trā) /'ɑntrey/ *n.* **1.** [*count*] a dish served as the main course of a meal. **2.** [*noncount*] the privilege or a means of entering; access: *gained entrée into the highest reaches of the government.*

en•trench (en trench′) /ɛn'trɛntʃ/ *v.* [~ + *obj*] to place in a position of strength; establish firmly: *The yearly marathon was firmly entrenched in the city.* —**en•trench′ment,** *n.* [*noncount*]

en•tre•pre•neur (än′trə prə nûr′, -nōōr′) /ˌɑntrəprə'nɜr, -'nʊr/ *n.* [*count*] a person who organizes and manages an enterprise, esp. a business, usually with considerable daring, skill, and financial risk. —**en′tre•pre•neur′i•al,** *adj.* —**en′tre•pre•neur′ship,** *n.* [*noncount*]

en•trust (en trust′) /ɛn'trʌst/ *v.* **1.** [~ + *obj* + *with* + *obj*] to give something for safekeeping to (someone): *She entrusted me with the money.* **2.** [~ + *obj* + *to* + *obj*] to place (something) in trust: *She entrusted the money to me.* —**en•trust′ment,** *n.* [*noncount*]

en•try (en′trē) /'ɛntriy/ *n.*, *pl.* **-tries. 1.** [*count*] the act of entering; entrance: *the country's entry into the war.* **2.** [*count*] a place of entrance, esp. an entrance hall. **3.** [*noncount*] entrée; access: *She has entry to the highest people in government.* **4.** [*count*] a statement, item, word, etc., entered or recorded in a book, register, list, or account: *The entries in her diary described every day she spent on her trip.* **5.** [*count*] a person or thing entered in a contest or competition: *a late entry into the race.*

en•twine (en twīn′) /ɛn'twayn/ *v.* **-twined, -twin•ing.** to twine about, around, or together: [*no obj*]: *Their arms entwined and they skipped off together to the park.* [~ + *obj*]: *She entwined her arm in mine and off we went.*

e•nu•mer•ate (i nōō′mə rāt′, i nyōō′-) /ɪ'nuwməˌreyt, ɪ'nyuw-/ *v.* [~ + *obj*], **-at•ed, -at•ing.** to name one by one; list: *He enumerated his friend's virtues.* —**e•nu•mer•a•ble** (i nōō′mər ə bəl) /ɪ'nuwmərəbəl/ *adj.* —**e•nu•mer•a•tion** (i nōō′mə rā′shən) /ɪˌnuwmə'reyʃən/ *n.* [*noncount*] —**e•nu′mer•a′tor,** *n.* [*count*] See -NUM-.

e•nun•ci•ate (i nun′sē āt′) /ɪ'nʌnsiyˌeyt/ *v.*, **-at•ed, -at•ing.** to utter or pronounce: [~ + *obj*]: *She enunciates her words clearly.* [*no obj*]: *trying to enunciate clearly.* —**e•nun•ci•a•tion** (e nun′sē ā′shən) /ɛˌnʌnsiy'eyʃən/ *n.* [*noncount*] See -NUNC-.

en•vel•op (en vel′əp) /ɛn'vɛləp/ *v.* [~ + *obj*] **1.** to wrap up in or as if in a covering: *She enveloped me in her arms.* **2.** to surround entirely: *Fog had enveloped the town.* —**en•vel′op•er,** *n.* [*count*] —**en•vel′op•ment,** *n.* [*noncount*]

en•ve•lope (en′və lōp′, än′-) /'ɛnvəˌlowp, 'ɑn-/ *n.* [*count*] a flat paper container, as for a letter.

en•vi•a•ble (en′vē ə bəl) /'ɛnviyəbəl/ *adj.* worthy of envy: *an enviable record of achievements.* —**en•vi•a•bly** (en′vē ə blē) /'ɛnviyəbliy/ *adv.*

en•vi•ous (en′vē əs) /'ɛnviyəs/ *adj.* full of, feeling, or expressing envy: *The losing players cast envious glances at the winning team.* [*be* + ~ + *of*]: *She was envious of her friend's good luck.* —**en′vi•ous•ly,** *adv.* —**en′vi•ous•ness,** *n.* [*noncount*]

en•vi•ron•ment (en vī′rən mənt, -vī′ərn-) /ɛn'vayrənmənt, -'vayərn-/ *n.* **1.** [*count*] social and cultural surroundings; milieu: *bringing up children in a safe environment.* **2.** the external factors and forces surrounding and affecting an organism, person, or population: [*count*] *Sharks have adapted to their environment.* [*noncount*] *Is evolution shaped by environment, or is environment shaped by evolution?* [*count: usually singular; the* + ~] *Legislation was enacted to save the environment from pollution.* —**Syn.** ENVIRONMENT, SURROUNDINGS, AMBIANCE, SETTING refer to the objects, conditions, or circumstances that influence the life of an individual or community. ENVIRONMENT may refer to physical or to social and cultural surroundings: *He grew up in* *an environment of affectionate adults.* SURROUNDINGS are the physical elements around a person, as the place where a person lives: *The inn was located in a town with mountainous surroundings.* AMBIANCE applies to the mood or tone of the surroundings: *The cozy restaurant had an ambiance of ease, friendliness, and elegance.* SETTING tends to highlight the person or thing surrounded by or set against a background: *The mansion was a lovely setting for a wedding.*

en•vi•ron•men•tal (en vī′rən men′təl, -vī′ərn-) /ɛnˌvayrən'mɛntəl, -ˌvayərn-/ *adj.* [*before a noun*] of or relating to the external environment: *environmental pollution.* —**en•vi′ron•men′tal•ly,** *adv.*

en•vi•ron•men•tal•ist (en vī′rən men′tl ist, -vī′ərn-) /ɛnˌvayrən'mɛntlɪst, -ˌvayərn-/ *n.* [*count*] **1.** an expert on environmental problems. **2.** a person who advocates protection of natural resources. —**en•vi′ron•men′tal•ism,** *n.* [*noncount*]

en•vi•rons (en vī′rənz, -vī′ərnz) /ɛn'vayrənz, -'vayərnz/ *n.* [*plural*] surrounding parts or districts: *New York City and its environs.*

en•vis•age (en viz′ij) /ɛn'vɪzɪdʒ/ *v.* [~ + *obj*], **-aged, -ag•ing.** to imagine happening; visualize; envision: *We envisage an era of great scientific discoveries.* See -VIS-.

en•vi•sion (en vizh′ən) /ɛn'vɪʒən/ *v.* [~ + *obj*] to picture in the mind, esp. some future event or events; imagine happening: *He envisioned a shopping mall taking over the park.* See -VIS-.

en•voy (en′voi, än′-) /'ɛnvɔy, 'ɑn-/ *n.* [*count*] **1.** a diplomatic representative ranking next below an ambassador. **2.** an official messenger or representative.

en•vy (en′vē) /'ɛnviy/ *n., pl.* **-vies,** *v.,* **-vied, -vy•ing.** —*n.* [*noncount*] **1.** a feeling of discontent caused by a desire for another's advantages or achievements; jealousy. **2.** [*the* + ~ + *of*] an object of envious feeling: *Her excellent grades made her the envy of her classmates.* —*v.* **3.** to look at with envy; be envious or jealous of: [~ + *obj* (+ *for* + *obj*)]: *We envied him for his success.* [~ + *obj* + *obj*]: *We envied them their wealth.* —**Syn.** ENVY and JEALOUSY are very close in meaning. ENVY denotes a longing to possess something awarded to or achieved by another: *to feel envy at another's good luck.* JEALOUSY, on the other hand, denotes a feeling of resentment because another has gained something that one more rightfully deserves: *to feel jealousy when a coworker receives a promotion.* JEALOUSY also refers to anguish that is caused by fear of losing someone or something to a rival: *a husband's jealousy of other men.*

en•zyme (en′zīm) /'ɛnzaym/ *n.* [*count*] a protein substance from living cells that is capable of producing certain chemical changes in plants and animals, as in digestion.

e•on (ē′ən, ē′on) /'iyən, 'iyɒn/ *n.* [*count*] an extremely long period of time.

EPA, an abbreviation of: Environmental Protection Agency.

ep•au•let or **ep•au•lette** (ep′ə let′, ep′ə let′) /'ɛpəˌlɛt, ˌɛpə'lɛt/ *n.* [*count*] an ornamental shoulder piece, esp. on a uniform.

e•phem•er•al (i fem′ər əl) /ɪ'fɛmərəl/ *adj.* lasting a very short time; short-lived; transitory: *the ephemeral joys of youth.*

ep•ic (ep′ik) /'ɛpɪk/ *adj.* **1.** of or relating to an epic. **2.** of unusually great size or extent: *an earthquake of epic dimensions.* —*n.* [*count*] **3.** a long poem in a formal style, usually about heroic events or great adventure. **4.** a novel, film, etc., resembling or suggesting an epic.

ep•i•cen•ter (ep′ə sen′tər) /'ɛpəˌsɛntər/ *n.* [*count*] **1.** a point, directly above the true center of an earthquake, from which its shock waves appear to spread. **2.** a point of focus, as of activity; center. Also, *esp. Brit.,* **ep′i•cen′tre.**

ep•i•cure (ep′i kyŏŏr′) /'ɛpɪˌkyʊr/ *n.* [*count*] a person who develops a careful, refined taste, esp. in food and wine.

ep•i•dem•ic (ep′i dem′ik) /ˌɛpɪ'dɛmɪk/ *n.* [*count*] **1.** an occurrence of a disease affecting many individuals and spreading from person to person quickly. **2.** a rapid increase in the occurrence of something: *an epidemic of brush fires.* —*adj.* **3.** [*before a noun*] of or resembling an epidemic: *a crime wave of epidemic proportions.*

ep′i•der′mis, *n.* [*noncount*] the outermost layer of the skin. —**ep′i•der′mal, ep′i•der′mic,** *adj.*

ep•i•gram (ep′i gram′) /'ɛpɪˌgræm/ *n.* [*count*] a short and witty saying or poem: *One of his favorite epigrams is "A picture is worth a thousand words."* See -GRAM-.

ep•i•lep•sy (ep′ə lep′sē) /'ɛpəˌlɛpsiy/ *n.* [*noncount*] a disorder of the nervous system in which the victim suffers from either mild, occasional loss of attention or sleepiness, or from severe convulsions with loss of consciousness.

ep•i•lep•tic (ep′ə lep′tik) /ˌɛpə'lɛptɪk/ *adj.* [*before a noun*] **1.** of or relating to epilepsy: *an epileptic seizure.* —*n.* [*count*] **2.** a person suffering from epilepsy.

ep•i•logue or **ep•i•log** (ep′ə lôg′, -log′) /'ɛpəˌlɔg, -ˌlɒg/ *n.* [*count*] a concluding part added to a book, story, or play. See -LOG-.

E•pis•co•pa•lian (i pis′kə pāl′yən) /ɪˌpɪskə'peylyən/ *adj.* **1.** of or relating to the Episcopal Church of the United States, descended from the Church of England. —*n.* [*count*] **2.** a member of the Episcopal Church. —**E•pis′co•pa′lian•ism,** *n.* [*noncount*]

ep•i•sode (ep′ə sōd′) /'ɛpəˌsowd/ *n.* [*count*] **1.** an incident in the course of a series of events, or in a person's life or experience: *His wife's death was a dark episode in his life.* **2.** an incident, scene, etc., within a story, usually fully developed and connected with the main story: *"The Adventures of Tom Sawyer" has many humorous episodes.* **3.** an individual program in a radio or television series.

ep•i•taph (ep′i taf′) /'ɛpɪˌtæf/ *n.* [*count*] words carved on a tomb or monument in memory of the person buried there.

ep•i•thet (ep′ə thet′) /'ɛpəˌθɛt/ *n.* [*count*] **1.** a characterizing word or phrase added to or used in place of the name of a person or thing: *William, Duke of Normandy, had the epithet "the Conqueror."* **2.** a word, phrase, or expression used as a term of abuse or contempt.

e•pit•o•me (i pit′ə mē) /ɪ'pɪtəmiy/ *n.* [*count; the* + ~ + *of*] a person or thing that is typical of a whole class of things: *She is the epitome of kindness.* See -TOM-.

ep•och (ep′ək; *esp. Brit.* ē′pok) /'ɛpək; *esp. Brit.* 'iypɒk/ *n.* [*count*] **1.** a period of time marked by noteworthy features or events: *an epoch of peace.* **2.** a division of geologic time. —**ep′och•al,** *adj.*

ep•ox•y (i pok′sē) /ɪ'pɒksiy/ *n., pl.* **-ox•ies,** *v.,* **-ox•ied, -ox•y•ing.** —*n.* [*count*] **1.** Also called **epox′y res′in.** a substance used chiefly in making strongly adhesive glue, coatings, and castings. —*v.* [~ + *obj*] **2.** to bond (two materials) by means of an epoxy resin.

eq., an abbreviation of: **1.** equal. **2.** equivalent.

-equa- or **-equi-,** *root. -equa-, -equi-* comes from Latin, where it has the meaning "equal; the same." This meaning is found in such words as: EQUABLE, EQUAL, EQUALIZE, EQUILIBRIUM, EQUINOX, EQUITY, EQUIVOCAL, INEQUALITY, INEQUITY.

eq•ua•ble (ek′wə bəl, ē′kwə-) /'ɛkwəbəl, 'iykwə-/ *adj.* **1.** changing very little; uniform: *an equable climate.* **2.** calm; even-tempered: *an equable disposition.* See -EQUA-.

e•qual (ē′kwəl) /'iykwəl/ *adj., n., v.,* **e•qualed, e•qual•ing** or (*esp. Brit.*) **e•qualled, e•qual•ling.** —*adj.* **1.** the same or alike in quantity, degree, value, etc.: *The two men were of equal height. Two plus two is equal to four.* **2.** evenly balanced: *an equal contest.* **3.** [*be* + ~ + *to*] having adequate powers, ability, or means; suited: *I'm sure she will be equal to the task.* —*n.* [*count*] **4.** a person or thing that is equal: *We always considered each other equals.* —*v.* [~ + *obj*] **5.** to be or become equal to: *Two plus two equals four.* **6.** to make or do something equal to: *The younger daughter tried hard to equal her older sister's achievements.* See -EQUA-.

e•qual•i•ty (i kwä′li tē) /ɪ'kwɑlɪtiy/ *n.* [*noncount*] the state or condition of being equal.

e•qual•ize (ē′kwə liz′) /'iykwəˌlayz/ *v.* [~ + *obj*], **-ized, -iz•ing.** to make equal. —**e•qual•i•za•tion** (ē′kwə lə zā′shən) /ˌiykwələ'zeyʃən/ *n.* [*noncount*] See -EQUA-.

e•qual•ly (ē′kwəl ē) /'iykwəliy/ *adv.* **1.** to the same degree: *They love their two children equally.* **2.** into parts that are equal: *We divided the candy equally.*

e′qual opportu′nity, *n.* [*noncount*] policies and practices, esp. in employment, that bar discrimination based on race, color, age, sex, religion, mental or physical handicap, or national origin.

e′qual sign′ or **e′quals sign′,** *n.* [*count*] the symbol (=) used, esp. in a mathematical or logical expression, to indicate that the terms it separates are equal.

e•qua•nim•i•ty (ē′kwə nim′i tē, ek′wə-) /ˌiykwə'nɪmɪtiy, ˌɛkwə-/ *n.* [*noncount*] composure, esp. under tension; evenness of temper.

e•quate (i kwāt′) /ɪ'kweyt/ *v.,* **e•quat•ed, e•quat•ing.** to consider or treat as equivalent: [~ + *obj* + *with* + *obj*]: *trying to equate experience with wisdom.* [~ + *obj* + *and* + *obj*]: *You can't equate profitability and investment.*

e•qua•tion (i kwā′zhən) /ɪ'kweyʒən/ *n.* [*count*] an expression or a proposition in mathematics or logic, stating that two quantities are equal. See -EQUA-.

e•qua•tor (i kwā′tər) /ɪ'kweytər/ *n.* [*count*] an imaginary line that is thought of as circling the earth and is the same distance from the North Pole and South Pole.

e•qua•to•ri•al (ē′kwə tôr′ē əl, -tōr′-, ek′wə-) /ˌiykwə'tɔriyəl, -'towr-, ˌɛkwə-/ *adj.* **1.** of or near the equator: *equatorial regions.* **2.** typical of the region around the equator: *equatorial heat.*

e•ques•tri•an (i kwes′trē ən) /ɪ'kwɛstriyən/ *adj.* [*before a noun*] of or relating to horseback riding or horseback riders: *equestrian skill.*

e•qui•dis•tant (ē′kwi dis′tənt, ek′wi-) /ˌiykwɪ'dɪstənt, ˌɛkwɪ-/ *adj.* [*usually: be* + ~] equally distant: *The two cities are equidistant from here.*

e•qui•lat•er•al (ē′kwə lat′ər əl, ek′wə-) /ˌiykwə'lætərəl, ˌɛkwə-/ *adj.* having all the sides equal: *an equilateral triangle.* See -LAT-[2].

e•qui•lib•ri•um (ē′kwə lib′rē əm, ek′wə-) /ˌiykwə'lɪbriyəm, ˌɛkwə-/ *n.* [*noncount*] **1.** a state of rest or balance between opposing forces, powers, or influences. **2.** mental or emotional balance; equanimity. See -EQUA-, -LIBRA-.

e•quine (ē′kwīn, ek′wīn) /'iykwayn, 'ɛkwayn/ *adj.* of or resembling a horse.

e•qui•nox (ē′kwə noks′, ek′wə-) /'iykwəˌnɒks, 'ɛkwə-/ *n.* [*count*] one of the times when the sun crosses the earth's equator, making night and day of approximately equal length all over the earth and occurring about March 21 and September 22. See -EQUA-, -NOC-.

e•quip (i kwip′) /ɪ'kwɪp/ *v.,* **e•quipped, e•quip•ping. 1.** to provide with what is needed for use or for an undertaking; supply (with); provide: [~ + *obj*] *to equip a safari.* [~ + *obj* + *with* + *obj*]: *The computer is equipped with a modem.* [~ + *obj* + *for* + *obj*]: *They are not properly equipped for a long climb.* **2.** to provide (someone) with adequate intellectual or emotional resources: [~ + *obj* + *for* + *obj*]: *Those children are not equipped for such difficult math.* [~ + *obj* + *to* + *verb*]: *Nothing in our experience has equipped us to deal with such misfortune.*

e•quip•ment (i kwip′mənt) /ɪ'kwɪpmənt/ *n.* [*noncount*] the articles and implements used or needed for a certain purpose or activity: *office equipment.*

eq•ui•ta•ble (ek′wi tə bəl) /'ɛkwɪtəbəl/ *adj.* fair and impartial; just: *equitable treatment of all citizens.* **—eq•ui•ta•bly** (ek′wi tə blē) /'ɛkwɪtəbliy/ *adv.*: *settled the argument equitably.* See -EQUA-.

eq•ui•ty (ek′wi tē) /'ɛkwɪtiy/ *n., pl.* **-ties. 1.** [*noncount*] the quality of being fair or impartial; fairness. **2.** the monetary value of a property or business beyond any amounts that are owed on it: [*noncount*]: *The landlord has more than $35,000 equity in that building.* [*count*]: *Since they paid off their mortgage, they now have an equity equal to the value of the house.* See -EQUA-.

equiv., an abbreviation of: **1.** equivalence. **2.** equivalent.

e•quiv•al•ence (i kwiv′ə ləns) /ɪ'kwɪvələns/ *n.* the act or condition of being the same or equal in value, measure, force: [*noncount*]: *demanding equivalence in treatment.* [*count*]: *An equivalence was found between the two chemical reactions.*

e•quiv•a•lent (i kwiv′ə lənt) /ɪ'kwɪvələnt / *adj.* **1.** having equivalence. **—*n.*** [*count*] **2.** something equivalent: *That car cost the equivalent of a year's salary.* **—e•quiv′a•lent•ly,** *adv.* See -EQUA-, -VAL-.

e•quiv•o•cal (i kwiv′ə kəl) /ɪ'kwɪvəkəl/ *adj.* **1.** deliberately vague; allowing the possibility of more than one meaning or interpretation: *an equivocal answer.* **2.** of doubtful nature or character; questionable: *Ours was an equivocal victory because we lost so many men.* See -EQUA-, -VOC-.

e•quiv•o•cate (i kwiv′ə kāt′) /ɪ'kwɪvəˌkeyt/ *v.* [*no obj*], **-cat•ed, -cat•ing.** to use ambiguous or unclear expressions, usually to mislead or to avoid commitment. **—e•quiv•o•ca•tion** (i kwiv′ə kā′shən) /ɪˌkwɪvə'keyʃən/ *n.* [*noncount; count*]

ER or **E.R.,** an abbreviation of: emergency room.

-er[1], *suffix.* **1.** *-er* is attached to verbs to form nouns with the meanings "a person, animal or thing that performs the action of the verb" or "the person, animal or thing used in performing the action of the verb": *teach* + *-er* → *teacher (= a person who teaches); fertilize* + *-er* → *fertilizer (= a thing that is used to fertilize)* **2.** *-er* is also attached to nouns to form new nouns that refer to the occupation, work, or labor of the root noun: *hat* + *-er* → *hatter (= one whose work is making hats); roof* + *-er* → *roofer (= one whose occupation is repairing roofs).* **3.** *-er* is also attached to nouns to form new nouns that refer to the place of origin, or the dwelling place, of the root noun: *Iceland* + *-er* → *Icelander (= a person who originally comes from Iceland); southern* + *-er* → *southerner (= a person who originally comes from, or lives in, the south).* Compare -IER, -OR.

-er[2], *suffix. -er* is regularly used to form the comparative form of short adjectives and adverbs: *hard* + *-er* → *harder; small* + *-er* → *smaller; fast* + *-er* → *faster.*

e•ra (ēr′ə, er′ə) /'ɪərə, 'ɛrə/ *n.* [*count*], *pl.* **e•ras. 1.** a period of time marked by special character, events, etc.; the period of time to which anything belongs. **2.** a system of chronologic notation reckoned from a given date: *The Christian era starts at the birth of Christ.* **3.** a major division of geologic time.

e•rad•i•cate (i rad′i kāt′) /ɪ'rædɪˌkeyt/ *v.* [~ + *obj*], **-cat•ed, -cat•ing.** to remove or destroy completely: *a new vaccine for eradicating measles.* **—e•rad•i•ca•tion** (i rad′i kā′shən) /ɪˌrædɪ'keyʃən/ *n.* [*noncount*] **—e•rad′i•ca′tor,** *n.* [*count*]

e•rase (i rās′) /ɪ'reys/ *v.* [~ + *obj*], **e•rased, e•ras•ing. 1.** to rub or scrape out: *to erase pencil marks.* **2.** to remove; eliminate: *couldn't erase the scene from her memory.* **—e•ras′a•ble,** *adj.* See -RASE-.

e•ras•er (i rā′sər) /ɪ'reysər/ *n.* [*count*] a device, as a piece of rubber or cloth, for erasing marks of pencil, chalk, etc. See illustration at SCHOOL.

e•rect (i rekt′) /ɪ'rɛkt/ *adj.* **1.** upright and straight in position or posture: *to sit erect.* **—*v.*** [~ + *obj*] **2.** to build; construct: *erected a monument to the founder in the town square.* **3.** to raise and set in an upright or vertical position: *to erect a tent.* **—e•rec•tion** (i rek′shən) /ɪ'rɛkʃən/ *n.* [*noncount; count*] **—e•rect′ly,** *adv.* **—e•rect′ness,** *n.* [*noncount*] See -RECT-.

er•mine (ûr′min) /'ɜrmɪn/ *n., pl.* **-mines,** (*esp. when thought of as a group*) **-mine** for 1. **1.** [*count*] a weasel having a white coat with a black-tipped tail in the winter. **2.** [*noncount*] the white winter fur of the ermine. **—er′mined,** *adj.*

e•rode (i rōd′) /ɪ'rowd/ *v.,* **e•rod•ed, e•rod•ing. 1.** to (cause to) be eaten into or worn away; to (cause to) be destroyed by slowly using up or disintegrating: [*no obj*]: *The bridge was eroding from the salt spray.* [~ + *obj*]: *Wind eroded the loose topsoil.* **2.** to (cause to) be destroyed or disappear gradually: [*no obj*]: *As the election drew near, support for the candidate was eroding.* [~ + *obj*]: *Scandals eroded his reputation.*

e•rog•e•nous (i roj′ə nəs) /ɪ'rɒdʒənəs/ *adj.* particularly sensitive to sexual excitement or pleasure: *erogenous zones of the body.* See -GEN-.

e•ro•sion (i rō′zhən) /ɪ'rowʒən/ *n.* [*noncount*] the act or process of eroding; the state of being eroded.

e•rot•ic (i rot′ik) /ɪ'rɒtɪk/ *adj.* **1.** of, relating to, or about sexual love: *erotic dreams.* **2.** tending to arouse sexual desire: *erotic dancing.* **—e•rot′i•cal•ly,** *adv.*

err (ûr, er) /ɜr, ɛr/ *v.* [*no obj*] **1.** to be mistaken or incorrect; make an error: *Banks rarely err in computing your balance.* **—*Idiom.* 2. to err on the side of,** [~ + *obj*] to act or behave in a certain way, and not its opposite: *It is better to err on the side of punctuality (= It is better to be early than late).*

er•rand (er′ənd) /'ɛrənd/ *n.* [*count*] a short trip to accomplish a certain purpose: *I have to do a few errands for my mother.*

er•rat•ic (i rat′ik) /ɪ'rætɪk/ *adj.* changeable in behavior or style; unpredictable: *behavior too erratic to trust.* **—er•rat′i•cal•ly,** *adv.*

er•ro•ne•ous (ə rō′nē əs, e rō′-) /ə'rowniyəs, ɛ'row-/ *adj.* containing error; mistaken; incorrect: *The facts are correct but your conclusion is erroneous.* **—er•ro′ne•ous•ly,** *adv.* **—er•ro′ne•ous•ness,** *n.* [*noncount*]

er•ror (er′ər) /'ɛrər/ *n.* **1.** [*count*] a mistake; inaccuracy: *made several errors in addition.* **2.** [*noncount*] the condition of being wrong: *I was in error about the date of the party.*

er•u•dite (er′yŏŏ dīt′, er′ŏŏ-) /'ɛryʊˌdayt, 'ɛrʊ-/ *adj.* characterized by great academic knowledge; learned; scholarly. **—er•u•di•tion** (er′yŏŏ dish′ən, er′ŏŏ-) /ˌɛryʊ'dɪʃən, ˌɛrʊ-/ *n.* [*noncount*]

e•rupt (i rupt′) /ɪ'rʌpt/ *v.* **1.** [*no obj*] to burst forth: *Molten lava erupted from the volcano.* **2.** (of a volcano, geyser, etc.) to throw out or eject matter violently: [*no obj*]: *Suddenly the volcano erupted.* [~ + *obj*]: *The volcano erupted lava and ash.* **3.** [*no obj*] to break out of a pent-up state, usually in a sudden and violent manner: *Words of anger erupted from her.* **—e•rup′tion,** *n.* [*noncount; count*] See -RUPT-.

-ery or **-ry,** *suffix.* **1.** *-ery* or *-ry* is used to form nouns that refer to **a.** things in a collection: *green + -ery → greenery (= green plants as a group); machine + -ery → machinery (= a group or collection of machines).* **b.** people in a collection: *Jew + -ry → Jewry (= Jews as a group); peasant + -ry → peasantry (= peasants as a group).* **c.** an occupation, activity, or condition: *dentist + -ry → dentistry (= occupation of a dentist); rival + -ry → rivalry (= condition of being a rival); rob + -ery → robbery (= activity of robbing or being robbed).* **2.** *-ery* is also used to form nouns that refer to a place where the activity of the root is done: *bake + -ery →bakery (= place where baking is done); wine + -ery → winery (= place where wine is made).*

es•ca•late (es′kə lāt′) /ˈɛskəˌleyt/ *v.,* **-lat•ed, -lat•ing.** to (cause to) increase in intensity, degree, or amount; to (cause to) rise: [*no obj*] *a time when the war escalated beyond control.* [~ + *obj*]: *The foes escalated the war.* —**es•ca•la•tion** (es′kə lā′shən) /ˌɛskəˈleyʃən/ *n.* [*noncount*]

es•ca•la•tor (es′kə lā′tər) /ˈɛskəˌleytər/ *n.* [*count*] a continuously moving stairway on an endless loop for carrying passengers up or down. See illustration at STORE.

es•ca•pade (es′kə pād′) /ˈɛskəˌpeyd/ *n.* [*count*] a reckless act or adventure; a wild or dangerous prank or trick.

es•cape (i skāp′) /ɪˈskeyp/ *v.,* **-caped, -cap•ing,** *n., adj.* —*v.* **1.** [~ (+ *from* + *obj*)] to slip or get away, as from confinement or jail: *How did the mice escape from their cage?* **2.** to avoid (capture, punishment, injury, or the like): [~ + *obj*]: *The town escaped the worst of the storm.* [*no obj*]: *managed to escape with only cuts and bruises.* **3.** [*no obj*] to issue from a confining enclosure, as a gas or liquid: *Air escaped from the balloon.* **4.** [~ + *obj*] to fail to remember or notice: *His name escapes me at the moment.* —*n.* **5.** [*count*] an act or instance of escaping. **6.** a way or means of escaping: [*count*]: *We used the tunnel as an escape.* [*noncount*]: *The back door is your only means of escape.* **7.** [*count*] a way or means of avoiding reality: *liked to read mystery stories as an escape.* —*adj.* [*before a noun*] **8.** for or providing an escape: *an escape hatch.* **9.** being a key on a microcomputer keyboard, often used to return to a previous program screen: *Hit the escape key.* —**Syn.** ESCAPE, ELUDE, EVADE mean to keep free of something. To ESCAPE is to succeed in keeping away from danger, from being chased or observed, etc.: *to escape punishment.* To ELUDE is to slip through an apparently tight net, thus avoiding, often by a narrow margin, whatever threatens; it implies using skill or cleverness to baffle or fool: *The fox eluded the hounds by his clever twists and turns.* To EVADE is to turn aside from or go out of reach of a person or thing, usually by using a trick to direct attention elsewhere: *to evade the police.*

es•cort (*n.* es′kôrt; *v.* i skôrt′) /*n.* ˈɛskɔrt; *v.* ɪˈskɔrt/ *n.* **1.** [*count*] a person or group accompanying another for protection, guidance, or courtesy. **2.** [*count*] an armed or protective guard, as a body of soldiers or ships: *The convoy had an escort of several destroyers and frigates.* **3.** [*count*] a man or woman who accompanies another person to a public event. **4.** [*noncount*] protection or supervision: *under police escort.* —*v.* [~ + *obj*] **5.** to attend or accompany as an escort: *I escorted her down the aisle.*

-ese, *suffix.* **1.** *-ese* is attached to nouns that refer to certain place names: **a.** to form adjectives that describe things made in or relating to the place: *Japan + -ese → Japanese (= of or relating to Japan or its people); Vienna + -ese → Viennese (= of or relating to Vienna or its people)* **b.** to form nouns with the meanings "the people living in (the place)" or "the language of (the place)": *Vietnam + -ese → Vietnamese (= the people living in/ the language spoken in Vietnam).* **2.** *-ese* is also used to form nouns that describe in an insulting or humorous way the language characteristic of or typical of the base word: *Brooklyn + -ese → Brooklynese (= the language characteristic of Brooklyn); journal + -ese → journalese (= the language typical of journalists).*

Es•ki•mo (es′kə mō′) /ˈɛskəˌmow/ *n., pl.* **-mo, -mos** for 1. **1.** [*count*] a member of a people living in regions from Greenland through Canada and Alaska to NE Siberia. **2.** [*noncount*] the group of languages spoken by the Eskimos.

ESL, an abbreviation of: English as a second language.

e•soph•a•gus (i sof′ə gəs) /ɪˈsɒfəgəs/ *n.* [*count*], *pl.* **-gi** (-jī′, gī′) /-ˌdʒay, ˌgay/. a muscular tube that allows food to pass from the back of the mouth to the stomach; gullet.

es•o•ter•ic (es′ə ter′ik) /ˌɛsəˈtɛrɪk/ *adj.* **1.** understood by or meant for only a small number of people who have special knowledge or interest: *poetry full of esoteric allusions.* **2.** private; secret: *an esoteric ritual.*

esp., an abbreviation of: especially.

es•pe•cial•ly (i spesh′ə lē) /ɪˈspɛʃəliy/ *adv.* **1.** to an exceptional degree; particularly; markedly: *Be especially watchful.* **2.** in particular; above all: *It is hot here, especially in July.* **3.** for a particular purpose; specifically: *These clothes were designed especially for you.*

es•pi•o•nage (es′pē ə näzh′, -nij) /ˈɛspiyəˌnɑʒ, -nɪdʒ/ *n.* [*noncount*] the act or practice of spying, as by one government or corporation against another.

es•pouse (i spouz′, i spous′) /ɪˈspawz, ɪˈspaws/ *v.* [~ + *obj*], **-poused, -pous•ing.** to support, as a cause; call for; promote; adopt: *espoused a philosophy of understanding.* —**es•pous′er,** *n.* [*count*]

es•pres•so (e spres′ō) /ɛˈsprɛsow/ *n., pl.* **-sos** for 2. **1.** [*noncount*] a strong coffee prepared by forcing steam through finely ground dark-roast coffee beans. **2.** [*count*] a cup of espresso.

es•prit de corps (e sprē′ də kôr′) /ɛˈspriyˈ də kɔr/ *n.* [*noncount*] a sense of unity and of common purpose among the members of a group.

es•py (i spī′) /ɪˈspay/ *v.* [~ + *obj*], **-pied, -py•ing.** to see at a distance; catch sight of.

Esq. or **Esqr.,** an abbreviation of: Esquire.

-esque, *suffix.* *-esque* is attached to nouns and proper names to form adjectives with the meanings "resembling," "in the style or manner of," "suggesting the work of" the person or thing denoted by the base word: *Kafka + -esque → Kafkaesque (= in the style or manner of Franz Kafka); Lincoln + -esque → Lincolnesque (= in the style of Abraham Lincoln); picture + -esque → picturesque (= resembling or suggesting a picture).*

Es•quire (es′kwīᵊr, e skwīᵊr′) /ˈɛskwayᵊr, ɛˈskwayᵊr/ *n.* a title of respect that is sometimes placed, esp. in its abbreviated form, Esq., after a man's last name in formal written address: in the U.S., chiefly applied to male or female lawyers.

-ess, *suffix.* *-ess* is used to form a feminine noun: *count + -ess → countess; god + -ess → goddess; lion + -ess → lioness.* —**Usage.** The use of words ending in -ESS has declined sharply in the latter half of the 20th century, but some are still current: *actress* (but some women prefer *actor*); *adventuress; enchantress; governess; heiress* (largely in journalistic writing); *hostess* (but women who conduct radio and television programs are *hosts*); *seamstress; seductress; temptress;* and *waitress.*

es•say (*n.* es′ā *or, for 2,* e sā′; *v.* e sā′) /*n.* ˈɛsey *or, for 2,* ɛˈsey; *v.* ɛˈsey/ *n.* [*count*] **1.** a short piece of writing on a particular theme or subject. **2.** an effort to perform or accomplish something; attempt. —*v.* [~ + *obj*] **3.** to try; attempt: *She essayed a short jump.*

es•say•ist (es′ā ist) /ˈɛseyɪst/ *n.* [*count*] a writer of essays.

es•sence (es′əns) /ˈɛsəns/ *n.* **1.** [*noncount*] the basic, unchanging nature of a thing; the substance that gives something identity: *The essence of civilized behavior is courtesy.* **2.** [*noncount*] the basic meaning of something; main point: *The essence of his speech was that we must all work harder.* **3.** [*count; noncount*] a concentrated substance made from a plant, drug, or the like: *essence of brandy.* —***Idiom.*** **4. in essence,** essentially; basically: *What she said, in essence, is that all will be well.* **5. of the essence,** absolutely essential; crucial: *It is of the essence that you attend that meeting.*

es•sen•tial (ə sen′shəl) /əˈsɛnʃəl/ *adj.* **1.** absolutely necessary; that cannot be done without; indispensable: *essential vitamins. Water is essential for life.* [*it + be + ~ + (that) clause*]: *It is essential that you be at the meeting.* **2.** [*before a noun*] relating to the essence of a thing: *The essential purpose of a vacation is to relax.* —*n.* [*count*] **3.** a basic or necessary element; chief point: *an essential of the job is promptness.* **4.** a basic or necessary item or thing: *bare essentials like food and water.* —**es•sen′tial•ly,** *adv.*

EST or **E.S.T.,** an abbreviation of: Eastern Standard Time.

-est, *suffix.* *-est* is regularly used to form the superlative form of short adjectives and adverbs: *fast + -est → fastest; soon + -est → soonest; warm + -est → warmest.*

est., an abbreviation of: **1.** established. **2.** estate. **3.** estimate. **4.** estimated.

estab., an abbreviation of: established.

es•tab•lish (i stab′lish) /ɪˈstæblɪʃ/ *v.* [~ + *obj*] **1.** to bring into being on a firm or permanent basis; set up; found: *to establish a university.* **2.** [~ + *oneself*] to install, put, or settle in a position, place, business, etc.:

They established themselves as founders of the society. **3.** to figure out; determine: *The coroner was able to establish the time of death.* [~ + *that clause*]: *The coroner was able to establish that death took place at about eight o'clock.* **4.** to cause to be accepted or recognized: *to establish a custom.* **5.** to enact, appoint, or ordain on a permanent basis: *The new parliament set about establishing laws to improve the economy.* See -STAB-.

es•tab•lish•ment (i stab′lish mənt) /ɪ'stæblɪʃmənt/ *n.* **1.** [*noncount*] the act of establishing or the state of being established. **2.** [*count*] a place of business: *That flour mill is the oldest establishment in town.* **3. the Establishment,** [*count; usually singular*] the people and institutions that control power in society.

es•tate (i stāt′) /ɪ'steyt/ *n.* **1.** [*count*] a piece of land as property, esp. one of large extent with a large house on it. **2.** [*noncount*] property or possessions, as the property of a deceased person. See -STAT-.

es•teem (i stēm′) /ɪ'stiym/ *v.* **1.** [~ + *obj*] to have high regard for: *She is esteemed for her fine qualities.* **2.** [~ + *obj* + *obj*] to consider as of a certain value or a certain type: *I would esteem it a great favor.* —*n.* [*noncount*] **3.** favorable opinion or judgment; respect or regard: *to hold a person in high esteem.* —**es•teemed′,** *adj.*: *an esteemed colleague.*

es•thete (es′thēt) /'ɛsθiyt/ *n.* AESTHETE.

es•thet•ics (es thet′iks) /ɛs'θɛtɪks/ *n.* AESTHETICS.

es•ti•mate (*v.* es′tə māt′; *n.* -mit) /*v.* 'ɛstəˌmeyt; *n.* -mɪt/ *v.*, **-mat•ed, -mat•ing,** *n.* —*v.* **1.** to form a judgment or opinion regarding the worth, amount, size, weight, etc., of; calculate approximately: [~ + *obj*]: *to estimate the cost of a college education.* [~ + *obj* + *at* + *obj*]: *estimated the cost at about $5,000.* [~ + *(that) clause*]: *Someone estimated that the cost of a college education has doubled in the last ten years.* **2.** to form an opinion of; judge: [~ + *obj*]: *She estimated his attitude was hostile.* [~ + *(that) clause*]: *I estimate that our candidate will win.* —*n.* [*count*] **3.** an approximate judgment or calculation, as of the value, amount, time, size, or weight of something: *The expert's estimate is that the painting is worth $5,000.* **4.** a judgment or opinion, as of the qualities of a person or thing: *My estimate of his character was incorrect.* **5.** a statement of the approximate charge for work to be done. —**es•ti•ma•tor** (es′tə-mā′tər) /'ɛstəˌmeytər/ *n.* [*count*]

es•ti•ma•tion (es′tə mā′shən) /ˌɛstə'meyʃən/ *n.* [*noncount*] judgment, impression, or opinion: *My estimation of his intelligence has just gone down.*

Es•to•ni•an (e stō′nē ən) /ɛ'stowniyən/ *adj.* **1.** of or relating to Estonia. —*n.* **2.** [*count*] a person born or living in Estonia. **3.** [*noncount*] the language spoken by many of the people living in Estonia.

es•tranged (i strānjd′) /ɪ'streyndʒd/ *adj.* unfriendly or hostile to (another); alienated from: *his estranged wife; estranged from her family.* —**es•trange′ment,** *n.* [*noncount*]

es•tro•gen (es′trə jən) /'ɛstrədʒən/ *n.* [*noncount*] a major female sex hormone that is produced in the ovaries and controls the reproductive cycle.

es•tu•ar•y (es′cho͞o er′ē) /'ɛstʃuwˌɛriy/ *n.* [*count*], *pl.* **-ar•ies.** the part of the mouth of a river in which its current meets the sea's tide.

ET or **E.T.,** an abbreviation of: Eastern time.

ETA or **E.T.A.,** an abbreviation of: estimated time of arrival.

et al. (et al′, äl′, ôl′) /ɛt æl, 'ɑl, 'ɔl/ a Latin abbreviation meaning: **1.** and others. **2.** and elsewhere.

etc., an abbreviation of: et cetera.

et cet•er•a (et set′ər ə, se′trə) /'ɛt sɛtərə, 'sɛtrə/ *adv.* and others; and so forth; and so on (used to indicate that more of the same sort or class have been omitted to save space or time). *Abbr.*: etc. —**Usage.** ET CETERA appears in English writing mostly in its abbreviated form, ETC. The expression *and et cetera* is redundant because *et* means *and* in Latin.

etch (ech) /ɛtʃ/ *v.* **1.** to engrave or cut into (a surface) with an acid, knife, or the like, esp. so as to form a design that can be transferred to paper: [*no obj*]: *She enjoys etching.* [~ + *obj*]: *The sculptor etched the gravestone with a chisel.* **2.** [~ + *obj*] to produce (a design, image, etc.) by this method, as on copper or glass: *The Swedish crystal was etched with a geometric design.* **3.** [~ + *obj*] to outline clearly or sharply: delineate: *His face was etched with lines of age and sorrow.* **4.** [~ + *obj*] to fix or imprint firmly: *His face is etched in my memory.* —**etch′er,** *n.* [*count*]

etch•ing (ech′ing) /'ɛtʃɪŋ/ *n.* **1.** [*noncount*] the act or process of making designs or pictures on a metal plate, glass, etc. **2.** [*count*] an impression, as on paper, that is made from an etched plate.

ETD or **E.T.D.,** an abbreviation of: estimated time of departure.

e•ter•nal (i tûr′nl) /ɪ'tɜrnl̩/ *adj.* **1.** having no beginning or end; lasting forever: *the eternal movement of the planets.* **2.** perpetual; constant: *This eternal chatter is driving me crazy.* **3.** enduring; long-lasting: *eternal principles of truth.* —**e•ter′nal•ly,** *adv.* —**Syn.** ETERNAL, ENDLESS, EVERLASTING, PERPETUAL imply lasting or going on without ceasing. That which is ETERNAL is, by its nature, without beginning or end: *God, the eternal Being.* That which is ENDLESS never stops but goes on continuously as if in a circle: *an endless succession of years.* That which is EVERLASTING will last through all future time: *a promise of everlasting life.* PERPETUAL implies continuous renewal, a starting again and again, far into the future: *perpetual strife between nations.*

e•ter•ni•ty (i tûr′ni tē) /ɪ'tɜrnɪtiy/ *n., pl.* **-ties. 1.** [*noncount*] infinite time; duration without beginning or end. **2.** [*noncount*] eternal existence, esp. the timeless state into which the soul is believed to pass at death. **3.** [*count, usually singular*] a period of time that seems endless: *I waited an eternity for a bus.*

e•ther (ē′thər) /'iyθər/ *n.* [*noncount*] **1.** a colorless, flammable liquid once used as an anesthetic in surgery. **2.** the upper regions of space; the clear sky.

e•the•re•al (i thēr′ē əl) /ɪ'θɪəriyəl/ *adj.* light; airy; extremely delicate: *ethereal beauty.*

eth•ic (eth′ik) /'ɛθɪk/ *n.* [*count; singular*] all the moral principles or values that are held by a culture, group, or individual, including concepts of right and wrong, rules of conduct, or the like: *a personal work ethic.* See ETHICS.

eth•i•cal (eth′i kəl) /'ɛθɪkəl/ *adj.* relating to or dealing with morality; relating to ethics: *an ethical question.* —**eth′i•cal•ly,** *adv.*

eth•ics (eth′iks) /'ɛθɪks/ *n.* **1.** [*plural; used with a plural verb*] a system or set of moral principles: *The ethics of one culture are not always shared by other cultures.* **2.** [*noncount; used with a singular verb*] a branch of philosophy dealing with issues like values in human conduct and questions of right and wrong. —**eth•i•cist** (eth′ə-sist) /'ɛθəsɪst/ *n.* [*count*]

E•thi•o•pi•an (ē′thē ō′pē ən) /ˌiyθiy'owpiyən/ *adj.* **1.** of or relating to Ethiopia. —*n.* [*count*] **2.** a person born or living in Ethiopia.

eth•nic (eth′nik) /'ɛθnɪk/ *adj.* **1.** [*before a noun*] relating to or characteristic of a people, esp. a group **(eth′nic group′)** sharing a common and distinctive culture. —*n.* [*count*] **2.** a member of an ethnic group or minority. —**eth′ni•cal•ly,** *adv.*: *ethnically diverse groups in the city.*

eth•nic•i•ty (eth nis′i tē) /ɛθ'nɪsɪtiy/ *n.* [*noncount*] ethnic characteristics, traits, or association: *The candidate made numerous appeals to the ethnicity of the voters.*

eth•no•cen•trism (eth′nō sen′triz əm) /ˌɛθ-now'sɛntrɪzəm/ *n.* [*noncount*] **1.** the belief that one's own ethnic group or culture is fundamentally superior to others. **2.** a tendency to view alien groups or cultures from the perspective of one's own. —**eth′no•cen′tric,** *adj.*

et•i•quette (et′i kit, -ket′) /'ɛtɪkɪt, -ˌkɛt/ *n.* [*noncount*] the rules of proper social or professional behavior; manners.

-ette, *suffix.* **1.** *-ette* is attached to nouns to form nouns that refer to a smaller version of the original noun or root: *kitchen* + *-ette* → *kitchenette (= small kitchen); novel* + *-ette* → *novelette (= smaller novel).* **2.** *-ette* is also attached to nouns to form nouns that refer specifically to a female: *major* + *-ette* → *majorette (= female leader of a band, or baton twirler); usher* + *-ette* → *usherette (= female usher in a movie theater).* **3.** *-ette* is attached to nouns to form nouns that refer to a name that is an imitation product of the root: *leather* + *-ette* → *leatherette (= imitation leather product).* —**Usage.** English nouns in which -ETTE signifies a feminine role or identity have been thought of as implying inferiority or unimportance and are now generally avoided. Only *(drum) majorette* is still widely used, usually indicating a young woman who twirls a baton with a marching band.

et•y•mol•o•gy (et′ə mol′ə jē) /ˌɛtə'mɒlədʒiy/ *n., pl.* **-gies. 1.** [*count*] the history of words or word elements: *a dictionary of etymology.* **2.** [*noncount*] the study of historical linguistic change in individual words. —**et•y•mo•log•i•cal** (et′ə mə loj′i kəl) /ˌɛtəmə'lɒdʒɪkəl/ *adj.* —**et•y•mol•o•gist** (et′ə mol′ə jist) /ˌɛtə'mɒlədʒɪst/ *n.* [*count*]

eu-, *prefix. eu-* comes from Greek, where it has the meaning "good, well". This meaning is found in such words as: EULOGIZE, EULOGY, EUPHEMISM, EUPHORIA, EUTHANASIA.

eu•ca•lyp•tus (yo͞o′kə lip′təs) /ˌyuwkə'lɪptəs/ *n.* [*count*], *pl.* **-ti** (-tī), **-tus•es.** a tree chiefly from Australia and nearby islands having sweet-smelling evergreen leaves.

Eu•cha•rist (yo͞o′kə rist) /'yuwkərɪst/ *n.* [*proper noun; often: the* + ~] **1.** the sacrament of Holy Communion. **2.** the bread and wine taken at Holy Communion, esp. the bread. **—Eu′cha•ris′tic,** *adj.*

eu•lo•gize (yo͞o′lə jīz′) /'yuwləˌdʒayz/ *v.* [~ + *obj*], **-gized, -giz•ing.** to praise in a eulogy; extol: *to eulogize the heroes of history.* **—eu′lo•giz′er,** *n.* [*count*] See -LOG-.

eu•lo•gy (yo͞o′lə jē) /'yuwlədʒiy/ *n., pl.* **-gies. 1.** [*count*] a speech or piece of writing in praise of a person or thing, esp. in honor of a deceased person. **2.** [*noncount*] high praise or commendation. See -LOG-.

eu•nuch (yo͞o′nək) /'yuwnək/ *n.* [*count*] a castrated man.

eu•phe•mism (yo͞o′fə miz′əm) /'yuwfəˌmɪzəm/ *n.* **1.** [*noncount*] the substitution of a mild, indirect, or vague expression for one thought to be offensive, harsh, or blunt. **2.** [*count*] word or expression so substituted: *"To pass away" is a euphemism for "to die."* **—eu′phe•mis′tic,** *adj.* **—eu′phe•mis′ti•cal•ly,** *adv.*

eu•pho•ri•a (yo͞o fôr′ē ə, -fōr′-) /yuw'fɔriyə, -'fowr-/ *n.* [*noncount*] a strong feeling of happiness, confidence, or well-being: *She was filled with euphoria over the news of her promotion.*

eu•phor•ic (yo͞o fôr′ik, -for′-) /yuw'fɔrɪk, -'fɒr-/ *adj.* filled with happiness, confidence, or well-being: *She felt euphoric over her promotion.* **—eu•phor′i•cal•ly,** *adv.*

Eur•a•sian (yo͝o rā′zhən) /yʊ'reyʒən/ *adj.* **1.** of mixed European and Asian descent. **—***n.* [*count*] **2.** a person who is of mixed European and Asian descent.

Euro-, *prefix. Euro-* is used with roots and means "Europe," "Western Europe," or "the European Community": *Euro-* + *-centric* → *Eurocentric (= centered on Europe); Euro-* + *-crat* → *Eurocrat (= bureaucrat in the European Community).* Also, *esp. before a vowel,* **Eur-.**

Eu•ro•dol•lar (yo͝or′ə dol′ər) /'yʊrəˌdɒlər/ *n.* [*count*] a U.S. dollar deposited in or credited to a European bank.

Eu•ro•pe•an (yo͝or′ə pē′ən) /ˌyʊrə'piyən/ *adj.* **1.** of or relating to Europe. **—***n.* [*count*] **2.** a person born or living in Europe.

Europe′an Econom′ic Commu′nity, *n.* [*proper noun; usually: the* + ~] an association of European nations for economic cooperation; the Common Market. *Abbr.:* EEC

Europe′an plan′, *n.* [*count*] a system of paying a fixed hotel rate that covers lodging only.

Eu•sta′chian tube′ (yo͞o stā′shən) /yuw'steyʃən/ *n.* [*count*] a tube or canal extending from the middle ear to the back of the throat.

eu•tha•na•sia (yo͞o′thə nā′zhə) /ˌyuwθə'neyʒə/ *n.* [*noncount*] painless killing of a person, usually when the person is suffering from an incurable, esp. a painful, disease or condition. Also called **mercy killing.**

e•vac•u•ate (i vak′yo͞o āt′) /ɪ'vækyuwˌeyt/ *v.* [~ + *obj*], **-at•ed, -at•ing.** to remove (persons or things) from a place, esp. for reasons of safety: *evacuated the people from the flooded village.* **—e•vac•u•a•tion** (i vak′yo͞o ā′shən) /ɪˌvækyuw'eyʃən/ *n.* [*count; noncount*] See -VAC-.

e•vac•u•ee (i vak′yo͞o ē′) /ɪˌvækyuw'iy/ *n.* [*count*] a person removed from a dangerous place.

e•vade (i vād′) /ɪ'veyd/ *v.* [~ + *obj*], **e•vad•ed, e•vad•ing.** to escape or avoid esp. by cleverness or trickery: *He managed to evade his pursuers.* See -VADE-. **—Syn.** See ESCAPE.

e•val•u•ate (i val′yo͞o āt′) /ɪ'vælyuwˌeyt/ *v.* [~ + *obj*], **-at•ed, -at•ing.** to determine the value, quality, or significance of; assess; appraise: *to evaluate property.* **—e•val•u•a•tion** (i val′yo͞o ā′shən) /ɪˌvælyuw'eyʃən/ *n.* [*count; noncount*] See -VAL-.

e•van•gel•i•cal (ē′van jel′i kəl, ev′ən-) /ˌiyvæn'dʒɛlɪkəl, ˌɛvən-/ *adj.* Also, **e′van•gel′ic. 1.** relating to or in keeping with the Gospels. **2.** belonging to or referring to the Christian churches that emphasize the authority of the Scriptures and personal conversion through faith in Christ. **3.** having strong or intense enthusiasm for a cause. **—***n.* [*count*] **4.** a person who belongs to an evangelical church or organization. **—e′van•gel′i•cal•ism,** *n.* [*noncount*]

e•van•ge•lism (i van′jə liz′əm) /ɪ'vændʒəˌlɪzəm/ *n.* [*noncount*] **1.** the preaching of the Christian gospel. **2.** missionary zeal, purpose, or activity. **—e•van′ge•list,** *n.* [*count*]

e•van•ge•lize (i van′jə līz′) /ɪ'vændʒəˌlayz/ *v.* [~ + *obj*], **-lized, -liz•ing.** to preach the Christian gospel to: *driving from town to town, evangelizing people.*

e•vap•o•rate (i vap′ə rāt′) /ɪ'væpəˌreyt/ *v.,* **-rat•ed, -rat•ing. 1.** to (cause to) change from a liquid or solid state into vapor or gas: [*no obj*]: *The dew evaporated in the hot sun.* [~ + *obj*]: *The hot sun evaporated the dew.* **2.** [*no obj*] to disappear; vanish: *His hopes evaporated.* **—e•vap•o•ra•tion** (i vap′ə rā′shən) /ɪˌvæpə'reyʃən/ *n.* [*noncount*]

e•va•sion (i vā′zhən) /ɪ'veyʒən/ *n.* **1.** an act or instance of evading: [*count*]: *an evasion of one's duty.* [*noncount*]: *guilty of fraud and tax evasion.* **2.** the avoiding of an accusation, question, or the like, as by a failing to tell the truth; subterfuge: [*count*]: *The jurors distrusted the witness for his many evasions.*

e•va•sive (i vā′siv) /ɪ'veysɪv/ *adj.* using evasion: *evasive answers; evasive maneuvers to escape.* **—e•va′sive•ly,** *adv.* **—e•va′sive•ness,** *n.* [*noncount*]

eve (ēv) /iyv/ *n.* [*count*] **1.** the evening or the day before an event, esp. a holiday. **2.** the evening.

e•ven (ē′vən) /'iyvən/ *adj.* **1.** without bumps on the surface; regular; smooth: *an even road.* **2.** on the same level; in the same plane or line; parallel: *even with the ground.* **3.** free from sudden changes; uniform; regular; constant: *a steady, even sound.* **4.** (of a number) that can be divided by two without a remainder: *1,024 is an even number.* **5.** [*before a noun*] denoted by or having such a number: *the even pages of a book.* **6.** [*before a noun*] exactly expressed in whole numbers. **7.** equal in measure or quantity: *even amounts of oil and vinegar.* **8.** equally balanced or divided; equal: *an even exchange.* **9.** [*be* + ~] leaving no balance of debt on either side: *I lent you my car last week; if you lend me yours this week we'll be even.* **10.** calm; not easily excited or angered; placid: *an even temper.* **11.** equitable or fair: *an even bargain.* **—***adv.* **12.** evenly; in an even manner; smoothly: *The road ran even over the fields.* **13.** (used with a comparative word to emphasize the comparison, or to mean "still" or "yet"): *That arrangement is acceptable, but this one is even more suitable.* **14.** (used with a superlative adjective, or with the conjunction *if,* to suggest that some possibility is unlikely to happen): [*before an adjective*]: *Even the slightest noise disturbs him.* [~ + *if*]: *Even if she comes, she may not stay.* **15.** (used to connect clauses to emphasize that the occurrence of one event is almost at the same time as the other): *Even as help was coming, the troops surrendered.* **16.** fully or quite: *ready to fight even unto death.* **17.** (used to stress or emphasize the truth of something): *He is willing, even eager.* **18.** exactly or precisely: *It was even so.* **—***v.* **19.** [~ + *obj*] to make level, smooth, or equal: *worked all day to even the pavement.* **20. even out,** to make or become level, smooth, or equal: [*no obj*]: *The wrinkles will even out when the suit dries.* [~ + *out* + *obj*]: *They need two home runs to even out the score.* **—*Idiom.* 21. break even,** [*no obj*] to have one's profits equal one's losses; to neither gain nor lose: *The company was managing only to break even.* **22. get even,** [*no obj*] to get revenge; retaliate; strike back: *to get even for the insult.* **—e′ven•ly,** *adv.* **—e′ven•ness,** *n.* [*noncount*]

e•ven•hand•ed (ē′vən han′did) /'iyvən'hændɪd/ *adj.* impartial; equitable: *even-handed justice.* **—e′ven•hand′ed•ly,** *adv.*

eve•ning (ēv′ning) /'iyvnɪŋ/ *n.* the latter part of the day and early part of the night.

eve′ning gown′, *n.* [*count*] a woman's formal dress, usually having a floor-length skirt.

eve′ning star′, *n.* [*count*] a bright planet, esp. Venus, seen in the western sky at or soon after sunset.

e•vent (i vent′) /ɪ'vɛnt/ *n.* [*count*] **1.** something that happens: *Winning the scholarship was an important event in her life.* **2.** something that occurs in a certain place during a particular time: *They went to all the planned events at their daughter's college.* **3.** a single sports contest within a scheduled program: *the figure-skating event.* **—*Idiom.* 4. in any event,** regardless of what happens; in any case: *In any event, I'll call you tomorrow.* **5. in the event of,** if there should be: *In the event of fire, stay calm while leaving the building.* **6. in the event that,** if it should happen that; in case: *In the event that I can't get the loans, I'll have to find some way to raise the money.* See -VEN-.

e•vent•ful (i vent′fəl) /ɪ'vɛntfəl/ *adj.* **1.** full of events or incidents, esp. of a striking character: *an eventful week-*

end. **2.** having important issues or results that come later; momentous: *an eventful meeting.* —**e•vent′ful•ly,** *adv.* —**e•vent′ful•ness,** *n.* [*noncount*] See -VEN-.

e•ven•tu•al (i ven′cho͞o əl) /ɪ'vɛntʃuwəl/ *adj.* [*before a noun*] happening at some time in the future; resulting; ultimate: *His mistakes led to his eventual dismissal.* —**e•ven′tu•al•ly,** *adv.* See -VEN-.

e•ven•tu•al•i•ty (i ven′cho͞o al′i tē) /ɪˌvɛntʃuw'ælɪtiy/ *n.* [*count*], *pl.* **-ties.** a possible event or circumstance; possibility.

ev•er (ev′ər) /'ɛvər/ *adv.* **1.** (used to mean "at any time" in questions, in sentences with negative words, with words expressing a condition, like *if,* with words expressing uncertainty, like *doubt,* and after a comparative adjective with *than*): *Did you ever go skiing? I hardly ever drink soda. If you ever see him, tell him to call me. I doubt that I'll ever see her again. She looks better than ever now.* **2.** (used to mean "at all times; always" before an adjective or another adverb): *an ever-present danger.* **3.** (used with *since* and the present perfect tense) starting in the past and going on continuously up to now: *Ever since then we've been best friends.* **4.** in any possible case; by any chance; at all: *How did you ever manage to do that?* —**Usage.** See STILL.

ev•er•glade (ev′ər glād′) /'ɛvərˌgleyd/ *n.* [*count*] Often, **everglades.** [*plural*] an area of low, swampy land.

ev•er•green (ev′ər grēn′) /'ɛvərˌgriyn/ *adj.* **1.** (of trees, shrubs, etc.) having green leaves throughout the year. —*n.* [*count*] **2.** an evergreen plant.

ev•er•last•ing (ev′ər las′ting, -lä′sting) /ˌɛvər'læstɪŋ, -'lɑstɪŋ/ *adj.* lasting forever; eternal: *everlasting life.* —**Syn.** See ETERNAL.

ev•er•more (ev′ər môr′, -mōr′) /ˌɛvər'mɔr, -'mowr/ *adv.* always; forever; from now on.

eve•ry (ev′rē) /'ɛvriy/ *adj.* **1.** being one of a group or series taken collectively; each (of a group): [*before a singular count noun*]: *We go to the office every day.* [*before a number*]: *Take these pills every two hours.* **2.** [*before a singular count noun*] all possible; the greatest possible degree of: *We wished him every chance of success.* —***Idiom.*** **3. every now and then** or **every so often,** on occasion; from time to time: *I see him every now and then.* **4. every other,** every second; every alternate: *every other day.* **5. every which way,** in all directions; in a disorganized fashion: *His hair stuck out every which way.* —**Syn.** See EACH.

eve•ry•bod•y (ev′rē bod′ē, -bud′ē) /'ɛvriyˌbɒdiy, -ˌbʌdiy/ *pron.* [*used with a singular verb*] every person: *Everybody wants another drink.* —**Usage.** See EACH.

eve•ry•day (ev′rē dā′; -dā′) /'ɛvriyˌdey; -'dey/ *adj.* [*before a noun*] **1.** of or relating to every day; daily: *an everyday occurrence.* **2.** of or for ordinary days, as contrasted with Sundays, holidays, or special occasions: *He changed into his everyday clothes.*

eve•ry•one (ev′rē wun′, -wən) /'ɛvriyˌwʌn, -wən/ *pron.* [*used with a singular verb*] every person; everybody: *Everyone wants to get ahead.* —**Usage.** See EACH.

eve•ry•place (ev′rē plās′) /'ɛvriyˌpleys/ *adv.* everywhere.

eve•ry•thing (ev′rē thing′) /'ɛvriyˌθɪŋ/ *pron.* every single thing; every particular of a total; all: *Put away everything on the floor.*

eve•ry•where (ev′rē hwâr′, -wâr′) /'ɛvriyˌhwɛər, -ˌwɛər/ *adv.* in every place or part; in all places: *She takes her baby with her everywhere.*

e•vict (i vikt′) /ɪ'vɪkt/ *v.* [~ + *obj*] to expel or force out (a person, esp. a tenant) from land, a building, etc., by legal process. —**e•vic•tion** (i vik′shən) /ɪ'vɪkʃən/ *n.* [*count; noncount*] See -VICT-.

ev•i•dence (ev′i dəns) /'ɛvɪdəns/ *n.* [*noncount*] **1.** that which tends to prove or disprove something; proof: *The play's long run is evidence of its great popularity.* **2.** something that makes plain; an indication or sign: *His flushed look was evidence of his fever.* See -VIDE-.

ev•i•dent (ev′i dənt) /'ɛvɪdənt/ *adj.* plain or clear to the sight or understanding: *his evident dismay at not being hired.* [*it + be +* ~ *+ that clause*]: *It was evident that the play was a big hit.* —**ev′i•dent•ly,** *adv.* See -VIDE-.

e•vil (ē′vəl) /'iyvəl/ *adj.* **1.** morally wrong or bad; immoral; wicked: *He led an evil life.* **2.** harmful; injurious: *evil pranks.* —*n.* **3.** [*count*] something evil; evil quality, intention, or conduct: *the lesser of two evils.*

e•vil•do•er (ē′vəl do͞o′ər, ē′vəl do͞o′ər) /'iyvəlˌduwər, ˌiyvəl'duwər/ *n.* [*count*] a person who does evil. —**e′vil•do′ing,** *n.* [*noncount*]

e′vil eye′, *n.* [*count*] a look believed capable of inflicting injury or bad luck on someone.

e•vince (i vins′) /ɪ'vɪns/ *v.* [~ + *obj*], **e•vinced** (i vinst′) /ɪ'vɪnst/ **e•vinc•ing.** to show clearly: *evinced regret by apologizing.* See -VINC-.

e•voc•a•tive (i vok′ə tiv, i vō′kə-) /ɪ'vɒkətɪv, ɪ'vowkə-/ *adj.* tending to call to the mind: *Her perfume is evocative of spring.* —**e•voc′a•tive•ly,** *adv.* See -VOC-.

e•voke (i vōk′) /ɪ'vowk/ *v.* [~ + *obj*], **e•voked, e•vok•ing.** to call up (memories, feelings, etc.): *The book evoked memories of her childhood.* See -VOC-.

ev•o•lu•tion (ev′ə lo͞o′shən; *esp. Brit.* ē′və-) /ˌɛvə'luwʃən; *esp. Brit.* ˌiyvə-/ *n.* [*noncount*] **1.** any process of formation or growth; development: *the evolution of the drama.* **2.** *Biol.* **a.** change in a population of living things by such processes as mutation and natural selection. **b.** the theory that all existing organisms developed from earlier forms by natural selection. —**ev•o•lu′tion•ar′y,** *adj.*

e•volve (i volv′) /ɪ'vɒlv/ *v.,* **e•volved, e•volv•ing. 1.** to (cause to) come forth gradually into being; develop: [*no obj*]: *The whole idea evolved from a casual remark.* [~ + *obj*]: *to evolve a scheme.* **2.** [*no obj*] (of a species or population) to undergo or develop by a process of evolution: *The human species evolved from an ancestor that probably dwelled in trees.* See -VOLV-.

ewe (yo͞o) /yuw/ *n.* [*count*] a female sheep, esp. when it is fully mature.

ew•er (yo͞o′ər) /'yuwər/ *n.* [*count*] a water pitcher or jug.

ex-, *prefix.* **1.** *ex-* comes from Latin, where it has the meaning "out, out of, away, forth." It is found in such words as: EXCLUDE, EXHALE, EXIT, EXPORT, EXTRACT. **2.** *ex-* is also used to mean "former; formerly having been": *ex-member (= former member).*

ex., an abbreviation of: **1.** examination. **2.** examined. **3.** example. **4.** except. **5.** exception. **6.** exchange.

ex•ac•er•bate (ig zas′ər bāt′, ek sas′-) /ɪg'zæsərˌbeyt, ɛk'sæs-/ *v.* [~ + *obj*] **-bat•ed, -bat•ing.** to make (something) worse: *If you try to argue now you'll only exacerbate the situation.* —**ex•ac•er•ba•tion** (ig zas′ər bā′shən, ek sas′-) /ɪgˌzæsər'beyʃən, ɛkˌsæs-/ *n.* [*noncount*] See -ACR-.

ex•act (ig zakt′) /ɪg'zækt/ *adj.* **1.** [*before a noun*] strictly accurate or correct: *an exact description.* **2.** characterized by, capable of, or using strict accuracy; precise: *an exact thinker.* —*v.* [~ + *obj* + *from* + *obj*] **3.** to call for, demand, or require: *parents who exact respect from their children.* —**ex•act′ness,** *n.* [*noncount*] See -ACT-.

ex•act•ing (ig zak′ting) /ɪg'zæktɪŋ/ *adj.* **1.** demanding or expecting much: *an exacting teacher.* **2.** requiring great effort; demanding: *an exacting task.* —**ex•act′ing•ly,** *adv.* See -ACT-.

ex•act•ly (ig zakt′lē) /ɪg'zæktliy/ *adv.* **1.** with great accuracy and precision; precisely: *Follow my directions exactly and you will find the airport.* **2.** completely; totally: *You got this exactly right.* **3.** absolutely; definitely: *"You mean we are going to stay for the whole year?" "Exactly!"* See -ACT-.

ex•ag•ger•ate (ig zaj′ə rāt′) /ɪg'zædʒəˌreyt/ *v.,* **-at•ed, -at•ing.** to magnify (something) beyond the limits of truth; overstate: [~ + *obj*]: *to exaggerate the difficulties of a situation.* [*no obj*]: *I think you are exaggerating when you say he is as tall as a tree.* —**ex•ag•ger•a•tion** (ig zaj′ə rā′shən) /ɪgˌzædʒə'reyʃən/ *n.* [*count; noncount*] See -AG-.

ex•alt (ig zôlt′) /ɪg'zɔlt/ *v.* [~ + *obj*] **1.** to raise in rank, power, or character; elevate. **2.** to praise highly; extol. —**ex•al•ta•tion** (eg′zôl tā′shən, ek′sôl-) /ˌɛgzɔl'teyʃən, ˌɛksɔl-/ *n.* [*noncount*] See -ALTI-.

ex•am (ig zam′) /ɪg'zæm/ *n.* [*count*] *Informal.* an examination: *a tough exam in physics.*

ex•am•i•na•tion (ig zam′ə nā′shən) /ɪgˌzæmə'neyʃən/ *n.* **1.** the act or process of examining: [*noncount*]: *picked up the object for closer examination.* [*count*]: *a complete physical examination.* **2.** [*count*] a test for knowledge of a subject.

ex•am•ine (ig zam′in) /ɪg'zæmɪn/ *v.* [~ + *obj*], **-ined, -in•ing. 1.** to inspect or look at carefully, closely, or officially so as to judge or discover something: *to examine merchandise.* **2.** to observe, test, or investigate (a person's body or any part of it), esp. in order to discover the state or condition of health or the cause of illness: *The doctor examined my eyes.* **3.** to test the knowledge, reactions, or qualifications of (a pupil, candidate, witness, etc.), as by questions: *to examine each applicant.* —**ex•am′in•er,** *n.* [*count*] See -AG-. —**Related Words.** EXAMINE is a verb, EXAMINATION and EXAM are nouns: *The doctor examined my leg. The doctor's examination was thorough. The math exam was hard.*

ex•am•ple (ig zam′pəl) /ɪg'zæmpəl/ *n.* [*count*] **1.** one of a number of things, or a part of something, that represents the whole thing or whole group: *This painting is an example of his early work.* **2.** a pattern or model, as of something to be imitated or avoided: *to set a good example.* **3. for example,** (used to mean that what follows is an instance or several instances of what has been spoken or written about); for instance: *The train I take is always late. For example, this morning it was a half an hour late.* See -AM-. **—Usage.** The expression FOR EXAMPLE stays the same if there is one example that follows, or if there are two or more examples: *There are several uses for computers. One, for example, is as a word processor.* (or) *There are several uses for computers. For example, they are used as word processors, teaching tools, and reference sources.*

ex•as•per•ate (ig zas′pə rāt′) /ɪg'zæspəˌreyt/ *v.* [~ + *obj*], **-at•ed, -at•ing.** to irritate or provoke to a high degree; annoy extremely: *Constant interruptions exasperate me.* **—ex•as′per•at′ing,** *adj.*

Exc., an abbreviation of: Excellency.

exc., an abbreviation of: **1.** except. **2.** exception.

ex•ca•vate (eks′kə vāt′) /'ɛkskəˌveyt/ *v.* [~ + *obj*], **-vat•ed, -vat•ing. 1.** to make hollow; make a hole or cavity in: *The ground was excavated for a foundation.* **2.** to make (a hole, tunnel, etc.) by removing material. **3.** to expose or lay bare by or as if by digging; unearth: *The archaeologist excavated the ruins of ancient Troy.* **—ex•ca•va•tion** (eks′kə vā′shən) /ˌɛkskə'veyʃən/ *n.* [*count; noncount*] **—ex′ca•va′tor,** *n.* [*count*]

ex•ceed (ik sēd′) /ɪk'siyd/ *v.* [~ + *obj*] **1.** [*not: be* + ~*-ing*] to be greater than, as in quantity or degree: *The price of the house could exceed $200,000.* **2.** to go beyond in quantity, degree, rate, etc.: *exceeding the speed limit.* See -CEED-.

ex•ceed•ing•ly (ik sē′ding lē) /ɪk'siydɪŋliy/ *adv.* to an unusual degree; very: *The day was exceedingly cold.* See -CEED-.

ex•cel (ik sel′) /ɪk'sɛl/ *v.* [~ *(+ in/at)* + *obj*] **-celled, -cel•ling.** to surpass others or be superior in some respect; do extremely well: *She excels in math.*

ex•cel•lence (ek′sə ləns) /'ɛksələns/ *n.* [*noncount*] the fact or state of excelling; superiority; high quality: *Swiss watches are famous for their excellence.*

Ex•cel•len•cy (ek′sə lən sē) /'ɛksələnsiy/ *n.* [*count*], *pl.* **-cies.** [*His/Her/Your/Their* + ~] a title of honor given to certain high officials, as governors, ambassadors, and Roman Catholic bishops and archbishops.

ex•cel•lent (ek′sə lənt) /'ɛksələnt/ *adj.* having outstanding quality or superior merit; extremely good: *an excellent meal.* **—ex′cel•lent•ly,** *adv.*

ex•cept[1] (ik sept′) /ɪk'sɛpt/ *prep.* **1.** with the exclusion of; other than; but: *They were all there except me.* **—*conj.*** **2.** [~ *(+ that)*] only; with the exception: *These are parallel cases except (that) one is younger than the other.* **3.** [~ + *adverb/phrase/clause*] otherwise than; but: *Our defenses were well fortified except in that corner.* **—*Idiom.*** **4. except for,** if it were not for: *They would travel more except for lack of money.*

ex•cept[2] (ik sept′) /ɪk'sɛpt/ *v.* [~ + *obj*] to exclude; leave out: *The A students were excepted from taking the exam.* See -CEP-.

ex•cept•ing (ik sep′ting) /ɪk'sɛptɪŋ/ *prep.* except: *All were killed, excepting the captain.* See -CEP-.

ex•cep•tion (ik sep′shən) /ɪk'sɛpʃən/ *n.* **1.** [*noncount*] the act of excepting or the fact of being excepted: *Fill in every line in this form without exception.* **2.** [*count*] something excepted: *I'll make an exception in your case.* **—*Idiom.*** **3. take exception to,** [~ + *obj*] **a.** to make an objection to: *She took exception to one point in the contract.* **b.** to take offense: *I took exception to those rude comments.* See -CEP-.

ex•cep•tion•al (ik sep′shə nl) /ɪk'sɛpʃənl̩/ *adj.* **1.** forming an exception or rare instance; unusual; out of the ordinary: *Getting snow on Halloween is exceptional.* **2.** unusually excellent; superior: *The movie was pretty good, but not exceptional.* **3.** (of a schoolchild) **a.** intellectually gifted. **b.** physically or esp. mentally handicapped to an extent that special schooling is required. **—ex•cep′tion•al•ly,** *adv.* See -CEP-.

ex•cerpt (ek′sûrpt) /'ɛksɜrpt/ *n.* [*count*] a passage or quotation taken or selected from a book, document, film, or the like; extract: *The pastor read excerpts from the Bible.*

ex•cess (ik ses′, ek′ses) /ɪk'sɛs, 'ɛksɛs/ *n.* **1.** [*noncount; in* + ~ + *of*] the fact of exceeding something else in amount or degree: *The cost was in excess of our original estimate.* **2.** [*count*] the amount or degree by which one thing exceeds another: *an excess of several hundred dollars.* **3.** [*noncount*] an extreme amount or degree; too much: *eating to excess.* **4.** [*count*] immoderate indulgence, as in eating, drinking, etc. **—*adj.*** [*before a noun*] **5.** more than or above what is necessary, usual, or specified; extra; surplus: *excess baggage.* **—ex•ces′sive,** *adj.* **—ex•ces′sive•ly,** *adv.* See -CESS-.

ex•change (iks chānj′) /ɪks'tʃeyndʒ/ *v.*, **-changed, -chang•ing,** *n.* **1.** to give up (something) for something else: [~ + *obj*]: *I went back to the store and exchanged the defective radio.* [~ + *obj* + *for* + *obj*]: *I exchanged the radio for a new one.* **2.** [~ + *obj*] to give and receive reciprocally; interchange: *We exchange gifts on the holiday.* **3.** [~ + *obj*] to transfer for money; barter; buy and sell; trade: *exchanged our dollars for French francs.* **—*n.*** **4.** the act, process, or an instance of exchanging: [*count*]: *an exchange of prisoners.* [*noncount; in* + ~]: *The trapper got some coffee, flour, and gunpowder in exchange for his furs.* **5.** [*count*] something given or received as a replacement or substitution for something else: *The car was a fair exchange.* **6.** [*count*] a place for buying and selling goods, commodities, securities, etc.: *a stock exchange.* **7.** [*count*] a central office or central station: *a telephone exchange.* **8.** [*count*] the transfer of equivalent sums of money, as in the currencies of two different countries: *We made an exchange of our dollars for Russian rubles.* **—ex•change′a•ble,** *adj.* **—ex•chang′er,** *n.* [*count*]

exchange′ rate′, *n.* [*count*] the ratio at which a unit of the currency of one country can be exchanged for that of another country: *The exchange rate was ten pesos for one U.S. dollar.*

ex•cise[1] (ek′sīz) /'ɛksayz/ *n.* [*noncount*] an internal tax on certain products or goods placed on their manufacture, sale, or use within the country. See -CISE-.

ex•cise[2] (ik sīz′) /ɪk'sayz/ *v.* [~ + *obj*], **-cised, -cis•ing.** to remove by or as if by cutting out or off: *The surgeons excised the tumor.* See -CISE-.

ex•cit•a•ble (ik sī′tə bəl) /ɪk'saytəbəl/ *adj.* easily excited: *The children get excitable at Christmas.* **—ex•cit′a•bil′i•ty,** *n.* [*noncount*] **—ex•cit′a•bly,** *adv.*

ex•cite (ik sīt′) /ɪk'sayt/ *v.* [~ + *obj*], **-cit•ed, -cit•ing. 1.** to arouse or stir up the emotions or feelings of: *The coming of Christmas excites the children.* **2.** to arouse or stir up (emotions or feelings); call forth; awaken: *The new book excited interest in the old case.* **—ex•ci•ta•tion** (ek′sī tā′shən, -sə-) /ˌɛksay'teyʃən, -sə-/ *n.* [*noncount*] **—Related Words.** EXCITE is a verb, EXCITED and EXCITING are adjectives, EXCITEMENT is a noun: *The news excited him. The excited children ran toward the door. The exciting news made them happy. The excitement was too much to bear.*

ex•cit•ed (ik sī′tid) /ɪk'saytɪd/ *adj.* full of emotions or feelings that have been stirred up or aroused: *Don't get so excited over such nonsense. The excited couple could hardly wait to move into their new house.* **—ex•cit•ed′ly,** *adv.*: *They pointed excitedly at the sky.* **—Usage.** See EXCITING.

ex•cite•ment (ik sīt′mənt) /ɪk'saytmənt/ *n.* [*noncount*] an excited state or condition: *a feeling of great excitement.*

ex•cit•ing (ik sī′ting) /ɪk'saytɪŋ/ *adj.* producing or causing excitement; stirring; thrilling: *an exciting novel.* **—ex•cit′ing•ly,** *adv.* **—Usage.** Compare EXCITED and EXCITING, which are both adjectives. EXCITING is used when the noun referred to is the person or thing that causes the excitement: *The movie is exciting (= the movie is causing excitement).* EXCITED is used when the noun referred to is the person (or rarely, the thing) that experiences the excitement: *the excited children (= the children experienced the excitement of Christmas, a party, etc.)*

excl., an abbreviation of: **1.** exclamation. **2.** excluding. **3.** exclusive.

ex•claim (ik sklām′) /ɪk'skleym/ *v.* to cry out or speak suddenly and vehemently: [*no obj*]: *We all exclaimed at how big the baby had grown in just a few weeks.* [*used with quotations*]: *"You're a liar!" she exclaimed.* See -CLAIM-.

ex•cla•ma•tion (ek′sklə mā′shən) /ˌɛksklə'meyʃən/ *n.* [*count*] the act of exclaiming: *an exclamation of shock.* See -CLAIM-.

exclama′tion point′, *n.* [*count*] the sign (!) used in writing after an exclamation or interjection, expressing strong emotion or astonishment, or to indicate a command. Also called **exclama′tion mark′.** See -CLAIM-.

ex•clude (ik sklōōd′) /ɪk'skluwd/ *v.* [~ + *obj*], **-clud•ed,**

-clud•ing. 1. to shut or keep out; prevent the entrance of: *That dining club still excludes women.* **2.** to shut out from consideration, privilege, etc.; disregard; discount: *The doctor excluded food poisoning as the cause of illness.*

ex•clu•sion (ik skloo͞′zhən) /ɪk'skluwʒən/ *n.* [*noncount*] the act of excluding or keeping out; the state of being excluded or kept out: *The court ruled that the exclusion of minority students from the school was illegal.*

ex•clu•sive (ik skloo͞′siv, -ziv) /ɪk'skluwsɪv, -zɪv/ *adj.* **1.** not fitting with another; unable to be used or held at the same time as; incompatible: *mutually exclusive plans of action.* **2.** [~ + *of*] omitting from consideration or account; excluding: *It was a profit of ten percent, exclusive of taxes.* **3.** limited to that which is designated: *exclusive attention to business.* **4.** [*before a noun*] shutting out all others from a part or share: *The movie company had the exclusive right to film the novel.* **5.** expensive or fashionable: *an exclusive shop downtown.* **6.** not allowing outsiders to be admitted to membership, association, friendship, etc.: *an exclusive circle of friends.* **—*n.*** [*count*] **7.** a news story obtained by a newspaper along with the right to use it first. **—ex•clu′sive•ly,** *adv.* **—ex•clu′sive•ness, ex•clu•siv•i•ty** (eks′kloo͞ siv′i tē) /ˌɛkskluw'sɪvɪtiy/ *n.* [*noncount*]

ex•com•mu•ni•cate (eks′kə myoo͞′ni kāt′) /ˌɛkskə'myuwnɪˌkeyt/ *v.* [~ + *obj*], **-cat•ed, -cat•ing.** to cut off from the rites of a church. **—ex•com•mu•ni•ca•tion** (eks′kə myoo͞′ni kā′shən) /ˌɛkskəˌmyuwnɪ'keyʃən/ *n.* [*count; noncount*]

ex•cre•ment (ek′skrə mənt) /'ɛkskrəmənt/ *n.* [*noncount*] waste matter discharged from the body, esp. feces.

ex•crete (ik skrēt′) /ɪk'skriyt/ *v.* [~ + *obj*], **-cret•ed, -cret•ing.** to separate and eliminate from the body: *excreting waste matter.* **—ex•cre•tion** (ik skrē′shən) /ɪk'skriyʃən/ *n.* [*noncount*]

ex•cru•ci•at•ing (ik skroo͞′shē ā′ting) /ɪk'skruwʃiyˌeytɪŋ/ *adj.* causing intense suffering; tormenting: *excruciating pain.*

ex•cur•sion (ik skûr′zhən) /ɪk'skɜrʒən/ *n.* [*count*] **1.** a short trip or outing to some place: *an excursion to the Statue of Liberty.* **2.** a deviation, digression, or change of direction into a new area: *a brief excursion into politics.*

ex•cus•a•ble (ik skyoo͞′zə bəl) /ɪk'skyuwzəbəl/ *adj.* that may be forgiven or excused: *an excusable error in judgment.* **—ex•cus′a•bly** (ik skyoo͞′zə blē) /ɪk'skyuwzəbliy/ *adv.*

ex•cuse (*v.* ik skyoo͞z′; *n.* -skyoo͞s′) /*v.* ɪk'skyuwz; *n.* -'skyuws/ *v.*, **-cused, -cus•ing,** *n.* **—*v.*** [~ + *obj*] **1.** to pardon or forgive; overlook: *Please excuse my child's rude behavior.* **2.** to offer an apology for: *She excused her son's absence by saying that he was ill.* **3.** to release from an obligation, responsibility, or duty: *to be excused from jury duty.* **—*n.*** [*count*] **4.** an instance or act of excusing: *I don't want to hear any more of your excuses.* **5.** a ground or reason for excusing or being excused: *Ignorance of the law is no excuse.* **—*Idiom.* 6. excuse me,** (used as a polite way to interrupt or disturb someone): *Excuse me, but may I talk to you for a moment?* **—Syn.** EXCUSE, FORGIVE, PARDON imply being lenient or giving up the wish to punish. EXCUSE means to overlook some (usually) slight offense: *I can excuse her rudeness because I don't think she meant it.* FORGIVE is applied to more serious offenses; the person who is wronged not only overlooks the offense but keeps no ill feelings against the offender: *to forgive and forget.* PARDON often applies to an act of leniency or mercy by an official or superior: *The governor pardoned the young offender.*

ex•ec (ig zek′) /ɪg'zɛk/ *n.* [*count*] *Informal.* an executive.

exec., an abbreviation of: **1.** executive. **2.** executor.

ex•e•cra•ble (ek′si krə bəl) /'ɛksɪkrəbəl/ *adj.* **1.** very bad; inferior: *an execrable performance.* **2.** completely detestable; abhorrent; *an execrable crime.*

ex•e•cute (ek′si kyoo͞t′) /'ɛksɪˌkyuwt/ *v.* [~ + *obj*], **-cut•ed, -cut•ing. 1.** to carry out; accomplish: *to execute a plan.* **2.** to perform or do: *to execute a handstand.* **3.** to put to death according to law: *The murderer was executed in the electric chair.* **4.** to murder; assassinate: *The rebel army leaders executed the general.* **5.** to run (a computer program) or process (a command): *The program is executed by typing RUN at the prompt.* **—ex•e•cu•tion** (ek′si kyoo͞′shən) /ˌɛksɪ'kyuwʃən/ *n.* [*count; noncount*] See -SEQ-.

ex•e•cu•tion•er (ek′si kyoo͞′shə nər) /ˌɛksɪ'kyuwʃənər/ *n.* [*count*] an official who puts someone to death legally by capital punishment. See -SEQ-.

ex•ec•u•tive (ig zek′yə tiv) /ɪg'zɛkyətɪv/ *n.* **1.** [*count*] a person or group having administrative or supervisory authority in an organization or government. **2.** [*noncount*] the executive branch of a government. **—*adj.*** [*before a noun*] **3.** of, related to, or suited to an executive: *executive duties.* **4.** for use by executives: *an executive jet.* See -SEQ-.

ex•ec•u•tor (ig zek′yə tər) /ɪg'zɛkyətər/ *n.* [*count*] a person who is named to carry out the terms of a will. See -SEQ-.

ex•ec•u•trix (ig zek′yə triks) /ɪg'zɛkyətrɪks/ *n.* [*count*], *pl.* **ex•ec•u•tri•ces** (ig zek′yə trī′sēz) /ɪgˌzɛkyə'traysiyz/ **ex•ec•u•trix•es.** a woman who is named to carry out the terms of a will. See -SEQ-.

ex•em•pla•ry (ig zem′plə rē) /ɪg'zɛmpləriy/ *adj.* **1.** so good or great as to be worthy of imitation; commendable: *exemplary bravery.* **2.** serving as an illustration or example: *The costumes were exemplary of Renaissance clothing.*

ex•em•pli•fy (ig zem′plə fī′) /ɪg'zɛmpləˌfay/ *v.* [~ + *obj*], **-fied, -fy•ing. 1.** to show or illustrate by example. **2.** to furnish or serve as an example of; typify.

ex•empt (ig zempt′) /ɪg'zɛmpt/ *v.* [~ + *obj*] **1.** to free from an obligation, rule, or duty. **—*adj.*** [*be* + ~ *(+ from)*] **2.** released from, or not subject to, an obligation, rule, or duty, etc.: *Charitable organizations are usually exempt from taxes.* **—ex•emp•tion** (ig zemp′shən) /ɪg'zɛmpʃən/ *n.* [*count; noncount*]

ex•er•cise (ek′sər siz′) /'ɛksərˌsayz/ *n., v.,* **-cised, -cis•ing. —*n.* 1.** [*noncount*] activity or exertion, esp. for the sake of practice, training, or improvement: *aerobic exercise.* **2.** [*count*] something done or performed as a means of practice or training: *dancing exercises.* **3.** [*noncount*] a putting into action, use, or effect: *the exercise of caution when driving.* **4.** [*count*] a written composition, musical piece, or artistic work done for practice or learning. **—*v.* 5.** to (cause to) go through exercises: [~ + *obj*]: *They exercised their muscles.* [*no obj*]: *We exercised for a full hour.* **6.** [~ + *obj*] to put into action, practice, or use: *They exercised their right to vote.* **—ex′er•cis′er,** *n.* [*count*]

ex•ert (ig zûrt′) /ɪg'zɜrt/ *v.* [~ + *obj*] **1.** to put into use; exercise: *a president exerting his authority.* **2.** [~ + *oneself*] to put (oneself) into vigorous action or effort: *If you exert yourself you can finish the task on time.* **—ex•er•tion** (ig zûr′shən) /ɪg'zɜrʃən/ *n.* [*noncount; count*]

ex•hale (eks hāl′, ek sāl′) /ɛks'heyl, ɛk'seyl/ *v.,* **-haled, -hal•ing.** to breathe out; emit (air, vapor, sound, etc.): [*no obj*]: *He exhaled through his teeth.* [~ + *obj*]: *She exhaled smoke in his face.* **—ex•ha•la•tion** (eks′hə lā′shən) /ˌɛkshə'leyʃən/ *n.* [*noncount; count*] See -HALE-.

ex•haust (ig zôst′) /ɪg'zɔst/ *v.* [~ + *obj*] **1.** to drain of strength or energy: *I have exhausted myself working. The children exhausted their babysitter.* **2.** to use up or consume completely: *The soldiers had exhausted their supply of ammunition.* **3.** to draw out all that is essential in; treat or study thoroughly: *They had completely exhausted the subject.* **—*n.*** [*noncount*] **4.** the steam or gases that escape or are sent out of an engine: *the exhaust from the car ahead.* **5.** Also called **exhaust system.** the parts of an engine through which the exhaust is ejected: *Check the exhaust for a leak.* **—ex•haus•tion** (ig zôs′chən) /ɪg'zɔstʃən/ *n.* [*noncount*] **—ex•haust′i•ble,** *adj.*

ex•haust•ed (ig zôs′tid) /ɪg'zɔstɪd/ *adj.* drained of strength or energy; greatly fatigued: *The exhausted runner stopped for a minute's rest.*

ex•haus•tive (ig zôs′tiv) /ɪg'zɔstɪv/ *adj.* very thorough; comprehensive; complete: *an exhaustive study of Greek vases.* **—ex•haus′tive•ly,** *adv.*

ex•hib•it (ig zib′it) /ɪg'zɪbɪt/ *v.* [~ + *obj*] **1.** to offer or expose to view; present for public inspection: *to exhibit Van Gogh's paintings.* **—*n.*** [*count*] **2.** something exhibited: *an exhibit of the artist's works.* **3.** a document or object exhibited in court as evidence: *The district attorney showed me several of the exhibits.* **—ex•hib′i•tor, ex•hib′it•er,** *n.* [*count*]

ex•hi•bi•tion (ek′sə bish′ən) /ˌɛksə'bɪʃən/ *n.* **1.** an exhibiting, showing, or presenting to view: [*noncount*]: *The sculptor earned the right of exhibition.* [*count*]: *an exhibition of temper.* **2.** [*count*] a public display, as of artistic works, factory products, performance skills, or objects of general interest: *an exhibition of Scandinavian crafts at the museum.*

ex•hi•bi•tion•ism (ek′sə bish′ə niz′əm) /ˌɛksə'bɪʃəˌnɪzəm/ *n.* [*noncount*] behavior that calls attention to oneself. **—ex′hi•bi′tion•ist,** *n.* [*count*], *adj.*

ex•hil•a•rate (ig zil′ə rāt′) /ɪg'zɪləˌreyt/ *v.* [~ + *obj*],

-rat•ed, -rat•ing. to make cheerful or merry; enliven: *The jog in the park exhilarated me.* **—ex•hil′a•rat′ing,** *adj.*

ex•hort (ig zôrt′) /ɪg'zɔrt/ *v.* to urge, advise, or persuade earnestly or urgently: [~ + *obj* + *to* + *verb*]: *The sergeant exhorted his men to try their best.* **—ex•hor•ta•tion** (eg′zôr tā′shən) /ˌɛgzɔr'teyʃən/ *n.* [*count; noncount*]

ex•hume (ig zo͞om′, -zyo͞om′, eks hyo͞om′) /ɪg'zuwm, -'zyuwm, ɛks'hyuwm/ *v.* [~ + *obj*], **-humed, -hum•ing.** to remove from the earth; disinter: *The judge ordered the corpse to be exhumed and re-examined.* **—ex•hu•ma•tion** (eks′hyo͝o mā′shən) /ˌɛkshyʊ'meyʃən/ *n.* [*count; noncount*] See -HUM-.

ex•i•gen•cy (ek′si jən sē, ig zij′ən-) /'ɛksɪdʒənsiy, ɪg'zɪdʒən-/ *n.* [*count*], *pl.* **-cies. 1.** Usually, **exigencies.** [*plural*] a need, demand, or requirement: *the exigencies of city life.* **2.** a case or situation which demands prompt action or remedy.

ex•ile (eg′zil, ek′sil) /'ɛgzayl, 'ɛksayl/ *n., v.,* **-iled, -il•ing.** **—*n.* 1.** [*noncount*] being sent out of one's native land; banishment. **2.** [*count*] a person who is banished or separated from his or her native land. **—*v.*** [~ + *obj*] **3.** to send out (a person) from his or her country; banish: *Napoleon was exiled to a small island near Italy.*

ex•ist (ig zist′) /ɪg'zɪst/ *v.* [*no obj*] **1.** to have actual being; be: *"I'm real— I exist," he said.* **2.** [*not: be + ~-ing*] to have life or animation; live: *Human beings could not exist without water.* **3.** [*not: be + ~-ing*] to continue to be or live: *Belief in magic still exists.* **4.** [*not: be + ~-ing*] be found; occur: *A life that is free from all worry doesn't exist.*

ex•ist•ence (ig zis′təns) /ɪg'zɪstəns/ *n.* **1.** [*noncount*] the state or fact of existing; being: *To prove his own existence, Descartes once said, "I think; therefore I am."* **2.** [*noncount*] continuance in being or life; life: *It was a constant struggle for existence.* **3.** [*count; usually singular*] mode or way of existing: *They were working for a better existence.* **4.** [*noncount*] all that exists: *Existence shows a universal order.*

ex•ist•ent (eg zis′tənt) /ɛg'zɪstənt/ *adj.* having existence.

ex•is•ten•tial (eg′zi sten′shəl, ek′si-) /ˌɛgzɪ'stɛnʃəl, ˌɛksɪ-/ *adj.* **1.** of or relating to existence. **2.** of, relating to, or characteristic of existentialism: *existential philosophy.* **—ex′is•ten′tial•ly,** *adv.*

ex•is•ten•tial•ism (eg′zi sten′shə liz′əm, ek′si-) /ˌɛgzɪ'stɛnʃəˌlɪzəm, ˌɛksɪ-/ *n.* [*noncount*] a philosophy that stresses the individual's position as an agent who determines what to do and who is responsible for his or her own choices. **—ex′is•ten′tial•ist,** *adj., n.* [*count*]

ex•ist•ing (eg zis′ting) /ɛg'zɪstɪŋ/ *adj.* [*before a noun*] being in use or in operation at the time of writing or speaking: *under the existing economic conditions.*

ex•it (eg′zit, ek′sit) /'ɛgzɪt, 'ɛksɪt/ *n.* [*count*] **1.** a way or passage out, as a door, stairs, etc.: *There is only one exit in this building.* **2.** a going out or away; departure: *He made a graceful exit.* **—*v.* 3.** to go out (of); leave (from); depart (from): [*no obj; (~ + from + obj)*]: *They exited from the room.* [~ + *obj*]: *To exit the building, follow these directions.*

exo-, *prefix. exo-* comes from Greek, where it means "outside, outer, external": *exocentric* (= *outside the center*). Also, *before a vowel,* **ex-.**

ex•o•dus (ek′sə dəs) /'ɛksədəs/ *n.* [*count; usually singular*] a mass departure or emigration: *The Israelite exodus from Egypt; the summer exodus to the shore.*

ex•on•er•ate (ig zon′ə rāt′) /ɪg'zɒnəˌreyt/ *v.* [~ + *obj*], **-at•ed, -at•ing.** to clear or free from an accusation, guilt, or blame: *The court exonerated him from any responsibility for the accident.* **—ex•on•er•a•tion** (ig zon′ə rā′shən) /ɪgˌzɒnə'reyʃən/ *n.* [*noncount*]

ex•or•bi•tant (ig zôr′bi tənt) /ɪg'zɔrbɪtənt/ *adj.* going beyond what is customary, proper, or reasonable in amount or extent: *exorbitant luxury.* **—ex•or′bi•tant•ly,** *adv.*

ex•or•cise or **ex•or•cize** (ek′sôr sīz′, -sər-) /'ɛksɔrˌsayz, -sər-/ *v.* [~ + *obj*], **-cised, -cis•ing** or **-cized, -ciz•ing. 1.** to expel (an evil spirit) by religious or solemn ceremonies. **2.** to dispel or get rid of (unpleasant memories). **—ex•or•cism** (ek′sôr siz′əm, -sər-) /'ɛksɔrˌsɪzəm, -sər-/ *n.* [*noncount; count*] **—ex′or•cist,** *n.* [*count*]

ex•ot•ic (ig zot′ik) /ɪg'zɒtɪk/ *adj.* **1.** not native; coming from abroad or outside a country; foreign: *The city has many restaurants with exotic foods.* **2.** strikingly unusual or strange in appearance or nature: *exotic solutions.* **—ex•ot′i•cal•ly,** *adv.*

exp., an abbreviation of: **1.** expenses. **2.** expired. **3.** export. **4.** exported. **5.** exporter. **6.** express.

ex•pand (ik spand′) /ɪk'spænd/ *v.* **1.** to increase in extent, size, scope, or volume: [*no obj*]: *The balloon expanded until it burst.* [~ + *obj*]: *The heat expanded the metal.* **2.** to stretch out; spread (out): [*no obj*]: *The snake expanded to its full length.* [~ + *obj*]: *A bird expands its wings.* **3.** to express more fully or in greater detail; develop: [~ + *obj*]: *The writer expanded her story into a novel.* [~ + *upon/on* + *obj*]: *The writer expanded on her story and wrote a full-fledged novel.* **—ex•pand′a•bil′i•ty, ex•pand′i•bil′i•ty,** *n.* [*noncount*] **—ex•pand′a•ble, ex•pand′i•ble,** *adj.* See -PAND-.

ex•panse (ik spans′) /ɪk'spæns/ *n.* [*count*] an uninterrupted space or area: *an expanse of water.* See -PAND-.

ex•pan•sion (ik span′shən) /ɪk'spænʃən/ *n.* **1.** [*noncount*] the act or process of expanding; the state or quality of being expanded: *Future expansion of the business will require us to build more factories. The runway is undergoing expansion to allow bigger planes to land there.* **2.** [*count*] an expanded portion or form of a thing: *The book is an expansion of a series of articles.* See -PAND-.

ex•pan•sive (ik span′siv) /ɪk'spænsɪv/ *adj.* **1.** having a wide range; extensive. **2.** cordially welcoming; outgoing: *an expansive host.* **3.** tending to expand or capable of expanding; causing expansion: *the expansive force of heat.* **—ex•pan′sive•ness,** *n.* [*noncount*] See -PAND-.

ex•pa•tri•ate (eks pā′trē it) /ɛks'peytriyɪt/ *adj.* **1.** dwelling in a foreign land: *The expatriate community, mostly British and Americans, was invited to the ambassador's residence.* **—*n.*** [*count*] **2.** a person dwelling in a foreign country. See -PATR-.

ex•pect (ik spekt′) /ɪk'spɛkt/ *v.* [~ + *obj*] **1. a.** to anticipate the occurrence or the coming of: *We are expecting fifty guests.* **b.** [*not: be + ~-ing*] to believe or think: [~ + *(that) clause*]: *We expect that fifty guests will come.* [~ + *obj* + *to* + *verb*]: *We expect fifty guests to come to the party.* [~ + *to* + *verb*]: *I expect to get there on time.* **2.** [*not: be + ~-ing; usually: I + ~; ~ + clause*] *Informal.* to suppose; guess; presume: *I expect you know who I'm talking about.* **—*Idiom.* 3. be expecting,** to be pregnant: *She's expecting and is due to give birth in August.* See -SPEC-.

ex•pect•an•cy (ik spek′tən sē) /ɪk'spɛktənsiy/ *n.* [*noncount*] the quality or state of expecting or of being expected: *There was a feeling of expectancy in the air.* See -SPEC-.

ex•pect•ant (ik spek′tənt) /ɪk'spɛktənt/ *adj.* **1.** having or marked by expectations: *an expectant audience.* **2.** [*before a noun*] pregnant: *an expectant mother.* **—ex•pect′ant•ly,** *adv.* See -SPEC-.

ex•pec•ta•tion (ek′spek tā′shən) /ˌɛkspɛk'teyʃən/ *n.* **1.** [*noncount*] the act or the state of expecting; anticipation. **2.** [*count*] something expected. **3.** Often, **expectations.** [*plural*] a prospect of future benefit or fortune: *to have great expectations.* See -SPEC-.

ex•pe•di•en•cy (ik spē′dē ən sē) /ɪk'spiydiyənsiy/ *n., pl.* **-cies. 1.** [*noncount*] the quality of being expedient. **2.** [*count*] something expedient. Often, **ex•pe′di•ence.**

ex•pe•di•ent (ik spē′dē ənt) /ɪk'spiydiyənt/ *adj.* **1.** fit or suitable for the purpose; proper; useful; worthwhile: *Sometimes I find it expedient to lecture from notes.* **2.** leading to advantage; done for self-interest; advantageous: *In an expedient move, the legislators voted themselves a pay raise.* **—*n.*** [*count*] **3.** a handy means to an end. **—ex•pe′di•ent•ly,** *adv.* See -PED-[1].

ex•pe•dite (ek′spi dīt′) /'ɛkspɪˌdayt/ *v.* [~ + *obj*], **-dit•ed, -dit•ing.** to speed up the progress of; perform promptly: *They promised to expedite payment.* **—ex′pe•dit′er, ex′pe•di′tor,** *n.* [*count*]

ex•pe•di•tion (ek′spi dish′ən) /ˌɛkspɪ'dɪʃən/ *n.* **1.** [*count*] a journey made for a specific purpose, as to explore or investigate: *an expedition to the South Pole.* **2.** [*count*] the group of persons or vehicles engaged in such a journey: *The expedition had to turn back when it ran out of food.* **3.** [*noncount*] promptness or speed in accomplishing something: *performed with expedition and efficiency.* **—ex′pe•di′tion•ar•y,** *adj.* See -PED-[1].

ex•pe•di•tious (ek′spi dish′əs) /ˌɛkspɪ'dɪʃəs/ *adj.* prompt; quick: *expeditious repairs.* **—ex′pe•di′tious•ly,** *adv.* **—ex′pe•di′tious•ness,** *n.* [*noncount*]

ex•pel (ik spel′) /ɪk'spɛl/ *v.* [~ + *obj*], **-pelled, -pel•ling.** to drive or force out or away; eject: *The army expelled the rebels from the region.* See -PEL-.

ex•pend (ik spend′) /ɪk'spɛnd/ *v.* [~ + *obj*] **1.** to use up: *expended much time and energy.* **2.** to pay out; spend: *He expends half his income on housing.* See -PEND-.

ex•pend•a•ble (ik spen′də bəl) /ɪk'spɛndəbəl/ *adj.* **1.** capable of being spent or expended: *The city has a million dollars of expendable funds for street repair.* **2.** not worth keeping or maintaining: *Lives must be saved, but the equipment is expendable.* **—*n.*** [*count*] **3.** Usually, **expendables.** [*plural*] an expendable person or thing. **—ex•pend•a•bil•i•ty** (ik spen′də bil′i tē) /ɪk,spɛndə'bɪlɪtiy/ *n.* [*noncount*] See -PEND-.

ex•pend•i•ture (ik spen′di chər) /ɪk'spɛndɪtʃər/ *n.* **1.** [*noncount*] the act of expending. **2.** [*count*] something expended.

ex•pense (ik spens′) /ɪk'spɛns/ *n.* **1.** [*noncount*] cost; charge: *Nine dollars for a complete dinner is a small expense.* **2.** [*count*] a cause or occasion of spending: *A car is a necessary expense.* **3. expenses,** [*plural*] **a.** charges incurred esp. during a business assignment: *used a credit card to pay his expenses.* **b.** money paid as reimbursement for charges: *salary and expenses.* **—*Idiom.*** **4. at the expense of,** at the sacrifice of; to the harm or detriment of: *The landlord was interested in saving money at the expense of providing adequate heat.* **5. at (someone's) expense, a.** with someone paying: *I flew to San Diego at the company's expense.* **b.** causing someone to look or feel foolish: *He felt confident enough to tell a joke at his own expense.* See -PEND-.

ex•pen•sive (ik spen′siv) /ɪk'spɛnsɪv/ *adj.* requiring great expense; costing a lot of money: *an expensive party.* **—ex•pen′sive•ly,** *adv.*

ex•pe•ri•ence (ik spēr′ē əns) /ɪk'spɪəriyəns/ *n., v.,* **-enced, -enc•ing. —*n.*** **1.** [*count*] something observed, lived through, or undergone: *That car crash was a frightening experience.* **2.** [*noncount*] the observing, living through, or undergoing of things in the course of time: *to learn from experience.* **3.** [*noncount*] knowledge or practical wisdom gained from what one has observed, lived through, or undergone: *a person of experience.* **—*v.*** [~ + *obj*] **4.** to have experience of; live through; undergo: *to experience the pleasure of a cruise.*

ex•pe•ri•enced (ik spēr′ē ənst) /ɪk'spɪəriyənst/ *adj.* wise or skillful in a particular field through experience: *an experienced teacher.*

ex•per•i•ment (*n.* ik sper′ə mənt; *v.* -ment′) /*n.* ɪk'spɛrəmənt; *v.* -,mɛnt/ *n.* **1.** [*count*] a test, trial, or set of actions, esp. one for the purpose of discovering something unknown or of testing a principle, law, or theory: *a laboratory experiment.* **2.** [*noncount*] the conducting of such tests, trials, etc.: *to prove by experiment.* **—*v.*** **3.** to try or test esp. in order to discover or prove something: [~ + *with* + *obj*]: *The chemist was experimenting with the formula.* [~ + *on* + *obj*]: *The scientists experimented on two groups of subjects.* **—ex•per′i•men′tal,** *adj.* **—ex•per′i•men′tal•ly,** *adv.* **—ex•per•i•men•ta•tion** (ik sper′ə men tā′shən) /ɪk,spɛrəmɛn'teyʃən/ *n.* [*noncount*]

ex•pert (ek′spûrt; *adj. also* ik spûrt′) /'ɛkspɜrt; *adj. also* ɪk'spɜrt/ *n.* [*count*] **1.** a person who has special skill or knowledge in a particular field: *a computer expert.* **—*adj.*** **2.** possessing special skill or knowledge; trained by practice: *She is an expert horseback rider.* **3.** [*before a noun*] relating to or characteristic of an expert: *expert advice.* **—ex•pert′ly,** *adv.* **—ex•pert′ness,** *n.* [*noncount*]

ex•per•tise (ek′spər tēz′) /,ɛkspər'tiyz/ *n.* [*noncount*] expert skill or knowledge.

ex•pir•a•tion (ek spə rā′shən) /ɛkspə'reyʃən/ *n.* [*noncount*] **1.** a coming to an end; termination: *the expiration of a contract.* **2.** the act of breathing out air from the lungs.

ex•pire (ik spīᵊr′) /ɪk'spayᵊr/ *v.,* **-pired, -pir•ing. 1.** [*no obj*] to come to an end; terminate: *The contract expired at the end of the month.* **2.** [*no obj*] to emit the last breath; die: *In the novel the hero expired after a long illness.* **3.** to breathe out (air) from the lungs: [*no obj*]: *still expiring irregularly.* [~ + *obj*]: *to expire air.* See -SPIR-.

ex•plain (ik splān′) /ɪk'spleyn/ *v.* **1.** to make clear or understandable: [~ + *obj*]: *Please explain your plan.* [~ + *(that) clause*]: *I explained that the mistakes were my own.* **2.** to give the cause or reason of; account for: [~ + *obj*]: *How do you explain such rude behavior?* [*no obj*]: *I asked her to explain.* **3. explain away,** [~ + *away* + *obj*] to lessen the importance or significance of through explanation; justify: *She explained away her rude behavior as a joke.*

ex•pla•na•tion (ek′splə nā′shən) /,ɛksplə'neyʃən/ *n.* **1.** [*noncount*] the act or process of explaining. **2.** [*count*] something that explains: *one of many explanations.*

ex•plan•a•to•ry (ik splan′ə tôr′ē, -tōr′ē) /ɪk'splænə,tɔriy, -,towriy/ *adj.* serving to explain: *an explanatory footnote.*

ex•ple•tive (ek′spli tiv) /'ɛksplɪtɪv/ *n.* [*count*] a word or expression, frequently profane, said suddenly to express anger, impatience, surprise, etc.: *He muttered an expletive when he stubbed his toe.*

ex•pli•ca•ble (ek′spli kə bəl, ik splik′ə bəl) /'ɛksplɪkəbəl, ɪk'splɪkəbəl/ *adj.* capable of being explained. **—ex•pli•ca•bly** (ek′spli kə blē) /'ɛksplɪkəbliy/ *adv.* See -PLIC-.

ex•pli•cate (ek′spli kāt′) /'ɛksplɪ,keyt/ *v.* [~ + *obj*], **-cat•ed, -cat•ing.** to explain in detail: *Can you explicate the theory?* **—ex•pli•ca•tion** (ek′spli kā′shən) /,ɛksplɪ'keyʃən/ *n.* [*noncount; count*] See -PLIC-.

ex•plic•it (ik splis′it) /ɪk'splɪsɪt/ *adj.* **1.** fully and clearly expressed or demonstrated: *explicit instructions.* **2.** unreserved in expression; outspoken: *explicit language.* **—ex•plic′it•ly,** *adv.* **—ex•plic′it•ness,** *n.* [*noncount*] See -PLIC-.

ex•plode (ik splōd′) /ɪk'splowd/ *v.,* **-plod•ed, -plod•ing. 1.** to (cause to) expand with force and noise; to (cause to) burst violently: [*no obj*]: *Suddenly the bomb exploded.* [~ + *obj*]: *The terrorists exploded the bomb.* **2.** to erupt energetically; to move or act suddenly and quickly with force: [*no obj*]: *to explode in laughter.* **3.** [~ + *obj*] to show to be wrong; discredit; disprove: *The new findings about the solar system explode the present theories.* See -PLAUD-, -PLOD-.

ex•ploit[1] (ek′sploit) /'ɛksplɔyt/ *n.* [*count*] a striking or notable deed; feat.

ex•ploit[2] (ik sploit′) /ɪk'splɔyt/ *v.* [~ + *obj*] **1.** to use for profit; turn to practical account: *to exploit a business opportunity.* **2.** to use selfishly for one's own ends: *a company that exploits its workers with low pay and no benefits.* **—ex•ploi•ta•tion** (ek′sploi tā′shən) /,ɛksplɔy'teyʃən/ *n.* [*noncount*]

ex•plore (ik splôr′, -splōr′) /ɪk'splɔr, -'splowr/ *v.,* **-plored, -plor•ing. 1.** to travel over (a region, area, etc.) for the purpose of discovery: [~ + *obj*]: *to explore an island.* [*no obj*]: *spent the day exploring.* **2.** [~ + *obj*] to look into closely; investigate: *We have to explore that idea.* **—ex•plor•a•tion** (ek′splə rā′shən) /,ɛksplə'reyʃən/ *n.* [*noncount; count*] **—ex•plor′a•to′ry,** *adj.*

ex•plo•sion (ik splō′zhən) /ɪk'splowʒən/ *n.* [*count*] **1.** an act or instance of exploding. **2.** the noise of an explosion. See -PLAUD-.

ex•plo•sive (ik splō′siv) /ɪk'splowsɪv/ *adj.* **1.** tending or serving to explode: *an explosive gas; an explosive temper.* **2.** relating to or of the nature of an explosion: *explosive violence.* **3.** likely to lead to violence, anger, or hostility: *That subject is an explosive issue for many.* **—*n.*** [*count; noncount*] **4.** an explosive agent or substance. **—ex•plo′sive•ly,** *adv.* **—ex•plo′sive•ness,** *n.* [*noncount*]

ex•po (ek′spō) /'ɛkspow/ *n.* [*count*], *pl.* **-pos.** an exposition.

ex•po•nent (ik spō′nənt *or, esp. for 3,* ek′spō nənt) /ɪk'spownənt *or, esp. for 3,* 'ɛkspownənt/ *n.* [*count*] **1.** a person or thing that supports or explains a cause: *The congressman is a leading exponent of free trade.* **2.** a person or thing that is a representative, advocate, or symbol of something: *an exponent of the new Europe.* **3.** a mathematical symbol or number placed above and after another symbol or number to denote the power to which the latter is to be raised. **—ex•po•nen•tial** (ek′spə nen′shəl) /,ɛkspə'nɛnʃəl/ *adj.* **—ex′po•nen′tial•ly,** *adv.* See -PON-.

ex•port (*v.* ik spôrt′, -spōrt′, ek′spôrt, -spōrt; *n., adj.* ek′spôrt, -spōrt) /*v.* ɪk'spɔrt, -'spowrt, 'ɛkspɔrt, -spowrt; *n., adj.* 'ɛkspɔrt, -spowrt/ *v.* **1.** to ship (commodities) to other countries: [~ + *obj*]: *The U.S. exports wheat to many countries.* **2.** [~ + *obj*] to transmit abroad: *exporting political ideologies.* **—*n.*** **3.** [*noncount*] the act or business of exporting. **4.** [*count*] something exported: *Our exports are down.* **—*adj.*** [*before a noun*] **5.** of or relating to the exporting of goods: *We had to pay very high export duties.* **—ex•port′a•ble,** *adj.* **—ex•por•ta•tion** (ek′spôr tā′shən, -spōr-) /,ɛkspɔr'teyʃən, -spowr-/ *n.* [*noncount*] **—ex•port′er,** *n.* [*count*] See -PORT-.

ex•pose (ik spōz′) /ɪk'spowz/ *v.* [~ + *obj*], **-posed, -pos•ing. 1.** to lay open to danger, attack, or harm: *the risk of exposing people to disease.* **2.** to uncover; bare: *to expose one's head to the rain.* **3.** to present to view; exhibit. See -POS-.

ex•po•sé (ek′spō zā′) /,ɛkspow'zey/ *n.* [*count*] a public revelation, as of something dishonest: *a magazine exposé on political corruption.* See -POS-.

ex•po•si•tion (ek′spə zish′ən) /ˌɛkspəˈzɪʃən/ *n.* [*count*] **1.** a large public exhibition: *an automobile exposition.* **2.** a detailed explanation: *gave an exposition of his views.* See -POS-.

ex•pos•i•to•ry (ik spoz′i tôr′ē, -tōr′ē) /ɪkˈspɒzɪˌtɔriy, -ˌtowriy/ *adj.* serving to explain something: *expository writing.* See -POS-.

ex•pos•tu•late (ik spos′chə lāt′) /ɪkˈspɒstʃəˌleyt/ *v.* [*no obj*], **-lat•ed, -lat•ing.** to reason earnestly with someone by way of warning or rebuke: *expostulated with the rebellious student.*

ex•po•sure (ik spō′zhər) /ɪkˈspowʒər/ *n.* **1.** [*noncount*] the act of exposing or the state of being exposed: *exposure to the effects of radiation.* **2.** an act or instance of revealing or unmasking something previously hidden: [*noncount*]: *exposure of graft and corruption.* [*count*]: *an exposure of the crime bosses in the city.* **3. a.** [*noncount*] the act of subjecting a photosensitive surface to light. **b.** [*count*] a photographic image that is produced: *A few of the exposures were blurred.* See -POS-.

ex•pound (ik spound′) /ɪkˈspawnd/ *v.* to make a detailed statement (about): [~ + *obj*]: *to expound theories.* [~ + *on* + *obj*]: *expounded on a favorite theory.* See -PON-.

ex•press (ik spres′) /ɪkˈsprɛs/ *v.* [~ + *obj*] **1.** to put into words: *to express an idea.* **2.** to show; reveal: *She expressed her anger.* **3.** [~ + *oneself*] to communicate one's opinions or feelings: *He expressed himself eloquently.* **4.** to represent by a symbol, figure, or formula: *to express water as H_2O.* **—*adj.*** [*before a noun*] **5.** clearly indicated; explicit: *She defied her parents' express command.* **6.** special; definite: *It was her express purpose not to get emotional.* **7.** direct or fast, esp. making few or no intermediate stops: *an express train.* **8.** sent faster than ordinary mail: *express mail.* **—*n.*** **9.** [*count*] an express vehicle: *The express whipped through the station.* **—*adv.*** **10.** by express: *to travel express.* See -PRESS-.

ex•pres•sion (ik spresh′ən) /ɪkˈsprɛʃən/ *n.* **1.** [*noncount*] the act of expressing or setting forth in words: *the free expression of opinions.* **2.** [*count*] a particular word, phrase, or form of words: *"Round the bend" is an old-fashioned expression meaning "crazy."* **3.** [*noncount*] the manner or form in which a thing is expressed: *delicacy of expression.* **4.** [*count*] a look on the face or a sound of the voice showing personal feeling: *She had a happy expression on her face.* **5.** [*count*] a mathematical symbol or set of symbols representing a value, relation, or the like: *$E = mc^2$ is an expression about the relationship of mass and energy.* **—ex•pres′sion•less,** *adj.* See -PRESS-.

ex•pres•sion•ism (ik spresh′ə niz′əm) /ɪkˈsprɛʃəˌnɪzəm/ *n.* [*often: Expressionism*] a style of art in which forms depict the personal view of the artist. **—ex•pres′sion•ist,** *n.* [*count*], *adj.* **—ex•pres′sion•is′tic,** *adj.*

ex•pres•sive (ik spres′iv) /ɪkˈsprɛsɪv/ *adj.* **1.** full of expression; meaningful: *an expressive shrug.* **2.** serving to express: *a look expressive of gratitude.* **—ex•pres′sive•ly,** *adv.* **—ex•pres′sive•ness,** *n.* [*noncount*]

ex•press•ly (ik spres′lē) /ɪkˈsprɛsliy/ *adv.* **1.** for the specific purpose; specially: *I came expressly to see you.* **2.** in an express manner; explicitly: *She expressly demanded an apology.*

ex•press•way (ik spres′wā′) /ɪkˈsprɛsˌwey/ *n.* [*count*] a highway for high-speed traffic, having limited access and a divider between lanes for traffic moving in opposite directions.

ex•pro•pri•ate (eks prō′prē āt′) /ɛksˈprowpriyˌeyt/ *v.* [~ + *obj*], **-at•ed, -at•ing.** to take possession of, esp. for public use: *The government expropriated the land.* **—ex•pro•pri•a•tion** (eks prō′prē ā′shən) /ɛksˌprowpriyˈeyʃən/ *n.* [*noncount*] See -PROPR-.

ex•pul•sion (ik spul′shən) /ɪkˈspʌlʃən/ *n.* [*noncount; count*] the act of expelling; the state of being expelled. See -PULS-.

ex•punge (ik spunj′) /ɪkˈspʌndʒ/ *v.* [~ + *obj*], **-punged, -pung•ing.** to take out; remove; erase: *to expunge a few lines from the script.* See -PUNCT-.

ex•pur•gate (ek′spər gāt′) /ˈɛkspərˌgeyt/ *v.* [~ + *obj*], **-gat•ed, -gat•ing.** to change by removing words or passages thought to be improper or objectionable: *The censors expurgated the documentary.* **—ex•pur•ga•tion** (ek′spûr gā′shən) /ˌɛkspɜrˈgeyʃən/ *n.* [*noncount; count*] See -PUR-.

ex•quis•ite (ik skwiz′it, ek′skwi zit) /ɪkˈskwɪzɪt, ˈɛkskwɪzɪt/ *adj.* **1.** of special beauty and appealing excellence: *an exquisite statuette.* **2.** intense; acute: *exquisite pain.* **3.** keenly sensitive or responsive: *She had an exquisite ear for music.* **4.** of particular refinement or elegance: *exquisite manners.* **—ex•quis′ite•ly,** *adv.* **—ex•quis′ite•ness,** *n.* [*noncount*] See -QUIS-.

ext., an abbreviation of: **1.** extension. **2.** exterior. **3.** external. **4.** extinct. **5.** extra. **6.** extract.

ex•tant (ek′stənt, ik stant′) /ˈɛkstənt, ɪkˈstænt/ *adj.* still existing: *There are three extant copies of the document.* See -STAT-.

ex•tem•po•ra•ne•ous (ik stem′pə rā′nē əs) /ɪkˌstɛmpəˈreyniyəs/ *adj.* spoken or performed without preparation; impromptu: *an extemporaneous speech.* **—ex•tem′po•ra′ne•ous•ly,** *adv.* See -TEMP-.

ex•tem•po•rize (ik stem′pə rīz′) /ɪkˈstɛmpəˌrayz/ *v.* [*no obj*], **-rized, -riz•ing.** to speak, perform, or do extemporaneously. See -TEMP-.

ex•tend (ik stend′) /ɪkˈstɛnd/ *v.* **1.** [~ + *obj*] to stretch or draw out or outward: *I extended my leg.* **2.** [~ + *obj*] to stretch forth; hold out; offer: *to extend one's hand in greeting.* **3.** to make longer; lengthen [~ + *obj*]: *The new section extended the highway.* [*no obj*]: *The road extends for another two miles.* **4.** to increase the duration or length of time (of); prolong: [~ + *obj*]: *I wish they didn't have to extend their visit.* [*no obj*]: *Their visit extended another hour.* **5.** to enlarge the area, scope, or application of: [~ + *obj*]: *The military powers extended their authority.* [*no obj*]: *Their authority extended into foreign countries.* **6.** [~ + *obj*] to grant or offer: *to extend aid to needy scholars.* See -TEND-.

extend′ed fam′ily, *n.* [*count*] a group that is related by blood or marriage, made up of a married couple, their children, and various close relatives. See -TEND-.

ex•ten•sion (ik sten′shən) /ɪkˈstɛnʃən/ *n.* **1.** [*count*] an addition: *added an extension to the house.* **2.** [*count*] an increase in length of time, area, duration, or scope: *an extension for filing our taxes.* **3.** [*count*] an additional telephone that operates on a principal line: *Pick up the extension in your room.* **4.** [*count*] a program by which an institution, such as a university, provides instruction or other services away from the regular location: *studying at an extension.* **—*adj.*** [*before a noun*] **5.** connecting two ends that would be otherwise too far away: *an extension cord.* **6.** of or being a program by which a university provides instruction away from the regular location or outside regular hours: *an extension course.* See -TEND-.

ex•ten•sive (ik sten′siv) /ɪkˈstɛnsɪv/ *adj.* of great extent; wide; broad: *The bomb destroyed an extensive area.* **—ex•ten′sive•ly,** *adv.* See -TEND-.

ex•tent (ik stent′) /ɪkˈstɛnt/ *n.* the space or degree to which a thing extends: *the extent of their property.* See -TEND-.

ex•ten•u•at•ing (ik sten′yo͞o āt′ing) /ɪkˈstɛnyuwˌeytɪŋ/ *adj.* that make something seem less serious by providing excuses: *He attributed his poor grades at school to extenuating circumstances.*

ex•te•ri•or (ik stēr′ē ər) /ɪkˈstɪəriyər/ *adj.* **1.** being on the outer side or the outside: *exterior surfaces.* **2.** intended or suitable for outdoor use: *exterior paint.* **—*n.*** [*count*] **3.** the outer surface or part; outside: *the exterior of the house.*

ex•ter•mi•nate (ik stûr′mə nāt′) /ɪkˈstɜrməˌneyt/ *v.* [~ + *obj*], **-nat•ed, -nat•ing.** to get rid of by destroying: *to exterminate insect pests.* **—ex•ter•mi•na•tion** (ik stûr′mə nā′shən) /ɪkˌstɜrməˈneyʃən/ *n.* [*noncount*] **—ex•ter′mi•na′tor,** *n.* [*count*] See -TERM-.

ex•ter•nal (ik stûr′nl) /ɪkˈstɜrnl/ *adj.* **1.** of or relating to the outside or outer part; outer. **2.** to be applied to the outside of a body: *The medicine says "for external use only."* **3.** located or being outside something; acting or coming from without: *external influences.* **—ex•ter′nal•ly,** *adv.*

ex•tinct (ik stingkt′) /ɪkˈstɪŋkt/ *adj.* **1.** no longer in existence: *an extinct species.* **2.** no longer in use; obsolete: *an extinct custom.* **3.** no longer active: *an extinct volcano.* **—ex•tinc•tion** (ik stingk′shən) /ɪkˈstɪŋkʃən/ *n.* [*noncount*]

ex•tin•guish (ik sting′gwish) /ɪkˈstɪŋgwɪʃ/ *v.* [~ + *obj*] **1.** to cause to stop burning; put out: *The firefighters extinguished the fire.* **2.** to put an end to or bring to an end: *extinguished his hopes.* **—ex•tin′guish•a•ble,** *adj.*

ex•tin•guish•er (ik sting′gwi shər) /ɪkˈstɪŋgwɪʃər/ *n.* [*count*] FIRE EXTINGUISHER.

ex•tol or **ex•toll** (ik stōl′, -stol′) /ɪkˈstowl, -ˈstɒl/ *v.* [~ + *obj*], **-tolled, -tol•ling** or **-toll•ing.** to praise highly; laud.

ex•tort (ik stôrt′) /ɪkˈstɔrt/ *v.* [~ + *obj*] to obtain (money) from a person by force, threats, violence, etc.: *The policeman extorted money from small shopkeepers.*

—**ex•tort′er,** *n.* [*count*] —**ex•tor•tion** (ik stôr′shən) /ɪk'stɔrʃən/ *n.* [*noncount*] —**ex•tor′tion•ist,** *n.* [*count*] See -TORT-.

ex•tor•tion•ate (ik stôr′shə nit) /ɪk'stɔrʃənɪt/ *adj.* excessive; too high; exorbitant: *extortionate prices.*

ex•tra (ek′strə) /'ɛkstrə/ *adj., n., pl.* **-tras,** *adv.* —*adj.* **1.** [*before a noun*] beyond, more, or better than what is usual: *Make an extra copy.* **2.** [*be* + ~] provided at an additional charge: *Home delivery is extra.* —*n.* **3.** an additional feature for which there is usually a charge: *We ordered a few extras for the car.* **4.** a special edition of a newspaper: *The "Daily News" put out an extra to report the election results.* —*adv.* **5.** in excess of, or beyond, the usual amount, size, or degree: *extra large galoshes.*

extra-, *prefix. extra-* comes from Latin, where it has the meaning "outside of; beyond": *extra-* + *galactic* → *extragalactic (= outside the galaxy); extra-* + *sensory* → *extrasensory (= beyond the senses).*

ex•tract (*v.* ik strakt′; *n.* ek′strakt) /*v.* ɪk'strækt; *n.* 'ɛkstrækt/ *v.* [~ + *obj*] **1.** to pull or draw out, esp. with effort: *The dentist extracted my tooth.* **2.** to draw forth: *extracting information from the prisoners.* **3.** to take or copy out (excerpts), as from a book: *They extracted a few examples from the text.* **4.** to separate or obtain from something: *The chemists extracted this substance from vanilla plants.* —*n.* **5.** [*count*] something extracted. **6.** [*count*] a passage taken from a written work; excerpt: *an extract from his play.* **7.** [*noncount*] a solid or liquid substance containing the essence of a food, plant, or drug in concentrated form: *beef extract; vanilla extract.* See -TRAC-.

ex•trac•tion (ik strak′shən) /ɪk'strækʃən/ *n.* **1.** [*noncount; count*] an act or instance of extracting something. **2.** [*noncount*] descent; ancestry: *of Greek extraction.* **3.** [*count*] something extracted; extract.

ex•tra•cur•ric•u•lar (ek′strə kə rik′yə lər) /ˌɛkstrəkə'rɪkyələr/ *adj.* outside the regular program of courses at a school: *extracurricular activities.*

ex•tra•dite (ek′strə dīt′) /'ɛkstrəˌdayt/ *v.* [~ + *obj*], **-dit•ed, -dit•ing. 1.** to formally surrender (an alleged fugitive or criminal) to another state, nation, or authority. **2.** to obtain the extradition of: *The U.S. finally succeeded in extraditing the spy from Mexico.*

ex•tra•di•tion (ek′strə dish′ən) /ˌɛkstrə'dɪʃən/ *n.* [*noncount*] the formal surrender of an alleged fugitive or criminal from one state or country to another.

ex•tra•mar•i•tal (ek′strə mar′i tl) /ˌɛkstrə'mærɪtl̩/ *adj.* [*usually: before a noun*] relating to sexual relations with someone other than one's spouse: *an extramarital affair.*

ex•tra•mu•ral (ek′strə myŏŏr′əl) /ˌɛkstrə'myʊrəl/ *adj.* involving representatives of more than one school: *extramural basketball games.*

ex•tra•ne•ous (ik strā′nē əs) /ɪk'streyniyəs/ *adj.* **1.** introduced or coming from without or outside: *extraneous substances in our water.* **2.** not pertinent; irrelevant: *The witness made several extraneous remarks that were stricken from the record.*

ex•traor•di•nar•y (ik strôr′dn er′ē, ek′strə ôr′-) /ɪk'strɔrdn̩ˌɛriy, ˌɛkstrə'ɔr-/ *adj.* **1.** being beyond what is usual; exceptional; remarkable: *extraordinary speed.* **2.** [*after a noun*] having a special, often temporary task or responsibility: *a minister extraordinary.* —**ex•traor′di•nar′i•ly,** *adv.* See -ORD-.

ex•trap•o•late (ik strap′ə lāt′) /ɪk'stræpəˌleyt/ *v.,* **-lat•ed, -lat•ing.** to figure out or infer (something unknown) from something known; conjecture: [~ + *obj*]: *We should be able to extrapolate our future costs for that program.* [*no obj*]: *Can you extrapolate from these figures?* —**ex•trap•o•la•tion** (ik strap′ə lā′shən) /ɪkˌstræpə'leyʃən/ *n.* [*noncount; count*]

ex•tra•sen•so•ry (ek′strə sen′sə rē) /ˌɛkstrə'sɛnsəriy/ *adj.* beyond one's normal sense perception. See -SENS-.

ex•tra•ter•res•tri•al (ek′strə tə res′trē əl) /ˌɛkstrətə'rɛstriyəl/ *adj.* **1.** existing, involving, or coming from outside the limits of the earth: *extraterrestrial biology.* —*n.* [*count*] **2.** an imagined extraterrestrial being. See -TERR-.

ex•trav•a•gance (ik strav′ə gəns) /ɪk'strævəgəns/ *n.* **1.** [*noncount*] the quality of being extravagant. **2.** [*count*] an example of being extravagant.

ex•trav•a•gant (ik strav′ə gənt) /ɪk'strævəgənt/ *adj.* **1.** spending much more than is necessary or wise: *an extravagant shopper.* **2.** exceeding the bounds of reason or moderation; excessive: *extravagant demands.* —**ex•trav′a•gant•ly,** *adv.*

ex•trav•a•gan•za (ik strav′ə gan′zə) /ɪkˌstrævə'gænzə/ *n.* [*count*], *pl.* **-zas.** a lavish or elaborate show, production, event, or entertainment.

ex•treme (ik strēm′) /ɪk'striym/ *adj.,* **-trem•er, -trem•est,** *n.* —*adj.* **1.** going beyond the ordinary or average: *extreme cold.* **2.** [*before a noun*] exceedingly great in degree or intensity: *extreme joy.* **3.** [*before a noun*] farthest from the center or middle: *the extreme limit of the city.* **4.** immoderate; radical: *the extreme right wing of the party.* **5.** last; final: *extreme hopes.* —*n.* [*count*] **6.** one of two things that are as different from each other as possible: *torn between the extremes of joy and grief.* —**ex•treme′ly,** *adv.*

ex•trem•ism (ik strē′miz əm) /ɪk'striymɪzəm/ *n.* [*noncount*] a tendency to go to extremes, esp. in politics. —**ex•trem′ist,** *n.* [*count*]

ex•trem•i•ty (ik strem′i tē) /ɪk'strɛmɪtiy/ *n., pl.* **-ties. 1.** [*count*] the terminal point, limit, or part of something. **2.** Usually, **extremities.** [*plural*] the end part of a limb, as a hand or foot. **3.** [*noncount*] an utmost degree: *the extremity of joy.*

ex•tri•cate (ek′stri kāt′) /'ɛkstrɪˌkeyt/ *v.* [~ + *obj*], **-cat•ed, -cat•ing.** to free or release from something that tangles or traps; disengage: *The fox tried desperately to extricate himself from the trap.* —**ex′tri•ca′tion,** *n.* [*noncount*]

ex•tro•vert (ek′strə vûrt′) /'ɛkstrəˌvɜrt/ *n.* [*count*] **1.** an outgoing person; an active, talkative, cheerful person. —*adj.* **2.** Also, **ex′tro•vert′ed.** marked by such a tendency to be outgoing. See -VERT-.

ex•trude (ik strōōd′) /ɪk'struwd/ *v.* [~ + *obj*], **-trud•ed, -trud•ing.** to force or press out, as through a small opening that gives shape: *The spaghetti-making machine extrudes dough through tiny holes.* —**ex•tru•sion** (ik-strōō′zhən) /ɪk'struwʒən/ *n.* [*noncount*] See -TRUDE-.

ex•u•ber•ance (ig zōō′bər əns) /ɪg'zuwbərəns/ *n.* [*noncount*] exuberant behavior or feeling.

ex•u•ber•ant (ig zōō′bər ənt) /ɪg'zuwbərənt/ *adj.* overflowing with enthusiasm, excitement, or cheerfulness; vigorous: *an exuberant welcome.* —**ex•u′ber•ant•ly,** *adv.*

ex•ude (ig zōōd′, ik sōōd′) /ɪg'zuwd, ɪk'suwd/ *v.,* **-ud•ed, -ud•ing. 1.** to (cause to) come out gradually in drops; (cause to) ooze out: [*no obj*]: *A sweet-smelling chemical exuded from the container.* [~ + *obj*]: *The animal exudes musk from special glands.* **2.** [~ + *obj*] to project (a quality or emotion) in great amount; radiate: *to exude cheerfulness.*

ex•ult (ig zult′) /ɪg'zʌlt/ *v.* [*no obj*] to show or feel a lively or triumphant joy: *The players exulted over their victory.* —**ex•ult′ant,** *adj.* —**ex•ul•ta•tion** (eg′zəl tā′-shən, ek′səl-) /ˌɛgzəl'teyʃən, ˌɛksəl-/ *n.* [*noncount*]

eye (ī) /ay/ *n., v.,* **eyed, ey•ing** or **eye•ing.** —*n.* [*count*] **1.** the organ of sight; in animals with backbones, one of a pair of rounded bodies in the skull with muscles and nerves. **2.** [*usually: singular*] sight; vision: *The marksman had a sharp eye.* **3.** [*usually: singular*] the power of seeing and appreciating something through vision: *an artistic eye.* **4.** a look, glance, or gaze: *to cast one's eye upon a scene.* **5.** an attentive look; observation: *under the watchful eyes of the guards.* **6.** point of view; intention: *through the eyes of a ten-year-old.* **7.** judgment; opinion: *innocent in the eyes of the law.* **8.** something suggesting the eye in appearance, as the opening in the lens of a camera or a hole in a needle. —*v.* [~ + *obj*] **9.** to look at; view; watch: *eyed the strangers with suspicion.* —***Idiom.*** **10. be all eyes,** to be extremely attentive; to pay great attention: *She was all eyes as the magician began his act.* **11. catch someone's eye,** to attract someone's attention: *She caught my eye as I moved toward the door.* **12. have an eye for,** [~ + *obj*] have good judgment about or appreciation for: *He has an eye for bargains.* **13. have eyes for,** [*have* + *-s* + *for* + *obj*] to be attracted to: *She only has eyes for you.* **14. keep one's eyes open,** [*no obj*] to be especially alert or observant: *The guards were told to keep their eyes open for a possible escape.* **15. make eyes at,** [*make* + ~*-s* + *at* + *obj*] to glance at in a flirting way; ogle. **16. see eye to eye,** to agree: *We finally see eye to eye after our misunderstanding.*

eye•ball (ī′bôl′) /'ayˌbɔl/ *n.* [*count*] **1.** the rounded part of the eye that is enclosed by the bony socket and eyelids. —*v.* [~ + *obj*] **2.** *Informal.* to look at carefully: *The two opponents eyeballed each other.*

eye•brow, *n.* [*count*] **1.** the fringe of hair growing on the bony arch or ridge above the top part of the eye. —***Idiom.*** **2. raise eyebrows,** to cause shock or surprise: *Your revolutionary proposal is sure to raise a few eyebrows.*

eye′-catch′ing, *adj.* attracting attention: *an eye-catching gown of red silk.*

eye•drop•per (ī′drop′ər) /'ay,drɒpər/ *n.* [*count*] DROPPER (def. 2).

eye•ful (ī′fo͝ol) /'ayfʊl/ *n.* [*count*], *pl.* **-fuls.** a thorough or complete view: *We got an eyeful of city life during our visit.*

eye•glass (ī′glas′) /'ay,glæs/ *n.* [*count*] **1. eyeglasses,** [*plural*] GLASS (def. 4). **2.** a single lens worn to aid vision; monocle.

eye•lash (ī′lash′) /'ay,læʃ/ *n.* [*count*] any of the short hairs growing in a fringe on the edge of an eyelid.

eye•let (ī′lit) /'aylɪt/ *n.* [*count*] **1.** a small hole for a cord or lace to pass through. **2.** a metal ring for lining a small hole; grommet.

eye•lid (ī′lid′) /'ay,lɪd/ *n.* [*count*] the movable lid of skin that covers and uncovers the eyeball.

eye•lin•er (ī′lī′nər) /'ay,laynər/ *n.* [*count*] a cosmetic applied in a line along the edge of the eyelids.

eye•o•pen•er (ī′ō′pə nər) /'ay,owpənər/ *n.* [*count; usually singular*] an experience or discovery that provides sudden knowledge about something: *Her book about the problems of teenagers was a real eyeopener.* **—eye′o′-pen•ing,** *adj.*

eye•piece (ī′pēs′) /'ay,piys/ *n.* [*count*] the lens or combination of lenses in an optical instrument such as a microscope through which the eye views the image.

eye′ shad′ow, *n.* [*noncount*] a cosmetic coloring material applied to the eyelids.

eye•sight (ī′sīt′) /'ay,sayt/ *n.* SIGHT (def. 1).

eye•sore (ī′sôr′, ī′sōr′) /'ay,sɔr, 'ay,sowr/ *n.* [*count*] something unpleasant to look at.

eye•strain (ī′strān′) /'ay,streyn/ *n.* [*noncount*] discomfort in the eyes produced by excessive or improper use.

eye•tooth (ī′to͞oth′) /'ay,tuwθ/ *n.* [*count*], *pl.* **-teeth** (-tēth′) /-,tiyθ/. **1.** a canine tooth of the upper jaw. **—*Idiom.* 2. give one's eyeteeth for,** [~ + *obj*] to want (something) very much: *I'd give my eyeteeth for a good job like that.*

eye•wit•ness (ī′wit′nis) /'ay'wɪtnɪs/ *n.* [*count*] a person who sees some act, occurrence, or the like, and can give a firsthand account of it.

F, f (ef) /ɛf/ *n.* [*count*], *pl.* **F's** or **Fs, f's** or **fs.** the sixth letter of the English alphabet, a consonant.

F, an abbreviation of: **1.** female. **2.** franc.

F, *Symbol.* **1.** the sixth in order or in a series. **2.** a grade indicating academic work of the lowest quality: *He got an F in chemistry.* **3.** Fahrenheit: *Water turns to ice at 32°F (said as "32 degrees Fahrenheit").*

F., an abbreviation of: **1.** Fahrenheit. **2.** February. **3.** franc. **4.** Friday.

f., an abbreviation of: **1.** feet. **2.** female. **3.** feminine. **4.** folio. **5.** following. **6.** foot. **7.** franc.

fa•ble (fā′bəl) /ˈfeybəl/ *n.* [*count*] **1.** a short tale used to teach a moral lesson, often with animals as characters: *Fables are found in many cultures, with different animals as the main characters.* **2.** a story not based on fact, such as a myth or legend.

fa•bled (fā′bəld) /ˈfeybəld/ *adj.* [*before a noun*] **1.** appearing in fables: *the fabled unicorn.* **2.** having no real existence; fictitious.

fab•ric (fab′rik) /ˈfæbrɪk/ *n.* **1.** [*count*] a cloth made by weaving or knitting threads or fibers. **2.** [*noncount*] framework; structure; makeup: *the fabric of family life.*

fab•ri•cate (fab′ri kāt′) /ˈfæbrɪˌkeyt/ *v.* [~ + *obj*], **-cat•ed, -cat•ing. 1.** to construct, esp. by assembling parts or sections; make. **2.** to invent; make up.

fab•ri•ca•tion (fab′rə kā′shən) /ˌfæbrəˈkeyʃən/ *n.* **1.** [*noncount*] the making up or inventing of false stories. **2.** [*count*] a false story that is made up or invented: *The story was a complete fabrication.* **3.** [*noncount*] the process of making, building, or of putting something together: *Our company is engaged in the fabrication of airplane parts.*

fab•u•lous (fab′yə ləs) /ˈfæbyələs/ *adj.* **1.** almost impossible to believe; incredible; astonishing: *fabulous adventures in Africa.* **2.** [*before a noun*] told about or known through fables: *the fabulous unicorn.* —**fab′u•lous•ly,** *adv.*

-fac-, *root.* *-fac-* comes from Latin, where it has the meaning "do; make." This meaning is found in such words as: BENEFACTOR, DE FACTO, FACSIMILE, FACT, FACTION, FACULTY, MANUFACTURE. See -FEC-, -FIC-.

fa•cade or **fa•çade** (fə säd′, fa-) /fəˈsɑd, fæ-/ *n.* [*count*] **1.** the front of a building. **2.** a superficial or false appearance: *a facade of self-confidence.* See -FACE-.

face (fās) /feys/ *n., v.,* **faced, fac•ing.** —*n.* **1.** [*count*] the front part of the head. **2.** [*count*] a look or expression on the face: *a sad face.* **3.** [*count; usually singular*] outward appearance: *The pioneers changed the face of the wilderness.* **4.** [*count; usually singular*] the surface of something: *The ship seems to have disappeared from the face of the earth.* —*v.* **5.** [~ + *obj*] to look toward: *She turned and faced the sea.* **6.** to have the front toward: [~ + *obj*]: *The barn faces the field.* [*no obj*]: *The barn faced south.* **7.** [~ + *obj*] to confront or meet directly or boldly: *You have to face facts.* **8. face up to,** [~ + *up* + *to* + *obj*] **a.** to admit: *You must face up to your mistake.* **b.** to meet courageously: *He had to face up to the possibility of losing his job.* —***Idiom.*** **9. face to face, a.** opposite one another; facing: *The dancers stood face to face with their partners.* **b.** confronting one another: *The two candidates finally met face to face.* **10. in the face of,** in spite of; notwithstanding: *He was steadfast in the face of many obstacles.* **11. lose face,** to be humiliated or embarrassed: *It was impossible to apologize publicly without losing face.* **12. make a face,** to put an exaggerated expression, as of dismay or disgust, on one's face: [*no obj*]: *After the teacher scolded her, the child made a face and sat down.* [*make* + *a* + ~ + *at* + *obj*]: *The child made a face at the dentist.* **13. to someone's face,** in one's very presence: *Tell her how you feel to her face.* See -FACE-.

-face-, *root.* *-face-* comes from Latin, where it has the meaning "form; face; make". It is related to -FAC-. This meaning is found in such words as: DEFACE, FACADE, FACE, FACET, FACIAL, SURFACE.

face•less (fās′lis) /ˈfeyslɪs/ *adj.* lacking distinction, personality, or identity: *A faceless mob attacked the parliament building.* —**face′less•ness,** *n.* [*noncount*]

face′-lift′ or **face′lift′,** *n.* [*count*] plastic surgery on the face to eliminate sagging and wrinkles.

fac•et (fas′it) /ˈfæsɪt/ *n.* [*count*] **1.** one of the small polished flat surfaces of a gem. **2.** aspect; side; part: *She was involved in all facets of the business.* See -FACE-.

fa•ce•tious (fə sē′shəs) /fəˈsiyʃəs/ *adj.* lacking seriousness; joking: *a facetious comment.* —**fa•ce′tious•ly,** *adv.* —**fa•ce′tious•ness,** *n.* [*noncount*]

fa•cial (fā′shəl) /ˈfeyʃəl/ *adj.* **1.** of the face: *a facial expression.* **2.** used to improve the condition or appearance of the face: *a facial cream.* —*n.* [*count*] **3.** a treatment to beautify the face: *She had a facial at the beauty parlor.* —**fa′cial•ly,** *adv.* See -FACE-.

fac•ile (fas′il) /ˈfæsɪl/ *adj.* **1.** quick in comprehension or action: *a facile mind in learning languages.* **2.** superficial; shallow: *facile answers to hard questions.* **3.** fluent; effortless: *a facile writing style.* —**fac′ile•ly,** *adv.*

fa•cil•i•tate (fə sil′i tāt′) /fəˈsɪlɪˌteyt/ *v.* [~ + *obj*], **-tat•ed, -tat•ing.** to make easier or less difficult; help forward. —**fa•cil•i•ta•tion** (fə sil i tā′shən) /fəsɪlɪˈteyʃən/ *n.* [*noncount*] —**fa•cil′i•ta′tor,** *n.* [*count*]

fa•cil•i•ty (fə sil′i tē) /fəˈsɪlɪtiy/ *n., pl.* **-ties. 1. a.** Often, **facilities.** [*count*] something designed, built, or installed to provide a specific convenience or service: *A new research facility.* **b.** Usually, **facilities.** [*count*] something that permits the easier performance of an action, course of conduct, etc.: *We chose that hotel because of its facilities for conferences.* **2.** [*noncount*] readiness or ease due to skill, aptitude, or practice; dexterity: *Mozart composed music with great facility.* **3.** Usually, **facilities.** [*plural*] a rest room: *There are no facilities on this highway.* **4.** [*noncount*] lack of difficulty; ease: *Modern stoves can be used with greater facility than the old, wood-burning types.*

fac•sim•i•le (fak sim′ə lē) /fækˈsɪməliy/ *n.* [*count*] **1.** an exact copy, such as of a book, painting, or manuscript: *a facsimile of the Declaration of Independence.* **2.** FAX. See -FAC-, -SIMIL-.

fact (fakt) /fækt/ *n.* **1.** [*noncount*] something that is real and actually exists; reality; truth: *Your fears have no basis in fact.* **2.** [*count*] something known to exist or to have happened: *It is a fact that an eclipse took place in that year.* **3.** [*count*] something known to be true: *scientific facts about plant growth.* —***Idiom.*** **4. after the fact,** done, made, or formulated after something has occurred: *We realized after the fact that she had been fooling us all along.* **5. in fact,** in truth; really; indeed; in reality: *They are, in fact, great patriots.* Also, **as a matter of fact.** See -FAC-.

fac•tion (fak′shən) /ˈfækʃən/ *n.* **1.** [*count*] a group within a larger group: *several factions of the Liberal Party.* **2.** [*noncount*] party strife and intrigue; discord; dissension. —**fac′tion•al,** *adj.* —**fac′tion•al•ism,** *n.* [*noncount*] See -FAC-.

fact′ of life′, *n.* [*count*] **1.** any aspect of human existence that must be acknowledged as unchangeable. —***Idiom.*** **2. facts of life,** information concerning sex, reproduction, and birth.

fac•tor (fak′tər) /ˈfæktər/ *n.* [*count*] **1.** one of the elements contributing to a particular result: *Various factors could be the cause of the disease.* **2.** one of two or more numbers, that when multiplied together produce a given product; a divisor: *6 and 3 are factors of 18.* **3.** an amount or degree on a scale of something: *We increased output by a factor of five (= We increased output by five times).* —*v.* [~ + *in/into* + *obj*] **4. factor in** or **into,** to include (something) as a contributing element; take into account: *We have to factor in the effects of advertising. You must factor the insurance payments into the cost of maintaining a car.* See -FAC-.

fac•to•ry (fak′tə rē) /ˈfæktəriy/ *n.* [*count*], *pl.* **-ries.** a building or group of buildings with facilities for the manufacture of goods. See -FAC-.

fac•tu•al (fak′cho͞o əl) /ˈfæktʃuwəl/ *adj.* **1.** of or relating to facts; concerning facts: *factual accuracy.* **2.** based on or restricted to facts: *a factual report.* —**fac′tu•al•ly,** *adv.* See -FAC-.

fac•ul•ty (fak′əl tē) /ˈfækəltiy/ *n.* [*count*], *pl.* **-ties. 1.** an ability for a particular kind of action: *He has a faculty for putting people at their ease.* **2.** one of the powers of the mind, such as memory, reason, or speech: *He is 90 years old but still has most of his faculties.* **3.** one of the departments of learning, such as theology, medicine, or law, in a university: *the medical faculty.* **4.** the people who teach at a university or college: [*plural*]: *The faculty sat as a group.* [*singular*]: *The faculty is paid well.* See -FAC-.

fad (fad) /fæd/ *n.* [*count*] a short-lived fashion, manner of conduct, etc., esp. one followed enthusiastically by a group. —**fad′dish,** *adj.* —**fad′dist,** *n.* [*count*]

fade (fād) /feyd/ *v.,* **fad•ed, fad•ing,** *n.* —*v.* **1.** to (cause to) lose brightness or vividness of color: [*no obj*]: *The green dress faded in the sun.* [~ + *obj*]: *The sun faded her green dress.* **2.** [*no obj*] to become dim or lose brightness: *The sunlight gradually faded.* **3.** [*no obj*] to lose freshness, vigor, strength, or health: *The tulips have faded.* **4. fade in** (or **out**), (of a film or television image) to (cause to) appear (or disappear) gradually: [*no obj*]: *The scene faded out and the screen was blank for a moment.* [~ + *out* + *obj*]: *The filmmaker faded out the last scene.* —*n.* [*count*] **5.** an act or instance of fading: *the fade of a car's brakes.*

fae•ces (fē′sēz) /ˈfiysiyz/ *n.* [*plural*] *Chiefly Brit.* FECES. —**fae•cal** (fē′kəl) /ˈfiykəl/ *adj.*

fag (fag) /fæg/ *n.* [*count*] **1.** *Slang.* a cigarette. **2.** *Slang* (*disparaging and offensive*). a male homosexual.

fag•got (fag′ət) /ˈfægət/ *n.* [*count*] *Slang* (*disparaging and offensive*). a male homosexual.

Fahr•en•heit (far′ən hīt′) /ˈfærənˌhayt/ *adj.* relating to or measured according to a temperature scale (**Fahr′enheit scale′**) in which 32° represents the point at which ice forms, and 212° represents the point at which steam forms. [*after a noun or number*]: *The temperature is seventy degrees Fahrenheit. Symbol:* F Compare CELSIUS.

fail (fāl) /feyl/ *v.* **1.** [*no obj*] to fall short of success or achievement; to be unsuccessful (in doing): *The experiment failed.* **2.** [~ + *obj*] (of some expected or usual resource) to turn out to be of no use or help to: *His friends failed him.* **3.** to receive less than the passing grade or mark in (an examination, class, or course of study): [*no obj*]: *After your last test I'm afraid you are failing.* [~ + *obj*]: *You are failing the course.* **4.** [~ + *obj*] to give less than a passing grade in a course of study to (someone): *The teacher failed him because he missed too many classes.* **5.** [*no obj*] to lose vigor; become weak: *The runner's strength failed.* **6.** [*no obj*] to become unable to meet or pay debts or business obligations: *The banks failed because of bad investments.* —***Idiom.* 7. without fail,** with certainty; positively: *Be in my office at nine o'clock without fail.*

fail•ing (fā′ling) /ˈfeylɪŋ/ *n.* [*count*] **1.** an act or instance of failing; failure. **2.** a defect or fault; shortcoming; weakness. —*prep.* **3.** in the absence or default of: *Failing payment, we shall sue.*

fail•ure (fāl′yər) /ˈfeylyər/ *n.* **1.** [*noncount*] a failing or proving unsuccessful; lack of success: *a life of failure.* **2.** [*count*] a person or thing that proves unsuccessful: *The meeting was a failure.* **3.** nonperformance of something due, required, or expected: [*count*]: *a failure to appear.* [*noncount*]: *failure to pay.* **4.** [*count*] a quantity or quality that is below normal; an insufficiency: *the failure of crops.* **5.** [*noncount*] deterioration or decay, esp. of vigor or strength: *kidney failure.* **6.** [*count*] a becoming insolvent or bankrupt: *the failure of a bank.*

faint (fānt) /feynt/ *adj.,* **-er, -est,** *v., n.* —*adj.* **1.** lacking brightness, vividness, clearness, loudness, strength, etc.: *a faint voice.* **2.** feeble or slight; lacking conviction or enough effort; weak: *faint encouragement.* —*v.* [*no obj*] **3.** to lose consciousness temporarily: *The boy wobbled unsteadily and fainted.* —*n.* [*count*] **4.** a temporary loss of consciousness resulting from a decreased flow of blood to the brain; swoon: *She fell to the floor in a faint.* —**faint′ly,** *adv.* —**faint′ness,** *n.* [*noncount*]

faint•heart•ed (fānt′här′tid) /ˈfeyntˈhɑrtɪd/ *adj.* lacking courage; cowardly.

fair[1] (fâr) /fɛər/ *adj.* and *adv.,* **-er, -est.** —*adj.* **1.** free from bias, dishonesty, or injustice: *a fair trial.* **2.** correctly or properly done, given, etc., according to the rules: *a fair fight.* **3.** [*before a noun*] somewhat large; ample: *a fair income.* **4.** neither excellent nor poor; moderately or tolerably good: *fair health.* **5.** (of the sky or the weather) bright; sunny: *fair skies overnight.* **6.** of a light hue or color; not dark: *fair skin.* **7.** pleasing in appearance; attractive: *a fair young face.* **8.** [*before a noun*] having or showing favorable or good conditions; likely; promising: *a fair chance of success.* —*adv.* **9.** in a fair manner: *He doesn't play fair.* —***Idiom.* 10. fair and square, a.** honestly; justly; straightforwardly: *She won the race fair and square.* **b.** honest; just; straightforward: *She was fair and square in all her dealings.* —**fair′ness,** *n.* [*noncount*]

fair[2] (fâr) /fɛər/ *n.* [*count*] **1.** an exhibition of farm products, livestock, etc., held annually by a county or state. **2.** a gathering of buyers and sellers in an appointed place: *a home-furnishings fair.* **3.** an exhibition and sale of articles to raise money, often for charity.

fair•ground (fâr′ground′) /ˈfɛərˌgrawnd/ *n.* [*count*] Often, **fairgrounds.** [*plural*] a place where fairs, horse races, etc., are held, esp. an area set aside by a county, city, or state for an annual fair.

fair′-haired′, *adj.* **1.** having light-colored hair. **2.** singled out for special favors: *We all waited for the boss's fair-haired lad to get yet another promotion.*

fair•ly (fâr′lē) /ˈfɛərliy/ *adv.* **1.** in a fair manner; justly; impartially: *We want you to judge fairly.* **2.** moderately; tolerably; to a large extent: *a fairly heavy rain.*

fair′ shake′, *n.* [*count*] a just and equal opportunity; fair treatment.

fair•way (fâr′wā′) /ˈfɛərˌwey/ *n.* [*count*] the part of a golf course where the grass is cut short between the tees and the putting greens.

fair•y (fâr′ē) /ˈfɛəriy/ *n.* [*count*], *pl.* **-ies. 1.** an imaginary being, generally thought of as having a tiny human form and possessing magical powers. **2.** *Slang* (*disparaging and offensive*). a male homosexual.

fair′y tale′, *n.* [*count*] **1.** a story, usually for children, about magical beings and creatures. **2.** an incredible or misleading story; lie. Also called **fair′y sto′ry.**

faith (fāth) /feyθ/ *n.* **1.** [*noncount*] confidence or trust in a person or thing: *I have faith that she'll do the right thing.* **2.** [*noncount*] belief in God or in the doctrines or teachings of religion: *It was a question of faith.* **3.** [*count*] a system of religious belief: *the Jewish faith.* **4.** [*noncount*] loyalty to a person, promise, engagement, etc.: *I signed the agreement in good faith.* —***Idiom.* 5. in faith,** in truth; indeed.

faith•ful (fāth′fəl) /ˈfeyθfəl/ *adj.* **1.** loyal in affection; constant: *faithful friends.* **2.** reliable, trusted, or believed: *faithful assurances of help.* **3.** loyal to one's partner by not having a sexual relationship with another. **4.** conscientious; regular: *a faithful worker.* —*n.* **5. the faithful,** [*plural; used with a plural verb*] **a.** the believers in a faith. **b.** the body of loyal members of any party or group: *a banquet for the party faithful.* —**faith′ful•ly,** *adv.* —**faith′ful•ness,** *n.* [*noncount*] —**faith′less,** *adj.*

fake (fāk) /feyk/ *v.,* **faked, fak•ing,** *n., adj.* —*v.* [~ + *obj*] **1.** to create or produce (something) in order to mislead, deceive, or cheat others: *The embezzler faked the report.* **2.** to pretend; simulate; feign: *faking illness.* **3.** to imitate convincingly or acceptably; counterfeit: *to fake some expensive paintings.* **4. fake it,** [*no obj*] to accomplish by trial and error or by improvising: *He doesn't know how to use that computer, he's just faking it.* —*n.* [*count*] **5.** anything that misleads, deceives, cheats, or fools others by seeming to be what it is not; counterfeit; sham: *The diamond was a fake.* **6.** a person who fakes; fraud: *That salesman is a fake.* —*adj.* **7.** designed to deceive or cheat; counterfeit: *a fake diamond.* —**fak′er,** *n.* [*count*]

fal•con (fôl′kən, fal′-) /ˈfɔlkən, ˈfæl-/ *n.* [*count*] a bird of prey having long pointed wings.

fall (fôl) /fɔl/ *v.,* **fell** (fel) /fɛl/ **fall•en, fall•ing,** *n.* —*v.* [*no obj*] **1.** to drop or come down under the force of gravity: *The apple fell from the tree.* **2.** to come or drop down suddenly to a lower position, esp. to leave a standing or erect position suddenly: *I fell to my knees.* **3.** to become less or lower; decline: *The temperature fell rapidly.* **4.** to grow less powerful or forceful; subside or abate: *The wind fell.* **5.** to extend downward; hang down: *Her hair fell to her waist.* **6.** to become lowered or directed downward: *Her eyes fell as she began to explain why she had stolen the money.* **7.** to give in to temptation or sin, esp. to become unchaste: *He had fallen into sin.* **8.** to give in and lose to an attack: *The city fell to the enemy.* **9.** to be overthrown, such as a government: *The dictatorship had finally fallen.* **10.** to drop down wounded or dead, esp. to be killed: *fallen in battle.* **11.** to pass into some physical, mental, or emotional condition: *to fall into a coma.* **12.** to come or occur as if by dropping, such as stillness or night: *The sun went down and night fell rapidly.* **13.** to come by lot or chance: *The chore fell to me.* See FALL TO below. **14.** to come to pass or occur at a certain time: *Christmas falls on a Monday this year.* **15.** to have its proper place: *The accent falls on the last syllable.* **16.** to come by right: *The inheritance fell to the only living relative.* **17.** to lose animation; appear disappointed or dismayed: *The child's face fell when the bird flew away.* **18.** to slope or extend in a downward direction: *The field falls gently to the river.* **19. fall back,** [*no obj*] to give way; retreat: *The troops fell back to their fortified positions.* **20. fall back on** or **upon,** [~ + *back* + *on/upon* + *obj*] to have recourse to; rely on: *We had no savings to fall back on.* **21. fall behind,** [*no obj*] **a.** to lag in pace or progress: *to fall behind in their studies.* **b.** to fail to pay one's debts on time. **22. fall for,** [~ + *for* + *obj*] *Slang.* **a.** to be deceived by: *I can't believe you would fall for an old trick like that.* **b.** to fall in love with: *He had fallen for her pretty badly.* **23. fall in with,** [~ + *in* + *with* + *obj*] to start to associate with: *to fall in with bad company.* **24. fall off,** [*no obj*] to decrease in number, amount, or intensity; diminish: *The winds fell off once the storm passed.* **25. fall on** or **upon,** [~ + *on/upon* + *obj*] **a.** to assault: *The gang fell on their rivals with knives and chains.* **b.** to become the obligation or duty of: *The welfare of the family fell on me.* **c.** to experience or come upon: *Once again we had fallen on bad times.* **26. fall out, a.** [~ + *out* (+ *with* + *obj*)] to quarrel; disagree: *They had fallen out only a week before their wedding.* **b.** [*no obj*] to come out: *His hair fell out after a few weeks of chemotherapy.* **27. fall over,** [*no obj*] to collapse: *fell over in a faint.* **28. fall through,** [*no obj*] to fail to be accomplished; collapse: *My plans kept falling through.* **29. fall to,** [~ + *verb-ing*] to apply oneself; begin: *They fell to bickering among themselves.* **30. fall under,** [~ + *under* + *obj*] **a.** to be the concern or responsibility of: *The ESL program fell under his jurisdiction.* **b.** to be classified as; be included within: *This crime falls under the category of murder.* **—*n.* 31.** [*count*] an act or instance of falling or dropping from a higher to a lower place or position: *a rapid fall in prices.* **32.** [*count*] something that falls or drops: *a heavy fall of rain.* **33.** [*noncount; often: the* + ~] the season of the year that comes after summer and before winter; autumn. **34.** [*count; usually singular*] a sinking to a lower level; decline: *the fall of an empire.* **35.** [*count*] the distance through which anything falls: *a long fall to the ground.* **36.** Usually, **falls.** [*plural*] a waterfall. **37.** [*count*] a downward slope: *the gentle rise and fall of the meadow.* **38.** [*count*] a falling from an erect position, such as to the ground: *She had a bad fall and broke her arm.* **39.** [*count; usually singular*] a succumbing to temptation; lapse into sin. **40.** [*count*] surrender or capture, such as of a city.

fal•la•cious (fə lā′shəs) /fəˈleyʃəs/ *adj.* **1.** logically unsound: *fallacious arguments.* **2.** deceptive; misleading: *fallacious testimony.* **—fal•la′cious•ly,** *adv.*

fal•la•cy (fal′ə sē) /ˈfæləsiy/ *n., pl.* **-cies. 1.** [*count*] a deceptive, misleading, or false notion; misconception: *It's a fallacy to think that government will solve all our problems.* **2.** [*noncount*] faulty or erroneous reasoning: *The statement was based on fallacy.* **3.** [*count*] a misleading or unsound argument: *A good logician would see the fallacies in your reasoning.*

fal•li•ble (fal′ə bəl) /ˈfæləbəl/ *adj.* **1.** able or likely to be deceived or mistaken: *People are fallible.* **2.** likely to be false or incorrect; not accurate: *fallible information.* **—fal•li•bil•i•ty** (fal′ə bil′i tē) /ˌfæləˈbɪlɪtiy/ **fal′li•ble•ness,** *n.* [*noncount*] **—fal′li•bly,** *adv.*

fall′ing-out′, *n.* [*count*], *pl.* **fall•ings-out, fall•ing-outs.** a quarrel or separation between persons formerly in close association.

fall′ing star′, *n.* [*count*] a meteor; shooting star.

fall•out or **fall-out** (fôl′out′) /ˈfɔlˌawt/ *n.* [*noncount*] **1.** the settling to the ground of particles ejected into the atmosphere from the earth by explosions, eruptions, forest fires, etc., esp. such settling from nuclear explosions. **2.** the particles themselves.

fal•low (fal′ō) /ˈfælow/ *adj.* **1.** (of land) plowed and left unseeded for a season or more; uncultivated. **2.** not in use; inactive: *Her creative energies were lying fallow.*

false (fôls) /fɔls/ *adj.,* **fals•er, fals•est. 1.** not true or correct; erroneous; wrong: *a false statement.* **2.** uttering or declaring what is untrue; lying: *a false witness.* **3.** not faithful or loyal: *a false friend.* **4.** tending to deceive or mislead; deceptive: *a false impression.* **5.** [*before a noun*] not genuine; counterfeit: *a false name.* **6.** [*before a noun*] not real; used as a substitute or aid, esp. temporarily; artificial: *false teeth.* **7.** [*before a noun*] based on mistaken, erroneous, or inconsistent impressions, ideas, or facts: *false pride.* **8.** [*before a noun*] wrong or not correct in pitch, such as a musical note: *He played several false notes.* **—false′ly,** *adv.* **—false′ness,** *n.* [*noncount*] **—Related Words.** FALSE is an adjective, FALSENESS and FALSITY are nouns, FALSIFY is a verb, FALSELY is an adverb: *His nervousness created a false impression during the job interview. She was discouraged by his falseness and cowardice. There was a good deal of falsity in the papers. He tried to falsify his passport. He was falsely accused of the murder.*

false•hood (fôls′ho͝od) /ˈfɔlshʊd/ *n.* **1.** [*count*] a false statement or lie; something false, such as an untrue idea or belief. **2.** [*noncount*] the act or practice of telling lies.

fal•set•to (fôl set′ō) /fɔlˈsɛtow/ *n.* [*count*], *pl.* **-tos.** an unnaturally or artificially high-pitched voice, esp. in a man.

fal•si•fy (fôl′sə fī) /ˈfɔlsəfay/ *v.* [~ + *obj*], **-fied, -fy•ing. 1.** to make false or incorrect, esp. so as to deceive: *to falsify income-tax reports.* **2.** to fashion or alter fraudulently: *He falsified the birthdate on his driver's license.* **3.** to represent falsely: *to falsify one's family history.* **—fal•si•fi•ca•tion** (fôl′sə fi kā′shən) /ˈfɔlsəfɪˈkeyʃən/ *n.* [*count; noncount*] **—fal′si•fi′er,** *n.* [*count*]

fal•si•ty (fôl′si tē) /ˈfɔlsɪtiy/ *n., pl.* **-ties. 1.** [*noncount*] the quality or condition of being false. **2.** [*count*] something false.

fal•ter (fôl′tər) /ˈfɔltər/ *v.* [*no obj*] **1.** to hesitate, be unsure, or fail in action, intent, endurance, etc.; give way: *She never faltered.* **2.** to speak with hesitation or uncertainty: *The boy faltered when the police demanded to know his name.* **3.** to move unsteadily; stumble: *She faltered toward the door.* **4.** to lose power; stop working smoothly: *The engine faltered and died.* **—fal′ter•ing,** *adj.*

fame (fām) /feym/ *n.* [*noncount*] the state or condition of being well or widely known, esp. favorable reputation; renown: *great fame as a painter.* **—famed,** *adj.*

fa•mil•ial (fə mil′yəl, -mil′ē əl) /fəˈmɪlyəl, -ˈmɪliyəl/ *adj.* of, relating to, or characteristic of a family: *familial ties.*

fa•mil•iar (fə mil′yər) /fəˈmɪlyər/ *adj.* **1.** commonly or generally known or seen: *a familiar sight.* **2.** well-acquainted; thoroughly conversant and knowledgeable: *She is thoroughly familiar with editing symbols.* **3.** informal; easygoing; without ceremony: *to write in a familiar style.* **4.** closely intimate or personal: *to be on familiar terms.* **5.** more intimate or personal than is proper; presuming: *familiar advances.* **—*n.*** [*count*] **6.** a familiar friend or associate. **—fa•mil′iar•ly,** *adv.*

fa•mil•i•ar•i•ty (fə mil′ē ar′i tē, -mil yar′-) /fəˌmɪliyˈærɪtiy, -mɪlˈyær-/ *n.* [*noncount*] **1.** thorough knowledge or mastery of something: *his familiarity with sports cars.* **2.** the state of being familiar; friendly relationship; intimacy: *has a familiarity with the mayor.* **3.** an absence of ceremony and formality; informality.

fa•mil•iar•ize (fə mil′yə rīz′) /fəˈmɪlyəˌrayz/ *v.* [~ + *obj*], **-ized, -iz•ing. 1.** to make (oneself or another) knowledgable; acquaint: *He familiarized us with the layout of the building.* **2.** to make (something) well-known; bring into common knowledge or use.

fam•i•ly (fam′ə lē, fam′lē) /ˈfæməliy, ˈfæmliy/ *n., pl.* **-lies,** *adj.* **—*n.*** [*count*] **1.** parents and their children thought of as a group: *How many people are in your family?* **2.** the spouse and child or children of one person. **3.** a group of persons sharing common ancestry, as parents, children, uncles, aunts, and cousins. **4.** a group of related things or individuals: *the halogen family of elements; The lion belongs to the cat family.* **—*adj.*** [*before a noun*] **5.** of, relating to, or characteristic of a family: *a family trait.* **6.** belonging to or used by a family: *the family automobile.* **—*Idiom.* 7. in a** or **the family way,** *Informal.* pregnant.

fam′ily plan′ning, *n.* [*noncount*] a program for planning the size of families through the spacing or prevention of pregnancies.

fam′ily tree′, *n.* [*count*] a chart showing the historical relationships within a family or group.

fam•ine (fam′in) /ˈfæmɪn/ *n.* extreme and general lack or scarceness of food, esp. within a large geographical area: [*noncount*]: *widespread famine.* [*count*]: a famine that killed thousands of people.

fam•ished (fam′isht) /ˈfæmɪʃt/ *adj.* very hungry.

fa•mous (fā′məs) /ˈfeyməs/ *adj.* **1.** having a widespread reputation, usually of a favorable nature; celebrated: *autographs of some of the famous people.* **2.** first-rate; excellent. **3.** [*usually: be* + ~ + *for*] notorious: *The movie star was famous for being late.* **—fa′mous•ly,** *adv.*

fan[1] (fan) /fæn/ *n., v.,* **fanned, fan•ning. —*n.*** [*count*] **1.** a device for producing a current of air by the revolving movement of one or more blades: *an electric fan.* See illustration at APPLIANCE. **2.** a flat object of plastic, paper, wood, etc., often in the shape of a triangle or a semicircle, for waving lightly in the hand to create a cooling current of air about the body: *a beautiful Chinese fan.* **—*v.* 3.** [~ + *obj*] to move or stir up (the air) with or as if with a fan. **4.** [~ + *obj*] to cause air to blow upon, such as from a fan: *When she fainted we fanned her face.* **5.** [~ + *obj*] to stir to activity; incite: *The story fanned the* *emotions of the voters.* **6.** to spread out like a fan: [*no obj*]: *The soldiers fanned out around the enemy.* [~ + *obj*]: *The magician fanned the cards expertly.*

fan[2] (fan) /fæn/ *n.* [*count*] an enthusiastic follower or admirer of a team, sport, celebrity, etc.; enthusiast: *hockey fans.*

fa•nat•ic (fə nat′ik) /fə'nætɪk/ *n.* [*count*] **1.** a person with extreme enthusiasm or zeal, such as in religion or politics; zealot. **—***adj.* Also, **fa•nat′i•cal. 2.** having extreme enthusiasm or zeal. **—fa•nat′i•cal•ly,** *adv.*

fan•ci•er (fan′sē ər) /'fænsiyər/ *n.* [*count*] a person having a liking for or interest in something; enthusiast.

fan•ci•ful (fan′si fəl) /'fænsɪfəl/ *adj.* **1.** characterized by or showing fancy; capricious in appearance: *fanciful designs.* **2.** suggested by fancy; imaginary; unreal: *the fanciful characters in his books for children.* **—fan′ci•ful•ly,** *adv.* **—fan′ci•ful•ness,** *n.* [*noncount*]

fan•cy (fan′sē) /'fænsiy/ *n., pl.* **-cies,** *adj.,* **-ci•er, -ci•est,** *v.,* **-cied, -cy•ing,** *interj.* **—***n.* **1.** [*noncount*] imagination or fantasy: *in a flight of fancy.* **2.** [*count*] a mental image or conception; notion: *happy fancies of being famous.* **3.** [*count*] a liking or preference; inclination: *a fancy for smoked oysters.* **—***adj.* **4.** of extra high quality or exceptional appeal: *fancy fruits.* **5.** ornamental; decorative; not plain: *a cake with a fancy icing.* **6.** much too costly; exorbitant: *a consultant who charges fancy fees.* **—***v.* [~ + *obj*] **7.** to picture to oneself; imagine: *Fancy her living with him.* **8.** [~ + *(that) clause*] to believe without being absolutely sure or certain: *I fancy my new neighbor is wealthy.* **9.** to take a liking to; like: *She fancies chocolates.* **—***interj.* **10.** (used to express mild surprise): *They invited you, too? Fancy (that)!* **—*Idiom.* 11. take a fancy to,** [~ + *obj*] to have a liking or preference for: *took a fancy to our style of living.* **12. take one's fancy,** to appeal or attract: *A chocolate dessert had taken his fancy.*

fan•fare (fan′fâr) /'fænfɛər/ *n.* **1.** [*count*] a short piece of music played on trumpets. **2.** [*noncount*] showy display, as of publicity or advertising.

fang (fang) /fæŋ/ *n.* [*count*] **1.** one of the long sharp teeth of a venomous snake by which poison is injected. **2.** a long sharp projecting tooth, esp. a canine tooth.

fan•ny (fan′ē) /'fæniy/ *n., pl.* **-nies.** *Informal.* BUTTOCKS.

fan′ny pack′, *n.* [*count*] a small zippered pouch hung from a belt around the waist.

fan•ta•size (fan′tə siz′) /'fæntə,sayz/ *v.,* **-sized, -siz•ing.** to daydream; imagine: [~ + *about* + *obj*]: *fantasizing about a perfect vacation.* [~ + *(that) clause*]: *fantasized that I would win a million dollars.*

fan•tas•tic (fan tas′tik) /fæn'tæstɪk/ *adj.* **1.** thought of and created by an unrestrained imagination; grotesque: *fantastic rock formations.* **2.** not based on reality; imaginary; irrational: *fantastic fears.* **3.** extremely great: *a fantastic salary.* **4.** extraordinarily good: *a fantastic musical.* **—fan•tas′ti•cal•ly,** *adv.*

fan•ta•sy (fan′tə sē, -zē) /'fæntəsiy, -ziy/ *n., pl.* **-sies. 1.** [*noncount*] imagination, esp. when it is let free and not held back: *indulging in fantasy from time to time.* **2.** [*count*] the succession of mental images formed in this way: *He had this fantasy about the tenant across the hall.* **3.** [*count*] a belief or notion based on no solid foundation; illusion: *She had a fantasy that he was trying to poison her.*

far (fär) /fɑr/ *adv., adj.,* **far•ther** or **fur•ther, far•thest** or **fur•thest. —***adv.* **1.** at or to a great distance or remote point; a long way off: *How far is it from here?* **2.** at or to a remote or advanced time; for a long time: *They stayed up talking far into the night.* **3.** at or to a great, advanced, or definite point or degree of progress: *You may have gone too far.* **4.** much or many: *I need far more time.* **—***adj.* **5.** being at a great distance; remote in time or place: *the far future.* **6.** [*before a noun*] more distant of the two: *The window is in the far corner.* **—*Idiom.* 7. a far cry, a.** quite some distance; removed: *a far cry from civilization.* **b.** very different; in sharp contrast: *This tiny apartment is a far cry from what she is accustomed to.* **8. by far, a.** by a great deal; very much: *That minivan is too expensive by far.* **b.** plainly; obviously: *This melon is by far the ripest of all.* **9. far and away,** without doubt; to a large extent: *This was far and away the best house we could find.* **10. far and wide,** to great lengths; over great distances: *The boy searched far and wide for his dog.* **11. far be it from me,** I do not wish or dare (to interrupt, criticize, etc.): *Far be it from me to complain.* **12. go far,** [*no obj*] to achieve a great deal: *She's a promising worker; I'm sure she'll go far.* **13. how far,** to what distance, extent, or degree: *How far can we go with this plan?* **14. so far, a.** up to now: *So far the budget cuts haven't hit us too badly.* **b.** up to a certain point or extent: *The road was built only so far before they ran out of money.* **15. the far side,** the farther or opposite side: *the far side of the moon.* **16. thus far,** so far: *Thus far we've been spared any crises.*

far•a•way (fär′ə wā′) /'fɑrə'wey/ *adj.* [*before a noun*] **1.** distant; remote: *faraway lands.* **2.** dreamy; preoccupied: *a faraway look in his eyes.* **—Usage.** After the verb *be*, use FAR AWAY (two words): *The lands were far away, over the ocean. My thoughts were far away; I had to snap out of it.* FARAWAY is usually the correct form before a noun.

farce (färs) /fɑrs/ *n.* [*count*] **1.** a comedy based on unlikely situations and exaggerated effects: *the latest farce on Broadway.* **2.** a foolish, false, or meaningless show; ridiculous sham; mockery: *dishonest politicians who make a farce of good government.*

fare (fâr) /fɛər/ *n., v.,* **fared, far•ing. —***n.* **1.** [*count*] the price of traveling in a bus, airplane, or other carrier: *special fares for senior citizens.* **2.** [*count*] a person who pays to travel in a vehicle: *The cab driver took her fare to the airport.* **3.** [*noncount*] food; diet: *The restaurant serves hearty fare.* **4.** [*noncount*] something offered to the public, as for entertainment: *musical fare of folk songs and country tunes.* **—***v.* [*no obj*] **5.** to experience good or bad fortune, treatment, etc.; get on: *He didn't fare too well on his own.*

fare•well (fâr′wel′) /,fɛər'wɛl/ *interj.* **1.** good-bye; may you stay well: *Farewell, friends.* **—***n.* [*count*] **2.** an expression of good wishes at parting: *The couple found their coats and said their farewells.* **3.** leave-taking; departure: *a friendly farewell.* **—***adj.* [*before a noun*] **4.** parting; final: *a farewell performance.*

far′-fetched′ or **far′fetched′,** *adj.* improbable; forced; strained: *a far-fetched example.*

far′-flung′, *adj.* [*before a noun*] extending over a great distance; widely distributed: *a far-flung empire.*

fa•ri•na (fə rē′nə) /fə'riynə/ *n.* [*noncount*] flour or meal made from cereal grains. **—far•i•na•ceous** (far′ə nā′shəs) /,færə'neyʃəs/ *adj.*

farm (färm) /fɑrm/ *n.* [*count*] **1.** a tract of land, usually with a house, barn, silo, etc., on which crops and often live animals are raised. See illustration at LANDSCAPE. **2.** land or water devoted to the raising of animals, fish, plants, etc. **—***v.* **3.** to cultivate land or soil to grow things: [*no obj*]: *The peasants have been farming on this land for many generations.* [~ + *obj*]: *peasants farming the land.* **4. farm out,** [~ + *out* + *obj*] to assign or send out (work) to another, esp. to a smaller business: *The company would farm out its smaller projects to reduce the time its own employees spent on minor work.* **—farm′er,** *n.* [*count*]

farm•house (färm′hous′) /'fɑrm,haws/ *n.* [*count*] a house on a farm, esp. the farmer's residence. See illustration at LANDSCAPE.

farm•land (färm′land′) /'fɑrm,lænd/ *n.* [*noncount*] land used to grow crops or that is suitable for growing crops.

far′-off′, *adj.* distant; remote: *far-off lands.*

far′-reach′ing, *adj.* extending far in influence, effect, etc.: *the far-reaching effect of the economic downturn.*

far•sight•ed (fär′si′tid, -si′tid) /'fɑr'saytɪd, -,saytɪd/ *adj.* **1.** seeing objects at a distance more clearly than those near at hand. **2.** wise, as in foreseeing future developments and planning for them. **—far′sight′ed•ness,** *n.* [*noncount*]

far•ther (fär′thər) /'fɑrðər/ *adv., comparative of* **far** *with* **farthest** *as superlative.* **1.** at or to a greater distance: *farther down the road.* **2.** at or to a more advanced point: *to go no farther in one's education.* **3.** at or to a greater degree or extent. **—***adj., compar. of* **far** *with* **farthest** *as superl.* **4.** more distant or remote: *the farther side of the mountain.*

far•ther•most (fär′thər mōst′) /'fɑrθər,mowst/ *adj.* farthest.

far•thest (fär′thist) /'fɑrðɪst/ *adj., superlative of* **far** *with* **farther** *as comparative.* **1.** most distant or remote: *Who came the farthest?* **2.** most extended; longest. **—***adv., superl. of* **far** *with* **farther** *as compar.* **3.** at or to the greatest distance or most advanced point: *This is the farthest I've been from home.* **4.** at or to the greatest degree or extent: *That is the farthest they have ever pushed my patience.*

far•thing (fär′thing) /'fɑrðɪŋ/ *n.* [*count*] a former British coin equal to 1/4th of a penny.

fas•ci•nate (fas′ə nāt′) /'fæsə,neyt/ *v.* [~ + *obj*], **-nat•ed, -nat•ing.** to attract and hold the attention of;

arouse the interest or curiosity of; allure: *Ancient Egypt has always fascinated me.* —**fas′ci•nated,** *adj.* —**fas′ci•nat•ing,** *adj.* —**fas•ci•na•tion** (fas′ə nā′shən) /ˌfæsəˈneyʃən/ *n.* [*noncount*] —**Related Words.** FASCINATE is a verb, FASCINATION is a noun, FASCINATING and FASCINATED are adjectives: *The magician fascinated the children with his tricks. Their faces showed their fascination. The fascinating tricks thrilled the children. The fascinated children talked about the magician all day.*

fas•cism (fash′iz əm) /ˈfæʃɪzəm/ *n.* [*noncount; sometimes: Fascism*] a governmental or political system that is led by a dictator and emphasizes nationalism, militarism, and often racism. —**fas′cist,** *n.* [*count*], *adj.*

fash•ion (fash′ən) /ˈfæʃən/ *n.* **1.** [*noncount*] a prevailing custom or style of dress, etiquette, socializing, etc. **2.** [*noncount*] the art, study, or business of designing clothing or appearance: *the fashion industry.* **3.** [*noncount*] conventional usage in dress, manners, etc. **4.** [*count*] manner; way of making or doing something: *in a warlike fashion.* —*v.* [~ + *obj*] **5.** to give a particular shape or form to; make; construct: *fashioned a necklace from paper clips.* —*Idiom.* **6. after** or **in a fashion,** to some small extent; in a rather poor way: *I spoke French after a fashion.*

fash•ion•a•ble (fash′ə nə bəl) /ˈfæʃənəbəl/ *adj.* **1.** observant of or conforming to the fashion; stylish: *fashionable clothes.* **2.** of, characteristic of, or used by the world of fashion: *a fashionable shop.* **3.** current; popular: *a fashionable topic of conversation.* —**fash′ion•a•bly,** *adv.*

fast[1] (fast) /fæst/ *adj.* and *adv.*, **-er, -est.** —*adj.* **1.** moving or able to move, operate, function, or take effect quickly; quick; swift; rapid: *a fast horse.* **2.** done in or taking comparatively little time: *a fast race.* **3.** (of a timepiece) indicating a time in advance of the correct time: *My watch is fast.* **4.** characterized by unrestrained or immoral conduct, esp. in sexual relations; wanton; loose: *a fast crowd.* **5.** characterized by extreme energy and activity, esp. in the pursuit of pleasure: *leading a fast life.* **6.** permanent, lasting, or unchangeable: *a fast color.* **7.** resistant (often used in combination): *acid-fast; Her clothes are color-fast (=won't lose color when washed).* **8.** firm; loyal; devoted: *fast friends.* **9. a.** (of money, profits, etc.) made quickly or easily and sometimes deviously: *They made a few fast profits.* **b.** cleverly quick and manipulative in making money: *a fast operator.* —*adv.* **10.** quickly, swiftly, or rapidly: *She drove very fast.* **11.** tightly; firmly: *held on fast to my hand; caught fast in a trap.* **12.** in a fixed and secure way, as a door, gate, or shutter: *The door was shut fast and locked.* **13.** soundly: *He was fast asleep.* **14.** ahead of the correct or announced time: *My alarm clock is running fast.* —*Idiom.* **15. pull a fast one,** to engage in unexpectedly unfair or deceitful behavior to achieve one's goal: *He pulled a fast one by sabotaging my computer files.*

fast[2] (fast) /fæst/ *v.* [*no obj*] **1.** to eat no food. **2.** to eat only a little or only certain kinds of food, esp. as a religious observance. —*n.* [*count*] **3.** an act or a period of not eating food, or a limiting of one's food.

fas•ten (fas′ən) /ˈfæsən/ *v.* **1.** [~ + *obj*] to attach firmly or securely in place or to something else; connect: *to fasten a light switch securely to the wall.* **2.** to (cause to) be secure, as an article of dress with buttons, clasps, etc., or a door with a lock, bolt, etc.: [~ + *obj*]: *Fasten the window.* [*no obj*]: *This clasp won't fasten.* **3.** to direct (the eyes, thoughts, etc.) intently; focus attention: [~ + *obj*]: *She fastened her eyes on him during the entire performance.* [~ + *on*]: *His gaze fastened on the jewels.* —**fas′ten•er,** *n.* [*count*]

fas•ten•ing (fas′ə ning) /ˈfæsənɪŋ/ *n.* [*count*] something that fastens, such as a lock or clasp.

fast′ food′, *n.* [*count; noncount*] food, as hamburgers or pizza, that can be prepared and served quickly. —**fast-food,** *adj: fast-food restaurants.*

fas•tid•i•ous (fa stid′ē əs) /fæˈstɪdiyəs/ *adj.* **1.** overly particular, critical, or demanding; hard to please: *a fastidious eater.* **2.** requiring or having excessive care or delicacy: *fastidious attention to detail.* —**fas•tid′i•ous•ly,** *adv.* —**fas•tid′i•ous•ness,** *n.* [*noncount*]

fat (fat) /fæt/ *n.*, *adj.*, **fat•ter, fat•test.** —*n.* **1.** an oily substance found in certain animal tissue and plant seeds, and used in cooking and in the manufacture of soaps and other products: [*noncount*]: *His diet was too rich in fat.* [*count*]: *Different fats are used in the preparation of this cooking oil.* **2.** [*noncount*] animal tissue containing much of this substance: *to have rolls of fat around one's waist.* **3.** [*noncount*] the richest or best part of anything: *the fat of the land.* —*adj.* **4.** having too much fat; corpulent: *a fat person.* **5.** plump; well-fed: *a fat chicken.* **6.** made up of or containing fat; greasy; oily; fatty: *fat meat.* **7.** profitable; providing a lot of money; lucrative: *a fat job in government.* —*Idiom.* **8. fat chance,** a very slight chance; small probability: *A fat chance we have of getting a raise!* **9. the fat is in the fire,** something has been done or started that cannot be reversed and will probably have dramatic or serious consequences: *Now that the enemy has begun its invasion, the fat is in the fire.* —**fat′ness,** *n.* [*noncount*] —**Related Words.** FAT is a noun and an adjective, FATNESS is a noun, FATTEN is a verb: *The meat has too much fat in it. You're too fat; you need to go on a diet. Unfortunately, fatness is bad for your health. The farmer wanted to fatten his pigs.*

fa•tal (fāt′l) /ˈfeytl̩/ *adj.* **1.** causing or capable of causing death; mortal; deadly: *a fatal accident; a fatal disease.* **2.** causing destruction, misfortune, or ruin; disastrous: *a fatal decision that ruined our hopes.* **3.** decisively important; fateful: *The fatal day was near.* —**fa′tal•ly,** *adv.*

fa•tal•ism (fāt′l iz′əm) /ˈfeytl̩ˌɪzəm/ *n.* [*noncount*] a belief that all events are inevitable and predetermined. —**fa′tal•ist,** *n.* [*count*] —**fa′tal•is′tic,** *adj.*

fa•tal•i•ty (fā tal′i tē) /feyˈtælɪtiy/ *n.*, *pl.* **-ties. 1.** [*count*] a death caused by a disaster: *highway fatalities.* **2.** [*noncount*] the quality of causing death or disaster; deadliness: *the fatality of cancer.* **3.** [*noncount*] the state or quality of being predetermined by or subject to fate.

fate (fāt) /feyt/ *n.* **1.** [*count; usually singular*] something that unavoidably happens to a person; one's fortune or lot: *The judge decided her fate.* **2.** [*noncount*] the power by which events are thought to be decided; destiny: *By a strange twist of fate, Thomas Jefferson and John Adams both died on July 4, 1826.* **3.** [*count*] ultimate outcome; final course or state: *the fate of a political campaign.* **4.** [*noncount*] death, destruction, or ruin: *They met their fate on the battlefield.*

fat•ed (fā′tid) /ˈfeytɪd/ *adj.* [*often: be* + ~ + *to* + *verb*] subject to, guided by, or decided by fate; destined: *was fated to be president.*

fate•ful (fāt′fəl) /ˈfeytfəl/ *adj.* **1.** having great significance or consequences; decisively important; critical: *a fateful meeting.* **2.** fatal, deadly, or disastrous: *that fateful day that started like any other.* —**fate′ful•ly,** *adv.*

fa•ther (fä′thər) /ˈfɑðər/ *n.* [*count*] **1.** a male parent. **2.** [*usually plural*] forefather: *Our fathers came from many different lands.* **3.** a person who has originated, started, or established something: *George Washington was the father of the American nation.* **4.** one of the leading men in a city, town, etc.: *the city fathers.* **5.** [*sometimes: Father*] a priest or a title for a priest. **6.** [*Father*] God. —*v.* [~ + *obj*] **7.** to cause a woman to become pregnant with (a child); beget: *He had fathered twins.* **8.** to be the creator, founder, or author of; originate: *He was thought to have fathered the atomic bomb.* —**fa′ther•hood′,** *n.* [*noncount*] —**fa′ther•less,** *adj.* —**fa′ther•ly,** *adj.*

fa′ther-in-law′, *n.* [*count*], *pl.* **fa•thers-in-law.** the father of one's husband or wife.

fa•ther•land (fä′thər land′) /ˈfɑðərˌlænd/ *n.* [*count*] **1.** one's native country. **2.** the land of one's ancestors.

fath•om (fath′əm) /ˈfæðəm/ *n.*, *pl.* **-oms,** (*esp. when thought of as a group*) **-om,** *v.* —*n.* [*count*] **1.** a nautical unit of length equal to 6 feet (1.8 m). —*v.* [~ + *obj*] **2.** to get to the truth of; comprehend; understand: *I couldn't fathom his motives.* —**fath′om•a•ble,** *adj.*

fa•tigue (fə tēg′) /fəˈtiyg/ *n.*, *v.*, **-tigued, -ti•guing.** —*n.* **1.** [*noncount*] weariness from exertion: *I had a feeling of great fatigue after that long trip.* **2.** [*noncount*] the weakening of material that has undergone stress, esp. repeated stress: *Metal fatigue is causing that bridge to crack.* **3. fatigues.** Also called **fatigue′ clothes′.** [*plural*] military clothing worn for routine jobs or in battle. —*v.* [~ + *obj*] **4.** to cause to be weary; exhaust; enervate: *Climbing the mountain fatigued the whole group.*

fat•ten (fat′n) /ˈfætn̩/ *v.* to (cause to) grow fat: [~ + *obj*]: *Certain foods will fatten livestock faster than others.* [*no obj*]: *The animals fattened and the land produced good crops.*

fat•ty (fat′ē) /ˈfætiy/ *adj.*, **-ti•er, -ti•est. 1.** [*before a noun*] made up of, containing, or resembling fat: *fatty tissue.* **2.** having too much fat: *fatty foods.* —**fat′ti•ness,** *n.* [*noncount*]

fat•u•ous (fach′o͞o əs) /ˈfætʃuwəs/ *adj.* foolish or inane; silly: *fatuous remarks.* —**fat′u•ous•ly,** *adv.* —**fat′u•ous•ness,** *n.* [*noncount*]

fau•cet (fô′sit) /ˈfɔsɪt/ *n.* [*count*] a device for controlling the flow of liquid from a pipe; tap: *The faucet with the 'C' on it is for cold water in the U.S. but for hot water in France.*

fault (fôlt) /fɔlt/ *n.* [*count*] **1.** a defect or imperfection; flaw; failing: *His only fault is that he lacks ambition.* **2.** [*usually: singular*] responsibility for failure or a wrongful act: *Whose fault was it?* **3.** an error or mistake; misdeed: *a fault in addition.* **4.** a break or crack in the continuity of a body of rock, or of the earth's surface: *huge faults in southern California.* **—***v.* [~ + *obj*] **5.** to accuse of error, misdeed, wrong, etc.; criticize; blame: *The boss can't fault you on inaccuracy.* **—*Idiom.* 6. at fault,** in the wrong; deserving blame: *She was at fault for lying.* **7. find fault,** [*find* + ~ (+ *with* + *obj*)] to complain or be critical: *always found fault with him no matter what he did.* **8. to a fault,** to an extreme degree; greatly; excessively: *She was generous to a fault.* —**fault′less,** *adj.* —**fault′less•ly,** *adv.*

fault•y (fôl′tē) /ˈfɔltiy/ *adj.,* **-i•er, -i•est.** having faults or defects; imperfect; defective: *faulty wiring.* —**fault′i•ly,** *adv.* —**fault′i•ness,** *n.* [*noncount*]

fau•na (fô′nə) /ˈfɔnə/ *n.* the animals of a given area or time period, thought of as a group: [*noncount; used with a singular verb*]: *African fauna was the subject of her study.* [*plural; used with a plural verb*]: *Some African faunas are endangered.*

faux pas (fō pä′) /ˈfow pɑ/ *n.* [*count*], *pl.* **faux pas** (fō päz′) /ˈfow pɑz/. an embarrassing social error.

fa•vor (fā′vər) /ˈfeyvər/ *n.* **1.** [*count*] something done or granted out of goodwill; a kind act: *to ask a favor of me.* **2.** [*noncount*] goodwill; friendly regard; approval: *I wanted to win her favor.* **3.** [*noncount*] special or preferential treatment; partiality: *The professor showed favor to certain students.* **4.** [*count*] a small gift or decorative item: *a party favor.* **5.** Usually, **favors.** [*plural*] sexual intimacy, esp. as permitted by a woman. **—***v.* [~ + *obj*] **6.** to regard with favor; approve; sanction: *How many favor Smith's proposal?* **7.** to prefer; treat with partiality: *The girl thought her father favored her sister.* **8.** [~ + *obj* (+ *with* + *obj*)] to show favor to; oblige: *Will you favor us with a reply?* **9.** to be favorable to; make easier: *The wind favored their journey.* **10.** to treat or use gently: *favors her sprained ankle.* **11.** to aid or support: *They favored the party's cause.* **12.** to bear a physical resemblance to: *He tends to favor his mother's family.* **—*Idiom.* 13. find favor with,** [~ + *obj*] to gain the approval of; be liked by: *The play found favor with the critics.* **14. in favor of, a.** on the side of; in support of: *in favor of aid to education.* **b.** to the advantage of: *She transferred out of a big college in favor of the smaller one in her neighborhood.* **15. in one's favor,** to one's credit or advantage: *comments made in your favor.* **16. out of favor,** no longer liked or approved of: *fashions now out of favor.* Also, *esp. Brit.,* **favour.**

fa•vor•a•ble (fā′vər ə bəl, fāv′rə-) /ˈfeyvərəbəl, ˈfeyvrə-/ *adj.* **1.** giving approval or support; positive: *a favorable report.* **2.** creating or winning favor; pleasing: *a favorable impression.* **3.** providing advantage, opportunity, or convenience; advantageous: *a favorable rate of interest.* **4.** promising; hopeful: *conditions favorable for employment.* —**fa′vor•a•bly,** *adv.*

fa•vor•ite (fā′vər it, fāv′rit) /ˈfeyvərɪt, ˈfeyvrɪt/ *n.* [*count*] **1.** a person or thing regarded with special preference, pleasure, or approval: *Vanilla is my favorite.* **2.** a competitor or contestant considered likely to win: *the favorite in the race.* **—***adj.* **3.** looked on with particular favor or preference; preferred: *my favorite movie star.*

fa•vor•it•ism (fā′vər i tiz′əm, fāv′ri-) /ˈfeyvərɪˌtɪzəm, ˈfeyvrɪ-/ *n.* [*noncount*] the unfair favoring of one person or group over others with equal claims; partiality.

fawn[1] (fôn) /fɔn/ *n.* **1.** [*count*] a young deer. **2.** [*noncount*] a light yellowish brown color.

fawn[2] (fôn) /fɔn/ *v.* [~ + *on/over* + *obj*] to seek (someone's) notice or try to gain (someone's) favor by flattery; toady: *The bellhop fawned over the guest.*

fax (faks) /fæks/ *n.* **1.** Also called **facsimile. a.** [*noncount*] a method for transmitting documents, drawings, photographs, or the like by telephone lines for exact reproduction elsewhere. **b.** [*count*] a machine **(fax′ machine′),** for doing this: *Our office has a fax.* See illustration at OFFICE. **c.** [*count*] an exact copy or reproduction transmitted in this way: *I got the fax.* **—***v.* **2.** to transmit (documents, drawings, photographs, or the like) by fax: [~ + *obj*]: *I'll fax the documents.* [~ + *obj* + *to* + *obj*]: *I'll fax the documents to you.* [~ + *obj* + *obj*]: *I'll fax you the documents.*

faze (fāz) /feyz/ *v.* [~ + *obj*], **fazed, faz•ing.** to cause to be disturbed or upset; to disconcert; fluster; daunt: *The roof could fall in and it wouldn't faze her.*

FBI, an abbreviation of: Federal Bureau of Investigation.

FCC, an abbreviation of: Federal Communications Commission.

F.D., an abbreviation of: **1.** fire department. **2.** focal distance.

FDA, an abbreviation of: Food and Drug Administration.

FDIC, an abbreviation of: Federal Deposit Insurance Corporation.

fear (fēr) /fɪər/ *n.* **1.** [*noncount*] a distressing emotion aroused by impending danger, evil, pain, etc.: *shaking in fear.* **2.** [*count*] a specific instance of such a feeling: *a fear of heights.* **3.** [*count*] concern or anxiety; worry; solicitude: *a fear for someone's safety.* **—***v.* [*not: be* + ~*-ing*] **4.** to look at with fear; be afraid of; dread: [~ + *obj*]: *She fears no one and nothing.* [~ + *verb-ing*]: *to fear flying.* **5.** [~ + *for* + *obj*] to have fear; be afraid: *feared for their safety.* **6.** [~ + *(that) clause*] to be worried or afraid: *I fear that I'll fail the test.* **7.** [~ + *obj*] to have reverence of: *to fear God.* —**fear′less,** *adj.* —**fear′less•ly,** *adv.* —**fear′less•ness,** *n.* [*noncount*] **—Syn.** See BRAVE.

fear•ful (fēr′fəl) /ˈfɪərfəl/ *adj.* **1.** causing fear; frightening: *fearful apparitions.* **2.** feeling fear, dread, or apprehension; anxious: *I was fearful about the exam.* **3.** [*before a noun*] extreme in size, intensity, or badness: *a fearful blizzard.* —**fear′ful•ly,** *adv.*

fear•some (fēr′səm) /ˈfɪərsəm/ *adj.* **1.** causing fear: *a fearsome dragon.* **2.** causing awe or respect: *fearsome intelligence.*

fea•si•ble (fē′zə bəl) /ˈfiyzəbəl/ *adj.* capable of being done or accomplished: *a feasible plan.* —**fea•si•bil•i•ty** (fē′zə bil′i tē) /ˌfiyzəˈbɪlɪtiy/ *n.* [*noncount*] —**fea′si•bly,** *adv.*

feast (fēst) /fiyst/ *n.* [*count*] **1.** any rich or large meal. **2.** something highly agreeable or satisfying: *a feast for the eyes.* **3.** Also, **feast day.** a celebration or time of celebration, usually of a religious nature, in honor of an event, person, etc. **—***v.* **4.** [*no obj*] to take part in a feast; eat a large or lavish meal: *They feasted for days when the war was over.* **5.** [~ + *obj*] to provide or entertain with a feast, so as to show honor to: *They feasted the victorious team.* **—*Idiom.* 6. feast one's eyes on,** [~ + *obj*] to look at with great pleasure. —**feast′er,** *n.* [*count*]

feat (fēt) /fiyt/ *n.* [*count*] a noteworthy act or achievement: *an athletic feat.*

feath•er (feth′ər) /ˈfɛðər/ *n.* **1.** [*count*] one of the light, horny structures that form the principal covering of birds. **2.** [*noncount*] condition, as of health, spirits, etc.: *feeling in fine feather after a vacation.* **—***v.* [~ + *obj*] **3.** to clothe or cover with or as if with feathers. **—*Idiom.* 4. a feather in one's cap,** a praiseworthy achievement; honor: *It was a feather in his cap to be named to the town council.* **5. feather one's nest,** to enrich oneself by using one's favorable or privileged position: *feathered her own nest instead of helping her clients.* —**feath′ered,** *adj.* —**feath′er•y,** *adj.,* **-i•er, -i•est.**

fea•ture (fē′chər) /ˈfiytʃər/ *n., v.,* **-tured, -tur•ing. —***n.* [*count*] **1.** an important part or characteristic: *an attractive feature of the house.* **2.** something offered as a special attraction: *The high-wire act is the feature of the circus.* **3.** any part of the face, such as the nose, chin, or eyes: *His eyes are his best feature.* **4. features,** [*plural*] the face; countenance: *The veil hid her features.* **5.** Also called **fea′ture film′.** the main motion picture in a movie program. **6.** a column, cartoon, etc., appearing regularly in a newspaper or magazine. **—***v.* [~ + *obj*] **7.** to make a feature of; give importance to: *The magazine featured a story on the hurricane.* **8.** to have or present (a performer) in a lead role or a prominent supporting role: *The movie will feature a rock star.* **9.** to show the main characteristics of; depict: *The publisher featured the new software.*

Feb or **Feb.,** an abbreviation of: February.

Feb•ru•ar•y (feb′ro͞o er′ē, feb′yo͞o-) /ˈfɛbruwˌɛriy, ˈfɛbyuw-/ *n.* [*proper noun; count*], *pl.* **-ar•ies.** the second month of the year, ordinarily containing 28 days, but containing 29 days in leap years. *Abbr.:* Feb.

-fec-, *root.* -fec- comes from Latin, where it has the meaning "do; make." It is related to the root -FAC-. This meaning is found in such words as: AFFECT, DEFECATE, DEFECT, EFFECT, INFECT.

fe•ces (fē′sēz) /ˈfiysiyz/ *n.* [*plural*] waste matter sent out of the intestines through the anus; excrement. Also, *esp. Brit.,* **faeces.** —**fe•cal** (fē′kəl) /ˈfiykəl/ *adj.*

feck•less (fek′lis) /ˈfɛklɪs/ *adj.* **1.** ineffective; incompetent. **2.** having no sense of responsibility; lazy.

fe•cund (fē′kənd, fek′ ənd) /ˈfiykənd, ˈfɛk ənd/ *adj.* fertile; prolific; fruitful: *fecund farmland.* —**fe•cun•di•ty** (fi-kun′di tē) /fɪˈkʌndɪtiy/ *n.* [*noncount*]

fed (fed) /fɛd/ *v.* **1.** pt. and pp. of FEED. —***Idiom.*** **2. fed up,** [*be* + ~] impatient; disgusted; bored: *I was fed up with his excuses.*

-fed-, *root.* -*fed-* comes from Latin, where it has the meaning "group; league; trust." This meaning is found in such words as: CONFEDERATE, FEDERAL, FEDERATION.

fed., an abbreviation of: **1.** federal. **2.** federated. **3.** federation.

fed•er•al (fed′ər əl) /ˈfɛdərəl/ *adj.* [*before a noun*] **1.** of, relating to, or of the nature of a union of states under a central government that is distinct from and above the governments of the separate states: *the federal government of the U.S.* **2.** of or involving such a central government: *federal laws.* —**fed′er•al•ly,** *adv.* See -FED-.

fed•er•al•ism (fed′ər ə liz′əm) /ˈfɛdərəˌlɪzəm/ *n.* [*noncount*] **1.** the federal principle of government. **2.** belief in this principle. —**fed′er•al•ist,** *n.* [*count*], *adj.* See -FED-.

fed•er•ate (*v.* fed′ə rāt′) / *v.* ˈfɛdəˌreyt / *v.,* **-at•ed, -at•ing.** to (cause to) unite or organize in a federation: [*no obj*]: *The states decided to federate while keeping many of their own rights.* [~ + *obj*]: *a leader who tried to federate the trade unions.* See -FED-.

fed•er•a•tion (fed′ə rā′shən) /ˌfɛdəˈreyʃən/ *n.* **1.** [*noncount*] the act of uniting or forming a union of states, societies, etc., each of which keeps control of its own internal affairs: *the parties opposing federation and in favor of separatism.* **2.** [*count*] a union of states, societies, etc., formed in this way: *The United States is a federation.* See -FED-.

fe•do•ra (fi dôr′ə, -dōr′ə) /fɪˈdɔrə, -ˈdowrə/ *n.* [*count*], *pl.* **-ras.** a soft felt hat with a curved brim.

fee (fē) /fiy/ *n.* [*count*] a sum charged or paid, as for professional services: *a doctor's fee.*

fee•ble (fē′bəl) /ˈfiybəl/ *adj.,* **-bler, -blest. 1.** physically weak; frail: *The sick child was still too feeble to walk on her own.* **2.** lacking in substance or effectiveness: *feeble arguments.* —**fee′ble•ness,** *n.* [*noncount*] —**fee′bly,** *adv.*

fee′ble-mind′ed, *adj.* mentally weak.

feed (fēd) /fiyd/ *v.,* **fed** (fed) /fɛd/ **feed•ing,** *n.* —*v.* **1.** [~ + *obj*] to give food to; supply with nourishment: *She liked to feed pigeons.* **2.** to provide as food: [~ + *obj* + *to* + *obj*]: *to feed breadcrumbs to pigeons.* [~ + *obj* + *obj*]: *to feed the pigeons some breadcrumbs.* **3.** [*no obj*] (esp. of animals) to take food; eat: *The cows were feeding.* **4.** [~ + *on* + *obj*] to be nourished; live by eating: *Those bats feed on fruit.* **5.** [~ + *obj*] to yield or serve as food for: *This land has fed ten generations.* —*n.* **6.** [*noncount*] food, esp. for farm animals: *grain feed.* **7.** [*count*] a meal, esp. a lavish one. **8.** [*count*] a feeding mechanism: *a printer tractor feed.* —**feed′er,** *n.* [*count*]

feed•back (fēd′bak′) /ˈfiydˌbæk/ *n.* [*noncount*] **1.** a reaction or response to a process or activity: *feedback from a speech.* **2.** information derived from such a reaction or response: *to use the feedback from an audience survey.*

feel (fēl) /fiyl/ *v.,* **felt** (felt) /fɛlt/ **feel•ing,** *n.* —*v.* **1.** [*not: be* + ~*-ing;* ~ + *obj*] to perceive (something) by direct physical contact: *I could feel a slight breeze.* **2.** to examine (something) by touch: [~ + *obj*]: *I felt her forehead to see if she had a fever.* [*no obj*]: *I felt around in my pocket for a dime.* **3.** [~ + *obj*] to find (one's way) by touching, groping, or cautious moves: *I felt my way through the darkened room.* **4.** [~ + *obj*] to experience the effects of; notice: *The whole region felt the storm.* **5.** [~ + *oneself* + *verb(-ing)*] to have a particular sensation or impression of: *I felt myself fly(ing) through the air. I felt my lips get(ting) dry.* **6.** [*not: be* + ~*-ing;* ~ + *(that) clause*] to have a belief in; think: *I feel he's guilty.* **7.** to perceive or experience a state of mind or a condition of body; to have a sensation of being; to become conscious of: [~ + *obj*]: *She felt pride in her accomplishments.* [~ + *adjective*]: *I'm feeling fine.* **8.** [*not: be* + ~*-ing;* ~ + *adjective*] to make itself felt, noticed, or apparent; seem; to give off sensations: *Her head feels cold.* **9. feel for,** [~ + *for* + *obj*] to feel sympathy for or compassion toward; empathize with: *I felt for you when your car was stolen.* **10. feel out,** to try to determine the mood or status of (a person or situation) by discreet, usually informal or unofficial inquiries: [~ + *out* + *obj*]: *We'll feel out the manager on your idea.* [~ + *obj* + *out*]: *to feel her out on the new idea.* —*n.* [*count; usually singular*] **11.** a quality of an object perceived by feeling or touching: *the feel of satin.* **12.** a sensation of something felt; vague mental impression or feeling: *a feel of sadness in the air.* **13.** the sense of touch: *soft to the feel.* **14.** native ability or acquired sensitivity: *to have a feel for teaching.* —***Idiom.*** **15. feel like, a.** to have a desire for; be favorably disposed toward: *I felt like screaming at them.* **b.** [*it* + ~ + *like* + *obj; not: be* + ~*-ing*] to appear or seem like: *It feels like rain.* **16. feel (like) oneself,** [*no obj*] to be in one's normal healthy and happy state: *You'll feel like yourself again tomorrow.* **17. feel up to,** [~ + *obj*] to feel strong or healthy enough to: *He's not feeling up to running today.*

feel•er (fē′lər) /ˈfiylər/ *n.* [*count*] **1.** a proposal, remark, hint, etc., designed to bring out the opinions of others: *The embassy was putting out feelers about a treaty.* **2.** an organ of touch, such as an antenna or a tentacle on an animal.

feel•ing (fē′ling) /ˈfiylɪŋ/ *n.* **1.** [*noncount*] the function or the power of perceiving by touch: *no feeling in his left hand.* **2.** [*count*] a particular sensation of this kind: *a feeling of warmth.* **3.** [*count*] a consciousness or awareness: *a feeling of inferiority.* **4.** [*count*] an emotion or emotional attitude: *a feeling of joy.* **5.** [*count*] idea; thought: *a feeling we were being watched.* **6.** [*count*] a sentiment; attitude; opinion: *a feeling in favor of the proposal.* **7. feelings,** [*plural*] the emotional side of a person; sensibilities: *I didn't intend to hurt her feelings.* **8.** [*noncount*] understanding; sympathetic perception: *a poem without feeling.* —*adj.* **9.** sensitive; readily affected by emotion; sympathetic: *a feeling heart.* **10.** indicating or characterized by emotion: *He gave a feeling reply to the charge.* —**feel′ing•ly,** *adv.*

feet (fēt) /fiyt/ *n.* **1.** pl. of FOOT. —***Idiom.*** **2. drag one's feet,** to act or proceed slowly or reluctantly: *They were dragging their feet when it came to refunding our money.* **3. get one's feet wet,** [*no obj*] to take the first step in an activity, venture, etc.: *He got his feet wet in the computer business working as a programmer.* **4. have one's feet on the ground,** [*no obj*] to have a realistic, sensible attitude or approach. **5. on one's feet, a.** in a standing position. **b.** in a secure, independent position or recovered state: *The loan helped me get on my feet again.* **6. stand on one's own (two) feet, a.** to be financially self-supporting. **b.** to be independent. **7. sweep off one's feet,** [*sweep* + *obj* + *off* + *one's* + ~] to impress or overwhelm by ability, enthusiasm, or charm.

feign (fān) /feyn/ *v.* [~ + *obj*] to pretend; put on an appearance of: *to feign sickness.*

feint (fānt) /feynt/ *n.* [*count*] **1.** a movement made to deceive an opponent. —*v.* [*no obj*] **2.** to make or deceive with a feint: *The boxer feinted with his left and threw a right.*

feist•y (fī′stē) /ˈfaystiy/ *adj.,* **-i•er, -i•est.** full of animation, energy, or courage; spirited; plucky: *The champion is faced with a feisty challenger.*

fe•lic•i•ty (fi lis′i tē) /fɪˈlɪsɪtiy/ *n., pl.* **-ties. 1.** [*noncount*] a state of being happy: *marital felicity.* **2.** [*noncount*] a skillful capacity: *poems with graceful felicity of expression.* **3.** [*count*] an instance or display of this: *The many felicities of a day in the country.*

fe•line (fē′lin) /ˈfiylayn/ *adj.* **1.** belonging or relating to the cat family; catlike: *feline agility.* **2.** sly, stealthy, or treacherous: *her slinky, feline quality on the movie screen.* —*n.* [*count*] **3.** an animal of the cat family; cat.

fell[1] (fel) /fɛl/ *v.* pt. of FALL.

fell[2] (fel) /fɛl/ *v.* [~ + *obj*] to knock, strike, shoot, or cut down; cause to fall: *to fell a tree.*

fell[3] (fel) /fɛl/ *adj.* **1.** fierce; cruel; deadly: *a fell disease.* —***Idiom.*** **2. at** or **in one fell swoop,** all at once or all together, as if by a single blow: *The tornado leveled the houses in one fell swoop.*

fel•low (fel′ō) /ˈfɛlow/ *n.* [*count*] **1.** a man or boy: *a handsome fellow.* **2.** *Informal.* a person; one: *They don't treat a fellow very well here.* **3.** a companion; comrade; associate: *his fellows at work.* **4.** a graduate student to whom an allowance is granted for special study. **5.** a member of any of certain learned societies: *a fellow of the British Academy.* —*adj.* [*before a noun*] **6.** belonging to the same class or group: *fellow students.*

fel•low•ship (fel′ō ship′) /ˈfɛlowˌʃɪp/ *n.* **1.** [*noncount*] friendly relationship; companionship; friendliness: *fellowship among old friends.* **2.** [*count*] an association or society: *a member of the youth fellowship.* **3.** [*count*] the position of, or the money given to, a fellow of a college or university: *a small fellowship for expenses and some tuition.*

fel•on (fel′ən) /ˈfɛlən/ *n.* [*count*] a person who has committed a felony.

fel•o•ny (fel′ə nē) /ˈfɛləniy/ *n.* [*count*], *pl.* **-nies.** an offense, such as murder or burglary, of serious character and usually punished by imprisonment for more than one year. —**fe•lo•ni•ous** (fə lō′nē əs) /fəˈlowniyəs/ *adj.*

felt[1] (felt) /fɛlt/ *v.* pt. and pp. of FEEL.

felt[2] (felt) /fɛlt/ *n.* [*noncount*] a nonwoven fabric of wool, fur, or hair, matted together by heat, moisture, and great pressure.

fem., an abbreviation of: **1.** female. **2.** feminine.

fe•male (fē′māl) /ˈfiymeyl/ *n.* [*count*] **1.** a person of the sex that bears young; a girl or woman. **2.** any organism of the sex or sexual phase that normally produces egg cells. **3.** a plant having a pistil or pistils. —*adj.* **4.** of, relating to, or being a female: *a female mammal.* **5.** [*before a noun*] of, relating to, or characteristic of a girl or woman; feminine: *female wisdom.* **6.** [*before a noun*] made up of females: *a wide female readership.* **7.** having a recessed part into which a corresponding part fits: *a female plug.*

fem•i•nine (fem′ə nin) /ˈfɛmənɪn/ *adj.* **1.** relating to or characteristic of women or girls: *feminine clothes.* **2.** belonging to the female sex; female: *a mostly feminine viewership.* **3.** of, relating to, or being the grammatical gender that has among its members most nouns referring to females, as well as other nouns, as Latin *stella* "star" or German *Zeit* "time." —**fem′i•nin′i•ty,** *n.* [*noncount*]

fem•i•nism (fem′ə niz′əm) /ˈfɛməˌnɪzəm/ *n.* [*noncount*] **1.** a doctrine advocating social, political, and economic rights for women equal to those of men. **2.** a movement for the attainment of such rights. —**fem′i•nist,** *n.* [*count*] *adj.*

fen (fen) /fɛn/ *n.* [*count*] low land covered wholly or partially with water; boggy land; marsh.

fence (fens) /fɛns/ *n., v.,* **fenced, fenc•ing.** —*n.* [*count*] **1.** a barrier enclosing or surrounding a field, yard, etc., usually made of posts and wire or wood. See illustration at HOUSE. **2.** a person who receives and disposes of stolen goods. —*v.* **3.** [~ + *obj*] to enclose by a fence: *to fence a farm.* **4.** [~ + (*in/off/out*) + *obj*] to separate by or as if by a fence: *to fence off a corner of a garden.* **5.** [~ + *obj*] to sell (stolen goods) to a fence: *The thieves weren't able to fence the stolen jewels.* **6.** [*no obj*] to practice the art or sport of fencing: *The two swordsmen were fencing.* —***Idiom.*** **7. on the fence,** uncommitted; neutral; undecided: *The party chairman stayed on the fence until the primaries were over.*

fenc•ing (fen′sing) /ˈfɛnsɪŋ/ *n.* [*noncount*] the art, practice, or sport in which a special sword is used for defense and attack.

fend (fend) /fɛnd/ *v.* **1.** [~ + *off* + *obj*] to ward off; keep or push away: *He used a stick to fend off his attackers.* **2.** [~ + *for* + *oneself*] to provide; manage; support: *He had to fend for himself after his father died.* See -FEND-.

-fend-, *root.* *-fend-* comes from Latin, where it has the meaning "strike." This meaning is found in such words as: DEFEND, DEFENSE, DEFENSIVE, FEND, INDEFENSIBLE, INOFFENSIVE, OFFEND, OFFENSE, OFFENSIVE.

fend•er (fen′dər) /ˈfɛndər/ *n.* [*count*] **1.** the part mounted over the wheels of an automobile, bicycle, etc., to reduce splashing. **2.** a low metal guard before an open fireplace to keep back falling coals.

fen•nel (fen′l) /ˈfɛnḷ/ *n.* [*noncount*] **1.** a plant of the parsley family, having sweet-smelling leaves and small yellow flowers. **2.** Also called **fen′nel seed′.** the seeds of this plant, used in cooking and medicine.

-fer-, *root.* *-fer-* comes from Latin, where it has the meaning "carry." This meaning is found in such words as: CONFER, DEFER, DIFFER, FERRY, INFER, PESTIFEROUS, PREFER, TRANSFER.

fer•ment (*n.* fûr′ment; *v.* fər ment′) / *n.* ˈfɜrmɛnt; *v.* fərˈmɛnt/ *n.* [*noncount*] **1.** agitation or excitement; commotion: *political ferment.* —*v.* **2.** to (cause to) undergo fermentation: [*no obj*]: *When wine ferments, it changes sugar to alcohol.* [~ + *obj*]: *This enzyme ferments the wine faster.*

fer•men•ta•tion (fûr′men tā′shən) /ˌfɜrmɛnˈteyʃən/ *n.* [*noncount*] the act or process of fermenting; a chemical change, such as the conversion of grape sugar into alcohol by yeast enzymes.

fern (fûrn) /fɜrn/ *n.* [*count*], *pl.* **ferns** or **fern.** a nonflowering plant having fronds and reproducing by spores.

fe•ro•cious (fə rō′shəs) /fəˈrowʃəs/ *adj.* **1.** savagely fierce or cruel; violently harsh; brutal: *ferocious animals.* **2.** extreme or intense: *a ferocious thirst.* —**fe•ro′cious•ly,** *adv.* —**fe•ro′cious•ness, fe•roc•i•ty** (fə ros′i tē) /fəˈrɒsɪtiy/ *n.* [*noncount*]

fer•ret (fer′it) /ˈfɛrɪt/ *n.* [*count*] **1.** a tame variety of the polecat, used esp. in Europe for driving rodents from their burrows. —*v.* **2.** to drive out by or as if by using a ferret: [~ + *obj*]: *to ferret rabbits from their burrows.* [~ + *out* + *obj*]: *to ferret out enemies.* [~ + *obj* + *out*]: *to ferret them out.* **3.** to search out; bring to light: [~ + *out* + *obj*]: *to ferret out the facts.* [~ + *obj* + *out*]: *to ferret it out.*

Fer′ris wheel′ (fer′is) /ˈfɛrɪs/ *n.* [*count*] an amusement ride made of a large upright wheel rotating on a fixed stand and having seats suspended freely from its rim.

fer•ry (fer′ē) /ˈfɛriy/ *n., pl.* **-ries,** *v.,* **-ried, -ry•ing.** —*n.* [*count*] **1.** a ferryboat. **2.** a service for flying airplanes over a particular route, esp. the delivery of airplanes to an overseas destination. —*v.* **3.** [~ + *obj*] to carry or convey back and forth over a fixed route in a boat or plane: *They ferried the passengers across the lake.* **4.** [*no obj*] to go in a ferry: *They ferried across the Hudson River.* **5.** [~ + *obj*] to fly (an airplane) over a particular route, esp. for delivery: *Women pilots in World War II ferried aircraft to Europe from the U.S.* See -FER-.

fer•ry•boat (fer′ē bōt′) /ˈfɛriyˌbowt/ *n.* [*count*] a boat used to transport passengers, vehicles, etc., across a river or the like. See -FER-.

fer•tile (fûr′tl) /ˈfɜrtḷ/ *adj.* **1.** bearing, producing, or capable of producing vegetation abundantly; productive: *fertile Illinois soil.* **2.** bearing or capable of bearing offspring. **3.** [*usually: before a noun*] abundantly productive; imaginative; creative: *a fertile imagination.* —**fer•til•i•ty** (fər til′i tē) /fərˈtɪlɪtiy/ *n.* [*noncount*] See -FER-.
—**Related Words.** FERTILE is an adjective, FERTILIZER and FERTILIZATION are nouns, FERTILIZE is a verb: *Many crops were grown on the fertile land. The farmer spread fertilizer on the land. Fertilization was necessary before planting. The farmer fertilized the land with chemicals.*

fer•ti•lize (fûr′tl īz′) /ˈfɜrtḷˌayz/ *v.* [~ + *obj*], **-lized, -liz•ing.** **1.** to make (the female sex cell) capable of development by uniting it with the male sex cell. **2.** to make fertile; enrich: *The farmers fertilized their farmland.* —**fer•ti•li•za•tion** (fûr′tl ə zā′shən) /ˌfɜrtḷəˈzeyʃən/ *n.* [*noncount*] See -FER-.

fer•ti•liz•er (fûr′tl ī′zər) /ˈfɜrtḷˌayzər/ *n.* [*count*] any substance used to fertilize the soil. See -FER-.

fer•vent (fûr′vənt) /ˈfɜrvənt/ *adj.* having or showing intense spirit or feeling; ardent; passionate: *a fervent admirer; He wrote a fervent plea.* —**fer′vent•ly,** *adv.*

fer•vor (fûr′vər) /ˈfɜrvər/ *n.* [*noncount*] great earnestness of feeling; passion. Also, *esp. Brit.,* **fer′vour.**

-fess-, *root.* *-fess-* comes from Latin, where it has the meaning "declare; acknowledge." This meaning is found in such words as: CONFESS, CONFESSION, CONFESSIONAL, PROFESS, PROFESSED, PROFESSION, PROFESSIONAL, PROFESSOR, UNPROFESSIONAL.

-fest, *suffix.* *-fest* is attached to nouns to form nouns with the meaning "an assembly of people engaged in a common activity" named by the first element of the compound: *gab + -fest → gabfest (= group of people gabbing or talking a lot); song + -fest → songfest (= assembly of people singing together).*

fes•ter (fes′tər) /ˈfɛstər/ *v.* [*no obj*] **1.** to form pus; putrefy: *a festering wound.* **2.** (of hatred, anger, jealousy, etc.) to grow stronger or worse gradually: *The desire for revenge festered in her heart.*

fes•ti•val (fes′tə vəl) /ˈfɛstəvəl/ *n.* [*count*] **1.** a day or time of religious or other celebration, marked by ceremonies and feasting: *the May festival.* **2.** a period or program of festive activities, cultural events, or entertainment: *a music and art festival.*

fes•tive (fes′tiv) /ˈfɛstɪv/ *adj.* relating to or suitable for a feast or festival; joyous; merry: *festive decorations; a festive mood.* —**fes′tive•ly,** *adv.*

fes•tiv•i•ty (fe stiv′i tē) /fɛˈstɪvɪtiy/ *n., pl.* **-ties. 1.** [*count*] a festive celebration, event, or occasion: *the Christmas festivities.* **2.** [*noncount*] festive character or quality; gaiety; merriment: *serious in the midst of festivity.*

fes•toon (fe sto͞on′) /fɛˈstuwn/ *n.* [*count*] **1.** a string or chain of flowers, leaves, ribbon, etc., hung in a curve between two points. —*v.* [~ + *obj*] **2.** to adorn or decorate with or as if with festoons: *to festoon a hall.*

fet•a (fet′ə) /ˈfɛtə/ *n.* [*noncount*] a soft, crumbly, white Greek cheese usually made from sheep's or goat's milk.

fe•tal or **foe•tal** (fēt′l) /ˈfiytḷ/ *adj.* of, relating to, or having the character of a fetus: *The doctor monitored the fetal heartbeat during labor.*

fetch (fech) /fɛtʃ/ *v.* **1.** to go and bring back; return with; get: [~ + *obj*]: *to fetch a glass of water.* [*no obj*]:

She taught the dog to fetch. **2.** [~ + *obj*] to cause to come; bring: *Go fetch a doctor.* **3.** [~ + *obj*] to sell for or bring (a price, financial return, etc.): *The horse fetched more money than it cost.* **—Idiom. 4. fetch and carry,** [*no obj*] to perform menial tasks: *I was pretty bored, fetching and carrying all day at the bazaar.* —**fetch′er,** *n.* [*count*]

fetch•ing (fech′ing) /ˈfɛtʃɪŋ/ *adj.* charming; captivating: *a fetching blue dress.* —**fetch′ing•ly,** *adv.*: *dressed fetchingly.*

fete or **fête** (fāt, fet) /feyt, fɛt/ *n., pl.* **fetes** or **fêtes,** *v.,* **fet•ed** or **fêt•ed, fet•ing** or **fêt•ing.** —*n.* [*count*] **1.** a festive celebration. —*v.* [~ + *obj*] **2.** to entertain at or honor with a fete: *The Nobel prize winner was feted at a gala luncheon.*

fet•id (fet′id, fē′tid) /ˈfɛtɪd, ˈfiytɪd/ *adj.* having an offensive odor.

fet•ish (fet′ish, fē′tish) /ˈfɛtɪʃ, ˈfiytɪʃ/ *n.* [*count*] **1.** an object regarded as having magical power; talisman. **2.** any object, idea, etc., that one gives reverence or devotion to; obsession: *The town makes a fetish of soccer.* —**fet′ish•ism,** *n.* [*noncount*] —**fet′ish•ist,** *n.* [*count*] —**fet′ish•is′tic,** *adj.*

fet•lock (fet′lok′) /ˈfɛtˌlɒk/ *n.* [*count*] the part of the leg of a horse above and behind the hoof that sticks out and has a tuft of hair.

fet•ter (fet′ər) /ˈfɛtər/ *n.* [*count*] **1.** a chain or shackle placed on the feet. **2.** Usually, **fetters.** [*plural*] anything that confines or restrains: *Education is supposed to remove fetters from the mind.* —*v.* [~ + *obj*] **3.** to put fetters upon: *The pirates fettered their slaves.* **4.** to confine; restrain; restrict: *fettered by a lack of self-confidence.*

fet•tle (fet′l) /ˈfɛtl̩/ *n.* [*noncount*] state; condition: *They felt in fine fettle.*

fet•tuc•ci•ne or **fet•tuc•ci•ni** (fet′ə chē′nē) /ˌfɛtəˈtʃiyniy/ *n.* [*noncount; used with a singular verb*] pasta cut in flat narrow strips: *This fettuccine is excellent.*

fe•tus (fē′təs) /ˈfiytəs/ *n.* [*count*], *pl.* **-tus•es.** unborn or unhatched young in the womb or egg, esp. in the later stages of development.

feud (fyo͞od) /fyuwd/ *n.* [*count*] **1.** a bitter quarrel or argument, esp. one that lasts for many generations between families, ethnic groups, etc. —*v.* [*no obj*] **2.** to engage in a feud: *The two groups had been feuding for years.*

feu•dal (fyo͞od′l) /ˈfyuwdl̩/ *adj.* [*before a noun*] of, relating to, or like feudalism, esp. of the Middle Ages.

feu•dal•ism (fyo͞od′l iz′əm) /ˈfyuwdl̩ˌɪzəm/ *n.* [*noncount*] the political, military, and social system of the Middle Ages in Western Europe, based on the work done by peasants for a landowner who gives protection in return. —**feu′dal•is′tic,** *adj.*

fe•ver (fē′vər) /ˈfiyvər/ *n.* **1.** an abnormally high body temperature: [*noncount*]: *Fever and chills are often symptoms of the flu.* [*count*]: *I was worried because she had a high fever.* **2.** [*count; usually singular*] intense nervous excitement: *in a fever of anticipation.* —**fe′ver•ish,** *adj.* —**fe′ver•ish•ly,** *adv.*

few (fyo͞o) /fyuw/ *adj.,* **-er, -est,** *n., pron.* —*adj.* [*before a plural noun*] **1.** not many but more than one; scarcely any; hardly any: *Few artists live luxuriously.* **2.** [*a* + ~] some; several: *A few artists did manage to live luxuriously.* —*n.* [*plural; used with a plural verb*] **3.** [*a* + ~] a small number or amount: *Did everyone go home? No, a few were still waiting.* **4. the few,** a special, limited number; the minority: *a concert that appeals to the few.* —*pron.* [*plural*] **5.** a small number of persons or things: *Many are called, but few are chosen.* **—Idiom. 6. few and far between,** placed at widely separated intervals; not frequent or plentiful: *Chances like this are few and far between.* **7. quite a few,** [*before a plural noun*] a fairly large number of; many: *He had quite a few girlfriends.* —**Usage.** When FEW is used with a noun, the noun is plural: *few speakers; a few speakers; quite a few speakers.* Note also the slight difference in meaning between FEW and A FEW. When FEW is used without *a* the meaning is "a small amount of; not as many as expected": *Few learners can hope to speak Chinese perfectly.* When A FEW is used, the meaning is more positive: "some, but not many": *A few learners can hope to speak Chinese perfectly.* See LITTLE. FEWER and LESS are opposed. FEWER should be used with plural count nouns: *fewer books,* while LESS is only to be used with noncount nouns: *less money.* In informal style, many speakers use LESS before plural nouns: *less books,* but never use FEWER before noncount nouns; no one would say: *fewer money.*

fey (fā) /fey/ *adj.* whimsical; strange: *in a fey manner.*

fez (fez) /fɛz/ *n.* [*count*], *pl.* **fez•zes.** a felt cap, usually red, shaped like a shortened cone and ornamented with a tassel, worn by men esp. in Egypt and formerly Turkey.

FHA, an abbreviation of: Federal Housing Administration.

fi•an•cé (fē′än sā′, fē än′sā) /ˌfiyɑnˈsey, fiyˈɑnsey/ *n.* [*count*] *pl.,* **-cēs.** a man who is engaged to be married.

fi•an•cée (fē′än sā′, fē än′sā) /ˌfiyɑnˈsey, fiyˈɑnsey/ *n.* [*count*] *pl.,* **-cées.** a woman who is engaged to be married.

fi•as•co (fē as′kō) /fiyˈæskow / *n.* [*count*], *pl.* **-cos, -coes.** a complete failure: *The debate was a total fiasco.*

fi•at (fē′ät, -at; fī′ət, -at) /ˈfiyɑt, -æt; ˈfayət, -æt/ *n.* an authoritative decree; an official order: [*count*]: *a royal fiat.* [*noncount*]: *to rule by fiat.*

fib (fib) /fɪb/ *n., v.,* **fibbed, fib•bing.** —*n.* [*count*] **1.** a small or trivial lie. —*v.* [*no obj*] **2.** to tell a fib: *Stop fibbing and tell me the truth.* —**fib′ber,** *n.* [*count*]

fi•ber (fī′bər) /ˈfaybər/ *n.* **1.** [*count*] a fine, threadlike piece, such as of cotton. **2.** matter or material made up of small thin threadlike pieces: [*noncount*]: *mats made of cotton fiber.* [*count*]: *plastic fibers.* **3.** [*noncount*] an essential or basic character, quality, or strength: *people of strong moral fiber.* **4.** [*count*] a thin, threadlike, or long cell or structure in the body that is combined in a bundle of tissue: *nerve fibers.* **5.** [*noncount*] Also called **bulk, roughage.** parts of plants that are hard or impossible to digest, eaten to aid the movement of food through the intestines: *a diet rich in fiber.* Also, *esp. Brit.,* **fi′bre.**

fi•ber•glass or **fi•ber glass** (fī′bər glas′) /ˈfayˌbər glæs/ *n.* [*noncount*] a material made up of fine threadlike pieces of glass.

fi′ber op′tics or **fi′ber•op′tics,** *n.* [*noncount; used with a singular verb*] the technology of sending computer data, video images, voice signals, etc., through transparent fibers that allow the light to be transmitted around curves. —**fi′ber•op′tic,** *adj.*

fib•ril•late (fib′rə lāt′, fī′brə-) /ˈfɪbrəˌleyt, ˈfaybrə-/ *v.,* **-lat•ed, -lat•ing.** (of muscular tissue) to twitch or quiver uncontrollably: [*no obj*]: *Suddenly the patient's heart began to fibrillate.* [~ + *obj*]: *The machine sent electrical shocks to the heart and fibrillated it.* —**fib•ril•la•tion** (fib′rə lā′shən, fī′brə-) /ˌfɪbrəˈleyʃən, ˌfaybrə-/ *n.* [*noncount*]

fi•brous (fī′brəs) /ˈfaybrəs/ *adj.* of, relating to, made of, or resembling fiber.

-fic-, *root.* *-fic-* comes from Latin, where it has the meaning "make, do." It is related to -FAC- and -FEC-. This meaning is found in such words as: BENEFICIAL, CERTIFICATE, FICTION, HONORIFIC, HORRIFIC, PACIFIC, PROLIFIC.

FICA or **F.I.C.A.** (fī′kə, fē′-) /ˈfaykə, ˈfiy-/ *n.* [*proper noun*] Federal Insurance Contributions Act, a system by which certain amounts are withheld from wages for taxes.

fiche (fēsh) /fiyʃ/ *n.* MICROFICHE.

fick•le (fik′əl) /ˈfɪkəl/ *adj.* not constant or loyal in affections or character. —**fick′le•ness,** *n.* [*noncount*]

fic•tion (fik′shən) /ˈfɪkʃən/ *n.* **1.** [*noncount*] literature that includes novels or short stories of events that are imagined: *I like to read fiction.* **2.** [*count; usually singular*] something invented or imagined, esp. a made-up story: *That story about her rich grandmother was just a fiction.* —**fic′tion•al,** *adj.* See -FIC-. —**Usage.** See FICTITIOUS.

fic•tion•al•ize (fik′shə nl iz′) /ˈfɪkʃənl̩ˌayz/ *v.* [~ + *obj*], **-ized, -iz•ing.** to make into fiction; give a fictional version of: *to fictionalize the life of a hero.* —**fic•tion•al•i•za•tion** (fik′shə nl ə zā′shən) /ˌfɪkʃənl̩əˈzeyʃən/ *n.* [*noncount; count*]

fic•ti•tious (fik tish′əs) /fɪkˈtɪʃəs/ *adj.* **1.** created, taken, or assumed for concealment; not genuine; false: *fictitious names.* **2.** of, relating to, or made up of fiction: *a fictitious heroine.* —**fic•ti′tious•ly,** *adv.* —**Usage.** FICTIONAL usually refers to events that are imaginary or made up: *a fictional tale.* FICTITIOUS more often implies that there was a deliberate effort to mislead or be false: *They used fictitious names on their gun permit applications.*

-fid-, *root.* *-fid-* comes from Latin, where it has the meaning "faith; trust." This meaning is found in such words as: CONFIDE, CONFIDENCE, FIDELITY.

fid•dle (fid′l) /ˈfɪdl̩/ *n., v.,* **-dled, -dling.** —*n.* [*count*] **1.** a violin. —*v.* **2.** to play (a tune) on the fiddle: [*no obj*]: *The emperor was said to have been fiddling while Rome burned.* [~ + *obj*]: *They fiddled a tune.* **3.** [~ + *with* + *obj*] to make fussing movements with the hands: *She fiddled nervously with her handkerchief.* **4.** [~ + *with* + *obj*] to touch or manipulate something, as to operate or adjust it; tinker: *I fiddled with the wires to the battery.*

—***Idiom.*** **5. (as) fit as a fiddle,** in perfect health; very fit: *fit as a fiddle after his vacation.* **6. play second fiddle to,** [~ + *obj*] to have or take a less important role than: *I was tired of playing second fiddle to him.* —**fid′dler,** *n.* [*count*]

fi•del•i•ty (fi del′i tē, fi-) /fɪˈdɛlɪtiy, fay-/ *n.* [*noncount*] **1.** loyalty: *Dogs are known for their fidelity to their masters.* **2.** faithfulness, esp. to one's spouse. **3.** accuracy; exactness. **4.** the degree of accuracy with which sound or images are recorded or reproduced. See -FID-.

fidg•et (fij′it) /ˈfɪdʒɪt/ *v.* [*no obj*] **1.** to move about restlessly, nervously, or impatiently: *fidgeting anxiously before being interviewed.* —*n.* [*count*] **2.** Often, **fidgets.** [*plural*] the condition or an instance of being nervously restless: *gets the fidgets during long meetings.* —**fidg′et•y,** *adj.,* **-i•er, -i•est.**

fie (fī) /fay/ *interj.* (used to express mild disgust, annoyance, or disapproval.)

field (fēld) /fiyld/ *n.* [*count*] **1.** a piece of open or cleared land, esp. one suitable for pasture or growing things: *The cows were grazing in the fields.* See illustration at LANDSCAPE. **2.** a piece of ground devoted to sports or contests; playing field: *The team took the field.* **3.** a particular branch of activity or interest: *the field of teaching.* **4.** [*usually singular*] a job or research location that is away from regular work or study facilities: *representatives in the field.* **5.** the scene or area of active military operations: *the killing fields.* **6.** a large area or expanse of anything: *a field of ice.* **7.** any region or area characterized by a particular feature, resource, activity, etc.: *an oil field.* **8.** the surface of a canvas, shield, flag, or coin on which something is portrayed: *a gold star on a field of blue.* **9.** all the competitors in a contest, or all the competitors except for the leader: *It's not a particularly strong field, so our team has a chance of advancing.* **10.** *Physics.* a region of space in which a force acts. —*v.* **11.** [~ + *obj*] (in baseball and cricket) to catch or pick up (the ball) in play: *The shortstop fielded the ball.* **12.** [~ + *obj*] to answer skillfully: *The president managed to field the question.* —***Idiom.*** **13. play the field,** *Informal.* **a.** to engage in a broad range of activities. **b.** to date a number of persons during the same period of time: *After she broke her engagement, she wanted to play the field for a while.* —**field′er,** *n.* [*count*]

field′ day′, *n.* [*count*] **1.** a day devoted to outdoor sports or athletic contests, such as at a school. **2.** a day for military exercises and display. **3.** an occasion or opportunity to enjoy or amuse oneself completely: *The children had a field day with their new toys.*

field′ glasses′, *n.* [*plural*] binoculars.

field′ hock′ey, *n.* [*noncount*] a field game in which two teams of 11 players each use curved sticks to try to drive a ball into a netted goal.

field′ mar′shal, *n.* [*count*] a military officer of the highest rank, such as in the British army.

field′-test′, *v.* [~ + *obj*] to test (a device or product) under conditions of actual use.

fiend (fēnd) /fiynd/ *n.* [*count*] **1.** any evil spirit; demon. **2.** an extremely cruel or wicked person. **3.** *Informal.* a person who is addicted or very attached to some habit, practice, condition, etc.: *a fiend for neatness.* —**fiend′ish,** *adj.* —**fiend′ish•ly,** *adv.*

fierce (fērs) /fɪərs/ *adj.,* **fierc•er, fierc•est. 1.** wild, savage, or hostile: *fierce beasts.* **2.** violent in force, intensity, etc.: *a fierce hurricane.* **3.** furiously eager or intense: *fierce competition.* **4.** *Informal.* extremely bad or severe: *a fierce cold.* —**fierce′ly,** *adv.* —**fierce′ness,** *n.* [*noncount*]

fier•y (fīᵊr′ē) /ˈfayᵊriy/ *adj.,* **-i•er, -i•est. 1.** made up of, characterized by, or containing fire; intensely hot: *the fiery pits of hell.* **2.** like or suggestive of fire: *a fiery chili sauce.* **3.** intensely ardent or passionate: *a fiery speech.* **4.** easily angered or provoked: *a fiery temper.* —**fier′i•ness,** *n.* [*noncount*]

fi•es•ta (fē es′tə) /fiyˈɛstə/ *n.* [*count*] ,*pl.* **-tas.** a festival or festive celebration.

fife (fīf) /fayf/ *n.* [*count*] a small flute used in marching bands. —**fif′er,** *n.* [*count*]

fif•teen (fif′tēn′) /ˈfɪfˈtiyn/ *n.* [*count*] **1.** a cardinal number, ten plus five. **2.** a symbol for this number, as 15 or XV. —*adj.* [*before a noun*] **3.** amounting to 15 in number. —**fif′teenth′,** *adj., n.* [*count*]

fifth (fifth) /fɪfθ/ *adj.* **1.** next after the fourth: *the fifth door on the right.* **2.** being one of five equal parts. —*n.* [*count*] **3.** a fifth part, esp. of one (⅕). **4.** [*usually: the* + ~] the fifth member of a series. **5.** a fifth part of a gallon of liquor or spirits (about 750 milliliters): *a fifth of his favorite Scotch whiskey.* —*adv.* **6.** in the fifth place. —**fifth′ly,** *adv.*

fif•ty (fif′tē) /ˈfɪftiy/ *n.* [*count*], *pl.* **-ties,** *adj.* **1.** a cardinal number, ten times five. **2.** a symbol for this number, as 50 or L. **3. fifties,** the numbers from 50 through 59, as in referring to the years of a lifetime or of a century or to degrees of temperature: *The temperature is in the fifties.* **4.** a fifty-dollar bill. —*adj.* [*before a noun*] **5.** amounting to 50 in number. —**fif′ti•eth,** *adj., n.* [*count*]

fif•ty-fif•ty or **50-50** (fif′tē fif′tē) /ˈfɪftiyˈfɪftiy/ *adj.* **1.** equally good and bad, likely and unlikely, favorable and unfavorable, etc.: *a fifty-fifty chance of success.* —*adv.* **2.** in an evenly or equally divided way: *The stolen money was divided fifty-fifty.*

fig (fig) /fɪg/ *n.* [*count*] **1.** a tree or shrub of the mulberry family that bears fruit that can be eaten. **2.** the pear-shaped fruit of such a tree or shrub.

fig., an abbreviation of: **1.** figurative. **2.** figuratively. **3.** figure.

fight (fīt) /fayt/ *n., v.,* **fought** (fôt) /fɔt/ **fight•ing.** —*n.* **1.** [*count*] a battle or combat: *a fight between the gangs.* **2.** [*count*] any contest or struggle: *a tough fight for reelection.* **3.** [*count*] an angry argument or disagreement: *a fight over who would use the car.* **4.** [*count*] a boxing bout: *the champ's first fight in almost a year.* **5.** [*noncount*] ability, will, or inclination to fight, keep trying, or resist: *She still had some fight left in her.* —*v.* **6.** to take part or contend in or as if in battle or in single combat: [~ + *obj*]: *The armies fought each other.* [*no obj*]: *They fought in World War II.* [~ + *with* + *obj*]: *The army fought with the enemy.* [~ + *against* + *obj*]: *The U.S. fought against Germany.* **7.** to contend in any manner; struggle vigorously for or against something: [~ + *obj*]: *He had to fight his despair. She fought back her tears.* [*no obj*]: *The candidates fought hard in the election.* [~ + *for* + *obj*]: *They fought hard for their rights.* **8.** [~ + *obj*] to make (one's way) by fighting or striving: *She had fought her way to the top.* —***Idiom.*** **9. fight it out,** [*no obj*] to fight until a decision is reached: *Both sides continued to fight it out.*

fight•er (fī′tər) /ˈfaytər/ *n.* [*count*] **1.** a boxer. **2.** an aircraft designed to seek out and destroy enemy aircraft. **3.** a person who fights, struggles, etc., esp. a person with the courage or disposition to fight, struggle, etc.

fig•ment (fig′mənt) /ˈfɪgmənt/ *n.* [*count*] a mere product of mental invention; a fantastic notion: *The noises in the attic were just a figment of his imagination.*

fig•ur•a•tive (fig′yər ə tiv) /ˈfɪgyərətɪv/ *adj.* **1.** of the nature of or involving a figure of speech, esp. a metaphor: *She used the word "dead" in a figurative sense to mean "tired."* **2.** characterized by or having figures of speech: *letters filled with figurative language.* —**fig′ur•a•tive•ly,** *adv.*

fig•ure (fig′yər) /ˈfɪgyər/ *n., v.,* **-ured, -ur•ing.** —*n.* [*count*] **1.** a symbol for a number. **2.** an amount or value expressed in numbers: *a figure that was more than we could afford.* **3. figures,** [*plural*] the use of numbers in calculating; arithmetic: *good at figures.* **4.** a written symbol other than a letter. **5.** the form or shape of something; outline: *a dim figure in the dark room.* **6.** the human bodily form or frame: *a graceful figure.* **7.** a character or personage, esp. one of distinction: *a well-known figure.* **8.** the appearance or impression made by a person or sometimes a thing: *a mother figure for the human race.* **9.** a diagram, illustration, map, or drawing in a text: *In the first figure you can see the statistics for the five most populous states.* **10.** a movement or series of movements in skating or dancing. —*v.* **11.** [~ + *(up* +*) obj*] to compute or calculate: *Let's figure (up) the total and split the bill.* **12.** [*not: be* + ~*-ing;* ~ + *(that) clause*] *Informal.* to conclude, judge, reason, or think: *I figured that you wanted me to stay.* **13.** [*no obj*] to be or appear in, esp. in an important, obvious, or prominent way: *Your name figures in my report.* **14.** [*not: be* + ~*-ing; it* + ~*; no obj*] *Informal.* (of a situation, act, request, etc.) to be logical, expected, or reasonable: *It figures: when I have the time to travel, I don't have the money.* **15. figure on,** [~ + *on* + *obj*] to count or rely on; take into consideration; plan on: *We had figured on Dad being able to baby-sit.* **16. figure out,** to understand; solve: [~ + *obj* + *out*]: *I can't figure her out; one minute she's happy, the next, sad.* [~ + *out* + *obj*]: *I can't figure out the directions.*

fig•ure•head (fig′yər hed′) /ˈfɪgyərˌhɛd/ *n.* [*count*] **1.** a person who is head of a group, country, etc., in title only: *The queen of England is a figurehead.* **2.** a carved figure built into the front of a sailing ship.

fig′ure of speech′, *n.* [*count*] an expression in which words are used in a nonliteral sense, as in metaphor, in order to suggest vivid images or to heighten effect: *When I said she was growing like a weed it was just a figure of speech.*

fig•ur•ine (fig′yə rēn′) /ˌfɪgyə'riyn/ *n.* [*count*] a small ornamental figure of pottery, metal, glass, etc.; statuette.

Fi•ji•an (fē′jē ən, fi jē′ən) /'fiydʒiyən, fɪ'dʒiyən/ *adj.* **1.** of or relating to Fiji. **2.** of or relating to the language spoken by many people living in Fiji. **—*n.* 3.** [*count*] a person born or living in Fiji. **4.** [*noncount*] the language spoken by many of the people in Fiji.

fil•a•ment (fil′ə mənt) /'fɪləmənt/ *n.* [*count*] **1.** a very fine thread or threadlike structure; a fiber or fibril: *filaments of gold.* **2.** (in a light bulb) the threadlike conductor that is heated and glows due to the passage of current. —**fil•a•men•tous** (fil′ə men′təs) /ˌfɪlə'mɛntəs/ *adj.*

filch (filch) /fɪltʃ/ *v.* [~ + *obj*] to steal (esp. something of small value); pilfer; swipe: *The children filched cookies.*

file[1] (fil) /fayl/ *n., v.,* **filed, fil•ing.** **—*n.*** [*count*] **1.** a cabinet or other container in which papers, letters, etc., are arranged in order. See illustration at OFFICE. **2.** a collection of papers, records, etc., arranged in order and often in a folder: *I would like to read my file.* **3.** a collection of related computer data or program records stored by name, such as on a disk: *When you type "dir" you will see a list or directory of the files on your disk.* **4.** a line of persons or things arranged one behind another: *a long file of people.* **—*v.* 5.** [~ + *obj*] to place in a file: *There were no jobs open, but they filed my resume.* **6.** [~ + *obj*] to arrange (papers, records, etc.) in convenient order for storage or reference: *asked his secretary to file the forms.* **7.** [~ + *obj*] to transmit (a news story), as by wire or telephone: *The correspondent filed his report.* **8.** [~ + *obj*] to initiate (legal proceedings): *to file charges against the driver.* **9.** [*no obj*] to march in a file or line, one after another: *The mourners filed by his coffin.* **10.** [*no obj*] to make application: *to file for divorce.* **—*Idiom.* 11. on file,** held in a file or record; filed for easy retrieval or as evidence of something: *They promised to keep my application on file.*

file[2] (fil) /fayl/ *n., v.,* **filed, fil•ing.** **—*n.*** [*count*] **1.** a metal tool, esp. of steel, having rough surfaces for reducing or smoothing metal, wood, etc. **2.** NAIL FILE. **—*v.*** [~ + *obj*] **3.** to reduce, smooth, or remove with or as if with a file: *She filed her nails.*

fi•let mi•gnon (fi lā′ min yon′) /fɪ'ley mɪn'yɒn/ *n.* [*count*] a small tender round piece of steak cut from the thick end of a beef tenderloin.

fil•i•al (fil′ē əl) /'fɪliyəl/ *adj.* of, relating to, or befitting a son or daughter: *filial obedience.*

fil•i•bus•ter (fil′ə bus′tər) /'fɪləˌbʌstər/ *n.* **1. a.** [*noncount*] the use of delaying tactics by a member of a legislative assembly to prevent the adoption of a measure: *Filibuster is likely if this bill reaches the Senate floor.* **b.** [*count*] an exceptionally long speech or other tactic used for this purpose: *a long filibuster.* **—*v.* 2.** to delay, slow down, or prevent the passage of (legislation) by tactics such as long speeches: [*no obj*]: *The senator was filibustering.* [~ + *obj*]: *The senators promised to filibuster that bill.*

fil•i•gree (fil′ə grē′) /'fɪləˌgriy/ *n.* [*noncount*] delicate ornamental work of fine silver, gold, or other metal wire.

Fil•i•pi•no (fil′ə pē′nō) /ˌfɪlə'piynow/ *n.* [*count*], *pl.* **-nos.** a person born or living in the Philippines.

fill (fil) /fɪl/ *v.* **1.** to (cause to) become full; put as much as can be held into: [~ + *obj*]: *to fill a jar with water.* [*no obj*]: *Her eyes filled with tears.* **2.** [~ + *obj*] to occupy to the full capacity: *The crowd filled the hall.* **3.** [~ + *obj*] to supply plentifully: *to fill a house with furniture.* **4.** [~ + *obj*] to penetrate to every part of: *Sunlight filled the room.* **5.** [~ + *obj*] to occupy and perform the duties of (a position, post, etc.): *The company has already filled the position you applied for.* **6.** [~ + *obj*] to supply the requirements or contents of (an order for goods, etc.): *We'll fill your order right away.* **7.** [~ + *obj*] to meet satisfactorily, as requirements: *to fill a need.* **8.** [~ + *obj*] to stop up or close (a cavity, hole, etc.): *to fill a tooth.* **9. fill in, a.** [~ + *in* + *obj*] to supply (missing information): *The spy filled in the names of the missing scientists.* **b.** to supply information to (someone): [~ + *obj* + *in*]: *Fill us in on your work experience.* [~ + *in* + *obj*]: *Fill in the boss about the plan.* **c.** to complete by adding detail or by inserting required information into: [~ + *in* + *obj*]: *I filled in the form on the typewriter. She'll fill in the background with diagonal lines.* [~ + *obj* + *in*]: *I filled the form in.* **d.** [*no obj*] to act as a substitute: *I filled in for him while he was on vacation.* **10. fill out, a.** to complete (a document or form) by supplying required information: [~ + *out* + *obj*]: *He filled out the form and signed it at the bottom.* [~ + *obj* + *out*]: *He filled it out.* **b.** [*no obj*] to become rounder and fuller, such as the human face or figure. **11. fill up, a.** to (cause to) become full to the top: [*no obj*]: *The tank filled up in no time.* [~ + *up* + *obj*]: *He filled up the tank with gas.* [~ + *obj* + *up*]: *He filled it up.* **b.** to take up (space) completely: [~ + *obj* + *up*]: *The huge football player seemed to fill the room up.* [~ + *up* + *obj*]: *He seemed to fill up the whole room.* **c.** to give a feeling of having eaten enough or too much: [~ + *obj* + *up*]: *Just a little of his chocolate cake always fills me up.* [~ + *up* + *obj*]: *Starchy food fills up the campers quickly.* **—*n.*** [*noncount*] **12.** a full supply; enough to satisfy want or desire: *to eat one's fill.* **13.** material such as earth or stones for building up the level of an area of ground.

fill•er (fil′ər) /'fɪlər/ *n.* **1.** [*count*] a person or thing that fills. **2.** [*noncount*] a substance used to fill cracks. **3.** [*count*] journalistic material of secondary importance used to fill out a column or page. **4.** [*noncount*] cotton, down, or other material used to stuff or pad something.

fil•let (fi lā′) / fɪ'ley / *n., v.,* **fil•leted** (fi lād′) /fɪ'leyd/ **fil•let•ing.** **—*n.* 1.** a boneless cut or slice of meat or fish, such as the beef tenderloin: [*noncount*]: *Fillet is usually very tender and very expensive.* [*count*]: *two fillets of beef.* **—*v.*** [~ + *obj*] **2.** to cut or prepare (meat or fish) as a fillet.

fill•ing (fil′ing) /'fɪlɪŋ/ *n.* **1.** [*count*] an act or instance of filling. **2.** something put in as a filler: [*noncount*]: *too much pie filling.* [*count*]: *delicious sandwich fillings.* **3.** [*count*] a substance such as cement or amalgam, used to fill a cavity in a tooth: *The dentist put in a temporary filling.*

fill′ing sta′tion, *n.* SERVICE STATION.

fil•ly (fil′ē) /'fɪliy/ *n.* [*count*], *pl.* **-lies.** a young female horse.

film (film) /fɪlm/ *n.* **1.** [*count*] a thin layer or coating: *a film of grease.* **2.** [*count*] a thin haze, blur, or mist: *There was a film in my eyes.* **3.** [*noncount*] a thin sheet or strip of specially treated plastic coated with a light-sensitive solution for taking photographs or motion pictures: *a roll of film.* **4.** MOTION PICTURE. **5. a.** Often, **films.** [*plural*] the motion-picture industry, or its productions, operations, etc.: *wanted to work in films.* **b.** [*noncount*] motion pictures as a form of art or entertainment: *a course on experimental film.* **—*v.* 6.** [~ + *obj*] to photograph with a motion-picture camera; to direct, make, or produce (a motion picture): *The cast and crew have been filming this movie for a year.* **7.** to (cause to) become covered by a film: [*no obj*]: *Her eyes filmed over.* [~ + *up* + *obj*]: *The steam filmed up the window.* —**film′y,** *adj.,* **-i•er, -i•est.**

fil•ter (fil′tər) /'fɪltər/ *n.* [*count*] **1.** any substance, such as cloth, paper, or charcoal, through which liquid or gas is passed to remove impurities or to trap solids: *The spring water goes through a filter before it is bottled.* **2.** any device containing a substance for filtering. **3.** a lens screen of colored glass used in photography to control the color or to diminish the intensity of light. **—*v.* 4.** [~ + *obj*] to remove by the action of a filter: *The dehumidifier filters moisture out of the air.* **5.** [~ + *obj*] to act as a filter for; to slow the passage of: *The dehumidifier filters the air.* **6.** [*no obj*] to pass or slip through slowly: *Sunlight was filtering through the trees.* **7.** [*no obj*] to reach gradually: *Day by day, news filtered out about the catastrophe.* —**fil′ter•a•ble, fil•tra•ble** (fil′trə bəl) /'fɪltrəbəl/ *adj.* —**fil′ter•er,** *n.* [*count*]

filth (filth) /fɪlθ/ *n.* [*noncount*] **1.** offensive or disgusting dirt or refuse; foul matter: *sidewalks covered with filth.* **2.** vulgar or obscene language or materials.

filth•y (fil′thē) /'fɪlθiy/ *adj.,* **-i•er, -i•est. 1.** very dirty: *The streets were filthy.* **2.** morally impure, obscene, or vulgar: *filthy language.* **—*Idiom.* 3. filthy rich,** extremely rich. —**filth′i•ness,** *n.* [*noncount*]

fil•tra•tion (fil trā′shən) /fɪl'treyʃən/ *n.* [*noncount*] the act or process of filtering.

fin (fin) /fɪn/ *n.* [*count*] **1.** a winglike or paddlelike part on the body of fishes and certain other water animals, used for movement, steering, or balancing. **2.** any part resembling a fin, such as part of a boat or an aircraft. **3.** Usually, **fins.** [*plural*] FLIPPER (def. 2). —**finned,** *adj.*

-fin- *root.* *-fin-* comes from Latin, where it has the meaning "end; complete; limit." This meaning is found in such words as: CONFINE, DEFINE, DEFINITE, DEFINITION, FINAL, FINALE, FINANCE, FINE, FINISH, FINITE, INDEFINITE.

fin., an abbreviation of: **1.** finance. **2.** financial. **3.** finish.

fi•na•gle (fi nā′gəl) /fɪ'neygəl/ *v.* [~ + *obj*], **-gled, -gl•ing.** to get or achieve (something) by guile or trickery: *to finagle an invitation.* —**fi•na′gler,** *n.* [*count*]

fi•nal (fīn′l) /'faynl̩/ *adj.* **1.** [*before a noun*] relating to or coming at the end; last in place, order, or time: *final meeting of the season.* **2.** conclusive or decisive; unchangeable: *That's my final offer.* **3.** being the end or purpose; ultimate: *a final result.* —*n.* [*count*] **4. a.** Often, **finals.** [*plural*] the last and decisive game, match, or round in a series: *Our team made it to the finals.* **b.** the last, usually long, examination in a course of study: *Do you have a final in history?* —**fi•nal•i•ty** (fī nal′i tē, fə-) /fay'nælɪtiy, fə-/ *n.* [*noncount*] —**fi′nal•ly,** *adv.* See -FIN-.

fi•na•le (fi nal′ē, -nä′lē) /fɪ'næliy, -'nɑliy/ *n.* [*count*], *pl.* **-les.** the concluding part of something; end. See -FIN-.

fi•nal•ist (fīn′l ist) /'faynl̩ɪst/ *n.* [*count*] a person who is participating in the final round of a contest. See -FIN-.

fi•na•lize (fīn′l iz′) /'faynl̩ˌayz/ *v.* [~ + *obj*], **-lized, -liz•ing.** to put into final form; complete all the details of (an agreement): *They finalized the deal.* See -FIN-.

fi•nance (fi nans′, fī′nans) /fɪ'næns, 'faynæns/ *n., v.,* **-nanced, -nanc•ing.** —*n.* **1.** [*noncount*] the management of money, as in banking and investment. **2. finances,** [*plural*] the monetary resources, such as of a company, individual, or government: *Our finances are in good shape.* —*v.* [~ + *obj*] **3.** to supply with money or capital; obtain money or credit for; fund: *How will we finance these expenses?* See -FIN-.

fi•nan•cial (fi nan′shəl, fī-) /fɪ'nænʃəl, fay-/ *adj.* **1.** relating to monetary income and expenses: *the candidate's financial affairs.* **2.** of or relating to those engaged in dealing with money and credit: *a financial advisor.* —**fi•nan′cial•ly,** *adv.* See -FIN-.

fin•an•cier (fin′ən sēr′, fī′nən-) /ˌfɪnən'sɪər, ˌfaynən-/ *n.* [*count*] **1.** a person skilled or engaged in managing large financial operations: *Wall Street financiers.* **2.** a financial backer: *financiers of the project.* See -FIN-.

finch (finch) /fɪntʃ/ *n.* [*count*] a small songbird having a short cone-shaped bill adapted for eating seeds.

find (find) /faynd/ *v.,* **found** (found) /fawnd/ **find•ing,** *n.* —*v.* **1.** [~ + *obj*] to come upon by chance; meet with: *to find a dime in the street.* **2.** [~ + *obj*] to locate by search or effort: *to find an apartment.* **3.** [~ + *obj*] to recover (something lost): *I found my watch under the clothes.* **4.** [*usually not: be* + ~*-ing*] to discover or perceive (something) after thinking about it or experiencing it: [~ + *obj* + *to* + *verb*]: *to find something to be true.* [~ + *obj* + *adjective* + *to* + *verb*]: *I found it hard to believe that they would betray me.* [~ + *(that) clause*]: *I found that money can't buy happiness.* **5.** [*not: be* + ~*-ing;* ~ + *obj*] (used with impersonal subjects like "one" or "you", or in the passive form, *be found*) exist: *One/You won't find much rainfall in the desert.* **6.** [*usually not: be* + ~*-ing;* ~ + *obj*] to gain or regain the use of: *Where does the school find the money to get computers every year?* **7.** [~ + *obj*] to figure out by study or calculation: *to find the sum of several numbers.* **8.** [~ + *obj*] to feel; perceive: *I found some peace at work.* **9.** [~ + *oneself*] to become aware of (oneself), as being in a certain condition or place: *She awoke to find herself back home.* **10.** [*not: be* + ~*-ing*] **a.** [~ + *obj* + *adjective*] to determine after judicial inquiry: *to find a person guilty.* **b.** [~ + *for* + *obj*] to determine or decide an issue after a trial: *The jury found for the defendant.* **11. find out, a.** to discover, expose, or confirm: [~ + *out* + *obj*]: *The detective couldn't find out anything about that suspect.* **b.** [~ + *obj* + *out*] to uncover and expose the true nature of (someone): *You will be found out if you lie.* —*n.* [*count*] **12.** something found, esp. a valuable or gratifying discovery: *What a find: gold, bullion, and old Spanish coins.* —***Idiom.*** **13. find oneself,** to discover and pursue one's genuine interests and talents: *He took a year off from school in order to find himself.* —**find′er,** *n.* [*count*]

find•ing (fin′ding) /'fayndɪŋ/ *n.* [*count*] **1.** Often, **findings.** [*plural*] something that is found out. **2. a.** a judicial decision or verdict. **b.** a U.S. presidential order authorizing an action.

fine[1] (fin) /fayn/ *adj.,* **fin•er, fin•est,** *adv.* —*adj.* **1.** [*often: before a noun*] of superior or best quality; excellent: *fine wine.* **2.** made up of tiny particles: *fine sand.* **3.** very thin; slender: *fine thread.* **4.** keen; sharp: *The knife needs a finer edge.* **5.** [*often: before a noun*] delicate in texture or workmanship: *fine silk; fine china.* **6.** highly skilled; accomplished: *a fine musician.* **7.** refined or elegant; polished: *fine manners.* **8.** delicate; subtle: *a fine distinction.* **9.** healthy; well: *She looks fine.* —*adv.* **10.** *Informal.* excellently; very well: *You did fine on the test.* —**fine′ly,** *adv.* See -FIN-.

fine[2] (fin) /fayn/ *n., v.,* **fined, fin•ing.** —*n.* [*count*] **1.** money imposed as a penalty for an offense: *a parking fine.* —*v.* [~ + *obj* (+ *obj*)] **2.** to punish by a fine: *fined him fifty dollars for littering.*

fine′ arts′ (fin) /fayn/ *n.* [*plural*] visual arts that are valued for beauty or expressiveness, such as painting, sculpture, or architecture. See -FIN-.

fin•er•y (fī′nə rē) /'faynəriy/ *n.* [*noncount*] beautiful, fine, or showy dress, ornaments, etc. See -FIN-.

fi•nesse (fi ness′) /fɪ'nɛs/ *n.* [*noncount*] extreme delicacy or subtlety in performance; skill in handling a difficult situation: *He handled the outburst with finesse.* See -FIN-.

fin•ger (fing′gər) /'fɪŋgər/ *n.* [*count*] **1.** any of the jointed end members of the hand, esp. one other than the thumb. **2.** something like a finger in form or use: *a finger of land.* —*v.* [~ + *obj*] **3.** to touch with the fingers; handle: *He fingered the gun.* **4.** *Slang.* to inform against or identify (someone) to the authorities: *The thief fingered his accomplice.* —***Idiom.*** **5. give (someone) the finger,** [*give* + *obj* + *the* + ~] *Slang.* to express contempt or indignation by extending the middle finger upward in an obscene gesture. **6. keep one's fingers crossed,** [*no obj*] to wish for good luck or success, esp. in a specific activity. **7. lay** or **put one's finger on,** [*used with negative words or in questions; lay/put* + *one's* + ~ + *on* + *obj*] **a.** to remember precisely or discover: *There's something about him that's familiar, but I can't lay my finger on it.* **b.** to locate exactly: *I've got the report somewhere; I just can't put my finger on it at the moment.* **8. twist** or **wrap around one's (little) finger,** [*twist/wrap* + *obj* + *around* + *one's* + ~] to exert complete control over: *She's got them wrapped around her little finger.*

fin•ger•ing (fing′gər ing) /'fɪŋgərɪŋ/ *n.* [*noncount*] **1.** the using of the fingers in playing on an instrument. **2.** the indication (on a sheet of music) of the fingering.

fin•ger•nail (fing′gər nāl′) /'fɪŋgərˌneyl/ *n.* [*count*] the nail at the end of a finger.

fin•ger•print (fing′gər print′) /'fɪŋgərˌprɪnt/ *n.* [*count*] **1.** an impression of the markings of the tip of the thumb or other finger, esp. for purposes of identification. —*v.* [~ + *obj*] **2.** to take or record the fingerprints of: *The police fingerprinted the suspect at headquarters.*

fin•ger•tip (fing′gər tip′) /'fɪŋgərˌtɪp/ *n.* [*count*] **1.** the tip or end of a finger: *His fingertips were dirty from the ink.* —***Idiom.*** **2. at one's fingertips,** immediately and easily available: *had all the information at his fingertips.* **3. to one's fingertips,** thoroughly; completely: *a politician all the way to his fingertips.*

fin•ick•y (fin′i kē) /'fɪnɪkiy/ *adj.* excessively particular; difficult to please; fussy: *a finicky eater.*

fin•ish (fin′ish) /'fɪnɪʃ/ *v.* **1.** to bring or come to an end or to completion: [~ + *obj*]: *We finished dinner at about 9 o'clock.* [~ + *verb-ing*]: *Have you finished reading all those books?* [*no obj*]: *When does school finish this year?* **2.** to use completely: [~ + *(up)* + *obj*]: *to finish (up) a can of paint.* [~ + *(off)* + *obj*]: *They finished (off) their beers.* **3.** to overcome completely; destroy or kill: [~ + *(off)* + *obj*]: *This spray will finish (off) the cockroaches.* [~ + *obj* + *off*]: *to finish them off.* **4.** [~ + *obj*] to put a finish on (wood, metal, etc.): *finished the chair with a glossy varnish.* —*n.* **5.** [*count*] the end or conclusion; the final part or last stage: *getting close to the finish now.* **6.** [*count; usually singular*] the surface coating or texture of wood, metal, etc.: *This old table has a beautiful hand-rubbed finish.* **7.** [*noncount*] a material for application in finishing: *If you get finish on your hands, maybe turpentine will remove it.* —**fin′ish•er,** *n.* [*count*] See -FIN-.

fi•nite (fī′nit) /'faynayt/ *adj.* **1.** having bounds or limits; not infinite; measurable. **2. a.** (of a verb form) distinguishing person, number, and tense, as well as mood or aspect, such as *opens* in *She opens the window.* **b.** (of a clause) containing a finite verb. —**fi′nite•ly,** *adv.* See -FIN-.

fink (fingk) /fɪŋk/ *n.* [*count*] *Slang.* **1.** an informer; stool pigeon. **2.** a contemptible person.

Finn (fin) /fɪn/ *n.* [*count*] a person born or living in Finland.

Fin•nish (fin′ish) /'fɪnɪʃ/ *n.* [*noncount*] **1.** the language spoken by many of the people in Finland. —*adj.* **2.** of or relating to Finland. **3.** of or relating to the language spoken by many of the people in Finland.

fiord (fyôrd, fyōrd) /fyɔrd, fyowrd/ *n.* FJORD.

fir (fûr) /fɜr/ *n.* **1.** [*count*] an evergreen tree of the pine family, having flat needles and erect cones. **2.** [*noncount*] the wood of such a tree.

fire (fīᵊr) /fayᵊr/ *n., v.,* **fired, fir•ing.** **—***n.* **1.** [*noncount*] a state, process, or instance of light, heat, and flame due to burning. **2.** [*count*] a burning mass of fuel, such as on a hearth. **3.** [*count*] the destructive burning of a building, town, forest, etc.; conflagration: *several brush fires.* **4.** [*noncount*] burning passion; ardor; excitement: *The general gave a speech that was full of fire and aroused his men.* **5.** [*noncount*] the shooting or discharge of firearms: *The enemy returned fire.* **—***v.* **6.** [~ + *obj*] to set on fire: *It took several matches to fire the wood.* **7.** [~ + *obj*] to bake (pottery) in a kiln. **8.** [~ + *obj*] to arouse: *a teacher who fired my interest in astronomy.* **9.** to discharge (a gun): [~ + *obj*]: *The officers fired their pistols at the suspect.* [*no obj*]: *Fire when ready.* **10.** [~ + *obj*] to dismiss from a job: *The boss fired her.* **—*Idiom.* 11. catch (on) fire,** [*no obj*] to become ignited; burn: *The wet logs just wouldn't catch (on) fire.* **12. play with fire,** [*no obj*] to trifle with a serious or dangerous matter. **13. under fire, a.** under attack, esp. by military forces. **b.** under censure or criticism: *a candidate under fire for allegations about his finances.*

fire•arm (fīᵊr′ärm′) /ˈfayᵊr,ɑrm/ *n.* [*count*] a weapon, such as a rifle, from which a projectile is fired by gunpowder.

fire•ball (fīᵊr′bôl′) /ˈfayᵊr,bɔl/ *n.* [*count*] **1.** a ball of fire, such as a large burst of flame from an explosive. **2.** a luminous meteor, sometimes exploding.

fire•bomb (fīᵊr′bom′) /ˈfayᵊr,bɒm/ *n.* [*count*] **1.** an explosive device that burns things near it. **—***v.* [~ + *obj*] **2.** to attack with firebombs: *firebombing the enemy.*

fire•brand (fīᵊr′brand′) /ˈfayᵊr,brænd/ *n.* [*count*] **1.** a piece of burning wood. **2.** a person who encourages unrest, argument, or strife.

fire•crack•er (fīᵊr′krak′ər) /ˈfayᵊr,krækər/ *n.* [*count*] a paper or cardboard tube filled with an explosive and discharged to make a noise, as during a celebration.

fire′ en′gine, *n.* [*count*] a truck equipped for firefighting.

fire′ escape′, *n.* [*count*] a metal stairway down an outside wall for escaping from a burning building.

fire′ extin′guisher, *n.* [*count*] a portable container filled with chemicals for putting out a fire.

fire•fight (fīᵊr′fīt′) /ˈfayᵊr,fayt/ *n.* [*count*] an exchange of gunfire between opposing forces.

fire•fight•er or **fire fight•er** (fīᵊr′fī′tər) /ˈfayᵊr,faytər/ *n.* [*count*] a person who fights fires: *The firefighters arrived at the scene.* **—fire′fight′ing,** *n.* [*noncount*], *adj.*

fire•fly (fīᵊr′flī′) /ˈfayᵊr,flay/ *n.* [*count*], *pl.* **-flies.** a beetle that comes out at night, having a light-producing organ at the rear of the abdomen. Also called **lightning bug.** Compare GLOWWORM.

fire•house (fīᵊr′hous′) /ˈfayᵊr,haws/ *n.* FIRE STATION.

fire′ hy′drant, *n.* HYDRANT.

fire•man (fīᵊr′mən) /ˈfayᵊrmən/ *n.* [*count*], *pl.* **-men.** a firefighter.

fire•place (fīᵊr′plās′) /ˈfayᵊr,pleys/ *n.* [*count*] **1.** the part of a chimney that opens into a room and in which fuel is burned; hearth. **2.** any open structure for keeping a fire, such as at a campsite.

fire•pow•er or **fire pow•er** (fīᵊr′pou′ər) /ˈfayᵊr,pawər/ *n.* [*noncount*] the capability of a military force or weapons system to deliver effective fire to a target.

fire•proof (fīᵊr′pro͞of′) /ˈfayᵊr,pruwf/ *adj.* **1.** resistant to fire: *fireproof gloves.* **—***v.* [~ + *obj*] **2.** to make fireproof: *to fireproof the school.*

fire•side (fīᵊr′sīd′) /ˈfayᵊr,sayd/ *n.* [*count; usually: the* + ~] the space around a fire or hearth: *to sit around the fireside and swap stories.*

fire′ sta′tion, *n.* [*count*] a building in which firefighting apparatus and usually fire department personnel are housed; firehouse.

fire•storm or **fire storm** (fīᵊr′stôrm′) /ˈfayᵊr,stɔrm/ *n.* [*count*] **1.** an enormous fire in which a rising column of air above the fire draws in strong winds often accompanied by rain. **2.** an intense outburst: *a firestorm of protest from the voters.*

fire′ tow′er, *n.* [*count*] a tower, such as on a mountain, from which a watch for fires is kept.

fire•trap (fīᵊr′trap′) /ˈfayᵊr,træp/ *n.* [*count*] a building that is esp. dangerous in case of fire.

fire•wood (fīᵊr′wo͝od′) /ˈfayᵊr,wʊd/ *n.* [*noncount*] wood suitable for fuel: *stacked his firewood by the campsite.*

fire•work (fīᵊr′wûrk′) /ˈfayᵊr,wɜrk/ *n.* [*count*] Often, **fireworks.** [*plural*] an explosive device for producing a display of light or a loud noise, used for signaling or as part of a celebration.

fir′ing squad′, *n.* [*count*] a detail of soldiers assigned to execute a condemned person by shooting.

firm[1] (fûrm) /fɜrm/ *adj.* and *adv.,* **-er, -est,** *v.* **—***adj.* **1.** not soft or not giving in when pressed: *a firm mattress.* **2.** securely in place: *Put another nail to make it firm.* **3.** not shaking or trembling; steady: *a firm handshake.* **4.** not giving in to change or fluctuation; fixed; steadfast: *a firm decision.* **5.** indicating firmness or determination: *a firm expression on his face.* **—***v.* [*no obj;* ~(+ *up*)] **6.** to become firm: *The pudding firmed up in the freezer.* **—***adv.* **7.** firmly: *Prices held firm today on the stock market.* **—firm′ly,** *adv.* **—firm′ness,** *n.* [*noncount*]

firm[2] (fûrm) /fɜrm/ *n.* [*count*] a commercial company; business: *She started her own firm.*

fir•ma•ment (fûr′mə mənt) /ˈfɜrməmənt/ *n.* [*count; usually singular: the* + ~] the arch of heaven; sky.

first (fûrst) /fɜrst/ *adj.* **1.** being before all others with respect to time, order, rank, importance, etc.: *I was the first guest to arrive.* **2.** [*before a noun*] LOW (def. 18): *When we put the car in first gear it stalls.* **—***adv.* **3.** before all others or anything else in time, order, rank, etc.: *We arrived first.* **4.** before some other thing, event, etc.: *Clean up your room first.* **5.** for the first time: *We first met in the library stacks.* **6.** in preference to something else; rather; sooner: *I'd die first.* **—***n.* **7.** [*count; singular: the* + ~] the person or thing that is first in time, order, rank, etc.: *I was the first to arrive.* **8.** [*noncount*] the beginning: *At first, we were nervous.* **9.** [*count; usually singular: a* + ~] something that happens for the first time: *It was a first for me.* **10.** [*noncount*] low gear in an automotive vehicle: *She shifted into first and drove off.* **—*Idiom.* 11. at first sight,** at once; immediately: *It was love at first sight.* **12. first off,** at the outset; immediately: *First off, why are you here?* **13. first thing,** before anything else: *We caught the train first thing in the morning.*

first′ aid′, *n.* [*noncount*] emergency treatment given to the sick or injured. **—first′-aid′,** *adj.* [*before a noun*]: *a first-aid worker.*

first•born (fûrst′bôrn′) /ˈfɜrstˈbɔrn/ *adj.* [*before a noun*] **1.** first in the order of birth; eldest: *the first-born son.* **—***n.* [*count; singular; the* + ~] **2.** a firstborn child.

first′ class′, *n.* [*noncount*] **1.** the best, finest, or highest class, grade, or rank. **2.** a class of mail consisting of materials, as letters, sealed against inspection. **—first′-class′,** *adj., adv.*

first•hand or **first-hand** (fûrst′hand′) /ˈfɜrst,hænd/ *adv.* **1.** from the source; directly: *I learned firsthand not to disagree.* **—***adj.* [*before a noun*] **2.** direct from the source: *firsthand knowledge.*

first′ la′dy, *n.* [*count*] **1.** [*often: First Lady*] the wife of the president of the U.S. or of the governor of a state: *The two First Ladies posed under flags of their states.* **2.** the foremost woman in any art, profession, or the like: *the first lady of the women's movement.*

first′ per′son, *n.* [*count; singular; usually: the* + ~] the form of a pronoun or verb that refers to the speaker, such as *I, we,* or *am.*

first′-rate′, *adj.* **1.** excellent; superb; of the highest rank, quality, or class: *a first-rate job.* **—***adv.* **2.** very well: *You did first-rate on the exam.*

first′-string′, *adj.* composed of regular members, participants, etc.: *a first-string team.* **—first′-string′er,** *n.* [*count*]

firth (fûrth) /fɜrθ/ *n.* [*count*] an indentation of the seacoast.

fis•cal (fis′kəl) /ˈfɪskəl/ *adj.* [*before a noun*] of or relating to the public treasury or to financial matters in general: *fiscal policies.* **—fis′cal•ly,** *adv.*

fish (fish) /fɪʃ/ *n., pl.* (*esp. when thought of as a group*) **fish,** (*esp. for kinds or species*) **fish•es,** *v.* **—***n.* **1.** [*count*] a cold-blooded animal living in water, having gills, fins, and usually a long body covered with scales. **2.** [*noncount*] the flesh of a fish used as food: *a recipe for fish with potatoes.* **—***v.* **3.** to go fishing (for): [~ + *obj*]: *to fish trout.* [*no obj*]: *I was fishing all day.* [~ + *for* + *obj*]: *fishing for salmon.* **4.** [~ + *obj (+ out of + obj)*] to draw or pull out as if fishing: *He fished a coin out of his pocket.* **5.** [~ + *for* + *obj*] to seek to obtain something indirectly: *fishing for a compliment.* **—*Idiom.* 6. fish**

out of water, a person who feels out of place: *felt like a fish out of water in the big city.*

fish′ cake′, *n.* [*count*] a fried patty of shredded fish, esp. salt codfish, and mashed potato.

fish•er (fish′ər) /ˈfɪʃər/ *n.* [*count*] **1.** a fisherman. **2.** a dark-furred North American marten.

fish•er•man (fish′ər mən) /ˈfɪʃərmən/ *n.* [*count*], *pl.* **-men.** a person who fishes for profit or pleasure.

fish•er•y (fish′ə rē) /ˈfɪʃəriy/ *n.* [*count*], *pl.* **-er•ies. 1.** a place where fish are grown. **2.** a place where fish or shellfish are caught.

fish•ing (fish′ing) /ˈfɪʃɪŋ/ *n.* [*noncount*] the technique, occupation, or sport of catching fish: *to go fishing.*

fish′ing rod′, *n.* [*count*] a long, slender, flexible rod for use with a reel and line in catching fish.

fish′ sto′ry, *n.* [*count*] a story that is difficult or impossible to believe.

fish•wife (fish′wif′) /ˈfɪʃˌwayf/ *n.* [*count*], *pl.* **-wives. 1.** a woman who sells fish. **2.** a coarse-mannered, loud woman.

fish•y (fish′ē) /ˈfɪʃiy/ *adj.*, **-i•er, -i•est. 1.** like a fish, esp. in smell or taste: *a fishy odor.* **2.** of questionable character; dubious; suspicious: *That excuse sounds fishy.*

fis•sion (fish′ən) /ˈfɪʃən/ *n.* [*noncount*] **1.** the splitting of the nucleus of an atom into nuclei of lighter atoms, accompanied by the release of energy. **2.** the division of a biological organism into new organisms as a process of reproduction.

fis•sure (fish′ər) /ˈfɪʃər/ *n.* [*count*] a narrow opening, division, or groove: *a fissure in the earth.*

fist (fist) /fɪst/ *n.* [*count*] the hand closed tightly with the fingers doubled into the palm.

fist•ful (fist′fo͝ol) /ˈfɪstfʊl/ *n.* [*count*], *pl.* **-fuls.** a handful.

fist•i•cuffs (fis′ti kufs′) /ˈfɪstɪˌkʌfs/ *n.* [*noncount*] combat with the fists.

fit[1] (fit) /fɪt/ *adj.*, **fit•ter, fit•test,** *v.*, **fit•ted** or **fit, fit•ting,** *n.* **—*adj.* 1.** [*be* + ~] adapted or suited; suitable; appropriate: [~ + *for*]: *The stormy night was not fit for man or beast.* [~ + *for* + *verb-ing*]: *This water isn't fit for drinking.* [~ + *to* + *verb*]: *water not fit to drink.* **2.** proper or becoming: *fit behavior.* **3.** prepared or ready: *crops fit for gathering.* **4.** in good physical condition; in good health: *She looked fit and trim.* **—*v.* 5.** to be adapted to or suitable for (a purpose, object, occasion, etc.): [*no obj*]: *The house fits nicely in that wooded area.* [~ + *obj*]: *Does a lunch at noontime fit your schedule?* **6.** [~ + *obj*] to be proper or becoming for: *Let the punishment fit the crime.* **7.** to be of the right size or shape (for): [~ + *obj*]: *The dress fitted her perfectly.* [*no obj*]: *Nothing she tried on would fit.* **8.** [~ + *obj*] to make (something) be of the right size or shape: *The tailor fitted the tuxedo on him.* **9.** [~ + *obj*] to make conform; adjust: *The jeweler fitted the ring to her finger.* **10.** [~ + *obj*] to prepare; make ready: *qualities that fit him for leadership.* **11.** [~ + *obj*] to put with precise placement or adjustment: *I fitted the key into the lock.* **12.** [~ + *obj*] to furnish; equip: *The car is fitted with air bags.* **13. fit out** or **up,** [~ + *out/up* + *obj*] to furnish with the necessary supplies; equip: *They fitted out an expedition.* **—*n.*** [*count*] **14.** the manner, fact, or condition of fitting or of being fitted: *The fit on the tuxedo was perfect. The coat is a poor fit.* **—*Idiom.* 15. fit to be tied,** extremely annoyed or angry. **—fit′ly,** *adv.* **—fit′ness,** *n.* [*noncount*] **—fit′ter,** *n.* [*count*]

fit[2] (fit) /fɪt/ *n.* [*count*] **1.** a sudden acute attack of a disease, esp. one with convulsions or unconsciousness: *a fit of epilepsy.* **2.** an onset or period of emotion, inclination, activity, etc.: *a fit of weeping.* **—*Idiom.* 3. by** or **in fits and starts,** at irregular periods; starting and stopping; intermittently: *We worked in fits and starts.* **4. throw a fit,** to become extremely excited or angry.

fit•ful (fit′fəl) /ˈfɪtfəl/ *adj.* having an irregular pattern of activity; spasmodic: *fitful sleep.* **—fit′ful•ly,** *adv.*

fit•ting (fit′ing) /ˈfɪtɪŋ/ *adj.* **1.** suitable or appropriate; proper or becoming: *a fitting role in the new company.* **—*n.*** [*count*] **2.** an act or instance of trying on clothes that are being made or altered: *Suits are made to order with only a few fittings.* **3.** a part needed to connect other parts: *the various fittings needed to install an air conditioner.* **—fit′ting•ly,** *adv.*

five (fīv) /fayv/ *n.* [*count*] **1.** a cardinal number, four plus one. **2.** a symbol for this number, as 5 or V. **3.** a five-dollar bill. **—*adj.*** [*before a noun*] **4.** amounting to five in number.

fix (fiks) /fɪks/ *v.* **1.** [~ + *obj*] to repair; mend: *If it's not broken, don't try to fix it.* **2.** [~ + *obj*] to put in order; adjust or arrange: *She fixed her hair in braids.* **3.** [~ + *obj*] to make fast, firm, or stable: *She fixed a poster on the wall.* **4.** [~ + *obj*] to settle definitely; determine: *We wanted to fix the price at $500.* **5.** [~ + *obj* + *on* + *obj*] to direct steadily: *His eyes fixed themselves on the distant ship.* **6.** [~ + *obj*] to make set or rigid; to put into permanent form: *What should we add to fix the cement?* **7.** [~ + *obj* + *on* + *obj*] to put or place (responsibility, blame, etc.) on a person: *fixed the blame for the fire on the prowler.* **8.** [~ + *obj*] to assign or refer to: *to fix a time for the meeting.* **9.** [~ + *obj*] to arrange or influence the outcome or action of, esp. dishonestly: *to fix a game.* **10.** to get (a meal) ready; prepare (food): [~ + *obj*]: *to fix dinner.* [~ + *obj* + *obj*]: *I'll fix you a drink.* **11.** [~ + *obj*] to get even with: *I'll fix you if you don't keep your promise.* **12.** [~ + *obj*] to castrate or spay: *The cat will have to be fixed so that it won't have kittens.* **13.** [*be* + ~*-ing* + *to* + *verb*] *Chiefly Southern U.S.* to prepare; plan: *I was just fixing to call you.* **14. fix on** or **upon,** [~ + *on* + *obj*] to decide on; determine: *We hadn't fixed on a date yet.* **15. fix up, a.** to make arrangements for: [~ + *obj* + *up*]: *We fixed him up to stay at a hotel.* **b.** to provide with an introduction to someone for a date: [~ + *obj* + *up*]: *I tried to fix him up with my cousin.* [~ + *up* + *obj*]: *fixed up several of the guys with dates.* **c.** [~ + *up* + *obj*] to mend or resolve: *Let's fix up our differences.* **—*n.*** [*count*] **16.** a position from which it is difficult to escape; predicament: *I'm in a bad fix.* **17.** a repair, adjustment, or solution, usually of an immediate nature: *a quick fix.* **18.** a charted position of a vessel or aircraft, determined by radar, or by taking bearings: *got a fix on the enemy vessel.* **19.** *Slang.* an injection of heroin or other narcotic.

-fix-, *root.* -*fix*- comes from Latin, where it has the meaning "fastened; put; placed." This meaning is found in such words as: AFFIX, FIXATION, INFIX, PREFIX, SUFFIX.

fix•ate (fik′sāt) /ˈfɪkseyt/ *v.* [~ + *on* + *obj*], **-at•ed, -at•ing.** to have a preoccupation with: *He has been fixating on becoming rich.* **—fix′at•ed,** *adj.*

fix•a•tion (fik sā′shən) /fɪkˈseyʃən/ *n.* [*count*] a preoccupation with one subject; obsession: *has a fixation about becoming fat.* See -FIX-.

fixed (fikst) /fɪkst/ *adj.* **1.** attached or placed so as to be firm and immovable; stationary: *fixed fortifications.* **2.** [*before a noun*] set or intent upon something; steadily directed: *a fixed stare.* **3.** not fluctuating or varying: *fixed income.* **4.** having the outcome arranged dishonestly in advance: *a fixed race.* **—fix•ed•ly** (fik′sid lē, fikst′lē) /ˈfɪksɪdliy, ˈfɪkstliy/ *adv.: I stared fixedly into the fire.*

fix•ings (fik′singz) /ˈfɪksɪŋz/ *n.* [*plural*] *Informal.* the necessary ingredients; the items to accompany something: *a turkey dinner with all the fixings.*

fix•i•ty (fik′si tē) /ˈfɪksɪtiy/ *n.* [*noncount*] the state or quality of being fixed; stability; permanence.

fix•ture (fiks′chər) /ˈfɪkstʃər/ *n.* [*count*] **1.** something securely attached or appended, such as to a wall: *a light fixture.* **2.** a person or thing long established in the same place or position: *She was a fixture at the license bureau for many years.*

fizz (fiz) /fɪz/ *v.* [*no obj*] **1.** to make a hissing or sputtering sound: *The soda fizzed in the glass.* **—*n.*** [*noncount*] **2.** a fizzing sound.

fiz•zle (fiz′əl) /ˈfɪzəl/ *v.*, **-zled, -zling,** *n.* **—*v.*** [*no obj*] **1.** to make a hissing or sputtering sound: *The wet match fizzled for a moment before expiring.* **2.** [~ (+ *out*)] to fail or expire feebly after a good start: *The enthusiasm soon fizzled (out).* **—*n.*** [*count*] **3.** an instance of fizzling: *The hot coals made a fizzle as they hit the water.* **4.** a failure; fiasco: *The play was a fizzle.*

fjord or **fiord** (fyôrd, fyōrd) /fyɔrd, fyowrd/ *n.* [*count*] a long narrow branch of the sea bordered by steep cliffs.

FL, an abbreviation of: Florida.

fl., an abbreviation of: **1.** floor. **2.** fluid.

Fla., an abbreviation of: Florida.

flab (flab) /flæb/ *n.* [*noncount*] loose, excessive flesh.

flab•ber•gast (flab′ər gast′) /ˈflæbərˌgæst/ *v.* [~ + *obj*] to overcome with surprise and bewilderment; astound: *The news of his promotion flabbergasted me.*

flab•by (flab′ē) /ˈflæbiy/ *adj.*, **-bi•er, -bi•est.** lacking firmness or tone; flaccid: *flabby muscles.* **—flab′bi•ness,** *n.* [*noncount*]

flac•cid (flak′sid, flas′id) /ˈflæksɪd, ˈflæsɪd/ *adj.* **1.** soft and limp: *flaccid skin.* **2.** weak: *a flaccid defense.*

flack (flak) /flæk/ *n.* *Slang.* **1.** [*count*] PRESS AGENT. **2.** [*noncount*] FLAK.

flag[1] (flag) /flæg/ *n.*, *v.*, **flagged, flag•ging. —*n.*** [*count*] **1.** a usually rectangular piece of cloth marked with distinctive colors or designs and used as a symbol, as of a nation, or as a means of signaling: *The American flag has both stars and stripes.* **—*v.*** [~ + *obj*] **2.** to signal or warn with or as if with a flag: [~ *(+ down) + obj*]: *to flag (down) a taxi.* [~ + *obj (+ down)*]: *to flag a taxi (down).* **3.** to mark (a page, file, card, etc.) for attention, as by attaching protruding tabs: *I flagged the section of the paper I thought you should read.*

flag[2] (flag) /flæg/ *v.* [*no obj*], **flagged, flag•ging.** to fall off in vigor, energy or interest; droop: *Attendance flagged after the team lost.*

flag•el•late (flaj′ə lāt′) /'flædʒəˌleyt/ *v.* [~ + *obj*], **-lat•ed, -lat•ing.** to punish with or as if with a whip: *flagellating his opponent.* —**flag•el•la•tion** (flaj′ə lā′shən) /ˌflædʒə'leyʃən/ *n.* [*noncount*]

flag•on (flag′ən) /'flægən/ *n.* [*count*] a container for holding liquids, esp. one with a handle, a spout, and a cover.

flag•pole (flag′pōl′) /'flægˌpowl/ *n.* [*count*] **1.** a staff or pole on which a flag is displayed. **—*Idiom.* 2. run (something) up the flagpole,** [*run + obj + up + the + ~*] to announce (a proposal or idea) as a test to gauge reactions: *Let's run the plan up the flagpole and see if the boss likes it.*

fla•grant (flā′grənt) /'fleygrənt/ *adj.* [*before a noun*] shockingly noticeable or evident; obvious; glaring: *a flagrant error.* —**fla′grant•ly,** *adv.*

fla•gran•te de•lic•to (flə gran′tē di lik′tō) /flə'græntiy dɪ'lɪktow/ *adv.* in the very act of committing an offense.

flag•ship (flag′ship′) /'flægˌʃɪp/ *n.* [*count*] **1.** a ship carrying the commander of a fleet, squadron, or the like. **2.** the best or most important one of a group or system: *The largest store is the flagship of the chain.*

flag•stone (flag′stōn′) /'flægˌstown/ *n.* [*count*] a flat stone slab used esp. for paving.

flail (flāl) /fleyl/ *n.* [*count*] **1.** an instrument for threshing grain by hand. **—*v.* 2.** to beat or swing as if with a flail: [*no obj*]: *The baby's arms were flailing about.* [~ + *obj*]: *The baby flailed his arms around. Her arms flailed the water.*

flair (flâr) /flɛər/ *n.* **1.** [*count*] a natural talent or ability; knack: *a flair for comedy.* **2.** [*noncount*] a sense of style: *She dresses with flair.*

flak or **flack** (flak) /flæk/ *n.* [*noncount*] **1.** antiaircraft fire. **2.** strong criticism or opposition: *The candidate took a lot of flak from the press.*

flake (flāk) /fleyk/ *n., v.,* **flaked, flak•ing. —*n.*** [*count*] **1.** a small, flat, thin piece: *a few flakes of snow.* **2.** *Slang.* an eccentric person; screwball. **—*v.*** [*no obj*] **3.** to peel off, fall in, or form into flakes: *Cook until the fish flakes easily with a fork.* —**flak′y,** *adj.,* **-i•er, -i•est.**

flam•bé (fläm bā′) /flɑm'bey/ *adj., v.,* **-béed, -bé•ing. —*adj.* 1.** (of food) served in flaming liquor. **—*v.*** [~ + *obj*] **2.** to pour liquor over and ignite: *The waiter flambéed the dessert and brought it flaming to the table.*

flam•boy•ant (flam boi′ənt) /flæm'bɔyənt/ *adj.* strikingly bold or brilliant; showy: *flamboyant clothes; flamboyant behavior.* —**flam•boy′ance,** *n.* [*noncount*] —**flam•boy′ant•ly,** *adv.*

flame (flām) /fleym/ *n., v.,* **flamed, flam•ing. —*n.*** [*count*] **1.** a portion of burning gas or vapor: *the flame of a match.* **2.** Often, **flames.** [*plural*] the state or condition of blazing combustion: *a house in flames.* **3.** intense ardor, zeal, or passion: *The flame of ambition.* **4.** sweetheart: *an old flame of mine from high school.* **—*v.*** [*no obj*] **5.** to burn with or burst into flames: *The gasoline flamed suddenly.* **6.** to glow like flame: *My face flamed scarlet.*

fla•men•co (flə meng′kō) /flə'mɛŋkow/ *n.* [*noncount*], *pl.* **-cos.** a Spanish dance marked by vigorous handclapping and stamping of the feet.

flame•throw•er (flām′thrō′ər) /'fleymˌθrowər/ *n.* [*count*] a device that sprays ignited fuel for some distance.

flam•ing (flā′ming) /'fleymɪŋ/ *adj.* [*before a noun*] **1.** burning; fiery: *flaming wreckage.* **2.** violent; intense: *a flaming rage.*

fla•min•go (flə ming′gō) /flə'mɪŋgow/ *n.* [*count*], *pl.* **-gos, -goes.** a wading bird having webbed feet, a bill bent downward at the tip, and pinkish to scarlet feathers.

flam•ma•ble (flam′ə bəl) /'flæməbəl/ *adj.* easily set on fire; combustible: *flammable rags.* —**flam•ma•bil•i•ty** (flam′ə bil′i tē) /ˌflæmə'bɪlɪtiy/ *n.* [*noncount*] **—Usage.** See INFLAMMABLE.

flange (flanj) /flændʒ/ *n.* [*count*] a projecting rim, collar, or ridge such as on a shaft, pipe, machine housing, etc., to give strength or support: *The flange of a train wheel keeps the wheel on the track.*

flank (flangk) /flæŋk/ *n.* [*count*] **1.** a side, esp. the side of an animal or a person between the ribs and hip. **2.** a cut of meat from the flank of an animal. **3.** the extreme right or left side of a military formation: *reinforced the left flank with more troops.* **—*v.*** [~ + *obj*] **4.** to stand or be placed at the flank or side of: *Two policemen flanked the mayor.* **5.** to pass around the flank of: *flanked his opponent's army and cut them off.*

flan•nel (flan′l) /'flænl/ *n.* **1.** [*noncount*] a warm, soft, napped fabric of wool or cotton. **2. flannels,** [*plural*] a garment, esp. trousers, made of flannel.

flan•nel•et or **flan•nel•ette** (flan′l et′) /ˌflænl'ɛt/ *n.* [*noncount*] a warm soft cotton fabric.

flap (flap) /flæp/ *v.,* **flapped, flap•ping,** *n.* **—*v.* 1.** to (cause to) swing back and forth loosely: [*no obj*]: *A loose shutter flapped noisily.* [~ + *obj*]: *The wind flapped the loose shutter.* **2.** to (cause to) move up and down, such as wings or arms: [*no obj*]: *The great bird's wings flapped.* [~ + *obj*]: *It flapped its wings once.* **—*n.*** [*count*] **3.** something flat and broad that is attached at one side only and hangs loosely or covers an opening: *the flap on a jacket pocket.* **4.** a flapping motion or sound: *the flap of wings.* **5.** *Informal.* a state of excitement: *The town was in a flap over the scandals.*

flap•jack (flap′jak′) /'flæpˌdʒæk/ *n.* [*count*] griddlecake; pancake.

flap•per (flap′ər) /'flæpər/ *n.* [*count*] **1.** something broad and flat used for striking or for making a noise by striking. **2.** a young woman who went against conventional behavior in the 1920's.

flare (flâr) /flɛər/ *v.,* **flared, flar•ing,** *n.* **—*v.*** [*no obj*] **1.** [~ *(+ up)*] to blaze with a burst of flame: *The fire flared (up) suddenly.* **2.** to burn unsteadily: *candles flaring in the wind.* **3.** [~ *(+ up/out)*] to burst out in sudden, fierce activity or emotion: *Tempers flared (up).* **4.** [~ *(+ out)*] to spread gradually outward: *bell-bottomed trousers that flare (out) at the ankles.* **—*n.* 5.** [*noncount*] a flaring or swaying flame or light. **6.** [*noncount*] a sudden blaze or burst of flame. **7. a.** [*noncount*] a blaze of fire or light used as a signal or for illumination. **b.** [*count*] a device or substance producing such a blaze: *The ship sent up warning flares.* **8.** [*count*] an outward curve or spread: *the flare of a skirt.*

flare•up (flâr′up′) /'flɛərˌʌp/ *n.* [*count*] **1.** a sudden flaring up of flame or light. **2.** a sudden outbreak: *a flareup of measles in the countryside.*

flash (flash) /flæʃ/ *n.* [*count*] **1.** a brief, sudden burst of bright light or flame: *a flash of lightning.* **2.** a sudden, brief outburst or display: *a flash of humor; a flash of anger.* **3.** a very brief moment; instant: *Quick as a flash, she was gone.* **4.** a sudden thought, insight, or vision: *a flash of inspiration.* **5.** a brief dispatch giving preliminary news of an important story: *a news flash from election headquarters.* **6.** FLASHLIGHT. **7. a.** bright artificial light thrown briefly upon a subject during a photographic exposure. **b.** the bulb or mechanism producing such light. **—*v.* 8.** to (cause to) break forth into sudden flame or light, esp. briefly or irregularly: [*no obj*]: *The light on the police car was flashing.* [~ + *obj*]: *The police car flashed its lights.* **9.** [*no obj*] to gleam: *The cat's eyes flashed in the darkness.* **10.** [~ + *obj*] to send forth like a flash: *She flashed a dazzling smile.* **11.** [*no obj*] to appear suddenly: *The answer flashed into his mind.* **12.** [~ + *obj*] to send a message quickly by electronic means: *The reporters flashed the story to the studio in New York.* **13.** [~ + *obj*] to display briefly: *She flashed her ID card at the guard.* **—*adj.* 14.** [*before a noun*] sudden and brief: *a flash fire; a flash flood.* **—*Idiom.* 15. flash in the pan,** [*count*] **a.** a brief, intense, but pointless effort that produces small and meaningless results: *The plan was no more than a flash in the pan.* **b.** one whose promise or success is temporary: *another politician who is just a flash in the pan.*

flash•back (flash′bak′) /'flæʃˌbæk/ *n.* **1. a.** [*noncount*] a technique in literature or film in which an earlier event is depicted after the time it actually occurred. **b.** [*count*] the scene so shown: *In a flashback we see her remembering that summer at the beach.* **2.** [*count*] a vivid recollection of a past event: *a sudden flashback of the accident.*

flash•bulb or **flash bulb** (flash′bulb′) /'flæʃˌbʌlb/ *n.* [*count*] a glass bulb, filled with oxygen and wire or foil, that when electrically ignited provides light for a photographic subject.

flash•card or **flash card** (flash′kärd′) /'flæʃˌkɑrd/ *n.* [*count*] a card bearing words, numerals, etc., displayed briefly to a student as a learning aid.

flash•er (flash′ər) /ˈflæʃər/ *n.* [*count*] a device that causes lights on a vehicle to flash, esp. as a warning.

flash•gun (flash′gun′) /ˈflæʃˌgʌn/ *n.* [*count*] a device that discharges a flashbulb and operates a camera shutter at the same time.

flash•ing (flash′ing) /ˈflæʃɪŋ/ *n.* [*noncount*] pieces of sheet metal or the like used to seal joints and angles, as on a roof.

flash•light (flash′līt′) /ˈflæʃˌlayt/ *n.* [*count*] Also called, *esp. Brit.,* **torch.** a small portable electric lamp powered by dry batteries.

flash′ point′ or **flash′point′,** *n.* [*count*] **1.** the lowest temperature at which a liquid will give off sufficient vapor to ignite when a flame is applied to it. **2.** a point at which a situation can flare up: *at a flashpoint in the budget crisis.*

flash•y (flash′ē) /ˈflæʃiy/ *adj.,* **-i•er, -i•est. 1.** briefly and superficially brilliant: *a flashy performance.* **2.** overly showy and tasteless: *flashy clothes.*

flask (flask) /flæsk/ *n.* [*count*] **1.** a bottle, usually of glass, having a rounded body and a narrow neck. **2.** a flat metal or glass bottle for carrying in the pocket.

flat[1] (flat) /flæt/ *adj.,* **flat•ter, flat•test,** *adv., n.* —*adj.* **1.** horizontally level: *flat, white roofs on the houses of the Greek town.* **2.** level, even, or smooth in surface, such as land or tabletops: *the flat prairie.* **3.** lying horizontally and at full length: *flat on the floor.* **4.** not deep, high, or thick: *stacks of flat boxes at the pizzeria.* **5.** spread out, as an unrolled map or the open hand: *The map was flat on the table.* **6.** with the air out; deflated; collapsed: *a flat tire.* **7.** [*before a noun*] absolute; downright; complete; definite: *issued a flat denial of the charges.* **8.** [*before a noun*] without the possibility of change or variation; fixed: *The hotel charged a flat rate.* **9.** lacking vitality or animation: *a flat play.* **10.** (of a carbonated beverage) having lost its bubbles: *The soda is flat.* **11.** pointless, as a remark or joke: *a flat joke.* **12.** (of paint) without gloss; not shiny; matte. **13.** lacking variation in pitch; monotonous: *answered in a flat, bored voice.* **14. a.** [*after a letter indicating tone*] (of a tone) lowered a half step in pitch: *B flat.* **b.** below an intended pitch, such as a note; too low (opposed to *sharp*): *The chorus was a little flat on that last song.* —*adv.* **15.** in a flat position; horizontally; levelly: *The trees had been laid flat by the hurricane.* **16.** completely; utterly: *flat broke until payday.* **17.** [*after a measurement of time*] exactly; precisely: *I got there in two minutes flat.* **18.** below the true pitch: *to sing flat.* —*n.* [*count*] **19.** a woman's shoe with a very low heel or no heel. **20.** a flat surface, side, or part of anything: *She held the stone in the flat of her hand.* **21.** flat or level ground: *salt flats.* **22. a.** (in musical notation) the character ♭, which indicates that the pitch of a note is lowered by one half step. **b.** a tone that is one half step below another. **23.** an automobile tire that has lost the air. —***Idiom.*** **24. fall flat,** [*no obj*] to fail completely and noticeably: *an attempt at humor that fell flat.* **25. flat out,** *Informal.* **a.** without hesitation; directly or openly: *The spy told us flat out he had been a double agent.* **b.** at full speed or with maximum effort: *We drove flat out to get there by afternoon.* —**flat′ly,** *adv.* —**flat′ness,** *n.* [*noncount*]

flat[2] (flat) /flæt/ *n.* [*count*] a residential apartment: *rented a flat in the city.*

-flat-, *root.* *-flat-* comes from Latin, where it has the meaning "blow; wind." This meaning is found in such words as: DEFLATE, INFLATE.

flat•bed (flat′bed′) /ˈflætˌbɛd/ *n.* [*count*] a truck or trailer having a body in the form of an open platform.

flat•boat (flat′bōt′) /ˈflætˌbowt/ *n.* [*count*] a large, flat-bottomed boat for use in shallow water, esp. on rivers.

flat•car (flat′kär′) /ˈflætˌkɑr/ *n.* [*count*] a railroad car made up of a platform without sides or top.

flat•fish (flat′fish′) /ˈflætˌfɪʃ/ *n., pl.* (*esp. when thought of as a group*) **-fish,** (*esp. for kinds or species*) **-fish•es.** any of various fishes, such as the flounders, that have as adults a greatly flattened body with both eyes on the upper side.

flat•foot (flat′fo͝ot′ *or, for 1,* -fo͝ot′) /ˈflætˌfʊt *or, for 1,* -ˈfʊt/ *n., pl.* **-feet** for 1, **-foots** for 2. **1. a.** [*noncount*] a condition in which the arch of the foot is flattened so that the entire sole rests upon the ground. **b.** [*count*] Also, **flat′ foot′.** a foot with such an arch. **2.** [*count*] *Slang.* a police officer.

flat•foot•ed (flat′fo͝ot′id) /ˈflætˌfʊtɪd/ *adj.* **1.** affected with flatfoot. **2.** firm; explicit; definite: *a flatfooted denial.* —***Idiom.*** **3. catch (someone) flatfooted,** catch someone unprepared or by surprise: *This latest scandal caught him flatfooted.*

flat•i•ron (flat′ī′ərn) /ˈflætˌayərn/ *n.* [*count*] an iron for pressing clothes.

flat′-out′, *adj.* *Informal.* **1.** using full speed or all of one's resources: *a flat-out effort.* **2.** complete: *a flat-out forgery.* See FLAT OUT under **flat**[1].

flat•ten (flat′n) /ˈflætn̩/ *v.* **1.** to (cause to) become flat: [~ (+ *out*) + *obj*]: *Flatten (out) the pizza dough with your hands.* [~ (+ *out*)]: *They flattened (out) against the wall and strained to see who was coming.* **2.** [~ + *obj*] to knock down: *The bulldozer flattened the barn.*

flat•ter (flat′ər) /ˈflætər/ *v.* **1.** to praise or compliment insincerely or excessively: [~ + *obj*]: *He always flatters her by constantly praising her looks.* **2.** [~ + *obj; usually: be* + ~*-ed*] to please or gratify by compliments or attentions: *I was flattered by the invitation.* **3.** [~ + *obj*] to represent or show favorably, esp. too favorably: *The portrait flatters her.* **4.** [~ + *oneself* + *that clause*] to feel satisfaction with (oneself), sometimes mistakenly: *He flattered himself that the speech had gone well.* —**flat′ter•ing,** *adj.*

flat•ter•y (flat′ə rē) /ˈflætəriy/ *n.* [*noncount*] **1.** the act of flattering. **2.** excessive or insincere praise.

flat•top (flat′top′) /ˈflætˌtɒp/ *n.* [*count*] **1.** *Informal.* an aircraft carrier. **2.** a crew cut in which the hair is cut flat across the top.

flaunt (flônt) /flɔnt/ *v.* [~ + *obj*] to show or display too much: *to flaunt her wealth by wearing flashy diamonds.*

flau•tist (flô′tist, flou′-) /ˈflɔtɪst, ˈflaw-/ *n.* FLUTIST.

fla•vor (flā′vər) /ˈfleyvər/ *n.* **1.** taste, esp. the distinctive taste of something in the mouth: [*count*]: *The shop sells ice cream in eight flavors.* [*noncount*]: *This stew has no flavor.* **2.** [*noncount*] the characteristic quality of a thing: *capturing the true flavor of your experience in the jungle.* **3.** [*count*] a particular quality that one notices in a thing: *language having a strong nautical flavor.* —*v.* [~ + *obj*] **4.** to give flavor to (something): *flavored the icing with vanilla.* Also, *esp. Brit.,* **flavour.** —**fla′vor•ful,** *adj.* —**fla′vor•less,** *adj.*

fla•vor•ing (flā′vər ing) /ˈfleyvərɪŋ/ *n.* [*noncount*] a substance used to give a particular flavor to food or drink.

flaw (flô) /flɔ/ *n.* [*count*] **1.** a feature that causes an imperfection in something; defect; blemish: *a flaw in the diamond.* **2.** an undesirable quality in character or personality: *a serious character flaw.* —**flawed,** *adj.* —**flaw′less,** *adj.* —**flaw′less•ly,** *adv.*

flax (flaks) /flæks/ *n.* [*noncount*] **1.** a plant with blue flowers that is cultivated for its fiber, used for making linen yarn. **2.** the fiber of this plant.

flax•en (flak′sən) /ˈflæksən/ *adj.* **1.** made of or resembling flax. **2.** pale yellow in color: *flaxen hair.*

flay (flā) /fley/ *v.* [~ + *obj*] **1.** to strip off the skin or outer covering of, such as by whipping: *flayed the prisoners with whips.* **2.** to criticize or scold harshly: *The critics flayed the movie.*

flea (flē) /fliy/ *n.* [*count*] a small, wingless, bloodsucking insect, noted for its ability to leap.

flea•bag (flē′bag′) /ˈfliyˌbæg/ *n.* [*count*] *Slang.* a cheap, run-down hotel or rooming house.

flea′ mar′ket, *n.* [*count*] a market, often outdoors, with a number of stalls selling old or used articles.

fleck (flek) /flɛk/ *n.* [*count*] **1.** a speck; a small bit: *a fleck of dirt.* **2.** a spot or small patch of color, light, etc.: *A few flecks of snow.* —*v.* [~ + *obj; usually: be* + ~*-ed*] **3.** to mark with flecks; spot: *The leaves were flecked with sunlight.*

-flect-, *root.* *-flect-* comes from Latin, where it has the meaning "bend." It is related to -FLEX-. This meaning is found in such words as: DEFLECT, GENUFLECT, INFLECT, REFLECT.

fledg•ling (flej′ling) /ˈflɛdʒlɪŋ/ *n.* [*count*] **1.** a young bird that has recently grown its feathers. **2.** an inexperienced person; beginner. —*adj.* [*before a noun*] **3.** new; inexperienced: *a fledgling pilot; a fledgling business.* Also, *esp. Brit.,* **fledge′ling.**

flee (flē) /fliy/ *v.,* **fled** (fled) /flɛd/ **flee•ing.** to run away (from), as from danger or pursuers; take flight (from); escape: [*no obj*]: *They fled by jumping on a boat.* [~ + *from* + *obj*]: *They fled from their home.* [~ + *to* + *obj*]: *tried to flee to a safe country.* [~ + *obj*]: *They fled the country.*

fleece (flēs) /fliys/ *n., v.,* **fleeced, fleec•ing.** —*n.* **1.** [*noncount*] the coat of wool that covers a sheep or a similar animal. **2.** [*count*] a piece of wool shorn from a sheep. —*v.* [~ + *obj* (+ *of*)] **3.** to take money or belongings by dishonesty, fraud, or deception; swindle:

The con artists fleeced the elderly couple of their savings. —**fleec′y,** *adj.,* **-i•er, -i•est**: *a blue sky with white, fleecy clouds.*

fleet[1] (flēt) /fliyt/ *n.* [*count*] **1.** a unit of naval ships grouped under one commander: *the Pacific fleet.* **2.** all the naval ships of a nation; navy: *the American fleet.* **3.** a group of vehicles under one management: *a fleet of cabs.*

fleet[2] (flēt) /fliyt/ *adj.,* **-er, -est.** swift; rapid: *a fleet horse.* —**fleet′ness,** *n.* [*noncount*]

fleet•ing (flē′ting) /ˈfliytɪŋ/ *adj.* passing swiftly; vanishing quickly: *a fleeting glance.* —**fleet′ing•ly,** *adv.*

flesh (flesh) /flɛʃ/ *n.* [*noncount*] **1.** the soft substance of an animal body between the skin and the skeleton, esp. muscular tissue. **2.** this substance used as an article of food, usually excluding fish and sometimes fowl; meat. **3.** [*the* + ~] the body, esp. as distinguished from the spirit or soul: *The spirit is willing but the flesh is weak.* **4.** humankind: *She said that to die was the way of all flesh.* **5.** the soft, pulpy portion of a fruit or vegetable: *the flesh of the peach.* —*v.* **6. flesh out, a.** to give dimension or substance to; develop: [~ + *out* + *obj*]: *Flesh out your essay with more details.* [~ + *obj* + *out*]: *to flesh the essay out.* **b.** [*no obj*] to become more fleshy or substantial: *He had fleshed out considerably over the years.* —***Idiom.*** **7. in the flesh,** present and alive before one's eyes; in person: *She is even more beautiful in the flesh.* **8. press the flesh,** *Informal.* to shake hands, as with voters during a political campaign.

flesh′ and blood′, *n.* [*noncount*] **1.** [*one's* + ~] close relatives: *my own flesh and blood.* **2.** the human body or nature: *more than flesh and blood can endure.* **3.** substance: *The concept lacks flesh and blood.*

flesh•ly (flesh′lē) /ˈflɛʃliy/ *adj.,* **-li•er, -li•est.** of or relating to the flesh or body, esp. to sensual or sexual aspects.

flesh•pot (flesh′pot′) /ˈflɛʃˌpɒt/ *n.* [*count*] a place offering luxurious and unrestrained pleasure or amusement.

flesh•y (flesh′ē) /ˈflɛʃiy/ *adj.,* **-i•er, -i•est. 1.** having much flesh; plump; fat: *fleshy cheeks.* **2.** pulpy, as a fruit, or thick and tender, as a succulent leaf: *fleshy fruit.*

fleur-de-lis also **fleur-de-lys** (flûr′dl ē′, -dl ēs′, flo͝or′-) /ˌflɜrdlˈiy, -dlˈiys, ˌflʊr-/ *n.* [*count*], *pl.* **fleurs-de-lis** or **fleurs-de-lys** (-dl ēz′) /-dlˈiyz/. a representation of an iris with three petals tied by a band, used as a design or symbol.

flew (flo͞o) /fluw/ *v.* a pt. of FLY[1].

flex (fleks) /flɛks/ *v.* **1.** to bend, as a part of the body: [~ + *obj*]: *I needed to flex my legs after the long drive.* [*no obj*]: *My fingers wouldn't flex.* **2.** [~ + *obj*] to tighten (a muscle) by contraction: *He flexed his biceps.* See -FLEX-.

-flex-, *root.* *-flex-* comes from Latin, where it has the meaning "bend." It is related to -FLECT-. This meaning is found in such words as: CIRCUMFLEX, FLEX, FLEXIBLE, REFLEX, REFLEXIVE.

flex•i•ble (flek′sə bəl) /ˈflɛksəbəl/ *adj.* **1.** capable of being bent without breaking: *That hose is flexible.* **2.** that can be changed; adaptable: *a flexible schedule.* **3.** willing to give in; accommodating: *a flexible personality.* —**flex•i•bil•i•ty** (flek′sə bil′i tē) /ˌflɛksəˈbɪlɪtiy/ *n.* [*noncount*] See -FLEX-.

flex•time (fleks′tīm′) /ˈflɛksˌtaym/ also **flex•i•time** (flek′si-) /ˈflɛksɪ-/ *n.* [*noncount*] a system that allows an employee to choose the hours for starting and leaving work.

flib•ber•ti•gib•bet (flib′ər tē jib′it) /ˈflɪbərtiyˌdʒɪbɪt/ *n.* [*count*] a flighty, silly person.

flick[1] (flik) /flɪk/ *n.* [*count*] **1.** a sudden light blow or tap, such as with a whip or the finger. **2.** the sound made by such a blow or tap. **3.** a light and rapid movement: *a flick of the wrist.* —*v.* **4.** [~ + *(away* +*) obj*] to strike, remove, propel, or operate with a sudden light, smart stroke: *flicked the horse with a whip; to flick (away) a crumb.* **5.** [~ + *obj*] to cause to move rapidly, suddenly, or jerkily: *a bird flicking its tail.* **6.** [~ + *through* + *obj*] to turn pages rapidly or idly: *to flick through a magazine.*

flick[2] (flik) /flɪk/ *n.* [*count*] *Slang.* a movie.

flick•er[1] (flik′ər) /ˈflɪkər/ *v.* [*no obj*] **1.** to burn unsteadily; shine with a wavering light: *The candle flickered in the wind.* **2.** to flutter: *Her eyelids flickered.* **3.** to appear quickly and briefly: *A smile flickered on his face.* —*n.* [*count*] **4.** an unsteady flame or light. **5.** a flickering movement. **6.** a brief appearance or feeling: *saw a flicker of interest in her eyes.*

flick•er[2] (flik′ər) /ˈflɪkər/ *n.* [*count*] a North American woodpecker having yellow or red underwings.

flied (flīd) /flayd/ *v.* a pt. and pp. of FLY[1].

fli•er or **fly•er** (flī′ər) /ˈflayər/ *n.* [*count*] **1.** a person, animal, or thing that flies. **2.** an aviator or pilot. **3.** a small piece of paper with a message or information on it, handed out or attached to a noticeboard.

flight[1] (flīt) /flayt/ *n.* **1.** [*noncount*] the act, manner, or power of flying. **2.** [*count*] the distance covered or the course taken by a flying object: *a 500-mile flight.* **3.** [*count*] a trip by or in an airplane, esp. a scheduled trip on an airline: *I had a long, rough flight.* **4.** [*count*] a number of beings or things flying or passing through the air together: *a flight of geese.* **5.** [*count*] a journey into or through outer space: *a space flight.* **6.** [*count*] swift movement, transition, or progression: *the flight of time.* **7.** [*count*] an act of going beyond the ordinary bounds of the mind: *a flight of the imagination.* **8.** [*count*] a series of steps, as between one floor or landing of a building and the next: *a flight of stairs.*

flight[2] (flīt) /flayt/ *n.* [*count*] **1.** an act or instance of fleeing or running away: *flight from persecution.* —***Idiom.*** **2. take flight,** [*no obj*] to retreat; run away; flee.

flight′ attend′ant, *n.* [*count*] an airline employee who attends to passengers' comfort on a flight.

flight′ bag′, *n.* [*count*] a lightweight shoulder bag for carrying small items aboard an aircraft.

flight′ deck′, *n.* [*count*] **1.** the upper deck of an aircraft carrier, designed as a runway. **2.** a compartment in certain aircraft containing the instruments and controls.

flight•less (flīt′lis) /ˈflaytlɪs/ *adj.* incapable of flying: *Penguins are flightless birds.*

flight•y (flī′tē) /ˈflaytiy/ *adj.,* **-i•er, -i•est.** unstable; skittish: *He's too flighty to deal with this problem.* —**flight′i•ness,** *n.* [*noncount*]

flim•flam (flim′flam′) /ˈflɪmˌflæm/ *n.* *Informal.* a deception; swindle: [*count*]: *a flimflam to defraud tourists of money.* [*noncount*]: *a master of flimflam.*

flim•sy (flim′zē) /ˈflɪmziy/ *adj.,* **-si•er, -si•est. 1.** without material strength or solidity: *a flimsy fabric.* **2.** inadequate; not convincing: *a flimsy excuse.* —**flim•si•ly** (flim′zə lē) /ˈflɪmzəliy/ *adv.* —**flim′si•ness,** *n.* [*noncount*]

flinch (flinch) /flɪntʃ/ *v.* to draw back or shrink, as from something dangerous, painful, or difficult: [*no obj*]: *The dog flinched at the noise.* [~ + *from* + *obj*]: *I won't flinch from hard work.*

fling (fling) /flɪŋ/ *v.,* **flung** (flung) /flʌŋ/ **fling•ing,** *n.* —*v.* [~ + *obj*] **1.** to throw or cast with force, violence, or without care: *flung the dishes to the floor.* **2.** [~ + *oneself*] to move (oneself) violently or abruptly: *flung herself from the room.* **3.** to put or send suddenly or without preparation: *to fling someone into jail.* **4.** [~ + *oneself*] to involve (oneself) actively in an undertaking: *He flung himself into writing the book.* **5.** [~ + *out* + *obj*] to throw aside or off: *We flung out a lot of old books.* **6. fling off** or **on,** to take off, or put on, (one's clothes) quickly and carelessly: [~ + *off/on* + *obj*]: *She flung off her clothes and jumped in the shower. I flung on a sweater and left.* [~ + *obj* + *off/on*]: *to fling it off.* —*n.* [*count*] **7.** an act or instance of flinging. **8.** a short period of unrestrained self-indulgence: *a last fling before marriage.* **9.** an attempt at something: *took a fling at playwriting.*

flint (flint) /flɪnt/ *n.* **1.** [*noncount*] a hard gray stone, a form of silica. **2.** [*count*] a piece of this, esp. when it is used for striking fire.

flint•lock (flint′lok′) /ˈflɪntˌlɒk/ *n.* [*count*] a gun used in former times, with a flint for igniting the charge.

flint•y (flin′tē) /ˈflɪntiy/ *adj.,* **-i•er, -i•est.** unmerciful; uncaring; hard: *He stared back at us with cold, flinty eyes.*

flip (flip) /flɪp/ *v.,* **flipped, flip•ping,** *n., adj.,* **flip•per, flip•pest.** —*v.* **1.** to turn over by or as if by tossing: [~ + *obj*]: *to flip a coin.* [~ + *obj* + *obj*]: *She flipped the dog a morsel.* **2.** [~ + *obj*] to move or activate with a sudden stroke: *to flip a switch.* **3.** to (cause to) turn over or do a somersault: [*no obj*]: *He rolled over the bar and flipped onto the floor.* [~ + *obj*]: *flipped her opponent over her shoulder.* **4.** to read or look at rapidly: [*no obj*]: *to flip through a magazine.* [~ + *obj*]: *He flipped the pages.* **5.** *Slang.* **a.** [*no obj*] to react with astonishment or delight: *I flipped when I heard the good news.* **b.** [~ + *for/over* + *obj*] to fall in love with (someone): *He really flipped over her.* **c. flip out,** to (cause to) become irrational, angry, or upset: [*no obj*]: *The boss flipped out when he heard you lost the account.* [~ + *obj* + *out*]: *This news will flip him out.* [~ + *out* + *obj*]: *That news would flip out anybody.* —*n.* [*count*] **6.** an act or instance of flipping. **7.** a somersault, esp. one performed in the air. —*adj.* **8.** flippant: *a flip answer.* —***Idiom.*** **9. flip one's lid** or **wig,** *Slang.* to lose control of one's temper.

flip′-flop′, *n., v.,* **-flopped, -flop•ping.** —*n.* [*count*] **1.** a sudden or unexpected reversal, such as of opinion or policy. **2.** a backward somersault. **3.** a flat rubber sandal with a thong fitting between the first two toes. —*v.* [*no obj*] **4.** to perform a flip-flop: *The president flip-flopped on the question.*

flip•pant (flip′ənt) /ˈflɪpənt/ *adj.* lacking in respect or seriousness: *a flippant answer.* —**flip′pant•ly,** *adv.*

flip•per (flip′ər) /ˈflɪpər/ *n.* [*count*] **1.** a broad flat limb, such as of a seal or whale, adapted for swimming. **2.** one of a pair of paddlelike devices worn on the feet in scuba diving and swimming.

flip′ side′, *n.* [*count*] **1.** the reverse and usually less popular side of a phonograph record. **2.** [*often: the* + ~] an opposite or reverse side or effect, often an undesirable one: *The flip side of fine dining is weight gain.*

flirt (flûrt) /flɜrt/ *v.* **1.** [*no obj*] to behave amorously toward someone in a casually playful manner. **2.** [~ + *with*] to consider without seriousness; trifle or toy with: *flirted with the idea of singing professionally* —*n.* [*count*] **3.** a person who is given to flirting; a tease. —**flir•ta′-tion,** *n.* [*noncount*]: *harmless office flirtation.* [*count*]: *minor flirtations with other workers.* —**flir•ta•tious** (flûr tā′-shəs) /flɜrˈteyʃəs/ *adj.* —**flir•ta′tious•ly,** *adv.*

flit (flit) /flɪt/ *v.* [*no obj*], **flit•ted, flit•ting.** to fly, move, or pass swiftly and lightly from one place or condition to another: *A smile flitted across his face.*

float (flōt) /flowt/ *v.* **1.** to (cause to) rest or remain on the surface of a liquid: [*no obj*]: *A ping-pong ball will float on water.* [~ + *obj*]: *Float the whipped cream on the coffee.* **2.** [*no obj*] to move gently on the surface of a liquid; drift along: *The raft floated downstream.* **3.** [*no obj*] to rest or move in a liquid, the air, etc.: *The balloon was floating away.* **4.** [*no obj*] to move lightly and gracefully: *She floated down the stairs.* **5.** [~ + *obj*] to issue (a security) on the stock market in order to raise money: *floating some bonds.* **6.** [~ + *obj*] to present for consideration: *I floated the idea to the committee.* —*n.* [*count*] **7.** something that floats, as a raft. **8.** (in a tank, cistern, etc.) a device, as a hollow ball, that automatically regulates the level, supply, or outlet of a liquid by floating. **9.** a piece of cork supporting a baited fishing line in the water. **10.** a vehicle bearing a display in a parade. **11.** a drink with ice cream floating in it: *a root-beer float.*

flock (flok) /flɒk/ *n.* [*count*] **1.** a group of animals, esp. sheep, goats, or birds, that live, travel, or feed together: *a flock of geese.* **2.** a large group of people or things: *flocks of sightseers.* **3.** a church congregation. —*v.* [*no obj*] **4.** to gather or go in a flock: *They flocked around the hero.*

flock•ing (flok′ing) /ˈflɒkɪŋ/ *n.* [*noncount*] a velvetlike pattern or coating on wallpaper, cloth, or metal.

floe (flō) /flow/ *n.* [*count*] a massive sheet of floating ice on the surface of the sea.

flog (flog, flôg) /flɒg, flɔg/ *v.* [~ + *obj*], **flogged, flog•ging.** **1.** to beat with or as if with a whip or stick: *flogging prisoners.* **2.** *Slang.* to sell, esp. aggressively: *flogged used cars for a living.*

flood (flud) /flʌd/ *n.* [*count*] **1.** a great flowing or overflowing of water, esp. over land not usually submerged. **2.** any great outpouring or stream: *a flood of tears.* **3.** **the Flood,** the great deluge recorded in the Bible as having occurred in the time of Noah. —*v.* **4.** to cover with or as if with a flood: [~ + *obj*]: *The river flooded the town.* [*no obj*]: *The basement flooded with water.* **5.** to overwhelm with an abundance of something: [~ + *obj*]: *flooded Congress with mail.* [*no obj*]: *Tourists flooded into town.*

flood•gate (flud′gāt′) /ˈflʌdˌgeyt/ *n.* [*count*] **1.** a gate regulating the flow of water. **2.** anything serving to control the passage of something: *opened (*or *closed) the floodgates to immigration.*

flood•light (flud′līt′) /ˈflʌdˌlayt/ *n., v.,* **-light•ed** or **-lit, -light•ing.** —*n.* [*count*] **1.** a lamp or projector that produces a light directed over a wide area. —*v.* [~ + *obj*] **2.** to illuminate with a floodlight: *to floodlight buildings.*

floor (flôr, flōr) /flɔr, flowr/ *n.* [*count*] **1.** the part of a room that forms its lower surface and upon which one walks: *The floor had a soft rug on it.* **2.** a continuous level surface extending horizontally throughout a building and making up one level or stage in the structure; story: *Our apartment is on the fifth floor.* **3.** the lower or bottom surface: *the ocean floor.* **4.** the part of a legislative chamber, meeting room, etc., where the members sit, and from which they speak: *on the Senate floor.* **5.** [*singular; the* + ~] the right of a member to speak at a meeting: *The senator from Alaska has the floor.* **6.** the area of a stock or commodity exchange, retail store, etc., where buying and selling or other business is conducted: *bought the sample off the showroom floor.* **7.** a base or minimum level: *The government established price and wage floors.* —*v.* [~ + *obj*] **8.** to cover or furnish with a floor. **9.** to knock down; flatten: *floored the bully with one punch.* **10.** to surprise and confuse; overwhelm: *I was floored by their generosity.* **11.** to push (the accelerator pedal) down to the floor of a vehicle, for maximum speed or power. —***Idiom.*** **12. mop** or **wipe the floor with,** [*mop/wipe* + *the* + ~ + *with* + *obj*] *Informal.* to overwhelm completely; defeat: *The team mopped the floor with their opponents.* **13. take the floor,** to arise to address a meeting: *The senator from Alaska took the floor.*

floor•board (flôr′bôrd′, flōr′bōrd′) /ˈflɔrˌbɔrd, ˈflowrˌbowrd/ *n.* [*count*] **1.** a board making up a wooden floor. **2.** the floor of an automobile.

floor•ing (flôr′ing, flōr′-) /ˈflɔrɪŋ, ˈflowr-/ *n.* **1.** [*count*] a floor. **2.** [*noncount*] materials for making floors: *pine flooring.*

floor′ show′, *n.* [*count*] a nightclub entertainment typically consisting of a series of singing, dancing, and often comedy acts.

floo•zy or **floo•zie** (flo͞o′zē) /ˈfluwziy/ *n.* [*count*], *pl.* **-zies.** *Slang.* a tawdry, usually immoral or promiscuous woman.

flop (flop) /flɒp/ *v.,* **flopped, flop•ping,** *n.* —*v.* **1.** to move, drop, or fall in a heavy, clumsy, or negligent manner: [*no obj*]: *The puppy just flopped around on the slippery floor. He flopped down on the couch.* [~ + *oneself*]: *He flopped himself down.* [~ + *obj*]: *He flopped the newspaper on my desk.* **2.** [*no obj*] to be a complete failure; fail: *The play flopped.* —*n.* [*count*] **3.** an act or sound of flopping. **4.** a complete failure: *The surprise party was a flop.*

flop•house (flop′hous′) /ˈflɒpˌhaws/ *n.* [*count*] a cheap, run-down hotel or rooming house.

flop•py (flop′ē) /ˈflɒpiy/ *adj.,* **-pi•er, -pi•est,** *n., pl.* **-pies.** —*adj.* **1.** tending to flop: *a dog with floppy ears.* —*n.* [*count*] **2.** FLOPPY DISK. —**flop•pi•ly** (flop′ə lē) /ˈflɒpəliy/ *adv.* —**flop′pi•ness,** *n.* [*noncount*]

flop′py disk′, *n.* [*count*] a thin, usually flexible plastic disk coated with magnetic material, for storing computer data and programs; diskette.

-flor-, *root.* *-flor-* comes from Latin, where it has the meaning "flower." This meaning is found in such words as: FLORA, FLORAL, FLORESCENCE, FLORID, FLORIST, FLOUR, FLOURISH, FLOWER.

flo•ra (flôr′ə, flōr′ə) /ˈflɔrə, ˈflowrə/ *n.* **1.** the plants of a particular region or time period, thought of as a group: [*noncount*]: *studying the flora of the desert.* [*plural*]: *The floras in this region are particularly varied.* **2.** [*noncount*] the microorganisms occurring on or within the human body: *intestinal flora.* See -FLOR-.

flo•ral (flôr′əl, flōr′-) /ˈflɔrəl, ˈflowr-/ *adj.* [*before a noun*] relating to or made up of flowers: *a floral wreath.* See -FLOR-.

flo•res•cence (flô res′əns, flō-, flə-) /flɔˈrɛsəns, flow-, flə-/ *n.* [*noncount*] the act, state, or period of flowering; bloom. —**flo•res′cent,** *adj.* See -FLOR-.

flor•id (flôr′id, flor′-) /ˈflɔrɪd, ˈflɒr-/ *adj.* **1.** reddish; ruddy; rosy: *a florid complexion.* **2.** flowery; excessively ornate; showy: *florid writing.* See -FLOR-.

flor•in (flôr′in, flor′-) /ˈflɔrɪn, ˈflɒr-/ *n.* [*count*] a former British coin equal to two shillings.

flo•rist (flôr′ist, flōr′-, flor′-) /ˈflɔrɪst, ˈflowr-, ˈflɒr-/ *n.* [*count*] a person who sells flowers and plants. See -FLOR-.

floss (flôs, flos) /flɔs, flɒs/ *n.* [*noncount*] **1.** embroidery thread of silk or cotton. **2.** strong thread used to clean between the teeth. —*v.* **3.** to use dental floss on (the teeth): [*no obj*]: *to floss regularly.* [~ + *obj*]: *flosses her teeth.*

flo•ta•tion (flō tā′shən) /flowˈteyʃən/ *n.* [*noncount*] the act or state of floating.

flo•til•la (flō til′ə) /flowˈtɪlə/ *n.* [*count*] **1.** a group of small ships. **2.** a group moving together: *a flotilla of cars.*

flot•sam (flot′səm) /ˈflɒtsəm/ *n.* [*noncount*] the part of the wreckage of a ship and its cargo found floating on the water. Compare JETSAM.

flounce[1] (flouns) /flawns/ *v.,* **flounced, flounc•ing,** *n.* —*v.* [*no obj*] **1.** to go with impatient, angry, exaggerated movements: *to flounce out of the room in a rage.* —*n.* [*count*] **2.** an act or instance of flouncing; a flouncing movement.

flounce[2] (flouns) /flawns/ *n.* [*count*] a strip of material gathered or pleated and attached along one edge, such as on the bottom of a skirt.

floun•der[1] (floun′dər) /ˈflawndər/ *v.* [*no obj*] **1.** to struggle to gain one's balance or move: *The cavalry began to flounder in the mud.* **2.** to act or speak clumsily or falteringly: *I floundered for an excuse.*

floun•der[2] (floun′dər) /ˈflawndər/ *n., pl.* (*esp. when thought of as a group*) **-der,** (*esp. for kinds or species*) **-ders.** any of various flatfishes valued as food.

flour (flouᵊr, flou′ər) /flawᵊr, ˈflawər/ *n.* [*noncount*] **1.** the finely ground meal of grain, esp. wheat, used in baking and cooking: *whole-wheat flour.* **—***v.* [~ + *obj*] **2.** to sprinkle or coat with flour. —**flour′y,** *adj.,* **-i•er, -i•est.** See -FLOR-.

flour•ish (flûr′ish, flur′-) /ˈflɜrɪʃ, ˈflʌr-/ *v.* **1.** [*no obj*] to be in a vigorous state; thrive: *a period in which art flourished.* **2.** [*no obj*] to be successful; prosper: *The business was flourishing.* **3.** [~ + *obj*] to hold (something) dramatically for all to see; brandish: *He flourished the trophy.* **—***n.* **4.** [*count*] a dramatic gesture: *With a flourish he placed the document in the attorney's hands.* **5.** [*count*] a decoration or extra feature added to writing: *Her signature has many flourishes.* **6.** [*count*] fanfare: *a flourish of trumpets.* **7.** [*noncount*] a condition or period of thriving: *a civilization in full flourish.* See -FLOR-.

flout (flout) /flawt/ *v.* [~ + *obj*] to treat with disdain or scorn; scoff at: *to flout the rules.*

flow (flō) /flow/ *v.* [*no obj*] **1.** to move in a stream: *The river flows to the sea.* **2.** to circulate: *Blood flows through our veins.* **3.** to stream or come forth: *Tears flowed from his eyes.* **4.** to issue or proceed from a source: *Orders flowed from the office.* **5.** to proceed continuously and easily: *The words flowed from his pen.* **6.** to hang loosely at full length: *her long hair flowing down her back.* **7.** to abound: *The land flowed with plentiful harvests.* **8.** to rise and advance, such as the tide (opposed to *ebb*). **—***n.* [*count; usually singular*] **9.** an act of flowing. **10.** movement in or as if in a stream: *the flow of traffic.* **11.** the rate or volume of flow: *an oil flow of 500 barrels a day.* **12.** an outpouring or discharge of something, as in a stream: *a flow of blood.* **13.** the rise of the tide (opposed to *ebb*). **14.** the transference of energy: *heat flow.* **—*Idiom.*** **15. go with the flow,** [*no obj*] to follow popular trends: *It's no use fighting these new ways; we may as well go with the flow.*

flow•er (flou′ər) /ˈflawər/ *n.* **1.** [*count*] the blossom of a plant; bloom. **2.** [*count*] a plant grown for its blossoms: *planting flowers in the spring.* **3.** [*noncount*] a state of bloom: *The peonies were in flower.* **4.** [*noncount*] the finest or most flourishing period: *when knighthood was in flower.* **5.** [*count; singular; the* + ~] the best or finest member, product, or example: *the flower of American youth.* **—***v.* [*no obj*] **6.** to produce flowers; blossom; come to full bloom: *These plants flower in the shade.* **7.** to come out into full development; flourish: *Her talent for writing flowered.* See -FLOR-.

flow•ered (flou′ərd) /ˈflawərd/ *adj.* [*before a noun*] printed with a pattern of flowers: *a flowered dress.* See -FLOR-.

flow′er girl′, *n.* [*count*] a young girl in a wedding procession.

flow•er•pot (flou′ər pot′) /ˈflawərˌpɒt/ *n.* [*count*] a container in which to grow and display plants.

flow•er•y (flou′ə rē) /ˈflawəriy/ *adj.,* **-i•er, -i•est. 1.** covered with or having many flowers; decorated with floral designs: *a flowery dress.* **2.** elaborate in speech or writing; too fancy in style: *a speech with flowery language.* **3.** typical of a flower: *a flowery fragrance.*

flown (flōn) /flown/ *v.* a pp. of FLY[1].

fl. oz., an abbreviation of: fluid ounce.

flu (flo͞o) /fluw/ *n.* [*noncount; often: the* + ~] influenza. See -FLU-.

-flu-, *root.* *-flu-* comes from Latin, where it has the meaning "flow." This meaning is found in such words as: AFFLUENCE, AFFLUENT, CONFLUENCE, FLU, FLUCTUATE, FLUE, FLUENT, FLUID, FLUME, FLUORIDE, FLUX, INFLUENCE, INFLUENZA.

flub (flub) /flʌb/ *v.,* **flubbed, flub•bing,** *n. Informal.* **—***v.* [~ + *obj*] **1.** to botch or bungle: *to flub a test in school.* **—***n.* [*count*] **2.** a mistake; bungle; blunder.

fluc•tu•ate (fluk′cho͞o āt′) /ˈflʌktʃuwˌeyt/ *v.* [*no obj*], **-at•ed, -at•ing.** to change continually; vary irregularly; shift back and forth or up and down: *Prices fluctuated wildly.* —**fluc•tu•a•tion** (fluk′cho͞o ā′shən) /ˌflʌktʃuwˈeyʃən/ *n.* [*count*] See -FLU-.

flue (flo͞o) /fluw/ *n.* [*count*] a passage or duct, as for smoke to escape from a chimney. See -FLU-.

flu•ent (flo͞o′ənt) /ˈfluwənt/ *adj.* **1.** spoken or written with ease: *spoke fluent French.* **2.** able to speak or write smoothly, easily, or readily: *fluent in three languages.* **3.** smooth; easy; graceful: *fluent motion.* —**flu′en•cy,** *n.* [*noncount*]: *fluency in French.* —**flu′ent•ly,** *adv.* See -FLU-.

fluff (fluf) /flʌf/ *n.* **1.** [*noncount*] light downy particles, such as of cotton. **2.** [*noncount*] something light or frivolous and not substantial: *The book is pure fluff, but fun to read.* **3.** [*count*] an error or blunder, esp. an actor's memory lapse in the delivery of lines. **—***v.* **4.** [~ + *up* + *obj*] to make fluffy: *He fluffed up his thinning hair.* **5.** [~ + *obj*] to make a mistake in: *fluffed his speech in the first act.*

fluff•y (fluf′ē) /ˈflʌfiy/ *adj.,* **-i•er, -i•est. 1.** of, resembling, or covered with fluff; downy: *a fluffy little chick.* **2.** light or airy: *a fluffy cake.* **3.** superficial: *fluffy thinking.* —**fluff′i•ness,** *n.* [*noncount*]

flu•id (flo͞o′id) /ˈfluwɪd/ *n.* **1.** a substance, such as a liquid or gas, that is capable of flowing and that changes its shape when acted upon by a force: [*noncount*]: *Fluid dripped from the tank.* [*count*]: *to drink fluids.* **—***adj.* **2.** flowing or capable of flowing: *a fluid substance.* **3.** changing easily or readily; not fixed, stable, or rigid: *Our plans are fluid.* **4.** smooth and flowing: *a dancer with fluid gestures.* **5.** convertible into cash; liquid: *fluid assets.* —**flu•id•i•ty** (flo͞o id′i tē) /fluwˈɪdɪtiy/ *n.* [*noncount*] —**flu′id•ly,** *adv.* See -FLU-.

flu′id ounce′, *n.* [*count*] a measure of capacity equal to 1/16 pint or 1.8047 cubic inches (29.573 milliliters) in the U.S., and equal to 1/20 of an imperial pint or 1.7339 cubic inches (28.413 milliliters) in Great Britain. *Abbr.*: fl. oz. *Symbol:* f.

fluke[1] (flo͝ok) /fluwk/ *n.* [*count*] **1.** the part of an anchor that catches in the ground. **2.** the barbed head of a harpoon, spear, arrow, etc. **3.** either half of the triangular tail of a whale.

fluke[2] (flo͝ok) /fluwk/ *n.* [*count*] a stroke of luck: *I got the job by a fluke.* —**fluk′ey, fluk′y,** *adj.,* **-i•er, -i•est.**

fluke[3] (flo͝ok) /fluwk/ *n.* [*count*] any of several American flounders of the Atlantic Ocean.

flume (flo͞om) /fluwm/ *n.* [*count*] **1.** a deep narrow passage containing a stream or torrent. **2.** an artificial channel for conducting water, such as one used to transport logs. **3.** an amusement park ride in which passengers are conveyed through a water-filled chute or over a water slide. See -FLU-.

flum•mox (flum′əks) /ˈflʌməks/ *v.* [~ + *obj*], *Informal.* to bewilder; confuse: *I was flummoxed by his odd behavior.*

flung (flung) /flʌŋ/ *v.* pt. and pp. of FLING.

flunk (flungk) /flʌŋk/ *v.* **1.** to fail (in) a course or examination: [*no obj*]: *You are in danger of flunking.* [~ + *obj*]: *He flunked math.* **2.** [~ + *obj*] to give a failing grade to: *The professor flunked nearly half the class.* **3. flunk out,** to (cause to) be dismissed from a school because of failing grades: [*no obj*]: *in danger of flunking out.* [~ + *out of* + *obj*]: *to flunk out of college.*

flun•ky or **flun•key** (flung′kē) /ˈflʌŋkiy/ *n.* [*count*], *pl.* **-kies** or **-keys. 1.** an assistant who does menial work. **2.** a person too eager to follow and obey someone powerful or important; toady; yes-man.

fluo•resce (flo͝o res′, flô-, flō-) /flʊˈrɛs, flɔ-, flow-/ *v.* [*no obj*], **-resced, -resc•ing.** to show fluorescence.

fluo•res•cence (flo͝o res′əns, flô-, flō-) /flʊˈrɛsəns, flɔ-, flow-/ *n.* [*noncount*] **1.** the giving off of radiation, esp. of visible light, by a substance exposed to light or x-rays. **2.** the radiation so produced. —**fluo•res′cent,** *adj.* See -FLU-.

fluores′cent lamp′, *n.* [*count*] a long, tube-shaped electric lamp in which light is produced by the fluorescence of the coating of the inside of the tube.

fluor•i•date (flo͝or′i dāt′, flôr′-, flōr′-) /ˈflʊrɪˌdeyt, ˈflɔr-, ˈflowr-/ *v.* [~ + *obj*], **-dat•ed, -dat•ing.** to add fluorides to (a water supply) to reduce tooth decay. —**fluor′i•da′tion,** *n.* [*noncount*]

fluor•ide (flo͝or′īd, flôr′-, flōr′-) /ˈflʊrayd, ˈflɔr-, ˈflowr-/ *n.* [*noncount*] a chemical compound containing fluorine. See -FLU-.

fluor•ine (flo͝or′ēn, -in, flôr′-, flōr′-) /ˈflʊriyn, -ɪn, ˈflɔr-, ˈflowr-/ *n.* [*noncount*] an element occurring as a pale yellow, poisonous gas. See -FLU-.

fluor•o•car•bon (flo͝or′ō kär′bən, flôr′-, flōr′-) /ˈflʊrowˌkɑrbən, ˈflɔr-, ˈflowr-/ *n.* [*count*] a compound containing fluorine and carbon and used chiefly as a lubricant, fire-extinguishing agent, and electrical insulator.

fluor•o•scope (flo͝or′ə skōp′, flôr′-, flōr′-) /ˈflʊrəˌskowp, ˈflɔr-, ˈflowr-/ *n.* [*count*] a screen coated with a fluorescent substance, used for viewing objects by means of x-ray. See -FLU-, -SCOPE-.

flur•ry (flûr′ē, flur′ē) /ˈflɜriy, ˈflʌriy/ *n., pl.* **-ries,** *v.,* **-ried, -ry•ing.** —*n.* [*count*] **1.** a brief shower of snow. **2.** [*usually singular*] sudden commotion, excitement, or activity: *a flurry of activity.* **3.** a gust of wind. —*v.* **4.** [~ + *obj*] to make confused or nervous; fluster: *Don't be flurried by the noise.* **5.** [*it* + ~; *no obj*] (of snow) to fall or be blown in a flurry: *It flurried all night.*

flush[1] (flush) /flʌʃ/ *n.* **1.** [*count*] a reddening of the skin, as from fever or from exercise. **2.** [*count; usually singular*] a sudden rise of emotion: *a flush of anger.* **3.** [*noncount*] glowing freshness or vigor: *a beautiful girl in the flush of youth.* —*v.* **4.** to (cause to) redden: [*no obj*]: *Her face flushed.* [~ + *obj*]: *Happiness flushed her face.* **5.** [~ *(+ out)* + *obj*] to flood or spray thoroughly with water: *to flush a pipe clean; flushed out the stables.* **6.** to (cause to) be washed with a sudden rush of water: [*no obj*]: *the sound of a toilet flushing.* [~ + *obj*]: *flushed the toilet.* **7.** [~ + *obj*] to animate; inflame: *flushed with success.*

flush[2] (flush) /flʌʃ/ *adj.* **1.** even or level with a surface: *The window frame is flush with the wall.* **2.** immediately next to: *The table was flush against the wall.* **3.** well-supplied; prosperous: *felt flush with so much money.* —*adv.* **4.** on the same level or plane; evenly: *The door shuts flush with the wall.* **5.** in direct contact: *set flush against the edge.*

flush[3] (flush) /flʌʃ/ *v.* [~ + *obj*] to cause to start up or fly off: *The hunters flushed quail.*

flush[4] (flush) /flʌʃ/ *n.* [*count*] a hand of cards all of one suit: *Your flush beats my straight.*

flus•ter (flus′tər) /ˈflʌstər/ *v.* to (cause to) become nervous or confused: [~ + *obj*]: *I was flustered by my unexpected visitor.* [*no obj*]: *He flusters too easily.*

flute (flo͞ot) /fluwt/ *n.* [*count*] **1.** a wind instrument with a high range, made of a tube with fingerholes or keys. **2.** a groove.

flut•ist (flo͞o′tist) /ˈfluwtɪst/ *n.* [*count*] a flute player.

flut•ter (flut′ər) /ˈflʌtər/ *v.* **1.** to (cause to) wave or flap about: [*no obj*]: *Banners fluttered in the breeze.* [~ + *obj*]: *The breeze fluttered the banners.* **2.** [*no obj*] to flap the wings rapidly or fly with flapping movements: *The pigeons fluttered away.* **3.** [*no obj*] to move in quick, irregular motions: *fluttered around the office looking for something to do.* **4.** [*no obj*] to beat rapidly: *Her heart fluttered for a moment.* —*n.* [*count*] **5.** a fluttering movement: *a flutter of wings.* **6.** [*usually: singular*] a state of nervous excitement or mental agitation: *in a flutter of anticipation.* **7.** [*usually: singular*] a stir; flurry: *That news caused quite a flutter.* —**flut′ter•y,** *adj.,* **-i•er, -i•est.**

flux (fluks) /flʌks/ *n.* **1.** [*count*] a flowing or flow: *a flux of traffic.* **2.** [*noncount*] continuous change or movement: *Our plans are in a state of flux.* See -FLU-.

fly[1] (flī) /flay/ *v.,* **flew** (flo͞o) /fluw/ or, for 11, **flied, flown** (flōn) /flown/, **fly•ing,** *n., pl.* **flies.** —*v.* **1.** [*no obj*] to move through the air using wings: *Outside the birds were flying.* **2.** [*no obj*] to be carried or move through the air or through space by any force or agency: *The jet can fly at the speed of sound.* **3.** [*no obj*] to travel in an aircraft or spacecraft: *The family flew to California.* **4.** to operate an aircraft or spacecraft: [*no obj*]: *The pilot flew to Hawaii.* [~ + *obj*]: *The pilot flew a variety of aircraft.* **5.** [~ + *obj*] to operate an aircraft or spacecraft over (an area): *to fly the Pacific.* **6.** [~ + *obj*] to transport or convey by air: *The army flew him to its secret base.* **7.** to (cause to) float or flutter in the air: [*no obj*]: *The king's banner flew over his tent.* [~ + *obj*]: *He tried to fly his kite.* **8.** [*no obj*] to pass swiftly: *How time flies!* **9.** [*no obj*] to move with often sudden swiftness: *cars flying by us; flew into a rage.* **10.** [*no obj*] to flee; escape: *He was warned to fly from the sheriff's wrath.* **11.** [*no obj*] to bat a fly ball in baseball: *The last hitter flied to right field.* **12.** [*no obj*] *Informal.* to be believable or feasible: *It seemed like a good idea, but it just wouldn't fly.* **13. fly at,** [~ + *at* + *obj*] to attack suddenly: *flew at him and scratched his face.* —*n.* [*count*] **14.** a fold of material that conceals fasteners in a garment opening. **15.** a flap forming the door of a tent. **16.** FLY BALL. —***Idiom.*** **17. fly high,** [*no obj*] to be full of happiness or excitement: *The workers were all flying high until the bad news arrived.* **18. fly in the face** or **teeth of,** [~ + *obj*] to act in defiance of: *to fly in the face of tradition.* **19. fly off the handle,** [*no obj*] *Informal.* to become very angry, esp. without warning. **20. let fly, a.** to hurl or propel (an object): [*no obj*]: *let fly with several snowballs.* [*let* + ~ + *obj*]: *She let fly a few snowballs.* **b.** [*no obj*] to let one's anger out: *let fly with an insult.* **21. on the fly,** hurriedly: *We had dinner on the fly.*

fly[2] (flī) /flay/ *n.* [*count*], *pl.* **flies. 1.** a two-winged insect, such as the common housefly. **2.** a fishing lure dressed to resemble an insect or small fish. —***Idiom.*** **3. fly in the ointment,** something that spoils an otherwise pleasant thing: *The fly in the ointment is that there is no money to finish the job.*

fly′ ball′, *n.* [*count*] a baseball batted high into the air.

fly•blown (flī′blōn′) /ˈflayˌblown/ *adj.* spoiled; contaminated.

fly•by or **fly-by** (flī′bī′) /ˈflayˌbay/ *n.* [*count*], *pl.* **-bys.** the flight of a spacecraft past a heavenly body.

fly′-by-night′, *adj.* [*before a noun*] **1.** not reliable and devoted to making a quick profit: *a fly-by-night business.* **2.** not lasting; transitory.

fly•er (flī′ər) /ˈflayər/ *n.* FLIER.

fly•ing (flī′ing) /ˈflayɪŋ/ *adj.* [*before a noun*] **1.** capable of flight: *Mosquitoes are flying insects.* **2.** made while moving swiftly: *a flying leap.* **3.** quick; brief: *a flying visit.* —*n.* [*noncount*] **4.** the act of traveling by aircraft.

fly′ing but′tress, *n.* [*count*] an arch or segment of an arch sticking out from and supporting a wall.

fly′ing col′ors, *n.* [*plural*] outstanding success; triumph: *He passed the test with flying colors.*

fly′ing fish′, *n.* [*count*] a warm-water sea fish having winglike fins that enable it to glide for some distance after leaping from the water.

fly′ing sau′cer, *n.* [*count*] a disk-shaped object reportedly seen flying at high speeds and altitudes; UFO.

fly′ing start′, *n.* [*count*] a favorable beginning to something.

fly•leaf (flī′lēf′) /ˈflayˌliyf/ *n.* [*count*], *pl.* **-leaves.** a blank page in the front or the back of a book.

fly•pa•per (flī′pā′pər) /ˈflayˌpeypər/ *n.* [*noncount*] paper with a sticky surface for catching flies.

fly•weight (flī′wāt′) /ˈflayˌweyt/ *n.* [*count*] a boxer weighing up to 112 lb. (51 kg).

fly•wheel (flī′hwēl′, -wēl′) /ˈflayˌhwiyl, -ˌwiyl/ *n.* [*count*] a heavy wheel that regulates the speed of the shaft and all connected machinery.

FM, an abbreviation of: **1.** frequency modulation: a method of broadcasting a signal on a radio carrier wave. **2.** a system of radio broadcasting using this method. Compare AM.

fm., an abbreviation of: **1.** fathom. **2.** from.

F.O., an abbreviation of: foreign office.

foal (fōl) /fowl/ *n.* [*count*] **1.** the young of any member of the horse family that is still nursing. —*v.* [~ + *obj*] **2.** to give birth to (a colt or filly): *a mare foaling a colt.*

foam (fōm) /fowm/ *n.* [*noncount*] **1.** a collection of tiny bubbles on the surface of a liquid: *beer with a head of foam.* **2.** a thick, frothy substance: *A special foam kept the wreckage from catching on fire.* **3.** a lightweight material in which gas bubbles are dispersed in a solid, used as insulation. —*v.* [*no obj*] **4.** to form foam; froth: *The boiling milk foamed.* —***Idiom.*** **5. foam at the mouth,** [*no obj*] to be extremely angry: *almost foaming at the mouth at the insult.* —**foam′y,** *adj.,* **-i•er, -i•est.**

foam′ rub′ber, *n.* [*noncount*] a light, spongy rubber used for mattresses, cushions, etc.

fob[1] (fob) /fɒb/ *n.* [*count*] **1.** a short chain or ribbon attached to a pocket watch. **2.** an ornament on a fob.

fob[2] (fob) /fɒb/ *v.,* **fobbed, fob•bing.** —***Idiom.*** **fob off,** to dispose of or induce someone to take (something inferior); palm off: [~ + *off* + *obj*]: *The car dealer fobbed off an inferior car on the buyer.* [~ + *obj* + *off*]: *He fobbed it off on the buyer.*

fo•cal (fō′kəl) /ˈfowkəl/ *adj.* [*before a noun*] of, relating to, or at a focus: *the focal length of a lens.* —**fo′cal•ly,** *adv.*

fo′cal point′, *n.* [*count*] the center of activity or attention; the principal point of interest: *The focal point of our discussion was the budget.*

fo•cus (fō′kəs) /ˈfowkəs/ *n., pl.* **-cus•es, -ci** (-sī, -kī) /-say, -kay/ *v.,* **-cused, -cus•ing** or (*esp. Brit.*) **-cussed, -cus•sing.** —*n.* **1.** [*count*] a central point, such as of attraction, attention, or activity: *His focus was on earning a living.* **2.** [*count*] a point at which rays of light, heat, or other radiation meet after being refracted or reflected. **3.** [*noncount*] the adjustment of an optical device that is necessary to produce a clear image: *The image is in focus.* —*v.* **4.** to (cause to) come to a focus or into focus: [~ + *obj*]: *to focus the lens of a camera.* [*no obj*]: *For a few moments my eyes wouldn't focus.* **5.** to concentrate:

[~ + *obj*]: *I tried to focus my thoughts.* [*no obj; (~ + on + obj)*]: *I tried to focus on the project.*

fod•der (fod′ər) /ˈfɒdər/ *n.* [*noncount*] **1.** coarse food for livestock. **2.** raw material: *Mothers-in-law are often fodder for comedy routines.*

foe (fō) /fow/ *n.* [*count*] **1.** a person who feels hatred toward another; enemy: *a bitter foe.* **2.** a military enemy. **3.** an opponent in a game or contest. **4.** a person who is opposed to something: *a foe to progress.*

foe•tus (fē′təs) /ˈfiytəs/ *n., pl.* **-tus•es.** FETUS. —**foe•tal** (fēt′l) /ˈfiytl̩/ *adj.*

fog (fog, fôg) /fɒg, fɔg/ *n., v.,* **fogged, fog•ging.** —*n.* **1.** [*noncount*] a cloudlike mass or layer of water droplets near the surface of the earth: *drove through heavy fog.* **2.** [*count; usually singular*] a state of mental confusion or unawareness: *lost in a fog, unable to concentrate.* —*v.* **3.** to (cause to) become covered or enveloped with or as if with fog: [~ + *obj*]: *The steam fogged his glasses.* [*no obj; (~ + up)*]: *The harbor fogged up. The windshield has fogged.* **4.** [~ + *obj*] to confuse or obscure: *The debate just fogged the issue.* —**fog′gy,** *adj.,* **-gi•er, -gi•est.**

fog•horn (fog′hôrn′, fôg′-) /ˈfɒg,hɔrn, ˈfɔg-/ *n.* [*count*] a deep, loud horn for sounding warnings to ships in foggy weather.

fo•gy or **fo•gey** (fō′gē) /ˈfowgiy/ *n.* [*count*], *pl.* **-gies** or **-geys.** an extremely old-fashioned or conservative person. —**fo′gy•ish,** *adj.*

foi•ble (foi′bəl) /ˈfɔybəl/ *n.* [*count*] a minor weakness or failing of character.

foil[1] (foil) /fɔyl/ *v.* [~ + *obj*] to prevent the success of; thwart: *Loyal troops foiled the revolt.*

foil[2] (foil) /fɔyl/ *n.* **1.** [*noncount*] metal in very thin sheets: *aluminum foil.* **2.** [*count*] a person or thing that serves as a contrast to another: *Goodness was a foil to their villainy.* See -FOLI-.

foil[3] (foil) /fɔyl/ *n.* [*count*] a flexible four-sided sword having a blunt point, used for fencing.

foist (foist) /fɔyst/ *v.* [~ + *obj (+ off) + on/upon + obj*] to force upon or impose dishonestly or unfairly: *to foist inferior goods (off) on a customer.*

fol., an abbreviation of: **1.** folio. **2.** followed. **3.** following.

fold[1] (fōld) /fowld/ *v.* **1.** [~ + *obj*] to bend (cloth, paper, etc.) over upon itself: *I folded the paper neatly in half.* **2.** to make or become compact by bending and laying parts together: [~ *(+ up) + obj*]: *I always have trouble folding (up) highway maps.* [~ + *obj (+ up)*]: *Sometimes I can't fold them (up) neatly.* [*no obj; (~ + up)*]: *The bed folds (up) to save space.* **3.** [~ + *obj*] to bring together and intertwine or cross: *folded his arms.* **4.** [~ + *obj*] to bring (the wings) close to the body: *The bird landed and folded its wings.* **5.** [~ + *obj*] to enclose; wrap; envelop: *She folded the apple in paper.* **6.** [~ + *obj*] to embrace or clasp; enfold: *to fold her in my arms.* **7. a.** to (cause to) go out of business: [*no obj*]: *The magazine folded after a few weeks.* [~ + *obj*]: *The publishers folded the magazine.* **b.** to (cause to) end a show; close: [*no obj*]: *The show will fold next week.* [~ + *obj*]: *The producers folded the show.* **8. fold in,** [~ + *in* + *obj*] to blend (a cooking ingredient) into a mixture by gently turning one part over another: *Fold in the egg whites.* **9. fold out** or **down,** [*no obj*] to spread or open up; unfold: *The couch folds out to a queen-size bed.* —*n.* [*count*] **10.** a part that is folded; pleat; layer: *folds of cloth.* **11.** a line, crease, or hollow made by folding.

fold[2] (fōld) /fowld/ *n.* [*count*] **1.** an enclosure for sheep. **2.** a group sharing common beliefs, values, etc.

-fold, *suffix. -fold* is attached to words that refer to a number or quantity to form adjectives with the meanings "having the number of kinds or parts" or "multiplied the number of times": *four + -fold → fourfold (= multiplied four times); many + -fold → manyfold (= having many parts or kinds).*

fold•a•way (fōld′ə wā′) /ˈfowldə,wey/ *adj.* [*before a noun*] designed to be folded out of the way when not in use: *a foldaway bed.*

fold•er (fōl′dər) /ˈfowldər/ *n.* [*count*] a folded sheet of light cardboard for holding papers, as in a file.

fold•out or **fold-out** (fōld′out′) /ˈfowld,awt/ *n.* [*count*] **1.** a page that is larger than the page size of a magazine or book, folded one or more times so as not to extend beyond the edges. —*adj.* [*before a noun*] **2.** designed to be unfolded for use, viewing, etc.

-foli-, *root. -foli-* comes from Latin, where it has the meaning "leaf." This meaning is found in such words as: DEFOLIATE, FOIL[2], FOLIAGE, FOLIO, PORTFOLIO.

fo•li•age (fō′lē ij) /ˈfowliyɪdʒ/ *n.* [*noncount*] leaves, as of a tree or plant: *beautiful autumn foliage in upstate New York.* See -FOLI-.

fo•li•o (fō′lē ō′) /ˈfowliy,ow/ *n.* [*count*], *pl.* **-li•os. 1.** a sheet of paper folded once to make two leaves, or four pages, of a book or manuscript. **2.** a book having pages of the largest size. See -FOLI-.

folk (fōk) /fowk/ *n.* **1.** Usually, **folks.** [*plural; used with a plural verb*] people in general: *Some folks simply won't take "no" for an answer.* **2.** Often, **folks.** [*plural; used with a plural verb*] people of a specified class or group: *Country folk are usually friendly.* **3.** [*plural; used with a plural verb*] people as the carriers of culture: *The folk are the bearers of oral tradition.* **4. folks,** [*plural*] *Informal.* **a.** members of one's family; one's relatives: *My wife's folks had a big reunion.* **b.** one's parents: *My folks won't let me go to the dance.* —*adj.* [*before a noun*] **5.** of or coming from the common people: *folk dances; folk music; folk songs; folk art.*

folk•lore (fōk′lôr′, -lōr′) /ˈfowk,lɔr, -,lowr/ *n.* [*noncount*] the traditional beliefs, legends, customs, etc., of a people. —**folk′lor′ic,** *adj.* —**folk′lor′ist,** *n.* [*count*]

folk•sy (fōk′sē) /ˈfowksiy/ *adj.,* **-si•er, -si•est.** very informal; easygoing: *the folksy style of a small town.* —**folk′si•ness,** *n.* [*noncount*]

folk•way (fōk′wā′) /ˈfowk,wey/ *n.* [*count*] a traditional way of living or thinking in a particular social group; custom.

foll., an abbreviation of: following.

fol•li•cle (fol′i kəl) /ˈfɒlɪkəl/ *n.* [*count*] a small cavity, sac, or gland.

fol•low (fol′ō) /ˈfɒlow/ *v.* **1.** to come after in sequence or order; succeed: [~ + *obj*]: *Night follows day, and day follows night.* [*no obj*]: *You lead and I'll follow.* **2.** to happen after something else; come next as an event or result: [*no obj*]: *After the defeat, great disorder followed.* [~ + *obj*]: *Flooding followed the storm.* **3.** to go or come after; move behind in the same direction: [~ + *obj*]: *Drive ahead, and I'll follow you.* [*no obj*]: *Drive ahead and I'll follow.* **4.** [~ + *obj*] to conform to, comply with, or act in accordance with; obey: *to follow orders.* **5.** [~ + *obj*] to move forward along: *We followed the road to Gaston.* **6.** [~ + *obj*] to go in pursuit of: *The police followed the fleeing suspects.* **7.** [~ + *obj*] to engage in or be concerned with as a pursuit: *to follow an ideal.* **8.** [~ + *obj*] to watch the development or progress of: *to follow the news.* **9.** [*not: be + ~-ing*] to keep up with and understand (an argument, story, etc.): [~ + *obj*]: *I can't follow your argument. Do you follow me?* [*no obj*]: *That's the explanation; can you follow?* **10.** [*not: be + ~-ing*] to result logically as an effect: [*no obj*]: *That can't be right —it just doesn't follow.* [~ + *from* + *obj*]: *That conclusion does not follow from your premise.* [*It + ~ + that clause*]: *It follows naturally that they must be innocent.* **11. follow through,** [*no obj*] **a.** to carry out fully, such as a stroke in golf or tennis. **b.** to continue an effort, plan, proposal, policy, etc., to its completion: *He followed through on every assignment we gave him.* **12. follow up, a.** to increase the effectiveness of by further action or repetition: [~ + *up* + *obj*]: *He followed up the aerobics with stretching exercises.* [~ + *obj* + *up*]: *followed them up with stretching exercises.* **b.** [~ + *up (+ on) + obj*] to pursue: *I'd like to follow up (on) that question.*

fol•low•er (fol′ō ər) /ˈfɒlowər/ *n.* [*count*] **1.** a person or thing that follows. **2.** a person who follows another in regard to his or her ideas or belief; disciple or adherent. **3.** a person who imitates, copies, or takes as a model or ideal: *a follower of current fashions.*

fol•low•ing (fol′ō ing) /ˈfɒlowɪŋ/ *n.* **1.** [*count*] a body of admirers, attendants, or patrons: *That television show has a large following.* **2. the following,** that which comes immediately after: *See the following for a list of exceptions.* [*used with a singular verb when singular noun follows*]: *The following is one reason only.* [*used with a plural verb when plural noun follows*]: *The following are several reasons for this discrepancy.* —*adj.* [*before a noun*] **3.** coming next in order or time; ensuing: *the following day.* **4.** that is now to follow: *Check the following report for details.* —*prep.* **5.** after: *Following the concert, there will be a champagne reception.*

fol′low-up′, *n.* [*count*] **1.** an action that serves to increase or monitor the effectiveness of a previous one: *Come back to the doctor's office for a follow-up.* **2.** a news story providing additional information on an earlier story: *wanted to do a follow-up but her editor said not to.* —*adj.* [*before a noun*] **3.** designed or serving to follow up: *a follow-up interview.*

fol•ly (fol′ē) /ˈfɒliy/ *n., pl.* **-lies. 1.** [*noncount*] the state or quality of being foolish: *to travel without money would be folly.* **2.** [*count*] a foolish action, practice, idea, etc. **3. follies,** [*plural*] a theatrical revue.

fo•ment (fō ment′) /fowˈmɛnt/ *v.* [~ + *obj*] to start or foster: *to foment distrust and rebellion.*

fond (fond) /fɒnd/ *adj.,* **-er, -est. 1.** [*be* + ~ + *of*] having a liking or affection for: *is fond of animals.* **2.** [*before a noun*] loving; affectionate: *a fond look.* **3.** [*before a noun*] excessively tender or indulgent; doting: *a fond parent.* **4.** [*before a noun*] hoped for foolishly or with strong feeling despite the unlikeliness of coming true: *to nourish fond hopes.* —**fond′ly,** *adv.: fondly stroked the cat.* —**fond′ness,** *n.* [*noncount*]

fon•dant (fon′dənt) /ˈfɒndənt/ *n.* **1.** [*noncount*] a thick, creamy sugar paste. **2.** [*count*] a candy made of this paste.

fon•dle (fon′dl) /ˈfɒndl̩/ *v.* [~ + *obj*], **-dled, -dling. 1.** to handle or touch lovingly, affectionately, or tenderly; caress: *fondled their newborn baby.* **2.** to molest sexually by touching, stroking, etc.

fon•due (fon do͞o′, -dyo͞o′) /fɒnˈduw, -ˈdyuw/ *n.* **1.** [*noncount*] a hot dish of melted cheese and wine. **2.** [*count*] a dish of hot liquid in which small pieces of food are cooked or dipped: *a chocolate fondue.*

font[1] (font) /fɒnt/ *n.* [*count*] **1.** a receptacle for the water used in baptism. **2.** a receptacle for holy water. **3.** someone or something providing useful information: *The book is a font of useful tips.*

font[2] (font) /fɒnt/ *n.* [*count*] a complete assortment of printing type of one style and size: *a gothic font.*

food (fo͞od) /fuwd/ *n.* **1.** [*noncount*] any nourishing substance eaten or drunk to sustain life, provide energy, and promote growth. **2.** [*noncount*] solid nourishment as distinguished from liquids: *food and drink.* **3.** [*count*] a particular kind of solid nourishment: *breakfast food; pet food.* **4.** [*noncount*] anything that nourishes: *food for thought.*

food′ chain′, *n.* [*count*] a series of interrelated organisms in which the smallest is fed upon by a larger one, which in turn feeds a still larger one.

food′ poi′soning, *n.* [*noncount*] an illness caused by eating contaminated or toxic food.

food′ proc′essor, *n.* [*count*] an electric appliance with a closed container and blades that can slice, chop, shred, or purée food at high speeds. See illustration at APPLIANCE.

food′ stamp′, *n.* [*count*] a coupon issued under a federal program to eligible needy persons and used to purchase food. Also called **food′ cou′pon.**

food•stuff (fo͞od′stuf′) /ˈfuwdˌstʌf/ *n.* a substance used or capable of being used as food: [*count; usually plural*]: *storing foodstuffs in case of a drought.* [*noncount*]: *meat by-products used as foodstuff for animals.*

fool (fo͞ol) /fuwl/ *n.* [*count*] **1.** a silly or stupid person; one who lacks sense: *I felt like a fool when I couldn't figure out how to use the fax machine.* **2.** a professional jester: *the court fool.* **3.** a person tricked or deceived into appearing silly or stupid: *tried to make a fool of him.* —*v.* **4.** [~ + *obj*] to trick, deceive, or impose on: *They tried to fool us.* **5.** [*no obj*] to jest; pretend; make believe: *I didn't mean it; I was only fooling.* **6. fool around,** [*no obj*] **a.** to waste time aimlessly: *He seems to be just fooling around and not taking his job seriously at all.* **b.** to be sexually promiscuous; engage casually in sexual activity: *He was fooling around with his neighbor's wife.* **7. fool with,** [~ + *obj*] to handle or play with idly or carelessly: *Don't fool with that vacuum cleaner.* —**Related Words.** FOOL is a noun and a verb, FOOLISH is an adjective, FOOLISHNESS is a noun: *He's a fool. They tried to fool me. What a foolish mistake! What foolishness are you up to now?*

fool•er•y (fo͞o′lə rē) /ˈfuwləriy/ *n., pl.* **-er•ies. 1.** [*noncount*] foolish conduct. **2.** [*count*] a foolish action, performance, or thing: *His fooleries are starting to annoy us.*

fool•har•dy (fo͞ol′här′dē) /ˈfuwlˌhɑrdiy/ *adj.,* **-di•er, -di•est.** recklessly or thoughtlessly bold; foolishly rash or taking unnecessary chances: *Driving in the blizzard was a foolhardy thing to do.*

fool•ish (fo͞o′lish) /ˈfuwlɪʃ/ *adj.* **1.** resulting from or showing a lack of good sense: *a foolish prank.* **2.** lacking forethought or caution; appearing like a fool: *felt foolish asking such a big favor.* —**fool′ish•ly,** *adv.* —**fool′ish•ness,** *n.* [*noncount*]

fool•proof (fo͞ol′pro͞of′) /ˈfuwlˌpruwf/ *adj.* **1.** easy to use, operate, or understand; involving no risk: *a foolproof VCR.* **2.** never-failing: *a foolproof method.*

fools•cap (fo͞olz′kap′) /ˈfuwlzˌkæp/ *n.* [*noncount*] inexpensive writing paper.

fool's′ gold′, *n.* [*noncount*] iron or copper pyrites.

fool's′ par′adise, *n.* [*count; usually singular*] a state of enjoyment based on false beliefs or hopes: *living in a fool's paradise.*

foot (fo͝ot) /fʊt/ *n., pl.* **feet** (fēt) /fiyt/. **1.** [*count*] the end of the leg, below the ankle joint, on which the body stands and moves. **2.** [*count*] a unit of length equal to 12 inches or 30.48 centimeters. **3.** [*count*] any part or thing resembling a foot, as in function, placement, or shape: *the foot of a couch; the foot of a stocking.* **4.** [*count; usually singular*] the lowest part, or bottom, such as of a hill, ladder, or page: *the foot of the mountain.* **5.** [*count; usually singular*] the part of anything opposite the top or head: *Her cat slept at the foot of her bed.* —*v.* [~ + *obj*] **6.** to pay or settle: *Who will foot the bill?* —*adj.* [*before a noun*] **7.** moving on foot: *a foot soldier.* **8.** operating by using the foot or feet: *a foot brake.* —***Idiom.*** **9. drag one's feet,** to delay unnecessarily. **10. foot it,** [~ + *it*] to walk; go on foot: *We'll have to foot it home.* **11. get off on the right** (or **wrong**) **foot,** to begin well (or badly): *I got off on the wrong foot by arriving late.* **12. on foot,** by walking or running: *to travel on foot.* **13. on one's feet, a.** standing: *The crowd was on their feet cheering.* **b.** in a good, healthy, or advantageous position: *Glad you're on your feet again after your illness.* **14. put one's foot down,** [*no obj*] to take a firm stand: *She put her foot down and didn't allow the children to watch television.* **15. put one's foot in one's mouth** or **put one's foot in it,** [*no obj*] to say something tactless. **16. set foot on** or **in,** [~ + *obj*] to enter: *Don't set foot in this office again!* **17. under foot,** in the way: *That cat is always under foot.*

foot•age (fo͝ot′ij) /ˈfʊtɪdʒ/ *n.* [*noncount*] **1.** length in feet. **2.** a material on film or videotape: *newsreel footage of the bombing.*

foot•ball (fo͝ot′bôl′) /ˈfʊtˌbɔl/ *n.* **1.** [*noncount*] a game in which two opposing teams of 11 players each defend goals at opposite ends of a field. **2.** [*count*] the ball used in this game, an inflated oval in a casing usually made of leather. **3.** [*noncount*] *Chiefly Brit.* RUGBY (def. 2). **4.** [*noncount*] *Chiefly Brit.* SOCCER.

foot•bridge (fo͝ot′brij′) /ˈfʊtˌbrɪdʒ/ *n.* [*count*] a bridge intended for people traveling on foot.

-footed, *suffix. -footed* is attached to nouns to form adjectives meaning "having (the kind of, number of, etc.) a foot or feet indicated": *a four-footed animal (= an animal having four feet).*

foot•fall (fo͝ot′fôl′) /ˈfʊtˌfɔl/ *n.* [*count*] the sound of a footstep.

foot•hill (fo͝ot′hil′) /ˈfʊtˌhɪl/ *n.* [*count*] a low hill at the base of a mountain range.

foot•hold (fo͝ot′hōld′) /ˈfʊtˌhowld/ *n.* [*count*] **1.** a place or support for the feet; a place where a person may stand or walk securely. **2.** a secure position, esp. a firm basis for further progress or development.

foot•ing (fo͝ot′ing) /ˈfʊtɪŋ/ *n.* **1.** [*count; usually singular*] the basis or foundation on which anything is established: *firm economic footing.* **2.** [*noncount*] a firm placing of the feet; stability: *to regain one's footing.* **3.** [*count; usually singular*] position or status assigned to a person, group, etc.; mutual standing: *on a friendly footing with the boss.*

foot•light (fo͝ot′līt′) /ˈfʊtˌlayt/ *n.* [*count*] **1.** Usually, **footlights.** [*plural*] the lights at the front of a stage that are nearly on a level with the feet of the performers. **2. the footlights,** [*plural*] the acting profession.

foot•loose (fo͝ot′lo͞os′) /ˈfʊtˌluws/ *adj.* free to go or travel about: *footloose vacationers.*

foot•man (fo͝ot′mən) /ˈfʊtmən/ *n.* [*count*], *pl.* **-men.** a male household servant.

foot•note (fo͝ot′nōt′) /ˈfʊtˌnowt/ *n.* [*count*] **1.** an explanatory note or reference at the bottom of a page. **2.** a minor comment or event added to a main statement or more important event. See -NOTA-.

foot•path (fo͝ot′path′) /ˈfʊtˌpæθ/ *n.* [*count*] a path for people going on foot.

foot•print (fo͝ot′print′) /ˈfʊtˌprɪnt/ *n.* [*count*] **1.** a mark left by a foot, as in earth or sand: *found footprints leading from the house.* **2.** the surface space, as of a desk, occupied by a piece of equipment, such as a microcomputer: *a bulky computer with a large footprint.*

foot•sie (fo͝ot′sē) /ˈfʊtsiy/ *n.* [*count*] *Informal.* —***Idiom.*** **play footsie(s) with,** [~ + *obj*] **1.** to flirt with, esp. by secretly touching someone's foot. **2.** to engage in secret or unlawful relations with.

foot•sore (fo͝ot′sôr′, -sōr′) /ˈfʊtˌsɔr, -ˌsowr/ *adj.* having sore feet.

foot•step (fo͝ot′step′) /ˈfʊtˌstɛp/ *n.* [*count*] **1.** the setting down of a foot, or the sound so produced; footfall; tread: *He heard footsteps behind him.* **2.** the distance covered by a step in walking; pace: *short footsteps.* —***Idiom.*** **3. follow in someone's footsteps,** [*no obj*] to imitate another person: *She was following in her father's footsteps as a lawyer.*

foot•stool (fo͝ot′sto͞ol′) /ˈfʊtˌstuwl/ *n.* [*count*] a low stool upon which to rest one's feet when seated. See illustration at APARTMENT.

foot•wear (fo͝ot′wâr′) /ˈfʊtˌwɛər/ *n.* [*noncount*] articles to be worn on the feet, such as shoes, slippers, or boots.

foot•work (fo͝ot′wûrk′) /ˈfʊtˌwɜrk/ *n.* [*noncount*] **1.** the use of the feet, as in tennis, boxing, or dancing: *His fatigue showed in his clumsy footwork.* **2.** travel from one place to another, as in gathering facts or fulfilling an assignment; legwork. **3.** the act of maneuvering, esp. in a skillful manner: *a bit of fancy footwork.*

fop (fop) /fɒp/ *n.* [*count*] a vain man who is overly concerned with his looks, clothes, and manners; dandy. —**fop′pish,** *adj.*

for (fôr; *unstressed* fər) /fɔr; *unstressed* fər/ *prep.* **1.** with the object or purpose of: *She likes to run for exercise.* **2.** intended to belong to, benefit, or be used by or with: *equipment for the army.* **3.** suiting the purposes or needs of: *medicine for the aged.* **4.** appropriate or adapted to: *a subject for speculation.* **5.** in consideration or payment of; in return for; in exchange for: *The tomatoes cost three for a dollar.* **6.** as an offset to; in response to: *medicine for your cold.* **7.** in order to obtain, gain, or acquire: *I had to work for decent wages.* **8.** (used to express a wish, as of something to be experienced, gained, or acquired): *O, for a cold drink!* **9.** sensitive or responsive to: *The art critic has an eye for beauty.* **10.** with regard or respect to: *I'm very pressed for time.* **11.** during the continuance of: *waiting for days.* **12.** to the extent or amount of: *to walk for a mile.* **13.** in favor of; on the side of; on behalf of: *My kids are all for saving the environment.* **14.** in place of; instead of: *a safe substitute for butter.* **15.** standing for; meaning the same as: *What is the Swahili word for "head?"* **16.** in punishment of: *payment for the crime.* **17.** in honor of: *a dinner for our guest.* **18.** with the purpose of reaching: *Let's start for London today.* **19.** in assignment or attribution to: *That's for you to decide.* **20.** such as to allow of or to require: *The reasons are just too many for separate mention.* **21.** such as results in: *My motive for going is clear.* **22.** as affecting the interests or circumstances of: *bad for your health.* **23.** in proportion or with reference to; as compared to others of: *tall for his age.* **24.** by reason of; because of: *to shout for joy.* **25.** in spite of: *They're decent people for all that.* **26.** (used to introduce a subject in a *to* + *verb* or infinitive phrase): *It's time for me to go.* —*conj.* **27.** seeing that; since; because: *I couldn't see them, for it was almost dark.*

for., an abbreviation of: **1.** foreign. **2.** forestry.

fo•ra (fôr′ə, fōr′ə) /ˈfɔrə, ˈfowrə/ *n.* [*plural*] a pl. of FORUM.

for•age (fôr′ij, for′-) /ˈfɔrɪdʒ, ˈfɒr-/ *n., v.,* **-aged, -ag•ing.** —*n.* [*noncount*] **1.** food for horses or cattle; fodder. —*v.* **2.** to wander or go in search of provisions: [*no obj*]: *foraging through the countryside for food.* [~ + *obj*]: *foraged the countryside for food.* **3.** [*no obj*] to search about: *foraging for supplies.* **4.** [~ + *obj*] to obtain by foraging: *to forage berries.* —**for′ag•er,** *n.* [*count*]

for•ay (fôr′ā, for′ā) /ˈfɔrey, ˈfɒrey/ *n.* [*count*] **1.** a quick raid or attack, usually for taking plunder; sortie: *a foray behind enemy lines.* **2.** a venture outside one's customary activity: *a brief foray into real estate.*

for•bade (fôr bad′) /fɔrˈbæd/ *v.* a pt. of FORBID.

for•bear[1] (fôr bâr′) /fɔrˈbɛər/ *v.,* **-bore, -borne, -bear•ing.** to refrain or abstain from: [*no obj*]: *I wanted to argue but decided to forbear.* [~ + *from* + *obj*]: *should forbear from saying cruel things.* [~ + *verb-ing*]: *He forbore smoking.*

for•bear[2] (fôr′bâr′) /ˈfɔrˌbɛər/ *n.* FOREBEAR.

for•bear•ance (fôr bâr′əns) /fɔrˈbɛərəns/ *n.* [*noncount*] patience or self-control when annoyed or provoked.

for•bid (fər bid′, fôr-) /fərˈbɪd, fɔr-/ *v.,* **-bade** or **-bad** or **-bid, -bid•den** or **-bid, -bid•ding. 1.** to command (a person) not to do something: [~ + *obj* + *obj*]: *I forbid you entry to this house.* [~ + *obj* + *to* + *verb*]: *forbade me to see him again.* **2.** [~ + *obj*] to prohibit (something): *to forbid smoking in public places.* **3.** [~ + *obj*] to prevent: *Loyalty forbids any further comment.*

for•bid•ding (fər bid′ing, fôr-) /fərˈbɪdɪŋ, fɔr-/ *adj.* grim; threatening: *a forbidding frown.* —**for•bid′ding•ly,** *adv.*

force (fôrs, fōrs) /fɔrs, fowrs/ *n., v.,* **forced, forc•ing.** —*n.* **1.** [*noncount*] physical power or strength: *to pull with all one's force.* **2.** [*noncount*] strength used upon an object; physical coercion; violence: *to use force to open a door.* **3.** [*noncount*] strength; energy; power: *the force of the waves.* **4.** [*noncount*] persuasive power; power to influence or convince: *the force of an argument.* **5.** Often, **forces.** [*plural*] the military or fighting strength, esp. of a nation: *armed forces.* **6.** [*count*] any body of persons combined for joint action: *a sales force.* **7.** *Physics.* **a.** [*noncount*] an influence on a body or system, producing or tending to produce a change in movement: *the measurement of the amount of force used.* **b.** [*count; usually singular*] the intensity of such an influence: *a force of 300 newtons.* **8.** [*count*] any influence or agency that is similar to physical force in having or producing change or movement: *social forces.* —*v.* [~ + *obj*] **9.** [~ + *obj* + *to* + *verb*] to compel, constrain, or make (someone) to do something: *The police forced him to confess.* **10.** to drive or propel against resistance: *to force one's way through a crowd.* **11.** to bring about or effect by force: *We'll have to force a solution.* **12.** to obtain or draw forth by or as if by force; extort: *to force a confession.* **13.** to break open (a door, lock, etc.): *The thieves forced the window.* —***Idiom.*** **14. in force, a.** in operation; effective: *a rule no longer in force.* **b.** in large numbers: *The army attacked in force.* —**Related Words.** FORCE is a noun and a verb, FORCEFUL is an adjective: *The police used force to subdue the prisoner. The police forced him to confess. She is a forceful speaker.*

forced (fôrst, fōrst) /fɔrst, fowrst/ *adj.* **1.** [*before a noun*] enforced; compulsory: *forced labor.* **2.** [*before a noun*] done suddenly of necessity: *a forced helicopter landing.* **3.** unnatural; false: *a forced smile.*

force′-feed′, *v.* [~ + *obj* (+ *obj*)], **-fed, -feed•ing. 1.** to force to ingest food. **2.** to force to learn: *force-fed military discipline.*

force•ful (fôrs′fəl, fōrs′-) /ˈfɔrsfəl, ˈfowrs-/ *adj.* powerful; vigorous: *a forceful blow; a forceful speech.* —**force′ful•ly,** *adv.* —**force′ful•ness,** *n.* [*noncount*]

for•ceps (fôr′səps, -seps) /ˈfɔrsəps, -sɛps/ *n.* [*plural*] an instrument for grasping objects firmly, as in surgical operations.

for•ci•ble (fôr′sə bəl, fōr′-) /ˈfɔrsəbəl, ˈfowr-/ *adj.* **1.** done or effected by force: *forcible entry.* **2.** powerfully effective: *a forcible response.* —**for′ci•bly,** *adv.*

ford (fôrd, fōrd) /fɔrd, fowrd/ *n.* [*count*] **1.** a place where a river can be crossed by wading. —*v.* [~ + *obj*] **2.** to cross (a river, stream, etc.) at a ford: *The wagons managed to ford the stream.*

fore[1] (fôr, fōr) /fɔr, fowr/ *adj.* [*before a noun*] **1.** situated in front: *the fore part of a boat.* —*adv.* **2.** at or toward the front of a vessel; forward. —*n.* [*count; usually singular*] **3.** the forepart of anything; front. —***Idiom.*** **4. fore and aft,** in, at, or to both ends of a ship. **5. to the fore,** into a conspicuous place or position.

fore[2] (fôr, fōr) /fɔr, fowr/ *interj.* (used as a cry of warning by a golfer to persons in danger of being struck by a ball in flight).

fore-, *prefix.* *fore-* is attached to nouns and means: **1.** before (in space, time, condition, etc.): *fore-* + *-cast* → *forecast (= prediction before weather comes); fore-* + *taste* → *foretaste (= a taste before the event takes place); fore-* + *warn* → *forewarn (= to warn ahead of time).* **2.** front: *fore-* + *head* → *forehead (= front of the head).* **3.** preceding: *fore-* + *father* → *forefather (= father that came before).* **4.** superior: *fore-* + *man* → *foreman (= superior to the other workers).*

fore•arm[1] (fôr′ärm′, fōr′-) /ˈfɔrˌɑrm, ˈfowr-/ *n.* [*count*] the part of the arm between the elbow and the wrist.

fore•arm[2] (fôr ärm′, fōr-) /fɔrˈɑrm, fowr-/ *v.* [~ + *obj*] to prepare beforehand, esp. for difficulties.

fore•bear or **for•bear** (fôr′bâr′, fōr′-) /ˈfɔrˌbɛər, ˈfowr-/ *n.* [*count*] ancestor; forefather.

fore•bod•ing (fôr bō′ding, fōr-) /fɔrˈbowdɪŋ, fowr-/ *n.* a strong inner feeling of future misfortune or evil: [*noncount*]: *It was a sense of foreboding.* [*count*]: *felt forebodings all day.*

fore•cast (fôr′kast′, fōr′-) /ˈfɔrˌkæst, ˈfowr-/ *v.,* **-cast** or **-cast•ed, -cast•ing,** *n.* —*v.* [~ + *obj*] **1.** to predict (a future condition or occurrence): *The weatherman had forecast a heavy snowfall.* **2.** to make a prediction about: *He forecast great problems for the future.* [~ + *(that) clause*]: *forecast that we would have great problems.* —*n.* [*count*] **3.** a prediction of future weather conditions.

4. a guess or prediction as to something in the future: *economic forecasts.* **—fore′cast′er,** *n.* [*count*]

fore•cas•tle (fōk′səl, fôr′kas′əl, fōr′-) /ˈfowksəl, ˈfɔrˌkæsəl, ˈfowr-/ *n.* [*count*] a structure sticking up at or immediately aft of the bow of a vessel.

fore•close (fôr klōz′, fōr-) /fɔrˈklowz, fowr-/ *v.,* **-closed, -clos•ing.** (of a bank) to take possession of (property or holdings bought with a mortgage): [*no obj*]: *The bank foreclosed on them.* [~ + *obj*]: *to foreclose a mortgage.*

fore•clo•sure (fôr klō′zhər, fōr-) /fɔrˈklowʒər, fowr-/ *n.* the act of foreclosing a mortgage or pledge: [*noncount*]: *risk of foreclosure.* [*count*]: *many foreclosures this year.*

fore•fa•ther (fôr′fä′thər, fōr′-) /ˈfɔrˌfɑðər, ˈfowr-/ *n.* [*count*] an ancestor; progenitor.

fore•fin•ger (fôr′fing′gər, fōr′-) /ˈfɔrˌfɪŋgər, ˈfowr-/ *n.* [*count*] the finger next to the thumb.

fore•foot (fôr′fo͝ot′, fōr′-) /ˈfɔrˌfʊt, ˈfowr-/ *n.* [*count*], *pl.* **-feet.** one of the front feet esp. of a four-legged animal.

fore•front (fôr′frunt′, fōr′-) /ˈfɔrˌfrʌnt, ˈfowr-/ *n.* [*count; usually singular*] the foremost part or place: *the forefront of a literary movement.*

fore•go (fôr gō′, fōr-) /fɔrˈgow, fowr-/ *v.,* **-went, -gone, -go•ing.** FORGO.

fore•go•ing (fôr gō′ing, fōr-) /fɔrˈgowɪŋ, fowr-/ *adj.* [*before a noun*] previously stated, written, or occurring: *mentioned in the foregoing paragraph.*

fore′gone′ conclu′sion, *n.* [*count*] a conclusion or result that will occur under any circumstances: *It's a foregone conclusion that you won't be hired since you are not qualified.*

fore•ground (fôr′ground′, fōr′-) /ˈfɔrˌgrawnd, ˈfowr-/ *n.* [*count; usually singular*] **1.** the portion of a scene nearest to the viewer. **2.** a prominent or important position; forefront.

fore•hand (fôr′hand′, fōr′-) /ˈfɔrˌhænd, ˈfowr-/ *adj.* **1.** (in tennis, squash, etc.) of, relating to, or being a stroke made with the palm of the hand facing the direction of movement. **—***n.* [*count*] **2.** (in tennis, squash, etc.) a forehand stroke.

fore•head (fôr′id, -hed′, for′-) /ˈfɔrɪd, -ˌhɛd, ˈfɒr-/ *n.* [*count*] the part of the face above the eyebrows; brow.

for•eign (fôr′in, for′-) /ˈfɔrɪn, ˈfɒr-/ *adj.* **1.** of or coming from another country or nation; not domestic or native: *foreign cars.* **2.** [*before a noun*] of or relating to contact or dealings with other countries: *foreign trade deficit.* **3.** [*before a noun*] not belonging to the place or body where found: *some foreign matter in my soup.* **4.** not related to or connected with the thing under consideration: *an issue foreign to our discussion.*

for•eign•er (fôr′ə nər, for′-) /ˈfɔrənər, ˈfɒr-/ *n.* [*count*] a person from a foreign country.

for′eign ex•change′, *n.* [*noncount*] the system under which the money of one country is exchanged for money from another.

fore•knowl•edge (fôr′nol′ij, fōr′-) /ˈfɔrˌnɒlɪdʒ, ˈfowr-/ *n.* [*noncount*] knowledge of something before it occurs.

fore•leg (fôr′leg′, fōr′-) /ˈfɔrˌlɛg, ˈfowr-/ *n.* [*count*] either of the front legs of a four-legged animal.

fore•limb (fôr′lim′, fōr′-) /ˈfɔrˌlɪm, ˈfowr-/ *n.* [*count*] a front limb of an animal.

fore•lock (fôr′lok′, fōr′-) /ˈfɔrˌlɒk, ˈfowr-/ *n.* [*count*] a lock of hair growing from the front part of the head.

fore•man (fôr′mən, fōr′-) /ˈfɔrmən, ˈfowr-/ or **-wom•an** (-wo͝om′ən) /-ˌwʊmən/ or **-per•son** (-pûr′sən) /-ˌpɜrsən/ *n.* [*count*], *pl.* **-men** or **-wom•en** or **-per•sons. 1.** a person in charge of a group of workers. **2.** the member of a jury who is selected to speak for all the jurors on the panel.

fore•mast (fôr′mast′, fōr′-; *Nautical.* -məst) /ˈfɔrˌmæst, ˈfowr-; *Nautical.* -məst/ *n.* [*count*] the mast nearest the bow of a vessel.

fore•most (fôr′mōst′, -məst, fōr′-) /ˈfɔrˌmowst, -məst, ˈfowr-/ *adj., adv.* first in place, rank, or importance: *brought in the foremost surgeons; to put one's studies foremost.*

fore•name (fôr′nām′, fōr′-) /ˈfɔrˌneym, ˈfowr-/ *n.* [*count*] a name that precedes the family name or surname; first name.

fo•ren•sic (fə ren′sik, -zik) /fəˈrɛnsɪk, -zɪk/ *adj.* **1.** relating to or used in legal proceedings or in debate: *forensic medicine; forensic evidence.* **—***n.* **2. forensics,** [*noncount; used with a singular verb*] the art of formal debate. **—fo•ren′si•cal•ly,** *adv.*

fore•part (fôr′pärt′, fōr′-) /ˈfɔrˌpɑrt, ˈfowr-/ *n.* [*count*] the first, front, or early part.

fore•play (fôr′plā′, fōr′-) /ˈfɔrˌpley, ˈfowr-/ *n.* [*noncount*] sexual activity preceding intercourse.

fore•run•ner (fôr′run′ər, fōr′-, fôr run′ər, fōr-) /ˈfɔrˌrʌnər, ˈfowr-, fɔrˈrʌnər, fowr-/ *n.* [*count*] **1.** person or thing that is similar to something that comes or happens after. **2.** a person or thing that is an omen, sign, or indication of something to follow; portent.

fore•see (fôr sē′, fōr-) /fɔrˈsiy, fowr-/ *v.* [~ + *obj*], **-saw, -seen, -see•ing.** to sense or know in advance: *foresaw no problems.* [~ + *(that) clause*]: *foresaw that there would be great famine.*

fore•see•a•ble (fôr sē′ə bəl, fōr-) /fɔrˈsiyəbəl, fowr-/ *adj.* that can be sensed or known in advance: *the foreseeable future.*

fore•shad•ow (fôr shad′ō, fōr-) /fɔrˈʃædow, fowr-/ *v.* [~ + *obj*] to show or indicate beforehand: *work that foreshadowed later inventions.*

fore•short•en (fôr shôr′tn, fōr-) /fɔrˈʃɔrtn̩, fowr-/ *v.* [~ + *obj*] to make more compact; shorten.

fore•sight (fôr′sīt′, fōr′-) /ˈfɔrˌsayt, ˈfowr-/ *n.* [*noncount*] **1.** care or provision for the future: *Through lack of foresight I had run out of money.* **2.** the act or power of foreseeing; knowledge or insight of the future; foreknowledge.

fore•skin (fôr′skin′, fōr′-) /ˈfɔrˌskɪn, ˈfowr-/ *n.* [*noncount*] the skin covering the tip of the penis.

for•est (fôr′ist, for′-) /ˈfɔrɪst, ˈfɒr-/ *n.* [*count*] **1.** a large area of land covered with trees and underbrush; woods. See illustration at LANDSCAPE. **—***v.* [~ + *obj*] **2.** to grow forest on: *to forest the land.* **—for′est•ed,** *adj.*

fore•stall (fōr stôl′, fôr-) /fowrˈstɔl, fɔr-/ *v.* [~ + *obj*] to prevent, hinder, or thwart by taking action in advance: *They forestalled a request for a raise by increasing medical benefits.*

for•est•a•tion (fôr′ə stā′shən, for′-) /ˌfɔrəˈsteyʃən, ˌfɒr-/ *n.* [*noncount*] the planting of forests.

for•est•er (fôr′ə stər, for′-) /ˈfɔrəstər, ˈfɒr-/ *n.* [*count*] an expert in forestry.

for′est rang′er, *n.* [*count*] a government officer who guards and cares for public forests.

for•est•ry (fôr′ə strē, for′-) /ˈfɔrəstriy, ˈfɒr-/ *n.* [*noncount*] the science of planting and taking care of trees and forests.

fore•taste (fôr′tāst′, fōr′-) /ˈfɔrˌteyst, ˈfowr-/ *n.* [*count; usually singular*] a sample of something to come in the future.

fore•tell (fôr tel′, fōr-) /fɔrˈtɛl, fowr-/ *v.,* **-told, -tell•ing.** to tell of beforehand; predict; prophesy: [~ + *obj*]: *Who can foretell the future?* [~ + *(that) clause*]: *The prophet foretold that the kingdom would be attacked.*

fore•thought (fôr′thôt′, fōr′-) /ˈfɔrˌθɔt, ˈfowr-/ *n.* [*noncount*] a thinking about a situation beforehand: *an escape plan prepared with forethought.*

for•ev•er (fôr ev′ər, fər-) /fɔrˈɛvər, fər-/ *adv.* **1.** without ending; for all time; eternally: *She's gone forever.* **2.** [*often: be* + ~ + *verb-ing*] continually; incessantly; always: *He is forever complaining.* **—***n.* [*noncount*] **3.** a seemingly endless period of time: *Don't spend forever on the phone.*

for•ev•er•more (fôr ev′ər môr′, -mōr′, fər-) /fɔrˌɛvərˈmɔr, -ˈmowr, fər-/ *adv.* forever hereafter.

fore•warn (fôr wôrn′, fōr-) /fɔrˈwɔrn, fowr-/ *v.* to warn in advance: [~ + *obj*]: *Thunder forewarned us of the coming storm.* [~ + *obj* + *of* + *obj*]: *We forewarned him of the danger.* [~ + *obj* + *(that) clause*]: *He was forewarned that his effort was useless.*

fore•word (fôr′wûrd′, -wərd, fōr′-) /ˈfɔrˌwɜrd, -wərd, ˈfowr-/ *n.* [*count*] an introductory statement in a book, esp. when written by someone other than the author. Compare AFTERWORD.

for•feit (fôr′fit) /ˈfɔrfɪt/ *n.* [*count*] **1.** an act of forfeiting. **—***v.* **2.** to (cause to) lose or become liable to lose, because of a failure to do something: [~ + *obj*]: *She forfeited the match by refusing to play.* [*no obj*]: *had to forfeit because she couldn't continue the match.*

for•fei•ture (fôr′fi chər) /ˈfɔrfɪtʃər/ *n.* [*noncount*] an act of forfeiting: *the forfeiture of his life.*

for•gave (fər gāv′) /fərˈgeyv/ *v.* pt. of FORGIVE.

forge[1] (fôrj, fōrj) /fɔrdʒ, fowrdʒ/ *v.,* **forged, forg•ing,** *n.* **—***v.* [~ + *obj*] **1.** to form by heating and hammering: *The blacksmith forged the horseshoe.* **2.** to form or make, esp. by concentrated effort; produce: *The two sides managed to forge a treaty.* **3.** to make a forgery of: *He forged our signatures.* **—***n.* [*count*] **4.** a fireplace or furnace in which metal is heated before shaping. **—forg′er,** *n.* [*count*]

forge[2] (fôrj, fōrj) /fɔrdʒ, fowrdʒ/ *v.* [*no obj*], **forged, forg•ing.** to move ahead slowly and steadily: *to forge through dense underbrush; forged ahead and finished the work.*

for•ger•y (fôr′jə rē, fōr′-) /'fɔrdʒəriy, 'fowr-/ *n., pl.* **-ger•ies. 1.** [*noncount*] the crime of falsely making or changing writing or a signature: *convicted of forgery.* **2.** [*count*] a piece of writing so made or altered: *That signature is an obvious forgery.* **3.** [*count*] any piece of work falsely claimed to be genuine: *Several paintings were forgeries.*

for•get (fər get′) /fər'gɛt/ *v.,* **-got** (-got′) /-'gɒt/ **got•ten** (-got′n) /-'gɒtn̩/ or **-got, -get•ting. 1.** [*usually not: be + ~-ing*] to cease to remember; be unable to recall: [~ + *obj*]: *I have forgotten your name.* [~ + *(that) clause*]: *I forgot that we had a meeting.* **2.** [*usually not: be + ~-ing*] to neglect unintentionally: [~ + *obj*]: *I'm sorry I forgot our appointment.* [~ + *about* + *obj*]: *I forgot about the meeting.* [~ + *to* + *verb*]: *I forgot to lock the gate.* **3.** [~ + *obj*] to leave behind unintentionally: *to forget the car keys.* **4.** [~ *(+ about)* + *obj*] to take no note of (often used in commands): *Forget (about) cooking; let's eat out.* **5.** to stop thinking of deliberately: [~ + *obj*]: *I tried to forget the past.* [~ + *about* + *obj*]: *I tried to forget all about her.* **—*Idiom.* 6. forget oneself,** [*no obj*] to say or do something improper: *I forgot myself and started shouting.*

for•get•ful (fər get′fəl) /fər'gɛtfəl/ *adj.* **1.** apt to forget; absent-minded: *got forgetful in old age.* **2.** [*be* + ~ + *of*] heedless; neglectful: *is forgetful of others.* **—for•get′ful•ly,** *adv.* **—for•get′ful•ness,** *n.* [*noncount*]

forget′-me-not′, *n.* [*count*] a plant having small light-blue flowers.

for•get•ta•ble (fər get′ə bəl) /fər'gɛtəbəl/ *adj.* apt to be or worthy of being forgotten: *a forgettable performance.*

for•give (fər giv′) /fər'gɪv/ *v.,* **-gave** (-gāv′) /-'geyv/ **-giv•en, -giv•ing. —***v.* [*usually not: be + ~-ing*] **1.** to grant pardon for (an offense); absolve: [~ + *obj*]: *to forgive a sin.* [*no obj*]: *Forgive and go forward.* **2.** to grant pardon to (a person): [~ + *obj*]: *forgave him and told him to repent.* [~ + *obj* + *obj*]: *forgave him his sins.* **3.** [~ + *obj*] to cease to feel resentment against: *to forgive one's enemies.* **4.** [~ + *obj*] to cancel or remit (a debt, obligation, etc.): *to forgive the interest owed on a loan.* **—for•give′ness,** *n.* [*noncount*] **—Syn.** See EXCUSE.

for•giv•ing (fər giv′ing) /fər'gɪvɪŋ/ *adj.* **1.** disposed to forgive: *in a forgiving mood.* **2.** [*be* + ~ + *of*] offering the chance to recover from mistakes: *a slope that was forgiving of inexperienced skiers.*

for•go or **fore•go** (fôr gō′) /fɔr'gow/ *v.* [~ + *obj*], **-went, -gone, -go•ing.** to give up; abstain from or refrain from: *I agreed to forgo a raise for this year for a larger one next year.*

fork (fôrk) /fɔrk/ *n.* [*count*] **1.** an instrument having two or more points or prongs for holding, lifting, etc., esp. one used for handling food: *knives, forks, and spoons.* See illustration at RESTAURANT. **2.** something resembling this in form, as a farm tool. **3.** the point or part at which a thing, such as a river or a road, divides into branches. **4.** either of the branches into which a thing divides: *When the road splits, take the left fork.* **—***v.* **5.** [*no obj*] to divide into branches: *The road forks up ahead.* **6.** *Informal.* **fork over, out,** or **up,** to deliver; pay; hand over: [~ + *over/out/up* + *obj*]: *Fork over the money now.* [~ + *obj* + *over/out/up*]: *Fork it over.* **—fork′ful** (-fo͝ol) /-fʊl/ *n.* [*count*], *pl.* **-fuls.**

forked (fôrkt, fôr′kid) /fɔrkt, 'fɔrkɪd/ *adj.* **1.** having a fork or forklike branches: *a snake's forked tongue.* **—*Idiom.* 2. to speak with** or **have a forked tongue,** [*no obj*] to speak untruthfully.

fork•lift (fôrk′lift′) /'fɔrk,lɪft/ *n.* [*count*] Also called **fork′lift truck′.** a small vehicle with two power-operated prongs at the front that can be slid under heavy loads in order to lift and move them, as in warehouses.

for•lorn (fôr lôrn′) /fɔr'lɔrn/ *adj.* **1.** miserable, as in condition or appearance: *a forlorn little cabin in the mountains.* **2.** lonely and sad: *gave her father a forlorn look.* **3.** despairing; with no hope: *a forlorn attempt to migrate.* **—for•lorn′ly,** *adv.*

form (fôrm) /fɔrm/ *n.* **1.** [*count*] the outside appearance of a clearly defined area: *a triangular form.* **2.** [*count*] the shape of a thing or person: *He could make out a dim form in the distance wearing a raincoat.* **3.** [*count*] a body, esp. that of a human being: *That suit really fits your form.* **4.** [*count*] something that gives or determines shape; a mold: *poured the cake mix into the forms.* **5.** [*count*] a particular condition, character, or mode in which something appears: *Ice is water in another form.* **6.** [*noncount*] the manner or style of performing, or coordinating parts for a pleasing result, as in musical composition; technique: *displayed excellent form.* **7.** [*count*] a document with blank spaces to be filled in with details before it is executed: *had to fill in a tax form.* **8.** [*count*] a formality or ceremony, often with implication of absence of real meaning: *He went through the forms of the service.* **9.** [*noncount*] procedure or conduct, as judged by social standards; custom: *Good form demands that we go to the wedding.* **10.** [*noncount*] physical condition or fitness, as for performing: *in peak form.* **11.** [*count*] **a.** a particular spelling of a word that occurs in more than one spelling: *In* I'm, 'm *is a form of* am. **b.** a word with a particular ending or other change: *The word* goes *is a form of* go. **12.** [*count*] a grade or class of pupils in a British secondary school or in certain U.S. private schools. **—***v.* **13.** [~ + *obj*] to construct or frame; put together: *Form the clay into a bowl.* **14.** [~ + *obj*] to make or produce: *The bitter cold formed ice on the window.* **15.** [*no obj*] to take or assume form; to be formed or produced: *Ice began to form on the window.* **16.** [~ + *obj*] to give form or shape to; shape; produce: *Form the dough into squares.* **17.** [*not: be + ~-ing; ~ + obj*] to serve to make up; compose; constitute: *Three citizens form the review board.* **18.** [~ + *obj*] to organize or start; initiate: *formed a civilian police board.* **19.** [~ + *obj*] to place in order; arrange: *The drill sergeant formed his men into a line.* **20.** [~ + *obj*] to shape in the mind: *She had formed the idea while waiting for a bus.* **21.** [~ + *obj*] to develop; establish: *He formed the habit of looking over the tops of his glasses.* **22.** [~ + *obj*] to mold or develop by discipline or instructions: *For some people the military forms character.* **23.** [~ + *obj*] to produce (a word or class of words) by adding a prefix or suffix, combining elements, or changing the shape of the word: *For many words in English we form the plural by adding* -s.

-form-, *root.* *-form-* comes from Latin, where it has the meaning "form, shape." This meaning is found in such words as: CONFORM, DEFORM, FORMALIZE, FORMAT, FORMULA, MALFORMATION, MULTIFORM, NONCONFORMIST, PERFORM, PLATFORM, REFORM, TRANSFORM, UNIFORM.

for•mal (fôr′məl) /'fɔrməl/ *adj.* **1.** [*before a noun*] being in accordance with accepted customs; conventional: *General Lee offered General Grant his sword as a formal act of surrender.* **2.** marked by form or ceremony: *The reception was a formal occasion.* **3.** designed for wear or use at elaborate ceremonial or social events: *The invitation specified formal attire.* **4.** requiring dress suitable for elaborate social events: *a formal dance.* **5.** too interested in ceremony; prim; decorous: *The boss is too formal on most occasions.* **6.** being a matter of form only: *more than just formal courtesy.* **7.** made or done in accordance with procedures that make sure something is valid or proper: *got the formal authorization.* **8.** [*before a noun*] of, relating to, or emphasizing the organization, form, or shape in the parts of a work of art, writing, or music: *The class analyzed the formal structure of the poem.* **9.** [*before a noun*] obtained in school; academic: *received a formal education.* **10.** of or relating to language use typical of impersonal and official situations, obeying standards of correctness, and the avoidance of colloquialisms: *formal English.* **11.** being such merely in appearance or name: *The queen was only the formal head of state.* **—***n.* [*count*] **12.** a dance or other social occasion that requires formal clothes. **13.** an evening gown: *spilling wine on her formal.* **—for′mal•ly,** *adv.* See -FORM-.

form•al•de•hyde (fôr mal′də hīd′, fər-) /fɔr'mældə,hayd, fər-/ *n.* [*noncount*] a toxic gas used chiefly in solution as a disinfectant and as a preservative.

for•mal•i•ty (fôr mal′i tē) /fɔr'mælɪtiy/ *n., pl.* **-ties. 1.** [*noncount*] the condition or quality of being formal; conventionality: *too much formality in the office.* **2.** [*count*] an established order or method of proceeding: *the formalities of the court process.* **3.** [*count*] a formal act or observance: *The receiving line was a necessary formality at the wedding.* See -FORM-.

for•mal•ize (fôr′mə līz′) /'fɔrmə,layz/ *v.* [~ + *obj*], **-ized, -iz•ing.** to make formal: *formalized their spoken agreement with a legal contract.* See -FORM-.

for•mat (fôr′mat) /'fɔrmæt/ *n., v.,* **-mat•ted, -mat•ting. —***n.* [*count*] **1.** the organization, plan, or style of something, such as the general appearance of a book, magazine, or newspaper. **2.** the arrangement of data for computer input or output. **—***v.* [~ + *obj*] **3.** to plan or provide a format for. **4. a.** to set the format of: *to format* *a computer document.* **b.** to prepare (a computer disk) for writing and reading. See -FORM-.

for•ma•tion (fôr mā′shən) /fɔr'meyʃən/ *n.* **1.** [*noncount*] the act or process of forming or the state of being formed: *the formation of ice.* **2.** the manner in which a thing is formed; formal structure or arrangement: [*count*]: *a formation of jet planes.* [*noncount*]: *planes flying in formation.* **3.** [*noncount*] development; creation; establishment: *The Pilgrims' goal was the formation of a colony in the New World.* See -FORM-.

form•a•tive (fôr′mə tiv) /'fɔrmətɪv/ *adj.* [*before a noun*] **1.** giving form or shape: *a formative process in manufacturing.* **2.** relating to formation, growth, or development: *a child's formative years.* See -FORM-.

for•mer (fôr′mər) /'fɔrmər/ *adj.* [*before a noun*] **1.** preceding in time; prior or earlier: *We had met on a former occasion.* **2.** being the first mentioned of two (distinguished from *latter*): *The former suggestion was better than the latter.* **3.** having once or previously been; erstwhile: *They welcomed the former president.* **—***n.* [*noncount; the* + ~] **4.** the one first mentioned: *We have two dogs, a collie and a beagle; the former is the older.*

for•mer•ly (fôr′mər lē) /'fɔrmərliy/ *adv.* in time past; in an earlier period or age; previously: *Zimbabwe was formerly known as Rhodesia.*

form•fit•ting (fôrm′fit′ing) /'fɔrm,fɪtɪŋ/ *adj.* designed to fit snugly: *a formfitting wet suit.*

For•mi•ca (fôr mī′kə) /fɔr'maykə/ *Trademark.* [*noncount*] a brand of laminated plastic typically used for countertops.

for•mi•da•ble (fôr′mi də bəl) /'fɔrmɪdəbəl/ *adj.* **1.** causing fear, awe, or concern: *a formidable opponent.* **2.** of awesome size, difficulty, etc.: *a formidable problem.* —**for′mi•da•bly,** *adv.*

form•less (fôrm′lis) /'fɔrmlɪs/ *adj.* lacking a definite form; shapeless. —**form′less•ness,** *n.* [*noncount*]

form′ let′ter, *n.* [*count*] a standardized letter that can be sent to any number of persons.

for•mu•la (fôr′myə lə) /'fɔrmyələ/ *n., pl.* **-las, -lae** (-lē′) /-,liy/. **1.** [*count*] a set form of words, as for stating something with authority, for indicating procedure to be followed, or for use on some ceremonial occasion. **2.** [*count*] fixed or conventional method or approach: *produced her popular novels by a formula.* **3.** [*count*] a mathematical rule or principle, frequently expressed in algebraic symbols: *$E = mc^2$ is a formula expressing the relationship between matter and energy.* **4.** [*count*] an expression of the parts or elements of a compound by symbols and figures: *H_2O is the molecular formula for water.* **5.** [*count*] a recipe or prescription: *The formula for making that new plastic is a closely kept secret.* **6.** [*noncount*] a special nutritive food mixture, esp. of milk or milk substitute, for feeding a baby. —**for•mu•la•ic** (fôr′myə lā′ik) /,fɔrmyə'leyɪk/ *adj.* See -FORM-.

for•mu•late (fôr′myə lāt′) /'fɔrmyə,leyt/ *v.* [~ + *obj*], **-lat•ed, -lat•ing. 1.** to express as a formula. **2.** to devise; develop: *managed to formulate a peace plan acceptable to both sides.* —**for•mu•la•tion** (fôr′mya lā′shən) /,fɔrmyæ'leyʃən/ *n.* [*noncount*]: *the formulation of policy.* [*count*]: *formulations of plots.* —**for′mu•la′tor,** *n.* [*count*]

for•ni•cate (fôr′ni kāt′) /'fɔrnɪ,keyt/ *v.* [*no obj*], **-cat•ed, -cat•ing.** (of two persons not married to each other) to have voluntary sexual intercourse. —**for•ni•ca•tion** (fôr′ni kā′shən) /,fɔrnɪ'keyʃən/ *n.* [*noncount*]

for•sake (fôr sāk′) /fɔr'seyk/ *v.* [~ + *obj*], **-sook, -sak•en, -sak•ing. 1.** to quit or leave entirely; abandon: *to forsake one's family.* **2.** to forgo: *persuaded him to forsake smoking.*

for•swear (fôr swâr′) /fɔr'swɛər/ *v.* [~ + *obj*], **-swore, -sworn, -swear•ing.** to promise not to do (something): *to forswear sinful ways.*

for•syth•i•a (fôr sith′ē ə, fər-) /fɔr'sɪθiyə, fər-/ *n.* [*count*], *pl.* **-syth•i•as.** a shrub having yellow flowers that blossom in early spring.

fort (fôrt, fōrt) /fɔrt, fowrt/ *n.* [*count*] **1.** a location occupied by troops and surrounded by defensive works. **2.** any permanent army post. **—*Idiom.* 3. hold the fort, a.** to defend one's position against attack or criticism: *held the fort against the attacks of the enemy.* **b.** to maintain the existing state of affairs: *Hold the fort until we get back from lunch.* See -FORT-.

-fort-, *root.* *-fort-* comes from Latin, where it has the meaning "strong; strength." This meaning is found in such words as: COMFORT, DISCOMFORT, EFFORT, FORT, FORTE, FORTIFY, FORTITUDE, FORTRESS, UNCOMFORTABLE.

forte[1] (fôrt, fōrt, fôr′tā) /fɔrt, fowrt, 'fɔrtey/ *n.* [*count; usually singular*] a field in which one excels; strong point: *His forte is mathematics.* See -FORT-.

for•te[2] (fôr′tā) /'fɔrtey/ *Music.* **—***adj.* **1.** loud (opposed to *piano*). **—***adv.* **2.** loudly. See -FORT-.

forth (fôrth, fōrth) /fɔrθ, fowrθ/ *adv.* **1.** onward or outward; forward or away: *rode forth to do battle.* **2.** out; into view: *Decency shines forth in his every action.*

forth•com•ing (fôrth′kum′ing, fōrth′-) /'fɔrθ'kʌmɪŋ, 'fowrθ-/ *adj.* **1.** [*before a noun*] about to appear; approaching in time: *the forthcoming concert.* **2.** [*be* + ~] ready or available: *Help will be forthcoming whenever you ask.* **3.** frank and cooperative: *She was forthcoming in her testimony.*

forth•right (fôrth′rīt′, fōrth′-) /'fɔrθ,rayt, 'fowrθ-/ *adj.* going straight to the point; direct: *forthright answers.* —**forth′right′ly,** *adv.* —**forth′right′ness,** *n.* [*noncount*]

forth•with (fôrth′with′, -wit͟h′, fōrth′-) /,fɔrθ'wɪθ, -'wɪð, ,fowrθ-/ *adv.* immediately: *The action is suspended forthwith.*

for•ti•fi•ca•tion (fôr′tə fi kā′shən) /,fɔrtəfɪ'keyʃən/ *n.* **1.** [*noncount*] the process or act of fortifying. **2.** [*count*] something that fortifies or protects. **3.** Often, **fortifications.** [*plural*] military works constructed in order to defend or strengthen a position.

for•ti•fy (fôr′tə fī′) /'fɔrtə,fay/ *v.* [~ + *obj*], **-fied, -fy•ing. 1.** to increase the defenses of: *They went about fortifying the besieged town.* **2.** to impart strength or vigor to: *had fortified myself with a good breakfast.* **3.** to increase the effectiveness of, such as by additional ingredients: *to fortify a diet with vitamins.* **4.** to strengthen mentally or morally: *fortified by faith.* See -FORT-.

for•tis•si•mo (fôr tis′ə mō′) /fɔr'tɪsə,mow/ *Music.* **—***adj.* **1.** very loud. **—***adv.* **2.** very loudly. See -FORT-.

for•ti•tude (fôr′ti to͞od′, -tyo͞od′) /'fɔrtɪ,tuwd, -,tyuwd/ *n.* [*noncount*] mental and emotional strength in facing difficulty and danger courageously: *It took fortitude to live on the frontier.* See -FORT-.

fort•night (fôrt′nīt′) /'fɔrt,nayt/ *n.* [*count*] a period of fourteen nights and days; two weeks. —**fort′night′ly,** *adj., adv.*

for•tress (fôr′tris) /'fɔrtrɪs/ *n.* [*count*] **1.** a fort or group of forts often including a town; citadel. **2.** any place of exceptional security; stronghold: *a little fortress of their own deep in the woods.* See -FORT-.

for•tu•i•tous (fôr to͞o′i təs, -tyo͞o′-) /fɔr'tuwɪtəs, -'tyuw-/ *adj.* **1.** happening or produced by chance; accidental: *a fortuitous encounter.* **2.** fortunate: *The money came at a fortuitous moment.* —**for•tu′i•tous•ly,** *adv.* —**for•tu′i•tous′ness,** *n.* [*noncount*] See -FORTUN-.

-fortun-, *root.* *-fortun-* comes from Latin, where it has the meaning "by chance; luck." This meaning is found in such words as: FORTUITOUS, FORTUNATE, FORTUNE, MISFORTUNE, UNFORTUNATE.

for•tu•nate (fôr′chə nit) /'fɔrtʃənɪt/ *adj.* **1.** receiving good from uncertain or unexpected sources; lucky: *You were very fortunate to escape from that explosion.* **2.** bringing or indicating good fortune: *a fortunate decision to buy.* —**for′tu•nate•ly,** *adv.* See -FORTUN-.

for•tune (fôr′chən) /'fɔrtʃən/ *n.* **1.** [*count*] wealth; riches: *inherited a fortune.* **2.** [*noncount*] chance; luck: *They had the bad fortune to go bankrupt.* **3. fortunes,** [*plural*] varied occurrences of a person's life: *a reversal of fortunes.* **4.** [*count*] fate; destiny; future. See -FORTUN-.

for′tune cook′ie, *n.* [*count*] a folded edible wafer containing a slip of paper with a printed saying or prediction.

for′tune-tell′er, *n.* [*count*] a person who claims the ability to predict the future. —**for′tune-tell′ing,** *n.* [*noncount*]

for•ty (fôr′tē) /'fɔrtiy/ *n., pl.* **-ties,** *adj.* **—***n.* [*count*] **1.** a cardinal number, ten times four. **2.** a symbol for this number, as 40 or XL. **3. forties,** the numbers from 40 through 49, as in referring to the years of a lifetime or of a century or to degrees of temperature. **—***adj.* [*before a noun*] **4.** amounting to 40 in number. —**for′ti•eth,** *adj., n.* [*count*]

for′ty-five′, *n.* [*count*] **1.** a .45-caliber handgun or its cartridge (often written as *.45*). **2.** a 7-inch phonograph record played at 45 r.p.m. (often written as *45*).

for•ty-nin•er (fôr′tē nī′nər) /,fɔrtiy'naynər/ *n.* [*count*] a person participating in the California gold rush in 1849.

for′ty winks′, *n.* [*noncount*] a short nap.

fo•rum (fôr′əm, fōr′əm) /'fɔrəm, 'fowrəm/ *n.* [*count*], *pl.* **fo•rums, fo•ra** (fôr′ə, fōr′ə) /'fɔrə, 'fowrə/. **1.** the marketplace or public square of an ancient Roman city. **2. a.** a meeting place for or a means through which discussion of matters of public interest can be conducted: *The magazine is a forum for various political views.* **b.** a public meeting or assembly for such discussion. **c.** a discussion of a public issue by a select group.

for•ward (fôr′wərd) /ˈfɔrwərd/ *adv.* Also, **forwards. 1.** toward or to what is in front, in the future, or in advance: *from this day forward.* **2.** into view or consideration; forth: *She brought forward a good suggestion.* **—*adj.* 3.** [*before a noun*] directed toward a point in advance: *a forward motion.* **4.** [*before a noun*] being in a condition of advancement: *a forward step in his career.* **5.** bold; unruly and impolite: *a rude, forward child.* **6.** [*before a noun*] situated in the front: *the forward part of the ship.* **7.** of, into, or for the future: *a forward price.* **—*n.*** [*count*] **8.** a player stationed in front of others on a team, as in basketball or hockey. **—*v.*** [~ + *obj*] **9.** to send onward, esp. to a new address: *The post office forwarded our letters.* **10.** to help onward; promote: *forwarding one's career.* **11.** to cause to advance: *to forward a tape on a VCR.* —**for′ward•ness,** *n.* [*noncount*]

for•went (fôr went′) /fɔrˈwɛnt/ *v.* pt. of FORGO.

fos•sil (fos′əl) /ˈfɒsəl/ *n.* [*count*] **1.** the preserved remains, or an imprint, of an organism from a former age. **2.** a very outdated or old-fashioned person or thing. **—*adj.*** [*before a noun*] **3.** of the nature of a fossil: *fossil insects.* **4.** formed from the remains of prehistoric life: *Coal and oil are fossil fuels.*

fos•sil•ize (fos′ə līz′) /ˈfɒsəˌlayz/ *v.*, **-ized, -iz•ing. 1.** to convert into or become a fossil: [*no obj*]: *Those specimens will fossilize.* [~ + *obj*]: *Those specimens were fossilized by the passing of time.* **2.** [~ + *obj; often: be* + ~*-ed*] to cause to become out-of-date: *fossilized social attitudes.* —**fos•sil•i•za•tion** (fos′ə lə zā′shən) /ˌfɒsələˈzeyʃən/ *n.* [*noncount*]

fos•ter (fô′stər, fos′tər) /ˈfɔstər, ˈfɒstər/ *v.* [~ + *obj*] **1.** to promote the growth or development of: *to foster new ideas.* **2.** to bring up; rear: *to foster an abandoned child.* **—*adj.*** [*before a noun*] **3.** providing or receiving parental care despite the absence of relationship by blood or law: *a foster home; foster children.*

fought (fôt) /fɔt/ *v.* pt. and pp. of FIGHT.

foul (foul) /fawl/ *adj.* **1.** offensive to the senses; disgusting: *a foul smell from the river.* **2.** marked by offensive matter or qualities: *The city air had become foul with pollution.* **3.** very dirty; filthy: *foul rags.* **4.** clogged with foreign matter: *a foul pipeline.* **5.** stormy; inclement: *foul weather.* **6.** angry; irritable: *in a foul temper.* **7.** morally offensive: *the foul crime of murder.* **8.** profane; obscene: *foul language.* **9.** contrary to the rules or practices, as in a sport or game. **—*adv.* 10.** in a foul manner. **—*n.*** [*count*] **11.** a violation of the rules of a sport or game: *disqualified for too many fouls.* **—*v.* 12.** [~ + *obj*] to make foul; defile; soil: *a river fouled with pollution.* **13.** [~ + *obj*] to clog; obstruct: *The valves were fouled with dirt.* **14.** to (cause to) become entangled or caught, such as a rope: [*no obj*]: *The ropes fouled in the wind.* [~ + *obj*]: *The wind and tides fouled the ropes.* **15.** [~ + *obj*] to dishonor; disgrace: *Scandal fouled his good name.* **16.** [*no obj*] to commit a foul in a sport or game. **17. foul up,** to make a mess; bungle: [*no obj*]: *really fouled up during the interview.* [~ + *up* + *obj*]: *really fouled up the interview.* [~ + *obj* + *up*]: *had really fouled it up this time.* —**foul′ly,** *adv.* —**foul′ness,** *n.* [*noncount*]

foul•mouthed (foul′mouthd′, -moutht′) /ˈfawlˈmawðd, -ˈmawθt/ *adj.* using obscene or profane language.

foul′ play′, *n.* [*noncount*] violent mischief, esp. murder.

foul′-up′, *n.* [*count*] **1.** a condition of disorder brought on by inefficiency or stupidity. **2.** failure of a mechanical part to operate correctly.

found[1] (found) /fawnd/ *v.* pt. and pp. of FIND.

found[2] (found) /fawnd/ *v.* [~ + *obj*] **1.** to establish on a firm or long-lasting basis: *She went on to found a new company.* **2.** to provide a firm basis for; ground: *a story founded on fact.*

foun•da•tion (foun dā′shən) /fawnˈdeyʃən/ *n.* **1.** the basis or groundwork of anything: [*noncount*]: *The criminal charges were without foundation.* [*count*]: *We need a foundation of trust.* **2.** [*count*] the base on which some structure rests: *They poured the concrete for the building foundation.* **3.** [*noncount*] the act of founding: *the events marking the foundation of the republic.* **4.** [*count*] an institution financed by a donation or money left after someone's death, such as one to aid research. **5.** [*count*] an undergarment worn to give shape to the body. **—Syn.** See BASE[1].

foun•der[1] (foun′dər) /ˈfawndər/ *v.* [*no obj*] **1.** to fill with water and sink: *The ship foundered during the typhoon.* **2.** to fail: *The project foundered when its supporters quit.*

foun•der[2] (foun′dər) /ˈfawndər/ *n.* [*count*] a person who founds: *the founders of the republic.*

found•ling (found′ling) /ˈfawndlɪŋ/ *n.* [*count*] an infant who is found abandoned; a child without a known parent or guardian.

found•ry (foun′drē) /ˈfawndriy/ *n.* [*count*], *pl.* **-ries.** an establishment for casting metal.

fount (fount) /fawnt/ *n.* [*count*] **1.** a spring of water; fountain. **2.** a source: *a fount of ideas.* See FONT[1].

foun•tain (foun′tn) /ˈfawntn̩/ *n.* [*count*] **1.** the source or origin of anything: *a fountain of wisdom.* **2.** an artificial jet or stream of water that spouts from an opening or structure.

foun•tain•head (foun′tn hed′) /ˈfawntn̩ˌhɛd/ *n.* [*count*] **1.** a spring from which a stream flows. **2.** a chief source: *a fountainhead of information.*

foun′tain pen′, *n.* [*count*] a pen with a refillable container holding ink that provides a continuous supply of ink to its point.

four (fôr, fōr) /fɔr, fowr/ *n.* [*count*] **1.** a cardinal number, three plus one. **2.** a symbol for this number, as 4 or IV. **—*adj.*** [*before a noun*] **3.** amounting to four in number. **—*Idiom.* 4. on all fours,** on one's hands and knees.

four•post•er (fôr′pō′stər, fōr′-) /ˈfɔrˈpowstər, ˈfowr-/ *n.* [*count*] a bed with four corner posts, such as for supporting a canopy.

four•score (fôr′skôr′, fōr′skōr′) /ˈfɔrˈskɔr, ˈfowrˈskowr/ *adj.* four times twenty; eighty.

four•some (fôr′səm, fōr′-) /ˈfɔrsəm, ˈfowr-/ *n.* [*count*] **1.** a company or set of four; two pairs. **2.** a golf match between two pairs of players.

four•square (fôr′skwâr′, fōr′-) /ˈfɔrˈskwɛər, ˈfowr-/ *adj.* **1.** firm; forthright: *foursquare dedication.* **—*adv.* 2.** without equivocation; forthrightly.

four•teen (fôr′tēn′, fōr′-) /ˈfɔrˈtiyn, ˈfowr-/ *n.* **1.** a cardinal number, ten plus four. **2.** a symbol for this number, as 14 or XIV. **—*adj.*** [*before a noun*] **3.** amounting to 14 in number. —**four′teenth′,** *adj., n.* [*count*]

fourth (fôrth, fōrth) /fɔrθ, fowrθ/ *adj.* **1.** next after the third; being the ordinal number for four. **2.** being one of four equal parts. **3.** relating to the gear transmission ratio at which the drive shaft speed is greater than that of third gear. **—*n.* 4.** [*count*] a fourth part, esp. of one (¼); QUARTER. **5.** [*count*] the fourth member of a series. **6.** [*noncount*] fourth gear. **7. the Fourth,** Independence Day; the Fourth of July. **—*adv.* 8.** in the fourth place. —**fourth′ly,** *adv.*

fourth′ class′, *n.* [*noncount*] a class of mail consisting of merchandise weighing one pound or more and not sealed against inspection. —**fourth′-class′,** *adj., adv.*

fourth′ dimen′sion, *n.* [*count; usually singular; usually: the* + ~] a dimension, usually time, in addition to length, width, and depth.

fourth′ estate′, *n.* [*noncount; often: the* + ~*; often: Fourth Estate*] the journalistic profession.

Fourth′ of July′, *n.* [*the* + ~*; proper noun*] INDEPENDENCE DAY.

four′-wheel′ also **four′-wheeled′,** *adj.* [*before a noun*] **1.** having four wheels. **2.** powered by four wheels: *four-wheel drive.*

fowl (foul) /fawl/ *n., pl.* **fowls,** (*esp. when thought of as a group*) **fowl. 1.** a domestic hen or rooster; chicken. **2.** any of several other similar birds, such as turkeys or pheasants.

fox (foks) /fɒks/ *n., pl.* **fox•es,** (*esp. when thought of as a group*) **fox,** *v.* **—*n.* 1.** [*count*] a small member of the dog family having a sharply pointed nose and face and a long bushy tail. **2.** [*noncount*] the fur of this animal. **3.** [*count*] a cunning or crafty person. **4.** [*count*] *Slang.* an attractive young woman. **—*v.*** [~ + *obj*] **5.** to trick: *foxed me out of $10.*

fox•glove (foks′gluv′) /ˈfɒksˌglʌv/ *n.* [*count*] a plant with purple flowers on tall spikes.

fox•hole (foks′hōl′) /ˈfɒksˌhowl/ *n.* [*count*] a pit for one or two soldiers dug as a shelter in a battle zone.

fox•hound (foks′hound′) /ˈfɒksˌhawnd/ *n.* [*count*] a breed of hound trained to hunt foxes.

fox′ ter′rier, *n.* [*count*] either of two breeds of small terriers with either a wiry or a smooth coat.

fox′ trot′, *n.* [*count*] a ballroom dance with various combinations of slow and quick steps. —**fox′-trot′,** *v.* [*no obj*], **-trot•ted, -trot•ting.**

fox•y (fok′sē) /ˈfɒksiy/ *adj.,* **-i•er, -i•est. 1.** slyly clever; cunning; crafty: *a foxy opponent.* **2.** *Slang.* physically attractive.

foy•er (foi′ər, foi′ā) /'fɔyər, 'fɔyey/ *n.* [*count*] **1.** the lobby of a theater, hotel, or apartment house. **2.** an entrance hall in a house or apartment.

fps, an abbreviation of: **1.** feet per second. **2.** foot-pound-second.

Fr., an abbreviation of: **1.** Father. **2.** France. **3.** French. **4.** Friar. **5.** Friday.

fr, an abbreviation of: **1.** fragment. **2.** *pl.* **fr, frs** franc. **3.** from.

-frac-, *root.* *-frac-* comes from Latin, where it has the meaning "break; broken." This meaning is found in such words as: **FRACTIOUS, FRACTURE, FRAGILE, FRAGMENT, FRAIL, INFRACTION, REFRACTION.**

fra•cas (frā′kəs, frak′əs) /'freykəs, 'frækəs/ *n.* [*count; usually singular*] a noisy disturbance; fight. See **-FRAC-.**

frac•tion (frak′shən) /'frækʃən/ *n.* [*count*] **1.** a number usually expressed in the form *a/b.* **2.** a part of a whole; portion: *Only a fraction of the members voted.* **3.** a very small part or segment: *You can now buy this software at only a fraction of the original cost.* —**frac′tion•al,** *adj.* See **-FRAC-.**

frac•tious (frak′shəs) /'frækʃəs/ *adj.* readily angered; quarrelsome; irritable. —**frac′tious•ly,** *adv.* —**frac′-tious•ness,** *n.* [*noncount*] See **-FRAC-.**

frac•ture (frak′chər) /'fræktʃər/ *n., v.,* **-tured, -tur•ing.** —*n.* [*count*] **1.** the breaking of a bone or cartilage, or the resulting condition: *a slight fracture of the wrist.* **2.** a break; split: *a fracture in relations between the two countries.* —*v.* **3.** to (cause to) become fractured or broken; to (cause to) suffer a fracture in: [*no obj*]: *The arm fractured when she fell.* [~ + *obj*]: *The bullet fractured his arm.* See **-FRAC-.**

frag•ile (fraj′əl) /'frædʒəl/ *adj.* **1.** easily broken or damaged: *a fragile vase.* **2.** delicate in appearance: *fragile beauty.* **3.** lacking in substance or force; flimsy: *a fragile excuse.* —**fra•gil•i•ty** (frə jil′i tē) /frə'dʒɪlɪtiy/ *n.* [*noncount*] See **-FRAC-.**

frag•ment (*n.* frag′mənt; *v.* frag′ment, frag ment′) / *n.* 'frægmənt; *v.* 'frægmɛnt, fræg'mɛnt/ *n.* [*count*] **1.** a part broken off or detached: *fragments of shattered glass.* **2.** an unfinished or isolated part: *He had written the book in fragments and now had to pull it together.* —*v.* **3.** to (cause to) collapse or break into pieces or fragments; disintegrate: [*no obj*]: *The parchment is likely to fragment if you touch it.* [~ + *obj*]: *Outside influences fragmented that culture.* **4.** [~ + *obj*] to divide into fragments: *The tactic was to fragment the opposition and have them fight among themselves.* —**frag•men•ta•tion** (frag′mən tā′shən) /ˌfrægmən'teyʃən/ *n.* [*noncount*] See **-FRAC-.**

frag•men•tar•y (frag′mən ter′ē) /'frægmənˌtɛriy/ *adj.* consisting of fragments; incomplete: *Only fragmentary evidence remained.* See **-FRAC-.**

fra•grance (frā′grəns) /'freygrəns/ *n.* [*count*] **1.** a sweet or pleasing scent: *the fragrance of roses.* **2.** something, as a perfume, having a pleasing scent.

fra•grant (frā′grənt) /'freygrənt/ *adj.* having a pleasing scent: *a fragrant rose.* —**fra′grant•ly,** *adv.*

frail (frāl) /freyl/ *adj.,* **-er, -est. 1.** having delicate health; weak: *He was old and frail.* **2.** easily broken or destroyed; fragile: *The climber dangled by one frail rope.* See **-FRAC-.**

frail•ty (frāl′tē, frā′əl-) /'freyltiy, 'freyəl-/ *n., pl.* **-ties. 1.** [*noncount*] the quality or state of being frail. **2.** [*count*] a fault resulting from moral weakness: *the silly human frailties.* See **-FRAC-.**

frame (frām) /freym/ *n., v.,* **framed, fram•ing.** —*n.* [*count*] **1.** a border or case for enclosing a picture, mirror, etc. **2.** a rigid structure formed of joined pieces and used as a major support, as in buildings, machinery, and furniture: *The frame of the car was rusting.* **3.** a body, esp. a human body, with reference to its size or build; physique: *a large frame.* **4.** a structure for letting something in or enclosing something: *a window frame.* **5.** a particular state: *an unhappy frame of mind.* **6.** one of the successive pictures on a strip of film: *Most of the frames came out all right.* —*v.* [~ + *obj*] **7.** to construct; shape; develop; devise; compose: *to frame a new constitution.* **8.** to cause (an innocent person) to seem guilty: *to invent false evidence and frame a defendant.* **9.** to provide with or put into a frame: *to frame the portrait.* —**fram′er,** *n.* [*count*]

frame′-up′, *n.* [*count*] an act of falsely incriminating an innocent person.

frame•work (frām′wûrk′) /'freymˌwɜrk/ *n.* [*count*] **1.** a skeletal structure designed to support something. **2.** a frame or structure composed of fitted parts.

franc (frangk) /fræŋk/ *n.* [*count*] the basic monetary unit of Belgium, Burundi, Djibouti, France, Guinea, Luxembourg, Madagascar, Rwanda, and Switzerland.

fran•chise (fran′chīz) /'fræntʃayz/ *n., v.,* **-chised, -chis•ing.** —*n.* **1.** [*count*] a privilege given to an individual or company by a government: *a franchise to operate a bus system.* **2.** [*count*] the right or license granted by an organization to an individual or group to market its products or services in a specific territory. **3.** [*noncount*] the right to vote. —*v.* [~ + *obj*] **4.** to grant a franchise to.

fran•chi•see (fran′chī zē′) /ˌfræntʃay'ziy/ *n.* [*count*] *pl.* **-sees.** a person or company to whom a franchise is granted.

fran•chis•er (fran′chī zər) /'fræntʃayzər/ *n.* [*count*] a person or company that grants a franchise. Also, **fran′-chi•sor.**

fran•gi•ble (fran′jə bəl) /'frændʒəbəl/ *adj.* easily broken. See **-FRAC-.**

frank[1] (frangk) /fræŋk/ *adj.,* **-er, -est. 1.** direct; holding nothing back: *frank criticism.* —*n.* [*count*] **2.** a stamp, printed marking, or signature on a piece of mail indicating that postal charges have been paid. —*v.* [~ + *obj*] **3.** to mark (mail) for transmission by a stamp, imprint, or signature: *Department mail was free and franked through the university.* —**frank′ly,** *adv.*: *They spoke freely and frankly.* —**frank′ness,** *n.* [*noncount*]

frank[2] (frangk) /fræŋk/ *n.* [*count*] a frankfurter.

frank•furt•er or **frank•fort•er** (frangk′fər tər) /'fræŋkfərtər/ *n.* [*count*] a cooked and smoked sausage usually of beef or beef and pork that is skinless or in a casing.

frank•in•cense (frang′kin sens′) /'fræŋkɪnˌsɛns/ *n.* [*noncount*] a sweet-smelling substance used chiefly as incense.

fran•tic (fran′tik) /'fræntɪk/ *adj.* **1.** desperate or wild with emotion; frenzied: *a mother frantic with worry.* **2.** marked by desperate urgency: *a frantic effort to rescue the mountain climbers.* —**fran′ti•cal•ly,** *adv.*

frap•pé (fra pā′) /fræ'pey/ *n.* [*count*] a fruit juice mixture frozen to a mush.

frat (frat) /fræt/ *n.* [*count*] a fraternity (def. 1).

-frat-, *root.* *-frat-* comes from Latin, where it has the meaning "brother." This meaning is found in such words as: **FRATERNAL, FRATERNITY, FRATRICIDE.**

fra•ter•nal (frə tûr′nl) /frə'tɜrnl̩/ *adj.* **1.** of or befitting a brother; brotherly. **2.** [*before a noun*] of or being a society of men who are associated in brotherly union, such as for mutual aid or benefit: *a fraternal order.* —**fra•ter′-nal•ly,** *adv.* See **-FRAT-.**

fra•ter•ni•ty (frə tûr′ni tē) /frə'tɜrnɪtiy/ *n., pl.* **-ties. 1.** [*count*] a social organization of male college students usually with secret initiation and rites and a name made from Greek letters. **2.** [*count*] a group of persons associated by or as if by ties of brotherhood: *the medical fraternity.* **3.** [*noncount*] the quality or state of being brotherly; brotherhood. See **-FRAT-.**

frat•er•nize (frat′ər nīz′) /'frætərˌnayz/ *v.* [*no obj*], **-nized, -niz•ing. 1.** to associate in a friendly way. **2.** to be friendly with members of a hostile group: *fraternizing with the enemy.* —**frat•er•ni•za•tion** (frat′ər nə zā′shən) /ˌfrætərnə'zeyʃən/ *n.* [*noncount*] —**frat′er•niz′er,** *n.* [*count*] See **-FRAT-.**

frat•ri•cide (fra′tri sīd′, frā′-) /'frætrɪˌsayd, 'frey-/ *n.* **1.** [*noncount*] the act of killing one's brother. **2.** [*count*] a person who kills his or her brother. —**frat′ri•cid′al,** *adj.* See **-FRAT-, -CIDE-.**

Frau (frou) /fraw/ *n.* [*count*], *pl.* **Frau•en** (frou′ən) /'frawən/ **Fraus.** a German title of respect and term of address for a married woman, corresponding to *Mrs.*

fraud (frôd) /frɔd/ *n.* **1.** [*noncount*] trickery carried out for profit or to gain some unfair or dishonest advantage: *mail fraud.* **2.** [*count*] something that is not what it pretends: *That charity is a fraud.* **3.** [*count*] a deceitful person; impostor.

fraud•u•lent (frô′jə lənt) /'frɔdʒələnt/ *adj.* characterized by, involving, or proceeding from fraud: *fraudulent schemes.* —**fraud′u•lence,** *n.* [*noncount*] —**fraud′u•lent•ly,** *adv.*

fraught (frôt) /frɔt/ *adj.* [*be* + ~ + *with*] filled with; accompanied by: *a scheme (that is) fraught with danger.*

Fräu•lein (froi′līn *or, often,* frô′-, frou′-) /'frɔylayn *or, often,* 'frɔ-, 'fraw-/ *n.* [*count*], *pl.* **-leins, -lein.** a German title of respect and term of address for an unmarried woman, equivalent to *Miss.*

fray[1] (frā) /frey/ *n.* [*count; usually singular*] a prolonged conflict, quarrel, or fight.

fray[2] (frā) /frey/ *v.* **1.** to (cause to) become worn into loose threads at the edge or end: [*no obj*]: *Sweaters of-*

ten fray at the elbows. [~ + *obj*]: *All that traffic frayed the carpet.* **2.** [~ + *obj*] to cause strain on: *The argument frayed everyone's nerves.*

fraz•zle (fraz′əl) /ˈfræzəl/ *v.*, **-zled, -zling,** *n.* **—***v.* [~ + *obj*] **1.** to make physically or mentally fatigued: *completely frazzled after the trip.* **2.** to fray. **—***n.* [*count; usually singular*] **3. worn to a frazzle,** completely exhausted: *worn to a frazzle from shopping.*

freak (frēk) /friyk/ *n.* [*count*] **1.** an abnormal, unusual, or strange person, animal, or thing; aberration. **2.** a sudden unexpected occurrence: *The snowstorm in July was a freak of nature.* **3.** *Slang.* **a.** a habitual user; addict: *a drug freak.* **b.** a devoted fan: *a baseball freak.* **—***adj.* [*before a noun*] **4.** unusual; odd; irregular: *a freak storm.* **—***v.* **5.** to (cause to) become frightened, nervous, or excited: [*no obj; (~ + out)*]: *I nearly freaked (out) when I heard the news.* [~ *(+ out) + obj*]: *That surprise test freaked (out) most of the students.* [~ + *obj (+ out)*]: *That test really freaked them (out).* **6. freak out,** [*no obj*] *Slang.* to hallucinate under the influence of a drug: *to freak out on LSD.* —**freak′ish, freak′y,** *adj.*, **-i•er, -i•est.**

freck•le (frek′əl) /ˈfrɛkəl/ *n.*, *v.*, **-led, -ling.** **—***n.* [*count*] **1.** a small brownish spot on the skin that may darken on exposure to sunlight. **—***v.* **2.** to (cause to) be covered with freckles: [*no obj*]: *She freckles easily.* [~ + *obj*]: *The sun freckled his skin.* —**freck′ly,** *adj.*, **-li•er, -li•est.**

free (frē) /friy/ *adj.*, **fre•er, fre•est,** *adv.*, *v.*, **freed, free•ing.** **—***adj.* **1.** enjoying personal rights or liberty: *free from bondage.* **2.** existing under, characterized by, or having civil and political liberties: *the free nations of the world.* **3.** exempt from outside authority, interference, or restriction; independent: *You have a free choice.* **4.** [*be + ~ + to + verb*] able to do something at will or as one wishes: *They were free to go at any time.* **5.** clear of obstructions or obstacles; not blocked: *a free flow of water.* **6.** without engagements or obligations: *have free time after class.* **7.** not occupied or in use: *The room is free now.* **8.** exempt or released; unburdened: *She seems so free from worry.* **9.** provided without a charge: *free parking.* **10.** loose; unattached: *Tie the free end of the rope to the dock.* **11.** lacking self-restraint; loose: *He was a little too free and easy toward women.* **12.** ready or generous in giving; not holding back: *free spending.* **13.** not literal; not exact; loose: *a free translation of the speech.* **—***adv.* **14.** in a free manner; freely. **15.** loose; no longer restrained or held back: *The button came free and fell off.* **—***v.* **16.** [~ + *obj*] to set at liberty: *The enemy freed the hostages.* **17.** [~ + *obj + from + obj*] to exempt or deliver: *hoped his new invention would free his people from hunger.* **18.** [~ + *obj + of + obj*] to relieve or rid: *to free oneself of responsibility.* **19.** to disengage; clear: [~ + *obj*]: *If you hold these packages I can free my arm and open the door.* [~ + *obj + from + obj*]: *freed the trapped victims from the wreckage.* **20. free up, a.** [~ + *up + obj*] to release, as from restrictions: *Can you free up some time to meet with us?* **b.** to disentangle: [~ + *up + obj*]: *to free up this stuck valve.* [~ + *obj + up*]: *to free it up.* **—*Idiom.* 21. for free,** without charge: *They mended my jacket for free.* **22. free and clear,** without any debt or restriction: *paid off the mortgage free and clear.* **23. set free,** to release; liberate: [*set + obj + ~*]: *set the hostages free.* [*set + ~ + obj*]: *to set free the hostages.* **24. with a free hand,** generously: *donated money with a free hand.* **—Related Words.** FREE is an adjective and a verb, FREELY is an adverb, FREEDOM is a noun: *Are you free tomorrow evening? He worked hard to free the slaves from captivity. You may speak freely; you're among friends. We need some freedom of choice.*

-free, *suffix.* *-free* is attached to nouns to form adjectives with the meaning "not containing (the noun mentioned); without": *sugar + -free → sugar-free (= not containing sugar); trouble + -free → trouble-free (= without trouble).*

free•base or **free-base** (frē′bās′) /ˈfriyˌbeys/ *v.*, **-based, -bas•ing 1.** [~ + *obj*] to purify (cocaine) by dissolving under heat with ether. **2.** [*no obj*] to smoke freebased cocaine.

free•bie or **free•bee** (frē′bē) /ˈfriybiy/ *n.* [*count*] *Informal.* something given for free.

free•dom (frē′dəm) /ˈfriydəm/ *n.* **1.** the state of being free or at liberty: [*noncount*]: *freedom of the press.* [*count*]: *They believe in the same freedoms as we do.* **2.** [*noncount*] political or national independence: *fighting for freedom.* **3.** [*noncount*] personal liberty: *stories of slaves who bought their freedom.* **4.** [*noncount*] the absence of or release from ties or obligations: *He wanted his freedom, but she wanted a commitment.* **5.** [*noncount*] ease or facility of movement or action: *This loose-fitting jacket gives the wearer more freedom.* **6.** [*noncount*] frankness of manner or speech: *They spoke with freedom about their love.* **7.** [*count*] a liberty taken: *You're taking some freedoms with the truth there (= You're not really telling the truth).* **8.** [*count; usually singular*] the right or access of use: *We gave them the freedom of our apartment during their stay.*

free′ en′terprise, *n.* [*noncount*] the doctrine or system that a capitalist economy can regulate itself in a competitive market on the basis of supply and demand with a minimum of governmental regulation.

free′ fall′, *n.* [*noncount*] the fall of a body such that the only force acting upon it is gravity.

free′-for-all′, *n.* [*count*] a fight, argument, or contest that is open to everyone and usually without rules.

free′ hand′, *n.* [*count; singular*] unrestricted freedom or authority: *They gave the director a free hand to cut the budget wherever she wanted.*

free•hand (frē′hand′) /ˈfriyˌhænd/ *adj.* **1.** drawn or done by hand without guiding instruments, measurements, or other aids: *a freehand map.* **—***adv.* **2.** in a freehand manner: *to draw freehand.*

free•lance or **free-lance** (frē′lans′) /ˈfriyˌlæns/ *n.*, *v.*, **-lanced, -lanc•ing,** *adj.*, *adv.* **—***n.* **1.** [*count*] Also, **free′-lanc′er.** a person who sells work or services to employers as needed. **—***v.* [*no obj*] **2.** to act or work as a freelance. **—***adj.* **3.** of or relating to a freelance or to freelancing: *freelance writing.* **—***adv.* **4.** as a freelance: *She works freelance.*

free•load (frē′lōd′) /ˈfriyˌlowd/ *v.* [*no obj*] *Informal.* to take advantage of the generosity of others: *freeloading off his friend.* —**free′load′er,** *n.* [*count*]

free′ love′, *n.* [*noncount*] sexual relations without commitment by the participants.

free•ly (frē′lē) /ˈfriyliy/ *adv.* **1.** frankly and without fear: *freely admitted he was the culprit.* **2.** without limiting or restraining: *He spent freely on the project.* **3.** not restricted: *Once I took the medicine I could move my arm freely.*

free•man (frē′mən) /ˈfriymən/ *n.* [*count*], *pl.* **-men. 1.** a person who is free; a person who enjoys personal, civil, or political liberty. **2.** a person who is entitled to citizenship.

free•stand•ing (frē′stan′ding) /ˈfriyˈstændɪŋ/ *adj.* unattached to a supporting unit or background; standing alone.

free•think•er (frē′thing′kər) /ˈfriyˈθɪŋkər/ *n.* [*count*] a person of independent opinions, esp. in religious matters. —**free′think′ing,** *adj.*, *n.* [*noncount*]

free′ trade′, *n.* [*noncount*] international trade that is free from protective duties and quotas and subject only to such tariffs as are needed for revenue.

free′ verse′, *n.* [*noncount*] verse with no fixed metrical pattern.

free•way (frē′wā′) /ˈfriyˌwey/ *n.* [*count*] an express highway with no intersections.

free•wheel•ing (frē′hwē′ling, -wē′-) /ˈfriyˈhwiylɪŋ, -ˈwiy-/ *adj.* [*before a noun*] not held back by rules or conventions: *a freewheeling lifestyle.*

free′ will′, *n.* [*noncount*] free and independent choice; voluntary decision.

free•will (frē′wil′) /ˈfriyˈwɪl/ *adj.* voluntary: *a freewill choice.*

freeze (frēz) /friyz/ *v.*, **froze** (frōz) /frowz/ **fro•zen** (frō′zən) /ˈfrowzən/ **freez•ing,** *n.* **—***v.* **1.** to (cause to) become hardened into ice or into a solid body: [*no obj*]: *Salt water freezes at a lower temperature than fresh water.* [~ + *obj*]: *The cold will freeze the pond.* **2.** to (cause to) become hard with cold: [*no obj*]: *The meat will freeze in a few hours.* [~ + *obj*]: *will freeze the meat solid.* **3.** to (cause to) suffer the effects or sensation of intense cold: [*no obj*]: *We froze until the heat came on.* [~ + *obj*]: *Those cold winter nights froze us.* **4.** [*no obj*] to be of the degree of cold at which water freezes: *It may freeze tonight if the temperature drops.* **5.** to lose warmth of feeling: [*no obj*]: *My heart froze when I heard the news.* [~ + *obj*]: *The news froze my heart.* **6.** [*no obj*] to become speechless or immobilized, as through fear: *When he got up in front of the huge audience he froze.* **7.** to (cause to) stop suddenly and remain motionless: [*no obj*]: *I froze when I heard the sound.* [~ + *obj*]: *The snap of a twig behind him froze him in his tracks.* **8.** to (cause to) become blocked or obstructed by the formation of ice: [*no obj*]: *The water pipes froze.* [~ + *obj*]: *The cold froze the pipes.* **9.** [*no obj*] to work or function badly because of cold: [*no obj*]: *The engine froze during* *the night and wouldn't start.* **10.** to (cause to) become fixed or stuck to something by or as if by the action of frost: [*no obj*]: *The sled froze to the sidewalk.* [~ + *obj*]: *The wiper was frozen to the windshield.* **11.** [*no obj;* ~ (+ *up*)] to become unfriendly or secretive: *She froze up when we questioned her.* **12.** [~ + *obj*] to fix (rents, prices, etc.) at a specific amount, usually by government order: *Why is it that wages are frozen while prices rise?* **13.** [~ + *obj*] to stop or limit production or use of: *an agreement to freeze nuclear weapons.* **14.** [~ + *obj*] to prevent (assets) from being sold or collected: *The government froze their accounts.* **15. freeze over,** [*no obj*] to become coated with ice: *The highway froze over.* **—*n.*** [*count; usually singular*] **16.** an act or instance of freezing; the state of being frozen. **17.** a period of very cold weather: *A freeze set in.* **18.** a legislative action to control prices, rents, production, etc.: *imposed a wage freeze.* **19.** a decision by one or more nations to stop or limit production or development of weapons: *calling for a freeze on nuclear weapons.*

freeze′-dry′, *v.* [~ + *obj*], **-dried, -dry•ing.** to preserve by freezing and then drying in a vacuum: *to freeze-dry coffee.*

freez•er (frē′zər) /ˈfriyzər/ *n.* [*count*] a refrigerator, refrigerator compartment, or room held at or below 32°F (0°C), used esp. for freezing food.

freez′ing point′, *n.* [*count*] the temperature at which a liquid freezes: *The freezing point of water is 32°F, or 0°C.*

freight (frāt) /freyt/ *n.* [*noncount*] **1.** goods or cargo transported for pay: *huge trucks carrying many tons of freight.* **2.** the transport of goods by common carriers. **3.** the charges for such transportation: *having to pay the freight.* **—*v.*** [~ + *obj*] **4.** to transport as freight. **5.** to fill or load; burden: *writings freighted with hidden meaning.*

freight•er (frā′tər) /ˈfreytər/ *n.* [*count*] a large ship or aircraft used mainly for carrying cargo.

French (french) /frɛntʃ/ *adj.* **1.** of or relating to France. **2.** of or relating to the language spoken in France. **—*n.*** **3.** [*plural; the* + ~*; used with a plural verb*] the people born or living in France. **4.** [*noncount*] the language spoken in France.

French′ door′, *n.* [*count*] a door having glass panes throughout its length.

French′ fry′, *n.* [*count*], *pl.* **French′ fries′.** a strip of potato that has been deep-fried. Also called **French′-fried′ pota′to.**

French′ horn′, *n.* [*count*] a brass wind instrument with a long coiled tube and an end that flares out.

French′ leave′, *n.* [*noncount*] an unauthorized departure.

French•man (french′mən) /ˈfrɛntʃmən/ *n.* [*count*], *pl.* **-men.** a person born or living in France.

French′ toast′, *n.* [*noncount*] bread dipped in a batter of egg and milk and sautéed until brown.

French•wom•an (french′wo͝om′ən) /ˈfrɛntʃˌwʊmən/ *n.* [*count*], *pl.* **-wom•en.** a woman born or living in France.

fre•net•ic (frə net′ik) /frəˈnɛtɪk/ also **fre•net′i•cal,** *adj.* wildly excited; frantic: *the frenetic activity of a political campaign.* —**fre•net′i•cal•ly,** *adv.*

fren•zied (fren′zēd) /ˈfrɛnziyd/ *adj.* marked by frenzy: *a frenzied mob.*

fren•zy (fren′zē) /ˈfrɛnziy/ *n., pl.* **-zies. 1.** [*count*] extreme mental agitation; wild or violent excitement: *In a sudden frenzy he hurled the chair through the window.* **2.** agitated or uncontrollable activity: [*noncount*]: *the frenzy of the mob.* [*count; usually singular*]: *in a frenzy.*

freq., an abbreviation of: **1.** frequency. **2.** frequent. **3.** frequently.

fre•quen•cy (frē′kwən sē) /ˈfriykwənsiy/ *n., pl.* **-cies. 1.** [*noncount*] the state or fact of being frequent; frequent occurrence. **2.** [*noncount*] rate of occurrence: *Similar crimes had decreased in frequency.* **3.** *Physics.* the number of cycles or times a wave vibrates in a given amount of time, often one second: [*noncount*]: *They played back the message at high frequency.* [*count*]: *sounds at high frequencies that can't be heard by humans.*

fre′quency modula′tion, *n.* [*noncount*] See FM.

fre•quent (*adj.* frē′kwənt; *v.* fri kwent′, frē′kwənt) / *adj.* ˈfriykwənt; *v.* frɪˈkwɛnt, ˈfriykwənt/ *adj.* **1.** happening at short intervals: *made frequent trips to Japan.* **2.** habitual or regular: *a frequent guest at our house.* **—*v.*** [~ + *obj*] **3.** to visit often: *frequented their neighborhood restaurant.* —**fre•quent′er,** *n.* [*count*] —**fre′quent•ly,** *adv.*

fres•co (fres′kō) /ˈfrɛskow/ *n., pl.* **-coes, -cos. 1.** [*noncount*] the art or technique of painting on a moist plaster surface. **2.** [*count*] a picture or design so painted.

fresh (fresh) /frɛʃ/ *adj.,* **-er, -est,** *adv.* **—*adj.*** **1.** newly made or obtained: *fresh footprints in the newly fallen snow.* **2.** [*be* + ~ + *from/out of*] recently arrived; just come: *was fresh out of military school.* **3.** not previously known, met with, etc.; new; novel: *to uncover fresh evidence.* **4.** [*before a noun*] additional or further: *The army needs fresh supplies.* **5.** [*often: before a noun*] (of water) not salty. **6.** not stale or spoiled: *fresh bread; fresh milk.* **7.** not preserved; recently harvested: *fresh vegetables.* **8.** not tired; vigorous: *felt fresh after that long walk.* **9.** not faded, worn, obliterated, etc.: *fresh paint.* **10.** pure, cool, or refreshing, such as air: *to breathe some fresh air.* **11.** *Informal.* rude; impolite: *a fresh brat.* **—*adv.*** **12.** newly; recently; just now: *We're fresh out of funds.* —**fresh′ly,** *adv.* —**fresh′ness,** *n.* [*noncount*]

fresh•en (fresh′ən) /ˈfrɛʃən/ *v.* **1.** to (cause to) become or grow fresh or refreshed: [*no obj*]: *Her interest in basketball freshened when she saw who was on the team.* [~ + *obj*]: *Freshen the air with flowers.* **2. freshen up,** to (cause to) become fresh in appearance: [*no obj*]: *to freshen up with a bath.* [~ + *obj* + *up*]: *freshened herself up and joined the party.* [~ + *up* + *obj*]: *The housekeeper freshened up the room.* —**fresh′en•er,** *n.* [*count*]: *an air freshener.*

fresh•et (fresh′it) /ˈfrɛʃɪt/ *n.* [*count*] a flooding of a stream from rain or melting snow.

fresh•man (fresh′mən) /ˈfrɛʃmən/ *n.* [*count*], *pl.* **-men. 1.** a student in the first year at a university, college, or high school. **2.** a beginner; someone lacking experience: *a freshman in politics.*

fresh•wa•ter or **fresh-wa•ter** (fresh′wô′tər, -wot′ər) /ˈfrɛʃˌwɔtər, -ˌwɒtər/ *adj.* [*before a noun*] of or living in or containing water that is not salty: *freshwater fish; a freshwater lake.*

fret[1] (fret) /frɛt/ *v.,* **fret•ted, fret•ting.** to feel or express worry, annoyance, discontent, or the like: [*no obj*]: *Don't fret; things will get better.* [~ + *about* + *obj*]: *fretting about the lost ring.* [~ + *at* + *obj*]: *He was fretting at the traffic delay in the tunnel.* [~ + *oneself*]: *Don't fret yourself over trifles.*

fret[2] (fret) /frɛt/ *n.* [*count*] any of the ridges of wood or metal set across the fingerboard of a stringed instrument, such as a guitar.

fret•ful (fret′fəl) /ˈfrɛtfəl/ *adj.* irritable; touchy; peevish: *a fretful baby.* —**fret′ful•ly,** *adv.*

Freud•i•an (froi′dē ən) /ˈfrɔydiyən/ *adj.* of or relating to the psychoanalytic theories of Sigmund Freud.

Fri., an abbreviation of: Friday.

fri•a•ble (frī′ə bəl) /ˈfrayəbəl/ *adj.* easily crumbled or reduced to powder; crumbly: *friable rock.*

fri•ar (frī′ər) /ˈfrayər/ *n.* [*count*] a man who is a member of a Roman Catholic mendicant order.

fric•as•see (frik′ə sē′) /ˌfrɪkəˈsiy/ *n., v.,* **-seed, -see•ing. —*n.*** **1.** chicken stewed and served in a sauce made with its own stock. **—*v.*** [~ + *obj*] **2.** to prepare as a fricassee: *to fricassee chicken.*

fric•tion (frik′shən) /ˈfrɪkʃən/ *n.* [*noncount*] **1.** surface resistance to relative motion, such as of a body sliding or rolling: *Friction will help slow down a car.* **2.** the rubbing of one surface against another: *friction on a rope.* **3.** disagreement; conflict: *friction between nations.*

Fri•day (frī′dā, -dē) /ˈfraydey, -diy/ *n.* the sixth day of the week, following Thursday: [*proper noun*]: *Can't we meet on Friday?* [*count*]: *Let's have the meeting two Fridays from today.*

fridge (frij) /frɪdʒ/ *n.* [*count*] a refrigerator.

fried (frīd) /frayd/ *adj.* **1.** cooked by frying: *fried chicken.* **2.** *Slang.* **a.** drunk; inebriated. **b.** intoxicated from drugs; high: *fried and disoriented.* **—*v.*** **3.** pt. and pp. of FRY[1].

friend (frend) /frɛnd/ *n.* [*count*] **1.** a person who is attached to another by feelings of affection or personal regard: *She was my best friend.* **2.** a person who gives assistance; supporter; patron: *supported by friends of the Boston Symphony.* **3.** a person who is not hostile: *Who goes there? Friend or foe?* **4.** [*Friend*] a member of the Society of Friends; a Quaker. **—*Idiom.*** **5. make friends with,** [*make* + ~*-s* + *with* + *obj*] to become a friend to: *made friends with the new neighbors.* —**friend′less,** *adj.*

friend•ly (frend′lē) /ˈfrɛndliy/ *adj.,* **-li•er, -li•est,** *adv., n., pl.* **-lies. —*adj.*** **1.** characteristic of or appropriate to a friend: *a friendly greeting.* **2.** kind; helpful: *a friendly passerby.* **3.** sympathetic: *nations who are friendly to our cause.* **4.** amicable; neighborly: *a friendly game of softball.* **5.** (used after a noun) made easy or pleasant to use, operate, understand, or experience: *visitor-friendly museums (= museums that are arranged to be easy or pleasant for visitors to use); a user-friendly computer (=*

a computer that is easy for the user to operate). **—*n.*** [*count*] **6.** a person or thing who is friendly. **—friend′li•ness,** *n.* [*noncount*]

friend•ship (frend′ship) /ˈfrɛndʃɪp/ *n.* **1.** [*noncount*] the state of being friends. **2.** [*count*] a friendly relation or intimacy: *friendships with people from her own culture.* **3.** [*noncount*] friendly feeling or disposition: *the long-standing friendship between Canada and the U.S.*

frieze (frēz) /friyz/ *n.* [*count*] a decorative, often carved band, as around the top of a wall or piece of furniture.

frig•ate (frig′it) /ˈfrɪgɪt/ *n.* [*count*] **1.** a fast ship of the late 18th and early 19th centuries. **2.** a modern warship smaller than a destroyer.

fright (frīt) /frayt/ *n.* **1.** sudden fear: [*noncount*]: *a feeling of fright.* [*count; usually singular*]: *You gave me quite a fright.* **2.** [*count*] something shocking, grotesque, or ridiculous in appearance: *My hair is a fright.* **—Related Words.** FRIGHT is a noun, FRIGHTFUL, FRIGHTENING are adjectives, FRIGHTEN is a verb: *You gave me quite a fright! It was a frightful sight. It was a frightening movie. You frightened me.*

fright•en (frīt′n) /ˈfraytn̩/ *v.* [~ + *obj*] **1.** to (cause to) become frightened: *Your story frightened me.* **2.** to drive or force to move by scaring: [~ + *away/off* + *obj*]: *to frighten off the pigeons.* [~ + *obj* + *away/off*]: *to frighten the pigeons away.*

fright•en•ing (frīt′ən ing) /ˈfraytənɪŋ/ *adj.* causing fear or anxiety.

fright•ful (frīt′fəl) /ˈfraytfəl/ *adj.* **1.** causing fright: *a frightful explosion.* **2.** horrible or shocking: *The storm did frightful damage.* **3.** unpleasant: *We had a frightful time.* **4.** very great; extreme: *That actor is a frightful ham.* **—fright′ful•ly,** *adv.*

frig•id (frij′id) /ˈfrɪdʒɪd/ *adj.* **1.** very cold in temperature: *a frigid climate.* **2.** lacking warmth of feeling: *a frigid reaction to the proposal.* **3.** (of a woman) sexually unresponsive. **—fri•gid•i•ty** (fri jid′i tē) /frɪˈdʒɪdɪtiy/ *n.* [*noncount*] **—frig′id•ly,** *adv.*

frill (fril) /frɪl/ *n.* [*count*] **1.** a trimming, such as a strip of cloth or lace, gathered at one edge; ruffle. **2.** something desirable but not essential: *a car with frills like a CD player.* **—frill′y,** *adj.,* **-i•er, -i•est.**

fringe (frinj) /frɪndʒ/ *n., v.,* **fringed, fring•ing.** **—*n.*** [*count*] **1.** a decorative border of short threads, cords, or loops: *fringe at the bottom edge of the curtain.* **2.** something resembling a fringe: *a fringe of grass.* **3.** a marginal part: *society's fringes.* **4.** a group with extremist views: *a radical fringe.* **—*v.*** [~ + *obj*] **5.** to furnish with or as if with a fringe. **6.** to be arranged in a fringe: *Guards fringed the building.*

fringe′ ben′efit, *n.* [*count*] a benefit, such as health insurance or a pension, received by an employee in addition to regular pay.

frip•per•y (frip′ə rē) /ˈfrɪpəriy/ *n.* [*noncount*] **1.** showy or gaudy dress. **2.** empty display; ostentation.

Fris•bee (friz′bē) /ˈfrɪzbiy/ *Trademark.* [*count*] a brand of plastic concave disk, used for various catching games: *He trained his dog to catch a Frisbee between its teeth.*

frisk (frisk) /frɪsk/ *v.* **1.** [*no obj*] to dance, leap, skip, or frolic: *The children frisked about.* **2.** [~ + *obj*] to search (a person) for concealed weapons, illegal possessions, etc.

frisk•y (fris′kē) /ˈfrɪskiy/ *adj.,* **-i•er, -i•est.** lively; playful: *a frisky kitten.* **—frisk•i•ly** (fris′kə lē) /ˈfrɪskəliy/ *adv.* **—frisk′i•ness,** *n.* [*noncount*]

frit•ter[1] (frit′ər) /ˈfrɪtər/ *v.* to (cause to) go to waste little by little: [~ + *away* + *obj*]: *to fritter away his money on useless items.* [~ + *obj* + *away*]: *to fritter money away.*

frit•ter[2] (frit′ər) /ˈfrɪtər/ *n.* [*count*] a small cake of fried batter, usually containing corn, fruit, or other food.

fri•vol•i•ty (fri vol′i tē) /frɪˈvɒlɪtiy/ *n., pl.* **-ties. 1.** [*noncount*] lighthearted or foolish activity: *A party is a time for frivolity.* **2.** [*count*] a frivolous act or thing.

friv•o•lous (friv′ə ləs) /ˈfrɪvələs/ *adj.* **1.** characterized by lack of seriousness or sense: *frivolous conduct.* **2.** not worthy of serious notice: *a frivolous suggestion.* **—friv′o•lous•ly,** *adv.*

frizz (friz) /frɪz/ *v.* **1.** to (cause to) form into small crisp curls: [*no obj*]: *Her hair frizzed when it rained.* [~ + *obj*]: *The hairdresser frizzed her hair.* **—*n.*** [*count*] **2.** hair that is frizzed. **—frizz′y,** *adj.,* **-i•er, -i•est**: *frizzy hair.*

friz•zle[1] (friz′əl) /ˈfrɪzəl/ *v.,* **-zled, -zling,** *n.* **—*v.*** [*no obj;* ~ + *obj*] **1.** to frizz. **—*n.*** [*count*] **2.** a short crisp curl.

friz•zle[2] (friz′əl) /ˈfrɪzəl/ *v.,* **-zled, -zling. 1.** [*no obj*] to make a sizzling noise while frying: *The bacon was frizzling.* **2.** [~ + *obj*] to make (food) crisp by frying.

fro (frō) /frow/ *adv.* from; back: *to and fro.*

frock (frok) /frɒk/ *n.* [*count*] **1.** a dress worn by a girl or woman. **2.** a smock worn by peasants and workers. **3.** a rough outer garment with large sleeves, worn by monks.

frock′ coat′, *n.* [*count*] a man's close-fitting, knee-length coat.

frog (frog, frôg) /frɒg, frɔg/ *n.* [*count*] **1.** a small tailless amphibian animal with smooth, moist skin and long hind legs for jumping. **2.** a slight hoarseness of the voice: *a frog in the throat.*

frog•man (frog′man′, -mən, frôg′-) /ˈfrɒgˌmæn, -mən, ˈfrɔg-/ *n.* [*count*], *pl.* **-men.** a swimmer who is equipped with air tanks, wet suit, diving mask, etc., for underwater activity.

frol•ic (frol′ik) /ˈfrɒlɪk/ *n., v.,* **-icked, -ick•ing.** **—*n.*** [*count*] **1.** merry play; fun; playful behavior or action: *a frolic in the park.* **—*v.*** [*no obj*] **2.** to play in a frisky, light-spirited manner; romp: *The family was frolicking in the snow.* **—frol′ic•some,** *adj.*

from (frum, from; *unstressed* frəm) /frʌm, frɒm; *unstressed* frəm/ *prep.* **1.** (used to specify a starting point in space or time): *a train running west from Chicago; from six o'clock to ten o'clock.* **2.** (used to specify a starting point in an expression of limits or amounts): *The number will be increased from 25 to 30.* **3.** (used to express the idea of being removed or separated): *The house is two miles from the shore.* **4.** (used to express discrimination or separation into different kinds): *excluded from membership in that private club.* **5.** (used to indicate the source or origin): *My wife comes from the Midwest.* **6.** (used to indicate agent, means, cause, or reason): *Death was from starvation.*

frond (frond) /frɒnd/ *n.* [*count*] an often large, finely divided leaf, esp. of ferns and certain palms.

front (frunt) /frʌnt/ *n.* [*count*] **1.** [*the* + ~] the forward part or surface of anything: *I sat in the front of the airplane.* **2.** the part or side of anything that faces forward: *I spilled some mustard on the front of my jacket.* **3.** the part or side of anything, as a building, that is situated or directed forward: *sat in the front of the restaurant.* See *in front* and *in front of* below. **4.** land facing a road, river, etc.; frontage. **5.** [*the* + ~] a line of battle; the place where combat operations are carried on: *The soldiers retreated from the front.* **6.** an area of activity, conflict, or competition: *news from the business front.* **7.** a person or thing that serves as a cover or disguise for some other activity, esp. one of a secret, dishonest, or illegal nature: *The store was a front for gamblers.* **8.** [*usually singular*] bearing, expression, or attitude in facing, confronting or dealing with anything: *She kept a calm front throughout the ordeal.* **9.** a zone or line between two different air masses: *a cold front coming from the north into our region.* **—*adj.*** [*before a noun*] **10.** of or relating to the front; situated in or at the front: *front seats.* **—*v.* 11.** [~ + *obj*] to have the front toward; face: *Our house fronts the lake.* **12.** [~ + *obj*] to furnish or supply a front to: *to front a building with sandstone.* **13.** [~ + *obj*] to serve as a front to: *A long, sloping lawn fronted their house.* **14. a.** [~ + *for* + *obj*] to serve as a cover or disguise: *The shop fronts for a narcotics ring.* **b.** [~ + *as* + *noun*] to be disguised as: *The drug warehouse fronted as a quiet little grocery store.* **—*Idiom.* 15. in front,** in a forward place or position: *My family was sitting in front, but I stayed in back.* **16. in front of, a.** ahead of: *They were sitting in front of me.* **b.** outside the entrance of: *We met in front of the hotel.* **c.** in the presence of: *Don't talk like that in front of the children.* **17. out front, a.** outside the entrance: *Let's meet out front.* **b.** ahead of competitors: *The runner from Kenya was out front for most of the race.* **18. up front,** *Informal.* **a.** in advance; before anything else: *You'll have to make a payment of $5,000 up front.* **b.** frank; honest: *to be up front in your answers.*

front•age (frun′tij) /ˈfrʌntɪdʒ/ *n.* [*count*] **1.** the front of a building or lot. **2.** the space lying between a building and the street, a body of water, etc.

fron•tal (frun′tl) /ˈfrʌntl̩/ *adj.* [*before a noun*] of, in, or at the front: *a frontal view.* **—front′al•ly,** *adv.*

front′ burn′er, *n.* [*count*] **—*Idiom.* on the front burner,** in a position of top priority: *kept the issue on the front burner.*

fron•tier (frun tēr′) /frʌnˈtɪər/ *n.* [*count*] **1.** the border between two countries: *the frontier crossing.* **2.** land that forms the furthest regions of a country or territory. **3.** Often, **frontiers.** the limit of knowledge or the most advanced achievement in a particular field: *the frontiers of medical research.* **—*adj.*** [*before a noun*] **4.** of, relating to, or located on a frontier: *a frontier town.* **—fron•tiers′man,** *n.* [*count*], *pl.* **-men.** **—Syn.** See BOUNDARY.

fron•tis•piece (frun′tis pēs′, fron′-) /ˈfrʌntɪsˌpiys, ˈfrɒn-/ *n.* [*count*] an illustrated page before the title page of a book.

front′ of′fice, *n.* [*count*] the executive or administrative officers of a company, organization, etc.

front′-run′ner or **front′run′ner,** *n.* [*count*] a person who leads in any competition: *That candidate quickly established himself as the front-runner.*

frost (frôst, frost) /frɔst, frɒst/ *n.* **1.** a degree or state of coldness that is enough to cause the freezing of water: [*noncount*]: *expecting frost tonight over most of the region.* [*count*]: *A slight frost will kill this plant.* **2.** [*noncount*] a covering of tiny ice crystals, formed from the atmosphere at night upon the ground when cooled below the dew point. **—*v.* 3.** to (cause to) become covered with frost: [*no obj;* ~ + *up/over*]: *The high school track frosted over last night.* [~ *(+ up/over)* + *obj*]: *The cold weather frosted up the track last night.* **4.** [~ + *obj*] to give a frostlike surface to (glass, metal, etc.). **5.** [~ + *obj*] to cover or decorate with frosting: *to frost a cake.* **6.** [~ + *obj*] to bleach some strands of (a person's hair).

frost•bite (frôst′bīt′, frost′-) /ˈfrɔstˌbayt, ˈfrɒst-/ *n., v.,* **-bit, -bit•ten, -bit•ing.** **—*n.*** [*noncount*] **1.** injury to any part of the body after long exposure to extreme cold. **—*v.*** [~ + *obj*] **2.** to injure by frost or extreme cold: *My toes were frostbitten from skating too long.*

frost•ed (frô′stid, fros′tid) /ˈfrɔstɪd, ˈfrɒstɪd/ *adj.* **1.** covered with frost. **2.** (of glass, metal, etc.) having a frostlike appearance. **3.** coated with frosting: *a frosted cake.* **4.** (of hair) having some strands bleached.

frost•ing (frô′sting, fros′ting) /ˈfrɔstɪŋ, ˈfrɒstɪŋ/ *n.* [*noncount*] **1.** a sweet, creamy mixture for coating or filling cakes, cookies, etc.; icing. **2.** a dull finish, such as on metal or glass.

frost•y (frô′stē, fros′tē) /ˈfrɔstiy, ˈfrɒstiy/ *adj.,* **-i•er, -i•est.** **1.** very cold; producing frost: *frosty weather.* **2.** covered with frost: *frosty ground.* **3.** unfriendly; cold in manner: *She gave a frosty reply to my request for a raise.* —**frost•i•ly** (frôs′tl ē, fros′-) /ˈfrɔstḷiy, ˈfrɒs-/ *adv.*: *She answered frostily that it was none of my business where she lived.* —**frost′i•ness,** *n.* [*noncount*]

froth (frôth, froth) /frɔθ, frɒθ/ *n.* [*noncount*] **1.** a mass of bubbles, such as on a liquid that has been shaken hard; foam. **2.** a foam of saliva or fluid resulting from disease. **3.** something trivial or unimportant; something not worth much: *The play was a charming bit of froth.* **—*v.*** [*no obj*] **4.** to give off froth: *The stew was frothing.* **—*Idiom.* 5. to froth at the mouth,** [*no obj*] **a.** to give out froth; foam: *The dog had rabies and frothed at the mouth.* **b.** to be extremely angry. —**froth′y,** *adj.,* **-i•er, -i•est.**

frown (froun) /frawn/ *v.* **1.** to wrinkle the forehead, such as when one is displeased or in deep thought: [*no obj*]: *She frowned when I gave the wrong answer.* [~ + *at* + *obj*]: *She frowned at the dog.* **2. frown on** or **upon,** [~ + *on/upon* + *obj*] to look on disapprovingly: *frowned on my idea to buy new computers because of the cost.* **—*n.*** [*count*] **3.** a disapproving look or expression on the face; scowl.

frowz•y (frou′zē) /ˈfrawziy/ *adj.,* **-i•er, -i•est.** dirty and untidy; slovenly: *frowzy run-down apartments.* —**frowz′i•ness,** *n.* [*noncount*]

froze (frōz) /frowz/ *v.* pt. of FREEZE.

fro•zen (frō′zən) /ˈfrowzən/ *v.* **1.** pp. of FREEZE. **—*adj.* 2.** congealed by cold; turned into ice. **3.** Also, **frozen over.** covered with ice, such as a stream: *They went skating on the frozen lake. The lake was frozen over.* **4.** frigid; very cold: *Let me in; I'm frozen.* **5.** chilly or cold in manner; unfeeling: *a frozen stare.* **6.** [*before a noun*] preserved or prepared by freezing: *frozen foods.* **7.** not permitted to be changed or incapable of being altered; fixed: *frozen rents.*

frt., an abbreviation of: freight.

fru•gal (froo′gəl) /ˈfruwgəl/ *adj.* **1.** economical in use or spending; sparing: *a frugal manager.* **2.** requiring little expense or few resources: *a frugal meal.* —**fru•gal•i•ty** (froo gal′i tē) /fruwˈgælɪtiy/ *n.* [*noncount*] —**fru′gal•ly,** *adv.* **—Syn.** See ECONOMICAL.

fruit (froot) /fruwt/ *n., pl.* **fruits,** (*esp. when thought of as a group*) **fruit,** *v.* **—*n.* 1.** the part of a plant that is developed from a flower, esp. when used as food: [*noncount*]: *Fruit provides vitamins.* [*count*]: *Apples and oranges are fruits.* See illustration at SUPERMARKET. **2.** [*count*] a product, result, or effect; return or profit: *the fruits of one's labors.* **—*Idiom.* 3. bear fruit,** to produce a result or profit: *The effort bore fruit.*

fruit•cake (froot′kāk′) /ˈfruwtˌkeyk/ *n.* **1.** a rich cake containing dried or candied fruit, nuts, spices, etc.: [*noncount*]: *Fruitcake is rich.* [*count*]: *Let's slice all the fruitcakes.* **2.** [*count*] *Slang.* a crazy or eccentric person.

fruit′ fly′, *n.* [*count*] a very small fly whose eggs are laid in fruit.

fruit•ful (froot′fəl) /ˈfruwtfəl/ *adj.* **1.** producing good results; profitable; useful: *a fruitful meeting.* **2.** producing a lot of growth. —**fruit′ful•ly,** *adv.* —**fruit′ful•ness,** *n.* [*noncount*]

fru•i•tion (froo ish′ən) /fruwˈɪʃən/ *n.* [*noncount*] the obtaining of something desired; accomplishment; realization: *to bring an idea to fruition.*

fruit•less (froot′lis) /ˈfruwtlɪs/ *adj.* not producing results or success: *a fruitless search.* —**fruit′less•ly,** *adv.* —**fruit′less•ness,** *n.* [*noncount*]

fruit•y (froo′tē) /ˈfruwtiy/ *adj.,* **-i•er, -i•est.** resembling fruit; having the taste or smell of fruit. —**fruit′i•ness,** *n.* [*noncount*]

frump (frump) /frʌmp/ *n.* [*count*] a dowdy or dull person. —**frump′y,** *adj.,* **-i•er, -i•est.**

frus•trate (frus′trāt) /ˈfrʌstreyt/ *v.* [~ + *obj*], **-trat•ed, -trat•ing.** **1.** to make (plans, efforts, etc.) worthless or of no use; defeat: *The steady rains frustrated our plans.* **2.** to disappoint; discourage; thwart: *If you give a child problems that are hard to solve, you may frustrate him.* —**frus•tra′tion,** *n.* [*noncount*]: *feelings of frustration.* [*count*]: *took his frustrations out on his staff.*

fry[1] (frī) /fray/ *v.,* **fried, fry•ing,** *n., pl.* **fries.** **—*v.* 1.** to (cause to) undergo cooking in fat or oil, usually over direct heat: [~ + *obj*]: *Let's fry some bacon and eggs.* [~ + *up* + *obj*]: *Let's fry up some bacon.* [~ + *obj* + *up*]: *Let's fry it up.* [*no obj*]: *The bacon and eggs fried.* **—*n.*** [*count*] **2.** a strip of French-fried potato. **3.** a social gathering at which food is fried.

fry[2] (frī) /fray/ *n.* [*count*], *pl.* **fry.** **1.** the young of fish. **2.** people, esp. children: *games for small fry.*

fry•er or **fri•er** (frī′ər) /ˈfrayər/ *n.* [*count*] **1.** something, such as a young chicken, to be cooked by frying: *a two-pound fryer.* **2.** a pan or appliance for frying foods.

ft., an abbreviation of: **1.** feet. **2.** foot. **3.** fort. **4.** fortification.

FTC, an abbreviation of: Federal Trade Commission.

fuch•sia (fyoo′shə) /ˈfyuwʃə/ *n.* [*count*], *pl.* **-sias.** **1.** a shrubby plant with pink to purplish drooping flowers. **2.** a bright purplish red color. **—*adj.* 3.** of the color fuchsia.

fud•dle (fud′l) /ˈfʌdl/ *v.,* **-dled, -dling,** *n.* **—*v.*** [~ + *obj*] **1.** to muddle or confuse: *That beer fuddled my brain.* **—*n.*** [*count; usually singular*] **2.** a confused state.

fud•dy-dud•dy (fud′ē dud′ē) /ˈfʌdiyˌdʌdiy/ *n.* [*count*], *pl.* **-dud•dies.** a person who is stuffy and old-fashioned.

fudge[1] (fuj) /fʌdʒ/ *n.* [*noncount*] a soft candy usually made with sugar, butter, milk, and flavoring.

fudge[2] (fuj) /fʌdʒ/ *v.,* **fudged, fudg•ing,** *adj.* **1.** [~ + *on* + *obj*] to behave in a dishonest way; cheat: *to fudge on an exam.* **2.** to avoid coming to grips with something; evade; dodge: [~ + *on* + *obj*]: *The president began to fudge on the issue.* [~ + *obj*]: *He began to fudge questions.* **3.** [*no obj*] to exaggerate a cost, estimate, etc., in order to allow for error. **4.** [~ + *obj*] to tamper with; falsify: *to fudge the company accounts.*

fu•el (fyoo′əl) /ˈfyuwəl/ *n., v.,* **-eled, -el•ing** or (*esp. Brit.*) **-elled, -el•ling.** **—*n.* 1.** matter that can be burned to create heat or power, such as coal, wood, oil, or gas: [*noncount*]: *ran out of fuel.* [*count*]: *Kerosene and gas are fuels.* **2.** [*noncount*] something that maintains, encourages, or stimulates: *The proposed amendment is fuel for debate.* **—*v.* 3.** [~ + *obj*] to supply with fuel: *fueled the plane.* **4.** [*no obj*] to obtain or replenish fuel: *The jet fighter fueled in midair.* **5.** [~ + *obj*] to encourage or stimulate: *to fuel suspicion.*

-fug-, *root.* *-fug-* comes from Latin, where it has the meaning "flee; move; run." This meaning is found in such words as: CENTRIFUGAL, CENTRIFUGE, FUGITIVE, FUGUE, REFUGE, SUBTERFUGE.

fu•gi•tive (fyoo′ji tiv) /ˈfyuwdʒɪtɪv/ *n.* [*count*] **1.** a person who is fleeing, as from prosecution or capture: *a fugitive from justice.* **—*adj.*** [*before a noun*] **2.** running away: *a fugitive convict.* **3.** fleeting; elusive: *fugitive thoughts.* See -FUG-.

fugue (fyoog) /fyuwg/ *n.* [*count*] a musical composition with two or more voices. —**fu′gal,** *adj.* See -FUG-.

-ful, *suffix.* **1.** *-ful* is attached to nouns to form adjectives with the meaning "full of; characterized by": *beauty* + *-ful* → *beautiful (= full of beauty); care* + *-ful* → *careful (= characterized by care).* **2.** *-ful* is attached to verbs to form adjectives with the meaning "tending to; able to": *harm* + *-ful* → *harmful (= tending to harm); wake* + *-ful* → *wakeful (= tending to stay awake).* **3.** *-ful* is attached to nouns to form nouns with the meaning "as much as will fill": *spoon* + *-ful* → *spoonful* (= *as much as will fill a spoon); cup* + *-ful* → *cupful* (= *as much as will fill a cup).*

ful•crum (fo͝ol′krəm, ful′-) /'fʊlkrəm, 'fʌl-/ *n.* [*count*], *pl.* **-crums, -cra** (-krə) /-krə/. the support, or point of rest, on which a lever turns in moving a body.

ful•fill or **ful•fil** (fo͝ol fil′) /fʊl'fɪl/ *v.* [~ + *obj*], **-filled, -fill•ing** or **-fil•ling. 1.** to carry out or bring to realization: *The dream of a world without war is yet to be fulfilled.* **2.** to perform or do, such as duty; obey or follow, such as commands: *ability to fulfill the job.* **3.** to satisfy (requirements, needs, obligations, etc.): *That book will fulfill a long-felt need.* **4.** [~ + *oneself*] to develop the full potential of (oneself). —**ful•fill′ment,** *n.* [*noncount*]

full (fo͝ol) /fʊl/ *adj.,* **-er, -est,** *adv.* —*adj.* **1.** completely filled: *a full cup.* **2.** [*be* + ~ + *of*] containing all that can be held: *eyes full of tears.* **3.** [*before a noun*] complete; entire; maximum: *a full supply of food; at full speed.* **4.** abundant; well-supplied: *a cabinet full of medicine.* **5.** (of garments, drapery, etc.) wide, ample, or having large folds; flowing out: *a full skirt.* **6.** filled or rounded out, as in form: *has a full figure.* **7.** [*be* + ~ + *of*] occupied with thinking of; having the mind focused on; engrossed with: *full of anxieties.* **8.** of the highest rank: *a full professor.* **9.** [*before a noun*] of the same parents: *full brothers, not half brothers.* **10.** ample and complete in volume or richness of sound: *a deep, full voice.* **11.** having eaten as much as one can: *feeling full from dinner.* —*adv.* **12.** exactly or directly; straight: *The blow struck him full in the face.* **13.** quite; very; perfectly: *You know full well what I mean.* —***Idiom.* 14. in full,** to or for the full or required amount: *We expect payment in full.* —**full′ness,** *n.* [*noncount*]

full•back (fo͝ol′bak′) /'fʊl,bæk/ *n.* **1.** [*count*] (in football) a running back who lines up behind the quarterback. **2.** [*count*] (in soccer, Rugby, and field hockey) a player stationed near the defended goal to carry out chiefly defensive duties. **3.** [*noncount*] the position played by a fullback.

full′-blood′ed, *adj.* [*before a noun*] **1.** of unmixed ancestry. **2.** vigorous; strong; hearty.

full′-blown′, *adj.* [*often: before a noun*] **1.** completely developed: *a full-blown war; full-blown disease.* **2.** in full bloom: *a full-blown rose.*

full′-bod′ied, *adj.* of full strength, flavor, richness, etc.: *full-bodied wine.*

full′ dress′, *n.* [*noncount*] attire customarily worn for formal or ceremonial occasions.

full-fledged (fo͝ol′flejd′) /'fʊl'flɛdʒd/ *adj.* [*before a noun*] **1.** of full rank or standing: *a full-fledged ambassador.* **2.** fully developed: *full-fledged adulthood.*

full′ moon′, *n.* [*count; singular*] the moon when the whole of its disk is showing.

full′-scale′, *adj.* [*before a noun*] **1.** having the exact size or proportions of the original: *a full-scale replica of the submarine.* **2.** using all possible means, facilities, etc.; complete: *a full-scale attack.*

full′-time′, *adj.* **1.** working or operating the customary number of hours in each day, week, or month: *a full-time employee.* Compare PART-TIME. —*adv.* **2.** on a full-time basis: *to work full-time.* —**full′-tim′er,** *n.* [*count*]

ful•ly (fo͝ol′ē) /'fʊliy/ *adv.* **1.** entirely or completely; to the greatest amount or degree: *Are you fully aware of what you have done?* **2.** quite; at least: *Fully half the class attended.*

ful•mi•nate (ful′mə nāt′) /'fʌlmə,neyt/ *v.* [*no obj*], **-nat•ed, -nat•ing.** to denounce strongly: *fulminating against the regulations.* —**ful•mi•na•tion** (ful′mi nā′shən) /,fʌlmɪ'neyʃən/ *n.* [*noncount*]

ful•some (fo͝ol′səm, ful′-) /'fʊlsəm, 'fʌl-/ *adj.* **1.** offensive to good taste; overdone: *fulsome décor.* **2.** excessively or insincerely lavish: *fulsome praise.*

fum•ble (fum′bəl) /'fʌmbəl/ *v.,* **-bled, -bling,** *n.* —*v.* **1.** [*no obj*] to feel or grope about clumsily: *He fumbled in his pocket for the keys.* **2.** to fail to hold a ball after having touched it or carried it, such as in a baseball or football game: [*no obj*]: *He has a reputation for fumbling in crucial situations.* [~ + *obj*]: *fumbled the ball.* **3.** to do (something) clumsily or unsuccessfully; blunder: [*no obj*]: *He fumbled for an answer.* [~ + *obj*]: *They fumbled an attempt to rescue the hostages.* —*n.* [*count*] **4.** an act or instance of fumbling. —**fum′bler,** *n.* [*count*] —**fum′bling•ly,** *adv.*

fume (fyo͞om) /fyuwm/ *n., v.,* **fumed, fum•ing.** —*n.* [*count*] **1.** Often, **fumes.** [*plural*] smoke, gas, or vapor, esp. of an irritating nature: *tobacco fumes.* —*v.* [*no obj*] **2.** to emit or give off fumes or vapor. **3.** to be fretful, irritated, or angry: *She always fumes when the mail is late.*

fu•mi•gate (fyo͞o′mi gāt′) /'fyuwmɪ,geyt/ *v.* [~ + *obj*], **-gat•ed, -gat•ing.** to expose to fumes in order to kill pests. —**fu•mi•ga•tion** (fyo͞o′mi gā′shən) /,fyuwmɪ'geyʃən/ *n.* [*noncount*] —**fu′mi•ga′tor,** *n.* [*count*]

fun (fun) /fʌn/ *n.,* [*noncount*] **1.** something that provides mirth or amusement: *A picnic would be fun.* **2.** enjoyment or playfulness: *She's full of fun.* —*adj.* **3.** [*before a noun*] *Informal.* providing pleasure or amusement; enjoyable: *That would be a fun thing to do.* —***Idiom.* 4. for** or **in fun,** as a joke; not seriously; playfully: *We played that prank on him for fun.* **5. make fun of,** [~ + *obj*] to make the object of jokes, insults, or ridicule; deride: *likes to make fun of the neighbors.*

-funct-, *root.* *-funct-* comes from Latin, where it has the meaning "perform, execute; purpose, use." This meaning is found in such words as: DEFUNCT, FUNCTION, FUNCTIONAL, MALFUNCTION, PERFUNCTORY.

func•tion (fungk′shən) /'fʌŋkʃən/ *n.* **1.** [*count*] action or activity thought of as proper to a person, thing, or institution; role: *The function of the kidneys is to purify the blood.* **2.** [*count*] a ceremonious public or social gathering or occasion: *a charity function.* **3.** [*count*] a factor related to or dependent upon other factors: *Price is a function of supply and demand.* **4.** [*noncount*] the way something works or operates: *They were testing him for heart function.* —*v.* [*no obj*] **5.** to operate: *The computer isn't functioning now.* **6.** to have or exercise a function; serve: *Let me function as your guide.* See -FUNCT-.

func•tion•al (fungk′shə nl) /'fʌŋkʃənḷ/ *adj.* **1.** of or relating to a function or functions. **2.** capable of functioning: *When will the ventilating system be functional again?* **3.** having or serving a useful purpose: *This screen is functional as well as decorative.* **4.** [*before a noun*] of or relating to improper function without known cause: *a functional disorder.* —**func•tion•al•i•ty** (fungk′shə nal′i tē) /,fʌŋkʃə'nælɪtiy/ *n.* [*noncount*] —**func′tion•al•ly,** *adv.* See -FUNCT-.

func•tion•ar•y (fungk′shə ner′ē) /'fʌŋkʃə,nɛriy/ *n.* [*count*], *pl.* **-ar•ies.** a person who functions in a specific position, esp. in government service; an official. See -FUNCT-.

fund (fund) /fʌnd/ *n.* [*count*] **1.** a sum of money set aside for a specific purpose: *a retirement fund.* **2.** an organization created to manage money contributed or invested. **3.** supply; stock: *a fund of knowledge.* **4. funds,** [*plural*] money immediately available: *Were enough funds allocated to our department this year?* —*v.* [~ + *obj*] **5.** to allocate or provide funds for (a program, project, etc.): *The government funded his research.*

fun•da•men•tal (fun′də men′tl) /,fʌndə'mɛntl/ *adj.* **1.** serving as, or being an essential part of, a foundation or basis; basic: *fundamental principles of physics.* **2.** of great importance; essential: *a fundamental revision of a theory.* **3.** being an original or primary source; being a starting point: *a fundamental idea.* —*n.* [*count*] **4.** a basic principle, rule, law, or the like: *the fundamentals of engineering.* —**fun′da•men′tal•ly,** *adv.*

fun•da•men•tal•ism (fun′də men′tl iz′əm) /,fʌndə'mɛntḷ,ɪzəm/ *n.* [*noncount*] **1.** [*sometimes: Fundamentalism*] a movement in American Protestantism that claims the Bible is literally infallible not only in faith and morals but also in history. **2.** the beliefs held by those in this movement. —**fun′da•men′tal•ist,** *n.* [*count*], *adj.*

fu•ner•al (fyo͞o′nər əl) /'fyuwnərəl/ *n.* [*count*] **1.** the ceremonies for a dead person before burial or cremation. —*adj.* [*before a noun*] **2.** of or relating to a funeral: *funeral services; funeral expenses.*

fu′neral home′, *n.* [*count*] an establishment where the dead are prepared for burial or cremation. Also called **fu′neral chap′el, fu′neral par′lor, mortuary.**

fu•ne•re•al (fyo͞o nēr′ē əl) /fyuw'nɪəriyəl/ *adj.* **1.** of or suitable for a funeral: *funereal music.* **2.** mournful; gloomy; dismal: *a funereal atmosphere of gloom.* —**fu•ne′re•al•ly,** *adv.*

fun•gi•cide (fun′jə sīd′, fung′gə-) /'fʌndʒə,sayd, 'fʌŋgə-/ *n.* [*count*] a substance that destroys fungi. —**fun′gi•cid′al,** *adj.* See -CIDE-.

fun•gus (fung′gəs) /'fʌŋgəs/ *n.* [*count*], *pl.* **fun•gi** (fun′ji, fung′gi) /'fʌndʒay, 'fʌŋgay/ **fun•gus•es.** a plant lacking chlorophyll, flowers, and leaves and that lives by decomposing and absorbing the organic material in which it grows: *Fungi include the mushrooms and molds.* —**fun′gal, fun′gous,** *adj.*

fu•nic•u•lar (fyo͞o nik′yə lər) /fyuw'nɪkyələr/ *n.* [*count*] a steep railway in which the cars are pulled up or down the tracks by steel cables. Also called **funic′ular rail′way.**

funk[1] (fungk) /fʌŋk/ *n.* [*count*] a dejected mood; depression: *been in a funk all day.*

funk[2] (fungk) /fʌŋk/ *n.* [*noncount*] **1.** music having a funky quality. **2.** the state or quality of being funky. **3.** a strong smell; stench.

funk•y[1] (fung′kē) /ˈfʌŋkiy/ *adj.*, **-i•er, -i•est.** depressed; unhappy; dejected: *in a foul, funky mood.*

funk•y[2] (fung′kē) /ˈfʌŋkiy/ *adj.*, **-i•er, -i•est. 1.** having an earthy, blues-based character: *funky jazz.* **2.** *Slang.* offbeat, odd, or quirky, such as in appearance or style: *funky clothes.* **3.** having an offensive smell; foul-smelling. —**funk′i•ness,** *n.* [*noncount*]

fun•nel (fun′l) /ˈfʌnl/ *n., v.,* **-neled, -nel•ing** or (*esp. Brit.*) **-nelled, -nel•ling.** —*n.* [*count*] **1.** a cone-shaped utensil with a tube at the point for channeling a substance through a small opening. **2.** a smokestack, esp. of a steamship. **3.** a shaft for ventilation. —*v.* **4.** [~ + *obj*] to pass along; channel: *funneled their profits into research.* **5.** to (cause to) pass through or as if through a funnel: [*no obj*]: *The group funneled out of the stadium.* [~ + *obj*]: *funneled the traffic around the overturned truck.*

fun•ny (fun′ē) /ˈfʌniy/ *adj.*, **-ni•er, -ni•est,** *n., pl.* **-nies,** *adv.* —*adj.* **1.** provoking laughter; amusing; comical: *a funny movie.* **2.** ill; slightly sick: *He felt funny so he sat down for a moment.* **3.** arousing suspicion; underhanded; deceitful: *There was something funny about those extra charges.* **4.** strange; peculiar; odd: *The car is making a funny noise.* —*n.* [*count*] **5. funnies,** [*plural*] comic strips or the section of a newspaper containing them. —*adv.* **6.** *Informal.* oddly; strangely; peculiarly: *a stranger who talked funny.* —**fun•ni•ly** (fun′l ē) /ˈfʌnl̩iy/ *adv.* —**fun′ni•ness,** *n.* [*noncount*]

fun′ny bone′, *n.* [*count*] **1.** the part of the elbow where a blow to the nerve causes a peculiar tingling sensation in the arm and hand. **2.** a sense of humor.

fun′ny mon′ey, *n.* [*noncount*] *Slang.* counterfeit or artificially inflated currency.

fur (fûr) /fɜr/ *n.* **1.** [*noncount*] the soft, thick, hairy coat of a mammal. **2.** [*noncount*] the processed pelt of certain animals, as minks or beavers, used esp. for jackets and coats. **3.** [*count*] a garment made of fur: *All the furs were on sale.* **4.** [*noncount*] a furlike coating. —*adj.* [*before a noun*] **5.** of, relating to, or dealing in fur or animal skins, etc.: *a fur coat; a fur trader.* —***Idiom.*** **6. make the fur fly,** to cause a lively disturbance. —**furred,** *adj.*

fur•bish (fûr′bish) /ˈfɜrbɪʃ/ *v.* [~ + *obj*] to restore to good condition, as by polishing.

fu•ri•ous (fyŏŏr′ē əs) /ˈfyʊriyəs/ *adj.* **1.** full of fury: *a furious accusation.* **2.** intensely violent: *a furious hurricane.* **3.** of great energy, speed, etc.: *furious activity.*

furl (fûrl) /fɜrl/ *v.* to (cause to) be gathered into a roll and bound securely: [*no obj*]: *the flag furled against its staff.* [~ + *obj*]: *furled the sails.*

fur•long (fûr′lông, -long) /ˈfɜrlɔŋ, -lɒŋ/ *n.* [*count*] a unit of distance equal to 220 yards (201 m) or ⅛ of a mile (0.2 km). *Abbr.:* fur.

fur•lough (fûr′lō) /ˈfɜrlow/ *n.* [*count*] **1.** a leave of absence granted to a person in military service; leave: *a two-week furlough.* **2.** a usually temporary layoff from work. **3.** a temporary leave of absence authorized for a prisoner from a prison. **4. on furlough,** granted permission to be temporarily absent from service, work, or prison. —*v.* [~ + *obj*] **5.** to give a furlough to.

fur•nace (fûr′nis) /ˈfɜrnɪs/ *n.* [*count*] a structure or apparatus in which heat is generated, such as for heating houses, melting metals, or producing steam.

fur•nish (fûr′nish) /ˈfɜrnɪʃ/ *v.* [~ + *obj*] **1.** to supply (a house, room, etc.) with what is needed, esp. with furniture: *to furnish an apartment.* **2.** to provide: *The delay furnished me with the time I needed.*

fur•nish•ings (fûr′ni shingz) /ˈfɜrnɪʃɪŋz/ *n.* [*plural*] **1.** furniture, carpeting, etc., for a house or room. **2.** articles or accessories of dress.

fur•ni•ture (fûr′ni chər) /ˈfɜrnɪtʃər/ *n.* [*noncount*] movable articles, such as tables, chairs, or cabinets, required for use or ornament in a house, office, or the like.

fu•ror (fyŏŏr′ôr, -ər) /ˈfyʊrɔr, -ər/ *n.* [*count; usually singular*] a general outburst of excitement or controversy: *a furor over health insurance.*

fur•ri•er (fûr′ē ər) /ˈfɜriyər/ *n.* [*count*] a person who sells, repairs, or cleans fur garments.

fur•row (fûr′ō, fur′ō) /ˈfɜrow, ˈfʌrow/ *n.* [*count*] **1.** a groove made in the ground, esp. by a plow. **2.** a groovelike depression in any surface: *the furrows of a wrinkled face.* —*v.* **3.** to (cause to) have wrinkles in (the face): [~ + *obj*]: *to furrow one's brow.* [*no obj*]: *His face furrowed in worry.*

fur•ry (fûr′ē) /ˈfɜriy/ *adj.*, **-ri•er, -ri•est.** made up of, resembling, or covered with fur. —**fur′ri•ness,** *n.* [*noncount*]

fur•ther (fûr′thər) /ˈfɜrðər/ *comparative adv. and adj. of* **far** *with superlative* **fur•thest,** *v.* —*adv.* **1.** at or to a greater distance; farther: *too tired to go further.* **2.** at or to a more advanced point: *Let's not discuss it further.* **3.** in addition; moreover: *Further, he should be here any minute.* —*adj.* **4.** more distant or remote; farther: *The map shows it to be further than I thought.* **5.** [*before a noun*] more extended: *a further delay.* **6.** [*before a noun*] additional; more: *Further meetings seem pointless.* —*v.* [~ + *obj*] **7.** to help forward (a work, etc.); promote; advance: *counted on her to further our cause.* —**fur′ther•ance,** *n.* [*noncount*]: *the furtherance of her aims.*

fur•ther•more (fûr′thər môr′, -mōr′) /ˈfɜrðərˌmɔr, -ˌmowr/ *adv.* moreover; besides; in addition.

fur•ther•most (fûr′thər mōst′) /ˈfɜrðərˌmowst/ *adj.* [*before a noun*] most distant.

fur•thest (fûr′thist) /ˈfɜrðɪst/ *adj., adv., superlative of* **far** *with* **fur•ther** *as comparative.* FARTHEST.

fur•tive (fûr′tiv) /ˈfɜrtɪv/ *adj.* **1.** taken, done, used, etc., secretly or without others noticing; stealthy; secret: *a furtive glance.* **2.** sly; shifty: *a furtive manner.* —**fur′tive•ly,** *adv.* —**fur′tive•ness,** *n.* [*noncount*]

fu•ry (fyŏŏr′ē) /ˈfyʊriy/ *n., pl.* **-ries. 1.** unrestrained or violent rage: [*noncount*]: *The soldiers were filled with fury.* [*count; usually singular*]: *felt a sudden fury.* **2.** [*noncount*] violence; fierceness: *the fury of a hurricane.*

-fus-, *root.* -*fus*- comes from Latin, where it has the meaning "pour, cast; join; blend." This meaning is found in such words as: CONFUSE, DEFUSE, DIFFUSE, EFFUSIVE, FUSE, FUSION, INFUSE, PROFUSE, SUFFUSE, TRANSFUSION.

fuse[1] (fyōōz) /fyuwz/ *n.* [*count*] **1.** a tube, cord, or the like, filled or saturated with matter that burns easily and rapidly, used for igniting an explosive. **2.** a mechanical or electronic device for detonating an explosive charge. —***Idiom.*** **3. have a short fuse,** [*no obj*] *Informal.* to anger easily; have a quick temper. —**fuse′less,** *adj.*

fuse[2] (fyōōz) /fyuwz/ *n., v.,* **fused, fus•ing.** —*n.* [*count*] **1.** a safety device containing a material that conducts electricity that will melt when too much current runs through an electric circuit, breaking the circuit. —*v.* **2.** to (cause to) combine or blend by melting together; melt: [*no obj*]: *The metal fused under the extreme heat.* [~ + *obj*]: *The extreme heat will fuse these elements together.* **3.** [~ + *obj*] to cause to unite; blend: *The author skillfully fuses these details into an interesting story.* —***Idiom.*** **4. blow a fuse,** *Informal.* to lose one's temper; become enraged. See -FUS-.

fu•se•lage (fyōō′sə läzh′, -lij) /ˈfyuwsəˌlɑʒ, -lɪdʒ/ *n.* [*count*] the central structure of an airplane.

fu•sil•lade (fyōō′sə läd′, -lād′) /ˈfyuwsəˌlɑd, -ˌleyd/ *n.* [*count*] **1.** a continuous discharge of firearms. **2.** a general outpouring: *a fusillade of questions.*

fu•sion (fyōō′zhən) /ˈfyuwʒən/ *n.* **1.** [*noncount*] the act or process of fusing or the state of being fused. **2.** [*count*] that which is fused; the result of fusing: *a fusion of the major political parties.* **3.** [*noncount*] the joining of atomic nuclei in a reaction that forms nuclei of heavier atoms. Compare FISSION (def. 2): *Fusion produces even greater energy than fission.* See -FUS-.

fuss (fus) /fʌs/ *n.* [*count*] **1.** an excessive display of attention or activity: *made a fuss over a little accident.* **2.** an argument or noisy dispute. **3.** a complaint or protest, esp. about something relatively unimportant. —*v.* [*no obj*] **4.** to care too much about small and unimportant things: *to fuss over details.* **5.** to behave in a busy or nervous manner; flutter about: *mothers fussing over their children.* **6.** to complain, esp. about something relatively unimportant: *to fuss and fume about the delay.*

fuss•budg•et (fus′buj′it) /ˈfʌsˌbʌdʒɪt/ *n.* [*count*] a fussy or needlessly fault-finding person.

fuss•y (fus′ē) /ˈfʌsiy/ *adj.*, **-i•er, -i•est. 1.** too busy with small, unimportant things; anxious or particular about petty details. **2.** hard to satisfy or please: *a fussy eater.* **3.** with too much decoration or too many elaborate designs: *a fussy hat.* —**fuss′i•ly,** *adv.* —**fuss′i•ness,** *n.* [*noncount*]

fus•ty (fus′tē) /ˈfʌstiy/ *adj.*, **-ti•er, -ti•est. 1.** stale; musty. **2.** old-fashioned: *fusty attitudes.*

fut., an abbreviation of: future.

fu•tile (fyōōt′l, fyōō′tīl) /ˈfyuwtl̩, ˈfyuwtayl/ *adj.* **1.** unable to produce any result; ineffective: *Attempts to swim across the stormy channel were futile.* **2.** trifling; frivolous; of little value: *futile remarks.* —**fu′tile•ly,** *adv.* —**fu•til•i•ty** (fyo͞o til′i tē) /fyuw'tılıtiy/ *n.* [*noncount*]

fu•ton (fo͞o′ton) /'fuwtɒn/ *n.* [*count*] a quiltlike mattress placed on a floor or a frame for sleeping, and folded and stored or used as seating.

fu•ture (fyo͞o′chər) /'fyuwtʃər/ *n.* **1.** [*count; singular; the* + ~] time that is to be or come hereafter: *some day in the future.* **2.** [*count; singular; the* + ~] something that will exist or happen in time to come. **3.** [*count*] events yet to happen: *to predict the future.* **4.** [*the* + ~] **a.** the future tense. **b.** a verb form or construction in the future tense. **5.** Usually, **futures.** [*plural*] commodities bought and sold to make a profit and intended for future delivery. —*adj.* [*before a noun*] **6.** being or coming hereafter: *future events.* **7.** of, relating to, or being a verb tense, form, or construction that refers to events or states in time to come.

fu•tur•is•tic (fyo͞o′chə ris′tik) /ˌfyuwtʃə'rıstık/ *adj.* **1.** of or relating to the future. **2.** ahead of the times; advanced: *futuristic technology.*

futz (futs) /fʌts/ *v.* [*no obj*] *Slang.* to pass time doing things of little importance: *futzing around.*

fuzz[1] (fuz) /fʌz/ *n.* [*noncount*] loose, light, fiberlike or fluffy matter; bits of thread.

fuzz[2] (fuz) /fʌz/ *n.* [*plural; used with a plural verb*] *Slang.* the police or a police officer.

fuzz•y (fuz′ē) /'fʌziy/ *adj.,* **-i•er, -i•est. 1.** resembling or covered with fuzz: *a fuzzy blanket.* **2.** indistinct; blurred: *a fuzzy photograph.* **3.** not logical: *a fuzzy thinker.* —**fuzz•i•ly** (fuz′ə lē) /'fʌzəliy/ *adv.* —**fuzz′i•ness,** *n.* [*noncount*]

fwd., an abbreviation of: **1.** foreword. **2.** forward.

-fy, *suffix.* **1.** *-fy* is found in loanwords from Latin and is attached to roots to form verbs with the meanings "to make; cause to be; render": *pure* + *-fy* → *purify (= to make pure); simple* + *-fy* → *simplify (= to make simple); liquid* + *-fy* → *liquefy (= to make into a liquid).* **2.** *-fy* is also used to mean "cause to conform to": *citify (= cause to conform to city ways).* Compare -IFY.

FYI, an abbreviation of: for your information.

G, g (jē) /dʒiy/ *n.* [*count*], *pl.* **Gs** or **G's, gs** or **g's.** the seventh letter of the English alphabet, a consonant.

G, an abbreviation of: **1.** general: a motion-picture rating advising that the film is suitable for general audiences, or for children as well as adults. **2.** good.

g, an abbreviation of: **1.** good. **2.** gram. **3.** the force of gravity exerted on an object at rest, equal to the acceleration of a falling body near the earth's surface.

GA or **Ga.,** an abbreviation of: Georgia.

gab (gab) /gæb/ *v.,* **gabbed, gab•bing,** *n. Informal.* **—***v.* [*no obj*] **1.** to talk or chat without purpose; chatter: *gabbing on the phone for hours.* **—***n.* [*noncount*] **2.** talk without purpose; chatter. **—*Idiom.* 3. have the gift of (the) gab,** to be able to talk glibly: *A good salesperson has the gift of gab.*

gab•ar•dine (gab′ər dēn′, gab′ər dēn′) /ˈgæbərˌdiyn, ˌgæbərˈdiyn/ *n.* [*noncount*] a firm, tightly woven fabric of wool, cotton, polyester, or other fiber, used for making coats and other garments. Also, **gaberdine.**

gab•ble (gab′əl) /ˈgæbəl/ *v.,* **-bled, -bling,** *n.* **—***v.* [*no obj*] **1.** to speak rapidly; jabber: *The children gabbled nervously.* **—***n.* [*noncount; singular*] **2.** rapid talk; a quick sequence of meaningless sounds: *the gabble of the crowd.*

gab•by (gab′ē) /ˈgæbiy/ *adj.,* **-bi•er, -bi•est.** talkative: *a gabby old cowboy relating one adventure after another.*

ga•ble (gā′bəl) /ˈgeybəl/ *n.* [*count*] the portion of the front or side of a building, usually three-sided in shape, enclosed by or hiding the end of a roof. **—ga′bled,** *adj.*

gad (gad) /gæd/ *v.* [*no obj,*] **gad•ded, gad•ding.** to move without purpose from one place to another in search of pleasure or amusement: *to gad about town.*

gad•a•bout (gad′ə bout′) /ˈgædəˌbawt/ *n.* [*count*] a person who moves about restlessly, as from one social activity to another.

gad•fly (gad′flī′) /ˈgædˌflay/ *n.* [*count*], *pl.* **-flies. 1.** a fly, such as a horsefly, that bites or annoys livestock. **2.** a person who persistently annoys or stirs up others, esp. with criticism.

gadg•et (gaj′it) /ˈgædʒɪt/ *n.* [*count*] a small mechanical apparatus or electronic device: *a gadget for peeling garlic.* **—gad•get•ry** (gaj′i trē) /ˈgædʒɪtriy/ *n.* [*noncount*]: *computer gadgetry.*

gaff (gaf) /gæf/ *n.* [*count*] **1.** an iron hook with a handle for pulling in or moving large fish. **—***v.* [~ + *obj*] **2.** to catch or hook (a fish) with a gaff.

gaffe (gaf) /gæf/ *n.* [*count*] a mistake or awkward remark or act in public that offends others; a social blunder; faux pas.

gaf•fer (gaf′ər) /ˈgæfər/ *n.* [*count*] **1.** the chief electrician on a motion-picture or television production. **2.** *Informal.* an old man.

gag[1] (gag) /gæg/ *v.,* **gagged, gag•ging,** *n.* **—***v.* **1.** [~ + *obj*] to stop up the mouth of (a person) by inserting a gag: *They gagged their prisoner.* **2.** [~ + *obj*] to prevent (a newspaper or writer) from exercising free speech: *The newspapers were gagged by government decree.* **3.** to (cause to) retch or choke: [*no obj*]: *She gagged on the strong whiskey.* [~ + *obj*]: *The strong whiskey gagged her.* **—***n.* [*count*] **4.** something put into a person's mouth to prevent speech, shouting, etc. **5.** any forced suppression of free speech: *a gag on war reporting.*

gag[2] (gag) /gæg/ *n.* [*count*] a joke or prank: *played a gag on him by pretending he had won the lottery.*

ga•ga (gä′gä) /ˈgɑgɑ/ *adj.* **1.** [*often: go/be* + ~] wildly enthusiastic: *went gaga over the new fashions.* **2.** [*often: go/be* + ~] madly in love; infatuated: *He's gaga about her.* **3.** showing mental deterioration from old age; senile.

gage (gāj) /geydʒ/ *n., v.,* **gaged, gag•ing.** (chiefly in technical use) GAUGE. **—gag′er,** *n.* [*count*]

gag•gle (gag′əl) /ˈgægəl/ *n.* [*count; usually singular*] **1.** a flock of geese when not flying. **2.** an often noisy group: *a gaggle of sightseers.*

gai•e•ty (gā′i tē) /ˈgeyɪtiy/ *n.* [*noncount*] the quality or state of being gay or cheerful; merriment.

gai•ly (gā′lē) /ˈgeyliy/ *adv.* **1.** merrily; cheerfully: *They waved gaily from the window.* **2.** brightly or showily: *gaily patterned dresses.*

gain (gān) /geyn/ *v.* **1.** [~ + *obj*] to get (something desired), esp. as a result of one's efforts; secure: *to gain possession of land.* **2.** [~ + *obj*] to acquire or get as an increase or addition: *The car gained speed.* **3.** [*no obj*] to improve; advance: *She's finally begun to gain in health.* **4.** [~ + *obj*] to obtain as a profit or advantage: *He didn't stand to gain much by the deal.* **5.** [~ + *obj*] to win (someone) to one's own side or point of view: *The candidate began to gain supporters.* **6.** (of a watch or clock) to run fast by (a specified amount): [~ + *obj*]: *My watch gains six minutes a day.* [*no obj*]: *Her watch gains.* **7.** [~ + *obj*] to get to; arrive at: *to gain one's destination.* **8. gain on/upon,** [~ + *obj*] to get nearer: *The police were gaining on the criminals.* **—***n.* **9.** [*noncount*] profit or advantage: *I see no gain in this plan.* **10.** [*count*] an increase: *showed a small gain in weight.* **11. gains,** [*plural*] profits or winnings.

gain•ful (gān′fəl) /ˈgeynfəl/ *adj.* [*before a noun*] profitable; lucrative: *looking for gainful employment.* **—gain′ful•ly,** *adv.*

gain•say (gān′sā′, gān sā′) /ˈgeynˌsey, geynˈsey/ *v.* [~ + *obj*], **-said** (-sed′, -sed′) /-ˌsɛd, -ˈsɛd/ **-say•ing.** to deny; contradict. **—gain′say′er,** *n.* [*count*]

gait (gāt) /geyt/ *n.* [*count*] **1.** a manner of walking or running: *a slow gait.* **2.** any of the ways in which a horse moves, as a walk, trot, canter, or gallop.

gait•er (gā′tər) /ˈgeytər/ *n.* [*count*] **1.** a cloth or leather covering for the ankle and instep and sometimes also the lower leg. **2.** a cloth or leather shoe with elastic insertions at the sides. **3.** an overshoe with a cloth top.

gal (gal) /gæl/ *n.* [*count*] *Informal.* a girl or woman.

gal., an abbreviation of: gallon.

ga•la (gā′lə, gal′ə) /ˈgeylə, ˈgælə/ *adj.* [*usually: before a noun*] **1.** marking or proper for a special occasion; festive; showy: *a gala affair.* **—***n.* [*count*] **2.** a celebration, often with entertainment: *a gala held at the concert hall.*

ga•lac•tic (gə lak′tik) /gəˈlæktɪk/ *adj.* [*usually: before a noun*] of or relating to a galaxy, as the Milky Way.

gal•ax•y (gal′ək sē) /ˈgæləksiy/ *n., pl.* **-ax•ies. 1. a.** [*count*] a large system of stars separated from similar systems by vast regions of space. **b.** [*proper noun; usually: the Galaxy*] MILKY WAY. **2.** [*count*] any large and brilliant or impressive group: *a galaxy of opera stars.*

gale (gāl) /geyl/ *n.* [*count*] **1.** a very strong wind. **2.** a wind of 32–63 mph (14–28 m/sec): *gales in the North Atlantic.* **3.** a noisy outburst: *a gale of laughter.*

gall[1] (gôl) /gɔl/ *n.* [*noncount*] **1.** rude boldness; nerve: *He has a lot of gall expecting me to finish his work.* **2.** BILE (def. 1).

gall[2] (gôl) /gɔl/ *v.* to annoy greatly: [~ + *obj*]: *His arrogant manner galls me.* [*It* + ~ + *obj* + *(that) clause*]: *It galls me that we can't fire him.* **—gall′ing,** *adj.*

gal•lant (gal′ənt *for 1,* gə lant′, -länt′, gal′ənt *for 2),* /ˈgælənt *for 1,* gəˈlænt, -ˈlɑnt, ˈgælənt *for 2), adj.* **1.** brave, heroic, spirited, or noble-minded: *a gallant knight.* **2.** exceptionally polite and attentive to women; chivalrous. **—gal′lant•ly,** *adv.*

gal•lant•ry (gal′ən trē) /ˈgæləntriy/ *n.* [*noncount*] **1.** great courage; heroic bravery; noble-minded behavior: *The army showed great gallantry.* **2.** polite attentiveness to women.

gall•bladder or **gall blad•der** (gôl′blad′ər) /ˈgɔlˌblædər/ *n.* [*count*] a pouch or sac attached to the liver, in which bile is stored and concentrated.

gal•le•on (gal′ē ən, gal′yən) /ˈgæliyən, ˈgælyən/ *n.* [*count*] a large sailing vessel of the 15th to the 17th centuries, used as a fighting or merchant ship.

gal•ler•y (gal′ə rē, gal′rē) /ˈgæləriy, ˈgælriy/ *n.* [*count*], *pl.* **-ler•ies. 1.** a raised area, often having a sloping floor, in a theater, church, or other public building, used as a place for spectators, exhibits, etc. **2.** the uppermost of such areas in a theater, usually containing the cheapest seats. **3.** the persons sitting in such an area in a theater: *a shout from the gallery.* **4.** any group of spectators or observers, as at a golf match or a legislative session. **5.** a room, series of rooms, or building for the showing and often the sale of works of art. **6.** a collection or group: *a gallery of misfits.* **7.** a long covered area, narrow and open at one or both sides, used esp. as a walkway or corridor. **8.** a large room or building used for a special purpose: *a shooting gallery.* **—*Idiom.* 9. play to the gallery,** to act in a manner intended to impress the general public.

gal•ley (gal′ē) /ˈgæliy/ *n.* [*count*], *pl.* **-leys. 1. a.** the kitchen area of a ship, plane, or camper. **b.** any small, narrow kitchen. **2.** a seagoing vessel propelled mainly by oars and used in ancient and medieval times.

gal•li•vant (gal′ə vant′, gal′ə vant′) /ˈgæləˌvænt,

ˌgælə'vænt/ *v.* [*no obj*] **1.** to wander about, seeking pleasure or entertainment; gad: *They gallivanted around town.* **2.** to go about with members of the opposite sex.

gal•lon (gal′ən) /'gælən/ *n.* [*count*] a common unit of liquid measurement in English-speaking countries, equal to four quarts, the U.S. standard gallon being equal to 231 cubic inches (3.7853 liters) and the British imperial gallon to 277.42 cubic inches (4.546 liters). *Abbr.*: gal.

gal•lop (gal′əp) /'gæləp/ *v.* **1.** to ride (a horse) at full speed: [*no obj*]: *The rider galloped away.* [~ + *obj*]: *The cavalry galloped their horses for hours.* **2.** [*no obj*] to run at a gallop: *The horses galloped away.* **3.** [*no obj*] to race; hurry: *She galloped out of the house.* **—*n.*** [*count*] **4.** a fast manner of moving for a horse or other four-legged animal in which, during each stride, all four feet are off the ground at once. **5.** a run or ride at this pace: *an early morning gallop.* **6.** a rapid rate of proceeding: *working at a gallop.*

gal•lows (gal′ōz) /'gælowz/ *n., pl.* **-lows, -lows•es. 1.** [*count*] a wooden frame made up of two upright pieces of wood with a crossbeam from which a person condemned to death is hanged. **2.** [*noncount*] execution by hanging: *sentenced to the gallows.*

gall•stone (gôl′stōn′) /'gɔl,stown/ *n.* [*count*] an abnormal stony mass in the gallbladder or the bile passages.

ga•lore (gə lôr′, -lōr′) /gə'lɔr, -'lowr/ *adj.* [*after a noun*] in great or plentiful amounts: *food galore at the party.*

ga•losh or **ga•loshe** (gə losh′) /gə'lɒʃ/ *n.* [*count; usually plural*] a waterproof overshoe, esp. a high one.

gal•va•nize (gal′və nīz′) /'gælvəˌnayz/ *v.* [~ + *obj*], **-nized, -niz•ing. 1.** to stimulate by an electric current: *to galvanize nerves.* **2.** to startle into sudden activity: *The news of the riots galvanized the police.* **3.** to coat (iron or steel) with zinc.

gal•va•nom•e•ter (gal′və nom′i tər) /ˌgælvə'nɒmɪtər/ *n.* [*count*] an instrument for detecting small electric currents and measuring their strength.

-gam-, *root. -gam-* comes from Greek, where it has the meaning "marriage." This meaning is found in such words as: BIGAMIST, BIGAMY, GAMETE, POLYGAMY.

gam•bit (gam′bit) /'gæmbɪt/ *n.* [*count*] **1.** an opening in chess in which a player seeks to obtain some advantage by sacrificing a pawn or piece. **2.** any action or maneuver by which one seeks an advantage; ploy: *an opening gambit in negotiations.* **3.** a remark made to open or redirect a conversation.

gam•ble (gam′bəl) /'gæmbəl/ *v.,* **-bled, -bling,** *n.* **—*v.* 1.** [*no obj*] to play at a game of chance for money or other stakes: *to gamble at cards.* **2.** to bet, wager, stake, or risk (something of value, as money) on the outcome of something involving chance or uncertainty; bet: [~ + *obj* + *on*]: *I'll gamble my life on his honesty.* [~ + *on* + *obj*]: *He gambled on that project's succeeding.* **3.** [~ + *(that) clause*] to take a chance; risk: *We're gambling that our new store will be a success.* **4.** to lose by betting: [~ + *obj* + *away*]: *gambled all his money away.* [~ + *away* + *obj*]: *gambled away all his money.* **—*n.*** [*count*] **5.** any matter or thing involving risk or hazardous uncertainty: *We took a gamble in hiring him.* **—gam′bler,** *n.* [*count*]

gam•bol (gam′bəl) /'gæmbəl/ *v.,* **-boled, -bol•ing** or (*esp. Brit.*) **-bolled, -bol•ling,** *n.* **—*v.*** [*no obj*] **1.** to skip about happily or merrily, as in dancing or playing; frolic. **—*n.*** [*count*] **2.** a skipping or leaping about; frolic.

game[1] (gām) /geym/ *n., adj.,* **gam•er, gam•est. —*n.* 1.** [*count*] an amusement or pastime: *children's games; card games.* **2.** [*count*] the equipment for a game: *Clean up the games from the floor.* **3.** [*count*] an activity in which players compete against others, involving skill, chance, or endurance and played according to a set of rules for the amusement of the players or of spectators. **4.** [*count*] a single occasion of such an activity: *a hockey game.* **5.** [*noncount*] the number of points required to win a game: *Game in table tennis is normally 21 points.* **6.** [*count*] the score at a particular stage in a game: *The game was seven to six at that point.* **7.** [*count*] a particular manner or style of playing a game: *He plays a fierce game.* **8.** [*count*] something resembling a game, as in requiring skill or endurance: *the game of diplomacy.* **9.** [*count*] *Informal.* a business or professional activity: *He's in the real-estate game.* **10.** [*count*] a trick or strategy: *We saw through his game.* **11.** [*count*] fun; sport; joke: *We have no time for your games.* **12.** [*noncount*] wild animals, including birds and fishes, such as are hunted for food or for sport or profit. **13.** [*noncount*] the flesh of such wild animals, used as food. **14.** [*noncount*] any object of pursuit, attack, abuse, etc.: *Any new student is fair game for the school bully.* **—*adj.* 15.** [*before a noun*] relating to animals viewed as game: *game laws.* **16.** having a fighting spirit; plucky: *a game fighter.* **17.** [*be* + ~] having the required spirit or will: [~ + *for*]: *Who's game for a hike?* [~ + *to* + *verb*]: *I'm game to try anything.* **—*Idiom.* 18. give the game away,** to reveal the truth about something. **19. play games,** to treat others manipulatively: *Stop playing games and tell us what you really want.* **20. play the game,** to act in accordance with rules, conventions, or standards. **—game′ly,** *adv.*: *The army fought gamely.* **—game′ness,** *n.* [*noncount*]

game[2] (gām) /geym/ *adj.* [*before a noun*] weak; lame: *a game leg.*

game•cock (gām′kok′) /'geymˌkɒk/ *n.* [*count*] a rooster trained for fighting.

game•keep•er (gām′kē′pər) /'geymˌkiypər/ *n.* [*count*] a person, as on an estate or game preserve, who cares for wild animals and prevents them from being illegally hunted.

game′ plan′, *n.* [*count*] **1.** a carefully planned strategy or course of action, as in politics or business. **2.** the strategy of an athletic team for winning a particular game.

game′ point′, *n.* [*count*] **1.** (in tennis, squash, handball, etc.) a situation in which the next point scored could decide the game. **2.** the point itself.

games•man•ship (gāmz′mən ship′) /'geymzmənˌʃɪp/ *n.* [*noncount*] **1.** skill in manipulating people or events so as to gain an advantage or outwit one's opponents or competitors. **2.** the use of methods in a sports contest that are not against the rules but are improper or unfair.

gam•ete (gam′ēt, gə mēt′) /'gæmiyt, gə'miyt/ *n.* [*count*] a mature sex cell, such as a sperm or egg, that unites with another such cell to form a new organism. See -GAM-.

gam•in (gam′in) /'gæmɪn/ *n.* [*count*] **1.** a boy who hangs around on the streets; urchin. **2.** GAMINE (def. 2).

gam•ine (gam′ēn, -in, ga mēn′) /'gæmiyn, -ɪn, gæ'miyn/ *n.* [*count*] **1.** a girl who hangs around on the streets. **2.** a small, playfully mischievous girl. **—*adj.* 3.** of or like a gamine: *clothes for the gamine figure.*

gam•ma (gam′ə) /'gæmə/ *n.* [*count*], *pl.* **-mas.** the third letter of the Greek alphabet (Γ, γ).

gam′ma ray′, *n.* [*count*] **1.** a particle of high-energy, high-frequency radiation given off by a radioactive atomic nucleus. **2.** a stream of such radiation.

gam•ut (gam′ət) /'gæmət/ *n.* [*count; usually singular: the* + ~ + *of*] **1.** an entire range: *the gamut of emotions, from grief to joy.* **2.** the whole series of recognized musical notes. **—*Idiom.* 3. run the gamut,** to extend across an entire range: *His emotions ran the gamut, from fear to joy.*

gam•y or **gam•ey** (gā′mē) /'geymiy/ *adj.,* **-i•er, -i•est.** having the tangy flavor of game esp. when slightly tainted. **—gam′i•ness,** *n.* [*noncount*]

gan•der (gan′dər) /'gændər/ *n.* [*count*] **1.** the male of the goose. Compare GOOSE (def. 2). **2.** *Slang.* a look: *Take a gander at his new shoes.*

gang (gang) /gæŋ/ *n.* [*count*] **1.** a group or band: *a gang of sightseers.* **2.** a group of youngsters who associate closely with each other, esp. such a group engaging in antisocial behavior: *street gangs.* **3.** a group of persons associated for some criminal purpose: *terrorist gangs.* **4.** a group of people with similar tastes or interests: *throwing a party for the gang I bowl with.* **5.** a group of persons working together: *a gang of laborers.* **—*v.* 6. gang up,** [~ + *on/against* + *obj*] to combine against: *Her three brothers were always ganging up on her.*

gan•gling (gang′gling) /'gæŋglɪŋ/ also **gan•gly, -gli•er, -gli•est,** *adj.* awkwardly and loosely built; lanky: *a tall, gangling youth.*

gan•gli•on (gang′glē ən) /'gæŋgliyən/ *n.* [*count*], *pl.* **-gli•a** (-glē ə) /-gliyə/ **-gli•ons.** a concentrated mass of nerve cells connected to each other.

gang•plank (gang′plangk′) /'gæŋˌplæŋk/ *n.* [*count*] a small movable bridge used for boarding or leaving a ship at a pier. Also called **gangway.**

gan•grene (gang′grēn, gang grēn′) /'gæŋgriyn, gæŋ'griyn/ *n.* [*noncount*] the death of body tissue due to blocked blood flow, usually followed by decay. **—gan•gre•nous** (gang′grə nəs) /'gæŋgrənəs/ *adj.*

gang•ster (gang′stər) /'gæŋstər/ *n.* [*count*] a member of a gang of criminals; mobster.

gang•way (*n.* gang′wā′; *interj.* gang′wā′) / *n.* 'gæŋˌwey; *interj.* 'gæŋ'wey/ *n.* [*count*] **1.** a passageway, esp. a narrow walkway. **2.** GANGPLANK. **3.** *Brit.* an aisle in the House of Commons separating the more influential members of the political parties from the younger, less influential members. —*interj.* **4.** Clear the way!—used as a warning or to ask for clear passage.

gan•try (gan′trē) /ˈgæntriy/ *n.* [*count*], *pl.* **-tries. 1.** a framework going high across a railroad track for displaying signals. **2.** a similar framework, as a bridgelike portion of certain cranes.

gaol (jāl) /dʒeyl/ *n., v. Brit.* JAIL. —**gaol′er,** *n.*

gap (gap) /gæp/ *n.* [*count*] **1.** a break or opening: *The animals escaped through a gap in the fence.* **2.** an incomplete area: *a gap in one's memory.* **3.** a wide or great difference between things: *a gap between the rich and the poor.* **4.** a great or wide disparity in attitudes, ways of thinking or seeing, character, or development: *a communications gap.* **5.** ravine. **6.** a mountain pass: *the Cumberland Gap.*

gape (gāp, gap) /geyp, gæp/ *v.,* **gaped** (gāpt, gapt) /geypt, gæpt/ **gap•ing. 1.** [~ + *at* + *obj*] to stare with the mouth wide open, as in shock, wonder, or surprise: *The tourists gaped at the tall buildings.* **2.** [*no obj*] to open or spread widely; split: *The canyon gaped before them.* —**gap′ing,** *adj.* [*before a noun*]

ga•rage (gə räzh′, -räj′) /gəˈrɑʒ, -ˈrɑdʒ/ *n., v.,* **-raged, -rag•ing.** —*n.* [*count*] **1.** a building or indoor area for parking motor vehicles. See illustration at HOUSE. **2.** a business for repairing and servicing motor vehicles. —*v.* [~ + *obj*] **3.** to put or keep in a garage: *They garaged their car.*

garb (gärb) /gɑrb/ *n.* [*noncount*] **1.** clothes; mode of dress, esp. when distinctive: *a nurse's garb.* —*v.* [~ + *obj*] **2.** to dress; clothe: *garbed in beautiful robes.*

gar•bage (gär′bij) /ˈgɑrbɪdʒ/ *n.* [*noncount*] **1.** matter that has been discarded, esp. food waste; refuse. **2.** anything contemptibly worthless, inferior, or vile. **3.** meaningless or unwanted computer data.

gar′bage can′, *n.* [*count*] a container, usually of metal or plastic, for the disposal of waste matter, esp. kitchen refuse.

gar•ble (gär′bəl) /ˈgɑrbəl/ *v.* [~ + *obj*], **-bled, -bling. 1.** to distort unintentionally or ignorantly; jumble: *to garble instructions.* **2.** to make unfair or misleading selections from or distort (facts, statements, writings, etc.) so as to change the meaning: *to garble a quotation.*

gar•çon (GAR SÔN′) /garˈsɔ̃/ *n.* [*count*], *pl.* **-çons** (-SÔN′) /-ˈsɔ̃/. *French.* waiter.

gar•den (gär′dn) /ˈgɑrdn̩/ *n.* [*count*] **1.** a plot or area of ground, usually near a house, where flowers, shrubs, vegetables, fruits, or herbs are grown. **2.** [*often plural*] a piece of ground or other space used as a park or other public recreation area. **3.** a fertile and delightful spot or region: *a garden in the wilderness.* —*adj.* [*before a noun*] **4.** relating to, produced in, or suitable for growing or use in a garden: *garden vegetables.* —*v.* [*no obj*] **5.** to cultivate a garden: *loves to garden.* —***Idiom.*** **6. lead (someone) down** or **up the garden path,** to mislead through false hopes or promises of reward; delude. —**gar′den•er,** *n.* [*count*]

gar•de•nia (gär dē′nyə, -nē ə) /gɑrˈdiynyə, -niyə/ *n.* [*count*], *pl.* **-nias. 1.** a subtropical evergreen tree or shrub of the madder family, having shiny leaves and fragrant white flowers. **2.** the flower of these plants.

gar′den-vari′ety, *adj.* common, usual, or ordinary; unexceptional: *just a garden-variety mistake.*

gar•gan•tu•an (gär gan′cho͞o ən) /gɑrˈgæntʃuwən/ *adj.* gigantic; enormous; colossal: *a gargantuan task.*

gar•gle (gär′gəl) /ˈgɑrgəl/ *v.,* **-gled, -gling,** *n.* —*v.* [*no obj*] **1.** to wash or rinse the throat or mouth with (a liquid held in the throat and kept in motion by a stream of air from the lungs). —*n.* [*count; usually singular*] **2.** a liquid used for gargling.

gar•goyle (gär′goil) /ˈgɑrgɔyl/ *n.* [*count*] a water spout in the form of a grotesque human or animal figure.

gar•ish (gâr′ish, gar′-) /ˈgɛərɪʃ, ˈgær-/ *adj.* **1.** overly or tastelessly colorful, showy, or elaborate: *garish Christmas decorations.* **2.** excessively bright; glaring: *the garish lights of the disco.* —**gar′ish•ly,** *adv.* —**gar′ish•ness,** *n.* [*noncount*]

gar•land (gär′lənd) /ˈgɑrlənd/ *n.* [*count*] a wreath of flowers, leaves, or other material, worn around the neck for an ornament or as an honor, or hung on something as a decoration.

gar•lic (gär′lik) /ˈgɑrlɪk/ *n.* [*noncount*] **1.** a hardy plant of the amaryllis family, having a strong-smelling and strong-tasting bulb. **2.** the bulb of this plant, consisting of smaller bulbs, or cloves, used in cooking. —*adj.* [*before a noun*] **3.** cooked, flavored, or seasoned with garlic: *garlic bread.* —**gar′lick•y,** *adj.,* **-i•er, -i•est.**

gar•ment (gär′mənt) /ˈgɑrmənt/ *n.* [*count*] any article of clothing: *flowing garments.*

gar•ner (gär′nər) /ˈgɑrnər/ *v.* [~ + *obj*] to get; acquire; earn; obtain: *The ballplayer had garnered a few trophies.*

gar•net (gär′nit) /ˈgɑrnɪt/ *n.* **1.** [*count*] a hard, deep red, glass-like mineral used as a gem. **2.** [*noncount*] a deep red color.

gar•nish (gär′nish) /ˈgɑrnɪʃ/ *v.* [~ + *obj*] **1.** to provide or supply with something ornamental; adorn; decorate. **2.** to provide (a food) with something that adds flavor, decorative color, etc.: *garnished the lamb chops with parsley.* **3.** GARNISHEE. —*n.* **4.** something placed around or on a food or in a beverage to add flavor, decorative color, etc.: [*count*]: *a garnish of parsley.* [*noncount*]: *Sprinkle some garnish on this salad.* **5.** [*noncount*] adornment; decoration.

gar•nish•ee (gär′ni shē′) /ˌgɑrnɪˈʃiy/ *v.,* **-eed, -ee•ing,** *n., pl.* **-ees.** *Law.* —*v.* [~ + *obj*] **1.** to make a claim to (money or property) by means of garnishment: *The government will garnishee your wages until the money is repaid.* —*n.* [*count*] **2.** a person told to hold money or property according to the terms of a garnishment.

gar•nish•ment (gär′nish mənt) /ˈgɑrnɪʃmənt/ *n.* [*count*] a warning given to a third party to hold wages, property, etc., belonging to someone else who owes money.

gar•ret (gar′it) /ˈgærɪt/ *n.* [*count*] an attic.

gar•ri•son (gar′ə sən) /ˈgærəsən/ *n.* [*count*] **1.** a body of troops stationed in a fortified place. **2.** any military post. —*v.* [~ + *obj*] **3.** to provide (a fort, town, etc.) with a garrison.

gar•rote or **ga•rote** or **ga•rotte** or **gar•rotte** (gə-rot′, -rōt′) /gəˈrɒt, -ˈrowt/ *n., v.,* **-rot•ed, -rot•ing** or **-rot•ted, -rot•ting.** —*n.* **1.** [*noncount*] a method of capital punishment in which an iron collar is tightened around a person's neck until death occurs. **2.** [*count*] a wire with a handle at each end, used for strangling a victim. —*v.* [~ + *obj*] **3.** to execute by the garrote. **4.** to kill or strangle with a garrote. —**gar•rot′er,** *n.* [*count*]

gar•ru•lous (gar′ə ləs, gar′yə-) /ˈgærələs, ˈgæryə-/ *adj.* endlessly talkative, esp. about unimportant matters: *a garrulous gossip.* —**gar•ru•li•ty** (gə ro͞o′li tē) /gəˈruwlɪtiy/ **gar′ru•lous•ness,** *n.* [*noncount*] —**gar′ru•lous•ly,** *adv.*

gar•ter (gär′tər) /ˈgɑrtər/ *n.* [*count*] an article of clothing for holding up a stocking, as an elastic band worn around the leg.

gar′ter snake′, *n.* [*count*] a harmless snake common in North and Central America, usually with three long stripes on the back.

gas (gas) /gæs/ *n., pl.* **gas•es,** *v.,* **gassed, gas•sing.** —*n.* **1.** a fluid substance with the ability to expand without limit, as opposed to a solid or a liquid: [*noncount*]: *huge clouds of gas in outer space.* [*count*]: *Some gases are lighter than air.* **2.** any such fluid or mixture of fluids, used as a fuel, anesthetic, choking agent, etc.: [*noncount*]: *The house is heated with natural gas.* [*count*]: *nerve gases.* **3.** [*noncount*] **a.** gasoline: *gas for a car.* **b.** [*usually: the* + ~] the foot-operated accelerator of an automotive vehicle: *put her foot on the gas.* **4.** [*noncount*] intestinal gas produced by bacterial action on waste matter in the intestines. **5.** *Slang.* **a.** [*noncount*] empty talk. **b.** [*count; usually singular*] a person or thing that is very pleasing: *This party is a gas.* —*v.* **6.** [~ + *obj*] to overcome, poison, or asphyxiate with gas or fumes: *Entire villages were gassed in the war.* **7.** [*no obj*] *Slang.* to indulge in idle talk. **8. gas up,** to fill the gasoline tank of a vehicle: [*no obj*]: *We last gassed up in San Diego.* [~ + *up* + *obj*]: *We gassed up the car.* [~ + *obj* + *up*]: *We gassed the car up an hour ago.* —***Idiom.*** **9. step on the gas,** *Informal.* to increase one's speed: *You'll have to step on the gas to finish the book in time.*

gas′ cham′ber, *n.* [*count*] a room used for executing prisoners by means of poison gas.

gas•e•ous (gas′ē əs, gash′əs) /ˈgæsiyəs, ˈgæʃəs/ *adj.* having the form or characteristics of gas: *a gaseous smell.*

gash (gash) /gæʃ/ *n.* [*count*] **1.** a long, deep wound or cut. —*v.* [~ + *obj*] **2.** to make a gash in: *The barbed wire gashed my leg.*

gas•ket (gas′kit) /ˈgæskɪt/ *n.* [*count*] a rubber, metal, or rope ring for placing around an opening or joint to make it close tight.

gas•light (gas′līt′) /ˈgæsˌlayt/ *n.* **1.** [*noncount*] light produced by the burning of special gas that shines brightly. **2.** [*count*] a gas burner, jet, or lamp for producing this kind of light.

gas′ mask′, *n.* [*count*] a masklike device that filters air through charcoal and chemicals to protect the wearer against harmful gases.

gas•o•hol (gas′ə hôl′, -hol′) /ˈgæsəˌhɔl, -ˌhɒl/ *n.* [*noncount*] a mixture of gasoline and ethyl alcohol, usually containing no more than 10 percent alcohol, used as an automobile fuel.

gas•o•line (gas′ə lēn′, gas′ə lēn′) /ˌgæsəˈliyn, ˈgæsəˌliyn/ *n.* [*noncount*] an easily ignited liquid mixture of hydrocarbons obtained from petroleum that burns rapidly and easily, used chiefly as a fuel for internal-combustion engines.

gasp (gasp) /gæsp/ *n.* [*count*] **1.** a sudden, short intake of breath, as in shock or surprise: *a gasp of horror.* **2.** a struggling effort to breathe: *gave a gasp for air.* **3.** a short, convulsive utterance: *The words came out as gasps.* —*v.* **4.** [*no obj*] to catch one's breath: *The audience gasped in horror.* **5.** [*no obj*] to struggle for breath: *He came out of the water and stood there gasping.* **6.** [~ + *out* + *obj*] to say or utter while struggling for breath: *was able to gasp out the name of his attacker.* —***Idiom.*** **7. last gasp,** dying moments: *the regime's last gasp.*

gas′ sta′tion, *n.* SERVICE STATION (def. 1).

gas•sy (gas′ē) /ˈgæsiy/ *adj.*, **-si•er, -si•est. 1.** full of or containing gas. **2.** resembling gas: *the gassy smell of car exhaust.* **3.** tending to have an accumulation of gas in the intestinal tract. **4.** *Slang.* talkative.

gas•tric (gas′trik) /ˈgæstrɪk/ *adj.* [*before a noun*] relating to the stomach: *a gastric ulcer.*

gas•tri•tis (ga stri′tis) /gæˈstraytɪs/ *n.* [*noncount*] a painful inflammation of the stomach.

gas•tro•en•ter•i•tis (gas′trō en′tə rī′tis) /ˌgæstrowˌɛntəˈraytɪs/ *n.* [*noncount*] a painful inflammation of the stomach and intestines.

gas•tro•in•tes•ti•nal (gas′trō in tes′tə nl) /ˌgæstrowɪnˈtɛstənl/ *adj.* of, relating to, or affecting the stomach and intestines.

gas•tron•o•my (ga stron′ə mē) /gæˈstrɒnəmiy/ *n.* [*noncount*] **1.** the art or activity of good eating. **2.** a style of eating: *French gastronomy.* —**gas•tro•nom•ic** (gas′trə-nom′ik) /ˌgæstrəˈnɒmɪk/ **gas′tro•nom′i•cal,** *adj.* See -NOM-[1].

gate (gāt) /geyt/ *n.* [*count*] **1.** a movable barrier, usually on hinges, closing an opening in a fence, wall, or other enclosure. See illustration at HOUSE. **2.** a tower for defending or decorating such an opening: *the palace gate.* **3.** any means of access or entrance: *the gate to success.* **4.** any movable barrier, as at a tollbooth or a railroad crossing. **5.** a passageway in a passenger terminal or pier that leads to a place for boarding a train, plane, or ship. **6.** [*usually singular; the* + ~] the total number of persons who pay for admission to an athletic contest, a performance, an exhibition, etc. **7.** [*usually singular; the* + ~] the total receipts from such admissions.

-gate, *suffix.* *-gate* was derived from *Watergate,* originally the name of a hotel complex where officials of the Republican party were caught trying to burglarize Democratic party headquarters. *Watergate* then came to be associated with "a political cover-up and scandal." The suffix is attached to some nouns to form nouns that refer to scandals resulting from concealed crime in government or business: *Iran* + *-gate* → *Irangate (= a scandal involving arms sales to Iran).*

gate′-crash′er, *n.* [*count*] a person who attends a party, social function, performance, or sports event without an invitation or a ticket.

gate•post (gāt′pōst′) /ˈgeytˌpowst/ *n.* [*count*] the vertical post on which a gate is hung by hinges, or the post against which the gate is closed.

gate•way (gāt′wā′) /ˈgeytˌwey/ *n.* [*count*] **1.** an entrance or passage that may be closed by a gate. **2.** a structure for enclosing such an opening or entrance. **3.** something that serves as a means of entry or access: *A good education can be a gateway to success.*

gath•er (gath′ər) /ˈgæðər/ *v.* **1.** to bring or come together into one group, collection, or place; collect; accumulate: [~ + *obj*]: *to gather firewood.* [*no obj*]: *A crowd gathered.* **2.** [~ + *obj*] to pick or harvest from a place of growth: *to gather vegetables from the garden.* **3.** [~ + *obj*] to pick up piece by piece: *Gather your toys from the floor.* **4.** [~ + *obj*] to scoop up: *She gathered the crying child in her arms.* **5.** [~ + *obj*] to increase: *The car quickly gathered speed.* **6.** to assemble or collect, as for an effort: [~ + *obj*]: *I gathered my energy for one last try.* [~ + *oneself* + *up*]: *He gathered himself up for the effort.* [~ + *up* + *obj*]: *She gathered up her courage.* **7.** to learn or conclude from observation; infer; deduce; understand: [~ + *(that) clause*]: *I gather that she is the real leader.* [~ + *obj*]: *He's rich? Yes, I gathered that.* **8.** [~ + *obj*] to wrap around or bring close to: *He gathered his scarf around his neck.* **9.** [~ + *obj*] to pull (cloth) along a thread in fine folds or puckers by means of even stitches: *She gathered the hem of the dress.* —*n.* [*count*] **10.** a drawing together; contraction. **11.** Often, **gathers.** [*plural*] a fold, pleat, or pucker, as in cloth. —**gath′er•er,** *n.* [*count*]

gath•er•ing (gath′ər ing) /ˈgæðərɪŋ/ *n.* [*count*] **1.** a group or meeting of people in one place; assembly: *A small gathering watched the game.* —*adj.* [*before a noun*] **2.** approaching: *a gathering storm.*

gauche (gōsh) /gowʃ/ *adj.* lacking social grace; awkward; tactless: *a gauche remark.* —**gauche′ly,** *adv.* —**gauche′ness,** *n.* [*noncount*]

gau•cho (gou′chō) /ˈgawtʃow/ *n.* [*count*], *pl.* **-chos.** a cowboy of the South American pampas.

gaud•y (gô′dē) /ˈgɔdiy/ *adj.*, **-i•er, -i•est.** showy in a tasteless way; flashy: *a gaudy display of wealth.* —**gaud•i•ly** (gôd′l ē) /ˈgɔdḷiy/ *adv.* —**gaud′i•ness,** *n.* [*noncount*]

gauge (gāj) /geydʒ/ *v.*, **gauged, gaug•ing,** *n.* —*v.* [~ + *obj*] **1.** to figure out or determine the exact dimensions, size, quantity, or force of; measure: *to gauge the thickness of a wall.* **2.** to estimate: *He tried to gauge the reaction of the crowd.* —*n.* [*count*] **3.** an instrument for measuring or testing something: *a pressure gauge.* **4.** a means of estimating or judging; criterion: *used opinion polls as a gauge of his popularity.* **5.** a unit of measure of the inner diameter of a shotgun barrel, equal to the number of lead bullets of such diameter required to make one pound: *a twelve-gauge shotgun.* **6.** the distance between the rails in a railroad track. **7.** the thickness of various, usually thin, objects, as sheet metal or wire. Also, *esp. in technical use,* **gage.**

gaunt (gônt) /gɔnt/ *adj.*, **-er, -est. 1.** extremely thin and bony; haggard: *He looked gaunt after his hospital stay.* **2.** bleak; desolate: *a gaunt landscape.* —**gaunt′ness,** *n.* [*noncount*]

gaunt•let[1] (gônt′lit, gänt′-) /ˈgɔntlɪt, ˈgɑnt-/ *n.* [*count*] **1.** a medieval glove made partly with metal, worn with a suit of armor to protect the hand. **2.** a glove with an extended, long cuff: *a police officer's motorcycle gauntlets.* —***Idiom.*** **3. take up the gauntlet,** to accept a challenge to fight. **4. throw down the gauntlet,** to challenge someone to fight.

gaunt•let[2] (gônt′lit, gänt′-) /ˈgɔntlɪt, ˈgɑnt-/ *n.* [*count*] **1.** a former punishment, chiefly military, in which the offender was made to run between two rows of men who struck at him with switches or weapons as he passed. **2.** an attack from two or more sides. —***Idiom.*** **3. run the gauntlet,** to suffer severe criticism or attacks. Also, **gantlet** (for def. 1).

gauze (gôz) /gɔz/ *n.* [*noncount*] any thin and often transparent fabric made from any fiber in a plain weave, esp. loosely woven cotton used as a dressing for wounds or surgery. —**gauz′y,** *adj.*, **-i•er, -i•est.**

gave (gāv) /geyv/ *v.* pt. of GIVE.

gav•el (gav′əl) /ˈgævəl/ *n.*, *v.*, **-eled, -el•ing** or (*esp. Brit.*) **-elled, -el•ling.** —*n.* [*count*] **1.** a small hammer or mallet used esp. by the officer leading a meeting or by a judge, usually to signal for attention or order. **2.** a similar mallet used by an auctioneer to indicate acceptance of the final bid. —*v.* [~ + *obj*] **3.** to begin or put into effect by striking a gavel: *to gavel the committee into session.*

gawk (gôk) /gɔk/ *v.* [~ + *at*] to stare stupidly or with astonishment: *onlookers gawking at the car accident.*

gawk•y (gô′kē) /ˈgɔkiy/ *adj.*, **-i•er, -i•est.** awkward; ungainly; clumsy. —**gawk′i•ly,** *adv.* —**gawk′i•ness,** *n.* [*noncount*]

gay (gā) /gey/ *adj.*, **-er, -est,** *n.* —*adj.* **1.** having or showing a merry, lively mood: *in gay spirits.* **2.** bright, showy, or attractive: *gay colors.* **3.** [*often: be* + ~] homosexual. **4.** [*before a noun*] indicating or relating to homosexual interests or issues: *a gay organization.* —*n.* [*count*] **5.** a homosexual person, esp. a male.

gay•ly (gā′lē) /ˈgeyliy/ *adv.* GAILY.

gaze (gāz) /geyz/ *v.*, **gazed, gaz•ing,** *n.* —*v.* [*no obj*] **1.** to look steadily and intently, as with great interest or wonder: *He gazed out the window at the sunset.* —*n.* [*count*] **2.** a steady or intent look: *an unwavering gaze.* —**gaz′er,** *n.* [*count*]

ga•ze•bo (gə zā′bō, -zē′-) /gəˈzeybow, -ˈziy-/ *n.* [*count*], *pl.* **-bos, -boes. 1.** a small roofed structure that is screened on all sides, used for outdoor entertaining and dining. **2.** an open structure built on a site that provides an attractive view.

ga•zelle (gə zel′) /gəˈzɛl/ *n.* [*count*], *pl.* **-zelles,** (*esp.

when thought of as a group) **-zelle.** any of various small graceful antelopes of Africa and Asia.

ga•zette (gə zet′) /gə'zɛt/ *n.* [*count*] **1.** a newspaper (now used chiefly in names): *The Phoenix Gazette.* **2.** an official journal.

gaz•et•teer (gaz′i tēr′) /ˌgæzɪ'tɪər/ *n.* [*count*] a geographical dictionary listing place names.

G.B., an abbreviation of: Great Britain.

gear (gēr) /gɪər/ *n.* **1. a.** [*count*] a part, as a disk, wheel, or other device, having teeth of such form, size, and spacing that they mesh with teeth in another part to carry or receive force and motion. **b.** [*count*] an assembly of such parts: *a car's reverse gear.* **c.** a range of speed governed by such machinery: [*noncount*]: *shifted to high gear.* [*count*]: *shifted to a lower gear.* **2.** [*noncount*] apparatus used for a particular purpose: *fishing gear.* **3.** [*noncount*] portable items of personal property, including clothing: *dressed in our hiking gear.* **—v. 4.** [~ + *obj* + *to*] to adjust or adapt to a particular situation in order to bring about satisfactory or suitable results: *geared their output to consumer demands.* **5. gear up,** [*no obj*] **a.** to get ready for a future event: *They were gearing up for the wedding reception.* **b.** to put on gear for a particular purpose: *The hikers geared up for the expedition.* **c.** to become excited: *We were all geared up for the big party.* **—*Idiom.* 6. in** or **into high gear,** in or into a state of the highest speed and efficiency: *went into high gear in an effort to finish.* **7. in gear, a.** in the state in which gears are connected or meshed: *The car is in gear.* **b.** in proper working order: *The office is in gear and working smoothly.* **8. out of gear,** in the state in which gears are not connected or meshed: *The engine is out of gear.* **9. shift** or **switch gears,** to alter or change one's strategy or thinking in a significant way.

gear•shift (gēr′shift′) /'gɪərˌʃɪft/ *n.* [*count*] a lever for shifting gears, esp. in a motor vehicle.

gee (jē) / dʒiy/ *interj.* This word is used to express surprise, disappointment, enthusiasm, or simple emphasis: *Gee, what a beautiful day it is!*

gee•gaw (jē′gô, gē′-) /' dʒiygɔ, 'giy-/ *n.* GEWGAW.

geese (gēs) /giys/ *n.* a pl. of GOOSE.

gee•zer (gē′zər) /'giyzər/ *n.* [*count*] *Slang.* a man who behaves strangely, esp. an elderly one.

Gei′ger count′er (gī′gər) /'gaygər/ *n.* [*count*] an instrument for detecting certain radiation, used chiefly to measure radioactivity.

gei•sha (gā′shə, gē′-) /'geyʃə, 'giy-/ *n.* [*count*], *pl.* **-sha, -shas.** a Japanese woman trained as a professional singer, dancer, and companion for men.

gel (jel) / dʒɛl/ *n., v.,* **gelled, gel•ling. —n. 1.** a partly solid, partly liquid substance, as jelly or glue, sometimes used in hair styling: [*noncount*]: *using gel to style her hair.* [*count*]: *There are a number of gels on the market.* **—v.** [*no obj*] **2.** to form or become a gel. **3.** JELL (def. 2).: *Most of my ideas need time to gel.*

gel•a•tin or **gel•a•tine** (jel′ə tn) /' dʒɛlətn̩/ *n.* [*noncount*] **1.** a nearly transparent, oily substance, obtained by boiling the bones, ligaments, etc., of animals and used in making jellies, glues, and the like. **2.** a preparation or product in which such a substance is the essential ingredient. **3.** jelly made of this substance: *gelatin for dessert.*

ge•lat•i•nous (jə lat′n əs) /dʒə'lætn̩əs/ *adj.* like a gel or gelatin; thick and sticky.

geld (geld) /gɛld/ *v.* [~ + *obj*], **geld•ed** or **gelt** (gelt) /gɛlt/ **geld•ing.** to remove the sex organs of (a horse or other animal); castrate: *to geld a stallion.*

geld•ing (gel′ding) /'gɛldɪŋ/ *n.* [*count*] a castrated male animal, esp. a horse.

gel•id (jel′id) /' dʒɛlɪd/ *adj.* very cold; icy.

gel•ig•nite (jel′ig nit′) /'dʒɛlɪgˌnayt/ *n.* [*noncount*] a powerful explosive substance made of glycerine and nitric acid.

gem (jem) / dʒɛm/ *n.* [*count*] **1.** a mineral, pearl, or other natural substance valued for its rarity and beauty and used in jewelry: *diamonds and other gems.* **2.** something prized because of its beauty or worth: *That new book is a gem.* **3.** a person held in great esteem or affection.

gem•stone (jem′stōn′) /' dʒɛmˌstown/ *n.* [*count*] a mineral or crystal that can be cut and polished for use as a gem.

-gen-, *root.* *-gen-* comes from Greek and Latin, where it has the meanings "race; birth; born; produced." These meanings are found in such words as: ANTIGEN, CARCINOGEN, CONGENITAL, DEGENERATE, ENGENDER, EROGENOUS, GENDER, GENE, GENERATE, GENUS, HOMOGENIZE.

gen•darme (zhän′därm, -därm′) /'ʒandarm, -'darm/ *n.* [*count*] a police officer in some European countries, esp. France.

gen•der (jen′dər) /' dʒɛndər/ *n.* **1. a.** [*noncount*] a set of grammatical categories applied to nouns, membership in a particular category being shown by the form of the noun itself or the choice of words that refer to or modify it: *Gender is often correlated in part with sex or animateness, as in the choice of* he *to replace* the man, she *to replace* the woman, *or* it *to replace* the table. *Gender is sometimes assigned without regard to the meaning of the noun, as in French* le livre (masculine) *"the book" or German* das Mädchen *(neuter) "the girl."* **b.** [*count*] one of the categories in such a set, as masculine, feminine, neuter, or common: *By some classifications, Swahili has as many as eleven genders or noun classes.* **2.** sex: [*noncount*]: *discrimination on the grounds of gender.* [*count*]: *the feminine and masculine genders.* See -GEN-.

gene (jēn) / dʒiyn/ *n.* [*count*] the basic physical unit of heredity; a part of cells that provides the coded instructions for the production of RNA, which, when translated into protein, controls how living things develop and grow. See -GEN-.

ge•ne•al•o•gy (jē′nē ol′ə jē, -al′-, jen′ē-) /ˌdʒiyniy'ɒlədʒiy, -'æl-, ˌdʒɛniy-/ *n., pl.* **-gies. 1.** [*count*] a record or account of the ancestry and descent of a person, family, group, etc. **2.** [*noncount*] the study of family ancestries and histories. **3.** [*count*] ancestry; descent from an original form: *the genealogy of certain plants.* **—ge•ne•a•log•i•cal** (jē′nē ə loj′i kəl, jen′ē-) /ˌdʒiyniyə'lɒdʒɪkəl, ˌdʒɛniy-/ **ge′ne•a•log′ic,** *adj.* **—ge′ne•al′o•gist,** *n.* [*count*]

gen•er•a (jen′ər ə) /' dʒɛnərə/ *n.* a pl. of GENUS.

gen•er•al (jen′ər əl) /' dʒɛnərəl/ *adj.* **1.** of, relating to, or affecting all persons or things belonging to a group, category, or system: *called a general meeting of union members.* **2.** [*before a noun*] of, relating to, or true of most persons or things: *the general mood of the people.* **3.** [*before a noun*] not limited to type; miscellaneous: *the general public.* **4.** considering or dealing with broad, universal, or important aspects: *issued general guidelines.* **5.** affecting the entire body: *general paralysis.* **6.** having extended command or superior or chief rank: [*before a noun*]: *a general manager.* [*after a noun*]: *the secretary general of the U.N.* **—n.** [*count*] **7.** an army, air force, or Marine Corps officer of high rank. **—*Idiom.* 8. in general, a.** with respect to the entirety; as a whole; for the most part: *He likes people in general.* **b.** as a rule; usually: *In general, the bus is on time.*

gen•er•al•is•si•mo (jen′ər ə lis′ə mō′) /ˌdʒɛnərə'lɪsəˌmow/ *n.* [*count*], *pl.* **-mos.** (in certain countries) the supreme commander of the armed forces.

gen•er•al•i•ty (jen′ə ral′i tē) /ˌdʒɛnə'rælɪtiy/ *n., pl.* **-ties. 1.** [*count*] an indefinite or unspecific statement, one lacking details: *talking in generalities.* **2.** [*count*] something usually true; truism: *It's a generality that people want to improve their lives.* **3.** [*noncount*] the greater part or majority: *the generality of people.* **4.** [*noncount*] the state or quality of being general.

gen•er•al•i•za•tion (jen′ər ə lə zā′shən) /ˌdʒɛnərələ'zeyʃən/ *n.* **1.** [*noncount*] the act or process of generalizing. **2.** [*count*] a statement that is a general idea or principle.

gen•er•al•ize (jen′ər ə līz′) /' dʒɛnərəˌlayz/ *v.,* **-ized, -iz•ing. 1.** [~ + *obj*] to figure out (a general principle) from particular facts or instances: *to generalize a scientific theory from observations.* **2.** [*no obj*] to form (a general opinion or conclusion) from only a few facts or cases: *We can't generalize from so little evidence.* **3.** [~ + *obj*] to bring into general use or knowledge. **4.** [*no obj*] to deal, think, or speak in generalities.

gen•er•al•ly (jen′ər ə lē) /'dʒɛnərəliy/ *adv.* **1.** usually; ordinarily: *He generally comes home at noon.* **2.** for the most part; widely: *a generally true statement.*

gen′eral practi′tioner, *n.* [*count*] a physician whose practice is not limited to any specialty. *Abbr.:* G.P.

gen′eral store′, *n.* [*count*] a store, usually in a country area, that sells a wide variety of merchandise.

gen•er•ate (jen′ə rāt′) /' dʒɛnəˌreyt/ *v.* [~ + *obj*], **-at•ed, -at•ing. 1.** to bring into existence; produce; originate: *to generate ideas.* **2.** to create by a natural or chemical process: *They used the waterfalls to generate power.* **3.** to inspire: *to generate enthusiasm.* See -GEN-.

gen•er•a•tion (jen′ə rā′shən) /ˌdʒɛnə'reyʃən/ *n.* **1.** [*count*] the entire group of individuals born and living at about the same time: *the postwar generation.* **2.** [*count*] a group of individuals most of whom are the same approximate age, having similar ideas, problems, attitudes, etc.: *referred to them as the "silent generation."* **3.** [*count*] the term of years accepted as the average period between the birth of parents and the birth of their offspring. **4.** [*count*] a stage of technological development or production: *a new generation of computers.* **5.** [*noncount*] the act or process of generating; the state of being generated. **—gen′er•a′tion•al,** *adj.*

gen•er•a•tive (jen′ər ə tiv) /'dʒɛnərətɪv/ *adj.* able to produce something; productive: *generative processes.*

gen•er•a•tor (jen′ə rā′tər) /'dʒɛnəˌreytər/ *n.* [*count*] a machine that converts one form of energy into another, esp. mechanical energy into electrical energy: *a car's generator.*

ge•ner•ic (jə ner′ik) /dʒə'nɛrɪk/ *adj.* **1.** of, relating to, or applying to all the members of a class, group, or kind: *a trait that is generic to humanity.* **2.** of, relating to, or making up a genus. **3.** (of a word) that may apply to, or refer to, both men and women: *A generic pronoun is "their."* **4.** not protected by trademark registration: *prescribed a generic drug.* **—ge•ner′i•cal•ly,** *adv.*

gen•er•os•i•ty (jen′ə ros′i tē) /ˌdʒɛnə'rɒsɪtiy/ *n.* [*noncount*] the quality of being generous; the act of being generous.

gen•er•ous (jen′ər əs) /'dʒɛnərəs/ *adj.* **1.** free in giving or sharing; unselfish: *generous with his money.* **2.** free from meanness or pettiness: *a generous attitude.* **3.** large; abundant; ample: *a generous portion of pie.* **—gen′er•ous•ly,** *adv.*

gen•e•sis (jen′ə sis) /'dʒɛnəsɪs/ *n.* [*count*], *pl.* **-ses** (-sēz′) /-ˌsiyz/. an origin; creation: *the genesis of an idea.* See -GEN-.

ge•net•ic (jə net′ik) /dʒə'nɛtɪk/ *adj.* of or relating to genes: *genetic differences between species.* **—ge•net′i•cal•ly,** *adv.* **—ge•net•i•cist** (jə net′ə sist) /dʒə'nɛtəsɪst/ *n.* [*count*] See -GEN-.

genet′ic engineer′ing, *n.* [*noncount*] **1.** the development and use of scientific methods, procedures, and technologies to change the genetic material of a cell, organism, or population. **2.** a technique producing unlimited amounts of an otherwise unavailable or scarce biological product by changing the genetic material of a cell or bacteria so that the cell or bacteria produce the desired product.

ge•net•ics (jə net′iks) /dʒə'nɛtɪks/ *n.* [*noncount; used with a singular verb*] **1.** the branch of biology that deals with the heredity of living things and how genes contribute to differences and similarities: *Genetics is a science that combines biology and statistics.* **2.** the genetic properties or makeup of an organism or group. See -GEN-.

gen•ial (jēn′yəl, jē′nē əl) /'dʒiynyəl, 'dʒiyniyəl/ *adj.* **1.** warmly and pleasantly cheerful; cordial: *a genial disposition.* **2.** pleasantly warm; comfortably mild: *a genial climate.* **—ge•ni•al•i•ty** (jē′nē al′i tē) /ˌdʒiyniy'ælɪtiy/ *n.* [*noncount*] **—gen′ial•ly,** *adv.*

ge•nie (jē′nē) /'dʒiyniy/ *n.* [*count*] **1.** JINN. **2.** a spirit, often appearing in human form, that when summoned by a person carries out the wishes of the summoner.

gen•i•tal (jen′i tl) /'dʒɛnɪtḷ/ *adj.* [*before a noun*] **1.** of or relating to reproduction. **2.** of or relating to the sexual organs. See -GEN-.

gen•i•ta•li•a (jen′i tā′lē ə, -tāl′yə) /ˌdʒɛnɪ'teyliyə, -'teylyə/ *n.* [*plural*] the organs of reproduction, esp. the external organs.

gen•i•tals (jen′i tlz) /'dʒɛnɪtlz/ *n.* [*plural*] GENITALIA. See -GEN-.

gen•i•tive (jen′i tiv) /'dʒɛnɪtɪv/ *adj.* **1.** of or naming a grammatical form that indicates possession, measure, origin, or other close association, such as *painter's,* in *the painter's brush; week's,* as in *a week's pay; author's,* as in *the author's book;* and *women's,* as in *women's colleges.* **—***n.* [*count; usually singular; the* + ~] **2.** the genitive case; a word or form in this case: *The genitive of the pronoun* me *is* my. See -GEN-.

gen•ius (jēn′yəs) /'dʒiynyəs/ *n., pl.* **-ius•es. 1.** an exceptional and natural capacity of intellect or ability, esp. as shown in creative and original work in science, art, music, etc.: [*noncount*]: *Mozart's genius.* [*count; usually singular*]: *a genius for leadership.* **2.** [*count*] a person having such capacity: *Einstein was a scientific genius.*

gen•o•cide (jen′ə sid′) /'dʒɛnəˌsayd/ *n.* [*noncount*] the deliberate and systematic killing or murdering of a national, racial, political, or cultural group. See -GEN-, -CIDE-.

gen•re (zhän′rə) /'ʒɑnrə/ *n.* [*count*] a class or category of art, music, or writing in which objects produced have a consistent form, content, or technique.

gent (jent) /dʒɛnt/ *n.* [*count*] a gentleman.

gen•teel (jen tēl′) /dʒɛn'tiyl/ *adj.* **1.** belonging or suited to polite society; well-bred: *genteel manners.* **2.** falsely polite or delicate.

gen•tile (jen′tīl) /'dʒɛntayl/ *adj.* (*sometimes: Gentile*) **1.** of or relating to any people not Jewish. **—***n.* [*count*] **2.** a person who is not Jewish, esp. a Christian.

gen•til•i•ty (jen til′i tē) /dʒɛn'tɪlɪtiy/ *n.* [*noncount*] good breeding or refinement; politeness and elegance.

gen•tle (jen′tl) /'dʒɛntḷ/ *adj.,* **-tler, -tlest. 1.** kindly; amiable; calm: *She had a soothing, gentle manner.* **2.** not severe, rough, or violent; mild; light: *a gentle tap on the arm.* **3.** moderate: *gentle heat.* **4.** not steep; gradual: *a gentle slope.* **5.** easily handled or managed: *a gentle animal.* **6.** soft or low: *a gentle sound.* **—gen′tle•ness,** *n.* [*noncount*] **—gen•tly** (jent′lē) /'dʒɛntliy/ *adv.*

gen•tle•man (jen′tl mən) /'dʒɛntḷmən/ *n.* [*count*], *pl.* **-men 1.** a man of good family, breeding, or social position. **2.** (used as a polite term) a man: *Do you know that gentleman in the tweed suit?* **3. gentlemen,** (used as a form of address): *Gentlemen, please come this way.* **4.** a civilized, educated, sensitive, or well-mannered man: *always a perfect gentleman.* **—gen′tle•man•ly,** *adj.*

gen•tri•fi•ca•tion (jen′trə fi kā′shən) /ˌdʒɛntrəfɪ'keyʃən/ *n.* [*noncount*] the buying and repair or replacement of houses or stores in poor, working-class, or run-down neighborhoods by more wealthy individuals.

gen•tri•fy (jen′trə fī′) /'dʒɛntrəˌfay/ *v.* [~ + *obj*], **-fied, -fy•ing.** to cause (a neighborhood) to undergo gentrification.

gen•try (jen′trē) /'dʒɛntriy/ *n.* [*plural*] wellborn and well-bred people, as of an aristocracy. See -GEN-.

gen•u•flect (jen′yŏŏ flekt′) /'dʒɛnyʊˌflɛkt/ *v.* [*no obj*] to bend the knee or touch one knee to the floor in reverence or worship. **—gen•u•flec•tion** (jen′yŏŏ flek′shən) /ˌdʒɛnyʊ'flɛkʃən/ *n.* [*count*] See -FLECT-.

gen•u•ine (jen′yōō in *or, sometimes,* -īn′) /'dʒɛnyuwɪn *or, sometimes,* -ˌayn/ *adj.* **1.** authentic; real; possessing the claimed character, quality, or origin; not counterfeit: *genuine leather.* **2.** free from pretending; sincere: *She has genuine admiration for talent.* **—gen′u•ine•ly,** *adv.* **—gen′u•ine•ness,** *n.* [*noncount*]

ge•nus (jē′nəs) /'dʒiynəs/ *n.* [*count*], *pl.* **gen•e•ra** (jen′ər ə) /'dʒɛnərə/ **ge•nus•es.** the major subdivision of a biological family or subfamily in the scientific system of classifying living things. See -GEN-.

-geo-, *root.* -*geo*- comes from Greek, where it has the meaning "the earth; ground". This meaning is found in such words as: APOGEE, GEOGRAPHY, GEOLOGY, GEOPOLITICS, PERIGEE.

ge•og•ra•phy (jē og′rə fē) /dʒiy'ɒgrəfiy/ *n., pl.* **-phies. 1.** [*noncount*] the science dealing with the areas of the earth's surface, as shown in the character and arrangement of and relations among such elements as climate, elevation, vegetation, population, and land use. **2.** [*count*] the arrangement and features of a given area on the earth: *the geography of a region.* **—ge•og′ra•pher,** *n.* [*count*] **—ge•o•graph•i•cal** (jē′ə graf′i kəl) /ˌdʒiyə'græfɪkəl/ **ge′o•graph′ic,** *adj.* **—ge′o•graph′i•cal•ly,** *adv.* See -GEO-, -GRAPH-.

ge•ol•o•gy (jē ol′ə jē) /dʒiy'ɒlədʒiy/ *n., pl.* **-gies. 1.** [*noncount*] the science that deals with the physical history of the earth, the rocks of which it is made up, and the physical, chemical, and biological changes that the earth has undergone or is undergoing. **2.** [*count*] the geologic features and processes occurring in a given region: *the geology of the Andes.* **3.** [*count; usually singular*] the study of the rocks and other physical features of a moon or another planet. **—ge•o•log•ic** (jē′ə loj′ik) /ˌdʒiyə'lɒdʒɪk/ **ge′o•log′i•cal,** *adj.* **—ge′o•log′i•cal•ly,** *adv.* **—ge•ol′o•gist,** *n.* [*count*] See -GEO-.

ge•om•e•try (jē om′i trē) /dʒiy'ɒmɪtriy/ *n.* **1.** [*noncount*] the branch of mathematics that deals with the properties, measurement, and relationships of points, lines, angles, and shapes in space by means of certain assumed properties of space. **2.** [*noncount*] any specific system of this that operates with a specific set of assumptions: *Euclidean geometry.* **3.** [*count*] the shape or form of a surface or solid: *the geometry of the room's outline.* **—ge•o•met•ric** (jē′ə me′trik) /ˌdʒiyə'mɛtrɪk/ **ge′o•met′ri•cal,** *adj.* **—ge′o•met′ri•cal•ly,** *adv.* See -METER-.

ge•o•phys•ics (jē′ō fiz′iks) /ˌdʒiyow'fɪzɪks/ *n.* [*noncount; used with a singular verb*] the branch of geology that deals with the physics of the earth and its atmosphere, including the study of oceans, earthquakes, volcanos, and the earth's magnetic field. **—ge′o•phys′i•cal,**

adj. —**ge•o•phys•i•cist** (jē′ō fiz′ə sist) /ˌdʒiyow'fɪzəsɪst/ *n.* [*count*] See -PHYS-.

ge•o•pol•i•tics (jē′ō pol′i tiks) /ˌdʒiyow'pɒlɪtɪks/ *n.* [*noncount; used with a singular verb*] the study of the influence of geography on the politics, national power, or foreign policy of a country. —**ge•o•po•lit•i•cal** (jē′ō pə-lit′i kəl) /ˌdʒiyowpə'lɪtɪkəl/ *adj.* See -GEO-.

ge•o•sta•tion•ar•y (jē′ō stā′shə ner′ē) /ˌdʒiyow'steyʃəˌnɛriy/ *adj.* of, relating to, or naming a satellite traveling in an orbit 22,300 mi. (35,900 km) above the earth's equator, where the satellite's rotation matches the earth's and the satellite always remains in the same spot over the earth. Also, **geosynchronous**.

ge•o•ther•mal (jē′ō thûr′məl) /ˌdʒiyow'θɜrməl/ also **ge•o•ther•mic** (jē′ō thûr′mik) /ˌdʒiyow'θɜrmɪk/ *adj.* of or relating to the heat of the earth's interior.

ge•ra•ni•um (ji rā′nē əm) /dʒɪ'reyniyəm/ *n.* [*count*] a common garden plant with small white, pink, or red flowers and rounded leaves.

ger•bil (jûr′bəl) /'dʒɜrbəl/ *n.* [*count*] a small rodent with long hind legs that is popular as a pet.

ger•i•at•rics (jer′ē a′triks, jēr′-) /ˌdʒɛriy'ætrɪks, ˌdʒɪər-/ *n.* [*noncount; used with a singular verb*] **1.** the branch of medicine dealing with the diseases and care of aged persons. **2.** the study of the physical processes and problems of aging. —**ger′i•at′ric,** *adj.*

germ (jûrm) /dʒɜrm/ *n.* [*count*] **1.** a living thing small enough to be visible only through a microscope, esp. such a living thing that produces disease; microbe. **2.** a source of development; origin; seed: *the germ of an idea.*

Ger•man (jûr′mən) /'dʒɜrmən/ *adj.* **1.** of or relating to Germany. **2.** of or relating to the language spoken in Germany. —*n.* **3.** [*count*] a person born or living in Germany. **4.** [*noncount*] the language spoken in Germany.

ger•mane (jər mān′) /dʒər'meyn/ *adj.* [*often: be + ~ (+ to)*] relevant; pertinent: *In your essay, please stick to points that are germane to the subject.*

Ger′man mea′sles, *n.* [*noncount; used with a singular verb*] a contagious disease in which red spots appear on the body; rubella.

Ger′man shep′herd, *n.* [*count*] one of a breed of large dogs with ears that stand up straight, a bushy tail, and a thick, usually gray or black-and-tan coat, often used in police work and as a guide dog.

ger•mi•cide (jûr′mə sīd′) /'dʒɜrməˌsayd/ *n.* [*count*] a solution for killing germs. —**ger′mi•cid′al,** *adj.* See -CIDE-.

ger•mi•nal (jûr′mə nl) /'dʒɜrmənl/ *adj.* being in the earliest stage of development: *germinal ideas.*

ger•mi•nate (jûr′mə nāt′) /'dʒɜrməˌneyt/ *v.,* **-nat•ed, -nat•ing. 1.** to (cause to) begin to grow or develop, as a seed into a plant: [*no obj*]: *The seeds germinated in the soil.* [*~ + obj*]: *germinated the seeds.* **2.** to (cause to) come into existence; begin: [*no obj*]: *a good place to let your ideas germinate.* [*~ + obj*]: *to germinate some unusual ideas.* —**ger•mi•na•tion** (jûr′mə nā′shən) /ˌdʒɜrmə'neyʃən/ *n.* [*noncount*]

ger•on•tol•o•gy (jer′ən tol′ə jē, jēr′-) /ˌdʒɛrən'tɒlədʒiy, ˌdʒɪər-/ *n.* [*noncount*] the study of aging and the problems of aged people. —**ge•ron•to•log•i•cal** (jə ron′tl oj′i kəl) /dʒəˌrɒntl'ɒdʒɪkəl/ *adj.* —**ger′on•tol′o•gist,** *n.* [*count*]

ger•ry•man•der (jer′i man′dər, ger′-) /'dʒɛrɪˌmændər, 'gɛr-/ *v.* [*~ + obj*] to divide (a state, county, etc.) into election districts so as to give one political party a majority in many districts while concentrating the voting strength of the other party into as few districts as possible: *gerrymandered the region into several smaller ones.* —**ger′ry•man′der•ing,** *n.* [*noncount*]

ger•und (jer′ənd) /'dʒɛrənd/ *n.* [*count*] a form of a verb that functions as a noun, such as the *-ing* form of an English verb: *The word* writing *is a gerund in the sentence* Writing is easy.

-gest-, *root.* *-gest-* comes from Latin, where it has the meaning "carry; bear." This meaning is found in such words as: CONGESTION, DIGEST, GESTATION, GESTICULATE, GESTURE, INGEST, SUGGEST.

ges•ta•tion (je stā′shən) /dʒɛ'steyʃən/ *n.* [*noncount*] **1.** the process, state, or period of time in which the female carries an unborn offspring before birth; the development of offspring in the womb: *Human gestation takes nine months.* **2.** the process, state, or period of time in which an idea is developed: *The plan was in gestation for years.* —**ges•ta′tion•al,** *adj.* See -GEST-.

ges•tic•u•late (je stik′yə lāt′) /dʒɛ'stɪkyəˌleyt/ *v.* [*no obj*], **-lat•ed, -lat•ing.** to make or use gestures, esp. in an excited manner with or instead of speech: *He gesticulated wildly.* —**ges•tic•u•la•tion** (je stik′yə lā′shən) /dʒɛˌstɪkyə'leyʃən/ *n.* [*count*]: *dramatic gesticulations.* [*noncount*]: *the uses of gesticulation.* See -GEST-.

ges•ture (jes′chər) /'dʒɛstʃər/ *n., v.,* **-tured, -tur•ing.** —*n.* **1.** [*count*] a movement or position of the hand, arm, body, head, or face that expresses an idea, opinion, emotion, etc.: *made a threatening gesture.* **2.** [*noncount*] the use of such movements to express thought, emotion, etc.: *the study of gesture among different cultures.* **3.** [*count*] any action, communication, etc., performed or intended for effect or as a formality; demonstration: *The donation was a gesture of friendship.* —*v.* **4.** to make or use a gesture or gestures (to express something): [*no obj*]: *She gestured to me.* [*~ + that clause*]: *He gestured that I could come in.* See -GEST-.

get (get) /gɛt/ *v.,* **got** (got) /gɒt/ or **got•ten** (got′n) /'gɒtn/ **get•ting,** *n.* —*v.* **1.** [*~ + obj*] to receive or come to have possession, use, or enjoyment of: *She got a lovely gift for her birthday.* **2.** [*~ + obj*] to cause to be in one's possession or be available for one's use: *I need to get some information.* **3.** [*~ + obj*] to earn: *I'm sure he gets fifty thousand a year.* **4.** [*~ + obj + obj*] to go after, take hold of, and bring (something) for oneself or another; fetch: *Please get me a cup of coffee.* **5.** to (cause to) become, to do, to move, etc., as mentioned: [*~ + obj*]: *We couldn't get the car into the garage.* [*~ + obj + verb-ed/-en*]: *We couldn't get the car started.* [*~ + verb-ed/-en*]: *He couldn't get started on his work.* [*~ + obj + verb-ing*]: *We finally got the car going.* [*~ + verb-ing*]: *I find it hard to get going in the morning.* [*~ + obj + to + verb*]: *We finally got the logs to burn.* [*~ + obj + adjective*]: *That gets me pretty angry.* [*no obj*]: *She'd like to get away for a while.* [*~ + adjective*]: *I get tired at night.* **6.** [*~ + obj*] to catch (a disease or sickness) or feel the bad effects of: *got malaria in the tropics; I got a headache from the noise.* **7.** [*~ + obj*] to communicate with over a distance; reach: *to get someone on the telephone.* **8.** [*~ + obj*] to hear or hear clearly: *I'm afraid I didn't get your last name.* **9.** [*not: be + ~-ing; ~ + obj*] to understand or comprehend: *I didn't get the joke.* **10.** [*~ + obj*] to capture; seize: *Get him before he escapes!* **11.** [*~ + obj*] to receive as a punishment or sentence: *The thief got a year in jail.* **12.** [*~ + obj + to + verb*] to influence or persuade: *We'll get him to go with us.* **13.** [*~ + obj*] to prepare; make ready: *to get dinner.* **14.** [*~ + obj*] to hit, strike, wound, or kill: *The bullet got him in the leg.* **15.** [*~ + obj*] to get revenge against: *I'll get you yet!* **16.** [*~ + one's*] to receive (one's fair reward or punishment): *Someday soon they'll get theirs.* **17.** [*~ + (to +) obj*] to puzzle; annoy; hurt: *Their nasty remarks get (to) me sometimes.* **18.** [*no obj*] to come to a specified place; arrive; reach: *to get home late.* **19.** [*~ + to + verb*] to succeed in something: *She gets to meet a lot of interesting people.* **20.** [*~ + verb-ed/-en*] The verb *get* may be used as an auxiliary verb (like BE) and be followed by a past participle to form the passive; it means almost the same as "become": *She got married when she was twenty-five.* **21. get about,** [*no obj*] **a.** to move around physically from one place to another: *He found it hard to get about after his leg injury.* **b.** to become known, as a rumor: *Soon the news got about.* **c.** to circulate: *She gets about a lot in her job as regional director.* **22. get across,** to (cause to) be or become clearly understood: [*~ + obj + across*]: *I tried to get my message across.* [*no obj*]: *The message got across.* **23. get ahead,** [*no obj*] to be successful, as in business or society: *She wants to get ahead in her job.* **24. get along,** [*no obj*] **a.** to go away; leave: *We must get along now; see you soon.* **b.** [*~ + along (+ with/without)*] to survive or continue to go on: *I can't get along without her.* **c.** [*~ + along (+ with)*] to be on good terms; agree: *He couldn't get along with his in-laws.* **25. get around, a.** [*~ + around + obj*] to overcome; circumvent; outwit: *found a way to get around the law.* **b.** [*no obj*] to travel from place to place; circulate: *I don't get around much anymore.* **26. get at,** [*~ + at + obj*] **a.** to reach; touch: *I can't get at that book on the shelf.* **b.** to suggest; hint at: *What are you getting at—do you think he's guilty?* **c.** to discover; determine: *to get at the root of the mystery.* **27. get away,** [*no obj*] **a.** to escape; flee: *The thieves got away.* **b.** to start out; leave: *Can you get away from the office by five o'clock?* **28. get away with,** [*~ + obj*] to do something without punishment: *She got away with a lot of mistakes.* **29. get back, a.** [*no obj*] to come back; return: *We got back home in June.* **b.** to recover; regain: [*~ + obj + back*]: *We got most of our money back.* [*~ + back + obj*]: *We got back most of our money.* **c.** [*~ + back + at*

+ *obj*] to punish another for harm or injury done to oneself; get revenge on: *Someday she'll get back at him for taking her money.* **30. get by, a.** to get beyond; pass: [*no obj*]: *I need to get by; please move a little.* [~ + *obj*]: *She couldn't get by us.* **b.** to escape the notice (of): [*no obj*]: *Somehow these errors got by.* [~ + *by* + *obj*]: *These errors got by our accountants.* **c.** [*no obj*] to survive or manage to live or continue: *couldn't get by on that low salary.* **31. get down, a.** to bring or come down; (cause to) descend: [*no obj*]: *The plane got down to about 500 feet.* [~ + *obj* + *down*]: *The pilot got the plane down safely.* **b.** [*no obj*] to concentrate; attend: *Get down to work.* **c.** [~ + *obj* + *down*] to cause to be depressed: *This cloudy weather gets me down.* **d.** [~ + *obj* + *down*] to swallow: *couldn't get any food down.* **32. get in, a.** [*no obj*] to enter: *The thieves got in through the window.* **b.** [*no obj*] to arrive at a destination: *The plane got in at noon.* **c.** [~ + *in* + *with* + *obj*] to enter into close association: *She got in with a bad crowd.* **33. get off, a.** [~ + *off* + *obj*] to dismount from or get out of: *The passengers got off the plane.* **b.** to (cause to) begin a journey: [*no obj*]: *We got off a few hours late.* [~ + *obj* + *off*]: *I got the kids off to school.* **c.** to (help someone to) escape punishment, esp. by providing legal assistance: [*no obj*]: *He got off with a very light sentence.* [~ + *obj* + *off*]: *The lawyer got his client off.* **d.** [*no obj*] to finish, as one's workday: *We get off at five o'clock.* **34. get off on,** [~ + *off* + *on* + *obj*] *Slang.* to enjoy: *gets off on baseball games.* **35. get on, a.** [*no obj*] to make progress; proceed; advance: *How are you getting on with your work?* **b.** to continue: *Let's get on with the trial, please.* **c.** [*be* + ~*-ing* + *on*] to advance in age: *He is getting on in years.* **36. get out, a.** to (cause to) leave or be removed: [*no obj*]: *Get out of this room.* [~ + *obj* + *out*]: *Get them out of this room.* **b.** to (cause to) become publicly known: [~ + *out* + *obj*]: *He got out the story to the papers.* [~ + *obj* + *out*]: *He got the news out.* [*no obj*]: *How did the news get out so fast?* **c.** to withdraw, leave, or retire: [~ + *of* + *obj*]: *He got out of the stock market before the collapse.* [*no obj*]: *We'll get out before the stock market collapses.* **d.** to produce or complete: [~ + *out* + *obj*]: *We can get out a thousand papers each day.* [~ + *obj* + *out*]: *We can get a thousand papers out each day.* **37. get over, a.** [~ + *over* + *obj*] to recover from: *to get over an illness.* **b.** [~ + *obj* + *over*] to get across: *I need to get my points over more convincingly.* **c.** [~ + *over* + *obj*] to overcome: *I got over that problem.* **38. get through, a.** [~ + *obj*] to finish: *I hope I can get through all this work.* **b.** [*no obj*] to reach someone, as by telephone: *I tried calling you, but I couldn't get through.* **c.** [~ *(+ to + obj)*] to make oneself clearly understood: *Am I getting through (to you)?* **d.** [~ + *obj*] to endure or survive: *They managed to get through the worst of the winter.* **39. get to,** [~ + *obj*] **a.** to get in touch or into communication with; contact: *I'll get to you by morning.* **b.** to make an impression on; affect emotionally: *That sad movie really got to me.* **c.** to begin: *Let's get to work.* **40. get together, a.** to (cause to) congregate, meet, or gather together: [*no obj*]: *We got together at the church.* [~ + *obj* + *together*]: *The minister got them together for a meeting.* [~ + *together* + *obj*]: *got together the best minds in the nation.* **b.** [*no obj*] to come to an accord; agree: *I'm sure we can get together on a price.* **c.** put together; organize: [~ + *obj* + *together*]: *He got a very good report together.* [~ + *together* + *obj*]: *He got together a good report.* **41. get up, a.** to (cause to) sit up or stand; arise: [*no obj*]: *The child got up from the floor.* [~ + *obj* + *up*]: *Get her up and bring her to the car.* **b.** to (cause to) rise from bed: [~ + *obj* + *up*]: *The radio got me up at six o'clock.* [*no obj*]: *I was so tired I couldn't get up on time.* **c.** [~ + *obj*] to ascend or mount: *We got up the mountain quickly.* **d.** [~ + *obj*] to draw upon; rouse: *He got up his courage.* —*n.* [*count*] **42.** a return of a ball, as in tennis, that would normally have resulted in a point for the opponent. —***Idiom.*** **43. get it, a.** to be punished or reprimanded: *You're going to get it if you're late.* **b.** to understand or grasp something: *You just don't get it, do you?* **44. get nowhere,** to make no progress despite much action and effort. **45. get off someone's back** or **case,** *Slang.* to stop nagging or criticizing someone. **46. has** or **have got,** [~ + *to* + *verb*] must: *He's got to see a doctor right away.*

get•a•way (get′ə wā′) /ˈgɛtəˌwey/ *n.* [*count*] **1.** an escape: *The thieves made a clean getaway.* **2.** a short vacation. **3.** a place for a vacation: *The shore is their favorite getaway.*

get′-togeth′er, *n.* [*count*] an informal, usually small social gathering or meeting.

get•up or **get-up** (get′up′) /ˈgɛtˌʌp/ *n.* [*count*] *Informal.* costume; outfit: *dressed in a weird getup.*

gew•gaw (gyo͞o′gô, go͞o′-) /ˈgyuwgɔ, ˈguw-/ also **gee•gaw** (gē′gô) /ˈgiygɔ/ *n.* [*count*] something gaudy and useless; trinket; bauble.

gey•ser (gī′zər, -sər *for 1;* gē′zər *for 2*) /ˈgayzər, -sər *for 1;* ˈgiyzər *for 2*/ *n.* [*count*] **1.** a hot spring that sends up fountainlike jets of water and steam into the air. **2.** *Brit.* a hot-water heater.

Gha•na•ian (gä′nē ən) /ˈgɑniyən/ or **Gha•ni•an** (gan′ē-ən) /ˈgæniyən/ *n.* [*count*] **1.** a person born or living in Ghana. —*adj.* **2.** of or relating to Ghana.

ghast•ly (gast′lē) /ˈgæstliy/ *adj.,* **-li•er, -li•est. 1.** shockingly frightful or dreadful; horrible: *a ghastly murder.* **2.** resembling a ghost: *a ghastly pallor.* **3.** serious; very bad: *a ghastly error.* —**ghast′li•ness,** *n.* [*noncount*]

gher•kin (gûr′kin) /ˈgɜrkɪn/ *n.* [*count*] the small, immature fruit of a kind of cucumber, used in pickling to make a small pickle eaten as a snack.

ghet•to (get′ō) /ˈgɛtow/ *n.* [*count*], *pl.* **-tos, -toes. 1.** a section of a city, esp. a thickly populated slum area, in which mostly members of a minority group live. **2.** (formerly, in most European countries) a section of a city in which all Jews were required to live: *the Warsaw ghetto.* **3.** an isolated or limiting environment in which a group has been put or has chosen to put itself: *a luxurious suburban ghetto for millionaires.*

ghet•to•ize (get′ō iz′) /ˈgɛtowˌayz/ *v.* [~ + *obj*], **-ized, -iz•ing.** to segregate in or as if in a ghetto.

ghost (gōst) /gowst/ *n.* [*count*] **1.** the disembodied soul of a dead person, imagined as nearly transparent and wandering among the living to haunt them. **2.** a weak or weakened version: *She's a ghost of her former self.* **3.** the slightest bit: *hadn't a ghost of a chance.* **4.** GHOSTWRITER. **5.** a secondary, usually faint or blurry image, as on a television screen or on a photographic negative or print. —*v.* **6.** to ghostwrite (a book, speech, etc.): [*no obj*]: *She ghosts for a living.* [~ + *obj*]: *She ghosted several books.* —***Idiom.*** **7. give up the ghost, a.** to die. **b.** to cease to function: *The old car gave up the ghost on our last trip.* —**ghost′ly,** *adj.,* **-li•er, -li•est.**

ghost•writ•er or **ghost writ•er** (gōst′rī′tər) /ˈgowstˌraytər/ *n.* [*count*] a person who writes a speech, book, article, etc., for another person who is named as the author. —**ghost′write′,** *v.,* **-wrote, -writ•ten, -writ•ing.** [*no obj*]: *He ghostwrites for a living.* [~ + *obj*]: *He ghostwrote several books.*

ghoul (go͞ol) /guwl/ *n.* [*count*] **1.** a legendary demon that robs graves and feeds on corpses. **2.** a grave robber. **3.** a person thought to resemble a ghoul. —**ghoul′ish,** *adj.*

GI or **G.I.** (jē′ī′) /ˈdʒiyˈay/ *n., pl.* **GIs** or **GI's** or **G.I.'s.** [*count*] a member or former member of the U.S. armed forces, esp. an enlisted soldier.

gi•ant (jī′ənt) /ˈdʒayənt/ *n.* [*count*] **1.** (in folklore) a being with human form but superhuman size and strength. **2.** a person or thing of unusually great size or power. **3.** a person or thing of extraordinary importance, achievement, etc.: *one of the giants of aviation.* —*adj.* [*before a noun*] **4.** unusually large; gigantic; huge: *a giant dinosaur.*

gi•ant•ess (jī′ən tis) /ˈdʒayəntɪs/ *n.* [*count*] **1.** (in folklore) a woman with human form but superhuman size and strength. **2.** a woman of unusually great size or power.

gib•ber (jib′ər, gib′-) /ˈdʒɪbər, ˈgɪb-/ *v.* [*no obj*] to speak meaninglessly or foolishly; chatter: *She was gibbering excitedly about nothing.*

gib•ber•ish (jib′ər ish, gib′-) /ˈdʒɪbərɪʃ, ˈgɪb-/ *n.* [*noncount*] **1.** meaningless or unintelligible talk or writing; nonsense. **2.** talk or writing containing many obscure or technical words: *a speech full of gibberish about the budget.*

gib•bet (jib′it) /ˈdʒɪbɪt/ *n.* [*count*] a gallows.

gib•bon (gib′ən) /ˈgɪbən/ *n.* [*count*] a small, slender tree-dwelling ape of S Asia.

gibe or **jibe** (jīb) /dʒayb/ *n.* [*count*] an insulting, taunting, or sarcastic remark.

gib•let (jib′lit) /ˈdʒɪblɪt/ *n.* Usually, **giblets.** [*plural*] the heart, liver, gizzard, or the like of a fowl.

gid•dy (gid′ē) /ˈgɪdiy/ *adj.,* **-di•er, -di•est. 1.** dizzy; feeling the effects of vertigo: *felt a little giddy at such a height.* **2.** [*before a noun*] causing dizziness: *a giddy climb.* **3.** frivolous and lighthearted: *He felt giddy and carefree.* —**gid′di•ness,** *n.* [*noncount*]

gift (gift) /gɪft/ *n.* [*count*] **1.** something given to another freely and without payment in return, as to honor a person or an occasion or to provide assistance; a present: *birthday gifts.* See illustration at STORE. **2.** something received without being earned: *This wonderful weather has been a gift.* **3.** a special ability; natural talent: *a gift for music.*

gift•ed (gif′tid) /ˈgɪftɪd/ *adj.* **1.** having special talent or ability: *She is a gifted storyteller.* **2.** having exceptional intelligence: *a program for gifted children.*

gig[1] (gig) /gɪg/ *n.* [*count*] **1.** a light, two-wheeled one-horse carriage. **2.** a light boat rowed with four, six, or eight long oars.

gig[2] (gig) /gɪg/ *n.* [*count*] *Slang.* **1.** a single engagement, as by jazz or rock musicians. **2.** any job, esp. one of brief duration.

gi•gan•tic (ji gan′tik, ji-) /dʒayˈgæntɪk, dʒɪ-/ *adj.* very large; huge: *We got lost in that gigantic airport.*

gig•gle (gig′əl) /ˈgɪgəl/ *v.*, **-gled, -gling,** *n.* —*v.* [*no obj*] **1.** to laugh in a silly, often high-pitched way, as from nervous embarrassment. —*n.* [*count*] **2.** a silly, often high-pitched laugh. —**gig′gler,** *n.* [*count*] —**gig′gly,** *adj.*, **-gli•er, -gli•est.**

gig•o•lo (jig′ə lō′, zhig′-) /ˈdʒɪgəˌlow, ˈʒɪg-/ *n.* [*count*], *pl.* **-los. 1.** a man, esp. a younger man supported by a usually older woman in return for his sexual attention and companionship. **2.** a male professional dancing partner or escort.

Gi′la mon′ster (hē′lə) /ˈhiylə/ *n.* [*count*] a large, poisonous lizard of the SW United States and NW Mexico, covered with beadlike scales of yellow, orange, and black.

gild (gild) /gɪld/ *v.* [~ + *obj*], **gild•ed** or **gilt** (gilt) /gɪlt/ **gild•ing. 1.** to coat with gold, gold leaf, or a gold-colored substance. —***Idiom.* 2. gild the lily,** to add unnecessary ornamental details to something already of great beauty. —**gild′er,** *n.* [*count*] —**gild′ing,** *n.* [*noncount*]

gill[1] (gil) /gɪl/ *n.* [*count*] **1.** the breathing organ of some water animals, as fish, that breathe oxygen dissolved in water. —***Idiom.* 2. green** or **white around the gills,** somewhat pale, as from sickness: *He looked a little green around the gills after that rough boat ride.* **3. to the gills,** *Informal.* as full as possible: *was filled to the gills with medications.*

gill[2] (jil) /dʒɪl/ *n.* [*count*] a unit of liquid measure equal to ¼ of a pint (118.2937 ml).

gilt (gilt) /gɪlt/ *v.* **1.** a pt. and pp. of GILD[1]. —*adj.* **2.** coated with or as if with gold; gilded; gold in color; golden. —*n.* [*noncount*] **3.** the thin layer of gold or other material applied in gilding.

gilt′-edged′ or **gilt′-edge′,** *adj.* **1.** having the edge or edges gilded: *gilt-edged paper.* **2.** of the highest or best quality, kind, rating, etc.: *gilt-edged securities.*

gim•crack (jim′krak′) /ˈdʒɪmˌkræk/ *n.* [*count*] **1.** a showy, useless thing; gewgaw; trinket. —*adj.* [*before a noun*] **2.** showy but useless: *gimcrack items at a flea market.* —**gim′crack′er•y,** *n.* [*noncount*]

gim•let (gim′lit) /ˈgɪmlɪt/ *n.* [*count*] **1.** a small, sharp tool for boring holes, made of a shaft with a pointed screw at one end and a handle at the other. **2.** a cocktail of gin or vodka, lime juice, and sometimes sugar. —*v.* [~ + *obj*] **3.** to pierce with or as if with a gimlet. —*adj.* [*before a noun*] **4.** sharp; piercing: *the old sailor's gimlet eyes.*

gim•mick (gim′ik) /ˈgɪmɪk/ *n.* [*count*] an ingenious or new device, plan, or action, esp. one used to draw attention or increase appeal; stunt; ploy: *They needed a gimmick to sell their cars.* —**gim•mick•ry** (gim′i krē) /ˈgɪmɪkriy/ *n.* [*noncount*] —**gim′mick•y,** *adj.*

gimp (gimp) /gɪmp/ *n.* [*count*] *Slang.* **1.** a limp. **2.** a person who limps. —*v.* [*no obj*] **3.** to limp. —**gimp′y,** *adj.*

gin[1] (jin) /dʒɪn/ *n.* a clear, colorless alcoholic liquor distilled with juniper berries and other flavorings: [*noncount*]: *bought some gin.* [*count*]: *bought a gin and tonic.*

gin[2] (jin) /dʒɪn/ *n.* [*noncount*] **1.** Also called **gin rummy.** a card game, a variety of rummy for two players. **2.** a hand in this game in which the cards are matched in sets, winning extra points.

gin•ger (jin′jər) /ˈdʒɪndʒər/ *n.* [*noncount*] **1.** a reedlike plant originally from SE Asia but now grown in most warm countries, having a strong-smelling and spicy root used in cookery and medicine. **2.** animation; excitement and vigor: *a performance full of ginger.* **3.** a yellowish or reddish brown. —*adj.* [*before a noun*] **4.** flavored or made with ginger. —**gin′ger•y,** *adj.*

gin′ger ale′, *n.* a bubbling soft drink flavored with ginger extract: [*noncount*]: *some homemade ginger ale.* [*count*]: *Please bring us two ginger ales.*

gin•ger•bread (jin′jər bred′) /ˈdʒɪndʒərˌbrɛd/ *n.* [*noncount*] a cake or cookie flavored with ginger and molasses.

gin•ger•ly (jin′jər lē) /ˈdʒɪndʒərliy/ *adv.* **1.** with great care or caution; warily: *I stepped gingerly over the broken glass.* —*adj.* **2.** cautious; careful: *walking in a gingerly manner.*

ging•ham (ging′əm) /ˈgɪŋəm/ *n.* [*noncount*] plain cotton cloth or fabric, usually striped or checked.

gin•gi•vi•tis (jin′jə vī′tis) /ˌdʒɪndʒəˈvaytɪs/ *n.* [*noncount*] inflammation and soreness of the gums.

gink•go or **ging•ko** (ging′kō, jing′-) /ˈgɪŋkow, ˈdʒɪŋ-/ *n.* [*count*], *pl.* **-goes** or **-koes.** a cultivated shade tree originally from China, having fan-shaped leaves and fleshy seeds with insides that can be eaten.

gin′ rum′my, *n.* GIN[2] (def. 1).

gin•seng (jin′seng) /ˈdʒɪnsɛŋ/ *n.* [*noncount*] **1.** the sweet-smelling root of a certain plant, used in medicine. **2.** a preparation, as tea or extract, made from this root.

gi•raffe (jə raf′) /dʒəˈræf/ *n.* [*count*] a tall, long-necked, spotted animal of Africa, the tallest living four-legged animal.

gird (gûrd) /gɜrd/ *v.* [~ + *obj*], **gird•ed** or **girt** (gûrt) /gɜrt/ **gird•ing. 1.** [~ + *oneself*] to put a belt or band around (oneself); bind with a belt or band: *They girded themselves with brightly colored cords.* **2.** [~ + *no obj*] to surround; enclose; hem in: *The enemy was girded by our troops.* **3.** [~ + *oneself*] to prepare (oneself) for action; brace: *girded themselves for battle.* —***Idiom.* 4. gird one's loins,** to prepare oneself for something requiring strength or endurance.

gird•er (gûr′dər) /ˈgɜrdər/ *n.* [*count*] a large beam, as of steel, reinforced concrete, or timber, used for supporting buildings, structures, etc.

gir•dle (gûr′dl) /ˈgɜrdl̩/ *n.*, *v.*, **-dled, -dling.** —*n.* [*count*] **1.** an undergarment, worn esp. by women, for giving a slimmer appearance to the abdomen, hips, and buttocks. **2.** a belt, cord, sash, or the like, worn about the waist. —*v.* [~ + *obj*] **3.** to encircle with or as if with a belt; gird. **4.** to encompass; enclose; encircle.

girl (gûrl) /gɜrl/ *n.* [*count*] **1.** a female child, from birth to full growth. **2.** a young, immature woman, esp., formerly, an unmarried one: *All the girls of the village came out to see the stranger.* **3.** a daughter: *My wife and I have two girls.* **4.** *Often Offensive.* a grown woman: *Who's the girl waiting on our table?* **5.** girlfriend; sweetheart: *had a girl in every port.* **6.** *Often Offensive.* **a.** a female servant. **b.** a female employee: *I'll have my girl call your office.* —**girl′hood′,** *n.* [*noncount*] —**girl′ish,** *adj.*

girl•friend (gûrl′frend′) /ˈgɜrlˌfrɛnd/ *n.* [*count*] **1.** a frequent or favorite female companion or lover. **2.** a woman's or girl's female friend.

girl′ scout′, *n.* [*count; sometimes: Girl Scout*] a member of an organization of girls **(Girl′ Scouts′)** that seeks to develop character and citizenship, promote health, and foster skills.

girt (gûrt) /gɜrt/ *v.* a pt. and pp. of GIRD.

girth (gûrth) /gɜrθ/ also **girt,** *n.* **1.** the measure around a body or object; circumference: [*count*]: *The girth of that huge tree was several yards.* [*noncount*]: *The tree was several yards in girth.* **2.** [*noncount*] size; bulk: *a man of huge girth.* **3.** [*count*] a band that passes underneath a horse or other animal to secure a saddle.

gis•mo or **giz•mo** (giz′mō) /ˈgɪzmow/ *n.* [*count*], *pl.* **-mos.** *Informal.* a gadget.

gist (jist) /dʒɪst/ *n.* [*noncount; the* + ~] the main or essential point of a matter: *the gist of a story.*

give (giv) /gɪv/ *v.*, **gave** (gāv) /geyv/ **giv•en, giv•ing,** *n.* —*v.* **1.** to present freely and without expecting something in return; make a gift of: [~ + *obj* + *to* + *obj*]: *to give a birthday present to my wife.* [~ + *obj* + *obj*]: *to give my wife a birthday present.* [*no obj*]: *The charity asked us to give generously.* **2.** to hand to someone: [~ + *obj* + *obj*]: *Give me that plate, please.* [~ + *obj* + *to* + *obj*]: *Give the book to your sister.* **3.** to place in someone's care: [~ + *obj* + *to* + *obj*]: *I gave the folders to your assistant.* [~ + *obj* + *obj*]: *Give the butler your coat.* **4.** to grant (permission, opportunity, etc.) to someone or something: [~ + *obj* + *obj*]: *Give me a chance.* [~ + (*to* +) *obj* + *obj*]: *Let's give (to) each candidate the same chance to speak.* [~ + *obj* + *to* + *obj*]: *You should give an opportunity to each candidate.* **5.** to convey by words: [~ + *obj*]: *to give advice.* [~ + *obj* + *obj*]: *I gave her my phone number.* **6.** to communicate (a disease); transmit: [~ + *obj* + *to* + *obj*]: *She gave* *her cold to her sister.* [~ + *obj* + *obj*]: *She gave her sister her cold.* **7.** to set forth or show; present; offer: [~ + *obj*]: *He wouldn't give a reason for his actions.* [~ + *obj* + *to* + *obj*]: *He wouldn't give any reason to his parents for his actions.* [~ + *obj* + *obj*]: *He wouldn't give his parents any reason for his actions.* **8.** to pay or transfer possession to another in exchange for something: [~ + *obj*]: *They gave five dollars for the picture.* [~ + *obj* + *obj*]: *They gave me five dollars for the picture.* **9.** to furnish, provide, or offer: [~ + *obj*]: *to give evidence in a court of law.* [~ + *obj* + *to* + *obj*]: *He gave testimony to the court.* [~ + *(to +) obj* + *obj*]: *He gave (to) the police the evidence they needed.* **10.** to provide as an entertainment or social function: [~ + *obj*]: *to give a Halloween party.* [~ + *obj* + *obj*]: *We gave them an anniversary party.* **11.** to deal or administer: [~ + *obj* + *to* + *obj*]: *to give medicine to a sick patient.* [~ + *obj* + *obj*]: *to give a sick patient medicine.* **12.** to assign, accept, or figure as a basis of calculation or reasoning: [~ + *obj*]: *Given these facts, the theory makes sense.* [~ + *obj* + *obj*]: *I give him two days before he quits.* **13.** to produce, yield, or cause: [~ + *obj*]: *This recipe gives good results.* [~ + *obj* + *obj*]: *The beer gave me a headache.* **14.** to make, do, or perform; put forth: [~ + *obj*]: *The car gave a lurch, then stalled.* [~ + *obj* + *obj*]: *Give me a little kiss.* **15.** [~ + *obj* + *to* + *verb*] to cause; be responsible for: *They gave me to understand that you would be there.* **16.** to care about something to the value or extent of: [~ + *obj*]: *I don't give a hoot about their opinion.* [~ + *obj* + *to* + *verb*]: *I'd give anything to be in bed asleep.* **17.** [~ + *obj*] to sacrifice: *He gave his life for his country.* **18.** [~ + *obj* + *obj*] to assign; allot: *They gave him the nickname "Scooter."* **19.** to acknowlege as deserving; attribute or ascribe: [~ + *obj* + *obj*]: *You've got to give him credit, he did a good job.* [~ + *obj* + *to* + *obj*]: *I have to give most of the credit to my teammates.* **20.** [~ + *obj* + *obj*] to connect with, as through a switchboard: *The operator gave me your office assistant's phone.* **21.** [*present tense only*] to present to an audience: [~ + *(to +) obj* + *obj*]: *Ladies and gentlemen, I give (to) you the governor.* **22.** to apply fully or freely; devote: [~ + *obj* + *to* + *obj*]: *I'll give my full attention to your problem.* [~ + *obj* + *obj*]: *I'll give it my full attention.* **23.** to inflict as a punishment on another; impose a sentence of: [~ + *obj* + *obj*]: *The judge gave him a sentence of ten years.* [~ + *(to +) obj* + *obj*]: *The judge gave (to) each defendant a sentence of ten years.* [~ + *obj* + *to* + *obj*]: *The judge gave the maximum sentence to each defendant.* **24.** to pledge, offer as a pledge, or deliver: [~ + *obj* + *obj*]: *She gave him her word.* [~ + *obj*]: *She gave her word.* **25.** [~ + *obj* + *obj*] to bear (a baby, children, etc.) to a man: *She gave him a beautiful baby boy.* **26.** [~ + *obj* + *obj*] to cause a woman to have (a baby or children); to father: *He gave her two children in four years.* **27.** [~ + *obj* + *obj*] to admit that (something) is true: *He's not handsome, I'll give you that.* **28.** [~ + *me* + *obj*] The expression *Give me* when followed by something as an object is used to mean "I would like to have (the object mentioned)": *Give me a house in the suburbs. (= I would like to have a house in the suburbs).* **29.** [*no obj*] to compromise or yield a little, as to influence or persuasion: *Each side in the dispute must give on some points.* **30.** [*no obj*] to sink in, bend, stretch, or yield a little under weight, force, pressure, etc.: *A horsehair mattress doesn't give much.* **31.** [*no obj*] to collapse; break down; fall apart: *The old chair gave when I sat on it.* **32.** [*no obj*] to be warm and open in relationships with others: *a withdrawn person who doesn't know how to give.* **33.** [*no obj*] *Informal.* to let out information: *Okay now, give! What happened?* **34.** [~ + *on/onto*] to provide a view or passage; face, open, or lead: *This door gives onto the hallway.* **35. give away, a.** to offer or donate as a present; bestow: [~ + *away* + *obj*]: *He gave away all his money to charity.* [~ + *obj* + *away*]: *He gave all his money away.* **b.** to present (the bride) to the bridegroom in a marriage ceremony: [~ + *away* + *obj*]: *The father gave away the bride.* [~ + *obj* + *away*]: *She asked him to give her away at the wedding.* **c.** to let out, disclose, betray, or expose: [~ + *away* + *obj*]: *giving away secrets.* [~ + *obj* + *away*]: *Would we be giving any secrets away?* **36. give back,** to return (something), as to the owner; restore: [~ + *back* + *obj*]: *I gave back the book.* [~ + *obj* + *back*]: *I gave the book back.* [~ + *back* + *obj* + *to* + *obj*]: *Give back the book to the owner.* [~ + *obj* + *back* + *to* + *obj*]: *Let's give the book back to the owner.* [~ + *obj* + *back* + *obj*]: *Give me back my money.* [~ + *obj* + *obj* + *back*]: *Give me my money back.* **37. give in, a.** to acknowledge defeat; admit a loss; surrender; yield: [*no obj*]: *was too tired to fight and gave in.* [~ + *in* + *to* + *obj*]: *She gave in to despair.* **b.** to hand in; deliver: [~ + *in* + *obj*]: *She gave in her timecard.* [~ + *obj* + *in*]: *She gave her timecard in.* **38. give of,** to devote or contribute generously of: [~ + *of* + *oneself*]: *She gives of herself at all times in her teaching.* [~ + *of* + *one's* + *obj*]: *She gave of her time freely.* **39. give off,** [~ + *obj*] to put forth; emit: *The gardenia gives off a strong fragrance.* **40. give out, a.** [~ + *obj*]: to send out; emit: *gave out a loud cry.* **b.** [~ + *obj*] to make public or make known; announce: *gave out the news.* **c.** to distribute; hand out; issue: [~ + *out* + *obj*]: *I gave out the test booklets.* [~ + *obj* + *out*]: *I gave the test booklets out.* **d.** [*no obj*] to become exhausted or used up: *The battery gave out.* **41. give over, a.** to put into the care or custody of; transfer: [~ + *over* + *obj*]: *She gave over all her property to her daughter.* [~ + *obj* + *over*]: *She gave it over to her daughter.* **b.** [~ + *oneself* + *over*] to submit fully; yield to: *She gave herself over to tears.* **c.** [~ + *obj* + *over*] to devote to a specified activity: *The day was given over to relaxing.* **42. give up, a.** [*no obj*] to abandon hope; despair: *After a while I just gave up; I thought I'd never see her again.* **b.** to stop; desist from; renounce: [*no obj*]: *After searching ten hours straight, we gave up.* [~ + *obj*]: *refused to give up politics.* [~ + *verb-ing*]: *to give up smoking.* **c.** to surrender; relinquish: [~ *(+ oneself)* + *up*]: *told the escaped convict to give (himself) up.* [~ + *up* + *obj*]: *Give up your hostages.* [~ + *obj* + *up*]: *Give the hostages up.* **d.** [~ + *oneself* + *up* + *to* + *obj*] to devote (oneself) entirely to: *She gave herself up to this project.* **—*n.*** [*noncount*] **43.** the quality or state of yielding or sinking under force or pressure; springiness: *There's not much give to this couch.* **—*Idiom.*** **44. give it to,** [~ + *obj*] *Informal.* to reprimand or punish: *His mom is really going to give it to him for breaking the window.* **45. give or take,** [~ + *obj*] plus or minus a specified amount: *in about an hour, give or take five minutes.* **—giv′er,** *n.* [*count*]

give′-and-take′, *n.* [*noncount*] **1.** the practice of dealing by compromise or with both sides giving in; cooperation. **2.** good-natured exchange of talk, ideas, etc.

give•a•way (giv′ə wā′) /ˈgɪvəˌwey/ *n.* [*count*] **1.** an act or instance of giving something away. **2.** something given away, esp. as a gift. **3.** an unintentional or accidental action that lets a secret be known or disclosed: *My embarrassed laugh was a dead giveaway.*

giv•en (giv′ən) /ˈgɪvən/ *v.* **1.** pp. of GIVE. **—*adj.*** **2.** [*before a noun*] stated, fixed, or made specific or certain: *a payment to be made at a given time.* **3.** [*be* + ~ + *to*] inclined; disposed: *He was given to making snide remarks.* **4.** This word is used to mean the same thing as "if (something) is true," or "assuming that (something is true)," followed by a conclusion: *Given A and B, C follows (= If A and B are true, then so is C).* **—*n.*** [*count; usually singular*] **5.** an established fact, condition, factor, etc.: *It was a given that the meetings were always late.*

giv′en name′, *n.* [*count*] the name given to one, as distinguished from an inherited family name; first name: *Her given name was Nancy.*

giz•mo (giz′mō) /ˈgɪzmow/ *n., pl.* **-mos.** GISMO.

giz•zard (giz′ərd) /ˈgɪzərd/ *n.* [*count*] the thick-walled, muscular lower stomach of many birds and reptiles, which grinds partially digested food.

gla•cial (glā′shəl) /ˈgleyʃəl/ *adj.* **1.** of or relating to glaciers or ice sheets; resulting from or associated with the action of ice or glaciers: *glacial terrain.* **2.** bitterly cold; icy: *a glacial winter wind.* **3.** happening or moving extremely slowly: *to work at a glacial pace.* **4.** coldly hostile: *glacial contempt.* **—gla′cial•ly,** *adv.*

gla•cier (glā′shər) /ˈgleyʃər/ *n.* [*count*] an extended mass of ice formed from snow falling and gathering over the years and moving very slowly downward or outward.

glad (glad) /glæd/ *adj.,* **glad•der, glad•dest. 1.** [*be* + ~] feeling joy or pleasure; delighted; pleased: *She was glad about the good news.* [~ + *to* + *verb*]: *He was glad to get a job.* [~ + *(that)clause*]: *We were glad that he finally got remarried.* **2.** [*before a noun*] accompanied by or causing joy or pleasure: *glad tidings.* **3.** [*be* + ~ + *to* + *verb*] very willing: *I'd be glad to help.* **—glad′ly,** *adv.* **—glad′ness,** *n.* [*noncount*]

glad•den (glad′n) /ˈglædn/ *v.* [~ + *obj*] to make glad: *gladdened hearts everywhere.*

glade (glād) /gleyd/ *n.* [*count*] an open space in a forest.

glad′ hand′, *n.* [*count; often: the*] **1.** a hearty, sometimes insincere welcome or greeting. **—glad′-hand′,** *v.*

2. to give a glad hand (to): [~ + *obj*]: *The candidate was out glad-handing local voters.* [*no obj*]: *out glad-handing and making speeches.*

glad•i•a•tor (glad′ē ā′tər) /ˈglædiyˌeytər/ *n.* [*count*] (in ancient Rome) a man armed with a sword or other weapon and forced to fight to the death in a public arena for the entertainment of spectators.

glad•i•o•lus (glad′ē ō′ləs) /ˌglædiyˈowləs/ *n.* [*count*], *pl.* **-lus, -li** (-lī) /-lay/ **-lus•es.** a plant of the iris family, native esp. to Africa, having erect, sword-shaped leaves and spikes of flowers in a variety of colors.

glam•or•ize or **glam•our•ize** (glam′ə rīz′) /ˈglæməˌrayz/ *v.* [~ + *obj*], **-ized, -iz•ing.** to make glamorous; romanticize: *a film that glamorizes violence.*

glam•or•ous (glam′ər əs) /ˈglæmərəs/ *adj.* **1.** full of glamour; charming and attractive: *a glamorous actress.* **2.** full of excitement, adventure, or unusual activity: *had a glamorous job.* —**glam′or•ous•ly,** *adv.*

glam•our or **glam•or** (glam′ər) /ˈglæmər/ *n.* **1.** the quality of fascinating or attracting, esp. by a combination of charm and good looks. **2.** excitement, adventure, and unusual activity: *the glamour of being an astronaut.* —*adj.* [*before a noun*] **3.** glamorous: *a glamour job.*

glance (glans) /glæns/ *v.,* **glanced, glanc•ing,** *n.* —*v.* **1.** [~ + *at*] to look quickly or briefly: *She glanced at the TV screen.* **2.** to look at or through something briefly and quickly: [~ + *through* + *obj*]: *She barely glanced through the newspaper.* [~ + *over* + *obj*]: *I glanced over the homework.* **3.** [~ + *on/off* + *obj*] to gleam or flash; shine brightly: *The sun glanced on the window.* **4.** [~ + *off* + *obj*] to strike a surface or object indirectly, esp. so as to bounce off at an angle: *The arrow glanced off his shield.* —*n.* [*count*] **5.** a quick or brief look: *loving glances.*

glanc•ing (glan′sing) /ˈglænsɪŋ/ *adj.* [*before a noun*] striking at an angle: *a glancing shot; a glancing blow.*

gland (gland) /glænd/ *n.* [*count*] an organ or group of cells specialized for producing liquid chemicals or secretions that are used by or released from the body: *sweat glands.* —**glan•du•lar** (glan′jə lər) /ˈglændʒələr/ *adj.*

glare (glâr) /glɛər/ *n., v.,* **glared, glar•ing.** —*n.* **1.** [*noncount*] a very harsh, bright, dazzling light: *the glare of sunlight.* **2.** [*count*] a fierce or angry stare. **3.** [*noncount*] dazzling public notice: *the glare of publicity.* —*v.* **4.** to shine with or reflect a very harsh, bright, dazzling light: [*no obj*]: *Headlights glared in the night.* [~ + *off*]: *The lights glared off our faces.* **5.** to stare with a fierce or angry look: [*no obj*]: *She glared angrily.* [~ + *at* + *obj*]: *She glared at him.*

glar•ing (glâr′ing) /ˈglɛərɪŋ/ *adj.* **1.** shining with or reflecting a harshly bright light. **2.** very conspicuous or obvious; flagrant: *a glaring error.* —**glar′ing•ly,** *adv.*

glas•nost (glaz′nost, gläz′-) /ˈglæznɒst, ˈglɑz-/ *n.* [*noncount*] the policy within the former Soviet Union of openly and frankly discussing economic and political realities.

glass (glas) /glæs/ *n.* **1.** [*noncount*] a hard, brittle, mostly transparent substance, usually produced by heating and melting sand, soda, and lime, as in the ordinary kind used for windows. **2.** [*count*] a tumbler or other drinking container without a handle: *a drinking glass.* See illustration at RESTAURANT. **3.** [*count*] a glassful: *drank two glasses of water.* **4.** **glasses,** Also called **eyeglasses.** [*plural*] two glass or plastic lenses set in a frame that includes two side pieces extending over and behind the ears, to help someone with defective vision see better or to protect the eyes from light, dust, etc. **5.** [*count*] a mirror. **6.** [*noncount*] things made of glass: *to collect old glass.* **7.** [*count*] any of various instruments for viewing, as a spyglass. —*adj.* **8.** made of glass: *a glass bead.* —*v.* [~ + *obj*] **9.** to cover or enclose with glass: *The room was glassed in.*

glass′ ceil′ing, *n.* [*count; usually singular*] an unacknowledged barrier to advancing to the highest positions in a profession, esp. as imposed upon women.

glass•ware (glas′wâr′) /ˈglæsˌwɛər/ *n.* [*noncount*] articles of glass, esp. drinking glasses.

glass•y (glas′ē) /ˈglæsiy/ *adj.,* **-i•er, -i•est.** **1.** resembling glass, as in smoothness: *a glassy surface of ice.* **2.** having no liveliness or expression: *a glassy stare.*

glau•co•ma (glô kō′mə, glou-) /glɔˈkowmə, glaw-/ *n.* [*noncount*] a condition of elevated fluid pressure within the eyeball, causing damage to the eye and steady loss of vision.

glaze (glāz) /gleyz/ *v.,* **glazed, glaz•ing,** *n.* —*v.* **1.** [~ + *obj*] to furnish or fit with glass: *to glaze a window.* **2.** [~ + *obj*] to give a glassy surface or coating to (a ceramic or the like), as by the application of a substance or by heating. **3.** [~ + *obj*] to coat (a food) with a liquid substance that sets to form a smooth, glossy surface: *glazed the ham with brown sugar.* **4.** [*no obj*] to become glassy: *Their eyes glazed over with boredom.* —*n.* **5.** [*count*] a smooth, glossy surface or coating, as on a piece of pottery. **6.** [*noncount*] the substance for producing such a coating. **7.** [*noncount*] a substance, as sugar syrup, used to form a glaze on food. —**glazed,** *adj.*

gla•zier (glā′zhər) /ˈgleyʒər/ *n.* [*count*] a person who fits windows or the like with glass or panes of glass.

gleam (glēm) /gliym/ *n.* [*count*] **1.** a flash or beam of light: *the gleam of a lantern.* **2.** a subdued or reflected light: *the gleam of the full moon.* **3.** a slight showing; trace: *a gleam of hope.* —*v.* [*no obj*] **4.** to send forth a gleam or gleams: *He polished the silver until it gleamed.* **5.** to appear suddenly: *A lantern gleamed in the darkness.*

glean (glēn) /gliyn/ *v.* [~ + *obj*] to gather or find out, usually bit by bit and with hard work: *to glean information.*

glee (glē) /gliy/ *n.* [*noncount*] delight; great joy: *The children were full of glee.* —**glee′ful,** *adj.* —**glee′ful•ly,** *adv.*

glen (glen) /glɛn/ *n.* [*count*] a small, narrow valley.

glib (glib) /glɪb/ *adj.,* **glib•ber, glib•best.** **1.** able to speak fluently, easily, and often insincerely and without thought: *a glib salesman.* **2.** said without thought; offhand: *a glib answer.* —**glib′ly,** *adv.* —**glib′ness,** *n.* [*noncount*]

glide (glīd) /glayd/ *v.,* **glid•ed, glid•ing,** *n.* —*v.* **1.** [*no obj*] to move smoothly, as if without effort: *skaters gliding over the ice.* **2.** [*no obj*] (of time) to elapse in a gradual way that goes unnoticed: *The years glided by.* **3.** [*no obj*] to move quietly or without being noticed: *He glided noiselessly into the room.* **4.** **a.** to move in the air, esp. at an easy angle downward, with little or no engine power: [*no obj*]: *The plane glided toward the runway.* [~ + *obj*]: *The pilot glided the plane to a safe landing.* **b.** [*no obj*] to fly in a glider. —*n.* [*count*] **5.** a gliding movement, as in dancing. **6.** an act or instance of gliding.

glid•er (glī′dər) /ˈglaydər/ *n.* [*count*] **1.** a heavier-than-air aircraft without a motor, launched by towing. **2.** a person or thing that glides. **3.** a porch swing made of an upholstered seat that hangs from a steel framework by links or springs.

glim•mer (glim′ər) /ˈglɪmər/ *n.* [*count*] **1.** a faint or unsteady light; gleam: *saw a glimmer in the woods.* **2.** a dim or faint perception; inkling: *a glimmer of hope.* —*v.* [*no obj*] **3.** to shine faintly or unsteadily; twinkle: *The lights glimmered in the distance.* —**glim′mer•ing,** *n.* [*count*]: *faint glimmerings of hope.*

glimpse (glimps) /glɪmps/ *n., v.,* **glimpsed, glimps•ing.** —*n.* [*count*] **1.** a very brief passing look, sight, or view: *caught only a quick glimpse of the gunmen.* **2.** a vague or incomplete idea; inkling: *had experienced a few glimpses of his bad temper.* —*v.* [~ + *obj*] **3.** to look briefly at: *barely glimpsed the thief.*

glint (glint) /glɪnt/ *n.* [*count*] **1.** a quick flash of light: *a glint from the shiny knife.* **2.** gleaming brightness: *a glint in his eye.* —*v.* [*no obj*] **3.** to shine with a glint: *Light glinted off his knife.*

glis•san•do (gli sän′dō) /glɪˈsɑndow/ *adj., adv., n., pl.* **-di** (-dē) /-diy/ **-dos.** *Music.* —*adj., adv.* **1.** performed by sliding one or more fingers rapidly over the keys of a piano or strings of a harp. —*n.* [*count*] **2.** a glissando passage.

glis•ten (glis′ən) /ˈglɪsən/ *v.* [*no obj*] **1.** to reflect a sparkling light or a faint, flickering glow, as a wet surface; shine: *The black street glistened in the rain.* —*n.* [*count*] **2.** a glistening; sparkle.

glitch (glich) /glɪtʃ/ *n.* [*count*] **1.** *Informal.* a minor defect or malfunction: *A computer glitch forced the space-flight cancellation.* **2.** a sudden interruption or surge in electric power.

glit•ter (glit′ər) /ˈglɪtər/ *v.* [*no obj*] **1.** to reflect light with a brilliant, sparkling luster; sparkle: *The gold glittered from her bracelets.* —*n.* **2.** [*count; usually singular*] a sparkling reflected brightness: *the glitter of sunlight on the ocean.* **3.** [*noncount*] showy splendor; false attractiveness: *the glitter of fame.* —**glit′ter•y,** *adj.*

glit•ter•ing (glit′ər ing) /ˈglɪtərɪŋ/ *adj.* [*before a noun*] brilliantly showy or successful: *a glittering performance.*

glitz (glits) /glɪts/ *n.* [*noncount*] tasteless showiness: *the glitz of a Vegas casino.* —**glitz′y,** *adj.,* **-i•er, -i•est.**

gloam•ing (glō′ming) /ˈglowmɪŋ/ *n.* [*count; singular: the* + ~] twilight; dusk.

gloat (glōt) /glowt/ *v.* [~ *(+ over)*] to take satisfaction in another's misfortune: *Our opponents gloated over our bad luck.*

glob (glob) /glɒb/ *n.* [*count*] **1.** a drop of a liquid. **2.** a usually rounded amount or lump of some liquid or soft substance: *a glob of whipped cream.*

glob•al (glō′bəl) /ˈglowbəl/ *adj.* **1.** relating to or involving the whole world; worldwide; universal: *global weather.* **2.** wide-ranging; comprehensive: *a global analysis of the problem.* **3.** globular; globe-shaped. —**glob′al•ly,** *adv.*

glob•al•ism (glō′bə liz′əm) /ˈglowbəˌlɪzəm/ *n.* [*noncount*] a policy of involving one's country internationally and of considering international as well as national goals and interests. —**glob′al•ist,** *n.* [*count*], *adj.*

globe (glōb) /glowb/ *n.* [*count*] **1.** [*singular; the* + ~] the planet Earth. **2.** a planet or other celestial body. **3.** a round ball or sphere on which is shown a map of the earth. **4.** a spherical body; sphere.

globe•trot•ter (glōb′trot′ər) /ˈglowbˌtrɒtər/ *n.* [*count*] a person who travels regularly to countries all over the world.

glob•u•lar (glob′yə lər) /ˈglɒbyələr/ *adj.* **1.** globe-shaped; spherical; rounded. **2.** made up of or having globules.

glob•ule (glob′yo͞ol) /ˈglɒbyuwl/ *n.* [*count*] a small spherical particle, like a drop: *a globule of sweat.*

gloom (glo͞om) /gluwm/ *n.* [*noncount*] **1.** total or partial darkness; dimness: *couldn't see in the gloom.* **2.** a state of sadness or depression: *I was filled with gloom.*

gloom•y (glo͞o′mē) /ˈgluwmiy/ *adj.,* **-i•er, -i•est. 1.** dark or dim; deeply shaded: *a gloomy prison cell.* **2.** causing sadness or depression: *a gloomy situation.* **3.** hopeless or pessimistic: *a gloomy view of the future.* —**gloom′i•ly,** *adv.* —**gloom′i•ness,** *n.* [*noncount*]

glop (glop) /glɒp/ *n.* [*noncount*] *Informal.* **1.** any gooey or gelatinous substance, esp. soft, unappetizing food. **2.** overly sentimental material: *The TV show was just some glop about happy families.* —**glop′py,** *adj.,* **-pi•er, -pi•est.**

glo•ri•fied (glôr′ə fīd′, glōr′-) /ˈglɔrəˌfayd, ˈglowr-/ *adj.* [*before a noun*] ordinary or simple, but treated as more splendid or excellent than would normally be considered: *The Assistant Manager was really just a glorified office boy.*

glo•ri•fy (glôr′ə fī′, glōr′-) /ˈglɔrəˌfay, ˈglowr-/ *v.* [~ + *obj*], **-fied, -fy•ing. 1.** to cause to be or treat as being more splendid, excellent, etc., than would normally be considered: *The commercials for the army try to glorify military life.* **2.** to honor with praise, admiration, or worship; extol: *to glorify a hero.* **3.** to praise the glory of (God), esp. as an act of worship. —**glor•i•fi•ca•tion** (glôr′ə fi kā′shən, glōr′-) /ˌglɔrəfɪˈkeyʃən, ˌglowr-/ *n.* [*noncount*]

glo•ri•ous (glôr′ē əs, glōr′-) /ˈglɔriyəs, ˈglowr-/ *adj.* **1.** delightful; wonderful: *had a glorious vacation.* **2.** magnificent; splendid: *a glorious summer day.* **3.** yielding glory: *won a glorious victory.* **4.** full of glory: *a glorious hero.* —**glo′ri•ous•ly,** *adv.*

glo•ry (glôr′ē, glōr′ē) /ˈglɔriy, ˈglowriy/ *n., pl.* **-ries,** *v.,* **-ried, -ry•ing.** —*n.* **1.** [*noncount*] very great praise, honor, fame, or distinction; renown: *He won great glory.* **2.** [*noncount*] wonderful beauty or magnificence; splendor: *the glory of autumn.* **3.** [*count*] something that is a source of honor, fame, or admiration; an object of pride or beauty: *the glories of ancient Greece.* —*v.* [~ + *in*] **4.** to rejoice proudly: *They gloried in their children's success.*

gloss[1] (glos, glôs) /glɒs, glɔs/ *n.* [*noncount*] **1.** a luster or shine on the surface of something; glaze: *the gloss of satin.* **2.** a falsely good appearance. **3.** a cosmetic that adds sheen or luster, esp. lip gloss —*v.* [~ + *obj*] **4.** to put a gloss on: *glossed her lips.* **5. gloss over,** to give a falsely good appearance to: *to gloss over someone's mistakes.*

gloss[2] (glos, glôs) /glɒs, glɔs/ *n.* [*count*] **1.** an explanation or translation, by means of a note in the margin of a text. —*v.* [~ + *obj*] **2.** to insert glosses on. See -GLOT-.

glos•sa•ry (glos′ə rē, glô′sə-) /ˈglɒsəriy, ˈglɔsə-/ *n.* [*count*], *pl.* **-ries.** a list of terms in a special subject, field, or area of usage, with definitions, esp. at the back of a book. See -GLOT-.

glos•sy (glos′ē, glô′sē) /ˈglɒsiy, ˈglɔsiy/ *adj.,* **-si•er, -si•est. 1.** having a shiny, bright surface: *glossy hair.* **2.** having an often superficial appearance of richness or attractiveness: *slick, glossy-looking fashion models.* **3.** [*before a noun*] printed on shiny paper: *glossy magazines.*

-glot-, *root.* *-glot-* comes from Greek, where it has the meaning "tongue." This meaning is found in such words as: GLOSS, GLOSSARY, GLOTTIS, POLYGLOT.

glot•tis (glot′is) /ˈglɒtɪs/ *n.* [*count*], *pl.* **glot•tis•es, glot•ti•des** (glot′i dēz′) /ˈglɒtɪˌdiyz/. the opening at the upper part of the vocal cords. —**glot′tal,** *adj.* See -GLOT.

glove (gluv) /glʌv/ *n.* [*count*] **1.** a covering for the hand made with a separate part for each finger and for the thumb. See illustration at CLOTHING. **2.** a similar covering made of padded leather, such as one having a pocket in the area over the palm for catching baseballs. **3.** a leather covering for the fist and sometimes the thumb, used in boxing. —**gloved,** *adj.*

glow (glō) /glow/ *n.* [*count; usually singular*] **1.** a light given off by or as if by a substance heated hot enough to do so; incandescence: *the glow of hot coals.* **2.** brightness of color: *the glow of the rubies.* **3.** a sensation or state of bodily heat: *a warm glow after exercising.* **4.** a warm, usually reddish color of the cheeks. **5.** warmth of emotion or passion; ardor: *felt the glow of love.* —*v.* [*no obj*] **6.** to give off a glow: *The coals glowed for hours.* **7.** to shine like something intensely heated: *The hands of the watch glow in the dark.* **8.** to have a healthy, reddish color: *Her face glowed.* **9.** to feel very warm: *His body was glowing after the exercise class.* **10.** to show happiness: *glowing with pride.*

glow•er (glou′ər) /ˈglawər/ *v.* [*no obj;* (~ + *at* + *obj*)] **1.** to look or stare with dislike, discontent, or anger; to glare. —*n.* [*count*] **2.** a look of dislike, discontent, or anger; a glare.

glow•ing (glō′ing) /ˈglowɪŋ/ *adj.* **1.** giving off bright light or heat without flame: *glowing coals.* **2.** showing good health or happy emotion. **3.** warmly praising: *a glowing account of her work.*

glow•worm (glō′wûrm′) /ˈglowˌwɜrm/ *n.* [*count*] the wingless female of a beetle, which gives off a continuing greenish light. Compare FIREFLY.

glu•cose (glo͞o′kōs) /ˈgluwkows/ *n.* [*noncount*] a simple sugar, $C_6H_{12}O_6$, that is produced by plants during the process of photosynthesis and is the principal source of energy for all living organisms.

glue (glo͞o) /gluw/ *n., v.,* **glued, glu•ing.** —*n.* [*noncount*] **1.** a hard protein gelatin substance, obtained naturally by boiling skins, hoofs, and other animal substances in water or prepared artificially, used as a strong adhesive. —*v.* [~ + *obj*] **2.** to join or attach firmly with or as if with glue: *to glue a label on a package; The kids' eyes were glued to the TV screen.* —**glue′y,** *adj.,* **-i•er, -i•est.**

glum (glum) /glʌm/ *adj.,* **glum•mer, glum•mest. 1.** sad and in low spirits; dejected: *feeling glum.* **2.** depressing: *a glum prospect for victory.* —**glum′ly,** *adv.* —**glum′ness,** *n.* [*noncount*]

glut (glut) /glʌt/ *v.,* **glut•ted, glut•ting,** *n.* —*v.* [~ + *obj*] **1.** to feed or fill too much: *to glut oneself with candy.* **2.** to flood (a market) with a particular item or service so that the supply greatly exceeds the demand: *The market was glutted with luxury cars.* —*n.* [*count*] **3.** an overly large supply or amount.

glu•ten (glo͞ot′n) /ˈgluwtn̩/ *n.* [*noncount*] a grayish, sticky protein substance, part of wheat flour and other grain flours.

glu•ti•nous (glo͞ot′n əs) /ˈgluwtn̩əs/ *adj.* gluey; sticky. —**glu′ti•nous•ly,** *adv.*

glut•ton (glut′n) /ˈglʌtn̩/ *n.* [*count*] **1.** a person who eats and drinks too much. **2.** a person with a remarkably great desire or capacity for something: *a glutton for work.* —**glut′ton•ous,** *adj.* —**glut′ton•ous•ly,** *adv.* —**glut′ton•y,** *n.* [*noncount*]

glyc•er•in (glis′ər in) /ˈglɪsərɪn/ also **glyc•er•ine** (glis′ər in, -ə rēn′) /ˈglɪsərɪn, -əˌriyn/ *n.* GLYCEROL.

glyc•er•ol (glis′ə rôl′, -rol′) /ˈglɪsəˌrɔl, -ˌrɒl/ *n.* [*noncount*] a colorless liquid used as a sweetener and preservative.

gnarled (närld) /nɑrld/ *adj.* twisted or knotted into a deformed condition: *gnarled tree roots; gnarled hands.*

gnash (nash) /næʃ/ *v.* [~ + *obj*] to grind or strike (the teeth) together, esp. in rage or pain.

gnat (nat) /næt/ *n.* [*count*] a very small fly, esp. one that bites, or the midge.

gnaw (nô) /nɔ/ *v.,* **gnawed, gnawed** or **gnawn, gnaw•ing. 1.** to bite or chew on, esp. for a long time without stopping: [~ + *obj*]: *The dog gnawed the bone.* [*no obj*]: *The dog gnawed at the bone.* **2.** [~ + *obj*] to wear away or remove by biting for a long time: *The mice gnawed the paint off the walls.* **3.** [~ + *obj*] to form or make by biting or chewing for a long time: *to gnaw a hole.* **4.** [~ + *at*] to trouble; vex; plague: *Her mistake gnawed at her conscience.*

gnome (nōm) /nowm/ *n.* [*count*] one of a group of beings like dwarfs, supposedly living in the interior of the earth. —**gnom′ish,** *adj.*

-gnos-, *root.* -*gnos*- comes from Greek and Latin, where it has the meaning "knowledge." This meaning is found in such words as: AGNOSTIC, COGNITION, COGNIZANT, DIAGNOSIS, DIAGNOSTIC, INCOGNITO, PRECOGNITION, PROGNOSIS, RECOGNIZE.

GNP or **G.N.P.,** an abbreviation of: gross national product.

gnu (no͞o, nyo͞o) /nuw, nyuw/ *n., pl.* **gnus,** (*esp. when thought of as a group*) **gnu.** either of two stocky, oxlike African antelopes, silvery gray or black. Also called **wildebeest.**

go (gō) /gow/ *v.,* **went** (went) /wɛnt/ **gone** (gôn, gon) /gɔn, gɒn/ **go•ing,** *n., pl.* **goes,** *adj.* —*v.* **1.** to move or proceed, esp. to or from something, or to do some activity or for some purpose: [*no obj*]: *to go home.* [~ + *obj*]: *Are you going my way?* [~ + *verb-ing*]: *They went shopping.* [~ + *to* + *verb*]: *We went to see her last week.* **2.** [*no obj*] to leave a place; depart: *Please go now; I'm getting tired.* **3.** [*no obj*] to keep or be in motion; function or operate; work: *I hear the engine going.* **4.** [~ + *adjective*] to become (the condition as stated): *He went mad.* **5.** to continue in a certain state or condition: [~ + *adjective*]: *to go barefoot.* [~ + *adverb phrase*]: *We went in shorts and tee shirts even in December.* **6.** [*no obj*] to act as specified: *go full speed ahead.* **7.** [~ + *to/into*] to act so as to come into a certain state or condition: *Let's go to sleep.* **8.** [~ + *by/under* + *obj*] to be known: *She went by a false name.* **9.** [*not: be* + ~*-ing; no obj*] to reach or give access to: *This road goes to the beach.* **10.** [*no obj*] to pass or elapse; pass by; slip away: *The time went fast.* **11.** [*no obj*] to be applied or allotted to or used for a particular recipient or purpose: *My money goes for food and rent.* **12.** [*no obj*] to be sold: *The house went for very little.* **13.** [*not: be* + ~*-ing; no obj*] to be considered generally or usually: *He's tall, as jockeys go.* **14.** [~ + *to* + *verb*] to tend: *This only goes to prove the point.* **15.** [*not: be* + ~*-ing; no obj*] to belong; have a place: *This book goes here.* **16.** [*not: be* + ~*-ing; no obj*] to harmonize; be compatible: *Your shirt and tie go well together.* **17.** [*not: be* + ~*-ing; no obj*] to fit or extend: *This belt won't go around my waist.* **18.** [*no obj*] to be or become consumed or used up: *The cake went fast.* **19.** [*no obj*] to be or become discarded, thrown away, dismissed, etc.: *That awful jacket has got to go.* **20.** [*no obj*] to result or end; turn out: *How did the game go?* **21.** [*no obj*] to develop or proceed: *How is your new job going?* **22.** [*no obj*] to move or proceed with remarkable speed or energy: *Look at that airplane go!* **23.** [*no obj*] to make a certain sound: *The gun goes bang.* **24.** to be phrased, written, or composed: [*no obj*]: *How does that song go?* [~ + *clause*]: *That saying went: "We have nothing to fear but fear itself."* **25.** [*no obj*] to fail or give way: *His eyesight is beginning to go.* **26.** [*no obj*] to die: *She went peacefully in her sleep last night.* **27.** [*no obj*] to come into action; begin: *Go when you hear the bell.* **28.** [*not: be* + ~*-ing; no obj*] to be or be able to be divided: *Three goes into fifteen five times.* **29.** The phrase *be* + *going* + *to* plus the root form of a verb is used to mean nearly the same things as the word WILL, that is "to do in the future; to have as one's goal in the future": *We're going to leave soon (= We will leave soon). Their daughter is going to be a doctor (= Their daughter's goal is to be a doctor).* **30.** [*not: be* + ~*-ing; no obj*] to be allowable: *Around here, anything goes.* **31.** [*not: be* + ~*-ing; no obj*] to be the final word: *Whatever I say goes!* **32.** [*no obj*] to put oneself through: *Don't go to any trouble.* **33.** The root form of *go* followed directly by the root form of another verb in informal contexts is used to mean "proceed to," with the meaning of greater feeling or emotion about the statement: *He had to go ask for a loan (= He had to proceed to ask for a loan).* **34.** [*no obj*] *Informal.* to urinate or defecate. **35.** [~ + *obj*] *Informal.* to risk, pay, afford, bet, or bid: *I'll go you one better.* **36. go about,** [~ + *obj*] to occupy oneself with; perform: *went about her work with a smile.* **37. go after,** [~ + *obj*] to attempt to obtain; try to accomplish; strive for: *He went after first prize in the contest.* **38. go against,** [~ + *obj*] to be in conflict with or opposed to: *Lateness goes against company policy.* **39. go ahead,** [*no obj*] to proceed without hesitation or delay: *Go ahead and use my car.* **40. go along,** [*no obj*] **a.** to agree; cooperate: *She'll go along with your decision.* **b.** to make progress; move along: *The project is going along quite well.* **41. go around,** [*no obj*] **a.** to be often in company: *went around with a bad crowd.* **b.** to pass or circulate: *A rumor is going around.* **c.** [*not: be* + ~*-ing*] to be sufficient for all: *There is enough to go around.* **d.** [~ + *verb-ing*] to do or perform (the action of the verb following) often: *likes to go around hurting people.* **42. go at,** [~ + *obj*] **a.** to assault; attack: *went at him with renewed strength.* **b.** to begin or proceed vigorously: *went at his new job with enthusiasm.* **c. go at it,** to fight; argue: *They're going at it again.* **43. go by, a.** [*no obj*] to pass: *Don't let this chance go by. Several months went by.* **b.** [~ + *obj*] to be guided by: *He always goes by the book (= He is always guided by the rules).* **44. go down,** [*no obj*] **a.** to decrease: *The inflation rate went down a little.* **b.** to sink: *The ship went down.* **c.** to suffer defeat: *Our team went down for the third time in a row.* **d.** to be accepted or believed: *His comment didn't go down well.* **e.** to be remembered in history or by posterity: *He wants to go down as a great leader.* **f.** *Slang.* to happen; occur: *What's been going down since I've been away?* **g.** *Brit.* to leave a university, permanently or at the end of a term. **h.** to stop functioning: *The computer went down.* **45. go for,** [~ + *obj*] **a.** to make an attempt at; try for: *to go for a win.* **b.** to assault: *He went for the man with the gun.* **c.** to favor; like: *went for him in a big way.* **46. go in for,** [~ + *obj*] to occupy oneself with: *He goes in for chess.* **47. go into,** [~ + *obj*] **a.** to discuss, examine, or investigate: *I don't want to go into your private life.* **b.** to begin or enter as one's field of study or work: *She went into physics quite by accident.* **48. go off,** [*no obj*] **a.** to explode: *The bomb went off.* **b.** to make a loud noise: *What time will the alarm go off?* **c.** (of what has been expected or planned) to happen: *The party went off exactly as we hoped.* **d.** to leave, esp. suddenly: *He went off with the money.* **49. go on, a.** [*no obj*] to happen or take place: *What's going on at the office?* **b.** [~ + *verb-ing*] to continue: *Go on working.* **c.** to progress; go forward: [*no obj*]: *The show must go on.* [~ + *to* + *obj*]: *Those trainees will go on to flying school.* [~ + *to* + *verb*]: *She went on to achieve great success on the stage.* **d.** [*no obj*] to behave; act: *If you go on like that, they'll fire you.* **e.** [*no obj*] to talk without stopping; chatter. **f.** The phrase *go on* is used to express disbelief: *Go on, you're kidding me.* **g.** [*no obj*] to appear onstage in a theatrical performance: *He went on as Othello.* **50. go out,** [*no obj*] **a.** to cease or fail to function: *The lights went out.* **b.** to participate in social activities: *We like to go out on weekends.* **c.** to take part in a strike: *The drivers' union went out (on strike) last week.* **51. go over, a.** [~ + *obj*] to repeat; review; examine: *Let's go over the examples one more time.* **b.** [*no obj*] to be effective or successful; to be accepted or believed: *The proposal just didn't go over.* **52. go through, a.** [~ + *obj*] to bear; experience: *didn't want to go through a divorce.* **b.** [~ + *obj*] to examine; search: *They went through our records very carefully.* **c.** [*no obj*] to be accepted or approved (by): *I hear your promotion just went through.* **d.** [~ + *obj*] to use up; spend: *We went through all this month's money.* **53. go through with,** [~ + *obj*] to stay with (something) to the end: *She went through with the divorce.* **54. go under,** [*no obj*] **a.** to be overwhelmed or ruined; fail: *Yet another business went under.* **b.** (of a ship) to sink. **55. go up,** [*no obj*] **a.** to be in the process of construction, as a building: *Another high-rise building is going up.* **b.** to increase in cost, value, etc.: *Prices went up again last year.* **c.** *Brit.* to go to a university at the beginning of a term. **56. go with,** [~ + *obj*] **a.** [*not: be* + ~*-ing*] to harmonize or match: *That hat goes with your dress.* See *go* (def. 16). **b.** to have a relationship with: *She's going with yet another movie star this month.* See GO OUT WITH below. —*n.* **57.** [*noncount*] energy or spirit: *She's got a lot of go.* **58.** [*count*] a try at something; attempt: *to have a go at the puzzle.* **59.** [*count; usually singular*] a successful accomplishment; success: *They made a go of it.* **60.** [*count; usually singular*] *Informal.* approval or permission, as to undertake something: *The astronauts were told it was a go.* —*adj.* [*be* + ~] **61.** (esp. in aerospace) functioning properly; ready: *All systems are go.* —***Idiom.*** **62. from the word go,** from the very start: *She was trouble from the word go.* **63. go all out,** [*no obj*] to give the greatest possible effort: *went all out to succeed.* **64. go and,** [*not: be* + ~*-ing;* ~ + *verb*] **a.** to be so thoughtless or unfortunate as to (do the action of the next verb): *went and lost her gloves.* **b.** to move or proceed to or from somewhere, and then do (the action of the next verb): *I'll go and see her tomorrow.* **65. go it alone,** to act or proceed without help or independently. **66. go (out) with,** [~ + *obj*] to have a relationship with; to date: *went out with her a few times.* **67. go to it,** to begin vigorously and at once: *Let's go to it so we can finish on time.* **68. let go, a.** [~ + *of* + *obj*] to free; release: *Let go of my hand.* **b.** to cease to employ; dismiss: [~ + *obj*]: *The company let go a hundred workers.* [*let* + *obj* + ~]: *They let a hundred of them go.* **c.** [~ (+ *oneself*) + *go*] to leave behind one's doubts or inhibitions: *Sometimes you just have to let (yourself) go.* **69. no go,** *Informal.* futile; useless: *It was no go; we couldn't convince them.* **70. on the go,** [*be* + ~] **a.** very busy; active: *on the go from morning to night.* **b.** while traveling: *luggage for the traveler (who is) on the go.* **71. to go,** for eating away from the place where sold: *pizza to go.*

goad (gōd) /gowd/ *n.* [*count*] **1.** a stick with a pointed or electrically charged end, for driving cattle, oxen, etc.; prod. **2.** anything that urges; a stimulus to action. **—***v.* [~ + *obj* (+ *into*)] **3.** to drive with or as if with a goad; incite: *actions meant to goad us into war.*

go′-a•head′, *n.* [*count; often singular*] **1.** permission or a signal to proceed: *They got the go-ahead on the building project.* **—***adj.* [*before a noun*] **2.** that puts a score or team ahead of another: *a go-ahead goal.*

goal (gōl) /gowl/ *n.* [*count*] **1.** the result or achievement toward which effort is directed; aim; end: *His goal was to become a famous statesman.* **2.** an area or point toward or into which players of various games attempt to propel a ball or puck to score points. **3.** the act of propelling a ball or puck toward or into such an area or object. **4.** the score made by achieving this.

goal•ie (gō′lē) /ˈgowliy/ *n.* GOALKEEPER.

goal•keep•er (gōl′kē′pər) /ˈgowl,kiypər/ *n.* [*count*] (in ice hockey, field hockey, lacrosse, soccer, etc.) a player whose chief duty is to prevent the ball or puck from crossing or entering the goal. **—goal′keep′ing,** *n.* [*noncount*]

goat (gōt) /gowt/ *n.* [*count*] **1.** an agile animal with hollow horns, closely related to sheep, usually found in mountainous regions. **2.** a man overly interested in sex. **3.** SCAPEGOAT. **—*Idiom.* 4. get someone's goat,** *Informal.* to anger, annoy, or frustrate someone.

goat•ee (gō tē′) /gowˈtiy/ *n.* [*count*], *pl.* **-ees.** a man's beard trimmed to a point on the chin.

goat•herd (gōt′hûrd′) /ˈgowt,hɜrd/ *n.* [*count*] a person who tends goats.

goat•skin (gōt′skin′) /ˈgowt,skɪn/ *n.* [*noncount*] **1.** the skin or hide of a goat. **2.** leather made from it.

gob (gob) /gɒb/ *n.* [*count*] **1.** a mass or lump: *He smeared a gob of plaster in the hole.* **2. gobs,** [*plural*] *Informal.* a large quantity: *gobs of money.*

gob•ble[1] (gob′əl) /ˈgɒbəl/ *v.,* **-bled, -bling. 1.** to swallow or eat quickly or hungrily in large pieces; gulp: [~ (+ *up/down*) + *obj*] *We gobbled (up) our lunch.* [~ + *obj* + *up/down*]: *We gobbled it down and ran back.* **2.** [~ + *up* + *obj*] to seize upon and read eagerly: *She would go and gobble up the books in the library.*

gob•ble[2] (gob′əl) /ˈgɒbəl/ *v.,* **-bled, -bling,** *n.* **—***v.* [*no obj*] **1.** to make the throaty sound or cry of a male turkey. **—***n.* [*count*] **2.** the cry itself.

gob•ble•dy•gook or **gob•ble•de•gook** (gob′əl dē-gŏŏk′) /ˈgɒbəldiy,gʊk/ *n.* [*noncount*] language that is full of needlessly difficult words or is otherwise hard to understand.

gob•bler (gob′lər) /ˈgɒblər/ *n.* [*count*] a male turkey.

go′-between′, *n.* [*count*] a person who acts as a messenger between persons or groups who will not or cannot meet.

gob•let (gob′lit) /ˈgɒblɪt/ *n.* [*count*] a drinking glass with a base and stem.

gob•lin (gob′lin) /ˈgɒblɪn/ *n.* [*count*] an evil spirit that is mischievous or harmful toward people.

God (god) /gɒd/ *n.* **1.** [*proper noun; no article*] the creator and ruler of the universe in certain religions, as Judaism, Christianity, or Islam; the Supreme Being. **2.** [*god; count*] one of several beings thought to live forever, esp. one that is male (opposed to *goddess*), having power over some portion of worldly affairs; deity: *the Greek and Roman gods.* **3.** [*god; count*] any person or object held in great reverence, awe, or respect, or one thought to be important: *His gods were money and power.* **—***interj.* **4.** *Sometimes Offensive.* This word is sometimes used to express disappointment, disbelief, frustration, or the like. **—god′like′,** *adj.*

god•child (god′chīld′) /ˈgɒd,tʃayld/ *n.* [*count*], *pl.* **-chil•dren.** a child for whom a godparent serves as a sponsor.

god•daugh•ter (god′dô′tər) /ˈgɒd,dɔtər/ *n.* [*count*] a female godchild.

god•dess (god′is) /ˈgɒdɪs/ *n.* [*count*] **1.** a female god: *the Greek and Roman goddesses.* **2.** a much admired woman. **3.** a woman of great beauty.

god•fa•ther (god′fä′thər) /ˈgɒd,fɑðər/ *n.* [*count*] **1.** a man who serves as sponsor for a child, such as at a baptism. **2.** the head of a Mafia family; don.

god′-fear′ing, *adj.* religious; devout; godly.

god•hood (god′hŏŏd) /ˈgɒdhʊd/ *n.* [*noncount*] divine character or condition; divinity.

god•less (god′lis) /ˈgɒdlɪs/ *adj.* **1.** acknowledging no god or deity; atheistic: *a godless society.* **2.** evil; sinful.

god•ly (god′lē) /ˈgɒdliy/ *adj.,* **-li•er, -li•est. 1.** obeying God or the rules of one's religion; devout. **2.** coming from God; divine. **—god′li•ness,** *n.* [*noncount*]

god•moth•er (god′muth′ər) /ˈgɒd,mʌðər/ *n.* [*count*] a woman who serves as sponsor for a child, such as at a baptism.

god•par•ent (god′pâr′ənt, -par′-) /ˈgɒd,pɛərənt, -,pær-/ *n.* [*count*] a godfather or godmother.

god•send (god′send′) /ˈgɒd,sɛnd/ *n.* [*count; usually singular; a* + ~] a needed thing that comes at the right moment: *The extra money is a godsend.*

god•son (god′sun′) /ˈgɒd,sʌn/ *n.* [*count*] a male godchild.

-goer, *suffix.* The suffix *-goer* is added to nouns to form nouns that mean "a person who (regularly) attends or goes to (the place mentioned)": *church* + *-goer* → *churchgoer* (= *a person who regularly attends church*).

go•fer or **go-fer** (gō′fər) /ˈgowfər/ *n.* [*count*] *Slang.* an employee whose chief duty is running errands.

go′-get′ter, *n.* [*count*] *Informal.* an aggressively energetic person who works hard to get ahead. **—go′-get′ting,** *adj.*

gog•gle (gog′əl) /ˈgɒgəl/ *n., v.,* **-gled, -gling,** *adj.* **—***n.* **1. goggles,** [*plural*] large glasses equipped with special lenses, protective rims, etc., to prevent injury to the eyes from strong wind, flying objects, blinding light, etc. **—***v.* [~ (+ *at*)] **2.** to stare with wide-open eyes: *We all goggled at the spectacle.* **—***adj.* [*before a noun*] **3.** bulging or staring: *goggle eyes.*

go′-go′, *adj.* [*before a noun*] **1.** disco: *go-go music.* **2.** performing at a discotheque or nightclub: *go-go dancers.*

go•ing (gō′ing) /ˈgowɪŋ/ *n.* **1.** [*count*] the act or fact of leaving: *comings and goings.* **2.** [*noncount*] the conditions that affect accomplishing something: *It was rough going.* **—***adj.* [*before a noun*] **3.** current; charged at the present time: *What is the going rate for babysitting nowadays?* **4.** working; thriving: *a going business.* **—*Idiom.* 5. have something going for (one),** to have an advantage: *She has a lot going for her: brains, education, and business contacts.* **6. while the going is good,** while it is advantageous: *I think we should get out while the going is good* (= *while we can still make a profit*).

-going, *suffix.* The suffix *-going* is added after nouns referring to places or events where people gather, to form adjectives that mean "attending or going regularly to (the place mentioned)": *church* + *-going* → *churchgoing* (= *regularly attending church*).

go′ings-on′, *n.* [*plural*] *Informal.* **1.** conduct or behavior, esp. when improper or dishonest: *strange goings-on.* **2.** happenings; events: *the goings-on of daily life.*

goi•ter (goi′tər) /ˈgɔytər/ *n.* [*count*] a swelling or enlargement of the thyroid gland on the front and sides of the neck. Also, *esp. Brit.,* **goi′tre.**

gold (gōld) /gowld/ *n.* **1.** [*noncount*] a precious yellow metal element that is easy to shape and does not corrode easily. **2.** [*noncount*] a quantity of gold coins: *to pay in gold.* **3.** [*noncount*] jewelry or other valuable items made of gold. **4.** [*noncount*] something considered to be like gold esp. in high value: *She has a heart of gold.* **5.** [*noncount*] a bright yellow color. **6.** [*count*] GOLD MEDAL: *The team won several golds.* **—***adj.* [*before a noun*] **7.** made of, relating to, or like gold. **8.** of the color of gold. **9.** (of a recording or record album) having sold at least one million single records or 500,000 long-playing albums.

gold•brick (gōld′brik′) /ˈgowld,brɪk/ *n.* [*count*] *Slang.* **1.** Also, **gold′brick′er.** a person who loafs on the job or avoids work. **—***v.* [*no obj*] **2.** to loaf or avoid work.

gold′ dig′ger, *n.* [*count*] **1.** a person who digs for gold. **2.** a person who feigns romantic interest in another while in fact looking for financial gain.

gold•en (gōl′dən) /ˈgowldən/ *adj.* **1.** of the color of gold: *golden hair.* **2.** made or consisting of gold: *golden earrings.* **3.** exceptionally valuable or advantageous: *a golden opportunity.* **4.** having glowing vitality: *golden youth.* **5.** of mellow, advanced age: *golden years.* **6.** highly talented and favored: *television's golden boy.* **7.**

richly resonant: *a golden voice.* **8.** indicating the 50th event of a series, as a wedding anniversary.

gold′en hand′shake, *n.* [*count*] a special reward, as a large sum of money, offered to employees so that they will retire early.

gold′en rule′, *n.* [*count; usually singular; the* + ~] a rule of correct or moral conduct, usually phrased "Do unto others as you would have others do unto you."

gold•finch (gōld′finch′) /ˈgowldˌfɪntʃ/ *n.* [*count*] a finch, the male of which has yellow colors in the summer.

gold•fish (gōld′fish′) /ˈgowldˌfɪʃ/ *n.* [*count*], *pl.* (*esp. when thought of as a group*) **-fish,** (*esp. for kinds or species*) **-fish•es.** a small, usually yellow or orange fish, originally from China and kept as a pet in glass bowls or garden ponds.

gold′ med′al, *n.* [*count*] a medal awarded to the competitor winning first place in a race, event, or other competition.

gold•smith (gōld′smith′) /ˈgowldˌsmɪθ/ *n.* [*count*] a person who makes or sells articles of gold, such as jewelry.

golf (golf, gôlf) /gɒlf, gɔlf/ *n.* [*noncount*] **1.** a game in which special sticks called clubs are used to hit a small, hard, usually white ball into a series of holes, usually 9 or 18, situated at various distances over a course. **—*v.*** [*no obj*] **2.** to play golf: *golfed on Sunday mornings.* —**golf′er,** *n.* [*count*]

golf′ club′, *n.* [*count*] **1.** a long stick, usually made of metal, with either a wooden or metal end used to strike a ball in the game of golf. **2.** a place where golf is played, consisting of a course or field for the holes and often a restaurant or other place to relax.

gol•ly (gol′ē) /ˈgɒliy/ *interj.* The word *golly* or the phrase *by golly* is used to express mild surprise, wonder, puzzlement, or the like: *"Golly!" she said, "I'm impressed."*

-gon, *suffix. -gon* comes from Greek, where it has the meaning "side; angle." This suffix is attached to roots to form nouns that refer to plane figures having the number of sides mentioned: *poly-* (*= many*) + *-gon* → *polygon* (*= a many-sided figure*).

go•nad (gō′nad, gon′ad) /ˈgownæd, ˈgɒnæd/ *n.* [*count*] an organ or gland in which sex cells are produced; an ovary or testis. —**go•nad′al,** *adj.*

gon•do•la (gon′dl ə *or, esp. for 1,* gon dō′lə) /ˈgɒndḷə *or, esp. for 1,* gɒnˈdowlə/ *n.* [*count*], *pl.* **-las. 1.** a long, narrow, flat-bottomed boat propelled by a gondolier and used on the canals in Venice, Italy. **2.** a passenger compartment that hangs beneath a balloon or airship. Compare CAR (def. 3). **3.** an enclosed cabin that hangs from an overhead cable and is used to transport passengers, as up and down a ski slope. **4.** Also called **gon′dola car′.** an open railroad freight car with low sides, for transporting freight and manufactured goods.

gon•do•lier (gon′dl ēr′) /ˌgɒndḷˈɪər/ *n.* [*count*] a person who uses a pole to propel a Venetian gondola.

gone (gôn, gon) /gɔn, gɒn/ *v.* **1.** pp. of GO[1]. **—*adj.*** [*be* + ~] **2.** departed; left: *When I looked up, the customer was gone.* **3.** past: *Two years were gone.* **—*Idiom.*** [*be* + ~] **4. far gone,** in an advanced or terminal state: *The patient was too far gone to save.*

gon•er (gô′nər, gon′ər) /ˈgɔnər, ˈgɒnər/ *n.* [*count*] *Informal.* a person or thing that is dead, lost, or past recovery.

gong (gông, gong) /gɔŋ, gɒŋ/ *n.* [*count*] **1.** a large bronze disk of Asian origin that produces a loud, hollow tone when struck. **2.** a simple bell struck by an electrically or mechanically operated hammer: *a fire gong.* **—*v.*** [*no obj*] **3.** to sound; ring: *The alarm gonged.*

gon•na (gô′nə, gun′ə) /ˈgɔnə, ˈgʌnə/ *v.* This word is used to represent "going to" as it is sometimes pronounced in fast or normal speech: *"I'm gonna get you," he shrieked.*

gon•or•rhe•a (gon′ə rē′ə) /ˌgɒnəˈriyə/ *n.* [*noncount*] a contagious disease of the urethra or the vagina, passed on during sexual activity. Also, *esp. Brit.,* **gon′or•rhoe′a.** —**gon′or•rhe′al,** *adj.*

goo (go͞o) /guw/ *n.* [*noncount*] *Informal.* a thick or sticky substance. —**goo′ey,** *adj.,* **-i•er, -i•est.**

goo•ber (go͞o′bər) /ˈguwbər/ *n.* [*count*] *South Midland and Southern U.S.* the peanut. Also called **goo′ber pea′.**

good (go͝od) /gʊd/ *adj.,* **bet•ter** (bet′ər) /ˈbɛtər/ **best** (best) /bɛst/ *n., interj., adv.* **—*adj.*** **1.** morally excellent; virtuous: *a wise and good man.* **2.** satisfactory or excellent in quality, quantity, or degree: *She was a good teacher.* **3.** [*It* + *be* + ~ + *(that) clause*] right; proper; fitting: *It is good that you are here.* **4.** well-behaved; easy to supervise: *What a good baby!* **5.** kind or friendly: *to do a good deed.* **6.** honorable or worthy: *the company's good name.* **7.** educated and refined: *comes from a good background.* **8.** financially sound or safe: *His credit is good.* **9.** genuine; valid: *My driver's license is good for another month.* **10.** sensible; sound: *to use good judgment.* **11.** healthful; beneficial: *Fresh fruit is good for you.* **12.** in excellent condition; healthy: *stays in good shape with exercise.* **13.** not spoiled; that can be eaten or enjoyed: *This food is still good.* **14.** favorable: *good news.* **15.** [*before a noun*] cheerful; amiable: *in good spirits.* **16.** [*before a noun*] agreeable; enjoyable: *Have a good time.* **17.** attractive: *has a good figure.* **18.** [*before a noun*] sufficient; enough: *a good supply.* **19.** advantageous; satisfactory for the purpose: *Yesterday was a good day for fishing.* **20.** skillful; clever: *He's good at arithmetic.* **21.** skillfully done: *a really good job.* **22.** conforming to rules of grammar, usage, etc.; correct: *He writes very good English.* **23.** socially proper: *good manners.* **24.** comparatively new or of relatively fine quality or condition: *She wore her good clothes.* **25.** [*before a noun*] full; complete; thorough: *a good day's journey from here.* **26.** fairly large: *a good amount.* **27.** free from precipitation or cloudiness: *good weather.* **28.** fertile; rich: *good soil.* **29.** loyal; dependable; reliable: *a good friend.* **30.** (of a return, service, or shot in tennis, handball, etc.) landing within the limits of a court or section of a court. **31.** [*before a noun*] favorably regarded (used with names): *the good ship* Syrena. **—*n.*** **32.** [*used with negative words, or in questions; noncount*] profit or advantage; worth; benefit: *What good will that do?* **33.** [*noncount*] excellence or merit; kindness: *to do good.* **34.** [*noncount*] morally right, correct, or proper behavior; goodness; virtue: *to be a power for good.* **35. goods,** [*plural*] **a.** possessions, esp. movable effects or personal property. **b.** articles of trade: *linen goods.* **c.** *Informal.* what has been promised or is expected: *to deliver the goods.* **d.** *Informal.* evidence of guilt, as stolen articles: *were caught with the goods.* **—*interj.*** **36.** This word is used to express approval or satisfaction: *Good! Now we can all go home.* **—*adv.*** **37.** *Informal.* well: *You did good; you should be proud.* **—*Idiom.*** **38. a good deal of,** [~ + *noncount noun*] quite a lot: *a good deal of money.* See DEAL. **39. come to no good,** to end in failure or as a failure: *She'll come to no good if she hangs around with that bad crowd.* **40. for good,** finally and permanently; forever: *We left that country for good.* **41. good and,** This phrase is used to mean "very" and comes before an adjective or adverb to express intensity: *The coffee is good and hot.* **42. good for,** [*be* + ~] **a.** certain to repay (money owed): *I'm sure she's good for that debt.* **b.** the equivalent in value of: *This pass is good for two free seats.* **c.** serviceable or useful for (a specified length of time or distance): *This warranty is only good for ninety days.* **43. make good,** to repay (money owed); to compensate for, as a loss; to fulfill, as a promise: *made good on the debt.* **44. no good,** without value or merit: *Face it, that car is no good.*

good-by or **good•by** or **good-bye** (go͝od′bī′) /ˌgʊdˈbay/ *interj., n., pl.* **-bys** or **-byes. —*interj.*** **1.** This word is used when the speaker is leaving someone, or being left by someone: *"Good-bye! See you tomorrow."* **—*n.*** [*count*] **2.** an act of saying "good-bye": *They made their good-byes.*

good′-for-noth′ing, *adj., n., pl.* **good-for-nothings. —*adj.*** **1.** worthless; of no use: *that good-for-nothing loafer.* **—*n.*** [*count*] **2.** a worthless or useless person.

good′-heart′ed or **good′heart′ed,** *adj.* kind or generous; benevolent. —**good′-heart′ed•ly,** *adv.* —**good′-heart′ed•ness,** *n.* [*noncount*]

good′-hu′mored, *adj.* cheerful; pleasant; amiable and friendly: *good-humored joking.*

good′-look′ing, *adj.* having a pleasingly attractive appearance; handsome or beautiful.

good•ly (go͝od′lē) /ˈgʊdliy/ *adj.* [*before a noun*], **-li•er, -li•est.** of substantial size or amount: *a goodly sum.*

good′-na′tured, *adj.* having or showing an agreeable disposition; amiable. —**good′-na′tured•ly,** *adv.*

good•ness (go͝od′nis) /ˈgʊdnɪs/ *n.* [*noncount*] **1.** the state or quality of being good. **2.** moral excellence; virtue. **3.** kindness; generosity: *volunteers out of the goodness of his heart.* **—*interj.*** **4.** This word is used to express surprise, alarm, etc.: *"Goodness! Late again!"*

good′ (or **Good′**) **Samar′itan** (sə mar′i tn) /səˈmærɪtn/ *n.* [*count*] a person who freely gives help to those in distress or need.

good•will or **good will** (go͝od′wil′) /ˈgʊdˈwɪl/ *n.* [*noncount*] **1.** friendly nature or behavior; kindness; good feelings toward another; benevolence. **2.** the good reputation of a business and the high quality of its relations with its customers, considered as part of its value.

good•y or **good•ie** (go͝od′ē) /ˈgʊdiy/ *n., pl.* **good•ies,** *interj.* —*n.* [*count*] Usually, **goodies.** [*plural*] **1.** something pleasing to eat, as candy. **2.** something esp. desirable: *all sorts of goodies, like money and cars and houses.* —*interj.* **3.** This word is used, as by children, to express childish delight, or is sometimes used ironically.

good′y-good′y, *n., pl.* **-good•ies,** *adj.* —*n.* [*count*] **1.** a person who is primly or smugly virtuous or proper. —*adj.* [*before a noun*] **2.** of or like a goody-goody.

goof (go͞of) /guwf/ *v. Informal.* **1.** [~ (+ *up*)] to make an error, misjudgment, etc.: *He goofed (up) when he bought that clunker.* **2.** [~ + *up* + *obj*] to spoil or make a mess of; botch; bungle: *He goofed up the job.* **3.** [~ + *around/off*] to waste time: *was always goofing around instead of studying.* —*n.* [*count*] **4.** a foolish or stupid person. **5.** a mistake, esp. one due to carelessness.

goof•ball (go͞of′bôl′) /ˈguwfˌbɔl/ *n.* [*count*] *Slang.* **1.** GOOF (def. 4). **2.** a pill that contains a tranquilizing drug.

goof′-off′, *n.* [*count*] *Informal.* a person who always avoids work or responsibility.

goof•y (go͞o′fē) /ˈguwfiy/ *adj.,* **-i•er, -i•est.** foolish; silly; ridiculous: *a goofy hat.*

gook (go͝ok, go͞ok) /gʊk, guwk/ *n.* [*noncount*] *Slang.* slime or oozy, wet dirt.

goon (go͞on) /guwn/ *n.* [*count*] **1.** a hired hoodlum or criminal. **2.** *Informal.* a stupid, foolish, or awkward person.

goose (go͞os) /guws/ *n., pl.* **geese** for 1, 2, 4. **1.** [*count*] a wild or farm bird, web-footed and able to swim well, larger and with a longer neck and legs than a duck. **2.** [*count*] the female of this bird. Compare GANDER (def. 1). **3.** [*noncount*] the flesh of a goose, used as food. **4.** [*count*] a silly or foolish person; simpleton. —***Idiom.*** **5. cook someone's goose,** *Informal.* to ruin someone's chances or future.

goose•ber•ry (go͞os′ber′ē, -bə rē) /ˈguwsˌbɛriy, -bəriy/ *n.* [*count*], *pl.* **-ries. 1.** the sour, sometimes prickly fruit of certain shrubs of the saxifrage family. **2.** any of these shrubs.

goose′ flesh′ or **goose′flesh′,** *n.* [*noncount*] a bristling of the hair on the skin, as from cold or fear. Also called **goose′ pim′ples, goose′ bumps′.** [*count; plural*]

GOP or **G.O.P.,** an abbreviation of: Grand Old Party, an earlier name for the Republican Party.

go•pher (gō′fər) /ˈgowfər/ *n.* [*count*] a burrowing rodent having a stout body, a short tail, and external cheek pouches.

gore[1] (gôr, gōr) /gɔr, gowr/ *n.* [*noncount*] **1.** blood that is shed, esp. when clotted. **2.** bloodshed; violence: *a movie full of gore.*

gore[2] (gôr, gōr) /gɔr, gowr/ *v.* [~ + *obj*], **gored, gor•ing.** to pierce with or as if with a horn or tusk: *The bull gored the bullfighter.*

gorge (gôrj) /gɔrdʒ/ *n., v.,* **gorged, gorg•ing.** —*n.* **1.** [*count*] a narrow canyon with steep, rocky walls, esp. one through which a stream runs. **2.** [*noncount*] a feeling of strong disgust or anger: *Their cruelty made his gorge rise.* —*v.* **3.** to stuff with food; glut: [~ + *oneself*]: *to gorge oneself.* [~ + *on* + *obj*]: *gorged on food.*

gor•geous (gôr′jəs) /ˈgɔrdʒəs/ *adj.* **1.** splendid in appearance; beautiful: *a gorgeous couple of actors.* **2.** extremely pleasant: *gorgeous weather.* —**gor′geous•ly,** *adv.*

go•ril•la (gə ril′ə) /gəˈrɪlə/ *n.* [*count*], *pl.* **-las. 1.** the largest manlike ape, from Africa near the equator, vegetarian and mainly living on the ground rather than in trees. **2.** an ugly or brutish man.

gorse (gôrs) /gɔrs/ *n.* [*noncount*] a spiny European evergreen shrub of the legume family, having primitive leaves and yellow flowers.

gor•y (gôr′ē, gōr′ē) /ˈgɔriy, ˈgowriy/ *adj.,* **-i•er, -i•est. 1.** covered or stained with gore; bloody: *a gory scene.* **2.** involving much bloodshed and violence: *a gory movie.* **3.** sensational: *Give us all the gory details.* —**gor′i•ness,** *n.* [*noncount*]

gosh (gosh) /gɒʃ/ *interj.* This word is used to express surprise or as a mild oath: *Gosh, that hurts!*

gos•ling (goz′ling) /ˈgɒzlɪŋ/ *n.* [*count*] a young goose.

gos•pel (gos′pəl) /ˈgɒspəl/ *n.* **1.** [*often: Gospel; noncount; often: the* + ~] the teachings of Jesus and the apostles; the Christian Bible, esp. the story of Jesus' life and teachings as contained in the first four books of the New Testament, namely Matthew, Mark, Luke, and John. **2.** [*usually: Gospel; count*] any of these four books. **3.** [*noncount*] Also called **gos′pel truth′.** something thought of as absolutely true and that cannot reasonably be questioned. **4.** [*count*] a doctrine regarded as of prime importance: *political gospel.* **5.** [*noncount*] music sung originally in American black Protestant churches and often characterized by responsive singing and a distinctive solo style. —*adj.* [*before a noun*] **6.** of, relating to, or proclaiming the gospel or its teachings; in accordance with the gospel; evangelical. **7.** of, relating to, employing, or performing gospel music.

gos•sa•mer (gos′ə mər) /ˈgɒsəmər/ *n.* [*noncount*] **1.** a fine, filmy cobweb found on grass or bushes or floating in the air in calm weather. **2.** any thin, light fabric, esp. one used for veils. **3.** something extremely light, flimsy, or delicate. —*adj.* **4.** Also, **gos•sa•mer•y** (gos′ə mə rē) /ˈgɒsəməriy/ **gos′sa•mered.** of or like gossamer; thin and light: *gossamer wings.*

gos•sip (gos′əp) /ˈgɒsəp/ *n., v.,* **-siped** or **-sipped, -sip•ing** or **-sip•ping.** —*n.* **1.** [*noncount*] idle talk, conversation, or rumor, esp. about the private affairs of others. **2.** [*count*] light, familiar writing of a similar kind: *a newspaper's gossip column.* **3.** [*count*] Also, **gos′sip•er, gos′sip•per.** a person who enjoys or indulges in gossip. —*v.* [*no obj*] **4.** to talk gossip. —**gos′sip•y,** *adj.*

got (got) /gɒt/ *v.* **1.** a pt. and pp. of GET. **2.** [~ + *obj*] *Informal.* have got; have: *I got a bad cold.* —*auxiliary verb.* [~ + *to* + *verb*] **3.** *Informal.* must; have got: *We got to get out of here.*

goth•ic (goth′ik) /ˈgɒθɪk/ *adj.* **1.** [*usually: Gothic*] of or relating to a style of architecture in W Europe from the mid-12th to the 16th century, characterized by pointed arches, high ceilings, tall columns, flying buttresses, and rich decoration **2.** [*often: Gothic*] of or relating to a style of literature characterized by a gloomy setting; mysterious, sinister, or violent events; and, in modern examples, a heroine in distress or danger: *a Gothic novel.* —*n.* **3.** [*noncount; usually: Gothic*] the arts, crafts, or architecture of the Gothic period. **4.** [*count; often: Gothic*] a novel, play, film, etc., in the gothic style.

got•ta (got′ə) /ˈgɒtə/ *v.* This word is used to represent "got to," as it is sometimes pronounced in informal, rapid, or regional conversational speech, when it means "have to, must": *We gotta go now (= We have got to go now = We have to/must go now).*

got•ten (got′n) /ˈgɒtn̩/ *v.* a pp. of GET.

gouge (gouj) /gawdʒ/ *v.,* **gouged, goug•ing. 1.** [~ + *obj*] to scoop out or turn with or as if with a pointed tool or object: *He gouged a hole in the rock with his chisel.* **2.** to dig or force out with or as if with a pointed object or tool: [~ + *out* + *obj*]: *He threatened to gouge out my eye.* [~ + *obj* + *out*]: *He threatened to gouge my eye out.* **3.** [~ + *obj*] to make a hole in (something) with or as if with a pointed object or tool: *The bullet fragments gouged his leg.* **4.** [~ + *obj*] to overcharge (someone) illegally or dishonestly: *They were gouging their customers in that store.* —**goug′er,** *n.* [*count*]

gou•lash (go͞o′läsh, -lash) /ˈguwlɑʃ, -læʃ/ *n.* a stew of beef or veal and vegetables, seasoned with paprika: [*noncount*]: *a bowl of goulash.* [*count*]: *a vegetable goulash.*

gourd (gôrd, gōrd, go͝ord) /gɔrd, gowrd, gʊrd/ *n.* [*count*] **1.** the hard-shelled fruit of a certain long, green plant, made into bowls, ladles, etc. **2.** a plant bearing such a fruit. **3.** a dried and dug out gourd shell used as a bottle, dipper, flask, etc. —***Idiom.*** [*be* + ~] **4. out of** or **off one's gourd,** *Slang.* out of one's mind; crazy.

gour•mand (go͝or mänd′, go͝or′mənd) /gʊrˈmɑnd, ˈgʊrmənd/ *n.* [*count*] **1.** one who is overly fond of good eating. **2.** a gourmet.

gour•met (go͝or mā′, go͝or′mā) /gʊrˈmey, ˈgʊrmey/ *n.* [*count*] **1.** one who is fond of fine food and drink. —*adj.* [*usually: before a noun*] **2.** of, characteristic of, or designed for gourmets: *gourmet cooking.* **3.** of or involving fancy or exotic foods: *a gourmet food store.*

gout (gout) /gawt/ *n.* [*noncount*] a painful swelling of the joints, esp. of the big toe, characterized by too much uric acid in the blood, which causes deposits in the small joints. —**gout•y,** *adj.,* **-i•er, -i•est.**

gov. or **Gov.,** an abbreviation of: **1.** government. **2.** governor.

gov•ern (guv′ərn) /ˈgʌvərn/ *v.* **1.** to rule by right of authority, as a king or queen or elected administrator does: [~ + *obj*]: *to govern a nation.* [*no obj*]: *I'm sure he governs fairly.* **2.** [~ + *obj*] to exercise a directing or restraining influence over; control: *the motives that govern a decision.* **3.** [~ + *obj*] to hold in check; control: *to govern one's temper.* —**gov′ern•a•ble,** *adj.* —**gov•ern•ance** (guv′ər nəns) /ˈgʌvərnəns/ *n.* [*noncount*]

gov•ern•ess (guv′ər nis) /ˈgʌvərnɪs/ *n.* [*count*] a woman employed in a private household to take charge of a child's upbringing and education.

gov•ern•ment (guv′ərn mənt, -ər mənt) /ˈgʌvərnmənt, -ərmənt/ *n.* **1.** [*noncount*] the political system by which direction and control over the actions of the members or citizens of a community, society, state, etc., is exercised; the direction of the affairs of a state, community, etc. **2.** [*count; usually singular; the* + ~] the governing body of persons in a state, community, etc. or a branch of this body. **3.** [*count*] (in some parliamentary systems, as that of the United Kingdom) **a.** the particular group of persons forming the cabinet at any given time: *The Prime Minister has formed a new government.* **b.** the parliament along with the cabinet. **4.** [*noncount*] direction; control; management; rule. —**gov•ern•men•tal** (guv′ərn-men′tl, guv′ər-) /ˌgʌvərnˈmɛntḷ, ˌgʌvər-/ *adj.*

gov•er•nor (guv′ər nər, -ə nər) /ˈgʌvərnər, -ənər/ *n.* [*count*] **1.** the executive head of a state in the U.S. **2.** a person charged with the direction or control of an institution, society, etc.: *the governor of a prison.* **3.** a ruler or chief magistrate appointed to govern a province, town, fort, or the like. **4.** a device for maintaining uniform speed (in a machine, engine, etc.), as by regulating the supply of fuel. —**gov′er•nor•ship′,** *n.* [*noncount*]

Govt. or **govt.,** government.

gown (goun) /gawn/ *n.* [*count*] **1.** a woman's dress or robe, esp. one that is full-length: *wedding gowns; evening gowns.* **2.** a nightgown or similar garment. **3.** a loose, flowing outer garment in any of various forms, worn by men and women as distinctive of office or profession: *academic gowns.* **4.** a protective garment worn over other clothes, as when performing surgery. —*v.* [~ + *obj*] **5.** to dress in a gown: *gowned in black.*

GP or **G.P.,** an abbreviation of: **1.** general practitioner. **2.** general purpose.

GPO or **G.P.O.,** an abbreviation of: **1.** general post office. **2.** Government Printing Office.

gr., an abbreviation of: **1.** grade. **2.** grain. **3.** gram. **4.** gravity. **5.** great. **6.** gross. **7.** group.

grab (grab) /græb/ *v.,* **grabbed, grab•bing,** *n.* —*v.* **1.** to seize suddenly, eagerly, or roughly; snatch: [~ + *obj*]: *He grabbed his hat and dashed off.* [~ + *at* + *obj*]: *She grabbed at the railing.* **2.** [~ + *obj*] to take possession of (something) illegally: *to grab land.* **3.** [~ + *obj*] to obtain and consume quickly: *Let's grab a sandwich.* **4.** [~ + *obj*] *Informal.* to arouse the interest or excitement of: *How does my idea grab you?* **5.** [*no obj*] (of brakes, a clutch, etc.) to take hold suddenly or with a jolting motion. —*n.* [*count*] **6.** a sudden, eager grasp or snatch: *I made a grab for my hat.* **7.** seizure or takeover by violent, illegal, or dishonest means: *land grabs.* —***Idiom.*** [*be* + ~] **8. up for grabs,** available for anyone to take, use, or buy. —**grab′ber,** *n.* [*count*]

grace (grās) /greys/ *n., v.,* **graced, grac•ing.** —*n.* **1.** [*noncount*] elegance or beauty of form, manner, motion, or action: *She moves with elegance and grace.* **2.** graceful, appealing, or proper behavior: [*noncount; sometimes: the* ~*s*]: *showed grace under pressure.* [*count*]: *the social graces.* **3.** Also, **grace period.** a period or allowance of time after a debt is technically payable, but before a penalty will be applied: [*noncount*]: *have 30 days' grace.* [*count*]: *We have a grace period of 30 days.* **4.** [*noncount*] favor or goodwill, or an expression of favor, esp. by a superior. **5.** [*noncount*] the freely given favor and love of God, esp. when unearned. **6.** [*noncount*] a short prayer before or after a meal, in which a blessing is asked and thanks are given: *Let's say grace.* **7.** [*proper noun; Your/His/Her* + *Grace*] a title used in addressing or mentioning a duke, duchess, or archbishop. —*v.* [~ + *obj*] **8.** to lend or add grace to; adorn: *Many paintings graced the walls.* **9.** [~ + *obj* + *with*] to favor or honor: *Will you grace us with your presence?* —***Idiom.*** **10. fall from grace,** [*no obj*] **a.** to become a wrongdoer; sin. **b.** to lose favor with those in power. **11. in someone's good (or bad) graces,** regarded with favor (or disfavor) by someone. **12. with good (or bad) grace,** without (or with) reluctance; willingly (or unwillingly): *congratulated the winner with good grace.* —**grace′less,** *adj.* —**grace′less•ly,** *adv.* —**grace′less•ness,** *n.* [*noncount*]

grace•ful (grās′fəl) /ˈgreysfəl/ *adj.* having grace of form, manner, movement, or speech. —**grace′ful•ly,** *adv.* —**grace′ful•ness,** *n.* [*noncount*]

gra•cious (grā′shəs) /ˈgreyʃəs/ *adj.* **1.** pleasantly kind; wishing well to others; courteous: *a gracious host.* **2.** characterized by good taste, comfort, ease, or luxury: *gracious suburban living.* —*interj.* **3.** This word is used to express surprise, relief, dismay, etc.: *Gracious! I've lost my purse.* —**gra′cious•ly,** *adv.* —**gra′cious•ness,** *n.* [*noncount*]

grack•le (grak′əl) /ˈgrækəl/ *n.* [*count*] a long-tailed blackbird having shining black feathers.

grad (grad) /græd/ *n.* [*count*] *Informal.* a graduate of a school. See -GRAD-.

-grad-, *root.* *-grad-* comes from Latin, where it has the meaning "step; degree; rank." This meaning is found in such words as: BIODEGRADABLE, CENTIGRADE, DEGRADE, GRAD, GRADATION, GRADIENT, GRADUAL, GRADUATE, RETROGRADE, UNDERGRADUATE, UPGRADE. See -GRESS-.

gra•da•tion (grā dā′shən) /greyˈdeyʃən/ *n.* [*count*] a process or change taking place through a series of stages or degrees; a stage or degree in such a series: *gradations of colors on the computer screen.* See -GRAD-.

grade (grād) /greyd/ *n., v.,* **grad•ed, grad•ing.** —*n.* **1.** [*count*] a degree or step in a scale of quality, rank, advancement, or value: *several grades of wool.* **2.** [*count*] a class of persons or things of the same relative rank, quality, etc. **3.** a single division of a school classified, usually by year, according to the age or progress of the pupils: [*noncount*]: *She was in third grade.* [*count*]: *students in seventh and eighth grades.* **4.** [*count*] the pupils in such a division, thought of as a group. **5.** [*count*] a letter or other symbol indicating the relative quality of a student's work; mark. **6.** [*count*] the degree at which a hill, mountain, etc., slopes up or down: *steep uphill grades.* —*v.* [~ + *obj*] **7.** to arrange in a series of grades; classify; sort: *a machine that grades eggs.* **8.** to assign a grade to (a student's work); mark. **9.** to reduce to a level that is less steep: *to grade a road.* —***Idiom.*** **10. make the grade,** to attain or reach a specific goal; succeed. See -GRAD-.

grade′ cross′ing, *n.* [*count*] a place where a railroad track and another track, a road, etc., meet at the same level.

grade′ school′, *n.* ELEMENTARY SCHOOL.

gra•di•ent (grā′dē ənt) /ˈgreydiyənt/ *n.* [*count*] **1.** the degree at which a highway, railroad, etc., slopes up or down: *a steep gradient.* **2.** the rate of change, as of distance, temperature, or pressure, as shown or represented by a curve in a graph. See -GRAD-.

grad•u•al (graj′o͞o əl) /ˈgrædʒuwəl/ *adj.* **1.** taking place, changing, moving, etc., by small degrees or little by little: *showed gradual improvement.* **2.** rising or going down at an even, moderate inclination: *a gradual slope.* —**grad′u•al•ly,** *adv.* See -GRAD-.

grad•u•ate (*n., adj.* graj′o͞o it, -āt′; *v.* -āt′) / *n., adj.* ˈgrædʒuwɪt, -ˌeyt; *v.* -ˌeyt/ *n., adj., v.,* **-at•ed, -at•ing.** —*n.* [*count*] **1.** a person who has received a degree or diploma on completing a course of study at a university, college, or school. **2.** Also, **graduate student.** a student who is studying for an advanced degree. —*adj.* [*before a noun*] **3.** of, relating to, or involved in academic study beyond a bachelor's or first professional degree: *graduate studies.* —*v.* **4.** to receive a degree or diploma (from), on completing a course of study: [*no obj;* ~ + *from*]: *to graduate with honors from college.* [~ + *obj*]: *She graduated college.* **5.** [~ + *obj*] to give a degree to or grant a diploma to: *The school graduates top scholars.* **6.** [*no obj*] to advance by degrees: *She graduated to a higher position in the company.* See -GRAD-.

grad•u•at•ed (graj′o͞o ā′tid) /ˈgrædʒuwˌeytɪd/ *adj.* arranged in steps, as the scale of a thermometer. See -GRAD-.

grad′uate school′ (graj′o͞o it) /ˈgrædʒuwɪt/ *n.* [*count*] a school, usually a division of a university, offering courses leading to degrees more advanced than the bachelor's degree.

grad•u•a•tion (graj′o͞o ā′shən) /ˌgrædʒuwˈeyʃən/ *n.* **1.** [*noncount*] an act of graduating from a college or school. **2.** the ceremony of conferring degrees or diplomas, as at a college or school: [*noncount*]: *Graduation is next week.* [*count*]: *We went to two graduations.*

graf•fi•ti (grə fē′tē) /grəˈfiytiy/ *n.* [*noncount*] drawings, writings, or marks made in public places, as walls, signs, or posters.

graft[1] (graft) /græft/ *n.* [*count*] **1.** a bud or small shoot of a plant placed into a groove, slit, or the like in a stem or trunk of another plant in which it continues to grow. **2.** a portion of living tissue removed during a medical operation from one part of an individual to another part, or from one individual to another individual. —*v.* [~ + *obj*] **3.** to insert (a graft) into a tree or other plant; insert a shoot of (one plant) into another plant. **4.** to transplant (a portion of living tissue) as a graft. —**graft′er,** *n.* [*count*]

graft[2] (graft) /græft/ *n.* [*noncount*] **1.** the obtaining of money or advantage by dishonest or unfair means, esp. through the abuse of one's position or influence, as in politics. **2.** the money or advantage so acquired. —**graft′er,** *n.* [*count*]

grain (grān) /greyn/ *n.* **1.** [*count*] a small, hard seed, esp. the seed of a food plant such as wheat, corn, rye, oats, rice, or millet. **2.** [*noncount*] the gathered seed of food plants, esp. of cereal plants: *shipped tons of grain.* **3.** [*count*] any small, hard particle, as of sand, gold, pepper, or gunpowder: *a few grains of salt.* **4.** [*count; usually singular*] the smallest possible amount: *There was a grain of truth in what she said.* **5.** [*noncount*] the arrangement or direction of the fibers in wood, meat, etc., or the pattern resulting from this: *the beautiful grain of walnut.* **6.** [*count*] a unit of weight equal to 50 milligrams or ¼ carat, used for pearls and sometimes diamonds. —***Idiom.*** **7. against one's** or **the grain,** in conflict with one's nature or beliefs: *It goes against her grain to spend more money than she has to.*

grain•y (grā′nē) /'greyniy/ *adj.,* **-i•er, -i•est. 1.** resembling grain; full of grains or grain. **2.** (of a photograph or picture) having an appearance resembling grain; granular. —**grain′i•ness,** *n.* [*noncount*]

gram (gram) /græm/ *n.* [*count*] a unit of mass or weight in the metric system, equal to 15.432 grains; 1/1000 of a kilogram. *Abbr.:* g, gr. Also, *esp. Brit.,* **gramme.**

-gram, *suffix. -gram* comes from Greek, where it has the meaning "what is written." It is attached to roots to form nouns that refer to something written or drawn, either by hand or machine: *cardio- (= of or relating to the heart) + -gram → cardiogram (= a recording and diagram of a heartbeat, drawn by a machine).* Compare -GRAPH-.

gram•mar (gram′ər) /'græmər/ *n.* **1.** [*noncount*] the study of the way that the sentences or words of a language are constructed, esp. the study of morphology and syntax. **2.** [*noncount*] these features or constructions themselves, characteristic of a given language: *English grammar.* **3.** [*count*] a theory or account of these features, as a set of rules governing a given language: *a grammar of English.* **4.** [*noncount*] the establishment of rules based on what is considered correct and incorrect language usage: *good grammar.* **5.** [*noncount*] usage of preferred or prescribed forms in speaking or writing: *She said his grammar was terrible.*

gram•mar•i•an (grə mâr′ē ən) /grə'mɛəriyən/ *n.* [*count*] a person who is an expert in grammar.

gram′mar school′, *n.* **1.** an elementary school, usually from kindergarten or first grade to grade five, six, or sometimes eight: [*count*]: *The district opened a new grammar school.* [*noncount*]: *children in grammar school.* **2.** *Brit.* a secondary school corresponding to a U.S. high school: [*count*]: *a new grammar school.* [*noncount*]: *attending grammar school.*

gram•ma•ti•cal (grə mat′i kəl) /grə'mætɪkəl/ *adj.* **1.** obeying the rules of grammar of a language: *a grammatical sentence.* **2.** of or relating to the study of grammar or language: *grammatical rules.* —**gram•mat′i•cal•ly,** *adv.*

gra•na•ry (grā′nə rē, gran′ə-) /'greynəriy, 'grænə-/ *n.* [*count*], *pl.* **-ries. 1.** a storehouse for grain. **2.** a region producing quantities of grain: *the nation's granary.*

grand (grand) /grænd/ *adj.,* **-er, -est,** *n.* —*adj.* **1.** impressive in size, appearance, or general effect: *grand mountain scenery.* **2.** stately; dignified: *a grand and regal manner.* **3.** highly ambitious or idealistic, often with unreal hopes of achieving success or anything important: *grand schemes.* **4.** respected; esteemed: *a grand old man.* **5.** [*before a noun*] complete; comprehensive: *the grand total.* **6.** first-rate; splendid: *We had a grand time.* —*n.* [*count*] **7.** GRAND PIANO. **8.** [*count; singular only*] *Informal.* a thousand dollars. —**grand′ly,** *adv.* —**grand′ness,** *n.* [*noncount*]

grand-, a combining form used in words describing family relationships, with the meaning "one generation different or removed" from the relation described by the base word: *grandmother (= the mother who is one generation before one's mother; one's mother's mother); grandnephew (= the nephew who is one generation after one's nephew).*

grand•child (gran′chīld′) /'græn,tʃayld/ *n.* [*count*], *pl.* **-chil•dren.** a child of one's son or daughter.

grand•daugh•ter (gran′dô′tər) /'græn,dɔtər/ *n.* [*count*] a daughter of one's son or daughter.

grande dame (grän′ däm′, gränd′) /'grɑn' dɑm, 'grɑnd/ *n.* [*count*], *pl.* **grandes dames** (grän′ dämz′, gränd′) /'grɑn' dɑmz, 'grɑnd/. an older woman, esp. of some distinction.

gran•deur (gran′jər) /'grændʒər/ *n.* [*noncount*] the quality or state of being grand, magnificent, or impressive: *the grandeur of the universe.*

grand•fa•ther (gran′fä′thər, grand′-) /'græn,fɑðər, 'grænd-/ *n.* [*count*] the father of one's father or mother.

grand′father (or **grand′father's**) **clock′,** *n.* [*count*] a large floor clock having a case as tall as or taller than a person.

gran•dil•o•quence (gran dil′ə kwəns) /græn'dɪləkwəns/ *n.* [*noncount*] speech that is overly obscure, lofty, or pompous in tone. —**gran•dil′o•quent,** *adj.* See -LOQ-.

gran•di•ose (gran′dē ōs′) /'grændiy,ows/ *adj.* **1.** falsely grand or affected; pompous: *grandiose words.* **2.** foolishly grand: *grandiose schemes.*

grand′ ju′ry, *n.* [*count*] a jury whose duty is to determine if a law has been violated and whether the evidence is strong enough to permit prosecution.

grand•ma (gran′mä′, -mô′, grand′-, gram′-) /'græn,mɑ, -,mɔ, 'grænd-, 'græm-/ *n.* [*count*], *pl.* **-mas.** *Informal.* GRANDMOTHER.

grand•moth•er (gran′muth′ər, grand′-, gram′-) /'græn,mʌðər, 'grænd-, 'græm-/ *n.* [*count*] the mother of one's father or mother.

grand•pa (gran′pä′, -pô′, grand′-, gram′-) /'græn,pɑ, -,pɔ, 'grænd-, 'græm-/ *n.* [*count*] *pl.* **-pas.** *Informal.* GRANDFATHER.

grand•par•ent (gran′pâr′ənt, -par′-, grand′-) /'græn,pɛərənt, -,pær-, 'grænd-/ *n.* [*count*] a parent of a parent; a grandmother or grandfather.

grand′ pian′o, *n.* [*count*] a large piano having the frame supported horizontally on three legs.

grand′ slam′, *n.* [*count*] **1.** the winning of or bid for all thirteen tricks of a deal in bridge. **2.** in baseball, a home run with all three runners on base. **3.** the winning by a single player of certain major championship contests in one season, as in tennis.

grand•son (gran′sun′, grand′-) /'græn,sʌn, 'grænd-/ *n.* [*count*] a son of one's son or daughter.

grand•stand (gran′stand′, grand′-) /'græn,stænd, 'grænd-/ *n.* [*count*] **1.** a main seating area, as of a stadium or racetrack. **2.** the people sitting in these seats, thought of as a group. —*v.* [*no obj*] **3.** to conduct oneself or perform so as to impress onlookers.

grange (grānj) /greyndʒ/ *n.* [*count*] a farm and its buildings.

gran•ite (gran′it) /'grænɪt/ *n.* [*noncount*] a coarse-grained stone, used chiefly in roads and in building. —**gra•nit•ic** (grə nit′ik) /grə'nɪtɪk/ *adj.*

gran•ny or **gran•nie** (gran′ē) /'græniy/ *n., pl.* **-nies,** *adj.* —*n.* [*count*] **1.** *Informal.* GRANDMOTHER. **2.** an elderly woman. —*adj.* [*before a noun*] **3.** (of clothing for women) loose-fitted, often with a high neckline, puff sleeves, and ruffles and lace trimmings: *a granny dress; a granny gown.*

gra•no•la (grə nō′lə) /grə'nowlə/ *n.* [*noncount*] a breakfast food of rolled oats, nuts, dried fruit, brown sugar, etc.

grant (grant) /grænt/ *v.* **1.** to give; confer; accord: [~ + *obj* + *to*]: *The teacher granted permission to leave.* [~ + *obj* + *obj*]: *He granted us permission to go ahead.* **2.** [~ + *obj*] to agree to: *to grant a request.* **3.** to accept for the sake of argument: [~ + *obj*]: *I grant that point.* [~ + *obj* + *obj*]: *I grant you that point.* [~ + *that clause*]: *I grant that what she did was silly.* [~ + *obj* + *(that) clause*]: *I grant you that the budget situation is grim.* —*n.* [*count*] **4.** something given or granted, as a privilege or right, a sum of money, or a tract of land. —***Idiom.*** **5. take for granted,** [*take* + *obj* + *for granted*] **a.** to assume without question: *I take his honesty for granted.* **b.** to treat with careless indifference: *You'll regret it if you take her for granted.* —**grant′er, gran′tor,** *n.* [*count*]

gran•tee (gran tē′) /græn'tiy/ *n.* [*count*], *pl.* **-tees.** the receiver of a grant.

gran•u•lar (gran′yə lər) /'grænyələr/ *adj.* **1.** of the nature of granules; grainy; composed of or having granules or grains. **2.** showing a grainy structure or surface: *a granular surface.* —**gran•u•lar•i•ty** (gran′yə lar′i tē) /,grænyə'lærɪtiy/ *n.* [*noncount*]

gran•u•lat•ed (gran′yə lā′tid) /'grænyə,leytɪd/ *adj.* made like or resembling grains: *granulated sugar.* —**gran•u•la•tion** (gran′yə lā′shən) /,grænyə'leyʃən/ *n.* [*noncount*]

gran•ule (gran′yo͞ol) /'grænyuwl/ *n.* [*count*] a little grain; a small particle; pellet: *granules of sand.*

grape (grāp) /greyp/ *n.* [*count*] the smooth-skinned, green or purple fruit that grows in clusters on vines, may be eaten, and is used to make wine.

grape•fruit (grāp′fro͞ot′) /ˈgreypˌfruwt/ *n.* **1.** a large, roundish, yellow-skinned citrus fruit that has a juicy, acid inside that may be eaten: [*count*]: *Grapefruits were plentiful.* [*noncount*]: *Grapefruit is high in vitamin C.* **2.** [*count*] the tropical or semitropical tree yielding this fruit.

grape•vine (grāp′vīn′) /ˈgreypˌvayn/ *n.* [*count*] **1.** a vine that bears grapes. **2.** an informal, person-to-person means of spreading gossip or information: *I heard it through the grapevine.*

graph (graf) /græf/ *n.* [*count*] **1.** a diagram representing a system of connections or relations among two or more things, as by a number of dots, shapes, or lines. **—***v.* [~ + *obj*] **2.** to represent by means of a graph: *The economists graphed the current trends.* See -GRAPH-.

-graph-, *root.* *-graph-* comes from Greek, where it has the meaning "written down, printed, drawn." This meaning is found in such words as: AUTOGRAPH, BIBLIOGRAPHY, BIOGRAPHY, CALLIGRAPHY, CARTOGRAPHY, CHOREOGRAPHY, CINEMATOGRAPHY, DIGRAPH, GEOGRAPHY, GRAPH, GRAPHIC, GRAPHITE, HAGIOGRAPHY, HOLOGRAPHY, IDEOGRAPH, LEXICOGRAPHY, LITHOGRAPHY, MIMEOGRAPH, MONOGRAPH, OCEANOGRAPHY, ORTHOGRAPHY, PARAGRAPH, PHONOGRAPH, PHOTOGRAPH, PICTOGRAPH, POLYGRAPH, PORNOGRAPHY, SEISMOGRAPH, TELEGRAPH, TYPOGRAPHY. See -GRAM.

graph•ic (graf′ik) /ˈgræfɪk/ *adj.* Also, **graph′i•cal.** **1.** giving a clear and effective picture; vivid: *a graphic account of the riots.* **2.** relating to the use of diagrams, graphs, mathematical curves, or the like. **3.** of, relating to, or expressed by writing: *graphic symbols.* **4.** [*before a noun*] relating to graphic arts. **—***n.* [*count*] **5.** a product of the graphic arts, as a drawing. **6.** a computer-generated image or picture. **—graph′i•cal•ly,** *adv.*: *graphically showing the destruction and disease in the war-torn region.* See -GRAPH-.

graph′ic arts′, *n.* [*plural*] **1.** Also called **graphics.** the techniques by which copies of a design are printed from a plate, block, or the like: *Engraving, etching, and lithography are graphic arts.* **2.** the techniques of drawing, painting, printmaking, and typography. See -GRAPH-.

graph•ics (graf′iks) /ˈgræfɪks/ *n.* **1.** [*noncount; used with a singular verb*] the art of drawing. **2.** [*plural; used with a plural verb*] GRAPHIC ARTS (def. 1). **3.** [*plural; used with a plural verb*] titles, credits, and other text shown on a motion-picture or television screen before, after, or during a film or program. See -GRAPH-.

graph•ite (graf′īt) /ˈgræfayt/ *n.* [*noncount*] a soft form of carbon occurring in black to dark gray masses, used for pencil leads and as a lubricant. See -GRAPH-.

graph•ol•o•gy (gra fol′ə jē) /græˈfɒlədʒiy/ *n.* [*noncount*] the study of handwriting, esp. when regarded as giving clues to the writer's character. **—graph•ol′o•gist,** *n.* [*count*]

grap•nel (grap′nl) /ˈgræpnḷ/ *n.* [*count*] **1.** a device consisting of one or more hooks or clamps for grasping or holding; grapple. **2.** a small anchor with three or more hooks.

grap•ple (grap′əl) /ˈgræpəl/ *v.*, **-pled, -pling,** *n.* **—***v.* **1.** to struggle with by holding, gripping, or wrestling; come to grips: [*no obj*]: *The two wrestlers grappled in the ring.* [~ + *with*]: *He grappled with his attacker.* **2.** [~ + *with*] to try to overcome or deal: *to grapple with a problem.* **—***n.* [*count*] **3.** GRAPNEL (def. 1).

grasp (grasp) /græsp/ *v.* **1.** [~ + *obj*] to seize and hold by or as if by clasping with the fingers or arms: *She grasped my arm and pulled me aside.* **2.** [~ + *for/at* + *obj*] to attempt seizing: *The baby grasped at the bottle.* **3.** [~ + *obj*] to comprehend; understand: *I grasp your meaning.* **—***n.* [*count; usually singular*] **4.** the act of grasping. **5.** [*within one's* + ~] reach; attainment; control: *The new promotion was within his grasp.* **6.** power to understand: *has a good grasp of math.* **—grasp′a•ble,** *adj.*

grasp•ing (gras′ping) /ˈgræspɪŋ/ *adj.* greedy; grabbing; avaricious.

grass (gras) /græs/ *n.* **1.** [*count*] a plant that has jointed stems and bladelike leaves and is grown for lawns, used as pasture, or cut for hay. **2.** [*noncount*] such plants thought of as a group: *Grass won't grow there.* **3.** [*noncount*] grass-covered ground: *a picnic on the grass.* **4.** [*noncount*] *Slang.* MARIJUANA. **—*Idiom.*** **5. let the grass grow under one's feet,** to delay action.

grass•hop•per (gras′hop′ər) /ˈgræsˌhɒpər/ *n.* [*count*] a plant-eating insect having large hind legs used for leaping.

grass′ roots′, *n.* [*plural; used with a plural verb but sometimes used with a singular verb*] **1.** ordinary citizens, esp. as contrasted with a leadership or elite. **—***adj.* [*grass-roots; before a noun*] **2.** of, from, or aimed at the grass roots: *grass-roots support.*

gras•sy (gras′ē) /ˈgræsiy/ *adj.*, **-si•er, -si•est.** covered with grass.

-grat-, *root.* *-grat-* comes from Latin, where it has the meaning "pleasing; thankful; favorable." This meaning is found in such words as: CONGRATULATE, GRATEFUL, GRATIFY, GRATIS, GRATITUDE, GRATUITOUS, GRATUITY, INGRATE, INGRATIATE, INGRATITUDE.

grate[1] (grāt) /greyt/ *n.* [*count*] **1.** a frame of metal bars for holding fuel when burning, as in a fireplace, furnace, or stove. **2.** a framework of parallel or crossed bars used as a guard, as over a window; grating.

grate[2] (grāt) /greyt/ *v.*, **grat•ed, grat•ing.** **1.** [~ + *on*] to have an irritating effect: *His constant chatter grates on my nerves.* **2.** to (cause to) make a sound of rough scraping or rubbing that is annoying or noisy; rasp: [*no obj*]: *The car fender grated against the fence.* [~ + *obj*]: *He grated the car fender against the fence.* **3.** [~ + *obj*] to make into small particles by rubbing against a rough surface: *to grate a carrot.* **—grat′er,** *n.* [*count*]

grate•ful (grāt′fəl) /ˈgreytfəl/ *adj.* **1.** thankful; appreciative: *I am grateful for your help.* **2.** expressing gratitude: *a grateful letter.* **—grate′ful•ly,** *adv.* **—grate′ful•ness,** *n.* [*noncount*] See -GRAT-.

grat•i•fy (grat′ə fī′) /ˈgrætəˌfay/ *v.*, **-fied, -fy•ing.** **1.** to give pleasure to (a person or persons): [~ + *obj*]: *Her praise gratified us all.* [*It* + ~ + *obj* + *that clause*]: *It gratified us that we were going home soon.* **2.** [~ + *obj*] to satisfy; indulge: *As a child she always wanted to gratify her desires instantly.* **—grat•i•fi•ca•tion** (grat′ə fi kā′shən) /ˌgrætəfɪˈkeyʃən/ *n.* [*noncount*] See -GRAT-.

grat•i•fy•ing (grat′ə fī′ing) /ˈgrætəˌfayɪŋ/ *adj.* giving pleasure or satisfaction: *gratifying news.* [*It* + *be* + ~ + *to* + *verb*]: *It is gratifying to see so many of you.* [*It* + *be* + ~ + *that clause*]: *It was gratifying that so many people could come.* [*that clause* + *be* + ~]: *That so many people could come was very gratifying.* See -GRAT-.

grat•ing[1] (grā′ting) /ˈgreytɪŋ/ *n.* [*count*] a fixed frame of bars or the like covering an opening, to keep things out while letting in light or air.

grat•ing[2] (grā′ting) /ˈgreytɪŋ/ *adj.* **1.** irritating; annoying: *a grating personality.* **2.** (of sound) harsh; discordant: *a grating voice.*

grat•is (grat′is, grä′tis) /ˈgrætɪs, ˈgrɑtɪs/ *adj.*, *adv.* without charge or payment; free: [*adj.; be* + ~]: *The books are gratis, compliments of your sales representative.* [*adverb*]: *The teachers got the books gratis.* See -GRAT-.

grat•i•tude (grat′i to͞od′, -tyo͞od′) /ˈgrætɪˌtuwd, -ˌtyuwd/ *n.* [*noncount*] the quality or feeling of being grateful. See -GRAT-.

gra•tu•i•tous (grə to͞o′i təs, -tyo͞o′-) /grəˈtuwɪtəs, -ˈtyuw-/ *adj.* **1.** given, done, received, or obtained without charge; free; voluntary: *gratuitous help.* **2.** being without apparent reason or cause; completely undeserved or unnecessary: *a gratuitous insult; gratuitous violence.* See -GRAT-.

gra•tu•i•ty (grə to͞o′i tē, -tyo͞o′-) /grəˈtuwɪtiy, -ˈtyuw-/ *n.* [*count*], *pl.* **-ties.** a gift of money over and above payment due for service; a tip. See -GRAT-.

grave[1] (grāv) /greyv/ *n.* [*count*] **1.** a place in the ground in which to bury a dead body. **2.** any place where a dead body rests: *The doomed ship's passengers went to a watery grave.* **—*Idiom.*** **3. have one foot in the grave,** to be so weak, sick, or old that death appears imminent. **4. make someone turn over in his** or **her grave,** to do something that would presumably have been very offensive, shocking, or insulting to a specified person who is now dead.

grave[2] (grāv) /greyv/ *adj.*, **grav•er, grav•est.** **1.** serious or solemn; sober: *filled with grave thoughts.* **2.** dangerous; threatening: *a grave international crisis.* **—grave′ly,** *adv.* **—grave′ness,** *n.* [*noncount*]

grav•el (grav′əl) /ˈgrævəl/ *n.*, *v.*, **-eled, -el•ing** or (*esp. Brit.*) **-elled, -el•ling,** *adj.* **—***n.* [*noncount*] **1.** small stones and pebbles or a mixture of these with sand. **—***v.* [~ + *obj*] **2.** to cover with gravel: *Graveled the roadbed.* **—***adj.* [*before a noun*] **3.** GRAVELLY (def. 2).

grav•el•ly (grav′əl ē) /ˈgrævəliy/ *adj.* **1.** covered with gravel; like gravel in texture: *a gravelly road.* **2.** sounding rough, harsh, or rasping: *a gravelly voice.*

grav•en (grā′vən) /ˈgreyvən/ *adj.* (of an image) carved.

grave•stone (grāv′stōn′) /ˈgreyvˌstown/ *n.* [*count*] a stone marking a grave and usually giving the name and birth and death dates of the person buried.

grave•yard (grāv′yärd′) /ˈgreyvˌyɑrd/ *n.* [*count*] **1.** CEMETERY. **2.** a place in which old or abandoned objects are kept: *an automobile graveyard.*

grave′yard shift′, *n.* [*count*] **1.** a work shift or schedule usually beginning at about midnight and continuing for about eight hours. **2.** those who work this shift. Also called **grave′yard watch′.**

grav•i•tate (grav′i tāt′) /ˈgrævɪˌteyt/ *v.* [~ + *to/toward* + *obj*], **-tat•ed, -tat•ing.** to be strongly drawn or attracted: *The press gravitated toward the celebrities.*

grav•i•ta•tion (grav′i tā′shən) /ˌgrævɪˈteyʃən/ *n.* [*noncount*] **1.** the force of attraction between any two masses. **2.** a movement or tendency toward something or someone: *the gravitation of people toward the suburbs.* —**grav′i•ta′tion•al,** *adj.* [*often: before a noun*]: *Gravitational force on the moon is less than on the earth.*

grav•i•ty (grav′i tē) /ˈgrævɪtiy/ *n.* [*noncount*] **1.** the force of attraction by which objects tend to fall toward the center of a mass, as that of objects falling on earth. **2.** serious or critical nature: *an illness of considerable gravity.*

gra•vy (grā′vē) /ˈgreyviy/ *n., pl.* **-vies. 1.** the fat and juices of cooked meat, often thickened and seasoned and used as a sauce: [*noncount*]: *served gravy with the roast.* [*count*]: *served two different gravies.* **2.** [*noncount*] *Slang.* **a.** profit or money easily, unexpectedly, or illegally obtained. **b.** something valuable obtained as a benefit beyond what is due or expected.

gray or **grey** (grā) /grey/ *adj.,* **gray•er, gray•est** or **grey•er, grey•est,** *n.* —*adj.* **1.** of a color between white and black; having a neutral hue. **2.** dull and dreary: *gray skies.* **3.** having gray hair: *was prematurely gray.* **4.** [*before a noun*] not clearly one thing or the other: *the gray area between realism and abstraction.* —*n.* **5.** [*noncount*] a color intermediate between white and black. **6.** gray material or clothing: [*noncount*]: *to dress in gray.* [*count*]: *dressed in grays and blues.* **7.** [*count*] a horse of a gray color. —**gray′ish,** *adj.* —**gray′ness,** *n.* [*noncount*]

gray•beard (grā′bērd′) /ˈgreyˌbɪərd/ *n.* [*count*] an old man.

gray′ mat′ter, *n.* [*noncount*] **1.** reddish gray nerve tissue of the brain and spinal cord, consisting chiefly of nerve cell bodies, with few nerve fibers. Compare WHITE MATTER. **2.** *Informal.* brains or intellect.

graze[1] (grāz) /greyz/ *v.,* **grazed, graz•ing. 1.** to feed on growing grass or other plant life, as cattle, sheep, etc., do: [~ + *on*]: *grazing on the grass in the field.* [~ + *obj*]: *The deer had grazed the area so thoroughly that there was nothing left.* **2.** [*no obj*] *Informal.* **a.** to eat small portions of food in place of regular meals. **b.** to sample small portions of a variety of foods at one meal. —**graz′er,** *n.* [*count*]

graze[2] (grāz) /greyz/ *v.,* **grazed, graz•ing,** *n.* —*v.* **1.** to touch or rub lightly in passing: [~ + *obj*]: *His knee grazed the chair.* [*no obj*]: *His knee grazed against the rough wall.* **2.** [~ + *obj*] to scrape the skin from: *The bullet just grazed his shoulder.* —*n.* [*count*] **3.** a touching or rubbing lightly in passing. **4.** a slight scratch; abrasion.

grease (*n.* grēs; *v.* grēs, grēz) / *n.* griys; *v.* griys, griyz/ *n., v.,* **greased, greasing.** —*n.* [*noncount*] **1.** the melted fat of animals, esp. when in a soft state. **2.** fatty or oily matter in general; lubricant: *grease for the axle of the car.* —*v.* [~ + *obj*] **3.** to put grease on; lubricate: *to grease the axle of a car.* **4.** to make smooth: *Money greased his way in society.* —***Idiom.*** **5. grease someone's palm** or **hand,** to give someone money as a bribe.

grease•paint or **grease paint** (grēs′pānt′) /ˈgriysˌpeynt/ *n.* [*noncount*] an oily mixture of melted wax or grease and a coloring substance, used by actors, clowns, etc., for making up or decorating their faces.

greas•y (grē′sē, -zē) /ˈgriysiy, -ziy/ *adj.,* **-i•er, -i•est. 1.** smeared or soiled with grease: *a greasy engine.* **2.** made up of or containing grease: *greasy food.* **3.** greaselike in appearance or to the touch: *greasy hair.* **4.** trying too hard to please; unctuous: *a greasy smile.* —**greas′i•ness,** *n.* [*noncount*]

great (grāt) /greyt/ *adj.,* **-er, -est,** *adv., n., pl.* **greats,** (*esp. when thought of as a group*) **great,** *interj.* —*adj.* **1.** unusually or comparatively large in size, dimensions, or number; big; numerous: *great herds of buffalo.* **2.** unusual or considerable in degree, power, or intensity: *great pain.* **3.** first-rate; excellent: *to have a great time.* **4.** healthy; well: *feeling great.* **5.** [*before a noun*] notable; remarkable: *a great occasion.* **6.** [*before a noun*] important; consequential: *the great issues in American history.* **7.** [*before a noun*] distinguished; famous: *a great inventor.* **8.** [*before a noun*] of noble character: *great thoughts.* **9.** [*before a noun*] of high rank or social standing: *a great lady.* **10.** having unusual merit; very admirable: *a great statesman.* **11.** [*before a noun*] of great or unusual length: *to wait a great while.* **12.** *Informal.* **a.** [*be* + ~ + *on/for*] enthusiastic about some specified activity: *She's a great one for talking.* **b.** [*be* + ~ + *at*] skillful; expert: *She's great at golf.* **13.** [*before a noun*] being of one generation older or younger than the family relative specified (used in combination): *a great-grandson.* —*adv.* **14.** *Informal.* very well: *Things are going great.* **15.** very: *a great big hole.* —*n.* **16.** [*count*] a person who has achieved distinction in a field: *one of the theater's greats.* **17.** [*part of a title; the* + ~] This word is used as part of the title of a king or ruler who is or was considered very important: *Alexander the Great.* —*interj.* **18.** This word is used to express acceptance, appreciation, approval, admiration, etc.: *You won the award? Great!* **19.** This word is used ironically to express disappointment, annoyance, distress, etc.: *Oh, great. Another visit from the in-laws.* —**great′ness,** *n.* [*noncount*]

great•coat (grāt′kōt′) /ˈgreytˌkowt/ *n.* [*count*] a heavy overcoat.

great•ly (grāt′lē) /ˈgreytliy/ *adv.* very much; to a great degree: *His health has greatly improved.*

greed (grēd) /griyd/ *n.* [*noncount*] excessive or overly strong desire, esp. for wealth, profit, or possessions; avarice.

greed•y (grē′dē) /ˈgriydiy/ *adj.,* **-i•er, -i•est. 1.** excessively or overly desiring wealth, possessions, etc.; avaricious. **2.** having a strong or great desire for food or drink. **3.** keenly desirous; eager: *greedy for love.* —**greed•i•ly** (grēd′l ē) /ˈgriydḷiy/ *adv.* —**greed′i•ness,** *n.* [*noncount*]

Greek (grēk) /griyk/ *adj.* **1.** of or relating to Greece. **2.** of or relating to the language spoken in Greece. —*n.* **3.** [*count*] a person born or living in Greece. **4.** [*noncount*] the language spoken in ancient or modern Greece. **5.** [*noncount*] something difficult to understand: *This contract is Greek to me.*

green (grēn) /griyn/ *adj.,* **-er, -est,** *n.* —*adj.* **1.** of the color of growing plants, between yellow and blue: *green leaves.* **2.** covered with growing plants or foliage: *green fields.* **3.** [*usually: before a noun*] consisting of green, usually leafy vegetables, as lettuce, spinach, or chicory: *a green salad.* **4.** not fully developed or matured; unripe: *green fruit.* **5.** immature in age or judgment; inexperienced: *green recruits.* **6.** having a sickly or pale appearance: *to turn green with nausea.* **7.** [*before a noun; often: Green*] advocating or promoting environmentalism: *a green political party.* —*n.* **8.** a color between yellow and blue, found in nature as the color of most grasses and leaves while growing: [*noncount*]: *The room was painted in green.* [*count*]: *The room was painted a pale green.* **9. greens,** [*plural*] **a.** the leaves and stems of certain plants, as spinach, kale, or lettuce, eaten as a vegetable. **b.** fresh leaves or branches of evergreen trees: *a room decorated with Christmas greens.* **10.** [*count*] grassy land; a plot of grassy ground, esp. in the center of a town. **11.** [*count*] Also called **putting green.** the area of closely cut grass surrounding each hole on a golf course. **12.** [*noncount; usually: the* + ~] *Slang.* money. —***Idiom.*** **13. green with envy,** [*be* + ~] extremely jealous. —**green′ish,** *adj.* —**green′ness,** *n.* [*noncount*]

green•back (grēn′bak′) /ˈgriynˌbæk/ *n.* [*count*] a U.S. bill of money, printed in green on the back.

green′ bean′, *n.* [*count*] the slender immature green pod of the kidney bean, eaten as a vegetable.

green•belt (grēn′belt′) /ˈgriynˌbɛlt/ *n.* [*count*] **1.** an area of woods, parks, or open land surrounding a community. **2.** Also, **green′ belt′.** a strip of land on the edge of a desert that has been planted and irrigated to keep the desert from spreading.

green•er•y (grē′nə rē) /ˈgriynəriy/ *n., pl.* **-er•ies.** [*noncount*] **1.** green foliage or vegetation. **2.** [*noncount*] greens used for decoration.

green′-eyed′, *adj.* jealous; envious.

green•gro•cer (grēn′grō′sər) /ˈgriynˌgrowsər/ *n.* [*count*] a seller of fresh vegetables and fruit.

green•horn (grēn′hôrn′) /ˈgriynˌhɔrn/ *n.* [*count*] **1.** an untrained or inexperienced person. **2.** a newly arrived immigrant; newcomer.

green•house (grēn′hous′) /ˈgriynˌhaws/ *n.* [*count*] a

building, room, or area, usually chiefly of glass, used for growing tender plants or plants out of season.

green′house effect′, *n.* [*count; usually singular: the* + ~] the long-term heating of the atmosphere resulting from the absorption of energy from the sun by certain gases in the atmosphere, as carbon dioxide and water vapor, which trap energy that normally would escape and allow cooling.

green′house gas′, *n.* [*count*] any of the gases that absorb energy from the sun and so contribute to the greenhouse effect, including carbon dioxide, methane, ozone, and the fluorocarbons.

green′ on′ion, *n.* [*count*] a young onion with a slender green stalk and a small bulb; scallion.

green′ pep′per, *n.* [*count*] the mild-flavored, unripe fruit of the bell or sweet pepper, used as a vegetable.

green•room (grēn′ro͞om′, -ro͝om′) /ˈgriynˌruwm, -ˌrʊm/ *n.* [*count*] a lounge in a theater, television studio, etc., for use by performers when they are not onstage or on the set.

green′ thumb′, *n.* [*count; usually singular; a* + ~] an exceptional skill for gardening or for growing plants successfully: *has a green thumb for indoor plants.*

Green′wich Time′ (gren′ich) /ˈgrɛnɪtʃ/ *n.* [*proper noun*] the time as measured on the prime meridian running through Greenwich, England, used in England and as a standard of calculation elsewhere. Also called **Green′wich Mean′ Time′.**

greet (grēt) /griyt/ *v.* [~ + *obj*] **1.** to speak or act in some form of welcome: *greeted us at the door.* **2.** to meet or receive: *greeted my suggestion with applause.* **3.** to make itself noticed to: *Music greeted our ears.*

greet•ing (grē′ting) /ˈgriytɪŋ/ *n.* **1.** an act or words of welcoming: [*noncount*]: *lifted her hand in greeting.* [*count*]: *We didn't get a very friendly greeting.* **2.** **greetings,** [*plural*] an expression of friendly or respectful regard: *sending our greetings.*

-greg-, *root.* *-greg-* comes from Latin, where it has the meaning "group; flock." This meaning is found in such words as: AGGREGATE, CONGREGATE, DESEGREGATE, GREGARIOUS, SEGREGATE.

gre•gar•i•ous (gri gâr′ē əs) /grɪˈgɛəriyəs/ *adj.* **1.** fond of the company of others; sociable: *A politician must be friendly and gregarious.* **2.** living in flocks or herds, as animals. —**gre•gar′i•ous•ly,** *adv.* —**gre•gar′i•ous•ness,** *n.* [*noncount*] See -GREG-.

grem•lin (grem′lin) /ˈgrɛmlɪn/ *n.* [*count*] an imaginary, mischievous being humorously accused of causing mechanical failures in aircraft or problems or disruptions in any activity.

gre•nade (gri nād′) /grɪˈneyd/ *n.* [*count*] a small shell containing an explosive or a chemical, as tear gas, and thrown by hand or fired from a rifle or launching device.

Gre•na•di•an (gri nā′dē ən) /grɪˈneydiyən/ *adj.* **1.** of or relating to Grenada. —*n.* [*count*] **2.** a person born or living in Grenada.

-gress-, *root.* *-gress-* comes from Latin, where it has the meaning "step; move." It is related to -GRAD-. This meaning is found in such words as: AGGRESSION, CONGRESS, DIGRESS, EGRESS, INGRESS, PROGRESS, REGRESS, TRANSGRESS.

grew (gro͞o) /gruw/ *v.* pt. of GROW.

grey (grā) /grey/ *adj.*, **-er, -est,** *n.*, *v.* GRAY.

grey•hound (grā′hound′) /ˈgreyˌhawnd/ *n.* [*count*] one of a breed of tall, slender shorthaired dogs noted for their keen sight and swiftness.

grid (grid) /grɪd/ *n.* [*count*] **1.** a grating of crossed bars; gridiron. **2.** a network of evenly spaced lines running up and down and left to right, for locating points on a map, chart, building plan, or aerial photograph by means of a system of coordinates. **3.** any network resembling this. **4.** a system of electrical distribution serving a large area, esp. by means of high-tension wires: *a power grid.* **5.** Also, **gridiron.** a municipal road plan in which all or most roads and streets cross at right angles. **6.** GRIDIRON (def. 1).

grid•dle (grid′l) /ˈgrɪdl̩/ *n.* [*count*] a flat pan for cooking pancakes, bacon, etc., over direct heat with little or no fat.

grid•dle•cake (grid′l kāk′) /ˈgrɪdl̩ˌkeyk/ *n.* [*count*] a pancake.

grid•i•ron (grid′ī′ərn) /ˈgrɪdˌayərn/ *n.* [*count*] **1.** a football field. **2.** a utensil consisting of parallel metal bars on which to broil meat or other food. **3.** any framework or network resembling a gridiron.

grid•lock (grid′lok′) /ˈgrɪdˌlɒk/ *n.* **1.** [*noncount*] a major traffic jam in which all movement comes to a stop because important intersections are blocked by traffic: *The city suffered from gridlock today for the third day in a row.* **2.** a complete stoppage of normal activity: [*count*]: *a financial gridlock resulting from high interest rates.* [*noncount*]: *complete gridlock, with no money coming in and none going out.* —*v.* **3.** to (cause to) undergo a gridlock: [*no obj*]: *Traffic gridlocked at key intersections today.* [~ + *obj*]: *Traffic was gridlocked all day.*

grief (grēf) /griyf/ *n.* **1.** [*noncount*] great mental suffering or distress over a loss or disappointment; sharp sorrow; painful regret. **2.** [*count; usually singular*] a cause or occasion of keen distress or sorrow: *His leaving was a great grief to her.* **3.** [*noncount*] *Informal.* trouble; difficulty; annoyance: *Don't let him give you any grief.* —***Idiom.*** **4.** **come to grief,** to suffer misfortune: *All his great ideas came to grief.* **5.** **good grief,** This phrase is used to express mild dismay or surprise: *Good grief, it's started to rain again!*

griev•ance (grē′vəns) /ˈgriyvəns/ *n.* **1.** [*count*] a wrong or unjust act considered as grounds for complaint. **2.** [*noncount*] a complaint: *She filed a grievance with her union.*

grieve (grēv) /griyv/ *v.*, **grieved, griev•ing.** to (cause to) feel grief, distress, or great sorrow: [*no obj*]: *She grieved for her lost dog.* [~ + *obj*]: *Her loss grieved me.* [*It* + ~ + *obj* + *to* + *verb*]: *It grieves me to refuse.* [*It* + ~ + *obj* + *that clause*]: *It grieves me deeply that she left.* —**griev′er,** *n.* [*count*]

griev•ous (grē′vəs) /ˈgriyvəs/ *adj.* **1.** causing grief or great sorrow: *a grievous loss.* **2.** causing serious harm; terrible: *a grievous offense.* **3.** characterized by great pain or suffering: *caused grievous bodily harm.* **4.** causing a great burden; oppressive: *a grievous tax.* —**griev′ous•ly,** *adv.*

grif•fin (grif′in) /ˈgrɪfɪn/ also **griffon, gryphon,** *n.* [*count*] an imaginary monster, usually having the head and wings of an eagle and the body of a lion.

grill[1] (gril) /grɪl/ *n.* [*count*] **1.** an apparatus with a grated metal framework for cooking food over direct heat, as a gas or charcoal fire. **2.** a metal grate for broiling food over a fire; gridiron. **3.** a dish of grilled meat, fish, vegetables, etc. **4.** a restaurant, or a part of a restaurant, where grilled food is served. —*v.* [~ + *obj*] **5.** to broil on a grill: *We'll grill a steak.* **6.** to ask (someone) questions in a hostile, severe, and persistent way: *The lawyer grilled the witness.*

grill[2] (gril) /grɪl/ *n.* GRILLE.

grille or **grill** (gril) /grɪl/ *n.* [*count*] **1.** a grating or barrier, as for a gate, usually of metal and often of decorative design. **2.** an opening covered by a grill for admitting air to cool the engine of an automobile or the like. **3.** a screen used to cover something, as a loudspeaker.

grim (grim) /grɪm/ *adj.*, **grim•mer, grim•mest.** **1.** stern; allowing no compromise; unyielding: *grim determination; a grim look.* **2.** of a sinister or ghastly character: *a grim murder mystery; a grim joke.* **3.** fierce, savage, or cruel: *War is a grim business.* **4.** unpleasant: *Things will get pretty grim for him if he doesn't change.* —**grim′ly,** *adv.* —**grim′ness,** *n.* [*noncount*]

grim•ace (grim′əs, gri mās′) /ˈgrɪməs, grɪˈmeys/ *n.*, *v.*, **-aced, -ac•ing.** —*n.* [*count*] **1.** a facial expression, often ugly or twisted, that indicates disapproval, pain, etc. —*v.* [*no obj*] **2.** to make grimaces: *She grimaced from the pain.*

grime (grīm) /graym/ *n.* [*noncount*] dirt or soot clinging to or embedded in a surface. —**grim′y,** *adj.*, **-i•er, -i•est.**

grin (grin) /grɪn/ *v.*, **grinned, grin•ning,** *n.* —*v.* **1.** to smile broadly: [*no obj*]: *He grinned delightedly.* [~ + *at* + *obj*]: *She grinned at her guest.* [~ + *obj*]: *He grinned his appreciation.* —*n.* [*count*] **2.** a broad smile. —***Idiom.*** **3.** **grin and bear it,** to suffer from something unpleasant without complaining.

grind (grind) /graynd/ *v.*, **ground** (ground) /grawnd/ **grind•ing,** *n.* —*v.* **1.** [~ + *obj*] to wear down, make smooth, or sharpen (something) by rubbing or friction: *to grind a lens; to grind knives.* **2.** to crush (something) into small particles, as by pounding; pulverize: [~ + *obj*]: *She accidentally ground the dirt into the rug.* [~ + *up* + *obj*]: *The glass bottles were ground up for recycling.* **3.** [~ + *down* + *obj*] to oppress, torment, or crush: *They were ground down by poverty.* **4.** [~ + *obj*] to grate together; grit: *She used to grind her teeth.* **5.** [~ + *obj*] to operate by turning a crank: *to grind a hand organ.* **6.** [~ + *obj*] to produce by crushing or hard rubbing: *The mill grinds flour.* **7.** to (cause to) rub harshly; grate: [*no obj*]: *The gears ground whenever I shifted.* [~ + *obj*]: *I kept grinding the gears.* **8.** [~ + *away*] to work or study hard or for long hours. **9.** [*no obj*] (in a dance) to rotate the hips in a suggestive manner. Compare BUMP (def. 9). **10. grind out, a.** to produce in a routine or mechanical way: [~ + *out* + *obj*]: *ground out another issue of the newspaper.* [~ + *obj* + *out*]: *Would they grind another issue out in time?* **b.** to extinguish (a cigarette or cigar) against a surface: [~ + *out* + *obj*]: *He ground out his cigarette.* [~ + *obj* + *out*]: *He ground his cigarette out.* —*n.* [*count*] **11.** a grade of fineness into which a substance is ground into particles: *That coffee is available in various grinds.* **12.** [*usually singular*] laborious, usually uninteresting work: *the daily grind.* **13.** *Informal.* a student who works and studies hard. **14.** a dance movement in which the hips are rotated in a suggestive manner. Compare BUMP (def. 16).

grind•er (grīn′dər) /ˈgrayndər/ *n.* [*count*] **1.** a person or thing that grinds, as an appliance for grinding food. **2.** a sharpener of tools. **3. a.** a molar tooth. **b. grinders,** [*plural*] *Slang.* the teeth. **4.** *Chiefly New England and Inland North.* HERO (def. 4).

grind•stone (grīnd′stōn′) /ˈgraynd,stown/ *n.* [*count*] **1.** a rotating solid stone wheel used for sharpening, shaping, etc. —***Idiom.*** **2. keep** or **put one's nose to the grindstone,** to work, study, or practice hard and steadily.

grip (grip) /grɪp/ *n., v.,* **gripped, grip•ping.** —*n.* [*count*] **1.** the act of grasping; a seizing and holding fast; firm grasp: *held the hammer securely in his grip.* **2.** the power of grasping or holding fast: *She has a strong grip when she shakes hands.* **3.** mental or intellectual grasp or hold or emotional control: *had a good grip on the problem.* **4.** competence or firmness in dealing with things: *He's beginning to lose his grip on reality.* **5.** a special mode of clasping hands: *a secret grip.* **6.** a handle or hilt: *a jeweled grip on a sword.* **7.** a suitcase. **8.** a stagehand. —*v.* [~ + *obj*] **9.** to grasp or seize firmly; hold fast: *I gripped the pole on the subway car to keep from falling.* **10.** to hold the interest of: *to grip the mind.* —***Idiom.*** **11. come to grips with,** [~ + *obj*] to face and cope with: *to come to grips with a problem.* —**grip′per,** *n.* [*count*]

gripe (grīp) /grayp/ *v.,* **griped, grip•ing,** *n.* —*v.* [*no obj*] **1.** *Informal.* to complain naggingly; grumble: *soldiers griping about mess-hall food.* —*n.* [*count*] **2.** *Informal.* a nagging complaint: *I've got a few gripes.* **3.** Usually, **the gripes.** [*plural*] spasmodic pain in the intestines. —**grip′er,** *n.* [*count*]

grippe (grip) /grɪp/ *n. Older Use.* INFLUENZA.

grip•ping (grip′ing) /ˈgrɪpɪŋ/ *adj.* holding one's interest intensely: *a gripping novel.*

gris•ly (griz′lē) /ˈgrɪzliy/ *adj.,* **-li•er, -li•est.** causing a feeling of horror; gruesome: *a grisly murder.*

grist (grist) /grɪst/ *n.* [*noncount*] **1.** grain to be ground, or that is ground. —***Idiom.*** **2. grist for** or **to one's mill,** something used to one's profit or advantage.

gris•tle (gris′əl) /ˈgrɪsəl/ *n.* [*noncount*] cartilage, esp. in meat. —**gris′tly,** *adj.,* **-tli•er, -tli•est:** *gristly beef.*

grit (grit) /grɪt/ *n., v.,* **grit•ted, grit•ting.** —*n.* [*noncount*] **1.** hard, abrasive particles, as of sand, stone, or gravel. **2.** firmness of character; pluck: *showed grit in the face of danger.* —***Idiom.*** **3. grit one's teeth,** to show forbearance or determination by or as if by clamping or grinding the teeth together.

grits (grits) /grɪts/ *n.* coarsely ground hominy, usually boiled and served as a breakfast cereal or a side dish: [*plural; used with a plural verb*]: *Grits make a hearty meal.* [*noncount; used with a singular verb*]: *Grits is quite nutritious.*

grit•ty (grit′ē) /ˈgrɪtiy/ *adj.,* **-ti•er, -ti•est. 1.** full of coarse particles, as of sand, stone, or gravel. **2.** showing determination and firmness: *a gritty fighter.*

griz•zled (griz′əld) /ˈgrɪzəld/ *adj.* having gray or partly gray hair: *the grizzled old war veteran.*

griz•zly (griz′lē) /ˈgrɪzliy/ *n., pl.* **-zlies.** GRIZZLY BEAR.

griz′zly bear′, *n.* [*count*] a large North American brown bear with rough, gray-tipped fur.

groan (grōn) /grown/ *n.* [*count*] **1.** a low, mournful sound made in response to pain or grief. **2.** a deeper, similar sound made to express contempt, dislike, disapproval, etc.: *Groans greeted the disappointing announcement.* **3.** a deep grating or creaking sound due to a continued heavy weight or strain: *The groan of the timbers in the wind.* —*v.* [*no obj*] **4.** to utter a deep, mournful sound that expresses pain or grief; moan: *He groaned from the pain.* **5.** to make a deep, similar sound to express contempt, dislike, disapproval, etc.: *The audience groaned at the joke.* **6.** to make a sound resembling a groan: *The steps of the old house groaned under my weight.*

gro•cer (grō′sər) /ˈgrowsər/ *n.* [*count*] the owner or operator of a store that sells groceries.

gro•cer•y (grō′sə rē, grōs′rē) /ˈgrowsəriy, ˈgrowsriy/ *n.* [*count*], *pl.* **-cer•ies. 1.** Also called **gro′cery store′.** a grocer's store. **2.** Usually, **groceries.** [*plural*] food and other commodities sold by a grocer.

grog (grog) /grɒg/ *n.* [*noncount*] **1.** a mixture of rum and water, often flavored with lemon, sugar, and spices and sometimes served hot. **2.** any alcoholic drink.

grog•gy (grog′ē) /ˈgrɒgiy/ *adj.,* **-gi•er, -gi•est. 1.** staggering, as from exhaustion or blows. **2.** dazed, as from lack of sleep. —**grog′gi•ly,** *adv.* —**grog′gi•ness,** *n.* [*noncount*]

groin (groin) /grɔyn/ *n.* [*count*] the place where the thigh joins the abdomen.

grom•met (grom′it, grum′-) /ˈgrɒmɪt, ˈgrʌm-/ *n.* [*count*] a ring or washer, esp. one used as a small hole protecting material where a rope passes.

groom (grōōm, grŏŏm) /gruwm, grʊm/ *n.* [*count*] **1.** BRIDEGROOM. **2.** a man or boy in charge of horses or a stable. —*v.* [~ + *obj*] **3.** to make (oneself or one's clothing) neat or tidy: *She groomed herself carefully before the meeting.* **4.** (of an animal) to tend (itself or another) by removing dirt or unwanted tiny organisms from the fur, skin, feathers, etc.: *Monkeys groom each other.* **5.** to clean, brush, and otherwise tend (a horse, dog, etc.). **6.** to prepare for a position, election, etc.: *The mayor is being groomed for higher office.* —**groom′er,** *n.* [*count*]

groove (grōōv) /gruwv/ *n., v.,* **grooved, groov•ing.** —*n.* [*count*] **1.** a long, narrow cut or indentation in a surface. **2.** a track or channel of a phonograph record for the needle or stylus to follow. **3.** [*usually singular*] a fixed routine: *to get into a groove.* —*v.* **4.** [~ + *obj*] to cut or make a groove in; furrow. **5.** [*no obj*] *Slang.* to enjoy oneself in a relaxed way: *grooving to the music.* —***Idiom.*** **6. in the groove,** *Slang.* in perfect form: *The tennis star is really in the groove now, hitting the ball well.*

groov•y (grōō′vē) /ˈgruwviy/ *adj.,* **-i•er, -i•est.** *Slang.* fashionably attractive; wonderful; great: *groovy music; a groovy car.*

grope (grōp) /growp/ *v.,* **groped, grop•ing,** *n.* —*v.* **1.** to feel about with the hands; feel one's way hesitantly: [*no obj*]: *to grope around in the darkness.* [~ + *obj*]: *I groped my way up the dark stairs.* **2.** [~ + *for*] to search uncertainly: *were groping for an answer to the latest crisis.* **3.** [~ + *obj*] *Slang.* to touch or handle (someone) sexually; fondle. —*n.* [*count*] **4.** an act or instance of groping. —**grop′er,** *n.* [*count*]

gross (grōs) /grows/ *adj.,* **-er, -est,** *n., pl.* **gross** for 7, **gross•es** for 8, *v.* —*adj.* **1.** without or before deductions; total (opposed to *net*): *gross earnings.* **2.** [*before a noun*] flagrant and extreme; glaring: *gross injustice.* **3.** indecent; vulgar: *gross language.* **4.** *Slang.* revolting; disgusting: *a really gross habit.* **5.** extremely or excessively fat. **6.** of or relating to only the broadest or most general considerations. —*n.* **7.** [*count*] a group of 12 dozen, or 144, things. *Abbr.:* gro.: *Bring in several gross of the pencils.* **8.** [*noncount*] total income, profits, etc., before any deductions (opposed to *net*). —*v.* [~ + *obj*] **9.** to earn as a total before any deductions: *The company grossed over three million dollars last year.* **10. gross out,** *Slang.* to disgust or offend: [~ + *obj* + *out*]: *That food really grossed me out.* [~ + *out* + *obj*]: *He tried to gross out the cheerleaders.* —**gross′ly,** *adv.* —**gross′ness,** *n.* [*noncount*]

gross′ na′tional prod′uct, *n.* [*count*] the total value of all goods and services produced in a country during one year. *Abbr.:* GNP

gro•tesque (grō tesk′) /growˈtɛsk/ *adj.* odd or unnatural in shape, appearance, or character; fantastically ugly or absurd; bizarre: *a grotesque statue of a human head on top of a lion's body.* —**gro•tesque′ly,** *adv.*

grot•to (grot′ō) /ˈgrɒtow/ *n.* [*count*], *pl.* **-toes, -tos. 1.** a cave or cavern. **2.** an artificial structure that resembles a small cave.

grouch (grouch) /grawtʃ/ *n.* [*count*] **1.** a complaining and continually unhappy person: *an old grouch.* —*v.* [*no obj*] **2.** to complain irritably or unhappily: *He grouched about his job.* —**grouch′i•ness,** *n.* [*noncount*] —**grouch′y,** *adj.,* **-i•er, -i•est.**

ground[1] (ground) /grawnd/ *n.* **1.** [*noncount; the* + ~] the solid surface of the earth; firm or dry land. **2.** [*noncount*] soil: *poor ground for growing crops.* **3.** [*noncount*] land having an indicated shape, quality, or character: *sloping ground.* **4.** [*count*] Often, **grounds.** [*plural*] an area of land put to a special use: *picnic grounds;*

hunting grounds. **5.** [*count*] Often, **grounds.** [*plural*] reason or cause; the foundation or basis on which a belief or action rests: *grounds for divorce.* **6.** [*noncount*] subject for or focus of discussion; topic: *We covered that ground in the last meeting.* **7.** [*noncount*] the main surface or background, as in a painting. **8. grounds,** [*plural*] leftover material, as from coffee that has been brewed: *coffee grounds.* **9. grounds,** [*plural*] the gardens, lawn, etc., surrounding and belonging to a building. **10.** [*noncount*] a conducting connection between an electric circuit or equipment and the earth or some other conducting body. *—adj.* [*before a noun*] **11.** operating on land: *ground forces; a ground attack.* *—v.* **12.** [~ + *obj*] to place (an idea, belief, or argument) on a firm or logical foundation: *an argument firmly grounded in logic.* **13.** [~ + *obj*] to instruct (someone) in basic principles: *to ground students in science.* **14.** [~ + *obj*] to establish a ground (def. 10) for (an electric circuit, device, etc.): *This appliance isn't grounded.* **15.** to (cause a vessel to) run aground: [*no obj*]: *The ship grounded on the sand bar.* [~ + *obj*]: *They accidentally grounded the boat on a sand bar.* **16.** [~ + *obj*] to restrict (an aircraft or pilot) to the ground; prevent from flying: *If the pilot used drugs, he was grounded.* **17.** [~ + *obj*] to restrict the activities, esp. the social activities, of usually as a punishment: *His parents grounded him for hitting another student.* **—*Idiom.*** **18. break ground, a.** to plow. **b.** to begin excavation for a construction project. **c.** Also, **break new ground.** to do something original or innovative. **19. cover (new) ground, a.** to travel over a certain area: *We covered a lot of ground in the car.* **b.** to deal with new material: *didn't cover any new ground in yesterday's class.* **20. cut the ground (out) from under,** [~ + *obj*] to make (someone or something) less effective or useful by some action taken ahead of time. **21. from the ground up, a.** gradually from the most elementary level to the highest level. **b.** extensively; thoroughly; completely: *knew his subject from the ground up.* **22. gain ground,** to make progress; advance. **23. give ground,** to retreat before a stronger force: *The weaker army began to give ground.* **24. hold** or **stand one's ground,** to maintain one's position. **25. into the ground,** beyond a reasonable or necessary point: *to run an argument into the ground.* **26. lose ground,** to lose one's advantage; fail to advance. **27. off the ground,** into action or well under way: *The plan never got off the ground.* **28. on one's own ground,** in an area or situation that one knows well. **29. shift ground,** to change position in an argument or situation.

ground[2] (ground) /grawnd/ *v.* **1.** a pt. and pp. of GRIND. *—adj.* **2.** reduced to fine particles or very small pieces by grinding: *ground beef.* **3.** having the surface roughened by or as if by grinding: *ground glass.*

ground′ ball′, *n.* [*count*] a batted baseball that rolls or bounces along the ground. Also called **grounder.**

ground′ floor′, *n.* [*count; often: the* + ~] **1.** the floor of a building at or nearest to ground level. **2.** *Informal.* a position or opportunity starting in a new enterprise that provides an advantage: *We got in on the ground floor of software development.*

ground•hog (ground′hôg′, -hog′) /ˈgrawndˌhɔg, -ˌhɒg/ *n.* WOODCHUCK.

ground•less (ground′lis) /ˈgrawndlɪs/ *adj.* without reasonable or rational basis; unfounded: *groundless fears.*

ground•nut (ground′nut′) /ˈgrawndˌnʌt/ *n.* [*count*] a peanut.

ground′ rule′, *n.* [*count*] **1.** a basic or governing principle of conduct in a situation, used in judging other cases: *the ground rules of the debate.* **2.** any of certain sports rules adopted, as in baseball, for playing in a particular stadium or field.

ground•swell (ground′swel′) /ˈgrawndˌswɛl/ *n.* [*count*] **1.** a broad, deep swell or rolling of the sea, due to a distant storm or gale. **2.** a surge or sudden outpouring of feelings, esp. among the general public: *a groundswell of support for the governor.*

ground•work (ground′wûrk′) /ˈgrawndˌwɜrk/ *n.* [*noncount*] foundation or basis: *to lay the groundwork for an alliance.*

group (gro͞op) /gruwp/ *n.* [*count*] **1.** any collection or assembly of persons or things, considered together as being related in some way: *a group of students.* **2.** a number of musicians who play together: *a rock group.* *—v.* **3.** to (cause to) place or form together in a group: [~ + *obj*]: *We grouped the students by age.* [~ + *obj* + *into*]: *grouped the errors into several types.* [*no obj*]: *The workers and their families grouped together to protest.*

group•ie (gro͞o′pē) /ˈgruwpiy/ *n.* [*count*] **1.** a person who is a fan of rock musicians and may follow them on tour. **2.** an ardent fan of a celebrity or of a particular activity: *a tennis groupie.*

group′ ther′apy, *n.* [*noncount*] psychotherapy in which a group of patients, led by a therapist, attempt to solve their problems.

grouse[1] (grous) /graws/ *n.* [*count*], *pl.* **grouse, grous•es.** a plump bird of the pheasant family, with a short bill and feathered legs.

grouse[2] (grous) /graws/ *v.*, **groused, grous•ing,** *n.* *Informal.* *—v.* **1.** to grumble; complain: [*no obj*]: *He was always grousing about his job.* [~ + *that clause*]: *He was always grousing that he hated his job.* *—n.* [*count*] **2.** a complaint. *—***grous′er,** *n.* [*count*]

grove (grōv) /growv/ *n.* [*count*] **1.** a small wood or forest-like area, usually with no undergrowth. **2.** a small orchard or stand of fruit-bearing trees, esp. citrus trees.

grov•el (grov′əl, gruv′-) /ˈgrɒvəl, ˈgrʌv-/ *v.* [*no obj*], **-eled, -el•ing** or (*esp. Brit.*) **-elled, -el•ling. 1.** to lie or crawl with the face downward and the body flat, as in fear. **2.** to humble oneself: *always groveling before the boss, begging for favors.* *—***grov′el•er,** *esp. Brit.,* **grov′el•ler,** *n.* [*count*]

grow (grō) /grow/ *v.*, **grew** (gro͞o) /gruw/ **grown, grow•ing.** *—v.* **1.** [*no obj*] to increase in size by a natural process of development: *The children have grown tall.* **2.** (of hair) to (cause to) become longer: [*no obj*]: *let her hair grow to her waist.* [~ + *obj*]: *I'm trying to grow a beard.* **3.** to (cause to) come into being and develop (as by planting and cultivating): [*no obj*]: *Several different kinds of plants grow wild here.* [~ + *obj*]: *The farmers grow corn in that region.* **4.** [*no obj*] to become stronger or more profound: *Our friendship grew.* **5.** [*no obj*] to increase gradually in size, amount, etc.; expand: *Her influence has grown.* **6.** [*no obj*] to become gradually attached (or apart) by or as if by growth: *We grew together as our common interests merged. The couple grew apart.* **7.** to come to be by degrees or gradually; become: [~ + *adj*]: *to grow old.* [~ + *to* + *verb*]: *I soon grew to love that job.* [~ + *into* + *obj*]: *The little girl grew into a fine young woman.* **8. grow into,** [~ + *obj*] **a.** to become large or tall enough to wear (an item of clothing): *The youngest daughter grew into her sister's clothes.* **b.** to become mature or experienced enough to handle: *He eventually grew into his job.* **9. grow on** or **upon,** [~ + *obj*] to become gradually more liked or accepted by: *His jokes will grow on you.* **10. grow out of,** [~ + *obj*] **a.** to become too large or mature for; outgrow: *has already grown out of her baby clothes.* **b.** to originate in; develop from: *The program grew out of a simple idea.* **11. grow up,** [*no obj*] **a.** to be or become fully grown; to attain maturity. **b.** to come into existence; arise: *New cities grew up in the desert.* *—***grow′er,** *n.* [*count*]

growl (groul) /grawl/ *v.* **1.** to utter a deep, throaty sound of anger or hostility: [*no obj*]: *The dog growled.* [~ + *obj*]: *The dog growled a warning.* **2.** [*no obj*] to murmur angrily; grumble: *He's been growling at his secretary.* **3.** [*no obj*] to rumble: *The thunder growled.* *—n.* [*count*] **4.** the act or sound of growling: *a loud growl.* *—***growl′er,** *n.* [*count*]

grown (grōn) /grown/ *adj.* **1.** arrived at full growth or maturity; adult: *a grown man.* *—v.* **2.** pp. of GROW.

grown′-up′, *adj.* **1.** having reached the age of maturity: *You look so grown-up in that suit!* **2.** characteristic of or suitable for adults: *a grown-up pastime.*

grown•up (grōn′up′) /ˈgrownˌʌp/ *n.* [*count*] a mature adult.

growth (grōth) /growθ/ *n.* **1.** [*noncount*] the act or process or a manner of growing; development; gradual increase: *to watch the growth of one's children.* **2.** [*noncount*] size or stage of development: *full growth.* **3.** [*noncount*] emotional and spiritual evolution: *felt stifled in her growth as a total human being.* **4.** [*noncount*] expansion; enlargement: *the growth of a business.* **5.** [*count; usually singular*] development from a simpler to a more complex stage: *the growth of language from a series of grunts to full sentences.* **6.** [*count*] something that has grown or developed, as a crop or harvest. **7.** [*count*] an abnormal increase in a mass of tissue, as a tumor. **8.** [*noncount*] origin or source: *tobacco of domestic growth.* *—adj.* [*before a noun*] **9.** growing or expected to grow in value or earnings at a rate higher than average: *a growth industry.*

grub (grub) /grʌb/ *n., v.,* **grubbed, grub•bing.** *—n.* **1.** [*count*] the thick-bodied, sluggish young of certain insects, esp. the beetle. **2.** [*noncount*] *Slang.* food: *How's the grub in that place?* **—*v.* 3.** to dig out of the ground: [~ + *obj*]: *The birds grubbed worms.* [*no obj*]: *They were grubbing for worms.* **4.** [~ + *obj*] *Slang.* to scrounge: *to grub a cigarette.* —**grub′ber,** *n.* [*count*]

grub•by (grub′ē) /ˈgrʌbiy/ *adj.,* **-bi•er, -bi•est. 1.** dirty; sloppy and filthy: *grubby work clothes.* **2.** contemptible; ignoble: *grubby political tricks.* —**grub′bi•ness,** *n.* [*noncount*]

grudge (gruj) /grʌdʒ/ *n., v.,* **grudged, grudg•ing. —*n.*** [*count*] **1.** a feeling of ill will or resentment because of some real or imagined wrong: *can really hold a grudge.* **—*v.*** [~ + *obj* + *obj*] **2.** to give or permit with reluctance: *They grudged us every day we were away.* **3.** to resent the good fortune of (another); begrudge: *I don't grudge her her good fortune.*

grudg•ing (gruj′ing) /ˈgrʌdʒɪŋ/ *adj.* reluctant; unwilling: *earned their grudging respect.* —**grudg′ing•ly,** *adv.*

gru•el (grōō′əl) /ˈgruwəl/ *n.* [*noncount*] a thin cooked cereal made by boiling meal, esp. oatmeal, in water or milk.

gru•el•ing (grōō′ə ling, grōō′ling) /ˈgruwəlɪŋ, ˈgruwlɪŋ/ *adj.* very tiring: *a grueling day at work.* Also, *esp. Brit.,* **gru′el•ling.**

grue•some (grōō′səm) /ˈgruwsəm/ *adj.* causing horror and disgust: *a gruesome murder.* —**grue′some•ly,** *adv.* —**grue′some•ness,** *n.* [*noncount*]

gruff (gruf) /grʌf/ *adj.,* **-er, -est. 1.** low and harsh; hoarse: *a gruff voice.* **2.** roughly stern; brusque: *a gruff manner.* —**gruff′ly,** *adv.* —**gruff′ness,** *n.* [*noncount*]

grum•ble (grum′bəl) /ˈgrʌmbəl/ *v.,* **-bled, -bling,** *n.* **—*v.* 1.** to murmur or mutter in discontent; complain unhappily: [*no obj*]: *All he did was grumble.* [*used with quotations*]: *"I hate that job," he grumbled.* **2.** [*no obj*] to rumble: *a volcano grumbling in the distance.* **—*n.*** [*count*] **3.** an expression of discontent; complaint. **4.** a rumble. —**grum′bler,** *n.* [*count*]

grump•y (grum′pē) /ˈgrʌmpiy/ *adj.,* **-i•er, -i•est.** unhappy and bad-tempered; grouchy: *She's always a little grumpy when she wakes up.* —**grump′i•ness,** *n.* [*noncount*]

grun•gy (grun′jē) /ˈgrʌndʒiy/ *adj.,* **-gi•er, -gi•est.** *Slang.* **1.** run-down; dilapidated: *a grungy old hotel.* **2.** dirty; filthy: *grungy clothes.*

grunt (grunt) /grʌnt/ *v.* [*no obj*] **1.** to make the deep, throaty sound that a hog or pig makes; to make a similar sound: *The usher just grunted and pointed to my seat.* **—*n.*** [*count*] **2.** a sound of grunting. **3.** *Slang.* an infantryman.

gryph•on (grif′ən) /ˈgrɪfən/ *n.* GRIFFIN.

gua•ca•mo•le (gwä kə mō′lē) /gwɑkəˈmowliy/ *n.* [*noncount*] a Mexican dip of mashed avocado mixed with lemon or lime juice, seasonings, and often tomato and onion.

guar•an•tee (gar′ən tē′) /ˌgærənˈtiy/ *n., pl.* **-tees,** *v.,* **-teed, -tee•ing. —*n.*** [*count*] **1.** an assurance, esp. one in writing, that something is of specified quality, content, benefit, etc., or will please the customer or perform satisfactorily for a given length of time. **2.** GUARANTY (defs. 1, 2). **3.** something that makes sure a particular outcome or condition will come to pass: *Wealth is not a guarantee of happiness.* **—*v.* 4.** [~ + *obj*] to offer a guarantee for: *The company guarantees its machines for ten years.* **5.** [~ + *obj*] to make oneself answerable for (something) on behalf of someone else; vouch for: *I guarantee his behavior.* **6.** [~ + *obj*] to protect against damage or loss: *This insurance guarantees a person against property loss.* **7.** to assure that a stated outcome is certain: [~ + *obj* + *to* + *verb*]: *That clown show is guaranteed to bring a smile to your face.* [~ + (*that*) *clause*]: *I guarantee that I'll be there.*

guar•an•tor (gar′ən tôr′, -tər) /ˈgærənˌtɔr, -tər/ *n.* [*count*] one that makes or gives a guarantee, guaranty, warrant, etc.

guar•an•ty (gar′ən tē′) /ˈgærənˌtiy/ *n., pl.* **-ties,** *v.,* **-tied, -ty•ing. —*n.*** [*count*] **1.** a pledge or formal assurance given as security that another's debt or obligation will be taken care of. **2.** something taken or presented as security. **—*v.* 3.** GUARANTEE.

guard (gärd) /gɑrd/ *v.* **1.** [~ + *obj*] to keep safe from harm or danger; protect: *The dog guarded the house when no one was home.* **2.** [~ + *obj*] to keep under close watch, as in order to prevent escape: *The police officers guarded the prisoner.* **3.** [~ + *obj*] to keep under control as a matter of caution: *to guard one's temper.* **4.** [~ + *obj*] to keep secret; protect or hide: *guarded the secrets of his business.* **5.** to provide or equip with some safeguard or protection: [~ + *obj*]: *This ingredient guards your teeth against decay.* [~ + *against*]: *The mouthwash guards against bad breath.* **6.** [~ (+ *against*) + *obj*] to position oneself in some sport so as to obstruct or impede the movement or progress of (an opponent on offense). **7.** [~ + *against*] to provide means of protection: *The computer program should guard against errors.* **—*n.* 8.** [*count*] a person or group that guards, as one that keeps watch over prisoners or property. **9.** [*noncount*] an act of guarding; a close watch: *under armed guard.* **10.** [*count*] a device, appliance, or attachment that prevents or minimizes injury, loss, etc.: *a guard for a goalie in hockey.* **11. a.** [*count*] either of the football linemen stationed between a tackle and the center, or either of the basketball players stationed in the backcourt. **b.** [*noncount*] the position played by this player: *He played guard.* **12.** [*count*] *Brit.* a railway conductor. **—*Idiom.* 13. off (one's) guard,** unprepared; unwary: *caught off guard.* **14. on (one's) guard,** watching; vigilant; wary. **15. stand guard over,** [~ + *obj*] to watch over; protect: *stood guard over their wounded comrade.* —**guard′er,** *n.* [*count*]

guard•ed (gär′did) /ˈgɑrdɪd/ *adj.* **1.** cautious; careful; prudent: *made a few guarded comments.* **2.** protected, watched, or restrained, as by a guard. —**guard′ed•ly,** *adv.*

guard•i•an (gär′dē ən) /ˈgɑrdiyən/ *n.* [*count*] **1.** a person who guards, upholds, or preserves: *the guardians of democracy.* **2.** a person legally entrusted with the care of another's person or property, as that of a child or of someone who is no longer capable of caring for himself or herself. **—*adj.*** [*before a noun*] **3.** guarding; protecting: *a guardian angel.* —**guard′i•an•ship′,** *n.* [*noncount*]

Gua•te•mal•an (gwä′tə mä′lən) /ˌgwɑtəˈmɑlən/ *adj.* **1.** of or relating to Guatemala. **—*n.*** [*count*] **2.** a person born or living in Guatemala.

gua•va (gwä′və) /ˈgwɑvə/ *n.* [*count*], *pl.* **-vas. 1.** a tropical American tree or shrub of the myrtle family. **2.** the large yellow fruit of this tree, used esp. for making jam.

gu•ber•na•to•ri•al (gōō′bər nə tôr′ē əl, -tōr′-, gyōō′-) /ˌguwbərnəˈtɔriyəl, -ˈtowr-, ˌgyuw-/ *adj.* of or relating to a state governor or the office of state governor: *a gubernatorial election.*

guer•ril•la or **gue•ril•la** (gə ril′ə) /gəˈrɪlə/ *n.* [*count*], *pl.* **-las.** a member of a band of unofficial soldiers that attacks an enemy in small groups, often without warning.

guess (ges) /gɛs/ *v.* **1.** to give an opinion about (something) without enough evidence or without knowing for certain if it is true; hazard: [~ + *obj*]: *to guess a person's weight.* [~ + *at*]: *I guessed at the weight of the package.* **2.** to give or figure out an answer correctly without knowing for certain: [*no obj*]: *I guessed and got it right.* [~ + *obj*]: *Somehow I guessed the right answer.* [~ + (*that*) *clause*]: *I guessed that the second choice would be correct.* **3.** [~ + (*that*) *clause*] to think, believe, or suppose: *I guess that I can manage alone.* **—*n.*** [*count*] **4.** an opinion that one reaches on the basis of guessing or in the absence of any or sufficient evidence. **5.** the act of forming such an opinion. —**guess′er,** *n.* [*count*]

guest (gest) /gɛst/ *n.* [*count*] **1.** a person who spends some time at another's home in a social activity, as a visit or party. **2.** a person who enjoys the hospitality of a club, a city, a country, or the like. **3.** a person who stays at or goes to a hotel, restaurant, etc. **4.** an often well-known person invited to appear in a television or other program. **—*adj.*** [*before a noun*] **5.** provided for a guest: *a guest towel.* **6.** participating or performing as a guest: *a guest conductor for the orchestra.*

guf•faw (gə fô′) /gəˈfɔ/ *n.* [*count*] **1.** a loud burst of laughter. **—*v.*** [*no obj*] **2.** to laugh loudly.

guid•ance (gīd′ns) /ˈgaydns/ *n.* [*noncount*] **1.** the act or function of guiding; leadership; direction. **2.** advice or counseling, esp. for students on educational or work-related matters. **3.** something that guides, as a system by which the flight of a missile may be changed by remote control.

guide (gīd) /gayd/ *v.,* **guid•ed, guid•ing,** *n.* **—*v.*** [~ + *obj*] **1.** to assist (a person) to travel through, or reach a destination in, an unfamiliar area, as by accompanying or giving directions to the person: *She guided us into the center of town.* **2.** to accompany (a sightseer) in order to show and comment upon points of interest. **3.** to direct the course of: *The pilot guided the plane to a safe landing.* **4.** to supply (a person) with advice: *guided me through many difficult times with his good advice.* **5.** to manage; supervise: *He guided the business to its most profitable year.* **—*n.*** [*count*] **6.** a person who guides, esp.

one hired to guide travelers, tourists, etc. **7.** a mark, tab, or the like to attract the eye and thus provide quick reference. **8.** a book, pamphlet, or the like with information, instructions, or advice; guidebook or handbook. **9.** a device that regulates or directs motion or action: *a sewing-machine guide.* **10.** something that influences one's actions: *Let your conscience be your guide.* —**guid′er,** *n.* [*count*]

guide•book (gīd′bo͝ok′) /ˈgaydˌbʊk/ *n.* [*count*] **1.** a book of directions, advice, and information for travelers or tourists: *a guidebook to downtown Copenhagen.* **2.** HANDBOOK (def. 1): *a guide to dieting.*

guid′ed mis′sile, *n.* [*count*] a rocket steered during its flight by radio signals, clockwork controls, etc.

guide•line (gīd′līn′) /ˈgaydˌlayn/ *n.* [*count*] any guide or indication of a future course of action, or of some course or set of steps to follow: *guidelines on tax reform.* See -LIN-.

guild or **gild** (gild) /gɪld/ *n.* [*count*] an organization of persons with related interests, goals, or jobs, etc., esp. one formed for mutual aid or protection: *a musicians' guild.*

guile (gīl) /gayl/ *n.* [*noncount*] slyness or cunning in reaching a goal; crafty or artful deception; duplicity. —**guile′ful,** *adj.* —**guile′less,** *adj.*

guil•lo•tine (gil′ə tēn′, gē′ə-) /ˈgɪləˌtiyn, ˈgiyə-/ *n., v.,* **-tined, -tin•ing.** —*n.* [*count*] **1.** a device for cutting off a person's head, consisting of a heavy blade that drops between two posts that guide its fall. —*v.* [~ + *obj*] **2.** to cut the head off (someone) by the guillotine.

guilt (gilt) /gɪlt/ *n.* [*noncount*] **1.** the fact or state of having committed an offense, crime, violation, or wrong, esp. against morals or against the law; culpability: *to admit one's guilt in a robbery.* **2.** a feeling of responsibility or remorse for the commission or consequences of some act of wrongdoing: *feelings of guilt.* **3.** responsibility; blame: *The guilt lies with those who would make false promises.* —**guilt′less,** *adj.* —**Related Words.** GUILT is a noun, GUILTY is an adjective: *He was filled with feelings of guilt. He felt very guilty about what he had done.*

guilt•y (gil′tē) /ˈgɪltiy/ *adj.,* **-i•er, -i•est. 1.** having committed an offense, crime, violation, or wrong, esp. against morals or against the law; culpable: *The jury found the defendant guilty of murder.* **2.** [*before a noun*] having or showing a feeling of guilt: *a guilty conscience.* —**guilt•i•ly** (gil′tl ē) /ˈgɪltḷiy/ *adv.* —**guilt′i•ness,** *n.* [*noncount*]

guin′ea fowl′ or **guin′ea•fowl′** (gin′ē) /ˈgɪniy/ *n.* [*count*] a large, plump bird originally of Africa, kept for food, having spotted gray coloring.

Guin•e•an (gin′ē ən) /ˈgɪniyən/ *adj.* **1.** of or relating to Guinea. —*n.* [*count*] **2.** a person born or living in Guinea.

guin′ea pig′, *n.* [*count*] **1.** a small, mildly fat, furry animal without a tail, raised as a pet and for use in laboratories. **2.** the subject of any sort of test or experiment.

guise (gīz) /gayz/ *n.* [*count*] general outside appearance, esp. a false or assumed appearance or disguise: *The king traveled in the guise of a beggar.*

gui•tar (gi tär′) /gɪˈtɑr/ *n.* [*count*] a stringed musical instrument with a long neck; a flat, somewhat violinlike body; and usually six strings. —**gui•tar′ist,** *n.* [*count*]

gulch (gulch) /gʌltʃ/ *n.* [*count*] a deep, narrow valley, esp. one marking the course of a stream.

gulf (gulf) /gʌlf/ *n.* [*count*] **1.** a portion of an ocean or sea partly enclosed by land. **2.** any wide gap or difference between two or more things, as between individuals with respect to social status, opinions, etc.

gull[1] (gul) /gʌl/ *n.* [*count*] a long-winged water-dwelling bird, typically white with gray or black upper wings and back.

gull[2] (gul) /gʌl/ *v.* [~ + *obj*] **1.** to deceive, trick, or cheat: *The crooks gulled him out of his life's savings.* —*n.* [*count*] **2.** a person who is easily deceived or cheated; dupe.

gul•let (gul′it) /ˈgʌlɪt/ *n.* [*count*] the tube that goes from the mouth to the stomach; esophagus.

gul•li•ble (gul′ə bəl) /ˈgʌləbəl/ *adj.* too willing to believe everything; naive; credulous: *selling junk to gullible consumers.* Sometimes, **gul′la•ble.** —**gul•li•bil•i•ty** (gul′ə bil′i tē) /ˌgʌləˈbɪlɪtiy/ *n.* [*noncount*]

gul•ly (gul′ē) /ˈgʌliy/ *n.* [*count*], *pl.* **-lies.** Also, **gulley. 1.** a small valley originally worn away by running water and serving to drain water away after long, heavy rains. **2.** a ditch or gutter: *a gully along the side of the road.*

gulp (gulp) /gʌlp/ *v.* **1.** [*no obj*] to gasp or swallow air, as if taking a large swallow of something liquid. **2.** to swallow eagerly, as in large amounts: [~ + *down* + *obj*]: *He gulped down lunch.* [~ + *obj*]: *I gulped three huge glasses of water.* **3.** [~ *(+ down)* + *obj*] to hold back; suppress: *He gulped (down) a sob.* —*n.* [*count*] **4.** the act of gulping. **5.** the amount swallowed at one time. —**gulp′er,** *n.* [*count*]

gum[1] (gum) /gʌm/ *n., v.,* **gummed, gum•ming.** —*n.* [*count*] **1.** a sticky substance that comes from plants and hardens when exposed to air. **2.** made from such a plant substance. **3.** chewing gum. —*v.* **4.** [~ + *obj*] to smear, stiffen, or stick together with gum. **5.** [~ *(+ up)* + *obj*] to clog with or as if with a gummy substance: *The engine was gummed (up) and wouldn't start.* **6. gum up,** *Slang.* to spoil or ruin: [~ + *up* + *obj*]: *You've really gummed up the project with that blunder.* [~ + *obj* + *up*]: *You've gummed it up now.*

gum[2] (gum) /gʌm/ *n.* [*count*] Often, **gums.** [*plural*] the firm, fleshy tissue covering the surfaces of the jaws and partly covering the bottom of the teeth.

gum•bo (gum′bō) /ˈgʌmbow/ *n., pl.* **-bos. 1.** a soup of chicken or seafood, greens, and seasonings, usually thickened with okra: [*count*]: *a hot gumbo.* [*noncount*]: *made some gumbo.* **2.** [*noncount*] OKRA.

gum•drop (gum′drop′) /ˈgʌmˌdrɒp/ *n.* [*count*] a small candy that is firm but chewy like gum.

gum•my (gum′ē) /ˈgʌmiy/ *adj.,* **-mi•er, -mi•est. 1.** sticky, as gum is: *a gummy surface.* **2.** covered with or clogged with a sticky substance.

gump•tion (gump′shən) /ˈgʌmpʃən/ *n.* [*noncount*] **1.** spirit; drive; resourcefulness: *It takes gumption to go to school and work too.* **2.** courage; guts: *It took a lot of gumption to stand up to her.*

gum•shoe (gum′sho͞o′) /ˈgʌmˌʃuw/ *n.* **1.** *Slang.* a detective. **2.** a rubber shoe worn over one's shoes; overshoe.

gun (gun) /gʌn/ *n., v.,* **gunned, gun•ning.** —*n.* [*count*] **1.** a weapon consisting of a metal tube from which projectiles are shot by the force of an explosive: *heavy artillery guns.* **2.** any firearm that may be carried, as a rifle, shotgun, or revolver. **3.** any device for shooting or ejecting something under pressure: *a staple gun.* **4.** the firing of a weapon as a signal or salute: *One runner started before the gun.* **5.** a person whose profession is killing: *a hired gun.* —*v.* **6.** [~ + *obj*] to cause (an engine or vehicle) to increase in speed very quickly by increasing the supply of fuel. **7. gun down,** to shoot with a gun: [~ + *down* + *obj*]: *The guards gunned down the fleeing convict.* [~ + *obj* + *down*]: *The guards gunned him down.* **8. gun for,** [~ + *obj*] **a.** to seek determinedly with hostile intent: *Watch out, the boss is gunning for you.* **b.** to try hard to obtain: *to gun for a raise.* —***Idiom.*** **9. stick to** or **stand by one's guns,** to keep steadfastly to one's position, opinion, belief, etc. **10. under the gun,** under pressure, as to meet a deadline or solve a problem. —**gun′ner,** *n.* [*count*]

gun•boat (gun′bōt′) /ˈgʌnˌbowt/ *n.* [*count*] a small armed warship used in ports where the water is shallow.

gun•fight (gun′fīt′) /ˈgʌnˌfayt/ *n.* [*count*] a battle between two or more people or groups using guns.

gun•fire (gun′fīᵊr′) /ˈgʌnˌfayᵊr/ *n.* [*noncount*] the firing of guns.

gung-ho (gung′hō′) /ˈgʌŋˈhow/ *adj. Informal.* strongly enthusiastic and loyal; zealous: *a gung-ho military outfit.*

gunk (gungk) /gʌŋk/ *n.* [*noncount*] *Slang.* any sticky, dirty, or greasy mass, as something left over or left on some part of machinery.

gun•man (gun′mən) /ˈgʌnmən/ *n.* [*count*], *pl.* **-men.** a person armed with or expert in the use of a gun, esp. one ready to use a gun unlawfully.

gun•ner•y (gun′ə rē) /ˈgʌnəriy/ *n.* [*noncount*] **1.** the art and science of making and operating guns, esp. large guns. **2.** the act of firing guns. **3.** guns thought of as a group.

gun•point (gun′point′) /ˈgʌnˌpɔynt/ *n.* [*noncount*] **1.** the point or aim of a gun. —***Idiom.*** **2. at gunpoint,** under threat of being shot: *held them up at gunpoint.*

gun•pow•der (gun′pou′dər) /ˈgʌnˌpawdər/ *n.* [*noncount*] an explosive mixture, as one made of potassium nitrate, sulfur, and charcoal, used in shells and cartridges, in fireworks, and for blasting.

gun•shot (gun′shot′) /ˈgʌnˌʃɒt/ *n.* **1.** [*count*] the shooting of a gun or the sound made by this. **2.** [*noncount*] a bullet, projectile, or other shot fired from a gun. **3.** [*noncount*] the range of a gun.

gun′-shy′, *adj.* **1.** frightened by the sound of a gun firing. **2.** distrustful because of some earlier unpleasant experience: *was gun-shy about dating again after the divorce.*

gun•smith (gun′smith′) /ˈgʌnˌsmɪθ/ *n.* [*count*] a person who makes or repairs firearms. —**gun′smith′ing,** *n.* [*noncount*]

gup•py (gup′ē) /ˈgʌpiy/ *n.* [*count*], *pl.* **-pies.** a small freshwater fish of the Caribbean often kept in aquariums.

gur•gle (gûr′gəl) /ˈgɜrgəl/ *v.,* **-gled, -gling,** *n.* —*v.* [*no obj*] **1.** to flow in a broken, irregular, noisy current: *The water gurgled down the drain.* **2.** to make or give off a sound as of water doing this; babble: *The baby was gurgling and cooing.* —*n.* [*count*] **3.** the act or noise of gurgling.

gur•ney (gûr′nē) /ˈgɜrniy/ *n.* [*count*], *pl.* **-neys.** a flat, padded table or stretcher with legs and wheels, for transporting patients or bodies. See illustration at HOSPITAL.

gu•ru (go͝or′o͞o, go͝o ro͞o′) /ˈgʊruw, gʊˈruw/ *n.* [*count*], *pl.* **-rus. 1.** a priest or teacher giving personal religious or spiritual instruction, esp. in Hinduism. **2.** advisor; mentor: *He's our computer guru.* **3.** a leader in a particular field: *the city's cultural gurus.*

gush (gush) /gʌʃ/ *v.* **1.** to (cause to) flow out suddenly, in great amounts, or forcefully, as a fluid from a place storing it; pour: [*no obj*]: *Oil gushed from the side of the crippled tanker.* [~ + *obj*]: *The crippled tanker gushed oil.* **2.** [*no obj*] to talk effusively: *gushing all night about his new job.* [*used with quotations*]: *"Gosh, this sure is an honor, sir!" the employee gushed.* —*n.* [*count; usually singular*] **3.** a sudden great outflow of a fluid: *a gush of blood.* **4.** an excessive outpouring: *a gush of praise.*

gush•er (gush′ər) /ˈgʌʃər/ *n.* [*count*] **1.** a person or thing that gushes. **2.** a flowing oil well, usually of large capacity.

gush•y (gush′ē) /ˈgʌʃiy/ *adj.,* **-i•er, -i•est.** effusively sentimental.

gus•set (gus′it) /ˈgʌsɪt/ *n.* [*count*] **1.** a small, triangular piece of material inserted into a shirt, shoe, etc., to improve the fit or for strengthening or reinforcement. **2.** a plate for uniting structural components at a joint, as in a steel frame or truss.

gus•sy (gus′ē) /ˈgʌsiy/ *v.,* **-sied, -sy•ing.** *Informal.* **1.** to adorn or decorate in a showy manner: [~ + *up* + *obj*]: *to gussy up a room with mirrors and lights.* [~ + *obj* + *up*]: *They gussied the room up with lots of mirrors and lights.* **2.** to dress in one's best clothes: [~ + *up*]: *She gussied up for the party.* [~ + *oneself* + *up*]: *She gussied herself up.*

gust (gust) /gʌst/ *n.* [*count*] **1.** a sudden strong blast of wind, water, fire, smoke, etc. **2.** a sudden burst of strong feeling: *a gust of anger.* —*v.* [*no obj*] **3.** to blow or rush in gusts: *The wind was gusting up to fifty miles per hour.* —**gust′y,** *adj.,* **-i•er, -i•est**: *a cold, gusty March day.*

gus•ta•to•ry (gus′tə tôr′ē, -tōr′ē) /ˈgʌstəˌtɔriy, -ˌtowriy/ *adj.* of or relating to taste or tasting.

gus•to (gus′tō) /ˈgʌstow/ *n.* [*noncount*] strong, hearty, or eager enjoyment, as in eating or drinking, or in action or speech in general; zest.

gut (gut) /gʌt/ *n., v.,* **gut•ted, gut•ting,** *adj.* —*n.* **1.** [*count*] the part of the body that carries food and digests it, esp. the intestines. **2. guts, a.** [*plural*] the inner organs of the body, esp. the bowels. **b.** [*noncount*] courage; nerve: *He didn't have the guts to defend them.* **c.** [*plural*] the inner working parts of a machine or device: *peered into the guts of the computer.* **3.** [*count*] the belly; abdomen: *a huge gut that draped over his waistband.* **4.** [*noncount*] intestinal tissue or fiber; catgut. —*v.* [~ + *obj*] **5.** to take out the inner organs of; disembowel: *to gut a fish.* **6.** to destroy the interior of: *Fire gutted the building.* **7.** to remove the vital or essential parts from: *Layoffs and firings gutted our department.* —*adj.* [*before a noun*] **8. a.** basic; essential: *gut issues.* **b.** based on instincts or emotions: *a gut reaction.* —***Idiom.* 9. hate someone's guts,** to hate or despise (someone) thoroughly. **10. spill one's guts,** to tell everything; reveal one's secret feelings. —**gut′less,** *adj.*

guts•y (gut′sē) /ˈgʌtsiy/ *adj.,* **-i•er, -i•est. 1.** daring or courageous; nervy: *a gutsy decision.* **2.** vigorous and earthy: *gutsy writing.*

gut•ter (gut′ər) /ˈgʌtər/ *n.* **1.** [*count*] a channel at the side or in the middle of a road or street, for carrying off surface water. **2.** [*count*] a channel at the edge of or on the roof of a building, for carrying off rainwater. **3.** [*count*] the lower channel along either side of a bowling alley. **4.** [*noncount*] the state or condition of those who live in squalid conditions: *He rose from the gutter to prominence.*

gut•ter•snipe (gut′ər snīp′) /ˈgʌtərˌsnayp/ *n.* [*count*] **1.** a person belonging to the lowest social group in a city. **2.** a street urchin.

gut•tur•al (gut′ər əl) /ˈgʌtərəl/ *adj.* as if pronounced in the back of the throat; throaty: *a hoarse, guttural voice.*

guy[1] (gī) /gay/ *n.* [*count*] **1.** a man or boy; fellow. **2. guys,** *Informal.* persons of either sex; people.

guy[2] (gī) /gay/ *n.* [*count*] a rope, cable, or device used to guide and steady an object being hoisted or lowered, or to secure anything likely to shift its position.

Guy•a•nese (gī′ə nēz′, -nēs′) /ˌgayəˈniyz, -ˈniys/ *n.* [*count*], *pl.* **-nese. 1.** a person born or living in Guyana. —*adj.* **2.** of or relating to Guyana.

guz•zle (guz′əl) /ˈgʌzəl/ *v.,* **-zled, -zling. 1.** to drink greedily or excessively: [*no obj*]: *been guzzling all evening.* [~ + *obj*]: *guzzled beer.* **2.** [~ + *obj*] to use in large quantities: *This car guzzles gas.* —**guz′zler,** *n.* [*count*]

gym (jim) /dʒɪm/ *n.* **1.** [*count*] a gymnasium: *The dance was held in the gym.* **2.** [*noncount*] PHYSICAL EDUCATION: *a course in gym.* —*adj.* [*before a noun*] **3.** of, relating to, or used for athletics or physical education: *gym clothes.*

gym•na•si•um (jim nā′zē əm) /dʒɪmˈneyziyəm/ *n.* [*count*], *pl.* **-si•ums, -si•a** (-zē ə, -zhə) /-ziyə, -ʒə/. a building or room designed and equipped for indoor sports, exercise, or physical education.

gym•nast (jim′nast, -nəst) /ˈdʒɪmnæst, -nəst/ *n.* [*count*] one who enjoys, or is trained in, gymnastics.

gym•nas•tics (jim nas′tiks) /dʒɪmˈnæstɪks/ *n.* **1.** [*plural; used with a plural verb*] physical exercises that develop and demonstrate strength, balance, and ability to move easily and smoothly, esp. such exercises performed mostly on special equipment. **2.** [*noncount; used with a singular verb*] the practice of such exercises: *Gymnastics is a demanding sport.* **3.** [*plural; used with a plural verb*] **a.** mental or creative feats of skill: *the lawyer's verbal gymnastics.* **b.** adroit, contorted physical movements: *performed all sorts of gymnastics to get the box onto the roof of the car.* —**gym•nas′tic,** *adj.*

-gyn-, *root. -gyn-* comes from Greek, where it has the meaning "wife; woman." This meaning is found in such words as: GYNECOLOGY, MISOGYNY.

gy•ne•col•o•gy (gī′ni kol′ə jē, jin′i-) /ˌgaynɪˈkɒlədʒiy, ˌdʒɪnɪ-/ *n.* [*noncount*] the branch of medicine that deals with the health and diseases of women, esp. of the reproductive organs. —**gy•ne•co•log•ic** (gī′ni kə loj′ik, jin′i-) /ˌgaynɪkəˈlɒdʒɪk, ˌdʒɪnɪ-/ **gy′ne•co•log′i•cal,** *adj.* [*before a noun*] —**gy′ne•col′o•gist,** *n.* [*count*] See -GYN-.

gyp (jip) /dʒɪp/ *v.,* **gypped, gyp•ping,** *n. Informal.* —*v.* [~ + *obj* (+ *out of*)] **1.** to cheat, defraud, or rob by some sharp practice; swindle: *gypped us out of our money.* —*n.* [*count*] **2.** a trick, swindle, or fraud.

gyp•sum (jip′səm) /ˈdʒɪpsəm/ *n.* [*noncount*] a soft white mineral, a form of calcium, used to make plaster of Paris and as a fertilizer.

gyp•sy (jip′sē) /ˈdʒɪpsiy/ *n., pl.* **-sies,** *adj.* —*n.* [*count*] **1.** [*Gypsy*] a member of a dark-haired, originally Indian people who traditionally traveled in covered carts carrying their possessions and now live mostly in permanent communities in many countries of the world. **2.** a person who is like the old idea of a Gypsy, wandering from place to place. **3.** a cab licensed to answer calls but not to pick up passengers directly from the street. —*adj.* [*before a noun*] **4.** [*Gypsy*] of or relating to the Gypsies.

gy•rate (jī′rāt, jī rāt′) /ˈdʒayreyt, dʒayˈreyt/ *v.,* **-rat•ed, -rat•ing.** to move in a circle or spiral or around a fixed point; whirl; revolve; rotate: [*no obj*]: *gyrated to the music.* [~ + *obj*]: *gyrated her hips to the music.* —**gy•ra•tion** (jī rā′shən) /dʒayˈreyʃən/ *n.* [*count*]

gy•ro (jēr′ō, yēr′ō) /ˈdʒɪərow, ˈyɪərow/ *n.* [*count*] pressed beef or lamb roasted on a vertical spit, thinly sliced, and usually served in a pita bread sandwich.

gy•ro•scope (jī′rə skōp′) /ˈdʒayrəˌskowp/ *n.* [*count*] a device consisting of a rotating wheel mounted so that its axis can turn freely in certain or all directions; it is capable of maintaining the same absolute direction in space in spite of movements of the mountings. See -SCOPE-.

H, h (āch) /eytʃ/ *n.* [*count*], *pl.* **Hs** or **H's, hs** or **h's.** the eighth letter of the English alphabet, a consonant.

H, an abbreviation of: **1.** hard. **2.** *Slang.* heroin. **3.** high.

h, an abbreviation of: **1.** hard. **2.** hardness.

h. or **H.,** an abbreviation of: **1.** hard. **2.** hardness. **3.** height. **4.** high. **5.** hour.

ha or **hah** (hä) /hɑ/ *interj.* This word is used to express surprise, questioning, suspicion, triumph, etc.

ha, an abbreviation of: hectare.

-hab-, *root.* -*hab*- comes from Latin, where it has the meaning "live, reside." This meaning is found in such words as: COHABIT, HABITABLE, HABITAT, HABITATION, INHABIT, INHABITANT.

ha•be•as cor•pus (hā′bē əs kôr′pəs) /ˈheybiyˈəs kɔrpəs/ *n.* [*noncount*] a law requiring that a person who has been detained by the authorities be brought before a court to determine if the detention is lawful.

hab•er•dash•er (hab′ər dash′ər) /ˈhæbərˌdæʃər/ *n.* [*count*] a dealer in men's clothing.

hab•er•dash•er•y (hab′ər dash′ə rē) /ˈhæbərˌdæʃəriy/ *n., pl.* **-er•ies. 1.** [*count*] a haberdasher's shop. **2.** [*noncount*] men's clothing.

-habil-, *root.* -*habil*- comes from Latin, where it has the meanings "handy; apt; able." These meanings are found in such words as: ABILITY, ABLE, REHABILITATE.

hab•it (hab′it) /ˈhæbɪt/ *n.* **1.** a pattern of behavior that is customary and regular, or that is repeated often: [*noncount*]: *I got up at 6 a.m. out of habit.* [*count*]: *Smoking had become a habit.* **2.** [*count*] an addiction, esp. to narcotics: *a serious drug habit.* **3.** [*count*] the dress of a particular rank, profession, etc., esp. the long garment worn by some clergy. **—Syn.** See CUSTOM.

hab•it•a•ble (hab′i tə bəl) /ˈhæbɪtəbəl/ *adj.* (of a place) that can be lived in: *Finally the renovated apartments were habitable.* **—hab•it•a•bil•i•ty** (hab′i tə bil′i tē) /ˌhæbɪtəˈbɪlɪtiy/ *n.* [*noncount*] See -HAB-.

hab•i•tat (hab′i tat′) /ˈhæbɪˌtæt/ *n.* [*count*] **1.** the natural environment of a living thing: *a jungle habitat.* **2.** HABITATION (def. 1). See -HAB-.

hab•i•ta•tion (hab′i tā′shən) /ˌhæbɪˈteyʃən/ *n.* **1.** [*count*] a place where one lives; residence; dwelling: *a mountain habitation far from the city.* **2.** [*noncount*] the act of inhabiting; occupancy by living creatures: *tenements unfit for human habitation.* See -HAB-.

hab′it-form′ing, *adj.* tending to cause addiction: *a habit-forming drug.*

ha•bit•u•al (hə bich′o͞o əl) /həˈbɪtʃuwəl/ *adj.* **1.** [*before a noun*] done by habit: *He's a habitual gossip.* **2.** commonly used, followed, observed, etc., by a particular person; customary. **—ha•bit′u•al•ly,** *adv.*

ha•bit•u•ate (hə bich′o͞o āt′) /həˈbɪtʃuˌweyt/ *v.* [~ + *obj* + *to* + *obj*], **-at•ed, -at•ing.** to cause (someone) to get used to a physical or mental situation; train: *Working on a farm had habituated him to waking up early. They became habituated to the constant rain.* **—ha•bit•u•a•tion** (hə bich′o͞o ā′shən) /həˌbɪtʃuˈweyʃən/ *n.* [*noncount*]

ha•bit•u•é (hə bich′o͞o ā′, -bich′o͞o ā′) /həˈbɪtʃuˌwey, -ˌbɪtʃuˈwey/ *n.* [*count*] a habitual visitor to a place: *a habitué of the café.*

ha•ci•en•da (hä′sē en′də) /ˌhɑsiyˈɛndə/ *n.* [*count*], *pl.* **-das.** (in Spanish America) **1.** a large land estate, esp. one used for ranching. **2.** the main house on such an estate.

hack[1] (hak) /hæk/ *v.* **1.** to cut, slice, chop, or sever with irregular blows: [~ *(+ away)* + *at* + *obj*]: *The rescue workers hacked away at the rubble all night.* [~ + *down* + *obj*]: *The timbermen hacked down the trees.* [~ + *obj*]: *hacked the timber to pieces.* **2.** [~ + *obj* + *through* + *obj*] to clear by cutting away vines, trees, or other growth: *hacked their way through the dense jungle.* [~ + *through* + *obj*]: *hacked through the jungle.* **3.** [~ + *obj*] to cut severely; trim: *to hack a budget.* **4.** [~ + *obj*] *Slang.* to cope with; tolerate: *I can't hack all this commuting.* **5.** [*no obj*] to cough in a short, raspy manner. **—***n.* [*count*] **6.** an act of cutting; cut, gash, or notch. **7.** a short, rasping dry cough. ***—Idiom.*** **8. hack it,** *Slang.* to deal with something successfully: *can't hack it as an executive.*

hack[2] (hak) /hæk/ *n.* [*count*] **1.** a hireling: *a political hack.* **2.** a person, esp. a writer, who produces mediocre work. **3.** an old or worn-out horse. **4. a.** a taxicab. **b.** a cabdriver. **—***v.* [*no obj*] **5.** to drive a taxi: *found a job hacking.* **—***adj.* [*before a noun*] **6.** working as a hack: *a hack writer.* **7.** suitable to or typical of a hack: *hack work.*

hack•er (hak′ər) /ˈhækər/ *n.* [*count*] **1.** a person or thing that hacks. **2.** a person unskilled in a sport. **3.** *Slang.* **a.** a person who is excellent at computer programming. **b.** a computer user who illegally gains access to restricted computer systems.

hack•le (hak′əl) /ˈhækəl/ *n., v.,* **-led, -ling. —***n.* [*count*] **1.** the neck feathers of a male bird, as the domestic rooster. **2. hackles,** [*plural*] hairs on the back of an animal's neck that can be made to stand up straight. ***—Idiom.*** **3. raise one's hackles,** to arouse one's anger.

hack•neyed (hak′nēd) /ˈhækniyd/ *adj.* commonplace or trite; very ordinary and uninteresting: *The play had a hackneyed plot.*

hack•saw or **hack saw** (hak′sô′) /ˈhækˌsɔ/ *n.* [*count*] a saw for cutting metal, usually made up of a narrow, fine-toothed blade attached to a frame.

had (had) /hæd/ *v.* pt. and pp. of HAVE.

had•dock (had′ək) /ˈhædək/ *n., pl.* (*esp. when thought of as a group*) **-dock,** (*esp. for kinds or species*) **-docks.** a food fish of the cod family, of the N Atlantic.

had•n't (had′nt) /ˈhædnt/ contraction of *had not.*

hadst (hadst) /hædst/ *v. Archaic.* a 2nd pers. sing. pt. of HAVE.

haft (haft) /hæft/ *n.* [*count*] a handle, esp. of a knife, sword, or dagger.

hag (hag) /hæg/ *n.* [*count*] an ugly old woman, esp. an evil or bad-tempered one. **—hag′gish,** *adj.*

hag•gard (hag′ərd) /ˈhægərd/ *adj.* tired or exhausted in appearance; worn; gaunt: *the haggard faces of refugees.* **—hag′gard•ly,** *adv.* **—hag′gard•ness,** *n.* [*noncount*]

hag•gle (hag′əl) /ˈhægəl/ *v.* [*no obj*], **-gled, -gling.** to bargain about the cost of something: *The tourists haggled for a better price.* **—hag•gler** (hag′lər) /ˈhæglər/ *n.* [*count*]

hag•i•og•ra•phy (hag′ē og′rə fē, hā′jē-) /ˌhægiyˈɒgrəfiy, ˌheydʒiy-/ *n.* [*count*], *pl.* **-phies.** biography of the lives of the saints. **—hag′i•og′ra•pher,** *n.* [*count*] See -GRAPH-.

hah (hä) /hɑ/ *interj.* HA.

ha-ha (hä′hä′, hä′hä′) /ˈhɑˈhɑ, ˌhɑˈhɑ/ *interj.* This word is used to express or represent laughter, amusement, scorn, etc.

hai•ku (hī′ko͞o) /ˈhaykuw/ *n.* [*count*], *pl.* **-ku.** a Japanese poem of 17 syllables divided into 3 lines of 5, 7, and 5 syllables.

hail[1] (hāl) /heyl/ *v.* **1.** [~ + *obj*] to greet or welcome: *to hail an old friend.* **2.** [~ + *obj* (+ *as* + *obj*)] to approve enthusiastically; praise: *hailed the new child care laws as a big step forward.* **3.** [~ + *obj*] to call out to, as in order to stop or to attract the attention of: *to hail a cab.* **4. hail from,** [~ + *from* + *obj; not: be* + ~*-ing* + *from*] to have as one's place of birth or residence: *hails from Indiana.* **—***interj.* **5.** This word is used as a greeting, or to express praise: *Hail, Caesar!* **—hail′er,** *n.* [*count*]

hail[2] (hāl) /heyl/ *n.* **1.** [*noncount*] a shower or storm of pellets of ice more than ⅕ in. (5 mm) in diameter: *golf-ball-sized hail.* **2.** [*count; usually singular*] a shower or large number of anything: *a hail of bullets.* **—***v.* **3.** [*it* + ~; *(no obj)*] to pour down hail: *It hailed all afternoon.* **4.** to (cause to) fall like hail: [*no obj*]: *Arrows hailed on the troops.* [~ + *obj*]: *The plane hailed leaflets on the city.*

hail•stone (hāl′stōn′) /ˈheylˌstown/ *n.* [*count*] a pellet of hail.

hail•storm (hāl′stôrm′) /ˈheylˌstɔrm/ *n.* [*count*] a storm with hail.

hair (hâr) /hɛər/ *n.* **1.** [*count*] any of many small, thin, tiny, threadlike pieces growing from the skin of mammals; a pilus: *She plucked a hair from her head.* **2.** [*noncount*] a mass of such pieces, such as that covering the human head or forming the coat of most mammals. **3.** [*count; usually singular; a* + ~] a very small amount or distance: *The falling rock missed him by a hair.* ***—Idiom.*** **4. get in someone's hair,** to annoy someone. **5. let one's hair down,** to behave in a relaxed, informal manner. **6. make one's hair stand on end,** to shock or frighten. **7. split hairs,** to make petty objections or distinctions: *splitting hairs about the rules.* **8. tear one's hair (out),** to behave frantically: *tearing my hair out with worry.* **—hair′less,** *adj.*

hair•ball (hâr′bôl′) /ˈhɛərˌbɔl/ *n.* [*count*] a ball of hair that has gathered in the stomach of a cat or other animal that licks its coat.

hair•breadth (hâr′bredth′, -breth′) /'hɛər,brɛdθ, -,brɛθ/ also **hairs•breadth** (hârz′-) /'hɛərz-/ *n.* [*count*] **1.** a very small space or distance: *to escape by a hairbreadth.* **—***adj.* **2.** extremely narrow or close: *a hairbreadth escape.*

hair•brush (hâr′brush′) /'hɛər,brʌʃ/ *n.* [*count*] a brush for grooming the hair.

hair•cut (hâr′kut′) /'hɛər,kʌt/ *n.* [*count*] **1.** an act or instance of cutting the hair. **2.** the style in which the hair is cut and worn: *a short haircut.*

hair•do (hâr′do͞o′) /'hɛər,duw/ *n.* [*count*], *pl.* **-dos.** the style in which a person's hair is worn.

hair•dress•er (hâr′dres′ər) /'hɛər,drɛsər/ *n.* [*count*] a person who arranges or cuts hair. **—hair′dress•ing,** *n.* [*noncount*]

haired (hârd) /hɛərd/ *adj.* This word is used in combination with other words to form adjectives that refer to a certain kind of hair: *a red-haired girl.*

hair•line (hâr′līn′) /'hɛər,layn/ *n.* [*count*] **1.** a very thin line. **2.** the border on the forehead where the hair starts to grow. **—***adj.* [*before a noun*] **3.** narrow or fine as a hair: *a hairline crack in the wall.* See -LIN-.

hair•piece (hâr′pēs′) /'hɛər,piys/ *n.* [*count*] a covering of false hair, as a toupee, for concealing baldness or adding to the existing hair.

hair•pin (hâr′pin′) /'hɛər,pɪn/ *n.* [*count*] **1.** a slender U-shaped piece of wire, etc., used to fasten the hair. **—***adj.* [*before a noun*] **2.** (of a road, etc.) curved like a hairpin.

hair′-rais′ing, *adj.* very frightening, shocking, or exciting: *hair-raising adventures.*

hairs•breadth or **hair's-breadth** (hârz′bredth′, -breth′) /'hɛərz,brɛdθ, -,brɛθ/ *n., adj.* HAIRBREADTH.

hair•split•ting (hâr′split′ing) /'hɛər,splɪtɪŋ/ *n.* [*noncount*] the making of trivial distinctions. **—hair′split′ter,** *n.* [*count*]

hair•style or **hair style** (hâr′stīl′) /'hɛər,stayl/ *n.* HAIRDO. **—hair′styl′ist,** *n.* [*count*]

hair′-trig′ger, *adj.* [*before a noun*] **1.** easily activated or set off: *a hair-trigger alarm.* **2.** reacting immediately to the slightest provocation: *a hair-trigger temper.*

hair•y (hâr′ē) /'hɛəriy/ *adj.,* **-i•er, -i•est. 1.** covered with hair: *hairy legs.* **2.** *Slang.* difficult, frightening, or risky: *a hairy mountain climb.* **—hair′i•ness,** *n.* [*noncount*]

Hai•tian (hā′shən) /'heyʃən/ *adj.* **1.** of or relating to Haiti. **2.** of or relating to the language spoken by many of the people in Haiti. **—***n.* **3.** [*count*] a person born or living in Haiti. **4.** [*noncount*] the language spoken by many of the people living in Haiti, also called Haitian Creole.

hajj or **hadj** (haj) /hædʒ/ *n.* [*count*], *pl.* **hajj•es** or **hadj•es.** a pilgrimage to Mecca, which every adult Muslim is supposed to make at least once.

haj•ji or **hadj•i** or **haj•i** (haj′ē) /'hædʒiy/ *n.* [*count*], *pl.* **haj•jis** or **hadj•is** or **haj•is.** one who has gone on a hajj.

hake (hāk) /heyk/ *n., pl.* (*esp. when thought of as a group*) **hake,** (*esp. for kinds or species*) **hakes.** a codlike saltwater fish.

hal•cy•on (hal′sē ən) /'hælsiyən/ *adj.* [*often: before a noun*] **1.** calm; tranquil: *halcyon weather.* **2.** happy; joyful; carefree: *the halcyon days of youth.*

hale (hāl) /heyl/ *adj.,* **hal•er, hal•est.** free from disease or weakness; robust: *hale and hearty old age.*

-hale-, *root.* -*hale*- comes from Latin, where it has the meaning "breathe." This meaning is found in such words as: EXHALE, HALITOSIS, INHALE.

half (haf) /hæf/ *n., pl.* **halves** (havz), *pron., adj., adv.* **—***n.* [*count*] **1.** one of two equal or nearly equal parts: *The two halves of the torn dollar bill fitted together perfectly.* **2.** either of two equal periods of play in a game. Compare QUARTER (def. 10). **3.** one of two; a part of a pair. **4.** [*usually singular*] the sum of 50 cents: *It cost a dollar and a half.* **—***adj.* [~ + *a/the* + *noun*] **5.** a quantity or amount equal to one half of something; (½): *half a loaf; half a dozen people.* **—***pron.* **6.** a quantity or amount equal to one half of (some group or thing): [*plural; used with a plural verb*]: *Of the passengers on the boat, half were American, half were Canadian.* [*singular; used with a singular verb*]: *The cake was delicious: half was vanilla and half was chocolate.* **—***adj.* [*before a noun*] **7.** being one of two equal or nearly equal parts of a whole: *a half quart.* **8.** being half in degree, amount, length, etc.: *travel at half speed.* **9.** partial or incomplete: *half measures.* **—***adv.* **10.** in or to the extent or measure of half: *Was the glass half full, or half empty?* **11.** in part; partly; incompletely: *half understood.* **—*Idiom.* 12. by half,** by a great deal; by far: *He is too clever by half.* **13. half again as much** or **as many,** as much as 50 percent more. **14. in half,** into two almost equal parts: *The vase broke in half.* **15. not (the) half of it,** a significant yet relatively minor part of something that remains to be described in full: *It's a shocking story, but you don't know the half of it.*

half•back (haf′bak′) /'hæf,bæk/ *n.* **1.** *Football.* **a.** [*count*] one of two backs who typically line up on each side of the fullback. **b.** [*noncount*] the position played by such a back. **2.** [*count*] (in soccer, etc.) a player stationed near the forward line to try to score points.

half′-baked′, *adj.* **1.** not baked enough. **2.** not planned or prepared well enough: *half-baked schemes.* **3.** unrealistic: *those half-baked theorists.*

half′-breed′, *n.* [*count*] *Often Disparaging and Offensive.* the child of parents of different races, esp. the child of an American Indian and a white person.

half′ broth′er, *n.* [*count*] a male having only one parent in common with another person.

half′-caste′, *n.* [*count*] a person whose parents are of different races.

half′-cocked′, *adj.* not having enough thought or preparation; ill-considered or ill-prepared; half-baked.

half•heart•ed (haf′här′tid) /'hæf'hɑrtɪd/ *adj.* having or showing little enthusiasm: *a half-hearted attempt.* **—half′heart′ed•ly,** *adv.* **—half′heart′ed•ness,** *n.* [*noncount*]

half′-life′ or **half′ life′,** *n.* [*count*], *pl.* **-lives.** the time required for one half the atoms of a given amount of a radioactive substance to decay: *a half-life of over 50,000 years.*

half′-mast′, *n.* [*noncount*] a position halfway between the top of a mast, staff, etc., and its base: *a flag flown at half-mast.*

half′ note′, *n.* [*count*] a musical note equivalent in time value to half a whole note.

half•pen•ny (hā′pə nē, hāp′nē) /'heypəniy, 'heypniy/ *n.* [*count*], *pl.* **half•pen•nies.** [*count*] a former British coin equal to half a penny.

half′ sis′ter, *n.* [*count*] a female having only one parent in common with another person.

half•time or **half-time** (haf′tīm′) /'hæf,taym/ *n.* **1.** the intermission between the two halves of a football, basketball, or other game: [*noncount*]: *During halftime we went for a walk.* [*count*]: *During halftimes the band plays.* **—***adj.* [*before a noun*] **2.** relating to or taking place during a halftime.

half′-truth′, *n.* [*count*] a statement that is only partly true, esp. one intended to deceive.

half•way (haf′wā′) /'hæf'wey/ *adv.* **1.** to half of the distance; to the midpoint: *to run halfway to town.* **2.** partially or nearly; almost: *He halfway surrendered to their demands.* **—***adj.* [*before a noun*] **3.** midway, as between two points. **4.** partial: *halfway measures.* **—*Idiom.* 5. meet (someone) halfway,** to compromise with: [~ + *obj*]: *The management met the ballplayer halfway in his salary demands.* [*no obj*]: *We met halfway on the salary dispute.*

half′way house′, *n.* [*count*] a residence in which persons newly released from psychiatric hospitals, prisons, or other institutions can readjust to society.

half′-wit′, *n.* [*count*] a stupid or foolish person. **—half′-wit′ted,** *adj.*: *a half-witted idea.*

hal•i•but (hal′ə bət, hol′-) /'hæləbət, 'hɒl-/ *n., pl.* (*esp. when thought of as a group*) **-but,** (*esp. for kinds or species*) **-buts.** any of various large flounders used for food.

hal•i•to•sis (hal′i tō′sis) /,hælɪ'towsɪs/ *n.* [*noncount*] a condition of having unpleasant-smelling breath; bad breath. See -HALE-.

hall (hôl) /hɔl/ *n.* [*count*] **1.** a corridor or passageway in a building: *She lived just down the hall from me.* **2.** the large entrance room of a building; vestibule; lobby. **3.** a large room or building for public gatherings; auditorium: *a concert hall.* **4.** a large building for living in, for instruction, or for other purposes at a college or university: *Over there is Lincoln Hall.* **5.** (in English colleges) **a.** a large room in which the members and students dine. **b.** dinner in such a room. **6.** the castle, house, or similar structure of a medieval noble.

hal•le•lu•jah or **hal•le•lu•iah** (hal′ə lo͞o′yə) /,hælə'luwyə/ *interj.* **1.** This word is used to express joy, praise, or gratitude; it means "Praise ye the Lord!" **—***n.* [*count*] **2.** a shout of joy, praise, or gratitude: *They greeted him with shouts and hallelujahs.*

hall•mark (hôl′märk′) /'hɔl,mɑrk/ *n.* [*count*] **1.** an official mark or stamp used in marking gold and silver articles that declares them to have pure gold or silver in them. **2.** any distinguishing feature or characteristic.

hal•low (hal′ō) /ˈhælow/ *v.* [~ + *obj*] to make or honor as holy; sanctify; consecrate: *to hallow the name of the Lord.* —**hal′lowed,** *adj.*

Hal•low•een or **Hal•low•e′en** (hal′ə wēn′, hol′-) /ˌhæləˈwiyn, ˌhɒl-/ *n.* [*noncount; count*] the evening of Oct. 31; the eve of All Saints' Day, observed esp. by children, who dress in costume and play trick or treat.

hal•lu•ci•nate (hə lo͞o′sə nāt′) /həˈluwsəˌneyt/ *v.* [*no obj*], **-nat•ed, -nat•ing.** to have hallucinations.

hal•lu•ci•na•tion (hə lo͞o′sə nā′shən) /həˌluwsəˈneyʃən/ *n.* [*count*] perception of something that does not exist, caused by various diseases, or by reaction to toxic substances or drugs: *This drug causes bizarre hallucinations.* —**hal•lu•ci•na•to•ry** (hə lo͞o′sə nə tôr′ē, -tōr′ē) /həˈluwsənəˌtɔriy, -ˌtowriy/ *adj.*

hal•lu•ci•no•gen (hə lo͞o′sə nə jən) /həˈluwsənədʒən/ *n.* [*count*] a substance that produces hallucinations. —**hal•lu•ci•no•gen•ic** (hə lo͞o′sə nə jen′ik) /həˌluwsənəˈdʒɛnɪk/ *adj.*

hall•way (hôl′wā′) /ˈhɔlˌwey/ *n.* [*count*] **1.** a corridor, as in a building. **2.** an entrance hall.

ha•lo (hā′lō) /ˈheylow/ *n.* [*count*], *pl.* **-los, -loes. 1.** Also called **nimbus.** the representation of a radiant light above or around the head of a holy person. **2.** any of a variety of bright circles or arcs centered on the sun or moon.

hal•o•gen (hal′ə jən, -jen′, hā′lə-) /ˈhælədʒən, -ˌdʒɛn, ˈheylə-/ *n.* any of various elements, as fluorine, chlorine, iodine, and bromine, that have properties in common: [*noncount*]: *the use of halogen in lamps.* [*count*]: *halogens as health hazards.*

hal′ogen lamp′, *n.* [*count*] a gas-filled, high-intensity lamp.

halt (hôlt) /hɔlt/ *v.* **1.** to (cause to) stop, cease moving, or operating: [*no obj*]: *The car halted in front of the house.* [~ + *obj*]: *He halted the car.* —*n.* [*count*] **2.** a temporary or permanent stop; standstill: *Work came to a halt.* —*interj.* **3.** This word is used to command someone to stop and stand motionless.

hal•ter (hôl′tər) /ˈhɔltər/ *n.* [*count*] **1.** a rope or strap with a noose for leading or restraining horses or cattle. **2.** a woman's upper garment, tied or fastened behind the neck and across the back, leaving the arms, shoulders, upper back, and often the midriff bare. —*v.* [~ + *obj*] **3.** to put a halter on; restrain as by a halter.

halt•ing (hôl′ting) /ˈhɔltɪŋ/ *adj.* faltering or hesitating, esp. in speech: *He asked in a halting voice if she would go out with him.* —**halt′ing•ly,** *adv.*

hal•vah (häl vä′, häl′vä) /hɑlˈvɑ, ˈhɑlvɑ/ *n.* [*noncount*] a sweet food of Turkish origin, made chiefly of ground sesame seeds and honey.

halve (hav) /hæv/ *v.* [~ + *obj*], **halved, halv•ing. 1.** to divide into two equal parts; to share equally: *Halve the apple so we can both eat it.* **2.** to reduce to half: *Profits were halved when the new tax was introduced.*

halves (havz) /hævz/ *n.* [*plural*] **1.** pl. of HALF. —***Idiom.*** **2. go halves,** to share equally; divide evenly: *We went halves on the dinner bill.*

ham[1] (ham) /hæm/ *n.* **1.** a cut of meat from a hog's hind quarter: [*noncount*]: *We had plenty of ham left over.* [*count*]: *fresh hams hanging in the butcher shop.* **2.** Often, **hams.** [*plural*] the back of the thigh, or the thigh and the buttock together.

ham[2] (ham) /hæm/ *n., v.,* **hammed, ham•ming.** —*n.* [*count*] **1.** an actor or performer who overacts. **2.** an operator of an amateur radio station: *The ham operators told the outside world about the revolution in their country.* —*v.* [*no obj*] **3.** Also, **ham it up.** to act with exaggerated expression of emotion; overact: *hamming (it up) for the camera.* —**ham′my,** *adj.,* **-mi•er, -mi•est.**

ham•burg•er (ham′bûr′gər) /ˈhæmˌbɜrgər/ *n.* **1.** [*noncount*] ground beef. **2.** [*count*] a rounded, flattened patty of ground beef. **3.** [*count*] a sandwich made up of such a patty.

ham•let (ham′lit) /ˈhæmlɪt/ *n.* [*count*] a small village.

ham•mer (ham′ər) /ˈhæmər/ *n.* [*count*] **1.** a tool consisting of a solid head set crosswise on a handle and used for driving nails, beating metals, etc. **2.** any of various instruments or devices resembling this in form, action, or use. **3.** a metal ball attached to a steel wire at the end of which is a grip, for throwing in the sport called the hammer throw. —*v.* **4.** to beat or drive (a nail, peg, etc.) with a hammer: [~ + *obj*]: *hammered a nail into the wall.* [~ + *in* + *obj*]: *hammered in a nail.* [~ + *obj* + *in*]: *The carpenter hammered a nail in.* **5.** to fasten by using hammer and nails; nail: [~ + *obj*]: *hammered the door shut.* **6.** to assemble or build with a hammer and nails: [~ + *together* + *obj*]: *to hammer together a small crate.* [~ + *obj* + *together*]: *to hammer a small crate together.* **7.** [~ + *obj*] to shape or ornament (metal or a metal object) by controlled blows of a hammer; beat out: *hammered the metal into a horseshoe.* **8.** [*no obj*] to strike blows with or as if with a hammer: *They hammered on the door.* **9. hammer away,** [~ + *at* + *obj*] **a.** to keep making hard-working attempts at something: *hammered away at her speech for days.* **b.** to repeat in order to persuade: *likes to hammer away at the importance of punctuality.* **10. hammer out, a.** to form or construct by repeated, vigorous, or strong effort: [~ + *out* + *obj*]: *to hammer out an agreement acceptable to both sides.* [~ + *obj* + *out*]: *They hammered it out in only a few hours.* **b.** to settle or resolve, as by vigorous or repeated effort: [~ + *out* + *obj*]: *hammered out their differences.* [~ + *obj* + *out*]: *hammered their differences out.* **c.** to hit with force: [~ + *out* + *obj*]: *to hammer out a tune on the piano.* [~ + *obj* + *out*]: *hammering it out over and over again.* —**ham′mer•er,** *n.* [*count*]

ham•mer•head (ham′ər hed′) /ˈhæmərˌhɛd/ *n.* [*count*] **1.** the crosswise top part of a hammer. **2.** a shark having a head shaped like a hammerhead with an eye at each end.

ham•mock (ham′ək) /ˈhæmək/ *n.* [*count*] a bed of canvas or cord that hangs between two supports, to which it is attached by cords or springs.

ham•per[1] (ham′pər) /ˈhæmpər/ *v.* [~ + *obj*] to get in the way of; interfere with: *Heavy rain hampered the flow of traffic.*

ham•per[2] (ham′pər) /ˈhæmpər/ *n.* [*count*] a large basket or wicker container, usually with a cover: *a picnic hamper filled with sandwiches.*

ham•ster (ham′stər) /ˈhæmstər/ *n.* [*count*] a short-tailed rodent with large cheek pouches, often kept as a pet.

ham•string (ham′string′) /ˈhæmˌstrɪŋ/ *n., v.,* **-strung** (-strung′) /-ˌstrʌŋ/ **-string•ing.** —*n.* [*count*] **1.** (in humans) a tendon behind the knee: *pulled a hamstring and couldn't play ball.* —*v.* [~ + *obj*] **2.** to disable by cutting the hamstring or hamstrings; cripple. **3.** to make powerless; thwart: *hamstrung by dozens of regulations.*

hand (hand) /hænd/ *n.* [*count*] **1.** the part at the end of the arm in humans, or in other animals, that consists of the wrist, knuckles, fingers, and thumb. **2.** something resembling a hand in shape or function, as the pointers on a timepiece: *The hands of the clock pointed to twelve.* **3.** a person performing manual labor or general duties: *a ranch hand.* **4.** a person, with reference to ability, knowledge, or experience: *an old hand at fund-raising.* **5.** skill: *The painting shows a master's hand.* **6.** a position, esp. one of control, used for bargaining, negotiating, etc.: *needed to strengthen our hand in the negotiations.* **7.** [*singular*] the means; agency: *Death occurred by his own hand.* **8.** [*singular*] assistance; aid: *Give me a hand with this ladder.* **9.** style of handwriting; penmanship: *a flowing hand.* **10.** [*singular*] a round or outburst of applause for a performer: *Let's give the singer a big hand.* **11.** a promise or pledge of marriage: *He asked for her hand in marriage.* **12.** a unit of measure equal to 4 inches (10.2 centimeters). **13. a.** the playing cards dealt to or held by each player at one time. **b.** a single round of a card game: *A few more hands and then we'll stop.* —*v.* **14.** to deliver or pass with or as if with the hand; offer: [~ + *obj* + *to* + *obj*]: *I handed the note to the ambassador.* [~ + *obj* + *obj*]: *She handed me the note.* **15.** [~ + *obj* + *obj*] to provide: *handed us a golden opportunity.* **16. hand down, a.** to deliver; pronounce: [~ + *down* + *obj*]: *The judge handed down the decision.* [~ + *obj* + *down*]: *He handed it down.* **b.** to transmit; pass along in turn: [~ + *down* + *obj*]: *She wanted to hand down the traditions of her church to her grandchildren.* [~ + *obj* + *down*]: *She handed them down to her children.* See HAND ON below. **17. hand in,** to submit; present for acceptance: [~ + *in* + *obj*]: *He handed in his resignation.* [~ + *obj* + *in*]: *handed the paper in late.* **18. hand off,** *Football.* to hand the ball to a member of one's team in the course of a play: [~ + *off* + *obj*]: *The quarterback handed off the ball to his halfback.* [~ + *obj* + *off*]: *He handed the ball off.* **19. hand on,** to hand down: [~ + *on* + *obj*]: *She handed on the leadership of the party to her successor.* [~ + *obj* + *on*]: *She handed it on to her successor.* **20. hand out,** to give or distribute; pass out: [~ + *out* + *obj*]: *She handed out the exam booklets to her class.* [~ + *obj* + *out*]: *She handed them out.* **21. hand over,** to deliver to another; surrender control of: [~ + *over* + *obj*]: *The kidnappers handed over the hostages.* [~ + *obj* + *over*]: *The kidnappers handed them over.* —***Idiom.*** **22. at hand, a.** within reach: *She* *picked up the first pencil at hand.* **b.** about to happen: *swore that the end of the world was at hand.* **c.** under consideration: *a discussion of the matter at hand.* **23. at the hand(s) of,** by or through the action of: *suffered at the hands of their captors.* **24. by hand,** by using the hands manually: *I wrote the whole report out by hand.* **25. change hands,** to pass from one owner to another: *changed hands eleven times in eleven years.* **26. eat out of someone's hand,** [*no obj*] to give in completely to someone: *That spoiled brat has his parents eating out of his hand.* **27. force someone's hand,** to compel a person to do or tell something before he or she is ready to do so: *You have forced my hand; I have no choice but to report you.* **28. from hand to mouth,** with nothing in reserve; with no savings; barely getting by: *to live from hand to mouth.* **29. hand and foot, a.** with the arms and legs restrained: *bound the bank employees hand and foot.* **b.** with slavish attentiveness: *to wait on someone hand and foot.* **30. hand in** or **and glove,** in close association or cooperation: *My boss and his superior were working hand in glove.* **31. hand in hand, a.** alongside one another while holding hands: *We walked hand in hand down by the beach.* **b.** hand in glove. **32. hand it to,** [~ + *obj*] to give deserved and proper credit to: *You've got to hand it to her, she made a great effort.* **33. hand over fist,** quickly and abundantly: *made money hand over fist.* **34. hands down, a.** without great effort; easily: *He won the championship hands down.* **b.** that cannot be argued about: *Hands down the best race I've ever seen.* **35. hand to hand,** in direct combat; at close quarters: *fighting hand to hand.* **36. have a hand in,** [~ + *obj*] to participate in: *Did you have a hand in this stupid business?* **37. have one's hands full,** [*no obj*] to be very busy: *had his hands full with five children.* **38. hold hands,** to join hands with another person, as in affection. **39. in hand, a.** under control: *has the situation well in hand.* **b.** in one's possession: *He's got enough cash in hand.* **40. in someone's hands,** in someone's possession, control, or care: *My fate is in your hands.* **41. join hands,** to unite in a common cause: *Will the former enemies now join hands?* **42. keep one's hand in,** [~ + *obj*] to continue to work at or practice: *Although he had officially retired he kept his hand in his former business.* **43. lay hands on,** [~ + *obj*] **a.** to obtain; acquire: *Where can I lay my hands on a good second-hand car?* **b.** to seize, esp. in order to punish. **44. on hand, a.** at one's disposal: *We don't have enough cash on hand.* **b.** present: *How many staff members are on hand?* **45. on one's hands,** as one's responsibility: *had a big problem on their hands.* **46. on the one hand.** This expression is used to introduce the first item to be presented: *On the one hand, we have to consider costs.* **47. on the other hand.** This expression is often used to introduce an item that opposes one that has just been introduced by the phrase *on the one hand*: *On the other hand, we have to consider the human factor.* **48. out of hand,** out of control: *The mob got completely out of hand.* **49. take (something** or **someone) in hand,** to take responsibility for; deal with: *The police took the situation in hand.* **50. throw up one's hands,** to stop trying; admit to failure: *At that point I threw up my hands; no one was listening.* **51. try one's hand at,** [~ + *obj*] to start (some activity) so as to test one's ability at: *tried my hand at car repair but couldn't get the hang of it.* **52. turn** or **put one's hand to,** [~ + *obj*] to set to work at: *He put his hand to gardening.* **53. wash one's hands of,** [~ + *obj*] to abandon any further responsibility for; to refuse to be involved with: *He washed his hands of the whole affair.*

hand•bag (hand′bag′) /ˈhænd,bæg/ *n.* [*count*] a woman's purse or pocketbook.

hand•ball (hand′bôl′) /ˈhænd,bɔl/ *n.* **1.** [*noncount*] a game played by two or four persons who strike a ball against a wall or walls with the hand. **2.** [*count*] the small, hard rubber ball used in this game.

hand•bill (hand′bil′) /ˈhænd,bɪl/ *n.* [*count*] a small printed advertisement usually for distribution by hand.

hand•book (hand′bo͝ok′) /ˈhænd,bʊk/ *n.* [*count*] a book of instruction or guidance, as for an occupation; manual.

hand•cart (hand′kärt′) /ˈhænd,kɑrt/ *n.* [*count*] a small cart pulled or pushed by hand.

hand•clasp (hand′klasp′) /ˈhænd,klæsp/ *n.* [*count*] a gripping of hands by two or more people, as in greeting.

hand•cuff (hand′kuf′) /ˈhænd,kʌf/ *n.* [*count*] **1.** a metal ring that can be locked around a prisoner's wrist, usually one of a pair connected by a chain or bar. **—*v.*** [~ + *obj*] **2.** to put handcuffs on: *handcuffed the suspect to the door handle.* **3.** to make ineffective or helpless: *They feel handcuffed by so many restrictions.*

hand•ful (hand′fo͝ol) /ˈhændfʊl/ *n.* [*count*], *pl.* **-fuls. 1.** the quantity or amount that the hand can hold: *a handful of sand.* **2.** [*singular; a* + ~ + *of*] a small quantity: *a handful of demonstrators.* **3.** [*singular*] a person or thing that is as much as one can control: *Those children are a handful.*

hand•gun (hand′gun′) /ˈhænd,gʌn/ *n.* [*count*] any firearm held and fired with one hand; a revolver or a pistol.

hand•i•cap (han′dē kap′) /ˈhændiy,kæp/ *n., v.,* **-capped, -cap•ping. —*n.*** [*count*] **1.** a contest in which a disadvantage or advantage, as of weight, is given to competitors to equalize their chances of winning. **2.** the disadvantage or advantage itself. **3.** any disadvantage that makes success more difficult. **4.** a physical or mental disability, esp. one that makes ordinary activities of daily living difficult: *The accident left him with a handicap.* **—*v.*** [~ + *obj*] **5.** to place at a disadvantage; burden: *The search was handicapped by the darkness.*

hand•i•capped (han′dē kapt′) /ˈhændiy,kæpt/ *adj.* **1.** physically or mentally disabled, as by accident, birth defect, etc.: *a handicapped person.* **—*n.*** **2. the handicapped,** [*plural; used with a plural verb*] handicapped persons thought of as a group.

hand•i•cap•per (han′dē kap′ər) /ˈhændiy,kæpər/ *n.* [*count*] **1.** an official who assigns handicaps to contestants. **2.** a person who makes predictions on the results of horse races.

hand•i•craft (han′dē kraft′) /ˈhændiy,kræft/ *n.* [*count; usually plural*] **1.** an art, craft, or trade in which manual skill is required. **2.** the articles made by handicraft.

hand•i•work (han′dē wûrk′) /ˈhændiy,wɜrk/ *n.* [*noncount*] work done by hand.

hand•ker•chief (hang′kər chif, -chēf′) /ˈhæŋkərtʃɪf, -,tʃiyf/ *n.* [*count*] a small piece of fabric used for wiping the nose, eyes, etc., or worn for decoration.

han•dle (han′dl) /ˈhændl̩/ *n., v.,* **-dled, -dling. —*n.*** [*count*] **1.** a part of a thing made to be taken or held by the hand: *I need the rake with the long handle.* **2.** *Slang.* a person's name. **—*v.*** **3.** [~ + *obj*] to touch, pick up, carry, or feel with the hand or hands; use the hands on; take hold of: *He handled the painting carefully.* **4.** [~ + *obj*] to manage, deal with, or be responsible for: *handled that angry customer with tact.* **5.** [~ + *obj*] to use or employ, esp. in a particular manner; manipulate: *That artist has learned to handle color expertly in his paintings.* **6.** [~ + *obj*] to manage, direct, train, or control: *The general could handle troops effectively.* **7.** [*no obj*] to behave or perform in a particular way when handled, directed, managed, etc: *The jet was handling poorly.* **8.** [~ + *obj*] to trade in: *That store doesn't handle computer software.* **—*Idiom.*** **9. get** or **have a handle on,** [~ + *obj*] to obtain or possess an understanding of: *He couldn't get a handle on their problems.*

han•dle•bar (han′dl bär′) /ˈhændl̩,bɑr/ *n.* [*count*] Usually, **handlebars.** [*plural*] the curved steering bar of a bicycle, motorcycle, etc., gripped by the hands.

han•dler (hand′lər) /ˈhændlər/ *n.* [*count*] **1.** a person or thing that handles. **2.** a person who trains a boxer or who trains dogs and exhibits them in dog shows. **3.** a person who manages and represents a public figure, esp. a political candidate: *The candidate was surrounded by his handlers and the news media.*

hand•made (hand′mād′) /ˈhændˈmeyd/ *adj.* made by hand.

hand•maid (hand′mād′) /ˈhænd,meyd/ also **hand•maid•en** (-mād′n) /-,meydn̩/ *n.* [*count*] a female servant or attendant.

hand′-me-down′, *n.* [*count*] **1.** a used item passed along for further use by another, esp. an article of clothing: *She was wearing her sister's hand-me-downs.* **—*adj.*** **2.** passed along for further use by another: *wearing hand-me-down shoes.*

hand•out (hand′out′) /ˈhænd,awt/ *n.* [*count*] **1.** food, clothing, or money given to a needy person, as a beggar. **2.** a free sample of a product. **3.** a press release. **4.** any copy of a speech, fact sheet, etc., distributed at a meeting.

hand•pick (hand′pik′) /ˈhændˈpɪk/ *v.* [~ + *obj*] **1.** to pick by hand. **2.** to select personally and with care: *She hand-picked her successor.*

hand•rail (hand′rāl′) /ˈhænd,reyl/ *n.* [*count*] a rail serving as a support or guard at the side of a stairway, platform, etc.

hand•shake (hand′shāk′) /ˈhænd,ʃeyk/ *n.* [*count*] **1.** a gripping and shaking of each other's hand, as in greeting, congratulation, or farewell. **2.** an exchange of signals in a computer system, making sure of a correct connection with another device.

hands′-off′, *adj.* characterized by not interfering: *a hands-off policy on privacy issues.*

hand•some (han′səm) /ˈhænsəm/ *adj.*, **-som•er, -som•est. 1.** having an attractive appearance; good-looking: *a handsome boy; a handsome couple.* **2.** having pleasing physical characteristics: *a handsome house.* **3.** [*usually before a noun*] considerable in amount: *a handsome salary.* —**hand′some•ly,** *adv.* —**hand′some•ness,** *n.* [*noncount*]

hands′-on′, *adj.* having, needing, or involving active personal participation: *hands-on experience with computers.*

hand•spring (hand′spring′) /ˈhænd,sprɪŋ/ *n.* [*count*] an acrobatic movement in which the upright body moves forward or backward in a complete circle, landing first on the hands and then on the feet.

hand•stand (hand′stand′) /ˈhænd,stænd/ *n.* [*count*] an act of supporting the body upside down in a vertical position by balancing on the palms of the hands.

hand′-to-hand′, *adj.* close to one's enemy or opponent; at close quarters: *hand-to-hand combat.*

hand′-to-mouth′, *adj., adv.* offering or providing barely enough to live on or to sustain one's existence; meager; precarious: *made a hand-to-mouth living; always living hand-to-mouth.*

hand•work (hand′wûrk′) /ˈhænd,wɜrk/ *n.* [*noncount*] work done by hand, as distinguished from work done by machine.

hand•writ•ing (hand′rī′ting) /ˈhænd,raytɪŋ/ *n.* [*noncount*] **1.** writing done with a pen or pencil in the hand. **2.** a style or manner of writing by hand. —***Idiom.*** **3. handwriting on the wall,** [*usually: the* + ~] a clear indication, esp. of failure or disaster: *This latest defeat was the handwriting on the wall that the war was lost.* —**hand•writ•ten** (hand′rit′n) /ˈhænd,rɪtn̩/ *adj.*: *a handwritten letter.*

hand•y (han′dē) /ˈhændiy/ *adj.*, **-i•er, -i•est. 1.** within easy reach; accessible: *kept supplies handy for an emergency.* **2.** convenient or useful: *a handy reference work.* **3.** skillful with the hands; dexterous: *He's handy with most tools.* —**hand′i•ness,** *n.* [*noncount*]

hand•y•man (han′dē man′) /ˈhændiy,mæn/ *n.* [*count*], *pl.* **-men.** a person hired to do small maintenance or repair jobs.

hang (hang) /hæŋ/ *v.*, **hung** (hung) /hʌŋ/ or (*esp. for 4*) **hanged, hang•ing,** *n.* —*v.* **1.** [~ + *obj*] to fasten (a thing) so that it is supported only from above or near its own top; suspend: *I hung a few pictures on the wall.* **2.** [*no obj*] to be suspended; dangle: *clothes hanging on the clothesline.* **3.** to (cause to) be placed in position or suspended so as to allow free movement: [~ + *obj*]: *The workmen hung the door of the new house.* [*no obj*]: *The door doesn't hang properly.* **4.** [~ + *obj*] to kill by suspending (someone) by the neck from a rope: *to hang a convicted murderer.* **5.** [~ + *obj*] to furnish or decorate with something suspended: *to hang a room with pictures.* **6.** [*no obj*] to stick out downward, jut out, or lean over or forward. **7. hang around,** *Informal.* **a.** [~ + *around* (+ *with*)] to spend time in a certain place or in certain company: *He's been hanging around with older kids.* **b.** [*no obj*] to linger about; remain in one place; loiter: *hung around until the bus left.* **8. hang back,** [*no obj*] to hesitate or be reluctant to move forward or take action: *She hung back from taking part in the game.* **9. hang in (there),** [*no obj*] *Informal.* to manage to go on or keep going; persevere or endure: *Hang in there; your hard work will pay off.* **10. hang on, a.** [*no obj*] to cling tightly: *My niece hung on tight to me.* **b.** [~ + *obj*] to be dependent on: *The future of our company may hang on this one deal.* **c.** [*no obj*] to continue; manage to keep going: *This job is so bad; how much longer can I hang on?* **d.** [*no obj*] to keep a telephone line open: *Hang on, I'll see if she's here.* **e.** [*no obj*] to wait briefly; keep calm: *"Hang on, we're almost home," he shouted.* **f.** [~ + *obj*] to listen very carefully or attentively to: *They hung on his every word.* **11. hang out, a.** to lean out, suspend, or be suspended: [*no obj*]: *He hung out the window, gulping in the fresh air.* [~ + *obj* + *out*]: *He hung his head out the window.* **b.** [*no obj*] *Informal.* to go often to or spend time at a certain place: *hanging out at the mall on weekends.* **c.** [*no obj*] *Informal.* to spend time in a casual way: *We were just hanging out and gossiping.* **12. hang up, a.** to suspend something on or as if on a hook: [~ + *up* + *obj*]: *I hung up my jacket on the hook.* [~ + *obj* + *up*]: *I hung it up.* **b.** to stop or delay the progress of: [~ + *up* + *obj*]: *This broken machine is hanging up the whole assembly line.* [~ + *obj* + *up*]: *You're hanging everybody up by not cooperating.* **c.** to end a telephone call by breaking the connection: [*no obj*]: *I hung up and wrote down the message.* [~ + *up* + *obj*]: *I hung up the phone.* —*n.* [*count; usually singular*] **13.** the way in which a thing hangs: *the hang of a jacket.* **14.** *Informal.* the precise manner of doing or using something; knack: *I've finally got the hang of programming a computer.* —***Idiom.*** **15. hang a left** (or **right**), *Slang.* to make a left (or right) turn, as while driving an automobile. **16. hang in the balance,** [*no obj*] to be in a dangerous, unsteady, or uncertain state or condition: *The fate of the world hung in the balance.* **17. hang it up,** *Informal.* to quit; resign: *He decided to hang it up after years on the job.* **18. hang loose,** [*no obj*] *Slang.* to remain relaxed or calm: *She's still hanging loose in spite of all the pressures of her new job.* **19. hang one on,** *Slang.* **a.** [*no obj*] to become extremely drunk. **b.** [~ + *obj*] to hit (someone): *He hung one on his tormentor.* **20. hang together,** [*no obj*] **a.** to be loyal to one another; remain united: *We must hang together to get out of this difficulty.* **b.** to be logical or consistent: *His research doesn't hang together.* **21. hang tough,** [*no obj*] *Informal.* to remain unchanging in one's attitude; to be unyielding: *The union has to hang tough during these negotiations.*

hang•ar (hang′ər) /ˈhæŋər/ *n.* [*count*] a shed or shelter, esp. for housing aircraft.

hang•dog (hang′dôg′, -dog′) /ˈhæŋ,dɔg, -,dɒg/ *adj.* looking defeated: *a hangdog expression.*

hang•er (hang′ər) /ˈhæŋər/ *n.* [*count*] **1.** a shoulder-shaped frame with a hook at the top, usually of wire, wood, or plastic, for draping and hanging a piece of clothing not in use: *Put the nice shirt on a hanger.* **2.** anything on which items are hung, such as a hook.

hang′er-on′, *n.* [*count*], *pl.* **hang•ers-on.** a person who remains in a place or with a group in the hope of personal gain: *The champ's hangers-on followed him everywhere.*

hang′ glid′er, *n.* [*count*] a large, kite-like device, from which a person is suspended, that glides through the air.

hang′ glid′ing, *n.* [*noncount*] the sport of launching oneself from a cliff or a steep incline and soaring through the air by means of a hang glider.

hang•ing (hang′ing) /ˈhæŋɪŋ/ *n.* **1.** the act or instance of executing a condemned prisoner by suspension by the neck from a noose until dead: [*noncount*]: *Public hanging was outlawed.* [*count*]: *to witness a hanging.* **2.** [*count*] something for hanging on a wall, as a tapestry: *a beautiful wall hanging.* —*adj.* [*before a noun*] **3.** punishable by or deserving death by hanging: *a hanging crime.* **4.** willing or likely to cause death by hanging: *a hanging jury; a hanging judge.* **5.** situated on a steep slope: *a hanging garden.*

hang•man (hang′mən) /ˈhæŋmən/ *n.* [*count*], *pl.* **-men.** a person who hangs criminals who are sentenced to death.

hang•nail (hang′nāl′) /ˈhæŋ,neyl/ *n.* [*count*] a small piece of partly detached skin next to a fingernail.

hang•out (hang′out′) /ˈhæŋ,awt/ *n.* [*count*] *Informal.* a place where a person frequently visits, esp. for seeing friends or for recreation: *Their favorite hangout was the disco.*

hang•o•ver (hang′ō′vər) /ˈhæŋ,owvər/ *n.* [*count*] **1.** the unpleasant physical aftereffects of consuming alcohol or drugs to excess. **2.** something remaining from a former time.

hang′-up′ or **hang′up′,** *n.* [*count*] *Slang.* **1.** something that a person worries about constantly or fears greatly: *had a hang-up about meeting new people.* **2.** problem; difficulty: *There's some hang-up about our plane reservation.*

hank (hangk) /hæŋk/ *n.* [*count*] a coil, knot, or loop: *a hank of hair.*

han•ker (hang′kər) /ˈhæŋkər/ *v.* to have a restless longing or desire for: [~ + *after* + *obj*]: *hankering after friendship.* [~ + *for* + *obj*]: *The nation hankered for peace.* [~ + *to* + *verb*]: *They hankered to have a place in the country.* —**han′ker•ing,** *n.* [*count*]: *a hankering for sweets.*

han•ky or **han•kie** (hang′kē) /ˈhæŋkiy/ *n.* [*count*], *pl.* **-kies.** a handkerchief.

han•ky-pan•ky or **han•key-pan•key** (hang′kē-pang′kē) /ˈhæŋkiyˈpæŋkiy/ *n.* [*noncount*] *Informal.* **1.** illegal or unethical behavior or dealings: *a little financial hanky-panky.* **2.** improper sexual relations.

han•som (han′səm) /ˈhænsəm/ *n.* [*count*] a low, two-wheeled, covered vehicle drawn by one horse, for two passengers, with the driver on an elevated seat behind.

Ha•nuk•kah or **Cha•nu•kah** (hä′nə kə, ᴋʜä′-) /ˈhɑnəkə, ˈxɑ-/ *n.* [*proper noun*] an eight-day Jewish festival celebrating the rededication of the Temple.

-hap-, *root.* *-hap-* comes from Old Norse, where it has the meaning "luck; chance." This meaning is found in such words as: HAPHAZARD, HAPLESS, HAPPEN, HAPPENING, HAPPENSTANCE, MISHAP, PERHAPS.

hap•haz•ard (hap haz′ərd) /hæpˈhæzərd/ *adj.* lacking order or planning; happening by chance: *the hotel's haphazard service.* —**hap•haz′ard•ly,** *adv.* See -HAP-.

hap•less (hap′lis) /ˈhæplɪs/ *adj.* [*before a noun*] unlucky; luckless; unfortunate: *hapless victims.* See -HAP-.

hap•pen (hap′ən) /ˈhæpən/ *v.* **1.** [*no obj*] to take place; come to pass; occur: *What happened after the accident?* **2.** [*not: be + ~-ing; It + ~ + (that) clause*] to come to pass by chance: *It just happened that a policeman was nearby.* **3.** [*not: be + ~-ing; ~ + to + verb*] to have the fortune or luck (to do something): *happened to see him there.* **4.** [*~ + to + obj*] to damage or be damaging to (a person or thing): *Nothing happened to her.* **5.** [*~ + on/upon + obj*] to meet, find, or discover by chance: *to happen upon a clue to a mystery.* **6.** [*~ + along*] to be, come, go, etc., casually or by chance: *happened along just in time.* See -HAP-.

hap•pen•ing (hap′ə ning) /ˈhæpənɪŋ/ *n.* [*count*] an occurrence or event, esp. one considered important: *an important happening that affected everyone.* See -HAP-.

hap•pen•stance (hap′ən stans′) /ˈhæpənˌstæns/ *n.* a chance happening or event: [*noncount*]: *Was it pure happenstance that you were present?* [*count*]: *an extraordinary happenstance.* See -HAP-, -STAN-..

hap•py (hap′ē) /ˈhæpiy/ *adj.,* **-pi•er, -pi•est. 1.** delighted; pleased; glad: *happy over the news.* **2.** characterized by or showing pleasure, contentment, or joy: *a happy baby.* **3.** [*be + ~ + to + verb*] pleased; willing: *I'll be happy to meet with you later.* **4.** apt; suitable; appropriate: *That remark was not a happy one.* —**hap•pi•ly** (hap′ə lē) /ˈhæpəliy/ *adv.*: *The kids were playing happily together.* —**hap′pi•ness,** *n.* [*noncount*]

hap′py-go-luck′y, *adj.* trusting cheerfully to luck; happily unworried.

hap′py hour′, *n.* [*noncount*] a period of time at a bar when drinks are sold at reduced prices:: *Are we too late for happy hour?*

ha•ra-ki•ri (här′ə kēr′ē, har′ə-, har′ē-) /ˈhɑrəˈkɪəriy, ˈhærə-, ˈhæriy-/ *n.* [*noncount*] ceremonial suicide by disembowelment.

ha•rangue (hə rang′) /həˈræŋ/ *n., v.,* **-rangued, -rangu•ing.** —*n.* [*count*] **1.** a long, passionate, and forceful speech, esp. one delivered in public. —*v.* [*~ + obj*] **2.** to address or speak to (someone) in a harangue: *haranguing the crowd into a frenzy.*

ha•rass (hə ras′, har′əs) /həˈræs, ˈhærəs/ *v.* [*~ + obj*], **1.** to annoy continuously; pester; persecute: *harassed the candidate about his war record.* **2.** to trouble by repeated attacks: *to harass enemy supply lines.* —**ha•rass′er,** *n.* [*count*] —**ha•rass′ment,** *n.* [*noncount*]

har•bin•ger (här′bin jər) /ˈhɑrbɪndʒər/ *n.* [*count*] someone or something that announces or signals the approach of someone or something; a forerunner.

har•bor (här′bər) /ˈhɑrbər/ *n.* [*count*] **1.** a body of water deep enough for anchoring a ship and providing protection from the weather. **2.** any place of shelter or safety. —*v.* [*~ + obj*] **3.** to give shelter to: *to harbor refugees.* **4.** to conceal; hide: *to harbor fugitives.* **5.** to keep or hold in the mind; entertain: *harbored suspicions.* Also, *esp. Brit.,* **harbour.**

hard (härd) /hɑrd/ *adj.* and *adv.,* **-er, -est.** —*adj.* **1.** not soft; solid and firm to the touch: *The rock felt hard in his fist.* **2.** firmly formed; tight: *a hard knot.* **3.** difficult to do or accomplish; troublesome: *a hard task.* [*It + be + ~ + to + verb*]: *It was hard to do that task.* [*be + ~ + to + verb*]: *You are hard to please.* **4.** involving a great deal of effort or energy: *hard labor.* **5.** performing or carrying on work with great effort or energy: *a hard worker.* **6.** violent in force; severe: *took a hard fall.* **7.** unfortunate: *hard luck.* **8.** harsh; rough; cruel: *hard treatment; a hard taskmaster.* [*be + ~ + on + obj*]: *Don't be so hard on your kids.* **9.** severe; austere: *a hard winter.* **10.** [*before a noun*] difficult to explain away: *hard facts.* **11.** [*before a noun*] factual or definitely true: *hard information.* **12.** [*before a noun*] resentful; bitter: *hard feelings.* **13.** [*before a noun*] examining closely; searching: *took a hard look at our finances.* **14.** lacking delicacy or softness; sharp: *a face with hard features.* **15.** [*before a noun*] severe or demanding in terms: *a hard bargain.* **16.** (of water) containing mineral salts that interfere with the action of soap. **17.** [*usually: before a noun*] in coins or paper money as distinguished from checks, etc.: *hard cash.* **18.** (of paper money) backed by gold reserves: *hard currency.* **19.** (of alcoholic beverages) containing more than 22.5 percent alcohol by volume. **20.** [*before a noun*] (of an illegal narcotic or drug) causing physical addiction. **21.** (of the letters *c* and *g*) pronounced as (k) in *come* and (g) in *go.* —*adv.* **22.** with great exertion: *to work hard.* **23.** intently or critically: *to look hard at a decision.* **24.** harshly or severely: *workers were hit hard by the recession.* **25.** so as to be solid, tight, or firm: *The ice was frozen hard.* **26.** in a deeply emotional manner: *He took the news very hard.* —***Idiom.*** **27. hard by,** near; in close proximity to. **28. hard put,** [*be + ~*] barely able: *We are hard put to pay the rent.* —**hard′ness,** *n.* [*noncount*]

hard′-and-fast′, *adj.* strict; binding: *hard-and-fast rules.*

hard•ball (härd′bôl′) /ˈhɑrdˌbɔl/ *n.* **1.** [*noncount*] baseball, as distinguished from softball. —***Idiom.*** **2. play hardball,** to be aggressive and ruthless in one's dealings: *played hardball in the election.*

hard′-bit′ten, *adj.* toughened by battle or struggle: *hard-bitten soldiers.*

hard′-boiled′, *adj.* **1.** (of an egg) boiled in the shell long enough for the yolk and white to solidify. **2.** not sentimental; realistic; tough: *a hard-boiled detective.*

hard′ cop′y, *n.* [*noncount*] computer output printed on paper; printout.

hard′-core′, *adj.* **1.** committed; uncompromising: *a hard-core conservative.* **2.** very realistic; explicit: *hard-core pornography.*

hard•cov•er (härd′kuv′ər) /ˈhɑrdˈkʌvər/ *n.* [*count*] **1.** a book bound in cloth, leather, or the like, over stiff material. —*adj.* **2.** bound as a hardcover. Compare PAPERBACK. Also, **hard•back** (härd′bak′) /ˈhɑrdˌbæk/.

hard′ disk′, *n.* [*count*] a rigid disk built into a personal computer for storing computer programs and relatively large amounts of data.

hard•en (här′dn) /ˈhɑrdn̩/ *v.* **1.** to (cause to) become hard or harder: [*no obj*]: *The ice cream hardened in the freezer.* [*~ + obj*]: *The freezer will harden the ice cream.* **2.** to (cause to) become pitiless, unfeeling, or less gentle and sympathetic: [*no obj*]: *His heart hardened with anger.* [*~ + obj*]: *His cruel life had hardened his heart.* **3.** [*~ + obj*] to cause to become stronger; toughen: *Battle had hardened the troops.* —**hard′en•er,** *n.* [*count*]

hard′ hat′ or **hard′hat′,** *n.* [*count*] **1.** a protective helmet of metal or plastic worn by construction workers. **2.** a construction worker. **3.** *Informal.* a conservative, intolerant person.

hard•head•ed or **hard-head•ed** (härd′hed′id) /ˈhɑrdˌhɛdɪd/ *adj.* **1.** not easily moved or deceived; shrewd: *too hardheaded to be fooled by flattery.* **2.** obstinate; stubborn; willful. —**hard′head′ed•ly,** *adv.* —**hard′head′ed•ness,** *n.* [*noncount*]

hard•heart•ed (härd′här′tid) /ˈhɑrdˈhɑrtɪd/ *adj.* unfeeling; unmerciful: *a hardhearted captor.* —**hard′heart′ed•ly,** *adv.* —**hard′heart′ed•ness,** *n.* [*noncount*]

hard′-line′ or **hard′line′,** *adj.* uncompromising; unyielding: *hard-line union demands.* —**hard′-lin′er,** *n.* [*count*]: *a hard-liner who would not give in to threats.*

hard•ly (härd′lē) /ˈhɑrdliy/ *adv.* **1.** only just; almost not; barely: *We hardly ever see you anymore.* **2.** not at all; scarcely: *It's hardly surprising that we lost money during the recession.* **3.** with little likelihood: *They will hardly come now.*

hard′-nosed′, *adj.* uncompromising; tough: *a hard-nosed negotiator.*

hard′ of hear′ing, *adj.* [*be + ~*] unable to hear well; deaf or almost deaf.

hard′ pal′ate, *n.* See PALATE (def. 1).

hard•press•ed (härd′prest′) /ˈhɑrdˈprɛst/ *adj.* in great difficulty; hard put: *was hardpressed for a good answer to the question.*

hard′ sell′, *n.* [*count*] an aggressive method of advertising, selling, or promoting.

hard•ship (härd′ship) /ˈhɑrdʃɪp/ *n.* **1.** [*noncount*] a condition that is difficult to live through; deprivation; oppression: *a life of hardship under that regime.* **2.** [*count*] an instance or cause of hardship: *endured many hardships in childhood.*

hard•tack (härd′tak′) /ˈhɑrdˌtæk/ *n.* [*noncount*] a hard, saltless biscuit.

hard′ up′, *adj. Informal.* **1.** in need of money: *too hard up to afford new shoes.* **2.** [*be* + ~ (+ *for*)] feeling a lack: *He's hard up for friends.*

hard•ware (härd′wâr′) /ˈhɑrdˌwɛər/ *n.* [*noncount*] **1.** articles made of metal, such as tools, locks, or machine parts. **2.** the mechanical equipment necessary for conducting an activity: *The theory is fine, but can the engineers construct the hardware?* **3.** the mechanical, magnetic, electronic, and electrical devices making up a computer system.

hard•wood (härd′wo͝od′) /ˈhɑrdˌwʊd/ *n.* **1.** [*noncount*] the hard, strong wood or timber of various broad-leaved deciduous trees: *a bureau made of hardwood.* **2.** [*count*] a tree yielding such wood.

har•dy (här′dē) /ˈhɑrdiy/ *adj.*, **-di•er, -di•est. 1.** capable of continuing in spite of fatigue, hardship, exposure, etc.; sturdy: *a hardy constitution.* **2.** requiring great physical courage, vigor, or endurance: *the hardiest sports.* **3.** (of plants) able to withstand the winter in the open air: *a hardy shrub.* **4.** bold or daring; courageous: *hardy explorers.* —**har•di•ly** (här′dl ē) /ˈhɑrdḷiy/ *adv.* —**har′di•ness,** *n.* [*noncount*]

hare (hâr) /hɛər/ *n.* [*count*], *pl.* **hares,** (*esp. when thought of as a group*) **hare.** a long-eared animal similar to a rabbit but usually larger.

hare•brained (hâr′brānd′) /ˈhɛərˌbreynd/ *adj.* silly; stupid; foolish: *a harebrained scheme.*

hare•lip (hâr′lip′) /ˈhɛərˌlɪp/ *n.* [*count*] a deformed lip, usually the upper one, in which there is a vertical split. —**hare′lipped′,** *adj.*

har•em (hâr′əm, har′-) /ˈhɛərəm, ˈhær-/ *n.* [*count*] **1.** the part of a Muslim palace or house reserved as a living place for women. **2.** the women dwelling in a harem.

hark (härk) /hɑrk/ *v.* **1.** [*no obj*] to listen attentively. **2. hark back,** [~ + *back* + *to* + *obj*] to remember or retell a previous event or topic: *always harking back to his army days.*

har•lot (här′lət) /ˈhɑrlət/ *n.* [*count*] a prostitute; whore. —**har•lot•ry** (här′lə trē) /ˈhɑrlətriy/ *n.* [*noncount*]

harm (härm) /hɑrm/ *n.* [*noncount*] **1.** injury or damage; hurt: *to do someone bodily harm.* **2.** moral injury; evil; wrong: *That proposal will do more harm than good.* —*v.* [~ + *obj*] **3.** to do or cause harm to: *to harm one's reputation.*

harm•ful (härm′fəl) /ˈhɑrmfəl/ *adj.* causing or capable of causing harm. —**harm′ful•ly,** *adv.* —**harm′ful•ness,** *n.* [*noncount*]

harm•less (härm′lis) /ˈhɑrmlɪs/ *adj.* without the power or desire to do harm; innocuous: *a harmless prank.* —**harm′less•ly,** *adv.*

har•mon•ic (här mon′ik) /hɑrˈmɒnɪk/ *adj.* of, having, or relating to musical harmony. —**har•mon′i•cal•ly,** *adv.*

har•mon•i•ca (här mon′i kə) /hɑrˈmɒnɪkə/ *n.* [*count*], *pl.* **-cas.** a small musical wind instrument containing a set of metal reeds. Also called **mouth organ.**

har•mo•ni•ous (här mō′nē əs) /hɑrˈmowniyəs/ *adj.* **1.** having or showing agreement in feeling, attitude, or action: *a harmonious group whose members got along well with each other.* **2.** forming a pleasingly consistent sound or appearance; pleasant to the sight or to the hearing: *harmonious colors; a harmonious tune.* —**har•mo′ni•ous•ly,** *adv.* —**har•mo′ni•ous•ness,** *n.* [*noncount*]

har•mo•nize (här′mə nīz′) /ˈhɑrməˌnayz/ *v.*, **-nized, -niz•ing. 1.** to (cause to) be harmonious: [~ + *obj*]: *to harmonize one's views with the facts.* [*no obj*]: *Their views harmonize neatly with ours.* **2.** [*no obj*] to sing or play with another in musical harmony. —**har•mo•ni•za•tion** (här′mə nə zā′shən) /ˌhɑrmənəˈzeyʃən/ *n.* [*noncount*] —**har′mo•niz′er,** *n.* [*count*]

har•mo•ny (här′mə nē) /ˈhɑrməniy/ *n.*, *pl.* **-nies. 1.** [*noncount*] a state or condition of agreement, cooperation, or peacefulness; accord: *lived in harmony.* **2.** a consistent, orderly, or pleasing arrangement of parts: [*noncount*]: *the beautiful harmony of color in that painting.* [*count*]: *the composer's beautiful harmonies in the last movement.*

har•ness (här′nis) /ˈhɑrnɪs/ *n.* [*count*] **1.** the parts other than the yoke that are attached to a horse's body or head to control it. **2.** something resembling a harness. —*v.* [~ + *obj*] **3.** to put a harness on; attach by a harness: *The horse was harnessed to the plow.* **4.** to gain control over for a particular end: *The hydroelectric plant harnesses water power.*

harp (härp) /hɑrp/ *n.* [*count*] **1.** a musical instrument having a triangular frame and strings plucked with the fingers. —*v.* **2. harp on** or **upon,** [~ + *on/upon* + *obj*] to repeat annoyingly over and over again: *kept harping on the details of his plan.* —**harp′ist,** *n.* [*count*]: *a harpist in the orchestra.*

har•poon (här po͞on′) /hɑrˈpuwn/ *n.* [*count*] **1.** a spear with a barbed edge attached to a rope, used in hunting whales and large fish. —*v.* [~ + *obj*] **2.** to spear with a harpoon.

harp•si•chord (härp′si kôrd′) /ˈhɑrpsɪˌkɔrd/ *n.* [*count*] a musical keyboard instrument whose strings are plucked by leather points. —**harp′si•chord′ist,** *n.* [*count*]

har•py (här′pē) /ˈhɑrpiy/ *n.* [*count*], *pl.* **-pies.** a bad-tempered woman.

har•ri•dan (här′i dn) /ˈhɑrɪdṇ/ *n.* [*count*] a harpy.

har•ried (har′ēd) /ˈhæriyd/ *adj.* beset by worry; harassed: *looked harried and tired.*

har•row (har′ō) /ˈhærow/ *n.* [*count*] a farm tool with spikelike teeth or upright disks, for leveling and breaking up clumps of earth after plowing.

har•row•ing (har′ō ing) /ˈhærowɪŋ/ *adj.* causing fright, upset, or pain: *a harrowing storm.*

har•ry (har′ē) /ˈhæriy/ *v.* [~ + *obj*], **-ried, -ry•ing.** to attack repeatedly; torment: *crows harrying a hawk.*

harsh (härsh) /hɑrʃ/ *adj.*, **-er, -est. 1.** not gentle or pleasant; severe: *received harsh treatment.* **2.** grim; stern: *a harsh master.* **3.** uncomfortable or irritating to the body or to the senses: *harsh detergents.* —**harsh′ly,** *adv.* —**harsh′ness,** *n.* [*noncount*]

hart (härt) /hɑrt/ *n.* [*count*], *pl.* **harts,** (*esp. when thought of as a group*) **hart.** a mature male European red deer with antlers.

har•um-scar•um (hâr′əm skâr′əm, har′əm skar′əm) /ˈhɛərəmˈskɛərəm, ˈhærəmˈskærəm/ *adj.* **1.** disorganized; uncontrolled: *a harum-scarum ball game.* —*adv.* **2.** wildly: *ran around harum-scarum.*

har•vest (här′vist) /ˈhɑrvɪst/ *n.* [*count*] **1.** Also, **har′vest•ing.** the gathering of crops: *helped with the harvest.* **2.** the season when ripened crops are gathered. **3.** a crop or yield of one growing season: *a harvest of wheat.* **4.** the result of any act, process, or event: *the harvest of twenty years of research.* —*v.* [~ + *obj*] **5.** to gather (a crop or the like); reap: *It was time to harvest the grain.* **6.** to gather the crop from: *to harvest the fields.* **7.** to accumulate; gather: *harvested the results of their research.* **8.** to take for use: *harvesting salmon from the river.*

har•ves•ter (här′və stər) /ˈhɑrvəstər/ *n.* [*count*] a special farm machine for harvesting crops.

has (haz; *unstressed* həz, əz) /hæz; *unstressed* həz, əz/ *v.* a 3rd pers. sing. pres. indic. of HAVE.

has′-been′, *n.* [*count*] a person or thing that is no longer effective, successful, or popular.

hash[1] (hash) /hæʃ/ *n.* **1.** cooked meat and potatoes cut in small pieces and browned together: [*noncount*]: *We're having hash for dinner.* [*count*]: *She makes a delicious hash.* **2.** [*count; usually singular*] a mess; jumble: *made a hash of his first job.* —*v.* **3.** [~ + *obj*] to make a mess or jumble of (things). **4. hash out** or **over,** [~ + *out/over* + *obj*] to discuss or review (something) thoroughly: *They hashed out their differences.*

hash[2] (hash) /hæʃ/ *n.* [*noncount*] *Slang.* hashish.

hash•ish or **hash•eesh** (hash′ēsh, hä shēsh′) /ˈhæʃiyʃ, hɑˈʃiyʃ/ *n.* [*noncount*] the flowering tops and leaves of Indian hemp, or the hardened juice of this plant, smoked, chewed, or drunk as a narcotic.

has•n't (haz′ənt) /ˈhæzənt/ contraction of *has not.*

hasp (hasp) /hæsp/ *n.* [*count*] a clasp for a door, lid, etc., esp. one passing over a staple and fastened by a pin or a padlock.

has•sle (has′əl) /ˈhæsəl/ *n.*, *v.*, **-sled, -sling.** *Informal.* —*n.* [*count*] **1.** a disorderly dispute or argument: *a hassle on the street that the cops broke up.* **2.** a difficult or trying situation; a bother: *a hassle to get to school so early.* —*v.* **3.** [*no obj*] to argue or quarrel: *children hassling over who has the most toys.* **4.** [~ + *obj*] to annoy or harass: *She'll hassle me until I agree to write the letter for her.*

has•sock (has′ək) /ˈhæsək/ *n.* [*count*] a thick, firm cushion used as a footstool or for kneeling.

hast (hast) /hæst/ *v. Archaic.* 2nd pers. sing. pres. indic. of HAVE.

haste (hāst) /heyst/ *n.* [*noncount*] **1.** unnecessarily quick action; thoughtless speed: *Haste makes waste.* —***Idiom.* 2. make haste,** [*no obj*] to hasten; hurry.

has•ten (hā′sən) /ˈheysən/ *v.* to (cause to) move or act with haste: [*no obj*]: *They hastened to the bus stop.* [~ + *obj*]: *to hasten the downfall of the dictatorship.*

hast•y (hā′stē) /ˈheystiy/ *adj.*, **-i•er, -i•est. 1.** moving, acting, or done with haste: *a hasty visit.* **2.** too quick;

rash: *regretted his hasty decision.* —**hast•i•ly** (hās′tl ē) /ˈheystḷiy/ *adv.*

hat (hat) /hæt/ *n., v.,* **hat•ted, hat•ting.** —*n.* [*count*] **1.** a shaped covering for the head, usually with a crown and often a brim. See illustration at CLOTHING. —*v.* [~ + *obj*] **2.** to provide with a hat; put a hat on. —***Idiom.*** **3. eat one's hat,** This phrase is used to express disbelief that something will happen: *If that train arrives on time, I'll eat my hat.* **4. hat in hand,** humbly and respectfully: *I asked for help, hat in hand.* **5. pass the hat,** to ask for contributions of money, as for charity: *They passed the hat and took in almost $500.* **6. take one's hat off to,** [~ + *obj*] to express high regard for; praise: *I take my hat off to her; she deserves the award.* **7. talk through one's hat,** [*no obj*] to make unsupported absurd statements. **8. throw** or **toss one's hat in** or **into the ring,** to declare one's candidacy: *He threw his hat in the ring and ran for the presidency.* **9. under one's hat,** secret; confidential: *Keep this information under your hat.* **10. wear two** or **several hats,** to work in more than one capacity: fill two or more positions: *He's wearing two hats: chairman of the department and assistant to the dean.* —**hat′less,** *adj.*

hatch[1] (hach) /hætʃ/ *v.* **1.** (of young birds) to (cause to) break out of an egg: [*no obj*]: *The young birds have hatched from their eggs.* [~ + *obj*]: *The birds were recently hatched from their eggs.* **2.** [*no obj*] (of eggs) to break open and allow a young bird to come out: *When will the eggs hatch?* **3.** [~ + *obj*] to cause young to emerge from (the egg): *The bird hatched its eggs.* **4.** [~ + *obj*] to bring forth; devise: *hatched a brilliant scheme.*

hatch[2] (hach) /hætʃ/ *n.* [*count*] **1. a.** Also called **hatchway.** an opening in the deck of a vessel, used as a passageway. **b.** the cover over such an opening: *Close the hatches.* **2.** a door in an aircraft: *an escape hatch.* —***Idiom.*** **3. down the hatch,** This expression is used as a toast before drinking something.

hatch[3] (hach) /hætʃ/ *v.* [~ + *obj*] **1.** to mark with closely drawn parallel lines, as for shading in drawing. —*n.* [*count*] **2.** a shading line in drawing or engraving. —**hatch′ing,** *n.* [*noncount*]

hatch•back (hach′bak′) /ˈhætʃˌbæk/ *n.* [*count*] an automobile in which the rear deck lid and the rear window lift and open as a unit.

hatch•er•y (hach′ə rē) /ˈhætʃəriy/ *n.* [*count*], *pl.* **-er•ies.** a place for hatching eggs of hens, fish, etc.

hatch•et (hach′it) /ˈhætʃɪt/ *n.* [*count*] **1.** a small, short-handled ax with one end of the head in a blade and the other in the shape of a hammer, made to be used with one hand. —***Idiom.*** **2. bury the hatchet,** to put aside one's differences or disagreements; stop fighting: *Let's bury the hatchet and be friends again.*

hatch′et job′, *n.* [*count*] a ruthless criticism or verbal attack.

hatch′et man′, *n.* [*count*] **1.** a professional murderer. **2.** a writer or speaker who specializes in verbal attacks. **3.** a person whose job it is to perform unpleasant tasks for a superior, as dismissing employees.

hatch•way (hach′wā′) /ˈhætʃˌwey/ *n.* HATCH[2] (def. 1a).

hate (hāt) /heyt/ *v.,* **hat•ed, hat•ing,** *n.* —*v.* **1.** [~ + *obj*] to dislike intensely; detest: *They hate violence.* **2.** [*not: be* + ~*-ing*] to be unwilling; dislike: [~ + *to* + *verb*]: *I hate to say I told you so.* [~ + *verb-ing*]: *I hate getting up so early.* —*n.* **3.** [*noncount*] intense dislike; extreme hostility: *enemies who are full of hate.* **4.** [*count*] the object of extreme dislike or hostility: *Murder and violence were his greatest hates.* —**hat′ed,** *adj.* —**hat′er,** *n.* [*count*]

hate•ful (hāt′fəl) /ˈheytfəl/ *adj.* **1.** arousing or deserving hate: *hateful oppression.* **2.** unpleasant; disliked; distasteful: *hateful chores.* **3.** full of or expressing hate: *a hateful speech.* —**hate′ful•ly,** *adv.* —**hate′ful•ness,** *n.* [*noncount*]

hath (hath) /hæθ/ *v. Archaic.* 3rd pers. sing. pres. indic. of HAVE.

ha•tred (hā′trid) /ˈheytrɪd/ *n.* [*noncount*] hate: *a look of pure hatred.*

hat•ter (hat′ər) /ˈhætər/ *n.* [*count*] **1.** a maker or seller of hats. —***Idiom.*** **2. mad as a hatter,** completely crazy.

haugh•ty (hô′tē) /ˈhɔtiy/ *adj.,* **-ti•er, -ti•est.** overly proud; arrogant: *haughty demeanor.* —**haugh•ti•ly** (hôt′l ē) /ˈhɔtḷiy/ *adv.* —**haugh′ti•ness,** *n.* [*noncount*]

haul (hôl) /hɔl/ *v.* **1.** to pull hard or draw with force; drag; tug: [~ + *obj*]: *They hauled the boat onto the beach.* [*no obj*]: *The rescue workers hauled on the ropes.* **2.** [~ + *obj*] to cart or transport; carry: *to haul freight.* **3.** [~ + *obj*] to arrest or bring before a judge or other authority: *The police hauled the pickpocket into court.* **4. haul off,** [*no obj*] **a.** to withdraw; leave: *They hauled off in a hurry.* **b.** to draw back the arm in order to strike: *hauled off and punched his tormenter.* —*n.* [*count*] **5.** an act or instance of hauling: *gave a haul on the fishing line.* **6.** the load hauled at one time: *a haul of logs.* **7.** [*usually singular*] the distance or route over which anything is hauled: *It was quite a haul home from Florida to California.* **8.** something taken or acquired: *The thieves made off with a haul of close to two million in jewels and cash.* —***Idiom.*** **9. long** (or **short**) **haul,** a relatively great (or small) period of time: *Over the long haul your investment will grow in value.* —**haul′er,** *n.* [*count*]

haul•age (hô′lij) /ˈhɔlɪdʒ/ *n.* [*noncount*] **1.** the act of hauling. **2.** a charge for hauling.

haunch (hônch, hänch) /hɔntʃ, hɑntʃ/ *n.* [*count*] **1.** the hip or the fleshy part of the body around the hip. **2.** the leg and loin of an animal.

haunt (hônt, hänt) /hɔnt, hɑnt/ *v.* [~ + *obj*] **1.** to visit or appear to frequently as a ghost: *to haunt a house.* **2.** to return often to the mind, memory, or consciousness of (someone): *Memories of love haunted me.* **3.** to visit frequently: *to haunt the art galleries.* **4.** to distress repeatedly: *a mistake that haunted him for years.* —*n.* [*count*] **5.** Often, **haunts.** [*plural*] a place frequently visited: *returned to his old haunts.*

haunt•ing (hôn′ting, hän′-) /ˈhɔntɪŋ, ˈhɑn-/ *adj.* remaining in the consciousness: *a haunting melody.* —**haunt′ing•ly,** *adv.*

haute cou•ture (ōt′ ko͞o to͝or′) /ˌowt kuwˈtʊr/ *n.* [*noncount*] **1.** fashionable clothing for women. **2.** the designers producing high fashion.

haute cui•sine (ōt′ kwi zēn′) /ˌowt kwɪˈziyn/ *n.* [*noncount*] artfully prepared food.

hau•teur (hō tûr′, ō tûr′) /howˈtɜr, owˈtɜr/ *n.* [*noncount*] haughty manner or spirit; arrogance.

have (hav; *unstressed* həv, əv; *for 25 usually* haf) /hæv; *unstressed* həv, əv; *for 25 usually* hæf/ *v.* and *auxiliary v., pres. sing. 1st* and *2nd pers.* **have,** *3rd* **has;** *pres. pl.* **have;** *past* and *past part.* **had;** *pres. part.* **hav•ing,** *n.* —*v.* [~ + *obj*] **1.** [*not: be* + ~*-ing*] to possess; own; hold for use; contain: *I have very little property. She has green eyes.* **2.** [*not: be* + ~*-ing*] to accept in some relation: *He wants to marry her, if she'll have him.* **3.** [*not: be* + ~*-ing*] to get; receive; take: *I have some bad news.* **4.** [*not: be* + ~*-ing*] to gain possession of: *There are no apples to be had at that price.* **5.** to experience, undergo, suffer, or endure: *Have a good time; had a bad cold.* [*not: be* + ~*-ing*] [~ + *obj* + *verb-ed/-en*]: *He had several cars stolen from him.* [~ + *obj* + *root form of verb*]: *It would be nice to have my children speak Italian.* [~ + *obj* + *verb-ing*]: *had the children speaking Italian in no time.* **6.** to cause to be done or to happen, as by command or invitation: [~ + *obj* + *root form of verb*]: *Have him come here at five.* [~ + *obj* + *verb-ed/-en*]: *We were having the kitchen redone.* [~ + *obj* + *verb-ing*]: *She had me running back and forth all day.* **7.** [~ + *obj* + *verb-ed/-en; not: be* + ~*-ing*] to hold or put in a certain position or situation: *The problem had me stumped.* **8.** [*not: be* + ~*-ing*] to be responsible for: *She has a lot of homework.* [~ + *obj* + *to* + *verb*]: *I have a letter to write.* **9.** to hold in mind, sight, etc.: *They were having doubts about his abilities.* **10.** [*not: be* + ~*-ing*] to be in a certain relation to: *She has three cousins.* **11.** [*not: be* + ~*-ing*] to show in action or words: *She had the nerve to refuse my invitation.* **12.** [*not: be* + ~*-ing*] to be distinguished by; characterized by: *This wool has a silky texture.* **13.** to engage in; carry on: *to have a conversation.* **14.** to eat or drink: *We had cake for dessert.* **15.** to permit; allow: *I will not have any talking during the concert.* **16.** [*often:* ~ + *it* + *(that) clause; not: be* + ~*-ing*] The word *have* is used with certain subjects, such as *rumor, gossip, and talk,* to mean that the following statement is an opinion or states a fact: *Rumor has it that she's moving.* **17.** The word *have* is used with certain subjects, such as *I, we, you, one,* and *they,* to mean much the same thing as the expression "there is" or "there are," namely, that the object after *have* exists, or that the object is under consideration for discussion: *Let's see what we have here (= Let's see what there is here).* Do not use the word *there* with the verb *have* for this meaning; *there* is used with the verb *be* to mean "exist." **18.** to beget or give birth to: *going to have a baby.* **19.** [*not: be* + ~*-ing*] to hold an advantage over: *He has you there.* **20.** to outwit; deceive; cheat: *We'd been had by a con artist.* **21.** to exercise; display; show:

Have pity on them. **22.** to invite or cause to be present as a companion or guest: *We had friends over for dinner.* **23.** to engage in sexual relations with. **—*auxiliary verb.*** **24.** The verb *have* is used as an auxiliary verb with a past participle of another verb to form: **a.** the present perfect tense, which, esp. with adverbs such as *just, already,* and *since,* shows that an action happened in the past, esp. the recent past, or its effects are still felt at the time of speaking or writing: *I have just eaten (= I ate in the very recent past). I've known her ever since she came to the United States (= I knew her when she came to the United States, and I still know her now).* **b.** the past perfect tense, which shows that the action of that verb happened earlier in time than another verb: *By the time the police came to the house, the crooks had already left (= The action of the crooks took place earlier than the action of the police).* **25.** The verb *have* is used with *to* and the root form of a main verb to mean "must; to be required, compelled, or under obligation": *I have to leave now (= I must leave now).* **26.** The verb *have* is used to stand for or replace another entire verb phrase that contains *have* in it **a.** when answering a question: *Have you been there before? —No, I haven't.* **b.** when asking for agreement from the listener: *We've been there before, haven't we?* **—*n.*** [*count*] **27.** Usually, **haves.** [*plural*] a person or group that has wealth or other material advantages (contrasted with *have-not*): *The haves in this society are not about to give up their wealth.* **—*Idiom.* 28. have done with,** [~ + *obj*] to cease; finish: *It seemed that they would never have done with their problems.* **29. have had it, a.** [~ *(+ with + obj)*] to be tired and disgusted: *I've had it with your excuses.* **b.** [*no obj*] to be ready for discarding, as something old or no longer useful or popular: *These old computers have had it.* **30. have it coming,** [~ *(+ to + obj)*] to deserve whatever one receives: *We weren't surprised by his sudden fall from power; he had it coming to him for a long time.* **31. have it in one,** to show (the ability or capability mentioned): *She never knew he had it in him to be so funny.* **32. have it in for,** [~ + *obj*] to wish harm to: *certain the boss had it in for her.* **33. have it out,** [~ *(+ with + obj)*] to reach an understanding through fighting or arguing freely: *had it out with his critics.* **34. have on, a.** [*not: be + ~-ing*] to wear: [~ + *obj* + *on*]: *She had a bathing suit on.* [~ + *on* + *obj*]: *He had on a wrinkled old shirt.* **b.** [*not: be + ~-ing*] to have (something) switched on: [~ + *obj* + *on*]: *They had their music on very loud.* [~ + *on* + *obj*]: *He had on the vacuum cleaner so he didn't hear the bell.* **c.** [~ + *obj* + *on*] *Chiefly Brit.* to tease or fool (a person): *We were having him on about the award.* **35. have to do with,** [~ + *obj*] **a.** to be associated with: *Your ambition had a lot to do with your success.* **b.** to deal with: *I won't have anything to do with her until she apologizes.*

ha•ven (hā′vən) /ˈheyvən/ *n.* [*count*] a place of shelter and safety; refuge.

have′-not′, *n.* [*count*] Usually, **have-nots.** [*plural*] a person or group that is without wealth or other material advantages.

have•n't (hav′ənt) /ˈhævənt/ contraction of *have not.*

hav•er•sack (hav′ər sak′) /ˈhævər,sæk/ *n.* [*count*] a bag with a single strap for wearing over one shoulder.

hav•oc (hav′ək) /ˈhævək/ *n.* [*noncount*] **1.** great destruction or devastation: *havoc caused by the bombing.* **—*Idiom.* 2. play havoc with** or **wreak havoc on,** [~ + *obj*] **a.** to create confusion or disorder in: *The plans for restructuring will play havoc with the town.* **b.** to destroy; ruin: *The tornado wreaked havoc on several towns in its path.*

haw (hô) /hɔ/ *v.* [*no obj*] to utter a sound representing a hesitation or pause in speech (usually in the expression: *hem and haw*): *He hemmed and hawed a bit before answering directly.*

Haw., an abbreviation of: Hawaii.

hawk¹ (hôk) /hɔk/ *n.* [*count*] **1.** a bird that catches animals for food, having a short, hooked beak, broad wings, and curved claws. **2.** a person who calls for aggressive action in settling disputes. —**hawk′ish,** *adj.*

hawk² (hôk) /hɔk/ *v.* [~ + *obj*] to offer for sale, esp. by calling out loud in public; peddle: *hawking souvenirs to tourists.* —**hawk′er,** *n.* [*count*]

hawk′-eyed′, *adj.* having very keen sight: *a hawk-eyed sentry.*

haw•ser (hô′zər, -sər) /ˈhɔzər, -sər/ *n.* [*count*] a heavy rope for holding a boat at a dock or for towing.

haw•thorn (hô′thôrn′) /ˈhɔ,θɔrn/ *n.* [*count*] a small tree of the rose family, with stiff thorns, white or red flowers, and bright-colored fruit.

hay (hā) /hey/ *n.* [*noncount*] **1.** grass cut and dried for use as food for animals: *gathering hay from the fields.* **2.** *Slang.* a small sum of money: *Twenty bucks for half an hour's work; that ain't hay!* **—*Idiom.* 3. make hay,** to make use of an opportunity: *Make hay while the sun shines.*

hay′ fe′ver, *n.* [*noncount*] allergic irritation of the mucous membranes of the nose, eyes, throat, and lungs, caused by plant pollen.

hay•seed (hā′sēd′) /ˈhey,siyd/ *n.* **1.** [*noncount*] grass seed, esp. that shaken out of hay. **2.** [*count*] an unsophisticated person from a rural area; yokel; hick.

hay•stack (hā′stak′) /ˈhey,stæk/ *n.* [*count*] **1.** a stack of hay built up in a field. **—*Idiom.* 2. a needle in a haystack,** something difficult to find: *Looking for someone in this mob is like trying to find a needle in a haystack.*

hay•wire (hā′wīᵊr′) /ˈhey,wayᵊr/ *adj.* [*be* + ~] **1.** not right; crazy: *There is something haywire about this situation.* **—*adv.*** **2.** out of control; in disorder: *Things went haywire when the storm struck.*

haz•ard (haz′ərd) /ˈhæzərd/ *n.* [*count*] **1.** something causing danger, peril, risk, or difficulty: *the many hazards of living in the big city.* **2.** a bunker, sand trap, or the like that is an obstacle on a golf course. **—*v.*** [~ + *obj*] **3.** to put forward; venture: *I'd hazard a guess that the loss is in the millions.* **4.** to expose to risk: *In making the investment he hazarded all his savings.*

haz•ard•ous (haz′ər dəs) /ˈhæzərdəs/ *adj.* full of risk; risky; dangerous: *a hazardous journey.* —**haz′ard•ous•ly,** *adv.*

haze¹ (hāz) /heyz/ *n., v.,* **hazed, haz•ing.** **—*n.*** **1.** a mass or collection in the atmosphere of very fine, widely spread solid or liquid particles that give the air a milky white appearance: [*count; usually singular*]: *a haze of smoke from his pipe.* [*noncount*]: *The mountain was barely visible through the haze.* **2.** [*count; singular*] a confused state of mind; daze: *After the accident the victims were still in a haze.* **—*v.*** [*no obj*] **3.** to become hazy: *The sky hazed over.*

haze² (hāz) /heyz/ *v.* [~ + *obj*], **hazed, haz•ing.** to force to perform pointless or humiliating tasks: *college seniors hazing freshmen.* —**haz′er,** *n.* [*count*]

ha•zel (hā′zəl) /ˈheyzəl/ *n.* **1.** [*count*] a small tree or shrub of the birch family, having toothed oval leaves and edible nuts. **—*adj.*** **2.** of a light golden- or greenish-brown color: *beautiful hazel eyes.*

ha•zel•nut (hā′zəl nut′) /ˈheyzəl,nʌt/ *n.* [*count*] the nut of the hazel; filbert.

ha•zy (hā′zē) /ˈheyziy/ *adj.,* **-zi•er, -zi•est.** **1.** having or showing haze; misty: *a hazy sky.* **2.** vague; indefinite; confused: *a few hazy ideas.* —**ha•zi•ly** (hā′zə lē) /ˈheyzəliy/ *adv.* —**ha′zi•ness,** *n.* [*noncount*]

H-bomb (āch′bom′) /ˈeytʃ,bɒm/ *n.* HYDROGEN BOMB.

hd., an abbreviation of: **1.** hand. **2.** head.

hdqrs., an abbreviation of: headquarters.

HDTV, an abbreviation of: high-definition television.

hdw. or **hdwe.,** an abbreviation of: hardware.

he (hē; *unstressed* ē) /hiy; *unstressed* iy/ *pron., nom.* **he,** *poss.* **his,** *obj.* **him;** *pl. nom.* **they,** *poss.* **their** or **theirs,** *obj.* **them;** *n., pl.* **hes;** *adj.* **—*pron.*** **1.** the male person or animal being discussed or last mentioned; that male: *Where did that man go? He's in the back of the room.* **2.** anyone (without reference to the person's sex); that person: *He who hesitates is lost.* **—*n.*** [*count*] **3.** any male person or animal: *Is that cat a he or a she?* **—*adj.*** **4.** male (usually used in combination with a noun): *a he-goat.* **—Usage.** In traditional grammar books, the word *he* and the other masculine pronouns HIS and HIM have been used when the sex of the person referred to was not known: *Everyone who wishes to vote 'yes' should raise his right hand.* This so-called "generic" use is often criticized as sexist, although many speakers and writers continue to use it. Other writers use the phrases *he or she, s/he, him or her,* and others to avoid favoring one sex: *Everyone who wishes to vote 'yes' should raise his or her right hand.* Another solution is to use THEY and the related forms THEM, THEIR: *Everyone who agrees should raise their right hand.* But this can create another problem, because *everyone* is technically singular and *they/them/their* is plural, and some writers dislike this "agreement" problem. To be safest, it is sometimes possible to change the main noun itself to the plural, so that the pronouns *they/them/their* can "agree:" *All who wish to vote 'yes' should raise their right hand.*

H.E., an abbreviation of: **1.** high explosive. **2.** His Eminence. **3.** His Excellency; Her Excellency.

head (hed) /hɛd/ *n.* [*count*] **1.** the upper part of the body, containing the skull with mouth, eyes, ears, nose, and brain: *Nod your head.* **2.** the head as the center of the intellect or as the controlling part of one's emotions; the mind: *a good head for mathematics.* **3.** the position or place of leadership, greatest authority, or honor: *at the head of her class.* **4.** a person in charge of others; chief: *the head of the household.* **5.** the part of anything thought of as forming the top or upper end: *the head of a pin.* **6.** the front end of something: *the head of a procession.* **7.** [*singular*] a person or animal considered as one of a number, herd, or group: *ten head of cattle.* **8.** a critical point in an activity where something must be done: *to bring matters to a head.* **9.** froth or foam at the top of a liquid: *the head on a glass of beer.* **10.** any dense flower cluster on a plant: *a head of cabbage.* **11.** the top part of an abscess, boil, etc. **12.** HEADLAND. **13.** Also, **heads.** the side of a coin that has a head or other principal figure (opposed to TAIL). **14.** the source of a river or stream: *The head of the Mississippi River is in Minnesota.* **15.** *Slang.* a habitual user of an illegal drug (often used in combination with a noun): *an acid-head.* **16.** a toilet, esp. on a boat or ship. **17.** pressure: *a head of steam.* **18.** any of the parts of a tape recorder that record, play back, or erase magnetic signals on audiotape or videotape. *—adj.* [*before a noun*] **19.** first in rank or position: *head cook.* **20.** of or for the head (often used in combination with a noun): *a head covering.* **21.** *Slang.* of or relating to drugs, drug paraphernalia, or drug users: *a head shop.* *—v.* **22.** [~ + *obj*] to go at the head of or in front of: *She headed the parade.* **23.** [~ *(+ up) + obj*] to be in charge of: *to head (up) a school.* **24.** to (cause to) move forward toward a point specified: [*no obj*]: *The bus headed out of town.* [~ + *obj*]: *I'll head the boat for shore.* **25. head for,** [~ + *for* + *obj*] to move toward (something): *heading for disaster.* **26. head off,** to get in the path of or in front of in order to stop or turn aside; intercept: [~ + *off* + *obj*]: *We headed off the robbers at the pass.* [~ + *obj* + *off*]: *We headed them off.* **—*Idiom.*** **27. come to a head,** to reach a critical point. **28. get one's head together,** [*no obj*] to get oneself under control: *Get your head together and stop dreaming.* **29. go over someone's head,** [*no obj*] to appeal to the superior of someone's own official superior: *He angered his boss by going over his head to the president about his troubles.* **30. go to one's head, a.** to overcome a person with a feeling of joy or drunkenness: *The liquor went straight to her head.* **b.** to fill one with conceit: *Don't let your recent success go to your head.* **31. hang** or **hide one's head,** to show a feeling of shame. **32. head and shoulders,** by an impressively great amount: *head and shoulders above the rest in talent.* **33. head over heels, a.** headlong, as in a somersault: *He fell head over heels into the pool.* **b.** intensely; completely: *head over heels in love.* **34. head to head,** in direct opposition or competition: *The two candidates went head to head in the primary.* **35. keep one's head,** to remain calm and effective: *The pilot kept her head when the plane lost power.* **36. keep one's head above water,** to have enough money to continue to live or survive. **37. lay** or **put heads together,** [*no obj*] to meet in order to consult or scheme: *Let's put our heads together and see if there's some way we can work out a solution.* **38. lose one's head,** to become uncontrolled or wildly excited. **39. make head(s) or tail(s) of,** [*with a negative word or phrase;* ~ + *obj*] to understand or interpret to even a small extent: *I can't make heads or tails of your message.* **40. make heads roll,** [*no obj*] to dismiss numbers of employees: *The boss is going to make heads roll unless she gets results.* **41. one's head off,** extremely; excessively: *to laugh one's head off.* **42. on one's head,** as one's responsibility or fault: *It will be on his head if the plan fails.* **43. out of one's head** or **mind,** insane; irrational; crazy. **44. over one's head,** beyond one's understanding, ability, or resources. —**head′ed,** *adj.* —**head′less,** *adj.*

head•ache (hed′āk′) /ˈhɛdˌeyk/ *n.* [*count*] **1.** a pain located in the head: *woke up with a throbbing headache.* **2.** an annoying or bothersome person, situation, etc.: *Another headache on the campaign trail was the reporters who wouldn't leave us alone.*

head•band (hed′band′) /ˈhɛdˌbænd/ *n.* [*count*] a band worn around the head.

head•board (hed′bôrd′, -bōrd′) /ˈhɛdˌbɔrd, -ˌbowrd/ *n.* [*count*] a board forming the head of something, as a bed.

head′ cold′, *n.* [*count*] a common cold esp. with nasal congestion and sneezing.

head•dress (hed′dres′) /ˈhɛdˌdrɛs/ *n.* [*count*] a covering or decoration for the head.

head•first (hed′fûrst′) /ˈhɛdˈfɜrst/ *adv.* **1.** with the head in front or bent forward: *to dive headfirst into the sea.* **2.** rashly: *plunged headfirst into the planning of the project.*

head•gear (hed′gēr′) /ˈhɛdˌgɪər/ *n.* [*noncount*] a covering for the head, as a hat or a helmet.

head•hunt•ing (hed′hun′ting) /ˈhɛdˌhʌntɪŋ/ *n.* [*noncount*] **1.** (among certain tribal peoples) the practice of cutting off and preserving the heads of enemies as trophies. **2.** the recruiting of executives for corporations. —**head′hunt′er,** *n.* [*count*]

head•ing (hed′ing) /ˈhɛdɪŋ/ *n.* [*count*] **1.** something that serves as a head, esp. a title or caption: *The heading was: "Verb tenses in English."* **2.** the compass direction toward which a traveler or vehicle is or should be moving; course.

head•land (hed′lənd) /ˈhɛdlənd/ *n.* [*count*] a piece of elevated land that extends into a large body of water.

head•light (hed′līt′) /ˈhɛdˌlayt/ *n.* [*count*] a light with a reflector, on the front of a vehicle.

head•line (hed′līn′) /ˈhɛdˌlayn/ *n., v.,* **-lined, -lin•ing.** *—n.* [*count*] Also called **head. 1.** a statement printed in large letters at the beginning of a newspaper article, summarizing the subject of the article. **2. headlines,** [*plural*] news stories important enough to appear on the front page of newspapers: *The peace conference has been in the headlines all week.* *—v.* **3.** [~ + *obj*] to furnish with a headline. **4.** [*no obj*] to be the star of a show, nightclub act, etc.

head•lock (hed′lok′) /ˈhɛdˌlɒk/ *n.* [*count*] a wrestling hold in which one arm is locked around the opponent's head.

head•long (hed′lông′, -long′) /ˈhɛdˌlɔŋ, -ˌlɒŋ/ *adv.* **1.** with the head going first; headfirst: *to plunge headlong into the water.* **2.** without delay; hastily; rashly: *to rush headlong into marriage.* *—adj.* **3.** hasty: *a headlong flight.* **4.** done or going with the head foremost: *a headlong dive.*

head•man (hed′man′, -man′) /ˈhɛdˈmæn, -ˌmæn/ *n.* [*count*], *pl.* **-men.** a chief or leader.

head•mas•ter or **-mis•tress** (hed′mas′tər) or (-mis′-tris) /ˈhɛdˌmæstər/ or /-ˈmɪstrɪs/ *n.* [*count*] the person in charge of a private school.

head′-on′, *adj.* **1.** meeting with the fronts or heads foremost: *a head-on collision.* **2.** characterized by direct opposition: *a head-on confrontation.* *—adv.* **3.** with the front or head foremost. **4.** in direct opposition.

head•phone (hed′fōn′) /ˈhɛdˌfown/ *n.* Usually, **headphones.** [*plural*] a headset designed for use with a stereo system.

head•quar•ter (hed′kwôr′tər, -kwô′-) /ˈhɛdˌkwɔrtər, -ˌkwɔ-/ *v.* to set up in headquarters: [*no obj*]: *The army headquartered in that small town before the invasion.* [~ + *obj*]: *The agency is headquartered in Fort Meade.*

head•quar•ters (hed′kwôr′tərz, -kwô′-) /ˈhɛdˌkwɔrtərz, -ˌkwɔ-/ *n.* [*count*], *pl.* **head•quar•ters.** a center of operations, as of a military commander or a business: *Their headquarters is in New York City.*

head•rest (hed′rest′) /ˈhɛdˌrɛst/ *n.* [*count*] **1.** a support for the head: *the headrest on a couch.* **2.** a padded extension at the top of a seat back, esp. in an automobile.

head•room (hed′ro͞om′, -ro͝om′) /ˈhɛdˌruwm, -ˌrʊm/ *n.* [*noncount*] **1.** the space between the top of a vehicle and the lowest part of a bridge or tunnel it is passing under. **2.** clear vertical space in which to move, stand, or sit: *There's a lot of headroom in this van.*

head•set (hed′set′) /ˈhɛdˌsɛt/ *n.* [*count*] a device consisting of one or two earphones, and sometimes a microphone, attached to a headband: *a portable stereo with headset.*

head′ start′, *n.* [*count*] **1.** an advantage in any competition, race, etc., such as allowing one or more competitors to start before the others. **2.** a productive beginning: *I'll get a head start on the paperwork.*

head•stone (hed′stōn′) /ˈhɛdˌstown/ *n.* [*count*] a stone marker set at the head of a grave; gravestone.

head•strong (hed′strông′, -strong′) /ˈhɛdˌstrɔŋ, -ˌstrɒŋ/ *adj.* determined to have one's own way; obstinate.

head•wait•er (hed′wā′tər) /ˈhɛdˈweytər/ *n.* [*count*] a waiter in charge of other staff, as in a restaurant.

head•way (hed′wā′) /ˈhɛdˌwey/ *n.* [*noncount*] forward movement; progress in a forward direction.

head•wind (hed′wind′) /ˈhɛdˌwɪnd/ *n.* [*count*] a wind

opposite to the course of a moving object (opposed to *tailwind*).

head•y (hed′ē) /ˈhɛdiy/ *adj.,* **-i•er, -i•est. 1.** giddy; dizzy: *She felt heady after her triumph in the race.* **2.** affecting the mind or senses greatly; exhilarating: *heady wine.*

heal (hēl) /hiyl/ *v.* **1.** to (cause to) become healthy or well again: [~ + *obj*]: *This medicine should heal that sore on your leg.* [*no obj*]: *When will my leg heal?* **2.** [~ + *obj*] to repair or take care of; settle: *Only time will heal my broken heart.* —**heal′er,** *n.* [*count*]

health (helth) /hɛlθ/ *n.* [*noncount*] **1.** the general condition of the body or mind: *She's in poor health at the moment.* **2.** the state of being fit; fitness of body or mind: *to lose his health.* —***Idiom.* 3. drink to one's health,** to offer a toast or a polite wish for a person's health, happiness, etc.: *We drank to her health.*

health•ful (helth′fəl) /ˈhɛlθfəl/ *adj.* bringing about or maintaining good health; wholesome: *a healthful diet.*

health•y (hel′thē) /ˈhɛlθiy/ *adj.,* **-i•er, -i•est. 1.** having or enjoying good health; fit: *looked so healthy after a week in the country.* **2.** relating to or having the appearance of good health: *healthy skin.* **3.** fostering good health; healthful: *a healthy climate.* **4.** prosperous or sound; successful: *a healthy business.* —**health•i•ly** (hel′thə lē) /ˈhɛlθəliy/ *adv.* —**health′i•ness,** *n.* [*noncount*]

heap (hēp) /hiyp/ *n.* [*count*] **1.** a group of things placed, thrown, or lying one on another; pile: *a heap of stones.* **2.** *Informal.* a great or large quantity or number: *a heap of trouble.* —*v.* **3.** to (cause to) become gathered or put in a heap: [*no obj;* (~ + *up*)]: *The snow had heaped up overnight.* [~ + *obj* (+ *up*)]: *The wind had heaped the snow (up) into drifts.* [~ (+ *up*) + *obj*]: *The wind had heaped (up) the snow.* **4.** [~ (+ *up/together*) + *obj*] to accumulate: *to heap up riches.* **5.** [~ + *obj* + *on/upon* + *obj*] to bestow in great quantity: *to heap blessings upon someone.* **6.** [~ + *obj*] to supply with a great deal of something: *to heap a plate with food.*

hear (hēr) /hɪər/ *v.,* **heard** (hûrd), **hear•ing. 1.** [*not: be* + *~-ing*] to become aware of (sounds, noises, etc.) by the ear: [~ + *obj*]: *to hear footsteps.* [~ + *obj* + *verb-ing*]: *I heard them singing.* [~ + *obj* + *root form of verb*]: *I didn't hear you speak.* **2.** [*no obj; not: be* + *~-ing*] to have the ability to be aware of sound by the ear: *He was unable to hear from birth.* **3.** [*not: be* + *~-ing*] to learn by hearing: [~ + *obj*]: *I hear you have a new job.* **4.** [~ + *from; not: be* + *~-ing*] to receive communication: *That letter was the last we heard from them.* **5.** [~ + *obj*] to give a formal hearing to (something); consider officially: *to hear a legal case.* **6. hear of,** [~ + *of* + *obj; not: be* + *~-ing*] **a.** to know of: *I have heard of one man who can help us.* **b.** [*with a negative word or phrase*] to listen with favor, assent, or agreement: *I will not hear of your going!* **7.** The expression *Hear! Hear!* is used to express approval, as of a speech: *A toast to our dear friend. — Hear! Hear!* —**hear′er,** *n.* [*count*] —**Usage.** The words HEAR and LISTEN have similar meanings, in that both involve the sense of hearing and the use of the ear. But HEAR is most often used when one simply experiences the sound; the sound comes to the hearer. For LISTEN the subject is more active and performs the action; one usually must concentrate when listening. For this reason, LISTEN may be used in the progressive tenses: *I was listening to the radio,* but HEAR for most of its meanings does not allow *be* + *~-ing* forms. Another difference between the two is that when there is an object, the verb LISTEN takes the preposition *to;* there may be no preposition after HEAR for most of its meanings. Compare SEE and LOOK.

hear•ing (hēr′ing) /ˈhɪərɪŋ/ *n.* **1.** [*noncount*] the sense making it possible to be aware of sound: *hard of hearing.* **2.** [*noncount*] the distance within which one can hear something; earshot: *Her complaint was loud enough to be within hearing of the waiter.* **3.** [*count*] opportunity to be heard: *Will the Board grant me a hearing?* **4.** [*count*] a session in which statements are made and arguments are presented, esp. before a judge, in a lawsuit.

hear′ing-ear′ dog′, *n.* [*count*] a dog trained to alert a person whose hearing is impaired to sounds, such as a telephone ringing.

heark•en or **hark•en** (här′kən) /ˈhɑrkən/ *v.* [~ + *to* + *obj*] to give heed or attention to what is said; listen: *Hearken to his words.*

hear•say (hēr′sā′) /ˈhɪərˌsey/ *n.* [*noncount*] information received from another that is not yet proved; rumor: *His court testimony was merely hearsay.*

hearse (hûrs) /hɜrs/ *n.* [*count*] a vehicle for conveying a dead person to the place of burial.

heart (härt) /hɑrt/ *n.* **1.** [*count*] a muscular organ in humans and many animals that receives blood from the veins and pumps it through the arteries to other parts of the body. **2.** [*count*] the center of a person's total personality, esp. of a person's intuition or sensibilities: *In your heart you know it's true.* **3.** [*count; usually singular*] capacity for sympathy; feeling; affection: *a very hard heart (= not having sympathy). His heart moved him to help the needy.* **4.** [*noncount*] spirit, courage, or enthusiasm: *no longer had the heart to argue.* See TAKE HEART below. **5.** [*count; usually singular*] the innermost or central part of anything: *We marched through the heart of town.* **6.** [*count*] the essential part; core: *Let's get to the heart of the matter.* **7.** [*count*] a shape with rounded sides meeting in a point at the bottom and curving inward to a cusp at the top. **8.** [*count*] a card of the suit that has such a shape as the symbol of the suit. **9. hearts, a.** the suit of cards so marked. **b.** [*noncount; used with a singular verb*] a game in which the players try to take all the hearts, or to avoid taking any of them. —***Idiom.* 10. after one's own heart,** agreeing with one's likes or one's preference: *a girl after his own heart.* **11. at heart,** in reality; basically: *very kind at heart.* **12. break someone's heart,** to cause someone to be deeply unhappy. **13. by heart,** entirely from memory: *recited the entire poem by heart.* **14. eat one's heart out,** to be very sorry about something; grieve: *I'm eating my heart out over losing you.* **15. from (the bottom of) one's heart,** with complete sincerity: *I wished her success from the bottom of my heart.* **16. have a heart,** to show compassion and mercy: *Have a heart and set the caged bird free.* **17. have one's heart in one's mouth,** to be extremely anxious or fearful: *My heart was in my mouth when I got up to speak to the crowd.* **18. have one's heart in the right place,** to wish to do the proper thing: *Yes, he's made mistakes, but his heart is in the right place.* **19. in one's heart of hearts,** in one's private thoughts or feelings: *In your heart of hearts you know she's the best for the job.* **20. lose one's heart to,** [~ + *obj*] to fall in love with. **21. near** or **close to one's heart,** of great interest or concern to one: *a project very close to her heart.* **22. set one's heart at rest,** to banish one's fears or anxieties: *The good economic news set the president's heart at rest.* **23. set one's heart on** or **have one's heart set on,** [~ + *obj*] to want (something) a great deal: *He set his heart on going to Tanzania. He had his heart set on that job.* **24. take heart,** [*no obj*] to regain one's courage or confidence: *He took heart when things began to improve.* **25. take to heart, a.** to consider seriously; to be affected deeply by: [~ + *to heart* + *obj*]: *He took to heart most of her comments.* [~ + *obj* + *to heart*]: *He took it to heart.* **b.** to grieve over: [~ + *obj* + *to heart*]: *He took the loss to heart.* [~ + *to heart* + *obj*]: *He took to heart her sudden death.* **26. to one's heart's content,** for as long as one wishes: *The children played to their heart's content.* **27. wear one's heart on one's sleeve,** to allow one's feelings, esp. of love, to show.

heart•ache (härt′āk′) /ˈhɑrtˌeyk/ *n.* emotional distress; anguish: [*count*]: *the joys and the heartaches of raising children.* [*noncount*]: *a life of heartache.*

heart′ attack′, *n.* [*count*] a sudden disruption of regular heart function because of an insufficient supply of oxygen to the heart muscle.

heart•beat (härt′bēt′) /ˈhɑrtˌbiyt/ *n.* [*count*] a single pulse of the heart as it takes in blood and pumps it out.

heart•break (härt′brāk′) /ˈhɑrtˌbreyk/ *n.* [*noncount*] great sorrow.

heart•break•ing (härt′brā′king) /ˈhɑrtˌbreykɪŋ/ *adj.* causing great sorrow, grief, or anguish: *a heartbreaking loss.*

heart•bro•ken (härt′brō′kən) /ˈhɑrtˌbrowkən/ *adj.* crushed by sorrow, grief, or anguish: *heartbroken by the news.*

heart•burn (härt′bûrn′) /ˈhɑrtˌbɜrn/ *n.* [*noncount*] an unpleasant burning feeling in the upper chest, usually caused by indigestion.

-hearted, *suffix.* *-hearted* is attached to adjectives to form adjectives with the meaning "having the character or personality of (the adjective mentioned)": *cold* + *-hearted* → *coldhearted (= having a cold heart; unkind or mean); light* + *-hearted* → *lighthearted (= feeling light and happy).*

heart•en (här′tn) /ˈhɑrtn̩/ *v.* [~ + *obj*] to give courage or confidence to (someone): *felt heartened by the good news.* —**heart′en•ing,** *adj.*

heart′ fail′ure, *n.* [*noncount*] **1.** a condition in which the heart fatally ceases to function. **2.** a condition in which the heart does not pump enough blood.

heart•felt (härt′felt′) /ˈhɑrtˌfɛlt/ *adj.* deeply or sincerely felt: *You have my heartfelt sympathy.*

hearth (härth) /hɑrθ/ *n.* **1.** [*count*] the floor of a fireplace, often extending into a room. **2.** [*noncount*] home and family life: *the joys of hearth and home.*

heart•i•ly (härt′l ē) /ˈhɑrtḷiy/ *adv.* **1.** deeply felt; with deep, genuine, sincere, or strong emotion; wholeheartedly: *They heartily dislike each other.* **2.** openly; without holding anything back: *laughed heartily.*

heart•less (härt′lis) /ˈhɑrtlɪs/ *adj.* unfeeling; unkind; harsh; cruel: *her cold, heartless attitude.* —**heart′less•ly,** *adv.* —**heart′less•ness,** *n.* [*noncount*]

heart•rend•ing (härt′ren′ding) /ˈhɑrtˌrɛndɪŋ/ *adj.* causing or expressing intense grief or distress: *a heartrending scream.* —**heart′rend′ing•ly,** *adv.*

heart•sick (härt′sik′) /ˈhɑrtˌsɪk/ *adj.* extremely unhappy. —**heart′sick′ness,** *n.* [*noncount*]

heart•strings (härt′stringz′) /ˈhɑrtˌstrɪŋz/ *n.* [*plural*] the deepest feelings: *a sad song that tugs at one's heartstrings.*

heart•throb (härt′throb′) /ˈhɑrtˌθrɒb/ *n.* [*count*] **1.** a heartbeat. **2.** a person who is the object of sentimental emotion, esp., a sweetheart.

heart′-to-heart′, *adj.* frank; sincere; intimate: *a heart-to-heart talk.*

heart•warm•ing (härt′wôr′ming) /ˈhɑrtˌwɔrmɪŋ/ *adj.* tenderly moving: *a heartwarming story of a boy and his dog.*

heart•y (här′tē) /ˈhɑrtiy/ *adj.*, **-i•er, -i•est. 1.** [*before a noun*] warmhearted; cordial: *a hearty welcome.* **2.** [*before a noun*] genuine; heartfelt: *had a hearty dislike for the in-laws.* **3.** [*before a noun*] wholehearted: *hearty support.* **4.** exuberant; unrestrained: *hearty laughter.* **5.** forceful; violent: *a hearty push.* **6.** strong and well; healthy: *You look hale and hearty.* **7.** [*before a noun*] large; substantial: *a hearty meal.* —**heart′i•ness,** *n.* [*noncount*]

heat (hēt) /hiyt/ *n.* **1.** [*noncount*] the condition or quality of being hot: *Heat rises.* **2.** [*noncount*] degree of hotness; temperature: *moderate heat.* **3.** [*noncount*] the sensation of warmth: *I could feel the heat from her skin.* **4.** [*noncount*] a source of warmth, as a stove: *Stand closer to the heat if you're cold.* **5.** [*noncount; often: the* + ~] hot weather or climate; a period of such hot weather: *The heat will be with us for a few days.* **6.** [*noncount*] sharp, pungent flavor; spiciness: *the heat of chili peppers.* **7.** [*noncount*] warmth or intensity of feeling; vehemence; passion: *He answered the charges with heat.* **8.** [*noncount; often: in* + *the* + ~ + *of*] a point of greatest intensity, excitement, or other emotion: *in the heat of battle.* **9.** [*noncount; the* + ~] *Slang.* **a.** pursuit or investigation by the police: *The criminals tried to get out of town because the heat was on.* **b.** the police: *Let's scram; here comes the heat!* **c.** intense pressure: *The heat is on now to find a replacement.* **d.** blame: *Who will take the heat for this mistake?* **10.** [*count*] a single division of a contest, esp. a race in which competitors qualify for entry in the final race or contest. —*v.* **11.** to (cause to) become hot or warm: [*no obj;* (~ + *up*)]: *The house is heating up in the sun.* [~ + *obj*]: *Heat the milk and let's have some cocoa.* [~ + *up* + *obj*]: *The sun is heating up the house.* [~ + *obj* + *up*]: *Heat the soup up.* **12. heat up,** to (cause to) become more active, intense, or excited: [*no obj*]: *The situation is heating up again.* [~ + *up* + *obj*]: *This crisis is bound to heat up the dispute.* [~ + *obj* + *up*]: *The terrorist attack heated things up again.* —***Idiom.*** **13. in heat,** in the period of time or state in which the female of certain mammals can mate or conceive young: *to be in heat.*

heat•ed (hē′tid) /ˈhiytɪd/ *adj.* excited or angry: *a heated argument.* —**heat′ed•ly,** *adv.: to argue heatedly.*

heat•er (hē′tər) /ˈhiytər/ *n.* [*count*] a device for heating water or air: *a gas heater.*

heath (hēth) /hiyθ/ *n.* **1.** [*count*] an area of open, uncultivated land. **2.** [*noncount*] a low-growing shrub common on such land.

hea•then (hē′*th*ən) /ˈhiyðən/ *n., pl.* **-thens, -then,** *adj.* —*n.* [*count*] **1.** an individual of a people that do not acknowledge the God of the Bible. **2.** an uncultured or uncivilized person. —*adj.* **3.** of or relating to heathens; pagan. **4.** uncultured or uncivilized. —**hea′then•dom,** *n.* [*noncount*] —**hea′then•ish,** *adj.* —**hea′then•ism,** *n.* [*noncount*]

heath•er (he*th*′ər) /ˈhɛðər/ *n.* [*noncount*] a heath plant having small pinkish purple flowers.

heat•ing (hē′ting) /ˈhiytɪŋ/ *n.* [*noncount*] a system, or the machines involved in the system, of keeping a room or a building warm.

heat′ light′ning, *n.* [*noncount*] lightning too distant for thunder to be heard.

heat•stroke (hēt′strōk′) /ˈhiytˌstrowk/ *n.* [*noncount*] a disturbance of the body's ability to control its temperature, caused by overexposure to too much heat, resulting in headache, fever, hot and dry skin, and rapid pulse.

heave (hēv) /hiyv/ *v.*, **heaved** or (*esp. Nautical*) **hove** (hōv) /howv/; **heav•ing;** *n.* —*v.* **1.** [~ + *obj*] to raise or lift with effort; hoist: *He heaved her to her feet.* **2.** [~ + *obj*] to lift and throw with effort: *to heave a stone through a window.* **3.** [~ + *obj*] to utter with great effort: *He heaved a sigh.* **4.** to (cause to) rise and fall with a swelling motion: [*no obj*]: *His chest was heaving from the effort.* [~ + *obj*]: *The rough seas heaved the boat about.* **5.** *Nautical.* to (cause to) move into a certain position or situation: [*no obj*]: *The boat hove into sight.* [~ + *obj*]: *The captain hove the boat closer to the lifeboats.* **6.** [*no obj*] to vomit; throw up. **7.** [*no obj*] to pull on: *The sailor heaved on the rope and pulled the box aboard.* **8. heave to,** [*no obj*] (of a ship) to come to a stop. —*n.* [*count*] **9.** an act or effort of heaving. **10. the heaves,** [*plural*] an episode of retching or vomiting.

heave′-ho′, *n.* [*count*], *pl.* **-hos.** *Informal.* an act of dismissing or throwing someone out of a place.

heav•en (hev′ən) /ˈhɛvən/ *n.* **1.** [*noncount*] the place where God, the angels, and the spirits of good people live after death: *children taught they must be good if they want to go to heaven some day.* **2.** Usually, **heavens.** [*plural*] the sky: *Ancient astronomers studied the heavens.* **3.** [*noncount*] a place or state of supreme happiness: *This tropical island is heaven.* **4.** Often, **heavens.** This word is used in phrases to express emphasis, surprise, or other emotion: *For heaven's sake, watch what you're doing!* —**heav′en•ly,** *adj.*, **-li•er, -li•est.** —**heav•en•ward** (hev′ən wərd) /ˈhɛvənwərd/ *adv., adj.*

heav•y (hev′ē) /ˈhɛviy/ *adj.*, **-i•er, -i•est,** *n., pl.* **heav•ies.** —*adj.* **1.** of great weight; hard to lift or carry: *a heavy load.* **2.** of great amount, quantity, or size: *a heavy vote.* **3.** [*often: before a noun*] of great force, strength, or intensity: *The ship plowed through the heavy seas.* **4.** of more than the usual or average weight: *He had a heavy build.* **5.** grave; serious: *a heavy punishment.* **6.** deep; profound: *a heavy sleep.* **7.** [*before a noun*] **a.** armed with weapons of large size: *a heavy cruiser.* **b.** (of guns) of the more powerful sizes: *heavy artillery.* **8.** having a large size or output: *heavy machinery.* **9.** producing or working with basic materials, as steel or coal, used in manufacturing: *heavy industry such as steelmaking.* **10.** burdensome; oppressive: *heavy taxes.* **11.** busy: *a heavy schedule.* **12.** being (the noun referred to) to an unusual degree: *a heavy drinker (= a drinker who drinks to an unusual degree).* **13.** thick; dense: *heavy cream.* **14.** [*be* + ~] full of; weighted or laden; loaded with: *words that are heavy with meaning.* **15.** depressed with trouble or sorrow; sad: *a heavy heart.* **16.** without excitement, spark, or interest; ponderous; dull: *a heavy style of writing.* **17.** slow in movement or action; clumsy: *a heavy walk.* **18.** loud and deep; sonorous: *heavy breathing.* **19.** overcast; threatening rain: *The sky is heavy and gray today.* **20.** (of food) not easily digested: *a heavy meal.* **21.** [*be* + ~] *Informal.* possessing or using in large quantities: *She was a bit heavy on the makeup.* **22.** *Slang.* very serious or important. —*n.* [*count*] **23.** a villainous character or role in a drama: *the scene where the heavy threatens the good guy's girlfriend.* **24.** *Slang.* **a.** HEAVYWEIGHT (def. 6). **b.** a person employed to use force; thug. —**heav•i•ly** (hev′ə lē) /ˈhɛvəliy/ *adv.* —**heav′i•ness,** *n.* [*noncount*]

heav′y-du′ty, *adj.* [*usually: before a noun*] **1.** made to undergo or withstand great strain or use: *heavy-duty machinery.* **2.** very important or intense: *heavy-duty competition.*

heav′y-hand′ed, *adj.* **1.** clumsy; without grace or sensitivity: *heavy-handed criticism.* **2.** oppressive; harsh: *a heavy-handed dictator.* —**heav′y-hand′ed•ly,** *adv.* —**heav′y-hand′ed•ness,** *n.* [*noncount*]

heav′y-heart′ed, *adj.* full of sorrow; melancholy.

heav′y met′al, *n.* [*noncount*] loud, highly amplified, often harsh rock music with a heavy beat. —**heav′y-met′al,** *adj.*

heav•y•set (hev′ē set′) /ˈhɛviyˈsɛt/ *adj.* having a large body; stocky; stout.

heav•y•weight (hev′ē wāt′) /ˈhɛviyˌweyt/ *adj.* [*before a noun*] **1.** of more than average weight or thickness. **2.** of or relating to heavyweights: *a heavyweight bout.* **3.** very powerful or important: *a team of heavyweight lawyers.* —*n.* [*count*] **4.** a person of more than average weight. **5.** a boxer weighing more than 175 lb. (79.4 kg). **6.** a very powerful, influential, or important person, company, etc.

He•brew (hē′bro͞o) /ˈhiybruw/ *n.* **1.** [*count*] a member of any of a group of Semitic peoples who claimed descent from Abraham, Isaac, and Jacob. **2.** [*noncount*] the Semitic language of the ancient Hebrews, revived as a vernacular in the 20th century. —*adj.* **3.** of the Hebrews or their language.

heck (hek) /hɛk/ *n., interj.* **1.** This word is used with words beginning with *wh-*, as *who, what,* etc., to express mild annoyance or disgust, etc.: *What the heck do you care?* **2.** This word is also used in the phrase *a heck of* to emphasize the speaker's feelings about the amount of or the quality of something: *a heck of a good speech.*

heck•le (hek′əl) /ˈhɛkəl/ *v.* [~ + *obj*], **-led, -ling.** to harass with impolite questions, insults, or the like: *The audience began to heckle the speaker.* —**heck•ler** (hek′lər) /ˈhɛklər/ *n.* [*count*]

hec•tare or **hek•tare** (hek′târ) /ˈhɛktɛər/ *n.* [*count*] a unit of surface or land measure equal to 100 ares, or 10,000 square meters (2.471 acres).

hec•tic (hek′tik) /ˈhɛktɪk/ *adj.* **1.** full of excitement or confused or hurried activity: *a hectic schedule.* **2.** feverish; flushed; red. —**hec′ti•cal•ly,** *adv.*

hec•tor (hek′tər) /ˈhɛktər/ *v.* [~ + *obj*] to harass (someone) by bullying: *always hectoring his students to perform better.*

he'd (hēd; *unstressed* ēd) /hiyd; *unstressed* iyd/ *contraction.* **1.** a shortened form of *he had: He'd been here before, hadn't he?* **2.** a shortened form of *he would: He'd be a great vice-president, wouldn't he?*

hedge (hej) /hɛdʒ/ *n., v.,* **hedged, hedg•ing.** —*n.* [*count*] **1.** a row of bushes or small trees forming a fence or boundary. **2.** an act or means of protecting oneself against unexpected occurrences: *bought gold as a hedge against inflation.* **3.** a statement that does not commit the speaker too deeply or does not answer a question directly. —*v.* **4.** [~ + *obj*] to enclose with or separate by a hedge: *They hedged their garden.* **5.** [~ + *obj*] to confine or restrict as if with a hedge: *felt hedged in by all the rules.* **6.** [~ + *obj*] to protect or lessen the bad effects of a possible loss by favoring or supporting more than one side: *hedged his investments by buying many different stocks.* **7.** [*no obj*] to refuse to answer a question directly. —**hedg′er,** *n.* [*count*]

hedge•hog (hej′hog′, -hôg′) /ˈhɛdʒˌhɒg, -ˌhɔg/ *n.* [*count*] an insect-eating animal with spiny hairs on the back and sides.

hedge•row (hej′rō′) /ˈhɛdʒˌrow/ *n.* HEDGE (def. 1).

he•don•ism (hēd′n iz′əm) /ˈhiydn̩ˌɪzəm/ *n.* [*noncount*] belief in or devotion to pleasure as a way of life. —**he′don•ist,** *n.* [*count*] —**he′don•is′tic,** *adj.*

hee•bie-jee•bies (hē′bē jē′bēz) /ˈhiybiyˈdʒiybiyz/ *n.* [*plural; usually: the* + ~] *Informal.* a feeling of nervousness; the jitters.

heed (hēd) /hiyd/ *v.* [~ + *obj*] **1.** to give careful attention to: *to heed a warning.* —*n.* [*noncount*] **2.** careful attention; notice: *Take heed my warnings.* —**heed′ful,** *adj.* —**heed′less,** *adj.*

hee•haw (hē′hô′) /ˈhiyˌhɔ/ *n.* [*count*] **1.** the sound made by a donkey. —*v.* [*no obj*] **2.** to make the sound of a donkey; bray.

heel[1] (hēl) /hiyl/ *n.* [*count*] **1.** the back part of the foot in humans, below and behind the ankle. **2.** the part of a stocking, shoe, etc., covering this part of the foot. **3.** a solid raised base attached to the sole of a shoe under the back part of the foot: *rubber heels.* **4. heels,** [*plural*] high-heeled shoes. **5.** the end part of a loaf of bread. **6.** the rear of the palm of the hand, next to the wrist. **7.** control; subjugation: *under the heel of the dictator.* —*v.* **8.** [~ + *obj*] to furnish or provide with heels: *The shoemaker heeled the shoes.* **9.** [*no obj*] (of a dog) to follow at one's heels on command. —***Idiom.*** **10. at one's heels,** close behind one: *The dogs were snapping at my heels, but I managed to get away.* **11. cool one's heels,** to wait or be kept waiting, esp. because of disdain or discourtesy: *I had to cool my heels until the boss found time to see me.* **12. down at (the) heel(s),** dressed shabbily. **13. kick up one's heels,** to have an unusually lively, entertaining time. **14. on** or **upon the heels of,** closely following: *The police were hot on the heels of the criminals.* **15. take to one's heels,** [*no obj*] to run away; take flight. **16. turn on one's heel,** to turn about suddenly, as in anger: *turned on her heel and stormed out of the room.* —**heel′less,** *adj.*

heel[2] (hēl) /hiyl/ *v.* [*no obj*] **1.** (esp. of a ship) to lean or incline to one side; tilt: *The torpedoed frigate was heeling to starboard.* **2.** a heeling movement; cant.

heel[3] (hēl) /hiyl/ *n.* [*count*] a dishonorable, dishonest, or contemptible person.

heft (heft) /hɛft/ *n.* [*noncount*] **1.** weight; heaviness. —*v.* [~ + *obj*] **2.** to test the weight of by lifting and balancing: *He hefted the spear.*

heft•y (hef′tē) /ˈhɛftiy/ *adj.,* **-i•er, -i•est. 1.** heavy; weighty: *a hefty dictionary.* **2.** mighty; powerful: *a hefty line of football players.* **3.** large; substantial: *a hefty increase in salary.* —**heft′i•ness,** *n.* [*noncount*]

he•gem•o•ny (hi jem′ə nē, hej′ə mō′nē) /hɪˈdʒɛməniy, ˈhɛdʒəˌmowniy/ *n.* [*noncount*] domination, esp. of one nation over others.

he•gi•ra (hi jī′rə, hej′ər ə) /hɪˈdʒayrə, ˈhɛdʒərə/ *n.* [*count*], *pl.* **-ras.** any flight to a more desirable place: *a hegira across the border to safety.*

heif•er (hef′ər) /ˈhɛfər/ *n.* [*count*] a young cow that is over a year old and has not produced a calf.

height (hīt) /hayt/ *n.* **1.** [*noncount*] extent or distance upward: *The plane gained height rapidly.* **2.** [*count*] distance upward between the lowest and highest points: *His height was about five feet, ten inches tall.* **3.** [*count; usually singular*] the quality or degree of being high, tall, elevated, or at a high altitude: *felt proud of her height.* **4.** Often, **heights.** [*plural*] **a.** a high place above a level; hill or mountain: *the heights overlooking the old city.* **b.** the highest part; apex; summit: *to reach the heights in one's profession.* **5.** [*count; usually singular; often: the* + ~] the highest or most intense point, amount, or degree; peak: *the height of pleasure; the height of rush hour.*

height•en (hīt′n) /ˈhaytn̩/ *v.* to increase (the degree of); strengthen or intensify: [~ + *obj*]: *to heighten one's awareness.* [*no obj*]: *The tension heightened in the room.*

Heim′lich maneu′ver (hīm′lik) /ˈhaymlɪk/ *n.* [*count; usually: the* + ~] an emergency procedure to aid a person choking on food by applying sudden pressure with an inward and upward thrust of the fist to the victim's upper abdomen in order to force out of the throat whatever is blocking it.

hei•nous (hā′nəs) /ˈheynəs/ *adj.* very evil and hateful: *Genocide is a heinous offense.* —**hei′nous•ly,** *adv.* —**hei′nous•ness,** *n.* [*noncount*]

heir (âr) /ɛər/ *n.* [*count*] **1.** a person who inherits or has a right to inherit from another person who dies: *sole heir to the millionaire's fortune; an heir to the throne.* **2.** a person or group considered as inheriting the qualities or endowments of those who went before: *He was the heir to the great tradition of epic poets.*

heir•ess (âr′is) /ˈɛərɪs/ *n.* [*count*] a woman who is an heir.

heir•loom (âr′lo͞om′) /ˈɛərˌluwm/ *n.* [*count*] a family possession handed down from generation to generation.

heist (hīst) /hayst/ *n.* [*count*] *Slang.* **1.** a robbery or holdup. —*v.* [~ + *obj*] **2.** to steal: *They heisted the gold and jewels from the vault.*

held (held) /hɛld/ *v.* pt. and pp. of HOLD[1].

hel•i•cal (hel′i kəl, hē′li-) /ˈhɛlɪkəl, ˈhiylɪ-/ *adj.* shaped like a helix; spiral.

hel•i•cop•ter (hel′i kop′tər, hē′li-) /ˈhɛlɪˌkɒptər, ˈhiylɪ-/ *n.* [*count*] **1.** a heavier-than-air craft that is lifted and kept in the air horizontally by rotating blades attached to its top. —*v.* **2.** to travel or transport in a helicopter: [*no obj*]: *The president helicoptered to the conference.* [~ + *obj*]: *She was helicoptered straight to the hospital.* See -PTER-.

-helio-, *root.* -*helio*- comes from Greek, where it has the meaning "sun." This meaning is found in such words as: APHELION, HELIUM, PERIHELION.

hel•i•port (hel′ə pôrt′, -pōrt′, hē′lə-) /ˈhɛləˌpɔrt, -ˌpowrt, ˈhiylə-/ *n.* [*count*] a takeoff and landing place for helicopters.

he•li•um (hē′lē əm) /ˈhiyliyəm/ *n.* [*noncount*] an inert, gaseous element present in natural gas. See -HELIO-.

he•lix (hē′liks) /ˈhiylɪks/ *n.* [*count*], *pl.* **hel•i•ces** (hel′ə sēz′) /ˈhɛləˌsiyz/ **he•lix•es.** a spiral.

hell (hel) /hɛl/ *n.* [*noncount*] **1.** the place or state of punishment where wicked people are believed to go after death; the place where evil and condemned spirits are sent. **2.** any place or state of suffering or misery: *This illness has made her life hell.* **3.** the place where dead people go. **4.** extreme disorder or confusion; chaos: *All hell broke loose.* **5.** a severe scolding or punishment: *I* *gave her hell for coming in so late.* **6.** This word is used in various phrases in swearing to express anger, dismissal, disgust, etc., or to express how strong one's feelings are about a situation: [*the* + ~ + *with*]: *The hell with it!* [*as* + ~]: *He's guilty as hell.* [*a* + ~ + *of*]: *He's a hell of a nice guy!* [*who/what/when/where/why/how* + *the* + ~]: *Who the hell was that?* —*interj.* **7.** This word is used alone in swearing to express irritation, disgust, surprise, etc.: *Hell! I've lost my wallet.* —*v.* **8. hell around,** [*no obj*] *Slang.* to live or act in a wild manner: *He helled around in Europe, then returned home.* —***Idiom.*** **9. be hell on,** [~ + *obj*] *Slang.* **a.** to be unpleasant to or painful for: *The news of her being fired will be hell on her family.* **b.** to be harmful to: *These roads are hell on tires.* **10. come hell or high water,** [*no obj*] whatever problem, obstacle, or difficulty may come: *You know I'll defend you come hell or high water.* **11. for the hell of it,** *Informal.* with no purpose other than sheer adventure or fun: *went for a long drive just for the hell of it.* **12. like hell,** *Informal.* **a.** with great speed, effort, intensity, etc.: *We ran like hell.* **b.** Also, **the hell.** This term is used to emphasize a speaker's denial or disagreement: *He says the motor is reliable? The hell it is.* **13. raise hell,** *Informal.* **a.** to indulge in wild celebration. **b.** to create an uproar; object violently: *If you fire the principal the whole town will raise hell.*

he'll (hēl; *unstressed* ēl, hil, il) /hiyl; *unstressed* iyl, hɪl, ɪl/ *contraction.* a shortened form of *he will: The doctor is in; he'll see you now.*

hell•bent (hel′bent′) /ˈhɛlˌbɛnt/ *adj.* [*be* + ~ + *on*] **1.** stubbornly determined: *He was hellbent on succeeding.* —*adv.* **2.** at terrific speed: *riding hellbent for the border.*

hell•hole (hel′hōl′) /ˈhɛlˌhowl/ *n.* [*count*] an extremely unpleasant place.

hel•lion (hel′yən) /ˈhɛlyən/ *n.* [*count*] a troublesome, wild, rowdy, or mischievous person.

hell•ish (hel′ish) /ˈhɛlɪʃ/ *adj.* extremely unpleasant or difficult; terrible: *the hot, hellish climate; a hellish year in a prison camp.* —**hell′ish•ly,** *adv.*

hel•lo (he lō′, hə-, hel′ō) /hɛˈlow, hə-, ˈhɛlow/ *interj., n., pl.* **-los.** —*interj.* **1.** This word is used to express a greeting, answer a telephone, or attract attention: *Hello, how are you?* **2.** This word is used to express surprise, wonder, etc.: *"Hello, what's this?" said the detective.* —*n.* [*count*] **3.** an act or instance of saying "hello"; greeting: *a mumbled hello.*

helm (helm) /hɛlm/ *n.* [*count*] **1.** a wheel, tiller, or apparatus by which a ship is steered. **2. at the helm,** in the position of control.

hel•met (hel′mit) /ˈhɛlmɪt/ *n.* [*count*] a usually strong and hard covering worn on the head for protection. —**hel′met•ed,** *adj.*

helms•man (helmz′mən) /ˈhɛlmzmən/ *n.* [*count*], *pl.* **-men.** a person who steers a ship.

help (help) /hɛlp/ *v.* **1.** to provide what is necessary to accomplish a task or satisfy a need; aid; assist: [~ + *obj*]: *He said he'd help me with my work.* [~ + *obj* (+ *to*) + *root form of verb*]: *We helped him (to) get settled in.* [~ (+ *to*) + *root form of verb*]: *I helped (to) carry the groceries.* [*no obj*]: *I hope this money will help.* **2.** [~ + *obj*] to save; rescue: *Help me, I'm falling!* **3.** [~ + *obj*] to be useful or profitable to: *Your knowledge of languages will help you in your career.* **4. cannot** or **can't help, a.** stop oneself from: [~ + *it*]: *I can't help it if I sneezed.* [~ + *verb-ing*]: *I can't help teasing him about it.* [~ + *but* + *root form of verb*]: *You can't help but admire her.* **b.** [~ + *obj; usually: be* + *helped*] to prevent or stop: *The disagreement could not be helped.* **5.** to (cause to) bring about improvement: [~ + *obj*]: *A new rug might help the room.* [*no obj*]: *I've tried those aspirins, but it doesn't help.* **6. a.** to serve oneself with: [~ + *oneself*]: *Do you want some cake? Help yourself.* [~ + *oneself* + *to* + *obj*]: *Help yourself to the cake.* **b.** [~ + *oneself* + *to* + *obj*] to take or use: *She helped herself to the pencils on my desk.* **c.** [~ + *oneself* + *to* + *obj*] to take or use without asking permission: *just helped himself to whatever money had been left around.* **7.** [~ + *obj*] to wait on (a customer): *"How may I help you?" asked the salesclerk.* **8. help out,** to assist during a time of need: [*no obj*]: *Maybe this money will help out a little.* [~ + *obj* + *out*]: *Can't you help him out?* [~ + *out* + *obj*]: *She helps out everyone who comes to her.* —*n.* **9.** [*noncount*] aid; assistance: *If she needs help, tell her to call me.* **10.** [*count*] a person or thing that helps: *You were a tremendous help after the fire.* **11.** [*noncount*] assistants or employees when thought of as a group: *hired new help at the shop.* **12.** [*noncount*] a means of dealing with something: *There is no help for the problem now.* —*interj.* **13.** The word is used to call for assistance or to attract attention: *"Help!" she called, "I can't get up."* —***Idiom.*** **14. so help me (God),** I am speaking the truth; on my honor. —**help′er,** *n.* [*count*] —**Usage.** See CANNOT.

help•ful (help′fəl) /ˈhɛlpfəl/ *adj.* giving aid or assistance: *helpful comments; a helpful person.* —**help′ful•ly,** *adv.* —**help′ful•ness,** *n.* [*noncount*]

help•ing (hel′ping) /ˈhɛlpɪŋ/ *n.* [*count*] a portion of food.

help•less (help′lis) /ˈhɛlplɪs/ *adj.* **1.** unable to help oneself; weak: *a helpless newborn baby.* **2.** without aid or protection: *The army was left helpless before the enemy bombardment.* **3.** weakened; powerless: *helpless with laughter.* —**help′less•ly,** *adv.* —**help′less•ness,** *n.* [*noncount*]

help′mate′ (-māt′) /-ˌmeyt/ or **-meet** (-mēt′) /-ˌmiyt/ *n.* [*count*] **1.** a companion and helper. **2.** a wife or husband.

hel•ter-skel•ter (hel′tər skel′tər) /ˈhɛltərˈskɛltər/ *adv.* **1.** in great haste; headlong: *running helter-skelter all over the house.* **2.** in a disorganized manner: *clothes scattered helter-skelter about the room.* —*adj.* [*before a noun*] **3.** carelessly hurried: *a helter-skelter rush.* **4.** disorganized; haphazard.

hem[1] (hem) /hɛm/ *v.,* **hemmed, hem•ming,** *n.* —*v.* **1.** [~ + *obj*] to form or sew a hem on: *She hemmed the skirt.* **2.** to enclose; surround: [~ + *in* + *obj*]: *The cavalry had managed to hem in the enemy infantry.* [~ + *obj* + *in*]: *A fence hemmed the sheep in.* —*n.* [*count*] **3.** the bottom edge or border of a garment, drape, etc., esp. one made by folding back an edge and sewing it down. —**hem′mer,** *n.* [*count*]

hem[2] (hem) /hɛm/ *interj., n., v.,* **hemmed, hem•ming.** —*interj.* **1.** This sound, resembling a slight clearing of the throat, is used esp. to attract attention or express doubt or hesitation. —*n.* [*count*] **2.** the sound or the saying of "hem." —*v.* [*no obj*] **3.** to utter the sound "hem." **4.** to hesitate in speaking: *He hemmed a few moments, then answered.* —***Idiom.*** **5. hem and haw,** [*no obj*] **a.** to hesitate or falter while speaking: *She hemmed and hawed a moment, nervous from all the pressure.* **b.** to avoid giving a direct answer: *The candidate hemmed and hawed when asked if he had ever used illegal drugs.*

he′-man′, *n.* [*count*], *pl.* **-men.** a virile man.

hem•i•sphere (hem′i sfēr′) /ˈhɛmɪˌsfɪər/ *n.* [*count*] **1.** [*often: Hemisphere*] half of the earth; one of the halves into which the earth may be divided: *the Western Hemisphere; the Southern Hemisphere.* **2.** a half of a sphere. —**hem•i•spher•ic** (hem′i sfer′ik) /ˌhɛmɪˈsfɛrɪk/ **hem′i•spher′i•cal,** *adj.*

hem•line (hem′lin′) /ˈhɛmˌlayn/ *n.* [*count*] the bottom edge of a coat, skirt, etc.

hem•lock (hem′lok′) /ˈhɛmˌlɒk/ *n.* **1.** [*count*] a poisonous plant of the parsley family. **2.** [*noncount*] a poisonous drink made from this plant. **3.** [*count*] Also called **hem′lock spruce′.** a tall cone-bearing tree of the pine family. **4.** [*noncount*] the soft, light wood of a hemlock tree.

hemo- or **hema-,** *prefix. hemo-* or *hema-* comes from Greek, where it has the meaning "blood." This meaning is found in such words as: HEMOGLOBIN, HEMOPHILIA, HEMORRHAGE, HEMORRHOID. Also, *esp. before a vowel,* **hem-.**

he•mo•glo•bin (hē′mə glō′bin, hem′ə-) /ˈhiyməˌglowbɪn, ˈhɛmə-/ *n.* [*noncount*] a protein appearing in red blood cells, which contains iron and carries oxygen from the lungs to the tissues of the body.

he•mo•phil•i•a (hē′mə fil′ē ə, -fēl′yə) /ˌhiyməˈfɪliyə, -ˈfiylyə/ *n.* [*noncount*] an inherited disorder that shows its effects only in males, in which too much bleeding occurs from minor injuries because blood fails to clot properly. —**he•mo•phil•i•ac** (hē′mə fil′ē ak′) /ˌhiyməˈfɪliyˌæk/ *n.* [*count*] See -PHIL-.

hem•or•rhage (hem′ər ij, hem′rij) /ˈhɛmərɪdʒ, ˈhɛmrɪdʒ/ *n., v.,* **-rhaged, -rhag•ing.** —*n.* **1.** a flow or giving off of blood, esp. in large amounts: [*noncount*]: *the danger of hemorrhage during the surgery.* [*count*]: *The hemorrhage can be prevented.* —*v.* **2.** to bleed a great deal; give off a great deal of blood: [*no obj*]: *The patient was hemorrhaging.* [~ + *obj*]: *hemorrhaging a great deal of blood.* **3.** [~ + *obj*] to lose in quantity: *The company was hemorrhaging cash.* —**hem•or•rhag•ic** (hem′ə raj′ik) /ˌhɛməˈrædʒɪk/ *adj.* [*before a noun*]: *hemorrhagic fever.*

hem•or•rhoid (hem′ə roid′, hem′roid) /ˈhɛməˌrɔyd, ˈhɛmrɔyd/ *n.* Usually, **hemorrhoids.** [*plural*] a swollen blood vessel in the region of the anus. Also called **pile.**

hemp (hemp) /hɛmp/ *n.* [*noncount*] **1.** marijuana, a tall Asian plant widely grown for its fiber and for the drugs that can be made from it. **2.** the tough fiber of this plant. **3.** an intoxicating drug, as marijuana, prepared from the hemp plant.

hen (hen) /hɛn/ *n.* [*count*] **1.** the female of the domestic fowl. **2.** the female of any bird.

hence (hens) /hɛns/ *adv.* **1.** for this reason; therefore: *The new secretary was caught stealing and hence must be fired.* **2.** from this time; from now: *in a month hence.* **3.** from this source or origin: *Hence the knight set forth on a quest.*

hence•forth (hens′fôrth′, -fōrth′; hens′fôrth′, -fōrth′) /ˌhɛns'fɔrθ, -'fowrθ;'hɛnsˌfɔrθ, -ˌfowrθ/ also **hence•for•ward** (-fôr′wərd, -fōr′-) /-'fɔrwərd, -'fowr-/ *adv.* from now on; from this point forward.

hench•man (hench′mən) /'hɛntʃmən/ *n.* [*count*], *pl.* **-men. 1.** a person hired by another to do dishonest or illegal acts, esp. a member of a criminal gang. **2.** a trusted supporter or follower.

hen•na (hen′ə) /'hɛnə/ *n.* [*noncount*] **1.** a reddish orange dye used esp. in coloring the hair. **2.** a color between red-brown and orange-brown. **—***v.* [~ + *obj*] **3.** to tint or dye with henna: *hennaed her hair.*

hen•peck (hen′pek′) /'hɛnˌpɛk/ *v.* [~ + *obj*] to find continual fault with (one's husband).

hep•a•ti•tis (hep′ə ti′tis) /ˌhɛpə'taytɪs/ *n.* [*noncount*] inflammation of the liver.

hep•ta•gon (hep′tə gon′) /'hɛptəˌgɒn/ *n.* [*count*] a shape having seven sides.

her (hûr; *unstressed* hər, ər) /hɜr; *unstressed* hər, ər/ *pron.* **1.** the form of the pronoun SHE, used as a direct or indirect object, or sometimes after the verb *be*: *We saw her this morning. I gave her the message.* **2.** a form of the pronoun SHE used to show possession or some relation: *Her coat is on the chair.* Compare HERS. **—***n.* [*count*] **3.** *Informal.* a female: *Is the new baby a him or a her?*

her•ald (her′əld) /'hɛrəld/ *n.* [*count*] **1.** a royal or official messenger. **2.** a person or thing that comes before; forerunner; harbinger: *The swallows are heralds of spring.* **—***v.* [~ + *obj*] **3.** to signal the coming of; usher in: *Daffodils herald the arrival of spring.*

he•ral•dic (he ral′dik, hə-) /hɛ'rældɪk, hə-/ *adj.* [*before a noun*] of or relating to heralds or heraldry.

her•ald•ry (her′əl drē) /'hɛrəldriy/ *n.* [*noncount*] **1.** the study of coats of arms and of noble families. **2.** heraldic designs.

herb (ûrb) /ɜrb/ *n.* [*count*] a plant whose stem above ground does not become woody, esp. one valued for the medicine made from it, for its flavor, or for its scent. —**her•ba•ceous** (hûr bā′shəs, ûr-) /hɜr'beyʃəs, ɜr-/ *adj.*

herb•al (ûr′bəl, hûr′-) /'ɜrbəl, 'hɜr-/ *adj.* [*before a noun*] of or relating to herbs; made from herbs: *herbal tea.*

herb•al•ist (hûr′bə list, ûr′-) /'hɜrbəlɪst, 'ɜr-/ *n.* [*count*] a person who collects or deals in medicinal herbs.

herb•i•cide (hûr′bə sīd′, ûr′-) /'hɜrbəˌsayd, 'ɜr-/ *n.* [*count*] a substance or chemical for killing plants, esp. weeds. —**her•bi•cid•al** (hûr′bə sīd′l, ûr′-) /ˌhɜrbə'saydl̩, ˌɜr-/ *adj.* See -CIDE-.

her•biv•ore (hûr′bə vôr′, -vōr′) /'hɜrbəˌvɔr, -ˌvowr/ *n.* [*count*] an animal that eats plants. See -VOR-.

her•biv•o•rous (hûr biv′ər əs, ûr-) /hɜr'bɪvərəs, ɜr-/ *adj.* feeding on plants. See -VOR-.

her•cu•le•an (hûr′kyə lē′ən, hûr kyo͞o′lē-) /ˌhɜrkyə'liyən, hɜr'kyuwliy-/ *adj.* requiring great strength: *a herculean task.*

herd (hûrd) /hɜrd/ *n.* [*count*] **1.** a number of animals feeding, traveling, or kept together; drove; flock: *a herd of zebras.* **2.** a cohesive group of people; crowd: *a herd of autograph seekers.* **3. the herd,** people in general; masses: *didn't associate with the common herd.* **—***v.* **4.** [*no obj*] to unite or move in a herd: *The tourists all herded into the tiny restaurant.* **5.** [~ + *obj*] to gather into or as if into a herd: *The guide herded her tourists into the ancient cathedral.* **—*Idiom.* 6. ride herd on,** [~ + *obj*] to maintain control or discipline over: *rode herd on the employees.* —**herd′er,** *n.* [*count*]

herds•man (hûrdz′mən) /'hɜrdzmən/ *n.* [*count*], *pl.* **-men.** the keeper of a herd, esp. of cattle or sheep; herder.

here (hēr) /hɪər/ *adv.* **1.** in or at this place: *Put the pen here.* **2.** to or toward this place: *Come here.* **3.** at this point in an action, speech, etc.: *Here the speaker paused.* **4.** in this instance or case; under consideration: *The matter here is of grave concern.* **5.** The word *here* is used as the first word in a sentence to call attention to some person or thing, or to what the speaker has, offers, or discovers. The verb of a sentence like this usually does not take an object, or else it is the verb BE. The subject of the verb is never the word *here*; the subject either comes after the verb, or, if it is a pronoun, it comes before the verb. It is the subject that decides which form of the verb, singular or plural, should be used: [~ + *verb* + *subject*]: *Here comes the bride. Here is your paycheck. Here come the boys. Here are the tickets.* [~ + *pronoun subject* + *verb*]: *Here she is! Here they are.* **6.** The word *here* is used to mean "present," as when the speaker is answering a roll call: *Please say "here" when your name is called.* **—***n.* [*noncount*] **7.** this place or point: *The next town is a long way from here.* **—***adj.* **8.** The word *here* is sometimes used for emphasis with a noun that has the word THIS or THESE before it. The word *here* may come after the noun (a usage considered standard), as in: *this package here,* or before the noun (a usage considered nonstandard): *this here package.* **—***interj.* **9.** The word *here* is used to command attention, give comfort, etc.: *Here, here, now, don't cry.* **—*Idiom.* 10. here and now,** without delay; immediately: *I want to know here and now what your plans are.* **11. here and there,** in or to this place and that; in or to various places; scattered about: *We looked here and there for her.* **12. here goes,** [*no obj*] This phrase is used to express the speaker's determination when beginning a bold or unpleasant action: *walked to the edge, said "Here goes," and jumped.* **13. here's to,** [~ + *obj*] This phrase is used in offering a toast to someone or something: *Here's to the New Year.* **14. neither here nor there,** unimportant: *Personal wants are neither here nor there in a national emergency.* **15. the here and now,** the immediate present: *It's the here and now, not the future, we're worried about.*

-here-, *root.* *-here-* comes from Latin, where it has the meaning "cling, stick tight." It is related to -HES-. This meaning is found in such words as: ADHERE, ADHERENT, COHERE, COHERENCE, COHERENT, INCOHERENCE, INCOHERENT. See -HES-.

here•a•bout (hēr′ə bout′) /'hɪərəˌbawt/ also **here′a•bouts′,** *adv.* about this place; in this neighborhood.

here•af•ter (hēr af′tər) /hɪər'æftər/ *adv.* **1.** in the future; from now on: *I'll forgive this one mistake, but hereafter there can be no more.* **—***n.* [*count; singular; the* + ~] **2.** a life or existence after death: *May we meet again in the hereafter.*

here•by (hēr bī′, hēr′bī′) /hɪər'bay, 'hɪərˌbay/ *adv.* by this action, document, etc.: *I hereby resign (= By saying or writing this, I resign).*

he•red•i•tar•y (hə red′i ter′ē) /hə'rɛdɪˌtɛriy/ *adj.* **1.** passing, or capable of passing, naturally from parent to young through the genes: *a hereditary disease.* **2.** of or relating to inheritance: *a hereditary title.* **3.** [*before a noun*] existing because of tradition: *hereditary enemies for centuries.* —**he•red•i•tar•i•ly** (hə red′i târ′ə lē) /hərɛdɪ'tɛərəliy/ *adv.*

he•red•i•ty (hə red′i tē) /hə'rɛdɪtiy/ *n.* [*noncount*] the passing on of qualities, characteristics, or traits from parents to their young through the genes.

here•in (hēr in′) /hɪər'ɪn/ *adv.* in or into this place, situation, circumstance, etc.: *all the words contained herein.*

here•of (hēr uv′, -ov′) /hɪər'ʌv, -'ɒv/ *adv.* of or concerning this: *more hereof later.*

her•e•sy (her′ə sē) /'hɛrəsiy/ *n., pl.* **-sies. 1.** religious opinion or doctrine that is different from or opposed to the accepted doctrine: [*count*]: *People used to be burned at the stake for such heresies.* [*noncount*]: *judged guilty of heresy.* **2.** [*noncount; count*] any belief or theory strongly different from or opposed to established beliefs, customs, etc.

her•e•tic (her′i tik) /'hɛrɪtɪk/ *n.* [*count*] **1.** a person who claims to believe in a church but holds opinions opposed to those of the church. **2.** a person who does not believe in an established view or doctrine. —**he•ret•i•cal** (hə-ret′i kəl) /hə'rɛtɪkəl/ *adj.*

here•to (hēr to͞o′) /hɪər'tuw/ also **here•un•to** (hēr-un′to͞o, hēr′un to͞o′) /hɪər'ʌntuw, ˌhɪərʌn'tuw/ *adv.* to this matter or document.

here•to•fore (hēr′tə fôr′, -fōr′) /ˌhɪərtə'fɔr, -'fowr/ *adv.* before this time.

here•with (hēr with′, -with′) /hɪər'wɪθ, -'wɪð/ *adv.* along with this; by means of this; hereby.

her•it•age (her′i tij) /'hɛrɪtɪdʒ/ *n.* [*count; usually singular*] something that comes or belongs to one by reason of being born to certain parents, born at a certain time, or in a certain country, esp. the traditions and ways of life.

her•maph•ro•dite (hûr maf′rə dīt′) /hɜr'mæfrəˌdayt/ *n.*

[*count*] a living thing in which reproductive organs of both sexes are present. —**her•maph•ro•dit•ic** (hûr maf′rə dit′ik) /hɜrˌmæfrə'dɪtɪk/ *adj.*

her•met•ic (hûr met′ik) /hɜr'mɛtɪk/ also **her•met′i•cal,** *adj.* made, sealed, or closed so tightly that no air can escape. —**her•met′i•cal•ly,** *adv.*

her•mit (hûr′mit) /'hɜrmɪt/ *n.* [*count*] a person who lives in solitude, esp. for reasons of religion.

her•mit•age (hûr′mi tij) /'hɜrmɪtɪdʒ/ *n.* [*count*] the place where a hermit lives.

her•ni•a (hûr′nē ə) /'hɜrniyə/ *n.* [*count*], *pl.* **-ni•as, -ni•ae** (-nē ē′) /-niyˌiy/. the sticking out of a body organ or tissue through an opening in its surrounding walls, esp. a part of the intestine sticking out. —**her′ni•al,** *adj.*

he•ro (hēr′ō) /'hɪərow/ *n.* [*count*], *pl.* **-roes;** for 4 also **-ros. 1.** a man who is famous for his courage or ability and admired for his brave deeds and noble qualities. **2.** any person who is thought of as a model to follow: *an athlete who is a hero to kids.* **3.** the principal male character in a story, play, film, etc. **4.** Also, **hero sandwich.** a sandwich made of a long roll cut lengthwise and containing such ingredients as meat, cheese, lettuce, and tomatoes.

he•ro•ic (hi rō′ik) /hɪ'rowɪk/ *adj.* Also, **he•ro′i•cal. 1.** of, relating to, or like a hero or heroine. **2.** having or involving daring or forceful action: *took heroic measures to save the child's life.* **3.** [*before a noun*] dealing with heroes and heroines: *heroic literature.* —*n.* **4. heroics,** [*plural*] language or behavior that is flamboyantly heroic: *Leave the heroics to the police.* —**he•ro′i•cal•ly,** *adv.*

her•o•in (her′ō in) /'hɛrowɪn/ *n.* [*noncount*] a white powder made from morphine that is narcotic and addictive.

her•o•ine (her′ō in) /'hɛrowɪn/ *n.* [*count*] **1.** a woman who is famous for her courage or ability and admired for her brave deeds and noble qualities. **2.** the principal female character in a story, play, film, etc.

her•o•ism (her′ō iz′əm) /'hɛrowˌɪzəm/ *n.* [*noncount*] **1.** the qualities of a hero or heroine; bravery. **2.** heroic conduct.

her•on (her′ən) /'hɛrən/ *n.* [*count*] a long-legged, long-necked wading bird usually having a long bill.

he′ro sand′wich, *n.* HERO (def. 4).

her•pes (hûr′pēz) /'hɜrpiyz/ *n.* [*noncount*] any of several viral diseases in which blisters appear on the skin or mucous membranes.

her•ring (her′ing) /'hɛrɪŋ/ *n., pl.* (*esp. when thought of as a group*) **-ring,** (*esp. for kinds or species*) **-rings.** an important food fish of the N Atlantic.

her•ring•bone (her′ing bōn′) /'hɛrɪŋˌbown/ *n.* [*noncount*] **1.** a pattern of vertical rows of slanting lines, either shaped in a V or an inverted V, used in bricks, fabrics, textiles, etc. —*adj.* [*before a noun*] **2.** woven in a pattern of herringbone: *herringbone tweed.*

hers (hûrz) /hɜrz/ *pron.* a form of the pronoun SHE used to show possession, or to mean "that or those belonging to her": *Are you a friend of hers?* [*be* + ~]: *The red umbrella is hers.*

her•self (hər self′) /hər'sɛlf/ *pron.* **1.** the form of the pronoun SHE, a reflexive pronoun, used to show that the subject of the sentence and this pronoun (a direct object, indirect object, or an object of a preposition) refer to the same female person: *Anne supports herself (= Anne supports Anne).* **2.** (used to give emphasis): *The queen herself wrote the letter.* **3.** (used in place of SHE or HER in various constructions where it is clear from some previous discussion who the female is): *The producer and herself were not on speaking terms. (= The producer and some female we were talking about recently were not on speaking terms).* **4.** her normal or customary self: *After a few weeks of rest, she will be herself again.*

he's (hēz; *unstressed* ēz) /hiyz; *unstressed* iyz/ *contraction.* **1.** a shortened form of *he is*: *He's late again.* **2.** a shortened form of *he has*: *He's already gone to bed.*

-hes-, *root.* *-hes-* comes from Latin, where it has the meaning "cling, stick to." It is related to -HERE-. This meaning is found in such words as: ADHESIVE, COHESIVE, HESITATE.

hes•i•tant (hez′i tənt) /'hɛzɪtənt/ *adj.* tending to hesitate; undecided or doubtful; uncertain: *a hesitant manner.* —**hes′i•tan•cy,** *n.* [*noncount*] —**hes′i•tant•ly,** *adv.* See -HES-.

hes•i•tate (hez′i tāt′) /'hɛzɪˌteyt/ *v.,* **-tat•ed, -tat•ing. 1.** [*no obj*] to wait or pause because of doubt, fear, or indecision; vacillate: *She hesitated before taking the job.* **2.** [~ + *to* + *verb*] to have doubts about; be uncertain about: *He hesitated to break the law.* —**hes′i•tat′ing•ly,** *adv.* See -HES-.

hes•i•ta•tion (hez′i tā′shən) /ˌhɛzɪ'teyʃən/ *n.* an act of hesitating: [*noncount*]: *a moment of hesitation.* [*count*]: *After a momentary hesitation, the general gave the command.* See -HES-.

het•er•o (het′ə rō) /'hɛtərow/ *n.* [*count*], *pl.* **-er•os. 1.** a heterosexual person. —*adj.* **2.** heterosexual.

-hetero-, *root.* *-hetero-* comes from Greek, where it has the meaning "the other of two; different." This meaning is found in such words as: HETEROGENEOUS, HETEROSEXUAL.

het•er•o•dox (het′ər ə doks′) /'hɛtərəˌdɒks/ *adj.* not agreeing with established doctrines, esp. in theology. —**het′er•o•dox′y,** *n.* [*noncount*] See -HETERO-, -DOX-.

het•er•o•ge•ne•ous (het′ər ə jē′nē əs, -jēn′yəs) /ˌhɛtərə'dʒiyniyəs, -'dʒiynyəs/ *adj.* composed of parts of different kinds; mixed. —**het•er•o•ge•ne•i•ty** (het′ə rō jə-nē′i tē) /ˌhɛtərowdʒə'niyɪtiy/ **het′er•o•ge′ne•ous•ness,** *n.* [*noncount*] —**het′er•o•ge′ne•ous•ly,** *adv.* See -HETERO-, -GEN-.

het•er•o•sex•u•al (het′ər ə sek′sho͞o əl) /ˌhɛtərə'sɛkʃuwəl/ *adj.* **1.** of, relating to, or showing behavior that indicates attraction to the opposite sex. **2.** of or relating to the opposite sex or to both sexes: *a heterosexual relationship.* —*n.* [*count*] **3.** a person attracted to the opposite sex. —**het•er•o•sex•u•al•i•ty** (het′ər ə sek′sho͞o al′i tē) /ˌhɛtərəˌsɛkʃuw'ælɪtiy/ *n.* [*noncount*] See -HETERO-.

heu•ris•tic (hyo͞o ris′tik) /hyʊ'rɪstɪk/ *adj.* **1.** encouraging a person to learn, discover, understand, or solve problems on his or her own, as by experimenting, evaluating possible answers or solutions, or by trial and error, and not by relying on rules or formulas: *a heuristic teaching method.* —*n.* [*count*] **2.** a heuristic method or argument. —**heu•ris′ti•cal•ly,** *adv.*

hew (hyo͞o) /hyuw/ *v.,* **hewed, hewed** or **hewn, hew•ing. 1.** [~ + *obj*] to strike forcibly with a cutting instrument, as an ax. **2.** [~ + *obj*] to shape or smooth with cutting blows: *to hew a statue from marble.* **3.** [~ *(+ down)* + *obj*] to cut down: *trees hewed down by the storm.* **4.** [~ + *to* + *obj*] to uphold or act in agreement with: *to hew to a party line.* —**hew′er,** *n.* [*count*]

hex (heks) /hɛks/ *v.* [~ + *obj*] **1.** to bewitch: *They were hexed by the wicked witch.* **2.** to bring bad luck to; jinx. —*n.* [*count*] **3.** a spell; charm; jinx.

-hexa-, *root.* *hexa-* comes from Greek, where it has the meaning "six." This meaning is found in such words as: HEXAGON, HEXAMETER.

hex•a•gon (hek′sə gon′, -gən) /'hɛksəˌgɒn, -gən/ *n.* [*count*] a figure having six angles and six sides. —**hex•ag•o•nal** (hek sag′ə nl) /hɛk'sægənl/ *adj.* See -HEXA-.

hex•am•e•ter (hek sam′i tər) /hɛk'sæmɪtər/ *n.* [*count*] a line of poetry having six important metrical feet. See -HEXA-.

hey (hā) /hey/ *interj.* This word is used to call attention or to express pleasure, surprise, bewilderment, etc.: *Hey, come back here, you!*

hey•day (hā′dā′) /'heyˌdey/ *n.* [*count; usually singular*] the stage or period of greatest strength, life, success, etc.; prime: *the heyday of the silent movies.*

HF, an abbreviation of: high frequency.

hgt., an abbreviation of: height.

hgwy., an abbreviation of: highway.

H.H., an abbreviation of: **1.** Her Highness; His Highness. **2.** His Holiness.

hi (hī) /hay/ *interj.* This word is used as an informal greeting: *Hi, how are you?*

HI, an abbreviation of: Hawaii.

hi•a•tus (hī ā′təs) /hay'eytəs/ *n.* [*count*], *pl.* **-tus•es, -tus.** a break or interruption in something, such as work, a series, or some action.

hi•ba•chi (hi bä′chē) /hɪ'bɑtʃiy/ *n.* [*count*], *pl.* **-chis.** a small cooking device consisting of a hollowed container for charcoal covered with a grill.

hi•ber•nate (hī′bər nāt′) /'haybərˌneyt/ *v.* [*no obj*], **-nat•ed, -nat•ing.** to spend the winter in a state resembling sleep, as bears do. —**hi•ber•na•tion** (hī′bər nā′shən) /ˌhaybər'neyʃən/ *n.* [*noncount*] —**hi′ber•na′tor,** *n.* [*count*]

hi•bis•cus (hī bis′kəs, hi-) /hay'bɪskəs, hɪ-/ *n.* [*count*], *pl.* **-cus•es.** a woody plant having large, showy yellow or red flowers.

hic•cup or **hic•cough** (hik′up, -əp) /'hɪkʌp, -əp/ *n., v.,* **hic•cuped** or **hic•cupped** or **hic•coughed** (hik′upt, -əpt) /'hɪkʌpt, -əpt/, **-cup•ing** or **-cup•ping** or **-cough•ing.** —*n.* [*count*] **1.** a sharp gulping sound in the throat caused by the rapid intake of air following a spasm of the muscle that causes breathing. **2.** Usually, **hiccups.** [*plural*] an attack of hiccups: *I have the hiccups.* **—***v.* [*no obj*] **3.** to make a hiccup. **4.** to make the sound like a hiccup: *The motor hiccuped as it started.*

hick (hik) /hɪk/ *n.* [*count*] **1.** an unsophisticated person from the country; rube. **—***adj.* [*before a noun*] **2.** UNSOPHISTICATED: *a hick town.*

hick•o•ry (hik′ə rē, hik′rē) /ˈhɪkəriy, ˈhɪkriy/ *n., pl.* **-ries. 1.** [*count*] a North American tree of the walnut family. **2.** [*noncount*] the wood of this tree.

hid (hid) /hɪd/ *v.* pt. or pp. of HIDE.

hide[1] (hīd) /hayd/ *v.,* **hid, hid•den** (hid′n) /ˈhɪdn̩/ or **hid, hid•ing. 1.** [~ + *obj*] to conceal (something) from sight: *Where did the crooks hide the money?* **2.** to conceal (oneself); remain so that one cannot be seen: [*no obj*]: *I hid in the closet.* [~ + *oneself*]: *I hid myself in the closet.* **3.** [~ + *obj*] to cover the view of: *The sun was hidden by the clouds.* **4.** [~ + *obj*] to conceal (something) from the knowledge of others; keep secret: *He was never able to hide his true feelings about her.* **5. hide out,** [*no obj*] to go into or remain in hiding: *The spies were hiding out in the farmhouse.* **—hid′er,** *n.* [*count*]

hide[2] (hīd) /hayd/ *n., v.,* **hid•ed, hid•ing. —***n.* [*count*] **1.** the raw skin of a large animal, as a cow or horse: *making hides into leather.* **2.** *Informal.* the life or welfare of a person: *turned informer to save his own hide.* **—***v.* [~ + *obj*] **3.** *Informal.* to give a beating to; thrash. **—*Idiom.* 4. hide (n)or hair,** This phrase is used in negative sentences or questions to mean "a trace or evidence, as of something missing": *I haven't seen hide nor hair of them since last week.* **5. tan one's hide,** to give a beating (to): *promised to tan his hide.*

hide′-and-seek′, *n.* [*noncount*] a children's game in which one player gives the other players a chance to hide and then tries to find them. Also called **hide′-and-go′-seek′.**

hide•a•way (hīd′ə wā′) /ˈhaydəˌwey/ *n.* [*count*] a place to which a person can retreat, as for relaxation or solitude.

hide•bound (hīd′bound′) /ˈhaydˌbawnd/ *adj.* narrow and rigid in opinion; inflexible: *hidebound board members who don't recognize innovation.*

hid•e•ous (hid′ē əs) /ˈhɪdiyəs/ *adj.* **1.** horrible or frightful to the senses; repulsive; very ugly: *a hideous monster.* **2.** shockingly bad or evil: *hideous crimes.* **3.** causing distress; appalling: *a hideous expense.* **—hid′e•ous•ly,** *adv.* **—hid′e•ous•ness,** *n.* [*noncount*]

hide•out or **hide-out** (hīd′out′) /ˈhaydˌawt/ *n.* [*count*] a safe place for hiding, esp. from the law.

hid•ing[1] (hī′ding) /ˈhaydɪŋ/ *n.* [*noncount*] the state of being hidden from others: *The crooks went into hiding.*

hid•ing[2] (hī′ding) /ˈhaydɪŋ/ *n.* [*count*] a beating.

hi•er•ar•chy (hī′ə rär′kē, hī′rär-) /ˈhayəˌrɑrkiy, ˈhayrɑr-/ *n.* [*count*], *pl.* **-chies. 1.** any system of persons or things ranked one above another. **2.** the persons in authority or having the highest power: *the party hierarchy.* **—hi•er•ar•chic** (hī′ə rär′kik) /ˌhayəˈrɑrkɪk/ **hi′er•ar′chi•cal,** *adj.* **—hi′er•ar′chi•cal•ly,** *adv.* See -ARCH-.

hi•er•o•glyph•ic (hī′ər ə glif′ik, hī′rə-) /ˌhayərəˈglɪfɪk, ˌhayrə-/ *adj.* Also, **hi′er•o•glyph′i•cal. 1.** of a type of writing in which pictures or symbols represent ideas: *The ancient Egyptians used a hieroglyphic system of writing.* **2.** hard to figure out; hard to read. **—***n.* [*count*] **3.** Also, **hi′er•o•glyph′.** a hieroglyphic symbol. **4.** Usually, **hieroglyphics.** [*plural*] hieroglyphic writing. **5. hieroglyphics,** [*plural*] characters or symbols that are difficult to understand.

hi-fi (hī′fī′) /ˈhayˈfay/ *n., pl.* **-fis,** *adj.* **—***n.* **1.** [*noncount*] HIGH FIDELITY. **2.** [*count*] a phonograph, radio, or other sound-reproducing apparatus that produces high quality sound: *an expensive hi-fi in the living room.* **—***adj.* [*before a noun*] **3.** of, relating to, or characteristic of hi-fi: *an expensive hi-fi radio.*

hig•gle•dy-pig•gle•dy (hig′əl dē pig′əl dē) /ˈhɪgəldiyˈpɪgəldiy/ *adv.* in a confused, disorderly manner: *papers scattered higgledy-piggledy.*

high (hī) /hay/ *adj.* and *adv.,* **-er, -est,** *n.* **—***adj.* **1.** (of things) having a considerable height; tall; lofty: *a high wall.* **2.** (of things) having a specified height: *The tree is 20 feet high.* **3.** located above the ground; elevated: *a high ledge.* **4.** greater than or going beyond the usual degree, measure, or amount: *high speed; high prices.* **5.** honorable; worthy of being admired; good: *high moral principles.* **6.** exalted or important, as in rank, station, or eminence: *a high government official.* **7.** of great consequence; grave: *guilty of high treason.* **8.** elevated in pitch: *high notes.* **9.** extending to or from an elevation: *a high dive.* **10.** [*before a noun*] extravagant; luxurious: *living the high life.* **11.** merry; happy: *They were in high spirits.* **12.** [*be* + ~] intoxicated, drunk, or under the influence of alcohol or narcotic drugs. **13.** [*before a noun*] complicated; advanced: *an expert in high finance.* **14.** relating to or being the gear of a transmission at which the drive shaft speed and the speed of the engine crankshaft correspond most closely. **—***adv.* **15.** at or to a high point, place, or level: *The hawk was circling high above the field.* **16.** richly; luxuriously; extravagantly: *to live high.* **—***n.* **17.** [*noncount*] the high gear of a transmission. **18.** [*count*] an atmospheric pressure system having relatively high pressure at its center. **19.** [*count*] a high or the highest point, place, or level; peak: *a record high for unemployment.* **20.** [*count*] **a.** an intoxicated state caused by alcohol or narcotic drugs: *on a high from the drug.* **b.** a period of sustained excitement: *They've been on a high ever since their engagement.* **—*Idiom.* 21. high and dry,** deserted; stranded; left alone: *was left high and dry without money or friends.* **22. high and low,** in every possible place: *to search high and low.* **23. high on,** [*be* + ~] enthusiastic about: *We're very high on the new executive we hired.* **24. high time,** [~ + *(that) clause*] a time or moment that is nearly too late: *It's high time (that) he got out of bed.* **25. on high, a.** above: *looking down from on high.* **b.** in heaven.

high•born (hī′bôrn′) /ˈhayˌbɔrn/ *adj.* of high rank by birth; noble.

high•boy (hī′boi′) /ˈhayˌbɔy/ *n.* [*count*] a tall chest of drawers on legs.

high•brow (hī′brou′) /ˈhayˌbraw/ *n.* [*count*] a person with superior intellectual or cultural interests and tastes.

high•chair (hī′châr′) /ˈhayˌtʃɛər/ *n.* [*count*] a tall chair with arms and long legs and usually a removable tray for food, for use by a very young child during meals.

high′er educa′tion, *n.* [*noncount*] education from a college or university.

high′er-up′, *n.* [*count*] a person of high authority in an organization.

high•fa•lu•tin (hī′fə lo͞ot′n) /ˌhayfəˈluwtn̩/ also **high•fa•lu•ting** (-lo͞o′ting, -lo͞ot′n) /-ˈluwtɪŋ, -ˈluwtn̩/ *adj. Informal.* acting as if one were superior to others; pompous; haughty; pretentious.

high′ fidel′ity, *n.* [*noncount*] sound reproduction over the full range of frequencies that can be heard by the human ear, with very little distortion of the signal. Also called **hi-fi. —high′-fi•del′i•ty,** *adj.*

high′-five′, *n., v.,* **-fived, -fiv•ing. —***n.* [*count*] **1.** a gesture of greeting, friendship, or triumph in which one person slaps the upraised palm of the hand against that of another. **—***v.* [~ + *obj*] **2.** to greet with a high-five.

high′-flown′, *adj.* **1.** extravagant: *some impossible, high-flown ideas.* **2.** (of language) pretentious; bombastic: *high-flown oratory.*

high′-hand′ed, *adj.* unfair or arbitrary, as from using one's power capriciously: *the boss's high-handed way of treating employees.* **—high′-hand′ed•ly,** *adv.* **—high′-hand′ed•ness,** *n.* [*noncount*]

high′ jinks′, *n.* [*plural*] wild or boisterous fun, celebration, or merrymaking.

high•land (hī′ləndz) /ˈhayləndz/ *n.* **1. highlands,** [*plural*] a mountainous region or elevated part of a country. **—***adj.* [*before a noun*] **2.** of, relating to, or characteristic of highlands: *danced a highland fling.*

high′-lev′el, *adj.* [*before a noun*] **1.** of or involving participants having high status: *a high-level meeting.* **2.** having high status: *high-level executives.* **3.** (of a computer programming language) based on a vocabulary of Englishlike statements for writing program code: *a high-level language like BASIC.*

high•light (hī′līt′) /ˈhayˌlayt/ *v.* [~ + *obj*] **1.** to emphasize or make (something) stand out: *The paper highlights the difficulties of the working poor.* **2.** to mark with a felt-tip pen that makes printed matter stand out: *highlighted important passages of the textbook.* **3.** to create highlights in: *The hairdresser highlighted her hair.* **—***n.* [*count*] **4.** Also, **high′ light′.** a memorable or enjoyable event, scene, etc.: *When she was promoted, it was the highlight of her career.* **5.** an area of contrasting lightness or brightness: *brown hair with blonde highlights.*

high•ly (hī′lē) /ˈhayliy/ *adv.* **1.** extremely: *highly amusing; highly spiced food.* **2.** with high appreciation or praise: *They spoke highly of you.* **3.** generously: *a highly paid consultant.*

high′-mind′ed, *adj.* having or showing high or strict

moral principles or feelings. —**high′-mind′ed•ly,** *adv.* —**high′-mind′ed•ness,** *n.* [*noncount*]

high•ness (hī′nis) /ˈhaynɪs/ *n.* **1.** [*noncount*] the quality or state of being high; loftiness. **2.** [*count; Highness*] This word is used as a title of honor for members of a royal family. It is usually preceded by the pronouns *His, Her, Your,* and more rarely *Our, Their*: *His Royal Highness, the Prince of Wales.*

high-pow•ered (hī′pou′ərd) /ˈhayˈpawərd/ *adj.* **1.** very energetic and capable: *high-powered executives.* **2.** forceful and aggressive: *high-powered sales tactics.* **3.** very powerful: *a high-powered telescope.*

high′-pres′sure, *adj., v.,* **-sured, -sur•ing.** —*adj.* **1.** having or involving a pressure above the normal: *a high-pressure weather front.* **2.** involving a high degree of stress; demanding: *a high-pressure job.* **3.** vigorous; persistent; aggressive: *a high-pressure sales pitch.* —*v.* [~ + *obj*] **4.** to use aggressive or forceful sales tactics on (someone): *high-pressured into buying a car.*

high′-rise′ or **high′rise′,** *adj.* [*before a noun*] **1.** (of a building) having many stories. —*n.* [*count*] **2.** Also, **high′ rise′, high-riser.** a high-rise building.

high•road (hī′rōd′) /ˈhay͵rowd/ *n.* [*count*] **1.** *Chiefly Brit.* HIGHWAY. **2.** an easy or ethical course: *the highroad to success.*

high′ school′, *n.* a school that usually has grades 9 or 10 through 12: [*count*]: *She went to a fairly good high school.* [*noncount*]: *went to high school for four years.*

high′ sea′, *n.* Usually, **high seas.** [*plural; usually: the* + ~] the open sea or ocean, esp. beyond the territorial waters of a country.

high′-sound′ing, *adj.* having an impressive or grand sound: *high-sounding titles.*

high′-spir′ited, *adj.* having or showing energy, enthusiasm, and eagerness.

high′-strung′, *adj.* being highly sensitive or nervous.

high•tail (hī′tāl′) /ˈhay͵teyl/ *v.* [*no obj*] *Informal.* **1.** to leave rapidly: *had hightailed out of town.* —***Idiom.*** **2.** **hightail it,** to hurry: *hightailed it out of here.*

high′-tech′, *n.* [*noncount*] **1.** HIGH TECHNOLOGY. **2.** a style of design for the interior of a house, apartment, office, etc., using or resembling materials or designs found in industry. —*adj.* [*before a noun*] **3.** relating to or suggesting high-tech: *high-tech office design.*

high′ technol′ogy, *n.* [*noncount*] technology that uses very advanced equipment and engineering techniques.

high′-ten′sion, *adj.* [*before a noun*] carrying or using high voltage: *high-tension wire.*

high′-test′, *adj.* (of gasoline) boiling at a relatively low temperature.

high′ tide′, *n.* the tide at its highest level of elevation: [*count*]: *High tides along the beaches vary.* [*noncount*]: *High tide is at 6 p.m.*

high•way (hī′wā′) /ˈhay͵wey/ *n.* [*count*] a main road, esp. one between towns or cities. See illustration at LANDSCAPE.

high•way•man (hī′wā′mən) /ˈhay͵weymən/ *n.* [*count*], *pl.* **-men.** a robber who holds up travelers on a public road.

hi•jack or **high•jack** (hī′jak′) /ˈhay͵dʒæk/ *v.* [~ + *obj*] **1.** to seize (an airplane or other vehicle) by threat or by force, esp. for ransom or political aims: *The terrorists hijacked the plane.* **2.** to steal (cargo) from a truck or other vehicle after forcing it to stop: *to hijack a load of whiskey.* —*n.* [*count*] **3.** an act or instance of hijacking. —**hi′jack′er,** *n.* [*count*]

hike (hīk) /hayk/ *v.,* **hiked, hik•ing,** *n.* —*v.* **1.** [*no obj*] to go on a hike: *to hike through the woods.* **2.** [~ + *up*] to move up out of place or position: *My shirt hikes up if I don't wear a belt.* **3.** to move or raise with a jerk: [~ + *up* + *obj*]: *to hike up one's socks.* [~ + *obj* + *up*]: *to hike one's socks up.* **4.** [~ + *obj*] to increase, often sharply and unexpectedly: *to hike the price of milk.* —*n.* [*count*] **5.** a long walk or march for pleasure, exercise, military training, or the like. **6.** an increase in quantity: *a hike in wages.* —**hik′er,** *n.* [*count*]

hi•lar•i•ous (hi lâr′ē əs, -lar′-) /hɪˈlɛəriyəs, -ˈlær-/ *adj.* extremely funny: *a hilarious joke.* —**hi•lar′i•ous•ly,** *adv.*

hi•lar•i•ty (hi lâr′i tē, -lar′-) /hɪˈlɛərɪtiy, -ˈlær-/ *n.* [*noncount*] the state or condition of being hilarious.

hill (hil) /hɪl/ *n.* [*count*] **1.** a natural elevation of the earth's surface, smaller than a mountain: *They learned to ski on a small hill.* See illustration at LANDSCAPE. **2.** an incline; slope: *a slight hill at the end of the street.* **3.** an artificial heap, pile, or mound: *a hill of trash.* —***Idiom.*** **4.** **over the hill,** advanced in age or no longer at one's best in performance: *a football player over the hill at 35 years of age.*

hill•bil•ly (hil′bil′ē) /ˈhɪl͵bɪliy/ *n., pl.* **-lies,** *adj.* —*n.* [*count*] **1.** *Often Disparaging.* a person from a backwoods area. —*adj.* **2.** of or relating to hillbillies: *hillbilly music.*

hill•ock (hil′ək) /ˈhɪlək/ *n.* [*count*] a small hill.

hill•side (hil′sīd′) /ˈhɪl͵sayd/ *n.* [*count*] the side of a hill.

hill•top (hil′top′) /ˈhɪl͵tɒp/ *n.* [*count*] the top of a hill.

hill•y (hil′ē) /ˈhɪliy/ *adj.,* **-i•er, -i•est.** full of hills.

hilt (hilt) /hɪlt/ *n.* [*count*] **1.** the handle of a sword, knife, or dagger. —***Idiom.*** **2.** **to the hilt,** completely; fully: *played the role to the hilt.*

him (him) /hɪm/ *pron.* **1.** the form of the pronoun HE, used as a direct or indirect object: *I'll see him tomorrow. Give him the message.* **2.** the form of the pronoun HE sometimes used after the verb *to be*, where strict formal usage requires *he*: *Who's at the door? —It's him again.* **3.** This form of HE is sometimes used instead of the pronoun *his* before the *-ing* form of a verb used as a noun or an adjective: *We were surprised by him wanting to leave.* —*n.* [*count*] **4.** *Informal.* a male: *Is the new baby a her or a him?*

him•self (him self′) /hɪmˈsɛlf / *pron.* **1.** the form of the pronoun HE, a reflexive pronoun, used to show that the subject of the sentence and this pronoun (a direct object, indirect object, or object of a preposition) refer to the same male person: *John cut himself (= John cut John). He wrote himself a note. He felt a conflict within himself.* **2.** (used to give emphasis to a male noun in the sentence and to point out something special about that person): *He himself told me. He took the subway there himself.* **3.** (used in place of HE or HIM in various constructions where it is clear from some previous discussion who the male is): *The producer and himself were involved (= The producer and some male we were talking about recently were involved).* **4.** his normal or customary self: *He is himself again.*

hind (hīnd) /haynd/ *adj.* [*before a noun*] situated in the rear or at the back; posterior: *the hind legs of an animal.* —**Syn.** See BACK.

hin•der[1] (hin′dər) /ˈhɪndər/ *v.* [~ + *obj*] to cause delay, interruption, or difficulty in; hamper: *Lack of money hindered completion of the project.*

hind•er[2] (hīn′dər) /ˈhayndər/ *adj.* situated at the rear or back.

hind•most (hīnd′mōst′) /ˈhaynd͵mowst/ *adj.* farthest behind; last.

hind•quar•ter (hīnd′kwôr′tər, -kwô′-) /ˈhaynd͵kwɔrtər, -͵kwɔ-/ *n.* **hindquarters,** [*plural*] the rear part of a four-legged animal.

hin•drance (hin′drəns) /ˈhɪndrəns/ *n.* **1.** [*noncount*] the act of hindering; the state of being hindered. **2.** [*count*] a person or thing that hinders.

hind•sight (hīnd′sīt′) /ˈhaynd͵sayt/ *n.* [*noncount*] the ability to understand something after it has occurred: *With the advantage of hindsight we now see our mistake.*

Hin•du (hin′do͞o) /ˈhɪnduw/ *n., pl.* **-dus,** *adj.* —*n.* [*count*] **1.** a person who believes in Hinduism. —*adj.* **2.** of or relating to Hindus or Hinduism.

Hin•du•ism (hin′do͞o iz′əm) /ˈhɪnduw͵ɪzəm/ *n.* [*noncount*] the common religion of India, based upon the religion set out in ancient texts which teach that one returns after death in another form.

hinge (hinj) /hɪndʒ/ *n., v.,* **hinged, hing•ing.** —*n.* [*count*] **1.** a jointed device or flexible piece on which a door or gate turns or moves. —*v.* [~ + *on/upon* + *obj*] **2.** to be dependent on; depend on: *Everything hinges on her decision.*

hint (hint) /hɪnt/ *n.* [*count*] **1.** an indirect, partly hidden, or helpful suggestion; clue: *Give me a hint as to his intentions.* **2.** a very slight amount that can barely be noticed: *a hint of garlic in the salad dressing.* —*v.* **3.** [~ + *obj*] to give a hint of: *The gray skies hinted a possible snowfall.* **4.** to make indirect suggestion; imply: [~ + *at* + *obj*]: *hinted at a solution to the problem.* [~ + *at* + *verb-ing*]: *She hinted at leaving but then never did.* [~ + *(that) clause*]: *hinted that changes were coming.* —**hint′er,** *n.* [*count*]

hin•ter•land (hin′tər land′) /ˈhɪntər͵lænd/ *n.* [*count*] **1.** Often, **hinterlands.** [*plural*] the remote parts of a country; back country. **2.** the land behind a coastal region.

hip[1] (hip) /hɪp/ *n.* [*count*] **1.** the part on each side of the body where the thigh bone meets the pelvis; haunch. **2.** the joint at this region of the body. —**hipped,** *adj.*: *wide-hipped.*

hip[2] (hip) /hɪp/ *n.* [*count*] the fleshy red fruit of a rose.

hip[3] (hip) /hɪp/ *adj.,* **hip•per, hip•pest.** *Slang.* **1.** familiar with or knowing about the latest ideas, styles, and developments: *parents trying to be hip.* —***Idiom.*** **2. hip to,** [*be* + ~] aware of or knowledgeable about: *is hip to what's happening.* —**hip′ness,** *n.* [*noncount*]

hip-hop (hip′hop′) /ˈhɪpˌhɒp/ *n. Slang.* RAP MUSIC.

hip•pie or **hip•py** (hip′ē) /ˈhɪpiy/ *n.* [*count*], *pl.* **-pies.** a young person of the 1960's who rejected established social values, called for the free expression of love, and often wore long hair and unconventional clothes.

hip•po (hip′ō) /ˈhɪpow/ *n.* HIPPOPOTAMUS.

Hip′pocrat′ic oath′ (hip′ə krat′ik) /ˌhɪpəˈkrætɪk/ *n.* [*count*] an oath that declares the obligations of doctors, usually taken by those about to start the practice of medicine.

hip•po•pot•a•mus (hip′ə pot′ə məs) /ˌhɪpəˈpɒtəməs/ *n.* [*count*], *pl.* **-mus•es, -mi** (-mī′) /-ˌmay/. a large African mammal with a hairless, thick body, short legs, and even-toed hoofs, living in and alongside rivers.

hip•ster (hip′stər) /ˈhɪpstər/ *n.* [*count*] *Slang.* a hip person.

hire (hīᵊr) /hayᵊr/ *v.,* **hired, hir•ing,** *n.* —*v.* **1.** [~ + *obj*] to employ (someone) for wages: *to hire a clerk.* **2.** [~ + *obj*] to pay for the temporary use of (something); rent: *hired a boat.* **3. hire on,** [*no obj*] to take a job: *hired on as wranglers with the rodeo.* **4. hire out,** to offer or exchange one's services for payment: [~ + *obj* + *out*]: *He hired himself out as a handyman.* [~ + *out* + *obj*]: *His office hired out skilled workers for a fee.* —*n.* **5.** [*noncount*] the act of hiring; the condition of being hired. **6.** [*count*] a person hired or to be hired: *the new hires on the job.* —***Idiom.*** **7. for hire,** available for use or service in exchange for payment: *limousines for hire.*

hire•ling (hīᵊr′ling) /ˈhayᵊrlɪŋ/ *n.* [*count*] a person who works merely for pay.

hir•sute (hûr′so͞ot, hûr so͞ot′) /ˈhɜrsuwt, hɜrˈsuwt/ *adj.* hairy; shaggy. —**hir′sute•ness,** *n.* [*noncount*]

his (hiz; *unstressed* iz) /hɪz; *unstressed* ɪz/ *pron.* **1.** the form of the pronoun HE used to show possession or some relation, used before a noun: *His coat is the brown one. Do you mind his speaking first?* **2.** the form of the pronoun HE used to show possession, or to mean "that or those belonging to him": *His was the strangest remark of all.* [*be* + ~]: *I borrowed a tie of his. I thought it was his.*

His•pan•ic (hi span′ik) /hɪˈspænɪk/ *adj.* **1.** of Spain or Spanish-speaking countries. **2.** of Hispanics. —*n.* [*count*] **3.** a U.S. citizen or resident of Spanish or Latin-American descent.

hiss (his) /hɪs/ *v.* **1.** [*no obj*] to make or give off a sharp sound like that of the letter *s*: *The snake hissed.* **2.** to express disapproval or contempt (for) by making this sound: [*no obj*]: *As the play got worse, the audience began to hiss and boo.* [~ + *at* + *obj*]: *The audience hissed at the villain.* [~ + *obj*]: *The audience hissed the actor off the stage.* —*n.* [*count*] **3.** a hissing sound.

hist., an abbreviation of: **1.** historian. **2.** historical. **3.** history.

his•to•ri•an (hi stôr′ē ən, -stōr′-) /hɪˈstɔriyən, -ˈstowr-/ *n.* [*count*] a writer of history.

his•tor•ic (hi stôr′ik, -stor′-) /hɪˈstɔrɪk, -ˈstɒr-/ *adj.* [*before a noun*] **1.** well-known or important in history: *a historic building.* **2.** HISTORICAL.

his•tor•i•cal (hi stôr′i kəl, -stor′-) /hɪˈstɔrɪkəl, -ˈstɒr-/ *adj.* [*before a noun*] **1.** of, relating to, or treating history or past events: *historical records.* **2.** based on or suggested by history: *a historical novel.* **3.** having once existed or lived, as opposed to being part of legend, fiction, or religious belief: *a study of the historical Jesus.* **4.** HISTORIC (def. 1).: *It was a historical event.* —**his•tor′i•cal•ly,** *adv.* —**his•tor′i•cal•ness,** *n.* [*noncount*]

his•to•ry (his′tə rē, his′trē) /ˈhɪstəriy, ˈhɪstriy/ *n., pl.* **-ries. 1.** [*noncount*] the branch of knowledge dealing with past events: *majoring in history.* **2.** [*count*] a continuous, systematic telling of past events: *a short history of the war.* **3.** [*count*] a record of past events and times, esp. of a particular person: *the patient's medical history.* **4.** [*count; usually singular*] a past that is special because of its interesting events: *a ship with an interesting history.* **5.** [*count*] events that are common in a person's life: *had a history of trouble with the police.* —***Idiom.*** **6. be history,** to be finished; be done for: *If they lose this game, they're history.*

his•tri•on•ic (his′trē on′ik) /ˌhɪstriyˈɒnɪk/ *adj.* [*before a noun*] **1.** overly dramatic; melodramatic: *a histrionic stage actor.* **2.** of or relating to actors or acting. —**his′tri•on′i•cal•ly,** *adv.*

his•tri•on•ics (his′trē on′iks) /ˌhɪstriyˈɒnɪks/ *n.* [*plural*] **1.** overly dramatic expression or behavior. **2.** dramatic representation; theatricals.

hit (hit) /hɪt/ *v.,* **hit, hit•ting,** *n.* —*v.* **1.** [~ + *obj*] to deal a blow or stroke to: *Hit the nail with the hammer.* **2.** to come against with an impact or with force: [~ + *obj*]: *The wheel of the car hit the curb.* [~ + *against* + *obj*]: *The car hit against the railing.* [~ + *on* + *obj*]: *Hailstones hit on the roof.* **3.** [~ + *obj*] to reach; strike: *Did the arrow hit the target?* **4.** [~ + *obj*] to drive or propel by a stroke: *to hit a ball onto the green.* **5.** [~ + *obj*] to have a significant effect or influence on; affect severely: *families hit hard by inflation.* **6.** [~ + *obj*] to come to (one's) mind: *Suddenly it hit us like a thunderbolt: the detective and the murderer were one and the same.* **7.** *Informal.* [~ + *obj*] to request of: *He hit me for a loan.* **8.** [~ + *obj*] to reach or attain (a level or amount): *Prices hit a new high.* **9.** [~ + *obj*] to be published in or on: *The story hit the front page.* **10.** [~ + *obj*] to land on or arrive in: *The troops hit the beach at dawn.* **11.** to come (upon) by accident or search: [~ + *obj*]: *to hit the right answer.* [~ + *on/upon* + *obj*]: *He finally hit on a solution to the problem.* **12.** [~ + *obj*] to succeed in attaining: *He hit just the right tone in his letter of apology.* **13.** [*no obj*] (of an engine) to ignite a mixture of air and fuel as designed: *not hitting on all cylinders.* **14. hit back,** [*no obj*] **a.** to strike or deal a blow: *just stood there and didn't hit back.* **b.** to make a verbal attack: *was advised to hit back against the false charges her opponent had made.* **15. hit out,** [*no obj*] **a.** to aim a blow: *hit out at his assailant.* **b.** to make a verbal attack: *to hit out angrily against his critics.* **16. hit up,** *Slang.* **a.** to ask to borrow money from: [~ + *obj* + *up*]: *hit me up for ten bucks.* [~ + *up* + *obj*]: *Can't we hit up your brother for the money?* **b.** [*no obj*] to inject a narcotic drug into a vein. —*n.* [*count*] **17.** an impact; strike; collision: *a sudden hit against a window.* **18.** a blow: *a direct hit.* **19.** critical comment: *The candidate took several hits from the press during the interview.* **20.** BASE HIT. **21.** a success: *The play is a big hit.* **22.** *Slang.* a dose of a narcotic drug. **23.** *Slang.* a gangland murder. —***Idiom.*** **24. hit it off,** to become friendly: *The two hit it off immediately.* **25. hit the books,** *Slang.* to study hard; cram. **26. hit the bottle,** to drink too much alcohol. **27. hit the ceiling** or **roof,** *Informal.* to lose one's temper; be enraged. **28. hit the hay** or **sack,** *Slang.* to go to bed; go to sleep: *Let's hit the sack.* **29. hit the nail on the head,** to say or do exactly the right thing. —**hit′ter,** *n.* [*count*]

hit′-and-run′, *adj.* [*before a noun*] **1.** guilty of fleeing the scene of an accident one has caused, esp. a road accident: *a hit-and-run driver.* **2.** resulting from such action or conduct: *hit-and-run fatalities.*

hitch[1] (hich) /hɪtʃ/ *v.* **1.** [~ + *obj*] to fasten or tie by means of a rope or strap; tether: *to hitch a horse to a post.* **2.** to harness (an animal) to a vehicle: [~ + *obj*]: *He hitched the horse to the carriage.* [~ + *up* + *obj*]: *He hitched up the horse to the carriage.* [~ + *obj* + *up*]: *He hitched the horse up to the carriage.* **3.** to hike up: [~ + *up* + *obj*]: *hitched up his trousers.* [~ + *obj* + *up*]: *hitched his trousers up.* **4.** [~ + *obj*] *Slang.* to marry: *He enjoyed dating but he wasn't going to get hitched.* —*n.* [*count*] **5.** an act of hitching or a state of being hitched. **6.** any of various knots or loops made to attach a rope to something in such a way as to be readily loosened. **7.** a period of military service: *a two-year hitch.* **8.** an unexpected difficulty, problem, obstacle, delay, etc.: *The rain was a hitch in our plans for the picnic.*

hitch[2] (hich) /hɪtʃ/ *v.* **1.** *Informal.* to hitchhike: [~ + *obj*]: *to hitch a ride from St. Louis to Chicago.* [*no obj*]: *You can get there by hitching.* —*n.* [*count*] **2.** a ride obtained by hitchhiking. —**hitch′er,** *n.* [*count*]

hitch•hike (hich′hīk′) /ˈhɪtʃˌhayk/ *v.,* **-hiked, -hik•ing,** *n.* —*v.* **1.** to travel by standing on the side of the road seeking free rides from passing vehicles: [*no obj*]: *hitchhiked from St. Louis to Chicago.* [~ + *obj*]: *He hitchhiked a ride from the beach.* —*n.* [*count*] **2.** an act of hitchhiking. —**hitch′hik′er,** *n.* [*count*]

hith•er (hith′ər) /ˈhɪðər/ *adv.* **1.** to or toward this place: *to come hither.* —*adj.* **2.** being on this or the closer side: *the hither side of the meadow.* —***Idiom.*** **3. hither and thither,** here and there; in all directions. **4. hither and yon,** in many places.

hith•er•to (hith′ər to͞o′) /ˈhɪðərˌtuw/ *adv.* up to this time; until now: *a fact hitherto unknown.*

hit′ list′, *n.* [*count*] *Informal.* **1.** a list of people that are targets for murder. **2.** a list of people, programs, etc., to be opposed.

hit′ man′ or **hit′man′,** *n.* [*count*] *Slang.* a hired killer.

hit′-or-miss′, *adj.* **1.** random; haphazard. —*adv.* **2.** haphazardly; randomly.

HIV, an abbreviation of: human immunodeficiency virus, a virus that is a cause of AIDS.

hive (hīv) /hayv/ *n., v.,* **hived, hiv•ing.** —*n.* [*count*] **1.** a shelter for housing a colony of honeybees; beehive. **2.** a colony of bees. **3.** a place swarming with busy occupants: *a hive of activity.* —*v.* [*no obj*] **4. hive off,** *Chiefly Brit.* to separate from a group: *The bombers hived off and went after their individual targets.*

hives (hīvz) /hayvz/ *n.* a disease that causes large, itchy patches to appear on the skin, usually caused by an allergic reaction: [*noncount; used with a singular verb*]: *Hives is sometimes a serious condition.* [*plural; used with a plural verb*]: *The hives on her skin weren't too bad this time.*

h'm or **hmm** (hmm) /hmm/ *interj.* This sound is used to express a pause, hesitation, doubt, or slight confusion: *Hmm, that's a tough question.*

HM, an abbreviation of: Her (or His) Majesty.

HMO, an abbreviation of: health maintenance organization.

HMS or **H.M.S.,** an abbreviation of: Her (or His) Majesty's Ship.

ho (hō) /how/ *interj.* This word is used to attract attention, and sometimes used after a word denoting a destination: *Westward ho! Land ho!*

hoa•gy or **hoa•gie** (hō′gē) /ˈhowgiy/ *n., pl.* **-gies.** *New Jersey and Pennsylvania.* HERO (def. 4).

hoard (hôrd, hōrd) /hɔrd, howrd/ *n.* [*count*] **1.** a supply of something gathered up and hidden for future use: *a hoard of money.* —*v.* **2.** to gather up and store a supply (of): [*no obj*]: *Anyone who was hoarding would be fined.* [~ + *obj*]: *hoarding food.* —**hoard′er,** *n.* [*count*]

hoar•frost (hôr′frôst′, -frost′, hōr′-) /ˈhɔrˌfrɔst, -ˌfrɒst, ˈhowr-/ *n.* FROST (def. 2).

hoarse (hôrs, hōrs) /hɔrs, howrs/ *adj.,* **hoars•er, hoars•est.** having a weak, rough, or unclear voice: *My voice was hoarse after lecturing.* —**hoarse′ly,** *adv.* —**hoarse′ness,** *n.* [*noncount*]

hoar•y (hôr′ē, hōr′ē) /ˈhɔriy, ˈhowriy/ *adj.,* **-i•er, -i•est. 1.** gray or white with age: *hoary hair.* **2.** ancient. **3.** stale because of being familiar: *a hoary joke.* —**hoar′i•ness,** *n.* [*noncount*]

hoax (hōks) /howks/ *n.* [*count*] **1.** something intended to deceive: *Was the bomb threat real or just another hoax?* —*v.* [~ + *obj*] **2.** to deceive by a hoax. —**hoax′er,** *n.* [*count*]

hob (hob) /hɒb/ *n.* [*count*] **1.** a hobgoblin or elf. —***Idiom.*** **2. play hob with,** [~ + *obj*] to do harm to: *That plays hob with our plans.*

hob•ble (hob′əl) /ˈhɒbəl/ *v.,* **-bled, -bling,** *n.* —*v.* **1.** [*no obj*] to walk lamely; limp: *After the accident I hobbled back to the lodge.* **2.** [~ + *obj*] to fasten together the legs of (a horse) by short lengths of rope to prevent free motion. **3.** [~ + *obj*] impede; hamper: *Those developments will hobble the plan, but not ruin it.* —*n.* [*count*] **4.** an uneven, halting way of walking; a limp. **5.** a rope, strap, etc., used to hobble. —**hob′bler,** *n.* [*count*]

hob•by (hob′ē) /ˈhɒbiy/ *n.* [*count*], *pl.* **-bies.** an activity engaged in for pleasure or relaxation: *stamp collecting and other hobbies.* —**hob′by•ist,** *n.* [*count*]

hob•by•horse (hob′ē hôrs′) /ˈhɒbiyˌhɔrs/ *n.* [*count*] **1.** a stick with a horse's head, or a rocking horse, ridden by children. **2.** a favorite idea or project.

hob•gob•lin (hob′gob′lin) /ˈhɒbˌgɒblɪn/ *n.* [*count*] **1.** something causing superstitious fear. **2.** a mischievous goblin.

hob•nail (hob′nāl′) /ˈhɒbˌneyl/ *n.* [*count*] a large-headed nail for protecting the soles of heavy boots and shoes. —**hob′nailed′,** *adj.*

hob•nob (hob′nob′) /ˈhɒbˌnɒb/ *v.* [*no obj*], **-nobbed, -nob•bing.** to associate on very friendly terms: *to hobnob with royalty.* —**hob′nob′ber,** *n.* [*count*]

ho•bo (hō′bō) /ˈhowbow/ *n.* [*count*], *pl.* **-bos, -boes. 1.** a tramp or vagrant. **2.** a migratory worker.

hock[1] (hok) /hɒk/ *n.* [*count*] the joint in the hind leg of a horse, cow, etc., corresponding to the ankle in humans.

hock[2] (hok) /hɒk/ *v.* [~ + *obj*] **1.** to pawn: *He had hocked his wife's jewelry to raise money to gamble.* —*n.* [*noncount*] **2.** the state of being deposited or held as security; pawn: *the jewelry was in hock.* **3.** the condition of owing; debt: *in hock to the amount of thirty thousand dollars.*

hock•ey (hok′ē) /ˈhɒkiy/ *n.* **1.** ICE HOCKEY. **2.** FIELD HOCKEY.

hock•shop (hok′shop′) /ˈhɒkˌʃɒp/ *n.* PAWNSHOP.

ho•cus-po•cus (hō′kəs pō′kəs) /ˈhowkəsˈpowkəs/ *n.* [*noncount*] **1.** meaningless words used in magic tricks. **2.** mysterious or meaningless activity or talk, esp. for covering up a deception.

hod (hod) /hɒd/ *n.* [*count*] a container attached to a pole and used for carrying bricks, mortar, etc.

hodge•podge (hoj′poj′) /ˈhɒdʒˌpɒdʒ/ *n.* [*count*] a mixture, esp., a disorganized mixture of very different things: *The essay is a hodgepodge of unrelated and unconnected ideas.*

Hodg′kin's disease′ (hoj′kinz) /ˈhɒdʒkɪnz/ *n.* [*noncount*] a malignant disease in which the lymph nodes and spleen become enlarged.

hoe (hō) /how/ *n., v.,* **hoed, hoe•ing.** —*n.* [*count*] **1.** a long-handled tool with a flat, square blade, used esp. in breaking up soil and in weeding. —*v.* **2.** to use a hoe: [~ + *obj*]: *hoeing the garden.* [*no obj*]: *out in the garden hoeing.* —**ho′er,** *n.* [*count*]

hoe•down (hō′doun′) /ˈhowˌdawn/ *n.* **1.** [*count*] a community party usually featuring folk and square dances. **2.** [*noncount*] a square dance.

hog (hôg, hog) /hɔg, hɒg/ *n., v.,* **hogged, hog•ging.** —*n.* [*count*] **1.** a pig or a swine, esp. one grown for eating. **2.** a selfish or filthy person. —*v.* [~ + *obj*] **3.** to take more than one's share of: *He hogged all the food at the cookout.* —***Idiom.*** **4. go (the) whole hog,** to do something thoroughly: *Let's go whole hog and re-do the entire kitchen.* **5. live** or **eat high off** or **on the hog,** [*no obj*] to live very comfortably and prosperously. —**hog′gish,** *adj.*

ho•gan (hō′gôn, -gən) /ˈhowgɔn, -gən/ *n.* [*count*] a Navajo dwelling made of logs and sticks covered with mud or sod.

hog•tie (hôg′tī′, hog′-) /ˈhɔgˌtay, ˈhɒg-/ *v.* [~ + *obj*], **-tied, -ty•ing. 1.** to tie (an animal) with all four feet together. **2.** to delay or prevent the progress of; thwart; hamper.

hog•wash (hôg′wosh′, -wôsh′, hog′-) /ˈhɔgˌwɒʃ, -ˌwɔʃ, ˈhɒg-/ *n.* [*noncount*] nonsense; bunk.

hog′-wild′, *adj.* wildly excited or enthusiastic: *We were hog-wild about the idea.*

hoi pol•loi (hoi′ pə loi′) /ˈhɔy pəˈlɔy/ *n.* [*plural; the* + ~] ordinary people; the masses.

hoist (hoist) /hɔyst/ *v.* [~ + *obj*] **1.** to raise or lift, esp. by a mechanical device: *to hoist the mainsail on a boat.* **2.** to raise to one's lips and drink: *to hoist a beer.* —*n.* [*count*] **3.** an apparatus for hoisting, as a block and tackle. **4.** the act of hoisting.

hoi•ty-toi•ty (hoi′tē toi′tē) /ˈhɔytiy ˈtɔytiy/ *adj.* pretentious; snobbish.

hok•ey (hō′kē) /ˈhowkiy/ *adj.,* **-i•er, -i•est. 1.** corny; sentimental: *a hokey love story.* **2.** false; phony: *a hokey gimmick designed to win votes.*

ho•kum (hō′kəm) /ˈhowkəm/ *n.* [*noncount*] utter nonsense; bunkum.

hold[1] (hōld) /howld/ *v.,* **held** (held) /hɛld/ **hold•ing,** *n.* —*v.* **1.** [~ + *obj*] to have or keep in the hand; grasp: *I held her hand as we crossed the street.* **2.** [~ + *obj*] to bear, sustain, or support with or as if with the hands or arms: *I held the baby gently.* **3.** [*no obj*] to maintain a grasp; remain together or supported: *The clamp held.* **4.** to (cause to) be, stay, or remain in a certain state: [~ + *obj* + *adjective*]: *The preacher held the audience spellbound.* [*no obj;* ~ + *adjective*]: *If you would just hold still, please.* [*no obj*]: *I hope our luck holds.* **5.** [~ + *obj*] to conduct; carry on: *to hold an interview.* **6.** to detain: [~ + *obj*]: *The police held her for questioning.* [~ + *obj* + *as* + *obj*]: *He was held as a hostage for five years.* [~ + *obj* + *obj*]: *They held him a prisoner.* **7.** [~ + *obj*] to hinder; restrain; keep back: *Please hold your applause.* **8.** [~ + *obj*] to set aside; reserve: *Your tickets are being held at the counter.* **9.** [~ + *obj*] to possess; occupy: *to hold a position of authority.* **10.** [~ + *obj; not: be* + *~-ing*] to contain or be capable of containing: *This bottle holds a quart.* **11.** [*not: be* + *~-ing*] to keep in the mind; believe; have or express the belief of: [~ + *obj*]: *He held an opposing view.* [~ + *that clause*]: *Copernicus held that the earth revolves around the sun.* **12.** [~ + *with* + *obj*] to agree; sympathize: *She doesn't hold with new ideas.* **13.** [~ + *(that) clause; not: be* + *~-ing*] to decide legally: *The court held that the law was valid.* **14.** [~ + *obj* + *adjective*] to regard; consider: *I hold you responsible for her safety.* **15.** [~ + *obj*] to make accountable: *We will hold you to your word.* **16.** [*no obj; not: be* + *~-ing*] to remain valid: *The argument still holds.* **17.** to keep by force: [~ + *obj*]: *Enemy forces held the hill.*

[*no obj*]: *In spite of the shelling their positions held.* **18.** [~ + *obj*] to point; aim: *held a gun on the prisoner.* **19.** [~ + *obj*] to keep going with; sustain: *The soprano held that high note for fifteen seconds.* **20.** [~ + *obj*] to omit, as from an order: *One burger — hold the pickle.* **21.** to keep (a telephone connection) open: [~ + *obj*]: *Can you hold the line for a moment?* [*no obj*]: *Please hold.* **22.** [~ + *obj*] to keep (a telephone call) from reaching someone: *She asked her secretary to hold all her calls.* **23.** [~ + *obj*] to control oneself in spite of drinking (liquor): *He can't hold his liquor.* **24. hold back, a.** to restrain; check; keep back; keep in control: [~ + *back* + *obj*]: *to hold back tears.* [~ + *obj* + *back*]: *couldn't hold the tears back any longer.* **b.** to slow down, prevent, or stop the advancement of: [~ + *obj* + *back*]: *Nothing could hold them back from success.* [~ + *back* + *obj*]: *What could hold back her career now?* **c.** to keep from giving or revealing; withhold: [~ + *back* + *obj*]: *to hold back information.* [~ + *obj* + *back*]: *holding information back.* **d.** [*no obj*] to keep from doing or taking action: *The police held back from attacking the rioters.* **25. hold down, a.** to keep under control or at a low level: [~ + *down* + *obj*]: *to hold down interest rates.* [~ + *obj* + *down*]: *to hold interest rates down.* **b.** [~ + *down* + *obj*] to continue to function in: *to hold down a job.* **26. hold forth,** [*no obj*] to speak at great length. **27. hold off, a.** to keep at a distance; keep back; repel: [~ + *off* + *obj*]: *The troops held off the latest assault.* [~ + *obj* + *off*]: *They held the enemy off.* **b.** [*no obj*] to postpone action; put off plans until later; defer: *Let's hold off on that proposal for now.* **28. hold on,** [*no obj*] **a.** to keep a firm grip on something: *He took my arm and held on tightly.* **b.** to keep going; continue: *The troops can hold on for another few days.* **c.** to keep a telephone connection open: *Can you hold on while I see if he's here?* **29. hold oneself in,** [*no obj*] to exercise control or restraint: *He held himself in and didn't show his real feelings.* **30. hold out, a.** [~ + *out* + *obj*] to present; offer: *When I said hello to them, they held out their hands in greeting.* **b.** [*no obj*] to continue to last: *Will the food hold out?* **c.** [*no obj*] to refuse to give in: *We are holding out for higher wages.* **d.** [*no obj*] to withhold something expected or due: *You'd better not be holding out on me.* **31. hold over, a.** to keep for future discussion, consideration, or action: [~ + *obj* + *over*]: *We'll hold that discussion over for our next meeting.* [~ + *over* + *obj*]: *We'll hold over that discussion for later.* **b.** to keep beyond the arranged period: [~ + *obj* + *over*]: *to hold a movie over for an extra week.* [~ + *over* + *obj*]: *held over the movie.* **32. hold up, a.** to support; uphold: [~ + *up* + *obj*]: *What holds up the bridge?* [~ + *obj* + *up*]: *What holds the bridge up?* **b.** to delay; bring to a stop: [~ + *up* + *obj*]: *Something is holding up the work.* [~ + *obj* + *up*]: *Something held the work up.* **c.** [*no obj*] to endure; last; continue without losing strength or ability; persevere: *How are you holding up under the strain?* **d.** to present for attention; display: [~ + *up* + *obj*]: *to hold up the youngest daughter as a model of good behavior.* [~ + *obj* + *up*]: *to hold her up as a model of good behavior.* **e.** to rob at gunpoint: [~ + *up* + *obj*]: *to hold up a store.* [~ + *obj* + *up*]: *He held them up and took their money.* **—*n.*** [*count*] **33.** an act of holding with the hand or other physical means: *a good hold on the rope.* **34.** something to hold a thing by: *climbing up using the toe holds on the mountainside.* **35.** something that holds fast or supports something else. **36.** an order reserving something: *to put a hold on a library book.* **37.** a controlling force or influence: *Drugs had a powerful hold on them.* **—*Idiom.*** **38. get hold of,** [~ + *obj*] **a.** to grasp; seize: *got hold of the line and pulled.* **b.** to find or obtain: *Where can they get hold of the art supplies they need?* **c.** to communicate with by telephone: *I couldn't get hold of you last week.* **39. no holds barred,** without limits: *It would be a fight to the finish, no holds barred.* **40. on hold, a.** into a state of interruption or waiting: *The plans were put on hold indefinitely.* **b.** into a state of being kept waiting by a telephone hold: *I've been on hold for a few minutes.* —**hold′er,** *n.* [*count*] **—Syn.** See CONTAIN.

hold[2] (hōld) /howld/ *n.* [*count*] **1.** the cargo space in the hull of a vessel. **2.** the cargo compartment of an aircraft.

hold•ing (hōl′ding) /ˈhowldɪŋ/ *n.* **1.** [*count*] the act of a person or thing that holds. **2.** [*count*] a section of land leased esp. for farming purposes. **3.** Often, **holdings.** [*plural*] legally owned property, as securities. **4. holdings,** [*plural*] the collection of books, periodicals, and other materials in a library: *with holdings in the millions.* **—*adj.*** [*before a noun*] **5.** used temporarily to delay something: *a holding action.*

hold′ing pat′tern, *n.* [*count*] **1.** a traffic course flown by aircraft at a specified location until cleared for landing. **2.** a condition of suspended activity: *We're in a holding pattern until we get a new director.*

hold•o•ver (hōld′ō′vər) /ˈhowldˌowvər/ *n.* [*count*] a person or thing remaining from a former period.

hold•up (hōld′up′) /ˈhowldˌʌp/ *n.* [*count*] **1.** a robbery of a person at gunpoint. **2.** a delay in the progress of something.

hole (hōl) /howl/ *n., v.,* **holed, hol•ing.** **—*n.*** [*count*] **1.** an opening through something; gap: *a hole in the roof.* **2.** a hollow place in a solid mass; cavity: *a hole in the ground.* **3.** a place dug out by an animal to live in; burrow: *a rabbit hole.* **4.** a cramped, small, uncomfortable, unpleasant place to live in: *living in an awful hole downtown.* **5.** an embarrassing position or predicament. **6.** a fault; flaw: *They pointed out the holes in your argument.* **7. a.** a circular opening in a golfing green into which the ball is to be played. **b.** a part of a golf course including fairway, rough, and hazards: *the eighteenth hole.* **—*v.*** [~ + *obj*] **8.** to make a hole in. **9.** to put or drive into a hole: *The golfer holed that last shot.* **10. hole up, a.** [*no obj*] to retire into a hole or cave for the winter. **b.** to hide from or as if from pursuers; take refuge: [*no obj*]: *They holed up in the old section of town.* [*be* + ~*-ed up*]: *They were holed up in the old hotel.* **—*Idiom.*** **11. hole in the wall,** a small or confining place. **12. in a** or **the hole,** in debt: *I'm in the hole for $300.* **13. pick a hole** or **holes in,** [~ + *obj*] to notice and point out errors in: *Go over this plan tonight and see if you can pick some holes in it.*

-holic, *suffix.* The suffix *-holic* is another form of -AHOLIC: *choco(late)* + *-holic* → *chocoholic* (= *person addicted to chocolate*).

hol•i•day (hol′i dā′) /ˈhɒlɪˌdey/ *n.* **1.** [*count*] a day on which business is not conducted in commemoration of an event or person. **2.** [*count*] any day of relaxation from work. **3.** Sometimes, **holidays.** *Chiefly Brit.* VACATION. **—*adj.*** [*before a noun*] **4.** festive; joyous: *in a holiday mood.* **5.** suitable for a holiday: *dressed in holiday attire.* **—*v.*** [*no obj*] **6.** to vacation: *to holiday at the shore.* **—Usage.** In British English, this word can be used either in the plural or in the singular, with no article *the,* to mean "vacation" (British English): *We went on holiday* = (American English): *We went on a holiday or a vacation.*

ho′lier-than-thou′, *adj.* overly pious; sanctimonious.

ho•li•ness (hō′lē nis) /ˈhowliynɪs/ *n.* **1.** [*noncount*] the quality or state of being holy; sanctity. **2.** [*His/Your* + *Holiness; proper noun*] a title of the pope.

hol•ler (hol′ər) /ˈhɒlər/ *v.* **1.** to cry aloud; shout; yell: [*no obj*]: *were hollering outside my window.* [~ + *obj*]: *Someone was hollering insults.* **—*n.*** [*count*] **2.** a loud cry; shout.

hol•low (hol′ō) /ˈhɒlow/ *adj.,* **-er, -est,** *n., v., adv.* **—*adj.*** **1.** having a space or cavity inside; empty: *a hollow sphere.* **2.** (of a surface) having a curve inward or downward: *a hollow surface.* **3.** sunken: *hollow cheeks.* **4.** (of a sound) not resonant; dull, muffled, or deep: *He answered in a hollow voice.* **5.** not having significance or importance; meaningless: *a hollow victory.* **6.** insincere; false: *a hollow laugh.* **—*n.*** [*count*] **7.** a shallow valley. **—*v.*** **8. hollow out,** [~ + *out* + *obj*] **a.** to make hollow: *to hollow out a log.* **b.** to form (something) by this action: *hollowed out a canoe from a log.* **—*adv.*** **9.** in a hollow manner. —**hol′low•ly,** *adv.* —**hol′low•ness,** *n.* [*noncount*]

hol•ly (hol′ē) /ˈhɒliy/ *n., pl.* **-lies.** **1.** [*count*] a tree or shrub with glossy leaves and red berries. **2.** [*noncount*] the leaves and berries of this tree or shrub.

hol•o•caust (hol′ə kôst′, hō′lə-) /ˈhɒləˌkɔst, ˈhowlə-/ *n.* [*count*] **1.** a great or complete destruction, esp. by fire: *a nuclear holocaust.* **2.** a sacrifice offered to God or to gods and burned. **3. the Holocaust,** the mass killing of European Jews and other civilians in Nazi concentration camps during World War II.

hol•o•gram (hol′ə gram′, hō′lə-) /ˈhɒləˌgræm, ˈhowlə-/ *n.* [*count*] a three-dimensional image of an object, produced by the patterns formed by a laser beam. Also called **holograph.**

hol•o•graph (hol′ə graf′, hō′lə-) /ˈhɒləˌgræf, ˈhowlə-/ *n.* HOLOGRAM. —**hol′o•graph′ic,** *adj.* See -GRAPH-.

ho•log•ra•phy (hə log′rə fē) /həˈlɒgrəfiy/ *n.* [*noncount*] the process or technique of making holograms. See -GRAPH-.

hol•ster (hōl′stər) /ˈhowlstər/ *n.* [*count*] **1.** a leather holder for a gun. **—*v.*** [~ + *obj*] **2.** to put in a holster: *The bandit holstered his gun.*

ho•ly (hō′lē) /ˈhowliy/ *adj.*, **-li•er, -li•est. 1.** recognized as or declared sacred by religious use or authority; consecrated: *holy ground.* **2.** saintly; pious; devout: *a holy nun.* **3.** [*usually: before a noun*] causing fear, awe, or distress: *He's a holy terror when he's angry.*

Ho′ly Commun′ion, *n.* [*proper noun*] COMMUNION (def. 1).

Ho′ly Ghost′, *n.* [*proper noun; usually: the* + ~] the third person of the Trinity. Also called **Holy Spirit.**

Ho′ly Spir′it, *n.* [*proper noun; usually: the* + ~] **1.** the spirit of God. **2.** HOLY GHOST.

ho′ly wa′ter, *n.* [*noncount*] water blessed by a priest.

hom•age (hom′ij, om′-) /ˈhɒmɪdʒ, ˈɒm-/ *n.* **1.** [*noncount*] respect; reverence: *to pay homage to one's ancestors.* **2.** [*count*] something acknowledging the high regard of another: *a book presented as an homage to a great teacher.*

hom•burg (hom′bûrg) /ˈhɒmbɜrg/ *n.* [*count*] a man's felt hat with a soft crown dented lengthwise and a rolled brim.

home (hōm) /howm/ *n., adj., adv., v.*, **homed, hom•ing. —*n.* 1.** a house or apartment that is the usual place where one lives: [*count*]: *bought a retirement home in Florida.* [*noncount*]: *He left home at six o'clock.* **2.** [*noncount*] the place in which one's family life and affections are centered: *thinking of home.* **3.** [*noncount*] a person's own country: *When we were in Uganda, we longed to hear the news from home.* **4.** [*count*] the place or region where something comes from or is most common: *Alaska is the home of Kodiak bears.* **5.** [*count*] headquarters: *The company's home is in Detroit.* **6.** [*count*] an institution for people with special needs: *a nursing home.* **7.** [*noncount*] HOME PLATE. **—*adj.*** [*before a noun*] **8.** of, relating to, or done or made in one's home or country; domestic: *home products.* **9.** principal: *the corporation's home office.* **10.** played in a team's own area: *a home game.* **—*adv.* 11.** to, toward, or at home: *I want to go home.* **12.** deep; to the heart: *The truth struck home.* **13.** to the point aimed at: *He drove the nail home.* **—*v.* 14. home in (on),** [~ + *in (on)* + *obj*] to go or move toward a specified target: *The missile homed in on the target.* **—*Idiom.* 15. at home, a.** in one's own house or place of residence: *It was good to be at home again.* **b.** comfortable; at ease: *Make yourself at home.* **c.** well-informed; knowledgeable about a subject: *a scholar at home in the classics.* **16. bring home,** to make clearly evident: [~ + *home* + *obj*]: *That defeat brought home to the team an awareness that they needed to practice.* [~ + *obj* + *home*]: *That defeat brought it home to me.* **17. home free,** in a position assured of success or out of danger or jeopardy: *Once we're past the guards we'll be home free.* —**home′like′,** *adj.* **—Usage.** Note that the word *home* usually does not take the preposition *to*: *I went home. I started home.*

home′ base′, *n.* **1.** [*noncount*] HOME PLATE. **2.** [*count*] HOME (def. 5).

home•bod•y (hōm′bod′ē) /ˈhowmˌbɒdiy/ *n.* [*count*], *pl.* **-bod•ies.** a person who prefers staying at home.

home•boy (hōm′boi′) /ˈhowmˌbɔy/ *n.* [*count*] **1.** a person from the same area as oneself. **2.** *Slang.* a close friend or fellow gang member.

home•com•ing (hōm′kum′ing) /ˈhowmˌkʌmɪŋ/ *n.* [*count*] **1.** a return to one's home. **2.** an annual event held by a college, university, or high school for visiting alumni.

home′ econom′ics, *n.* [*noncount; used with a singular verb*] the study and practice of managing a home and family.

home•grown (hōm′grōn′) /ˈhowmˈgrown/ *adj.* **1.** grown or produced at home or in a particular region for local consumption: *homegrown tomatoes.* **2.** native to or characteristic of a region: *both homegrown and visiting musicians.*

home•land (hōm′land′, -lənd) /ˈhowmˌlænd, -lənd/ *n.* [*count*] **1.** one's native land. **2.** a region created or considered as a state by or for a particular ethnic group: *the Palestinian homeland.*

home•less (hōm′lis) /ˈhowmlɪs/ *adj.* **1.** having nowhere to live; living on the streets: *homeless people.* **2.** of or serving people having nowhere to live: *homeless shelters.* **—*n.* the homeless.** [*plural; used with a plural verb*] **3.** people who have nowhere to live, or who live on the streets.

home•ly (hōm′lē) /ˈhowmliy/ *adj.*, **-li•er, -li•est. 1.** unattractive; plain: *a homely but lovable puppy.* **2.** simple; unpretentious: *homely food.* —**home′li•ness,** *n.* [*noncount*]

home•made (hōm′mād′) /ˈhowmˈmeyd/ *adj.* **1.** made or prepared at home, locally, or at the place bought: *homemade pastry.* **2.** made in one's own country; domestic.

home•mak•er (hōm′mā′kər) /ˈhowmˌmeykər/ *n.* [*count*] a person who manages the household of his or her own family, esp. doing so as a principal occupation. —**home′-mak′ing,** *n.* [*noncount*], *adj.*

ho•me•op•a•thy (hō′mē op′ə thē) /ˌhowmiyˈɒpəθiy/ *n.* [*noncount*] a method of treating disease by giving very small doses of drugs that in a healthy person would produce symptoms similar to those of the disease. —**ho•me•o•path** (hō′mē ə path′) /ˈhowmiyəˌpæθ/ *n.* [*count*] —**ho′me•o•path′ic,** *adj.* See -HOMO-, -PATH-.

hom•er (hō′mər) /ˈhowmər/ *n.* [*count*] **1.** HOME RUN. **—*v.*** [*no obj*] **2.** to hit a home run.

home•room or **home room** (hōm′ro͞om′, -ro͝om′) /ˈhowmˈruwm, -ˈrʊm/ *n.* [*count*] a classroom in which a group of pupils in the same grade meet at the beginning of the day.

home′ run′, *n.* [*count*] a hit in baseball allowing the batter to circle the bases and score a run.

home•sick (hōm′sik′) /ˈhowmˌsɪk/ *adj.* feeling sad because of a longing for home or family while away from them. —**home′sick′ness,** *n.* [*noncount*]

home•spun (hōm′spun′) /ˈhowmˌspʌn/ *adj.* **1.** spun or made at home: *homespun cloth.* **2.** made of homespun cloth: *homespun clothing.* **3.** plain; simple: *homespun amusements.* **—*n.*** [*noncount*] **4.** a plain-weave cloth originally made at home.

home•stead (hōm′sted, -stid) /ˈhowmstɛd, -stɪd/ *n.* [*count*] **1.** a dwelling with its land and buildings occupied by the owner as a home. **2.** an area of land given by the government to someone who promises to farm it for a period of time. **—*v.* 3.** to acquire or settle on (land) as a homestead: [~ + *obj*]: *They homesteaded the land.* [*no obj*]: *They homesteaded for a year.* —**home′stead′er,** *n.* [*count*]

home•stretch (hōm′strech′) /ˈhowmˈstrɛtʃ/ *n.* [*count*] **1.** the straight part of a racetrack from the last turn to the finish line. **2.** the final phase of any work or project.

home•ward (hōm′wərd) /ˈhowmwərd/ *adv.* **1.** Also, **home′wards.** toward home: *heading homeward.* **—*adj.* 2.** directed toward home: *a homeward journey.*

home•work (hōm′wûrk′) /ˈhowmˌwɜrk/ *n.* [*noncount*] **1.** schoolwork assigned to be done outside the classroom: *complaining about too much homework.* **2.** thorough study of a subject by way of preparation: *You'd better do your homework for the next committee meeting.*

hom•ey or **hom•y** (hō′mē) /ˈhowmiy/ *adj.*, **-i•er, -i•est.** comfortably informal; cozy: *a homey inn.* —**hom′ey•ness, hom′i•ness,** *n.* [*noncount*]

hom•i•cide (hom′ə sīd′, hō′mə-) /ˈhɒməˌsayd, ˈhowmə-/ *n.* **1.** the killing of one human being by another: [*noncount*]: *guilty of homicide.* [*count*]: *There were two homicides last year.* **2.** [*count*] a person who kills another. —**hom′i•cid′al,** *adj.* See -CIDE-.

hom•i•ly (hom′ə lē) /ˈhɒməliy/ *n.* [*count*], *pl.* **-lies. 1.** a sermon. **2.** a moralistic or inspirational talk or observation: *a homily on the virtues of clean living.*

hom′ing pi′geon, *n.* [*count*] a pigeon trained to carry messages and return home.

hom•i•ny (hom′ə nē) /ˈhɒməniy/ *n.* [*noncount*] hulled corn prepared by bleaching the whole kernels or by crushing and sifting.

-homo-, *root.* -*homo-* comes from Greek, where it has the meaning "same, identical". This meaning is found in such words as: HOMOGENEOUS, HOMOGENIZE, HOMONYM.

ho•mo•ge•ne•ous (hō′mə jē′nē əs, -jēn′yəs, hom′ə-) /ˌhowməˈdʒiyniyəs, -ˈdʒiynyəs, ˌhɒmə-/ *adj.* made up of parts or elements that are all of the same kind or nature, or are essentially alike: *Japan has a largely homogeneous population.* —**ho•mo•ge•ne•i•ty** (hō′mə jə nē′i tē, -nā′-, hom′ə-) /ˌhowmədʒəˈniyɪtiy, -ˈney-, ˌhɒmə-/ *n.* [*noncount*] —**ho′mo•ge′ne•ous•ly,** *adv.* See -GEN-, -HOMO-.

ho•mog•e•nize (hə moj′ə nīz′) /həˈmɒdʒəˌnayz/ *v.* [~ + *obj*], **-nized, -niz•ing. 1.** to make homogeneous. **2.** to break up the fat in (milk or cream) causing it to be evenly distributed throughout. —**ho•mog•e•ni•za•tion** (hə moj′ə ni zā′shən) /həˌmɒdʒənɪˈzeyʃən/ *n.* [*noncount*] See -HOMO-, -GEN-.

hom•o•nym (hom′ə nim) /ˈhɒmənɪm/ *n.* [*count*] **1.** HOMOPHONE (def. 1). **2.** a word that is the same as another in sound and spelling but different in meaning, such as *bear* "to carry" and *bear* "large, brown or black furry animal." See -HOMO-, -ONYM-.

ho•mo•pho•bi•a (hō′mə fō′bē ə) /ˌhowmə'fowbiyə/ *n.* [*noncount*] fear of or hatred toward homosexuals and homosexuality. See -HOMO-, -PHOBIA-.

hom•o•phone (hom′ə fōn′, hō′mə-) /'hɒməˌfown, 'howmə-/ *n.* [*count*] a word pronounced the same as another but different in meaning, whether spelled the same or not, such as *heir* and *air.* See -HOMO-, -PHON-.

Ho•mo sa•pi•ens (hō′mō sā′pē ənz) /'how'mow seypiyənz/ *n.* [*noncount*] **1.** the species to which modern humans belong. **2.** HUMANKIND.

ho•mo•sex•u•al (hō′mə sek′shōō əl) /ˌhowmə'sɛkʃuwəl/ *adj.* **1.** attracted sexually to members of one's own sex. **2.** of or relating to homosexuality. **—*n.*** [*count*] **3.** a homosexual person. —**ho•mo•sex•u•al•i•ty** (hō′mə sek′shōō al′i tē) /ˌhowməˌsɛkʃuw'ælɪtiy/ *n.* [*noncount*] See -HOMO-.

hom•y (hō′mē) /'howmiy/ *adj.,* **hom•i•er, hom•i•est.** HOMEY.

hon (hun) /hʌn/ *n. Informal.* HONEY (def. 2).

Hon., an abbreviation of: **1.** Honorable. **2.** Honorary.

hon•cho (hon′chō) /'hɒntʃow/ *n.* [*count*], *pl.* **-chos.** *Slang.* a boss; chief: *Get the head honcho on the phone.*

Hon•du•ran (hon dŏŏr′ən, -dyŏŏr′-) /hɒn'dʊrən, -'dyʊr-/ *adj.* **1.** of or relating to Honduras. **—*n.*** [*count*] **2.** a person born or living in Honduras.

hone (hōn) /hown/ *v.* [~ + *obj*], **honed, hon•ing. 1.** to sharpen: *He honed his sword on a nearby rock.* **2.** to make more adroit or effective: *honed her technique as a pianist.* —**hon′er,** *n.* [*count*]

hon•est (on′ist) /'ɒnɪst/ *adj.* **1.** honorable in principles, intentions, and actions; upright: *decent, honest folk.* **2.** showing fairness and trustworthiness: *honest business dealings.* **3.** gained fairly: *to earn an honest living.* **4.** sincere; open: *an honest face.* **5.** truthful or creditable: *He gave an honest account of how he had received the money.* —**hon′es•ty,** *n.* [*noncount*]

hon•est•ly (on′ist lē) /'ɒnɪstliy/ *adv.* **1.** in an honest way: *He earned his money honestly.* **2.** really; truthfully; in truth: *I honestly don't understand.*

hon•ey (hun′ē) /'hʌniy/ *n., pl.* **hon•eys,** *adj., v.,* **hon•eyed** or **hon•ied, hon•ey•ing. —*n.* 1.** [*noncount*] a sweet, sticky fluid produced by bees from nectar. **2.** [*count*] *Informal.* **a.** sweetheart; darling. **b.** [*sometimes: Honey*] an affectionate or familiar term of address: *"Did you have a rough day at work, honey?" he asked.* **c.** a term of address sometimes considered offensive when used to strangers or subordinates: *"Get me a cup of coffee, will you, honey."* **3.** [*count*] *Informal.* something esp. good of its kind: *That's a honey of a car.* **—*adj.*** [*before a noun*] **4.** of, like, relating to, or containing honey. **—*v.*** [~ + *obj*] **5.** to talk flatteringly to (often followed by *up*). **6.** to sweeten with honey: *honeyed tea.*

hon•ey•bee or **hon•ey bee** (hun′ē bē′) /'hʌnˌiy biy/ *n.* [*count*] any bee that collects and stores honey.

hon•ey•comb (hun′ē kōm′) /'hʌniyˌkowm/ *n.* [*count*] **1.** a structure made of rows of six-sided wax holes or compartments, formed by bees in their hive for storing honey, pollen, and their eggs. **—*adj.*** [*before a noun*] **2.** having the structure or appearance of a honeycomb: *a honeycomb pattern.* **—*v.*** [~ + *obj*] **3.** to cause to be full of holes or cavities. **4.** to penetrate in all parts, esp. so as to weaken: *The agency was honeycombed with spies.*

hon•ey•dew (hun′ē dōō′, -dyōō′) /'hʌniyˌduw, -ˌdyuw/ *n.* a winter melon having a smooth, greenish rind and sweet, light green flesh: [*noncount*]: *slices of honeydew.* [*count*]: *The honeydews were on sale.*

hon•eyed or **hon•ied** (hun′ēd) /'hʌniyd/ *adj.* **1.** containing honey. **2.** flattering: *honeyed words.* **3.** pleasantly soft, as the voice.

hon•ey•moon (hun′ē mōōn′) /'hʌniyˌmuwn/ *n.* [*count*] **1.** a vacation or trip taken by a newly married couple. **2.** any new relationship in which there is an initial period of harmony and goodwill. **—*v.*** [*no obj*] **3.** to spend one's honeymoon: *They honeymooned in Paris.* —**hon′ey•moon′er,** *n.* [*count*]

hon•ey•suck•le (hun′ē suk′əl) /'hʌniyˌsʌkəl/ *n.* [*noncount*] an upright or climbing shrub grown for its sweet-smelling, tube-like flowers.

honk (hongk, hôngk) /hɒŋk, hɔŋk/ *n.* [*count*] **1.** the cry of a goose. **2.** any similar sound, as of an automobile horn. **—*v.* 3.** to (cause to) give off a honk: [*no obj*]: *geese honking in flight.* [~ + *obj*]: *The driver honked his horn impatiently.* —**honk′er,** *n.* [*count*]

hon•ky or **hon•kie** or **hon•key** (hong′kē, hông′-) /'hɒŋkiy, 'hɔŋ-/ *n.* [*count*], *pl.* **-kies** or **-keys.** *Slang* (*disparaging and offensive*). a white person.

honk•y-tonk (hong′kē tongk′, hông′kē tôngk′) /'hɒŋkiyˌtɒŋk, 'hɔŋkiyˌtɔŋk/ *n.* [*count*] **1.** a cheap, noisy nightclub or dance hall. **—*adj.*** Also, **honk′y-tonk′y. 2.** of, relating to, or characterized by honky-tonks: *a honky-tonk part of town.* **3.** of or relating to ragtime piano music.

hon•or (on′ər) /'ɒnər/ *n.* **1.** [*noncount*] honesty, fairness, high standards or integrity in one's beliefs and actions: *a code of honor.* **2.** [*count; usually singular*] a source of credit or distinction: *to be an honor to one's country.* **3.** [*noncount*] high respect, as for worth, merit, or rank: *The president dedicated a memorial in honor of the dead.* **4.** [*noncount*] fame; glory: *to earn a position of honor.* **5.** [*count; usually singular*] the privilege of being associated with or receiving a favor from a respected person, group, etc.: *the honor of serving on a panel.* **6.** Usually, **honors.** [*plural*] evidence, as a special ceremony, decoration, scroll, or title, of high rank or distinction: *a funeral with full military honors.* **7.** [*proper noun; His/Her/Your* + ~] a title of respect for judges and mayors: *"Your Honor, I object," the lawyer protested to the judge.* **8. honors,** [*plural*] **a.** special rank, award, or recognition given by a school to an outstanding student: *graduated with honors.* **b.** a class or course for advanced students, usually involving advanced or independent work: *an honors course in linguistics.* **—*v.*** [~ + *obj*] **9.** to hold in honor or high respect; revere: *to honor one's ancestors.* **10.** to treat with honor; give honor or distinction to: *Will you honor us with your presence tonight?* **11.** to keep to the terms of: *to honor a treaty.* **12.** to accept or pay (a credit card, check, etc.): *Most major credit cards are honored at this restaurant.* **—*adj.*** [*before a noun*] **13.** of, relating to, or noting honor: *an honor guard of three soldiers carrying flags in the parade.* **—*Idiom.* 14. do honor to,** [~ + *obj*] **a.** to bring respect to: *You do honor to our college.* **b.** to be a credit to: *He did honor to his country.* **15. do the honors,** to act as host, as in serving at the dinner table: *Please do the honors and carve the roast.* **16. on** or **upon one's honor,** bound by one's word or good name: *You are on your honor not to cheat.* Also, *esp. Brit.,* **honour.** —**hon′or•ee′,** *n.* [*count*], *pl.* **-ees.** —**hon′or•er,** *n.* [*count*]

hon•or•a•ble (on′ər ə bəl) /'ɒnərəbəl/ *adj.* **1.** having or showing principles of honor; upright: *an honorable and forthright leader.* **2.** indicating the recipient's good record of conduct: *an honorable discharge from the army.* **3.** meriting high respect: *honorable mention in the competition.* **4.** [*Honorable; often: the* + ~ + *name*] a title of respect used before the names of certain ranking government officials or as a title of courtesy for certain British nobility: *The Honorable Jane Seymour. Abbr.*: Hon. —**hon′or•a•bly,** *adv.*

hon•o•rar•i•um (on′ə râr′ē əm) /ˌɒnə'rɛəriyəm/ *n.* [*count*], *pl.* **-rar•i•ums, -rar•i•a** (-râr′ē ə) /-'rɛəriyə/. a payment for acts or professional services for which a fee is not usually paid.

hon•or•ar•y (on′ə rer′ē) /'ɒnəˌrɛriy/ *adj.* [*usually: before a noun*] **1.** given for honor only, without the usual requirements or privileges: *an honorary degree from a university.* **2.** holding a title or position without salary or payment: *an honorary president.*

hon•or•if•ic (on′ə rif′ik) /ˌɒnə'rɪfɪk/ *adj.* **1.** carrying or signaling honor, such as a title or a grammatical form used in speaking to or about a superior, an elder, etc.: *Japanese uses honorific words depending on the status of the person speaking and of the person spoken to.* **—*n.*** [*count*] **2.** (in certain languages, as Chinese and Japanese) a class of grammatical words or forms of words used to show respect: *the complicated use of honorifics.* **3.** a title or term of respect. See -FIC-.

hooch or **hootch** (hōōch) /huwtʃ/ *n.* [*noncount*] *Slang.* alcoholic liquor.

hood[1] (hŏŏd) /hʊd/ *n.* [*count*] **1.** a soft or flexible covering for the head and neck: *I pulled up my hood when it started to snow.* **2.** something resembling this, esp. in shape, as the covering of a baby carriage. **3.** the hinged movable part at the front of an automobile body covering the engine. **—*v.*** [~ + *obj*] **4.** to cover with or as if with a hood. —**hood′ed,** *adj.*

hood[2] (hŏŏd) /hʊd/ *n.* [*count*] *Slang.* a hoodlum.

hood[3] (hŏŏd) /hʊd/ *n.* [*count*] *Slang.* a neighborhood.

-hood, *suffix.* **1.** *-hood* is used to form nouns with the meaning "the state or condition of": *likely* + *-hood* → *likelihood (= the state or condition of being likely); child* + *-hood* → *childhood (= the state or period of time of* *being a child).* **2.** *-hood* is also used to form nouns with the meaning "a body or group of persons of a particular character or class": *priest* + *-hood* → *priesthood* (= *a body of priests).*

hood•lum (ho͞od′ləm, ho͝od′-) /ˈhuwdləm, ˈhʊd-/ *n.* [*count*] **1.** a criminal or thug: *the crime boss and his hoodlums.* **2.** a young street criminal, esp. one belonging to a gang.

hood•wink (ho͝od′wingk′) /ˈhʊdˌwɪŋk/ *v.* [~ + *obj*] to trick; fool; deceive: *We were hoodwinked by a con artist.*

hoo•ey (ho͞o′ē) /ˈhuwiy/ *n.* [*noncount*] *Informal.* nonsense.

hoof (ho͝of, ho͞of) /hʊf, huwf/ *n., pl.* **hoofs** or **hooves** (ho͝ovz, ho͞ovz) /hʊvz, huwvz/ for 1, 2; *v.,* **hoofed, hoof•ing.** —*n.* [*count*] **1.** the hard, horny covering protecting the ends of the foot in certain animals, such as the ox and horse. **2.** the entire foot of a horse, donkey, etc. —*v.* **3.** [~ + *it*] *Slang.* to walk: *Let's hoof it from here.* **4.** [*no obj*] *Slang.* to dance: *started out hoofing in school shows.* —***Idiom.*** **5. on the hoof,** (of livestock) before butchering; alive: *Cattle were shipped on the hoof to Chicago.* —**hoofed,** *adj.: hoofed animals.*

hook (ho͝ok) /hʊk/ *n.* [*count*] **1.** a curved or angled piece of metal or other hard substance for catching, pulling, or suspending something: *I hung my coat up on the hook.* **2.** a fishhook. **3.** something that attracts attention: *Their sales hook was the promise of easy payments.* **4.** something having a sharp curve, bend, or angle at one end: *a hook in the road.* **5. a.** the path of a ball, as in baseball, that curves in a direction opposite to the throwing hand or to the side of the ball from which it was struck. **b.** a ball moving in such a path. **6.** (in boxing) a short circular punch delivered with the elbow bent: *a left hook to the jaw.* —*v.* **7.** to seize, fasten, or catch hold of with or as if with a hook: [~ + *obj*]: *She hooked her arm through mine.* [*no obj*]: *The buttons hook easily to their fastenings.* **8.** [~ + *obj*] to catch (fish) with a fishhook: *I had hooked a huge trout.* **9.** [~ + *obj*] *Slang.* to steal or seize secretly: *hooked a few watches before the manager returned.* **10.** to hit or throw (a ball) so that a hook results: [*no obj*]: *The next pitch hooked over the plate for a strike.* [~ + *obj*]: *The pitcher hooked the next pitch outside.* **11.** [*no obj*] to curve or bend like a hook: *The road hooked to the left and then sharply to the right.* **12. hook up,** to connect to a power source: [~ + *up* + *obj*]: *I hooked up the computer.* [~ + *obj* + *up*]: *I hooked the computer up.* —***Idiom.*** **13. by hook or (by) crook,** by any means whatsoever: *By hook or by crook he'll be there.* **14. hook, line, and sinker,** *Informal.* entirely; completely: *believed the story hook, line, and sinker.* **15. off the hook, a.** released from some difficulty, problem, or obligation: *You're off the hook: if things go wrong, you won't be blamed.* **b.** (of a telephone receiver) not resting on the cradle.

hook•ah or **hook•a** (ho͝ok′ə) /ˈhʊkə/ *n.* [*count*], *pl.* **hook•ahs** or **hook•as.** a water pipe with a long easily bent tube by which the smoke is drawn through a jar of water and thus cooled.

hook′ and eye′, *n.* [*count*] a two-piece clothes fastener, made up of a hook and a loop or bar caught by the hook.

hooked (ho͝okt) /hʊkt/ *adj.* **1.** bent like a hook; hook-shaped. **2.** having a hook or hooks. **3.** made by hooking: *a hooked rug.* **4.** *Informal.* [*be* + ~ (+ *on*)] **a.** addicted to narcotic drugs: *was hooked on cocaine.* **b.** very enthusiastic about something: *He's so hooked on computers that he won't stop even to eat.*

hook•er (ho͝ok′ər) /ˈhʊkər/ *n.* [*count*] *Slang.* a prostitute.

hook•up (ho͝ok′up′) /ˈhʊkˌʌp/ *n.* [*count*] **1.** an act or instance of hooking up. **2.** a device or connection, as a plug, for bringing electricity, water, etc., from a source to a user.

hook•worm (ho͝ok′wûrm′) /ˈhʊkˌwɜrm/ *n.* **1.** [*count*] a worm with hooks around its mouth that lives in the intestines of humans and other animals. **2.** [*noncount*] a disease caused by hookworms.

hook•y or **hook•ey** (ho͝ok′ē) /ˈhʊkiy/ *n.* [*noncount*] —***Idiom.*** **play hooky** or **hookey,** [*no obj*] to be absent from school or work without permission.

hoo•li•gan (ho͞o′li gən) /ˈhuwlɪgən/ *n.* [*count*] a young hoodlum. —**hoo′li•gan•ism,** *n.* [*noncount*]

hoop (ho͞op, ho͝op) /huwp, hʊp/ *n.* [*count*] **1.** a circular band or ring, as one of metal or wood. **2.** such a band for holding together the sides of a container. **3.** the metal ring from which a basketball net is suspended, or the ring and net together. —*v.* [~ + *obj*] **4.** to bind or fasten with or as if with a hoop.

hoop•la (ho͞op′lä) /ˈhuwplɑ/ *n.* [*noncount*] *Informal.* **1.** commotion; noise and activity; to-do: *the hoopla of a political convention.* **2.** sensational publicity; ballyhoo: *a lot of advertising hoopla.*

hoo•ray (ho͝o rā′) /hʊˈrey/ also **hoo•rah** (-rä′) /-ˈrɑ/ *interj., v., n.* HURRAH.

hoot (ho͞ot) /huwt/ *v.* **1.** to cry out or shout: [*no obj*]: *The fans hooted at the umpire unmercifully.* [~ + *obj*]: *The fans hooted the umpire.* **2.** [*no obj*] to make the cry of an owl, or a sound similar to it: *In the night an owl hooted from a distance.* —*n.* [*count*] **3.** the cry of an owl. **4.** any similar sound: *the hoot of the train in the distance.* **5.** a shout, esp. of disapproval or mockery. **6.** [*in questions or with a negative word*] *Informal.* the least bit: *didn't care a hoot about that.* **7.** *Slang.* an extremely funny person or thing: *That sitcom is a real hoot.* —**hoot′er,** *n.* [*count*]

hoot•en•an•ny (ho͞ot′n an′ē, ho͞ot′nan′-) /ˈhuwtn̩ˌæniy, ˈhuwtˌnæn-/ *n.* [*count*], *pl.* **-nies.** an informal session or concert at which folk musicians perform, often with audience participation.

hooves (ho͝ovz, ho͞ovz) /hʊvz, huwvz/ *n.* a pl. of HOOF.

hop[1] (hop) /hɒp/ *v.,* **hopped, hop•ping,** *n.* —*v.* **1.** [*no obj*] to make a short, bouncing leap, as a rabbit does: *The canary hopped on to her finger.* **2.** [~ + *obj*] to jump over; clear with a hop: *hopped the fence and was gone.* **3.** [*no obj*] to move quickly as if jumping: *hopped into bed.* **4.** to board or get onto (a vehicle): [~ + *obj*]: *to hop a train to Peoria.* [*no obj*]: *He hopped into his car.* **5.** [*no obj*] to travel or move frequently from one place or situation to another: *to party-hop* (= *to go from one party to another).* —*n.* [*count*] **6.** a short leap on one foot. **7.** a short, quick movement or action: *a quick hop into bed.* **8.** a journey, esp. a short trip by air: *a quick hop from London to Paris.* **9.** a dance or dancing party: *the school hop.* **10.** a bounce or rebound, as of a ball.

hop[2] (hop) /hɒp/ *n., v.,* **hopped, hop•ping.** —*n.* **1. hops,** [*plural*] the dried ripe cones of the female flowers of a twining plant of the hemp family, used in brewing beer. —*v.* **2. hop up,** *Slang.* **a.** [~ + *up* + *obj*] to excite; make enthusiastic: *The demonstrators hopped up the crowd with their fiery speeches.* **b.** [~ + *up* + *obj*] to add to the power of: *They hopped up the engine of their car.* **c.** [*usually: be* + *hopped up*] to stimulate by narcotics: *hopped up on drugs.*

hope (hōp) /howp/ *n., v.,* **hoped, hop•ing.** —*n.* **1.** [*noncount*] a feeling that events will turn out well: *lost all hope of success.* **2.** [*count*] a particular instance of this feeling: *the hope of winning.* **3.** [*noncount*] a thing that provides a reason for this feeling in a particular instance: *The medicine is her last hope.* **4.** [*count*] something hoped for: *Our only hope is that the Coast Guard heard our SOS.* —*v.* **5.** to look forward (to) with desire and reasonable confidence: [*no obj*]: *We can only wait and hope.* [~ + *for* + *obj*]: *Hope for the best.* [~ + *to* + *verb*]: *I hope to see you again some time.* [~ + *(that) clause*]: *I hope she sees us. We hope that you will come again.* —***Idiom.*** **6. hope against hope,** [~ + *(that) clause*] to continue to hope when the situation appears very bad: *hoped against hope that someone survived the crash.*

hope•ful (hōp′fəl) /ˈhowpfəl/ *adj.* **1.** full of hope; expressing hope; optimistic: *hopeful about getting into college.* **2.** causing a feeling of hope: *The new pitcher is a hopeful prospect.* —*n.* [*count*] **3.** a person who wants to be a success: *major league hopefuls.* —**hope′ful•ness,** *n.* [*noncount*]

hope•ful•ly (hōp′fə lē) /ˈhowpfəliy/ *adv.* **1.** in a hopeful manner: *The dog sat hopefully, waiting for dinner.* **2.** it is hoped; if all goes well: *Hopefully, we will get to the show on time.*

hope•less (hōp′lis) /ˈhowplɪs/ *adj.* **1.** without hope or beyond help: *a hopeless situation.* **2.** despairing: *I felt hopeless when I saw how slim my chances were.* **3.** useless; inept: *He's hopeless at the computer.* —**hope′less•ly,** *adv.* —**hope′less•ness,** *n.* [*noncount*]

hop•per (hop′ər) /ˈhɒpər/ *n.* [*count*] **1.** a person or thing that hops. **2.** any jumping insect. **3.** a funnel-shaped bin in which loose material, as grain or coal, is stored temporarily. **4.** a box into which a proposed legislative bill is dropped and thereby officially introduced.

hop•ping (hop′ing) /ˈhɒpɪŋ/ *adj.* **1.** busy: *He kept his staff hopping.* —***Idiom.*** **2. hopping mad,** very angry; furious.

hop•scotch (hop′skoch′) /ˈhɒpˌskɒtʃ/ *n.* [*noncount*] **1.** a game in which a child hops around a diagram drawn on the pavement to pick up a small object, as a stone or stick, that was previously thrown down in one part of the diagram. —*v.* **2.** to jump, move, pass, or journey quickly and directly, as from one place to another: [*no obj*]: *They hopscotched around the country in their small plane.* [~ + *obj*]: *They hopscotched the area looking for survivors.*

horde (hôrd, hōrd) /hɔrd, howrd/ *n.* [*count*] a large group, number, or crowd: *hordes of grasshoppers.*

ho•ri•zon (hə rī′zən) /hə'rayzən/ *n.* **1.** [*count*] the line or circle that forms what seems to be the boundary between earth and sky. **2. on the horizon,** at the limit or range of knowledge, progress, or the like: *A cure for that disease is now on the horizon.* **3.** Usually, **horizons.** [*plural*] the scope or range of a person's interest: *Her horizons expanded when she lived abroad for a year.*

hor•i•zon•tal (hôr′ə zon′tl, hor′-) /ˌhɔrə'zɑntl̩, ˌhɒr-/ *adj.* parallel to level ground; flat or level: *a horizontal position.* —**hor′i•zon′tal•ly,** *adv.*

hor•mone (hôr′mōn) /'hɔrmown/ *n.* [*count*] **1.** a chemical that the body releases that affects how certain organs or tissues grow or develop. **2.** an artificially made substance that acts like a hormone. —**hor•mo•nal** (hôr-mōn′l) /hɔr'mownl̩/ *adj.*

horn (hôrn) /hɔrn/ *n.* **1.** [*count*] one of the hard, permanent, hollow, and usually paired growths that stick out from the heads of cows, goats, sheep, etc. **2.** [*count*] a similar growth, as an antler. **3.** [*noncount*] the hard substance of which horn growths are made: *a handle made of horn.* **4.** [*count*] a wind instrument in music, as a trumpet. **5.** [*count*] an instrument for sounding a warning signal: *an automobile horn.* **6.** [*count; usually: the* + ~] *Slang.* a telephone: *been on the horn all morning.* —*v.* **7. horn in,** *Informal.* to intrude: [*no obj*]: *He was always horning in when I tried to talk to her.* [~ + *in* + *on* + *obj*]: *He was horning in on our conversation.* —*adj.* [*before a noun*] **8.** made of horn: *a horn handle.* —***Idiom.*** **9. blow** or **toot one's own horn,** to boast about oneself. **10. on the horns of a dilemma,** facing and forced to choose between two equally difficult choices. —**horned,** *adj.: a great horned owl.* —**horn′less,** *adj.*

hor•net (hôr′nit) /'hɔrnɪt/ *n.* [*count*] a large stinging wasp.

horn′ of plen′ty, *n.* CORNUCOPIA.

horn•pipe (hôrn′pīp′) /'hɔrnˌpayp/ *n.* [*count*] **1.** a musical wind instrument having one ox horn hiding the reed and another forming the bell. **2.** a lively jiglike dance, originally to music played on a hornpipe.

horn•y (hôr′nē) /'hɔrniy/ *adj.,* **-i•er, -i•est. 1.** made up of a horn or a hornlike substance: *the horny covering of a turtle.* **2.** having a horn or horns. **3.** made hard like a horn; rough: *The farmer had strong, horny hands.* **4.** *Slang* (*vulgar*). sexually excited.

hor•o•scope (hôr′ə skōp′, hor′-) /'hɔrəˌskowp, 'hɒr-/ *n.* [*count*] **1.** a diagram of the heavens showing the position of planets and the signs of the zodiac, as at the moment of a person's birth, used esp. to predict events in a person's life. **2.** predictions based on such a diagram. See -SCOPE-.

-horr-, *root.* *-horr-* comes from Latin, where it has the meaning "shake, tremble." This meaning is found in such words as: ABHOR, ABHORRENT, HORRENDOUS, HORRIBLE, HORRID, HORRIFIC, HORRIFY, HORROR.

hor•ren•dous (hə ren′dəs) /hə'rɛndəs/ *adj.* shockingly dreadful; horrible; terrible: *a horrendous crime.* —**hor•ren′dous•ly,** *adv.* See -HORR-.

hor•ri•ble (hôr′ə bəl, hor′-) /'hɔrəbəl, 'hɒr-/ *adj.* **1.** causing horror; shockingly dreadful: *a horrible crime.* **2.** extremely unpleasant; deplorable; disgusting: *a horrible smell.* —**hor′ri•ble•ness,** *n.* [*noncount*] —**hor′ri•bly,** *adv.* See -HORR-.

hor•rid (hôr′id, hor′-) /'hɔrɪd, 'hɒr-/ *adj.* **1.** such as to cause horror. **2.** extremely unpleasant; nasty: *horrid table manners.* —**hor′rid•ly,** *adv.* See -HORR-.

hor•rif•ic (hô rif′ik, ho-) /hɔ'rɪfɪk, hɒ-/ *adj.* causing horror. See -FIC-, -HORR-.

hor•ri•fy (hôr′ə fī′, hor′-) /'hɔrəˌfay, 'hɒr-/ *v.* [~ + *obj*], **-fied, -fy•ing.** to cause to feel horror; to distress greatly; shock: *The accident horrified the onlookers.* See -HORR-.

hor•ror (hôr′ər, hor′-) /'hɔrər, 'hɒr-/ *n.* **1.** [*noncount*] overwhelming distress caused by something shocking, terrifying, or revolting. **2.** [*count*] anything that causes such a feeling: *the horrors of trench warfare.* **3.** [*count*] a strong fear or dislike of something: *a horror of firearms.* **4.** [*count*] something that inspires revulsion: *That wallpaper is a horror.* —*adj.* [*before a noun*] **5.** inspiring horror: *a horror movie.* —*interj.* **6. horrors,** This word is used to express mild dismay, surprise, disappointment, etc.: *Horrors! Back again, eh?* See -HORR-.

hors d'oeuvre (ôr dûrv′) /ɔr dɜrv/ *n.* [*count*], *pl.* **hors d'oeuvre** (ôr dûrv′) /ɔr dɜrv/ **hors d'oeuvres** (ôr dûrvz′, dûrv′) /ɔr dɜrvz, 'dɜrv/. food served as an appetizer.

horse (hôrs) /hɔrs/ *n., pl.* **hors•es,** (*esp. when thought of as a group*) **horse,** *v.,* **horsed, hors•ing,** *adj.* —*n.* **1.** [*count*] a large mammal with solid hooves, used for carrying or pulling loads and for riding. **2.** [*count*] something on which a person rides, sits, or exercises, as if riding on the back of such an animal: *a rocking horse.* **3.** [*count*] a wooden apparatus for exercising or performing gymnastics; vaulting horse. **4.** [*noncount*] *Slang.* HEROIN —*v.* [*no obj*] **5. horse around,** *Informal.* to fool around; play roughly. —***Idiom.*** **6. eat like a horse,** to eat a great deal. **7. from the horse's mouth,** from a source that can be trusted or believed: *I got the news straight from the horse's mouth.* **8. hold one's horses,** *Informal.* to be patient: *Hold your horses; we'll be there in a minute.* **9. look a gift horse in the mouth,** to be critical of a gift.

horse•back (hôrs′bak′) /'hɔrsˌbæk/ *n.* [*noncount*] **1.** the back of a horse: *They came on horseback.* —*adv.* **2.** on the back of a horse: *to ride horseback.* —*adj.* [*before a noun*] **3.** on the back of a horse: *horseback riding.*

horse′ chest′nut, *n.* [*count*] **1.** a shrub or tree with large leaves and upright clusters of white flowers. **2.** the shiny brown nutlike seed of this tree.

horse•flesh (hôrs′flesh′) /'hɔrsˌflɛʃ/ *n.* [*noncount*] horses thought of as a group, esp. for riding or racing: *He's a good judge of horseflesh.*

horse′ fly′ or **horse′fly′,** *n.* [*count*] a bloodsucking, usually large fly, a pest of horses, cattle, etc.

horse•hair (hôrs′hâr′) /'hɔrsˌhɛər/ *n.* [*noncount*] the hair of a horse, esp. from the mane or tail, once used to stuff furniture.

horse•hide (hôrs′hīd′) /'hɔrsˌhayd/ *n.* [*noncount*] the hide of a horse; leather made from the hide of a horse.

horse•man or **-wo•man** (hôrs′mən) or (-wŏŏm′ən) /'hɔrsmən/ or /-ˌwʊmən/ *n.* [*count*], *pl.* **-men** or **-wo•men. 1.** a person who is skilled in managing or riding a horse. **2.** a person who rides on horseback. —**horse′man•ship′,** *n.* [*noncount*]

horse•play (hôrs′plā′) /'hɔrsˌpley/ *n.* [*noncount*] rough, loud, or noisy play.

horse•pow•er (hôrs′pou′ər) /'hɔrsˌpawər/ *n.* [*noncount*] **1.** a foot-pound-second unit of power, equivalent to 550 foot-pounds per second, or 745.7 watts. **2.** usable or effective power: *a computer with a lot of horsepower.*

horse•rad•ish (hôrs′rad′ish) /'hɔrsˌrædɪʃ/ *n.* [*noncount*] **1.** a plant of the mustard family, having small white flowers, grown for its root. **2.** the strong-smelling root of this plant, used as a condiment.

horse′ sense′, *n.* COMMON SENSE.

horse•shoe (hôrs′shōō′, hôrsh′-) /'hɔrsˌʃuw, 'hɔrʃ-/ *n.* **1.** [*count*] a U-shaped metal plate nailed to a horse's hoof to protect it. **2.** [*count*] something U-shaped, as a valley. **3. horseshoes,** [*noncount; used with a singular verb*] a game in which horseshoes or other U-shaped objects are tossed at an iron stake.

horse′shoe crab′, *n.* [*count*] a large marine arthropod having a brown covering curved like a horseshoe and a stiff tail.

horse•whip (hôrs′hwip′, -wip′) /'hɔrsˌhwɪp, -ˌwɪp/ *n., v.,* **-whipped, -whip•ping.** —*n.* [*count*] **1.** a whip for controlling horses. —*v.* [~ + *obj*] **2.** to flog with a horsewhip.

hors•y or **hors•ey** (hôr′sē) /'hɔrsiy/ *adj.,* **-i•er, -i•est. 1.** of, relating to, or like a horse. **2.** dealing with or interested in horses, horse racing, or horse shows: *the horsy set.* **3.** heavy and awkward.

hort., an abbreviation of: horticulture.

hor•ti•cul•ture (hôr′ti kul′chər) /'hɔrtɪˌkʌltʃər/ *n.* [*noncount*] the science or art of growing flowers, fruits, vegetables, or plants used as decorations. —**hor′ti•cul′tur•al,** *adj.* —**hor′ti•cul′tur•ist,** *n.* [*count*]

ho•san•na (hō zan′ə) /how'zænə/ *interj.* This word is used to express praise of God.

hose (hōz) /howz/ *n., pl.* **hos•es** for 1; **hose** for 2, *v.,* **hosed, hos•ing.** —*n.* [*count*] **1.** a flexible tube for carrying a liquid, such as water, to a desired point: *a garden hose.* **2.** [*plural; used with a plural verb*] stockings or socks for the foot. See illustration at CLOTHING. —*v.* **3.** to water, wash, spray, or pour water on with a hose: [~ + *obj*]: *He hosed the sidewalk.* [~ + *off* + *obj*]: *He hosed off the car.* [~ + *obj* + *off*]: *He hosed the car off.* [~ + *down* + *obj*]: *He hosed down the lawn.* [~ + *obj* + *down*]: *hosed the kids down for fun.*

ho•sier•y (hō′zhə rē) /'howʒəriy/ *n.* [*noncount*] stockings or socks of any kind.

hospital

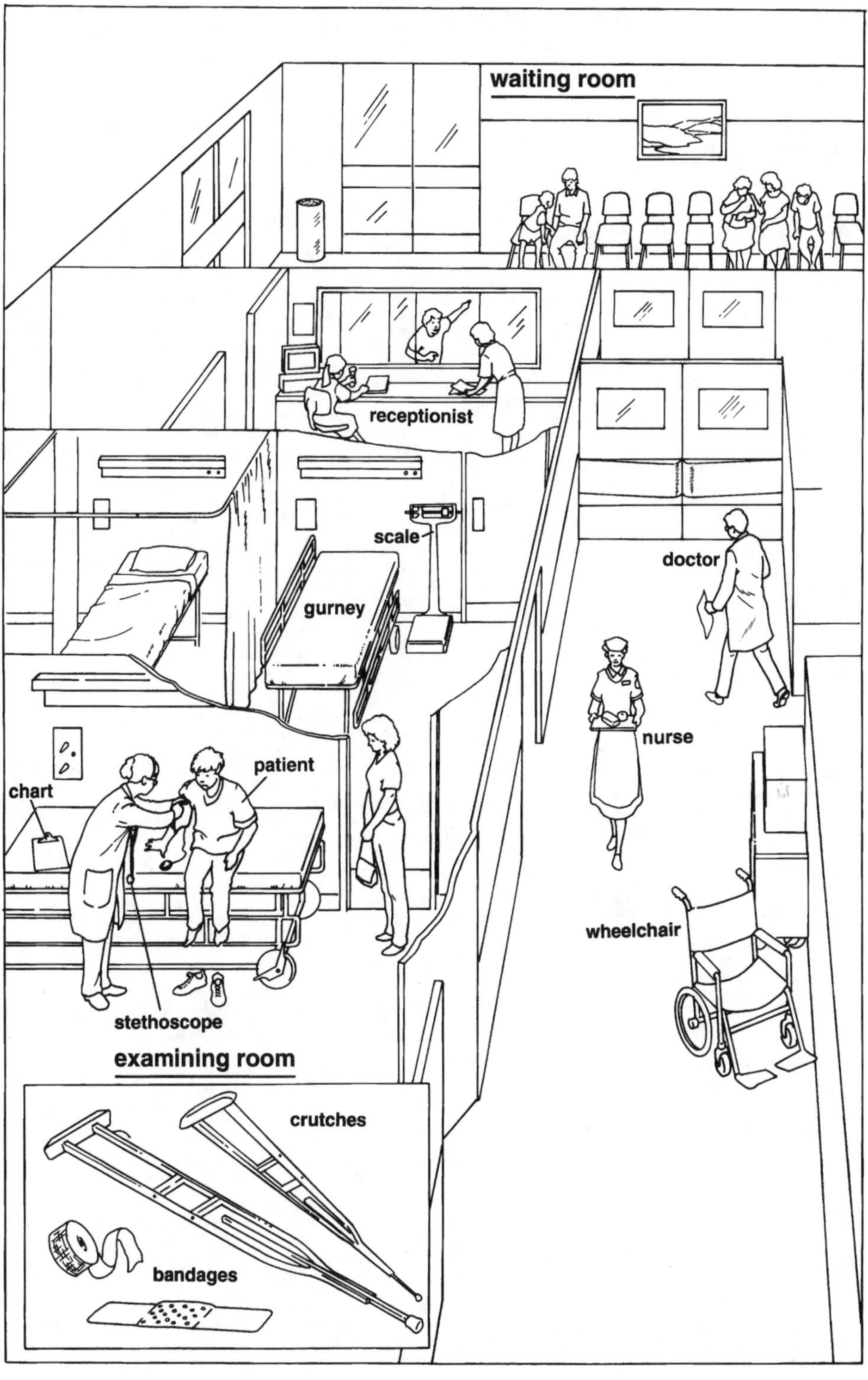
waiting room
receptionist
scale
gurney
doctor
nurse
patient
chart
wheelchair
stethoscope
examining room
crutches
bandages

hosp., an abbreviation of: hospital.

hos•pice (hos′pis) /ˈhɒspɪs/ *n.* [*count*] a health care facility, or a system of professional home visits and care, for people who are dying.

hos•pi•ta•ble (hos′pi tə bəl, ho spit′ə bəl) /ˈhɒspɪtəbəl, hɒˈspɪtəbəl/ *adj.* **1.** treating guests or strangers warmly: *a hospitable family.* **2.** showing a welcoming warmth: *a hospitable smile.* **3.** favorable toward; receptive to: *He was hospitable to new ideas.* —**hos′pi•ta•bly,** *adv.*

hos•pi•tal (hos′pi tl) /ˈhɒspɪtl̩/ *n.* [*count*] an institution in which the sick or injured are given medical and surgical treatment. SEE ILLUSTRATION. —**Usage.** In British English, the word HOSPITAL can appear as a noncount noun, without the article *a* or *the* before it, in certain phrases: (British English): *He's in hospital.* = (American English): *He's in a hospital* or *He's in the hospital.*

hos•pi•tal•i•ty (hos′pi tal′i tē) /ˌhɒspɪˈtælɪtiy/ *n.* [*noncount*] the friendly reception and treatment of guests or strangers.

hos•pi•tal•ize (hos′pi tl īz′) /ˈhɒspɪtl̩ˌayz/ *v.* [~ + *obj*], **-ized, -iz•ing.** to place in a hospital for medical care or observation. —**hos•pi•tal•i•za•tion** (hos′pi tl i zā′shən) /ˌhɒspɪtl̩ɪˈzeyʃən/ *n.* [*noncount*]: *His injuries did not require hospitalization.* [*count*]: *The number of hospitalizations actually decreased.*

host[1] (hōst) /howst/ *n.* [*count*] **1.** a person who receives or entertains guests. **2.** a person who introduces a television or radio show, or one who interviews guests. **3.** one that provides resources, as for a convention: *The host country for the Olympics was Spain.* **4.** the owner or manager of a hotel. **5.** a living animal or plant from which a parasite obtains nutrition. **6.** Also, **host computer.** a computer to which other computers are connected and from which data and programs are used. —*v.* [~ + *obj*] **7.** to be the host at (a dinner, reception, etc.): *The chairman hosted the party for her staff.*

host[2] (hōst) /howst/ *n.* [*count*] **1.** [*usually:* ~ + *of*] a great number of persons or things; multitude: *a host of details.* **2.** an army.

hos•tage (hos′tij) /ˈhɒstɪdʒ/ *n.* [*count*] a person captured or kept by another so that certain terms will be met by the person's family, government, etc.

hos•tel (hos′tl) /ˈhɒstl̩/ *n., v.,* **-teled, -tel•ing** or (*esp. Brit.*) **-telled, -tel•ling.** —*n.* [*count*] **1.** Also called **youth hostel.** an inexpensive, supervised place to live, esp. for young travelers. —*v.* [*no obj*] **2.** to stay at hostels while traveling. —**hos′tel•er,** *n.* [*count*]

hos•tel•ry (hos′tl rē) /ˈhɒstl̩riy/ *n.* [*count*], *pl.* **-ries.** an inn or hotel.

host•ess (hō′stis) /ˈhowstɪs/ *n.* [*count*] **1.** a woman who is a host. **2.** a woman who is employed in a restaurant or the like to take guests to their seats. **3.** a woman working for an airline who sees to the passengers' comfort. —*v.* [~ + *obj*] **4.** to be or serve as hostess to or at: *hostessing the party.*

hos•tile (hos′tl) /ˈhɒstl̩/ *adj.* **1.** of or relating to an enemy: *The army encountered hostile forces.* **2.** disagreeing or disapproving; antagonistic: *He faced hostile criticism.* **3.** not friendly or hospitable: *She was hostile to the teacher.* —**hos′tile•ly,** *adv.*

hos•til•i•ty (ho stil′i tē) /hɒˈstɪlɪtiy/ *n., pl.* **-ties.** **1.** [*noncount*] a hostile state or attitude; enmity: *Hostility between the two countries eased.* **2.** [*count*] a hostile act, as of war: *Hostilities broke out.* **3.** [*noncount*] opposition or resistance to an idea: *The plan met with much hostility.*

hot (hot) /hɒt/ *adj.,* **hot•ter, hot•test,** *n.* —*adj.* **1.** having or giving off heat; having a high temperature: *hot coffee.* **2.** [*be* + ~] having or causing a feeling of great bodily heat: *He was hot with fever.* **3.** peppery; spicy: *Is this mustard hot?* **4.** [*usually: before a noun*] having or showing strong, intense, or violent feeling: *has a hot temper.* **5.** *Slang.* **a.** sexually aroused. **b.** sexy; attractive. **6.** violent, furious, or intense: *the hottest battle of the war.* **7.** strong or fresh, as a scent or trail. **8.** new; fresh: *news hot off the press.* **9.** [*usually: be* + ~] following very closely; close: *The search party was hot on their trail.* **10.** *Informal.* very good: *The movie was not so hot; a hot new idea.* **11.** [*be* + ~ + *on/at*] knowing a lot about something; expert: *She was pretty hot on computer programming.* **12.** [*before an adjective of color*] extremely intense: *a hot pink bathrobe.* **13.** *Informal.* currently popular or in demand: *the hottest new styles of clothing.* **14.** *Slang.* performing well or winningly: *He was on a hot streak (= He was winning because he was lucky).* **15.** *Slang.* funny; laughable; absurd: *That's a hot one!* **16.** *Slang.* **a.** stolen recently or otherwise illegal and dangerous to possess: *hot jewels.* **b.** [*usually: be* + ~] wanted by the police. **c.** [*be* + ~] dangerous; risky: *That deal is too hot for me to handle.* **d.** [*be* + ~] unpleasant: *The cops have made things hot for him.* **17.** [*be* + ~ + *to* + *verb*] *Informal.* eager: *hot to get started.* **18.** actively conducting an electric current or containing a high voltage: *a hot wire.* **19.** RADIOACTIVE. —*adv.* **20.** while hot: *Serve the fish hot from the oven.* —*n.* **21. the hots,** [*plural*] [~ *(+ for + obj)*] *Slang.* strong sexual desire or attraction. —***Idiom.*** **22. (all) hot and bothered,** *Informal.* excited, aroused, or confused and worried. **23. hot and heavy,** *Informal.* in an intense, vehement manner: *arguing hot and heavy.* **24. hot under the collar,** *Informal.* angry; upset. —**hot′ness,** *n.* [*noncount*]

hot′ air′, *n.* [*noncount*] *Informal.* meaningless or exaggerated talk or writing.

hot•bed (hot′bed′) /ˈhɒtˌbɛd/ *n.* [*count*] **1.** a glass structure covering a bed of earth that is heated, used for growing plants. **2.** a place, condition, situation, or environment that favors rapid growth or spread.

hot′-blood′ed, *adj.* **1.** excitable; impetuous: *hot-blooded adventurers.* **2.** showing or feeling emotions deeply; passionate: *their hot-blooded love for each other.*

hot′ cake′ or **hot′cake′,** *n.* [*count*] **1.** a pancake or griddlecake. —***Idiom.*** **2. sell** or **go like hot cakes,** [*no obj*] to be bought, taken, or used up very quickly.

hot′ dog′,[1] *n.* [*count*] **1.** a frankfurter. **2.** a sandwich of a frankfurter in a split roll. **3.** Also, **hot′dog′.** *Slang.* a person who hot-dogs; hot-dogger. —*interj.* **4.** This word is used to express delight: *Hot dog! I got the raise!*

hot′-dog′[2] or **hot′dog′,** *v.* [*no obj*], **-dogged, -dog•ging.** *Slang.* to perform difficult, showy actions in a sport or other activity: *surfers hot-dogging in the heavy surf.* —**hot′-dog′ger,** *n.* [*count*]

ho•tel (hō tel′) /howˈtɛl/ *n.* [*count*] a building that offers a temporary place to stay for travelers. SEE ILLUSTRATION.

ho•te•lier (ō′tl yā′, hōt′l ēr′, hō tel′yər) /ˌowtl̩ˈyey, ˌhowtl̩ˈɪər, howˈtɛlyər/ *n.* [*count*] a manager or owner of a hotel or inn.

hot′ flash′, *n.* [*count*] a sudden, temporary feeling of heat experienced by some women during menopause. Also called **hot′ flush′.**

hot•foot (hot′fo͝ot′) /ˈhɒtˌfʊt/ *n., pl.* **-foots,** *v.,* **-foot•ed, -foot•ing.** —*n.* [*count*] **1.** a practical joke in which a match is secretly put into the victim's shoe and then lighted. —*v.* [~ *(+ it)*] **2.** to go in a great hurry or quickly: *to hotfoot (it) to the bank.*

hot•head (hot′hed′) /ˈhɒtˌhɛd/ *n.* [*count*] a person who acts without thinking or with too much emotion, or is quick to anger. —**hot′head′ed,** *adj.* —**hot′head′ed•ly,** *adv.* —**hot′head′ed•ness,** *n.* [*noncount*]

hot•house (hot′hous′) /ˈhɒtˌhaws/ *n.* [*count*] **1.** an artificially heated building, esp. a greenhouse, for the growing of tender plants. —*adj.* [*before a noun*] **2.** grown in a hothouse: *hothouse tomatoes.* **3.** overprotected: *a spoiled, hothouse child.* **4.** favoring rapid development: *a hothouse environment for new ideas.*

hot′ line′, *n.* [*count*] **1.** a direct telephone or other link that provides immediate communication between heads of state in crisis. **2.** Also, **hot′line′.** a telephone number providing direct access to a company, professional service, or agency, so as to get information, make a complaint, or receive counseling.

hot•ly (hot′lē) /ˈhɒtliy/ *adv.* **1.** angrily or forcefully: *arguing hotly.* **2.** closely: *The convict was hotly pursued.*

hot′ plate′, *n.* [*count*] a portable appliance having an electrical unit for cooking.

hot′ pota′to, *n.* [*count*] a situation or issue that is difficult, unpleasant, or risky to deal with.

hot′ rod′, *n.* [*count*] an automobile specially built or altered for increased speed and fast starts.

hot′-rod′, *v.,* **-rod•ded, -rod•ding.** [*no obj*] to drive a vehicle very fast. —**hot′ rod′der,** *n.* [*count*]

hot′ seat′, *n.* [*count; usually singular; often: the* + ~] *Slang.* **1.** ELECTRIC CHAIR. **2.** a highly uncomfortable or embarrassing situation.

hot•shot (hot′shot′) /ˈhɒtˌʃɒt/ *Slang.* —*adj.* [*before a noun*] **1.** successful and aggressive: *a hotshot sales manager.* **2.** displaying attention-getting skill: *a hotshot ballplayer.* —*n.* [*count*] **3.** Also, **hot′ shot′.** an impressively successful or skillful person.

hot′ spot′ or **hot′spot′,** *n.* [*count*] **1.** a country or region where dangerous or difficult political situations exist or may develop. **2.** a place of lively activity.

hot′ tub′, *n.* [*count*] a wooden tub, usually big enough to hold several persons, filled with hot water and often equipped with a whirlpool.

hotel

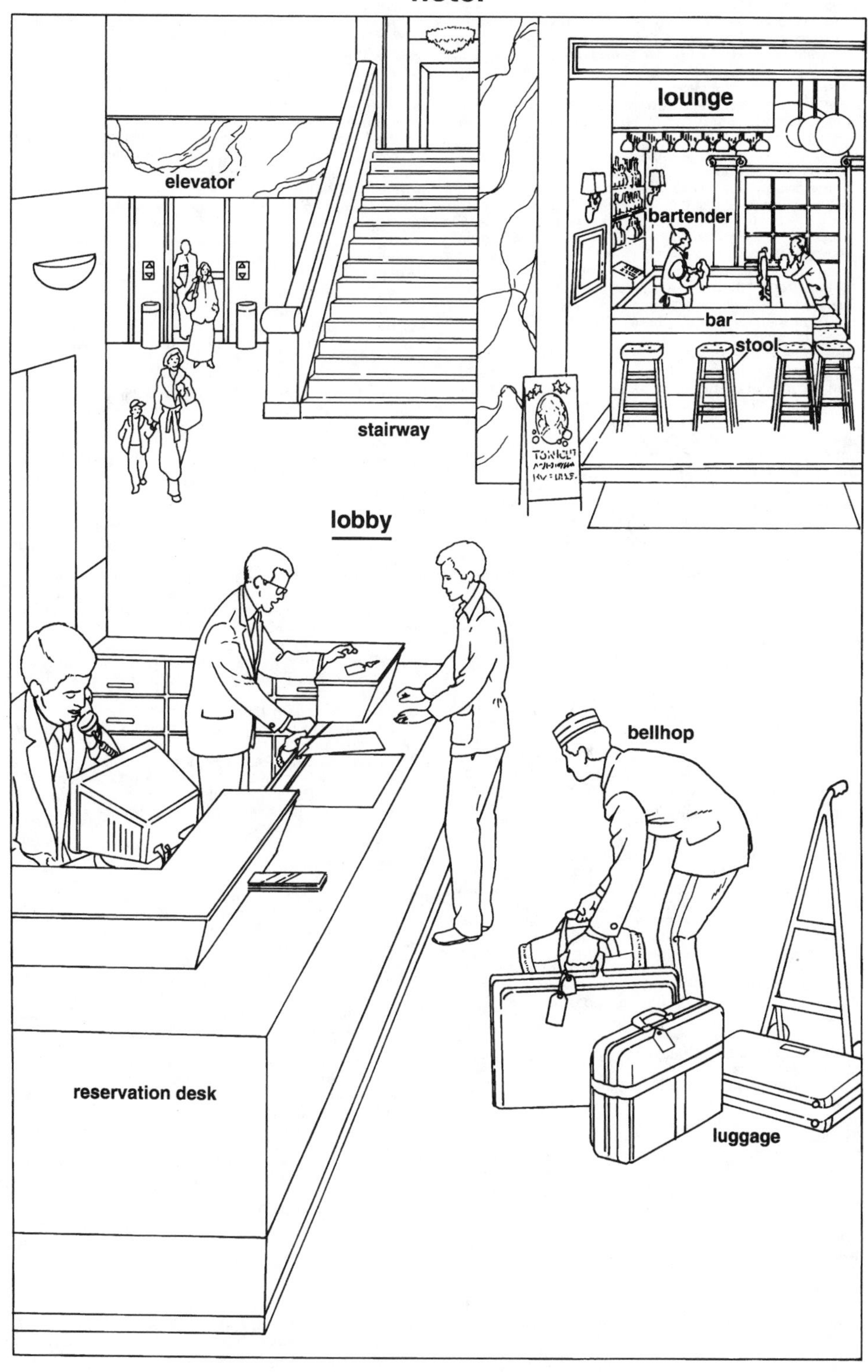

elevator
lounge
bartender
bar
stool
stairway
lobby
bellhop
reservation desk
luggage

hot′ wa′ter, *n.* [*noncount*] a difficult situation; trouble: *was in hot water with the police.*

hound (hound) /hawnd/ *n.* [*count*] **1.** a breed of dog used in hunting, esp. such a dog having a long face and large drooping ears. **2.** any dog. **3.** a mean, contemptible person. **4.** enthusiast; devotee: *an autograph hound (= one who is greatly interested in obtaining autographs).* —*v.* [~ + *obj*] **5.** to persecute; harass: *hounded him to get the work done.*

hour (ouᵊr, ou′ər) /awᵊr, ˈawər/ *n.* [*count*] **1.** a period of time equal to 1/24 of a day or 60 minutes. **2.** any specific one of these 24 periods. **3.** a particular or appointed time: *At what hour do you open? (= At what time do you open?)* **4.** a customary or usual time: *at the dinner hour.* **5.** the present time: *news of the hour.* **6. hours,** [*plural*] **a.** time spent working, etc.: *The doctor's hours were from 10 to 4.* **b.** the usual time of going to bed and getting up: *likes to keep late hours.* **7.** the distance normally covered in an hour's traveling: *We live about an hour from the city.* **8.** a single period, as of instruction, usually lasting from 40 to 55 minutes: *The class meets four hours a week.* **9.** CREDIT HOUR. —*Idiom.* **10. on the hour,** at the start of each hour: *The shuttle leaves every hour on the hour.*

hour•glass (ouᵊr′glas′, ou′ər-) /ˈawᵊr,glæs, ˈawər-/ *n.* [*count*] **1.** an instrument for measuring time, made of two sections of glass joined by a narrow passage through which an amount of sand or mercury runs in just an hour. —*adj.* [*before a noun*] **2.** having the shape of an hourglass: *an hourglass figure.*

hour•ly (ouᵊr′lē, ou′ər-) /ˈawᵊrliy, ˈawər-/ *adj.* [*before a noun*] **1.** occurring or done each hour: *The TV channel had hourly news reports.* **2.** using an hour as a basic unit for counting or figuring (some amount): *hourly wages.* **3.** hired to work for wages by the hour: *hourly workers.* —*adv.* **4.** at or during every hour; once an hour.

house (*n., adj.* hous; *v.* houz) / *n., adj.* haws; *v.* hawz/ *n., pl.* **hous•es** (hou′ziz) /ˈhawzɪz/ *v.,* **housed, hous•ing,** *adj.* —*n.* [*count*] **1.** a building in which people live; residence. SEE ILLUSTRATION. **2.** household: *In our house, my parents make decisions together.* **3.** [*often: House*] a family, including ancestors and descendants: *the House of Hapsburg.* **4.** [*used with a noun in combination*] a building, enclosure, or other construction for any of various purposes: *a clubhouse (= a house for the members of a club); a doghouse (= a house for a dog).* **5.** a theater, concert hall, or auditorium, or the audience in it: *There was a full house for his performance.* **6. a.** [*often: House*] a law-making body or branch of government: *the House of Representatives.* **b.** the building in which such a body meets. **7.** [*often: House*] a commercial establishment; business firm: *a publishing house.* —*v.* [~ + *obj*] **8.** to put or receive into a house: *to house students in a dormitory.* **9.** to provide with a place, as to work or study: *This floor houses our executive staff.* **10.** to contain; hold; be a place for taking or holding: *This casing houses the batteries.* —*adj.* [*before a noun*] **11.** suitable for or customarily kept in a house: *house paint; house cats.* **12.** served by a restaurant as its customary brand: *the house wine; the house salad dressing.* —*Idiom.* **13. bring down the house,** to win the enthusiasm of a live audience. **14. keep house,** to maintain a home. **15. on the house,** as a gift from the management; free: *drinks on the house.* —**house•ful** (hous′fəl) /ˈhawsfəl/ *n.* [*count*], *pl.* **-fuls.**

house′ arrest′, *n.* [*noncount*] confinement of an arrested person in his or her home or in a public place, as a hospital, instead of a jail.

house•boat (hous′bōt′) /ˈhaws,bowt/ *n.* [*count*] a flat-bottomed bargelike boat fitted for use as a place to live.

house•boy (hous′boi′) /ˈhaws,bɔy/ *n.* [*count*] a boy or young man employed as a houseman.

house•break (hous′brāk′) /ˈhaws,breyk/ *v.* [~ + *obj*], **-broke, -bro•ken, -break•ing.** to train (a pet) to excrete outdoors or in a specific place.

house•break•er (hous′brā′kər) /ˈhaws,breykər/ *n.* [*count*] a person who breaks into and enters a house with the intention to rob or steal something.

house•coat (hous′kōt′) /ˈhaws,kowt/ *n.* [*count*] a woman's robe or dresslike garment for casual wear about the house.

house•fa•ther (hous′fä′thər) /ˈhaws,fɑðər/ *n.* [*count*] a man who supervises a group of young people, such as students, living in a dormitory, hostel, etc.

house•fly or **house fly** (hous′flī′) /ˈhaws,flay/ *n.* [*count*], *pl.* **-flies.** a medium-sized fly common wherever humans live.

house•hold (hous′hōld′, -ōld′) /ˈhaws,howld, -,owld/ *n.* [*count*] **1.** the people of a house taken as a group. —*adj.* [*before a noun*] **2.** of or relating to a household. **3.** for use in the home, esp. for cooking, cleaning, or laundering: *household bleach.* **4.** widely familiar: *a household name in men's fashions.*

house′hold word′, *n.* [*count*] a familiar name, phrase, or saying; byword.

house•hus•band (hous′huz′bənd) /ˈhaws,hʌzbənd/ *n.* [*count*] a married man who stays at home to manage the household while his spouse goes out to work.

house•keep•er (hous′kē′pər) /ˈhaws,kiypər/ *n.* [*count*] a person, often hired, who does housekeeping for a home. —**house′keep′ing,** *n.* [*noncount*]

house•maid (hous′mād′) /ˈhaws,meyd/ *n.* [*count*] a female servant employed in a home to do housework.

house•man (hous′man′, -mən) /ˈhaws,mæn, -mən/ *n.* [*count*], *pl.* **-men.** a male servant who performs general duties in a home, hotel, etc.

house•moth•er (hous′muth′ər) /ˈhaws,mʌðər/ *n.* [*count*] a woman who supervises a group of young people, such as students, living in a dormitory, hostel, etc.

house•par•ent (hous′pâr′ənt, -par′-) /ˈhaws,pɛərənt, -,pær-/ *n.* [*count*] a housemother or housefather.

house•plant (hous′plant′) /ˈhaws,plænt/ *n.* [*count*] a plant grown indoors, used for decoration.

house•sit or **house-sit** (hous′sit′) /ˈhaws,sɪt/ *v.* [*no obj*], **-sat, -sit•ting.** to take care of a home while the regular owner or occupant is away. —**house′ sit′ter, house′-sit′ter,** *n.* [*count*]

house•top (hous′top′) /ˈhaws,tɒp/ *n.* [*count*] **1.** a roof. —*Idiom.* **2. from the housetops,** so that all can hear: *He wanted to shout his joy from the housetops.*

house•wares (hous′wârz′) /ˈhaws,wɛərz/ *n.* [*plural*] things used in the home, such as household equipment, kitchen utensils or devices, glasses, etc. See illustration at STORE.

house•warm•ing (hous′wôr′ming) /ˈhaws,wɔrmɪŋ/ *n.* [*count*] a party to celebrate a move to a new home.

house•wife (hous′wīf′) /ˈhaws,wayf/ *n.* [*count*], *pl.* **-wives.** a married woman who manages her own household. —**house′wife′ly,** *adj.*

house•work (hous′wûrk′) /ˈhaws,wɜrk/ *n.* [*noncount*] the work of cleaning, cooking, etc., to be done in the home.

hous•ing (hou′zing) /ˈhawzɪŋ/ *n.* **1.** [*noncount*] houses or dwelling places thought of as a group. **2.** [*noncount*] the providing of houses or shelter: *housing of the poor.* **3.** [*count*] anything that covers or protects, such as a casing or enclosed case and support for a mechanism.

HOV, an abbreviation of: high-occupancy vehicle, a vehicle carrying a sufficient number of passengers to be allowed to use certain highway lanes.

hove (hōv) /howv/ *v.* a pt. and pp. of HEAVE.

hov•el (huv′əl, hov′-) /ˈhʌvəl, ˈhɒv-/ *n.* [*count*] a small, shabby house.

hov•er (huv′ər, hov′-) /ˈhʌvər, ˈhɒv-/ *v.* [*no obj*] **1.** to hang fluttering or suspended in the air: *a kite hovering over the yard.* **2.** to remain near someone or something: *He kept hovering outside my office.* **3.** to remain in an uncertain state: *to hover between life and death.*

hov•er•craft (huv′ər kraft′, hov′-) /ˈhʌvər,kræft, ˈhɒv-/ *n.* [*count*], *pl.* **-craft.** [*sometimes: Hovercraft*] a passenger craft that rides on a cushion of air, kept in the air by fans and driven forward by propellers.

how (hou) /haw/ *adv.* **1.** [*used in questions*] **a.** in what way or manner; by what means: *How did the fire start?* **b.** to what extent, degree, etc.: *How difficult was the test?* **c.** at what amount or rate or in what measure or quantity: *How much is this? How are these tomatoes sold?* **d.** in what state or condition: *How is the baby?* **e.** for what reason; why: *How can you say that?* **f.** to what effect; with what meaning: *How is one to interpret such actions?* **g.** what: *How do you mean?* **h.** by what title or name: *How does one address the president?* **i.** in what form or shape: *How does the demon appear in the first act?* **2.** This word is used to express strong feeling: *How sweet it is! How I love this mountain scenery!* —*conj.* **3.** the manner or way in which: *I couldn't figure out how to solve the problem.* **4.** about the manner or condition in which: *Be careful how you act.* **5.** in whatever manner or way; however: *You can dress how you please.* **6.** that: *She told us how he was honest and could be trusted.* —*n.* [*count*] **7.** a question concerning manner or method: *too many hows about the way this happened.* —*Idiom.* **8. and how!** *Informal.* certainly: *Am I happy? And how!* **9. how about?** This phrase is used to mean "What do you think

house

antenna
chimney
roof
window
garage
door
porch
shrubs
driveway
walk
lawn
gate
fence

or feel regarding (the next thing mentioned)?" or "What is your response to (the next thing mentioned)?": *If they don't have pumpkin pie, how about apple?* **10. how are you?** This phrase is used as a greeting to someone already known to the speaker: *I haven't seen you lately; how are you?* **11. how come?** *Informal.* This phrase introduces a question meaning "how is it that? why?," but, unlike similar questions, there is not a change in word order: *How come you don't visit us anymore?* **12. how do you do?** This expression is used when one is introduced to someone in a formal situation: *"This is my husband, Mr. Smith."— "How do you do, Mr. Smith?"* **13. how so?** how does it happen to be so? why?: *You left early? How so?* **—Usage.** Compare the use of *how* in questions (def. 1) and in emphasizing (def. 2). In the questions, the subject comes after the verb: *How **did the fire** start?* In emphasizing statements, the subject comes before the verb: *How sweet **it is!*** Also, compare the use of *How is/are...?* with a similar construction involving WHAT, as in *What is/are...like?* Both ask a question about a noun or about some state or condition. The expression *How is/are...?* is used to ask about temporary or changing states or conditions of things: *How is your arm? —A little sore. How is your sister? She looks a little tired today.* The expression *What is/are...like?* is used to ask questions about the permanent state, nature, or condition of someone or something: *What is school like in your country?—Well, there is elementary school, what they call gymnasium, and then college or university. What is your sister like?—She is tough, smart, and works hard.*

how•ev•er (hou ev′ər) /haw'ɛvər/ *adv.* **1.** nevertheless; yet; on the other hand; in spite of that: *We have not yet won; however, we shall keep trying.* **2.** to whatever extent or degree; no matter how: *However much you spend, I will reimburse you.* **3.** [*used in questions*] how; how under the circumstances: *However did you escape?* *—conj.* **4.** in whatever way, manner, or state: *Arrange your work hours however you like.*

how•itz•er (hou′it sər) /'hawɪtsər/ *n.* [*count*] a cannon with a short barrel, used esp. for firing shells at a steep upward angle.

howl (houl) /hawl/ *v.* [*no obj*] **1.** (of a dog, wolf, or the like) to make a loud, long, mournful cry: *The coyote was howling at the moon.* **2.** to make a similar cry, as in pain or rage; wail: *She howled as the dentist began to pull the tooth.* **3.** to make a sound like an animal howling: *The wind howls through the trees.* **4.** to laugh uproariously. *—n.* [*count*] **5.** the cry of a dog, wolf, or the like. **6.** a cry, as of pain or rage. **7.** a sound like wailing: *the howl of the wind.* **8.** a loud outburst; yell: *howls of laughter.* **9.** something that causes hilarity.

howl•er (hou′lər) /'hawlər/ *n.* [*count*] **1.** someone or something that howls. **2.** a funny and absurd mistake: *The essay was filled with grammatical howlers.*

howl•ing (hou′ling) /'hawlɪŋ/ *adj.* [*before a noun*] complete; great; total: *The party was a howling success.*

how′-to′, *adj., n., pl.* **-tos.** *—adj.* [*before a noun*] **1.** giving basic instructions to the nonexpert for doing or making something: *a how-to book on photography.* *—n.* [*count*] **2.** the guidelines for doing something: *the how-tos of gardening.*

hp, an abbreviation of: horsepower.

H.P. or **h.p.** or **HP,** an abbreviation of: **1.** high pressure. **2.** horsepower.

H.Q. or **h.q.** or **HQ,** an abbreviation of: headquarters.

hr., an abbreviation of: hour.

H.S., an abbreviation of: high school.

ht., an abbreviation of: height.

Hts., an abbreviation of: Heights (used in place names).

hua•ra•che (wə rä′chē, -chā) /wə'rɑtʃiy, -tʃey/ *n.* [*count*], *pl.* **-ches** (-chēz, -chāz) /-tʃiyz, -tʃeyz/. a Mexican sandal having the upper part woven of leather strips.

hub (hub) /hʌb/ *n.* [*count*] **1.** the central part of a wheel, fan, propeller, etc. **2.** a focus of activity or authority; core: *The city was the manufacturing hub.*

hub•bub (hub′ub) /'hʌbʌb/ *n.* [*count; usually singular*] a loud, confused noise, as of many voices; tumult; uproar.

hub•cap (hub′kap′) /'hʌbˌkæp/ *n.* [*count*] a removable cover for the center of the exposed side of an automobile wheel, covering the axle.

hu•bris (hyo͞o′bris, ho͞o′-) /'hyuwbrɪs, 'huw-/ *n.* [*noncount; used with a singular verb*] exaggerated pride or self-confidence; arrogance.

huck•le•ber•ry (huk′əl ber′ē) /'hʌkəlˌbɛriy/ *n.* [*count*], *pl.* **-ries. 1.** a dark blue or black berry that may be eaten, coming from a shrub of the heath family. **2.** a shrub bearing huckleberries.

huck•ster (huk′stər) /'hʌkstər/ *n.* [*count*] **1.** a person who uses showy methods of promoting or advertising things. **2.** a person who sells small items; hawker. **—huck′ster•ish,** *adj.* **—huck′ster•ism,** *n.* [*noncount*]

hud•dle (hud′l) /'hʌdl/ *v.,* **-dled, -dling,** *n.* *—v.* **1.** to (cause to) gather or crowd together: [*no obj*]: *They huddled around the stove to get warm.* [~ + *obj*]: *The counselers huddled the children round the campfire.* **2.** [*no obj*] to meet together and discuss; confer or consult: *The union negotiators huddled for a few moments.* *—n.* [*count*] **3.** a closely gathered group, mass, or heap; bunch. **4.** a close gathering of football players before a play to hear instructions for the next play. **5.** a conference or consultation.

hue (hyo͞o) /hyuw/ *n.* [*count*] **1.** a gradation or shade of a color; tint: *pale hues.* **2.** color: *all the hues of the rainbow.* **—hued,** *adj.*

hue′ and cry′, *n.* [*count; usually singular*] public clamor, protest, or alarm.

huff (huf) /hʌf/ *n.* [*count; usually singular*] **1.** a mood of quiet and barely held back anger; a fit of resentment. *—v.* [*no obj*] **2.** to show or express anger: *He huffed about the unfairness of the press.* **3.** to puff or blow; breathe heavily.

huf•fy (huf′ē) /'hʌfiy/ *adj.,* **-fi•er, -fi•est.** annoyed; offended: *got huffy when I asked his age.* **—huff•i•ly** (huf′ə lē) /'hʌfəliy/ *adv.*

hug (hug) /hʌg/ *v.,* **hugged, hug•ging,** *n.* *—v.* **1.** to hold or clasp tightly in the arms; embrace: [~ + *obj*]: *to hug one's child.* [*no obj*]: *They were hugging and crying.* **2.** [~ + *obj*] to keep close to: *The boat hugged the shore.* *—n.* [*count*] **3.** a tight clasp with the arms; embrace. **—hug′ger,** *n.* [*count*]

huge (hyo͞oj) /hyuwdʒ/ *adj.,* **hug•er, hug•est. 1.** extraordinarily large in size, weight, quantity, or area; gigantic: *a huge ship.* **2.** very great; extraordinary: *The book was a huge success.* **—huge′ly,** *adv.* **—huge′ness,** *n.* [*noncount*]

huh (hu) /hʌ/ *interj.* This word is used to express surprise, disbelief, dislike, or to ask a question: *Huh! Look at that! You're OK, huh?*

hu•la (ho͞o′lə) /'huwlə/ *n.* [*count*], *pl.* **-las.** a Hawaiian native dance marked by swaying of the hips and sliding motions of the feet and complicated arm movements that tell a story in pantomime. Also called **hu′la-hu′la.**

hulk (hulk) /hʌlk/ *n.* [*count*] **1.** the body of an old ship. **2.** the shell of something wrecked, burned-out, or abandoned: *the abandoned hulk of a military tank.* **3.** a large, clumsy-looking person.

hulk•ing (hul′king) /'hʌlkɪŋ/ *adj.* [*before a noun*] heavy; ponderous; massive.

hull¹ (hul) /hʌl/ *n.* [*count*] **1.** the outer covering of a seed or fruit. *—v.* [~ + *obj*] **2.** to remove the hull of; skin, peel, shell, or shuck.

hull² (hul) /hʌl/ *n.* [*count*] the hollow lowermost portion of a ship.

hul•la•ba•loo (hul′ə bə lo͞o′) /'hʌləbəˌluw/ *n.* [*count*], *pl.* **-loos.** a large or great noise or disturbance; uproar.

hum (hum) /hʌm/ *v.,* **hummed, hum•ming,** *n., interj.* *—v.* **1.** [*no obj*] to make a low, continuous sound; drone: *bees humming in the garden.* **2.** to sing with closed lips, without pronouncing words: [*no obj*]: *He was humming quietly to himself.* [~ + *obj*]: *He hummed a tune.* **3.** [*no obj*] to give forth an unclear sound of mixed voices or noises: *The crowded room was humming.* **4.** [*no obj*] to be in a state of busy activity: *The household was humming with wedding preparations.* *—n.* [*count*] **5.** the act or sound of humming. *—interj.* **6.** This word is used to express hesitation, dissatisfaction, doubt, a moment of thinking, etc. **—hum′mer,** *n.* [*count*]

-hum-, *root.* *-hum-* comes from Latin, where it has the meaning "ground." This meaning is found in such words as: EXHUME, HUMBLE, HUMILIATE, HUMILITY, HUMUS, POSTHUMOUS.

hu•man (hyo͞o′mən) /'hyuwmən/ *adj.* **1.** [*before a noun*] of, relating to, characteristic of, or having the nature of people: *human weakness.* **2.** [*before a noun*] made up of people: *the human race.* **3.** [*before a noun*] of or relating to the social aspect of people: *human affairs.* **4.** sympathetic; kind; humane: *a warmly human understanding.* *—n.* [*count*] **5.** Also called **hu′man be′ing.** a person; a man, woman, or child. **—hu′man•ness,** *n.* [*noncount*]

hu•mane (hyo͞o mān′) /hyuw'meyn/ *adj.* **1.** having or showing the qualities of tenderness, kindness, and compassion: *was humane in his treatment of the prisoners.* **2.** of or relating to humanistic studies. **—hu•mane′ly,** *adv.* **—hu•mane′ness,** *n.* [*noncount*]

hu•man•ism (hyōō′mə niz′əm) /ˈhyuwmə,nɪzəm/ *n.* [*noncount*] **1.** [*often: Humanism*] a system or manner of thinking or action in which human interests, values, and dignity are most important, often rejecting the importance of a belief in God or in religion. **2.** devotion to or study of the humanities. —**hu′man•ist,** *n.* [*count*], *adj.* —**hu′man•is′tic,** *adj.*

hu•man•i•tar•i•an (hyōō man′i târ′ē ən) /hyuw,mænɪˈtɛəriyən/ *adj.* **1.** having concern for or helping to improve the welfare and happiness of people, as by eliminating poverty. —*n.* [*count*] **2.** a person who promotes humanitarian causes. —**hu•man′i•tar′i•an•ism,** *n.* [*noncount*]

hu•man•i•ty (hyōō man′i tē) /hyuwˈmænɪtiy/ *n., pl.* **-ties. 1.** [*noncount*] all human beings thought of as a group; the human race. **2.** [*noncount*] the quality or condition of being human; human nature: *We share a common humanity.* **3.** [*noncount*] the quality of being humane; goodwill; benevolence: *Your humanity toward us in our time of suffering will never be forgotten.* **4. the humanities,** [*plural*] literature, languages, philosophy, art, etc., as distinguished from the sciences.

hu•man•ize (hyōō′mə nīz′) /ˈhyuwmə,nayz/ *v.* [~ + *obj*], **-ized, -iz•ing. 1.** to make humane. **2.** to attribute human qualities to: *Some people tend to humanize their pets.* —**hu•man•i•za•tion** (hyōō′mə ni zā′shən) /,hyuwmənɪˈzeyʃən/ *n.* [*noncount*] —**hu′man•iz′er,** *n.* [*count*]

hu•man•kind (hyōō′mən kīnd′) /ˈhyuwmən,kaynd/ *n.* [*noncount*] human beings thought of as a group; the human race; humanity; mankind.

hu•man•ly (hyōō′mən lē) /ˈhyuwmənliy/ *adv.* **1.** in a human manner: *was humanly subject to occasional weakness.* **2.** with regard to human needs or concerns; humanely: *to deal humanly with the homeless.* **3.** within the limits of human ability: *It's not humanly possible to do that.*

hu•man•oid (hyōō′mə noid′) /ˈhyuwmə,nɔyd/ *adj.* **1.** having human characteristics or form: *a humanoid robot.* —*n.* [*count*] **2.** a humanoid being or creature.

hu′man rights′, *n.* [*plural*] basic and fundamental rights, esp. those believed to belong to an individual and with which a government may not interfere, such as the right to speak, the right to associate with anyone else, and the right to work.

hum•ble (hum′bəl) /ˈhʌmbəl/ *adj.,* **-bler, -blest,** *v.,* **-bled, -bling.** —*adj.* **1.** not proud or arrogant; modest. **2.** low in importance, status, or condition; lowly: *began his career in a very humble position.* —*v.* [~ + *obj*] **3.** to lower in condition, importance, or dignity: *The politician was humbled by defeat in the last election.* —**hum′ble•ness,** *n.* [*noncount*] —**hum′bler,** *n.* [*count*] —**hum′bly,** *adv.* See -HUM-.

hum•bug (hum′bug′) /ˈhʌm,bʌg/ *n.* **1.** [*noncount*] something intended to fool, trick, or deceive others. **2.** [*count*] a person who is not what he or she claims to be; an impostor. **3.** [*noncount*] meaningless or empty talk; nonsense.

hum•ding•er (hum′ding′ər) /ˈhʌmˈdɪŋər/ *n.* [*count*] *Informal.* a remarkable person or thing.

hum•drum (hum′drum′) /ˈhʌm,drʌm/ *adj.* lacking variety; boring; dull.

hu•mer•us (hyōō′mər əs) /ˈhyuwmərəs/ *n.* [*count*], *pl.* **-mer•i** (-mə rī′) /-mə,ray/. the long upper bone extending from the shoulder to the elbow. —**hu′mer•al,** *adj.*

hu•mid (hyōō′mid) /ˈhyuwmɪd/ *adj.* containing a high amount of water vapor: *humid air.* —**hu′mid•ly,** *adv.*

hu•mid•i•fy (hyōō mid′ə fī′) /hyuwˈmɪdə,fay/ *v.* [~ + *obj*], **-fied, -fy•ing.** to make humid. —**hu•mid•i•fi•ca•tion** (hyōō mid′ə fi kā′shən) /hyuw,mɪdəfɪˈkeyʃən/ *n.* [*noncount*] —**hu•mid′i•fi′er,** *n.* [*count*]

hu•mid•i•ty (hyōō mid′i tē) /hyuwˈmɪdɪtiy/ *n.* [*noncount*] the amount of water vapor in the air.

hu•mi•dor (hyōō′mi dôr′) /ˈhyuwmɪ,dɔr/ *n.* [*count*] a container specially made to keep cigars or other items of tobacco properly moist.

hu•mil•i•ate (hyōō mil′ē āt′) /hyuwˈmɪliy,eyt/ *v.* [~ + *obj*], **-at•ed, -at•ing.** to cause (a person) a painful loss of pride, self-respect, or dignity: *The mishap humiliated her in front of her friends.* See -HUM-.

hu•mil•i•at•ing (hyōō mil′ē āt′ing) /hyuwˈmɪliy,eytɪŋ/ *adj.* causing a feeling of humiliation: *That humiliating defeat crushed the team.* —**hu•mil′i•at′ing•ly,** *adv.*: *The team was humiliatingly defeated.* See -HUM-.

hu•mil•i•a•tion (hyōō mil′ē ā′shən) /hyuw,mɪliyˈeyʃən/ *n.* **1.** [*noncount*] a feeling of great embarrassment because of a painful loss of pride, self-respect, or dignity. **2.** [*count*] a particular instance, experience, or event that causes such embarrassment: *suffered one humiliation after another.* See -HUM-.

hu•mil•i•ty (hyōō mil′i tē) /hyuwˈmɪlɪtiy/ *n.* [*noncount*] the quality or state of being humble. See -HUM-.

hum•ming•bird (hum′ing bûrd′) /ˈhʌmɪŋ,bɜrd/ *n.* [*count*] a tiny, usually colorful bird having a long, slender bill for sipping nectar.

hu•mon•gous (hyōō mung′gəs, -mong′-) /hyuwˈmʌŋgəs, -ˈmɒŋ-/ also **humungous,** *adj. Slang.* extraordinarily large.

hu•mor (hyōō′mər) /ˈhyuwmər/ *n.* [*noncount*] **1.** a funny, comic, or absurd quality causing amusement. **2.** the ability or faculty of seeing and knowing what is amusing or comical, and being able to express it or appreciate it: *a keen sense of humor.* **3.** something that causes humor: *The story had no humor in it.* **4.** mental temperament; a temporary mood or frame of mind: *in sulky humor; in good humor.* —*v.* [~ + *obj*] **5.** to go along with the humor or mood of (someone) in order to soothe, cheer up, calm down, etc.: *to humor a child.* Also, *esp. Brit.,* **humour.** —**hu′mor•ist,** *n.* [*count*] —**hu′mor•less,** *adj.* —**hu′mor•less•ly,** *adv.* —**hu′mor•less•ness,** *n.* [*noncount*]

hu•mor•ous (hyōō′mər əs) /ˈhyuwmərəs/ *adj.* **1.** having humor; funny; comical: *a humorous little story.* **2.** having the ability to make people laugh: *a humorous person.* —**hu′mor•ous•ly,** *adv.* —**hu′mor•ous•ness,** *n.* [*noncount*]

hump (hump) /hʌmp/ *n.* [*count*] **1.** a rounded lump that sticks out noticeably, as on the back of a camel. —*v.* **2.** [~ + *obj*] to raise (the back) in a hump; hunch. **3.** [~ + *obj; no obj*] *Slang* (*vulgar*). to have sexual intercourse (with). **4.** [*no obj*] *Slang.* to hurry; rush. —***Idiom.*** **5. over the hump,** past the worst part of something.

hump•back (hump′bak′) /ˈhʌmp,bæk/ *n.* [*count*] **1.** a back that is humped. **2.** a whale noted for the way it arches its back as it dives. —**hump′backed′,** *adj.*

humph (*an expression resembling a snort or grunt; spelling pron.* humf) /*an expression resembling a snort or grunt; spelling pron.* hʌmf/ *interj.* **1.** This sound is used to express disbelief, dislike, etc.: *"Humph," she said, "your promises mean nothing."* —*v.* [*no obj*] **2.** to make the sound "humph."

hu•mus (hyōō′məs) /ˈhyuwməs/ *n.* [*noncount*] the dark material in soils, produced by the decay of vegetable or animal matter. See -HUM-.

hunch (hunch) /hʌntʃ/ *v.* [~ + *obj*] **1.** to thrust out or up in a hump; arch: *He hunched his shoulders.* —*n.* [*count*] **2.** a feeling or guess about the future; a suspicion: *I had a hunch you wouldn't show up on time.* **3.** a hump.

hunch•back (hunch′bak′) /ˈhʌntʃ,bæk/ *n.* [*count*] **1.** a person whose back is humped because of abnormal spinal curvature. **2.** HUMPBACK (def. 1). —**hunch′backed′,** *adj.*

hun•dred (hun′drid) /ˈhʌndrɪd/ *n., pl.* **-dreds,** (*as after a numeral*) **-dred,** *adj.* —*n.* [*count*] **1.** a cardinal number, ten times ten. **2.** a symbol for this number, such as 100 or C. **3. hundreds,** [*plural*] **a.** a number between 100 and 999, such as in referring to an amount of money: *We spent hundreds extra on those options for the new car.* **b.** a generally large number: *Hundreds came to the funeral.* **4.** a hundred-dollar bill. —*adj.* [*after a number and before a noun*] **5.** amounting to 100 in number: *Two hundred dollars is a lot to pay.* —**hun′dred•fold′,** *adv.* —**hun′dredth,** *adj., n.* [*count*] —**Usage.** The word *hundred* and a few other words of higher numbers like THOUSAND, MILLION, and BILLION stay in the singular form when a number comes before them, even when that number is greater than one: *two hundred people, three million soldiers, four thousand planes, five billion dollars.* But if no number comes before these words they may be plural: *hundreds of people, millions of soldiers, thousands of planes, billions of dollars.*

hun•dred•weight (hun′drid wāt′) /ˈhʌndrɪd,weyt/ *n.* [*count*], *pl.* **-weights,** (*as after a numeral*) **-weight.** a unit of weight commonly equivalent to 100 pounds (45. 359 kilograms) in the U.S. *Abbr.:* cwt

hung (hung) /hʌŋ/ *v.* **1.** pt. and pp. of HANG. —***Idiom.*** **2. hung over,** [*usually: be* + ~] suffering the effects of a hangover: *hung over from the vodka.* **3. hung up,** [*usually: be* + ~] *Slang.* **a.** unavoidably detained: *were hung up by the traffic jam.* **b.** [~ (+ *on* + *obj*)] baffled by a problem: *was hung up on how to end his novel.* **c.** Also, **hung-up.** having psychological problems. **4. hung up on,** [*usually: be* + ~ + *obj*] *Slang.* **a.** thinking about something all the time: *hung up on petty details.* **b.** infatuated with; in love with.

Hun•gar•i•an (hung gâr′ē ən) /hʌŋ'gɛəriyən/ *adj.* **1.** of or relating to Hungary. **2.** of or relating to the language spoken in Hungary. **—***n.* **3.** [*count*] a person born or living in Hungary. **4.** [*noncount*] the language spoken in Hungary.

hun•ger (hung′gər) /'hʌŋgər/ *n.* [*noncount*] **1.** a strong need or desire for food: *The meal should satisfy his hunger.* **2.** the painful sensation or state of weakness caused by the need of food: *to collapse from hunger.* **3.** a shortage of food; famine: *a concert to aid the fight against hunger.* **4.** a strong desire or craving for anything; lust: *his hunger for power.* **—***v.* **5.** to have a strong desire: [~ + *for* + *obj*]: *They hungered for justice.* [~ + *after* + *obj*]: *He hungered after power.*

hun′ger strike′, *n.* [*count*] a deliberate refusal to eat, done as protest: *a hunger strike against injustice.* **—hun′ger strik′er,** *n.* [*count*]

hung′ ju′ry, *n.* [*count*] a jury that cannot agree on a verdict.

hun•gry (hung′grē) /'hʌŋgriy/ *adj.,* **-gri•er, -gri•est. 1.** having a desire or need for food. **2.** [*be* + ~ + *for* + *obj*] eager; desirous: *She was hungry for success.* **3.** indicating hunger or strong desire: *a hungry look in a person's eyes.* **4. go hungry,** to lack enough food: *Many of the poor went hungry.* **—hun•gri•ly** (hung′grə lē) /'hʌŋgrəliy/ *adv.*

hunk (hungk) /hʌŋk/ *n.* [*count*] **1.** a large piece: *a hunk of meat.* **2.** *Slang.* a handsome man with a well-developed body.

hun•ker (hung′kər) /'hʌŋkər/ *v.* [*no obj;* ~ + *down*] **1.** to squat; crouch: *They hunkered down and drew diagrams on the sand.* **2.** to settle in for a length of time: *The troops hunkered down to wait out the air raid. The dictator hunkered down in his bomb shelter and escaped the shelling.*

hunk•y-do•ry (hung′kē dôr′ē, -dōr′ē) /'hʌŋkiy'dɔriy, -'dowriy/ *adj. Informal.* fine; pleasing: *Things are just hunky-dory.*

hunt (hunt) /hʌnt/ *v.* **1.** to chase or search for (game or other wild animals) for the purpose of catching or killing: [~ + *obj*]: *Do you need a license to hunt pheasant?* [*no obj*]: *They hunt in the spring.* **2.** [~ (+ *down*) + *obj*] to chase (a person) in order to capture: *to hunt down a kidnapper.* **3.** to search thoroughly: [~ + *obj*]: *They were hunting the area for a new house.* [*no obj*]: *They were hunting for a new house.* **4.** [~ + *obj*] to pursue or take game in: *Poachers have been hunting the woods.* **—***n.* [*count*] **5.** the act or practice of hunting. **6.** a search or pursuit; a seeking to find: *The hunt for the house took a year.*

hunt•er (hun′tər) /'hʌntər/ *n.* [*count*] **1.** a person who chases or searches for wild animals. **2.** a person who tries to get something: *a fortune hunter (= someone trying to get a fortune).*

hunt•ress (hun′tris) /'hʌntrɪs/ *n.* [*count*] a female hunter.

hunts•man (hunts′mən) /'hʌntsmən/ *n.* [*count*], *pl.* **-men.** a hunter.

hur•dle (hûr′dl) /'hɜrdl̩/ *n., v.,* **-dled, -dling. —***n.* **1.** [*count*] a fencelike barrier or frame over which racers or horses must jump in certain races. **2. hurdles,** [*noncount; used with a singular verb*] a track race in which racers leap hurdles. **3.** [*count*] a difficulty to be overcome; obstacle. **—***v.* [~ + *obj*] **4.** to leap over (a barrier), as in a race: *He hurdled the bars easily.* **5.** to overcome; surmount: *He hurdled the last obstacle to success.* **—hur′dler,** *n.* [*count*]

hur•dy-gur•dy (hûr′dē gûr′dē, -gûr′-) /'hɜrdiy'gɜrdiy, -ˌgɜr-/ *n.* [*count*], *pl.* **-gur•dies.** a kind of musical instrument played by turning a crank.

hurl (hûrl) /hɜrl/ *v.* [~ + *obj*] **1.** to throw or fling with great force or strength: *hurled a brick through the window.* **2.** to say with force, as by shouting: *to hurl insults at the umpire.* **—***n.* [*count*] **3.** a powerful throw; pitch. **—hurl′er,** *n.* [*count*]

hurl•y-burl•y (hûr′lē bûr′lē, -bûr′-) /'hɜrliy'bɜrliy, -ˌbɜr-/ *n.* [*noncount*] noisy disorder and confusion; commotion; uproar.

hur•rah (hə rä′, -rô′) /hə'rɑ, -'rɔ/ also **hur•ray** (-rā′) /-'rey/ *interj., v.,* **-rahed, -rah•ing** also **-rayed, -ray•ing,** *n.* **—***interj.* **1.** This word is used to express joy, exultation, appreciation, encouragement, or the like: *Hurray! You did it!* **—***v.* [*no obj*] **2.** to shout "hurrah." **—***n.* [*count*] **3.** an exclamation of "hurrah." **—*Idiom.* 4. last** or **final hurrah,** a final moment of glory.

hur•ri•cane (hûr′i kān′, hur′-) /'hɜrɪˌkeyn, 'hʌr-/ *n.* [*count*] a violent tropical storm, esp. of the W North Atlantic, having wind speeds of or greater than 74 mph (33 m/sec).

hur•ried (hûr′ēd, hur′ēd) /'hɜriyd, 'hʌriyd/ *adj.* done with often excessive haste: *had a hurried meal.* **—hur′ried•ly,** *adv.*

hur•ry (hûr′ē, hur′ē) /'hɜriy, 'hʌriy/ *v.,* **-ried, -ry•ing,** *n.* **—***v.* **1.** to (cause to) move, proceed, or act with haste: [*no obj*]: *He hurried into town.* [~ + *to* + *verb*]: *She hurried to help him when he fell.* [~ + *up*]: *Could you please hurry up?* [~ + *obj*]: *The outfielder hurried his throw to first base.* **2.** [~ + *obj*] to cause to be hasty; rush: *We don't want to hurry them into a decision.* **—***n.* [*noncount*] **3.** a state of urgency or eagerness: *There's no hurry; take your time.* **4.** hurried movement or action; haste. **—*Idiom.* 5. in a hurry, a.** quickly: *She finished in a hurry.* **b.** wanting to act quickly: *in a hurry to go home.*

hurt (hûrt) /hɜrt/ *v.,* **hurt, hurt•ing,** *n., adj.* **—***v.* **1.** [~ + *obj*] to cause bodily injury to; injure: *That fall hurt his leg.* **2.** to cause a feeling of bodily pain to or in: [~ + *obj*]: *The old wound still hurts him.* [~ + *oneself*]: *He hurt himself long ago.* [*no obj*]: *The old wound still hurts.* **3.** [~ + *obj*] to damage or ruin (a material object) by rough use, improper care, etc.: *Stains can't hurt this fabric.* **4.** [~ + *obj*] to affect in a bad way; harm: *Those lies hurt his reputation.* **5.** to offend or cause sorrow to: [~ + *obj*]: *She hurt his feelings with those unkind remarks.* [*no obj*]: *The blow to her pride really hurts.* **6.** [*usually: be* + ~*-ing; no obj*] to suffer from not having enough of something: *are still hurting from the effects of the famine.* **—***n.* **7.** [*noncount*] mental distress: *feelings of hurt.* **8.** [*count*] a bodily wound or injury. **—***adj.* **9.** physically injured: *a badly hurt leg.* **10.** offended: *hurt pride.* **11.** suggesting that one has been offended: *had a hurt look on her face.* **—*Idiom.* 12. It does/would/will not hurt.** This phrase is used to suggest that what follows is a good idea: [~ + *to* + *verb*]: *It doesn't hurt to change your car's oil (= It is a good idea to change your car's oil).* [~ + *obj* + *to* + *verb*]: *It wouldn't hurt you to apologize to her (= It would be a good idea for you to apologize to her).*

hurt•ful (hûrt′fəl) /'hɜrtfəl/ *adj.* causing hurt, distress, or injury.

hur•tle (hûr′tl) /'hɜrtl̩/ *v.* [*no obj*], **-tled, -tling.** to move with great speed: *The car hurtled down the road.*

hus•band (huz′bənd) /'hʌzbənd/ *n.* [*count*] **1.** a married man. **—***v.* [~ + *obj*] **2.** to manage or use carefully: *to husband one's resources.*

hus•band•ry (huz′bən drē) /'hʌzbəndriy/ *n.* [*noncount*] **1.** the growing of crops and the raising of farm animals. **2.** careful management of resources.

hush (hush) /hʌʃ/ *interj.* **1.** This word is used as a command to be silent or quiet: *Hush, child, they'll hear you.* **—***v.* **2.** [~ + *obj*] to cause to become silent or quiet: *We hushed the children when the mayor began his speech.* **3.** to suppress mention of; keep concealed: [~ + *up* + *obj*]: *to hush up a scandal.* [~ + *obj* + *up*]: *to hush it up quickly.* **4.** [~ + *obj*] to make calm: *to hush someone's fears.* **—***n.* [*count; usually singular*] **5.** silence or quiet, esp. after noise; stillness: *A hush fell over the crowd.*

hushed (husht) /hʌʃt/ *adj.* quiet: *the hushed countryside.*

hush′-hush′, *adj.* highly secret or confidential.

hush′ pup′py, *n.* [*count*] *Southern U.S.* a small, deep-fried ball of cornmeal dough.

husk (husk) /hʌsk/ *n.* [*count*] **1.** the dry outer covering of certain fruits or seeds, esp. of an ear of corn. **—***v.* [~ + *obj*] **2.** to remove the husk from: *husking corn.* **—husk′er,** *n.* [*count*]

husk•y[1] (hus′kē) /'hʌskiy/ *adj.,* **-i•er, -i•est,** *n.* **—***adj.* **1.** big and strong; burly; brawny: *husky football players.* **2.** (of the voice) somewhat hoarse. **—***n.* [*noncount*] **3.** a size of garments for boys who are heavier than average. **—husk•i•ly** (hus′kə lē) /'hʌskəliy/ *adv.* **—husk′i•ness,** *n.* [*noncount*]

husk•y[2] (hus′kē) /'hʌskiy/ *n.* [*count*], *pl.* **husk•ies.** (*sometimes: Husky.*) a furry, strong dog used to pull sleds in cold climates.

hus•sy (hus′ē, huz′ē) /'hʌsiy, 'hʌziy/ *n.* [*count*], *pl.* **-sies.** a woman or girl who is considered somewhat immoral.

hus•tings (hus′tingz) /'hʌstɪŋz/ *n.* **1.** [*noncount*] any place from which political campaign speeches are made: *out on the hustings.* **2.** [*plural*] the speeches and political activities given or done during a campaign.

hus•tle (hus′əl) /ˈhʌsəl/ *v.*, **-tled, -tling,** *n.* **—***v.* **1.** to (cause to) move, esp. to leave, roughly or hurriedly: [*no obj*]: *She hustled off to work.* [~ + *obj*]: *He hustled the kids to school.* **2.** [*no obj*] to proceed or work rapidly or energetically: *I hustled and finished the report.* **3.** [*no obj*] to be aggressively energetic: *He really hustled and signed up a lot of clients.* **4.** [~ + *obj*] to promote aggressively: *The author went on TV talk shows to hustle his newest book.* **5.** [~ + *obj*] to pressure (a person) to buy or do something unwise: *The car salesman tried to hustle us into a bad deal.* **6.** [~ + *obj*] to obtain by often dishonest or illegal means: *to hustle money from unsuspecting tourists.* **7.** *Slang.* to earn one's living by illegal means: [*no obj*]: *out hustling on the streets.* [~ + *obj*]: *out hustling drugs.* **—***n.* **8.** [*noncount*] energetic or hurried activity. **9.** [*noncount*] discourteous shoving or jostling: *the hustle and bustle of the big city.* **10.** [*count*] *Slang.* a scheme of persuading someone to buy something unprofitable or participate in a dishonest scheme: *The con artists tried another hustle.* **—hus•tler** (hus′lər) /ˈhʌslər/ *n.* [*count*]

hut (hut) /hʌt/ *n.* [*count*] a small dwelling or building of simple construction.

hutch (huch) /hʌtʃ/ *n.* [*count*] **1.** a pen or enclosed coop for small animals: *a rabbit hutch.* **2.** a chestlike cabinet with doors or drawers, usually with open shelves above.

hutz•pa or **hutz•pah** (KHŏŏt′spə, hŏŏt′-) /ˈxʊtspə, ˈhʊt-/ *n. Slang.* CHUTZPA.

hwy or **hwy.,** an abbreviation of: highway.

hy•a•cinth (hī′ə sinth) /ˈhayəsɪnθ/ *n.* [*count*] a plant grown from a bulb, of the lily family, with a rounded cluster of sweet-smelling, colorful flowers.

hy•brid (hī′brid) /ˈhaybrɪd/ *n.* [*count*] **1.** the offspring of two animals or plants of different breeds, varieties, or species. **2.** anything of blended origins: *The work is a hybrid of classical and rock music styles.* **—***adj.* [*before a noun*] **3.** bred or descended from two distinct breeds, varieties, or species. **4.** formed or made up of very different or unlike elements or parts. **—hy′brid•ism,** *n.* [*noncount*]

-hydr-, *root. -hydr-* comes from Greek, where it has the meaning "water." This meaning is found in such words as: CARBOHYDRATE, DEHYDRATION, HYDRANT, HYDRAULIC, HYDROCARBON, HYDROELECTRIC, HYDROFOIL, HYDROGEN, HYDROPHOBIA, HYDROPLANE, HYDROPONICS, HYDROTHERAPY.

hy•drant (hī′drənt) /ˈhaydrənt/ *n.* [*count*] an upright pipe with a spout or nozzle for drawing water from a water main, esp. for fighting fires. See illustration at STREET. See -HYDR-.

hy•drau•lic (hī drô′lik, -drol′ik) /hayˈdrɔlɪk, -ˈdrɒlɪk/ *adj.* operated by, moved by, or relating to the pressure of water or other liquids in motion: *hydraulic brakes.* **—hy•drau′li•cal•ly,** *adv.* See -HYDR-.

hy•drau•lics (hī drô′liks, -drol′iks) /hayˈdrɔlɪks, -ˈdrɒlɪks/ *n.* [*noncount; used with a singular verb*] the science that deals with the laws governing water or other liquids in motion, and how these laws are used in engineering. See -HYDR-.

hy•dro•car•bon (hī′drə kär′bən, hī′drə kär′-) /ˌhaydrəˈkɑrbən, ˈhaydrəˌkɑr-/ *n.* [*count*] a group of chemical compounds containing only hydrogen and carbon, such as methane or benzene. See -HYDR-.

hy•dro•e•lec•tric (hī′drō i lek′trik) /ˌhaydrowɪˈlɛktrɪk/ *adj.* of or relating to the production and distribution of electricity taken from the energy of falling water or any other hydraulic source. **—hy•dro•e•lec•tric•i•ty** (hī′drō-i lek tris′i tē, -ē′lek-) /ˌhaydrowɪlɛkˈtrɪsɪtiy, -ˌiylɛk-/ *n.* [*noncount*] See -HYDR-.

hy•dro•foil (hī′drə foil′) /ˈhaydrəˌfɔyl/ *n.* [*count*] **1.** a winglike structure fitted near the bottom of a boat to lift the hull while the boat is moving. **2.** a vessel equipped with a hydrofoil. See -HYDR-.

hy•dro•gen (hī′drə jən) /ˈhaydrədʒən/ *n.* [*noncount*] a colorless, odorless gas that burns easily, and combines chemically with oxygen to form water. See -HYDR-.

hy′drogen bomb′, *n.* [*count*] a bomb that takes its explosive energy from the fusion of hydrogen atoms. Also called **H-bomb.** See -HYDR-.

hy′drogen perox′ide, *n.* [*noncount*] a colorless liquid which is used chiefly as an antiseptic and to bleach or whiten objects. See -HYDR-.

hy•dro•pho•bi•a (hī′drə fō′bē ə) /ˌhaydrəˈfowbiyə/ *n.* [*noncount*] **1.** RABIES. **2.** a fear of water. See -HYDR-.

hy•dro•phone (hī′drə fōn′) /ˈhaydrəˌfown/ *n.* [*count*] a device for detecting sounds sent through water, as for locating submarines. See -HYDR-, -PHON-.

hy•dro•plane (hī′drə plān′) /ˈhaydrəˌpleyn/ *n., v.,* **-planed, -plan•ing.** **—***n.* [*count*] **1.** a seaplane. **2.** a light, high-powered boat designed to skim along the surface of the water at high speeds. **—***v.* [*no obj*] **3.** to skim over water in the manner of a hydroplane. **4.** to travel in or pilot a hydroplane. See -HYDR-.

hy•dro•pon•ics (hī′drə pon′iks) /ˌhaydrəˈpɒnɪks/ *n.* [*noncount; used with a singular verb*] the growing of plants by placing the roots in liquid solutions rather than in soil. **—hy′dro•pon′ic,** *adj.* See -HYDR-.

hy•dro•ther•a•py (hī′drə ther′ə pē) /ˌhaydrəˈθɛrəpiy/ *n.* [*noncount*] the use of water in the treatment of disease or injury, such as with soothing baths or sprays for wounds or heated pools for stiffened joints. See -HYDR-.

hy•e•na (hī ē′nə) /hayˈiynə/ *n.* [*count*], *pl.* **-nas.** a large, wolf-like, meat-eating animal with a laugh-like cry.

hy•giene (hī′jēn) /ˈhaydʒiyn/ *n.* [*noncount*] **1.** the scientific study of how to preserve health and prevent disease. **2.** cleanliness, esp. so as to preserve health and prevent disease. **—hy•gi•en•ic** (hī′jē en′ik, hī jen′-) /ˌhaydʒiyˈɛnɪk, hayˈdʒɛn-/ *adj.* **—hy′gi•en′i•cal•ly,** *adv.*

hy•gien•ist (hī jē′nist, -jen′ist, hī′jē nist) /hayˈdʒiynɪst, -ˈdʒɛnɪst, ˈhaydʒiynɪst/ *n.* [*count*] **1.** an expert in hygiene. **2.** DENTAL HYGIENIST.

hy•men (hī′mən) /ˈhaymən/ *n.* [*count*] a membrane partly closing the opening of the vagina in a girl or woman who has not had sex.

hymn (him) /hɪm/ *n.* [*count*] a song of praise, esp. to God.

hym•nal (him′nl) /ˈhɪmnḷ/ *n.* [*count*] Also called **hymn•book** (-bŏŏk′) /-ˌbʊk/. a book of hymns for use in a religious service.

hyp., an abbreviation of: **1.** hypotenuse. **2.** hypothesis. **3.** hypothetical.

hype (hīp) /hayp/ *v.,* **hyped, hyp•ing,** *Informal.* **—***v.* [~ + *obj*] **1.** to stimulate; excite: *The kids were all hyped about going to Disneyland.* **2.** to create interest in or publicize in a showy way; tout: *The car was hyped as America's answer to foreign imports.* **—***n.* [*noncount*] **3.** exaggerated publicity, advertising, or promotion: *a lot of sales hype.*

hy•per (hī′pər) /ˈhaypər/ *adj. Informal.* **1.** overexcited; keyed up: *acting hyper after staying inside for five days.* **2.** overly concerned about something: *hyper about proper pronunciation.*

hyper-, *prefix.* **1.** *hyper-* is attached to nouns and adjectives and means "excessive; overly; too much; unusual:" *hyper- + critical → hypercritical (= overly critical); hyper- + inflation → hyperinflation (= inflation that is unusual or too high).* Compare SUPER-. **2.** *hyper-* is also used in computer words to refer to anything not rigidly connected in a step-by-step manner: *hyper- + text → hypertext (= text or information that the user can gain access to in the order he or she chooses).*

hy•per•ac•tive (hī′pər ak′tiv) /ˌhaypərˈæktɪv/ *adj.* unusually or abnormally active. **—hy•per•ac•tiv•i•ty** (hī′pər-ak tiv′i tē) /ˌhaypəræk'tɪvɪtiy/ *n.* [*noncount*]

hy•per•bo•le (hī pûr′bə lē) /hayˈpɜrbəliy/ *n.* [*noncount*] obvious and intentional exaggeration: *a campaign full of hyperbole; an example of hyperbole, such as "to wait an eternity."* **—hy•per•bol•ic** (hī′pər bol′ik) /ˌhaypərˈbɒlɪk/ *adj.*

hy•per•crit•i•cal (hī′pər krit′i kəl) /ˌhaypərˈkrɪtɪkəl/ *adj.* harshly critical; overcritical. **—hy′per•crit′i•cal•ly,** *adv.*

hy•per•sen•si•tive (hī′pər sen′si tiv) /ˌhaypərˈsɛnsɪtɪv/ *adj.* **1.** too sensitive: *The actor was hypersensitive to criticism.* **2.** allergic to a substance to which most people do not normally react. **—hy′per•sen′si•tive•ness, hy•per•sen•si•tiv•i•ty** (hī′pər sen′si tiv′i tē) /ˌhaypərˌsɛnsɪˈtɪvɪtiy/ *n.* [*noncount*]

hy•per•ten•sion (hī′pər ten′shən) /ˌhaypərˈtɛnʃən/ *n.* [*noncount*] high blood pressure. **—hy•per•ten•sive** (hī′-pər ten′siv) /ˌhaypərˈtɛnsɪv/ *adj., n.* [*count*]

hy•per•ven•ti•late (hī′pər ven′tl āt′) /ˌhaypərˈvɛntḷˌeyt/ *v.,* **-lat•ed, -lat•ing.** [*no obj*] to undergo hyperventilation.

hy•per•ven•ti•la•tion (hī′pər ven′tl ā′shən) /ˌhaypərˌvɛntḷˈeyʃən/ *n.* [*noncount*] abnormally rapid or deep breathing that goes on too long, resulting in too much oxygen in the blood.

hy•phen (hī′fən) /ˈhayfən/ *n.* [*count*] a short line (-) used to connect the parts of a compound word or the parts of a word divided for any purpose.

hy•phen•ate (hī′fə nāt′) /ˈhayfəˌneyt/ *v.,* **-at•ed, -at•ing,** *adj., n.* **—***v.* [~ + *obj*] **1.** to join by a hyphen: *How do you decide whether to hyphenate two words, or to spell them as two separate words?* **2.** to write or divide with a hyphen. **—***adj.* **3.** hyphenated. **—***n.* [*count*] **4.** a person working in more than one craft or occupation: *She was a* *hyphenate who had gained fame as a writer-director-producer.* **5.** a person of mixed national origin or identity: *A Korean-American is a hyphenate.* —**hy•phen•a•tion** (hī′fə nā′shən) /ˌhayfə'neyʃən/ *n.* [*noncount*]

hyp•no•sis (hip nō′sis) /hɪp'nowsɪs/ *n., pl.* **-ses** (-sēz) /-siyz/. **1.** [*noncount*] a trance-like state in which a person is more likely to respond to suggestions from someone else than when fully awake and aware. **2.** HYPNOTISM (defs. 1, 2).

hyp•not•ic (hip not′ik) /hɪp'nɒtɪk/ *adj.* **1.** of, relating to, or resembling hypnosis or hypnotism: *a hypnotic trance.* **2.** causing or bringing about sleep: *hypnotic drugs.* —*n.* [*count*] **3.** a drug or other substance or thing that brings about sleep; sedative. —**hyp•not′i•cal•ly,** *adv.*

hyp•no•tism (hip′nə tiz′əm) /'hɪpnəˌtɪzəm/ *n.* **1.** [*noncount*] the study or practice of causing hypnosis. **2.** [*count*] the act of hypnotizing: *The hypnotism took only moments.* **3.** HYPNOSIS (def. 1). —**hyp′no•tist,** *n.* [*count*]

hyp•no•tize (hip′nə tiz′) /'hɪpnəˌtayz/ *v.* [~ + *obj*], **-tized, -tiz•ing. 1.** to put in a state of hypnosis. **2.** to fascinate: *The cat was hypnotized by the string I dangled before her.*

hy•po (hī′pō) /'haypow/ *n.* [*count*], *pl.* **-pos.** *Informal.* a hypodermic syringe or injection.

hypo-, *prefix. hypo-* is attached to roots and means "under, below:" *hypo- + dermic → hypodermic (= under the skin); hypo- + thermia → hypothermia (= heat or temperature below what it should be).* Also, *esp. before a vowel,* **hyp-.**

hy•po•al•ler•gen•ic (hī′pō al′ər jen′ik) /ˌhaypowˌælər'dʒɛnɪk/ *adj.* made or designed to lessen the likelihood of an allergic reaction: *hypoallergenic cosmetics.*

hy•po•chon•dri•a (hī′pə kon′drē ə) /ˌhaypə'kɒndriyə/ *n.* [*noncount*] unnecessary worry or preoccupation with one's health. —**hy•po•chon•dri•ac** (hī′pə kon′drē ak′) /ˌhaypə'kɒndriyˌæk/ *n.* [*count*]

hy•poc•ri•sy (hi pok′rə sē) /hɪ'pɒkrəsiy/ *n.* [*noncount; count*], *pl.* **-sies.** an act or instance of pretending to have desirable qualities or views that one does not really possess.

hyp•o•crite (hip′ə krit) /'hɪpəkrɪt/ *n.* [*count*] a person who practices hypocrisy. —**hyp′o•crit′i•cal,** *adj.* —**hyp′o•crit′i•cal•ly,** *adv.*

hy•po•der•mic (hī′pə dûr′mik) /ˌhaypə'dɜrmɪk/ *adj.* **1.** of or relating to the process of injecting medicine or drugs under the skin: *a hypodermic injection.* —*n.* [*count*] **2.** an injection (of a drug) under the skin. **3.** a syringe or needle used in giving an injection under the skin. See -DERM-.

hy•po•gly•ce•mi•a (hī′pō glī sē′mē ə) /ˌhaypowglay'siymiyə/ *n.* [*noncount*] an abnormally low level of a blood sugar, glucose, in the blood. —**hy•po•gly•ce•mic** (hī′pō glī sē′mik) /ˌhaypowglay'siymɪk/ *adj., n.* [*count*]

hy•pot•e•nuse (hī pot′n o͞os′, -yo͞os′) /hay'pɒtn̩ˌuws, -ˌyuws/ also **hypothenuse,** *n.* [*count*] the side of a right triangle opposite the right angle.

hy•po•ther•mi•a (hī′pə thûr′mē ə) /ˌhaypə'θɜrmiyə/ *n.* [*noncount*] body temperature that is below normal. See -THERM-.

hy•poth•e•sis (hī poth′ə sis, hi-) /hay'pɒθəsɪs, hɪ-/ *n.* [*count*], *pl.* **-ses** (-sēz′) /-ˌsiyz/. a theory or idea that is put forth to explain something, and that is either accepted as a guide for future investigation or is assumed for the sake of argument and testing. See -THES-.

hy•poth•e•size (hī poth′ə sīz′, hi-) /hay'pɒθəˌsayz, hɪ-/ *v.,* **-sized, -siz•ing. 1.** [*no obj*] to form a hypothesis. **2.** [~ + *(that) clause*] to assume by hypothesis: *We hypothesized that she was really a spy.* See -THES-.

hy•po•thet•i•cal (hī′pə thet′i kəl) /ˌhaypə'θɛtɪkəl/ *adj.* Also, **hy′po•thet′ic. 1.** assumed to exist by hypothesis; supposed: *a hypothetical situation.* **2.** of, relating to, involving, or characterized by hypothesis: *hypothetical reasoning.* —**hy′po•thet′i•cal•ly,** *adv.* See -THES-.

hys•ter•ec•to•my (his′tə rek′tə mē) /ˌhɪstə'rɛktəmiy/ *n.* [*count*], *pl.* **-mies.** surgical removal of the uterus. See -TOM-.

hys•te•ri•a (hi ster′ē ə, -stēr′-) /hɪ'stɛriyə, -'stɪər-/ *n.* [*noncount*] a wild, violent, or uncontrollable emotional behavior, as from fear or grief.

hys•ter•ic (hi ster′ik) /hɪ'stɛrɪk/ *n.* [*count*] **1.** Usually, **hysterics.** [*plural*] a fit of uncontrollable laughter or weeping. **2.** a person susceptible to hysteria. —*adj.* **3.** hysterical.

hys•ter•i•cal (hi ster′i kəl) /hɪ'stɛrɪkəl/ *adj.* **1.** of, relating to, characterized by, or suffering from hysteria: *a hysterical patient.* **2.** uncontrollably emotional or agitated: *nearly hysterical after the accident.* **3.** very funny; hilarious: *a hysterical movie.* —**hys•ter′i•cal•ly,** *adv.*

Hz, an abbreviation of: hertz.

I

I, i (ī) /ay/ *n.* [*count*], *pl.* **I's** or **Is, i's** or **is.** the ninth letter of the English alphabet, a vowel.

I (ī) /ay/ *pron., nom.* **I,** *poss.* **my** or **mine,** *obj.* **me;** *pl. nom.* **we,** *poss.* **our** or **ours,** *obj.* **us;** *n., pl.* **I's.** *—pron.* **1.** (used as the singular subject pronoun by a speaker or writer in referring to himself or herself): *I'll be happy to see you. Am I glad to see her!* *—n.* [*count*] **2.** the ego; the self: *the "I" of the narrator.*

I, an abbreviation of: interstate (used with a number to designate an interstate highway): *I-95.*

IA or **Ia.,** an abbreviation of: Iowa.

-ial, *suffix. -ial* is used after some roots to form adjectives from nouns, with the meaning "relating to, of the kind of": *manor + -ial → manorial (= relating to a manor).* See -AL[1].

-ian, *suffix. -ian* is used to form nouns and adjectives with the meanings of -AN: *Orwell + -ian → Orwellian (= interested in, or relating to, the writing of George Orwell); Washington + -ian → Washingtonian (= a person who lives in Washington).*

-iatrics, *suffix. -iatrics* comes from Greek, and is attached to some roots to form nouns with the meaning "healing; the medical practice of": *ger- (= old people) + -iatrics → geriatrics (= the healing of older people); ped- (= child) + -iatrics → pediatrics (= medical practice involving children).*

-iatry, *suffix. -iatry* comes from Greek, and is attached to some roots to form nouns with the meaning "healing; the medical practice of": *pod- (= foot) + -iatry → podiatry (= the healing of the foot); psych- (= the mind) + -iatry → psychiatry (= the medical practice dealing with the mind).*

i•bex (ī′beks) /ˈaybɛks/ *n.* [*count*], *pl.* **i•bex•es, ib•i•ces** (ib′ə sēz′, ī′bə-) /ˈɪbəˌsiyz, ˈaybə-/ (*esp. when thought of as a group*) **i•bex.** a wild mountain goat of Eurasia and N Africa, having long curved horns.

ibid. (ib′id) /ˈɪbɪd/ an abbreviation of: *ibidem,* a Latin expression used in footnotes to mean "in the same book, chapter, page, etc., as previously mentioned."

-ibility, *suffix. -ibility* is used to form nouns from adjectives that end in *-ible*: *reducible (adjective) → reducibility (= the state or condition of being reducible, of being able to be reduced); flexible (adjective) → flexibility (= the state or condition of being able to move smoothly).* See -ABILITY, -ABLE, -IBLE.

i•bis (ī′bis) /ˈaybɪs/ *n.* [*count*], *pl.* **i•bis•es,** (*esp. when thought of as a group*) **i•bis.** a large wading bird of warm regions.

-ible, *suffix. -ible,* a variant form of -ABLE, is attached to roots, mostly of verbs, to form adjectives with the meaning "capable of, fit for, tending to": *cred- (= believe) + -ible → credible (= that can be believed); vis- (= see) + -ible → visible (= that can be seen); reduce + -ible → reducible (= that can be reduced).* See -ABILITY, -ABLE, -IBILITY.

i•bu•pro•fen (ī′byo͞o prō′fən) /ˌaybyuwˈprowfən/ *n.* [*noncount*] a non-aspirin drug used esp. for reducing pain and swelling.

-ic, *suffix. -ic* is attached to nouns to form adjectives with the meaning "of or relating to:" *metal + -ic → metallic; poet + -ic → poetic.* This suffix is also attached to nouns to form adjectives with the meaning "having some characteristics of; in the style of:" *ballet + -ic → balletic; sophomore + -ic → sophomoric; Byron + -ic → Byronic (= in the style of Byron).*

-ical, *suffix. -ical,* a combination of -IC and-AL[1], is attached to roots to form adjectives with the meaning "of or relating to": *rhetor- + -ical → rhetorical.* This suffix originally provided synonyms to adjectives that ended in -IC: *poet + -ic → poetic; poet + -ical → poetical.* But some of these pairs of words or formations are now different in meaning: *econom- + -ic → economic (= of or relating to economics); econom- + -ical → economical (= being careful in spending money); histor- + -ic → historic (= having a long history; important); histor- + -ical → historical (= happening in the past).*

ice (īs) /ays/ *n., v.,* **iced, ic•ing.** *—n.* **1.** [*noncount*] the solid form of water; frozen water: *skating on the ice.* **2.** [*noncount*] pieces of this frozen water, used to keep things cool or cold: *I'll have some ice with my soda, please.* **3.** [*noncount*] any substance resembling frozen water: *Dry ice is frozen carbon dioxide.* **4.** [*count*] a frozen dessert made of sweetened water and fruit juice: *a cherry ice.* **5.** [*count*] *Brit.* a portion or serving of ice cream. **6.** [*noncount*] *Slang.* diamonds. *—v.* **7. ice up or over,** to cover or to become covered with ice: [*no obj*]: *The airport runway iced over.* [~ + *obj* + *up*]: *The cold has iced the windshield up.* [~ + *up* + *obj*]: *to ice up the windshield.* **8.** [~ + *obj*] to make cool or cold with or as if with ice: *Ice the area of the sprain with an ice pack.* **9.** [~ + *obj*] to cover with icing; frost: *to ice a cake.* *—Idiom.* **10. break the ice,** to act in a friendly way, as by overcoming awkwardness or formality: *His joke broke the ice.* **11. on ice,** in a state of being held back: *Let's put that plan on ice for now.* **12. (skating) on thin ice,** in a dangerous, difficult, or delicate situation: *You'll be on very thin ice if you fail the course.*

ice′ bag′, *n.* [*count*] a waterproof bag filled with ice and applied to a part of the body to reduce pain or swelling.

ice•berg (īs′bûrg) /ˈaysbɜrg/ *n.* [*count*] **1.** a large floating mass of ice. **2.** an emotionally cold person. *—Idiom.* **3. tip of the iceberg,** the first hint of something larger or more complicated: *Our problems with that are just the tip of the iceberg; the whole system is faulty.*

ice•bound (īs′bound′) /ˈaysˌbawnd/ *adj.* stuck, closed off, held, or hemmed in by ice: *an icebound ship.*

ice•box (īs′boks′) /ˈaysˌbɒks/ *n.* [*count*] a refrigerator.

ice•break•er (īs′brā′kər) /ˈaysˌbreykər/ *n.* [*count*] **1.** a ship for breaking through ice and making passages. **2.** something that eases tension: *His joke was an icebreaker at the party.*

ice•cap (īs′kap′) /ˈaysˌkæp/ *n.* [*count*] a thick cover of ice over an area, sloping in all directions from the center.

ice′ cream′, *n.* **1.** [*noncount*] a frozen mixture eaten as a dessert, made with cream or milk, sugar, and flavoring: *He likes vanilla ice cream best.* **2.** [*count*] a portion or serving of this dessert: *Two ice creams, please.*

iced (īst) /ayst/ *adj.* [*before a noun*] **1.** made cold: *She made some iced tea.* **2.** covered or decorated with icing: *little iced cupcakes.*

ice′ hock′ey, *n.* [*noncount*] a game played on ice between two teams of six skaters each.

Ice•land•er (īs′lan′dər, -lən dər) /ˈaysˌlændər, -ləndər/ *n.* [*count*] a person born or living in Iceland.

Ice•land•ic (īs lan′dik) /aysˈlændɪk/ *adj.* **1.** of or relating to Iceland. **2.** of or relating to the language spoken in Iceland. *—n.* [*noncount*] **3.** the language spoken in Iceland.

ice′ milk′, *n.* **1.** [*noncount*] a frozen mixture similar to ice cream but made with skim milk: *two scoops of ice milk.* **2.** [*count*] a portion or serving of this food: *Two ice milks, please.*

ice′ pick′, *n.* [*count*] a sharp-pointed tool for chipping ice.

ice′ skate′, *n.* [*count*] a shoe fitted with a metal blade for skating on ice.

ice′-skate′, *v.* [*no obj*], **-skat•ed, -skat•ing.** to skate on ice. —**ice′ skat′er,** *n.* [*count*]

-ician, *suffix. -ician* is attached to nouns or roots to form nouns with the meaning "the person having the occupation or work of": *beauty + -ician → beautician (= person who works in a beauty shop); mort- (= death) + -ician → mortician (= person working to prepare dead people for burial).*

i•ci•cle (ī′si kəl) /ˈaysɪkəl/ *n.* [*count*] a hanging, pointed mass of ice formed by the freezing of dripping water.

ic•ing (ī′sing) /ˈaysɪŋ/ *n.* [*noncount*] **1.** a sweet mixture of sugar, butter, and flavoring, used as a coating on cakes, cookies, etc.; frosting **2.** the freezing of moisture from the air on the surface of an aircraft: *Icing on the wings was a cause of the air crash.* **3. icing on the cake,** an extra, unnecessary detail that makes something better or more desirable: *A new car for graduation was the icing on the cake.*

ick•y (ik′ē) /ˈɪkiy/ *adj.,* **-i•er, -i•est.** *Informal.* **1.** causing a feeling of strong distaste; repulsive: *"Ooh, those icky worms!" the kids exclaimed.* **2.** too sweet or sentimental: *a few icky scenes in the play.*

i•con (ī′kon) /ˈaykɒn/ *n.* [*count*] **1.** a picture, esp. of Christ, a saint, etc., painted on a wooden panel and venerated in the Eastern Church. **2.** a representation that stands for something it resembles; symbol. **3.** a small graphic image on a computer screen representing a disk drive, a file, a command, etc.: *The icon of a wastebasket represents deleting a file.* —**i•con′ic,** *adj.* —**i•co•nic•i•ty** (ī′kə nis′i tē) /ˌaykəˈnɪsɪtiy/ *n.* [*noncount*]

i•con•o•clast (ī kon′ə klast′) /ayˈkɒnəˌklæst/ *n.* [*count*] a person who attacks accepted beliefs and considers them to be based on error or superstition; dissenter: *an iconoclast who will have nothing to do with organized religion.* —**i•con′o•clas′tic,** *adj.*

-ics, *suffix.* *-ics* is attached to roots to form nouns with the meaning "a body of facts, knowledge, or principles." Such nouns usually correspond to adjectives ending in -IC or -ICAL: *eth-* (= *custom; character*) + *-ics* → *ethics* (= *the principles of good character*).

ICU, an abbreviation of: intensive care unit.

i•cy (ī′sē) /'aysiy/ *adj.,* **i•ci•er, i•ci•est. 1.** made of, resembling, or covered with ice: *icy runways at the snowbound airport.* **2.** very cold: *Her hands were icy from the cold.* **3.** showing anger or dislike in a quiet way; hostile; unfriendly: *an icy stare.* —**i′ci•ness,** *n.* [*noncount*]

id (id) /ɪd/ *n.* [*count; usually singular; usually: the* + ~] the part of mind that is the source of unconscious and instinctive drives that seek satisfaction and pleasure. Compare EGO (def. 2), SUPEREGO.

ID (ī′dē′) /'ay'diy/ *n., pl.* **ID's, IDs.** a means of identification, as a document containing information regarding the bearer's identity: [*noncount*]: *Stores need two forms of ID, a driver's license and a credit card.* [*count*]: *The bartender refused to accept the teenager's ID.* Also, **I.D.**

ID or **Id.,** an abbreviation of: Idaho.

I'd (id) /ayd/ **1.** contraction of *I would*: *I'd be there sooner if I could.* **2.** contraction of *I had*: *I'd been there many times.*

I.D., an abbreviation of: **1.** identification. **2.** identity.

i•de•a (ī dē′ə, ī dē^{ə}′) /ay'diyə, ay'diy^{ə}/ *n.* [*count*] **1.** a thought that comes as a result of mental activity: *Einstein's ideas about time and space.* **2.** [*usually singular*] an opinion, view, or belief: *His idea of a good time is relaxing at home.* **3.** a plan of action; intention; suggestion: *had the idea of becoming an engineer; What a great idea!* **4.** [*usually singular*] a purpose or guiding principle: *The idea was to make money.*

i•de•al (ī dē′əl, ī dēl′) /ay'diyəl, ay'diyl/ *n.* [*count*] **1.** an idea or notion of something perfect: *democracy existing as an ideal.* **2.** a person or thing thought of as being a perfect example of something: *I thought of him as the ideal of teachers everywhere.* **3.** an ultimate object, esp. one of high or noble character: *Don't compromise your ideals.* **4.** something that exists only in the imagination. —*adj.* **5.** [*before a noun*] being or making up a standard of excellence: *ideal beauty.* **6.** perfect of its kind: *an ideal spot for a home.* **7.** wonderful; excellent; best: *It would be ideal if you could stay.*

i•de•al•ism (ī dē′ə liz′əm) /ay'diyə,lɪzəm/ *n.* [*noncount*] the belief that one should follow or try to achieve ideals: *youthful idealism.* —**i•de′al•ist,** *n.* [*count*] —**i•de′al•is′tic,** *adj.*

i•de•al•ize (ī dē′ə līz′) /ay'diyə,layz/ *v.,* **-ized, -iz•ing.** to consider or represent (someone or something) as ideal: [~ + *obj*]: *She idealized her successful mother.* [*no obj*]: *his tendency to idealize about retirement.* —**i•de•al•i•za•tion** (ī dē′ə li zā′shən) /ay,diyəlɪ'zeyʃən/ *n.* [*noncount*]

i•de•al•ly (ī dē′ə lē) /ay'diyəliy/ *adv.* **1.** according to an ideal; perfectly: *ideally graceful and beautiful.* **2.** according to one's wishes, even if impossible: *Ideally I'd like to finish by next month.*

i•dée fixe (ē dā fēks′) /iy'dey fiyks/ *n.* [*count*], *pl.* **i•dées fixes** (ē dā fēks′) /iy'dey fiyks/. an idea that one thinks about for a long time, esp. one not likely to be real or practical: *The dictator's idée fixe was that he should have nuclear weapons.*

i•dem (ī′dem, id′em) /'aydɛm, 'ɪdɛm/ *pron., adj.* [*used in footnotes when writing papers or articles*] the same (piece of writing, etc.) as was already written or referred to.

i•den•ti•cal (ī den′ti kəl, i den′-) /ay'dɛntɪkəl, ɪ'dɛn-/ *adj.* **1.** alike in every way; exactly alike: *No two people have identical fingerprints.* **2.** being the very same; self-same: *It's the identical house the famous actress lived in.* —**i•den′ti•cal•ly,** *adv.*

i•den•ti•fi•a•ble (ī den′ti fī′ə bl) /ay,dɛntɪ'fayəbl/ *adj.* **1.** that can be used to identify someone: *an identifiable birthmark on her forearm.* **2.** that can be named.

i•den•ti•fi•ca•tion (ī den′tə fi kā′shən, i den′-) /ay,dɛntəfɪ'keyʃən, ɪ,dɛn-/ *n.* [*noncount*] **1.** an act or instance of identifying; the state of being identified: *Positive identification of the accident victim was impossible.* **2.** something, as a birth certificate or driver's license, that identifies a person. **3.** a process by which one person comes to believe he or she has the qualities of another: *the audience's identification with the main character.*

i•den•ti•fy (ī den′tə fī′, i den′-) /ay'dɛntə,fay, ɪ'dɛn-/ *v.,* **-fied, -fy•ing. 1.** [~ + *obj*] to prove or verify the identity of: *Can you identify the body?* **2.** [~ + *obj*] to serve as a means of identification for: *Her birthmark identifies her.* **3.** [~ + *obj* + *with* + *obj*] to associate or connect closely: *The voters identified the vice-president with the old regime.* **4.** to associate (one or oneself) with another person or a group by identification: [~ + *oneself* + *with* + *obj*]: *The audience identified itself with the main character.* [~ + *with* + *obj*]: *The audience could identify with the main character.* **5.** [~ + *obj*] to notice the importance of (some facts): *The paper identifies three important factors in economic depressions.*

i•den•ti•ty (ī den′ti tē, i den′-) /ay'dɛntɪtiy, ɪ'dɛn-/ *n., pl.* **-ties. 1.** [*noncount*] the state or fact of remaining the same; the condition of being oneself or itself, and not another: *After his amnesia he doubted his own identity.* **2.** condition or character as to who a person is or what a thing is: [*noncount*]: *a case of mistaken identity.* [*count*]: *the identity of the rape victim.* **3.** [*noncount*] the sense of self, providing a feeling of sameness and continuity; individuality: *the searching for cultural identity.* **4.** the state or fact of being the same one as described: [*noncount*]: *to establish identity of stolen property.* [*count*]: *an identity of interests.*

id•e•o•gram (id′ē ə gram′, ī′dē-) /'ɪdiyə,græm, 'aydiy-/ *n.* [*count*] a written symbol that represents a thing directly rather than a word or sound.

id•e•o•graph (id′ē ə graf′, ī′dē-) /'ɪdiyə,græf, 'aydiy-/ *n.* [*count*] an ideogram. See -GRAPH-.

i•de•o•log•i•cal (ī′dē ə loj′ik əl, id′ē-) /,aydiyə'lɒdʒɪkəl, ,ɪdiy-/ *adj.* of or relating to ideology: *ideological commitment to capitalism.* —**i•de′o•log′ic•al•ly,** *adv.*: *ideologically opposed to accepting aid.*

i•de•ol•o•gy (ī′dē ol′ə jē, id′ē-) /,aydiy'ɒlədʒiy, ,ɪdiy-/ *n., pl.* **-gies.** the body of belief, doctrine, or thought that guides an individual, movement, or group: [*noncount*]: *communist ideology.* [*count*]: *numerous ideologies of social behavior.* See -LOG-.

id•i•o•cy (id′ē ə sē) /'ɪdiyəsiy/ *n., pl.* **-cies. 1.** completely senseless or foolish behavior: [*noncount*]: *What idiocy is this? A new computer?* [*count*]: *new idiocies that will lose money.* **2.** [*noncount*] the state of being an idiot; extreme mental deficiency: *congenital idiocy.*

id•i•om (id′ē əm) /'ɪdiyəm/ *n.* [*count*] **1.** an expression or phrase that does not follow regular rules of grammar, or one whose meaning cannot be predicted from the meaning of its individual parts: *The expression* kick the bucket, *meaning "to die," is an idiom in English.* **2.** a language, dialect, or style of speaking typical of a person or of a group: *the idiom of the arts folk.*

id•i•o•mat•ic (id′ē ə mat′ik) /,ɪdiyə'mætɪk/ *adj.* that sounds natural and correct to a native speaker of a language: *answered in fluent, idiomatic German.* —**id′i•o•mat′i•cal•ly,** *adv.*

id•i•o•syn•cra•sy (id′ē ə sing′krə sē, -sin′-) /,ɪdiyə'sɪŋkrəsiy, -'sɪn-/ *n.* [*count*], *pl.* **-sies.** a characteristic, a habit, a particular like or dislike, etc., special to or distinctive of an individual: *a few little idiosyncrasies, like wearing earmuffs inside and outside on cold days.* —**id•i•o•syn•crat•ic** (id′ē ō sin krat′ik, -sing-) /,ɪdiyowsɪn'krætɪk, -sɪŋ-/ *adj.*: *her idiosyncratic ways.*

id•i•ot (id′ē ət) /'ɪdiyət/ *n.* [*count*] **1.** a completely stupid or foolish person: *He was a total idiot to squander his life savings.* **2.** formerly, a person classified in the lowest rank of mental retardation.

i•di•ot•ic (id′ē ot′ik) /,ɪdiy'ɒtɪk/ *adj.* completely stupid or foolish: *What an idiotic idea that was!* —**id′i•ot′i•cal•ly,** *adv.*

i•dle (īd′l) /'aydl/ *adj.,* **i•dler, i•dlest,** *v.,* **i•dled, i•dling,** *n.* —*adj.* **1.** not working or active; doing nothing: *idle machinery; Most of the men were idle during the depression.* **2.** not filled with activity: *idle hours.* **3.** habitually avoiding work; lazy: *She's been idle ever since she came back from college.* **4.** [*usually: before a noun*] of no real worth or purpose: *idle threats.* —*v.* **5.** to pass time doing nothing; waste time: [*no obj*]: *They appeared to be idling near the doorway.* [~ + *away* + *obj*]: *idled away the afternoon.* [~ + *obj* + *away*]: *They idled the afternoon away, playing cards.* **6.** (of a machine or mechanism) to (cause to) operate at a low speed, not connected to a load: [*no obj*]: *The car idled at the red light.* [~ + *obj*]: *The driver idled his car's engine.* **7.** [~ + *obj*] to cause to be out of work or unemployed: *The strike idled many workers.* —**i′dle•ness,** *n.* [*noncount*] —**i′dler,** *n.* [*count*] —**id′ling,** *adj.* [*before a noun*]: *an engine at idling speed.* —**i′dly,** *adv.*: *chatted idly.*

i•dol (īd′l) /'aydl/ *n.* [*count*] **1.** an image worshiped as a god: *idol worship.* **2.** a person or thing greatly admired or loved: *the newest teen idol.*

i•dol•a•trous (ī dol′ə trəs) /ɪ'dɒlətrəs/ *adj.* **1.** worshiping idols. **2.** admiring or loving excessively: *young fans idolatrous of the rock star.*

i•dol•a•try (ī dol′ə trē) /ay'dɒlətriy/ *n.* [*noncount*] idolatrous behavior. —**i•dol′a•ter,** *n.* [*count*]

i•dol•ize (id′l īz′) /'aydl̩ˌayz/ *v.*, **-ized, -iz•ing. 1.** [~ + *obj*] to treat with adoration or great devotion: *idolizes her father.* **2.** [~ + *obj*] to worship as a god.

i•dyll or **i•dyl** (id′l) /'aydl̩/ *n.* [*count*] **1.** a poem or a prose composition describing country scenes or any charmingly simple episode. **2.** an episode or scene that is charmingly simple. —**i•dyl•lic** (ī dil′ik) /ay'dɪlɪk/ *adj.*: *an idyllic scene of cows and rolling hills.*

i.e., an abbreviation of: Latin *id est* that is.

-ier, *suffix. -ier* is attached to nouns or roots to form nouns with the meaning "person or thing that does (the action of the word mentioned); person or thing in charge of (the word mentioned)": *finance + -ier → financier (= person doing finance); cour- (= run) + -ier → courier (= messenger); hotel + -ier → hotelier (= person in charge of hotels).* Compare -ER[1].

if (if) /ɪf/ *conj.* **1.** The word *if* is used with a clause to mean "in case that; granting or supposing that; on condition that." **a.** It is used with most tenses of verbs to describe two events, one depending on the other: *If you have no electricity, the computer doesn't work.* **b.** It is used to describe two connected events that will occur in the future. The verb in the *if* clause does not take *will* or *shall*, but the main clause verb does: *If we have enough money, we will send you to a good college* (not: *If we will have enough money...).* **2.** The word *if* is used to mean "in case that; supposing that," when describing an unreal or imaginary situation. Special verb tenses are used. **a.** for unreal or imaginary present time situations. The structure is: the past tense in the *if* clause + the modal verb would with the main verb: *If I were you, I wouldn't worry. If I had lots of money I would buy you a nice house.* **b.** for unreal or imaginary past time situations. The structure is: HAD + the past participle form in the *if* clause + the modal verb would, and HAVE, and the past participle of the main verb: *If she had worked harder on the drums, she would have played for that band. If I had only started sooner, I would have finished the book by now.* **3.** The word *if* is used to mean "even though:" *It was an enthusiastic, if small, audience.* **4.** The word *if* is used to mean "whether" in structures of indirect speech, after such verbs as *ask, wonder, tell, know,* and certain others: *She asked if I spoke Spanish. I wonder if she will be able to come with us.* **5.** The word *if* is used to indicate politeness by the speaker: *If you will, please come forward and stand by my side. If you would just step this way, madam, we'll help you right away.* **6.** The word *if* is used to introduce a phrase that the speaker wishes could be true at the moment: *If only Dad could see me now!* **7.** The word *if* is used to mean "that": *I'm sorry if you don't agree.* —*n.* [*count*] **8.** an uncertain possibility. **9.** a condition: *There are too many ifs in his agreement.* —***Idiom.*** **10. ifs, ands, or buts,** [*usually with a negative word*] reasons or excuses given: *You'd better have this finished on time, no ifs, ands, or buts about it.*

if•fy (if′ē) /'ɪfiy/ *adj.*, **-fi•er, -fi•est.** full of unresolved points or unanswered questions; uncertain: *an iffy situation.* —**if′fi•ness,** *n.* [*noncount*]

-ify, *suffix. -ify* is used to form verbs with the meaning "cause to be in (a stated condition); to make or cause to become (a certain condition)": *intense + -ify → intensify (= cause to be intense); speechify (= make speeches).* See -FY.

ig•loo (ig′lo͞o) /'ɪgluw/ *n.* [*count*], *pl.* **-loos.** a dome-shaped Eskimo dwelling of blocks of hard snow.

ig•ne•ous (ig′nē əs) /'ɪgniyəs/ *adj.* (of rocks) formed under intense heat, as from volcanos.

ig•nite (ig nīt′) /ɪg'nayt/ *v.*, **-nit•ed, -nit•ing.** to (cause to) catch fire; (cause to) begin to burn: [*no obj*]: *Gasoline will ignite when the spark is fired.* [~ + *obj*]: *They ignited the bonfire.*

ig•ni•tion (ig nish′ən) /ɪg'nɪʃən/ *n.* **1.** [*noncount*] the act of igniting or the state of being ignited: *The Space Center announced, "We have ignition; we have liftoff."* **2.** [*count; usually singular*] (in an engine) the process, spark, or switch that ignites the fuel in the cylinder: *The ignition isn't working well.*

ig•no•ble (ig nō′bəl) /ɪg'nowbəl/ *adj.* of low character; dishonorable; worthy of shame; base: *ignoble purposes.* —**ig•no′bly,** *adv.*: *to go down ignobly in defeat.*

ig•no•min•i•ous (ig′nə min′ē əs) /ˌɪgnə'mɪniyəs/ *adj.* of or relating to ignominy: *an ignominious retreat.* —**ig′no•min′i•ous•ly,** *adv.* See -NOM-[2].

ig•no•min•y (ig′nə min′ē, ig nom′ə nē) /'ɪgnəˌmɪniy, ɪg'nɒməniy/ *n.*, *pl.* **-ies. 1.** [*noncount*] disgrace; shame; dishonor: *The traitor lived a life of ignominy in his adopted country, never trusted by his new countrymen.* **2.** [*count*] an act or instance of such disgraceful or shameful conduct: *the ignominies of a spy.* See -NOM-[2].

ig•no•ra•mus (ig′nə rā′məs, -ram′əs) /ˌɪgnə'reyməs, -'ræməs/ *n.* [*count*], *pl.* **-mus•es.** an extremely ignorant person. See -GNOS-.

ig•no•rance (ig′nər əns) /'ɪgnərəns/ *n.* [*noncount*] lack of knowledge about something: *My ignorance of literature is deep.* See -GNOS-.

ig•no•rant (ig′nər ənt) /'ɪgnərənt/ *adj.* **1.** of or relating to ignorance: *How can you blame the ignorant masses?* **2.** [*be* + ~ + *of*] uninformed; unaware: *ignorant of most of the charges brought against her.* —**ig′no•rant•ly,** *adv.* See -GNOS-.

ig•nore (ig nôr′, -nōr′) /ɪg'nɔr, -'nowr/ *v.* [~ + *obj*], **-nored, -nor•ing.** to keep oneself from noticing or recognizing; disregard: *We taught her to ignore insulting remarks.* See -GNOS-.

i•gua•na (i gwä′nə) /ɪ'gwɑnə/ *n.* [*count*], *pl.* **-nas.** a lizard with a large stout body and a fringe from neck to tail.

i•kon (ī′kon) /'aykɒn/ *n.* ICON (defs. 1, 2).

IL, an abbreviation of: Illinois.

il-[1], *prefix. il-* is another form of IN-[2] that is attached to roots beginning with *l*; it means "not:" *il- + legible → illegible (= that cannot be easily read).*

il-[2], *prefix. il-* is another form of IN-[1] that is attached to roots beginning with *l*; it means "in, into:" *il- + -luminate (= light) → illuminate (= shine on or into).*

ilk (ilk) /ɪlk/ *n.* [*count; usually singular*] family, class, group, or kind: *to distrust politicians and all their ilk.*

ill (il) /ɪl/ *adj.*, **worse** (wûrs) /wɜrs/ **worst** (wûrst) /wɜrst/ *n.*, *adv.* —*adj.* **1.** [*be* + ~] sick; unwell; of poor health: *She's ill and won't be in today.* **2.** [*before a noun*] hostile; unkind: *ill feeling.* **3.** [*before a noun*] evil; wicked: *ill deeds.* **4.** [*before a noun*] unfavorable: *ill fortune.* —*n.* **5.** [*noncount*] an unfavorable opinion or statement: *I can speak no ill of her.* **6.** [*noncount*] harm or injury: *His remarks did much ill.* **7.** [*count*] trouble; misfortune: *Many ills befell him.* —*adv.* **8.** unsatisfactorily; poorly; badly: *It ill befits a person to betray friends.* **9.** faultily; improperly: *an ill-constructed house.* **10.** with difficulty or inconvenience: *an expense we can ill afford.* **11.** The word *ill* can be used in combination with other adjectives or participles to mean "badly, improperly; inadequately:" *ill- + considered → ill-considered (= not thought out well in advance; inappropriate); ill- + defined → ill-defined (= not well defined or clearly set out).* —***Idiom.*** **12. ill at ease,** uncomfortable; uneasy: *When I first arrived at the party I felt very ill at ease because I didn't know anyone.* **13. speak ill of,** [~ + *obj*] to say unfriendly or unpleasant things about: *unwise to speak ill of the dead.* —**Related Words.** ILL is an adjective, ILLNESS is a noun: *He was feeling ill. He had a strange illness.*

I'll (īl) /ayl/ contraction of *I will; I shall.*

Ill., an abbreviation of: Illinois.

ill., an abbreviation of: **1.** illustrated. **2.** illustration. **3.** illustrator.

ill′-advised′, *adj.* marked by a lack of forethought; unwise: *an ill-advised remark.* —**ill′-advis′edly,** *adv.*

ill′-bred′, *adj.* showing lack of good manners.

il•le•gal (i lē′gəl) /ɪ'liygəl/ *adj.* **1.** against the law; forbidden by law or statute: *illegal possession of marijuana.* [*It + be + ~ + (for + noun +) to + verb*]: *It is illegal (for drivers) to park on this street.* **2.** forbidden by official rules or regulations: *an illegal forward pass in football.* —*n.* [*count*] **3.** a person who has entered a country without official legal permission: *captured a number of illegals at the border.* —**il•le′gal•ly,** *adv.* See -LEG-.

il•le•gal•i•ty (il′ē gal′i tē) /ˌɪliy'gælɪtiy/ *n.* **1.** [*noncount*] the act or state of being illegal: *a question of illegality.* **2.** [*count*] an illegal action: *illegalities that added up to a number of crimes.* See -LEG-.

il•leg•i•ble (i lej′ə bəl) /ɪ'lɛdʒəbəl/ *adj.* not legible; impossible or hard to read: *to scrawl an illegible message.* —**il•leg•i•bil•i•ty** (i lej′ə bil′i tē) /ɪˌlɛdʒə'bɪlɪtiy/ *n.* [*noncount*] —**il•leg′i•bly,** *adv.*: *She wrote illegibly.* See -LEG-.

il•le•git•i•ma•cy (il′i jit′ə mə sē) /ˌɪlɪ'dʒɪtəməsiy/ *n.* [*noncount*] the state or condition of being illegitimate. See -LEG-.

il•le•git•i•mate (il′i jit′ə mit) /ˌɪlɪ'dʒɪtəmɪt/ *adj.* **1.** born of parents who are not married to each other: *an illegitimate child.* **2.** not allowed by rules or custom; unlawful; illegal. —**il′le•git′i•mate•ly,** *adv.* See -LEG-.

ill′-fat′ed, *adj.* having an unhappy fate or ending: *The crew set out on its ill-fated voyage, never to return.*

ill′-got′ten, *adj.* taken, received, or acquired by dishonest, improper, or evil means: *his ill-gotten gains.*

ill′-hu′mor, *n.* [*noncount*] a disagreeable or surly mood. —**ill′-hu′mored,** *adj.: in an ill-humored mood.*

il•lib•er•al (i lib′ər əl, i lib′rəl) /ɪ'lɪbərəl, ɪ'lɪbrəl/ *adj.* narrow-minded; bigoted; not allowing freedom of choice. See -LIBER-.

il•lic•it (i lis′it) /ɪ'lɪsɪt/ *adj.* **1.** not legally permitted; unlawful: *illicit drugs.* **2.** disapproved of or not permitted for ethical reasons: *an illicit love affair.* —**il•lic′it•ly,** *adv.* —**il•lic′it•ness,** *n.* [*noncount*]

il•lit•er•a•cy (i lit′ər ə sē) /ɪ'lɪtərəsiy/ *n.* [*noncount*] the state or condition of being illiterate: *a crusade against illiteracy.*

il•lit•er•ate (i lit′ər it) /ɪ'lɪtərɪt/ *adj.* **1.** unable to read and write: *Many adults in this country are still illiterate.* **2.** having or demonstrating a lack of knowledge in a particular field: *musically illiterate.* —*n.* [*count*] **3.** an illiterate person: *helped illiterates learn to read.* See -LIT-.

ill′-man′nered, *adj.* having bad or poor manners; impolite.

ill′-na′tured, *adj.* having or showing an unpleasant manner. —**ill′-na′tured•ly,** *adv.* —**ill′-na′tured•ness,** *n.* [*noncount*] See -NAT-.

ill•ness (il′nis) /'ɪlnɪs/ *n.* **1.** [*noncount*] poor health; sickness: *He retired early because of illness.* **2.** [*count*] an example of such poor health: *an illness that can't be treated.*

il•log•i•cal (i loj′i kəl) /ɪ'lɒdʒɪkəl/ *adj.* not logical; unreasoning: *an illogical reply.* —**il•log′i•cal•ly,** *adv.* See -LOG-.

ill′-starred′, *adj.* unlucky; ill-fated: *an ill-starred voyage.*

ill′-treat′, *v.* [~ + *obj*] to treat badly; abuse: *ill-treated as a girl.* —**ill′-treat′ment,** *n.* [*noncount*]: *to suffer from ill-treatment in prison.*

il•lu•mi•nate (i lo͞o′mə nāt′) /ɪ'luwməˌneyt/ *v.* [~ + *obj*], **-nat•ed, -nat•ing. 1.** to supply or brighten with light; light up: *The streets were well illuminated.* **2.** to decorate with lights: *streets illuminated for the holidays.* **3.** to make clear; clear up; clarify: *illuminated many difficult points.*

il•lu•mi•nat•ing (i lo͞o′mə nā′ting) /ɪ'luwməˌneytɪŋ/ *adj.* helping to make clear or understandable: *an illuminating lecture on mathematics.* —**il•lu′mi•nat′ing•ly,** *adv.*

il•lu•mi•na•tion (i lo͞o′mə nā′shən) /ɪˌluwmə'neyʃən/ *n.* [*noncount*] **1.** the act of illuminating; the state of being illuminated: *proper illumination of the photographer's subject.* **2.** the act of making something clear; the state of having understood: *His face lit up with sudden illumination.*

il•lu•mine (i lo͞o′min) /ɪ'luwmɪn/ *v.* [~ + *obj*], **-mined, -min•ing.** to illuminate. —**il•lu′mi•na•ble,** *adj.*

illus., an abbreviation of: **1.** illustrated. **2.** illustration.

il•lu•sion (i lo͞o′zhən) /ɪ'luwʒən/ *n.* **1.** [*count*] something that deceives one by producing a false impression of what is real: *The puddle of water on the dry road ahead was just an optical illusion.* **2.** [*noncount*] the state or condition of being deceived or fooled; false belief in something not true or real: *I was under the illusion you really cared for me.* **3.** [*count*] an instance of being deceived or of believing something false: *has no illusions about her chances of getting the job.* —**il•lu′sion•al, il•lu′sion•ar′y,** *adj.* —**il•lu′sioned,** *adj.* —**Usage.** Compare ILLUSION and DELUSION, both of which refer to false judgments or ideas. An ILLUSION is a false mental picture of something that really exists: *A mirage is an illusion produced by the reflection of light against the sky.* In other words, the light really exists, but we interpret what we see incorrectly. A DELUSION is something that we believe in but for which there is no real basis: *He was suffering from delusions from the drug. He had delusions that people were chasing him.* See -LUD-.

il•lu•so•ry (i lo͞o′sə rē, -zə-) /ɪ'luwsəriy, -zə-/ *adj.* causing or like an illusion; deceptive: *illusory hopes of success.* —**il•lu•so•ri•ly** (i lo͞o′sər ə lē) /ɪ'luwsərəliy/ *adv.* —**il•lu′so•ri•ness,** *n.* [*noncount*] See -LUD-.

il•lus•trate (il′ə strāt′, i lus′trāt) /'ɪləˌstreyt, ɪ'lʌstreyt/ *v.* [~ + *obj*], **-trat•ed, -trat•ing. 1.** to provide (a book, etc.) with artwork: *to illustrate a book.* **2.** to make clear or understandable by providing examples: *illustrated his point with statistics.* —**il′lus•tra′tor,** *n.* [*count*]

il•lus•tra•tion (il′ə strā′shən) /ˌɪlə'streyʃən/ *n.* **1.** [*count*] something that illustrates: *lots of colorful illustrations in each chapter.* **2.** [*count*] an example that explains a point: *He used the statistics of newly arrived immigrants as an illustration.* **3.** [*noncount*] the act of making something clear or of explaining; elucidation: *By way of illustration, let's consider how the typical accountant begins tax preparation.*

il•lus•tra•tive (i lus′trə tiv) /ɪ'lʌstrətɪv/ *adj.* serving to illustrate: *illustrative examples.* —**il•lus′tra•tive•ly,** *adv.*

il•lus•tri•ous (i lus′trē əs) /ɪ'lʌstriyəs/ *adj.* famous; highly distinguished: *an illustrious leader.* —**il•lus′tri•ous•ly,** *adv.* —**il•lus′tri•ous•ness,** *n.* [*noncount*]

ill′ will′, *n.* [*noncount*] hostile feeling; hatred or enmity: *ill will between them.* —**ill′-willed′,** *adj.*

I'm, contraction of *I am*: *I'm here. I'm hungry.*

im-[1], *prefix. im-* is another form of IN-[2] that is attached to roots beginning with *p, b,* and *m;* it means "not:" *im-* + *possible* → *impossible (= not possible).*

im-[2], *prefix. im-* is another form of IN-[1] that is attached to roots beginning with *p, b,* and *m;* it means "in, into:" *im-* + *-migrate* → *immigrate (= travel into).*

im•age (im′ij) /'ɪmɪdʒ/ *n.* [*count*] **1.** a visible representation of a person, animal, or thing: *an image of dark, dismal high-rises in the distance.* **2.** an optical appearance of an object, as one produced by reflection from a mirror, etc.: *The lens takes the image and focuses it on the film.* **3.** a mental representation; idea; conception: *a clear image in the mind.* **4.** form; appearance; semblance: *created in God's image.* **5.** copy: *That child is the image of his mother.* **6.** a general opinion of someone or something, as of a candidate, etc., esp. when achieved by advertising: *The company's image needed improvement.* **7.** the perfect example or type of something: *Biting his nails and pulling at his hair, he was the image of worry.* **8.** a figure of speech used to describe something.

im•age•ry (im′ij rē) /'ɪmɪdʒriy/ *n.* [*noncount*] **1.** mental images thought of as a group; pictorial images. **2.** the use of images or illustration in writing or in art: *effective imagery in poetry.*

im•ag•i•na•ble (i maj′ə nə bəl) /ɪ'mædʒənəbəl/ *adj.* **1.** capable of being imagined: *Einstein used thought experiments to try to come up with imaginable events to test his theory.* **2.** [*used with superlative words*] the most extreme possible: [*before a noun*]: *the best imaginable circumstances.* [*after a noun*]: *the worst conditions imaginable.* —**i•mag′i•na•bly,** *adv.*

im•ag•i•nar•y (i maj′ə ner′ē) /ɪ'mædʒəˌnɛriy/ *adj.* **1.** existing only in the imagination: *imaginary monsters.* —*n.* [*noncount; the* + ~] **2.** that which exists only in the mind: *confusing the imaginary with the real.*

im•ag•i•na•tion (i maj′ə nā′shən) /ɪˌmædʒə'neyʃən/ *n.* **1.** the action of forming or ability to imagine: [*count*]: *Fairy tales help develop children's imaginations.* [*noncount*]: *has lots of imagination.* **2.** [*noncount*] creative talent, esp. the ability to take care of difficulties; resourcefulness: *a job that requires imagination.* **3.** [*noncount*] the product of imagining; a mental creation: *In his imagination the old man was young and strong again.*

im•ag•i•na•tive (i maj′ə nə tiv, -ə nā′tiv) /ɪ'mædʒənətɪv, -əˌneytɪv/ *adj.* **1.** of or relating to imagination: *a very imaginative person.* **2.** showing the results of imagination: *an imaginative advertising campaign.* —**im•ag′i•na•tive•ly,** *adv.*

im•ag•ine (i maj′in) /ɪ'mædʒɪn/ *v.,* **-ined, -in•ing. 1.** to form a mental image of (something not actually present to the senses): [~ + *obj*]: *I imagined her standing before me.* [~ + *(that) clause*]: *I imagined that my grandmother was there before us.* [*no obj*]: *He's just imagining; no one is really chasing him.* **2.** [~ + *(that) clause; not: be* + ~*-ing*] to believe; suppose; think: *He imagined the house was haunted.* **3.** [~ + *clause; not: be* + ~*-ing*] to guess: *I can't imagine what you mean.*

i•mam (i mäm′) /ɪ'mɑm/ *n.* [*count*] **1.** a Muslim official, esp. one in charge of a mosque. **2.** the title for a Muslim leader.

im•bal•ance (im bal′əns) /ɪm'bæləns/ *n.* [*count*] the state or condition of lacking balance: *an imbalance of trade payments.*

im•be•cile (im′bə sil, -səl) /'ɪmbəsɪl, -səl/ *n.* [*count*] **1.** formerly, a person classified in a low rank of mental retardation. **2.** a stupid person; fool; idiot: *Some imbecile smashed our car.* —**im•be•cil•ic** (im′bə sil′ik) /ˌɪmbə'sɪlɪk/ *adj.* —**im•be•cil•i•ty** (im′bə sil′i tē) /ˌɪmbə'sɪlɪtiy/ *n., pl.* **-ties:** [*noncount*]: *a condition of imbecility.* [*count*]: *One of his newest imbecilities was trying to hitch a cat to a cart.*

im•bed (im bed′) /ɪm'bɛd/ *v.,* **-bed•ded, -bed•ding.** EMBED.

im•bibe (im bīb′) /ɪm'bayb/ *v.,* **-bibed, -bib•ing. 1.** to drink (liquids, esp. alcohol): [*no obj*]: *too early to be imbibing.* [~ + *obj*]: *imbibing some beer.* **2.** [~ + *obj*] to absorb or soak up: *Plants imbibe light from the sun.* **3.** [~ + *obj*] to receive into the mind: *to imbibe a sermon.* **—im•bib′er,** *n.* [*count*]

im•bro•glio (im brōl′yō) /ɪm'browlyow/ *n.* [*count*], *pl.* **-glios. 1.** a bitter, complicated disagreement: *embroiled in an imbroglio.* **2.** a complicated and perplexing state of affairs.

im•bue (im byōō′) /ɪm'byuw/ *v.* [~ + *obj*], **-bued, -bu•ing.** to fill (a person) with a strong feeling or opinion: *to be imbued with patriotism.*

IMF or **I.M.F.,** an abbreviation of: International Monetary Fund.

im•i•tate (im′i tāt′) /'ɪmɪ,teyt/ *v.* [~ + *obj*], **-tat•ed, -tat•ing. 1.** to follow as a model or example: *to imitate an author's style.* **2.** to copy the way someone speaks, acts, etc.; to mimic: *My daughters imitated my scolding voice.* **—im′i•ta′tor,** *n.* [*count*]

im•i•ta•tion (im′i tā′shən) /,ɪmɪ'teyʃən/ *n.* **1.** [*noncount*] a result or product of imitating: *Imitation is supposed to be a form of flattery.* **2.** [*count*] the act of imitating; an impersonation: *does imitations of famous political figures.* **3.** [*count*] a counterfeit; copy: *That jewel is just an imitation.* **—*adj.*** [*before a noun*] **4.** designed to imitate a genuine or superior article or thing: *imitation leather.*

im•i•ta•tive (im′i tā′tiv) /'ɪmɪ,teytɪv/ *adj.* imitating; copying. **—im′i•ta′tive•ly,** *adv.* **—im′i•ta′tive•ness,** *n.* [*noncount*]

im•mac•u•late (i mak′yə lit) /ɪ'mækyəlɪt/ *adj.* **1.** free from stain; clean: *immaculate linen.* **2.** free from errors: *an immaculate text.* **—im•mac′u•late•ly,** *adv.* **—im•mac′u•late•ness,** *n.* [*noncount*]

im•ma•te•ri•al (im′ə tēr′ē əl) /,ɪmə'tɪəriyəl/ *adj.* **1.** unimportant: *What people wear to the party is immaterial.* **2.** not material; not in the physical world; spiritual. **—im′ma•te′ri•al•ly,** *adv.* **—im′ma•te′ri•al•ness,** *n.* [*noncount*]

im•ma•ture (im′ə chŏŏr′, -tŏŏr′) /'ɪmə'tʃʊr, -'tʊr/ *adj.* **1.** not mature or ripe: *the immature seeds of a plant.* **2.** emotionally undeveloped; childish; juvenile: *immature temper tantrums.* **—im′ma•ture′ly,** *adv.: acting immaturely and selfishly.* **—im′ma•tur′i•ty,** *n.* [*noncount*]

im•meas•ur•a•ble (i mezh′ər ə bəl) /ɪ'mɛʒərəbəl/ *adj.* that cannot be measured; limitless. **—im•meas′ur•a•bly,** *adv.*

im•me•di•a•cy (i mē′dē ə sē) /ɪ'miydiyəsiy/ *n., pl.* **-cies. 1.** [*noncount*] the state or quality of being immediate: *recognized the immediacy of our problem and ran to get a doctor.* **2.** Often, **immediacies.** [*plural*] immediate needs: *the immediacies of everyday living.* See -MEDI-.

im•me•di•ate (i mē′dē it) /ɪ'miydiyɪt/ *adj.* [*before a noun*] **1.** occurring or done without delay: *an immediate reply.* **2.** having no object or space in between: *lives in the immediate vicinity.* **3.** with nothing coming between to interfere; direct: *an immediate cause.* **4.** of or relating to the present time: *What are your immediate plans?* **5.** very close in relationship: *My immediate family consists of my wife, children, father, and sisters.* See -MEDI-.

im•me•di•ate•ly (i mē′dē it lē) /ɪ'miydiyɪtliy/ *adv.* **1.** instantly; at once: *Please telephone him immediately.* **2.** with no object or space in between: *The mayor sat immediately to my left.* See -MEDI-.

im•me•mo•ri•al (im′ə môr′ē əl, -mōr′-) /,ɪmə'mɔriyəl, -'mowr-/ *adj.* **from time immemorial,** from a period of time extending back beyond memory: *From time immemorial these mountains have stood.* **—im′me•mo′ri•al•ly,** *adv.* See -MEM-.

im•mense (i mens′) /ɪ'mɛns/ *adj.* so large as to be impossible to measure: *an immense territory.* **—im•mense′ly,** *adv.: We enjoyed the party immensely.* **—im•men′si•ty,** *n.* [*noncount*]: *the immensity of the galaxy and the universe.*

im•merse (i mûrs′) /ɪ'mɜrs/ *v.* [~ + *obj*], **-mersed, -mers•ing. 1.** to plunge into or place under a liquid: *Do not immerse this electrical coffee pot in water.* **2.** to involve deeply; absorb: *deeply immersed in her law practice.* **—im•mers′i•ble,** *adj.: That electrical coffee pot is not immersible.* See -MERG-.

im•mer•sion (i mûr′zhən, -shən) /ɪ'mɜrʒən, -ʃən/ *n.* **1.** [*count*] the act of immersing: *a quick immersion into local politics.* **2.** [*noncount*] the state of being immersed. See -MERG-.

im•mi•grant (im′i grənt) /'ɪmɪgrənt/ *n.* [*count*] **1.** one who immigrates: *laws against immigrants who tried to get work.* **—*adj.*** [*before a noun*] **2.** of or relating to immigrants and immigration: *a department of immigrant affairs.* See -MIGR-.

im•mi•grate (im′i grāt′) /'ɪmɪ,greyt/ *v.* [~ + *to* + *obj*], **-grat•ed, -grat•ing.** to come to a country of which one is not a native, usually to live there permanently: *They immigrated to the United States in the 1850's.* See -MIGR-. **—Usage.** Note carefully the difference between EMIGRATE and IMMIGRATE, both of which involve travel and a country. When you EMIGRATE you come out of a country, or leave it; the preposition to use is FROM: *She found it hard to emigrate from her home country.* With IMMIGRATE the action is to the new country you are going toward or entering; the preposition is usually TO: *She immigrated to the United States in 1907.*

im•mi•gra•tion (im′ə grā′shən) /,ɪmə'greyʃən/ *n.* [*noncount*] the act of immigrating: *Immigration to that country rose in the early part of the century.* See -MIGR-.

im•mi•nent (im′ə nənt) /'ɪmənənt/ *adj.* likely to occur at any moment: *the imminent collapse of communism.* **—im′mi•nence,** *n.* [*noncount*] **—im′mi•nent•ly,** *adv.*

im•mo•bile (i mō′bəl, -bēl) /ɪ'mowbəl, -biyl/ *adj.* **1.** incapable of moving or being moved: *The straps kept him immobile on the operating table.* **2.** not mobile or moving; motionless: *He stood immobile and unseeing.* **—im•mo•bil•i•ty** (im′ō bil′i tē) /,ɪmow'bɪlɪtiy/ *n.* [*noncount*] See -MOB-.

im•mo•bil•ize (i mō′bə līz) /ɪ'mowbəlayz/ *v.* [~ + *obj*], **-lized, -liz•ing.** to cause to be immobile: *The drug immobilized his arms and legs.* **—im•mo•bi•li•za•tion** (i mō′bə li zā′shən) /ɪ,mowbəlɪ'zeyʃən/ *n.* [*noncount*] See -MOB-.

im•mod•er•ate (i mod′ər it) /ɪ'mɒdərɪt/ *adj.* going beyond what is proper; excessive: *immoderate eating.* **—im•mod′er•ate•ly,** *adv.* **—im•mod•er•a•tion** (i mod′ə-rā′shən) /ɪ,mɒdə'reyʃən/ *n.* [*noncount*] See -MOD-.

im•mod•est (i mod′ist) /ɪ'mɒdɪst/ *adj.* **1.** indecent; shameless: *wouldn't let her wear that bathing suit because it was immodest for a teenager.* **2.** not modest; claiming to be important: *made immodest statements about his own talent.* **—im•mod′est•ly,** *adv.* See -MOD-.

im•mo•late (im′ə lāt′) /'ɪmə,leyt/ *v.* [~ + *obj*], **-lat•ed, -lat•ing.** to kill (someone or some animal) as a victim in a sacrifice, as by fire; offer in sacrifice: *The young students immolated themselves to protest the repressive regime.* **—im•mo•la•tion** (im′ə lā′shən) /,ɪmə'leyʃən/ *n.* [*noncount*]

im•mor•al (i môr′əl, i mor′-) /ɪ'mɔrəl, ɪ'mɒr-/ *adj.* **1.** going against moral principles: *The protesters considered the war immoral.* **2.** not moral, esp. in sexual matters: *an immoral movie.* **—im•mor′al•ly,** *adv.* See -MOR-.

im•mo•ral•i•ty (im′ə ral′i tē, im′ô-) /,ɪmə'rælɪtiy, ,ɪmɔ-/ *n., pl.* **-ties. 1.** [*noncount*] immoral quality or conduct: *the immorality of the war.* **2.** [*noncount*] sexual misconduct: *His immorality was frowned on by the church members.* **3.** [*count*] an immoral act. See -MOR-.

im•mor•tal (i môr′tl) /ɪ'mɔrtl/ *adj.* **1.** not mortal; not liable or subject to death: *immortal souls.* **2.** that will not decay; everlasting: *immortal wisdom.* **3.** perpetual; constant: *an immortal enemy.* **—*n.*** [*count*] **4.** an immortal being: *"I want to be an immortal and live forever," she exclaimed.* **5.** a person of long-lasting fame: *one of baseball's immortals.* **—im•mor′tal•ly,** *adv.* See -MORT-.

im•mor•tal•i•ty (im′ôr tal′i tē) /,ɪmɔr'tælɪtiy/ *n.* [*noncount*] **1.** immortal condition or quality: *Most religions say something about immortality.* **2.** long-lasting fame: *achieved immortality on the Hollywood screen.* See -MORT-.

im•mor•tal•ize (i môr′tl iz′) /ɪ'mɔrtl̩,ayz/ *v.* [~ + *obj*], **-ized, -iz•ing. 1.** to bestow immortality: *Tom and Huck were immortalized in the writings of Mark Twain.* **2.** to make immortal; give (someone) immortality: *Did the Greek gods have the power to immortalize the figures in mythology?* See -MORT-.

im•mov•a•ble or **im•move•a•ble** (i mōō′və bəl) /ɪ'muwvəbəl/ *adj.* **1.** incapable of being moved: *The chairs and desks in that classroom were immovable.* **2.** not moving; motionless; immobile: *stood immovable in the forest.* **3.** unaffected by feeling; unyielding: *an immovable heart.* See -MOV-.

im•mune (i myōōn′) /ɪ'myuwn/ *adj.* **1.** [*be/become* + ~ + *to*] protected from a disease, as by an injection: *had to take yellow fever shots to become immune to that disease.* **2.** [*before a noun*] of or relating to the production of special cells in the body that combat disease: *an im-*

mune reaction. **3.** [*be* + ~ + *from*] exempt; protected; able to escape: *promised he would be immune from prosecution.* **4.** [*be* + ~ + *to*] not responsive to or affected by something: *has to be immune to harsh words and criticism in his job.* —**im•mu′ni•ty,** *n.* [*noncount*]: *promised immunity in exchange for his testimony.*

im•mu•nize (im′yə nīz′, i myōō′nīz) /ˈɪmyəˌnayz, ɪˈmyuwnayz/ *v.* [~ + *obj*], **-nized, -niz•ing.** to make immune: *The vaccine immunized her against measles.* —**im•mu•ni•za•tion** (im′yə ni zā′shən, i myōō′-) /ˌɪmyənɪˈzeyʃən, ɪˌmyuw-/ *n.* [*noncount*]: *Immunization just wasn't practical.* [*count*]: *The doctors continued with the immunizations.*

im•mu•ta•ble (i myōō′tə bəl) /ɪˈmyuwtəbəl/ *adj.* unchangeable: *the immutable laws of physics.* —**im•mu•ta•bil•i•ty** (i myōō′tə bil′i tē) /ɪˌmyuwtəˈbɪlɪtiy/ *n.* [*noncount*] —**im•mu′ta•bly,** *adv.* See -MUT-.

imp (imp) /ɪmp/ *n.* [*count*] **1.** a small devil or demon. **2.** a mischievous child: *That little imp spilled his cereal all over the floor!*

imp., an abbreviation of: **1.** imperative. **2.** imperfect. **3.** imperial. **4.** import. **5.** imprint.

im•pact (*n.* im′pakt; *v.* im pakt′) / *n.* ˈɪmpækt; *v.* ɪmˈpækt/ *n.* **1.** the striking of one thing against another; collision: [*noncount*]: *The atomic particles break apart on impact with others.* [*count*]: *The bullet struck with a tremendous impact.* **2.** [*noncount*] influence, as the force carried by a new idea, etc.: *the impact of Einstein on modern physics.* —*v.* **3.** [~ + *obj*] to drive or press (something) closely or firmly into something. **4.** [~ + *obj*] to collide with: *The rocket was designed to impact the planet Mars.* **5.** to have an impact or effect on; influence: [~ + *obj*]: *The decision may impact your whole career.* [~ + *on* + *obj*]: *Increased demand will impact on sales.* See -PACT-.

im•pact•ed (im pak′tid) /ɪmˈpæktɪd/ *adj.* **1.** (of a tooth) so positioned that normal growth out of the gum is impossible: *impacted wisdom teeth.* **2.** driven together; tightly packed. **3.** densely populated; overcrowded: *an impacted school district.* See -PACT-.

im•pair (im pâr′) /ɪmˈpɛər/ *v.* [~ + *obj*] to make worse; damage: *Smoking can impair your health.* —**im•pair′ment,** *n.* [*noncount*]: *impairment of the learning process.* [*count*]: *a hearing impairment.*

im•pal•a (im pal′ə, -pä′lə) /ɪmˈpælə, -ˈpɑlə/ *n.* [*count*], *pl.* **-pal•as,** (*esp. when thought of as a group*) **-pal•a.** an African antelope, the male of which has ringed horns.

im•pale (im pāl′) /ɪmˈpeyl/ *v.* [~ + *obj*], **-paled, -pal•ing.** to pierce through (something or someone's body): *The spear impaled his wrist.*

im•pal•pa•ble (im pal′pə bəl) /ɪmˈpælpəbəl/ *adj.* **1.** incapable of being felt; intangible: *Impalpable gloom fell over the room.* **2.** difficult for the mind to grasp easily: *impalpable theories.* —**im•pal′pa•bly,** *adv.*

im•pan•el (im pan′l) /ɪmˈpænl/ also **empanel,** *v.* [~ + *obj*], **-eled, -el•ing** or (*esp. Brit.*) **-elled, -el•ling. 1.** to enter on a panel for jury duty: *She was impaneled on her first day of jury duty.* **2.** to select (a jury) from a panel: *The jury was impaneled and the trial began.*

im•part (im pärt′) /ɪmˈpɑrt/ *v.* [~ + *obj* (+ *to* + *obj*)] **1.** to make known; disclose: *to impart the findings.* **2.** to give; bestow: *Those spices impart a real sense of India to this food.* See -PAR-.

im•par•tial (im pär′shəl) /ɪmˈpɑrʃəl/ *adj.* fair; just; not partial or biased: *Stay impartial until you have heard both sides.* —**im•par•ti•al•i•ty** (im pär′shē al′i tē) /ɪmˌpɑrʃiyˈælɪtiy/ *n.* [*noncount*] —**im•par′tial•ly,** *adv.*: *The judge decided the case impartially.*

im•pass•a•ble (im pas′ə bəl) /ɪmˈpæsəbəl/ *adj.* not allowing passage: *Snow made the highways impassable.* See -PASS[1]-.

im•passe (im′pas) /ˈɪmpæs/ *n.* [*count; usually singular*] a situation from which there is no escape: *The discussions reached an impasse.* See -PASS-[1].

im•pas•sioned (im pash′ənd) /ɪmˈpæʃənd/ *adj.* filled with intense feeling or passion: *an impassioned plea for forgiveness.* —**im•pas′sioned•ly,** *adv.* See -PASS-[2].

im•pas•sive (im pas′iv) /ɪmˈpæsɪv/ *adj.* showing or feeling no emotion: *remained impassive in spite of our pleas for help.* —**im•pas′sive•ly,** *adv.*: *watched impassively as they led her son to the gallows.* —**im•pas•siv•i•ty** (im′pa siv′i tē) /ˌɪmpæˈsɪvɪtiy/ *n.* [*noncount*] See -PASS-[2].

im•pa•tience (im pā′shəns) /ɪmˈpeyʃəns/ *n.* [*noncount*] **1.** unwillingness to tolerate anything that hinders; irritation at having to wait for something: *My impatience grew as the train was delayed more and more.* **2.** eager desire for relief or change; restlessness. See -PAT-.

im•pa•tient (im pā′shənt) /ɪmˈpeyʃənt/ *adj.* **1.** of or relating to impatience: *The impatient teacher demanded that we answer her questions immediately.* **2.** indicating lack of patience: *an impatient answer.* **3.** [*be* + ~ + *to* + *verb*] eagerly desirous: *was impatient to finish her dinner and go out and play.* —**im•pa′tient•ly,** *adv.*: *waited impatiently in the car.* See -PAT-.

im•peach (im pēch′) /ɪmˈpiytʃ/ *v.* [~ + *obj*] **1.** to accuse (a public official) of misconduct in office by bringing charges before an appropriate court or place of hearing: *The Judiciary Committee would have voted to impeach the president.* **2.** to challenge whether (a person) is telling the truth: *to impeach a witness.* —**im•peach′a•ble,** *adj.*: *an impeachable offense.* —**im•peach′er,** *n.* [*count*] —**im•peach′ment,** *n.* [*noncount*]: *Was the crime really worthy of impeachment?* [*count*]: *The country hasn't had an impeachment in decades.*

im•pec•ca•ble (im pek′ə bəl) /ɪmˈpɛkəbəl/ *adj.* faultless; flawless: *impeccable manners.* —**im•pec•ca•bil•i•ty** (im-pek′ə bil′i tē) /ɪmˌpɛkəˈbɪlɪtiy/ *n.* [*noncount*] —**im•pec′ca•bly,** *adv.*: *The children behaved impeccably.*

im•pe•cu•ni•ous (im′pi kyōō′nē əs) /ˌɪmpɪˈkyuwniyəs/ *adj.* having little or no money; penniless. —**im′pe•cu′ni•ous•ly,** *adv.* —**im′pe•cu′ni•ous•ness,** *n.* [*noncount*]

im•pede (im pēd′) /ɪmˈpiyd/ *v.* [~ + *obj*], **-ped•ed, -ped•ing.** to cause to slow down in movement or progress: *A lumber shortage impeded construction of the new house.* See -PED-[1].

im•ped•i•ment (im ped′ə mənt) /ɪmˈpɛdəmənt/ *n.* [*count*] **1.** something that impedes; a hindrance: *impediments to the peace process.* **2.** a physical problem that interferes with normal speech: *a speech impediment.* See -PED-[1].

im•pel (im pel′) /ɪmˈpɛl/ *v.* [~ + *obj*], **-pelled, -pel•ling. 1.** to urge forward; to force (to some action): *The economic conditions impelled us.* [~ + *obj* + *to* + *verb*]: *Financial problems impelled the firm to cut its budget.* **2.** to impart motion to: *The wheel acts to impel the shaft.* —**im•pel′ler,** *n.* [*count*] See -PEL-.

im•pend•ing (im pend′ing) /ɪmˈpɛndɪŋ/ *adj.* [*before a noun*] about to happen: *the impending crisis.* See -PEND-.

im•pen•e•tra•ble (im pen′i trə bəl) /ɪmˈpɛnɪtrəbəl/ *adj.* **1.** that cannot be penetrated: *an impenetrable barrier.* **2.** that cannot be understood: *an impenetrable mystery.* —**im•pen•e•tra•bil•i•ty** (im pen′i trə bil′i tē) /ɪmˌpɛnɪtrəˈbɪlɪtiy/ *n.* [*noncount*] —**im•pen′e•tra•bly,** *adv.*

im•pen•i•tent (im pen′i tənt) /ɪmˈpɛnɪtənt/ *adj.* feeling no regret about one's sins. —**im•pen′i•tence,** *n.* [*noncount*] See -PEN-.

imper., an abbreviation of: imperative.

im•per•a•tive (im per′ə tiv) /ɪmˈpɛrətɪv/ *adj.* **1.** [*usually: It* + *be* + ~ + *(that) clause*] absolutely necessary: *It is imperative that we leave.* **2.** of the nature of, or expressing, a command; of or naming a grammatical mood used in commands, as in *Listen! Go!* Compare INDICATIVE (def. 2), SUBJUNCTIVE (def. 1). —*n.* **3.** [*count*] a command; order. **4.** [*count*] an unavoidable requirement: *the imperatives of leadership.* **5.** [*noncount; usually: the* + ~] the imperative mood; a verb form in this mood: *Use the imperative in this sentence.* —**im•per′a•tive•ly,** *adv.*

im•per•cep•ti•ble (im′pər sep′tə bəl) /ˌɪmpərˈsɛptəbəl/ *adj.* very difficult to notice; subtle; not able to be easily perceived: *At first the uphill slope of the road was imperceptible, but it became steeper.* —**im•per•cep•ti•bil•i•ty** (im′pər sep′tə bil′i tē) /ˌɪmpərˌsɛptəˈbɪlɪtiy/ *n.* [*noncount*] —**im′per•cep′ti•bly,** *adv.* See -CEP-.

imperf., an abbreviation of: imperfect.

im•per•fect (im pûr′fikt) /ɪmˈpɜrfɪkt/ *adj.* **1.** of, relating to, or having defects or weaknesses: *imperfect vision.* **2.** lacking completeness: *imperfect knowledge.* **3.** of or naming a verb tense or form that shows a repeated, habitual, or continuing action or state in the past, or an action or state that was in progress at a point of reference in the past: *The Spanish verb form* hablaban, *which means "they used to speak" or "they were speaking," is in the imperfect tense.* —*n.* [*noncount; usually: the* + ~] **4.** the imperfect tense; a verb form in this tense: *Use the imperfect in the next two sentences.* —**im•per′fect•ly,** *adv.*: *I spoke English imperfectly at first.* —**im•per′fect•ness,** *n.* [*noncount*] See -FEC-.

im•per•fec•tion (im′pər fek′shən) /ˌɪmpərˈfɛkʃən/ *n.* **1.** [*count*] a fault; flaw: *These shirts are cheaper because of a few minor imperfections.* **2.** [*noncount*] the quality or state of being imperfect: *Don't settle for imperfection; try for perfection.* See -FEC-.

im•pe•ri•al (im pēr′ē əl) /ɪmˈpɪəriyəl/ *adj.* [*before a* *noun*] **1.** of, relating to, or characteristic of an empire or emperor: *the imperial powers of the nineteenth century.* **2.** (of weights and measures) agreeing with or using standards legally established in Great Britain: *An imperial gallon equals roughly five American quarts.* —**im•pe′ri•al•ly,** *adv.*

im•pe•ri•al•ism (im pēr′ē ə liz′əm) /ɪm'pɪəriyəˌlɪzəm/ *n.* [*noncount*] the policy of extending the rule or authority of an empire over foreign countries: *The loss of India was a blow to British imperialism.* —**im•pe′ri•al•ist,** *n.* [*count*], *adj.*: *the imperialist forces against the socialist forces.* —**im•pe′ri•al•is′tic,** *adj.*

im•per•il (im per′əl) /ɪm'pɛrəl/ *v.* [~ + *obj*], **-iled, -il•ing** or (*esp. Brit.*) **-illed, -il•ling.** to put in peril or danger; endanger. —**im•per′il•ment,** *n.* [*noncount*]

im•pe•ri•ous (im pēr′ē əs) /ɪm'pɪəriyəs/ *adj.* domineering; having a manner of acting that looks down at others: *The vice-president's imperious manner annoyed her subordinates.* —**im•pe′ri•ous•ly,** *adv.*: *She gestured imperiously at me to leave her room.* —**im•pe′ri•ous•ness,** *n.* [*noncount*]

im•per•ish•a•ble (im per′i shə bəl) /ɪm'pɛrɪʃəbəl/ *adj.* **1.** that will not perish: *some imperishable foods, like canned goods.* —*n.* [*count*] **2.** food that is not subject to decay or that does not spoil easily: *had to stock up on imperishables for the long winter ahead.*

im•per•ma•nent (im pûr′mə nənt) /ɪm'pɜrmənənt/ *adj.* not permanent: *impermanent physical beauty.* —**im•per′ma•nence,** *n.* [*noncount*]: *the impermanence of physical beauty.* —**im•per′ma•nent•ly,** *adv.* See -MAN-[2].

im•per•me•a•ble (im pûr′mē ə bəl) /ɪm'pɜrmiyəbəl/ *adj.* (of porous substances, etc.) not permitting a fluid to pass through: *The tree cells have an impermeable membrane.* —**im•per•me•a•bil•i•ty** (im pûr′mē ə bil′i tē) /ɪmˌpɜrmiyə'bɪlɪtiy/ *n.* [*noncount*] —**im•per′me•a•bly,** *adv.*

im•per•mis•si•ble (im′pər mis′ə bəl) /ˌɪmpər'mɪsəbəl/ *adj.* not permissible: *impermissible crimes.* See -MIS-.

im•per•son•al (im pûr′sə nl) /ɪm'pɜrsənl̩/ *adj.* **1.** lacking reference to a person: *impersonal remarks.* **2.** without human traits: *an impersonal god.* **3.** lacking human emotion or warmth: *a cold, impersonal letter of rejection.* **4.** [*before a noun*] **a.** (of a verb) having only third person singular forms and used without an expressed subject, as Latin *pluit* "it is raining," or occurring with an empty subject word, as the English verb *rain* in *It is raining.* **b.** (of a pronoun) indefinite, as French *on* "one." —**im•per′son•al•ly,** *adv.*

im•per•son•ate (im pûr′sə nāt′) /ɪm'pɜrsəˌneyt/ *v.* [~ + *obj*], **-at•ed, -at•ing. 1.** to assume the character or appearance of (someone else); pretend to be: *arrested for impersonating a police officer.* **2.** to imitate the voice, behavior, etc., of (another person) to entertain: *When he impersonates the president the audience laughs hysterically.* —**im•per•son•a•tion** (im pûr′sə nā′shən) /ɪmˌpɜrsə'neyʃən/ *n.* [*noncount*]: *Impersonation of a police officer is against the law.* [*count*]: *Her impersonations of me had me laughing uncontrollably.* —**im•per′son•a′tor,** *n.* [*count*]: *a female impersonator.*

im•per•ti•nent (im pûr′tn ənt) /ɪm'pɜrtn̩ənt/ *adj.* rude; disrespectful: *an impertinent reply.* —**im•per′ti•nence,** *n.* [*noncount*] —**im•per′ti•nent•ly,** *adv.* See -TEN-.

im•per•turb•a•ble (im′pər tûr′bə bəl) /ˌɪmpər'tɜrbəbəl/ *adj.* incapable of being upset; calm: *remained his usual imperturbable self during the crisis.* —**im•per•turb•a•bil•i•ty** (im′pər tûr′bə bil′i tē) /ˌɪmpərˌtɜrbə'bɪlɪtiy/ *n.* [*noncount*] —**im′per•turb′a•bly,** *adv.*: *sitting there imperturbably through the uproar.* See -TURB-.

im•per•vi•ous (im pûr′vē əs) /ɪm'pɜrviyəs/ *adj.* **1.** not permitting passage through: *The raincoat is impervious to rain.* **2.** incapable of being injured or impaired: *impervious to wear and tear.* **3.** incapable of being influenced: *impervious to reason.* —**im•per′vi•ous•ly,** *adv.*

im•pe•ti•go (im′pi tī′gō) /ˌɪmpɪ'taygow/ *n.* [*noncount*] a skin infection with red swelling spots that form crusts. See -PET-.

im•pet•u•ous (im pech′o͞o əs) /ɪm'pɛtʃuwəs/ *adj.* of, relating to, or characterized by sudden or rash action or emotion; impulsive: *an impetuous youth.* —**im•pet•u•os•i•ty** (im pech′o͞o os′i tē) /ɪmˌpɛtʃuw'ɒsɪtiy/ *n.* [*noncount*] —**im•pet′u•ous•ly,** *adv.* See -PET-.

im•pe•tus (im′pi təs) /'ɪmpɪtəs/ *n., pl.* **-tus•es. 1.** [*count*] a force that moves one to action; impulse: *Some children need an impetus to study.* **2.** [*noncount*] the momentum of a moving body: *The sled zoomed downhill under its own impetus.* See -PET-.

im•pi•e•ty (im pī′i tē) /ɪm'payɪtiy/ *n., pl.* **-ties. 1.** [*noncount*] the quality or state of being impious. **2.** [*count*] an impious act or practice: *forgiveness for my impieties.*

im•pinge (im pinj′) /ɪm'pɪndʒ/ *v.* [~ + *on/upon*], **-pinged, -ping•ing. 1.** to intrude on; infringe: *to impinge on another's rights.* **2.** to strike; collide: *light that impinges on the lens.* **3.** to make an impression; have an effect. —**im•pinge′ment,** *n.* [*noncount*]

im•pi•ous (im′pē əs, im pī′-) /'ɪmpiyəs, ɪm'pay-/ *adj.* not pious; lacking reverence or respect for God or religion; irreligious. —**im′pi•ous•ly,** *adv.*

imp•ish (im′pish) /'ɪmpɪʃ/ *adj.* of, relating to, or like an imp; mischievous: *gave me an impish grin.* —**imp′ish•ly,** *adv.*: *grinning impishly.* —**imp′ish•ness,** *n.* [*noncount*]

im•plac•a•ble (im plak′ə bəl, -plā′kə-) /ɪm'plækəbəl, -'pleykə-/ *adj.* impossible to placate; not to be pacified or stopped: *an implacable enemy.* —**im•plac•a•bil•i•ty** (im plak′ə bil′i tē, -plā′kə-) /ɪmˌplækə'bɪlɪtiy, -ˌpleykə-/ *n.* [*noncount*] —**im•plac′a•bly,** *adv.*: *The enemy advanced implacably.* See -PLAC-.

im•plant (*v.* im plant′; *n.* im′plant′) / *v.* ɪm'plænt; *n.* 'ɪmˌplænt/ *v.* [~ + *obj*] **1.** to establish or fix firmly in the mind: *to implant principles of behavior.* **2.** to plant securely (in something): *to implant a post in the soil.* **3.** to insert or graft (a substance) into the body: *The doctors implanted the new heart in the patient.* —*n.* [*count*] **4.** a device or material used for repairing or replacing part of the body: *an organ implant.* —**im•plant′a•ble,** *adj.* —**im•plant′er,** *n.* [*count*]

im•plau•si•ble (im plô′zə bəl) /ɪm'plɔzəbəl/ *adj.* not plausible; unlikely: *the student's implausible story about a dog eating the computer disk.* —**im•plau•si•bil•i•ty** (im plô′zə bil′i tē) /ɪmˌplɔzə'bɪlɪtiy/ *n.* [*noncount*] —**im•plau′si•bly,** *adv.* See -PLAUD-.

im•ple•ment (*n.* im′plə mənt; *v.* also -ment′) / *n.* 'ɪmpləmənt; *v.* ælsɒ -ˌmɛnt/ *n.* [*count*] **1.** a tool or utensil for doing work: *household implements such as pots and pans.* —*v.* [~ + *obj*] **2.** to fulfill; carry out: *to implement campaign reform.* —**im•ple•men•ta•tion** (im′plə mən tā′shən) /ˌɪmpləmən'teyʃən/ *n.* [*noncount*]: *asking for assistance in the implementation of reforms.*

im•pli•cate (im′pli kāt′) /'ɪmplɪˌkeyt/ *v.* [~ + *obj*], **-cat•ed, -cat•ing.** to show or declare (someone else) to be involved, usually in committing a crime: *He was implicated in the robbery.* See -PLIC-.

im•pli•ca•tion (im′pli kā′shən) /ˌɪmplɪ'keyʃən/ *n.* **1.** [*count*] something implied: *The reporters discussed the implications of the president's speech.* **2.** [*noncount*] the state of being implicated: *his implication in the crime.* **3. by implication,** following from or implied by something else: *That policy was a failure, and so, by implication, was the president who had proposed it.* See -PLIC-.

im•plic•it (im plis′it) /ɪm'plɪsɪt/ *adj.* **1.** not stated directly; implied: *an implicit agreement.* **2.** [*usually: before a noun*] unquestioning; absolute; complete: *implicit trust.* **3.** potentially contained; part of a situation or circumstance that might be revealed; inherent: *aware of the drama implicit in the occasion of his death.* —**im•plic′it•ly,** *adv.*: *We agreed implicitly on most of the issues.* —**im•plic′it•ness,** *n.* [*noncount*] See -PLIC-.

im•plode (im plōd′) /ɪm'plowd/ *v.* [*no obj*], **-plod•ed, -plod•ing.** to burst inward (opposed to *explode*). —**im•plo•sion** (im plō′zhən) /ɪm'plɒʒən/ *n.* [*noncount*]: *the likelihood of implosion.* [*count*]: *An implosion would wreck most of the stabilizing gear.* —**im•plo•sive** (im plō′siv) /ɪm'plowsɪv/ *adj.* See -PLOD-.

im•plore (im plôr′, -plōr′) /ɪm'plɔr, -'plowr/ *v.*, **-plored, -plor•ing.** to beg urgently (for); beseech: [~ + *obj*]: *He implored her forgiveness.* [~ + *obj* + *to* + *verb*]: *They implored him not to go.* —**im•plor′ing,** *adj.*: *an imploring look.* —**im•plor′ing•ly,** *adv.*: *The dog looked imploringly at me.*

im•ply (im plī′) /ɪm'play/ *v.*, **-plied, -ply•ing. 1.** to indicate or suggest (something) without its being stated in words: [~ + *obj*]: *His actions implied a lack of faith.* [~ + *(that) clause*]: *The doctor's frown implied that something was wrong.* **2.** [~ + *obj*] to involve as a necessary circumstance; presuppose: *A fair trial implies a jury that is not biased.* See -PLIC-.

im•po•lite (im′pə līt′) /ˌɪmpə'layt/ *adj.* not polite; rude: *In the Japanese culture it is impolite to open a gift immediately.* —**im′po•lite′ly,** *adv.* See -POLI-.

im•pol•i•tic (im pol′i tik) /ɪm'pɒlɪtɪk/ *adj.* not politic; not expedient: *It was impolitic to complain about our situation, because others were suffering even more.* See -POLIS-.

im•pon•der•a•ble (im pon′dər ə bəl) /ɪm'pɒndərəbəl/ *adj.* **1.** that cannot be precisely measured or evaluated:

Imponderable factors may influence the results. —*n.* [*count*] **2.** something imponderable: *Her candidacy in the presidential race is another imponderable.* See -PEND-.

im•port (*v.* im pôrt′, -pōrt′; *n.* im′pôrt, -pōrt) / *v.* ɪm'pɔrt, -'powrt; *n.* 'ɪmpɔrt, -powrt/ *v.* [~ + *obj*] **1.** to bring in from a foreign country: *to import cars and computer parts.* **2.** to introduce from one use into another: *The word* input *was imported to computer usage to mean "type in to the computer."* **3.** to mean or signify; imply: *Her words imported a change of attitude.* —*n.* **4.** [*count*] something imported: *Imports rose again.* **5.** [*noncount*] the act of importing: *the import of cars.* **6.** [*noncount*] importance; consequence: *matters of great import.* **7.** [*noncount*] meaning; implication: *He felt the import of her words.* —**im•port′a•ble,** *adj.* —**im•port′er,** *n.* [*count*] See -PORT-.

im•por•tance (im pôr′tns) /ɪm'pɔrtns/ *n.* [*noncount*] the quality or state of being important: *the importance of brushing one's teeth every day.* See -PORT-.

im•por•tant (im pôr′tnt) /ɪm'pɔrtnt/ *adj.* **1.** of much or great effect, significance, or consequence: *an important event in history.* [*It* + *be* + ~ + *that clause*]: *It's important that you understand our position.* **2.** of great distinction, rank, or power: *an important scientist.* —**im•por′tant•ly,** *adv.*: *She works well with others, but more importantly, her record is the best in the company.* See -PORT-. —**Related Words.** IMPORTANT is an adjective, IMPORTANCE is a noun: *You missed a very important meeting. Was anything of importance discussed there?*

im•por•ta•tion (im′pôr tā′shən, -pōr-) /,ɪmpɔr'teyʃən, -powr-/ *n.* **1.** [*noncount*] the act of importing: *He fought against the importation of cheaper steel.* **2.** [*count*] something imported.

im•por•tu•nate (im pôr′chə nit) /ɪm'pɔrtʃənɪt/ *adj.* overly urgent in asking so as to be annoying: *importunate whining for video games.* —**im•por′tu•nate•ly,** *adv.*

im•por•tune (im′pôr to͞on′, -tyo͞on′) /,ɪmpɔr'tuwn, -'tyuwn/ *v.*, **-tuned, -tun•ing,** *adj.* —*v.* **1.** to urge with too much persistence so as to be annoying: [~ + *obj*]: *importuning him for a raise.* [*no obj*]: *importuning for a raise every day.* —*adj.* **2.** importunate. —**im′por•tun′i•ty,** *n.* [*noncount*]: *continuing importunity.* [*count*]: *obnoxious importunities on the streets.*

im•pose (im pōz′) /ɪm'powz/ *v.*, **-posed, -pos•ing. 1.** [~ + *obj*] to apply by authority; force the acceptance of: *to impose taxes.* **2.** to thrust (oneself) impolitely upon others: [*no obj*]: *Are you sure I'm not imposing, because I can come back later.* [~ + *on* + *obj*]: *She imposed on the boss for some help.* [~ + *oneself*]: *to impose oneself uninvited.* —**im•pos′er,** *n.* [*count*] See -POS-.

im•pos•ing (im pō′zing) /ɪm'powzɪŋ/ *adj.* impressive because of size, dignity, power, etc.: *The Empire State Building in New York is an imposing skyscraper.* —**im•pos′ing•ly,** *adv.* See -POS-.

im•po•si•tion (im′pə zish′ən) /,ɪmpə'zɪʃən/ *n.* **1.** [*noncount*] the act of imposing: *the imposition of a new sales tax.* **2.** [*count*] the act of pushing oneself on others: *It was a big imposition to drive her fifty miles just for a pizza.* See -POS-.

im•pos•si•ble (im pos′ə bəl) /ɪm'pɒsəbəl/ *adj.* **1.** not possible: *Traveling faster than the speed of light is impossible.* [*It* + *be* + ~ (+ *for* + *obj*) + *to* + *verb*]: *It's impossible (for anything) to travel faster than the speed of light.* **2.** extremely difficult: *in the impossible situation of having to increase output, cut workers, and reduce costs.* **3.** completely impractical: *an impossible plan.* **4.** hopelessly unsuitable, undesirable, or objectionable: *The kids have been impossible all day.* —**im•pos•si•bil•i•ty** (im pos′ə bil′i tē) /ɪm,pɒsə'bɪlɪtiy/ *n.* [*count*]: *the impossibility of arriving somewhere before you start to go there.* —**im•pos′si•bly,** *adv.* [*before an adjective or adverb*]: *The jet shot up into the sky impossibly fast.*

im•pos•tor or **im•post•er** (im pos′tər) /ɪm'pɒstər/ *n.* [*count*] one who pretends to be another in order to deceive someone: *One of these is an impostor; can you figure out which?* See -POS-.

im•po•tence (im′pə təns) /'ɪmpətəns/ *n.* [*noncount*] **1.** the lack of power to do what is necessary: *The general raged at his impotence as he watched the enemy blow up his bridges.* **2.** the condition in which a male is unable to make or keep the penis erect during sex. Also, **im′po•ten•cy.** See -POT-.

im•po•tent (im′pə tənt) /'ɪmpətənt/ *adj.* **1.** of or relating to impotence: *The police were impotent in the face of such large-scale rioting.* **2.** (of a male) unable to make or keep the penis erect during sex. —**im′po•tent•ly,** *adv.* See -POT-.

im•pound (im pound′) /ɪm'pawnd/ *v.* [~ + *obj*] to seize and keep (possessions, etc.) in the custody of the law: *a new law to impound any property owned by aliens.* See -POUND-.

im•pov•er•ish (im pov′ər ish, -pov′rish) /ɪm'pɒvərɪʃ, -'pɒvrɪʃ/ *v.* [~ + *obj*] **1.** to reduce to poverty: *The family was impoverished because neither parent could find work.* **2.** to exhaust the strength or vitality of: *Excessive farming impoverished the soil.* —**im•pov′er•ished,** *adj.*: *We lived in an impoverished African country.* —**im•pov′er•ish•ment,** *n.* [*noncount*]

im•prac•ti•ca•ble (im prak′ti kə bəl) /ɪm'præktɪkəbəl/ *adj.* not practicable: *Your idea to give everyone a computer workstation is impracticable.* —**im•prac′ti•ca•bly,** *adv.*

im•prac•ti•cal (im prak′ti kəl) /ɪm'præktɪkəl/ *adj.* **1.** not practical or useful: *Running a household without a budget is impractical.* [*it* + *be* + ~ (+ *for* + *obj*) + *to* + *verb*]: *It's impractical (for us) to run our household without a budget.* **2.** incapable of dealing sensibly with ordinary matters: *What an impractical professor; he can't even change a light bulb.* **3.** idealistic: *an impractical belief that everyone is good.* [*it* + *be* + ~ (+ *for* + *obj*) + *to* + *verb*]: *It's a bit impractical (for you) to hope that everyone will be nice to you.* **4.** IMPRACTICABLE. —**im•prac•ti•cal•i•ty** (im prak′ti kal′i tē) /ɪm,præktɪ'kælɪtiy/ *n.* [*noncount*]

im•pre•ca•tion (im′pri kā′shən) /,ɪmprɪ'keyʃən/ *n.* [*count*] **1.** the act of cursing or calling down evil on someone. **2.** a curse.

im•pre•cise (im′prə sīs′) /,ɪmprə'says/ *adj.* not precise: *imprecise when it came to explaining how many people would be fired.* —**im′pre•cise′ly,** *adv.* —**im•pre•ci•sion** (im′prə sizh′ən) /,ɪmprə'sɪʒən/ **im′pre•cise′ness,** *n.* [*noncount*]

im•preg•na•ble[1] (im preg′nə bəl) /ɪm'prɛgnəbəl/ *adj.* **1.** strong enough to withstand attack; unconquerable: *an impregnable fort.* **2.** that cannot be argued against or shown to be wrong: *impregnable proof.* —**im•preg•na•bil•i•ty** (im preg′nə bil′i tē) /ɪm,prɛgnə'bɪlɪtiy/ *n.* [*noncount*] —**im•preg′na•bly,** *adv.*

im•preg•na•ble[2] (im preg′nə bəl) /ɪm'prɛgnəbəl/ *adj.* that may become pregnant.

im•preg•nate (im preg′nāt) / ɪm'prɛgneyt / *v.* [~ + *obj*], **-nat•ed, -nat•ing. 1.** to make pregnant: *The dog was impregnated several months ago.* **2.** to fertilize: *The flower was impregnated with pollen.* **3.** to cause to enter and be spread or permeated throughout: *to impregnate a handkerchief with perfume.* —**im•preg•na•tion** (im′preg nā′shən) /,ɪmprɛg'neyʃən/ *n.* [*noncount*]

im•pre•sa•ri•o (im′prə sär′ē ō′, -sâr′-) /,ɪmprə'sɑriy,ow, -'sɛər-/ *n.* [*count*], *pl.* **-ri•os.** one who manages operas or concerts: *an impresario of rock concerts to raise money for charity.*

im•press (*v.* im pres′; *n.* im′pres) / *v.* ɪm'prɛs; *n.* 'ɪmprɛs/ *v.* **1.** [~ + *obj*] to affect (someone) deeply; influence: *impressed us as sincere.* **2.** [~ + *obj*] to create a favorable impression on (someone): *Her excellent work impressed me.* **3.** [~ + *on* + *obj* + *obj*] to establish firmly in the mind: *We impressed on her the necessity of being honest.* **4.** [~ + *obj*] to produce (a mark) by pressure as from a stamp; imprint: *to impress a picture of a duck by using a stamp pad and some ink.* **5.** [~ + *obj*] to furnish with a mark by or as if by stamping: *to impress the page with his seal.* —*n.* [*count*] **6.** a mark made by or as if by pressure. See -PRESS-.

im•pres•sion (im presh′ən) /ɪm'prɛʃən/ *n.* [*count*] **1.** a strong effect produced on the mind, feelings, or sense: *What were your impressions of Denmark after living there a year?* **2.** an image in the mind caused by something external: *the impression of sadness from a painting.* **3.** a somewhat vague awareness: *a general impression of distant voices.* **4.** a mark produced by pressure: *The dog's paws made cute little impressions in the sand.* **5.** an imitation of a famous person by an entertainer. —***Idiom.*** **6. be under the impression,** [~ + *(that) clause*] to have the (perhaps mistaken) opinion, belief, or feeling that: *I was under the impression that you were working for him.* See -PRESS-.

im•pres•sion•a•ble (im presh′ə nə bəl, -presh′nə-) /ɪm'prɛʃənəbəl, -'prɛʃnə-/ *adj.* capable of being easily impressed: *a young, impressionable mind.* See -PRESS-.

im•pres•sion•ism (im presh′ə niz′əm) /ɪm'prɛʃə,nɪzəm/ *n.* [*noncount*] **1.** [*usually: Impressionism*] a style of late 19th-century painting with short brush strokes of bright colors next to each other to represent the effect of light on objects. **2.** a style of literature or of musical composition that emphasizes mood and sensory impressions. See -PRESS-.

im•pres•sion•ist (im presh′ə nist) /ɪm'prɛʃənɪst/ *n.* [*count*] **1.** an artist who practices impressionism. **2.** an entertainer who does impressions: *the impressionist doing his imitations of the president.* **—***adj.* [*before a noun*] **3.** of or relating to artistic impressionism. See -PRESS-.

im•pres•sion•is•tic (im presh′ə nis′tik) /ɪmˌprɛʃə'nɪstɪk/ *adj.* **1.** of or relating to impressionism. **2.** relying on or based on images or effects produced on the mind; based on feelings or emotions rather than on facts: *In science you must avoid impressionistic statements and stick to observations.* See -PRESS-.

im•pres•sive (im pres′iv) /ɪm'prɛsɪv/ *adj.* causing admiration because of size, conduct, manner, etc.: *the impressive old castles of Ireland.* —**im•pres′sive•ly,** *adv.*: *The huge crater stretched out impressively before us.* —**im•pres′sive•ness,** *n.* [*noncount*] See -PRESS-.

im•pri•ma•tur (im′pri mä′tər, -mā′-, im prim′ə to͝or′, -tyo͝or′) /ˌɪmprɪ'mɑtər, -'mey-, ɪm'prɪməˌtʊr, -ˌtyʊr/ *n.* **1.** [*noncount*] permission to print or publish a book, etc., granted by a church authority. **2.** [*count; usually singular*] sanction; approval; permission: *Get the boss's imprimatur on that project.*

im•print (*n.* im′print; *v.* im print′) / *n.* 'ɪmprɪnt; *v.* ɪm'prɪnt/ *n.* [*count*] **1.** a mark impressed on something: *an imprint of shoes on wet concrete.* **2.** a long-lasting effect: *That tragic childhood incident left a strong imprint on him.* **—***v.* [~ + *obj*] **3.** to mark by or as if by pressure: *to imprint a book with a mark.* **4.** to produce (a mark) by pressure: *to imprint the seal on the document.* **5.** to fix firmly on the mind: *That day is imprinted on his memory forever.* —**im•print′er,** *n.* [*count*]

im•pris•on (im priz′ən) /ɪm'prɪzən/ *v.* [~ + *obj*] to confine in a prison: *They imprisoned him in a dark dungeon.* —**im•pris′on•ment,** *n.* [*noncount*]: *Imprisonment seemed so cruel.* [*count*]: *an imprisonment of a few years.*

im•prob•a•ble (im prob′ə bəl) /ɪm'prɒbəbəl/ *adj.* not probable; unlikely to be true or to happen: *an improbable ending to a story.* [*it* + *be* + ~ + *that clause*]: *It's improbable that we should win ten straight games.* —**im•prob•a•bil•i•ty** (im prob′ə bil′i tē) /ɪmˌprɒbə'bɪlɪtiy/ *n.* [*count*] —**im•prob′a•bly,** *adv.* See -PROB-.

im•promp•tu (im promp′to͞o, -tyo͞o) /ɪm'prɒmptuw, -tyuw/ *adj.* **1.** done without preparation: *an impromptu party.* **—***adv.* **2.** without preparation: *to deliver a speech impromptu.*

im•prop•er (im prop′ər) /ɪm'prɒpər/ *adj.* **1.** not belonging or applicable: *drew some improper conclusions.* **2.** not agreeing with what is proper: *improper conduct.* [*it* + *be* + ~ (+ *for* + *obj*) + *to* + *verb*]: *It was improper (for you) to make that offer.* **3.** abnormal; irregular: *signs of improper functioning.* **4.** not correct: *improper laboratory procedures.* —**im•prop′er•ly,** *adv.* See -PROPR-.

im•pro•pri•e•ty (im′prə prī′i tē) /ˌɪmprə'prayɪtiy/ *n., pl.* **-ties. 1.** [*noncount*] the quality or condition of being improper. **2.** [*count*] an improper act: *accused of financial improprieties.* See -PROPR-.

im•prove (im pro͞ov′) /ɪm'pruwv/ *v.,* **-proved, -prov•ing. 1.** to (cause to) become better: [~ + *obj*]: *Exercise improves one's health.* [*no obj*]: *His health seems to be improving.* **2.** [~ + *obj*] to increase the value of (real property) by remodeling or adding features: *improved the property by remodeling the bathroom.* **3. improve on,** [~ + *obj*] to produce something better than: *tried to improve on my previous supervisor's work by adding to what she had started.* —**im•prov′a•ble,** *adj.* See -PROV-.

im•prove•ment (im pro͞ov′mənt) /ɪm'pruwvmənt/ *n.* **1.** [*noncount*] an act of improving or the state of being improved: *signs of economic improvement.* **2.** [*count*] a change or addition by which a thing is improved: *to make improvements on a house.* See -PROV-.

im•prov•i•dent (im prov′i dənt) /ɪm'prɒvɪdənt/ *adj.* neglecting to provide for future needs. —**im•prov′i•dence,** *n.* [*noncount*] —**im•prov′i•dent•ly,** *adv.*

im•pro•vise (im′prə vīz′) /'ɪmprəˌvayz/ *v.,* **-vised, -vis•ing. 1.** to perform without preparation: [~ + *obj*]: *The teacher stood before his class and improvised a lecture.* [*no obj*]: *Good jazz musicians can improvise for any length of time.* **2.** to make, provide, or arrange (something) from available materials: [~ + *obj*]: *to improvise a dinner from the leftovers.* [*no obj*]: *Good teachers know how to improvise.* —**im•prov′i•sa′tion** (-prov′ə zā′shən) /-ˌprɒvə'zeyʃən/ *n.* [*noncount*]: *The comedian was good at improvisation.* [*count*]: *The musician performed a few improvisations on a theme.* —**im•prov•i•sa•tion•al** (im-prov′ə zā′shə nl) /ɪmˌprɒvə'zeyʃənl̩/ *adj.*: *improvisational humor.* —**im′pro•vis′er, im′pro•vi′sor,** *n.* [*count*]

im•pru•dent (im pro͞od′nt) /ɪm'pruwdnt/ *adj.* not prudent; lacking discretion: *imprudent behavior.* —**im•pru′dence,** *n.* [*noncount*]

im•pu•dent (im′pyə dənt) /'ɪmpyədənt/ *adj.* rude; very disrespectful: *an impudent child.* —**im′pu•dence,** *n.* [*noncount*]: *sent to the principal's office for impudence.* —**im′pu•dent•ly,** *adv.*

im•pugn (im pyo͞on′) /ɪm'pyuwn/ *v.* [~ + *obj*] to cast doubt upon: *The lawyer impugned the witness's story.* —**im•pugn′er,** *n.* [*count*] See -PUGN-.

im•pulse (im′puls) /'ɪmpʌls/ *n.* **1.** [*count*] the influence of a particular feeling, etc., to do something: *a sudden impulse to quit his job.* **2.** [*noncount*] sudden desire leading to action: *swayed by impulse.* **3.** [*count*] a pushing force that causes motion. **4.** [*count*] a single, usually sudden, flow of electric current or signal from the nerves to a muscle, in one direction: *to send out radio impulses that are picked up by the circling aircraft.* See -PULS-.

im•pul•sive (im pul′siv) /ɪm'pʌlsɪv/ *adj.* caused by or swayed by impulse: *an impulsive action.* —**im•pul′sive•ly,** *adv.*: *reached out impulsively and took his hand.* —**im•pul′sive•ness,** *n.* [*noncount*] See -PULS-.

im•pu•ni•ty (im pyo͞o′ni tē) /ɪm'pyuwnɪtiy/ *n.* [*noncount*] avoidance of punishment: *able to steal money with impunity.*

im•pure (im pyo͝or′) /ɪm'pyʊr/ *adj.* **1.** of or relating to impurity: *impure water.* **2.** not chaste: *He was having impure thoughts about his girlfriend.* —**im•pure′ly,** *adv.* See -PUR-.

im•pu•ri•ty (im pyo͝or′i tē) /ɪm'pyʊrɪtiy/ *n.* **1.** [*count*] a substance mixed with some other substance, making the other substance no longer pure: *Remove the impurities from the gasoline before it is ignited.* **2.** [*noncount*] the quality or state of being impure: *the sin of impurity.* See -PUR-.

im•pute (im pyo͞ot′) /ɪm'pyuwt/ *v.* [~ + *obj* + *to* + *obj*], **-put•ed, -put•ing. 1.** to believe that someone has (a quality, etc.): *The children imputed magical powers to the old woman.* **2.** to believe that someone or something is responsible for (something); to attribute (something) to someone or something: *The critics imputed the failure of the play to the director.* —**im•put′a•ble,** *adj.* —**im•pu•ta•tion** (im′pyo͞o tā′shən) /ˌɪmpyʊ'teyʃən/ *n.* [*noncount*] See -PUTE-.

in (in) /ɪn/ *prep.* **1.** This word is used before a noun that refers to space, a place, or to something that puts limits on something else, to show that the following noun includes something within it, contains something within it, or surrounds something: *They were walking in the park (= The park limits where they were walking, and surrounds them or contains them). The horses were galloping in the field. She was still in bed when I came home. The doll is in the box; leave it there.* **2.** This word is used before a noun that is abstract, cannot be touched, or refers to an occupation, interest, quality, characteristic, etc. It is used to show that the following noun includes or contains someone or something: *He was an important character in the play (= The play includes this character). She worked in politics. In the last section of the book we list irregular verbs. There was a lot of evil in his personality.* **3.** This word is used to show motion or direction from outside to a point within, and to mean "into": *Let's go in the house. Put the doll in the box.* **4.** This word is used before a noun that refers to a period of time, to show that something happens during that time, or occurs within a period or limit of that time: *in ancient times (= something happened during ancient times). We did the task in only ten minutes. I love Paris in the autumn. We will be there in an hour. She is an actress in her twenties.* **5.** This word is used with a following noun to show that the action, situation, condition, or manner of action is limited or described by that noun: *to speak in a whisper. They are similar in appearance. He was dressed in a kilt; she was in her pajamas. We were not afraid to meet in public. Smith shook his head in amazement.* **6.** This word is used with a noun to show that the action described is accomplished with the use of, or by means of, that noun: *speaking in French; written in ink.* **7.** This word is used with a noun, or a present participle form of a verb, to show what will result from some other action: *In showing his emotions so clearly, he risked losing his advantage.* **8.** This word is used to indicate a change from one state to another: *to break in half.* **9.** This word is used with a noun to indicate the aim or purpose of something: *speaking in honor of the event.* **10.** This word is used with a noun that describes the color of something: *The walls were in yellow.* —*adv.* **11.** in or into some place, position, state, relation, etc.: *Please come in. Have your papers handed in by Tuesday.* **12.** having arrived: *Her plane isn't in yet.* **13.** in one's house or office: *I wasn't in all day; I had to go to court.* **14.** in office or power: *That party has been voted in, but it may soon be voted out.* **15.** in possession or occupancy: *The doctor is in.* **16.** on good terms; in favor: *She got in good with her boss.* **17.** in season: *Watermelons will soon be in.* —*adj.* **18.** inner; internal: *the in part of a mechanism.* **19. a.** fashionable; stylish; in style: *It was the in place to dine. Wild, colorful hats are definitely in this year.* **b.** [*before a noun*] understood only by a special group: *an in joke.* **20.** [*before a noun*] included in a favored group: *She was never part of the in crowd.* **21.** plentiful; available. **22.** being in power: *the in party during the crisis.* —*n.* [*count*] **23.** Usually, **the ins.** persons who are in power: *The ins will continue to dominate.* **24.** pull or influence: *He's got an in with the senator.* —***Idiom.*** **25. in for,** certain to undergo (a disagreeable experience): *It looks as if we're in for stormy weather. The economy is in for another tough six months.* **26. in for it,** *Slang.* about to suffer punishment or unpleasant consequences: *We're in for it now, unless we can escape through the back before they catch us.* **27. have it in for,** [~ + *obj*] to cause difficulty for; to make trouble for: *That teacher seems to have it in for him; she's always picking on him.* **28. in that,** because; inasmuch as: *I expected a better price from that store in that I'd bought all my other computer equipment from them previously.* **29. the ins and outs of,** all the details or parts of: *a book on the ins and outs of photography.* —**Usage.** The most basic meaning of this word is that of general limits or boundaries put on places and actions. In referring to place and to time, *in* is the preposition that is more general and less specific in its meaning than AT and ON. Thus, we have *in Russia; in the autumn,* both of which are more general than *on Avenue C, on the twelfth of June and at 23rd Street and Lexington Avenue; at eight o'clock.* See the note under AT.

IN, an abbreviation of: Indiana.

in-[1], *prefix. in-* is attached to verbs and nouns and means "in; into; on:" *in- + come → income (= money coming in); in- + corporate (= body) → incorporate (= make into one body); in- + land → inland (= in the land).*

in-[2], *prefix. in-* is attached to adjectives and means "not:" *in- + accurate → inaccurate (= not accurate); in- + capable → incapable (= not capable); in- + direct → indirect (= not direct).* For variants before other sounds, see IM-, IL-, IR-.

-in, *suffix. -in* is attached to some verbs to form nouns that refer to organized protests through, using, or in support of the named activity: *sit + -in → sit-in (= a protest in which participants sit and block passage).*

in., an abbreviation of: inch.

in•a•bil•i•ty (in′ə bil′i tē) /ˌɪnəˈbɪlɪtiy/ *n.* lack of ability: [*noncount*]: *failed through obvious inability.* [*count; usually singular*]: *an obvious inability to deal with the facts.*

in ab•sen•tia (in ab sen′shə, -shē ə) /ɪn æbˈsɛnʃə, -ʃiyə/ *adv. Latin.* in absence: *to be tried for his crimes in absentia.*

in•ac•ces•sible (in′ək ses′ə bl) /ˌɪnəkˈsɛsəbl/ *adj.* that cannot be reached: *an inaccessible hideaway in the mountains.* —**in•ac•ces•si•bil•i•ty** (in ək ses′ə bil′i tē) /ɪnəkˌsɛsəˈbɪlɪtiy/ *n.* [*noncount*] —**in•ac•ces′si•bly,** *adv.*

in•ac•cu•ra•cy (in ak′yər ə sē) /ɪnˈækyərəsiy/ *n., pl.* **-cies. 1.** [*count*] something inaccurate; an error: *He complained about the inaccuracies in the report about him.* **2.** [*noncount*] the act or state of being inaccurate: *He couldn't tolerate inaccuracy in his newspaper.* See -CURA-.

in•ac•cu•rate (in ak′yər it) /ɪnˈækyərɪt/ *adj.* not accurate; incorrect: *an inaccurate statement.* —**in•ac′cu•rate•ly,** *adv.* See -CURA-.

in•ac•tion (in ak′shən) /ɪnˈækʃən/ *n.* [*noncount*] absence of action or of activity; idleness.

in•ac•ti•vate (in ak′tə vāt′) /ɪnˈæktəˌveyt/ *v.* [~ + *obj*], **-vat•ed, -vat•ing.** to make inactive. —**in•ac•ti•va•tion** (in ak′tə vā′shən) /ɪnˌæktəˈveyʃən/ *n.* [*noncount*]

in•ac•tive (in ak′tiv) /ɪnˈæktɪv/ *adj.* **1.** not active: *an inactive volcano.* **2.** quiet; not doing much: *an inactive, boring retirement.* **3.** *Military.* not on active duty. —**in•ac•tiv•i•ty** (in′ak tiv′i tē) /ˌɪnækˈtɪvɪtiy/ *n.* [*noncount*]: *a boring inactivity once he retired.*

in•ad•e•qua•cy (in ad′ə kwə sē) /ɪnˈædəkwəsiy/ *n., pl.* **-cies. 1.** [*noncount*] the state or condition of being inadequate: *fearing inadequacy in dealing with people.* **2.** [*count*] something inadequate; a defect: *There are several obvious inadequacies in your plan.*

in•ad•e•quate (in ad′i kwit) /ɪnˈædɪkwɪt/ *adj.* not adequate or sufficient. —**in•ad′e•quate•ly,** *adv.*

in•ad•mis•si•ble (in əd mis′ə bəl) /ɪnədˈmɪsəbəl/ *adj.* that cannot be used as evidence in a court of law. See -MIS-.

in•ad•vert•ent (in′əd vûr′tnt) /ˌɪnədˈvɜrtnt/ *adj.* **1.** unintentional: *an inadvertent insult.* **2.** not attentive: *He was inadvertent and knocked over his glass.* —**in′ad•vert′•ence,** *n.* [*noncount*] —**in′ad•vert′ent•ly,** *adv.*: *I inadvertently overheard her conversation.* See -VERT-.

in•ad•vis•a•ble (in′əd vī′zə bəl) /ˌɪnədˈvayzəbəl/ *adj.* not advisable; unwise; not sensible: *an inadvisable plan.* [*it + be + ~ (+ for + obj) + to + verb*]: *It would be inadvisable (for me) to approach him while he's still angry.* See -VIS-.

in•al•ien•a•ble (in āl′yə nə bəl, -ā′lē ə-) /ɪnˈeylyənəbəl, -ˈeyliyə-/ *adj.* not alienable; that cannot be taken away; not transferable to another: *inalienable rights.* —**in•al•ien•a•bil•i•ty** (in āl′yə nə bil′i tē, -ā′lē ə-) /ɪnˌeylyənəˈbɪlɪtiy, -ˌeyliyə-/ *n.* [*noncount*] —**in•al′ien•a•bly,** *adv.* See -ALI-.

in•am•o•ra•ta (in am′ə rä′tə, in′am-) /ɪnˌæməˈrɑtə, ˌɪnæm-/ *n.* [*count*], *pl.* **-tas.** a woman who loves or is loved; a female lover. See -AM-.

in•ane (i nān′) /ɪˈneyn/ *adj.* **1.** lacking sense, significance, or ideas; silly: *inane questions.* **2.** empty; pointless: *an inane remark about the weather.* —**in•ane′ly,** *adv.* —**in•an•i•ty** (i nan′i tē) /ɪˈnænɪtiy/ *n.* [*noncount*]: *a moment of sheer inanity.* [*count*]: *some inanities about the weather.*

in•an•i•mate (in an′ə mit) /ɪnˈænəmɪt/ *adj.* not animate; lifeless: *inanimate objects such as stones, cement, and logs.* —**in•an′i•mate•ly,** *adv.* —**in•an′i•mate•ness, in•an•i•ma•tion** (in an′ə mā′shən) /ɪnˌænəˈmeyʃən/ *n.* [*noncount*] See -ANIMA-.

in•ap•pli•ca•ble (in ap′li kə bəl, in′ə plik′ə bəl) /ɪnˈæplɪkəbəl, ˌɪnəˈplɪkəbəl/ *adj.* not suited; irrelevant: *Your idea is exciting but inapplicable.*

in•ap•pro•pri•ate (in′ə prō′prē it) /ˌɪnəˈprowpriyɪt/ *adj.* not appropriate; unsuited; improper: *thought wearing shorts to church was inappropriate.* [*it + be + ~ (+ for + obj) + to + verb*]: *It is inappropriate for his lawyer to make any public comments on the case.* —**in′ap•pro′•pri•ate•ly,** *adv.* See -PROPR-.

in•ar•tic•u•late (in′är tik′yə lit) /ˌɪnɑrˈtɪkyəlɪt/ *adj.* **1.** lacking the ability to express oneself clearly: *an inarticulate speaker.* **2.** unable to use words in speech: *inarticulate with rage.* **3.** not uttered or pronounced to express meaning: *a baby's inarticulate sounds.* —**in′ar•tic′u•late•ly,** *adv.* —**in′ar•tic′u•late•ness,** *n.* [*noncount*]

in•as•much as (in′əz much′ əz, az′) /ˌɪnəzˈmʌtʃ əz, ˌæz/ *conj.* **1.** in view of the fact that; since: *We might as well go in, inasmuch as we have come all this distance to be here.* **2.** insofar as; to such a degree as: *She'll help us, inasmuch as she is able.*

in•at•ten•tion (in′ə ten′shən) /ˌɪnəˈtɛnʃən/ *n.* [*noncount*] lack of attention; negligence. —**in•at•ten•tive** (in′ə ten′tiv) /ˌɪnəˈtɛntɪv/ *adj.*

in•aud•i•ble (in ô′də bəl) /ɪnˈɔdəbəl/ *adj.* that cannot be heard. —**in•au′dib•ly,** *adv.* See -AUD-.

in•au•gu•ral (in ô′gyər əl, -gər əl) /ɪnˈɔgyərəl, -gərəl/ *adj.* [*before a noun*] **1.** of or relating to an inauguration: *the president's inaugural address.* **2.** marking the beginning of a new business, etc.: *the inaugural run of the pony express.* —*n.* [*count*] **3.** an address at the beginning of a term of office. **4.** an inaugural ceremony.

in•au•gu•rate (in ô′gyə rāt′, -gə-) /ɪnˈɔgyəˌreyt, -gə-/ *v.* [~ + *obj*], **-rat•ed, -rat•ing. 1.** to make a formal beginning of; begin: *The end of World War II inaugurated the era of nuclear power.* **2.** to put (someone) into office with formal ceremonies; install: *He was inaugurated in January.* **3.** to introduce or cause to begin: *Airmail service was inaugurated in 1918.* —**in•au•gu•ra•tion** (in ô′gyə-rā′shən, -gə-) /ɪnˌɔgyəˈreyʃən, -gə-/ *n.* [*noncount*]: *inauguration of the new space flights.* [*count*]: *Inaugurations are held in January.*

in•aus•pi•cious (in′ô spish′əs) /ˌɪnɔˈspɪʃəs/ *adj.* not auspicious; unfavorable: *an inauspicious moment to arrive.* —**in′aus•pi′cious•ly,** *adv.* —**in′aus•pi′cious•ness,** *n.* [*noncount*]

in•board (in′bôrd′, -bōrd′) /ˈɪnˌbɔrd, -ˌbowrd/ *adj.* **1.** located inside a hull or aircraft. **2.** located nearer the center, as of an airplane. —*adv.* **3.** inside or toward the center of a machine, etc.

in•born (in′bôrn′) /ˈɪnˈbɔrn/ *adj.* naturally present at birth; innate: *the inborn ability to learn.*

in•bound (in′bound′) /ˈɪnˈbawnd/ *adj.* inward bound: *inbound ships.*

in•bred (in′bred′) /ˈɪnˈbrɛd/ *adj.* **1.** innate: *an inbred grace.* **2.** resulting from or involved in inbreeding.

in•breed•ing (in′brē′ding) /ˈɪnˌbriydɪŋ/ *n.* [*noncount*] the breeding or mating of closely related individuals.

inc., an abbreviation of: **1.** incomplete. **2.** incorporated. **3.** increase.

in•cal•cu•la•ble (in kal′kyə lə bəl) /ɪnˈkælkyələbəl/ *adj.* **1.** unable to be calculated: *the incalculable number of stars.* **2.** uncertain; unpredictable: *The future is incalculable.* —**in•cal′cu•la•bly,** *adv.: the incalculably many stars in the galaxy.*

in•can•des•cent (in′kən des′ənt) /ˌɪnkənˈdɛsənt/ *adj.* **1.** glowing or white with heat: *an incandescent lamp bulb.* **2.** extremely bright; brilliant: *incandescent wit.* —**in′can•des′cence,** *n.* [*noncount*] —**in′can•des′cent•ly,** *adv.*

in•can•ta•tion (in′kan tā′shən) /ˌɪnkænˈteyʃən/ *n.* the chanting or saying of magical words: [*noncount*]: *the incantation of odd-sounding syllables to ward off evil.* [*count*]: *prayers and incantations to the gods.*

in•ca•pa•ble (in kā′pə bəl) /ɪnˈkeypəbəl/ *adj.* **1.** [*be* + ~ + *of*] not having the necessary ability, qualification, or strength to perform some function: *incapable of doing such a difficult thing.* **2.** lacking ordinary capability; incompetent: *incapable management.* —**in•ca•pa•bil•i•ty** (in kā′pə bil′i tē) /ɪnˌkeypəˈbɪlɪtiy/ *n.* [*noncount*] —**in•ca′pa•bly,** *adv.*

in•ca•pac•i•tate (in′kə pas′i tāt′) /ˌɪnkəˈpæsɪˌteyt/ *v.* [~ + *obj*], **-tat•ed, -tat•ing. 1.** to deprive of ability; disable: *physically incapacitated as a result of his fall.* **2.** to deprive of legal power.

in•ca•pac•i•ty (in′kə pas′i tē) /ˌɪnkəˈpæsɪtiy/ *n.* [*noncount*] **1.** lack of ability or strength. **2.** lack of legal power to act.

in•car•cer•ate (in kär′sə rāt′) /ɪnˈkɑrsəˌreyt/ *v.* [~ + *obj*], **-at•ed, -at•ing.** to put in prison; confine. —**in•car′cer•a′tion,** *n.* [*noncount*]

in•car•nate (*adj.* in kär′nit, -nāt; *v.* -nāt) / *adj.* ɪnˈkɑrnɪt, -neyt; *v.* -neyt/ *adj., v.,* **-nat•ed, -nat•ing.** —*adj.* [*after a noun*] **1.** given a bodily, esp. a human, form: *a devil incarnate.* **2.** personified; typified: *The alien monster represents evil incarnate.*

in•car•na•tion (in′kär nā′shən) /ˌɪnkɑrˈneyʃən/ *n.* **1.** [*count; usually singular; usually: the* + ~] a person or thing personified: *That dancer is the incarnation of beauty and grace.* **2.** [*count*] the act or state of being given a bodily form: *She thought they had known each other in a previous incarnation.*

in•cen•di•ar•y (in sen′dē er′ē) /ɪnˈsɛndiyˌɛriy/ *adj., n., pl.* **-ar•ies.** —*adj.* [*before a noun*] **1.** used for setting property on fire: *incendiary bombs.* **2.** tending to arouse strife between groups; inflammatory: *incendiary speeches.* —*n.* [*count*] **3.** a device containing a substance that burns quickly with an intense heat: *flung incendiaries at the soldiers.*

in•cense[1] (in′sens) /ˈɪnsɛns/ *n.* [*noncount*] **1.** a substance producing a sweet odor when burned. **2.** the perfume or smoke arising from incense.

in•cense[2] (in sens′) /ɪnˈsɛns/ *v.* [~ + *obj*], **-censed, -cens•ing.** to arouse the anger of; enrage: *incensed that his friend had approached the boss without consulting him.* —**in•cense′ment,** *n.* [*noncount*]

in•cen•tive (in sen′tiv) /ɪnˈsɛntɪv/ *n.* something that arouses someone to action: [*noncount*]: *very little incentive to work.* [*count*]: *gave incentives to the farmers.*

in•cep•tion (in sep′shən) /ɪnˈsɛpʃən/ *n.* [*count*] beginning: *He's been on the TV show since its inception.*

in•cer•ti•tude (in sûr′ti to͞od′, -tyo͞od′) /ɪnˈsɜrtɪˌtuwd, -ˌtyuwd/ *n.* [*noncount*] uncertainty; doubtfulness. See -CERT-.

in•ces•sant (in ses′ənt) /ɪnˈsɛsənt/ *adj.* unending: *incessant noise.* —**in•ces′sant•ly,** *adv.: The music blared incessantly.* See -CESS-.

in•cest (in′sest) /ˈɪnsɛst/ *n.* [*noncount*] sexual relations between persons so closely related that they are forbidden to marry. —**in•ces′tu•ous** (in ses′cho͞o əs) /ɪnˈsɛstʃuwəs/ *adj.*

inch (inch) /ɪntʃ/ *n.* [*count*] **1.** a unit of length, 1⁄12 of a foot, equivalent to 2.54 centimeters. **2.** a very small amount, degree, or distance: *avoiding disaster by inches.* —*v.* **3.** to move by small degrees: [*no obj*]: *We inched slowly through the traffic.* [~ + *obj*]: *The driver inched her truck carefully into the spot.* —***Idiom.* 4. every inch,** in every respect; completely: *She's every inch a lady.* **5. within an inch of,** nearly; close to: *We came within an inch of being drowned.*

in•cho•ate (in kō′it, -āt) /ɪnˈkowɪt, -eyt/ *adj.* just beginning to exist or appear: *a child's inchoate social awareness.*

in•ci•dence (in′si dəns) /ˈɪnsɪdəns/ *n.* [*count; usually singular*] the rate or range of occurrence of something: *a high incidence of flu.* See -CIDE-.

in•ci•dent (in′si dənt) /ˈɪnsɪdənt/ *n.* [*count*] **1.** an occurrence or event: *an unpleasant incident at the office.* **2.** a minor event leading to serious consequences: *a minor border incident that erupted into a war.* —*adj.* **3.** likely to happen, often as a side effect: *hazards incident to the job.* **4.** falling or striking on something, such as light rays do. See -CIDE-.

in•ci•den•tal (in′si den′tl) /ˌɪnsɪˈdɛntl̩/ *adj.* **1.** likely to happen in an unplanned manner: *Incidental expenses were paid for by his employer.* —*n.* [*count*] **2.** something incidental. **3. incidentals,** [*plural*] minor expenses. See -CIDE-.

in•ci•den•tal•ly (in′si den′tl ē -dent′lē) /ˌɪnsɪˈdɛntl̩iy -ˈdɛntliy/ *adv.* apart or aside from the main subject; by the way: *Incidentally, if you want to see her again, let me know.* See -CIDE-.

in•cin•er•ate (in sin′ə rāt′) /ɪnˈsɪnəˌreyt/ *v.* [~ + *obj*], **-at•ed, -at•ing.** to burn to ashes: *The garbage was incinerated in the building.* —**in•cin•er•a•tion** (in sin′ə rā′shən) /ɪnˌsɪnəˈreyʃən/ *n.* [*noncount*]

in•cin•er•a•tor (in sin′ə rā′tər) /ɪnˈsɪnəˌreytər/ *n.* [*count*] a furnace or device for burning materials.

in•cip•i•ent (in sip′ē ənt) /ɪnˈsɪpiyənt/ *adj.* [*before a noun*] beginning to appear: *an incipient cold.* —**in•cip′i•ent•ly,** *adv.* See -CEP-.

in•cise (in sīz′) /ɪnˈsayz/ *v.* [~ + *obj*], **-cised, -cis•ing.** to cut into; cut marks upon: *to incise a wound.* See -CISE-.

in•ci•sion (in sizh′ən) /ɪnˈsɪʒən/ *n.* [*count*] **1.** a cut or gash. **2.** a surgical cut into tissue. See -CISE-.

in•ci•sive (in sī′siv) /ɪnˈsaysɪv/ *adj.* **1.** penetrating; cutting: *an incisive tone of voice.* **2.** clear and direct; keen: *an incisive analysis; incisive wit.* —**in•ci′sive•ly,** *adv.* —**in•ci′sive•ness,** *n.* [*noncount*] See -CISE-.

in•ci•sor (in sī′zər) /ɪnˈsayzər/ *n.* [*count*] any of the four frontmost teeth in each jaw, used for cutting and gnawing. See -CISE-.

in•cite (in sīt′) /ɪnˈsayt/ *v.,* **-cit•ed, -cit•ing.** to stimulate to action; stir up: [~ + *obj*]: *sentenced for inciting a riot.* [~ + *obj* + *to* + *verb*]: *The union incited the workers to strike.* —**in•cite′ment,** *n.* [*noncount*]: *No more incitement to riot was necessary.* [*count*]: *an incitement to riot.* —**in•cit′er,** *n.* [*count*]

in•ci•vil•i•ty (in′sə vil′i tē) /ˌɪnsəˈvɪlɪtiy/ *n., pl.* **-ties. 1.** [*noncount*] the quality or state of being uncivil or impolite: *no need for incivility.* **2.** [*count*] an uncivil or impolite act. —**in•civ•il** (in siv′əl) /ɪnˈsɪvəl/ *adj.*

incl., an abbreviation of: including.

in•clem•ent (in klem′ənt) /ɪnˈklɛmənt/ *adj.* **1.** stormy; bad: *inclement weather.* **2.** not kind or merciful. —**in•clem′en•cy,** *n.* [*noncount*]

in•cli•na•tion (in′klə nā′shən) /ˌɪnkləˈneyʃən/ *n.* [*count*] **1.** a special liking or feeling for something: *a great inclination for sports.* **2.** the act of moving from a higher place down; the state of being moved this way: *an inclination of the head.* **3.** an inclined surface.

in•cline (*v.* in klīn′; *n.* in′klīn, in klīn′) / *v.* ɪnˈklayn; *n.* ˈɪnklayn, ɪnˈklayn/ *v.,* **-clined, -clin•ing,** *n.* —*v.* **1.** to (cause to) slant, lean, or bend: [*no obj*]: *His head inclined toward me.* [~ + *obj*]: *He inclined his head toward me.* **2.** [*no obj*] to have a preference: *inclines toward mysticism.* **3.** [~ + *obj* + *to* + *verb*] to persuade; dispose: *Her attitude did not incline me to help her.* See INCLINED. —*n.* [*count*] **4.** an inclined surface; slant: *The truck could hardly make it up the incline.*

in•clined (in klīnd′) /ɪnˈklaynd/ *adj.* **1.** [*be* + ~ + *to* + *verb*] wanting to: *I'm inclined to believe you.* **2.** [*be* + ~ + *to* + *verb*] likely; having a tendency: *She's inclined to be very active.* **3.** [*be* + *adverb* + ~] naturally skilled; adept: *He's athletically inclined.* **4.** sloping; slanted: *an inclined plane; an inclined roof.*

in•clude (in klo͞od′) /ɪnˈkluwd/ *v.* [~ + *obj*], **-clud•ed, -clud•ing. 1.** [*not: be* + ~*-ing*] to contain or have as part of a whole: *The meal includes dessert and coffee.* **2.** to place (something) in a category: *Whom would you include in your list?* —**in•clu•sion** (in klo͞o′zhən) /ɪnˈkluwʒən/ *n.* [*noncount*]

in•clud•ed (in klo͞o′did) /ɪnˈkluwdɪd/ *adj.* [*after a noun*] being part of the whole; including: *The terrorists wanted everyone as hostages, children included.*

in•clud•ing (in klo͞o′ding) /ɪn'kluwdɪŋ/ *prep.* having as part of a whole; containing: *The terrorists wanted everyone as hostages, including the children.*

in•clu•sive (in klo͞o′siv) /ɪn'kluwsɪv/ *adj.* **1.** [*after a noun*] including the limit or extremes of (usually two numbers): *from 6 to 37 inclusive (= including 6 and 37).* **2.** including everything: *an inclusive fee.* ***—Idiom.*** **3. inclusive of,** [*after a noun*] including: *the plan involving Europe inclusive of Britain.* **—in•clu′sive•ly,** *adv.* **—in•clu′sive•ness,** *n.* [*noncount*]

in•cog•ni•to (in′kog nē′tō, in kog′ni tō′) /ˌɪnkɒg'niytow, ɪn'kɒgnɪˌtow/ *adj., adv.* with one's identity hidden or unknown: *The former president was incognito on the airplane. He was traveling incognito.* See -GNOS-.

in•co•her•ence (in′kō hēr′əns, -her′-) /ˌɪnkow'hɪərəns, -'hɛr-/ *n.* [*noncount*] the state or condition of being incoherent: *a speech full of incoherence.* See -HERE-.

in•co•her•ent (in′kō hēr′ənt, -her′-) /ˌɪnkow'hɪərənt, -'hɛr-/ *adj.* lacking logical connections; disorganized: *a lot of incoherent thoughts.* **—in′co•her′ent•ly,** *adv.* See -HERE-.

in•com•bus•ti•ble (in′kəm bus′tə bəl) /ˌɪnkəm'bʌstəbəl/ *adj.* not combustible; incapable of being burned.

in•come (in′kum) /'ɪnkʌm/ *n.* payment for goods or for services, or from rents or investments: [*count*]: *an annual income of $25,000.* [*noncount*]: *low income.*

in′come tax′, *n.* a tax on the incomes of individuals and corporations: [*noncount*]: *How much income tax did you pay?* [*count*]: *How much did you pay in state and federal income taxes last year?*

in•com•ing (in′kum′ing) /'ɪnˌkʌmɪŋ/ *adj.* [*before a noun*] **1.** coming in; arriving: *the incoming tide.* **2.** newly arrived: *incoming mail.* **3.** about to take office: *the incoming mayor.*

in•com•men•su•rate (in′kə men′sər it, -shər-) /ˌɪnkə'mɛnsərɪt, -ʃər-/ *adj.* not enough; inadequate; *income incommensurate with needs.* **—in′com•men′su•rate•ly,** *adv.*

in•com•mu•ni•ca•do (in′kə myo͞o′ni kä′dō) /ˌɪnkəˌmyuwnɪ'kɑdow/ *adj., adv.* without means of communicating with others: *was incommunicado for days; held him incommunicado.*

in•com•pa•ra•ble (in kom′pər ə bəl, -prə bəl) /ɪn'kɒmpərəbəl, -prəbəl/ *adj.* **1.** fine beyond comparison: *incomparable beauty.* **2.** not fit for comparison: *The two jobs are really incomparable.* See -PAR-.

in•com•pat•i•ble (in′kəm pat′ə bəl) /ˌɪnkəm'pætəbəl/ *adj.* **1.** unable to exist together in harmony: *incompatible roommates.* **2.** clashing; discordant: *incompatible colors.* **3.** unable to be used with another: *That computer is incompatible with mine.* **—*n.*** [*count*] **4.** Usually, **incompatibles.** [*plural*] an incompatible person or thing. **—in•com•pat•i•bil•i•ty** (in′kəm pat′ə bil′i tē) /ˌɪnkəmˌpætə'bɪlɪtiy/ *n.* [*noncount*]: *Computer manufacturers should solve the problem of incompatibility between systems.* **—in′com•pat′i•bly,** *adv.* See -PAT-.

in•com•pet•ence (in kom′pi təns) /ɪn'kɒmpɪtəns/ *n.* [*noncount*] **1.** the quality or condition of being incompetent: *transferred because of his incompetence.* **2.** the condition of being unable to act with legal effectiveness: *incompetence to stand trial.* See -PET-.

in•com•pe•tent (in kom′pi tənt) /ɪn'kɒmpɪtənt/ *adj.* **1.** lacking qualification or ability; incapable: *incompetent to do that work.* **2.** not legally qualified: *incompetent to stand trial.* **—*n.*** [*count*] **3.** an incompetent person, as one who is mentally deficient. **—in•com′pe•tent•ly,** *adv.* : *For years the company was incompetently managed.* See -PET-.

in•com•plete (in′kəm plēt′) /ˌɪnkəm'pliyt/ *adj.* lacking some part; not complete. **—in′com•plete′ly,** *adv.* **—in′com•plete′ness,** *n.* [*noncount*]

in•com•pre•hen•si•ble (in′kom pri hen′sə bəl, in-kom′-) /ˌɪnkɒmprɪ'hɛnsəbəl, ɪnˌkɒm-/ *adj.* impossible to comprehend or understand. **—in•com•pre•hen•si•bil•i•ty** (in′kom pri hen′sə bil′i tē) /ˌɪnkɒmprɪˌhɛnsə'bɪlɪtiy/ *n.* [*noncount*]: *the incomprehensibility of the universe.* **—in′com•pre•hen′si•bly,** *adv.* See -PREHEND-.

in•con•ceiv•a•ble (in′kən sē′və bəl) /ˌɪnkən'siyvəbəl/ *adj.* **1.** that cannot be imagined: *inconceivable distances.* [*it + be + ~ + that clause*]: *It's inconceivable that we'll travel to distant galaxies.* **2.** incredible: *inconceivable blunders.* [*it + be + ~ + that clause*]: *It's inconceivable that these things should happen.* **—in′con•ceiv′ab•ly,** *adv.*

in•con•clu•sive (in′kən klo͞o′siv) /ˌɪnkən'kluwsɪv/ *adj.* not proving something beyond doubt: *The results of the tests were inconclusive.* **—in′con•clu′sive•ly,** *adv.* **—in′con•clu′sive•ness,** *n.* [*noncount*]

in•con•gru•ous (in kong′gro͞o əs) /ɪn'kɒŋgruwəs/ *adj.* **1.** out of place; inappropriate. **2.** not harmonious in character. **3.** inconsistent: *an incongruous alibi.* **—in•con•gru•i•ty** (in′kən gro͞o′i tē) /ˌɪnkən'gruwɪtiy/ *n.* [*noncount*]: *the incongruity of meeting my neighbor on Mt. Kilimanjaro.* [*count*]: *incongruities among the students.* **—in•con′gru•ous•ly,** *adv.*

in•con•se•quen•tial (in′kon si kwen′shəl, in kon′-) /ˌɪnkɒnsɪ'kwɛnʃəl, ɪnˌkɒn-/ *adj.* having little importance; unimportant: *inconsequential gossip.* **—in′con•se•quen′tial•ly,** *adv.* See -SEQ-.

in•con•sid•er•a•ble (in′kən sid′ər ə bəl) /ˌɪnkən'sɪdərəbəl/ *adj.* small, as in value, or size: *inconsiderable resources.*

in•con•sid•er•ate (in′kən sid′ər it) /ˌɪnkən'sɪdərɪt/ *adj.* lacking proper feeling for others; thoughtless: *inconsiderate of her husband not to phone ahead.* **—in′con•sid′er•ate•ly,** *adv.* **—in′con•sid′er•ate•ness, in•con•sid•er•a•tion** (in′kən sid′ə rā′shən) /ˌɪnkənˌsɪdə'reyʃən/ *n.* [*noncount*]

in•con•sist•ent (in′kən sis′tənt) /ˌɪnkən'sɪstənt/ *adj.* **1.** not consistent: *an inconsistent argument.* **2.** not keeping to the same principles, course, etc.: *an inconsistent hitter.* **—in′con•sist′ent•ly,** *adv.* See -SIST-.

in•con•sol•a•ble (in′kən sō′lə bəl) /ˌɪnkən'sowləbəl/ *adj.* not consolable; very sad: *She was inconsolable after his death.* See -SOLA-.

in•con•spic•u•ous (in′kən spik′yo͞o əs) /ˌɪnkən'spɪkyuwəs/ *adj.* not easily seen or noticed: *an inconspicuous little spy.* **—in′con•spic′u•ous•ly,** *adv.*: *hovered inconspicuously in the background.* **—in′con•spic′u•ous•ness,** *n.* [*noncount*]

in•con•stant (in kon′stənt) /ɪn'kɒnstənt/ *adj.* not constant; changeable: *an inconstant breeze.* **—in•con′stan•cy,** *n.* [*noncount*] **—in•con′stant•ly,** *adv.* See -STAN-.

in•con•test•a•ble (in′kən tes′tə bəl) /ˌɪnkən'tɛstəbəl/ *adj.* not open to argument. **—in•con•test•a•bil•i•ty** (in′kən tes′tə bil′i tē) /ˌɪnkənˌtɛstə'bɪlɪtiy/ *n.* [*noncount*] **—in′con•test′a•bly,** *adv.* See -TEST-.

in•con•ti•nent (in kon′tn ənt) /ɪn'kɒntn̩ənt/ *adj.* lacking self-control, esp. in the discharge of urine or feces. **—in•con′ti•nence,** *n.* [*noncount*] See -TEN-.

in•con•tro•vert•i•ble (in′kon trə vûr′tə bəl, in kon′-) /ˌɪnkɒntrə'vɜrtəbəl, ɪnˌkɒn-/ *adj.* that cannot be argued; indisputable: *incontrovertible evidence of guilt.* See -VERT-.

in•con•ven•ience (in′kən vēn′yəns) /ˌɪnkən'viynyəns/ *n., v.,* **-ienced, -ienc•ing.** **—*n.*** **1.** [*noncount*] the quality or state of being inconvenient: *put him through a lot of inconvenience to get to the airport.* **2.** [*count*] an inconvenient circumstance or thing: *a real inconvenience to live there without a car.* **—*v.*** [~ + *obj*] **3.** to make things inconvenient for (someone): *Sorry to inconvenience you, but can you take care of this problem?* See -VEN-.

in•con•ven•ient (in′kən vēn′yənt) /ˌɪnkən'viynyənt/ *adj.* **1.** not easily reachable or close at hand: *The computer was at an inconvenient angle on the table.* **2.** not at a time that suits one: *The funeral was at an inconvenient time.* **3.** not suiting one's needs or purposes: *Being without a car was inconvenient.* [*it + be + ~ (+ for + obj) + to + verb*]: *It was inconvenient for me to be without a car.* **—in′con•ven′ient•ly,** *adv.* See -VEN-.

in•cor•po•rate (in kôr′pə rāt′) / ɪn'kɔrpəˌreyt/ *v.,* **-rat•ed, -rat•ing.** **1.** to form (into) a corporation: [*no obj*]: *The business incorporated and called itself Handelman's, Inc.* [~ + *obj*]: *He decided to incorporate his business.* **2.** [~ + *obj* + *into* + *obj*] to introduce (something) as a basic part: *Use the word processor to incorporate any revisions into your text.* **3.** [~ + *obj*] to include as a part: *His book incorporates his earlier essay.* **4.** [~ + *obj*] to make or gather into something real; to embody: *This essay incorporates all her thinking on the subject.* **—in•cor′po•ra′tion,** *n.* [*noncount*]: *the incorporation of those states into one country.* See -CORP-.

in•cor•po•rat•ed (in kôr′pə rā′tid) /ɪn'kɔrpəˌreytɪd/ *adj.* formed into a legal corporation: *an incorporated business.* [*after a noun*]: usually part of the name of the corporation, in abbreviated form: *Whitehall Industries, Inc.* See -CORP-.

in•cor•po•re•al (in′kôr pôr′ē əl, -pōr′-) /ˌɪnkɔr'pɔriyəl, -'powr-/ *adj.* not corporeal; not material: *incorporeal ghosts.* See -CORP-.

in•cor•rect (in′kə rekt′) /ˌɪnkə'rɛkt/ *adj.* **1.** not correct as to fact; inaccurate: *an incorrect answer on a test.* **2.** improper; inappropriate: *incorrect attire at the wedding.* **3.** not correct in form, use, or manner: *incorrect English.* —**in′cor•rect′ly,** *adv.* See -RECT-.

in•cor•ri•gi•ble (in kôr′i jə bəl, -kor′-) /ɪnˈkɔrɪdʒəbəl, -ˈkɒr-/ *adj.* **1.** impossible to reform: *an incorrigible liar.* **2.** unruly; uncontrollable: *an incorrigible child.* **3.** firmly fixed; not easily changed: *an incorrigible optimist.* —**in•cor•ri•gi•bil•i•ty** (in kôr′i jə bil′i tē, -kor′-) /ɪnˌkɔrɪdʒəˈbɪlɪtiy, -ˌkɒr-/ *n.* [*noncount*] —**in•cor′ri•gi•bly,** *adv.*

in•cor•rupt•i•ble (in′kə rup′tə bəl) /ˌɪnkəˈrʌptəbəl/ *adj.* **1.** not corruptible; honest: *an incorruptible customs official.* **2.** that will not decay. —**in•cor•rupt•i•bil•i•ty** (in′kə-rup′tə bil′i tē) /ˌɪnkəˌrʌptəˈbɪlɪtiy/ *n.* [*noncount*] See -RUPT-.

in•crease (*v.* in krēs′; *n.* in′krēs) / *v.* ɪnˈkriys; *n.* ˈɪn-kriys/ *v.*, **-creased, -creas•ing,** *n.* —*v.* **1.** to (cause to) become greater: [*no obj*]: *Her knowledge increased daily.* [~ + *obj*]: *went to school to increase his knowledge of business.* —*n.* **2.** [*noncount*] growth in size, strength, or quality: *The economy is on the increase.* **3.** [*count*] an amount by which something is increased: *an increase of 12%.*

in•creased (in′krēst, in krēst′) /ˈɪnkriyst, ɪnˈkriyst/ *adj.* [*before a noun*] having grown in size or strength: *increased use of handguns in violent crimes.*

in•creas•ing (in krē′sing) /ɪnˈkriysɪŋ/ *adj.* [*often: before a noun*] growing larger or greater: *the increasing use of computers in the schools.* —**in•creas′ing•ly,** *adv.: increasingly easy to purchase handguns.*

in•cred•i•ble (in kred′ə bəl) /ɪnˈkrɛdəbəl/ *adj.* impossible or hard to believe: *We got there with incredible speed.* [*it + be +* ~ *+ that clause*]: *It is incredible that we won the championship.* —**in•cred•i•bil•i•ty** (in kred′-ə bil′i tē) /ɪnˌkrɛdəˈbɪlɪtiy/ *n.* [*noncount*] —**in•cred′i•bly,** *adv.: incredibly huge.* See -CRED-.

in•cred•u•lous (in krej′ə ləs) /ɪnˈkrɛdʒələs/ *adj.* **1.** unbelieving; skeptical: *He's incredulous about the claims of budget cuts.* **2.** indicating or showing one's disbelief: *gave me an incredulous look when I accused her of stealing.* —**in•cre•du•li•ty** (in kri do͞o′li tē, -dyo͞o′-) /ɪn-krɪˈduwlɪtiy, -ˈdyuw- / *n.* [*noncount*] —**in•cred′u•lous•ly,** *adv.* See -CRED-.

in•cre•ment (in′krə mənt, ing′-) /ˈɪnkrəmənt, ˈɪŋ-/ *n.* [*count*] **1.** something added or gained. **2.** an amount by which something increases: *salary increments of $1,000 a month.* **3.** one of a series of regular additions: *deposits in increments of $500.* —**in•cre•men•tal** (in′krə men′tl, ing′-) /ˌɪnkrəˈmɛntl, ɪŋ-/ *adj.: There were small, incremental changes in that stock.*

in•crim•i•nate (in krim′ə nāt′) /ɪnˈkrɪməˌneyt/ *v.* [~ + *obj*], **-nat•ed, -nat•ing.** to accuse (someone) of a crime: *The testimony of the defendant incriminated the others.* —**in•crim′i•nat′ing,** *adj.: incriminating evidence.* —**in•crim•i•na•tion** (in krim′ə nā′shən) /ɪnˌkrɪməˈneyʃən/ *n.* [*noncount*] —**in•crim•i•na•to•ry** (in krim′ə nə tôr′ē, -tōr′ē) /ɪnˈkrɪmənəˌtɔriy, -ˌtowriy/ *adj.*

in•cu•bate (in′kyə bāt′, ing′-) /ˈɪnkyəˌbeyt, ˈɪŋ-/ *v.*, **-bat•ed, -bat•ing.** **1.** [~ + *obj*] to sit on (eggs) for hatching: *The bird incubated its eggs.* **2.** to (cause eggs to) hatch, as by artificial heat: [~ + *obj*]: *incubated the eggs by warming them.* [*no obj*]: *The eggs were incubating in that warm environment.* **3.** [~ + *obj*] to keep in a favorable condition to promote development, as for prematurely born infants. —**in•cu•ba•tion** (in′kyə bā′shən, ing′-) /ˌɪnkyəˈbeyʃən, ˌɪŋ-/ *n.* [*noncount*]: *That disease has a long incubation period.*

in•cu•ba•tor (in′kyə bā′tər, ing′-) /ˈɪnkyəˌbeytər, ˈɪŋ-/ *n.* [*count*] **1.** an apparatus for incubation. **2.** an apparatus in which prematurely born infants are cared for.

in•cul•cate (in kul′kāt, in′kul kāt′) /ɪnˈkʌlkeyt, ˈɪnk-ʌlˌkeyt/ *v.* [~ + *obj*], **-cat•ed, -cat•ing.** to fix in the mind by repeated statements: *to inculcate virtue in the young.* —**in•cul•ca•tion** (in′kul kā′shən) /ˌɪnkʌlˈkeyʃən/ *n.* [*noncount*]

in•cul•pa•ble (in kul′pə bəl) /ɪnˈkʌlpəbəl/ *adj.* not culpable; blameless; without fault. See -CULP-.

in•cul•pate (in kul′pāt, in′kul pāt) /ɪnˈkʌlpeyt, ˈɪnkʌl-peyt/ *v.* [~ + *obj*], **-pat•ed, -pat•ing.** to incriminate. See -CULP-.

in•cum•ben•cy (in kum′bən sē) /ɪnˈkʌmbənsiy/ *n.*, *pl.* **-cies.** **1.** [*noncount*] the quality or state of being incumbent: *the power of incumbency.* **2.** [*count*] the position or term of an incumbent: *an incumbency of one term.*

in•cum•bent (in kum′bənt) /ɪnˈkʌmbənt/ *adj.* **1.** currently holding an office: *the incumbent president.* **2.** [*be* + ~ + *upon/on*] obligatory: *a duty that was incumbent upon me.* —*n.* [*count*] **3.** the holder of an office: *Incumbents have advantages at election time.* —**in•cum′-bent•ly,** *adv.*

in•cur (in kûr′) /ɪnˈkɜr/ *v.* [~ + *obj*], **-curred, -cur•ring.** **1.** to become liable for: *to incur debts.* **2.** to bring upon oneself: *incurred her displeasure.* See -CUR-.

in•cur•a•ble (in kyo͝or′ə bəl) /ɪnˈkyʊrəbəl/ *adj.* **1.** not curable: *an incurable disease.* **2.** not likely or easily able to change: *incurable pessimism.* —**in•cur′a•bly,** *adv.: incurably optimistic.* See -CURA-.

in•cu•ri•ous (in kyo͝or′ē əs) /ɪnˈkyʊriyəs/ *adj.* not curious; indifferent: *gave an incurious glance my way.*

in•cur•sion (in kûr′zhən, -shən) /ɪnˈkɜrʒən, -ʃən/ *n.* [*count*] a hostile invasion of another's territory; a raid: *enemy incursions during the night.* See -CUR-.

Ind., an abbreviation of: Indiana.

ind., an abbreviation of: **1.** independent. **2.** index. **3.** industry.

in•debt•ed (in det′id) /ɪnˈdɛtɪd/ *adj.* **1.** [*be* + ~ + *to*] obligated to repay money; in debt: *is indebted to the amount of several thousand dollars.* **2.** grateful for favors, kindness, or help: *feels indebted to his professor of linguistics.*

in•de•cen•cy (in dē′sən sē) /ɪnˈdiysənsiy/ *n.*, *pl.* **-cies.** **1.** [*noncount*] the quality or condition of being indecent: *indecency in the movies.* **2.** [*count*] an indecent act: *accused of all sorts of indecencies.* See -DECE-.

in•de•cent (in dē′sənt) /ɪnˈdiysənt/ *adj.* **1.** not decent; offending standards of what is right or proper, esp. in matters dealing with sex: *indecent language.* **2.** lacking common decency; in bad taste: *After the funeral he tried with indecent haste to get the inheritance money.* —**in•de′cent•ly,** *adv.: indecently exposed.* See -DECE-.

in•de•ci•pher•a•ble (in′di sī′fər ə bəl) /ˌɪndɪˈsayfərəbəl/ *adj.* that cannot be deciphered: *indecipherable handwriting.*

in•de•ci•sion (in′di sizh′ən) /ˌɪndɪˈsɪʒən/ *n.* [*noncount*] lack of ability to decide: *Because of his indecision we missed our big chance.* See -CISE-.

in•de•ci•sive (in′di sī′siv) /ˌɪndɪˈsaysɪv/ *adj.* **1.** characterized by indecision: *indecisive about what to do next.* **2.** not clear as to outcome; inconclusive: *an indecisive battle.* —**in′de•ci′sive•ly,** *adv.* —**in′de•ci′sive•ness,** *n.* [*noncount*] See -CISE-.

in•deed (in dēd′) /ɪnˈdiyd/ *adv.* **1.** This word is used to express emphasis about something, and to mean "in fact; in truth:" *It did indeed rain.* —*interj.* **2.** This word is used to express surprise or scorn about something: *That's a fine excuse indeed.*

in•de•fat•i•ga•ble (in′di fat′i gə bəl) /ˌɪndɪˈfætɪgəbəl/ *adj.* incapable of being tired out: *an indefatigable worker.* —**in′de•fat′i•ga•bly,** *adv.: worked indefatigably.*

in•de•fen•si•ble (in′di fen′sə bəl) /ˌɪndɪˈfɛnsəbəl/ *adj.* **1.** not justifiable: *indefensible treatment.* **2.** incapable of being defended: *We are in an indefensible position, unless we can call in air strikes.* —**in′de•fen′si•bly,** *adv.* See -FEND-.

in•de•fin•a•ble (in′di fī′nə bəl) /ˌɪndɪˈfaynəbəl/ *adj.* not easily identified: *had some indefinable quality.* See -FIN-.

in•def•i•nite (in def′ə nit) /ɪnˈdɛfənɪt/ *adj.* **1.** having no fixed or specified limit: *an indefinite number.* **2.** not clearly defined: *an indefinite boundary between the two countries.* **3.** not firmly decided; vague: *was indefinite about joining us for lunch.* —**in•def′i•nite•ly,** *adv.* See -FIN-.

indef′inite ar′ticle, *n.* [*count*] an article, as English *a* or *an,* that does not particularize the noun modified.

in•del•i•ble (in del′ə bəl) /ɪnˈdɛləbəl/ *adj.* **1.** [*before a noun*] making marks that cannot be removed: *indelible pens.* **2.** not removable: *indelible stains.* **3.** memorable; unforgettable: *indelible memories.* —**in•del′i•bly,** *adv.*

in•del•i•cate (in del′i kit) /ɪnˈdɛlɪkɪt/ *adj.* rather offensive; rude: *indelicate language.* —**in•del•i•ca•cy** (in del′i-kə sē) /ɪnˈdɛlɪkəsiy/ *n.* [*noncount*]: *showing his indelicacy by telling a dirty joke at the table.* [*count*]: *his many indelicacies in public.* —**in•del′i•cate•ly,** *adv.*

in•dem•ni•fy (in dem′nə fī′) /ɪnˈdɛmnəˌfay/ *v.* [~ + *obj*], **-fied, -fy•ing.** **1.** to compensate for loss sustained, etc. **2.** to protect against possible loss. —**in•dem•ni•fi•ca•tion** (in dem′nə fi kā′shən) /ɪnˌdɛmnəfɪˈkeyʃən/ *n.* [*noncount*]

in•dem•ni•ty (in dem′ni tē) /ɪnˈdɛmnɪtiy/ *n.*, *pl.* **-ties.** **1.** [*noncount*] security against damage or loss. **2.** [*count*] money as payment for loss sustained.

in•dent (in dent′) /ɪnˈdɛnt/ *v.* to set in from the margin:

[~ + *obj*]: *Indent the first line of a paragraph.* [*no obj*]: *You forgot to indent.* See -DENT-.

in•den•ta•tion (in′den tā′shən) /ˌɪndɛn'teyʃən/ *n.* [*count*] **1.** a recess on the surface of something: *small indentations where a mouse had chewed the diskette.* **2.** a series of notches: *the indentation of a maple leaf.* **3.** the space from the margin to where writing begins; amount that has been indented. See -DENT-.

in•de•pend•ence (in′di pen′dəns) /ˌɪndɪ'pɛndəns/ *n.* [*noncount*] the quality, state, or condition of being independent; freedom; liberty. See -PEND-.

in•de•pend•ent (in′di pen′dənt) /ˌɪndɪ'pɛndənt/ *adj.* **1.** not ruled by another country; self-governing: *That country is independent.* **2.** not influenced or controlled by others: *an independent inquiry.* **3.** not depending or contingent upon something else: *Those budget changes are independent of anything the financial division might put forward.* **4.** not relying on another for aid or support. **5.** refusing to be under obligation to others. **6.** [*before a noun*] sufficient to support one without the need to work: *an independent income.* **7.** not belonging to a political party: *independent voters.* **8.** capable of standing as a complete sentence: *an independent clause.* Compare DEPENDENT (def. 3), MAIN (def. 2). **—*n.*** [*count*] **9.** an independent person or thing. **10.** a small, privately owned business: *The independents were in an economic war with the multinational oil companies.* **11.** [*sometimes: Independent*] a person who does not belong to a particular political party. **—*Idiom.*** **12. independent of,** [*be* + ~] irrespective of; regardless of: *That finding was independent of anyone else's study.* **—in′de•pend′ent•ly,** *adv.*: *worked independently.* See -PEND-.

in′-depth′, *adj.* intensive; thorough: *an in-depth study.*

in•de•scrib•a•ble (in′di skrī′bə bəl) /ˌɪndɪ'skraybəbəl/ *adj.* not describable: *a scene of indescribable confusion.* **—in′de•scrib′a•bly,** *adv.*: *indescribably delicious.* See -SCRIB-.

in•de•struct•i•ble (in′di struk′tə bəl) /ˌɪndɪ'strʌktəbəl/ *adj.* that cannot be destroyed; not destructible. **—in•de•struct•i•bil•i•ty** (in′di struk′tə bil′i tē) /ˌɪndɪˌstrʌktə'bɪlɪtiy/ **in′de•struct′i•ble•ness,** *n.* [*noncount*] **—in′de•struct′i•bly,** *adv.* See -STRU-.

in•de•ter•mi•na•ble (in′di tûr′mə nə bəl) /ˌɪndɪ'tɜrmənəbəl/ *adj.* that cannot be determined: *The distance to the ship was indeterminable.*

in•de•ter•mi•nate (in′di tûr′mə nit) /ˌɪndɪ'tɜrmənɪt/ *adj.* **1.** not precisely fixed or determined: *an indeterminate shape in the distance.* **2.** not settled in advance: *The acting principal will serve for an indeterminate time.* **—in•de•ter•mi•na•cy** (in′di tûr′mə nə sē) /ˌɪndɪ'tɜrmənəsiy/ *n.* [*noncount*] **—in•de•ter•mi•nate•ly,** *adv.* **—in′de•ter′mi•nate•ness,** *n.* [*noncount*] **—in•de•ter•mi•na•tion** (in′di tûr′mə nā′shən) /ˌɪndɪˌtɜrmə'neyʃən/ *n.* [*noncount*] See -TERM-.

in•dex (in′deks) /'ɪndɛks/ *n., pl.* **-dex•es, -di•ces** (-də sēz′) /-dəˌsiyz/ *v.* **—*n.*** [*count*] **1.** (in a printed work) an alphabetical listing of names and topics with the numbers of the pages on which they are discussed: *An index is usually at the back of a book.* **2.** an ordered arrangement of material, as in a library: *Look in the index to authors in the card catalog.* **3.** something used to point out; an indication: *a true index of his character.* **4.** a number or formula expressing a property or ratio: *an index of growth.* **—*v.*** [~ + *obj*] **5.** to provide with an index: *The book is fully indexed.* **6.** to enter in an index: *That item is indexed on page 445.* **7.** to adjust, as wages: *Salaries were indexed to inflation.* **—in′dex•er,** *n.* [*count*]

in′dex fin′ger, *n.* FOREFINGER.

In′dia ink′ (in′dē ə) /'ɪndiyə/ *n.* [*noncount*]; [*sometimes: india ink*] a black ink made of lampblack and glue.

In•di•an (in′dē ən) /'ɪndiyən/ *n.* **1.** [*count*] Also called **Native American.** a member of any of the original peoples of North and South America. **2.** [*count*] a person born or living in India. **—*adj.*** **3.** of or relating to American Indians, or to any of the languages spoken by them. **4.** of or relating to India.

In′dian corn′, *n.* [*noncount*] **1.** CORN[1] (def. 1). **2.** any corn with kernels of different colors.

In′dian sum′mer, *n.* a period of mild, dry weather occurring in mid or late autumn: [*noncount*]: *a bit of Indian summer for the next few days.* [*count*]: *an Indian summer that went quickly.*

in•di•cate (in′di kāt′) /'ɪndɪˌkeyt/ *v.,* **-cat•ed, -cat•ing.** **1.** to be a sign of; show: [~ + *obj*]: *Snow indicates winter.* [~ + *(that) clause*]: *The patient's pale skin indicates that he may have anemia.* **2.** to point out or point to: [~ + *obj*]: *to indicate a place on a map.* [~ + *(that) clause*]: *used his finger to indicate that the pain was in his chest.* **3.** to express: [~ + *obj*]: *indicated his disapproval.* [~ + *(that) clause*]: *I indicated that I would go on with my talk.*

in•di•ca•tion (in′di kā′shən) /ˌɪndɪ'keyʃən/ *n.* something serving to indicate: [*count*]: *some indications this morning that it would rain.* [*noncount*]: *no indication that things would be this bad.*

in•dic•a•tive (in dik′ə tiv) /ɪn'dɪkətɪv/ *adj.* **1.** [*be* + ~ (+ *of*)] pointing out; expressing; suggestive: *Her behavior was indicative of a mental disorder.* **2.** of or naming the grammatical mood used for ordinary statements and questions, as the mood of the verb *plays* in *She plays tennis.* Compare IMPERATIVE (def. 3), SUBJUNCTIVE (def. 1). **—*n.*** [*count; usually singular; usually: the* + ~] **3.** the indicative mood; a verb in this form: *The verb* was *is in the indicative in the sentence:* He was at home. **—in•dic′a•tive•ly,** *adv.*

in•di•ca•tor (in′di kā′tər) /'ɪndɪˌkeytər/ *n.* [*count*] **1.** a person or thing that indicates. **2.** a pointing device, as a needle on the dial of a measuring instrument: *The indicator showed 120 miles an hour.* **3.** a light on a car that flashes to show which way the car will turn.

in•dict (in dīt′) /ɪn'dayt/ *v.* [~ + *obj*] **1.** to charge with a crime: *indicted him for rape.* **2.** to accuse of wrongdoing, etc.: *indicted the administration as being unsympathetic to the needs of the cities.* **—in•dict′a•ble,** *adj.* See -DICT-.

in•dict•ment (in dīt′mənt) /ɪn'daytmənt/ *n.* **1.** a formal charge of a crime: [*count*]: *The judge handed down an indictment.* [*noncount*]: *The criminal is now under indictment.* **2.** [*count*] a statement or sign that something is wrong, etc.: *The fact that so many children still can't read is a serious indictment.* See -DICT-.

in•dif•fer•ence (in dif′ər əns) /ɪn'dɪfərəns/ *n.* [*noncount*] **1.** lack of interest or concern: *shocked by the indifference shown toward the poor.* **2.** unimportance: *a matter of indifference to me.* See -FER-.

in•dif•fer•ent (in dif′ər ənt, -dif′rənt) /ɪn'dɪfərənt, -'dɪfrənt/ *adj.* **1.** without interest or concern: *once interested in the trombone, but now seems indifferent.* **2.** not particularly good: *an indifferent performance.* **—in•dif′fer•ent•ly,** *adv.* See -FER-.

in•dig•e•nous (in dij′ə nəs) /ɪn'dɪdʒənəs/ *adj.* coming from a particular region or country; native: *the indigenous peoples of southern Africa.* [*be* + ~ + *to*]: *plants that are indigenous to Canada.*

in•di•gent (in′di jənt) /'ɪndɪdʒənt/ *adj.* **1.** needy; poor; impoverished. **—*n.*** **the indigent** [*plural; used with a plural verb*] **2.** people who are indigent: *a desire to do something for the indigent.* **—in′di•gent•ly,** *adv.*

in•di•gest•i•ble (in′di jes′tə bəl, -dī-) /ˌɪndɪ'dʒɛstəbəl, -day-/ *adj.* not digestible; not easily digested.

in•di•ges•tion (in′di jes′chən, -dī-) /ˌɪndɪ'dʒɛstʃən, -day-/ *n.* [*noncount*] a feeling of discomfort after eating, as of heartburn or nausea, due to inadequate digestion.

in•dig•nant (in dig′nənt) /ɪn'dɪgnənt/ *adj.* feeling, characterized by, or showing indignation: *gave me an indignant look.* **—in•dig′nant•ly,** *adv.*

in•dig•na•tion (in′dig nā′shən) /ˌɪndɪg'neyʃən/ *n.* [*noncount*] strong displeasure at something unjust or offensive: *righteous indignation.*

in•dig•ni•ty (in dig′ni tē) /ɪn'dɪgnɪtiy/ *n., pl.* **-ties.** **1.** [*noncount*] an injury to a person's dignity: *the indignity of a strip search.* **2.** [*count*] an example of such injury or insult: *to suffer many indignities as a hostage.*

in•di•go (in′di gō′) /'ɪndɪˌgow/ *n.* [*noncount*] **1.** a blue dye obtained from various plants. **2.** a deep violet blue color. **—*adj.*** **3.** of the color indigo.

in•di•rect (in′də rekt′, -dī-) /ˌɪndə'rɛkt, -day-/ *adj.* **1.** not following a straight line: *an indirect route.* **2.** not intended; incidental: *an indirect outcome.* **3.** not direct in action or procedure; roundabout: *The politician's indirect answers were frustrating.* **4.** not direct in bearing, force, etc.: *indirect evidence.* **—in′di•rect′ly,** *adv.* **—in′di•rect′ness,** *n.* [*noncount*] See -RECT-.

in′direct ob′ject, *n.* [*count*] a word or group of words representing the person or thing to which or for which the action of a verb is performed: *In the sentence* She gave the boy the book, *the noun* the boy *is the indirect object.*

in′direct tax′, *n.* [*count*] a tax on something that is paid by the consumer as part of the market price.

in•dis•creet (in′di skrēt′) /ˌɪndɪ'skriyt/ *adj.* not discreet; lacking prudence or good judgment: *overheard your in-*

discreet remark about her. —**in′dis•creet′ly,** *adv.* See -CERN-.

in•dis•cre•tion (in′di skresh′ən) /ˌɪndɪ'skrɛʃən/ *n.* **1.** [*noncount*] lack of discretion; bad judgment: *indiscretion in dealing with people.* **2.** [*count*] an indiscreet act, remark, etc.: *his indiscretions with prostitutes.* See -CERN-.

in•dis•crim•i•nate (in′di skrim′ə nit) /ˌɪndɪ'skrɪmənɪt/ *adj.* not discriminating; lacking in care or judgment: *the indiscriminate slaughter of innocent people.* —**in′dis•crim′i•nate•ly,** *adv.*: *The terrorists shot everyone indiscriminately.* See -CERN-.

in•dis•pen•sa•ble (in′di spen′sə bəl) /ˌɪndɪ'spɛnsəbəl/ *adj.* necessary or essential: *A computer is indispensable to many writers.* —**in•dis•pen•sa•bil•i•ty** (in′di spen′sə-bil′i tē) /ˌɪndɪˌspɛnsə'bɪlɪtiy/ *n.* [*noncount*] —**in′dis•pen′-sa•bly,** *adv.* See -PEND-.

in•dis•posed (in′di spōzd′) /ˌɪndɪ'spowzd/ *adj.* [*be* + ~] **1.** sick or ill, esp. slightly: *He's indisposed and won't be at the meeting.* **2.** [~ + *to* + *verb*] not inclined (to do something); unwilling: *indisposed to helping.* —**in•dis•po•si•tion** (in′dis pə zish′ən) /ˌɪndɪspə'zɪʃən/ *n.* [*noncount*] See -POS-.

in•dis•put•a•ble (in′di spyōō′tə bəl, in dis′pyə-) /ˌɪndɪ'spyuwtəbəl, ɪn'dɪspyə-/ *adj.* that cannot be denied: *indisputable evidence.* [*it* + *be* + ~ + *that clause*]: *It is indisputable that he is the guilty man.* —**in′dis•put′a•bly,** *adv.* See -PUTE-.

in•dis•sol•u•ble (in′di sol′yə bəl) /ˌɪndɪ'sɒlyəbəl/ *adj.* not dissoluble; that cannot be dissolved: *indissoluble links between Canada and the United States.* See -SOLV-.

in•dis•tinct (in′di stingkt′) /ˌɪndɪ'stɪŋkt/ *adj.* **1.** not distinct: *indistinct markings.* **2.** not clearly distinguishable: *an indistinct shape.* —**in′dis•tinct′ly,** *adv.* See -STIN-.

in•di•vid•u•al (in′də vij′ōō əl) /ˌɪndə'vɪdʒuwəl/ *n.* [*count*] **1.** a single human being, as distinguished from a group: *the freedom of each individual.* **2.** a person: *Several unidentified individuals approached the speaker.* —*adj.* [*before a noun*] **3.** single; particular; separate: *each individual child.* **4.** intended for the use of one person only: *individual portions.* **5.** of or characteristic of a particular person or thing: *individual tastes.* —**in′di•vid′u•al•ly,** *adv.*: *individually wrapped pieces of chocolate.*

in•di•vid•u•al•ism (in′də vij′ōō ə liz′əm) /ˌɪndə'vɪdʒuwəˌlɪzəm/ *n.* [*noncount*] **1.** a social theory calling for the liberty of the individual. **2.** the principle or habit of independent thought or action. —**in′di•vid′u•al•ist,** *n.* [*count*] —**in′di•vid′u•al•is′tic,** *adj.*

in•di•vid•u•al•i•ty (in′də vij′ōō al′i tē) /ˌɪndəˌvɪdʒuw'ælɪtiy/ *n.* [*noncount*] the uniqueness that makes one person or thing different from others.

in•di•vid•u•al•ize (in′də vij′ōō ə līz′) /ˌɪndə'vɪdʒuwəˌlayz/ *v.* [~ + *obj*], **-ized, -iz•ing.** to make (something) individual: *individualized his greeting cards with a personal message in each one.* —**in•di•vid•u•al•i•za•tion** (in′də vij′ōō ə lə zā′shən) /ˌɪndəˌvɪdʒuwələ'zeyʃən/ *n.* [*noncount*]

in•di•vis•i•ble (in′də viz′ə bəl) /ˌɪndə'vɪzəbəl/ *adj.* not divisible: *The pledge of allegiance to the flag says, "..one nation, indivisible, with liberty and justice for all."* —**in•di•vis•i•bil•i•ty** (in′də viz′ə bil′i tē) /ˌɪndəˌvɪzə'bɪlɪtiy/ *n.* [*noncount*] —**in′di•vis′i•bly,** *adv.*

in•doc•tri•nate (in dok′trə nāt′) /ɪn'dɒktrəˌneyt/ *v.* [~ + *obj*], **-nat•ed, -nat•ing. 1.** to instruct (someone) in a doctrine in a way not allowing for dissent: *indoctrinated to love their country and to hate the West.* **2.** to teach thoroughly: *indoctrinated the recruits in the ways of army life.* —**in•doc•tri•na•tion** (in dok′trə nā′shən) /ɪnˌdɒktrə'neyʃən/ *n.* [*noncount*] See -DOC-.

in•do•lent (in′dl ənt) /'ɪndḷənt/ *adj.* lazy; slothful. —**in′-do•lence,** *n.* [*noncount*]

in•dom•i•ta•ble (in dom′i tə bəl) /ɪn'dɒmɪtəbəl/ *adj.* that cannot be easily overcome: *an indomitable fighter.* —**in•dom′i•ta•bly,** *adv.* See -DOMIN-.

In•do•ne•sian (in′də nē′zhən, -shən) /ˌɪndə'niyʒən, -ʃən/ *n.* **1.** [*count*] a person born or living in Indonesia. **2.** [*noncount*] the language spoken by many of the people in Indonesia. —*adj.* **3.** of or relating to Indonesia. **4.** of or relating to the language spoken by many of the people in Indonesia.

in•door (in′dôr′, -dōr′) /'ɪnˌdɔr, -ˌdowr/ *adj.* located, used, or existing inside a building: *indoor plumbing.*

in•doors (in dôrz′, -dōrz′) /ɪn'dɔrz, -'dowrz/ *adv.* in or into a building: *Let's go indoors.*

in•du•bi•ta•ble (in dōō′bi tə bəl, -dyōō′-) /ɪn'duwbɪtəbəl, -'dyuw-/ *adj.* not to be doubted; unquestionable: *indubitable sincerity.* —**in•du′bi•ta•bly,** *adv.*: *indubitably correct.*

in•duce (in dōōs′, -dyōōs′) /ɪn'duws, -'dyuws/ *v.*, **-duced, -duc•ing. 1.** to move (someone) by persuasion: [~ + *obj*]: *The unsuccessful job interview induced a sense of failure in him.* [~ + *obj* + *to* + *verb*]: *See if you can induce him to stay.* **2.** [~ + *obj*] to bring about or cause: *Carbohydrates eaten in the late evening induce sleep.* **3.** [~ + *obj*] to produce (an electric current) by induction. —**in•duc′er,** *n.* [*count*] See -DUC-.

in•duce•ment (in dōōs′mənt, -dyōōs′-) /ɪn'duwsmənt, -'dyuws-/ *n.* **1.** [*count*] something that induces: *What inducements did they offer you?* **2.** [*noncount*] the act of inducing; the state of being induced. See -DUC-.

in•duct (in dukt′) /ɪn'dʌkt/ *v.* **1.** [~ + *obj* + *into* + *obj*] to install in an office, place of honor, etc., esp. with formal ceremonies: *to be inducted into baseball's Hall of Fame.* **2.** [~ + *obj* + *into/to* + *obj*] to introduce, esp. to something requiring special knowledge: *They inducted him into the mystic rites.* **3.** [~ + *obj*] to take (a draftee) into military service; draft. See -DUC-.

in•duct•ance (in duk′təns) /ɪn'dʌktəns/ *n.* [*noncount*] the property of an electrical circuit by which a change in current causes force.

in•duc•tee (in′duk tē′, in duk-) /ˌɪndʌk'tiy, ɪn dʌk-/ *n.* [*count*], *pl.* **-tees.** one who is inducted into the military: *Will the inductees step forward?*

in•duc•tion (in duk′shən) /ɪn'dʌkʃən/ *n.* **1.** [*noncount*] the act of inducing. **2.** formal installation in an office, position, etc.: [*noncount*]: *Induction will take place next week.* [*count*]: *Inductions normally take place during the spring.* **3.** [*noncount*] (in logic) a process of reasoning in which individual facts are used to arrive at a general statement or conclusion: *If you reason that Mary is dark-haired and Greek, and Bob is dark-haired and Greek, that therefore all Greeks are dark-haired, that is an example of induction.* **4.** [*noncount*] the process by which a body having electric or magnetic properties produces magnetism or an electric charge in a neighboring body without touching it. See -DUC-.

in•duc•tive (in duk′tiv) /ɪn'dʌktɪv/ *adj.* **1.** of or relating to electrical or magnetic induction. **2.** of, relating to, or employing logical induction: *inductive reasoning.* See -DUC-.

in•dulge (in dulj′) /ɪn'dʌldʒ/ *v.*, **-dulged, -dulg•ing. 1.** [~ + *obj*] to yield to (desires, etc.): *indulged his passion for flying.* **2.** [~ + *obj*] to yield to the wishes of (someone): *Her parents indulge her too much.* **3.** to allow (oneself) to follow one's will, wishes, or desires: [~ + *oneself*]: *She indulged herself in reckless spending.* [~ + *in*]: *She indulged in some humor.* **4.** [*no obj*] to drink alcoholic liquor: *He indulged too much that night.*

in•dul•gence (in dul′jəns) /ɪn'dʌldʒəns/ *n.* **1.** [*noncount*] the act or practice of indulging: *Too much indulgence can spoil your children.* **2.** [*count*] something indulged in: *Rich desserts are an indulgence.* **3.** [*noncount*] understanding; tolerance; forgiveness: *The pilot asked for the passengers' indulgence during the delay.*

in•dul•gent (in dul′jənt) /ɪn'dʌldʒənt/ *adj.* characterized by or showing indulgence: *indulgent parents.* —**in•dul′-gent•ly,** *adv.*

in•dus•tri•al (in dus′trē əl) /ɪn'dʌstriyəl/ *adj.* [*before a noun*] **1.** of or relating to industry: *industrial pollution.* **2.** having many industries; industrialized: *a well-developed, industrial country.* **3.** characterized by heavy, harsh-sounding pounding: *industrial rock music.* —*n.* **4. industrials,** [*plural*] stocks and bonds of industrial companies. —**in•dus′tri•al•ly,** *adv.*

indus′trial arts′, *n.* [*plural*] the techniques of using tools and machinery, as taught in secondary and technical schools.

in•dus•tri•al•ism (in dus′trē ə liz′əm) /ɪn'dʌstriyəˌlɪzəm/ *n.* [*noncount*] the economic system of a society in which industry, esp. heavy industry, plays a large role.

in•dus•tri•al•ist (in dus′trē ə list) /ɪn'dʌstriyəlɪst/ *n.* [*count*] **1.** one who owns an industrial enterprise. —*adj.* [*before a noun*] **2.** of or relating to industrialism.

in•dus•tri•al•ize (in dus′trē ə līz′) /ɪn'dʌstriyəˌlayz/ *v.*, **-ized, -iz•ing. 1.** [~ + *obj*] to introduce industry into (a country, etc.) on a large scale: *industrialized the entire valley.* **2.** [*no obj*] to undergo the introduction of such industry: *The valley industrialized rapidly.* —**in•dus•tri•al•i•za•tion** (in dus′trē ə li zā′shən) /ɪnˌdʌstriyəlɪ'zeyʃən/ *n.* [*noncount*]: *Industrialization came too fast.*

indus′trial park′, *n.* [*count*] a set of industrial companies placed in parklike surroundings in a suburban area.

indus′trial-strength′, *adj.* [*usually: before a noun*] unusually strong or effective: *industrial-strength soap.*

in•dus•tri•ous (in dus′trē əs) /ɪn'dʌstriyəs/ *adj.* hard-working; diligent: *an industrious person.* —**in•dus′tri•ous•ly,** *adv.* —**in•dus′tri•ous•ness,** *n.* [*noncount*]

in•dus•try (in′də strē) /ˈɪndəstriy/ *n., pl.* **-tries. 1.** [*count*] the group of manufacturing businesses in a particular field: *the steel industry.* **2.** [*count*] any general business activity: *the tourist industry.* **3.** [*noncount*] manufacture in general: *Will industry be welcome in a farming community?* **4.** [*noncount*] energetic activity at a task; diligence: *working with great industry.*

-ine[1], *suffix. -ine* is attached to some roots or nouns to form adjectives with the meaning "of, relating to, or characteristic of; of the nature of; made of:" *crystal + -ine → crystalline (= of, like, or made of crystal); equ- (= horse) + -ine → equine (= of or relating to horses).*

-ine[2], *suffix. -ine* is attached to some roots to form nouns that name chemical substances and elements: *caffe- (= coffee) + -ine → caffeine (= a chemical substance found in coffee); chlor- + -ine → chlorine.*

in•e•bri•ate (*v.* in ē′brē āt′, *n., adj.* -it) / *v.* ɪnˈiybriyˌeyt, ɪˈniy-; *n., adj.* -ɪt/ *v.,* **-at•ed, -at•ing,** *n., adj.* —*v.* [~ + *obj*] **1.** to make drunk: *Drinking too much alcohol inebriated him.* —*n.* [*count*] **2.** an intoxicated person, esp. a drunkard. —*adj.* **3.** Also, **in•e′bri•at′ed.** drunk; intoxicated: *completely inebriated.* —**in•e•bri•a•tion** (in ē′brē ā′shən) /ɪnˌiybriyˈeyʃən/ *n.* [*noncount*]: *total inebriation.*

in•ed•i•ble (in ed′ə bəl) /ɪnˈɛdəbəl/ *adj.* not fit to be eaten: *inedible berries.* —**in•ed•i•bil•i•ty** (in ed′ə bil′i tē) /ɪnˌɛdəˈbɪlɪtiy/ *n.* [*noncount*]

in•ed•u•ca•ble (in ej′o͝o kə bəl) /ɪnˈɛdʒʊkəbəl/ *adj.* incapable of being educated. See -DUC-.

in•ef•fa•ble (in ef′ə bəl) /ɪnˈɛfəbəl/ *adj.* that cannot be expressed in words: *ineffable joy.* —**in•ef′fa•bly,** *adv.*

in•ef•fec•tive (in′i fek′tiv) /ˌɪnɪˈfɛktɪv/ *adj.* **1.** not effective: *an ineffective air conditioner.* **2.** inefficient or incompetent: *an ineffective manager.* See -FEC-.

in•ef•fec•tu•al (in′i fek′cho͞o əl) /ˌɪnɪˈfɛktʃuwəl/ *adj.* **1.** producing no satisfactory effect: *an ineffectual remedy.* **2.** not worthwhile: *ineffectual efforts.* See -FEC-.

in•ef•fi•cient (in′i fish′ənt) /ˌɪnɪˈfɪʃənt/ *adj.* **1.** not efficient: *an old, inefficient heating system.* **2.** lacking in ability; incompetent. —**in′ef•fi′cien•cy,** *n.* [*count*], *pl.* -cies: *There are many inefficiencies in the way that office is run.* —**in′ef•fi′cient•ly,** *adv.* See -FEC-.

in•el•e•gant (in el′i gənt) /ɪnˈɛlɪgənt/ *adj.* lacking in gracefulness: *inelegant writing.* —**in•el′e•gant•ly,** *adv.*

in•el•i•gi•ble (in el′i jə bəl) /ɪnˈɛlɪdʒəbəl/ *adj.* **1.** not eligible: *ineligible for citizenship.* —*n.* [*count*] **2.** a person who is ineligible. —**in•el•i•gi•bil•i•ty** (in el′i jə bil′i tē) /ɪnˌɛlɪdʒəˈbɪlɪtiy/ *n.* [*noncount*] —**in•el′i•gi•bly,** *adv.* See -LEC-.

in•e•luc•ta•ble (in′i luk′tə bəl) /ˌɪnɪˈlʌktəbəl/ *adj.* that cannot be avoided; inescapable. —**in′e•luc′ta•bly,** *adv.*: *The journalist was ineluctably drawn to solving the murder.*

in•ept (in ept′) /ɪnˈɛpt/ *adj.* **1.** lacking skill or ability; incompetent: *inept handling of the crisis.* **2.** inappropriate; unsuitable; out of place: *embarrassed by an inept remark.* —**in•ept•i•tude** (in ep′ti to͞od′, -tyo͞od′) /ɪnˈɛptɪˌtuwd, -ˌtyuwd/ *n.* [*noncount*] —**in•ept′ly,** *adv.* —**in•ept′ness,** *n.* [*noncount*] See -APT-.

in•e•qual•i•ty (in′i kwol′i tē) /ˌɪnɪˈkwɒlɪtiy/ *n., pl.* **-ties. 1.** [*noncount*] the condition of being unequal: *As president, he fought against inequality.* **2.** [*count*] an instance of being unequal: *the many inequalities women confront in business.* **3.** [*count*] a statement in mathematics that two quantities are unequal. See -EQUA-.

in•eq•ui•ty (in ek′wi tē) /ɪnˈɛkwɪtiy/ *n.* **1.** [*noncount*] unfairness; lack of equity. **2.** [*count*] an act or instance of this: *the inequities of the tax system.* See -EQUA-.

in•ert (in ûrt′) /ɪnˈɜrt/ *adj.* **1.** having no power of action (opposed to *active*): *inert matter.* **2.** (of chemical substances) having little or no ability to react in a chemical reaction: *Nitrogen is an inert gas.* **3.** inactive or sluggish: *He stood inert as we rushed toward her.* —**in•ert′ly,** *adv.* —**in•ert′ness,** *n.* [*noncount*]

in•er•tia (in ûr′shə) /ɪnˈɜrʃə/ *n.* [*noncount*] **1.** a feeling of inertness; sluggishness: *was filled with inertia and had no desire to get out of bed.* **2.** the property of matter by which it keeps its state so long as it is not acted upon by an external force: *to overcome the inertia of such a huge mass.* —**in•er′tial,** *adj.*: *inertial guidance systems.*

in•es•cap•a•ble (in′ə skā′pə bəl) /ˌɪnəˈskeypəbəl/ *adj.* that cannot be escaped or avoided: *an inescapable conclusion.* —**in′es•cap′a•bly,** *adv.*

in•es•ti•ma•ble (in es′tə mə bəl) /ɪnˈɛstəməbəl/ *adj.* **1.** that cannot be estimated; incalculable: *inestimable harm.* **2.** too precious to be estimated; priceless: *of inestimable value.* —**in•es′ti•ma•bly,** *adv.*

in•ev•i•ta•ble (in ev′i tə bəl) /ɪnˈɛvɪtəbəl/ *adj.* **1.** unable to be avoided or escaped: *an inevitable conclusion.* [*it + be + ~ + that clause*]: *It was inevitable that we would lose.* **2.** that which always happens: *smoking his usual, inevitable, foul-smelling cigar.* —*n.* [*count; usually singular; the + ~*] **3.** something unavoidable: *We must accept the inevitable.* —**in•ev•i•ta•bil•i•ty** (in ev′i tə bil′i tē) /ɪnˌɛvɪtəˈbɪlɪtiy/ *n.* [*noncount*]: *the inevitability of death.* [*count*]: *An inevitability of owning a foreign car is the difficulty in getting spare parts.* —**in•ev′i•ta•bly,** *adv.*

in•ex•act (in′ig zakt′) /ˌɪnɪgˈzækt/ *adj.* not exact: *Psychology is an inexact science.* —**in′ex•act′ly,** *adv.* See -ACT-.

in•ex•cus•a•ble (in′ik skyo͞o′zə bəl) /ˌɪnɪkˈskyuwzəbəl/ *adj.* that may not be excused: *inexcusable behavior.* —**in′ex•cus′a•bly,** *adv.*

in•ex•haust•i•ble (in′ig zôs′tə bəl) /ˌɪnɪgˈzɔstəbəl/ *adj.* **1.** not exhaustible: *an inexhaustible supply of energy.* **2.** untiring; tireless: *an inexhaustible runner.* —**in′ex•haust′i•bly,** *adv.*

in•ex•o•ra•ble (in ek′sər ə bəl) /ɪnˈɛksərəbəl/ *adj.* **1.** not able to be changed: *the inexorable future.* **2.** not to be affected by requests; merciless: *The judge was inexorable and passed the maximum sentence.* —**in•ex′o•ra•bly,** *adv.*: *The torpedo moved inexorably toward its target.*

in•ex•pen•sive (in′ik spen′siv) /ˌɪnɪkˈspɛnsɪv/ *adj.* not expensive; not high in price. —**Syn.** See CHEAP.

in•ex•pe•ri•ence (in′ik spēr′ē əns) /ˌɪnɪkˈspɪəriyəns/ *n.* [*noncount*] lack of experience: *inexperience in dealing with people from different cultures.* —**in′ex•pe′ri•enced,** *adj.*: *inexperienced first-year players.*

in•ex•pert (in eks′pûrt, in′ik spûrt′) /ɪnˈɛkspɜrt, ˌɪnɪkˈspɜrt/ *adj.* not expert; unskilled.

in•ex•pli•ca•ble (in ek′spli kə bəl, in′ik splik′ə-) /ɪnˈɛksplɪkəbəl, ˌɪnɪkˈsplɪkə-/ *adj.* incapable of being explained: *She's always been very quiet, so her outburst is all the more inexplicable.* —**in•ex′pli•ca•bly,** *adv.*: *inexplicably delayed.* See -PLIC-.

in•ex•press•i•ble (in′ik spres′ə bəl) /ˌɪnɪkˈsprɛsəbəl/ *adj.* that cannot be described in words: *inexpressible joy.* See -PRESS-.

in•ex•tin•guish•a•ble (in′ik sting′gwi shə bəl) /ˌɪnɪkˈstɪŋgwɪʃəbəl/ *adj.* not extinguishable: *an inextinguishable fire.*

in ex•tre•mis (in ik strē′mis) /ɪn ɪkˈstriymɪs/ *adv.* **1.** in a very difficult situation: *a company that was in extremis.* **2.** near death.

in•ex•tri•ca•ble (in ek′stri kə bəl, in′ik strik′ə-) /ɪnˈɛkstrɪkəbəl, ˌɪnɪkˈstrɪkə-/ *adj.* **1.** from which one cannot escape: *an inextricable maze.* **2.** that cannot be untangled: *an inextricable knot.* **3.** very complicated or intricate: *The movie had an inextricable plot.* —**in•ex′tri•ca•bly,** *adv.*: *Your salary is inextricably linked to our budget concerns.*

inf., an abbreviation of: **1.** inferior. **2.** infinitive. **3.** infirmary. **4.** information.

in•fal•li•ble (in fal′ə bəl) /ɪnˈfæləbəl/ *adj.* **1.** absolutely sure: *an infallible rule.* **2.** that never fails in operating; certain: *had an infallible remedy for the hiccups.* **3.** not fallible; free from error, as applied to persons, their judgment, or what they say: *thought he was infallible.* —**in•fal•li•bil•i•ty** (in fal′ə bil′i tē) /ɪnˌfæləˈbɪlɪtiy/ **in•fal′li•ble•ness,** *n.* [*noncount*]: *They believe in the infallibility of the Pope in faith and morals.* —**in•fal′li•bly,** *adv.*

in•fa•mous (in′fə məs) /ˈɪnfəməs/ *adj.* **1.** of or relating to infamy: *infamous for the disgraceful way he treated women.* **2.** deserving of or causing an evil reputation: *an infamous deed.*

in•fa•my (in′fə mē) /ˈɪnfəmiy/ *n., pl.* **-mies. 1.** [*noncount*] strong condemnation due to a shameful or criminal act: *That day of the sneak attack would live in infamy.* **2.** [*count*] an infamous act or circumstance.

in•fan•cy (in′fən sē) /ˈɪnfənsiy/ *n.* [*noncount*] **1.** the state or period of being an infant: *remembers nothing of his infancy.* **2.** a very early stage: *Space science is still in its infancy.*

in•fant (in′fənt) /ˈɪnfənt/ *n.* [*count*] **1.** a child during the earliest period of its life. —*adj.* [*before a noun*] **2.** of or relating to infants or infancy: *infant mortality rates.* **3.** being in the earliest stage: *a technology in its infant stages.*

in•fan•ti•cide (in fan′tə sīd′) /ɪnˈfæntəˌsayd/ *n.* **1.** the act of killing an infant: [*noncount*]: *That culture practiced infanticide of girls.* [*count*]: *the number of infanticides.* **2.** [*count*] a person who kills an infant.

in•fan•tile (in′fən tīl′, -til) /ˈɪnfənˌtayl, -tɪl/ *adj.* **1.** characteristic of or behaving like an infant: *infantile temper tantrums.* **2.** of or relating to infants or infancy: *infantile sicknesses.*

in•fan•try (in′fən trē) /ˈɪnfəntriy/ *n., pl.* **-tries.** soldiers or military units that fight on foot: [*noncount*]: *In the infantry he was forced to forget his past training.* [*count*]: *We have two infantries ready to move forward.* —**in′fan•try•man,** *n.* [*count*], *pl.* **-men.**

in•fat•u•at•ed (in fach′o͞o ā′tid) /ɪnˈfætʃuw͵eytɪd/ *adj.* having a foolish or excessive admiration for someone: *completely infatuated with her.* —**in•fat•u•a•tion** (in-fach′o͞o ā′shən) /ɪn͵fætʃuwˈeyʃən/ *n.* [*noncount*]: *an extreme case of infatuation.* [*count*]: *She was his latest infatuation.*

in•fect (in fekt′) /ɪnˈfɛkt/ *v.* [~ + *obj*] **1.** to affect with disease-producing germs: *The germs had infected his wound.* **2.** to affect the morals, opinions, emotions, etc., of others: *His courage infected the other soldiers.* See -FEC-.

in•fec•tion (in fek′shən) /ɪnˈfɛkʃən/ *n.* **1.** [*noncount*] the state of being infected: *If you leave that wound untreated, infection will result.* **2.** [*count*] an infectious disease: *an ear infection.*

in•fec•tious (in fek′shəs) /ɪnˈfɛkʃəs/ *adj.* **1.** (of a disease) spread by infection, as from one person to another or from one part of the body to another: *If you have an infectious disease you really should not go to work.* **2.** tending to spread quickly and to many people: *infectious laughter.* —**in•fec′tious•ly,** *adv.*: *grinned infectiously.* —**in•fec′tious•ness,** *n.* [*noncount*] See -FEC-.

in•fe•lic•i•tous (in′fə lis′i təs) /͵ɪnfəˈlɪsɪtəs/ *adj.* not fitting or appropriate: *an infelicitous remark about his weight.* —**in•fe•lic•i•ty** (in′fə lis′i tē) /͵ɪnfəˈlɪsɪtiy/ *n.* [*count*], *pl.* **-ties**: *guilty of many infelicities during the interview.* [*noncount*]: *writing that was marked by infelicity.*

in•fer (in fûr′) /ɪnˈfɜr/ *v.,* **-ferred, -fer•ring.** to conclude from evidence: [~ + *obj*]: *You can infer that fact from the others.* [~ + *that clause*]: *He inferred that you are opposed to the treaty.* See -FER-.

in•fer•ence (in′fər əns, in′frəns) /ˈɪnfərəns, ˈɪnfrəns/ *n.* **1.** [*count*] an act or instance of inferring: *Don't make such rash inferences from such small evidence.* **2.** [*noncount*] the process of drawing a conclusion from reasoning: *Deductive inference can sometimes lead to the wrong conclusion.* —**in•fer•en•tial** (in′fə ren′shəl) /͵ɪnfəˈrɛnʃəl/ *adj.* See -FER-.

in•fe•ri•or (in fēr′ē ər) /ɪnˈfɪəriyər/ *adj.* **1.** low or lower in rank, degree, or position: *felt inferior to his coworkers.* **2.** low or lower in place or position: *the inferior regions of the earth.* **3.** of low grade or worse condition; poor in quality: *That inferior product ranked well below the others.* —*n.* [*count*] **4.** a person inferior to another or others, as in rank or merit: *His inferiors treated him as badly as his superiors did.* —**in•fe•ri•or•i•ty** (in fēr′ē ôr′i tē, -or′-) /ɪn͵fɪəriyˈɔrɪtiy, -ˈɒr-/ *n.* [*noncount*]

in•fer•nal (in fûr′nl) /ɪnˈfɜrnl̩/ *adj.* **1.** fiendish; diabolical: *an infernal plot.* **2.** very troublesome; outrageous: *an infernal nuisance.* **3.** of, living in, or fit for hell or the underworld.

in•fer•no (in fûr′nō) /ɪnˈfɜrnow/ *n.* [*count*], *pl.* **-nos.** a place that resembles hell, esp. in heat: *The flaming skyscraper had become a towering inferno.*

in•fer•tile (in fûr′tl) /ɪnˈfɜrtl̩/ *adj.* not fertile; barren: *infertile soil.* —**in•fer•til•i•ty** (in′fər til′i tē) /͵ɪnfərˈtɪlɪtiy/ *n.* [*noncount*]: *drugs to combat infertility.* See -FER-.

in•fest (in fest′) /ɪnˈfɛst/ *v.* [~ + *obj*] to overrun (a place) in a troublesome manner; cause hardship to (a place) by great numbers: *The mice infested the farmhouse.* —**in•fes•ta•tion** (in′fe stā′shən) /͵ɪnfɛˈsteyʃən/ *n.* [*count*]: *infestations of bees in their roof.* [*noncount*]: *the infestation of the roof.*

in•fi•del (in′fi dl, -del′) /ˈɪnfɪdl̩, -͵dɛl/ *n.* [*count*] **1.** one who does not accept a particular religion, esp. Christianity or Islam. **2.** a person who has no religious faith; an unbeliever. —*adj.* [*usually: before a noun*] **3.** of or concerning infidels; heathen.

in•fi•del•i•ty (in′fi del′i tē) /͵ɪnfɪˈdɛlɪtiy/ *n., pl.* **-ties. 1.** [*noncount*] unfaithfulness to one's partner in marriage; adultery: *guilty of infidelity.* **2.** [*count*] an act of adultery: *could no longer overlook his infidelities.* **3.** [*noncount*] disloyalty: *acts of infidelity against our organization.* **4.** [*count*] an act of disloyalty: *some business infidelities.* See -FID-.

in•field (in′fēld′) /ˈɪn͵fiyld/ *n.* **1. a.** [*count*] the area of a baseball field bounded by the base lines: *an infield of artificial turf.* **b.** [*noncount*] the positions played by players in this area: *played well in the infield.* **c.** [*count*] the players at these positions thought of as a group (contrasted with *outfield*): *one of the best infields in the league.* **2.** [*count*] the area enclosed by a racetrack or running track. —**in′field′er,** *n.* [*count*]

in•fight•ing (in′fī′ting) /ˈɪn͵faytɪŋ/ *n.* [*noncount*] **1.** fighting at close range. **2.** fighting between people closely associated: *political infighting.* —**in′fight′er,** *n.* [*count*]

in•fil•trate (in fil′trāt, in′fil trāt′) /ɪnˈfɪltreyt, ˈɪnfɪl͵treyt/ *v.,* **-trat•ed, -trat•ing.** to move into (an enemy country, etc.) secretly to do harm: [~ + *obj*]: *Spies had infiltrated enemy headquarters.* [*no obj*]: *They had infiltrated into enemy territory.* —**in•fil•tra•tion** (in′fil trā′shən) /͵ɪnfɪlˈtreyʃən/ *n.* [*noncount*]: *infiltration behind enemy lines.* —**in′fil•tra′tor,** *n.* [*count*]: *The infiltrator had penetrated the high command.*

in•fi•nite (in′fə nit) /ˈɪnfənɪt/ *adj.* **1.** great beyond measure: *infinite patience with her unruly students.* **2.** without limits; boundless: *God's infinite mercy.* —*n.* **3.** [*noncount; the* + ~] something infinite: *afraid of confronting the infinite in death.* —**in′fi•nite•ly,** *adv.*: *Retyping his paper was infinitely easier than learning a new word-processing program.* See -FIN-.

in•fin•i•tes•i•mal (in′fin i tes′ə məl) /͵ɪnfɪnɪˈtɛsəməl/ *adj.* so small as to be incapable of being measured: *to an infinitesimal degree.* —**in′fin•i•tes′i•mal•ly,** *adv.*: *reduced the volume of her headset infinitesimally.* See -FIN-.

in•fin•i•tive (in fin′i tiv) /ɪnˈfɪnɪtɪv/ *n.* [*count*] **1.** This word is the name of a verb form that in many languages names the action of a verb but is separate from the verb; it may function as a noun, adjective, or adverb. It is often translated into English with the word "to" before it: *The Spanish infinitive* hablar *means "to speak."* **2.** This word, when referring to English verb forms, is used **a.** in some grammar books to mean "the root form of the verb; the form that follows certain modal verbs, or that comes after (but does not include) the word TO:" *We use the infinitive without to after words like* must *and* should, *as in "We must go; we should leave," where* go *and* leave *are the infinitives.* **b.** in this dictionary and in many grammar books, to mean "the word TO, followed by the root form of the verb:" *We can use the infinitive of the verb as the subject of a sentence; the phrase* to err *is the infinitive and is the subject of the sentence "To err is human."* —*adj.* [*before a noun*] **3.** consisting of or containing an infinitive: *an infinitive clause.* —**in•fin•i•ti•val** (in′fi ni tī′vəl), *adj.* /͵ɪnfɪnɪˈtayvəl/, *adj.* —**Usage.** In this book, the term ROOT is used for the basic form of a verb, esp. the form that appears after the word TO and in commands (compare IMPERATIVE). The term INFINITIVE is used in this book for the construction made up of TO and a following ROOT form of a verb. Thus, the word *take* is called the ROOT, and the construction *to take* is called the INFINITIVE.

in•fin•i•ty (in fin′i tē) /ɪnˈfɪnɪtiy/ *n., pl.* **-ties. 1.** [*noncount*] the quality or state of being infinite. **2.** [*noncount*] infinite space, time, distance, or amount: *The new telescope gave us a glimpse into infinity.* **3.** [*count*] an infinite extent, amount, or number: *an infinity of stars.* **4.** [*count; usually singular*] a great amount, extent, or number: *waited an infinity for her to come back.* See -FIN-.

in•firm (in fûrm′) /ɪnˈfɜrm/ *adj.* **1.** feeble or weak because of age: *The old man was too infirm to walk.* —*n.* **the infirm,** [*plural; used with a plural verb*] **2.** infirm people: *care of the infirm.*

in•fir•ma•ry (in fûr′mə rē) /ɪnˈfɜrməriy/ *n.* [*count*], *pl.* **-ries.** a place for the care of the infirm, sick, or injured: *went to the school infirmary and the nurse gave her an aspirin.*

in•fir•mi•ty (in fûr′mi tē) /ɪnˈfɜrmɪtiy/ *n., pl.* **-ties. 1.** [*count*] a physical weakness: *the infirmities of age.* **2.** [*noncount*] the quality or state of being infirm: *suffering from physical infirmity.*

in•flame (in flām′) /ɪnˈfleym/ *v.* [~ + *obj*], **-flamed, -flam•ing. 1.** to kindle or excite (people, passions, etc.): *The speaker inflamed (the passions of) the crowd with his angry words.* **2.** to cause inflammation in: *The infection inflamed her lungs.* —**in•flamed′,** *adj.*: *eyes inflamed from tear gas.*

in•flam•ma•ble (in flam′ə bəl) /ɪnˈflæməbəl/ *adj.* **1.** capable of being set on fire; combustible; flammable: *Don't light matches near inflammable liquids.* **2.** easily aroused to passion or anger: *an inflammable temper.* —**in•flam•ma•bil•i•ty** (in flam′ə bil′i tē) /ɪn͵flæməˈbɪlɪtiy/ *n.* [*noncount*] —**Usage.** Note that INFLAMMABLE and FLAMMABLE may mean the same thing. That is because the prefix in

INFLAMMABLE is IN[1]-, meaning "in; into;" it is not the prefix IN[2]-, meaning "not."

in•flam•ma•tion (in′flə mā′shən) /ˌɪnflə'meyʃən/ *n.* redness, swelling, and fever in an area of the body, in reaction to an infection or injury: [*noncount*]: *Exposure to chemical weapons may lead to inflammation.* [*count*]: *an inflammation in the liver.*

in•flam•ma•to•ry (in flam′ə tôr′ē, -tōr′ē) /ɪn'flæməˌtɔriy, -ˌtowriy/ *adj.* **1.** causing or arousing anger, etc.: *A few inflammatory speeches and the mob was off.* **2.** of or caused by inflammation: *inflammatory reactions to the medicine.*

in•flate (in flāt′) /ɪn'fleyt/ *v.,* **-flat•ed, -flat•ing.** **1.** to (cause to) be expanded with air or gas: [~ + *obj*]: *Did you inflate the tires to the proper pressure?* [*no obj*]: *Those balloons inflate easily.* **2.** [~ + *obj*] to puff up with pride, vanity, etc.: *He will try to inflate your ego.* **3.** [~ + *obj*] to increase too much, such as the level of prices: *The company inflated its prices during the oil shortage.* **—in•flat′a•ble,** *adj.*: *an inflatable life raft.* See -FLAT-.

in•flat•ed (in flā′tid) /ɪn'fleytɪd/ *adj.* **1.** expanded or filled with air: *properly inflated tires.* **2.** filled with pride or vanity: *an inflated opinion of his own importance.* **3.** increased too much: *grossly inflated charges.*

in•fla•tion (in flā′shən) /ɪn'fleyʃən/ *n.* [*noncount*] a steady rise in the level of prices: *During inflation money does not buy as much as it once did.* **—in•fla•tion•ar•y** (in flā′shə ner′ē) /ɪn'fleyʃəˌnɛriy/ *adj.*: *inflationary pressures.*

in•flect (in flekt′) /ɪn'flɛkt/ *v.* **1.** [~ + *obj*] to change (the voice) when pronouncing: *When you inflect your voice in English you can make a difference in meaning; there is a difference, as between "You are coming" spoken with little change in stress or pitch, and "**You** are coming?".* **2.** [~ + *obj*] to change the form of (a word) by inflection; conjugate or decline: *The computer program can inflect that verb, producing the forms talk, talks, talked, and talking.* **3.** [*no obj*] to be able to undergo such a change: *In English the verb* must *does not inflect; it stays the same.* See -FLECT-.

in•flec•tion (in flek′shən) /ɪn'flɛkʃən/ *n.* **1.** [*noncount*] change in pitch or tone of voice: *He spoke with very little inflection in his voice.* **2. a.** [*noncount*] the process of adding an affix to a base or root of a word, or otherwise changing the shape of a base or root to give it a different syntactic function without changing its form class, as in forming the past tense *served* from *serve,* or in forming the present tense, third person singular form *sings* from *sing,* or in forming *harder* from *hard.* **b.** [*count*] an affix added in this process, as the *-s* in *sings* or the *-ed* in *played.* **c.** an inflected form of a word, as *sings* from *sing.* Also, *esp. Brit.,* **inflexion. —in•flec′tion•al,** *adj.*: *inflectional endings in English, such as* -est *in* fastest, *or* -ing *in* running. Compare DERIVATION.

in•flex•i•ble (in flek′sə bəl) /ɪn'flɛksəbəl/ *adj.* **1.** not flexible; rigid: *an inflexible plastic rod.* **2.** (of people) unyielding; stubborn: *an inflexible determination.* **3.** not permitting variation; unalterable: *inflexible rules.* **—in•flex•i•bil•i•ty** (in flek′sə bil′i tē) /ɪnˌflɛksə'bɪlɪtiy/ *n.* [*noncount*] **—in•flex′i•bly,** *adv.*

in•flict (in flikt′) /ɪn'flɪkt/ *v.* [~ + *obj* (+ *on* + *obj*)] **1.** to impose something to be suffered: *to inflict punishment (on a wrongdoer).* **2.** to deliver, such as a blow: *The hurricane inflicted severe damage (on the crops).*

in′-flight′ or **in′flight′,** *adj.* [*usually: before a noun*] done, served, or shown during flight in an aircraft: *an in-flight movie.*

in•flo•res•cence (in′flô res′əns, -flō-, -flə-) /ˌɪnflɔ'rɛsəns, -flow-, -flə-/ *n.* [*noncount*] **1.** a flowering or blossoming. **2.** flowers thought of as a group. **—in′flo•res′cent,** *adj.* See -FLOR-.

in•flu•ence (in′flo͞o əns) /'ɪnfluwəns/ *n., v.,* **-enced, -enc•ing.** **—***n.* **1.** [*noncount*] the power to produce effects by indirect means: *the influence of religion in politics.* **2.** [*count*] a person or thing that exerts influence: *Is he a good influence on her behavior?* **3.** [*noncount*] the power to persuade, or to obtain advantages due to one's status, rank, etc.: *Thanks to his uncle's influence he was able to get a job.* **—***v.* [~ + *obj*] **4.** to cause an effect on (someone); affect: *The job market influenced his decision to relocate.* **5.** to persuade; to move (someone) to some action: *Don't let me influence you; you make your own decision.* [~ + *obj* + *to* + *verb*]: *My father influenced me to accept the job.* **—*Idiom.*** **6. under the influence,** *Law.* less than drunk but feeling the effects of alcohol or drugs: *arrested for driving while under the influence.* See -FLU-.

in•flu•en•tial (in′flo͞o en′shəl) /ˌɪnfluw'ɛnʃəl/ *adj.* of or relating to influence: *an influential congresswoman in the caucus.* See -FLU-.

in•flu•en•za (in′flo͞o en′zə) /ˌɪnfluw'ɛnzə/ *n.* [*noncount*] a serious, easily spread disease caused by different viruses and characterized by sneezing, coughing, fever, and exhaustion; the flu. See -FLU-.

in•flux (in′fluks′) /'ɪnˌflʌks/ *n.* [*count*] **1.** an act of flowing in; inflow. **2.** the arrival of people or things, esp. in large numbers: *an influx of tourists.* See -FLU-.

in•fo (in′fō) /'ɪnfow/ *n.* [*noncount*] *Informal.* information: *Do you have any info on the new job postings?*

in•fo•mer•cial (in′fō mûr′shəl) /ˌɪnfow'mɜrʃəl/ *n.* [*count*] a program-length television commercial made to appear as a documentary or a talk show. See -MERC-.

in•form (in fôrm′) /ɪn'fɔrm/ *v.* **1.** to give knowledge of a fact to (someone); tell: [~ + *obj*]: *We informed them, so they should have come.* [~ + *obj* + *of/about* + *obj*]: *We informed them of our arrival. We informed them about our plans.* [~ + *obj* + (*that*) *clause*]: *We informed the press that the president had arrived.* **2.** [~ + *on/against* + *obj*] to give information indicating that someone has committed a crime, as to the police: *informed on the other members of the gang.* See -FORM-.

in•for•mal (in fôr′məl) /ɪn'fɔrməl/ *adj.* **1.** without formality; casual: *an informal visit.* **2.** not according to the official manner: *informal proceedings.* **3.** suitable to or characteristic of casual speech or writing: *an informal use of a word.* **—in•for′mal•ly,** *adv.*: *dressed informally for the party.* See -FORM-. **—Syn.** See COLLOQUIAL.

in•for•mal•i•ty (in′fôr mal′i tē) /ˌɪnfɔr'mælɪtiy/ *n., pl.* **-ties.** **1.** [*noncount*] the condition of being informal: *The informality of the party was welcome after a day of formal interviews.* **2.** [*count*] an act of being informal: *lighthearted informalities.* See -FORM-.

in•form•ant (in fôr′mənt) /ɪn'fɔrmənt/ *n.* [*count*] a person who informs or gives information, esp. secretly; an informer. See -FORM-.

in•for•ma•tion (in′fər mā′shən) /ˌɪnfər'meyʃən/ *n.* [*noncount*] **1.** knowledge gained through study, instruction, etc.: *There is very little information about that culture.* **2.** knowledge given or received about a particular fact; news: *information about the missing hostages.* **3.** computer data at any stage of processing, such as input, output, storage, or transmission. See -FORM-.

in•form•a•tive (in fôr′mə tiv) /ɪn'fɔrmətɪv/ *adj.* giving information; instructive: *an informative book.* **—in•form′a•tive•ly,** *adv.* **—in•form′a•tive•ness,** *n.* [*noncount*] See -FORM-.

in•form•er (in fôr′mər) /ɪn'fɔrmər/ *n.* [*count*] one who gives information, esp. secretly, as to the police.

in•fo•tain•ment (in′fō tān′mənt) /ˌɪnfow'teynmənt/ *n.* [*noncount*] broadcasting that treats factual matter in an entertaining way.

in•fra (in′frə) /'ɪnfrə/ *adv.* (used in writing to refer to parts of a text that come below the point of reading). Compare SUPRA.

in•frac•tion (in frak′shən) /ɪn'frækʃən/ *n.* [*count*] a breaking of the rules or of the law; violation: *Too many infractions of school rules will result in your dismissal.* See -FRAC-.

in•fra•red (in′frə red′) /ˌɪnfrə'rɛd/ *n.* [*noncount*] **1.** electromagnetic radiation or light that is invisible, near the red end of the spectrum. **—*adj.*** **2.** of, relating to, or using infrared rays: *infrared radiation.* Compare ULTRAVIOLET.

in•fra•struc•ture (in′frə struk′chər) /'ɪnfrəˌstrʌktʃər/ *n.* [*noncount*] **1.** the framework or features of a system or organization: *the infrastructure of the department.* **2.** the basic facilities serving a country, city, or area, such as transportation and communication systems: *bridges and roads and other parts of the country's infrastructure.* See -STRU-.

in•fre•quent (in frē′kwənt) /ɪn'friykwənt/ *adj.* **1.** happening or occurring rarely: *infrequent visits.* **2.** not habitual or regular: *an infrequent visitor.* **—in•fre′quen•cy, in•fre′quence,** *n.* [*noncount*] **—in•fre′quent•ly,** *adv.*: *My grandmother complained that I visited her too infrequently.*

in•fringe (in frinj′) /ɪn'frɪndʒ/ *v.,* **-fringed, -fring•ing.** **1.** [~ + *obj*] to break a rule or regulation; violate: *By copying my programs and selling them they were infringing my copyright.* **2.** [~ + *on/upon* + *obj*] to interfere with: *to infringe on someone's privacy.* See -FRACT-.

in•fringe•ment (in frinj′mənt) /ɪn'frɪndʒmənt/ *n.* [*count*] **1.** an act of infringing: *numerous infringements against* *the law.* **2.** an act of interfering with someone's rights: *infringements on our right to privacy.* See -FRACT-.

in•fu•ri•ate (in fyŏŏr′ē āt′) /ɪn'fyʊriy,eyt/ *v.* [~ + *obj*], **-at•ed, -at•ing.** to make very angry; enrage: *The child's stubbornness infuriated his mother.* [*it* + ~ + *obj* + *that clause*]: *It infuriated us that our plane was delayed.* —**in•fu′ri•at′ed,** *adj.*: *infuriated passengers.* —**in•fu′ri•at′ing,** *adj.*: *an infuriating delay.* [*it* + *be* + ~ + *that clause*]: *It was infuriating that we had to wait.* [*it* + *be* + ~ + *to* + *verb*]: *It was infuriating to wait so long.* —**in•fu′ri•at′ing•ly,** *adv.*: *computer manuals infuriatingly difficult to understand.*

in•fuse (in fyōōz′) /ɪn'fyuwz/ *v.*, **-fused, -fus•ing. 1.** [~ + *obj* + *into* + *obj*] to introduce, as if by pouring: *to infuse new life into industry.* **2.** [~ + *obj* + *with* + *obj*] to inspire; fill (someone) with emotion: *infused the team with enthusiasm.* —**in•fus′er,** *n.* [*count*] See -FUS-.

in•fu•sion (in fyōō′zhən) /ɪn'fyuwʒən/ *n.* [*count*] the act or instance of infusing: *an infusion of new ideas.*

-ing[1], *suffix.* **1.** *-ing* is attached to verbs to form nouns that express the action of the verb or its result, product, material, etc.: *build* + *-ing* → *building: the art of building; a new building.* **2.** *-ing* is also attached to roots (other than verb roots) to form nouns: *off* + *-ing* → *offing.*

-ing[2], *suffix.* *-ing* is attached to verbs to form the present participle of verbs: *walk* + *-ing* → *walking: Is the baby walking yet?* These participles are often used as adjectives: *war* + *-ing* → *warring: warring factions.*

in•gen•ious (in jēn′yəs) /ɪn'dʒiynyəs/ *adj.* showing cleverness; resourceful: *an ingenious mechanic.* —**in•gen′ious•ly,** *adv.* —**in•gen′ious•ness,** *n.* [*noncount*] See -GEN-.

in•gé•nue or **in•ge•nue** (an′zhə nōō′) /'ænʒə,nuw/ *n.* [*count*] **1.** the role of an innocent, unworldly young woman, esp. as represented on the stage. **2.** an actress who plays such a role. See -GEN-.

in•ge•nu•i•ty (in′jə nōō′i tē, -nyōō′-) /,ɪndʒə'nuwɪtiy, -'nyuw-/ *n.* [*noncount*] the quality of being ingenious: *a device of great ingenuity.* See -GEN-.

in•gen•u•ous (in jen′yōō əs) /ɪn'dʒɛnyuwəs/ *adj.* apparently sincere and truthful: *That crook had the ingenuous eyes of a young schoolboy.* —**in•gen′u•ous•ly,** *adv.* —**in•gen′u•ous•ness,** *n.* [*noncount*] See -GEN-.

in•gest (in jest′) /ɪn'dʒɛst/ *v.* [~ + *obj*] to take into the body, as food or liquid: *ingested a rich, heavy meal.* —**in•ges•tion** (in jes′chən) /ɪn'dʒɛstʃən/ *n.* [*noncount*] See -GEST-.

in•glo•ri•ous (in glôr′ē əs, -glōr′-) /ɪn'glɔriyəs, -'glowr-/ *adj.* shameful; disgraceful: *an inglorious defeat.* —**in•glo′ri•ous•ly,** *adv.*

in•got (ing′gət) /'ɪŋgət/ *n.* [*count*] a mass of metal made into a convenient form for shaping, remelting, or refining: *an ingot of gold in the shape of a bar.*

in•grained (in grānd′, in′grānd′) /ɪn'greynd, 'ɪn,greynd/ also **engrained,** *adj.* **1.** fixed deep in one's mind: *ingrained superstition.* **2.** forced deeply into or through something, as through the grain or fiber of something: *deeply ingrained dirt and stains.*

in•grate (in′grāt) /'ɪngreyt/ *n.* [*count*] an ungrateful person: *What an ingrate!* See -GRAT-.

in•gra•ti•ate (in grā′shē āt′) /ɪn'greyʃiy,eyt/ *v.* [~ + *oneself*], **-at•ed, -at•ing.** to make (oneself) favored by others, esp. by falsely acting pleasant: *trying to ingratiate himself with the boss.* —**in•gra′ti•a′ting,** *adj.*: *an ingratiating smile.* —**in•gra•ti•a•tion** (in grā′shē ā′shən) /ɪn,greyʃiy'eyʃən/ *n.* [*noncount*] See -GRAT-.

in•grat•i•tude (in grat′i tōōd′, -tyōōd′) /ɪn'grætɪ,tuwd, -,tyuwd/ *n.* [*noncount*] the state of being ungrateful; ungratefulness. See -GRAT-.

in•gre•di•ent (in grē′dē ənt) /ɪn'griydiyənt/ *n.* [*count*] **1.** something that is an element of a mixture: *The ingredients of a cake typically include eggs, milk, flour, and sugar.* **2.** an important part of anything: *the ingredients of a good marriage.* See -GRAD-. —**Syn.** See ELEMENT.

in•gress (in′gres) /'ɪngrɛs/ *n.* **1.** [*noncount*] the act of going in or entering: *Ingress was impossible because the whole place was sealed off.* **2.** [*count*] a means or place of entering: *An ingress was blocked.* See -GRESS-.

in•grown (in′grōn′) /'ɪn,grown/ *adj.* having grown into the flesh: *His ingrown toenail was so painful he couldn't walk.*

in•hab•it (in hab′it) /ɪn'hæbɪt/ *v.* [*not: be* + ~*-ing;* ~ + *obj*] to live in (a place), as people or animals do: *That town is inhabited by 600 people.* —**in•hab′it•a•ble,** *adj.*: *According to the myth, the earth was not inhabitable until fire was given by the gods.* See -HAB-.

in•hab•it•ant (in hab′i tənt) /ɪn'hæbɪtənt/ *n.* [*count*] a person or animal that inhabits: *The inhabitants of that remote village never experience crime.* See -HAB-.

in•hal•ant (in hā′lənt) /ɪn'heylənt/ *n.* [*count*] a medicine inhaled for the effect of its vapor. See -HALE-.

in•ha•la•tor (in′hə lā′tər) /'ɪnhə,leytər/ *n.* [*count*] **1.** an apparatus used to help a patient inhale. **2.** an apparatus for giving artificial respiration; respirator. See -HALE-.

in•hale (in hāl′) /ɪn'heyl/ *v.*, **-haled, -hal•ing.** to breathe in or draw in (smoke, air, etc.) by breathing: [~ + *obj*]: *to inhale air; to inhale the fumes.* [*no obj*]: *inhaled deeply on her cigarette.* See -HALE-.

in•hal•er (in hā′lər) /ɪn'heylər/ *n.* [*count*] **1.** an apparatus or device used in inhaling medicine; inhalator. **2.** a person who inhales. See -HALE-.

in•her•ent (in hēr′ənt, -her′-) /ɪn'hɪərənt, -'hɛr-/ *adj.* existing as a permanent part or quality that cannot be taken out: *Freedom of religion is an inherent part of the bill of rights.* —**in•her′ent•ly,** *adv.*: *inherently lazy.*

in•her•it (in her′it) /ɪn'hɛrɪt/ *v.* **1.** to take or receive (property, etc.) that is left to one after the death of someone or by someone's will, as an heir: [~ + *obj*]: *hopes to inherit her father's business.* [*no obj*]: *On his death, will she inherit?* **2.** [~ + *obj*] to receive from a past situation or from someone who has gone before: *inherited many of the problems of the previous administration.* **3.** [~ + *obj*] to receive (a genetic trait, etc.) from a parent or ancestor: *inherited her beauty from her grandmother.*

in•her•it•ance (in her′i təns) /ɪn'hɛrɪtəns/ *n.* **1.** something inherited; legacy: [*count*]: *a large inheritance from her mother's estate.* [*noncount*]: *the rules governing inheritance of cattle.* **2.** [*noncount*] the receiving of a genetic characteristic or trait: *the inheritance of blue eyes.* **3.** [*noncount*] something received from a predecessor: *the inheritance of a budget deficit.*

in•hib•it (in hib′it) /ɪn'hɪbɪt/ *v.* [~ + *obj*] **1.** to hold back (an action, impulse, etc.): *This jacket inhibits free movement.* **2.** to restrain (one's feelings, etc.): *The way she leaned over my shoulder when I worked really inhibited me.* See -HAB-.

in•hib•it•ed (in hib′i tid) /ɪn'hɪbɪtɪd/ *adj.* overly restrained in the acting of or the expressing of one's real feelings: *He was very inhibited, especially about sex.* See -HAB-.

in•hi•bi•tion (in′i bish′ən, in′hi-) /,ɪnɪ'bɪʃən, ,ɪnhɪ-/ *n.* **1.** [*noncount*] the act of inhibiting; the state of being inhibited: *a life of inhibition.* **2.** [*count*] something that inhibits: *a lot of inhibitions about socializing.* See -HAB-.

in•hib•i•tor or **in•hib•it•er** (in hib′i tər) /ɪn'hɪbɪtər/ *n.* [*count*] **1.** one that inhibits. **2.** a substance that slows down or stops a chemical reaction. See -HAB-.

in-house (*adj.* in′hous′; *adv.* -hous′) / *adj.* 'ɪn,haws; *adv.* -'haws/ *adj.* **1.** using an organization's own staff rather than someone from outside: *in-house research.* —*adv.* **2.** within an organization's own staff, rather than from outside: *The ad campaign was created in-house.*

in•hu•man (in hyōō′mən) /ɪn'hyuwmən/ *adj.* **1.** cruel; brutal; unfeeling: *an inhuman master.* **2.** not human; strange: *inhuman forms peering through the windows.*

in•hu•mane (in′hyōō mān′) /,ɪnhyuw'meyn/ *adj.* not humane: *suffered from inhumane and brutal treatment.* —**in′hu•mane′ly,** *adv.*: *They were treated inhumanely.*

in•hu•man•i•ty (in′hyōō man′i tē) /,ɪnhyuw'mænɪtiy/ *n.* [*noncount*] the state or quality of being inhuman or inhumane; cruelty: *man's inhumanity to man.*

in•im•i•cal (i nim′i kəl) /ɪ'nɪmɪkəl/ *adj.* **1.** harmful; causing injury: *conditions inimical to health.* **2.** unfriendly; hostile: *a cold, inimical gaze.* —**in•im′i•cal•ly,** *adv.*

in•im•i•ta•ble (i nim′i tə bəl) /ɪ'nɪmɪtəbəl/ *adj.* that cannot be imitated; matchless: *the painter's inimitable style.* —**in•im•i•ta•bil•i•ty** (i nim′i tə bil′i tē) /ɪ,nɪmɪtə'bɪlɪtiy/ **in•im′i•ta•ble•ness,** *n.* [*noncount*] —**in•im′i•ta•bly,** *adv.*

in•iq•ui•ty (i nik′wi tē) /ɪ'nɪkwɪtiy/ *n.*, *pl.* **-ties. 1.** [*noncount*] great and harmful injustice or wickedness. **2.** [*count*] a wicked act; sin. —**in•iq′ui•tous,** *adj.* See -EQUA-.

in•i•tial (i nish′əl) /ɪ'nɪʃəl/ *adj.*, *n.*, *v.*, **-tialed, -tial•ing** or (*esp. Brit.*) **-tialled, -tial•ling.** —*adj.* [*usually: before a noun*] **1.** of, relating to, or occurring at the beginning; first: *the initial step in a process.* —*n.* [*count*] **2.** an initial letter, as of a proper name: *Your initials are the first letters of your first and last name.* —*v.* [~ + *obj*] **3.** to mark or sign with the initials of one's name: *initialed the report and filed it away.* —**in•i′tial•ly,** *adv.*: *Initially we didn't hear anything.*

in•i•ti•ate (*v.* i nish′ē āt′; *n.* -it, -āt′) / *v.* ɪ'nɪʃiy,eyt; *n.* -ɪt, -,eyt/ *v.*, **-at•ed, -at•ing,** *n.* —*v.* [~ + *obj*] **1.** to begin: *initiated major social reforms.* **2.** to introduce into the knowledge of a subject: *He initiated her into calligraphy.* **3.** to admit into the membership of a group: *The club initiated twelve new members.* **—*n.*** [*count*] **4.** a person who has been initiated: *The new initiates had to demonstrate their allegiance to the club.* **—in•i•ti•a•tion** (i nish′ē ā′shən) /ɪ,nɪʃiy'eyʃən/ *n.* [*noncount*]: *Initiation into that club is expensive.* [*count*]: *Initiations into the club usually take place in December.* **—in•i′ti•a′tor,** *n.* [*count*] **—Syn.** See BEGIN.

in•i•ti•a•tive (i nish′ē ə tiv, i nish′ə-) /ɪ'nɪʃiyətɪv, ɪ'nɪʃə-/ *n.* **1.** [*count*] a first act or step in a process: *to take the initiative in making friends.* **2.** [*noncount*] readiness in initiating action: *to lack initiative.* **3.** [*noncount; usually: one's* + ~] one's personal, responsible decision: *The teens decided to act on their own initiative.* **4.** [*count*] a procedure by which a certain number of voters may propose a law, etc., and have a popular vote on its adoption.

in•ject (in jekt′) /ɪn'dʒɛkt/ *v.* **1.** to force (a fluid) into a part of the body with a special needle: [~ + *obj* + *into* + *obj*]: *The nurse injected the drug into the patient.* [~ + *obj* + *with* + *obj*]: *She injected the patient with the drug.* **2.** [~ + *obj* + *into* + *obj*] to introduce (something different): *The host tried to inject some humor into the situation.* **3.** [~ + *obj*] to interject (a remark, etc.), as into conversation: *had remarks that he wished to inject at that moment.* **—in•jec′tor,** *n.* [*count*] See -JEC-.

in•jec•tion (in jek′shən) /ɪn'dʒɛkʃən/ *n.* **1.** the act of injecting: [*noncount*]: *The drug must be administered by injection.* [*count*]: *Injections can be given under the skin.* **2.** [*count*] the act of bringing something (into something else): *an injection of financial support.* See -JEC-.

in•ju•di•cious (in′jo͞o dish′əs) /,ɪndʒuw'dɪʃəs/ *adj.* not wise; showing lack of judgment: *an injudicious decision.* See -JUD-.

in•junc•tion (in jungk′shən) /ɪn'dʒʌŋkʃən/ *n.* [*count*] an order by a court requiring a person or persons to do, or to keep from doing, a particular act: *an injunction to prevent the father from visiting.* See -JUNC-.

in•jure (in′jər) /'ɪndʒər/ *v.* [~ + *obj*], **-jured, -jur•ing. 1.** to do or cause harm of any kind to: *injured his hand.* **2.** to wound or offend: *to injure a friend's feelings.* **—in′-jur•er,** *n.* [*count*] See -JUR-.

in•ju•ry (in′jə rē) /'ɪndʒəriy/ *n., pl.* **-ries. 1.** [*noncount*] harm, damage, or wrong done or suffered: *to escape without injury.* **2.** [*count*] a particular form or instance of harm: *an injury to one's shoulder.* **—in•ju•ri•ous** (in-jo͝or′ē əs) /ɪn'dʒʊriyəs/ *adj.*

in•jus•tice (in jus′tis) /ɪn'dʒʌstɪs/ *n.* **1.** [*noncount*] the quality or fact of being unjust: *fighting against injustice.* **2.** [*count*] an unjust act; a wrong: *to suffer many injustices.*

ink (ingk) /ɪŋk/ *n.* **1.** a fluid used for writing or drawing: [*noncount*]: *My pen has run out of ink.* [*count*]: *The artist works with inks.* **—*v.*** [~ + *obj*] **2.** to mark, stain, cover, draw, or smear with ink: *to ink the paper.* **—ink′less,** *adj.*

ink•ling (ingk′ling) /'ɪŋklɪŋ/ *n.* [*count*] **1.** a slight suggestion; hint: *They gave us no inkling of what was going to happen.* **2.** a slight understanding: *I don't have an inkling of how it works.*

ink•y (ing′kē) /'ɪŋkiy/ *adj.*, **-i•er, -i•est. 1.** black as ink: *inky shadows.* **2.** resembling ink. **3.** stained with ink. **—ink′i•ness,** *n.* [*noncount*]

in•laid (in′lād′, in lād′) /'ɪn,leyd, ɪn'leyd/ *adj.* decorated with a design set into the surface: *an inlaid table.*

in•land (*adj.* in′lənd; *adv., n.* -land′, -lənd) / *adj.* 'ɪnlənd; *adv., n.* -,lænd, -lənd/ *adj.* [*before a noun*] **1.** relating to or located in the inside part of a region: *inland cities.* **2.** *Chiefly Brit.* domestic; internal: *inland revenue.* **—*adv.* 3.** in or toward the interior of a country: *The expedition traveled inland.*

in′-law′, *n.* [*count*] a relative by marriage: *In-laws may present problems in a marriage.* **—Usage.** As the example above shows, the word IN-LAW has as its plural form IN-LAWS. But when a compound noun is formed with -IN-LAW, such as *brother-in-law, sister-in-law, mother-in-law,* etc., its plural is formed by making the first part of the compound plural, and leaving -IN-LAW unchanged: *brothers-in-law, sisters-in-law, mothers-in-law.*

in•lay (*v.* in′lā′, in′lā′; *n.* in′lā′) / *v.* 'ɪn,ley, ,ɪn'ley; *n.* 'ɪn,ley/ *v.*, **-laid, -lay•ing,** *n.* **—*v.*** [~ + *obj*] **1.** to decorate (an object) with shaped pieces of contrasting material set in its surface, so that the surface is flat: *inlaid the table with brass and ivory.* **2.** to put (pieces of wood, etc.) onto the surface of an object: *inlaid the ivory and brass into the table.* **—*n.*** [*count*] **3.** inlaid work. **4.** a tooth filling of hard, long-lasting material first shaped to fit a prepared cavity: *an inlay of gold.*

in•let (in′let, -lit) /'ɪnlɛt, -lɪt/ *n.* [*count*] **1.** a small bay that reaches into land along the shoreline. **2.** a narrow passage between islands.

in•mate (in′māt′) /'ɪn,meyt/ *n.* [*count*] a person who is kept in a prison, hospital, etc.

in me•mo•ri•am (in mə môr′ē əm, -mōr′-) /ɪn mə'mɔriyəm, -'mowr-/ *prep.* This phrase appears before a name on a gravestone, and means "in memory (of); to the memory (of); as a memorial (to)" the person named.

in•most (in′mōst′) /'ɪn,mowst/ *adj.* [*before a noun*] **1.** located farthest within or inside: *the inmost recesses of the forest.* **2.** most secret; intimate: *to guess at his inmost thoughts.*

inn (in) /ɪn/ *n.* [*count*] **1.** a small hotel; lodge: *a cozy little New England inn.* **2.** a place where liquor is served; a tavern.

in•nards (in′ərdz) /'ɪnərdz/ *n.* [*plural*] **1.** the inside parts of the body, esp. of an animal. **2.** the inside mechanism, etc., of something: *If we can get to the engine's innards we might find out what's making that noise.*

in•nate (i nāt′, in′āt) /ɪ'neyt, 'ɪneyt/ *adj.* **1.** existing from birth; inborn; native: *innate talents.* **2.** existing in the nature of something: *an innate defect in the hypothesis.* **3.** arising from the intellect rather than learned through experience: *an innate knowledge of good and evil.* **—in•nate′ly,** *adv.* **—in•nate′ness,** *n.* [*noncount*] See -NAT-.

in•ner (in′ər) /'ɪnər/ *adj.* [*before a noun*] **1.** situated within or farther within; more inside: *an inner room.* **2.** private or intimate: *to learn the inner workings of the organization.* **3.** of or relating to the mind or spirit: *the inner life.*

in′ner cit′y, *n.* [*count*] a central part of a city, often deteriorating, populated mainly by poor people: *the problems of the nation's inner cities.* **—in′ner-cit′y,** *adj.* [*before a noun*]: *inner-city crime.*

in′ner ear′, *n.* [*count*] the inner, liquid-filled portion of the ear, involved in hearing and balance.

in•ner•most (in′ər mōst′) /'ɪnər,mowst/ *adj.* **1.** farthest inward; inmost: *the innermost reaches of the jungle.* **2.** most private, secret, or intimate: *my innermost thoughts.*

in•ning (in′ing) /'ɪnɪŋ/ *n.* [*count*] **1.** a division of a baseball game during which each team has an opportunity to score: *He scored a home run in the bottom of the ninth inning.* **2. innings,** [*plural*] [*count; but used with a singular verb in the singular form*] *Cricket.* a unit of play in which each team has a turn at bat. **3.** an opportunity for activity; a turn: *You've had your innings, now it's my chance.*

inn•keep•er (in′kē′pər) /'ɪn,kiypər/ *n.* [*count*] a person who owns or manages an inn or, sometimes, a hotel.

in•no•cence (in′ə səns) /'ɪnəsəns/ *n.* [*noncount*] **1.** the quality or condition of being innocent: *A trial starts out by assuming the defendant's innocence.* **2.** the absence of cunning or dishonesty: *the innocence of youth.*

in•no•cent (in′ə sənt) /'ɪnəsənt/ *adj.* **1.** free from moral wrong; without sin; pure: *the innocent children.* **2.** free from legal wrong; guiltless: *innocent until proven guilty.* **3.** not involving evil intent or motive; harmless: *an innocent mistake.* **4.** showing the simplicity of someone not accustomed to recognizing evil; ingenuous: *gave her father a wide-eyed, innocent look.* **—*n.*** [*count*] **5.** an innocent person, esp. one who has the simplicity of not recognizing evil. **—in′no•cent•ly,** *adv.* See -NOC-, -NOX-.

in•noc•u•ous (i nok′yo͞o əs) /ɪ'nɒkyuwəs/ *adj.* **1.** not harmful; harmless: *innocuous home medicine.* **2.** not likely to irritate; inoffensive: *just an innocuous remark about the weather.* **—in•noc′u•ous•ly,** *adv.* **—in•noc′u•ous•ness,** *n.* [*noncount*] See -NOC-, -NOX-.

in•no•vate (in′ə vāt′) /'ɪnə,veyt/ *v.*, **-vat•ed, -vat•ing.** to introduce something new; make changes: [~ + *on/in* + *obj*]: *to innovate on another's creation.* [~ + *obj*]: *to innovate a computer operating system.* **—in′no•va′tion,** *n.* [*count; noncount*] **—in′no•va′tion•al,** *adj.* **—in′no•va′-tive,** *adj.* See -NOV-.

in•nu•en•do (in′yo͞o en′dō) /,ɪnyuw'ɛndow/ *n., pl.* **-dos, -does.** an indirect hint, esp. of an offensive or derogatory nature: [*noncount*]: *There was plenty of innuendo in that newspaper article.* [*count*]: *The article was simply a list of innuendos.*

in•nu•mer•a•ble (i no͞o′mər ə bəl, i nyo͞o′-) /ɪ'nuwmərəbəl, ɪ'nyuw-/ *adj.* too numerous to be counted: *his innumerable excuses and missed assignments.* See -NUM-.

in•oc•u•late (i nok′yə lāt′) /ɪ'nɒkyə,leyt/ *v.* [~ + *obj*], **-lat•ed, -lat•ing.** to inject a vaccine, microorganism, etc., in order to protect against, treat, or study a disease: *inoculated me against yellow fever.* —**in•oc•u•la•tion** (i nok′yə lā′shən) /ɪˌnɒkyə'leyʃən/ *n.* [*count*]: *After three inoculations I was beginning to feel like a pin cushion.* [*noncount*]: *Inoculation is not the best way to prevent this disease.*

in•of•fen•sive (in′ə fen′siv) /ˌɪnə'fɛnsɪv/ *adj.* causing no harm, trouble, or annoyance: *an inoffensive manner; an inoffensive odor.* —**in′of•fen′sive•ly,** *adv.* See -FEND-.

in•op•er•a•ble (in op′ər ə bəl, -op′rə bəl) /ɪn'ɒpərəbəl, -'ɒprəbəl/ *adj.* **1.** not operable; that cannot be made practical: *an inoperable plan.* **2.** that cannot be treated by surgery: *an inoperable brain tumor.* See -OPER-.

in•op•er•a•tive (in op′ər ə tiv, -op′rə tiv) /ɪn'ɒpərətɪv, -'ɒprətɪv/ *adj.* **1.** not in operation; not working: *The machine is inoperative.* **2.** without effect; not in effect: *inoperative remedies.* See -OPER-.

in•op•por•tune (in op′ər to͞on′, -tyo͞on′) /ɪnˌɒpər'tuwn, -'tyuwn/ *adj.* not at a good time; untimely: *It's an inopportune time to talk to him.*

in•or•di•nate (in ôr′dn it) /ɪn'ɔrdn̩ɪt/ *adj.* not within proper limits: *to drink an inordinate amount of wine.* —**in•or′di•nate•ly,** *adv.*: *inordinately expensive.* See -ORD-.

in•or•gan•ic (in′ôr gan′ik) /ˌɪnɔr'gænɪk/ *adj.* **1.** not having the characteristics of living things: *inorganic rocks.* **2.** of or relating to chemical compounds that are not hydrocarbons: *inorganic chemistry.* See -ORGA-.

in•pa•tient (in′pā′shənt) /'ɪnˌpeyʃənt/ *n.* [*count*] a patient who stays in a hospital.

in•put (in′po͝ot′) /'ɪnˌpʊt/ *n., adj., v.,* **-put•ted** or **-put, -put•ting.** —*n.* **1.** [*count*] something put in. **2.** [*noncount*] the act or process of putting in. **3.** [*noncount*] the energy supplied to a machine. **4.** [*noncount*] data entered into a computer for processing. **5.** [*noncount*] contribution of information, ideas, etc.: *Before making a decision we need your input.* —*adj.* [*before a noun*] **6.** of or relating to data or equipment used for input: *a computer's main input device.* —*v.* [~ + *obj*] **7.** to enter (data) into a computer for processing: *You simply input the customer's name and address here.*

in•quest (in′kwest) /'ɪnkwɛst/ *n.* [*count*] a legal inquiry made by a coroner to find out the cause of death of a murder victim. See -QUES-.

in•qui•e•tude (in kwī′i to͞od′, -tyo͞od′) /ɪn'kwayɪˌtuwd, -ˌtyuwd/ *n.* [*noncount*] restlessness or uneasiness.

in•quire (in kwīᵊr′) /ɪn'kwayᵊr/ also **enquire,** *v.,* **-quired, -quir•ing. 1.** to seek information by questioning; ask: [*no obj*]: *to inquire about a person.* [~ + *obj*]: *to inquire a person's name.* [*used with quotations*]: *"Why are you searching for that planet?" he inquired.* **2.** [~ + *into* + *obj*] to make an investigation: *decided to inquire further into the incident.* **3. inquire after,** [~ + *obj*] to ask about the health of (someone not present): *politely inquired after each other's families.* —**in•quir′er,** *n.* [*count*] See -QUIR-.

in•quir•ing (in kwīᵊr′ing) /ɪn'kwayᵊrɪŋ/ *adj.* [*before a noun*] **1.** seeking information: *an inquiring mind.* **2.** showing a wish to seek information: *an inquiring expression on his face.* —**in•quir′ing•ly,** *adv.* See -QUIR-.

in•quir•y (in kwīᵊr′ē, in′kwə rē) /ɪn'kwayᵊriy, 'ɪnkwəriy/ also **enquiry,** *n., pl.* **-quir•ies. 1.** a seeking or request for truth, information, or knowledge: [*noncount*]: *Further inquiry turned up no new evidence.* [*count*]: *Additional inquiries on the computer show no more sources on that topic.* **2.** [*count*] an investigation, as into an incident: *ordered an inquiry into the death of his previous wife.* **3.** [*count*] a question; query: *inquiries as to her name and address.* See -QUIR-.

in•qui•si•tion (in′kwə zish′ən, ing′-) /ˌɪnkwə'zɪʃən, ˌɪŋ-/ *n.* [*count*] **1.** an official investigation lacking regard for individual rights and showing prejudice on the part of the examiners. **2.** any harsh, difficult, or prolonged questioning. —**in•quis•i•tor** (in kwiz′i tər, ing-) /ɪn'kwɪzɪtər,ɪŋ-/ *n.* [*count*]: *The chief inquisitor badgered his witnesses.* See -QUIS-.

in•quis•i•tive (in kwiz′i tiv) /ɪn'kwɪzɪtɪv/ *adj.* **1.** eager for knowledge; curious: *an inquisitive mind.* **2.** overly curious; prying: *That inquisitive child is always listening in to private conversations.* —**in•quis′i•tive•ly,** *adv.* —**in•quis′i•tive•ness,** *n.* [*noncount*] See -QUIS-.

in re (in rē′, rā′) /'ɪn riy, 'rey/ *prep.* in the matter of.

in•road (in′rōd′) /'ɪnˌrowd/ *n.* [*count; usually: inroads, plural*] something that affects something else: *The unexpected expenses have made serious inroads on our savings.*

ins., an abbreviation of: **1.** inches. **2.** inspector.

in•sane (in sān′) /ɪn'seyn/ *adj.* **1.** [*not in technical use*] mentally unsound; mad. **2.** of or characteristic of the mentally deranged: *insane actions.* **3.** utterly senseless; irrational; foolish: *You're insane if you think you can jump off that bridge and live.* —**in•sane′ly,** *adv.* —**in•sane′ness,** *n.* [*noncount*] —**in•san•i•ty** (in san′i tē) /ɪn'sænɪtiy/ *n.* [*noncount*] See -SAN-.

in•sa•tia•ble (in sā′shə bəl, -shē ə-) /ɪn'seyʃəbəl, -ʃiyə-/ *adj.* that cannot be satisfied: *insatiable ambition.* —**in•sa•tia•bil•i•ty** (in sā′shə bil′i tē, -shē ə-) /ɪnˌseyʃə'bɪlɪtiy, -ʃiyə-/ **in•sa′tia•ble•ness,** *n.* [*noncount*] —**in•sa′tia•bly,** *adv.* See -SAT-.

in•scribe (in skrīb′) /ɪn'skrayb/ *v.* [~ + *obj*], **-scribed, -scrib•ing. 1.** to address (a book, etc.) to a person, esp. by writing a brief personal note in or on it: *The ballplayer inscribed the boy's book.* **2.** to mark (a surface) with words, etc., esp. in a way that will be noticeable and last a long time. **3.** to write or engrave (words, etc.): *inscribed his initials on the statue.* —**in•scrib′er,** *n.* [*count*] See -SCRIB-.

in•scrip•tion (in skrip′shən) /ɪn'skrɪpʃən/ *n.* [*count*] the words, characters, or letters inscribed on a surface: *an inscription on the ring.* See -SCRIB-.

in•scru•ta•ble (in skro͞o′tə bəl) /ɪn'skruwtəbəl/ *adj.* **1.** incapable of being analyzed. **2.** not easily understood: *an inscrutable smile.* —**in•scru•ta•bil•i•ty** (in skro͞o′tə bil′i tē) /ɪnˌskruwtə'bɪlɪtiy/ **in•scru′ta•ble•ness,** *n.* [*noncount*] —**in•scru′ta•bly,** *adv.*

in•seam (in′sēm′) /'ɪnˌsiym/ *n.* [*count*] an inside or inner seam of a piece of clothing, esp. the seam of a trouser leg.

in•sect (in′sekt) /'ɪnsɛkt/ *n.* [*count*] **1. a.** a member of a class of animals that are small, air-breathing arthropods having a body divided into three parts and having two antennae, three pairs of legs, and usually two pairs of wings: *insects such as beetles, ants, and flies.* **b.** any small arthropod, such as a spider, that looks somewhat like such an animal. **2.** one who deserves hate or contempt; an unimportant person. —*adj.* [*before a noun*] **3.** of, relating to, or used against insects: *insect spray.*

in•sec•ti•cide (in sek′tə sīd′) /ɪn'sɛktəˌsayd/ *n.* a substance for killing insects: [*noncount*]: *spraying crops with insecticide.* [*count*]: *many insecticides to choose from.* —**in•sec•ti•cid•al** (in sek′tə sīd′l) /ɪnˌsɛktə'saydl̩/ *adj.* See -CIDE-.

in•sec•tiv•o•rous (in′sek tiv′ər əs) /ˌɪnsɛk'tɪvərəs/ *adj.* feeding chiefly on insects. —**in•sec•ti•vore** (in sek′tə-vôr′, -vōr′) /ɪn'sɛktəˌvɔr, -ˌvowr/ *n.* [*count*] See -VOR-.

in•se•cure (in′si kyo͝or′) /ˌɪnsɪ'kyʊr/ *adj.* **1.** subject to fears, doubts, etc.: *an insecure person.* **2.** not safe; exposed to risk or danger: *fortified the defenses of their insecure borders.* **3.** not firmly or safely fastened; not secure: *an insecure ladder.* —**in′se•cure′ly,** *adv.*: *The seatbelt was insecurely fastened.* —**in•se•cu•ri•ty** (in′si-kyo͝or′i tē) /ˌɪnsɪ'kyʊrɪtiy/ *n., pl.* **-ties:** [*noncount*]: *Her fear of asking questions in class is a sign of insecurity.* [*count*]: *Deal with your insecurities by confronting them.* See -CURA-.

in•sem•i•nate (in sem′ə nāt′) /ɪn'sɛməˌneyt/ *v.* [~ + *obj*], **-nat•ed, -nat•ing.** to put semen into (the female reproductive area) so as to make pregnant; impregnate: *The veterinarian inseminated the cows.* —**in•sem•i•na•tion** (in sem′ə nā′shən) /ɪnˌsɛmə'neyʃən/ *n.* [*noncount*]: *artificial insemination.*

in•sen•sate (in sen′sāt, -sit) /ɪn'sɛnseyt, -sɪt/ *adj.* **1.** not able to feel things: *insensate rocks.* **2.** without emotional sensitivity; cold: *a harsh, insensate boss.* See -SENS-.

in•sen•si•ble (in sen′sə bəl) /ɪn'sɛnsəbəl/ *adj.* [*not: be* + ~] **1.** incapable of feeling; unconscious: *rendered insensible before the operation.* **2.** without a particular feeling or sensation: *insensible to shame.* **3.** unaware; not appreciative: *The family was not insensible of your kindness.* —**in•sen•si•bil•i•ty** (in sen′sə bil′i tē) /ɪnˌsɛnsə'bɪlɪtiy/ *n.* [*noncount*] —**in•sen′si•bly,** *adv.* See -SENS-. —**Usage.** In many cases, pairs of words with the same root and the prefix *in-* in one of them are opposite in meaning. However, the words SENSIBLE and INSENSIBLE are not opposites for all the meanings of the root, -SENS-. Thus, one of the meanings of SENSIBLE is "showing good sense or judgment; wise; not foolish." But INSENSIBLE cannot be used for the opposite of that meaning.

in•sen•si•tive (in sen′si tiv) /ɪn'sɛnsɪtɪv/ *adj.* **1.** not emotionally sensitive or sympathetic; callous: *He has an insensitive nature.* **2.** not physically sensitive: *insensitive skin.* —**in•sen′si•tive•ly,** *adv.* —**in•sen•si•tiv•i•ty** (in-sen′si tiv′i tē) /ɪnˌsɛnsɪ'tɪvɪtiy/ *n.* [*noncount*] See -SENS-.

in•sen•ti•ent (in sen′shē ənt, -shənt) /ɪn'sɛnʃiyənt, -ʃənt/ *adj.* not sentient; without sensation or feeling. —**in•sen′ti•ence,** *n.* [*noncount*] See -SENS-.

in•sep•a•ra•ble (in sep′ər ə bəl, -sep′rə-) /ɪn'sɛpərəbəl, -'sɛprə-/ *adj.* that cannot be separated, parted, or disjoined: *The two sisters were inseparable.*

in•sert (*v.* in sûrt′; *n.* in′sûrt) / *v.* ɪn'sɜrt; *n.* 'ɪnsɜrt/ *v.* [~ + *obj*] **1.** to put or place in: *to insert a key in a lock.* **2.** to introduce into the body of something: *to insert a new paragraph in an article.* —*n.* [*count*] **3.** something inserted or to be inserted for advertising: *a sales insert.* —**in•ser′tion,** *n.* [*noncount*]: *careful insertion of the needle into the vein.* [*count*]: *a few insertions into the main part of your essay.*

in•set (*n.* in′set′; *v.* in set′) / *n.* 'ɪn,sɛt; *v.* ɪn'sɛt/ *n., v.,* **-set, -set•ting.** —*n.* [*count*] **1.** something inserted, such as a small map, etc., within the border of a larger one: *The inset shows a close-up of the city streets.* **2.** a piece of cloth set into a garment. —*v.* [~ + *obj*] **3.** to set in or insert: *to inset a panel in a dress.*

in•shore (in′shôr′, -shōr′) /'ɪn'ʃɔr, -'ʃowr/ *adj.* **1.** situated close to the shore: *inshore waters.* —*adv.* **2.** toward the shore.

in•side (in′sīd′, in′sīd′) /,ɪn'sayd, 'ɪn,sayd/ *prep.* **1.** on the inner side or part of; within: *inside the circle.* **2.** before; within: *to arrive inside an hour.* —*adv.* **3.** in or into the inner part: *Look inside.* **4.** indoors: *to play inside on rainy days.* **5.** by true nature; in one's mind or soul: *Inside, she's really very shy.* —*n.* [*count*] **6.** the inner part; interior: *the inside of the house.* **7.** the inner side or surface: *the inside of the hand.* **8. insides,** [*plural*] *Informal.* the inner parts of the body, esp. the stomach and intestines. **9.** a position within a circle of power, etc.: *to be on the inside in the administration.* **10.** [*count; usually singular*] inward nature, thoughts, feelings, etc.: *I smile that way on the outside, but on the inside I'm really upset.* —*adj.* [*before a noun*] **11.** located or being on or in the inside: *an inside seat on the airplane.* **12.** located close to the side of the road: *tried to pass on the inside lane.* **13.** private; confidential: *inside information.* —***Idiom.*** **14. inside of,** within the space or period of; before: *We'll reach the city inside of twenty minutes.* **15. inside out, a.** with the inner side reversed to face the outside: *Turn that shirt inside out when you wash it.* **b.** thoroughly; completely: *She knew me inside out.*

in•sid•er (in′sī′dər) /,ɪn'saydər/ *n.* [*count*] **1.** one belonging to a chosen circle of power, etc., esp. one who knows or can find out confidential information: *insiders in the White House.* **2.** a person with special knowledge or influence: *It's another job for insiders; why even apply for it?*

in•sid•i•ous (in sid′ē əs) /ɪn'sɪdiyəs/ *adj.* **1.** treacherous; sneaky and dishonest: *an insidious plan.* **2.** operating or proceeding without being noticed but with serious effect: *an insidious disease.* See -SID-.

in•sight (in′sīt′) /'ɪn,sayt/ *n.* an act or instance of perceiving the true nature of a thing, esp. through intuitive understanding: [*noncount*]: *The seminar provided insight into how computer programs could work for students.* [*count*]: *gave us valuable insights.* —**in•sight′ful,** *adj.*: *an insightful article on marriage.*

in•sig•ni•a (in sig′nē ə) /ɪn'sɪgniyə/ *n.* [*count*], *formally a pl. of* **insigne,** *which is seldom used; used as sing. or pl.; pl. also* **-ni•as. 1.** a badge that shows office or rank: *military insignia.* **2.** a distinguishing mark: *A black armband may be an insignia of mourning.* Sometimes, **in•sig•ne** (in sig′nē) /ɪn'sɪgniy/. See -SIGN-.

in•sig•nif•i•cant (in′sig nif′i kənt) /,ɪnsɪg'nɪfɪkənt/ *adj.* unimportant; without value or consequence: *Omit the insignificant details.* —**in′sig•nif′i•cance,** *n.* [*noncount*] See -SIGN-.

in•sin•cere (in′sin sēr′) /,ɪnsɪn'sɪər/ *adj.* not sincere; hypocritical: *an insincere apology.* —**in′sin•cere′ly,** *adv.* —**in•sin•cer•i•ty** (in′sin ser′i tē) /,ɪnsɪn'sɛrɪtiy/ *n.* [*noncount*]

in•sin•u•ate (in sin′yo͞o āt′) /ɪn'sɪnyuw,eyt/ *v.,* **-at•ed, -at•ing. 1.** [~ + *that clause*] to suggest slyly (usually referring to something negative): *He insinuated that they were lying without actually saying so.* **2.** [~ + *obj*] to put or introduce (doubt, etc.), as into the mind: *to insinuate doubt.* **3.** [~ + *obj*] to bring or introduce (someone) into a position by indirect methods: *He insinuated her into the top echelons.* —**in•sin•u•a•tive** (in sin′yo͞o ā′tiv, -ə-tiv) /ɪn'sɪnyuw,eytɪv, -ətɪv/ *adj.* —**in•sin′u•a′tor,** *n.* [*count*]

in•sin•u•a•tion (in sin′yo͞o ā′shən) /ɪn,sɪnyuw'eyʃən/ *n.* **1.** the act or state of insinuating: [*noncount*]: *When direct methods failed he tried insinuation.* [*count*]: *made several nasty insinuations about me.* **2.** [*count*] a statement that insinuates something: *ridiculous insinuations about his sexuality.*

in•sip•id (in sip′id) /ɪn'sɪpɪd/ *adj.* **1.** not having stimulating qualities; vapid: *a boring, insipid personality.* **2.** without enough taste to be pleasing; bland: *insipid soup.*

in•sist (in sist′) /ɪn'sɪst/ *v.* **1.** [~ + *on/upon* + *obj*] to continue to stress the importance of: *to insist upon a point.* **2.** to demand firmly or without stopping: [~ + *(that) clause*]: *I insist that you go.* [*used with quotations*]: *"But you must help me," she insisted.* —**in•sist′ing•ly,** *adv.*: *insistingly asking for clarification.* See -SIST-.

in•sis•tence (in sis′təns) /ɪn'sɪstəns/ *n.* [*noncount*] **1.** the act of insisting: *She finished the work at the boss's insistence.* **2.** the state or quality of being insistent: *The insistence in her voice made me look up.*

in•sist•ent (in sis′tənt) /ɪn'sɪstənt/ *adj.* **1.** stating something firmly; persistent: *He's insistent about getting her to stop smoking.* **2.** that causes someone to notice: *the insistent ringing of the alarm clock.*

in si•tu (in sī′to͞o, -tyo͞o, sē′-) /'ɪn saytuw, -tyuw, 'siy-/ *adj., adv.* situated in its original or natural place or position.

in•so•far (in′sə fär′, -sō-) /,ɪnsə'fɑr, -sow-/ *adv.* [~ + *as*] to such an extent: *I will do the work insofar as I am able.*

in•sole (in′sōl′) /'ɪn,sowl/ *n.* [*count*] **1.** the inner sole of a shoe or boot. **2.** material used as an inner sole within a shoe, esp. for comfort.

in•so•lent (in′sə lənt) /'ɪnsələnt/ *adj.* boldly rude or disrespectful; insulting: *He gave an insolent reply to her question.* —**in′so•lence,** *n.* [*noncount*] —**in′so•lent•ly,** *adv.*

in•sol•u•ble (in sol′yə bəl) /ɪn'sɒlyəbəl/ *adj.* **1.** (of a substance) that cannot be dissolved: *insoluble salts.* **2.** (of a problem, crime, etc.) that cannot be solved: *an insoluble mystery.* —**in•sol•u•bil•i•ty** (in sol′yə bil′i tē) /ɪn,sɒlyə'bɪlɪtiy/ *n.* [*noncount*] See -SOLV-.

in•sol•ven•cy (in sol′vən sē) /ɪn'sɒlvənsiy/ *n.* [*noncount*] the state or condition of being insolvent. See -SOLV-.

in•sol•vent (in sol′vənt) /ɪn'sɒlvənt/ *adj.* **1.** not solvent; unable to pay money to creditors. —*n.* [*count*] **2.** a person who is insolvent. See -SOLV-.

in•som•ni•a (in som′nē ə) /ɪn'sɒmniyə/ *n.* [*noncount*] difficulty in falling or staying asleep, esp. when habitual. —**in•som•ni•ac** (in som′nē ak′) /ɪn'sɒmniy,æk/ *n.* [*count*], *adj.*

in•sou•ci•ant (in so͞o′sē ənt) /ɪn'suwsiyənt/ *adj.* free of concern; nonchalant. —**in•sou′ci•ance,** *n.* [*noncount*]

in•spect (in spekt′) /ɪn'spɛkt/ *v.* [~ + *obj*] **1.** to look carefully at or over: *to inspect every part of a motor.* **2.** to examine officially: *The general inspected the troops.* —**in•spec′tor,** *n.* [*count*] See -SPEC-.

in•spec•tion (in spek′shən) /ɪn'spɛkʃən/ *n.* **1.** the act of inspecting: [*noncount*]: *a look of careful inspection.* [*count*]: *A quick inspection of the hands proved that she hadn't washed.* **2.** an act of officially inspecting something: [*noncount*]: *the queen's inspection of the troops.* [*count*]: *I took my car in for an inspection.* See -SPEC-.

in•spi•ra•tion (in′spə rā′shən) /,ɪnspə'reyʃən/ *n.* **1.** [*count*] anything that inspires: *The painter's inspiration came from nature.* **2.** [*count*] something inspired: *She got a sudden inspiration to reverse the wires, and it worked.* **3.** [*noncount*] *Theol.* a divine influence felt directly by the soul: *divine inspiration for writing the books of the Bible.* **4.** [*noncount*] the drawing of air into the lungs; inhalation. See -SPIR-.

in•spi•ra•tion•al (in′spə rā′shən əl) /,ɪnspə'reyʃənəl/ *adj.* providing inspiration: *inspirational passages from the Bible.* See -SPIR-.

in•spire (in spīᵊr′) /ɪn'spayᵊr/ *v.,* **-spired, -spir•ing. 1.** [~ + *obj*] to fill or affect (someone) with a strong or uplifting influence: *Her courage inspired her followers.* **2.** [~ + *obj* + *with* + *obj*] to fill or affect (someone) with any feeling, etc.: *Their teacher inspired them with respect.* **3.** [~ + *obj* + *(in* + *obj)*] to produce (a feeling, etc.): *A good leader inspires confidence in his or her followers.* **4.** to influence or impel (someone to do something): [~ + *obj* + *to* + *obj*]: *Competition inspired them to greater efforts.* [~ + *obj* + *to* + *verb*]: *Her criticisms inspired him to try harder.* **5.** [~ + *obj*] to communicate or suggest by a divine influence: *Christians believe that the New Testament was inspired by God.* See -SPIR-.

in•spir•ed (in spīᵊrd′) /ɪn'spayᵊrd/ *adj.* **1.** accomplished beautifully or performed well: *an inspired piece of writ-*

ing. **2.** clever; correct; accurate: *an inspired guess.* **3.** communicated, guided, or influenced by God: *the divinely inspired books of the Bible.* See -SPIR-.

in•spir•ing (in spīᵊr ing) /ɪnspayᵊrɪŋ/ *adj.* causing inspiration: *an inspiring speech.* See -SPIR-.

inst., an abbreviation of: **1.** institute. **2.** institution. **3.** instructor. **4.** instrument. **5.** instrumental.

in•sta•bil•i•ty (in′stə bil′i tē) /ˌɪnstəˈbɪlɪtiy/ *n.* [*noncount*] **1.** the quality or state of being unstable; lack of stability: *Political instability led to a revolution.* **2.** the tendency to behave in an unpredictable manner: *emotional instability.* See -STAB-.

in•stall or **in•stal** (in stôl′) /ɪnˈstɔl/ *v.* [~ + *obj*], **-stalled, -stall•ing** or **-stal•ling. 1.** to place in position for use: *to install a heating system.* **2.** to establish (someone) in an office or place: *to install the vice-president in her new office.* **3.** to bring (someone) into an office with ceremonies: *He was installed as the archbishop.* —**in•stall′er,** *n.* [*count*]

in•stal•la•tion (in′stə lā′shən) /ˌɪnstəˈleyʃən/ *n.* **1.** [*count*] an area with equipment to do a particular task: *a chemical-weapons installation.* **2.** [*noncount*] the act or process of installing: *Installation of your new satellite dish takes only a few hours.*

in•stall•ment[1] or **in•stal•ment** (in stôl′mənt) /ɪnˈstɔlmənt/ *n.* [*count*] **1.** any of several parts into which a debt is divided for regular payment. **2.** a single portion of something issued or published in parts at fixed times: *a magazine serial in six installments.*

in•stall•ment[2] or **in•stal•ment** (in stôl′mənt) /ɪnˈstɔlmənt/ *n.* [*noncount*] **1.** the act of installing: *Installment of the bishop was a six-hour ceremony.* **2.** the fact of being installed; installation: *Installment takes an hour.*

install′ment plan′, *n.* [*count*] a system for paying for an item in fixed amounts at specified times.

in•stance (in′stəns) /ˈɪnstəns/ *n.* [*count*] **1.** an occurrence of something: *allegations of new instances of oppression.* **2.** an example put forth in proof or illustration: *to cite a few instances.* —***Idiom.*** **3. for instance,** as an example; for example: *There are many different breeds of dogs; for instance, there are collies, dachshunds, and terriers.* See -STAN-.

in•stant (in′stənt) /ˈɪnstənt/ *n.* **1.** [*count*] a very short space of time; moment: *In an instant they were whisked away.* **2.** [*count*] the point of time now present: *Come here this instant!* **3.** [*count*] a particular moment: *at the instant of contact.* **4.** [*noncount*] an instant beverage, esp. instant coffee: *I don't mind a cup of instant if you've got it.* —*adj.* **5.** happening without any interval of time; immediate: *instant relief.* **6.** pressing or urgent: *instant need.* **7.** (of a food or beverage) specially made so as to require very little time and effort to prepare: *Just add boiling water to the instant coffee.* **8.** [*before a noun*] appearing rapidly and with little preparation: *no instant answers to these problems.* —*adv.* **9.** instantly.

in•stan•ta•ne•ous (in′stən tā′nē əs) /ˌɪnstənˈteyniyəs/ *adj.* occurring or completed in an instant; immediate: *an instantaneous response.* —**in′stan•ta′ne•ous•ly,** *adv.*: *The image of the explosion was transmitted instantaneously all over the world.*

in•stan•ter (in stan′tər) /ɪnˈstæntər/ *adv.* immediately; at once.

in•stant•ly (in′stənt lē) /ˈɪnstəntliy/ *adv.* immediately; at once: *He was killed instantly in the crash.*

in′stant re′play, *n.* **1. a.** [*noncount*] the recording and immediate rebroadcasting of a part of a live television broadcast, esp. of a sports event: *Some umpires don't like the use of instant replay.* **b.** [*count*] the segment recorded this way: *Different instant replays were not conclusive in judging whether the goal should have been allowed.* **2.** [*count*] any immediate repetition of an event, showing, etc.

in•state (in stāt′) /ɪnˈsteyt/ *v.* [~ + *obj*], **-stat•ed, -stat•ing.** to place in a state, position, or office; install: *He was instated in the job.* See -STAT-.

in•stead (in sted′) /ɪnˈstɛd/ *adv.* **1.** as a substitute; in place of someone or something: *The roast beef is gone, so we'll have steak instead.* —***Idiom.*** **2. instead of,** in place of: *Instead of meat, how about fish?*

in•step (in′step′) /ˈɪnˌstɛp/ *n.* [*count*] **1.** the arched, upper surface of the human foot. **2.** the part of a shoe, stocking, etc., covering this surface.

in•sti•gate (in′sti gāt′) /ˈɪnstɪˌgeyt/ *v.*, **-gat•ed, -gat•ing. 1.** [~ + *obj*] to cause (something) to happen by urging; foment: *to instigate a quarrel.* **2.** [~ + *obj* + *to* + *verb*/ *obj*] to urge or provoke to some action: *to instigate people to revolt.* —**in•sti•ga•tion** (in′sti gā′shən) /ˌɪnstɪˈgeyʃən/ *n.* [*noncount*] —**in′sti•ga′tor,** *n.* [*count*]: *Blame the riot on those instigators.*

in•still or **in•stil** (in stil′) /ɪnˈstɪl/ *v.* [~ + *obj* (+ *in/into* + *obj*)], **-stilled, -still•ing** or **-stil•ling.** to cause (some quality, etc.) to enter the mind of someone, by a long process: *to instill a sense of decency in his children.*

in•stinct (in′stingkt) /ˈɪnstɪŋkt/ *n.* **1.** an inborn pattern of activity: [*count*]: *mating instincts.* [*noncount*]: *Wolves hunt in packs by instinct.* **2.** a natural or innate impulse without needing to think or consider: [*noncount*]: *He knew by instinct that he should keep quiet.* [*count*]: *She has an instinct to make money.* —**in•stinc•tu•al** (in stingk′cho͞o əl) /ɪnˈstɪŋktʃuwəl/ *adj.* See -STIN-.

in•stinc•tive (in stink′təv) /ɪnˈstɪnktəv/ *adj.* **1.** done or felt without thinking or considering: *an instinctive feeling of distrust; Babies have an instinctive fear of falling.* **2.** done or performed by instinct: *instinctive mating patterns.* See -STIN-.

in•sti•tute (in′sti to͞ot′, -tyo͞ot′) /ˈɪnstɪˌtuwt, -ˌtyuwt/ *v.*, **-tut•ed, -tut•ing,** *n.* —*v.* [~ + *obj*] **1.** to set up; establish; organize: *The colony quickly instituted rules.* **2.** to start; set in operation; initiate: *He instituted a lawsuit against his old company.* —*n.* [*count*] **3.** a society, etc., for carrying on a particular work, as of a literary, scientific, or educational character: *a research institute.* —**in′sti•tut′er, in′sti•tu′tor,** *n.* [*count*] See -STIT-.

in•sti•tu•tion (in′sti to͞o′shən, -tyo͞o′-) /ˌɪnstɪˈtuwʃən, -ˈtyuw-/ *n.* **1.** [*count*] an organization devoted to the promotion of a cause, program, etc., esp. one of a public or educational character: *Large institutions have big bureaucracies.* **2.** [*count*] the building for such work. **3.** [*count*] a place for the care or confinement of people, as mental patients: *a mental institution.* **4.** [*count*] an established custom or law accepted as a basic part of a culture: *still has great respect for the institution of marriage.* **5.** [*count*] any familiar, long-established person, thing, or practice: *The elderly business professor had become an institution in the college.* **6.** [*noncount*] the act of instituting: *the institution of new organizations.* —**in′sti•tu′tion•al,** *adj.*: *Institutional inertia is the tendency to keep repeating procedures that have outlived their usefulness.* See -STIT-.

in•sti•tu•tion•al•ize (in′sti to͞o′shə nl iz′, -tyo͞o′-) /ˌɪnstɪˈtuwʃənl̩ˌayz, -ˈtyuw-/ *v.* [~ + *obj*], **-ized, -iz•ing. 1.** to make (something) into an institution; treat (something) as an institution: *institutionalizing racism.* **2.** to place or confine (someone) in an institution: *The deranged criminal was institutionalized for several years.* —**in•sti•tu•tion•al•i•za•tion** (in′sti to͞o′shə nl i zā′shən, -tyo͞o′-) /ˌɪnstɪˌtuwʃənl̩ɪˈzeyʃən, -ˌtyuw-/ *n.* [*noncount*]

instr., an abbreviation of: **1.** instructor. **2.** instrument. **3.** instrumental.

in•struct (in strukt′) /ɪnˈstrʌkt/ *v.* **1.** [~ + *obj* (+ *in* + *obj*)] to provide (someone) with knowledge, esp. by a systematic method: *The teacher instructed her students in mathematics.* **2.** to give (someone) orders or directions; direct; order; command: [~ + *obj* + *to* + *verb*]: *She instructed us to leave one by one.* [~ (+ *obj*); *used in quotations*)]: *"Concentrate," he instructed her, "and think about what to do next."* See -STRU-.

in•struc•tion (in struk′shən) /ɪnˈstrʌkʃən/ *n.* **1.** [*noncount*] the act or practice of instructing: *methods of instruction using computers.* **2.** [*noncount*] knowledge or information imparted: *The course gives you a lot of instruction but not very much that is useful.* **3.** [*count*] Usually, **instructions.** [*plural*] orders, directions, or advice: *The book was entitled "Instructions for the Lonely."* —**in•struc′tion•al,** *adj.*: *instructional materials for the classroom, such as overhead projectors.* See -STRU-.

in•struc•tive (in struk′tiv) /ɪnˈstrʌktɪv/ *adj.* serving to instruct: *an instructive lesson on hotel management.* See -STRU-.

in•struc•tor (in struk′tər) /ɪnˈstrʌktər/ *n.* [*count*] **1.** a person who instructs; teacher. **2.** a teacher in a college or university who ranks below an assistant professor. See -STRU-.

in•stru•ment (in′strə mənt) /ˈɪnstrəmənt/ *n.* [*count*] **1.** a mechanical implement, esp. one used for delicate work: *surgical instruments.* **2.** a device for producing musical sounds: *Her instrument is the trombone.* **3.** a means by which something is done: *an instrument of government.* **4.** a device for measuring the value of something watched, esp. one used in navigation of aircraft: *Suddenly the instruments went dead.* **5.** a formal legal document, such as a draft or bond: *negotiable instruments.* See -STRU-.

in•stru•men•tal (in′strə men′tl) /ˌɪnstrəˈmɛntl̩/ *adj.* **1.**

serving or acting as an instrument: *Your linguistics professor was instrumental in getting me that job.* **2.** performed on a musical instrument, and not including the voice: *an instrumental piece for piano.* **—*n.*** [*count*] **3.** a piece of music played by instruments, and not including the voice: *The band played a short instrumental.* See -STRU-.

in•stru•men•tal•ist (in′strə men′tl ist) /ˌɪnstrəˈmɛntl̩ɪst/ *n.* [*count*] a person who plays a musical instrument. See -STRU-.

in•stru•men•ta•tion (in′strə men tā′shən) /ˌɪnstrəmɛnˈteyʃən/ *n.* [*noncount*] **1.** the arranging of music for instruments. **2.** the use of instruments. **3.** an arrangement of instruments, as on a car's dashboard: *The instrumentation on this year's model is efficient.* See -STRU-.

in•sub•or•di•nate (in′sə bôr′dn it) /ˌɪnsəˈbɔrdn̩ɪt/ *adj.* not obeying superiors; disobedient: *fired for being insubordinate.* —**in•sub•or•di•na•tion** (in′sə bôr′dn ā′shən) /ˌɪnsəˌbɔrdn̩ˈeyʃən/ *n.* [*noncount*]: *fired for insubordination.* See -ORD-.

in•sub•stan•tial (in′səb stan′shəl) /ˌɪnsəbˈstænʃəl/ *adj.* **1.** not substantial; not real: *The experience now seems as insubstantial as a dream.* **2.** not solid or firm; weak; flimsy: *an insubstantial support on a chair.* See -STAN-.

in•suf•fer•a•ble (in suf′ər ə bəl) /ɪnˈsʌfərəbəl/ *adj.* not to be endured; intolerable: *an insufferable, spoiled brat.* —**in•suf′fer•a•bly,** *adv.*: *kids behaving insufferably all day.*

in•suf•fi•cient (in′sə fish′ənt) /ˌɪnsəˈfɪʃənt/ *adj.* not sufficient; lacking in what is necessary or required: *insufficient funds.* —**in′suf•fi′cient•ly,** *adv.*

in•su•lar (in′sə lər, ins′yə-) /ˈɪnsələr, ˈɪnsyə-/ *adj.* **1.** of or relating to an island or islands: *Japan's insular possessions.* **2.** narrow-minded; provincial: *their insular attitudes toward education.* —**in•su•lar•i•ty** (in′sə lar′i tē, ins′yə-) /ˌɪnsəˈlærɪtiy, ˌɪnsyə-/ *n.* [*noncount*]

in•su•late (in′sə lāt′, ins′yə-) /ˈɪnsəˌleyt, ˈɪnsyə-/ *v.* [~ + *obj*], **-lat•ed, -lat•ing. 1.** to cover or separate with a material that prevents or reduces the passage of heat, electricity, or sound: *They insulated the pipes and windows.* **2.** to protect (someone) too much: *You can't insulate your children from evil forever.* —**in′su•la′tor,** *n.* [*count*]: *The cord acts as an insulator.*

in•su•la•tion (in′sə lā′shən, ins′yə-) /ˌɪnsəˈleyʃən, ˌɪnsyə-/ *n.* [*noncount*] **1.** material used for insulating: *used fiberglass insulation in their attic.* **2.** the act of insulating; the state of being insulated.

in•su•lin (in′sə lin, ins′yə-) /ˈɪnsəlɪn, ˈɪnsyə-/ *n.* [*noncount*] **1.** a hormone that controls how glucose is absorbed and used by the body. **2.** any of several preparations of this substance, used for treating diabetes.

in•sult (*v.* in sult′; *n.* in′sult) / *v.* ɪnˈsʌlt; *n.* ˈɪnsʌlt/ *v.* [~ + *obj*] **1.** to treat (someone) with deep contempt; be rude to: *insulted him with her remarks about his waistline.* **2.** to offend or demean: *a TV sitcom that insults my intelligence.* **—*n.*** [*count*] **3.** a rude action or remark: *traded insults with his rival.* **4.** something having the effect of an insult: *That show is an insult to my intelligence.* —**in•sult′ing,** *adj.*: *insulting remarks.*

in•su•per•a•ble (in so͞o′pər ə bəl) /ɪnˈsuwpərəbəl/ *adj.* that cannot be overcome: *insuperable difficulties right at the beginning.*

in•sup•port•a•ble (in′sə pôr′tə bəl, -pōr′-) /ˌɪnsəˈpɔrtəbəl, -ˈpowr-/ *adj.* **1.** that cannot be endured; unbearable: *insupportable stress.* **2.** that cannot be justified, as by evidence: *The paper's account was full of insupportable accusations.*

in•sur•ance (in sho͝or′əns, -shûr′-) /ɪnˈʃʊrəns, -ˈʃɜr-/ *n.* **1.** [*noncount*] the act, system, or business of insuring property, life, etc., against loss or harm in return for payment. **2.** [*noncount*] coverage under a contract in which one party agrees to compensate another for a loss: *He had life insurance that was enough to support his children.* **3.** [*noncount*] the amount for which anything is insured: *His insurance was $50,000.* **4.** any means of guaranteeing against loss or harm: [*noncount*]: *to take vitamin C as insurance against colds.* [*count; usually singular*]: *As an insurance against being swindled, they examined the car carefully before buying.* See -CURA-.

in•sure (in sho͝or′, -shûr′) /ɪnˈʃʊr, -ˈʃɜr/ *v.* [~ + *obj*], **-sured, -sur•ing. 1.** to guarantee (someone or something) against death, loss, or damage: *The car was insured.* **2.** ENSURE. —**in•sur′a•ble,** *adj.* —**in•sur′er,** *n.* [*count*] See -CURA-.

in•sured (in sho͝ord′, -shûrd′) /ɪnˈʃʊrd, -ˈʃɜrd/ *n., pl* **insured.** [*count; usually: the* + ~] a person whose life or property is covered by an insurance policy: *The insured has a chance to get his or her money back.* See -CURA-.

in•sur•gent (in sûr′jənt) /ɪnˈsɜrdʒənt/ *n.* [*count*] **1.** a person who takes part in armed resistance to an established government; a rebel. **—*adj.*** [*before a noun*] **2.** rising in revolt; rebellious. —**in•sur′gence,** *n.* [*count*]: *an insurgence in the mountainous regions by rebels.* [*noncount*]: *government troops trying to fight against insurgence from the north.*

in•sur•mount•a•ble (in′sər moun′tə bəl) /ˌɪnsərˈmawntəbəl/ *adj.* that cannot be overcome: *facing insurmountable problems.*

in•sur•rec•tion (in′sə rek′shən) /ˌɪnsəˈrɛkʃən/ *n.* an act or instance of rising in rebellion against an established government: [*noncount*]: *The slightest hint of insurrection would not be tolerated by the government.* [*count*]: *The government fought two insurrections.* —**in′sur•rec′tion•ist,** *n.* [*count*] See -RECT-.

int., an abbreviation of: **1.** interest. **2.** interim. **3.** interior. **4.** interjection. **5.** internal. **6.** international. **7.** intransitive.

in•tact (in takt′) /ɪnˈtækt/ *adj.* not changed, broken, reduced in ability, or diminished: *In spite of falling, the vase was still intact. Despite misfortune, my faith remained intact.* See -TACT-. **—Syn.** See COMPLETE.

in•take (in′tāk′) /ˈɪnˌteyk/ *n.* [*count*] **1.** the opening at which a fluid is taken into a channel, etc. **2.** an act or instance of taking in. **3.** [*count; usually singular*] something taken in: *an intake of several thousand dollars a month.*

in•tan•gi•ble (in tan′jə bəl) /ɪnˈtændʒəbəl/ *adj.* **1.** that cannot be touched or felt; impalpable: *an intangible presence in the spooky room.* **—*n.*** [*count*] **2.** something intangible, esp. an asset, as goodwill: *We hired him because of several intangibles he seemed to possess.*

in•te•ger (in′ti jər) /ˈɪntɪdʒər/ *n.* [*count*] one of the positive or negative numbers 1, 2, 3, etc., or zero, not a fraction; a whole number. See -TACT-.

in•te•gral (in′ti grəl, in teg′rəl) /ˈɪntɪgrəl, ɪnˈtɛgrəl/ *adj.* **1.** [*usually: before a noun*] of or belonging as an essential part of the whole; necessary to completeness: *an integral part.* **2.** relating to or being an integer; not a fraction. **—*n.*** [*count*] **3.** an integral whole. See -TACT-.

in•te•grate (in′ti grāt′) /ˈɪntɪˌgreyt/ *v.*, **-grat•ed, -grat•ing. 1.** [~ + *obj* (+ *into* + *obj*)] to bring together, combine, or incorporate into a whole or into a larger unit: *He integrated several ideas from that novelist into his writing.* **2.** to (cause to) become part of a larger unit, as by giving equal opportunity and consideration to: [~ + *obj*]: *to integrate an individual into society.* [*no obj*]: *My immigrant grandmother lived in this country for eighty years but she never integrated into the society.* **3.** [~ + *obj*] to make (a school, etc.) open or available to all racial and ethnic groups: *By the end of the sixties the restaurants were integrated.* —**in′te•gra′ted,** *adj.*: *to fight for a fully integrated school.* —**in•te•gra•tion** (in′ti grā′shən) /ˌɪntɪˈgreyʃən/ *n.* [*noncount*]: *fought for integration for all races.* —**in′te•gra′tive,** *adj.* See -TACT-.

in•teg•ri•ty (in teg′ri tē) /ɪnˈtɛgrɪtiy/ *n.* [*noncount*] **1.** honesty; soundness of moral quality: *The judge is a man of integrity.* **2.** the state of being whole or entire: *to preserve the integrity of the empire.* See -TACT-.

in•tel•lect (in′tl ekt′) /ˈɪntl̩ˌɛkt/ *n.* [*count*] **1.** [the part of the mind by which one knows or understands. **2.** a person who has a great capacity for learning. See -LEG-.

in•tel•lec•tu•al (in′tl ek′cho͞o əl) /ˌɪntl̩ˈɛktʃuwəl/ *adj.* **1.** appealing to the intellect: *intellectual pursuits.* **2.** of or relating to the intellect: *The intellectual powers of the mind conflict with the emotional part.* **3.** placing a high value on the intellect: *an intellectual fellow, always reading philosophy and physics.* **—*n.*** [*count*] **4.** a person who values or pursues intellectual interests: *an intellectual who liked to keep up with many different subjects.* —**in′tel•lec′tu•al•ly,** *adv.* See -LEG-.

in•tel•li•gence (in tel′i jəns) /ɪnˈtɛlɪdʒəns/ *n.* [*noncount*] **1.** capacity for learning, reasoning, and understanding: *Do computers have any intelligence?* **2.** mental alertness or quickness of understanding: *writes with intelligence and wit.* **3.** news received or given, esp. about an enemy. **4.** an organization that gathers such information: *military intelligence.* See -LEG-.

in•tel•li•gent (in tel′i jənt) /ɪnˈtɛlɪdʒənt/ *adj.* **1.** having strong intelligence: *an intelligent student.* **2.** displaying quickness of intelligence: *His intelligent replies impressed the questioners.* **3.** (of an electronic device) containing built-in processing power: *an intelligent terminal, not a dumb one.* —**in•tel′li•gent•ly,** *adv.* See -LEG-.

in•tel•li•gent•si•a (in tel′i jent′sē ə, -gent′-) /ɪn,tɛlɪ'dʒɛntsiyə, -'gɛnt-/ *n.* [*plural; used with a plural verb; often: the* + ~] intellectuals thought of as a group or class, esp. as an elite: *The intelligentsia are often distrusted.*

in•tel•li•gi•ble (in tel′i jə bəl) /ɪn'tɛlɪdʒəbəl/ *adj.* capable of being understood; comprehensible: *dialects that are mutually intelligible.* —**in•tel•li•gi•bil•i•ty** (in tel′i jə bil′i tē) /ɪn,tɛlɪdʒə'bɪlɪtiy/ *n.* [*noncount*] —**in•tel′li•gi•bly,** *adv.*

in•tem•per•ate (in tem′pər it, -prit) /ɪn'tɛmpərɪt, -prɪt/ *adj.* **1.** uncontrolled in one's drinking habits: *his intemperate consumption of alcohol.* **2.** uncontrolled in other habits: *intemperate criticism.* **3.** extreme in temperature, as climate: *the intemperate climate of Greenland.* —**in•tem•per•ance** (in tem′pər əns, -prəns) /ɪn'tɛmpərəns, -prənshyphnb/ *n.* [*noncount*]

in•tend (in tend′) /ɪn'tɛnd/ *v.* **1.** [*usually not: be* + ~*-ing*] to have in mind as something to be done; aim: [~ + *to* + *verb*]: *We intend to leave in a month.* [~ + *verb-ing*]: *He had not intended staying for another week.* **2.** [*not: be* + ~*-ing*] to mean for a particular purpose: [~ + *obj*]: *The fund was intended for emergency use only.* [~ + *obj* + *as* + *obj*]: *I intended the computer programs as aids to the teacher.* [~ + *obj* + *to* + *verb*]: *I intended the programs to be aids to the teacher.* [~ + *that clause*]: *I intended that the programs should be used as teaching aids.* **3.** [~ + *obj; not: be* + ~*-ing; often: be* + ~*-ed* + *by*] (of words, terms, statements, etc.) to mean or signify: *I'm sorry about those remarks; no insult was intended by them.* See -TEND-.

in•tend•ed (in ten′did) /ɪn'tɛndɪd/ *adj.* **1.** proposed; desired: *the intended effect.* **2.** done purposely; intentional: *an intended snub.* **3.** [*usually; before a noun*] prospective; expected to be: *his intended wife.* —*n.* [*count; singular*] **4.** *Informal.* the person one plans to marry; one's fiancé or fiancée: *She's my intended.* See -TEND-.

in•tense (in tens′) /ɪn'tɛns/ *adj.* **1.** occurring in a high degree: *a wall of intense heat from the blazing building.* **2.** strong in feeling or emotion; ardent: *an intense dislike for each other.* **3.** concentrated and strenuous: *intense thought.* **4.** showing seriousness, strong feeling, or tension: *He's very intense during interviews.* —**in•tense′ly,** *adv.* See -TEND-.

in•ten•si•fi•er (in ten′sə fī′ər) /ɪn'tɛnsə,fayər/ *n.* [*count*] **1.** a person or thing that intensifies, or makes more intense. **2.** a word, esp. an adverb, that increases the strength of or emphasis on the word or phrase it is used with: *Words like* very, quite, completely, amazingly, *and* extremely *are intensifiers: She is very/quite beautiful. He is completely crazy.* See -TEND-.

in•ten•si•fy (in ten′sə fī′) /ɪn'tɛnsə,fay/ *v.*, **-fied, -fy•ing.** to (cause to) become intense or more intense: [*no obj*]: *The pain in my back seemed to intensify.* [~ + *obj*]: *Stretching out on the floor intensified the pain.* —**in•ten•si•fi•ca•tion** (in ten′sə fi kā′shən) /ɪn,tɛnsəfɪ'keyʃən/ *n.* [*noncount*] See -TEND-.

in•ten•si•ty (in ten′si tē) /ɪn'tɛnsɪtiy/ *n., pl.* **-ties. 1.** [*noncount*] the quality of being intense. **2.** [*noncount*] great energy, strength, or force, as of activity or feeling: *He answered with intensity that he hated materialism.* **3.** [*noncount*] the strength or sharpness of a color. **4.** [*count*] *Physics.* magnitude, as of energy or a force per unit of area, volume, time, etc. See -TEND-.

in•ten•sive (in ten′siv) /ɪn'tɛnsɪv/ *adj.* **1.** of or characterized by intensity: *The witness had to undergo intensive questioning.* **2.** This word is used after nouns and other roots to mean "requiring or having a high amount or concentration of" the quality or element mentioned: *labor-intensive (= requiring a high amount of labor).* **3.** (of a grammatical form or construction) showing increased emphasis or force: *The adverb* certainly *is an intensive adverb. In the sentence* I did it myself *the pronoun* myself *is an intensive pronoun but in the sentence* I hurt myself *the word* myself *is a reflexive pronoun.* —*n.* [*count*] **4.** an intensive form or construction. —**in•ten′sive•ly,** *adv.* —**in•ten′sive•ness,** *n.* [*noncount*] See -TEND-.

inten′sive care′, *n.* [*noncount*] the use of specialized equipment and personnel for continuous care of someone critically ill, usually in a special area in a hospital (an **inten′sive care′ u′nit).**

in•tent[1] (in tent′) /ɪn'tɛnt/ *n.* **1.** [*count; usually singular*] something intended; intention: *The original intent was to raise funds.* **2.** [*noncount*] the act or fact of intending, as to do something: *The burglar entered the house with criminal intent.* **3.** [*noncount*] meaning; significance; basic idea. —***Idiom.* 4. to** or **for all intents and purposes,** for all practical purposes; practically speaking: *His adoptive father was for all intents and purposes his real father.*

in•tent[2] (in tent′) /ɪn'tɛnt/ *adj.* **1.** firmly fixed or directed: *gave us an intent stare.* **2.** [*be* + ~] having the attention sharply fixed on something: *I was intent on my work and didn't hear you.* **3.** [*be* + ~] determined or resolved: *was intent on revenge.* —**in•tent′ly,** *adv.* —**in•tent′ness,** *n.* [*noncount*]

in•ten•tion (in ten′shən) /ɪn'tɛnʃən/ *n.* **1.** [*noncount*] an act or instance of deciding upon an action; plan: *His intention was to spend a month in Spain.* **2. intentions,** [*plural*] **a.** general purposes; attitude toward the effect of one's actions: *He's constantly making mistakes, but at least he has good intentions.* **b.** purpose or attitude with respect to marrying someone: *Are his intentions serious?*

in•ten•tion•al (in ten′shə nl) /ɪn'tɛnʃənl/ *adj.* done with intention; deliberate; planned: *an intentional insult.* —**in•ten′tion•al•ly,** *adv.*: *dropped the plate intentionally.*

in•ter (in tûr′) /ɪn'tɜr/ *v.* [~ + *obj*], **-terred, -ter•ring.** to place (a dead body) in a grave or tomb; bury.

inter-, *prefix. inter-* comes from Latin, where it has the meaning "between, among": *intercity (= between cities); interdepartmental (= between or among departments).*

inter., an abbreviation of: intermediate.

in•ter•act (in′tər akt′) /,ɪntər'ækt/ *v.* to act upon one another: [*no obj*]: *When the two chemicals interact they form a gas.* [~ + *with* + *obj*]: *One chemical interacts with the other.* —**in′ter•ac′tion,** *n.* [*noncount*]: *social interaction between men and women.* [*count*]: *day-to-day interactions.* —**in′ter•ac′tive,** *adj.*: *Interactive video lets the user decide what to see on the screen.*

in•ter•cede (in′tər sēd′) /,ɪntər'siyd/ *v.* [*no obj*], **-ced•ed, -ced•ing. 1.** to speak in behalf of someone, esp. so as to gain a favor or save from harm: *to intercede with the governor for a condemned man.* **2.** to try to settle differences between two groups; mediate: *Switzerland was willing to intercede in the dispute.* See -CEDE-.

in•ter•cept (*v.* in′tər sept′; *n.* in′tər sept′) / *v.* ,ɪntər'sɛpt; *n.* 'ɪntər,sɛpt/ *v.* [~ + *obj*] **1.** to seize or halt (someone or something on the way from one place to another): *to intercept a messenger.* **2.** to take possession of (a ball or puck) during a pass by the opposing team: *intercepted three of his first five passes.* —*n.* [*count*] **3.** an act of intercepting. **4.** an intercepted message. —**in′ter•cep′tion,** *n.* [*noncount*]: *More interception of enemy signals is now possible.* [*count*]: *three interceptions out of his first five passes.* —**in′ter•cep′tor,** *n.* [*count*] See -CEP-.

in•ter•ces•sion (in′tər sesh′ən) /,ɪntər'sɛʃən/ *n.* **1.** [*noncount*] an act or instance of interceding. **2.** [*count*] an act of pleading on behalf of another person: *intercessions on behalf of the condemned criminal.* See -CEDE-.

in•ter•change (*v.* in′tər chānj′; *n.* in′tər chānj′) / *v.* ,ɪntər'tʃeyndʒ; *n.* 'ɪntər,tʃeyndʒ/ *v.*, **-changed, -chang•ing,** *n.* —*v.* **1.** to cause (one thing) to change places with another: [~ + *obj*]: *to interchange pieces of modular furniture.* [*no obj*]: *The two sides interchange every other game.* —*n.* [*count*] **2.** an act or instance of interchanging: *the free interchange of ideas.* **3.** a highway intersection in which vehicles may move from one road to another without crossing traffic: *an accident at the last interchange.*

in•ter•change•a•ble (in′tər chān′jə bəl) /,ɪntər'tʃeyndʒəbəl/ *adj.* that can be interchanged: *The two parts are interchangeable, so it doesn't matter which one you use.*

in•ter•com (in′tər kom′) /'ɪntər,kɒm/ *n.* [*count*] a communication system within a building, etc., with a receiver for listening and a microphone for speaking at two or more points.

in•ter•con•nect (in′tər kə nekt′) /,ɪntərkə'nɛkt/ *v.* to (cause to) be or become connected: [*no obj*]: *The bedroom and bathroom interconnect.* [~ + *obj*]: *Try to interconnect the various ideas.* See -NEC-.

in•ter•con•ti•nen•tal (in′tər kon′tn en′tl) /,ɪntər,kɒntn̩'ɛntl̩/ *adj.* **1.** between or among continents: *intercontinental travel.* **2.** capable of traveling between continents: *intercontinental ballistic missiles.*

in•ter•course (in′tər kôrs′, -kōrs′) /'ɪntər,kɔrs, -,kowrs/ *n.* [*noncount*] **1.** dealings or communication between individuals, groups, etc.: *social intercourse.* **2.** sexual relations. See -COUR-.

in•ter•cul•tur•al (in′tər kul′chər əl) /,ɪntər'kʌltʃərəl/ *adj.* relating to two or more cultures.

in•ter•de•part•men•tal (in′tər dē′pärt men′tl, -di-pärt-) /ˌɪntərˌdiypɑrtˈmɛntḷ, -dɪpɑrt-/ *adj.* involving two or more departments: *interdepartmental rivalry.*

in•ter•de•pend•ent (in′tər di pen′dənt) /ˌɪntərdɪˈpɛndənt/ *adj.* depending on each other. —**in′ter•de•pend′ence,** *n.* [*noncount*] See -PEND-.

in•ter•dict (*n.* in′tər dikt′; *v.* in′tər dikt′) / *n.* ˈɪntərˌdɪkt; *v.* ˌɪntərˈdɪkt/ *n.* [*count*] **1.** any act or decree that prohibits: *an interdict by the church officials.* —*v.* [~ + *obj*] **2.** to forbid or cut off by decree: *The country was interdicted.* **3.** to cut off or reduce the flow of (troops, etc.) or hinder the use of (a road, etc.) by ground fire or bombing. —**in′ter•dic′tion,** *n.* [*noncount*] See -DICT-.

in•ter•dis•ci•pli•nar•y (in′tər dis′ə plə ner′ē) /ˌɪntərˈdɪsəpləˌnɛriy/ *adj.* involving two or more disciplines or fields.

in•ter•est (in′tər ist, -trist) /ˈɪntərɪst, -trɪst/ *n.* **1.** a feeling of having one's attention attracted by something: [*count*]: *an interest in architecture.* [*noncount*]: *I lost interest in the movie.* **2.** [*count*] something that arouses such feelings: *Chess is his only interest.* **3.** [*noncount*] the power to excite such feelings: *a subject that holds little interest for me.* **4.** [*noncount*] concern or importance: *a matter of great interest.* **5.** [*count*] a cause, etc., in which a person has a concern: *made that slow business a going interest.* **6.** [*count*] a legal share, right, or title, as in the ownership of property: *a small interest in the property he inherited from his mother.* **7.** [*count*] Often, **interests.** [*plural*] a group having influence on and often financially involved in an area of activity: *Big Oil interests in congressional races.* **8.** benefit; advantage: [*often: interests; plural*]: *We have your best interests in mind.* [*noncount*]: *It's in your best interest.* **9.** [*noncount*] money paid or charged for a loan (often expressed as a percent): *borrowed at 8 percent interest.* **10.** [*noncount*] something added to be more than an exact equivalent: *returned the insult with interest.* —*v.* [~ + *obj; not: be* + ~*-ing*] **11.** to excite the attention of: *Nothing interests her anymore.* [*it* + ~ + *obj* + *that clause*]: *It interests me that you want to see him.* **12.** to concern (a person, etc.); to be in the interests of: *The fight for peace interests most nations.* **13.** to cause to participate: *Can I interest you in dinner and a movie?* —***Idiom.*** **14. in the interest(s) of,** for the sake of; on behalf of: *acting in the interests of good government.*

in•ter•est•ed (in′trə stid, -tə res′tid) /ˈɪntrəstɪd, -təˌrɛstɪd/ *adj.* **1.** having an interest in something: *He was interested in what I had to say.* **2.** having one's attention attracted by something: *The interested fan never noticed the pickpocket at work on his wallet.* **3.** [*usually: before a noun*] influenced by personal reasons to act or believe in a certain way: *I am not an interested witness; I'm completely neutral.*

in′terest group′, *n.* [*count*] a group of people acting together for a common interest.

in•ter•est•ing (in′tər ə sting, -trə sting) /ˈɪntərəstɪŋ, -trəstɪŋ/ *adj.* exciting the attention; intriguing: *an interesting book.* [*it* + *be* + ~ + *(that) clause*]: *It was interesting that she should return to the scene of the murder.*

in•ter•face (*n.* in′tər fās′; *v.* also in′tər fās′) / *n.* ˈɪntərˌfeys; *v.* ælsɒ ˌɪntərˈfeys/ *n., v.,* **-faced, -fac•ing.** —*n.* [*count*] **1.** the area linking several disciplines or fields of study. **2.** something that makes it possible for separate elements to work together or communicate: *A new computer interface allows these machines to communicate.* —*v.* **3.** to (cause to) be brought into an interface: [*no obj*]: *The systems could not interface.* [~ + *obj*]: *to interface the two systems.* **4.** [~ + *with* + *obj*] to meet or communicate directly: *His job required him to interface with the Art Department.* See -FACE-.

in•ter•fere (in′tər fēr′) /ˌɪntərˈfɪər/ *v.* [*no obj; often;* ~ + *with* + *obj*], **-fered, -fer•ing. 1.** to hamper, hinder, or block someone or something: *The television interferes with his studying.* **2.** to take part in the affairs of others; meddle: *His in-laws were always interfering in his life.* **3.** (in a game or sport) to get in the way of an opposing player illegally. **4.** *Physics.* to cause interference: *My computer monitor interferes with the television reception.* See -FER-.

in•ter•fer•ence (in′tər fēr′əns) /ˌɪntərˈfɪərəns/ *n.* [*noncount*] **1.** an act or an instance of interfering: *constant interference in trying to finish his work.* **2.** the mixed-up sounds or images resulting when a radio or television picks up unwanted signals: *We could not watch Channel 5 last night; there was too much interference.* See -FER-.

in•ter•fer•on (in′tər fēr′on) /ˌɪntərˈfɪərɒn/ *n.* [*noncount*] any of various proteins that interfere with reproduction of an invading virus.

in•ter•im (in′tər əm) /ˈɪntərəm/ *n.* [*noncount*] **1. in the interim,** in the time period between another time; meantime: *In the interim, we'll wait for an answer.* —*adj.* [*before a noun*] **2.** temporary; provisional: *An interim government was appointed.*

in•te•ri•or (in tēr′ē ər) /ɪnˈtɪəriyər/ *adj.* [*before a noun*] **1.** located within or inside; inner: *an interior view.* **2.** situated inland from the coast or border: *the interior regions of Tanzania.* —*n.* [*count*] **3.** the internal or inner part; inside: *the interior of a watermelon.* **4.** the inside of a building, etc.: *roomy interiors.* **5.** [*usually singular; usually: the* + ~] the inland parts of a region, etc.: *How far into the interior should we go?*

inte′rior decora′tion, *n.* [*noncount*] the planning of the color schemes and other decorative parts of the insides of a house, etc. —**inte′rior dec′orator,** *n.* [*count*]

interj., an abbreviation of: interjection.

in•ter•ject (in′tər jekt′) /ˌɪntərˈdʒɛkt/ *v.* to insert or make (a remark), often suddenly: [*no obj*]: *May I interject for just a moment?* [~ + *obj*]: *to interject a remark.* [*used with quotations*]: *"Just a minute, Mr. Chairman, I object!" he interjected.* See -JEC-.

in•ter•jec•tion (in′tər jek′shən) /ˌɪntərˈdʒɛkʃən/ *n.* **1.** [*noncount*] the act of interjecting. **2.** [*count*] something interjected, as a remark. **3.** [*count*] a word or short phrase used to express emotion, such as *Hey! Oh! Ouch! Ugh! Good grief! Indeed! Abbr.:* interj. See -JEC-.

in•ter•lace (in′tər lās′, in′tər lās′) /ˌɪntərˈleys, ˈɪntərˌleys/ *v.,* **-laced, -lac•ing. 1.** to cross one another as if woven together: [*no obj*]: *Their hands interlaced.* [~ + *obj*]: *They interlaced their hands together.* **2.** [~ + *obj* + *with*] to mix together: *She interlaced her lecture on Schubert with some of his music.*

in•ter•leu•kin (in′tər lo͞o′kin) /ˈɪntərˌluwkɪn/ *n.* [*noncount*] a protein in the body's defense system that stimulates the growth and action of white blood cells.

in•ter•lock (in′tər lok′) /ˌɪntərˈlɒk/ *v.* **1.** to fit into each other, as in machinery, so that various parts work together: [*no obj*]: *The gears interlock with the teeth and turn the wheels at different speeds.* [~ + *obj*]: *to interlock the parts together.* **2.** to interweave, interlace, or interrelate, one with another: [*no obj*]: *The branches of the trees interlock to form an archway.* [~ + *obj*]: *They interlocked their arms and walked off.*

in•ter•loc•u•tor (in′tər lok′yə tər) /ˌɪntərˈlɒkyətər/ *n.* [*count*] a person who takes part in a conversation. —**in•ter•loc•u•to•ry** (in′tər lok′yə tôr′ē, -tōr′-) /ˌɪntərˈlɒkyəˌtɔriy, -ˌtowr-/ *adj.* See -LOQ-.

in•ter•lop•er (in′tər lō′pər) /ˈɪntərˌlowpər/ *n.* [*count*] a person who intrudes on the field of interest or business of others.

in•ter•lude (in′tər lo͞od′) /ˈɪntərˌluwd/ *n.* [*count*] **1.** an episode, period, or space that comes between others: *a quiet interlude between storms.* **2.** a short musical piece between the acts of a play. See -LUD-.

in•ter•mar•ry (in′tər mar′ē) /ˌɪntərˈmæriy/ *v.* [*no obj*], **-ried, -ry•ing. 1.** to become connected by marriage, as two families, tribes, or religions: *To end the feud, the two tribes intermarried.* **2.** to marry within a group. —**in•ter•mar•riage** (in′tər mar′ij) /ˌɪntərˈmærɪdʒ/ *n.* [*noncount*]

in•ter•me•di•ar•y (in′tər mē′dē er′ē) /ˌɪntərˈmiydiyˌɛriy/ *n., pl.* **-ies,** *adj.* —*n.* [*count*] **1.** a person who comes between two groups and acts as a mediator to bring them into agreement; a go-between. —*adj.* **2.** being between: *an intermediary stage in development.* **3.** serving as an intermediary between persons or parties: *an intermediary diplomatic attaché.*

in•ter•me•di•ate (in′tər mē′dē it) /ˌɪntərˈmiydiyɪt/ *adj.* **1.** being, located, or acting between two points, stages, things, persons, etc.: *intermediate steps in a procedure.* **2.** of or relating to an intermediate school or grade, between primary school and high school. **3.** between the levels of beginner and advanced: *an intermediate-level textbook.* See -MEDI-.

in•ter•ment (in tûr′mənt) /ɪnˈtɜrmənt/ *n.* [*noncount*] the act or ceremony of interring; burial.

in•ter•mi•na•ble (in tûr′mə nə bəl) /ɪnˈtɜrmənəbəl/ *adj.* seeming to last forever; endless: *his interminable chatter about his accomplishments.* —**in•ter′mi•na•bly,** *adv.* See -TERM-.

in•ter•min•gle (in′tər ming′gəl) /ˌɪntərˈmɪŋgəl/ *v.,* **-gled, -gling.** to mingle, one with another; intermix: [*no obj*]: *The two groups intermingled during the coffee break, then separated.* [~ + *obj*]: *to intermingle the groups.*

in•ter•mis•sion (in′tər mish′ən) /ˌɪntərˈmɪʃən/ *n.* an interval, as between acts of a play, parts of a performance, or periods of play in a sport: [*count*]: *After a short intermission the play continued.* [*noncount*]: *During intermission they serve drinks and snacks.* See -MIS-.

in•ter•mit•tent (in′tər mit′nt) /ˌɪntərˈmɪtnt/ *adj.* stopping for a time, then starting again: *intermittent pain.* —**in′ter•mit′tent•ly,** *adv.: During the earthquake the lights flickered intermittently.* See -MIT-.

in•ter•mix (in′tər miks′) /ˌɪntərˈmɪks/ *v.* to mix together; intermingle: [*no obj*]: *If the two groups intermix they may find solutions for each other's problems.* [~ + *obj*]: *Let's intermix the two groups.*

in•tern[1] (in tûrn′) /ɪnˈtɜrn / *v.* [~ + *obj*] to imprison or keep (someone) within certain limits, as prisoners of war or enemy aliens. —**in•tern′ment,** *n.* [*noncount*]

in•tern[2] (in′tûrn) /ˈɪntɜrn/ *n.* [*count*] **1.** a resident member of the medical staff of a hospital, usually a recent medical school graduate, serving as a trainee under the supervision of a fully qualified doctor. **2.** anyone working as a trainee, (sometimes without pay) to gain practical experience in an occupation. —*v.* [*no obj*] **3.** to serve as an intern: *journalism students interning on a newspaper.* —**in′tern•ship′,** *n.* [*count*]

in•ter•nal (in tûr′nl) /ɪnˈtɜrnl̩/ *adj.* **1.** situated or existing in the interior of something; of or relating to the inside or inner part: *the internal organs of the body.* **2.** [*before a noun*] of or relating to the domestic affairs of a country: *a bureau of internal affairs.* **3.** relating to or occurring within an organization, as a corporation: *an internal memo from one department head to another.* **4.** [*before a noun*] to be taken into the body, esp. orally: *medicine for internal use only.* —**in•ter′nal•ly,** *adv.*

inter′nal-combus′tion en′gine, *n.* [*count*] an engine in which the process of combustion or the burning of fuel takes place within the engine's cylinders.

in•ter•nal•ize (in tûr′nl īz) /ɪnˈtɜrnl̩ˌayz/ *v.* [~ + *obj*], **-ized, -iz•ing.** to take in (something from outside, as culture or moral values) and make it one's own: *She has internalized many of the values of her parents.*

in•ter•na•tion•al (in′tər nash′ə nl) /ˌɪntərˈnæʃənl̩/ *adj.* **1.** involving two or more nations: *international trade.* **2.** of or relating to two or more nations or their citizens: *a matter of great international concern.* **3.** thinking in ways that go beyond national boundaries or the viewpoints of individual countries: *Living abroad gave them a more international outlook.* —*n.* [*count*] **4.** an organization, business, or group having branches, dealings, or members in several countries. —**in′ter•na′tion•al•ly,** *adv.*: *internationally famous.* See -NAT-.

in•ter•na•tion•al•ism (in′tər nash′ə nl iz′əm) /ˌɪntərˈnæʃənl̩ˌɪzəm/ *n.* [*noncount*] the principle of cooperation among nations to achieve the common good.

Interna′tional Phonet′ic Al′phabet, *n.* [*proper noun; the* + ~] a set of symbols created by the International Phonetic Association to provide a consistent system for writing down the speech sounds of any language. *Abbr.:* IPA

in•ter•ne•cine (in′tər nē′sēn, -sin, -nes′ēn, -nes′in) /ˌɪntərˈniysiyn, -sayn, -ˈnɛsiyn, -ˈnɛsayn/ *adj.* [*usually: before a noun*] **1.** of or relating to conflict or struggle within a group: *an internecine feud.* **2.** having or resulting in great destruction or slaughter: *an internecine battle.*

in•tern•ee (in′tûr nē′) /ˌɪntɜrˈniy/ *n.* [*count*], *pl.* **-ees.** a person who is or has been interned, as a prisoner of war.

in•tern•ist (in′tûr nist, in tûr′nist) /ˈɪntɜrnɪst, ɪnˈtɜrnɪst/ *n.* [*count*] a physician specializing in the diagnosis and treatment of diseases not requiring surgery.

in•ter•of•fice (in′tər ô′fis, -of′is) /ˌɪntərˈɔfɪs, -ˈɒfɪs/ *adj.* [*before a noun*] functioning or communicating between the offices of a company or organization: *an interoffice memo.*

in•ter•per•son•al (in′tər pûr′sə nl) /ˌɪntərˈpɜrsənl̩/ *adj.* of, relating to, or involving relations between persons: *skilled in resolving interpersonal conflicts.*

in•ter•plan•e•tar•y (in′tər plan′i ter′ē) /ˌɪntərˈplænɪˌtɛriy/ *adj.* being or occurring between planets: *interplanetary travel.*

in•ter•play (in′tər plā′) /ˈɪntərˌpley/ *n.* [*noncount*] interaction: *the clever interplay of color, sound, and image in that video.*

in•ter•po•late (in tûr′pə lāt′) /ɪnˈtɜrpəˌleyt/ *v.* [~ + *obj*], **-lat•ed, -lat•ing.** to introduce (something additional or extra) between other things or parts; insert; interject; interpose: *to interpolate an unwanted comment.* —**in•ter•po•la•tion** (in tûr′pə lā′shən) /ɪnˌtɜrpəˈleyʃən/ *n.* [*count*]

in•ter•pose (in′tər pōz′) /ˌɪntərˈpowz/ *v.* [~ + *obj*], **-posed, -pos•ing. 1.** to place between; step in; intervene: *She interposed herself between her arguing brothers.* **2.** to put in (a remark, question, etc.) in the middle of a conversation or discussion: *He interposed a wry observation.* —**in•ter•po•si•tion** (in′tər pə zish′ən) /ˌɪntərpəˈzɪʃən/ *n.* [*noncount*] See -POS-.

in•ter•pret (in tûr′prit) /ɪnˈtɜrprɪt/ *v.* **1.** [~ + *obj*] to give or provide the meaning of; explain: *to interpret a fable.* **2.** [~ + *obj (+ as)*] to understand (something said, ordered, or done) in a particular way: *We chose to interpret the reply as favorable.* **3.** to translate what is said in a foreign language: [*no obj*]: *He interprets at the UN.* [~ + *obj*]: *He interpreted the speech for us.* **4.** [~ + *obj*] to bring out the meaning of (a dramatic work, a piece of music, etc.), as by performance or explanation: *The student interpreted the symbolism in Yeats' poem.* —**in•ter′pret•er,** *n.* [*count*]

in•ter•pre•ta•tion (in tûr′pri tā′shən) /ɪnˌtɜrprɪˈteyʃən/ *n.* **1.** the act of interpreting; the result or product of interpreting; explanation: [*noncount*]: *The message's meaning is open to interpretation.* [*count*]: *many different interpretations of his speech.* **2.** [*count*] an adaptation or version of a creative work or style: *a modern designer's interpretation of Renaissance clothing.*

in•ter•pre•ta•tive (in tûr′pri tā′tiv) /ɪnˈtɜrprɪˌteytɪv/ *adj.* giving or providing an interpretation.

in•ter•ra•cial (in′tər rā′shəl) /ˌɪntərˈreyʃəl/ *adj.* of, involving, or for members of different races: *interracial friendship.*

in•ter•re•late (in′tər ri lāt′) /ˌɪntərrɪˈleyt/ *v.*, **-lat•ed, -lat•ing.** to bring or enter into a relation or connection: [~ + *obj*]: *Try to interrelate the two issues.* [*no obj*]: *The two issues do not interrelate.* —**in′ter•re•lat′ed,** *adj.*

in•ter•ro•gate (in ter′ə gāt′) /ɪnˈtɛrəˌgeyt/ *v.* [~ + *obj*], **-gat•ed, -gat•ing.** to ask questions of (a person), esp. formally and thoroughly: *The police interrogated them for hours.* —**in•ter•ro•ga•tion** (in ter′ə gā′shən) /ɪnˌtɛrəˈgeyʃən/ *n.* [*count*]: *The interrogations could go on for days.* [*noncount*]: *Under interrogation he is likely to tell the police everything.* —**in•ter′ro•ga′tor,** *n.* [*count*] See -ROGA-.

in•ter•rog•a•tive (in′tə rog′ə tiv) /ˌɪntəˈrɒgətɪv/ *adj.* **1.** of, relating to, forming, making up, or used in a question: *There is an interrogative pronoun,* what, *in the interrogative sentence:* What do you want? —*n.* [*count*] **2.** an interrogative word, particle, or construction, as *who, what, which.*

in•ter•rog•a•to•ry (in′tə rog′ə tôr′ē, -tōr′ē) /ˌɪntəˈrɒgəˌtɔriy, -ˌtowriy/ *adj., n., pl.* **-to•ries.** —*adj.* **1.** expressing a question; interrogative. —*n.* [*count*] **2.** a question; inquiry.

in•ter•rupt (*v.* in′tə rupt′; *n.* in′tə rupt′) / *v.* ˌɪntəˈrʌpt; *n.* ˈɪntəˌrʌpt/ *v.* **1.** [~ + *obj*] to cause or make a break in the continuing progress of (a course, process, condition, etc.): *The flow of the river is interrupted by a waterfall.* **2.** [~ + *obj*] to break off or cause to stop: *He interrupted his work to answer the bell.* **3.** to stop (a person) while speaking or working, esp. by a remark added in: [*no obj*]: *Please don't interrupt.* [~ + *obj*]: *He kept interrupting the boss whenever she spoke.* [*used with quotations*]: *"Wait a minute," she interrupted, "I don't agree."* —*n.* [*count*] **4.** a hardware or software signal that temporarily stops the working of a program in a computer so that another procedure can be carried out. —**in′ter•rup′tion,** *n.* [*count*]: *We should be safe from all interruptions.* [*noncount*]: *working without interruption for hours.* See -RUPT-.

in•ter•sect (in′tər sekt′) /ˌɪntərˈsɛkt/ *v.* **1.** [~ + *obj*] to cut or divide by passing through or across: *The highway intersects the town.* **2.** [*no obj*] to meet and cross: *The two streets intersect at the red light.* See -SECT-.

in•ter•sec•tion (in′tər sek′shən) /ˌɪntərˈsɛkʃən/ *n.* **1.** [*count*] a place where two or more roads meet; junction: *There have been many accidents at that intersection.* **2.** [*noncount*] the act or fact of intersecting: *the angle formed at the point of intersection.* See -SECT-.

in•ter•ses•sion (in′tər sesh′ən) /ˈɪntərˌsɛʃən/ *n.* a period between two academic terms, sometimes used for brief supplementary courses: [*count*]: *This year we have an intersession that lasts two weeks.* [*noncount*]: *What will you do during intersession?* See -SESS-.

in•ter•sperse (in′tər spûrs′) /ˌɪntərˈspɜrs/ *v.*, **-spersed, -spers•ing. 1.** [~ + *obj*] to scatter or place at intervals among other things: *to intersperse flowers among shrubs.* **2.** [~ + *obj* + *with* + *obj*] to vary with something scattered or placed at intervals: *to intersperse a speech with anecdotes.*

in•ter•state (*adj.* in′tər stāt′; *n.* in′tər stāt′) / *adj.* ˌɪntər'steyt; *n.* 'ɪnˌtər steyt/ *adj.* [*before a noun*] **1.** connecting or involving different states: *an interstate highway; interstate trade.* **—***n.* [*count*] **2.** [*sometimes: Interstate*] a highway that is part of a nationwide U.S. system of highways connecting major cities. See -STAT-.

in•ter•stel•lar (in′tər stel′ər) /ˌɪntər'stɛlər/ *adj.* located or occurring between stars: *interstellar dust.*

in•ter•stice (in tûr′stis) /ɪn'tɜrstɪs/ *n.* [*count*], *pl.* **-stic•es** (-stə sēz′, -stə siz) /-stəˌsiyz, -stəsɪz/. a small or narrow space between things or parts: *the interstices between the slats of a fence.* See -STIT-.

in•ter•twine (in′tər twīn′) /ˌɪntər'twayn/ *v.*, **-twined, -twin•ing.** to twine together: [~ + *obj*]: *They intertwined their arms and walked off together.* [*no obj*]: *Their arms intertwined as they walked off together.*

in•ter•ur•ban (in′tər ûr′bən) /ˌɪntər'ɜrbən/ *adj.* of, located in, or operating between two or more cities: *an interurban transit system.*

in•ter•val (in′tər vəl) /'ɪntərvəl/ *n.* [*count*] **1.** a period of time coming between two others: *An interval of 50 years of peace then followed.* **2.** a space between things, points, limits, etc.: *The workers planned an interval of ten feet between each fence post.* **3.** the difference in pitch between two musical tones sounded at the same time or one after the other. **4.** *Brit.* INTERMISSION. **—*Idiom.* 5. at intervals, a.** now and then: *We met at intervals over the years.* **b.** here and there: *We'd see scrub grass and trees growing at intervals.*

in•ter•vene (in′tər vēn′) /ˌɪntər'viyn/ *v.* [*no obj*], **-vened, -ven•ing. 1.** to come between people, groups, etc. who are disagreeing, in order to help make an agreement possible; intercede: *His daughters would keep fighting until he intervened.* **2.** to occur or be between two things: *A few years intervened before they met again.* **3.** to occur between other events or periods: *Nothing important has intervened since then.* **4.** to interfere with force or a threat of force: *to intervene in the affairs of another country.* **—in•ter•ven•tion** (in′tər ven′shən) /ˌɪntər'vɛnʃən/ *n.* [*noncount*] See -VEN-.

in•ter•view (in′tər vyōō′) /'ɪntərˌvyuw/ *n.* [*count*] **1.** a formal meeting in which one or more persons question, consult, or judge the worth of another person: *an interview for a job.* **2. a.** a conversation or meeting in which a writer, reporter, or television host seeks information from one or more persons for a news story, broadcast, etc. **b.** the report of such a conversation. **—***v.* **3.** to give or conduct an interview (with): [~ + *obj*]: *The reporter interviewed several witnesses.* [*no obj*]: *The committee has been interviewing all day, but doesn't like any of the candidates.* **4.** [*no obj*] to have an interview; be interviewed: *The candidate interviewed with several companies before she chose ours.* **—in′ter•view•ee′,** *n.* [*count*], *pl.* **-ees**: *An interviewee may feel nervous when being interviewed.* **—in′ter•view′er,** *n.* [*count*]

in•ter•weave (in′tər wēv′) /ˌɪntər'wiyv/ *v.*, **-wove** or **-weaved, -wo•ven** or **-wove** or **-weaved, -weav•ing.** to weave together; intermingle: [*no obj*]: *The melodies interweaved throughout the work.* [~ + *obj*]: *interweaving truth with fiction.*

in•tes•tate (in tes′tāt, -tit) /ɪn'tɛsteyt, -tɪt/ *adj.* **1.** not having made a will: *to die intestate.* **2.** not taken care of or distributed to heirs by means of a will: *Her property remains intestate.* **—in•tes•ta•cy** (in tes′tə sē) /ɪn'tɛstəsiy/ *n.* [*noncount*] See -TEST-.

in•tes•ti•nal (in tes′tə nl) /ɪn'tɛstənl/ *adj.* [*usually before a noun*] **1.** of or relating to the intestines: *intestinal flu.* **—*Idiom.* 2. intestinal fortitude,** courage; willingness to continue in spite of unpleasantness; guts.

in•tes•tine (in tes′tin) /ɪn'tɛstɪn/ *n.* [*count*] **1.** Usually, **intestines.** [*plural*] the lower part of the tube in the body that carries food, extending from the stomach to the anus. **2.** Also called **small intestine.** the narrow, longer part of the intestines that serves to digest and absorb nutrients. **3.** Also called **large intestine.** the broad, shorter part of the intestines that absorbs water from digested food and eliminates the rest.

in•ti•ma•cy (in′tə mə sē) /'ɪntəməsiy/ *n.*, *pl.* **-cies. 1.** [*noncount*] the state of being intimate: *Their intimacy was something she could never intrude on.* **2.** [*count*] an act that shows close feeling or intimate association: *their little intimacies, like holding hands.*

in•ti•mate[1] (in′tə mit) /'ɪntəmɪt/ *adj.* **1.** associated in close personal relationship: *intimate friends.* **2.** [*before a noun*] private; personal: *an intimate secret.* **3.** offering privacy; cozy: *We had a romantic lunch at an intimate café.* **4.** [*before a noun*](of knowledge, understanding, etc.) coming from close personal connection, study, or familiar experience; deep and detailed: *intimate knowledge of a subject.* **5.** engaging in or characterized by sexual relations: *had been intimate more than once.* **6.** [*before a noun*] (of clothing) worn next to the skin: *intimate lingerie.* **—***n.* [*count*] **7.** an intimate friend or associate. **—in′ti•mate•ly,** *adv.*

in•ti•mate[2] (in′tə māt′) /'ɪntəˌmeyt/ *v.*, **-mat•ed, -mat•ing.** to indicate or make known indirectly; hint; imply; suggest: [~ + *obj*]: *He intimated his dislike.* [~ + *(that) clause*]: *He intimated that he would accept if certain conditions were met.*

in•ti•ma•tion (in′tə mā′shən) /ˌɪntə'meyʃən/ *n.* [*count*] a hint or suggestion: *gave few intimations about his intentions.*

in•tim•i•date (in tim′i dāt′) /ɪn'tɪmɪˌdeyt/ *v.* [~ + *obj*], **-dat•ed, -dat•ing. 1.** to make timid; fill with fear: *The bullies intimidated the new kids at school.* **2.** to cause a feeling of great awe in (someone): *was not intimidated by the huge room where she had to give her speech.* **3.** [~ + *obj* + *into* + *verb-ing*] to force into or deter from some action by inducing fear: *to intimidate a voter into staying away from the polls.* **—in•tim•i•da•tion** (in tim′i-dā′shən) /ɪnˌtɪmɪ'deyʃən/ *n.* [*noncount*]

in•tim•i•dat•ing (in tim′ə dā′ting) /ɪn'tɪməˌdeytɪŋ/ *adj.* causing a feeling of fright, or of great awe: *The building was designed to be intimidating.* **—in•tim′i•dat′ing•ly,** *adv.*

in•to (in′tōō; *unstressed* -tŏŏ, -tə) /'ɪntuw; *unstressed* -tʊ, -tə/ *prep.* **1.** to the inside of; in toward: *He walked into the room.* **2.** toward or in the direction of: *Are you going into town?* **3.** to a point of contact with; against: *He accidentally backed his truck into a parked car.* **4.** This word is used to indicate insertion in: *The computer wasn't plugged into the socket.* **5.** This word is used to indicate entry, inclusion, or introduction in a place or condition: *She was received into the church.* **6.** to a certain condition or form: *The road has lapsed into disrepair.* **7.** to an occupation, action, possession, or acceptance of: *He went into banking.* **8.** This word is used to indicate a continuing extent in time or space: *The noise of the dog barking lasted well into the night.* **9.** This word is used between two numbers to indicate that the second number is to be divided by the first number: *2 into 20 equals 10.* **10.** *Informal.* interested or absorbed in, esp. obsessively; hooked on: *She's into yoga.* **11.** *Informal.* in debt to: *I'm into him for ten dollars.*

in•tol•er•a•ble (in tol′ər ə bəl) /ɪn'tɒlərəbəl/ *adj.* that cannot be tolerated; so great that it cannot be endured: *intolerable pain.* **—in•tol′er•a•bly,** *adv.*

in•tol•er•ant (in tol′ər ənt) /ɪn'tɒlərənt/ *adj.* **1.** not tolerating or respecting beliefs, opinions, usages, manners, etc., that are different from one's own: *Some of those churchgoers are intolerant of other religions.* **2.** [*usually: be* + ~ + *of*] unable or unwilling to endure: *That young child is intolerant of heat.* **—in•tol′er•ance,** *n.* [*noncount*]

in•to•na•tion (in′tō nā′shən, -tə-) /ˌɪntow'neyʃən, -tə-/ *n.* the pattern or melody of rising or falling pitch changes in the voice when used in speaking, esp. the pitch pattern of a sentence, which distinguishes kinds of sentences or speakers of different language cultures: [*noncount*]: *The sentence* You're crazy *has different meanings depending on intonation.* [*count*]: *Swedish and Norwegian intonations.* [*count*] the act of intoning: *intonation of a prayer.* See -TON-.

in•tone (in tōn′) /ɪn'town/ *v.*, **-toned, -ton•ing.** to speak or recite in a singing voice or with a particular tone, esp. with a slow, even tone with little change in pitch: [~ + *obj*]: *to intone prayers for the dead.* [*used with quotations*]: *"Welcome to the Department of Motor Vehicles," the recording intoned.* **—in•ton′er,** *n.* [*count*] See -TON-.

in to•to (in tō′tō) /'ɪn towtow/ *adv.* in all; completely; entirely.

in•tox•i•cate (in tok′si kāt′) /ɪn'tɒksɪˌkeyt/ *v.*, **-cat•ed, -cat•ing. 1.** to affect the body's physical and mental control by means of alcoholic liquor, a drug, or another substance; to cause to become drunk: [~ + *obj*]: *Alcohol intoxicates you faster if you weigh less.* [*no obj*]: *All alcohol intoxicates.* **2.** [~ + *obj*] to make enthusiastic; delight; exhilarate: *The beauty of the summer night intoxicated her.* **—in•tox•i•cant** (in tok′si kənt) /ɪn'tɒksɪkənt/ *n.* [*count*]: *Beer is an intoxicant.* **—in•tox•i•ca•tion** (in tok′si kā′shən) /ɪnˌtɒksɪ'keyʃən/ *n.* [*noncount*] See -TOX-.

in•tox•i•cated (in tok′si kā′tid) /ɪn'tɒksɪˌkeytɪd/ *adj.* **1.** drunk; inebriated. **2.** enchanted; mentally or emotionally thrilled or excited: *intoxicated by his success.* See -TOX-.

in•tox•i•cat•ing (in tok′si kā′ting) /ɪn'tɒksɪˌkeytɪŋ/ *adj.* **1.** causing or that can cause intoxication or drunkenness: *intoxicating beverages like beer and wine.* **2.** mentally or emotionally thrilling or exciting: *an intoxicating ride in a hot-air balloon.* —**in•tox′i•cat′ing•ly,** *adv.* See -TOX-.

intra-, *prefix. intra-* comes from Latin, where it has the meaning "within": *intraspecies (= within species).* Compare INTRO-, INTER-.

in•trac•ta•ble (in trak′tə bəl) /ɪn'træktəbəl/ *adj.* **1.** not easily managed; stubborn: *an intractable child.* **2.** hard to treat, relieve, or cure: *an intractable disease.* —**in•trac•ta•bil•i•ty** (in trak′tə bil′i tē) /ɪnˌtræktə'bɪlɪtiy/ *n.* [*noncount*] See -TRAC-.

in•tra•mu•ral (in′trə myŏŏr′əl) /ˌɪntrə'myʊrəl/ *adj.* **1.** involving only students at the same school or college: *intramural basketball.* **2.** being or occurring within the walls, boundaries, or confines of an institution or organization.

in•tran•si•gent or **in•tran•si•geant** (in tran′si jənt) /ɪn'trænsɪdʒənt/ *adj.* refusing to agree or compromise; inflexible: *The sick man was intransigent about accepting treatment.* —**in•tran′si•gence,** *n.* [*noncount*] See -ACT-.

in•tran•si•tive (in tran′si tiv) /ɪn'trænsɪtɪv/ *adj.* of or being a verb that indicates a complete action without a direct object, as *sit* or *lie,* and that in English does not form a passive. In this book the symbol for an intransitive verb is: [*no obj*] —**in•tran′si•tive•ly,** *adv.*

in•tra•u′ter•ine device′ (in′trə yōō′tər in, -tə rīn′) /ˌɪntrə'yuwtərɪn, -təˌrayn/ *n.* [*count*] a device, as a loop or coil, for insertion into the uterus as a contraceptive. *Abbr.:* IUD

in•tra•ve•nous (in′trə vē′nəs) /ˌɪntrə'viynəs/ *adj.* **1.** of, relating to, being, or occurring within a vein: *an intravenous injection.* —*n.* [*count*] **2.** an intravenous injection or feeding. *Abbr.:* IV —**in′tra•ve′nous•ly,** *adv.: being fed intravenously.* See -VEN-.

in•trep•id (in trep′id) /ɪn'trɛpɪd/ *adj.* fearless; dauntless: *an intrepid explorer.* —**in•trep′id•ly,** *adv.*

in•tri•ca•cy (in′tri kə sē) /'ɪntrɪkəsiy/ *n., pl.* **-cies. 1.** [*noncount*] the state or quality of being intricate. **2.** [*count*] an intricate part, action, detail, etc.: *I couldn't figure out some of the intricacies of the plot.*

in•tri•cate (in′tri kit) /'ɪntrɪkɪt/ *adj.* **1.** having many interconnected or interrelated parts: *an intricate maze.* **2.** complex; complicated: *an intricate political issue.*

in•trigue (*v.* in trēg′; *n. also* in′trēg) /*v.* ɪn'triyg; *n. also* 'ɪntriyg/ *v.,* **-trigued, -tri•guing,** *n.* —*v.* **1.** [~ + *obj*] to arouse the curiosity or interest of by unusual, new, or otherwise fascinating qualities: *Fairy tales intrigue many children.* **2.** [*no obj*] to plan or plot secretly or in a dishonest way: *The dukes intrigued against the king.* —*n.* **3.** [*noncount*] the use of dishonest or secret plots or plans: *The king's court was full of intrigue.* **4.** [*count*] such a plot or plan: *political intrigues.* —**in•tri′guer,** *n.* [*count*]

in•tri•guing (in trē′ging) /ɪn'triygɪŋ/ *adj.* very interesting; fascinating: *an intriguing mystery.* —**in•tri′guing•ly,** *adv.*

in•trin•sic (in trin′sik, -zik), /ɪn'trɪnsɪk, -zɪk/ *adj.* belonging to or being part of a thing by its very nature: *A good education has intrinsic value.* —**in•trin′si•cal•ly,** *adv.*

intro-, *prefix. intro-* comes from Latin, where it has the meaning "inside, within": *intro- + -duce (= lead) → introduce (= bring inside or within to meet someone); intro- + -version (= a turning) → introversion (= a turning inside or within).* Compare INTRA-.

in•tro•duce (in′trə dōōs′, -dyōōs′) /ˌɪntrə'duws, -'dyuws/ *v.* [~ + *obj* (+ *to* + *obj*)], **-duced, -duc•ing. 1.** to present (a person) to another so as to make acquainted and so they know each other's name: *I would like to introduce you to my father.* **2.** to acquaint (two or more persons) with each other personally, so that they know each other's names: *Will you introduce us?* **3.** to present (a person, product, etc.) for or as if for the first time by a formal act, announcement, etc.: *to introduce a debutante to society.* **4.** to bring (a person) to first knowledge or experience of something: *He introduced me to skiing.* **5.** to create, propose, bring into notice, use, etc., for the first time; institute: *to introduce a new procedure.* **6.** to present for official consideration or action: *introduced a bill to outlaw radar detectors in cars.* **7.** to begin; start; preface: *to introduce a speech with an anecdote.* **8.** to put or place into something for the first time; insert. **9.** [~ + *obj* + *into* + *from*] to bring in or establish, as something foreign or not native: *a plant introduced into America from Africa.* **10.** to present (a speaker, performer, etc.) to an audience. See -DUC-.

in•tro•duc•tion (in′trə duk′shən) /ˌɪntrə'dʌkʃən/ *n.* **1.** [*noncount*] the act of introducing or the state of being introduced. **2.** [*count*] a formal personal presentation of one person to another or others. **3.** [*count*] a preliminary part, as of a book, musical composition, or the like, leading up to the main part. **4.** [*count*] a book, lecture, etc., that provides basic knowledge of a subject: *an introduction to music history.* See -DUC-.

in•tro•duc•to•ry (in′trə duk′tə rē) /ˌɪntrə'dʌktəriy/ *adj.* relating to or providing general or basic information: *an introductory course in English composition.* See -DUC-.

in•tro•spec•tion (in′trə spek′shən) /ˌɪntrə'spɛkʃən/ *n.* [*noncount*] the habit or act of studying one's own mental and emotional state and processes. —**in•tro•spec•tive** (in′trə spek′tiv) /ˌɪntrə'spɛktɪv/ *adj.* See -SPEC-.

in•tro•vert (in′trə vûrt′) /'ɪntrəˌvɜrt/ *n.* [*count*] a shy or retiring person. —**in•tro•ver•sion** (in′trə vûr′zhən, -shən) /ˌɪntrə'vɜrʒən, -ʃən/ *n.* [*noncount*] —**in′tro•vert′ed,** *adj.* See -VERT-.

in•trude (in trōōd′) /ɪn'truwd/ *v.,* **-trud•ed, -trud•ing.** to push, thrust, or force upon someone or something without invitation, permission, or welcome: [~ + *on* + *obj*]: *I don't want to intrude on you if you're busy.* [*no obj*]: *I hope I'm not intruding.* [~ + *obj*]: *The judge intruded her prejudices into the case.* See -TRUDE-.

in•trud•er (in trōōd′ər) /ɪn'truwdər/ *n.* [*count*] a person who enters a place secretly or illegally: *The alarms go off if an intruder enters the house.* See -TRUDE-.

in•tru•sion (in trōō′zhən) /ɪn'truwʒən/ *n.* an act or instance of intruding: [*noncount*]: *She hated the intrusion into her private life.* [*count*]: *The press made intrusions into his private life.* —**in•tru•sive** (in trōō′siv) /ɪn'truwsɪv/ *adj.: an intrusive question.* —**in•tru′sive•ly,** *adv.* —**in•tru′sive•ness,** *n.* [*noncount*] See -TRUDE-.

in•tu•it (in tōō′it, -tyōō′-) /ɪn'tuwɪt, -'tyuw-/ *v.* to know or sense by intuition: [~ + *obj*]: *He intuited the reason for her behavior.* [~ + *that clause*]: *She intuited almost immediately that something was wrong at home.*

in•tu•i•tion (in′tōō ish′ən, -tyōō-) /ˌɪntuw'ɪʃən, -tyuw-/ *n.* **1.** [*noncount*] direct perception of, or the power of understanding, a fact, the truth, a conclusion, etc., without any reasoning process or analysis: *Your argument is based on intuition, not logic.* **2.** [*count*] a fact, truth, etc., perceived in this way: *His intuitions were usually right.*

in•tu•i•tive (in tōō′i tiv, -tyōō′-) /ɪn'tuwɪtɪv, -'tyuw-/ *adj.* resulting from, having, or involving intuition: *She's an intuitive person.* —**in•tu′i•tive•ly,** *adv.: He seemed to know intuitively what to do.* —**in•tu′i•tive•ness,** *n.* [*noncount*]

in•un•date (in′ən dāt′) /'ɪnənˌdeyt/ *v.* [~ + *obj*], **-dat•ed, -dat•ing. 1.** to overspread with water; flood: *Heavy rains inundated the town.* **2.** to overwhelm: *inundated by telephone calls.* —**in•un•da•tion** (in′ən dā′shən) /ˌɪnən'deyʃən/ *n.* [*count*]

in•ure (in yŏŏr′, i nŏŏr′) /ɪn'yʊr, ɪ'nʊr/ *v.* [~ + *obj* + *to* + *obj*], **-ured, -ur•ing.** to toughen by use or exposure; accustom: *He was inured to the cold.*

in•vade (in vād′) /ɪn'veyd/ *v.,* **-vad•ed, -vad•ing. 1.** to enter forcefully as an enemy; go into with hostile intent: [~ + *obj*]: *The dictator invaded his neighboring states.* [*no obj*]: *He was ready to invade.* **2.** [~ + *obj*] to enter and affect in a harmful or destructive way: *viruses that invade the bloodstream.* **3.** [~ + *obj*] to intrude upon; encroach or infringe on: *to invade someone's privacy.* **4.** [~ + *obj*] to enter or penetrate: *City dwellers invaded the suburbs.* —**in•vad′er,** *n.* [*count*] See -VADE-.

in•va•lid[1] (in′və lid) /'ɪnvəlɪd/ *n.* [*count*] **1.** an unhealthy person, esp. one who is too sick or weak to care for himself or herself. —*adj.* **2.** unable to care for oneself, as through ill health. **3.** of or for invalids. —*v.* [~ + *obj*] **4.** to make (someone) an invalid. **5.** *Chiefly Brit.* to evacuate (military personnel) from an area of fighting because of injury or illness.

in•val•id[2] (in val′id) /ɪn'vælɪd/ *adj.* **1.** not valid; without force or a firm foundation; that cannot be defended; weak in logic: *an invalid conclusion.* **2.** empty or without legal force: *The contract was declared invalid.* —**in•va•lid•i•ty** (in′və lid′i tē) /ˌɪnvə'lɪdɪtiy/ *n.* [*noncount*]

in•val•i•date (in val′i dāt′) /ɪn'vælɪˌdeyt/ *v.* [~ + *obj*], **-dat•ed, -dat•ing. 1.** to discredit; show that (something) is incorrect: *This new finding invalidates his previous argument.* **2.** to deprive of legal force; nullify: *The judge invalidated the guilty verdict and set the defendant free.* —**in•val•i•da•tion** (in val′i dā′shən) /ɪnˌvælɪ'deyʃən/ *n.* [*noncount*]

in•val•u•a•ble (in val′yōō ə bəl) /ɪn'vælyuwəbəl/ *adj.* beyond a value that can be determined or calculated; of great worth; priceless: *Your assistance was invaluable.* —**in•val′u•a•bly,** *adv.*

in•var•i•a•ble (in vâr′ē ə bəl) /ɪn'vɛəriyəbəl/ *adj.* **1.** not variable; not able to be changed; staying the same; static. —*n.* [*count*] **2.** something invariable; a constant. —**in•var′i•a•bly,** *adv.*: *was invariably late to class.* See -VAR-.

in•va•sion (in vā′zhən) /ɪn'veyʒən/ *n.* [*count*] **1.** an act or instance of invading, esp. by an army. **2.** the entrance or coming of anything troublesome or harmful, as disease. **3.** entrance so as to overrun: *the annual invasion of tourists.* **4.** infringement; intrusion: *an invasion of one's privacy.* See -VADE-.

in•vec•tive (in vek′tiv) /ɪn'vɛktɪv/ *n.* [*noncount*] great and forceful denunciation or reproach, esp. with abusive language: *a politician who specialized in invective against his opponents.*

in•veigh (in vā′) /ɪn'vey/ *v.* [~ + *against* + *obj*] to protest strongly or complain bitterly: *The clergy inveighed against immorality.*

in•vei•gle (in vā′gəl, -vē′-) /ɪn'veygəl, -'viy-/ *v.* [~ + *obj*], **-gled, -gling. 1.** to lure (someone) by clever talk or promises: *managed to inveigle us into lending her money.* **2.** to obtain by clever talk or methods: *He inveigled a door pass from the usher.* —**in•vei•gler** (in vā′glər, -vē′-) /ɪn'veyglər, -'viy-/ *n.* [*count*]

in•vent (in vent′) /ɪn'vɛnt/ *v.* [~ + *obj*] **1.** to produce for the first time, as a result of one's own ingenuity and effort: *Edison is usually credited with inventing the light bulb.* **2.** to make up or think up (something false): *quick at inventing excuses* —**in•ven′tor,** *n.* [*count*] See -VEN-. —**Syn.** See DISCOVER.

in•ven•tion (in ven′shən) /ɪn'vɛnʃən/ *n.* **1.** [*noncount*] the act of inventing: *the invention of the computer chip.* **2.** [*count*] anything invented or devised. **3.** [*noncount*] inventiveness; imagination. **4.** [*count*] something made up: *another of his inventions about having oil on his land.* See -VEN-.

in•ven•tive (in ven′tiv) /ɪn'vɛntɪv/ *adj.* **1.** skilled or apt at inventing, thinking up, or making something: *She was very inventive, creating toys from any material at hand.* **2.** apt at creating with the imagination: *an inventive storyteller.* **3.** relating to, involving, or showing invention; clever: *an inventive excuse.* —**in•ven′tive•ness,** *n.* [*noncount*]

in•ven•to•ry (in′vən tôr′ē, -tōr′ē) /'ɪnvən,tɔriy, -,towriy/ *n., pl.* **-ries,** *v.,* **-ried, -ry•ing.** —*n.* [*count*] **1.** a complete listing of merchandise or stock on hand, work in progress, raw materials, etc., esp. a list made regularly by a business. **2.** the items on such a list; a merchant's stock of goods. —*v.* [~ + *obj*] **3.** to make an inventory of; catalog: *They inventoried all stock.* See -VENT-.

in•verse (in vûrs′, in′vûrs) /ɪn'vɜrs, 'ɪnvɜrs/ *adj.* **1.** reversed in position, order, direction, or tendency; opposite: *Read the numbers in inverse order.* **2.** (of a proportion) having two terms of which one increases as the other decreases. —*n.* [*noncount*] **3.** something that is the direct opposite: *The outcome was the inverse of what was supposed to happen.* —**in•verse′ly,** *adv.* See -VERT-.

in•ver•sion (in vûr′zhən, -shən) /ɪn'vɜrʒən, -ʃən/ *n.* **1.** [*noncount*] an act or instance of inverting; the state of being inverted. **2.** [*count*] anything inverted. **3.** [*count*] a reversal of the usual order of words, as in the placement of the subject after an auxiliary verb in a question. **4.** [*count*] a reversal in the normal atmospheric conditions affecting temperature rate, in which the temperature rises at higher altitudes rather than falling. See -VERT-.

in•vert (in vûrt′) /ɪn'vɜrt/ *v.* [~ + *obj*] **1.** to turn upside down. **2.** to reverse in position, order, direction, or relationship. **3.** to turn inward or back upon itself; to turn inside out. See -VERT-.

in•ver•te•brate (in vûr′tə brit, -brāt′) /ɪn'vɜrtəbrɪt, -,breyt/ *adj.* **1.** without a backbone or spinal column; not vertebrate. **2.** without strength of character. —*n.* [*count*] **3.** an invertebrate animal. **4.** a person who lacks strength of character. See -VERT-.

in•vest (in vest′) /ɪn'vɛst/ *v.* **1.** to put up or spend (money) in hopes of making a profit: [~ + *obj*]: *They invested their money in stocks and bonds.* [*no obj*]: *They decided to invest in stocks and bonds.* **2.** [~ + *obj*] to use (money), as in accumulating something: *to invest large sums in books.* **3.** [~ + *obj*] to use, give, or devote (time, talent, etc.), as to achieve something: *She invested years of her life in writing that book.* **4.** [~ + *obj*] to provide with power, authority, or rank: *Feudalism invested the lords with authority over their vassals.* —**in•ves′tor,** *n.* [*count*]

in•ves•ti•gate (in ves′ti gāt′) /ɪn'vɛstɪ,geyt/ *v.,* **-gat•ed, -gat•ing.** to look into or examine the particulars of (something) carefully so as to discover something hidden, unique, or complex: [*no obj*]: *The police were called in to investigate.* [~ + *obj*]: *The scientists were investigating the behavior of dolphins.* —**in•ves′ti•ga′tor,** *n.* [*count*]

in•ves•ti•ga•tion (in ves′ti gā′shən) /ɪn,vɛstɪ'geyʃən/ *n.* the act or process of investigating or the condition of being investigated: [*noncount*]: *a matter for investigation.* [*count*]: *police investigations.*

in•ves•ti•ga•tive (in ves′ti gā′tiv) /ɪn'vɛstɪ,geytɪv/ *adj.* of, like, or relating to an investigation: *investigative reporting.*

in•ves•ti•ture (in ves′ti chər, -chŏŏr′) /ɪn'vɛstɪtʃər, -,tʃʊr/ *n.* [*count*] the act, ceremony or process of investing, as with a rank, office, or title.

in•vest•ment (in vest′mənt) /ɪn'vɛstmənt/ *n.* **1.** [*noncount*] the investing of money in order to make a profit. **2.** [*count*] a thing invested in, as a business or a product: *Computers are usually a good investment for business.* **3.** [*count*] something invested, as a sum of money: *Each partner's investment was $5,000.* **4.** [*count*] the investing of time and effort in order to achieve something: *The two years he spent writing the book were an investment in his future career.* **5.** [*count*] the act of formally investing, as with a title or office.

in•vet•er•ate (in vet′ər it) /ɪn'vɛtərɪt/ *adj.* [*before a noun*] **1.** habitual; constant: *an inveterate gambler.* **2.** firmly established and continuing for a long time: *an inveterate back problem.* —**in•vet•er•a•cy** (in vet′ər ə sē) /ɪn'vɛtərəsiy/ *n.* [*noncount*]

in•vid•i•ous (in vid′ē əs) /ɪn'vɪdiyəs/ *adj.* **1.** creating ill will; causing resentment or envy: *an invidious job of evaluating teachers.* **2.** offensively or unfairly pointing up similarities or differences: *an invidious comparison.* —**in•vid′i•ous•ly,** *adv.* —**in•vid′i•ous•ness,** *n.* [*noncount*]

in•vig•or•ate (in vig′ə rāt′) /ɪn'vɪgə,reyt/ *v.* [~ + *obj*], **-at•ed, -at•ing.** to give vigor to; fill with life and energy; energize: *A quick walk in the park will invigorate you on this cold morning.* —**in•vig′or•at′ing•ly,** *adv.* —**in•vig•or•a•tion** (in vig′ə rā′shən) /ɪn,vɪgə'reyʃən/ *n.* [*noncount*]

in•vin•ci•ble (in vin′sə bəl) /ɪn'vɪnsəbəl/ *adj.* **1.** that cannot be conquered or defeated: *an invincible army.* **2.** that cannot be overcome: *invincible difficulties.* —**in•vin•ci•bil•i•ty** (in vin′sə bil′i tē) /ɪn,vɪnsə'bɪlɪtiy/ *n.* [*noncount*] See -VINC-.

in•vi•o•la•ble (in vī′ə lə bəl) /ɪn'vayələbəl/ *adj.* **1.** prohibiting violation; free and safe from destruction, violence, or misuse: *an inviolable sanctuary.* **2.** that cannot be violated: *inviolable secrecy.* —**in•vi′o•la•bil′i•ty,** *n.* [*noncount*]

in•vi•o•late (in vī′ə lit, -lāt′) /ɪn'vayəlɪt, -,leyt/ *adj.* free from violation or injury; not affected or disturbed: *The castle was left inviolate after the long attack.*

in•vis•i•ble (in viz′ə bəl) /ɪn'vɪzəbəl/ *adj.* **1.** not visible: *organisms invisible to the naked eye.* **2.** out of sight; hidden: *an invisible seam in a garment.* **3.** not ordinarily found in financial statements: *Goodwill is an invisible asset to a business.* —**in•vis•i•bil•i•ty** (in viz′ə bil′i tē) /ɪn,vɪzə'bɪlɪtiy/ *n.* [*noncount*] —**in•vis′i•bly,** *adv.* See -VIS-.

in•vi•ta•tion (in′vi tā′shən) /,ɪnvɪ'teyʃən/ *n.* **1.** [*noncount*] the act of inviting. **2.** [*count*] the written or spoken form with which a person is invited: *a wedding invitation.* **3.** [*count*] something that attracts or encourages an action; incentive; provocation: *an invitation to disaster.*

in•vi•ta•tion•al (in′vi tā′shə nl) /,ɪnvɪ'teyʃənl/ *adj.* restricted to participants who have been invited.

in•vite (*v.* in vīt′; *n.* in′vīt) / *v.* ɪn'vayt; *n.* 'ɪnvayt/ *v.,* **-vit•ed, -vit•ing,** *n.* —*v.* **1.** [~ + *obj*] to request the presence or participation of in a kindly or courteous way: *to invite friends to dinner.* **2.** to request politely or formally: [~ + *obj*]: *to invite donations to a charity.* [~ + *obj* + *to* + *verb*]: *I invited him to say a few words to the audience.* **3.** [~ + *obj*] to bring on, call forth, or make likely (some action or reaction), often unintentionally: *to invite trouble.* **4.** [~ + *obj*] to encourage, attract, or provide an incentive for: *His proposal invited great interest.* —*n.* [*count*] **5.** *Informal.* an invitation: *Didn't you get an invite?* —**in•vi•tee** (in′vi tē′, -vī-) /,ɪnvɪ'tiy, -vay-/ *n.* [*count*] *pl.,* **-tees.**

in•vit•ing (in vī′ting) /ɪn'vaytɪŋ/ *adj.* attractive, alluring, or tempting: *an inviting job offer.*

in vi•tro (in vē′trō) /'ɪn viytrow/ *adj.* [*before a noun*] developed or kept alive or growing in a controlled, non-living environment, as in a laboratory test tube: *In vitro fertilization is the fertilization of cells in a test tube.*

in•vo•ca•tion (in′və kā′shən) /ˌɪnvəˈkeyʃən/ *n.* **1.** [*noncount*] the act of praying to or calling upon a god, spirit, etc., for aid, protection, inspiration, or the like. **2.** [*count*] a prayer invoking God's presence, said at the beginning of a ceremony or public occasion. See -VOC-.

in•voice (in′vois) /ˈɪnvɔys/ *n., v.,* **-voiced, -voic•ing.** **—*n.*** [*count*] **1.** a bill, typically listing the goods sold or services provided, along with prices, the total charge, and the terms. **—*v.*** [~ + *obj*] **2.** to present an invoice to or for: *They invoiced the company for the delivery.*

in•voke (in vōk′) /ɪnˈvowk/ *v.* [~ + *obj*], **-voked, -vok•ing.** **1.** to call for with earnest desire; pray for: *to invoke God's mercy.* **2.** to call on (a deity, spirit, etc.), as in prayer: *The minister invoked the Holy Spirit in the confirmation service.* **3.** to declare to be in effect: *to invoke the law.* **4.** to cause, call forth, or bring about: *The poem invoked powerful feelings.* See -VOC-.

in•vol•un•tar•y (in vol′ən ter′ē) /ɪnˈvɒlənˌtɛriy/ *adj.* **1.** not voluntary; independent of one's will: *an involuntary witness to the crime.* **2.** unintentional; unconscious: *an involuntary gesture.* **3.** [*usually: before a noun*] *Physiol.* acting or functioning without the will: *an involuntary muscular response.* **—in•vol•un•tar•i•ly** (in vol′ən ter′ə lē, -vol′ən târ′-) /ɪnˈvɒlənˌtɛrəliy, -ˌvɒlənˈtɛər-/ *adv.* **—in•vol′un•tar′i•ness,** *n.* [*noncount*] See -VOL-.

in•volve (in volv′) /ɪnˈvɒlv/ *v.* [*not usually: be + ~-ing; ~ + obj*], **-volved, -volv•ing.** **1.** to include or use (something) as a necessary part, circumstance, condition, or end result: *This job involves long hours.* **2.** to cause (someone) to be connected with, associated with, or otherwise concerned with: *Don't involve me in your quarrel.* **3.** to stimulate or engage the interests or emotions of: *The play involved the audience deeply.*

in•volved (in volvd′) /ɪnˈvɒlvd/ *adj.* **1.** [*be/become* + ~] associated in a relationship, esp. a sexual relationship: *They dated before becoming seriously involved.* **2.** [*be* + ~] interested in, preoccupied with, or enthusiastic about something: *was very involved in his work.* **3.** [*be* + ~] being a part of something; taking part in something: *A lot of workers are involved in the strike.* **4.** complicated; complex: *an involved argument.* See -VOLV-.

in•volve•ment (in volv′mənt) /ɪnˈvɒlvmənt/ *n.* **1.** [*noncount*] the act of involving or the state of being involved. **2.** [*noncount*] absorption in something: *total involvement in community affairs.* **3.** [*count*] a relationship, esp. a close one, between people; an affair: *We had a brief involvement.*

in•vul•ner•a•ble (in vul′nər ə bəl) /ɪnˈvʌlnərəbəl/ *adj.* incapable of being wounded, hurt, or damaged: *an invulnerable fortress.* **—in•vul•ner•a•bil•i•ty** (in vul′nər ə bil′i tē) /ɪnˌvʌlnərəˈbɪlɪtiy/ *n.* [*noncount*]

in•ward (in′wərd) /ˈɪnwərd/ *adv.* Also, **in′wards.** **1.** toward the inside, interior, or center, as of a place, space, or body: *The window swung inward on its hinges.* **2.** into or toward the mind or soul: *Let us turn our thoughts inward.* **—*adj.*** **3.** proceeding or directed toward the inside or interior. **4.** located within or in or on the inside; inner; relating to the inside or inner part. **5.** mental or spiritual; inner: *inward thoughts.*

in•ward•ly (in′wərd lē) /ˈɪnwərdliy/ *adv.* **1.** in or on, or relating to, the inside or inner part; internally. **2.** privately; secretly: *Inwardly, he disliked his guest.* **3.** within the self; mentally or spiritually: *He promised to stay inwardly calm.*

Io., an abbreviation of: Iowa.

i•o•dine (ī′ə dīn′, -din; *in Chemistry also* -dēn′) /ˈayəˌdayn, -dɪn; *in Chemistry also* -ˌdiyn/ also **i•o•din** (-din) /-dɪn/ *n.* [*noncount*] a dense, violet-colored substance used as an antiseptic on wounds, as a nutritional supplement, and in photography.

i•o•dize (ī′ə dīz′) /ˈayəˌdayz/ *v.* [~ + *obj*], **-dized, -diz•ing.** to treat or affect with iodine.

i•on (ī′ən, ī′on) /ˈayən, ˈayɒn/ *n.* [*count*] an atom or atom group that is electrically charged by the loss or gain of electrons, represented by a plus or a minus sign, as Na^{+}, Ca^{++}, or Cl^{-}. **—i•on′ic,** *adj.*

-ion, *suffix. -ion* is attached to some roots to form nouns that refer to action or condition: *uni- (= one) + -ion → union (= condition of being one).* Compare -TION.

i•on•ize (ī′ə nīz′) /ˈayəˌnayz/ *v.,* **-ized, -iz•ing.** **1.** [~ + *obj*] to separate or change into ions. **2.** [*no obj*] to become changed into ions. **—i•on•i•za•tion** (ī′ə ni zā′shən) /ˌayənɪˈzeyʃən/ *n.* [*noncount*]

i•o•ta (ī ō′tə) /ayˈowtə/ *n.* [*count*], *pl.* **-tas.** **1.** [*used with a negative word, or in questions*] a very small amount or quantity; a jot; a whit: *Why should I care an iota about that?* **2.** the ninth letter of the Greek alphabet (Ι, ι).

IOU or **I.O.U.,** *n.* [*count*], *pl.* **IOUs, IOU's,** or **I.O.U.'s.** an informal note acknowledging a debt and consisting only of the letters *IOU,* the sum owed, and the signature of the person who owes the money: *The letters IOU are from the pronunciation of the phrase "I owe you".*

-ious, *suffix. -ious,* a variant form of -OUS, is attached to roots to form adjectives: *hilar- (= cheerful) + -ious → hilarious (= very funny).*

IPA, an abbreviation of: International Phonetic Alphabet.

ip•so fac•to (ip′sō fak′tō) /ˈɪpˈsow fæktow/ *adv.* by the fact itself: *to be condemned ipso facto as a murderer.*

IQ, an abbreviation of: intelligence quotient.

ir-¹, *prefix. ir-* is another form of IN-¹ that is attached to roots beginning with *r: ir- + radiate → irradiate.*

ir-², *prefix. ir-* is another form of IN-² that is attached to roots beginning with *r: ir- + reducible → irreducible.*

IRA or **I.R.A.** (ī′är′ā′; *for 1 also* ī′rə) /ˈayˈɑrˈey; *for 1 also* ˈayrə/ an abbreviation of: **1.** individual retirement account. **2.** Irish Republican Army.

I•ra•ni•an (i rā′nē ən, i rä′-, ī rā′-) /ɪˈreyniyən, ɪ ˈrɑ-, ayˈrey-/ *adj.* **1.** of or relating to Iran. **—*n.*** [*count*] **2.** a person born or living in Iran.

I•ra•qi (i rak′ē, i rä′kē) /ɪˈrækiy, ɪˈrɑkiy/ *n., pl.* **-qis.** **1.** [*count*] a person born or living in Iraq. **2.** [*noncount*] the language spoken by many of the people living in Iraq. **—*adj.*** **3.** of or relating to Iraq. **4.** of or relating to the language spoken by many of the people in Iraq.

i•ras•ci•ble (i ras′ə bəl) /ɪˈræsəbəl/ *adj.* **1.** easily made angry; very irritable: *an irascible city bus driver.* **2.** showing or produced by anger: *an irascible response.* **—i•ras•ci•bil•i•ty** (i ras′ə bil′i tē) /ɪˌræsəˈbɪlɪtiy/ *n.* [*noncount*]

i•rate (ī rāt′, ī′rāt) /ayˈreyt, ˈayreyt/ *adj.* **1.** angry; enraged; furious; annoyed: *She grew very irate when I asked her to explain the mistake on my bill.* **2.** arising from or showing anger: *an irate letter to the editor.* **—i•rate′ly,** *adv.* **—i•rate′ness,** *n.* [*noncount*]

ire (īᵉr) /ayᵉr/ *n.* [*noncount*] deep anger; rage; wrath: *The garbage strike stirred the neighborhood's ire.*

ir•i•des•cent (ir′i des′ənt) /ˌɪrɪˈdɛsənt/ *adj.* displaying bright, strong, shifting colors: *the iridescent feathers of the peacock.* **—ir′i•des′cence,** *n.* [*noncount*]

i•rid•i•um (i rid′ē əm) /ɪˈrɪdiyəm/ *n.* [*noncount*] a precious metal resembling platinum.

i•ris (ī′ris) /ˈayrɪs/ *n.* [*count*], *pl.* **i•ris•es;** esp. for 1 **ir•i•des** (ir′i dēz′, ī′ri-) /ˈɪrɪˌdiyz, ˈayrɪ-/. **1.** the round, colored, front part of the eye that contains an opening, the pupil, in its center. **2.** a plant having showy, colorful flowers.

I•rish (ī′rish) /ˈayrɪʃ/ *adj.* **1.** of or relating to Ireland. **2.** of or relating to the language spoken by many of the people in Ireland. **—*n.*** **3.** [*plural; the + ~; used with a plural verb*] the people born or living in Ireland. **4.** [*noncount*] a language spoken by many of the people in Ireland.

I•rish•man (ī′rish mən) /ˈayrɪʃmən/ *n.* [*count*], *pl.* **-men.** a person born or living in Ireland.

I•rish•wom•an (ī′rish wo͝om′ən) /ˈayrɪʃˌwʊmən/ *n.* [*count*], *pl.* **-wom•en.** a woman born or living in Ireland.

irk (ûrk) /ɜrk/ *v.* to irritate, annoy, or bother:[~ + *obj*]: *The continual delays on the trains irked the passengers.* [*it* ~ + *obj* + *to* + *verb*]: *It irks me to have to pay your way.* [*it* + ~ + *obj* + *that clause*]: *It irks me that I have to pay your way.*

irk•some (ûrk′səm) /ˈɜrksəm/ *adj.* annoying; irritating; tiresome: *irksome restrictions.* **—irk′some•ness,** *n.* [*noncount*]

i•ron (ī′ərn) /ˈayərn/ *n.* **1.** [*noncount*] a silver-white metallic element, used in some forms for making steel, tools, implements, machinery, etc., and also found in tiny quantities in food and in blood. **2.** [*noncount*] a part of a person's nature that does not bend or yield easily: *She had a will of iron.* **3.** [*count*] an electrical appliance with a flat metal bottom, used when heated to press or smooth clothes, linens, etc. See illustration at APPLIANCE. **4.** [*count*] golf clubs with iron heads. Compare WOOD¹ (def. 6). **5. irons,** [*plural*] a set of rings or other fastenings for the ankles or wrists, used to chain up a person or animal. **—*adj.*** [*before a noun*] **6.** of, containing, or made of iron: *an iron skillet.* **7.** resembling iron in firmness, strength, character, etc.: *an iron will.* **8.** holding strongly and tightly: *shakes hands with an iron grip.* **—*v.*** **9.** to smooth or press with a heated iron, as clothes or linens: [~ + *obj*]: *to iron shirts.* [*no obj*]: *He was ironing when you called.* **10. iron out,** to clear away (difficulties): [~ + *out* + *obj*]: *to iron out any problems you may* *have.* [~ + *obj* + *out*]: *Let's iron your problems out.* —***Idiom.*** **11. irons in the fire,** undertakings; projects: *He still has plenty of irons in the fire concerning finding a job.* **12. strike while the iron is hot,** to take advantage quickly of an opportunity by taking immediate action.

i•ron•clad (*adj.* i′ərn klad′; *n.* -klad′) / *adj.* 'ayərn'klæd; *n.* -ˌklæd/ *adj.* **1.** covered with iron plates, as a vessel; armor-plated. **2.** inflexible; unbreakable: *an ironclad contract.* —*n.* [*count*] **3.** a wooden warship of the middle or late 19th century having iron or steel armor plating.

i′ron cur′tain, *n.* [*the* + ~; *sometimes: Iron Curtain*] a barrier to understanding and the exchange of information created by the hostility of one country toward another, esp. the barrier that existed between the former Soviet Union or its allies and other countries.

i•ron•ic (i ron′ik) /ay'rɒnɪk/ also **i•ron′i•cal,** *adj.* **1.** of, relating to, containing, or showing irony or mockery: *an ironic smile.* [*it* + *be* + ~ + *that clause*]: *It is ironic that in peacetime they spent more on the military than during wartime.* **2.** using irony: *an ironic writer.* —**i•ron′i•cal•ly,** *adv.*

i•ron•ing (i′ər ning) /'ayərnɪŋ/ *n.* [*noncount*] **1.** the act or process of smoothing or pressing clothes, linens, etc., with a heated iron. **2.** articles of clothing, linens, etc., that have been or are to be ironed.

i′ron lung′, *n.* [*count*] a rigid machine that encloses the whole body except the head and in which pulses of high and low pressure cause normal breathing movements or force air into and out of the lungs.

i•ron•ware (i′ərn wâr′) /'ayərnˌwɛər/ *n.* [*noncount*] articles of iron, as pots, kettles, or tools.

i•ron•work (i′ərn wûrk′) /'ayərnˌwɜrk/ *n.* [*noncount*] objects or parts of objects made of iron: *ornamental ironwork.*

i•ro•ny (i′rə nē, i′ər-) /'ayrəniy, 'ayər-/ *n., pl.* **-nies. 1.** [*noncount*] the use of words to convey a meaning that is the opposite of their literal or actual meaning. **2.** an outcome opposite to what was, or might have been, expected: [*noncount*]: *What irony to be offered three jobs after having none for so long.* [*count*]: *It was a real irony that my former boss was asking me for a job.*

ir•ra•di•ate (*v.* i rā′dē āt′; *adj.* -it, -āt′) / *v.* ɪ'reydiyˌeyt; *adj.* -ɪt, -ˌeyt/ *v.* [~ + *obj*], **-at•ed, -at•ing,** *adj.* **1.** to shed rays of light on; illuminate. **2.** to heat with radiant energy. **3.** to expose to radiation, as for medical treatment. —**ir•ra•di•a•tion** (i rā′dē ā′shən) /ɪˌreydiy'eyʃən/ *n.* [*noncount*]

ir•ra•tion•al (i rash′ə nl) /ɪ'ræʃənḷ/ *adj.* **1.** lacking sound judgment or logic: *an irrational argument.* **2.** not controlled or governed by reason: *irrational behavior.* **3.** not having the power of reason: *Brute animals are irrational beings.* **4.** (of a number) that cannot be expressed exactly as a ratio of two integers: *The value of* pi *is an irrational number.* —**ir•ra′tion•al•ly,** *adv.* **See -RATIO-.**

ir•rec•on•cil•a•ble (i rek′ən sī′lə bəl, i rek′ən sī′-) /ɪ'rɛkənˌsayləbəl, ɪˌrɛkən'say-/ *adj.* that cannot be brought into harmony or agreement; incompatible: *irreconcilable differences.*

ir•re•cov•er•a•ble (ir′i kuv′ər ə bəl) /ˌɪrɪ'kʌvərəbəl/ *adj.* that cannot be recovered or regained: *an irrecoverable loss.*

ir•re•deem•a•ble (ir′i dē′mə bəl) /ˌɪrɪ'diyməbəl/ *adj.* **1.** not redeemable; that cannot be bought back or paid off: *an irredeemable bond.* **2.** irreparable; hopeless.

ir•ref•u•ta•ble (i ref′yə tə bəl, ir′i fyōō′tə bəl) /ɪ'rɛfyətəbəl, ˌɪrɪ'fyuwtəbəl/ *adj.* not refutable; that cannot be disproved or argued successfully against: *an irrefutable argument.*

ir•re•gard•less (ir′i gärd′lis) /ˌɪrɪ'gardlɪs/ *adv.* [*often:* ~ + *of*] *Nonstandard.* regardless; without concern for; without taking into acount: *The kids are going to disobey you irregardless of the punishment you threaten them with.*

ir•reg•u•lar (i reg′yə lər) /ɪ'rɛgyələr/ *adj.* **1.** lacking an even shape, formal arrangement, balance, or harmony; uneven: *irregular patterns.* **2.** varied in timing or rhythm; erratic: *He worked very irregular hours.* **3.** not according to or conforming to established rules, principles, manners, morals, standards, etc.: *The judge ruled that the lawyer's request was highly irregular.* **4.** not following the more normal or usual pattern of formation, word changes, etc., in a language, as English verbs that do not form the past tense by adding *-ed: the irregular verbs* keep *and* see, *with their irregular past tense forms* kept *and* saw. —*n.* [*count*] **5.** one that is irregular, such as a product or material that does not meet standards of the manufacturer. **6.** a soldier or fighter who does not belong to an official military force, as a guerrilla. —**ir•reg•u•lar•i•ty** (i reg′yə lar′i tē) /ɪˌrɛgyə'lærɪtiy/ *n.* [*count*]: *Because there were several irregularities in the arrest the prisoner will probably go free.* [*noncount*]: *a degree of irregularity in every language.* —**ir•reg′u•lar′ly,** *adv.* See -REG-.

ir•rel•e•vance (i rel′ə vəns), /ɪ'rɛləvəns/ *n.* **1.** [*noncount*] the state or condition of being irrelevant. **2.** Also, **ir•rel′e•van•cy,** *pl.* **-cies.** [*count*] a statement, fact, or act that is irrelevant: *His argument is full of irrelevancies.*

ir•rel•e•vant (i rel′ə vənt) /ɪ'rɛləvənt/ *adj.* not relevant; not applicable or pertinent: *The complaints raised against the proposal were really irrelevant, so we ignored them.*

ir•re•li•gious (ir′i lij′əs) /ˌɪrɪ'lɪdʒəs/ *adj.* not religious; not practicing a religion; feeling no religious impulses, or feeling hostile to religion.

ir•re•me•di•a•ble (ir′i mē′dē ə bəl) /ˌɪrɪ'miydiyəbəl/ *adj.* that cannot be remedied, cured, or repaired: *irremediable damage to the child's learning ability.* —**ir′re•me′di•a•bly,** *adv.*

ir•rep•a•ra•ble (i rep′ər ə bəl) /ɪ'rɛpərəbəl/ *adj.* that cannot be repaired, rectified, remedied, or made good: *an irreparable mistake.* See -PARE-.

ir•re•place•a•ble (ir′i plā′sə bəl) /ˌɪrɪ'pleysəbəl/ *adj.* that cannot be replaced; unique: *an irreplaceable vase.*

ir•re•press•i•ble (ir′i pres′ə bəl) /ˌɪrɪ'prɛsəbəl/ *adj.* that cannot be held back or restrained; uncontrollable: *irrepressible laughter.* —**ir′re•pres′sib•ly,** *adv.* See -PRESS-.

ir•re•proach•a•ble (ir′i prō′chə bəl) /ˌɪrɪ'prowtʃəbəl/ *adj.* that cannot be criticized or blamed.

ir•re•sist•i•ble (ir′i zis′tə bəl) /ˌɪrɪ'zɪstəbəl/ *adj.* **1.** that cannot be resisted or withstood: *an irresistible force* **2.** desirable; enticing; attractive; tempting: *found the necklace irresistible.* —**ir′re•sist′i•bly,** *adv.: was irresistibly attracted to her.* See -SIST-.

ir•res•o•lute (i rez′ə lōōt′) /ɪ'rɛzəˌluwt/ *adj.* not resolute; doubtful; hesitating; unsure: *He was irresolute about his choice of a career.* —**ir•res′o•lute′ly,** *adv.* —**ir•res•o•lu•tion** (i rez′ə lōō′shən) /ɪˌrɛzə'luwʃən/ *n.* [*noncount*] See -SOLV-.

ir•re•spec•tive of (ir′i spek′tiv) /ˌɪrɪ'spɛktɪv/ *prep.* without regard to; ignoring or not concerned about or concerned with: *We'll be there, irrespective of the weather.* See -SPEC-.

ir•re•spon•si•ble (ir′i spon′sə bəl) /ˌɪrɪ'spɒnsəbəl/ *adj.* **1.** showing or characterized by a lack of a sense of responsibility: *irresponsible sexual behavior.* **2.** not capable of or qualified for responsibility: *The children are just too irresponsible to be left alone* —**ir•re•spon•si•bil•i•ty** (ir′i-spon′sə bil′i tē) /ˌɪrɪˌspɒnsə'bɪlɪtiy/ *n.* [*noncount*] —**ir′re•spon′si•bly,** *adv.* See -SPOND-.

ir•re•triev•a•ble (ir′i trē′və bəl) /ˌɪrɪ'triyvəbəl/ *adj.* not retrievable; that cannot be recovered or retrieved.

ir•rev•er•ence (i rev′ər əns) /ɪ'rɛvərəns/ *n.* [*noncount*] the quality of being irreverent; lack of reverence or respect.

ir•rev•er•ent (i rev′ər ənt) /ɪ'rɛvərənt/ *adj.* not reverent; not showing respect or reverence for something: *an irreverent attitude toward religion.* —**ir′rev′er•ent•ly,** *adv.*

ir•re•vers•i•ble (ir′i vûr′sə bəl) /ˌɪrɪ'vɜrsəbəl/ *adj.* not reversible; that cannot be changed: *His refusal is irreversible.* —**ir′re•vers′i•bly,** *adv.: He is irreversibly opposed to your nomination.* See -VERT-.

ir•rev•o•ca•ble (i rev′ə kə bəl) /ɪ'rɛvəkəbəl/ *adj.* that cannot be changed or taken back: *an irrevocable commitment to quality.* —**ir•rev′o•ca•bly,** *adv.* See -VOC-.

ir•ri•gate (ir′i gāt′) /'ɪrɪˌgeyt/ *v.* [~ + *obj*], **-gat•ed, -gat•ing. 1.** to supply (land) with water by artificial means, such as by changing the course of streams, by flooding, or by spraying. **2.** to supply or wash (an opening in the body, a wound, etc.) with liquid. —**ir•ri•ga•ble** (ir′i gə bəl) /'ɪrɪgəbəl/ *adj.* —**ir•ri•ga•tion** (ir′i gā′shən) /ˌɪrɪ'geyʃən/ *n.* [*noncount*]

ir•ri•ta•ble (ir′i tə bəl) /'ɪrɪtəbəl/ *adj.* easily irritated or annoyed; readily becoming impatient or angry: *was irritable with fatigue and worry.* —**ir•ri•ta•bil•i•ty** (ir′i tə bil′i tē) /ˌɪrɪtə'bɪlɪtiy/ *n.* [*noncount*] —**ir′ri•ta•bly,** *adv.*

ir•ri•tant (ir′i tənt) /'ɪrɪtənt/ *n.* [*count*] **1.** anyone or anything that causes a feeling of impatience or anger: *A lazy worker is an irritant to colleagues.* **2.** a substance that causes a feeling of itching or other irritation on the skin or some part of the body.

ir•ri•tate (ir′i tāt′) /'ɪrɪˌteyt/ *v.,* **-tat•ed, -tat•ing. 1.** [~ + *obj*] to cause (someone) to have a feeling of impatience or anger; annoy: *Her whining really irritates me.* **2.** to cause (someone to have) a feeling of itching or other irritation on the skin or on a part of the body: [*no obj*]: *That chemical irritates if it gets on your skin.* [~ + *obj*]: *Harsh soap irritates her skin.*

ir•ri•tat•ed (ir′i tā′tid) /ˈɪrɪˌteytɪd/ *adj.* **1.** annoyed; angered; made impatient: *I soon became irritated by her grouchiness.* **2.** showing signs of irritation: *the baby's irritated skin.*

ir•ri•tat•ing (ir′i tā′ting) /ˈɪrɪˌteytɪŋ/ *adj.* **1.** causing a feeling of annoyance, anger, or impatience: *his irritating whining.* **2.** causing an irritation to the skin or other part of the body: *the irritating effects of soot on the eyes.*

ir•ri•ta•tion (ir′i tā′shən) /ˌɪrɪˈteyʃən/ *n.* **1.** [*noncount*] a feeling of annoyance, anger, or impatience. **2.** [*count*] something that causes such a feeling of anger, annoyance, or impatience: *Those troublemakers are just minor irritations.* **3.** [*noncount*] a feeling of scratchiness, itchiness, or other discomfort on the skin or some part of the body. **4.** [*count*] an area of soreness or inflammation: *an irritation on my leg.*

IRS, an abbreviation of: Internal Revenue Service.

is (iz) /ɪz/ *v.* 3rd pers. sing. pres. indic. of BE.

is., an abbreviation of: **1.** island. **2.** isle.

-ise, *suffix. Chiefly Brit.* See -IZE.

-ish, *suffix.* **1.** *-ish* is attached to nouns or roots to form adjectives with the meaning: **a.** relating to; in the same manner of; having the characteristics of: *brute + -ish → brutish.* **b.** of or relating to the people or language of: *Brit- + -ish → British; Swede + -ish → Swedish.* **c.** like; similar to: *baby + -ish → babyish; mule + -ish → mulish; girl + -ish → girlish.* **d.** addicted to; inclined or tending to: *book + -ish → bookish (= tending to read books a great deal).* **e.** near or about: *fifty + -ish → fiftyish (nearly fifty years old).* **2.** *-ish* is also attached to adjectives to form adjectives with the meaning "somewhat, rather": *old + -ish → oldish (= somewhat old); red + -ish → reddish (= somewhat red); sweet + -ish → sweetish.*

Is•lam (is läm′, is′läm, -ləm, iz′-) /ɪsˈlɑm, ˈɪslɑm, -ləm, ˈɪz-/ *n.* **1.** [*proper noun*] the religion of the Muslims, as set forth in the Koran, which teaches that there is only one God, Allah, and that Muhammad is His prophet. **2.** [*noncount*] the culture or civilization of Muslim believers, or regions where theirs is the leading religion. —**Is•lam′ic,** *adj.*

is•land (i′lənd) /ˈaylənd/ *n.* [*count*] **1.** an area of land completely surrounded by water but not large enough to be called a continent. **2.** something resembling an island, esp. in being isolated: *Her desk was an island of tranquillity in all the hubbub and chaos around her.* **3.** a freestanding unit with a counter on top, located so as to permit access from all sides.

is•land•er (i′lən dər) /ˈayləndər/ *n.* [*count*] a native of an island; someone who lives on an island.

isle (īl) /ayl/ *n.* [*count*] **1.** a small island. **2.** any island.

is•let (i′lit) /ˈaylɪt/ *n.* [*count*] a very small island.

ism (iz′əm) /ˈɪzəm/ *n.* [*count*] a distinctive belief, theory, system, or practice; anything that could be referred to by a word with the suffix -ISM: *capitalism, socialism, and other isms.*

-ism, *suffix.* **1.** *-ism* is attached to verb roots to form action nouns: *baptize → bapt- + -ism → baptism.* **2.** *-ism* is used to form nouns showing action or practice: *adventure + -ism → adventurism (= the action or practice of taking risks in intervening in international affairs).* **3.** *-ism* is used to form nouns showing state or condition: *alcoholism (= disease or condition in which alcohol is involved).* **4.** *-ism* is attached to roots to form nouns showing the names of principles or doctrines: *Darwinism (= principles of Darwin's theory of evolution); despotism.* **5.** *-ism* is used to form nouns showing an example of a use: *witticism (= example of something witty); Africanism (= word from Africa or from an African language).* Compare -IST, -IZE.

isn't (iz′ənt) /ˈɪzənt/ contraction of *is not.*

iso-, *prefix. iso-* comes from Greek, where it has the meaning "equal". This meaning is found in such scientific and chemical words as: ISOSCELES, ISOTOPE.

i•so•late (*v.* i′sə lāt′; *n., adj.* -lit, -lāt′) / *v.* ˈaysəˌleyt; *n., adj.* -lɪt, -ˌleyt/ *v.* [~ + *obj*], **-lat•ed, -lat•ing. 1.** to set or place apart; separate so as to be alone: *He was isolated in a little cubicle by himself.* **2.** to keep (an infected person) from contact with noninfected persons; quarantine. **3.** to obtain (a chemical substance or microorganism) in a separate or pure state, not in combination with other substances. —**i•so•la•tion** (ī′sə lā′shən) /ˌaysəˈleyʃən/ *n.* [*noncount*]: *a desperate feeling of isolation in the big city.*

i•so•la•tion•ism (ī′sə lā′shə niz′əm) /ˌaysəˈleyʃəˌnɪzəm/ *n.* [*noncount*] the policy or doctrine that calls for isolating one's country from alliances with and commitments to other countries. —**i′so•la′tion•ist,** *n.* [*count*], *adj.*

i•so•met•ric (ī′sə me′trik) /ˌaysəˈmɛtrɪk/ *adj.* Also, **i′so•met′ri•cal. 1.** of or relating to isometric exercises. —*n.* **2. isometrics,** [*plural*] exercises in which a muscle or muscle group is tensed against another muscle or something that cannot move. —**i′so•met′ri•cal•ly,** *adv.*

i•sos•ce•les (ī sos′ə lēz′) /ayˈsɒsəˌliyz/ *adj.* (of a two-dimensional figure in geometry) having two straight sides equal: *an isosceles triangle; an isosceles trapezoid.*

i•so•tope (ī′sə tōp′) /ˈaysəˌtowp/ *n.* [*count*] one of two or more forms of a chemical element having the same number of protons, or the same atomic number, but having different numbers of neutrons, or different atomic weights. —**i•so•top•ic** (ī′sə top′ik) /ˌaysəˈtɒpɪk/ *adj.*

Is•rae•li (iz rā′lē) /ɪzˈreyliy/ *n.* [*count*], *pl.* **-lis** or **-li. 1.** a person born or living in Israel. —*adj.* **2.** of or relating to Israel.

is•su•ance (ish′o͞o əns) /ˈɪʃuwəns/ *n.* [*noncount*] the act of issuing.

is•sue (ish′o͞o) /ˈɪʃuw/ *n., v.,* **-sued, -su•ing.** —*n.* [*count*] **1.** the act of sending out or putting forth; distribution. **2.** a series of things or one of a series of things printed, published, or given out at one time: *a new bond issue; a magazine issue.* **3.** a point in question or a matter that is in dispute or may be argued about because of its importance: *His age isn't the issue.* **4.** a point at which a matter is ready for decision: *to bring a case to an issue.* **5.** [*noncount; used with a singular or plural verb*] offspring; child or children. —*v.* **6.** [~ + *obj*] to publish, mint, deliver for use, sale, etc.; put into circulation: *The magazine was first issued in the early seventies.* **7.** [~ + *obj*] to distribute (food, clothing, supplies, etc.) officially, as to military personnel or students: *Each soldier was issued a bedroll.* **8.** [~ + *obj*] to send out; release, as a statement: *to issue a denial of the charges.* **9.** to (cause to) go, pass, be sent out, or flow out; (cause to) emerge: [*no obj*]: *to issue forth to battle.* [~ + *obj*]: *The nuclear power plant issued contaminated water into the river.* —***Idiom.* 10. at issue,** being argued about and not yet decided: *At issue were salary increases, work hours, and benefits.* **11. make an issue,** [~ + *over/of/about* + *obj*] to cause a disagreement about; make a fuss over: *Don't make such an issue of that report.* **12. take issue,** [~ + *with* + *obj*] to disagree; dispute: *He took issue with those who disagreed with him.*

-ist, *suffix. -ist* forms nouns usually corresponding to verbs ending in *-ize* and nouns ending in *-ism*, and referring to a person who practices or is concerned with something: *novel + -ist → novelist (= someone writing a novel); terrorist (= one who practices terrorism, one who terrorizes).*

isth•mus (is′məs) /ˈɪsməs/ *n.* [*count*], *pl.* **-mus•es, -mi** (-mī) /-may/. a narrow strip of land, bordered on both sides by water, connecting two larger bodies of land: *The isthmus of Panama is between North and South America.*

it (it) /ɪt/ *pron., nom.* **it,** *poss.* **its,** *obj.* **it,** *pl. nom.* **they,** *poss.* **their** or **theirs,** *obj.* **them,** *n.* —*pron.* This pronoun is used **1.** to represent a physical thing, a thought or idea, or anything not a person, that is understood, was previously mentioned, is about to be mentioned, or is present in the immediate context of speaking or writing: *It was broken. You can't tell a book by its cover. Since you don't like it, you don't have to go skiing. It all started with Adam and Eve. It's a long way to the moon.* **2.** to represent a person or animal that is understood, was previously mentioned, or about to be mentioned, and whose gender is unknown or not considered: *Who was it? It was John. That baby is cute; it has such pretty blue eyes.* **3.** to represent a group that is understood, was previously mentioned, or is about to be mentioned: *The judge told the jury it could recess.* **4.** as the impersonal subject of the verb *to be,* esp. to refer to time, distance, or the weather: *It is six o'clock. It was foggy outside. It's raining again. It's so hot here. It's six miles from my house to the post office. It's June 20.* **5.** in statements expressing an action, condition, fact, circumstance, or situation, without reference to someone performing an action: *If it weren't for her, I wouldn't go.* **6.** in referring to something as the origin or cause of pain, pleasure, etc.: *Where does it hurt?* **7.** in referring to a source not specifically named or described: *It is said that love is blind.* **8.** in referring to the general state of affairs or life in general: *How's it going with you?* **9.** as an anticipatory subject or object to make a sentence more full of suspense or to shift emphasis: *It is necessary that you do your duty. It* *was a gun that he was carrying. I didn't like it that she had tricked us.* **10.** in referring to a critical event that has finally happened or is about to happen: *Suddenly the lights went out, and we thought, this is it!* **11.** informally, instead of the pronoun *its* before a gerund or present participle: *It having rained for only one hour didn't help the crops.* **—*n.*** [*noncount*] **12.** (in children's games) the player who is to perform some task, as, in tag, the one who must catch the others: *If I catch you, you're it!* **13.** *Slang.* **a.** a desirable personal attribute, as talent or sex appeal: *If you've got it, flaunt it.* **b.** sexual intercourse: *After months of dating they finally did it.*

I•tal•ian (i tal′yən) /ɪ'tælyən/ *adj.* **1.** of or relating to Italy. **2.** of or relating to the language spoken in Italy. **—*n.*** **3.** [*count*] a person born or living in Italy. **4.** [*noncount*] the language spoken in Italy.

i•tal•ic (i tal′ik, ī tal′-) /ɪ'tælɪk, ay'tæl-/ *adj.* **1.** being or relating to a style of printing types in which the letters usually slope to the right: *This sentence is in italic type.* **—*n.*** **2.** Often, **italics.** italic type: [*plural*]: *She printed the report completely in italics.* [*noncount*]: *It was in italic.*

i•tal•i•cize (i tal′ə sīz′, ī tal′-) /ɪ'tælə,sayz, ay'tæl-/ *v.*, **-cized, -ciz•ing.** to print in italic type; to use italic print: [~ + *obj*]: *to italicize a line.* [*no obj*]: *The laser printer italicizes.* —**i•tal•i•ci•za•tion** (i tal′ə sə zā′shən, ī tal′-) /ɪ,tæləsə'zeyʃən, ay,tæl-/ *n.* [*noncount*]

itch (ich) /ɪtʃ/ *v.* **1.** [*no obj*] to have or feel a tingling irritation of the skin that causes a desire to scratch the part affected: *My skin itches.* **2.** to cause such a feeling: [*no obj*]: *This shirt itches.* [~ + *obj*]: *This shirt itches me.* **3.** *Informal.* to scratch a part that itches: [~ + *obj*]: *Even though the poison ivy is driving you mad, don't itch it!* [*no obj*]: *Don't itch; just try to think of something else.* **4.** to have a desire to do or get something: [*no obj*]: *to itch after fame.* [~ + *to* + *verb*]: *He was itching to get back to his home town.* **—*n.*** [*count*] **5.** the sensation of itching: *a bad itch.* **6.** a restless desire or longing: *an itch for excitement.* —**itch′y,** *adj.*, **-i•er, -i•est.**

it'd (it′əd) /'ɪtəd/ *contraction.* This word is a shortened form of: **1.** it would: *It'd be great to see you again.* **2.** it had: *It'd been cloudy and dark all day.*

-ite, *suffix.* *-ite* is attached to nouns and roots to form nouns with the meanings: **1.** a person associated with or living in a place; a person connected with a tribe, leader, set of beliefs, system, etc.: *Manhattan + -ite → Manhattanite; Israel + -ite → Israelite; Labor + -ite → Laborite (= someone following the Labor Party).* **2.** mineral or fossil; explosive; chemical compound or drug product: *anthracite; cordite; dynamite; sulfite.*

i•tem (*n.* ī′təm; *adv.* ī′tem) / *n.* 'aytəm; *adv.* 'aytɛm/ *n.* [*count*] **1.** a separate thing or particular article: *There were at least 50 items on the list.* **2.** a piece of information: *a news item.* **3.** *Slang.* a topic of gossip: *The new couple in the neighborhood are a hot item.* **—*adv.*** **4.** This word is used to introduce each article or statement in a list or series and means "also, likewise".

i•tem•ize (ī′tə mīz′) /'aytə,mayz/ *v.*, **-ized, -iz•ing.** **1.** [~ + *obj*] to list by items; give the particulars of: *to itemize an account.* **2.** to list separately (all allowable deductions) in computing income tax: [*no obj*]: *You'll need fifteen forms if you want to itemize.* [~ + *obj*]: *We should itemize those expenses as deductions.* —**i•tem•i•za•tion** (ī′tə mə zā′shən) /,aytəmə'zeyʃən/ *n.* [*noncount*] —**ī′tem•ized′,** *adj.*: *an itemized bill.*

it•er•ate (it′ə rāt′) /'ɪtə,reyt/ *v.* [~ + *obj*], **-at•ed, -at•ing.** to say or do (something) again or over and over: *He iterated his objections.* —**it•er•a•tion** (it′ə rā′shən) /,ɪtə'reyʃən/ *n.* [*noncount*]: *constant iteration.* [*count*]: *The computer can perform repeated iterations of that function for days.*

i•tin•er•ant (ī tin′ər ənt, i tin′-) /ay'tɪnərənt, ɪ'tɪn-/ *adj.* [*before a noun*] **1.** working in one place for a short time and then moving on to another place, as a physical or outdoor laborer: *itinerant workers.* **2.** traveling from place to place, esp. on a circuit, as a minister or judge. **—*n.*** [*count*] **3.** a person who alternates between working and wandering. **4.** a person who travels from place to place, for business.

i•tin•er•ar•y (ī tin′ə rer′ē, i tin′-) /ay'tɪnə'rɛriy, ɪ'tɪn-/ *n.* [*count*], *pl.* **-ar•ies.** **1.** a detailed plan for a journey, esp. a list of places to visit. **2.** a line of travel; route. **3.** a traveler's guidebook.

-itis, *suffix.* **1.** *-itis* is attached to roots to form nouns that refer to an inflammation or disease affecting a certain part of the body: *appendix + -itis → appendicitis; bronchi (= part of the lungs) + -itis → bronchitis.* **2.** *-itis* is also used to form nouns made up for a particular occasion to refer to something comparable in a funny way to a disease: *The teenagers seem to be suffering from telephonitis (= excessive use of the telephone, as if using it were a disease).*

it'll (it′l) /'ɪtl̩/ *contraction.* This word is a shortened form of *it will*: *"It'll be a long time before you see me back here again," she promised.*

its (its) /ɪts/ *adj.* This word is the possessive form of IT, and is used to show possession by something that was referred to earlier: *The book has lost its jacket.*

it's (its) /ɪts/ *contraction.* **1.** a shortened form of *it is*: *It's starting to rain.* **2.** a shortened form of *it has*: *It's been a long time since we saw each other.*

it•self (it self′) /ɪt'sɛlf/ *pron.* **1.** This pronoun, a reflexive form of IT ,is used as the direct or indirect object of a verb or the object of a preposition to refer to the same thing as the subject: *The battery recharges itself (= The battery recharges the same battery). The bird built a nest for itself.* **2.** This pronoun is used to give emphasis to a noun or pronoun, not a person: *which itself is a fact; The land itself was not for sale.* **3.** This pronoun is used to refer to the normal or usual self (when not a person): *The injured cat was never quite itself again.*

it•ty-bit•ty (it′ē bit′ē) /'ɪtiy'bɪtiy/ also **it•sy-bit•sy** (it′sē bit′sē) /'ɪtsiy'bɪtsiy/ *adj. Informal.* very small; tiny.

IUD, an abbreviation of: intrauterine device.

IV (ī′vē′) /'ay'viy/ *n.* [*count*], *pl.* **IVs, IV's.** an apparatus for intravenous delivery of electrolyte solutions, medicines, and nutrients.

IV, an abbreviation of: intravenous.

I've (īv) /ayv/ *contraction.* a shortened form of *I have*: *I've been working on the railroad for a long time.*

-ive, *suffix.* *-ive* is attached to roots or nouns to form adjectives with the meaning "having a tendency or connection with; like": *act(ion) + -ive → active (= tending to be full of action or activity); sport + -ive → sportive (= like sports).*

i•vo•ry (ī′və rē, ī′vrē) /'ayvəriy, 'ayvriy/ *n.*, *pl.* **-ries,** *adj.* **—*n.*** **1.** [*noncount*] the hard white substance similar to dentine that makes up the main part of the tusks, esp. of the elephant and walrus. **2.** [*count*] a tusk yielding ivory. **3.** [*count*] *Slang.* a tooth. **4.** **ivories,** [*plural*] *Slang.* **a.** the keys of a piano. **b.** dice. **5.** [*noncount*] a creamy or yellowish white. **—*adj.*** **6.** [*before a noun*] consisting or made of ivory: *an ivory carving.* **7.** of the color ivory.

ī′vory tow′er, *n.* [*count*] a place, situation, or attitude that is removed or kept apart from worldly, everyday, or practical affairs.

i•vy (ī′vē) /'ayviy/ *n.*, *pl.* **i•vies.** a climbing vine of the ginseng family, from Eurasia and N Africa, having smooth, shiny evergreen leaves: [*noncount*]: *beautiful ivy growing up the sides of the building.* [*count*]: *replanting a few ivies.*

-ize, *suffix.* **1.** *-ize* is used to form verbs with the meaning "to make; cause to become:" *fossil + -ize → fossilize (= to make something into a fossil); sterile + -ize → sterilize (= to make something sterile).* **2.** *-ize* is also used to form verbs with the meaning "to convert into, give a specified character or form to; change to a state of:" *computer + -ize → computerize (= make an office use computers); dramat- + -ize → dramatize (= give the form of a drama to some other piece of work); American + -ize → Americanize (= convert to an American character).* **3.** *-ize* is also used to form verbs with the meaning "to subject to; cause to undergo or suffer from (an emotion or a process, sometimes named after its originator)": *hospital + -ize → hospitalize (= cause to undergo treatment in a hospital); terror + -ize → terrorize (= cause to suffer terror); galvan- + -ize → galvanize (= to coat metal or stimulate electrically, as by the experiments of L. Galvani, Italian physicist).* Also, *chiefly British,* **-ise.**

J

J, j (jā) / dʒey/ *n., pl.* **Js** or **J's, js** or **j's.** the tenth letter of the English alphabet, a consonant.

J or **j,** an abbreviation of: joule.

J., an abbreviation of: **1.** Journal. **2.** Judge. **3.** Justice.

JA or **J.A.,** an abbreviation of: joint account.

jab (jab) / dʒæb/ *v.,* **jabbed, jab•bing,** *n.* **—***v.* **1.** to poke sharply or quickly, as with an end or point: [~ + *obj*]: *He jabbed his elbow into my side.* [*no obj*]: *to jab at a fire with a stick.* **—***n.* [*count*] **2.** a sharp, quick thrust; a short, quick boxing punch.

jab•ber (jab′ər) /ˈdʒæbər/ *v.* **1.** to speak rapidly, unclearly, or in a foolish way; chatter: [*no obj*]: *What are you jabbering about?* [~ + *obj*]: *They were jabbering some nonsense again.* **—***n.* [*noncount*] **2.** rapid, unclear, or foolish talk; talk with no meaning; gibberish. **—jab′ber•er,** *n.* [*count*]

jac•a•ran•da (jak′ə ran′də) /ˌdʒækəˈrændə/ *n.* [*count*], *pl.* **-das.** a tropical tree, having bright clusters of usually purplish flowers.

jack (jak) / dʒæk/ *n.* **1.** [*count*] any of various portable devices for raising or lifting heavy objects a short distance off the ground: *an automobile jack.* **2.** [*count*] Also called **knave.** a playing card with the picture of a soldier or servant: *a pair of jacks.* **3.** [*count*] a connecting device in an electrical circuit designed so that a plug can be attached to it: *a telephone jack.* **4. a.** [*count*] one of a set of small, six-pointed metal objects or pebbles used in the game of jacks. **b. jacks,** [*noncount; used with a singular verb*] a children's game in which a player tosses and gathers these objects usually while bouncing a small rubber ball. **—***v.* **5.** to lift or move (something) with or as if with a jack: [~ + *obj*]: *to jack the car on the soft grass.* [~ + *up* + *obj*]: *to jack up a car.* [~ + *obj* + *up*]: *to jack it up.* **6.** to increase, raise, or accelerate (prices, wages, speed, etc.): [~ + *up* + *obj*]: *The landlord jacked up rent illegally.* [~ + *obj* + *up*]: *They jacked oil prices up.* **—*Idiom.* 7. every man jack,** everyone without exception: *The killers managed to escape, every man jack.*

jack•al (jak′əl, -ôl) /ˈdʒækəl, -ɔl/ *n.* [*count*] a wild dog of Asia and Africa that hunts in packs, often at night.

jack•ass (jak′as′) /ˈdʒækˌæs/ *n.* [*count*] **1.** a male donkey. **2.** a very foolish or stupid person; blockhead; dolt.

jack•boot (jak′bo͞ot′) /ˈdʒækˌbuwt/ *n.* [*count*] **1.** a man's sturdy leather boot reaching up over the knee. **2.** authority or rule based on the power of the military; totalitarian rule: *living under the jackboots.*

jack•daw (jak′dô′) /ˈdʒækˌdɔ/ *n.* [*count*] a small crow.

jack•et (jak′it) /ˈdʒækɪt/ *n.* [*count*] **1.** a short coat, in any of various forms, usually opening down the front. See illustration at CLOTHING. **2.** an article like a piece of clothing, designed to be placed around the body, but used for some purpose other than as clothing. Compare LIFE JACKET, STRAITJACKET. **3.** a protective outer covering, as the plastic around a wire, a casing for a bullet, or a wrapper for a book. **4.** the skin of a potato, esp. when it has been cooked. **—jack′et•ed,** *adj.*

Jack′ Frost′, *n.* [*proper noun*] frost or freezing cold thought of as a person: *Jack Frost nipping at your nose.*

jack•ham•mer (jak′ham′ər) /ˈdʒækˌhæmər/ *n.* [*count*] a portable drill operated by compressed air and used to drill rock, break up pavement, etc.: *the pounding noise of the jackhammers.*

jack′-in-the-box′ or **jack′-in-a-box′,** *n.* [*count*], *pl.* **-box•es.** a toy made up of a box from which an enclosed doll springs up when the lid is opened.

jack′-in-the-pul′pit, *n.* [*count*], *pl.* **-pul•pits.** a North American plant of the arum family having an upright spike with an arch over it that resembles a pulpit in a church.

jack•knife (jak′nīf′) /ˈdʒækˌnayf/ *n., pl.* **-knives,** *v.,* **-knifed, -knif•ing. —***n.* [*count*] **1.** a large pocketknife. **2.** a dive in which the diver bends in midair to touch the toes, keeping the legs straight, and then straightens out. **—***v.* **3.** (of a trailer truck) to have the cab and trailer swivel at the point where they meet until they form a V shape: [*no obj*]: *A tractor trailer truck had jackknifed and rolled over.* [~ + *obj*]: *The trailer was jackknifed across all four lanes of traffic.* **4.** [*no obj*] (in diving) to perform a jackknife: *The diver jackknifed cleanly into the water.*

jack′-of-all′-trades′, *n.* [*count*], *pl.* **jacks-of-all-trades.** a person who is skilled at many different kinds of work.

jack-o'-lan•tern (jak′ə lan′tərn) /ˈdʒækəˌlæntərn/ *n.* [*count*] a pumpkin that has been hollowed out and cut with openings to represent a human face, traditionally displayed at Halloween, often with a candle or light inside.

jack•pot (jak′pot′) /ˈdʒækˌpɒt/ *n.* [*count; usually singular; often: the* + ~] **1.** the chief prize, or all the prizes or money to be won in a game, contest, lottery, or the like: *a jackpot of one million dollars.* **2.** an outstanding reward or success: *Getting that new account was the jackpot.* **—*Idiom.* 3. hit the jackpot, a.** to achieve sudden success: *She felt she'd hit the jackpot when she got the job.* **b.** to win a jackpot: *hit the jackpot on a slot machine.*

jack′ rab′bit, *n.* [*count*] a large hare of W North America, having long hind legs and long ears.

Ja•cuz•zi (jə ko͞o′zē) / dʒəˈkuwziy/ *pl.* **zis.** [*count*] *Trademark.* a brand name for a device for a whirlpool bath and related products.

jade (jād) / dʒeyd/ *n.* [*noncount*] **1.** a mineral, sometimes green, considered valuable as an ornament for carvings, jewelry, etc. **2.** Also called **jade′ green′.** a color varying from bluish green to yellowish green.

jad•ed (jā′did) /ˈdʒeydɪd/ *adj.* dulled or made weary by boredom, overwork, or worldly experience. **—jad′ed•ly,** *adv.* **—jad′ed•ness,** *n.* [*noncount*]

jag (jag) / dʒæg/ *n.* [*count*] a prolonged period of some activity; spree: *a crying jag; a laughing jag.*

jag•ged (jag′id) /ˈdʒægɪd/ *adj.* **1.** raggedly uneven on the edges, with sharply irregular notches on the surface or at the borders: *the knife's jagged edge.* **2.** having a harsh, rough, or uneven quality: *a jagged scream.* **—jag′ged•ly,** *adv.* **—jag′ged•ness,** *n.* [*noncount*]

jag•uar (jag′wär, -yo͞o är′) /ˈdʒægwɑr, -yuwˌɑr/ *n.* [*count*] a large powerful cat of tropical America, having a tan coat with black rose-shaped spots.

jai a•lai (hī′ lī′, hī′ ə lī′, hī′ ə lī′) /ˈhay, lay, ˈhay əˌlay, ˌhay əˈlay/ *n.* [*noncount*] a game played on a three-walled court by two, four, or six players using a curved wicker basket strapped to the wrist to catch and throw a small, hard ball against the front wall.

jail (jāl) / dʒeyl/ *n.* **1.** a prison, esp. one for holding persons who are awaiting trial or are convicted of minor offenses: [*count*]: *The jails were crowded and filthy.* [*noncount*]: *He was taken directly to jail. He was in jail for several months.* **—***v.* [~ + *obj*] **2.** to take into or hold in lawful custody; imprison: *He was jailed on a lesser charge.*

jail•bird (jāl′bûrd′) /ˈdʒeylˌbɜrd/ *n.* [*count*] a person kept in jail.

jail•break (jāl′brāk′) /ˈdʒeylˌbreyk/ *n.* [*count*] an escape from prison, esp. by force.

jail•er or **jail•or** (jā′lər) /ˈdʒeylər/ *n.* [*count*] a person in charge of a jail or section of a jail.

ja•la•pe•ño or **ja•la•pe•no** (hä′lə pān′yō) /ˌhɑləˈpeynyow/ *n., pl.* **-ños** or **-nos.** a hot-tasting, green or orange-red pepper used esp. in Mexican cooking: [*noncount*]: *The sauce is too spicy; maybe there's too much jalapeño.* [*count*]: *The jalapeños are hot.* Also called **ja′lape′ño pep′per.**

ja•lop•y (jə lop′ē) / dʒəˈlɒpiy/ *n.* [*count*], *pl.* **-lop•ies.** an old, broken-down, or otherwise poorly functioning car.

jal•ou•sie (jal′ə sē′) /ˈdʒæləˌsiy/ *n.* [*count*] a window blind or shutter made with horizontal strips adjustable for admitting light and air but keeping out rain and sun.

jam[1] (jam) / dʒæm/ *v.,* **jammed, jam•ming,** *n.* **—***v.* **1.** to press, squeeze, or push into a confined space; fill tightly: [~ + *obj* (+ *in/into* + *obj*)]: *He jammed his socks into a drawer.* [~ + *in/into* + *obj*]: *The commuters jammed into the packed subway car.* **2.** [~ + *obj*] to bruise or crush by squeezing: *She jammed her hand in the door.* **3.** to push or thrust violently on or against something: [~ + *obj* + *on* + *obj*]: *Jam your foot on the brake.* [~ + *on* + *obj*]: *Jam on the brakes, quick!* **4.** [~ + *obj*] to block up by crowding: *Crowds jammed the doors.* **5.** to put or place in position with a quick or violent gesture: [~ + *obj* (+ *on* + *obj*)]: *He jammed his hat on his head.* [~ + *on* + *obj*]: *He jammed on his hat.* [~ + *obj* + *on*]: *He jammed his hat on.* **6.** (of a machine, part, etc.) to (cause to) become unworkable, as through parts being moved out of place, becoming stuck, etc.: [*no obj*]: *The lock jammed and I couldn't open it.* [~ + *obj*]: *I jammed the lock.* **7.** [~ + *obj*] to interfere with (radio signals or the like) by sending out other signals of approximately the same frequency: *The government* *jammed broadcasts from the rebels.* **8.** [*no obj*] to participate in a jam session: *The musicians jammed for a few hours.* **—***n.* [*count*] **9.** the act of jamming or the state of being jammed: *a huge jam of people; a traffic jam.* **10.** *Informal.* a difficult or embarrassing situation; predicament; fix.

jam² (jam) /dʒæm/ *n.* [*noncount; count*] a food made from crushed fruit boiled with sugar.

Ja•mai•can (jə māʹkən) /dʒəˈmeykən/ *adj.* **1.** of or relating to Jamaica. **—***n.* [*count*] **2.** a person born or living in Jamaica.

jamb (jam) /dʒæm/ *n.* [*count*] either of the sides of a doorway, window, or other opening: *a door jamb.*

jam•bo•ree (jamʹbə rēʹ) /ˌdʒæmbəˈriy/ *n.* [*count*], *pl.* **-rees. 1.** a party; any merrymaking. **2.** a large social gathering, often including speeches and entertainment.

jamʹ-packʹed, *adj.* packed as tightly or fully as possible: *The city is jam-packed with tourists.*

jamʹ sesʹsion, *n.* [*count*] an informal performance of a group of musicians, esp. jazz musicians.

Jan or **Jan.,** an abbreviation of: January.

Janeʹ Doeʹ (jānʹ dōʹ) /ˈdʒeynˈ dow/ *n.* [*count*] a made-up or pretended name used in legal proceedings for a female person whose true name is not known: *the defendant known as Jane Doe.* Compare JOHN DOE.

jan•gle (jangʹgəl) /ˈdʒæŋgəl/ *v.,* **-gled, -gling,** *n.* **—***v.* **1.** to (cause to) make a harsh ringing or clattering sound: [*no obj*]: *Suddenly the alarm jangled and I woke up.* [~ + *obj*]: *He jangled coins together in his pocket.* **2.** [~ + *obj*]to cause to become irritated; to jar: *a loud noise that jangles the nerves.* **—***n.* [*count*] **3.** a harsh ringing or clattering sound. **—jan•gler** (jangʹglər) /ˈdʒæŋglər/ *n.* [*count*] **—jan•gly** (jangʹglē) /ˈdʒæŋgliy/ *adj.*

jan•i•tor (janʹi tər) /ˈdʒænɪtər/ *n.* [*count*] a person who is employed in an apartment house, office building, school, etc., to keep the public areas clean and do minor repairs; caretaker. **—jan•i•to•ri•al** (janʹi tôrʹē əl, -tōrʹ-) /ˌdʒænɪˈtɔriyəl, -ˈtowr-/ *adj.: janitorial duties.*

Jan•u•ar•y (janʹyo͞o erʹē) /ˈdʒænyuwˌɛriy/ *n.* [*proper noun*], *pl.* **-ar•ies.** the first month of the year, containing 31 days. *Abbr.:* Jan.

Jap•a•nese (japʹə nēzʹ, -nēsʹ) /ˌdʒæpəˈniyz, -ˈniys/ *adj., n., pl.* **-nese. —***adj.* **1.** of or relating to Japan. **2.** of or relating to the language spoken in Japan. **—***n.* **3.** [*count*] a person born or living in Japan. **4.** [*noncount*] the language spoken in Japan.

jar¹ (jär) /dʒɑr/ *n.* [*count*] **1.** a container with a wide or broad opening, usually shaped like a cylinder and made of glass or earthenware. **2.** the quantity such a container can hold: *add a jar of spaghetti sauce.*

jar² (jär) /dʒɑr/ *v.,* **jarred, jar•ring,** *n.* **—***v.* **1.** to have a sudden and unpleasant effect on one's nerves, feelings, etc.: [~ + *obj*]: *The loud bang jarred my nerves. Her refusal jarred me.* [~ + *on* + *obj*]: *Her squeaky voice jarred on me after a while.* [*no obj*]: *After a very short while his voice jars.* **2.** [~ + *obj*] to cause to vibrate or shake: *The explosion jarred several buildings.* **3.** [*no obj*] to conflict; clash: *I think those colors jar.* **—***n.* [*count*] **4.** a jolt or shake. **5.** a sudden unpleasant effect upon the mind, feelings, or senses; shock: *The disagreement comes as a jar to our belief in harmony.* **—jarʹring,** *adj.: a jarring noise.* **—jarʹring•ly,** *adv.*

jar•gon (järʹgən) /ˈdʒɑrgən/ *n.* [*noncount*] **1.** the specialized language used by a particular trade, profession, or group that is difficult for outsiders to understand: *medical jargon; legal jargon.* **2.** language that is overly complicated: *The tax form was full of jargon.* **—jarʹgon•y, jarʹgon•isʹtic,** *adj.*

jas•mine (jazʹmin, jasʹ-) /ˈdʒæzmɪn, ˈdʒæs-/ *n.* [*noncount*] **1.** a shrub or vine of the olive family, having sweet-smelling flowers used in perfumes and teas. **2.** a pale yellow color.

jaun•dice (jônʹdis, jänʹ-) /ˈdʒɔndɪs, ˈdʒɑn-/ *n.* [*noncount*] a disease in which the skin and the whites of the eyes become yellow because of an increase of bile in the blood.

jaun•diced (jônʹdist, jänʹ-) /ˈdʒɔndɪst, ˈdʒɑn-/ *adj.* **1.** affected with or colored by or as if by jaundice: *jaundiced skin.* **2.** affected with or showing prejudice, distaste, or doubt: *takes a jaundiced view of politics.*

jaunt (jônt, jänt) /dʒɔnt, dʒɑnt/ *n.* [*count*] **1.** a short journey, esp. one taken for pleasure. **—***v.* [*no obj*] **2.** to make a short journey.

jaun•ty (jônʹtē, jänʹ-) /ˈdʒɔntiy, ˈdʒɑn-/ *adj.,* **-ti•er, -ti•est. 1.** easy and lighthearted in manner or bearing; lively; perky: *to walk with a jaunty step.* **2.** smartly trim, as clothing: *a jaunty hat.* **—jaun•ti•ly** (jônʹtl ē, jänʹ-) /ˈdʒɔntḷiy, ˈdʒɑn-/ *adv.* **—jaunʹti•ness,** *n.* [*noncount*]

ja•va (jäʹvə, javʹə) /ˈdʒɑvə, ˈdʒævə/ *n.* [*noncount*] *Slang.* coffee: *a cup of java.*

jave•lin (javʹlin, javʹə-) /ˈdʒævlɪn, ˈdʒævə-/ *n.* [*count*] a spear thrown by hand, esp. a long metal spear used in throwing for distance as a sport.

jaw (jô) /dʒɔ/ *n.* [*count*] **1.** either of two bones or bony structures that form the frame of the mouth and that hold the teeth. **2.** the part of the face covering these bones. **3. jaws,** [*plural*] anything resembling a pair of jaws in shape or in power to grasp or hold: *the jaws of a pair of pliers.* **—***v.* [*no obj*] **4.** *Slang.* to talk; chat: **—jawed,** *adj.: firm-jawed.*

jaw•bone (jôʹbōnʹ) /ˈdʒɔˌbown/ *n., v.,* **-boned, -bon•ing. —***n.* [*count*] **1.** any bone of a jaw, esp. the lower bone. **—***v.* [~ + *obj*] **2.** to seek to influence by persuasion, esp. by public appeal: *The president tried to jawbone the unions into agreement.*

jaw•break•er (jôʹbrāʹkər) /ˈdʒɔˌbreykər/ *n.* [*count*] **1.** a word that is hard to pronounce. **2.** a very hard candy.

jay (jā) /dʒey/ *n.* [*count*] a noisy, blue and gray bird.

jay•walk (jāʹwôkʹ) /ˈdʒeyˌwɔk/ *v.* [*no obj*] to cross a street in disregard of traffic rules or at a place other than a proper crosswalk. **—jayʹwalkʹer,** *n.* [*count*]

jazz (jaz) /dʒæz/ *n.* [*noncount*] **1.** music originating from black songs in New Orleans around the beginning of the 20th century and over time developing many different and complicated styles, characterized by strong rhythms and improvisation. **2.** *Slang.* liveliness; spirit; excitement. **3.** *Slang.* similar or related but unnamed things: *We like sightseeing, museums, and all that jazz.* **—***v.* **4. jazz up,** *Slang.* to make something exciting or interesting: [~ + *up* + *obj*]: *jazzed up the book with pictures.* [~ + *obj* + *up*]: *tried to jazz the party up.*

jazz•y (jazʹē) /ˈdʒæziy/ *adj.,* **-i•er, -i•est. 1.** relating to or suggesting jazz music: *a bluesy, jazzy sound.* **2.** *Slang.* fancy or flashy: *a jazzy sweater.* **—jazz•i•ly** (jazʹə-lē) /ˈdʒæzəliy/ *adv.* **—jazzʹi•ness,** *n.* [*noncount*]

jct. or **jctn.,** an abbreviation of: junction.

JD, an abbreviation of: **1.** juvenile delinquency. **2.** juvenile delinquent.

jeal•ous (jelʹəs) /ˈdʒɛləs/ *adj.* **1. a.** full of a feeling of resentment or anger about someone's success, achievements, advantages, etc.; envious: *a jealous colleague.* [*be* + ~ + *of* + *obj*]: *to be jealous of a rich brother.* **b.** aroused or caused by such feeling: *a jealous rage.* **2.** overly watchful in guarding something, so as to be suspicious of unfaithfulness: *a jealous husband.* **3.** alertly watchful in guarding possessions: *squirrels jealous of their winter supply of nuts.* **—jealʹous•ly,** *adv.*

jeal•ous•y (jelʹə sē) /ˈdʒɛləsiy/ *n., pl.* **-ous•ies. 1.** [*noncount*] the quality or state of being jealous. **2.** [*count*] an instance of being jealous: *forgot their petty jealousies.* **—Syn.** See ENVY.

jean (jēn) /dʒiyn/ *n.* **1.** [*noncount*] Sometimes, **jeans** [*plural*]. a strong fabric, usually of cotton: *blue jean(s) material.* **2. jeans,** [*plural; used with a plural verb*] BLUE JEANS: *His jeans were covered with paint.*

-jec-, *root.* -*jec*- comes from Latin, where it has the meaning "throw; be near; place." This meaning is found in such words as: ABJECT, ADJACENT, ADJECTIVE, CONJECTURE, EJACULATE, EJECT, INJECT, INTERJECT, OBJECT, PROJECT, REJECT, SUBJECT, TRAJECTORY.

Jeep (jēp) /dʒiyp/ *Trademark.* [*count*] a small, rugged vehicle with four-wheel drive, originally developed for military use.

jeer (jēr) /dʒɪər/ *v.* **1.** to speak or shout with rudeness or mockery; taunt; ridicule: [~ + *at* + *obj*]: *The crowd began to jeer at the speaker.* [~ + *obj*]: *The crowd jeered the speaker.* **2.** [~ + *obj*] to drive (someone) away by rude shouts and laughter: *The audience jeered the actors off the stage.* **—***n.* [*count*] **3.** a rude or sneering comment or noise. **—jeerʹer,** *n.* [*count*] **—jeerʹing•ly,** *adv.*

Je•ho•vah (ji hōʹvə) /dʒɪˈhowvə/ *n.* [*proper noun*] a name of God in the Old Testament.

je•june (ji jo͞onʹ) /dʒɪˈdʒuwn/ *adj.* **1.** lacking interest or meaning; insignificant; insipid: *a jejune novel.* **2.** lacking maturity; childish: *jejune behavior.*

jell (jel) /dʒɛl/ *v.* **1.** to (cause to) become firmer, more like jelly, to the touch; gel: [*no obj*]: *The pudding had begun to jell.* [~ + *obj*]: *The cold will jell the dessert.* **2.** to (cause to) become clear, substantial, or definite; crystallize: [*no obj*]: *My ideas began to jell into a good plan.* [~ + *obj*]: *Talking with you helped jell my ideas.*

jel•lied (jel′ēd) /ˈdʒɛliyd/ *adj.* prepared with, or made like, jelly: *jellied candy; jellied salads.*

Jell-O (jel′ō) /ˈdʒɛlow/ *Trademark.* [*noncount*] a dessert made from a mixture of gelatin, sugar, and fruit flavoring.

jel•ly (jel′ē) /ˈdʒɛliy/ *n., pl.* **-lies. 1.** a sweet, soft, sticky food spread on bread, etc., made of fruit juice boiled with sugar and sometimes pectin, then cooled: [*noncount*]: *a sandwich made of peanut butter and jelly.* [*count*]: *some different jellies: orange, strawberry, and grape.* **2.** [*noncount*] any substance having such consistency: *petroleum jelly for burned skin.* **—jel′ly•like′,** *adj.*

jel•ly•bean (jel′ē bēn′) /ˈdʒɛliyˌbiyn/ *n.* [*count*] a small, bean-shaped, chewy candy.

jel•ly•fish (jel′ē fish′) /ˈdʒɛliyˌfɪʃ/ *n., pl.* (*esp. when thought of as a group*) **-fish,** (*esp. for kinds or species*) **-fish•es. 1.** a stinging, jellylike sea creature. **2.** a person who cannot or will not make a decision; a weak person.

jeop•ard•ize (jep′ər dīz′) /ˈdʒɛpərˌdayz/ *v.* [~ + *obj*], **-ized, -iz•ing.** to put in jeopardy; cause danger, risk, or peril to; imperil: *Don't jeopardize your career with a foolish gamble like that.*

jeop•ard•y (jep′ər dē) /ˈdʒɛpərdiy/ *n.* [*noncount*] risk of or exposure to loss, harm, death, or injury; danger: *to put one's life in jeopardy.*

jer•e•mi•ad (jer′ə mī′əd, -ad) /ˌdʒɛrəˈmayəd, -æd/ *n.* [*count*] a long complaint, esp. a sad or mournful one.

jerk (jûrk) /dʒɜrk/ *n.* [*count*] **1.** a quick, sharp pull, push, twist, throw, or the like; sudden movement: *The train started with a jerk.* **2.** a sudden movement of a muscle, esp. when involuntary. **3.** *Slang.* a foolish, stupid person; an idiot; a dope. **—*v.* 4.** [~ + *obj*] to pull, twist, move, push, or throw with a quick, sudden motion: *She jerked the child by the hand.* **5.** [*no obj*] to move with a quick, sharp motion, as if uncontrolled: *His arms and legs jerked in spasm.* **6.** [~ + *obj*] *Informal.* to prepare and serve (sodas, ice cream, etc.) at a soda fountain: *He jerked sodas for a few years.* **7. jerk off,** [*no obj*] *Slang* (*vulgar*). to masturbate.

jer•kin (jûr′kin) /ˈdʒɜrkɪn/ *n.* [*count*] a close-fitting jacket or short coat, usually sleeveless, often of leather.

jerk•wa•ter (jûrk′wô′tər, -wot′ər) /ˈdʒɜrkˌwɔtər, -ˌwɒtər/ *adj.* [*before a noun*] small, unimportant, and out-of-the-way: *a jerkwater town.*

jerk•y[1] (jûr′kē) /ˈdʒɜrkiy/ *adj.,* **-i•er, -i•est. 1.** having or moving with jerks or sudden starts: *In a series of jerky movements the train stopped.* **2.** *Slang.* silly; foolish: *a jerky thing to do.*

jer•ky[2] (jûr′kē) /ˈdʒɜrkiy/ *n.* [*noncount*] meat that has been smoked and dried so that it is hard to chew.

jer•ry-built (jer′ē bilt′) /ˈdʒɛriyˌbɪlt/ *adj.* **1.** built cheaply and not skillfully; shoddy: *jerry-built housing.* **2.** put together or developed in a disorganized way: *a jerry-built motor.*

jer•sey (jûr′zē) /ˈdʒɜrziy/ *n., pl.* **-seys. 1.** [*noncount*] a plain-knit, machine-made fabric of wool, silk, nylon, etc., that is usually soft and elastic, used for garments. **2.** [*count*] a close-fitting knitted sweater or shirt. **3.** [*count; Jersey*] one of a breed of dairy cattle, raised originally on the British island of Jersey in the English Channel.

jest (jest) /dʒɛst/ *n.* **1.** [*count*] a joke or witty remark. **2.** [*noncount*] sport or fun: *to speak half in jest, half in earnest.* **—*v.*** [*no obj*] **3.** to speak in a joking or playfully teasing way. **—jest′ing•ly,** *adv.*

jest•er (jes′tər) /ˈdʒɛstər/ *n.* [*count*] **1.** a person who is given to jesting. **2.** a professional fool or clown, esp. at a court in medieval times.

Jes•u•it (jezh′o͞o it, -yo͞o it, jez′-) /ˈdʒɛʒuwɪt, -yuwɪt, ˈdʒɛz-/ *n.* [*count*] a member of a Roman Catholic religious order for men **(Society of Jesus)** that was founded in 1534. **—Jes′u•it′ic, Jes′u•it′i•cal,** *adj.*

Je•sus (jē′zəs, -zəz) /ˈdʒiyzəs, -zəz/ *n.* [*proper noun*] Also called **Je′sus Christ′, Je′sus of Naz′areth.** born 4? B.C., crucified A.D. 29?, the source of the Christian religion.

jet[1] (jet) /dʒɛt/ *n., v.,* **jet•ted, jet•ting,** *adj.* **—*n.*** [*count*] **1.** a stream of a liquid, gas, or small solid particles forcefully shooting out from a nozzle, opening, etc.: *Jets of water were aimed at the blazing fire.* **2.** a spout or nozzle that lets out liquid or gas: *The gas was escaping from the jet on the stove.* **3.** Also, **jet plane.** an airplane moved by jet propulsion. **4.** JET ENGINE. **—*v.* 5.** to (cause to) move or travel in or as if in a jet plane: [*no obj*]: *diplomats jetting to Europe.* [~ + *obj*]: *to jet a messenger to Washington.* **—*adj.*** [*before a noun*] **6.** relating to, associated with, or involving a jet, jet engine, or jet plane: *jet aircraft.*

jet[2] (jet) /dʒɛt/ *n.* [*noncount*] **1.** a hard black coal that can be highly polished, sometimes used in jewelry. **2.** a deep black. **—*adj.*** [*before a noun*] **3.** of the color jet: *jet black hair.*

jet′ en′gine, *n.* [*count*] an engine, such as of an aircraft, that produces forward motion by pushing out backwards a jet of fluid or heated air and gases.

jet′ lag′ or **jet′lag′,** *n.* [*noncount*] a feeling of fatigue or confusion when the body's normal biological rhythms have been affected after a long flight through several time zones.

jet′ propul′sion, *n.* [*noncount*] the propulsion of something by its reaction to a force ejecting a gas or a liquid from it. **—jet′-propelled′,** *adj.*

jet•sam (jet′səm) /ˈdʒɛtsəm/ *n.* [*noncount*] cargo, supplies, goods, etc., from a boat that are thrown overboard deliberately to lighten it or make it stable in an emergency. Compare FLOTSAM.

jet′ set′, *n.* [*count; usually singular; usually: the* + ~] an international social set of wealthy people who travel frequently by jet to parties and resorts. **—jet′-set′ter,** *n.* [*count*]

jet′ stream′, *n.* [*count; usually singular; usually: the* + ~] strong, usually westerly winds in a relatively narrow and shallow stream in the upper atmosphere of the earth.

jet•ti•son (jet′ə sən, -zən) /ˈdʒɛtəsən, -zən/ *v.* [~ + *obj*] **1.** to throw (cargo, supplies, etc.) overboard from a boat or aircraft to lighten it or make it stable in an emergency: *The crew jettisoned some of the cargo as the plane lost altitude.* **2.** to throw off (something) that seems to be an obstacle or burden; discard: *We quickly jettisoned our idea as impractical.*

jet•ty (jet′ē) /ˈdʒɛtiy/ *n.* [*count*], *pl.* **-ties. 1.** a structure or the like, sticking out into a body of water, as to protect a harbor. **2.** a landing pier.

Jew (jo͞o) /dʒuw/ *n.* [*count*] **1.** a member of a people now living in many countries of the world who trace their descent from the Israelites of the Bible. **2.** a person whose religion is Judaism. **—*adj.*** [*before a noun*] **3.** *Offensive.* of Jews; Jewish. **—*v.* 4.** [*jew*] *Offensive.* to bargain sharply with; beat down in price: [~ + *down* + *obj*]: *to jew down the price.* [~ + *obj* + *down*]: *to jew the price down.*

jew•el (jo͞o′əl) /ˈdʒuwəl/ *n.* [*count*] **1.** a cut and polished precious stone; gem. **2.** an ornament worn for beauty that is made of or with such a cut and polished stone. **3.** a person or thing that is treasured: *She was a jewel to work with.*

jew•eled (jo͞o′əld) /ˈdʒuwəld/ *adj.* made or set with jewels.

jew•el•er (jo͞o′ə lər) /ˈdʒuwələr/ *n.* [*count*] a person who designs, makes, sells, or repairs jewelry, watches, etc. Also, *esp. Brit.,* **jew′el•ler.**

jew•el•ry (jo͞o′əl rē) /ˈdʒuwəlriy/ *n.* [*noncount*] objects used to decorate a person, as necklaces, rings, bracelets, or brooches, esp. when made of precious metals, gemstones, pearls, etc.: *articles of jewelry.* See illustration at STORE. Compare COSTUME JEWELRY. Also, *esp. Brit.,* **jew′el•ler•y.** **—Usage.** The word JEWELRY is a non-count noun in English, and does not have a plural form. We speak of *articles of jewelry* or *pieces of jewelry,* as *rings, bracelets,* or *necklaces,* but we cannot make a plural of the word JEWELRY itself.

Jew•ish (jo͞o′ish) /ˈdʒuwɪʃ/ *adj.* **1.** of, relating to, or characteristic of the Jews or Judaism: *Jewish custom and tradition.* **—*n.*** [*noncount*] **2.** *Informal.* Yiddish. **—Jew′ish•ness,** *n.* [*noncount*]

Jew•ry (jo͞o′rē) /ˈdʒuwriy/ *n.* [*noncount*] the Jewish people thought of as a group.

jez•e•bel (jez′ə bel′, -bəl) /ˈdʒɛzəˌbɛl, -bəl/ *n.* [*count*] a wicked, shameless woman.

jib or **jibb** (jib) /dʒɪb/ *n.* [*count*] **1.** a triangular sail set in front of other sails on a ship. **—*Idiom.* 2. cut of one's jib,** style; appearance: *I could tell by the cut of his jib that he was important.*

jibe[1] (jīb) /dʒayb/ *v.,* **jibed, jib•ing,** *n.* GIBE.

jibe[2] (jīb) /dʒayb/ *v.,* **jibed, jib•ing.** to be in harmony or agreement with; agree; correspond: [*no obj*]: *These measurements don't jibe; someone has made an error.* [~ + *with* + *obj*]: *Your observations don't jibe with the facts as we know them.*

jif•fy (jif′ē) /ˈdʒɪfiy/ also **jiff** (jif) /dʒɪf/ *n.* [*count; usually singular*], *pl.* **jif•fies** also **jiffs.** *Informal.* a very short time; moment; instant: *to get dressed in a jiffy.*

jig[1] (jig) /dʒɪg/ *n.* [*count*] a plate, box, or frame for holding work and guiding a machine tool to it.

jig[2] (jig) /dʒɪg/ *n., v.,* **jigged, jig•ging.** —*n.* [*count*] **1.** a rapid, lively, springy, irregular dance for one or more persons. **2.** a piece of music for such a dance. —*v.* **3.** [*no obj*] to dance a jig or any lively dance. **4.** to (cause to) move with quick jerky or bobbing motions: [~ + *obj*]: *jigging his son on his knee.* [*no obj*]: *His knees began to jig nervously.*

jig•ger[1] (jig′ər) /ˈdʒɪgər/ *n.* [*count*] **1.** a person or thing that jigs. **2.** a device that one cannot or does not name more precisely: *Where does this little jigger go, and what does it do?* **3. a.** a measure of 1½ oz. (45 ml) used in cocktail recipes. **b.** a small whiskey glass holding this amount.

jig•ger[2] (jig′ər) /ˈdʒɪgər/ *v.* [~ + *obj*] **1.** to jerk rapidly; jig: *jiggered the light switch up and down.* **2.** to change or manipulate, esp. for illegal or dishonest purposes: *The accountant jiggered the figures to hide the theft.*

jig•gle (jig′əl) /ˈdʒɪgəl/ *v.,* **-gled, -gling,** *n.* —*v.* **1.** to move up and down or back and forth with short, quick jerks: [~ + *obj*]: *You have to jiggle the handle to get the machine started.* [*no obj*]: *His fat stomach jiggled as he walked.* —*n.* [*count*] **2.** a jiggling movement. —**jig′gly,** *adj.,* **-gli•er, -gli•est.**

jig•saw (jig′sô′) /ˈdʒɪgˌsɔ/ *n., v.,* **-sawed, -sawed** or **-sawn, -saw•ing.** —*n.* [*count*] **1.** Also, **jig′ saw′.** an electric saw with a narrow, vertically mounted blade, for cutting curves, complicated patterns, etc. —*v.* [~ + *obj*] **2.** to cut or form with or as if with a jigsaw.

jig′saw puz′zle, *n.* [*count*] **1.** a game that is a set of irregularly cut pieces of pasteboard, wood, or the like that form a picture or design when fitted together. **2.** a complicated, confusing situation or condition: *the jigsaw puzzle of ethnic neighborhoods.*

ji•had or **je•had** (ji häd′) /dʒɪˈhɑd/ *n.* [*count*] a holy war undertaken as a sacred duty by Muslims.

jilt (jilt) /dʒɪlt/ *v.* [~ + *obj*] to reject (a lover or sweetheart), esp. suddenly and without care for feelings. —**jilt′er,** *n.* [*count*]

Jim′ Crow′ (jim) /dʒɪm/ *adj.* [*before a noun*] [sometimes: *jim crow*] of or relating to a practice or policy of segregating or discriminating against black people. —**Jim′ Crow′ism, jim′ crow′ism,** *n.* [*noncount*]

jim′-dan′dy, *adj., n., pl.* **-dies.** *Informal.* —*adj.* **1.** of high or outstanding quality; excellent: *a jim-dandy idea.* —*n.* [*count*] **2.** something of high or outstanding quality: *That new computer is a real jim-dandy.*

jim•my (jim′ē) /ˈdʒɪmiy/ *n., pl.* **-mies,** *v.,* **-mied, -my•ing.** —*n.* [*count*] **1.** a short crowbar; a metal bar used to pry open something closed or locked, as a door or window. —*v.* [~ + *obj*] **2.** to force open with or as if with a jimmy: *The thief must have jimmied the door.*

jin•gle (jing′gəl) /ˈdʒɪŋgəl/ *v.,* **-gled, -gling,** *n.* —*v.* **1.** to (cause to) make clinking or tinkling sounds, like the sounds from a small bell: [*no obj*]: *The coins jingled in her purse.* [~ + *obj*]: *He jingled the coins in his pocket.* —*n.* [*count*] **2.** a tinkling or clinking sound: *the jingle of house keys.* **3.** a group of words or a short song with catchy sounds, usually of a light or humorous character, used for advertising. —**jin′gly,** *adj.,* **-gli•er, -gli•est.**

jin•go•ism (jing′gō iz′əm) /ˈdʒɪŋgowˌɪzəm/ *n.* [*noncount*] the spirit, policy, or practice of extreme love of one's country, often calling for constant preparation for war and a desire to interfere in foreign affairs of other nations. —**jin′go•ist,** *n.* [*count*], *adj.* —**jin′go•is′tic,** *adj.*

jink (jink) /dʒɪnk/ *v.* to move up or down or side to side, suddenly and rapidly, esp. to avoid something: [*no obj*]: *The pilots jinked to avoid the missiles.* [~ + *obj*]: *jinked their planes to avoid the missiles.*

jinn (jin) /dʒɪn/ also **jin•ni** (ji nē′, jin′ē) /dʒɪˈniy, ˈdʒɪniy/ *n.* [*count*], *pl.* **jinns** also **jin•nis,** (*esp. as a group*) **jinn** also **jin•ni.** (in Islamic myth) a spirit capable of appearing in human and animal forms and influencing people for good or evil.

jin•rik•i•sha or **jin•rik•sha** (jin rik′shô, -shä) /dʒɪnˈrɪkʃɔ, -ʃɑ/ *n.* [*count*], *pl.* **-shas.** a small, two-wheeled passenger vehicle pulled by one person, formerly used widely in Japan and China. Also called **rick-sha, rickshaw.**

jinx (jingks) /dʒɪŋks/ *n.* [*count*] **1.** one thought to bring bad luck: *You're a jinx; every time you come to a game, we lose.* —*v.* [~ + *obj*] **2.** to bring bad luck to: *Acting too hastily might jinx the deal.*

jit•ney (jit′nē) /ˈdʒɪtniy/ *n.* [*count*], *pl.* **-neys.** a small bus or car following a regular route along which it picks up and discharges passengers.

jit•ter (jit′ər) /ˈdʒɪtər/ *n.* **1. jitters,** [*plural; usually: the* + ~] a feeling of fright or uneasiness: *to get the jitters in an empty house on a stormy night.* —*v.* [*no obj*] **2.** to behave nervously: *an actor jittering before going on stage.*

jit•ter•bug (jit′ər bug′) /ˈdʒɪtərˌbʌg/ *n., v.,* **-bugged, -bug•ging.** —*n.* [*count*] **1.** a fast-paced dance of twirls, splits, and somersaults, performed to swing music. —*v.* [*no obj*] **2.** to dance the jitterbug. —**jit′ter•bug′ger,** *n.* [*count*]

jit•ter•y (jit′ər ē) /ˈdʒɪtəriy/ *adj.,* **-i•er, -i•est.** very tense; nervous; afraid or uneasy: *The students were very jittery before their exam.*

jive (jiv) /dʒayv/ *n., v.,* **jived, jiv•ing,** *adj.* —*n.* [*noncount*] **1.** swing music. **2.** *Slang.* talk that deceives, exaggerates, or is otherwise meaningless: *Don't give me any jive, just give me the facts.* —*v.* **3.** *Slang.* to tease, fool, kid, or exaggerate: [~ + *obj*]: *Quit jiving me and give me a straight answer.* [*no obj*]: *They were just jiving.* —*adj.* **4.** *Slang.* intended to deceive: *jive talk.* —**jiv′er,** *n.* [*count*] —**jiv′ey,** *adj.,* **-i•er, -i•est.**

job (job) /dʒɒb/ *n.* [*count*] **1.** a piece of work to do, esp. a specific task done as part of one's occupation or for an agreed price: *had the job of mowing the lawn every Saturday.* **2.** a position one holds as one's occupation or employment: *landed a good job.* **3.** a responsibility; duty: *It is your job to be on time.* **4.** the performance of a task: *to do a good job.* **5.** a state of affairs; matter: *to make the best of a bad job.* **6.** a difficult task: *We had quite a job getting him to agree.* **7.** *Informal.* an example of a specific type: *That little sports job is a great car.* **8.** *Slang.* a theft or similar crime: *pulled off a job.* **9.** a unit of work for a computer printer: *a print job.* —*adj.* [*before a noun*] **10.** of or relating to employment: *job security.* —***Idiom.*** **11. do a job on,** [~ + *obj*] to affect destructively: *the loss of his wife really did a job on him.* **12. on the job,** while working; at work: *He got that injury on the job.* —**job′less,** *adj.* —**job′less•ness,** *n.* [*noncount*]

job′ ac′tion, *n.* [*count*] a work slowdown or other organized action used by employees as a means of protest or to force an employer to give in to demands.

job′ lot′, *n.* [*count*] a large, often assorted group of goods sold or handled together.

jock[1] (jok) /dʒɒk/ *n.* [*count*] **1.** a jockstrap. **2.** *Informal.* a person who enjoys or is good at sports; athlete. **3.** *Informal.* someone who enjoys a specific activity; enthusiast: *a computer jock (= someone who enjoys operating computers); science jocks.*

jock[2] (jok) /dʒɒk/ *n.* [*count*] a jockey.

jock•ey (jok′ē) /ˈdʒɒkiy/ *n., pl.* **-eys,** *v.,* **-eyed, -ey•ing.** —*n.* [*count*] **1.** a person who rides horses professionally in races. —*v.* **2.** to ride (a horse) as a jockey: [~ + *obj*]: *She jockeyed the horse to a victory.* [*no obj*]: *quit jockeying after his fall.* **3.** [~ + *obj*] *Informal.* to operate or guide the movement of, esp. skillfully; pilot; drive: *He jockeyed the ship skillfully into port.* **4. jockey for position,** to try to get an advantage by acting in a tricky manner.

jock•strap (jok′strap′) /ˈdʒɒkˌstræp/ *n.* [*count*] an elastic belt with a pouch for supporting the genitals, worn by men esp. while participating in athletics. Also called **athletic supporter.**

jo•cose (jō kōs′, jə-) /dʒowˈkows, dʒə-/ *adj.* given to joking; playful. —**jo•cose′ly,** *adv.* —**jo•cos•i•ty** (jō kos′i tē) /dʒowˈkɒsɪtiy/ **jo•cose′ness,** *n.* [*noncount*]

joc•u•lar (jok′yə lər) /ˈdʒɒkyələr/ *adj.* given to or characterized by joking or jesting. —**joc•u•lar•i•ty** (jok′yə lar′i tē) /ˌdʒɒkyəˈlærɪtiy/ *n.* [*noncount*] —**joc′u•lar•ly,** *adv.*

joc•und (jok′ənd, jō′kənd) /ˈdʒɒkənd, ˈdʒowkənd/ *adj.* cheerful; merry; jolly. —**jo•cun•di•ty** (jō kun′di tē) /dʒowˈkʌndɪtiy/ *n.* [*noncount*] —**joc′und•ly,** *adv.*

jodh•purs (jod′pərz) /ˈdʒɒdpərz/ *n.* [*plural*] trousers used when riding horses, cut very full over the hips and tapering at the knees to become tightfitting from the knees to the ankles.

jog[1] (jog) /dʒɒg/ *v.,* **jogged, jog•ging,** *n.* —*v.* **1.** [~ + *obj*] to move or shake with a push or jerk: *He jogged my arm as he walked past.* **2.** [~ + *obj*] to rouse (the memory) to alertness: *hearing the name jogged his memory of an earlier time.* **3.** to (cause a horse to) go at a steady trot, or at a slow, steady pace: [~ + *obj*]: *The jockey jogged the horse.* [*no obj*]: *The horse jogged around the track.* **4.** [*no obj*] to run at a slow, steady pace: *He liked to jog in the park every morning.* —*n.* [*count*] **5.** a shake; slight push; nudge: *a little jog from behind.* **6.** a reminder: *a jog to the memory.* **7.** an act or instance of jogging: *to go for a jog.* **8.** a jogging pace: *proceeding at a slow jog.* —**jog′ger,** *n.* [*count*]

jog² (jog) / dʒɒg/ *n., v.,* **jogged, jog•ging.** —*n.* [*count*] **1.** a bend or turn. —*v.* [*no obj*] **2.** to bend or turn: *The road jogs to the left up ahead.*

jog•gle (jog′əl) /ˈdʒɒgəl/ *v.,* **-gled, -gling,** *n.* —*v.* **1.** to (cause to) move or shake slightly; move one way or another, as by repeated jerks; jiggle: [~ + *obj*]: *Don't joggle the cart.* [*no obj*]: *The cart joggled along.* —*n.* [*count*] **2.** the act of joggling; a slight shake or jolt.

john (jon) / dʒɒn/ *n.* [*count*] **1.** *Informal.* a toilet or bathroom. **2.** *Slang.* [*sometimes: John*] a prostitute's customer.

John′ Doe′ (dō) /dow/ *n.* [*count*] **1.** an unnamed, but average person: *Your regular John Doe doesn't want more taxes and less service.* **2.** a made-up or pretended name used in legal proceedings for a male person whose true name is not known: *the defendant known as John Doe.* Compare Jane Doe.

joie de vi•vre (zhwädᵊ vē′vrᵊ) /ʒwɑdᵊ ˈviyvrᵊ/ *n.* [*noncount*] *French.* a delight in being alive; carefree enjoyment of living.

join (join) / dʒɔyn/ *v.* **1.** to (cause to) come into or be in contact or connection with; connect: [~ + *obj*]: *They all joined hands.* [*no obj*]: *Their hands joined and they formed a circle.* [~ + *up* + *obj*]: *joined up the hose with the faucet.* [~ + *obj* + *up*]: *joined the parts up into a whole.* **2.** to come into contact or union with: [~ + *obj*]: *The brook joins the river.* [*no obj*]: *The two rivers joined before they reached the sea.* **3.** to (cause to) come together in a particular relation or for a specific purpose; unite: [~ + *obj*]: *Join us and help fight poverty.* [~ + *with* + *obj*]: *Join with us in our campaign.* **4.** [~ + *obj*] to become a member of: *to join a club.* **5.** to enlist (in), as a branch of the armed forces: [~ + *obj*]: *to join the Navy.* [~ + *up*]: *joined up and went to sea.* **6.** [~ + *obj*] to come into the company of; meet or accompany (someone), so as to participate with or in some activity: *Can you join us for a drink?* **7.** [~ + *obj*] to bring into close relationship: *joined them in matrimony.* **8. join in,** to take part in; become involved in: [*no obj*]: *was too shy to join in.* [~ + *in* + *obj*]: *Wouldn't you like to join in the fun?* See -junc-.

join•er (joi′nər) /ˈdʒɔynər/ *n.* [*count*] **1.** a person who joins, esp. a person who likes to join groups or organizations. **2.** a carpenter, esp. one who constructs doors, paneling, and other permanent woodwork.

joint (joint) / dʒɔynt/ *n.* [*count*] **1.** the place at which two things or parts are joined. **2.** the place where two bones or other elements of a skeleton meet, whether tightly or so as to permit free movement: *the joint of the elbow.* **3.** a large piece of meat, usually with a bone: *a joint of beef.* **4.** *Slang.* a marijuana cigarette. **5.** *Slang.* **a.** a disreputable place of public entertainment: *a strip joint.* **b.** a dwelling or place of business: *Let's go to his joint and see if he's been there.* **c.** [*often: the* + ~] prison. —*adj.* [*before a noun*] **6.** shared by or common to two or more: *joint authorship.* **7.** undertaken or produced by two or more in connection or in common: *a joint effort.* —***Idiom.*** **8. out of joint, a.** dislocated: *knocked his shoulder out of joint.* **b.** in an unfavorable or disordered state: *The flood threw their lives out of joint.* —**joint′ly,** *adv.: worked jointly on the proposal.* See -junc-.

joist (joist) / dʒɔyst/ *n.* [*count*] one of a number of small parallel beams of wood, steel, or reinforced concrete that support a floor or ceiling.

joke (jōk) / dʒowk/ *n., v.,* **joked, jok•ing.** —*n.* [*count*] **1.** a short, humorous story with a word or phrase that ends it and causes laughter. **2.** something amusing or ridiculous: *thought the whole episode was a joke.* **3.** something not taken seriously: *That law is just a joke: no one obeys it.* **4. no joke,** a matter of great seriousness: *That loss we took was no joke.* [*it* + *be* + ~]: *It's no joke exercising every day on that sore leg.* —*v.* [*no obj*] **5.** to speak or act in a playful or merry way: *He was joking around instead of working.* **6.** to say something in fun or teasing: *I was only joking.* —**jok′ey, jok′y,** *adj.,* **-i•er, -i•est.** —**jok′ing•ly,** *adv.*

jok•er (jō′kər) /ˈdʒowkər/ *n.* [*count*] **1.** a person who jokes. **2.** one of two extra playing cards in a pack, usually having the figure of a jester, used in some games as the highest card or as a wild card. **3.** *Informal.* a person; fellow: *Some joker left the refrigerator door open.*

jol•li•ty (jol′i tē) /ˈdʒɒlɪtiy/ *n.* [*noncount*] a jolly or merry mood or condition; gaiety: *holiday jollity.*

jol•ly (jol′ē) /ˈdʒɒliy/ *adj.,* **-li•er, -li•est,** *v.,* **-lied, -ly•ing,** *n., pl.* **-lies,** *adv.* —*adj.* **1.** being in good spirits; merry. **2.** cheerfully festive: *a jolly party.* —*v.* **3.** to try to keep (a person) happy or in good humor, esp. in order to gain something: [~ + *obj*]: *The workers jollied the boss into giving them extra time off.* [~ + *obj* + *along*]: *They were just jollying the boss along.* —*n.* **4.** Usually, **jollies.** [*plural*] *Informal.* thrills; kicks: *getting their jollies from other people's misfortune.* —*adv.* **5.** *Brit.* very: *jolly good.* —**jol′li•ness,** *n.* [*noncount*]

jolt (jōlt) / dʒowlt/ *v.* **1.** to (cause to) move by or as if by sudden rough jerks or bumps; shake up roughly: [*no obj*]: *The bus jolted along the bumpy road.* [~ + *obj*]: *The driver jolted the bus down the bumpy road.* **2.** [~ + *obj*] to knock sharply so as to move or dislodge; jar: *The champion jolted the challenger with an uppercut.* **3.** [~ + *obj*] to shock or startle: *We were jolted by the news of her sudden death.* —*n.* [*count*] **4.** a jolting movement or blow. **5.** a psychological shock: *The news of his death was a jolt to her.* —**jolt′er,** *n.* [*count*]

jon•quil (jong′kwil, jon′-) /ˈdʒɒŋkwɪl, ˈdʒɒn-/ *n.* [*count*] a plant of the narcissus family having long, narrow leaves and yellow or white flowers.

Jor•da•ni•an (jôr dā′nē ən) /dʒɔrˈdeyniyən/ *n.* [*count*] **1.** a person born or living in Jordan. —*adj.* **2.** of or relating to Jordan.

josh (josh) / dʒɒʃ/ *v.* to tease in a cheerful, light way: [*no obj*]: *We were only joshing.* [~ + *obj*]: *We joshed him for his mistake.* —**josh′er,** *n.* [*count*] —**josh′ing•ly,** *adv.*

jos•tle (jos′əl) /ˈdʒɒsəl/ *v.,* **-tled, -tling,** *n.* —*v.* **1.** to bump against, push, or elbow roughly or rudely: [~ + *obj*]: *The crowd pushed and jostled her.* [*no obj*]: *didn't like it if people jostled against her.* **2.** to compete or contend with: [~ + *obj*]: *jostling each other for the chairmanship.* [*no obj*]: *jostling for advantage.* —*n.* [*count*] **3.** the act of jostling; a rough bump or push.

jot (jot) / dʒɒt/ *v.,* **jot•ted, jot•ting,** *n.* —*v.* **1.** to write or mark down quickly or briefly: [~ + *obj*]: *to jot a note to a friend.* [~ + *down* + *obj*]: *Jot down the license number.* [~ + *obj* + *down*]: *Jot it down before you forget it.* —*n.* [*count; singular; usually a* + ~]; [*often with a negative word or phrase*] **2.** the least amount; a little bit: *I don't care a jot.*

joule (jo͞ol, joul) / dʒuwl, dʒawl/ *n.* [*count*] a unit of work or energy, equal to the work done by a force of one newton when moved through a distance of one meter in the direction of the force.

jounce (jouns) / dʒawns/ *v.,* **jounced, jounc•ing,** *n.* —*v.* [*no obj*] **1.** to move joltingly up and down: *The bus jounced along.* —*n.* [*count*] **2.** a jouncing movement. —**jounc′y,** *adj.,* **-i•er, -i•est.**

-jour-, *root.* *-jour-* comes from French and ultimately from Latin, where it has the meaning "daily; of or relating to one day." This meaning is found in such words as: adjourn, journal, journey, sojourn.

jour., an abbreviation of: journal.

jour•nal (jûr′nl) /ˈdʒɜrnl̩/ *n.* [*count*] **1.** a daily record that is written down, usually in a small book, of things that happen, things one sees, or things one thinks about: *to keep a journal.* **2.** a daily newspaper. **3.** a periodical or magazine, esp. one devoted to a special interest: *a business journal.* See -jour-.

jour•nal•ese (jûr′nl ēz′, -ēs′) /ˌdʒɜrnl̩ˈiyz, -ˈiys/ *n.* [*noncount*] a style of writing thought of as typical of newspapers and magazines. See -jour-.

jour•nal•ism (jûr′nl iz′əm) /ˈdʒɜrnl̩ˌɪzəm/ *n.* [*noncount*] **1.** the work of gathering, writing, editing, and publishing or broadcasting news. **2.** material written for a newspaper or magazine: *an example of good journalism.* **3.** a course of study for a career in journalism. —**jour′nal•ist,** *n.* [*count*] —**jour′nal•is′tic,** *adj.* See -jour-.

jour•ney (jûr′nē) /ˈdʒɜrniy/ *n., pl.* **-neys,** *v.,* **-neyed, -ney•ing.** —*n.* [*count*] **1.** a traveling from one place to another, usually taking a rather long time; trip: *a journey to China.* **2.** a distance or period of time traveled: *It's an hour's journey from here.* **3.** passage or progress from one stage to another: *the journey from poverty to success.* —*v.* [*no obj*] **4.** to make a journey; travel: *They journeyed through the night.* —**jour′ney•er,** *n.* [*count*] See -jour-.

jour•ney•man (jûr′nē mən) /ˈdʒɜrniymən/ *n.* [*count*], *pl.* **-men. 1.** a person who has served an apprenticeship to learn a trade or craft and is certified to work at it. **2.** a worker or performer who does good or competent work but is not exceptional: *a journeyman actor.* See -jour-.

joust (joust) / dʒawst/ *n.* [*count*] **1.** a combat for two mounted knights armed with lances, with each attempting to knock the other from his horse. —*v.* [*no obj*] **2.** to engage in a joust. **3.** to contend or compete: *The two were jousting for the lead role.* —**joust′er,** *n.* [*count*]

jo•vi•al (jō′vē əl) /ˈdʒowviyəl/ *adj.* showing hearty good humor or a spirit of friendliness; cheerful; jolly: *a jovial smile.* —**jo•vi•al•i•ty** (jō′vē al′i tē) /ˌdʒowviyˈælɪtiy/ *n.* [*noncount*] —**jo′vi•al•ly,** *adv.*: *He greeted her jovially.*

jowl (joul) /dʒawl/ *n.* [*count; usually plural*] a fold of flesh hanging from the jaw: *His jowls quivered with greed.* —**jowled,** *adj*: *a heavily jowled politician.* —**jowl′y,** *adj.*, **-i•er, -i•est.**

joy (joi) /dʒɔy/ *n.* **1.** [*noncount*] a feeling or state of great delight or happiness; gladness; elation: *He was filled with joy at the birth of his daughter. He jumped for joy at the news.* **2.** [*count*] a source or cause of great pleasure: *a book that was a joy to read.* —**joy′less,** *adj.* —**joy′less•ness,** *n.* [*noncount*]

joy•ful (joi′fəl) /ˈdʒɔyfəl/ *adj.* **1.** full of joy; glad; delighted: *She was joyful when she heard the news.* [*be* + ~ + *to* + *verb*]: *He was joyful to see his brother again.* **2.** showing, or expressing, or causing joy: *a joyful look; a joyful event.* —**joy′ful•ly,** *adv.* —**joy′ful•ness,** *n.* [*noncount*]

joy•ous (joi′əs) /ˈdʒɔyəs/ *adj.* joyful; happy; jubilant: *a joyous shout.* —**joy′ous•ly,** *adv.* —**joy′ous•ness,** *n.* [*noncount*]

joy•ride (joi′rīd′) /ˈdʒɔyˌrayd/ *n., v.,* **-rode, -rid•den, -rid•ing.** —*n.* [*count*] **1.** a pleasure ride in an automobile, esp. when the vehicle is driven recklessly or used without the owner's permission. **2.** a brief, exciting, or reckless period of time: *The economic joyride is over.* —*v.* [*no obj*] **3.** to go on a joyride. —**joy′rid′er,** *n.* [*count*]

joy•stick (joi′stik′) /ˈdʒɔyˌstɪk/ *n.* [*count*] **1.** *Informal.* the control stick of an airplane, tank, or other vehicle. **2.** a lever used to control the movement of a computer's cursor, as in a video game.

JP or **J.P.,** an abbreviation of: Justice of the Peace.

Jr. or **jr.,** an abbreviation of: Junior.

ju•bi•lant (jo͞o′bə lənt) /ˈdʒuwbələnt/ *adj.* showing great joy, satisfaction, or triumph; overjoyed: *He was jubilant at winning first prize in the contest.* —**ju′bi•lant•ly,** *adv.*

ju•bi•la•tion (jo͞o′bə lā′shən) /ˌdʒuwbəˈleyʃən/ *n.* [*noncount*] a feeling of, or the expression of, joy, satisfaction, triumph, or great happiness; the act of rejoicing: *a moment of jubilation when they won the championship.*

ju•bi•lee (jo͞o′bə lē′, jo͞o′bə lē′) /ˈdʒuwbəˌliy, ˌdʒuwbəˈliy/ *n.* [*count*], *pl.* **-lees. 1.** the celebration of an anniversary, esp. a 50th anniversary. —*adj.* [*often: after a noun*] **2.** FLAMBÉ: *cherries jubilee.*

-jud-, *root.* -jud- comes from Latin, where it has the meaning "judge." It is related to -JUR- and -JUS-. This meaning is found in such words as: ADJUDGE, ADJUDICATE, INJUDICIOUS, JUDGE, JUDICIAL, MISJUDGE, PREJUDICE.

Ju•da•ic (jo͞o dā′ik) /dʒuwˈdeyɪk/ also **Ju•da′i•cal,** *adj.* of or relating to Judaism or the Jews; Jewish.

Ju•da•ism (jo͞o′dē iz′əm, -də-) /ˈdʒuwdiyˌɪzəm, -də-/ *n.* [*noncount*] **1.** the religion of the Jews, based on the Old Testament and the teachings and commentaries of the rabbis as found chiefly in the Talmud. **2.** belief in this religion, its practices, and ceremonies. **3.** this religion thought of as forming the basis of the cultural and social identity of the Jews. **4.** Jews thought of as a group; Jewry.

Ju•das (jo͞o′dəs) /ˈdʒuwdəs/ *n.* **1.** [*proper noun*] Judas Iscariot, the disciple who betrayed Jesus. **2.** [*count*] a person who betrays a friend; traitor. **3.** [*count; usually: judas; before a noun*] Also called **ju′das hole′.** a peephole, as in the door of a prison cell.

judge (juj) /dʒʌdʒ/ *n., v.,* **judged, judg•ing.** —*n.* [*count*] **1.** a public officer with the authority to hear and decide cases in a court of law. **2.** a person who makes a decision in a competition, contest, or matter at issue: *the judges of a contest.* **3.** a person qualified to pass critical judgment: *a good judge of horses.* —*v.* **4.** to pass legal judgment on (someone) in a court of law: [~ + *obj* + *to* + *be* + *adjective/noun*]: *The court judged him to be the guilty party.* **5.** [~ + *obj*] to hear evidence or legal arguments in (a case) in order to pass judgment; try: *to judge a case.* **6.** to form a judgment or opinion of; decide upon critically: [~ + *obj*]: *to judge a book by its cover.* [~ + *clause*]: *Can you judge if he'll make a good teacher or not?* [~ + *obj* (+ *to* + *be*) + *adjective*]: *judged him (to be) ready for the contest.* [*no obj*]: *You're not in a position to judge in the matter.* **7.** [~ + *obj* (+ *to* + *be*) + *adjective*] to decide or settle authoritatively: *The censor judged the book (to be) obscene.* **8.** to infer, think, or hold as an opinion; make a careful guess about; estimate: [~ + *obj* + *to* + *verb*]: *I judged the distance to be about two miles.* [~ + (*that*) *clause*]: *I judged that the distance was about two miles.* **9.** [~ + *obj*] to act as a judge in (a competition). —**judge′ship,** *n.* [*noncount*] See -JUD-.

judg•ment (juj′mənt) /ˈdʒʌdʒmənt/ *n.* **1.** [*noncount*] the ability to judge, make a decision, or form an opinion wisely: *showed good judgment in choosing friends.* **2.** [*count*] an opinion, conclusion, or belief based on the circumstances before one's view: *It was the reviewer's judgment that the play would not be a success.* **3.** [*count*] **a.** a judicial decision given by a judge or court. **b.** the obligation, esp. a sum of money to be paid, arising from or resulting from a judicial decision: *a judgment of one million dollars in damages.* **4.** [*count*] a misfortune believed to be punishment from God for sins committed: *Some thought the plagues and earthquakes were a divine judgment.* Also, *esp. Brit.,* **judge′ment.** See -JUD-.

judg•men•tal (juj men′tl) /dʒʌdʒˈmɛntl̩/ *adj.* tending to make judgments, esp. harsh moral judgments. See -JUD-.

judg′ment call′, *n.* [*count*] **1.** a decision made by a referee or umpire in a sporting event based on personal observation of a disputed play. **2.** any determination or judgment based on feeling or personal views.

ju•di•cial (jo͞o dish′əl) /dʒuwˈdɪʃəl/ *adj.* [*before a noun*] **1.** relating to judgment in courts of justice or to the administration of justice; relating to courts of law or to judges; judiciary: *judicial proceedings.* **2.** characteristic of a judge or the judiciary: *judicial solemnity.* —**ju•di′cial•ly,** *adv.* See -JUD-.

ju•di•ci•ar•y (jo͞o dish′ē er′ē, -dish′ə rē) /dʒuwˈdɪʃiyˌɛriy, -ˈdɪʃəriy/ *n., pl.* **-ar•ies,** *adj.* —*n.* [*count; usually singular; often: the* + ~] **1.** the judicial branch of government. **2.** the system of courts of justice in a country. **3.** judges thought of as a group. —*adj.* **4.** relating to the judicial branch or system or to judges: *the judiciary functions of the Supreme Court.*

ju•di•cious (jo͞o dish′əs) /dʒuwˈdɪʃəs/ *adj.* having, exercising, or characterized by sound judgment: *He made judicious use of his money.* —**ju•di′cious•ly,** *adv.* —**ju•di′cious•ness,** *n.* [*noncount*] See -JUD-.

ju•do (jo͞o′dō) /ˈdʒuwdow/ *n.* [*noncount*] a sport or martial art based on jujitsu but differing from it in banning dangerous throws and blows and stressing the athletic or sport element.

jug (jug) /dʒʌg/ *n.* [*count*] **1.** a large container for liquids, usually having a handle and a narrow neck. **2.** the contents of or the amount in such a container.

jug•ger•naut (jug′ər nôt′, -not′) /ˈdʒʌgərˌnɔt, -ˌnɒt/ *n.* [*count*] any massive, overpowering force or object: *an economic juggernaut.*

jug•gle (jug′əl) /ˈdʒʌgəl/ *v.,* **-gled, -gling,** *n.* —*v.* **1.** to keep (several objects, as balls, knives, plates, etc.) in continuous motion in the air at the same time by tossing and catching: [*no obj*]: *The clown learned how to juggle.* [~ + *obj*]: *He juggled oranges and apples.* **2.** [~ + *obj*] to alter, fix, change, or manipulate (accounts, business figures, etc.) in order to deceive: *to juggle the firm's accounts to hide the theft.* **3.** [~ + *obj*] to manage or switch rapidly between the requirements of (two or more activities) so as to handle each adequately: *Many students must juggle the requirements of work and school.* —*n.* [*count*] **4.** the act or fact of juggling. —**jug′gler,** *n.* [*count*]

jug•u•lar (jug′yə lər) /ˈdʒʌgyələr/ *adj.* [*before a noun*] **1.** of or relating to any of several veins of the neck that carry blood from the head to the heart. —*n.* [*count*] **2.** a jugular vein. —***Idiom.*** **3. go for the jugular,** to attack a vital part or area that is weak or particularly open to attack.

juice (jo͞os) /dʒuws/ *n., v.,* **juiced, juic•ing.** —*n.* **1.** the natural fluid or liquid that can be taken, squeezed, or removed from a plant or one of its parts, esp. a fruit: [*noncount*]: *She likes orange juice.* [*count*]: *contains natural fruit juices.* **2.** [*count*] the liquid part or contents of a plant or animal substance: *Use the juice from the roast to make gravy.* **3.** [*count*] the natural fluids of an animal body: *Gastric juices help us digest food.* **4.** [*noncount*] strength or vitality; force; vigor. **5.** [*noncount*] *Informal.* electricity; gasoline; fuel: *It takes a lot of juice to run this machine.* **6.** [*noncount*] *Slang.* influence; power: *He must have a lot of juice to get an appointment with the top person.* —*v.* **7.** [~ + *obj*] to remove the juice from: *to juice oranges.* **8. juice up,** to add power, energy, or speed to; strengthen: [~ + *up* + *obj*]: *He juiced up the engine.* [~ + *obj* + *up*]: *He juiced it up.* —**juice′less,** *adj.*

juic•er (jo͞o′sər) /ˈdʒuwsər/ *n.* [*count*] **1.** a kitchen appliance for removing the juice from fruits and vegetables. **2.** *Slang.* a heavy drinker of alcohol.

juic•y (jo͞o′sē) /ˈdʒuwsiy/ *adj.,* **-i•er, -i•est. 1.** full of juice: *a juicy pear.* **2.** very profitable, satisfying, or important: *a juicy contract.* **3.** very interesting or colorful, esp. when slightly scandalous or improper: *juicy gossip; juicy details.* —**juic•i•ly** (jo͞o′sə lē) /ˈdʒuwsəliy/ *adv.* —**juic′i•ness,** *n.* [*noncount*]

ju•jit•su (jo͞o jit′so͞o) /dʒuwˈdʒɪtsuw/ also **ju•jut•su** (-jut′-, -jo͞ot′-) /-ˈdʒʌt-, -ˈdʒuwt-/ *n.* [*noncount*] a Japanese method of defending oneself without weapons by using the strength and weight of one's adversary to disable him or her.

ju•jube (jo͞o′jo͞ob, *also* jo͞o′jo͞o bē′) /ˈdʒuwdʒuwb, *also* ˈdʒuwdʒuwˌbiy/ *n.* [*count*] a small, chewy, fruit-flavored candy or lozenge.

juke•box (jo͞ok′boks′) /ˈdʒuwkˌbɒks/ *n.* [*count*] a coin-operated phonograph, typically in a brightly lit cabinet, having a variety of records that can be selected by pushing a button or buttons.

Jul or **Jul.,** an abbreviation of: July.

ju•lep (jo͞o′lip) /ˈdʒuwlɪp/ *n.* MINT JULEP.

ju•li•enne (jo͞o′lē en′) /ˌdʒuwliyˈɛn/ *adj.* Also, **ju′li•enned′.** (of food, esp. vegetables) cut into thin strips or small, matchlike pieces: [*before a noun*]: *We had julienne potatoes.* [*after a noun*]: *They served potatoes julienne.*

Ju•ly (jo͝o lī′) /dʒʊˈlay/ *n.* [*proper noun*], *pl.* **-lies.** the seventh month of the year, containing 31 days. *Abbr.:* Jul.

jum•ble (jum′bəl) /ˈdʒʌmbəl/ *v.,* **-bled, -bling,** *n.* —*v.* **1.** to mix in a confused mass; put or throw together without order: [~ + *obj*]: *The clothes were all jumbled together.* [~ + *up* + *obj*]: *Someone jumbled up the files.* [~ + *obj* + *up*]: *Someone jumbled them up.* —*n.* [*count*] **2.** a mixed, disordered, or confused heap or mass: *the clothes in a jumble on the floor.* **3.** a state of confusion or disorder: *My mind's in a jumble.*

jum•bo (jum′bō) /ˈdʒʌmbow/ *n., pl.* **-bos,** *adj.* —*n.* [*count*] **1.** one that is very large of its kind, as a very large jet airplane. —*adj.* [*usually: before a noun*] **2.** very large: *a jumbo box of cereal.*

jump (jump) /dʒʌmp/ *v.* **1.** [*no obj*] to leap or spring off the ground or other support by a sudden muscular effort; leap: *to jump into the air; to jump out a window.* **2.** [~ + *obj*] to leap, spring, or go off or over: *to jump a stream.* **3.** [~ + *obj*] to cause to leap: *The rider jumped her horse cleanly over a fence.* **4.** [*no obj*] to move suddenly or quickly: *to jump out of bed.* **5.** [*no obj*] to move or jerk involuntarily, as from shock: *I jumped when the firecracker exploded.* **6.** [*usually: be* + *~-ing; no obj*] *Informal.* to be full of activity; bustle: *The town is jumping with excitement.* **7.** [*no obj*] to rise or increase suddenly in amount: *Oil prices jumped during this quarter.* **8.** [*no obj*] to proceed suddenly, ignoring the steps that should come between (something) or the thinking that should come before it: *to jump to a conclusion.* **9.** [*no obj*] to move or change suddenly: *was always jumping from one topic to another.* **10.** [~ + *at* + *obj*] to take eagerly; seize: *We jumped at the offer.* **11.** to enter into something with strength and enthusiasm: [~ + *into* + *obj*]: *She jumped right into the discussion.* [~ + *in*]: *Feel free to jump in and disagree.* **12.** to (cause to) advance rapidly or suddenly, esp. in rank: [*no obj*]: *to jump from clerk to manager in six months.* [~ + *obj*]: *The army jumped him from second lieutenant straight to captain.* **13.** [~ + *obj*] to act or start before (a signal); anticipate: *The driver jumped the green light.* **14.** [~ + *obj*] to attack or pounce upon without warning: *The gang jumped him in a dark alley.* **15.** [~ + *obj*] to flee without notification or permission: *jumped ship.* **16.** to get on board hastily or with little preparation: [~ + *obj*]: *He jumped a plane for Chicago.* [~ + *on* + *obj*]: *He jumped on a plane for Chicago.* **17.** [~ + *obj*] to connect (a dead battery) to a live battery by attaching booster cables between the two terminals. **18. jump on** or **jump all over,** [~ + *on* + *obj;* ~ + *all* + *over* + *obj*] to scold or criticize suddenly and severely: *jumped on him for being late.* —*n.* [*count*] **19.** an act or instance of jumping; leap: *a jump of several yards.* **20.** a space, obstacle, or apparatus that is cleared or to be cleared in a leap. **21.** a sudden rise in amount, price, etc.: *last year's jump in oil prices.* **22.** a sudden switch from one topic, idea, point, or thing to another. **23.** a move or one of a series of moves: *to stay a jump ahead of the police.* **24.** a sudden movement, often involuntary, as from nervous excitement. **25. the jumps,** [*plural*] *Informal.* restlessness; nervousness; anxiety. —***Idiom.* 26. get** or **have the** or **a jump on,** [~ + *obj*] to have an initial advantage over: *to get a jump on your competitor with an early start.*

jump•er[1] (jum′pər) /ˈdʒʌmpər/ *n.* [*count*] **1.** a person or thing that jumps. **2.** a shot in basketball made while leaping in the air. **3.** a short length of cable used to make an electrical connection or to bypass a circuit.

jump•er[2] (jum′pər) /ˈdʒʌmpər/ *n.* [*count*] **1.** a sleeveless dress, or a skirt with a bib and straps or with an open-sided bodice, usually worn over a blouse. **2.** a loose outer jacket worn esp. by workers and sailors. **3.** *Brit.* a pullover sweater.

jump′-start′, *n.* [*count*] **1.** the starting by means of booster cables of an internal-combustion engine that has a discharged or weak battery. —*v.* [~ + *obj*] **2.** to give a jump-start to: *to jump-start the car's engine.* **3.** to give new energy to; revive: *to jump-start the sluggish economy.*

jump•suit (jump′so͞ot′) /ˈdʒʌmpˌsuwt/ *n.* [*count*] **1.** a one-piece suit worn by parachutists for jumping. **2.** a similar garment, usually combining a shirt with shorts or trousers in one piece.

jump•y (jum′pē) /ˈdʒʌmpiy/ *adj.,* **-i•er, -i•est. 1.** nervous or apprehensive; jittery: *The long wait is making me jumpy.* **2.** characterized by sudden starts, jerks, or jumps: *a jumpy TV picture.* —**jump′i•ness,** *n.* [*noncount*]

Jun or **Jun.,** an abbreviation of: June.

Jun., an abbreviation of: Junior.

-junc-, *root.* *-junc-* comes from Latin, where it has the meaning "join; connect." This meaning is found in such words as: ADJOIN, ADJUNCT, CONJUNCTION, DISJOINTED, INJUNCTION, JOIN(T), REJOIN, REJOINDER, SUBJUNCTIVE.

jun•co (jung′kō) /ˈdʒʌŋkow/ *n.* [*count*], *pl.* **-cos.** a small gray or gray and brown North American finch. Also called **snowbird.**

junc•tion (jungk′shən) /ˈdʒʌŋkʃən/ *n.* [*count*] a place or point where two or more things meet or are joined, such as a station where railroad lines meet, cross, or diverge, or an intersection of roads. See -JUNC-.

junc•ture (jungk′chər) /ˈdʒʌŋktʃər/ *n.* [*count*] **1.** a point of time, esp. one made important or critical by circumstances that come together: *At this juncture, we must decide whether to continue negotiations.* **2.** a place where two things are joined. See -JUNC-.

June (jo͞on) /dʒuwn/ *n.* [*proper noun*] the sixth month of the year, containing 30 days. *Abbr.:* Jun.

jun•gle (jung′gəl) /ˈdʒʌŋgəl/ *n.* **1.** wild land overgrown with thick, dense plant life, often nearly impossible to penetrate: [*noncount*]: *The country is all jungle.* [*count*]: *the jungles of the world.* **2.** [*count*] something that causes confusion: *a jungle of rules and regulations.* **3.** [*count*] a place of violent struggle: *the jungle of the ghetto streets.*

jun•ior (jo͞on′yər) /ˈdʒuwnyər/ *adj.* **1. a.** younger: *your junior brother.* **b.** This word is used to name a son after his father; it is often written as *Jr.* following the name: *Edward Hansen, Jr.* **2.** [*before a noun*] of more recent election, appointment, or admission: *the junior senator from Michigan.* **3.** of lower rank or standing: *a junior law partner.* **4.** of or relating to juniors in high school or college: *junior year.* **5.** [*before a noun*] being smaller than the usual size: *junior clothes.* —*n.* [*count*] **6.** a person who is younger than another: *She is my junior.* **7.** a person who is newer or of lower rank, as in a profession; subordinate: *a junior in the firm.* **8.** a student in the next to the last year at a high school, college, or university. **9. a.** Often, **juniors.** [*plural*] a clothing size for garments for women with short waists and narrow shoulders. **b.** a garment in this size range. **10.** This word is used as a term of address for a boy; or youth; or son: *Get out there, Junior, and show us what you can do.*

jun′ior col′lege, *n.* an institution offering courses only through the first two years of college instruction and granting an associate's degree or a certificate of title: [*count*]: *The junior colleges of that system are funded by the City.* [*noncount*]: *two years of junior college.*

jun′ior high′ school′, *n.* a school attended after elementary school and usually for grades seven through nine: [*count*]: *The district changed from a junior high school to a middle school.* [*noncount*]: *is attending junior high school.*

ju•ni•per (jo͞o′nə pər) /ˈdʒuwnəpər/ *n.* [*count*] an evergreen shrub or tree of the cypress family having scaly leaves and berrylike cones that provide an oil used in flavoring gin.

junk[1] (jungk) /dʒʌŋk/ *n.* [*noncount*] **1.** old, mostly useless material or objects, such as metal, paper, or rags:

junk accumulating in the attic. **2.** something thought of as worthless, meaningless, or useless; trash: *junk found in a garage sale.* **—*v.*** [~ + *obj*] **3.** to discard as no longer of use; scrap: *They had to junk the car after thirteen years.* —**junk′y,** *adj.,* **-i•er, -i•est.**

junk[2] (jungk) /dʒʌŋk/ *n.* [*count*] a seagoing ship used primarily in Chinese waters, having square sails, a high stern, and usually a flat bottom.

junk′ bond′, *n.* [*count*] a corporate bond with a low rating and a high yield and usually involving high risk.

junk•er (jung′kər) /ˈdʒʌŋkər/ *n.* [*count*] *Informal.* a car that is old or in bad enough repair to be scrapped.

jun•ket (jung′kit) /ˈdʒʌŋkɪt/ *n.* **1.** [*noncount*] a custardlike dessert of flavored milk and rennet. **2.** [*count*] a pleasure trip or excursion: *a junket down the Mississippi.* **3.** [*count*] a trip taken by a government official at public expense. **—*v.*** [*no obj*] **4.** to go on a junket: *The Congressmen were junketing in Asia.* —**jun•ke•teer** (jung′ki-tēr′) /ˌdʒʌŋkɪˈtɪər/ **jun′ket•er,** *n.* [*count*]

junk′ food′, *n.* food, as potato chips or candy, that is high in calories but of little nutritional value: [*noncount*]: *feasting on junk food.* [*count*]: *ate junk foods instead of fruits and vegetables.*

junk•ie or **junk•y** (jung′kē) /ˈdʒʌŋkiy/ *n.* [*count*], *pl.* **junk•ies.** *Informal.* **1.** a drug addict. **2.** a person with a strong craving for something: *a chocolate junkie.* **3.** a follower; devotee: *a baseball junkie.*

junk′ mail′, *n.* [*noncount*] advertisements and requests for donations, mailed in bulk.

jun•ta (hŏŏn′tə, jun′-, hun′-) /ˈhʊntə, ˈdʒʌn-, ˈhʌn-/ *n.* [*count*], *pl.* **-tas.** a small group ruling, or planning to rule, a country, esp. immediately after a coup d'état and before a legal government has been set up.

-jur-, *root.* *-jur-* comes from Latin, where it has the meaning "swear." It is related to the root -JUS-, meaning "law; rule." This meaning is found in such words as: **ABJURE, CONJURE, INJURE, JURIDICAL, JURISDICTION, JURY, PERJURE.**

ju•rid•i•cal (jŏŏ rid′i kəl) /dʒʊˈrɪdɪkəl/ also **ju•rid′ic,** *adj.* **1.** of or relating to the administration of justice. **2.** of or relating to law or jurisprudence; legal. See -JUR-.

ju•ris•dic•tion (jŏŏr′is dik′shən) /ˌdʒʊrɪsˈdɪkʃən/ *n.* [*noncount*] **1.** the right, power, or authority to administer justice by hearing and determining controversies: *to have military jurisdiction over the occupied territories.* **2.** the extent or range of judicial, law-enforcement, or other authority: *a case under local jurisdiction.* —**ju′ris•dic′tion•al,** *adj.* See -JUR-, -DICT-.

ju•ris•pru•dence (jŏŏr′is prōōd′ns) /ˌdʒʊrɪsˈpruwdns/ *n.* [*noncount*] **1.** the science or philosophy of law. **2.** a system of laws. **3.** a branch of law: *medical jurisprudence.* See -JUR-.

ju•rist (jŏŏr′ist) /ˈdʒʊrɪst/ *n.* [*count*] a person who knows a lot about the law, esp. a judge. Compare JUROR. See -JUR-.

ju•ris•tic (jŏŏ ris′tik) /dʒʊˈrɪstɪk/ also **ju•ris′ti•cal,** *adj.* of or relating to a jurist or to jurisprudence; juridical. See -JUR-.

ju•ror (jŏŏr′ər, -ôr) /ˈdʒʊrər, -ɔr/ *n.* [*count*] **1.** a member of a jury. **2.** a person summonded to serve as a juror. See -JUR-.

ju•ry (jŏŏr′ē) /ˈdʒʊriy/ *n.* [*count*], *pl.* **-ries. 1.** a group of persons who are sworn to decide a case or give a verdict by examining the evidence in a court. **2.** a group of persons who are chosen to decide on who is to receive prizes, awards, etc., as in a competition. See -JUR-.

ju′ry-rig′, *v.* [~ + *obj*], **-rigged, -rig•ging.** to assemble hastily or from whatever is at hand, esp. for temporary use: *to jury-rig stage lights using car headlights.* —**ju′ry-rigged′,** *adj.: the jury-rigged booby traps.*

-jus-, *root.* *-jus-* comes from Latin, where it has the meaning "law; rule; fair; just." It is related to the root -JUR-. This meaning is found in such words as: **ADJUST, JUST, JUSTICE, MALADJUSTED, READJUST, UNJUST.**

just (just) /dʒʌst/ *adv.* **1.** within a brief preceding time; only a moment before: *The sun just came out.* **2.** at this moment: *The movie is just ending.* **3.** exactly or precisely: *That's just what I mean.* **4.** by a narrow margin; barely: *She's just over six feet tall.* **5.** only or merely: *I was just a child.* **6.** simply: *We'll just have to wait and see.* **7.** quite; really; positively: *I'm feeling just fine.* **—*adj.*** **8.** guided by reason, justice, and fairness: *a just society.* **9.** done or made according to principle; equitable; proper: *a just reply.* **10.** based on right; rightful; lawful: *a just claim to the land.* **11.** given or awarded rightly; deserved: *The criminal received a just punishment.* **—*Idiom.*** **12. just about,** almost; nearly: *Dinner was just about ready.* —**just′ly,** *adv.* —**just′ness,** *n.* [*noncount*] See -JUS-..

jus•tice (jus′tis) /ˈdʒʌstɪs/ *n.* **1.** [*noncount*] the quality of being just; righteousness, fairness, or moral rightness: *If there is any justice in this world, you'll be rewarded for your hard work.* **2.** [*noncount*] rightfulness: *There's justice in what he says.* **3.** [*noncount*] judgment of individuals or causes by judicial process: *The courts administer justice.* **4.** [*count*] a judicial officer; a judge or magistrate. **—*Idiom.*** **5. bring (someone) to justice,** [*bring* + *obj* + *to* + ~] to cause to come before a court for trial or to receive punishment for one's crimes. **6. do justice, a.** to appreciate properly: [*do* + *justice to* + *obj*]: *We'll have to see the play again if we want to do justice to it.* [*do* + *obj (pronoun)* + *justice*]: *If you want to do it justice, you'll just have to see it again.* **b.** to reflect or express the worth of properly: [*do* + *justice* + *to* + *obj*]: *That gown simply doesn't do justice to your figure.* [*do* + *obj (pronoun)* + *justice*]: *That gown doesn't do you justice.* See -JUS-.

jus′tice of the peace′, *n.* [*count*] a local public officer having authority to decide minor civil and criminal cases in court, to administer oaths, to perform marriages, etc.

jus•ti•fi•a•ble (jus′tə fī′ə bəl, jus′tə fī′-) /ˈdʒʌstəˌfayəbəl, ˌdʒʌstəˈfay-/ *adj.* that can be justified: *a case of justifiable homicide.* —**jus′ti•fi′a•bly,** *adv.* See -JUS-.

jus•ti•fi•ca•tion (jus′tə fi kā′shən) /ˌdʒʌstəfɪˈkeyʃən/ *n.* a reason, fact, circumstance, or explanation that justifies: [*noncount*]: *His treatment of you was all the justification you needed to leave.* [*count*]: *He was looking for any justification to fire her.* See -JUS-.

jus•ti•fy (jus′tə fī′) /ˈdʒʌstəˌfay/ *v.* [~ + *obj*], **-fied, -fy•ing. 1.** to show or prove to be just, right, or reasonable: *The pleasure these paintings give justifies their high cost.* **2.** to defend as permitted or allowable: *I can't justify my actions.* **3.** to space out words or characters in (lines of type) to produce an even margin. See -JUS-.

jut (jut) /dʒʌt/ *v.* [*no obj;* (~ + *out*)], **jut•ted, jut•ting.** to stick out beyond the main body or line; to project; protrude: *a strip of land jutting (out) into the bay.*

jute (jōōt) /dʒuwt/ *n.* [*noncount*] **1.** a strong, rough, coarse fiber used for making burlap, gunny, cordage, etc. **2.** a plant of the linden family from which this fiber is made.

ju•ve•nile (jōō′və nl, -nīl′) /ˈdʒuwvənl̩, -ˌnayl/ *adj.* **1.** of, characteristic of, or suitable for children or young people: *juvenile books.* **2.** young; youthful. **3.** immature; childish: *juvenile temper tantrums.* **—*n.*** [*count*] **4.** a young person; youth. **5.** a person not old enough to be thought of, or treated as, an adult: *a court for juveniles.* —**ju′ve•nile•ly,** *adv.*

ju′venile delin′quency, *n.* [*noncount*] illegal or criminal behavior by a minor or someone not old enough to be treated as an adult in a court of law. —**ju′venile delin′quent,** *n.* [*count*]

jux•ta•pose (juk′stə pōz′, juk′stə pōz′) /ˈdʒʌkstəˌpowz, ˌdʒʌkstəˈpowz/ *v.* [~ + *obj*], **-posed, -pos•ing.** to place close together or side by side, esp. for comparison or contrast: *juxtaposed the left view with the right.* —**jux•ta•po•si•tion** (juk′stə pə zish′ən) /ˌdʒʌkstəpəˈzɪʃən/ *n.* [*noncount*] See -POS-.

JV or **J.V.,** an abbreviation of: **1.** joint venture. **2.** junior varsity.

K, k (kā) /key/ *n.* [*count*], *pl.* **Ks** or **K's, ks** or **k's.** the 11th letter of the English alphabet, a consonant.

K, an abbreviation of: **1.** *Computers.* **a.** the number 1024 or 2^{10}: *A binary 32K memory has 32,768 positions.* **b.** kilobyte. **2.** the number 1000: *a $20K salary.* **3.** kindergarten. **4.** kitchen.

k. or **k,** an abbreviation of: **1.** karat. **2.** kilogram.

ka•bob (kə bob′) /kə'bɒb/ *n.* KEBAB.

ka•bu•ki (kə bo͞o′kē, kä′bo͞o kē′) /kə'buwkiy, 'kɑbuwˌkiy/ *n.* [*noncount*] a popular drama of Japan in which male actors perform all the roles, wearing very fancy costumes and acting according to certain styles and patterns.

kaf•fee•klatsch or **kaf•fee klatsch** (kä′fē kläch′, -klach′, kô′-) /'kɑfiyˌklɑtʃ, -ˌklætʃ, 'kɔ-/ also **coffee klatsch,** *n.* [*count*] a social gathering for informal conversation at which coffee is served.

kale (kāl) /keyl/ *n.* [*noncount*] a cabbagelike plant of the mustard family, having wrinkled leaves and used as a vegetable: *a salad with kale.*

ka•lei•do•scope (kə lī′də skōp′) /kə'laydəˌskowp/ *n.* [*count*] **1.** a tube-shaped instrument in which loose bits of colored glass at the end of the tube are reflected in mirrors so as to display changing patterns as the tube is rotated. **2.** [*usually singular*] a continually shifting pattern, scene, or the like. **—ka•lei•do•scop•ic** (kə lī′də-skop′ik) /kəˌlaydə'skɒpɪk/ *adj.*

ka•mi•ka•ze (kä′mi kä′zē) /ˌkɑmɪ'kɑziy/ *n., pl.* **-zes,** *adj.* **—***n.* [*count*] **1.** (during World War II) a member of a special group of Japanese airmen flying suicidal missions against U.S. warships. **2.** an airplane filled with explosives and flown by a kamikaze. **—***adj.* [*before a noun*] **3.** of or resembling a kamikaze; wildly reckless; suicidal: *a kamikaze attack.*

kan•ga•roo (kang′gə ro͞o′) /ˌkæŋgə'ruw/ *n.* [*count*], *pl.* **-roos,** (*esp. when thought of as a group*) **-roo.** a plant-eating animal of Australia and nearby islands, that jumps with powerful hind legs, and carries its young in its pouch.

kan′garoo court′, *n.* [*count*] a self-appointed or otherwise irregularly operated court or trial that disregards existing principles of law or human rights and thus makes a fair trial impossible.

Kans., an abbreviation of: Kansas.

ka•pok (kā′pok) /'keypɒk/ *n.* [*noncount*] the silky down material that covers the seeds of a tropical tree, and is used for stuffing life jackets, etc., and for insulation.

ka•put (kä po͝ot′, -po͞ot′, kə-) /kɑ'pʊt, -'puwt, kə-/ *adj.* [*be* + ~] *Slang.* ruined; demolished; unable to operate or continue; broken: *The TV is kaput.*

Kar•a•kul (kar′ə kəl) /'kærəkəl/ *n.* [*noncount*] an Asian breed of sheep having curly fleece that is black in the young and brown or gray in the adult.

kar•at or **car•at** (kar′ət) /'kærət/ *n.* [*count*] a unit for measuring the amount of pure gold in a mixture of gold, pure gold being 24 karats: *fourteen karats of gold.* [*singular before a noun*]: *eighteen-karat gold.*

ka•ra•te (kə rä′tē) /kə'rɑtiy/ *n.* [*noncount*] a Japanese method of self-defense using fast, hard blows with the hands, elbows, knees, or feet.

kar•ma (kär′mə) /'kɑrmə/ *n.* [*noncount*] **1.** (in Hinduism and Buddhism) action seen as bringing upon oneself results that will be felt either in this life or in a reincarnation. **2.** the good or bad feelings felt to be generated by someone or something: *bad karma.*

ka•sha (kä′shə) /'kɑʃə/ *n.* [*noncount*] **1.** a soft food prepared from crushed grain with the hulls removed, esp. buckwheat. **2.** such grain before cooking.

ka•ty•did (kā′tē did) /'keytiydɪd/ *n.* [*count*] a large, usually green, long-horned American grasshopper, the males of which produce a characteristic song resembling the phrase "Katey did."

kay•ak (kī′ak) /'kayæk/ *n.* [*count*] **1.** an Eskimo canoe with a skin cover on a light framework and a flexible opening at the center. **2.** a small boat resembling this. **—***v.* [*no obj*] **3.** to go or travel by kayak.

kay•o (kā′ō′, kā′ō′) /'key'ow, 'keyˌow/ *n., pl.* **-os,** *v.,* **-oed, -o•ing.** See KO.

ka•zoo (kə zo͞o′) /kə'zuw/ *n.* [*count*], *pl.* **-zoos.** a musical toy made up of a tube that is open at both ends and has a hole in the side covered with something like paper, which produces a buzzing sound when the performer hums into one end.

ke•bab or **ka•bob** (kə bob′) /kə'bɒb/ *n.* [*count*] small pieces of meat or seafood that are seasoned and put on a thin metal or wooden rod, then broiled or grilled, often with peppers, onions, or other vegetables.

keel (kēl) /kiyl/ *n.* [*count*] **1.** the base at the bottom of the hull of a boat, usually a long metal or wooden bar, that extends from the back to the front and from which the sides are built. **—***v.* **2. keel over,** [*no obj*] **a.** to capsize or overturn: *The boat keeled over in the hurricane.* **b.** to fall in or as if in a faint: *to keel over from the heat.* **—*Idiom.*** **3. on an even keel,** in a steady or stable state: *to keep things on an even keel.*

keen (kēn) /kiyn/ *adj.,* **-er, -est. 1.** finely sharpened; so shaped as to cut or pierce readily: *a razor with a keen edge.* **2.** sharp, piercing, or biting: *a keen wind.* **3.** very sensitive, responsive, or alert: *a keen sense of hearing; a keen mind.* **4.** having great ability to see clearly and understand; astute: *a keen observer of human nature.* **5.** intense: *keen competition for the job.* **6.** [*usually: be* + ~] eager; interested; enthusiastic: [~ + *to* + *verb*]: *I was very keen to go swimming.* [~ + *on/about*]: *He was very keen on football.* **7.** [*be* + ~ + *on*] interested in romantically: *not keen on anyone special at the moment.* **8.** *Slang.* great; wonderful: *a keen new bike.* **—keen′ly,** *adv.: felt the loss keenly.* **—keen′ness,** *n.* [*noncount*]

keep (kēp) /kiyp/ *v.,* **kept, keep•ing,** *n.* **—***v.* **1.** [~ + *obj*] to hold or cause to remain in one's possession: *kept the change from a ten-dollar bill.* **2.** [~ + *obj*] to hold or cause to remain in a given place; put or store: *I keep the car in the garage.* **3.** to (cause to) continue or stay in a certain position, state, course, condition, or action: [~ + *obj* + *verb-ing*]: *to keep a light burning.* [~ + *verb-ing*]: *I kept trying to reach her by phone.* [~ (+ *obj*) + *adjective*]: *Keep the children quiet during the ceremony.* [~ + *obj* + *verb-ed/-en*]: *You have to keep your lawn mowed in that neighborhood.* [~ + *obj*]: *vowed to keep his silence.* **4.** to maintain or cause to stay fresh or in usable or edible condition; (cause to) be preserved: [~ + *obj*]: *to keep meat by freezing it.* [*no obj*]: *How long will this meat keep in hot weather?* **5.** [~ + *obj*] to cause to stay or remain in a particular place; detain: *They kept me in prison for days.* **6.** to remain in (a place, spot, etc.); stay: [~ + *obj*]: *Please keep your seats.* [*no obj*]: *Keep off the grass.* **7.** [~ + *obj*] to have readily available for use or sale: *to keep machine parts in stock.* **8.** [~ + *obj*] to maintain in one's service or for one's use: *She can no longer afford to keep a car and a driver.* **9.** [~ + *obj*] to associate with: *to keep bad company.* **10.** to (cause to) be held back from disclosing: [~ + *obj*]: *keeping secrets.* [*no obj*]: *The rest of the story will have to keep until the next time.* **11.** [~ + *obj*] to withhold, as from use; reserve; save: *to keep the best wine for guests.* **12.** to restrain or prevent, as from an action: [~ + *obj* + *from* + *verb-ing*]: *to keep the warmth from escaping.* [~ + *oneself* + *from* + *verb-ing*]: *couldn't keep herself from smiling.* [~ + *from* + *verb-ing*]: *Can you keep from smiling?* **13.** [~ + *obj*] to control; maintain: *police officers keeping the peace.* **14.** [~ + *obj*] to maintain by writing; to record regularly: *to keep a diary.* **15.** [~ + *obj*] to observe; obey or fulfill: *She always keeps her promises.* **16.** [~ + *obj*] to observe (a season, festival, etc.) with formalities or rites: *to keep Christmas.* **17.** [~ + *obj*] to maintain; manage: *to keep a small grocery store.* **18.** [~ + *obj*] to guard; protect: *He kept her from harm.* **19.** [~ + *obj*] to maintain or support: *Can you keep a family on those wages?* **20.** [~ + *obj*] to maintain one's position in or on: *to keep a job.* **21.** [*no obj*] to continue to follow a path, course, etc.: *Keep on this road; keep left.* **22. keep at,** to (cause to) continue (working, etc.); persevere in: [~ + *at* + *obj*]: *She just kept at the task.* [~ + *obj* + *at* + *obj*]: *The boss kept us at it all night.* **23. keep back, a.** to hold in check; restrain: [~ + *obj* + *back*]: *The police kept the crowd back.* [~ + *back* + *obj*]: *They kept back the crowd.* **b.** [*no obj*] to stay away from: *The firefighters at first kept back from the fire.* **c.** to withhold; not to tell: [~ + *obj* + *back*]: *Don't keep any information back.* [~ + *back* + *obj*]: *She's keeping back the news from us.* **24. keep down, a.** to maintain at an acceptable level; control: [~ + *obj* + *down*]: *The store kept the temperature down.* [~ + *down* + *obj*]: *They kept down the temperature.* **b.** to prevent from advancing or flourishing: [~ + *obj* + *down*]: *It's hard to keep a good person down.* [~ + *down* + *obj*]: *The company shouldn't keep down dedicated workers.* **c.** to avoid vomiting (food): [~ + *down* + *obj*]: *The patient managed to keep* down the meal. [~ + *obj* + *down*]: *wondered if he could keep it down.* **25. keep on,** [~ + *on* + *verb-ing*] to continue; persist: *The train kept right on going.* **26. keep to,** [~ + *to* + *obj*] **a.** to obey; conform to; go along with: *to keep to the rules.* **b.** to confine oneself to: *to keep to one's bed.* **27. keep up, a.** [~ + *up* + *with* + *obj*] to perform as swiftly or successfully as others: *She easily kept up with the rest of the runners.* **b.** to persevere; continue: [~ + *up* + *obj*]: *kept up a continuous groaning.* [~ + *up* (+ *with*) + *obj*]: *kept up (with) the payments; told her to keep up the good work.* [*no obj*]: *How long will that horrible music keep up?* **c.** [~ + *up* + *obj*] to maintain in good condition or repair: *He liked to keep up old cars.* **d.** [~ + *up* + *with* + *obj*] to stay informed: *He kept up with all the latest sports events.* —*n.* [*count*] **28.** [*usually singular*] the cost of food and a place to live or stay; subsistence; support: *had to work for his keep.* **29.** the innermost and strongest structure or central tower of a medieval castle; dungeon. —***Idiom.*** **30. for keeps, a.** with the understanding that winnings are retained by the winner: *playing poker for keeps.* **b.** with serious intent or purpose: *We're all in this effort for keeps.* **c.** permanently; forever. **31. keep to oneself, a.** to remain apart from the society of others. **b.** [~ + *obj* + *to* + *oneself*] to hold (something) as secret or not to be told to another: *You can't keep that information to yourself any longer.* [~ + *to* + *oneself* + *obj*]: *Keep to yourself any information you receive.*

keep•er (kē′pər) /ˈkiypər/ *n.* [*count*] **1.** a person who guards or watches, as a prison warden. **2.** a person who owns or operates a business, or one who is responsible for the maintenance of something: *hotelkeeper; zookeeper.* **3.** a person responsible for the preservation and conservation of something valuable, as a curator at a museum.

keep•ing (kē′ping) /ˈkiypɪŋ/ *n.* [*noncount*] **1. in keeping with,** in agreement with things that are usually associated together or connected: *Her actions were not in keeping with her words.* **2.** the act of a person or thing that keeps; observance, custody, or care: *We put the jewels in your keeping.*

keep•sake (kēp′sāk′) /ˈkiypˌseyk/ *n.* [*count*] anything kept, or given to be kept, as a memento; remembrance.

keg (keg) /kɛg/ *n.* [*count*] **1.** a small cask or barrel. **2.** a unit of weight equal to 100 pounds (45 kg), used for nails.

kelp (kelp) /kɛlp/ *n.* [*noncount*] a large brown seaweed used as food and in manufacturing processes.

kel•vin (kel′vin) /ˈkɛlvɪn/ *n.* [*count*] **1.** a standard unit of temperature. *Abbr.:* K —*adj.* **2.** of or relating to an absolute scale of temperature **(Kel′vin scale′)** based on the kelvin in which the degree intervals are equal to those of the Celsius scale: *converting to kelvin temperatures.* [*after a noun*]: *thirty degrees kelvin.*

ken (ken) /kɛn/ *n., v.,* **kenned** or **kent** (kent) /kɛnt/ **ken•ning.** —*n.* [*noncount*] **1.** knowledge or understanding: *an idea beyond one's ken.* —*v.* [~ + *obj*] **2.** *Chiefly Scottish.* to have knowledge (about); know.

ken•nel (ken′l) /ˈkɛnl̩/ *n., v.,* **-neled, -nel•ing** or (*esp. Brit.*) **-nelled, -nel•ling.** —*n.* [*count*] **1.** a small house for a dog. **2.** Often, **kennels.** [*plural*] a business or establishment where dogs or cats are bred, trained, or kept for a fee. —*v.* [~ + *obj*] **3.** to put or keep in or as if in a kennel.

Ken•yan (ken′yən, kēn′-) /ˈkɛnyən, ˈkiyn-/ *adj.* **1.** of or relating to Kenya. —*n.* [*count*] **2.** a person born or living in Kenya.

kept (kept) /kɛpt/ *v.* **1.** pt. and pp. of KEEP. —*adj.* **2.** financially supported by another in exchange for something, as sexual services: *a kept woman.*

ker•a•tin (ker′ə tin) /ˈkɛrətɪn/ *n.* [*noncount*] a tough protein that is the main part of hair, nails, horn, hoofs, etc., and of the outermost layer of skin.

kerb (kûrb) /kɜrb/ *n., v., Brit.* CURB (defs. 1, 5, 9).

ker•chief (kûr′chif, -chēf) /ˈkɜrtʃɪf, -tʃiyf/ *n.* [*count*] **1.** a woman's square scarf worn as a covering for the head or sometimes the shoulders. **2.** HANDKERCHIEF.

ker•nel (kûr′nl) /ˈkɜrnl̩/ *n., v.,* **-neled, -nel•ing** or (*esp. Brit.*) **-nelled, -nel•ling.** —*n.* [*count*] **1.** the soft part in the shell of a nut or the stone of a fruit that can usually be eaten. **2.** an essential part; germ: *There was hardly a kernel of truth in what you told him.*

ker•o•sene (ker′ə sēn′) /ˈkɛrəˌsiyn/ *n.* [*noncount*] a liquid made from petroleum or shale, used as a fuel and cleaning solvent.

kes•trel (kes′trəl) /ˈkɛstrəl/ *n.* [*count*] a small falcon that hovers as it hunts.

ketch (kech) /kɛtʃ/ *n.* [*count*] a sailing vessel with two masts, the larger, forward one being the mainmast.

ketch•up (kech′əp, kach′-) /ˈkɛtʃəp, ˈkætʃ-/ *n.* [*noncount*] a thick sauce made of tomatoes, onions, vinegar, sugar, and spices.

ket•tle (ket′l) /ˈkɛtl̩/ *n.* [*count*] a pot, usually of metal, with a spout, handle, and lid used mainly to boil water.

ket•tle•drum (ket′l drum′) /ˈkɛtl̩ˌdrʌm/ *n.* [*count*] a large drum consisting of a hollow curved bottom of brass, copper, or fiberglass over which is stretched a skin, the tension of which can be adjusted by screws or foot pedals to vary the pitch. Compare TIMPANI.

key[1] (kē) /kiy/ *n., pl.* **keys,** *adj., v.,* **keyed, key•ing.** —*n.* [*count*] **1.** a small metal instrument specially cut to fit into a lock and move its bolt: *the house keys.* **2.** any of various devices resembling or functioning as a key: *The key of an old-fashioned clock is used to wind it up.* **3.** something that provides a means to achieve, become skilled at, or understand something else: *the key to a secret code; the key to happiness.* **4.** a book or other text containing the solutions or answers for material given elsewhere, as testing exercises. **5.** an explanation of abbreviations, symbols, and the like used in a dictionary, map, etc.: *a pronunciation key.* **6.** one of the buttons or levers on the keyboard of a typewriter, computer, piano, or the like, that are pressed to operate the device. **7.** the principal tonality of a piece of music: *a symphony in the key of C minor.* **8.** mood or characteristic style, as of expression or thought: *He writes in a melancholy key.* **9.** a hand-operated switching device capable of switching one or more parts of a circuit. —*adj.* [*before a noun*] **10.** chief; major; essential; crucial; fundamental; pivotal: *a key industry.* —*v.* **11.** [~ + *obj*] to bring into a state of agreement, conformity, or harmony; coordinate: *The commercials should be keyed to the audience who will be viewing them.* **12.** [~ + *obj*] to regulate the musical pitch of. **13.** [~ + *obj*] to set with or as if with a key: *He keyed the alarm.* **14.** to type (data) into a computer: [~ + *in* + *obj*]: *He keyed in all the data.* [~ + *obj* + *in*]: *He keyed the data in.* **15. key (in) on,** [~ + *in* + *on* + *obj*] to single out as important: *The basketball team keyed in on their opponent's star player.*

key[2] (kē) /kiy/ *n.* [*count*], *pl.* **keys.** a reef or low island; cay.

key•board (kē′bôrd′, -bōrd′) /ˈkiyˌbɔrd, -ˌbowrd/ *n.* [*count*] **1.** the row or set of keys on a piano, organ, typewriter, computer, etc. See illustration at OFFICE. **2.** any of various musical instruments played by means of a piano-like keyboard. —*v.* [~ + *obj*] **3.** to enter (data) into a computer by means of a keyboard: *keyboarded all the data.* —**key′board′er,** *n.* [*count*]

keyed′ up′, *adj.* tense; very nervous or stimulated: *a keyed up boxing crowd.*

key•hole (kē′hōl′) /ˈkiyˌhowl/ *n.* [*count*] a hole for inserting a key in a lock, esp. one in the shape of a circle with a narrow rectangle beneath it.

key•note (kē′nōt′) /ˈkiyˌnowt/ *n., v.,* **-not•ed, -not•ing.** —*n.* [*count*] **1.** the note or tone on which a key or system of tones is based; tonic. **2.** the central idea, as of a speech or political campaign: *The keynote of his campaign was the economy.* **3.** KEYNOTE ADDRESS. —*v.* [~ + *obj*] **4.** to deliver a keynote address (at): *He will keynote the conference.* —**key′not′er,** *n.* [*count*] See -NOTA-.

key′note address′, *n.* [*count*] a speech, as at a political convention or other gathering, that presents important issues, principles, policies, etc. Also called **key′note speech′.**

key•punch (kē′punch′) /ˈkiyˌpʌntʃ/ *n.* [*count*] **1.** a machine, operated by a keyboard, for coding information by punching holes in cards or paper tape in certain patterns. —*v.* [~ + *obj*] **2.** to punch holes in (a punch card or paper tape) using a keypunch. —**key′punch′er,** *n.* [*count*]

key•stone (kē′stōn′) /ˈkiyˌstown/ *n.* [*count*] **1.** the wedge-shaped piece at the top of an arch that holds the other pieces in place. **2.** something on which associated things depend; basis; foundation: *the keystone of one's philosophy.*

kg, an abbreviation of: kilogram.

khak•i (kak′ē, kä′kē) /ˈkækiy, ˈkɑkiy/ *n., pl.* **khak•is,** *adj.* —*n.* **1.** [*noncount*] dull yellowish brown. **2.** [*noncount*] a strong, usually twilled fabric of this color, used esp. in making uniforms. **3.** Usually, **khakis.** [*plural*] **a.** a uniform made of this cloth. **b.** a garment made of this cloth. —*adj.* **4.** of the color khaki. **5.** made of khaki.

kHz, an abbreviation of: kilohertz.

KIA or **K.I.A.,** an abbreviation of: killed in action.

kib•butz (ki bo͝ots′, -bo͞ots′) /kɪˈbʊts, -ˈbuwts/ *n.* [*count*], *pl.* **-but•zim** (-bo͝ot sēm′) /-but'siym/. (in Israel) a community settlement or farm in which the people living there share the work, property, and profits from any business.

ki•bosh (kī′bosh, ki bosh′) /'kaybɒʃ, kɪ'bɒʃ/ *n.* [*noncount*] *Slang.* **—*Idiom.* put the kibosh on,** [~ + *obj*] to put an end to; check: *put the kibosh on excessive spending.*

kick (kik) /kɪk/ *v.* **1.** to strike with the foot or feet; to make a rapid, forceful move with the feet: [~ + *obj*]: *to kick a ball.* [*no obj*]: *The baby was laughing and kicking in delight.* **2.** [~ + *obj*] to drive, force, thrust, etc., by or as if by kicks: *He kicked a hole in the door.* **3.** [~ + *obj*] *Football.* to score (a field goal) by kicking the ball. **4.** [~ + *obj*] *Slang.* to give up or break (a drug addiction): *He kicked his habit.* **5.** [*no obj*] to resist, object, or complain: *All she did was kick about her new job.* **6.** [*no obj*] to recoil on firing: *The heavy rifle kicked against his shoulder.* **7.** [*no obj*] to be actively or vigorously involved: *alive and kicking.* **8. kick around, a.** [~ + *obj* + *around*] to treat harshly: *Don't kick the staff around like that.* **b.** to speculate about; discuss: [~ + *around* + *obj*]: *We kicked around a few ideas.* [~ + *obj* + *around*]: *We kicked a few ideas around.* **c.** [*no obj*] to move frequently from place to place; roam; wander: *They kicked around for a few years, then settled down.* **d.** [*no obj*] to linger or remain for a long interval without being used, noticed, or resolved: *The old bike's just been kicking around in the garage.* **9. kick back, a.** [*no obj*] to recoil: *The gun kicked back hard against his shoulder.* **b.** to give someone a kickback: [~ + *back* + *obj*]: *had to kick back some $30,000.* [~ + *obj* + *back*]: *Kick something back to the mob boss.* **10. kick in, a.** to contribute one's share: [~ + *in* + *obj*]: *We kicked in a few dollars for the fund.* [~ + *obj* + *in*]: *We kicked a few dollars in.* **b.** [*no obj*] to go into effect; become operational: *Next year the new tax code kicks in.* **11. kick off, a.** [*no obj*] *Football.* to begin or resume play by a kickoff. **b.** [*no obj*] *Slang.* to die. **c.** to start or begin (a project, undertaking, etc.): [~ + *off* + *obj*]: *The company kicked off its ad campaign.* [~ + *obj* + *off*]: *They kicked it off with a great celebration.* **12. kick out,** throw out; get rid of: [~ + *out* + *obj*]: *The voters wanted to kick out all the do-nothing politicians.* [~ + *obj* + *out*]: *The voters want to kick them out.* **13. kick over,** (of an engine) to begin ignition; turn over; start: [*no obj*]: *See if it will kick over.* [~ + *obj* + *over*]: *Kick the engine over.* [~ + *over* + *obj*]: *Kick over the engine.* **14. kick up, a.** [~ + *up* + *obj*] to stir up: *spending more time kicking up trouble than working.* **b.** [*no obj*] to become evident or active: *My rheumatism is kicking up again.* **—*n.*** [*count*] **15.** the act of kicking. **16.** an objection or complaint: *What's your kick?* **17. a.** a thrill; excitement that gives pleasure: *What a kick it is to see you again!* **b.** a strong but temporary interest, often an activity: *Photography is his latest kick.* **18.** a stimulating or intoxicating quality in alcoholic drink or certain drugs: *a strong kick to this wine.* **19.** a recoil, as of a gun. **—kick′er,** *n.* [*count*]

kick•back (kik′bak′) /'kɪk,bæk/ *n.* [*count*] a portion of one's income or profit given to someone as payment for having made the income possible, esp. as in a dishonest or illegal scheme involving the use of political or professional influence.

kick•off or **kick-off** (kik′ôf′, -of′) /'kɪk,ɔf, -,ɒf/ *n.* [*count*] **1.** a kick that puts the ball into play in football or soccer. **2.** start; beginning: *Tonight is the campaign kick-off.*

kick•stand (kik′stand′) /'kɪk,stænd/ *n.* [*count*] a device for supporting a bicycle or motorcycle when not in use, usually a bar on a spring that can be swung up toward the rear or down to rest on the ground.

kick•y (kik′ē) /'kɪkiy/ *adj.,* **-i•er, -i•est.** *Slang.* pleasurably amusing or exciting: *a kicky dance club.*

kid[1] (kid) /kɪd/ *n.* **1.** [*count*] *Informal.* **a.** a child or young person. **b.** This word is used as a familiar form of address: *"Hey kid, come here," he yelled.* **2.** [*count*] a young goat. **3.** [*noncount*] leather made from the skin of a kid or goat. **—*adj.*** [*before a noun*] **4.** made of kidskin. **5.** *Informal.* younger: *my kid sister.*

kid[2] (kid) /kɪd/ *v.,* **kid•ded, kid•ding.** *Informal.* **1.** to talk or deal jokingly with; tease; jest with: [*no obj*]: *We were just kidding; we didn't mean those things we said about you.* [~ + *obj*]: *We were just kidding you about your clothes.* **2.** to fool; deceive: [~ + *obj*]: *You're not kidding me this time, it's for real, isn't it?* [*no obj*]: *Stop kidding around and tell me the truth.* **—kid′der,** *n.* [*count*]

kid•die or **kid•dy** (kid′ē) /'kɪdiy/ *n.* [*count*], *pl.* **-dies.** *Informal.* a child; youngster; tot.

kid•nap (kid′nap) /'kɪdnæp/ *v.* [~ + *obj*], **-napped** or **-naped, -nap•ping** or **-nap•ing.** to carry off (a person) by force or trickery, esp. for use as a hostage or to get money; abduct. **—kid′nap•per, kid′nap•er,** *n.* [*count*]

kid•ney (kid′nē) /'kɪdniy/ *n.* [*count*], *pl.* **-neys.** one of a pair of organs in the rear of the upper abdomen that filter waste from the blood, produce uric acid or urea, and maintain water balance in the body.

kid′ney bean′, *n.* [*count*] **1.** a bean plant grown in many varieties for its seeds and pods which can be eaten. **2.** its mature seed, esp. the dark red, kidney-shaped seed of some varieties.

kid′ney stone′, *n.* [*count*] a stony mineral mass formed abnormally in the kidney.

kiel•ba•sa (kil bä′sə, kēl-) /kɪl'bɑsə, kiyl-/ *n., pl.* **-sas, -sy** (-sē) /-siy/. a smoked sausage flavored with garlic: [*noncount*]: *served us kielbasa.* [*count*]: *We had two kielbasas.*

kill (kil) /kɪl/ *v.* **1.** to deprive of life; cause the death of; cause to die; slay: [~ + *obj*]: *soldiers killing the enemy.* [*no obj*]: *had to kill or be killed.* **2.** [~ + *obj*] to destroy; do away with; extinguish: *His negative response killed our hopes.* **3.** [~ + *obj*] to cause (time) to pass with a minimum of boredom: *killed time by reading a novel.* **4.** *Informal.* to overcome completely; produce an effect that is overwhelming: [~ + *obj*]: *That comedian just kills me.* [*no obj*]: *dressed to kill.* **5.** [~ + *obj*] *Informal.* to cause distress, pain, discomfort, or exhaustion to: *My feet are killing me.* **6.** [~ + *obj*] *Informal.* to consume completely: *They killed a bottle of bourbon.* **7.** [~ + *obj*] to cancel publication of (a word, item, etc.) in something written; delete or remove (something typed or entered into a computer): *killed the last few sentences of his essay.* **8.** [~ + *obj*] to defeat or veto (a legislative bill, etc.): *The bill was killed before it even got to the floor of the Senate.* **9.** [~ + *obj*] to turn off; switch off: *Kill the engine.* **10.** [~ + *obj*] to hit (a tennis ball, volleyball, etc.) with such force that it cannot be returned. **11. kill off,** to destroy completely: [~ + *off* + *obj*]: *to kill off an infestation of termites.* [~ + *obj* + *off*]: *to kill the termites off.* **—*n.*** [*count*] **12.** [*usually singular*] the act of killing, esp. game. **13.** [*usually singular*] an animal or animals killed. **—kill′er,** *n.* [*count*]

kill•deer (kil′dēr′) /'kɪl,dɪər/ *n.* [*count*], *pl.* **-deers, -deer.** a common bird, a plover, having two black bands around the upper breast.

kill′er whale′, *n.* [*count*] a large, black-and-white whale that feeds chiefly on fish.

kill•ing (kil′ing) /'kɪlɪŋ/ *n.* **1.** the act of one that kills: [*noncount*]: *Killing is frowned on in most cultures.* [*count*]: *two gangland-style killings.* **2.** [*count*] a quick and unusually large profit or financial gain: *They made quite a killing on that last deal.* **—*adj.*** **3.** [*before a noun*] fatal or destructive: *striking with killing force.* **4.** exhausting: *a killing pace.*

kill′-joy′ or **kill′joy′,** *n.* [*count*] a person who spoils the joy or pleasure of others; spoilsport.

kiln (kil, kiln) /kɪl, kɪln/ *n.* [*count*] a furnace or oven for burning, baking, or drying something, esp. one for pottery or for bricks.

ki•lo (kē′lō) /'kiylow/ *n.* [*count*], *pl.* **-los.** a kilogram.

kilo-, *prefix. kilo-* is attached to quantities and means "thousand": *kilo-* + *liter* → *kiloliter (= one thousand liters); kilo-* + *watt* → *kilowatt (= one thousand watts).*

kil•o•gram (kil′ə gram′) /'kɪlə,græm/ *n.* [*count*] a unit of mass equal to 1000 grams or approximately 2.2 pounds; the base unit of mass. *Abbr.:* kg Also, *esp. Brit.,* **kil′o•gramme′.**

kil•o•hertz (kil′ə hûrts′) /'kɪlə,hɜrts/ *n.* [*count*], *pl.* **-hertz, -hertz•es.** a unit of frequency equal to 1000 cycles per second. *Abbr.:* kHz Formerly, **kilocycle.**

kil•o•me•ter (ki lom′i tər, kil′ə mē′-) /kɪ'lɒmɪtər, 'kɪlə,miy-/ *n.* [*count*] a unit of length, the common measure of distances, equal to 1000 meters (3280.8 feet or 0.621 mile). *Abbr.:* km Also, *esp. Brit.,* **kil′o•me′tre.** See -METER-.

kil•o•ton (kil′ə tun′) /'kɪlə,tʌn/ *n.* [*count*] **1.** a unit of weight equal to 1000 tons. **2.** an explosive force equal to that of 1000 tons of TNT.

kil•o•watt (kil′ə wot′) /'kɪlə,wɒt/ *n.* [*count*] a unit of power equal to 1000 watts. *Abbr.:* kW, kw

kilt (kilt) /kɪlt/ *n.* [*count*] **1.** a knee-length plaid skirt with folds, worn by Scotsmen in the Highlands or in some military regiments **2.** a skirt modeled on this.

kil•ter (kil′tər) /'kɪltər/ *n.* [*noncount*] good condition; order: *The engine was out of kilter.*

ki•mo•no (kə mō′nə, -nō) /kə'mownə, -now/ *n.* [*count*], *pl.* **-nos. 1.** a loose, wide-sleeved Japanese robe, fastened at the waist with a broad sash. **2.** a loose dressing gown, esp. for women.

kin (kin) /kɪn/ *n.* [*plural*] all of a person's relatives.

kind[1] (kīnd) /kaynd/ *adj.,* **-er, -est. 1.** having a good nature or way of behaving; compassionate: *a kind, helpful man.* [*It + be + ~ + of + obj* (+ *to + verb*)]: *It was kind of her to visit him in the hospital.* **2.** considerate or helpful; humane: *to be kind to animals.*

kind[2] (kīnd) /kaynd/ *n.* **1.** [*count*] a class or group of animals, people, objects, etc., that are classified on the basis of traits, appearance, or characteristics that they have in common; category; variety; sort: *What kind of dog is that?* **2.** [*noncount*] nature or character: *to differ in degree rather than kind.* **3.** [*count; a + ~ + of + noun*] a more or less adequate example of something: *The vines formed a kind of roof.* **—*Idiom.* 4. in kind, a.** with something of the same kind as that received: *She answered his insults in kind (= by giving back insults).* **b.** in goods, commodities, or services rather than money: *payment in kind.* **5. kind of,** *Informal.* to some extent; somewhat; rather: *It's kind of dark in here.* **6. of a kind,** of the same class, nature, character, etc.: *They were two of a kind.*

kin•der•gar•ten (kin′dər gär′tn, -dn) /ˈkɪndərˌgɑrtn̩, -dn̩/ *n.* a class or school for young children, usually five-year-olds: [*count*]: *The district consolidated its kindergartens under one roof.* [*noncount*]: *started kindergarten when she was five.* **—kin•der•gart•ner, kin•der•gar•ten•er** (kin′dər gärt′nər, -gärd′-) /ˈkɪndərˌgɑrtnər, -ˌgɑrd-/ *n.* [*count*]

kind•heart•ed (kīnd′här′tid) /ˈkaynd'hɑrtɪd/ *adj.* having or showing sympathy or kindness. **—kind′heart′ed•ly,** *adv.* **—kind′heart′ed•ness,** *n.* [*noncount*]

kin•dle (kin′dl) /ˈkɪndl̩/ *v.,* **-dled, -dling. 1.** to start (a fire); cause (a flame or blaze) to begin burning: [*~ + obj*]: *to kindle a fire.* [*no obj*]: *The wood did not kindle easily.* **2.** to (cause to) become aroused, excited, animated, or stirred up: [*~ + obj*]: *The promise of a bonus kindled their interest.* [*no obj*]: *Their interest kindled and grew.*

kin•dling (kind′ling) /ˈkɪndlɪŋ/ *n.* [*noncount*] materials used in lighting a fire.

kind•ly (kīnd′lē) /ˈkayndliy/ *adj.,* **-li•er, -li•est,** *adv.* **—*adj.*** [*usually before a noun*] **1.** having, showing, or proceeding from a kind disposition: *kindly people.* **—*adv.* 2.** in a kind manner. **3.** cordially or heartily: *We thank you kindly.* **4.** This word is used in requests to mean "please": *Kindly close the door.* **5.** with liking; favorably: *to take kindly to an idea.* **—kind′li•ness,** *n.* [*noncount*]

kind•ness (kīnd′nis) /ˈkayndnɪs/ *n.* **1.** [*noncount*] the state or quality of being kind; kind behavior: *Show a little kindness.* **2.** [*count*] a kind act; favor: *Please, do me a kindness and leave.*

kin•dred (kin′drid) /ˈkɪndrɪd/ *n.* [*noncount*] **1.** a person's relatives thought of as a group; kin; kinfolk. **2.** relationship by birth or descent; kinship. **—*adj.* 3.** closely similar: *kindred spirits.*

ki•net•ic (ki net′ik, kī-) /kɪˈnɛtɪk, kay-/ *adj.* **1.** of, related to, or caused by motion: *kinetic energy.* **—*n.* 2. kinetics,** [*noncount; used with a singular verb*] the science or study of motion or movement.

kin•folk (kin′fōk′) /ˈkɪnˌfowk/ *n.* [*plural; used with a plural verb*] relatives; kin. Sometimes, **kin′folks′.**

king (king) /kɪŋ/ *n.* [*count*] **1.** a male sovereign who usually has inherited the position from his parents: *the king of Sweden.* [*used as a title*]: *King Henry VIII ruled England in the 16th century.* **2.** a person or thing best in its class: *The king of the jungle is supposed to be the lion.* **3.** a playing card with a picture of a king. **4.** the chief chess piece of each color, whose capture is the object of the game. **5.** a checker piece that has been moved entirely across the board and has been crowned, thus allowing it to be moved in any direction. **—king′ly,** *adj.,* **-li•er, -li•est,** *adv.* **—king′ship,** *n.* [*noncount*]

king•dom (king′dəm) /ˈkɪŋdəm/ *n.* [*count*] **1.** a state or government having a king or queen as its head. **2.** anything making up an area or domain (as of study, thought, etc.): *the kingdom of thought.* **3.** any of one of the three broad divisions of natural objects: *the animal, vegetable, and mineral kingdoms.*

king•fish•er (king′fish′ər) /ˈkɪŋˌfɪʃər/ *n.* [*count*] a brightly colored bird found worldwide, with a large head and big bill.

king•pin (king′pin′) /ˈkɪŋˌpɪn/ *n.* [*count*] **1.** *Informal.* a person or thing of chief importance: *He's the kingpin of the entire organization.* **2.** the central pin in bowling.

king′-size′ or **king′-sized′,** *adj.* **1.** larger or longer than the usual size: *king-size cigarettes.* **2.** (of a bed) extra large, usually 76–78 in. (193–198 cm) wide and 80–84 in. (203–213 cm) long; of or for a bed with such measurements: *king-size sheets.*

kink (kingk) /kɪŋk/ *n.* [*count*] **1.** a twist or curl, as in a thread, rope, wire, or hair: *a kink in the telephone cord.* **2.** a muscular stiffness or soreness: *He woke up with a kink in his neck.* **3.** a flaw or imperfection likely to get in the way of the smooth operation of something, as a machine or plan: *We have to iron out a few kinks in the plan.* **—*v.* 4.** to (cause to) form a kink or kinks, as a rope: [*no obj*]: *The string seems to kink just when the kite is up in the air.* [*~ + obj*]: *to kink a wire.*

kin•ship (kin′ship) /ˈkɪnʃɪp/ *n.* [*noncount*] **1.** the state of being kin: *a close feeling of kinship with his ancestors.* **2.** relationship because of similar nature, qualities, or characteristics; affinity; likeness: *felt kinship with fellow sufferers.*

kins•man or **-wom•an** (kinz′mən) or (-wo͝om′ən) /ˈkɪnzmən/ or /-ˌwʊmən/ *n.* [*count*], *pl.* **-men** or **-wom•en. 1.** a relative. **2.** a person of the same nationality or ethnic group.

ki•osk (kē′osk, kē osk′) /ˈkiyɒsk, kiyˈɒsk/ *n.* [*count*] **1.** a small building or structure open on one or more sides, used as a newsstand, refreshment stand, etc. **2.** a thick, columnlike structure on which notices and advertisements are posted. **3.** *Brit.* a telephone booth.

kip•per (kip′ər) /ˈkɪpər/ *n.* [*count*] **1.** a fish, esp. a herring, that has been kippered. **—*v.*** [*~ + obj*] **2.** to prepare or cure fish by splitting, salting, drying, and smoking.

kis•met (kiz′mit, -met, kis′-) /ˈkɪzmɪt, -mɛt, ˈkɪs-/ *n.* [*noncount*] fate; destiny.

kiss (kis) /kɪs/ *v.* **1.** to touch or press with the lips slightly pushed out, to show affection, greeting, reverence, etc.: [*~ + obj*]: *She kissed him.* [*no obj*]: *They kissed briefly.* **2.** [*~ + obj*] to touch gently or lightly: *The breeze kissed her face.* **3.** [*~ + obj*] to put, bring, take, or express by kissing: *She kissed the baby's tears away.* **4. kiss off,** *Slang.* to reject or dismiss openly and without feeling: [*~ + off + obj*]: *kissed off a promising job.* [*~ + obj + off*]: *just kissed it off.* **—*n.*** [*count*] **5.** an act or instance of kissing: *a quick kiss for luck.* **6.** a slight touch or contact: *the kiss of the sunlight.* **—*Idiom.* 7. blow** or **throw a kiss,** to indicate a kiss from a distance by kissing one's own fingertips and moving the hand forward toward the person greeted, usually used to signal farewell: *She blew a kiss to the crowd.* **8. kiss of death,** [*usually: the + ~*] something that causes or is thought to cause destruction, failure, disaster, or the like: *Hiring him was the kiss of death for this project.* **—kiss′a•ble,** *adj.*

kiss′-and-tell′, *adj.* [*before a noun*] disclosing secrets or private matters to the public; gossipy: *a kiss-and-tell Hollywood memoir.*

kiss•er (kis′ər) /ˈkɪsər/ *n.* [*count*] **1.** a person who kisses. **2.** *Slang.* **a.** the face. **b.** the mouth.

kit[1] (kit) /kɪt/ *n., v.,* **kit•ted, kit•ting. —*n.* 1.** [*count*] a set of tools, supplies, or materials used for a specific purpose: *a first-aid kit.* **2.** [*count*] a case or container for these. **3.** [*count*] a set of materials or parts from which something can be assembled: *a model airplane kit.* **4.** [*noncount*] *Chiefly Brit.* gear: *battle kit.* **—*v.* 5. kit out,**[*no obj*] *Chiefly Brit.* to outfit or equip. **—*Idiom.* 6. the whole kit and caboodle,** all the persons or things concerned: *bought the whole kit and caboodle for $500.*

kit[2] (kit) /kɪt/ *n.* [*count*] **1.** a kitten. **2.** a young fox, beaver, or other small animal that has fur.

kitch•en (kich′ən) /ˈkɪtʃən/ *n.* [*count*] **1.** a room or place equipped for cooking or preparing food, washing dishes, and the like. See illustration at APARTMENT. **—*adj.*** [*before a noun*] **2.** of or resembling a language used for communication between employers and employees who do not speak the same language: *knew enough kitchen English to understand simple orders.*

kitch•en•ette (kich′ə net′) /ˌkɪtʃəˈnɛt/ *n.* [*count*] a small, compact kitchen.

kitch′en police′, *n.* [*plural*] See KP.

kite (kīt) /kayt/ *n., v.,* **kit•ed, kit•ing. —*n.*** [*count*] **1.** a light frame of wood or plastic, covered with some thin material, as paper, cloth, or plastic, to be flown in the wind at the end of a long string. **2.** a slim, graceful bird (a hawk) with long, pointed wings and usually a notched or forked tail. **—*v.*** [*~ + obj*] **3.** to write (a bad check) to obtain money or credit.

kith (kith) /kɪθ/ *n.* **—*Idiom.* kith and kin,** [*plural*] relatives, or acquaintances and relatives together.

kitsch (kich) /kɪtʃ/ *n.* [*noncount*] something of overly sentimental style, created to appeal to popular or unselective taste: *The lamp in the shape of a mermaid was definitely kitsch.* —**kitsch′y,** *adj.,* **-i•er, -i•est.**

kit•ten (kit′n) /ˈkɪtn̩/ *n.* [*count*] a young cat. —**kit′ten•ish,** *adj.*

kit•ty[1] (kit′ē) /ˈkɪtiy/ *n., pl.* **-ties. 1.** [*count*] a kitten. **2.** [*proper noun*] a pet name for a cat.

kit•ty[2] (kit′ē) /ˈkɪtiy/ *n.* [*count*], *pl.* **-ties. 1.** a pool or reserve of money, often collected from a number of people or sources and meant for a particular purpose: *a kitty for the widow's fund.* **2.** (in poker) the pot.

kit′ty-cor′nered or **kit′ty-cor′ner,** *adj., adv.* CATERCORNERED.

ki•wi (kē′wē) /ˈkiywiy/ *n.* [*count*], *pl.* **-wis. 1.** a bird like an ostrich that cannot fly and that is active during the night. **2.** Also called **ki′wi•fruit′** (-frōōt′) /-ˌfruwt/. the egg-sized berry of the Chinese gooseberry, having fuzzy brownish skin and tasty green flesh. **3.** *Informal.* a New Zealander.

Kleen•ex (klē′neks) /ˈkliynɛks/ *pl.* **-ex•es.** *Trademark.* thin soft paper used in place of a handkerchief: [*noncount*]: *went through a whole box of Kleenex.* [*count*]: *There are some wadded-up Kleenexes to be thrown away.*

klep•to•ma•ni•a (klep′tə mā′nē ə, -mān′yə) /ˌklɛptəˈmeyniyə, -ˈmeynyə/ *n.* [*noncount*] an uncontrollable desire to steal things, without regard for need or the monetary value of the object. —**klep•to•ma•ni•ac** (klep′tə mā′nē ak′) /ˌklɛptəˈmeyniyˌæk/ *n.* [*count*], *adj.*

kludge (klōōj) /kluwdʒ/ *n.* [*count*] *Slang.* a poorly designed or patched together solution to a problem in computer hardware or software.

klutz (kluts) /klʌts/ *n.* [*count*] *Slang.* a clumsy person. —**klutz′y,** *adj.,* **-i•er, -i•est.** —**klutz′i•ness,** *n.* [*noncount*]

km, an abbreviation of: kilometer.

kn, an abbreviation of: knot.

knack (nak) /næk/ *n.* [*count; usually singular*] a special skill, talent, or ability: *a knack for making clothes.*

knack•wurst (näk′wûrst) /ˈnɑkwɜrst/ also **knock•wurst,** *n.* a short, thick, highly seasoned sausage: [*noncount*]: *He ordered knackwurst for lunch.* [*count*]: *See if the knackwursts are cooked yet.*

knap•sack (nap′sak′) /ˈnæpˌsæk/ *n.* [*count*] a canvas, nylon, or leather bag for clothes or other supplies, carried on the back by soldiers, hikers, etc.

knave (nāv) /neyv/ *n.* [*count*] **1.** an untrustworthy or dishonest person. **2.** (in cards) the jack. —**knav′ish,** *adj.*

knav•er•y (nā′və rē) /ˈneyvəriy/ *n., pl.* **-er•ies. 1.** [*noncount*] action or practice characteristic of a knave, as dishonest dealing; trickery. **2.** [*count*] a knavish act or practice.

knead (nēd) /niyd/ *v.* [~ + *obj*] **1.** to make (dough, clay, etc.) into a uniform mixture by pressing, folding, and stretching. **2.** to press, stretch, or move by similar movements: *The masseur kneaded his client's sore shoulder.* —**knead′er,** *n.* [*count*]

knee (nē) /niy/ *n., v.,* **kneed, knee•ing.** —*n.* [*count*] **1.** the joint of the human leg between the thigh and the lower leg. **2.** the area of the leg between this joint and the hip when sitting down: *bounced her little nephew on her knee.* **3.** the part of a garment covering the knee: *grass stains on the knees of my trousers.* —*v.* [~ + *obj*] **4.** to strike with the knee: *kneed his attacker in the stomach.* —***Idiom.* 5. bring someone to his** or **her knees,** to force someone to do one's will. **6. on** or **to one's knees,** kneeling: *fell to his knees in prayer.*

knee•cap (nē′kap′) /ˈniyˌkæp/ *n., v.,* **-capped, -cap•ping.** —*n.* [*count*] **1.** the patella, the bone that is in front of the knee and protects it. —*v.* [~ + *obj*] **2.** to cripple (a person) by shooting in the knee.

knee′-deep′, *adj.* **1.** reaching the knees: *knee-deep mud.* **2.** [*be* + ~] covered up to the knees: *We were knee-deep in the river.* **3.** [*be* + ~] deeply involved: *was knee-deep in debt.*

kneel (nēl) /niyl/ *v.* [*no obj*], **knelt** (nelt) /nɛlt/ or **kneeled, kneel•ing.** to go down or rest on the knees or a knee: *She knelt down and began to pray.*

knell (nel) /nɛl/ *n.* [*count*] **1.** the sound made by a bell rung slowly, esp. for a death or a funeral. **2.** an indication of the end or failure of something: *The death knell of Western Communism was the collapse of the Berlin Wall.* —*v.* **3.** [*no obj*] (of a bell) to sound, as at a funeral. **4.** [*no obj*] to give forth a mournful or warning sound. **5.** [~ + *obj*] to proclaim or summon by or as if by a bell.

knelt (nelt) /nɛlt/ *v.* a pt. and pp. of KNEEL.

knew (nōō, nyōō) /nuw, nyuw/ *v.* pt. of KNOW.

knick•ers (nik′ərz) /ˈnɪkərz/ *n.* [*plural*] **1.** loose-fitting short trousers gathered in to fit tightly at the knees. **2.** *Brit.* women's underpants.

knick•knack (nik′nak′) /ˈnɪkˌnæk/ *n.* [*count*] a small item used mostly for ornament; a piece of bric-a-brac.

knife (nīf) /nayf/ *n., pl.* **knives** (nīvz) /nayvz/ *v.,* **knifed, knif•ing.** —*n.* [*count*] **1.** an instrument for cutting, made of a sharp-edged metal blade fitted with a handle: *steak knives.* See illustration at RESTAURANT. **2.** a knifelike weapon; *The man was dead, with a knife sticking out of him.* —*v.* **3.** [~ + *obj*] to cut, stab, etc., with a knife: *had been knifed and left to die.* **4.** [*no obj*] to move through something with or as if with a knife: *The ship knifed through the water.* —***Idiom.* 5. knife (someone) in the back,** to attempt to defeat, weaken, or ruin someone in a secret or dishonest way.

knight (nīt) /nayt/ *n.* [*count*] **1.** (in the Middle Ages) a mounted soldier serving under a lord or king and having an honorable rank. **2.** a man who is given a title of knighthood by a king, in Great Britain ranking next below a baronet. **3.** a member of any order or association that designates its members as knights: *the Knights of Columbus.* **4.** a chess piece shaped like a horse's head. —*v.* [~ + *obj*] **5.** to dub or make (a man) a knight: *He was knighted by King Arthur himself.*

knight•hood (nīt′hŏŏd′) /ˈnaytˌhʊd/ *n.* **1.** the rank or title of a knight: [*noncount*]: *conferred knighthood upon him.* [*count*]: *each received a knighthood.* **2.** [*noncount*] the state of being a knight: *when knighthood was in flower.*

knight•ly (nīt′lē) /ˈnaytliy/ *adj.* of, belonging to, or characteristic of a knight. —**knight′li•ness,** *n.* [*noncount*]

knish (knish) /knɪʃ/ *n.* [*count*] a baked pastry filled usually with potatoes, sausage, or meat.

knit (nit) /nɪt/ *v.,* **knit•ted** or **knit, knit•ting,** *n.* —*v.* **1.** to make (a garment, fabric, etc.) by joining or interlocking loops of yarn by hand with knitting needles or by machine: [~ + *obj*]: *knitted her own sweater.* [~ + *obj* + *obj*]: *She knit me a beautiful sweater.* [*no obj*]: *sat knitting quietly.* **2.** to cause to contract and be shaped into folds or wrinkles: [~ + *obj*]: *to knit one's brow (= to frown) in concentration.* [*no obj*]: *Her brows knit as she concentrated.* **3.** to (cause to) become closely and firmly joined together; grow together: [*no obj*]: *The broken bones would knit in about a month.* [~ + *obj*]: *a tightly knit group of professionals.* —*n.* [*count*] **4.** a fabric or garment produced by knitting: *winter knits.* —**knit′ter,** *n.* [*count*]

knit•ting (nit′ing) /ˈnɪtɪŋ/ *n.* [*noncount*] **1.** something being knitted. **2.** the act of knitting.

knit•wear (nit′wâr′) /ˈnɪtˌwɛər/ *n.* [*noncount*] clothing made of knitted fabric.

knob (nob) /nɒb/ *n.* [*count*] **1.** a part, usually rounded, that forms a handle, as on a door or drawer, or forms a control device, as on a radio. **2.** a rounded lump sticking out on the surface or at the end of something.

knock (nok) /nɒk/ *v.* **1.** [*no obj*] to strike a blow that makes noise, as in seeking admittance, calling attention, or giving a signal: *She knocked loudly at the door.* **2.** to give a forceful blow to; strike: [*no obj*]: *He knocked against the table and fell.* [~ + *obj*]: *The muggers knocked him senseless.* **3.** [*no obj*] to make a banging noise: *The car's engine is knocking.* **4.** [~ + *obj*] to make by striking a blow or blows: *to knock a hole in the wall.* **5.** [~ + *obj*] *Informal.* to criticize or find fault with: *Don't knock that new shampoo until you have tried it.* **6. knock around** or **about, a.** [*no obj*] to wander, esp. living briefly in one place after another. **b.** to mistreat; manhandle; beat: [~ + *around* + *obj*]: *knocking around the suspect.* [~ + *obj* + *around*]: *knocked the suspect around.* **7. knock down, a.** to cause to fall by striking: [~ + *obj* + *down*]: *The police knocked him down.* [~ + *down* + *obj*]: *Lightning knocked down the tree.* **b.** to (cause to) be dismantled for ease of handling: [*no obj*]: *The tent knocks down quickly and easily.* [~ + *down* + *obj*]: *They knocked down the crate and unpacked it.* [~ + *obj* + *down*]: *They knocked it down.* **c.** to lower the price of: [~ + *obj* + *down*]: *to knock the price down by $500.* [~ + *down* + *obj*]: *to knock down the price by $500.* **8. knock off, a.** to cease or stop an activity, esp. the day's work: [*no obj*]: *The boss let us knock off a little early today.* [~ + *off* + *obj*]: *We knocked off work a little early today.* **b.** Also, **knock out.** *Informal.* to do, produce, or finish quickly or with ease: [~ + *off* + *obj*]: *to knock off a couple of projects a day.* [~ + *obj* + *off*]: *He* *knocked two chapters off by mid morning.* **c.** *Slang.* to murder: [~ + *obj* + *off*]: *The mob knocked him off.* [~ + *off* + *obj*]: *The mob knocks off anyone who gets in their way.* **d.** to reduce a price by the amount of: [~ + *off* + *obj*]: *Knock off $500 and I'll buy it.* [~ + *obj* + *off*]: *Knock $500 off.* **e.** *Slang.* to defeat: [~ + *off* + *obj*]: *Our team knocked off our rivals in the first match.* [~ + *obj* + *off*]: *We knocked them off in the first match.* **f.** *Slang.* to rob; steal or burglarize: [~ + *off* + *obj*]: *The thieves knocked off a few of the richer houses.* [~ + *obj* + *off*]: *They knocked this one off first.* **9. knock out, a.** to defeat (an opponent) in a boxing match by striking such a blow that the opponent is unable to rise within the specified time: [~ + *out* + *obj*]: *knocked out the challenger in the fourth round.* [~ + *obj* + *out*]: *knocked him out in the fourth round.* **b.** to make unconscious: [~ + *out* + *obj*]: *The gas knocked out the entire household.* [~ + *obj* + *out*]: *The pills knocked him out at once.* **c.** to make tired or exhausted: [~ + *obj* + *out*]: *This work knocks me out.* [~ + *out* + *obj*]: *This work could knock out anyone.* **d.** to damage or destroy: [~ + *out* + *obj*]: *The storm knocked out the power lines.* [~ + *obj* + *out*]: *The hurricane knocked the electricity out.* **10. knock over, a.** to strike (someone or something) from a standing position to one that is down: [~ + *over* + *obj*]: *He knocked over the glasses as he squeezed by the table.* [~ + *obj* + *over*]: *He knocked my glass over as he squeezed by.* **b.** *Slang.* to rob, burglarize, or hijack: [~ + *over* + *obj*]: *The gang knocked over a bank.* [~ + *obj* + *over*]: *The gang knocked it over and fled.* **11. knock up, a.** *Slang* (*vulgar*). to make pregnant. **b.** [~ + *obj* + *up*] *Brit.* to wake up; rouse: *Knock them up when you're ready to leave.* **—***n.* **12.** [*count*] an act or instance of knocking: *a knock on the head.* **13.** [*count*] *Informal.* negative criticism: *The knock on him is that he can't handle stress.* **14.** [*noncount*] the noise resulting from faulty firing of an engine: *the gasoline that takes care of engine knock.* **—*Idiom.*** **15. knock it off,** to cease doing or saying something.

knock•er (nok′ər) /ˈnɒkər/ *n.* [*count*] **1.** someone or something that knocks. **2.** a hinged knob, bar, etc., on a door, to use for knocking.

knock′-knee′, *n.* **knock-knees,** [*plural*] a condition in which the legs of a person curve inward at the knees. —**knock′-kneed′,** *adj.*

knock•out (nok′out′) /ˈnɒkˌawt/ *n.* [*count*] **1.** an act or instance of knocking out. **2.** the state or fact of being knocked out. **3.** *Informal.* a person or thing overwhelmingly attractive, appealing, or successful: *That car is a knockout.* **—***adj.* [*before a noun*] **4.** serving to knock out: *a knockout punch.*

knock•wurst (nok′wûrst) /ˈnɒkwɜrst/ *n.* KNACKWURST.

knoll (nōl) /nowl/ *n.* [*count*] a small, rounded hill.

knot (not) /nɒt/ *n., v.,* **knot•ted, knot•ting.** **—***n.* [*count*] **1.** a tying tightly together of the two ends of a cord, rope, or the like into a knob: *to tie a knot securely.* **2.** a lump of something formed by tying into this shape: *a knot of hair on the top of her head.* **3.** a tangled mass; snarl: *combed out the knots in the dog's fur.* **4.** a group or cluster of persons or things: *a knot of spectators.* **5.** the hard, cross-grained mass of wood at the place where a branch joins a tree trunk; a part of this mass showing in a piece of lumber. **6.** a cramping, as of a muscle. **7. a.** a unit of speed equal to one nautical mile or about 1.15 statute miles per hour. **b.** a nautical mile. **8.** a bond or tie: *the knot of matrimony.* **—***v.* **9.** to (cause to) become tied or tangled in a knot: [~ + *obj*]: *He knotted the rope.* [*no obj*]: *The rope is too wet to knot easily.* **10.** to (cause to) have a feeling of tension or nervousness (in): [*no obj*]: *His stomach knotted in fear.* [~ + *obj*]: *The excitement knotted his stomach.*

knot•hole (not′hōl′) /ˈnɒtˌhowl/ *n.* [*count*] a hole in a plank formed by the falling out of a knot or a portion of a knot.

knot•ty (not′ē) /ˈnɒtiy/ *adj.,* **-ti•er, -ti•est.** **1.** having or full of knots: *knotty wood.* **2.** very involved, intricate, or difficult: *a knotty problem.*

know (nō) /now/ *v.,* **knew** (no͞o, nyo͞o) /nuw, nyuw/ **known** (nōn) /nown/ **know•ing,** *n.* **—***v.* [*not: be* + *~-ing*] **1.** to perceive or understand as fact or truth; to have in the mind clearly and with certainty: [~ + *obj*]: *I don't know your name.* [~ + *(that) clause*]: *She knows that he is the crook.* [~ + *about* + *obj*]: *She knows about your bad habits.* **2.** [~ + *obj*] to have (something) fixed in the mind or memory: *to know a poem by heart.* **3.** [~ + *obj*] to be acquainted or familiar with: *I know the mayor well. I knew my way around town fairly well.* **4.** [~ + *how clause*] to understand from experience or practice: *knows how to make gingerbread.* **5.** [~ + *obj* + *from* + *obj*] to be able to distinguish: *old enough to know right from wrong* **6.** [~ + *obj*] to recognize: *I'd know her if I saw her again.* **7.** [~ + *obj*] (of a language) to be able to speak: *He knows Swahili, Spanish, and Swedish.* **8. know of,** [~ + *of* + *obj*] to have heard about: *Do you know of any computer stores in this neighborhood?* **—*Idiom.*** **9. in the know,** in possession of special knowledge or information; well-informed. —**know′a•ble,** *adj.*

know′-how′, *n.* [*noncount*] knowledge of how to do something; expertise: *financial know-how; electronics know-how.*

know•ing (nō′ing) /ˈnowɪŋ/ *adj.* **1.** showing shrewd knowledge of secret or private information: *gave me a knowing glance.* **2.** conscious; intentional; deliberate: *a knowing lie.* —**know′ing•ly,** *adv.*

know′-it-all′, *n.* [*count*] a person who acts as though he or she knows everything.

knowl•edge (nol′ij) /ˈnɒlɪdʒ/ *n.* **1.** [*noncount*] acquaintance with facts, truths, or principles in the mind. **2.** [*count; singular; often: a* + ~] familiarity with an area of study, as by study or experience: *His knowledge of Chinese is very good.* **3.** [*noncount*] the sum of what is known; information: *Knowledge of the situation is limited.* **—*Idiom.*** **4. to one's knowledge,** according to the information available to one: *To my knowledge, he never worked here.*

knowl•edge•a•ble or **knowl•edg•a•ble** (nol′i jə bəl) /ˈnɒlɪdʒəbəl/ *adj.* possessing or showing knowledge, insight, or understanding; well-informed; perceptive: *to be knowledgeable about the enemy's tactics.*

knuck•le (nuk′əl) /ˈnʌkəl/ *n., v.,* **-led, -ling.** **—***n.* **1.** [*count*] any joint of a finger, esp. where a finger bends, or where a finger meets the hand. **—***v.* **2. knuckle down,** [*no obj*] **a.** to apply oneself with energy; to work earnestly; become serious. **b.** Also, **knuckle under.** [*no obj*] to admit that one is defeated; to submit; yield: *He won't ever knuckle under to your threats.*

knuck•le•head (nuk′əl hed′) /ˈnʌkəlˌhɛd/ *n.* [*count*] *Informal.* a stupid or foolish person. —**knuck′le•head′ed,** *adj.*

KO (*n.* kā′ō′, kā′ō′; *v.* kā′ō′) / *n.* ˈkeyˈow, ˈkeyˌow; *v.* ˈkeyˈow/ *n., pl.* **KOs** or **KO's,** *v.,* **KO'd, KO'•ing.** **—***n.* **1.** a knockout in boxing: [*count*]: *five KOs to his credit.* [*noncount*]: *winner by KO.* **—***v.* [~ + *obj*] **2.** to knock unconscious in boxing; knock out: *KO'd in one round.* Often, **K.O., k.o.**

ko•a•la (kō ä′lə) /kowˈɑlə/ *n.* [*count*], *pl.* **-las.** a gray-furred, tree-dwelling Australian animal resembling a teddy bear.

kohl•ra•bi (kōl rä′bē, -rab′ē) /kowlˈrɑbiy, -ˈræbiy/ *n., pl.* **-bies.** a cabbage of the mustard family, with a bulblike stem that can be eaten: [*count*]: *two kohlrabies.* [*noncount*]: *a head of kohlrabi.*

ko•la (kō′lə) /ˈkowlə/ *n., pl.* **-las.** [*count*] **1.** an African tree that grows in warm climates, grown for kola nuts. **2.** COLA[1].

ko′la nut′, *n.* [*count*] the large brown seed of the kola tree.

kook (ko͝ok) /kuwk/ *n.* [*count*] *Slang.* an eccentric person. —**kook′y,** *adj.,* **-i•er, -i•est.** —**kook′i•ness,** *n.* [*noncount*]

kook•a•bur•ra (ko͝ok′ə bûr′ə, -bur′ə) /ˈkʊkəˌbɜrə, -ˌbʌrə/ *n.* [*count*], *pl.* **-ras.** an Australian bird of the kingfisher family, having a call that resembles raucous laughter.

ko•peck or **ko•pek** (kō′pek) /ˈkowpɛk/ *n.* [*count*] a monetary unit of the former Soviet Union, equal to 1/100 of the ruble.

Ko•ran (kə rän′, -ran′, kô-, kō-) /kəˈrɑn, -ˈræn, kɔ-, kow-/ *n.* [*proper noun; the* + ~] the sacred text of Islam, divided into 114 chapters, believed by Muslims to be the word of God, dictated to Muhammad by the archangel Gabriel. Often, **Qur'an.** —**Ko•ran′ic,** *adj.*

Ko•re•an (kə rē′ən, kô-, kō-) /kəˈriyən, kɔ-, kow-/ *adj.* **1.** of or relating to either North Korea or South Korea. **2.** of or relating to the language spoken in North Korea or South Korea. **—***n.* **3.** [*count*] a person born or living in North Korea or South Korea. **4.** [*noncount*] the language spoken in North Korea or South Korea.

ko•sher (kō′shər) /ˈkowʃər/ *adj.* **1. a.** fit or allowed to be eaten or used, according to certain laws of Judaism: *kosher food.* **b.** subject to or obeying such laws: *a kosher restaurant.* **2.** *Informal.* proper; obeying the rules; legitimate: *Cheating them wouldn't be kosher.* [*It* + *be* + ~

+ *to* + *verb*]: *It wouldn't be kosher to sneak around behind his back.* **—***v.* [~ + *obj*] **3.** to make kosher.

kow•tow (kou′tou′, -tou′) /ˈkawˈtaw, -ˌtaw/ *v.* **1.** [~ + *to* + *obj*] to act in a subservient way: *kowtowing to one's superiors.* **2.** [*no obj*] to touch the forehead to the ground while kneeling, as an act of worship, respect, etc., esp. in former Chinese custom. **—kow′tow′er,** *n.* [*count*]

KP (kā′pē′) /ˈkeyˈpiy/ *n., pl.* **KPs, KP's**. **1.** [*noncount*] military duty as a kitchen helper: *assigned to KP.* **2.** [*count*] a soldier detailed to work as kitchen help.

Krem•lin (krem′lin) /ˈkrɛmlɪn/ *n.* [*proper noun; the* + ~] **1.** the government of the former Soviet Union or, now, of Russia. **2.** the citadel of Moscow, containing within its walls some of the offices of the former Soviet government and, now, the Russian government.

Krem•lin•ol•o•gy (krem′li nol′ə jē) /ˌkrɛmlɪˈnɒlədʒiy/ *n.* [*noncount*] the study of the government and policies of the former Soviet Union. —**Krem′lin•ol′o•gist,** *n.* [*count*]

kryp•ton (krip′ton) /ˈkrɪptɒn/ *n.* [*noncount*] a gaseous element, present in very small amounts in the atmosphere, that does not react easily with other elements.

KS, an abbreviation of: Kansas.

kt., an abbreviation of: **1.** karat. **2.** kiloton. **3.** knot.

ku•dos (ko͞o′dōz, -dōs, -dos, kyo͞o′-) /ˈkuwdowz, -dows, -dɒs, ˈkyuw-/ *n.* [*noncount; used with a singular verb*] honor; glory; praise: *kudos for a job well done.*

kud•zu (ko͝od′zo͞o) /ˈkʊdzuw/ *n.* [*count*], *pl.* **-zus.** a fast-growing vine of the legume family, planted esp. for animal food and to retain soil.

kum•quat (kum′kwot) /ˈkʌmkwɒt/ *n.* [*count*] **1.** a small, orange-colored citrus fruit with a sweet skin and acid flesh, eaten chiefly as a preserve. **2.** a shrub that bears this fruit.

kung fu (kung′ fo͞o′, ko͝ong′) /ˈkʌŋˈ fuw, ˈkʊŋ/ *n.* [*noncount*] a Chinese style of self-defense or martial art based on the use of smooth movements of the arms and legs.

Ku•wai•ti (ko͞o wā′tē) /kʊˈweytiy/ *n.* [*count*] **1.** a person born or living in Kuwait. **—***adj.* **2.** of or relating to Kuwait.

kvetch (kvech) /kvɛtʃ/ *v., Slang.* [*no obj*] **1.** to complain, esp. continually: *Stop kvetching about things you can't change.* **—***n.* [*count*] **2.** Also, **kvetch′er.** a person who kvetches.

KY or **Ky.,** an abbreviation of: Kentucky.

L, l (el) /ɛl/ *n.* [*count*], *pl.* **Ls** or **L's, ls** or **l's.** the 12th letter of the English alphabet, a consonant.

L, an abbreviation of: **1.** large. **2.** left. **3.** length. **4.** long. **5.** longitude.

L, *Symbol.* (*sometimes l.c.*) the Roman numeral for 50.

l, an abbreviation of: **1.** large. **2.** liter.

L., an abbreviation of: **1.** lady. **2.** lake. **3.** large. **4.** latitude. **5.** left. **6.** Liberal. **7.** low.

l., an abbreviation of: **1.** left. **2.** length. **3.** *pl.* **ll.,** line. **4.** liter.

la (lä) /lɑ/ *n.* [*count*] the musical syllable used for the sixth tone in an ascending scale.

LA, an abbreviation of: Louisiana.

lab (lab) /læb/ *n.* [*count*] laboratory: *biology lab.*

-lab-, *root.* *-lab-* comes from Latin, where it has the meaning "work." This meaning is found in such words as: BELABOR, COLLABORATE, ELABORATE, LABOR, LABORIOUS.

la•bel (lā′bəl) /'leybəl/ *n., v.,* **-beled, -bel•ing** or (*esp. Brit.*) **-belled, -bel•ling.** **—***n.* [*count*] **1.** a slip of paper, cloth, or other material, attached to something to indicate its manufacturer, the kind of thing it is, its ownership, etc. **2.** a descriptive word or phrase: *She wasn't happy with the "yuppie" label they applied to her.* **3.** a word or phrase indicating that what follows belongs in a particular category or classification, as the word *Physics* before a dictionary definition. **4.** a brand or trademark, esp. of a manufacturer of compact discs, tape cassettes, etc. **—***v.* **5.** to mark with a label: [~ + *obj*]: *to label all the shirts according to size.* [~ + *obj* + *obj*]: *The bottle was labeled poison.* **6.** to put in a certain class; classify: [~ + *obj* + *obj*]: *They labeled her an executive assistant. He was labeled a rebel by the town.* [~ + *obj* + *adjective*]: *That teacher was labeled tough by the students.*

la•bi•al (lā′bē əl) /'leybiyəl/ *adj.* **1.** of or relating to the lips. **2.** (of a speech sound) made or pronounced using one or both lips, as the sounds (p), (v), (m), (w), or (o͞o). **—***n.* [*count*] **3.** a labial speech sound, esp. a consonant.

la•bor (lā′bər) /'leybər/ *n.* **1.** [*noncount*] activity to produce something: *Much labor went into making that book.* **2.** [*noncount*] the body of persons doing such activity, esp. those working for wages: *a meeting between labor and management to avoid a strike.* **3.** [*noncount*] physical or mental work, esp. of a hard or tiring kind; toil: *manual labor, like digging ditches.* **4.** [*count*] a job or task done or to be done: *the labors of Hercules.* **5.** the last part of pregnancy, beginning with contractions in the uterus, up to the moment of giving birth: [*count*]: *a difficult labor.* [*noncount*]: *Labor can take hours.* **—***v.* **6.** [*no obj*] to perform labor; work; toil: *laboring in the fields.* **7.** [~ + *for*] to try to achieve something, as a goal; work hard for: *The negotiators labored for peace tirelessly.* **8.** [*no obj*] to move slowly and with effort: *The truck labored up the hill.* **9.** [~ + *under* + *obj*] to continue to believe something that is not true or likely: *to labor under a misapprehension.* **10.** [~ + *obj*] to dwell on at length or in detail: *Don't labor the point.* Compare BELABOR. **—***adj.* [*usually before a noun*] **11.** of or relating to workers, their associations, or working conditions: *labor reforms; labor unions.* Also, *esp. Brit.,* **labour.** See -LAB-.

lab•o•ra•to•ry (lab′rə tôr′ē, -tōr′ē, lab′ər ə-) /'læbrə,tɔriy, -,towriy, 'læbərə-/ *n.* [*count*], *pl.* **-ries.** **1.** a place with equipment to conduct scientific experiments or tests, or in which to manufacture chemicals, medicines, or the like. **2.** a building or room in a school or university with equipment for certain subjects: *a language learning laboratory.* See -LAB-.

La′bor Day′, *n.* [*proper noun*] a legal holiday in the U.S. and Canada observed on the first Monday in September in honor of labor.

la•bored (lā′bərd) /'leybərd/ *adj.* done or made with difficulty: *labored breathing.* See -LAB-.

la•bor•er (lā′bər ər) /'leybərər/ *n.* [*count*] a worker whose work requires bodily strength rather than mental skill or learning.

la•bo•ri•ous (lə bôr′ē əs, -bōr′-) /lə'bɔriyəs, -'bowr-/ *adj.* requiring much work or effort; needing much work; difficult; hard; arduous: *a laborious undertaking.* **—la•bo′ri•ous•ly,** *adv.* See -LAB-.

la•bor•sav•ing or **la•bor-sav•ing** (lā′bər sā′ving) /'ley,bər seyvɪŋ/ *adj.* [*before a noun*] designed to reduce human labor: *The dishwasher is a laborsaving device.*

la′bor un′ion, *n.* [*count*] an organization of wage earners or workers for support and protection, and for dealing as a group with employers.

Lab′ra•dor retriev′er (lab′rə dôr′) /'læbrə,dɔr/ *n.* [*count*] one of a breed of solidly-built retrievers with a short, dense black, yellow, or chocolate coat and a thick tail.

lab•y•rinth (lab′ə rinth) /'læbərɪnθ/ *n.* [*count*] **1.** a complicated combination of paths or passages in which it is difficult to find one's way or to reach the exit: *a labyrinth of small winding streets in the Old Quarter.* **2.** a complicated arrangement or state of things or events: *a labyrinth of government red tape.* **—lab•y•rin•thine** (lab′ə-rin′thin, -thīn) /,læbə'rɪnθɪn, -θayn/ *adj.*

lace (lās) /leys/ *n., v.,* **laced, lac•ing.** **—***n.* **1.** [*noncount*] a netlike fabric of threads made by hand or machine, often used for decoration. **2.** [*count*] a cord or string for holding or drawing together, esp., a shoelace. **—***v.* **3.** to fasten, draw together, or compress by or as if by means of a lace: [~ + *obj*]: *He laced the canopy onto the tent.* [~ + *up* + *obj*]: *She laced up her ice skates.* [~ + *obj* + *up*]: *She laced the skates up.* **4.** [~ + *obj*] to add a small amount of alcoholic liquor or other substance to: *laced the coffee with a little brandy.* **5.** [~ + *into* + *obj*] to attack physically or verbally: *The candidate laced into her opponent.*

lac•er•ate (*v.* las′ə rāt′; *adj.* -ə rāt′, -ər it) / *v.* 'læsə,reyt; *adj.* -ə,reyt, -ərɪt/ *v.* [~ + *obj*], **-at•ed, -at•ing.** **1.** to tear roughly; cut; mangle: *The bull's leg had been lacerated by the barbed wire.* **2.** to distress or torture mentally or emotionally: *His criticism lacerated my heart.* **—lac•er•a•tion** (las′ə rā′shən) /,læsə'reyʃən/ *n.* [*noncount*]: *treatment for laceration.* [*count*]: *He suffered numerous lacerations from the broken glass.*

lace•wing (lās′wing′) /'leys,wɪŋ/ *n.* [*count*] a slender green insect with delicate transparent wings.

lach•ry•mal or **lac•ri•mal** (lak′rə məl) /'lækrəməl/ *adj.* **1.** of, relating to, or characterized by tears. **2.** of, relating to, or having glands that produce tears.

lach•ry•mose (lak′rə mōs′) /'lækrə,mows/ *adj.* **1.** tending to cause tears; mournful: *a lachrymose story.* **2.** often or easily shedding tears; tearful: *lachrymose mourners.*

lack (lak) /læk/ *n.* **1.** absence of something needed or desirable; not enough of something needed or desired: [*noncount*]: *There is no lack of talent on this team.* [*count; usually singular*]: *The team has a lack of skill.* **2.** [*noncount*] something missing or wanted: *felt the lack of a steady income.* **—***v.* [*not: be* + *~-ing;* see LACKING] **3.** [~ + *obj*] to be without; have need of: *You lack common sense.* **4.** [~ + *obj*] to fall short in: *He lacks three votes to win.* **5.** [*no obj*] to be absent or missing: *Nothing lacks but their full agreement.* **6.** [~ + *for* + *obj*] to not have enough of something: *She will never lack for friends.* **—Related Words.** LACK is a noun and a verb, LACKING is an adjective: *A lack of money prevented us from buying a house. We lacked enough money to buy a house. You are lacking in many important skills.*

lack•a•dai•si•cal (lak′ə dā′zi kəl) /,lækə'deyzɪkəl/ *adj.* being without life or spirit; listless: *was lackadaisical about keeping appointments.* **—lack′a•dai′si•cal•ly,** *adv.*

lack•ey (lak′ē) /'lækiy/ *n.* [*count*], *pl.* **-eys.** a follower who obeys orders without questioning; a toady.

lack•ing (lak′ing) /'lækɪŋ/ *adj.* [*be* + ~] **1.** [~ + *in* + *obj*] deficient; not having or not having enough: *was lacking in stamina.* **2.** missing; absent: *Air support was lacking.* **—***prep.* **3.** being without: *Lacking equipment, the scientists gave up.*

lack•lus•ter (lak′lus′tər) /'læk,lʌstər/ *adj.* **1.** lacking sheen; dull: *lackluster eyes.* **2.** lacking liveliness: *a lackluster performance.* Also, *esp. Brit.,* **lack′lus′tre.**

la•con•ic (lə kon′ik) /lə'kɑnɪk/ *adj.* using few words; terse; concise: *His laconic reply to our appeal for help was "Look elsewhere."* **—la•con′i•cal•ly,** *adv.*

lac•quer (lak′ər) /'lækər/ *n.* [*noncount*] **1.** a varnish made of resin and painted or sprayed on a surface for protection or to give it a shiny coating. **—***v.* [~ + *obj*] **2.** to coat with lacquer: *to lacquer the wood.*

lac•ri•mal (lak′rə məl) /'lækrəməl/ *adj.* lachrymal.

la•crosse (lə krôs′, -kros′) /lə'krɔs, -'krɑs/ *n.* [*noncount*] a game in which two 10-member teams attempt to send a small ball into each other's netted goal, each player carrying a stick at the end of which is a netted pocket for catching, carrying, or throwing the ball.

lac•tate (lak′tāt) /ˈlækteyt/ *v.* [*no obj*], **-tat•ed, -tat•ing.** to release milk through special glands. —**lac•ta•tion** (lak tā′shən) /lækˈteyʃən/ *n.* [*noncount*]

lac•tic (lak′tik) /ˈlæktɪk/ *adj.* of or obtained from milk.

lac′tic ac′id, *n.* [*noncount*] a syrupy liquid produced by the fermentation of bacteria in carbohydrate matter.

lac•tose (lak′tōs) /ˈlæktows/ *n.* [*noncount*] **1.** a sugar present in milk that yields glucose and galactose. **2.** a white, crystal-like, sweet commercial form of this compound.

la•cu•na (lə kyōō′nə) /ləˈkyuwnə/ *n.* [*count*], *pl.* **-nae** (-nē) /-niy/ **-nas.** a gap or missing part, as in a manuscript.

lac•y (lā′sē) /ˈleysiy/ *adj.*, **-i•er, -i•est.** of or like lace.

lad (lad) /læd/ *n.* [*count*] a boy or youth; young man.

lad•der (lad′ər) /ˈlædər/ *n.* [*count*] **1.** a structure of wood, metal, or rope having two side pieces between which a series of steps or rungs are set to provide a means of climbing up or down. **2.** a means of rising, as to importance or fame: *the ladder of success.* **3.** a graded series of stages or levels in status: *high on the political ladder.* **4.** *Chiefly Brit.* a run in a stocking.

lad•die (lad′ē) /ˈlædiy/ *n.* [*count*] *Chiefly Scottish.* a lad; boy.

lad•en (lād′n) /ˈleydn̩/ *adj.* [*usually: be + ~ + with + obj*] burdened; heavily loaded: *vines laden with grapes.*

la-di-da (lä′dē dä′) /ˈlɑdiyˈdɑ/ *Informal.* —*adj.* **1.** affected; foppish: *a la-di-da manner.* —*adv.* **2.** in an affected manner: *acting la-di-da.*

la′dies′ man′, *n.* [*count*] a man who tries to please women and to attract their attention.

la′dies′ room′, *n.* [*count*] a public bathroom for women.

lad•ing (lā′ding) /ˈleydɪŋ/ *n.* [*noncount*] the act of loading cargo or the load or cargo so loaded.

la•dle (lād′l) /ˈleydl̩/ *n., v.,* **-dled, -dling.** —*n.* [*count*] **1.** a long-handled utensil with a cup-shaped bowl at the end, used for dipping and pouring liquids. —*v.* [*~ + obj*] **2.** to serve with or as if with a ladle: *to ladle soup into bowls.*

la•dy (lā′dē) /ˈleydiy/ *n., pl.* **-dies,** *adj.* —*n.* [*count*] **1.** a woman who is refined, polite, and well-spoken. **2.** a woman of high social position or economic class. **3.** any woman; female: *the lady who answered the phone.* **4.** This word is used as a term of address for a woman, **a.** as a polite term; usually in the plural: *Ladies and gentlemen, welcome.* **b.** as an offensive term (usually in the singular): *"Hey, lady, you're in my way!" he hollered.* **5.** wife: *The ambassador and his lady arrived late.* **6.** *Slang.* a female lover or companion. **7.** [*Lady*] (in Great Britain) the title of a woman of rank, or the wife of a man of certain rank: [*proper noun*]: *Lady Huxtable.* [*count*]: *Lords and Ladies filled the hall.* **8.** [*usually: Lady; proper noun*] a quality or abstract idea thought of as a female person: *Lady Luck.* —*adj.* [*before a noun*] **9.** *Sometimes Offensive.* female: *a lady cabdriver.*

la•dy•bug (lā′dē bug′) /ˈleydiyˌbʌg/ *n.* [*count*] a small, round, often brightly colored and spotted beetle feeding chiefly on small insects and also on plants. Also, **la•dy•bird** (lā′dē bûrd′) /ˈleydiyˌbɜrd/.

la•dy•fin•ger (lā′dē fing′gər) /ˈleydiyˌfɪŋgər/ *n.* [*count*] a small finger-shaped sponge cake.

la′dy-in-wait′ing, *n.* [*count*], *pl.* **la•dies-in-wait•ing.** a lady who waits on a queen or princess.

la•dy•kill•er (lā′dē kil′ər) /ˈleydiyˌkɪlər/ *n.* [*count*] *Informal.* a man who is very attractive to women.

la•dy•like (lā′dē līk′) /ˈleydiyˌlayk/ *adj.* of, relating to, or befitting a lady; proper: *ladylike manners.*

la•dy•love (lā′dē luv′) /ˈleydiyˌlʌv/ *n.* [*count*] a female sweetheart.

la•dy•ship (lā′dē ship′) /ˈleydiyˌʃɪp/ *n.* [*count*] **1.** [*often: Ladyship; often: Her/Your + ~*] This form is used in speaking of or to a woman having the title of "Lady": *Bow to Her Ladyship.* **2.** the rank of a lady.

la′dy's-slip′per or **la′dy-slip′per,** *n.* [*count*] an orchid that has a slipper-shaped lip.

la•e•trile (lā′i tril) /ˈleyɪtrɪl/ *n.* [*noncount*] a controversial drug prepared chiefly from apricot pits and believed by some to cure cancer.

lag (lag) /læg/ *v.,* **lagged, lag•ging,** *n.* —*v.* **1.** to fail to keep up or maintain a desired pace or speed: [*no obj*]: *to lag behind in production.* [*~ + obj*]: *The construction industry still lags the economy.* **2.** [*no obj*] to decrease gradually: *Interest lagged as the meeting dragged on.* —*n.* [*count*] **3.** a lagging behind: *a lag in production.* **4.** a period of time in which there is a delay or slowing down: *a lag of ten minutes.*

la•ger (lä′gər, lô′-) /ˈlɑgər, ˈlɔ-/ *n.* a light beer aged at low temperatures from six weeks to six months: [*noncount*]: *some cold lager.* [*count*]: *Two lagers, please.* Also called **la′ger beer′.**

lag•gard (lag′ərd) /ˈlægərd/ *n.* [*count*] a person or thing that lags or is slow and delays something, esp. work.

la•gniappe (lan yap′, lan′yap) /lænˈyæp, ˈlænyæp/ *n.* [*count*] **1.** a small gift given by a merchant to a customer for making a purchase; bonus. **2.** a gratuity; tip.

la•goon (lə gōōn′) /ləˈguwn/ *n.* [*count*] an area of shallow water separated from the sea by sandy dunes or coral reefs.

laid (lād) /leyd/ *v.* pt. and pp. of LAY[1].

laid′-back′, *adj. Informal.* relaxed; easygoing.

lain (lān) /leyn/ *v.* pp. of LIE[2].

lair (lâr) /lɛər/ *n.* [*count*] **1.** a den or resting place of a wild animal. **2.** a secret hiding place or base of operations; hideout: *a pirate's lair.*

lais•sez faire or **lais•ser faire** (les′ā fâr′) /ˌlɛsˈey fɛər/ *n.* [*noncount*] **1.** the theory or system of government that holds that the government should intervene in or interfere with economic affairs as little as possible. **2.** the practice or doctrine of not interfering in the affairs of others.

la•i•ty (lā′i tē) /ˈleyɪtiy/ *n.* [*plural; used with a plural verb; usually: the + ~*] **1.** the body of religious worshipers that are not clergy. **2.** the people outside of a particular profession, as distinguished from those belonging to it.

lake (lāk) /leyk/ *n.* [*count*] a body of fresh or salt water of considerable size, surrounded by land.

lal•ly•gag (lä′lē gag′, lal′ē-) /ˈlɑliyˌgæg, ˈlæliy-/ also **lol•ly•gag** (lä′lē gag′) /ˈlɑliyˌgæg/ *v.* [*no obj*], **-gagged, -gag•ging.** *Informal.* to spend time idly.

lam (lam) /læm/ *n., v.,* **lammed, lam•ming.** *Slang.* —*n.* [*count*] **1.** a hasty escape; flight. —*v.* [*no obj*] **2.** to run away quickly; escape; flee: *The crooks lammed out of there as fast as they could.* —***Idiom.*** **3. on the lam,** *Slang.* hiding or in flight from the police.

la•ma (lä′mə) /ˈlɑmə/ *n.* [*count*], *pl.* **-mas.** a Buddhist monk or priest, esp. in Tibet or Mongolia.

la•ma•ser•y (lä′mə ser′ē) /ˈlɑməˌsɛriy/ *n.* [*count*], *pl.* **-ser•ies.** a monastery of lamas.

lamb (lam) /læm/ *n.* **1.** [*count*] a young sheep. **2.** [*noncount*] the meat of a young sheep: *a leg of lamb.* **3.** a person who is gentle, meek, or easily cheated. —*v.* [*no obj*] **4.** to give birth to a lamb.

lam•baste or **lam•bast** (lam bāst′, -bast′) /læmˈbeyst, -ˈbæst/ *v.* [*~ + obj*], **-bast•ed, -bast•ing.** *Informal.* **1.** to beat or whip severely: *lambasted the prisoners.* **2.** to scold or reprimand harshly; berate: *She lambasted me for being late.*

lamb•kin (lam′kin) /ˈlæmkɪn/ *n.* [*count*] a little lamb.

lame (lām) /leym/ *adj.,* **lam•er, lam•est,** *v.,* **lamed, lam•ing.** —*adj.* **1.** crippled or physically disabled, esp. in the foot or leg so as to cause limping. **2.** being stiff and sore: *a lame arm from tennis.* **3.** weak; inadequate: *a lame excuse.* **4.** *Slang.* out of touch; square: *That music is so lame.* —*v.* [*~ + obj*] **5.** to make lame or defective: *The bullet lamed him for life.* —**lame′ly,** *adv.* —**lame′ness,** *n.* [*noncount*]

la•mé (la mā′, lä-) /læˈmey, lɑ-/ *n.* [*noncount*] a fabric in which metallic threads, as of gold or silver, are woven with silk, wool, rayon, or cotton: *a dress with silver lamé.*

lame•brain (lām′brān′) /ˈleymˌbreyn/ *n.* [*count*] *Informal.* a stupid person; dunce; fool. —**lame′brained′,** *adj.*

lame′ duck′, *n.* [*count*] **1.** an elected official or group continuing in office during the time between an election defeat and when the new person takes office. **2.** anyone or anything soon to be replaced by another. **3.** an ineffective person or thing. —**lame-duck,** *adj.*: *a lame-duck president.*

la•ment (lə ment′) /ləˈmɛnt/ *v.* **1.** to express mourning or grief for or over someone or something: [*~ + obj*]: *The entire country lamented the death of their leader.* [*no obj*]: *The nation lamented in unity.* **2.** to be very sorry for; regret: [*~ + the fact + that clause*]: *We lament the fact that this company cannot continue to make a profit.* [*~ + obj*]: *lamented the news.* —*n.* [*count*] **3.** an expression of grief, mourning, or sadness: *a lament over the death of the leader.*

lam•en•ta•ble (lam′ən tə bəl, lə men′tə bəl) /ˈlæməntəbəl, ləˈmɛntəbəl/ *adj.* that is to be lamented; regrettable; unfortunate: *His death was lamentable.* —**lam′en•ta•bly,** *adv.*

lam•en•ta•tion (lam′ən tā′shən) /ˌlæmən'teyʃən/ *n.* the act of lamenting or of expressing grief: [*noncount*]: *wails of lamentation.* [*count*]: *lamentations for the death of the children.*

lam•i•nat•ed (lam′ə nāt′id) /'læməˌneytɪd/ *adj.* **1.** made or constructed from layers of material bonded together: *laminated wood.* **2.** covered over with a layer or layers, usually of plastic: *His diploma was laminated.* —**lam•i•na•tion** (lam′ə nā′shən) /ˌlæmə'neyʃən/ *n.* [*noncount*]

lamp (lamp) /læmp/ *n.* [*count*] **1.** a device that provides artificial light, as by electricity or gas: *a fluorescent lamp; a kerosene lamp.* See illustration at APARTMENT. **2.** a device that provides heat or other radiation: *an infrared lamp.*

lam•poon (lam po͞on′) /læm'puwn/ *n.* [*count*] **1.** a broad, often harsh satire of an individual or institution. —*v.* [~ + *obj*] **2.** to ridicule in a lampoon.

lamp•post (lamp′pōst′) /'læmpˌpowst/ *n.* [*count*] a pole supporting a lamp that lights a street or other outdoor area. See illustration at STREET.

lam•prey (lam′prē) /'læmpriy/ *n.* [*count*], *pl.* **-preys.** an eellike, jawless fish that attaches itself to other fishes with its round, sucking mouth.

lamp•shade (lamp′shād) /'læmpʃeyd/ *n.* [*count*] a cover for a lamp put over the bulb to make the light less harsh or to direct the light in a certain direction.

lance (lans) /læns/ *n., v.,* **lanced, lanc•ing.** —*n.* [*count*] **1.** a long wooden shaft with a pointed metal head, esp. one used by a knight. **2.** LANCER. **3.** LANCET. —*v.* [~ + *obj*] **4.** to open or pierce with or as if with a lancet: *The nurse lanced the boil.*

lance′ cor′poral, *n.* [*count*] an enlisted person in the U.S. Marine Corps ranking above a private first class.

lanc•er (lan′sər) /'lænsər/ *n.* [*count*] a cavalry soldier armed with a lance.

lan•cet (lan′sit) /'lænsɪt/ *n.* [*count*] a sharp-pointed instrument used in medical operations, usually with two edges, for making small openings.

land (land) /lænd/ *n.* **1.** [*noncount*] any part of the earth's surface, as a continent or an island, not covered by a body of water. **2.** [*noncount*] an area of ground with reference to its nature: *land good for farming.* **3.** [*noncount*] an area of ground with specific boundaries: *to buy land in Florida.* **4.** [*noncount*] rural or farming areas (contrasted with urban areas): *They left the land for the city.* **5.** [*count*] *Law.* any part of the earth's surface that can be owned as property, and everything connected to it: *You're on his lands.* **6.** [*count*] a region or country: *Immigrants came from many lands.* **7.** realm or domain; world: *still in the land of the living.* —*v.* **8.** to (cause to) come to land or shore: [*no obj*]: *The boat lands at Cherbourg.* [~ + *obj*]: *We managed to land the boat at the shoreline.* **9.** [*no obj*] to go or come ashore from a ship or boat: *The Pilgrims landed in 1620.* **10.** to (cause to) come down upon or strike a surface: [*no obj*]: *The plane landed on time.* [~ + *obj*]: *The pilot managed to land the crippled plane.* **11.** to (cause to) arrive or come in a particular place, position, or condition: [~ + *obj*]: *His behavior will land him in jail.* [*no obj*]: *to land in trouble.* **12.** [~ + *obj*] *Informal.* to catch or capture; gain; win: *to land a high-paying job.* **13.** [~ + *obj*] to bring (a fish) onto land or into a boat, as with rod and reel.

lan•dau (lan′dô, -dou) /'lændɔ, -daw/ *n.* [*count*] a four-wheeled, two-seated carriage with a top made in two parts that may be let down or folded back.

land•ed (lan′did) /'lændɪd/ *adj.* [*before a noun*] **1.** owning land, esp. a large amount of land, as an estate: *landed gentry.* **2.** consisting of land: *landed property.*

land•fall (land′fôl′) /'lændˌfɔl/ *n.* [*noncount*] **1.** an approach to or sighting of land. **2.** the land sighted.

land•fill (land′fil′) /'lændˌfɪl/ *n.* **1.** [*count*] a low area of land built up from deposits of solid garbage in layers and covered by soil. **2.** [*noncount*] the solid garbage itself.

land•ing (lan′ding) /'lændɪŋ/ *n.* [*count*] **1.** the act of a person or thing that lands: *The plane made a perfect landing.* **2.** a place where persons or goods are landed: *a boat landing.* **3.** the level floor between flights of stairs or at the head or foot of a flight of stairs.

land′ing gear′, *n.* [*noncount*] the wheels, floats, etc., of an aircraft, upon which it lands and moves on ground or water.

land′la′dy, *n.* [*count*], *pl.* **-dies.** a woman who owns and leases apartments, houses, land, etc., to others.

land•locked (land′lokt′) /'lændˌlɒkt/ *adj.* **1.** shut in completely, or almost completely, by land: *a landlocked bay.* **2.** having no direct means of reaching the sea: *a landlocked country.*

land•lord (land′lôrd′) /'lændˌlɔrd/ *n.* [*count*] **1.** a person or organization that owns and leases apartments, a building, land, etc., to others. **2.** an innkeeper.

land•lub•ber (land′lub′ər) /'lændˌlʌbər/ *n.* [*count*] someone unfamiliar with the sea or seamanship.

land•mark (land′märk′) /'lændˌmɑrk/ *n.* [*count*] **1.** a feature in the landscape or an object in an area that is easily noticed or that serves as a guide, as to ships at sea or to travelers on a road: *The tower is a local landmark.* **2.** something used to mark the boundary of land. **3.** a building or other place of outstanding historical or cultural importance: *The president's birthplace has been designated a landmark.* **4.** a very important, significant, or historic event, time, achievement, etc.: *The decision is a landmark in constitutional law.*

land•mass (land′mas′) /'lændˌmæs/ *n.* [*count*] a part of the earth's crust standing above sea level and having a distinct identity, as a continent or large island.

land′ mine′, *n.* [*count*] an explosive device set into the ground, designed to explode when walked on or ridden over.

land′-of′fice busi′ness, *n.* [*count*] lively or very profitable business.

land•scape (land′skāp′) /'lændˌskeyp/ *n., v.,* **-scaped, -scap•ing.**. —*n.* [*count*] **1.** a section or area of natural scenery that can be seen from a single viewpoint. SEE ILLUSTRATION. **2.** a picture depicting such scenery. **3.** an area of action or of activity; arena; scene: *the political landscape.* —*v.* **4.** [~ + *obj*] to improve the appearance of (an area of land) by planting trees, shrubs, grass, or the like. **5.** [*no obj*] to do such work as a profession. —**land′scap′er,** *n.* [*count*]

land•slide (land′slīd′) /'lændˌslayd/ *n.* [*count*] **1.** the falling or sliding of a mass of soil or rock on or from a steep slope. **2.** an election in which a particular candidate or party receives an overwhelming number of votes. **3.** any overwhelming victory.

land•ward (land′wərd) /'lændwərd/ *adv.* **1.** Also, **land′-wards.** toward the land. —*adj.* [*before a noun*] **2.** facing or tending toward the land. **3.** being in the direction of the land: *a landward breeze.*

lane (lān) /leyn/ *n.* [*count*] **1.** a narrow, often winding road in the country. **2.** any narrow or well-defined passage, track, channel, or course: *sea lanes.* **3.** a part of a highway or road wide enough for one vehicle, often marked off by painted lines. **4.** (in a running or swimming race) the marked-off space or path within which a competitor must remain.

lan•guage (lang′gwij) /'læŋgwɪdʒ/ *n.* **1.** [*count*] a body of words, sounds, and the systems for their use common to a people of the same community or nation, the same geographical area, or the same cultural tradition. **2.** [*noncount*] communication using a system of vocal sounds, written symbols, signs, or gestures: *spoken language; sign language.* **3.** [*noncount*] any set or system of special symbols, signs, sounds, or gestures used as a means of communicating: *the language of mathematics.* **4.** [*noncount*] communication of thought, feeling, etc., without using words: *body language.* **5.** [*noncount*] the study of language; linguistics. **6.** [*noncount*] a particular manner of verbal expression: *flowery language.* **7.** [*count*] a set of symbols and syntactic rules for their combination and use, by means of which a computer can be given directions: *a computer language like BASIC or FORTRAN.* See -LING-.

lan•guid (lang′gwid) /'læŋgwɪd/ *adj.* **1.** lacking in liveliness or interest; slack; listless: *a languid effort.* **2.** drooping or slowing down from weakness or fatigue; faint: *feeling languid from the heat.*

lan•guish (lang′gwish) /'læŋgwɪʃ/ *v.* [*no obj*] **1.** to be or become feeble; droop; fade: *languishing from the heat.* **2.** to lose liveliness or the will to do things: *He languished in his dull job.* **3.** to suffer neglect: *to languish in prison.* **4.** to suffer from a feeling of longing: *languishing for her love.*

lan•guor (lang′gər) /'læŋgər/ *n.* [*noncount*] **1.** lack of energy or vitality; sluggishness. **2.** lack of spirit or interest; listlessness: *a feeling of utter languor.* **3.** pleasant laziness or relaxation.

lan•guor•ous (lang′ər əs) /'læŋərəs/ *adj.* **1.** causing a feeling of pleasant laziness or relaxation: *a languorous breeze.* **2.** showing a feeling of pleasant laziness or relaxation: *a languorous wave of the hand.* —**lan′guor•ous•ly,** *adv.*

lank (langk) /læŋk/ *adj.,* **-er, -est.** (of hair) straight and limp; without spring or curl.

lank•y (lang′kē) /'læŋkiy/ *adj.,* **-i•er, -i•est.** ungracefully

landscape

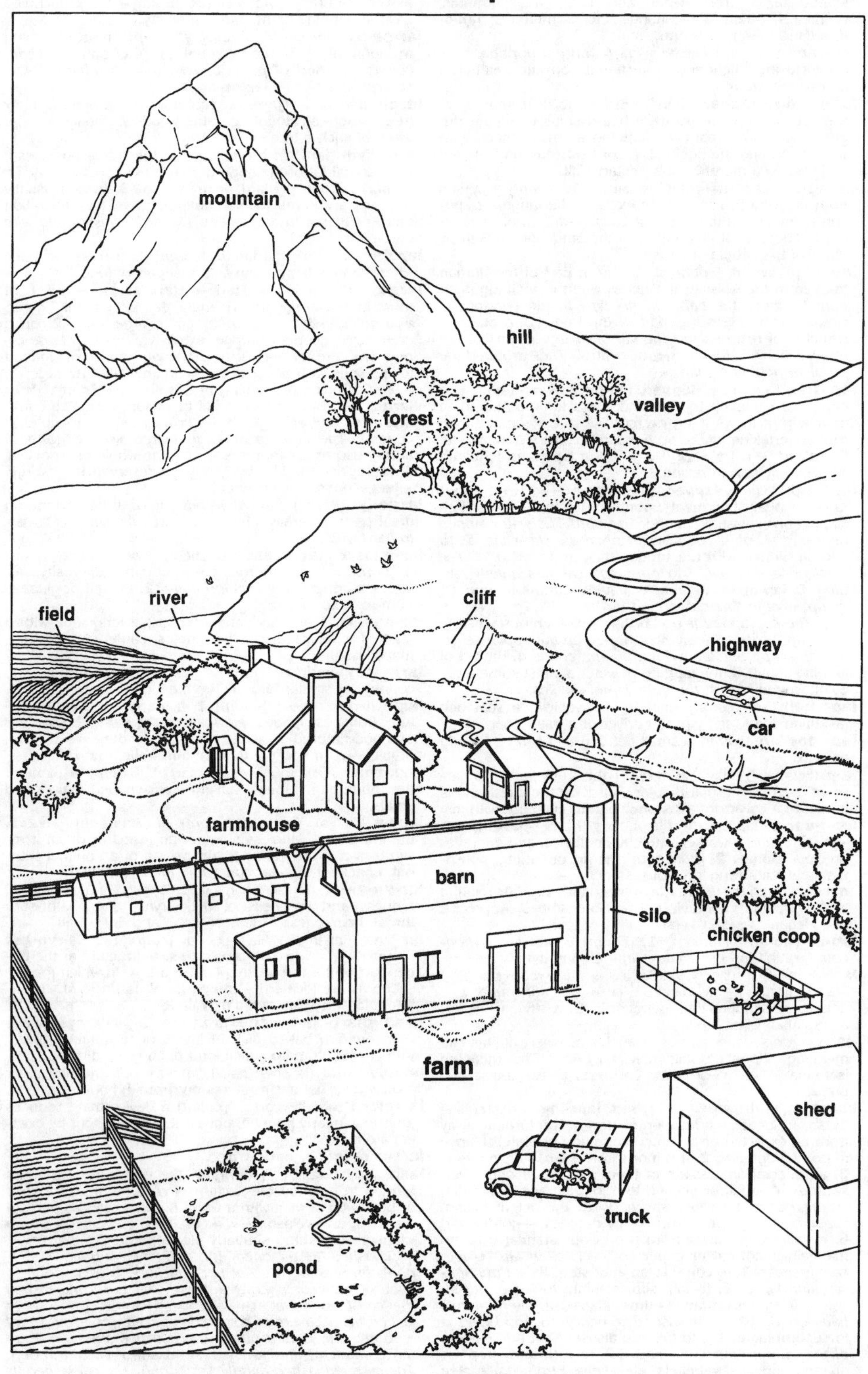
mountain
hill
forest
valley
river
field
cliff
highway
car
farmhouse
barn
silo
chicken coop
farm
shed
truck
pond

tall and thin: *a lanky teenager.* —**lank′i•ness,** *n.* [*noncount*]

lan•o•lin (lan′l in) /ˈlænlɪn/ *n.* [*noncount*] a fatty substance taken from wool and used in ointments, cosmetics, waterproof coatings, etc. Sometimes, **lan•o•line** (lan′l in, -ēn′) /ˈlænlɪn, -ˌiyn/.

lan•tern (lan′tərn) /ˈlæntərn/ *n.* [*count*] a portable case for enclosing a light and protecting it from the weather: *a kerosene lantern.*

lan•yard or **lan•iard** (lan′yərd) /ˈlænyərd/ *n.* [*count*] **1.** a short rope or wire used on board ships to secure riggings. **2.** a small cord for hanging a small object, as a whistle, around the neck. **3.** a cord worn around the left shoulder by a member of a military unit.

La•o•tian (lā ō′shən) /leyˈowʃən/ *n.* **1.** [*count*] a person born or living in Laos. **2.** [*noncount*] the language spoken by many of the people in Laos. —*adj.* **3.** of or relating to Laos. **4.** of or relating to the language spoken by many of the people in Laos.

lap¹ (lap) /læp/ *n.* [*count*] **1.** the front part of the human body from the waist to the knees when in a sitting position: *balanced the baby on his lap.* **2.** the part of the clothing that covers this part of the body. **3.** a place or situation of rest or care: *the lap of luxury.* **4.** an area of responsibility, care, charge, or control: *They dropped the problem right in my lap.*

lap² (lap) /læp/ *n., v.,* **lapped, lap•ping.** —*n.* [*count*] **1.** a complete circle or trip around a track or a unit of a course in racing or in an exercise. **2.** one stage of a long trip, undertaking, etc.: *The first lap was from New York to Cleveland.* —*v.* [~ + *obj*] **3.** to get a lap or more ahead of (a competitor) in racing.

lap³ (lap) /læp/ *v.,* **lapped, lap•ping,** *n.* —*v.* **1.** (of water) to wash against or beat upon (something) with a light slapping or splashing sound: [*no obj*]: *The water lapped gently.* [~ + *obj*]: *The waves lapped the shoreline.* **2.** to take in (liquid) with the tongue; lick in: [~ + *obj*]: *The cat lapped the milk.* [*no obj*]: *The cat was quietly lapping.* **3. lap up, a.** to take up (liquid) with the tongue: [~ + *up* + *obj*]: *The cat lapped up her milk.* [~ + *obj* + *up*]: *The cat lapped it up.* **b.** to receive enthusiastically: [~ + *up* + *obj*]: *The actress lapped up the applause.* [~ + *obj* + *up*]: *She lapped it up.* —*n.* [*count*] **4.** the act of lapping liquid. **5.** the lapping of water against something. **6.** the sound of this: *the quiet lap of the sea.*

lap′ belt′, *n.* [*count*] (in a motor vehicle) a seat belt fastening across the lap of a driver or a passenger.

lap′ dog′, *n.* [*count*] a small pet dog that can be held in the lap.

la•pel (lə pel′) /ləˈpɛl/ *n.* [*count*] the front part of a garment, as a jacket, that is folded back on the chest and is joined to a collar or forms one continuous piece with it.

lap•i•dar•y (lap′i der′ē) /ˈlæpɪˌdɛriy/ *n., pl.* **-dar•ies,** *adj.* —*n.* **1.** [*count*] a worker who cuts, polishes, and engraves precious stones. **2.** [*noncount*] the art of cutting, polishing, and engraving precious stones. —*adj.* Also, **lap•i•dar•i•an** (lap′i dâr′ē ən) /ˌlæpɪˈdɛəriyən/. **3.** of or relating to the cutting or engraving of precious stones. **4.** precise and elegant: *lapidary verse.*

lap•in (lap′in) /ˈlæpɪn/ *n.* **1.** [*count*] a rabbit. **2.** [*noncount*] rabbit fur, esp. when trimmed and dyed.

lap•is laz•u•li (lap′is laz′o͝o lē, -lī′, laz′yo͝o-, lazh′o͝o-) /ˈlæpˈɪs læzʊliy, -ˌlay, ˈlæzyʊ-, ˈlæʒʊ-/ *n.* [*noncount*] **1.** a deep blue semiprecious gemstone. **2.** a sky-blue color; azure. Also called **lapis.**

-laps-, *root.* *-laps-* comes from Latin, where it has the meaning "slip; slide; fall; make an error." This meaning is found in such words as: COLLAPSE, ELAPSE, LAPSE, RELAPSE.

lapse (laps) /læps/ *n., v.,* **lapsed, laps•ing.** —*n.* [*count*] **1.** an accidental or temporary decline or turning away from an expected or accepted condition or state: *a lapse in good judgment.* **2.** a minor error: *a lapse of memory.* **3.** an interval or passage of time: *a lapse of only a few seconds.* **4.** a fall or decline to a lower grade, condition, or degree: *a lapse into savagery.* **5.** the act of falling, slipping, sliding, etc., slowly or by degrees. —*v.* [*no obj*] **6.** to fall or turn away from a previous standard; fail to maintain a normal or expected level: *often lapsed into carelessness.* **7.** to come to an end; stop: *We let our subscription lapse.* **8.** to fall, slip, or sink: *to lapse into silence.* **9.** to pass away, as time; elapse: *A few moments had lapsed.* **10.** (of an insurance policy) to stop being in force; terminate. **11.** to fall into disuse: *That odd custom of the tribe eventually lapsed.* **12.** to turn away from or abandon principles, beliefs, etc.: *lapsed from grace.* See -LAPS-.

lap•top (lap′top′) /ˈlæpˌtɒp/ *n.* [*count*] a portable microcomputer small enough to rest on the lap.

lap•wing (lap′wing′) /ˈlæpˌwɪŋ/ *n.* [*count*] a bird, a large plover of Eurasia and N Africa, having a long, upcurved crest, a flopping flight, and a shrill cry.

lar•ce•ny (lär′sə nē) /ˈlɑrsəniy/ *n., pl.* **-nies.** *Law.* the wrongful taking of the personal goods of another: [*noncount*]: *accused of petty larceny.* [*count*]: *charged with several larcenies.* —**lar′ce•nous,** *adj.*

larch (lärch) /lɑrtʃ/ *n.* **1.** [*count*] a cone-bearing leafy tree that gives a tough, durable wood. **2.** [*noncount*] the wood of such a tree.

lard (lärd) /lɑrd/ *n.* [*noncount*] **1.** the fat of hogs, esp. the internal fat of the abdomen, used in cooking. —*v.* [~ + *obj*] **2.** to apply lard or grease to. **3.** to add usually unnecessary items to (something), more for decoration than for actual improvement: *He larded his writing with metaphors.*

lar•der (lär′dər) /ˈlɑrdər/ *n.* [*count*] **1.** a room or place where food is kept; pantry. **2.** a supply of food.

large (lärj) /lɑrdʒ/ *adj.,* **larg•er, larg•est,** *n.* —*adj.* **1.** of more than average size, quantity, degree, etc.; big; great: *a large house; a large number; a large shirt.* **2.** on a great scale, scope, or range; extensive; broad: *a large variety of interests.* —*n.* **3. a.** [*noncount*] a size of clothing for persons who are heavier or broader than average. **b.** [*count*] a piece of clothing in this size. —***Idiom.*** **4. at large, a.** [*be* + ~] not in jail or prison; free: *The criminals were still at large.* **b.** [*after a noun*] as a whole; in general: *The country at large feared war.* **c.** [*after a noun*] Also **at-large.** representing the whole of a political division or similar body: *a representative at-large.* —**large′ness,** *n.* [*noncount*]

large•ly (lärj′lē) /ˈlɑrdʒliy/ *adv.* to a great extent; in great part; generally; chiefly: *He owes his success largely to hard work.*

lar•gess or **lar•gesse** (lär zhes′, -jes′) /lɑrˈʒɛs, -ˈdʒɛs/ *n.* [*noncount*] **1.** generous giving of gifts; generosity: *Her largesse benefits the less fortunate.* **2.** the gift or gifts, as of money, so given.

lar•i•at (lar′ē ət) /ˈlæriyət/ *n.* [*count*] a long rope with a knotted loop, used to catch horses, cattle, or other animals; lasso.

lark¹ (lärk) /lɑrk/ *n.* [*count*] a songbird living in the open country, or similar bird, as the meadowlark.

lark² (lärk) /lɑrk/ *n.* [*count*] **1.** a merry, carefree adventure; frolic; escapade: *had a lark at the party.* **2.** innocent or good-natured mischief; something done as a joke; prank. —*v.* [*no obj*] **3.** to have fun; frolic; romp.

lark•spur (lärk′spûr′) /ˈlɑrkˌspɜr/ *n.* [*count*] a plant of the buttercup family, having spur-shaped calyx and petals.

lar•va (lär′və) /ˈlɑrvə/ *n.* [*count*], *pl.* **-vae** (-vē) /-viy/. **1.** the immature, wingless stage of an insect in which it resembles a short worm. **2.** the young of an animal without a backbone. —**lar′val,** *adj.*: *the larval stage.*

lar•yn•gi•tis (lar′ən jī′tis) /ˌlærənˈdʒaytɪs/ *n.* [*noncount*] redness and soreness of the larynx, often with sore throat, hoarseness or loss of voice, and dry cough.

lar•ynx (lar′ingks) /ˈlærɪŋks/ *n.* [*count*], *pl.* **la•ryn•ges** (lə rin′jēz) /ləˈrɪndʒiyz/ **lar•ynx•es.** a structure at the upper part of the throat, shaped like a box, in which the vocal cords are located. —**la•ryn•ge•al** (lə rin′jē əl, lar′ən-jē′əl) /ləˈrɪndʒiyəl, ˌlærənˈdʒiyəl/ *adj.*

la•sa•gna or **la•sa•gne** (lə zän′yə, lä-) /ləˈzɑnyə, lɑ-/ *n.* [*noncount*] a baked dish of layers of rectangular pasta, with cheese, tomato sauce, and often ground meat.

las•civ•i•ous (lə siv′ē əs) /ləˈsɪviyəs/ *adj.* inclined to or arousing sexual desire. —**las•civ′i•ous•ly,** *adv.*

la•ser (lā′zər) /ˈleyzər/ *n.* [*count*] a device that produces a narrow, nearly parallel, powerful beam of light by exciting atoms.

la′ser disc′, *n.* OPTICAL DISC.

lash¹ (lash) /læʃ/ *n.* [*count*] **1.** the end part of a whip, formed from a flexible section of cord. **2.** a swift stroke or blow with or as if with a whip: *twenty lashes as punishment.* **3.** an eyelash. —*v.* **4.** to strike or beat, as with a whip or something similarly slender and flexible: [~ + *obj*]: *lashed the prisoners.* [*no obj;* (~ + *out*); (~ + *at* + *obj*)]: *She lashed (out) at her attackers.* **5.** [~ + *obj*] to beat violently or sharply against: *The hurricane lashed the coast.* **6.** to attack with harsh words: [~ + *obj*]: *lashed his accusers in a stinging speech.* [~ + *out* (+ *at* + *obj*)]: *She lashed out at the injustice she saw.* **7.** to move suddenly and swiftly; rush, dash, or flash: [*no obj*]: *The cat's tail lashed angrily.* [~ + *obj*]: *The cat lashed its tail in anger.*

lash[2] (lash) /læʃ/ *v.* [~ + *obj*] to bind or fasten with a rope, cord, etc.: *The campers lashed their tent to a tree during the hurricane.*

lass (las) /læs/ *n.* [*count*] a girl or young woman.

las•sie (las′ē) /ˈlæsiy/ *n.* [*count*] a lass.

las•si•tude (las′i to͞od′, -tyo͞od′) /ˈlæsɪˌtuwd, -ˌtyuwd/ *n.* [*noncount*] weariness of body or mind; listlessness: *a feeling of lassitude in the humid climate.*

las•so (las′ō, la so͞o′) /ˈlæsow, læˈsuw/ *n., pl.* **-sos, -soes,** *v.,* **-soed, -so•ing.** —*n.* [*count*] **1.** a long rope or line of hide or other material with a knotted loop at one end, used for roping horses, cattle, etc. —*v.* [~ + *obj*] **2.** to catch with or as if with a lasso.

last[1] (last) /læst/ *adj., a superlative of* **late** *with* **later** *as comparative.* **1.** being or occurring or coming after all others, with respect to time, order, rank, place, or importance: *the last line on a page; the last person to get on stage; last in line.* **2.** [*before a noun indicating time*] most recent; next before the present; immediately before: *I saw her last week.* **3.** [*before a noun*] being the only one remaining: *It's my last dollar.* **4.** [*before a noun*] final: *one's last hours.* **5.** [*before a noun*] ultimate or conclusive; definitive: *in the last analysis.* **6.** [*before a noun*] least desirable or likely: *He's the last person we'd want to represent us.* **7.** [*before a noun*] individual; single: *Don't start until every last person is present.* —*adv.* **8.** after all others in time, order, rank, etc.; latest: *Do this last.* **9.** on the most recent occasion: *He was alone when last seen.* **10.** in conclusion: *Last, I want to thank my wife.* —*n.* **11.** [*count; singular: the* + ~] a person or thing that is last: *drank the last of the brandy.* **12.** [*noncount; the* + ~] a final appearance or mention: *That's the last we'll hear of it.* **13.** [*noncount; the* + ~] the end or conclusion: *the last of September.* —***Idiom.*** **14. at (long) last,** after a lot of delay; finally: *At long last we had finished the job.* **15. breathe one's last,** to die. **16. to the last,** to the end: *To the last he told everyone he was innocent.* —**Usage.** When the word LAST is used before an expression of time, like *week, month, year,* etc., it is more usual not to use a preposition (such as *in, on,* or *at*), and not to include the article *the*: *We saw her last week/last month/last year.* The use of the word *the* with LAST refers to a period of time that continues up to the present time: *for the last week (= for the seven days up to now),* as opposed to *last week (= the week before this week).* The word LAST is also different from LATEST. LAST can be used to refer to a thing before another: *He played great tennis in his last appearance at Wimbledon (= the time before now). The last I heard, they were getting a divorce (= the last time I heard anything).* The word LATEST means "newest": *He has been playing great tennis in his latest appearance at Wimbledon (= in his most recent, newest appearance at Wimbledon). Here is the latest news — They are getting a divorce (= the latest or "newest" news).*

last[2] (last) /læst/ *v.* [*not: be* + ~*-ing*] **1.** [*no obj*] to go on or continue in time: *The festival lasted for three weeks.* **2.** [*no obj*] to continue without running out; be enough: *Enjoy it while the money lasts.* **3.** [*no obj*] to continue or remain in usable condition: *The car won't last if you don't take care of it.* **4.** [~ *(+ out) + obj*] to continue to survive for the time or duration of: *can't last (out) another day without food.*

last′ hurrah′, *n.* [*count*] any final attempt, competition, performance, or the like: *her last hurrah as a candidate for senator.*

last•ing (las′ting) /ˈlæstɪŋ/ *adj.* [*before a noun*] enduring for a long time: *our lasting friendship.* —**last′ing•ly,** *adv.*

Last′ Judg′ment, *n.* [*proper noun; the* + ~] the final judgment by God of all people at the end of the world.

last•ly (last′lē) /ˈlæstliy/ *adv.* in conclusion; finally: *Lastly, I'd like to thank my wife.*

last′ straw′, *n.* [*count; usually singular; usually: the* + ~] the last of a number of irritations or troubles coming one after the other, that leads to a loss of patience, to a disaster, etc.

-lat-[1], *root. -lat-* comes from Latin, where it has the meaning "carried." This meaning is found in such words as: ABLATIVE, COLLATE, CORRELATE, DILATORY, ELATED, OBLATE, PRELATE, RELATE, RELATIVE, SUPERLATIVE.

-lat-[2], *root. -lat-* comes from Latin, where it has the meaning "line; side." This meaning is found in such words as: BILATERAL, COLLATERAL, DILATE, EQUILATERAL, LATERAL, LATITUDE, QUADRILATERAL, TRILATERAL, UNILATERAL.

lat., an abbreviation of: latitude.

latch (lach) /lætʃ/ *n.* [*count*] **1.** a device for holding a door, gate, or the like closed, with a bar that falls or slides into a catch, groove, or hole. **2.** a lock on a door that can be opened with a key. —*v.* **3.** to close or fasten (with a latch): [~ + *obj*]: *He latched the barn door shut.* [*no obj*]: *The door would not latch.* **4. latch on** or **onto,** [~ + *on* or *onto* + *obj*] **a.** to obtain; get. **b.** to attach oneself to: *The stray dog latched onto the children and followed them home.*

latch•key (lach′kē′) /ˈlætʃˌkiy/ *n.* [*count*], *pl.* **-keys.** a key for releasing a latch or lock, esp. a lock on an outer door.

latch′key child′, *n.* [*count*] a child who spends part of the day alone and unsupervised, esp. one who has a key to his or her home for entrance after school while the parents are at work.

late (lāt) /leyt/ *adj.,* **lat•er** or **lat•ter, lat•est** or **last** (last) /læst/ *adv.,* **lat•er, lat•est.** —*adj.* **1.** occurring after the usual or proper time: *a late spring.* **2.** continued until after the usual time or hour: *a late business meeting.* **3.** near or at the end of the day or well into the night: *a late hour.* **4.** [*before a noun*] most recent: *Here is a late news bulletin.* **5.** [*before a noun*] recently deceased: *the late John and Jane Doe.* **6.** [*before a noun*] belonging to an advanced period or stage in the history or development of something: *the late phase of feudalism.* **7.** [*before a noun*] belonging in or near the end of a stage or period in a life: *in his late twenties.* —*adv.* **8.** after the usual or proper time, or after delay: *to arrive twenty minutes late.* **9.** until after the usual time or hour, esp. of the night: *to work late.* **10.** recently but no longer; lately. —***Idiom.*** **11. of late,** lately; recently: *He seems tired of late.* —**late′ness,** *n.* [*noncount*]: *Please excuse the lateness of the hour.* [*count*]: *Two latenesses count as one absence.*

late•com•er (lāt′kum′ər) /ˈleytˌkʌmər/ *n.* [*count*] one that arrives late: *Latecomers may be seated during the hymn.*

late•ly (lāt′lē) /ˈleytliy/ *adv.* of late; recently; not long since; in the recent past: *Lately I haven't been feeling well.*

la•tent (lāt′nt) /ˈleytnt/ *adj.* **1.** present but not visible; not apparent: *a latent talent.* **2.** (of a disease, or something causing a disease) remaining in an inactive or hidden phase; dormant. —**la′ten•cy,** *n.* [*noncount*]

lat•er•al (lat′ər əl) /ˈlætərəl/ *adj.* **1.** of or related to the side; located at, proceeding from, or directed to a side: *a lateral pass in football.* **2.** relating to a new but equivalent or similar position, office, etc.: *The company offered her a lateral move but not a promotion.* **3.** (of a speech sound) produced so that the breath passes on either or both sides of the tongue: *The sound (l) is a lateral sound in English.* —*n.* [*count*] **4.** a pass in football that is to the side, not forward. **5.** a lateral speech sound. —*v.* **6.** [*no obj*] to throw a lateral in football. —**lat′er•al•ly,** *adv.* See -LAT-[2].

lat•est (lā′tist) /ˈleytɪst/ *adj.* **1.** most recent; current: *the latest fashions.* **2.** last. —*adv.* **3. at the latest,** not any later than (a time mentioned): *I'll be there at 3:00 at the latest.* —*n.* [*noncount; the* + ~] **4.** the most recent news, development, etc.: *Here's the latest from our news bureau.* —**Usage.** See LAST[1].

la•tex (lā′teks) /ˈleytɛks/ *n.* [*noncount*] a milky liquid in certain plants, as milkweeds, poppies, or the plants yielding rubber, that thickens on exposure to air, used in making rubber and adhesives.

lath (lath) /læθ/ *n., pl.* **laths** (la*th*z, laths). **1.** [*count*] a thin, narrow strip of wood used with other strips to form a backing for plaster or as a support for slates and other roofing materials, etc. **2.** [*noncount*] any building material, such as wire mesh, used in place of wooden laths.

lathe (lā*th*) /leyð/ *n., v.,* **lathed, lath•ing.** —*n.* [*count*] **1.** a machine used in cutting or forming a piece of wood, metal, etc., by holding and rotating it against a tool that shapes it. —*v.* [~ + *obj*] **2.** to cut, shape, or treat on a lathe.

lath•er (la*th*′ər) /ˈlæðər/ *n.* **1.** foam or froth made by a detergent, esp. soap, stirred or rubbed in water: [*noncount*]: *soapy lather.* [*count; singular*]: *work the soap into a good lather.* **2.** foam or froth formed by sweating a great deal, as a horse does: [*noncount*]: *Wipe down the horse's lather.* [*count; singular*]: *The horse was in a lather after the race.* **3.** [*count; singular*] *Informal.* a state of excitement, agitation, or the like: *She's in a lather because the taxi is late.* —*v.* **4.** [*no obj*] to form a lather: *a soap that lathers well.* **5.** [~ + *obj*] to apply lather to; cover with lather: *Lather your face before shaving.* —**lath′er•y,** *adj.*

Lat•in (lat′n) /ˈlætn̩/ *n.* **1.** [*noncount*] the language of ancient Rome, kept through the Middle Ages and into modern times as the church language of Western Christianity and once as an international language among universities, learned societies, etc. **2.** [*count*] **a.** a member of any people speaking a language descended from Latin, as French, Spanish, Italian, or Portuguese. **b.** a native or inhabitant of any country in Latin America; Latin American. *—adj.* **3. a.** of or relating to a country in Latin America; Latin American. **b.** of or pertaining to any of the peoples of Europe or North or South America speaking languages descended from Latin.

La•ti•no (lə tē′nō, la-) /lə'tiynow, læ-/ *n., pl.* **-nos.** HISPANIC.

lat•i•tude (lat′i to͞od′, -tyo͞od′) /'lætɪ,tuwd, -,tyuwd/ *n.* **1. a.** the angular distance, measured north or south from the equator, of a point on the earth's surface, expressed in degrees: [*noncount*]: *at twenty degrees latitude.* [*count; usually singular*]: *drifting at a latitude of fifteen degrees.* **b.** [*plural*] a place or region as marked by this distance: *at tropical latitudes.* **2.** [*noncount*] freedom from narrow restrictions; freedom of action, opinion, etc.: *They allow their children plenty of latitude in choosing friends.* See -LAT-[2].

la•trine (lə trēn′) /lə'triyn/ *n.* [*count*] a communal bathroom, esp. in a military base.

lat•ter (lat′ər) /'lætər/ *adj.* **1.** being the second mentioned of two (distinguished from *former*): *Of the two I prefer the latter version.* **2.** more advanced in time; later: *in these latter days of human progress.* **3.** near or somewhat near to the end: *the latter part of the century.* *—n.* [*noncount; the* + ~] **4.** the second thing mentioned of two: *Of your two examples, I prefer the latter.* —**lat′ter•ly,** *adv.*

lat′ter-day′, *adj.* [*before a noun*] **1.** of a later or following period: *latter-day pioneers.* **2.** of the present period or time; modern: *chivalrous, latter-day knights.*

lat•tice (lat′is) /'lætɪs/ *n.* [*count*] **1.** a structure or framework of crossed wooden or metal strips usually arranged to form a diagonal pattern of open spaces between the strips. **2.** an arrangement in space of isolated points in a regular pattern, showing the positions of atoms, molecules, or ions in the structure of a crystal. —**lat′ticed,** *adj.* [*before a noun*]

lat•tice•work (lat′is wûrk′) /'lætɪs,wɜrk/ *n.* work made up of crossed strips usually arranged in a diagonal pattern of open spaces; a lattice: [*noncount*]: *beautiful latticework.* [*count*]: *an imposing latticework.*

Lat•vi•an (lat′vē ən) /'lætviyən/ *adj.* **1.** of or relating to Latvia. **2.** of or relating to the language spoken by many of the people living in Latvia. *—n.* **3.** [*count*] a person born or living in Latvia. **4.** [*noncount*] the language spoken by many of the people living in Latvia.

laud (lôd) /lɔd/ *v.* [~ + *obj*] to praise; extol: *They lauded the decision.*

laud•a•ble (lô′də bəl) /'lɔdəbəl/ *adj.* deserving praise; commendable: *a laudable effort to cut costs.* —**laud′a•bly,** *adv.*

lau•da•num (lôd′n əm) /'lɔdn̩əm/ *n.* [*noncount*] a drug made from opium.

laud•a•to•ry (lô′də tôr′ē, -tōr′ē) /'lɔdə,tɔriy, -,towriy/ also **laud•a•tive** (lô′də tiv) /'lɔdətɪv/ *adj.* expressing praise: *laudatory remarks.*

laugh (laf) /læf/ *v.* **1.** [*no obj*] to express amusement, mirth, pleasure, happiness, and sometimes disrespect or nervousness with a sound or sounds ranging from a loud burst to a series of quiet chuckles: *He laughed loudly.* **2.** [~ + *obj*] to drive, put, bring, etc., by or with laughter: *The audience laughed him off the stage.* **3.** [~ + *obj*] to utter with laughter: *He laughed his agreement.* **4. laugh at,** [~ + *at* + *obj*] **a.** to make fun of; ridicule: *They laughed at his attempts to dance.* **b.** to find amusing: *I always laugh at her jokes.* **5. laugh off,** to dismiss as unimportant: [~ + *obj* + *off*]: *The president laughed the criticism off.* [~ + *off* + *obj*]: *He laughed off the threats.* *—n.* [*count*] **6.** the act or sound of laughing; laughter: *The joke was worth a few laughs.* **7.** a person or thing that causes laughter, amusement, or ridicule: *That exam was a laugh; it was so easy.* **8. laughs,** [*plural*] *Informal.* fun; amusement: *played a trick just for laughs.* **—*Idiom.*** **9. have the last laugh,** to prove successful despite the doubts of others. **10. laugh up** or **in one's sleeve,** [*no obj*] to be secretly amused; to make fun of something privately or secretly. **11. no laughing matter,** something serious and not to be joked about or ridiculed. —**laugh′ing•ly,** *adv.*

laugh•a•ble (laf′ə bəl) /'læfəbəl/ *adj.* causing laughter; funny; amusing. —**laugh′a•bly,** *adv.*

laugh′ing gas′, *n.* NITROUS OXIDE.

laugh•ing•stock (laf′ing stok′) /'læfɪŋ,stɒk/ *n.* [*count*] an object of ridicule: *The team became a laughingstock by losing every game.*

laugh•ter (laf′tər) /'læftər/ *n.* [*noncount*] the action or sound of laughing.

launch[1] (lônch, länch) /lɔntʃ, lɑntʃ/ *v.* **1.** [~ + *obj*] to set (a boat or ship) afloat. **2.** [~ + *obj*] to send forth, catapult, or release: *to launch a spacecraft.* **3.** [~ + *obj*] to start (a person) on a course, career, etc.: *launched herself in advertising.* **4.** [~ + *obj*] to get going; start; initiate: *to launch a scheme.* **5.** [~ + *obj*] to throw; hurl: *launching spears at the explorers.* **6.** [~ + *into* + *obj*] to burst out or plunge boldly or directly into action, speech, etc.: *She launched into her speech.* *—n.* [*count*] **7.** the act of launching.

launch[2] (lônch, länch) /lɔntʃ, lɑntʃ/ *n.* [*count*] a heavy motorboat used to carry people.

launch•er (lôn′chər, län′-) /'lɔntʃər, 'lɑn-/ *n.* [*count*] a person or thing that launches, esp. a device for holding a rocket or grenade in position for firing.

launch′ (or **launch′ing**) **pad′** or **launch′pad′,** *n.* [*count*] the platform from which a rocket, missile, etc., is launched.

laun•der (lôn′dər, län′-) /'lɔndər, 'lɑn-/ *v.* **1.** to wash (clothes, linens, etc.); to wash and iron (clothes): [~ + *obj*]: *She laundered the sheets.* [*no obj*]: *He spent the whole day laundering.* **2.** [*no obj*] to undergo washing and ironing: *The shirt didn't launder well.* **3.** [~ + *obj*] to disguise the source of (illegal or secret funds or profits), as by sending through a foreign bank. —**laun′der•er,** *n.* [*count*] —**laun•dress** (lôn′dris, län′-) /'lɔndrɪs, 'lɑn-/ *n.* [*count*]

laun•der•ette (lôn′də ret′, län′-) /,lɔndə'rɛt, ,lɑn-/ also **laun•drette** (lôn dret′, län-) /lɔn'drɛt, lɑn-/ *n.* [*count*] a self-service laundry having coin-operated washers, dryers, etc.

Laun•dro•mat (lôn′drə mat′, län′-) /'lɔndrə,mæt, 'lɑn-/ *Trademark.* [*count*] a launderette.

laun•dry (lôn′drē, län′-) /'lɔndriy, 'lɑn-/ *n., pl.* **-dries. 1.** [*noncount*] articles of clothing or linens that have been or are to be washed: *enough laundry for a full load.* **2.** [*count*] a room or business establishment where things are laundered. —**laun′dry•man′** or **-wom′an,** *n.* [*count*], *pl.* **-men** or **-wom•en.**

laun′dry list′, *n.* [*count*] a lengthy, esp. random list of items: *submitted our laundry list of requests.*

lau•re•ate (lôr′ē it, lor′-) /'lɔriyɪt, 'lɒr-/ *n.* [*count*] **1.** a person who has been honored for achieving distinction in a particular field or with a particular award: *a Nobel laureate.* *—adj.* [*after a noun*] **2.** deserving or having special recognition for achievement: *a poet laureate.*

lau•rel (lôr′əl, lor′-) /'lɔrəl, 'lɒr-/ *n.* [*count*] **1.** Also called **bay.** a small European evergreen tree, having dark, glossy green leaves. **2.** a leaf or branch of laurel, or a wreath made of these, used as a sign of victory or distinction. **3.** Usually, **laurels.** [*plural*] honor won, as for achievement in a field or activity. **—*Idiom.*** **4. rest on one's laurels,** to stop trying for further successes.

la•va (lä′və, lav′ə) /'lɑvə, 'lævə/ *n.* [*noncount*] **1.** the hot, melted, fluid rock that comes out of a volcano. **2.** the rock formed when this becomes solid and cools.

la•vage (lə väzh′, lav′ij) /lə'vɑʒ, 'lævɪdʒ/ *n.* [*noncount*] the washing of an organ of the body by flooding with water.

lav•a•to•ry (lav′ə tôr′ē, -tōr′ē) /'lævə,tɔriy, -,towriy/ *n.* [*count*], *pl.* **-ries. 1.** a room fitted with washbowls and toilets. **2.** a flush toilet.

lav•en•der (lav′ən dər) /'lævəndər/ *n.* **1.** [*noncount*] a pale bluish purple. **2.** [*count*] a plant of the mint family having spikes of sweet-smelling, pale purple flowers, that produces an oil used in making perfume. **3.** [*noncount*] the dried flowers or other parts of this plant used as scent or as a preservative.

lav•ish (lav′ish) /'lævɪʃ/ *adj.* **1.** spent, given, produced, or occurring in great amounts: *a lavish serving of food.* **2.** generous: *to be lavish with one's time or money.* *—v.* [~ + *obj* + *on* + *obj*] **3.** to expend or give in great amounts or without limit: *to lavish gifts on one's children.* —**lav′ish•ly,** *adv.*

law (lô) /lɔ/ *n.* **1.** [*noncount*] the principles, rules, and regulations set up by a government, other authority, or by custom, that apply to all the people of a group; a system or collection of such principles and rules: *a country that is ruled by law.* **2.** [*count*] a single rule or principle from this collection: *They passed a law to punish terrorist acts.* **3.** [*noncount*] the field of knowledge concerned with these rules, or the profession that deals with law and legal procedure: *to study law; to practice law.* **4.** [*count; the* + ~] the police, or the people whose job it is to enforce the law: *in trouble with the law.* **5.** a rule or principle of proper conduct that reflects the rules of one's conscience, the concepts of natural justice, or the will of God: [*count*]: *a moral law.* [*noncount*]: *divine law.* **6.** [*count*] a rule or manner of behavior that is instinctive: *the law of self-preservation.* **7.** [*count*] (in philosophy, science, etc.) a statement of a relation or sequence of events that will always occur under the same conditions: *the laws of motion.* **8.** [*count*] a rule or principle thought of as regulating or governing the structure of something, or how its parts are put together: *the laws of grammar.* —***Idiom.*** **9. be a law to** or **unto oneself,** to act without regard for established controls, customs, or principles. **10. lay down the law,** to issue orders in a firm way.

law′-abid′ing, *adj.* keeping to or obeying the law.

law′ and or′der, *n.* [*noncount*] the rule of law as accepted and obeyed by citizens: *keeping respect for law and order.*

law•break•er (lô′brā′kər) /ˈlɔˌbreykər/ *n.* [*count*] one who breaks the law. —**law′break′ing,** *n.* [*noncount*], *adj.*

law•ful (lô′fəl) /ˈlɔfəl/ *adj.* **1.** allowed by law: *a lawful enterprise.* **2.** recognized by law; legally qualified; legitimate: *a lawful king.* —**law′ful•ly,** *adv.*

law•less (lô′lis) /ˈlɔlɪs/ *adj.* **1.** lacking regard for the law: *a lawless country.* **2.** unruly; disorderly; *a lawless crew.* **3.** illegal: *lawless activities.* —**law′less•ness,** *n.* [*noncount*]

law•mak•er (lô′mā′kər) /ˈlɔˌmeykər/ *n.* [*count*] a person who makes a law or laws; a legislator.

law•man (lô′man′, -mən) /ˈlɔˌmæn, -mən/ *n.* [*count*], *pl.* **-men.** an officer of the law, as a sheriff.

lawn (lôn) /lɔn/ *n.* [*count*] a stretch of open, grass-covered land, esp. one closely mowed and near a house. See illustration at HOUSE.

lawn′ bowl′ing, *n.* [*noncount*] a game played on a bowling green by rolling a ball toward a stationary ball.

lawn′ mow′er, *n.* [*count*] a hand-operated or motor-driven machine for cutting the grass of a lawn.

law•suit (lô′so͞ot′) /ˈlɔˌsuwt/ *n.* [*count*] a case in a court of law involving one party against another.

law•yer (lô′yər, loi′ər) /ˈlɔyər, ˈlɔyər/ *n.* [*count*] a person whose profession is to represent clients in a court of law or to advise or act for them in other legal matters.

lax (laks) /læks/ *adj.*, **-er, -est. 1.** not strict or severe; careless: *lax morals.* **2.** slack; not tense: *a lax rope.* **3.** not rigidly exact or precise; vague: *lax thinking.* —**lax•i•ty** (lak′si tē) /ˈlæksɪtiy/ **lax′ness,** *n.* [*noncount*] —**lax′ly,** *adv.* See -LAX-.

-lax-, *root. -lax-* comes from Latin, where it has the meaning "loose, slack." This meaning is found in such words as: LAX, LAXATIVE, RELAX.

lax•a•tive (lak′sə tiv) /ˈlæksətɪv/ *n.* [*count*] **1.** a medicine for relieving constipation. —*adj.* [*before a noun*] **2.** of, relating to, or being such a medicine. See -LAX-.

lay[1] (lā) /ley/ *v.*, **laid, lay•ing,** *n.* —*v.* **1.** [~ + *obj*] to put or place in a position that is flat; set down: *to lay a book on a desk.* **2.** [~ + *obj*] to knock or beat down: *One punch laid him low.* **3.** [~ + *obj*] to put or place in a particular position: *The dog laid its ears back.* **4.** [~ + *obj*] to cause to be in a particular state or condition: *Their motives were laid bare.* **5.** [~ + *obj*] to set, place, or apply: *Don't you lay a hand on her.* **6.** [~ + *obj*] to place in proper position or in an orderly fashion: *to lay bricks.* **7.** [~ + *obj*] to establish as a basis; set up: *These talks will lay the foundation for further negotiations.* **8.** [~ + *obj*] to submit for someone's consideration: *I laid my case before the commission.* **9.** [~ + *obj* (+ *on* + *obj*)] to charge someone as being responsible for (something): *to lay the blame on the inspector.* **10.** [~ + *obj*] to bury: *They laid him to rest in the old churchyard.* **11.** to bring forth and deposit (an egg or eggs): [~ + *obj*]: *The hens laid an egg every day.* [*no obj*]: *The hens weren't laying.* **12.** [~ + *obj*] to impose as a burden, duty, penalty, or the like: *voted to lay an embargo on oil shipments.* **13.** [~ + *obj*] to place food, plates, knives, forks, spoons, etc., on (a table); set. **14.** [~ + *obj*] to devise or arrange: *They laid their plans carefully.* **15.** [~ + *obj (+ on)*] to bet (money); stake: *He laid $10 on the horse.* **16.** [~ + *obj* + *obj*] to bet (someone): *I'll lay you ten to one that we win.* **17.** [~ + *obj*] to place, set, or locate: *The scene is laid in France.* **18.** [~ + *obj*] *Slang (vulgar).* to have sexual intercourse with. **19.** [*no obj*] *Nonstandard.* LIE[2]: *just laying around the house.* **20. lay aside, a.** to abandon; reject: [~ + *aside* + *obj*]: *They laid aside his plan.* [~ + *obj* + *aside*]: *They laid it aside.* **b.** to save for use at a later time; store: [~ + *aside* + *obj*]: *She had laid aside some money.* [~ + *obj* + *aside*]: *How had she laid it aside?* **21. lay away, a.** to reserve for later use; save: [~ + *obj* + *away*]: *She laid the money away.* [~ + *away* + *obj*]: *She had laid away a fair amount of money.* **b.** [~ + *away* + *obj*] to hold merchandise until final payment or request for delivery: *to lay away a winter coat.* **22. lay back,** [*no obj*] *Slang.* to relax. **23. lay down,** [~ + *down* + *obj*] **a.** to give up: *The troopers laid down their guns.* **b.** to state authoritatively: *Their parents finally laid down the rules.* **c.** to stock; store: *to lay down wine.* **24. lay for,** [~ + *for* + *obj*] to lie in wait for: *The cops are laying for the thief.* **25. lay in,** [~ + *in* + *obj*] to store away for future use: *to lay in a supply of food.* **26. lay into,** [~ + *into* + *obj*] to attack physically or with words. **27. lay off, a.** to dismiss (an employee), often temporarily: [~ + *obj* + *off*]: *The boss laid him off after only a few days.* [~ + *off* + *obj*]: *The company laid off hundreds of workers.* **b.** *Slang.* to stop annoying or teasing: [~ + *off* + *obj*]: *I told you to just lay off your brother.* [*no obj*]: *Just lay off, leave me alone!* **c.** [*no obj*] *Informal.* to stop work: *Let's lay off early.* **d.** [~ + *off* + *obj*] to stop or stop using: *to lay off drinking.* **28. lay on,** [~ + *on* + *obj*] to cover with; apply: *to lay on a coat of wax.* **29. lay open, a.** to cut open: [~ + *open* + *obj*]: *The surgeon laid open the area of the infection.* [~ + *obj* + *open*]: *She laid it open and began to operate.* **b.** to expose; reveal: [~ + *open* + *obj*]: *The news story laid open a whole new set of allegations against him.* [~ + *obj* + *open*]: *The news story laid it all open.* **c.** [~ + *obj* + *open*] to expose (someone) to criticism, blame, or suspicion: *This new charge lays him open to a criminal indictment.* **30. lay out, a.** to spread out in order; arrange; prepare: [~ + *out* + *obj*]: *She laid out her pens and paper and set to work.* [~ + *obj* + *out*]: *She laid them out and set to work.* **b.** to plan; plot; design; to make a layout of: [~ + *out* + *obj*]: *She laid out the design on paper.* [~ + *obj* + *out*]: *Lay it out on paper first.* **c.** to ready (a corpse) for burial: [~ + *obj* + *out*]: *The undertaker laid the body out.* [~ + *out* + *obj*]: *The undertaker laid out the body.* **d.** [~ + *out* + *obj*] *Informal.* to spend or contribute (money): *He laid out $50 for each ticket.* **e.** [~ + *obj* + *out*] *Slang.* to knock (someone) down or unconscious: *laid him out with one punch.* **31. lay over,** [*no obj*] to make a short stopover: *The plane laid over in Albany.* **32. lay up,** to cause to be kept in one's bed or indoors: [~ + *obj* + *up*]: *was laid up with the flu.* [~ + *up* + *obj*]: *This flu has laid up the entire crew.* —*n.* [*count*] **33.** the way or position in which a thing is laid or lies: *the lay of the south pasture.* **34.** *Slang* (*vulgar*). **a.** a partner in sexual intercourse. **b.** an instance of sexual intercourse. —***Idiom.*** **35. get laid,** *Slang* (*vulgar*). to have sexual intercourse. **36. lay it on (thick),** to flatter someone or boast extravagantly; exaggerate. **37. lay of the land,** [*the* + ~] the conditions, circumstances, or situation: *Let's get the lay of the land before proceeding.* —**Usage.** For many speakers, the verbs LAY, LIE[2] and LIE[1] are confused. LAY and LIE[2] are confused because both have the sense of "in a flat position." The verb LAY in most of its meanings takes an object, and a general rule to remember is that if the word "put, place," can be substituted in a sentence, then LAY is the verb to use: *Lay (= put, place) the books on the table. She laid (= put, placed) the baby in the cradle.* But the verb LIE[2] does not take an object: *Lie down and rest a moment. The baby is lying down.* For many speakers, the problem comes in the past tense for these two verbs, because the past tense of LIE[2] is *lay,* which looks like, but is not, the present form of LAY: *The dog will want to lie in the shade; yesterday he lay in the grass.* Note that we can *lay* something, as a baby, down on a bed; the baby will then *lie* there until we pick it up. Finally, the verb LIE[1] meaning "to tell a lie or make a false statement" is regular: its past tense is *lied.*

lay[2] (lā) /ley/ *v.* pt. of LIE[2].

lay[3] (lā) /ley/ *adj.* [*before a noun*] **1.** belonging to, involving, or performed by someone not a member of the clergy: *a lay sermon.* **2.** not belonging to or proceeding from a profession, esp. the law or medicine: *a lay opinion.*

lay[4] (lā) /ley/ *n.* [*count*] **1.** a short narrative or other poem. **2.** a song.

lay′a•way plan′ (lā′ə wā′) /ˈleyəˌwey/ *n.* [*count*] a method of buying something by which an item is kept by the store until the customer has completed payments.

lay•er (lā′ər) /ˈleyər/ *n.* [*count*] **1.** a thickness of some material laid on or spread over a surface: *a layer of soot on the window sill.* **2.** a bed; stratum: *alternating layers of basalt and sandstone.* **3.** a person or thing that lays: *a carpet layer.* **4.** a hen kept for egg production. **5.** one of several items of clothing worn one on top of the other: *wore layers of warm clothing.* **—***v.* [~ + *obj*] **6.** to make a layer of. **7.** to form, put down, or arrange in layers. **8.** to arrange or wear (clothing) in layers.

lay•ette (lā et′) /leyˈɛt/ *n.* [*count*] an outfit of clothing, bedding, etc., for a newborn baby.

lay•man (lā′mən) /ˈleymən/ *n.* [*count*], *pl.* **-men. 1.** a person who is not a member of the clergy; one of the laity. **2.** a person who is not a member of a given profession, as law or medicine.

lay•off (lā′ôf′, -of′) /ˈleyˌɔf, -ˌɒf/ *n.* [*count*] **1.** the act of dismissing employees, esp. temporarily. **2.** a period of unemployment imposed on a worker: *a layoff of several months.*

lay•out (lā′out′) /ˈleyˌawt/ *n.* **1.** [*count*] an arrangement or plan: *the layout of a house.* **2.** [*count*] the act of laying or spreading out. **3.** [*count*] a plan or sketch showing the arrangement of stories, pictures, illustrations, and artwork in an advertisement, newspaper, or magazine page, etc.; the arrangement itself. **4.** [*noncount*] the technique, process, or occupation of making layouts. **5.** [*count*] *Informal.* a place and the features that go with it: *a fancy layout with a swimming pool and a tennis court.* **6.** [*count*] *Informal.* a display: *an appetizing layout of food.*

lay•o•ver (lā′ō′vər) /ˈleyˌowvər/ *n.* [*count*] STOPOVER: *a layover each way in Las Vegas.*

laze (lāz) /leyz/ *v.*, **lazed, laz•ing. 1.** [*no obj*] to relax or lounge lazily. **2.** to pass (time, life, etc.) lazily: [~ + *obj* + *away*]: *He's just been lazing his days away.* [~ + *away* + *obj*]: *to laze away the days.*

la•zy (lā′zē) /ˈleyziy/ *adj.*, **-zi•er, -zi•est. 1.** unwilling to work or perform effort, activity, or exertion; indolent: *too lazy to get up in the morning.* **2.** causing or encouraging idleness: *a lazy afternoon.* **3.** slow-moving; sluggish: *a lazy stream.* —**la•zi•ly** (lā′zə lē) /ˈleyzəliy/ *adv.* —**la′zi•ness,** *n.* [*noncount*]

la•zy•bones (lā′zē bōnz′) /ˈleyziyˌbownz/ *n.* [*count*], *pl.* **-bones.** *Informal.* a lazy person.

la′zy Su′san (so͞o′zən) /ˈsuwzən/ *n.* [*count*] a revolving tray for food.

lb., an abbreviation of Latin *libra*: pound.

l.c., an abbreviation of: lowercase.

LCD, *n.* [*count*], *pl.* **LCDs, LCD's.** liquid-crystal display: a display of information, as on digital watches, portable computers, and calculators, using a liquid-crystal film that changes when voltage is applied.

Ld., an abbreviation of: limited.

lead[1] (lēd) /liyd/ *v.*, **led** (led) /lɛd/ **lead•ing,** *n.*, *adj.* **—***v.* **1.** to go before or with to show the way; conduct or escort; guide: [~ + *obj*]: *The captain led his troops over the hill.* [*no obj*]: *If you lead, I will follow.* **2.** [~ + *obj*] to conduct by guiding: *to lead a horse by a rope.* **3.** [~ + *obj*] to influence (the thoughts); cause: *What led her to change her mind?* **4.** [~ + *to* + *obj*] to result in; tend toward: *The incident led to her resignation.* **5.** [~ + *obj*] to guide in direction, course, action, opinion, etc.; bring: *You can lead him around to your point of view.* **6.** [~ + *obj*] to go through or pass (time, life, etc.): *to lead a full and happy life.* **7.** [~ + *obj*] to conduct in a particular course: *The pipes led the water directly to the sewer.* **8.** (of a road, passage, etc.) to serve to bring (a person) to a place: [~ + *obj*]: *The next street will lead you to the post office.* [~ + *to* + *obj*]: *That path leads directly to the house.* **9.** [~ + *obj*] to take or bring: *The visitors were led into the senator's office.* **10.** [~ + *obj*] to be in command of; direct: *He led the British forces during the war.* **11.** [~ + *obj*] to go at the head of or in advance of: *The mayor will lead the parade.* **12.** to have first place in: [~ + *obj*]: *Iowa leads the nation in corn production.* [*no obj*]: *His party was leading in the polls.* **13.** [~ + *obj*] to direct or have the principal part in: *Who is going to lead the discussion?* **14.** [~ + *obj*] to act as leader of (an orchestra, band, etc.); conduct. **15.** to begin a hand in a card game (with a card or suit specified): [~ + *obj*]: *I'll lead diamonds.* [*no obj*]: *The player to the dealer's left is supposed to lead.* **16. lead off, a.** to begin; start: [~ + *off* + *obj*]: *Let's lead off the meeting with a prayer.* [*no obj*]: *The meeting led off with a prayer.* **b.** *Baseball.* to be the first player in (the batting order) or the first batter in (an inning): [~ + *off* + *obj*]: *He led off the game with a home run.* [*no obj*]: *He led off, and promptly singled.* **17. lead on,** to mislead: [~ + *obj* + *on*]: *led him on into thinking he had the job.* [~ + *on* + *obj*]: *He'd led on dozens of customers.* **—***n.* [*count*] **18.** the first or foremost place: *to take the lead in the race.* **19.** the extent of such an advance position: *a lead of several yards.* **20.** a person or thing that leads. **21.** a leash: *The dog was on a short lead.* **22.** a piece of useful information: *The reporter got a lead on the story from a bystander.* **23.** example; leadership: *He took the lead in the charity drive.* **24. a.** the principal part in a play. **b.** the person who plays it. **25. a.** the act or right of playing first in a card game. **b.** the card, suit, etc., so played. **26.** the opening paragraph of a newspaper story, serving as a summary. **27.** an insulated single wire used as a conductor in electrical connections. **—***adj.* [*before a noun*] **28.** most important; principal; leading; first: *a lead editorial.* **—*Idiom.* 29. lead up to,** [~ + *obj*] **a.** to prepare the way for: *A number of events led up to the stock market crash.* **b.** to approach gradually: *He was slowly leading up to a request for a raise.*

lead[2] (led) /lɛd/ *n.* [*noncount*] **1.** a heavy, soft, bluish-gray metal that can be shaped easily. **2.** bullets; shot: *shot the victim full of lead.* **3.** graphite, esp. a thin stick of graphite used in a pencil. **—***v.* [~ + *obj*] **4.** to cover, line, weight, or treat with lead or one of its compounds. **—*Idiom.* 5. get the lead out,** [*no obj*] *Slang.* to move or work faster; hurry up.

lead•ed (led′id) /ˈlɛdɪd/ *adj.* (of gasoline) containing lead.

lead•en (led′n) /ˈlɛdn̩/ *adj.* **1.** very heavy; ponderous: *leaden feet.* **2.** dull; spiritless; gloomy: *a leaden conversation.* **3.** of a dull gray color: *leaden skies.* **4.** made of lead.

lead•er (lē′dər) /ˈliydər/ *n.* [*count*] one that leads.

lead•er•ship (lē′dər ship′) /ˈliydərˌʃɪp/ *n.* **1.** [*noncount*] the position or function of a leader. **2.** [*noncount*] ability to lead: *She demonstrated qualities of leadership.* **3.** [*count; usually singular*] the leaders of a group: *the government leadership.*

lead•ing (lē′ding) /ˈliydɪŋ/ *adj.* [*before a noun*] **1.** principal; foremost: *a leading authority.* **2.** coming in advance of others; first: *We rode in the leading car.* **3.** directing; guiding.

lead′ing ques′tion *n.* [*count*] a question worded in a way that suggests the proper or desired answer: *to ask leading questions of a witness.*

lead′ time′ (lēd) /liyd/ *n.* the period of time between the start or first phase of a process and the point where results are seen: [*count*]: *a lead time of about fifty days for the project.* [*noncount*]: *not enough lead time.*

leaf (lēf) /liyf/ *n.*, *pl.* **leaves** (lēvz) /liyvz/ *v.* **—***n.* **1.** [*count*] one of the usually green, flat parts at the end of a stem on a plant. **2.** [*count*] a sheet of paper or other writing material, one side of each sheet making up a page. **3.** [*noncount*] a thin sheet of metal: *decorated with silver leaf.* **4.** [*count*] a flat part of a table that slides, is hinged, or detaches from the main piece: *the leaves of a dining room table.* **—***v.* **5. leaf through,** [~ + *obj*] to turn pages of: *leafing through a book.* **—*Idiom.* 6. take a leaf out of** or **from someone's book,** to use someone as an example: *The company took a leaf out of Japan's book on how to mass-produce automobiles efficiently.* **7. turn over a new leaf,** to begin new; make a fresh start. —**leaf′less,** *adj.*

leaf•let (lēf′lit) /ˈliyflɪt/ *n.*, *v.*, **-let•ed** or **-let•ted, -let•ing** or **-let•ting. —***n.* [*count*] **1.** a small flat or folded sheet of printed matter, as an advertisement or notice, usually intended for free distribution. **2.** one of the separate parts or divisions of certain leaves. **—***v.* [~ + *obj*] **3.** to distribute leaflets to or among: *The student government leafleted the entire campus.*

leaf•y (lē′fē) /ˈliyfiy/ *adj.*, **-i•er, -i•est.** full of leaves.

league[1] (lēg) /liyg/ *n.*, *v.*, **leagued, lea•guing. —***n.* [*count*] **1.** a group of persons, parties, organizations, countries, etc., who join to promote common interests or to provide assistance or service to each of its members. **2.** a group of athletic teams organized to compete chiefly among themselves: *a bowling league.* **3.** group; class; category: *As a pianist he simply isn't in your league.* **—***v.* [*no obj*] **4.** to unite in a league; combine: *They leagued together.* **—*Idiom.* 5. in league (with),** working together, esp. secretly; conspiring: *They were in league with the enemy.*

league[2] (lēg) /liyg/ *n.* [*count*] a unit of distance usually roughly 3 miles (4.8 kilometers).

leak (lēk) /liyk/ *n.* [*count*] **1.** an unintended hole, crack, or the like, through which liquid, gas, light, etc., enters or escapes: *a leak in the roof.* **2.** a spreading or release of secret information by an unnamed source: *a leak to the* *press about his role in the conspiracy.* **—***v.* **3.** [*no obj*] to let a liquid, gas, light, etc., enter or escape, as through a hole or crack: *The boat leaks.* **4.** to (cause to) pass in or out in this manner, as liquid, gas, or light: [*no obj*]: *Gas was leaking from a pipe.* [~ + *obj*]: *The brakes are leaking fluid.* **5.** to (cause or allow to) become known: [*no obj*]: *The news leaked to the public.* [~ + *obj*]: *Who leaked that story to the press?* **—*Idiom.* 6. take a leak,** *Slang* (*vulgar*). to urinate. —**leak′y,** *adj.*, **-i•er, -i•est.**

leak•age (lē′kij) /ˈliykɪdʒ/ *n.* an act of leaking; a leak; an amount of such leaking: [*noncount*]: *to prevent leakage.* [*count*]: *leakages all through the ship's hull.*

lean[1] (lēn) /liyn/ *v.*, **leaned** or (*esp. Brit.*) **leant** (lent) /lɛnt/ **lean•ing. 1.** to bend or tilt (the body) from a vertical position: [*no obj*]: *She leaned out the window.* [~ + *obj*]: *He leaned his head forward.* **2.** to bend or slant in a particular direction: [*no obj*]: *The post leans to the left.* [~ + *obj*]: *He leaned the bike to the left.* **3.** to rest or lie on something for support: [*no obj*]: *She leaned against a wall.* [~ + *obj*]: *He leaned the bike against the railing.* **4.** [~ + *on/upon*] to depend or rely: *He could always lean on them in an emergency.* **5.** [*no obj*] to tend to agree with or be in favor of: *They're leaning toward our point of view.* **6. lean on,** [~ + *on* + *obj*] *Informal.* to pressure or threaten: *The gangster was leaning on the small businesses for more money.*

lean[2] (lēn) /liyn/ *adj.*, **-er, -est,** *n.* **—***adj.* **1.** (of persons or animals) without much flesh or fat; thin: *lean cattle.* **2.** (of meat) containing little or no fat: *lean beefsteak.* **3.** lacking in richness, fullness, quantity, etc.; poor: *a number of very lean years.* **4.** spare; economical: *Our business has to become leaner if we are to survive.* **—***n.* [*noncount*] **5.** the part of flesh that consists of muscle rather than fat. —**lean′ness,** *n.* [*noncount*]

lean•ing (lē′ning) /ˈliynɪŋ/ *n.* [*count*] a tendency; inclination: *literary leanings.*

lean′-to′, *n.* [*count*], *pl.* **-tos.** a shack or shed supported at one side by trees or posts and that has a slanted roof.

leap (lēp) /liyp/ *v.*, **leaped** or **leapt** (lept, lēpt) /lɛpt, liypt/ **leap•ing,** *n.* **—***v.* **1.** to spring through the air from one point or position to another; jump (over): [*no obj*]: *to leap over a ditch.* [~ + *obj*]: *to leap a fence.* **2.** [~ + *obj*] to cause to jump this way: *The rider leaped her horse over the obstacles.* **3.** [*no obj*] to move or act quickly or suddenly: *to leap aside.* **4.** [*no obj*] to pass, come, rise, etc., as if with a jump: *Suddenly an idea leaped to her mind.* **—***n.* [*count*] **5.** a springing movement. **6.** the distance covered in a leap; jump: *a leap of three feet.* **7.** an abrupt change, usually for the better: *a leap in profits.* **—*Idiom.* 8. by leaps and bounds,** very rapidly: *The baby seemed to be growing by leaps and bounds.* **9. leap in the dark,** [*count*] an action that risks results that cannot be predicted. —**leap′er,** *n.* [*count*]

leap•frog (lēp′frog′, -frôg′) /ˈliypˌfrɒg, -ˌfrɔg/ *n.*, *v.*, **-frogged, -frog•ging. —***n.* [*noncount*] **1.** a game in which a player jumps over another player bent over from the waist. **—***v.* **2.** to jump over or pass (a person or thing) in or as if in leapfrog: [*no obj*]: *leapfrogging past the opposition.* [~ + *obj*]: *leapfrogged the fence.*

leap′ year′, *n.* [*count*] **1.** (in the Western calendar) a year that contains 366 days, with February 29 as an additional day; it occurs every four years: *A leap year occurs in years whose last two digits are evenly divisible by four, except for years marking a century that are not divisible by 400.* **2.** a year containing an extra day in any calendar.

learn (lûrn) /lɜrn/ *v.*, **learned** (lûrnd) /lɜrnd/ or **learnt** (lûrnt) /lɜrnt/ **learn•ing. —***v.* **1.** to gain or acquire knowledge of or skill in (something) by study, instruction, or experience: [~ + *obj*]: *to learn a new language.* [~ + (*how*) *to* + *verb*]: *Where did you learn (how) to throw a ball like that?* [*no obj*]: *She learns quickly.* **2.** to become informed of or acquainted with; find out: [~ + *obj*]: *to learn the truth.* [~ + (*that*) *clause*]: *I learned that he was a sailor only last week.* [~ + *about/of* + *obj*]: *When did you learn about his past?* **3.** [~ + *obj*] to memorize: *He learned the poem in ten minutes.* **4.** [~ + *obj*] to gain by experience, exposure to example, or the like: *She learned patience from her father.* **5.** [~ + *obj* + *obj*] *Nonstandard.* to teach: *learned him a lesson he won't forget.* —**learn′er,** *n.* [*count*]

learn•ed (lûr′nid *for 1-3;* lûrnd *for 4*) /ˈlɜrnɪd *for 1-3;* lɜrnd *for 4*/ *adj.* **1.** having much knowledge; scholarly: *learned professors.* **2.** [*before a noun*] of a scholarly nature: *a learned journal.* **3.** well-informed: *very learned in the ways of the world.* **4.** obtained or acquired by experience, study, etc., and not inborn: *learned behavior.*

learn•ing (lûr′ning) /ˈlɜrnɪŋ/ *n.* [*noncount*] **1.** knowledge obtained by careful study in any field of scholarly work. **2.** the act or process of acquiring knowledge or skill.

learn′ing disabil′ity, *n.* [*count*] any of several conditions esp. in school-aged children in which there is evidence of difficulty in accomplishing specific tasks, as reading and writing. —**learn′ing-disa′bled,** *adj.*

lease (lēs) /liys/ *n.*, *v.*, **leased, leas•ing. —***n.* [*count*] **1.** a contract allowing the use of land, renting property, etc., to another for a certain period in exchange for rent or other payment. **2.** the period of time for which a lease is made: *a five-year lease.* **—***v.* **3.** to grant the temporary possession or use of (lands, property, etc.) to another, usually for compensation at a fixed rate; to let: [~ + *obj* (+ *to* + *obj*)]: *to lease one's apartment to a friend.* [~ + *obj* + *obj*]: *We leased him the apartment.* [*no obj*]: *to lease at a lower rate.* **4.** [~ + *obj* (+ *from* + *obj*)] to take or hold by lease: *He leased the farm from the sheriff.* **—*Idiom.* 5. a new lease on life,** [*count*] a chance to improve one's situation or to live longer or more happily: *After his heart operation he felt he had a new lease on life.* —**leas′er,** *n.* [*count*]

leash (lēsh) /liyʃ/ *n.* **1.** [*count*] a chain, strap, etc., for controlling or leading a dog or other animal; a lead. **2.** [*noncount*] control; restraint: *to keep one's temper in leash.* **—***v.* [~ + *obj*] **3.** to secure or control by or as if by a leash: *Leash your dog.*

least (lēst) /liyst/ *adj.*, *a superlative of* **little** *with* **less** *or* **lesser** *as comparative.* **1.** smallest in size, amount, degree, etc.; slightest; lowest in amount: *wasn't paying the least attention.* **—***n.* [*noncount; the* + ~] **2.** something that is least: *Your little problem is the least of my worries right now.* **—***adv.* **3.** *superl. of* **little** *with* **less** *as compar.* to the smallest extent, amount, or degree: *That's the least important question of all.* **—*Idiom.* 4. at least, a.** at the lowest estimate or figure: *We'll have to pay $500 at least to cover that damage.* **b.** at any rate; in any case: *At least she wasn't hurt.* **5. not in the least,** not in the smallest degree: *not worried in the least.* **6. to say the least,** This expression is used to express the belief that a situation or circumstance is even worse than stated: *The result will be terrible inflation, to say the least.*

leath•er (leth′ər) /ˈlɛðər/ *n.* [*noncount*] **1.** the skin of an animal in which the hair has been removed and prepared by tanning or a similar process to preserve it and make it soft and easily shaped when dry. **—***adj.* [*before a noun*] **2.** relating to or made of leather. —**leath′er•y,** *adj.*

leath•er•neck (leth′ər nek′) /ˈlɛðərˌnɛk/ *n.* [*count*] *Informal.* a U.S. marine.

leave[1] (lēv) /liyv/ *v.*, **left** (left) /lɛft/ **leav•ing. 1.** to go out of or away from, as a place: [~ + *obj*]: *to leave the house.* [*no obj*]: *We left for the airport.* **2.** [~ + *obj*] to quit: *to leave a job.* **3.** [~ + *obj*] to let remain behind: *The bear left tracks in the snow.* **4.** [~ + *obj*] to let stay or be in the condition stated: *Leave the motor running.* **5.** [~ + *obj*] to let remain in a position to do something without being bothered: *We left him to his work.* **6.** [~ + *obj*] to let (a thing) remain for another's action or decision: *We left the details to the lawyer.* **7.** [~ + *obj*] to give in charge; entrust: *Leave the package with my neighbor.* **8.** [~ + *obj*] to turn aside from; abandon or disregard: *She left music to study engineering.* **9.** to give for use after one's death or departure: [~ + *obj* + *to* + *obj*]: *to leave one's money to charity.* [~ + *obj* + *obj*]: *She left him a lot of money.* **10.** [~ + *obj*] to have remaining after death: *He leaves a wife and three children.* **11.** [*not: be* + ~*-ing;* ~ + *obj*] to have as a remainder after subtraction: *2 from 4 leaves 2.* **12. leave off, a.** [*no obj*] to stop; cease; discontinue: *The professor couldn't remember where she had left off from the previous lecture.* **b.** to omit: [~ + *obj* + *off*]: *We left him off the list.* [~ + *off* + *obj*]: *We left off too many of her relatives from the list.* **13. leave out,** to omit; exclude: [~ + *out* + *obj*]: *She left out a few important statistics.* [~ + *obj* + *out*]: *You left them out of your report.* —**leav′er,** *n.* [*count*]

leave[2] (lēv) /liyv/ *n.* **1.** [*noncount*] permission to do something: *to beg leave to go.* **2.** permission to be absent, as from work or military duty: [*noncount*]: *to ask for leave.* [*count*]: *allowed us a leave to visit home during Christmas.* **3.** [*count*] the time this permission lasts: *30 days' leave.* **—*Idiom.* 4. take leave of,** [~ + *obj*] to part or separate from: *Have you taken leave of your senses? (= Are you crazy?)* **5. take one's leave,** to depart: *We should take our leave before the speeches begin.*

leav•en (lev′ən) /ˈlɛvən/ *n.* [*noncount*] **1.** a substance, as yeast or baking powder, that causes fermentation and expansion of dough or batter. **2.** an element that produces a change, as by making something dull become more lively. —*v.* [~ + *obj*] **3.** to add leaven to (dough or batter). **4.** to fill (a situation) with something that produces or causes a change.

leav•en•ing (lev′ə ning) /ˈlɛvənɪŋ/ *n.* [*noncount*] **1.** Also called **leav′ening a′gent.** a substance used to produce fermentation in dough or batter; leaven. **2.** the process of causing fermentation by leaven.

leaves (lēvz) /liyvz/ *n.* pl. of LEAF.

Leb•a•nese (leb′ə nēz′, -nēs′) /ˌlɛbəˈniyz, -ˈniys/ *adj., n., pl.* **-nese.** —*adj.* **1.** of or relating to Lebanon. —*n.* [*count*] **2.** a person born or living in Lebanon.

-lec-, *root.* *-lec-* comes from Latin (and sometimes Greek), where it has the meaning "gather; choose." This meaning is found in such words as: COLLECT, ELECTION, ELIGIBLE, ELITE, INELIGIBLE, LECTERN, LECTURE, RECOLLECT, SELECT. See -LEG-.

lech•er (lech′ər) /ˈlɛtʃər/ [*count*] Also, **lech** (lech) /lɛtʃ/. a man who engages in lechery.

lech•er•ous (lech′ər əs) /ˈlɛtʃərəs/ *adj.* (usually of a man) continually thinking of or wanting to have sex. —**lech′er•ous•ly,** *adv.*

lech•er•y (lech′ə rē) /ˈlɛtʃəriy/ *n.* [*noncount*] (usually of a man) constant indulgence in sexual activity.

lec•tern (lek′tərn) /ˈlɛktərn/ *n.* [*count*] a stand with a slanted top, used to hold a book, speech, etc., at the proper height for a standing reader or speaker. See -LEC-.

lec•ture (lek′chər) /ˈlɛktʃər/ *n., v.,* **-tured, -tur•ing.** —*n.* [*count*] **1.** a talk delivered before an audience or a class, esp. for instruction or to set forth some subject: *a lecture on modern art.* **2.** a speech of warning or scolding; a long reprimand: *got a stern lecture on being responsible.* —*v.* **3.** to give a lecture or series of lectures: [*no obj*]: *He lectured to a number of student groups.* [~ + *obj*]: *She lectured the students on diplomacy.* **4.** to scold or warn, esp. at some length: [~ + *obj*]: *She lectured her children on good table manners.* [*no obj*]: *She lectured to them.* —**lec′tur•er,** *n.* [*count*] See -LEC-.

led (led) /lɛd/ *v.* pt. and pp. of LEAD[1].

LED (el′ē dē′) /ˌɛliyˈdiy/ *n.* [*count*], *pl.* **LEDs, LED's.** light-emitting diode: a device that gives off light when current goes through it, used esp. for displaying readings on digital watches, calculators, etc.

ledge (lej) /lɛdʒ/ *n.* [*count*] a narrow, flat, shelflike part sticking out from a wall, cliff, or other upright structure.

ledg•er (lej′er) /ˈlɛdʒɛr/ *n.* [*count*] an account book in which money amounts coming into and going out of a business are recorded.

lee (lē) /liy/ *n.* [*count; usually singular; often: the* + ~] **1.** protective shelter: *the lee of a rock in a storm.* **2.** the side or part that is sheltered or turned away from the wind: *the huts that were erected under the lee of the mountain.* **3.** *Chiefly Nautical.* the quarter or region toward which the wind blows. —*adj.* **4.** of, on, or moving toward the lee.

leech (lēch) /liytʃ/ *n.* [*count*] **1.** a bloodsucking worm once used widely for letting out blood in medical treatments. **2.** a person who clings to another for personal gain; parasite. —*v.* **3.** to cling to and feed upon, drain, use up (someone, or someone's resources): [~ + *obj*]: *Her companion leeched her of all the money she had.* [*no obj*]: *constantly leeching from his relations.*

leek (lēk) /liyk/ *n.* [*count*] a plant of the amaryllis family, related to the onion, having a rounded bulb and leaves used in cooking.

leer (lēr) /lɪər/ *v.* [*no obj*] **1.** to look with a sideways glance, esp. one suggesting sexual interest. —*n.* [*count*] **2.** a sly look, or one that suggests sexual interest.

leer•y (lēr′ē) /ˈlɪəriy/ *adj.* [*be* + ~ + *of*], **-i•er, -i•est.** careful; suspicious; not trusting: *I'm leery of his financial advice.* —**leer′i•ness,** *n.* [*noncount*]

lees (lēz) /liyz/ *n.* [*plural*] the grounds or sediment that collects at the bottom of a bottle of wine, beer, etc.

lee•ward (lē′wərd; *Nautical.* lo͞o′ərd) /ˈliywərd; *Nautical.* ˈluwərd/ *adj.* **1.** relating to, in, or moving toward the direction toward which the wind blows (opposed to *windward*). —*n.* [*count; usually singular; usually: the* + ~] **2.** the lee side; the point or direction toward which the wind blows. —*adv.* **3.** toward the lee.

lee•way (lē′wā′) /ˈliyˌwey/ *n.* [*noncount*] **1.** extra time, space, materials, etc., within which to act: *a leeway of two weeks.* **2.** a degree of freedom of action or thought: *plenty of leeway to make a choice.*

left[1] (left) /lɛft/ *adj.* **1.** of, relating to, or located on or near the side of a person or thing that is turned toward the west when the person or thing is facing north (opposed to *right*): *He uses his left hand to hold his fork.* **2.** (*often: Left*) of or belonging to the political left wing or side; having liberal or radical views in politics. —*n.* **3.** [*noncount*] the left side, or something on the left side: *Look to your left.* **4.** [*count*] a turn toward the left: *Make a left at the next corner.* **5. the Left,** [*noncount*] **a.** individuals or organized groups calling for liberal reform or revolutionary change in the social, political, or economic scheme. **b.** the liberal position held by these people. —*adv.* **6.** toward the left: *We turned left.*

left[2] (left) /lɛft/ *v.* **1.** pt. and pp. of LEAVE[1]. —*adj.* [*be* + ~] **2.** remaining after something has been used, taken away, etc.; not used: *Only one quart of juice is left.*

left′-hand′, *adj.* [*before a noun*] **1.** on or to the left: *a left-hand turn.* **2.** of, for, or with the left hand.

left′-hand′ed, *adj.* **1.** having the left hand more in control or effective than the right; preferring to use the left hand: *a left-handed pitcher.* **2.** fitted to or performed by the left hand: *a left-handed tool.* **3.** having more than one meaning and therefore doubtful and possibly insulting: *a left-handed compliment.* —*adv.* **4.** with the left hand: *to write left-handed.*

left•ist (lef′tist) /ˈlɛftɪst/ *n.* [*count; sometimes: Leftist*] **1.** a member of the political Left; liberal or radical. —*adj.* **2.** of, relating to, or called for by the political Left. —**left′-ism,** *n.* [*noncount*]

left•o•ver (left′ō′vər) /ˈlɛftˌowvər/ *n.* [*count*] **1.** Usually, **leftovers.** [*plural*] food remaining uneaten at the end of a meal, esp. when saved for later use. **2.** anything left or remaining from a larger amount; remainder. —*adj.* [*before a noun*] **3.** being left or remaining: *leftover meatloaf.*

left′ wing′, *n.* [*count; usually: the* + ~] the liberal or radical element in a political party or other organization. —**left′-wing′,** *adj.*: *left-wing politics.* —**left′-wing′er,** *n.* [*count*]

left•y or **left•ie** (lef′tē) /ˈlɛftiy/ *n.* [*count*], *pl.* **-ies.** *Informal.* a left-handed person.

leg (leg) /lɛg/ *n., v.,* **legged, leg•ging.** —*n.* [*count*] **1.** either of the two lower limbs of a two-footed animal, as a human being, or any of the paired limbs of an animal, that support and move the body. **2.** something resembling or suggesting a leg in use, position, or appearance, as one of the sides of a triangle. **3.** the part of a piece of clothing, boot, or the like that covers the leg. **4.** one of usually several relatively slender supports for a piece of furniture. **5.** one of the separate parts or sections of anything: *on the last leg of a trip.* —*v.* [*no obj*] **6.** to use the legs in walking or running: *We were legging back to the store.* —***Idiom.*** **7. a leg to stand on,** [*usually used with a negative word*] facts or proof to support one's claims or arguments: *With such skimpy evidence against us the police don't have a leg to stand on.* **8. a leg up,** an advantage: *Our new product gave us a leg up on our competition.* **9. on one's** or **its last legs,** just short of collapse: *The failing business was on its last legs when he took it over.* **10. stretch one's legs,** to move or walk around after a long time sitting.

-leg-, *root.* *-leg-* comes from Latin, where it has the meanings "law" and "to gather; read." It is related to -LEC-. These meanings are found in such words as: DELEGATE, ILLEGAL, ILLEGIBLE, INTELLECT, INTELLIGENT, LEGACY, LEGAL, LEGATE, LEGEND, LEGIBLE, LEGION, LEGISLATE, LEGITIMATE, PARALEGAL, PRIVILEGE, RELEGATE, SACRILEGE.

leg•a•cy (leg′ə sē) /ˈlɛgəsiy/ *n.* [*count*], *pl.* **-cies. 1.** (in a will) a gift of money or other personal property to someone. **2.** anything handed down from the past, as if from an ancestor: *left a legacy of debt.* See -LEG-.

le•gal (lē′gəl) /ˈliygəl/ *adj.* **1.** permitted by law; lawful: *Theft is not legal.* **2.** [*before a noun*] of or relating to law: *the legal system.* **3.** [*before a noun*] of, relating to, or befitting the profession of law or lawyers: *She has a sharp legal mind.* —*n.* [*count*] **4.** a person who acts in a legal manner. —**le′gal•ly,** *adv.* See -LEG-.

le′gal age′, *n.* the age, 18 in most states, at which a person is legally responsible and may enter into contracts: [*count*]: *a legal age of twenty-one.* [*noncount*]: *under legal age.*

le•gal•ese (lē′gə lēz′, -lēs′) /ˌliygəˈliyz, -ˈliys/ *n.* [*noncount*] language containing many legal terms or much legal jargon.

le′gal hol′iday, *n.* [*count*] a public holiday established by law, during which certain work, government business, etc., is cut short or suspended.

le•gal•ism (lē′gə liz′əm) /ˈliygəˌlɪzəm/ *n.* **1.** [*noncount*] strict adherence to the law. **2.** [*count*] an example of such strict following of the rules. **—le′gal•is′tic,** *adj.* See -LEG-.

le•gal•i•ty (lē gal′i tē) /liy'gælɪtiy/ *n.* [*noncount*] the state or condition of being legal. See -LEG-.

le•gal•ize (lē′gə līz′) /'liygəˌlayz/ *v.* [~ + *obj*], **-ized, -iz•ing.** to make legal; authorize. **—le•gal•i•za•tion** (lē′gə li-zā′shən) /ˌliygəlɪ'zeyʃən/ *n.* [*noncount*] See -LEG-.

le′gal ten′der, *n.* [*noncount*] currency or money that may be lawfully used in payment of money debts and that must be accepted when offered for payment: *The two-dollar bill is still legal tender in the United States.*

leg•ate (leg′it) /'lɛgɪt/ *n.* [*count*] **1.** a member of the clergy sent or appointed by the pope as his representative. **2.** a usually official representative or envoy. See -LEG-.

leg•a•tee (leg′ə tē′) /ˌlɛgə'tiy/ *n.* [*count*], *pl.* **-tees.** a person to whom a legacy is assigned or left. See -LEG-.

le•ga•tion (li gā′shən) /lɪ'geyʃən/ *n.* [*count*] **1.** a diplomatic minister and staff in a foreign mission. **2.** the official headquarters of a diplomatic minister. See -LEG-.

le•ga•to (lə gä′tō) /lə'gɑtow/ *adj., adv. Music.* without breaks between successive tones: *a legato passage; The passage was played legato.*

leg•end (lej′ənd) /'lɛdʒənd/ *n.* **1.** [*count*] an unproved story handed down by tradition from earlier times and popularly accepted as historical: *the legend of King Arthur.* **2.** [*noncount*] a body of stories of this kind: *the winning of the West in American legend.* **3.** [*count*] a table on a map, chart, or the like, listing and explaining the symbols used. **4.** [*count*] a person who is very famous, well-known, liked, or admired in some areas. See -LEG-.

leg•end•ar•y (lej′ən der′ē) /'lɛdʒənˌdɛriy/ *adj.* of, relating to, or of the nature of a legend: *a legendary hero.* See -LEG-.

leg•er•de•main (lej′ər də mān′) /ˌlɛdʒərdə'meyn/ *n.* [*noncount*] **1.** the ability to fool people with hand tricks, as by making objects disappear; sleight of hand. **2.** trickery; deception: *some financial legerdemain to fool the accountants.* See -MAN-[1].

leg•ged (leg′id, legd) /'lɛgɪd, lɛgd/ *adj.* This word is used after some words to form adjectives indicating a certain number or a certain kind of legs: *two-legged; long-legged.*

leg•ging (leg′ing) /'lɛgɪŋ/ *n.* [*count*] **1.** Also, **leg•gin** (leg′in) /'lɛgɪn/. a covering, as of leather or canvas, for the leg. **2. leggings,** [*plural*] close-fitting trousers worn outdoors in the winter.

leg•gy (leg′ē) /'lɛgiy/ *adj.,* **-gi•er, -gi•est. 1.** having unnaturally long legs. **2.** having long, attractively shaped legs: *leggy dancers.*

leg•i•ble (lej′ə bəl) /'lɛdʒəbəl/ *adj.* capable of being read, esp. with ease, as writing or printing; easily readable. **—leg•i•bil•i•ty** (lej′ə bil′i tē) /ˌlɛdʒə'bɪlɪtiy/ *n.* [*noncount*] **—leg′i•bly,** *adv.* See -LEG-.

le•gion (lē′jən) /'liydʒən/ *n.* [*count*] **1.** the largest unit of the Roman army, numbering at different periods from about 4000 to 6000 foot soldiers. **2.** a military or semimilitary unit. **3.** any large group of armed men. **4.** any great number of persons or things; multitude; throng: *legions of admirers.* **—***adj.* [*be* + ~] **5.** very great in number: *The holy man's followers were legion.* **—le•gion•ar•y** (lē′jə ner′ē) /'liydʒəˌnɛriy/ *adj., n.* [*count*], *pl.* **-ar•ies.** See -LEG-.

le•gion•naire (lē′jə nâr′) /ˌliydʒə'nɛər/ *n.* **1.** (*often cap.*) a member of the American Legion. **2.** a member of any legion.

le•gion•naires′′ disease′, *n.* [*noncount*] a form of pneumonia caused by bacteria, typically caught by breathing in droplets from a contaminated water supply.

leg•is•late (lej′is lāt′) /'lɛdʒɪsˌleyt/ *v.,* **-lat•ed, -lat•ing. 1.** [*no obj*] to make or create laws: *It is Congress's responsibility to legislate effectively for the people.* **2.** [~ + *obj*] to create or control by legislation: *attempts to legislate morality.* **—leg′is•la′tor,** *n.* [*count*] See -LEG-.

leg•is•la•tion (lej′is lā′shən) /ˌlɛdʒɪs'leyʃən/ *n.* [*noncount*] **1.** the act of making or creating laws. **2.** a law or a body of laws created. See -LEG-.

leg•is•la•tive (lej′is lā′tiv) /'lɛdʒɪsˌleytɪv/ *adj.* **1.** having the function of making laws: *a legislative body.* **2.** of or relating to the creation of laws or to a legislature. See -LEG-.

leg•is•la•ture (lej′is lā′chər) /'lɛdʒɪsˌleytʃər/ *n.* [*count*] a body or group of persons, usually elected to the position, who are given the power to make, change, or take back the laws of a country or state. See -LEG-.

le•git (lə jit′) /lə'dʒɪt/ *adj. Informal.* legitimate.

le•git•i•mate (*adj.* li jit′ə mit; *v.* -māt′) / *adj.* lɪ'dʒɪtəmɪt; *v.* -ˌmeyt/ *adj., v.,* **-mat•ed, -mat•ing. —***adj.* **1.** according to law; lawful: *the property's legitimate owner.* **2.** following established rules, principles, or standards. **3.** born of legally married parents: *legitimate children.* **4.** valid; logical: *a legitimate conclusion.* **5.** justified; genuine; reasonable: *had a legitimate complaint.* **—***v.* [~ + *obj*] **6.** to make legitimate: *Parliament legitimated her accession to the throne.* **—le•git•i•ma•cy** (li jit′ə mə sē) /lɪ'dʒɪtəməsiy/ *n.* [*noncount*] **—le•git′i•mate•ly,** *adv.* See -LEG-.

le•git•i•mize (li jit′ə mīz′) /lɪ'dʒɪtəˌmayz/ *v.* [~ + *obj*], **-mized, -miz•ing.** to legitimate. **—le•git•i•mi•za•tion** (li-jit′ə mə zā′shən) /lɪˌdʒɪtəmə'zeyʃən/ *n.* [*noncount*] See -LEG-.

leg•man (leg′man′, -mən) /'lɛgˌmæn, -mən/ *n.* [*count*], *pl.* **-men. 1.** a person who works as an assistant to gather information, run errands, etc. **2.** a reporter who gathers news firsthand.

leg•ume (leg′yōōm, li gyōōm′) /'lɛgyuwm, lɪ'gyuwm/ *n.* [*count*] **1.** a plant, esp. one used for feed, food, or as a soil-improving crop; it is part of a family that includes peas, beans, alfalfa, clover, peanuts, and acacia. **2.** the pod, bean, or seed of such a plant. **—le•gu•mi•nous** (li-gyōō′mə nəs) /lɪ'gyuwmənəs/ *adj.*

leg•work (leg′wûrk′) /'lɛgˌwɜrk/ *n.* [*noncount*] work or research involving extensive walking or traveling from one place to another.

lei (lā) /ley/ *n.* [*count*], *pl.* **leis.** (in Hawaii) a wreath of flowers, leaves, etc., worn around the neck.

lei•sure (lē′zhər, lezh′ər) /'liyʒər, 'lɛʒər/ *n.* [*noncount*] **1.** freedom from the demands of work or duty: *a life of leisure.* **2.** time free from the demands of work or duty: *the leisure to pursue hobbies.* **—***adj.* **3.** free or unoccupied: *leisure hours.* **4.** having leisure; not required to work for a living: *the leisure class.* **5.** designed for entertainment or recreation: *video games and other leisure products.* **—*Idiom.* 6. at leisure, a.** with free time: *Do it when you're at leisure.* **b.** without haste or pressure; slowly: *He finished the book at leisure.* **7. at one's leisure,** when one has free time; at one's convenience: *Reply at your leisure.*

lei•sured (lē′zhərd, lezh′ərd) /'liyʒərd, 'lɛʒərd/ *adj.* [*before a noun*] **1.** having leisure: *the leisured classes.* **2.** leisurely; unhurried; relaxed: *leisured activities.*

lei•sure•ly (lē′zhər lē, lezh′ər-) /'liyʒərliy, 'lɛʒər-/ *adj.* **1.** unhurried; deliberate: *a leisurely conversation.* **—***adv.* **2.** in a leisurely manner: *to travel leisurely through Europe.*

leit•mo•tif (līt′mō tēf′) /'laytmowˌtiyf/ *n.* [*count*] a theme associated throughout a music drama with a particular person, situation, or idea.

lem•ming (lem′ing) /'lɛmɪŋ/ *n.* [*count*] a small, mainly arctic animal like a rat, noted for its mass migrations that sometimes result in mass drownings in the sea.

lem•on (lem′ən) /'lɛmən/ *n.* **1.** the yellowish, acid fruit of a subtropical citrus tree: [*noncount*]: *Would you like lemon with your tea?* [*count*]: *Lemons cost a dollar each there.* **2.** [*count*] the tree itself. **3.** [*noncount*] a color of yellow much like that of the outside of a lemon. **4.** [*count*] *Informal.* one that proves to be faulty or unsatisfactory; dud: *Our new car turned out to be a lemon.* **—***adj.* [*before a noun*] **5.** made of or with lemon: *lemon pie.* **6.** having the color, taste, or odor of lemon. **—lem′on•y,** *adj.*

lem•on•ade (lem′ə nād′, lem′ə nād′) /ˌlɛmə'neyd, 'lɛməˌneyd/ *n.* [*noncount*] a beverage made up of lemon juice, sweetener, and water.

le•mur (lē′mər) /'liymər/ *n.* [*count*] a small monkeylike animal that lives in trees and hunts at night, having large eyes and a foxlike face.

lend (lend) /lɛnd/ *v.,* **lent** (lent) /lɛnt/ **lend•ing. 1.** to grant the use of (something) on condition that it or its equivalent will be returned: [~ + *obj*]: *He doesn't like to lend things.* [~ + *obj* + *to* + *obj*]: *He lent his lawnmower to me.* [~ + *obj* + *obj*]: *He lent me his lawnmower.* **2.** to give (money) on condition that it is returned and that interest is paid for its temporary use: [~ + *obj*]: *The bank lends money at high interest rates.* [~ + *obj* + *to* + *obj*]: *The bank wouldn't lend the money to him.* [~ + *obj* + *obj*]: *The bank refused to lend him money.* **3.** (of a library) to allow the use of (books and other materials) outside library premises for a certain period: [~ + *obj*]: *The library lends videotapes.* [~ + *obj* + *to* + *obj*]: *That library will lend videotapes to anyone living in the vicinity.* [~ + *obj* + *obj*]: *The library will lend you the videotapes.* **4.** to give or contribute willingly or helpfully: [~ + *obj*]: *always there lending support.* [~ + *obj* + *to* + *obj*]: *lent their support to the cause.* [~ + *obj* + *obj*]: *He lent their cause his support.* **5.** [*not: be* + ~*-ing;* ~ + *oneself* + *to*] to adapt (itself or oneself) to something; be suitable for: *The building lends itself to inexpensive remodeling.* **6.** to give, confer, furnish, or impart (a quality) to something: [~ + *obj* + *to* + *obj*]: *A fireplace lends coziness to a room.* [~ + *obj* + *obj*]: *The use of a warm color there lends the room cheeriness.* **—*Idiom.* 7. lend a hand,** to give help; aid: [*no obj*]: *Can you lend a hand with this job?* [~ + *obj* + *a hand*]: *Can you lend us a hand?* [~ + *to* + *obj*]: *Lend a hand to the others.* —**lend′er,** *n.* [*count*] **—Usage.** See BORROW.

length (lengkth, lenth) /lɛŋkθ, lɛnθ/ *n.* **1.** [*noncount*] the longest extent of anything as measured from end to end: *The length of the yard was three hundred feet.* **2.** [*noncount*] extent from beginning to end of a series, account, book, etc.: *a novel 300 pages in length.* **3.** [*noncount*] extent in time; amount of time something lasts; duration: *the length of a visit.* **4.** [*count*] a distance figured by the extent of something specified: *Hold the picture at arm's length.* **5.** [*count*] a piece or portion of a certain or a known amount or distance measured: *He cut off a length of rope.* **6.** [*noncount*] the quality or state of being long rather than short: *a journey remarkable for its length.* **7.** Usually, **lengths.** [*plural*] the extent to which one would go to reach or accomplish a desired end: *to go to great lengths to get what one wants.* **—*Idiom.* 8. at length, a.** after a considerable time; finally: *He ran for most of the morning; at length he stopped.* **b.** fully; in detail: *went on at length about her family.*

length•en (lengk′thən, len′-) /ˈlɛŋkθən, ˈlɛn-/ *v.* to (cause to) become greater in length; (cause to) grow longer: [*no obj*]: *Her hair lengthened gradually.* [~ + *obj*]: *They had to lengthen the road.*

length•wise (lengkth′wīz′, lenth′-) /ˈlɛŋkθˌwayz, ˈlɛnθ-/ also **length•ways** (lengkth′wāz′, lenth′-) /ˈlɛŋkθˌweyz, ˈlɛnθ-/ *adj., adv.* in the direction of the length: *a lengthwise cut; She cut the material lengthwise.*

length•y (lengk′thē, len′-) /ˈlɛŋkθiy, ˈlɛn-/ *adj.,* **-i•er, -i•est.** of great length; very long: *a lengthy journey; a lengthy explanation.*

le•ni•en•cy (lē′nē ən sē, lēn′yən sē) /ˈliyniyənsiy, ˈliynyənsiy/ *n.* [*noncount*] the quality or state of being lenient: *The judge was known for his leniency toward first-time offenders.*

le•ni•ent (lē′nē ənt, lēn′yənt) /ˈliyniyənt, ˈliynyənt/ *adj.* not strict or severe; kind; indulgent: *to be lenient toward the children.* —**le′ni•ent•ly,** *adv.*

lens (lenz) /lɛnz/ *n.* [*count*], *pl.* **lens•es. 1.** a piece of glass or other transparent substance, curved on one or both surfaces and used in eyeglasses to correct vision problems, or in devices such as microscopes or binoculars to make things appear clearer, closer, or larger. **2.** a part of the eye behind the pupil that focuses images on the retina. **3.** CONTACT LENS.

lent (lent) /lɛnt/ *v.* pt. and pp. of LEND.

Lent (lent) /lɛnt/ *n.* [*proper noun*] (in many Christian churches) an annual season of fasting and asking forgiveness in preparation for Easter. —**Lent•en, lent•en** (lent′n) /ˈlɛntn̩/ *adj.: the Lenten season.*

len•til (len′til, -tl) /ˈlɛntɪl, -tl̩/ *n.* [*count*] **1.** a plant of the legume family, having flattened seeds used as food. **2.** the seed itself.

le•o•nine (lē′ə nin′) /ˈliyəˌnayn/ *adj.* of, relating to, resembling, or suggestive of a lion: *a leonine head.*

leop•ard (lep′ərd) /ˈlɛpərd/ *n.* [*count*] **1.** a large, powerful, spotted Asian or African cat, usually yellowish brown with black markings. **2.** any similar cat, as the snow leopard.

le•o•tard (lē′ə tärd′) /ˈliyəˌtɑrd/ *n.* [*count*] a skintight, single piece of clothing for the chest and trunk of the body, worn by acrobats, dancers, etc.

lep•er (lep′ər) /ˈlɛpər/ *n.* [*count*] **1.** a person who has leprosy. **2.** a person who is shut out of a group, as for unacceptable behavior; an outcast.

lep•re•chaun (lep′rə kôn′, -kon′) /ˈlɛprəˌkɔn, -ˌkɒn/ *n.* [*count*] a small elflike creature of Irish folklore, often represented as a little old man who will reveal the location of a crock of gold to anyone who catches him.

lep•ro•sy (lep′rə sē) /ˈlɛprəsiy/ *n.* [*noncount*] an infectious disease in which the skin and tissue of the body is destroyed and there is a loss of sensation. —**lep′rous,** *adj.*

les•bi•an (lez′bē ən) /ˈlɛzbiyən/ *n.* [*count*] a female homosexual. —**les′bi•an•ism,** *n.* [*noncount*]

le•sion (lē′zhən) /ˈliyʒən/ [*count*] any single, usually well-defined area of diseased or injured tissue.

less (les) /lɛs/ *adv., a comparative of* **little** *with* **least** *as superlative.* **1.** to a smaller length, amount, or degree: *a less-developed country.* **2.** [*much/still* + ~] to say nothing of: *I could barely pay for my own meal, much less hers.* **3.** [*with a negative word or phrase*] in any way different; other: *He's nothing less than a thief.* **—*adj., a compar. of*** **little** *with* **least** *as superl.* **4.** smaller in size, amount, degree, etc.: *He has less money than before.* **5.** lower in consideration, rank, or importance: *complained to no less a person than the mayor (= to no one ranking lower than the mayor).* **6.** fewer: *There were less than ten speakers before me.* **—*n.*** [*noncount*] **7.** a smaller amount or quantity: *She eats less every day.* **8.** something not as important: *People have been imprisoned for less.* **—*prep.* 9.** minus; without; subtracting: *a year less two days.* **—*Idiom.* 10. less and less,** to a decreasing extent or degree: *I see less and less of my sister these days.*

-less, *suffix.* **1.** *-less* is attached to nouns to form adjectives with the meaning "without, not having (the thing or quality named by the noun)": *care* + *-less* → *careless; shame* + *-less* → *shameless* **2.** *-less* is also attached to verbs to form adjectives with the meaning "that cannot be" plus the *-ed/en* form of the verb; or "that never" plus the *-s* form of the verb: *tire* + *-less* → *tireless (= that never tires); count* + *-less* → *countless (= that cannot be counted).*

les•see (le sē′) /lɛˈsiy/ *n.* [*count*], *pl.* **sees.** a person to whom a lease is granted.

less•en (les′ən) /ˈlɛsən/ *v.* to (cause to) become less; reduce: [*no obj*]: *His shyness lessened as he grew older.* [~ + *obj*]: *Cold lessens feeling.*

less•er (les′ər) /ˈlɛsər/ *adj., a comparative of* **little** *with* **least** *as superlative.* **1.** smaller, as in size, value, or importance: *a lesser evil.* **—*adv., a compar. of*** **little** *with* **least** *as superl.* **2.** less.

les•son (les′ən) /ˈlɛsən/ *n.* [*count*] **1.** a section into which a course of study is divided: *to take driving lessons.* **2.** a unit of a book, an exercise, etc., that is assigned to a student for study. **3.** something to be learned or studied: *Have we learned anything from the lessons of history?* **4.** a useful piece of practical wisdom coming from one's experience or study: *The accident taught him a lesson.* **5.** a punishment intended to teach one better ways: *If she does that again, he'll give her a good lesson.* **6.** a portion of Scripture read at a church service.

les•sor (les′ôr, le sôr′) /ˈlɛsɔr, lɛˈsɔr/ *n.* [*count*] a person who grants a lease.

lest (lest) /lɛst/ *conj.* **1.** for fear that; so that (one) should not: *I used notes lest faulty memory should lead me astray.* **2.** that (used after words expressing fear, danger, anxiety, etc.): *We worried lest the secret become known.*

let[1] (let) /lɛt/ *v.,* **let, let•ting,** *n.* **—*v.* 1.** to allow or permit: [~ + *obj* + *root form of verb*]: *Don't let her see our faces.* [~ + *obj*]: *Can you come out? No, my parents won't let me.* **2.** [~ + *obj*] to allow to pass, go, or come: *He let us into the house.* **3.** [~ + *obj* + *root form of verb*] to cause to; make: *to let her know the truth.* **4.** [~ + *obj* + *root form of verb*] This word is used in the command forms *Let* or *Let us* (or *Let's,* which is short for *Let us*): **a.** to make a request: *Let's try to get along, please.* **b.** to give a command: *Let me see what's in your hand.* **c.** to express a warning about someone else doing something: *If they think they can just take over, just let them try.* **d.** to make a suggestion: *Why not let her drive?* **e.** to express one's indifference to some situation; to show that one does not care about something: *If she wants to gamble, let her do it.* **5.** [~ + *obj*] to grant the use of for rent or hire: *to let rooms.* **6.** [*no obj*] to allow to be leased: *an apartment to let.* **—*v.* 7. let down, a.** to disappoint or betray: [~ + *obj* + *down*]: *She really let me down when she didn't come to our party.* [~ + *down* + *obj*]: *He let down the whole team.* **b.** [~ + *obj* + *down*] to lower: *He let the car down off the lift.* **c.** to make (a garment) longer: [~ + *down* + *obj*]: *Can you let down this dress a few inches?* [~ + *obj* + *down*]: *He let the dress down a few inches.* **8. let in,** to admit: [~ + *in* + *obj*]: *This place lets in all kinds of people.* [~ + *obj* + *in*]: *Let me in.* **9. let in on,** [~ + *obj* + *in* + *on* + *obj*] to allow to share in: *I'll let you in on a secret.* **10. let off, a.** to release like an explosion: [~ + *off* + *obj*]: *to let off steam.* [~ + *obj* + *off*]: *to let steam off.* **b.** to excuse from work or responsibility: [~ + *obj* + *off*]: *The boss let us off early.* [~ + *off* + *obj*]: *The boss let off his workers early.* **c.** to release with little or no punishment: [~ + *obj* + *off*]: *The judge let him off with probation.* [~

+ *off* + *obj*]: *That judge lets off too many criminals.* **11. let on, a.** to reveal: [~ + *on* + *(that) clause*]: *He didn't let on that he knew about the party.* [*no obj*]: *She knew where they were going, but she never let on.* [~ + *on* + *about* + *obj*]: *She never let on about it.* **b.** [~ + *on* + *(that) clause*] to pretend: *He tried to let on that he didn't care.* **12. let out, a.** [~ + *out* + *obj*] to make known; express: *He let out a doubt.* **b.** to release from confinement, restraint, etc.: [~ + *obj* + *out*]: *to let air out of a tire.* **c.** to alter (a garment) so as to make larger or looser: [~ + *out* + *obj*]: *to let out a dress a few inches.* [~ + *obj* + *out*]: *to let a dress out a few inches.* **d.** [*no obj*] to be finished or dismissed: *School lets out in May.* **13. let up,** [*no obj*] **a.** to grow less powerful; lessen; abate; diminish: *The hurricane let up gradually.* **b.** to cease; stop: *At last, the rain is letting up.* **14. let up on,** [~ + *up on* + *obj*] to become more lenient with; to treat less strictly: *Let up on her; she's just a child.* **—*n.*** [*count; usually singular*] **15.** *Brit.* a housing rental. **—*Idiom.*** **16. let be,** [~ + *obj* + *be*] to refrain from interfering with or bothering: *Those boys wouldn't let him be, with their constant teasing.* **17. let go, a.** [~ + *obj* + *go*] to allow to escape: *She let the fish go because it was too small to keep.* **b.** to stop holding on to: [~ + *go* + *of* + *obj*]: *let go of the rope and fell.* [*no obj*]: *Hold on, don't let go.* **18. let oneself in for,** [~ + *obj* + *in* + *for*] to allow oneself to become involved in: *He didn't know what he was letting himself in for when he started the new job.* **19. let (someone) have it,** [~ + *obj* + *have it*] *Informal.* to attack; assault.

let[2] (let) /lɛt/ *n.* [*count*] (in tennis, badminton, etc.) any shot or action that must be replayed, esp. an otherwise valid serve that has hit the top of the net.

-let, *suffix.* **1.** *-let* is attached to a noun to form a noun that is a smaller version of the original noun or root: *book* + *-let* → *booklet (= a smaller book); pig* + *-let* → *piglet (= a smaller pig).* **2.** *-let* is also attached to a noun to form a noun that is a band, ornament, or article of clothing worn on the part of the body mentioned: *ankle* + *-let* → *anklet (= piece of clothing like a sock worn on the ankle); wrist* + *-let* → *wristlet (= ornament like a bracelet worn on the wrist).*

let•down (let′doun′) /ˈlɛtˌdawn/ *n.* [*count*] **1.** a disappointment; a disillusionment: *The news was a letdown.* **2.** a decrease in force or energy; depression: *I felt a terrible letdown after the party.*

le•thal (lē′thəl) /ˈliyθəl/ *adj.* of or causing death; deadly; fatal: *a lethal weapon; a lethal injection.* **—le′thal•ly,** *adv.*

le•thar•gic (lə thär′jik) /ləˈθɑrdʒɪk/ *adj.* **1.** drowsy; sluggish: *He's always lethargic after little sleep.* **2.** causing lethargy: *a lethargic day.* **—le•thar′gi•cal•ly,** *adv.*

leth•ar•gy (leth′ər jē) /ˈlɛθərdʒiy/ *n.* [*noncount*] the quality or state of being drowsy or dull; listlessness.

let's (lets) /lɛts/ contraction of *let us*: *Let's go home now.*

let•ter (let′ər) /ˈlɛtər/ *n.* **1.** a written or printed message or communication addressed to a person or organization and usually sent by mail: [*count*]: *Her letters went unanswered.* [*noncount; by* + ~]: *The news came by letter.* **2.** [*count*] a symbol or character that is used in writing and printing to represent a speech sound and is part of an alphabet: *The letter L is the twelfth letter in the English alphabet.* **3.** [*singular; often: the* + ~] literal meaning, as distinct from implied meaning (opposed to *spirit*): *the letter of the law.* **4. letters,** [*used with a singular or plural verb*] literature or learning in general: *a man of letters.* **—*v.*** **5.** [~ + *obj*] to mark or write with letters; inscribe: *The sign was beautifully lettered.* **—*Idiom.*** **6. to the letter,** to the last particular; precisely: *I followed your instructions to the letter.* **—let′ter•er,** *n.* [*count*] See -LIT-.

let′ter car′rier, *n.* MAIL CARRIER.

let•tered (let′ərd) /ˈlɛtərd/ *adj.* **1.** educated or able to read; literate. **2.** marked with or as if with letters.

let•ter•head (let′ər hed′) /ˈlɛtərˌhɛd/ *n.* **1.** [*count*] a printed heading on stationery giving the name and address of a person or organization. **2.** [*noncount*] a sheet of paper with such a heading.

let•ter•ing (let′ər ing) /ˈlɛtərɪŋ/ *n.* [*noncount*] **1.** the act or process of writing or forming letters. **2.** the letters written.

let′ter-per′fect, *adj.* precise or exact in every detail.

let′ter-qual′i•ty, *adj.* (of a computer printer) producing type that is equal in sharpness and thickness to that produced by an electric typewriter.

let•tuce (let′is) /ˈlɛtɪs/ *n.* **1.** a plant having large green leaves used in salads: [*noncount*]: *They grew lettuce in their backyard.* [*count*]: *Some lettuces were ruined.* **2.** [*noncount*] the leaves of this plant.

let•up (let′up′) /ˈlɛtˌʌp/ *n.* a stopping of activity, work, etc.: [*noncount*]: *rained without letup.* [*count*]: *raining without a letup.*

leu•ke•mi•a (lo͞o kē′mē ə) /luwˈkiymiyə/ *n.* [*noncount*] an often fatal disease in which the blood-forming organs produce too many of a certain type of white blood cell.

-lev-, *root.* *-lev-* comes from Latin, where it has the meaning "lift; be light." This meaning is found in such words as: ALLEVIATE, CANTILEVER, ELEVATE, ELEVATOR, LEVEE, LEVER, LEVERAGE, LEVITATE, LEVITY, LEVY, RELEVANT, RELIEVE.

lev•ee (lev′ē) /ˈlɛviy/ *n.* [*count*] *pl.* **-ees. 1.** a mound, bank, or other raised area designed to prevent the flooding of a river. **2.** a landing place for ships. See -LEV-.

lev•el (lev′əl) /ˈlɛvəl/ *adj., n., v.,* **-eled, -el•ing** or (*esp. Brit.*) **-elled, -el•ling. —*adj.*** **1.** having a flat or even surface: *level land.* **2.** equal, as in height, condition, rank, state, or advancement: *Their abilities were about level.* **3.** [*before a noun*] filled to a height even with the rim of a container: *a level teaspoon of salt.* **4.** steady; not changing: *to speak in a level voice.* **5.** sensible; rational: *to keep a level head in a crisis.* **6.** of or relating to a particular rank or involving members of such a rank (usually used in combination): *high-level discussions.* **—*n.*** **7.** a position with respect to a given or specified height: [*noncount*]: *a shelf built at eye level.* [*count*]: *The water rose to a level of 30 feet.* **8.** [*count*] a position in a graded scale of values, amount, or quantity: *an average level of skill.* **9.** [*count*] rank or status: *the top levels of government.* **10.** [*count*] a horizontal surface: *the upper level of the bridge.* **11.** [*count*] a device used to determine if a surface is flat or even. **—*v.*** **12.** [~ + *obj*] to make (a surface) level: *They leveled the ground before planting corn.* **13.** [~ + *obj*] to bring (something) to the level of the ground: *to level trees.* **14.** [~ + *obj*] *Informal.* to knock down (a person): *The champ leveled the challenger.* **15.** [~ + *obj* (+ *at/against* + *obj*)] to aim or point (a weapon, criticism, etc.) at a mark or objective: *Charges have been leveled against you.* **16. level off, a.** (of an aircraft, etc.) to (cause to) stay at a constant altitude or depth after a climb or descent: [*no obj*]: *The plane leveled off.* [~ + *obj* + *off*]: *The pilot leveled the plane off.* [~ + *off* + *obj*]: *The captain leveled off the submarine.* **b.** [*no obj*] to become stable; reach a constant amount or limit: *Unemployment hasn't leveled off.* **c.** to make even or smooth: [~ + *off* + *obj*]: *leveled off the ground.* [~ + *obj* + *off*]: *Maybe we can level it off.* **17. level with,** [~ + *with* + *obj*] to speak truthfully and openly with: *Level with me; how much will it cost?* **—*Idiom.*** **18. one's level best,** one's very best: *did her level best to help.* **19. on the level,** honest; sincere; reliable: *Is this offer on the level?* **—lev′el•er,** *n.* [*count*] **—lev′el•ly,** *adv.* **—lev′el•ness,** *n.* [*noncount*]

lev•el•head•ed (lev′əl hed′id) /ˈlɛvəlˈhɛdɪd/ *adj.* having common sense and sound judgment; sensible: *a level-headed manager.* **—lev′el•head′ed•ness,** *n.* [*noncount*]

lev•er (lev′ər, lē′vər) /ˈlɛvər, ˈliyvər/ *n.* [*count*] **1.** a handle used to operate something, as a piece of machinery. **2.** a stiff, rigid bar used to move or lift something heavy, by placing one end of it under the heavy object, resting the middle of it over some other object, and by pushing down on the other end. **3.** a means of persuasion: *used money as a political lever.* **—*v.*** [~ + *obj*] **4.** to move or lift with or as if with a lever. See -LEV-.

lev•er•age (lev′ər ij, lev′rij; lē′vər ij, -vrij) /ˈlɛvərɪdʒ, ˈlɛvrɪdʒ; ˈliyvərɪdʒ, -vrɪdʒ/ *n., v.,* **-aged, -ag•ing. —*n.*** [*noncount*] **1.** the action of a lever; the mechanical advantage gained by using a lever. **2.** power to act effectively or to influence people: *has leverage with the police.* **—*v.*** [~ + *obj*] **3.** to speculate in (invested funds) by using borrowed money to buy controlling interest in a company. See -LEV-.

le•vi•a•than (li vī′ə thən) /lɪˈvayəθən/ *n.* [*count*] **1.** a huge sea animal, as a whale. **2.** something of immense size or power.

Le•vi's (lē′vīz) /ˈliyvayz/ *Trademark.* [*plural; used with a plural verb*] a brand of jeans, esp. blue jeans.

lev•i•tate (lev′i tāt′) /ˈlɛvɪˌteyt/ *v.,* **-tat•ed, -tat•ing.** to (cause to) rise or float in the air as if defying gravity: [*no obj*]: *The dancer seemed to levitate in the air.* [~ + *obj*]: *The magician appeared to levitate several people.* **—lev•i•ta•tion** (lev′i tā′shən) /ˌlɛvɪˈteyʃən/ *n.* [*noncount*] See -LEV-.

lev•i•ty (lev′i tē) /ˈlɛvɪtiy/ *n.* [*noncount*] lack of proper seriousness; frivolousness: *The situation is too serious for levity.* See -LEV-.

lev•y (lev′ē) /ˈlɛviy/ *n., pl.* **lev•ies,** *v.,* **lev•ied, lev•y•ing.** —*n.* [*count*] **1.** a collecting of a tax by authority or force; a demand of such tax. **2.** the amount owed or collected. —*v.* [~ + *obj* (+ *on* + *obj*)] **3.** to impose (a tax, fine, etc.): *to levy a duty on imports.* —**lev′i•er,** *n.* [*count*] See -LEV-.

lewd (lo͞od) /luwd/ *adj.,* **-er, -est. 1.** sexually crude; lustful: *lewd behavior.* **2.** obscene or indecent: *lewd gestures.* —**lewd′ly,** *adv.* —**lewd′ness,** *n.* [*noncount*]

lex•i•cal (lek′si kəl) /ˈlɛksɪkəl/ *adj.* of or relating to the words or vocabulary of a language. See -LEG-.

lex•i•cog•ra•phy (lek′si kog′rə fē) /ˌlɛksɪˈkɒgrəfiy/ *n.* [*noncount*] the writing or editing of dictionaries. —**lex′i•cog′ra•pher,** *n.* [*count*] —**lex•i•co•graph•ic** (lek′si kə-graf′ik) /ˌlɛksɪkəˈgræfɪk/ **lex′i•co•graph′i•cal,** *adj.* See -GRAPH-, -LEG-.

lex•i•con (lek′si kon′, -kən) /ˈlɛksɪˌkɒn, -kən/ *n.* [*count*], *pl.* **-ca** (-kə) /-kə/ **-cons. 1.** a list, wordbook, or dictionary of a language. **2.** the vocabulary of a particular language, field, social class, person, etc.

LF, an abbreviation of: low frequency.

lg., an abbreviation of: **1.** large. **2.** long.

lge., an abbreviation of: large.

li•a•bil•i•ty (lī′ə bil′i tē) /ˌlayəˈbɪlɪtiy/ *n., pl.* **-ties. 1. liabilities,** [*plural*] money owed; debts (opposed to *assets*): *a company's huge liabilities.* **2.** [*count*] something that is a disadvantage: *His lack of education is a liability.* **3.** [*noncount*] the state or quality of being liable.

li•a•ble (lī′ə bəl) /ˈlayəbəl/ *adj.* [*be* + ~] **1.** legally responsible: *You are liable for the damage.* **2.** exposed or subject to something generally negative: *If you jump, you're liable to hurt yourself.* **3.** [~ + *to* + *verb*] likely; apt: *She's liable to get angry.*

li•ai•son (lē ā′zən, lē′ə zon′) /liyˈeyzən, ˈliyəˌzɒn/ *n.* **1.** [*noncount*] the contact kept in place by communication between parts of a group, as between units of the armed forces, in order to maintain cooperation. **2.** [*count*] a person who begins and maintains such a contact. **3.** [*count*] a love affair.

li•ar (lī′ər) /ˈlayər/ *n.* [*count*] a person who tells lies.

lib (lib) /lɪb/ *n.* [*noncount*] *Informal.* liberation: *women's lib; men's lib.* See -LIBER-.

li•ba•tion (lī bā′shən) /layˈbeyʃən/ *n.* [*count*] **1.** a pouring out of wine or other liquid in honor of a god. **2.** the liquid poured out. **3.** an intoxicating beverage.

lib•ber (lib′ər) /ˈlɪbər/ *n.* [*count*] *Informal.* a follower or member of a group seeking social equality: *a women's libber.* See -LIBER-.

li•bel (lī′bəl) /ˈlaybəl/ *n., v.,* **-beled, -bel•ing** or (*esp. Brit.*) **-belled, -bel•ling.** —*n.* **1.** [*noncount*] damage to the character or name of another by written or printed words, pictures, or the like, rather than by spoken words: *sued for libel.* **2.** [*count*] something that deliberately or harmfully misrepresents the character or name of another: *That charge was simply a libel put out by my opponent.* —*v.* [~ + *obj*] **3.** to print or publish a libel against (someone). —**li′bel•er,** *n.* [*count*] —**li′bel•ous,** *adj.* See -LIBR-.

-liber-, *root.* *-liber-* comes from Latin, where it has the meaning "free." This meaning is found in such words as: DELIVER, ILLIBERAL, LIBERAL, LIBERATE, LIBERTINE, LIBERTY, LIVERY.

lib•er•al (lib′ər əl, lib′rəl) /ˈlɪbərəl, ˈlɪbrəl/ *adj.* **1.** favorable to progress, change, or reform, as in political or religious affairs: *establishing a liberal democracy in the former totalitarian regime.* **2.** [*often: Liberal*] of or relating to a political party calling for measures favorable to progress, change, or reform. **3.** free from prejudice or bigotry; tolerant; open-minded: *liberal views on child-raising.* **4.** generous: *a liberal donation.* **5.** free; not literal: *a liberal interpretation of the rules.* **6.** of, relating to, or based on the liberal arts: *a liberal education.* —*n.* [*count*] **7.** a person of liberal principles or views. **8.** [*often: Liberal*] a member of a liberal political party. —**lib•er•al•i•ty** (lib′ə ral′i tē) /ˌlɪbəˈrælɪtiy/ *n.* [*noncount*] —**lib′er•al•ly,** *adv.* See -LIBER-.

lib′eral arts′, *n.* [*plural*] academic college courses providing education in the arts, humanities, natural sciences, and social sciences.

lib•er•al•ism (lib′ər ə liz′əm, lib′rə-) /ˈlɪbərəˌlɪzəm, ˈlɪbrə-/ *n.* [*noncount*] **1.** the quality or state of being liberal. **2.** a political and social philosophy calling for individual freedom, democratic government, progress and reform, and protection of civil liberties. **3.** [*sometimes: Liberalism*] the principles and practices of a liberal party in politics. See -LIBER-.

lib•er•al•ize (lib′ər ə līz′, lib′rə-) /ˈlɪbərəˌlayz, ˈlɪbrə-/ *v.,* **-ized, -iz•ing.** to (cause to) become liberal: [*no obj*]: *After the death of the dictator the country began to liberalize.* [~ + *obj*]: *The new president liberalized many of the old policies.* —**lib•er•al•i•za•tion** (lib′ər ə lə zā′shən, lib′rə-) /ˌlɪbərələˈzeyʃən, ˌlɪbrə-/ *n.* [*noncount*] See -LIBER-.

lib•er•ate (lib′ə rāt′) /ˈlɪbəˌreyt/ *v.* [~ + *obj*], **-at•ed, -at•ing. 1.** to set free, as from imprisonment. **2.** to free (a nation or area) from control by a foreign or oppressive government. **3.** to free (a group or individual) from social or economic discrimination, esp. arising from traditional role expectations or bias. **4.** *Informal.* to steal or take over illegally: *The prisoners liberated several shipments of chocolate.* —**lib•er•a•tion** (lib′ə rā′shən) /ˌlɪbəˈreyʃən/ *n.* [*noncount*] —**lib′er•a′tor,** *n.* [*count*] See -LIBER-.

Li•be•ri•an (lī bēr′ē ən) /layˈbɪəriyən/ *adj.* **1.** of or relating to Liberia. —*n.* [*count*] **2.** a person born or living in Liberia.

lib•er•tine (lib′ər tēn′) /ˈlɪbərˌtiyn/ *n.* [*count*] **1.** a person who is morally or sexually uncontrolled. —*adj.* **2.** licentious; dissolute. See -LIBER-.

lib•er•ty (lib′ər tē) /ˈlɪbərtiy/ *n., pl.* **-ties. 1.** [*noncount*] freedom from government or control that is oppressive and that denies rights. **2.** [*noncount*] freedom from external or foreign rule; independence: *The American colonies fought for liberty from Great Britain.* **3.** [*noncount*] power or right to act according to choice: *You have some liberty to choose among the courses you take.* **4.** [*noncount*] freedom from being held captive, confined, or otherwise kept in slavery: *gave an enslaved people their liberty.* **5.** [*noncount*] permission granted to a sailor to go ashore, usually for less than 24 hours. **6.** [*count*] an instance of being improper in action or speech: *taking liberties as a guest.* —***Idiom.*** **7. at liberty, a.** free from captivity or restraint. **b.** free to do or be as specified: *You are at liberty to leave.* See -LIBER-.

li•bid•i•nous (li bid′n əs) /lɪˈbɪdn̩əs/ *adj.* full of lust or sexual desire; lustful; lascivious.

li•bi•do (li bē′dō) /lɪˈbiydow/ *n.* [*count*], *pl.* **-dos.** sexual drive. —**li•bid•i•nal** (li bid′n l) /lɪˈbɪdn̩l/ *adj.*

-libr-, *root.* *-libr-* comes from Latin, where it has the meaning "book." This meaning is found in such words as: LIBEL, LIBRARY, LIBRETTO.

-libra-, *root.* *-libra-* comes from Latin, where it has the meaning "balance; weigh." This meaning is found in such words as: DELIBERATE, EQUILIBRIUM.

li•brar•i•an (lī brâr′ē ən) /layˈbrɛəriyən/ *n.* [*count*] a person specializing in library work. See illustration at SCHOOL. See -LIBR-.

li•brar•y (lī′brer′ē) /ˈlayˌbrɛriy/ *n.* [*count*], *pl.* **-brar•ies. 1. a.** a place, as a building or set of rooms, containing books, recordings, or other reading, viewing, or listening materials arranged and cataloged in a fixed way. See illustration at SCHOOL. **b.** such a place together with the staff maintaining it: *a public library.* **2.** any collection of books or set of items resembling a library in appearance, organization, or purpose. See -LIBR-.

li•bret•to (li bret′ō) /lɪˈbrɛtow/ *n.* [*count*], *pl.* **-bret•tos, -bret•ti** (-bret′ē) /-ˈbrɛtiy/. **1.** the text of an opera or similar work. **2.** a book or booklet containing such a text. —**li•bret′tist,** *n.* [*count*] See -LIBR-.

Lib•y•an (lib′ē ən) /ˈlɪbiyən/ *adj.* **1.** of or relating to Libya. —*n.* [*count*] **2.** a person born or living in Libya.

lice (līs) /lays/ *n.* [*plural*] a pl. of LOUSE.

li•cense (lī′səns) /ˈlaysəns/ *n., v.,* **-censed, -cens•ing.** —*n.* **1.** [*count*] a certificate, tag, plate, etc., giving proof of permission from a government or other authority to do something: *a driver's license.* **2.** [*noncount*] deliberate moving away from or exaggeration of a rule, principle, or standard, as for the sake of literary or artistic effect: *poetic license.* —*v.* [~ + *obj*] **3.** to issue or grant a license to: *The city licenses those hot dog stands.* —**li′censed,** *adj.*

li•cen•see or **li•cen•cee** (lī′sən sē′) /ˌlaysənˈsiy/ *n.* [*count*] one to whom a license is granted or issued.

li•cen•tious (lī sen′shəs) /layˈsɛnʃəs/ *adj.* sexually uncontrolled; lascivious; lewd. —**li•cen′tious•ly,** *adv.* —**li•cen′tious•ness,** *n.* [*noncount*]

li•chen (lī′kən) /ˈlaykən/ *n.* [*count*] an organism made of a fungus and an alga, most commonly forming crusty patches on rocks and trees.

lic•it (lis′it) /ˈlɪsɪt/ *adj.* legal; lawful. —**lic′it•ly,** *adv.*

lick (lik) /lɪk/ *v.* **1.** to pass the tongue over the surface of, as to moisten, taste, or eat: [~ + *obj*]: *to lick a postage stamp.* [*no obj*]: *The cat was licking at its fur.* **2.** [~ + *obj*] to cause to become by stroking with the tongue: *to lick a spoon clean.* **3.** (of waves, flames, etc.) to pass or play lightly over: [~ + *obj*]: *The waves licked the shore.* [*no obj*]: *The flames licked at the roof.* **4.** [~ + *obj*] *Informal.* **a.** to hit or beat, esp. as a punishment; thrash. **b.** to defeat: *We licked their team fair and square.* **5. lick up,** to lap up: [~ + *up* + *obj*]: *The cat licked up her milk.* [~ + *obj* + *up*]: *She licked it up.* **—***n.* [*count*] **6.** a stroke of the tongue over something: *a quick lick of the tongue.* **7.** *Informal.* **a.** a blow: *a few licks with a cane.* **b.** a brief, brisk burst of activity or energy. **c.** a small amount: *haven't done a lick of work.* **8.** Usually, **licks.** [*plural*] a musical phrase, as by a jazz soloist in improvising. **—*Idiom.*** **9. last licks,** a final turn or opportunity. **10. lick and a promise,** a quick and usually sloppy or not careful performance of a chore. **11. lick one's lips,** to move the tongue over one's lips in greedy anticipation. **12. lick one's wounds,** to attempt to heal or comfort oneself after injury or defeat.

lick′e•ty-split′ (lik′i tē) /ˈlɪkɪtiy/ *adv. Informal.* at great speed; rapidly: *to travel lickety-split.*

lic•o•rice (lik′ər ish, lik′rish, lik′ə ris) /ˈlɪkərɪʃ, ˈlɪkrɪʃ, ˈlɪkərɪs/ *n.* **1.** [*count*] a plant of the legume family. **2.** [*noncount*] the sweet-tasting, dried root of this plant, or an extract made from it, used in medicine, candy, cooking, etc. **3.** a candy flavored with licorice root: [*noncount*]: *eating licorice.* [*count*]: *A licorice cost only two cents back then.*

lid (lid) /lɪd/ [*count*] **1.** a removable or hinged cover for closing the opening, usually at the top, of a pot, jar, trunk, etc.; a movable cover. **2.** an eyelid. **3.** a restraint, ceiling, or curb, as on prices or news: *a lid on costs.* **—lid′ded,** *adj.*

lie[1] (lī) /lay/ *n., v.,* **lied, ly•ing.** **—***n.* [*count*] **1.** a false statement made knowingly and on purpose with the intention of deceiving; a falsehood. **2.** something intended or serving to give a false impression. **—***v.* **3.** to speak falsely, knowing that what one says is not true, as with intent to deceive: [*no obj*]: *lied about his age.* [~ + *obj*]: *lying his way out of difficulty.* [*used with quotations*]: *"Of course I love you," he lied.*

lie[2] (lī) /lay/ *v.,* **lay** (lā) /ley/ **lain** (lān) /leyn/ **ly•ing,** *n.* **—***v.* **1.** [*no obj*] to be in a horizontal or flat position, as on a bed or the ground; recline (often fol. by *down*): *I had to lie down after driving all day.* **2.** [*no obj*] (of objects) to rest in a horizontal or flat position: *The book lies on the table.* **3.** [*no obj*] to be or remain in the position, condition, or state (that is mentioned in the next phrase): *The troops lay in ambush.* **4.** [*no obj*] to rest, press, or weigh: *many worries lay on my mind.* **5.** [*no obj*] to be situated or extended: *the land lying along the coast.* **6.** [*no obj; not: be* + *~-ing*] to be in or have a specified direction; extend: *The trail from here lies to the west.* **7.** [*no obj; not: be* + *~-ing*] to be found or located in a particular area or place; occur: *The fault lies with us.* **8.** [*no obj*] to be buried in a particular spot: *Here lies the late hero.* **9. lie behind,** [~ + *behind* + *obj*] to be the real reason for something: *What lies behind her decision to quit?* **10. lie in,** [*no obj*] to be kept in bed, or to stay in bed, as in childbirth. **11. lie with,** [*not: be* + *~-ing; ~* + *with* + *obj*] to be the duty or function of: *The blame lies with the parents.* **—***n.* [*count*] **12.** the manner, relative position, or direction in which something lies, as the position of the ball in golf compared to how easy it is to play. **—*Idiom.*** **13. lie down on the job,** *Informal.* to do less than one could or should do. **14. take lying down,** [*take* + *obj* + *lying down*] to accept or give in to (something) without resistance: *Are you going to take that insult lying down?* **—Usage.** See LAY.

lie′ detec′tor, *n.* [*count*] an instrument that records the changes in certain activities of a person's body that may indicate when a lie is being told. Also called **polygraph.**

lien (lēn) /liyn/ *n.* [*count*] the legal right to hold another's property or to have it sold or applied for payment of a claim, esp. to satisfy a debt.

lieu (lo͞o) /luw/ *n.* [*noncount*] **1.** place; stead. **—*Idiom.*** **2. in lieu of,** instead of: *gave us an IOU in lieu of cash.*

lieu•ten•ant (lo͞o ten′ənt) /luwˈtɛnənt/ *n.* [*count*] **1.** a rank in the armed forces above a sergeant and below a captain. **2.** a commissioned officer in the U.S. Navy or Coast Guard ranking above a lieutenant junior grade. **3.** an aide; assistant: *If she can't attend, she will send her lieutenant.* **—lieu•ten′an•cy,** *n.* [*noncount*] See -TEN-.

life (līf) /layf/ *n., pl.* **lives** (līvz), *adj.* **—***n.* **1.** [*noncount*] the general condition, quality, or force that separates organisms from objects and from dead organisms, and that shows itself in the ability of organisms to grow, reproduce, and change in response to the environment: *There are many forms of life on earth.* **2.** [*count*] the period or amount of time of living existence of an individual; lifetime: *She led a long life.* **3.** [*count*] the period of existence, activity, or effectiveness of something not living or inanimate: *The life of a new car is quite a few years.* **4.** [*noncount*] the course of existence or sum of experiences and actions that make up a person's existence: *Life is full of ups and downs.* **5.** [*count*] a living being: *Several lives were lost in the fire.* **6.** [*noncount*] living things thought of as a group: *insect life.* **7.** [*count*] a biography: *a life of Willa Cather.* **8.** [*noncount*] liveliness; spirit; activity: *The party was full of life.* **9.** [*count; usually singular*] a person or thing that enlivens: *the life of the party.* **10.** [*noncount*] a manner of existing characteristic of a particular group, time, place, etc.: *He enjoyed the bustle of city life.* **11.** [*noncount*] a prison sentence of spending one's life in prison. **12.** [*count; usually singular*] anything or anyone considered to be as precious as life: *She was his life.* **—***adj.* [*before a noun*] **13.** for or lasting a lifetime; lifelong: *life imprisonment.* **14.** of or relating to living, animate existence: *life functions.* **—*Idiom.*** **15. bring to life, a.** [~ + *obj* + *to life*] to restore to consciousness; bring to. **b.** [~ + *obj* + *to life*] to make animated, lively, and interesting: *He brought the party to life.* **c.** to give or represent with characteristics that are like life: [~ + *to life* + *obj*]: *The movie brings to life a great historical event.* [~ + *obj* + *to life*]: *It brings it all to life.* **16. come to life, a.** to recover consciousness; come to. **b.** to become animated, lively, and interesting. **c.** to appear lifelike: *The sculptor made the ancient god come to life.* **17. for dear life,** with the most desperate effort possible: *He hung on to the slippery rope for dear life.* **18. for life,** for as long as one lives: *friends for life.* **19. for the life of one,** [*with a negative word*] even with the greatest effort: *I can't solve that problem for the life of me.* **20. not on your life,** absolutely not: *Want to go back to that nightclub?— Not on your life, pal!* **21. take one's life in one's hands,** to risk death by knowingly doing something very dangerous. **22. take (someone's) life,** to kill.

life′ belt′, *n.* [*count*] a beltlike life preserver.

life•blood (līf′blud′) /ˈlayfˌblʌd/ *n.* [*noncount*] **1.** the blood, esp. when it is considered as essential to maintain life. **2.** a crucial force or resource: *Agriculture is the lifeblood of that country.*

life•boat (līf′bōt′) /ˈlayfˌbowt/ *n.* [*count*] a ship's boat designed to be used to rescue persons from a sinking vessel.

life•guard (līf′gärd′) /ˈlayfˌgɑrd/ *n.* [*count*] an expert swimmer employed to protect bathers from drowning.

life′ jack′et, *n.* [*count*] a life preserver in the form of a sleeveless jacket. Also called **life vest.**

life•less (līf′lis) /ˈlayflɪs/ *adj.* **1.** without life; dead: *a lifeless body.* **2.** not animated, lively, or interesting: *a lifeless performance.*

life•like (līf′līk′) /ˈlayfˌlayk/ *adj.* resembling or simulating real life.

life•line (līf′līn′) /ˈlayfˌlayn/ *n.* [*count*] **1.** a line or rope for saving life, as one attached to a lifeboat. **2.** a route over which supplies must be sent to help an area or group of persons stay alive.

life•long (līf′lông′, -long′) /ˈlayfˌlɔŋ, -ˌlɒŋ/ *adj.* [*before a noun*] lasting through much of one's life: *lifelong regret.*

life′ net′, *n.* [*count*] a strong net or the like held by firefighters or others to catch persons jumping from a burning building.

life′ preserv′er, *n.* [*count*] **1.** a jacket, belt, or other device that keeps a person afloat in water. **2.** *Brit. Slang.* a blackjack.

lif•er (lī′fər) /ˈlayfər/ *n.* [*count*] *Informal.* **1.** a person sentenced to or serving a term of life imprisonment. **2.** a person who has devoted a lifetime to a certain profession, occupation, or interest.

life′ raft′, *n.* [*count*] an often inflatable raft for use in emergencies, as when a ship must be abandoned.

life•sav•er (līf′sā′vər) /ˈlayfˌseyvər/ *n.* [*count*] **1.** one who rescues another from danger of death, esp. from drowning. **2.** one that provides timely aid in a difficult situation.

life′-size′ or **life′-sized′,** *adj.* of the size of the original: *life-size statues of warriors.*

life′ style′ or **life′-style′,** *n.* [*count*] the typical way of living, reflecting attitudes, preferences, opinions, etc., of an individual or group.

life•time (līf′tīm′) /ˈlayfˌtaym/ *n.* [*count*] **1.** the amount of time that a person stays alive or that something continues; the term of a life: *hoped to see peace within our lifetime.* **2.** a very long time: *We waited a lifetime for the* *doctor's report.* **—***adj.* [*before a noun*] **3.** for the length of a person's life: *a lifetime membership.* **—*Idiom.* 4. of a lifetime,** [*after a noun*] most memorable: *the vacation of a lifetime.*

life•work (līf′wûrk′) /ˈlayfˈwɜrk/ *n.* [*count; usually singular*] the complete or principal work, labor, or task of a lifetime: *Her lifework was fighting poverty.*

lift (lift) /lɪft/ *v.* **1.** [~ + *obj*] to move or bring (something) from a lower to a higher position; hoist: *She lifted the child onto the chair.* **2.** [*no obj*] to go up; rise: *The fog lifted.* **3.** [~ + *obj*] to raise or direct upward: *lifted her eyes to the heavens.* **4.** [~ + *obj*] to stop or put an end to: *lifted the blockade.* **5.** [~ + *obj*] to hold up or display on high: *lifted his trophy to the crowd.* **6.** [~ + *obj*] to raise in rank, condition, status, fame, etc.: *They lifted themselves from poverty.* **7.** [~ + *obj*] *Informal.* to plagiarize: *The author lifted the characters and plot from another writer's novel.* **8.** [~ + *obj*] *Informal.* to steal: *caught trying to lift someone's wallet.* **9.** (of a pain, burden, sadness) to (cause to) be removed: [~ + *obj*]: *He took drugs to lift his depression.* [*no obj*]: *His depression lifted quickly.* **—***n.* **10.** [*count*] the act of lifting, raising, or rising. **11.** [*noncount*] a lifting or raising force, as upward pressure on an airplane wing in flight. **12.** [*count*] the weight, load, or quantity lifted: *The weightlifter did a lift of 500 pounds.* **13.** [*count*] a ride in a vehicle, esp. one given to a pedestrian. **14.** [*count*] a feeling of happiness, excitement, encouragement, or uplift: *Praise from the boss gave the staff a much-needed lift.* **15.** [*count*] a device for lifting: *The mechanic moved the car onto a hydraulic lift.* **16.** [*count*] **a.** SKI LIFT. **b.** CHAIR LIFT. **17.** [*count*] *Brit.* ELEVATOR (def. 2). **—*Idiom.* 18. lift a finger** or **hand,** [*with a negative word or in a question*] to exert any effort at all: *They won't lift a finger to help you.*

lift•off or **lift-off** (lift′ôf′, -of′) /ˈlɪftˌɔf, -ˌɒf/ *n.* [*count*] **1.** the action of an aircraft in rising into the air, or of a rocket in rising from its launching site under its own power. **2.** the instant when such action occurs.

-lig-, *root.* *-lig-* comes from Latin, where it has the meaning "to tie; bind." This meaning is found in such words as: LIGAMENT, LIGATURE, OBLIGATE, OBLIGE, RELIGION.

lig•a•ment (lig′ə mənt) /ˈlɪgəmənt/ *n.* [*count*] a band of strong tissue that connects bones or holds organs in place. See -LIG-.

lig•a•ture (lig′ə chər, -cho͝or′) /ˈlɪgətʃər, -ˌtʃʊr/ *n.* **1.** [*noncount*] the act of binding or tying up. **2.** [*count*] anything that serves for binding or tying up, as a band, bandage, or cord. **3.** [*count*] a stroke or bar connecting two letters; a character or type combining two or more letters, as *fl* and *ffl.* See -LIG-.

light[1] (līt) /layt/ *n., adj.,* **light•er, light•est,** *v.,* **light•ed** or **lit** (lit) /lɪt/ **light•ing.** **—***n.* **1.** [*noncount*] the brightness that makes things visible, made up of a form of radiation to which the eyes react: *The sun gives off light.* **2.** [*count*] something giving off such brightness, as the sun or a lamp. **3.** [*noncount*] the brightness from the sun; daylight, daybreak, dawn, or daytime: *at first light (= at dawn).* **4.** [*count*] a device for or means of starting a fire, as a spark, flame, or match. **5.** [*count*] a traffic light: *went through a red light.* **6.** [*count; usually singular*] the way in which a thing appears or is looked at: *He saw things in a new light.* **7.** [*count*] a gleam or sparkle: *a fierce light in her eyes.* **8.** [*noncount*] insight; understanding; awareness: *These new facts throw some light on the mystery.* **9.** [*count*] a person who is an important figure: *one of the leading lights of the Broadway stage.* **10. lights,** [*plural*] the information, ideas, background, or mental ability one has: *According to his lights, he acted correctly.* **—***adj.* **11.** having light; bright; well-lighted: *The room was light enough to read in.* **12.** pale; not deep in color: *a light blue.* **13.** (of coffee or tea) containing enough milk or cream to produce a light color. **—***v.* **14.** to (cause to) burn: [~ + *obj*]: *They lit the fire.* [~ *(+ up)* + *obj*]: *She lit (up) a cigarette.* [~ *(+ up)*]: *These wet logs won't light (up). She took the cigarette and lit up.* **15.** to (cause to) become bright when switched on: [*no obj*]: *This table lamp won't light.* [~ + *obj*]: *to light the lamp.* **16.** to (cause to) be brightened, esp. with joy, excitement, or the like: [~ *(+ up)* + *obj*]: *A smile lit (up) her face.* [*no obj*]: *Her face lit up with the good news.* **17.** to (cause to) become bright: [*no obj;* (~ + *up*)]: *The sky lights up at sunrise.* [~ *(+ up)* + *obj*]: *to light up a room.* [~ + *up* + *obj*]: *The car's headlights lit up the area ahead.* **—*Idiom.* 18. bring to light,** to discover or reveal: [~ + *obj*]: *The investigation brought to light new facts about the case.* [~ + *obj* + *to light*]: *The investigation brought new facts to light.* **19. come to light,** to be discovered or revealed: *New facts came to light.* **20. in (the) light of,** taking into account; because of; considering: *In the light of these new charges, perhaps we'd better re-open the investigation.* **21. light at the end of the tunnel,** a possibility of success, relief, or of being saved that is not yet present but that will come about: *We still have problems, but at least we can see some light at the end of the tunnel.* **22. see the light,** to understand something at last. —**light′ness,** *n.* [*noncount*]

light[2] (līt) /layt/ *adj.* and *adv.,* **-er, -est.** **—***adj.* **1.** of little weight; not heavy: *a light load.* **2.** of low specific gravity: *a light metal.* **3.** of less than the usual or average weight: *Wear light clothing in the summer to stay cool.* **4.** of small amount, force, intensity, pressure, etc.: *a light rain.* **5.** easy to endure, deal with, or perform: *light duties.* **6.** not very serious; entertaining: *Mystery stories make light reading.* **7.** trivial: *The loss of a job is no light matter.* **8.** easily digested; not rich or heavy: *a light meal.* **9.** (of alcoholic beverages) **a.** not heavy or strong: *a light apéritif.* **b.** (esp. of beer and wine) having fewer calories and usually a lower alcohol content than the standard product. **10.** airy in movement; agile: *light on one's feet.* **11.** cheerful; carefree: *a light heart.* **12.** dizzy or somewhat faint: *I felt light in the head.* **13.** (of soldiers) lightly armed or equipped: *light cavalry.* **14.** made to carry small loads swiftly: *a light truck.* **15.** using small-scale machinery for the production of consumer goods: *light industry.* **—***adv.* **16.** without much or extra baggage: *He prefers to travel light, with just a backpack.* —**light′ly,** *adv.* —**light′ness,** *n.*

light[3] (līt) /layt/ *v.* [*no obj*], **light•ed** or **lit** (lit) /lɪt/ **light•ing.** **1.** [~ + *on/upon*] to come down to rest; fall or settle (upon): *The bird lighted on the branch.* **2.** [~ + *on/upon*] to come by chance; happen; hit: *to light on a clue.* **3. light into,** [~ + *into* + *obj*] to attack physically or verbally: *He lit into the next speaker with criticism.* **4. light out,** [*no obj*] *Informal.* to depart quickly: *He lit out for the coast.*

light•en[1] (līt′n) /ˈlaytn̩/ *v.* to (cause to) become lighter or less dark; brighten: [*no obj*]: *The sky lightened at dawn.* [~ + *obj*]: *The sun lightened her hair.*

light•en[2] (līt′n) /ˈlaytn̩/ *v.* **1.** [~ + *obj*] to make lighter in weight: *They lightened the sinking lifeboat by throwing off extra weight.* **2.** to (cause to) become less of a burden: [~ + *obj*]: *to lighten taxes.* [*no obj*]: *Our responsibilities have begun to lighten somewhat.* **3.** to (cause to) become cheery or glad: [~ + *obj*]: *Such news lightens my heart.* [*no obj*]: *His heart lightened at the thought.* **4. lighten up,** to (cause to) become less serious or earnest: [*no obj*]: *needs to lighten up.* [~ + *obj* + *up*]: *Only she can lighten him up.*

light•er (lī′tər) /ˈlaytər/ *n.* [*count*] a mechanical device used in lighting cigarettes, cigars, or pipes.

light′-fin′gered, *adj.* skillful at stealing.

light′-foot′ed, *adj.* stepping lightly or nimbly.

light•head•ed (līt′hed′id) /ˈlaytˈhɛdɪd/ *adj.* **1.** giddy; dizzy. **2.** frivolous; foolish.

light•heart•ed (līt′här′tid) /ˈlaytˈhɑrtɪd/ *adj.* carefree; cheerful. —**light′heart′ed•ly,** *adv.* —**light′heart′ed•ness,** *n.* [*noncount*]

light′ heav′yweight, *n.* [*count*] a boxer weighing up to 175 lb. (80 kg).

light•house (līt′hous′) /ˈlaytˌhaws/ *n.* [*count*] a tower or other building displaying a bright light or lights to guide ships.

light•ing (lī′ting) /ˈlaytɪŋ/ *n.* [*noncount*] **1.** the act of igniting or brightening. **2.** the arrangement of lights to achieve particular effects.

light′-mind′ed, *adj.* frivolous; silly.

light•ning (līt′ning) /ˈlaytnɪŋ/ *n., v.,* **-ninged, -ning,** *adj.* **—***n.* [*noncount*] **1.** a brilliant flash in the sky, caused by an electric spark in the atmosphere, occurring within one thundercloud, between clouds, or between a cloud and the ground. **—***v.* [*it* + ~*; no obj*] **2.** to give off a flash or flashes of lightning: *Go inside if it starts to lightning.* **—***adj.* [*before a noun*] **3.** of, relating to, or resembling lightning: *moved with lightning speed.*

light′ning bug′, *n.* FIREFLY.

light′ning rod′, *n.* [*count*] **1.** a metal rod that conducts electricity, installed to attract lightning away from a structure by providing a direct path to the ground. **2.** a person or thing that attracts negative feelings, opinions, etc., thereby keeping them from other targets.

light′ pen′, *n.* [*count*] a light-sensitive device used for pointing at characters or objects on a computer screen.

light•weight (līt′wāt′) /ˈlaytˌweyt/ *adj.* **1.** light in weight: *a lightweight topcoat.* **2.** of little importance or consequence: *a lightweight novelist.* **3.** of or relating to a lightweight boxer: *the new lightweight contender.* **—*n.*** [*count*] **4.** a person of less than average weight. **5.** *Informal.* a person who is of little importance or consequence. **6.** a boxer weighing up to 135 lb. (61 kg).

light′-year′, *n.* [*count*] **1.** the distance that light can travel in one year, about 5.88 trillion mi. (9.46 trillion km); it is used as a unit in measuring distances among stars. **2. light-years,** [*plural*] **a.** a very great measure of comparison: *Today's computers are light-years ahead of older ones in power and memory.* **b.** a very long time: *Vacation already seemed light-years away.*

lik•a•ble or **like•a•ble** (lī′kə bəl) /ˈlaykəbəl/ *adj.* readily or easily liked; pleasing: *a likeable fellow.* **—lik′a•ble•ness, lik•a•bil•i•ty** (lī′kə bil′i tē) /ˌlɪkəˈbɪlɪtiy/ *n.* [*noncount*]

like[1] (līk) /layk/ *adj.*, (*Poetic*) **lik•er, lik•est,** *prep.*, *adv.*, *conj.*, *n.*, *interj.* **—*adj.*** [*before a noun*] **1.** of the same form, appearance, kind, character, amount, etc.: *I cannot remember a like instance.* **2.** corresponding to or agreeing with in general or in some respect; similar: *drawing, painting, and like arts.* **—*prep.*** **3.** in a manner characteristic of: *She works like a beaver.* **4.** resembling; similar to: *Your necklace is like mine.* **5.** characteristic of: *It would be like him to forget our appointment.* **6.** as if there is promise of; indicative of: *It looks like rain.* **7.** [*usually: feel + ~ + verb-ing*] willing to; disposed or inclined to: *I don't feel like going to bed.* **8.** This word is used with certain words or expressions to indicate a comparison, and sometimes to indicate feeling or attitude about the comparison: *Like father, like son (= The way a father behaves is the way a son will behave). He ran like hell (= He ran very fast).* **9.** such as; for example: *I want to do something really different, like skydiving.* **—*adv.*** **10.** nearly; approximately: *The house is more like 40 years old.* **11.** *Informal.* likely or probably: *Like enough he'll come with us.* **—*conj.*** **12.** in the same way as; just as; as: *It happened like you said it would.* **13.** as if: *He acted like he was afraid.* **—*n.*** **14.** [*an adjective showing possession + ~*] a similar or comparable person or thing, or persons or things; match or equal: *No one has seen her like in a long time.* **15.** [*an adjective showing possession + ~*] kind; sort; type: *He despised bigots and their like.* **16. the like,** something of a similar nature: *They grow oranges, lemons, and the like.* **—*interj.*** **17.** *Informal.* This word is used to focus attention on a word asking a question, or before an answer to a question, or with some other information in a sentence: *Like, why didn't you write to me?* **—*Idiom.*** **18. like anything, blazes, crazy, hell,** or **mad,** *Informal.* to the greatest extent or degree possible: *I ran like crazy.* **19. like to** or **liked to,** *Nonstandard.* This phrase is used to mean "was on the verge of or came close to (doing something)": *The poor kid like to froze.* **20. something like,** approximately the same as. **21. the like** or **likes of,** the equal of: *I have never seen the like(s) of her since.*

like[2] (līk) /layk/ *v.*, **liked, lik•ing,** *n.* **—*v.*** [*not: be + ~-ing*] **1.** to take pleasure in; find agreeable to one's taste; enjoy: [*~ + obj*]: *to like opera.* [*~ + verb-ing*]: *She likes playing baseball.* [*~ + to + verb*]: *She likes to play baseball.* **2.** [*~ + obj*] to regard with favor: *I like you as a friend.* **3.** [*often: would + ~*] to wish or want; prefer: [*~ + obj*]: *I'd like a piece of cake.* [*~ + to + verb*]: *I'd really like to go home now.* [*no obj*]: *Stay if you like.* **—*n.*** [*count*] **4.** Usually, **likes.** [*plural*] the things a person likes: *Find out about his likes and dislikes.* **—lik′er,** *n.* [*count*] **—Usage.** See DISLIKE, ENJOY.

-like, *suffix.* -*like* is attached to nouns to form adjectives with the meaning "of or resembling (the noun base)": *child + -like → childlike; life + -like → lifelike.*

like•li•hood (līk′lē ho͝od′) /ˈlaykliyˌhʊd/ also **like′li•ness,** *n.* the state of being likely or probable; probability: [*noncount*]: *the likelihood of rain.* [*count*]: *a likelihood of rain.*

like•ly (līk′lē) /ˈlaykliy/ *adj.*, **-li•er, -li•est,** *adv.* **—*adj.*** **1.** probable; fairly sure; expected: [*be + ~ + to + verb*]: *An earthquake is not likely to happen here.* [*It + be + ~ + (that) clause*]: *It's likely that she will win.* **2.** [*before a noun*] believable: *It was a likely enough excuse.* **3.** [*before a noun*] suitable; promising: *We found a likely place to pitch the tent.* **—*adv.*** **4.** probably: *We will most likely stay home.*

like′-mind′ed, *adj.* having the same or a similar opinion, way of thinking or acting, etc.

lik•en (lī′kən) /ˈlaykən/ *v.* [*~ + obj + to + obj*] to compare and claim (someone or something) to be similar or like (another): *The cartoon likened the senator to a money-grubbing weasel.*

like•ness (līk′nis) /ˈlayknɪs/ *n.* **1.** [*count*] a portrait; copy: *He drew a beautiful likeness of her.* **2.** [*noncount*] the state or fact of being like or similar.

like•wise (līk′wīz′) /ˈlaykˌwayz/ *adv.* **1.** moreover; in addition; also; too: *She is likewise a fine lawyer.* **2.** in like manner; in the same way; similarly: *I'm tempted to do likewise.*

lik•ing (lī′king) /ˈlaykɪŋ/ *n.* [*count; usually singular*] preference; taste: *We found the beach there much to our liking.*

li•lac (lī′lək, -läk, -lak) /ˈlaylək, -lɑk, -læk/ *n.* **1.** a shrub of the olive family, having large clusters of fragrant purple or white flowers: [*noncount*]: *the smell of lilac.* [*count*]: *pruning the lilacs.* **2.** [*noncount*] pale reddish purple. **—*adj.*** **3.** having the color lilac.

Lil•li•pu•tian (lil′i pyo͞o′shən) /ˌlɪlɪˈpyuwʃən/ *adj.* **1.** extremely small; tiny. **2.** petty; unimportant; trivial.

lilt (lilt) /lɪlt/ *n.* [*count*] rhythmic rising or falling in the voice; cadence. **—lilt′ing,** *adj.*

lil•y (lil′ē) /ˈlɪliy/ *n.*, *pl.* **lil•ies,** *adj.* **—*n.*** [*count*] **1.** a scaly-bulbed plant having showy, funnel-shaped or bell-shaped flowers. **2.** the flower or the bulb of such a plant. **3.** a related or similar plant or flower. **—*adj.*** **4.** white as a lily: *her lily hands.*

lil•y-liv•ered (lil′ē liv′ərd) /ˈlɪliyˌlɪvərd/ *adj.* cowardly.

lil′y of the val′ley, *n.* [*count*], *pl.* **lilies of the valley.** a plant of the lily family, having a long cluster of small, drooping, bell-shaped, fragrant white flowers.

lil′y pad′, *n.* [*count*] the large, floating leaf of a water lily.

-lim-, *root.* -*lim*- comes from Latin, where it has the meaning "line; boundary; edge; threshold." This meaning is found in such words as: ELIMINATE, LIMBO, LIMIT, PRELIMINARY, SUBLIME, SUBLIMINAL, UNLIMITED. See -LIN-.

li′ma bean′ (lī′mə) /ˈlaymə/ *n.* [*count*] **1.** a bean having a broad, flat seed that can be eaten. **2.** the seed.

limb (lim) /lɪm/ *n.* [*count*] **1.** one of the paired bodily parts of animals, used esp. for moving or grasping; a leg, arm, or wing. **2.** a large or main branch of a tree. **—*Idiom.*** **3. out on a limb,** in a risky or dangerous situation. **4. risk life and limb,** to take a dangerous risk or chance that could result in physical injury or harm. **—limb′less,** *adj.*

lim•ber (lim′bər) /ˈlɪmbər/ *adj.* **1.** able to bend the body easily; supple: *a limber athlete.* **2.** able to bend easily; flexible; pliant: *limber joints.* **—*v.*** **3.** to make (cause to) become limber: [*~ + up*]: *to limber up before a game.* [*~ + up + obj*]: *She limbered up her arm before throwing the ball.* [*~ + obj + up*]: *She limbered her arm up.* **—lim′ber•ness,** *n.* [*noncount*]

lim•bo[1] (lim′bō) /ˈlɪmbow/ *n.* [*noncount*], *pl.* **-bos.** **1.** [*proper noun; often: Limbo*] a region on the border of hell or heaven in Roman Catholic teaching, serving as the place after death of unbaptized infants and of righteous people who died before the coming of Christ. **2.** a place or state that is intermediate, transitional, or uncertain: *Negotiations were in limbo again, neither side wishing to compromise.* See -LIM-.

lim•bo[2] (lim′bō) /ˈlɪmbow/ *n.* [*count*], *pl.* **-bos.** a dance from the West Indies in which the dancer bends backward from the knees and moves with a shuffling step under a horizontal bar that is lowered after each pass.

lime[1] (līm) /laym/ *n.* [*noncount*] a white or grayish white, odorless, lumpy solid used chiefly in mortar, plaster, and cement, in bleaching powder, and in various compounds for improving crops. **—lim′y,** *adj.*, **-i•er, -i•est.**

lime[2] (līm) /laym/ *n.* **1.** the small, greenish yellow, acid fruit of a citrus tree related to the lemon: [*count*]: *two limes.* [*noncount*]: *a taste of lime.* **2.** [*count*] the tree that bears this fruit. **3.** [*noncount*] a greenish yellow. **—*adj.*** **4.** of the color lime. **5.** made with limes.

lime•ade (lim′ād′, līm′ād′) /ˌlaymˈeyd, ˈlaymˌeyd/ *n.* a beverage of lime juice, sugar, and water: [*noncount*]: *a drink of limeade.* [*count*]: *We'll have two limeades.*

lime•light (līm′līt′) /ˈlaymˌlayt/ *n.* [*noncount; the + ~*] a position at the center of public attention: *always trying to steal the limelight.*

lim•er•ick (lim′ər ik) /ˈlɪmərɪk/ *n.* [*count*] a kind of humorous poem in which lines one, two, and five rhyme, and lines three and four rhyme.

lime•stone (līm′stōn′) /ˈlaymˌstown/ *n.* [*noncount*] a rock made up mostly of calcium carbonate, some of which is formed from the skeletons of tiny sea organisms and coral.

lim•it (lim′it) /ˈlɪmɪt/ *n.* [*count*] **1.** the furthest boundary, point, or edge of the extent or amount of something: *had reached the limit of their endurance.* **2. the limit,** [*sin-*

gular] *Informal.* something very annoying or amazing: *Their weird stunts are the limit!* **—***v.* [~ + *obj*] **3.** to restrict by or as if by limits: *to limit spending.* **—lim′it•er,** *n.* [*count*] **—lim′it•less,** *adj.* See **-LIM-**.

lim•i•ta•tion (lim′i tā′shən) /ˌlɪmɪ'teyʃən/ *n.* **1.** [*count*] a lack of capacity or ability; shortcoming: *He's aware of his own limitations.* **2.** [*noncount*] the act of limiting; the state of being limited. **3.** [*count*] a period of time, defined by law, during which legal action may be taken: *statute of limitations.* See **-LIM-**.

lim•it•ed (lim′i tid) /'lɪmɪtɪd/ *adj.* **1.** confined within limits; restricted: *a train making limited stops.* **2.** (of trains, buses, etc.) making only a limited number of stops: *a limited express.* **3.** restricted in the power to govern by limitations written in a country's laws and in a constitution: *a limited monarchy.* See **-LIM-**.

lim•o (lim′ō) /'lɪmow/ *n.* [*count*], *pl.* **-os.** *Informal.* a limousine.

lim•ou•sine (lim′ə zēn′, lim′ə zēn′) /'lɪməˌziyn, ˌlɪmə'ziyn/ *n.* [*count*] **1.** a large, luxurious automobile, esp. one driven by a chauffeur. **2.** a large sedan or small bus for transporting passengers to and from an airport, train station, etc.

limp[1] (limp) /lɪmp/ *v.* [*no obj*] **1.** to walk with difficult movement, with one leg or foot dragging behind: *The injured player limped off the field.* **2.** to progress with great difficulty, hesitation, or slowness: *The economy limps along.* **—***n.* [*count*] **3.** a lame movement or way of walking.

limp[2] (limp) /lɪmp/ *adj.,* **-er, -est. 1.** lacking stiffness, as of substance or structure; too soft: *a limp rag.* **2.** tired; fatigued: *I was limp with exhaustion.* **3.** without firmness, force, energy, etc.: *limp writing.* **—limp′ly,** *adv.* **—limp′ness,** *n.* [*noncount*]

lim•pet (lim′pit) /'lɪmpɪt/ *n.* [*count*] a sea animal with a low cone-shaped shell that usually attaches itself to rocks.

lim•pid (lim′pid) /'lɪmpɪd/ *adj.* **1.** clear or transparent, as water, crystal, or air. **2.** lucid; clear; easily understood: *limpid prose.* **3.** completely calm: *a limpid gaze.* **—lim•pid•i•ty** (lim pid′i tē) /lɪm'pɪdɪtiy/ **lim′pid•ness,** *n.* [*noncount*] **—lim′pid•ly,** *adv.*

-lin-, *root.* *-lin-* comes from Latin, where it has the meaning "string; line." This meaning is found in such words as: CRINOLINE, DELINEATE, LINE, LINEAGE, LINEAL, LINEAMENT, LINEAR, LINEN, LINGERIE. The meaning is also found in many compound words with *line* as the last part, such as BASELINE, GUIDELINE, HAIRLINE, PIPELINE, SIDELINE, UNDERLINE. See **-LIM-**.

lin., an abbreviation of: linear.

linch•pin (linch′pin′) /'lɪntʃˌpɪn/ *n.* [*count*] **1.** a pin inserted through the end of part of an axle to keep a wheel on. **2.** something that holds the various parts or elements of a complicated structure together: *The linchpin of the campaign was the heavy use of advertising.*

lin•den (lin′dən) /'lɪndən/ *n.* **1.** [*count*] a tree of North America or Europe, having sweet-smelling yellowish white flowers and heart-shaped leaves. **2.** [*noncount*] the wood of any of the lindens.

line[1] (līn) /layn/ *n., v.,* **lined, lin•ing.** **—***n.* [*count*] **1.** a long mark of very slight thickness or breadth: *notebook paper with blue lines.* **2.** something arranged along a line, esp. a straight line; a row: *hid behind a line of trees.* **3.** a number of persons standing one behind the other: *a long line for tickets to the play.* See IN LINE, ON LINE below. **4.** a mark or wrinkle on the face, neck, etc. **5.** an indication of a boundary; limit: *the international date line.* **6.** a row of written or printed letters, words, etc. **7.** a unit in the structure of a poem: *a line of poetry.* **8.** Usually, **lines.** [*plural*] the words of an actor's part in a drama, musical comedy, etc. **9.** a short written message: *Drop me a line when you're on vacation.* **10.** a system of transportation: *a steamship line; a subway line.* **11.** a course of direction; route: *the line of flight.* **12.** a course of action, procedure, thought, policy, etc.: *That newspaper follows a conservative line.* **13.** a piece of useful information: *I've got a line on a good used car.* **14.** a series of generations descended from a common ancestor: *a line of kings.* **15.** [*usually singular*] a person's occupation: *What line are you in?* **16.** *Informal.* conversation or a story intended to impress or influence: *He handed us a line about his rich relatives.* **17.** outline or contour: *That ship has fine lines.* **18. lines,** [*plural*] a plan of construction, action, or procedure: *The two books were written along the same lines.* **19.** a circuit or connection, as a telephone connection: *Please hold the line.* **20.** a stock of goods of the same general class but having a range of styles, sizes, prices, or quality: *introduced a new line of beauty products.* **21. a.** a series of fortifications: *the Maginot line.* **b.** Often, **lines.** a distribution of troops, ships, etc., arranged for defense or drawn up for battle: *behind enemy lines.* **22.** a thread, string, cord, rope, cable, etc., as a clothesline, or a cord with a hook for fishing. **23.** a pipe or hose: *A steam line had ruptured in the submarine's engine room.* **24.** either of the two front rows of football players who are lined up opposite each other at the start of a play. **—***v.* **25.** *Baseball.* to hit a line drive: [~ + *obj*]: *He lined the ball into left field.* [*no obj*]: *He lined to left his next time at bat.* **26.** [~ + *obj*] to mark with a line or lines. **27.** [~ + *obj*] to form a line along: *Rocks lined the drive.* **28.** [~ + *obj*] to apply liner to (the eyes). **29. line up, a.** to obtain for use; secure; make available: [~ + *up* + *obj*]: *What entertainment did you line up?* [~ + *obj* + *up*]: *He lined them up six months ago.* **b.** to (cause to) take a position in a line:[*no obj*]: *We lined up at the ticket office.* [~ + *up* + *obj*]: *The sergeant lined up his troops.* [~ + *obj* + *up*]: *The sergeant lined his troops up.* **—*Idiom.* 30. down the line, a.** in every way; thoroughly; completely: *They promised to back me down the line.* **b.** in the future: *We'll use your plan down the line when things improve financially.* **31. draw the line,** to impose or establish a restriction or limit: *They draw the line at drinking before noon.* **32. hold the line,** to maintain the current situation: *to hold the line on price increases.* **33. in line, a.** in the proper direction or alignment; straight: *The four wheels are in line.* **b.** in agreement with or in proportion to (some standard): *brought our inflation rate in line with the rest of Europe.* **c.** under control: *kept his squirming children in line during the long opera.* **d.** arranged one behind the other; in a row: *We have been waiting in line since six in the morning.* **34. in line for,** in a position to become: *She was in line for president.* **35. into line, a.** into a straight row: *Get your soldiers into line.* **b.** into agreement with or in proportion to (some standard): *to bring manufacturing prices into line.* **36. lay it on the line,** *Informal.* to say, tell, or give information directly and honestly. **37. off line, a.** occurring or functioning away from the central work location, as an assembly line. **b.** not in operation; not functioning. **c.** not actively linked to a computer or central computer. **38. on line, a.** on or part of an assembly line. **b.** in or into operation. **c.** actively linked to a computer. **39. on the line,** in a dangerous or risky position: *He had put his reputation on the line.* **40. out of line, a.** not in a straight line: *The tires had worn and were now out of line.* **b.** disrespectful; behaving badly: *You're way out of line, criticizing his wife like that.* **41. read between the lines,** to understand, uncover, or discover a meaning hinted at but not said directly. See **-LIN-**.

line[2] (līn) /layn/ *v.* [~ + *obj*], **lined, lin•ing. 1.** to cover the inner side or surface of: *to line a coat with blue silk.* **2.** to cover: *Bookcases lined the wall.* See **-LIN-**.

lin•e•age (lin′ē ij) /'lɪniyɪdʒ/ *n.* the line of descendants of a particular ancestor; family; race: [*noncount*]: *a family of ancient lineage.* [*count*]: *noble lineages.* See **-LIN-**.

lin•e•al (lin′ē əl) /'lɪniyəl/ *adj.* [*before a noun*] **1.** being in the direct line: *a lineal descendant.* **2.** LINEAR. See **-LIN-**.

lin•e•a•ment (lin′ē ə mənt) /'lɪniyəmənt/ *n.* [*count*] Usually, **lineaments.** [*plural*] features that distinguish one from another, esp. of the face or body. See **-LIN-**.

lin•e•ar (lin′ē ər) /'lɪniyər/ *adj.* **1.** of, made up of, resembling, or using lines: *linear design.* **2.** extended or arranged in a line: *a linear series.* **3.** involving length only: *linear measurements.* **—lin′e•ar•ly,** *adv.* See **-LIN-**.

line•back•er (līn′bak′ər) /'laynˌbækər/ *n.* **1.** [*count*] a football player on defense who takes a position close behind the linemen. **2.** [*noncount*] the position played by this player.

line′ drive′, *n.* [*count*] a batted baseball that travels low and straight. Also called **liner.**

line•man (līn′mən) /'laynmən/ *n.* [*count*], *pl.* **-men. 1.** a person who installs or repairs telephone, telegraph, or other wires. **2.** one of the players in the line of a football team, as a center, guard, tackle, or end.

lin•en (lin′ən) /'lɪnən/ *n.* **1.** [*noncount*] fabric woven from flax yarns. **2.** Often, **linens.** bedding, tablecloths, shirts, etc., made of linen cloth or a similar fabric, as cotton: [*plural*]: *a sale on linens.* [*noncount*]: *a sale on bed linen.* See illustration at STORE. **—***adj.* **3.** made of linen: *a linen jacket.* **—*Idiom.* 4. wash** or **air one's dirty linen in public,** to reveal one's embarrassing secrets to outsiders. See **-LIN-**.

lin•er[1] (lī′nər) /'laynər/ *n.* [*count*] **1.** a ship or airplane operated by a transportation company. **2.** EYELINER. **3.** LINE DRIVE.

lin•er[2] (lī′nər) /'laynər/ *n.* [*count*] **1.** something serving as a lining. **2.** a person who fits or provides linings.

lines•man (līnz′mən) /'laynzmən/ *n.* [*count*], *pl.* **-men.** an official in tennis, soccer, football, or ice hockey who keeps track of boundaries, distances, or the like.

line•up (līn′up′) /'layn,ʌp/ *n.* [*count*] **1.** an orderly arrangement of persons or things in, or as if in, a line: *the fall lineup of TV programs.* **2.** a group of persons lined up by the police to allow identification by a witness to or a victim of a crime. **3.** a list of the players in a game, as of baseball, together with their positions.

-ling, *suffix.* **1.** *-ling* is used to form a noun that indicates a feeling of distaste or disgust for the person or thing named: *hire + -ling → hireling (= someone hired to do menial or distasteful tasks); under + -ling → underling.* **2.** *-ling* is also used to form a noun that is a smaller version or example of the base word: *prince + -ling → princeling; duck + -ling → duckling.*

-ling-, *root.* *-ling-* comes from Latin, where it has the meaning "tongue." This meaning is found in such words as: BILINGUAL, LANGUAGE, LINGO, LINGUINE, LINGUISTIC/S, MONOLINGUAL.

lin•ger (ling′gər) /'lɪŋgər/ *v.* [*no obj*] **1.** to remain in a place longer than is usual or expected: *They lingered over their coffee for a few minutes.* **2.** to continue to exist but with lessened strength: *Old hatreds lingered after the war.* —**lin′ger•er,** *n.* [*count*] —**lin′ger•ing•ly,** *adv.*

lin•ge•rie (län′zhə rā′, lan′zhə rē′) /,lɑnʒə'rey, 'lænʒə,riy/ *n.* [*noncount*] underwear, sleepwear, and other items of clothing worn close to the body by women. See -LIN-.

lin•go (ling′gō) /'lɪŋgow/ *n.* [*count*], *pl.* **-goes. 1.** the language or vocabulary, esp. the jargon or slang, of a particular field, group, or individual: *"Pre-owned" is car-salesman lingo for "used."* **2.** language or speech, esp. if strange or foreign: *Can you speak the local lingo?* See -LING-.

lin′gua fran′ca (ling′gwa frang′kə) /'lɪŋ'gwæ fræŋkə/ *n.* [*count*], *pl.* **lingua fran•cas, lin•guae fran•cae** (ling′gwē fran′sē, frang′kē) /'lɪŋ'gwiy frænsiy, 'fræŋkiy/. any language that is widely used as a means of communication among speakers of other languages.

lin•gual (ling′gwəl) /'lɪŋgwəl/ *adj.* of or relating to the tongue or some tonguelike part. See -LING-.

lin•gui•ne or **lin•gui•ni** (ling gwē′nē) /lɪŋ'gwiyniy/ *n.* [*noncount; used with a singular verb*] a type of pasta in long, slender, flat strips: *The linguine is very good there.* See -LING-.

lin•guist (ling′gwist) /'lɪŋgwɪst/ *n.* [*count*] **1.** a specialist in linguistics. **2.** a person who is skilled in several languages; polyglot. See -LING-.

lin•guis•tics (ling gwis′tiks) /lɪŋ'gwɪstɪks/ *n.* [*noncount; used with a singular verb*] the study of language: *Linguistics includes the areas of phonetics, morphology, syntax, and semantics.* —**lin•guis′tic,** *adj.* See -LING-.

lin•i•ment (lin′ə mənt) /'lɪnəmənt/ *n.* a liquid preparation for rubbing on the skin, esp. to relieve soreness: [*count*]: *various liniments.* [*noncount*]: *smelled of liniment.*

lin•ing (lī′ning) /'laynɪŋ/ *n.* [*count*] something used to line another thing; a layer of material on the inner side or surface of something.

link (lingk) /lɪŋk/ *n.* [*count*] **1.** one of the rings or separate pieces that form a chain. **2.** anything that connects one part or thing with another; a bond or tie: *The locket was a link with her past.* **3.** any of a number of connected sausages. **4.** CUFF LINK. —*v.* **5.** to join by or as if by a link or links; unite: [~ + *obj* + *to* + *obj*]: *The new bridge will link the island to the mainland.* [~(+ *up*) + *obj* + *and/with* + *obj*]: *The new bridge will link (up) the island and the mainland.* [~ (+ *up*)]: *The company will soon link up with a hotel chain.*

link•age (ling′kij) /'lɪŋkɪdʒ/ *n.* **1.** [*noncount*] the act of linking, or the state or manner of being linked. **2.** [*count*] a system of links: *a linkage between cause and effect.*

link′ing verb′, *n.* COPULA.

links (lingks) /lɪŋks/ *n.,* [*count*] *pl.* **links.** a golf course.

link•up (lingk′up′) /'lɪŋk,ʌp/ *n.* [*count*] **1.** a linkage established, as between military units or two spacecraft. **2.** a connection or hookup.

li•no•le•um (li nō′lē əm) /lɪ'nowliyəm/ *n.* [*noncount*] a hard, washable floor covering.

lin′seed oil′, *n.* [*noncount*] an oil made by pressing seeds from flax, used in making paints, printing inks, linoleum, etc.

lint (lint) /lɪnt/ *n.* [*noncount*] tiny shreds of yarn; bits of thread. —**lint′y,** *adj.,* **-i•er, -i•est.**

lin•tel (lin′tl) /'lɪntḷ/ *n.* [*count*] a piece of wood or stone supporting the weight above an opening, as a door.

li•on (lī′ən) /'layən/ *n.* [*count*] **1.** a large, usually yellowish-brown member of the cat family, of Africa and S Asia, having a tufted tail and, in the male, a large mane. **2.** a person of great strength or courage. **3.** a famous or influential celebrity: *a literary lion.*

li•on•ess (lī′ə nis) /'layənɪs/ *n.* [*count*] a female lion.

li•on•heart•ed (lī′ən här′tid) /'layən,hɑrtɪd/ *adj.* exceptionally brave.

li•on•ize (lī′ə nīz′) /'layə,nayz/ *v.* [~ + *obj*], **-ized, -iz•ing.** to treat (a person) as a celebrity: *was lionized by the press.* —**li•on•i•za•tion** (lī′ə nə zā′shən) /,layənə'zeyʃən/ *n.* [*noncount*]

li′on's share′, *n.* [*count; usually singular*] the largest part or share, esp. an unfairly large portion.

lip (lip) /lɪp/ *n.* **1.** [*count*] either of the two fleshy parts or folds forming the outside edges of the mouth. **2.** [*count*] Usually, **lips.** [*plural*] these parts as organs of speech: *The news was on everyone's lips.* **3.** [*count*] any edge or rim: *the lip of the canyon wall.* **4.** [*count*] any part or structure of the body that resembles a lip. **5.** [*noncount*] *Slang.* impudent talk: *Don't give me any lip.* —*adj.* [*before a noun*] **6.** of or for the lips: *lip salve.* —***Idiom.* 7. keep a stiff upper lip,** [*no obj*] to maintain a determined attitude when facing difficulty. **8. smack one's lips,** to indicate one's keen enjoyment, or that one is looking forward to something: *He smacked his lips at the thought of salmon steaks.* —**lipped,** *adj.: thin-lipped.* —**lip′py,** *adj.,* **-pi•er, -pi•est.**

lip•o•suc•tion (lip′ə suk′shən, lī′pə-) /'lɪpə,sʌkʃən, 'laypə-/ *n.* [*noncount*] the surgical removal of excess fat from areas under the skin by means of vacuum suctioning.

lip•read•ing (lip′rē′ding) /'lɪp,riydɪŋ/ *n.* [*noncount*] a method of understanding spoken words by interpreting the movements of a speaker's lips without hearing the sounds made. —**lip′read′,** *v.,* **-read** (-red′) /-,rɛd/ **-read•ing:** [*no obj*]: *learning to lipread.* [~ + *obj*]: *She could lipread his words.* —**lip′read′er,** *n.* [*count*]

lip′ serv′ice, *n.* [*noncount*] insincere claims of friendship, admiration, support, etc.

lip•stick (lip′stik′) /'lɪp,stɪk/ *n.* **1.** [*noncount*] a waxy, crayonlike cosmetic for coloring the lips. **2.** [*count*] a tube containing this cosmetic.

lip-sync or **lip-synch** (lip′singk′) /'lɪp,sɪŋk/ *v.,* **-synced, -sync•ing** or **-synched, -synch•ing.** to synchronize or match lip movements and recorded sound: [*no obj*]: *There was a contest to see who could lip-sync the best.* [~ + *obj*]: *He lip-synced all his favorite pop songs.*

liq., an abbreviation of: **1.** liquid. **2.** liquor.

liq•ue•fy (lik′wə fī′) /'lɪkwə,fay/ *v.,* **-fied, -fy•ing.** to (cause to) become liquid: [*no obj*]: *The mixture liquefied.* [~ + *obj*]: *The blender will liquefy the mix.* —**liq•ue•fac•tion** (lik′wə fak′shən) /,lɪkwə'fækʃən/ *n.* [*noncount*]

li•queur (li kûr′, -kyŏŏr′) /lɪ'kɜr, -'kyʊr/ *n.* a strong, sweet, flavored alcoholic liquor: [*noncount*]: *served liqueur after dinner.* [*count*]: *an after-dinner liqueur.*

liq•uid (lik′wid) /'lɪkwɪd/ *adj.* **1.** made up of molecules that move freely among themselves but do not tend to separate like those of gases; neither gaseous nor solid: *liquid nitrogen.* **2.** of, relating to, or made up of liquids: *a liquid diet.* **3.** clear and bright: *soft, liquid eyes.* **4.** smooth; flowing freely: *liquid dance steps; liquid song.* **5.** in cash or easily changed into cash: *liquid assets.* —*n.* **6.** a liquid substance: [*noncount*]: *needs more liquid.* [*count*]: *Drink plenty of liquids.* —**li•quid•i•ty** (li kwid′i tē) /lɪ'kwɪdɪtiy/ *n.* [*noncount*]: *the liquidity of his stocks and bonds.*

liq•ui•date (lik′wi dāt′) /'lɪkwɪ,deyt/ *v.* [~ + *obj*], **-dat•ed, -dat•ing. 1.** to settle or pay (a debt): *to liquidate a claim.* **2.** to convert (property or other assets) into cash: *to liquidate an estate.* **3.** to get rid of, esp. by killing: *The regime liquidated enemies.* **4.** to break up or do away with: *to liquidate a partnership.* —**liq•ui•da•tion** (lik′wi dā′shən) /,lɪkwɪ'deyʃən/ *n.* [*noncount*] —**liq′ui•da′tor,** *n.* [*count*]

liq•uid•ize (lik′wi dīz′) /'lɪkwɪ,dayz/ *v.* [~ + *obj*], **-ized, -iz•ing.** to make liquid. —**liq′uid•iz′er,** *n.* [*count*]

liq′uid meas′ure, *n.* [*noncount*] the system of units for measuring the volume of liquid products, as milk.

liq•uor (lik′ər) /'lɪkər/ *n.* [*noncount*] **1.** an alcoholic beverage that has undergone a process of heating, evaporating, and condensing back to a liquid, as brandy or whiskey, as distinguished from a fermented beverage, as wine or beer. **—v.** [~ + *obj* (+ *up*)] **2.** *Informal.* to make (someone) drunk with liquor: *They liquored him up.*

li•ra (lēr′ə) /ˈlɪərə/ *n.* [*count*], *pl.* **li•re** (lēr′ā) /ˈlɪərey/ **li•ras.** the basic monetary units of Italy, Malta, and Turkey.

lisp (lisp) /lɪsp/ *n.* [*count*] **1.** a speech defect in which *s* and *z* are pronounced like or nearly like the *th-* sounds of *thin* and *this,* respectively; any slightly different pronunciation of speech sounds like (s) and (z). **—v. 2.** to pronounce or speak with a lisp: [*no obj*]: *has been lisping since childhood.* [~ + *obj*]: *He lisps his s sounds.* **3.** to speak imperfectly, esp. in a childish manner: [*no obj*]: *Stop lisping.* [~ + *obj*]: *He lisped some s sounds.*

lis•some or **lis•som** (lis′əm) /ˈlɪsəm/ *adj.* graceful; supple.

list[1] (list) /lɪst/ *n.* **1.** [*count*] a series of items written or printed together in a grouping or sequence so as to make up a record: *a shopping list.* **2.** [*noncount*] LIST PRICE. **—v. 3.** [~ + *obj*] to make a list of: *He listed the items they would need.* **4.** [~ + *obj*] to enter in a list, directory, catalog, etc.: *to list him among the members.* **5.** [*no obj*] to be offered for sale at a specified price: *This radio lists at $49.95.*

list[2] (list) /lɪst/ *n.* [*count*] **1.** a leaning to one side, as of a ship: *a heavy list to starboard.* **—v.** [*no obj*] **2.** to lean to one side: *The boat listed to starboard.*

lis•ten (lis′ən) /ˈlɪsən/ *v.* **1.** to give attention with the ear; pay attention for the purpose of hearing: [~ + *to* + *obj*]: *He listened to every word.* [*no obj*]: *I wasn't listening.* **2.** [~ + *to* + *obj*] to obey; take advice from: *Children don't always listen to their parents.* **3.** [~ + *for* + *obj*] to wait attentively in order to hear a sound or signal: *listening for the phone to ring.* **4. listen in, a.** [*no obj*] to listen to a broadcast, as on the radio. **b.** to listen to a conversation without joining it: [*no obj*]: *He sat in the back, listening in.* [~ + *on* + *obj*]: *wanted to listen in on the talks.* **—lis′ten•er,** *n.* [*count*] **—Usage.** See HEAR.

list•ing (lis′ting) /ˈlɪstɪŋ/ *n.* [*count*] **1.** a list: *a listing of the courses for the fall semester.* **2.** something listed or included in a list: *a listing in the telephone directory.*

list•less (list′lis) /ˈlɪstlɪs/ *adj.* having or showing little or no interest in anything; spiritless. **—list′less•ly,** *adv.* **—list′less•ness,** *n.* [*noncount*]

list′ price′, *n.* the price at which a product is usually sold to the public, from which discounts may be made: [*noncount*]: *to pay list price for goods.* [*count*]: *List prices are down.*

lit (lit) /lɪt/ *v.* **1.** a pt. and pp. of LIGHT[1]. **—adj. 2.** *Slang.* under the influence of liquor; drunk.

-lit-, *root.* *-lit-* comes from Latin, where it has the meaning "letter; read; word." This meaning is found in such words as: ALLITERATION, ILLITERATE, LETTER, LITERACY, LITERAL, LITERARY, OBLITERATE, UNLETTERED.

lit., an abbreviation of: **1.** liter. **2.** literal. **3.** literally. **4.** literary. **5.** literature.

lit•a•ny (lit′n ē) /ˈlɪtn̩iy/ *n.* [*count*], *pl.* **-nies. 1.** a form of prayer consisting of a series of prayers by a priest or leader, with responses from the congregation that are the same for a number in succession. **2.** a long list of anything repetitious: *a litany of complaints.*

li•tchi (lē′chē) /ˈliytʃiy/ *n.*, *pl.* **-tchis. 1.** the fruit of a Chinese tree made up of a thin, brittle shell around a sweet, jellylike pulp and a single seed: [*noncount*]: *some sweet litchi.* [*count*]: *Bring back four litchis.* **2.** [*count*] the tree itself.

li•ter (lē′tər) /ˈliytər/ *n.* [*count*] a unit of liquid measure equal to the volume of one kilogram of water or 1.0567 U.S. liquid quarts. *Abbr.:* l Also, *esp. Brit.,* **litre.**

lit•er•a•cy (lit′ər ə sē) /ˈlɪtərəsiy/ *n.* [*noncount*] **1.** the quality or state of being literate, esp. the ability to read and write. **2.** a person's knowledge of a particular subject or field: *computer literacy.* See -LIT-.

lit•er•al (lit′ər əl) /ˈlɪtərəl/ *adj.* **1.** being in accordance with the primary or strict meaning of a word or words; not figurative or metaphorical: *a savior of his people in the literal sense.* **2.** following the words of the original exactly: *a literal translation from Russian to English.* **3.** true to fact; without exaggeration: *a literal description of the horrors of war.* **4.** tending to understand words in the strict sense or in an unimaginative way: *He's so literal that he never knows when we're joking.* **—lit′er•al•ness,** *n.* [*noncount*] See -LIT-.

lit•er•al•ly (lit′ər ə lē) /ˈlɪtərəliy/ *adv.* **1.** in the literal or strict sense: *deciding what the word meant literally.* **2.** in a literal manner; word for word: *to translate literally.* **3.** actually; without exaggeration or inaccuracy: *The city was literally destroyed.* **4.** This word is sometimes used to add emphasis to a statement and means "in effect; very nearly": *The senator was literally buried alive in the primary (= The senator lost the election badly).* See -LIT-. **—Usage.** The last meaning of LITERALLY is sometimes criticized as incorrect, since it appears to be the opposite of definitions 1 and 3. Nevertheless, many speakers use this last sense of LITERALLY to add emphasis to a statement.

lit•er•ar•y (lit′ə rer′ē) /ˈlɪtəˌrɛriy/ *adj.* **1.** relating to or of the nature of books and writings, esp. those classed as literature: *literary history.* **2.** educated; well-read: *a literary person.* See -LIT-.

lit•er•ate (lit′ər it) /ˈlɪtərɪt/ *adj.* **1.** able to read and write. **2.** educated; well-read. **3.** having knowledge or skill in a specified field: *computer-literate.* **—lit′er•ate•ly,** *adv.* See -LIT-.

lit•e•ra•ti (lit′ə rä′tē) /ˌlɪtəˈrɑtiy/ *n.* [*plural*], *sing.* **-ra•tus** (-rä′təs) /-ˈrɑtəs/. persons interested in scholarly or literary affairs; intellectuals. See -LIT-.

lit•er•a•ture (lit′ər ə chər, li′trə-) /ˈlɪtərətʃər, ˈlɪtrə-/ *n.* [*noncount*] **1.** writing in prose or poetry thought of as having permanent value or excellence. **2.** the entire body of writings of a specific language, period, people, etc.: *French literature.* **3.** the writings dealing with a particular subject: *the literature of biology.* **4.** any kind of printed material, as circulars, leaflets, or handbills: *company literature describing new products.* See -LIT-.

-lith-, *root.* *-lith-* comes from Greek, where it has the meaning "stone." This meaning is found in such words as: LITHIUM, LITHOGRAPHY, MONOLITH, NEOLITHIC.

lithe (līth) /layð/ *adj.,* **lith•er, lith•est.** limber; supple; flexible: *a lithe dancer; lithe bodies.*

lithe•some (līth′səm) /ˈlayðsəm/ *adj.* lithe; lissome.

lith•i•um (lith′ē əm) /ˈlɪθiyəm/ *n.* [*noncount*] a soft, silver-white metallic element, the lightest of all metals. See -LITH-.

lith•o•graph (lith′ə graf′) /ˈlɪθəˌgræf/ *n.* [*count*] **1.** a print produced by lithography. **—v.** [~ + *obj*] **2.** to produce or copy by lithography. **—li•thog•ra•pher** (li thog′rə fər) /lɪˈθɒgrəfər/ *n.* [*count*] See -GRAPH-, -LITH-.

li•thog•ra•phy (li thog′rə fē) /lɪˈθɒgrəfiy/ *n.* [*noncount*] a printing technique in which a stone or metal plate is treated so that ink attaches to it only in the areas that contain the image to be printed. **—lith•o•graph•ic** (lith′ə graf′ik) /ˌlɪθəˈgræfɪk/ *adj.* See -GRAPH-, -LITH-.

Lith•u•a•ni•an (lith′o͞o ā′nē ən) /ˌlɪθuwˈeyniyən/ *adj.* **1.** of or relating to Lithuania. **2.** of or relating to the language spoken by many of the people in Lithuania. **—n. 3.** [*count*] a person born or living in Lithuania. **4.** [*noncount*] the language spoken by many of the people in Lithuania.

lit•i•gant (lit′i gənt) /ˈlɪtɪgənt/ *n.* [*count*] a person engaged in a lawsuit.

lit•i•gate (lit′i gāt′) /ˈlɪtɪˌgeyt/ *v.,* **-gat•ed, -gat•ing. 1.** [~ + *obj*] to make the subject of a lawsuit; contest at law: *Who is litigating the case?* **2.** [*no obj*] to carry on a lawsuit: *They're still litigating.* **—lit•i•ga•tion** (lit′i gā′shən) /ˌlɪtɪˈgeyʃən/ *n.* [*noncount*]: *involved in litigation.* [*count*]: *a lengthy litigation.* **—lit′i•ga′tor,** *n.* [*count*]

li•ti•gious (li tij′əs) /lɪˈtɪdʒəs/ *adj.* **1.** of or relating to litigation. **2.** inclined to or willing to litigate: *a litigious person.* **—li•ti′gious•ness,** *n.* [*noncount*]

lit•mus (lit′məs) /ˈlɪtməs/ *n.* [*noncount*] coloring matter that turns blue in alkaline solution and red in acid solution, used as a chemical indicator.

lit′mus pa′per, *n.* [*noncount*] a strip of paper with litmus, used as a chemical indicator.

lit′mus test′, *n.* [*count*] **1.** a test for acidity or alkalinity using litmus paper. **2.** a crucial test using a single issue or factor as the basis for judgment: *A candidate's honesty is the litmus test for the voters.*

li•tre (lē′tər) /ˈliytər/ *n.* *Chiefly Brit.* LITER.

lit•ter (lit′ər) /ˈlɪtər/ *n.* **1.** [*noncount*] rubbish scattered about: *streets full of litter.* **2.** [*noncount*] a condition of disorder or untidiness: *We were appalled at the litter in the room.* **3.** [*count*] the group of young born to an animal at one birth: *a litter of six kittens.* **4.** [*count*] a framework of cloth stretched between two parallel bars, for carrying a sick or wounded person; stretcher. **5.** [*count*] a vehicle carried by people or animals, made up of a couch hung between two parallel bars. **6.** [*noncount*] straw, hay, or the like, used as bedding for animals or as protection for plants. **7.** [*noncount*] any of various absorbent materials, as clay pellets, used for lining a box in which a cat can eliminate waste. **—v. 8.** to throw scattered objects, rubbish, etc., on (a place): [~ + *obj*]: *to be fined for littering the sidewalk.* [*no obj*]: *He was given a fine for littering.* **9.** [~ + *obj*] to scatter (objects) in disorder. **10.** [~ + *obj*] to be scattered about (a place) in disorder: *Bits of paper littered the floor.* —**lit′ter•er,** *n.* [*count*]

lit•té•ra•teur also **lit•te•ra•teur** (lit′ər ə to͝or′) /ˌlɪtərə'tʊr/ *n.* [*count*] a literary person, esp. a writer of literary works. See -LIT-.

lit•ter•bug (lit′ər bug′) /'lɪtərˌbʌg/ *n.* [*count*] a person who litters public places with trash.

lit•tle (lit′l) /'lɪtl/ *adj.,* **lit•tler** or **less** (les) /lɛs/ or **less•er, lit•tlest** or **least** (lēst) /liyst/ *adv.,* **less, least,** *n.* —*adj.* **1.** [*before a noun*] small in size, amount, or scale; not big: *a little desk; a little voice.* **2.** [*before a noun*] short in length, duration, or extent; brief: *Give me a little time.* **3.** [*before a noun*] small in number: *a little group of scientists.* **4.** [*before a noun*] This word is used before a noun and without the article *a* to mean "small in amount or degree; not much," and is used to emphasize the feeling that the amount is not as much as one would like: *There is little hope of victory. I have very little money left.* **5.** [*before a noun; a* + ~ + *noun*] This word, when preceded by the article *a,* is used to mean "of a certain amount; some; more than expected, appreciable," and is used to emphasize the feeling that the amount is enough or sufficient, though perhaps just barely so: *I have a little money left; maybe it's enough for the movies. We're having a little difficulty.* **6.** [*before a noun*] younger or youngest: *her little brother.* **7.** minor; unimportant: *life's little pleasures.* **8.** mean, narrow, or not willing to understand others: *little minds.* **9.** [*before a noun*] This word is sometimes used before a noun to indicate feelings of affection or amusement: *Bless your little heart!* —*adv.* **10.** [*before a verb*] not at all: *He little knows what awaits him.* **11.** This word is used with or without the article *a* to mean "in only a small amount or degree; not much; slightly," and emphasizes the feeling that the action or the amount indicated is not very much and is perhaps less than would be best: *a little known work of art; She's little better than she was before the treatment.* —*n.* **12.** [*noncount*] This word is used without the article *a* as a noncount noun to mean "a small amount, quantity, or degree," and to emphasize the feeling that the amount is less than might be expected or proper: *They did little to make us comfortable.* **13.** [*count; singular; a* + ~] This word, when preceded by the article *a,* is used to mean "a certain amount; some; an amount perhaps more than expected," and is used to emphasize the feeling that the amount is enough or sufficient, though perhaps just barely so: *Save a little for me.* **14.** [*count; singular; a* + ~] a short distance: *It's down the road a little.* **15.** [*count; singular; a* + ~] a short time: *Stay here for a little.* —***Idiom.*** **16. little by little,** by small degrees; gradually: *Little by little he was improving.* —**lit′tle•ness,** *n.* [*noncount*]

lit′tle fin′ger, *n.* [*count*] the smallest finger on the hand; the pinky.

lit•to•ral (lit′ər əl) /'lɪtərəl/ *adj.* [*before a noun*] of or relating to the shore of a lake, sea, or ocean.

li•tur•gi•cal (li tûr′ji kəl) /lɪ'tɜrdʒɪkəl/ *adj.* of or relating to liturgy.

lit•ur•gy (lit′ər jē) /'lɪtərdʒiy/ *n., pl.* **-gies. 1.** [*count*] a form of public worship; ritual according to a fixed pattern. **2.** [*noncount*] a collection of forms for public worship. —**lit′ur•gist,** *n.* [*count*]

liv•a•ble or **live•a•ble** (liv′ə bəl) /'lɪvəbəl/ *adj.* **1.** suitable for living in; habitable: *to make an old house livable.* **2.** worth living; endurable: *making life more livable.* —**liv′a•ble•ness, liv•a•bil•i•ty** (liv′ə bil′i tē) /ˌlɪvə'bɪlɪtiy/ *n.* [*noncount*]

live[1] (liv) /lɪv/ *v.,* **lived** (livd), **liv•ing. 1.** [*no obj*] to be alive; to have life: *Elephants live for many years.* **2.** [*no obj*] to continue to have life; remain alive: *to live to a ripe old age.* **3.** [*no obj*] to continue in existence, operation, memory, etc.; last: *a book that lives in my memory.* **4.** [~ + *on* + *obj*] to have enough for one's existence; provide for oneself: *He can't live on his salary.* **5.** [~ + *on* + *obj*] to eat (something) in order to stay alive or to subsist: *lived on nuts and bananas.* **6.** [*no obj*] to dwell or reside: *to live in a cottage.* **7.** to pass (life) in a specified manner: [*no obj*]: *They lived happily ever after.* [~ + *obj*]: *to live a life of ease.* **8.** [~ + *obj*] to practice or represent in one's life: *to live a philosophy of nonviolence.* **9.** [*no obj*] to enjoy life to the full: *At 50 she was just beginning to live.* **10. live down,** to cause to be forgotten or forgiven through one's future behavior: [~ + *down* + *obj*]: *She'll never live down that horrible moment of failure.* [~ + *obj* + *down*]: *She'll never live it down.* **11. live in** (or **out**), [*no obj*] to reside at (or away from) the place of one's employment, esp. as a domestic servant. **12. live out,** [~ + *out* + *obj*] to continue to the end of: *They lived out their lives in peaceful contentment.* **13. live together,** [*no obj*] to dwell or live in the same place while having a sexual relationship but without being married. **14. live up to,** [~ + *up* + *to* + *obj*] to behave so as to satisfy or represent (ideals, standards, etc.): *living up to the high standards of his father.* **15. live with,** [~ + *with* + *obj*] **a.** to dwell in the same place with, sometimes in a sexual relationship. **b.** to endure: *We'll just have to live with that noise.* —***Idiom.*** **16. live it up,** *Informal.* to live in a wild manner; pursue pleasure. —**Related Words.** LIVE is a verb and an adjective, LIFE is a noun, ALIVE, LIVELY, and LIFELIKE are adjectives: *He lives in Manhattan. It was a live show. His life was almost over. She was barely alive. It was a lively TV show, full of fun. He sculpted a lifelike statue.*

live[2] (līv) /layv/ *adj.,* **liv•er, liv•est** for 4–6, 11, *adv.* —*adj.* **1.** [*before a noun*] being alive; living: *live animals.* **2.** [*before a noun*] of, relating to, or during the life of a living being: *an animal's live weight.* **3.** characterized by or indicating the presence of living creatures: *the live sounds of the forest.* **4.** energetic; alert; lively; full of life: *His approach is live and fresh.* **5.** burning or glowing: *live coals.* **6.** having bounce: *a live tennis ball.* **7.** being in play, as a baseball or football. **8.** loaded but unexploded: *live ammunition.* **9.** made up of people who are actually present: *a live audience.* **10.** broadcast while happening or being performed: *a live telecast.* **11.** of current interest or importance; unsettled: *live issues.* **12.** connected to a source of electricity: *a live outlet.* —*adv.* **13.** by transmission at the actual moment of occurrence or performance: *a program broadcast live.*

live-in (liv′in′) /'lɪvˌɪn/ *adj.* [*before a noun*] **1.** dwelling or living at the same place as one works: *a live-in maid.* **2.** living at the same place as a sexual partner to whom one is not married: *a live-in boyfriend.* —*n.* [*count*] **3.** a live-in person.

live•li•hood (līv′lē ho͝od′) /'layvliyˌhʊd/ *n.* [*count; usually singular*] a means of supporting one's existence: *Teaching is his livelihood.*

live•long (liv′lông′, -long′) /'lɪvˌlɔŋ, -ˌlɒŋ/ *adj.* (of time) whole; entire: *to complain the livelong day.*

live•ly (līv′lē) /'layvliy/ *adj.* and *adv.,* **-li•er, -li•est.** —*adj.* **1.** full or suggestive of life or vital energy: *a lively discussion.* **2.** animated; spirited: *a lively tune.* **3.** eventful or exciting: *The opposition gave us a lively time.* **4.** keen; vivid: *took a lively interest in us.* **5.** rebounding quickly: *a lively tennis ball.* —*adv.* **6.** with briskness: *Please step lively.* —**live′li•ness,** *n.* [*noncount*]

liv•en (lī′vən) /'layvən/ *v.* to (cause to) become more lively: [~ *(+ up)* + *obj*]: *Can we liven (up) the party?* [~ + *obj (+ up)*]: *Can we liven the party (up)?* [~ + *up*]: *The party livened up.*

liv•er (liv′ər) /'lɪvər/ *n.* **1.** [*count*] a large organ in animals with backbones, located in the upper abdomen, releasing bile and cleansing the blood. **2.** this organ of an animal, as a calf, used as food: [*noncount*]: *having liver for dinner.* [*count*]: *chicken livers.*

liv•er•wurst (liv′ər wûrst′, -wo͝osht′) /'lɪvərˌwɜrst, -ˌwʊʃt/ *n.* [*noncount*] a cooked sausage containing a large percentage of pork liver and pork meat.

liv•er•y (liv′ə rē, liv′rē) /'lɪvəriy, 'lɪvriy/ *n., pl.* **-er•ies. 1.** [*count*] a uniform worn by servants. **2.** [*noncount*] the care, stabling, etc., of horses for pay. **3.** [*count*] a company that rents out vehicles. —**liv′er•ied,** *adj.* See -LIBER-.

lives (līvz) /layvz/ *n.* pl. of LIFE.

live•stock (līv′stok′) /'layvˌstɒk/ *n.* the horses, cattle, sheep, and other useful animals kept or raised on a farm or ranch: [*noncount; used with a singular verb*]: *The livestock is worth a lot.* [*plural; used with a plural verb*]: *The livestock were grazing.*

live′ wire′ (līv) /layv/ *n.* [*count*] *Informal.* an energetic, very alert person.

liv•id (liv′id) /'lɪvɪd/ *adj.* **1.** having a discolored, bluish, bruised appearance. **2.** enraged; furiously angry: *Her insulting remark made him livid.* —**liv′id•ly,** *adv.*

liv•ing (liv′ing) /'lɪvɪŋ/ *adj.* **1.** having life; being alive; not dead: *one's nearest living relatives.* **2.** in actual existence or use: *living languages.* **3.** vigorous; strong: *a living faith.* **4.** [*before a noun*] relating to or suitable for human activity or existence: *not enough living space.* **5.** [*before a noun*] of or relating to living persons: *the worst flood in living memory.* **6.** [*before a noun*] lifelike; true to life:

The statue is the living image of the general. **7.** [*before a noun*] This word is used to mean "very; absolute" and to express strong feeling: *to scare the living daylights out of someone.* **—***n.* **8.** [*noncount*] the act or condition of a person or thing that lives: *a poor standard of living.* **9.** [*count; singular*] livelihood: *to earn a living.* **10. the living,** [*plural*] living persons considered as a group: *the living and the dead.*

liv′ing room′, *n.* [*count*] a room in a home used by the members of the household for leisure activities, entertaining guests, etc. See illustration at APARTMENT.

liv′ing wage′, *n.* [*count*] a wage or a salary on which it is possible to live at least according to minimum customary standards.

liv′ing will′, *n.* [*count*] a document in which a person states that no special and extraordinary measures are to be used to prolong his or her life in the event of a terminal illness.

liz•ard (liz′ərd) /ˈlɪzərd/ *n.* [*count*] a reptile with scales, typically having a long body, long tail, and four legs, as the chameleon, iguana, or gecko.

′ll (əl, l) /əl, l/ **1.** a contraction of *shall* or *will*: *I'll answer the phone. What'll we do?* **2.** a contraction of *till*[1] (used when the preceding word ends in *t*): *Wait'll you see this!*

lla•ma (lä′mə, yä′-) /ˈlɑmə, ˈyɑ-/ *n.* [*count*], *pl.* **-mas.** a woolly-haired South American animal related to the camel.

lla•no (lä′nō, yä′-) /ˈlɑnow, ˈyɑ-/ *n.* [*count*], *pl.* **-nos.** (in the southwestern U.S. and Spanish America) a wide, long grassy plain with few trees.

LNG, an abbreviation of: liquefied natural gas.

lo (lō) /low/ *interj.* This word is used to mean "look! see!" and to express surprise, as in the phrase *lo and behold.*

load (lōd) /lowd/ *n.* [*count*] **1.** anything put in or on something to be carried somewhere; freight; cargo: *a truck with a load of watermelons.* **2.** the quantity that can be or usually is carried at one time, taken as a unit of measure or weight (usually used in combination after a noun): *a carload of people.* **3.** workload: *The professor was carrying a load of twenty-one class hours a year.* **4.** burden; onus: *That's a load off my mind.* **5. loads of,** or **a load of,** *Informal.* a great quantity or number: *There were loads of people there.* **—***v.* **6.** [~ + *obj*] to put a load on or in (something); fill: *to load a ship.* **7.** [*no obj*] to put on or take on a load, as of passengers or goods: *All buses load at the platform.* **8.** [~ + *obj*] to take on as a load: *The ship loaded coal.* **9.** [*no obj*] to enter a bus, ship, etc., so that it is filled. **10.** [~ + *obj (+ down)*] to give a great supply of something: *They loaded us down with gifts.* **11.** [~ + *obj* + *down*] to weigh down; oppress: *to load oneself down with obligations.* **12.** to insert a bullet, etc., into (a firearm): [~ + *obj*]: *He loaded the gun and fired.* [*no obj*]: *He loaded quickly.* **13.** [~ + *obj*] to place (film, tape, etc.) into (a camera or other device): *He loaded the film into the camera. He loaded the camera with film.* **14.** [~ + *obj*] **a.** to transfer (data) into a computer's memory, as from a disk. **b.** to place (a disk) into a device, as a disk drive. **—***adv.* **15. loads,** *Informal.* very much; a great deal: *It would help loads if you could send some money.* **—*Idiom.* 16. get a load of,** [~ + *obj*] *Slang.* to look at or listen to; notice: *Get a load of this car.* —**load′er,** *n.* [*count*]

load•ed (lō′did) /ˈlowdɪd/ *adj.* **1.** carrying or having a load; full: *a loaded bus.* **2.** containing ammunition or an explosive charge: *a loaded rifle.* **3.** filled with hidden meaning: *a loaded statement; a loaded question.* **4.** [*be* + ~] *Slang.* **a.** wealthy; rich. **b.** under the influence of alcohol; drunk. **5.** (of dice) dishonestly weighted so as to increase the chances that certain combinations will appear face up when the dice are thrown.

loaf[1] (lōf) /lowf/ *n.* [*count*] *pl.* **loaves** (lōvz). **1.** a shaped or molded mass of bread. **2.** a similar shaped or molded mass of food: *a meat loaf.*

loaf[2] (lōf) /lowf/ *v.* to pass time idly: [*no obj*]: *He loafed during the summer.* [~ + *obj*]: *to loaf the afternoon away.* —**loaf′er,** *n.* [*count*]

Loaf•er (lō′fər) /ˈlowfər/ *Trademark.* [*count*] a slip-on shoe similar to a moccasin.

loam (lōm) /lowm/ *n.* [*noncount*] a rich soil containing a relatively equal mixture of sand and silt and a somewhat smaller amount of clay. —**loam′y,** *adj.,* **-i•er, -i•est.**

loan (lōn) /lown/ *n.* [*count*] **1.** the act of lending: *the loan of a book.* **2.** something lent, esp. a sum of money lent at interest: *a loan of $25,000.* **—***v.* **3.** to make a loan of; lend: [~ + *obj* + *obj*]: *Loan me your umbrella.* [~ + *obj* + *to* + *obj*]: *Loan your umbrella to him.* [~ + *obj*]: *The bank loans money.* **—*Idiom.* 4. on loan,** loaned for temporary use: *The books are on loan.*

loan•er (lō′nər) /ˈlownər/ *n.* [*count*] **1.** one that loans. **2.** something, as a car or appliance, that is lent to replace an item being serviced or repaired.

loan′ shark′, *n.* [*count*] *Informal.* a person who lends money at rates of interest that are too high. —**loan′-shark′ing,** *n.* [*noncount*]

loan•word (lōn′wûrd′) /ˈlownˌwɜrd/ *n.* [*count*] a word in one language that has been borrowed from another language and usually changed to fit the new language, as *macho,* taken into Modern English from Spanish.

loath (lōth, lōth) /lowθ, lowð/ *adj.* [*be* + ~ + *to* + *verb*] unwilling; reluctant: *is loath to admit a mistake.*

loathe (lōth) /lowð/ *v.,* **loathed, loath•ing.** to feel disgust or intense hatred of; abhor; dislike strongly: [~ + *obj*] *She positively loathes him.* [~ + *verb-ing*]: *He loathes going to the dentist.* —**loath′er,** *n.* [*count*]

loath•ing (lō′thing) /ˈlowðɪŋ/ *n.* strong dislike or aversion: [*noncount*]: *a feeling of loathing.* [*count*]: *a loathing of spiders.*

loath•some (lōth′səm, lōth′-) /ˈlowðsəm, ˈlowθ-/ *adj.* causing feelings of loathing; disgusting; revolting: *a loathsome skin disease.* —**loath′some•ness,** *n.* [*noncount*]

loaves (lōvz) /lowvz/ *n.* pl. of LOAF[1].

lob (lob) /lɒb/ *v.,* **lobbed, lob•bing,** *n.* **—***v.* **1.** to hit (a ball) in a high curve to the back of the opponent's court in tennis: [~ + *obj*]: *lobbed the ball.* [*no obj*]: *lobbing five times in the first set.* **2.** [~ + *obj*] to fire or hurl (something, as a missile or a shell) in a high curve so that it drops onto a target. **—***n.* [*count*] **3.** a lobbed ball: *a shallow lob.* —**lob′ber,** *n.* [*count*]

lob•by (lob′ē) /ˈlɒbiy/ *n., pl.* **-bies,** *v.,* **-bied, -by•ing.** **—***n.* [*count*] **1.** an entrance hall or corridor, as in a public building, often serving as an anteroom; foyer. See illustration at HOTEL. **2.** a group of persons who try to influence legislators or other public officials to vote or act in favor of a special interest. **—***v.* **3.** to try to influence the actions or votes of: [~ + *obj*]: *lobbied a few key senators.* [*no obj*]: *lobbied for the bill.* **4.** [~ + *obj*] to urge the passage of by lobbying: *to lobby a bill.* —**lob′by•ist,** *n.* [*count*]

lobe (lōb) /lowb/ *n.* [*count*] a roundish part that sticks out, as of an organ or a leaf. —**lobed,** *adj.*

lo•bot•o•my (lə bot′ə mē, lō-) /ləˈbɒtəmiy, low-/ *n.* [*count*], *pl.* **-mies.** a surgical operation into or across a lobe, esp. a lobe of the brain, in order to treat a mental disorder. See -TOM-.

lob•ster (lob′stər) /ˈlɒbstər/ *n., pl.* (*esp. when thought of as a group*) **-ster,** (*esp. for kinds or species*) **-sters.** **1.** [*count*] a saltwater crustacean that can be eaten, having eyes on stalks, eight legs, and two large pincers. **2.** [*noncount*] the edible meat of the lobster.

-loc-, *root.* *-loc-* comes from Latin, where it has the meaning "location; place." This meaning is found in such words as: ALLOCATE, DISLOCATE, LOCAL, LOCALE, LOCATE, LOCOMOTIVE, LOCUS, RELOCATE.

lo•cal (lō′kəl) /ˈlowkəl/ *adj.* **1.** relating to, characteristic of, or restricted to a particular place: *a local custom; a local hospital.* **2.** [*before a noun*] of or relating to a city, town, or small district rather than an entire state or country: *local town government.* **3.** stopping at most or all stations: *a local train.* **4.** affecting only a particular part or area of the body without loss of consciousness: *a local anesthetic.* **—***n.* [*count*] **5.** a local train, bus, etc.: *Take the local to 23rd Street.* **6.** a local anesthetic. **7.** Often, **locals.** [*plural*] a local person or resident: *The locals don't like newcomers.* —**lo′cal•ly,** *adv.* See -LOC-.

lo•cale (lō kal′) /lowˈkæl/ *n.* [*count*] a place or locality: *to move to a warmer locale.* See -LOC-.

lo•cal•i•ty (lō kal′i tē) /lowˈkælɪtiy/ *n.* [*count*], *pl.* **-ties.** a specific place or area; location: *They moved to another locality.*

lo•cal•ize (lō′kə līz′) /ˈlowkəˌlayz/ *v.* [~ + *obj*], **-ized, -iz•ing.** to make local; keep, confine, or restrict to a particular place: *The anesthetic will localize the pain.* —**lo•cal•i•za•tion** (lō′kə lə zā′shən) /ˌlowkələˈzeyʃən/ *n.* [*noncount*] See -LOC-.

lo•cate (lō′kāt, lō kāt′) /ˈlowkeyt, lowˈkeyt/ *v.,* **-cat•ed, -cat•ing.** **—***v.* **1.** [~ + *obj*] to identify or discover the location of; find: *to locate a missing book.* **2.** to establish (one's business or home) in a locality; settle: [~ + *obj*]: *They located their offices downtown.* [*no obj*]: *decided to locate in New Mexico.* **3.** [~ + *obj*] to assign a particular location to, as by knowledge or opinion: *Some scholars* *locate the Garden of Eden in Babylonia.* —**lo•cat′a•ble,** *adj.* —**lo′cat•er, lo′ca•tor,** *n.* [*count*] See -LOC-.

lo•ca•tion (lō kā′shən) /low'keyʃən/ *n.* [*count*] **1.** a place or situation occupied: *a house in a fine location.* **2.** a place of activity or residence: *This town is a good location for a young doctor.* **3.** a site outside a movie studio used for filming. —***Idiom.*** **4. on location,** engaged in filming at a place away from the studio, esp. one that is or is like the setting of the screenplay. See -LOC-.

loch (lok, loKH) /lɒk, lɒx/ *n.* [*count*] *Scottish.* **1.** a lake. **2.** a partially landlocked or protected bay or arm of the sea.

lock[1] (lok) /lɒk/ *n.* [*count*] **1.** a device for keeping a door, gate, lid, drawer, or the like securely closed or fastened, made up of a bolt or system of bolts moved by a key, dial, etc. **2.** (in a firearm) the mechanism that explodes the charge. **3.** an enclosed chamber in a canal, dam, etc., with gates at each end, for raising or lowering vessels from one level to another by increasing or decreasing water in the chamber. **4.** complete and unchallenged control or an unbreakable hold: *to have a lock on the senatorial nomination.* **5.** *Slang.* a sure thing: *The team is a lock to win the championship.* —*v.* **6.** to (cause a door, window, building, etc., to) become fastened or made secure by the operation of a lock or locks: [~ + *obj*]: *I locked the car doors.* [*no obj*]: *The car doors lock automatically.* **7.** [~ + *obj*] to shut in a place by or as if by means of a lock: *We locked the hamster in its cage.* **8.** to (cause to) become fastened, fixed, interlocked, or jammed by or as if by a lock: [~ + *obj*]: *to lock the steering wheel on a car to prevent theft.* [*no obj*]: *The gears locked into place.* **9.** [~ + *obj*] to unite firmly by linking: *to lock arms.* **10.** [~ + *obj*] to hold fast in an embrace: *She locked him in her arms.* **11. lock in, a.** to (cause to) be aimed at (a target or goal) and be unable to change: [~ + *in* + *obj*]: *The pilot locked in his target.* [~ + *obj* + *in*]: *The pilot locked it in and fired.* [~ + *in* + *on* + *obj*]: *The missiles locked in on the target.* **b.** to put into a place, room, etc., and lock its doors: [~ + *obj* + *in*]: *They locked him in with the other prisoners.* [~ + *in* + *obj*]: *The guard locked in the prisoners every night.* **12. lock out, a.** [~ + *obj* + *out*] to keep out by or as if by a lock: *I was locked out of my car.* **b.** to subject (employees) to a lockout: [~ + *out* + *obj*]: *The boss locked out the striking employees.* [~ + *obj* + *out*]: *to lock them out if they don't negotiate.* **13. lock up, a.** to imprison for a crime: [~ + *obj* + *up*]: *took him away and locked him up.* [~ + *up* + *obj*]: *locking up criminals.* **b.** to make secure with a lock: [~ + *up* + *obj*]: *locked up the money in his safe.* [~ + *obj* + *up*]: *locked the money up in his safe.* [*no obj*]: *The watchman locked up for the night.* **c.** to fasten or fix firmly, as by engaging parts: [*no obj*]: *The car's brakes locked up.* [~ + *up* + *obj*]: *Slamming on the brakes will lock up your wheels.* [~ + *obj* + *up*]: *Something locked the gears up.* —***Idiom.*** **14. lock horns,** [~ (+ *with* + *obj*)] to come into conflict; clash: *They locked horns with their critics.* **15. lock, stock, and barrel,** with every part or item included; completely: *He'll sue you lock, stock, and barrel.* **16. under lock and key,** securely locked up: *to keep important papers under lock and key.*

lock[2] (lok) /lɒk/ *n.* [*count*] **1.** a tuft or ringlet of hair. **2. locks,** [*plural*] the hair of the head: *golden locks.*

lock•er (lok′ər) /'lɒkər/ *n.* [*count*] **1.** a chest, compartment, or closet in which clothing and valuables may be locked for safekeeping: *a gym locker.* **2.** a large, typically room-size compartment for keeping frozen foods.

lock•et (lok′it) /'lɒkɪt/ *n.* [*count*] a small case for a miniature portrait, a lock of hair, or other keepsake, usually worn on a necklace.

lock•jaw (lok′jô′) /'lɒk,dʒɔ/ *n.* [*noncount*] a condition in which the jaws become locked together, caused by tetanus.

lock•out (lok′out′) /'lɒk,awt/ *n.* [*count*] the temporary closing of a business or the refusal by an employer to allow employees to come to work until they accept the employer's terms.

lock•smith (lok′smith′) /'lɒk,smɪθ/ *n.* [*count*] a person who makes, repairs, and installs locks.

lock•step (lok′step′) /'lɒk,stɛp/ *n.* [*noncount*] **1.** a way of marching in which the leg of each person moves with and closely behind the corresponding leg of the person ahead. **2.** a rigid and inflexible pattern or process: *to be in lockstep to the old way of doing things.* —*adj.* [*before a noun*] **3.** rigid and inflexible: *lockstep educational procedures.*

lock•up (lok′up′) /'lɒk,ʌp/ *n.* [*count*] **1.** a jail, esp. a local one for temporary detention. **2.** the act of locking up or the state of being locked up.

lo•co (lō′kō) /'lowkow/ *adj. Slang.* insane; crazy.

lo•co•mo•tion (lō′kə mō′shən) /,lowkə'mowʃən/ *n.* [*noncount*] the act or power of moving from place to place: *Most plants lack locomotion.* See -LOC-, -MOT-.

lo•co•mo•tive (lō′kə mō′tiv) /,lowkə'mowtɪv/ *n.* [*count*] **1.** a self-propelled railroad engine for pulling or pushing railroad cars. —*adj.* **2.** [*before a noun*] of or relating to locomotives. **3.** of, relating to, producing, or aiding in locomotion. See -LOC-, -MOT-.

lo•cus (lō′kəs) /'lowkəs/ *n.* [*count*], *pl.* **-ci** (-sī, -kē, -ki) /-say, -kiy, -kay/. **1.** a place; locality. **2.** a center or source, as of activities or power: *The locus of control is headquarters.* See -LOC-.

lo•cust (lō′kəst) /'lowkəst/ *n.* [*count*] **1.** a grasshopper having short antennae and commonly migrating in swarms that strip the vegetation from large areas. **2.** any of various cicadas, as the seventeen-year locust. **3.** a North American tree of the legume family, having clusters of fragrant white flowers.

lo•cu•tion (lō kyōō′shən) /low'kyuwʃən/ *n.* [*count*] **1.** a word, phrase, or expression, esp. as used by a particular person, group, etc. **2.** a style of speech or verbal expression. See -LOQ-.

lode (lōd) /lowd/ *n.* [*count*] **1.** a veinlike deposit, usually one that contains metal. **2.** a rich supply or source.

lode•stone (lōd′stōn′) /'lowd,stown/ *n.* **1.** [*noncount*] a mineral that possesses magnetism. **2.** [*count*] something that attracts like a magnet.

lodge (loj) /lɒdʒ/ *n., v.,* **lodged, lodg•ing.** —*n.* [*count*] **1.** a house or cabin, esp. one used as a temporary residence by hunters, skiers, hikers, or campers. **2.** a resort hotel, motel, or inn: *a fancy lodge near the sea.* **3.** the meeting place of a branch of certain fraternal organizations: *the Elks Club lodge.* **4.** the members of such a branch: *The lodge made a large donation.* **5.** a dwelling for North American Indians, as a wigwam or long house. —*v.* **6.** [*no obj*] to stay in a living space or quarters, esp. temporarily: *We lodged in a guest house for the night.* **7.** [*no obj*] to live in rented quarters in another's house: *He lodged with us last year.* **8.** [~ + *obj*] to have as a lodger: *The family agreed to lodge the foreign student for the summer.* **9.** to (cause to) be fixed, implanted, or caught in a place or position; (cause to) come to rest; stick: [*no obj*]: *The bullet lodged in the wall.* [~ + *obj*]: *He lodged his finger in the hole.* **10.** [~ + *obj*] to put or bring before a court or other authority: *She lodged a complaint with the union.*

lodg•er (loj′ər) /'lɒdʒər/ *n.* [*count*] a person who rents quarters in another's house; roomer.

lodg•ing (loj′ing) /'lɒdʒɪŋ/ *n.* **1.** [*noncount*] accommodation in a house, esp. in rooms for rent: *to furnish board and lodging.* **2. lodgings,** [*plural*] a room or rooms rented for residence: *found lodgings for the night.*

loft (lôft, loft) /lɔft, lɒft/ *n.* [*count*] **1.** an upper room or storage area beneath a sloping roof; attic; garret. **2.** a gallery or upper level in a church, hall, etc., for a special purpose: *a choir loft.* **3.** an upper story of a business building, warehouse, or factory, usually an open floor area. **4.** such an upper story converted or adapted to any of various uses, as quarters for living or studios for artists or dancers. **5.** Also called **loft′ bed′.** a balcony or platform built over a living area and used for sleeping. —*v.* [~ + *obj*] **6.** to hit or throw aloft: *He lofted a fly ball into center field.*

loft•y (lôf′tē, lof′-) /'lɔftiy, 'lɒf-/ *adj.,* **-i•er, -i•est. 1.** extending high in the air; towering: *lofty mountains.* **2.** elevated in style or tone: *lofty sentiments.* **3.** arrogant in manner; haughty: *a rather lofty butler.* —**loft•i•ly** (lôf′tə lē, lof′-) /'lɔftəliy, 'lɒf-/ *adv.* —**loft′i•ness,** *n.* [*noncount*]

log[1] (lôg, log) /lɔg, lɒg/ *n., v.,* **logged, log•ging.** —*n.* [*count*] **1.** a portion or length of the trunk or of a large limb of a tree that has fallen. **2.** any detailed, usually sequential record, as of the progress of an activity or of the trip of a ship or aircraft. —*v.* **3.** [~ + *obj*] to cut (trees) into logs. **4.** to cut down the trees or timber on (land): [~ + *obj*]: *logging the mountain behind our house.* [*no obj*]: *They have logged in that area for generations.* **5.** [~ + *obj*] to enter in a log; compile: *The captain logged the ship's position.* **6.** [~ + *obj*] to travel at or for (a certain speed, time, or distance): *logged 10,000 hours flying time.* **7. log in** or **on,** [*no obj*] to gain access to a secured computer system or on-line service by keying in personal identification information. **8. log off** or **out,** to terminate a session on such a system or service: [*no* obj]: *He logs off at night.* [~ + obj]: *He logged off the system.* —**log′ger,** *n.* [count]

log² (lôg, log) /lɔg, lɒg/ *n.* LOGARITHM.

-log-, *root.* *-log-* comes from Greek, where it has the meaning "speak; word; speech." This meaning is found in such words as: ANALOG, APOLOGY, CHRONOLOGY, DECALOGUE, DIALOGUE, DOXOLOGY, EPILOGUE, EULOGY, IDEOLOGY, LOGARITHM, LOGIC, LOGO, MONOLOGUE, NEOLOGISM, PHILOLOGY, SYLLOGISM, TAUTOLOGY, TERMINOLOGY. See -LOGY.

lo•gan•ber•ry (lō′gən ber′ē) /ˈlowgən,bɛriy/ *n.* [count], *pl.* **-ries. 1.** a dark red, tart-tasting, long berry of a blackberry bush of the rose family. **2.** the bush itself.

log•a•rithm (lô′gə rith′əm, log′ə-) /ˈlɔgə,rɪðəm, ˈlɒgə-/ *n.* [count] the exponent of the power to which a base number must be raised to equal a given number; log: *2 is the logarithm of 100 to the base 10 (2 =* log_{10} *100).* —**log′a•rith′mic,** *adj.* See -LOG-.

loge (lōzh) /lowʒ/ *n.* [count] (in a theater) a box or the front section of the lowest balcony, separated from the back section by an aisle or railing or both.

log•ger•head (lô′gər hed′, log′ər-) /ˈlɔgər,hɛd, ˈlɒgər-/ *n.* [count] **1.** a stupid person; blockhead. —***Idiom.*** **2. at loggerheads with,** [~ + obj] in conflict with: *two nations at loggerheads with each other.*

log•ic (loj′ik) /ˈlɒdʒɪk/ *n.* [noncount] **1.** the science that studies the principles governing correct or reliable ways of reasoning. **2.** a particular method or way of reasoning or presenting arguments. **3.** reason or sound judgment: *There is no logic in such foolish statements.* See -LOG-.

log•i•cal (loj′i kəl) /ˈlɒdʒɪkəl/ *adj.* **1.** according to or agreeing with the principles of logic: *a logical conclusion.* **2.** reasoning in agreement with the principles of logic: *a logical thinker.* **3.** reasonable; to be expected: *The idea sounds logical to me.* —**log′i•cal•ly,** *adv.* See -LOG-.

lo•gi•cian (lō jish′ən) /lowˈdʒɪʃən/ *n.* [count] a person who is skilled in logic. See -LOG-.

lo•gis•tics (lō jis′tiks, lə-) /lowˈdʒɪstɪks, lə-/ *n.* **1.** the branch of military science dealing with obtaining equipment, moving personnel, providing facilities, etc.: [*noncount; used with a singular verb*]: *Logistics is a complex field.* [*plural; used with a plural verb*]: *Logistics aren't going to assist you here.* **2.** the planning and coordination of the details of any operation: [*noncount; used with a singular verb*]: *The logistics of the office move is the problem.* [*plural; used with a plural verb*]: *The logistics are a nightmare.* —**lo•gis′tic, lo•gis′ti•cal,** *adj.* [*before a noun*] —**lo•gis′ti•cal•ly,** *adv.* See -LOG-.

log•jam (lôg′jam′, log′-) /ˈlɔg,dʒæm, ˈlɒg-/ *n.* [count] **1.** a pileup or tangle of logs, causing a blockage, as in a river. **2.** any blockage: *a logjam of bills before Congress.*

lo•go (lō′gō) /ˈlowgow/ *n.* [count], *pl.* **-gos.** Also called **lo•go•type.** (lō′gō tīp′) /ˈlowgow,tayp/. a graphic representation or a symbol of a company name, trademark, etc., esp. one designed to be recognized easily. See -LOG-.

-logue or **-log,** See -LOG-.

-logy, *suffix.* *-logy* comes from Greek, where it has the meaning "word." It is attached to roots to form nouns with the meanings: "field of study, discipline; list of": *astro- (= star) + -logy → astrology (= study of the influence of stars on events); bio- (= life) + -logy → biology (= study of living things).* See -LOG-.

loin (loin) /lɔyn/ *n.* **1.** Usually, **loins.** [*plural*] the parts of the body of animals that lie on either side of the spine between the ribs and the hipbones. **2.** [*count*] a cut of meat from this region, esp. one including the adjacent bone. **3. loins,** [*plural*] **a.** the parts of the human body between the hips and the lower ribs, esp. regarded as the seat of physical strength and reproductive power. **b.** the genital area; the sex organs.

loin•cloth (loin′klôth′, -kloth′) /ˈlɔyn,klɔθ, -,klɒθ/ *n.* [*count*] a cloth worn around the loins or hips, esp. in tropical regions.

loi•ter (loi′tər) /ˈlɔytər/ *v.* [*no obj*] to remain in an area without obvious purpose; hang around: *two men loitering suspiciously by the entrance to the hotel.* —**loi′ter•er,** *n.* [*count*]

loll (lol) /lɒl/ *v.* [*no obj*] **1.** to lie or lean in a relaxed or indolent manner; lounge: *to loll on a sofa.* **2.** to hang loosely: *His head lolled forward.*

lol•li•pop or **lol•ly•pop** (lol′ē pop′) /ˈlɒliy,pɒp/ *n.* [*count*] a piece of hard candy attached to the end of a small stick.

lol•ly•gag (lol′ē gag′) /ˈlɒliy,gæg/ *v.*, **-gagged, -gag•ging.** LALLYGAG.

Lon′don broil′ (lun′dən) /ˈlʌndən/ *n.* a cut of beef broiled and served in thin, crosscut slices: [*count*]: *a three-pound London broil.* [*noncount*]: *serving London broil.*

lone (lōn) /lown/ *adj.* [*before a noun*] being alone; standing by itself or apart; isolated; sole: *a lone traveler.*

lone•ly (lōn′lē) /ˈlownliy/ *adj.*, **-li•er, -li•est. 1.** having or suffering from a depressing feeling caused by being alone; lonesome: *felt lonely and without friends.* **2.** causing such a feeling: *a lonely room.* **3.** lone; solitary: *a lonely tower on the plain.* —**lone′li•ness,** *n.* [*noncount*]

lon•er (lō′nər) /ˈlownər/ *n.* [*count*] a person who is or prefers to be alone.

lone•some (lōn′səm) /ˈlownsəm/ *adj.* **1.** depressed or sad because of the lack of friends or companionship; lonely. **2.** marked by or causing such a feeling: *a lonesome evening at home.*

long¹ (lông, long) /lɔŋ, lɒŋ/ *adj.*, **long•er** (lông′gər, long′-) /ˈlɔŋgər, ˈlɒŋ-/ **long•est** (lông′gist, long′-) /ˈlɔŋgɪst, ˈlɒŋ-/ *n., adv.* —*adj.* **1.** having considerable or greater than usual measurement in length or distance: *a long table; a long way to travel.* **2.** lasting a considerable length of time: *a long story; a long trip.* **3.** [*after a noun*] extending, lasting, measuring, or totaling a number of specified units: *The river was eight miles long.* **4.** containing many items: *a long list.* **5.** extending beyond normal, moderate, or desired limits: *He's been working long hours.* **6.** reaching well into the past: *a long record of hatred.* **7.** taking a long time; slow: *He was long in getting here.* **8.** forward-looking; long-range: *taking the long view.* **9.** intense, thorough, or critical; seriously examining: *took a long look at his life.* **10.** having a good or large supply or endowment: *He's long on brains.* **11.** being against great odds; unlikely: *a long chance.* **12. a.** (of a speech sound) lasting a relatively long time: *long vowels.* **b.** having the sound of the English vowels in *mate, meet, mite, mote, moot,* and *mute*: *The long vowels are sometimes written with a macron on top of them, as ā, ē, ī, and ō.* —*n.* **13.** [*noncount*] a comparatively long time: *They haven't been gone for long.* **14. a.** [*noncount*] a size of garments for men who are taller than average. **b.** [*count*] a garment in this size. —*adv.* **15.** for or through a great extent of space or, esp., time: *a reform that has long been needed.* **16.** for or throughout a period or extent, esp. of time: *How long did he stay?* **17.** at a point of time far distant from the time indicated: *long before now.* —***Idiom.*** **18. as long as, a.** provided that: *You can watch television as long as you have finished your homework.* **b.** seeing that; since: *As long as you're going, I'll go too.* **c.** Also, **so long as.** during the time that; while: *As long as he has been in charge that division has done well.* **19. before long,** soon: *I hope I get to see you before long.* **20. the long and (the) short of it,** [~ + *be* + (*that*) *clause*] the essential point or end result: *The long and short of it is that they'll have to sell the house.*

long² (lông, long) /lɔŋ, lɒŋ/ *v.* to have an earnest or strong desire or craving; yearn: [~ + *for* + *obj*]: *to long for spring.* [~ + *to* + *verb*]: *He longed to return home.* [~ + *for* + *obj* + *to* + *verb*]: *longed for her to kiss him.*

long•boat (lông′bōt′, long′-) /ˈlɔŋ,bowt, ˈlɒŋ-/ *n.* [*count*] a large oared boat carried by a sailing ship.

long′ dis′tance, *n.* [*noncount*] telephone service between distant places. —**long′-dis′tance,** *adj.* [*usually before a noun*]: *a long-distance call.* —*adv.*: *to call long-distance.*

long′-drawn′-out′, *adj.* lasting a very long time: *a long-drawn-out explanation.* Often, **long′-drawn′.**

lon•gev•i•ty (lon jev′i tē, lôn-) /lɒnˈdʒɛvɪtiy, lɔn-/ *n.* [*noncount*] **1.** long life: *a family known for longevity.* **2.** length of life: *research in longevity.* **3.** length of service; seniority: *promotions based on longevity.*

long′ face′, *n.* [*count*] an unhappy or gloomy facial expression.

long•hair (lông′hâr′, long′-) /ˈlɔŋ,hɛər, ˈlɒŋ-/ *n.* [*count*] *Informal.* **1.** an intellectual. **2.** a person devoted to the arts, esp. a lover of classical music. —*adj.* Also, **long′-haired′. 3.** having long hair: *a longhair cat.* **4.** of or characteristic of longhairs.

long•hand (lông′hand′, long′-) /ˈlɔŋ,hænd, ˈlɒŋ-/ *n.* [*noncount*] writing of the ordinary kind, in which words are written out in full: *His longhand was hardly readable.*

long•ing (lông′ing, long′-) /ˈlɔŋɪŋ, ˈlɒŋ-/ *n.* **1.** [*noncount*] strong, lasting desire, esp. for something hard to reach or distant: *filled with longing for the past.* **2.** [*count*] an instance of this: *a sudden longing to see old friends.* —*adj.* **3.** characterized by earnest desire: *a longing look.* —**long′ing•ly,** *adv.*

lon•gi•tude (lon′ji to͞od′, -tyo͞od′) /ˈlɒndʒɪ,tuwd, -,tyuwd/

n. the distance east or west on the earth's surface, as measured in degrees from the meridian of some particular place to the prime meridian at Greenwich, England: [*noncount*]: *sixty degrees in longitude.* [*count*]: *measuring longitudes.*

lon•gi•tu•di•nal (lon′ji to͞od′n l, -tyo͞od′-) /ˌlɒndʒɪ'tuwdn̩l, -'tyuwd-/ *adj.* **1.** of or relating to longitude or length: *longitudinal measurement.* **2.** extending in the direction of the length; lengthwise. **—lon′gi•tu′di•nal•ly,** *adv.*

long′ jump′, *n.* [*count; singular; usually: the* + ~] an athletic field event featuring competition in a jump from a running start.

long′-lived′ (-līvd′, -livd′) /-'layvd, -'lɪvd/ *adj.* **1.** having a long life: *a long-lived animal.* **2.** lasting or functioning a long time: *a long-lived battery.*

long′-play′ing, *adj.* [*before a noun*] of or relating to phonograph records played at 33⅓ revolutions per minute.

long′-range′, *adj.* [*before a noun*] **1.** considering or extending into the future: *a long-range weather forecast.* **2.** designed to cover or operate over a long distance: *long-range rockets.*

long•shore•man (lông′shôr′mən, -shōr′-, long′-) /'lɔŋ'ʃɔrmən, -'ʃowr-, 'lɒŋ-/ *n.* [*count*], *pl.* **-men.** a person who works on the docks or wharves of a port, as in loading and unloading vessels.

long′ shot′, *n.* [*count*] **1.** a horse in a race, or a team, etc., that has little chance of winning and carries long odds. **2.** an undertaking that is unlikely to be successful. ***—Idiom.*** **3. by a long shot,** by any means: *You aren't finished by a long shot.*

long•stand•ing (lông′stan′ding, long′-) /'lɔŋ'stændɪŋ, 'lɒŋ-/ *adj.* existing for a long time: *a longstanding disagreement.*

long′-suf′fering, *adj.* patiently or stoically enduring injury, trouble, or pain: *a long-suffering, abused spouse.*

long′-term′, *adj.* **1.** covering or involving a relatively long period of time: *long-term effects of a drug.* **2.** maturing after a relatively long period of time: *a long-term bond.*

long•time (lông′tīm′, long′-) /'lɔŋˌtaym, 'lɒŋ-/ *adj.* [*before a noun*] existing or continuing as such for a long period of time; longstanding: *longtime friends.*

long′-wind′ed (-win′did) /'wɪndɪd/ *adj.* talking or writing at a length that is boring and tiresome: *long-winded speakers.* **—long′-wind′ed•ness,** *n.* [*noncount*]

look (lo͝ok) /lʊk/ *v.* **1.** to turn one's eyes toward something or in some direction in order to see: [~ + *at*]: *I'm looking at this book.* [*no obj*]: *She looked out the window.* **2.** [*no obj*] to use one's sight in seeking, searching, examining, watching, etc.: *to look through the papers.* **3.** [~ + *adjective*] to appear to the eye as specified: *You look pale.* See LOOK LIKE below. **4.** to appear to the mind; seem: [~ + *adjective*]: *Things are looking pretty grim.* [~ + *noun*]: *He looked a perfect fool.* See LOOK LIKE below. **5.** [~ + *at*] to direct attention or consideration: *Let's look at the facts.* **6.** [*not: be* + ~*-ing; no obj*] to face or give a view: *The room looks on the garden.* **7.** [~ + *obj*] to give (someone) a look: *Can you look me in the eye and say that?* **8.** [~ + *obj*] to have an appearance appropriate to or that fits (one's age, circumstances, etc.): *began to look his age.* **9.** (used in the imperative form, and sometimes followed by a word like "who, what, when, where, how" etc.) to observe or pay attention to: [~ + *obj*]: *Now look what you've done! Look how beautifully he skates.* [*no obj*]: *Look, I'm tired of this!* [~ + *at*]: *Look at what's happened.* **10. look after,** [~ + *after* + *obj*] to take care of: *a babysitter to look after the kids.* **11. look ahead,** [*no obj*] to think about or plan for the future: *Our leaders have to look ahead.* **12. look back,** [*no obj*] **a.** to review past events: *looking back to his childhood.* **b. never look back,** to have great success: *started her own business and never looked back.* **13. look down on** or **upon,** [~ + *down* + *on/upon* + *obj*] to regard with a feeling of superiority or contempt. **14. look for,** [~ + *for* + *obj*] **a.** to seek; search for: *I've been looking for you.* **b.** to anticipate; expect: *I'll look for you at the reception.* **15. look forward to,** [~ + *forward* + *obj*] to anticipate with eagerness or pleasure: *She's looking forward to working here.* **16. look in (on),** [~ + *in* + *(on)* + *obj*] to visit briefly: *The doctor looked in on her patient.* **17. look into,** [~ + *into* + *obj*] to inquire into; investigate; examine: *The detective was looking into the kidnapping.* **18. look like,** [*not: be* + ~*-ing*] **a.** [~ + *obj*] to resemble: *She looks just like her father.* **b.** [~ + *clause*] to have the appearance of; seem to the eye to be: *He looks like he's working.* **c.** [~ + *clause*] to seem to the mind to be: *Things look like they can't get much worse.* **d.** [*It* + ~ + *clause*] to be probable that: *It looks like we'll be late.* **19. look on, a.** [*no obj*] to be a spectator; watch. **b.** Also, **look upon.** [~ + *upon* + *obj* + *as* + *obj*] to consider; regard: *She looked on him as a son.* **20. look out,** [*no obj*] to be alert to danger; be careful: *Look out; here she comes.* **21. look out for,** [~ + *out* + *for* + *obj*] to take watchful care of: *My boss was always looking out for me.* **22. look over,** to examine, esp. briefly: [~ + *over* + *obj*]: *I looked over your term paper.* [~ + *obj* + *over*]: *I looked it over.* **23. look to,** [~ + *to* + *obj*] **a.** to depend on: *to look to the president for leadership.* **b.** to expect or anticipate: *We look to a brighter future for our children.* **24. look up, a.** [*no obj*] to become better or more prosperous; improve: *The business is looking up.* **b.** to search for, as an item of information, in a reference book or the like: [~ + *obj* + *up*]: *looking words up in the dictionary.* [~ + *up* + *obj*]: *Don't look up every word.* **c.** to seek out, esp. to visit: [~ + *up* + *obj*]: *to look up an old friend.* [~ + *obj* + *up*]: *to look him up next time.* **25. look up to,** [~ + *up* + *to* + *obj*] to regard with admiration or respect: *A lot of people look up to you, so don't let them down.* **—*n.*** [*count*] **26.** the act of looking: *Have a look at these figures.* **27.** the way in which a person or thing appears; aspect: *the look of an honest man.* **28.** fashion; style: *the latest look in furniture.* **29. looks,** [*plural*] **a.** general aspect; appearance: *We didn't like the looks of the place.* **b.** physical appearance esp. when attractive: *all looks and no brains.* **—Usage.** See SEE.

look-a•like (lo͝ok′ə līk′) /'lʊkəˌlayk/ *n.* [*count*] a person or thing that resembles another closely; a double.

look′ing glass′, *n.* [*count*] a mirror.

look•out (lo͝ok′out′) /'lʊkˌawt/ *n.* [*count*] **1.** the act of looking out or keeping watch: *kept a sharp lookout in case they came back.* **2.** a person or group keeping a watch: *The lookouts were asleep.* **3.** a station or place from which a watch is kept. **4.** a matter of care or concern: *That problem's not my lookout.*

look′-see′, *n.* [*count*] *Informal.* a usually quick inspection or survey; look: *to have a look-see.*

loom[1] (lo͞om) /luwm/ *n.* [*count*] **1.** a hand-operated or power-driven device for weaving fabrics. **—*v.*** [~ + *obj*] **2.** to weave (something) on a loom.

loom[2] (lo͞om) /luwm/ *v.* [*no obj*] **1.** to come into view in indistinct and enlarged form: *Suddenly the mountain loomed over them.* **2.** to assume form as an event about to happen: *A battle looms at the border.*

loon[1] (lo͞on) /luwn/ *n.* [*count*] a large, ducklike diving bird of the Northern Hemisphere.

loon[2] (lo͞on) /luwn/ *n.* [*count*] a crazy or simple-minded person.

loon•y or **loon•ey** (lo͞o′nē) /'luwniy/ *adj.*, **-i•er, -i•est,** *n., pl.* **-ies** or **-eys.** *Informal.* **—*adj.*** **1.** lunatic; insane. **2.** extremely foolish. **—*n.*** [*count*] **3.** a lunatic.

loon′y bin′, *n.* [*count*] *Informal.* an insane asylum.

loop (lo͞op) /luwp/ *n.* [*count*] **1.** a portion of a cord, ribbon, etc., folded or doubled upon itself so as to leave an opening between the parts. **2.** anything shaped more or less like a loop. **3.** INTRAUTERINE DEVICE. **4.** the repeating of a set of instructions in a computer routine or program. **5. the loop,** a group or network of people who have inside information or who are influential or powerful; inner circle: *He was kept out of the loop on policy decisions.* **—*v.*** **6.** [~ + *obj*] to form into a loop: *looping his shoelaces.* **7.** to make or form a loop: [*no obj*]: *The river loops around the two counties.* [~ + *obj*]: *The pilot looped her plane.* ***—Idiom.*** **8. throw** or **knock (someone) for a loop,** to overwhelm with surprise or confusion.

loop•hole (lo͞op′hōl′) /'luwpˌhowl/ *n.* [*count*] **1.** a narrow opening in the wall of a fort or protected area for looking through or firing weapons. **2.** a means of escape or of avoiding something, esp. a means or opportunity of avoiding following a law, fulfilling a contract, etc.: *loopholes in the tax code.*

loop•y (lo͞o′pē) /'luwpiy/ *adj.*, **-i•er, -i•est. 1.** full of loops. **2.** *Slang.* crazy; confused: *loopy after a few drinks.*

loose (lo͞os) /luws/ *adj.*, **loos•er, loos•est,** *adv., v.,* **loosed, loos•ing. —*adj.*** **1.** free or released from being fastened or attached: *a loose rope; a loose tooth.* **2.** free from confinement or restraint: *The loose papers flew off his desk.* **3.** not fitting closely or tightly: *a loose sweater.* **4.** relaxed or limber in nature: *to run with a loose, open stride.* **5.** not close or tight in structure or arrangement: *a cloth with a loose weave.* **6.** allowing freedom for independent action: *a loose federation of city-states.* **7.** not strict, exact, or precise: *a loose interpretation of the law.* **8.** unable to be held in check: *a loose tongue.* **9.** sexually immoral; dissolute: *loose living.* **—***adv.* **10.** in a loose manner; loosely (often used in combination): *loose-fitting.* **—***v.* [~ + *obj*] **11.** to let loose; set free: *He loosed the animals from the house.* **12.** to unfasten: *to loose a boat from its moorings.* **13.** to shoot; discharge; let fly: *to loose missiles at the invaders.* **—*Idiom.* 14. break loose,** [*no obj*] to free oneself; escape: *The circus animals broke loose.* **15. cast loose,** [~ + *obj* + *loose*] to unfasten; set adrift; free: *He cast the boat loose.* **16. cut loose,** [*no obj*] to behave wildly; carouse: *The team needed to cut loose after all that tension.* **17. hang** or **stay loose,** [*no obj*] *Informal.* to remain relaxed and calm. **18. let loose, a.** [~ + *obj* + *loose*] to free: *The children were let loose to run around.* **b.** [*no obj*] to yield; give way: *The guardrail let loose and the bus plunged down the canyon.* **c.** [*no obj*] to speak or act with unrestricted freedom: *to let loose with a few swearwords.* **19. on the loose,** free; unconfined: *Several escaped convicts were on the loose.* **20. turn** or **set loose,** [~ + *obj* + *loose*] to free from confinement: *turned the prisoners loose one by one.* —**loose′ly,** *adv.* —**loose′ness,** *n.* [*noncount*]

loose′ end′, *n.* [*count*] **1.** Usually, **loose ends.** [*plural*] an unsettled or unfinished detail. **—*Idiom.* 2. at loose ends,** in an uncertain or unsettled state: *felt at loose ends with the family away.*

loose′-leaf′, *adj.* [*before a noun*] having individual pieces of paper held in a binder **(loose′-leaf′ bind′er),** as by rings that open and close, in such a way as to allow removal or replacement of a piece of paper without tearing.

loos•en (lo͞o′sən) /ˈluwsən/ *v.* **1.** to (cause to) become less tight: [~ + *obj*]: *to loosen a belt.* [*no obj*]: *His grip loosened.* **2.** to (cause to) become less firmly fixed in place: [~ + *obj*]: *She twisted the tooth, trying to loosen it.* [*no obj*]: *The tooth loosened on its own.* **3.** [~ + *obj*] to unfasten or undo: *He loosened the ropes.* **4.** [~ + *obj*] to relax in strictness: *loosening admission standards.* **5. loosen up,** [*no obj*] to become less tense or formal; relax: *His doctor advised him to loosen up a bit.*

loot (lo͞ot) /luwt/ *n.* [*noncount*] **1.** money, goods, property, etc., taken by force during war. **2.** anything taken by dishonesty or force: *a burglar's loot.* **3.** *Slang.* money or gifts. **—***v.* **4.** [~ + *obj*] to take as loot: *to loot a nation's art treasures.* **5.** to take loot from (a place) in or as if in war: [~ + *obj*]: *The rioters looted several stores.* [*no obj*]: *Rioters were looting all night.* —**loot′er,** *n.* [*count*]

lop (lop) /lɒp/ *v.,* **lopped, lop•ping. 1.** to cut off (a limb or part) from something: [~ + *obj* + *off*]: *lopped the villain's head off.* [~ + *off* + *obj*]: *lopped off a few branches.* **2.** to eliminate as unnecessary: [~ + *off* + *obj*]: *We had to lop off pages of the report.* [~ + *obj* + *off*]: *We had to lop them off.*

lope (lōp) /lowp/ *v.,* **loped, lop•ing,** *n.* **—***v.* [*no obj*] **1.** to move or run with bounding steps or with a long, easy stride. **—***n.* [*count*] **2.** the act of loping.

lop•sid•ed (lop′sī′did) /ˈlɒpˈsaydɪd/ *adj.* heavier, larger, or more developed on one side than the other; unevenly balanced. —**lop′sid′ed•ly,** *adv.* —**lop′sid′ed•ness,** *n.* [*noncount*]

-loq-, *root.* *-loq-* comes from Latin, where it has the meaning "speak; say." This meaning is found in such words as: CIRCUMLOCUTION, ELOQUENT, LOCUTION, LOQUACIOUS, SOLILOQUY.

lo•qua•cious (lō kwā′shəs) /lowˈkweyʃəs/ *adj.* talking or tending to talk much or freely; talkative; garrulous: *a loquacious dinner guest.* —**lo•qua′cious•ness, lo•quac•i•ty** (lō kwas′i tē) /lowˈkwæsɪtiy/ *n.* [*noncount*] See -LOQ-.

lord (lôrd) /lɔrd/ *n.* **1.** [*count*] a person who has authority, control, or power over others; master or ruler. **2.** [*count*] a nobleman or peer. **3.** [*proper noun; Lord*] (in Great Britain) **a.** the title of certain high officials: *Lord Mayor of London.* **b.** the formally polite title of a bishop: *Lord Bishop of Durham.* **4.** [*proper noun; Lord*] the Supreme Being; God. **5.** [*proper noun; Lord*] Jesus Christ. **—***interj.* **6.** [*often: Lord*] This word is sometimes used to express surprise, delight, dismay, etc.: *Lord, what a beautiful day!* **—***v.,* ***Idiom.*** **7. lord it over,** [~ + *obj*] to behave arrogantly toward (someone): *to lord it over one's friends with one's new wealth.*

lord•ly (lôrd′lē) /ˈlɔrdliy/ *adj.,* **-li•er, -li•est,** *adv.* **—***adj.* **1.** suitable for or like a lord; grand. **2.** arrogant; superior. **—***adv.* **3.** in the manner of a lord.

lord•ship (lôrd′ship) /ˈlɔrdʃɪp/ *n.* **1.** [*count; often: Your/His + Lordship*] (in Great Britain) a term of respect used when speaking of or to judges or certain noblemen. **2.** [*noncount*] the rank or dignity of a lord.

Lord's′ Prayer′ (prâr) /prɛər/ *n.* [*proper noun; the* ~] the prayer given by Jesus to his disciples, beginning with the words *Our Father.*

lore (lôr, lōr) /lɔr, lowr/ *n.* [*noncount*] the body of knowledge or learning, esp. of a traditional or popular nature, on a particular subject: *nature lore.*

lor•gnette (lôrn yet′) /lɔrnˈyɛt/ *n.* [*count*] a pair of eyeglasses or opera glasses mounted on a handle.

lor•ry (lôr′ē, lor′ē) /ˈlɔriy, ˈlɒriy/ *n.* [*count*], *pl.* **-ries.** *Chiefly Brit.* a large motor truck.

lose (lo͞oz) /luwz/ *v.,* **lost** (lôst, lost) /lɔst, lɒst/ **los•ing.** **—***v.* **1.** [~ + *obj*] to come to be without, as through accident: *They lost all their belongings in the storm.* **2.** [~ + *obj*] to fail to keep, as by accident, usually temporarily: *I just lost a dime under this sofa.* **3.** [~ + *obj*] to suffer the taking away of: *to lose one's job.* **4.** [*not: be + ~-ing; ~ + obj*] to experience the death of (someone): *He had just lost his wife to cancer.* **5.** [~ + *obj*] (of a physician) to fail to preserve the life of (a patient): *The doctor lost a young patient.* **6.** [~ + *obj*] to fail to keep, preserve, or maintain: *to lose a fortune by gambling.* **7.** [~ + *obj*] (of a timepiece) to run slower by: *The watch loses three minutes a day.* **8.** to come to have less (money) than before: [~ + *obj*]: *lost a million dollars on the deal.* [*no obj*]: *We lost on that deal.* **9.** [~ + *obj*] to get rid of: *to lose weight.* **10.** [~ + *obj; usually: be + lost*] to bring to destruction: *Ship and crew were lost.* **11.** [~ + *obj*] to have (someone) slip from sight or awareness: *The detective lost the man she was following.* **12.** [~ + *obj*] to stray from: *to lose one's way.* **13.** [~ + *obj*] to waste: *We have lost enough time waiting.* **14.** [~ + *obj*] to fail to gain or win: *He lost the bet.* **15.** to be defeated (in): [~ + *obj*]: *They lost four games in a row.* [*no obj*]: *Our team lost again, 6-0.* **16.** to cause the loss of: [~ + *obj* + *for* + *obj*]: *The delay lost the battle for them.* [~ + *obj* + *obj*]: *That delay lost them the battle.* **17.** [~ + *oneself*] to allow (oneself) to be absorbed in something: *I had lost myself in thought.* **18.** [~ + *obj*] **a.** to fail to hear, understand, comprehend, or see: *I've lost you; do you mind going over it again for me?* **b.** to cause this to happen: *I'm afraid you've lost me; do you mind going over it one more time?* **19. lose out,** [*no obj*] to suffer defeat or loss: *Our company lost out on the deal.* **—*Idiom.* 20. lose it,** to fail to maintain one's temper, composure, or control. **—Related Words.** LOSE is a verb, LOST is an adjective, LOSS is a noun: *I lost my keys. The lost sheep was found again. The company announced a small loss for the computer division.*

los•er (lo͞oz′ər) /ˈluwzər/ *n.* [*count*] **1.** a person or thing that loses. **2.** a person or thing who constantly loses, fails to perform well, or is unsuccessful. **—*Idiom.* 3. born loser,** [*count*] a person who always loses or is unsuccessful. **4. good** (or **bad) loser,** [*count*] a person who takes defeat or failure in a positive (or negative) way, without (or with) complaining.

loss (lôs, los) /lɔs, lɒs/ *n.* **1.** the act of losing possession of something: [*noncount*]: *bearing the loss of property.* [*count*]: *a temporary loss of hearing.* **2.** [*count*] something that is lost: *suffered huge losses in the market crash.* **3.** [*count*] the death of a person: *to mourn the loss of a grandparent.* **4.** [*count*] a losing by defeat: *Another two losses and our team will be eliminated.* **5.** [*noncount*] decrease: *loss of engine speed.* **—*Idiom.* 6. at a loss, a.** at less than cost: *selling everything at a loss.* **b.** in a state of bewilderment or uncertainty: *I'm at a complete loss to understand what she's doing.* **7. dead loss,** [*count*] a completely useless or worthless person or thing: *That decrepit old car is a dead loss.*

lost (lôst, lost) /lɔst, lɒst/ *adj.* **1.** [*before a noun*] no longer possessed: *lost friendships.* **2.** no longer to be found: *lost articles.* **3.** unable to find one's way: *There are two lost children at the information booth.* **4.** not used to good purpose: *a lost advantage.* **5.** not won: *a lost prize.* **6.** followed by defeat: *a lost battle.* **7.** [*be* + ~] preoccupied: *He was lost in thought.* **8.** distraught; overwhelmed: *the lost look of a man trapped.* **9.** [*be* + ~ + *on* + *obj*] wasted: *Your jokes were lost on him; he has no sense of humor.* **—***v.* **10.** pt. and pp. of LOSE. **—*Idiom.* 11. get lost,** [*no obj*] *Slang.* **a.** to leave, esp. so as to avoid trouble or conflict: *Get lost; I'll take care of the boss.* **b.** to stop being a nuisance: *If he calls again, tell him to get lost.*

lot (lot) /lɒt/ *n.* **1.** [*count*] one of a set of objects, as straws or pebbles, drawn or thrown from a container to decide a question or choice by chance. **2.** [*noncount*] the casting or drawing of such objects: *to choose a person by lot.* **3.** [*count; usually singular*] fate; fortune; destiny: *Her lot was not a happy one.* **4.** [*count*] a distinct piece of land: *a building lot.* **5.** [*count*] a distinct piece or parcel, as of merchandise: *The furniture was auctioned off in 20 lots.* **6.** [*noncount; the + ~; usually used with a plural verb*] the whole number or amount of things or persons: *The whole lot of them are missing.* **7.** [*count; usually singular; usually: a + ~*] kind; sort: *That group's a bad lot.* **8.** [*count*] a great many: [*a + ~ + of + plural noun*]: *a lot of books.* [*lots + of + plural noun*]: *She had lots of books.* **9.** [*count*] a great deal: [*a + ~ + of + noncount noun*]: *They had a lot of money.* [*lots + of + noncount noun*]: *She had lots of money.* —***Idiom.*** **10. a lot,** to a great degree; much: *I feel a lot better.* **11. draw** or **cast lots,** to settle a question by the use of lots: *They drew lots to decide.*

lo•tion (lō′shən) /ˈlowʃən/ *n.* a liquid preparation used for medicines and for protecting and soothing the skin: [*noncount*]: *Pour some lotion on your arms.* [*count*]: *lotions for dry skin.*

lot•ter•y (lot′ə rē) /ˈlɒtəriy/ *n.* [*count*], *pl.* **-ter•ies. 1.** a gambling game or method of raising money in which a large number of tickets are sold and a drawing is held for prizes. **2.** a drawing of lots. **3.** something whose outcome appears to be determined by chance: *Life is a lottery.*

lot•to (lot′ō) /ˈlɒtow/ *n.* [*count*], *pl.* **-tos. 1.** a game of chance similar to bingo. **2.** a lottery, esp. one operated by a state government.

lo•tus (lō′təs) /ˈlowtəs/ *n., pl.* **-tus•es. 1.** [*count*] a plant in Greek legend having a fruit that caused a state of dreamy and happy forgetfulness in those who ate it. **2.** [*noncount*] the fruit of this plant. **3.** [*count*] a plant of the water lily family having shieldlike leaves and showy, single flowers usually sticking out above the water.

loud (loud) /lawd/ *adj.,* **-er, -est,** *adv.* —*adj.* **1.** marked by high volume of sound: *loud peals of thunder.* **2.** clamorous; noisy: *a loud party.* **3.** too brightly colored; ostentatious: *loud colors; a loud tie.* —*adv.* **4.** in a loud manner: loudly: *Don't talk so loud.* —***Idiom.*** **5. out loud,** aloud; so as to be heard: *spoke out loud.* —**loud′ly,** *adv.* —**loud′ness,** *n.* [*noncount*]

loud•mouth (loud′mouth′) /ˈlawdˌmawθ/ *n.* [*count*] a person who talks in a loud obnoxious manner. —**loud′-mouthed′,** *adj.*

loud•speak•er (loud′spē′kər) /ˈlawdˌspiykər/ *n.* [*count*] a device that changes amplified electronic signals into sound. See illustration at TERMINAL.

lounge (lounj) /lawndʒ/ *v.,* **lounged, loung•ing,** *n.* —*v.* [*no obj*] **1.** to pass time lazily or in doing nothing. **2.** to rest or lie down lazily; lean lazily; loll. —*n.* [*count*] **3.** an often backless sofa having a headrest at one end. **4.** a usually public room for relaxing or waiting: *the VIP lounge at the airport.* See illustration at HOTEL. **5.** a section on a train, plane, or ship for socializing.

loupe (lo͞op) /luwp/ *n.* [*count*] a magnifying glass used by jewelers and watchmakers, esp. one designed to fit in the eye socket.

louse (*n.* lous; *v.* also louz) / *n.* laws; *v.* ælsɒ lawz/ *n., pl.* **lice** (lis) for 1 **lous•es** for 2, *v.,* **loused, lous•ing.** —*n.* [*count*] **1.** a small, flat, wingless insect with sucking mouthparts, that lives on humans and animals. **2.** *Slang.* a mean, contemptible person. —*v.* **3. louse up,** *Slang.* to fail to do successfully; botch: [*~ + up + obj*]: *He loused up his opportunity.* [*~ + obj + up*]: *It's your big chance; don't louse it up.* [*no obj*]: *He's going to louse up again.*

lous•y (lou′zē) /ˈlawziy/ *adj.,* **-i•er, -i•est. 1.** infested with lice. **2.** *Informal.* **a.** mean; contemptible: *That was a lousy thing to do.* **b.** wretchedly bad; miserable: *lousy weather.* —***Idiom.*** **3. lousy with,** [*be + ~*] *Slang.* well supplied with: *is lousy with money.* —**lous•i•ly** (lou′zə lē) /ˈlawzəliy/ *adv.* —**lous′i•ness,** *n.* [*noncount*]

lout (lout) /lawt/ *n.* [*count*] a clumsy, bad-mannered, boorish person; an oaf. —**lout′ish,** *adj.*

lou•ver or **lou•vre** (lo͞o′vər) /ˈluwvər/ *n.* [*count*] **1.** any of a series of narrow openings on a door or window, produced by slanting, overlapping fins or slats of wood or glass, that can be adjusted for letting in light and air while shutting out rain. **2.** a fin or slat from such an opening. —**lou′vered,** *adj.*

lov•a•ble or **love•a•ble** (luv′ə bəl) /ˈlʌvəbəl/ *adj.* of such a nature as to attract or deserve love.

love (luv) /lʌv/ *n., v.,* **loved, lov•ing.** —*n.* **1.** [*noncount*] a deep, tender, passionate affection for another person, esp. when based on sexual attraction. **2.** [*noncount*] a feeling of warm personal attachment or deep affection: *a mother's love for her child; love of one's country.* **3.** [*count*] a person toward whom love is felt: *He is the love of my life.* **4.** [*count*] a love affair. **5.** [*count*] a strong enthusiasm or liking: *a love of books.* **6.** [*count*] the object of such liking or enthusiasm: *The theater was her first love.* **7.** [*noncount*] a score of zero, as in tennis. —*v.* **8.** [*~ + obj*] to have love or affection for: *He loves her dearly.* **9.** to have a strong liking for: [*~ + obj*]: *to love music.* [*~ + verb-ing*]: *She loves playing tennis.* [*~ + to + verb*]: *They love to go camping.* **10.** [*no obj*] to feel the emotion of love: *After the tragedy he felt he couldn't love again.* —***Idiom.*** **11. in love (with),** having or feeling deep affection or passion (for): [*no obj*]: *I'm glad you're in love.* [*~ + obj*]: *She's in love with me.* **12. make love,** [*no obj*] to have sexual relations. —**love′less,** *adj.*

love•bird (luv′bûrd′) /ˈlʌvˌbɜrd/ *n.* [*count*] **1.** a small parrot of Africa, known for the affection shown between mates. **2. lovebirds,** [*plural*] a pair of lovers.

love•lorn (luv′lôrn′) /ˈlʌvˌlɔrn/ *adj.* being without love or a lover.

love•ly (luv′lē) /ˈlʌvliy/ *adj.,* **-li•er, -li•est. 1.** having a beauty that appeals to the heart or mind as well as to the eye; charmingly or gracefully beautiful: *The bride looks lovely.* **2.** highly pleasing; delightful: *We had a lovely time.* —**love′li•ness,** *n.* [*noncount*]

love•mak•ing (luv′mā′king) /ˈlʌvˌmeykɪŋ/ *n.* [*noncount*] sexual activity.

lov•er (luv′ər) /ˈlʌvər/ *n.* [*count*] **1.** a person who is in love with another. **2.** a person who has a sexual or romantic relationship with another. **3.** a devotee of something: *a music lover.*

love′ seat′, *n.* [*count*] a chair or small sofa for two persons.

love•sick (luv′sik′) /ˈlʌvˌsɪk/ *adj.* filled with longing for one's beloved: *a lovesick adolescent.*

lov•ing (luv′ing) /ˈlʌvɪŋ/ *adj.* warmly affectionate: *He gave his child a loving embrace.* —**lov′ing•ly,** *adv.*

low[1] (lō) /low/ *adj.* and *adv.,* **-er, -est,** *n.* —*adj.* **1.** situated, placed, or occurring not far above the ground, floor, or base: *a low shelf that the baby could reach.* **2.** of small extent upward: *a low fence that he could jump over easily.* **3.** not far above the horizon; not high in the sky: *The moon was low in the sky.* **4.** lying below the general level: *low, marshy ground.* **5.** bending downward; deep: *He gave a low bow.* **6.** aimed down; held or pointed down: *His head was low in prayer.* **7.** leaving much of the upper part of the chest bare: *a low neckline.* **8.** of less than average or normal height or depth: *The river is low.* **9.** ranked near the beginning or bottom on a scale of measurement: *a low income bracket.* **10.** most discouraging: *a low point in life.* **11.** [*be + ~*] depressed or dejected: *feeling low.* **12.** of or having a small number, amount, degree, force, or intensity (sometimes used in combination): *low visibility; a low-cholesterol diet.* **13.** soft: subdued; not loud: *a low murmur.* **14.** deep in pitch: *a low voice.* **15.** disapproving; disliking: *had a low opinion of the book.* **16.** near the bottom in rank or status: *of low birth.* **17.** of inferior quality: *a low grade of fabric.* **18.** relating to the gear transmission ratio at which the drive shaft moves at the slowest speed when compared to the speed of the engine crankshaft; first: *Put the car in low gear.* —*adv.* **19.** in or to a low position, point, or degree: *The plane flew low.* **20.** in or to a condition of being used up: *We're running low on fuel.* —*n.* **21.** [*count*] something that is low; a low or the lowest point, place, or level: *recent lows in the stock market.* **22.** [*noncount*] a low transmission gear: *Put the car in low.* **23.** [*count*] a low-pressure system in the atmosphere: *a low over the Caribbean.* —***Idiom.*** **24. lay low, a.** [*lay + obj + ~*] to overpower or kill: *to lay one's attackers low.* **b.** [*lay + obj + ~*] to knock down: *He laid his opponent low with one punch.* **c.** [*no obj*] *Informal.* to lie low: *We were laying low, waiting for our chance.* **25. lie low,** [*no obj*] **a.** to hide oneself. **b.** to wait quietly before acting: *The guerrillas were lying low, waiting to attack.* —**low′ness,** *n.* [*noncount*]

low[2] (lō) /low/ *v.* [*no obj*] **1.** to make the deep sound of cattle; moo. —*n.* [*count*] **2.** the act or the sound of lowing.

low•brow (lō′brou′) /ˈlowˌbraw/ *n.* [*count*] **1.** a person with little interest in matters of intellect or culture. —*adj.* **2.** of or being a lowbrow. See HIGHBROW.

low-cal (lō′kal′, -kal′) /ˈlowˈkæl, -ˌkæl/ *adj.* containing fewer calories than usual or standard: *a low-cal diet; a low-cal beverage.*

low•down (*n.* lō′doun′; *adj.* -doun′) / *n.* ˈlowˌdawn; *adj.*

-'dawn/ *n.* [*count; usually singular; the* + ~] **1.** the real and plain facts or the truth: *Give me the lowdown on the situation.* **—*adj.*** **2.** [*before a noun*] contemptible; base; mean: *an awful, lowdown trick.* **3.** FUNKY[2] (def. 1).

low•er[1] (lō′ər) /'lowər/ *v.* **1.** to (cause to) descend; (cause to) be let or put down: [~ + *obj*]: *to lower a flag.* [*no obj*]: *The sun lowered in the west.* **2.** to (cause to) become lower in height or level: [~ + *obj*]: *to lower the water in a canal.* [*no obj*]: *The water level lowered.* **3.** [~ + *obj*] to reduce in amount, price, degree, or force: *lowered the amount of salt in our diet.* **4.** to make or become less loud or lower in pitch: [~ + *obj*]: *He lowered his voice.* [*no obj*]: *Her voice lowered and she spoke softly in my ear.* **5.** [~ + *obj*] to bring down in rank or status: *wouldn't lower himself to beg.* **—*adj.*** **6.** comparative of LOW[1]. **7.** [*before a noun*] of or relating to the parts of a river farthest from the source: *the lower Mississippi.* **—low′er•most′,** *adj.*

low•er[2] (lou′ər) /'lawər/ *v.* [*no obj*] to be dark and threatening: *The sky lowered just before the storm.*

low•er•case (lō′ər kās′) /'lowər'keys/ *adj.* **1.** (of an alphabetical letter) of a particular form often different from and smaller than its corresponding capital letter, as a, b, q, r. **—*n.*** [*noncount*] **2.** a lowercase letter: *written in lowercase.*

low′er class′ (lō′ər) /'lowər/ *n.* [*count*] a class of people below the middle class in social standing and usually having low income and lacking education. **—low′er-class′,** *adj.*

low′est com′mon denom′inator, *n.* [*count*] **1.** the smallest number that is a common denominator of a certain group of fractions. **2.** something understood by or acceptable to the largest number of people.

low′-key′ or **low′-keyed′,** *adj.* of reduced strength, amount, power, or intensity; restrained: *a low-key reception.*

low•land (lō′lənd) /'lowlənd/ *n.* [*noncount*] **1.** land that is low or level in comparison with the nearby country. **—*adj.*** [*before a noun*] **2.** of, relating to, or characteristic of a lowland or lowlands.

low•life (lō′lif′) /'low,layf/ *n.* [*count*], *pl.* **-lifes.** a contemptible or disreputable person.

low•ly (lō′lē) /'lowliy/ *adj.*, **-li•er, -li•est,** *adv.* **—*adj.*** **1.** humble in status or condition; simple: *a lowly cottage.* **2.** humble in attitude or behavior; meek. **—*adv.*** **3.** in a low position, manner, or degree. **—low′li•ness,** *n.* [*noncount*]

low′-mind′ed, *adj.* having or showing coarse or vulgar taste or interests.

low′ pro′file, *n.* [*count*] a deliberately inconspicuous, quiet, or anonymous way of behaving: *After his last big mistake, he kept a low profile around the office.*

low′-rise′, *adj.* [*before a noun*] **1.** having few floors and usually no elevator: *low-rise apartment buildings.* **—*n.*** [*count*] **2.** a low-rise building.

low′-spir′ited, *adj.* depressed; saddened; dejected.

low′ tide′, *n.* [*noncount*] the tide at the point where the sea is at its lowest.

lox (loks) /lɒks/ *n.* [*noncount*] smoked salmon.

loy•al (loi′əl) /'lɔyəl/ *adj.* **1.** faithful to one's government or one's country: *a loyal subject.* **2.** faithful to one's oath or obligations: *loyal to a vow.* **3.** faithful to a person or thing thought to deserve it: *a loyal friend.* **—loy′al•ly,** *adv.*

loy•al•ist (loi′ə list) /'lɔyəlɪst/ *n.* [*count*] **1.** a person who remains loyal, esp. to a king, queen, or government. **2.** [*sometimes: Loyalist*] a person who remained loyal to the British during the American Revolution.

loy•al•ty (loi′əl tē) /'lɔyəltiy/ *n.*, *pl.* **-ties.** **1.** [*noncount*] the state or condition of being loyal or faithful. **2.** [*count*] an instance of faithfulness: *felt a loyalty to old friends.*

loz•enge (loz′inj) /'lɒzɪndʒ/ *n.* [*count*] a small flavored tablet made from sugar or syrup and often containing medication: *throat lozenges.*

LP, *n.* [*count*], *pl.* **LPs, LP's.** a long-playing record.

LPG, an abbreviation of: liquefied petroleum gas.

LPN, an abbreviation of: licensed practical nurse.

LR, an abbreviation of: living room.

LSD, *n.* [*noncount*] lysergic acid diethylamide: a drug that produces temporary hallucinations and a psychotic state.

Lt., an abbreviation of: lieutenant.

lt., an abbreviation of: light.

Ltd. or **ltd.,** an abbreviation of: limited.

lu•au (lo͞o′ou) /'luwaw/ *n.* [*count*], *pl.* **-aus.** an outdoor feast of Hawaiian food.

lub•ber (lub′ər) /'lʌbər/ *n.* [*count*] **1.** a big, clumsy person. **2.** an awkward or unskilled sailor.

lube (lo͞ob) /luwb/ *n.* *Informal.* **1.** [*noncount*] lubricant. **2.** [*count*] an application of a lubricant to a vehicle: *The car needs a lube.*

lu•bri•cant (lo͞o′bri kənt) /'luwbrɪkənt/ *n.* **1.** a substance, as oil or grease, for lessening friction, esp. in the working parts of a mechanism: [*count*]: *Lubricants loosened the jammed gears.* [*noncount*]: *A little lubricant loosened the gears.* **2.** [*count*] something that increases ease of functioning: *alcohol as a social lubricant.* **—*adj.*** **3.** capable of or used in lubricating.

lu•bri•cate (lo͞o′bri kāt′) /'luwbrɪ,keyt/ *v.* [~ + *obj*], **-cat•ed, -cat•ing.** **1.** to apply an oily or greasy substance to (something) in order to reduce friction; make slippery: *lubricated the gears.* **2.** to cause to run smoother; ease: *to lubricate relations between enemies.* **3.** *Slang.* to provide with liquor: *They lubricated their guests with gin.* **—lu•bri•ca•tion** (lo͞o′bri kā′shən) /,luwbrɪ'keyʃən/ *n.* [*noncount*] **—lu′bri•ca′tor,** *n.* [*count*]

-luc-, *root.* *-luc-* comes from Latin, where it has the meaning "light." This meaning is found in such words as: ELUCIDATE, LUCID, LUCITE, LUCUBRATE, PELLUCID, TRANSLUCENT.

lu•cid (lo͞o′sid) /'luwsɪd/ *adj.* **1.** easily understood; intelligible: *a lucid explanation.* **2.** rational; sane: *a few lucid moments in his madness.* **3.** glowing with light. **—lu•cid•i•ty** (lo͞o sid′i tē) /luw'sɪdɪtiy/ **lu′cid•ness,** *n.* [*noncount*] **—lu′cid•ly,** *adv.* See -LUC-.

Lu•cite (lo͞o′sīt) /'luwsayt/ *Trademark.* [*noncount*] a transparent or translucent plastic. See -LUC-.

luck (luk) /lʌk/ *n.* [*noncount*] **1.** the force that seems to operate for good or ill in a person's life: *success that owes a lot to luck.* **2.** good fortune; success: *He had no luck finding work.* **—*v.*** *Informal.* **3. luck into** or **onto,** [~ + *obj*] to meet or obtain through accidental good fortune: *He just lucked into the job.* **4. luck out,** [*no obj*] to have an occasion of very good luck; be lucky: *You really lucked out when you found that ten-dollar bill.* **—*Idiom.*** **5. down on one's luck,** in unfortunate circumstances. **6. in luck,** lucky; fortunate: *You're in luck—you won the lottery.* **7. out of luck,** unlucky; unfortunate: *You're out of luck; the boss isn't in.* **8. push** or **crowd one's luck,** to threaten one's success by taking further risks; go too far. **—luck′less,** *adj.*

luck•y (luk′ē) /'lʌkiy/ *adj.*, **-i•er, -i•est.** **1.** having good luck; fortunate: *That was my lucky day.* **2.** happening by good fortune: *a lucky accident.* **3.** believed to bring good luck: *a lucky penny.* **—luck•i•ly** (luk′ə lē) /'lʌkəliy/ *adv.* **—luck′i•ness,** *n.* [*noncount*]

lu•cra•tive (lo͞o′krə tiv) /'luwkrətɪv/ *adj.* profitable; making money or a profit: *a lucrative business.* **—lu′cra•tive•ly,** *adv.* **—lu′cra•tive•ness,** *n.* [*noncount*]

lu•cre (lo͞o′kər) /'luwkər/ *n.* [*noncount*] monetary reward or gain; money.

lu•cu•brate (lo͞o′kyo͝o brāt′) /'luwkyʊ,breyt/ *v.* [*no obj*], **-brat•ed, -brat•ing.** to study hard and for long hours. **—lu•cu•bra•tion** (lo͞o′kyo͝o brā′shən) /,luwkyʊ'breyʃən/ *n.* [*noncount*] See -LUC-.

-lud-, *root.* *-lud-* comes from Latin, where it has the meaning "to play." This meaning is found in such words as: ALLUDE, ALLUSION, COLLUDE, COLLUSION, DELUDE, DELUSION, ELUDE, ELUSIVE, ILLUSION, ILLUSORY, INTERLUDE, LUDICROUS, PRELUDE.

Lud•dite (lud′īt) /'lʌdayt/ *n.* [*count*] **1.** a member of any of various bands of workers in England (1811–16) who destroyed industrial machinery in the belief that its use reduced the number of jobs. **2.** any opponent of new technologies or of technological change.

lu•di•crous (lo͞o′di krəs) /'luwdɪkrəs/ *adj.* causing or deserving laughter because of being absurd; ridiculous; laughable: *a ludicrous failure.* **—lu′di•crous•ly,** *adv.* **—lu′di•crous•ness,** *n.* [*noncount*] See -LUD-.

lug[1] (lug) /lʌg/ *v.*, **lugged, lug•ging,** *n.* **—*v.*** **1.** [~ + *obj*] to pull or carry with effort or difficulty: *lugging heavy rocks.* **2.** [*no obj*] (of an engine or machine) to jerk, hesitate, or strain. **—*n.*** [*count*] **3.** an act or instance of lugging.

lug[2] (lug) /lʌg/ *n.* [*count*] **1.** a projecting piece by which anything is held or supported. **2.** *Slang.* an awkward fellow.

lug•gage (lug′ij) /'lʌgɪdʒ/ *n.* [*noncount*] suitcases, trunks, etc.; baggage: *He had five pieces of luggage.* See illustration at HOTEL.

lu•gu•bri•ous (lo͞o go͞o′brē əs, -gyo͞o′-) /lʊ'guwbriyəs, -'gyuw-/ *adj.* mournful, dismal, or gloomy, esp. in an exaggerated manner: *lugubrious songs of lost love.* —**lu•gu′bri•ous•ly,** *adv.* —**lu•gu′bri•ous•ness,** *n.* [*noncount*]

luke•warm (lo͞ok′wôrm′) /ˈluwkˈwɔrm/ *adj.* **1.** moderately warm; tepid: *lukewarm water.* **2.** having or expressing little interest or enthusiasm: *a lukewarm greeting.* —**luke′warm′ly,** *adv.* —**luke′warm′ness,** *n.* [*noncount*]

lull (lul) /lʌl/ *v.* **1.** [~ + *obj*] to put to sleep or rest by soothing means: *to lull a child to sleep with singing.* **2.** [~ + *obj*] to soothe or make quiet: *lulled his fears.* **3.** [*no obj*] to quiet down; let up; subside: *furious activity that finally lulled.* —*n.* [*count; usually singular*] **4.** a temporary calm or stillness: *a lull in a storm.* —**lull′ing•ly,** *adv.*

lull•a•by (lul′ə bī′) /ˈlʌləˌbay/ *n.* [*count*], *pl.* **-bies.** a song used to lull a child to sleep.

lum•ba•go (lum bā′gō) /lʌmˈbeygow/ *n.* [*noncount*] pain in the lower, side region of the back.

lum•bar (lum′bər, -bär) /ˈlʌmbər, -bɑr/ *adj.* of or relating to the loin or loins.

lum•ber[1] (lum′bər) /ˈlʌmbər/ *n.* [*noncount*] timber or wood from a tree sawed or split into planks, boards, etc. —**lum′ber•er,** *n.* [*count*] —**lum′ber•man,** *n.* [*count*], *pl.* **-men.**

lum•ber[2] (lum′bər) /ˈlʌmbər/ *v.* [*no obj*] to move clumsily or heavily, esp. from great weight or size: *The huge truck lumbered onto the highway.*

lum•ber•jack (lum′bər jak′) /ˈlʌmbərˌdʒæk/ *n.* [*count*] a person who works at cutting down trees; logger.

lum•ber•yard (lum′bər yärd′) /ˈlʌmbərˌyɑrd/ *n.* [*count*] a yard where lumber is stored for sale.

lu•mi•nar•y (lo͞o′mə ner′ē) /ˈluwməˌnɛriy/ *n.* [*count*], *pl.* **-ar•ies. 1.** a luminous heavenly body, as the sun. **2.** a person who has gained fame and importance.

lu•mi•nes•cence (lo͞o′mə nes′əns) /ˌluwməˈnɛsəns/ *n.* [*noncount*] **1.** the giving off of light not caused by something burning, occurring at a temperature below that of burning. **2.** the light produced in this way. —**lu′mi•nes′cent,** *adj.*

lu•mi•nous (lo͞o′mə nəs) /ˈluwmənəs/ *adj.* **1.** radiating or reflecting light; shining; bright: *luminous eyes.* **2.** clear; enlightening: *a luminous explanation.* —**lu•mi•nos•i•ty** (lo͞o′mə nos′i tē) /ˌluwməˈnɒsɪtiy/ *n.* [*noncount*] —**lu′mi•nous•ly,** *adv.*

lum•mox (lum′əks) /ˈlʌməks/ *n.* [*count*] a clumsy person.

lump[1] (lump) /lʌmp/ *n.* [*count*] **1.** a piece or mass of solid matter without regular shape: *a lump of coal.* **2.** a swelling: *A blow to his head raised a lump there.* **3.** *Informal.* a clumsy, dull person. —*adj.* [*before a noun*] **4.** not divided or separated: *to pay a debt in a lump sum.* —*v.* **5.** to (cause to) be united into one collection or mass: [~ + *obj* + *together*]: *We lumped the red and blue marbles together.* [~ + *together* + *obj*]: *We lumped together the red and blue marbles.* [~ + *together*]: *The red blood cells lumped together.* **6.** to deal with, consider, etc., in a lump or mass: [~ + *together* + *obj*]: *to lump together unrelated matters.* [~ + *obj* + *together*]: *lumps unrelated matters together.* **7.** [*no obj*] to move heavily and awkwardly: *The heavy tanks lumped along.* —***Idiom.* 8. get** or **take one's lumps,** to receive or endure hardship, punishment, criticism, etc. —**lump′i•ness,** *n.* [*noncount*] —**lump′ish,** *adj.* —**lump′y,** *adj.,* **-i•er, -i•est.**

lump[2] (lump) /lʌmp/ *v.* [~ + *obj*] *Informal.* to put up with; accept and endure: *If you don't like it, you can lump it.*

lu•na•cy (lo͞o′nə sē) /ˈluwnəsiy/ *n., pl.* **-cies. 1.** [*noncount*] insanity; mental disorder. **2.** extreme foolishness or an instance of it: [*noncount*]: *The decision to resign was sheer lunacy.* [*count*]: *sick of their lunacies.*

lu•nar (lo͞o′nər) /ˈluwnər/ *adj.* [*before a noun*] of or relating to the moon: *lunar orbit; a lunar month.*

lu•na•tic (lo͞o′nə tik) /ˈluwnətɪk/ *n.* [*count*] **1.** an insane person. **2.** a person who is extremely foolish or who takes dangerous, unnecessary chances. —*adj.* **3.** insane; crazy. **4.** wildly or dangerously foolish. **5.** designated for or used by the insane: *a lunatic asylum.*

lu′natic fringe′, *n.* [*count*] members on the outer edges of any group, as in politics or religion, who hold extreme or fanatical views.

lunch (lunch) /lʌntʃ/ *n.* **1.** a light midday meal between breakfast and dinner; luncheon: [*count*]: *a lunch of sandwiches.* [*noncount*]: *went out for lunch.* —*v.* [*no obj*] **2.** to eat lunch. —***Idiom.* 3. out to lunch,** *Slang.* in a daze; not attentive or aware.

lunch•eon (lun′chən) /ˈlʌntʃən/ *n.* [*count*] lunch, esp. one that is formal: *a political luncheon.*

lunch•eon•ette (lun′chə net′) /ˌlʌntʃəˈnɛt/ *n.* [*count*] a small restaurant where light meals are served; lunch counter.

lunch′eon meat′, *n.* any of various sausages or molded loaf meats, usually sliced and served cold, as in sandwiches: [*noncount*]: *buying some luncheon meat.* [*count*]: *different luncheon meats.*

lunch•room (lunch′ro͞om′, -ro͝om′) /ˈlʌntʃˌruwm, -ˌrʊm/ *n.* [*count*] a room, as in a school or workplace, where light meals or snacks can be bought or where food brought from home may be eaten.

lung (lung) /lʌŋ/ *n.* [*count*] either of the two saclike organs used for breathing in the chest of humans and air-breathing animals.

lunge (lunj) /lʌndʒ/ *n., v.,* **lunged, lung•ing.** —*n.* [*count*] **1.** a sudden forward thrust, as with a sword or knife; stab. —*v.* [*no obj*] **2.** to make a lunge or thrust; move with a lunge: *He lunged for the knife but missed it.*

lunk•head (lungk′hed′) /ˈlʌŋkˌhɛd/ *n.* [*count*] *Slang.* a dull or stupid person; blockhead. Also called **lunk** (lungk) /lʌŋk/.

lu•pus (lo͞o′pəs) /ˈluwpəs/ *n.* [*noncount*] any of several diseases characterized by skin eruptions or inflammation.

lurch[1] (lûrch) /lɜrtʃ/ *n.* [*count*] **1.** an act or instance of swaying abruptly; a sudden tip or roll to one side, as of a ship or a person losing his or her balance. —*v.* [*no obj*] **2.** (of a ship) to roll or pitch suddenly: *The ship lurched in the storm.* **3.** to stagger or sway: *He lurched out of the bar.*

lurch[2] (lûrch) /lɜrtʃ/ *n.* —***Idiom.* leave (someone) in the lurch,** to leave behind or desert (someone) when help is needed most: *He left his family in the lurch and took off with his secretary.*

lure (lo͝or) /lʊr/ *n., v.,* **lured, lur•ing.** —*n.* [*count*] **1.** anything that attracts or tempts: *the lure of the big city.* **2.** a live or esp. plastic or metal object used as bait in fishing or trapping. —*v.* [~ + *obj*] **3.** to attract or tempt: *Can we lure you away from your present job?*

lu•rid (lo͝or′id) /ˈlʊrɪd/ *adj.* **1.** shocking; gruesome: *the lurid details of the accident.* **2.** shining with an unnatural, fiery glow: *a lurid sunset.* —**lu′rid•ly,** *adv.* —**lu′rid•ness,** *n.* [*noncount*]

lurk (lûrk) /lɜrk/ *v.* [*no obj*] **1.** to lie or wait in hiding: *lurked in the bushes waiting to pounce.* **2.** to exist without being seen, suspected, or detected: *We didn't see the dangers that lurked in our experiments.*

lus•cious (lush′əs) /ˈlʌʃəs/ *adj.* **1.** highly pleasing to the taste or smell: *sweet, luscious peaches.* **2.** richly satisfying to the senses or the mind: *the luscious style of his poetry.* **3.** sexually attractive: *a luscious body.* —**lus′cious•ly,** *adv.* —**lus′cious•ness,** *n.* [*noncount*]

lush[1] (lush) /lʌʃ/ *adj.,* **-er, -est. 1.** (of plants, vegetation, etc.) growing in great number or amount: *lush grass in the meadow.* **2.** showing or having an abundant supply of riches, wealth, comfort, or luxury: *a lush life.* —**lush′ness,** *n.* [*noncount*]

lush[2] (lush) /lʌʃ/ *n.* [*count*] *Slang.* a drunkard.

lust (lust) /lʌst/ *n.* **1.** [*noncount*] very strong sexual desire or appetite. **2.** [*noncount*] a passionate or overwhelming desire or craving: *lust for power.* **3.** [*count*] strong enthusiasm; zest; relish: *a lust for life.* —*v.* **4.** [*no obj*] to have intense sexual desire: *He lusted in his heart for her.* **5.** [~ + *for/after* + *obj*] to have a strong wish or desire: *He lusted for power.* —**lust′ful,** *adj.* —**lust′ful•ly,** *adv.*

lus•ter (lus′tər) /ˈlʌstər/ *n.* [*noncount*] **1.** the state or quality of shining by reflecting light: *the luster of satin.* **2.** radiant brightness; brilliance; radiance: *the luster in her eyes.* **3.** distinction; glory: *achievements that add luster to one's name.* Also, *esp. Brit.,* **lustre.** —**lus′ter•less,** *adj.*

lus•trous (lus′trəs) /ˈlʌstrəs/ *adj.* **1.** having luster; shining: *lustrous hair.* **2.** illustrious: *a lustrous career.*

lust•y (lus′tē) /ˈlʌstiy/ *adj.,* **-i•er, -i•est.** full of energy; hearty: *a lusty enthusiasm.* —**lust•i•ly** (lus′tl ē) /ˈlʌstl̩iy/ *adv.: singing lustily.* —**lust′i•ness,** *n.* [*noncount*]

lute (lo͞ot) /luwt/ *n.* [*count*] a musical instrument with strings, a long neck with frets, and a hollow, typically pear-shaped body.

Lux•em•bourg•er (luk′səm bûr′gər) /ˈlʌksəmˌbɜrgər/ *n.* [*count*] a person born or living in Luxembourg.

Lux•em•bourg•i•an (luk′səm bûr′jē ən, luk′səm bûr′jē ən) /ˈlʌksəmˌbɜrdʒiyən, ˌlʌksəmˈbɜrdʒiyən/ *adj.* of or relating to Luxembourg.

lux•u•ri•ant (lug zho͝or′ē ənt, luk sho͝or′-) /lʌgˈʒʊriyənt, lʌkˈʃʊr-/ *adj.* **1.** showing a great amount of growth or growing things, as vegetation; lush. **2.** producing abundantly, as soil; fertile. **3.** rich or great in amount; abundant. —**lux•u′ri•ance,** *n.* [*noncount*] —**lux•u′ri•ant•ly,** *adv.*

lux•u•ri•ate (lug zhŏŏr′ē āt′, luk shŏŏr′-) /lʌg'ʒʊriy,eyt, lʌk'ʃʊr-/ *v.* [*no obj*], **-at•ed, -at•ing. 1.** to enjoy oneself without holding back; indulge in luxury. **2.** to grow fully; thrive. **3.** to take great delight: *luxuriated in the warm bath.*

lux•u•ri•ous (lug zhŏŏr′ē əs, luk shŏŏr′-) /lʌg'ʒʊriyəs, lʌk'ʃʊr-/ *adj.* **1.** characterized by luxury: *a luxurious hotel.* **2.** given or inclined to luxury: *luxurious tastes.* **3.** of the richest or finest quality: *luxurious shampoos.* —**lux•u′ri•ous•ly,** *adv.* —**lux•u′ri•ous•ness,** *n.* [*noncount*]

lux•u•ry (luk′shə rē, lug′zhə-) /'lʌkʃəriy, 'lʌgʒə-/ *n., pl.* **-ries,** *adj.* **—*n.* 1.** [*count*] a material object, service, etc., that brings physical comfort or rich living, but is not a necessity of life: *swimming pool, tennis court, and other luxuries.* **2.** [*noncount*] indulgence in the comforts and pleasures provided by such things: *a taste for luxury.* **3.** [*count; usually singular; usually: the + ~ + of*] a means of using such pleasure or comfort: *This travel plan gives you the luxury of choosing which countries you can visit.* **4.** [*count; usually singular; the + ~ + of*]: a foolish or worthless form of giving in to one's desires: *We cannot afford the luxury of self-pity.* **—*adj.*** [*before a noun*] **5.** of, relating to, or providing luxury: *a luxury hotel.*

-ly, *suffix.* **1.** *-ly* is attached to adjectives to form adverbs: *glad + -ly → gladly; gradual + -ly → gradually.* **2.** *-ly* is also attached to nouns that refer to units of time, to form adjectives and adverbs with the meaning "at or for every (such unit of time)": *hour + -ly → hourly (= at every hour); day + -ly → daily (= on or for every day).* **3.** *-ly* is also attached to nouns to form adjectives with the meaning "like (the noun mentioned):" *saint + -ly → saintly; coward + -ly → cowardly.*

ly•ce•um (lī sē′əm) /lay'siyəm/ *n.* [*count*] **1.** an institution for popular education, providing discussions, lectures, concerts, etc. **2.** a building for such activities.

lye (lī) /lay/ *n.* [*noncount*] a substance used for washing and for making soap.

ly•ing[1] (lī′ing) /'layɪŋ/ *n.* [*noncount*] the telling of lies.

ly•ing[2] (lī′ing) /'layɪŋ/ *v.* pres. part. of LIE[2].

ly′ing-in′, *n., pl.* **ly•ings-in, ly•ing-ins,** *adj.* **—*n.*** [*noncount*] **1.** the act or state of a woman staying in a bed awaiting birth of her child. **—*adj.*** [*before a noun*] **2.** of, relating to, or providing facilities for childbirth: *a lying-in hospital.*

Lyme′ disease′ (līm) /laym/ *n.* [*noncount*] a serious, recurrent disease characterized by pains in the joints, fatigue, and sometimes problems in the nervous system, caused by a microorganism carried by a tick.

lymph (limf) /lɪmf/ *n.* [*noncount*] a clear, yellowish fluid in the blood that contains special blood cells that fight infection.

lym•phat•ic (lim fat′ik) /lɪm'fætɪk/ *adj.* of, relating to, containing, or carrying lymph.

lym•pho•ma (lim fō′mə) /lɪm'fowmə/ *n.* [*count*], *pl.* **-mas, -ma•ta** (-mə tə) /-mətə/. a tumor in any of the areas where lymph is made or stored in the body.

lynch (linch) /lɪntʃ/ *v.* [~ + *obj*] to put to death, esp. by hanging, by the action of a mob that does not have legal authority. —**lynch′er,** *n.* [*count*]

lynx (lingks) /lɪŋks/ *n.* [*count*], *pl.* **lynx•es,** (*esp. when thought of as a group*) **lynx.** a wildcat having long limbs, a short tail, and usually tufted ears.

lyre (lī^ə^r) /lay^ə^r/ *n.* [*count*] a small harplike musical instrument of ancient Greece.

lyr•ic (lir′ik) /'lɪrɪk/ *adj.* Also, **lyr′i•cal. 1.** (of a poem) having the general effect of a song, esp. in expressing emotions. **2.** characterized by or expressing strong, spontaneous feeling: *lyric writing.* **—*n.*** [*count*] **3.** a lyric poem. **4.** Usually, **lyrics.** [*plural*] the words of a song. —**lyr′i•cal•ly,** *adv.*

lyr•i•cist (lir′ə sist) /'lɪrəsɪst/ *n.* [*count*] **1.** a person who writes the lyrics for songs. **2.** a lyric poet. —**lyr′i•cism,** *n.* [*noncount*]

-lys-, *root.* *-lys-* comes from Greek and Latin, where it has the meaning "to break down, loosen, dissolve." This meaning is found in such words as: ANALYSIS, ANALYTIC, CATALYST, DIALYSIS, ELECTROLYSIS, ELECTROLYTE, PALSY, PARALYSIS, PARALYTIC.

ly•ser′gic ac′id di•eth•yl•am′ide (lī sûr′jik, li-; dī-eth′ə lam′īd, -eth′ə lə mīd′) /lay'sɜrdʒɪk, lɪ-; day,ɛθə'læmayd, -'ɛθələ,mayd/ *n.* [*noncount*] See LSD.

M, m (em) /ɛm/ *n.* [*count*], *pl.* **Ms** or **M's, ms** or **m's.** the 13th letter of the English alphabet, a consonant.

M, an abbreviation of: **1.** mach. **2.** married. **3.** medium. **4.** mega-.

M, *Symbol.* **1.** the 13th in order or in a series. **2.** the Roman numeral for 1000.

m, an abbreviation of: **1.** mass. **2.** medium. **3.** meter. **4.** middle.

M., an abbreviation of: **1.** majesty. **2.** measure. **3.** medicine. **4.** medium. **5.** meridian. **6.** Monday. **7.** *pl.* **MM.** messieurs.

m., an abbreviation of: **1.** male. **2.** married. **3.** masculine. **4.** *Physics.* mass. **5.** medium. **6.** Latin *merīdiēs* noon. **7.** meter. **8.** middle. **9.** mile. **10.** minute. **11.** morning.

ma (mä) /mɑ/ *n.* [*count*], *pl.* **mas.** mother.

MA, an abbreviation of: Massachusetts.

M.A., an abbreviation of: Master of Arts.

ma'am (mam, mäm; *unstressed* məm) /mæm, mɑm; *unstressed* məm/ *n.* [*often: Ma'am*] MADAM (def. 1).

ma•ca•bre (mə kä′brə, -käb′) /mə'kɑbrə, -'kɑb/ *adj.* gruesome; ghastly, esp. relating to death: *eerie, macabre tales of violence.*

ma•caque (mə kak′, -käk′) /mə'kæk, -'kɑk/ *n.* [*count*] a monkey, chiefly of Asia, having cheek pouches.

mac•a•ro•ni (mak′ə rō′nē) /ˌmækə'rowniy/ *n.,* [*noncount*], *pl.* **-nis, -nies.** a kind of tube-shaped pasta made of wheat flour.

mac•a•roon (mak′ə ro͞on′) /ˌmækə'ruwn/ *n.* [*count*] a cookie made of beaten egg whites, sugar, and almond paste.

ma•caw (mə kô′) /mə'kɔ/ *n.* [*count*] an extremely large, long-tailed parrot of the tropics.

mace[1] (mās) /meys/ *n.* [*count*] **1.** a clublike weapon, often with a spiked metal head. **2.** a ceremonial staff that symbolizes the office of an official, used in processions.

mace[2] (mās) /meys/ *n.* [*noncount*] a spice made from the inner husk of the nutmeg.

Mace (mās) /meys/ *Trademark.* **Maced, Mac•ing.** [*noncount*] **1.** a chemical spray that causes severe eye irritation, used against rioters or an attacker. **—***v.* [~ + *obj*] **2.** [*sometimes: mace*] to spray with Mace: *He maced his assailant.*

mach or **Mach** (mok) /mɒk/ *n.* [*noncount*] the speed of an aircraft in relation to the speed of sound: *The plane flew at Mach 3, three times the speed of sound.*

ma•chet•e (mə shet′ē, -chet′ē) /mə'ʃɛtiy, -'tʃɛtiy/ *n.* [*count*], *pl.* **-chet•es.** a heavy swordlike knife used as a cutting tool in farming: *to hack through the grasses with a machete.*

Mach•i•a•vel•li•an (mak′ē ə vel′ē ən) /ˌmækiyə'vɛliyən/ *adj.* characterized by dishonesty, trickery, cunning, or lies: *the Machiavellian way he won the nomination and destroyed his opponent.* Sometimes, **Mach′i•a•vel′i•an.**

mach•i•na•tion (mak′ə nā′shən) /ˌmækə'neyʃən/ *n.* [*count*] Usually, **machinations.** [*plural*] a crafty, clever course of action to gain power; an intrigue: *his machinations to win the election.* See -MECH-.

ma•chine (mə shēn′) /mə'ʃiyn/ *n., v.,* **-chined, -chin•ing.** **—***n.* [*count*] **1.** an apparatus made of connected parts having separate functions, used to accomplish work: *a sewing machine.* **2.** a device that carries, sends, or changes force or motion, such as a lever, pulley, or inclined plane. **3.** any of various devices that dispense things: *a vending machine for hot coffee or tea.* **4.** a group of persons that controls a political party: *the Democratic party machine.* **—***v.* [~ + *obj*] **5.** to make or finish with a machine: *to machine the parts so they fitted together.* See -MECH-.

machine′ gun′, *n.* [*count*] a firearm capable of shooting a continuous stream of bullets.

ma•chin•er•y (mə shē′nə rē) /mə'ʃiynəriy/ *n.* [*noncount*] **1.** a collection of machines: *the machinery humming along in the factory.* **2.** the parts of a machine thought of as a group. **3.** a system that obtains results: *the criminal justice machinery.* See -MECH-.

ma•chin•ist (mə shē′nist) /mə'ʃiynɪst/ *n.* [*count*] one who operates, makes, or repairs machines.

ma•chis•mo (mä chēz′mō, mə chiz′-) /mɑ'tʃiyzmow, mə'tʃɪz-/ *n.* [*noncount*] an exaggerated sense of manliness: *a cowboy full of machismo.*

ma•cho (mä′chō) /'mɑtʃow/ *adj.* **1.** having or showing machismo: *had to display a macho attitude.* **—***n.* [*noncount*] **2.** MACHISMO.

mack•er•el (mak′ər əl, mak′rəl) /'mækərəl, 'mækrəl/ *n., pl.* (*esp. when thought of as a group*) **-el,** (*esp. for kinds or species*) **-els.** a food fish of the N Atlantic.

mack•i•naw (mak′ə nô′) /'mækəˌnɔ/ *n.* [*count*] a short, double-breasted coat of woolen material.

mack•in•tosh or **mac•in•tosh** (mak′in tosh′) /'mækɪnˌtɒʃ/ *n.* [*count*] *Chiefly Brit.* RAINCOAT.

mac•ra•mé or **mac•ra•me** (mak′rə mā′) /'mækrəˌmey/ *n.* [*noncount*] **1.** Also called **mac′ramé lace′.** lacelike webbing made of cord tied in knots. **2.** the technique of producing macramé.

macro-, *prefix. macro-* comes from Greek, where it has the meaning "large (or long), esp. in comparison with others of its kind." This meaning is found in such words as: MACROBIOTIC, MACROCOSM, MACRON. Compare MICRO-.

mac•ro•bi•ot•ics (mak′rō bī ot′iks) /ˌmækrowbay'ɒtɪks/ *n.* [*noncount; used with a singular verb*] a program that emphasizes harmony with nature, esp. through diet. **—mac′ro•bi•ot′ic,** *adj.*

mac•ro•cosm (mak′rə koz′əm) /'mækrəˌkɒzəm/ *n.* [*count*] the universe, or any system, considered as a whole or a single unit (opposed to *microcosm*).

ma•cron (mā′kron, mak′ron) /'meykrɒn, 'mækrɒn/ *n.* [*count*] a horizontal line used over a vowel to show that the vowel is long or has a specific pronunciation, as (ā) in *fate* (fāt).

mad (mad) /mæd/ *adj.,* **mad•der, mad•dest. 1.** mentally disturbed or mentally ill; deranged. **2.** [*be* + ~] angry; greatly irritated; enraged: *He's really mad at his daughter.* **3.** affected with rabies; rabid: *a mad dog.* **4.** extremely foolish: *a mad scheme.* [*be* + ~ + *to* + *verb*]: *You're mad to go out in such weather.* **5.** [*before a noun*] very hurried and disorganized: *mad haste.* **6.** [*be* + ~] full of enthusiasm; infatuated: *He's mad about opera.* **7.** [*before a noun*] wildly fun-loving; hilarious: *a mad time at the party.* **—*Idiom.*** **8. drive someone mad,** to cause someone to be furious or irritated: *Rush hour traffic always drives her mad.* **9. like mad,** at a furious pace: *rushing around like mad.* **—mad′ly,** *adv.*: *madly in love with her.* **—mad′ness,** *n.* [*noncount*]: *suffering from madness.*

Mad•a•gas•can (mad′ə gas′kən) /ˌmædə'gæskən/ *n.* [*count*] **1.** a person born or living in Madagascar. **—***adj.* **2.** of or relating to Madagascar.

mad•am (mad′əm) /'mædəm/ *n.* [*count*], *pl.* **mes•dames** (mā dam′, -däm′) /mey'dæm, -'dɑm/ for 1; **mad•ams** for 2. **1.** [*often: Madam*] a respectful term of address to a woman: *Please step this way, Madam.* **2.** a woman in charge of a brothel.

mad•ame (mad′əm, mə dam′, -däm′, ma-) /'mædəm, mə'dæm, -'dɑm, mæ-/ *n.* [*count*], *pl.* **mes•dames** (mā-dam′, -däm′) /mey'dæm, -'dɑm/. [*often: Madame*] a French title equivalent to Mrs.: *Madame Curie. Abbr.:* Mme.

mad•cap (mad′kap′) /'mædˌkæp/ *adj.* [*before a noun*] **1.** recklessly foolish; impulsive; rash: *madcap schemes.* **—***n.* [*count*] **2.** a madcap person.

mad•den (mad′n) /'mædn̩/ *v.* [~ + *obj*] to cause anger; infuriate. **—mad′den•ing,** *adj.*: *a maddening itch.*

mad•der (mad′ər) /'mædər/ *n.* **1.** [*count*] a plant of Europe having clusters of small yellowish flowers. **2.** [*noncount*] the root of this plant, once used in dyeing. **3.** [*noncount*] a dye derived from madder.

mad•ding (mad′ing) /'mædɪŋ/ *adj.* [*before a noun*] noisy; tumultuous: *far from the madding crowd.*

made (mād) /meyd/ *v.* **1.** pt. and pp. of MAKE. **—***adj.* **2.** This word is often used in combination with another word, often a noun, to mean "produced, made (in the particular place or way)": *machine-made clothes.* **—*Idiom.*** **3. have it made,** [*no obj*] *Informal.* to be assured of success: *Now that he's president, he has it made.*

mad•e•moi•selle (mad′ə mə zel′, mad′mwə-, mam-zel′) /ˌmædəmə'zɛl, ˌmædmwə-, mæm'zɛl/ *n.* [*count*], *pl.* **mademoiselles, mes•de•moi•selles** (mā′də mə zel′, -zelz′, mād′mwə-) /ˌmeydəmə'zɛl, -'zɛlz, ˌmeydmwə-/. [*often: Mademoiselle*] a French title equivalent to Miss. *Abbr.:* Mlle.

made′-to-or′der, *adj.* **1.** made to fit an individual's particular measurements or the like: *made-to-order shoes.* **2.** perfectly suited: *a made-to-order candidate.*

made′-up′, *adj.* **1.** fabricated; concocted: *a made-up story.* **2.** [*usually: be* + ~] wearing facial makeup: *She was heavily made-up.*

mad•house (mad′hous′) /ˈmæd,haws/ *n.* [*count*] (-hou′-ziz) /-ˌhawzɪz/. **1.** a hospital for the mentally disturbed. **2.** a disorderly, noisy place: *The train station was a madhouse.*

mad•man or **-wom•an** (mad′man′, -mən) or (-wŏŏm′-ən) /ˈmæd,mæn, -mən/ or /-ˈwˌʊmən/ *n.* [*count*], *pl.* **-men** or **-wom•en.** one who is or appears to be insane: *Some madman on the street started screaming at me.*

Ma•don•na (mə don′ə) /məˈdɒnə/ *n.* **1.** [*proper noun; usually: the* + ~] Mary, the mother of Jesus; the Virgin Mary. **2.** [*count*] an image of the Virgin Mary.

mad•ras (mad′rəs, mə dras′, -dräs′) /ˈmædrəs, məˈdræs, -ˈdrɑs/ *n.* [*noncount*] a light cotton fabric, esp. one in multicolored plaid.

mad•ri•gal (mad′ri gəl) /ˈmædrɪgəl/ *n.* [*count*] a song sung without musical instruments, usually having many parts.

mael•strom (māl′strəm) /ˈmeylstrəm/ *n.* [*count*] **1.** a powerful whirlpool often dangerous to approach. **2.** a disorderly, stormy, tumultuous condition: *the maelstrom of a presidential election.*

maes•tro (mī′strō) /ˈmaystrow/ *n.* [*count*], *pl.* **-tros. 1.** a famous composer or conductor of music. **2.** a master of any art.

Ma•fi•a (mä′fē ə, maf′ē ə) /ˈmɑfiyə, ˈmæfiyə/ *n.* **1.** [*count; usually: the* + ~] a secret criminal organization originating in Sicily. **2.** [*mafia; count*] any powerful, secret group: *the union mafia.*

ma•fi•o•so (mä′fē ō′sō) /ˌmɑfiyˈowsow/ *n.* [*count*], *pl.* **-si** (-sē) /-siy/ **-sos.** [*often: Mafioso*] a member of the Mafia.

mag•a•zine (mag′ə zēn′, mag′ə zēn′) /ˌmægəˈziyn, ˈmægəˌziyn/ *n.* [*count*] **1.** a publication published at regular periods, containing essays, etc., and often illustrations: *a news magazine.* See illustration at SCHOOL. **2.** a room for keeping gunpowder and other explosives. **3.** a building where the military keeps arms or provisions. **4.** a receptacle on a gun for holding cartridges.

ma•gen•ta (mə jen′tə) /məˈdʒɛntə/ *n.* [*noncount*] a purplish red color.

mag•got (mag′ət) /ˈmægət/ *n.* [*count*] a soft-bodied, wormlike creature that grows into certain flies.

Ma•gi (mā′jī) /ˈmeydʒay/ *n.* [*plural*], *sing.* **-gus** (-gəs) /-gəs/. [*sometimes: magi*] the wise men, three by tradition, who visited the infant Jesus and left gifts.

mag•ic (maj′ik) /ˈmædʒɪk/ *n.* [*noncount*] **1.** the art of producing illusions or tricks that fool or deceive an audience. **2.** the practice of using various techniques, as special words or gestures, to control events: *sorcerers using black magic.* **3.** any extraordinary influence or power: *the magic of fame.* **—*adj.*** [*before a noun*] **4.** done by or used in magic: *a magic trick; a magic wand.* **5.** mysteriously enchanting, skillful, or effective. **—mag′i•cal,** *adj.* **—mag′i•cal•ly,** *adv.*

ma•gi•cian (mə jish′ən) /məˈdʒɪʃən/ *n.* [*count*] **1.** one who performs illusions that fool the audience: *The magician waved her magic wand and the bird disappeared.* **2.** someone using various techniques to control events; a sorcerer.

mag•is•te•ri•al (maj′ə stēr′ē əl) /ˌmædʒəˈstɪəriyəl/ *adj.* **1.** acting like a master or as if in a position of authority: *His magisterial tone only made me angrier.* **2.** [*before a noun*] of or relating to a magistrate or the office of a magistrate.

mag•is•trate (maj′ə strāt′, -strit) /ˈmædʒə,streyt, -strɪt/ *n.* [*count*] **1.** a civil officer who administers the law. **2.** a judicial officer, as a justice of the peace.

mag•ma (mag′mə) /ˈmægmə/ *n.* [*noncount*] extremely hot, melted material beneath or within the earth's crust.

mag•na•nim•i•ty (mag′nə nim′i tē) /ˌmægnəˈnɪmɪtiy/ *n.* [*noncount*] the quality or condition of being magnanimous.

mag•nan•i•mous (mag nan′ə məs) /mægˈnænəməs/ *adj.* generous and gracious in forgiving an insult or harm done to one: *magnanimous after his victory.* **—mag•nan′i•mous•ly,** *adv.*

mag•nate (mag′nāt, -nit) /ˈmægneyt, -nɪt/ *n.* [*count*] a person of great influence or importance in a particular field: *an oil magnate.*

mag•ne•sia (mag nē′zhə, -shə) /mægˈniyʒə, -ʃə/ *n.* [*noncount*] a white tasteless substance, magnesium oxide, used as an antacid and laxative.

mag•ne•si•um (mag nē′zē əm, -zhəm, -shē əm) /mægˈniyziyəm, -ʒəm, -ʃiyəm/ *n.* [*noncount*] a light, silver-white element that burns with a dazzling light, used in fireworks and flashbulbs.

mag•net (mag′nit) /ˈmægnɪt/ *n.* [*count*] **1.** a body, as a piece of iron or steel, that has the property of attracting certain substances, as iron. **2.** one that attracts: *He's a magnet to women.*

mag•net•ic (mag net′ik) /mægˈnɛtɪk/ *adj.* **1.** of or relating to a magnet or magnetism: *the magnetic properties of the solar wind.* **2.** capable of being magnetized or attracted by a magnet: *Rubber is not magnetic.* **3.** having a strong attractive charm: *a magnetic personality.* **—mag•net′i•cal•ly,** *adv.*

magnet′ic field′, *n.* [*count*] a region of space in which a magnetic force acts: *You can create a magnetic field by wrapping coils of wire around a nail and attaching the ends to a battery.*

magnet′ic res′onance im′aging, *n.* [*noncount*] a process of producing images of the body by means of a strong magnetic field and low-energy radio waves: *Using high-speed magnetic resonance imaging, researchers are discovering how the brain works. Abbr.:* MRI

magnet′ic tape′, *n.* a ribbon of material coated with a substance sensitive to electromagnets and used to record sound, images, or data: [*noncount*]: *The data was recorded on magnetic tape.* [*count*]: *The magnetic tapes, with all the back-up information, were also destroyed.*

mag•net•ism (mag′ni tiz′əm) /ˈmægnɪ,tɪzəm/ *n.* [*noncount*] **1.** the properties of attraction that magnets possess: *weakened magnetism.* **2.** strong attractive power or charm.

mag•net•ite (mag′ni tīt′) /ˈmægnɪ,tayt/ *n.* [*noncount*] a common black mineral that is the most magnetic mineral and an important iron ore.

mag•net•ize (mag′ni tīz′) /ˈmægnɪ,tayz/ *v.* [~ + *obj*], **-ized, -iz•ing.** to make a magnet of: *Rubbing the nail with a magnet will magnetize it.* **—mag•net•i•za•tion** (mag′ni ti zā′shən) /ˌmægnɪtɪˈzeyʃən/ *n.* [*noncount*]: *Magnetization stops when the electrical current is removed.*

mag•ne•to (mag nē′tō) /mægˈniytow/ *n.* [*count*], *pl.* **-tos.** a small electric generator in which magnets provide the magnetic field: *The magneto was dead and so the mobile phone wouldn't work.*

mag•ne•tom•e•ter (mag′ni tom′i tər) /ˌmægnɪˈtɒmɪtər/ *n.* [*count*] an instrument for measuring a magnetic field.

mag•ni•fi•ca•tion (mag′nə fi kā′shən) /ˌmægnəfɪˈkeyʃən/ *n.* **1.** [*noncount*] the act of magnifying or the state of being magnified. **2.** the amount or power by which something may be magnified, as by a microscope: [*count*]: *a magnification of one hundred.* [*noncount*]: *The captain ordered full magnification on the viewing screen.*

mag•nif•i•cent (mag nif′ə sənt) /mægˈnɪfəsənt/ *adj.* **1.** splendid or impressive in appearance: *a magnificent palace.* **2.** very fine; superb: *magnificent weather.* **—mag•nif′i•cence,** *n.* [*noncount*]: *the magnificence of the Taj Mahal.* **—mag•nif′i•cent•ly,** *adv.*: *played magnificently in the tournament.*

mag•ni•fy (mag′nə fī′) /ˈmægnə,fay/ *v.* [~ + *obj*], **-fied, -fy•ing. 1.** to increase the apparent size of: *Binoculars magnify images.* **2.** to exaggerate; overstate: *to magnify one's difficulties.* **—mag′ni•fi′er,** *n.* [*count*]

mag′nifying glass′, *n.* [*count*] a lens that makes an object appear larger.

mag•ni•tude (mag′ni to͞od′, -tyo͞od′) /ˈmægnɪ,tuwd, -ˌtyuwd/ *n.* [*noncount*] **1.** greatness of size or amount. **2.** great importance or consequence: *an event of great magnitude to the world.* **—*Idiom.* 3. of the first magnitude,** of greatest significance.

mag•no•lia (mag nōl′yə, -nō′lē ə) /mægˈnowlyə, -ˈnowliyə/ *n.* [*count*], *pl.* **-lias.** a shrub or tree having large usually fragrant flowers, grown for ornament.

mag•num (mag′nəm) /ˈmægnəm/ *n.* [*count*] **1.** a large wine bottle holding the same amount as two ordinary bottles. **2.** a firearm that uses cartridges of a larger charge than others of the same size. **—*adj.*** [*before a noun*] **3.** of or relating to such a firearm or cartridge.

mag′num o′pus, *n.* [*count*] a great work, esp. the chief work of a writer or artist.

mag•pie (mag′pī′) /ˈmæg,pay/ *n.* [*count*] a bird of the jay family, having long, black-and-white feathers and noisy habits.

ma•ha•ra•jah or **ma•ha•ra•ja** (mä′hə rä′jə, -zhə) /ˌmɑhəˈrɑdʒə, -ʒə/ *n.* [*count*], *pl.* **-jahs** or **-jas.** a former ruling prince in India, esp. of one of the major states.

ma•ha•ra•nee or **ma•ha•ra•ni** (mä′hə rä′nē) /ˌmɑhəˈrɑniy/ *n.* [*count*], *pl.* **-nees** or **-nis. 1.** the wife of a maharajah. **2.** a former Indian princess who was a sovereign in her own right.

ma•ha•ri•shi (mä hə rē′shē, mə här′ə-) /mɑhə'riyʃiy, mə'hɑrə-/ *n.* [*count*], *pl.* **-shis.** a Hindu religious wise person.

mah-jongg or **mah•jong** (mä′jông′, -jong′, -zhông′, -zhong′) /'mɑ'dʒɔŋ, -'dʒɒŋ, -'ʒɔŋ, -'ʒɒŋ/ *n.* [*noncount*] a game of Chinese origin played by four persons with dominolike tiles. Also, **mah′-jong′.**

ma•hog•a•ny (mə hog′ə nē) /mə'hɒgəniy/ *n., pl.* **-nies. 1.** [*count*] a tropical American tree giving hard, reddish brown wood. **2.** [*noncount*] the wood itself. **3.** [*noncount*] a reddish brown color.

maid (mād) /meyd/ *n.* [*count*] **1.** a female servant. **2.** a girl or young unmarried woman.

maid•en (mād′n) /'meydn̩/ *n.* [*count*] **1.** a girl or young unmarried woman; maid. **—*adj.*** [*before a noun*] **2.** of, relating to, or befitting a maiden. **3. a.** unmarried: *a maiden aunt.* **b.** virgin. **4.** first: *a maiden flight.* **—maid′-en•hood′,** *n.* [*noncount*] **—maid′en•ly,** *adj.*

maid′en name′, *n.* [*count*] a woman's family name before marriage.

maid′ of hon′or, *n.* [*count*] an unmarried woman who is the chief attendant of a bride.

maid•serv•ant (mād′sûr′vənt) /'meyd,sɜrvənt/ *n.* [*count*] a female servant.

mail[1] (māl) /meyl/ *n.* **1.** [*noncount*] letters, etc., sent or delivered by the postal service: *The mail is sorted electronically.* **2.** [*noncount*] a single collection or delivery of such postal matter: *Was there mail today?* **3.** Also, **mails.** the system for sending or delivering such postal matter: [*count; usually singular*]: *The mail is very slow in this area.* [*plural*]: *The mails are slow in this area.* [*noncount; by* + ~]: *It came by mail last week.* **—*adj.*** [*before a noun*] **4.** of or relating to mail. **—*v.* 5.** to send by mail: [~ + *obj*]: *Mail the package tomorrow.* [~ + *obj* + *to* + *obj*]: *Mail your complaint to me.* [~ + *obj* + *obj*]: *Mail me the proposal.*

mail[2] (māl) /meyl/ *n.* [*noncount*] flexible armor of metal rings or plates.

mail•box (māl′boks′) /'meyl,bɒks/ *n.* [*count*] **1.** a public box in which mail is placed for pickup. See illustration at STREET. **2.** a private box into which mail is delivered. **3.** a file in a computer for the storage of electronic mail.

mail′ car′rier, *n.* [*count*] one employed to deliver the mail.

mail•er (mā′lər) /'meylər/ *n.* [*count*] **1.** one who sends mail. **2.** a special envelope designed to prevent damage to its contents.

mail•lot (mä yō′) /mɑ'yow/ *n.* [*count*] **1.** a close-fitting, one-piece bathing suit for women. **2.** tights for dancers, acrobats, etc.

mail•man (māl′man′) /'meyl,mæn/ *n., pl.* **-men.** MAIL CARRIER.

mail′ or′der, *n.* [*noncount*] an order for goods received or shipped through the mail.

maim (mām) /meym/ *v.* [~ + *obj; usually: be* + ~*-ed*], to injure (someone) so that part of the body can no longer be used: *was badly maimed in the fire.*

main (mān) /meyn/ *adj.* [*before a noun*] **1.** chief in size, extent, or importance: *He had the main part in a play.* **2.** (in a sentence) of or relating to the clause that can stand by itself; independent: *In the sentence* I'll see you when I get home, *the main clause is* I'll see you. **—*n.*** [*count*] **3.** a principal pipe in a system used to carry and send water, gas, etc. **—*Idiom.* 4. in the main,** most importantly: *In the main, she has proposed a very good plan.* **5. with might and main,** with strength or force. **—main′ly,** *adv.: He got rich mainly from government contracts.*

main•frame (mān′frām′) /'meyn,freym/ *n.* [*count*] a large computer, often the center of a system serving many users. Compare MICROCOMPUTER, MINICOMPUTER.

main•land (mān′land′, -lənd) /'meyn,lænd, -lənd/ *n.* [*count; usually singular; usually: the* + ~] the principal land of a region, etc., as distinguished from nearby islands: *ferried back to the mainland.*

main′ line′, *n.* [*count*] **1.** a principal highway or railway line. **2.** *Slang.* a vein that can be easily reached, used for injection of a narcotic.

main•line (mān′līn′, -līn′) /'meyn,layn, -'layn/ *v.,* **-lined, -lin•ing,** *adj.* **—*v.* 1.** *Slang.* to inject a narcotic directly into a vein: [*no obj*]: *He was mainlining at $500 a day.* [~ + *obj*]: *mainlined heroin for several months.* **—*adj.* 2.** having a principal or established position: *mainline churches.*

main•mast (mān′mast′, -məst) /'meyn,mæst, -məst/ *n.* [*count*] the principal mast on a sailing ship.

main•sail (mān′sāl′, -səl) /'meyn,seyl, -səl/ *n.* [*count*] the lowermost sail on a mainmast.

main•spring (mān′spring′) /'meyn,sprɪŋ/ *n.* [*count*] **1.** the principal spring in a mechanism, as in a watch. **2.** the chief force that causes movement, action, etc.: *Unemployment was the mainspring of the discontent.*

main•stay (mān′stā′) /'meyn,stey/ *n.* [*count*] a person or thing that acts as a chief support or part: *She's so active, she's the mainstay of the company.*

main•stream (mān′strēm′) /'meyn,striym/ *n.* [*count*] **1.** the principal or most usual course of action or way of thinking: *That political party must return to the mainstream of American values.* **—*adj.*** [*before a noun*] **2.** of or relating to a principal or widely accepted group, style, etc.: *The party platform appealed to mainstream America.* **—*v.*** [~ + *obj*] **3.** to send into the mainstream, as by placing (special students) in regular school classes: *to mainstream handicapped children.*

main•tain (mān tān′) /meyn'teyn/ *v.* **1.** [~ + *obj*] to keep in existence; preserve: *maintained their friendship for over forty years.* **2.** [~ + *obj*] to keep in a certain condition, operation, or force: *to maintain an even temperature.* **3.** [~ + (*that*) *clause*] to state or declare: *maintained that he had been home all night.* **4.** [~ + *obj*] to support in argument: *maintained her innocence in spite of the evidence.* **5.** [~ + *obj*] to provide for the upkeep or support of: *Is that salary enough to maintain a family?* **—main•tain′a•ble,** *adj.* **—main′te•nance** (mān′tə nəns) /'meyntənəns/ *n.* [*noncount*] See -TAIN-, -MAN-[1].

maî•tre (or **mai•tre**) **d′** (mā′tər dē′, mā′trə) /,mey'tər diy, ,meytrə/ *n., pl.* **maître** (or **maitre**) **d's.** MAÎTRE D'HÔTEL.

maî•tre d'hô•tel (mā′trə dō tel′) /'meytrə dow'tɛl/ *n.* [*count*], *pl.* **maî•tres d'hôtel** (mā′trəz, -trə) /'meytrəz, -trə/. **1.** a headwaiter. **2.** a steward or butler.

maize (māz) /meyz/ *n.* CORN[1] (def. 1).

ma•jes•tic (mə jes′tik) /mə'dʒɛstɪk/ *adj.* impressive; grand: *majestic mountains.* **—ma•jes′ti•cal•ly,** *adv.*

maj•es•ty (maj′ə stē) /'mædʒəstiy/ *n., pl.* **-ties. 1.** [*noncount*] high and noble dignity; grandeur: *the majesty of the plains sweeping into the distance.* **2.** [*count; usually Majesty; often: Your/His/Her* + ~] a title of a king, queen, or sovereign: *Her Majesty, the Queen.*

ma•jor (mā′jər) /'meydʒər/ *n.* [*count*] **1.** a military officer ranking below a lieutenant colonel and above a captain. **2. a.** a field of study in which a student specializes: *a major in botany.* **b.** a student specializing in such a field: *a history major.* **3. the majors,** [*plural*] the major leagues. **—*adj.*** [*before a noun*] **4.** greater in size, extent, or importance: *a major part in the play.* **5.** of great risk; serious: *a major operation.* **6.** *Music.* based on a major scale: *a major key.* **7.** relating to the subject in which a student specializes: *major courses.* **—*v.*** [~ + *in* + *obj*] **8.** to follow an academic major: *majoring in physics.*

ma′jor-do′mo (dō′mō) /'dowmow/ *n.* [*count*], *pl.* **-mos. 1.** a man in charge of a great household, as that of a king or queen. **2.** a steward. **3.** one who makes arrangements for another.

ma•jor•ette (mā′jə ret′) /,meydʒə'rɛt/ *n.* [*count*] a girl or woman who twirls a baton or leads a marching band.

ma′jor gen′eral, *n.* [*count*] a military officer ranking below a lieutenant general and above a brigadier.

ma•jor•i•ty (mə jôr′i tē, -jor′-) /mə'dʒɔrɪtiy, -'dʒɒr-/ *n., pl.* **-ties. 1.** [*count*] a number, part, or amount forming more than half of the whole or total: *the majority of the population; She got a majority of the votes in the election.* **2.** [*noncount*] the amount by which the greater number, as of votes, exceeds the remainder. **3.** [*noncount*] the state or time of being of full legal age: *to attain one's majority.* **4.** [*noncount*] the military rank or office of a major.

ma′jor scale′, *n.* [*count*] a musical scale consisting of a series of whole steps except for half steps between the third and fourth and seventh and eighth degrees.

make (māk) /meyk/ *v.,* **made** (mād) /meyd/ **mak•ing,** *n.* **—*v.* 1.** to bring into existence by combining material; produce: [~ + *obj*]: *to make a dress.* [~ + *obj* + *obj*]: *I'll make the kids some breakfast.* **2.** [~ + *obj*] to cause to exist or happen; produce: *Why is he always making trouble?* **3.** to cause to be or become; transform: [~ + *obj* + *adjective*]: *This news will make her happy.* [~ + *adjective* + (*that*) *clause*]: *He tried to make sure that everything was OK.* [~ + *obj* + *into* + *obj*]: *The talent agent says he made her into a star.* [~ + *obj* + *obj*]:

The evidence makes you the chief suspect. **4.** [*not: be + ~-ing; ~ + obj*] to become; develop into: *Someday you'll make a good lawyer.* **5.** [*not: be + ~-ing; ~ + obj*] to be adequate or suitable for: *This table will make a good lectern.* **6.** [*~ + obj + obj*]: to appoint; name: *made her chairwoman.* **7.** [*~ + obj + root form of verb*] to force or cause (someone to do something); compel: *The pain made her cry out.* **8.** [*~ + obj*] to put in the proper condition or state; prepare: *to make a bed.* **9.** [*~ + obj*] to earn for oneself: *to make a good salary.* **10.** [*~ + obj*] to write; compose: *to make a will.* **11.** [*~ + obj*] to agree upon; arrange: *to make a deal.* **12.** [*~ + obj*] to establish; enact: *to make laws.* **13.** [*~ + obj*] to form in the mind: *to make a decision.* **14.** [*~ + obj + at + obj*] to estimate; figure: *I make the value at $1,000.* **15.** [*~ + obj*] to put together; form: *to make a matched set.* **16.** [*~ + obj; not: be + ~-ing*] to amount to; total: *Two plus two makes four.* **17.** [*~ + obj; not: be + ~-ing*] to provide: *That book makes good reading.* **18.** [*not: be + ~-ing; ~ + obj*] to be enough so as to become: *One story does not make a writer.* **19.** [*~ + obj; not: be + ~-ing*] to assure the success or fame of: *Her last book really made her reputation as a scholar.* **20.** [*~ + obj*] to reach; attain: *made admiral just before he retired from the Navy.* **21.** [*~ + obj*] to arrive in time for; catch: *I just made the plane.* **22.** [*~ + obj*] to attain a position in or on: *The novel made the bestseller list.* **23.** [*~ + obj*] to receive notice in or on: *The murder made the evening news.* **24.** [*~ + obj*] *Slang.* to have sexual intercourse with. **25.** [*~ + obj*] to score: *She made 40 points.* **26. make away with,** [*~ + away + with + obj*] to carry off; steal: *The thieves made away with all the money.* **27. make for,** [*~ + for + obj*] **a.** to move toward: *We made for shelter when we saw the clouds.* **b.** [*not: be + ~-ing*] to bring about or keep going: *A calm manner in a police officer makes for fewer arguments.* **28. make of,** [*~ + of + obj*] to judge the truth or nature of: *What do you make of that remark?* **29. make off,** [*no obj*] to run away: *The thieves made off before the police arrived.* **30. make off with,** [*~ + off + with + obj*] to carry away; steal: *The robbers made off with a million dollars in cash.* **31. make out, a.** to write out or complete, as a bill or check: [*~ + out + obj*]: *I made out the check.* [*~ + obj + out*]: *I made it out and sealed it in the envelope.* **b.** to understand; figure out the meaning of; fathom: [*~ + out + obj*]: *I can't make out this last equation.* [*~ + obj + out*]: *I can't make this out.* **c.** to see clearly enough so as to be able to read: [*~ + out + obj*]: *I can't make out his handwriting.* [*~ + obj + out*]: *I can't make it out.* **d.** to suggest or pretend (to be, or that something is the case): [*~ + obj + out + to + verb*]: *He made me out to be a liar.* [*~ + out + that clause*]: *He makes out that he is a successful businessman.* **e.** [*no obj*] to manage; succeed: *How are you making out in school?* **f.** [*no obj*] *Slang.* to engage in kissing and caressing: *making out in the back seat.* **32. make over,** to remodel; fix, change, or alter: [*~ + over + obj*]: *The carpenters made over the room as a gym.* [*~ + obj + over*]: *The beautician made her face over.* **33. make up, a.** [*~ + up + obj; usually: not: be + ~-ing*] to form; constitute: *Immigrants make up a large part of our school's population.* **b.** to prepare by putting together; compile: [*~ + up + obj*]: *Make up a list of what you'll need.* [*~ + obj + up*]: *Make a list up and send it to me.* **c.** to invent (a story or tale); concoct: [*~ + up + obj*]: *She made up that whole story.* [*~ + obj + up*]: *She made that whole story up.* **d.** [*~ + up + for + obj*] to repay; compensate: *Perhaps $50 will make up for your trouble.* **e.** [*~ + up + obj; not: be ~-ing*] to complete: *The two couples made up a foursome at golf.* **f.** to put in order; arrange: [*~ + up + obj*]: *She made up the bed.* [*~ + obj + up*]: *Make the bed up before you watch TV.* **g.** to settle; decide: [*~ + up + obj*]: *Make up your mind.* [*~ + obj + up*]: *You'll have to make your mind up soon.* **h.** to (cause to) become friends again; to (cause to) be reconciled: [*no obj*]: *finally made up after years of quarreling.* [*~ + up + obj*]: *They made up their argument.* **i.** to dress in costume and makeup: [*~ + up + obj*]: *She made up the children and sent them onstage.* [*~ + obj + up*]: *She made herself up and dashed onstage.* **j.** to provide enough so that (something) is no longer lacking: [*~ + up + obj*]: *The college will make up the difference between your loan and your tuition.* [*~ + obj + up*]: *In such cases the college will make it up.* —*n.* [*count*] **34.** the style in which something is made; form. **35.** brand: *a foreign make of car.* —***Idiom.*** **36. make as if** or **as though,** [*~ + clause*] *Informal.* pretend: *He made as if nothing bothered him.* **37. make believe,** imagine: [*no obj*]: *Kids like to make believe.* [*~ + (that) clause*]: *She made believe (that) he had won the lottery.* **38. make do,** [*no obj*] to manage with whatever is available: *If those are the only tools we have, we'll just have to make do with them.* **39. make good, a.** [*no obj*] to succeed: *These graduates will make good.* **b.** [*~ + on + obj*] to compensate for: *Will he make good on the purchases?* **c.** Also, **make good on.** [*~ + obj*] to fulfill, as a promise: *Is he someone who will make good on his promises?* **40. make it, a.** to achieve success: *He really seems to have made it: big house, good job, beautiful family.* **b.** to arrive on time: *I just made it to that meeting!* **41. make light of,** [*~ + obj*] to treat as unimportant or insignificant. **42. make like,** [*~ + obj*] *Informal.* to pretend to be or to be like: *Stop making like a clown!* **43. make love,** to have sexual relations (with): [*no obj*]: *How often couples make love is their own business.* [*~ + to + obj*]: *He wanted to make love to her right then and there.* **44. make much of,** [*~ + obj*] to treat as important: *The press tried to make much of his past.* **45. make short work of,** [*~ + obj*] to finish or dispose of quickly: *You made short work of that apple pie.* **46. on the make, a.** in pursuit of gain: *a young executive on the make.* **b.** *Slang.* in search of sexual activity: *He was constantly on the make at singles bars.* —**mak′er,** *n.* [*count*]

make′-believe′, *n.* [*noncount*] **1.** a state of pretense, esp. of an innocent kind: *a world of make-believe.* —*adj.* [*before a noun*] **2.** pretended; imaginary.

make•shift (māk′shift′) /ˈmeykˌʃɪft/ *adj.* used temporarily because nothing better is available: *a makeshift classroom.*

make•up or **make-up** (māk′up′) /ˈmeykˌʌp/ *n.* **1.** [*noncount*] cosmetics, esp. for the face or some part of it: *wearing a lot of eye makeup.* **2.** [*count; usually singular*] the manner in which someone or something is put together; composition; constitution: *the makeup of a criminal.* **3.** [*count*] an examination or the like given to compensate for a student's previous absence or failure: *The make-up was held in a huge auditorium.*

make′-work′, *n.* [*noncount*] work created to keep a person from being idle or unemployed: *Some companies give their employees make-work rather than lay them off.*

mak•ing (mā′king) /ˈmeykɪŋ/ *n.* **1.** [*noncount*] the act of a person or thing that makes, produces, etc.: *the making of dresses.* **2.** Usually, **makings.** [*plural*] the qualities necessary to develop into or become something: *has the makings of a first-rate officer.* —***Idiom.*** **3. in the making, a.** nearly ready, completed, or finished: *The experimental design is still in the making.* **b.** ready to be obtained or taken: *There is a fortune in the making for anyone who creates good software.* **4. of one's own making,** caused by oneself and not by another or others: *His problems are of his own making.*

mal-, *prefix.* *mal-* is attached to nouns and adjectives and means "bad; wrongful; ill". This meaning is found in such words as: MALADROIT, MALCONTENT, MALFUNCTION.

mal•a•chite (mal′ə kīt′) /ˈmæləˌkayt/ *n.* [*noncount*] a green mineral, an ore of copper, used for making ornaments.

mal•ad•just•ed (mal′ə jus′tid) /ˌmæləˈdʒʌstɪd/ *adj.* badly or poorly adjusted, esp. to one's social circumstances, etc.: *maladjusted to society.* —**mal′ad•just′ment,** *n.* [*noncount*] See -JUS-.

mal•a•droit (mal′ə droit′) /ˌmæləˈdrɔyt/ *adj.* lacking in skill, smoothness, or politeness; awkward. —**mal′a•droit′ly,** *adv.* —**mal′a•droit′ness,** *n.* [*noncount*]

mal•a•dy (mal′ə dē) /ˈmælədiy/ *n.* [*count*], *pl.* **-dies.** a disorder or disease of the body.

ma•laise (ma lāz′, -lez′, mə-) /mæˈleyz, -ˈlɛz, mə-/ *n.* [*noncount*] a condition of general bodily weakness or unease: *suffering from the malaise of a long, boring summer.*

mal•a•prop•ism (mal′ə prop iz′əm) /ˈmæləprɒpˌɪzəm/ *n.* **1.** [*noncount*] a confused use of words in which an appropriate word is replaced by one with similar sound but foolishly wrong meaning. **2.** [*count*] an instance of this, as in "Lead the way and we'll precede."

ma•lar•i•a (mə lâr′ē ə) /məˈlɛəriyə/ *n.* [*noncount*] a disease characterized by attacks of chills, fever, and sweating, caused by microorganisms that enter the bloodstream from the bite of a certain mosquito. —**ma•lar′i•al,** *adj.*

ma•lar•key (mə lär′kē) /məˈlɑrkiy/ *n.* [*noncount*] *Informal.* speech or writing designed to fool, mislead, or impress.

Ma•lay•sian (mə lā′zhən) /məˈleyʒən/ *n.* [*count*] **1.** a person born or living in Malaysia. *—adj.* **2.** of or relating to Malaysia.

mal•con•tent (mal′kən tent′) /ˌmælkən'tɛnt/ *adj.* **1.** not satisfied with current conditions. *—n.* [*count*] **2.** a malcontent person.

male (māl) /meyl/ *n.* [*count*] **1.** a person bearing an X and Y chromosome pair in the cells and normally having a penis, scrotum, and testicles and developing hair on the face at adolescence; a boy or man: *Males outnumber females in my school.* **2.** an organism of the sex or sexual phase that normally produces a sperm cell. *—adj.* [*usually: before a noun*] **3.** of, relating to, or being a male: *a male choir.* **4.** of or relating to a boy or man; masculine: *the male ego.* **5.** made to fit into a corresponding open or recessed part: *a male plug.* —**male′ness,** *n.* [*noncount*]

mal•e•dic•tion (mal′i dik′shən) /ˌmælɪ'dɪkʃən/ *n.* [*count*] a curse. See -DICT-.

mal•e•fac•tor (mal′ə fak′tər) /'mæləˌfæktər/ *n.* [*count*] **1.** a criminal. **2.** a person who does evil.

ma•lev•o•lent (mə lev′ə lənt) /mə'lɛvələnt/ *adj.* **1.** wishing evil or harm to others; malicious. **2.** producing harm or evil; injurious. —**ma•lev′o•lence,** *n.* [*noncount*] —**ma•lev′o•lent•ly,** *adv.* See -VOL-.

mal•fea•sance (mal fē′zəns) /mæl'fiyzəns/ *n.* [*noncount*] misconduct or wrongdoing committed esp. by a public official.

mal•for•ma•tion (mal′fôr mā′shən, -fər-) /ˌmælfɔr'meyʃən, -fər-/ *n.* [*noncount*] improper formation: *braces for malformation of the teeth.* —**mal•formed** (mal fôrmd′) /mæl'fɔrmd/ *adj.* See -FORM-.

mal•func•tion (mal fungk′shən) /mæl'fʌŋkʃən/ *n.* [*count*] **1.** failure to function properly: *They aborted the mission because of a malfunction in the torpedo.* *—v.* [*no obj*] **2.** to fail to function properly: *The torpedo malfunctioned and failed to explode.* See -FUNCT-.

mal•ice (mal′is) /'mælɪs/ *n.* [*noncount*] a desire to inflict harm or suffering on another: *His malice toward his opponent did not stop after the election.* —**ma•li•cious** (mə lish′əs) /mə'lɪʃəs/ *adj.: His malicious attempts to discredit her backfired.* —**ma•li′cious•ly,** *adv.*

ma•lign (mə lin′) /mə'layn/ *v.* [~ + *obj*] to speak harmful lies about; to slander; defame: *She maligned her ex-husband whenever she could.*

ma•lig•nan•cy (mə lig′nən sē) /mə'lɪgnənsiy/ *n.* [*noncount*] the state or condition of being malignant.

ma•lig•nant (mə lig′nənt) /mə'lɪgnənt/ *adj.* **1.** inclined to cause harm, suffering, or distress: *malignant remarks.* **2.** very dangerous in effect. **3.** tending to produce death: *a malignant tumor.*

ma•lin•ger (mə ling′gər) /mə'lɪŋgər/ *v.* [*no obj*] to pretend illness, esp. in order to avoid duty or work. —**ma•lin′ger•er,** *n.* [*count*]

mall (môl) /mɔl/ *n.* [*count*] **1.** a large area with many shops and restaurants in nearby buildings or in a single large building. **2.** a city street lined with shops and closed off to motor vehicles. **3.** a large area with shade trees used as a public walk. **4.** a strip of land separating two roadways.

mal•lard (mal′ərd) /'mælərd/ *n.* [*count*], *pl.* **-lards,** (*esp. when thought of as a group*) **-lard.** a common wild duck from which the domestic ducks are descended.

mal•le•a•ble (mal′ē ə bəl) /'mæliyəbəl/ *adj.* **1.** capable of being shaped by hammering or by pressure from rollers. **2.** adaptable; able to change or adjust: *Young children have malleable personalities.* —**mal•le•a•bil•i•ty** (mal′ē ə bil′i tē) /ˌmæliyə'bɪlɪtiy/ *n.* [*noncount*]

mal•let (mal′it) /'mælɪt/ *n.* [*count*] **1.** a hammerlike tool with an enlarged head, typically of wood, used for driving another tool. **2.** the wooden implement used to strike a ball in croquet or polo.

mal•nour•ished (mal nûr′isht, -nur′-) /mæl'nɜrɪʃt, -'nʌr-/ *adj.* poorly or improperly nourished; suffering from malnutrition.

mal•nu•tri•tion (mal′nōō trish′ən, -nyōō-) /ˌmælnuw'trɪʃən, -nyuw-/ *n.* [*noncount*] lack of proper nutrition; inadequate or unbalanced nutrition: *starving children suffering from malnutrition.*

mal•oc•clu•sion (mal′ə klōō′zhən) /ˌmælə'kluwʒən/ *n.* [*noncount*] irregular contact of opposite teeth in the upper and lower jaws: *The orthodontist said she needed braces to correct the malocclusion.*

mal•o•dor•ous (mal ō′dər əs) /mæl'owdərəs/ *adj.* having a very unpleasant odor.

mal•prac•tice (mal prak′tis) /mæl'præktɪs/ *n.* [*noncount*] behavior by a professional that is against the rules of that profession, or that causes injury or loss.

malt (môlt) /mɔlt/ *n.* **1.** [*noncount*] grain prepared by boiling and drying, used in brewing beer. **2.** [*noncount*] an alcoholic beverage, as beer, fermented from malt. **3.** [*count*] MALTED MILK (def. 2): *a vanilla malt and a chocolate malt.*

malt′ed milk′, *n.* **1.** [*noncount*] a powder made of dehydrated milk and malted cereals that can be added to water and dissolved. **2.** a beverage made from malted milk, ice cream, and flavoring: [*noncount*]: *a glass of malted milk.* [*count*]: *They ordered two malted milks, one vanilla and one chocolate.*

Mal•tese (môl tēz′, -tēs′) /mɔl'tiyz, -'tiys/ *adj., n., pl.* **-tese.** *—adj.* **1.** of or relating to Malta. **2.** of or relating to the language spoken by many of the people in Malta. *—n.* **3.** [*count*] a person born or living in Malta. **4.** [*noncount*] the language spoken by many of the people in Malta.

Mal•thu•sian (mal thōō′zhən, -zē ən) /mæl'θuwʒən, -ziyən/ *adj.* **1.** of or relating to the theories of Thomas R. Malthus, an English economist, which state that population increases faster than the means of providing food unless war, famine, or disease occurs first, or efforts are made to limit population. *—n.* [*count*] **2.** a follower of Malthus.

malt•ose (môl′tōs) /'mɔltows/ *n.* [*noncount*] a white, crystallike sugar, used chiefly as a nutrient or sweetener.

mal•treat (mal trēt′) /mæl'triyt/ *v.* [~ + *obj*] to treat or handle badly or roughly; abuse. —**mal•treat′ment,** *n.* [*noncount*]

ma•ma or **mam•ma** (mä′mə, mə mä′) /'mɑmə, mə'mɑ/ *n., pl.* **-mas.** MOTHER[1].

mam•bo (mäm′bō) /'mɑmbow/ *n., pl.* **-bos,** *v.,* **-boed, -bo•ing.** *—n.* [*count*] **1.** a ballroom dance of Caribbean origin similar to the rumba and cha-cha. *—v.* [*no obj*] **2.** to dance the mambo.

mam•mal (mam′əl) /'mæməl/ *n.* [*count*] a warm-blooded animal with a backbone, having a covering of hair on some or most of the body, a heart with four chambers, and nourishing its newborn with its milk. —**mam•ma•li•an** (mə mā′lē ən, -māl′yən) /mə'meyliyən, -'meylyən/ *adj.*

mam•ma•ry (mam′ə rē) /'mæməriy/ *adj.* [*before a noun*] of or relating to the breasts, or the glands that a female mammal uses to feed her young with milk.

mam•mo•gram (mam′ə gram′) /'mæməˌgræm/ *n.* [*count*] an x-ray photograph obtained by mammography.

mam•mog•ra•phy (ma mog′rə fē) /mæ'mɒgrəfiy/ *n.* [*noncount*] x-ray photography of a breast, esp. to detect tumors.

mam•moth (mam′əth) /'mæməθ/ *n.* [*count*] **1.** an extinct elephant with long hair and tusks. *—adj.* [*often: before a noun*] **2.** very large; enormous: *a mammoth budget.*

man (man) /mæn/ *n., pl.* **men** (men) /mɛn/ *v.,* **manned, man•ning,** *interj.* *—n.* **1.** [*count*] an adult male person, as distinguished from a boy or a woman: *The little boy had grown up to be a handsome man.* **2.** [*count*] a human being, or a person without regard to sex: *All men are created equal in the eyes of the law.* **3.** [*noncount*] the human individual as representing the species, without reference to sex; the human race; humankind: *It is written that man does not live by bread alone.* **4.** [*count*] a husband. **5.** [*count*] a male lover or sweetheart. **6.** [*count*] a male having qualities considered properly masculine: *The four years in the army made a man of him.* **7.** [*count*] a male servant or attendant. **8.** [*count*] *Slang.* male friend; ally: *Hey, it's my main man.* **9.** [*count*] *Slang.* (used as a term of familiar address): *Hey, man, take it easy.* **10.** [*count*] a playing piece used in certain games, as checkers. *—interj.* **11.** used to express astonishment, delight, or other strong emotion: *Man, what a car!* *—v.* [~ + *obj*] **12.** to supply with people, as for service: *to man the ship.* **13.** to take one's place at, as to defend or operate: *There were enough volunteers to man the phones.* ***—Idiom.*** **14. man to man,** speaking freely or honestly: [*adverb*]: *They spoke man to man.* [*adjective*]: *They had a man-to-man talk.* **15. one's own man,** free from restrictions; independent: *Now that he has a business he feels he is his own man.* **16. to a man,** including everyone: *The battalion was annihilated to a man.*

-man, *suffix.* *-man* is used to form nouns with the meaning "person, or man, who is or does (something connected with the noun base)": *mail + -man → mailman (= person who delivers mail).*

-man-[1], *root.* *-man-* comes from Latin, where it has the meaning "hand." This meaning is found in such words as: AMANUENSIS, LEGERDEMAIN, MAINTAIN, MANACLE, MANAGE, MANEUVER, MANUAL, MANUFACTURE, MANURE, MANUSCRIPT.

-man-², *root.* *-man-* comes from Latin, where it has the meaning "stay; to last or remain." This meaning is found in such words as: IMPERMANENT, PERMANENT, REMAIN.

man•a•cle (man′ə kəl) /ˈmænəkəl/ *n., v.,* **-cled, -cling.** —*n.* [*count*] **1.** a handcuff. —*v.* [~ + *obj*] **2.** to handcuff; fetter. **3.** to keep held back; restrain. See -MAN-¹.

man•age (man′ij) /ˈmænɪdʒ/ *v.,* **-aged, -ag•ing. 1.** to succeed in dealing with; contrive: [~ + *to* + *verb*]: *They managed to see the governor.* [~ + *obj*]: *I don't know how, but he managed it.* **2.** [~ + *obj*] **a.** to take charge of; supervise; control: *to manage a business.* **b.** to handle the career or functioning of: *to manage a performer.* **3.** [*no obj*] to function; get along: *We managed without a car during our stay in the city.* —**man′age•a•ble,** *adj.: Those children are old enough to be easily manageable.* See -MAN-¹.

man•age•ment (man′ij mənt) /ˈmænɪdʒmənt/ *n.* **1.** [*noncount*] the act or process of managing: *courses in management.* **2.** [*count*] the persons directing a business; executives: *Upper management should trim its staff.* See -MAN-¹.

man•ag•er (man′i jər) /ˈmænɪdʒər/ *n.* [*count*] **1.** one who manages a business or one of its parts. **2.** one who directs or assists in the activities of an athlete or team. **3.** a person who manages another's career: *the rock star's manager.*

man•a•ge•ri•al (man′ə jēr′ē əl) /ˌmænəˈdʒɪəriyəl/ *adj.* [*before a noun*] of or relating to a manager or to management: *a managerial post.* See -MAN-¹.

ma•ña•na (mä nyä′nä) /mɑˈnyɑnɑ/ *n.* [*count*], *pl.* ***-nas,*** *adv. Spanish.* tomorrow: *You'll wind up spending a lot of mañanas worrying about the yesterdays you never had.*

man•a•tee (man′ə tē′, man′ə tē′) /ˈmænəˌtiy, ˌmænəˈtiy/ *n.* [*count*], *pl.* **-tees.** a plant-eating water mammal of the Caribbean and W Africa, having front flippers and a broad, spoon-shaped tail.

-mand-, *root.* *-mand-* comes from Latin, where it has the meaning "order." This meaning is found in such words as: COMMAND, COUNTERMAND, DEMAND, MANDATE, MANDATORY, REMAND.

man•da•rin (man′də rin) /ˈmændərɪn/ *n.* [*count*] **1.** a member of an influential class; a government official or bureaucrat: *The mandarins guessed wrong about the reaction of the people to a tax cut.* **2. a.** a small, spiny citrus tree of China, bearing flattish, orange-yellow loose-skinned fruit. **b.** this fruit, some varieties of which are called tangerines.

man•date (man′dāt) /ˈmændeyt/ *n., v.,* **-dat•ed, -dat•ing.** —*n.* [*count*] **1.** authorization to act in a particular way given by the people to an elected representative: *The new president received a clear mandate to spend money.* **2.** any authoritative order or command: *a royal mandate.* —*v.* [~ + *obj*] **3.** to authorize (a particular action): *The principal mandated the new dress code.* See -MAND-.

man•da•to•ry (man′də tôr′ē, -tōr′ē) /ˈmændəˌtɔriy, -ˌtowriy/ *adj.* ordered by an authority: *mandatory budget cuts.* See -MAND-.

man•di•ble (man′də bəl) /ˈmændəbəl/ *n.* [*count*] the bone part of the lower jaw of animals with backbones. —**man•dib•u•lar** (man dib′yə lər) /mænˈdɪbyələr/ *adj.*

man•do•lin (man′dl in, man′dl in′) /ˈmændl̩ɪn, ˌmændl̩ˈɪn/ *n.* [*count*] an eight-stringed musical instrument with a pear-shaped wooden body and a neck with frets.

man•drake (man′drāk, -drik) /ˈmændreyk, -drɪk/ *n.* [*count*] a narcotic plant with a fleshy, forked root somewhat resembling a human body.

man•drill (man′dril) /ˈmændrɪl/ *n.* [*count*] a large W African baboon.

mane (mān) /meyn/ *n.* [*count*] **1.** the long thick hair around or at the back of the neck of some animals, as the horse or lion. **2.** long luxuriant hair on the head of a person: *Her mane of black hair flowed in the wind.*

man′-eat′er, *n.* [*count*] **1.** an animal that eats or is said to eat human flesh. **2.** a cannibal. —**man′-eat′ing,** *adj.* [*before a noun*]

ma•nège or **ma•nege** (ma nezh′, -nāzh′) /mæˈnɛʒ, -ˈneyʒ/ *n.* [*noncount*] the art of training and riding horses. See -MAN-¹.

ma•neu•ver (mə noo͞′vər) /məˈnuwvər/ *n.* [*count*] **1.** a planned movement of troops, warships, etc. **2. maneuvers,** [*plural*] a series of military exercises used as practice for war: *The troops are out on maneuvers.* **3.** a clever or skillful movement, action, or trick; a crafty tactic; a ploy: *another maneuver to gain control of the company.* —*v.* **4.** to move or change the position of by a maneuver: [~ + *obj*]: *She maneuvered the truck around the fallen tree.* [*no obj*]: *He maneuvered out of the way of the fallen tree.* **5.** [*no obj*] to scheme; make a plot; intrigue: *He maneuvered for the job for a year.* Also, *esp. Brit.,* **manoeuvre.** See -MAN-¹.

ma•neu•ver•a•ble (mə noo͞′vər ə bəl) /məˈnuwvərəbəl/ *adj.* that can be maneuvered: *a maneuverable car that is easy to park in tight spaces.* —**ma•neu•ver•a•bil•i•ty** (mə noo͞′vər ə bil′i tē) /məˌnuwvərəˈbɪlɪtiy/ *n.* [*noncount*]: *Maneuverability has been improved with the new steering mechanism.* See -MAN-¹.

man•ful (man′fəl) /ˈmænfəl/ *adj.* [*before a noun*] having or showing boldness, courage, or strength. —**man′ful•ly,** *adv.: He struggled manfully with the huge load.*

man•ga•nese (mang′gə nēs′, -nēz′) /ˈmæŋgəˌniys, -ˌniyz/ *n.* [*noncount*] a hard, easily broken, grayish white, metallic element used chiefly in strengthening steel.

mange (mānj) /meyndʒ/ *n.* [*noncount*] a skin disease affecting animals, causing scabs on the skin and loss of hair.

man•ger (mān′jər) /ˈmeyndʒər/ *n.* [*count*] a box or open container in a stable or barn from which animals eat.

man•gle (mang′gəl) /ˈmæŋgəl/ *v.* [~ + *obj*], **-gled, -gling. 1.** [*usually: be* + ~] to injure severely or mutilate by cutting, tearing, or crushing: *mangled bodies in the wreckage.* **2.** to spoil; ruin; mar badly: *to mangle a paper by careless editing.*

man•go (mang′gō) /ˈmæŋgow/ *n., pl.* **-goes, -gos. 1.** the sweet yellow or orange fruit of a tree of the cashew family that grows in hot climates: [*count*]: *Each mango costs a few cents in the tropics.* [*noncount*]: *Blend the mango into the juice.* **2.** [*count*] the tree itself.

man•grove (mang′grōv, man′-) /ˈmæŋgrowv, ˈmæn-/ *n.* [*count*] a tree or shrub growing in hot climates, often a low tree growing in marshes or swamps, noted for its roots that grow above ground and interlace with others.

man•gy (mān′jē) /ˈmeyndʒiy/ *adj.,* **-gi•er, -gi•est. 1.** having, caused by, or like the disease mange: *a mangy dog.* **2.** dirty and run-down; unclean: *a mangy cabin.* —**man′gi•ness,** *n.* [*noncount*]

man•han•dle (man′han′dl, man han′dl) /ˈmænˌhændl̩, mænˈhændl̩/ *v.* [~ + *obj*], **-dled, -dling. 1.** to handle roughly. **2.** to move by human strength alone: *We manhandled the piano up the five flights of stairs and into the tiny apartment.*

man•hole (man′hōl′) /ˈmænˌhowl/ *n.* [*count*] a hole, usually with a cover, giving access to a sewer, drain, steam boiler, etc.

man•hood (man′ho͝od) /ˈmænhʊd/ *n.* [*noncount*] **1.** the state or time of being a man. **2.** men thought of as a group.

man′-hour′, *n.* [*count*] a unit of measurement based on an ideal amount of work accomplished by one person in one hour: *increases in man-hours during the holiday seasons.*

man•hunt (man′hunt′) /ˈmænˌhʌnt/ *n.* [*count*] an intensive search for a person, esp. a criminal.

ma•ni•a (mā′nē ə, mān′yə) /ˈmeyniyə, ˈmeynyə/ *n., pl.* **-ni•as. 1.** excitement for something; craze: [*count*]: *a mania for rock stars.* [*noncount*]: *car mania.* **2.** [*noncount*] a mental illness in which the victim suffers from over-excitedness, too much activity and talkativeness, and confused judgment.

-mania, *suffix.* *-mania* is attached to roots to form nouns with the meaning "great or strong enthusiasm for (the element of the root)": *biblio-* (= *book*) + *-mania* → *bibliomania (= excessive or strong interest in or enthusiasm for books).*

ma•ni•ac (mā′nē ak′) /ˈmeyniyˌæk/ *n.* [*count*] **1.** an insane person; lunatic. **2.** a person who is very enthusiastic or overly excited (about something): *a maniac about neatness.* —**ma•ni•a•cal** (mə nī′ə kəl) /məˈnayəkəl/ *adj.* —**ma•ni′a•cal•ly,** *adv.*

man•ic (man′ik) /ˈmænɪk/ *adj.* **1.** relating to or affected by mania: *manic behavior during a crisis.* **2.** overly excited or enthusiastic: *a manic person when it comes to details.*

man′ic-de•pres′sive (də pres′iv) /dəˈprɛsɪv/ *adj.* **1.** suffering from a condition in which there are periods of excitement and confidence followed by depression and anxiety. —*n.* [*count*] **2.** a person suffering from such a disorder.

man•i•cure (man′i kyo͝or′) /ˈmænɪˌkyʊr/ *n., v.,* **-cured, -cur•ing.** —*n.* [*count*] **1.** a cosmetic treatment of the hands or fingernails. —*v.* [~ + *obj*] **2.** to apply manicure treatment to. **3.** to trim or cut very carefully: *to manicure a lawn.* —**man′i•cur′ist,** *n.* [*count*] See -CURA-, -MAN-[1].

man•i•fest (man′ə fest′) /ˈmænəˌfɛst/ *adj.* **1.** readily and easily seen; evident; plain: *a manifest error.* —*v.* [~ + *obj*] **2.** to make clear or evident: *Hepatitis manifests itself with yellowed eyes and skin, and darkened urine.* —*n.* [*count*] **3.** a list of the cargo or passengers carried by a vessel. —**man′i•fest′ly,** *adv.*

man•i•fes•ta•tion (man′ə fə stā′shən, -fe-) /ˌmænəfəˈsteyʃən, -fɛ-/ *n.* **1.** [*noncount*] an act of manifesting; the state of being manifested. **2.** [*count*] outward or visible indication of something: *a manifestation of the disease.*

man•i•fes•to (man′ə fes′tō) /ˌmænəˈfɛstow/ *n.* [*count*], *pl.* **-tos, -toes.** a public statement of one's intentions or purposes: *His party manifesto called for increased military spending.*

man•i•fold (man′ə fōld′) /ˈmænəˌfowld/ *adj.* **1.** of many kinds; having many different parts: *manifold duties.* —*n.* [*count*] **2.** a fitting with openings for directing the flow of liquids or gases, as in the exhaust system of an automobile.

man•i•kin or **man•ni•kin** (man′i kin) /ˈmænɪkɪn/ *n.* [*count*] **1.** a very little man; dwarf; pygmy. **2.** MANNEQUIN.

ma•nil•a (mə nil′ə) /məˈnɪlə/ *adj.* [*before a noun*] made of strong, often light brownish-yellow paper or fiber: *Put the report in a manila folder.*

man′ in the street′, *n.* [*count*] an ordinary person; average citizen: *Ask the man in the street this question: are you better off than you were four years ago?*

man•i•oc (man′ē ok′, mā′nē-) /ˈmæniyˌɒk, ˈmeyniy-/ *n.* CASSAVA.

ma•nip•u•la•ble (mə nip′yə lə bəl) /məˈnɪpyələbəl/ *adj.* capable of being manipulated: *manipulable children who are eager to please adults.* See -MAN-[1].

ma•nip•u•late (mə nip′yə lāt′) /məˈnɪpyəˌleyt/ *v.* [~ + *obj*], **-lat•ed, -lat•ing. 1.** to manage or influence skillfully and often unfairly: *He could manipulate people's feelings to get his way.* **2.** to handle or use, esp. with skill: *He manipulated a large tractor easily by the age of ten.* **3.** to adapt or change (accounts, etc.) to suit one's purpose: *manipulated the sales figures to "create" a huge profit last year.* —**ma•nip•u•la•tion** (mə nip′yə lā′shən) /məˌnɪpyəˈleyʃən/ *n.* [*noncount*]: *capable of manipulation to get what he wants.* [*count*]: *the craftsman's manipulations of his tools.* —**ma•nip•u•la•tive** (mə nip′yə lā′tiv, -lə tiv) /məˈnɪpyəˌleytɪv, -lətɪv/ *adj.* —**ma•nip′u•la′tor,** *n.* [*count*] See -MAN-[1].

man•kind (man′kīnd′) /ˈmænˈkaynd/ *n.* [*noncount*] **1.** human beings thought of as a group without reference to sex; humankind: *Mankind is not ready to explore the stars.* **2.** men as distinguished from women.

man•ly (man′lē) /ˈmænliy/ *adj.,* **-li•er, -li•est. 1.** having qualities traditionally thought of as belonging to or relating to men; not feminine or boyish: *manly acts of courage.* **2.** relating to or suitable for males: *manly sports.* —**man′li•ness,** *n.* [*noncount*]

man′-made′, *adj.* produced by humans; not resulting from natural processes: *man-made pollution.*

man•na (man′ə) /ˈmænə/ *n.* [*noncount*] **1.** (in the Bible) the food miraculously supplied to the Israelites in the wilderness. **2.** a sudden or unexpected source of help or good fortune.

manned (mand) /mænd/ *adj.* carrying or operated by one or more persons: *a manned spacecraft.*

man•ne•quin or **man•i•kin** or **man•ni•kin** (man′i-kin) /ˈmænɪkɪn/ *n.* [*count*] **1.** a solid representation of the human form used in window displays, etc.; a dummy. **2.** one employed to model clothing.

man•ner (man′ər) /ˈmænər/ *n.* [*count*] **1.** a way of doing, being done, or happening: *In what manner were you notified?* **2. manners,** [*plural*] **a.** the ways of living of a people, class, or period: *Victorian manners.* **b.** ways of behaving with reference to polite standards: *She has such good manners.* **3.** a person's outward appearance when doing or behaving: *a charming manner.* **4.** a characteristic or customary style; fashion: *built in the 19th-century manner.* **5.** [*singular; but used with a singular or plural verb*] kind; sort: *What manner of man is he? All manner of things were happening.*

man•nered (man′ərd) /ˈmænərd/ *adj.* **1.** having manners of a specific kind (usually used in combination): *ill-mannered.* **2.** affected; having a false appearance: *a mannered walk.*

man•ner•ism (man′ə riz′əm) /ˈmænəˌrɪzəm/ *n.* [*count*] a habitual or characteristic manner or way of doing something: *his annoying mannerism of picking at his teeth while talking.*

man•ner•ly (man′ər lē) /ˈmænərliy/ *adj.* having or showing good manners; courteous.

man•nish (man′ish) /ˈmænɪʃ/ *adj.* being typical or suggestive of a man rather than a woman. —**man′nish•ly,** *adv.: She was dressed mannishly in a suit and tie.* —**man′nish•ness,** *n.* [*noncount*]

ma•noeu•vre (mə nōō′vər) /məˈnuwvər/ *n., v.,* **-vred, -vring.** *Chiefly Brit.* MANEUVER.

man•or (man′ər) /ˈmænər/ *n.* [*count*] **1.** an estate owned by a king or nobleman. **2.** (in England) the house and land of a lord. **3.** the main house on an estate, etc. —**ma•nor•i•al,** (mə nôr′ē əl, -nōr-), /məˈnɔriyəl -nowr-/ *adj.*

man•pow•er (man′pou′ər) /ˈmænˌpawər/ *n.* [*noncount*] power in terms of people available for work or military service.

man•qué (mäng kā′) /mɑŋˈkey/ *adj.* [*after a noun*] unsuccessful; unfulfilled: *a poet manqué.*

manse (mans) /mæns/ *n.* [*count*] **1.** the house occupied by a minister or parson. **2.** a handsome, stately mansion.

man•serv•ant (man′sûr′vənt) /ˈmænˌsɜrvənt/ *n.* [*count*], *pl.* **men•serv•ants.** a male servant.

man•sion (man′shən) /ˈmænʃən/ *n.* [*count*] **1.** a very large or stately house as a place to live. **2.** Often, **mansions.** [*plural*] *Chiefly Brit.* APARTMENT HOUSE.

man′-sized′ or **man′-size′,** *adj.* big; generous: *a man-sized sandwich.*

man•slaugh•ter (man′slô′tər) /ˈmænˌslɔtər/ *n.* [*noncount*] the unlawful killing of a human being in which there is no prior intent to kill.

man•tel or **man•tle** (man′tl) /ˈmæntl̩/ *n.* [*count*] **1.** a construction that frames the opening of a fireplace. **2.** a shelf above a fireplace opening. Also called **man•tel•piece, man•tle•piece** (man′tl pēs′) /ˈmæntl̩ˌpiys/.

man•til•la (man til′ə, -tē′ə) /mænˈtɪlə, -ˈtiyə/ *n.* [*count*], *pl.* **-las.** a woman's head scarf worn over the back and shoulders, esp. in Spain or Latin America.

man•tis (man′tis) /ˈmæntɪs/ *n.* [*count*], *pl.* **-tis•es, -tes** (-tēz). /-tiyz/ an insect having a long body and typically holding the forelegs in an upraised position as if in prayer.

man•tle (man′tl) /ˈmæntl̩/ *n.* [*count*] **1.** a cloak without sleeves. **2.** something that covers, surrounds, or conceals: *the mantle of darkness.* **3.** the portion of the earth, about 1800 mi. (2900 km) thick, between the crust and the core. **4.** a small hood that does not burn, used in certain lanterns, that gives off a brilliant light when placed around a flame. **5.** [*usually singular*] the responsibility or duties of a certain position: *assumed the mantle of leadership.* **6.** MANTEL.

man•tra (man′trə, män′-) /ˈmæntrə, ˈmɑn-/ also **man•tram** (-trəm) /-trəm/ *n.* [*count*], *pl.* **-tras** also **-trams. 1.** (in Hinduism and Buddhism) a sacred word or formula repeated as a prayer or to help one meditate. **2.** any often repeated word or phrase; a slogan. —**man•tric** (man′trik) /ˈmæntrɪk/ *adj.*

man•u•al (man′yōō əl) /ˈmænyuwəl/ *adj.* **1.** [*before a noun*]operated by hand rather than mechanically: *a manual gearshift.* **2.** involving or requiring human effort; physical: *manual labor.* **3.** of or relating to the hands. —*n.* [*count*] **4.** a book giving instructions on how something works or on how to do something: *a computer manual.* —**man′u•al•ly,** *adv.: When the automatic devices for the landing gear failed, he tried to lower it manually.* See -MAN-[1].

man•u•fac•ture (man′yə fak′chər) /ˌmænyəˈfæktʃər/ *v.,* **-tured, -tur•ing,** *n.* —*v.* [~ + *obj*] **1.** to make or produce by hand or machinery, esp. on a large scale: *The company manufactures hundreds of handguns every day.* **2.** to work up (material) into form for use: *to manufacture cotton.* **3.** to make up (something untrue): *to manufacture an excuse.* —*n.* [*noncount*] **4.** the making of goods or products by manual labor or by machinery, esp. on a large scale: *the manufacture of cars.* **5.** the making of something: *the manufacture of body cells.* —**man′u•fac′tur•er,** *n.* [*count*] See -FAC-, -MAN-[1].

ma•nure (mə nŏŏr′, -nyŏŏr′) /məˈnʊr, -ˈnyʊr/ *n.* [*noncount*] solid waste material from animals, used as a substance to fertilize soil. See -MAN-[1].

man•u•script (man′yə skript′) /ˈmænyəˌskrɪpt/ *n.* [*count*] **1.** a written, typewritten, or computer-produced piece of writing before being set in type: *handed in his manuscript late.* **2.** a piece of writing on parchment or paper before books were invented: *ancient and forgotten manuscripts.* See -MAN-[1], -SCRIB-.

man•y (men′ē) /'mɛniy/ *adj.,* **more** (môr, mōr) /mɔr, mowr/ **most** (mōst) /mowst/ *n., pron.* **—adj. 1.** [*before a plural noun*] forming a large number; numerous: *many people.* **2.** [*~ + a + singular count noun*] noting each one of a large number: *For many a day it rained.* **—n.** [*count*] **3.** [*a + adjective + ~ + of the + plural noun*] a large number of persons or things: *A good many of the beggars were blind.* **4. the many,** [*plural; used with a plural verb*] the greater part of humankind: *The needs of the many outweighed the needs of the few.* **—pron.** [*used with a plural verb*] **5.** many persons or things: *Many were unable to attend. Many of us dislike your new policies.* **—*Idiom.* 6. many a time,** again and again; frequently.

map (map) /mæp/ *n., v.,* **mapped, map•ping.** **—n.** [*count*] **1.** a drawing on a flat surface, of parts or features of a place, as of the earth: *The map showed all the city streets.* See illustration at SCHOOL. **—v. 2.** [*~ + obj*] to represent or draw on or as if on a map: *He mapped the surrounding terrain.* **3. map out,** to sketch or plan (something) out in detail: [*~ + out + obj*]: *to map out a new career.* [*~ + obj + out*]: *took some time to map it out.* **—*Idiom.* 4. off the map,** out of existence: *Whole cities were wiped off the map by the tidal wave.* **5. on the map,** in or into a position of importance: *The new casino put our town on the map.* **—map′mak•er,** *n.* [*count*]

ma•ple (mā′pəl) /'meypəl/ *n.* **1.** [*count*] any of numerous trees or shrubs grown for ornament, for timber, or for sap. **2.** [*noncount*] the wood of the maple. **3.** [*noncount*] the flavor of maple syrup or maple sugar.

ma′ple sug′ar, *n.* [*noncount*] a yellowish brown sugar produced by boiling down maple syrup.

ma′ple syr′up, *n.* [*noncount*] a syrup produced by partially boiling down the sap of the sugar maple.

mar (mär) /mɑr/ *v.* [*~ + obj*], **marred, mar•ring.** to damage the attractiveness of; spoil: *The strip mining area mars the beauty of the mountains.*

Mar or **Mar.,** an abbreviation of: March.

mar•a•bou also **mar•a•bout,** (mar′ə bo͞o′) /'mærə,buw/ *n., pl.* **-bous. 1.** [*count*] a stork of sub-Saharan Africa that eats dead animals. **2.** [*noncount*] material made from the feathers of marabous and used to trim women's hats and clothing.

ma•rac•a (mə rä′kə, -rak′ə) /mə'rɑkə, -'rækə/ *n.* [*count*], *pl.* **-rac•as.** a gourd-shaped rattle filled with seeds or pebbles and used as a rhythm instrument.

mar′a•schi′no cher′ry (mar′ə skē′nō, -shē′-) /,mærə'skiynow, -'ʃiy-/ *n.* [*count*] a cherry kept in sweet syrupy water, used esp. in cocktails.

mar•a•thon (mar′ə thon′, -thən) /'mærə,θɒn, -θən/ *n.* [*count*] **1.** a foot race over a course measuring 26 mi. 385 yd. (42 km 352 m). **2.** any long-distance race. **3.** a long contest or event requiring great endurance: *a dance marathon.* **—mar′a•thon′er,** *n.* [*count*]

ma•raud (mə rôd′) /mə'rɔd/ *v.* to carry out raids: [*no obj*]: *Vikings marauding along the coasts of England.* [*~ + obj*]: *They marauded villages along the coast.* **—ma•raud′er,** *n.* [*count*] **—ma•raud′ing,** *adj.* [*before a noun*]: *marauding pirates.*

mar•ble (mär′bəl) /'mɑrbəl/ *n.* **1.** [*noncount*] limestone that has been changed into a hard rock, used in sculpture and in buildings: *columns of beautiful marble.* **2.** [*noncount*] something resembling marble, as in hardness: *a heart of marble.* **3.** [*count*] a little ball usually made of glass for use in games: *The marbles spilled onto the floor.* **4. marbles,** [*noncount; used with a singular verb*] a game for children played with marbles in a marked area on the ground. **5. marbles,** [*plural*] *Slang.* wits; common sense: *Have you lost all your marbles?* **—adj.** [*before a noun*] **6.** consisting of or resembling marble: *marble statues.*

mar•bled (mär′bəld) /'mɑrbəld/ *adj.* having a pattern of, or colored like, the grainy or streaked colors of marble.

mar•bling (mär′bling) /'mɑrblɪŋ/ *n.* [*noncount*] **1.** patterns or markings that resemble those of marble. **2.** the intermixture of fat with lean in a cut of meat.

march (märch) /mɑrtʃ/ *v.* **1.** [*no obj*] to walk with regular steps, esp. in step with others: *The soldiers marched down the street.* **2.** [*no obj*] to proceed in a deliberate manner: *She marched off to bed.* **3.** [*no obj*] to go forward or advance: *Time marches on.* **4.** [*no obj*] to take part in an organized march: *They marched for civil rights.* **5.** [*~ + obj*] to cause to march: *took her arm and marched her out the door.* **—n.** [*count*] **6.** the act of marching: *daily marches in the Army.* **7.** the distance covered in a single period of marching: *a day's march.* **8.** [*usually singular*] advance; progress: *the march of science.* **9.** a piece of music with a rhythm suited to go with marching. **10.** a procession organized as a protest or demonstration: *a march on Washington.* **—march′er,** *n.* [*count*]

March (märch) /mɑrtʃ/ *n.* [*proper noun*] the third month of the year, containing 31 days. *Abbr.:* Mar.

mar•chion•ess (mär′shə nis, mär′shə nes′) /'mɑrʃənɪs, ,mɑrʃə'nɛs/ *n.* [*count*] **1.** the wife or widow of a marquess. **2.** a woman holding a rank equal to that of a marquess.

mare[1] (mâr) /mɛər/ *n.* [*count*] a female horse or donkey.

ma•re[2] (mär′ā, mâr′ē) /'mɑrey, 'mɛəriy/ *n.* [*count*], *pl.* **ma•ri•a** (mär′ē ə, mâr′-) /'mɑriyə, 'mɛər-/. a large, dark plain found on the moon.

mar•ga•rine (mär′jər in, -jə rēn′) /'mɑrdʒərɪn, -dʒə,riyn/ *n.* [*noncount*] a butterlike product made of vegetable oils: *spread some margarine on his toast.*

mar•gin (mär′jin) /'mɑrdʒɪn/ *n.* [*count*] **1.** the blank space around the printed matter on a page: *Leave a margin of one inch on each side of your essay.* **2.** a border; edge: *the margin of the forest; living on the margins of society.* **3.** an amount allowed beyond what is necessary: *no margin for error.* **4.** an amount or degree of difference: *to win by a margin of three votes.*

mar•gin•al (mär′jə nəl) /'mɑrdʒənəl/ *adj.* **1.** of, relating to, or located in a margin: *marginal notes.* **2.** barely adequate: *a marginal student.* **—mar′gin•al•ly,** *adv.*: *He improved only marginally.*

mar•gi•na•li•a (mär′jə nā′lē ə, -nāl′yə) /,mɑrdʒə'neyliyə, -'neylyə/ *n.* [*plural; used with a plural verb*] marginal notes, as in a manuscript.

ma•ri•a•chi (mär′ē ä′chē) /,mɑriy'ɑtʃiy/ *n., pl.* **-chis. 1.** [*count*] a Mexican band made up of street musicians. **2.** [*count*] a member of a mariachi. **3.** [*noncount*] the traditional Mexican music played by a mariachi.

mar•i•gold (mar′i gōld′) /'mærɪ,gowld/ *n.* [*count*] a plant having golden or orange flowers and strong-scented leaves.

ma•ri•jua•na or **ma•ri•hua•na** (mar′ə wä′nə) /,mærə'wɑnə/ *n.* [*noncount*] **1.** the dried leaves and flowers of the hemp plant used esp. as a drug. **2.** HEMP (def. 1).

ma•rim•ba (mə rim′bə) /mə'rɪmbə/ *n.* [*count*], *pl.* **-bas.** a musical instrument made up of a set of different-sized wooden bars that are struck with small hammers.

ma•ri•na (mə rē′nə) /mə'riynə/ *n.* [*count*], *pl.* **-nas.** a boat basin where small boats can dock and be serviced.

mar•i•nade (*n.* mar′ə nād′; *v.* mar′ə nād′) / *n.* ,mærə'neyd; *v.* 'mærə,neyd/ *n., v.,* **-nad•ed, -nad•ing.** **—n. 1.** a liquid mixture in which food is soaked before cooking: [*noncount*]: *chicken marinade.* [*count*]: *a marinade of olive oil and wine vinegar.* **—v. 2.** to marinate.

mar•i•nate (mar′ə nāt′) /'mærə,neyt/ *v.,* **-nat•ed, -nat•ing.** (of food) to (cause to) be soaked in a marinade: [*~ + obj*]: *Marinate the stew meat overnight.* [*no obj*]: *Allow the meat to marinate overnight.* **—mar•i•na•tion** (mar′ə-nā′shən) /,mærə'neyʃən/ *n.* [*noncount*]

ma•rine (mə rēn′) /mə'riyn/ *adj.* [*before a noun*] **1.** of or relating to the sea: *marine vegetation.* **2.** of or relating to shipping by sea. **—n.** [*count; sometimes: Marine*] **3.** a member of the U.S. Marine Corps.

Marine′ Corps′, *n.* [*proper noun; usually: the + ~*] a branch of the U.S. Navy trained to make sea-launched assaults on land targets: *The Marine Corps made its first landing on this beach.*

mar•i•ner (mar′ə nər) /'mærənər/ *n.* [*count*] a person who directs or assists in the sailing of a ship; a sailor.

mar•i•on•ette (mar′ē ə net′) /,mæriyə'nɛt/ *n.* [*count*] a puppet moved by strings attached to its jointed limbs.

mar•i•tal (mar′i tl) /'mærɪtl/ *adj.* [*before a noun*] of or relating to marriage: *marital vows.* **—mar′i•tal•ly,** *adv.*

mar•i•time (mar′i tim′) /'mærɪ,taym/ *adj.* [*before a noun*] **1.** of or relating to navigation. **2.** of or relating to the sea: *maritime weather.*

mar•jo•ram (mär′jər əm) /'mɑrdʒərəm/ *n.* [*noncount*] a sweet-smelling herb of the mint family.

mark[1] (märk) /mɑrk/ *n.* [*count*] **1.** a visible impression on a surface, as a line or spot: *had a mark on her face from the scratch.* **2.** a symbol used in writing or printing: *a punctuation mark.* **3.** something that indicates something else; a token: *to bow as a mark of respect.* **4.** a noticeable influence; imprint: *The experience left its mark on her.* See *make one's mark* below. **5.** something typical or characteristic of something else; a trait: *a mark of nobility.* **6.** a device or symbol serving to identify, etc.: *The peasant put his mark on the document.* **7.** TRADE-

MARK. **8. a.** a symbol used in rating a student's achievement; grade: *Her mark was an A.* **b.** Often, **marks.** [*plural*] any evaluative rating: *We gave him high marks for trying so hard.* **9.** an object or sign serving to indicate position, as a point reached on a scale: *I finally reached the halfway mark of the book.* **10.** a standard of merit: *His work was clearly not up to the mark.* **11.** a target; goal: *to miss the mark.* **12. a.** an object of cruel laughter: *The short, pudgy boy was an easy mark for bullies.* **b.** the victim of a swindle: *The banker was the mark for the con artists.* **13.** the starting line in a race: *"On your mark...get set...go!"* **—v. 14.** [~ + *obj*] to be a distinguishing feature of: *a day marked by sadness.* **15.** to make or put a mark or marks (on): [~ + *obj*]: *She marked the wall with her greasy glove.* [*no obj*]: *That soft wood surface marks too easily.* **16.** [~ + *obj*] to give a grade to: *When will you mark the exams?* **17.** [~ + *obj*] to serve as a sign or signal of; to indicate: *That day marked the end of a career.* **18.** [~ + *obj*] to label with indications of quality: *to mark merchandise.* **19.** [~ + *obj*] to form by or as if by marks: *to mark out a plan of attack.* **20.** [~ + *obj*] to designate by or as if by marks: *He marked the sections that he wanted to delete.* **21.** [~ + *obj*] to set apart beforehand: *clearly marked for greatness.* **22.** [~ + *obj*] to give attention to: *Mark my words; she'll be famous one day.* **23. mark down, a.** to reduce the price of: [~ + *down* + *obj*]: *marked down the prices almost 30%.* [~ + *obj* + *down*]: *They had marked the prices down.* **b.** to make a note of in writing: [~ + *down* + *obj*]: *We'd better mark down the sizes.* [~ + *obj* + *down*]: *We'd better mark them down.* **24. mark off, a.** to mark the dimensions or boundaries of: [~ + *off* + *obj*]: *marked off the parade route with stripes.* [~ + *obj* + *off*]: *They marked it off with yellow tape.* **b.** to write a line on or through some item: [~ + *off* + *obj*]: *He marked off each name on the list.* [~ + *obj* + *off*]: *He marked them off one by one.* **25. mark up, a.** to mar or ruin the appearance of with marks: [~ + *up* + *obj*]: *Don't mark up the wall!* [~ + *obj* + *up*]: *Someone marked the painting up when they vandalized the museum.* **b.** to mark with notations or symbols: [~ + *up* + *obj*]: *Teachers shouldn't mark up a student's paper too much.* [~ + *obj* + *up*]: *Don't mark it up with so much red ink!* **c.** to raise the price of: [~ + *up* + *obj*]: *The store marked up its inventory.* [~ + *obj* + *up*]: *The store marked prices up almost 50%.* **—*Idiom.* 26. beside the mark,** not on the subject at hand; not relevant. **27. make one's mark,** to achieve success: *to make one's mark in show business.* **28. mark time, a.** to function at a job without making progress or advancing: *He was just marking time until retirement.* **b.** to move the feet one after the other as if marching but without moving forward. **29. wide of the mark,** far from the target or one's aim: *comments wide of the mark.*

mark[2] (märk) /mark/ *n.* [*count*] the basic monetary unit of Germany and certain other countries.

mark•down (märk′doun′) /'mark,dawn/ *n.* [*count*] **1.** a reduction in the price of an item: *a markdown on sofas.* **2.** the amount by which a price is reduced: *a markdown of 30%.*

marked (märkt) /markt/ *adj.* **1.** striking; conspicuous: *showed marked improvements in all the tests.* **2.** watched as someone suspected of something, or as the object of revenge: *The accountant is a marked man.* **3.** having a mark or marks. **—mark•ed•ly** (mär′kid lē) /'markɪdliy/ *adv.*: *His grades improved markedly after tutoring.*

mark•er (märk′ər) /'markər/ *n.* [*count*] **1.** a thing that marks a place or shows the position of something: *left a piece of paper in the book as a marker.* **2.** a tool for making marks: *He used a yellow marker.*

mar•ket (mär′kit) /'markɪt/ *n.* [*count*] **1.** a place where buyers and sellers meet for the sale of goods: *We went to the market for vegetables.* **2.** a store for selling food: *Go to the market for milk.* **3.** a meeting of people for buying and selling: *a market day.* **4.** trade in a particular product: *the cotton market.* **5.** demand for an item or a product: *The health-food market is expanding.* **6.** a region in which goods and services are bought or used: *the foreign market.* **7.** [*usually: the* + ~] STOCK MARKET. **—v. 8.** [*no obj*] to buy provisions for the home: *They were out marketing when their house was robbed.* **9.** [~ + *obj*] to offer in a market for sale; to sell: *Can they market their computers as being better than the competition?* **—*Idiom.* 10. in the market for,** interested in buying: *He's in the market for a good used car.* **11. on the market,** for sale; available: *How long has their house been on the market?* **—mar′ket•a•ble,** *adj.* **—mar′ket•er,** *n.* [*count*]

mar•ket•ing (mär′ki ting) /'markɪtɪŋ/ *n.* [*noncount*] **1.** the act or practice of advertising and selling a product: *She majored in marketing.* **2.** shopping for food: *Her husband did the marketing on Fridays.*

mar•ket•place (mär′kit plās′) /'markɪt,pleys/ *n.* [*count*] **1.** an area in a town where a market is held. **2.** the world of business and trade: *In a free, open marketplace our goods can compete.* **3.** any sphere in which people or things compete: *a marketplace for ideas.*

mark•ka (märk′kä) /'markka/ *n., pl.* **-kaa** (-kä) /-ka/. the basic monetary unit of Finland.

marks•man (märks′mən) /'marksmən/ *n.* [*count*], *pl.* **-men.** one who is skilled in shooting at a target. **—marks′man•ship′,** *n.* [*noncount*]

mark•up (märk′up′) /'mark,ʌp/ *n.* [*count*] an increase in the price of an item.

mar•lin (mär′lin) /'marlɪn/ *n., pl.* (*esp. when thought of as a group*) **-lin,** (*esp. for kinds or species*) **-lins.** a large saltwater game fish.

mar•ma•lade (mär′mə lād′, mär′mə lād′) /'marmə,leyd, ,marmə'leyd/ *n.* [*noncount*] a jelly made from boiled fruit, containing pieces of citrus fruit: *marmalade on toast.*

mar•mo•set (mär′mə zet′, -set′) /'marmə,zɛt, -,sɛt/ *n.* [*count*] a squirrel-sized monkey having soft fur and a long tail.

mar•mot (mär′mət) /'marmət/ *n.* [*count*] a short, stout, burrowing animal, as the woodchuck.

ma•roon[1] (mə ro͞on′) /mə'ruwn/ *n.* [*noncount*] **1.** a dark brownish red color. **—*adj.* 2.** of the color maroon.

ma•roon[2] (mə ro͞on′) /mə'ruwn/ *v.* [~ + *obj; usually be* + *~-ed*] to put ashore and abandon on an isolated island or coast: *was marooned on an island.*

mar•quee (mär kē′) /mar'kiy/ *n.* [*count*], *pl.* **-quees. 1.** a cover that sticks out over the entrance to a building. **2.** a large outdoor tent for sheltering a party.

mar•quess (mär′kwis) /'markwɪs/ *n.* [*count*] **1.** a British nobleman ranking below a duke and above an earl. **2.** MARQUIS.

mar•quis (mär′kwis, mär kē′) /'markwɪs, mar'kiy/ *n.* [*count*], *pl.* **-quis•es, -quis** (-kēz′) /-'kiyz/. a European nobleman ranking below a duke and above a count.

mar•quise (mär kēz′) /mar'kiyz/ *n.* [*count*], *pl.* **-quis•es. 1.** the wife or widow of a marquis. **2.** a woman holding a rank equal to that of a marquis.

mar•riage (mar′ij) /'mærɪdʒ/ *n.* **1.** [*noncount*] the institution under which a man and woman live as husband and wife under law: *different customs of marriage.* **2.** the state or relationship of being married: [*noncount*]: *a happy state of marriage.* [*count*]: *Her last two marriages were unhappy.* **3.** [*count*] the ceremony that formalizes marriage: *The marriage took place in her old parish church.* **4.** [*count*] an intimate living arrangement without permission from the law: *a trial marriage.* **5.** [*count*] a close association in which there is blending of different elements: *The car is a perfect marriage of power and performance.*

mar•riage•a•ble (mar′ij ə bəl) /'mærɪdʒəbəl/ *adj.* suitable, as in age, for marriage: *a daughter of marriageable age.*

mar•ried (mar′ēd) /'mæriyd/ *adj.* **1.** united in marriage: *a happily married couple.* **2.** [*before a noun*]of or relating to marriage or married persons: *Married life isn't easy.* **—*n.*** [*count*] **3.** Usually, **marrieds.** [*plural*] married people.

mar•row (mar′ō) /'mærow/ *n.* [*noncount*] the soft fatty tissue in the cavities of bones where blood cells are produced.

mar•ry (mar′ē) /'mæriy/ *v.*, **-ried, -ry•ing. 1.** [~ + *obj*] to take (someone) as a husband or wife: *He married her when he was eighteen.* **2.** [*no obj*] to take a husband or wife; wed: *In some countries girls can marry when they are fourteen.* **3.** [~ + *obj*] to perform the marriage ceremony for (a couple): *The priest married them in the old church.* **4.** to arrange the marriage of: [~ + *obj*]: *He wanted to marry his daughter into a rich family.* [~ + *off* + *obj*]: *They married off all their children.* [~ + *obj* + *off*]: *married them off quickly.* **5.** to gain through marriage: [~ + *obj*]: *to marry money.* [*no obj*]: *to marry into money.* **6.** to join or unite closely: [~ + *obj*]: *marrying the two disciplines of study.* [*no obj*]: *This wine and cheese marry well.* **—Related Words.** MARRY is a verb, MARRIAGE is a noun, MARRIED is an adjective: *She wants to marry you. They had a difficult marriage. A married man can't have another wife in this culture.*

marsh (märsh) /mɑrʃ/ *n.* [*count*] an area of waterlogged soil covered with tall grasses. —**marsh′y,** *adj.,* **-i•er, -i•est.**

mar•shal (mär′shəl) /ˈmɑrʃəl/ *n., v.,* **-shaled, -shal•ing** or (*esp. Brit.*) **-shalled, -shal•ling.** —*n.* [*count*] **1.** an administrative officer of a U.S. court with duties similar to a sheriff's. **2.** the chief of a police or fire department. **3.** an official who leads special ceremonies, as a parade. **4.** an army officer of the highest rank, as in France. —*v.* [~ + *obj*] **5.** to arrange in proper or effective order: *to marshal facts.* **6.** to usher or show the way to (someone) ceremoniously.

marsh′ gas′, *n.* [*noncount*] methane formed from decayed organic matter.

marsh•mal•low (märsh′mel′ō, -mal′ō) /ˈmɑrʃˌmɛlow, -ˌmælow/ *n.* **1.** [*noncount*] a spongy candy substance made from gelatin, corn syrup, and flavoring: *cookies filled with marshmallow.* **2.** [*count*] a piece of this, eaten as a candy: *roasting marshmallows over the campfire.*

marsh′ mar′igold, *n.* [*count*] a yellow-flowered plant of the buttercup family, growing in marshes.

mar•su•pi•al (mär so͞o′pē əl) /mɑrˈsuwpiyəl/ *n.* [*count*] **1.** an animal that gives birth to immature young that complete their development in a pouch on the mother's abdomen: *Marsupials include opossums and kangaroos.* —*adj.* [*before a noun*] **2.** of or relating to the marsupials.

mart (märt) /mɑrt/ *n.* [*count*] **1.** market; trading center. **2.** a place for selling goods wholesale.

mar•ten (mär′tn) /ˈmɑrtn̩/ *n., pl.* **-tens,** (*esp. when thought of as a group*) **-ten. 1.** [*count*] a mainly tree-dwelling animal of the weasel family. **2.** [*noncount*] the fur of such an animal.

mar•tial (mär′shəl) /ˈmɑrʃəl/ *adj.* [*before a noun*] relating to or suitable for war: *martial music.* —**mar′tial•ly,** *adv.*

mar′tial art′, *n.* [*count*] Often, **martial arts.** [*plural*] a traditional form of self-defense of East Asia: *martial arts such as judo and kung fu.*

mar′tial law′, *n.* [*noncount*] law or control temporarily imposed upon an area by military forces: *to declare martial law.*

Mar•tian (mär′shən) /ˈmɑrʃən/ *adj.* **1.** of or relating to the planet Mars or its hypothetical inhabitants. —*n.* [*count*] **2.** a suppposed inhabitant of Mars.

mar•tin (mär′tn) /ˈmɑrtn̩/ *n.* [*count*] a bird having a wedge-shaped or notched tail.

mar•ti•net (mär′tn et′, mär′tn et′) /ˌmɑrtn̩ˈɛt, ˈmɑrtn̩ˌɛt/ *n.* [*count*] **1.** someone who demands overly strict discipline, esp. a military person. **2.** someone who sticks to rules and demands this of others: *Her teacher was a martinet.*

mar•ti•ni (mär tē′nē) /mɑrˈtiyniy/ *n.* [*count*], *pl.* **-nis.** a cocktail made with gin or vodka and dry vermouth.

mar•tyr (mär′tər) /ˈmɑrtər/ *n.* [*count*] **1.** one who willingly suffers death rather than give up his or her religion: *early Christian martyrs.* **2.** one who suffers for a cause. **3.** one who undergoes suffering. —*v.* [~ + *obj*] **4.** to make a martyr of, esp. by putting to death. **5.** to torment; torture. —**mar•tyr•dom** (mär′tər dəm) /ˈmɑrtərdəm/ *n.* [*noncount*]

mar•vel (mär′vəl) /ˈmɑrvəl/ *n., v.,* **-veled, -vel•ing** or (*esp. Brit.*) **-velled, -vel•ling.** —*n.* [*count*] **1.** something that causes wonder or astonishment: *an engineering marvel.* —*v.* **2.** to be filled with wonder (at): [~ + *at* + *obj*]: *I marveled at her ability to charm.* [~ + *that clause*]: *They marveled that you won.*

mar•vel•ous (mär′və ləs) /ˈmɑrvələs/ *adj.* **1.** superbly fine; wonderful: *a marvelous show.* **2.** tending to cause a feeling of marvel: *a marvelous view of the ruins.* Also, *esp. Brit.,* **mar′vel•lous.** —**mar′vel•ous•ly,** *adv.: did marvelously well in the stock market.*

Marx•ism (märk′siz əm) /ˈmɑrksɪzəm/ also **Marx•i•an•ism** (märk′sē ə niz′əm) /ˈmɑrksiy ə ˌnɪzəm/ *n.* [*noncount*] the system of thought developed by Karl Marx and Friedrich Engels, esp. that struggle among the social classes has been the main force of historical change and that capitalism will be replaced by a socialist order and a classless society. —**Marx′ist, Marx′i•an,** *n.* [*count*], *adj.*

mar•zi•pan (mär′zə pan′) /ˈmɑrzəˌpæn/ *n.* [*noncount*] a molded candy substance made of almond paste.

masc., an abbreviation of: masculine.

mas•car•a (ma skar′ə) /mæˈskærə/ *n.* [*noncount*] a cosmetic applied to the eyelashes.

mas•cot (mas′kot, -kət) /ˈmæskɒt, -kət/ *n.* [*count*] something adopted by a group as its symbol to bring good luck: *took in the stray dog and made it their mascot.*

mas•cu•line (mas′kyə lin) /ˈmæskyəlɪn/ *adj.* **1.** of or relating to a man or men. **2.** having qualities traditionally thought of as belonging to men, as strength. **3.** of, relating to, or being the grammatical gender that has among its members most nouns referring to males, as well as other nouns, as Spanish *dedo* "finger" or German *Bleistift* "pencil." **4.** (of a woman) mannish. —*n.* **5.** [*noncount; singular; usually the* + ~] the masculine gender in grammar. **6.** [*count*] a word or other form in or marking the masculine gender. —**mas•cu•lin•i•ty** (mas′kyə lin′i tē) /ˌmæskyəˈlɪnɪtiy/ *n.* [*noncount*]

mash (mash) /mæʃ/ *v.* [~ + *obj*] **1.** to change (something) into a soft pulpy mass by beating: *mashed the potatoes.* **2.** to crush: *He mashed his fingers when the door closed on them.* —*n.* [*noncount*] **3.** a soft pulpy mass. **4.** a mixture of boiled grain, bran, etc., fed to livestock.

mash•er[1] (mash′ər) /ˈmæʃər/ *n.* [*count*] a person or thing that mashes: *a potato masher.*

mash•er[2] (mash′ər) /ˈmæʃər/ *n.* [*count*] a man who tries to attract women, often in a bothersome or annoying way: *a masher at a subway station.*

mask (mask) /mæsk/ *n.* [*count*] **1.** a covering for the face, worn to hide one's identity, to frighten, or to cause laughter. **2.** anything that disguises: *His politeness is a mask for anger.* **3.** a covering, as of wire or gauze, worn over all or part of the face, for protection, etc.: *a catcher's mask.* —*v.* [~ + *obj*] **4.** to disguise; hide: *to mask one's intentions.* **5.** to cover, hide, or shield with or as if with a mask: *eyes masked by reflecting sunglasses.* —**masked,** *adj.: a masked robber.*

mas•och•ism (mas′ə kiz′əm, maz′-) /ˈmæsəˌkɪzəm, ˈmæz-/ *n.* [*noncount*] **1.** a psychological disorder in which sexual pleasure is derived from pain. **2.** the tendency to find pleasure in submissiveness, etc. —**mas′och•ist,** *n.* [*count*] —**mas′och•is′tic,** *adj.* —**mas′och•is′ti•cal•ly,** *adv.*

ma•son (mā′sən) /ˈmeysən/ *n.* [*count*] one whose trade is building with stones or bricks.

ma•son•ry (mā′sən rē) /ˈmeysənriy/ *n.* [*noncount*] **1.** work constructed by a mason, esp. stonework: *admiring the masonry in that cathedral.* **2.** the craft of a mason.

mas•quer•ade (mas′kə rād′) /ˌmæskəˈreyd/ *n., v.,* **-ad•ed, -ad•ing.** —*n.* [*count*] **1.** a party of people wearing masks and costumes. **2.** a costume worn at such a gathering. **3.** false outward show: *a masquerade of his true feelings.* —*v.* **4.** [~ + *as* + *obj*] to represent oneself falsely: *masqueraded as a surgeon.* **5.** to disguise oneself: [~ + *as* + *obj*]: *The spy masqueraded as an old peddler.* [*no obj*]: *He could be masquerading; who knows?* —**mas′quer•ad′er,** *n.* [*count*]

mass[1] (mas) /mæs/ *n.* **1.** [*count*] a body of matter, usually of indefinite shape: *took a mass of dough and spread it on the pan.* **2.** [*count*] a collection of particles thought of as forming one body: *a mass of sand.* **3.** [*count*] a large number; a great deal of: *a mass of errors.* **4.** [*count; usually singular*] the greater part of something: *the great mass of American films.* **5.** [*noncount*] the entire collection (of something); aggregate; whole: *People, in the mass, mean well.* **6.** [*noncount*] bulk; massiveness: *towers of great mass.* **7.** [*noncount*] *Physics.* the quantity or amount of physical matter of a thing as figured from its weight or from Newton's second law of motion. *Abbr.:* m **8. the masses,** [*plural*] common people thought of as a whole: *an appeal to the masses.* —*adj.* [*before a noun*] **9.** of or relating to a large number of people: *mass unemployment.* **10.** done on a large scale: *weapons of mass destruction.* —*v.* **11.** to (cause to) come together in or form a mass: [*no obj*]: *Clouds were massing in the west.* [~ + *obj*]: *The general massed his troops for battle.*

mass[2] (mas) /mæs/ *n.* [*often: Mass*] the ceremony of the Eucharist: [*noncount*]: *Mass is held on Sunday.* [*count*]: *The priest performed two Masses each Sunday.*

Mass., an abbreviation of: Massachusetts.

mas•sa•cre (mas′ə kər) /ˈmæsəkər/ *n., v.,* **-cred, -cring.** —*n.* [*count*] **1.** the violent killing of a large number of esp. helpless human beings: *a massacre of civilians.* **2.** a general slaughter. **3.** the inflicting of great damage or defeat: *another massacre for our team.* —*v.* [~ + *obj*] **4.** to kill in a massacre; slaughter: *Thousands of people were massacred.* **5.** to defeat thoroughly: *massacred yet again by our rivals.*

mas•sage (mə säzh′) /məˈsɑʒ/ *n., v.,* **-saged, -sag•ing.** —*n.* **1.** the skill of treating the body by rubbing, squeezing, etc., so as to stimulate circulation or take away pain: [*count*]: *He went to the trainer's room for a massage.* [*noncount*]: *treatment with massage and hot water bot-*

tles. —*v.* [~ + *obj*] **2.** to treat by massage: *massaged his stiff neck.* **3.** to persuade by flattery: *massaged his ego.* **4.** to manipulate to produce a desired result: *The accountants massaged the data to make it look like there were net losses.*

massage′ par′lor, *n.* [*count*] **1.** an establishment providing massages. **2.** a similar establishment that also provides sexual services.

mas•seur (mə sûr′, -sŏŏr′) /mə'sɜr, -'sʊr/ *n.* [*count*] a man who provides massage as a profession.

mas•seuse (mə sōōs′, -sōōz′) /mə'suws, -'suwz/ *n.* [*count*] a woman who provides massage as a profession.

mas•sive (mas′iv) /'mæsɪv/ *adj.* **1.** made up of or forming a large mass: *the massive columns of the ancient temple.* **2.** large or prominent: *a massive forehead.* **3.** large in amount or degree: *a massive dose of medicine.* —**mas′sive•ly,** *adv.* —**mas′sive•ness,** *n.* [*noncount*]

mass′ me′dia, *n.* the means of communication, as newspapers, that reach great numbers of people: [*noncount; used with a singular verb*]: *The mass media is not responsible for the decline in values.* [*plural; used with a plural verb*]: *The mass media are no longer as responsible as they once were.*

mass′ noun′, *n.* [*count*] a noun that refers to a quantity or mass of things seen as a whole or collection, and therefore not normally having a plural. A mass noun like *sugar* or *sand* does not have a plural, unless we refer to a measure or type or kind of such a thing: *The noncount meaning of the mass noun* sugar *appears in "I like sugar." The count meaning of the mass noun* sugar *appears in: "How many sugars (= spoons, packets, or lumps of sugar) do you want in your coffee?"*

mass′ num′ber, *n.* [*count*] the number of protons and neutrons in the nucleus of an atom.

mass′-produce′, *v.* [~ + *obj*], **-duced, -duc•ing.** to produce (goods) in large amounts, esp. by machinery: *When cars could be mass-produced, prices for them fell.* —**mass′ produc′tion,** *n.* [*noncount*]

mast (mast) /mæst/ *n.* [*count*] **1.** a polelike structure rising above a ship to hold sails **2.** any upright pole, as a support for an aerial, etc.: *television masts.*

mas•tec•to•my (ma stek′tə mē) /mæ'stɛktəmiy/ *n.* [*count*], *pl.* **-mies.** the surgical removal of all or part of the breast. See -TOM-.

mas•ter (mas′tər) /'mæstər/ *n.* [*count*] **1.** a person with the ability or power to control: *She simply wanted to be the master of her own fate.* **2.** an owner of a slave or animal: *The dog followed its master everywhere she went.* **3.** a person very skilled or famous in a discipline, as an art or science: *one of the great masters of modern art; a Zen master.* **4.** *Chiefly Brit.* a male teacher. **5.** an original document, drawing, manuscript, tape, or disk, etc., from which copies are made. —*adj.* [*before a noun*] **6.** chief; principal: *a master list; The house has a large master bedroom.* **7.** controlling others of its type: *a master switch.* **8.** being a master from which copies can be made: *a master tape.* **9.** very skilled: *a master designer.* —*v.* [~ + *obj*] **10.** to make oneself master of; to learn to use or control: *to master a foreign language.* **11.** to conquer; overcome: *He soon mastered the difficulties of his new job.* **12.** to produce a master tape, disk, or record of.

mas•ter•ful (mas′tər fəl) /'mæstərfəl/ *adj.* **1.** having or showing the qualities of a master; authoritative. **2.** done well; showing mastery; masterly: *a masterful performance.* —**mas′ter•ful•ly,** *adv.*

mas′ter key′, *n.* [*count*] a key that will open a number of different locks.

mas•ter•ly (mas′tər lē) /'mæstərliy/ *adj.* **1.** very skillful: *a masterly job of fixing the wiring.* —*adv.* **2.** in a masterly manner.

mas•ter•mind (mas′tər mīnd′) /'mæstər,maynd/ *v.* [~ + *obj*] **1.** to plan and direct skillfully: *to mastermind the theft.* —*n.* [*count*] **2.** one who is responsible for the performance of a project: *a mastermind behind the plot.*

mas′ter of cer′emonies, *n.* [*count*] one who conducts events, as a television broadcast, acting as host and introducing the speakers. *Abbr.:* MC

mas•ter•piece (mas′tər pēs′) /'mæstər,piys/ *n.* [*count*] **1.** a person's greatest piece of work, as in an art. **2.** a fine example of excellence: *That speech was a masterpiece of quick thinking.*

mas′ter ser′geant, *n.* [*count*] a noncommissioned officer in the armed forces ranking above certain sergeants.

mas•ter•stroke (mas′tər strōk′) /'mæstər,strowk/ *n.* [*count*] an extremely skillful or effective action: *planned his masterstroke to catch his opponent off guard.*

mas•ter•work (mas′tər wûrk′) /'mæstər,wɜrk/ *n.* MASTERPIECE.

mas•ter•y (mas′tə rē) /'mæstəriy/ *n.* [*noncount*] **1.** knowledge or skill: *His mastery of Italian was complete.* **2.** superiority; control; dominance: *mastery over their enemies.* **3.** expert skill or knowledge.

mast•head (mast′hed′) /'mæst,hɛd/ *n.* [*count*] **1.** a box or column, usually on the editorial page of a newspaper or magazine, giving the names of the owners, staff members, etc. **2.** the top part of a ship's mast.

mas•ti•cate (mas′ti kāt′) /'mæstɪ,keyt/ *v.,* **-cat•ed, -cat•ing.** to chew (food): [~ + *obj*]: *masticating their crunchy cereal noisily.* [*no obj*]: *noisily masticating during breakfast.* —**mas•ti•ca•tion** (mas′ti kā′shən) /,mæstɪ'keyʃən/ *n.* [*noncount*]

mas•tiff (mas′tif) /'mæstɪf/ *n.* [*count*] a breed of large, powerful shorthaired dogs having a spotted coat and a dark muzzle.

mas•to•don (mas′tə don′) /'mæstə,dɒn/ *n.* [*count*] an extinct elephantlike mammal.

mas•tur•bate (mas′tər bāt′) /'mæstərbeyt/ *v.,* **-bat•ed, -bat•ing.** to stimulate the genitals of (oneself or someone else) for sexual pleasure: [*no obj*]: *Masturbating is normal.* [~ + *obj*]: *masturbating one another.* —**mas•tur•ba•tion** (mas′tər bā′shən) /,mæstər'beyʃən/ *n.* [*noncount*] See -TURB-.

mat[1] (mat) /mæt/ *n., v.,* **mat•ted, mat•ting.** —*n.* [*count*] **1.** a piece of fabric used on a floor as a covering: *a floor mat.* **2.** a piece of material set under an object, as a dish: *a place mat.* **3.** a thick pad placed on a floor to protect wrestlers and gymnasts. **4.** a thick tangled mass, as of weeds or hair. —*v.* **5.** to form into a tangled mass: [*no obj*]: *Her hair matted from the sweat.* [~ + *obj*]: *The rain matted his hair.* **6. go to the mat,** [~ (+ *for* + *obj*)] to support or defend a person or cause with determination: *promised he'd go to the mat for her when she came up for review.*

mat[2] (mat) /mæt/ *n., v.,* **mat•ted, mat•ting.** —*n.* [*count*] **1.** material serving as a frame or border for a picture. —*v.* [~ + *obj*] **2.** to provide (a picture) with a mat.

mat[3] (mat) /mæt/ *adj., n., v.,* **mat•ted, mat•ting.** MATTE.

mat•a•dor (mat′ə dôr′) /'mætə,dɔr/ *n.* [*count*] one who traditionally kills the bull in a bullfight.

match[1] (mach) /mætʃ/ *n.* [*count*] a slender piece of wood or cardboard with a tip having a chemical substance that produces fire when rubbed on a rough or chemically prepared surface.

match[2] (mach) /mætʃ/ *n.* [*count*] **1.** a person or thing that equals or resembles another in some respect. **2.** a person or thing able to deal with another as an equal: *met his match in the debate.* **3.** a pair of persons or things that go together well: *They are a perfect match.* **4.** a game or competition in which two or more contestants oppose each other: *a tennis match.* —*v.* **5.** [~ + *obj*] to equal: *He couldn't match his earlier score.* **6.** to go harmoniously with or correspond because of color or design: [~ + *obj*]: *The skirt matches the jacket perfectly.* [*no obj*]: *The skirt and jacket match perfectly.* **7.** to (cause to) correspond: [~ + *obj*]: *has to match his actions with his beliefs.* [*no obj*]: *His actions and his beliefs match.* **8.** to fit together; to find a connection to or with: [*no obj*]: *See if the puzzle pieces match.* [~ + *obj*]: *Match the puzzle pieces to the clues at the bottom.* **9.** [~ + *obj*] to place in conflict; to provide with an opponent or competitor, often of equal power: *The teams were well matched.*

match•book (mach′bŏŏk′) /'mætʃ,bʊk/ *n.* [*count*] a small folder into which matches are stapled or glued.

match•less (mach′lis) /'mætʃlɪs/ *adj.* having no equal: *matchless courage.*

match•mak•er (mach′mā′kər) /'mætʃ,meykər/ *n.* [*count*] **1.** one who arranges marriages by introducing possible mates. **2.** one who arranges any possible alliance.

mate (māt) /meyt/ *n., v.,* **mat•ed, mat•ing.** —*n.* [*count*] **1.** a husband or wife; spouse. **2.** a sexual partner of an animal: *studying how baboons and their mates interact.* **3.** one of a pair: *a mate of a glove.* **4.** *Chiefly Brit.* friend; buddy; chum (often used as a friendly term of address): *Well, mate, let's get going.* **5.** a rank below a ship's captain: *the first mate.* **6.** This word is used after a root or word with the meaning "a person who shares": *an officemate (= someone sharing an office); a roommate (= someone sharing a room).* —*v.* **7.** to (cause to) have sexual relations in order to breed, as animals: [*no obj*]:

Those animals mate in the fall. [~ + *obj*]: *Researchers tried to mate the female with the male.* —**mat′ing,** *adj.* [*before a noun*]: *the mating season, when animals display their courtship behavior.*

-mater-, *root.* *-mater-* comes from Latin, where it has the meaning "mother." This meaning is found in such words as: MATERNAL, MATERNITY, MATRIARCH, MATRICIDE, MATRIMONY, MATRIX, MATRON.

ma•te•ri•al (mə tēr′ē əl) /mə'tɪəriyəl/ *n.* **1.** [*noncount*] the substance of which something is made: *the basic material of our bodies.* **2.** [*noncount*] something, esp. a solid, that serves as raw matter to be made into something: *building material.* **3. materials,** [*plural*] the apparatus needed to make something: *writing materials.* **4.** a textile fabric, as cloth: [*noncount*]: *She bought some material to make a dress.* [*count*]: *She used a light material to make her dress.* **5.** [*noncount*] ideas or facts that can provide the basis for some work: *material for a book.* **6.** [*noncount*] a person considered as suited to a particular activity: *She's certainly college material.* —*adj.* [*before a noun*] **7.** formed of matter; physical; corporeal; of or relating to matter: *the material world.* **8.** relating to the physical world rather than the spiritual or intellectual: *material comforts.* **9.** of or relating to materialism; materialistic. **10.** important: *a material difference.* **11.** to the point; pertinent; essential: *asked a material question.* —**ma•te′ri•al•ly,** *adv.*

ma•te•ri•al•ism (mə tēr′ē ə liz′əm) /mə'tɪəriyə,lɪzəm/ *n.* [*noncount*] too much emphasis on material objects, comforts, and considerations, as opposed to spiritual or intellectual values: *the materialism of the 1970's and 1980's.* —**ma•te′ri•a•list,** *n.* [*count*], *adj.* —**ma•ter′i•a•list′ic,** *adj.*

ma•te•ri•al•ize (mə tēr′ē ə līz′) /mə'tɪəriyə,layz/ *v.* [*no obj*], **-ized, -iz•ing. 1.** to become real: *Our ideas never materialized.* **2.** to assume material form: *materialized suddenly out of thin air.* —**ma•te•ri•al•i•za•tion** (mə tēr′ē ə li zā′shən) /mə,tɪəriyəlɪ'zeyʃən/ *n.* [*noncount*]

ma•té•ri•el or **ma•te•ri•el** (mə tēr′ē el′) /mə,tɪəriy'ɛl/ *n.* [*noncount*] all the equipment used by an organization, as the military: *a depot for war matériel.*

ma•ter•nal (mə tûr′nl) /mə'tɜrnḷ/ *adj.* **1.** of or relating to a mother: *maternal instincts.* **2.** [*before a noun*] related through a mother's side of the family: *a maternal aunt.* —**ma•ter′nal•ly,** *adv.* See -MATER-.

ma•ter•ni•ty (mə tûr′ni tē) /mə'tɜrnɪtiy/ *n.* [*noncount*] **1.** the state of being a mother; motherhood. —*adj.* [*before a noun*] **2.** applying to mothers before, during, and after childbirth: *maternity leave.* **3.** suitable for wear by pregnant women: *maternity clothes.* See -MATER-.

math (math) /mæθ/ *n.* [*noncount*] mathematics.

math•e•mat•i•cal (math′ə mat′ik əl) /,mæθə'mætɪkəl/ *adj.* [*before a noun*] of or relating to mathematics: *mathematical equations.* —**math′e•mat′i•cal•ly,** *adv.*: *mathematically inclined.*

math•e•ma•ti•cian (math′ə mə tish′ən) /,mæθəmə'tɪʃən/ *n.* [*count*] a specialist in mathematics.

math•e•mat•ics (math′ə mat′iks) /,mæθə'mætɪks/ *n.* **1.** [*noncount; used with a singular verb*] the systematic study of numbers and the relations between quantities expressed by symbols: *Mathematics deals with counting and with areas of circles and volumes.* **2.** [*plural; used with a plural verb*] mathematical procedures, operations, or properties: *The mathematics are tricky in that equation.*

mat•i•née or **mat•i•nee** (mat′n ā′) /,mætṇ'ey/ *n.* [*count*] a performance held in the daytime, usually in the afternoon.

ma•tri•arch (mā′trē ärk′) /'meytriy,ɑrk/ *n.* [*count*] **1.** the female head of a family or tribal line. **2.** a woman who is the founder or most important member of a group. See -ARCH-, -MATER-.

ma•tri•ar•chal (mā′trē är′kəl) /,meytriy'ɑrkəl/ *adj.* of or relating to a matriarch or to a matriarchy.

ma•tri•ar•chy (mā′trē är′kē) /'meytriy,ɑrkiy/ *n., pl.* **-chies. 1.** a family, society, or state governed by women: [*count*]: *a matriarchy deep in the jungle.* [*noncount*]: *men's inherent fear of matriarchy.* **2.** a form of social organization in which the mother is head of the family and women have considerable power and property: [*count*]: *Were matriarchies more stable than patriarchies?* [*noncount*]: *the notion of matriarchy in anthropology.* See -MATER-.

mat•ri•cide (ma′tri sīd′, mā′-) /'mætrɪ,sayd, 'mey-/ *n.* **1.** the act of killing one's mother: [*noncount*]: *the horror of matricide.* [*count*]: *the number of reported matricides.* **2.** [*count*] one who kills his or her mother. —**mat•ri•cid•al,** (ma′tri sīd′l, mā′-) /,mætrɪ'saydḷ, ,mey-/ *adj.* See -MATER-, -CIDE-.

ma•tric•u•late (mə trik′yə lāt′) /mə'trɪkyə,leyt/ *v.,* **-lat•ed, -lat•ing.** to (cause to) be enrolled as a student in a college or university: [~ + *obj*]: *The college matriculated over 1200 new students.* [*no obj*]: *He took enough courses to matriculate.* —**ma•tric•u•la•tion** (mə trik′yə-lā′shən) /mə,trɪkyə'leyʃən/ *n.* [*noncount*]

mat•ri•mo•ny (ma′trə mō′nē) /'mætrə,mowniy/ *n.* [*noncount*] the state of being married; marriage. —**mat•ri•mo•ni•al** (ma′trə mō′nē əl) /,mætrə'mowniyəl/ *adj.* [*before a noun*]: *matrimonial bliss.* See -MATER-.

ma•trix (mā′triks, ma′-) /'meytrɪks, 'mæ-/ *n.* [*count*], *pl.* **ma•tri•ces** (mā′tri sēz′, ma′-) /'meytrɪ,siyz, 'mæ-/ **ma•trix•es. 1.** something that makes up the point from which something else comes; the basis of something. **2.** a rectangular arrangement of symbols. See -MATER-.

ma•tron (mā′trən) /'meytrən/ *n.* [*count*] **1.** a married woman, esp. one who is mature and dignified. **2.** a woman officer, as in a prison for women. —**ma′tron•ly,** *adj.* See -MATER-.

ma′tron of hon′or, *n.* [*count*] a married woman who is the principal attendant of the bride at a wedding.

matte or **mat** or **matt** (mat) /mæt/ *adj., n., v.,* **mat•ted** or **matt•ed, mat•ting** or **matt•ing.** —*adj.* **1.** having a dull surface; not shiny or glossy: *matte paint.* —*n.* [*count*] **2.** a dull surface, as on metals, paint, paper, or glass. —*v.* [~ + *obj*] **3.** to finish with a matte surface.

mat•ter (mat′ər) /'mætər/ *n.* **1.** [*noncount*] the material of which any physical object is composed; physical substance, as distinguished from the spirit or the mind. **2.** [*noncount*] a particular kind of substance: *coloring matter.* **3.** [*count*] a situation; affair; circumstance; event: *a trivial matter.* **4.** [*noncount*] importance; significance: *decisions of little matter.* **5.** [*count; singular; a* + ~ + *of*] an amount counted approximately: *It's only a matter of time before the police get you* (= *It's only a short time before they get you*). **6.** [*count; singular; a* + ~ + *of*] This phrase is used to introduce the thing needed in order to do or to accomplish something already mentioned: *Using a computer is just a matter of patience and training* (= *Patience and training are needed to use a computer*). **7. the matter,** [*count; singular; the* + ~] something troubling: *Is something the matter?* **8.** [*noncount*] something written or printed: *reading matter.* **9.** [*noncount*] things sent by mail: *postal matter.* **10.** [*noncount*] a substance given off by a living body, esp. pus: *grayish matter oozing from the wound.* —*v.* [*not: be* + ~*-ing*] **11.** to be of importance: [*no obj*]: *The cost doesn't matter to him.* [*It* + ~ + *that clause*]: *It doesn't matter that your hair is too long.* —***Idiom.*** **12. a matter of opinion,** a topic on which there may be different opinions: *a matter of opinion which of the two dogs is cuter.* **13. as a matter of fact,** in reality; actually: *As a matter of fact, I don't care.* **14. for that matter,** as far as that is concerned; as for that: *I don't want you going out with him, or, for that matter, talking to him.* **15. no matter,** [~ + *who / what / when / where / how / why*] regardless of; not making a difference: *No matter how hard we try, we always lose.* **16. no matter what,** definitely; certainly; regardless: *We'll be there no matter what.*

mat′ter-of-fact′, *adj.* **1.** concerned with fact alone. **2.** not showing emotions; nonchalant: *tried to be very matter-of-fact, but my heart was breaking.* —**mat′ter-of-fact′ly,** *adv.*

mat•ting (mat′ing) /'mætɪŋ/ *n.* [*noncount*] **1.** material for mats. **2.** mats thought of as a group.

mat•tress (ma′tris) /'mætrɪs/ *n.* [*count*] a large pad used on a bed for support.

ma•ture (mə to͝or′, -tyo͝or′, -cho͝or′) /mə'tʊr, -'tyʊr, -'tʃʊr/ *adj.,* **-tur•er, -tur•est,** *v.,* **-tured, -tur•ing.** —*adj.* **1.** fully developed in body or mind: *mature enough to take care of herself when she came home from school.* **2.** complete in development: *The wine is fully mature.* **3.** [*before a noun*] intended for or composed of adults: *mature subjects; a movie for mature audiences.* **4.** payable; due: *a mature bond.* —*v.* **5.** to (cause to) become mature: [*no obj*]: *The wine had matured beautifully.* [~ + *obj*]: *Experience has matured him.* **6.** [*no obj*] to become due: *The bond had matured and was worth $50.* —**mat•u•ra•tion** (mach′ə rā′shən) /,mætʃə'reyʃən/ *n.* [*noncount*] —**ma•ture′ly,** *adv.* —**Related Words.** MATURE is an adjective and a verb, MATURITY is a noun: *She's very mature for her age. The plants matured and grew. Face your problems with maturity.*

ma•tu•ri•ty (mə to͝or′i tē, -tyo͝or-′, -cho͝or-′) /mə'tʊrɪtiy, -tyʊr-', -tʃʊr-'/ *n.* **1.** [*noncount*] the quality or state of being mature: *to show great maturity in handling an emergency.* **2.** [*noncount*] full development: *to bring a plan to maturity.* **3.** [*count*] the time when a note or bill of exchange becomes due.

maud•lin (môd′lin) /ˈmɔdlɪn/ *adj.* embarrassingly sentimental or foolishly sad: *a maudlin story about a lost dog.*

maul (môl) /mɔl/ *n.* **mauled, maul•ing.** [*count*] **1.** a heavy hammer used esp. for driving stakes or wedges. —*v.* [~ + *obj*] **2.** to handle or use roughly: *The gang was mauling her in the parking lot.* **3.** to injure by rough treatment: *The lion tamer was mauled by one of the lions.* —**maul′er,** *n.* [*count*]

maun•der (môn′dər) /ˈmɔndər/ *v.* [*no obj*] to talk ramblingly or without making much sense: *maundering about his difficult life during the war.*

mau•so•le•um (mô′sə lē′əm, -zə-) /ˌmɔsəˈliyəm, -zə-/ *n.* [*count*], *pl.* **-le•ums, -le•a** (-lē′ə) /-ˈliyə/. a large, impressive tomb.

mauve (mōv, môv) /mowv, mɔv/ *n.* [*noncount*] a pale purple.

ma•ven or **ma•vin** (mā′vən) /ˈmeyvən/ *n.* [*count*] an expert: *a word maven.*

mav•er•ick (mav′ər ik, mav′rik) /ˈmævərɪk, ˈmævrɪk/ *n.* [*count*] **1.** an animal that has been branded, esp. a motherless calf. **2.** one who thinks and acts independently: *a political maverick against business as usual.* —*adj.* [*before a noun*] **3.** of or relating to such a person: *a maverick politician.*

maw (mô) /mɔ/ *n.* [*count*] the mouth, throat, or stomach, esp. of a creature devouring everything: *The huge maw of the monster opened wide.*

mawk•ish (mô′kish) /ˈmɔkɪʃ/ *adj.* overly emotional or sad; maudlin: *gets to be a little mawkish when he talks about his childhood.* —**mawk′ish•ly,** *adv.*

max (maks) /mæks/ *n.* [*noncount*] *Slang.* **1.** maximum: *The max for this old crate is about fifty miles an hour.* —***Idiom.*** **2. to the max,** to the greatest or furthest degree; totally: *We drove her car to the max.*

max•i (mak′sē) /ˈmæksiy/ *n.* [*count*], *pl.* **max•is. 1.** an ankle-length coat or skirt. **2.** MAXISKIRT.

maxi-, *prefix. maxi-* is attached to nouns and means "very large or long in comparison with others of its kind". This meaning is found in such words as: MAXISKIRT.

max•il•la (mak sil′ə) /mækˈsɪlə/ *n.* [*count*], *pl.* **max•il•lae** (mak sil′ē) /mækˈsɪliy/. an upper jaw or jawbone. —**max•il•lar•y** (mak′sə ler′ē) /ˈmæksəˌlɛriy/ *adj.*

max•im (mak′sim) /ˈmæksɪm/ *n.* [*count*] a proverb: *His maxim was "Seize the day."*

max•i•mal (mak′sə məl) /ˈmæksəməl/ *adj.* [*usually before a noun*] greatest possible; highest: *making maximal use of the opportunity.* —**max′i•mal•ly,** *adv.*

max•i•mize (mak′sə miz′) /ˈmæksəˌmayz/ *v.* [~ + *obj*], **-mized, -miz•ing. 1.** to increase to the greatest possible amount: *to maximize profits.* **2.** to make fullest use of: *to maximize one's potential.*

max•i•mum (mak′sə məm) /ˈmæksəməm/ *n.*, *pl.* **-mums, -ma** (-mə) /-mə/ *adj.* —*n.* [*count*] **1.** the highest amount, value, or degree that can be reached: *At a maximum, we have twenty students in each class.* **2.** an upper limit allowed by regulation: *raising the maximums of permitted imports.* —*adj.* [*before a noun*] **3.** being the greatest, largest, or highest that can be reached: *a maximum prison sentence of 50 years.*

max•i•skirt (mak′sē skûrt′) /ˈmæksiyˌskɜrt/ *n.* [*count*] a long skirt ending below the calf, usually nearer the ankle.

may (mā) /mey/ *auxiliary (modal) v.* [~ + *root form of a verb*], *pres.* **may;** *past* **might;** *imperative, infinitive, and participles lacking.* **1. a.** (used to express the possibility or the chances of the occurrence of the main verb): *It may rain. You may have been right. He might have been here before us. Her weight may have gone down.* **b.** (used to express the willingness of the subject to receive or grant permission or have the opportunity): *You may see the doctor now. May we have a word with you? If you fail three times, you may appeal to the academic department that offered the course.* **2.** (used with another phrase or clause to express that something else follows another idea, esp. in clauses that indicate the condition, purpose, or result of something): *Let's agree on this so that (as a result) we may go home early. Difficult as it may seem, I know it can be done.* **3.** (used to express a wish or prayer appearing before its subject in an unusual word order): *Long may you live! May the couple always be happy and healthy. May we yet see the light of day. Long may the banner wave.* —***Idiom.*** **4. may as well.** (used to express an opinion about a reason for doing or not doing the action of the main verb): *I can't stay awake, so I may as well go to bed.* See CAN. —**Usage.** See CAN.[1]

May (mā) /mey/ *n.* [*proper noun*] the fifth month of the year, containing 31 days.

may•be (mā′bē) /ˈmeybiy/ *adv., n., pl.* **-bes.** —*adv.* **1.** perhaps; possibly: *Maybe I'll go too.* —*n.* [*count*] **2.** a possibility or uncertainty: *There are too many maybes in his plan.* —**Usage.** The word MAYBE is much more informal than the word PERHAPS: *Our teacher's sick; maybe she'll be better tomorrow. The report said that perhaps the economy would improve.*

may•day (mā′dā′) /ˈmeyˌdey/ *n.* [*count*] an internationally accepted call for help or to indicate distress, used in radio messages: *We heard several maydays from the area.*

may•fly (mā′flī′) /ˈmeyˌflay/ *n.* [*count*], *pl.* **-flies.** an insect with large clear wings and a threadlike tail.

may•hem (mā′hem, mā′əm) /ˈmeyhɛm, ˈmeyəm/ *n.* [*noncount*] **1.** the crime of deliberately injuring another so as to cripple or mutilate. **2.** random or deliberate violence or damage.

mayn't (mā′ənt, mānt) /ˈmeyənt, meynt/ *Brit.* a contraction of "may not."

may•o (mā′ō) /ˈmeyow/ *n.* MAYONNAISE.

may•on•naise (mā′ə nāz′, mā′ə nāz′) /ˌmeyəˈneyz, ˈmeyəˌneyz/ *n.* [*noncount*] a thick sauce made of egg yolks, lemon juice, oil, and seasonings.

may•or (mā′ər, mâr) /ˈmeyər, mɛər/ *n.* [*count*] the chief executive of a city or town. —**may′or•al,** *adj.* [*before a noun*]: *a mayoral candidate.* —**may′or•al•ty,** *n.* [*noncount*]

maze (māz) /meyz/ *n.* [*count*] **1.** a confusing network of paths; labyrinth: *a maze of corridors.* **2.** a complicated, perplexing system: *a maze of bureaucratic red tape.*

ma•zur•ka (mə zûr′kə, -zŏŏr′-) /məˈzɜrkə, -ˈzʊr-/ *n.* [*count*], *pl.* **-kas. 1.** a lively Polish dance in triple meter. **2.** music for this dance.

MBA or **M.B.A.,** *n.* [*count*], *pl.* **MBA's** or **M.B.A.'s. 1.** an academic degree, Master of Business Administration: *has an MBA from Wharton.* **2.** one who has earned this degree: *a lot of MBA's looking for jobs.*

MC, an abbreviation of: master of ceremonies.

Mc•Coy (mə koi′) /məˈkɔy/ *n.* [*count*], *pl.* **McCoys.** the real thing or person as promised or stated (usually used in the phrase *the real McCoy*): *That wasn't an imitation; it was the real McCoy.*

MD, an abbreviation of: **1.** Doctor of Medicine. **2.** Maryland.

Md., an abbreviation of: Maryland.

mdse., an abbreviation of: merchandise.

me (mē) /miy/ *pron.* **1.** This pronoun is used as the direct or indirect object of the pronoun *I*: *They asked me to the party. Give me your hand.* **2.** This pronoun is used instead of the pronoun *I* after the verb *to be* in many non-formal instances: *Who is it? --It's me.* **3.** This pronoun is used instead of the pronoun *I* after the word *as, than,* and in certain constructions in non-formal instances: *She's a lot smarter than me (= than I am). He's as smart as me.* **4.** This pronoun is used instead of the pronoun *my* before an *-ing* form of a verb in many non-formal instances: *Did you hear about me getting promoted?* —*adj.* [*before a noun*] **5.** of or involving too much interest in one's own satisfaction: *The 1980's were considered the me decade.*

ME, an abbreviation of: Maine.

Me., an abbreviation of: Maine.

mead (mēd) /miyd/ *n.* [*noncount*] an alcoholic drink of fermented honey and water.

mead•ow (med′ō) /ˈmɛdow/ *n.* [*count*] a grassy, flat area.

mead•ow•lark (med′ō lärk′) /ˈmɛdowˌlɑrk/ *n.* [*count*] a North American songbird having a brown-streaked back.

mea•ger (mē′gər) /ˈmiygər/ *adj.* **1.** not enough in quantity or quality; insufficient: *a meager salary.* **2.** having little flesh; lean. Also, *esp. Brit.,* **mea′gre.** —**mea′ger•ly,** *adv.* —**mea′ger•ness,** *n.* [*noncount*]

meal[1] (mēl) /miyl/ *n.* [*count*] **1.** food served and eaten at one time: *The children were served a hot meal.* **2.** one such regular time or occasion for eating: *too many snacks between meals.*

meal[2] (mēl) /miyl/ *n.* [*noncount*] **1.** a coarse powder ground from the seeds of any grain: *barley meal.* **2.** any ground substance, as of nuts or seeds. —**meal′y,** *adj.,* **-i•er, -i•est**: *a mealy taste.*

meal•time (mēl′tīm′) /ˈmiylˌtaym/ *n.* [*count*] the usual time for a meal: *We barely met during mealtimes.*

meal′y-mouthed′ or **meal′y•mouthed′,** *adj.* avoiding plain, simple, or honest language: *mealy-mouthed politicians.*

mean[1] (mēn) /miyn/ *v.,* **meant** (ment) /mɛnt/ **mean•ing. 1.** [*not: be + ~-ing*] to have as its meaning or its sense; to signify: [*~ + obj*]: *The word "klock" in Swedish means "smart; wise."* [*~ + (that) clause*]: *That gesture means that the person hates you.* **2.** [*not: be + ~-ing*] to desire to express or indicate; to refer: [*~ + obj*]: *Which book did you mean?* [*~ + (that) clause*]: *By "perfect" I mean there should be no mistakes.* **3.** to have in mind as one's purpose or intention; intend: [*~ + obj*]: *She meant no harm.* [*~ + to + verb*]: *I've been meaning to call you, but things got too busy.* [*no obj*]: *I'm sure they meant well, but they didn't finish the job.* **4.** [*be + meant; not: be + ~-ing*] to be expected to happen in a certain way: *The couple were meant for each other.* **5.** [*not: be + ~-ing*] to produce (something) as a result: [*~ + obj*]: *Further budget cuts will mean more layoffs.* [*~ + (that) clause*]: *Does this traffic jam mean we'll be late?* **6.** [*not: be + ~-ing*] to show that something exists as a cause: [*~ + obj*]: *A grinding noise could mean a damaged disk drive.* [*~ + (that) clause*]: *A flickering screen could mean that your computer cables are not connected tightly.* **7.** [*not: be + ~-ing; ~ + obj*] to have the value of; to have the importance of: *Money means everything to them.*

mean[2] (mēn) /miyn/ *adj.,* **-er, -est. 1.** having evil or unkind intentions; malicious: *a mean, cruel remark.* **2.** small-minded: *mean motives.* **3.** stingy; miserly: *mean with one's money.* **4.** low in status: *of mean and humble birth.* **5.** bad-tempered: *a mean old horse.* **6.** excellent; topnotch: *plays a mean game of tennis.* —**mean′ly,** *adv.* —**mean′ness,** *n.* [*noncount*]

mean[3] (mēn) /miyn/ *n.* [*count*], *pl.* **means. 1.** Usually, **means.** [*plural*] an instrument, thing, or method used to achieve something: *They have the means, but do they have the will?* [*count; singular; used with a singular verb*]: *The quickest means of travel into the jungle is by canoe.* [*plural; used with a plural verb*]: *The means of winning that election are many: bribery, threats, and smear tactics.* **2. means,** [*plural*] **a.** available resources, esp. money: *We don't have sufficient means to send our children to college.* **b.** considerable financial resources: *a person of means.* **3.** something located in the middle between two extremes: *in the mean.* **4.** an average, esp. the arithmetic mean. —*adj.* [*before a noun*] **5.** occupying a middle position: *the mean amount of rainfall for that region.* —***Idiom.*** **6. by all means,** certainly: *By all means, help yourself, but save some for me.* **7. by means of,** by the way or method of; by the use of or by using. **8. by no means** or **not by any means,** not at all; definitely not: *By no means is he ready to retire. He is not by any means ready to retire.*

me•an•der (mē an′dər) /miy'ændər/ *v.* [*no obj*] **1.** to proceed by a winding course: *a stream meandering through the valley.* **2.** to wander aimlessly. —*n.* [*count*] **3.** a winding path.

mean•ing (mē′ning) /'miynɪŋ/ *n.* **1.** what is intended to be or is expressed: [*count*]: *Most meanings of a word are given in the dictionary.* [*noncount*]: *Did you understand the meaning of that play?* **2.** [*noncount*] the end, purpose, or significance of something: *His life no longer had meaning after his children died.* —**mean′ing•less,** *adj.*

mean•ing•ful (mē′ning fəl) /'miynɪŋfəl/ *adj.* **1.** having meaning: *a meaningful sentence.* **2.** expressing or showing an opinion, attitude, etc.: *exchanged meaningful glances.* **3.** serious; significant; important: *She wanted a meaningful relationship.* —**mean′ing•ful•ly,** *adv.*: *glanced meaningfully at each other.* —**mean′ing•ful•ness,** *n.* [*noncount*]

meant (ment) /mɛnt/ *v.* pt. and pp. of MEAN[1].

mean•time (mēn′tīm′) /'miyn,taym/ *n.* [*noncount*] **1.** the time between two events: *We have to leave at seven; in the meantime, let's have a drink.* —*adv.* **2.** MEANWHILE.

mean•while (mēn′hwīl′, -wīl′) /'miyn,hwayl, -,wayl/ *n.* [*noncount*] **1.** MEANTIME. —*adv.* **2.** in the time between: *The party is Tuesday, so meanwhile I have to shop and cook.* **3.** at the same time: *Meanwhile, I was enjoying myself.*

mea•sles (mē′zəlz) /'miyzəlz/ *n.* [*noncount; used with a singular verb*] an acute infectious disease characterized by small red spots on the skin, fever, and coldlike symptoms.

mea•sly (mē′zlē) /'miyzliy/ *adj.,* **-sli•er, -sli•est.** so little or small as to be inadequate: *a measly salary.*

meas•ur•a•ble (mezh′ər ə bəl) /'mɛʒərəbəl/ *adj.* **1.** that can be measured. **2.** large or significant enough to be measured: *a measurable difference between the two experiments.* —**meas′ur•a•bly,** *adv.*

meas•ure (mezh′ər) /'mɛʒər/ *n., v.,* **-ured, -ur•ing.** —*n.* **1.** [*count*] a unit or standard of measurement: *A second is a measure of time.* **2.** [*noncount*] a system of measurement: *an ounce in liquid measure.* **3.** [*count*] an instrument, as a container, that holds a certain amount and has marks indicating the amounts: *a one-cup measure.* **4.** [*count; singular*] the extent, dimensions, etc., of something, figured by comparison with a standard, or by judging against others: *to take the measure of a room.* **5.** [*count*] a known amount measured out: *a measure of brandy.* **6.** [*noncount*] reasonable limits: *spending without measure.* **7.** [*count*] a legislative bill: *a measure to limit campaign spending.* **8.** Usually, **measures.** [*plural*] actions to achieve an end: *took several measures to divert suspicion.* **9.** [*count*] a short rhythmical arrangement, as in poetry. —*v.* **10.** [*~ + obj*] to figure out the size, dimensions, etc., of (something), esp. with a standard: *measured the floor with a ruler.* **11.** [*~ + obj*] (of an instrument) to mark off or record the size, amount, or capacity of: *A clock measures time.* **12.** [*~ + obj*] to judge by comparison with something or someone else: *How do we measure pain and suffering?* **13.** [*not: be + ~-ing; ~ + obj*] to be of a certain size, amount, etc.: *The yard measured 100 feet by 200 feet.* **14. measure out,** Also, **measure off,** to mark off or deal out by measuring: [*~ + out/off + obj*]: *to measure out a cup of flour.* [*~ + obj + out/off*]: *He measured it out and handed it to her.* **15. measure up, a.** [*~ + up + to + obj*] to reach the same level as (something else): *The exhibition didn't measure up to last year's.* **b.** [*no obj*] to have the right qualifications: *He didn't quite measure up, so we didn't hire him.* —***Idiom.*** **16. beyond** or **above measure,** too great or too much to be counted, figured, etc.: *loved her beyond measure.* **17. for good measure,** as an extra: *In addition to dessert, they served chocolates for good measure.* **18. have** or **take someone's measure,** to judge someone's worth: *They eyed each other warily, each taking the measure of the other.* —**meas′ure•less,** *adj.*

meas•ured (mezh′ərd) /'mɛʒərd/ *adj.* slow, careful, and deliberate; even: *He spoke in soft, measured tones.*

meas•ure•ment (mezh′ər mənt) /'mɛʒərmənt/ *n.* **1.** [*noncount*] the act of measuring. **2.** [*count*] the number representing the extent, size, etc., determined by measuring: *The measurements of the house are 100 feet by 200 feet.* **3.** [*noncount*] a system of measuring: *liquid measurement.* **4.** [*plural*] the size of parts of the body, esp. of the chest, waist, and hips: *Her measurements were 36-24-34.*

meas•ur•ing (mezh′ər ing) /'mɛʒərɪŋ/ *adj.* [*before a noun*] used for making a measurement: *a measuring spoon.*

meat (mēt) /miyt/ *n.* **1.** the flesh of animals used for food: [*noncount*]: *Is the meat fresh?* [*count*]: *Different meats were displayed behind the counter.* **2.** the part of something that can be eaten, as a nut. **3.** [*noncount*] important or valuable content, points, or part (of something): *Her article had some clever phrases but no meat, nothing substantial.*

meat•ball (mēt′bôl′) /'miyt,bɔl/ *n.* [*count*] **1.** a small ball of seasoned ground meat. **2.** *Slang.* a clumsy, fat, or useless person.

meat•y (mē′tē) /'miytiy/ *adj.,* **-i•er, -i•est. 1.** of or relating to meat: *a meaty dinner.* **2.** (of a body) resembling meat; fat; heavy: *his meaty arms.* **3.** having substance, importance, or value: *some meaty proposals.*

mec•ca (mek′ə) /'mɛkə/ *n.* [*count*] a place that attracts many people with interests in common: *a mecca for the film industry.*

-mech-, *root.* *-mech-* comes from Greek (but for some words comes through Latin), where it has the meaning "machine," and therefore "instrument or tool." This meaning is found in such words as: MACHINATION, MACHINE, MACHINERY, MECHANIC, MECHANICAL, MECHANIZE.

me•chan•ic (mə kan′ik) /mə'kænɪk/ *n.* [*count*] one who repairs machinery, or who is skilled in the use of tools and equipment: *an auto mechanic.* See -MECH-.

me•chan•i•cal (mə kan′i kəl) /mə'kænɪkəl/ *adj.* **1.** of or relating to machinery or tools: *He has no mechanical skills.* **2.** operated or produced by machinery: *a mechanical snow blower.* **3.** lacking freshness; dull or done by habit: *a mechanical job that required no thinking.* **4.** of or relating to the study of mechanics. —**me•chan′i•cal•ly,** *adv.* See -MECH-.

me•chan•ics (mə kan′iks) /mə'kænɪks/ *n.* **1.** [*noncount; used with a singular verb*] the branch of physics that deals with the action of forces on bodies and with motion: *Mechanics includes the study of kinetics.* **2.** [*noncount; used with a singular verb*] the theoretical and practical application of this science to making or working with machinery and mechanical tools or instruments. **3.** [*plural; the + ~ + of; used with a plural verb*] routine or basic methods, procedures, or techniques of doing things: *The practical mechanics of running a household are difficult for him.*

mech•an•ism (mek′ə niz′əm) /'mɛkə,nɪzəm/ *n.* [*count*] **1.** an assembly of moving parts performing a function: *The alarm mechanism is jammed.* **2.** the way or means by which an effect is produced: *the language learning mechanism in the human brain.* **3.** a procedure within an organization: *What is the mechanism for adjusting the bylaws?* **4.** a manner of behaving that helps one deal with the environment: *His amnesia was a defense mechanism.* See -MECH-.

mech•a•nis•tic (mek′ə nis′tik) /,mɛkə'nɪstɪk/ *adj.* of or relating to mechanics.

mech•a•nize (mek′ə nīz′) /'mɛkə,nayz/ *v.* [~ + *obj*], **-nized, -niz•ing. 1.** to make mechanical; to operate by machinery. **2.** to introduce machinery into, esp. in order to replace manual labor. **3.** to equip with tanks or other armored vehicles: *a mechanized division.* —**mech•a•ni•za•tion** (mek′ə ni zā′shən) /,mɛkənɪ'zeyʃən/ *n.* [*noncount*]: *Will mechanization result in a loss of jobs?* See -MECH-.

med•al (med′l) /'mɛdl̩/ *n.* [*count*] **1.** a flat piece of metal with a design on it, awarded as a sign of victory or for bravery, merit, or the like: *loved to wear a chestful of medals during parades.* **2.** a similar object bearing a religious image, as of a saint: *a St. Christopher medal.*

med•al•ist (med′l ist) /'mɛdl̩ɪst/ *n.* [*count*] a person to whom a medal has been awarded: *an Olympic gold medalist from the 1992 games.* Also, *esp. Brit.,* **med′al•list.**

me•dal•lion (mə dal′yən) /mə'dælyən/ *n.* [*count*] **1.** a large medal. **2.** an ornament resembling a medal.

med•dle (med′l) /'mɛdl/ *v.* [*no obj*], **-dled, -dling.** to involve oneself in a matter without right or invitation: *Stop meddling in our affairs and leave us alone!* —**med′dler,** *n.* [*count*] —**med•dle•some** (med′l səm) /'mɛdl̩səm/ *adj.*

-medi-, *root.* *-medi-* comes from Latin, where it has the meaning "middle." This meaning is found in such words as: IMMEDIATE, INTERMEDIATE, MEDIA, MEDIAL, MEDIAN, MEDIATE, MEDIATOR, MEDIEVAL, MEDIOCRE, MEDIUM, MULTIMEDIA.

me•di•a (mē′dē ə) /'miydiyə/ *n.* **1.** [*plural*] a pl. of MEDIUM. **2.** [*the* + ~] means of communication, as radio, television, and magazines, with wide reach and influence: [*noncount; used with a singular verb*]: *The media is to blame for the defeat of our candidate.* [*plural; used with a plural verb*]: *The media have too much influence over elections.* —*adj.* [*before a noun*] **3.** of or relating to the media: *media research.* See -MEDI-.

me•di•al (mē′dē əl) /'miydiyəl/ *adj.* **1.** of, relating to, or in the middle. **2.** relating to a mean or average. See -MEDI-.

me•di•an (mē′dē ən) /'miydiyən/ *adj.* [*usually: before a noun*] **1.** situated in or relating to the middle: *a low median income.* —*n.* [*count*] **2.** the middle number in a sequence of numbers, or the average of the middle two numbers of an even-numbered sequence: *4 is the median of 1, 3, 4, 8, 9.* **3.** a straight line from an angle of a triangle to the midpoint of the opposite side. **4.** Also called **me′dian strip′.** a strip in the middle of a highway to separate opposite lanes of traffic. See -MEDI-.

me•di•ate (mē′dē āt′) /'miydiy,eyt/ *v.,* **-at•ed, -at•ing. 1.** to attempt to settle (a dispute) between two opposing sides: [*no obj*]: *The UN president agreed to mediate.* [~ + *obj*]: *She agreed to mediate the dispute.* **2.** [~ + *obj*] to bring about a solution between two opposing sides: *to mediate a settlement.* —**me•di•a•tion** (mē′dē ā′shən) /,miydiy'eyʃən/ *n.* [*noncount*]: *trained in diplomatic mediation.* —**me′di•a′tor,** *n.* [*count*]: *experienced mediators.* See -MEDI-.

med•ic (med′ik) /'mɛdɪk/ *n.* [*count*] **1.** a military medical corpsman. **2.** a doctor; intern.

Med•i•caid (med′i kād′) /'mɛdɪ,keyd/ *n.* [*proper noun; no article*] a government program of medical insurance for the poor: *When was Medicaid instituted?*

med•i•cal (med′i kəl) /'mɛdɪkəl/ *adj.* [*before a noun*] of or relating to medicine. —**med′i•cal•ly,** *adv.*

Med•i•care (med′i kâr′) /'mɛdɪ,kɛər/ *n.* [*proper noun; no article*] a government program of medical insurance for the aged or disabled: *When was Medicare established?*

med•i•cate (med′i kāt′) /'mɛdɪ,keyt/ *v.* [~ + *obj*], **-cat•ed, -cat•ing. 1.** to treat with medicine: *The doctor medicated him with a drug.* **2.** [*usually: be + ~ + -ed*] to include a medicine in (something): *The cough drops were medicated with a decongestant.*

med•i•ca•tion (med′i kā′shən) /,mɛdɪ'keyʃən/ *n.* a medicine: [*noncount*]: *prescribed medication for the pain.* [*count*]: *Her medications did not agree with her.*

me•dic•i•nal (mə dis′ə nl) /mə'dɪsənl̩/ *adj.* of or relating to a medicine: *That soda has a medicinal taste.* —**me•dic′i•nal•ly,** *adv.*

med•i•cine (med′ə sin) /'mɛdəsɪn/ *n.* **1.** [*count*] a substance used in treating disease or illness. **2.** [*noncount*] the art or science of preserving health and treating disease.

med′icine ball′, *n.* [*count*] a solid, heavy, leather-covered ball used for exercise.

med′icine man′, *n.* [*count*] a person believed to possess magical powers, esp. among North American Indians; shaman.

me•di•e•val or **me•di•ae•val** (mē′dē ē′vəl, med′ē-, mid′ē-, mid ē′vəl) /,miydiy'iyvəl, ,mɛdiy-, ,mɪdiy-, mɪd'iyvəl/ *adj.* of, relating to, or characteristic of the Middle Ages: *medieval architecture.* —**me′di•e′val•ist,** *n.* [*count*] See -MEDI-.

me•di•o•cre (mē′dē ō′kər) /,miydiy'owkər/ *adj.* of ordinary or moderate quality: *gets mediocre grades.* —**me•di•oc•ri•ty** (mē′dē ok′ri tē) /,miydiy'ɒkrɪtiy/ *n.* [*noncount*]: *was not satisfied with mediocrity.* See -MEDI-.

med•i•tate (med′i tāt′) /'mɛdɪ,teyt/ *v.,* **-tat•ed, -tat•ing. 1.** [*no obj*] to think calmly, carefully, and thoroughly about something. **2.** [*no obj*] to try to achieve a calm, relaxed state of mind, as by deep breathing or repeating a mantra: *meditated as part of his yoga training.* **3.** [~ + *obj*] to plan in the mind: *to meditate revenge.*

med•i•ta•tion (med′i tā′shən) /,mɛdɪ'teyʃən/ *n.* the act of meditating: [*noncount*]: *a state of meditation.* [*count*]: *In my meditations I came across that idea.*

med•i•ta•tive (med′i tā′tiv) /'mɛdɪ,teytɪv/ *adj.* **1.** of or relating to meditating: *the meditative disciplines.* **2.** thinking or planning carefully. —**med′i•ta′tive•ly,** *adv.*

me•di•um (mē′dē əm) /'miydiyəm/ *n., pl.* **-di•a** (-dē ə) /-diyə/ for 1–5, 7 **-di•ums** for 1–7, *adj.* —*n.* [*count*] **1.** a middle state or condition: *He had reached a happy medium: not too rich, not too poor.* **2.** a substance, as air, through which a force acts or is carried: *the medium of air through which sound waves travel.* **3.** a means by which something is accomplished: *Words are a medium of expression.* **4.** one of the means or channels of general communication or entertainment in society, as newspapers or television. **5.** surrounding conditions or influences; environment: *In the air the bird was in its natural medium.* **6.** one who claims to be able to contact the spirits of the dead. **7.** the material or technique with which an artist works. —*adj.* [*usually: before a noun*] **8.** halfway between extremes in degree, quantity, position, or quality: *He was of medium build.* See -MEDI-.

med•ley (med′lē) /'mɛdliy/ *n.* [*count*], *pl.* **-leys. 1.** a mixture, esp. of different elements; jumble. **2.** a piece of music combining passages from various sources: *a medley of songs from the 1950's.*

me•dul•la (mə dul′ə) /mə'dʌlə/ *n.* [*count*], *pl.* **-dul•las, -dul•lae** (-dul′ē) /-'dʌliy/. the lowest or hindmost part of the brain of humans and of animals with backbones.

meek (mēk) /miyk/ *adj.,* **-er, -est. 1.** humbly patient. **2.** timid; spiritless; tame. —**meek′ly,** *adv.* —**meek′ness,** *n.* [*noncount*]

meet (mēt) /miyt/ *v.,* **met** (met) /mɛt/ **meet•ing,** *n.* —*v.* **1.** to come into the presence of; encounter: [~ + *obj*]: *met him on the street yesterday.* [*no obj*]: *met at the train station.* **2.** to become acquainted (with): [~ + *obj*]: *I've never met your cousin.* [*no obj*]: *"Yes, we've already met," she said.* **3.** to come together at an agreed place or time: [~ + *obj*]: *Meet me at noon, the usual place.* [*no obj*]: *The directors will meet on Tuesday.* **4.** [~ + *obj*] to be present at the arrival of: *to meet a train.* **5.** [~ + *obj*] to come to the notice of: *A strange sight met my eyes.* **6.** to come into physical contact with: [~ + *obj*]: *The car met the bus head-on.* [*no obj*]: *The car and the bus met head-on.* **7.** to form a connection: [*no obj*]: *The two streets meet in front of our house.* [~ + *obj*]: *His eyes met hers.* **8.** to encounter in opposition, conflict, or contest: [~ + *obj*]: *Our proposal met a lot of opposition.* [*no obj*]: *The rival teams meet next week.* **9.** [~ + *obj*] to deal effectively with: *met the challenge.* **10.** [~ + *obj*] to comply with: *to meet a deadline.* **11. meet up,** [*no obj*] to come together after going in different directions: *After shopping, they met up for pizza.* **12. meet with,** [~ + *obj*] to encounter; experience: *Your proposal was met with a lot of opposition.* **—*n.*** [*count*] **13.** an assembly for athletic or sports competition, as for racing: *a track meet.*

meet•ing (mē′ting) /'miytɪŋ/ *n.* [*count*] **1.** the act of coming together: *Our meeting was a complete accident.* **2.** an assembly or conference: *the last meeting of the parents' group.* **3.** a point of contact: *the meeting of two roads.* **—*Idiom.* 4. meeting of minds,** [*count*] agreement; accord: *finally came to a meeting of minds regarding the firing of faculty.*

mega-, *prefix. mega-* comes from Greek, where it has the meaning: **1.** extremely large, huge: *megalith (= extremely large stone or rock); megastructure (= a huge structure).* **2.** *mega-* is also used to mean one million of the units of (the base root or word): *megahertz (= one million hertz); megaton (= one million tons).* **3.** *mega-* also means very large quantities or amounts: *megabucks (= a great deal of money); megadose (= a large dose of medicine).* **4.** *mega-* also means things that are extraordinary examples of their kind: *megahit (= a smash movie or stage hit); megatrend (= important, very popular trend).*

meg•a•cy•cle (meg′ə sī′kəl) /'mɛgəˌsaykəl/ *n.* MEGAHERTZ.

meg•a•hertz (meg′ə hûrts′) /'mɛgəˌhɜrts/ *n.* [*count*], *pl.* **-hertz, -hertz•es.** a unit of frequency equal to one million cycles per second.

meg•a•lo•ma•ni•a (meg′ə lō mā′nē ə) /ˌmɛgəlow'meyniyə/ *n.* [*noncount*] an exaggerated, mistaken belief in one's own importance. **—meg•a•lo•ma•ni•ac** (meg′ə lō mā′nē ak′) /ˌmɛgəlow'meyniyˌæk/ *n.* [*count*]

meg•a•lop•o•lis (meg′ə lop′ə lis) /ˌmɛgə'lɒpəlɪs/ also **me•gap•ol•is** (mə gap′ə lis) /mə'gæpəlɪs/ *n.* [*count*] **1.** a very large city. **2.** an urban region that contains more than one large city. See -POLIS-.

meg•a•phone (meg′ə fōn′) /'mɛgəˌfown/ *n.* [*count*] a cone-shaped device for making the voice louder. See -PHON-.

meg•a•ton (meg′ə tun′) /'mɛgəˌtʌn/ *n.* [*count*] **1.** one million tons. **2.** an explosive force equal to that of one million tons of TNT.

mel•an•cho•li•a (mel′ən kō′lē ə, -kōl′yə) /ˌmɛlən'kowliyə, -'kowlyə/ *n.* [*noncount*] a severe form of depression. **—mel•an•chol•ic** (mel′ən kol′ik) /ˌmɛlən'kɒlɪk/ *adj.*

mel•an•chol•y (mel′ən kol′ē) /'mɛlənˌkɒliy/ *n.* [*noncount*] **1.** a gloomy state of mind; depression or dejection. **—*adj.* 2.** affected with melancholy; depressed: *a melancholy mood.* **3.** causing melancholy: *a melancholy occasion.*

mé•lange (mā länzh′, -länj′) /mey'lɑ̃ʒ, -'lɑndʒ/ *n.* [*count*], *pl.* **-langes** (-länzh′, -län′jiz) /-'lɑ̃ʒ, -'lɑndʒɪz/. a mixture; a medley: *an odd mélange of artists and police officers.*

mel•a•nin (mel′ə nin) /'mɛlənɪn/ *n.* [*noncount*] coloring matter found in animal life, making up the dark color of skin, hair, fur, scales, and feathers.

mel•a•no•ma (mel′ə nō′mə) /ˌmɛlə'nowmə/ *n.* [*count*], *pl.* **-mas, -ma•ta** (-mə tə) /-mətə/. a skin tumor.

me•lee or **mê•lée** (mā′lā, mā lā′, mel′ā) /'meyley, mey'ley, 'mɛley/ *n.* [*count*] **1.** a confused hand-to-hand fight: *waded into the melee and started hitting.* **2.** a state of confusion: *a wild melee of shouting and screaming.*

mel•lif•lu•ous (mə lif′lo͞o əs) /mə'lɪfluwəs/ *adj.* sweetly or smoothly flowing: *a mellifluous voice.* **—mel•lif′lu•ous•ly,** *adv.*

mel•low (mel′ō) /'mɛlow/ *adj.,* **-er, -est,** *v.* **—*adj.* 1.** sweet and full-flavored from ripeness. **2.** soft and rich, as sound or colors: *the mellow sound of the muted trumpet.* **3.** made gentle by age or maturity: *became mellow after his retirement.* **4.** pleasantly intoxicated: *mellow after a few drinks.* **5.** free from tension; pleasantly agreeable: *a mellow neighborhood.* **—*v.* 6.** to (cause to) become mellow: [*no obj*]: *The music mellowed as the band settled into a quiet mood.* [~ + *obj*]: *The years have mellowed her.* **7. mellow out,** [*no obj*] *Slang.* to relax: *The kids urged their parents to "mellow out."*

me•lod•ic (mə lod′ik) /mə'lɒdɪk/ *adj.* **1.** [*before a noun*] of or relating to a melody: *a melodic line.* **2.** having a pleasant tune. **—me•lod′i•cal•ly,** *adv.*

me•lo•di•ous (mə lō′dē əs) /mə'lowdiyəs/ *adj.* **1.** of or relating to melody; tuneful. **2.** producing melody; musical. **—me•lo′di•ous•ly,** *adv.* **—me•lo′di•ous•ness,** *n.* [*noncount*]

mel•o•dra•ma (mel′ə drä′mə, -dram′ə) /'mɛləˌdrɑmə, -ˌdræmə/ *n., pl.* **-mas. 1.** [*count*] a play or story that exaggerates emotion and emphasizes plot or action: *TV soap operas are melodramas that never seem to end.* **2.** [*noncount*] melodramatic behavior or events: *The trial had more than its share of melodrama.*

mel•o•dra•mat•ic (mel′ə drə mat′ik) /ˌmɛlədrə'mætɪk/ *adj.* **1.** of or relating to or fitting a melodrama: *a melodramatic performance.* **—*n.* 2. melodramatics,** [*plural*] melodramatic writing or behavior: *Stop the melodramatics; you've only scraped your knee.*

mel•o•dy (mel′ə dē) /'mɛlədiy/ *n.* [*count*], *pl.* **-dies.** a pleasing sequence; a tune.

mel•on (mel′ən) /'mɛlən/ *n.* the fruit of any of various plants of the gourd family, as the watermelon: [*noncount*]: *I had some melon for breakfast.* [*count*]: *Melons were unavailable at that time of year.*

melt (melt) /mɛlt/ *v.* **1.** to (cause to) become liquid by heat: [*no obj*]: *In just a few hours the snow melted.* [~ + *obj*]: *The hot sun melted the snow.* **2.** [*no obj*] to dissolve: *Melt 1/4 cup of sugar in 2 cups of boiling water.* **3.** to (cause to) become less or nothing: [*no obj*]: *His fortune slowly melted away.* [~ + *obj* + *away*]: *The cost of her medicine melted their savings away.* [~ + *away* + *obj*]: *The cost melted away their savings.* **4.** [*no obj*] to pass; blend: *Night melted into day.* **5.** to (cause to) become softened in feeling: [*no obj*]: *His heart melted when he heard about her problems.* [~ + *obj*]: *a story that would melt your heart.*

melt•down (melt′doun′) /'mɛltˌdawn/ *n.* [*count*] **1.** the melting of the core of a nuclear reactor, due to inadequate cooling of the fuel elements. **2.** any quickly developing breakdown, mishap, or accident.

melt′ing pot′, *n.* [*count*] **1.** a container in which metals or other substances are heated until they fuse. **2.** a country or situation in which a blending of races, peoples, etc., takes place: *the traditional description of the United States as a melting pot.*

-mem-, *root. -mem-* comes from Latin, where it has the meaning "mind; memory." This meaning is found in such words as: COMMEMORATE, IMMEMORIAL, MEMENTO, MEMO, MEMOIR, MEMORABILIA, MEMORANDUM, MEMORIAL, MEMORIZE, MEMORY, REMEMBER, REMEMBRANCE.

mem•ber (mem′bər) /'mɛmbər/ *n.* [*count*] **1.** an individual forming part of a group: *a member of the House of Representatives.* **2.** a part or organ of an animal body; a limb, as a leg, arm, or wing.

mem•ber•ship (mem′bər ship′) /'mɛmbərˌʃɪp/ *n.* **1.** [*noncount*] the state of being a member: *Membership provides you with free parking.* **2.** [*count; usually singular*] the total number of members belonging to an organization: *The membership of the group has declined in recent years.*

mem•brane (mem′brān) /'mɛmbreyn/ *n.* [*count*] a thin layer of tissue that covers an organ, etc. **—mem•bra•nous** (mem′brə nəs) /'mɛmbrənəs/ *adj.*

me•men•to (mə men′tō) /mə'mɛntow/ *n.* [*count*], *pl.* **-tos, -toes.** something that serves as a reminder of what is past or gone; a souvenir: *mementos of her time in Brazil.* See -MEM-.

mem•o (mem′ō) /'mɛmow/ *n.* [*count*], *pl.* **mem•os.** memorandum: *sent a memo about expense accounts.* See -MEM-.

mem•oir (mem′wär, -wôr) /'mɛmwɑr, -wɔr/ *n.* [*count*] **1.** a record of events based on the writer's personal observation. **2.** Usually, **memoirs.** [*plural*] an autobiography: *The general retired and began to write his memoirs.* See -MEM-.

mem•o•ra•bil•i•a (mem′ər ə bil′ē ə, -bil′yə) /ˌmɛmərə'bɪliyə, -'bɪlyə/ *n.* [*plural*] mementos or souvenirs that are collected and kept. See -MEM-.

mem•o•ra•ble (mem′ər ə bəl) /'mɛmərəbəl/ *adj.* worth remembering: *a memorable performance.* **—mem′o•ra•bly,** *adv.* See -MEM-.

mem•o•ran•dum (mem′ə ran′dəm) /ˌmɛmə'rændəm/ *n.* [*count*], *pl.* **-dums, -da** (-də) /-də/. **1.** a record or a written statement of something. **2.** a written message, esp. one between employees of a company; memo. See -MEM-.

me•mo•ri•al (mə môr′ē əl, -mōr′-) /mə'mɔriyəl, -'mowr-/ *n.* [*count*] **1.** something designed to preserve the memory of a person, etc., as a monument: *a memorial to the war dead.* **—*adj.* 2.** serving to preserve the memory; commemorative: *memorial services.* See -MEM-.

mem•o•rize (mem′ə rīz′) /'mɛməˌrayz/ *v.* [~ + *obj*], **-rized, -riz•ing.** to learn (something) completely so that it can be repeated exactly: *to memorize a poem.*

—**mem•o•ri•za•tion** (mem′ə ri zā′shən) /ˌmɛmərɪˈzeyʃən/ *n.* [*noncount*]: *excellent powers of memorization.* See -MEM-.

mem•o•ry (mem′ə rē) /ˈmɛməriy/ *n., pl.* **-ries. 1.** [*noncount*] the mental ability of keeping and recalling facts, events, or experiences: *long- and short-term memory.* **2.** [*count*] this ability as possessed by an individual: *to have a good memory.* **3.** [*count*] the length of time over which remembering extends: *within living memory.* **4.** [*count*] a mental picture kept in the mind; a recollection: *memories of summer at the beach.* **5.** [*noncount*] the state or fact of being remembered, esp. to commemorate someone or something: *bowed their heads in memory of their parents.* **6.** [*noncount*] Also called **storage. a.** the capacity of a computer to store information: *random access memory.* **b.** the components of the computer in which such information is stored: *He bought extra memory and installed it in his computer.* See -MEM-.

men (men) /mɛn/ *n.* pl. of MAN.

-men-, *root.* *-men-* comes from Latin, where it has the meaning "mind." This meaning is found in such words as: COMMENTARY, MENTAL, MENTALITY, MENTION, REMINISCENT.

men•ace (men′is) /ˈmɛnɪs/ *n., v.,* **-aced, -ac•ing.** —*n.* **1.** [*count*] someone or something that threatens to cause evil, etc.; a threat: *He is a menace to society and should be locked away.* **2.** [*noncount*] the quality of such danger or behavior: *said with quiet menace, "No one is leaving."* —*v.* [~ + *obj*] **3.** to threaten; put in danger: *A gang menaced the students.*

men•ac•ing (men′ə sing) /ˈmɛnəsɪŋ/ *adj.* threatening: *menacing looks.* —**men′ac•ing•ly,** *adv.*

mé•nage or **me•nage** (mā näzh′) /meyˈnɑʒ/ *n.* [*count*] a household; a group of people living in a household.

me•nag•er•ie (mə naj′ə rē, -nazh′-) /məˈnædʒəriy, -ˈnæʒ-/ *n.* [*count*] **1.** a collection of animals, esp. for displaying. **2.** an unusual group of people.

mend (mend) /mɛnd/ *v.* **1.** [~ + *obj*] to make (something damaged) better by repairing: *to mend torn clothes.* **2.** [~ + *obj*] to set right; improve: *See if you can mend matters between them.* **3.** to (cause to) progress toward recovery: [*no obj*]: *His broken arm is mending.* [~ + *obj*]: *The treatment mended his broken arm.* —*n.* [*count*] **4.** the act of mending. **5.** a mended place or part. —***Idiom.* 6. mend one's fences,** to strengthen or establish again one's position by negotiation, discussing, or explaining: *mended his fences with his wife's family.* **7. mend one's ways,** to improve one's way of behaving: *As he grew older he mended his ways and became a useful citizen.* **8. on the mend,** improving, esp. in health: *The patient was on the mend.* —**mend′er,** *n.* [*count*]

men•da•cious (men dā′shəs) /mɛnˈdeyʃəs/ *adj.* **1.** telling lies, esp. as one's habit: *a mendacious official.* **2.** untrue: *a mendacious report.* —**men•da′cious•ly,** *adv.*

men•dac•i•ty (men das′i tē) /mɛnˈdæsɪtiy/ *n.* [*noncount*] the act or state of telling lies: *known for his mendacity.*

men•di•cant (men′di kənt) /ˈmɛndɪkənt/ *n.* [*count*] **1.** one who lives by begging; beggar. **2.** a member of a religious order who begs or lives on alms.

mend•ing (men′ding) /ˈmɛndɪŋ/ *n.* [*noncount*] **1.** the act of repairing clothes, as by sewing. **2.** clothes to be repaired.

men•folk (men′fōk′) /ˈmɛnˌfowk/ also **men•folks** (men′fōks) /ˈmɛnfowks/ *n.* [*plural; used with a plural verb*] men, esp. those of a family.

me•ni•al (mē′nē əl, mēn′yəl) /ˈmiyniyəl, ˈmiynyəl/ *adj.* **1.** degrading; low or unimportant: *menial work.* —*n.* [*count*] **2.** a domestic servant. —**me′ni•al•ly,** *adv.*

men•in•gi•tis (men′in jī′tis) /ˌmɛnɪnˈdʒaytɪs/ *n.* [*noncount; used with a singular verb*] a severe illness affecting the membranes covering the brain and spinal cord.

men•o•pause (men′ə pôz′) /ˈmɛnəˌpɔz/ *n.* [*noncount*] the time when a woman's menstruation naturally stops. —**men′o•pau′sal,** *adj.*

me•nor•ah (mə nôr′ə, -nōr′ə) /məˈnɔrə, -ˈnowrə/ *n.* [*count*] a special candelabrum used during the Jewish festival of Hanukkah.

men's′ room, *n.* [*count*] a public bathroom for men.

men•stru•al (men′strōō əl) /ˈmɛnstruwəl/ *adj.* [*before a noun*] of or relating to menstruation: *the menstrual flow.*

men•stru•ate (men′strōō āt′) /ˈmɛnstruwˌeyt/ *v.* [*no obj*], **-at•ed, -at•ing.** to undergo menstruation.

men•stru•a•tion (men′strōō ā′shən, -strā′-) /ˌmɛnstruwˈeyʃən, -ˈstrey-/ *n.* [*noncount*] the periodic flow of blood and tissue from a woman's uterus.

mens•wear (menz′wâr′) /ˈmɛnzˌwɛər/ *n.* [*noncount*] Also, **men's′ wear′.** items that go with clothing for men.

-ment, *suffix.* **1.** *-ment* is attached to verbs to form nouns that refer to the action of the verb: *govern + -ment → government.* **2.** *-ment* is also attached to verbs to form nouns that refer to a state or condition resulting from the action of a verb: *refresh + -ment → refreshment.* **3.** *-ment* is attached to verbs to form nouns that refer to a product resulting from the action of a verb: *frag- + -ment → fragment (= a piece resulting from the breaking off of something).*

men•tal (men′tl) /ˈmɛntl̩/ *adj.* [*before a noun*] **1.** of or relating to the mind: *mental capacity; mental arithmetic.* **2.** of or relating to a disorder of the mind: *a mental patient.* **3.** for persons with such a disorder: *a mental institution.* **4.** *Informal.* insane; crazy: *a real mental case.* —**men′tal•ly,** *adv.: tried to compute the odds mentally.* See -MEN-.

men•tal•ist (men′tl ist) /ˈmɛntl̩ɪst/ *n.* [*count*] a mind reader or fortune-teller.

men•tal•i•ty (men tal′i tē) /mɛnˈtælɪtiy/ *n., pl.* **-ties. 1.** [*noncount*] mental capacity; the ability of the mind: *superior mentality.* **2.** [*count*] a person's mental outlook: *a bossy mentality.* See -MEN-.

men′tal retarda′tion, *n.* [*noncount*] a developmental disorder affecting the ability of a person to learn.

men•thol (men′thôl, -thol) /ˈmɛnθɔl, -θɒl/ *n.* [*noncount*] an alcohol that dissolves in water, obtained from peppermint oil. —**men•tho•lat•ed** (men′thə lā′tid) /ˈmɛnθəˌleytɪd/ *adj.: mentholated cigarettes.*

men•tion (men′shən) /ˈmɛnʃən/ *v.* **1.** to refer briefly to; speak of: [~ + *obj*]: *Did she mention this to her husband?* [~ + (*that*) *clause*]: *Did I mention that we're leaving in five minutes?* —*n.* [*noncount*] **2.** an incidental reference: *The dog barked at the mention of her master's name.* **3.** formal recognition for a noteworthy act: *to receive honorable mention for her essay.* —***Idiom.* 4. Don't mention it.** This phrase is used as a polite answer to someone who has thanked you for your help: *"Thanks for everything." "--Don't mention it; I was glad to help."* **5. not to mention,** in addition to: *They own two houses, not to mention a boat.* See -MEN-.

men•tor (men′tôr, -tər) /ˈmɛntɔr, -tər/ *n.* [*count*] **1.** a trusted counselor or teacher: *Two of his professors were his mentors.* —*v.* [~ + *obj*] **2.** to act as a mentor (to): *He mentored several bright young students.*

men•u (men′yōō) /ˈmɛnyuw/ *n.* [*count*], *pl.* **men•us. 1.** a list of the dishes served at a meal. See illustration at RESTAURANT. **2.** the dishes served. **3.** a list of items from which to choose, as of options available to a computer user: *From the menu select S, N, or D.*

me•ow (mē ou′) /miyˈaw/ *n.* [*count*] **1.** the sound a cat makes. —*v.* [*no obj*] **2.** to make the sound of a cat.

-merc-, *root.* *-merc-* comes from Latin, where it has the meaning "trade." This meaning is found in such words as: COMMERCE, COMMERCIAL, INFOMERCIAL, MERCANTILE, MERCENARY, MERCHANT.

mer•can•tile (mûr′kən tēl′, -tīl′, -til) /ˈmɜrkənˌtiyl, -ˌtayl, -tɪl/ *adj.* [*before a noun*] of or relating to merchants or trade. See -MERC-.

mer•ce•nar•y (mûr′sə ner′ē) /ˈmɜrsəˌnɛriy/ *adj., n., pl.* **-nar•ies.** —*adj.* **1.** working for money and not for ideals: *She'd become mercenary and no longer cared about the underprivileged.* **2.** hired to serve in a foreign army: *mercenary forces.* —*n.* [*count*] **3.** a professional soldier hired to serve in a foreign army: *The mercenaries decided to surrender.* See -MERC-.

mer•chan•dise (*n.* mûr′chən dīz′, -dīs′; *v.* -dīz′) / *n.* ˈmɜrtʃənˌdayz, -ˌdays; *v.* -ˌdayz/ *n., v.,* **-dised, -dis•ing.** —*n.* [*noncount*] **1.** goods bought and sold. **2.** the stock of goods in a store: *took an inventory of all the merchandise.* —*v.* **3.** [*no obj*] to carry on trade: *trained in merchandising.* **4.** [~ + *obj*] to promote the sales of: *busy merchandising the new T-shirts.* —**mer′chan•dis′er,** *n.* [*count*] See -MERC-.

mer•chant (mûr′chənt) /ˈmɜrtʃənt/ *n.* [*count*] **1.** one whose business is buying and selling goods for profit. **2.** a storekeeper; retailer. **3.** one who indulges in something undesirable: *the merchants of gloom and doom.* —*adj.* [*before a noun*] **4.** used for trade or commerce: *a merchant ship.* See -MERC-.

mer•chant•a•ble (mûr′chən tə bəl) /ˈmɜrtʃəntəbəl/ *adj.* marketable.

mer′chant marine′, *n.* [*noncount*] **1.** the ships of a nation that work in commerce. **2.** the officers and crews of such ships.

mer•ci•ful (mûr′si fəl) /ˈmɜrsɪfəl/ *adj.* **1.** showing mercy to another: *a merciful judge.* **2.** fortunate: *a merciful release from the pain.* —**mer′ci•ful′ly,** *adv.*: *It was mercifully quiet.*

mer•ci•less (mûr′si lis) /'mɜrsɪlɪs/ *adj.* **1.** having or showing no mercy: *merciless to his enemies.* **2.** harsh; difficult: *merciless snowstorms.* —**mer′ci•less•ly,** *adv.*

mer•cu•ri•al (mər kyŏŏr′ē əl) /mər'kyʊriyəl/ *adj.* changeable; varying; erratic: *a mercurial nature; a mercurial mood.*

mer•cu•ry (mûr′kyə rē) /'mɜrkyəriy/ *n.* [*noncount*] **1.** a heavy, silver-white element, liquid at room temperature; quicksilver: *Mercury is used in thermometers.* **2.** temperature: *The mercury climbed to a hundred today.*

mer•cy (mûr′sē) /'mɜrsiy/ *n., pl.* **-cies. 1.** [*noncount*] compassion or kindness shown toward an offender or an enemy; benevolence: *to show no mercy toward enemies.* **2.** [*count*] an act of kindness or compassion. **3.** [*count*] something of good fortune; blessing: *It was a mercy that they weren't hurt.* —***Idiom.* 4. at the mercy of,** in the power of; subject to: *The little boat was completely at the mercy of the hurricane.*

mer′cy kill′ing, *n.* EUTHANASIA.

mere (mēr) /mɪər/ *adj.* [*before a noun*], *superlative* **mer•est.** being nothing more than what is specified; minor or unimportant: *A mere child couldn't defeat him.*

mere•ly (mēr′lē) /'mɪərliy/ *adv.* only (and nothing more); just; simply: *Instead of making a fuss, he merely raised an eyebrow.*

mer•e•tri•cious (mer′i trish′əs) /ˌmɛrɪ'trɪʃəs/ *adj.* appearing to be attractive but without value; tawdry. —**mer′e•tri′cious•ly,** *adv.* —**mer′e•tri′cious•ness,** *n.* [*noncount*]

-merg-, *root.* *-merg-* comes from Latin, where it has the meaning "plunge; dip; mix." This meaning is found in such words as: EMERGE, EMERGENCY, IMMERSE, IMMMERSION, MERGE, MERGER, SUBMERGE.

merge (mûrj) /mɜrdʒ/ *v.,* **merged, merg•ing. 1.** to (cause to) become combined; (cause to) lose identity by blending: [*no obj*]: *The two rivers merge at that city.* [~ + *obj*]: *In the story he merged his mind with the robot's and shared its thoughts.* **2.** to combine into a single body, etc.: [*no obj*]: *The two firms merged.* [~ + *obj*]: *She merged the two firms together.* See -MERG-.

merg•er (mûr′jər) /'mɜrdʒər/ *n.* [*count*] **1.** a combining of corporations by transferring the properties to one corporation. **2.** an act or instance of merging. See -MERG-.

me•rid•i•an (mə rid′ē ən) /mə'rɪdiyən/ *n.* [*count*] **1. a.** a great circle of the earth passing from one pole to another. **b.** the half of such a circle between the poles. —*adj.* [*before a noun*] **2.** of or relating to a meridian.

me•ringue (mə rang′) /mə'ræŋ/ *n.* **1.** [*noncount*] a pie topping made of stiffly beaten egg whites. **2.** [*count*] a pie topped with meringue.

mer•it (mer′it) /'mɛrɪt/ *n.* **1.** [*noncount*] claim to respect and praise; excellence; worth: *received a pay raise on the basis of merit.* **2.** [*count*] something that deserves praise: *Its chief merit is simplicity.* **3. merits,** [*plural*] the basic rights and wrongs of a matter: *The jury was instructed to decide the case on its merits.* —*v.* [*not: be* + ~*-ing;* ~ + *obj*] **4.** to be worthy of; deserve: *Do you think this case merits further discussion?*

mer•i•toc•ra•cy (mer′i tok′rə sē) /ˌmɛrɪ'tɒkrəsiy/ *n., pl.* **-cies.** a system in which talented persons are rewarded and advanced: [*noncount*]: *The concept of meritocracy was foreign to our company.* [*count*]: *Meritocracies exist in some companies.* See -CRACY.

mer•i•to•ri•ous (mer′i tôr′ē əs, -tōr′-) /ˌmɛrɪ'tɔriyəs, -'towr-/ *adj.* deserving praise; praiseworthy. —**mer′i•to′ri•ous•ly,** *adv.*

mer•maid (mûr′mād′) /'mɜrˌmeyd/ *n.* [*count*] (in folklore) a female creature of the sea, having the head and torso of a woman and the tail of a fish.

mer•man (mûr′man′) /'mɜrˌmæn/ *n.* [*count*], *pl.* **-men.** (in folklore) a male creature of the sea, having the head and torso of a man and the tail of a fish.

mer•ri•ment (mer′i mənt) /'mɛrɪmənt/ *n.* [*noncount*] cheerful or joyful behavior; enjoyment; mirth.

mer•ry (mer′ē) /'mɛriy/ *adj.,* **-ri•er, -ri•est. 1.** full of cheerfulness or joy; joyous in spirit: *He was a merry soul that evening.* **2.** having much festiveness: *a merry party.* —**mer′ri•ly,** *adv.*: *merrily rejoicing.*

mer′ry-go-round′, *n.* [*count*] **1.** a revolving circular platform with wooden horses, benches, etc., on which people ride, as at an amusement park. **2.** a busy round of events: *The candidate has been on a merry-go-round of speeches, banquets, and press conferences.*

mer•ry•mak•ing (mer′ē mā′king) /'mɛriyˌmeykɪŋ/ *n.* [*noncount*] the act of taking part gaily or joyfully in some festivity. —**mer′ry•mak′er,** *n.* [*count*]

me•sa (mā′sə) /'meysə/ *n.* [*count*], *pl.* **-sas.** a land formation having steep sides and a relatively flat top, common in the southwestern U.S.

mes•ca•line (mes′kə lēn′, -lin) /'mɛskəˌliyn, -lɪn/ *n.* [*noncount*] a white, crystallike powder that produces hallucinations.

mes•dames (mā däm′, -dämz′, -dam′, -damz′) /mey'dɑm, -'dɑmz, -'dæm, -'dæmz/ *n.* [*plural*] **1.** a pl. of MADAM. **2.** a pl. of MADAME.

mes•de•moi•selles (mā′də mə zel′, -zelz′, mād′mwə-) /ˌmeydəmə'zɛl, -'zɛlz, ˌmeydmwə-/ *n.* [*plural*] a pl. of MADEMOISELLE.

mesh (mesh) /mɛʃ/ *n.* [*noncount*] **1.** an arrangement of interlocking metal links used in jewelry, sieves, etc. **2.** any fabric of open texture resembling a net: *stockings of mesh.* **3.** an intertwined structure resembling a net; network. —*v.* **4.** to (cause to) become or be engaged, as the teeth of gears: [*no obj*]: *The gears meshed smoothly.* [~ + *obj*]: *He meshed the gears smoothly.* **5.** to (cause to) match, coordinate, or fit together: [*no obj*]: *Her ideas meshed with mine.* [~ + *obj*]: *meshed the ideas into one proposal.*

mes•mer•ize (mez′mə rīz′, mes′-) /'mɛzməˌrayz, 'mɛs-/ *v.* [~ + *obj*], **-ized, -iz•ing.** to keep the attention of; fascinate or spellbind: *The TV mesmerizes the children.* —**mes•mer•ism** (mez′mə riz′əm, mes′-) /'mɛzməˌrɪzəm, 'mɛs-/ *n.* [*noncount*] —**mes′mer•iz′er,** *n.* [*count*]

mes•quite or **mes•quit** (me skēt′, mes′kēt) /mɛ'skiyt, 'mɛskiyt/ *n.* **1.** [*count*] a spiny tree or shrub of W North America. **2.** [*noncount*] the wood of such a tree or shrub.

mess (mes) /mɛs/ *n.* **1.** a dirty or disorderly state: [*count; singular*]: *Things are in a mess here.* [*noncount*]: *How much mess did they make?* **2.** [*count*] a dirty or disorderly person or thing: *The room is a mess. Look at your clothes; you're a mess.* **3.** [*count*] a dirty or untidy mass; jumble: *a mess of papers.* **4.** [*count; usually singular*] an unpleasant situation; trouble: *Look at the mess you've gotten us into now.* **5.** [*count*] a group, as in the military, regularly taking their meals together. **6.** [*noncount*] the meal so taken. **7.** [*count*] MESS HALL. —*v.* **8.** to make dirty or untidy: [~ + *obj*]: *Please, you're messing my hair.* [~ + *up* + *obj*]: *Don't mess up the room!* [~ + *obj* + *up*]: *Don't mess it up!* **9. mess around** or **about, a.** [*no obj*] to busy oneself without purpose; waste time: *He was just messing around.* **b.** [~ + *around/about* + *with* + *obj*] to involve oneself, esp. for unlawful purposes, or in some dangerous way: *to mess around with gamblers.* **c.** [~ + *around/about* (+ *with* + *obj*)] to have sexual affairs: *to mess around (with other women).* **10. mess in** or **with,** [~ + ~ + *in/with* + *obj*] to interfere with (someone); meddle: *Stop messing in my affairs.* **11. mess up, a.** [*no obj*] to perform poorly; produce errors or confusion: *It's your big chance, so don't mess up.* **b.** to make a mess of (affairs, etc.); spoil or ruin: [~ + *up* + *obj*]: *to mess up all our plans.* [~ + *obj* + *up*]: *to mess things up.* **c.** to treat roughly; beat up: [~ + *obj* + *up*]: *The gang messed him up.* [~ + *up* + *obj*]: *promised to mess up anyone who got in his way.* **12. mess with,** [~ + *with* + *obj*] to become involved with (someone or something dangerous): *Don't mess with drugs.*

mes•sage (mes′ij) /'mɛsɪdʒ/ *n.* [*count*] **1.** a communication delivered in writing, speech, etc.: *There was a message at the hotel for me.* **2.** the main point of something, as of a speech or book: *The message of the movie was clear: war is horrible.* **3.** a warning: *He was sending a clear message to us: they are prepared to fight to the end.* —***Idiom.* 4. get the message,** to understand a warning sent: *doesn't get the message that her work is not satisfactory.*

mes•sei•gneurs (mā se nyŏŏr′), /meysɛ'nyʊr/. *n.* [*plural*] (*sometimes cap.*) pl. of MONSEIGNEUR.

mes•sen•ger (mes′ən jər) /'mɛsəndʒər/ *n.* [*count*] a person who carries messages or parcels.

mess′ hall′, *n.* [*count*] a dining hall, esp. at a military base.

Mes•si•ah (mi sī′ə) /mɪ'sayə/ *n.* **1.** [*proper noun; often: the* + ~] the promised deliverer of the Jewish people. **2.** [*proper noun; usually: the* + ~] Jesus Christ, regarded by Christians as fulfilling this promise. —**Mes•si•an•ic** (mes′ē an′ik) /ˌmɛsiy'ænɪk/ *adj.* [*before a noun*]

mes•sieurs (me syœ′), /mɛ'syœ/. *n.* [*plural*] pl. of MONSIEUR.

Messrs. (mes′ərz) /'mɛsərz/ pl. of MR.

mess•y (mes′ē) /'mɛsiy/ *adj.,* **-i•er, -i•est. 1.** dirty, untidy, or disorderly: *very messy in his personal habits.* **2.**

jumbled; confused; involving trouble or danger: *a difficult, messy situation.* —**mess•i•ly** (mes′ə lē) /ˈmɛsəliy/ *adv.* —**mess′i•ness,** *n.*

mes•ti•zo (me stē′zō) /mɛˈstiyzow/ *n.* [*count*], *pl.* **-zos, -zoes.** a person of different races, esp., of mixed American Indian and European ancestry.

met (met) /mɛt/ *v.* pt. and pp. of MEET[1].

meta-, *prefix. meta-* comes from Greek, where it has the meanings "after, along with, beyond, among, behind." These meanings are found in such words as: METABOLISM, METAMORPHOSIS, METAPHOR, METAPHYSICS.

met•a•bol•ic (met′ə bol′ik) /ˌmɛtəˈbɒlɪk/ *adj.* [*before a noun*] of or relating to metabolism: *a high metabolic rate.*

me•tab•o•lism (mə tab′ə liz′əm) /məˈtæbəˌlɪzəm/ *n.* the physical and chemical processes in a living body by which it is produced and maintained: [*noncount*]: *studying the metabolism of dolphins.* [*count*]: *He has a very active metabolism.*

me•tab•o•lize (mə tab′ə līz′) /məˈtæbəˌlayz/ *v.,* **-lized, -liz•ing.** to perform the process of metabolism: [*no obj*]: *He wasn't metabolizing as well as he should.* [∼ + *obj*]: *Can the body metabolize these proteins efficiently?*

met•a•car•pus (met′ə kär′pəs) /ˌmɛtəˈkɑrpəs/ *n., pl.* **-pi** (-pī) /-pay/. the bones between the wrist and the fingers. —**met′a•car′pal,** *adj., n.* [*count*]

met•al (met′l) /ˈmɛtl̩/ *n.* **1.** a usually solid, shiny, basic substance, as gold, silver, or copper, that can be used to conduct electricity or heat: [*noncount*]: *Early man learned how to use metal for weapons.* [*count*]: *Gold is a valuable metal.* **2.** an alloy or mixture of such substances, as brass, etc.: [*noncount*]: *Instead of metal, this car was made of fiberglass.* [*count*]: *They tried many different metals before they found aluminum.*

me•tal•lic (mə tal′ik) /məˈtælɪk/ *adj.* of, made of, or resembling metal: *a loud metallic clang.*

met•al•lur•gy (met′l ûr′jē) /ˈmɛtl̩ˌɜrdʒiy/ *n.* [*noncount*] the science of metals, including their properties and uses. —**met′al•lur′gist,** *n.* [*count*]

met•a•mor•phism (met′ə môr′fiz əm) /ˌmɛtəˈmɔrfɪzəm/ *n.* [*noncount*] a natural change in the structure of a rock, as from heat. —**met′a•mor′phic,** *adj.*: *metamorphic rocks.* See -MORPH-.

met•a•mor•phose (met′ə môr′fōz, -fōs) /ˌmɛtəˈmɔrfowz, -fows/ *v.,* **-phosed, -phos•ing. 1.** to subject to metamorphosis or metamorphism: [∼ + *obj*]: *The heat metamorphosed those rocks.* [*no obj*]: *Over thousands of years the rocks metamorphosed.* **2.** to (cause to) undergo a change in form or nature: [*no obj*]: *She metamorphosed into a lovely creature when she matured.* [∼ + *obj*]: *Living in the city metamorphosed him into an unfeeling killer.* See -MORPH-.

met•a•mor•pho•sis (met′ə môr′fə sis) /ˌmɛtəˈmɔrfəsɪs/ *n., pl.* **-ses** (-sēz′) /-ˌsiyz/. **1.** a significant change in form from one stage to the next in the life history of a living thing, as from the caterpillar to the pupa to the butterfly: [*noncount*]: *the study of metamorphosis.* [*count*]: *a late metamorphosis.* **2.** [*count*] any complete change in appearance, character, etc.: *Politics is undergoing an important metamorphosis.* See -MORPH-.

met•a•phor (met′ə fôr′, -fər) /ˈmɛtəˌfɔr, -fər/ *n.* **1.** [*count*] a way of describing another object or thing by suggesting a comparison of it to something else, but without using the word "like" or "as": *The rose is often a metaphor of love in poetry.* **2.** [*noncount*] the use of such a way of describing things: *examples of metaphor in the* Iliad. **3.** [*count*] a symbol or sign of something else: *That crime story is a metaphor of the times.*

met•a•phor•i•cal (met′ə fôr′i kəl, -for′-) /ˌmɛtəˈfɔrɪkəl, -ˈfɒr-/ *adj.* using or described by metaphor: *a metaphorical statement.* —**met′a•phor′i•cal•ly,** *adv.*: *I was speaking metaphorically when I said that, not literally.*

met•a•phys•i•cal (met′ə fiz′i kəl) /ˌmɛtəˈfɪzɪkəl/ *adj.* **1.** of or relating to metaphysics: *the metaphysical notions of meaning, truth, and beauty.* **2.** highly abstract, subtle, or difficult to understand: *You've become too metaphysical for me at this point.*

met•a•phys•ics (met′ə fiz′iks) /ˌmɛtəˈfɪzɪks/ *n.* [*noncount; used with a singular verb*] the branch of philosophy that deals with questions of knowledge and the existence of the world: *Metaphysics was influenced greatly by Einstein's theories.* See -PHYS-.

me•tas•ta•sis (mə tas′tə sis) /məˈtæstəsɪs/ *n., pl.* **-ses** (-sēz′) /-ˌsiyz/. **1.** [*count*] the spread of disease-producing organisms or of cancer cells to other parts of the body. **2.** [*noncount*] the condition produced by this: *The X-rays showed the areas of metastasis.* —**met•a•stat•ic** (met′ə stat′ik) /ˌmɛtəˈstætɪk/ *adj.*

me•tas•ta•size (mə tas′tə sīz′) /məˈtæstəˌsayz/ *v.* [*no obj*], **-sized, -siz•ing.** to spread by means of metastasis.

mete (mēt) /miyt/ *v.* [∼ + *out* + *obj*], **met•ed, met•ing. 1.** to distribute by measure; allot: *to mete out praise.* **2.** to give out or order (punishment) officially: *The judge meted out a prison term.*

me•te•or (mē′tē ər, -ôr′) /ˈmiytiyər, -ˌɔr/ *n.* [*count*] **1.** a meteoroid that has entered the earth's atmosphere. **2.** a short-lasting, fiery streak in the sky produced by a meteoroid passing through the earth's atmosphere.

me•te•or•ic (mē′tē ôr′ik, -or′-) /ˌmiytiyˈɔrɪk, -ˈɒr-/ *adj.* **1.** of or relating to meteors. **2.** resembling a meteor in quick brilliance, suddenness of appearance, etc.: *a meteoric rise to fame.*

me•te•or•ite (mē′tē ə rīt′) /ˈmiytiyəˌrayt/ *n.* [*count*] **1.** the remains of a meteoroid that has reached the earth from outer space: *The tip of the meteorite was still glowing from the heat.* **2.** a meteoroid.

me•te•or•oid (mē′tē ə roid′) /ˈmiytiyəˌrɔyd/ *n.* [*count*] any of the small bodies of rock or metal traveling through space that, upon entering the earth's atmosphere, are heated to glowing and become meteors.

me•te•or•ol•o•gy (mē′tē ə rol′ə jē) /ˌmiytiyəˈrɒlədʒiy/ *n.* [*noncount*] the science dealing with the atmosphere, weather, and climate. —**me•te•or•o•log•ic** (mē′tē ər ə-loj′ik) /ˌmiytiyərəˈlɒdʒɪk/ **me′te•or•o•log′i•cal,** *adj.* —**me′te•or•ol′o•gist,** *n.* [*count*]: *TV weather forecasters prefer to be called meteorologists.*

me•ter[1] (mē′tər) /ˈmiytər/ *n.* [*count*] a unit of length, equivalent to 39.37 U.S. inches; now defined as 1/299,792,458 of the distance light travels in a vacuum in one second. *Abbr.*: m See -METER-.

me•ter[2] (mē′tər) /ˈmiytər/ *n.* **1. a.** [*noncount*] the rhythmic element in music. **b.** [*count*] the unit of measurement adopted for a given piece of music. **2.** [*noncount*] the arrangement of words in poetic rhymes. See -METER-.

me•ter[3] (mē′tər) /ˈmiytər/ *n.* [*count*] **1.** an instrument for measuring and recording the quantity of something, as of water, miles, or time: *an electric meter.* **2.** PARKING METER: *a few more minutes left on the meter.* —*v.* [∼ + *obj*] **3.** to measure by means of a meter: *The gas was metered.* **4.** to process (mail) by means of a postage meter. See -METER-.

-meter-, *root. -meter-* comes from Greek, where it has the meaning "measure." This meaning is found in such words as: ANEMOMETER, BAROMETER, CENTIMETER, DIAMETER, GEOMETRY, KILOMETER, METER, METRIC, METRONOME, ODOMETER, PARAMETER, PEDOMETER, PERIMETER, SYMMETRY.

me′ter maid′, *n.* [*count*] a woman who is a member of a police or traffic department who issues tickets for parking violations.

meth•a•done (meth′ə dōn′) /ˈmɛθəˌdown/ also **meth•a•don** (meth′ə don′) /ˈmɛθəˌdɒn/ *n.* [*noncount*] an artificially produced narcotic similar to morphine but taken orally: *Methadone is used as a heroin substitute.*

meth•ane (meth′ān) /ˈmɛθeyn/ *n.* [*noncount*] a colorless, odorless gas that can be burned, the main part of marsh gas.

meth•a•nol (meth′ə nôl′, -nol′) /ˈmɛθəˌnɔl, -ˌnɒl/ *n.* METHYL ALCOHOL.

me•thinks (mi thingks′) /mɪˈθɪŋks/ *v. impers.; pt.* **me•thought** (mi thôt′) /mɪˈθɔt/ *Archaic.* it seems to me.

meth•od (meth′əd) /ˈmɛθəd/ *n.* **1.** [*count*] a procedure, technique, or planned way of doing something: *There are several methods we could use to recover your lost data.* **2.** [*noncount*] order or system in doing anything: *There's no method to your work.*

me•thod•i•cal (mə thod′i kəl) /məˈθɒdɪkəl/ *adj.* done with method; orderly, systematic, or careful: *A methodical search of the surrounding area failed to turn up any clues.* —**me•thod′i•cal•ly,** *adv.*

Meth•od•ism (meth′ə diz′əm) /ˈmɛθəˌdɪzəm/ *n.* [*noncount*] the religion of Methodists.

Meth•od•ist (meth′ə dist) /ˈmɛθədɪst/ *n.* [*count*] a member of a Christian group founded by John Wesley.

meth•od•ol•o•gy (meth′ə dol′ə jē) /ˌmɛθəˈdɒlədʒiy/ *n., pl.* **-gies.** a set or system of methods or principles used in a discipline, as in the sciences: [*noncount*]: *the methodology used in her research.* [*count*]: *experience with several methodologies.* —**meth•od•o•log•i•cal** (meth′ə-dl oj′i kəl) /ˌmɛθədl̩ˈɒdʒɪkəl/ *adj.*

meth•yl al′cohol (meth′əl) /ˈmɛθəl/ *n.* [*noncount*] a colorless poisonous liquid used as a solvent, a fuel, or in antifreeze. Also called **methanol**.

me•tic•u•lous (mə tik′yə ləs) /məˈtɪkyələs/ *adj.* **1.** taking or showing extreme care about small details: *He was very meticulous in his figures.* **2.** finicky; fussy: *a meticulous dresser.* **—me•tic′u•lous•ly,** *adv.* **—me•tic′u•lous•ness,** *n.* [*noncount*]

mé•tier or **me•tier** (mā′tyā, mā tyā′) /ˈmeytyey, meyˈtyey/ *n.* [*count*] **1.** a field of work; profession. **2.** a field of activity in which one has special ability or training: *Learning languages is his métier.*

me•tre (mē′tər) /ˈmiytər/ *n., v.,* **-tred, -tring.** *Chiefly Brit.* METER.

met•ric (me′trik) /ˈmɛtrɪk/ *adj.* [*before a noun*] relating to the meter or to the metric system. See -METER-.

met•ri•cal (me′tri kəl) /ˈmɛtrɪkəl/ also **metric,** *adj.* **1.** relating to or composed in meter. **2.** relating to measurement. **—met′ri•cal•ly,** *adv.* See -METER-.

met•ri•ca•tion (me′tri kā′shən) /ˌmɛtrɪˈkeyʃən/ *n.* [*noncount*] the process or result of establishing the metric system as the standard system of measurement.

met•ri•cize (me′trə sīz′) /ˈmɛtrəˌsayz/ *v.* [~ + *obj*], **-cized, -ciz•ing.** to express in terms of the metric system.

met′ric sys′tem, *n.* [*count*] a decimal system of weights and measures, universally used in science, and the official system of measurement in many countries: *the metric system of milliliters, centiliters, and liters.*

met′ric ton′, *n.* [*count*] a unit of 1000 kilograms, equivalent to 2204.62 pounds.

met•ro (me′trō) /ˈmɛtrow/ *n., pl.* **-ros.** [*often: Metro*] the underground railway of certain cities, as Washington, D.C., and Paris, France: [*count*]: Compare the metros in both cities. [*noncount*]: *You can get there by metro.*

met•ro•nome (me′trə nōm′) /ˈmɛtrəˌnowm/ *n.* [*count*] an instrument that makes repeated clicks, used to mark rhythm in practicing music. See -METER-.

me•trop•o•lis (mi trop′ə lis) /mɪˈtrɒpəlɪs/ *n.* [*count*], *pl.* **-lis•es.** the chief city of a country or region. See -POLIS-.

met•ro•pol•i•tan (me′trə pol′i tn) /ˌmɛtrəˈpɒlɪtn̩/ *adj.* **1.** of or relating to a metropolis: *Storms are expected in the metropolitan area tonight.* **2.** of or like a metropolis in being sophisticated: *a metropolitan outlook.* See -POLIS-.

met•tle (met′l) /ˈmɛtl̩/ *n.* [*noncount*] **1.** courage or willingness to do a task: *a man of mettle.* **2.** disposition or temperament: *of fine mettle.*

met•tle•some (met′l səm) /ˈmɛtl̩səm/ *adj.* spirited; courageous.

mew (myōō) /myuw/ *n.* [*count*] **1.** the high-pitched cry of a cat. **—v.** [*no obj*] **2.** to make a mew or similar sound.

mewl (myōōl) /myuwl/ *v.* [*no obj*] to cry, as a baby, young child, or the like; whimper.

Mex•i•can (mek′si kən) /ˈmɛksɪkən/ *adj.* **1.** of or relating to Mexico. **—n.** [*count*] **2.** a person born or living in Mexico.

mez•za•nine (mez′ə nēn′, mez′ə nēn′) /ˈmɛzəˌniyn, ˌmɛzəˈniyn/ *n.* [*count*] **1.** the lowest balcony in a theater: *seats in the mezzanine.* **2.** a low-ceilinged story between two other stories, usually immediately above the ground floor: *room 535 on the mezzanine.*

mez′zo-sopran′o (met′sō, med′zō, mez′ō) /ˈmɛtsow, ˈmɛdzow, ˈmɛzow/ *n., pl.* **-pran•os,** *adj.* **—n.** [*count*] **1.** a voice or voice part which has a range between that of a soprano and a contralto. **2.** a person having such a voice. **—adj.** [*before a noun*] **3.** of, relating to, characteristic of, or suitable to a mezzo-soprano.

mfg., an abbreviation of: manufacturing.

mfr., an abbreviation of: **1.** manufacture. **2.** *pl.* **mfrs.** manufacturer.

mg, an abbreviation of: milligram.

mgr or **Mgr,** an abbreviation of: **1.** manager. **2.** Monseigneur. **3.** Monsignor.

MHz, an abbreviation of: megahertz.

mi (mē) /miy/ *n. Music.* the syllable used for the name of the third tone in the Western musical scale.

MI, an abbreviation of: Michigan.

mi, an abbreviation of: mile.

mi., an abbreviation of: **1.** mile. **2.** mill.

MIA or **M.I.A.,** an abbreviation of: missing in action.

mi•as•ma (mī az′mə, mē-) /mayˈæzmə, miy-/ *n.* [*count*], *pl.* **-mas, -ma•ta** (-mə tə) /-mətə/. **1.** unpleasant or harmful fumes: *a miasma rising from the backed-up sewer.* **2.** a dangerous deathlike influence: *The room had a miasma of evil.*

mi•ca (mī′kə) /ˈmaykə/ *n.* [*noncount*] a mineral that can be easily separated into thin transparent sheets.

mice (mīs) /mays/ *n.* pl. of MOUSE.

Mich., an abbreviation of: Michigan.

micro-, *prefix.* **1.** *micro-* comes from Greek, where it has the meaning: small or very small in comparison with others of its kind: *micro- + organism → microorganism (= very small living creature).* **2.** *micro-* also means restricted in scope: *micro- + habitat → microhabitat; micro- + economics → microeconomics.* **3.** *micro-* also means containing or dealing with texts that require enlargement to be read: *micro- + film → microfilm.* **4.** *micro-* is used to mean one millionth: *micro- + gram → microgram.* Also, *esp. before a vowel,* **micr-.**

mi•crobe (mī′krōb) /ˈmaykrowb/ *n.* [*count*] a microorganism, esp. a disease-causing bacterium.

mi•cro•bi•ol•o•gy (mī′krō bī ol′ə jē) /ˌmaykrowbayˈɒlədʒiy/ *n.* [*noncount*] the branch of biology dealing with microscopic organisms. **—mi′cro•bi•ol′o•gist,** *n.* [*count*]

mi•cro•chip (mī′krō chip′) /ˈmaykrowˌtʃɪp/ *n.* CHIP[1] (def. 5).

mi•cro•com•put•er (mī′krō kəm pyōō′tər) /ˈmaykrowkəmˌpyuwtər/ *n.* [*count*] a compact computer having less power than a minicomputer: *a lab full of microcomputers.*

mi•cro•cosm (mī′krə koz′əm), /ˈmaykrəˌkɒzəm/ *n.* [*count*] a world in miniature that has all the features of a larger world: *The problems in our community are a microcosm of what is happening around the country.* See -COSM-.

mi•cro•fiche (mī′krə fēsh′) /ˈmaykrəˌfiyʃ/ *n., pl.* **-fiche, -fich•es.** a flat sheet of microfilm: [*noncount*]: *documents available on microfiche.* [*count*]: *a machine to read microfiches.* Also called **fiche.**

mi•cro•film (mī′krə film′) /ˈmaykrəˌfɪlm/ *n.* **1.** a film having a miniature photographic copy of printed matter: [*noncount*]: *The data's on microfilm in the safe.* [*count*]: *The microfilms are cracked with age.* **—v.** [~ + *obj*] **2.** to make a microfilm of: *The secret formula was microfilmed and smuggled out of the country.*

mi•crom•e•ter[1] (mī krom′i tər) /mayˈkrɒmɪtər/ *n.* [*count*] any of various devices for measuring very small distances, angles, etc. See -METER-.

mi•cro•met•er[2] (mī′krō mē′tər) /ˈmaykrowˌmiytər/ *n.* [*count*] a micron.

mi•cron (mī′kron) /ˈmaykrɒn/ *n.* [*count*], *pl.* **-crons, -cra** (-krə) /-krə/. the millionth part of a meter.

mi•cro•or•gan•ism (mī′krō ôr′gə niz′əm) /ˌmaykrowˈɔrgəˌnɪzəm/ *n.* [*count*] any organism too small to be viewed by the unaided eye, as bacteria or some fungi and algae. See -ORGA-.

mi•cro•phone (mī′krə fōn′) /ˈmaykrəˌfown/ *n.* [*count*] an instrument that changes sound waves into electric currents, used in recording or transmitting sound. See -PHON-.

mi•cro•proc•es•sor (mī′krō pros′es ər, -ə sər) /ˈmaykrowˌprɒsɛsər, -əsər/ *n.* [*count*] a small computer circuit that performs all the functions of a CPU.

mi•cro•scope (mī′krə skōp′) /ˈmaykrəˌskowp/ *n.* [*count*] an instrument having a magnifying lens, used for viewing objects too small to be seen by the unaided eye. **—mi•cros•co•py** (mī kros′kə pē) /mayˈkrɒskəpiy/ *n.* [*noncount*] See -SCOPE-.

mi•cro•scop•ic (mī′krə skop′ik) /ˌmaykrəˈskɒpɪk/ also **mi•cro•scop•i•cal** (mī′krə skop′i kəl) /ˌmaykrəˈskɒpɪkəl/ *adj.* **1.** too small to be visible without a microscope. **2.** very small; tiny: *He brushed a microscopic fleck of dust off his jacket.* **3.** very detailed; meticulous: *a microscopic analysis.* **—mi′cro•scop′i•cal•ly,** *adv.* See -SCOPE-.

mi•cro•sur•ger•y (mī′krō sûr′jə rē, mī′krō sûr′-) /ˈmaykrowˌsɜrdʒəriy, ˌmaykrowˈsɜr-/ *n.* [*noncount*] a surgical procedure performed under magnification and with specialized instruments.

mi•cro•wave (mī′krō wāv′) /ˈmaykrowˌweyv/ *n., v.,* **-waved, -wav•ing.** **—n.** [*count*] **1.** an electromagnetic wave of extremely high frequency. **2.** a microwave oven: *Put it in the microwave and defrost it.* **—v.** [~ + *obj*] **3.** to cook or heat in a microwave oven: *He microwaved dinner because he was in a hurry.* **—mi′cro•wav′a•ble,** *adj.: a microwavable plastic tray.*

mi′crowave ov′en, *n.* [*count*] an electrically operated oven that uses microwaves to generate heat. See illustration at APPLIANCE.

mid[1] (mid) /mɪd/ *adj.* [*before a noun*] being at or near the middle point of: *in mid autumn.*

mid[2] or **'mid** (mid) /mɪd/ *prep.* AMID.

mid-, *prefix. mid-* is attached to nouns and means "being at or near the middle point of": *midday; mid-Victorian; mid-twentieth century.*

mid•air (mid âr′) /mɪdˈɛər/ *n.* [*noncount*] **1.** any point in the air not touching the earth: *The helicopter pivoted in midair.* **—***adj.* [*before a noun*] **2.** occurring in midair: *a midair collision.*

mid•day (*n.* mid′dā′, -dā′; *adj.* -dā′) / *n.* ˈmɪdˈdey, -ˌdey; *adj.* -ˌdey/ *n.* [*noncount*] **1.** the middle of the day: *The sun is highest at midday.* **—***adj.* [*before a noun*] **2.** of or relating to the middle part of the day: *a midday news broadcast.*

mid•dle (mid′l) /ˈmɪdl̩/ *adj.* [*before a noun*] **1.** in or near the center; central: *the middle part of a room.* **2.** intermediate or intervening: *We could see them in the middle distance.* **—***n.* [*count*] **3.** [*usually singular*] the point, part, time, etc., that is at the same distance from extremes, limits, or starting and ending points: *in the middle of the pool.* **4.** the central part of the human body, esp. the waist: *He bent at the middle.* **—*Idiom.* 5. in the middle of,** while doing something: *I'm in the middle of an interview.*

mid′dle age′, *n.* [*noncount*] the period of human life between youth and old age, usually considered as the years between 45 and 65. —**mid′dle-aged′,** *adj.*: *a middle-aged tennis player.*

Mid′dle Ag′es, *n.* [*plural; the* + ~] the time in European history from the late 5th century to about 1350.

Mid′dle Amer′ica, *n.* **1.** [*noncount*] conventional middle-class Americans as a group: *Could he persuade Middle America to vote for him?* **2.** [*proper noun; no article*] the Midwest: *his bus tour of Middle America.* —**Mid′dle Amer′ican,** *n.* [*count*], *adj.*

mid•dle•brow (mid′l brou′) /ˈmɪdl̩ˌbraw/ *n.* [*count*] **1.** a person of ordinary tastes and interests: *A middlebrow is between a highbrow and a lowbrow.* **—***adj.* **2.** characteristic of middlebrows.

mid′dle class′, *n.* [*count*] a class of people intermediate between those of higher and lower economic or social standing. —**mid′dle-class′,** *adj.*: *criticizing her parents for their middle-class values.*

mid′dle ear′, *n.* [*count*] the middle portion of the ear made up of the eardrum and an air-filled chamber.

mid•dle•man (mid′l man′) /ˈmɪdl̩ˌmæn/ *n.* [*count*], *pl.* **-men. 1.** one who buys goods from the producer and resells them to the consumer. **2.** a person who goes between disputing parties to try to settle a conflict: *a middleman between the two factions.*

mid•dle•most (mid′l mōst′) /ˈmɪdl̩ˌmowst/ *adj.* MIDMOST.

mid′dle-of-the-road′, *adj.* favoring an intermediate position between two extremes, esp. in politics: *The candidate's middle-of-the-road position was favored by most voters.* —**mid′dle-of-the-road′er,** *n.* [*count*]

mid′dle school′, *n.* a school for grades five or six through eight: [*count*]: *a principal at two different middle schools.* [*noncount*]: *the first year of middle school.*

mid•dle•weight (mid′l wāt′) /ˈmɪdl̩ˌweyt/ *n.* [*count*] **1.** a boxer weighing up to 160 pounds (72.5 kg). **—***adj.* [*before a noun*] **2.** of or relating to middleweights: *the middleweight division.*

mid•dling (mid′ling) /ˈmɪdlɪŋ/ *adj.* **1.** average in size, quantity, or quality. **2.** mediocre; ordinary; commonplace. **—***adv.* **3.** moderately; fairly: *doing middling well.*

mid•dy (mid′ē) /ˈmɪdiy/ *n.* [*count*], *pl.* **-dies.** *Informal.* a midshipman.

midge (mij) /mɪdʒ/ *n.* [*count*] **1.** a very small, two-winged insect resembling a mosquito. **2.** a tiny person.

midg•et (mij′it) /ˈmɪdʒɪt/ *n.* [*count*] **1.** (not in technical use) an extremely small person having normal physical proportions. **2.** any animal or thing that is very small for its kind. **—***adj.* [*before a noun*] **3.** very small or of a class below the usual size; miniature.

mid•i (mid′ē) /ˈmɪdiy/ *n.* [*count*], *pl.* **mid•is.** a garment, as a coat, extending to the middle of the calf.

mid•land (mid′lənd) /ˈmɪdlənd/ *n.* [*count; usually: the* + ~] **1.** the middle or interior part of a country. **—***adj.* [*before a noun*] **2.** in or of the midland; inland.

mid•most (mid′mōst′) /ˈmɪdˌmowst/ *adj.* **1.** being in or near the very middle; middle. **2.** most private; innermost. **—***adv.* **3.** in the middle.

mid•night (mid′nīt′) /ˈmɪdˌnayt/ *n.* [*noncount; usually: no article*] **1.** the middle of the night, esp. twelve o'clock at night: *to stay up past midnight.* **—***adj.* [*before a noun*] **2.** of or relating to midnight: *a midnight swim in the ocean.* **—Usage.** The word MIDNIGHT, like the word NOON, is not normally used with *the*: *We met at midnight. The appointment was for midnight at the secret hideout.*

mid′night sun′, *n.* [*noncount; the* + ~] the sun that is visible at midnight during the summer in the arctic and antarctic.

mid•point (mid′point′) /ˈmɪdˌpɔynt/ *n.* [*count*] a point at or near the middle of something, as a line: *the midpoint of a line; the midpoint of the trip.* See -POINT-.

mid•riff (mid′rif) /ˈmɪdrɪf/ *n.* [*count*] **1.** DIAPHRAGM (def. 1). **2.** the middle portion of the human body, between the chest and the waist. **3.** the part of a dress or bodice that covers this area of the body.

mid•ship•man (mid′ship′mən, mid ship′-), /ˈmɪdˌʃɪpmən, mɪdˈʃɪp-/ *n.* [*count*], *pl.* **-men.** a student, as at the U.S. Naval Academy, in training for commission.

midst (midst) /mɪdst/ *n.* [*noncount*] **1.** [*often: in* + *the* + ~ + *of*] the position of being among other things or parts: *in the midst of the crowd.* **2.** [*often: in* + *the* + ~ + *of*] the position of occurring in the middle of a period of time, etc; the middle point or part: *got up in the midst of the concert and walked out.* **3.** [*often: in* + *the* + ~ + *of*] the state of being engaged in: *He was in the midst of work when the phone rang.* **4.** the middle or central point or part.

mid•stream (mid′strēm′) /ˈmɪdˈstriym/ *n.* [*noncount*] **1.** the middle of a stream. **2.** the middle period of a process or course: *in the midstream of her career.*

mid•sum•mer (mid′sum′ər, -sum′-) /ˈmɪdˈsʌmər, -ˌsʌm-/ *n.* [*noncount*] **1.** the middle of summer. **2.** the summer solstice, around June 21. **—***adj.* [*before a noun*] **3.** of, relating to, or occurring in the middle of the summer.

mid•term (mid′tûrm′) /ˈmɪdˌtɜrm/ *n.* **1.** [*noncount*] the halfway point of a term, as a term of office: *Our next project is due at midterm.* **2.** [*count*] an examination given halfway through a school term. **—***adj.* [*before a noun*] **3.** of or relating to a term: *midterm exams.*

mid•town (mid′toun′, -toun′) /ˈmɪdˈtawn, -ˌtawn/ *n.* [*noncount*] **1.** the central part of a city between uptown and downtown: *Most of midtown was closed to traffic.* **—***adj.* [*before a noun*] **2.** of or relating to this part: *a midtown café.*

mid•way (*adv., adj.* mid′wā′; *n.* -wā′) / *adv., adj.* ˈmɪdˈwey; *n.* -ˌwey/ *adj., adv.* **1.** in the middle of the way; halfway: [*adjective; before a noun*]: *the midway point of the project.* [*adverb*]: *to be positioned midway between the two warring sides.* **—***n.* [*count*] **2.** [*often: Midway*] a place or way, as at a carnival, having sideshows, games, and food stands.

mid•week (*n.* mid′wēk′, -wēk′; *adj.* -wēk′) / *n.* ˈmɪdˈwiyk, -ˌwiyk; *adj.* -ˌwiyk/ *n.* **1.** the middle of the week: [*count*]: *Midweeks I'm too busy to see you.* [*noncount*]: *Come midweek if you have the chance.* **—***adj.* [*before a noun*] **2.** relating to or occurring in the middle of the week: *a midweek conference.*

mid•wife (mid′wīf′) /ˈmɪdˌwayf/ *n., pl.* **-wives,** *v.,* **-wifed** or **-wived, -wif•ing** or **wiv•ing.** **—***n.* [*count*] **1.** one who assists women during childbirth. **2.** a person or thing that assists in producing something new: *a midwife in the creation of a new product.* **—***v.* [~ + *obj*] **3.** to assist in the birth of (a baby). **4.** to assist in producing or bringing about (something new): *She midwifed the new telephone mechanism.* —**mid•wife•ry** (mid wif′ə rē) /mɪdˈwɪfəriy/ *n.* [*noncount*]

mid•win•ter (*n.* mid′win′tər, -win′-; *adj.* -win′-) / *n.* ˈmɪdˈwɪntər, -ˌwɪn-; *adj.* -ˌwɪn-/ *n.* [*noncount*] **1.** the middle of winter. **2.** the winter solstice, around December 22. **—***adj.* [*before a noun*] **3.** of, relating to, or occurring in the middle of the winter.

mid•year (mid′yēr′, -yēr′) /ˈmɪdˈyɪər, -ˌyɪər/ *n.* **1.** [*noncount*] the middle of the year: *economic conditions at midyear.* **2.** [*count*] Often, **midyears.** [*plural*] an examination at the middle of a school year. **—***adj.* [*before a noun*] **3.** of or relating to midyear.

mien (mēn) /miyn/ *n.* [*count*] the face or manner of a person, esp. as it shows character, feeling, etc.

miff (mif) /mɪf/ *v.* to put (someone) into an irritable mood; offend: [*usually* ~ + *-ed*]: *miffed at not being invited to the party.* [*It* + ~ + *obj* + *that clause*]: *It miffed her that her friend did not invite her to his party.*

might[1] (mīt) /mayt/ *auxiliary (modal) v.* [~ + *root form of a verb*], *pres. sing. and pl.* **might;** *past* **might. 1. a.** (used to express the speaker's uncertainty about the possibility of the occurrence of the main verb): *It might rain. You might be right.* **b.** (used to express an opinion about something that did not happen, but for which there was a strong possibility): *I can't believe he did that; he might have been killed! (= There was a possibility, but in fact he was not killed)* **c.** (used to express that some action is or would have been a good idea): *They might at least have tried to get there on time.* **d.** (used to suggest some action): *You might begin by apologizing to her.* **e.** (used to express politeness when asking for something or for permission): *Might I speak to you for a moment?* **2.** pt. of MAY[1]: *I asked if we might borrow their car.* **3.** (used with another phrase or clause to express the condition, purpose, or result of something): *Let's agree on this so that (as a result) we might go home early. Difficult as it might be, we managed to do it.* **—*Idiom.* 4. might as well.** (used to express an opinion that there is no good reason for not doing the action of the main verb): *I can't stay awake so I might as well go to bed.*

might[2] (mīt) /mayt/ *n.* [*noncount*] **1.** physical strength: *He swung with all his might.* **2.** superior strength; force: *didn't believe that might makes right.* **3.** power to be effective: *the might of the ballot box.*

might•y (mī′tē) /ˈmaytiy/ *adj.*, **-i•er, -i•est,** *adv.*, *n.* **—*adj.* 1.** having or showing might: *mighty rulers.* **2.** of great size; huge: *the mighty Mississippi River.* **3.** great in amount, extent, or importance: *a mighty accomplishment.* **—*adv.* 4.** *Informal.* very; extremely: *I'm mighty pleased.* **—*n.* 5. the mighty,** [*plural; used with a plural verb*] mighty people thought of as a group. **—might•i•ly** (mīt′l ē) /ˈmaytḷiy/ *adv.* **—might′i•ness,** *n.* [*noncount*]

-migr-, *root.* -*migr*- comes from Latin, where it has the meaning "move to a new place; migrate." This meaning is found in such words as: EMIGRANT, EMIGRATE, IMMIGRATE, MIGRANT, MIGRATE, TRANSMIGRATION.

mi•graine (mī′grān) /ˈmaygreyn/ *n.* a severe, repeated headache, with pressure or throbbing: [*count*]: *a bad migraine after working late hours.* [*noncount*]: *the symptoms of migraine.*

mi•grant (mī′grənt) /ˈmaygrənt/ *adj.* [*before a noun*] **1.** migrating: *migrant workers.* **—*n.*** [*count*] **2.** a person or animal that migrates. **3.** Also called **mi′grant work′er.** one who moves from place to place to get work. See -MIGR-.

mi•grate (mī′grāt) /ˈmaygreyt/ *v.*, **-grat•ed, -grat•ing. 1.** [~ + *from/to* + *obj*] to move from one country, region, or place to another: *migrated from the farms to the cities.* **2.** [*no obj*] to pass at regular periods from one region to another, as certain birds: *The birds migrated south for the winter.* **—mi•gra•tion** (mī grā′shən) /mayˈgreyʃən/ *n.* [*count*]: *Some birds begin their migrations early.* [*noncount*]: *large-scale migration from the farms to the cities.* **—mi•gra•to•ry** (mī′grə tôr′ē, -tōr′ē) /ˈmaygrəˌtɔriy, -ˌtowriy/ *adj.*: *migratory birds.* See -MIGR-.

mike (mīk) /mayk/ *n.*, *v.*, **miked, mik•ing. —*n.*** [*count*] **1.** a microphone. **—*v.*** [~ + *obj*] **2.** to supply with a microphone: *to mike a singer.*

mil (mil) /mɪl/ *n.* [*count*] a unit of length equal to 0.001 of an inch (0.0254 mm), used in measuring the diameter of wires.

mild (mīld) /mayld/ *adj.*, **-er, -est. 1.** gentle or soft in feeling, manner, etc.: *a mild disposition.* **2.** not severe or extreme; temperate: *a mild winter.* **3.** not sharp in taste or smell: *a mild cheese.* **4.** moderate in strength, degree, or force: *a mild drug; a mild fever.* **—mild′ly,** *adv.*: *He spoke mildly to us.* **—mild′ness,** *n.* [*noncount*]: *the relative mildness of the infection.*

mil•dew (mil′do͞o′, -dyo͞o′) /ˈmɪlˌduw, -ˌdyuw/ *n.* [*noncount*] **1.** a cottony coating on plants, fabrics, etc., caused by fungi: *mildew on the pages of the old diary.* **—*v.* 2.** to (cause to) become affected with mildew: [*no obj*]: *The book had mildewed over the years.* [~ + *obj*]: *The book had been mildewed by moisture.*

mile (mīl) /mayl/ *n.* [*count*] **1.** a unit of distance on land in English-speaking countries equal to 5280 feet, or 1760 yards (1.609 kilometers). *Abbr.*: mi, mi. **2.** NAUTICAL MILE. **3.** any of various other units of distance used at different times in different countries: *A Swedish mile equals ten English miles.* **4.** a substantial distance: *She missed it by a mile.*

mile•age or **mil•age** (mī′lij) /ˈmaylɪdʒ/ *n.* [*noncount*] **1.** the total number of miles traveled in a given time: *The mileage for our trip was over 2,000.* **2.** the number of miles or average distance that a vehicle can travel on a quantity of fuel: *The mileage is about 20 miles per gallon.* **3.** wear, use, or profit: *to get good mileage out of an old coat.*

mile•post (mīl′pōst′) /ˈmaylˌpowst/ *n.* [*count*] any one of a series of posts set up to mark distance by miles, as along a highway.

mil•er (mī′lər) /ˈmaylər/ *n.* [*count*] a participant in a one-mile race.

mile•stone (mīl′stōn′) /ˈmaylˌstown/ *n.* [*count*] **1.** a stone that functions as a milepost. **2.** a significant or important event in history: *The fall of Communism was one of the milestones of the twentieth century.*

mi•lieu (mil yo͞o′) /mɪlˈyʊ/ *n.* [*count*], *pl.* **mi•lieus** (mil-yo͞oz′) /mɪlˈyʊz, miyl-/ **mi•lieux** (*Fr.* mē lyœ′) /*Fr.* miyˈlyœ/. surroundings; environment: *a poor social milieu.*

mil•i•tan•cy (mil′i tən sē) /ˈmɪlɪtənsiy/ *n.* [*noncount*] the actions of militant people: *The police weren't prepared for the militancy of the demonstrators.*

mil•i•tant (mil′i tənt) /ˈmɪlɪtənt/ *adj.* **1.** strongly aggressive and often combative, esp. in support of a cause: *militant reformers.* **2.** engaged in warfare; fighting. **—*n.*** [*count*] **3.** a militant person: *Militants staged violent demonstrations.* **—mil′i•tant•ly,** *adv.*

mil•i•ta•rism (mil′i tə riz′əm) /ˈmɪlɪtəˌrɪzəm/ *n.* [*noncount*] a strong military spirit or policy; maintenance of a large military establishment. **—mil′i•ta•rist,** *n.* [*count*] **—mil′i•ta•ris′tic,** *adj.*

mil•i•ta•rize (mil′i tə rīz′) /ˈmɪlɪtəˌrayz/ *v.* [~ + *obj*], **-rized, -riz•ing. 1.** to equip with armed forces, etc.: *The former buffer zone had become fully militarized again.* **2.** to fill (someone) with a feeling of militarism. **—mil•i•ta•ri•za•tion** (mil′i tər i zā′shən) /ˌmɪlɪtərɪˈzeyʃən/ *n.* [*noncount*]

mil•i•tar•y (mil′i ter′ē) /ˈmɪlɪˌtɛriy/ *adj.*, *n.*, *pl.* **-tar•y,** sometimes **-tar•ies. —*adj.*** [*before a noun*] **1.** of or relating to the army, armed forces, soldiers, or war-making: *military preparedness.* **—*n.* 2. the military, a.** [*noncount; used with a singular verb*] the armed forces of a nation; the military establishment: *The military does not want him to become president.* **b.** [*plural; used with a plural verb*] military personnel: *The military were not treating civilians kindly.*

mil′itary police′, *n.* [*plural; used with a plural verb*] soldiers who perform police duties within the army: *The military police were at the scene. Abbr.*: MP

mil•i•tate (mil′i tāt′) /ˈmɪlɪˌteyt/ *v.* [~ + *against* + *obj*], **-tat•ed, -tat•ing.** to have a substantial effect; weigh heavily; hinder: *His prison record militated against him.*

mi•li•tia (mi lish′ə) /mɪˈlɪʃə/ *n.* [*count*] a body of citizens enrolled for military service, called out at regular periods for drill but serving full time only in emergencies. **—mi•li′tia•man,** *n.* [*count*], *pl.* **-men.**

milk (milk) /mɪlk/ *n.* **1.** [*noncount*] a white liquid produced by the mammary glands of female mammals, serving to nourish their young: *fed by mother's milk.* **2.** this liquid from cows or other animals, used by humans for food or to make butter, cheese, etc.: [*noncount*]: *a glass of milk.* [*count*]: *He took two milks with his coffee (= two measures of milk).* **3.** [*noncount*] any liquid resembling this, as the liquid within a coconut. **—*v.*** [~ + *obj*] **4.** to draw milk from the udder or breast of: *milked the cows twice every day.* **5.** to take out or extract something from, as if by milking: *The snake handler carefully milked the rattlesnake of its venom.* **6.** to get something from; steal from: *milked her of all her savings.* **7.** to extract; draw out; obtain: *to milk laughs from the audience.* **—milk′er,** *n.* [*count*] **—milk′i•ness,** *n.* [*noncount*] **—milk′y,** *adj.*, **-i•er, -i•est.**

milk•maid (milk′mād′) /ˈmɪlkˌmeyd/ *n.* [*count*] a woman who milks cows or is employed in a dairy; dairymaid.

milk•man (milk′man′) /ˈmɪlkˌmæn/ *n.* [*count*], *pl.* **-men.** a person who sells or delivers milk.

milk′ of magne′sia, *n.* [*noncount*] a milky white liquid of magnesium hydroxide, used as an antacid or laxative.

milk′ shake′ or **milk′shake′,** *n.* [*count*] a beverage blended of milk, flavoring, and ice cream.

milk•sop (milk′sop′) /ˈmɪlkˌsɒp/ *n.* [*count*] a weak, feeble, ineffective, or useless person.

milk′ tooth′, *n.* [*count*] one of the temporary teeth that are later replaced by permanent teeth.

milk•weed (milk′wēd′) /ˈmɪlkˌwiyd/ *n.* [*count*] a plant having a milky juice and clusters of white-to-purple flowers.

Milk′y Way′, *n.* [*proper noun; usually: the* + ~] the spiral-shaped galaxy containing our solar system.

mill[1] (mil) /mɪl/ *n.* [*count*] **1.** a factory for certain kinds of manufacture, as steel or textiles: *the cotton mills of the Old South.* **2.** a building with machinery for grinding grain into flour. **3.** a machine for grinding or crushing any solid substance: *a coffee mill.* **4.** a business that gives out products in an impersonal or mechanical manner: *The school was a diploma mill.* **—*v.* 5.** [~ + *obj*] to grind, work, or shape in or with a mill: *The men milled the wheat into flour.* **6.** [*no obj*] to move slowly around without aim or purpose, or in confusion: *After the accident the crowd milled around.* **—*Idiom.* 7. through the mill,** through a set of difficult or painful experiences: *really been through the mill with three divorces.*

mill[2] (mil) /mɪl/ *n.* [*count*] a unit of money used in accounting, equal to .001 of a U.S. dollar.

mil•len•ni•um (mi len′ē əm) /mɪˈlɛniyəm/ *n.* [*count*], *pl.* **-ni•ums, -ni•a** (-nē ə) /-niyə/. a period of 1000 years: *to view history through the millenia.* —**mil•len′ni•al,** *adj.*

mill•er (mil′ər) /ˈmɪlər/ *n.* [*count*] a person who owns or operates a mill, esp. a mill that grinds grain into flour.

mil•let (mil′it) /ˈmɪlɪt/ *n.* [*noncount*] **1.** a grass grown as a food-grain crop. **2.** the grain of such a grass.

milli-, *prefix. milli-* comes from Latin, where it has the meanings: **1.** one thousand: *milli- + -pede (= foot) → millipede (= a small creature with very many legs).* **2.** (in the metric system) equal to 1/1000 of the unit mentioned: *milli- + meter → millimeter (= 1/1000 of a meter).*

mil•liard (mil′yərd, -yärd) /ˈmɪlyərd, -yɑrd/ *n.* [*count*] *Brit.* one thousand millions; equivalent to U.S. billion.

mil•li•gram (mil′i gram′) /ˈmɪlɪˌgræm/ *n.* [*count*] a unit of mass or weight equal to 1/1000 of a gram. *Abbr.:* mg Also, *esp. Brit.,* **mil′li•gramme′.**

mil•li•li•ter (mil′ə lē′tər) /ˈmɪləˌliytər/ *n.* [*count*] a unit of volume equal to 1/1000 of a liter, equivalent to 0.033815 fluid ounce. *Abbr.:* ml

mil•li•me•ter (mil′ə mē′tər) /ˈmɪləˌmiytər/ *n.* [*count*] a unit of length equal to 1/1000 of a meter, equivalent to 0. 03937 inch. *Abbr.:* mm

mil•li•ner (mil′ə nər) /ˈmɪlənər/ *n.* [*count*] a person who creates or sells hats for women.

mil•li•ner•y (mil′ə ner′ē, -nə rē) /ˈmɪləˌnɛriy, -nəriy/ *n.* [*noncount*] **1.** women's hats and related articles. **2.** the business or trade of a milliner.

mil•lion (mil′yən) /ˈmɪlyən/ *n., pl.* **-lions,** (*as after a numeral*) **-lion,** *adj.* —*n.* [*count*] **1.** a number, 1000 times 1000. **2.** a symbol for this number, as 1,000,000 or M̅. **3. millions,** [*plural*] a number between 1,000,000 and 999,999,999. **4.** the amount of a thousand thousand units of money: *The painting fetched a million.* **5.** a very great number or amount: *Thanks a million.* —*adj.* [*after a number and before a noun*] **6.** amounting to one million in number: *Two million dollars is a lot to pay.* —**mil′lionth,** *adj., n.* [*count*]

mil•lion•aire or **mil•lion•naire** (mil′yə nâr′, mil′yə-nâr′) /ˌmɪlyəˈnɛər, ˈmɪlyəˌnɛər/ *n.* [*count*] one whose wealth amounts to a million or more in currency.

mil•li•pede or **mil•le•pede** (mil′ə pēd′) /ˈmɪləˌpiyd/ *n.* [*count*] a small creature having a long, rounded body of many segments, each with two pairs of legs. See -PED-[1].

mill•stone (mil′stōn′) /ˈmɪlˌstown/ *n.* [*count*] **1.** either of a pair of circular stones between which grain is ground, as in a mill. **2.** anything that grinds or crushes. **3. a millstone around one's neck,** any heavy mental or emotional burden: *The debt had become a giant millstone around his neck.*

milque•toast (milk′tōst′) /ˈmɪlkˌtowst/ *n.* [*often: Milquetoast*] [*count*] a timid person: *a milquetoast at the office, never taking a chance or daring to disagree.*

mime (mīm) /maym/ *n., v.,* **mimed, mim•ing.** —*n.* **1.** [*noncount*] the art or technique of portraying a character, mood, or story by body movements without words; pantomime. **2.** [*count*] an actor who specializes in this art. —*v.* **3.** [~ + *obj*] to mimic; show by actions one's meaning: *I mimed turning a steering wheel to indicate I wanted to rent a car.* **4.** [*no obj*] to act in mime.

mim•e•o•graph (mim′ē ə graf′) /ˈmɪmiyəˌgræf/ *n.* [*count*] **1.** a printing machine with an ink-fed drum, around which a stencil is placed and which rotates as successive sheets of paper are fed into it. **2.** a copy made from a mimeograph. —*v.* [~ + *obj*] **3.** to duplicate (something) by means of a mimeograph. See -GRAPH-.

mi•met•ic (mi met′ik, mī-) /mɪˈmɛtɪk, may-/ *adj.* of, relating to, or using mimicry: *mimetic gestures.*

mim•ic (mim′ik) /ˈmɪmɪk/ *v.,* **-icked, -ick•ing,** *n.* —*v.* [~ + *obj*] **1.** to imitate or copy in action, speech, etc., often playfully, sometimes to insult another: *He mimicked the teacher's scolding.* **2.** to resemble closely: *This virus mimics the effects of the other.* —*n.* [*count*] **3.** a person or thing that mimics, esp. a performer. —**mim′ick•er,** *n.* [*count*]

mim•ic•ry (mim′ik rē) /ˈmɪmɪkriy/ *n., pl.* **-ries. 1.** [*noncount*] the act, practice, or art of mimicking. **2.** [*noncount*] the close outside resemblance of one organism to a different organism: *an insect's mimicry of a dead leaf.* **3.** [*count*] an instance or result of mimicking.

mi•mo•sa (mi mō′sə, -zə) /mɪˈmowsə, -zə/ *n.* [*count*], *pl.* **-sas.** a plant, shrub, or tree of warm regions, having small flowers in rounded heads.

min., an abbreviation of: **1.** minimum. **2.** minor. **3.** minute.

-min-, *root. -min-* comes from Latin, where it has the meaning "least; smallest." This meaning is found in such words as: DIMINISH, DIMINUTIVE, MINIATURE, MINIMAL, MINIMUM, MINOR, MINORITY, MINUEND, MINUS, MINUTE.

min•a•ret (min′ə ret′, min′ə ret′) /ˌmɪnəˈrɛt, ˈmɪnəˌrɛt/ *n.* [*count*] a high, slender tower attached to a mosque, from which the muezzin calls the people to prayer.

mince (mins) /mɪns/ *v.,* **minced, minc•ing,** *n.* —*v.* **1.** [~ + *obj*] to chop into very small pieces: *meat that has been minced.* **2.** [~ + *obj*] to soften, esp. for the sake of politeness: *He was angry and didn't mince his words.* **3.** to move with short, unnaturally dainty steps: [*no obj*]: *He minced across the room.* [~ + *obj*]: *He minced his way across the room.* —*n.* [*noncount*] **4.** mincemeat. —**minc′ing,** *adj.: short, mincing steps.*

mince•meat (mins′mēt′) /ˈmɪnsˌmiyt/ *n.* [*noncount*] **1.** a finely chopped mixture, as of minced apples, fat, raisins, and sometimes meat, for filling a pie. **2.** meat that has been chopped in very fine pieces. —***Idiom.*** **3. make mincemeat of,** [~ + *obj*] to destroy or defeat completely: *They made mincemeat of us, beating us 50-0.*

mind (mīnd) /maynd/ *n.* **1.** [*count*] the part in a conscious being that reasons, thinks, feels, wills, perceives, judges, etc.: *If we could record the activity of every brain cell, we could glimpse the workings of the mind.* **2.** [*count*] intellect or understanding; intelligence: *a sharp mind.* **3.** [*count*] a person considered with reference to intellectual power: *the great minds of the day.* **4.** [*count*] sanity or a sound, healthy mental condition: *losing his mind.* **5.** [*count*] a way of thinking and feeling; temper: *a liberal mind.* **6.** [*count*] opinion, view, or sentiments: *In my mind he's the best for the job.* **7.** [*noncount*] remembrance or recollection; memory: *to call to mind.* **8.** [*count*] attention; thoughts: *to keeps his mind on his studies.* —*v.* **9.** [~ + *obj*] to pay attention to: *Don't mind me; just pretend I'm not here.* **10.** [~ + *obj*] to attend to (one's affairs): *Mind your own business!* **11.** [~ + *obj*] to look after; take care of; tend: *Who's minding the children?* **12.** [*often in commands*] to be cautious (about); take (something) into account: [~ + *obj*]: *"Mind the step," he warned.* [~ + *clause*]: *Mind what you say.* [*no obj*]: *Mind now, I want you home by twelve.* [~ + *you*]: *Mind you, I still have a right to my opinion.* **13.** [*not: be + ~-ing; often with a negative word or phrase, or in questions*] to feel concern at; care about; object to: [~ + *obj*]: *I wouldn't mind a drink right about now. (= I would like to have a drink).* [~ + *verb-ing*]: *You know, I wouldn't mind having that drink now.* [~ + *clause*]: *Do you mind if I smoke?* [*no obj*]: *No, I don't mind.* **14.** to obey: [~ + *obj*]: *Mind your parents.* [*no obj*]: *If he didn't mind, he was punished.* —***Idiom.*** **15. bear** or **keep (something) in mind,** to hold in one's memory; remember: *Keep that fact in mind.* [~ + (*that*) *clause*]: *Bear in mind that your taxes are due.* **16. be of one mind,** to share an opinion: *The soldiers were of one mind: to get to the top of the hill.* **17. be of two minds,** to be unable to decide. **18. have (half) a mind to,** [~ + *root form of verb*] to be (almost) decided to; be inclined to: *I have (half) a mind to quit early.* **19. never mind,** This phrase is used to express: **a.** comfort to another after something unfortunate has happened: *Never mind about that broken window.* **b.** the attitude that something is not important: *She still owes me money, but never mind.* **20. on one's mind,** in one's thoughts; of concern to one: *The economy has been on his mind lately.* **21. out of one's mind, a.** insane; mad. **b.** emotionally overwhelmed; frantic: *out of my mind with worry.* **22. to mind,** to one's memory or awareness: *Any suggestions?-- Nothing comes immediately to mind.* **23. to one's mind,** in one's opinion: *He's the best candidate to my mind, at least right now.*

mind′-blow′ing, *adj.* **1.** overwhelming; astounding: *a mind-blowing experience.* **2.** producing a hallucinogenic effect: *LSD and other mind-blowing drugs.*

mind•ed (mīn′did) /ˈmayndɪd/ *adj.* **1.** having a certain kind of mind (usually used in combination): *strong-minded; sports-minded.* **2.** [*be* + ~] inclined or disposed: *She can order another dress if she is so minded.*

mind•ful (mīnd′fəl) /ˈmayndfəl/ *adj.* [*usually: be* + ~ + *of*] attentive; aware: *Be mindful of the consequences.* —**mind′ful•ly,** *adv.* —**mind′ful•ness,** *n.* [*noncount*]

mind•less (mīnd′lis) /ˈmayndlɪs/ *adj.* **1.** showing, using, or requiring no intelligence: *a boring, mindless job.* **2.** [*be* + ~ + *of*] refusing to worry or think about; heedless: *mindless of all the dangers.* **3.** stupid; thoughtless: *mindless violence.*

mind's′ eye′, *n.* [*noncount*] the imagination: *In my mind's eye I can still see her.*

mine[1] (mīn) /mayn/ *pron.* **1.** the form of the pronoun *I* used to show possession after the verb *be*: *The yellow sweater is mine.* **2.** the form of the pronoun *I* used to refer to a thing or things that belong to the speaker: *Mine is on the left. He was a good friend of mine.*

mine[2] (mīn) /mayn/ *n., v.,* **mined, min•ing.** **—***n.* [*count*] **1.** an area dug up for minerals, as ore, coal, or precious stones: *the diamond mines of South Africa.* **2.** an abundant source; store: *a mine of information.* **3.** an explosive device placed in the ground or in the water that is designed to blow up when enemy troops, vehicles, or ships pass near it. **—***v.* **4.** to dig in (the earth) for extracting a mineral substance: [*no obj*]: *to mine for a year before striking gold.* [~ + *obj*]: *to mine an area for years.* **5.** to dig out (a mineral) from a mine: [*no obj*]: *to mine for gold.* [~ + *obj*]: *to mine gold, diamonds, and silver.* **6.** [~ + *obj*] to place mines, as in military or naval operations: *to mine the entrance to the harbor.* **7.** [~ + *obj*] to use for extracting material from: *to mine every reference book available.* —**min′er,** *n.* [*count*]: *miners out on strike.*

mine•field (min′fēld) /'maynfiyld/ *n.* [*count*] **1.** an area of land or water where mines have been put: *The submarine slid carefully through the minefield.* **2.** any extremely dangerous situation: *a political minefield.*

min•er•al (min′ər əl, min′rəl) /'mɪnərəl, 'mɪnrəl/ *n.* [*count*] **1.** a substance occurring in nature, of definite chemical composition and usually of definite crystal structure: *Coal, iron, salt, and tin are minerals.* **2.** an inorganic element, as calcium, etc., essential to the functioning of the human body: *vitamins and minerals.* **3.** a substance neither animal nor vegetable. **—***adj.* [*before a noun*] **4.** of, relating to, or of the nature of a mineral.

min•er•al•o•gy (min′ə rol′ə jē, -ral′ə-) /ˌmɪnə'rɒlədʒiy, -'rælə-/ *n.* [*noncount*] the study of minerals. —**min′er•al′o•gist,** *n.* [*count*]

min′eral oil′, *n.* [*noncount*] a colorless, oily, almost tasteless oil obtained from petroleum.

min′eral wa′ter, *n.* [*noncount*] water containing dissolved mineral salts or gases.

min•e•stro•ne (min′ə strō′nē) /ˌmɪnə'strowniy/ *n.* [*noncount*] a thick vegetable soup.

mine•sweep•er (mīn′swē′pər) /'maynˌswiypər/ *n.* [*count*] a ship used for removing or destroying explosive mines.

min•gle (ming′gəl) /'mɪŋgəl/ *v.,* **-gled, -gling.** **1.** [*no obj*] to mix in company: *He wandered around, trying to mingle with the guests.* **2.** to mix or combine; put together in a mixture; blend: [*no obj*]: *His shouts mingled with those of other survivors.* [~ + *obj*]: *His account mingled truth with exaggerations.* —**min′gled,** *adj.*: *a look of mingled despair and hopefulness.*

min•i (min′ē) /'mɪniy/ *n.* [*count*], *pl.* **min•is.** **1.** MINISKIRT. **2.** MINICOMPUTER. **3.** anything small of its kind.

mini-, *prefix. mini-* is attached to nouns and means: **1.** of a small or reduced size in comparison with others of its kind: *mini-* + *car* → *minicar; mini-* + *gun* → *minigun.* **2.** limited in scope, intensity, or duration: *mini-* + *boom (= economic upturn)* → *miniboom (= short-lived economic boom); mini-* + *course* → *minicourse (= short course of study).* **3.** (of clothing) short; not reaching the knee: *mini-* + *dress* → *minidress; mini-* + *skirt* → *miniskirt.* See -MIN-.

min•i•a•ture (min′ē ə chər, min′ə chər) /'mɪniyətʃər, 'mɪnətʃər/ *n.* [*count*] **1.** a copy of something on a small scale. **2.** something small of its class or kind. **3.** a very small painting, esp. on ivory. **—***adj.* [*before a noun*] **4.** represented on a small scale: *a miniature poodle.* **—*Idiom.*** **5. in miniature,** of a reduced size; on a small scale. —**min′i•a•tur•ist,** *n.* [*count*] See -MIN-.

min•i•a•tur•ize (min′ē ə chə rīz′, min′ə-) /'mɪniyətʃəˌrayz, 'mɪnə-/ *v.* [~ + *obj*], **-ized, -iz•ing.** to make in reduced size: *to miniaturize electronic equipment.* —**min•i•a•tur•i•za•tion** (min′ē ə chər i zā′shən, min′ə-) /ˌmɪniyətʃərɪ'zeyʃən, ˌmɪnə-/ *n.* [*noncount*] See -MIN-.

min•i•bike (min′ē bīk′) /'mɪniyˌbayk/ *n.* [*count*] a small, lightweight motorcycle with a low frame.

min•i•bus (min′ē bus′) /'mɪniyˌbʌs/ *n.* [*count*] a small bus typically used for transporting people short distances.

min•i•com•put•er (min′ē kəm pyōō′tər) /'mɪniykəmˌpyuwtər/ *n.* [*count*] a computer with processing and storage capabilities smaller than those of a mainframe but larger than those of a microcomputer.

min•im (min′əm) /'mɪnəm/ *n.* [*count*] the smallest unit of liquid measure, 1/60 of a fluid dram, roughly equivalent to one drop. *Abbr.*: min, min. See -MIN-.

min•i•mal (min′ə məl) /'mɪnəməl/ *adj.* **1.** making up or being a minimum: *a minimal weight loss of two pounds a week.* **2.** [*before a noun*] of or relating to minimalism. —**min′i•mal•ly,** *adv.* See -MIN-.

min•i•mal•ism (min′ə mə liz′əm) /'mɪnəməˌlɪzəm/ *n.* [*noncount*] a style or method in literature, art, dance, or music that is simple, plain, and often repetitious and impersonal in tone. —**min′i•mal•ist,** *n.* [*count*] See -MIN-.

min•i•mize (min′ə mīz′) /'mɪnəˌmayz/ *v.* [~ + *obj*], **-mized, -miz•ing.** **1.** to reduce to the smallest possible amount or degree: *to minimize losses.* **2.** to make something seem of low value; belittle: *kept minimizing my accomplishments.* —**min•i•mi•za•tion** (min′ə mi zā′shən) /ˌmɪnəmɪ'zeyʃən/ *n.* [*noncount*] —**min′i•miz′er,** *n.* [*count*] See -MIN-.

min•i•mum (min′ə məm) /'mɪnəməm/ *n., pl.* **-mums, -ma** (-mə) /-mə/ *adj.* **—***n.* [*count*] **1.** the least amount possible, allowable, or needed: *to work a minimum of six hours a day.* **2.** the lowest amount, value, or degree attained: *the lowest minimums ever recorded for summer temperatures.* **—***adj.* [*before a noun*] **3.** of or relating to a minimum: *a minimum stay of five days.* See -MIN-.

min•ion (min′yən) /'mɪnyən/ *n.* [*count*] a low-ranking worker who follows blindly his or her superior.

min•is•cule (min′ə skyōōl′) /'mɪnəˌskyuwl/ *adj.* MINUSCULE. See -MIN-.

min•i•se•ries (min′ē sēr′ēz) /'mɪniyˌsɪəriyz/ *n.* [*count*], *pl.* **-ries.** a television program broadcast in parts over several days.

min•i•skirt (min′ē skûrt′) /'mɪniyˌskɜrt/ *n.* [*count*] a short skirt ending several inches above the knee.

min•is•ter (min′ə stər) /'mɪnəstər/ *n.* [*count*] **1.** a person with authority to conduct religious worship. **2.** a person appointed to a high office of state, esp. as head of an administrative department: *moved from foreign minister to prime minister.* **3.** a diplomatic representative ranking below an ambassador. **—***v.* **4. minister to,** [~ + *obj*] to give service, care, or aid: *to minister to the needs of the hungry.*

min•is•te•ri•al (min′ə stēr′ē əl) /ˌmɪnə'stɪəriyəl/ *adj.* [*before a noun*] of or relating to a government minister: *a ministerial staff.*

min•is•tra•tion (min′ə strā′shən) /ˌmɪnə'streyʃən/ *n.* **1.** [*noncount*] the giving of care, aid, or help: *ministration to the sick.* **2.** [*count*] an act or instance of this: *brushed aside the ministrations of his nurse.*

min•is•try (min′ə strē) /'mɪnəstriy/ *n., pl.* **-tries.** **1.** [*count*] the service or functions of a minister of religion: *Her first ministry was a small Midwestern town.* **2.** [*count; usually singular; the* + ~] the body or class of ministers of religion; clergy: *decided to enter the ministry of her church.* **3.** [*count*] an administrative department headed by a government minister: *a ministry of defense.*

mink (mingk) /mɪŋk/ *n., pl.* **minks,** (*esp. when thought of as a group*) **mink.** **1.** [*count*] a weasel of N. America and of Eurasia. **2.** [*noncount*] the soft, shiny fur of this animal: *a coat of mink.* **3.** [*count*] a piece of clothing, esp. a coat or stole, made of this fur.

Minn., an abbreviation of: Minnesota.

min•now (min′ō) /'mɪnow/ *n.* [*count*], pl. (*esp. for kinds or species*) **-nows,** (*esp. when thought of as a group; rare*) **-now.** a small fish of fresh waters.

mi•nor (mī′nər) /'maynər/ *adj.* **1.** lesser, as in size, extent, or rank: *a minor role.* **2.** under full legal age. **3.** of or relating to a student's academic minor: *minor subjects.* **4.** (in music) based on a scale in which the third note is one half step smaller than the corresponding major scale: *a minor key.* **—***n.* [*count*] **5.** a person under full legal age: *corrupting the morals of a minor.* **6. a.** a subject or course of knowledge studied secondarily to a major subject or course. **b.** a student studying such a subject: *the number of physics majors and English minors.* **7.** a minor musical scale, chord, etc. **—***v.* [*no obj*] **8.** to choose or study as a secondary academic subject: *to minor in biology.* See -MIN-.

mi•nor•i•ty (mi nôr′i tē, -nor′-, mī-) /mɪ'nɔrɪtiy, -'nɒr-, may-/ *n., pl.* **-ties,** *adj.* **—***n.* **1.** [*count*] a number, part, or amount forming less than half of the whole: *He got a minority of the votes in the first election.* **2.** [*count*] a smaller group opposed to a majority: *a minority of stockholders.* **3.** [*count*] Also called **minor′ity group′.** a group differing, esp. in race, religion, or ethnic background, from the majority of a population: *Can the rights of minorities be guaranteed?* **4.** [*count*] a member of such a group: *made an effort to hire more minorities.* **5.** [*non-*

count] the state or period of being under full legal age. **—***adj.* [*before a noun*] **6.** of or relating to a minority: *a minority opinion.* See -MIN-.

min•strel (min′strəl) /ˈmɪnstrəl/ *n.* [*count*] **1.** a medieval poet, singer, and musician, who either traveled from place to place to perform, or was a member of a noble household. **2.** a musician, singer, or poet.

mint[1] (mint) /mɪnt/ *n.* **1.** [*noncount*] a sweet-smelling herb, such as the spearmint and peppermint. **2.** [*count*] a mint-flavored candy: *He chewed on a mint to settle his stomach.* **—***adj.* [*before a noun*] **3.** flavored with mint: *mint tea.* —**mint′y,** *adj.*, **-i•er, -i•est.**

mint[2] (mint) /mɪnt/ *n.* [*count*] **1.** a place where coins, etc., are produced under government authority. **2.** [*singular; a* + ~] a vast amount, esp. of money: *That car must have cost a mint!* **—***adj.* **3.** being in its original condition, as if newly made: *an old car in mint condition.* **—***v.* [~ + *obj*] **4.** to make (money) by stamping metal: *to mint coins.* **5.** to make or invent: *to mint words.* —**mint′er,** *n.* [*count*]

mint′ ju′lep, *n.* [*count*] an alcoholic drink traditionally made with bourbon, sugar, and sprigs of mint.

min•u•et (min′yo͞o et′) /ˌmɪnyuwˈɛt/ *n.* [*count*] **1.** a slow, stately dance in triple meter. **2.** a piece of music for such a dance.

mi•nus (mī′nəs) /ˈmaynəs/ *prep.* **1.** less by the subtraction of: *Ten minus six is four.* **2.** lacking or without: *a book minus a page.* **—***adj.* **3.** signaling subtraction: *a minus sign.* **4.** algebraically negative: *a minus quantity.* **5.** [*after a noun*](in school grades) less than; just below: *to get a C minus on a test (= to get a grade just below a C).* **6.** [*before a number*] (in stating a temperature) the number of degrees below zero: *a temperature of minus 40 (= a temperature of 40 degrees below zero).* **—***n.* [*count*] **7.** MINUS SIGN. **8.** a minus quantity. **9.** a deficiency or loss. See -MIN-.

mi•nus•cule (min′ə skyo͞ol′, mi nus′kyo͞ol) /ˈmɪnəˌskyuwl, mɪˈnʌskyuwl/ *adj.* very small. See -MIN-.

mi′nus sign′, *n.* [*count*] the symbol (−) that indicates subtraction or a negative quantity.

min•ute[1] (min′it) /ˈmɪnɪt/ *n.* [*count*] **1.** the sixtieth part (1/60) of an hour; 60 seconds. **2.** a short space of time: *Give me a few minutes; I'll be right there.* **3.** an exact point in time; instant; moment: *Come here this minute!* **4. minutes,** [*plural*] the official record of the proceedings at a meeting of a group: *The minutes have several errors.* **5.** *Geometry.* the sixtieth part of a degree in measuring angles, often represented by the sign ′. **—***adj.* [*before a noun*] **6.** done or prepared in a very short time: *minute pudding.* **—*Idiom.* 7. the last minute,** the last moment of time: *waited until the last minute before handing in her test.* **8. the minute (that),** as soon as; at the same time as: *Let me know the minute (that) they get here.* **9. up to the minute,** modern; up-to-date: *His clothes were always up to the minute.* See -MIN-.

mi•nute[2] (mī no͞ot′, -nyo͞ot′, mi-) /mayˈnuwt, -ˈnyuwt, mɪ-/ *adj.*, **-nut•er, -nut•est. 1.** extremely small, as in size or degree: *minute differences.* **2.** of minor importance; insignificant. **3.** concerned about even the smallest details: *a minute examination.* —**mi•nute′ly,** *adv.* —**mi•nute′ness,** *n.* [*noncount*] See -MIN-.

min′ute steak′ (min′it) /ˈmɪnɪt/ *n.* a thin slice of beefsteak, sautéed briefly on each side: [*count*]: *preparing a few minute steaks for dinner.* [*noncount*]: *Next time buy minute steak that isn't so tough.*

mi•nu•ti•a (mi no͞o′shē ə, -shə, -nyo͞o′-) /mɪˈnuwʃiyə, -ʃə, -ˈnyuw-/ *n.* [*count*], *pl.* **-ti•ae** (-shē ē′) /-ʃiyˌiy/. Usually, **minutiae.** [*plural*] small or unimportant matters: *got bogged down in the minutiae.*

minx (mingks) /mɪŋks/ *n.* [*count*] a bold or impolite girl; a girl who likes to flirt or tease.

-mir-, *root. -mir-* comes from Latin, where it has the meaning "to wonder." This meaning is found in such words as: ADMIRABLE, ADMIRATION, ADMIRE, MIRACLE, MIRACULOUS, MIRAGE, MIRROR.

mir•a•cle (mir′ə kəl) /ˈmɪrəkəl/ *n.* [*count*] **1.** a supernatural or divine event or happening: *Jesus performed a number of miracles.* **2.** a superb or extraordinary example of something; a marvel: *It was a miracle that the pilot landed the plane in that snowstorm.* See -MIR-.

mi•rac•u•lous (mi rak′yə ləs) /mɪˈrækyələs/ *adj.* **1.** of or relating to a miracle: *the miraculous healing powers of the water at Lourdes.* **2.** wonderful or marvelous: *a miraculous recovery from his illness.* —**mi•rac′u•lous•ly,** *adv.* See -MIR-.

mi•rage (mi räzh′) /mɪˈrɑʒ/ *n.* [*count*] **1.** an image one sees, esp. in the desert, of an object that is not present; an illusion: *saw mirages of lakes that vanished as they approached.* **2.** anything that seems to be within reach but that proves unreal, etc.: *The promises of promotion turned out to be a mirage.* See -MIR-.

mire (mīᵊr) /mayᵊr/ *n., v.,* **mired, mir•ing. —***n.* [*count*] **1.** an area of wet, swampy ground; bog. **2.** a difficult or unpleasant situation that one cannot escape from: *the mire of poverty.* **—***v.* [*usually: be* + ~ + *-ed*] **3.** to become stuck in mire: *The troops were mired in the mud.* **4.** to involve; entangle; trap: *mired in lawsuits.*

mir•ror (mir′ər) /ˈmɪrər/ *n.* [*count*] **1.** a reflecting surface, usually of glass with a silvery backing: *looked in the mirror to comb her hair.* **2.** something that gives a faithful representation of something else: *music that was a mirror of its time.* **—***v.* [~ + *obj*] **3.** to reflect as if in a mirror: *The grey sea mirrored the rainy sky.* **4.** to show or imitate: *The poll's findings mirror the opinions of many Americans.* See -MIR-.

mirth (mûrth) /mɜrθ/ *n.* [*noncount*] amusement, esp. with laughter: *He laughed softly, but with no real mirth.* —**mirth′ful,** *adj.*

mis-, *prefix. mis-* is attached to nouns, verbs, and adjectives and means: **1.** mistaken; wrong; wrongly; incorrectly: *mis-* + *trial* → *mistrial (= a trial conducted improperly); mis-* + *print* → *misprint (= something incorrectly printed); mis-* + *fire* → *misfire: (= fail to fire properly).* **2.** the opposite of: *mis-* + *trust* → *mistrust (= the opposite of trust).*

-mis-, *root. -mis-* comes from Latin, where it has the meaning "send." It is related to -MIT-. This meaning is found in such words as: ADMISSION, COMMISSAR, COMMISSARY, COMMISSION, COMPROMISE, DEMISE, DISMISS, EMISSARY, IMPERMISSIBLE, INTERMISSION, MISSAL, MISSILE, MISSION, MISSIONARY, MISSIVE, OMISSION, PERMISSION, PERMISSIVE, PROMISE, PROMISSORY, REMISS, SUBMISSION, SUBMISSIVE, SURMISE, TRANSMISSION.

mis•ad•ven•ture (mis′əd ven′chər) /ˌmɪsədˈvɛntʃər/ *n.* misfortune; mishap: [*noncount*]: *death by misadventure, or accidental death.* [*count*]: *his misadventures in Africa.* See -VEN-.

mis•an•dry (mis′an drē) /ˈmɪsændriy/ *n.* [*noncount*] hatred of or hostility toward men. See -ANDRO-.

mis•an•thrope (mis′ən thrōp′, miz′-) /ˈmɪsənˌθrowp, ˈmɪz-/ also **mis•an•thro•pist** (mis an′thrə pist, miz-) /mɪsˈænθrəpɪst, mɪz-/ *n.* [*count*] one who hates all human beings. —**mis•an•throp•ic** (mis′ən throp′ik, miz′-) /ˌmɪsənˈθrɒpɪk, ˌmɪz-/ *adj.* —**mis•an•thro•py** (mis an′thrə pē) /mɪsˈænθrəpiy/ *n.* [*noncount*] See -ANTHRO-.

mis•ap•pre•hend (mis′ap ri hend′) /ˌmɪsæprɪˈhɛnd/ *v.* [~ + *obj*] to misunderstand. —**mis•ap•pre•hen•sion** (mis′ap ri hen′shən) /ˌmɪsæprɪˈhɛnʃən/ *n.* [*count*]: *under a grave misapprehension that things were proceeding smoothly.* [*noncount*]: *blaming mistakes on misapprehension.* See -PREHEND-.

mis•ap•pro•pri•ate (mis′ə prō′prē āt′) /ˌmɪsəˈprowpriyˌeyt/ *v.* [~ + *obj*], **-at•ed, -at•ing.** to apply wrongfully or dishonestly, as funds that were placed in one's care: *The dishonest manager misappropriated funds.* —**mis•ap•pro•pri•a•tion** (mis′ə prō′prē ā′shən) /ˌmɪsəˌprowpriyˈeyʃən/ *n.* [*noncount*]: *guilty of misappropriation of funds.* [*count*]: *More misappropriations were discovered before the trial began.* See -PROPR-.

mis•be•got•ten (mis′bi got′n) /ˌmɪsbɪˈgɒtn̩/ *adj.* **1.** born of parents who are not married to each other; illegitimate: *his misbegotten son.* **2.** badly planned, made, or carried out: *a misbegotten plan.*

mis•be•have (mis′bi hāv′) /ˌmɪsbɪˈheyv/ *v.,* **-haved, -hav•ing.** to behave badly or improperly: [*no obj*]: *misbehaving in church.* [~ + *oneself*]: *misbehaving himself at parties.*

mis•be•hav•ior (mis′bi hāv′yər) /ˌmɪsbɪˈheyvyər/ *n.* [*noncount*] bad behavior: *misbehavior during mass.*

misc., an abbreviation of: **1.** miscellaneous. **2.** miscellany.

-misc-, *root. -misc-* comes from Latin, where it has the meaning "mix." This meaning is found in such words as: MISCELLANEOUS, MISCELLANY, PROMISCUOUS.

mis•cal•cu•late (mis′kal′kyə lāt′) /ˌmɪsˈkælkyəˌleyt/ *v.,* **-lated, -lat•ing. 1.** to make a mistake in counting: [*no obj*]: *miscalculated when adding the figures.* [~ + *obj*]: *He miscalculated the total.* **2.** to make an error in judging: [*no obj*]: *The candidate miscalculated badly.* [~ + *obj*]: *She miscalculated the opposition to her proposal.* —**mis•cal•cu•la•tion** (mis′kal kyə lā′shən) /ˌmɪskælkyəˈleyʃən/ *n.* [*count*]: *A few miscalculations and your career could be over.* [*noncount*]: *no room for miscalculation in the Olympics.*

mis•call (mis kôl′) /mɪs'kɔl/ *v.* [~ + *obj*] **1.** to call by a wrong name. **2.** to make an error in judging a game or other situation: *The referee miscalled that play.*

mis•car•riage (mis′kar′ij, mis′kar′-) /ˌmɪs'kærɪdʒ, 'mɪsˌkær-/ *n.* [*count*] **1.** the birth of a dead offspring: *suffered a miscarriage during her last pregnancy.* **2.** a failure to attain one's end: *a miscarriage of justice.*

mis•car•ry (mis kar′ē) /mɪs'kæriy/ *v.* [*no obj*], **-ried, -ry•ing. 1.** to have a miscarriage of a fetus: *When she miscarried for the third time she wondered if she should adopt a child.* **2.** to fail to attain one's end; be unsuccessful: *The plan miscarried.*

mis•cast (mis kast′) /mɪs'kæst/ *v.* [~ + *obj*], **-cast, -cast•ing. 1.** to cast (an actor) in an unsuitable role: *The directors miscast the comedian in a serious role.* **2.** to cast (a play, etc.) with unsuitable actors.

mis•ceg•e•na•tion (mi sej′ə nā′shən, mis′i jə-) /mɪˌsɛdʒə'neyʃən, ˌmɪsɪdʒə-/ *n.* [*noncount*] intercourse involving a man and a woman of different races. See -MISC-.

mis•cel•la•ne•ous (mis′ə lā′nē əs) /ˌmɪsə'leyniyəs/ *adj.* made up of parts of different kinds; of or having mixed character, kinds, etc.: *The party attracted a miscellaneous group of people.* See -MISC-.

mis•cel•la•ny (mis′ə lā′nē) /'mɪsəˌleyniy/ *n.* [*count*], *pl.* **-nies.** a collection or mixture of various items or parts. See -MISC-.

mis•chance (mis chans′) /mɪs'tʃæns/ *n.* **1.** [*count*] an occurrence of bad luck: *An odd mischance brought him face to face with his enemy.* **2.** [*noncount*] bad luck: *It was by mischance that the car ran off the road.*

mis•chief (mis′chif) /'mɪstʃɪf/ *n.* [*noncount*] **1.** conduct or activity that causes slight annoyance: *The children were always getting into mischief.* **2.** a tendency to tease or annoy: *Her eyes were full of mischief.* **3.** harm or trouble: *to come to mischief.*

mis•chie•vous (mis′chə vəs) /'mɪstʃəvəs/ *adj.* **1.** maliciously or playfully annoying: *The mischievous boys stole apples from the neighbor's tree.* **2.** slyly teasing: *a mischievous look.* **3.** harmful; causing trouble. —**mis′chie•vous•ly,** *adv.* —**mis′chie•vous•ness,** *n.* [*noncount*]

mis•con•ceived (mis′kən sēvd′) /ˌmɪskən'siyvd/ *adj.* poorly planned; not carefully or properly thought about: *the government's misconceived foreign policy.*

mis•con•cep•tion (mis′kən sep′shən) /ˌmɪskən'sɛpʃən/ *n.* [*count*] something not carefully or properly thought about or planned; a mistaken or erroneous idea: *a major misconception about AIDS.*

mis•con•duct (*n.* mis kon′dukt; *v.* mis′kən dukt′) / *n.* mɪs'kɒndʌkt; *v.* ˌmɪskən'dʌkt/ *n.* [*noncount*] **1.** improper behavior, esp. by an official in office, or in the administration of justice: *official misconduct as mayor.* —*v.* [~ + *obj*] **2.** to misbehave (oneself).

mis•con•struc•tion (mis′kən struk′shən) /ˌmɪskən'strʌkʃən/ *n.* **1.** [*noncount*] the state or condition of being mistaken: *a law not open to misconstruction.* **2.** [*count*] an act or example of such misunderstanding. See -STRU-.

mis•con•strue (mis′kən strōō′) /ˌmɪskən'struw/ *v.* [~ + *obj*], **-strued, -stru•ing.** to misunderstand the meaning of; misinterpret: *I don't want my words to be misconstrued.* See -STRU-.

mis•count (*v.* mis kount′; *n.* mis′kount′) / *v.* mɪs'kawnt; *n.* 'mɪsˌkawnt/ *v.* **1.** to count incorrectly: [*no obj*]: *The census miscounted by as much as 20%.* [~ + *obj*]: *The minority population was miscounted in the last census.* —*n.* [*count*] **2.** an incorrect counting: *a miscount by as much as 20%.*

mis•cre•ant (mis′krē ənt) /'mɪskriyənt/ *adj.* **1.** evil and villainous. —*n.* [*count*] **2.** a vicious or evil person.

mis•cue (mis kyōō′) /mɪs'kyuw/ *n., v.,* **-cued, -cu•ing.** —*n.* [*count*] **1.** an error, mistake, or blunder: *several miscues on the last bill.* —*v.* [*no obj*] **2.** to make a mistake: *He miscued again and the ball got past him.*

mis•deed (mis dēd′) /mɪs'diyd/ *n.* [*count*] an immoral deed.

mis•de•mean•or (mis′di mē′nər) /ˌmɪsdɪ'miynər/ *n.* [*count*] **1.** a criminal offense less serious than a felony. **2.** an instance of misbehavior. Also, *esp. Brit.,* **mis′de•mean′our.**

mis•di•rect (mis′di rekt′) /ˌmɪsdɪ'rɛkt/ *v.* [~ + *obj*] **1.** to direct, instruct, or address wrongly: *to misdirect a person to the wrong office.* **2.** to make use of wrongly or incorrectly: *misdirected all his energy.* See -RECT-.

mis•do•ing (mis dōō′ing) /mɪs 'duwɪŋ/ *n.* [*count*] Often, **misdoings.** [*plural*] a wrong, improper, or mistaken act.

mise-en-scène (mē zäɴ sen′) /miyzɑ̃'sɛn/ *n.* [*count*], *pl.* **-scènes** (-sens′, -sen′) /-'sɛns, -'sɛn/. **1.** the process of setting a stage. **2.** the stage setting or scenery of a play. See -MIS-.

mi•ser (mī′zər) /'mayzər/ *n.* [*count*] a person who saves money and is reluctant to spend it. —**mi′ser•li•ness,** *n.* [*noncount*] —**mi′ser•ly,** *adj.* See -MISER-.

-miser-, *root.* -*miser*- comes from Latin, where it has the meaning "wretched." This meaning is found in such words as: COMMISERATE, MISER, MISERABLE, MISERLY, MISERY.

mis•er•a•ble (miz′ər ə bəl, miz′rə-) /'mɪzərəbəl, 'mɪzrə-/ *adj.* **1.** unfortunate, unhappy, or uncomfortable: *a miserable beggar.* **2.** evil; hateful; contemptible: *a miserable villain.* **3.** having, showing, or causing misery: *a miserable failure.* —**mis′er•a•bly,** *adv.*: *He failed miserably in his last few games.* See -MISER-.

mis•er•y (miz′ə rē) /'mɪzəriy/ *n., pl.* **-er•ies.** wretched, unfortunate, or unhappy conditions: [*noncount*]: *the misery he felt after his defeat.* [*count*]: *home and job miseries.* See -MISER-.

mis•fea•sance (mis fē′zəns) /mɪs'fiyzəns/ *n.* [*noncount*] the wrongful use of one's legal or lawful authority. —**mis•fea•sor** (mis fē′zər) /mɪs'fiyzər/ *n.* [*count*]

mis•fire (*v.* mis fīər′; *n.* mis′fīər′) / *v.* mɪs'fɪər; *n.* 'mɪsˌfayər/ *v.,* **-fired, -fir•ing,** *n.* —*v.* [*no obj*] **1.** to fail to fire or ignite properly: *The engine was sputtering and misfiring.* **2.** to fail to achieve the desired result: *His criticisms misfired completely.* —*n.* [*count*] **3.** an act or instance of misfiring.

mis•fit (mis fit′, mis′fit′ *for 1;* mis′fit′ *for 2*) / mɪs'fɪt, 'mɪsˌfɪt *for 1;* 'mɪsˌfɪt *for 2*/ *n.* [*count*] **1.** something, as a piece of clothing, that fits badly. **2.** one not suited or unable to adjust to a situation: *a social misfit.*

mis•for•tune (mis fôr′chən) /mɪs'fɔrtʃən/ *n.* **1.** [*noncount*] bad fortune; bad luck: *That failure was more a result of misfortune than of bad judgment.* **2.** [*count*] an instance of this: *some misfortunes of the business downturn.* See -FORTUN-.

mis•giv•ing (mis giv′ing) /mɪs'gɪvɪŋ/ *n.* [*count*] Often, **misgivings.** [*plural*] a feeling of doubt: *He had a few misgivings about the plan.*

mis•guide (mis gīd′) /mɪs'gayd/ *v.* [~ + *obj*], **-guid•ed, -guid•ing.** to guide wrongly; misdirect. —**mis•guid•ance** (mis gīd′ns) /mɪs'gaydns/ *n.* [*noncount*]

mis•guid•ed (mis gī′did) /mɪs'gaydɪd/ *adj.* wrong because of bad judgment: *a few misguided attempts to take over the business.*

mis•han•dle (mis han′dl) /mɪs'hændl̩/ *v.* [~ + *obj*], **-dled, -dling.** to manage badly; deal with poorly: *to mishandle a business account.*

mis•hap (mis′hap, mis hap′) /'mɪshæp, mɪs'hæp/ *n.* an unfortunate event: [*count*]: We had a little mishap on the way over here. [*noncount*]: *They flew through the snowstorm without mishap.* See -HAP-.

mish•mash (mish′mäsh′, -mash′) /'mɪʃˌmɑʃ, -ˌmæʃ/ also **mish•mosh** (mish′mosh′) /'mɪʃˌmɒʃ/ *n.* [*count*] a confused mess; hodgepodge: *a mishmash of wild opinions.*

mis•in•form (mis′in fôrm′) /ˌmɪsɪn'fɔrm/ *v.* [~ + *obj*] to give false or misleading information to: *Whoever told you I was dead misinformed you.*

mis•in•for•ma•tion (mis′in fər mā′shən) /ˌmɪsɪnfər'meyʃən/ *n.* [*noncount*] false information deliberately given: *The spy was given misinformation to bring back to his country.*

mis•in•ter•pret (mis′in tûr′prit) /ˌmɪsɪn'tɜrprɪt/ *v.* [~ + *obj*] to interpret incorrectly: *to misinterpret her quiet anger as agreement with the plan.* —**mis•in•ter•pre•ta•tion** (mis′in tûr′pri tā′shən) /ˌmɪsɪnˌtɜrprɪ'teyʃən/ *n.* [*noncount*]: *a speech open to much misinterpretation.* [*count*]: *numerous misinterpretations to be cleared up.*

mis•judge (mis juj′) /mɪs'dʒʌdʒ/ *v.* [~ + *obj*], **-judged, -judg•ing.** to judge or form an opinion incorrectly or unjustly: *If I misjudged you, I'm sorry.* —**mis•judg′ment,** *n.* [*count; noncount*] See -JUD-.

mis•lay (mis lā′) /mɪs'ley/ *v.* [~ + *obj*], **-laid, -lay•ing. 1.** to lose temporarily; misplace: *I mislaid my keys.* **2.** to lay or place (something) wrongly: *to mislay linoleum on the kitchen floor.*

mis•lead (mis lēd′) /mɪs'liyd/ *v.* [~ + *obj*], **-led, -lead•ing. 1.** to lead or guide in the wrong direction. **2.** to lead (someone) into error; lead astray: *I was misled into believing he was honest.*

mis•lead•ing (mis′lē′ding) /ˌmɪs'liydɪŋ/ *adj.* intended to deceive: *fed the spy misleading information.*

mis•man•age (mis man′ij) /mɪs'mænɪdʒ/ *v.* [~ + *obj*], **-aged, -ag•ing.** to manage poorly or dishonestly: *had* *mismanaged the funds.* —**mis•man′age•ment,** *n.* [*noncount*]

mis•match (mis mach′; *for 2 also* mis′mach′) /mɪsˈmætʃ; *for 2 also* ˈmɪsˌmætʃ/ *v.* [~ + *obj*] **1.** to match badly or unsuitably: *The two were completely mismatched and never should have gotten married.* —*n.* [*count*] **2.** a bad or unsuitable match: *The game was a complete mismatch.*

mis•no•mer (mis nō′mər) /mɪsˈnowmər/ *n.* [*count*] a name (of something) that is inappropriate because it fails to describe it properly: *Calling that company a "business" is really a misnomer; it is badly managed and has never made a profit.* See -NOM-².

mi•sog•a•my (mi sog′ə mē, mī-) /mɪˈsɒgəmiy, may-/ *n.* [*noncount*] hatred of marriage. —**mi•sog′a•mist,** *n.* [*count*] See -GAM-.

mi•sog•y•ny (mi soj′ə nē, mī-) /mɪˈsɒdʒəniy, may-/ *n.* [*noncount*] hatred of or hostility toward women. Compare MISANDRY. —**mi•sog′y•nist,** *n.* [*count*] —**mi•sog′y•nous,** *adj.* See -GYN-.

mis•place (mis plās′) /mɪsˈpleys/ *v.* [~ + *obj*], **-placed, -plac•ing. 1.** to put in a wrong place. **2.** to put in a place afterward forgotten: *I seem to have misplaced my keys.* **3.** to place or bestow improperly or unwisely: *to misplace his trust in someone.* —**mis•placed′,** *adj.*: *misplaced loyalties.* Compare MISLAY.

mis•play (*n.* mis plā′, mis′plā′; *v.* mis plā′) / *n.* mɪsˈpley, ˈmɪsˌpley; *v.* mɪsˈpley/ *n.* [*count*] **1.** a wrong or bad play in a sport: *A few more misplays like that one and our team will be eliminated.* —*v.* **2.** to play wrongly or badly: [~ + *obj*]: *to misplay the last three balls.* [*no obj*]: *The team has been misplaying all day.*

mis•print (*n.* mis′print′, mis print′; *v.* mis print′) / *n.* ˈmɪsˌprɪnt, mɪsˈprɪnt; *v.* mɪsˈprɪnt/ *n.* [*count*] **1.** a mistake in printing: *The misprints in the headline were pretty obvious.* —*v.* [~ + *obj*] **2.** to print incorrectly: *They misprinted all the signs.*

mis•pro•nounce (mis′prə nouns′) /ˌmɪsprəˈnawns/ *v.* [~ + *obj*], **-nounced, -nounc•ing.** to pronounce incorrectly: *always mispronounces my name.* —**mis•pro•nun•ci•a•tion** (mis′prə nun′sē ā′shən) /ˌmɪsprəˌnʌnsiyˈeyʃən/ *n.* [*noncount*]: *mispronunciation of the French vowels.* [*count*]: *a list of common mispronunciations.* See -NOUNCE-.

mis•quote (mis kwōt′) /mɪsˈkwowt/ *v.*, **-quot•ed, -quot•ing,** *n.* —*v.* [~ + *obj*] **1.** to quote incorrectly: *claimed he had been misquoted.* —*n.* [*count*] **2.** Also, **mis•quo•ta•tion** (mis′kwō tā′shən) /ˌmɪskwowˈteyʃən/. an incorrect quotation: *several misquotes and outright distortions of my position.* See -QUOT-.

mis•read (mis rēd′) /mɪsˈriyd/ *v.* [~ + *obj*], **-read** (red), **-read•ing. 1.** to read wrongly: *I misread the date.* **2.** to misunderstand: *misread the dictator's intentions.*

mis•rep•re•sent (mis′rep ri zent′) /ˌmɪsrɛprɪˈzɛnt/ *v.* [~ + *obj*], **1.** to represent incorrectly or falsely: *The candidate's position was misrepresented in her opponent's TV ads.* **2.** to represent in an unsatisfactory manner: *He misrepresents the stockholder's views.* —**mis•rep•re•sen•ta•tion** (mis′rep ri zən tā′shən) /ˌmɪsrɛprɪzənˈteyʃən/ *n.* [*noncount*]: *comments open to misrepresentation.* [*count*]: *distortions and misrepresentations of my position.*

mis•rule (mis ro͞ol′) /mɪsˈruwl/ *n.*, *v.*, **-ruled, -rul•ing.** —*n.* [*noncount*] **1.** bad or unwise rule; misgovernment. —*v.* [~ + *obj*] **2.** to rule badly; misgovern.

miss[1] (mis) /mɪs/ *v.* **1.** to fail to hit: [~ + *obj*]: *missed the first pitch.* [*no obj*]: *He swung and missed.* **2.** [~ + *obj*] to fail to meet, catch, etc.: *to miss a train.* **3.** [~ + *obj*] to fail to take advantage of: *I missed a chance to meet him.* **4.** [~ + *obj*] to fail to be present for: *to miss school.* **5.** [*not: be* + ~*-ing;* ~ + *obj*] to notice the absence or loss of: *When did you first miss your wallet?* **6.** to regret the absence or loss of: [~ + *obj*]: *I miss you all dreadfully.* [~ + *verb-ing*]: *He missed watching the African sunsets.* **7.** [*not: be* + ~*-ing;* ~ + *verb-ing*] to escape or avoid: *He just missed being caught.* **8.** [~ + *obj*] to fail to understand: *to miss the point of a remark.* **9.** [*no obj*] (of a car, etc.) to misfire: *The car was missing on all four cylinders.* **10. miss out,** [*no obj*] to fail to experience or take advantage of something: *They missed out on a golden opportunity to improve their financial situation.* —*n.* [*count*] **11.** a failure of any kind, esp. to hit something: *a couple of swings and misses and the game is over.* **12.** a misfire. —***Idiom.* 13. miss the boat,** *Informal.* to fail to take advantage of an opportunity: *He missed the boat by failing to apply for the grant.*

miss[2] (mis) /mɪs/ *n.*, *pl.* **miss•es. 1.** [*Miss*] This word is used as a title of respect before the name of an unmarried woman: *Miss Mary Jones.* **2.** [*Miss*] This word is used as a polite form of address to a young woman: *Miss, please bring me some ketchup.* **3.** [*Miss*] This word is used as a title before the name of a place, or a quality, that a young woman has been selected to represent: *Miss America.* **4.** [*count*] a young unmarried woman; girl. **5. misses,** [*plural*] **a.** a range of sizes, chiefly from 6 to 20, for garments that fit women of average height and build. **b.** a garment in this size range.

Miss., an abbreviation of: Mississippi.

mis•sal (mis′əl) /ˈmɪsəl/ *n.* [*count*] [*sometimes: Missal*] a book containing the prayers used in the Roman Catholic mass over the course of the year. See -MIS-.

mis•shape (mis shāp′, mish-) /mɪsˈʃeyp, mɪʃ-/ *v.* [~ + *obj*], **-shaped, -shaped** or **-shap•en, -shap•ing.** to shape badly or wrongly; deform. —**mis•shap′en,** *adj.*: *His craggy face had become misshapen with age and disease.*

mis•sile (mis′əl) /ˈmɪsəl/ *n.* [*count*] **1.** an object or weapon propelled at a target, as a stone, bullet, etc.: *Rocks, stones, and other flying missiles came down on their heads.* **2.** a rocket-propelled weapon: *Missiles from both sides filled the air.* See -MIS-.

mis•sile•ry or **mis•sil•ry** (mis′əl rē) /ˈmɪsəlriy/ *n.* [*noncount*] **1.** the science of the construction and use of missiles, esp. guided missiles: *advances in rocketry and missilery.* **2.** missiles, esp. guided missiles, thought of as a group: *The missilery of both sides goes far beyond what is needed for defensive purposes.* See -MIS-.

miss•ing (mis′ing) /ˈmɪsɪŋ/ *adj.* lacking, absent, or not found: *the missing murder weapon.*

mis•sion (mish′ən) /ˈmɪʃən/ *n.* [*count*] **1.** a committee sent to a foreign country to conduct negotiations, establish relations, etc.: *a fact-finding mission to the Caribbean.* **2.** a permanent diplomatic establishment in another country: *the Cuban mission to the UN.* **3.** a group of people sent by a church to carry on religious and other work in other countries. **4.** a specific task that one is sent to perform: *on a mission of mercy.* **5.** one's chosen duty or task: *His mission in life was to educate the illiterate.* **6.** a place providing charity, as food or shelter, for the poor: *ran a small mission with a soup kitchen.* See -MIS-.

mis•sion•ar•y (mish′ə ner′ē) /ˈmɪʃəˌnɛriy/ *n.*, *pl.* **-ar•ies,** *adj.* —*n.* Also, **mis•sion•er** (mish′ə nər) /ˈmɪʃənər/. [*count*] **1.** one sent by a church into an area to carry on religious or humanitarian work: *a missionary in Africa.* —*adj.* [*before a noun*] **2.** of or relating to religious missions. See -MIS-.

mis•sive (mis′iv) /ˈmɪsɪv/ *n.* [*count*] a written message; letter. See -MIS-.

mis•spell (mis spel′) /mɪsˈspɛl/ *v.* [~ + *obj*], **-spelled** or **-spelt, -spell•ing.** to spell incorrectly: *misspelling simple words.* —**mis•spell′ing,** *n.* [*count*]: *Many of his misspellings involved simple words.* [*noncount*]: *too much misspelling.*

mis•spend (mis spend′) /mɪsˈspɛnd/ *v.* [~ + *obj*], **-spent, -spend•ing.** to spend wrongly or unwisely: *misspent his inheritance.*

mis•state (mis stāt′) /mɪsˈsteyt/ *v.* [~ + *obj*], **-stat•ed, -stat•ing.** to tell lies: *misstated your true intentions.* —**mis•state′ment,** *n.* [*count*] See -STAT-.

mis•step (mis step′) /mɪsˈstɛp/ *n.* [*count*] **1.** a wrong step: *One misstep and you'll fall down the mountain.* **2.** an error in conduct: *some missteps during his interview.*

mist (mist) /mɪst/ *n.* **1.** a mass of tiny drops of water, resembling fog: [*noncount*]: *driving through mist.* [*count*]: *the mists of Avalon.* **2.** [*count*] a cloud of particles resembling this: *a mist of perfume.* **3.** [*count*] something that dims or blurs: *a mist of tears.* —*v.* **4.** to (cause to) become misty: [*no obj;* (~ + *up/over*)] *His eyes misted (over) when he told us about his dead son.* [~ + *obj*]: *The humidity misted the car window.* **5.** [*no obj; it* + ~] to rain in very fine drops; drizzle: *It was misting, not quite raining.* —**mist′i•ness,** *n.* [*noncount*] —**mist′y,** *adj.*, **-i•er, -i•est.**

mis•take (mi stāk′) /mɪˈsteyk/ *n.*, *v.*, **-took, -tak•en, -tak•ing.** —*n.* [*count*] **1.** an error in action or judgment caused by poor reasoning, carelessness, etc.: *too many mistakes in grammar.* —*v.* **2.** [~ + *obj* + *for* + *obj*] to identify wrongly as something or someone else: *I mistook her for the mayor.* **3.** [~ + *obj*] to understand or judge wrongly: *I must have mistaken the date.* —***Idiom.* 4. by mistake,** accidentally: *set off the alarm by mistake.*

mis•tak•en (mi stā′kən) /mɪˈsteykən/ *adj.* **1.** wrongly thought or done: *a mistaken notion.* **2.** being in error;

wrong: *If you think you'll get away with this, you are mistaken.* **—mis•tak′en•ly,** *adv.: mistakenly assumed that you would be here.*

mis•ter (mis′tər) /'mɪstər/ *n.* **1.** [*Mister*] This word is used as a title of respect before a man's name or position, and is usually written as *Mr.*: *Mr. Jones. "Mr. Mayor, what is your opinion?" they shouted.* **2.** [*singular*] This word is used as an informal term of address to a man: *Watch out, mister!*

mis•time (mis′tīm′) /,mɪs'taym/ *v.* [~ + *obj*], **-timed, -tim•ing.** to do or say at the wrong time: *The pilot mistimed his landing.*

mis•tle•toe (mis′əl tō′) /'mɪsəl,tow/ *n.* [*noncount*] a plant having yellowish flowers and white berries used in Christmas decorations: *If you stand under mistletoe, anyone wishing to do so may kiss you.*

mis•treat (mis trēt′) /mɪs'triyt/ *v.* [~ + *obj*] to treat badly or harmfully: *The dog's owner mistreats him terribly.* **—mis•treat′ment,** *n.* [*noncount*]: *to suffer mistreatment.*

mis•tress (mis′tris) /'mɪstrɪs/ *n.* [*count*] **1.** a woman who has authority, esp. the female head of a household: *The servant did whatever the mistress of the house ordered.* **2.** a woman who has a continuing sexual relationship with a man not married to her: *He had mistresses in several cities.* **3.** a woman who has control of something: *the mistress of a great fortune.* **4.** [*sometimes: Mistress*] something thought of as feminine that has control: *Great Britain, mistress of the seas.* **5.** *Brit.* a female schoolteacher; schoolmistress.

mis•tri•al (mis trī′l, mis′trī′l) /mɪs'trayl, 'mɪstrayl/ *n.* [*count*] a trial forced to end without a decision, esp. because of error in the proceedings: *The judge declared a mistrial.*

mis•trust (mis trust′) /mɪs'trʌst/ *n.* [*noncount*] **1.** lack of trust or confidence; distrust: *eyes full of mistrust.* **—***v.* [~ + *obj*] **2.** to look at or think about (someone) with suspicion; distrust: *I mistrust anyone who uses an initial for his first name.* **—mis•trust′ful,** *adj.*: *staring with mistrustful eyes.*

mis•un•der•stand (mis′un dər stand′) /,mɪsʌndər'stænd/ *v.* [*not: be* + ~*-ing*], **-stood, -stand•ing. 1.** to interpret incorrectly; attach a wrong meaning to: [~ + *obj*]: *The radar operators misunderstood his orders.* [*no obj*]: *I think you misunderstood; repeat the instructions.* **2.** [~ + *obj*] to fail to understand the character, nature, etc., of (someone): *He continually misunderstands his children.*

mis•un•der•stand•ing (mis′un dər stan′ding) /,mɪsʌndər'stændɪŋ/ *n.* **1.** a failure to understand: [*noncount*]: a source of mistrust and misunderstanding. [*count*]: *a major misunderstanding during the peace talks.* **2.** [*count*] a disagreement or quarrel: *had a misunderstanding but now we're friends again.*

mis•use (*n.* mis yo͞os′; *v.* -yo͞oz′) / *n.* mɪs'yuws; *v.* -'yuwz/ *n., v.,* **-used, -us•ing.** **—***n.* **1.** wrong or improper use: [*noncount*]: *The principal was dismissed for misuse of school funds.* [*count*]: *a misuse of the word "appropriately."* **—***v.* [~ + *obj*] **2.** to use incorrectly: *to misuse a word.* **3.** to treat harmfully; mistreat: *to misuse a friend.*

-mit-, *root.* *-mit-* comes from Latin, where it has the meaning "send." It is related to -MIS-. This meaning is found in such words as: ADMIT, COMMIT, COMMITTEE, EMIT, INTERMITTENT, NONCOMMITTAL, OMIT, PERMIT, REMIT, REMITTANCE, SUBMIT, TRANSMIT.

mite[1] (mīt) /mayt/ *n.* [*count*] a small, sometimes microscopic, creature, often living on other animals.

mite[2] (mīt) /mayt/ *n.* [*count*] **1.** [*usually singular; a* + ~ + *of*] a very small amount: *a mite of difficulty.* **2.** a coin of very small value. **3.** a very small creature, person, or thing. **—*Idiom.*** **4. a mite,** somewhat; a bit: *could be a mite snappy and angry if he hadn't slept well.*

mi•ter (mī′tər) /'maytər/ *n.* [*count*] the official headdress of a bishop, having an outline resembling a pointed arch in the front and back. Also, *esp. Brit.,* **mitre.**

mit•i•gate (mit′i gāt′) /'mɪtɪ,geyt/ *v.* [~ + *obj*] **-gat•ed, -gat•ing.** to lessen in force or intensity; make less severe: *to mitigate the harshness of a punishment.* **—mit•i•ga•tion** (mit i gā′shən) /mɪtɪ'geyʃən/ *n.* [*noncount*]

mitt (mit) /mɪt/ *n.* [*count*] **1. a.** a rounded, thickly padded, mittenlike glove used by catchers in baseball. **b.** a similar glove used by first basemen. **2.** *Slang.* a hand. **3.** a mitten for a particular use: *an oven mitt.* **4.** a glove that leaves the lower ends of the fingers bare.

mit•ten (mit′n) /'mɪtn̩/ *n.* [*count*] **1.** a hand covering that surrounds the four fingers together and the thumb separately. **2.** MITT (def. 4).

mix (miks) /mɪks/ *v.* **1.** to (cause to) become combined into one mass: [*no obj*]: *a paint that mixes with water.* [~ + *obj*]: *You can mix this paint with water.* **2.** [~ + *obj*] to put together in a confused way: *He mixed everything in a heap and tossed it into the washing machine.* **3.** [~ + *obj*] to combine or unite: *to mix business and pleasure.* **4.** [~ + *obj*] to form or make by combining ingredients: *to mix mortar; mixed some concrete and poured it into the frame.* **5.** [*no obj*] to enjoy the company of people: *He stood alone and refused to mix with the other guests.* **6. mix up, a.** to confuse completely: [*be* + ~*-ed* + *up*]: *He's all mixed up and doesn't know which way to go.* [~ + *obj* + *up*]: *He mixed me up by calling the meeting for today.* [~ + *up* + *obj*]: *He mixed up a lot of people by changing the date.* **b.** to mistake (one thing) for another: [~ + *obj* + *up*]: *He's always mixing the two of us up.* [~ + *up* + *obj*]: *He always mixes up the two of us.* **c.** to rearrange the order of: [~ + *up* + *obj*]: *She mixed up the cards and dealt them.* [~ + *obj* + *up*]: *She mixed them up and dealt them out.* **—***n.* [*count*] **7.** an act or instance of mixing; mixture: *a mix of concrete.* **8.** a commercial preparation to which usually only a liquid must be added before cooking or baking: *a cake mix.* **—*Idiom.*** **9. mix it up,** [*no obj*] *Slang.* **a.** to engage in a quarrel. **b.** to fight with the fists: *eager to mix it up with the gang down the road.* **—mix′a•ble,** *adj.* **—mix′er,** *n.* [*count*] See -MISC-.

mixed (mikst) /mɪkst/ *adj.* [*before a noun*] **1.** made up of things that are different but of the general type: *ate some mixed nuts.* **2.** of or relating to persons of different religions or races: *a mixed marriage.* **3.** including contrasting, sometimes opposite elements or parts: *mixed emotions about going abroad.* **4.** of or intended for people of different sexes: *the mixed doubles tennis matches.*

mixed′ num′ber, *n.* [*count*] a number made up of a whole number and a fraction or decimal, as $4\frac{1}{2}$ or 4.5.

mixed′-up′, *adj.* confused or unstable: *a mixed-up kid.*

mix•er (mik′sər) /'mɪksər/ *n.* [*count*] an electrical machine used for mixing things together.

mix•ture (miks′chər) /'mɪkstʃər/ *n.* [*count*] **1.** a product of mixing: *Pour the mixture into the mold.* **2.** any blend of different elements: *a mixture of reggae and classical music.* **3.** the act of mixing or the state of being mixed.

mix-up (miks′up′) /'mɪks,ʌp/ *n.* [*count*] a state of confusion or disorder; a mistake: *There must be a mix-up; we were told we didn't need reservations.*

ml, an abbreviation of: milliliter.

Mlle., an abbreviation of: Mademoiselle.

mm, an abbreviation of: millimeter.

MM., an abbreviation of: Messieurs.

Mme., an abbreviation of: Madame.

MN, an abbreviation of: Minnesota.

-mne-, *root.* *-mne-* comes from Greek, where it has the meaning "mind; remembering." This meaning is found in such words as: AMNESIA, AMNESTY, MNEMONIC.

mne•mon•ic (ni mon′ik) /nɪ'mɒnɪk/ *adj.* **1.** assisting the memory: *He used a mnemonic device—a song—to memorize the names of the chemical elements.* **—***n.* [*count*] **2.** something intended to assist the memory, as a song or formula. **3.** a symbol or other short form used as a computer code or function, as in programming. See -MNE-.

MO, an abbreviation of: **1.** method or mode of operation. **2.** Missouri.

Mo., an abbreviation of: **1.** Missouri. **2.** Monday.

mo., *pl.* **mos.** an abbreviation of: month.

M.O., an abbreviation of: **1.** method or mode of operation. **2.** modus operandi. **3.** money order.

m.o., an abbreviation of: **1.** mail order. **2.** modus operandi. **3.** money order.

moan (mōn) /mown/ *n.* [*count*] **1.** a low, sad, or miserable sound expressing suffering or complaint: *more moans about low pay.* **2.** any similar sound: *the moan of the wind.* **—***v.* **3.** [*no obj*] to utter moans: *He moaned softly with pain.* **4.** [*no obj*] (of the wind, etc.) to make a sound like such moans: *Outside the wind moaned and howled.* **5.** to complain; grumble: [*no obj*]: *She's always moaning about some little pain.* [~ + (*that*) *clause*]: *He moaned that his salary was too low.* [*used with quotations*]: *"I feel awful," he moaned.*

moat (mōt) /mowt/ *n.* [*count*] a deep, wide trench, usually filled with water, esp. one surrounding a fortified place.

mob (mob) /mɒb/ *n., adj., v.,* **mobbed, mob•bing.** **—***n.* [*count*] **1.** a disorderly crowd of people: *angry mobs of protesters.* **2.** [*singular; the* + ~] the common people: *rule by the mob.* **3.** *Informal.* a criminal gang involved in organized crime: *the most powerful mob in the area.* **—adj.** [*before a noun*] **4.** of or by the common people: *degenerated into mob rule.* **—v.** [~ + *obj*] **5.** to crowd around noisily, as from curiosity or hostility: *Fans mobbed the actor.* **6.** to attack in a riotous mob: *The crowd mobbed the consulate.* **7.** to fill with people; crowd: *The theater was mobbed with people trying to get in.*

-mob-, *root.* *-mob-* comes from Latin, where it has the meaning "move." It is related to -MOT- and -MOV-. This meaning is found in such words as: AUTOMOBILE, DEMOBILIZE, IMMOBILE, IMMOBILIZE, MOBILE, MOBILITY, MOBILIZE, SNOWMOBILE.

mo•bile (mō′bəl, -bēl) /ˈmowbəl, -biyl/ *adj.* **1.** capable of moving or being moved easily or quickly: *My grandmother was still mobile when she was 99.* **2.** using a motor vehicle for easy movement from place to place: *a mobile x-ray unit.* **3.** changing easily in expression, mood, etc.: *a mobile face.* **4.** permitting the moving from one social group, class, or level to another: *The society was upwardly mobile.* **—n.** [*count*] **5.** a sculpture or other hanging device, usually having delicately balanced parts that can move independently, as when stirred by a breeze. **—mo•bil•i•ty** (mō bil′i tē) /mowˈbɪlɪtiy/ *n.* [*noncount*] See -MOB-.

mo′bile home′, *n.* [*count*] a large house trailer, designed for year-round living in one place.

mo•bi•lize (mō′bə līz′) /ˈmowbəˌlayz/ *v.,* **-lized, -liz•ing. 1.** to (cause to) assemble and get ready for action or war: [~ + *obj*]: *Would the president mobilize troops?* [*no obj*]: *The whole country mobilized for war.* **2.** [~ + *obj*] to bring together for action or use: *mobilized voter support.* **—mo•bi•li•za•tion** (mō′bə li zā′shən) /ˌmowbəlɪˈzeyʃən/ *n.* [*noncount*]: *large-scale mobilization of troops.* [*count*]: *Mobilizations were scheduled one right after the other.* **—mo′bi•liz′er,** *n.* [*count*]. See -MOB-.

mob•ster (mob′stər) /ˈmɒbstər/ *n.* [*count*] a member of a criminal mob.

moc•ca•sin (mok′ə sin, -zən) /ˈmɒkəsɪn, -zən/ *n.* [*count*] **1.** a shoe without a heel, made entirely of soft leather, as deerskin, worn originally by American Indians. **2.** a hard-soled shoe or slipper resembling this. **3.** COTTONMOUTH.

mo•cha (mō′kə) /ˈmowkə/ *n.* [*noncount*] **1.** a variety of coffee, originally grown in Arabia. **2.** a flavoring obtained by blending coffee with chocolate. **3.** a brownish chocolate color.

mock (mok) /mɒk/ *v.* [~ + *obj*] **1.** to make fun of; to treat with ridicule or contempt: *They mocked him and called him a coward.* **2.** to imitate or mimic: *mocked the way his teacher spoke.* **—adj.** [*before a noun*] **3.** deliberately pretended, as for demonstration purposes: *a mock examination.* **—mock′er,** *n.* [*count*] **—mock′ing•ly,** *adv.*

mock•er•y (mok′ə rē) /ˈmɒkəriy/ *n., pl.* **-er•ies. 1.** [*noncount*] ridicule; contempt: *a target of mockery.* **2.** [*count*] something done poorly or badly: *The trial was a mockery of justice.* **—*Idiom.* 3. make a mockery of,** [~ + *obj*] to make (something) seem foolish: *The criminal made a mockery of all the attempts to grant him leniency, because he went right out and committed more crimes.*

mock•ing•bird (mok′ing bûrd′) /ˈmɒkɪŋˌbɜrd/ *n.* [*count*] a New World songbird that uses the calls of other bird species, esp. one having gray, white, and black coloring.

mock′-up′ or **mock′up′,** *n.* [*count*] a model, often full-size, for study, testing, or teaching: *They strapped the pilot into a mock-up of the experimental aircraft.*

mod (mod) /mɒd/ *adj.* **1.** very modern in style, etc. **2.** [*sometimes: Mod*] of or relating to a style of dress of the 1960's, with miniskirts and bell-bottom trousers. **—n.** [*count*] **3.** a person who is very modern in style, dress, etc.

-mod-, *root.* *-mod-* comes from Latin, where it has the meaning "manner; kind; measured amount." This meaning is found in such words as: ACCOMMODATE, COMMODIOUS, IMMODERATE, IMMODEST, MODAL, MODE, MODEL, MODERN, MODICUM, MODULE, MOOD, OUTMODED, REMODEL.

mod•al (mōd′l) /ˈmowdl̩/ *adj.* **1.** of or relating to a mode or way of doing something. **2.** A *modal verb* is used before an auxiliary, or a main verb to indicate the speaker's attitude toward the action expressed by the main verb. Modal verbs in English are: CAN, COULD, MAY, MIGHT, MUST, OUGHT, SHALL, SHOULD, WILL and WOULD. Some characteristics of these verbs are: **a.** Modal verbs do not change in the present tense, third person singular form: *I can run. He can run (He runs).* **b.** Modal verbs are followed by the root form of the next verb: *I can swim. She could have walked. He might be staying.* **c.** Modal verbs come before the word NOT in negative sentences: *I will not see you today. She won't be home.* **d.** Modal verbs come before the subject in questions: *Can I see you in your office? Will you be home tomorrow?* **e.** Modal verbs can stand alone when another main verb is understood but has been left out: *I'd like to talk with you now but I can't (= can't talk with you now). He'll be there, won't he? (= won't he be there?)* **f.** Modal verbs express different attitudes toward the action of the main verb. Some of these feelings include: possibility: *It might rain tomorrow;* ability: *He could lift a hundred pounds;* permission: *May I go home now? Can she come in, please?;* necessity: *It must be here somewhere!;* suggestions: *We could have pizza tonight, I guess.* See each verb for more details. **—n.** [*count*] **3.** a modal verb: *For your homework, find all the modals on this page and underline them.* See -MOD-.

mode[1] (mōd) /mowd/ *n.* [*count*] **1.** a manner of acting or doing; method: *modes of transportation.* **2.** a particular type or form of something: *Heat is a mode of motion.* **3.** a certain condition or status, as for performing a task: *a machine in the automatic mode.* See -MOD-.

mode[2] (mōd) /mowd/ *n.* [*count*] fashion or style in manners, dress, etc.

mod•el (mod′l) /ˈmɒdl̩/ *n., adj., v.,* **-eled, -el•ing** or (*esp. Brit.*) **-elled, -el•ling. —n.** [*count*] **1.** a standard or example of something that can be used for imitation or comparison: *He is a model of hard work.* **2.** a copy, usually in miniature, to show appearance of something: *a model of a house.* **3.** a person or thing that serves as a subject for an artist, etc.: *the model for the art class.* **4.** a style of a particular product, as a car, machine, etc.: *a new car model.* **5.** a simplified representation of a system or of some event or action, as in the sciences, proposed by scientists to explain or describe the event or action: *a model of the universe.* **—adj.** [*before a noun*] **6.** serving as an example or model: *They went through the model home.* **7.** worthy to serve as a model; exemplary: *a model student.* **8.** being a miniature version of something: *model ships.* **—v. 9.** [~ + *obj*] to make a model of: *to model airplanes out of wood.* **10.** [~ + *obj*] to display to other persons, esp. by wearing: *modeled expensive dresses.* **11.** [*no obj*] to serve or be employed as a model: *modeled for some big-name companies.* **12.** [~ + *obj* + *on* + *obj*] to copy the qualities or character of another: *The scientists modeled the robots on an old science fiction story.* **—mod′el•er;** *esp. Brit.,* **mod′el•ler,** *n.* [*count*] See -MOD-.

mo•dem (mō′dəm, -dem) /ˈmowdəm, -dɛm/ *n.* [*count*] an electronic device that makes possible the transmission of data to or from a computer through telephone lines. See -MOD-.

mod•er•ate (*adj., n.* mod′ər it, mod′rit; *v.* -ə rāt′) / *adj., n.* ˈmɒdərɪt, ˈmɒdrɪt; *v.* -əˌreyt/ *adj., n., v.,* **-at•ed, -at•ing. —adj. 1.** keeping within reasonable or proper limits: *moderate prices.* **2.** of medium quantity, extent, or amount: *a moderate income.* **3.** mediocre or fair: *moderate talent.* **4.** of or relating to moderates, as in politics: *the moderate wing of the party.* **—n.** [*count*] **5.** one who is moderate in opinion or who is opposed to extreme views, as in politics. **—v. 6.** to be at the head of or preside over (a public forum, etc.): [~ + *obj*]: *He moderated the last town meeting.* [*no obj*]: *He's good at moderating: he keeps things moving.* **7.** to (cause to) become less violent or extreme: [~ + *obj*]: *moderated her criticism of the plan.* [*no obj*]: *The storm moderated.* **—mod′er•ate•ness,** *n.* [*noncount*]

mod•er•ate•ly (mod′ər it lē, mod′rit lē) /ˈmɒdərɪtliy, ˈmɒdrɪtliy/ *adv.* fairly; somewhat: *moderately happy with his new car.*

mod•er•a•tion (mod′ə rā′shən) /ˌmɒdəˈreyʃən/ *n.* [*noncount*] **1.** control, esp. over one's behavior or emotions: *Moderation in eating should keep your weight down.* **2.** reduction or reducing; lessening: *The drug brought some moderation of the pain.* **—*Idiom.* 3. in moderation,** within reasonable or sensible limits: *Drinking in moderation will not affect his health.* See -MOD-.

mod•er•a•tor (mod′ə rā′tər) /ˈmɒdəˌreytər/ *n.* [*count*] **1.** a person or thing that moderates. **2.** a person in charge of a group event or meeting: *As the moderator he decides who speaks and for how long.* See -MOD-.

mod•ern (mod′ərn) /ˈmɒdərn/ *adj.* **1.** of or relating to present and recent time; contemporary. **2.** [*before a noun*] of or relating to certain styles of art, literature, etc., that reject older, traditional forms: *modern art.* **3.** using the latest techniques or ideas: *a modern city with efficient subways.* **—mo•der•ni•ty** (mo dûr′ni tē) /mɒˈdɜrnɪtiy/ *n.* [*noncount*] **—mod′ern•ness,** *n.* [*noncount*] See -MOD-.

mod•ern•ism (mod′ər niz′əm) /ˈmɒdərˌnɪzəm/ *n.* [*noncount*] **1.** modern character, tendencies, or values; belief in or sympathy with what is modern. **2.** [*sometimes: Modernism*] a movement in the arts and literature rejecting the past. —**mod′ern•ist,** *n.* [*count*], *adj.* —**mod′ern•is′tic,** *adj.*: *modernistic sculpture.* See -MOD-.

mod•ern•ize (mod′ər nīz′) /ˈmɒdərˌnayz/ *v.*, **-ized, -iz•ing.** to (cause to) become modern: [~ + *obj*]: *Our competitors modernized their equipment.* [*no obj*]: *If we hope to compete today we have to modernize.* —**mod•ern•i•za•tion** (mod′ər ni zā′shən) /ˌmɒdərnɪˈzeyʃən/ *n.* [*noncount*] —**mod′ern•iz′er,** *n.* [*count*] See -MOD-.

mod•est (mod′ist) /ˈmɒdɪst/ *adj.* **1.** having or showing a moderate opinion of one's merits, importance, etc.; not boasting: *She was very modest about the award.* **2.** free from obvious displays of showiness: *a modest house in the country.* **3.** showing regard for the decencies of behavior, dress, etc.: *She was too modest to wear a revealing swimsuit in public.* **4.** limited in amount, extent, etc.: *a modest salary.* —**mod′est•ly,** *adv.*: *He answered modestly that a team effort had helped him win the award.*

mod•es•ty (mod′ə stē) /ˈmɒdəstiy/ *n.* [*noncount*] **1.** the quality or state of being modest: *answered the questions with modesty.* **2.** the quality or state of being modest about sexual matters: *Her modesty prevented her from talking about sex in any detail.* See -MOD-.

mod•i•cum (mod′i kəm) /ˈmɒdɪkəm/ *n.* [*count; usually singular; a* + ~] a moderate amount: *displays a modicum of good sense.* See -MOD-.

mod•i•fy (mod′ə fī′) /ˈmɒdəˌfay/ *v.* [~ + *obj*], **-fied, -fy•ing. 1.** to change somewhat the form or qualities of; amend: *to modify a contract.* **2.** (of a word, phrase, or clause) to describe, limit, or qualify (another word, phrase, or clause): *In the phrase* a good cook, *the word* good *modifies the word* cook. —**mod•i•fi•ca•tion** (mod′ə fi kā′shən) /ˌmɒdəfɪˈkeyʃən/ *n.* [*noncount*]: *to accept a contract without modification.* [*count*]: *The modifications were completed in a week.* —**mod′i•fi′er,** *n.* [*count*]: *When the word* model *is used as a modifier, it goes before the noun it modifies, as in* a model home. See -MOD-.

mod•ish (mō′dish) /ˈmowdɪʃ/ *adj.* fashionable; stylish. —**mod′ish•ly,** *adv.* —**mod′ish•ness,** *n.* [*noncount*] See -MOD-.

mod•u•lar (moj′ə lər) /ˈmɒdʒələr/ *adj.* **1.** of or relating to a module. **2.** made up of standardized units for easy construction or arrangement: *a series of modular boxes that fit into each other.*

mod•u•late (moj′ə lāt′) /ˈmɒdʒəˌleyt/ *v.* [~ + *obj*], **-lat•ed, -lat•ing. 1.** to regulate by a certain measure or amount **2.** to alter (the voice) according to the situation, one's listener, etc.: *modulated his voice instantly when he realized that his boss was listening.* —**mod•u•la•tion** (moj′ə lā′shən) /ˌmɒdʒəˈleyʃən/ *n.* [*noncount*] —**mod′u•la′tor,** *n.* [*count*]

mod•ule (moj′o͞ol) /ˈmɒdʒuwl/ *n.* [*count*] **1.** a part that can be separated from the rest, frequently one that may be exchanged with or used in place of others: *The kit contained modules that could be put together to form various toys.* **2.** any of the parts of a spacecraft that may stand alone or be used independently: *The lunar module detached itself and headed toward the surface.* See -MOD-.

mo•dus op•e•ran•di (mō′dəs op′ə ran′dē, -dī), *n.* {*count*} /ˈmowˌdəs ɒpəˈrændiy, -day/, *n.* {*count*} *pl.* **mo•di operandi** (mō′dē, -dī) /ˈmowdiy, -day/. method of working or operating: *The burglars had a modus operandi that led the detectives to them.* See -MOD-.

mo•gul (mō′gəl) /ˈmowgəl/ *n.* [*count*] a bump or mound of hard snow on a ski slope.

Mo•gul (mō′gəl, mō gul′) /ˈmowgəl, mowˈgʌl/ *n.* [*count*] **1.** a Muslim ruler from a dynasty that dominated N India from the 16th to the early 18th centuries. **2.** [*mogul*] a powerful or influential person: *a mogul of the movie industry.*

mo•hair (mō′hâr′) /ˈmowˌhɛər/ *n.* [*noncount*] **1.** the hair of an Angora goat. **2.** a fabric made wholly or partly of yarn from this hair, used in clothing and upholstery.

Mo•ham•med (mo͝o ham′id, -hä′mid, mō-) /moʊˈhæmɪd, -ˈhɑmɪd, mow-/ *n.* MUHAMMAD.

Mo•ham•med•an (mo͝o ham′i dn, mō-) /moʊˈhæmɪdn̩, mow-/ *adj.* **1.** of or relating to Muhammad or Islam; Islamic; Muslim. —*n.* [*count*] **2.** a follower of Islam; Muslim. —**Mo•ham′med•an•ism,** *n.* [*noncount*]

moi•e•ty (moi′i tē) /ˈmɔyɪtiy/ *n.* [*count*], *pl.* **-ties. 1.** a half. **2.** a portion, part, or share of any size.

moi•ré (mwä rā′ mô-) /mwɑˈrey, mɔ-/ *adj.*, *n.*, *pl.* **-rés.** —*adj.* **1.** (of silks) presenting a watery or wavelike appearance. —*n.* **2.** [*count*] a design pressed on silk, rayon, etc., by engraved rollers. **3.** [*noncount*] a fabric of silk, rayon, etc., with a watery or wavelike appearance.

moist (moist) /mɔyst/ *adj.*, **-er, -est. 1.** slightly wet; damp: *a moist rag.* **2.** (of the eyes) tearful: *His eyes grew moist.* —**moist′ly,** *adv.* —**moist′ness,** *n.* [*noncount*]

mois•ten (moi′sən) /ˈmɔysən/ *v.* to (cause to) become moist: [~ + *obj*]: *moistened her lips before speaking.* [*no obj*]: *Her lips moistened.* —**moist′en•er,** *n.* [*count*]

mois•ture (mois′chər) /ˈmɔystʃər/ *n.* [*noncount*] liquid, esp. water, that has turned into steam or a fine mist: *a thin layer of moisture on his forehead.*

mois•tur•ize (mois′chə rīz′) /ˈmɔystʃəˌrayz/ *v.* [~ + *obj*], **-ized, -iz•ing.** to add or restore moisture to: *The suntan lotion is supposed to moisturize the skin.* —**mois′tur•iz′er,** *n.* [*noncount*]: *Rub some moisturizer on the skin.* [*count*]: *many moisturizers to choose from.* —**mois′tur•iz′ing,** *adj.* [*before a noun*]: *Rub some moisturizing cream on the skin.*

mo•lar (mō′lər) /ˈmowlər/ *n.* [*count*] Also called **mo′lar tooth′.** a tooth having a broad biting surface for grinding.

mo•las•ses (mə las′iz) /məˈlæsɪz/ *n.* [*noncount*] a thick syrup produced during the refining of sugar.

mold[1] (mōld) /mowld/ *n.* [*count*] **1.** a hollow form for giving a particular shape to a liquid: *pouring the concrete into a mold.* **2.** something formed in a mold: *a mold of gelatin.* **3.** a special or distinctive nature, character, or type: *a person of a simple mold.* —*v.* [~ + *obj*] **4.** to work into a required shape or form; shape: *to mold a figure in clay.* **5.** to shape or form in or on a mold: *The car body is molded in Japan.* **6.** to produce by or as if by shaping material; form. **7.** to have influence in forming, as of the character of someone or something: *Parents mold their children more by example than by preaching.* Also, *esp. Brit.*, **mould.** —**mold′a•ble,** *adj.* —**mold′er,** *n.* [*count*]

mold[2] (mōld) /mowld/ *n.* **1.** [*noncount*] a growth of very small fungi on vegetable or animal matter. **2.** any of the fungi that produce such a growth; mildew: [*noncount*]: *Mold grows rapidly in damp places.* [*count*]: *The molds grow rapidly in the dark.* —*v.* **3.** to (cause to) become overgrown with mold: [*no obj*]: *The bread had molded.* [~ + *obj*]: *Mildew had molded the bread.* Also, *esp. Brit.*, **mould.**

mold•er (mōl′dər) /ˈmowldər/ *v.* [*no obj*] to turn to dust by natural decay: *The books were left moldering in the library for decades before anyone discovered them.*

mold•ing (mōl′ding) /ˈmowldɪŋ/ *n.* **1.** [*noncount*] the act or process of shaping into a mold. **2.** something molded, esp. a long, narrow ornamental strip, as of wood, for decoration on furniture and buildings: [*noncount*]: *strips of rotten molding.* [*count*]: *He cut and fitted the moldings over the doorway.*

mold•y (mōl′dē) /ˈmowldiy/ *adj.*, **-i•er, -i•est. 1.** overgrown or covered with mold. **2.** musty, as from age: *a moldy old attic.* **3.** *Informal.* old-fashioned; outmoded: *moldy, boring professors.* —**mold′i•ness,** *n.* [*noncount*]

mole[1] (mōl) /mowl/ *n.* [*count*] **1.** a small, insect-eating mammal living chiefly underground. **2.** a spy who becomes part of and works from within the ranks of an enemy intelligence agency.

mole[2] (mōl) /mowl/ *n.* [*count*] a small spot or blemish on the human skin, present from birth, usually of a dark color: *a small mole on her cheek.*

mo•lec•u•lar (mə lek′yə lər) /məˈlɛkyələr/ *adj.* [*usually before a noun*] of or relating to molecules.

mol•e•cule (mol′ə kyo͞ol′) /ˈmɒləˌkyuwl/ *n.* [*count*] **1.** the smallest physical unit of an element or compound, made up of one or more similar atoms in an element and two or more different atoms in a compound. **2.** any very small particle.

mole•hill (mōl′hil′) /ˈmowlˌhɪl/ *n.* [*count*] a small ridge of earth raised up by a mole burrowing under the ground.

mole•skin (mōl′skin′) /ˈmowlˌskɪn/ *n.* **1.** [*noncount*] the soft, deep gray fur of the mole. **2.** [*noncount*] a strong, heavy cotton fabric with a suedelike finish. **3. moleskins,** [*plural*] a garment, esp. trousers, of this fabric. **4.** [*noncount*] an adhesive-backed material resembling felt, applied to parts of the feet that are rubbed too much by shoes, etc.

mo•lest (mə lest′) /məˈlɛst/ *v.* [~ + *obj*] **1.** to bother or annoy: *The bully always molested him when he walked home from school.* **2.** to make indecent sexual advances to: *molesting children in a day-care center.* —**mo•les•ta•tion** (mō′le stā′shən, mol′e-) /ˌmowlɛˈsteyʃən, ˌmɒlɛ-/ *n.* [*noncount*]: *child molestation.* —**mo•lest′er,** *n.* [*count*]: *mandatory prison for child molesters.*

moll (mol) /mɒl/ *n.* [*count*] *Slang.* a gangster's girlfriend.

mol•li•fy (mol′ə fī′) /ˈmɒləˌfay/ *v.* [~ + *obj*], **-fied, -fy•ing. 1.** to cause to calm down: *The lollipop seemed to mollify the crying child.* **2.** to reduce: *to mollify one's demands.* —**mol•li•fi•ca•tion** (mol′ə fi kā′shən) /ˌmɒləfɪˈkeyʃən/ *n.* [*noncount*]

mol•lusk or **mol•lusc** (mol′əsk) /ˈmɒləsk/ *n.* [*count*] an animal without a backbone, having a soft body enclosed by a shell: *Mollusks include snails and octopuses.* —**mol•lus•kan, mol•lus•can** (mə lus′kən) /məˈlʌskən/ *adj., n.* [*count*]

mol•ly•cod•dle (mol′ē kod′l) /ˈmɒliyˌkɒdl/ *v.,* **-dled, -dling,** *n.* —*v.* [~ + *obj*] **1.** to spoil (someone) by treating him or her like a baby: *They mollycoddle that boy.* —*n.* [*count*] **2.** one who is spoiled, pampered, or coddled.

molt (mōlt) /mowlt/ *v.* **1.** (of an animal) to cast off or shed skin, etc., in the process of growth: [*no obj*]: *The bird had molted and was growing new feathers.* [~ + *obj*]: *The bird had molted its feathers.* —*n.* [*noncount*] **2.** an act or instance of molting. **3.** something dropped in molting. Also, *esp. Brit.,* **moult.**

mol•ten (mōl′tn) /ˈmowltn̩/ *v.* **1.** a pp. of MELT. —*adj.* **2.** liquefied by heat: *molten rocks pouring from the volcano.* **3.** produced by melting and casting: *a molten image.*

mo•lyb•de•num (mə lib′də nəm) /məˈlɪbdənəm/ *n.* [*noncount*] a silver-white metal element, used with iron in making hard, high-speed cutting tools.

mom (mom) /mɒm/ *n.* [*count*] *Informal.* mother.

mo•ment (mō′mənt) /ˈmowmənt/ *n.* **1.** [*count*] an indefinitely short period of time; instant: *Moments later, the thief vanished.* **2.** [*count*] the particular time when something happens: *The moment he began speaking, boos and catcalls filled the room.* **3.** [*noncount*] importance or consequence: *a decision of great moment.* —***Idiom.* 4. at the moment,** at the present moment: *The boss is busy at the moment.* **5. have one's** or **its moments,** to have a time or period of success, etc.: *My job has its moments.*

mo•men•tar•i•ly (mō′mən târ′ə lē, mō′mən ter′-) /ˌmowmənˈtɛərəliy, ˈmowmənˌtɛr-/ *adv.* **1.** for a moment; briefly: *Flames escaped from the capsule momentarily, then all was quiet.* **2.** at any moment; soon: *She'll be here momentarily.* **3.** instantly.

mo•men•tar•y (mō′mən ter′ē) /ˈmowmənˌtɛriy/ *adj.* **1.** lasting only a moment; very brief: *a momentary lull in the fighting.* **2.** that might occur at any moment: *momentary annihilation.* —**mo′men•tar′i•ness,** *n.* [*noncount*]

mo•men•tous (mō men′təs) /mowˈmɛntəs/ *adj.* of great importance: *The fall of Rome was a momentous event.* —**mo•men′tous•ly,** *adv.* —**mo•men′tous•ness,** *n.* [*noncount*]

mo•men•tum (mō men′təm) /mowˈmɛntəm/ *n.* [*noncount*] **1.** force or speed of movement; impetus, as of a physical object: *The car gained momentum as it hurtled down the street.* **2.** force or speed, as of events: *a career that had lost momentum.*

mom•ma (mom′ə) /ˈmɒmə/ *n.* [*count*], *pl.* **-mas.** *Informal.* MOTHER (defs. 1, 2).

mom•my or **mom•mie** (mom′ē) /ˈmɒmiy/ *n.* [*count*], *pl.* **-mies.** *Informal.* MOTHER (defs. 1, 2).

Mon., an abbreviation of: Monday.

-mon-, *root.* *-mon-* comes from Latin, where it has the meaning "warn." This meaning is found in such words as: ADMONISH, ADMONITION, MONITOR, MONITORY, MONSTER, MONSTROUS, MONUMENT, PREMONITION, SUMMON.

mon•arch (mon′ərk, -ärk) /ˈmɒnərk, -ɑrk/ *n.* [*count*] a ruler, as a king, queen, or emperor; the sole ruler of a state or nation. —**mo•nar•chic** (mə när′kik) /məˈnɑrkɪk/ **mo•nar′chi•cal,** *adj.* See -ARCH-.

mon•ar•chism (mon′ər kiz′əm) /ˈmɒnərˌkɪzəm/ *n.* [*noncount*] **1.** the principles of monarchy. **2.** the calling for or favoring of monarchical rule. —**mon′ar•chist,** *n.* [*count*], *adj.* —**mon′ar•chist′ic,** *adj.* See -ARCH-.

mon•ar•chy (mon′ər kē) /ˈmɒnərkiy/ *n., pl.* **-chies. 1.** [*count*] a government or state in which the supreme power is held by a monarch: *The three monarchies joined together to form one kingdom.* **2.** [*noncount*] the fact or state of being a monarchy: *Some consider monarchy to be the best form of government.* See -ARCH-.

mon•as•ter•y (mon′ə ster′ē) /ˈmɒnəˌstɛriy/ *n.* [*count*], *pl.* **-ter•ies. 1.** a place where a community of monks lives. **2.** the community itself.

mo•nas•tic (mə nas′tik) /məˈnæstɪk/ *adj.* Also, **mo•nas′ti•cal. 1.** of or relating to monks or monasteries: *monastic vows.* —*n.* [*count*] **2.** a member of a monastic community or order, esp. a monk. —**mo•nas′ti•cism,** *n.* [*noncount*]

mon•au•ral (mon ôr′əl) /mɒnˈɔrəl/ *adj.* MONOPHONIC: *monaural records.*

Mon•day (mun′dā, -dē) /ˈmʌndey, -diy/ *n.* the second day of the week, following Sunday: [*count*]: *a cold and gray Monday.* [*proper noun*]: *Can we meet on Monday?*

Mon•e•gasque (mon′i gask′) /ˌmɒnɪˈgæsk/ *adj.* **1.** of or relating to Monaco. —*n.* [*count*] **2.** a person born or living in Monaco.

mon•e•ta•rism (mon′i tə riz′əm, mun′-) /ˈmɒnɪtəˌrɪzəm, ˈmʌn-/ *n.* [*noncount*] an economic doctrine holding that changes in the money supply determine the direction of a nation's economy. —**mon′e•ta•rist,** *n.* [*count*], *adj.*

mon•e•tar•y (mon′i ter′ē, mun′-) /ˈmɒnɪˌtɛriy, ˈmʌn-/ *adj.* of or relating to the coinage or money supply of a country: *monetary policy.* —**mon•e•tar•i•ly** (mon′i târ′ə lē, mun′-) /ˌmɒnɪˈtɛərəliy, ˌmʌn-/ *adv.*

mon•ey (mun′ē) /ˈmʌniy/ *n., pl.* **mon•eys, mon•ies,** *adj.* —*n.* [*noncount*] **1.** the coins and bills issued by a country to buy something: *He doesn't have a lot of money with him.* **2.** wealth: *Money can't buy love.* —*adj.* [*before a noun*] **3.** of or relating to money or finance: *a money drawer.* —***Idiom.* 4. for my money,** according to my opinion: *For my money, she'd make a perfect president.* **5. in the money,** *Informal.* financially successful: *Once the deal was completed his company was clearly in the money.* **6. make money,** to get money by earning it: *makes good money as an accountant.* **7. one's money's worth,** a value equal to what one spends or has paid for something: *We got our money's worth on that car.* **8. (right) on the money,** *Informal.* done expertly or with great accuracy: *His weather forecasts are always right on the money.* See MONIES.

mon•ey•bag (mun′ē bag′) /ˈmʌniyˌbæg/ *n.* **1.** [*count*] a bag for money. **2. moneybags,** [*count; singular; used with a singular verb*] a very wealthy person: *a real moneybags.*

mon•eyed (mun′ēd) /ˈmʌniyd/ *adj.* **1.** wealthy. **2.** of or relating to the wealthy: *the politician's moneyed interests.*

mon•ey•mak•er (mun′ē mā′kər) /ˈmʌniyˌmeykər/ *n.* [*count*] **1.** one who is successful at making money. **2.** something that provides a large profit. —**mon′ey•mak′ing,** *adj.* [*before a noun*], *n.* [*noncount*]

mon′ey or′der, *n.* [*count*] an order for the payment of money, as one issued by one bank or post office and payable at another: *sent him a money order.*

mon•ger (mung′gər, mong′-) /ˈmʌŋgər, ˈmɒŋ-/ *n.* [*count; often used in combination with another word*] **1.** a person involved with something in a low or mean way: *a gossipmonger (= someone involved in gossiping).* **2.** *Chiefly Brit.* a dealer in or trader of a product: *fishmonger (= someone dealing in or trading fish).* —*v.* [~ + *obj*] **3.** to sell.

Mon•go•li•an (mong gō′lē ən) /mɒŋˈgowliyən/ *adj.* **1.** of or relating to Mongolia. **2.** of or relating to the languages spoken by many of the people in Mongolia. —*n.* **3.** [*count*] a person born or living in Mongolia. **4.** [*noncount*] one of the languages spoken by many of the people in Mongolia.

mon•gol•ism (mong′gə liz′əm) /ˈmɒŋgəˌlɪzəm/ *n.* [*noncount*] [*sometimes: Mongolism*] (no longer in technical use; sometimes considered offensive) DOWN'S SYNDROME.

mon•gol•oid (mong′gə loid′) /ˈmɒŋgəˌlɔyd/ *adj.* (no longer in technical use; sometimes considered offensive) **1.** of, affected with, or characteristic of Down's syndrome. —*n.* [*count*] **2.** a person affected with Down's syndrome.

mon•goose (mong′gōōs′, mon′-) /ˈmɒŋˌguws, ˈmɒn-/ *n.* [*count*], *pl.* **-goos•es.** a slender meat-eating animal noted for its ability to kill cobras.

mon•grel (mung′grəl, mong′-) /ˈmʌŋgrəl, ˈmɒŋ-/ *n.* [*count*] **1.** an animal or plant, but esp. a dog, of mixed breed. —*adj.* [*before a noun*] **2.** being a mongrel.

mon•ied (mun′ēd) /ˈmʌniyd/ *adj.* MONEYED.

mon•ies (mun′ēz) /ˈmʌniyz/ *n.* [*plural*] money, esp. when thought of as a particular amount set aside for a certain purpose: *tax-levy monies.*

mon•i•ker or **mon•ick•er** (mon′i kər) /ˈmɒnɪkər/ *n.* [*count*] *Slang.* name; nickname: *His teammates gave him the moniker "Smilin' Jack."*

mon•i•tor (mon′i tər), /ˈmɒnɪtər/ *n.* [*count*] **1.** a student appointed to assist a teacher. **2.** a device for observing or recording the operation of a machine or system, esp.

an automatic control system: *The monitors showed the patient's heartbeat to be above normal.* **3.** *Radio and Television.* a large television receiver used in a control room or studio for monitoring transmissions. **4.** a component with a display screen for viewing computer data, etc.: *The monitor wasn't hooked up correctly to the computer.* **5.** a large lizard of Africa, S Asia, the East Indies, and Australia. **—*v.*** [~ + *obj*] **6.** to observe or detect (an operation) with instruments: *to monitor the patient's heartbeat.* **7.** to supervise or watch closely; keep track of: *to monitor the progress of the committee carefully.* See -MON-.

mon•i•to•ry (mon′i tôr′ē, -tōr′ē) /ˈmɒnɪˌtɔriy, -ˌtowriy/ *adj.* providing or carrying a warning. See -MON-.

monk (mungk) /mʌŋk/ *n.* [*count*] a man who is a member of a religious order, usually living in a monastery.

mon•key (mung′kē) /ˈmʌŋkiy/ *n., pl.* **-keys,** *v.* **—*n.*** [*count*] **1.** a primate having a tail. **—*v.*** **2.** [~ + *around*] *Informal.* to play idly or foolishly: *The boys were just monkeying around.* **3.** [~ + *with/around with* + *obj*] to tamper or meddle: *Quit monkeying with the antenna.*

mon′key busi′ness, *n.* [*noncount*] **1.** foolish, playful, or mischievous behavior: *schoolboys up to some monkey business.* **2.** dishonest conduct; trickery.

mon•key•shines (mung′kē shīnz′) /ˈmʌŋkiyˌʃaynz/ *n.* [*plural*] MONKEY BUSINESS (def. 1).

mon′key wrench′, *n.* [*count*] **1.** a wrench having a movable opening that can be adjusted for grasping nuts of different sizes. **2.** something that interferes: *That throws a monkey wrench into our plans.*

mon•o[1] (mon′ō) /ˈmɒnow/ *n.* MONONUCLEOSIS: *a bad case of mono.*

mon•o[2] (mon′ō) /ˈmɒnow/ *adj.* MONOPHONIC: *The old mono records were scratchy and worn.*

mono-, *prefix. mono-* comes from Greek, where it has the meaning "one, single, lone." This meaning is found in such words as: MONARCH, MONASTERY, MONOCHROME, MONOCLE, MONOGAMY, MONOGRAM, MONOGRAPH, MONOLINGUAL, MONOLITH, MONOLOGUE, MONONUCLEOSIS, MONOPOLY, MONORAIL, MONOSYLLABLE, MONOTONOUS.

mon•o•chro•mat•ic (mon′ə krō mat′ik) /ˌmɒnəkrowˈmætɪk/ *adj.* **1.** of or having one color. **2.** of or relating to light of one color or to radiation of a single wavelength. See -CHROM-.

mon•o•chrome (mon′ə krōm′) /ˈmɒnəˌkrowm/ *n.* [*count*] **1.** a painting or drawing in different shades of a single color. **—*adj.*** **2.** being or made in the shades of a single color: *old monochrome TV screens.* See -CHROM-.

mon•o•cle (mon′ə kəl) /ˈmɒnəkəl/ *n.* [*count*] an eyeglass for one eye. **—mon′o•cled,** *adj.* See -OCUL-.

mo•noc•u•lar (mə nok′yə lər) /məˈnɒkyələr/ *adj.* of or relating to only one eye: *a monocular lens.* See -OCUL-.

mo•nog•a•my (mə nog′ə mē) /məˈnɒgəmiy/ *n.* [*noncount*] the having of only one spouse at a time. **—mo•nog′a•mous,** *adj.* **—mo•nog′a•mous•ly,** *adv.* See -GAM-.

mon•o•gram (mon′ə gram′) /ˈmɒnəˌgræm/ *n., v.,* **-grammed, -gram•ming.** **—*n.*** [*count*] **1.** a design made up of combined alphabetic letters, commonly one's initials. **—*v.*** [~ + *obj*] **2.** to decorate with a monogram: *a shirt that was monogrammed.* See -GRAM-.

mon•o•graph (mon′ə graf′) /ˈmɒnəˌgræf/ *n.* [*count*] a learned piece of writing or detailed study, usually on a single topic or subject. See -GRAPH-.

mon•o•lin•gual (mon′ə ling′gwəl) /ˌmɒnəˈlɪŋgwəl/ *adj.* **1.** knowing or able to use only one language. **2.** spoken or written in only one language. **—*n.*** [*count*] **3.** a monolingual person. See -LING-.

mon•o•lith (mon′ə lith) /ˈmɒnəlɪθ/ *n.* [*count*] **1.** a column, etc., formed of a single block of stone. **2.** something having a large, unchanging quality or character: *the monolith of the bureaucracy.* **—mon′o•lith′ic,** *adj.* See -LITH.

mon•o•logue or **mon•o•log** (mon′ə lôg′, -log′) /ˈmɒnəˌlɔg, -ˌlɒg/ *n.* [*count*] **1.** a dramatic piece spoken by a single performer. **2.** a long speech by a single speaker. **—mon•o•log•ist** (mon′ə lô′gist, -log′ist, mənol′ə jist) /ˈmɒnəˌlɔgɪst, -ˌlɒgɪst, məˈnɒlədʒɪst/ **mon•o•logu•ist** (mon′ə lô′gist, -log′ist) /ˈmɒnəˌlɔgɪst, -ˌlɒgɪst/ *n.* [*count*] See -LOG-.

mon•o•ma•ni•a (mon′ə mā′nē ə, -mān′yə) /ˌmɒnəˈmeyniyə, -ˈmeynyə/ *n.* [*noncount*] an overwhelming interest or zeal in a single thing: *The captain's monomania was authority.* **—mon•o•ma•ni•ac** (mon′ə mā′nē ak′) /ˌmɒnəˈmeyniyˌæk/ *n.* [*count*]

mon•o•nu•cle•o•sis (mon′ə nōō′klē ō′sis, -nyōō′-) /ˌmɒnəˌnuwkliyˈowsɪs, -ˌnyuw-/ *n.* [*noncount*] a disease with a high, sudden fever and fatigue, that is easily transmitted to others.

mon•o•phon•ic (mon′ə fon′ik) /ˌmɒnəˈfɒnɪk/ *adj.* [*before a noun*] of or naming a system of sound recording and reproduction using only a single channel. See -PHON-.

mo•nop•o•lize (mə nop′ə līz′) /məˈnɒpəˌlayz/ *v.* [~ + *obj*], **-lized, -liz•ing.** **1.** to have sole power over: *A few large companies have monopolized the oil industry.* **2.** to take up or take over completely: *to monopolize all of someone's time.*

mo•nop•o•ly (mə nop′ə lē) /məˈnɒpəliy/ *n., pl.* **-lies.** **1.** the exclusive and complete control (as by a business) of a product, service, or invention that makes it possible to control prices: [*noncount*]: *the power of monopoly over the oil industry.* [*count*]: *a virtual monopoly of machinery.* **2.** [*count*] the exclusive possession or control of something: *He doesn't have a monopoly on brain power.* **3.** [*count*] a company or group that has such control: *He ran a monopoly in the shipping business.* **—mo•nop′o•list,** *n.* [*count*] **—mo•nop′o•lis′tic,** *adj.* **—mo•nop•o•li•za•tion** (mə nop′ə li zā′shən) /məˌnɒpəlɪˈzeyʃən/ *n.* [*noncount*]: *the monopolization of his attentions.*

mon•o•rail (mon′ə rāl′) /ˈmɒnəˌreyl/ *n.* **1.** [*count*] a single rail functioning as a track for wheeled vehicles, such as railroad cars, balanced upon or hanging from it. **2.** a transportation system using such a rail: [*count*]: *the future of the monorail.* [*noncount*]: *by monorail.*

mon•o•so•di•um glu•ta•mate (mon′ə sō′dē əm glōō′tə māt′) /ˌmɒnəˈsowdiyˈəm gluwtəˌmeyt/ *n.* [*noncount*] a white, crystallike powder used to intensify the flavor of foods: *allergic reactions to monosodium glutamate.* Also called **MSG.**

mon•o•syl•la•ble (mon′ə sil′ə bəl) /ˈmɒnəˌsɪləbəl/ *n.* [*count*] a word of one syllable: *The words* yes *and* no *are monosyllables.* **—mon•o•syl•lab•ic** (mon′ə si lab′ik) /ˌmɒnəsɪˈlæbɪk/ *adj.*

mon•o•the•ism (mon′ə thē iz′əm) /ˈmɒnəθiyˌɪzəm/ *n.* [*noncount*] the belief that there is only one God. **—mon′o•the′ist,** *n.* [*count*], *adj.* **—mon•o•the•is•tic** (mon′ə thē is′tik) /ˌmɒnəθiyˈɪstɪk/ *adj.* See -THEO-.

mon•o•tone (mon′ə tōn′) /ˈmɒnəˌtown/ *n.* [*count; usually singular*] a sound of one unchanging tone or pitch: *speaking in a boring monotone.* See -TON-.

mo•not•o•nous (mə not′n əs) /məˈnɒtn̩əs/ *adj.* **1.** lacking in variety: *a boring, monotonous job.* **2.** said in one unchanging tone. **—mo•not′o•nous•ly,** *adv.* **—mo•not′o•nous•ness, mo•not•o•ny** (mə not′n ē) /məˈnɒtn̩iy/ *n.* [*noncount*]: *a life of monotony.* See -TON-.

mon•sei•gneur (môn se nyœr′) /mɔ̃sɛˈnyœr/ *n.* [*proper noun; no article*], *pl.* **mes•sei•gneurs** (mā se nyœr′) /meysɛˈnyœr/. a French title of honor for princes and bishops.

mon•sieur (mə syœ′) /məˈsyœ/ *n.* [*proper noun; no article; often: Monsieur*], *pl.* **mes•sieurs** (me syœ′) /mɛˈsyœ/. the French title of respect and term of address for a man, corresponding to *Mr.* or *sir.* See -SENE-.

mon•si•gnor (mon sē′nyər, mon′sē nyôr′) /mɒnˈsiynyər, ˌmɒnsiyˈnyɔr/ *n., pl.* **mon•si•gnors, mon•si•gno•ri** (môn′sē nyôr′ē) /ˌmɔnsiyˈnyɔriy/. **1.** [*proper noun; no article: Monsignor*] a title for certain Roman Catholic priests: *Will Monsignor Kelly please step forward?* **2.** [*count*] a person bearing this title: *a monsignor from Rome.* See -SENE-.

mon•soon (mon sōōn′) /mɒnˈsuwn/ *n.* [*count*] **1.** the seasonal wind of the Indian Ocean and S Asia, blowing from the SW in summer and from the NE in winter. **2.** (in India and nearby lands) the season during which the SW monsoon blows, usually having heavy rains. **3.** (loosely) a heavy rain or rainstorm. **—mon•soon′al,** *adj.*

mon•ster (mon′stər) /ˈmɒnstər/ *n.* [*count*] **1.** any animal or human that is different from a normal shape or character; any creature ugly enough to frighten people: *monsters of myth and legend.* **2.** one who causes horror by wickedness, cruelty, etc.: *Those monsters slaughter innocent people!* **3.** any animal or thing huge in size. **—*adj.*** [*before a noun*] **4.** huge; enormous; gigantic; monstrous: *monster truck races.* See -MON-.

-monstr-, *root. -monstr-* comes from Latin, where it has the meaning "show; display." This meaning is found in such words as: DEMONSTRATE, MONSTRANCE, MUSTER, REMONSTRATE.

mon•strance (mon′strəns) /ˈmɒnstrəns/ *n.* [*count*] a special holder used in the Roman Catholic Church for the display of the Host. See -MONSTR-.

mon•stros•i•ty (mon stros′i tē) /mɒnˈstrɒsɪtiy/ *n.*

[*count*], *pl.* **-ties.** something monstrous: *That monstrosity blocks our view of the river.* See -MON-.

mon•strous (mon′strəs) /ˈmɒnstrəs/ *adj.* **1.** of or relating to a monster: *Beowulf fought the monstrous creature and managed to pull off its arm.* **2.** large; huge; gigantic: *The huge ship cast a monstrous shadow.* **3.** horribly wicked or cruel: *monstrous acts of murder.* See -MON-.

Mont., an abbreviation of: Montana.

mon•tage (mon täzh′) /mɒnˈtɑʒ/ *n.* [*count*], *pl.* **-tag•es** (-tä′zhiz) /-ˈtɑʒɪz/. **1.** the combining of images from different sources into a single composition, as a picture, film, or piece of music: *a montage of different camera shots creating a dizzying effect on the viewer.* **2.** any combination of widely differing elements forming a unified whole.

month (munth) /mʌnθ/ *n.* [*count*] **1.** any of the 12 parts, as January or February, into which the calendar year is divided. **2.** the time from any day of one calendar month to the corresponding day of the next, or a period of four weeks or 30 days. —***Idiom.*** **3. a month of Sundays,** any long period of time: *It's been a month of Sundays since you've called.*

month•ly (munth′lē) /ˈmʌnθliy/ *adj., n., pl.* **-lies,** *adv.* —*adj.* **1.** of or relating to a month, or to each month: *a monthly salary.* **2.** done, happening, appearing, etc., once a month: *a monthly magazine.* —*n.* [*count*] **3.** a periodical published once a month. —*adv.* **4.** once a month.

mon•u•ment (mon′yə mənt) /ˈmɒnyəmənt/ *n.* [*count*] **1.** something erected in memory of a person, event, etc., as a pillar or statue: *The arch in St. Louis is a monument to the pioneers.* **2.** any building from a past age, thought of as having importance. **3.** anything that has lasted a long time and is evidence of something noteworthy: *The canal and hydroelectric plant remain a monument to human ingenuity.* See -MON-.

mon•u•men•tal (mon′yə men′tl) /ˌmɒnyəˈmɛntl̩/ *adj.* **1.** of or relating to a monument. **2.** exceptionally great, as in quality or degree: *a monumental book.* **3.** of historical or lasting importance or significance: *a monumental victory.* —**mon′u•men′tal•ly,** *adv.* See -MON-.

moo (mo͞o) /muw/ *n., pl.* **moos,** *v.,* **mooed, moo•ing.** —*n.* [*count*] **1.** the deep, low sound a cow makes. —*v.* [*no obj*] **2.** to make such a sound.

mooch (mo͞och) /muwtʃ/ *Slang.* —*v.* **1.** to borrow without intending to return or repay: [*no obj*]: *always mooching off his friends.* [~ + *obj*]: *Stop mooching cigarettes and just buy your own.* **2.** [*no obj*] to loiter or wander about: *mooching around her old neighborhood.* —*n.* [*count*] **3.** Also, **mooch′er.** a person who mooches.

mood[1] (mo͞od) /muwd/ *n.* [*count*] **1.** a person's emotional state at a particular time: *What kind of mood is she in now?* **2.** a feeling or emotion held by a large number of people at a time: *the country's distrustful mood.* **3.** a state of sullenness or bad temper: *He's in one of his moods again.* See -MOD-.

mood[2] (mo͞od) /muwd/ *n.* [*count*] a category or set of categories of a verb that indicate the attitude of the speaker toward what is being said, as in expressing a fact, a question, a possibility, a wish, or a command, and indicated by some change in the form of the verb, or by the use of modal verbs: *The indicative mood is used in statements ("He wasn't there."), the imperative mood in commands ("Be there!"), and the subjunctive mood in certain kinds of wishes ("If only he were here!").* See -MOD-.

mood•y (mo͞o′dē) /ˈmuwdiy/ *adj.,* **-i•er, -i•est. 1.** (of a person) changing one's moods: *She's very moody: one minute she's happy, the next minute, sad.* **2.** unhappy; gloomy or sullen; depressed: *moody since he lost his job.* **3.** expressing such a mood: *a moody silence.* —**mood•i•ly** (mo͞od′l ē) /ˈmuwdl̩iy/ *adv.*: *answered moodily that she didn't care one way or the other.* —**mood′i•ness,** *n.* [*noncount*]

moon (mo͞on) /muwn/ *n.* [*count*] **1.** [*singular; the* + ~] the earth's natural satellite. **2.** a natural satellite that goes around any planet: *the moons of Jupiter.* —*v.* [*no obj*] **3.** to act or wander dreamily or without energy: *He's been mooning about her all day.* —***Idiom.*** **4. blue moon,** a very long time: *Once in a blue moon such a chance comes along.*

moon•beam (mo͞on′bēm′) /ˈmuwnˌbiym/ *n.* [*count*] a ray of moonlight.

moon•light (mo͞on′līt′) /ˈmuwnˌlayt/ *n.* [*noncount*] **1.** the light of the moon: *dancing in the moonlight.* —*adj.* [*before a noun*] **2.** occurring by moonlight, or at night: *a moonlight swim.* —*v.* [*no obj*] **3.** to work at an additional job after one's regular employment, as at night: *As a firefighter he was not supposed to moonlight.* —**moon′light′er,** *n.* [*count*]: *As a moonlighter he wasn't getting enough sleep.* —**moon•lit** (mo͞on′lit′) /ˈmuwnˌlɪt/ *adj.*

moon•scape (mo͞on′skāp′) /ˈmuwnˌskeyp/ *n.* [*count*] **1.** the general appearance of the surface of the moon. **2.** an artistic representation of this.

moon•shine (mo͞on′shīn′) /ˈmuwnˌʃayn/ *n.* [*noncount*] **1.** *Informal.* smuggled or illegally produced liquor. **2.** empty or foolish talk; nonsense.

moon•shot or **moon shot** (mo͞on′shot′) /ˈmuwnˌʃɒt/ *n.* [*count*] the launching of a rocket or spacecraft to the moon.

moon•struck (mo͞on′struk′) /ˈmuwnˌstrʌk/ also **moon•strick•en** (mo͞on′strik′ən) /ˈmuwnˌstrɪkən/ *adj.* **1.** mentally unbalanced, supposedly by the influence of the moon. **2.** dreamily romantic: *moonstruck after meeting the movie star.*

moor[1] (mo͝or) /mʊr/ *n.* [*count*] an area of open wasteland, often overgrown with grass and heath.

moor[2] (mo͝or) /mʊr/ *v.* **1.** to hold and attach (a ship, etc.) in a particular place, as by ropes or anchors: [~ + *obj*]: *The crew moored the ship to the dock.* [*no obj*]: *We moored next to the dock.* **2.** [~ + *obj*] to attach firmly; secure.

moor•ing (mo͝or′ing) /ˈmʊrɪŋ/ *n.* [*count*] **1.** Usually, **moorings.** [*plural*] the means by which a ship, boat, or aircraft is moored: *Ships were torn from their moorings.* **2. moorings,** [*plural*] a place where a ship, boat, or aircraft may be moored: *The safest moorings were on the mainland.* **3.** Usually, **moorings.** a source of stability or security: *Would he lose his moorings if he began to doubt his religion?*

moose (mo͞os) /muws/ *n.* [*count*], *pl.* **moose.** a large, long-headed deer of the Northern Hemisphere, the male of which has enormous, flat antlers.

moot (mo͞ot) /muwt/ *adj.* **1.** that may be discussed and debated. **2.** of little or no practical value or meaning; interesting only from the point of view of theory: *a moot question; a moot point.*

mop (mop) /mɒp/ *n., v.,* **mopped, mop•ping.** —*n.* [*count*] **1.** a device consisting of absorbent material, as a sponge, fastened to a handle and used esp. for washing floors. **2.** a thick mass of hair. —*v.* **3.** to wipe with or as if with a mop: [~ + *obj*]: *mopped his brow with a handkerchief.* [~ + *up* + *obj*]: *They mopped up the water.* [~ + *obj* + *up*]: *They mopped the water up.* [~ (+ *up*)]: *You vacuum while I mop (up).* **4. mop up, a.** to clear (an area, etc.) of remaining enemy soldiers following a victory: [~ + *up* + *obj*]: *Their squad mopped up the area.* [*no obj*]: *Their squad was ordered to mop up.* **b.** [~ + *up* + *obj*] to complete, as by finishing the remaining details of a task: *mopped up the rest of her business and went on a vacation.*

mope (mōp) /mowp/ *v.,* **moped, mop•ing,** *n.* —*v.* [*no obj*] **1.** to be sunk in dejection; brood: *moping and feeling sorry for herself.* —*n.* [*count*] **2.** a person who mopes. —**mop′er,** *n.* [*count*] —**mop′ey, mop′y,** *adj.* **-i•er, -i•est.** —**mop′ish,** *adj.,*

mo•ped (mō′ped′) /ˈmowˌpɛd/ *n.* [*count*] a motorized bicycle with pedals, designed for low-speed operation. See -PED-[1].

mop•pet (mop′it) /ˈmɒpɪt/ *n.* [*count*] a young child.

-mor-, *root.* -*mor*- comes from Latin, where it has the meaning "custom; proper." This meaning is found in such words as: AMORAL, DEMORALIZE, IMMORAL, MORAL, MORALE, MORALITY, MORES.

mor•al (môr′əl, mor′-) /ˈmɔrəl, ˈmɒr-/ *adj.* **1.** [*before a noun*] of or relating to the principles of right conduct, or with the distinction between right and wrong; ethical: *Abortion is a difficult moral choice.* **2.** agreeing with accepted principles of conduct; upright: *A moral man wouldn't threaten a child.* **3.** [*before a noun*] based on principles of right conduct, rather than on law, custom, etc.: *He has a moral obligation to care for his own flesh and blood.* **4.** virtuous in sexual matters; chaste: *He was too moral to cheat on his wife.* **5.** [*before a noun*] of or relating to the mind, feelings, etc., but not anything physical or material: *We could not send troops; all we could give was moral support.* **6.** [*before a noun*] based on strong probability; virtual: *a moral certainty.* —*n.* [*count*] **7.** the lesson contained in a fable, etc.: *The moral of the story was to do what you can today, and not to put it off until tomorrow.* **8. morals,** [*plural*] principles, standards, or habits with respect to right or wrong conduct: *He acts without morals.* See -MOR-.

mo•rale (mə ral′) /məˈræl/ *n.* [*noncount*] emotional or mental condition with respect to cheerfulness, confidence, etc., esp. in the face of opposition, etc.: *The morale of the troops was high.* See -MOR-.

mor•al•ist (môr′ə list, mor′-) /'mɔrəlɪst, 'mɒr-/ *n.* [*count*] **1.** one who practices or teaches morality. **2.** a person concerned with regulating the morals of others, as by censorship. —**mor′al•is′tic,** *adj.* See -MOR-.

mo•ral•i•ty (mə ral′i tē, mô-) /mə'rælɪtiy, mɔ-/ *n., pl.* **-ties** for 3. **1.** [*noncount*] agreement with the rules of conduct; moral conduct: *the decline of morality on TV shows.* **2.** [*noncount*] moral quality or character: *questioning his morality.* **3.** [*count*] a system of ethical principles. See -MOR-.

mor•al•ize (môr′ə līz′, mor′-) /'mɔrə,layz, 'mɒr-/ *v.* [*no obj*], **-ized, -iz•ing.** to express opinions about matters of right and wrong, esp. in a tiresome way or when intolerant of other's views: *moralizing about what TV shows our children should watch.* See -MOR-.

mor•al•ly (môr′ə lē, mor′-) /'mɔrəliy, 'mɒr-/ *adv.* **1.** with regard to principles of right conduct: *Is it morally justifiable to participate in a sport in which the aim is to injure another?* **2.** correctly, properly, or virtuously: *thought he had acted morally but his doubts remained.* See -MOR-.

mo•rass (mə ras′) /mə'ræs/ *n.* [*count*] **1.** a marsh or bog. **2.** something confusing or troublesome or from which it is difficult to free oneself: *a morass of details.*

mor•a•to•ri•um (môr′ə tôr′ē əm, -tōr′-, mor′-) /,mɔrə'tɔriyəm, -'towr-, ,mɒr-/ *n.* [*count*], *pl.* **-to•ri•a** (-tôr′ē ə, -tōr′-) /-'tɔriyə, -'towr-/ **-to•ri•ums.** a stopping, usually temporary, of some activity: *a moratorium on rent increases.*

mo•ray (môr′ā, mōr′ā; mô rā′, mō-) /'mɔrey, 'mowrey; mə'rey, mow-/ *n.* [*count*], *pl.* **-rays.** a tropical eel. Also called **mo′ray eel′.**

mor•bid (môr′bid) /'mɔrbɪd/ *adj.* suggesting an unhealthy mental state because of too much gloominess, gruesomeness, etc.: *a morbid interest in horror movies.* —**mor•bid•i•ty, mor′bid•ness,** (môr bid′i tē) /mɔr'bɪdɪtiy/ *n.* [*noncount*] —**mor′bid•ly,** *adv.*

mor•dant (môr′dnt) /'mɔrdnt/ *adj.* sharply critical or sarcastic; biting; cutting: *mordant wit.* —**mor′dant•ly,** *adv.*

more (môr, mōr) /mɔr, mowr/ *adj., comparative of* **much** *or* **many** *with* **most** *as superlative.* **1.** in greater quantity, amount, or number: *I need more money. She had more coins than I did.* **2.** additional or further: *Do you need more time?* —*n.* [*noncount*] **3.** an additional quantity, amount, or number: *Would you like more?* **4.** a greater quantity, amount, or degree: *The price is more than I thought. Their report is more than just a survey.* —*pron.* **5.** [*used with a plural verb*] a greater number of persons or of a specified class: *More have been injured than ever.* —*adv., compar. of* **much** *with* **most** *as superl.* **6.** [*often used before adjectives and adverbs, and regularly before those of more than two syllables*] in or to a greater extent or degree: *Things have become more interesting. The car moved more slowly.* **7.** in addition; further; again: *Let's talk more tomorrow.* —***Idiom.*** **8. more and more,** to an increasing extent or degree: *I love you more and more every day.* **9. more or less,** to some extent; somewhat: *We came to more or less the same conclusion.* **10. what is more,** (used to introduce information that supports the truth of what has been said): *This airline is terrible: the planes are always late and what is more, they're hot and uncomfortable.*

more•o•ver (môr ō′vər, mōr-, môr′ō′vər, mōr′-) /mɔr'owvər, mowr-, 'mɔr,owvər, 'mowr-/ *adv.* in addition to what has been said; further; besides: *We're late and, moreover, we're lost.*

mo•res (môr′āz, -ēz, mōr′-) /'mɔreyz, -iyz, 'mowr-/ *n.* [*plural*] customs held to be of central importance and accepted without question: *Violations of social mores are becoming more frequent.* See -MOR-.

morgue (môrg) /mɔrg/ *n.* [*count*] **1.** a place in which dead bodies are kept until they have been identified or disposed of. **2.** a reference file of old clippings, etc., esp. in a newspaper office. See -MORT-.

mor•i•bund (môr′ə bund′, mor′-) /'mɔrə,bʌnd, 'mɒr-/ *adj.* **1.** near death. **2.** not progressing; near the end of usefulness: *The move to restrict the number of terms a Congressperson could serve was moribund.* See -MORT-.

Mor•mon (môr′mən) /'mɔrmən/ *n.* [*count*] **1.** a member of the Church of Jesus Christ of Latter-day Saints (**Mor′mon Church′**), founded in the U.S. in 1830 by Joseph Smith. —*adj.* **2.** of or relating to the Mormons or their beliefs. —**Mor′mon•ism,** *n.* [*noncount*]

morn (môrn) /mɔrn/ *n.* [*noncount*] morning: *in the morn.*

morn•ing (môr′ning) /'mɔrnɪŋ/ *n.* **1.** the first period of the day, usually from dawn, but sometimes considered from midnight, up to noon: [*noncount*]: *On Monday morning we arrived at work.* [*count*]: *On Monday mornings she usually comes to work late.* **2.** [*count*] the early period of anything; beginning: *the morning of life.* —*adj.* [*before a noun*] **3.** of or in the morning: *a morning call to be awakened at 5 a.m.*

morn′ing glo′ry or **morn′ing-glo′ry,** *n.* [*count*] a twining plant having funnel-shaped flowers of various colors, often opening only in the morning.

morn′ing sick′ness, *n.* [*noncount*] nausea occurring esp. in the early part of the day during the first months of pregnancy.

morn′ing star′, *n.* [*count*] a bright planet, esp. Venus, seen in the E immediately before sunrise.

Mo•roc•can (mə rok′ən) /mə'rɒkən/ *adj.* **1.** of or relating to Morocco. —*n.* [*count*] **2.** a person born or living in Morocco.

mo•ron (môr′on, mōr′-) /'mɔrɒn, 'mowr-/ *n.* [*count*] **1.** a person who is stupid or lacking in good judgment: *Put that knife down, you moron!* **2.** a person of borderline intelligence in a former classification of mental retardation, having an intelligence quotient of 50 to 69.

mo•ron•ic (mə ron′ik) /mə'rɒnɪk/ *adj.* stupid or lacking in judgment: *a moronic thing to do.* —**mo•ron′i•cal•ly,** *adv.*

mo•rose (mə rōs′) /mə'rows/ *adj.* **1.** angrily gloomy, often in a quiet way: *a morose and grouchy mood.* **2.** characterized by or expressing gloom: *a morose silence.* —**mo•rose′ly,** *adv.*: *He looked at us morosely.* —**mo•rose′ness,** *n.* [*noncount*]

-morph-, *root.* *-morph-* comes from Greek, where it has the meaning "form; shape." This meaning is found in such words as: AMORPHOUS, ANTHROPOMORPHISM, METAMORPHOSIS, MORPHEME, MORPHINE.

mor•pheme (môr′fēm) /'mɔrfiym/ *n.* [*count*] a basic grammatical unit of a language that makes up a word or meaningful part of a word that cannot be divided into smaller meaningful parts, as *the, write,* the *-s* of *books,* or the *-ed* of *waited.* See -MORPH-.

mor•phine (môr′fēn) /'mɔrfiyn/ also **mor•phi•a** (môr′fē ə) /'mɔrfiyə/ *n.* [*noncount*] a drug made from opium and used chiefly in medicine as a pain reliever. See -MORPH-.

mor•phol•o•gy (môr fol′ə jē) /mɔr'fɒlədʒiy/ *n.* [*noncount*] **1.** the branch of biology that deals with the form and structure of organisms. **2.** the study of how words are formed in a particular language, as plurals, past tenses, possessives, compounds, etc., in English. —**mor•pho•log•i•cal** (môr′fə loj′i kəl) /,mɔrfə'lɒdʒɪkəl/ *adj.* See -MORPH-.

mor•row (môr′ō, mor′ō) /'mɔrow, 'mɒrow/ *n.* [*count; usually singular; usually: the* + ~] *Literary.* the next day; tomorrow.

Morse′ code′ (môrs) /mɔrs/ *n.* [*noncount*] either of two systems of clicks and spaces, short and long sounds, or flashes of light, used to represent letters, numerals, etc. Also called **Morse′ al′phabet.**

mor•sel (môr′səl) /'mɔrsəl/ *n.* [*count*] a small piece or amount of anything, esp. food; scrap; bit: *to eat a few morsels.*

-mort-, *root.* *-mort-* comes from Latin, where it has the meaning "death." This meaning is found in such words as: AMORTIZE, IMMORTAL, IMMORTALITY, IMMORTALIZE, MORGUE, MORTAL, MORTALITY, MORTGAGE.

mor•tal (môr′tl) /'mɔrtl/ *adj.* **1.** that will suffer death: *mortal creatures.* **2.** of or relating to human beings who must die someday: *this mortal life.* **3.** [*before a noun*] never giving up or surrendering; relentless: *a mortal enemy.* **4.** severe; extreme: *in mortal danger.* **5.** causing or liable to cause death; fatal: *a mortal wound.* **6.** [*before a noun*] to the death: *mortal combat.* **7.** involving spiritual death: *a mortal sin.* —*n.* [*count*] **8.** a human being: *In this story earth mortals must face immortal aliens from outer space.* —**mor′tal•ly,** *adv.*: *He fell, mortally wounded.* See -MORT-.

mor•tal•i•ty (môr tal′i tē) /mɔr'tælɪtiy/ *n.* [*noncount*] **1.** the state or condition of being mortal: *views his mortality without fear.* **2.** the frequency of deaths in a certain population; death rate: *a study of infant mortality in poor countries.* See -MORT-.

mor•tar[1] (môr′tər) /'mɔrtər/ *n.* [*count*] **1.** a bowl-shaped container in which substances can be pounded or ground with a pestle. **2.** a very short cannon for throwing shells at high angles: *shells from the enemy mortars.*

mor•tar[2] (môr′tər) /ˈmɔrtər/ *n.* [*noncount*] **1.** a mixture of lime or cement with sand and water, used to hold stones, etc., together. **—***v.* [~ + *obj*] **2.** to plaster or fix with mortar.

mor•tar•board (môr′tər bôrd′, -bōrd′) /ˈmɔrtərˌbɔrd, -ˌbowrd/ *n.* [*count*] **1.** a board, usually square, used by masons to hold mortar. **2.** a close-fitting cap with a square, flat top and a tassel, worn at formal academic ceremonies by graduates or faculty.

mort•gage (môr′gij) /ˈmɔrgɪdʒ/ *n., v.,* **-gaged, -gag•ing.** **—***n.* [*count*] **1.** an amount of money loaned to buy a house: *a mortgage of over $200,000.* **2.** an agreement to give up property if one is unable to pay back the money loaned. **—***v.* [~ + *obj*] **3.** to place (property) under an agreement: *had to mortgage their house to pay the bill.* **4.** to pledge; risk (something) for future gain: *to mortgage the company's future.* **—mort′ga•gor, mort′gag•er,** *n.* [*count*] See -MORT-.

mort•ga•gee (môr′gə jē′) /ˌmɔrgəˈdʒiy/ *n.* [*count*], *pl.* **-gees.** a person to whom property is mortgaged. See -MORT-.

mor•ti•cian (môr tish′ən) /mɔrˈtɪʃən/ *n.* [*count*] one who conducts the preparation of a dead person's body for burial and directs funeral services. See -MORT-.

mor•ti•fy (môr′tə fī′) /ˈmɔrtəˌfay/ *v.* [~ + *obj*], **-fied, -fy•ing.** to humiliate (someone), as by an injury to self-respect: *He was mortified when he forgot his speech.* —**mor•ti•fi•ca•tion** (môr′tə fi kā′shən) /ˌmɔrtəfɪˈkeyʃən/ *n.* [*noncount*] See -MORT-.

mor•tise or **mor•tice** (môr′tis) /ˈmɔrtɪs/ *n., v.,* **-tised, -tis•ing.** **—***n.* [*count*] **1.** a notch or slot made in a piece of wood or the like, esp. in a wall near a door to attach a lock. **—***v.* [~ + *obj*] **2.** to cut or form a mortise in.

mor•tu•ar•y (môr′cho͞o er′ē) /ˈmɔrtʃuwˌɛriy/ *n.* [*count*], *pl.* **-ar•ies.** a building or business where the bodies of the dead are prepared for burial or cremation and for viewing, and where services are often held.

mos., an abbreviation of: months.

mo•sa•ic (mō zā′ik) /mowˈzeyɪk/ *n.* **1.** [*count*] a picture made of small colored pieces of stone, etc., fitted together in a flat surface: *a hand-made mosaic.* **2.** [*noncount*] the process of producing such a decoration. **3.** [*count*] something resembling a mosaic, esp. in being made up of many distinct, different elements: *The city has become a cultural mosaic.* **—***adj.* [*before a noun*] **4.** of or relating to a mosaic or mosaic work: *a mosaic tile.* **5.** made up of a combination of diverse elements.

mo•sey (mō′zē) /ˈmowziy/ *v.* [*no obj*], **-seyed, -sey•ing.** *Informal.* to wander without hurrying; stroll; saunter.

Mos•lem (moz′ləm, mos′-) /ˈmɒzləm, ˈmɒs-/ *adj., n., pl.* **-lems, -lem.** MUSLIM.

mosque (mosk, môsk) /mɒsk, mɔsk/ *n.* [*count*] a Muslim place of public worship.

mos•qui•to (mə skē′tō) /məˈskiytow/ *n.* [*count*], *pl.* **-toes, -tos.** a two-winged insect, the female of which sucks the blood of animals and humans: *Some mosquitoes transmit diseases such as malaria and yellow fever.*

moss (môs, mos) /mɔs, mɒs/ *n.* [*noncount*] a tiny, leafy-stemmed plant that grows in a thick mass on moist ground, tree trunks, rocks, etc. **—moss′y,** *adj.,* **-i•er, -i•est.**

most (mōst) /mowst/ *adj., superlative of* **much** *or* **many** *with* **more** *as comparative.* [*before a noun*] **1.** [*the* + ~] in the greatest number, amount, or degree: [*before a plural noun*]: *He received the most votes.* [*before a noncount noun*]: *She has the most talent.* **2.** [*before a plural noun*] in the majority of instances; more than half: *Most operations are successful.* **—***n.* [*noncount*] **3.** [*the* + ~] the greatest quantity, amount, or degree: *The most I can hope for is a passing grade.* **4.** [~ + *of*] the greatest number or greater part of what is specified: *Most of his writing is rubbish.* **5.** [*the* + ~] the greatest number: *The most this room will seat is 150.* **6.** the majority of persons: *to be happier than most.* **7. the most,** *Slang.* the very best of something: *thought her boyfriend was the most.* **—***adv., superl. of* **much** *with* **more** *as compar.* **8.** [*often used before adjectives and adverbs, and regularly before those of more than two syllables*] in or to the greatest extent or degree: *most rapid; the most popular kid in the class; She behaved most wisely; He worked most carefully.* **9.** very: *This murder is a most puzzling case.* **10.** *Informal.* almost or nearly: *Most everyone around here shops at this place.* **—*Idiom.* 11. at (the) most,** at the maximum: *Jog for one hour at (the) most.* **12. for the most part,** on the whole; generally; usually: *For the most part we walked, but occasionally we biked.* **13. make the most of,** [~ + *obj*] to use to greatest advantage: *Make the most of your opportunities.*

most•ly (mōst′lē) /ˈmowstliy/ *adv.* for the most part; in the main; chiefly; generally; customarily: *The guests are mostly friends of the bride. The train is mostly on time.*

-mot-, *root.* *-mot-* comes from Latin, where it has the meaning "move." It is related to -MOV-. This meaning is found in such words as: AUTOMOBILE, AUTOMOTIVE, COMMOTION, DEMOTE, DEMOTION, EMOTE, EMOTION, LOCOMOTIVE, MOTEL, MOTIF, MOTION, MOTIVATE, MOTIVE, MOTOCROSS, MOTOR, PROMOTE, PROMOTION, REMOTE.

mo•tel (mō tel′) /mowˈtɛl/ *n.* [*count*] a hotel designed for motorists. See -MOT-.

moth (môth, moth) /mɔθ, mɒθ/ *n.* [*count*], *pl.* **moths** (mô*th*z, mo*th*z, môths, moths). an insect that resembles a butterfly and is active mostly at night: *Moths are attracted to light.*

moth•ball (môth′bôl′, moth′-) /ˈmɔθˌbɔl, ˈmɒθ-/ *n.* [*count*] **1.** a small, strong-smelling ball of naphthalene for placing in storage areas to repel moths. **2. in mothballs,** in a state of storage; no longer used: *The fleet was in mothballs.* **—***v.* [~ + *obj*] **3.** to put into storage; make (something) no longer active: *agreed to mothball their most dangerous missiles.*

moth•er (mu*th*′ər) /ˈmʌðər/ *n.* [*count*] **1.** a female parent: *His mother died when he was young.* **2.** [*often: Mother; no article*] one's own mother. **3.** a woman looked upon as a mother, or who exercises authority like that of a mother. **4.** something that gives rise to something else: *Necessity is the mother of invention.* **5. the mother of,** the greatest, most powerful, most outstanding example of (something mentioned next): *the mother of all wars.* **—***adj.* [*before a noun*] **6.** being a mother: *a mother bird.* **7.** relating to or characteristic of a mother: *mother love.* **8.** derived from or as if from one's mother; native: *his mother culture.* **—***v.* [~ + *obj*] **9.** to care for or protect like a mother: *She mothered her children wisely.* **—moth′er•less,** *adj.*

moth•er•hood (mu*th*′ər ho͝od) /ˈmʌðərhuwd/ *n.* [*noncount*] the state of being a mother: *the joys of motherhood.*

moth′er-in-law′, *n.* [*count*], *pl.* **mothers-in-law.** the mother of one's husband or the mother of one's wife.

moth•er•land (mu*th*′ər land′) /ˈmʌðərˌlænd/ *n.* [*count; usually: the/one's* + ~] **1.** one's native land. **2.** the land of one's ancestors: *great respect for the motherland.*

moth•er•ly (mu*th*′ər lē) /ˈmʌðərliy/ *adj.* **1.** of or relating to a mother: *motherly care.* **—***adv.* **2.** in the manner of a mother. —**moth′er•li•ness,** *n.* [*noncount*]

moth′er-of-pearl′, *n.* [*noncount*] **1.** a hard, shiny substance that forms the inner layer of certain shells, used for making buttons, beads, etc. **—***adj.* [*before a noun*] **2.** made of or resembling mother-of-pearl.

mo•tif (mō tēf′) /mowˈtiyf/ *n.* [*count*] a subject, theme, etc., that repeats in a literary, artistic, or musical work: *a flower motif in the wallpaper pattern.* See -MOT-.

mo•tile (mōt′l, mō′til) /ˈmowtl̩, ˈmowtɪl/ *adj.* *Biology.* moving or capable of moving by itself: *motile cells or motile spores.* —**mo•til•i•ty** (mō til′i tē) /mowˈtɪlɪtiy/ *n.* [*noncount*] See -MOT-.

mo•tion (mō′shən) /ˈmowʃən/ *n.* **1.** [*noncount*] the action or process of moving; movement: *the effects of energy on motion.* **2.** [*noncount*] power of movement, as of a living body: *Most plants are incapable of motion.* **3.** [*count*] the manner of moving the body while walking; gait: *walked with a curious, swaying motion.* **4.** [*count*] a bodily movement or change of posture; gesture: *He made motions to indicate eating.* **5.** [*count*] a formal proposal, esp. one made to a group deciding an issue: *Her motion was defeated.* **6. in motion,** in active operation; moving: *We can't stop now, the procedures are already in motion.* **—***v.* **7.** to make a motion or gesture, as with the hand: [*no obj*]: *At last the king motioned to us.* [~ + *obj*]: *He motioned his approval.* [~ + *obj* + *to* + *verb*]: *He motioned us to come forward.* See -MOT-.

mo•tion•less (mō′shən ləs) /ˈmowʃənləs/ *adj.* showing or having no motion; without motion: *a motionless statue.* **—mo′tion•less•ly,** *adv.* **—mo′tion•less•ness,** *n.* [*noncount*] See -MOT-.

mo′tion pic′ture, *n.* [*count*] **1.** a story, incident, or message presented in film. **2. motion pictures,** [*plural*] MOVIE (def. 3).

mo′tion sick′ness, *n.* [*noncount*] nausea resulting from the effect of motion, as during car or plane travel.

mo•ti•vate (mō′tə vāt′) /ˈmowtəˌveyt/ *v.,* **-vat•ed, -vat•ing.** to provide (someone) with a motive or motives; impel: [~ + *obj*]: *A good teacher will motivate his or her students.* [~ + *obj* + *to* + *verb*]: *The death of his wife and children motivated him to seek revenge.* —**mo′ti•va′tor,** *n.* [*count*] See -MOT-.

mo•ti•va•tion (mō′tə vā′shən) /ˌmowtə'veyʃən/ *n.* **1.** [*count*] an act or instance of motivating: *A good teacher will provide motivations for his or her students.* **2.** [*noncount*] the state or condition of being motivated; desire: *Motivation was a key to their success.* —**mo′ti•va′tion•al,** *adj.* See -MOT-.

mo•tive (mō′tiv) /'mowtɪv/ *n.* [*count*] **1.** something that causes a person to act in a certain way; incentive: *What could possibly be the motive for such a crime?* —*adj.* **2.** of or relating to motion: *motive forces at work.* See -MOT-.

mot•ley (mot′lē) /'mɒtliy/ *adj.* **1.** showing greatly different elements or parts that make up the whole; heterogeneous: *a motley crowd of spectators.* **2.** being of different colors combined.

mo•to•cross (mō′tō krôs′, -kros′) /'mowtowˌkrɔs, -ˌkrɒs/ *n.* [*count*] a motorcycle race over a course of very rough terrain. See -MOT-.

mo•tor (mō′tər) /'mowtər/ *n.* [*count*] **1.** a small engine, esp. an internal-combustion engine in an automobile, etc.: *The motor won't start.* **2.** a machine that changes electrical energy into mechanical energy: *a little electric motor that burns out if it is overloaded.* —*adj.* [*before a noun*] **3.** of or relating to a motor. **4.** of, by, or for motor vehicles or for motorists: *a motor inn.* **5.** of or relating to muscular movement: *a motor response.* —*v.* **6.** to ride in an automobile; drive: [*no obj*]: *They motored quietly into town.* [~ + *obj*]: *She motored them to the train station.* See -MOT-.

mo•tor•bike (mō′tər bīk′) /'mowtərˌbayk/ *n., v.,* **-biked, -bik•ing.** —*n.* [*count*] **1.** a small, lightweight motorcycle. **2.** a bicycle propelled by an attached motor. —*v.* [*no obj*] **3.** to drive or ride a motorbike.

mo•tor•boat (mō′tər bōt′) /'mowtərˌbowt/ *n.* [*count*] **1.** a boat powered by a motor. —*v.* [*no obj*] **2.** to travel in or operate a motorboat.

mo•tor•cade (mō′tər kād′) /'mowtərˌkeyd/ *n.* [*count*] a parade of automobiles: *the president's motorcade.*

mo•tor•car (mō′tər kär′) /'mowtərˌkɑr/ *n.* AUTOMOBILE.

mo•tor•cy•cle (mō′tər sī′kəl) /'mowtərˌsaykəl/ *n., v.,* **-cled, -cling.** —*n.* [*count*] **1.** a motor vehicle similar to a bicycle but usually larger and heavier. —*v.* [*no obj*] **2.** to ride on a motorcycle. —**mo′tor•cy′clist,** *n.* [*count*] See -CYCLE-.

mo′tor home′, *n.* [*count*] a vehicle with living quarters, used for camping or taking long trips.

mo•tor•ist (mō′tər ist) /'mowtərɪst/ *n.* [*count*] one who drives or travels in a privately owned automobile.

mo•tor•ize (mō′tə rīz′) /'mowtəˌrayz/ *v.* [~ + *obj*], **-ized, -iz•ing.** **1.** to furnish with a motor. **2.** to supply (soldiers) with motor vehicles: *a motorized division.* —**mo•tor•i•za•tion** (mō′tər i zā′shən) /ˌmowtərɪ'zeyʃən/ *n.* [*noncount*]

mo•tor•man (mō′tər mən) /'mowtərmən/ *n.* [*count*], *pl.* **-men.** one who drives an electrically operated vehicle, as a subway train: *The motorman was responsible for the crash.*

mo′tor scoot′er, *n.* SCOOTER (def. 2).

mo′tor ve′hicle, *n.* [*count*] an automobile, truck, bus, or similar motor-driven vehicle: *Interstate highways are reserved for motor vehicles only.*

mot•tled (mot′ld) /'mɒtld/ *adj.* marked with blotches of different colors: *The foreman's face was mottled with anger.*

mot•to (mot′ō) /'mɒtow/ *n.* [*count*], pl. **-toes, -tos.** **1.** a word, phrase, or sentence adopted as an expression of one's guiding principle: *"Preparedness, that's my motto," she declared.* **2.** a sentence, phrase, or word expressing the spirit or purpose of an organization or group, often on a banner, etc.: *the state motto "Excelsior," meaning "ever upward."*

moue (mo͞o) /muw/ *n.* [*count*], *pl.* **moues** (mo͞o) /muw/. a pouting expression on the face, indicating pain, disgust, etc.

mould (mōld) /mowld/ *n., v. Chiefly Brit.* MOLD.

moult (mōlt) /mowlt/ *v., n. Chiefly Brit.* MOLT.

mound (mound) /mawnd/ *n.* [*count*] **1.** an elevation of earth: *Native Americans raised special burial mounds in southern Illinois.* **2.** a heap or raised mass: *two mounds of mashed potatoes.* **3.** the slightly raised ground from which a baseball pitcher delivers the ball.

mount[1] (mount) /mawnt/ *v.* **1.** to go up; climb; ascend: [~ + *obj*]: *She mounted the stairs.* [*no obj*]: *I approached the stairs and mounted carefully.* **2.** to get up on (a platform, a horse, etc.): [~ + *obj*]: *He mounted the stage and strode to the podium.* [*no obj*]: *mounted smoothly and galloped off.* **3.** [~ + *obj*] to set (a person) on horseback: *She mounted her daughter on the horse next to hers.* **4.** [~ + *obj*] to set or place at a higher position: *The Greeks mounted their wooden horse on a platform.* **5.** [~ + *obj*] to organize and launch (an attack, etc.): *A search was mounted the next day.* **6.** [~ + *obj*] to put (a sentry) on guard: *to mount a 24-hour watch.* **7.** [~ + *obj*] to fix on or in a frame, etc.: *to mount a photograph on cardboard.* **8.** [~ + *obj*] to provide (a play, etc.) with scenery, costumes, etc., for production: *The school managed to mount quite a performance for their end-of-year play.* **9.** [~ + *obj*] (of an animal) to climb upon (another animal) for sexual relations. **10.** [~(+ *up*)] to increase in amount or intensity: *The tension mounted (up) as the two old enemies began their debate.* —*n.* [*count*] **11.** an animal, or sometimes a vehicle, as a bicycle, used for riding: *an easy-going mount for a child to ride.* **12.** a support, backing, etc., on or in which something is mounted. —**mount′a•ble,** *adj.* —**mount′er,** *n.* [*count*]

mount[2] (mount) /mawnt/ *n.* a mountain: [*count*]: *to climb a mount.* [*often: Mount; no article; part of the name of a mountain*]: *climbing Mount Kilimanjaro.*

moun•tain (moun′tn) /'mawntn̩/ *n.* [*count*] **1.** a natural high piece of land rising more or less quickly to a high point: *We climbed up the mountain for several days.* See illustration at LANDSCAPE. **2.** a large mass or heap; pile: *a mountain of papers on my desk.* **3.** a huge amount: *a mountain of work to do.* —*adj.* [*before a noun*] **4.** of or relating to mountains: *The mountain people are fiercely independent.* —***Idiom.*** **5. make a mountain out of a molehill,** to make a minor difficulty seem much worse than it really is: *It's only a small bruise; don't make a mountain out of a molehill.*

moun•tain•eer (moun′tn ēr′) /ˌmawntn̩'ɪər/ *n.* [*count*] **1.** someone who lives in a mountainous area. **2.** a climber of mountains, esp. for sport. —*v.* [*no obj*] **3.** to climb mountains: *They enjoy mountaineering.*

moun′tain li′on, *n.* COUGAR.

moun•tain•ous (moun′tn əs) /'mawntn̩əs/ *adj.* **1.** (of a region) having many mountains: *We'll never be able to land in that mountainous region.* **2.** [*before a noun*] resembling a mountain, as being very large: *mountainous difficulties.*

moun•tain•top (moun′tn top′) /'mawntn̩ˌtɒp/ *n.* [*count*] the top of a mountain.

moun•te•bank (moun′tə bangk′) /'mawntəˌbæŋk/ *n.* [*count*] a person who tries to fool or deceive people.

mount•ed (moun′tid) /'mawntɪd/ *adj.* [*before a noun*] riding on horses or motorcycles: *mounted police.*

mount•ing (moun′ting) /'mawntɪŋ/ *n.* **1.** [*noncount*] the act of a person or thing that mounts. **2.** [*count*] a mount, support, or setting: *a mounting of black stone.*

mourn (môrn, mōrn) /mɔrn, mowrn/ *v.* **1.** to feel or express grief (for): [*no obj*]: *He still mourns for the old days.* [~ + *obj*]: *mourned her lost youth.* **2.** to grieve or express sadness over the death of (someone): [*no obj*]: *She still mourns for her son.* [~ + *obj*]: *We barely had time to mourn our dead.* —**mourn′er,** *n.* [*count*]

mourn•ful (môrn′fəl, mōrn′-) /'mɔrnfəl, 'mowrn-/ *adj.* **1.** feeling or expressing grief: *mournful visitors to the funeral home.* **2.** gloomy, sad, or dreary, as in appearance or sound: *the mournful sound of the foghorn.* —**mourn′ful•ly,** *adv.* —**mourn′ful•ness,** *n.* [*noncount*]

mourn•ing (môr′ning, mōr′-) /'mɔrnɪŋ, 'mowr-/ *n.* [*noncount*] **1.** the act of a person who mourns; sorrowing: *a time for mourning.* **2.** the conventional signs of sorrow for a person's death, esp. the wearing of black, etc.: *The whole country is still in mourning over her death.*

mouse (*n.* mous; *v.* mouz) / *n.* maws; *v.* mawz/ *n., pl.* **mice** (mīs) /mays/ *v.,* **moused, mous•ing.** —*n.* [*count*] **1.** a small rodent having a long, thin tail. **2.** a quiet, timid person: *"Are you a man or a mouse?" she yelled.* **3.** a palm-sized device equipped with one or more buttons, used to point at and select items on a computer display screen and to control the movement of the cursor: *He used the mouse to move the cursor.* —*v.* [*no obj*] **4.** to prowl about, as if in search of something: *mousing around.* **5.** to hunt for or catch mice.

mouse•trap (mous′trap′) /'mawsˌtræp/ *n., v.,* **-trapped, -trap•ping.** —*n.* [*count*] **1.** a trap for mice, esp. a wooden one with a metal spring. **2.** a device or trick for trapping someone. —*v.* [~ + *obj*] **3.** to trap, trick, or catch, esp. unexpectedly or cleverly.

mousse (mōōs) /muws/ *n., v.,* **moussed, mouss•ing.** —*n.* **1.** a sweetened dessert usually made with gelatin and whipped cream or beaten egg whites and chilled in a mold: [*noncount*]: *some delicious chocolate mousse.* [*count*]: *a mousse of chocolate and vanilla.* **2.** [*noncount*] a foamy preparation used to set or style the hair. —*v.* [~ + *obj*] **3.** to set or style (the hair) with mousse.

mous•tache (mus′tash, mə stash′) /'mʌstæʃ, mə'stæʃ/ *n.* MUSTACHE.

mous•y or **mous•ey** (mou′sē, -zē) /'mawsiy, -ziy/ *adj.,* **-i•er, -i•est. 1.** resembling a mouse, as in being drab and colorless or meek and timid: *mousy brown hair; a mousy little worker.* **2.** infested with mice. —**mous′i•ness,** *n.* [*noncount*]

mouth (*n.* mouth; *v.* mouth) / *n.* mawθ; *v.* mawð/ *n., pl.* **mouths** (mouthz), *v.* —*n.* **1.** [*count*] the opening through which a person or animal takes in food: *The baby closed his mouth and wouldn't eat.* **2.** [*count*] a person or animal who depends on someone for food or shelter: *another mouth to feed.* **3.** [*count*] the opening in the face thought of as the source of speaking: *Secrets came tumbling out of his mouth.* **4.** [*noncount*] talk, esp. loud, empty, or boastful talk, or disrespectful talk or language: *I won't take any more mouth from you!* **5.** [*count*] an opening leading out of or into a hole or a hollow thing: *the mouth of the jar.* **6.** [*count*] the lower end of a river or stream, where flowing water is discharged: *at the mouth of the river.* —*v.* **7.** [~ + *obj*] to say (something) without believing or understanding: *mouthed the usual empty promises for reform.* **8.** to form (a word, etc.) silently in one's mouth: [~ + *obj*]: *He mouthed a few words at me, but I couldn't figure them out.* [*used with quotations*]: *She mouthed "I can't" at me from across the room.* **9. mouth off,** [*no obj*] *Slang.* **a.** to talk disrespectfully to someone; sass. **b.** to express one's opinions forcefully or without holding oneself back: *He's always mouthing off at our meetings.* —***Idiom.*** **10. down in** or **at the mouth,** greatly saddened; dejected: *In the last week of summer vacation she looked down in the mouth.*

mouth•ful (mouth′fōōl′) /'mawθ,fʊl/ *n.* [*count*], *pl.* **-fuls. 1.** the amount a mouth can hold; the amount taken into the mouth at one time: *She explained the plan between mouthfuls of dessert.* **2.** [*singular; a* + ~] a spoken remark of great truth, relevance, etc.: *You just said a mouthful.* **3.** [*singular; a* + ~] a long word or phrase, esp. one hard to pronounce: *Her Polish name is quite a mouthful for her American teacher.*

mouth′ or′gan, *n.* HARMONICA.

mouth•piece (mouth′pēs′) /'mawθ,piys/ *n.* [*count*] **1.** a piece placed at or forming the mouth, as of a telephone, etc. **2.** a piece or part, as of a musical instrument, applied to or held in the mouth. **3.** a person, newspaper, etc., that expresses the opinions of others: *That newspaper is a mouthpiece of the union.* **4.** *Slang.* a lawyer, esp. a criminal lawyer.

mouth•wash (mouth′wôsh′, -wosh′) /'mawθ,wɔʃ, -,wɒʃ/ *n.* a liquid solution for cleaning or refreshing the mouth: [*noncount*]: *He brushed his teeth and used mouthwash.* [*count*]: *a new mouthwash on the market.*

mouth′-wa′tering, *adj.* very appetizing in appearance, aroma, or description: *a mouth-watering dish.*

-mov-, *root.* -*mov*- comes from Latin, where it has the meaning "move." It is related to -MOT-. This meaning is found in such words as: IMMOVABLE, MOVABLE, MOVE, MOVEMENT, REMOVABLE, REMOVAL, REMOVE.

mov•a•ble or **move•a•ble** (mōō′və bəl) /'muwvəbəl/ *adj.* **1.** capable of being moved: *The doll's arms, legs, hands, and head were movable.* **2.** changing from one date to another in different years: *Easter is a movable feast.* —*n.* [*count*] **3.** an article of furniture that is not fixed in place. See -MOV-.

move (mōōv) /muwv/ *v.,* **moved, mov•ing,** *n.* —*v.* **1.** to (cause to) pass from one position to another; to change one's place: [*no obj*]: *She fell down and didn't move.* [~ + *obj*]: *Can you move some books off your desk?* **2.** to (cause to) change the place where one lives or does business; relocate: [*no obj*]: *She moved to Illinois.* [~ + *obj*]: *The company moved him to Dallas.* **3.** to (cause to) progress: [*no obj*]: *Work on the project is moving well.* [~ + *obj*]: *The coach really moved his team ahead.* **4.** [*no obj*] to have a regular motion, as a part of a machine: *The clock doesn't move.* **5.** to sell or be sold: [*no obj*]: *Sales show that the new minivans are moving well.* [~ + *obj*]: *The car dealer had to move all of last year's models.* **6.** [*no obj*] to start off or leave: *I think we'd better be moving.* **7.** to transfer a piece in a game, as chess: [*no obj*]: *Whenever she moved, she always captured one of my pieces.* [~ + *obj*]: *He moved the piece slowly forward and said, "Checkmate."* **8.** (of the bowels) to (cause to) discharge the feces: [*no obj*]: *His bowels wouldn't move unless he took a laxative.* [~ + *obj*]: *He couldn't move his bowels without taking a laxative.* **9.** [*no obj*] to be active in a particular area: *She moves in the best circles of society.* **10.** [~ + *obj* + *to* + *verb*] to cause (someone) to do some action: *Curiosity moved me to open the box.* **11.** to affect (someone) with tender emotion or feeling; to arouse or touch: [~ + *obj*]: *I was moved by your troubles, so I decided to help you.* [~ + *obj* + *to* + *obj*]: *Her words moved me to anger.* **12.** to propose (a motion, etc.) formally, as to a court or judge: [~ + (*that*) *clause*]: *I move (that) we all get big raises.* [*no obj*]: *He moved for adjournment.* [~ + *obj*]: *The proposal was moved and seconded.* **13. move along,** to move from one place to another: [*no obj*]: *The police urged the crowd to move along.* [~ + *obj* + *along*]: *The police moved the demonstrators along.* **14. move in,** [*no obj*] **a.** to begin to occupy a place, esp. by bringing in one's possessions: *You can move in any time after September 1st.* **b.** to move toward, often in preparation for an attack: *The troops quickly moved in opposite the demonstrators.* **15. move in on,** [~ + *in* + *on* + *obj*] to make threatening and aggressive movements or actions toward: *If the giant computer companies move in on our market, we'll be in big trouble.* **16. move off,** [*no obj*] to move away from; to depart: *The enemy troops moved off when the fighter planes came.* **17. move on, a.** [~ + *on* + *obj*] to attack as a military target. **b.** [*no obj*] to begin action on something new: *We've debated this for hours; it's time to move on.* **c.** to leave a position or place: [*no obj*]: *He moved on to another job.* [~ + *obj* + *on*]: *The police moved the demonstrators on.* **18. move over,** [*no obj*] to shift to a nearby place, as to make room for another: *Could you please move over; I need to reach my seat.* **19. move up,** to (cause to) advance to a higher level: [*no obj*]: *She moved up quickly in the company.* [~ + *obj* + *up*]: *His father moved him up quickly through the ranks.* —*n.* [*count*] **20.** an act or instance of moving; movement: *stood still and didn't make a move.* **21.** a change of location or residence: *to make a move to Los Angeles.* **22.** an action toward an objective or goal; step: *He made several moves to take over the company.* **23.** (in chess, etc.) a player's right or turn to make a play: *It's your move.* —***Idiom.*** **24. get a move on,** [*no obj*] *Informal.* to hasten to act; hurry up: *Get a move on or we'll be late!* **25. move heaven and earth,** to do everything in one's power to bring something about. **26. on the move, a.** busy; active. **b.** going from place to place: *We were always on the move in those days because Mom was transferred so often.* **c.** advancing; progressing: *young executives on the move.* See -MOV-.

move•ment (mōōv′mənt) /'muwvmənt/ *n.* **1.** the act or result of moving: [*noncount*]: *In the last stages of the disease, movement is painful.* [*count*]: *nervous movements of his hands and arms.* **2.** Usually, **movements.** [*plural*] actions or activities, as of a person, or a change of position or location, as of troops or ships. **3.** [*noncount*] a great number of events or incidents; rapid progress of events. **4.** the direction, course, or trend of affairs in a field: [*noncount*]: *movement in education toward more computer use.* [*count*]: *a movement away from established traditions.* **5.** [*count*] a series of actions directed toward a particular end: *a gradual movement toward greater equality.* **6.** [*count*] a loosely organized group favoring a common goal: *the women's movement.* **7.** the price change in the market of some product or security: [*noncount*]: *little movement in stocks.* [*count*]: *slight movements in the Tokyo market.* **8.** [*count*] BOWEL MOVEMENT. **9.** [*count*] the working parts of a mechanism, as of a watch: *The watch has a Swiss movement.* **10.** [*count*] *Music.* a principal division or section of a sonata, symphony, or the like. See -MOV-.

mov•er (mōō′vər) /'muwvər/ *n.* [*count*] **1.** one that moves. **2.** Often, **movers.** [*plural*] a person or company that moves household effects, etc. **3. movers and shakers,** influential people, as in business: *Will the movers and shakers go along with this plan?*

mov•ie (mōō′vē) /'muwviy/ *n.* [*count*] **1.** MOTION PICTURE: *They stayed up to watch a late-night movie.* **2.** Usually, **the movies.** [*plural*] a motion-picture theater: *We went to the movies last night.* **3. the movies,** [*plural*] the business of making motion pictures; the motion-picture industry: *a producer who made his fortune in the movies.* See -MOV-.

mov•ing (mōō′ving) /'muwvɪŋ/ *adj.* **1.** [*before a noun*] capable of or having motion: *A moving body tends to* *stay in motion.* **2.** [*before a noun*] involving a motor vehicle in motion: *If you receive another moving violation, you'll lose your license.* **3.** causing or stirring strong emotions or feelings: *a moving, powerful performance.* —**mov′ing•ly,** *adv.*: *She spoke movingly about the refugees.* See -MOV-.

mow (mō) /mow/ *v.*, **mowed, mowed** or **mown** (mōn) /mown/ **mow•ing. 1.** to cut down (grass, etc.), esp. with a machine: [~ + *obj*]: *He earned money mowing lawns.* [*no obj*]: *She was out mowing all morning.* **2. mow down, a.** to destroy or kill in great numbers, as in a battle: [~ + *obj* + *down*]: *mowed them down with the machine gun.* [~ + *down* + *obj*]: *mowed down the advancing troops.* **b.** to overwhelm or defeat: [~ + *down* + *obj*]: *The pitcher mowed down one batter after another.* [~ + *obj* + *down*]: *The pitcher mowed them down.* —**mow′er,** *n.* [*count*]

Mo•zam•bi•can (mō′zəm bē′kən) /ˌmowzəm'biykən/ *n.* [*count*] **1.** a person born or living in Mozambique. —*adj.* **2.** of or relating to Mozambique.

moz•za•rel•la (mot′sə rel′lə, mōt′-) /ˌmɒtsə'rɛlə, ˌmowt-/ *n.* [*noncount*] a mild, white, semisoft Italian cheese.

MP, an abbreviation of: **1.** Member of Parliament. **2.** Military Police.

mp or **m.p.,** an abbreviation of: melting point.

mpg or **m.p.g.,** an abbreviation of: miles per gallon.

mph or **m.p.h.,** an abbreviation of: miles per hour.

Mr. (mis′tər) /'mɪstər/ *pl.* **Messrs.** (mes′ərz) /'mɛsərz/. **1.** mister; a title of respect used before a man's name, or sometimes before a position: *Mr. Jones is here. Mr. President, what are your views on the situation?* **2.** (used before an imagined name to express the opinion that the man so named possesses a particular quality, characteristic, identity, etc.): *She's waiting for Mr. Right.*

Mrs. (mis′iz, miz′iz) /'mɪsɪz, 'mɪzɪz/ *pl.* **Mmes.** (mā däm′, -dam′) /mey'dɑm, -'dæm/. **1.** a title of respect used before the name of a married woman: *Mrs. Jones.* **2.** (used before an imagined name to express the opinion that the woman so named possesses a particular quality, characteristic, identity, etc.): *Mrs. Punctuality is right on time, as usual.*

MS, an abbreviation of: **1.** Mississippi. **2.** multiple sclerosis.

Ms. (miz) /mɪz/ *pl.* **Mses.** (miz′əz) /'mɪzəz/. **1.** a title of respect used before a woman's name: *"Come in, Miss Jones." "It's Ms. Jones," she corrected.* **2.** (used before an imagined name to express the opinion that the woman so named possesses a particular quality, characteristic, identity, etc.): *I see that Ms. Perfect got 100% on the test again.* —**Usage.** Unlike *Miss* or *Mrs., Ms.* does not depend upon or indicate marital status.

MS., *pl.* **MSS.** an abbreviation of: manuscript.

ms., *pl.* **mss.** an abbreviation of: manuscript.

M.S., Master of Science.

MSG, an abbreviation of: monosodium glutamate.

MST or **M.S.T.,** an abbreviation of: Mountain Standard Time.

MT, an abbreviation of: **1.** Montana. **2.** Mountain Time.

Mt. or **mt.,** an abbreviation of: **1.** mount. **2.** mountain.

mtg., an abbreviation of: **1.** meeting. **2.** Also, **mtge.** mortgage.

much (much) /mʌtʃ/ *adj.*, **more** (môr, mōr) /mɔr, mowr/ **most** (mōst) /mowst/ *n., pron., adv.*, **more, most.** —*adj.* **1.** [*before a noncount noun*] great in amount, measure, or degree: *much wasted effort.* —*n.* [*noncount*], *pron.* **2.** a great quantity, measure, or degree: *not much to do; He owed much of his success to his family.* **3.** a great, important, or notable thing or matter: *He isn't much to look at.* **4.** an amount or degree of something: *How much does it cost?* —*adv.* **5.** to a great extent or degree: *to talk too much.* **6.** nearly, approximately, or about: *That book is much like the others.* **7. much as, a.** almost to the same degree as: *Babies need love, much as they need food.* **b.** (used to express a contrast between one clause and another) even though; although: *Much as he wants to go to Iceland, he won't.* —***Idiom.*** **8. I thought as much,** (used to express the speaker's belief that what precedes was expected): *"The police haven't found your stolen car yet." --"I thought as much; it will probably never turn up."* **9. make much of,** [+ *obj*] to treat or consider (something) as being important: *Her opponent tried to make much of the fact that she had tried marijuana as a college student.* **10. not much of a,** not a very good example of (something): *We didn't have much of a holiday: rain, cold weather, and flu.* **11. so much for,** (used to express the speaker's belief that the next thing mentioned is finished, or has no chance of being successful): *Look at this traffic jam; so much for arriving on time!*

muck (muk) /mʌk/ *n.* [*noncount*] **1.** animal waste matter used as fertilizer; manure. **2.** mud, filth, dirt, or slime. **3.** insulting remarks to hurt the reputation of another: *stirring up muck about his political opponent.* —*v.* **4.** [~ + *up* + *obj*] *Informal.* to make dirty; soil: *He had mucked up his clothes in the barnyard.* **5. muck about** or **around,** [*no obj*] *Informal.* to waste time: *He was mucking about the house all summer.* **6. muck up,** *Informal.* to make a mess of; fail badly at; bungle: [~ + *up* + *obj*]: *He had mucked up the whole report.* [~ + *obj* + *up*]: *He must have mucked it all up.* —**muck′y,** *adj.*, **-i•er, -i•est.**

muck•rake (muk′rāk′) /'mʌkˌreyk/ *v.* [*no obj*], **-raked, -rak•ing.** to search for and bring to public knowledge wrongdoing, corruption, etc., whether real or imagined, esp. in politics. —**muck′rak′er,** *n.* [*count*]

mu•cous (myo͞o′kəs) /'myuwkəs/ *adj.* [*before a noun*] **1.** of or resembling mucus. **2.** containing or releasing mucus: *a mucous membrane.*

mu•cus (myo͞o′kəs) /'myuwkəs/ *n.* [*noncount*] a watery, slippery substance produced in the body and that serves to protect and lubricate certain surfaces: *mucus in his nose.*

mud (mud) /mʌd/ *n.* [*noncount*] **1.** wet, soft dirt: *He slipped in the mud.* **2.** scandalous or false and harmful claims or information: *His campaign team began slinging mud at his opponent.*

mud•dle (mud′l) /'mʌdl̩/ *v.*, **-dled, -dling,** *n.* —*v.* **1.** to mix up in a confused manner: [~ + *obj*]: *Most of my papers had been muddled during my absence.* [~ + *up* + *obj*]: *Someone had muddled up the papers in his office.* [~ + *obj* + *up*]: *Someone had muddled them up.* **2.** [~ + *obj*] to cause to become mentally confused: *The five strong drinks had muddled him.* **3. muddle along,** [*no obj*] to think or act without planning or direction: *Our company is just muddling along.* **4. muddle through,** [*no obj*] to reach a goal despite lack of knowledge, skill, or direction: *We'll just have to muddle through as best we can.* —*n.* [*count; singular*] **5.** the state of being confused: *in a muddle and unable to figure out which way to go.* **6.** a confused or disordered state of affairs: *a muddle of insurance forms.*

mud•dle•head•ed (mud′l hed′id) /'mʌdl̩ˌhɛdɪd/ *adj.* confused in one's thinking; blundering.

mud•dy (mud′ē) /'mʌdiy/ *adj.*, **-di•er, -di•est,** *v.*, **-died, -dy•ing.** —*adj.* **1.** covered or filled with mud. **2.** not clear or pure: *muddy colors.* **3.** hidden or vague, as in thought or expression. —*v.* [~ + *obj*] **4.** to make muddy: *Your boots have muddied the carpet.* **5.** to cause to be confused: *to muddy our thinking by appealing to our emotions.* —**mud′di•ness,** *n.* [*noncount*]

mud•sling•ing (mud′sling′ing) /'mʌdˌslɪŋɪŋ/ *n.* [*noncount*] efforts or actions to damage one's opponent by harmful, false, or scandalous attacks. —**mud′sling′er,** *n.* [*count*]

muen•ster (mun′stər, mo͝on′-) /'mʌnstər, 'mʊn-/ *n.* [*noncount; often Muenster*] a semisoft cheese made from whole milk.

mu•ez•zin (myo͞o ez′in, mo͞o-) /myuw'ɛzɪn, muw-/ *n.* [*count*] a person who calls Muslims to prayer.

muff (muf) /mʌf/ *n.* [*count*] **1.** a thick, tube-shaped case for the hands that is covered with fur. —*v.* [~ + *obj*] **2.** to handle badly; miss: *The shortstop muffed the throw to first base.*

muf•fin (muf′in) /'mʌfɪn/ *n.* [*count*] a small round bread made with flour or cornmeal, eggs, milk, etc., and baked in a pan containing a series of cuplike molds.

muf•fle (muf′əl) /'mʌfəl/ *v.* [~ + *obj*], **-fled, -fling. 1.** to wrap with something to deaden sound: *to muffle drums.* **2.** to deaden (sound) by or as if by wrappings: *His voice was muffled over the phone.* **3.** to wrap or cover in a shawl, etc., esp. to keep warm or protect the face and neck: *muffled in a scarf and heavy coat.*

muf•fler (muf′lər) /'mʌflər/ *n.* [*count*] **1.** a scarf worn around the neck for warmth. **2.** a device for deadening sound: *With the muffler loose, the car rumbled noisily down the street.*

mug (mug) /mʌg/ *n., v.*, **mugged, mug•ging.** —*n.* [*count*] **1.** a rounded drinking cup with a handle: *a coffee mug.* **2.** the amount it holds: *spilled a mug of coffee on the papers.* **3.** *Slang.* a person's face or mouth: *Get your ugly mug out of here!* —*v.* **4.** [~ + *obj*] to assault or attack, usually in order to rob: *He was mugged in a dark street.* **5.** [*no obj*] to make faces: *to mug for the camera.*

—**mug′ger,** *n.* [*count*] —**mug′ging,** *n.* [*count*]: *a savage mugging on a dark and deserted street.* [*noncount*]: *a short prison term for mugging.*

mug•gy (mug′ē) /ˈmʌgiy/ *adj.,* **-gi•er, -gi•est.** (of the weather, etc.) uncomfortably humid; damp and close: *a hot, muggy day.* —**mug′gi•ness,** *n.* [*noncount*]

Mu•ham•mad (mo͝o ham′əd, -hä′məd) /mʊˈhæməd, -ˈhɑməd/ *n.* [*proper noun; no article*] Also, **Mohammed.** A.D. 570–632, an Arab prophet and the founder of Islam.

Mu•ham•mad•an (mo͝o ham′ə dn) /mʊˈhæmədn̩/ *adj.* **1.** of or relating to Muhammad or Islam. —*n.* [*count*] **2.** a follower of Muhammad; a believer in Islam. —**Mu•ham′mad•an•ism,** *n.* [*noncount*]

muk•luk or **muc•luc** or **muck•luck** (muk′luk) /ˈmʌklʌk/ *n.* [*count*] **1.** a soft boot worn by Eskimos. **2.** a slipper or boot resembling this.

mu•lat•to (mə lat′ō, -lä′tō, myo͞o-) /məˈlætow, -ˈlɑtow, myuw-/ *n., pl.* **-toes,** *adj.* —*n.* [*count*] **1.** the offspring of one white parent and one black parent. **2.** a person whose ancestry is a mixture of this type. —*adj.* **3.** of a light brown color.

mul•ber•ry (mul′ber′ē, -bə rē) /ˈmʌlˌbɛriy, -bəriy/ *n.* [*count*], *pl.* **-ries. 1.** a purplish berrylike fruit that can be eaten. **2.** a tree giving or growing this fruit.

mulch (mulch) /mʌltʃ/ *n.* **1.** a covering, as of straw, spread on the ground around plants to prevent loss of water or soil, etc.: [*noncount*]: *Spread mulch around the plants.* [*count*]: *a good, solid mulch.* —*v.* [~ + *obj*] **2.** to cover with mulch.

mule (myo͞ol) /myuwl/ *n.* [*count*] **1.** an animal produced by a female horse and a male donkey: *A mule is sterile and cannot produce offspring.* **2.** a stubborn person. **3.** *Slang.* a person paid to carry illegal goods, esp. drugs, for a smuggler.

mul•ish (myo͞o′lish) /ˈmyuwlɪʃ/ *adj.* very stubborn; not giving in. —**mul′ish•ly,** *adv.* —**mul′ish•ness,** *n.* [*noncount*]

mull[1] (mul) /mʌl/ *v.* to think about carefully: [~ + *obj* + *over*]: *mulled the plan over first.* [~ + *over* + *obj*]: *mulled over the idea for weeks.*

mull[2] (mul) /mʌl/ *v.* [~ + *obj*] to heat, sweeten, and flavor (ale or wine) with spices.

mul•lah (mul′ə, mo͝ol′ə, mo͞o′lə) /ˈmʌlə, ˈmʊlə, ˈmuwlə/ *n.* [*count*], *pl.* **-lahs.** a Muslim teacher of the sacred law.

mul•let (mul′it) /ˈmʌlɪt/ *n., pl.* (*esp. when thought of as a group*) **-let,** (*esp. for kinds or species*) **-lets.** a fish with spiny fins.

mul′li•gan stew′ (mul′i gən) /ˈmʌlɪgən/ *n.* [*noncount*] a stew made up of any ingredients that are available. Also called **mulligan.**

multi-, *prefix. multi-* comes from Latin, where it has the meaning "many, much": *multi-* + *colored* → *multicolored* (= *having many colors*); *multi-* + *vitamin* → *multivitamin* (= *composed of many vitamins*).

mul•ti•cul•tur•al (mul′tē kul′chər əl, mul′tī-) /ˌmʌltiyˈkʌltʃərəl, ˌmʌltay-/ *adj.* of or relating to different cultures or cultural elements: *multicultural studies.* —**mul′ti•cul′tur•al•ism,** *n.* [*noncount*]

mul•ti•dis•ci•pli•nar•y (mul′tē dis′ə plə ner′ē, mul′tī-) /ˌmʌltiyˈdɪsəpləˌnɛriy, ˌmʌltay-/ *adj.* combining several special branches of learning or fields of expertise.

mul•ti•far•i•ous (mul′tə fâr′ē əs) /ˌmʌltəˈfɛəriyəs/ *adj.* having many different parts; varied: *multifarious activities.* —**mul′ti•far′i•ous•ly,** *adv.* —**mul′ti•far′i•ous•ness,** *n.* [*noncount*]

mul•ti•form (mul′tə fôrm′) /ˈmʌltəˌfɔrm/ *adj.* having many shapes or kinds. See -FORM-.

mul•ti•lat•er•al (mul′tē lat′ər əl, mul′tī-) /ˌmʌltiyˈlætərəl, ˌmʌltay-/ *adj.* **1.** having several or many sides. **2.** involving more than two opposing sides: *multilateral agreements to stop the spread of nuclear arms.* See -LAT-[2].

mul•ti•lin•gual (mul′tē ling′gwəl, mul′tī-) /ˌmʌltiyˈlɪŋgwəl, ˌmʌltay-/ *adj.* **1.** using or able to speak several languages with some ease or ability: *One has to be multilingual in many countries of Asia and Africa.* **2.** spoken or written in several languages: *a multilingual broadcast.* **3.** of, involving, or dealing with several different languages: *a multilingual dictionary.* —**mul′ti•lin′gual•ism,** *n.* [*noncount*]

mul•ti•me•di•a (mul′tē mē′dē ə, mul′tī-) /ˌmʌltiyˈmiydiyə, ˌmʌltay-/ *n.* [*noncount; used with a singular verb*] **1.** the combined use of several media, as films, video, etc. —*adj.* **2.** of or relating to the use of several media simultaneously: *a multimedia presentation with slides, sounds, and graphics.* See -MEDI-.

mul•ti•na•tion•al (mul′tē nash′ə nl, mul′tī-) /ˌmʌltiyˈnæʃənl̩, ˌmʌltay-/ *n.* [*count*] **1.** a large corporation with operations and branches in several countries: *The huge multinationals have cornered the market.* —*adj.* **2.** of, relating to, or involving several nations or multinationals: *the UN and multinational peacekeeping forces in the region.* See -NAT-.

mul•ti•ple (mul′tə pəl) /ˈmʌltəpəl/ *adj.* [*before a noun*] **1.** consisting of, having, or involving several individuals, parts, etc.; manifold: *suffered multiple injuries in the car wreck.* —*n.* [*count*] **2.** a number that contains another, smaller number an exact number of times without a remainder: *12 is a multiple of 3.* See -PLIC-.

mul′tiple-choice′, *adj.* providing several possible answers from which the correct one must be selected: *a multiple-choice question.*

mul′tiple sclero′sis, *n.* [*noncount*] a serious disease that destroys part of the nerves and causes mild to severe muscular problems.

mul•ti•plex (mul′tə pleks′) /ˈmʌltəˌplɛks/ *adj.* **1.** having many parts or aspects. **2.** of, relating to, or using equipment permitting the sending of two or more signals over a single channel at the same time. —*n.* [*count*] **3.** a multiplex electronics system. **4.** a building containing a number of movie theaters: *a multiplex at the shopping mall.* See -PLEX-.

mul•ti•pli•cand (mul′tə pli kand′) /ˌmʌltəplɪˈkænd/ *n.* [*count*] a number to be multiplied by another. See -PLIC-.

mul•ti•pli•ca•tion (mul′tə pli kā′shən) /ˌmʌltəplɪˈkeyʃən/ *n.* [*noncount*] **1.** the act or process of multiplying or the state of being multiplied. **2.** a mathematical operation, symbolized by *a* × *b*, *a* · *b*, *a* * *b*, or *ab*, in which *a* is to be added to itself as many times as there are units in *b*. See -PLIC-.

multiplica′tion sign′, *n.* [*count*] the symbol (·), (×), or (*) between two numbers, meaning that the first number is to be added to itself as often as is indicated by the second number.

mul•ti•plic•i•ty (mul′tə plis′i tē) /ˌmʌltəˈplɪsɪtiy/ *n.* [*count*], *pl.* **-ties. 1.** a large number: *a multiplicity of new problems.* **2.** the state of having many parts.

mul•ti•pli•er (mul′tə plī′ər) /ˈmʌltəˌplayər/ *n.* [*count*] **1.** a person or thing that multiplies. **2.** a number by which another is multiplied.

mul•ti•ply (mul′tə plī′) /ˈmʌltəˌplay/ *v.,* **-plied, -ply•ing. 1.** to find the product (of numbers) by multiplication: [~ + *obj* + *and* + *obj*]: *Multiply the length and width.* [~ + *obj* + *by* + *obj*]: *Multiply the length by the width to get the area.* [*no obj*]: *You made a mistake when you multiplied; you should have divided.* **2.** [*no obj*] to increase in number by giving birth to offspring: *Soon the insects multiplied and destroyed all the crops.* **3.** to (cause to) grow in number, etc.; increase: [*no obj*]: *Our problems have multiplied under your leadership.* [~ + *obj*]: *The problems are multiplied when we consider the cost overruns.* See -PLIC-.

mul•ti•ra•cial (mul′tē rā shəl, mul′tī-) /ˌmʌltiyreyʃəl, ˌmʌltay-/ *adj.* of, relating to, or made up of several races: *a multiracial society.*

mul•ti•stage (mul′ti stāj′) /ˈmʌltɪˌsteydʒ/ *adj.* [*before a noun*] (of a rocket or guided missile) having more than one stage.

mul•ti•sto•ry (mul′tē stôr′ē, -stōr′ē, mul′tī-) /ˌmʌltiyˈstɔriy, -ˈstowriy, ˌmʌltay-/ *adj.* [*before a noun*] (of a building) made up of several stories: *housed in a huge multistory apartment complex.*

mul•ti•tude (mul′ti to͞od′, -tyo͞od′) /ˈmʌltɪˌtuwd, -ˌtyuwd/ *n.* [*count*] **1.** a great number: *a multitude of problems.* **2.** a great number of people gathered together; a crowd; throng: *the multitudes who tried to see him.* —**Syn.** See CROWD.

mul•ti•tu•di•nous (mul′ti to͞od′n əs, -tyo͞od′-) /ˌmʌltɪˈtuwdn̩əs, -ˈtyuwd-/ *adj.* **1.** existing in great numbers; very numerous. **2.** containing or extending over many parts or elements.

mul•ti•vi•ta•min (mul′ti vī′tə min, mul′ti vī′-) /ˌmʌltɪˈvaytəmɪn, ˈmʌltɪˌvay-/ *adj.* **1.** containing or made up of several vitamins: *a multivitamin supplement.* —*n.* [*count*] **2.** a compound of several vitamins. See -VIT-.

mum[1] (mum) /mʌm/ *adj.* silent: *to keep mum.*

mum[2] (mum) /mʌm/ *n.* CHRYSANTHEMUM.

mum•ble (mum′bəl) /ˈmʌmbəl/ *v.,* **-bled, -bling,** *n.* —*v.* **1.** to say or speak in a soft manner that is hard to understand: [*no obj*]: *He tended to mumble.* [~ + *obj*]: *He mumbled a few words that I couldn't understand.* [*used with quotations*]: *"I'm sorry," he mumbled.* —*n.* [*count*] **2.** a soft, indistinct utterance or sound. —**mum′bler,** *n.* [*count*]

mum•bo jum•bo (mum′bō jum′bō) /ˈmʌmˈbow dʒʌmbow/ *n.* [*noncount*] senseless or meaningless language or words, usually designed to hide or confuse.

mum•mi•fy (mum′ə fī′) /ˈmʌmə,fay/ *v.* [~ + *obj*], **-fied, -fy•ing.** to make (a dead body) into a mummy. —**mum•mi•fi•ca•tion** (mum′ə fi kā′shən) /ˌmʌməfɪˈkeyʃən/ *n.* [*noncount*]

mum•my (mum′ē) /ˈmʌmiy/ *n.* [*count*], *pl.* **-mies.** the dead body of a human being or animal that has been preserved from decay by an ancient Egyptian process or some similar method.

mumps (mumps) /mʌmps/ *n.* [*noncount; often: the* + ~; *used with a singular verb*] an infectious disease in which certain glands in the throat, neck, and mouth swell: *The mumps is sometimes a serious disease.*

mun., an abbreviation of: municipal.

munch (munch) /mʌntʃ/ *v.* to chew steadily or strongly and often loudly enough to be heard: [*no obj*]: *He munched on an apple.* [~ + *obj*]: *He munched his cornflakes.*

mun•dane (mun dān′, mun′dān) /mʌnˈdeyn, ˈmʌndeyn/ *adj.* **1.** of or relating to this world or earth as compared with heaven; worldly; earthly: *mundane affairs.* **2.** common; ordinary; uninteresting; banal: *to bring some excitement to our mundane lives.* —**mun•dane′ly,** *adv.*

mu•nic•i•pal (myo͞o nis′ə pəl) /myuwˈnɪsəpəl/ *adj.* [*before a noun*] **1.** of or relating to a city, etc., or its local government: *municipal elections.* —*n.* [*count*] **2.** a bond issued by a municipal government. —**mu•nic′i•pal•ly,** *adv.*

mu•nic•i•pal•i•ty (myo͞o nis′ə pal′i tē) /myuw,nɪsəˈpælɪtiy/ *n.* [*count*], *pl.* **-ties.** a city, town, or borough having its own government: *Small municipalities are looking for financial help from the state.*

mu•nif•i•cent (myo͞o nif′ə sənt) /myuwˈnɪfəsənt/ *adj.* having or showing great generosity. —**mu•nif′i•cence,** *n.* [*noncount*] —**mu•nif′i•cent•ly,** *adv.*

mu•ni•tion (myo͞o nish′ən) /myuwˈnɪʃən/ *n.* [*count*] **1.** Usually, **munitions.** [*plural*] materials used in war, esp. weapons and ammunition. —*v.* [~ + *obj*] **2.** to provide with munitions.

mu•ral (myo͝or′əl) /ˈmyʊrəl/ *n.* [*count*] a large picture painted directly on a wall or ceiling. —**mu′ral•ist,** *n.* [*count*]

mur•der (mûr′dər) /ˈmɜrdər/ *n.* **1.** the unlawful killing of a person, esp. when done deliberately: [*noncount*]: *guilty of murder.* [*count*]: *an increase in the number of murders.* **2.** [*noncount; be* + ~] *Informal.* something extremely difficult or unpleasant: *The final exam was murder!* —*v.* **3.** to kill (a person) unlawfully and deliberately: [~ + *obj*]: *He murdered his wife and children.* [*no obj*]: *The troops murdered and looted as they swept through the towns.* **4.** [~ + *obj*] to spoil or mar through incompetence: *The singer murdered that last song.* **5.** [~ + *obj*] *Informal.* to defeat thoroughly: *The home team murdered their opponents 60-0.* —***Idiom.*** **6. get away with murder,** to do something very harmful, damaging, immoral, etc., and not to be punished: *Just because she's famous, she thinks that she can get away with murder.* —**mur′der•er,** *n.* [*count*] —**mur′der•ess,** *n.* [*count*]

mur•der•ous (mûr′dər əs) /ˈmɜrdərəs/ *adj.* **1.** of the nature of or involving murder: *a murderous deed.* **2.** guilty of or capable of murder: *a murderous dictator.* **3.** (of expressions on the face) showing great anger: *a murderous expression.* **4.** *Informal.* very difficult, dangerous, or unpleasant: *murderous heat.* —**mur′der•ous•ly,** *adv.*: *a murderously hot day.*

murk (mûrk) /mɜrk/ *n.* [*noncount*] darkness; gloom.

murk•y (mûr′kē) /ˈmɜrkiy/ *adj.*, **-i•er, i•est. 1.** dark, gloomy, and cheerless: *a murky, dark cave.* **2.** thick and heavy, as with mist: *murky streets.* **3.** muddy; hard to see through: *Fish were dying in the murky ponds.* **4.** vague; unclear: *a murky statement.* —**murk•i•ly** (mûr′kə lē) /ˈmɜrkəliy/ *adv.* —**murk′i•ness,** *n.* [*noncount*]

mur•mur (mûr′mər) /ˈmɜrmər/ *n.* [*count*] **1.** a low, soft, continuous sound, as of a brook or of distant voices: *the murmur of the ocean waves.* **2.** a mumbled, low, soft sound made by a person, as in complaining: *She went to bed without a murmur of protest.* **3.** an abnormal sound heard within the body, esp. one coming from the heart valves: *a heart murmur.* —*v.* **4.** [*no obj*] to make a low, soft, continuous sound: *The brook murmured in the distance.* **5.** to express in murmurs: [*no obj*]: *The villagers murmured among themselves.* [~ + *obj*]: *He murmured his approval.* [*used with quotations*]: *She murmured "I love you" in his ear as he slept.* —**mur′mur•er,** *n.* [*count*]

mus•cle (mus′əl) /ˈmʌsəl/ *n., v.,* **-cled, -cling.** —*n.* **1.** a tissue in the body made up of long cells that can contract, causing movement of the body: [*count*]: *His leg muscles had grown weak from his stay in the hospital.* [*noncount*]: *to cut through muscle to get to the diseased organ.* **2.** [*noncount*] muscular strength; brawn. **3.** [*noncount*] power or force: *to put muscle into our foreign policy.* —*v.* **4.** [~ + *in on* + *obj*] *Informal.* to make one's way by force: *Our competitors are muscling in on our territory.* **5.** [~ + *obj*] *Informal.* to push or move by force: *to muscle the car out of the ditch.*

mus•cle•bound (mus′əl bound′) /ˈmʌsəl,bawnd/ *adj.* **1.** having enlarged muscles, as from too much exercise. **2.** rigid; inflexible: *a musclebound foreign policy.*

mus•cu•lar (mus′kyə lər) /ˈmʌskyələr/ *adj.* **1.** of or relating to muscle or the muscles. **2.** having well-developed muscles; brawny: *muscular lifeguards.* —**mus•cu•lar•i•ty** (mus′kyə lar′i tē) /ˌmʌskyəˈlærɪtiy/ *n.* [*noncount*]

mus′cular dys′trophy (dis′trə fē) /ˈdɪstrəfiy/ *n.* [*noncount*] an inherited disease in which the muscles gradually waste away.

muse[1] (myo͞oz) /myuwz/ *v.,* **mused, mus•ing.** to think about or ponder quietly: [*no obj*]: *He sat by the window, musing about the world.* [*used with quotations*]: *"Maybe God doesn't play dice with the universe," he mused.*

muse[2] (myo͞oz) /myuwz/ *n.* [*count*] the imaginary force thought to provide inspiration to poets, writers, artists, etc.: *waiting for the muse.*

mu•sette (myo͞o zet′) /myuwˈzɛt/ *n.* [*count*] Also called **musette′ bag′.** a small leather or canvas bag with a shoulder strap.

mu•se•um (myo͞o zē′əm) /myuwˈziyəm/ *n.* [*count*] a building where works of art or other objects of value are kept and displayed.

mush[1] (mush *or, esp. for 2–4* mo͝osh) /mʌʃ *or, esp. for 2–4* mʊʃ/ *n.* [*noncount*] **1.** a thick mixture made by boiling meal, esp. cornmeal, in water or milk. **2.** any thick, soft mass. **3.** anything lacking force, substance, or strength: *His arguments are nothing but mush.* —*v.* [~ + *obj*] **4.** to squeeze or crush; crunch.

mush[2] (mush) /mʌʃ/ *v.* [*no obj*] **1.** to go or travel, esp. over snow with a dog team and sled. —*interj.* **2.** (used as an order to start or speed up a dog team): *"Mush!" she cried, and the team leaped ahead.* —*n.* [*count*] **3.** a trip or journey, esp. across snow and ice with a dog team.

mush•room (mush′ro͞om, -ro͝om) /ˈmʌʃruwm, -rʊm/ *n.* [*count*] **1.** a fungus that includes the toadstools and puffballs. **2.** anything of similar shape or rapid growth, as a mushroom-shaped cloud of smoke from a nuclear explosion. —*adj.* [*before a noun*] **3.** of or containing mushrooms. **4.** resembling a mushroom in shape or rapid growth. —*v.* [*no obj*] **5.** to spread, grow, or develop quickly: *Sales began to mushroom.* **6.** to gather mushrooms: *to go mushrooming in the woods.*

mush•y (mush′ē, mo͝osh′ē) /ˈmʌʃiy, ˈmʊʃiy/ *adj.*, **-i•er, -i•est. 1.** resembling mush; pulpy: *mushy oatmeal.* **2.** overly emotional or sentimental: *mushy love letters.* —**mush′i•ness,** *n.* [*noncount*]

mu•sic (myo͞o′zik) /ˈmyuwzɪk/ *n.* [*noncount*] **1.** sounds arranged to have melody, rhythm, or harmony: *music to soothe the soul.* **2.** the art of producing this: *to study music.* **3.** the written or printed set of musical notes for a composition: *She tried to play from memory, but found that she needed the music.* **4.** musical quality: *the music of words.*

mu•si•cal (myo͞o′zi kəl) /ˈmyuwzɪkəl/ *adj.* **1.** [*before a noun*] of or relating to music: *musical entertainment.* **2.** of the nature of or resembling music; tuneful: *a sweet, musical voice.* **3.** fond of or skilled in music: *My daughters are both very musical.* —*n.* [*count*] **4.** Also called **musical comedy.** a play or motion picture in which the story line is interrupted by or developed by songs, dances, etc.: *He starred in several musicals on Broadway.* —**mu•si•cal•i•ty** (myo͞o′zi kal′i tē) /ˌmyuwzɪˈkælɪtiy/ *n.* [*noncount*] —**mu′si•cal•ly,** *adv.*

mu•si•cale (myo͞o′zi kal′) /ˌmyuwzɪˈkæl/ *n.* [*count*] a social occasion featuring music.

mu•si•cian (myo͞o zish′ən) /myuwˈzɪʃən/ *n.* [*count*] one who performs music, esp. professionally. —**mu•si′cian•ship′,** *n.* [*noncount*]

mu•si•col•o•gy (myo͞o′zi kol′ə jē) /ˌmyuwzɪˈkɒlədʒiy/ *n.* [*noncount*] the study of music, as in historical research or musical theory. —**mu′si•col′o•gist,** *n.* [*count*]

musk (musk) /mʌsk/ *n.* [*noncount*] **1.** a strong-smelling substance obtained from a certain deer and used to make perfumes. **2.** an artificial imitation of this substance. —**musk′i•ness,** *n.* [*noncount*] —**musk′y,** *adj.,* **-i•er, -i•est.**

mus•ket (mus′kit) /ˈmʌskɪt/ *n.* [*count*] a heavy, large-caliber gun with a long barrel, once used by infantry soldiers. —**mus•ket•eer** (mus′ki tēr′) /ˌmʌskɪˈtɪər/ *n.* [*count*] —**mus•ket•ry** (mus′ki trē) /ˈmʌskɪtriy/ *n.* [*noncount*]

musk•mel•on (musk′mel′ən) /ˈmʌskˌmɛlən/ *n.* [*count*] **1.** a round melon having a juicy, sweet-smelling and sweet-tasting, yellow, white, or green edible flesh. **2.** the plant of the gourd family bearing this fruit. **3.** CANTALOUPE (def. 1).

musk•rat (musk′rat′) /ˈmʌskˌræt/ *n., pl.* **-rats,** (*esp. when thought of as a group*) **-rat. 1.** [*count*] a large, North American rodent that lives in water. **2.** [*noncount*] its glossy, dark brown fur, used for coats, trimming, etc.

Mus•lim (muz′lim, mo͝oz′-, mo͝os′-) /ˈmʌzlɪm, ˈmʊz-, ˈmʊs-/ also **Mos•lem** (moz′ləm, mos′-), /ˈmɒzləm, ˈmɒs-/ *adj., n., pl.* **-lims, -lim.** —*adj.* **1.** of or relating to the religion, law, or civilization of Islam. —*n.* [*count*] **2.** a follower of Islam. **3.** BLACK MUSLIM.

mus•lin (muz′lin) /ˈmʌzlɪn/ *n.* [*noncount*] a cotton fabric made in various degrees of fineness, used esp. for sheets.

muss (mus) /mʌs/ *v.* **1.** to put into disorder; make messy: [~ + *obj*]: *She mussed his hair a little.* [~ + *up* + *obj*]: *She mussed up his hair.* [~ + *obj* + *up*]: *She mussed her hair up.* —*n.* [*count; singular; a* + ~] **2.** a state of disorder or untidiness. —**muss′y,** *adj.,* **-i•er, -i•est.**

mus•sel (mus′əl) /ˈmʌsəl/ *n.* [*count*] a two-shelled water creature, a mollusk, the soft body of which can be eaten.

must (must) /mʌst/ *auxiliary v., pres. sing.* and *pl. 1st, 2nd,* and *3rd pers.* **must,** *past* **must;** *adj.; n.* —*auxiliary (modal) verb.* [~ + *root form of a verb*] **1.** (used to express that the action of the next verb is something that will have to be done): *I must keep my promise.* **2.** (used to express that the action of the next verb is a requirement or is felt to be necessary by law, by religious or moral rule, or by some social agreement): *The rules must be obeyed.* **3.** (used to express that the action of the next verb is desirable, advisable, or a good idea): *You really must read this book; you'll really like it.* **4.** (used to express that the action of the next verb cannot be avoided, or that it is necessary because of natural laws or the way the universe is): *All good things must come to an end.* **5.** (used to express that logically there is a need for the action or state of the next verb to be true): *There must be some mistake (= there cannot be any other explanation possible). She must have had a very good reason for what she did.* **6.** (used to express that the action of the next verb is very likely to happen or to be true, or that it is reasonable to expect that action to happen or to be true): *You must be joking. He must be at least 70 years old.* **7.** (used in clauses with "if," and in certain questions, to express annoyance): *If you must know, your teacher is late (= I wish you wouldn't keep asking me). Must you repeat everything I say? (= You repeat everything so often it has become annoying.)* —*adj.* [*before a noun*] **8.** necessary; vital: *A raincoat is must clothing in this area.* —*n.* [*count; singular; a* + ~] **9.** something necessary, vital, or required: *Getting enough sleep is a must.*

mus•tache (mus′tash, mə stash′) /ˈmʌstæʃ, məˈstæʃ/ *n.* [*count*] the hair growing on the upper lip. —**mus′tached,** *adj.*

mus•tang (mus′tang) /ˈmʌstæŋ/ *n.* [*count*] a small, strong horse of the American plains.

mus•tard (mus′tərd) /ˈmʌstərd/ *n.* [*noncount*] **1.** a strong-smelling and strong-tasting condiment prepared from the seed of a plant, used esp. as a food seasoning: *Will you have mustard on your hot dog?* **2.** the plant that gives this seed.

mus′tard gas′, *n.* [*noncount*] an oily liquid, used, esp. in World War I, as a chemical-warfare gas.

mus•ter (mus′tər) /ˈmʌstər/ *v.* **1.** to assemble (troops, etc.), as for battle or inspection: [~ + *obj*]: *The ship's company was mustered on the main deck.* [*no obj*]: *The ship's company mustered on the main deck.* **2.** [~ + *obj*] to gather or summon: *He mustered all his courage.* **3. muster out,** [*no obj*] to discharge from military service: *He was mustered out before the war.* —*n.* [*count*] **4.** an assembling of troops or persons for formal inspection or other purposes. —*Idiom.* **5. pass muster,** to be judged acceptable: *Does his work pass muster, or should he be asked to do it again?* See -MONSTR-.

must•n't (mus′ənt) /ˈmʌsənt/ a contraction of *must not.*

mus•ty (mus′tē) /ˈmʌstiy/ *adj.,* **-ti•er, -ti•est.** having an odor or flavor that suggests mold: *a musty old library.* —**mus•ti•ly** (mus′tl ē) /ˈmʌstḷiy/ *adv.* —**mus′ti•ness,** *n.* [*noncount*]

-mut-, *root.* -*mut*- comes from Latin, where it has the meaning "change." This meaning is found in such words as: COMMUTATION, COMMUTE, IMMUTABLE, MUTABLE, MUTATE, MUTATION, MUTUAL, PERMUTATION, PERMUTE, TRANSMUTE.

mu•ta•ble (myo͞o′tə bəl) /ˈmyuwtəbəl/ *adj.* **1.** allowing change: *mutable laws of nature.* **2.** likely to change: *the mutable ways of fortune.* —**mu•ta•bil•i•ty** (myo͞o′tə bil′i tē) /ˌmyuwtəˈbɪlɪtiy/ *n.* [*noncount*] —**mu′ta•bly,** *adv.* See -MUT-.

mu•tant (myo͞ot′nt) /ˈmyuwtnt/ *n.* [*count*] **1.** a new type of organism produced by mutation: *The plant must have been a mutant; it was huge.* —*adj.* [*usually: before a noun*] **2.** undergoing or resulting from mutation: *a mutant species.* See -MUT-.

mu•tate (myo͞o′tāt) /ˈmyuwteyt/ *v.,* **-tat•ed, -tat•ing.** to (cause to) undergo mutation: [*no obj*]: *The plant must have mutated.* [~ + *obj*]: *Radiation can mutate plant life by affecting the genes.* See -MUT-.

mu•ta•tion (myo͞o tā′shən) /myuwˈteyʃən/ *n.* **1.** *Biology.* **a.** sudden departure or change from the parent type, seen in offspring in one or more characteristics that have been inherited, caused by a change in a gene or a chromosome: [*noncount*]: *Mutation can sometimes benefit a species.* [*count*]: *Some mutations may result in a change of color.* **b.** [*count*] an individual, species, or the like resulting from such a change: *a mutation that was much bigger than the rest.* **2.** a change or alteration, as in form or nature: [*noncount*]: *the possibility of social mutation.* [*count*]: *economic mutations and other financial shifts.* —**mu•ta′tion•al,** *adj.* See -MUT-.

mute (myo͞ot) /myuwt/ *adj.,* **mut•er, mut•est,** *n., v.,* **mut•ed, mut•ing.** —*adj.* **1.** silent; not having or giving off any sound: *They were mute when I asked them who was the thief.* **2.** incapable of speech; dumb: *mute from birth.* **3.** (of letters) silent; not pronounced: *The letter "e" is mute in the word "come."* —*n.* [*count*] **4.** a person incapable of speech. **5.** a mechanical device for muffling the tone of a musical instrument. —*v.* [~ + *obj*] **6.** to deaden or muffle the sound of. **7.** to reduce the intensity of (a color) by the addition of another color: *The colors are more muted in the bedroom.* —**mute′ly,** *adv.: They stood by mutely, unable or unwilling to answer.* —**mute′ness,** *n.* [*noncount*]

mu•ti•late (myo͞ot′l āt′) /ˈmyuwtḷˌeyt/ *v.* [~ + *obj*], **-lat•ed, -lat•ing.** to injure the appearance of, by damaging parts: *to mutilate a painting.* —**mu•ti•la•tion** (myo͞ot′l ā′shən) /ˌmyuwtḷˈeyʃən/ *n.* [*noncount*] —**mu′ti•la′tor,** *n.* [*count*]

mu•ti•ny (myo͞ot′n ē) /ˈmyuwtṇiy/ *n., pl.* **-nies,** *v.,* **-nied, -ny•ing.** —*n.* **1.** rebellion against legal authority, esp. by sailors or soldiers against their officers: [*noncount*]: *guilty of mutiny.* [*count*]: *a short mutiny on board the ship.* —*v.* [*no obj*] **2.** to commit mutiny: *The crew mutinied because of bad food.* —**mu′ti•neer′,** *n.* [*count*] —**mu′ti•nous,** *adj.: a mutinous crew with no sense of morals.*

mutt (mut) /mʌt/ *n.* [*count*] *Slang.* **1.** a dog of mixed breeds: *Spot was just a mutt, but the children loved him.* **2.** a stupid or foolish person; simpleton.

mut•ter (mut′ər) /ˈmʌtər/ *v.* **1.** to say words, or to make sounds, in a low tone hard to understand or hear; murmur: [*no obj*]: *He sat, muttering quietly to himself.* [~ + *obj*]: *He muttered a few words of greeting.* [*used with quotations*]: *"That's it," he muttered, "no more."* —*n.* [*count*] **2.** the act or sound of a person who mutters: *answering in low mutters.*

mut•ton (mut′n) /ˈmʌtṇ/ *n.* [*noncount*] the flesh of a mature sheep, used as food. —**mut′ton•y,** *adj.*

mu•tu•al (myo͞o′cho͞o əl) /ˈmyuwtʃuwəl/ *adj.* **1.** possessed, felt, or performed by each of two with respect to the other; reciprocal: *mutual respect.* **2.** having the same relation each toward the other: *mutual enemies.* **3.** held or having in common; shared: *mutual interests.* —**mu•tu•al•i•ty** (myo͞o′cho͞o al′i tē) /ˈmyuwtʃuwˈælɪtiy/ *n.* [*noncount*] —**mu′tu•al•ly,** *adv.: If two events or circumstances are mutually exclusive, only one can happen or be true, but not both.* See -MUT-.

mu′tual fund′, *n.* [*count*] an investment company that constantly sells its stock, which it is obligated to repurchase from its shareholders when asked to do so.

muu•muu (mo͞o′mo͞o′) /ˈmuwˌmuw/ *n.* [*count*], *pl.* **-muus. 1.** a long, loose-hanging dress, usually brightly colored or patterned, worn esp. by Hawaiian women. **2.** a similar dress worn as a housedress.

muz•zle (muz′əl) /ˈmʌzəl/ *n., v.,* **-zled, -zling.** —*n.* [*count*] **1.** the part of the head of an animal that comprises the jaws, mouth, and nose. **2.** the mouth of the barrel of a gun, etc. **3.** a device, usually an arrangement of straps or wires, placed over an animal's mouth to prevent the animal from biting, etc. —*v.* [~ + *obj*] **4.** to put a muzzle on (an animal or its mouth). **5.** to hold back from or prevent speech or the expression of opinion: *to muzzle the press by violence.*

my (mī) /may/ *pron.* **1.** a form of the possessive case of the pronoun I, used as an adjective before a noun: *My soup is cold.* **2.** (used in forms of address before titles, names, etc.): *Yes, my lord, I'll see to it right away. My dear Mrs. Adams, won't you come this way.* **3.** (used in exclamations of surprise, dismay, disagreement, etc., before certain nouns): *You got a perfect score? My foot! (= I don't believe it).* —*interj.* **4.** (used as an exclamation of mild surprise or dismay): *My, my, what have we here — a broken foot and possible fractured leg?*

My•lar (mī′lär) /ˈmaylɑr/ *Trademark.* [*noncount*] a brand of strong, thin polyester film used in photography, recording tapes, and insulation.

my•na or **my•nah** or **mi•na** (mī′nə) /ˈmaynə/ *n.* [*count*], *pl.* **-nas** or **-nahs.** an Asian bird of the starling family, some of which have the ability to mimic speech as pets.

my•o•pi•a (mī ō′pē ə) /mayˈowpiyə/ *n.* [*noncount*] **1.** a condition of the eye in which objects can be seen clearly only when near to the eye; nearsightedness. **2.** lack of foresight or ability to understand something obvious: *to demonstrate myopia by not adjusting to the changing student population.* —**my•op•ic** (mī op′ik), /mayˈɒpɪk/ *adj.* —**my•op′i•cal•ly,** *adv.* See -OPTI-.

myr•i•ad (mir′ē əd) /ˈmɪriyəd/ *n.* [*count*] **1.** a great number of persons or things: *a myriad of problems.* —*adj.* [*before a noun*] **2.** of a great number; innumerable.

myrrh (mûr) /mɜr/ *n.* [*noncount*] **1.** a sweet-smelling, bitter substance from Arabian and E African plants, used chiefly in making incense. **2.** a plant giving this substance.

myr•tle (mûr′tl) /ˈmɜrtl̩/ *n.* [*count*] **1.** a plant of S Europe, having evergreen leaves, fragrant white flowers, and sweet-smelling berries. **2.** an unrelated plant, as the periwinkle.

my•self (mī self′) /mayˈsɛlf/ *pron.* **1.** a form of the pronoun ME, a reflexive pronoun, used as the direct or indirect object of a verb or as the object of a preposition, when the subject is *I*: *I excused myself from the table. I gave myself a pat on the head. I was pretty happy with myself for the moment.* **2.** (used to add emphasis to the pronouns I or ME): *I myself don't like it. I did it all myself.* **3.** (used in certain constructions without a verb): *Myself a parent, I understand their concern.* **4.** (used in place of I or ME in some special constructions with words like "and," "as," and "than"): *My wife and myself agree. He knows as much about the case as myself. No one is more to blame than myself.* **5.** my usual, normal, healthy, or customary self: *I wasn't myself when I said that.*

mys•te•ri•ous (mi stēr′ē əs) /mɪˈstɪəriyəs/ *adj.* involving or full of mystery: *a mysterious phone call; a mysterious smile.* —**mys•te′ri•ous•ly,** *adv.* —**mys•te′ri•ous•ness,** *n.* [*noncount*]

mys•ter•y (mis′tə rē, -trē) /ˈmɪstəriy, -triy/ *n., pl.* **-er•ies. 1.** [*count*] anything kept secret or unexplained or unknown: *the mysteries of nature.* **2.** [*count*] a person or thing that arouses curiosity or wonder: *The guest was a mystery to everyone.* **3.** [*count*] a novel, film, or the like with a plot involving the solving of a puzzle, esp. a crime. **4.** [*noncount*] the quality of being hidden, hard to understand, or puzzling: *The place has an air of mystery about it.*

mys•tic (mis′tik) /ˈmɪstɪk/ *adj.* [*before a noun*] **1.** mystical. —*n.* [*count*] **2.** one who claims to have insight into mysteries beyond ordinary human knowledge.

mys•ti•cal (mis′ti kəl) /ˈmɪstɪkəl/ *adj.* **1.** [*before a noun*] occult; of or relating to a mystic. **2.** of or relating to mystics or mysticism. —**mys′ti•cal•ly,** *adv.*

mys•ti•cism (mis′tə siz′əm) /ˈmɪstəˌsɪzəm/ *n.* [*noncount*] **1.** the beliefs, ideas, or way of thought of mystics. **2.** the belief that it is possible to gain knowledge of spiritual truths beyond ordinary human understanding, through a direct union with God that occurs after fasting, praying, or meditating. **3.** ideas or thoughts that are difficult or impossible to understand or prove: *The physicist's ideas about the beginning of the universe are more mysticism than true science.*

mys•ti•fy (mis′tə fī′) /ˈmɪstəˌfay/ *v.* [~ + *obj*], **-fied, -fy•ing.** to cause confusion; to perplex or bewilder: *completely mystified by his decision not to take such a good job.* —**mys•ti•fi•ca•tion** (mis′tə fi kā′shən) /ˌmɪstəfɪˈkeyʃən/ *n.* [*noncount*]

mys•tique (mi stēk′) /mɪˈstiyk/ *n.* [*noncount*] a feeling or aura of mystery surrounding a particular occupation, activity, etc.: *the mystique of appearing in a Broadway show.*

myth (mith) /mɪθ/ *n.* **1.** [*count*] a traditional story, esp. one that involves gods and heroes and explains a practice or some natural object or phenomenon: *Greek, Roman, Chinese, Japanese, African, and Indian myths.* **2.** [*noncount*] stories of this kind thought of as a group; mythology: *the study of ancient myth.* **3.** an invented story, fictitious person, etc.: [*noncount*]: *His account of the event is pure myth.* [*count*]: *Her story is just a myth.* **4.** [*count*] a belief or set of beliefs that surround a person, a phenomenon, or an institution: *myths of racial superiority.*

myth•i•cal (mith′i kəl) /ˈmɪθɪkəl/ *adj.* **1.** of or relating to a myth: *mythical heroes.* **2.** untrue; false: *mythical superiority of one race over another.* **3.** unreal; not existing: *mythical salary increases that never really happen.*

my•thol•o•gy (mi thol′ə jē) /mɪˈθɒlədʒiy/ *n., pl.* **-gies. 1.** [*count*] a body of myths, as that of a particular people. **2.** [*noncount*] myths thought of as a group. **3.** [*noncount*] the science or study of myths. **4.** [*count*] a set of stories, traditions, or beliefs that surround a particular person, event, or institution: *An entire mythology has grown around the dead movie star.* —**myth•o•log•i•cal** (mith′ə loj′i kəl) /ˌmɪθəˈlɒdʒɪkəl/ *adj.* —**my•thol′o•gist,** *n.* [*count*]

N

N, n (en) /ɛn/ *n.* [*count*], *pl.* **Ns** or **N's, ns** or **n's.** the 14th letter of the English alphabet, a consonant.

N, an abbreviation of: **1.** north. **2.** northern.

N., an abbreviation of: **1.** north. **2.** northern. **3.** November.

n., an abbreviation of: **1.** name. **2.** neuter. **3.** new. **4.** north. **5.** northern. **6.** noun. **7.** number.

N.A., an abbreviation of: **1.** North America. **2.** not applicable.

nab (nab) /næb/ *v.* [~ + *obj*], **nabbed, nab•bing.** *Informal.* **1.** to arrest or capture: *The police nabbed the crooks.* **2.** to catch or seize, esp. suddenly: *The kidnappers nabbed him as he got into his car.*

na•bob (nā′bob) /ˈneybɒb/ *n.* [*count*] a very wealthy, influential, or powerful person.

na•dir (nā′dər) /ˈneydər/ *n.* [*count*] the lowest point: *The loss of his job and his wife marked the nadir of his life.*

nag[1] (nag) /næg/ *v.,* **nagged, nag•ging,** *n.* **—***v.* **1.** to annoy by continuously finding fault or making demands: [~ + *obj* (+ *into* + *verb*)]: *nagged them into contributing money.* [*no obj*]: *He kept nagging about needing money.* **2.** to be a constant source of unease or irritation to: [~ + *obj*]: *Her doubts nagged her.* [*no obj*]: *The debt kept nagging at his conscience.* **—***n.* [*count*] **3.** a person who nags.

nag[2] (nag) /næg/ *n.* [*count*] a horse, esp. one that is old or worn out.

nag•ging (nag′ing) /ˈnægɪŋ/ *adj.* persistently bothersome: *a nagging backache.*

nail (nāl) /neyl/ *n.* [*count*] **1.** a thin, rod-shaped piece of metal, usually having a pointed tip and a flattened head, made to be hammered into wood or other material as a fastener or support. **2.** a thin, hard, horny area on the upper side of the end of a finger or toe. **—***v.* **3.** to fasten with a nail or nails: [~ + *obj*]: *to nail a picture to the wall.* [~ + *up* + *obj*]: *to nail up the demands on the wall.* [~ + *obj* + *up*]: *to nail the demands up.* **4.** to enclose or shut by nailing: [~ + *obj*]: *He nailed the door closed.* [~ + *obj* + *up*]: *He nailed the door up.* [~ + *up* + *obj*]: *They nailed up the door.* **5.** [~ + *obj*] *Informal.* **a.** to catch; seize: *The police nailed him as he was trying to escape.* **b.** to hit successfully: *The batter nailed the ball for a home run.* **6. nail down,** to make final; settle once and for all: [~ + *down* + *obj*]: *to nail down an agreement.* [~ + *obj* + *down*]: *Nail it down before you sign anything.* **—*Idiom.*** **7. hit the nail on the head,** to say or do exactly the right thing; to be exactly right.

nail′ brush′, *n.* [*count*] a small, usually tough, stiff brush for cleaning the fingernails or hands.

nail′ file′, *n.* [*count*] a small, thin bar of metal or sometimes plastic with a rough surface, used for shaping the fingernails.

nail′ pol′ish, *n.* [*noncount*] a lacquer for painting the fingernails or toenails.

na•ive or **na•ïve** (nä ēv′) /nɑˈiyv/ *adj.* **1.** childlike and innocent. **2.** showing a lack of experience, wisdom, or judgment; gullible. **—na•ive′ly,** *adv.* See -NAT-.

na•ive•té or **na•ïve•té** or **na•ive•te** (nä ēv tā′, -ē′və-tā′, -ēv′tā, -ē′və-) /nɑiyvˈtey, -ˌiyvəˈtey, -ˈiyvtey, -ˈiyvə-/ *n.* [*noncount*] the quality or state of being naive; innocence; lack of experience. See -NAT-.

na•ked (nā′kid) /ˈneykɪd/ *adj.* **1.** being without clothing; nude. **2.** [*before a noun*] lacking the customary or usual covering or protection: *a naked sword; naked light bulbs.* **3.** lacking furnishings or decoration: *the empty house with its naked walls.* **4.** [*before a noun*] not assisted by the use of a microscope, telescope, or other instrument: *a planet barely visible to the naked eye.* **5.** defenseless; unprotected: *a town left naked to the invasions of the enemy.* **6.** [*before a noun*] plain; simple; unadorned: *the naked truth.* **7.** [*before a noun*] plainly revealed; obvious: *a naked threat.* **—na′ked•ly,** *adv.* **—na′ked•ness,** *n.* [*noncount*]

nam•by-pam•by (nam′bē pam′bē) /ˈnæmbiyˈpæmbiy/ *adj., n., pl.* **-bies.** **—***adj.* **1.** indecisive; irresolute: *a namby-pamby personality.* **2.** sentimental; insipid: *namby-pamby greeting cards.* **—***n.* [*count*] **3.** one that is namby-pamby.

name (nām) /neym/ *n., v.,* **named, nam•ing,** *adj.* **—***n.* [*count*] **1.** a word or phrase by which a person or thing is identified or known: *Please state your name and address.* **2.** an often insulting description: *He called her names.* **3.** [*usually singular*] **a.** reputation: *These bad loans gave him a bad name.* **b.** a reputation of fame or distinction: *made a name for herself in politics.* **—***v.* **4.** to give a name to; call: [~ + *obj*]: *to name a baby.* [~ + *obj* + *obj*]: *They named their baby Frederick.* **5. name (someone or something) after/for (someone or something else),** to give a name to (someone or something) in memory of or tribute to someone or something else: [~ + *obj* + *after* + *obj*]: *They named him after his father.* [~ + *obj* + *obj* + *after* + *obj*]: *They named him Frederick after his father.* **6.** [~ + *obj*] **a.** to accuse by name: *She named the thief.* **b.** to identify by name: *Name all the state capitals.* **7.** [~ + *obj* + (*as* +) *obj*] to designate or nominate for duty or office: *They named him (as) campaign manager.* **8.** [~ + *obj*] to specify; say what something should be: *Name your price.* **—***adj.* [*before a noun*] **9.** famous; well-known: *a (big) name author.* **10.** designed for or bearing a name: *name tags.* **—*Idiom.*** **11. by name,** using the name of someone directly: *I mentioned you by name.* **12. by (the) name (of),** having the name of: *an interesting fellow by the name of David Jones.* **13. in name only,** having a title or position but not the power or status to go with it: *a king in name only, powerless to rule.* **14. in the name of,** with appeal to or by authority of: *Open, in the name of the law.* **15. name names,** to specify or accuse people by name: *The informant began naming names to the police.* **16. to one's name,** within one's resources: *not a penny to his name.* **—name′a•ble,** *adj.* **—nam′er,** *n.* [*count*]

name′-drop′, *v.* [*no obj*], **-dropped, -drop•ping.** to mention the names of famous or important people in order to impress others. **—name′drop•per,** *n.* [*count*]

name•less (nām′lis) /ˈneymlɪs/ *adj.* **1.** having no name. **2.** not referred to by name. **3.** anonymous: *a nameless source of information.* **4.** too shocking or vile to be specified: *a nameless crime.*

name•ly (nām′lē) /ˈneymliy/ *adv.* that is to say; specifically: *a new item of legislation, namely, the housing bill.*

name•plate (nām′plāt′) /ˈneymˌpleyt/ *n.* [*count*] a piece of metal, wood, or plastic on which the name of a person, company, etc., is printed or engraved.

name•sake (nām′sāk′) /ˈneymˌseyk/ *n.* [*count*] **1.** a person named after another. **2.** a person having the same name as another.

Na•mib•i•an (nə mib′ē ən) /nəˈmɪbiyən/ *adj.* **1.** of or relating to Namibia. **—***n.* [*count*] **2.** a person born or living in Namibia.

nan•ny (nan′ē) /ˈnæniy/ *n.* [*count*], *pl.* **-nies.** NURSEMAID.

nan′ny goat′, *n.* [*count*] a female goat.

nan•o•sec•ond (nan′ə sek′ənd) /ˈnænəˌsɛkənd/ *n.* [*count*] one billionth of a second. *Abbr.:* ns nsec

nap[1] (nap) /næp/ *v.,* **napped, nap•ping,** *n.* **—***v.* [*no obj*] **1.** to sleep for a short time; doze. **2.** to be off one's guard: *The question caught him napping.* **—***n.* [*count*] **3.** a brief period of sleep, esp. one taken during daytime. **—nap′per,** *n.* [*count*]

nap[2] (nap) /næp/ *n., v.,* **napped, nap•ping.** **—***n.* [*count*] **1.** the short fuzzy ends of fibers on the surface of cloth. **—***v.* [~ + *obj*] **2.** to raise a nap on. **—napped,** *adj.*

na•palm (nā′päm) /ˈneypɑm/ *n.* [*noncount*] **1.** a jellylike substance that burns quickly and easily, used in fire bombs, flamethrowers, etc. **—***v.* [~ + *obj*] **2.** to bomb or attack with napalm.

nape (nāp, nap) /neyp, næp/ *n.* [*count*] the back of the neck.

naph•tha (naf′thə, nap′-) /ˈnæfθə, ˈnæp-/ *n.* [*noncount*] a colorless, flammable liquid used to dissolve other substances and as a fuel.

nap•kin (nap′kin) /ˈnæpkɪn/ *n.* [*count*] **1.** a piece of cloth or paper for use in wiping the lips and fingers and to protect the clothes while eating. See illustration at RESTAURANT. **2.** *Chiefly Brit.* DIAPER.

na•po•le•on (nə pō′lē ən, -pōl′yən) /nəˈpowliyən, -ˈpowlyən/ *n.* [*count*] a pastry made of thin layers of puff paste and custard or cream filling.

nap•py (nap′ē) /ˈnæpiy/ *n.* [*count*], *pl.* **-pies.** *Brit.* a diaper.

narc or **nark** (närk) /nɑrk/ *n.* [*count*] *Slang.* an agent who investigates narcotics violations.

nar•cis•sism (när′sə siz′əm) /ˈnɑrsəˌsɪzəm/ *n.* [*noncount*] excessive love or admiration for oneself. **—nar′cis•sist,** *n.* [*count*] **—nar′cis•sis′tic,** *adj.*

nar•cis•sus (när sis′əs) /nɑrˈsɪsəs/ *n.* [*count*], pl. **-cis•sus, -cis•sus•es, -cis•si** (-sis′ē, -sis′ī) /-ˈsɪsiy, -ˈsɪsay/. a plant having yellow or white flowers with a cup-shaped crown.

nar•co•sis (när kō′sis) /nɑr'kowsɪs/ *n.* [*noncount*] a state of deep drowsiness caused by drugs.

nar•cot•ic (när kot′ik) /nɑr'kɒtɪk/ *n.* [*count*] **1.** an addictive or nearly addictive substance that blunts the senses causing sleep or relief from pain, also capable of causing confusion, inability to think or feel, and possibly coma and death. **2.** anything that exercises a soothing or numbing effect or influence: *Her narcotic was music.* **—***adj.* [*before a noun*] **3.** of or having the power to produce narcosis: *a narcotic drug.* **4.** of or relating to narcotics or their use: *narcotic addicts.*

nark (närk) /nɑrk/ *n.* NARC.

nar•rate (nar′āt, na rāt′) /'næreyt, næ'reyt/ *v.* [~ + *obj*], **-rat•ed, -rat•ing. 1.** to give an account of (events, experiences, etc.). **2.** to add a spoken background or commentary to (a film, television program, etc.). **—nar•ra•tion** (na rā′shən) /næ'reyʃən/ *n.* [*noncount*]: *the skill of narration.* [*count*]: *narrations of his experiences.* **—nar′ra•tor,** *n.* [*count*]

nar•ra•tive (nar′ə tiv) /'nærətɪv/ *n.* **1.** [*count*] a story or account of events, experiences, or the like, whether true or fictional. **2.** [*noncount*] the art, technique, or process of narrating: *the use of narrative in poetry.* **—***adj.* [*before a noun*] **3.** of, relating to, consisting of, or being a narrative: *narrative poetry.*

nar•row (nar′ō) /'nærow/ *adj.*, **-er, -est,** *v.* **—***adj.* **1.** of little width; not wide or broad: *a narrow alley.* **2.** limited in range or scope: *a narrow view of right and wrong.* **3.** [*before a noun*] barely adequate or successful; close: *a narrow escape.* **—***v.* **4.** to (cause to) decrease in width: [*no obj*]: *The road narrows ahead.* [~ + *obj*]: *She narrowed her eyes.* **5.** to (cause to) be reduced or smaller: [*no obj*]: *The gap between the rich and the poor is not narrowing.* [~ + *obj*]: *to narrow the gap between them.* **6.** to limit or restrict: [~ + *down* + *obj*]: *The detectives narrowed down the search to just two suspects.* [~ + *obj* (+ *down*)]: *They narrowed the search (down) to just two suspects.* **—***n.* [*count*] **7. narrows,** [*used with a singular or plural verb*] a narrow part of a river, ocean current, etc. **—nar′row•ness,** *n.* [*noncount*]

nar•row•ly (nar′ō lē) /'nærowliy/ *adv.* **1.** hardly; nearly; only just: *narrowly avoided being captured.* **2.** closely; with close attention: *She watched them narrowly.*

nar′row-mind′ed, *adj.* having a mind that is unwilling to accept or consider; intolerant. **—nar′row-mind′ed•ness,** *n.* [*noncount*]

nar•whal or **nar•wal** (när′wəl) /'nɑrwəl/ also **nar•whale** (-hwāl′, -wāl′) /-ˌhweyl, -ˌweyl/ *n.* [*count*] a small arctic whale, the male of which has a long, spiral-shaped, twisted tusk extending forward from the upper jaw.

nar•y (nâr′ē) /'nɛəriy/ *adj.* not any: *nary a sound.*

NASA (nas′ə) /'næsə/ *n.* [*proper noun; no article*] National Aeronautics and Space Administration.

na•sal (nā′zəl) /'neyzəl/ *adj.* **1.** of or relating to the nose: *nasal congestion.* **2.** making use of or pronounced through the nose: *nasal vowels.* **—na•sal•i•ty** (nā zal′i tē) /ney'zælɪtiy/ *n.* [*noncount*] **—na′sal•ly,** *adv.*

nas•cent (nas′ənt, nā′sənt) /'næsənt, 'neysənt/ *adj.* beginning to exist or develop. **—nas′cence,** *n.* [*noncount*] See -NAT-.

nas•tur•tium (nə stûr′shəm, na-) /nə'stɜrʃəm, næ-/ *n.* [*count*], *pl.* **-tiums.** a garden plant having shield-shaped leaves and colorful flowers.

nas•ty (nas′tē) /'næstiy/ *adj.*, **-ti•er, -ti•est,** *n.*, *pl.* **-ties.** **—***adj.* **1.** offensive to taste, smell, or the senses in general; nauseating: *a nasty smell of garbage.* **2.** indecent or obscene: *nasty language.* **3.** highly objectionable or unpleasant: *a nasty habit.* **4.** vicious, angry, threatening, or ugly: *A nasty dog guards his store at night.* **5.** bad to deal with or experience: *a nasty accident.* **—nas•ti•ly** (nas′tl ē) /'næstl̩iy/ *adv.* **—nas′ti•ness,** *n.* [*noncount*]

-nat-, *root.* *-nat-* comes from Latin, where it has the meaning "born; birth." This meaning is found in such words as: COGNATE, ILL-NATURED, INNATE, INTERNATIONAL, MULTINATIONAL, NAIVE, NASCENT, NATAL, NATION, NATIONAL, NATIVE, NATIVITY, NATURE, SUPERNATURAL.

na•tal (nāt′l) /'neytl̩/ *adj.* of or relating to birth: *natal care.* See -NAT-.

na•tion (nā′shən) /'neyʃən/ *n.* [*count*] **1.** a body of people, living in a particular territory, that is unified by birth, culture, race, language, or society, and often has its own government. **2.** the territory or country itself. **3.** an American Indian group or tribe, esp. a member tribe of an American Indian confederation. **—na′tion•hood′,** *n.* [*noncount*] See -NAT-.

na•tion•al (nash′ə nl, nash′nəl) /'næʃənl̩, 'næʃnəl/ *adj.* **1.** of, relating to, or belonging to a nation: *a national anthem.* **2.** [*before a noun*] typical of or common to the people of a nation: *national customs.* **—***n.* [*count*] **3.** a citizen of a particular nation under recognized law. **4.** a national company, business, or organization. Compare MULTINATIONAL. **—na′tion•al•ly,** *adv.* See -NAT-.

Na′tional Guard′, *n.* [*proper noun; often: the* + ~] a state military force that may be called upon by the state or federal government in emergencies.

na•tion•al•ism (nash′ə nl iz′əm, nash′nə liz′-) /'næʃənl̩ˌɪzəm, 'næʃnəˌlɪz-/ *n.* [*noncount*] **1.** devotion and loyalty to one's own nation; patriotism. **2.** the desire for national independence. **—na′tion•al•ist,** *adj.*, *n.* [*count*] **—na′tion•al•is′tic,** *adj.* See -NAT-.

na•tion•al•i•ty (nash′ ə nal′i tē) /ˌnæʃ ə'nælɪtiy/ *n.*, *pl.* **-ties. 1.** [*noncount*] the state of belonging to a particular nation, whether by birth or naturalization. **2.** [*count*] people who belong to a nation: *Many different nationalities came to the U.S.* See -NAT-.

na•tion•al•ize (nash′ə nl īz′, nash′nə līz′) /'næʃənl̩ˌayz, 'næʃnəˌlayz/ *v.* [~ + *obj*], **-ized, -iz•ing.** to bring (an industry, or land) under the ownership or control of a government: *That country has nationalized its airlines.* **—na•tion•al•i•za•tion** (nash′ə nl i zā′shən) /ˌnæʃənl̩ɪ'zeyʃən/ *n.* [*noncount*] See -NAT-.

na•tion•wide (nā′shən wīd′) /'neyʃən'wayd/ *adj.* extending throughout a nation: *a nationwide search.* See -NAT-.

na•tive (nā′tiv) /'neytɪv/ *adj.* **1.** [*before a noun*] being the place or environment in which a person was born, or the place or environment in which a thing came into being: *returned to his native land.* **2.** [*before a noun*] belonging to a person by birth or to a thing by nature; inherent: *the desert's native beauty.* **3.** belonging to or originating in a certain place; local: *The dancers wore their native dress.* **4.** [*before a noun*] born in a particular place: *a native New Yorker.* **5.** of or relating to something first learned by a person: *English is his native language.* **—***n.* [*count*] **6.** a person born in a particular place or country: *a native of Ohio.* **7.** one who lived in a place originally or has lived there a long time, esp. as distinguished from temporary residents. **8.** an animal, plant, etc., originating in a particular region. **—*Idiom.* 9. go native,** [*no obj*] to adopt the behavior and dress of a surrounding culture. See -NAT-.

Na′tive Amer′ican, *n.* AMERICAN INDIAN.

na•tiv•i•ty (nə tiv′i tē, nā-) /nə'tɪvɪtiy, ney-/ *n.*, *pl.* **-ties. 1.** [*count*] a birth. **2.** [*proper noun; the Nativity*] the birth of Christ. See -NAT-.

natl., an abbreviation of: national.

NATO (nā′tō) /'neytow/ *n.* [*proper noun; no article*] North American Treaty Organization.

nat•ter (nat′ər) /'nætər/ *v.* [*no obj*] to talk idly and without stopping.

nat•ty (nat′ē) /'nætiy/ *adj.*, **-ti•er, -ti•est.** neat and tidy; spruce: *a natty uniform.* **—nat•ti•ly** (nat′l ē) /'nætl̩iy/ *adv.*

nat•u•ral (nach′ər əl, nach′rəl) /'nætʃərəl, 'nætʃrəl/ *adj.* **1.** existing in or formed by nature and not by humans; not artificial: *The valley made a natural amphitheater.* **2.** of or relating to nature: *the natural world.* **3.** having undergone little or no processing and containing no chemical additives: *natural foods.* **4.** having a real or physical existence: *the natural, not the supernatural, world.* **5.** [*before a noun*] of, relating to, or belonging to one's nature; inborn; innate: *natural athletes.* **6.** behaving normally; appearing normal: *Please relax and look natural for the photographer.* **7.** in agreement with the nature of people or things; to be expected: *a natural result.* [*It* + *be* + ~ + *that clause*]: *It's natural that the parents should miss their children.* **8.** happening in the ordinary or usual course of things, without accident, violence, etc.: *to die a natural death.* **9.** [*before a noun*] ILLEGITIMATE: *a natural child.* **10.** [*before a noun*] related by blood rather than by adoption; biological: *searching for his natural parents.* **11.** [*after a noun*] *Music.* neither sharp nor flat: *That note is a G natural.* **—***n.* [*count*] **12.** any person or thing that is or is likely to be suitable to or successful in an endeavor: *He's a natural for that new position as supervisor.* **13. a.** a white key on a piano, organ, or the like. **b.** the sign ♮, placed before a note that would otherwise be understood as sharp or flat. **—nat′u•ral•ness,** *n.* [*noncount*] See -NAT-.

nat′ural child′birth, *n.* childbirth involving little or no use of drugs or painkilling medication: [*noncount*]: *classes to prepare for natural childbirth.* [*count*]: *the second natural childbirth today.*

nat′ural gas′, *n.* [*noncount*] a gas that is found underground and under the sea, and is used as a fuel for heating and cooking.

nat′ural his′tory, *n.* [*noncount*] the study of plants, animals, rocks, and other natural objects.

nat•u•ral•ism (nach′ər ə liz′əm, nach′rə-) /ˈnætʃərəˌlɪzəm, ˈnætʃrə-/ *n.* [*noncount*] (in a work of art or a piece of writing) treatment of forms, colors, space, events, and people as they appear or might appear in nature or real life. —**nat′u•ral•is′tic,** *adj.* See -NAT-.

nat•u•ral•ist (nach′ər ə list, nach′rə-) /ˈnætʃərəlɪst, ˈnætʃrə-/ *n.* [*count*] **1.** a person who studies or is an expert in natural history, esp. a zoologist or a botanist. **2.** a follower of naturalism in literature or art. See -NAT-.

nat•u•ral•ize (nach′ər ə līz′, nach′rə-) /ˈnætʃərəˌlayz, ˈnætʃrə-/ *v.* [~ + *obj*], **-ized, -iz•ing.** to make (someone) a citizen: *He was naturalized after having lived in that country for ten years.* —**nat•u•ral•i•za•tion** (nach′ər ə lizā′shən) /ˌnætʃərəlɪˈzeyʃən/ *n.* [*noncount*]

nat•u•ral•ly (nach′ər ə lē, -əl lē, nach′rə lē, -rəl lē) /ˈnætʃərəliy, -əlliy, ˈnætʃrəliy, -rəlliy/ *adv.* **1.** in a natural manner: *Just smile naturally.* **2.** being in a certain way by nature: *She has naturally curly hair.* **3.** of course; as would be expected; needless to say: *Naturally, you'll have to pay in advance.* —***Idiom.*** **4. come naturally,** [*not: be* + *~-ing; no obj*] to be easy for someone to do or learn: *Playing the violin comes naturally to her.*

nat′ural sci′ence, *n.* a science or knowledge of objects, events, or processes in nature: [*count*]: *The natural sciences include biology, physics, chemistry, and geology.* [*noncount*]: *to major in natural science.*

nat′ural selec′tion, *n.* [*noncount*] the process in nature by which some forms of life that are best able to function or adapt to changes in climate, to competition for food or mates, etc., tend to survive, reproduce in greater numbers, and pass on their characteristics to later generations.

na•ture (nā′chər) /ˈneytʃər/ *n.* **1.** [*noncount*] the natural world as it exists without human beings or civilization; the elements of the natural world, as mountains, trees, animals, or rivers. **2.** [*noncount*] the laws and principles that guide the universe or an individual. **3.** [*count*] the native character that is part of someone or something: *It is a cat's nature to keep itself clean.* **4.** character, kind, type, or sort: [*count; usually singular*]: *What is the nature of your business here?* [*noncount; often: in* + ~]: *The problems are economic in nature.* **5.** [*count*] disposition; temperament: *an evil nature; a kind, loving nature.* **6.** [*noncount*] the simple or primitive condition of humankind before modern civilization: *to return to nature to live.* —***Idiom.*** **7. by nature,** as a result of inborn or inherent qualities; innately. **8. call of nature,** [*count*] the need to urinate or defecate. **9. second nature,** [*noncount*] a habit or way of acting or thinking that has become part of the character of a person: *He has been a police officer for so long that dealing with emergencies has become second nature to him.* See -NAT-.

Nau•ga•hyde (nô′gə hīd′) /ˈnɔgəˌhayd/ *Trademark.* [*noncount*] a brand of strong vinyl-coated fabric made to look like leather.

naught or **nought** (nôt) /nɔt/ *n.* [*noncount*] **1.** nothing. **2.** a cipher (0); zero: *a score of ten to naught.* —***Idiom.*** **3. come to naught,** [*no obj*] to end in failure: *His plans came to naught.*

naugh•ty (nô′tē) /ˈnɔtiy/ *adj.,* **-ti•er, -ti•est. 1.** disobedient; mischievous: *naughty children.* **2.** improper or indecent: *a naughty word.* —**naugh•ti•ly** (nô′tlē) /ˈnɔtliy/ *adv.* —**naugh′ti•ness,** *n.* [*noncount*]

nau•se•a (nô′zē ə, -zhə, -sē ə, -shə) /ˈnɔziyə, -ʒə, -siyə, -ʃə/ *n.* [*noncount*] sickness in the stomach, esp. when accompanied by a need or desire to vomit.

nau•se•ate (nô′zē āt′, -zhē-, -sē-, -shē-) /ˈnɔziyˌeyt, -ʒiy-, -siy-, -ʃiy-/ *v.* [~ + *obj*], **-at•ed, -at•ing. 1.** to cause (someone) to feel nausea: *The rolling of the ship nauseated him.* **2.** to cause to feel extreme disgust: *was nauseated by such cruelty.*

nau•se•at•ing (nô′zē āt′ ing, -zhē-, -sē-, -shē-) /ˈnɔziyˌeytɪŋ, -ʒiy-, -siy-, -ʃiy-/ *adj.* causing a feeling of nausea: *a nauseating smell.* —**nau′se•at′ing•ly,** *adv.*

nau•seous (nô′shəs, -zē əs) /ˈnɔʃəs, -ziyəs/ *adj.* **1.** affected with nausea or disgust: *I feel nauseous.* **2.** causing nausea or disgust: *a nauseous smell.* —**nau′seous•ness,** *n.* [*noncount*]

-naut-, *root. -naut-* comes from Greek, where it has the meaning "sailor;" it has become generalized to mean "traveler." These meanings are found in such words as: ASTRONAUT, COSMONAUT, NAUTICAL, NAUTILUS.

nau•ti•cal (nô′ti kəl, not′i-) /ˈnɔtɪkəl, ˈnɒtɪ-/ *adj.* of or relating to sailors, ships, or navigation. —**nau′ti•cal•ly,** *adv.* See -NAUT-.

nau′tical mile′, *n.* [*count*] a unit of distance at sea, equal to 1.852 kilometers.

nau•ti•lus (nôt′l əs, not′-) /ˈnɔtl̩əs, ˈnɒt-/ *n.* [*count*], *pl.* **nau•ti•lus•es, nau•ti•li** (nôt′l ī′, not′-). /ˈnɔtl̩ˌay, ˈnɒt-/ a sea creature living in a shell shaped like a spiral, with a pearly interior. See -NAUT-.

-nav-, *root. -nav-* comes from Latin, where it has the meaning "boat, ship." It is related to -NAUT-. This meaning is found in such words as: CIRCUMNAVIGATE, NAVAL, NAVE, NAVIGABLE, NAVIGATE, NAVY.

na•val (nā′vəl) /ˈneyvəl/ *adj.* [*before a noun*] **1.** of or relating to ships. **2.** relating to a navy. See -NAV-.

nave (nāv) /neyv/ *n.* [*count*] the principal, longer area of a church, from the main entrance to the space around the altar, with aisles of less height on the sides. See -NAV-.

na•vel (nā′vəl) /ˈneyvəl/ *n.* [*count*] the hollow part of the surface of the abdomen where the umbilical cord was connected with the fetus; bellybutton.

na′vel or′ange, *n.* [*count*] a seedless or nearly seedless orange having a small hollow part at the top that contains a small secondary fruit.

nav•i•ga•ble (nav′i gə bəl) /ˈnævɪgəbəl/ *adj.* **1.** deep and wide enough for ships to pass through: *a navigable river.* **2.** capable of being steered or guided, as a ship, aircraft, or missile. —**nav′i•ga•bil′i•ty,** *n.* [*noncount*] See -NAV-.

nav•i•gate (nav′i gāt′) /ˈnævɪˌgeyt/ *v.,* **-gat•ed, -gat•ing. 1.** to move on, over, or through (water, air, or land) in a ship or aircraft: [~ + *obj*]: *The ship easily navigated the river.* [*no obj*]: *The ship could navigate through the marshes at high tide.* **2.** to direct or manage (a ship, aircraft, spacecraft, etc.) on its course: [~ + *obj*]: *The pilot navigated the plane through the snowstorm.* [*no obj*]: *to navigate in the snow and cold.* **3.** to walk or find one's way on, in, or across: [~ + *obj*]: *It was hard to navigate the stairs in the dark.* [*no obj*]: *Do you think you can navigate through the downtown area safely?* See -NAV-.

nav•i•ga•tion (nav′i gā′shən) /ˌnævɪˈgeyʃən/ *n.* [*noncount*] **1.** the act or process of navigating. **2.** the art or science of directing the course of a ship, aircraft, spacecraft, etc. See -NAV-.

nav•i•ga•tor (nav′i gā′tər) /ˈnævɪˌgeytər/ *n.* [*count*] a person who navigates. See -NAV-.

na•vy (nā′vē) /ˈneyviy/ *n., pl.* **-vies. 1.** [*count*] the warships and supplies used for fighting at sea, belonging to a country or ruler. **2.** [*noncount; often: the* + *Navy*] the complete body of such warships, together with the people, equipment, etc., that make up the sea power of a nation: *joined the Navy.* **3.** [*noncount*] Also, **navy blue.** dark blue in color. See -NAV-.

na′vy bean′, *n.* [*count*] a small, white kidney bean.

nay (nā) /ney/ *adv.* **1.** (used to contrast, correct, and emphasize a statement following another) and not only so but; only that but also; indeed: *She has many good, nay, noble qualities.* —*n.* [*count*] **2.** a denial or refusal. **3.** a negative vote or voter: *The vote is ten nays, one aye.*

nay•say•er (nā′sā′ər) /ˈneyˌseyər/ *n.* [*count*] a person who by habit expresses negative or pessimistic views.

Na•zi (nät′sē, nat′-) /ˈnɑtsiy, ˈnæt-/ *n., pl.* **-zis,** *adj.* —*n.* [*count*] **1.** a member of the German fascist party that controlled Germany from 1933 to 1945 under Adolf Hitler. **2.** [*often: nazi*] a person regarded as fascistic in views or behavior. —*adj.* [*before a noun*] **3.** of or relating to the Nazis. —**Na′zism** (nät′siz əm, nat′-) /ˈnɑtsɪzəm, ˈnæt-/ **Na′zi•ism,** *n.* [*noncount*]

NB or **N.B.,** an abbreviation of Latin *nota bene*: note well (look at this carefully).

N-bomb (en′bom′) /ˈɛnˌbɒm/ *n.* NEUTRON BOMB.

n/c, an abbreviation of: no charge.

NC, an abbreviation of: **1.** no charge. **2.** Also, **N.C.** North Carolina.

NCO, an abbreviation of: noncommissioned officer.

ND or **N.D.,** an abbreviation of: North Dakota.

N.Dak., an abbreviation of: North Dakota.

NE, an abbreviation of: **1.** Nebraska. **2.** New England. **3.** northeast. **4.** northeastern.

n.e., an abbreviation of: **1.** northeast. **2.** northeastern.

Ne•an•der•thal (nē an′dər thôl′, nā än′dər täl′) /niyˈændərˌθɔl, neyˈɑndərˌtɑl/ *adj.* **1.** Also, **Ne•an•der•tal** (nē an′dər tôl′, -täl′) /niyˈændərˌtɔl, -ˌtɑl/. of or relating to a now extinct human people of Europe and Asia who lived from around 100,000 B.C. to 40,000 B.C. **2.** [*often:*

neanderthal] crude; primitive. —*n.* [*count*] **3.** a member of the Neanderthal people. **4.** [*often: neanderthal*] a person of crude or primitive behavior or mode of thought.

neap (nēp) /niyp/ *adj.* **1.** designating those tides, midway between spring tides, that attain the least height. —*n.* [*count*] **2.** neap tide.

near (nēr) /nɪər/ *adv.* and *adj.*, **-er, -est,** *prep., v.* —*adv.* **1.** close in space or time: *Come nearer. The wedding day was drawing near.* **2.** closely with respect to connection or similarity: *a near-fatal accident.* **3.** almost; nearly: *He was near dead from cold.* —*adj.* **4.** being close by in space or time: *the near fields; the near future.* **5.** being the lesser in distance: *the near side of the moon.* **6.** [*before a noun*] closely related or connected, as in a family: *near relatives.* **7.** [*before a noun*](used to describe something that is almost the same as something else, the difference between them being narrow or close): *That was a near miss; the bullets flew just inches over our heads.* —*prep.* [*(~ + to)*] **8.** at, to, or within a short distance from: *regions near (to) the equator.* **9.** close to in time: *Let's meet again near the beginning of the year.* **10.** close to a condition, state, action, or amount; close in relationship: *She came near to hitting him.* —*v.* **11.** to come or draw near; approach: [*~ + obj*]: *The boat neared the dock.* [*no obj*]: *Storm clouds neared.* —***Idiom.*** **12. near at hand, a.** close in space; in the immediate area. **b.** soon; in the near future: *The end was near at hand.* **13. nowhere near,** not nearly: *The car is nowhere near big enough for all of us.* —**near′ness,** *n.* [*noncount*]

near•by (nēr′bī′) /ˈnɪərˈbay/ *adj.* **1.** close at hand; next to; neighboring; adjacent: *This drug can be bought at your nearby pharmacy.* —*adv.* **2.** in the area close by: *The race was held nearby.*

near•ly (nēr′lē) /ˈnɪərliy/ *adv.* **1.** all but; almost: *a plan very nearly like our own.* **2.** not far from: *a nearly perfect likeness.*

near•sight•ed (nēr′sī′tid, -sī′-) /ˈnɪərˌsaytɪd, -ˈsay-/ *adj.* able to see clearly at a short distance only; myopic. —**near′sight′ed•ly,** *adv.* —**near′sight′ed•ness,** *n.* [*noncount*]

neat (nēt) /niyt/ *adj.*, **-er, -est,** *adv.* —*adj.* **1.** in a pleasingly orderly and clean condition: *a neat room.* **2.** having a trim and graceful appearance, shape, style, etc.: *a neat figure.* **3.** cleverly effective; skillful; adroit: *a neat solution to the problem.* **4.** *Slang.* great; wonderful; fine: *What a neat car!* **5.** (of alcoholic drinks) with no ice or water added or any other liquid mixed. —**neat′ly,** *adv.* —**neat′ness,** *n.* [*noncount*]

neath or **'neath** (nēth, nēth) /niyθ, niyð/ *prep. Chiefly Literary.* BENEATH.

Neb., an abbreviation of: Nebraska.

Nebr., an abbreviation of: Nebraska.

neb•u•la (neb′yə lə) /ˈnɛbyələ/ *n.* [*count*], *pl.* **-lae** (-lē′, -lī′) /-ˌliy, -ˌlay/ **-las.** a cloud of gas and dust in outer space between stars. —**neb′u•lar,** *adj.*

neb•u•lous (neb′yə ləs) /ˈnɛbyələs/ *adj.* **1.** hazy, vague, unclear, indistinct, or confused: *his nebulous theories that couldn't easily be explained or defended.* **2.** of or resembling a nebula or nebulae.

-nec-, *root.* -*nec*- comes from Latin, where it has the meaning "tie; weave; bind together." This meaning is found in such words as: ANNEX, CONNECT, DISCONNECT, INTERCONNECT, NEXUS.

nec•es•sar•i•ly (nes′ə sâr′ə lē, -ser′-) /ˌnɛsəˈsɛərəliy, -ˈsɛr-/ *adv.* **1.** by or of necessity: *You don't necessarily have to attend.* **2.** as a necessary or logical result; unavoidably; inevitably: *That conclusion doesn't necessarily follow.*

nec•es•sar•y (nes′ə ser′ē) /ˈnɛsəˌsɛriy/ *adj.* essential; needed; unavoidable: *a small but necessary change in our plans.* [*It + be + ~ + that clause*]: *It is necessary that you stay until the end of the meeting.* [*It + be + ~(+ for + obj) + to + verb*]: *It isn't necessary (for you) to stay.* —**Related Words.** NECESSARY is an adjective, NECESSITY is a noun, NECESSITATE is a verb: *He carried only what was necessary for survival. He carried a few necessities with him. The invasion necessitates a quick response on our part.*

ne•ces•si•tate (nə ses′i tāt′) /nəˈsɛsɪˌteyt/ *v.*, **-tat•ed, -tat•ing.** to make necessary: [*~ + obj*]: *These comments don't necessitate a response.* [*~ + verb-ing*]: *The extra guests necessitated our taking two cars.*

ne•ces•si•ty (nə ses′i tē) /nəˈsɛsɪtiy/ *n., pl.* **-ties. 1.** [*count*] something necessary: *The poor lacked food, shelter, and other necessities of life.* **2.** [*noncount*] the fact of being necessary or needed; indispensability: *the necessity of adequate housing.* **3.** [*count*] requirement; need: *a necessity for a quick decision.* **4.** [*noncount*] an unavoidable need to do something: *not by choice but by necessity.* —***Idiom.*** **5. of necessity,** unavoidably; necessarily: *The report we wrote was of necessity rushed and full of errors.*

neck (nek) /nɛk/ *n.* [*count*] **1.** the part of the body that connects the head and the trunk. **2.** the part of a garment around, partly covering, or closest to the neck; neckline: *a blouse with a low neck.* **3.** a slender part that resembles a neck: *a bottle with a narrow neck; a guitar with a slender neck.* **4.** a narrow strip of land, or a channel for water. —*v.* [*no obj*] **5.** *Informal.* to engage in kissing and caressing. —***Idiom.*** **6. neck and neck,** just even or very close: *The candidates were neck and neck in the polls.* **7. neck of the woods,** neighborhood or surrounding area: *In his neck of the woods he was considered a good salesman.* **8. stick one's neck out,** [*no obj*] *Informal.* to make oneself vulnerable by taking a risk: *willing to stick his neck out if it meant saving his friends.*

neck•er•chief (nek′ər chif, -chēf′) /ˈnɛkərtʃɪf, -ˌtʃiyf/ *n.* [*count*] a cloth worn around the neck.

neck•lace (nek′lis) /ˈnɛklɪs/ *n.* [*count*] a piece of jewelry worn around the neck, as a string of pearls.

neck•line (nek′līn′) /ˈnɛkˌlayn/ *n.* [*count*] the opening at the neck of a garment.

neck•tie (nek′tī′) /ˈnɛkˌtay/ *n.* [*count*] a band of decorative fabric worn around the neck under the collar and knotted in front with the ends hanging down.

nec•ro•man•cy (nek′rə man′sē) /ˈnɛkrəˌmænsiy/ *n.* [*noncount*] magic, esp. evil magic practiced by a witch or sorcerer. —**nec′ro•man′cer,** *n.* [*count*]

ne•crop•o•lis (nə krop′ə lis) /nəˈkrɒpəlɪs/ *n.* [*count*], *pl.* **-lis•es.** a cemetery, esp. one of large size and of an ancient city. See -POLIS-.

ne•cro•sis (nə krō′sis) /nəˈkrowsɪs/ *n.* [*noncount*] death of a certain portion of animal or plant tissue. —**ne•crot•ic** (nə krot′ik) /nəˈkrɒtɪk/ *adj.*

nec•tar (nek′tər) /ˈnɛktər/ *n.* [*noncount*] **1.** the sweet liquid of a plant that attracts the bees, insects, or birds that pollinate the flower. **2.** (in Greek myth) the life-giving drink of the gods. **3.** any delicious drink.

nec•tar•ine (nek′tə rēn′, nek′tə rēn′) /ˌnɛktəˈriyn, ˈnɛktəˌriyn/ *n.* [*count*] a variety of peach having a smooth, shiny skin.

née or **nee** (nā) /ney/ *adj.* (used to introduce the maiden name of a married woman) born with the name of: *Mrs. Jones, née Berg.*

need (nēd) /niyd/ *n., v., auxiliary v., pres. sing. 3rd pers.* **need.** —*n.* **1.** [*count*] a necessary duty or obligation: *There is no need to go there.* **2.** [*count*] a lack of something wanted or necessary: *the needs of the poor.* **3.** [*noncount*] urgent want: *They have need of your charity.* **4.** [*noncount*] a situation or time of difficulty: *to help a friend in need.* **5.** [*noncount*] great or extreme poverty: *The family's need is acute.* —*v.* [*not: be + ~-ing*] **6.** to have need of; require: [*~ + obj*]: *Fish need water.* [*~ + verb-ing*]: *The lawn needed mowing.* [*~ + to + verb*]: *You need to mow the lawn.* [*~ + obj + to + verb*]: *Do you need me to help with the dishes?* —*auxiliary v.* [*~ + root form of a verb*] **7.** [*with a negative word or phrase, or in a question*] (used to express an obligation or necessity of the action of the main verb): *Need I say more? (= Should I say more?). You needn't drive so fast.* —***Idiom.*** **8. if need be,** should the necessity come about: *We'll simply buy more if need be.* —**Related Words.** NEED is a verb and a noun, NEEDY is an adjective: *I need a few good soldiers to volunteer. His needs are simple: food, clothing, and shelter. The organization helps needy people.*

need•ful (nēd′fəl) /ˈniydfəl/ *adj.* necessary or required: *a needful hurry.* [*It + be + ~(+ for + obj) + to + verb*]: *It's needful for us to hurry.*

nee•dle (nēd′l) /ˈniydl/ *n., v.,* **-dled, -dling.** —*n.* [*count*] **1.** a small, rodlike instrument, usually of steel, with a sharp point at one end and a hole for thread at the other end, used for passing thread through cloth to make stitches in sewing. **2.** any of various related, usually larger, instruments for making stitches, as a knitting needle. **3.** *Med.* a hypodermic needle. **4.** any long, thin, pointed object that resembles a needle, as a stylus used in engraving and etching, or a thin leaf of a pine tree. **5. the needle,** [*singular*] *Informal.* teasing remarks: *They gave him the needle after he tripped over his girlfriend's feet while dancing.* —*v.* [*~ + obj*] **6.** to sew or pierce with or as if with a needle. **7.** *Informal.* **a.** to prod or persuade (someone) to a certain action: *We needled her into going with us.* **b.** to tease; make fun of: *His friends needled him about his bad driving.*

nee•dle•point (nēd′l point′) /ˈniydḷˌpɔynt/ *n.* [*noncount*] **1.** embroidery done on canvas. **—*adj.* 2.** done in needlepoint: *a needlepoint cushion.*

need•less (nēd′lis) /ˈniydlɪs/ *adj.* **1.** unnecessary: *a needless waste of food.* **—*Idiom.* 2. needless to say,** (used to emphasize that what is about to be said is clear and obvious): *We played the champions and, needless to say, lost again.* —**need′less•ly,** *adv.* —**need′less•ness,** *n.* [*noncount*]

nee•dle•work (nēd′l wûrk′) /ˈniydḷˌwɜrk/ *n.* [*noncount*] the art, process, or product of working with a needle, esp. in embroidery, needlepoint, sewing, tapestry, quilting, etc.

need•n't (nēd′nt) /ˈniydnt/ a contraction of *need not.*

need•y (nē′dē) /ˈniydiy/ *adj.,* **-i•er, -i•est,** *n.* **—*adj.* 1.** poor; destitute: *donations to help needy families.* **—*n.* 2. the needy,** [*plural*] needy persons thought of as a group. —**need′i•ness,** *n.* [*noncount*]

ne'er (nâr) /nɛər/ *adv. Literary.* never.

ne'er′-do-well′, *n.* [*count*] **1.** an idle, worthless person. **—*adj.* 2.** worthless; good-for-nothing.

ne•far•i•ous (ni fâr′ē əs) /nɪˈfɛəriyəs/ *adj.* extremely wicked, evil, or villainous: *a nefarious plot.* —**ne•far′i•ous•ly,** *adv.* —**ne•far′i•ous•ness,** *n.* [*noncount*]

-neg-, *root.* -*neg*- comes from Latin, where it has the meaning "deny; nothing." This meaning is found in such words as: ABNEGATE, ABNEGATION, NEGATE, NEGATION, NEGATIVE, NEGLECT, NEGLIGEE, NEGLIGENCE, NEGLIGENT, NEGLIGIBLE, RENEGADE, RENEGE.

ne•gate (ni gāt′, neg′āt) /nɪˈgeyt, ˈnɛgeyt/ *v.* [~ + *obj*], **-gat•ed, -gat•ing. 1.** to deny the existence, evidence, or truth of (something): *negated our beliefs.* **2.** to cause to be ineffective or useless: *He negated all attempts to help.* See -NEG-.

ne•ga•tion (ni gā′shən) /nɪˈgeyʃən/ *n.* **1.** the act of denying: [*noncount*]: *shook his head in negation.* [*count*]: *a negation of one's former beliefs.* **2.** [*count; usually singular*] the absence or opposite of something considered positive or affirmative: *Darkness is the negation of light.* **3.** [*count*] a negative statement, idea, concept, doctrine, etc.; a contradiction: *A negation of the statement "It is raining" is the statement "It is not the case that it is raining."* See -NEG-.

neg•a•tive (neg′ə tiv) /ˈnɛgətɪv/ *adj.* **1.** expressing, containing, or suggesting the word "no" or "not;" expressing denial: *a negative response to the question; Negative words in English include* nobody, nor, *and* nothing. **2.** refusing consent or permission: *a negative reply to my request.* **3.** showing an attitude of refusal; unwilling: *a negative attitude about cooperating.* **4.** unfavorable: *negative criticism.* **5.** lacking positive qualities: *a negative advertising campaign.* **6.** being without rewards or results: *A search for drugs proved negative.* **7.** *Math.* **a.** involving or noting subtraction; minus. **b.** measured or proceeding in the direction opposite to positive; less than zero. **8.** *Photography.* being an image in which the lightest areas are shown as the darkest. **9.** of or relating to the electric charge of a body that has more electrons, having lower potential and drawing the flow of current. **10.** *Med.* failing to show a positive result in a diagnostic test: *The test results were negative, which meant that she didn't have the disease.* **—*n.*** [*count*] **11.** a negative statement, answer, word, gesture, etc.: *to answer a request with a negative; Words such as* no, not, nor, *and* nobody *are negatives.* See IN THE NEGATIVE below. **12.** the negative form of a statement: *The negative of the clause* I am running *is* I am not running. **13.** one or more persons arguing against a statement in a formal debate, esp. a team arguing this way. Compare AFFIRMATIVE. **14.** a negative quality or characteristic: *a plan with only one negative.* **15.** *Math.* **a.** a minus sign. **b.** a negative amount or symbol. **16.** *Photography.* a negative image, as on a film, used chiefly for making positives. **—*interj.* 17.** (used often in official situations, to indicate disagreement, denial of permission, etc., esp. as a response); no: *"You won't come with us?" "Negative."* **—*Idiom.* 18. in the negative,** in the form of a negative response: *to answer in the negative.* —**neg′a•tive•ly,** *adv.* —**neg′a•tive•ness, neg•a•tiv•i•ty** (neg′ə tiv′i tē) /ˌnɛgəˈtɪvɪtiy/ *n.* [*noncount*] See -NEG-.

neg•a•tiv•ism (neg′ə ti viz′əm) /ˈnɛgətɪˌvɪzəm/ *n.* [*noncount*] a negative attitude; a way of thinking that expects the worst. See -NEG-.

ne•glect (ni glekt′) /nɪˈglɛkt/ *v.* **1.** [~ + *obj*] to pay no attention or too little attention to: *They neglected their children.* **2.** [~ + *obj*] to fail to give enough care to: *She neglected her health.* **3.** to fail to carry out or perform: [~ + *obj*]: *to neglect the household chores.* [~ + *to* + *verb*]: *He neglected to answer your invitation* **—*n.*** [*noncount*] **4.** an act or instance of neglecting; negligence: *The neglect of the property was shameful.* **5.** the fact or state of being neglected: *a house left in total neglect.* —**ne•glect′ful,** *adj.*: *neglectful of her duties.* —**ne•glect′ful•ly,** *adv.* See -LEG-, -NEG-.

neg•li•gee or **neg•li•gée** (neg′li zhā′, neg′li zhā′) /ˌnɛglɪˈʒey, ˈnɛglɪˌʒey/ *n.* [*count*], *pl.* **-gees** or **-gées.** a woman's loose, sheer dressing gown. See -LEG-, -NEG-.

neg•li•gence (neg′li jəns) /ˈnɛglɪdʒəns/ *n.* [*noncount*] the quality or state of being negligent: *negligence in doing one's duties.* See -LEG-, -NEG-.

neg•li•gent (neg′li jənt) /ˈnɛglɪdʒənt/ *adj.* **1.** guilty of or characterized by neglect, as of duty: *negligent officials.* **2.** careless and indifferent; offhand: *He gave a negligent shrug of unconcern.* —**neg′li•gent•ly,** *adv.* See -LEG-, -NEG-.

neg•li•gi•ble (neg′li jə bəl) /ˈnɛglɪdʒəbəl/ *adj.* so small or unimportant as to be safely disregarded or ignored: *negligible expenses.* See -LEG-, -NEG-.

ne•go•ti•a•ble (ni gō′shē ə bəl, -shə bəl) /nɪˈgowʃiyəbəl, -ʃəbəl/ *adj.* **1.** capable of being discussed, argued about, bargained over, or negotiated: *Most of their demands are not negotiable.* **2.** (esp. of securities) that can be transferred or exchanged for money: *negotiable stocks and bonds.* **3.** that can be easily or safely crossed or traveled on: *negotiable roads.* **—*n.*** [*count*] **4. negotiables,** [*plural*] negotiable securities. —**ne•go•ti•a•bil•i•ty** (ni gō′shē ə bil′i tē, -shə bil′-) /nɪˌgowʃiyəˈbɪlɪtiy, -ʃəˌbɪl-/ *n.* [*noncount*]

ne•go•ti•ate (ni gō′shē āt′) /nɪˈgowʃiyˌeyt/ *v.,* **-at•ed, -at•ing. 1.** to deal, discuss, argue, or bargain with another or others, as in working out the terms of a contract: [*no obj*]: *The union is negotiating with management.* [~ + *obj*]: *to negotiate a better deal.* **2.** [~ + *obj*] to move through, around, or over in an effective, correct, or safe way: *The car had trouble negotiating sharp curves.*

ne•go•ti•a•tion (ni gō′shē ā′shən, -sē-) /nɪˌgowʃiyˈeyʃən, -siy-/ *n.* discussion, argument, or bargaining with others in search of an agreement: [*noncount*]: *The contract is under negotiation.* [*count; usually plural*]: *negotiations to reach a settlement.*

ne•go•ti•a•tor (ni gō′shē ā′tər, -sē-) /nɪˈgowʃiyˌeytər, -siy-/ *n.* [*count*] a person who takes part in negotiations.

Neg•ress (nē′gris) /ˈniygrɪs/ *n.* [*count*] *Usually Offensive.* a black woman or girl.

Neg•ri•tude (neg′ri to͞od′, -tyo͞od′, nē′gri-) /ˈnɛgrɪˌtuwd, -ˌtyuwd, ˈniygrɪ-/ *n.* [*noncount; sometimes: negritude*] pride taken by black people in their historical, cultural, and physical heritage.

Ne•gro (nē′grō) /ˈniygrow/ *adj., n., pl.* **-groes. —*adj.* 1.** characteristic of one of the traditional racial divisions of humankind, the people of which generally have brown to black skin, dark eyes, and woolly or crisp hair; including esp. the peoples who first lived in sub-Saharan Africa. **—*n.*** [*count*] **2.** a member of the peoples traditionally classified as the Negro race. **—Usage.** See BLACK.

Ne•groid (nē′groid) /ˈniygrɔyd/ *adj.* **1.** of, relating to, or characteristic of the people traditionally classified as the Negro race. **—*n.*** [*count*] **2.** a member of such peoples.

neigh (nā) /ney/ *n.* [*count*] **1.** the high-pitched, snorting sound of a horse. **—*v.*** [*no obj*] **2.** to make such a sound.

neigh•bor (nā′bər) /ˈneybər/ *n.* [*count*] **1.** a person who lives near another. **2.** a person or thing that is near or next to another: *Canada, America's neighbor to the North.* **3.** one's fellow human being: *The golden rule asks that we love our neighbors as we love ourselves.* **4.** (once frequently used informally as a term of address, esp. in greeting a stranger): *Howdy, neighbor.* **—*adj.*** [*before a noun*] **5.** located near or living near another: *The two neighbor nations were constantly at war.* **—*v.* 6.** to live or be situated near to; adjoin: [~ + *on* + *obj*]: *The two nations neighbored on each other.* [~ + *obj*]: *They neighbored each other.* Also, *esp. Brit.,* **neigh′bour.**

neigh•bor•hood (nā′bər ho͝od′) /ˈneybərˌhʊd/ *n.* [*count*] **1.** the area or region around or near some place or thing; vicinity: *This is a safe neighborhood.* **2.** a number of persons living in a particular area or place: *The whole neighborhood showed up for the funeral.* **—*adj.*** [*before a noun*] **3.** in, of, located in, or relating to a particular area where people live: *the neighborhood council.* **—*Idiom.* 4. in the neighborhood of,** approximately;

nearly; about: *The job will pay in the neighborhood of six thousand dollars.*

neigh•bor•ing (nā′bər ing) /ˈneybərıŋ/ *adj.* [*before a noun*] near; close to; nearby: *a neighboring village.*

neigh•bor•ly (nā′bər lē) /ˈneybərliy/ *adj.* having or showing qualities of a good neighbor; friendly; helpful to neighbors: *Helping them out was a neighborly thing to do.* —**neigh′bor•li•ness,** *n.* [*noncount*]

nei•ther (nē′thər, nī′-) /ˈniyðər, ˈnay-/ *conj.* **1.** [~ + *phrase* + *nor* + *phrase*] (used before a noun or phrase and combined with the word NOR and another noun or phrase) not either, (in reference to the noun or phrase mentioned): *Neither John nor Betty is at home; both have gone shopping.* **2.** (used after a negative phrase or clause; the subject and verb after it are reversed) nor; nor yet; no more: *He can't be there; neither can I.* —*adj.* [*before a noun*] **3.** not either; not the one or the other: *We'll take neither path; instead, we'll rest under this tree.* —*pron.* [*usually considered singular and used with a singular verb*] **4.** not either; not one person or thing or the other: *Neither is to be trusted. Neither of the keys fits the lock.* —***Idiom.*** **5. neither here nor there,** not important or relevant: *Whether they come is neither here nor there; what matters is that we invite them.* —**Usage.** The expected and strict rule for subject-verb agreement for two nouns joined by NEITHER followed by NOR as a conjunction is that the noun closer to the verb decides the agreement pattern: *Neither the mayor nor the council* ***members are*** *willing to give in on the issue. Neither the council members nor the* ***mayor is*** *willing to give in on the issue.* When NEITHER is used as a pronoun, strict usage demands that the verb following it be singular: *Neither is likely to succeed.*

nel•son (nel′sən) /ˈnɛlsən/ *n.* [*count*] a wrestling hold in which pressure is applied to the head, back of the neck, and one or both arms of the opponent.

nem•e•sis (nem′ə sis) /ˈnɛməsıs/ *n.* [*count*], *pl.* **-ses** (-sēz′) /-ˌsiyz/. **1.** a source or cause of harm or failure: *The driving test was her nemesis; she failed it repeatedly.* **2.** an opponent or rival that cannot be overcome: *That pitcher was our team's nemesis; every time he faced us we lost.* **3.** an agent of punishment for wrongdoing.

neo-, *prefix. neo-* comes from Greek, where it has the meaning "new." It has come to mean "new, recent, revived, changed": *neo-* + *colonialism* → *neocolonialism (= colonialism that has been revived); neo-* + *-lithic* → *neolithic (= of a recent Stone Age).* Also, *esp. before a vowel,* **ne-.**

ne•o•clas•sic (nē′ō klas′ik) /ˌniyowˈklæsık/ also **ne′o•clas′si•cal,** *adj.* of, relating to, or naming revival or slight changing of ancient classical styles, forms, principles, etc., as in art, literature, music, or architecture. —**ne•o•clas•si•cism** (nē′ō klas′ə siz′əm) /ˌniyowˈklæsəˌsızəm/ *n.* [*noncount*]

ne•o•co•lo•ni•al•ism (nē′ō kə lō′nē ə liz′əm) /ˌniyowkəˈlowniyəˌlızəm/ *n.* [*noncount*] a policy by which a nation exerts political and economic control over a less powerful independent nation or region.

Ne•o•lith•ic (nē′ə lith′ik) /ˌniyəˈlıθık/ *adj.* [*often: neolithic*] of, naming, or characteristic of the last phase of the Stone Age, commonly thought to have begun c9000–8000 B.C. in the Middle East, when people used stone tools and began to form villages and raise crops. Compare MESOLITHIC, PALEOLITHIC. See -LITH-.

ne•ol•o•gism (nē ol′ə jiz′əm) /niyˈɒləˌdʒızəm/ *n.* [*count*] a new word or phrase or an existing word used in a new sense: *Some neologisms have entered the language from computers, such as the word* mouse *meaning "pointing device."* See -LOG-.

ne•on (nē′on) /ˈniyɒn/ *n.* [*noncount*] **1.** a colorless, odorless gas used in a type of electrical lamp. **2.** a sign or advertising sign formed from a type of electrical lamp containing neon: *His name was in neon everywhere in the theater district.*

ne•o•nate (nē′ə nāt′) /ˈniyəˌneyt/ *n.* [*count*] a newborn child, or one in its first 28 days. —**ne•o•na•tal** (nē′ə-nāt′l) /ˌniyəˈneytḷ/ *adj.*: *neonatal care.* See -NAT-.

ne•o•phyte (nē′ə fīt′) /ˈniyəˌfayt/ *n.* [*count*] someone just learning an activity, occupation, etc.: *She was a neophyte in politics.*

ne•o•plasm (nē′ə plaz′əm) /ˈniyəˌplæzəm/ *n.* [*count*] a new growth of abnormal tissue; tumor.

neph•ew (nef′yo͞o) /ˈnɛfyuw/ *n.* [*count*] **1.** a son of one's brother or sister. **2.** a son of one's spouse's brother or sister.

ne•phri•tis (nə frī′tis) /nəˈfraytıs/ *n.* [*noncount*] disease of the kidneys. —**ne•phrit′ic** (nə frit′ik) /nəˈfrıtık/ *adj.*

nep•o•tism (nep′ə tiz′əm) /ˈnɛpəˌtızəm/ *n.* [*noncount*] favoritism based on family relationship: *He was accused of nepotism when he hired his daughter as vice president.* —**nep′o•tist,** *n.* [*count*]

nerd (nûrd) /nɜrd/ *n.* [*count*] *Slang.* a socially backward person, esp. one preoccupied with intellectual matters or with technology: *a computer nerd.* —**nerd′y,** *adj.*, **-i•er, -i•est:** *She thought the boy's glasses were nerdy.*

nerve (nûrv) /nɜrv/ *n.*, *v.*, **nerved, nerv•ing.** —*n.* **1.** [*count*] one or more bundles of long, thin fibers forming part of a system that carries messages of feeling, motion, etc., between the brain or spinal cord and other parts of the body. **2.** [*noncount*] courage under difficult circumstances: *It took nerve to enter the burning building.* **3.** [*noncount*] boldness; impudent behavior: *You have a lot of nerve, insulting us like that.* **4. nerves,** [*plural*] nervousness: *a bad attack of nerves.* **5. nerves,** [*plural*] ability to remain calm: *The noise of the battle had left his nerves shot.* —*v.* [~ + *obj*] **6.** to give strength, life, or courage to: *He nerved himself for the attack.* —***Idiom.*** **7. get on someone's nerves,** to irritate or annoy someone. —**Related Words.** NERVE is a noun, NERVOUS and NERVY are adjectives: *You have a lot of nerve. He was nervous before the test. That was a nervy thing to say to your parents.*

nerve′ cell′, *n.* NEURON.

nerve′ cen′ter, *n.* [*count*] a source of information, control, or activity: *City hall was the nerve center of the town.*

nerve′ gas′, *n.* [*noncount*] a poison gas that interferes with the sending and receiving of nerve messages and with breathing, used as a chemical weapon.

nerve•less (nûrv′lis) /ˈnɜrvlıs/ *adj.* **1.** without nervousness; calm: *She stood nerveless and unafraid.* **2.** lacking strength, feeling, or power; weak: *nerveless limbs that no longer supported him.* **3.** lacking courage. —**nerve′-less•ly,** *adv.* —**nerve′less•ness,** *n.* [*noncount*]

nerve′-rack′ing or **nerve′-wrack′ing,** *adj.* producing great anxiety, tension, or irritation: *Driving with him was a nerve-racking experience.* [*It* + *be* + ~ + *to* + *verb*]: *It was nerve-racking to wait for the news.*

nerv•ous (nûr′vəs) /ˈnɜrvəs/ *adj.* **1.** [*be* + ~] very uneasy or apprehensive; fearful; timid: *He's very nervous about the results of the election.* **2.** highly excitable or upset; jumpy: *a nervous crowd.* **3.** [*before a noun*] of, relating to, or affecting the nerves: *a nervous disease.* **4.** [*before a noun*] suffering from, characterized by, or coming from a condition of disordered nerves that affects one's thinking or emotional state: *been under a nervous strain.* **5.** [*before a noun*] bringing, caused by, or having sharp uneasiness or worry: *a nervous moment of anticipation.* —**nerv′ous•ly,** *adv.* —**nerv′ous•ness,** *n.* [*noncount*]

nerv′ous break′down, *n.* [*count*] a severe but unspecific mental or emotional disorder.

nerv′ous sys′tem, *n.* [*count*] the system of nerve cells, chemicals, and structures that work to receive messages from outside the body, and in sending messages that result in movement and other responses, including the brain, spinal cord, and nerves.

nerv•y (nûr′vē) /ˈnɜrviy/ *adj.*, **-i•er, -i•est. 1.** brash; pushy: *a nervy request for a free ticket.* **2.** having or showing courage. —**nerv•i•ly** (nûr′və lē) /ˈnɜrvəliy/ *adv.* —**nerv′i•ness,** *n.* [*noncount*]

-ness, *suffix. -ness* is attached to adjectives and verbs ending in *-ing* or *-ed/-en* to form nouns that refer to the quality or state of the adjective or verb: *dark* + *-ness* → *darkness; prepared* + *-ness* → *preparedness (= a state of being prepared).*

nest (nest) /nɛst/ *n.* [*count*] **1.** a bowl-shaped or pocket-like structure, often of twigs, grasses, and mud, prepared by a bird for holding eggs until they hatch and for caring for young. **2.** any structure or shelter used for keeping eggs and raising young: *a wasps' nest.* **3.** a snug retreat; refuge. **4.** a set of items that fit close together or one within another: *a nest of tables.* **5.** a place where something bad is kept or grows: *a nest of thieves.* —*v.* **6.** [*no obj*] to build or have a nest: *Many birds nest in trees.* **7.** to fit together or one within another: [*no obj*]: *The plastic bowls nest for storage.* [~ + *obj*]: *You can nest one bowl within another.*

nest′ egg′, *n.* [*count*] money saved and held as a reserve for emergencies, retirement, etc.

nes•tle (nes′əl) /ˈnɛsəl/ *v.*, **-tled, -tling. 1.** to lie close and snug; snuggle; cuddle: [*no obj*]: *They were nestling in bed.* [~ + *obj*]: *She nestled herself in the chair.* **2.** [*no* *obj*] to be located in a sheltered spot: *a cottage nestling in a grove of leafy trees.*

nest•ling (nest′ling, nes′ling) /ˈnɛstlɪŋ, ˈnɛslɪŋ/ *n.* [*count*] **1.** a bird too young to leave the nest. **2.** a young child or infant.

net[1] (net) /nɛt/ *n., v.,* **net•ted, net•ting.** —*n.* **1.** [*noncount*] a fabric made up of evenly sized open mesh: *curtains of net.* **2.** [*count*] a bag or other piece of such meshed fabric, for catching fish or other animals: *a butterfly net.* **3.** [*count*] a piece of net designed for another specific purpose, as to divide a court in racket games, or to protect against insects. **4.** [*count*] the goal in hockey or soccer. **5.** [*count*] a computer or telecommunications network. —*v.* [~ + *obj*] **6.** to take with a net: *to net fish.* **7.** to catch: *The police netted one of the criminals trying to escape.* **8.** (in racket games) to hit (the ball) into the net.

net[2] (net) /nɛt/ *adj., n., v.,* **net•ted, net•ting.** —*adj.* **1.** (of an amount of money) remaining after nothing further needs to be subtracted or allowed for (opposed to *gross*): [*before a noun*]: *net price; net earnings.* [*after a noun*]: *earned $200 net.* **2.** [*before a noun*] final; ultimate; after all events have taken place: *a net result.* **3.** (of weight) after deducting the amount of weight for the container or wrapping: [*before a noun*]: *The net weight is six grams.* [*after a noun*]: *weighs six grams net.* —*n.* [*count; usually singular*] **4.** net income, profit, etc. (opposed to *gross*): *What's your net after taxes?* —*v.* [~ + *obj*] **5.** to gain or produce as clear profit: *netted over $150 million.*

neth•er (neth′ər) /ˈnɛðər/ *adj.* [*before a noun*] **1.** lying beneath the earth's surface: *the nether regions.* **2.** lower or under: *his nether lip.*

Neth•er•land•er (neth′ər lan′dər, -lən-) /ˈnɛθərˌlændər, -lən-/ *n.* [*count*] a person born or living in the Netherlands.

neth•er•most (neth′ər mōst′, -məst) /ˈnɛðərˌmowst, -məst/ *adj.* lowest; farthest down.

net•ting (net′ing) /ˈnɛtɪŋ/ *n.* [*noncount*] net fabric.

net•tle (net′l) /ˈnɛtl̩/ *n., v.,* **-tled, -tling.** —*n.* [*count*] **1.** a plant covered with stinging hairs. —*v.* [~ + *obj*] **2.** to irritate; annoy: *nettled by the criticisms.*

net•tle•some (net′l səm) /ˈnɛtl̩səm/ *adj.* causing irritation or annoyance: *nettlesome problems.*

net•work (net′wûrk′) /ˈnɛtˌwɜrk/ *n.* [*count*] **1.** any combination of interconnecting pieces, strings, lines, passages, etc.: *a network of veins.* **2. a.** a group of radio or television stations linked by wire or microwaves. **b.** a company or organization that provides the programs for these stations. **3.** any system or group of interrelated or interconnected elements esp. over a large area: *a network of supply depots.* **4.** a computer or telecommunications system linked to permit exchange of information. **5.** an association of individuals having a common interest and often providing mutual assistance, information, etc. —*v.* **6.** [*no obj*] to engage in networking, so as to advance, esp. one's career. **7.** [~ + *obj*] to link (computers) in a network. —**net′work′er,** *n.* [*count*]

net•work•ing (net′wûr′king) /ˈnɛtˌwɜrkɪŋ/ *n.* [*noncount*] **1.** the informal sharing of information and services among individuals or groups that have a common interest. **2.** the design, establishment, or use of a computer network.

neu•ral (no͝or′əl, nyo͝or′-) /ˈnʊrəl, ˈnyʊr-/ *adj.* [*before a noun*] of or relating to a nerve or the nervous system: *neural connections.* —**neu′ral•ly,** *adv.*

neu•ral•gia (no͝o ral′jə, nyo͝o-) /nʊˈrældʒə, nyʊ-/ *n.* [*noncount*] sharp pain along the length of a nerve. —**neu•ral′gic,** *adj.* See -ALG-.

neur•as•the•ni•a (no͝or′əs thē′nē ə, nyo͝or′-) /ˌnʊrəsˈθiyniyə, ˌnyʊr-/ *n.* [*noncount*] a pattern of fatigue, sleep disturbances, and long-lasting aches, often linked with depression. —**neur•as•then•ic** (no͝o′əs then′ik, nyo͝or′-) /ˌnʊəsˈθɛnɪk, ˌnyʊr-/ *adj.*

neu•ri•tis (no͝o ri′tis, nyo͝o-) /nʊˈraytɪs, nyʊ-/ *n.* [*noncount*] a nerve disorder, often marked by pain, numbness or tingling, or paralysis. —**neu•rit•ic** (no͝o rit′ik, nyo͝o-) /nʊˈrɪtɪk, nyʊ-/ *adj.*

neuro-, *prefix. neuro-* comes fom Greek, where it has the meaning "nerve, nerves." Its meaning now includes "nervous system," and this meaning is found in such words as: *neurology, neurotic.*

neu•rol•o•gy (no͝o rol′ə jē, nyo͝o-) /nʊˈrɒlədʒiy, nyʊ-/ *n.* [*noncount*] the branch of medicine dealing with the nervous system. —**neu•ro•log•i•cal** (no͝or ə loj′i kəl, nyo͝or-) /nʊrəˈlɒdʒɪkəl, nyʊr-/ *adj.* —**neu′ro•log′i•cal•ly,** *adv.* —**neu•rol′o•gist,** *n.* [*count*]

neu•ron (no͝or′on, nyo͝or′-) /ˈnʊrɒn, ˈnyʊr-/ *n.* [*count*] a special cell in the body that is capable of sending along messages that represent feelings, commands to muscles, etc. Also called **nerve cell.** Also, *esp. Brit.,* **neu•rone** (no͝or′ōn, nyo͝or′-) /ˈnʊrown, ˈnyʊr-/. —**neu•ron•al** (no͝or′ə nl, nyo͝or′-, no͝o rōn′l, nyo͝o-) /ˈnʊrənl̩, ˈnyʊr-, nʊˈrownl̩, nyʊ-/ *adj.*

neu•ro•sis (no͝o rō′sis, nyo͝o-) /nʊˈrowsɪs, nyʊ-/ *n.* [*count*], *pl.* **-ses** (-sēz) /-siyz/. a disorder of the mind in which feelings of anxiety, fears, obsessions, etc., may occur in various degrees and patterns and control the personality.

neu•rot•ic (no͝o rot′ik, nyo͝o-) /nʊˈrɒtɪk, nyʊ-/ *adj.* **1.** of, relating to, or showing the characteristics of neurosis: *a neurotic personality.* —*n.* [*count*] **2.** a neurotic person. —**neu•rot′ic•al•ly,** *adv.* —**neu•rot•i•cism** (no͝o rot′ə siz′əm, nyo͝o-) /nʊˈrɒtəˌsɪzəm, nyʊ-/ *n.* [*noncount*]

neu•ter (no͞o′tər, nyo͞o′-) /ˈnuwtər, ˈnyuw-/ *adj.* **1.** of, relating to, or being a grammatical gender that refers to things classed as neither masculine nor feminine: *In Latin nouns may be masculine, feminine, or neuter in gender.* **2.** *Biology.* having no or imperfectly developed organs of reproduction: *Worker bees are neuter.* —*n.* **3. a.** [*noncount*] the neuter gender. **b.** [*count*] a word or other linguistic form in or marking the neuter gender. **4.** [*count*] an animal made sterile by having its organs of reproduction removed or altered. —*v.* [~ + *obj*] **5.** to remove the organs of reproduction of (a dog, cat, etc.).

neu•tral (no͞o′trəl, nyo͞o′-) /ˈnuwtrəl, ˈnyuw-/ *adj.* **1.** not taking part or giving assistance in a disagreement, dispute, or war between others: *a neutral nation.* **2.** of no particular kind, characteristics, etc.: *a neutral personality.* **3.** (of a color or shade) having no hue; being black, gray, beige, or white in color. **4.** (of particles) having no electric charge. **5.** being in the position or state of not being attached to wheels or of not providing moving power to another part: *the neutral gear in a car's transmission.* —*n.* **6.** [*count*] a person or nation that is neutral: *Sweden was a neutral during World War II.* **7.** [*noncount*] a neutral gear. **8.** [*count*] a neutral color. —**neu′tral•ly,** *adv.*

neu•tral•i•ty (no͞o tral′i tē, nyo͞o-) /nuwˈtrælɪtiy, nyuw-/ *n.* [*noncount*] **1.** the state of being neutral. **2.** the policy or status of a nation that remains neutral in a dispute.

neu•tral•ize (no͞o′trə līz′, nyo͞o′-) /ˈnuwtrəˌlayz, ˈnyuw-/ *v.* [~ + *obj*], **-ized, -iz•ing.** **1.** to make neutral. **2.** to make (something) have no or little effect; counteract; nullify: *His campaign team tried to neutralize the bad effects of the debate.* —**neu•tral•i•za•tion** (no͞o′trə li zā′shən, nyo͞o′-) /ˌnuwtrəlɪˈzeyʃən, ˌnyʊ-/ *n.* [*noncount*] —**neu′tral•iz′er,** *n.* [*count*]

neu•tri•no (no͞o trē′nō, nyo͞o-) /nuwˈtriynow, nyuw-/ *n.* [*count*], *pl.* **-nos.** a subatomic particle with no mass or very little mass, that is electrically neutral.

neu•tron (no͞o′tron, nyo͞o′-) /ˈnuwtrɒn, ˈnyuw-/ *n.* [*count*] a particle found in the nucleus of most atoms, having no charge, and a mass slightly greater than that of a proton.

neu′tron bomb′, *n.* [*count*] a nuclear weapon designed to release a powerful burst of neutrons and gamma rays, with a weaker blast wave than other nuclear bombs.

Nev., an abbreviation of: Nevada.

nev•er (nev′ər) /ˈnɛvər/ *adv.* **1.** not ever; at no time; not at any time: *It never happened. He never knew what hit him.* **2.** not at all; absolutely not: *This will never do.* —***Idiom.*** **3. never mind,** don't bother; don't concern yourself: *Never mind about your mistake.*

nev•er•more (nev′ər môr′, -mōr′) /ˌnɛvərˈmɔr, -ˈmowr/ *adv.* never again.

nev′er-nev′er land′, *n.* [*noncount*] an unreal, imaginary, or ideal state, condition, place, etc.

nev•er•the•less (nev′ər thə les′) /ˌnɛvərðəˈlɛs/ *adv.* nonetheless; notwithstanding; however; in spite of that: *a small but nevertheless important improvement.*

new (no͞o, nyo͞o) /nuw, nyuw/ *adj.,* **-er, -est,** *adv., n.* —*adj.* **1.** of recent creation, production, purchase, etc.: *a new book.* **2.** [*before a noun*] of a kind now existing or appearing for the first time; novel: *a new concept of the universe.* **3.** [*before a noun*] having only lately become known, discovered, or invented: *discovered a new comet.* **4.** different from what one has had or seen: *The spacecraft explored new planetary worlds.* **5.** [*before a noun*] having lately or recently come to a place, position, status, etc.: *a new baby.* **6.** [*be* + ~ + *to*] unaccustomed; just learning or beginning to know about: *He was new to the job.* **7.** [*before a noun*] further; additional: *new gains.* **8.** [*before a noun*] fresh or unused: *a new sheet of paper.* **9.** [*before a noun*] improved in physical or moral quality: *Exercise made a new man of him.* **10.** [*before a noun*] other than the former or the old: *the beginning of a new era in politics.* **11.** [*New*] (of a language) in its latest known period, esp. as a living language at the present time: *New High German.* **—***adv.* **12.** (used with an adjective or participle of a verb) recently; freshly: *a new-found friend (= a friend who has recently been found).* **—***n.* [*noncount*] **13.** something that is new: *Ring out the old, ring in the new.* —**new′ness,** *n.* [*noncount*]

New′ Age′, *adj.* **1.** of or relating to a movement with a broad range of philosophies and practices having mysterious, occult, or paranormal aspects. **2.** of or relating to a mild, easygoing style of instrumental music drawing on classical music, jazz, and rock. **—***n.* [*noncount*] **3.** New Age movement or music.

new•born (no͞o′bôrn′, nyo͞o′-) /'nuw'bɔrn, 'nyuw-/ *adj., n., pl.* **-born, -borns. —***adj.* **1.** recently or only just born. **—***n.* [*count*] **2.** a newborn infant.

new•com•er (no͞o′kum′ər, nyo͞o′-) /'nuw,kʌmər, 'nyuw-/ *n.* [*count*] a person or thing that has recently arrived; new arrival.

new•fan•gled (no͞o′fang′gəld, -fang′-, nyo͞o′-) /'nuw'fæŋgəld, -,fæŋ-, 'nyuw-/ *adj.* of a new kind or fashion: *a newfangled contraption for peeling vegetables.*

new′-fash′ioned, *adj.* **1.** made in a new style, fashion, etc. **2.** up-to-date; modern.

new•ly (no͞o′lē, nyo͞o′-) /'nuwliy, 'nyuw-/ *adv.* [*often: before the -ed/-en form of a verb*] recently; lately: *a newly arrived professor; the newly risen moon.*

new•ly•wed (no͞o′lē wed′, nyo͞o′-) /'nuwliy,wɛd, 'nyuw-/ *n.* [*count*] a person who has recently married.

new′ moon′, *n.* [*count; usually singular*] the moon when it is almost invisible or visible only as a slender crescent.

news (no͞oz, nyo͞oz) /nuwz, nyuwz/ *n.* [*noncount; used with a singular verb*] **1.** a report of a recent event; information: *to hear news of a relative.* **2.** [*the* + ~] a report on recent or new events in a newspaper or magazine, or on radio or television: *the six o'clock news.* **3.** such reports thought of as a group: *good at his job of gathering news.* **4.** a person, event, etc., thought of as worth reporting: *This scandal is news.*

news•boy (no͞oz′boi′, nyo͞oz′-) /'nuwz,bɔy, 'nyuwz-/ *n.* [*count*] a person, typically a boy, who sells or delivers newspapers.

news•cast (no͞oz′kast′, nyo͞oz′-) /'nuwz,kæst, 'nyuwz-/ *n.* [*count*] a broadcast of news on radio or television. —**news′cast′er,** *n.* [*count*]

news•let•ter (no͞oz′let′ər, nyo͞oz′-) /'nuwz,lɛtər, 'nyuwz-/ *n.* [*count*] a printed report, usually issued at regular times by an organization or agency to present information to employees, contributors, stockholders, or the public.

news•man (no͞oz′man′, -mən, nyo͞oz′-) /'nuwz,mæn, -mən, 'nyuwz-/ *n.* [*count*], *pl.* **-men.** a person whose work is to gather and report news; a reporter or correspondent.

news•pa•per (no͞oz′pā′pər, nyo͞oz′-, no͞os′-, nyo͞os′-) /'nuwz,peypər, 'nyuwz-, 'nuws-, 'nyuws-/ *n.* **1.** [*count*] a publication, usually issued daily or weekly and containing news, comments on the news, features, and advertising. See illustration at SCHOOL. **2.** [*count*] a business organization that prints and distributes such a publication. **3.** [*count*] a single issue of such a publication: *bought today's newspaper.* **4.** [*noncount*] the paper on which a newspaper is printed: *wrapped the fish in newspaper.*

news′pa′per•man′ or **-wom′an,** *n.* [*count*], *pl.* **-men** or **-wom•en.** **1.** a person working for a newspaper or wire service as a reporter, writer, or editor. **2.** the owner or operator of a newspaper or news service.

new•speak (no͞o′spēk′, nyo͞o′-) /'nuw,spiyk, 'nyuw-/ *n.* [*noncount; sometimes: Newspeak*] a style of language using ambiguity, false or confusing statements, and contradictions: *Newspeak was invented by the writer George Orwell in his novel* 1984.

news•print (no͞oz′print′, nyo͞oz′-) /'nuwz,prɪnt, 'nyuwz-/ *n.* [*noncount*] paper made mainly from wood pulp and used chiefly for newspapers.

news•reel (no͞oz′rēl′, nyo͞oz′-) /'nuwz,riyl, 'nyuwz-/ *n.* [*count*] a short motion picture giving recent news.

news•stand (no͞oz′stand′, nyo͞oz′-) /'nuwz,stænd, 'nyuwz-/ *n.* [*count*] a stall or other place at which newspapers, often magazines, and sometimes candy and other items are sold. See illustration at TERMINAL.

news•wor•thy (no͞oz′wûr′t͟hē, nyo͞oz′-) /'nuwz,wɜrðiy, 'nyuwz-/ *adj.* of enough interest to be presented as news: *a newsworthy event.* —**news′wor′thi•ness,** *n.* [*noncount*]

news•y (no͞o′zē, nyo͞o′-) /'nuwziy, 'nyuw-/ *adj.,* **-i•er, -i•est.** full of news: *wrote a long, newsy letter.*

newt (no͞ot, nyo͞ot) /nuwt, nyuwt/ *n.* [*count*] a brightly colored salamander that can live on land and in water.

New′ Tes′tament, *n.* [*proper noun; often: the* + ~] the collection of the books of the Christian Bible, focusing on the life and teachings of Jesus Christ and his disciples.

new′ wave′, *n.* [*count*] **1.** a movement, esp. in art, literature, or politics, that breaks with traditional values, techniques, or the like. **2.** [*often: New Wave*] **a.** a movement in filmmaking that started in France in the 1950's. **b.** the members of this movement.

new′ year′, *n.* **1.** [*count; singular; usually: the* + ~] the year approaching or newly begun. **2.** [*noncount; New Year*] **a.** NEW YEAR'S DAY. **b.** the first few days of any year. **c.** ROSH HASHANAH.

New′ Year's′ Day′, *n.* [*proper noun; no article*] January 1, a day celebrated as a holiday in many countries.

New′ Year's′ Eve′, *n.* [*proper noun; no article*] the night of December 31.

New Zea•land•er (no͞o′ zē′lənd ər, nyo͞o′) /,nuw ,ziyləndər, ,nyuw/ *n.* [*count*] a person born or living in New Zealand.

next (nekst) /nɛkst/ *adj.* **1.** immediately following in time, order, importance, etc.: *the next day; the next flight for the Bahamas.* **2.** [*before a noun; usually: the* + ~] nearest or closest in place or position: *She lived in the next house over.* **—***adv.* **3.** in the place, time, order, etc., nearest or immediately following: *We're going to London next.* **4.** on the first occasion to follow: *When next we meet.* **5.** [*before an adjective*] having more (of some quality) than all others except one: *If we can't go swimming, the next best thing would be to walk on the beach.* **—*Idiom.* 6. next door to,** close to or near to another; adjacent to: *She lived next door to us for five years.* **7. next to, a.** near or close to: *Sit next to me.* **b.** almost; nearly: *Climbing that mountain was next to impossible.* **c.** aside from: *Next to me, you're the best.*

next-door (*adv.* neks′dôr′, -dōr′, nekst′-; *adj.* -dôr′, -dōr′) / *adv.* 'nɛks'dɔr, -'dowr, 'nɛkst-; *adj.* -,dɔr, -,dowr/ *adv.* **1.** Also, **next′ door′.** to, at, or in the next house, building, apartment, etc.: *They live next door.* **—***adj.* [*before a noun*] **2.** located or living in the next house, building, apartment, etc.: *next-door neighbors.*

next′ of kin′, *n.* [*count*], *pl.* **next of kin.** the person who is most closely related to another.

nex•us (nek′səs) /'nɛksəs/ *n.* [*count*], *pl.* **nex•us.** a means of connection; a tie or link. See -NEC-.

NH or **N.H.,** an abbreviation of: New Hampshire.

nib (nib) /nɪb/ *n.* [*count*] **1.** the point of a pen **2.** any pointed end.

nib•ble (nib′əl) /'nɪbəl/ *v.,* **-bled, -bling,** *n.* **—***v.* **1.** to bite off; eat or chew in small bits (of): [*no obj*]: *to nibble on a cracker.* [~ + *obj*]: *nibbling a cracker.* **2.** to bite lightly or gently: [*no obj*]: *The puppy nibbled at his ear.* [~ + *obj*]: *She nibbled his ear.* **3. nibble (away) at,** [~ + *obj*] to cause to decrease or become less bit by bit: *Tax increases are nibbling away at our profits.* **—***n.* [*count*] **4.** a small piece bitten off; a morsel or bite. **5.** an act or instance of nibbling. **6.** a response by a fish to bait on a fishing line: *I thought I felt a nibble.* **7.** a show of interest that is not definite: *We had the house up for sale for months before we got a nibble from a possible buyer.* —**nib′bler,** *n.* [*count*]

nibs (nibz) /nɪbz/ *n.* **his** or **her nibs,** [*used as a title; no article*] *Informal.* a person in authority, esp. one who is self-important: *Will you be seeing her nibs today?*

Nic•a•ra•guan (nik′ə räg′wən) /,nɪkə'rɑgwən/ *n.* [*count*] **1.** a person born or living in Nicaragua. **—***adj.* **2.** of or relating to Nicaragua.

nice (nīs) /nays/ *adj.,* **nic•er, nic•est. 1.** pleasing; agreeable; delightful: *We had a nice visit.* [*It* + *be* + ~ + *to* + *verb*]: *It was so nice to see you again.* **2.** [*be* + ~ (+ *to*)] kind; thoughtful: *Be nice to guests.* **3.** requiring or showing great skill, care, or tact: *a nice handling of a crisis.* **4.** fine; subtle: *a nice distinction.* **5.** refined; discriminating: *a nice sense of color.* **—*Idiom.* 6. nice and,** (used with an adjective to express stronger sufficiency, pleasure, comfort, or the like): *It's nice and warm in here.* —**nice′ness,** *n.* [*noncount*]

nice•ly (nis′lē) /'naysliy/ *adv.* **1.** in a pleasing, agreeable, or delightful way: *behaved nicely.* **2.** correctly; properly: *Five dollars should do quite nicely for a tip for the waiter.*

ni•ce•ty (ni′si tē) /'naysɪtiy/ *n., pl.* **-ties. 1.** [*count*] a delicate or fine point; a detail or subtlety: *observing the* *niceties of polite behavior.* **2.** [*noncount*] exactness or preciseness, as in workmanship; detail. **3.** Usually, **niceties.** [*plural*] fine things: *enjoying the niceties of life.*

niche (nich) /nɪtʃ/ *n.* [*count*] **1.** a recess in a wall or the like, usually in the shape of a half circle with an arch, as for a statue or other decorative object. **2.** a suitable place or position: *trying to find his niche in the world.*

nick (nik) /nɪk/ *n.* [*count*] **1.** a small notch, groove, chip, or the like: *some nicks on the car door.* **2.** a small dent or wound: *a couple of nicks on his face from shaving.* —*v.* [~ + *obj*] **3.** to cut into or through: *He nicked his face shaving.* **4.** to make a nick in (something); notch: *The rocks must have nicked the car door.* **5.** *Brit. Slang.* **a.** to arrest (a criminal or suspect). **b.** to steal. —***Idiom.*** **6. in the nick of time,** at the right moment and no sooner; at the last possible moment: *arrived in the nick of time.*

nick•el (nik′əl) /ˈnɪkəl/ *n.* **1.** [*noncount*] a hard, silvery white metallic element, used in combinations of metals. **2.** [*count*] a coin of the U.S., equal to five cents. —*adj.* [*before a noun*] **3.** *Slang.* costing five dollars: *a nickel bag of heroin.*

nick•name (nik′nām′) /ˈnɪkˌneym/ *n., v.,* **-named, -nam•ing.** —*n.* [*count*] **1.** a descriptive name added to or used in place of the proper name of a person, place, etc.: *Abraham Lincoln's nickname was Honest Abe.* **2.** a familiar, informal form of a proper name, as *Jim* for *James* and *Peg* for *Margaret.* —*v.* [~ + *obj* + *obj*] **3.** to give a nickname to; call by a nickname: *He was nicknamed Honest Abe.*

nic•o•tine (nik′ə tēn′, -tin, nik′ə tēn′) /ˈnɪkəˌtiyn, -tɪn, ˌnɪkəˈtiyn/ *n.* [*noncount*] a colorless, oily, poisonous toxic liquid substance, found in tobacco.

niece (nēs) /niys/ *n.* [*count*] **1.** a daughter of one's brother or sister. **2.** a daughter of one's spouse's brother or sister.

nif•ty (nif′tē) /ˈnɪftiy/ *adj.,* **-ti•er, -ti•est.** *Informal.* **1.** very good; fine; excellent: *a nifty idea.* **2.** attractively stylish or smart: *a nifty new suit.*

Ni•ge•ri•an (nī jēr′ē ən) /nayˈdʒɪəriyən/ *adj.* **1.** of or relating to Nigeria. —*n.* [*count*] **2.** a person born or living in Nigeria.

nig•gard•ly (nig′ərd lē) /ˈnɪgərdliy/ *adj.* very stingy: *a niggardly donation.* —**nig′gard•li•ness,** *n.* [*noncount*]

nig•ger (nig′ər) /ˈnɪgər/ *n.* [*count*] *Disparaging and Offensive.* **1.** a black person. **2.** a member of any dark-skinned people.

nig•gle (nig′əl) /ˈnɪgəl/ *v.* [*no obj*], **-gled, -gling. 1.** to spend too much time on trivial things: *to niggle over every detail in a contract.* **2.** to cause worry: *Something was niggling at the back of her mind.*

nig•gling (nig′ling) /ˈnɪglɪŋ/ *adj.* **1.** not important; petty: *niggling doubts.* **2.** demanding too much care, time, attention, etc.: *a thousand niggling details.*

nigh (nī) /nay/ *adv., adj.,* **-er, -est,** *prep.* —*adv.* **1.** near in space, time, or relation: *The ship drew nigh to the dock.* **2.** nearly; almost: *arrived nigh onto midnight.* —*adj.* **3.** near; approaching. —*prep.* **4.** near: *She's nigh fifty now.*

night (nīt) /nayt/ *n.* **1.** the period of darkness between sunset and sunrise: [*count*]: *cold winter nights.* [*noncount*]: *can't see well at night.* **2.** [*count*] the earlier part of this period: *We had a night of theater and dinner.* **3.** [*noncount*] the darkness of this time; the dark: *Night is falling.* **4.** [*noncount*] a condition or time of ignorance, sinfulness, misfortune, etc.: *the black night of despair.* **5.** [*count*] an evening used or set aside for a particular event or purpose: *It was the Junior Prom night.* —*adj.* [*before a noun*] **6.** of, relating to, occurring, or used at night: *the night hours; a night vision scope.* **7.** active or working at night: *night watchmen.* —***Idiom.*** **8. night and day,** without stopping; continually: *worked night and day on the problem.*

night′ blind′ness, *n.* [*noncount*] a condition in which vision is less acute in dim light.

night•cap (nīt′kap′) /ˈnaytˌkæp/ *n.* [*count*] **1.** an alcoholic drink taken at the end of the day. **2.** a cap for the head, intended to be worn in bed. **3.** *Informal.* the last of a day's sports events, esp. the second game of a doubleheader in baseball.

night•clothes (nīt′klōz′, -klōt͟hz′) /ˈnaytˌklowz, -ˌklowðz/ *n.* [*plural*] clothes for wearing in bed, as pajamas.

night•club (nīt′klub′) /ˈnaytˌklʌb/ *n., v.,* **-clubbed, -club•bing.** —*n.* [*count*] **1.** Also, **night′ club′.** an establishment open at night, offering food, drink, floor shows, dancing, etc. —*v.* [*no obj*] **2.** to visit nightclubs.

night′ crawl′er, *n.* [*count*] a large earthworm that comes to the surface of the ground at night.

night•fall (nīt′fôl′) /ˈnaytˌfɔl/ *n.* [*noncount*] the coming of night; dusk.

night•gown (nīt′goun′) /ˈnaytˌgawn/ *n.* [*count*] a loose gown, worn in bed esp. by women or children.

night•ie or **night•y** (nī′tē) /ˈnaytiy/ *n., pl.* **-ies.** *Informal.* NIGHTGOWN.

night•in•gale (nīt′n gāl′, nī′ting-) /ˈnaytn̩ˌgeyl, ˈnaytɪŋ-/ *n.* [*count*] a small European bird noted for the melodious song of the male, often heard at night.

night•ly (nīt′lē) /ˈnaytliy/ *adj.* [*often: before a noun*] **1.** coming or occurring each night or at night. **2.** appearing or active at night. **3.** of, relating to, or characteristic of night. —*adv.* **4.** on every night: *Performances are given nightly.* **5.** at or by night.

night•mare (nīt′mâr′) /ˈnaytˌmɛər/ *n.* [*count*] **1.** a frightening or terrifying dream that produces feelings of great fear and anxiety. **2.** a condition, thought, or experience that is very unpleasant: *Driving through that city at rush hour is a nightmare.* —**night′mar′ish,** *adj.*

night′ owl′, *n.* [*count*] a person who often stays up late at night.

night′ school′, *n.* school or classes held in the evening, such as for people who work in the day: [*noncount*]: *He went to night school.* [*count*]: *a nearby night school.*

night•shade (nīt′shād′) /ˈnaytˌʃeyd/ *n.* [*count*] **1.** a weed that has poisonous leaves, white flowers, and black berries. **2.** BELLADONNA (def. 1).

night•shirt (nīt′shûrt′) /ˈnaytˌʃɜrt/ *n.* [*count*] a nightgown cut like a long shirt.

night•spot (nīt′spot′) /ˈnaytˌspɒt/ *n.* NIGHTCLUB.

night′ stick′, *n.* [*count*] a police officer's club.

night′ ta′ble, *n.* [*count*] a small table put next to a bed.

night•time (nīt′tīm′) /ˈnaytˌtaym/ *n.* NIGHT (def. 1).

ni•hil•ism (nī′ə liz′əm, nē′-) /ˈnayəˌlɪzəm, ˈniy-/ *n.* [*noncount*] **1.** a doctrine of rejecting established laws, authority, and the basic institutions of society. **2.** the view that existence makes no sense or that there is no point in acting morally. —**ni′hil•ist,** *n.* [*count*], *adj.* —**ni′hil•is′tic,** *adj.*

nil (nil) /nɪl/ *n.* [*noncount*] **1.** nothing; naught; zero: *Our profits were nil.* —*adj.* **2.** having no value or existence.

nim•ble (nim′bəl) /ˈnɪmbəl/ *adj.,* **-bler, -blest. 1.** quick and light in movement; agile: *nimble feet.* **2.** quick to understand, think, plan, etc.: *a nimble mind.* —**nim′ble•ness,** *n.* [*noncount*] —**nim′bly,** *adv.*

nim•bus (nim′bəs) /ˈnɪmbəs/ *n.* [*count*], *pl.* **-bi** (-bī) /-bay/ **-bus•es. 1.** HALO (def. 1). **2.** a dense rain cloud.

nin•com•poop (nin′kəm po͞op′, ning′-) /ˈnɪnkəmˌpuwp, ˈnɪŋ-/ *n.* [*count*] a fool or stupid person; a simpleton.

nine (nīn) /nayn/ *n.* [*count*] **1.** a cardinal number, equal to eight plus one. **2.** a symbol for this number, as 9 or IX. **3.** a set of this many persons or things. **4.** a baseball team. —*adj.* [*before a noun*] **5.** amounting to nine in number. —***Idiom.*** **6. dressed to the nines,** dressed very well or splendidly, esp. in formal clothing.

nine•pin (nīn′pin′) /ˈnaynˌpɪn/ *n.* **1. ninepins,** [*noncount; used with a singular verb*] a game of bowling played without the head pin. **2.** [*count*] a pin used in this game.

nine•teen (nīn′tēn′) /ˈnaynˈtiyn/ *n.* [*count*] **1.** a cardinal number, equal to ten plus nine. **2.** a symbol for this number, as 19 or XIX. **3.** a set of this many persons or things. —*adj.* [*before a noun*] **4.** amounting to 19 in number. —**nine′teenth′,** *adj., n.* [*count*]

nine•ty (nīn′tē) /ˈnayntiy/ *n., pl.* **-ties,** *adj.* —*n.* [*count*] **1.** a cardinal number, equal to ten times nine. **2.** a symbol for this number, such as 90 or XC. **3.** a set of this many persons or things. **4. nineties,** [*usually: the* + ~] the numbers from 90 through 99, as in referring to the years of a lifetime or of a century or to degrees of temperature. —*adj.* [*before a noun*] **5.** amounting to 90 in number. —**nine′ti•eth,** *adj., n.* [*count*]

nin•ny (nin′ē) /ˈnɪniy/ *n.* [*count*], *pl.* **-nies.** a simpleton.

ninth (nīnth) /naynθ/ *adj.* **1.** next after the eighth. —*n.* [*count*] **2.** a ninth part, esp. of one; 1/9. **3.** the ninth number of a series; the one counted as the number nine.

nip[1] (nip) /nɪp/ *v.,* **nipped, nip•ping,** *n.* —*v.* **1.** to squeeze tightly between two surfaces or points; pinch; bite: [~ + *obj*]: *The dog nipped my leg.* [*no obj*]: *The dog nipped at her heels.* **2.** [~ + *obj*] to cut off by pinching, biting, or snipping: *She nipped a few hairs from his head.* **3.** [~ + *obj*] to check in growth or development: *He nipped that rumor quickly.* **4.** to affect sharply and painfully, as extreme cold does: [*no obj*]: *The cold was nipping at our faces.* [~ + *obj*]: *The cold nipped our faces.* **5.** [~ + *obj*] to steal: *nipped a few coins from my desk.* **6.** [*no obj*] *Chiefly Brit.* to move quickly: *I'll just nip out and be right back.* **—*n.*** [*count*] **7.** an act of nipping: *The dog gave her a few nips on the leg.* **8.** a biting quality, as of frosty or sharply cold air: *quite a nip in the air tonight.* **—*Idiom.* 9. nip and tuck,** (of a contest or competition) closely fought right to the end, esp. with each side gaining then losing the advantage. **10. nip in the bud,** [~ + *obj* + *in the bud*] to stop (something) before it can develop or grow fully: *to nip a plan in the bud.*

nip[2] (nip) /nɪp/ *n.* [*count*] a small drink of alcoholic liquor.

nip•per (nip′ər) /ˈnɪpər/ *n.* [*count*] **1.** a person or thing that nips. **2.** Usually, **nippers.** [*plural*] a device for nipping, such as pincers or forceps. **3.** a claw of a crab or lobster. **4.** *Informal.* a child, esp. a small boy.

nip•ple (nip′əl) /ˈnɪpəl/ *n.* [*count*] **1.** the dark part of the breast where, in the female, milk is sucked by a baby; teat. **2.** something resembling it, such as the mouthpiece of a nursing bottle or a pacifier.

nip•py (nip′ē) /ˈnɪpiy/ *adj.*, **-pi•er, -pi•est. 1.** chilly; cold: *a nippy wind.* **2.** sharp tasting or smelling. **—nip′pi•ness,** *n.* [*noncount*]

nir•va•na (nir vä′nə, -van′ə, nər-) /nɪrˈvɑnə, -ˈvænə, nər-/ *n.* [*noncount*] **1.** [*often: Nirvana*] (in Buddhism) the final release from the cycle of being reborn again, that comes as a result of the ending of individual passion and hatred; salvation. **2.** a place or state in which there is freedom from pain and worry.

Ni•sei (nē′sā, nē sā′) /ˈniysey, niyˈsey/ *n.* [*count; sometimes: nisei*], *pl.* **-sei.** a child of Japanese immigrants, born and educated in North America.

nit[1] (nit) /nɪt/ *n.* [*count*] **1.** the egg of an insect that lives off a larger animal, esp. of a louse. **2.** the young of such an insect.

nit[2] (nit) /nɪt/ *n.* [*count*] *Brit.* a nitwit.

nit•pick or **nit-pick** (nit′pik′) /ˈnɪtˌpɪk/ *v.* to complain about petty details; niggle: [*no obj*]: *He wasted time nitpicking.* [~ + *obj*]: *He nitpicked the report to pieces.* **—nit′pick′er,** *n.* [*count*]

ni•trate (ni′trāt, -trit) /ˈnaytreyt, -trɪt/ *n.* [*count*] **1.** a chemical compound with nitrogen and oxygen in it. **2.** fertilizer made up of potassium nitrate or sodium nitrate.

ni′tric ac′id (ni′trik) /ˈnaytrɪk/ *n.* [*noncount*] a colorless or yellowish, strong-smelling, corrosive liquid used chiefly in the manufacture of explosives and fertilizers.

ni•tro•gen (ni′trə jən) /ˈnaytrədʒən/ *n.* [*noncount*] a colorless, odorless, gaseous element that makes up about four-fifths of the earth's atmosphere and is found in animal and vegetable tissues. **—ni•trog•e•nous** (nī troj′ə-nəs) /nayˈtrɒdʒənəs/ *adj.*

ni•tro•glyc•er•in (ni′trə glis′ər in) /ˌnaytrəˈglɪsərɪn/ also **ni•tro•glyc•er•ine** (ni′trə glis′ər in, -ə rēn′) /ˌnaytrəˈglɪsərɪn, -əˌriyn/ *n.* [*noncount*] an oily liquid used in explosives and as a medicine to make the blood vessels wider.

ni•trous ox′ide (nī′trəs) /ˈnaytrəs/ *n.* [*noncount*] a colorless, sweet-smelling gas that often produces a pleasant feeling when inhaled and is used esp. in dentistry for reducing pain. Also called **laughing gas.**

nit•ty-grit•ty (nit′ē grit′ē) /ˈnɪtiyˈgrɪtiy/ *n.* [*count*], *pl.* **-grit•ties.** the essential or fundamental parts or details of a matter: *The discussion got down to the nitty-gritty.*

nit•wit (nit′wit′) /ˈnɪtˌwɪt/ *n.* [*count*] a scatterbrained, stupid, or foolish person.

nix (niks) /nɪks/ *Slang.* **—*n.*** [*noncount*] **1.** nothing: *got nix for our trouble.* **—*adv.* 2.** no: *They said nix to our proposal.* **—*v.*** [~ + *obj*] **3.** to veto: *He nixed the plan.*

NJ or **N.J.,** an abbreviation of: New Jersey.

NM or **N.M.,** an abbreviation of: New Mexico.

N. Mex., an abbreviation of: New Mexico.

no[1] (nō) /now/ *adv., n., pl.* **noes, nos. —*adv.* 1.** (used to express dissent, disagreement, denial, or refusal, as in response to a question or request, or in giving a command): *"Can we leave now?"—"No, stay here."* **2.** (used to emphasize or introduce a negative statement): *No, not one of them came.* **3.** [*before an adjective or adverb that is comparative, or ending in -er*] not in any degree or manner; not at all: *She's no better today than she was yesterday.* **4.** not: *whether or no.* **—*n.*** [*count*] **5.** an instance of saying the word "no." **6.** a denial or refusal: *a definite no to our request.* **7.** a negative vote or voter: *Five noes against two yeses.*

no[2] (nō) /now/ *adj.* **1.** not any: [*before a noncount noun*]: *He had no money.* [*before a plural noun*]: *I had no books.* [*before a count noun*]: *I had no way of knowing who would be there.* **2.** [*before a noun*] (used before a noun to suggest the opposite of that noun) not at all; far from being: *He is no genius.*

no. or **No.,** an abbreviation of: **1.** north. **2.** northern. **3.** number.

no•bil•i•ty (nō bil′i tē) /nowˈbɪlɪtiy/ *n.* [*noncount*] **1.** the noble, or highest social, class, or the body of nobles in a country. **2.** the state or quality of being noble. **3.** nobleness of mind, character, or spirit.

no•ble (nō′bəl) /ˈnowbəl/ *adj.*, **-bler, -blest,** *n.* **—*adj.* 1.** having a high rank or title, esp. of or belonging to a class with special social or political status given by birth. **2.** of a high moral character or excellence: *It was very noble of him to accept the blame.* **3.** grand in appearance; magnificent: *a noble mansion.* **4.** [*before a noun*] (of chemicals) inert; chemically inactive; seldom combining with other substances: *the noble gases.* **—*n.*** [*count*] **5.** a nobleman or noblewoman. **—no′ble•ness,** *n.* [*noncount*] **—no′bly,** *adv.*

no•ble•man or **-wom•an** (nō′bəl mən) or (-wo͝om′ən) /ˈnowbəlmən/ or /-ˌwʊmən/ *n.* [*count*], *pl.* **-men** or **-wom•en.** a person of noble birth or rank; a noble.

no•blesse o•blige (nō bles′ ō blēzh′) /nowˈblɛs owˈbliyʒ/ *n.* [*noncount*] the responsibility of people of privilege to display honorable and generous conduct toward all. See -LIG-.

no•bod•y (nō′bod′ē, -bud′ē, -bə dē) /ˈnowˌbɒdiy, -ˌbʌdiy, -bədiy/ *pron., n., pl.* **-bod•ies. —*pron.* 1.** no person; not anyone; no one: *Nobody is home.* **—*n.*** [*count*] **2.** a person of no importance: *treated their part-time staff like nobodies.*

-noc-, *root.* *-noc-* comes from Latin, where it has the meaning "harm; kill." This meaning is found in such words as: INNOCENT, INNOCUOUS, NOXIOUS, OBNOXIOUS.

-noct-, *root.* *-noct-* comes from Latin, where it has the meaning "night." This meaning is found in such words as: NOCTURNAL, NOCTURNE.

noc•tur•nal (nok tûr′nl) /nɒkˈtɜrnl̩/ *adj.* **1.** of or relating to the night. **2.** active at night (opposed to *diurnal*): *nocturnal animals.* **—noc•tur′nal•ly,** *adv.* See -NOCT-, -NOX-.

noc•turne (nok′tûrn) /ˈnɒktɜrn/ *n.* [*count*] an artistic work appropriate to the night, esp. a dreamy piece of music for the piano. See -NOCT-, -NOX-.

nod (nod) /nɒd/ *v.*, **nod•ded, nod•ding,** *n.* **—*v.* 1.** to make a slight, quick bending movement of the head, as in agreement, greeting, or command: [*no obj*]: *She nodded at us and we stood up.* [~ + *obj*]: *He nodded his head in approval.* **2.** [~ + *obj*] to express or show by such a movement: *He nodded his approval.* **3.** [*no obj*] to let the head fall slightly forward with a sudden movement, as from sleepiness. **4. nod off,** [*no obj*] to fall asleep. **—*n.*** [*count*] **5.** a short, quick bending of the head: *At a nod from the teacher they all began to sing.* **—*Idiom.* 6. give the nod to,** [~ + *obj*] to express approval of: *He gave the nod to our proposal.*

node (nōd) /nowd/ *n.* [*count*] **1.** a knot or knob of something that sticks up or out. **2.** a centering point of parts, lines, etc., that come together. **3.** *Anat.* a knotlike mass of tissue: *a lymph node.* **4.** *Botany.* a part of a stem from which a leaf or branch grows. **—nod′al,** *adj.*

nod•ule (noj′o͞ol) /ˈnɒdʒuwl/ *n.* [*count*] a small node. **—nod′u•lar,** *adj.*

No•el (nō el′) /nowˈɛl/ *n.* **1.** CHRISTMAS. **2.** [*count: noel*] a Christmas carol.

no′-fault′, *n.* [*noncount*] **1.** a form of automobile insurance in which the person holding the policy may collect money in case of an accident without the need to determine which driver is at fault. **—*adj.*** [*before a noun*] **2.** of or relating to no-fault insurance: *a no-fault policy.* **3.** holding neither party responsible: *a no-fault divorce.*

nog•gin (nog′ən) /ˈnɒgən/ *n.* [*count*] **1.** a small mug. **2.** a small amount of liquor. **3.** *Informal.* a person's head.

no-good (*adj.* nō′go͝od′; *n.* nō′go͝od′) / *adj.* ˈnowˈgʊd; *n.* ˈnowˌgʊd/ *adj.* **1.** lacking worth or value; useless; bad: *He's a no-good cheat.* **—*n.*** [*count*] **2.** a no-good person or thing.

noise (noiz) /nɔyz/ *n., v.*, **noised, nois•ing. —*n.* 1.** [*noncount*] sound, esp. of a loud, harsh, or confused kind. **2.** [*count*] a sound of any kind: *strange noises coming from the engine.* **3.** [*noncount*] loud shouting or calling for something; clamor; uproar: *couldn't hear over the noise of the crowd.* **4.** [*noncount*] an electric disturbance in a communications system that interferes with or prevents reception of a signal or of information: *background noise.* **—*v.*** [~ + *about/abroad; usually: It* + *be* + *noised* + *about* + *that clause*] **5.** to spread, as a report or rumor: *It was noised about that he would dump his vice president in the upcoming election.* —**noise′less,** *adj.* —**noise′less•ly,** *adv.*

noise•mak•er (noiz′mā′kər) /ˈnɔyzˌmeykər/ *n.* [*count*] one that makes noise, esp. a rattle, horn, or other device used for making noise at festive occasions.

noi•some (noi′səm) /ˈnɔysəm/ *adj.* **1.** offensive or disgusting, as an odor. **2.** harmful to health; noxious.

nois•y (noi′zē) /ˈnɔyziy/ *adj.,* **-i•er, -i•est. 1.** making much noise: *noisy children.* **2.** full of noise: *a noisy party.* —**nois•i•ly** (noi′zə lē) /ˈnɔyzəliy/ *adv.* —**nois′i•ness,** *n.* [*noncount*]

no•lo con•ten•de•re (nō′lō kən ten′də rē) /ˈnowlow kənˈtɛndəriy/ *n.* [*noncount*] a plea in a court of law that allows for the defendant to be punished without admitting guilt.

-nom-¹, *root. -nom-* comes from Greek, where it has the meaning "custom; law; manage; control." This meaning is found in such words as: AGRONOMY, ANOMALOUS, ANOMALY, ASTRONOMY, AUTONOMOUS, AUTONOMY, ECONOMY, GASTRONOMY, TAXONOMY.

-nom-², *root. -nom-* comes from Latin and from Greek, where it has the meaning "name." This meaning is found in such words as: BINOMIAL, DENOMINATION, IGNOMINY, MISNOMER, NOMENCLATURE, NOMINAL, NOMINATE, NOMINATION, NOMINATIVE, NOUN, ONOMATOPOEIA, POLYNOMIAL, PRONOUN.

nom., an abbreviation of: nominative.

no•mad (nō′mad) /ˈnowmæd/ *n.* [*count*] **1.** a member of a people who have no permanent single place for living but move from place to place, usually within an established area. **2.** any wanderer; itinerant. —**no•mad′ic,** *adj.: nomadic tribes.*

no′ man's′ land′, *n.* **1.** [*noncount*] an area between warring armies that no one controls. **2.** [*count; usually singular*] an area where guidelines and authority are not clear or definite: *a no man's land between right and wrong.*

nom de guerre (nom′ də gâr′) /ˌnɒmdəˈgɛər/ *n.* [*count*], *pl.* **noms de guerre.** a fictitious name; pseudonym. See -NOM-².

nom de plume (nom′ də plōōm′) /ˌnɒm′ də pluwm/ *n.* [*count*], *pl.* **noms de plume.** a pen name: *Mark Twain was the nom de plume of Samuel Clemens.* See -NOM-².

no•men•cla•ture (nō′mən klā′chər, nō men′klə chər, -chŏŏr′) /ˈnowmənˌkleytʃər, nowˈmɛnklətʃər, -ˌtʃʊr/ *n.* [*noncount*] a set or system of terms for things in a particular science or art: *the nomenclature of physics.* See -NOM-².

nom•i•nal (nom′ə nl) /ˈnɒmənl/ *adj.* **1.** being such in name only; so-called: *He was only the nominal head of the country.* **2.** being small or low in amount when compared with the actual value: *He offered them the house for a nominal price.* **3.** of, relating to, or being a name or names. **4.** of, relating to, functioning as, or producing a noun: *The suffix* -ness *in the word* liveliness *is a nominal suffix.* —**nom′i•nal•ly,** *adv.: He's only nominally in charge here.* See -NOM-².

nom•i•nate (nom′ə nāt′) /ˈnɒməˌneyt/ *v.,* **-nat•ed, -nat•ing. 1.** [~ + *obj* (+ *for* + *obj*)] to propose (someone) for appointment or election to an office or duty: *The party nominated her for vice-president.* [~ + *obj* (+ *as*) + *obj*]: *She nominated him (as) her representative to the peace talks.* **2.** [~ + *obj* (+ *for* + *obj*)] to propose for an honor: *They nominated her for the award.* —**nom′i•na′tor,** *n.* [*count*] See -NOM-².

nom•i•na•tion (nom′ə nā′shən) /ˌnɒməˈneyʃən/ *n.* **1.** [*count*] an act or instance of nominating: *There are two nominations for the award.* **2.** [*noncount*] the state or condition of being nominated: *His nomination was assured.* See -NOM-².

nom•i•na•tive (nom′ə nə tiv, nom′nə-) /ˈnɒmənətɪv, ˈnɒmnə-/ *adj.* **1.** of, relating to, or being a grammatical form or category that shows the noun or pronoun is the subject of a verb: *The pronoun* he *in the sentence "Is he there?" is in the nominative case; the pronoun* him *in the sentence "Did you see him?" is in the objective case.* **2.** nominated; appointed by nomination. —*n.* [*count*] **3.** the nominative case. **4.** a word or phrase in the nominative case, as the English pronoun *I* or the Latin word *nauta* "sailor" in *Nauta bonus est* "The sailor is good." See -NOM-².

nom•i•nee (nom′ə nē′) /ˌnɒməˈniy/ *n.* [*count*] a person who has been nominated, as to run for elective office.

non-, *prefix. non-,* usually meaning "not," is attached **1.** to adjectives and adverbs and means a simple negative or absence of something: *non- + violent → nonviolent.* **2.** to a noun of action and means the failure of such action: *non- + payment → nonpayment (= failure to pay).* **3.** to a noun to suggest that the thing mentioned is not true, real, or worthy of the name: *nonevent.*

non•a•ge•nar•i•an (non′ə jə nâr′ē ən, nō′nə-) /ˌnɒnədʒəˈnɛəriyən, ˌnownə-/ *adj.* **1.** of the age of 90 years, or between 90 and 100 years old. —*n.* [*count*] **2.** a nonagenarian person.

non•al•co•hol•ic (non′al kə hô′lik, -hol′ik) /ˌnɒnælkəˈhɔlɪk, -ˈhɒlɪk/ *adj.* not being or containing alcohol: *nonalcoholic drinks.*

non•a•ligned (non′ə līnd′) /ˌnɒnəˈlaynd/ *adj.* not taking sides in political matters, not allied, esp. with either one of two opposing powers or ideologies: *nonaligned nations.* —**non•a•lign•ment** (non′ə līn′mənt) /ˌnɒnəˈlaynmənt/ *n.* [*noncount*]

non•ap•pear•ance (non′ə pēr′əns) /ˌnɒnəˈpɪərəns/ *n.* failure to appear: [*noncount*]: *Nonappearance means you'll lose your chance to win.* [*count*]: *His continual nonappearances at meetings began to annoy everyone.*

nonce (nons) /nɒns/ *n.* [*noncount; usually: the* + ~] the immediate occasion or purpose: *We'll stay, for the nonce.*

nonce′ word′, *n.* [*count*] a word coined and used only for a particular occasion.

non•cha•lant (non′shə länt′, non′shə länt′, -lənt) /ˌnɒnʃəˈlɑnt, ˈnɒnʃəˌlɑnt, -lənt/ *adj.* coolly unconcerned; indifferent; offhand. —**non′cha•lance′,** *n.* [*noncount*] —**non′cha•lant′ly,** *adv.*

non•com (non′kom′) /ˈnɒnˌkɒm/ *n.* NONCOMMISSIONED OFFICER.

non•com•bat•ant (non′kəm bat′nt, non kom′bə tnt) /ˌnɒnkəmˈbætnt, nɒnˈkɒmbətnt/ *n.* [*count*] **1.** a member of a military force who is not a fighter, as a surgeon, nurse, or chaplain. **2.** a person who is not a combatant in wartime; a civilian. —*adj.* [*before a noun*] **3.** not making up, designed for, or engaged in combat.

non′com•mis′sioned of′ficer (non′kə mish′ənd, non′-) /ˈnɒnkəˈmɪʃənd, ˌnɒn-/ *n.* [*count*] an officer, as a sergeant or corporal, holding a rank below a commissioned officer in a branch of the armed forces.

non•com•mit•tal (non′kə mit′l) /ˌnɒnkəˈmɪtl/ *adj.* having or giving no particular view, feeling, character, or the like: *a noncommittal answer.* —**non′com•mit′tal•ly,** *adv.* See -MIT-.

non•com•pli•ance (non′kəm plī′əns) /ˌnɒnkəmˈplayəns/ *n.* [*noncount*] failure or refusal to go along with or obey a law, rule, or regulation. See -PLET-.

non com•pos men•tis (non′ kom′pəs men′tis) /ˈnɒnˈkɒmˈpəs mɛntɪs/ *adj.* not of sound mind; mentally incompetent.

non•con•duc•tor (non′kən duk′tər) /ˌnɒnkənˈdʌktər/ *n.* [*count*] a substance that does not easily conduct heat, sound, or electricity. See -DUC-.

non•con•form•ist (non′kən fôr′mist) /ˌnɒnkənˈfɔrmɪst/ *n.* [*count*] **1.** a person who refuses to conform to established customs, attitudes, or ideas. —*adj.* [*before a noun*] **2.** of or relating to this kind of person or behavior. —**non′con•form′i•ty,** *n.* [*noncount*] See -FORM-.

non•co•op•er•a•tion or **non•co-op•er•a•tion** (non′kō op′ə rā′shən) /ˌnɒnkowˌɒpəˈreyʃən/ *n.* [*noncount*] **1.** failure or refusal to cooperate. **2.** a method of showing opposition to a government by refusing to participate in civic and political life or to obey governmental regulations. See -OPER-.

non•cred•it (non kred′it) /nɒnˈkrɛdɪt/ *adj.* [*usually: before a noun*] (of a course in school) not given for credit; not counted for credit toward graduation. See -CRED-.

non•dair•y (non dâr′ē) /nɒnˈdɛəriy/ *adj.* [*usually: before a noun*] being a substitute for milk or milk products; containing no dairy ingredients: *nondairy creamer.*

non•de•script (non′di skript′) /ˌnɒndɪˈskrɪpt/ *adj.* undistinguished or dull; without interest or character; not easily noticed: *nondescript clothes.* See -SCRIB-.

none (nun) /nʌn/ *pron.* [*often:* ~ + *of*] **1.** no one; not one: *None of the members is going.* **2.** not any: *That is none of your business.* **3.** no part; nothing: *I'll have none of that.* **4.** [*used with a plural verb*] not any persons or things: *There were many and now there are none.* —*adv.* **5. none but,** only; nothing less than: *He had none but the best wishes for her.* **6. none the,** to no extent; not at all: *We are none the worse after all we've been through.* **7. none too,** not very: *We could hear none too well from the back.*

non•en•ti•ty (non en′ti tē) /nɒnˈɛntɪtiy/ *n.* [*count*], *pl.* **-ties.** a person or thing of no importance.

non•es•sen•tial (non′ə sen′shəl) /ˌnɒnəˈsɛnʃəl/ *adj.* not necessary; that can be done without: *nonessential personnel.*

none•such (nun′such′) /ˈnʌnˌsʌtʃ/ *n.* [*count; usually singular*] a person or thing without equal.

none•the•less (nun′thə les′) /ˌnʌnðəˈlɛs/ *adv.* nevertheless; in spite of that: *He had a learning disability but became a great scientist nonetheless.*

non•e•vent (non′i vent′) /ˌnɒnɪˈvɛnt/ *n.* [*count*] a planned event for which there is much publicity but that occurs with little impact.

non•ex•is•tent (non′ig zis′tənt) /ˌnɒnɪgˈzɪstənt/ *adj.* **1.** not existing: *Basic services were nonexistent in the poorer parts of the country.* **2.** false; fictitious: *The spy's passport had the name of a nonexistent company as his address.* **—non′ex•is′tence,** *n.* [*noncount*]

non•fat (non′fat′) /ˈnɒnˈfæt/ *adj.* [*usually: before a noun*] having the fat or fat solids removed: *nonfat milk.*

non•fic•tion (non fik′shən) /nɒnˈfɪkʃən/ *n.* [*noncount*] writing that is not fictional. **—non•fic′tion•al,** *adj.*

non•flam•mable (non′flam′ə bəl) /ˌnɒnˈflæməbəl/ *adj.* not burning or catching fire easily. Compare INFLAMMABLE.

non•in•ter•ven•tion (non′in tər ven′shən) /ˌnɒnɪntərˈvɛnʃən/ *n.* [*noncount*] a policy of not intervening in the affairs of others. See -VEN-.

non•met•al (non met′l) /nɒnˈmɛtl/ *n.* [*count*] an element not having the characteristics of a metal, as nitrogen.

non•na•tive (non′nā′tiv) /ˌnɒnˈneytɪv/ *adj.* **1.** (of a person) not being a native of a place. **2.** [*before a noun*] (of a language) not spoken as a person's first language.

no′-no′, *n.* [*count*], *pl.* **-nos, -no's.** *Informal.* something that is forbidden or unacceptable.

no′-non′sense, *adj.* [*before a noun*] **1.** serious; businesslike: *He gave a no-nonsense explanation.* **2.** economical; practical: *a no-nonsense economy car.*

non•pa•reil (non′pə rel′) /ˌnɒnpəˈrɛl/ *adj.* **1.** having no equal; peerless. **—*n.*** [*count*] **2.** a person or thing having no equal. **3.** a pellet of colored sugar for decorating candy, cakes, or cookies. **4.** a bite-sized disk of chocolate covered with white nonpareil pellets.

non•par•ti•san (non pär′tə zən) /nɒnˈpɑrtəzən/ *adj.* **1.** not supporting or controlled by one particular group, such as a political party; objective. **—*n.*** [*count*] **2.** a person who is nonpartisan. See also BIPARTISAN.

non•pay•ment (non′pā′mənt) /ˌnɒnˈpeymənt/ *n.* [*noncount*] failure to pay an amount of money owed.

non•per•son (non pûr′sən) /nɒnˈpɜrsən/ *n.* [*count*] **1.** a person whose existence is not recognized. **2.** UNPERSON.

non•plus (non plus′, non′plus) /nɒnˈplʌs, ˈnɒnplʌs/ *v.* [~ + *obj*], **-plussed** or **-plused, -plus•sing** or **-plus•ing.** to make (someone) completely confused, puzzled, or unsure; baffle: *The child was nonplussed by the bright lights.*

non•pre•scrip•tion (non′pri skrip′shən) /ˌnɒnprɪˈskrɪpʃən/ *adj.* [*before a noun*] (of drugs, medication, etc.) that may be obtained legally without a doctor's prescription.

non•prof•it (non prof′it) /nɒnˈprɒfɪt/ *adj.* not established for the purpose of making a profit: *a nonprofit organization.*

non•pro•lif•er•a•tion (non′prə lif′ə rā′shən) /ˌnɒnprəˌlɪfəˈreyʃən/ *n.* [*noncount*] **1.** the action or practice of slowing or stopping the spread of something, esp. of nuclear weapons. **—*adj.*** [*before a noun*] **2.** of or relating to this practice: *a nonproliferation treaty.*

non•res•i•dent (non rez′i dənt) /nɒnˈrɛzɪdənt/ *adj.* **1.** not living permanently in a particular place: *a nonresident visa.* **—*n.*** [*count*] **2.** a person who is nonresident.

non•re•stric•tive (non′ri strik′tiv) /ˌnɒnrɪˈstrɪktɪv/ *adj.* **1.** not restrictive or limiting: *nonrestrictive regulations for certain industries.* **2.** of or being a word, phrase, or clause that modifies another word but does not limit, or restrict, what that word refers to: *The relative clause* which was very dry *is nonrestrictive in the sentence* The summer of 1894, which was very dry, was bad for crops. *In English a nonrestrictive clause is usually set off by commas.*

non•re•turn•able (non′ri tûrn′ə bəl) /ˌnɒnrɪˈtɜrnəbəl/ *adj.* **1.** (of bottles, cans, containers, etc.) that cannot be returned to the place where purchased for a deposit or refund. **2.** that cannot be returned or exchanged. **—*n.*** [*count*] **3.** an item purchased, esp. a bottle, can, or container, that cannot be returned for a deposit refund.

non•rig•id (non rij′id) /nɒnˈrɪdʒɪd/ *adj.* **1.** not rigid. **2.** having a flexible gas container without a supporting structure and held in shape only by the pressure of the gas that is inside: *A blimp is a nonrigid airship.*

non•sched•uled (non skej′o͞old, -o͞o əld) /nɒnˈskɛdʒuwld, -uwəld/ *adj.* (of an airline or plane) allowed to carry passengers or freight between points when there is demand, rather than on a schedule.

non•sec•tar•i•an (non′sek târ′ē ən) /ˌnɒnsɛkˈtɛəriyən/ *adj.* not associated with or limited to a certain religion or to a particular group or sect within a particular religion.

non•sense (non′sens, -səns) /ˈnɒnsɛns, -səns/ *n.* [*noncount*] **1.** words without sense; gibberish. **2.** words, or a position, that is foolish or ridiculous: *a lot of nonsense about how women can't do as good a job as men.* **3.** conduct or action that is senseless or foolish: *Stop this nonsense at once!* **4.** impolite, rude, or otherwise objectionable behavior: *Don't take any nonsense from him.* See -SENS-.

non•sen•si•cal (non sen′si kəl) /nɒnˈsɛnsɪkəl/ *adj.* full of nonsense: *nonsensical ideas.* **—non•sen′si•cal•ly,** *adv.*

non seq., non sequitur.

non se•qui•tur (non sek′wi tər, -to͝or′) /ˈnɒn ˈsɛkwɪtər, -ˌtʊr/ *n.* [*count*] **1.** a statement, as a conclusion, that does not follow logically from what has been said before. **2.** a comment that is unrelated to one that went before.

non•sex•ist (non sek′sist) /nɒnˈsɛksɪst/ *adj.* not showing, calling for, promoting, or involving sexism: *nonsexist language.*

non•skid (non′skid′) /ˈnɒnˈskɪd/ *adj.* [*before a noun*] resistant to skidding: *nonskid tires.*

non•stand•ard (non′stan′dərd) /ˈnɒnˈstændərd/ *adj.* **1.** not standard. **2.** not agreeing with the pronunciation, grammar, vocabulary, etc., that is felt to be the usage considered acceptable by most educated native speakers: *nonstandard English.* Compare STANDARD (def. 11).

non•stick (non′stik′) /ˈnɒnˈstɪk/ *adj.* having a type of finish on the surface designed to prevent food from sticking during cooking or baking: *a nonstick pan.*

non•stop (non′stop′) /ˈnɒnˈstɒp/ *adj.* **1.** being without a single stop on the way: *a nonstop flight from New York to Dallas.* **2.** happening, done, or held without a pause or without stopping in between: *held nonstop meetings.* **—*adv.*** **3.** without a single stop on the way: *flew nonstop from San Diego to New York.* **4.** without interruption: *talking nonstop.*

non•sup•port (non′sə pôrt′, -pōrt′) /ˌnɒnsəˈpɔrt, -ˈpowrt/ *n.* [*noncount*] failure to provide financial support for a spouse, child, or other dependent.

non•un•ion (non yo͞on′yən) /nɒnˈyuwnyən/ *adj.* **1.** not belonging to a labor union: *nonunion workers.* **2.** not recognizing or accepting labor unions: *a nonunion factory.* **3.** not produced by union workers: *nonunion goods.*

non•ver•bal (non vûr′bəl) /nɒnˈvɜrbəl/ *adj.* [*often: before a noun*] **1.** not using words to express meaning: *nonverbal signals like nodding or shaking the head.* **2.** not using or involving the use of language: *The test measures nonverbal abilities in reasoning.*

non•vi•o•lence (non vī′ə ləns) /nɒnˈvayələns/ *n.* [*noncount*] **1.** absence or lack of violence. **2.** the policy or practice of deliberately avoiding or opposing the use of violence. **—non•vi′o•lent,** *adj.*

non•white (non hwīt′, -wīt′) /nɒnˈhwayt, -ˈwayt/ *adj.* **1.** not belonging to the white race. **—*n.*** [*count*] **2.** a person not belonging to the white race.

noo•dle[1] (no͞od′l) /ˈnuwdl/ *n.* [*count*] a dried strip of egg dough boiled and served as a side dish or in soups, casseroles, etc.

noo•dle[2] (no͞od′l) /ˈnuwdl/ *n.* [*count*] *Slang.* the head.

nook (no͝ok) /nʊk/ *n.* [*count*] **1.** a corner, as in a room: *a breakfast nook.* **2.** any hidden corner or area hard to reach. **3.** a sheltered spot: *a shady nook.*

noon (no͞on) /nuwn/ *n.* [*noncount*] midday; twelve o'clock in the daytime. **—Usage.** See MIDNIGHT.

no′ one′, *pron.* no person: *No one is home.*

noose (no͞os) /nuws/ *n.* [*count*] a loop in a rope or cord that tightens as part of it is pulled, as in a lasso or a rope to hang someone.

nope (nōp) /nowp/ *adv. Informal.* no.

nor (nôr; *unstressed* nər) /nɔr; *unstressed* nər/ *conj.* **1.** (used in negative phrases, esp. after *neither,* to introduce new items in a list or series): *Neither he nor I will be there.* **2.** (used to express a connection plus a continuing of the force of a negative word coming before it, such as *not, no, never,* etc.): *I never saw him again, nor did I regret it. She couldn't make it to the party, nor could we. She had no way of knowing, nor did we, that her husband was injured.* **—Usage.** Notice that in the examples for definition 2 an auxiliary verb like DID, or a modal verb like COULD, comes after *nor,* and the subject follows the auxiliary or modal:*..nor did I..; nor could we..*

Nor•dic (nôr′dik) /ˈnɔrdɪk/ *adj.* **1.** of or relating to the area of Northern Europe called Scandinavia. **2.** having or suggesting the physical features associated with the peoples of northern Europe, typically tall stature, blond hair, and blue eyes. **3.** [*sometimes: nordic*] of or relating to sporting events involving ski jumping and cross-country skiing.

norm (nôrm) /nɔrm/ *n.* [*count*] **1.** a standard, model, or pattern, esp. a rule or standard of behavior that is considered normal in society. **2.** the expected or usual number, level, amount, or average: *For many students it is no longer the norm to finish college in four years.* See -NORM-.

-norm-, *root.* *-norm-* comes from Latin, where it has the meaning "a carpenter's square; a rule or pattern." This meaning is found in such words as: ABNORMAL, ENORMITY, ENORMOUS, NORM, NORMAL, NORMALCY, NORMALIZE, SUBNORMAL.

nor•mal (nôr′məl) /ˈnɔrməl/ *adj.* **1.** conforming to or agreeing with the standard or the common type; usual; regular; natural: *a normal height for his age.* **2.** nearly average in one's mental or emotional state; rational; sane. **—*n.*** [*noncount*] **3.** the normal form or state: *Things returned to normal after the war.* See -NORM-.

nor•mal•cy (nôr′məl sē) /ˈnɔrməlsiy/ *n.* [*noncount*] the state or condition of being normal. See -NORM-.

nor•mal•i•ty (nôr mal′i tē) /nɔrˈmælɪtiy/ *n.* [*noncount*] the state or condition of being normal. See -NORM-.

nor•mal•ize (nôr′məl īz) /ˈnɔrməlayz/ *v.,* **-ized, -iz•ing.** to (cause to) become normal; to (cause to) come back to a previous state, esp. of friendliness: [~ + *obj*]: *to normalize relations between the two countries.* [*no obj*]: *The situation seems to have normalized.* —**nor•mal•i•za•tion** (nôr′məl i zā′shən) /ˌnɔrməlɪˈzeyʃən/ *n.* [*noncount*] See -NORM-.

nor•mal•ly (nôr′mə lē) /ˈnɔrməliy/ *adv.* **1.** in a normal manner or a normal way: *breathing normally.* **2.** in a usual manner or usual way; usually: *Normally we wouldn't ask such a question.* See -NORM-.

nor•ma•tive (nôr′mə tiv) /ˈnɔrmətɪv/ *adj.* of, relating to, or tending to establish a norm: *a normative rule of conduct.* See -NORM-.

north (nôrth) /nɔrθ/ *n.* [*noncount; usually: the* + ~] **1.** one of the four main points of the compass, to the left of a person facing the rising sun. *Abbr.:* N **2.** the direction in which this point lies: *Look to the north.* **3.** [*usually: North*] a region or territory in this direction. **4. the North,** the northern area of the United States, esp. the states that fought to preserve the Union in the Civil War. **—*adj.*** [*before a noun*] **5.** in, toward, or facing the north: *the north gate.* **6.** directed or going toward the north: *The tanks were taking a north course.* **7.** coming from the north: *a north wind.* **8.** [*usually: North*] naming the northern part of a region, nation, country, etc.: *the North Atlantic.* **—*adv.*** **9.** to, toward, or in the north: *sailing north.*

north•bound (nôrth′bound′) /ˈnɔrθˌbawnd/ *adj.* moving or going in a north direction: *a northbound train.*

north•east (nôrth′ēst′; *Nautical.* nôr′-) /ˌnɔrθˈiyst; *Nautical.* ˌnɔr-/ *n.* [*noncount*] **1.** a point on the compass midway between north and east. *Abbr.:* NE **2.** a region in this direction. **3. the Northeast,** the northeastern part of the United States. **—*adj.*** **4.** in, toward, or facing the northeast: *a northeast course.* **5.** coming from the northeast: *a northeast wind.* **—*adv.*** **6.** toward the northeast: *sailing northeast.* —**north′east′er•ly,** *adv.* —**north′east′ern,** *adj.*

north•east•er (nôrth′ē′stər; *Nautical.* nôr′-) /ˌnɔrθˈiystər; *Nautical.* ˌnɔr-/ *n.* [*count*] a storm from the northeast.

north•er (nôr′thər) /ˈnɔrðər/ *n.* [*count*] a storm from the north.

north•er•ly (nôr′thər lē) /ˈnɔrðərliy/ *adj., adv., n., pl.* **-lies.** **—*adj.*** **1.** moving, directed, or located toward the north. **2.** (esp. of a wind) coming from the north. **—*adv.*** **3.** toward the north. **4.** from the north. **—*n.*** [*count*] **5.** a wind that blows from the north.

north•ern (nôr′thərn) /ˈnɔrðərn/ *adj.* **1.** lying toward or located in the north. **2.** directed or going northward. **3.** coming from the north, as a wind. **4.** [*often: Northern*] of or relating to the North: *the northern U.S.*

north•ern•er (nôr′thər nər) /ˈnɔrðərnər/ *n.* [*count*] [*often: Northerner*] someone born in, or living in, the north, esp. the northern U.S.

north′ern lights′, *n.* [*plural*] the aurora of the Northern Hemisphere: *We watched the northern lights descend like sheets of color in the skies of Norway.*

North′ Pole′, *n.* [*proper noun; the* + ~] the northern end of the earth's axis; the northernmost point on earth.

north•ward (nôrth′wərd; *Nautical.* nôr′thərd) /ˈnɔrθwərd; *Nautical.* ˈnɔrðərd/ *adv.* **1.** Also, **north′wards.** toward the north: *The tanks continued to sweep northward.* **—*adj.*** **2.** moving, bearing, facing, or located toward the north: *the northward flank of the army.* Also, **north′ward•ly.**

north•west (nôrth′west′; *Nautical.* nôr′-) /ˌnɔrθˈwɛst; *Nautical.* ˌnɔr-/ *n.* [*noncount*] **1.** a point on the compass midway between north and west. *Abbr.:* NW **2.** a region in this direction. **3. the Northwest, a.** the northwestern part of the United States when its western boundary was the Mississippi River. **b.** the northwestern part of Canada. **—*adj.*** **4.** in, toward, or facing the northwest: *the northwest corner.* **5.** coming from the northwest: *a northwest wind.* **—*adv.*** **6.** toward the northwest: *sailing northwest.* —**north′west′er•ly,** *adv.* —**north′west′ern,** *adj.*

Nor•we•gian (nôr wē′jən) /nɔrˈwiydʒən/ *adj.* **1.** of or relating to Norway. **2.** of or relating to the language spoken in Norway. **—*n.*** **3.** [*count*] a person born or living in Norway. **4.** [*noncount*] the language spoken in Norway.

nos. or **Nos.,** an abbreviation of: numbers.

nose (nōz) /nowz/ *n., v.,* **nosed, nos•ing.** **—*n.*** [*count*] **1.** the part of the face above the mouth that contains the nostrils and organs of smell and through which a person breathes. **2.** the sense of smell: *Certain breeds of dog have a good nose.* **3.** anything that resembles a nose: *the nose of a plane.* **4.** an ability to understand, interpret, find out about (something): *had a nose for a good story.* **5.** the human nose as a symbol of interfering or prying: *Keep your nose out of my business!* **—*v.*** **6.** to move or push forward with or as if with the nose: [~ + *obj*]: *The boat nosed its way toward shore.* [*no obj*]: *The plane nosed forward cautiously.* **7.** [~ + *about/around*] to meddle or pry: *nosing around asking questions.* **8. nose out,** to defeat, esp. by a narrow margin: [~ + *out* + *obj*]: *She nosed out her opponent in the election.* [~ + *obj* + *out*]: *She nosed him out in the election.* **—*Idiom.*** **9. follow one's nose, a.** to go forward in a straight course: *Just follow your nose and you'll see the church straight ahead.* **b.** to guide oneself by instinct: *He followed his nose on negotiating that deal.* **10. keep one's nose clean,** to behave properly; avoid trouble. **11. lead (around) by the nose,** [*lead* + *obj* + *(around) by the nose*] to control (someone); dominate. **12. look down one's nose at,** [~ + *obj*] to consider (someone or something) as inferior or less acceptable. **13. on the nose,** precisely; exactly: *We arrived at 3 o'clock on the nose.* **14. put** or **keep one's nose to the grindstone,** to work intensely and persistently at a task. **15. put someone's nose out of joint,** to annoy; irritate. **16. turn up one's nose at,** [~ + *obj*] to reject (something) contemptuously: *turned up his nose at the pitiful offer.* **17. under someone's nose,** plainly visible; in full view: *It was right under my nose all the time.*

nose•bleed (nōz′blēd′) /ˈnowzˌbliyd/ *n.* [*count*] bleeding from the nostrils.

nose′ cone′, *n.* [*count*] the cone-shaped forward section of a rocket or guided missile.

nose•dive (nōz′dīv′) /ˈnowzˌdayv/ *n., v.,* **-dived** or **-dove, -dived, -div•ing.** **—*n.*** Also, **nose′ dive′.** [*count*] **1.** a fast downward motion of an aircraft with the forward part pointing downward. **2.** a sudden sharp drop or rapid decline: *Stock prices took a nosedive.* **—*v.*** [*no obj*] Also, **nose′-dive′.** **3.** to go into a nosedive: *Stocks nosedived for the fifth week in a row.*

nose•gay (nōz′gā′) /ˈnowzˌgey/ *n.* [*count*] a small bouquet of flowers.

nosh (nosh) /nɒʃ/ *Informal.* **—*v.*** **1.** to snack or eat (something) between meals: [*no obj*]: *noshing on peanuts.* [~ + *obj*]: *to nosh potato chips.* **—*n.*** [*count*] **2.** a snack. —**nosh′er,** *n.* [*count*]

no′-show′, *n.* [*count*] **1.** a person who has a reservation or ticket and does not use it or cancel it: *a few no-shows on the last flight.* **2.** a person who fails to show up, as for an appointment, esp. without warning.

nos•tal•gia (no stal′jə, nə-) /nɒˈstældʒə, nə-/ *n.* [*noncount*] a sentimental longing for places, things, friends, or conditions belonging to the past. See -ALG-.

nos•tal•gic (no stal′jik, nə-) /nɒˈstældʒɪk, nə-/ *adj.* having a feeling of nostalgia: *nostalgic for the past.* —**nos•tal′gi•cal•ly,** *adv.* See -ALG-.

nos•tril (nos′trəl) /ˈnɒstrəl/ *n.* [*count*] either of the two outer openings of the nose.

nos•trum (nos′trəm) /ˈnɒstrəm/ *n.* [*count*] **1.** a medicine sold with false or exaggerated claims. **2.** a favorite scheme or plan to correct social or political problems; cure-all.

nos•y or **nos•ey** (nō′zē) /ˈnowziy/ *adj.*, **-i•er, -i•est.** overly curious about the affairs of others; prying. —**nos•i•ly** (nō′zl ē) /ˈnowzliy/ *adv.* —**nos′i•ness,** *n.* [*noncount*]

not (not) /nɒt/ *adv.* **1.** (used with verbs like *be, have,* and *do,* and with modal verbs, to express the opposite of the main verb, and also to express denial, refusal, prohibiting, etc.: *I do not remember the answer. You must not think about it. It's not far from here. They are not coming.* **2.** (used with verbs like *think, want, seem, appear, expect,* and others that have another verb in a phrase or clause following, to express the opposite of the verb that follows): *He did not seem to be ready (= It did not seem that he was ready). He did not want to go (= He wanted not to go.) I did not expect to see you here (= I expected that I wouldn't see you here).* **3.** [~ + *a/one* + *noun*] (used before a singular count noun) not even one (expressing emphasis about the lack of something): *He had not a penny to his name. Not a single missile got through the defense system. Not one student could name the president.* —***Idiom.*** **4. not at all, a.** (used as an answer to someone else's thanks): *"I appreciate your help." —"Not at all."* **b.** (used to emphasize an answer of "no"): *"Did you like the show?" —"Not at all!"*

-nota-, *root.* *-nota-* comes from Latin, where it has the meaning "note." This meaning is found in such words as: ANNOTATE, ANNOTATION, CONNOTATION, CONNOTE, DENOTATION, DENOTE, FOOTNOTE, KEYNOTE, NOTABLE, NOTARIZE, NOTARY, NOTATION, NOTE, NOTORIETY, NOTORIOUS.

no•ta be•ne (nō′tä be′ne; *Eng.* nō′tə ben′ē, bē′nē) /ˈnowˈtɑ bɛnɛ; *Eng.* ˈnowˈtə bɛniy, ˈbiyniy/ *Latin.* (used in writing or formal speech) note well; take careful notice of what has been said or written. See -NOTA-.

no•ta•ble (nō′tə bəl) /ˈnowtəbəl/ *adj.* **1.** worthy of notice: *a notable success.* **2.** distinguished; prominent; eminent: *notable artists.* —*n.* [*count*] **3.** an important, distinguished, or eminent person. See -NOTA-.

not•ab•ly (nō′tə blē) /ˈnowtəbliy/ *adv.* **1.** in a way that is worthy of being noticed: *The audience was notably small.* **2.** especially; particularly: *a notably fine meal.* See -NOTA-.

no•ta•rize (nō′tə rīz′) /ˈnowtəˌrayz/ *v.* [~ + *obj*], **-rized, -riz•ing.** to make (a document) legal, as by signing it before a notary public. —**no•ta•ri•za•tion** (nō′tər i zā′shən) /ˌnowtərɪˈzeyʃən/ *n.* [*noncount*] See -NOTA-.

no•ta•ry (nō′tə rē) /ˈnowtəriy/ *n.* [*count*], *pl.* **-ries.** a person who is authorized to witness the signing of documents and make them official by placing a special stamp on them. Also, **notary public.** See -NOTA-.

no•ta•tion (nō tā′shən) /nowˈteyʃən/ *n.* **1.** [*noncount*] a system of special symbols or signs for a particular use: *musical notation.* **2.** [*noncount*] the act, process, or method of writing down by means of such a system. **3.** [*count*] a short note; annotation. See -NOTA-.

notch (noch) /nɒtʃ/ *n.* [*count*] **1.** an angled or V-shaped cut in the edge or top of something. **2.** an amount within a scale; degree: *She's a notch above the average.* —*v.* **3.** [~ + *obj*] to make a notch or notches in. **4.** [~ *(+ up)* + *obj*] to score; to add to one's record: *The pitcher notched (up) another win.*

note (nōt) /nowt/ *n., v.,* **not•ed, not•ing.** —*n.* [*count*] **1.** a brief written record of something to help someone remember something for future reference: *She took notes in her English class.* **2.** a brief written or printed statement giving information: *I left you a note on the refrigerator door.* **3.** a short letter: *a note of apology.* **4.** a reference or comment added to a passage of writing, to give one's source, more information, etc.; a footnote. **5.** an expression of a quality, emotion, etc., that is part of the surroundings; a hint: *a note of fear in his voice.* **6.** *Music.* a tone of a certain pitch, or a sign or character used to represent it in a piece of music. **7.** a sound of musical quality: *the beautiful notes of the nightingale.* **8.** a certificate, as of a government or a bank, accepted as money; a bill: *a bundle of fifty-dollar notes.* —*v.* **9.** to write or mark down briefly; make a record or note of so as to remember later: [~ + *obj*]: *He noted the professor's comments in the margins.* [~ + *down* + *obj*]: *Note down this name.* **10.** to make particular or special mention of (something): [~ + *obj*]: *noted the heroic efforts of her staff.* [~ + *that clause*]: *noted that her staff had done a fine job.* **11.** to take notice of; perceive: [~ + *obj*]: *We noted his reluctance to testify.* [~ + *that clause*]: *She noted that some people left early.* —***Idiom.*** **12. compare notes (on),** to share information about: *They compared notes on the experience.* **13. of note,** having fame or importance: *writers of note.* **14. take note (of),** to notice: [*no obj*]: *The sign warned trespassers to take note.* [*take note of* + *obj*]: *He failed to take note of the warning lights.* See -NOTA-.

note•book (nōt′bo͝ok′) /ˈnowtˌbʊk/ *n.* [*count*] **1.** a book of or for notes and other writing, esp. a book or binder of blank pages with straight lines in it. See illustration at SCHOOL. **2.** a small, lightweight laptop computer about the size of a notebook. See -NOTA-.

not•ed (nō′tid) /ˈnowtɪd/ *adj.* well-known; celebrated; famous: *a noted scholar.* [*be* + ~ + *for*]: *The town is noted for its hills.* See -NOTA-.

note•pap•er (nōt′pā′pər) /ˈnowtˌpeypər/ *n.* [*noncount*] writing paper suitable for notes. See -NOTA-.

note•wor•thy (nōt′wûr′thē) /ˈnowtˌwɜrðiy/ *adj.* worthy of notice; notable: *a noteworthy success.* See -NOTA-.

noth•ing (nuth′ing) /ˈnʌθɪŋ/ *pron.* **1.** not anything: *He was warned to say nothing about the affair.* **2.** no trace: *The house showed nothing of its former splendor.* **3.** something of no importance, significance, or value: *Money means nothing to him.* **4.** (used to express the opinion that some action is not a great effort, or is no trouble, etc.): *Carry four bags? Nothing to it.* —*n.* **5.** [*count*] an unimportant action, matter, circumstance, thing, or remark: *whispering sweet nothings.* **6.** [*count*] a person of little or no importance; a nobody. **7.** [*noncount*] zero; a cipher: *Five minus five leaves nothing.* —*adv.* **8.** in no respect or degree; not at all: *It was nothing like that.* —*adj.* [*before a noun*] **9.** amounting to nothing: *He did a nothing job on that last report.* —***Idiom.*** **10. for nothing, a.** free of charge: *He towed the car for nothing.* **b.** for no apparent reason or motive: *flew into a rage for nothing.* **c.** for no gain: *We went to all that trouble for nothing.* **11. in nothing flat,** in very little time: *He drove the twenty miles in nothing flat.* **12. make nothing of,** [~ + *obj*] to fail to understand or comprehend: *I can make nothing of this handwriting.* **13. nothing but,** only; just: *I could see nothing but corn everywhere I looked.* **14. nothing doing,** *Informal.* certainly not: *"So do I get the raise?" —"Nothing doing!"* **15. think nothing of,** [~ + *obj*] to regard or consider as unimportant, insignificant, or easy: *thought nothing of running ten miles a day.*

noth•ing•ness (nuth′ing nis) /ˈnʌθɪŋnɪs/ *n.* [*noncount*] **1.** the state or quality of being nothing. **2.** absence of meaning or worth; emptiness: *the nothingness of my job.*

no•tice (nō′tis) /ˈnowtɪs/ *n., v.,* **-ticed, -tic•ing.** —*n.* **1.** [*noncount*] information, warning, or announcement of something coming or about to happen; notification: *to give notice of one's intentions.* **2.** [*noncount*] a notification by one of the parties to an agreement, as for working at a job, that the agreement will end at a certain time: *She gave her employer two-weeks' notice.* **3.** [*count*] a written or printed statement with information or warning: *to post a notice against trespassers.* **4.** [*noncount*] observation, attention, or heed; note: *to take notice of one's surroundings.* **5.** [*noncount*] interested or favorable attention: *She was singled out for notice because of her charitable work.* **6.** [*count*] a brief published review or criticism of a book, play, etc. —*v.* **7.** to become aware of or pay attention to; observe; note: [~ + *obj*]: *I suddenly noticed her at the door.* [~ + *(that) clause*]: *She noticed that I frowned whenever I typed fast.* [~ + *obj* + *verb-ing*]: *She noticed him standing at the door.* [~ + *obj* + *root*]: *She noticed him leave exactly at eight o'clock.* —***Idiom.*** **8. at** or **on short** or **a moment's notice,** with very little advance warning: *Firefighters have to be ready to act at a moment's notice.* See -NOTA-.

no•tice•a•ble (nō′ti sə bəl) /ˈnowtɪsəbəl/ *adj.* capable of being noticed: *a noticeable change in the weather.* —**no′tice•a•bly,** *adv.* See -NOTA-.

no•ti•fy (nō′tə fī′) /ˈnowtəˌfay/ *v.,* **-fied, -fy•ing.** to inform; give notice to; tell: [~ + *obj*]: *to notify the police.* [~ + *obj* + *of*]: *to notify the police of a crime.* [~ + *obj* + *that clause*]: *You'll have to notify him that there's been an accident.* —**no•ti•fi•ca•tion** (nō′tə fi kā′shən) /ˌnowtəfɪˈkeyʃən/ *n.* [*count*]: *a notification of our intent to sell the house.* [*noncount*]: *to give sufficient notification of your intention.* —**no′ti•fi′er,** *n.* [*count*] See -NOTA-.

no•tion (nō′shən) /ˈnowʃən/ *n.* [*count*] **1.** an idea or view, esp. one's own view: *His notion of comfort meant comfortable shoes.* **2.** a foolish idea; whim: *had some weird notion about space creatures.* **3. notions,** [*plural*] small articles, as buttons, thread, or ribbon, displayed together for sale. —**no′tion•al,** *adj.* See -NOTA-.

no•to•ri•e•ty (nō′tə rī′ə tē) /ˌnowtəˈrayətiy/ *n.* [*noncount*] the state or condition of being widely known, esp. for something unfavorable. See -NOTA-.

no•to•ri•ous (nō tôr′ē əs, -tōr′-, nə-) /nowˈtɔriyəs, -ˈtowr-, nə-/ *adj.* widely known esp. for something unfavorable: *a notorious thief.* —**no•to′ri•ous•ly,** *adv.: He's a notoriously slow driver.* See -NOTA-.

not•with•stand•ing (not′with stan′ding, -with-) /ˌnɒtwɪð'stændɪŋ, -wɪθ-/ *prep.* **1.** in spite of: *Notwithstanding a brilliant defense, he was found guilty.* [*after a noun*]: *The doctor's orders notwithstanding, she returned to work.* —*adv.* **2.** nevertheless; anyway.

nou•gat (no͞o′gət) /'nuwgət/ *n.* [*count*] a candy containing nuts and sometimes fruit in a sugar or honey paste.

nought (nôt) /nɔt/ *n., adj., adv.* NAUGHT.

noun (noun) /nawn/ *n.* [*count*] a member of a class of words that can function as the subject or object in a sentence or phrase, and typically refer to persons, places, animals, things, states, or qualities, as *cat, desk, Ohio, darkness*: *Count nouns can usually take a plural ending.* *Abbr.*: n. See -NOM-².

-nounce-, *root.* *-nounce-* comes from Latin, where it has the meaning "call; say." It is related to -NUNC-. This meaning is found in such words as: ANNOUNCE, DENOUNCE, MISPRONOUNCE, PRONOUNCE, RENOUNCE.

nour•ish (nûr′ish, nur′-) /'nɜrɪʃ, 'nʌr-/ *v.* [~ + *obj*] **1.** to supply with what is necessary for life, health, and growth: *This food will nourish the sick infants.* **2.** to keep alive; cause to grow: *still nourished the hope of peace.* **3.** to strengthen; promote; foster: *to nourish talent.*

nour•ish•ing (nûr′ish ing, nur′-) /'nɜrɪʃɪŋ, 'nʌr-/ *adj.* providing food, or what is necessary for life, health, and growth: *nourishing foods.*

nour•ish•ment (nûr′ish mənt, nur′-) /'nɜrɪʃmənt, 'nʌr-/ *n.* [*noncount*] **1.** something that nourishes; food; sustenance. **2.** the act of nourishing; the state of being nourished.

nou•veau riche (no͞o′vō rēsh′) /'nuw'vow riyʃ/ *n.* [*count*], *pl.* **nou•veaux riches** (no͞o′vō rēsh′) /'nuw'vow riyʃ/. a person who is newly rich, esp. one thought of as being showy, vulgar, or lacking culture. See -NOV-.

nou•velle′ cuisine′ (no͞o vel′) /nuw'vɛl/ *n.* [*noncount*] a style of cooking that emphasizes the use of fresh ingredients, light sauces, and artful presentation of the food. See -NOV-.

-nov-, *root.* *-nov-* comes from Latin, where it has the meaning "new." This meaning is found in such words as: INNOVATE, INNOVATION, NOVA, NOVEL, NOVELETTE, NOVELIST, NOVELLA, NOVELTY, NOVICE, NOVITIATE, RENOVATE, RENOVATION.

Nov or **Nov.,** an abbreviation of: November.

no•va (nō′və) /'nowvə/ *n.* [*count*], *pl.* **-vas, -vae** (-vē) /-viy/. a star that suddenly becomes thousands of times brighter and then fades to its original brightness. See -NOV-.

nov•el¹ (nov′əl) /'nɒvəl/ *n.* [*count*] a long written story, usually fairly complicated, about characters and events that have been invented by the writer. See -NOV-.

nov•el² (nov′əl) /'nɒvəl/ *adj.* of a new kind; different from anything seen or known before: *novel solutions to old problems.* See -NOV-.

nov•el•ette (nov′ə let′) /ˌnɒvə'lɛt/ *n.* [*count*] a brief novel or long short story. See -NOV-.

nov•el•ist (nov′əl ist) /'nɒvəlɪst/ *n.* [*count*] a person who writes novels. See -NOV-.

no•vel•la (nō vel′ə) /now'vɛlə/ *n.* [*count*], *pl.* **-las.** a written story, longer and more complex than a short story; a short novel. See -NOV-.

nov•el•ty (nov′əl tē) /'nɒvəltiy/ *n., pl.* **-ties,** *adj.* —*n.* **1.** [*noncount*] the state or quality of being novel: *brought novelty to the old way of doing business.* **2.** [*count*] a novel event, occurrence, experience, etc. **3.** [*count*] a small, cheap, decorative or amusing article, usually mass-produced. —*adj.* [*before a noun*] **4.** of or relating to novelties as articles of trade: *some cheap little novelty items.* See -NOV-.

No•vem•ber (nō vem′bər) /now'vɛmbər/ *n.* [*proper noun*] the 11th month of the year, containing 30 days. *Abbr.*: Nov.

nov•ice (nov′is) /'nɒvɪs/ *n.* [*count*] **1.** a person who is new to the circumstances, work, etc., in which he or she is placed; beginner. **2.** a person admitted into a religious order for a period of testing before taking vows. See -NOV-.

no•vi•ti•ate (nō vish′ē it, -āt′) /now'vɪʃiyɪt, -ˌeyt/ *n.* **1.** [*noncount*] the state or period of being a religious novice. **2.** [*count*] the housing in which religious novices live. **3.** [*count*] a religious novice. See -NOV-.

No•vo•caine (nō′və kān′) /'nowvəˌkeyn/ *Trademark.* [*noncount*] a brand of anesthetic drug used esp. in dentistry.

now (nou) /naw/ *adv.* **1.** at the present time or moment: *I am now reading this definition.* **2.** without further delay; immediately: *Do it now or not at all.* **3.** at the time being referred to: *The case was now ready for the jury.* **4.** in the very recent past: *I saw them just now.* **5.** in these times; nowadays: *Now we have luxuries unknown to our ancestors.* **6.** (used to introduce a statement or question, esp. when starting a new topic): *Now, may I ask you something?* **7.** (used to strengthen a command, request, or the like): *Now stop that!* **8.** (used to hesitate while the speaker thinks of something): *Now, let me think.* —*conj.* **9.** Also, **now that.** inasmuch as; since: *Now that you're here, why not stay for dinner.* —*n.* [*noncount; no article*] **10.** the present time or moment: *Up to now no one has volunteered.* —*adj.* **11.** current; very fashionable: *the now look in clothes.* —***Idiom.*** **12. now and again,** occasionally. Also, **now and then.**

now•a•days (nou′ə dāz′) /'nawəˌdeyz/ *adv.* **1.** at the present time; these days: *Nowadays I hardly ever see her.* —*n.* [*noncount; no article*] **2.** the present: *The kitchens of nowadays are more efficient than those of yesterday.*

no′ way′, *adv. Informal.* absolutely not; no: *No way will I be there.*

no•way (nō′wā′) /'nowˌwey/ also **no•ways** (nō′wāz′) /'nowˌweyz/ *adv. Informal.* in no way; not at all: *He was noway responsible.*

no•where (nō′hwâr′, -wâr′) /'nowˌhwɛər, -ˌwɛər/ *adv.* **1.** in, or at, no place; not anywhere; to no place: *We went nowhere last weekend.* —*n.* [*noncount*] **2.** the state of nonexistence or seeming nonexistence: *Thieves appeared from nowhere.* **3.** a state of not being well-known: *She came out of nowhere and won the nomination.* **4.** an unknown, faraway, remote, or nonexistent place or region: *got lost in the middle of nowhere.* —*adj.* [*usually: before a noun*] *Informal.* **5.** being or leading nowhere; pointless; worthless: *stuck in a nowhere job.* —***Idiom.*** **6. nowhere near,** not nearly: *We have nowhere near enough food.*

no′-win′, *adj.* not likely to yield benefit, success, or victory: *a no-win situation.*

no•wise (nō′wīz′) /'nowˌwayz/ *adv.* not at all.

-nox-, *root.* *-nox-* comes from Latin, where it has the meaning "night." This meaning is found in such words as: EQUINOX, NOCTAMBULISM, NOCTURNAL, NOCTURNE.

nox•ious (nok′shəs) /'nɒkʃəs/ *adj.* harmful to the health: *noxious fumes.* See -NOC-.

noz•zle (noz′əl) /'nɒzəl/ *n.* [*count*] a spout of a pipe, hose or the like, used to direct the flow of something passing through it, as water.

-n't, a contraction of *not: didn't; hadn't; couldn't; shouldn't; won't; mustn't.*

nth (enth) /ɛnθ/ *adj.* **1.** being the last in a series of values, amounts, etc., that increase or decrease: *This is the nth time I've told you.* **2.** utmost; extreme: *the nth degree.*

nt. wt., an abbreviation of: net weight.

nu•ance (no͞o′äns, nyo͞o′-, no͞o äns′, nyo͞o-) /'nuwɑns, 'nyuw-, nuw'ɑns, nyuw-/ *n.* [*count*] a slight difference or distinction, as in expression, meaning, color, tone, etc.: *nuances of feeling in a poem.* —**nu′anced,** *adj.*

nub (nub) /nʌb/ *n.* [*count*] **1.** [*usually singular*] the main point or heart of something; gist: *The nub of the matter is money.* **2.** a knob; a lump or small piece. —**nub′by,** *adj.,* **-bi•er, -bi•est.**

nu•bile (no͞o′bil, -bīl, nyo͞o′-) /'nuwbɪl, -bayl, 'nyuw-/ *adj.* **1.** (of a young woman) sexually developed and physically attractive. **2.** (of a young woman) suitable for marriage.

nu•cle•ar (no͞o′klē ər, nyo͞o′-) /'nuwkliyər, 'nyuw-/ *adj.* **1.** relating to or involving atomic weapons: *a nuclear war.* **2.** operated or powered by atomic energy: *a nuclear power plant; a nuclear submarine.* **3.** [*before a noun*] of, relating to, or forming a nucleus: *nuclear particles.*

nu′clear en′ergy, *n.* [*noncount*] energy released by reactions within atomic nuclei, as in nuclear fission or fusion; atomic energy.

nu′clear fam′ily, *n.* [*count*] a family group that includes only father, mother, and children.

nu′clear reac′tor, *n.* REACTOR (def. 2). Also called **nu′clear pile′.**

nu′clear win′ter, *n.* [*count*] worldwide darkness and cold that some believe could result from extensive dust clouds produced by nuclear war.

nu•cle′ic ac′id (no͞o klē′ik, -klā′-, nyo͞o-) /nuw'kliyɪk, -'kley-, nyuw-/ *n.* [*count*] one of a group of long molecules, either DNA or various types of RNA, carrying genetic information that directs functions of a living cell.

nu•cle•us (no͞o′klē əs, nyo͞o′-) /'nuwkliyəs, 'nyuw-/ *n.* [*count*], *pl.* **-cle•i** (-klē ī′) /-kliyˌay/ **-cle•us•es.** **1.** a central part about which other parts are grouped or gathered; core: *The police managed to arrest some members of the gang, but none that make up its nucleus.* **2.** a special, usually round mass of material in a cell that directs its growth and reproduction and contains most of the genetic material. **3.** the central, positively charged mass within an atom, made up of neutrons and protons and making up most of the atom's mass.

nude (no͞od, nyo͞od) /nuwd, nyuwd/ *adj.,* **nud•er, nud•est,** *n.* **—***adj.* **1.** being without clothing or covering; naked; bare. **2.** (of a photograph, painting, statue, etc.) depicting the nude human figure. **—***n.* **3.** [*count*] a sculpture, painting, etc., of a nude human figure. **4.** [*noncount*] the condition of being unclothed: *to sleep in the nude.*

nudge (nuj) /nʌdʒ/ *v.,* **nudged, nudg•ing,** *n.* **—***v.* [~ + *obj*] **1.** to push slightly or gently, esp. with the elbow to get someone's attention. **2.** to come close to reaching: *The thermometer was nudging 80° F.* **—***n.* [*count*] **3.** a slight or gentle push esp. with the elbow.

nud•ism (no͞o**′**diz əm, nyo͞o**′**-) /ˈnuwdɪzəm, ˈnyuw-/ *n.* [*noncount*] the practice of going nude in public, esp. in secluded places that allow sexually mixed groups. **—nud′ist,** *n.* [*count*], *adj.*

nu•di•ty (no͞o**′**di tē, nyo͞o**′**-) /ˈnuwdɪtiy, ˈnyuw-/ *n.* [*noncount*] the state or condition of being nude.

nug•get (nug**′**it) /ˈnʌgɪt/ *n.* [*count*] **1.** a lump, esp. of gold or other precious metal. **2.** anything small but of great value or significance: *nuggets of wisdom.*

nui•sance (no͞o**′**səns, nyo͞o**′**-) /ˈnuwsəns, ˈnyuw-/ *n.* [*count*] one that is unpleasant, inconvenient, or annoying: *Ants are a nuisance at a picnic.*

nuke (no͞ok, nyo͞ok) /nuwk, nyuwk/ *n., v.,* **nuked, nuk•ing.** *Slang.* **—***n.* [*count*] **1.** a nuclear weapon. **2.** a nuclear power plant or nuclear reactor. **—***v.* [~ + *obj*] **3.** to attack with nuclear weapons. **4.** to heat or cook in a microwave oven: *nuking some leftovers.*

null (nul) /nʌl/ *adj.* **1.** lacking value or significance. **2.** being or amounting to nothing; nil. **3.** *Math.* (of a set) empty: *A null set is a collection that has no members in it.* **—*Idiom.* 4. null and void,** without force or effect; not valid: *The contract is now null and void.* **—nul′li•ty,** *n.* [*noncount*] See -NULL-.

-null-, *root. -null-* comes from Latin, where it has the meaning "none; not one." This meaning is found in such words as: ANNUL, NULL, NULLIFY.

nul•li•fy (nul**′**ə fī**′**) /ˈnʌləˌfay/ *v.* [~ + *obj*], **-fied, -fy•ing. 1.** to make or declare legally no longer binding: *to nullify a contract.* **2.** to deprive (something) of value or effectiveness: *The budget cuts nullified all plans.* **—nul•li•fi•ca•tion** (nul**′**ə fi kā**′**shən) /ˌnʌləfɪˈkeyʃən/ *n.* [*noncount*] See -NULL-.

-num-, *root. -num-* comes from Latin, where it has the meaning "number." This meaning is found in such words as: ENUMERATE, INNUMERABLE, NUMBER, NUMERAL, NUMERATOR, NUMEROUS, OUTNUMBER, SUPERNUMERARY.

numb (num) /nʌm/ *adj.,* **-er, -est,** *v.* **—***adj.* **1.** incapable of feeling sensations, as if under the effects of anesthesia: *fingers that were numb with cold.* **2.** empty of emotion; stunned: *felt numb with grief.* **—***v.* [~ + *obj*] **3.** to make numb. **—numb′ing,** *adj.* **—numb′ly,** *adv.* **—numb′ness,** *n.* [*noncount*]

num•ber (num**′**bər) /ˈnʌmbər/ *n.* **1.** [*count*] a mathematical unit used to count or express an amount, quantity, etc.: *Six is an even number; one, three, and five are odd numbers.* **2.** [*count*] a numeral or group of numerals; a written number. **3.** the total of a group or of a collection of units: [*count*]: *What is the number of people with reserved seats?* [*noncount*]: *Rivers are few in number in that state.* **4.** [*count; usually singular; often:* ~ + *of*] an indefinite quantity; several: *I've been there a number of times.* **5.** [*count*] the particular numeral that is given or assigned to an object so as to distinguish it or show its place in a series: *a house number; a license number; a telephone number.* [*before a numeral*]: *We took the number 113 bus to the station.* **6. numbers,** [*plural*] **a.** a considerable amount or quantity; many: *arrived in large numbers.* **b.** numerical strength; a greater amount: *There is strength in numbers.* **c.** [*the* + ~] a lottery in which bets are placed on numbers chosen at random and published or broadcast. **d.** *Informal.* the figures representing the actual cost, expense, profit, etc.: *The numbers didn't really add up, so the accountant went back over them.* **e.** arithmetic: *Are you any good at numbers?* **7.** [*count*] a tune or arrangement for singing or dancing; a piece of music: *The next number they played was "Sunshine of Your Love."* **8.** [*count*] a certain performance within a show, as a song or dance: *Don't miss the number that opens the second act.* **9.** [*noncount*] a category of change in the form of a word which indicates whether the word refers to one or to more than one thing, in the distinction between singular and plural: *In English, number is represented by the ending -s for many nouns in the plural, such as* boys, books, clothes, *and* dolls. **10.** [*count; usually singular*] *Informal.* person; individual: *The girls think he's a pretty hot number. One of our number is no longer with us; Bob died suddenly last week.* **—***v.* **11.** [~ + *obj*] to mark with or distinguish by numbers, usually in a series: *He numbered the examples one through ten on the board.* **12.** to amount to or reach in number; total: [~ + *obj*]: *Our air force numbers one thousand bombers.* [*no obj*]: *Our army numbers in the thousands.* **13.** [~ + *obj*] to consider or include in a number: *I number myself among his friends. He was numbered among their enemies.* **14.** [~ + *obj; usually: be* + ~*ed*] to be close to the end of something: *He knew his hours were numbered after he took three bullets in the chest.* **15.** [~ + *obj*] to figure out the amount or quantity of; count: *We numbered the days until we could go home again.* **—*Idiom.* 16. by the numbers,** according to standard procedures. **17. do a number on,** [~ + *obj*] *Slang.* to defeat or humiliate: *Their team did a number on us, beating us 55-0.* **18. get** or **have someone's number,** *Informal.* to figure out or understand someone's character, intentions, or any hidden motives or plans they may have: *She thinks she's fooling them, but in fact they have her number. She's got my number all right; she knew just what I would do.* **19. without number,** of unknown or countless number; vast: *Stars and galaxies without number fill the universe.* See -NUM-.

num•ber•less (num**′**bər lis) /ˈnʌmbərlɪs/ *adj.* too many to be counted: *numberless grains of sand.* See -NUM-.

nu•mer•a•ble (no͞o**′**mər ə bəl, nyo͞o**′**-) /ˈnuwmərəbəl, ˈnyuw-/ *adj.* that can be counted, totaled, or numbered. See -NUM-.

nu•mer•al (no͞o**′**mər əl, nyo͞o**′**-; no͞om**′**rəl, nyo͞om**′**-) /ˈnuwmərəl, ˈnyuw-; ˈnuwmrəl, ˈnyuwm-/ *n.* [*count*] a word, letter, symbol, or figure representing a number: *the Roman numeral X for 10.* See -NUM-.

nu•mer•ate (*v.* no͞o**′**mə rāt**′**, nyo͞o**′**-; *adj.* -mər it) / *v.* ˈnuwməˌreyt, ˈnyuw-; *adj.* -mərɪt/ *v.,* **-at•ed, -at•ing,** *adj.* **—***v.* [~ + *obj*] **1.** to enumerate. **—***adj.* **2.** able to use or understand numerical techniques of mathematics. **—nu•mer•a•cy** (no͞o**′**mər ə sē, nyo͞o**′**-) /ˈnuwmərəsiy, ˈnyuw-/ *n.* [*noncount*] See -NUM-.

nu•mer•a•tor (no͞o**′**mə rā**′**tər, nyo͞o**′**-) /ˈnuwməˌreytər, ˈnyuw-/ *n.* [*count*] the term of a fraction, usually written above or before the line, that indicates the number of equal parts that are to be added together: *In the number three-fifths, three is the numerator.* Compare DENOMINATOR. See -NUM-.

nu•mer•i•cal (no͞o mer**′**i kəl, nyo͞o-) /nuwˈmɛrɪkəl, nyuw-/ also **nu•mer′ic,** *adj.* **1.** of or relating to numbers; of the nature of a number: *Put them in numerical order.* **2.** expressed in numbers: *numerical equations.* **—nu•mer′i•cal•ly,** *adv.* See -NUM-.

nu•mer•ol•o•gy (no͞o**′**mə rol**′**ə jē, nyo͞o**′**-) /ˌnuwməˈrɒlədʒiy, ˌnyuw-/ *n.* [*noncount*] the study of numbers, as the figures designating the year of one's birth, to determine their secret meaning. **—nu′mer•ol′o•gist,** *n.* [*count*]

nu•mer•ous (no͞o**′**mər əs, nyo͞o**′**-) /ˈnuwmərəs, ˈnyuw-/ *adj.* **1.** very many; existing in great quantity: *We have been there on numerous occasions.* **2.** large in number: *Recent audiences have been more numerous.* See -NUM-.

num•skull or **numb•skull** (num**′**skul**′**) /ˈnʌmˌskʌl/ *n.* [*count*] a dull-witted or stupid person.

nun (nun) /nʌn/ *n.* [*count*] a woman who is a member of a religious order, esp. one who observes vows of poverty, chastity, and obedience.

-nunc-, *root. -nunc-* comes from Latin, where it has the meaning "call; say." It is related to -NOUNCE-. This meaning is found in such words as: ANNUNCIATION, DENUNCIATION, ENUNCIATE, NUNCIO, PRONUNCIATION, RENUNCIATION.

nun•ci•o (nun**′**shē ō**′**, -sē ō**′**, no͝on**′**-) /ˈnʌnʃiyˌow, -siyˌow, ˈnʊn-/ *n.* [*count*], *pl.* **-ci•os.** a permanent diplomatic representative of the pope at a foreign capital. See -NUNC-.

nun•ner•y (nun**′**ə rē) /ˈnʌnəriy/ *n.* [*count*], *pl.* **-ner•ies.** a residence for nuns; convent.

nup•tial (nup**′**shəl, -chəl) /ˈnʌpʃəl, -tʃəl/ *adj.* **1.** of or relating to marriage or the marriage ceremony: *nuptial vows.* **—***n.* **2.** Usually, **nuptials.** [*plural*] a wedding or marriage: *The nuptials were held in a beautiful old cathedral.*

nurse (nûrs) /nɜrs/ *n., v.,* **nursed, nurs•ing. —***n.* [*count*]

1. a person trained in the care of the sick, esp. a registered nurse. See illustration at HOSPITAL. **2.** a woman who has the general care of a child or children; dry nurse. **3.** a woman who feeds someone else's baby from her own breast; wet nurse. **—***v.* **4.** [~ + *obj*] to tend to or take care of (someone) in sickness: *She nursed him back to health.* **5.** [~ + *obj*] to try to cure (an ailment) by taking care of oneself: *She was nursing a cold.* **6.** (of a woman) to feed (an infant) at the breast: [~ + *obj*]: *The mother nursed her baby.* [*no obj*]: *She was nursing.* **7.** [*no obj*] (of an infant) to feed at the breast. **8.** [~ + *obj*] to handle carefully or fondly, esp. to consume slowly: *to nurse a cup of tea.* **9.** [~ + *obj*] to keep steadily in one's mind or memory: *He nursed a grudge.* **—nurs′er,** *n.* [*count*]

nurse•maid (nûrs′mād′) /ˈnɜrsˌmeyd/ *n.* [*count*] a woman or girl whose job is to care for children, esp. in a household. Also called **nurs′er•y•maid′.**

nurs•er•y (nûr′sə rē) /ˈnɜrsəriy/ *n.* [*count*], *pl.* **-er•ies. 1.** a room or place set apart for infants or very young children. **2.** a nursery school or day nursery. **3.** a place where young trees or other plants are raised.

nurs′ery rhyme′, *n.* [*count*] a short, simple poem or song for very young children.

nurs′ery school′, *n.* a school for children before they attend kindergarten: [*count*]: *a new nursery school.* [*noncount*]: *attending nursery school.*

nurs′ing home′, *n.* [*count*] **1.** an institution caring for older or sick people where the patients can live. **2.** *Chiefly Brit.* a small private hospital.

nurs•ling or **nurse•ling** (nûrs′ling) /ˈnɜrslɪŋ/ *n.* [*count*] a nursing infant or young animal.

nur•ture (nûr′chər) /ˈnɜrtʃər/ *v.,* **-tured, -tur•ing,** *n.* **—***v.* [~ + *obj*] **1.** to feed; supply with nourishment. **2.** to encourage or provide moral support: *He nurtured his students in their studies.* **3.** to bring up; train; educate. **—***n.* [*noncount*] **4.** upbringing; training; education; development: *providing for the nurture of young artists.* **5.** something that nourishes; nourishment; food. **—nur′tur•er,** *n.* [*count*]

nut (nut) /nʌt/ *n.* [*count*] **1.** a dry fruit made up of a kernel that may be eaten, and enclosed in a woody or leathery shell. **2.** the kernel itself. **3.** a hard, one-seeded fruit, as the chestnut or the acorn. **4.** a block, usually of metal, made with a threaded hole so that it can be screwed down on a bolt to hold together objects through which the bolt passes. **5.** *Slang.* a person who is greatly interested in or enthusiastic about something; devotee: *She's a sports nut.* **6.** *Slang.* **a.** a foolish, silly, or eccentric person. **b.** an insane person. **—*Idiom.* 7. a hard** or **tough nut to crack, a.** a difficult problem: *Getting a tax refund this year is going to be a tough nut to crack.* **b.** a person difficult to understand or convince.

nut•crack•er (nut′krak′ər) /ˈnʌtˌkrækər/ *n.* [*count*] an instrument for cracking the shells of nuts.

nut•hatch (nut′hach′) /ˈnʌtˌhætʃ/ *n.* [*count*] a small, sharp-beaked bird that seeks food along tree trunks and branches.

nut•meat (nut′mēt′) /ˈnʌtˌmiyt/ *n.* [*count*] the kernel of a nut, usually one that can be eaten.

nut•meg (nut′meg) /ˈnʌtmɛg/ *n.* **1.** [*count*] the hard, strong-smelling seed of an East Indian tree. **2.** [*noncount*] the powder made from this seed and used as a spice.

nu•tri•a (no͞o′trē ə, nyo͞o′-) /ˈnuwtriyə, ˈnyuw-/ *n.* **1.** [*count*] a large South American animal that is related to the rat and is at home in water. **2.** [*noncount*] the fur of this animal, used for garments.

nu•tri•ent (no͞o′trē ənt, nyo͞o′-) /ˈnuwtriyənt, ˈnyuw-/ *adj.* [*before a noun*] **1.** nourishing; providing nourishment. **—***n.* [*count*] **2.** a nutrient substance.

nu•tri•ment (no͞o′trə mənt, nyo͞o′-) /ˈnuwtrəmənt, ˈnyuw-/ *n.* [*count*] any substance that when taken into a living organism serves to keep it alive.

nu•tri•tion (no͞o trish′ən, nyo͞o-) /nuwˈtrɪʃən, nyuw-/ *n.* [*noncount*] **1.** the study or science of the food and diet requirements of humans and animals for proper health and development: *majoring in nutrition.* **2.** the process by which living things take in and use food material. **3.** food; nutriment. **—nu•tri′tion•al,** *adj.* **—nu•tri′tion•al•ly,** *adv.* **—nu•tri′tion•ist,** *n.* [*count*] **—nu•tri•tive** (no͞o′tri tiv, nyo͞o′-) /ˈnuwtrɪtɪv, ˈnyuw-/ *adj.*

nu•tri•tious (no͞o trish′əs, nyo͞o-) /nuwˈtrɪʃəs, nyuw-/ *adj.* providing nourishment; nourishing: *Vegetables and grains are nutritious foods.* **—nu•tri′tious•ly,** *adv.* **—nu•tri′tious•ness,** *n.* [*noncount*]

nuts (nuts) /nʌts/ *Slang.* **—***interj.* **1.** (used to express feelings of disgust, defiance, disapproval, despair, etc.): *"Nuts; late again," he groaned.* **—***adj.* [*be* + ~] **2.** insane; crazy: *I'm going nuts with all this work.* **—*Idiom.* 3. be nuts about,** [~ + *obj*] to admire fervently; love deeply: *He's nuts about baseball.*

nut•shell (nut′shel′) /ˈnʌtˌʃɛl/ *n.* [*count*] **1.** the shell of a nut. **—*Idiom.* 2. in a nutshell,** briefly; in a few words: *That, in a nutshell, is our story.*

nut•ty (nut′ē) /ˈnʌtiy/ *adj.,* **-ti•er, -ti•est. 1.** nutlike, esp. in flavor. **2.** *Slang.* **a.** silly or ridiculous: *a nutty idea.* **b.** peculiar, odd, strange; eccentric: *I saw this nutty old man walking around the park talking to lamp posts.* **—nut′ti•ness,** *n.* [*noncount*]

nuz•zle (nuz′əl) /ˈnʌzəl/ *v.,* **-zled, -zling,** *n.* **—***v.* **1.** [~ + *obj*] to touch or rub with the nose, snout, muzzle, etc.: *The deer nuzzled her neck.* **2.** to lie very close (to); cuddle or snuggle up (to): [*no obj*]: *They nuzzled under the covers.* [~ + *obj*]: *He nuzzled her under the covers.* **—***n.* [*count*] **3.** an affectionate embrace or cuddle.

NV, an abbreviation of: Nevada.

NW or **N.W.** or **n.w.,** an abbreviation of: **1.** northwest. **2.** northwestern.

NY or **N.Y.,** an abbreviation of: New York.

ny•lon (nī′lon) /ˈnaylɒn/ *n.* **1.** [*noncount*] a substance like thin plastic, made into fibers and sheets, usually tough, strong, and easily stretched, used esp. for yarn, fabrics, and bristles. **2. nylons,** [*plural*] stockings made of nylon.

nymph (nimf) /nɪmf/ *n.* [*count*] **1.** any of various minor divinities of mythology thought of as beautiful young women living in the sea, a river, a tree, or a mountain. **2.** a beautiful or graceful young woman. **3.** the young of an insect.

nym•pho•ma•ni•a (nim′fə mā′nē ə, -mān′yə) /ˌnɪmfəˈmeyniyə, -ˈmeynyə/ *n.* [*noncount*] overwhelmingly strong sexual desire in a female. Compare SATYRIASIS. **—nym•pho•ma•ni•ac** (nim′fə mā′nē ak′) /ˌnɪmfəˈmeyniyˌæk/ *n.* [*count*], *adj.*

O, o (ō) /ow/ *n.* [*count*], *pl.* **O's** or **Os; o's** or **os** or **oes.** the 15th letter of the English alphabet, a vowel.

O (ō) /ow/ *interj., n., pl.* **O's.** —*interj.* **1.** (used before a person's name when speaking to that person directly, esp. in solemn or poetic language): *Hear, O Great King, the plea of your subjects.* **2.** (used to express strong emotion, such as surprise, pain, annoyance, desire, or gladness): *"O, no, they're back!" "O, now you want to go."* —*n.* [*count*] **3.** the exclamation "O": *A series of O's occurred in his speech to the king.*

O, *Symbol.* **1.** the 15th in order or in a series. **2.** the Arabic numeral zero; cipher. **3.** a major blood group. **4.** oxygen.

-o, *suffix.* **1.** *-o* is used as the final element in certain nouns that are shortened from longer nouns: *ammo* (from "ammunition"); *combo* (from "combination"); *promo* (from "promotion"). **2.** *-o* is also attached to certain adjectives and nouns to form nouns that have an unfavorable or insulting meaning: *weird* + *-o* → *weirdo (= a very weird person); wine* + *-o* → *wino (= someone who drinks too much wine).* **3.** *-o* is attached to certain nouns and adjectives to form informal nouns or adjectives; these are often used when speaking directly to another: *kid* + *-o* → *kiddo (= a kid or person); neat* + *-o* → *neato (= an informal use of "neat"); right* + *-o* → *righto (= an informal use of "right").*

O., an abbreviation of: **1.** October. **2.** Ohio.

oaf (ōf), *n.* [*count*] a crudely clumsy or stupid person. —**oaf′ish,** *adj.* —**oaf′ish•ly,** *adv.*

oak (ōk) /owk/ *n.* **1.** [*count*] a tree or shrub of the beech family, which bears the acorn as its fruit. **2.** [*noncount*] the hard, long-lasting wood of such a tree. —**oak′en,** *adj.*

oar (ôr, ōr), *n.* [*count*] **1.** a long pole with a broad, wide blade at one end, used as a lever for rowing or otherwise moving or steering a boat: *dipping the oars into the water and stroking.* —*v.* **2.** to (cause to) row with or as if with oars: [~ + *obj*]: *He oared the boat downstream.* [*no obj*]: *She oared on the lake.* —**oars′man,** *n.* [*count*], *pl.* **-men.**

o•a•sis (ō ā′sis) /ow'eysɪs/ *n.* [*count*], *pl.* **-ses** (-sēz) /-siyz/. **1.** an area in a desert region where plants and trees can grow, usually having a spring or well. **2.** a safe, quiet, or welcoming place, usually away from work or stress; haven.

oat (ōt), *n.* **1.** [*noncount*] a cereal grass grown for its grain. **2.** Usually, **oats.** [*plural*] the grain of this plant. —***Idiom.* 3. feel one's oats,** to have a strong sense of self-confidence. —**oat′en,** *adj.*

oath (ōth) /owθ/ *n.* [*count*], *pl.* **oaths** (ōthz, ōths). **1.** a solemn declaration to God, a god, or some person or thing that is sacred, that what one says is the truth, or that what one promises will be done. **2.** an irreverent use of the name of God or of anything sacred. **3.** a curse word. —***Idiom.* 4. take an oath,** to swear solemnly; vow: *He took an oath to care for his niece.* [~ + *that clause*]: *He took an oath that he would care for his niece.* **5. under oath,** [*noncount*] solemnly bound by the obligations of an oath.

oat•meal (ōt′mēl′) /'owt,miyl/ *n.* [*noncount*] **1.** meal made from ground or rolled oats. **2.** a cooked breakfast food made from this.

ob-, *prefix. ob-* is attached to roots and means "toward," "to," "on," "over," "against": *object, obligate.*

ob•du•ra•cy (ob′dŏŏ rə sē, -dyŏŏ-) /'ɒbdʊrəsiy, -dyʊ-/ *n.* [*noncount*] the state or condition of being obdurate. See -DUR-.

ob•du•rate (ob′dŏŏ rit, -dyŏŏ-) /'ɒbdʊrɪt, -dyʊ-/ *adj.* not moved by persuasion or pity; not giving in; unyielding: *an obdurate opponent.* —**ob′du•rate•ness,** *n.* [*noncount*] See -DUR-.

o•be•di•ence (ō bē′dē əns) /ow'biydiyəns/ *n.* [*noncount*] the state or condition of being obedient.

o•be•di•ent (ō bē′dē ənt) /ow'biydiyənt/ *adj.* complying with authority; willing to obey: *an obedient child.* [*be* + ~ + *to* + *obj*]: *She is obedient to her parents.*

o•bei•sance (ō bā′səns, ō bē′-) /ow'beysəns, ow'biy-/ *n.* **1.** [*count*] a movement of the body, as a bow, expressing respect or submissiveness. **2.** [*noncount*] deference; homage. —**o•bei′sant,** *adj.*

ob•e•lisk (ob′ə lisk) /'ɒbəlɪsk/ *n.* [*count*] a tall, pointed, four-sided pillar of stone.

o•bese (ō bēs′) /ow'biys/ *adj.* extremely fat. —**o•be•si•ty** (ō bē′si tē) /ow'biysɪtiy/ *n.* [*noncount*]

o•bey (ō bā′) /ow'bey/ *v.* **1.** [~ + *obj*] to do or follow the wishes or instructions of: *She always obeyed her parents.* **2.** [*no obj*] to be obedient: *Teach your dog to obey.* **3.** [~ + *obj*] to comply with; follow: *to obey orders.* **4.** [~ + *obj*] to respond quickly to: *The car obeys my slightest touch on the steering wheel.* **5.** [*usually not: be* + *~-ing;* ~ + *obj*] to conform to; be subject to: *All objects obey the law of gravity.* —**Related Words.** OBEY is a verb, OBEDIENT is an adjective, OBEDIENCE is a noun: *These children obey their parents. These children are obedient to their parents. These children have learned obedience.*

ob•fus•cate (ob′fə skāt′, ob fus′kāt) /'ɒbfə,skeyt, ɒb'fʌskeyt/ *v.* [~ + *obj*], **-cat•ed, -cat•ing.** to confuse; make unclear: *You are deliberately obfuscating the issue.* —**ob′fus•ca′tion,** *n.* [*noncount*] —**ob•fus•ca•to•ry** (ob-fus′kə tôr′ē, -tōr′ē) /ɒb'fʌskə,tɔriy, -,towriy/ *adj.*

o•bit (ō bit′) /ow'bɪt/ *n.* [*count*] an obituary.

o•bit•u•ar•y (ō bich′ŏŏ er′ē) /ow'bɪtʃuw,ɛriy/ *n.* [*count*], *pl.* **-ar•ies.** a written notice of the death of a person, as in a newspaper, often with a biographical sketch.

obj., an abbreviation of: **1.** object. **2.** objective.

ob•ject (*n.* ob′jikt, -jekt; *v.* əb jekt′) / *n.* 'ɒbdʒɪkt, -dʒɛkt; *v.* əb'dʒɛkt/ *n.* [*count*] **1.** anything that can be seen or touched and is for the most part stable or lasting in form, and is usually not alive: *to collect small objects.* **2.** a thing, person, or matter to which thought or action is directed; the cause of such thought or action: *the object of her desires.* **3.** the purpose toward which effort or action is directed; goal; objective: *His main object was to take over the company.* **4.** a noun, noun phrase, or pronoun in a phrase or sentence that represents either the goal or the thing receiving the action of a verb, or that represents the goal of a preposition: *The word* ball *in* I hit the ball *is an object. The words* her *and* question *in* He asked her a question *are objects. The word* table *in the phrase* under the table *is also an object.* Compare DIRECT OBJECT, INDIRECT OBJECT. **5.** [*noncount*] a cause for worry or restraint: *Money is no object, so spend all you want.* —*v.* **6.** to express or feel disapproval, dislike, or opposition: [~ + *to* + *obj*]: *They objected to my proposal.* [*no obj*]: *They wanted to sell the property, but we objected strongly.* **7.** [~ + *that clause*] to state or present (some fact or opinion, etc.) as the thing that one opposes: *They objected that the rules were unfair.* —**ob•jec′tor,** *n.* [*count*] See -JEC-.

ob•jec•tion (əb jek′shən) /əb'dʒɛkʃən/ *n.* [*count*] **1.** a reason or argument offered in opposition: *raised an objection to the proposal.* **2.** the act of objecting. **3.** a feeling of disapproval or disagreement: *Despite her family's objection, she married him.* See -JEC-.

ob•jec•tion•a•ble (əb jek′shə nə bəl) /əb'dʒɛkʃənəbəl/ *adj.* causing a feeling of disapproval; offensive; unacceptable: *objectionable behavior.* See -JEC-.

ob•jec•tive (əb jek′tiv) /əb'dʒɛktɪv/ *n.* [*count*] **1.** a purpose; aim; goal: *The army's objective was to seize the town before the invaders did.* —*adj.* **2.** not influenced by personal feelings or prejudice: *an objective opinion.* **3.** of, relating to, or being a grammatical case that typically indicates the object of a transitive verb or of a preposition (contrasted with *subjective*). —**ob•jec′tive•ly,** *adv.* —**ob•jec•tiv•i•ty** (ob′jik tiv′i tē, -jek-) /,ɒbdʒɪk'tɪvɪtiy, -dʒɛk-/ **ob•jec′tive•ness,** *n.* [*noncount*] See -JEC-.

ob′ject les′son, *n.* [*count*] a practical or concrete demonstration or example of a principle: *Watching him run that meeting was an object lesson in leadership.*

ob•jet d'art (ob′zhā där′) /,ɒb'ʒey dɑr/ *n.* [*count*], *pl.* **ob•jets d'art** (ob′zhā där′) /,ɒb'ʒey dɑr/. an object of artistic worth or interest. Also called **ob•jet′.**

ob•late (ob′lāt, o blāt′) /'ɒbleyt, ɒ'bleyt/ *adj.* flattened at the top. See -LAT-[1].

ob•li•gate (ob′li gāt′) /'ɒblɪ,geyt/ *v.* [~ + *obj* + *to* + *verb*], **-gat•ed, -gat•ing.** to make (someone) feel or understand that some action is morally or legally necessary: *The contract obligates you to pay on time.* See -LIG-.

ob•li•ga•tion (ob′li gā′shən) /,ɒblɪ'geyʃən/ *n.* **1.** something that a person feels morally or legally bound to do: [*count*]: *to feel an obligation to help one's parents.* [*noncount*]: *a strong sense of family obligation.* **2.** [*noncount*] a binding promise or contract: *Try our product, with no obligation to buy.* See -LIG-.

o•blig•a•to•ry (ə blig′ə tôr′ē, -tōr′ē, ob′li gə-) /ə'blɪgə,tɔriy, -,towriy, 'ɒblɪgə-/ *adj.* required; necessary;

mandatory; compulsory: *obligatory payment of taxes.* See -LIG-.

o•blige (ə blīj′) /ə'blaydʒ/ *v.,* **o•bliged, o•blig•ing. 1.** to require, as by law, contrast, conscience, or force; bind: [*be* + ~-*ed* + *to* + *verb*]: *After having been invited to their party, we were obliged to invite them to ours.* [~ + *obj* + *to* + *verb*]: *The will obliges the heirs to live in the family mansion.* **2.** [~ + *obj; usually: be* + ~-*ed*] to place under a debt of gratitude for a favor or service: *We are much obliged for the ride.* **3.** to do a favor or perform some service for (another): [~ + *obj*]: *The singer obliged us with a song.* [*no obj*]: *He would be happy to oblige.* —**o•blig′ing,** *adj.: He's very obliging and will certainly help you.* See -LIG-.

o•blique (ə blēk′, ō blēk′; *Military.* ə blīk′, ō blīk′) /ə'bliyk, ow'bliyk; *Military.* ə'blayk, ow'blayk/ *adj.* **1.** slanting; sloping; sideways: *an oblique line.* **2.** not straight or direct, such as a course. **3.** indirectly expressed: *an oblique reference to the queen.*

ob•lit•er•ate (ə blit′ə rāt′) /ə'blɪtə,reyt/ *v.* [~ + *obj*], **-at•ed, -at•ing. 1.** to remove or destroy all traces of: *The bombardment obliterated the village.* **2.** to make (something) impossible to read or decipher; blot out; efface. —**ob•lit′er•a′tion,** *n.* [*noncount*] —**ob•lit′er•a′tor,** *n.* [*count*] See -LIT-.

ob•liv•i•on (ə bliv′ē ən) /ə'blɪviyən/ *n.* [*noncount*] **1.** the state of being completely forgotten: *All their bright plans have faded into oblivion.* **2.** the state of forgetting or of being not aware of what is going on around oneself: *the oblivion of sleep.*

ob•liv•i•ous (ə bliv′ē əs) /ə'blɪviyəs/ *adj.* **1.** [*be* + ~ + *to/of* + *obj*] unaware of what is around oneself: *oblivious to the danger.* **2.** [*usually: be* + ~; *sometimes: after a noun*] forgetful; unable to remember: *Some survivors just sat and stared, oblivious.* —**ob•liv′i•ous•ness,** *n.* [*noncount*]

ob•long (ob′lông′, -long′) /'ɒb,lɔŋ, -,lɒŋ/ *adj.* **1.** in the form of a rectangle one of whose dimensions is much greater than the other. —*n.* [*count*] **2.** an oblong figure.

ob•lo•quy (ob′lə kwē) /'ɒbləkwiy/ *n.* [*noncount*] **1.** blame or verbal abuse. **2.** discredit or disgrace. See -LOQ-.

ob•nox•ious (əb nok′shəs) /əb'nɒkʃəs/ *adj.* very objectionable or offensive: *an obnoxious bore.* See -NOC-.

o•boe (ō′bō) /'owbow/ *n.* [*count*] a woodwind instrument having a slender, cone-shaped, tubelike body and a double-reed mouthpiece. —**o′bo•ist,** *n.* [*count*]

ob•scene (əb sēn′) /əb'siyn/ *adj.* **1.** offensive to people's feelings about what is moral or decent: *obscene language.* **2.** intended to excite or stimulate sexual appetite; lewd: *obscene movies.* **3.** terrible; disgusting; abominable; repulsive: *obscene cruelty.* —**ob•scene′ness,** *n.* [*noncount*]

ob•scen•i•ty (ob sen′i tē, -sē′ni-) /ɒb'sɛnɪtiy, -'siynɪ-/ *n.* **1.** [*noncount*] the state or condition of being obscene. **2.** [*count*] an act, word, or statement that is considered obscene.

ob•scure (əb skyŏŏr′) /əb'skyʊr/ *adj.,* **-scur•er, -scur•est,** *v.,* **-scured, -scur•ing,** —*adj.* **1.** not clear or plain; ambiguous, vague, or uncertain: *an obscure message; obscure motives.* **2.** not easily noticed: *the obscure beginnings of a revolutionary movement.* **3.** of little or no fame or distinction; unknown: *an obscure artist.* **4.** dark; dim; murky; hard to see, as if hidden by darkness: *An obscure figure loomed out of the shadows.* —*v.* [~ + *obj*] **5.** to conceal; cover; mask: *Poets sometimes try to obscure their message.* **6.** to make dark or indistinct: *The darkness obscured his features.* —**ob•scure′ly,** *adv.*

ob•scur•i•ty (ob skyŏŏr′ə tē) /ɒb'skyʊrətiy/ *n.* [*noncount*] **1.** the condition or state of being hard to see because of darkness or dimness. **2.** the condition or state of being unknown or not famous: *He rose from obscurity to sudden fame.*

ob•se•qui•ous (əb sē′kwē əs) /əb'siykwiyəs/ *adj.* slavishly attentive; servile; fawning: *The waiter gave an obsequious bow to the duchess.* See -SEQ-.

ob•serv•ance (əb zûr′vəns) /əb'zɜrvəns/ *n.* [*noncount*] **1.** the action of following, obeying, or complying with a law, custom, etc. **2.** a celebration by ceremonies, practices, etc.: *the observance of the Sabbath.* **3.** an act or instance of watching; observation. See -SERV-[2].

ob•serv•ant (əb zûr′vənt) /əb'zɜrvənt/ *adj.* **1.** quick to notice; alert: *Be observant for signs of danger.* **2.** careful in the observing of a law, religious ritual, custom, or the like: *an observant Catholic.* See -SERV-[2].

ob•ser•va•tion (ob′zûr vā′shən) /,ɒbzɜr'veyʃən/ *n.* **1.** [*count*] an act or instance of watching attentively. **2.** [*noncount*] the ability or habit of observing or noticing things: *powers of observation.* **3.** an act or instance of watching carefully or noting something for a scientific or other special purpose: [*count*]: *a classroom observation of a teacher by the headmaster.* [*noncount; under* + ~]: *to keep the patient under observation until he recovers.* **4.** [*count*] a judgment made on the basis of what one has observed: *He shared her observations on how people behaved.* **5.** [*count*] a remark; comment. See -SERV-[2].

ob•serv•a•to•ry (əb zûr′və tôr′ē, -tōr′ē) /əb'zɜrvə,tɔriy, -,towriy/ *n.* [*count*], *pl.* **-ries.** a building equipped for studying the heavens or other natural phenomena, esp. a place equipped with a powerful telescope. See -SERV-[2].

ob•serve (əb zûrv′) /əb'zɜrv/ *v.,* **-served, -serv•ing. 1.** to see, watch, or notice: [~ + *obj*]: *I observed a person dashing across the field.* [*no obj*]: *I'm just observing; I'm not participating.* **2.** to look at with attention: [~ + *obj*]: *The scientists observed the eclipse.* [*no obj*]: *to observe and learn.* **3.** [*used with quotations*] to state by way of comment; remark: *"You're simply not ready," he quietly observed.* **4.** [~ + *obj*] to keep or maintain in one's action, conduct, etc.: *to observe silence.* **5.** [~ + *obj*] to obey, comply with, or conform to: *to observe the law.* **6.** [~ + *obj*] to celebrate, as a holiday, in a customary way. —**ob•serv′er,** *n.* [*count*] See -SERV-[2].

ob•sess (əb ses′) /əb'sɛs/ *v.* **1.** [~ + *obj*] to dominate the thoughts of; preoccupy: *Revenge obsessed him.* **2.** [*no obj*] to think about something without stopping: *He obsessed about his old girlfriend for years.* See -SESS-.

ob•ses•sion (əb sesh′ən) /əb'sɛʃən/ *n.* **1.** [*noncount*] the intense preoccupation of one's thoughts by a single, continuous idea or feeling; the state of being obsessed. **2.** [*count*] the idea, image, desire, etc., itself. See -SESS-.

ob•sess•ive (ob ses′iv) /ɒb'sɛsɪv/ *adj.* **1.** of, being, or resembling an obsession: *an obsessive fear of disease.* **2.** possessed or tending to be possessed by obsessions: *an obsessive personality.* —**ob•sess′ive•ly,** *adv.* See -SESS-.

ob•sid•i•an (əb sid′ē ən) /əb'sɪdiyən/ *n.* [*noncount*] a hard, dark, glasslike substance formed when volcanic eruptions cool.

ob•so•les•cence (ob′sə les′əns) /,ɒbsə'lɛsəns/ *n.* [*noncount*] the state or quality of becoming obsolescent or obsolete.

ob•so•les•cent (ob′sə les′ənt) /,ɒbsə'lɛsənt/ *adj.* becoming obsolete; passing out of use, as a word or a product.

ob•so•lete (ob′sə lēt′, ob′sə lēt′) /,ɒbsə'liyt, 'ɒbsə,liyt/ *adj.* **1.** no longer in general use; fallen into disuse: *obsolete customs.* **2.** no longer useful; out-of-date: *an obsolete battleship.*

ob•sta•cle (ob′stə kəl) /'ɒbstəkəl/ *n.* [*count*] something that prevents or slows progress; an obstruction; hindrance. See -STAN-.

ob•ste•tri•cian (ob′sti trish′ən) /,ɒbstɪ'trɪʃən/ *n.* [*count*] a doctor who is a specialist in obstetrics. See -STAN-.

ob•stet•rics (əb ste′triks) /əb'stɛtrɪks/ *n.* [*noncount; used with a singular verb*] the branch of medical science dealing with pregnancy and childbirth. —**ob•stet′ri•cal, ob•stet′ric,** *adj.* See -STAN-.

ob•sti•na•cy (ob′stə nə sē) /'ɒbstənəsiy/ *n.* [*noncount*] the quality or state of being obstinate. See -STAN-.

ob•sti•nate (ob′stə nit) /'ɒbstənɪt/ *adj.* firmly or stubbornly unwilling to change one's purpose, opinion, or course of action: *Our neighbors were so obstinate they refused to evacuate their house even during the flood.* See -STAN-.

ob•strep•er•ous (əb strep′ər əs) /əb'strɛpərəs/ *adj.* **1.** resisting control or restraint; unruly: *obstreperous demonstrators.* **2.** noisy, clamorous, or boisterous: *an obstreperous party.*

ob•struct (əb strukt′) /əb'strʌkt/ *v.* [~ + *obj*] **1.** to block or close up, as by being in the way: *The fallen rocks obstructed the road.* **2.** to interrupt, slow down, or prevent the progress of: *to face charges of obstructing justice.* —**ob•struc′tive,** *adj.* —**ob•struc′tive•ness,** *n.* [*noncount*] See -STRU-.

ob•struc•tion (ob struk′shən) /ɒb'strʌkʃən/ *n.* **1.** [*count*] something that obstructs something else: *The tanks rolled over the obstructions the farmers had placed in their path.* **2.** [*noncount*] the act of obstructing something: *obstruction of justice.* See -STRU-.

ob•struc•tion•ist (əb struk′shə nist) /əb'strʌkʃənɪst/ *n.* [*count*] a person who deliberately delays or prevents progress. —**ob•struc′tion•ism,** *n.* [*noncount*] See -STRU-.

ob•tain (əb tān′) /əb'teyn/ *v.* **1.** [~ + *obj*] to come into possession of; acquire: *to obtain a driver's license.* **2.** [*no obj; usually: not be + ~ -ing*] to be common or customary, esp. so as to be in force or to exist in a particular place or time: *the morals that obtained in ancient Rome.* —**ob•tain′a•ble,** *adj.* —**ob•tain′ment,** *n.* [*noncount*] See -TAIN-.

ob•trude (əb trōōd′) /əb'truwd/ *v.,* **-trud•ed, -trud•ing.** **1.** to thrust forward; impose without invitation or need: [*~ + obj*]: *obtruding his opinion on others.* [*~ + on/ upon + obj*]: *to obtrude on someone's privacy.* **2.** [*no obj*] to (cause to) push or stick out: *The veins on his forearms obtruded like wires.* [*~ + obj*]: *The plastic material was obtruded through small holes in the metal plate.* See -TRUDE-.

ob•tru•sive (ob trōō′siv) /ɒb'truwsɪv/ *adj.* causing attention in an unpleasant way: *obtrusive gold decoration.* —**ob•tru′sive•ly,** *adv.* —**ob•tru′sive•ness,** *n.* [*noncount*] See -TRUDE-.

ob•tuse (əb tōōs′, -tyōōs′) /əb'tuws, -'tyuws/ *adj.* **1.** not quick or alert in the ability to understand or feel; insensitive; dull: *an obtuse mind.* **2.** (of an angle) greater than 90° but less than 180°. —**ob•tuse′ness,** *n.* [*noncount*]

ob•verse (*n.* ob′vûrs; *adj.* ob vûrs′, ob′vûrs) / *n.* 'ɒbvɜrs; *adj.* ɒb'vɜrs, 'ɒbvɜrs/ *n.* [*count*] **1.** the side of a coin, medal, flag, etc., that bears the principal design (opposed to *reverse*). **2.** the front or principal surface of anything. **3.** an opposite or contrary side, position, or aspect: *Your opinion is the obverse of ours.* —*adj.* **4.** facing the observer: *the obverse side.* See -VERT-.

ob•vi•ate (ob′vē āt′) /'ɒbviyˌeyt/ *v.* [*~ + obj*], **-at•ed, -at•ing.** to think about (something) ahead of time and prevent or make unnecessary: *Their plan to go south will obviate the need for warm clothes.* —**ob•vi•a•tion** (ob′-vē ā′shən) /ˌɒbviy'eyʃən/ *n.* [*noncount*] See -VIA-.

ob•vi•ous (ob′vē əs) /'ɒbviyəs/ *adj.* **1.** easily or clearly comprehended; evident: *an obvious solution to a problem.* [*It + be + ~ + that clause*]: *It must be obvious to everyone that he's lying.* **2.** [*usually: be + ~*] not subtle or restrained: *That tight dress is too obvious to wear on a first date.* See -VIA-.

ob•vi•ous•ly (ob′vē əs lē) /'ɒbviyəsliy/ *adv.* **1.** used to express the opinion that what follows is, or should be, clearly understood or known about: *Obviously we'll have to finish this part of the course before we can begin the next one.* **2.** plainly; easily seen or recognized: *The men had obviously not slept well: there were dark circles under their eyes.* See -VIA-.

oc•a•ri•na (ok′ə rē′nə) /ˌɒkə'riynə/ *n.* [*count*], *pl.* **-nas.** a simple musical wind instrument shaped somewhat like an egg, with a mouthpiece and finger holes.

oc•ca•sion (ə kā′zhən) /ə'keyʒən/ *n.* **1.** [*count*] a particular time, esp. when certain events or circumstances take place: *On several occasions he was seen leaving the spy's apartment.* **2.** [*count*] a special or important time, event, ceremony, etc.: *The party was quite an occasion.* **3.** a convenient or favorable time; opportunity: [*count*]: *a good occasion to take inventory of our stock.* [*noncount*]: *We never had occasion to take that highway.* **4.** [*count*] the immediate cause; reason: *What is the occasion for this uproar?* —*v.* [*~ + obj*] **5.** to give cause for; bring about: *Those actions occasioned hostility and eventually war.* —***Idiom.*** **6. on occasion,** [*noncount*] once in a while; occasionally: *to drink on occasion.*

oc•ca•sion•al (ə kā′zhə nl) /ə'keyʒənl̩/ *adj.* [*before a noun*] occurring or appearing at irregular times or not very often: *an occasional headache.* —**oc•ca′sion•al•ly,** *adv.*

oc•ci•den•tal (ok′si den′tl) /ˌɒksɪ'dɛntl̩/ *adj.* of or relating to the West, or the countries of Europe and America. See -CIDE-.

oc•clude (ə klōōd′) /ə'kluwd/ *v.,* **-clud•ed, -clud•ing.** **1.** to (cause to) be closed, shut, or stopped up, as a passage or opening: [*~ + obj*]: *Something occluded the drainpipe.* [*no obj*]: *The drainpipe occluded.* **2.** [*no obj*] (of a tooth) to make contact with the surface of an opposite tooth when the jaws are closed. —**oc•clu•sion** (ə-klōō′zhən) /ə'kluwʒən/ *n.* [*count*]: *an occlusion of the teeth.* [*noncount*]: *improper occlusion.* —**oc•clu•sive** (ə-klōō′siv) /ə'kluwsɪv/ *adj.*

oc•cult (ə kult′, ok′ult) /ə'kʌlt, 'ɒkʌlt/ *adj.* **1.** of or relating to any system claiming use or knowledge of secret, magical, or supernatural powers. **2.** beyond ordinary knowledge or understanding. —*n.* [*noncount; the + ~*] **3.** supernatural, secret, or magical powers or affairs. —**oc•cult′ism,** *n.* [*noncount*]

oc•cu•pan•cy (ok′yə pən sē) /'ɒkyəpənsiy/ *n.* [*noncount*] the condition, state, or fact of occupying something or of having living quarters in some place: *Occupancy by more than 250 persons is dangerous and illegal.* See -CEP-.

oc•cu•pant (ok′yə pənt) /'ɒkyəpənt/ *n.* [*count*] **1.** a person or group that occupies something: *He robbed the occupants of a taxicab.* **2.** a tenant or resident: *the occupants of a house.* See -CEP-.

oc•cu•pa•tion (ok′yə pā′shən) /ˌɒkyə'peyʃən/ *n.* [*count*] **1.** a person's usual or principal work, esp. in earning a living. **2.** any activity that a person does. **3.** the act of occupying an area, esp. by military forces. See -CEP-.

oc•cu•pa•tion•al (ok′yə pā′shə nl) /ˌɒkyə'peyʃənl̩/ *adj.* [*before a noun*] of, relating to, or caused by one's occupation: *occupational stress.* See -CEP-.

oc•cu•py (ok′yə pī′) /'ɒkyəˌpay/ *v.* [*~ + obj*], **-pied, -py•ing.** **1.** to have, hold, or take as a separate space: *The orchard occupies half the farm.* **2.** to be a resident or tenant of: *Our company occupied the three top floors of that building.* **3.** to fill up with some activity; spend: *to occupy time reading.* **4.** to get the interest or attention of; involve: *We occupied the children with a game.* **5.** to take possession and control of (a place), such as by military invasion: *The enemy forces occupied the town.* **6.** to hold (a position, office, etc.): *He occupies the key position of advisor to the president.* See -CEP-.

oc•cur (ə kûr′) /ə'kɜr/ *v.* [*no obj*], **-curred, -cur•ring.** **1.** to happen; take place; come to pass: *The accident occurred last night.* **2.** [*not: be + ~ -ing*] to be met with or found; present itself; turn up; appear; exist: *Crime and disease occur in all countries of the world.* **3.** [*not: be + ~ -ing; usually: ~ + to + obj*] to come to mind: *An idea just occurred to me.* [*~ + to + obj + that clause*]: *The thought occurred to me that we should save money.* [*It + ~ + to + obj + (that) clause*]: *It never occurred to me (that) we would not have enough money.* See -CUR-.

oc•cur•rence (ə kûr′əns, ə kur′-) /ə'kɜrəns, ə'kʌr-/ *n.* **1.** [*noncount*] a process or instance of occurring. **2.** [*count*] something that occurs: *unexpected occurrences.* See -CUR-.

o•cean (ō′shən) /'owʃən/ *n.* **1.** [*noncount; the + ~*] the vast body of salt water that covers almost three-fourths of the earth's surface. **2.** [*count*] any of the divisions of this body, commonly known as the Atlantic, the Pacific, the Indian, the Arctic, and the Antarctic oceans. **3.** [*count*] a vast quantity: *oceans of tears.*

o•cean•go•ing or **o•cean-go•ing** (ō′shən gō′ing) /'owʃənˌgowɪŋ/ *adj.* [*before a noun*] (of a ship) designed and equipped to travel on the open sea.

o•ce•an•ic (ō′shē an′ik) /ˌowʃiy'ænɪk/ *adj.* [*before a noun*] of or relating to an ocean: *oceanic depths.*

o•cea•nog•ra•phy (ō′shə nog′rə fē, ō′shē ə-) /ˌowʃə'nɒgrəfiy, ˌowʃiyə-/ *n.* [*noncount*] the branch of physical geography dealing with the ocean. —**o′cea•nog′ra•pher,** *n.* [*count*] —**o•cea•no•graph•ic** (ō′shə-nə graf′ik) /ˌowʃənə'græfɪk/ *adj.* See -GRAPH-.

oc•e•lot (os′ə lot′, ō′sə-) /'ɒsəˌlɒt, 'owsə-/ *n.* [*count*] a spotted wildcat of Texas and Central and South America.

o•cher or **o•chre** (ō′kər) /'owkər/ *n.* [*noncount*] **1.** a mixture of iron with various earthy materials, ranging in color from pale yellow to orange and red, and used as pigment. **2.** the color of this; pale to reddish yellow.

o'clock (ə klok′) /ə'klɒk/ *adv.* **1.** (used after a number, from 1 to 12, to specify the hour of the day): *11 o'clock in the morning.* **2.** (used after a number to indicate a position in space in front of one's view, as if one could see a clock and the numbers of the clock's face with 12 o'clock directly ahead in horizontal position or straight up in vertical position): *The pilot called out, "Enemy planes approaching at ten o'clock."*

Oct or **Oct.,** an abbreviation of: October.

octa-, *prefix.* *octa-* comes from Greek, where it has the meaning "eight": *octa- + -gon → octagon (= eight-sided figure).*

oc•ta•gon (ok′tə gon′, -gən) /'ɒktəˌgɒn, -gən/ *n.* [*count*] a flat, geometrical shape or figure having eight angles and eight sides. —**oc•tag•o•nal** (ok tag′ə nl) /ɒk'tægənl̩/ *adj.* See -GON-.

oc•tane (ok′tān) /'ɒkteyn/ *n.* [*noncount; often: after a word that names degree*] a chemical substance, a hydrocarbon that is found in petroleum and is used to indicate the level of quality of gasoline: *high-octane fuel.*

oc•tave (ok′tiv, -tāv) /'ɒktɪv, -teyv/ *n.* [*count*] **1. a.** a tone on the eighth degree from a given musical tone. **b.** the interval between such tones. **2.** a series or group of eight.

oc•tet (ok tet′) /ɒk'tɛt/ *n.* [*count*] **1.** a company of eight singers or musicians. **2.** a musical composition for eight voices or instruments.

Oc•to•ber (ok tō′bər) /ɒk'towbər/ *n.* the tenth month of the year, containing 31 days. *Abbr.:* Oct.

oc•to•ge•nar•i•an (ok′tə jə nâr′ē ən) /ˌɒktədʒə'nɛəriyən/ *n.* [*count*] one between 80 and 90 years old.

oc•to•pus (ok′tə pəs) /'ɒktəpəs/ *n.* [*count*], *pl.* **-pus•es, -pi** (-pī′) /-ˌpay/. **1.** a sea creature having a soft, oval body and eight tentacles with suckers on them. **2.** something like an octopus, as an organization having many branches.

-ocul-, *root.* *-ocul-* comes from Latin, where it has the meaning "eye." This meaning is found in such words as: BINOCULAR, MONOCLE, OCULAR, OCULIST.

oc•u•lar (ok′yə lər) /'ɒkyələr/ *adj.* **1.** of, relating to, or for the eyes. **2.** performed or seen by the eye or eyesight. See -OCUL-.

oc•u•list (ok′yə list) /'ɒkyəlɪst/ *n.* [*count*] (formerly) **1.** OPHTHALMOLOGIST. **2.** OPTOMETRIST. See -OCUL-.

OD (ō′dē′) /'ow'diy/ *n., pl.* **ODs** or **OD's,** *v.,* **OD'd** or **ODed, OD'•ing.** —*n.* [*count*] **1.** an overdose of a drug, esp. a fatal one. **2.** a person who has become seriously ill or has died from a drug overdose. —*v.* [*no obj*] **3.** to take a drug overdose. **4.** to die from a drug overdose. **5.** to have or take too much of something: *I was OD'ing on caffeine.*

odd (od) /ɒd/ *adj.,* **-er, -est. 1.** differing in nature from what is usual or expected: *an odd choice for ambassador.* **2.** peculiar, weird, bizarre, or strange: *odd taste in clothing.* **3.** leaving a remainder when divided by 2, as a number: *3, 15, and 181 are odd numbers.* **4.** [*after a number*] more or less, esp. a little more than: *I owe the dentist three hundred-odd dollars.* **5.** [*before a noun*] being part of a pair, set, or series of which the rest is lacking: *an odd glove.* **6.** [*before a noun*] remaining after all others are paired, grouped, or divided into equal numbers or parts: *Who gets the odd hamburger?* **7.** [*before a noun*] of various or different types or sorts: *odd bits of information.* **8.** [*before a noun*] not regular or full-time; occasional: *did odd jobs.*

odd•ball (od′bôl′) /'ɒdˌbɔl/ *Informal.* —*n.* [*count*] **1.** a peculiar person; eccentric. —*adj.* [*before a noun*] **2.** peculiar; weird: *oddball behavior.*

odd•i•ty (od′i tē) /'ɒdɪtiy/ *n., pl.* **-ties. 1.** [*count*] a peculiar person, thing, or event. **2.** [*count*] an odd characteristic, trait, or element; peculiarity. **3.** [*noncount*] the quality of being odd.

odd•ment (od′mənt) /'ɒdmənt/ *n.* [*count*] an odd article; a bit; something remaining; a remnant.

odds (odz) /ɒdz/ *n.* [*plural*] **1.** the probability that something is so or that it is more likely to occur than something else: *The odds are that it will rain today.* **2.** this probability, expressed as a number: *The odds are two-to-one that it will rain today.* **3.** an allowance to make something more equal, as that given to the weaker player in a contest; handicap. —***Idiom.*** **4. against all odds,** in spite of all likelihood against one: *He somehow managed to succeed against all odds.* **5. at odds,** [*be* + ~ (+ *with* + *obj*)] in disagreement: *They were at odds (with each other) over politics.*

odds′ and ends′, *n.* [*plural*] small, unimportant things, matters, articles, items, etc.

odds′-on′, *adj.* [*usually: before a noun*] being the one more or most likely to achieve something: *an odds-on favorite to win.*

ode (ōd) /owd/ *n.* [*count*] a lyric poem, typically with an irregular meter, rhyme, or form, and expressing praise or enthusiastic emotion. —**od′ic,** *adj.*

o•di•ous (ō′dē əs) /'owdiyəs/ *adj.* **1.** deserving or causing hatred; hateful: *the odious Nazi concentration camps.* **2.** highly offensive; disgusting: *odious remarks.*

o•di•um (ō′dē əm) /'owdiyəm/ *n.* [*noncount*] **1.** intense hatred or dislike. **2.** the blame, disapproval, etc., attached to some discreditable action.

o•dom•e•ter (ō dom′i tər) /ow'dɒmɪtər/ *n.* [*count*] an instrument for measuring distance traveled, as by an automobile. See -METER-.

o•dor (ō′dər) /'owdər/ *n.* the property of a substance that acts on the sense of smell; scent: [*count*]: *an unpleasant odor.* [*noncount*]: *full of odor.* Also, *esp. Brit.,* **odour.**

o•dor•if•er•ous (ō′də rif′ər əs) /ˌowdə'rɪfərəs/ *adj.* giving off a usually strong odor. See -FER-.

o•dor•ous (ō′dər əs) /'owdərəs/ *adj.* odoriferous.

Od•ys•sey (od′ə sē) /'ɒdəsiy/ *n., pl.* **-seys. 1.** [*proper noun; often: the* + ~] an epic poem believed to have been written by Homer, describing the adventures of Odysseus, an ancient king of Greece, in his ten-year attempt to return home after the Trojan War. **2.** [*count; often: odyssey*] any long journey, esp. when filled with adventure, hardships, etc.

o'er (ôr, ōr) /ɔr, owr/ *prep., adv.* OVER.

oeu•vre (o͞ov′rə) /'uwvrə/ *n.* [*count*], *pl.* **oeu•vres** the works of a writer, painter, or the like, viewed as a whole.

of (uv, ov; *unstressed* əv *or, esp. before consonants,* ə) /ʌv, ɒv; *unstressed* əv *or, esp. before consonants,* ə/ *prep.* **1.** (used to indicate distance or direction from something, separation from something, or the condition of having been deprived of something): *We came within a mile of the house. He was robbed of all his money.* **2.** by; coming from: *the songs of Gershwin.* **3.** (used to indicate that the preceding noun concerns or is about the following noun): *a book of mythology (= the book is about/concerns mythology).* **4.** resulting from, caused by, or in connection with: *He was dead of hunger.* **5.** containing; made up of: *a dress of silk.* **6.** (used to indicate that the preceding noun and the following noun are considered to be the same): *Only a genius of a pilot could have saved us.* **7.** owned by, possessed by, or closely associated with: *the property of the church (= The property is owned by the church).* **8.** having; possessing: *a woman of courage (= The woman possesses courage).* **9.** (used to indicate that a noun is included, or to show a part of an amount): *You are now one of us. Three-fifths of a cup should be enough.* **10.** (used to indicate that the following noun is the object or receiver of the action of the *-ing* form of the verb that precedes): *the bombing of the city (= The city is being bombed.)* **11.** (used to indicate that the following noun is the subject or doer of the action of the *-ing* form of the verb that precedes): *the crying of the baby (= It is the baby who does the crying).* **12.** before the hour of; until: *at ten minutes of one.* **13.** (used to indicate a certain time): *It was the autumn of 1941.* **14.** on the part of: *It was nice of you to come.* **15.** set aside for or devoted to: *a moment of prayer.*

off (ôf, of) /ɔf, ɒf/ *adv.* **1.** so as to be no longer supported or attached: *This button is about to come off.* **2.** so as to be no longer covering or enclosing: *Pull the wrapping off.* **3.** in a direction that is away from a place: *to look off toward the west.* **4.** away from a path, course, etc.: *The road branches off to Grove City.* **5.** so as to be away or on one's way: *Let's start off early on our trip.* **6.** away from what is considered normal, standard, or the like: *He's always going off on some strange line of thinking.* **7.** so as to go from one condition or state to another: *drifted off to sleep.* **8.** from a charge or price: *took 10 percent off.* **9.** at a distance in space or future time: *Summer is only a week off.* **10.** out of operation: *Turn the lights off.* **11.** into operation or action; on: *The whistle goes off at noon.* **12.** in absence from work, service, etc.: *got a day off.* **13.** completely; utterly: *Finish off that last piece of meat.* **14.** into effect: *The contest went off as planned.* **15.** so as to be divided or separated into parts: *Mark off the paper into sections.* —*prep.* **16.** so as no longer to be supported by, resting on, etc.: *Wipe the dirt off your shoes.* **17.** deviating from: *The ship is 50 miles off course.* **18.** below the usual level or standard: *This dress was marked 20 percent off.* **19.** away or resting from: *He's off duty on Tuesdays.* **20.** abstaining from: *off drugs.* **21.** located apart from: *a village off the main road.* **22.** leading away from: *an alley off 12th Street.* **23.** *Informal.* from (a certain source): *I bought this watch off a street vendor.* **24.** by means of; using (someone or something) as the source: *He was living off his parents.* —*adj.* **25.** [*be* + ~] in error; wrong: *You are off on that point.* **26.** [*be* + ~] less than normal or sane: *Sometimes he's a little off, but he's harmless.* **27.** [*before a noun*] not up to the usual or expected standard: *The play has its off moments.* **28.** [*be* + ~] affected by spoilage; bad: *The cream is a bit off.* **29.** [*be* + ~] no longer in effect, in operation, or in process: *The deal is off.* **30.** [*be* + ~] in a certain state, circumstance, etc.: *to be badly off for money.* **31.** free from work or duty: *He's off tomorrow.* **32.** [*before a noun*] of less than the ordinary activity; slack: *the off season at the beach.* **33.** [*before a noun*] unlikely; remote: *We stopped by on the off chance that we'd find her at home.* **34.** [*be* + ~] starting on one's way; leaving: *I'm off to Europe on Monday.* **35.** [*be* + ~] lower in price or value; down: *Stock prices were off this morning.* —*v.* [~ + *obj*] **36.** *Slang.* to kill: *They were ready to off the cops.* —***Idiom.*** **37. off and on,** with periods of time in between: *to work off and on.* Also, **on and off. 38. off of,** off: *Take your feet off of the table!* **39. off with,** [~ + *with* + *obj; usually as a command*]

a. take away; remove: *Off with those muddy boots!* **b.** cut off: *Off with his head!*

-off, *suffix. -off* is used to form nouns that name or refer to a competition or contest, esp. between finalists or to break a tie: *cook + -off → cookoff (= a cooking contest); runoff (= a deciding final contest).*

of•fal (ô′fəl, of′əl) /'ɔfəl, 'ɒfəl/ *n.* [*noncount*] **1.** waste parts that cannot be eaten of an animal killed for food. **2.** rubbish; garbage.

off•beat (*adj.* ôf′bēt′, of′-; *n.* -bēt′) / *adj.* 'ɔf'biyt, 'ɒf-; *n.* -ˌbiyt/ *adj.* **1.** not usual; unconventional: *an offbeat comedian; a little offbeat restaurant.* **—n.** [*count*] **2.** an unaccented beat of a measure in music.

off′-col′or, *adj.* **1.** not having the usual or standard color. **2.** containing slightly offensive language, actions, etc.; risqué: *off-color jokes.* Also, **off′-col′ored.**

of•fend (ə fend′) /ə'fɛnd/ *v.* **1.** [~ + *obj*] to irritate, annoy, or anger; cause resentful displeasure in; insult: *His impolite remarks offended the audience.* **2.** [~ + *obj*] to affect (the sense, taste, etc.) in an unpleasant or disagreeable way: *That odor offends my nose.* **3.** to violate (a criminal, religious, or moral law): [~ + *obj*]: *The movie offends the morals of the community.* [~ + *against* + *obj*]: *The movie offends against our principles.* **4.** [*no obj*] to cause displeasure or resentment: *words that offend.* **—of•fend′er,** *n.* [*count*] See -FEND-.

of•fend•ing (ə fend′ing) /ə'fɛndɪŋ/ *adj.* causing a feeling of offense: *The writers removed the offending lines from the speech.* See -FEND-.

of•fense or **of•fence** (ə fens′ *or, for 6* ô′fens, of′ens) /ə'fɛns *or, for 6* 'ɔfɛns, 'ɒfɛns/ *n.* **1.** [*count*] a violation or breaking of a social or moral rule; sin: *an offense against God.* **2.** [*count*] a crime or act of breaking the law; misdemeanor: *a traffic offense.* **3.** something that offends, displeases, or causes hurt feelings, disrespect, or insult: [*noncount*]: *to avoid giving offense.* [*count*]: *an offense against decency.* **4.** attack or assault: [*noncount*]: *weapons of offense.* [*count*]: *The best defense is a strong offense.* **5.** [*count*] a person, army, etc., that is attacking. **6. a.** [*count*] the team or unit responsible for scoring points in a game. **b.** [*count*] a pattern or style of scoring attack: *The coach had designed several new offenses.* **c.** [*noncount*] effectiveness or ability to score points: *Offense was my weak point.* See -FEND-. **—Syn.** See CRIME.

of•fen•sive (ə fen′siv *or, for 4* ô′fen-, of′en-) /ə'fɛnsɪv *or, for 4* 'ɔfɛn-, 'ɒfɛn-/ *adj.* **1.** causing resentful displeasure; highly irritating or annoying: *His remarks were highly offensive.* **2.** unpleasant or disagreeable to the senses; disgusting: *offensive odors.* **3.** disgusting to one's moral sense or to good taste; repulsive: *offensive language.* **4.** [*usually: before a noun*] of or relating to offense or attack, as in war or games, etc.: *a good offensive strategy.* **—n. 5.** [*noncount; usually: the* + ~] the position or strategy of attacking: *to take the offensive; The army went on the offensive.* **6.** [*count*] an attacking movement or strategy; attack: *launching an offensive against the enemy lines.* See -FEND-.

of•fer (ô′fər, of′ər) /'ɔfər, 'ɒfər/ *v.* **1.** to present or hold out (something) for acceptance or rejection: [~ + *obj*]: *to offer a drink.* [~ + *obj* + *to* + *obj*]: *He offered a drink to his guests.* [~ + *obj* + *obj*]: *He offered his guests a drink.* **2.** to propose or put forward for others to consider: [~ + *obj*]: *I offered a suggestion.* [~ + *obj* + *to* + *obj*]: *I offered a suggestion to them.* [~ + *obj* + *obj*]: *I offered them a suggestion.* [*used with quotations*]: *"We could cut back on costs," I offered.* **3.** [~ + *to* + *verb*] to show willingness (to do something): *I offered to go first.* **4.** to present solemnly as an act of worship to God or to a god: [~ + *obj*]: *Let us offer thanks.* [~ + *obj* + *to* + *obj*]: *In the Eucharist, the priest offered the bread and wine to God.* [~ + *obj* + *obj*]: *They offered the gods sacrifices.* [~ + *obj* + *up* + *to* + *obj*]: *offering their prayers up to God.* [~ + *up* + *obj* + *to* + *obj*]: *offering up their prayers to God.* **5.** to present or provide, as for sale: [~ + *obj*]: *This car offers anti-lock brakes at a low price.* [~ + *obj* + *obj*]: *Our company offers you low prices.* [~ + *obj* + *to* + *obj*]: *The company offers high quality to its customers.* **6.** to propose or present as a price for buying something: [~ + *obj*]: *They offered a low bid of $50,000.* [~ + *obj* + *obj*]: *They offered us a low price of $50,000.* [~ + *obj* + *to* + *obj*]: *They offered $100,000 to the homeowners.* **7.** to put forth; do or perform: [~ + *obj*]: *to offer resistance.* [~ + *obj* + *obj*]: *He offered the police no resistance.* [~ + *obj* + *to* + *obj*]: *He offered no resistance to the police.* **8.** [~ + *obj*] to give, make, or promise: *offered no response to the question.* **9.** [*no obj*] to present itself; occur: *A sudden opportunity offered.* **—n.** [*count*] **10.** an act or instance of offering. **11.** a proposal or bid to give or pay something. **—of′fer•er, of′fer•or,** *n.* [*count*] See -FER-.

of•fer•ing (ô′fər ing, of′ər-) /'ɔfərɪŋ, 'ɒfər-/ *n.* [*count*] **1.** something offered in devotion to a deity or a church: *collected the offerings from the congregation.* **2.** something presented for inspection or sale. See -FER-.

off•hand (ôf′hand′, of′-) /'ɔf'hænd, 'ɒf-/ *adj.* without thought beforehand; unplanned; casual: *offhand remarks.* Also, **off′hand′ed.** **—off′hand′ed•ly,** *adv.* **—off′hand′ed•ness,** *n.* [*noncount*]

off′-hour′, *n.* [*count*] **1.** a period when a person is not at a job. **2.** a period outside of rush hour. **—adj.** [*usually: before a noun*] **3.** of, relating to, or during an off-hour: *off-hour traffic.*

of•fice (ô′fis, of′is) /'ɔfɪs, 'ɒfɪs/ *n.* **1.** [*count*] a place where business, work, or one's job is conducted or accomplished. SEE ILLUSTRATION. **2.** [*count*] a group of persons in a place where business is conducted: *The whole office contributed.* **3.** [*count*] a business or professional organization: *a law office.* **4.** [*noncount*] a position of duty, trust, or authority: *the office of president.* **5.** employment or position as an official: [*noncount*]: *to seek political office.* [*count*]: *He had never held a political office before this one.* **6.** [*count; usually: Office; often: the* + ~] a government agency, or a division of a government department: *the Foreign Office.* **7.** Often, **offices.** [*plural*] something done for another: *Through the good offices of a friend I was hired.* See -OPER-, -FAC-.

of•fice•hold•er (ô′fis hōl′dər, of′is-) /'ɔfɪsˌhowldər, 'ɒfɪs-/ *n.* [*count*] a person filling a governmental position; public official. See -OPER-, -FAC-.

of•fi•cer (ô′fə sər, of′ə-) /'ɔfəsər, 'ɒfə-/ *n.* [*count*] **1.** a person who holds a position of rank or authority in the armed services, esp. one holding a commission. **2.** a member of a police department. **3.** a person who is appointed or elected to a position of responsibility or authority in an organization. See -OPER-, -FAC-.

of•fi•cial (ə fish′əl) /ə'fɪʃəl/ *n.* [*count*] **1.** a person who is appointed or elected to an office or is charged with certain duties: *an official of the court.* **—adj. 2.** [*before a noun*] of or relating to an office or to a position of duty, trust, or authority: *official powers.* **3.** appointed, authorized, recognized, or approved by a government or organization: *an official flag.* **4.** [*before a noun*] formal; ceremonial: *an official visit by the head of state.* **—of•fi′cial•ism,** *n.* [*noncount*] **—of•fi′cial•ly,** *adv.* See -OPER-, -FAC-.

of•fi•cial•dom (ə fish′əl dəm) /ə'fɪʃəldəm/ *n.* [*noncount*] officials thought of as a group or whole. See -OPER-, -FAC-.

of•fi•ci•ate (ə fish′ē āt′) /ə'fɪʃiyˌeyt/ *v.*, **-at•ed, -at•ing.** **1.** [*no obj*] to perform the duties or function of some office or position. **2.** [*no obj*] to perform the official duties of a member of the clergy: *The pastor officiated at their wedding.* **3.** to serve as referee, umpire, etc., in (a contest or game): [*no obj*]: *officiating at baseball games.* [~ + *obj*]: *officiated a game.* **—of•fi′ci•a′tor,** *n.* [*count*] See -OPER-, -FAC-.

of•fi•cious (ə fish′əs) /ə'fɪʃəs/ *adj.* too willing to offer help or advice that is not asked for and not wanted; interfering in the affairs of others; meddlesome. See -OPER-, -FAC-.

off•ing (ô′fing, of′ing) /'ɔfɪŋ, 'ɒfɪŋ/ *n.* [*count; usually: the* + ~] **1.** the more distant part of the sea seen from the shore. **—*Idiom.* 2. in the offing,** [*noncount*] in the near future: *A surprise is in the offing.*

off′-key′, *adj.* **1.** out of tune: *an off-key song.* **2.** somewhat irregular, abnormal, or unsuitable. **—adv. 3.** out of tune: *sang off-key.*

off′-lim′its, *adj.* [*be* + ~] forbidden to be visited, used, etc., by certain persons: *The downtown area was off-limits to enlisted men.*

off′-line′ or **off′line′,** *adj.* operating independently of, or no longer connected to, another computer: *I was off-line when your message came through (= My computer was off-line).* Compare ON-LINE.

off′-load′ or **off′load′,** *v.* to unload.

off-peak (ôf′pēk′, of′-) /'ɔf'piyk, 'ɒf-/ *adj.* [*usually: before a noun*] of or relating to a time of day or a period of time other than the regular or busiest time: *off-peak tourist season.*

off•print (ôf′print′, of′-) /'ɔfˌprɪnt, 'ɒf-/ *n.* [*count*] a reprint of an article from a larger publication.

off′-put′ting, *adj.* causing a feeling of uneasiness or dislike: *an off-putting manner.*

off′-sea′son, *n.* [*count*] **1.** a time of year other than the regular or busiest one for something. **—adj.** [*usually:*

office

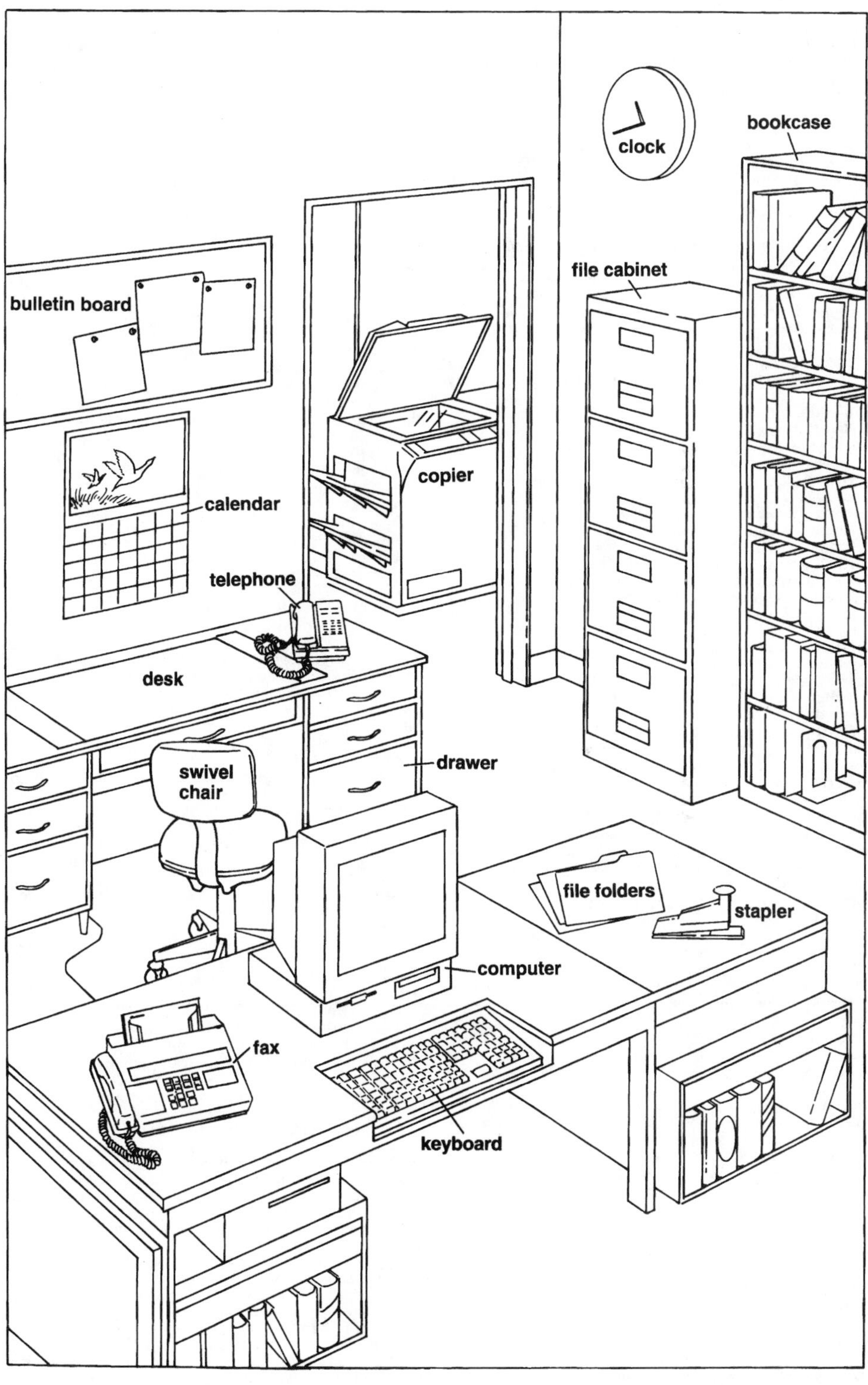
clock
bookcase
file cabinet
bulletin board
copier
calendar
telephone
desk
drawer
swivel chair
file folders
stapler
computer
fax
keyboard

before a noun] **2.** of, relating to, or during the off-season: *tickets at off-season prices.* **—*adv.*** **3.** in or during the off-season: *traveled off-season.*

off•set (*n., adj.* ôf′set′, of′-; *v.* ôf′set′, of′-) / *n., adj.* ˈɔfˌsɛt, ˈɒf-; *v.* ˌɔfˈsɛt, ˌɒf-/ *n., adj., v.,* **-set, -set•ting.** **—*n.*** [*count*] **1.** something that makes up for something else. **2.** the start, beginning, or outset. **3. a.** a process in which a metal or paper plate is used to make an inked imprint or mark on a piece of rubber that then transfers the mark or imprint to the paper being printed. **b.** the imprint or mark itself. **—*adj.*** **4.** of, noting, or relating to an offset. **5.** related to, printed by, or suitable for printing by offset. **6.** placed away from a center line; off-center. **7.** placed at an angle to something. **—*v.*** [~ + *obj*] **8.** to make up for: *The gains offset the losses.* **9.** *Print.* to make an offset of.

off•shoot (ôf′sho͞ot′, of′-) /ˈɔfˌʃuwt, ˈɒf-/ *n.* [*count*] **1.** a branch of a main stem, as of a plant. **2.** anything thought of as developing from a main source: *an offshoot of medical science.*

off•shore (ôf′shôr′, -shōr′, of′-) /ˈɔfˈʃɔr, -ˈʃowr, ˈɒf-/ *adv.* **1.** off or away from the shore: *drifting slowly offshore.* **2.** at a distance from the shore: *anchored five miles offshore.* **3.** in a foreign country. **—*adj.*** **4.** moving away from the shore: *an offshore wind.* **5.** located or operating at some distance from the shore: *offshore oil-drilling rigs.* **6.** located or operating in a foreign country: *offshore companies.*

off•side (ôf′sīd′, of′-) /ˈɔfˈsayd, ˈɒf-/ *adj., adv. Sports.* illegally beyond a certain line or area or in advance of the ball or puck at the beginning of or during play: *an offside tackle; playing offside.*

off•spring (ôf′spring′, of′-) /ˈɔfˌsprɪŋ, ˈɒf-/ *n.* [*count*], *pl.* **-spring. 1.** children or young of a particular parent; descendants. **2.** a child or animal in relation to its parent or parents. **3.** product; result: *That device is the offspring of her inventive mind.*

off•stage (ôf′stāj′, of′-) /ˈɔfˈsteydʒ, ˈɒf-/ *adv.* **1.** away from the part of the stage that the audience sees (opposed to *onstage*): *could hear whispering offstage.* **2.** in private life. **—*adj.*** **3.** being or occurring offstage: *offstage whispers.* **4.** private: *an unglamorous offstage life.*

off′-the-cuff′, *adj.* with little or no preparation; impromptu: *off-the-cuff remarks.*

off′-the-rec′ord, *adj.* **1.** not for publication; not to be quoted. **—*adv.*** **2.** unofficially; not to be quoted or published: *speaking off-the-record.*

off′-the-shelf′, *adj.* **1.** readily available from merchandise in stock. **2.** made according to a standard format; ready-made: *off-the-shelf computer programs.*

off′-the-wall′, *adj.* very unusual; bizarre: *unpredictable, off-the-wall behavior.*

off•track (ôf′trak′, of′-) /ˈɔfˈtræk, ˈɒf-/ *adj.* [*before a noun*] away from a racetrack: *offtrack betting.*

off′-white′, *adj.* **1.** white mixed with a small amount of gray, yellow, or other light color. **—*n.*** [*noncount*] **2.** an off-white color.

off′ year′, *n.* [*count*] **1.** a year without a major, esp. presidential, election. **2.** a year that has reduced production or lower, poorer activity in a particular field.

oft (ôft, oft) /ɔft, ɒft/ *adv.* OFTEN.

of•ten (ô′fən, of′ən; ôf′tən, of′-) /ˈɔfən, ˈɒfən; ˈɔftən, ˈɒf-/ *adv.* many times; frequently; on numerous occasions: *I've been to their home often.*

o•gle (ō′gəl) /ˈowgəl/ *v.,* **o•gled, o•gling,** *n.* **—*v.*** **1.** to look at with esp. sexual interest: [~ + *obj*]: *They ogled any woman who walked by.* [*no obj*]: *The workers stood there ogling.* **—*n.*** [*count*] **2.** a look that indicates sexual interest.

o•gre (ō′gər) /ˈowgər/ *n.* [*count*] **1.** a monster in fairy tales usually represented as a frightening giant who eats people. **2.** a frightening or menacing person.

oh (ō) /ow/ *interj., n., pl.* **oh's, ohs. —*interj.*** **1.** (used to express surprise, pain, disapproval, sympathy, agreement, and other emotions): *Oh! What's that noise?* **2.** (used when speaking to another to attract that person's attention): *Oh, waiter!* **3.** (used when the speaker is hesitating, thinking, guessing, etc.: *The fish must have weighed, oh, six or seven pounds.* **—*n.*** [*count*] **4.** the saying of the word "oh."

OH, an abbreviation of: Ohio.

ohm (ōm) /owm/ *n.* [*count*] the international unit or measure of electrical resistance.

o•ho (ō hō′) /owˈhow/ *interj.* (used to express surprise, triumph, etc.): *Oho! We found it!*

-oid, *suffix. -oid* is used to form adjectives and nouns with the meaning "resembling, like," with the suggestion of an incomplete or imperfect similarity to the root element: *human* + *-oid* → *humanoid* (= *resembling a human, but not quite the same*).

oil (oil) /ɔyl/ *n.* **1.** any of a large group of liquid substances that are thick, smooth, sticky, and sometimes easy to burn, taken from the ground, or from the fat of animals, or from plants, used variously in cooking, heating, and providing power in engines, and to make connecting parts run smoother: [*noncount*]: *cooking oil.* [*count*]: *vegetable oils.* **2. a.** a paint made of oil, esp. of linseed oil and used by artists for painting on canvas or other surfaces: [*count*]: *bought some bright oils to use in class.* [*noncount*]: *working in oil.* **b.** [*count*] an oil painting. **—*v.*** [~ + *obj*] **3.** to smear, lubricate, or supply with oil. **—*adj.*** [*before a noun*] **4.** of or relating to oil: *oil heat.* **5.** using oil: *an oil lantern.*

oil•cloth (oil′klôth′, -kloth′) /ˈɔylˌklɔθ, -ˌklɒθ/ *n.* [*noncount*] a cotton fabric made waterproof by treatment with oil.

oil′ paint′ing, *n.* **1.** [*noncount*] the art or technique of painting with oils. **2.** [*count*] a painting made in oils.

oil•skin (oil′skin′) /ˈɔylˌskɪn/ *n.* **1.** [*noncount*] a cotton fabric made waterproof by treatment with oil and used to make clothing for wear in the rain, at sea, etc. **2.** [*count*] Often, **oilskins.** [*plural*] a piece of clothing made of this, as a long, full raincoat.

oil′ slick′, *n.* [*count*] a layer of oil on the surface of a body of water.

oil′ well′, *n.* [*count*] a well drilled to obtain petroleum.

oil•y (oi′lē) /ˈɔyliy/ *adj.,* **-i•er, -i•est. 1.** smeared, covered, or soaked with oil; greasy: *an oily rag.* **2.** of, relating to, or made of oil: *rubbed an oily lotion on her skin.* **3.** smooth and too polite: *an oily smile.* —**oil′i•ness,** *n.* [*noncount*]

oink (oingk) /ɔyŋk/ *n.* [*count*] **1.** the grunting sound made by a hog. **—*v.*** [*no obj*] **2.** to make such a sound.

oint•ment (oint′mənt) /ˈɔyntmənt/ *n.* a soft, smooth, oily or slightly greasy preparation, often medicated, for application to the skin; salve: [*noncount*]: *put ointment on the burn.* [*count*]: *ointments to relieve itching.*

OK or **O.K.** or **o•kay** (ō′kā′, ō′kā′, ō′kā′) /ˈowˈkey, ˌowˈkey, ˈowˌkey/ *adj., adv., n., pl.* **OKs** or **OK's** or **O.K.'s** or **o•kays,** *v.,* **OK'd** or **O.K.'ed** or **o•kayed, OK′•ing** or **O.K.′•ing** or **o•kay•ing,** *interj.* **—*adj.*** **1.** [*be/seem* + ~] all right; satisfactory: *Is everything OK? Things seem OK at the moment.* **2.** [*usually: be* + ~] correct, permissible, or acceptable: *Let's leave, if that's OK with you.* **3.** [*be* + ~] feeling well: *The patient's OK now.* **4.** [*be* + ~] safe: *Stay behind me and you'll be OK.* **5.** good enough; adequate: *an OK speech; The play was just OK.* **—*adv.*** **6.** all right; well enough; successfully; fine: *We got along OK.* **—*n.*** [*count*] **7.** an approval: *Do you have an OK to do this?* **—*v.*** [~ + *obj*] **8.** to approve; authorize: *O.K.'ed the plan.* **—*interj.*** **9.** (used to express the speaker's agreement with what has been said): *"Will you come with me now?"—"OK, I guess so."* **10.** (used to express the speaker's desire to see if the person spoken to understands what has been said): *Turn the ignition on when I signal, OK?* **11.** (used to express the desire to be finished with one subject and move to a new one): *OK, let's turn now to Chapter 10.*

OK, an abbreviation of: Oklahoma.

Okla., an abbreviation of: Oklahoma.

o•kra (ō′krə) /ˈowkrə/ *n., pl.* **o•kras. 1.** [*count*] a shrub of the mallow family with green seed pods that have a sticky liquid inside them. **2.** [*noncount*] the pods, used esp. in soups and stews. Also called **gumbo.**

old (ōld) /owld/ *adj.,* **old•er, old•est** or **eld•er, eld•est,** *n.* **—*adj.*** **1.** having lived or existed for a long time; advanced in years: *an old man; an old building.* **2.** [*before a noun*] of or relating to the later part of life or existence: *old age.* **3.** [*after a number or phrase indicating amount of time*] having lived or existed for a certain time: *a six-month-old company.* **4.** [*before a noun*] of long standing: *an old friend.* **5.** [*before a noun*] long known or in use: *the same old excuses.* **6.** [*before a noun*] having been replaced by something newer or more recent: *We sold our old house.* **7.** [*before a noun*] former: *tried to get my old job back.* **8.** [*before a noun*] belonging to the past: *the good old days.* **9.** of or started at an earlier period or date: *old maps.* **10.** having been in existence since the distant past: *an old family.* **11.** prehistoric; ancient: *old civilizations.* **12.** sensible, mature, or wise: *old beyond her years.* **13.** (used to emphasize feeling or emotion toward, or an attitude about, the following noun): *We had a high old time.* **—*n.*** **14. the old,** [*plural; used with a plural verb*] old persons thought of as a group. **15.** [*count; used after a word or phrase indicating amount of time*] a person or animal of a specified age or age group: *a program for six-year-olds.* **16.** [*noncount*] earlier times: *in days of old.*

old•en (ōl′dən) /ˈowldən/ *adj.* [*before a noun*] ancient; old.

old′-fash′ioned, *adj.* **1.** of a kind that is no longer in style; out-of-date: *an old-fashioned bathing suit.* **2.** having, accepting, or choosing the conservative behavior, ways, beliefs, or tastes of earlier times: *old-fashioned ideas.*

old′ fo′gy (or **fo′gey**), *n.* FOGY.

old′ guard′, *n.* [*count; usually singular; often: the* + ~] **1.** the members of a group, as a political party, who resist change. **2.** persons who have been associated with a place, organization, company, etc., for a long time.

old′ hand′, *n.* [*count*] a specialist or veteran in a subject: *an old hand at politics.*

old′ hat′, *adj.* [*be* + ~] old-fashioned; out-of-date; no longer used; dated: *That slang word is old hat.*

old•ie (ōl′dē) /ˈowldiy/ *n.* [*count*] *Informal.* a song, joke, movie, etc., that was popular at a time in the past.

old′ la′dy, *n.* [*count*], *pl.* **old ladies.** *Slang.* **1.** one's mother. **2.** one's wife. **3.** one's girlfriend or female lover.

old′ maid′, *n.* **1.** [*count*] a spinster. **2.** [*count*] a fussy, cautious, timid person. **3.** [*noncount*] a simple card game, played with a deck having one card removed, in which players match pairs, the loser being the holder of the odd card, usually a queen.

old′ mas′ter, *n.* [*count*] **1.** an important artist of an earlier period, esp. the 15th to 18th centuries. **2.** a work by such an artist.

old′ school′, *n.* [*noncount; usually: the* + ~] persons calling for or supporting established custom or tradition, generally against change or modern trends.

Old′ Tes′tament, *n.* [*proper noun; the* + ~] the complete Bible of the Jews, including the Law, the Prophets, and the Hagiographa, being the first of the two main divisions of the Christian Bible.

old′-time′, *adj.* [*before a noun*] **1.** belonging to old or former times, methods, ideas, etc. **2.** being long established: *old-time residents.*

old′-tim′er, *n.* [*count*] **1.** a person who has lived in a place, belonged to an organization, or worked at something for a long time. **2.** an elderly person.

old′-world′, *adj.* **1.** of or relating to the ancient world or to a former period of history. **2.** of or relating to Europe, Asia, Africa, or the eastern half of the globe.

o•lé (ō lā′) /owˈley/ *interj., n., pl.* **o•lés.** —*interj.* **1.** (a Spanish cheer used to express approval, triumph, or encouragement). —*n.* [*count*] **2.** a cry of "olé."

o•le•ag•i•nous (ō′lē aj′ə nəs) /ˌowliyˈædʒənəs/ *adj.* **1.** having the nature or qualities of oil; containing oil. **2.** offensively fawning; smarmy.

o•le•an•der (ō′lē an′dər, ō′lē an′-) /ˈowliyˌændər, ˌowliyˈæn-/ *n.* [*count*] a poisonous evergreen shrub of Eurasia, having bright clusters of pink, red, or white flowers.

o•le•o (ō′lē ō) /ˈowliyow/ *n.* MARGARINE.

o•le•o•mar•ga•rine (ō′lē ō mär′jər in, -jə rēn′) /ˌowliyowˈmɑrdʒərɪn, -dʒəˌriyn/ *n. Older Use.* MARGARINE.

ol•fac•to•ry (ol fak′tə rē, -trē, ōl-) /ɒlˈfæktəriy, -triy, owl-/ *adj., n., pl.* **-ries.** —*adj.* [*before a noun*] **1.** of or relating to the sense of smell. —*n.* [*count*] **2.** Usually, **olfactories.** [*plural; usually: the* + ~] an organ of the body connected with the sense of smell.

ol•i•gar•chy (ol′i gär′kē) /ˈɒlɪˌgɑrkiy/ *n., pl.* **-chies. 1.** [*noncount*] a form of government in which power is held by a few persons or by a dominant class or group. **2.** [*count*] a state or organization ruled this way: *corrupt oligarchies.* **3.** [*count*] the persons or class that rules this way: *the ageing oligarchy.* —**ol′i•gar′chic,** *adj.* See -ARCH-.

ol•ive (ol′iv) /ˈɒlɪv/ *n.* **1.** [*count*] an evergreen tree of the Mediterranean and other warm regions, grown chiefly for its fruit. **2.** [*count*] the small, oval-shaped fruit of this tree, eaten as a food and used as a source of oil. **3.** [*noncount*] the wood of this tree. **4.** [*noncount*] the green or dull yellow green color of the unripe olive fruit. —*adj.* **5.** [*before a noun*] of, relating to, or made of olive or olives. **6.** of the color olive.

ol′ive branch′, *n.* [*count*] a branch of the olive tree as a sign or token of peace.

O•lym•pic Games′, (ə lim′pik, ō lim′-) /əˈlɪmpɪk, owˈlɪm-/ *n.* [*plural; usually: the* + ~] Also, **Olympics.** a modern international sports competition traditionally held every four years but after 1992 with Summer Games and Winter Games alternating every two years. —**O•lym′pic,** *adj.* [*before a noun*]: *Olympic athletes.*

om•buds•man (om′bədz mən, om bŏŏdz′-) /ˈɒmbədzmən, ɒmˈbʊdz-/ *n.* [*count*], *pl.* **-men 1.** a public official, esp. in Scandinavian countries, who investigates complaints by private citizens against government agencies or officials. **2.** a person who investigates and tries to resolve complaints, as from employees or students.

o•me•ga (ō mē′gə, ō mā′-, ō meg′ə) /owˈmiygə, owˈmey-, owˈmɛgə/ *n.* [*count*], *pl.* **-gas. 1.** the 24th and last letter of the Greek alphabet (Ω, ω). **2.** the last of a series; the end.

om•e•let or **om•e•lette** (om′lit, om′ə-) /ˈɒmlɪt, ˈɒmə-/ *n.* [*count*] beaten eggs cooked until set and often served folded around a filling, as of cheese.

o•men (ō′mən) /ˈowmən/ *n.* [*count*] any event believed to signal the coming of something good or evil.

om•i•nous (om′ə nəs) /ˈɒmənəs/ *adj.* foreboding; threatening: *ominous black clouds.* —**om′i•nous•ly,** *adv.* —**om′i•nous•ness,** *n.* [*noncount*]

o•mis•sion (ō mish′ən) /owˈmɪʃən/ *n.* **1.** [*noncount*] the act of omitting or the state of being omitted. **2.** [*count*] something left out, not done, or neglected. See -MIS-.

o•mit (ō mit′) /owˈmɪt/ *v.,* **o•mit•ted, o•mit•ting. 1.** [~ + *obj*] to leave out; fail to include: *omitted a few details from the report.* **2.** [~ + *to* + *verb*] to fail (to do, make, use, send, etc): *He omitted to tell us his lawyer would be at the meeting.* See -MIT-.

omni-, *prefix. omni-* comes from Latin, where it has the meaning "all": *omni-* + *directional* → *omnidirectional* (= *in all directions*).

om•ni•bus (om′nə bus′, -bəs) /ˈɒmnəˌbʌs, -bəs/ *n., pl.* **-bus•es** or **bus•ses,** *adj.* —*n.* [*count*] **1.** BUS[1] (def. 1). —*adj.* [*before a noun*] **2.** relating to, including, or dealing with many items at once: *an omnibus legislative bill.*

om•ni•po•tence (om nip′ə təns) /ɒmˈnɪpətəns/ *n.* [*noncount*] the state or condition of having infinite or unlimited power. See -POT-.

om•nip•o•tent (om nip′ə tənt) /ɒmˈnɪpətənt/ *adj.* infinite in power, such as God. See -POT-.

om•ni•pres•ent (om′nə prez′ənt) /ˌɒmnəˈprɛzənt/ *adj.* present everywhere at the same time. —**om′ni•pres′ence,** *n.* [*noncount*]

om•nis•cient (om nish′ənt) /ɒmˈnɪʃənt/ *adj.* having complete or unlimited knowledge, awareness, or understanding. —**om•nis′cience,** *n.* [*noncount*] See -SCI-.

om•niv•o•rous (om niv′ər əs) /ɒmˈnɪvərəs/ *adj.* **1.** feeding on both animals and plants. **2.** eating all kinds of foods. **3.** taking in everything, such as with the mind: *an omnivorous reader.* —**om•ni•vore** (om′nə vôr′, -vōr′) /ˈɒmnəˌvɔr, -ˌvowr/ *n.* [*count*] See -VOR-.

on (on, ôn) /ɒn, ɔn/ *prep.* **1.** so as to be or to remain supported by: *Put the package on the table.* **2.** so as to be attached to or unified with: *There is a label on the jar.* **3.** so as to be a covering or wrapping for: *Put the blanket on the baby.* **4.** in connection, association, or cooperation with: *to serve on a jury.* **5.** so as to be a supporting part or base of: *legs on a chair.* **6.** (used to show that the preceding noun has the following noun as its place, location, situation, etc.): *an ugly scar on the face.* **7.** very close to; at the edge of: *a house on the lake.* **8.** in the direction of: *to sail on a southerly course.* **9.** using as a means of carrying or of supporting or providing movement: *arrived on the noon plane.* **10.** by the agency or means of: *drunk on wine.* **11.** directed against or toward: *She played a joke on him.* **12.** having as a subject; being about (something): *a new book on dogs.* **13.** in a state, condition, or process of: *The workers are on strike.* **14.** engaged in or involved with: *I'm on the second chapter of the book.* **15.** subject to: *If there is a doctor on call it means that a doctor can be summoned quickly in an emergency.* **16.** having as a source or agent: *He came to depend on his friends.* **17.** having as a basis or ground: *on my word of honor.* **18.** assigned to or working at: *Who's on duty today?* **19.** (used with days and dates) at the time mentioned: *The train arrives every hour on the hour (= at one, two, three o'clock, etc.)* **20.** at the time or occasion of: *You have to pay cash on delivery (= at the time delivery is made).* **21.** within the required limits of: *The train arrived on time.* **22.** having as the object or end of motion: *The demonstrators marched on the capital.* **23.** having as the object or the goal of action, thought, desire, etc.: *to gaze on a scene.* **24.** having as the subject or reference; with respect to: *What are your views on rock music?* **25.** paid for by, esp. as a treat or gift: *Dinner is on me.* **26.** taking or using as a measure or cure to improve one's health, energy, etc.: *He's on a low-salt diet.* **27.** regularly taking or addicted to: *She's not on drugs anymore.* **28.** with; carried by: *I have no money on me.* **29.** so as to disturb or affect in a bad way: *My hair dryer broke on me.* **30.** having as a risk or unfortunate result: *on pain of death.* **31.** in addition to: *millions on millions of stars.* **—*adv.*** **32.** in, into, or onto a position of being supported or attached: *Sew the buttons on.* **33.** in, into, or onto a position of covering or wrapping: *Put your raincoat on.* **34.** tightly attached to a thing, such as for support: *Hold on!* **35.** toward a place, point, activity, or object: *to look on while others work.* **36.** forward, onward, or along, such as in any course or process later on: *further on.* **37.** with continuous activity: *continued on with his job.* **38.** into or in active operation or performance: *Turn the gas on.* **—*adj.*** [*be* + ~] **39.** operating or in use: *Is the radio on?* **40.** taking place; occurring: *Don't you know there's a war on?* **41.** being broadcast: *What's on tonight, anything interesting to watch?* **42.** scheduled or planned: *Do you have anything on for tomorrow?* **43. a.** behaving in a very animated or theatrical manner: *He never stops and just relaxes; he's always on.* **b.** functioning or performing at one's best: *The pitcher is really on today.* **—*Idiom.*** **44. on and off,** with periods of time in between; intermittently. **45. on and on,** at great length: *to chatter on and on.* Compare AT, IN. **—Usage.** See ABOUT.

once (wuns) /wʌns/ *adv.* **1.** formerly: *a once powerful nation.* **2.** a single time: *We eat out once a week.* **3.** at any time; ever: *If the facts once became known, we'd be in trouble.* **4.** by a single step, degree, or grade: *She's my first cousin once removed.* **—*n.*** [*noncount*] **5.** a single occasion; one time only: *Once is enough.* **—*conj.*** **6.** if or when at any time; if ever: *Once the news is out, they'll hunt us down.* **7.** whenever; as soon as: *Once you're finished, you can leave.* **—*adj.*** **8.** former; one-time: *the once and future king.* **—*Idiom.*** **9. all at once,** suddenly: *All at once it started to rain.* **10. at once, a.** immediately; promptly: *left at once.* **b.** at the same time; simultaneously: *They all sprang up at once.* **11. once (and) for all,** decisively; finally: *Let's settle this argument once and for all.* **12. once in a while,** sometimes; occasionally. **13. once or twice,** a very few times; not frequently: *I've only seen her once or twice.* **14. once upon a time,** (used as an opening phrase to give the setting for a fairy tale or similar story in the distant, imaginary past): *Once upon a time there was a giant.*

once′-o′ver, *n.* [*count*] a quick look or examination of something: *He gave the report the once-over.*

on•col•o•gy (ong kol′ə jē) /ɒŋ'kɒlədʒiy/ *n.* [*noncount*] the study of tumors, including cancers. **—on•co•log•ic** (ong′kə loj′ik) /ˌɒŋkə'lɒdʒɪk/ **on′co•log′i•cal,** *adj.* **—on•col′o•gist,** *n.* [*count*]

on•com•ing (on′kum′ing, ôn′-) /'ɒnˌkʌmɪŋ, 'ɔn-/ *adj.* [*before a noun*] **1.** approaching; nearing: *an oncoming train.* **2.** emerging: *the oncoming generation.*

one (wun) /wʌn/ *adj.* [*before a noun*] **1.** being or amounting to a single unit or individual or entire thing; equal to the number 1: *one child; only one piece of cake left.* **2.** being an individual instance, example, or member of a number, kind, or group indicated: *one member of the team.* **3.** of the same or having a single kind, nature, or condition: *We are of one mind.* **4.** (used to refer to an unspecified or imprecise day or time): *one evening last week.* **5.** [*before a proper noun or name*] (used to name a person otherwise unknown or not yet described): *One John Smith was chosen.* **6.** [*before a singular count noun*] being a particular or only individual, item, or unit: *She's the one person I can trust.* **7.** (used to show strong feeling about the noun or adjective that follows) a or an: *That is one smart dog.* **—*n.*** [*count*] **8.** the first and lowest whole number, being a cardinal number; a unit: *Ten minus nine leaves one.* **9.** a symbol of this number, as 1 or I. **10.** a single person or thing: *Let's do one at a time.* **11.** a one-dollar bill. **—*pron.*** **12.** (used to stand for a person or thing of a number or kind that is about to be indicated): *He is one of the Elizabethan poets.* **13.** (used to stand for a person or thing that has just been mentioned or indicated, or is already understood from the context): *The portraits are good ones.* **14.** a person, or a personified being: *Satan, the evil one.* **15.** any person or thing; people in general: *One shouldn't cry over spilled milk (= People in general, including the speaker, shouldn't get upset about things that can't be fixed.)* **—*Idiom.*** **16. all one,** the same: *You can stay or go; it's all one to me. (= It doesn't matter to me which action you take.)* **17. as one, a.** with complete agreement; unanimously: *They voted as one.* **b.** all at the same time; in unison: *We rose to our feet as one.* **18. at one,** united in thought or feeling; attuned: *to feel at one with the world.* **19. one and all,** everyone. **20. one by one,** singly and following after another.

one′ anoth′er, *pron.* EACH OTHER. **—Usage.** See EACH OTHER.

one′-dimen′sional, *adj.* **1.** having one dimension only: *A line is one-dimensional.* **2.** having no depth, scope, interesting qualities, etc: *a novel full of one-dimensional characters.*

one′-lin′er, *n.* [*count*] a brief joke or witty remark.

one•ness (wun′nis) /'wʌnnɪs/ *n.* [*noncount*] **1.** the quality of being one; singleness. **2.** unity of thought, feeling, purpose, etc.; harmony; concord.

one′-on′-one′, *adj.* **1.** made up of or involving direct, individual communication or competition; person-to-person: *a one-on-one interview.* **—*adv.*** **2.** directly to or with each other: *They argued one-on-one.* **—*n.*** [*count*] **3.** a direct meeting between two persons. **—*Idiom.*** **4. go one-on-one with,** [~ + *obj*] *Sports.* to play directly against (an opposing player).

on•er•ous (on′ər əs, ō′nər-) /'ɒnərəs, 'ownər-/ *adj.* being a burden; troublesome: *an onerous task.*

one•self or **one's self** (wun self′, wunz-) /wʌn'sɛlf, wʌnz-/ *pron.* **1.** (used when the subject of a sentence is ONE and the object of the verb or a preposition also refers to the same individual): *One should be able to laugh at oneself.* **2.** (used when the subject or object of a sentence is ONE and the speaker wishes to emphasize that subject or object): *To do something oneself brings great joy.* **—*Idiom.*** **3. be oneself,** [*no obj*] **a.** to be in one's normal state of mind or physical condition: *was himself again after a nap.* **b.** to be sincere: *Just be yourself during the interview.* **4. by oneself, a.** without a companion; alone. **b.** through one's own efforts and without help: *Did you draw this picture by yourself?*

one′-shot′, *adj.* [*usually: before a noun*] **1.** occurring, appearing, done, etc., only once: *a one-shot deal.* **2.** achieved or accomplished with a single try: *a one-shot solution.*

one′-sid′ed, *adj.* **1.** partial; unfair: *a one-sided judgment.* **2.** with one side much better than the other; unequal: *a one-sided fight.* **—one′-sid′ed•ness,** *n.* [*noncount*]

one′-time′ or **one′time′,** *adj.* [*before a noun*] **1.** former; sometime: *was a one-time ski instructor.* **2.** occurring, done, etc., only once: *a one-time offer.*

one′-track′, *adj.* [*before a noun*] unable or unwilling to deal or work with more than one idea, subject, etc., at one time: *a one-track mind.*

one′-up′, *v.* [~ + *obj*], **-upped, -up•ping.** to gain an advantage over: *With this new plan, we can one-up the competition.*

one′-up′man•ship or **one′-ups′man•ship** (wun′up′mən ship′, -ups′-) /'wʌn'ʌpmənˌʃɪp, -'ʌps-/ *n.* [*noncount*] the art or practice of trying for or gaining the advantage in a competitive relationship.

one′-way′, *adj.* [*before a noun*] **1.** moving or allowing movement in one direction only: *a one-way street.* **2.** used or usable for travel in one direction only: *a one-way ticket.* **3.** without returning the same feeling, without equal responsibility, etc.: *a one-way friendship.*

on•go•ing (on′gō′ing, ôn′-) /'ɒnˌgowɪŋ, 'ɔn-/ *adj.* continuing without ending or without interruption: *ongoing research.*

on•ion (un′yən) /'ʌnyən/ *n.* [*count*] **1.** a plant of the amaryllis family, having a white or yellow, strong-smelling bulb that can be eaten. **2.** this bulb, used in cooking.

on•ion•skin (un′yən skin′) /'ʌnyənˌskɪn/ *n.* [*noncount*] a thin, strong, lightweight paper.

on′-line′ or **on′line′,** *adj.* operating under the direct control of, or connected to, a main computer: *If you are not getting any messages back, make sure you are still on-line (= Make sure your computer is still on-line).* Compare OFF-LINE.

on•look•er (on′lo͝ok′ər, ôn′-) /'ɒnˌlʊkər, 'ɔn-/ *n.* [*count*] a person watching or looking at some action; spectator: *onlookers to an accident.* **—on′look′ing,** *adj.*

on•ly (ōn′lē) /'ownliy/ *adv.* **1.** without others or anything further; exclusively: *This information is for your eyes only.* **2.** no more than; just: *We get away from the city only on weekends.* **3.** as recently as: *I read that article only yesterday.* **4.** in the final outcome or decision: *That will only make matters worse.* **5.** (used after a clause and before a phrase with *to* and a verb, to indicate that the verb happens immediately after the first action described): *The scout tried to creep up silently behind the enemy agent,* *only to sneeze suddenly.* —*adj.* [*before a noun*] **6.** being the single one or the relatively few of the kind; lone; sole: *Is this the only seat left?* **7.** alone of its kind: *an only child.* —*conj.* **8.** (used between clauses or phrases to limit the degree of the first clause or phrase); but; except: *I would have gone, only you objected.* —***Idiom.*** **9. only too,** very; extremely: *only too happy to help.*

on•o•mat•o•poe•ia (on′ə mat′ə pē′ə, -mä′tə-) /ˌɒnəˌmætə'piyə, -ˌmɑtə-/ *n.* [*noncount*] **1.** the formation of a word, as *cuckoo* or *boom,* by imitating the sound made by or associated with the thing the noun refers to: *In English, onomatopoeia is found in words like* tweet, zap, flick, *and* hiss. **2.** the use of such imitative words, as in poetry. —**on′o•mat′o•poe′ic, on•o•mat•o•po•et•ic** (on′ə mat′ə pō et′ik, -mä′tə-) /ˌɒnəˌmætəpow'ɛtɪk, -ˌmɑtə-/ *adj.* See -NOM-², -ONYM-.

on•rush (on′rush′, ôn′-) /'ɒnˌrʌʃ, 'ɔn-/ *n.* [*count*] a strong forward rush, flow, movement, etc. —**on′rush′-ing,** *adj.* [*before a noun*]: *onrushing traffic.*

on•set (on′set′, ôn′-) /'ɒnˌsɛt, 'ɔn-/ *n.* [*count*] **1.** a beginning or start: *the onset of winter.* **2.** an assault or attack: *the onset of the enemy.*

on•slaught (on′slôt′, ôn′-) /'ɒnˌslɔt, 'ɔn-/ *n.* [*count*] a fierce attack.

on•to (on′to͞o, ôn′-; *unstressed* on′tə, ôn′-) /'ɒntuw, 'ɔn-; *unstressed* ˈɒntə, ˈɔn-/ *prep.* **1.** to a place or position on; upon; on: *They pulled him onto his feet.* **2.** *Informal.* aware of the true nature, motive, or meaning of: *I'm onto your tricks.*

on•tol•o•gy (on tol′ə jē) /ɒn'tɒlədʒiy/ *n.* [*noncount*] the branch of metaphysics that studies the question of what it means to exist. —**on•to•log•i•cal** (on′tl oj′i kəl) /ˌɒntl̩'ɒdʒɪkəl/ *adj.*

o•nus (ō′nəs) /'ownəs/ *n., pl.* **o•nus•es. 1.** [*count*] a difficult or disagreeable obligation or task. **2.** [*noncount*] burden of proof: *The onus is on you to show you really want to improve.* **3.** [*noncount*] blame; responsibility.

on•ward (on′wərd, ôn′-) /'ɒnwərd, 'ɔn-/ *adv.* Also, **on′-wards. 1.** toward a point ahead or in front; forward, as in space or time: *The army marched onward into the setting sun.* —*adj.* [*before a noun*] **2.** directed or moving onward; forward: *the onward flight to freedom.*

-onym-, *root.* *-onym-* comes from Greek, where it has the meaning "name." This meaning is found in such words as: ACRONYM, ANONYMOUS, ANTONYM, HOMONYM, ONOMATOPOEIA, PATRONYMIC, PSEUDONYM, SYNONYM.

on•yx (on′iks) /'ɒnɪks/ *n.* **1.** a mineral stone, a form of quartz, having straight parallel bands of alternating colors: [*count*]: *a bright onyx.* [*noncount*]: *a statue of onyx.* **2.** [*noncount*] black, esp. a pure or jet black. —*adj.* **3.** black, esp. jet black.

oo•dles (o͞od′lz) /'uwdlz/ *n.* [*plural; sometimes used with a singular verb*] *Informal.* a large amount or quantity: *oodles of information; oodles of fun.*

ooze[1] (o͞oz) /uwz/ *v.,* **oozed, ooz•ing,** *n.* —*v.* [*no obj*] **1.** (of moisture, liquid, etc.) to flow or pass slowly or gradually: *Water was oozing from her sneakers.* **2.** [~ + *obj*] to give off or allow (moisture, liquid, etc.) to exude: *The wound began to ooze blood.* **3.** [*no obj; (~ out/away)*] to appear or disappear slowly or gradually: *His confidence began to ooze (out). You sensed his courage oozing (away).* **4.** [~ + *obj*] to display or show falsely: *oozing charm.* —*n.* [*noncount*] **5.** the act of oozing. **6.** something that oozes.

ooze[2] (o͞oz) /uwz/ *n.* [*noncount*] **1.** a type of mud made chiefly of the shells of one-celled organisms, found on the ocean bottom. **2.** soft mud or slime.

o•pac•i•ty (ō pas′i tē) /ow'pæsɪtiy/ *n.* [*noncount*] **1.** the state or quality of being difficult to see through. **2.** the state or quality of being difficult to understand or unclear in meaning.

o•pal (ō′pəl) /'owpəl/ *n.* a mineral, a form of silica, found in many varieties and colors, including milky white, sometimes made into a gemstone with many shining colors in it: [*count*]: *a ring with two beautiful, shiny opals.* [*noncount*]: *a necklace of opal.*

o•paque (ō pāk′) /ow'peyk/ *adj.* **1.** not allowing light to pass through; difficult to see through. **2.** hard to understand; not clear: *opaque arguments.* **3.** dull, stupid, or unintelligent.

op′ art′ (op) /ɒp/ *n.* [*noncount*] abstract art in which lines, forms, and space are arranged to produce visual effects, as apparent movement.

op. cit. (op′ sit′) /'ɒp' sɪt/ an abbreviation of Latin *opere citato:* in the work cited.

OPEC (ō′pek) /'owpɛk/ *n.* [*proper noun; noncount; no article*] Organization of Petroleum Exporting Countries, an organization of countries that produce oil and establish prices for it on the world market.

op′-ed′ (op′ed′) /'ɒpˌɛd/ *n.* [*proper noun; noncount; sometimes Op-Ed*] a newspaper page or section with signed articles by commentators and essayists, opposite the editorial page.

o•pen (ō′pən) /'owpən/ *adj.* **1.** not closed or barred at the time mentioned: *She left the windows open at night.* **2.** (of a door, window sash, etc.) set so as to permit passage through the opening that it can be used to close; not locked: *The door is open; come in.* **3.** arranged so that the inside is easy to reach: *The dresser drawer was open.* **4.** mostly free of things that block or that prevent movement through: *an open floor plan.* **5.** [*before a noun*] built or designed so as not to be fully enclosed: *an open staircase.* **6.** [*before a noun*] having mostly large or numerous empty spaces, gaps, or intervals: *open ranks of soldiers.* **7.** not covered or closed: *His eyes were open.* **8.** without a covering, esp. a covering that protects: *an open wound.* **9.** extended, unfolded, or arranged: *an open newspaper; The book was open on the desk.* **10.** without restrictions or limits as to who may participate: *open enrollment.* **11.** available: *Which job is open?* **12.** [*be* + ~ + *to*] available or possible for one to do: *What course of action is open to us now?* **13.** ready for or carrying on normal trade or business: *The new store is now open.* **14.** not reserved, engaged, or committed: *open time on the calendar.* **15.** [*before a noun*] so clear that all can see or know: *open disregard of the rules.* **16.** truthful; honest; candid: *always open and fair in his dealings with others.* **17.** generous: *to give with an open hand.* **18.** [*be* + ~ + *to* + *obj*] likely to receive: *He left himself open to criticism.* **19.** [*be* + ~ + *to*] willing to receive or accept: *open to suggestions.* **20.** undecided; unsettled: *several open questions.* **21.** (in sports) unguarded by an opponent: *An open receiver caught the pass.* —*v.* **22.** to (cause to) be moved from a shut or closed position, such as a door, window, etc.: [~ + *obj*]: *He opened the door.* [*no obj*]: *The door slowly opened.* **23.** [~ + *obj*] to remove a blockage or barrier from: *to open the road after a snowstorm.* **24.** [*no obj*] (of a road, pass, etc.) to have a blockage or barrier removed: *The road finally opened when the blizzard stopped.* **25.** to (cause to) be not covered or closed; (cause to) have certain parts apart: [~ + *obj*]: *He opened his mouth to speak.* [*no obj*]: *His eyes opened suddenly.* **26.** [~ + *obj*] to arrange so that the inside of (a box, drawer, etc.) is easily reached: *Open the toolbox.* **27.** [~ + *obj*] to make available: *to open a port for trade.* **28.** to (cause to) be made ready for customers or normal work activity: [~ + *obj*]: *They open the store at nine o'clock.* [*no obj*]: *They open at nine o'clock.* **29.** to (cause to) be established or set up for business purposes or for public use: [~ + *obj*]: *The company will open an office in Singapore.* [*no obj*]: *A new store opened on Main Street last week.* **30.** to (cause to) be set in action, begun, or started: [~ + *obj*]: *opened the meeting with a short speech.* [*no obj*]: *The meeting opened with a short speech.* **31.** [~ + *obj*] **a.** to expose to view: *The surgeon opened the chest cavity.* **b.** to disclose; reveal; show: *He opened his heart to her* (= *He let her see his true feelings*). **32.** to (cause to) be expanded, unfolded, spread out; (cause to) be turned or arranged to be read: [~ + *obj*]: *to open a map.* [*no obj*]: *The map opened easily.* **33.** to (cause to) be less tight, less compact, or less closely spaced: [~ + *obj*]: *The soldiers began to open ranks.* [*no obj*]: *The ranks of the soldiers began to open.* **34.** to make (the mind) ready to receive knowledge, sympathy, etc.: [~ + *obj*]: *College opened his mind.* [*no obj*]: *His mind opened when he went to college.* **35.** [~ + *obj*] to make or produce (a way or path): *to open a way through a crowd.* **36.** [*no obj*] to provide a way of approaching a place: *a door that opens into a garden.* **37.** [*no obj*] to part or seem to part: *The clouds opened.* **38.** to (cause to) spread out: [~ + *obj*]: *He opened his hand and revealed a shiny new quarter.* [*no obj*]: *His hand opened.* **39.** to (cause to) spread or expand: [*no obj*]: *The flower opened in the sunlight.* [~ + *obj*]: *The fisherman opened the oysters with a sharp knife.* **40.** to (cause to) be created: [~ + *up* + *obj*]: *The new program opens (up) new possibilities.* [~(+ *up*)]: *New possibilities open (up) thanks to this proposal.* **41. open up, a.** to make or become open: [*no obj*]: *The flower opened up in the sun.* [~ + *up* + *obj*]: *They opened up their shops.* [~ + *obj* + *up*]: *It was too early to open the shops up.* **b.** [*no obj*] to begin firing a gun or the like: *The infantry opened up with their automatic weapons.* **c.** [*no obj*] to share or become willing to share one's feelings, confidences, etc.: *had to learn to open up to others.* —*n.* **42.** [*noncount; the* + ~] an open or clear space: *was out in the open where he could be seen.* **43.** [*noncount; the* + ~] the open air; outdoors: *They slept out in the open.* **44.** [*noncount; the* + ~] open water, as of the sea. **45.** [*count*] a contest or tournament in which both amateurs and professionals may compete: *tennis opens.* —***Idiom.*** **46. open someone's eyes,** to make someone alert to a situation. **47. out in** or **in the open,** not hidden; not concealed: *The secret is finally out in the open.* —**o′pen•ness,** *n.* [*noncount*]

o′pen air′, *n.* [*noncount*] the outdoors. —**o′pen-air′,** *adj.* [*before a noun*]: *an open-air market; an open-air museum.*

o′pen-and-shut′, *adj.* immediately or clearly obvious; straightforward: *an open-and-shut case of larceny.*

o′pen-end′ed, *adj.* **1.** not having fixed limits: *a wide-ranging, open-ended discussion.* **2.** having no fixed answer: *an open-ended test question.*

o•pen•er (ō′pə nər) /ˈowpənər/ *n.* [*count*] **1.** a person or thing that opens. **2.** a device for opening sealed containers or cans: *a can opener.* **3.** the first of several theatrical numbers, sports events, etc. —***Idiom.*** **4. for openers,** to begin with: *For openers, we need to discuss the plans.*

o′pen-faced′, *adj.* **1.** having a face that seems innocent or truthful and not ready to deceive. **2.** [*before a noun*] Also, **o′pen-face′.** (of a sandwich) made with the filling lying on a single slice of bread.

o•pen•hand•ed (ō′pən han′did) /ˈowpənˈhændɪd/ *adj.* generous.

o′pen-heart′ed, *adj.* **1.** candid or frank: *an open-hearted discussion.* **2.** kindly; wishing for good; benevolent: *a friendly, open-hearted man.*

o′pen-heart′ sur′gery, *n.* [*count*] an operation performed on the exposed heart with the aid of a special machine to keep the blood circulating.

o′pen house′, *n.* **1.** [*count*] a party or reception during which a person's home is open to visitors. **2.** a time during which a school, institution, etc., is open to the public: [*count*]: *an annual open house.* [*noncount*]: *On what night is open house this year?* **3.** [*count*] a house or apartment for sale or rent that is available for viewing.

o•pen•ing (ō′pə ning) /ˈowpənɪŋ/ *n.* [*count*] **1.** an act or instance of making or becoming open. **2.** an unoccupied space or place: *an opening in the woods.* **3.** a hole in something solid. **4. a.** start: *The opening of the play will be delayed for 15 minutes.* **b.** the first part or initial stage of anything: *The opening of the movie gives us a glimpse of the future.* **5.** a vacancy for a job. **6.** an opportunity; chance: *a rare opening to meet the boss.* **7.** the formal or official beginning of an activity, event, presentation, etc.: *The mayor was present for the opening of the new highway.* —*adj.* [*before a noun*] **8.** coming first; beginning: *opening remarks.*

o′pen let′ter, *n.* [*count*] a letter, often of protest, addressed to a specific person, but also intended to be brought to public attention.

o•pen•ly (ō′pən lē) /ˈowpənliy/ *adv.* without hiding or without trying to deceive; not secretly; plainly; clearly: *They discussed their problems openly.*

o′pen mar′riage, *n.* a marriage in which the partners are free to have close friendships or sexual relationships with other persons: [*noncount*]: *thought about the idea of open marriage.* [*count*]: *They had an open marriage.*

o′pen-mind′ed, *adj.* **1.** willing to receive or consider new ideas or arguments. **2.** not having or showing prejudice; not bigoted; impartial.

o′pen se′cret, *n.* [*count*] something that is supposed to be a secret but is actually known by others.

o′pen shop′, *n.* [*count*] a business establishment in which a union acts as a representative of all the employees but in which union membership is not a condition for employment.

-oper-, *root.* *-oper-* comes from Latin, where it has the meaning "work." This meaning is found in such words as: COOPERATE, INOPERATIVE, OPERA, OPERATE, OPUS.

op•er•a (op′ər ə, op′rə) /ˈɒpərə, ˈɒprə/ *n., pl.* **-er•as.** a long dramatic musical work similar to a play but in which the parts are sung: [*count*]: *sang in many operas.* [*noncount*]: *has a love of opera.* See -OPER-.

op•er•a•ble (op′ər ə bəl, op′rə-) /ˈɒpərəbəl, ˈɒprə-/ *adj.* **1.** able to be treated by a surgical operation. **2.** capable of being put into use, operation, or practice: *an operable plan.* See -OPER-.

op•er•ate (op′ə rāt′) /ˈɒpəˌreyt/ *v.,* **-at•ed, -at•ing. 1.** [*no obj*] to work; function: *This coffee machine is not operating properly.* **2.** [~ + *obj*] to manage or use: *could operate farm machinery.* **3.** [*no obj*] to carry on business: *The company operates in southern California.* **4.** [~ + *obj*] to put or keep in operation: *operated a factory in the midwest.* **5.** to perform a medical procedure in which the body is cut open and a part is removed or adjusted: [*no obj*]: *The surgeon is ready to operate.* [~ + *on* + *obj*]: *The surgeon operated on several patients.* **6.** [*no obj*] *Informal.* to put oneself into a position of favor, advantage, etc., in a cunning way: *really knows how to operate in the halls of government.* See -OPER-.

op•er•at•ic (op′ə rat′ik) /ˌɒpəˈrætɪk/ *adj.* of or relating to opera. See -OPER-.

op•er•a•tion (op′ə rā′shən) /ˌɒpəˈreyʃən/ *n.* **1.** [*count*] an act, instance, process, or manner of working. **2.** [*noncount*] the state of being operative: *a rule no longer in operation.* **3.** [*noncount*] the using of force, power, or influence; agency: *the operation of alcohol on the brain.* **4.** [*count*] a process of a practical or mechanical nature: *a delicate operation in watchmaking.* **5.** [*count*] a business transaction: *a shady operation.* **6.** [*count*] a business, esp. one run on a large scale. **7.** [*count*] a medical procedure of cutting open the body to restore or improve the health of a patient, as by removing a diseased part. **8.** [*count*] a mathematical process, as addition or multiplication. See -OPER-.

op•er•a•tion•al (op′ə rā′shə nəl) /ˌɒpəˈreyʃənəl/ *adj.* **1.** able to be used; working; usable. **2.** [*before a noun*] of or relating to an operation or operations: *the operational costs of the project.*

op•er•a•tive (op′ər ə tiv, op′rə tiv, op′ə rā′tiv) /ˈɒpərətɪv, ˈɒprətɪv, ˈɒpəˌreytɪv/ *n.* [*count*] **1.** a person engaged or skilled in some branch of work, esp. productive or industrial work; worker. **2.** a detective. **3.** a secret agent: *an FBI operative.* —*adj.* **4. a.** being in operation: *The plant was fully operative.* **b.** being in force: *The regulation became operative last month.* **5.** [*before a noun*] most important or significant; key: *The operative word is "caution."* See -OPER-.

op•er•a•tor (op′ə rā′tər) /ˈɒpəˌreytər/ *n.* [*count*] **1.** a person who operates a machine or apparatus, esp. a telephone switchboard. **2.** a person who manages an industrial establishment or a business: *a hotel operator.* **3.** a person who accomplishes his or her purposes by cleverness or in slightly dishonest ways: *He's a smooth operator.* See -OPER-.

op•er•et•ta (op′ə ret′ə) /ˌɒpəˈrɛtə/ *n.* [*count*], *pl.* **-tas.** a short opera usually of light character. See -OPER-.

oph•thal•mol•o•gy (of′thəl mol′ə jē, -thə-, op′-) /ˌɒfθəlˈmɒlədʒiy, -θə-, ˌɒp-/ *n.* [*noncount*] the branch of medicine dealing with the physical structure, functions, and diseases of the eye. —**oph′thal•mol′o•gist,** *n.* [*count*]: *An ophthalmologist treats diseases of the eye; an optometrist tests your eyes and measures them for glasses.* See -OPTI-.

o•pi•ate (ō′pē it, -āt′) /ˈowpiyɪt, -ˌeyt/ *n.* [*count*] **1.** a drug containing opium. **2.** a drug that calms one or makes one sleepy. **3.** anything that brings on a feeling of laziness or soothes the feelings.

o•pine (ō pin′) /owˈpayn/ *v.* [*used with quotations*], **o•pined, o•pin•ing.** to express an opinion about (something).

o•pin•ion (ə pin′yən) /əˈpɪnyən/ *n.* **1.** [*noncount*] a belief or judgment based on information that one cannot be certain about. **2.** [*count*] a personal view or belief. **3.** [*count*] the formal expression of a professional judgment: *got a second medical opinion.* **4.** [*count*] the formal statement by a judge or a court of the principles used in reaching a decision on a case.

o•pin•ion•at•ed (ə pin′yə nā′tid) /əˈpɪnyəˌneytɪd/ *adj.* stubbornly believing in or declaring the correctness of one's own opinions; close-minded; dogmatic.

o•pi•um (ō′pē əm) /ˈowpiyəm/ *n.* [*noncount*] **1.** a narcotic drug made from the dried, condensed juice of the seed capsules of a poppy. **2.** OPIATE (def. 3).

o•pos•sum (ə pos′əm, pos′əm) /əˈpɒsəm, ˈpɒsəm/ *n.* [*count*], *pl.* **-sums,** (*esp. when thought of as a group*) **-sum.** a small animal with a long tail, of the eastern U.S., that carries its young in a pouch and is noted for pretending to be dead when it is in danger.

op•po•nent (ə pō′nənt) /əˈpownənt/ *n.* [*count*] a person who is on an opposing side in a game, argument, controversy, or the like; adversary. See -PON-.

op•por•tune (op′ər to͞on′, -tyo͞on′) /ˌɒpərˈtuwn, -ˈtyuwn/ *adj.* **1.** correct or right for a certain purpose or aim; suitable; apt: *an opportune comment.* **2.** occurring or happening at a good or appropriate time; well-timed: *an opportune appearance at the press conference.* See -PORT-.

op•por•tun•ism (op′ər tōō′niz əm, -tyōō′-) /ˌɒpər'tuwnɪzəm, -'tyuw-/ *n.* [*noncount*] the policy or practice, as in politics or business, of taking actions or making decisions based on whether they will bring success and gain, rather than on whether they are moral or good. —**op′por•tun′ist,** *n.* [*count*] See -PORT-.

op•por•tun•is•tic (op′ər tōō nis′tik, -tyōō-) /ˌɒpər-tuw'nɪstɪk, -tyuw-/ *adj.* **1.** following a policy of opportunism. **2.** (of a disease or infection) caused by an organism that flourishes only in certain circumstances, as when the body is already weakened by another condition. See -PORT-.

op•por•tu•ni•ty (op′ər tōō′ni tē, -tyōō′-) /ˌɒpər'tuwnɪtiy, -'tyuw-/ *n., pl.* **-ties. 1.** [*count*] a favorable or good occasion or time (to do something): *an opportunity to apologize.* **2.** [*noncount*] a situation, state, or condition that is favorable for attaining or achieving a goal, or that provides a good position or chance for success: *a land of opportunity.* **3.** [*count*] a good chance or prospect: *has many opportunities to succeed.* See -PORT-.

op•pose (ə pōz′) /ə'powz/ *v.* [~ + *obj*], **-posed, -pos•ing. 1. a.** to act against; combat: *The two boxers had opposed each other several times before* **b.** to resist; be against: *Several senators opposed the project.* **2.** to set (something) opposite something else, or to set (two things) so as to be opposite one another. —***Idiom.* 3. as opposed to,** [~ + *obj*] in contrast to; instead of: *I'd rather have a small computer as opposed to a big one.* **4. be opposed to,** [~ + *obj*] to be against: *was opposed to a tax hike.* See -POS-.

op•pos•ing (ə pō′zing) /ə'powzɪŋ/ *adj.* opposite; contrary: *The two speakers took opposing viewpoints.* See -POS-.

op•po•site (op′ə zit, -sit) /'ɒpəzɪt, -sɪt/ *adj.* **1.** [*sometimes: after a noun*] located or lying face to face with something else or each other, or placed in corresponding positions across a line, space, etc.: *They sat at opposite ends of the room.* [*be* + ~ + *to/from* + *obj*]: *We were opposite to each other on the train.* **2.** very or totally different: *opposite sides in a controversy.* —*n.* [*count*] **3.** a person or thing that is opposite in character. **4.** ANTONYM: *The words* friend *and* enemy *are opposites.* —*prep.* **5.** across from; facing: *He sat opposite me on the train.* —*adv.* **6.** on or to the opposite side: *I was at one end and she sat opposite.* See -POS-.

op•po•si•tion (op′ə zish′ən) /ˌɒpə'zɪʃən/ *n.* **1.** [*noncount*] the action of opposing. **2.** [*count; usually singular; usually: the* + ~] a person or group of people opposing something or someone. **3.** [*count; usually singular; sometimes: the Opposition*] the major political party opposed to the party in power and seeking to replace it. See -POS-.

op•press (ə pres′) /ə'prɛs/ *v.* [~ + *obj*] **1.** to use harsh authority or power over (others): *The dictator oppressed his countrymen.* **2.** to lie heavily upon (the mind, a person, etc.); weigh down: *She's oppressed with worry.* —**op•pres′sion,** *n.* [*noncount*] —**op•pres′sor,** *n.* [*count*] See -PRESS-.

op•pres•sive (ə pres′iv) /ə'prɛsɪv/ *adj.* **1.** unfairly or unjustly harsh, difficult, or cruel: *an oppressive government.* **2.** causing discomfort: *oppressive heat.* **3.** causing anxiety or depression: *an oppressive sense of failure.* —**op•pres′sive•ly,** *adv.* —**op•pres′sive•ness,** *n.* [*noncount*] See -PRESS-.

op•pro•bri•ous (ə prō′brē əs) /ə'prowbriyəs/ *adj.* **1.** showing or expressing opprobrium: *an opprobrious attack on immorality.* **2.** deserving opprobrium: *opprobrious conduct.* —**op•pro′bri•ous•ness,** *n.* [*noncount*] See -PROB-.

op•pro•bri•um (ə prō′brē əm) /ə'prowbriyəm/ *n.* [*noncount*] **1.** disgrace or reproach brought on by shameful conduct. **2.** the cause of such disgrace or reproach. **3.** criticism; reproach; scorn. See -PROB-.

opt (opt) /ɒpt/ *v.* **1.** to make a choice; choose: [~ + *for* + *obj*]: *Voters opted for the new candidate.* [~ + *to* + *verb*]: *They opted to retire early.* **2. opt out,** [~ *(+ of + obj)*] to decide not to participate in something: *opted out of attending the show.* See -OPT-.

-opt-, *root. -opt-* comes from Latin, where it has the meaning "choose; choice." This meaning is found in such words as: ADOPT, CO-OPT, OPT, OPTION, OPTIONAL.

-opti-, *root. -opti-* comes from Greek, where it has the meaning "light; sight." This meaning is found in such words as: AUTOPSY, BIOPSY, MYOPIA, OPHTHALMOLOGY, OPTIC, OPTICAL, OPTICIAN, OPTOMETRY, SYNOPTIC.

op•tic (op′tik) /'ɒptɪk/ *adj.* [*before a noun*] **1.** of or relating to the eye or to eyesight: *affecting the optic nerve.* —*n.* [*count*] **2.** a lens of an optical instrument. See -OPTI-.

op•ti•cal (op′ti kəl) /'ɒptɪkəl/ *adj.* [*before a noun*] **1.** of, relating to, or applying optics. **2.** of or relating to the eye or eyesight: *an optical illusion (= something that is not really the way the eye perceives it).* —**op′ti•cal•ly,** *adv.* See -OPTI-.

op′tical disc′, *n.* [*count*] **1.** Also called **laser disc.** a plastic disk on which digital data, as music or pictures, are stored as tiny pits in the surface and read by using a laser. **2.** VIDEODISC. Compare COMPACT DISC.

op•ti•cian (op tish′ən) /ɒp'tɪʃən/ *n.* [*count*] a person who makes or sells eyeglasses and contact lenses. See -OPTI-.

op•tics (op′tiks) /'ɒptɪks/ *n.* [*noncount; used with a singular verb*] the branch of physical science that deals with the properties and actions of both visible and invisible light and with vision. See -OPTI-.

op•ti•mism (op′tə miz′əm) /'ɒptəˌmɪzəm/ *n.* [*noncount*] **1.** a tendency to look on the more favorable side or to expect the most favorable outcome or result of events or conditions. **2.** the belief that good will ultimately triumph over evil and that virtue will be rewarded. —**op′ti•mist,** *n.* [*count*] —**op′ti•mis′tic,** *adj.* —**op′ti•mis′ti•cal•ly,** *adv.*

op•ti•mum (op′tə məm) /'ɒptəməm/ *n., pl.* **-ma** (-mə) /-mə/ **-mums,** *adj.* —*n.* [*count*] **1.** the most favorable point, degree, or amount of something for obtaining a certain result. —*adj.* [*before a noun*] **2.** most favorable or desirable; best: *optimum conditions for growth.* —**op′ti•mal,** *adj.*

op•tion (op′shən) /'ɒpʃən/ *n.* **1.** [*noncount*] the power or right of choosing: *to have no option but to stay.* **2.** [*count*] something that may be chosen; choice: *Your options are law school or taking a job.* **3.** [*count*] an item of equipment or an extra feature that may be chosen: *The car had several options like power windows and a CD player.* —*v.* [~ + *obj*] **4.** to take or grant an option on. —**op′tion•al,** *adj.* —**op′tion•al•ly,** *adv.* See -OPT-. —**Syn.** See CHOICE.

op•tom•e•try (op tom′i trē) /ɒp'tɒmɪtriy/ *n.* [*noncount*] the profession of examining the eyes for defects of vision and for eye disorders. —**op•tom′e•trist,** *n.* [*count*] See -OPTI-.

op•u•lence (op′yə ləns) /'ɒpyələns/ *n.* [*noncount*] the state or condition of being or appearing very wealthy; richness: *a home of great opulence.*

op•u•lent (op′yə lənt) /'ɒpyələnt/ *adj.* **1.** characterized by opulence: *an opulent lifestyle.* **2.** wealthy, rich, or affluent. —**op′u•lent•ly,** *adv.*

o•pus (ō′pəs) /'owpəs/ *n.* [*count*], *pl.* **o•pus•es** or, esp. for 1, **o•pe•ra** (ō′pər ə, op′ər ə) /'owpərə, 'ɒpərə/. **1.** one of the musical works of a composer. **2.** a literary or artistic work. See -OPER-.

or (ôr; *unstressed* ər) /ɔr; *unstressed* ər/ *conj.* **1.** (used to connect words, phrases, or clauses that represent or stand for choices, alternatives, or options): *to be or not to be; Do you want vanilla or chocolate?* **2.** (used to connect different words or names that refer to the same thing): *the Hawaiian, or Sandwich, Islands.* **3.** (used with the word EITHER to connect two clauses showing one choice followed by another): *Either we go now or we wait till tomorrow.* **4.** (used to correct or rephrase what was previously said): *His autobiography, or rather his memoirs, will be published soon.* **5.** otherwise; or else: *Be here on time, or we'll leave without you.*

OR, an abbreviation of: **1.** operating room. **2.** Oregon.

-or, *suffix. -or* is used to form nouns that are agents, or that do or perform a function: *debtor; tailor; traitor; projector; repressor; sensor; tractor.*

or•a•cle (ôr′ə kəl, or′-) /'ɔrəkəl, 'ɒr-/ *n.* [*count*] **1.** (in the ancient world) **a.** a shrine at which questions are asked of a particular god or goddess through some means of communication: *the Delphic oracle.* **b.** the priest, priestess, or other person or sign through which the questions are answered. **c.** an answer given by an oracle. **2.** a person who makes statements that are thought to be wise. —**o•rac•u•lar** (ô rak′yə lər, ō rak′-) /ɔ'rækyələr, ow'ræk-/ *adj.*

o•ral (ôr′əl, ōr′-) /'ɔrəl, 'owr-/ *adj.* **1.** made or expressed by the mouth; spoken: *oral testimony; oral exams.* **2.** of, using, or carried by speech: *oral teaching methods.* **3.** involving the mouth: *oral hygiene.* —*n.* [*count*] Usually, **orals.** [*plural*] **4.** an oral examination in a school, college, or university. —**o′ral•ly,** *adv.*

or•ange (ôr′inj, or′-) /'ɔrɪndʒ, 'ɒr-/ *n.* **1.** [*count*] a rounded, reddish yellow, bitter or sweet citrus fruit that can be eaten. **2.** [*count*] a white-flowered evergreen tree carrying such fruit. **3.** [*noncount*] a reddish yellow color. *—adj.* **4.** [*before a noun*] of, relating to, or containing the orange or its juice or flavor: *orange sherbet.* **5.** of the color orange.

or•ange•ade (ôr′inj ād′, or′-) /ˌɔrɪndʒ'eyd, ˌɒr-/ *n.* a beverage of orange juice, sugar, and plain or carbonated water: [*noncount*]: *I don't like orangeade.* [*count*]: *I'll have two orangeades.*

o•rang•u•tan (ô rang′o͞o tan′, ō rang′-, ə rang′-) /ɔ'ræŋʊˌtæn, ow'ræŋ-, ə'ræŋ-/ also **o•rang′u•tang′** (-tang′) /-ˌtæŋ/ *n.* [*count*] a large, mostly tree-dwelling, long-armed, humanlike ape of Borneo and Sumatra.

o•rate (ô rāt′, ō rāt′, ôr′āt, ōr′āt) /ɔ'reyt, ow'reyt, 'ɔreyt, 'owreyt/ *v.*,[*no obj*] **-rat•ed, -rat•ing.** to speak pompously or in a dramatic manner: *He was orating at length about his new invention.*

o•ra•tion (ô rā′shən, ō rā′-) /ɔ'reyʃən, ow'rey-/ *n.* [*count*] a formal public speech, esp. for a special occasion.

or•a•tor (ôr′ə tər, or′-) /'ɔrətər, 'ɒr-/ *n.* [*count*] a person noted for giving public speeches.

or•a•to•ri•o (ôr′ə tôr′ē ō′, -tōr′-, or′-) /ˌɔrə'tɔriyˌow, -'towr-, ˌɒr-/ *n.* [*count*], *pl.* **-ri•os.** a long musical work usually based upon a religious idea, for solo voices, chorus, and orchestra.

or•a•to•ry (ôr′ə tôr′ē, -tōr′ē, or′-) /'ɔrəˌtɔriy, -ˌtowriy, 'ɒr-/ *n.* [*noncount*] skill or ability in public speaking; the art of public speaking, esp. in a formal and eloquent manner. —**or•a•tor•i•cal** (ôr′ə tôr′i kəl, or′ə tor′-) /ˌɔrə'tɔrɪkəl, ˌɒrə'tɒr-/ *adj.*

orb (ôrb) /ɔrb/ *n.* [*count*] a round object, as a sphere or globe. —**or•bic•u•lar** (ôr bik′yə lər) /ɔr'bɪkyələr/ *adj.*

or•bit (ôr′bit) /'ɔrbɪt/ *n.* **1.** the curved path, usually rounded, that a planet, satellite, spaceship, etc., follows around a heavenly body: [*count*]: *a comet with a very irregular orbit.* [*noncount; in/into* + ~]: *a spacecraft in orbit.* **2.** [*count*] the area of a nation's or a person's influence: *within England's orbit.* *—v.* **3.** to move or travel around in an orbital or rounded path: [~ + *obj*]: *The satellite orbited the earth.* [*no obj*]: *The moon orbited above the horizon.* **4.** [~ + *obj*] to send into orbit, as a satellite. —**or•bit•al** (ôr′bit l) /'ɔrbɪtl/ *adj.*

or•chard (ôr′chərd) /'ɔrtʃərd/ *n.* [*count*] **1.** an area of land used for the growing of fruit or nut trees. **2.** a group or collection of such trees.

or•ches•tra (ôr′kə strə, -kes trə) /'ɔrkəstrə, -kɛs trə/ *n.* [*count*], *pl.* **-tras.** **1.** a group of performers on various musical instruments, including esp. strings, winds, and drums, who play music together. **2. a.** the space reserved for the musicians, usually the front part of the main floor **(or′chestra pit′)**. **b.** the entire main-floor space for the audience. **c.** the front section of seats on the main floor. **3.** (in ancient theaters) the circular space in front of the stage, used for the chorus or reserved for important persons. —**or•ches•tral** (ôr kes′trəl) /ɔr'kɛstrəl/ *adj.* [*before a noun*]

or•ches•trate (ôr′kə strāt′) /'ɔrkəˌstreyt/ *v.* [~ + *obj*], **-trat•ed, -trat•ing.** **1.** to compose or arrange (music) for an orchestra. **2.** to arrange, coordinate, or organize the elements of (something) in order to achieve a goal, result, or effect: *to orchestrate negotiations behind the scenes.* —**or•ches•tra•tion** (ôr′kə strā′shən) /ˌɔrkə'streyʃən/ *n.* [*count*] —**or′ches•tra′tor, or′ches•trat′er,** *n.* [*count*]

or•chid (ôr′kid) /'ɔrkɪd/ *n.* [*count*] **1.** a plant that grows in temperate and tropical regions, having usually showy flowers. **2.** the flower of this plant.

-ord-, *root.* *-ord-* comes from Latin, where it has the meaning "order; fit." This meaning is found in such words as: COORDINATE, EXTRAORDINARY, INORDINATE, INSUBORDINATE, ORDAIN, ORDER, ORDINAL, ORDINANCE, ORDINARY, ORDINATION, SUBORDINATE.

or•dain (ôr dān′) /ɔr'deyn/ *v.* **1.** [~ + *obj*] to make (someone) a priest, minister, or rabbi. **2.** (of someone in authority) to order, enact, or establish by law, command, etc.: [~ + *that clause*]: *The king ordained that everyone should pay tax.* [~ + *obj*]: *Had this law been ordained?* **3.** [~ + *clause*] to decide or determine (the fate of someone or something): *The fates ordained whether he would live or die.* See -ORD-.

or•deal (ôr dēl′, -dē′əl) /ɔr'diyl, -'diyəl/ *n.* [*count*] any very severe, difficult, or trying test, experience, or trial.

or•der (ôr′dər) /'ɔrdər/ *n.* **1.** a command or instruction to do something, given by someone in authority: [*count*]: *gave orders not to be disturbed.* [*noncount; by* + ~]: *We're here to arrest you by order of the High Command.* **2.** [*noncount*] the way or manner of arranging things to follow one after another; succession; sequence: *words in alphabetical order.* **3.** [*noncount*] good or harmonious arrangement: *Can you put this room in better order?* **4.** [*noncount*] proper, satisfactory, or working condition: *got the motorcycle in working order again.* **5.** [*noncount*] agreement with or obedience to law, regulations, or established authority: *to keep order in the classroom.* **6.** [*noncount*] established and correct practice: *parliamentary rules of order.* **7.** [*count*] the current or established arrangement: *The old world order is changing.* **8.** [*count*] a direction or request to make, provide, send, or give someone something: *sent in an order for shirts.* **9.** [*count*] an amount of goods or items purchased or sold: *Your order hasn't been delivered yet.* **10.** [*count*] a portion of food requested or served in a restaurant: *an order of french fries.* **11.** [*count*] a class, kind, or sort distinguished from others by character or rank: *talents of a high order.* **12.** [*count*] a major subdivision of a class or subclass in a classification of living things, made up of one or more families. **13.** [*count; sometimes: Order*] a group, body of persons, or organization of the same profession, occupation, or interests: *the Order of the Garter.* **14.** [*count*] a body or society of persons who agree to live under the same religious, moral, or social regulations, such as a society in a monastery: *the Franciscan order of monks.* **15.** [*count*] a written direction to pay money or deliver goods: *a money order.* **16. orders,** [*plural*] the rank or status of an ordained Christian minister. **17.** [*count; Order*] **a.** a special honor or rank given by a king, queen, or other ruler to a person for distinguished achievement. **b.** the insignia worn by such a person. *—v.* **18.** to give an order or command to: [~ + *obj* + *to* + *verb*]: *She ordered them to leave at once.* [*used with quotations*]: *"Sit down at once!" he ordered.* [~ + *obj*]: *She ordered them out of her house.* **19. a.** to direct (someone or something) to be made, done, brought, obtained, etc.: [~ + *obj*]: *to order a copy of a book.* [~ + *obj* + *to* + *verb*]: *She ordered them to investigate.* [~ + *obj* + *verb-ed/-en*]: *She ordered the flags flown at half mast.* [*no obj*]: *"Are you ready to order?" the waiter asked.* [~ + *obj* + *obj*]: *He ordered us a delicious dinner.* **b.** [~ + *obj*] to give an order or command to: *The teacher ordered the children to be quiet.* **20.** [~ + *obj*] to arrange in a suitable way: *to order one's work day.* **21. order around** or **about,** [~ + *obj* + *around/about*] to give orders to (someone) in an unpleasant, rude, or bossy way. —***Idiom.*** **22. a tall** or **large order,** a difficult or nearly impossible task. **23. call to order,** [*call* + *obj* + *to* + ~] to begin (a meeting): *They called the meeting to order.* **24. in order, a.** right and proper; appropriate: *An apology is certainly in order.* **b.** properly arranged or prepared; ready: *Everything's in order, so we can go now.* **c.** correct according to the rules of parliamentary procedure. **25. in order that,** (used to introduce a clause that explains the reason for something) so that; to the end that: *These pupils are studying business in order that they might become better accountants.* **26. in order to,** (used to introduce a phrase to explain the reason for something) as a means to; with the purpose of: *The exchange students are studying here in order to get a better understanding of how American business works.* **27. in short order,** with promptness or speed; rapidly; quickly: *She had her homework done in short order.* **28. on order,** ordered but not yet received: *That part you need is on order.* **29. on the order of,** [~ + *obj*] approximately; about: *That house must be worth on the order of three million dollars.* **30. out of order, a.** not in correct sequence or arrangement: *These pages are out of order.* **b.** not appropriate or suitable: *Your remarks are out of order.* **c.** not operating properly; in disrepair: *The elevators are out of order again.* **d.** incorrect according to the rules of parliamentary procedure. **31. to order,** according to the needs or request of the person buying something: *The curtains were made to order.* See -ORD-.

or•dered (ôr′dərd) /'ɔrdərd/ *adj.* orderly: *an ordered life of work and relaxation.*

or•der•ly (ôr′dər lē) /'ɔrdərliy/ *adj., n., pl.* **-lies.** *—adj.* **1.** arranged or organized in a neat manner or in a regular sequence: *orderly closets.* **2.** willing or liking to organize things in a neat manner: *an orderly housekeeper.* **3.** observing or obeying laws, rules, or discipline; well-behaved; law-abiding: *an orderly crowd.* *—n.* [*count*] **4.** a hospital attendant having general, nonmedical duties. **5.** an enlisted soldier assigned to perform various chores for a commanding officer or group of officers. —**or′der•li•ness,** *n.* [*noncount*] See -ORD-.

or•di•nal (ôr′dn əl) /'ɔrdnəl/ *adj.* [*before a noun*] **1.** of or relating to order, rank, or position in a series. **—*n.*** [*count*] **2.** an ordinal number or numeral: *The word "second" is an ordinal.* See -ORD-.

or′dinal num′ber, *n.* [*count*] a number that expresses position in a series, as *first, second,* or *third.*

or•di•nance (ôr′dn əns) /'ɔrdṇəns/ *n.* [*count*] a public regulation, rule, or order: *a city ordinance.* See -ORD-.

or•di•nar•i•ly (ôr′dn âr′ə lē, ôr′dn er′ə lē) /ˌɔrdṇ'ɛərəliy, 'ɔrdṇˌɛrəliy/ *adv.* **1.** most of the time; generally; usually: *Ordinarily this train is on time.* **2.** in an ordinary manner or fashion: *dressed ordinarily.*

or•di•nar•y (ôr′dn er′ē) /'ɔrdṇˌɛriy/ *adj., n., pl.* **-nar•ies.** **—*adj.*** **1.** of no special quality or interest; commonplace; unexceptional: *not a hero but a plain, ordinary man.* **2.** customary; usual; normal: *wore their ordinary clothes.* **—*n.*** [*noncount; the* + ~] **3.** customary or average condition, degree, etc.: *ability far above the ordinary.* **—*Idiom.*** **4. out of the ordinary, a.** unusual. **b.** unusually good: *She wanted to get him a birthday present that was out of the ordinary this year.* **—or′di•nar′i•ness,** *n.* [*noncount*] See -ORD-.

or•di•na•tion (ôr′dn ā′shən) /ˌɔrdṇ'eyʃən/ *n.* **1.** [*count*] the act of ordaining. **2.** [*noncount*] the state of being ordained. See -ORD-.

ord•nance (ôrd′nəns) /'ɔrdnəns/ *n.* [*noncount*] **1.** cannon or artillery. **2.** military weapons with their equipment, ammunition, etc. See -ORD-.

ore (ôr, ōr) /ɔr, owr/ *n.* a metal-bearing mineral that can be mined at a profit, or a mineral or natural product serving as a source of some nonmetallic substance, as sulfur: [*noncount*]: *searching for iron ore.* [*count*]: *different ores.*

Ore., an abbreviation of: Oregon.

Oreg., an abbreviation of: Oregon.

o•reg•a•no (ə reg′ə nō′, ô reg′-) /ə'rɛgəˌnow, ɔ'rɛg-/ *n.* [*noncount*] a sweet-smelling herb of the mint family having leaves used as seasoning in cooking.

-orga-, *root.* *-orga-* comes from Greek, where it has the meanings "tool; body organ; musical instrument." These meanings are found in such words as: DISORGANIZE, INORGANIC, MICROORGANISM, ORGAN, ORGANIZE, REORGANIZE.

or•gan (ôr′gən) /'ɔrgən/ *n.* [*count*] **1. a.** Also called **pipe organ.** a musical instrument having one or more sets of pipes, played by a keyboard that controls compressed air which sounds the pipes. **b.** a similar musical instrument having the tones produced electronically: *an electronic organ.* **2.** a grouping of tissues into a distinct structure that performs a special task, as a heart or kidney in animals or a leaf or stamen in plants. **3.** a newspaper, magazine, or other means of communicating information esp. in behalf of some organization. **4.** an instrument or means, as of action: *the organs of government.* See -ORGA-.

or•gan•dy (ôr′gən dē) /'ɔrgəndiy/ *n., pl.* **-dies.** a fine, thin cotton fabric usually having a crisp finish, used for dresses, curtains, etc.: [*noncount*]: *a dress of organdy.* [*count*]: *organdies on sale.*

or•gan•elle (ôr′gə nel′, ôr′gə nel′) /ˌɔrgə'nɛl, 'ɔrgəˌnɛl/ *n.* [*count*] a structure within a living cell that has a specific function; cell organ. See -ORGA-.

or•gan•ic (ôr gan′ik) /ɔr'gænɪk/ *adj.* **1.** [*before a noun*] of or relating to a class of chemical compounds that was formerly made up of only those existing in, or derived from, plants or animals, but that now includes all other compounds of carbon. Compare INORGANIC (def. 2). **2.** [*before a noun*] relating to, characteristic of, or coming from living things. **3.** of, relating to, or involving animals, produce, etc., raised or grown without artificial or synthetic fertilizers, pesticides, or drugs: *organic farming.* **4.** of or relating to an organ or the organs of an animal, plant, or fungus. **5.** having or showing a systematic arrangement of parts; organized; systematic: *a view of language as a unified, organic whole.* **—*n.*** [*count*] **6.** a substance, as a fertilizer or pesticide, of animal or vegetable origin: *tomatoes grown only with organics.* **—or•gan′i•cal•ly,** *adv.* See -ORGA-.

or•gan•ism (ôr′gə niz′əm) /'ɔrgəˌnɪzəm/ *n.* [*count*] **1.** any individual life form thought of as a single unit. **2.** any complex, organized system like a living being: *the organism that is society.* See -ORGA-.

or•gan•ist (ôr′gə nist) /'ɔrgənɪst/ *n.* [*count*] a person who plays the organ. See -ORGA-.

or•gan•i•za•tion (ôr′gə nə zā′shən) /ˌɔrgənə'zeyʃən/ *n.* **1.** [*noncount*] the act or process of organizing, planning, or working to put something together: *the organization of a committee to run the banquet.* **2.** [*noncount*] the state or manner of being organized. **3.** [*noncount*] the structure of something: *the organization of brain cells to perform a function.* **4.** [*count*] a group of persons grouped together or organized for some purpose or work; an association: *a national organization devoted to women's rights.* **—or•gan•i•za•tion•al** (ôr′gə nə zā′shə-nl) /ˌɔrgənə'zeyʃənḷ/ *adj.* See -ORGA-.

or•gan•ize (ôr′gə nīz′) /'ɔrgəˌnayz/ *v.,* **-ized, -iz•ing. 1.** [~ + *obj*] to form (a group) as or into a whole or single body that is made up of parts that depend on each other or that work with each other, esp. for united action: *to organize a committee.* **2.** [~ + *obj*] to make (something that lacks order) into something with a system or logical structure: *organizing her classroom notes.* **3.** [~ + *obj*] to call together (workers, employees, etc., of a business or workplace) so as to form a labor union. **4.** [*no obj*] to come together and form a labor union: *The workers organized.* **—or′gan•iz′er,** *n.* [*count*] See -ORGA-.

or•gan•ized (ôr′gə nīzd′) /'ɔrgəˌnayzd/ *adj.* [*before a noun*] **1.** grouped or associated with an organization, esp. with a union: *organized labor.* **2.** having an organization or structure for directing many activities over a wide area: *organized crime.* See -ORGA-.

or•gasm (ôr′gaz əm) /'ɔrgæzəm/ *n.* the intense physical and emotional feeling experienced at the peak of sexual excitement; climax: [*count*]: *experiencing an orgasm.* [*noncount*]: *achieving orgasm.* **—or•gas•mic** (ōr gaz′-mik) /owr'gæz'mɪkgæs-/ *adj.*

or•gy (ôr′jē) /'ɔrdʒiy/ *n.* [*count*], *pl.* **-gies. 1.** a drunken party, esp. a party with wild sexual activity. **2.** any actions or proceedings that are uncontrolled or wild: *an orgy of killing.*

-ori-, *root.* *-ori-* comes from Latin, where it has the meaning "rise; begin; appear." This meaning is found in such words as: ABORIGINAL, ABORIGINE, ABORT, ABORTION, DISORIENT, ORIENT, ORIENTATE, ORIENTATION, ORIGIN, ORIGINAL.

o•ri•ent (*n.* ôr′ē ənt, -ē ent′, ōr′-; *v.* ôr′ē ent′, ōr′-) / *n.* 'ɔriyənt, -iyˌɛnt, 'owr-; *v.* 'ɔriyˌɛnt, 'owr-/ *n.* **1. Orient,** [*proper noun; the* + ~] **a.** the countries of Asia, esp. East Asia, such as China, Japan, and India. **b.** (formerly) the countries to the E of the Mediterranean. **—*v.*** [~ + *obj*] **2.** to find or figure out for (oneself or another) one's location or place by referring to one's surroundings, circumstances, facts, etc. **3.** to make (someone) familiar with new surroundings or circumstances: *to orient new students to the campus.* **4.** to place (something) in a position that relates or refers to the points of the compass or other locations: *to orient a building north and south.* See -ORI-.

o•ri•en•tal (ôr′ē en′tl, ōr′-) /ˌɔriy'ɛntḷ, ˌowr-/ *adj.* **1.** [*usually: Oriental*] of, relating to, or characteristic of the Orient, or the East; Eastern. **2.** eastern. **—*n.*** [*count; usually: Oriental*] **3.** *Usually considered offensive.* a native or inhabitant of East Asia, or a person of East Asian descent. See -ORI-.

o•ri•en•tate (ôr′ē ən tāt, ōr′-, -en-) /'ɔriyənteyt, 'owr-, -ɛn-/ *v.* [~ + *obj*], **-tat•ed, -tat•ing.** to orient (oneself). See -ORI-.

o•ri•en•ta•tion (ôr′ē ən tā′shən, -en-, ōr′-) /ˌɔriyən'teyʃən, -ɛn-, ˌowr-/ *n.* **1.** [*noncount*] the act or process of orienting; the state of being oriented. **2.** an introduction, as a tour, that helps one to adjust to new surroundings: [*count*]: *a twenty-minute orientation to the library facilities.* [*noncount*]: *two days of orientation.* **3.** [*count*] direction, aims, goals, etc., with respect to one's attitudes or judgment: *His political orientation is clearly radical.* See -ORI-.

o•ri•ent•ed (ôr′ē ən tid, ōr′-, -en-) /'ɔriyəntɪd, 'owr-, -ɛn-/ *adj.* **1.** (usually used after another word, usually a noun, adjective, or adverb) interested in, aimed at, or believing in (the noun, adjective, or adverb mentioned): *a child-oriented business (= a business interested in children); businesses oriented toward children; socially oriented agencies (= agencies that are aimed at improving social conditions).* **2.** [*be* + ~ + *to/toward*] showing or having an interest in: *The school was oriented to helping foreign students succeed.* See -ORI-.

or•i•fice (ôr′ə fis, or′-) /'ɔrəfɪs, 'ɒr-/ *n.* [*count*] an opening, as of a tube or pipe; a mouthlike opening or hole.

o•ri•ga•mi (ôr′i gä′mē) /ˌɔrɪ'gɑmiy/ *n.* [*noncount*] the Japanese art of folding paper into decorative or representational forms, such as of animals or flowers.

or•i•gin (ôr′i jin, or′-) /'ɔrɪdʒɪn, 'ɒr-/ *n.* **1.** [*count; usually: singular*] a source from which anything arises or comes. **2.** [*count; often: plural*] the first years or stage of existence: *a woman of mysterious origins.* **3.** [*noncount*] descent: *was clearly of Scandinavian origin.* See -ORI-.

o•rig•i•nal (ə rij′ə nl) /ə'rɪdʒənl̩/ *adj.* **1.** [*before a noun*] belonging or relating to the origin or beginning of something; earliest: *the original source of the problem.* **2.** arising or proceeding independently; inventive: *an original idea.* **3.** thinking or acting in an independent, creative, or individual manner: *an original thinker.* **4.** [*before a noun*] created, undertaken, or presented for the first time: *the original performance of a play.* **5.** being that from which a copy, translation, or the like is made: *The original document is in Washington.* **—***n.* [*count*] **6.** a primary form or type from which other, different types come. **7.** an original work, document, or the like, as opposed to a copy or imitation. **8.** a person whose ways of thinking or acting are original. **—o•rig•i•nal•i•ty** (ə rij′ə nal′i tē) /ə,rɪdʒə'nælɪtiy/ *n.* [*noncount*] See -ORI-.

o•rig•i•nal•ly (ə rij′ə nl ē) /ə'rɪdʒənl̩iy/ *adv.* **1.** by origin: *My husband's family was originally French Canadian.* **2.** at first: *Originally the book was going to be much longer.* **3.** in a way that is new or original. See -ORI-.

o•rig•i•nate (ə rij′ə nāt′) /ə'rɪdʒə,neyt/ *v.,* **-nat•ed, -nat•ing. 1.** to (cause to) take or have origin; (cause to) arise or begin: [*no obj*]: *Where did this idea originate?* [~ + *obj*]: *Who originated this scheme?* **2.** [*no obj*] (of a bus, train, subway, etc.) to begin a scheduled run at a certain place: *Our train originates at the eastern part of town.* **—o•rig•i•na•tion** (ə rij′ə nā′shən) /ə,rɪdʒə'neyʃən/ *n.* [*noncount*] **—o•rig′i•na′tor,** *n.* [*count*] See -ORI-.

o•ri•ole (ôr′ē ōl′, ōr′-) /'ɔriy,owl, 'owr-/ *n.* [*count*] a songbird, the male of which is typically black and orange or black and yellow.

Or•lon (ôr′lon) /'ɔrlɒn/ *Trademark.* [*noncount*] a brand of acrylic textile fiber.

or•na•ment (*n.* ôr′nə mənt; *v.* -ment′, -mənt) / *n.* 'ɔrnəmənt; *v.* -,mɛnt, -mənt/ *n.* **1.** [*count*] an object, piece, or feature intended to add beauty to the appearance of something; embellishment; decoration. **2.** [*noncount*] a group or style of such objects or features; ornamentation. **3.** [*count*] a person or thing that adds to the credit or glory of a society, a period of time, an organization, etc. **—***v.* [~ + *obj*] **4.** to furnish with ornaments; embellish; decorate. **5.** to serve as an ornament to. **—or•na•men•tal** (ôr′nə men′tl) /,ɔrnə'mɛntl̩/ *adj.* **—or•na•men•ta•tion** (ôr′nə mən tā′shən, -men-) /,ɔrnəmən'teyʃən, -mɛn-/ *n.* [*noncount*]

or•nate (ôr nāt′) /ɔr'neyt/ *adj.* **1.** overly decorated, often showily so: *an ornate hotel lobby.* **2.** using words or phrases that are too flowery: *ornate writing.* **—or•nate′ly,** *adv.* **—or•nate′ness,** *n.* [*noncount*]

or•ner•y (ôr′nə rē) /'ɔrnəriy/ *adj.,* **-i•er, -i•est. 1.** disagreeable; bad-tempered. **2.** stubborn. **—or′ner•i•ness,** *n.* [*noncount*]

or•ni•thol•o•gy (ôr′nə thol′ə jē) /,ɔrnə'θɒlədʒiy/ *n.* [*noncount*] the branch of zoology that deals with birds. **—or′ni•thol′o•gist,** *n.* [*count*]

o•ro•tund (ôr′ə tund′, ōr′-) /'ɔrə,tʌnd, 'owr-/ *adj.* **1.** (of the voice or speech) having strength, fullness, and clearness. **2.** (of speech or writing) showing self-importance; overly dramatic. **—o•ro•tun•di•ty** (ôr′ə tun′di tē) /,ɔrə'tʌndɪtiy/ *n.* [*noncount*] See -ROTA-.

or•phan (ôr′fən) /'ɔrfən/ *n.* [*count*] **1.** a child who has lost both parents or, less commonly, one parent through death. **2.** the first line of a paragraph when it appears alone at the bottom of a printed page. **—***adj.* [*before a noun*] **3.** having lost his or her parents: *an orphan child.* **4.** of or for orphans. **—***v.* [~ + *obj*] **5.** to cause to become an orphan.

or•phan•age (ôr′fə nij) /'ɔrfənɪdʒ/ *n.* [*count*] a place or institution for the housing and care of orphans.

ortho-, *prefix. ortho-* comes from Greek, where it has the meaning "straight, upright, right, correct": *ortho- + graph → orthography (= correct writing); ortho- + dontics → orthodontics (= dentistry dealing with straightening teeth); ortho- + pedic → orthopedic (= correction of improper bone structure from childhood).*

or•tho•don•tics (ôr′thə don′tiks) /,ɔrθə'dɒntɪks/ *n.* [*noncount; used with a singular verb*] the branch of dentistry dealing with the prevention and correction of crooked teeth. **—or•tho•don•tia** (ôr′thə don′shə) /,ɔrθə'dɒnʃə/ *n.* [*noncount*]: *orthodontia for their two children.* **—or′tho•don′tic, or′tho•don′tal,** *adj.* [*before a noun*] **—or′tho•don′tist,** *n.* [*count*]

or•tho•dox (ôr′thə doks′) /'ɔrθə,dɒks/ *adj.* **1.** agreeing with or following the approved or officially accepted form of any belief, religion, system, philosophy, etc., esp. the older, more traditional form. **2.** customary or normal; generally accepted: *an orthodox viewpoint.* See -DOX-.

or•tho•dox•y (ôr′thə dok′sē) /'ɔrθə,dɒksiy/ *n., pl.* **-dox•ies. 1.** [*count*] a principle or practice that most people agree with or follow for a particular belief, religion, system, philosophy, etc. **2.** [*noncount*] orthodox character: *questioned the orthodoxy of his opinions.* See -DOX-.

or•thog•ra•phy (ôr thog′rə fē) /ɔr'θɒgrəfiy/ *n., pl.* **-phies. 1.** [*noncount*] the way of writing words with the proper letters according to accepted usage; correct spelling. **2.** [*count*] a method or system of spelling, as by the use of an alphabet or other system of symbols. **—or•tho•graph•ic** (ôr′thə graf′ik) /,ɔrθə'græfɪk/ *adj.* [*before a noun*]: *One orthographic convention in English is that "qu" is pronounced like "kw."* See -GRAPH-.

or•tho•pe•dics or **or•tho•pae•dics** (ôr′thə pē′diks) /,ɔrθə'piydɪks/ *n.* [*noncount; used with a singular verb*] the branch of medicine dealing esp. with the correction of improperly formed or injured parts of the human skeleton. **—or′tho•pe′dic,** *adj.* **—or′tho•pe′dist,** *n.* [*count*] See -PED-.

-ory[1], *suffix.* **1.** *-ory* is attached to nouns and verbs that end in *-e* to form adjectives with the meaning "of or relating to (the noun or verb mentioned)": *excrete + -ory → excretory (= of or relating to excreting); sense + -ory → sensory (= of or relating to the senses).* **2.** *-ory* is also attached to certain roots to form adjectives with the meaning "providing or giving": *satisfact- + -ory → satisfactory (= giving satisfaction).*

-ory[2], *suffix. -ory* is attached to roots to form nouns that refer to places or things that hold (the root), or places that are used for (the root): *cremat- + -ory → crematory (= a place where bodies are cremated); observat(ion) + -ory → observatory (= place where observations of the heavens are made).*

or•zo (ôr′zō) /'ɔrzow/ *n.* [*noncount*] pasta in the form of small ricelike grains.

os•cil•late (os′ə lāt′) /'ɒsə,leyt/ *v.* [*no obj*], **-lat•ed, -lat•ing. 1.** to swing or move to and fro, forward and back, or side to side: *The pendulum oscillated.* **2.** to vary, change, or switch between differing or opposite beliefs, conditions, moods, etc.; vacillate. **—os′cil•la′tor,** *n.* [*count*]

os•cil•la•tion (os′ə lā′shən) /,ɒsə'leyʃən/ *n.* the change or switch in something, such as a decrease or increase, or the single swing in one direction of something that is oscillating; fluctuation: [*noncount*]: *unexplainable oscillation in the stock market.* [*count*]: *wild oscillations of the pointer on the temperature gauge.*

-ose[1], *suffix. -ose* is attached to roots to form adjectives with the meaning "full of, abounding in, given to, or like (the root):" *verb- (= word) + -ose → verbose (= full of words); bellic- (= war) + -ose → bellicose (= eager for fighting or war).*

-ose[2], *suffix. -ose* is attached to roots to form nouns that name sugars, carbohydrates, and substances that are formed from proteins: *fruct- + -ose → fructose (= a fruit sugar); lact- + -ose → lactose (= a milk sugar); prote- + ose → proteose (= a compound made from protein).*

o•sier (ō′zhər) /'owʒər/ *n.* [*count*] **1.** a willow tree having tough, flexible twigs used for wickerwork. **2.** a twig from such a willow.

os•mo•sis (oz mō′sis, os-) /ɒz'mowsɪs, ɒs-/ *n.* [*noncount*] **1.** the tendency of a fluid, usually water, to pass through a membrane, causing the concentrations of materials on either side of the membrane to become equal: *Water seeps into the roots because of osmosis.* **2.** a process of gradual absorption: *to learn French by osmosis.*

os•prey (os′prē, -prā) /'ɒspriy, -prey/ *n.* [*count*], *pl.* **-preys.** a large hawk that feeds on fish.

os•si•fy (os′ə fī′) /'ɒsə,fay/ *v.,* **-fied, -fy•ing. 1.** to (cause to) become bone or be hardened like bone: [*no obj*]: *Over time the soft substances ossified.* [~ + *obj*]: *Dry, extreme heat ossified these clam shells.* **2.** [*no obj*] to become rigid or unchangeable in one's habits, opinions, etc.: *had ossified in his attitudes.* **—os•si•fi•ca•tion** (os′ə fi kā′shən) /,ɒsəfɪ'keyʃən/ *n.* [*noncount*]

os•ten•si•ble (o sten′sə bəl) /ɒ'stɛnsəbəl/ *adj.* [*before a noun*] outwardly appearing a certain way; professed; pretended: *an ostensible reason.* **—os•ten′si•bly,** *adv.* See -TEND-.

os•ten•ta•tion (os′ten tā′shən, -tən-) /,ɒstɛn'teyʃən, -tən-/ *n.* [*noncount*] a false or overly grand display of wealth meant to impress others.

os•ten•ta•tious (os′ten tā′shəs, -tən-) /,ɒstɛn'teyʃəs, -tən-/ *adj.* **1.** marked by a false or overly grand display of wealth: *ostentatious jewelry.* **2.** overly dramatic; done in an exaggerated way that draws attention to oneself: *gave* *an ostentatious bow to the audience.* **—os′ten•ta′tious•ly,** *adv.*

os•te•op•a•thy (os′tē op′ə thē) /ˌɒstiyˈɒpəθiy/ *n.* [*noncount*] a system of medical practice emphasizing the massage and manipulation of muscles and bones to promote strength and relieve certain disorders. **—os•te•o•path** (os′tē ə path′) /ˈɒstiyəˌpæθ/ *n.* [*count*]

os•te•o•po•ro•sis (os′tē ō pə rō′sis) /ˌɒstiyowpəˈrowsɪs/ *n.* [*noncount*] a disorder in which the bones become increasingly brittle and break easily because of loss of calcium and other minerals.

os•tra•cism (os′trə siz′əm) /ˈɒstrəˌsɪzəm/ *n.* [*noncount*] the state or condition of being excluded from society, privileges, membership, etc.

os•tra•cize (os′trə sīz′) /ˈɒstrəˌsayz/ *v.* [∼ + *obj*], **-cized, -ciz•ing.** to exclude (someone) from society, privileges, membership, etc.

os•trich (ô′strich, os′trich) /ˈɔstrɪtʃ, ˈɒstrɪtʃ/ *n.* [*count*] a two-toed, swift-footed bird that cannot fly, originally of Africa and SW Asia.

OT or **o.t.,** an abbreviation of: overtime.

OTB, an abbreviation of: offtrack betting.

OTC, 1. Also, **O.T.C.** Officers' Training Corps. **2.** over-the-counter.

oth•er (uth′ər) /ˈʌðər/ *adj.* [*before a noun*] **1.** additional: *I made one other purchase.* **2.** different from the one mentioned: *Some other player might be better at the game.* **3.** [*the* + ∼] (used to refer to the remaining or second one of two persons or things, as when the person or thing is known from the discussion or context, or has already been mentioned): *wore no rings on the other hand.* **4.** [∼ + *plural noun*] being the remaining ones of a number: *Some other countries may join the boycott.* **5.** former; earlier: *sailing ships of other days.* **6.** [*the* + ∼] not long past: *I saw her the other night.* **—***n.* [*count*] **7.** the other one: *Each praises the other.* **—***pron.* **8.** Usually, **others.** [*plural*] other persons or things: *Others in the medical profession may not like this.* **9.** [*singular*] some person or thing else: *Surely some friend or other will help me.* **—***adv.* **10. other than,** otherwise; differently: *We can't collect the rent other than by suing the tenant.* **—*Idiom.* 11. every other,** the first or the second of a pair: *skipping every other page.* **12. on the other (hand),** (used to introduce the second of two ideas that contrast with each other): *On the one hand, we could go; on the other (hand), we could stay.* **13. the other side of the coin,** the second, different choice or point of view to consider.

oth•er•wise (uth′ər wīz′) /ˈʌðərˌwayz/ *adv.* **1.** under other circumstances: *With this chip the computer runs faster than it would otherwise.* **2.** in another manner or way; differently: *Could he do otherwise than smile?* **3.** in other respects: *an otherwise happy and uneventful life.* **—***conj.* **4.** or else: *Button up your coat, otherwise you'll catch cold.* **—***adj.* **5.** of a different kind: *We hoped his behavior would be otherwise.*

oth•er•world•ly (uth′ər wûrld′lē) /ˈʌðərˈwɜrldliy/ *adj.* concerned with the world of imagination or the world to come.

ot•ter (ot′ər) /ˈɒtər/ *n., pl.* **-ters,** (*esp. when thought of as a group*) **-ter. 1.** [*count*] a furry, water-dwelling, weasel-like mammal having webbed feet and a long, slightly flattened tail. **2.** [*noncount*] the fur of an otter.

ouch (ouch) /awtʃ/ *interj.* (used to express sudden pain or dismay): *Ouch, that needle hurt!*

ought (ôt) /ɔt/ *auxiliary (modal) verb.* [∼ + *to* + *root form of a verb*] **1.** (used to express the opinion that the action of the main verb is one's duty or moral obligation): *Every citizen ought to help.* **2.** (used to express the opinion that the action of the main verb is one of justice, moral rightness, or the like): *He ought to be punished.* **3.** (used to express the opinion that the action of the main verb is proper, correct, or appropriate for the situation): *We ought to bring her some flowers.* **4.** (used to express the opinion that the action of the main verb is probable, that it follows naturally from the circumstances, or that it is expected): *That ought to be our train now.*

ounce (ouns) /awns/ *n.* [*count*] **1.** a unit of weight equal to 437.5 grains or 1/16 of a pound (28.349 grams) avoirdupois. **2.** a unit of weight equal to 480 grains or 1/12 of a pound (31.103 grams) troy or apothecaries' weight. **3.** a fluid ounce: *Thirty-two ounces make a quart.* **4.** a small quantity or portion: *doesn't have an ounce of sense.*

our (ouᵊr, ou′ər; *unstressed* är) /awᵊr, ˈawər; *unstressed* ɑr/ *pron.* [*before a noun*] a form of the pronoun WE used to show possession: *Our team won.* Compare OURS.

ours (ouᵊrz, ou′ərz *or, often,* ärz) /awᵊrz, ˈawərz *or, often,* ɑrz/ *pron.* **1.** [*be* + ∼] a form of the pronoun WE used to show possession: *Which house is ours?* **2.** that or those belonging to us: *Ours are the pink ones. She's a cousin of ours.*

our•selves (är selvz′, ouᵊr-, ou′ər-) /ɑrˈsɛlvz, awᵊr-, ˌawər-/ *pron.pl.* **1.** a form of the pronoun WE, a reflexive pronoun used as the direct or indirect object of a verb or the direct object of a preposition when the subject is *we*: *We may be deceiving ourselves. We don't dare vote ourselves a big pay raise.* **2.** (used to add emphasis to the pronouns WE and US): *We ourselves would never say such a thing.* **3.** (used in place of WE or US in certain constructions with "and" and "more than"): *The children and ourselves want to thank you. No one is more fortunate than ourselves.* **4.** our normal, healthy, or customary selves: *We were ourselves again after a nap.*

-ous, *suffix.* **1.** *-ous* is attached to roots to form adjectives with the meaning "possessing, full of (a given quality)": *glory* + *-ous* → *glorious; wonder* + *ous* → *wondrous; covet* + *-ous* → *covetous; nerve* + *-ous* → *nervous.* **2.** *-ous* is also attached to roots to form adjectives referring to the names of chemical elements: *stannous chloride,* $SnCl_2$.

oust (oust) /awst/ *v.* [∼ + *obj*] to expel, remove, or force (someone) from a place or position occupied: *He ousted her from the job and took over.*

oust•er (ou′stər) /ˈawstər/ *n.* [*count*] the removal or forcing of someone from a place or position occupied: *an ouster from political office.*

out (out) /awt/ *adv.* **1.** not in the usual place, position, state, etc.: *Those books are out of alphabetical order.* **2.** away from one's home, country, work, etc., as specified: *to go out of town.* **3.** in or into the outdoors: *to go out for a walk; Take the dog out.* **4.** to a state of exhaustion; to a condition in which everything is totally used up: *to pump a well out.* **5.** to the end or conclusion, a final decision, etc.: *to say it all out.* **6.** to a point or state of dying out or fading away: *That practice is on the way out.* **7.** not burning or lit: *The lights went out. Put that cigarette out.* **8.** in or into a state of neglect, disuse, etc.: *That style is out.* **9.** so as not to be in the normal or proper position or state; out of joint: *Her back went out after her fall.* **10.** in or into public notice or knowledge: *Her story has come out at last.* **11.** so as to extend or project: *Let's stretch out on the grass. A nail was sticking out.* **12.** from a certain source or material: *made out of scraps.* **13.** so as to deprive or be deprived: *to be cheated out of one's money.* **14.** aloud or loudly: *to cry out.* **15.** thoroughly; completely; entirely: *The children tired me out. Clean out the room.* **16.** so as to make impossible to see, read, or understand: *to cross out a misspelling.* **—***adj.* **17.** [*be* + ∼] not at one's home or place of employment; absent: *will be out all week.* **18.** [*be* + ∼] not open to consideration: *She gets airsick, so flying is out.* **19.** [*be* + ∼] wanting; lacking; without: *We had some tickets but now we're out.* **20.** [*be* + ∼] removed from or not in effective operation, play, etc.: *He's out for the season with a leg injury.* **21.** [*be* + ∼ + *of* + *obj*] no longer holding a job, public office, etc.; unemployed: *to be out of work.* **22.** [*be* + ∼] no longer working or operating; extinguished: *Are the lights out?* **23.** [*be* + ∼] finished; ended: *before the week is out.* **24.** [*be* + ∼] not currently fashionable or in style: *Fitted waistlines are out this season.* **25.** [*be* + ∼] unconscious; senseless: *A few drinks and he's out.* **26.** not in power, authority, or the like: *a member of the out party.* **27.** *Baseball.* [*be* + ∼] (of a batter) not succeeding in getting or staying on base: *Two men are out but the bases are loaded.* **28.** [*be* + ∼] outside of official limits or the prescribed area, as in the playing of a game on a marked court or field; out of bounds. **29.** [*be* + ∼] having a financial loss to an indicated extent: *They were out millions.* **30.** [*be* + ∼] not correct or accurate: *The builder's estimate was out by ten thousand dollars.* **31.** [*before a noun*] located at a distance; outlying: *the out islands.* **32.** *Slang.* publicly acknowledged: *an out lesbian.* **—***prep.* **33.** (used to indicate movement or direction from the inside to the outside of something): *She ran out the door.* **34.** (used to indicate location): *The car is out back.* **35.** (used to indicate movement away from a central point): *Let's drive out the old parkway.* **—***interj.* **36.** begone! Go away!: *Out! And don't come back!* **37.** (used in radio communications to signal that the sender has finished the message and is not expecting a reply). Compare OVER (def. 32). **—***n.* [*count*] **38.** a means of escape from responsibility, embarrassment, argument, confrontation, etc.: *If we just give him an out, maybe he'll resign.* **39.** Usually, **outs.** [*plural*] persons or groups not in office or lacking status, power, or authority. **40.** *Baseball.* an instance of putting out a batter or base runner. **—*v.*** [*no obj*] **41.** to come out; become public: *The truth will out.* **—*Idiom.*** **42. all out,** with the highest or greatest effort: *They went all out to finish by Friday.* **43. on the outs,** in a state of disagreement; quarreling; at odds. **44. out for,** [*be* + ~ + *obj*] strongly or eagerly determined to acquire, achieve, etc.: *He was out for money.* **45. out from under,** [*be* + ~ (+ *obj*)] no longer having burdens or responsibilities, esp. free of debt. **46. out of,** [~ + *obj*] **a.** not within: *They ran out of the house.* **b.** beyond the reach of: *out of sight.* **c.** not in a condition of: *out of danger.* **d.** without; lacking: *We're out of milk.* **e.** from within or among: *Take the jokers out of the pack of cards.* **f.** because of; owing to: *They did that out of spite.* **g.** made of; constructed from: *a kite made out of string, paper, and glue.* **47. out of it,** *Informal.* [*usually: be* + ~] **a.** not participating: *I'm out of it these days; tell me what's been going on.* **b.** not conscious: *The sedative worked; he's out of it.* **c.** confused; muddled: *too out of it to remember his own name.* **48. out of place, a.** not in the correct position or order. **b.** not suitable to the circumstances or surroundings: *behavior out of place in church.*

out-, *prefix.* **1.** *out-* is attached to verbs and means "going beyond, surpassing, or outdoing (the action of the verb)": *out-* + *bid* → *outbid; out-* + *do* → *outdo; out-* + *last* → *outlast.* **2.** *out-* is also attached to nouns to form certain compounds, and means "outside; out": *out-* + *cast* → *outcast; out-* + *come* → *outcome; out-* + *side* → *outside.*

out•age (ou′tij) /ˈawtɪdʒ/ *n.* [*count*] an interruption or failure in the supply of power, esp. electricity.

out′-and-out′, *adj.* [*before a noun*] complete; absolute: *He told an out-and-out lie.*

out•back (out′bak′) /ˈawtˌbæk/ *n.* **1.** [*count; usually singular; usually: the* + ~; *sometimes: Outback*] the country far away from cities, towns, or villages esp. in Australia; the bush. **—*adj.*** [*before a noun*] **2.** of, relating to, or located in an outback: *outback settlements.*

out•bal•ance (out′bal′əns) /ˌawtˈbæləns/ *v.* [~ + *obj*], **-anced, -anc•ing.** to have greater importance or weight than; outweigh: *Those considerations outbalance our needs.*

out•board (out′bôrd′, -bōrd′) /ˈawtˌbɔrd, -ˌbowrd/ *adj.* **1.** located on the outside of a ship's hull or aircraft: *an outboard motor.* **2.** having a motor located on the outside of the hull: *an outboard boat.* **3.** located farther from the center, as an engine of an aircraft: *a fire on the outboard engine.* **—*adv.*** **4.** away from the center of a hull, aircraft, etc. **—*n.*** [*count*] **5.** Also called **outboard motor**. a motor located on the outside of a ship or aircraft. **6.** a boat equipped with such a motor.

out•bound (out′bound′) /ˈawtˈbawnd/ *adj.* headed, sailing, or going outward: *an outbound freighter.*

out•break (out′brāk′) /ˈawtˌbreyk/ *n.* [*count*] a sudden occurrence or appearance; eruption: *the outbreak of disease.*

out•build•ing (out′bil′ding) /ˈawtˌbɪldɪŋ/ *n.* [*count*] a building apart from and usually secondary to a main building.

out•burst (out′bûrst′) /ˈawtˌbɜrst/ *n.* [*count*] a sudden and often violent release, outpouring, or eruption: *an outburst of tears; an outburst of machine gun fire.*

out•cast (out′kast′) /ˈawtˌkæst/ *n.* [*count*] **1.** a person who is rejected or cast out, as from home or society. **—*adj.*** [*before a noun*] **2.** cast out, as from one's home or society: *an outcast son.*

out•class (out′klas′) /ˌawtˈklæs/ *v.* [~ + *obj*] to go beyond in excellence; be superior to: *outclassed the competition.*

out•come (out′kum′) /ˈawtˌkʌm/ *n.* [*count*] a final product or end result: *What was the outcome of your interview?*

out•crop (*n.* out′krop′; *v.* out′krop′) / *n.* ˈawtˌkrɒp; *v.* ˌawtˈkrɒp/ *n., v.,* **-cropped, -crop•ping.** **—*n.*** [*count*] **1. a.** an area where something has risen to the surface of the earth, as a layer of bedrock. **b.** the exposed portion of such a layer. **—*v.*** [*no obj*] **2.** to rise suddenly to the surface of the earth, as layers of bedrock.

out•cry (out′krī′) /ˈawtˌkray/ *n.* [*count*], *pl.* **-cries.** **1.** a strong and usually public expression of protest or anger. **2.** a loud cry.

out•dat•ed (out′dā′tid) /ˌawtˈdeytɪd/ *adj.* out-of-date; not modern; outmoded: *outdated clothes.*

out•dis•tance (out′dis′təns) /ˌawtˈdɪstəns/ *v.* [~ + *obj*], **-tanced, -tanc•ing.** to go far ahead of, as in running: *She outdistanced him by about 100 yards.*

out•do (out′do͞o′) /ˌawtˈduw/ *v.* [~ + *obj*], **-did, -done, -do•ing.** **1.** to perform better than; do better than: *They outdid our team in every category.* **2.** [~ + *oneself*] to perform better than one's usually high standard.

out•door (out′dôr′, -dōr′) /ˈawtˌdɔr, -ˌdowr/ *adj.* [*before a noun*] **1.** located, occurring, or belonging outdoors: *outdoor activities.* **2.** fond of things done outdoors: *She's the outdoor type, fond of hiking and skiing.*

out•doors (out′dôrz′, -dōrz′) /ˌawtˈdɔrz, -ˈdowrz/ *adv.* **1.** outside; in the open air: *They stood outdoors in the rain.* **—*n.*** [*noncount; used with a singular verb; usually: the* + ~] **2.** the world outside of or away from houses; open air: *to live in the outdoors.*

out•er (ou′tər) /ˈawtər/ *adj.* [*before a noun*] **1.** located on or toward the outside; exterior: *an outer wall.* **2.** located farther out or farther from the center: *the outer planets of the solar system.*

out•er•most (ou′tər mōst′) /ˈawtərˌmowst/ *adj.* [*before a noun*] farthest out; farthest from the inside or center: *the outermost limits of the galaxy.*

out′er space′, *n.* [*noncount*] **1.** space beyond the atmosphere of the earth. **2.** space beyond the solar system; deep space.

out•er•wear (ou′tər wâr′) /ˈawtərˌwɛər/ *n.* [*noncount; used with a singular verb*] **1.** clothing, such as overcoats, worn over other clothing for warmth or protection outdoors; overclothes. **2.** clothing, such as dresses, sweaters, or suits, worn over undergarments.

out•field (out′fēld′) /ˈawtˌfiyld/ *n.* **1.** [*count; usually: the* + ~] the part of a baseball field beyond the diamond-shaped infield. **2.** [*noncount*] the positions played by the right, center, and left fielders. **3.** [*count*] the fielders playing in those positions (contrasted with *infield*). **—out′field′er,** *n.* [*count*]

out•fit (out′fit′) /ˈawtˌfɪt/ *n., v.,* **-fit•ted, -fit•ting.** **—*n.*** [*count*] **1.** a collection of gear, esp. clothes, used for a particular task or role: *a cowboy's outfit.* **2.** a set of clothes and other items worn together as an ensemble: *a new spring outfit.* **3.** a set of items used for any purpose: *a ski outfit of poles, skiis, boots, and goggles.* **4.** a group or team of people, as a business or military unit. **—*v.*** [~ + *obj*] **5.** to furnish; supply: *They outfitted him with a gun.* **—out′fit′ter,** *n.* [*count*]

out•flank (out′flangk′) /ˌawtˈflæŋk/ *v.* [~ + *obj*] **1.** to get around the flank or side of (an enemy force): *outflanked by superior forces.* **2.** to outmaneuver: *The candidate was outflanked on the issues.*

out•fox (out′foks′) /ˌawtˈfɒks/ *v.* [~ + *obj*] to be cleverer than (someone); outsmart: *He outfoxed his opponents in the campaign and managed to win.*

out•go•ing (out′gō′ing) /ˈawtˌgowɪŋ/ *adj.* **1.** going out; departing: *outgoing trains.* **2.** [*before a noun*] leaving or retiring from a position or office: *the outgoing mayor.* **3.** friendly; sociable: *a cheerful, outgoing child.*

out•grow (out′grō′) /ˌawtˈgrow/ *v.* [~ + *obj*], **-grew, -grown, -grow•ing.** **1.** to grow too large for: *had outgrown last year's boots.* **2.** to cast aside, lose, or forget about as one develops or grows older; grow out of: *to outgrow a fear of the dark.* **3.** to grow or increase faster than.

out•growth (out′grōth′) /ˈawtˌgrowθ/ *n.* [*count*] a natural development or result: *Success was an outgrowth of their hard work.*

out•house (out′hous′) /ˈawtˌhaws/ *n.* [*count*], *pl.* **-hous•es.** **1.** PRIVY. **2.** OUTBUILDING.

out•ing (ou′ting) /ˈawtɪŋ/ *n.* [*count*] **1.** a pleasure trip, picnic, or the like: *an outing to the beach.* **2.** a public appearance, as by a player in an athletic contest.

out•land•ish (out lan′dish) /awtˈlændɪʃ/ *adj.* strange or odd, esp. in a way that is displeasing, freakish, or grotesque.

out•last (out′last′) /ˌawtˈlæst/ *v.* [~ + *obj*] **1.** to endure or last longer than: *The champion outlasted his opponent.* **2.** to live longer than; outlive.

out•law (out′lô′) /ˈawtˌlɔ/ *n.* [*count*] **1.** a criminal, esp. one who is running away and hiding to avoid being captured by legal authorities. **—*v.*** [~ + *obj*] **2.** to make unlawful or illegal: *Abortion was outlawed in that state.* **3.** to prohibit: *to outlaw smoking in a theater.* **—*adj.*** [*before a noun*] **4.** of, relating to, or characteristic of an outlaw: *the outlaw society in the early days of the Old West; the dictator's outlaw regime.*

out•lay (*n.* out′lā′; *v.* out′lā′) / *n.* ˈawtˌley; *v.* ˌawtˈley/ *n., v.,* **-laid, -lay•ing.** **—*n.*** [*count*] **1.** an act of spending something, as money: *outlays for new equipment.* **2.** an amount spent: *an outlay of several thousand dollars.* —*v.* [~ + *obj*] **3.** to spend or expend, as money.

out•let (out′let, -lit) /'awtlɛt, -lɪt/ *n.* [*count*] **1.** an opening or passage by which anything is let out; vent; exit. **2.** a point on a wiring system at which current may be taken to supply electric devices; plug: *an electrical wall outlet.* **3.** a means of expression, release, or satisfaction: *an outlet for one's artistic impulses.* **4.** a store selling the goods of a particular manufacturer or wholesaler: *a clothing outlet.*

out•line (out′līn′) /'awt,layn/ *n., v.,* **-lined, -lin•ing.** —*n.* [*count*] **1.** the line by which a figure or object is defined or bounded; contour: *We could just see an outline of the shore in the distance.* **2.** a drawing that is only a line, without shading or modeling of the form. **3.** a general account, description, or report, indicating only the main features of a subject: *an outline of a book.* **4. outlines,** [*plural*] the most basic features or main aspects of something under discussion: *Just give us the outlines of your plan.* —*v.* [~ + *obj*] **5.** to draw the outline of (something), or draw (something) in outline. **6.** to indicate the main features of: *outlined his strategy.*

out•live (out′liv′) /,awt'lɪv/ *v.* [~ + *obj*], **-lived, -liv•ing.** **1.** to live longer than; survive: *She outlived all her old classmates.* **2.** to outlast; live through: *He outlived the war.*

out•look (out′lo͝ok′) /'awt,lʊk/ *n.* **1.** [*count*] the view from a particular place: *The outlook from the terrace is magnificent.* **2.** [*count*] the place from which an observer looks out: *We drove up to the outlook to the Mississippi River.* **3.** mental attitude or view; point of view: [*count*]: *a very gloomy outlook.* [*noncount; in* + ~]: *became philosophical in outlook.* **4.** [*count*] prospect for the future: *The political outlook is grim.*

out•ly•ing (out′lī′ing) /'awt,layɪŋ/ *adj.* [*before a noun*] lying or located at a distance from the center or the main area; remote: *the outlying districts of the town.*

out•ma•neu•ver (out′mə no͞o′vər) /,awtmə'nuwvər/ *v.* [~ + *obj*] **1.** to outwit or defeat by tricks, cleverness, or skill: *outmaneuvered her rivals to win the election.* **2.** to surpass in the ability of maneuvering: *This boat can outmaneuver the other boats.* See -MAN[1]-.

out•mod•ed (out′mō′did) /,awt'mowdɪd/ *adj.* **1.** no longer fashionable: *an outmoded style.* **2.** no longer acceptable or usable: *outmoded teaching methods.* See -MOD-.

out•num•ber (out′num′bər) /,awt'nʌmbər/ *v.* [~ + *obj*] to be greater than in number: *Our forces outnumber theirs by over two to one.* See -NUM-.

out′-of-bod′y, *adj.* [*before a noun*] of, relating to, or characterized by the sensation of viewing oneself from the outside, as though the consciousness has left the body and is acting on its own: *an out-of-body experience.*

out′-of-date′, *adj.* outmoded; obsolete: *out-of-date technology.*

out′-of-doors′, *adj.* **1.** Also, **out′-of-door′.** outdoor: *out-of-doors activities.* —*n.* **2.** OUTDOORS.

out′-of-the-way′, *adj.* **1.** away from where people travel through or live: *an out-of-the-way cabin in the woods.* **2.** seldom encountered; unusual: *out-of-the-way facts.*

out•pa•tient or **out–pa•tient** (out′pā′shənt) /'awt,peyʃənt/ *n.* [*count*] a person who receives treatment at a hospital but does not stay there overnight. See -PAT-.

out•place (out′plās′) /,awt'pleys/ *v.* [~ + *obj*], **-placed, plac•ing.** to provide outplacement to.

out•place•ment (out′plās′mənt) /'awt,pleysmənt/ *n.* [*noncount*] assistance in finding a new job, provided by a company for an employee who is being let go.

out•post (out′pōst′) /'awt,powst/ *n.* [*count*] **1.** a station established at a distance from an army to protect it from a surprise attack. **2.** the body of troops stationed there. **3.** a post or settlement in a foreign place or in foreign surroundings.

out•pour•ing (out′pôr′ing, -pōr′-) /'awt,pɔrɪŋ, -,powr-/ *n.* [*count*] something that pours out: *an outpouring of sympathy.*

out•put (out′po͝ot′) /'awt,pʊt/ *n., v.,* **-put•ted** or **-put, -put•ting.** —*n.* **1.** the quantity or amount of something produced, esp. in a specified period: [*count; usually singular*]: *an output of over 500 computers a day.* [*noncount*]: *Output increased.* **2.** [*noncount*] the material produced; product; yield. **3.** the current, voltage, power, or signal produced by an electrical or electronic device, or by a machine: [*count*]: *an output of energy.* [*noncount*]: *too much output from the generator.* **4. a.** any information made available by computer, as on a printout, display screen, or disk: [*noncount*]: *Let's scroll through the output.* [*count; usually singular*]: *an unwanted output on the printer.* **b.** [*noncount*] the process of transferring such information from computer memory to or by means of an output device. —*v.* [~ + *obj*] **5.** to transfer (computer output): *Output the data to the printer.* **6.** to produce; yield; turn out.

out•rage (out′rāj) /'awtreydʒ/ *n., v.,* **-raged, -rag•ing.** —*n.* **1.** [*count*] an act of great cruelty or violence that strongly offends the feelings. **2.** [*count*] any act that strongly offends the feelings: *It's an outrage that she was fired.* **3.** [*noncount*] a strong, powerful feeling of resentment or anger aroused by an injury, insult, or injustice. —*v.* [~ + *obj*] **4.** to anger or offend; shock.

out•ra•geous (out rā′jəs) /awt'reydʒəs/ *adj.* **1.** of or involving great injury or wrong: *outrageous crimes.* **2.** strongly offensive to the sense of right or decency: *his outrageous behavior.* **3.** passing reasonable bounds: *an outrageous price.* **4.** remarkable; fantastic: *She looks absolutely outrageous in red.*

out•rank (out′rangk′) /,awt'ræŋk/ *v.* [~ + *obj*] to have a higher rank than.

ou•tré (o͞o trā′) /uw'trey/ *adj.* unconventional; bizarre: *extreme and outré clothing designs.*

out•reach (*v.* out′rēch′; *n., adj.* out′rēch′) / *v.* ,awt'riytʃ; *n., adj.* 'awt,riytʃ/ *v.* [~ + *obj*] **1.** to reach beyond; exceed: *Demand has outreached supply.* —*n.* [*noncount*] **2.** an act or instance of reaching out. **3.** the act of extending community services to a wider section of the population: *programs of community outreach to the poor.* —*adj.* [*before a noun*] **4.** concerned with extending community services: *outreach programs.*

out•rig•ger (out′rig′ər) /'awt,rɪgər/ *n.* [*count*] **1.** a frame that supports a float that sticks out from the side of a boat and rests on the water, used to help keep the boat stable. **2.** a boat with such a supporting frame.

out•right (*adj.* out′rīt′; *adv.* out′rīt′, -rīt′) / *adj.* 'awt,rayt; *adv.* 'awt'rayt, -,rayt/ *adj.* [*before a noun*] **1.** complete; total: *an outright victory.* **2.** open; direct; not hiding or holding something back: *He issued an outright denial.* —*adv.* **3.** completely; entirely: *We own the house outright.* **4.** without holding anything back: *Ask her outright for a raise.* **5.** at once; instantly: *Three were killed outright.*

out•run (out′run′) /,awt'rʌn/ *v.* [~ + *obj*], **-ran, -run, -run•ning.** **1.** to run faster or farther than: *The kids outran the teacher to the playground.* **2.** to grow faster than; exceed; surpass: *Production is outrunning sales.*

out•sell (out′sel′) /,awt'sɛl/ *v.* [~ + *obj*], **-sold, -sell•ing.** **1.** to surpass (a competitor) in salesmanship or selling. **2.** to exceed (another product) in number of sales.

out•set (out′set′) /'awt,sɛt/ *n.* [*count; usually singular; usually: the* + ~] beginning; start: *at the outset of the war.*

out•shine (out′shīn′) /,awt'ʃayn/ *v.* [~ + *obj*], **-shone** or **shined, -shin•ing.** **1.** to shine more brightly than. **2.** to go beyond (another) in excellence, achievement, etc.: *She worked hard to outshine the other designers.*

out•side (*n.* out′sīd′, -sīd′; *adj.* out′sīd′, out′-; *adv.* out′sīd′; *prep.* out′sīd′, out′sīd′) / *n.* 'awt'sayd, -,sayd; *adj.* ,awt'sayd, 'awt-; *adv.* ,awt'sayd; *prep.* ,awt'sayd, 'awt,sayd/ *n.* [*count*] **1.** the outer side, surface, or part; exterior: *painted the outside of the house.* **2.** [*often: singular, the* + ~] the outer appearance: *He was smiling on the outside but angry on the inside.* **3.** [*often: singular, the* + ~] the space beyond a boundary or beyond some fence or enclosure: *The prisoner had no idea of life on the outside.* —*adj.* **4.** [*before a noun*] of, situated in, or coming from an area beyond an enclosed place, fence, boundary, etc.: *news from the outside world.* **5.** [*before a noun*] located on, or relating to, the outer side; exterior: *the outside walls.* **6.** [*before a noun*] situated away from the inside or center: *the outside lane on a highway.* **7.** [*before a noun*] not belonging to a specified group or the group in question: *outside agitators.* **8.** [*before a noun*] extremely unlikely or remote: *an outside chance for recovery.* **9.** [*before a noun*] extreme or maximum: *an outside estimate.* **10.** [*before a noun*] being in addition to one's regular work or duties: *an outside job as a waiter.* **11.** *Baseball.* (of a pitched ball) passing, but not going over, home plate on the side opposite the batter. —*adv.* **12.** on or to the outside: *Take the dog outside.* **13.** in or to an area beyond a given place: *Citizens are forbidden to travel outside.* —*prep.* **14.** on the outside of: *a noise outside the door.* **15.** beyond the limits or borders of: *visitors from outside the country.* **16.** aside from: *She* *has no interests outside her work.* **—*Idiom.* 17. at the outside,** [*noncount*] at the highest limit; at the maximum: *We could expect to get, at the outside, about $100,000 for the house.* **18. outside of,** [~ + *obj*] other than; excepting: *She has no interests outside of her work.*

out•sid•er (out′sī′dər) /ˌawt'saydər/ *n.* [*count*] **1.** a person not part of a particular group. **2.** *Chiefly Brit.* a competitor not considered likely to win.

out•size (out′sīz′) /'awtˌsayz/ *n.* [*count*] **1.** an uncommon or irregular size, esp. one larger than average. *—adj.* [*before a noun*] **2.** Also, **out′sized′.** being unusually large, heavy, extensive, etc.: *an outsize uniform.*

out•skirt (out′skûrt′) /'awtˌskɜrt/ *n.* [*count*] Often, **outskirts.** [*plural*] the outlying district or region, as of a city.

out•smart (out′smärt′) /ˌawt'smɑrt/ *v.* [~ + *obj*] **1.** to defeat or gain an advantage over (someone), as by being more clever or intelligent; outwit. **—*Idiom.* 2. outsmart oneself,** to defeat oneself through the same schemes one has planned to use for gain or profit.

out•spo•ken (out′spō′kən) /'awt'spowkən/ *adj.* **1.** said or expressed with honesty and openness: *outspoken criticism.* **2.** unreserved in speech; unafraid to say what one believes. **—out′spo′ken•ness,** *n.* [*noncount*]

out•spread (out′spred′) /'awtˌsprɛd/ *adj.* [*sometimes: after a noun*] spread or stretched out; extended: *outspread arms; with arms outspread.*

out•stand•ing (out′stan′ding) /ˌawt'stændɪŋ/ *adj.* **1.** [*before a noun*] obvious; conspicuous; striking: *outstanding courage.* **2.** superior; excellent; distinguished: *an outstanding student who finished at the top of her class.* **3.** continuing in existence; remaining unpaid, unresolved, etc.; not taken care of or solved: *outstanding debts; Several questions are still outstanding.* **4.** standing out; projecting: *a stiff, outstanding fabric.* **—out•stand′ing•ly,** *adv.: an outstandingly fine restaurant.*

out•stretch (out′strech′) /ˌawt'strɛtʃ/ *v.* [~ + *obj*] **1.** to stretch forth; extend: *to outstretch one's hand.* **2.** to pass or stretch beyond the limits of: *His behavior outstretches my patience.*

out•stretched (out′strecht′) /'awt'strɛtʃt/ *adj.* [*sometimes: after a noun*] stretched out: *an outstretched hand.*

out•strip (out′strip′) /ˌawt'strɪp/ *v.* [~ + *obj*], **-stripped, -strip•ping. 1.** to outdo; surpass; excel over: *He has outstripped his competition.* **2.** to pass in running or swift travel. **3.** to be greater than; exceed: *a demand that outstrips the supply.*

out•take (out′tāk′) /'awtˌteyk/ *n.* [*count*] a segment of film or videotape or a part of a recording that is edited out of the final version.

out•ward (out′wərd) /'awtwərd/ *adj.* [*before a noun*] **1.** moving or directed toward the outside or away from a center: *the outward flow of water.* **2.** relating to or being what is seen or apparent and not what is on the inside; relating to surface qualities only; superficial: *an outward show of grief.* **3.** lying toward or on the outside; exterior; of or relating to the outside or the outer surface: *an outward court.* **4.** belonging or relating to what is external to or outside of oneself: *Outward influences affected her deeply.* *—adv.* Also, **out′wards. 5.** toward the outside; out: *The door opened outward.* **6.** away from port. **7.** toward the world outside of or external to oneself: *His country needed to look outward.* **—out′ward•ly,** *adv.*

out•weigh (out′wā′) /ˌawt'wey/ *v.* [~ + *obj*] **1.** to be greater than in value or importance: *The safety of her crew outweighed all other considerations.* **2.** [*not: be + ~-ing*] to exceed in weight: *The champ outweighed his opponent by about twenty pounds.*

out•wit (out′wit′) /ˌawt'wɪt/ *v.* [~ + *obj*], **-wit•ted, -wit•ting.** to defeat or gain an advantage over (another) by greater cleverness; outsmart.

out•worn (out′wôrn′, -wōrn′) /'awt'wɔrn, -'wowrn/ *adj.* out-of-date; no longer modern or useful: *outworn economic theories.*

ou•zo (o͞o′zō) /'uwzow/ *n.* [*noncount*] a clear, anise-flavored liqueur of Greece.

o•va (ō′və) /'owvə/ *n.* [*plural; used with a plural verb*] pl. of OVUM.

o•val (ō′vəl) /'owvəl/ *adj.* **1.** having the general form or outline of an egg; egg-shaped. **2.** shaped like a flattened circle. *—n.* [*count*] **3.** something oval in shape or outline, such as a field on which an oval track is laid out for athletic contests.

O′val Of′fice, *n.* [*proper noun; the* + ~] **1.** the office of the president of the U.S., located in the White House. **2.** this office thought of as the seat of executive power in the federal government.

o•va•ry (ō′və rē) /'owvəriy/ *n.* [*count*], *pl.* **-ries. 1.** an organ that is the part of the female reproductive system in which the ova and the female sex hormones develop. **2.** the larger, lower part of the pistil in flowering plants that surrounds the ovules or new seeds. **—o•var•i•an** (ō-vâr′ē ən) /ow'vɛəriyən/ *adj.*

o•va•tion (ō vā′shən) /ow'veyʃən/ *n.* [*count*] long, loud applause or other expression of great approval.

ov•en (uv′ən) /'ʌvən/ *n.* [*count*] a small box-shaped area with a door, as a part of a stove, for baking, roasting, heating, or drying; or an appliance in this shape.

o•ver (ō′vər) /'owvər/ *prep.* **1.** above in place or position: *the roof over one's head.* **2.** above and to the other side of: *The car went over the guard rail.* **3.** above in authority, rank, power, etc.: *They have control over the news media.* **4.** so as to rest on or cover; on or upon: *She pulled the blankets over her head and fell asleep.* **5.** on top of: *She hit the intruder over the head with a frying pan.* **6.** across; throughout: *They hitchhiked all over Europe.* **7.** from one side to the other of; on or to the other side of; across: *lands over the sea; If you go over the bridge you will be in Illinois.* **8.** in excess of; more than: *Both children read over twenty books last summer.* **9.** above in degree, quantity, etc.: *a big improvement over last year's numbers.* **10.** in preference to: *He was chosen over another applicant.* **11.** throughout the length of; during; until the end of: *We wrote to each other over a long period of years.* **12.** in reference to, concerning, or about: *to quarrel over a matter.* **13.** while doing or attending to: *to discuss the situation over lunch.* **14.** via; by means of: *I heard it over the radio.* **15.** because of; caused by: *I don't want an argument over this.* *—adv.* **16.** beyond the top or upper part of something: *The soup boiled over.* **17.** so as to cover or affect the whole surface: *The furniture was covered over with dust.* **18.** through a region, area, etc.: *He is known the world over.* **19.** at some distance, such as in a direction indicated: *They live over by the hill.* **20.** from one side or place to another or across an intervening space: *to sail over; Toss the ball over, will you?* **21.** from beginning to end; throughout: *Think it over carefully.* **22.** from one person, party, etc., to another: *He handed the property over to his brother.* **23.** on the other side, as of a sea, a river, or any space: *Next time we'll come over to Japan.* **24.** so as to be moved from a standing or straight position: *to knock over a glass; to fall over.* **25.** so as to put or be in the reversed position: *The dog rolled over.* **26.** once more; again: *Do the work over.* **27.** in repetition: *20 times over.* **28.** in excess or addition: *to pay the full sum and something over.* **29.** divided by: *48 over 2 is 24.* *—adj.* [*be* + ~] **30.** ended; done; past; finished: *They became friends when the war was over.* *—n.* [*count*] **31.** an amount in excess or addition; extra. *—interj.* **32.** (used in radio communications to signal that the sender is waiting for a reply to or an acknowledgment of a message just sent): *Tower, this is Flight 77 requesting permission to land, over.* Compare OUT (def. 37). **—*Idiom.* 33. all over, a.** throughout; everywhere: *They traveled all over when they visited Australia.* **b.** ended; finished; over with: *The season was all over when they lost that game.* **34. over and above,** [~ + *obj*] in addition to; besides: *These expenses are over and above our initial estimates.* **35. over and over,** many times; repeatedly: *We thanked him over and over.* **36. over the hill,** [*noncount*] past one's prime: *That quarterback is over the hill and should retire.* **37. over with,** finished; ended; done: *Their relationship was over with.* **—Usage.** See ABOVE.

over-, *prefix.* **1.** *over-* is attached to nouns and verbs and means the same as the adverb or adjective OVER, as in: *overboard; overcoat; overhang; overlord; overthrow.* **2.** *over-* is also used to mean "over the limit; to excess; too much; too": *overact (= to act too much); overcrowd (= to crowd too many people or things into); overaggressive (= too aggressive); overfull; overweight.* **3.** *over-* is also used to mean "outer," as when referring to an outer covering: *overskirt (= a skirt worn over something, such as a gown).*

o•ver•a•chieve (ō′vər ə chēv′) /ˌowvərə'tʃiyv/ *v.* [*no obj*], **-chieved, -chiev•ing. 1.** to perform, esp. in school, better than the potential indicated by tests of one's mental ability or aptitude. **2.** to perform better or achieve more than is usual or expected, esp. in pursuing one's career. **—o′ver•a•chiev′er,** *n.* [*count*]

o•ver•act (ō′vər akt′) /ˌowvər'ækt/ *v.* to perform (a role) in an exaggerated manner: [~ + *obj*]: *The hero in the play overacted the role.* [*no obj*]: *guilty of overacting.*

o•ver•age[1] (ō′vər āj′) /ˈowvərˈeydʒ/ *adj.* beyond the acceptable, desired, or usual age.

o•ver•age[2] (ō′vər ij) /ˈowvərɪdʒ/ *n.* [*count*] an excess supply of merchandise.

o•ver•all (*adv.* ō′vər ôl′; *adj., n.* ō′vər ôl′) / *adv.* ˈowvərˈɔl; *adj., n.* ˈowvərˌɔl/ *adj., adv.* **1.** from one end or limit to the other: *The overall length is 15 feet. The computer takes up three square feet overall.* **2.** covering or including everything: *The overall pattern is one of growth and success. Overall, things have become better.* —*n.* [*count*] **3. overalls,** [*plural*] **a.** loose, sturdy trousers, usually having a bib with attached shoulder straps, originally worn over other trousers to protect them while working. See illustration at CLOTHING. **b.** long waterproof leggings. **4.** *Brit.* a smock or loose-fitting housedress.

o•ver•awe (ō′vər ô′) /ˌowvərˈɔ/ *v.* [~ + *obj*], **-awed, -aw•ing.** to fill (someone) with a feeling of awe, fear, or respect; intimidate: *He was overawed by the huge office.*

o•ver•bal•ance (*v.* ō′vər bal′əns; *n.* ō′vər bal′əns) / *v.* ˌowvərˈbæləns; *n.* ˈowvərˌbæləns/ *v.,* **-anced, -anc•ing,** *n.* —*v.* **1.** [~ + *obj*] to outweigh. **2.** to (cause to) lose balance or fall or turn over: [*no obj*]: *He overbalanced and toppled backwards.* [~ + *obj*]: *The weight of the rail car overbalanced the crane attempting to lift it.* —*n.* [*count*] **3.** a weight or amount that is too much. **4.** something that more than equals.

o•ver•bear•ing (ō′vər bâr′ing) /ˌowvərˈbɛərɪŋ/ *adj.* very rude in the way one gives orders or demands; dictatorial: *an overbearing boss.*

o•ver•bite (ō′vər bīt′) /ˈowvərˌbayt/ *n.* [*count*] a condition of the teeth in which the upper front teeth stick out too far over the lower ones.

o•ver•blown (ō′vər blōn′) /ˈowvərˈblown/ *adj.* **1.** overdone or excessive: *overblown praise.* **2.** self-important; pretentious: *What an overblown old windbag the club's president is!*

o•ver•board (ō′vər bôrd′, -bōrd′) /ˈowvərˌbɔrd, -ˌbowrd/ *adv.* **1.** over the side of a ship or boat, esp. into or in the water: *His canoe rocked suddenly and he fell overboard.* —***Idiom.*** **2. go overboard,** [*no obj*] to be unrestrained or excessive: *certainly went overboard with the decorations.*

o•ver•bur•den *v.* ō′vər bûr′dən, *n.* ō′vər bûr′dən), *v.* [~ + *obj*] to load too much; put a burden on.

o•ver•cast (*adj.* ō′vər kast′, -kast′; *v.* ō′vər kast′, ō′vər-kast′,; *n.* ō′vər kast′) / *adj.* ˈowvərˈkæst, -ˌkæst; *v.* ˌowvərˈkæst, ˈowvərˌkæst,; *n.* ˈowvərˌkæst/ *adj., v.,* **-cast, -cast•ing,** *n.* —*adj.* **1.** overspread with clouds; cloudy. —*v.* [~ + *obj*] **2.** to cause to be overclouded or darkened: *Clouds began to overcast the sky.* —*n.* [*noncount*] **3.** the condition of the sky when it is covered or overspread with clouds.

o•ver•charge (*v.* ō′vər chärj′; *n.* ō′vər chärj′) / *v.* ˌowvərˈtʃɑrdʒ; *n.* ˈowvərˌtʃɑrdʒ/ *v.,* **-charged, -charg•ing,** *n.* —*v.* **1.** to charge (a purchaser) too high a price: [~ + *obj*]: *He deliberately overcharges tourists.* [*no obj*]: *The merchant was always overcharging.* **2.** [~ + *obj*] to overload. —*n.* [*count*] **3.** a charge or fee that is higher than a stated or fair price.

o•ver•coat (ō′vər kōt′) /ˈowvərˌkowt/ *n.* [*count*] a coat worn over one's ordinary indoor clothing, as in cold weather.

o•ver•come (ō′vər kum′) /ˌowvərˈkʌm/ *v.,* **-came, -come, -com•ing. 1.** to defeat or gain an advantage over (someone or something) in a struggle or conflict; gain the victory over (someone or something); conquer: [~ + *obj*]: *We overcame the enemy on the last attack.* [*no obj*]: *vowed to overcome.* **2.** [~ + *obj*] to succeed in controlling: *to overcome the temptation to smoke.* **3.** [~ + *obj*] to overpower or overwhelm in body or mind: *The firefighters were overcome by smoke.*

o•ver•crowd (ō′vər kroud′) /ˌowvərˈkrawd/ *v.* [~ + *obj*] to cause to have too many people in (a room, building, etc.); crowd or fill too much.

o•ver•do (ō′vər do͞o′) /ˌowvərˈduw/ *v.* [~ + *obj*], **-did, -done, -do•ing. 1.** to do too much of or to; overindulge in; be extreme about: *to overdo the charm with the boss.* **2.** to overact (a part); exaggerate. **3.** [~ + *it/things*] **a.** to strain (oneself); make too many demands on (one's physical strength): *He overdid it with all those exercises.* **b.** to do (something) in an exaggerated or self-important way. **4.** to cook too much; overcook: *The meat had been overdone.*

o•ver•dose (*n.* ō′vər dōs′, *v.* ō′vər dōs, ō′vər dōs′) / *n.* ˈowvərˌdows, *v.* ˈowvərdows, ˌowvərˈdows/ *n., v.,* **-dosed, dos•ing.** —*n.* [*count*] **1.** a dose of a drug that is too great: *an overdose of sleeping pills.* **2.** a person who has become seriously ill or has died from taking too much of a drug. —*v.* [*no obj*] **3.** to take too much of a drug: *He overdosed on cocaine.* **4.** to die from taking too much of a drug: *He overdosed last week from cocaine.* **5.** to have or take too much of anything: *You're overdosing on chocolate again.*

o•ver•draft (ō′vər draft′) /ˈowvərˌdræft/ *n.* [*count*] **1.** an act of overdrawing. **2.** the amount overdrawn.

o•ver•draw (ō′vər drô′) /ˌowvərˈdrɔ/ *v.,* **-drew, -drawn, -draw•ing.** to try to draw or to spend an amount from (one's bank account, an allowance, etc.) that is greater than the money available to one: [*no obj*]: *Your bank won't allow you to overdraw.* [~ + *obj*]: *You can't overdraw your account.*

o•ver•dress (*v.* ō′vər dres′, *n.* ō′vər dres′) / *v.* ˌowvərˈdrɛs, *n.* ˈowvərˌdrɛs/ *v.* **1.** to dress too formally or elaborately for the occasion: [*no obj*]: *was overdressed for the beach.* [~ + *obj*]: *The costume designer overdressed the actors.* **2.** to dress with too much clothing: [~ + *obj*]: *Sometimes he overdresses the kids on winter days.* [*no obj*]: *I think they overdress on these cool days; it's not winter yet, after all.* —*n.* [*count*] **3.** a dress worn over another.

o•ver•drive (ō′vər drīv′) /ˈowvərˌdrayv/ *n.* [*noncount*] **1.** a device in a motor vehicle containing a gear that provides a drive shaft speed greater than the engine crankshaft speed. **2.** a state of great activity or productivity: *We went into overdrive to finish the project on time.*

o•ver•due (ō′vər do͞o′, -dyo͞o′) /ˌowvərˈduw, -ˈdyuw/ *adj.* **1.** having passed the time when due or expected: *two overdue library books.* **2.** needed or expected for some time but not yet having been done: *Improvements in the mass transit system are long overdue.* **3.** [*be* + ~; *sometimes: after a noun*] advanced or ready more than enough: *Her baby is overdue by at least three weeks.*

o•ver•es•ti•mate (*v.* ō′vər es′tə māt′; *n.* ō′vər es′tə-mit) / *v.* ˌowvərˈɛstəˌmeyt; *n.* ˈowvərˈɛstəmɪt/ *v.,* **-mated, mat•ing,** *n.* —*v.* [~ + *obj*] **1.** to form a judgment or opinion about (the value or worth of someone or something) that is too high or good: *We overestimated the cost of the dental treatment; to overestimate an employee's ability.* —*n.* [*count*] **2.** a judgment or guess about value, worth, cost, etc., that is too high or too great.

o•ver•flow (*v.* ō′vər flō′; *n.* ō′vər flō′) / *v.* ˌowvərˈflow; *n.* ˈowvərˌflow/ *v.* **1.** to flow or run over, such as rivers or water: [*no obj*]: *After the earthquake rivers overflowed at their banks.* [~ + *obj*]: *The rivers overflowed their banks.* **2.** [*no obj*] to have the contents flowing or spilling over an edge, rim, etc.: *The jar overflowed.* **3.** [~ + *obj*] to cause the contents of to flow or spill over: *He overflowed the bathtub.* **4.** to pass from one part to another of (something) as if flowing from a place or space that is too full: [*no obj*]: *The joyous crowd overflowed into the street.* [~ + *obj*]: *The crowd overflowed the auditorium.* **5.** [*no obj*] to be supplied with something in great amount or measure: *His heart was overflowing with gratitude.* —*n.* [*count*] **6.** an overflowing, or something that flows or spills over. **7.** an excess; too great an amount or quantity: *an overflow of applicants for the job.* **8.** an outlet, pipe, opening, etc., for any extra or overflowing liquid to pass through.

o•ver•fly (ō′vər flī′) /ˌowvərˈflay/ *v.* [~ + *obj*], **-flew, -flown, -fly•ing. 1.** to fly over (a specified area, country, etc.): *The plane lost its way and overflew enemy territory.* **2.** to fly farther than or beyond; overshoot. —**o′ver•flight′,** *n.* [*count*]

o•ver•grown (ō′vər grōn′, ō′vər grōn′) /ˌowvərˈgrown, ˈowvərˌgrown/ *adj.* **1.** covered with a growth of something: *overgrown with moss.* **2.** having grown too much: *overgrown weeds.*

o•ver•hand (ō′vər hand′) /ˈowvərˌhænd/ *adj.* **1.** thrown or performed with the hand and often part or all of the arm raised over the shoulder; overarm: *an overhand return in tennis.* —*adv.* **2.** with the hand raised above the shoulder: *to pitch overhand.* —*n.* [*count*] **3.** an overhand stroke, throw, or delivery. Also, **o′ver•hand′ed** (for defs. 1, 2).

o•ver•hang (*v.* ō′vər hang′; *n.* ō′vər hang′) / *v.* ˌowvərˈhæŋ; *n.* ˈowvərˌhæŋ/ *v.,* **-hung, -hang•ing,** *n.* —*v.* **1.** to hang over (something); stick out over (something below): [*no obj*]: *pools of water where trees overhang.* [~ + *obj*]: *The tree branches overhang the water.* —*n.* [*count*] **2.** something that sticks out over something below, such as an upper part of a building, a roof, or a balcony.

o•ver•haul (*v.* ō′vər hôl′, ō′vər hôl′; *n.* ō′vər hôl′) / *v.* ˌowvərˈhɔl, ˈowvərˌhɔl; *n.* ˈowvərˌhɔl/ *v.* [~ + *obj*] **1.** to make necessary repairs on (something): *to overhaul an old engine.* **2.** to examine completely and revise: *to overhaul a school curriculum.* **3.** to come closer to, catch up with, or overtake: *The police tried desperately to overhaul the fleeing assassin.* **—*n.*** **4.** Also, **o′ver•haul′ing.** a complete and general examination of something, with repairs or changes if necessary: [*noncount*]: *The old engines were in need of overhaul.* [*count*]: *a simple overhaul of the procedures.*

o•ver•head (*adv.* ō′vər hed′; *adj., n.* ō′vər hed′) / *adv.* 'owvər'hɛd; *adj., n.* 'owvər,hɛd/ *adv.* **1.** above one's head; up in the air or sky, esp. high in the sky: *The planes circled overhead.* **—*adj.*** **2.** [*often: be +* ~] located, operating, or passing above or over the head: *Do we need to have all the overhead lights on?* **3.** [*before a noun*] of or relating to the general costs of running a business: *large overhead expenses.* **—*n.*** **4.** [*noncount*] the general, steady costs of running a business, as for rent, lighting, and heating, that cannot be charged to a specific product or part of the work operation. **5.** [*count*] a stroke in tennis or badminton in which the ball or shuttlecock is hit with a downward motion from above the head; smash. **6.** [*count*] Also called **o′verhead projec′tor.** an apparatus that sends an image above and behind the operator when a transparent picture is placed horizontally on its surface and lighted from below.

o•ver•hear (ō′vər hēr′) /,owvər'hɪər/ *v.*, **-heard, -hear•ing.** to hear (speech or a speaker) without the speaker's intention or knowledge: [~ + *obj*]: *I hope he didn't overhear us talking about him.* [*no obj*]: *I couldn't help overhearing.*

o•ver•heat (ō′vər hēt′) /,owvər'hiyt/ *v.* to (cause to) become too hot or be heated too much: [~ + *obj*]: *Driving in the desert can rapidly overheat any car's engine.* [*no obj*]: *The car overheated before we went five miles.*

o•ver•joy (ō′vər joi′) /,owvər'dʒɔy/ *v.* [~ + *obj*] to cause to feel great joy or delight: *news that did not exactly overjoy the boss.* —**o′ver•joyed′,** *adj.*

o•ver•kill (ō′vər kil′) /'owvər,kɪl/ *n.* [*noncount*] **1.** the ability of a nation to destroy by nuclear weapons more of an enemy than would be necessary for a victory. **2.** an instance in which there is too much of what is required or suitable: *publicity overkill.*

o•ver•land (ō′vər land′, -lənd) /'owvər,lænd, -lənd/ *adv.* **1.** by, over, or across land: *The army swept overland, across the Russian steppes.* **—*adj.*** **2.** proceeding, performed, or carried on overland: *an overland journey.*

o•ver•lap (*v.* ō′vər lap′; *n.* ō′vər lap′) / *v.* ,owvər'læp; *n.* 'owvər,læp/ *v.*, **-lapped, -lap•ping,** *n.* **—*v.*** **1. a.** to stretch over and cover a part of (something else): [~ + *obj*]: *Each piece of tile overlaps the next one.* [*no obj*]: *The pieces of tile overlap.* **b.** (of two things) to come or fit together so that one partially covers (the other): [~ + *obj*]: *The tiles overlap each other.* [*no obj*]: *The edges overlap at a slight angle.* **2.** to have something in common or come together partly with (another): [~ + *obj*]: *My work days overlapped his.* [*no obj*]: *Our workdays overlapped.* **—*n.*** **3.** [*noncount*] an act or instance of overlapping: *overlap between two theories.* **4.** [*count*] an overlapping part.

o•ver•lay (*v.* ō′vər lā′; *n.* ō′vər lā′) / *v.* ,owvər'ley; *n.* 'owvər,ley/ *v.*, **-laid, -lay•ing,** *n.* **—*v.*** [~ + *obj*] **1.** to lay or place (one thing) over or upon another: *to overlay fertilizer on the soil.* **2.** to cover with something: *to overlay the soil with fertilizer.* **3.** to finish or decorate with an overlay: *The wood was overlaid with gold.* **—*n.*** [*count*] **4.** something laid over something else. **5.** a decorative layer put on top of something.

o•ver•load (*v.* ō′vər lōd′, *n.* ō′vər lōd′) / *v.* ,owvər'lowd, *n.* 'owvər,lowd/ *v.* **1.** [~ + *obj*] to load too much: *The bus was overloaded with passengers.* **2.** to (cause to) use too much electricity: [*no obj*]: *The circuits overloaded.* [~ + *obj*]: *You overloaded the circuits.* **3.** [~ + *obj*] to give too much work, too many problems, too much stress, etc., to (someone): *He was overloaded with the demands of his job.* **—*n.*** [*count*] **4.** a load or burden that is too much.

o•ver•look (*v.* ō′vər lo͝ok′; *n.* ō′vər lo͝ok′) / *v.* ,owvər'lʊk; *n.* 'owvər,lʊk/ *v.* [~ + *obj*] **1.** to fail to notice or think about; not see the importance of: *overlooked several important facts.* **2.** to disregard in a kind way; forgive, excuse, or pardon: *I'll overlook your mistake this time.* **3.** to look over, such as from a higher position: *a room that overlooks the ocean.* **—*n.*** [*count*] **4.** a piece of ground or land that provides a good view below.

o•ver•lord (ō′vər lôrd′) /'owvər,lɔrd/ *n.* [*count*] a lord over other lords.

o•ver•ly (ō′vər lē) /'owvərliy/ *adv.* excessively: *overly curious.*

o•ver•much (ō′vər much′) /'owvər'mʌtʃ/ *adj., n., adv.* too much.

o•ver•night (*adv.* ō′vər nīt′; *adj., n.* ō′vər nīt′) / *adv.* 'owvər'nayt; *adj., n.* 'owvər,nayt/ *adv.* **1.** for or during the night: *We'll stay overnight and leave early tomorrow morning.* **2.** very quickly; suddenly: *New suburbs sprang up overnight.* **3.** on the previous evening: *Preparations were made overnight.* **—*adj.*** [*before a noun*] **4.** done, made, occurring, or continuing during the night: *an overnight flight.* **5.** staying for one night: *overnight guests.* **6.** being or intended for delivery on the next day: *overnight mail.* **7.** occurring suddenly or within a very short time: *an overnight success.* **—*n.*** [*count*] **8.** an overnight stay or trip.

o•ver•pass (ō′vər pas′) / 'owvər,pæs / *n.* [*count*] a road, walkway, or bridge that provides a means of travel above another route.

o•ver•play (ō′vər plā′) /,owvər'pley/ *v.* [~ + *obj*] **1.** to exaggerate or emphasize too much (one's role in a play, an emotion one feels, an effect, etc.): *The actor overplayed the bad guy in that movie.* **—*Idiom.*** **2. overplay one's hand,** to overestimate the strength of one's position.

o•ver•pop•u•late (ō′vər pop′yə lāt′) /,owvər'pɒpyə,leyt/ *v.* [~ + *obj*], **-lat•ed, -lat•ing.** to fill with too many people or inhabitants and thus cause a strain on resources: *refugees overpopulating the border towns.* —**o•ver•pop•u•la•tion** (ō′vər pop′yə lā′shən) /'owvər,pɒpyə'leyʃən/ *n.* [*noncount*]

o•ver•pow•er (ō′vər pou′ər) /,owvər'pawər/ *v.* [~ + *obj*] **1.** to overcome (someone or something) by superior force; subdue; hold down; defeat: *She overpowered her attacker.* **2.** to affect or impress deeply or powerfully and sometimes unpleasantly or negatively; overwhelm: *The evidence will overpower you.* —**o′ver•pow′er•ing,** *adj.*: *an overpowering smell; overpowering arguments.*

o•ver•price (ō′vər prīs′) /,owvər'prays/ *v.* [~ + *obj*], **-priced, -pric•ing.** to put too high a price on (an item for sale).

o•ver•qual•i•fied (ō′vər kwol′ə fīd′) /'owvər'kwɒlə,fayd/ *adj.* having more education, training, or experience than is required for a job.

o•ver•rate (ō′vər rāt′) /,owvər'reyt/ *v.*, **-rat•ed, -rat•ing.** [~ + *obj*] to rate or classify too highly or favorably.

o•ver•reach (ō′vər rēch′) /,owvər'riytʃ/ *v.* [~ + *obj*] **1.** to reach or extend over or beyond. **2.** [~ + *oneself*] to defeat (oneself) by trying too hard or by being too eager.

o•ver•re•act (ō′vər rē akt′) /,owvərriy'ækt/ *v.* [*no obj*] to react or respond to something more strongly than is necessary.

o•ver•ride (*v.* ō′vər rīd′; *n.* ō′vər rīd′) / *v.* ,owvər'rayd; *n.* 'owvər,rayd/ *v.*, **-rode, -rid•den, -rid•ing,** *n.* **—*v.*** [~ + *obj*] **1.** to give a command that cancels the effect of something; set aside; overrule: *She overrode our objections and went ahead with the plan.* **2.** to replace (something) in importance; be more important than (something): *The need for food and shelter overrides most other concerns.* **—*n.*** [*count*] **3.** an act or instance of overriding. **4.** budgetary or expense increase; exceeding of an estimate: *The cost overrides run into the millions.* **5.** a system or device for interrupting and changing an operation that is normally automatic: *a manual override.*

o•ver•rid•ing (ō′vər rī′ding) /,owvər'raydɪŋ/ *adj.* [*before a noun*] most important; primary; major; main; principal: *The overriding consideration is the safety of the children.*

o•ver•rule (ō′vər ro͞ol′) /,owvər'ruwl/ *v.* [~ + *obj*], **-ruled, -rul•ing.** **1.** to rule against or disallow the arguments of: *The judge overruled the lawyer.* **2.** to rule against; reject: *The judge overruled the objection.*

o•ver•run (*v.* ō′vər run′; *n.* ō′vər run′) / *v.* ,owvər'rʌn; *n.* 'owvər,rʌn/ *v.*, **-ran, -run, -run•ning,** *n.* **—*v.*** [~ + *obj*] **1.** to spread over or cover (an area or place) quickly and in great numbers: *Weeds are overrunning the garden.* **2.** to attack and defeat completely and occupy the position of; overwhelm: *The army overran our position.* **3.** to run past or go beyond: *to overrun the finish line.* **4.** to exceed: *to overrun the budget.* **5.** to overflow: *The stream overran its banks.* **—*n.*** [*count*] **6.** an act, instance, or amount of overrunning, esp. the process of exceeding the costs of production: *cost overruns.*

o•ver•seas (*adv.* ō′vər sēz′; *adj.* ō′vər sēz′) / *adv.* ,owvər'siyz; *adj.* 'owvər'siyz/ also **o′ver•sea′,** *adv.* **1.** over, across, or beyond the sea; abroad: *lived overseas.* **—*adj.*** [*before a noun*] **2.** of or relating to passage over the sea: *overseas shipments.* **3.** of, from, or located in places across the sea; foreign: *overseas competition.*

o•ver•see (ō′vər sē′) /ˌowvər'siy/ *v.* [~ + *obj*], **-saw, -seen, -see•ing.** to supervise; manage: *He oversaw the project.* —**o′ver•se′er,** *n.* [*count*]

o•ver•sell (ō′vər sel′) /ˌowvər'sɛl/ *v.* [~ + *obj*], **-sold, -sell•ing.** to make claims about (something) that are extreme or exaggerated and that may not be believed.

o•ver•sexed (ō′vər sekst′) /'owvər'sɛkst/ *adj.* having an unusually strong sexual drive.

o•ver•shad•ow (ō′vər shad′ō) /ˌowvər'ʃædow/ *v.* [~ + *obj*] **1.** to be greater than in importance, interest, or significance: *She was overshadowed by her famous sister.* **2.** to cast a shadow over; darken: *Clouds overshadowed the moon.* **3.** to make (someone) sad: *The tragic death of their children overshadowed their lives.*

o•ver•shoe (ō′vər sho͞o′) /'owvərˌʃuw/ *n.* [*count*] an outer shoe or boot worn for protection in wet weather.

o•ver•shoot (ō′vər sho͞ot′) /ˌowvər'ʃuwt/ *v.,* **-shot, -shoot•ing. 1.** [~ + *obj*] to shoot or go over, beyond, or above so as to miss: *The missile overshot its target.* **2.** to pass or go by or beyond (a landing or stopping place) unintentionally: [~ + *obj*]: *The plane overshot the runway.* [*no obj*]: *On his landing the pilot overshot and crashed.*

o•ver•sight (ō′vər sīt′) /'owvərˌsayt/ *n.* **1.** [*noncount*] failure to notice or consider something: *guilty of oversight.* **2.** [*count*] a careless mistake or error: *Her mistake was a minor oversight.* **3.** [*noncount*] the act of watching over work, proceedings, etc.; supervision: *the joint House and Senate committee on oversight.*

o•ver•sim•pli•fy (ō′vər sim′plə fī′) /ˌowvər'sɪmpləˌfay/ *v.,* **-fied, -fy•ing.** to make (something) seem simpler than it really is and therefore distort or represent it incorrectly: [~ + *obj*]: *He oversimplified the statistics.* [*no obj*]: *You are oversimplifying.*

o•ver•size (ō′vər sīz′) /'owvər'sayz/ also **o′ver•sized′,** *adj.* of a size larger than is usual: *oversize tires.*

o•ver•sleep (ō′vər slēp′) /ˌowvər'sliyp/ *v.* [*no obj*], **-slept, -sleep•ing.** to sleep beyond the proper or intended time of waking up: *I was late to work because I overslept.*

o•ver•state (ō′vər stāt′) /ˌowvər'steyt/ *v.* [~ + *obj*], **-stat•ed, -stat•ing.** to state too strongly; exaggerate: *to overstate a problem.* See -STAT-.

o•ver•stay (ō′vər stā′) /ˌowvər'stey/ *v.* [~ + *obj*] to stay beyond the proper time, limit, or extent of: *The guests have overstayed their welcome (= they have stayed longer than they were welcome to stay).*

o•ver•step (ō′vər step′) /ˌowvər'stɛp/ *v.* [~ + *obj*], **-stepped, -step•ping.** to go beyond: *The officer overstepped his authority.*

o•ver•stuffed (ō′vər stuft′) /'owvərˌstʌft/ *adj.* **1.** stuffed or filled to excess. **2.** (of furniture) having the entire frame covered by stuffing and upholstery: *an overstuffed sofa.*

o•ver•sub•scribe (ō′vər səb skrīb′) /ˌowvərsəb'skrayb/ *v.* [~ + *obj*], **-scribed, -scrib•ing.** to subscribe for more of (something) than is available or required. See -SCRIB-.

o•vert (ō vûrt′, ō′vûrt) /ow'vɜrt, 'owvɜrt/ *adj.* open to view or knowledge; not hidden or secret (opposed to *covert*): *a look of overt hostility.* —**o•vert′ly,** *adv.*

o•ver•take (ō′vər tāk′) /ˌowvər'teyk/ *v.* [~ + *obj*], **-took, -tak•en, -tak•ing. 1.** to come alongside or catch up with and pass: *We overtook that slow truck.* **2.** to befall or happen to (someone) suddenly: *Bad luck overtook them.*

o•ver•tax (ō′vər taks′) /ˌowvər'tæks/ *v.* [~ + *obj*] **1.** to make demands on (someone or something) that are too great. **2.** to demand too much tax from.

o′ver-the-count′er, *adj.* [*usually: before a noun*] **1.** not listed on or not bought and sold through an organized securities exchange: *over-the-counter stocks.* **2.** sold legally without a prescription: *over-the-counter drugs.*

o•ver•throw (*v.* ō′vər thrō′; *n.* ō′vər thrō′) / *v.* ˌowvər'θrow; *n.* 'owvərˌθrow/ *v.,* **-threw, -thrown, -throw•ing,** *n.* —*v.* [~ + *obj*] **1.** to remove (a leader, dictator, king, queen, etc.) from a position of power. **2.** to put an end to by force: *to overthrow tyranny.* **3.** to throw past or over: *to overthrow first base.* —*n.* [*count*] **4.** an act or instance of overthrowing or of being overthrown.

o•ver•time (ō′vər tīm′) /'owvərˌtaym/ *n.* [*noncount*] **1.** time spent working that is before or after one's regularly scheduled working hours. **2.** pay for such time: *got overtime for the extra hours.* **3.** an additional period in a game played when the score is tied at the end of the regular playing period. —*adv.* **4.** during overtime: *to work overtime.* —*adj.* [*before a noun*] **5.** of or for overtime: *overtime pay.*

o•ver•tone (ō′vər tōn′) /'owvərˌtown/ *n.* [*count*] an additional meaning or quality, as in someone's speech or behavior, that is not openly expressed but can be understood or felt by others. See -TON-.

o•ver•ture (ō′vər chər, -cho͝or′) /'owvərtʃər, -ˌtʃʊr/ *n.* [*count*] **1.** Often, **overtures.** [*plural*] an initial move in discussing or working on an agreement or a joint action; a proposal; offer. **2.** a piece of music that introduces another musical work, such as an opera or musical comedy. **3.** an introductory part: *The small attacks were an overture to the full-scale assault.*

o•ver•turn (ō′vər tûrn′) / ˌowvər'tɜrn / *v.* **1.** to (cause to) turn over on the side, face, or back: [*no obj*]: *The truck skidded and overturned.* [~ + *obj*]: *The burglars had overturned the furniture.* **2.** [~ + *obj*] to destroy the power of; overthrow: *tried to overturn the government.*

o•ver•view (ō′vər vyo͞o′) /'owvərˌvyuw/ *n.* [*count*] a general outline of a subject or situation; survey; summary.

o•ver•ween•ing (ō′vər wē′ning) /'owvər'wiynɪŋ/ *adj.* **1.** too proud or confident. **2.** exaggerated; excessive: *overweening pride.*

o•ver•weight (ō′vər wāt′) / 'owvər'weyt / *adj.* weighing too much; weighing more than is normal, proper, or allowed: *an aging, overweight prizefighter; He had become overweight because he had no time to exercise. The letter was overweight and needed extra postage.*

o•ver•whelm (ō′vər hwelm′, -welm′) /ˌowvər'hwɛlm, -'wɛlm/ *v.* [~ + *obj*] **1.** to overpower or overcome in mind or feeling: *She was overwhelmed by remorse.* **2.** to overpower or defeat (a group) with greater force or numbers: *The enemy battalion overwhelmed our defenders.* **3.** to burden excessively: *He was overwhelmed with work, illness, and family problems.*

o•ver•whelm•ing (ō′vər hwel′ming, -wel′-) /ˌowvər'hwɛlmɪŋ, -'wɛl-/ *adj.* **1.** very large, such as in amount or size; very great: *an overwhelming victory of over one hundred thousand votes.* **2.** very powerful: *an overwhelming feeling of guilt; an overwhelming desire to help.* —**o′ver•whelm′ing•ly,** *adv.*

o•ver•work (*v.* ō′vər wûrk′, *n.* ō′vər wûrk′) / *v.* ˌowvər'wɜrk, *n.* 'owvərˌwɜrk/ *v.* **1.** to (cause to) work too hard, too much, or too long: [~ + *obj*]: *I think your boss overworks you and the whole staff.* [*no obj*]: *You look very tired, as if you've been overworking.* **2.** [~ + *obj*] to use too often or too much: *You are overworking the phrase "for these reasons" in your essay; try some different words for variety.* —*n.* [*noncount*] **3.** a condition of overworking or of having been overworked.

o•ver•wrought (ō′vər rôt′, ō′vər-) /'owvər'rɔt, ˌowvər-/ *adj.* extremely excited, nervous, or upset.

o•vi•duct (ō′vi dukt′) /'owvɪˌdʌkt/ *n.* [*count*] a tube through which the eggs of a female, the ova, are carried from the ovary to the outside or into the uterus. See -DUC-.

o•void (ō′void) /'owvɔyd/ *adj.* egg-shaped; having the solid form of an egg.

ov•u•late (ov′yə lāt′, ō′vyə-) /'ɒvyəˌleyt, 'owvyə-/ *v.* [*no obj*], **-lat•ed, -lat•ing.** to produce and discharge eggs from an ovary. —**ov•u•la•tion** (ov′yə lā′shən, ō′vyə-) /ˌɒvyə'leyʃən, ˌowvyə-/ *n.* [*noncount*]

o•vum (ō′vəm) /'owvəm/ *n.* [*count*], *pl.* **o•va** (ō′və) /'owvə/. the female reproductive cell, developed in the ovary.

ow (ou) /aw/ *interj.* (used esp. to express sharp or sudden pain): *Ow! I stepped on a nail.*

owe (ō) /ow/ *v.,* **owed, ow•ing.** [*not: be* + ~*-ing*] **1. a.** to be obligated to pay, repay, or give (something): [~ + *obj*]: *They still owe a hundred thousand dollars on their house.* [~ + *obj* + *obj*]: *I owe him a dollar.* [*no obj*]: *Do you still owe on that boat?* **b.** [~ + *obj*] to be in debt to: *I still owe my brother for the money I borrowed.* **2.** [~ + *obj* + *to* + *obj*] to be thankful and grateful to someone or something for making (something) possible: *owed his success to his wife.*

ow•ing (ō′ing) /'owɪŋ/ *adj.* [*be* + ~] **1.** owed, unpaid, or due for payment: *to pay what is owing.* —***Idiom.* 2. owing to,** [~ + *obj*] because of; as a result of: *We were delayed owing to the bad weather at the airport.*

owl (oul) /awl/ *n.* [*count*] a bird chiefly active at night, that hunts small animals for food, and that has a broad head with large, forward-directed eyes. —**owl′ish,** *adj.*

own (ōn) /own/ *adj.* **1.** (used after a possessive pronoun to emphasize the idea of ownership of, interest in, or relation to the next noun); of, relating to, or belonging to oneself or itself: *He spent only his own money.* **2.** (used after a possessive pronoun to emphasize that the subject is the only doer or performer of an action): *She insists on being her own doctor.* **—*pron.*** **3.** something that belongs to oneself: *He thought the office computer was his own.* **—*v.*** **4.** [*not: be + ~-ing*] to have or hold as one's own; possess: *She owns several cars.* **5.** to acknowledge or admit; confess: [*~ + that clause*]: *He owned that he might have been at fault.* [*~ + up to + obj*]: *He owned up to stealing the car.* [*~ + up*]: *Won't anyone own up?* **—*Idiom.*** **6. come into one's own,** to achieve the recognition, standing, or self-respect that one deserves. **7. hold one's own, a.** to keep one's position or condition steady or unchanged. **b.** to be equal to the opposition: *He's holding his own in the 25-mile race.* **8. of one's own,** belonging to oneself: *They wanted a home of their own.* **9. on one's own, a.** through one's own efforts or resources: *did the job on her own.* **b.** living or functioning independently: *was on her own at the age of 17.* **c.** *Chiefly Brit.* by oneself; without company: *walked home on his own.* **—own′er,** *n.* [*count*] **—own′er•ship′,** *n.* [*noncount*]

ox (oks) /ɒks/ *n.* [*count*], *pl.* **ox•en. 1.** a large, bulky animal belonging to the same family as domestic cows, water buffaloes, and yaks, esp. an adult male with its sex organs removed, used as a draft animal. **2.** any of the cattlelike animals of this group.

ox•i•da•tion (ok′si dā′shən) /ˌɒksɪ'deyʃən/ also **ox•i•di•za•tion** (ok′si də zā′shən) /ˌɒksɪdə'zeyʃən/ *n.* [*noncount*] the process or result of oxidizing.

ox•ide (ok′sīd, -sid) /'ɒksayd, -sɪd/ *n.* [*count*] a chemical compound in which oxygen is bonded to one or more atoms.

ox•i•dize (ok′si dīz′) /'ɒksɪˌdayz/ *v.*, **-dized, -diz•ing. 1.** [*~ + obj*] to combine chemically with oxygen; convert into an oxide. **2.** [*~ + obj*] to cover with a coating of oxide or rust. **3.** [*no obj*] to become oxidized. **—ox′i•diz′er,** *n.* [*count*]

ox•y•a•cet•y•lene (ok′sē ə set′l ēn′, -in) /ˌɒksiyə'sɛtḷˌiyn, -ɪn/ *n.* [*noncount*] a mixture of oxygen and acetylene, used in a blowtorch for cutting steel plates or the like.

ox•y•gen (ok′si jən) /'ɒksɪdʒən/ *n.* [*noncount*] a colorless, odorless gas, an element that is about one-fifth of the volume of the atmosphere and is present in a combined state in nature.

ox•y•gen•ate (ok′si jə nāt′) /'ɒksɪdʒəˌneyt/ *v.* [*~ + obj*], **-at•ed, -at•ing.** to treat, combine, or enrich with oxygen: *to oxygenate blood.*

ox•y•mo•ron (ok′si môr′on, -mōr′-) /ˌɒksɪ'mɔrɒn, -'mowr-/ *n.* [*count*], *pl.* **-mo•ra** (-môr′ə, -mōr′ə) /-'mɔrə, -'mowrə/. a figure of speech that uses two words or phrases that seem to be contradictory or opposite, such as "cruel kindness."

oys•ter (oi′stər) /'ɔystər/ *n.* [*count*] a sea animal that may be eaten, having two shells that enclose it.

oz., an abbreviation of Italian *onza*: ounce.

o•zone (ō′zōn, ō zōn′) /'owzown, ow'zown/ *n.* [*noncount*] **1.** a form of oxygen, O_3, produced when ultraviolet light passes through air or oxygen. **2.** OZONE LAYER.

o′zone hole′, *n.* [*count*] any part of the ozone layer that has become reduced in size by pollution in the atmosphere, resulting in too much ultraviolet radiation passing through, and therefore warming, the atmosphere.

o′zone lay′er, *n.* [*count; usually: the + ~*] the layer of the upper atmosphere where most of the ozone is concentrated, from about 8 to 30 mi. (12 to 48 km) above the earth.

P, p (pē) /piy/ *n.* [*count*], *pl.* **Ps** or **P's, ps** or **p's.** the 16th letter of the English alphabet, a consonant.

p., an abbreviation of: **1.** page. **2.** part. **3.** penny; pence. **4.** pint.

PA, an abbreviation of: **1.** Pennsylvania. **2.** public-address system.

Pa., an abbreviation of: Pennsylvania.

P.A., an abbreviation of: public-address system.

-pac-, *root. -pac-* comes from Latin, where it has the meaning "peace." This meaning is found in such words as: PACIFIC, PACIFY, PACT.

pace (pās) /peys/ *n., v.,* **paced, pac•ing.** **—***n.* [*count*] **1.** [*usually singular*] a rate of movement, esp. in walking, etc.; speed: *to set a rapid pace.* **2.** [*usually singular*] a rate of doing something, of activity, etc.; tempo: *The number of students grew at a very rapid pace last year.* **3.** a single step: *took a few paces toward her.* **4.** the distance covered in a step: *standing only a few paces apart.* **—***v.* **5.** [~ + *obj*] to regulate the speed of, as in racing: *That runner paced the others for the first ten miles of the marathon.* **6.** to cross with regular, sometimes slow, steps: [~ + *obj*]: *paced the floor nervously.* [*no obj*]: *paced up and down.* **7.** [~ + *off* + *obj*] to measure by paces: *He paced off a few feet from the wall.* **—*Idiom.*** **8. keep pace,** to do or work at the same rate (as): [*no obj*]: *They were working too fast for me to keep pace.* [~ + *with* + *obj*]: *Newspapers could hardly keep pace with developments during the war.* **9. put through one's paces,** to cause to demonstrate a set of practiced routines: *The teacher put us through our paces when the parents came to visit the class.* **10. set the pace,** to act as an example for others to equal; be first or first-rate: *We want our company to set the pace for sales in the whole region.* **—pac′er,** *n.* [*count*]

pace•mak•er (pās′mā′kər) /ˈpeysˌmeykər/ *n.* [*count*] **1.** PACESETTER. **2.** an electronic device surgically placed beneath the skin to provide a normal heartbeat by electrically stimulating the heart muscle.

pace•set•ter (pās′set′ər) /ˈpeysˌsɛtər/ *n.* [*count*] **1.** a person or group that serves as a model to be imitated. **2.** a person, animal, or thing that sets the pace, as in racing. Also called **pacemaker.**

pach•y•derm (pak′i dûrm′) /ˈpækɪˌdɜrm/ *n.* [*count*] a large, thick-skinned mammal with hoofs, as the elephant, hippopotamus, or rhinoceros. See -DERM-.

pa•cif•ic (pə sif′ik) /pəˈsɪfɪk/ *adj.* **1.** tending to make or preserve peace; peaceable. **2.** at peace; peaceful; tranquil. **—pa•cif′i•cal•ly,** *adv.* See -FIC-, -PAC-.

pac•i•fi•er (pas′ə fī′ər) /ˈpæsəˌfayər/ *n.* [*count*] **1.** a person or thing that pacifies. **2.** a device, often shaped like a nipple, for a baby to suck or bite on. See -PAC-.

pac•i•fism (pas′ə fiz′əm) /ˈpæsəˌfɪzəm/ *n.* [*noncount*] the belief that war or violence should never be used to settle disputes. See -PAC-.

pac•i•fist (pas′ə fist) /ˈpæsəfɪst/ *n.* [*count*] **1.** a person who believes in pacifism. **2.** a person who refuses to participate in military activity because of his or her beliefs regarding war. See -PAC-.

pac•i•fy (pas′ə fī′) /ˈpæsəˌfay/ *v.* [~ + *obj*], **-fied, -fy•ing.** **1.** to bring or restore to a state of peace: *The babysitter tried to pacify the screaming child.* **2.** to bring to a state of order, often by force; subdue: *The army was ordered to pacify the surrounding area.* **—pac•i•fi•ca•tion** (pas′ə fi kā′shən) /ˌpæsəfɪˈkeyʃən/ *n.* [*noncount*] See -PAC-.

pack[1] (pak) /pæk/ *n.* [*count*] **1.** a number of things wrapped together for easy handling; a bundle: *We loaded several packs on the donkeys.* **2.** BACKPACK. **3.** a definite amount of something sold, with its package: *a pack of cigarettes.* **4.** a group of things: *a pack of lies.* **5.** a group of animals of the same kind, esp. animals that hunt together: *a pack of wolves.* **6.** a set of playing cards; a deck. **7.** a cloth or small package used to wrap an injured part of the body for healing: *put an ice pack on the bee sting.* **—***v.* **8.** [~ + *obj*] to make into a pack or bundle: *He packed the snow into a hard ball.* **9.** [*no obj*] to be easily made into a pack or any small, tight mass: *Wet snow packs easily.* **10.** [~ + *obj*] to fill (something) with suitable objects: *to pack a trunk with clothes for the trip.* **11.** to put (clothes, etc.) into a case, etc., as for traveling or storage: [~ + *obj*]: *to pack clothes for a trip.* [*no obj*]: *Haven't you packed yet?* **12.** to crowd together within; cram: [~ + *obj*]: *The crowd packed the gallery.* [~ + *into* + *obj*]: *Thousands packed into the stadium to hear his farewell concert.* **13.** [~ + *obj*] to carry or wear as part of one's usual equipment: *In the U.S., police officers usually pack a gun.* **14.** [*not: be* + ~*-ing;* ~ + *obj*] *Informal.* to be able to deliver; to possess: *This champion packs a mean punch.* **15. pack in,** [~ + *obj* + *in*] to attract (people) in large numbers: *The new movie was packing them in during its first week of showing.* **16. pack in** or **up,** to give up or give in; to abandon: [~ + *in/up* + *obj*]: *to pack in one's career at age 35.* [~ + *obj* + *in/up*]: *deciding to pack it all in and retire.* **17. pack off** or **away,** to send away, often with speed or eagerness: [~ + *obj* + *off/away*]: *to pack the kids off to camp.* [~ + *off/away* + *obj*]: *to pack off the kids to camp.* **—***adj.* [*before a noun*] **18.** used for carrying a pack or load: *a sturdy pack horse.*

pack[2] (pak) /pæk/ *v.* [~ + *obj*] to choose, collect, or organize (cards, persons, etc.) so as to serve one's own purposes: *to pack the jury with women jurors.*

pack•age (pak′ij) /ˈpækɪdʒ/ *n., v.,* **-aged, -ag•ing.** **—***n.* [*count*] **1.** a bundle packed and wrapped or put in a box; parcel: *Could someone help me carry the packages in from the car?* **2.** a container in which something is packed: *Take the wrapping off the package.* **3.** a group or combination of related parts offered as a unit: *The president vetoed the new tax package.* **—***v.* [~ + *obj*] **4.** to make or put into a package. **5.** to design and manufacture a package for (a product): *packaged in eye-catching containers.* **6.** to combine or offer (related elements) into or as a unit. **7.** to present (something) in a way that disguises its true nature: *trying to package himself as someone concerned with the environment and education.* **—***adj.* [*before a noun*] **8.** offered as a unit combining a number of goods or services: *a package tour, including sightseeing, hotels, and airfare.*

packed (pakt) /pækt/ *adj.* **1.** very full; crowded to overflowing: *playing to a packed house.* **2.** [*be* + ~] having put one's clothes, belongings, etc., into a suitcase, bag, or trunk in preparation for a trip, for storage, etc.: *We're all ready to go and you're not even packed yet?*

pack•er (pak′ər) /ˈpækər/ *n.* [*count*] a person or thing that packs, esp. a person or company that packs food for market: *a meat packer.*

pack•et (pak′it) /ˈpækɪt/ *n.* [*count*] a small package or parcel: *a packet of letters.*

pack•ing (pak′ing) /ˈpækɪŋ/ *n.* [*noncount*] **1.** the act or work of a packer. **2.** material used to cushion goods packed in a container: *Save the boxes and packing in case you have to return the computer.*

pack′ rat′, *n.* [*count*] **1.** an American rat noted for carrying off shiny articles to its nest. **2.** *Informal.* one who saves useless small items.

pact (pakt) /pækt/ *n.* [*count*] an agreement, treaty, or compact: *a trade pact.* See -PAC-.

-pact-, *root. -pact-* comes from Latin, where it has the meaning "fasten." This meaning is found in such words as: COMPACT, IMPACT, IMPACTED, SUBCOMPACT.

pad[1] (pad) /pæd/ *n., v.,* **pad•ded, pad•ding.** **—***n.* [*count*] **1.** a mass of soft material used for comfort or protection, for applying medicine, or for stuffing: *The roller skaters wore knee pads.* **2.** a number of sheets of paper glued together at one edge, used for writing, drawing, etc.: *Bring in a pad and pencil.* **3.** the fleshy, cushionlike mass of tissue on the underside of each finger and toe. **4.** *Slang.* one's living quarters: *Come up to my pad for the weekend.* **—***v.* [~ + *obj*] **5.** to provide with a pad or padding: *The dress was padded at the shoulders.* **6.** to expand or add to without need or in a dishonest way: *padded his expense account.* **—*Idiom.*** **7. on the pad,** *Slang.* (of a police officer) receiving bribes, esp. on a regular basis.

pad[2] (pad) /pæd/ *n., v.,* **pad•ded, pad•ding.** **—***n.* [*count*] **1.** a dull, soft sound: *the pad of our daughter's little feet as she came into the room.* **—***v.* [*no obj*] **2.** to travel on foot; walk: *He padded off into the distance.* **3.** to walk so that one's footsteps make a dull, soft sound: *He padded softly behind her.*

pad•ding (pad′ing) /ˈpædɪŋ/ *n.* [*noncount*] **1.** material, as cotton or straw, used to pad something. **2.** something added but not needed.

pad•dle (pad′l) /ˈpædl/ *n., v.,* **-dled, -dling.** **—***n.* [*count*] **1.** a short, flat-bladed oar for moving and steering a canoe or small boat. **2.** any similar item used for mixing, stirring, or beating. **3.** a racket with a short handle and a wide, rounded front surface, used in table tennis, etc. **4.** a blade or part of a wheel moved by the action of water rushing past it, or by an engine that pushes it through water: *a paddle wheel boat.* **—v. 5.** to (cause to) move in a canoe or the like by using a paddle: [*no obj*]: *paddled across the lake in the canoe.* [~ + *obj*]: *He paddled the canoe across the lake.* **6.** [~ + *obj*] to spank with or as if with a paddle: *threatened to paddle the naughty child.* **—pad′dler,** *n.* [*count*]

pad′dle wheel′, *n.* [*count*] a wheel for moving a ship through the water, having a number of paddles entering the water at right angles and pushing the ship.

pad•dock (pad′ək) /ˈpædək/ *n.* [*count*] **1.** a small field, closed off with a fence, near a barn, used for letting animals out to pasture or to exercise. **2.** the closed area in which horses are saddled and mounted before a race. **—v.** [~ + *obj*] **3.** to confine in a paddock.

pad•dy (pad′ē) /ˈpædiy/ *n.* [*count*], *pl.* **-dies.** a rice field.

pad′dy wag′on, *n.* [*count*] an enclosed truck or van used by the police to carry prisoners.

pad•lock (pad′lok′) /ˈpæd,lɒk/ *n.* [*count*] **1.** a small lock made of a U-shaped bar that can be opened and swung away. **—v.** [~ + *obj*] **2.** to fasten with or as if with a padlock: *The file cabinet was padlocked.*

pa•dre (pä′drā, -drē) /ˈpɑdrey, -driy/ *n.* [*count*], *pl.* **-dres.** a priest or clergyman.

pae•an (pē′ən) /ˈpiyən/ *n.* [*count*] a song of praise, joy, thanksgiving, or triumph.

pa•gan (pā′gən) /ˈpeygən/ *n.* [*count*] **1.** one of a people or community following a polytheistic religion, as the ancient Greeks. **2.** one who is not a believer in one of the monotheistic religions. **3.** one who is not religious, esp. a hedonist or sensualist. **—adj. 4.** of or relating to pagans or their religion: *pagan rituals and sacrifices.* **5.** not religious. **—pa′gan•ism,** *n.* [*noncount*]

page[1] (pāj) /peydʒ/ *n., v.,* **paged, pag•ing.** **—n.** [*count*] **1.** one side, or both sides, of a sheet of something printed or written, as a book or letter: *How many pages are there in this book?* **2.** an important event or period: *a bright page in English history.* **3.** a block of computer memory up to 4,096 bytes long. **—v. 4. page through,** [~ + *through* + *obj*] to turn pages of (a book).

page[2] (pāj) /peydʒ/ *n., v.,* **paged, pag•ing.** **—n.** [*count*] **1.** a boy servant or attendant. **2.** an employee who carries messages, etc., as in a legislature. **—v.** [~ + *obj*] **3.** to summon (a person) by calling out his or her name, as over a public-address system: *He must be somewhere at the airport; let's see if we can page him.* **4.** to summon or alert by electronic pager: *The doctor was paged repeatedly.*

pag•eant (paj′ənt) /ˈpædʒənt/ *n.* [*count*] **1.** a parade in which the participants wear fancy, decorative costumes. **2.** a show that portrays scenes about the history of a place, institution, etc.: *a medieval pageant.* **3.** a show or exhibition: *a beauty pageant.*

pag•eant•ry (paj′ən trē) /ˈpædʒəntriy/ *n.* [*noncount*] spectacular display; a show of grandness and splendor: *the pageantry of the Olympics.*

page′ print′er, *n.* [*count*] a high-speed computer printer that uses a laser beam to print a full page of text at a time.

pag•er (pā′jər) /ˈpeydʒər/ *n.* [*count*] a pocket-sized electronic device that notifies the person carrying it of telephone calls.

pag•i•na•tion (paj′ə nā′shən) /,pædʒəˈneyʃən/ *n.* [*noncount*] the act or an arrangement of numbering pages.

pa•go•da (pə gō′də) /pəˈgowdə/ *n.* [*count*], *pl.* **-das.** a temple or sacred building of the Far East, usually a tower having an upward-curving roof over each story.

paid (pād) /peyd/ *v.* a pt. and pp. of PAY[1].

pail (pāl) /peyl/ *n.* [*count*] **1.** a container with a handle; bucket. **2.** the amount filling a pail: *dumping pails of water on them.* **—pail′ful′,** *n.* [*count*], *pl.* **-fuls.**

pain (pān) /peyn/ *n.* **1.** [*noncount*] physical suffering; great discomfort: *maintained that pain existed only in the mind.* **2.** [*count*] an instance of such suffering: *a back pain.* **3.** [*noncount*] severe mental or emotional distress: *the pain of loneliness.* **4. pains,** [*plural*] **a.** great care: *Take pains with your work.* **b.** the contractions in the uterus during childbirth. **5.** [*count*] Also called **pain in the neck.** an annoying person or thing: *She can be a real pain (in the neck), always bothering people with her problems.* **—v. 6.** to cause pain to: [~ + *obj*] *Your dishonesty pained me.* [*It* + ~ + *obj* + *to* + *verb*]: *It pains me to tell you this, but you're wrong.* **—*Idiom.* 7. go to great pains,** [~ + *to* + *verb*] to make a great effort to do something: *He went to great pains to avoid the draft.* **8. on** or **under pain of,** resulting in; risking: *You can't bring whiskey into that country on pain of death.*

pain•ful (pān′fəl) /ˈpeynfəl/ *adj.* **1.** causing or characterized by pain: *a painful wound.* **2.** difficult to endure; agonizing: *a painful life.* **—pain′ful•ly,** *adv.*

pain•kill•er (pān′kil′ər) /ˈpeyn,kɪlər/ *n.* [*count*] something, as a drug or treatment, that relieves pain: *Some narcotic drugs are painkillers.* **—pain′kill′ing,** *adj.*

pain•less (pān′ləs) /ˈpeynləs/ *adj.* **1.** not causing or involving pain: *wanted to die a painless death.* **2.** simple; not demanding effort: *a painless way of learning a language.* **—pain′less•ly,** *adv.*

pains•tak•ing (pānz′tā′king, pān′stā′-) /ˈpeynz,teykɪŋ, ˈpeyn,stey-/ *adj.* taking pains; showing great care and effort; careful: *a painstaking craftsman.* **—pains′tak′ing•ly,** *adv.*: *He had painstakingly gone through every word in the dictionary.*

paint (pānt) /peynt/ *n.* **1.** a liquid substance made of solid coloring matter and applied to a surface for protection or decoration: [*noncount*]: *two gallons of paint.* [*count*]: *He used both latex and oil-based paints in his apartment.* **2.** [*noncount*] this substance when it has dried on a surface: *peeling, flaking paint.* **—v. 3.** to coat, cover, or decorate with paint: [~ + *obj*]: *She paints houses for a living.* [*no obj*]: *They painted all day.* **4.** to produce (a picture, etc.) in paint: [~ + *obj*]: *The artist painted a beautiful landscape.* [*no obj*]: *The child likes to paint.* **5.** [~ + *obj*] to represent in paint: *to paint a sunset.* **6.** [~ + *obj* + *as* + *obj*] to describe vividly in words: *The ads painted the resort as a paradise.* **7.** [~ + *obj*] to coat or brush, as with a liquid medicine or a cosmetic: *painted her fingernails bright purple.* **—*Idiom.* 8. paint the town (red),** to go out and celebrate, esp. without restraint: *She promised him that on the night she finished the book they would paint the town red.*

paint•brush (pānt′brush′) /ˈpeynt,brʌʃ/ *n.* [*count*] a brush for applying paint.

paint•er (pān′tər) /ˈpeyntər/ *n.* [*count*] **1.** one who paints pictures: *That painter does landscapes.* **2.** one who paints houses, rooms, etc.: *The painters came and redid the walls.*

paint•ing (pān′ting) /ˈpeyntɪŋ/ *n.* **1.** [*count*] a picture, design, or piece of art done in paints: *His best paintings hung in the National Museum.* **2.** [*noncount*] the act, art, or work of one who paints pictures: *Painting did not bring in a lot of money for him.* **3.** [*noncount*] the act or work of one who paints houses, rooms, etc.

pair (pâr) /pɛər/ *n., pl.* **pairs, pair,** *v.,* **paired, pair•ing.** **—n.** [*count*] **1.** two things that are the same or similar, that correspond to each other, or that are matched together: *a pair of matching bookends.* **2.** something made of two parts joined together: *a pair of scissors.* **3.** two similar or associated individuals: *a pair of oxen.* **4.** a married, engaged, or dating couple: *the happy pair.* **5.** two playing cards having the same number or same level, but not the same suit: *a pair of jacks and another pair of eights.* **—v. 6.** to arrange or group in pairs or groups of two: [~ + *obj*]: *to pair socks.* [~ + *off* + *obj*]: *The teacher paired off each student with a partner.* [~ + *obj* + *off*]: *The teacher paired them off.* [*no obj;* ~ + *off*]: *to pair off for a dance.* **7. pair up,** to unite in a close relationship with another, as in a business partnership or marriage: [*no obj*]: *If they paired up they would make a powerful team.* [~ + *obj* + *up*]: *If we could pair them up they would make a strong team.* [~ + *up* + *obj*]: *Pair up the two of them.* See -PAR-. **—Usage.** See COUPLE.

pais•ley (pāz′lē) /ˈpeyzliy/ *n.* [*noncount*] **1.** a pattern of colorful, very detailed, usually curving figures. **—adj.** [*before a noun*] **2.** having the pattern of paisley.

pa•ja•mas (pə jä′məz, -jam′əz) /pəˈdʒɑməz, -ˈdʒæməz/ *n.* [*plural*] clothing worn for sleeping, made of loose-fitting trousers and a top: *These pajamas don't fit.* Also, *esp. Brit.,* **pyjamas.**

Pa•ki•sta•ni (pak′ə stan′ē, pä′kə stä′nē) /,pækəˈstæniy, ,pɑkəˈstɑniy/ *n.* [*count*], *pl.* **-nis, -ni.** **1.** a person born or living in Pakistan. **—adj. 2.** of or relating to Pakistan.

pal (pal) /pæl/ *n., v.,* **palled, pal•ling.** *Informal.* **—n.** [*count*] **1.** a close friend; comrade; chum: *His pal would always come to his rescue.* **—v.** [*no obj*] **2.** to do something together as friends: *They were always palling around.*

pal•ace (pal′is) /ˈpælɪs/ *n.* [*count*] **1.** the place that is the official home of a king, queen, or other high-ranking person: *the marble steps of the royal palace.* **2.** a luxurious mansion: *Their home was a palace, stretching for what seemed like miles.*

pal′ace guard′, *n.* [*count*] **1.** the guard protecting a palace. **2.** a group of trusted advisers of a head of state: *We can't get through his palace guard to alert him of the danger.*

pal•at•a•ble (pal′ə tə bəl) /'pælətəbəl/ *adj.* **1.** acceptable or agreeable to the taste: *Ethiopian food is quite palatable.* **2.** agreeable to the mind or feelings: *Is the revised plan more palatable to the chief?*

pal•ate (pal′it) /'pælɪt/ *n.* [*count*] **1.** the inside top part, or roof, of the mouth in mammals: *He got peanut butter stuck on his palate.* **2.** the sense of taste: *a dinner to delight the palate.*

pa•la•tial (pə lā′shəl) /pə'leyʃəl/ *adj.* **1.** of, relating to, or resembling a palace: *a palatial house.* **2.** suitable for a palace; magnificent.

pa•lav•er (pə lav′ər, -lä′vər) /pə'lævər, -'lɑvər/ *n.* **1.** [*noncount*] meaningless talk; chatter. **2.** [*count*] a conference: *The explorers arranged for a palaver with the chief of the village.* **—***v.* [*no obj*] **3.** to talk a great deal about meaningless things. **4.** to confer or meet with someone.

pale[1] (pāl) /peyl/ *adj.*, **pal•er, pal•est,** *v.*, **paled, pal•ing.** **—***adj.* **1.** lacking strong or natural color; colorless or whitish: *a pale complexion.* **2.** of a color that is near to white or gray: *pale yellow.* **3.** not bright or brilliant; dim: *the pale moon.* **—***v.* [*no obj*] **4.** to become pale: *to pale at the sight of blood.* **5.** to become or seem less important: *My problems with my children pale in comparison to hers.* —**pale′ness,** *n.* [*noncount*]

pale[2] (pāl) /peyl/ *n.* **1.** a stake or picket, as of a fence. **2.** limits; bounds: *outside the pale of my jurisdiction.* **—*Idiom.*** **3. beyond the pale,** beyond the limits of proper behavior, courtesy, etc.: *Holding children hostage for political purposes is behavior beyond the pale.*

pale•face (pāl′fās′) /'peyl,feys/ *n.* [*count*] *Slang (sometimes offensive).* a white person, esp. as distinct from a North American Indian.

pa•le•on•tol•o•gy (pā′lē ən tol′ə jē) /,peyliyən'tɒlədʒiy/ *n.* [*noncount*] the science that deals with the forms of life existing long ago, as represented by their fossils. —**pa′le•on•tol′o•gist,** *n.* [*count*]

pal•ette (pal′it) /'pælɪt/ *n.* [*count*] **1.** a thin board or tablet used by painters for holding and mixing colors. **2.** the set of colors on such a board. **3.** the variety of techniques of an art: *a composer's musical palette.*

pal•i•mo•ny (pal′ə mō′nē) /'pælə,mowniy/ *n.* [*noncount*] a form of alimony awarded to one member of an unmarried couple who separated after a period of living together.

pal•in•drome (pal′in drōm′) /'pælɪn,drowm/ *n.* [*count*] a word, line, verse, number, etc., reading the same backward and forward, as *Madam, I'm Adam.* See -DROM-.

pal•i•sade (pal′ə sād′) /,pælə'seyd/ *n.* [*count*] **1.** a fence or stakes set firmly in the ground to defend an area. **2. palisades,** [*plural*] a line of cliffs.

pall[1] (pôl) /pɔl/ *n.* [*count*] **1.** [*usually singular*] something that covers over, esp. with darkness: *A pall of smoke hung over the site of the explosion.* **2.** [*usually singular*] a feeling of gloom, sadness, mystery, etc., that seems to spread over a group of people: *A deep pall of gloom hung over the room when we heard the news of the election.* **3.** a cloth for spreading over a coffin or tomb. **4.** a coffin.

pall[2] (pôl) /pɔl/ *v.* [*no obj*] to cause tiredness or weariness; to become dull or uninteresting: *The pleasures of that nightclub began to pall after a few months.*

pall•bear•er (pôl′bâr′ər) /'pɔl,beərər/ *n.* [*count*] one of several persons who carry or walk near the coffin during a procession at a funeral.

pal•let[1] (pal′it) /'pælɪt/ *n.* [*count*] **1.** a mattress of straw. **2.** a small bed.

pal•let[2] (pal′it) /'pælɪt/ *n.* [*count*] **1.** a small, low, flat platform on which goods are placed for storage or moving: *The workers loaded the pallets into the warehouse.* **2.** a painter's palette.

pal•li•ate (pal′ē āt′) /'pæliy,eyt/ *v.* [~ + *obj*], **-at•ed, -at•ing.** **1.** to relieve (pain, etc.) without curing; alleviate: *to palliate a chronic disease.* **2.** to try to make (a wrong act or an offense) seem less serious by giving excuses, etc.: *to palliate his crime by claiming it was necessary in order to feed his family.* —**pal•li•a•tion** (pal′ē ā′shən) /,pæliy'eyʃən/ *n.* [*noncount*]

pal•li•a•tive (pal′ē ā′tiv, -ē ə tiv) /'pæliy,eytɪv, -iyətɪv/ *adj.* of or relating to palliation: *palliative measures.*

pal•lid (pal′id) /'pælɪd/ *adj.* **1.** pale; faint or lacking in color; wan: *a pallid face.* **2.** lacking in liveliness or interest: *a pallid performance by the exhausted cast.*

pal•lor (pal′ər) /'pælər/ *n.* [*noncount*] paleness in a person's face, as from fear, ill health, or death.

palm[1] (päm) /pɑm/ *n.* [*count*] **1.** the part of the inner surface of the hand that reaches from the wrist to the bases of the fingers. **2.** the corresponding part of an animal. **3.** the part of a glove covering this part of the hand. **—***v.* **4.** [~ + *obj*] to hide in the palm, as in doing a magic trick: *The magician palmed the quarter and then made it "appear" in your ear.* **5.** [~ + *obj*] to pick up (something) in the hand without others noticing: *The crook managed to palm a few rings from the display area.* **6. palm off,** to sell (something) to someone by falsely describing it as something that it is not: [~ + *off* + *obj* + *on* + *obj*]: *to palm off the stolen jewels on tourists.* [~ + *off* + *obj*]: *He palmed off the cheap jewelry as twenty-four carat gold.* [~ + *obj* + *off*]: *He palmed the cheap jewelry off as genuine.*

palm[2] (päm) /pɑm/ *n.* [*count*] **1.** a tall tree without branches, with a mass of leaves at the top: *palms waving gently in the Indian Ocean breeze.* **2.** a leaf of such a tree, once carried as a sign of victory.

palm•is•try (pä′mə strē) /'pɑməstriy/ *n.* [*noncount*] the practice of claiming to know one's future or character by examining the lines on the palm of one's hand. —**palm•ist** (pä′mist) /'pɑmɪst/ *n.* [*count*]

pal•o•mi•no (pal′ə mē′nō) /,pælə'miynow/ *n.* [*count*], *pl.* **-nos.** a horse with a golden coat and a white mane and tail.

pal•pa•ble (pal′pə bəl) /'pælpəbəl/ *adj.* **1.** plainly seen or felt; obvious: *Her disgust was palpable when her former boyfriend walked in.* **2.** capable of being touched or felt; tangible: *could sense a palpable presence in the spooky, dark hotel room.* —**pal′pa•bly,** *adv.*: *a story that was palpably untrue.*

pal•pate (pal′pāt) /'pælpeyt/ *v.* [~ + *obj*], **-pat•ed, -pat•ing.** to examine by touch, esp. for the purpose of seeing if there is disease or illness: *The doctor palpated my stomach to see if the tumor had grown.* —**pal•pa•tion** (pal pā′shən) /pæl'peyʃən/ *n.* [*noncount*]

pal•pi•tate (pal′pi tāt′) /'pælpɪ,teyt/ *v.*, **-tat•ed, -tat•ing.** **1.** to (cause to) beat very fast, as the heart; flutter: [*no obj*]: *His heart palpitated madly when he realized he had forgotten his speech.* [~ + *obj*]: *drugs that palpitate the heart.* **2.** [*no obj*] to tremble; quiver; throb. —**pal•pi•ta•tion** (pal′pi tā′shən) /,pælpɪ'teyʃən/ *n.* [*count*]: *palpitations of the heart.* [*noncount*]: *The drug causes palpitation.*

pal•sy (pôl′zē) /'pɔlziy/ *n.*, *pl.* **-sies,** *v.*, **-sied, -sy•ing.** **—***n.* **1.** paralysis or trembling of the muscles: [*noncount*]: *suffering from palsy.* [*count*]: *several different palsies.* **—***v.* [~ + *obj*] **2.** to paralyze. —**pal′sied,** *adj.*: *palsied hands.* See -LYS-.

pal•try (pôl′trē) /'pɔltriy/ *adj.*, **-tri•er, -tri•est.** **1.** ridiculously or insultingly small: *a paltry wage.* **2.** completely worthless: *paltry clothes.* —**pal′tri•ness,** *n.* [*noncount*]

pam•pas (pam′pəz; *before a noun:* pam′pəs) /'pæmpəz; *before a noun:* 'pæmpəs/ *n.* [*plural*], *sing.* **-pa.** the wide, large, grassy plains of S South America, esp. in Argentina.

pam•per (pam′pər) /'pæmpər/ *v.* [~ + *obj*] to treat with too much kindness or care: *to pamper a child.*

pam•phlet (pam′flit) /'pæmflɪt/ *n.* [*count*] a short, small publication, usually containing factual information or dealing with an important, current, or controversial topic or subject. —**pam•phlet•eer** (pam′fli tēr′) /,pæmflɪ'tɪər/ *n.* [*count*]

pan[1] (pan) /pæn/ *n.*, *v.*, **panned, pan•ning.** **—***n.* [*count*] **1.** a wide or broad, usually shallow metal container used for frying, baking, washing, etc.: *a frying pan.* **2.** a similar container or part, as one of the scales of a balance: *In one pan he placed the weight and in the other he measured out a kilo of flour.* **3.** a container in which gold is separated from gravel by shaking, stirring, or moving through water. **—***v.* **4.** [~ + *obj*] *Informal.* to criticize harshly, as in a review: *The critics panned the new play.* **5.** to wash (gravel, etc.) in a pan to separate gold: [*no obj*]: *The prospectors were panning for gold in the stream.* [~ + *obj*]: *to pan the gravel near Sutter's Mill.* **6. pan out,** [*no obj*] *Informal.* to have an end or outcome, esp. a successful one: *Things did not pan out well at his new job when he lost the report.*

pan[2] (pan) /pæn/ *v.*, **panned, pan•ning,** *n.* **—***v.* **1.** to move a camera from one side to another to follow a moving subject or keep a wide scene in view: [*no obj*]: *The camera operator panned from one end of the field to the other.* [~ + *obj*]: *She panned the camera to the left.* **2.** [*no obj*] (of a camera) to be moved in such a manner: *The camera panned back to show the captain and his men surrounded by enemy soldiers.* **—*n.*** [*count*] **3.** the act of panning a camera.

pan-, *prefix. pan-* comes from Greek, where it has the meaning "all." This meaning is found in such words as: PANORAMA; PANTHEISM. It is also used esp. in terms that imply or suggest the union of all branches of a group: *Pan-American; Pan- + hellenic (Greek) → Panhellenic (= all Greeks united in one group); Pan-Slavism (= all the people of Slavic background united).*

pan•a•ce•a (pan′ə sē′ə) /ˌpænəˈsiyə/ *n.* [*count*], *pl.* **-ce•as. 1.** something that can cure all ills; a cure-all. **2.** a solution for all difficulties. **—pan′a•ce′an,** *adj.*

pa•nache (pə nash′, -näsh′) /pəˈnæʃ, -ˈnɑʃ/ *n.* [*noncount*] a grand, somewhat showy manner: *doffed his hat with panache.*

Pan•a•ma hat (pan′ə mä) /ˈpænəmɑ/ *n.* [*count*] Also, **Pan′a•ma.** a hat made of finely folded young leaves of a palmlike plant of Central America.

Pan•a•ma•ni•an (pan′ə mā′nē ən) /ˌpænəˈmeyniyən/ *adj.* **1.** of or relating to Panama. **—*n.*** [*count*] **2.** a person born or living in Panama.

Pan-A•mer•i•can (pan′ə mer′i kən) /ˌpænəˈmɛrɪkən/ *adj.* of, relating to, or representing all the countries or people of North, Central, and South America.

pan•cake (pan′kāk′) /ˈpænˌkeyk/ *n., v.,* **-caked, -cak•ing. —*n.*** [*count*] **1.** a thin, flat cake of flour, eggs, and milk, fried on both sides in a frying pan; a griddlecake or flapjack. **—*v.* 2.** (of an airplane) to (cause to) drop flat to the ground after leveling off a few feet above it: [*no obj*]: *The plane pancaked down the runway.* [~ + *obj*]: *The pilot pancaked his airplane.* **3.** [~ + *obj*] *Informal.* to flatten, esp. as the result of an accident: *pancaked the car into an oncoming truck.*

pan•chro•mat•ic (pan′krō mat′ik, -krə-) /ˌpænkrowˈmætɪk, -krə-/ *adj.* (of photographic film) sensitive to all visible colors. See -CHROM-.

pan•cre•as (pan′krē əs, pang′-) /ˈpænkriyəs, ˈpæŋ-/ *n.* [*count*] a large gland located near the stomach, which releases digestive enzymes into the intestine and insulin into the bloodstream. **—pan•cre•at•ic** (pan′krē at′ik) /ˌpænkriyˈætɪk/ *adj.*

-pand-, *root. -pand-* comes from Latin, where it has the meaning "spread; get larger." This meaning is found in such words as: EXPAND, EXPANSE, EXPANSION, EXPANSIVE.

pan•da (pan′də) /ˈpændə/ *n.* [*count*], *pl.* **-das.** a white-and-black bearlike mammal.

pan•dem•ic (pan dem′ik) /pænˈdɛmɪk/ *adj.* **1.** (of a disease) having spread among humans throughout an entire country or continent or the whole world. **—*n.*** [*count*] **2.** a pandemic disease.

pan•de•mo•ni•um (pan′də mō′nē əm) /ˌpændəˈmowniyəm/ *n.* [*noncount*] **1.** wild or noisy uproar or disorder: *Pandemonium erupted in the hall after her racist remarks.* **2.** a place or scene of complete chaos, uproar, or disorder: *The room was pandemonium.*

pan•der (pan′dər) /ˈpændər/ *n.* [*count*] Also, **pan′der•er. 1.** one who finds clients for a prostitute; pimp; procurer. **2.** one who appeals to or profits from the weaknesses of others. **—*v.* 3. pander to,** [~ + *to* + *obj*] to provide or furnish (a person or people) with something that satisfies their low desires or that appeals to their prejudices or fears: *Those newspapers pander to the public's lowest desires: greed and sex.*

P. and L. or **p. and l.,** an abbreviation of: profit and loss.

pane (pān) /peyn/ *n.* [*count*] one of the divisions of a window, made of a single plate of glass in a frame.

pan•e•gyr•ic (pan′i jir′ik, -jī′rik) /ˌpænɪˈdʒɪrɪk, -ˈdʒayrɪk/ *n.* **1.** [*count*] a formal, elaborate speech or writing that praises a person or thing; a eulogy. **2.** [*noncount*] formal or elaborate praise.

pan•el (pan′l) /ˈpænl/ *n., v.,* **-eled, -el•ing** or (*esp. Brit.*) **-elled, -el•ling. —*n.*** [*count*] **1.** a section or part of a wall, etc., esp. one sunk below or raised above the surface. **2.** a thin, flat piece of wood or the like, as a large piece of plywood: *mounted panels on the wall to reduce noise.* **3.** a group conducting a public discussion, judging a contest, etc.: *a panel of experts.* **4.** (a list of) people summoned for service as jurors. **5.** a surface on a machine on which dials and controls are mounted: *The control panel on that new car looks like one for a spaceship.* **—*v.*** [~ + *obj*] **6.** to arrange in (a wall, etc.) with a panel or panels.

pan•el•ing (pan′l ing) /ˈpænlɪŋ/ *n.* [*noncount*] **1.** panels of wood, thought of as a group or put on a wall. **2.** material made into panels. Also, *esp. Brit.,* **pan′el•ling.**

pan•el•ist (pan′l ist) /ˈpænlɪst/ *n.* [*count*] a member of a panel.

pan′el truck′, *n.* [*count*] a small truck having a long, fully closed body.

pang (pang) /pæŋ/ *n.* [*count*] **1.** a sudden feeling of distress in the mind or in the feelings: *a pang of guilt.* **2.** a sudden, brief, and sharp pain: *the pangs of childbirth.*

pan•han•dle[1] (pan′han′dl) /ˈpænˌhændl/ *n.* [*count*] **1.** the handle of a pan. **2.** a long, narrow strip of land that sticks out from a larger territory: *the Texas panhandle.*

pan•han•dle[2] (pan′han′dl) /ˈpænˌhændl/ *v.,* **-dled, -dling.** to approach people passing by on the street and beg (something) from (them): [*no obj*]: *panhandling on the streets.* [~ + *obj*]: *panhandling the businessmen; panhandled a few dollars.* **—pan′han′dler,** *n.* [*count*]

pan•ic (pan′ik) /ˈpænɪk/ *n., adj., v.,* **-icked, -ick•ing. —*n.* 1.** [*noncount*] a sudden, great fear: *Panic seized the demonstrators when the police attacked.* **2.** [*count*] an instance, outbreak, or period of such fear: *A sudden panic seized him.* **3.** [*count*] a sudden widespread fear that the economy is in trouble, causing stock values to fall and some banks to fail. **4.** [*count; usually singular; usually: a* + ~] *Informal.* someone or something considered very funny: *That new show is a panic; we were gasping from laughing so hard.* **—*adj.*** [*before a noun*] **5.** of, relating to, or caused by panic: *panic selling of stocks.* **—*v.* 6.** to (cause to) have a feeling of panic: [*no obj*]: *He panicked at the thought of asking her for a date.* [~ + *obj*]: *Something must have panicked the burglars, because they dropped the loot and ran.* **—pan′ick•y,** *adj.*

pan•nier or **pan•ier** (pan′yər, -ē ər) /ˈpænyər, -iyər/ *n.* [*count*] **1.** a basket for carrying supplies, etc. **2.** one of a pair of baskets to be slung across the back of a pack animal, a bicycle, etc.

pan•o•ply (pan′ə plē) /ˈpænəpliy/ *n.* [*count*], *pl.* **-plies.** a large, magnificent, impressive arrangement, collection, or display.

pan•o•ram•a (pan′ə ram′ə, -rä′mə) /ˌpænəˈræmə, -ˈrɑmə/ *n.* [*count*], *pl.* **-ram•as. 1.** a wide view of a large area. **2.** a large picture display of a landscape or other scene, often shown one part at a time before spectators. **3.** a continuous unfolding of events: *the panorama of Chinese history.* **—pan•o•ram•ic** (pan′ə ram′ik) /ˌpænəˈræmɪk/ *adj.*

pan•sy (pan′zē) /ˈpænziy/ *n.* [*count*], *pl.* **-sies. 1.** a violet grown in many kinds, having flowers in many different, rich colors. **2.** *Slang* (*disparaging and offensive*). **a.** a male homosexual. **b.** an effeminate man.

pant[1] (pant) /pænt/ *v.* **1.** [*no obj*] to breathe hard and quickly, as after hard work: *He ran up seven flights of stairs, panting and gasping for air.* **2.** [*used with quotations*] to breathe or say rapidly or with gasps: *"Look out," she panted, "he's after us."* **3.** [*no obj*] to wish for or desire with strong eagerness; yearn: *to pant for revenge.* **—*n.*** [*count*] **4.** a short, quick effort to breathe; gasp.

pant[2] (pant) /pænt/ *adj.* [*before a noun*] of or relating to pants: *a pant leg; pant cuffs.*

pan•ta•loons (pan′tl o͞onz′) /ˌpæntlˈuwnz/ *n.* [*plural*] a man's close-fitting garment for the hips and legs, worn esp. in the 19th century.

pan•the•ism (pan′thē iz′əm) /ˈpænθiyˌɪzəm/ *n.* [*noncount*] any religious belief or position in philosophy that claims that God is part of or inside of the universe. **—pan′the•ist,** *n.* [*count*] **—pan′the•is′tic, pan′the•is′ti•cal,** *adj.*

pan•the•on (pan′thē on′, -ən) /ˈpænθiyˌɒn, -ən/ *n.* [*count*] **1.** a public building containing tombs or memorials of the famous dead people of a nation. **2.** the heroes or idols of any group, movement, etc., thought of as a group or collection: *had earned her place in the pantheon of American literature.* **3.** all the gods of a particular mythology, thought of as a group. See -THEO-.

pan•ther (pan′thər) /ˈpænθər/ *n., pl.* **-thers,** (*esp. when thought of as a group*) **-ther. 1.** the cougar. **2.** the leopard.

pant•ies (pan′tēz) /ˈpæntiyz/ *n.* [*plural*] short underpants for women and children: *Her panties were lacy, frilly things.* See illustration at CLOTHING. Often, **pant′ie, panty** [*count*]: *She rewashed one panty and rinsed the others.*

pan•to•mime (pan′tə mīm′) /ˈpæntəˌmaym/ *n., v.,* **-mimed, -mim•ing. —*n.* 1.** [*noncount*] the art of conveying actions and thoughts by movements without speech. **2.** [*count*] a play or entertainment in which the performers express themselves by gesture alone. **—*v.* 3.** to represent or express in pantomime: [~ + *obj*]: *He pantomimed hunger by rubbing his belly and groaning.* [*no obj*]: *He pantomimed by rubbing his stomach and groaning.* —**pan•to•mim•ist** (pan′tə mi′mist) /'pæntə,maymɪst/ *n.* [*count*]

pan•try (pan′trē) /'pæntriy/ *n.* [*count*], *pl.* **-tries.** a small room near a kitchen, in which food, dishes, etc., are kept.

pants (pants) /pænts/ *n.* [*plural*] **1.** TROUSERS: *His pants were too short.* See illustration at CLOTHING. **2.** underpants, esp. for women and children; panties. **3.** *Brit.* men's underpants, esp. long drawers. —***Idiom.*** **4. wear the pants,** to have the dominant role: *Who wears the pants in that family, the husband or wife?*

pant•suit (pant′so͞ot′) /'pænt,suwt/ also **pants suit,** *n.* [*count*] a woman's suit consisting of trousers and a matching jacket.

pant•y•hose (pan′tē hōz′) /'pæntiy,howz/ *n.* [*plural; used with a plural verb*] a one-piece, skintight piece of clothing worn by women, combining panties and stockings: *Her pantyhose were too tight.*

pant•y•waist (pan′tē wāst′) /'pæntiy,weyst/ *n.* [*count*] *Informal.* an effeminate man; sissy.

pap (pap) /pæp/ *n.* [*noncount*] **1.** soft food for infants or sick people. **2.** ideas, writings, etc., having no real content, worth, or value: *The book was full of pap.*

pa•pa (pä′pə, pə pä′) /'pɑpə, pə'pɑ/ *n.* [*count*], *pl.* **-pas.** *Informal.* father.

pa•pa•cy (pā′pə sē) /'peypəsiy/ *n.* [*count*], *pl.* **-cies. 1.** the office, position, power, or rank of the pope. **2.** the period during which a certain pope is in office.

pa•pal (pā′pəl) /'peypəl/ *adj.* [*before a noun*] **1.** of or relating to the pope or the papacy. **2.** of or relating to the Roman Catholic Church.

pa•pa•ya (pə pä′yə) /pə'pɑyə/ *n., pl.* **-yas. 1.** [*count*] a small tropical American tree, bearing a yellow, melonlike fruit. **2.** the fruit itself: [*count*]: *Several papayas fell from the tree.* [*noncount*]: *Papaya is sweet when ripe.*

pa•per (pā′pər) /'peypər/ *n.* **1.** [*noncount*] a substance made from wood pulp, rags, or other fiber, used to write or print on, for wrapping, etc.: *a few sheets of paper; wrapping paper.* **2.** [*count*] a piece, sheet, or leaf of this: *a few papers lying on the floor.* **3.** [*count*] a written or printed document or the like: *He went through the papers on his desk.* **4.** [*count*] a newspaper or journal: *the tabloid papers.* **5.** [*count*] an essay, article, or scholarly piece of writing, usually intended to be published. **6.** [*count*] a written piece of schoolwork, as a composition or report: *The sixth-grade class had to do a paper on a science project.* **7.** Often, **papers.** [*plural*] a document establishing a person's identity, status, or the like: *citizenship papers.* **8.** [*noncount*] money in the form of bills. **9.** [*noncount*] wallpaper. —*v.* [~ + *obj*] **10.** to cover with wallpaper: *They papered the walls with a beautiful pattern.* **11.** to line or cover with paper: *to paper the shelves.* **12. paper over,** to conceal or cover up (disagreement, trouble, etc.), esp. to keep up a false appearance of agreement: [~ + *over* + *obj*]: *tried to paper over their marital problems for the children's sake.* [~ + *obj* + *over*]: *The conflict is obvious now; you can't paper it over anymore.* —*adj.* [*before a noun*] **13.** made of paper: *a paper bag.* **14.** existing on paper only; claimed to exist (as on official documents) but not real: *the company's paper profits.* —***Idiom.*** **15. on paper, a.** in written or printed form: *Let's get down on paper everything that happened.* **b.** claimed to exist but not real; existing in theory only: *The plan looks good on paper, but will it work?* —**pa′per•er,** *n.* [*count*]

pa•per•back (pā′pər bak′) /'peypər,bæk/ *n.* **1.** a book bound in a flexible paper cover: [*count*]: *paperbacks on every imaginable topic.* [*noncount; in* + ~]: *That dictionary is now available in paperback.* —*adj.* [*before a noun*] **2.** (of a book) bound in a flexible paper cover. **3.** of or relating to paperbacks: *a paperback book club.*

pa•per•board (pā′pər bôrd′, -bōrd′) /'peypər,bɔrd, -,bowrd/ *n.* [*noncount*] **1.** thick, stiff cardboard composed of layers of paper; pasteboard. —*adj.* [*before a noun*] **2.** of, relating to, or made of paperboard.

pa•per•boy or **-girl,** (pā′pər boi′) or (-gûrl′) /'peypər,bɔy/ or /-,gɜrl/ *n.* [*count*] a young person who sells newspapers on the street or delivers them to homes.

pa′per clip′, *n.* [*count*] a flat clip that holds sheets of paper between two loops.

pa′per ti′ger, *n.* [*count*] a person, nation, etc., that has the appearance of power but is actually weak.

pa′per trail′, *n.* [*count*] a written or printed record, as of memos, court opinions, etc., esp. when used to incriminate someone: *searching for a paper trail that would prove his guilt.*

pa•per•weight (pā′pər wāt′) /'peypər,weyt/ *n.* [*count*] a small, heavy object placed on papers to keep them in place.

pa•per•work (pā′pər wûrk′) /'peypər,wɜrk/ *n.* [*noncount*] clerical work not in itself important but still a necessary part of some job.

pa•per•y (pā′pə rē) /'peypəriy/ *adj.* like paper; thin and easily broken.

pa•pier-mâ•ché (pā′pər mə shā′, pä pyā′-) /,peypərmə'ʃey, pɑ,pyey-/ *n.* [*noncount*] **1.** moistened paper pulp mixed with glue, made into shapes when moist, and becoming hard and strong when dry: *a box of papier-mâché.* —*adj.* [*before a noun*] **2.** made of papier-mâché.

pa•pist (pā′pist) /'peypɪst/ *n.* [*count*], *adj.* *Usually Disparaging.* Roman Catholic. —**pa′pism,** *n.* [*noncount*]

pa•poose or **pap•poose** (pa po͞os′, pə-) /pæ'puws, pə-/ *n.* [*count*] a North American Indian baby or young child.

pap•ri•ka (pa prē′kə, pə-, pä-, pap′ri kə) /pæ'priykə, pə-, pɑ-, 'pæprɪkə/ *n.* [*noncount*] a red powder made from dried, ripe sweet peppers, used as a spice in cooking.

Pap′ (or **pap′**) **test′** (pap) /pæp/ *n.* [*count*] a test for cancer of the cervix.

pa•py•rus (pə pī′rəs) /pə'payrəs/ *n., pl.* **-py•ri** (-pī′rī, -rē) /-'payray, -riy/ **-py•rus•es. 1.** [*noncount*] a tall water plant, originally from the Nile valley. **2.** [*noncount*] a material on which to write, prepared from thin strips of this plant pressed together. **3.** [*count*] a document written on this material.

par (pär) /pɑr/ *n., adj., v.,* **parred, par•ring.** —*n.* **1.** [*count; usually singular; on/at* + *a* + ~] an equality in value; a level of equality: *The company saw its gains rise on a par with losses.* **2.** [*noncount*] an average or normal amount, degree, etc.: *He doesn't look up to par these days; maybe he's tired.* **3.** [*noncount*] the number of golf strokes set as a standard for a certain hole or a complete course. —*v.* [~ + *obj*] **4.** *Golf.* to hit the number of strokes that equals par on (a hole or course): *parred the last two holes.* —***Idiom.*** **5. par for the course,** [*be* + ~] exactly what one might expect; typical: *His nasty behavior is par for the course in that company.* See -PAR-.

-par-, *root.* *-par-* comes from Latin, where it has the meaning "equal; a piece." This meaning is found in such words as: APART, APARTHEID, BIPARTISAN, COMPARABLE, COMPARE, COMPARTMENT, COUNTERPART, DEPART, DEPARTMENT, DEPARTURE, DISPARAGE, IMPART, INCOMPARABLE, PAIR, PAR, PARENTHESIS, PART, PARTIAL, PARTICIPLE, PARTICLE, PARTICULAR, PARTISAN, PARTITION, PARTY, REPARTEE.

par., an abbreviation of: **1.** paragraph. **2.** parallel. **3.** parenthesis.

para-[1], *prefix.* **1.** *para-* comes from Greek, where it has the meaning "at or to one side of, beside, side by side." This meaning is found in such words as: PARABOLA; PARAGRAPH. **2.** *para-* is also used to mean "beyond, past, by": PARADOX. **3.** *para-* also has the meaning "abnormal, defective": PARANOIA. **4.** *para-* is also attached to names of jobs or occupations to mean "ancillary, subsidiary, assisting." This meaning is found in such words as: PARALEGAL; PARAPROFESSIONAL. Also, *esp. before a vowel,* **par-.**

para-[2], *prefix.* *para-* is taken from PARACHUTE, and is used to form compounds that refer to persons or things that use parachutes or that are landed by parachute: *paratrooper.*

par•a•ble (par′ə bəl) /'pærəbəl/ *n.* [*count*] a short story that illustrates some truth or lesson.

pa•rab•o•la (pə rab′ə lə) /pə'ræbələ/ *n.* [*count*], *pl.* **-las.** a curve that is the same shape as the path of an object thrown into the air and landing in another place. —**par•a•bol•ic** (par′ə bol′ik) /,pærə'bɒlɪk/ *adj.*

par•a•chute (par′ə sho͞ot′) /'pærə,ʃuwt/ *n., v.,* **-chut•ed, -chut•ing.** —*n.* [*count*] **1.** a folding, circular, fabric device with cords to attach to a person or thing in order to allow it to descend slowly from a height, esp. from an aircraft: *The parachute opened and he drifted slowly down to the ground.* —*v.* **2.** to (cause or allow to) let drop or land (troops, etc.) by parachute: [~ + *obj*]: *to parachute supplies into the region.* [*no obj*]: *The wounded pilot parachuted slowly down.* —**par′a•chut′ist,** *n.* [*count*]

pa•rade (pə rād′) /pə'reyd/ *n., v.,* **-rad•ed, -rad•ing.** —*n.* [*count*] **1.** a public procession in honor of an event, person, etc., or to celebrate something: *a parade down Main Street.* **2.** a military ceremony involving the marching of troops. **3.** a continual passing by, as of people, etc.: *the parade of the seasons.* —*v.* **4.** to (cause to) march in a procession: [*no obj*]: *The police officers paraded on St.*

Patrick's Day. [~ + *obj*]: *The hostages were paraded through the city streets.* **5.** [~ + *obj*] to show in an obvious way, as to gain attention: *paraded her former boyfriends in front of him.* **6.** [*no obj*] to walk in a public place, so as to be noticed: *teenagers parading in the park.* **—*Idiom.* 7. on parade,** marching in a parade, as at a formal occasion. **—pa•rad′er,** *n.* [*count*]

par•a•digm (par′ə dīm′, -dim) /ˈpærəˌdaym, -dım/ *n.* [*count*] **1.** a set of all the inflected forms of a word based on a single stem or root, as *boy, boy's, boys, boys'.* **2.** an example serving as a model; pattern: *a paradigm of virtue.* **—par•a•dig•mat•ic** (par′ə dig mat′ik) /ˌpærədıgˈmætık/ *adj.*

par•a•dise (par′ə dis′, -dīz′) /ˈpærəˌdays, -ˌdayz/ *n.* **1.** [*proper noun; no article*] heaven, the final resting place of good people when they die. **2.** [*count*] a place of great beauty or happiness: *went to an island paradise for our vacation.* **3.** [*noncount*] a state of supreme happiness: *All the boys thought a date with her would be paradise.*

par•a•dox (par′ə doks′) /ˈpærəˌdɒks/ *n.* [*count*] **1.** a seemingly contradictory statement that expresses a possible truth. **2.** a person or thing that seems to contain two parts that are opposite or that cannot both be true, but that are true nevertheless: *the paradox of American society, where enough food is grown to feed the world and yet where people still go hungry.* **—par′a•dox′i•cal,** *adj.* **—par′a•dox′i•cal•ly,** *adv.* See -DOX-.

par•af•fin (par′ə fin) /ˈpærəfın/ *n.* [*noncount*] **1.** a colorless, tasteless, odorless, waxy substance, used esp. in candles. **2.** Also called **par′affin oil′.** *Brit.* KEROSENE.

par•a•gon (par′ə gon′, -gən) /ˈpærəˌgɒn, -gən/ *n.* [*count*] a model or pattern of excellence: *a paragon of virtue, who was not capable of committing a crime.*

par•a•graph (par′ə graf′) /ˈpærəˌgræf/ *n.* [*count*] a distinct portion of written matter that deals with a particular idea, usually containing several sentences and beginning with a new line that is usually indented. See -GRAPH-.

Par•a•guay•an (par′ə gwī′ən, -gwā′-) /ˌpærəˈgwayən, -ˈgwey-/ *adj.* **1.** of or relating to Paraguay. **—*n.*** [*count*] **2.** a person born or living in Paraguay.

par•a•keet (par′ə kēt′) /ˈpærəˌkiyt/ *n.* [*count*] a small- to medium-sized parrot having a long tail.

par•a•le•gal (par′ə lē′gəl) /ˌpærəˈliygəl/ *n.* [*count*] an attorney's assistant trained to perform certain legal tasks but not licensed to practice law. See -LEG-.

par•al•lel (par′ə lel′, -ləl) /ˈpærəˌlɛl, -ləl/ *adj., n., v.,* **-leled, -lel•ing** or (*esp. Brit.*) **-lelled, -lel•ling,** *adv.* **—*adj.* 1.** (of two or more items) lined up in the same direction, never meeting or spreading apart: *parallel rows of chairs.* [*be* + ~ + *to*]: *The highway was parallel to the old country road for a few miles.* **2.** having the same direction, tendency, or course: *parallel interests.* **3. a.** of or relating to operations within a computer performed at the same time: *parallel processing.* **b.** relating to or supporting the transfer of electronic data by several bits at a time: *a parallel printer.* **—*n.* 4.** [*count*] a parallel line or plane. **5.** anything parallel or comparable in direction, course, nature, or tendency to something else: [*count*]: *parallels between human sacrifice and the Christian rite of Holy Communion.* [*noncount*]: *a case that has no parallel.* **6.** [*count*] any of the imaginary lines on the earth's surface, parallel to the equator, that mark latitude. **7.** [*noncount*] an arrangement of an electrical circuit in which all positive terminals are connected to one point and all negative ones to another: *batteries arranged in parallel.* **—*v.*** [~ + *obj*] **8.** to provide a parallel for; match; equal: *The rate of inflation paralleled the price of oil.* **9.** to be in a parallel course to: *The road parallels the river.* **—*adv.* 10.** in a parallel course or manner: *The river runs parallel to the main street.* **—par′al•lel•ism,** *n.* [*noncount*]

par•al•lel•o•gram (par′ə lel′ə gram′) /ˌpærəˈlɛləˌgræm/ *n.* [*count*] a four-sided figure having both pairs of opposite sides parallel to each other.

pa•ral•y•sis (pə ral′ə sis) /pəˈræləsıs/ *n., pl.* **-ses** (-sēz′) /-ˌsiyz/. **1.** [*count*] a loss of or reduction in the ability to move or to feel a sensation in a body part, caused by injury to or disease of the brain or spinal cord. **2.** [*noncount*] a state of helpless inability to act: *The department drifted in paralysis until new management took over.* See -LYS-.

par•a•lyt•ic (par′ə lit′ik) /ˌpærəˈlıtık/ *n.* [*count*] **1.** a person suffering from paralysis. **—*adj.* 2.** affected with paralysis; of or relating to paralysis. See -LYS-.

par•a•lyze (par′ə līz′) /ˈpærəˌlayz/ *v.* [~ + *obj*], **-lyzed, -lyz•ing. 1.** to affect with paralysis: *The injury to his spine paralyzed him from the waist down.* **2.** to bring to a condition of helpless inability to act: *The strike paralyzed shipping.* Also, *esp. Brit.,* **par′a•lyse′. —par′a•lyz′er,** *n.* [*count*] **—par′a•lyz′ing•ly,** *adv.* See -LYS-.

par•a•med•ic[1] (par′ə med′ik) /ˌpærəˈmɛdık/ *n.* [*count*] one who is trained to assist a doctor or to give health care in the absence of a doctor.

par•a•med•ic[2] (par′ə med′ik, par′ə med′-) /ˌpærəˈmɛdık, ˈpærəˌmɛd-/ *n.* [*count*] **1.** a medic in the paratroops. **2.** a physician who parachutes into remote areas to give medical care.

pa•ram•e•ter (pə ram′i tər) /pəˈræmıtər/ *n.* [*count*] **1.** Usually, **parameters.** [*plural*] limits or boundaries; guidelines: *Let's try to keep within the parameters of the discussion.* **2.** something that helps one measure or determine how good, useful, worthwhile, etc., something else is; factor: *Stock prices during a recession are a useful parameter for judging long-term success.* See -METER-.

par•a•mil•i•tar•y (par′ə mil′i ter′ē) /ˌpærəˈmılıˌtɛriy/ *adj., n., pl.* **-tar•ies. —*adj.*** [*before a noun*] **1.** of or relating to an organization resembling a regular military force: *paramilitary uniforms worn by the terrorists.* **—*n.*** [*count*] **2.** Also, **par•a•mil•i•ta•rist** (par′ə mil′i tər ist) /ˌpærəˈmılıtərıst/. a person employed in such a force.

par•a•mount (par′ə mount′) /ˈpærəˌmawnt/ *adj.* **1.** chief in importance or effect or impact: *a question of paramount importance.* **2.** above others in rank or authority; superior: *the paramount leader.*

par•a•mour (par′ə mo͝or′) /ˈpærəˌmʊr/ *n.* [*count*] a lover whom one is not supposed to have: *His wife found out about his paramour.* See -AM-.

par•a•noi•a (par′ə noi′ə) /ˌpærəˈnɔyə/ *n.* [*noncount*] **1.** a mental disorder in which the victim believes that actions done by others are hostile to him or her. **2.** too much distrust of others, without reason or cause.

par•a•noid (par′ə noid′) /ˈpærəˌnɔyd/ *adj.* **1.** of or relating to paranoia. **—*n.*** [*count*] **2.** a person suffering from paranoia.

par•a•pet (par′ə pit, -pet′) /ˈpærəpıt, -ˌpɛt/ *n.* [*count*] **1.** a wall or elevation in a fort, esp. one at the outer edge of a rampart. **2.** any low protective wall at the edge of a balcony, roof, etc.

par•a•pher•na•lia (par′ə fər nāl′yə, -fə nāl′-) /ˌpærəfərˈneylyə, -fəˈneyl-/ *n.* **1.** equipment or items necessary for a particular activity: [*plural; used with a plural verb*]: *All the maps and travel paraphernalia were stored in the glove compartment.* [*noncount; used with a singular verb*]: *Is all this paraphernalia necessary to take a simple picture?* **2.** [*plural; used with a plural verb*] personal belongings: *Their paraphernalia were stored in trunks.*

par•a•phrase (par′ə frāz′) /ˈpærəˌfreyz/ *n., v.,* **-phrased, -phras•ing. —*n.* 1.** [*count*] a restatement of a passage giving the meaning in another form, so as to make the meaning clear: *a paraphrase of an English proverb.* **—*v.* 2.** to give the meaning of (something) in a paraphrase: [~ + *obj*]: *If I may paraphrase his polite remarks, they were, quite simply, an order for you to get out.* [*no obj*]: *If I may paraphrase, we should get out of here as fast as possible.*

par•a•ple•gi•a (par′ə plē′jē ə, -jə) /ˌpærəˈpliydʒiyə, -dʒə/ *n.* [*noncount*] paralysis of both legs due to spinal disease or injury. **—par•a•ple•gic** (par′ə plē′jik) /ˌpærəˈpliydʒık/ *adj., n.* [*count*]

par•a•pro•fes•sion•al (par′ə prə fesh′ə nl) /ˌpærəprəˈfɛʃənl̩/ *n.* [*count*] **1.** one trained to assist a doctor, lawyer, teacher, or other professional. **—*adj.*** [*before a noun*] **2.** of or relating to paraprofessionals.

par•a•psy•chol•o•gy (par′ə sī kol′ə jē) /ˌpærəsayˈkɒlədʒiy/ *n.* [*noncount*] the branch of psychology that studies events or abilities that cannot be proved to exist, like clairvoyance and telepathy. **—par′a•psy•chol′o•gist,** *n.* [*count*]

par•a•site (par′ə sīt′) /ˈpærəˌsayt/ *n.* [*count*] **1.** a living being that lives on or within a different plant or animal, from which it obtains nutrients (opposed to *host*). **2.** one who receives support from another without giving anything in return. **—par•a•sit•ic** (par′ə sit′ik) /ˌpærəˈsıtık/ *adj.*

par•a•sol (par′ə sôl′, -sol′) /ˈpærəˌsɔl, -ˌsɒl/ *n.* [*count*] a lightweight umbrella used by women as a sunshade.

par•a•troop•er (par′ə tro͞op′ər) /ˈpærəˌtruwpər/ *n.* [*count*] a member of a military unit who is trained to land in combat areas by parachute.

par•boil (pär′boil′) /ˈpɑrˌbɔyl/ *v.* [~ + *obj*] to boil partially, esp. before further cooking.

par•cel (pär′səl) /ˈpɑrsəl/ *n., v.,* **-celed, -cel•ing** or (*esp. Brit.*) **-celled, -cel•ling,** *adv.* **—*n.*** [*count*] **1.** an object wrapped up to form a small bundle; a package: *stored most of our belongings in parcels.* **2.** a distinct, continuous piece of land: *a parcel in the backwoods.* **—*v.* 3.** to divide into or give out in portions: [~ + *obj*]: *He parceled the land among his three sons.* [~ + *out* + *obj*]: *He parceled out the land among his three sons.* [~ + *obj* + *out*]: *He parceled the land out.*

par′cel post′, *n.* [*noncount*] **1.** (in the U.S. Postal Service) parcels weighing one pound or more, sent at fourth-class rates. **2.** the mail service for delivering such parcels.

parch (pärch) /pɑrtʃ/ *v.* [~ + *obj*] **1.** to make (something) too dry, as heat, sun, and wind do: *The hot sun soon parched the desert.* **2.** to make thirsty: *That hard work in the sun parched us.*

parch•ed (pärcht) /pɑrtʃt/ *adj.* **1.** [*usually: be* + ~] very thirsty: *I was parched after the race and drank a quart of water.* **2.** made completely dry: *the parched desert sand.*

parch•ment (pärch′mənt) /ˈpɑrtʃmənt/ *n.* **1.** [*noncount*] the skin of sheep, goats, etc., prepared so as to be written on: *scrolls of parchment.* **2.** [*count*] something written, as a manuscript, on such material: *ancient parchments with odd symbols on them.* **3.** [*noncount*] a kind of stiff, off-white paper treated so as to be like this material. **4.** [*count*] a diploma.

par•don (pär′dn) /ˈpɑrdn/ *n.* [*count*] **1.** forgiveness for a wrong done to one: *I beg your pardon.* **2.** a legal release from the punishment for an unlawful act, given by a government official: *The president issued him a full and complete pardon.* **—*v.*** [~ + *obj*] **3.** (used without a subject as a polite command) to excuse; forgive: *Pardon me for interfering.* **4.** to release (a person) from the penalty for an unlawful act. **—*interj.* 5.** (used with a rise in the voice at the end, when asking another speaker to repeat something): *Pardon? I didn't quite catch that.* —**par′don•a•ble,** *adj.* —**par′don•er,** *n.* [*count*] —**Syn.** See EXCUSE.

pare (pâr) /pɛər/ *v.* [~ + *obj*], **pared, par•ing. 1.** to cut off or trim the outer coating or layer of, so as to prepare for something: *to pare an apple.* **2.** to reduce or remove by or as if by cutting; diminish or decrease gradually: *to pare (down) expenses.* —**par′er,** *n.* [*count*] See -PARE-[1].

-pare-[1], *root.* *-pare-* comes from Latin, where it has the meaning "prepare." This meaning is found in such words as: APPARATUS, DISPARATE, PARE, PREPARATION, PREPARE, RAMPART, REPAIR, SEPARATE.

-pare-[2], *root.* *-pare-* comes from Latin, where it has the meaning "to bring forth; breed." This meaning is found in such words as: PARENT, PARTURITION, POSTPARTUM.

par•ent (pâr′ənt, par′-) /ˈpɛərənt, ˈpær-/ *n.* [*count*] **1.** a father or a mother: *a parent's concern for his children.* **2.** any living thing that produces another: *The parents of the yellow-white corn must have been yellow and white.* **—*adj.*** [*before a noun*] **3.** of or relating to a living thing that produces another. **4.** of or referring to a corporation that owns controlling interests in lesser companies: *The parent company was a huge conglomerate.* **—*v.*** [~ + *obj*] **5.** to be or act as a parent of. —**par′ent•hood′,** *n.* [*noncount*]: *Parenthood is tough for sixteen-year-old mothers.* See -PARE-[2].

par•ent•age (pâr′ən tij, par′-) /ˈpɛərəntɪdʒ, ˈpær-/ *n.* [*noncount*] descent from parents or ancestors. See -PARE-[2].

pa•ren•tal (pə ren′tl) /pəˈrɛntl/ *adj.* [*before a noun*] of or relating to the parent or parents of a child: *some firm parental discipline; parental guidance.* See -PARE-[2].

paren′tal leave′, *n.* a leave of absence enabling a parent to care for a new baby: [*noncount*]: *parental leave for up to one year.* [*count*]: *That company allows only one parental leave per family.*

pa•ren•the•sis (pə ren′thə sis) /pəˈrɛnθəsɪs/ *n.* [*count*], *pl.* **-ses** (-sēz′) /-ˌsiyz/. **1.** either or both of a pair of signs () used in writing to mark off an extra remark that interrupts, explains, or adds to what was said. **2.** a word or phrase that interrupts, or adds something in this way, signaled in speech by intonation and in writing by commas, parentheses, or dashes, as *Bill Smith—you've met him—is coming tonight.* —**par•en•thet•ic** (par′ən thet′ik) /ˌpærənˈθɛtɪk/ **par′en•thet′i•cal,** *adj.*: *He made a parenthetic(al) remark about how he never made good speeches, then continued with his speech.* See -PAR-, -THES-.

par•ent•ing (pâr′ən ting, par′-) /ˈpɛərəntɪŋ, ˈpær-/ *n.* [*noncount*] the rearing of children by parents. See -PARE-[2].

par ex•cel•lence (pär ek′sə läns′, ek′sə lans′) /ˌpɑr ɛksəˈlɑns, ˈɛksəˌlæns/ *adj.* [*after a noun*] being an example of excellence; superior: *an orator par excellence.*

par•fait (pär fā′) /pɑrˈfey/ *n.* [*count*] **1.** a dessert of layered ice cream, fruit, or syrup and whipped cream. **2.** a frozen dessert of flavored whipped cream or custard.

pa•ri•ah (pə rī′ə) /pəˈrayə/ *n.* [*count*] an outcast; any person that is avoided or is not accepted.

par•ing (pâr′ing) /ˈpɛərɪŋ/ *n.* [*count*] **1.** the act of a person or thing that pares: *a drastic paring of the school budget.* **2.** a piece or part pared off: *apple parings.*

par•ish (par′ish) /ˈpærɪʃ/ *n.* [*count*] **1.** a local church and the area or neighborhood assigned to it. **2.** (in Louisiana) a county.

pa•rish•ion•er (pə rish′ə nər) /pəˈrɪʃənər/ *n.* [*count*] one of the members or inhabitants of a parish.

par•i•ty (par′i tē) /ˈpærɪtiy/ *n.* [*noncount*] **1.** equality, as in status or character: *parity in pay scales.* **2.** equivalent value in the currency of another country. **3.** a system of regulating prices of farm products, usually by means of government price supports, so as to provide farmers with the same purchasing power they had in a specified year. **4.** *Computers.* (of the total number of bits for each byte) the state of being even or odd, used to detect errors in a computer system or in data communications. See -PAR-.

park (pärk) /pɑrk/ *n.* **1.** [*count*] a public area of land having areas or facilities for sports, relaxation, etc. **2.** [*count*] a closed area or a stadium used for sports. **3.** [*count*] a space where automobiles may be stationed: *a car park.* **4.** [*noncount*] a setting in an automatic transmission in which the transmission is in neutral and the brake is locked: *Put the car in park.* **—*v.* 5.** to leave (a vehicle) in a certain place for a period of time: [~ + *obj*]: *He parked the car in a tow-away zone.* [*no obj*]: *You can park over there.* **6.** [~ + *obj*] *Informal.* to put, leave, or settle: *He parked his bulk on the bar stool.*

par•ka (pär′kə) /ˈpɑrkə/ *n.* [*count*], *pl.* **-kas.** a hooded coat made of materials that protect against very cold temperatures.

park′ing me′ter, *n.* [*count*] a mechanical device for receiving and registering payment for the length of time that a vehicle is to occupy a parking space.

Par′kin•son's disease′ (pär′kin sənz) /ˈpɑrkɪnsənz/ *n.* [*noncount*] a disease of the nerves believed to be caused by the breakdown of certain brain cells: *Parkinson's disease involves tremors of the fingers and hands.* Also called **par•kin•son•ism** (pär′kin sə niz′əm) /ˈpɑrkɪnsəˌnɪzəm/.

Par′kinson's law′ (or **Law′**), *n.* [*noncount*] any of various statements about business and office management expressed in a joking way, as if they were laws of physics: *An example of Parkinson's law is the statement that work expands to fill the time allotted for it.*

park•way (pärk′wā′) /ˈpɑrkˌwey/ *n.* [*count*] a wide, broad road with a dividing strip or strips planted with grass, trees, etc.: *All the parkways into the city were jammed.*

par•lance (pär′ləns) /ˈpɑrləns/ *n.* [*noncount*] a manner of speaking: *In legal parlance, the judge is the adjudicator.*

par•lay (pär′lā, -lē) /ˈpɑrley, -liy/ *v.*, **-layed, -lay•ing,** *n.*, *pl.* **-lays. —*v.*** [~ + *obj*] **1.** to gamble (an original amount and its winnings) on a later betting event. **2.** to use (something, as assets) to get a relatively great gain: *to parlay a modest inheritance into a huge fortune.* **—*n.*** [*count*] **3.** a bet of an original sum and its winnings.

par•ley (pär′lē) /ˈpɑrliy/ *n.*, *pl.* **-leys,** *v.*, **-leyed, -ley•ing. —*n.*** [*count*] **1.** a discussion; conference: *a short parley to plan strategy.* **2.** a conference between enemies under a truce. **—*v.*** [*no obj*] **3.** to hold a conference: *They parleyed only three miles from the war zone.*

par•lia•ment (pär′lə mənt; *sometimes* pärl′yə-) /ˈpɑrləmənt; *sometimes* ˈpɑrlyə-/ *n.* **1.** [*Parliament; proper noun*] the national law-making body of Great Britain, made up of the House of Commons and the House of Lords. **2.** [*sometimes: Parliament*] the national law-making body of certain other countries: [*proper noun*]: *He reconvened Parliament.* [*count*]: *Parliaments often seem to be very inefficient governing bodies.*

par•lia•men•tar•i•an (pär′lə men târ′ē ən, -mən-) /ˌpɑrləmɛnˈtɛəriyən, -mən-/ *n.* [*count*] an expert in parliamentary rules and procedures.

par•lia•men•ta•ry (pär′lə men′tə rē, -trē) /ˌpɑrləˈmɛntəriy, -triy/ *adj.* **1.** of or relating to a parliament: *parliamentary maneuvering.* **2.** of or relating to procedures of running a meeting: *parliamentary procedures of nominating, seconding, and making motions.*

par•lor (pär′lər) /ˈpɑrlər/ *n.* [*count*] **1.** a room in a home for receiving visitors: *a front parlor.* **2.** a shop or business establishment: *a funeral parlor; a beauty parlor.* Also, *esp. Brit.,* **parlour.**

Par•me•san (pär′mə zän′, -zan′, -zən; pär′mə zän′, -zan′) /ˈpɑrməˌzɑn, -ˌzæn, -zən; ˌpɑrməˈzɑn, -ˈzæn/ *n.* [*noncount*] [*sometimes: parmesan*] a hard, dry Italian cheese made from skim milk, usually grated. Also called **Par′mesan cheese′.**

par•mi•gia•na (pär′mə zhä′nə, -zhän′, -jä′nə, -jän′) /ˌpɑrməˈʒɑnə, -ˈʒɑn, -ˈdʒɑnə, -ˈdʒɑn/ also **par•mi•gia•no** (-zhä′nō, -jä′-) /-ˈʒɑnow, -ˈdʒɑ-/ *adj.* [*after a noun*] cooked with Parmesan cheese: *veal parmigiana.*

pa•ro•chi•al (pə rō′kē əl) /pəˈrowkiyəl/ *adj.* **1.** of or relating to a parish or parishes. **2.** [*before a noun*] of or relating to parochial schools. **3.** very limited or narrow in viewpoint, opinions, scope, or outlook: *the teacher's parochial attitudes toward foreign students.* —**pa•ro′chi•al•ism,** *n.* [*noncount*] See -PAR-.

paro′chial school′, *n.* a primary or secondary school run by a religious organization: [*noncount*]: *He went to parochial school for eight years.* [*count*]: *Are there any parochial schools in that neighborhood?*

par•o•dy (par′ə dē) /ˈpærədiy/ *n., pl.* **-dies,** *v.,* **-died, -dy•ing.** —*n.* **1.** [*count*] a humorous imitation of a serious piece of literature, intended to make fun of such writing: *a parody of* War and Peace. **2.** [*noncount*] this kind of writing thought of as a style: *the role of parody in modern literature.* **3.** [*count*] any funny imitation, as of a person, show, etc., intended to make fun of its target: *The skit was a parody of a popular TV show.* **4.** [*count*] a poorly done, weak, worthless, or useless imitation of something: *The bill was a parody of an attempt at genuine reform.* —*v.* [~ + *obj*] **5.** to imitate (a piece of literature, an author, etc.) for making fun of something: *to parody horror movies.* **6.** to imitate in a weak or useless way. See -PAR-. —**Syn.** See BURLESQUE.

pa•role (pə rōl′) /pəˈrowl/ *n., v.,* **-roled, -rol•ing,** *adj.* —*n.* [*noncount*] **1.** the release of a person from prison before the end of the sentence imposed, with a promise or condition that no more crimes will be committed: *The prisoner was granted parole but had to report to the authorities every few weeks.* —*v.* [~ + *obj*] **2.** to place or release on parole: *He was paroled but then later caught and convicted for another crime.* —*adj.* [*before a noun*] **3.** of or relating to parole or parolees: *a parole violation.*

pa•rol•ee (pə rō lē′, -rō′lē) /pərowˈliy, -ˈrowliy/ *n.* [*count*], *pl.* **-ees.** one who has been released from prison on parole.

par•ox•ysm (par′ək siz′əm) /ˈpærəkˌsɪzəm/ *n.* [*count*] **1.** any sudden, violent, or uncontrolled outburst, as of action or emotion: *paroxysms of laughter.* **2.** a severe attack, or a sudden increase in the intensity, of a disease.

par•quet (pär kā′) /pɑrˈkey/ *n.* [*noncount*] **1.** a floor made of short strips of wood forming a pattern: *a floor of parquet.* —*v.* [~ + *obj*] **2.** to construct (a floor) in this way.

par•ri•cide (par′ə sīd′) /ˈpærəˌsayd/ *n.* **1.** [*noncount*] the killing of one's father, mother, or other close relative: *guilty of parricide.* **2.** [*count*] a person who commits such an act. —**par•ri•cid•al** (par′ə sīd′l) /ˌpærəˈsaydḷ/ *adj.* See -CIDE-.

par•rot (par′ət) /ˈpærət/ *n.* [*count*] **1.** a noisy, often brightly colored bird, principally of the tropics: *Some parrots can imitate human speech.* **2.** one who, without thought or understanding, repeats the words of another. —*v.* [~ + *obj*] **3.** to repeat without thought or understanding: *The students parroted the answers back.*

par•ry (par′ē) /ˈpæriy/ *v.,* **-ried, -ry•ing,** *n., pl.* **-ries.** —*v.* **1.** to turn aside or push aside (a sword attack, a blow, etc.): [~ + *obj*]: *parried the first attack with a quick move to the side.* [*no obj*]: *As the attacker swung, she parried, then sidestepped his charge.* **2.** to dodge; avoid dealing with: [~ + *obj*]: *The senator parried that embarrassing question by raising a similar issue about his opponent.* [*no obj*]: *The senator could only parry and try to cover up.* —*n.* [*count*] **3.** an act or instance of parrying: *thrust and parry.* —**par′ri•er,** *n.* [*count*]

parse (pärs, pärz) /pɑrs, pɑrz/ *v.* [~ + *obj*], **parsed, pars•ing.** to analyze (a sentence) in terms of its grammatical parts. See -PAR-.

par•si•mo•ni•ous (pär′sə mō′nē əs) /ˌpɑrsəˈmowniyəs/ *adj.* of or relating to parsimony.

par•si•mo•ny (pär′sə mō′nē) /ˈpɑrsəˌmowniy/ *n.* [*noncount*] great or extreme unwillingness to spend money; frugality; stinginess.

pars•ley (pär′slē) /ˈpɑrsliy/ *n.* [*noncount*] an herb from the Mediterranean, used in cooking as flavoring or decoration.

pars•nip (pär′snip) /ˈpɑrsnɪp/ *n.* [*count*] **1.** a plant of the parsley family, grown for its white root, which can be eaten. **2.** the root of this plant.

par•son (pär′sən) /ˈpɑrsən/ *n.* [*count*] a member of the clergy, esp. a Protestant minister; pastor; rector.

par•son•age (pär′sə nij) /ˈpɑrsənɪdʒ/ *n.* [*count*] the house or home provided by a parish for its pastor.

part (pärt) /pɑrt/ *n.* **1.** a separate or distinct portion of a whole; a piece; constituent: [*count*]: *the rear part of the house.* [*noncount*]: *Part of the problem is your lack of organization.* **2.** [*noncount*] an essential, necessary, or basic quality: *A sense of humor is part of a healthy personality.* **3.** [*count*] a portion, piece, or organ of an animal body: *learning the names of body parts in English.* **4.** [*count*] any of a number of quantities or proportions that make up a whole: *Use three parts olive oil and one part wine vinegar.* **5.** [*count*] a portion given out; a share: *This part is mine; you can't have it.* **6.** [*count*] either of the opposing sides in a contest, contract, etc.: *The party of the first part —that's me— promises to pay the party of the second part —that's you— a just and fair price.* **7.** [*count*] the dividing line formed in separating the hair of the head when combing it: *His part was crooked.* **8.** [*count*] a basic piece of a machine or tool, esp. a replacement for the original piece: *harder to get parts for foreign cars.* **9.** [*count*] the written section of a piece of music assigned by the composer or arranger to a single performer or section of the band, orchestra, or chorus: *an interesting trombone part in that jazz piece.* **10.** a section or division of a written work: [*count*]: *a history of the world in six parts.* [*noncount; before a number*]: *Part 1 is very interesting, but Part 2 puts me right to sleep.* **11.** a person's participation, contribution, or concern in something: [*noncount*]: *I had no part in hiring her.* [*count; usually singular*]: *Is there a useful part I can play in her life?* **12.** [*count*] a role in a play or the lines that make up the role: *That actress is fabulous playing the part of Lady Macbeth.* —*v.* **13.** to (cause to) be or become divided into parts; break up: [*noncount*]: *Finally the storm clouds parted and the sun shone through.* [~ + *obj*]: *Moses lifted his staff, and God parted the Red Sea.* **14.** to (cause to) go apart from, or leave one another, as persons: [~ + *obj*]: *till death do us part.* [*no obj*]: *We ought to be able to part as friends.* **15.** to (cause to) break or become torn apart, as a cable: [*no obj*]: *The cable parted, and the tram slid back down the hill.* [~ + *obj*]: *He parted the cable with his knife.* **16.** [~ + *obj*] to comb (the hair) away from a dividing line: *He parted his hair on the right.* **17. part with,** [~ + *with* + *obj*] to give up, hand over, or relinquish: *She couldn't bear to part with her favorite toy.* —*adj.* [*before a noun*] **18.** partial; not total or complete: *part payment.* —*adv.* **19.** in part; partly: *He's part crazy, part mean.* —***Idiom.*** **20. for one's part,** as far as (something) concerns one: *For my part, you can do whatever you please.* **21. in part,** in some measure or degree: *We're losing money — in part because, with our ancient computers, we can't stay competitive.* **22. on the part of,** as done by; by (someone): *too much rowdiness on the part of the class.* **23. part and parcel,** an essential part that must not be ignored: *Unemployment is part and parcel of the bigger problem, a sagging economy.* **24. take part,** [~ (+ *in* + *obj*)] to participate; share or partake: *He refused to take part in the festivities.* **25. take someone's part,** to support or defend someone: *I'll take your part when times get rough.* See -PAR-.

par•take (pär tāk′) /pɑrˈteyk/ *v.* [*no obj*], **-took, -tak•en, -tak•ing. 1.** to take part in something with others: *to partake in a celebration.* **2.** to have a portion: *to partake of a meal.* —**par•tak′er,** *n.* [*count*]

par•tial (pär′shəl) /ˈpɑrʃəl/ *adj.* **1.** being in part only; incomplete: *partial payment.* **2.** biased or prejudiced in favor of one person, etc., over another: *The judge was partial.* See IMPARTIAL. —***Idiom.*** **3. partial to,** [*be* + ~] favoring; especially fond of: *is partial to vanilla ice cream.* —**par•ti•al•i•ty** (pär shē al′i tē) /pɑrʃiyˈælɪtiy/ *n.* [*noncount*]: *showed partiality in hiring his friend's son for the position.* —**par′tial•ly,** *adv.*: *The sun was partially blocked by the clouds.* See -PAR-.

par•tic•i•pant (pär tis′ə pənt) /pɑrˈtɪsəpənt/ *n.* [*count*] a person or group who participates in something: *a willing participant in the crime.* See -CEP-, -PAR-.

par•tic•i•pate (pär tis′ə pāt′) /pɑrˈtɪsəˌpeyt/ *v.* [*no obj*], **-pat•ed, -pat•ing.** to take part or have a share, as with others: *to participate in a conversation.* —**par•tic•i•pa•tion** (pär tis′ə pā′shən) /pɑrˌtɪsəˈpeyʃən/ *n.* [*noncount*]: *active participation in the project.* —**par•tic′i•pa′tive,** *adj.* —**par•tic′i•pa′tor,** *n.* [*count*] See -CEP-, -PAR-.

par•tic•i•pa•to•ry (pär tis′ə pə tôr′ē, -tōr′ē) /pɑrˈtɪsəpəˌtɔriy, -ˌtowriy/ *adj.* [*before a noun*] of or relating to participation: *seeing a participatory democracy at work in the small New England town meetings.* See -CEP-, -PAR-.

par•ti•ci•ple (pär′tə sip′əl, -sə pəl) /ˈpɑrtəˌsɪpəl, -səpəl/ *n.* [*count*] a verbal form that can function as an adjective or be used with auxiliaries to make compound verb forms, as *burning* in *a burning candle* or *running* in *She was running.* In English, participles are the *-ing* or *-ed/ -en* forms of verbs. Compare PAST PARTICIPLE, PRESENT PARTICIPLE. See -CEP-, -PAR-.

par•ti•cle (pär′ti kəl) /ˈpɑrtɪkəl/ *n.* [*count*] **1.** a tiny portion or amount; a very small bit: *a particle of dust.* **2.** one of the extremely small, most basic pieces of matter, as an atom, proton, or quark. **3.** a small, usually unchanging word or affix, often a preposition or conjunction, having a functional or relational significance rather than an intrinsic meaning: *In English the particles include words like* to *when used in forming the infinitive, as in* to go, *or the word following the verb in a phrasal verb, as* up *in* get up. See -PAR-.

par•tic•u•lar (pər tik′yə lər, pə tik′-) /pərˈtɪkyələr, pəˈtɪk-/ *adj.* **1.** [*before a noun*] relating to a single or specific person, thing, group, etc.; not general: *one's particular interests.* **2.** [*before a noun*] considered separately from others; specific; distinct: *a particular item on a list.* **3.** [*before a noun*] greater or stronger than usual; unusual: *Take particular pains with this job.* **4.** [*be* + ~] overly selective; fussy; hard to please: *He is very particular about his food.* **—***n.* [*count*] **5.** an individual or distinct part, as an item in a series: *In at least one particular the lawyer had caught her in a lie.* **6.** Usually, **particulars.** [*plural*] specific points, details, or circumstances: *the particulars of a case.* **—*Idiom.* 7. in particular,** particularly; especially: *Are you doing anything in particular at the moment?* See -PAR-.

par•tic•u•lar•ize (pər tik′yə lə rīz′, pə tik′-) /pərˈtɪkyələˌrayz, pəˈtɪk-/ *v.,* **-ized, -iz•ing. 1.** [~ + *obj*] to state or treat in detail. **2.** [*no obj*] to give details; be specific. **—par•tic•u•lar•i•za•tion** (pər tik′yə lər i zā′shən, pə tik′-) /pərˌtɪkyələrɪˈzeyʃən, pəˌtɪk-/ *n.* [*noncount*] See -PAR-.

par•tic•u•lar•ly (pər tik′yə lər lē, pə tik′-) /pərˈtɪkyələrliy, pəˈtɪk-/ *adv.* **1.** to a special degree; especially: *It was done particularly well.* **2.** specifically; individually: *No one, particularly not the boss, is going to like this presentation.* **3.** in detail. See -PAR-.

part•ing (pär′ting) /ˈpɑrtɪŋ/ *n.* [*noncount*] **1.** a division; separation: *the parting of the Red Sea.* **2.** leave-taking; an occasion of one person leaving another: *the heartbreak of parting from the one she loved.* **—***adj.* **3.** given, taken, or done when leaving another: *a parting glance.* **4.** departing: *parting flights.*

par•ti•san (pär′tə zən, -sən) /ˈpɑrtəzən, -sən/ *n.* [*count*] **1.** a believer in, or follower of, a person or cause, esp. one who shows an unthinking loyalty. **2.** a member of a guerrilla group of soldiers fighting an occupying army: *The partisans were able to escape into the surrounding hills.* **—***adj.* [*before a noun*] **3.** of, relating to, or characteristic of partisans: *partisan bickering over the trade bill.* **—par′ti•san•ship′,** *n.* [*noncount*]: *Partisanship kept the new trade bill from being passed.* See -PAR-.

par•ti•tion (pär tish′ən, pər-) /pɑrˈtɪʃən, pər-/ *n.* **1.** [*noncount*] a division into portions; a separation, as of two or more things: *the partition of the former Communist empire into dozens of independent states.* **2.** [*count*] a wall or barrier within a space, dividing it into separate areas: *A partition in your apartment would provide privacy.* **—***v.* [~ + *obj*] **3.** to divide into parts or portions. **4.** to divide or separate by a partition [~ *(+ off)* + *obj*]: *to partition (off) a dining area.* [~ + *obj (+ off)*]: *to partition the area (off).* **5.** to divide (a territory) into separate political parts: *The defeated country was partitioned and governed by the UN.* **—par•ti′tioned,** *adj.* See -PAR-.

part•ly (pärt′lē) /ˈpɑrtliy/ *adv.* in part; not wholly or completely: *partly made of iron.* See -PAR-.

part•ner (pärt′nər) /ˈpɑrtnər/ *n.* [*count*] **1.** one who is associated with another; an associate: *his partner in crime.* **2.** one of two or more persons who have a business and share in the risks and profits: *My business partners think your company is a good investment.* **3.** a husband, wife, or lover: *If you or your partner is infected with the HIV virus, contact a doctor at once.* **4.** either of two people who dance together, etc.: *an ice-skating partner.* **—part′ner•ship′,** *n.* [*noncount*]: *promises of partnership.* [*count*]: *a partnership in the new company.*

part′ of speech′, *n.* [*count*] a class of words in a language, often based on their meaning, form, or use in a sentence: *In English, some parts of speech are the noun, pronoun, verb, adverb, adjective, preposition, conjunction, and interjection.*

par•tridge (pär′trij) /ˈpɑrtrɪdʒ/ *n.,* [*count*] *pl.* **-tridg•es,** (*esp. when thought of as a group*) **-tridge. 1.** a plump bird of the pheasant family. **2.** a bird resembling the partridge, as the ruffed grouse.

part′-song′, *n.* [*count*] a song with parts for several voices meant to be sung without accompaniment.

part-time (*adj.* pärt′tīm′; *adv.* pärt′tīm′) / *adj.* ˈpɑrtˌtaym; *adv.* ˈpɑrtˈtaym/ *adj.* **1.** working or attending school on less than a full-time schedule: *The number of part-time students has increased.* **2.** relating to such work or study: *part-time employment.* **—***adv.* **3.** on a part-time basis: *was working part-time.* **—part′-tim′er,** *n.* [*count*]

par•tu•ri•tion (pär′to͝o rish′ən, -tyo͝o-, -cho͝o-) /ˌpɑrtʊˈrɪʃən, -tyʊ-, -tʃʊ-/ *n.* [*noncount*] the act or process of bringing forth young; childbirth. See -PARE-[2].

part•way (pärt′wā′, -wā′) /ˈpɑrtˈwey, -ˌwey/ *adv.* **1.** at a part of the way: *I'm already partway home.* **2.** in or to some degree; partially: *The window was partway open.*

par•ty (pär′tē) /ˈpɑrtiy/ *n., pl.* **-ties,** *adj., v.,* **-tied, -ty•ing. —***n.* [*count*] **1.** a social gathering for conversation, refreshments, etc.: *an all-night party at his friend's house.* **2.** a group gathered for some special purpose or task: *a search party.* **3.** a political group seeking political power for directing government policy: *the two main parties in American politics, the Democrats and the Republicans.* **4.** a person or group that participates in some action: *He was a party to the merger deal.* **5.** one of the litigants in a legal proceeding; a plaintiff or defendant. **—***adj.* [*before a noun*] **6.** of or relating to a party or faction; partisan: *party politics.* **7.** of or for a social gathering: *a party dress.* **—***v.* [*no obj*] **8.** to go to or give parties: *On graduation night they partied at as many different houses as they could.* See -PAR-.

par′ty line′, *n.* [*count*] **1.** the declared policies of a group, esp. of the Communist Party, binding on its members and adherents: *was always careful to follow the party line.* **2.** the guiding policy or practices of a political party: *The delegates voted along party lines.* **3.** a telephone line connecting the telephones of a number of different people via one circuit to a central office.

par•ve•nu (pär′və no͞o′, -nyo͞o′, pär′və no͞o′, -nyo͞o′) /ˈpɑrvəˌnuw, -ˌnyuw, ˌpɑrvəˈnuw, -ˈnyuw/ *n., pl.* **-nus,** *adj.* **—***n.* [*count*] **1.** one who has attained wealth or influence, but has not yet gained the acceptance or the social graces associated with it. **—***adj.* [*before a noun*] **2.** characteristic of a parvenu.

pas•cal (pa skal′, pä skäl′) /pæˈskæl, pɑˈskɑl/ *n.* a unit of pressure or stress, equal to one newton per square meter. *Abbr.:* Pa

Pas•cal (pa skal′) /pæˈskæl/ *n.* [*proper noun; no article*] Also, **PASCAL .** a high-level computer language, designed to make structured programming easier.

pas•chal (pas′kəl) /ˈpæskəl/ *adj.* **1.** of or relating to Easter. **2.** of or relating to Passover.

pa•sha (pä′shə, pash′ə, pə shä′, -shô′) /ˈpɑʃə, ˈpæʃə, pəˈʃɑ, -ˈʃɔ/ *n.* [*count*], *pl.* **-shas.** a former title placed after the name of high officials in countries under Turkish rule.

pass (pas) /pæs/ *v.* **1.** to move past; go by: [~ + *obj*]: *to pass a car on the side of the road.* [*no obj*]: *Several cars passed before I realized we were slowing down.* **2.** [*no obj*] to go across or over an entrance, etc.; cross: *The burglar stood in the hallway, then passed into the next room.* **3.** to let something go without taking notice, etc.; disregard: [*no obj*]: *let her offensive remarks pass.* [~ + *obj*]: *Pass chapter two and go on to chapter three.* **4.** to (cause to) allow to go through a barrier, etc.: [~ + *obj*]: *The guard passed the visitor after examining his papers.* [*no obj*]: *"Your papers are in order; you may pass," the guard said.* **5.** [~ + *obj*] to endure or undergo: *passed the worst night of their lives.* **6.** to (cause to) elapse or go through a period of time: [~ + *obj*]: *How did you pass the time in Finland in winter?* [*no obj*]: *Actually, the days passed quickly.* **7.** [*no obj*] to come to an end: *The crisis soon passed.* **8.** [*no obj*] to go away; depart: *The feeling will pass.* **9.** to undergo or complete successfully: [~ + *obj*]: *to pass an examination.* [*no obj*]: *Two students passed, but many more failed.* **10.** [~ + *obj*] to permit (a person) to complete an examination, course, etc., successfully: *The teacher passed all of her students.* **11.** [*no obj*] to be something not very good but still acceptable: *This copy isn't very good, but it will pass.* **12.** [*no obj*] to live or be known as a member of a racial, religious, or ethnic group not one's own. **13.** [~ + *obj*] to convey, transfer, or transmit: *Please pass the salt.* **14.** to (cause to) go or move onward: [~ + *obj*]: *to pass a rope through a hole.* [*no obj*]: *Can the rope pass through this hole?* **15.** [~ + *obj*] to cause to be accepted: *trying to pass a bad check.* **16.** [*no obj*] to be exchanged or conveyed, as between two persons: *Sharp words passed between them.* **17.** to discharge or excrete from the body: [~ + *obj*]: *He passed a kidney stone in his urine.* [*no obj*]: *Don't worry, the kidney stones will pass normally through your urine.* **18.** [~ + *obj*] to approve, esp. by vote: *Congress passed the bill.* **19.** to obtain the approval of: [~ + *obj*]: *The bill passed the Senate.* [*no obj*]: *The bill didn't pass.* **20.** [~ + *obj*] to express, as an opinion: *to pass judgment without knowing the facts.* **21.** to transfer (a ball or puck) to a teammate: [~ + *obj*]: *He passed the ball to his teammate.* [*no obj*]: *He couldn't pass to anyone, so he shot.* **22.** [*no obj; usually:* ~ + *on* + *obj*] to express or pronounce an opinion or judgment: *Will you pass on the authenticity of this drawing?* **23. pass away** or **on,** [*no obj*] to die: *She passed away quietly in her sleep.* **24. pass down,** [~ + *down* + *obj*] to tell or teach (traditions, etc.) to one's descendants; hand down: *passing down important traditions to the next generation.* **25. pass off, a.** to present or sell (something) deceptively or under false pretenses: [~ + *off* + *obj*]: *The used car salesman tried to pass off this cheap car as a more expensive model.* [~ + *obj* + *off*]: *He tried to pass it off as a new model.* **b.** [~ + *oneself* + *off* + *as*] to cause to be accepted under a false identity: *He passed himself off as a doctor.* **26. pass on, a.** [*no obj*] Also, **pass away,** to die. **b.** to give something to someone; tell information to someone: [~ + *obj* + *on*]: *passed the latest gossip on.* [~ + *on* + *obj*]: *Pass on the information to your co-workers.* **27. pass out,** [*no obj*] to faint: *He passed out from all the drinking.* **28. pass over, a.** [~ + *over* + *obj*] to disregard; ignore: *I will pass over the fact that my opponent is a liar.* **b.** to fail to notice or consider; overlook: [~ + *over* + *obj*]: *The company passed over several qualified women and hired a man.* [~ + *obj* + *over*]: *They passed him over for the promotion again.* **29. pass up,** to refuse or neglect to take advantage of, as an opportunity: [~ + *up* + *obj*]: *When he turned down that job offer, he passed up a golden opportunity.* [~ + *obj* + *up*]: *The offer was so good she just couldn't pass it up.* **—*n.*** [*count*] **30.** an act of passing. **31.** a narrow route or way across a low area in a mountain range. **32.** a permission to pass, or enter: *He showed his pass and the guard let him into the building.* **33.** written permission given a soldier to be absent briefly from a station: *He had a three-day pass to Seoul.* **34.** a free ticket or permit: *a pass to get into the show.* **35.** a particular stage or state of affairs: *The situation came to a dreadful pass.* **36.** a single movement, effort, etc.: *The bombers had only enough fuel for one pass at the target.* **37.** a gesture, action, or remark intended to be sexually inviting: *He made several passes at her.* **38.** the transfer of a ball or puck from one teammate to another: *threw a perfect pass to him for the touchdown.* **—*Idiom.* 39. come to pass,** [*It* + ~ + *(that) clause*]: to happen; occur: *It came to pass that a babe was born in a manger.* See -PASS-[1].

-pass-[1], *root.* *-pass-* comes from Latin, where it has the meaning "step; pace." This meaning is found in such words as: BYPASS, COMPASS, ENCOMPASS, IMPASSE, PASS, PASSABLE, PASSAGE, PASSAGEWAY, PASSPORT, SURPASS, TRESPASS, UNDERPASS.

-pass-[2], *root.* *-pass-* comes from Latin, where it has the meaning "suffer; experience." It is related to -PAT-. This meaning is found in such words as: COMPASSION, DISPASSIONATE, IMPASSIONED, IMPASSIVE, PASSION, PASSIVE.

pass•a•ble (pas′ə bəl) /ˈpæsəbəl/ *adj.* **1.** that can be passed, gone or traveled through, or crossed: *The road is barely passable.* **2.** barely acceptable; adequate: *a passable knowledge of Albanian.* **—pass′a•bly,** *adv.* See -PASS-[1].

pas•sage (pas′ij) /ˈpæsɪdʒ/ *n.* **1.** [*count*] a section of a written, spoken, or musical work: *a passage of Scripture.* **2.** [*noncount*] an act or instance of passing from one place, etc., to another: *the passage of motor vehicles.* **3.** [*noncount*] the permission, right, or freedom to pass: *promised safe passage out of his country.* **4.** [*count*] a hall or corridor; passageway. **5.** [*count*] an opening or entrance into, through, or out of something: *the nasal passages.* **6.** [*count; usually singular*] a progress or course, as of events: *the slow passage of time.* **7.** [*noncount*] the process of making a bill into a law: *Passage of the bill into law is by no means assured.* See -PASS-[1].

pas•sage•way (pas′ij wā′) /ˈpæsɪdʒˌwey/ *n.* [*count*] a way that provides passage through, as a corridor or an alley. See -PASS-[1].

pass•book (pas′bŏŏk′) /ˈpæsˌbʊk/ *n.* [*count*] a book held by a depositor in which the bank records deposits and withdrawals. See illustration at BANK.

pas•sé (pa sā′) /pæˈsey/ *adj.* old-fashioned; out-of-date; outmoded. See -PASS-[1].

pas•sen•ger (pas′ən jər) /ˈpæsəndʒər/ *n.* [*count*] a person traveling in an automobile, train, etc., esp. one who is not the operator: *One passenger refused to show his ticket, so the whole train was stopped.* See illustration at TERMINAL. See -PASS-[1].

pass•er•by or **pass•er-by** (pas′ər bī′, -bī′) /ˈpæsərˈbay, -ˌbay/ *n.* [*count*], *pl.* **pass•ers•by** or **pass•ers-by** (pas′ərz bī′, -bī′) /ˈpæsərzˈbay, -ˌbay/. a person passing by: *A group of passers-by formed around the accident victim.* See -PASS-[1].

pas•sim (pas′im) /ˈpæsɪm/ *adv.* (used in bibliographic references, such as indexes or notes) here and there; appearing frequently (in the source cited).

pass•ing (pas′ing) /ˈpæsɪŋ/ *adj.* [*before a noun*] **1.** going past, as in time; elapsing: *Each passing day her love grew stronger.* **2.** brief; not lasting long: *a passing fancy.* **3.** superficial; not detailed: *He made only passing mention of her work.* **4.** indicating satisfactory performance, as in a test: *a passing grade of 45 out of 50.* **—*n.*** [*noncount*] **5.** the act of a person or thing that passes or causes to pass: *the passing of time.* **6.** death: *Her passing will not go unnoticed or be forgotten.* **—*Idiom.* 7. in passing,** by the way; incidentally: *Let me mention, in passing, the marvelous help I received from the police.* **—pass′ing•ly,** *adv.* See -PASS-[1].

pas•sion (pash′ən) /ˈpæʃən/ *n.* **1.** (an instance or an experience of) strong feeling: [*noncount*]: *an actress of strong passion.* [*count*]: *Sometimes his passions got the better of him.* **2.** [*noncount*] (an instance or an experience of) strong feeling of love: *his overwhelming passion for her.* **3.** [*noncount*] (an instance or feeling of) strong sexual desire; lust: *Passion swept through them.* **4.** [*count; usually singular*] a strong fondness or desire for something: *a passion for music.* See -PASS-[2].

pas•sion•ate (pash′ə nit) /ˈpæʃənɪt/ *adj.* **1.** of or relating to passion: *a passionate defense of the rights of the oppressed.* **2.** easily aroused to or influenced by sexual desire: *a passionate lover.* **—pas′sion•ate•ly,** *adv.*: *He believed passionately in his cause.* See -PASS-[2].

pas•sive (pas′iv) /ˈpæsɪv/ *adj.* **1.** not reacting to something expected to produce signs of feeling: *He was passive enough to accept the boss's abuse in front of everyone in the office.* **2.** not acting or participating much; inactive: *a passive member of a committee.* **3.** (opposed to *active*) of, relating to, or being a voice, verb form, or construction that expresses an action that is done to rather than by the subject: *In a passive sentence, the subject undergoes the action of the verb but does not perform it. In the passive sentence* The letter was written last week, *the subject* letter *does not perform the action, but receives the action of writing.* **—*n.*** **4.** [*noncount*] the passive voice. **5.** [*count*] a passive verb form or construction. **—pas′sive•ly,** *adv.*: *He stood there passively accepting the abuse from his partner.* See -PASS-[2].

pas′sive resist′ance, *n.* [*noncount*] the action of resisting a government or laws by not cooperating or by other nonviolent methods.

pas′sive smok′ing, *n.* [*noncount*] the inhaling of the cigarette, cigar, or pipe smoke of others.

pas•siv•i•ty (pa siv′i tē) /pæˈsɪvɪtiy/ *n.* [*noncount*] the state or condition of being passive. See -PASS[2]-.

Pass•o•ver (pas′ō′vər) /ˈpæsˌowvər/ *n.* [*proper noun*] a Jewish festival held in March or April and celebrated for either seven or eight days in memory of the Exodus of the Israelites from Egypt.

pass•port (pas′pôrt, -pōrt) /ˈpæspɔrt, -powrt/ *n.* [*count*] **1.** a document issued by a government to a citizen, establishing his or her identity and right to travel to and return from other countries. **2.** anything that provides admission: *Education is no longer a passport to success.* See -PASS-[2], -PASS-[1], -PORT-.

pass•word (pas′wûrd′) /ˈpæsˌwɜrd/ *n.* [*count*] a secret word or expression used to gain entrance, access to an automatic teller machine, etc. See -PASS[2]-.

past (past) /pæst/ *adj.* **1.** gone by in time: *The bad times are all past now.* **2.** [*before a noun*] of or having occurred during a previous time; bygone: *past glories.* **3.**

[*before a noun*] gone by just before the present time: *during the past year.* **4.** [*after a noun*] ago: *six days past.* **5.** [*before a noun*] having once been; having formerly served as: *three past presidents of the club.* **6.** [*before a noun*] of or relating to a verb tense or form referring to events or states in times gone by: *the irregular past tense of some English verbs, like* go *and* is. **—*n.*** **7.** [*noncount; the* + ~] time gone by: *far back in the distant past.* **8.** [*noncount*] the history of a person, nation, etc.: *our country's glorious past.* **9.** [*noncount; the* + ~] what happened at some earlier time: *Try to learn from the past.* **10.** [*count*] an earlier period of a person's life, career, etc.: *He's got a very interesting past; read this report from the police.* **11.** [*noncount; the* + ~] the past tense. **—*adv.*** **12.** so as to pass by or beyond; by: *The troops marched past.* **—*prep.*** **13.** beyond in time; later than; after: *It's already past noon.* **14.** beyond in space or position; farther on than: *Go to the house just past the church.* **15.** beyond in amount, number, etc.; over: *past the maximum age.* **16.** beyond the reach, influence, or power of: *That patient is past hope of recovery.*

pas•ta (pä′stə) /ˈpɑstə/ *n., pl.* **-tas.** a food made of thin dough in a variety of shapes, as spaghetti or ravioli: [*noncount*]: *a serving of pasta on the side.* [*count*]: *cooks various pastas.*

paste (pāst) /peyst/ *n., v.,* **past•ed, past•ing.** **—*n.*** [*noncount*] **1.** a mixture of flour and water, used for causing material to stick to something: *The kids put paste on the cardboard pieces and stuck them together.* **2.** dough, esp. when prepared with shortening. **3.** a soft mixture of crushed food and a liquid that can be spread on food and eaten: *almond paste.* **4.** any mixture of some powdery substance, as clay, with a liquid: *paste for making pottery.* **—*v.*** [~ + *obj*] **5.** to fasten or stick with paste: *pasted the children's pictures on the wall.* **6.** to cover with something applied by paste. **7.** *Slang.* to hit (a person) hard: *She pasted him one across the mouth.*

paste•board (pāst′bôrd′, -bōrd′) /ˈpeystˈbɔrd, -ˌbowrd/ *n.* [*noncount*] **1.** a stiff board made from sheets of paper pasted together. **—*adj.*** [*before a noun*] **2.** made of pasteboard.

pas•tel (pa stel′) /pæˈstɛl/ *n.* **1.** [*count*] a color having a soft, pale, light shade. **2.** [*noncount*] a dried paste made of coloring matter. **3.** [*count*] a crayon made from such paste. **4.** [*noncount*] the art of drawing with such crayons. **5.** [*count*] a drawing so made. **—*adj.*** [*before a noun*] **6.** having a soft, pale, light color or shade. **7.** drawn with pastels.

pas•teur•ize (pas′chə rīz′) /ˈpæstʃəˌrayz/ *v.* [~ + *obj*], **-ized, -iz•ing.** to heat (a food, as milk, beer, or wine) to a high temperature to destroy bacteria without changing taste or quality. —**pas•teur•i•za•tion** (pas′chə ri zā′shən) /ˌpæstʃərɪˈzeyʃən/ *n.* [*noncount*]

pas•tiche (pa stēsh′, pä-) /pæˈstiyʃ, pɑ-/ *n.* [*count*] **1.** a piece of writing, music, or art that consists of ideas or techniques borrowed from other sources. **2.** a hodgepodge; a patchwork: *Their new proposal is just a pastiche of old ideas thrown together.*

pas•time (pas′tīm′) /ˈpæsˌtaym/ *n.* [*count*] something, as a game, sport, or hobby, that serves to make time pass agreeably: *Baseball used to be the great American pastime.*

past′ mas′ter, *n.* [*count*] a person who is very skilled in a profession or art; expert.

pas•tor (pas′tər) /ˈpæstər/ *n.* [*count*] a minister or priest in charge of a church.

pas•to•ral (pas′tər əl) /ˈpæstərəl/ *adj.* **1.** having the simplicity, peacefulness, etc., associated with rural areas. **2.** relating to the country or to life in the country; rural; rustic. **3.** of or relating to a pastor or the duties of a pastor: *pastoral visits.*

past′ par′ticiple, *n.* [*count*] a verb form, a participle, with past, perfect, or passive meaning, as *fallen, sung,* or *defeated,* used in English and other languages in forming the present perfect, past perfect, and passive, and also as an adjective and a noun: *She has* ***fallen*** *and can't get up. The crook had* ***left*** *before the police arrived. The sheriff was* ***shot*** *trying to rescue the hostage. The* ***fallen*** *rocks blocked the road. He showed no mercy for the* ***crippled*** *and the* ***maimed.***

past′ per′fect, *adj.* **1.** relating to or being a verb tense or form in English made up of *had* followed by the past participle, and indicating **a.** that the action or state expressed by the verb was completed before some other point of reference in the past: *Long before the police arrived (= reference point in the past), the burglar had left the scene of the crime (= the leaving was completed).* **b.** that the action or state expressed by the verb extended up to, or had results continuing up to, some point of reference in the past: *I had never seen anything like it (= from before that time in the past, and up until that time the speaker had not seen such a thing).* **—*n.*** **2.** [*noncount*] the past perfect tense. **3.** [*count*] a form in this tense.

pas•tra•mi (pə strä′mē) /pəˈstrɑmiy/ *n.* [*noncount*] beef left in a mixture of seasonings and smoked before cooking.

pas•try (pā′strē) /ˈpeystriy/ *n., pl.* **-tries.** **1.** a sweet baked food made of dough: [*noncount*]: *Coffee and pastry is all we had for breakfast.* [*count*]: *The bakery sells delicious little pastries; try one.* **2.** [*noncount*] dough used to enclose food: *The pie was delicious, but the pastry was a bit hard and crunchy.*

pas•ture (pas′chər) /ˈpæstʃər/ *n., v.,* **-tured, -tur•ing.** **—*n.*** **1.** Also called **pas′ture•land′** (-land′) /-ˌlænd/. an area of ground covered with grass plants that cattle may eat; grassland: [*noncount*]: *The farm has twenty acres of pasture.* [*count*]: *driving past green pastures and white farmhouses.* **2.** [*noncount*] grass or other plants for feeding livestock. **—*v.*** [~ + *obj*] **3.** to feed (farm animals, etc.) by putting (them) out so that they may eat the grass in a pasture. **—*Idiom.*** **4. put out to pasture,** [*put* + *obj* + *out to pasture*] **a.** to put (cattle) in a pasture so they can eat the grass there: *The farmer put his cows out to pasture.* **b.** to dismiss or retire (someone) as being too old: *Some of these old professors should be put out to pasture.*

past•y (pā′stē) /ˈpeystiy/ *adj.,* **-i•er, -i•est,** *n., pl.* **past•ies.** **—*adj.*** **1.** of or like paste, as in texture or color: *His face had a pasty complexion after that bouncy flight.* **—*n.*** [*count*] **2. pasties,** [*plural*] a pair of small, cuplike coverings for a woman's nipples, used by nude dancers, etc. —**past′i•ness,** *n.* [*noncount*]

pat[1] (pat) /pæt/ *v.,* **pat•ted, pat•ting,** *n.* **—*v.*** [~ + *obj*] **1.** to strike lightly, as with the hand, to flatten, smooth, or shape: *She patted her hair.* **2.** to stroke or tap gently as an expression of affection, pity, etc.: *She patted her dog on the head.* **—*n.*** [*count*] **3.** a light stroke, tap, or blow, as with the hand. **4.** a small piece, usually flat and square, formed by patting, cutting, etc.: *a pat of butter.* **—*Idiom.*** **5. pat on the back, a.** [*count*] praise, congratulations, or encouragement: *She just needed a pat on the back.* **b.** [~ + *obj* + *on the back*] to praise, congratulate, or encourage: *The boss patted him on the back for his fine work.*

pat[2] (pat) /pæt/ *adj.* **1.** exactly to the point or purpose: *a pat solution to the problem.* **2.** unconvincing because it seems to have been rehearsed, practiced, or memorized; shallow: *gave his usual pat answers to difficult questions.* **—*adv.*** **3.** exactly or perfectly: *He had those answers down pat.* **—*Idiom.*** **4. stand pat,** [*no obj*] to cling firmly to one's decision or beliefs: *The boss stood pat and would not budge from his position.*

-pat-, *root.* *-pat-* comes from Latin, where it has the meaning "suffer; experience." It is related to -PASS-[2]. This meaning is found in such words as: COMPATIBLE, IMPATIENCE, IMPATIENT, INCOMPATIBLE, OUTPATIENT, PATIENCE, PATIENT, SIMPATICO.

pat., an abbreviation of: **1.** patent. **2.** patented.

patch (pach) /pætʃ/ *n.* [*count*] **1.** a small piece of material used to repair a tear, cover a hole, or strengthen a weak place. **2.** a piece of material used to cover or protect an injured part, as an eye. **3.** a small piece, scrap, or area of anything: *a patch of ice.* **4.** a small area of land for growing something: *a cabbage patch.* **5.** a cloth emblem worn on one's clothing to identify one's military unit, school, etc. **—*v.*** **6.** [~ + *obj*] to mend or strengthen with or as if with a patch: *He patched the pants with some scraps of denim.* **7.** to repair or restore, esp. in a quick way: [~ + *obj*]: *The army doctor patched wounded soldiers together.* [~ + *obj* + *up*]: *The doctor patched them up.* [~ + *up* + *obj*]: *patching up soldiers so they could be sent out to fight again.* **8.** [~ + *obj*] to make by joining patches together: *to patch a quilt.* **9. patch up,** to settle or smooth over (a quarrel): [~ + *up* + *obj*]: *The husband and wife tried to patch up their differences.* [~ + *obj* + *up*]: *They tried to patch things up.*

patch•work (pach′wûrk′) /ˈpætʃˌwɜrk/ *n.* **1.** [*count*] something made up of pieces that do not go together; mélange: *That speech was a patchwork of unconnected clichés.* **2.** [*noncount*] sewn work made of pieces of material in many different colors or shapes. **—*adj.*** [*before a noun*] **3.** resembling a patchwork: *a patchwork repair job.*

patch•y (pach′ē) /ˈpætʃiy/ *adj.,* **-i•er, -i•est.** **1.** of or relating to patches. **2.** not regular in quality, texture, or distribution: *patchy fog.* —**patch′i•ness,** *n.* [*noncount*]

pate (pāt) /peyt/ *n.* [*count*] the top of the head.

pâ•té (pä tā′, pa-) /pɑ'tey, pæ-/ *n., pl.* **-tés.** a paste made of meat, served as an appetizer: [*noncount*]: *delicious liver paté.* [*count*]: *Different patés were set out on the head table.*

pa•tel•la (pə tel′ə) /pə'tɛlə/ *n.* [*count*], *pl.* **-tel•las, -tel•lae** (-tel′ē) /-'tɛliy/. the bone at the front of the knee; kneecap.

pat•ent (pat′nt; *for 4* pāt′-) /'pætnt; *for 4* 'peyt-/ *n.* **1.** [*count*] the right granted to an inventor to be the only manufacturer or seller of an invention for a specified number of years: *She applied to the government for a patent.* **2.** PATENT LEATHER. —*adj.* **3.** [*before a noun*] protected by a patent; dealing with patents: *patent law.* **4.** easily open to notice; plain to see: *a patent absurdity.* **5.** made of patent leather: *patent shoes.* —*v.* [~ + *obj*] **6.** to obtain a patent on (an invention): *to patent a new invention; to patent her software.*

pat′ent leath′er (pat′nt, pat′n; *esp. Brit.* pāt′nt) /'pætnt, 'pætn̩; *esp. Brit.* 'peytnt/ *n.* [*noncount*] hard, shiny, smooth leather used esp. for shoes and handbags.

pat•ent•ly (pat′nt lē) /'pætntliy/ *adv.* clearly; obviously; openly; plainly: *patently false remarks.*

pa•ter•fa•mil•i•as (pā′tər fə mil′ē əs, pä′-, pat′ər-) /ˌpeytərfə'mɪliyəs, ˌpɑ-, ˌpætər-/ *n.* [*count*] the male head of a household or family, usually the father. See -PATR-.

pa•ter•nal (pə tûr′nl) /pə'tɜrnl̩/ *adj.* **1.** of, relating to, characteristic of, or befitting a father; fatherly: *paternal advice.* **2.** related on the father's side: *his paternal grandfather.* **3.** derived or inherited from a father. —**pa•ter′nal•ly,** *adv.* See -PATR-.

pa•ter•nal•ism (pə tûr′nl iz′əm) /pə'tɜrnl̩ˌɪzəm/ *n.* [*noncount*] the principle or practice of managing or governing workers, citizens, individuals, etc., in the manner of a father dealing with his children. —**pa•ter•nal•is•tic** (pə-tûr′nl is′tik) /pəˌtɜrnl̩'ɪstɪk/ *adj.*: *a paternalistic manner of governing, doling out favors the way a father would.* See -PATR-.

pa•ter•ni•ty (pə tûr′ni tē) /pə'tɜrnɪtiy/ *n.* [*noncount*] **1.** the state of being a father; fatherhood. **2.** origin or descent from a father. —*adj.* [*before a noun*] **3.** of or relating to a legal dispute in which a woman accuses a man of having fathered her child: *a paternity suit.* See -PATR-.

path (path) /pæθ/ *n.* [*count*], *pl.* **paths** (pat͟hz, paths). **1.** a way or small passage on the ground beaten by human or animal feet: *a path through the woods.* **2.** a narrow walk or way: *a bicycle path.* **3.** a route, course, or track along which something moves: *the path of a hurricane.* **4.** a course or direction of action, conduct, or procedure: *What path should we follow in hiring a new secretary?* **5.** (in computer operating systems) a listing of the route through directories that locates and names a certain file or program on a disk drive.

-path-, *root.* *-path-* comes from Greek, where it has the meaning "suffering; disease; feeling." This meaning is found in such words as: ANTIPATHY, APATHETIC, APATHY, EMPATHY, HOMEOPATHY, PATHETIC, PATHOLOGY, PATHOS, PSYCHOPATH, SYMPATHETIC, SYMPATHIZE, SYMPATHY, TELEPATHY.

pa•thet•ic (pə thet′ik) /pə'θɛtɪk/ *adj.* **1.** causing or evoking pity, either through concern, compassion, or contempt; pitiful; pitiable: *The sick, homeless man was a pathetic sight.* **2.** sad; sorrowful; mournful: *a pathetic tone of voice.* —**pa•thet′i•cal•ly,** *adv.* See -PATH-.

path•find•er (path′fīn′dər) /'pæθˌfayndər/ *n.* [*count*] one who finds a way, esp. through a wilderness or an unexplored area. —**path′find′ing,** *n.* [*noncount*], *adj.*

path•o•gen (path′ə jən, -jen′) /'pæθədʒən, -ˌdʒɛn/ *n.* [*count*] any disease-producing agent, esp. a microorganism. —**path′o•gen′ic,** *adj.* See -PATH-, -GEN-.

pa•thol•o•gy (pə thol′ə jē) /pə'θɒlədʒiy/ *n., pl.* **-gies. 1.** [*noncount*] the study of diseases. **2.** [*count*] any condition that is not healthy or normal. —**path•o•log•i•cal** (path′ə loj′i kəl) /ˌpæθə'lɒdʒɪkəl/ *adj.*: *a pathological liar.* —**pa•thol′o•gist,** *n.* [*count*] See -PATH-.

pa•thos (pā′thos, -thōs, -thôs) /'peyθɒs, -θows, -θɔs/ *n.* [*noncount*] the quality or power in life or art of causing a feeling of pity or compassion. See -PATH-.

path•way (path′wā′) /'pæθˌwey/ *n.* [*count*] a path, course, route, or way.

pa•tience (pā′shəns) /'peyʃəns/ *n.* [*noncount*] **1.** the ability to control one's feelings in spite of misfortune or pain, without complaining: *has the patience of Job.* **2.** an ability or willingness to suppress feelings of annoyance when faced with delay: *The airline said it appreciated our patience in waiting for our flight.* **3.** the ability to work quietly and steadily; diligence. See -PAT-.

pa•tient (pā′shənt) /'peyʃənt/ *n.* [*count*] **1.** one under medical care or treatment: *The patients in this ward all have cancer.* See illustration at HOSPITAL. —*adj.* **2.** able to control one's feelings in spite of annoyance, misfortune, etc., without complaining. **3.** continuing to work steadily; diligent; steady. —**pa′tient•ly,** *adv.*: *The dog sat patiently.* See -PAT-. —**Related Words.** PATIENT is an adjective and a noun, PATIENTLY is an adverb, PATIENCE is a noun: *Be patient with the baby. That doctor has many patients. That teacher treats his class patiently. Don't lose your patience with the baby.*

pat•i•na (pat′n ə, pə tē′nə) /'pætn̩ə, pə'tiynə/ *n.* [*count*], *pl.* **-nas. 1.** a film or coating, usually green, on the surface of something, esp. old bronze. **2.** an aura surrounding something, esp. one associated with antiquity or beauty or history.

pat•i•o (pat′ē ō′) /'pætiyˌow/ *n.* [*count*], *pl.* **-i•os. 1.** a paved area, connected to a house and used for outdoor lounging, etc.: *a barbecue on the patio.* **2.** a courtyard, esp. of a house, enclosed by low buildings or walls.

pat•ois (pat′wä, pä′twä, pa twä′) /'pætwɑ, 'pɑtwɑ, pæ'twɑ/ *n.* [*count*], *pl.* **pat•ois** (pat′wäz, pä′twäz, pa-twäz′) /'pætwɑz, 'pɑtwɑz, pæ'twɑz/. a form of a language distinctive to and spoken in a given area, differing from the standard, literary form of the language.

pat. pend., an abbreviation of: patent pending.

-patr-, *root.* *-patr-* comes from Latin, where it has the meaning "father." This meaning is found in such words as: COMPATRIOT, EXPATRIATE, PATERFAMILIAS, PATERNAL, PATERNITY, PATRICIAN, PATRICIDE, PATRON.

pa•tri•arch (pā′trē ärk′) /'peytriyˌɑrk/ *n.* [*count*] **1.** the male head of a family or tribal line. **2.** one regarded as the father or founder of an order, class, etc. **3.** a bishop of an Eastern Orthodox church. **4.** a respected old man: *a patriarch of the village.* —**pa′tri•ar′chal,** *adj.* See -PATR-, -ARCH-.

pa•tri•arch•y (pā′trē är′kē) /'peytriyˌɑrkiy/ *n., pl.* **-arch•ies. 1. a.** [*noncount*] a form of social organization in which the father is the head of the family, clan, or tribe and descent is established through the male line. **b.** [*count*] a society based on this social organization. **2. a.** [*noncount*] the principles or philosophy upon which control by male authority is based. **b.** [*count*] an institution or organization in which power is held by and transferred through males. See -PATR-.

pa•tri•cian (pə trish′ən) /pə'trɪʃən/ *n.* [*count*] **1.** a person of noble or high rank; aristocrat. **2.** a person of culture, education, and refinement. —*adj.* **3.** of high social rank or noble family; aristocratic. See -PATR-.

pat•ri•cide (pa′trə sīd′, pā′-) /'pætrəˌsayd, 'pey-/ *n.* **1.** the act of killing one's own father: [*noncount*]: *The hero of the tragedy* Oedipus *is guilty of patricide.* [*count*]: *an increase in the number of patricides.* **2.** [*count*] a person who commits such an act. See -PATR-, -CIDE-.

pat•ri•mo•ny (pa′trə mō′nē) /'pætrəˌmowniy/ *n.* [*count*], *pl.* **-nies.** an estate or possessions inherited from one's father or ancestors. —**pat′ri•mo′ni•al,** *adj.* See -PATR-.

pa•tri•ot (pā′trē ət, -ot′) /'peytriyət, -ˌɒt/ *n.* [*count*] one who loves and defends his or her country: *Is someone who disagrees with one's government any less a patriot?* —**pa′tri•ot′ic,** *adj.* —**pa′tri•ot′ic•al•ly,** *adv.* —**pa′tri•ot•ism,** *n.* [*noncount*] See -PATR-.

pa•trol (pə trōl′) /pə'trowl/ *v.,* **-trolled, -trol•ling,** *n.* —*v.* **1.** (of a police officer, etc.) to pass regularly along (a route) or through (an area) to maintain order and security: [~ + *obj*]: *patrolling the downtown area.* [*no obj*]: *When they are out patrolling they need a partner for back-up.* —*n.* **2.** [*count*] a person or group that patrols. **3.** [*noncount*] the act of patrolling: *The cops were out on patrol.*

patrol′ car′, *n.* SQUAD CAR.

pa•trol•man or **-wom•an** (pə trōl′mən) or (-wo͝om′ən) /pə'trowlmən/ or /-ˌwʊmən/ *n.* [*count*], *pl.* **-men** or **-wom•en.** a police officer assigned to patrol.

pa•tron (pā′trən) /'peytrən/ *n.* [*count*] **1.** one who is a customer, esp. a regular one, of a store, etc.: *Patrons must leave the hotel by 3:00 p.m.* **2.** one who supports an artist, charity, etc., with money, etc.: *a patron of the arts.* See -PATR-.

pa•tron•age (pā′trə nij, pa′-) /'peytrənɪdʒ, 'pæ-/ *n.* [*noncount*] **1.** the financial support or business provided to a store, hotel, etc., by customers or paying guests: *The management thanks you for your patronage.* **2. a.** the power of public officials to appoint their supporters, etc., to government jobs or to grant them favors. **b.** the jobs or favors so given. **3.** the support a patron gives to an artist, a charity, etc. See -PATR-.

pa•tron•ize (pā′trə nīz′, pa′-) /ˈpeytrəˌnayz, ˈpæ-/ *v.* [~ + *obj*], **-ized, -iz•ing. 1.** to give (a store, hotel, etc.) one's regular business: *He patronizes the same coffee shop daily.* **2.** to behave in an arrogant, proud, or condescending manner toward: *"Stop patronizing me," she complained to her boss.* **3.** to act as a patron toward (an artist, etc.); support. —**pa′tron•iz′er,** *n.* [*count*] See -PATR-.

pa•tron•iz•ing (pā′trə nī′zing, pa′-) /ˈpeytrəˌnayzɪŋ, ˈpæ-/ *adj.* behaving in an arrogant, proud, or condescending manner toward someone. See -PATR-.

pa′tron saint′, *n.* [*count*] a saint who is the guardian of a person, group, etc. See -PATR-.

pat•ro•nym•ic (pa′trə nim′ik) /ˌpætrəˈnɪmɪk/ *n.* [*count*] **1.** a name formed from the name of a father or ancestor, esp. by the addition of a suffix or prefix indicating descent, as *Stevenson* (son of *Steven*); *Browning* (son of *Brown*); or *Macdonald* (son of *Donald*). —*adj.* [*before a noun*] **2.** (of a family name) formed from the name of a father or ancestor. **3.** (of a suffix or prefix) indicating descent from a father or ancestor. —**pat′ro•nym′i•cal•ly,** *adv.* See -PATR-, -ONYM-.

pat•sy (pat′sē) /ˈpætsiy/ *n.* [*count*], *pl.* **-sies.** *Slang.* **1.** one who is easily fooled or lets himself be badly treated. **2.** a person who takes the blame for something; fall guy.

pat•ter¹ (pat′ər) /ˈpætər/ *v.* [*no obj*] **1.** to make a sound of many quick, light taps: *The rain pattered on the tin roof.* **2.** to walk somewhere in tiny, quick, light steps: *The child's feet pattered down the hall.* —*n.* [*count*] **3.** a rapid series of light tapping sounds.

pat•ter² (pat′ər) /ˈpætər/ *n.* [*noncount*] rapid talk used to attract attention, etc.: *the patter of the auctioneer.*

pat•tern (pat′ərn) /ˈpætərn/ *n.* [*count*] **1.** a decorative design, as for wallpaper, made up of elements in a regular arrangement: *children's wallpaper with a pattern of rainbows.* **2.** a recognizable combination of actions, qualities, etc., characteristic of a particular person or population: *the behavior patterns of teenagers.* **3.** an original used as a guide: *The U.S. Constitution has been a pattern for many newly independent countries.* **4.** anything designed to serve as a model or guide: *a pattern for the dress.* —*v.* [~ + *obj*] **5.** to make, put together, or design (something) according to a pattern: *He patterned his writing on his favorite author.*

pat•ty (pat′ē) /ˈpætiy/ *n.* [*count*], *pl.* **-ties. 1.** a thin, round piece of ground-up food, as of meat: *hamburger patties on the grill.* **2.** a little pie; pastry.

pau•ci•ty (pô′si tē) /ˈpɔsɪtiy/ *n.* [*noncount*] smallness of quantity; scarcity; scantiness: *a paucity of funds.*

paunch (pônch, pänch) /pɔntʃ, pɑntʃ/ *n.* [*count*] **1.** a large belly, or one that sticks out; a potbelly. **2.** the belly or abdomen. —**paunch′y,** *adj.,* **-i•er, -i•est.**: *getting paunchy from lack of exercise.*

pau•per (pô′pər) /ˈpɔpər/ *n.* [*count*] a person without any means of support; a poor person. —**pau′per•ism,** *n.* [*noncount*]

pause (pôz) /pɔz/ *n., v.,* **paused, paus•ing.** —*n.* [*count*] **1.** a temporary stop or rest: *After a brief pause, he resumed his speech.* —*v.* [*no obj*] **2.** to make a brief stop or delay: *The pilot paused, then dove toward the target.* —***Idiom.*** **3. give pause,** to cause to hesitate or reconsider, as from surprise or doubt: [*give + obj + pause*]: *The presence of the bodyguards and their two machine guns gave him pause.* [~ + *pause* + *to* + *obj*]: *The bitter cold gave pause to even the most curious onlooker.*

pave (pāv) /peyv/ *v.* [~ + *obj*], **paved, pav•ing. 1.** to cover or lay (a road, etc.) with concrete, stones, etc., to make a firm, level surface: *They always seem to pave the roads in hot weather.* —***Idiom.*** **2. pave the way for,** [~ + *obj*] to prepare the way for; make possible: *The negotiations should pave the way for more business for us.*

pave•ment (pāv′mənt) /ˈpeyvmənt/ *n.* **1.** [*count*] a paved road, highway, etc. **2.** [*noncount*] a paved surface or floor: *streets with cracked and broken pavement.*

pa•vil•ion (pə vil′yən) /pəˈvɪlyən/ *n.* [*count*] **1.** a light, usually open building, used for concerts, etc. **2.** any of a number of buildings forming a hospital or the like. **3.** a tent, esp. a large and elaborate one.

pav•ing (pā′ving) /ˈpeyvɪŋ/ *n.* [*noncount*] **1.** a pavement. **2.** material for paving.

paw (pô) /pɔ/ *n.* [*count*] **1.** the foot of an animal that has claws or nails: *The dog held up its sore paw.* **2.** *Informal.* the human hand, esp. one that is large, rough, or clumsy: *"Keep your paws off me!" she screamed at him.* —*v.* **3.** to strike or scrape with the paws or feet: [~ + *obj*]: *The cat pawed the door.* [~ + *at* + *obj*]: *The cat pawed at the door, trying to get in.* **4.** [~ + *obj*] to handle (someone) clumsily, rudely, or without permission; grope: *She testified that he first pawed her, then tried to rip off her clothes.*

pawn¹ (pôn) /pɔn/ *v.* [~ + *obj*] to deposit (something valuable) as security, as for money borrowed, esp. with a pawnbroker: *He pawned his watch to raise the money.*

pawn² (pôn) /pɔn/ *n.* [*count*] **1.** one of eight chess pieces of one color and of the lowest value. **2.** one used to further another person's purposes: *an unwitting pawn in the power game.*

pawn•bro•ker (pôn′brō′kər) /ˈpɔnˌbrowkər/ *n.* [*count*] one whose business is lending money at interest on personal property deposited with the lender until claimed later. —**pawn′bro′king, pawn′bro′ker•age,** *n.* [*noncount*]

pawn•shop (pôn′shop′) /ˈpɔnˌʃɒp/ *n.* [*count*] the shop of a pawnbroker.

paw•paw or **pa•paw** (pô′pô′, pə pô′) /ˈpɔˌpɔ, pəˈpɔ/ *n.* **1.** [*count*] a tree of the eastern U.S., having large, oblong leaves and purplish flowers. **2.** [*noncount*] the fleshy fruit of this tree, which can be eaten. **3.** PAPAYA.

pay (pā) /pey/ *v.,* **paid** or **payed, pay•ing,** *n., adj.* —*v.* **1.** to settle (a debt, etc.) by handing over money or goods, or by doing something: [~ + *obj*]: *He paid the bill promptly.* [*no obj*]: *Can I pay by credit card?* **2.** to give over (money) (to someone) in exchange for something: [~ + *obj*]: *She paid him for the yard work.* [~ + *obj* + *obj*]: *She paid him fifty dollars for the yard work.* [~ + *obj* + *to* + *verb*]: *She paid him to clean up the yard.* [~ + *obj* + *obj* + *to* + *verb*]: *She paid him fifty dollars to clean up the yard.* [*no obj*]: *Teaching pays poorly.* **3.** [*not: be* + ~ *-ing*] to be worthwhile (to): [*no obj*]: *Crime does not pay.* [*It* + ~ + *to* + *verb*]: *Sometimes it pays to be courteous.* **4.** [~ + *obj*] to give back or yield as a return: *The stock paid six percent last year.* **5.** to give (attention, etc.), when it is proper to do so: [~ + *obj*]: *At the funeral I paid my respects and left.* [~ + *obj* + *to* + *obj*]: *The class was not paying attention to the teacher.* [~ + *obj* + *obj*]: *She paid him a nice compliment.* **6.** to make (a call, etc.): [~ + *obj* + *to* + *obj*]: *I paid a visit to the widow's house.* [~ + *obj* + *obj*]: *She paid us a visit but then wouldn't leave.* **7.** to suffer in punishment; undergo: [~ + *obj*]: *to pay the penalty for his crimes.* [*no obj*]: *I'll make him pay for his treachery.* **8. pay back, a.** to repay or return: [~ + *back* + *obj*]: *He paid back every cent he owed.* [~ + *obj* + *back*]: *I lent him money but he hasn't paid me back.* [~ + *obj* + *back* + *obj*]: *He paid me back the money he owed.* **b.** [~ + *obj* + *back*] to take action against another in return for some hurt or offense; punish: *She paid him back for cheating on her by finding a new boyfriend.* **9. pay off, a.** to pay (someone) everything due that person, esp. wages: [~ + *obj* + *off*]: *The company paid him off and he left.* [~ + *off* + *obj*]: *The company paid off as many workers as it could before bankruptcy.* **b.** to pay (a debt) in full: [~ + *off* + *obj*]: *He paid off the debt.* [~ + *obj* + *off*]: *He paid the debt off.* **c.** *Informal.* to bribe: [~ + *obj* + *off*]: *When the guard asks for your papers, see if you can pay him off.* [~ + *off* + *obj*]: *to pay off the border guard.* **d.** [*no obj*] to result in success: *That last move just didn't pay off.* **10. pay out, a.** to distribute (money, etc.); disburse: [~ + *out* + *obj*]: *The insurance companies are paying out a lot of money to settle their claims.* [~ + *obj* + *out*]: *They paid the money out in small amounts.* **b.** to let out (a rope) by slackening: [~ + *out* + *obj*]: *paid out a few more yards of rope.* [~ + *obj* + *out*]: *had only paid a yard or two out when the rope tightened.* **11. pay up,** [*no obj*] to pay fully: *I won the bet; pay up!* —*n.* [*noncount*] **12.** the act of paying or being paid; payment: *They'll do anything for pay.* **13.** wages or salary paid for work: *The pay isn't so good.* —*adj.* **14.** operated by depositing coins: *a pay phone.* **15.** relating to or requiring payment. —***Idiom.*** **16. pay through the nose,** to pay a price that is much too high: *They wound up paying through the nose for that car.* —**pay′er,** *n.* [*count*]

pay•a•ble (pā′ə bəl) /ˈpeyəbəl/ *adj.* [*be* + ~] that should or must be paid; due: *The dentist's bill is payable on the first of the month.*

pay′ dirt′, *n.* [*noncount*] **1.** soil, gravel, or ore that can be mined at a profit. **2.** *Informal.* any source of success or wealth: *to hit pay dirt.*

pay•ee (pā ē′) /peyˈiy/ *n.* [*count*], *pl.* **-ees.** one to whom money is paid: *Endorse the check by signing it over to the payee.*

pay•load (pā′lōd′) /ˈpeyˌlowd/ *n.* [*count*] **1.** the part of a cargo that produces income, usually expressed in weight.

2. the bomb load, warhead, cargo, or passengers of an aircraft, rocket, missile, etc.

pay•mas•ter (pā′mas′tər) /ˈpeyˌmæstər/ *n.* [*count*] one whose job in a company, etc., is to pay out wages.

pay•ment (pā′mənt) /ˈpeymənt/ *n.* **1.** [*count*] something paid; an amount paid: *payments of several million dollars.* **2.** [*noncount*] the act of paying.

pay•off (pā′ôf′, -of′) /ˈpeyˌɔf, -ˌɒf/ *n.* [*count*] **1.** [*usually singular*] the payment of a salary, debt, etc.; the time at which such payment is made. **2.** *Informal.* the outcome of a series of events; climax. **3.** a settlement, as in punishment or reward. **4.** *Informal.* BRIBE: *payoffs to investors and contractors.*

pay′ phone′, *n.* [*count*] a public telephone requiring that the caller deposit coins to pay for a call.

pay•roll (pā′rōl′) /ˈpeyˌrowl/ *n.* [*count*] **1.** a list of employees to be paid, with the amount owed to each. **2.** [*usually singular*] the sum total of these amounts.

PC or **P.C.,** an abbreviation of: **1.** Peace Corps. **2.** *pl.* **PCs** or **PC's** or **P.C.'s.** personal computer. **3.** *Brit.* Police Constable. **4.** political correctness; politically correct.

PCB, *n.* [*count*], *pl.* **PCB's, PCBs.** a highly poisonous compound, formerly used in industry.

pct., an abbreviation of: percent.

pd., an abbreviation of: paid.

pea (pē) /piy/ *n., pl.* **peas,** *adj.* **—***n.* [*count*] **1.** the round, edible seed of a widely grown plant of the legume family: *peas and carrots as a side dish.* **2.** the plant itself. **3.** any of different but similar plants or their seed, as the chickpea. **—***adj.* **4.** [*before a noun*] of or relating to peas: *pea soup.*

peace (pēs) /piys/ *n.* **1.** [*noncount*] freedom from war; absence of fighting between nations. **2.** [*noncount*] a state of harmony between people: *Why can't we just live in peace?* **3.** [*noncount*] freedom from civil commotion; public order and security: *The police keep the peace.* **4.** [*noncount*] freedom from anxiety or annoyance: *peace of mind.* **5.** [*noncount*] a state of tranquillity or serenity: *a feeling of peace after prayer.* **6.** [*noncount*] silence; stillness: *some peace and quiet in the countryside.* **7.** [*count*] a treaty that ends a war or fighting: *an honorable peace.* **—*Idiom.*** **8. at peace,** [*be* + ~] **a.** in a state of not fighting; not at war: *a nation once again at peace.* **b.** untroubled; peaceful; tranquil. **c.** having died; deceased. **9. hold** or **keep one's peace,** to keep from, or stop, speaking; keep silent: *He kept his peace and waited for me to speak first.* **10. make one's peace with,** [~ + *obj*] to stop arguing with (someone): *She had made her peace with him years ago.* **11. make peace,** to arrange an end of fighting or antagonism.

peace•a•ble (pē′sə bəl) /ˈpiysəbəl/ *adj.* willing to avoid fighting or quarreling.

peace•ful (pēs′fəl) /ˈpiysfəl/ *adj.* **1.** free from war or fighting: *a peaceful decade.* **2.** peaceable; not willing or eager to fight: *a peaceful man.* —**peace′ful•ly,** *adv.*

peace•mak•er (pēs′mā′kər) /ˈpiysˌmeykər/ *n.* [*count*] a person, group, or nation that tries to make peace. —**peace′mak′ing,** *n.* [*noncount*], *adj.*

peace•time (pēs′tīm′) /ˈpiysˌtaym/ *n.* [*noncount*] a period of freedom from war: *During peacetime he flew commercial airliners.*

peach (pēch), *n.* **1.** the round, pink-to-yellow, fuzzy-skinned fruit of a tree of the rose family: [*count*]: *a couple of peaches.* [*noncount*]: *pies with fillings of peach or pear.* **2.** [*count*] the tree itself. **3.** [*count*] *Informal.* a person or thing that is attractive and liked.

pea•cock (pē′kok′) /ˈpiyˌkɒk/ *n.* [*count*], *pl.* **-cocks,** (*esp. when thought of as a group*) **-cock. 1.** a male bird known for its long, erect, bright, shining tail feathers that are marked with eyelike spots and can be spread in a fan. **2.** one too interested in his or her appearance.

pea′ jack′et, *n.* [*count*] a short, double-breasted coat of navy-blue wool, originally worn by seamen. Also called **pea•coat** (pē′kōt′) /ˈpiyˌkowt/.

peak (pēk) /piyk/ *n.* [*count*] **1.** the pointed top of a mountain or ridge. **2.** a mountain with a pointed top. **3.** the pointed top of anything. **4.** the most important level; the maximum point or volume of anything: *at the peak of her career.* **5.** the front piece of a cap that sticks out over the eyes. **—***v.* [*no obj*] **6.** to stick out or forward in a peak. **7.** to reach a peak of activity, development, etc.: *His popularity peaked after the convention.* **—***adj.* [*before a noun*] **8.** attaining the highest level, point, etc.: *peak performance.* **9.** of or being the time when traffic, use, or demand is greatest and charges, etc., are highest: *during the peak travel season.*

peak•ed (pē′kid) /ˈpiykɪd/ *adj.* pale and tired-looking.

peal (pēl) /piyl/ *n.* [*count*] **1.** a loud, long ringing of bells. **2.** any loud, long sound or series of sounds, as of thunder or laughter: *peals of laughter.* **—***v.* **3.** to (cause to) make a loud, ringing sound: [*no obj*]: *The church bells pealed after the news of the peace treaty.* [~ + *obj*]: *They pealed the church bells joyously.*

pea•nut (pē′nut′, -nət) /ˈpiyˌnʌt, -nət/ *n.* [*count*] **1.** the pod or nut of a plant of the legume family. **2.** the plant itself. **3.** any small or insignificant person or thing. **4. peanuts,** [*plural*] *Informal.* a very small amount of money: *got peanuts for our old car.*

pea′nut but′ter, *n.* [*noncount*] a paste made from ground, roasted peanuts: *a sandwich of peanut butter and jelly.*

pear (pâr) /pɛər/ *n.* **1.** the rounded fruit of a tree of the rose family: [*count*]: *Pears were fifty cents each.* [*noncount*]: *a filling of pear and peach in the pie.* **2.** [*count*] the tree itself.

pearl (pûrl) /pɜrl/ *n.* **1.** [*count*] a smooth, rounded bead, formed within the shells of oysters, valued as a gem. **2.** [*count*] something resembling this, as in costume jewelry. **3.** [*count*] something precious or choice: *pearls of wisdom.* **4.** [*noncount*] a pale gray, often with a bluish tinge. **5.** MOTHER-OF-PEARL. **—***adj.* [*before a noun*] **6.** of or resembling a pearl. —**pearl′y,** *adj.,* **-i•er, -i•est.**

peas•ant (pez′ənt) /ˈpɛzənt/ *n.* [*count*] **1.** a member of a class of small farmers of low social rank, as in Europe: *tried to unify the workers and peasants.* **2.** an uneducated person lacking in good manners. **—***adj.* [*before a noun*] **3.** of or relating to peasants.

peas•ant•ry (pez′ən trē) /ˈpɛzəntriy/ *n.* [*noncount*] peasants thought of as a group: *The peasantry is afraid to go against the dictator's policies.*

peat (pēt) /piyt/ *n.* [*noncount*] **1.** material found in marshy regions, made of partially decayed vegetable matter. **2.** such vegetable matter used as fertilizer or fuel.

peat′ moss′, *n.* [*noncount*] **1.** any moss from which peat may form. **2.** such moss when dried, used chiefly as a place where seeds may be planted.

peb•ble (peb′əl) /ˈpɛbəl/ *n.* [*count*] a small, rounded stone, esp. one worn down by the action of water. —**peb′bly,** *adj.,* **-bli•er, -bli•est.**

pe•can (pi kän′, -kan′, pē′kan) /pɪˈkɑn, -ˈkæn, ˈpiykæn/ *n.* [*count*] **1.** a tall hickory tree of the southern U.S. and Mexico, grown for its smooth-shelled, edible nuts. **2.** a nut of this tree.

pec•ca•dil•lo (pek′ə dil′ō) /ˌpɛkəˈdɪlow/ *n.* [*count*], *pl.* **-loes, -los.** a minor or slight fault or offense.

peck[1] (pek) /pɛk/ *n.* [*count*] **1.** a unit of measurement for dry goods, equal to 8 quarts; the fourth part of a bushel, equal to 537.6 cubic inches (8.81 liters). **2.** a container for measuring this quantity. **3.** a considerable quantity: *a peck of trouble.*

peck[2] (pek) /pɛk/ *v.* **1.** to strike or pierce with the beak, as a bird does: [~ + *obj*]: *The birds pecked a hole in the bag of seed.* [*no obj*]: *birds pecking at the ground.* **2.** [~ + *obj*] to kiss (someone) lightly on the cheek: *She pecked him quickly on the cheek.* **3. peck at,** [~ + *at* + *obj*] **a.** to nibble at (food) without much interest: *sat there pecking at his meal.* **b.** to nag: *kept pecking at him to load the dishwasher.* **—***n.* [*count*] **4.** a quick stroke, as in pecking. **5.** a quick, light kiss: *a little peck on the cheek.*

peck′ing or′der, *n.* [*count*] **1.** Also, **peck′ or′der.** the order of dominance among certain birds in which each bird's social position is maintained by pecking a bird of lower status. **2.** an order or hierarchy of position or authority in a human group.

pec•tin (pek′tin) /ˈpɛktɪn/ *n.* [*noncount*] a white substance present in ripe fruits, used to thicken fruit jellies. —**pec•tic** (pek′tik) /ˈpɛktɪk/ **pec′tin•ous,** *adj.*

pec•to•ral (pek′tər əl) /ˈpɛktərəl/ *adj.* **1.** of, in, on, or relating to the chest or breast: *large pectoral muscles.* **—***n.* [*count*] **2.** a pectoral body part or organ, as a pectoral muscle.

pe•cu•liar (pi kyōōl′yər) /pɪˈkyuwlyər/ *adj.* **1.** strange; queer; odd: *a peculiar noise coming from the car engine.* **2.** characteristic of some person, group, or thing: *the peculiar properties of that drug.* [*be* + ~ + *to*]: *an expression that is peculiar to Canadians.* —**pe•cu′liar•ly,** *adv.*

pe•cu•li•ar•i•ty (pi kyōō′lē ar′i tē) /pɪˌkyuwliyˈærɪtiy/ *n., pl.* **-ties. 1.** [*noncount*] the quality or condition of being peculiar. **2.** [*count*] a manner or way of thinking that is odd or strange: *has some funny peculiarities, like standing on one foot while she talks.* **3.** [*count*] a quality distinctive to only one group or thing: *the peculiarities of her Midwestern dialect.*

pe•cu•ni•ar•y (pi kyōō′nē er′ē) /pɪ'kyuwniyˌɛriy/ *adj.* of, relating to, or consisting of money.

-ped-[1], *root. -ped-* comes from Latin, where it has the meaning "foot." This meaning is found in such words as: BIPED, CENTIPEDE, EXPEDIENT, EXPEDITE, EXPEDITION, IMPEDE, IMPEDIMENT, MILLIPEDE, MOPED, PEDAL, PEDESTAL, PEDESTRIAN, PEDICURE, PEDOMETER, QUADRUPED.

-ped-[2], *root. -ped-* comes from Greek, where it has the meaning "child." This meaning is found in such words as: ENCYCLOPEDIA, ORTHOPEDIC, PEDAGOGUE, PEDAGOGY, PEDERASTY, PEDIATRICIAN, PEDIATRICS.

ped•a•gogue or **ped•a•gog** (ped′ə gog′, -gôg′) /'pɛdəˌgɒg, -ˌgɔg/ *n.* [*count*] **1.** a teacher; schoolteacher. **2.** one who is overly formal or pays too much attention to small, unimportant details. See -PED-[2].

ped•a•go•gy (ped′ə gō′jē, -goj′ē) /'pɛdəˌgowdʒiy, -ˌgɒdʒiy/ *n.* [*noncount*] **1.** the work of a teacher; teaching. **2.** the art or science of teaching. —**ped•a•gog•ic** (ped′ə goj′ik, -gō′jik) /ˌpɛdə'gɒdʒɪk, -'gowdʒɪk/ **ped′a•gog′i•cal,** *adj.* See -PED-[2].

ped•al (ped′l; *for also* pēd′l) /'pɛdl̩; *for also* 'piydl̩/ *n., v.,* **-aled, -al•ing** or (*esp. Brit.*) **-alled, -al•ling.** —*n.* [*count*] **1.** a foot-operated lever to control, activate, or power various mechanisms: *got her feet tangled on the bicycle pedals.* **2.** a foot-operated lever on a keyboard musical instrument. —*v.* **3.** to work or use pedals, as in riding a bicycle: [*no obj*]: *He pedaled furiously up the hill.* [~ + *obj*]: *He could hardly pedal the bike up the hill.* See -PED-[1].

ped•ant (ped′nt) /'pɛdnt/ *n.* [*count*] **1.** one who enjoys displaying learning. **2.** one too concerned with minor details, esp. in teaching: *a boring, uninspiring pedant whose students fall asleep in his classes.* **3.** one too concerned with book knowledge without regard to common sense. —**pe•dan•tic** (pə dan′tik) /pə'dæntɪk/ *adj.* —**ped′ant•ry,** *n.* [*noncount*] See -PED[2]-.

ped•dle (ped′l) /'pɛdl̩/ *v.,* **-dled, -dling. 1.** to go with or carry (goods, esp. small articles) from place to place for sale; hawk: [~ + *obj*]: *peddling some useless medicine.* [*no obj*]: *peddling on the Lower East Side.* **2.** [~ + *obj*] to deal out or attempt to spread: *to peddle radical ideas.* —**ped′dler,** *n.* [*count*] See -PED[1]-.

ped•er•as•ty (ped′ə ras′tē, pē′də-) /'pɛdəˌræstiy, 'piydə-/ *n.* [*noncount*] sexual relations between a man and a boy. —**ped′er•ast′,** *n.* [*count*] See -PED-[2].

ped•es•tal (ped′ə stl) /'pɛdəstl̩/ *n.* [*count*] **1.** a supporting base esp. for a column, statue, etc. —***Idiom.*** **2. set** or **put on a pedestal,** [*set/put + obj + on a pedestal*] to believe (someone) to be great; to glorify; idealize: *tended to put women on a pedestal.* See -PED-[1].

pe•des•tri•an (pə des′trē ən) /pə'dɛstriyən/ *n.* [*count*] **1.** one who travels on foot: *Pedestrians have to dodge cars, buses, and bicycles.* See illustration at STREET. —*adj.* **2.** going or performed on foot. **3.** of or intended for walking: *a pedestrian crossing.* **4.** lacking in liveliness or imagination; commonplace: *a pedestrian account of the leader's rise to power.* See -PED-[1].

pe•di•at•rics (pē′dē a′triks) /ˌpiydiy'ætrɪks/ *n.* [*noncount; used with a singular verb*] the branch of medicine concerned with the development, care, and diseases of babies and children: *Pediatrics was his specialty.* —**pe′di•at′ric,** *adj.* —**pe•di•a•tri•cian** (pē′dē ə trish′ən) /ˌpiydiyə'trɪʃən/ *n.* [*count*] See -PED-[2].

ped•i•cure (ped′i kyŏŏr′) /'pɛdɪˌkyʊr/ *n.* **1.** [*noncount*] professional care of the feet, as removal of corns and trimming of toenails. **2.** [*count*] a single such treatment. —**ped′i•cur′ist,** *n.* [*count*] See -PED-[1], -CURA-.

ped•i•gree (ped′i grē′) /'pɛdɪˌgriy/ *n.* **1.** one's ancestral line; lineage; ancestry: [*noncount*]: *a study of their pedigree.* [*count*]: *a pedigree spanning centuries.* **2.** a record of the ancestry of an animal, esp. of a purebred animal: [*noncount*]: *great pedigree.* [*count*]: *the pedigree of a collie.* **3.** [*noncount*] distinguished or pure ancestry. —*adj.* Also, **ped′i•greed′. 4.** having established purebred ancestry: *a pedigree collie.*

pe•dom•e•ter (pə dom′i tər) /pə'dɒmɪtər/ *n.* [*count*] an instrument that measures the distance walked or run, by recording the number of steps taken. See -PED-[1], -METER-.

pee (pē) /piy/ *v.,* **peed, pee•ing,** *n. Slang (sometimes considered vulgar).* —*v.* [*no obj*] **1.** to urinate. —*n.* **2.** [*noncount*] urine. **3.** [*count*] an act of urinating.

peek (pēk) /piyk/ *v.* [*no obj*] **1.** to glance quickly or secretly; peep: *Can't we peek at the presents?* —*n.* [*count*] **2.** a quick or secret look or glance; peep: *a quick peek at the document on her desk.*

peel (pēl) /piyl/ *v.* **1.** [~ + *obj*] to strip (something) of its skin, rind, etc.: *to peel and boil some potatoes.* **2.** [*no obj*] (of skin, paint, etc.) to come off in pieces: *My skin peeled after the sunburn.* **3.** [~ + *obj*] to strip away from something: *to peel paint from a car.* **4. peel off,** [*no obj*] to make a turn away from a group: *One by one the jets peeled off from the formation and dove for their targets.* —*n.* [*noncount*] **5.** the skin or rind of a fruit or vegetable: *grated lemon peel.* —***Idiom.*** **6. keep one's eyes peeled,** [*no obj*] to watch carefully; be alert: *Keep your eyes peeled for the turnoff.* —**peel′er,** *n.* [*count*]

peel•ing (pē′ling) /'piylɪŋ/ *n.* [*count*] a piece, as of skin or rind, peeled off: *potato peelings.*

peep[1] (pēp) /piyp/ *v.* [*no obj*] **1.** to look through a small opening or from a hidden or secret location: *peeping through the curtains.* **2.** to come partly into view; begin to appear: *The winter sun peeped briefly over the mountaintop.* —*n.* [*count*] **3.** a quick or secret look. **4.** the first appearance, as of dawn. —**peep′er,** *n.* [*count*]

peep[2] (pēp) /piyp/ *n.* [*count*] **1.** a short, high-pitched, shrill little cry or sound, as of a young bird. **2.** a slight sound or remark, as of complaint: *I don't want to hear a peep out of you!* —*v.* [*no obj*] **3.** to make a short, high-pitched, shrill little cry.

peep•hole (pēp′hōl′) /'piypˌhowl/ *n.* [*count*] a small hole, as in a door, through which to look.

Peep′ing Tom′, *n.* [*count*] one who receives sexual pleasure by watching others secretly: *The police discovered that the Peeping Tom had a telescope.*

peer[1] (pēr) /pɪər/ *n.* [*count*] **1.** one who is the equal of another in abilities or social status: *a jury of his peers.* **2.** a member of any of the five degrees of the nobility in Great Britain and Ireland.

peer[2] (pēr) /pɪər/ *v.* [*no obj*] **1.** to look searchingly, as in making an effort to see clearly: *He peered at the computer screen, wondering what his programming mistake was.* **2.** to appear slightly; come into view: *The sun peered briefly out of the leaden skies.*

peer•age (pēr′ij) /'pɪərɪdʒ/ *n.* **1.** [*noncount*] the body of the peers of a country. **2.** [*count*] the rank of a peer: *He was hoping for a peerage by Christmas.*

peer•less (pēr′lis) /'pɪərlɪs/ *adj.* having no equal; unrivaled: *played the cello with peerless skill.*

peeve (pēv) /piyv/ *v.,* **peeved, peev•ing,** *n.* —*v.* **1.** to annoy: [~ + *obj*]: *Their last loss really peeved the coach.* [*It + ~ + obj + that clause*]: *It really peeved the coach that his team lost again.* —*n.* [*count*] **2.** something causing annoyance or irritation: *His pet peeve was that no one made their beds in the morning.*

pee•vish (pē′vish) /'piyvɪʃ/ *adj.* irritable, grouchy, or cranky: *When he doesn't get enough sleep he is peevish all day.* —**pee′vish•ly,** *adv.: peevishly refused to help.* —**pee′vish•ness,** *n.* [*noncount*]

pee•wee, *pl.* **- wees.** (pē′wē′) /'piyˌwiy/ *n.* [*count*] *Informal.* a person or thing that is unusually small.

peg (peg) /pɛg/ *n., v.,* **pegged, peg•ging,** *adj.* —*n.* [*count*] **1.** a shaped pin of wood, metal, etc., driven into something as a fastening, support, stopper, etc.: *hung his coat on the peg by the door.* **2.** a notch, level, or degree: *to come down a peg.* **3.** *Informal.* a hard throw, esp. as to a base in baseball: *His peg to the plate beat the runner trying to score.* **4.** *Brit.* CLOTHESPIN. —*v.* **5.** to fasten with or as if with pegs: [~ (+ *down*) + *obj*]: *worked quickly to peg down the canopy.* [~ + *obj* (+ *down*)]: *quickly pegged it down.* **6.** [~ + *obj*] to keep (a price, etc.) at a set level: *The dollar was no longer pegged to the British pound.* **7.** [~ + *obj*] *Informal.* to throw (a ball) forcefully: *pegged the ball to second base.* **8.** [~ + *obj* + *as* + *obj*] *Informal.* to identify; label; classify: *She pegged him as a loser.* **9. peg away,** [*no obj*] to work continuously or for a long time at something: *pegging away at his homework.*

peg′ leg′, *n.* [*count*] **1.** an artificial leg, esp. a wooden one. **2.** a person with an artificial leg.

peign•oir (pān wär′, pen-, pān′wär, pen′-) /peyn'wɑr, pɛn-, 'peynwɑr, 'pɛn-/ *n.* [*count*] a woman's loose dressing gown.

pe•jo•ra•tive (pi jôr′ə tiv, -jor′-) /pɪ'dʒɔrətɪv, -'dʒɒr-/ *adj.* **1.** (of a word) having a disparaging, derogatory, or belittling force. —*n.* [*count*] **2.** a pejorative form or word.

Pe•king•ese or **Pe•kin•ese** (pē′kə nēz′, -nēs′) /ˌpiykə'niyz, -'niys/ *n., pl.* **-ese** for 1, *adj.* —*n.* [*count*] **1.** one of a Chinese breed of small dogs having a long, silky coat and a flat, wrinkled muzzle. —*adj.* **2.** of or relating to this breed.

-pel-, *root. -pel-* comes from Latin, where it has the meaning "drive; push." It is related to the root -PULS-.

This meaning is found in such words as: COMPEL, DISPEL, EXPEL, IMPEL, PROPEL, PROPELLER, REPEL, REPELLANT.

pel•i•can (pel′i kən) /ˈpɛlɪkən/ *n.* [*count*] a large, web-footed bird of warmer regions of the world, having a throat pouch that expands.

pel•la•gra (pə lag′rə, -lā′grə, -lä′-) /pəˈlægrə, -ˈleygrə, -ˈlɑ-/ *n.* [*noncount*] a disease caused by a lack of niacin in the diet, characterized by skin changes, neurological problems, and diarrhea.

pel•let (pel′it) /ˈpɛlɪt/ *n.* [*count*] **1.** a small, rounded body, as of food or medicine: *They fed their pet little green pellets of food.* **2.** a small ball of metal, like a bullet, made to be shot from a shotgun. **—*v.*** [~ + *obj*] **3.** to hit with pellets.

pell-mell or **pell•mell** (pel′mel′) /ˈpɛlˈmɛl/ *adv.* **1.** done too fast and without enough care or thinking: *ran pell-mell into the crowd.* **—*adj.*** **2.** disorderly or confused. **3.** in too much of a hurry; rash.

pel•lu•cid (pə lo͞o′sid) /pəˈluwsɪd/ *adj.* **1.** allowing light to pass most easily, as glass; translucent. **2.** clear in meaning or expression. See -LUC-.

pelt[1] (pelt) /pɛlt/ *v.* **1.** [~ + *obj*] to attack (someone) with repeated blows: *The crowd began to pelt him with rocks.* **2.** [~ + *obj*] to attack (someone) with shouting, etc.: *pelted with questions about his new policy.* **3.** [*no obj*] to beat or pound without stopping: *rain pelting down.*

pelt[2] (pelt) /pɛlt/ *n.* [*noncount*] the untanned hide or skin of an animal.

pel•vis (pel′vis) /ˈpɛlvɪs/ *n.* [*count*], *pl.* **-vis•es, -ves** (-vēz) /-viyz/. **1.** the bowl-like space in the lower trunk of the body at the hips and the end of the spine. **2.** the bones forming this cavity. **—pel′vic,** *adj.*

pen[1] (pen) /pɛn/ *n., v.,* **penned, pen•ning. —*n.*** [*count*] **1.** any of various instruments for writing or drawing with ink. See illustration at SCHOOL. **2.** the pen as a symbol of writing; authorship: *The pen is mightier than the sword.* **—*v.*** [~ + *obj*] **3.** to write or draw with or as if with a pen: *to pen an essay.*

pen[2] (pen) /pɛn/ *n., v.,* **penned, pen•ning. —*n.*** [*count*] **1.** a small fenced-in area for domestic animals. **2.** a playpen. **3.** BULLPEN (defs. 1, 2). **—*v.*** [~ + *obj*] **4.** to confine in or as if in a pen: *The animals were penned there for weeks.*

pen[3] (pen) /pɛn/ *n. Slang.* PENITENTIARY.

-pen-, *root.* *-pen-* comes from Latin and Greek, where it has the meanings "penalty; wrong," and hence "repent." These meanings are found in such words as: IMPENITENT, PENAL, PENALIZE, PENITENCE, PENOLOGY, REPENT, SUBPOENA.

Pen. or **pen.,** an abbreviation of: peninsula.

pe•nal (pēn′l) /ˈpiynl̩/ *adj.* of or relating to punishment, as for crimes or offenses: *a penal code.* See -PEN-.

pe•nal•ize (pēn′l īz′, pen′-) /ˈpiynl̩ˌayz, ˈpɛn-/ *v.* [~ + *obj*], **-ized, -iz•ing. 1.** to punish (someone) with a penalty: *You will be penalized if you come in late to class.* **2.** to punish (someone) by putting him or her under a handicap: *penalized the Giants fifteen yards on that play.* **—pe•nal•i•za•tion** (pēn′l i zā′shən, pen′-) /ˌpiynl̩ɪˈzeyʃən, ˌpɛn-/ *n.* [*noncount*] See -PEN-.

pen•al•ty (pen′l tē) /ˈpɛnl̩tiy/ *n.* [*count*], *pl.* **-ties. 1.** a punishment for breaking a law or violating a rule: *stiff penalties for insider trading.* **2.** a loss because of failing to fulfill some obligation, as a sum of money: *substantial penalties for withdrawing your money early from this kind of account.* See -PEN-.

pen•ance (pen′əns) /ˈpɛnəns/ *n.* **1.** a punishment to show sorrow for one's sins: [*noncount*]: *For every sin you must do penance.* [*count*]: *a penance of a rosary for your sins.* **2.** [*proper noun; often: Penance*] a sacrament, as in the Roman Catholic Church, of confession, repentance, and forgiveness for one's sins. See -PEN-.

pence (pens) /pɛns/ *n.* [*plural*] *Brit.* (used after a number in referring to a sum of money, rather than to the coins themselves) pl. of PENNY: *sixpence.*

pen•chant (pen′chənt) /ˈpɛntʃənt/ *n.* [*count*] a strong desire, interest, taste, or liking for something: *a penchant for fast cars.* See -PEND-.

pen•cil (pen′səl) /ˈpɛnsəl/ *n., v.,* **-ciled, -cil•ing** or (*esp. Brit.*) **-cilled, -cil•ling. —*n.*** **1.** a slender tube of wood, metal, etc., containing a thin piece of graphite, etc., used for writing or drawing: [*count*]: *broke the point on his pencil.* [*noncount; in* + ~]: *Write your answers in pencil.* See illustration at SCHOOL. **2.** [*count*] a stick of cosmetic coloring material for use on the eyebrows: *an eyebrow pencil.* **—*v.*** **3.** [~ + *obj*] to write, draw, or mark with or as if with a pencil: *penciled a note at the end of the memo.* **4. pencil in,** to add, schedule, or list (something) that may be changed, by or as if by writing down in pencil: [~ + *in* + *obj*]: *penciled in the names of several players who might be needed if the star was too ill.* [~ + *obj* + *in*]: *I'll pencil you in for ten o'clock.*

-pend-, *root.* *-pend-* comes from Latin, where it has the meaning "hang; be suspended or weighed." This meaning is found in such words as: APPEND, APPENDAGE, APPENDIX, COMPENDIUM, DEPEND, EXPEND, IMPENDING, INDEPENDENT, PENDANT, PENDING, PENDULOUS, PENDULUM, SPEND, STIPEND, SUSPEND.

pend•ant (pen′dənt) /ˈpɛndənt/ *n.* [*count*] Also, **pendent. 1.** a hanging ornament on a necklace. **—*adj.*** **2.** PENDENT. See -PEND-.

pend•ent (pen′dənt) /ˈpɛndənt/ *adj.* Also, **pendant. 1.** hanging or suspended. **2.** overhanging; jutting. **3.** (esp. of a lawsuit) undecided; pending. **—*n.*** **4.** PENDANT.

pend•ing (pen′ding) /ˈpɛndɪŋ/ *prep.* **1.** while awaiting; until: *We'll do this work pending his return.* **2.** during: *pending the trial.* **—*adj.*** **3.** awaiting decision or settlement: *That case is still pending.* **4.** about to happen; impending: *Dad knew the driving test was pending; why was he late?* See -PEND-.

pen•du•lous (pen′jə ləs, pen′dyə-, -də-) /ˈpɛndʒələs, ˈpɛndyə-, -də-/ *adj.* hanging down loosely: *pendulous blossoms.* See -PEND-.

pen•du•lum (pen′jə ləm, pen′dyə-, -də-) /ˈpɛndʒələm, ˈpɛndyə-, -də-/ *n.* [*count*] **1.** a weight hanging from a fixed point so as to move back and forth by the action of gravity and momentum. **2.** something that may change from one position to another and back again: *the pendulum of public opinion.* See -PEND-.

pen•e•trate (pen′i trāt′) /ˈpɛnɪˌtreyt/ *v.,* **-trat•ed, -trat•ing. 1.** to pierce or pass into or through: [~ + *obj*]: *The bullet penetrated the wall.* [*no obj*]: *Maybe the bullet didn't penetrate.* **2.** to enter the interior of: [~ + *obj*]: *to penetrate a forest.* [*no obj*]: *The explorers penetrated into the interior.* **3.** to spread through; seem to be everywhere in; permeate: [~ + *obj*]: *The tobacco smoke penetrated the room.* [*no obj*]: *That cigarette smoke really penetrates, doesn't it?* **4.** [~ + *obj*] to arrive at the meaning of; comprehend: *to penetrate the mysteries of Einstein's theories.* **5.** [~ + *obj*] to obtain a share of (a market): *to penetrate the coffee market.* **—pen•e•tra•ble** (pen′i trə bəl) /ˈpɛnɪtrəbəl/ *adj.*

pen•e•trat•ing (pen′i trā′ting) /ˈpɛnɪˌtreytɪŋ/ *adj.* **1.** able or tending to penetrate. **2.** acute; showing great ability to notice or understand: *a penetrating remark.*

pen•e•tra•tion (pen′i trā′shən) /ˌpɛnɪˈtreyʃən/ *n.* **1.** the act or power of penetrating: [*count*]: *enemy penetrations into our territory.* [*noncount*]: *a fighter capable of penetration of enemy defenses.* **2.** [*noncount*] the ability to understand quickly and easily; insight: *the student's penetration of this theorem.*

pen•guin (peng′gwin, pen′-) /ˈpɛŋgwɪn, ˈpɛn-/ *n.* [*count*] a flightless water-dwelling bird of the Southern Hemisphere, having webbed feet and flipperlike wings.

pen•i•cil•lin (pen′ə sil′in) /ˌpɛnəˈsɪlɪn/ *n.* [*noncount*] an antibiotic produced from molds.

pen•in•su•la (pə nin′sə lə, -nins′yə lə) /pəˈnɪnsələ, -ˈnɪnsyələ/ *n.* [*count*], *pl.* **-las.** an area of land almost surrounded by water. **—pen•in′su•lar,** *adj.*

pe•nis (pē′nis) /ˈpiynɪs/ *n.* [*count*], *pl.* **-nis•es, -nes** (-nēz) /-niyz/. the male sex organ, and, in mammals, the organ through which urine is released from the body. **—pe•nile** (pēn′l, pē′nīl) /ˈpiynl̩, ˈpiynayl/ *adj.*

pen•i•tent (pen′i tənt) /ˈpɛnɪtənt/ *adj.* **1.** expressing sorrow for wrongdoing and desiring to make up for the wrong; repentant; contrite. **—*n.*** [*count*] **2.** a penitent person. **—pen′i•tence,** *n.* [*noncount*] **—pen•i•ten•tial** (pen′i ten′shəl) /ˌpɛnɪˈtɛnʃəl/ *adj.* **—pen′i•tent•ly,** *adv.* See -PEN-.

pen•i•ten•tia•ry (pen′i ten′shə rē) /ˌpɛnɪˈtɛnʃəriy/ *n.* [*count*], *pl.* **-ries.** a place for imprisonment or punishment. See -PEN-.

pen•knife (pen′nīf′) /ˈpɛnˌnayf/ *n.* [*count*], *pl.* **-knives.** a small pocketknife.

pen•man•ship (pen′mən ship′) /ˈpɛnmənˌʃɪp/ *n.* [*noncount*] **1.** the art of handwriting; use of the pen in writing. **2.** a person's style or manner of handwriting: *My penmanship was always the worst in the class.*

Penn. or **Penna.,** an abbreviation of: Pennsylvania.

pen′ name′, *n.* [*count*] a name used by a writer that is not his or her real name; nom de plume.

pen•nant (pen′ənt) /ˈpɛnənt/ *n.* [*count*] **1.** a long flag that gradually tapers toward one end. **2.** a flag serving as an emblem of victory or championship, esp. in baseball.

pen•ni•less (pen′i lis) /ˈpɛnɪlɪs/ *adj.* totally without money; destitute.

pen•ny (pen′ē) /ˈpɛniy/ *n.,* [*count*] *pl.* **pen•nies,** (*esp. when thought of as a group* for 2–4) **pence. 1.** a unit of money of different nations, as Australia, Canada, and the U.S., a coin equal to 1/100 of a dollar; one cent. **2.** Also called **new penny.** a unit of money of the United Kingdom, a coin equal to 1/100 of a pound. **3.** a unit of money equal to 1/240 of the former British pound or to 1/12 of the former British shilling. **4.** a unit of money of Ireland, equal to 1/100 of the Irish pound. **5.** a sum of money: [*every* + ~]: *to spend every penny to send his kids to college (= to spend all of one's money).* [*with a negative word or phrase*]: *He hasn't got a penny to his name (= He has no money).* —***Idiom.*** **6. a bad penny,** someone or something undesirable. **7. a penny for your thoughts,** (used to ask the listener what he or she is thinking about): *"A penny for your thoughts?"— "Oh, I was thinking of the last time we were in Paris."* **8. a pretty penny,** a great sum of money: *spent a pretty penny fixing up their house.*

pen′ny pinch′er, *n.* [*count*] a stingy person; a person not willing to spend money. —**pen′ny-pinch′ing,** *n.* [*noncount*]: *It's a bit late for penny-pinching now; the deficit is too huge.*

pen•ny•weight (pen′ē wāt′) /ˈpɛniyˌweyt/ *n.* [*count*] (in certain systems of measurement or weight) a unit of 24 grains or 1/20 of an ounce (1.555 grams). *Abbr.:* dwt, pwt

pe•nol•o•gy (pē nol′ə jē) /piyˈnɒlədʒiy/ *n.* [*noncount*] **1.** the study of the punishment of crime. **2.** the study of the management of prisons. —**pe•nol′o•gist,** *n.* [*count*] See -PEN-.

pen′ pal′, *n.* [*count*] a person with whom one keeps up an exchange of letters, usually someone far away: *My daughter's pen pal is a girl her age in Uganda.*

pen•sion (pen′shən; *Fr.* päɴ syôɴ′ *for* 2) /ˈpɛnʃən; *Fr.* pɑ̃ˈsyɔ̃ *for 2*/ *n., pl.* **-sions** (-shənz; *Fr.* -syôɴ′ *for* 2) /-ʃənz; *Fr.* -ˈsyɔ̃ *for 2*/ *v.* —*n.* [*count*] **1.** a fixed amount of money paid regularly to one who no longer works for a company, for past services, etc.: *He watched his pension dwindle.* **2.** (in Europe) a boardinghouse or small hotel: *a small pension in Barcelona.* —*v.* **3.** [~ + *obj*] to grant or pay a pension to: *The company will pension you at age 55.* **4.** to cause (someone) to retire on a pension: [~ + *off* + *obj*]: *The company pensioned off most of its workers.* [~ + *obj* + *off*]: *The company pensioned us off.* —**pen′sion•er,** *n.* [*count*]: *pensioners and others on fixed incomes.* See -PEND-.

pen•sive (pen′siv) /ˈpɛnsɪv/ *adj.* dreamily thoughtful; thinking deeply or sadly: *He was pensive, looking out the window, thinking about her.* —**pen′sive•ly,** *adv.*: *gazing pensively out the window.* See -PEND-.

pent (pent) /pɛnt/ *adj.* shut in; confined: *pent cattle; pent emotions.* See PENT-UP.

penta-, *prefix. penta-* comes from Greek, where it has the meaning "five": *penta-* + *-gon* → *pentagon (= five-sided figure).*

pen•ta•gon (pen′tə gon′) /ˈpɛntəˌgɒn/ *n.* **1.** [*count*] a flat figure having five angles and five sides. **2. the Pentagon, a.** [*proper noun; the* + ~] a building in Arlington, Va., built in the form of a pentagon and containing the U.S. Department of Defense. **b.** [*noncount*] the U.S. Department of Defense; the U.S. military establishment. —**pen•tag•o•nal** (pen tag′ə nl) /pɛnˈtægənl/ *adj.*

pen•ta•gram (pen′tə gram′) /ˈpɛntəˌgræm/ *n.* [*count*] a five-pointed, star-shaped figure.

pen•tam•e•ter (pen tam′i tər) /pɛnˈtæmɪtər/ *n.* **1.** [*count*] a line of verse having five metrical feet. **2.** [*noncount*] unrhymed verse having five iambic feet. See -METER-.

Pen•te•cos•tal (pen′ti kô′stl, -kos′tl) /ˌpɛntɪˈkɔstl̩, -ˈkɒstl̩/ *adj.* **1.** of or relating to Pentecost, a Christian festival, or to Shavuoth, a Jewish holy day. **2.** of or relating to any of various Christian groups, usually fundamentalist, that emphasize the activity of the Holy Spirit.

pent•house (pent′hous′) /ˈpɛntˌhaws/ *n.* [*count*], *pl.* **-hous•es. 1.** an apartment on the roof of a building. **2.** any specially designed apartment on the top floor of a building.

pent′-up′, *adj.* confined; held in; restrained; not let out or expressed; curbed: *pent-up rage.*

pe•nul•ti•mate (pi nul′tə mit) /pɪˈnʌltəmɪt/ *adj.* [*usually: before a noun*] next to the last: *the penultimate syllable.* See -ULT-.

pe•nu•ri•ous (pə nŏŏr′ē əs, -nyŏŏr′-) /pəˈnʊriyəs, -ˈnyʊr-/ *adj.* **1.** very stingy. **2.** extremely poor. —**pe•nu′ri•ous•ly,** *adv.* —**pe•nu′ri•ous•ness,** *n.* [*noncount*]

pen•u•ry (pen′yə rē) /ˈpɛnyəriy/ *n.* [*noncount*] great, deep poverty; destitution.

pe•on (pē′ən, pē′on) /ˈpiyən, ˈpiyɒn/ *n.* [*count*] **1.** (in Spanish America) a farm worker or unskilled laborer. **2.** a person of low social status who does unskilled work. —**pe•on•age** (pē′ə nij) /ˈpiyənɪdʒ/ *n.* [*noncount*]

pe•o•ny (pē′ə nē) /ˈpiyəniy/ *n.* [*count*], *pl.* **-nies.** a plant having large, round, pink or white showy flowers.

peo•ple (pē′pəl) /ˈpiypəl/ *n., pl.* **-ples** for 2 *v.,* **-pled, -pling.** —*n.* **1.** [*plural*] persons as a group; persons in general: *There were too many people in the room.* **2.** [*plural*] human beings, as distinguished from animals or other beings: *All people have names.* **3.** [*count*] the entire body of persons who make up a community, tribe, etc., in that they have a common culture, religion, or the like: *a hard-working, industrious people; the Jewish people.* **4.** [*plural; the* + ~] the ordinary persons of a community, country, etc., as distinguished from those who have wealth, rank, etc.; the citizens of a state who are allowed to vote: *the common people; a man of the people; a people's army.* **5.** [*plural*] the followers of, or the persons working for, a ruler, employer, etc.: *The tycoon promised that his people would look at our proposals.* **6.** [*plural*] a person's family or relatives: *Her people have lived here for generations.* **7.** (added to words or roots to make nouns that refer to the persons of any particular group, profession, etc.; it is sometimes used to avoid making reference to the sex or gender of the persons designated: *sales* + *people* → *salespeople (not: salesmen).* —*v.* [~ + *obj*] **8.** to fill with people; populate: *The area was first peopled by nomads.*

pep (pep) /pɛp/ *n., v.,* **pepped, pep•ping.** —*n.* [*noncount*] **1.** lively spirits or energy: *After her coffee she felt full of pep again.* —*v.* **2. pep up,** to make or become spirited: [~ + *up* + *obj*]: *something to pep up his students.* [~ + *obj* + *up*]: *Perhaps this movie will pep them up.* —**pep′pi•ness,** *n.* [*noncount*] —**pep′py,** *adj.,* **-pi•er, -pi•est.**

pep•per (pep′ər) /ˈpɛpər/ *n.* **1.** [*noncount*] the strong-smelling, dried berries of a tropical shrub, used as a spice. **2.** [*count*] **a.** a plant belonging to the nightshade family. **b.** the fruit of this plant, ranging from mild to very strong in flavor. —*v.* [~ + *obj*] **3.** to season, sprinkle, cover, or pelt with or as if with pepper, or missiles or small objects: *The side of the ship was peppered with gunshots.*

pep•per•corn (pep′ər kôrn′) /ˈpɛpərˌkɔrn/ *n.* [*count*] **1.** the dried berry of the pepper plant. **2.** anything very small or unimportant. —*adj.* **3.** (of hair) growing in tight spirals.

pep•per•mint (pep′ər mint′, -mənt) /ˈpɛpərˌmɪnt, -mənt/ *n.* **1.** [*noncount*] a sweet-smelling herb of the mint family. **2.** [*noncount*] the strong-smelling oil of this plant, used as a flavoring. **3.** [*count*] a candy drop or confection flavored with peppermint: *asked for a peppermint for his throat.*

pep•per•o•ni (pep′ə rō′nē) /ˌpɛpəˈrowniy/ *n., pl.* **-nis.** (a piece of) highly seasoned, spicy, hard sausage: [*noncount*]: *pizza with cheese and pepperoni.* [*count*]: *She would peel off the pepperonis from her pizza.*

pep•per•y (pep′ə rē) /ˈpɛpəriy/ *adj.* **1.** of, full of, or tasting like pepper. **2.** sharp or stinging: *a peppery speech.* **3.** easily angered.

pep′ talk′, *n.* [*count*] a lively, emotional talk intended to inspire enthusiasm, etc.: *The coach gave his team a pep talk during halftime.*

pep•tic (pep′tik) /ˈpɛptɪk/ *adj.* **1.** relating to or associated with digestion; digestive. **2.** promoting digestion. —*n.* [*count*] **3.** a substance promoting digestion.

per (pûr; *unstressed* pər) /pɜr; *unstressed* pər/ *prep.* **1.** for or in each or every; a or an: *Membership costs $100 per year.* **2.** according to; in accordance with: *I delivered the box per your instructions.* —*adv.* **3.** *Informal.* each; for each one: *The charge was five dollars per.*

per-, *prefix. per-* comes from Latin, is attached to roots and means "through, thoroughly, completely, very": *per-* + *-vert* → *pervert (= a person completely turned away from the normal); per-* + *-fect* → *perfect (= thoroughly or completely done).*

per•am•bu•late (pər am′byə lāt′) /pərˈæmbyəˌleyt/ *v.,* **-lat•ed, -lat•ing.** to walk through, about, or over; traverse: [*no obj*]: *They perambulated about the park for a while.* [~ + *obj*]: *They perambulated the fields.*

per•am•bu•la•tor (pər am′byə lā′tər) /pərˈæmbyəˌleytər/ *n.* BABY CARRIAGE.

per an•num (pər an′əm) /ˈpər ænəm/ *adv.* by the year; yearly.

per•cale (pər kāl′) /pər'keyl/ *n.* [*noncount*] a smooth cotton cloth, used esp. for bedsheets.

per cap•i•ta (pər kap′i tə) /'pər kæpɪtə/ *adj., adv.* by or for each individual person: *—adv.: income per capita. —adj.* [*before a noun*]: *Per capita income has fallen in the last decade.*

per•ceive (pər sēv′) /pər'siyv/ *v.,* **-ceived, -ceiv•ing.** [*not: be + ~-ing*] **1.** [*~ + obj*] to become aware of or identify by the senses: *Some artists perceive very subtle differences in shade and tone.* **2.** to recognize or understand: [*~ + obj*]: *I perceive difficulties in putting your idea into practice.* [*~ + that clause*]: *He perceived that there would be difficulties.* **—per•ceiv′a•ble,** *adj.* See -CEIVE-.

per•cent or **per cent** (pər sent′) /pər'sɛnt/ *n.* **1.** [*noncount; usually after a number*] one one-hundredth part; 1/100: *reduced our workload by fifty percent.* **2.** [*count; usually singular*] PERCENTAGE (defs. 1, 3): *What percent of the people will still vote for him? —adj.* [*before a noun*] **3.** figured or expressed on the basis of a rate per hundred: *a six percent interest rate. Symbol:* % See -CENT-.

per•cent•age (pər sen′tij) /pər'sɛntɪdʒ/ *n.* **1.** [*count*] a rate per hundred: *A high percentage of our students go on to college.* **2.** [*count*] an amount of money calculated by percent: *high percentages in mortgage rates.* **3.** [*count*] a part in general; portion: *increasing percentages of happy campers every year.* **4.** [*count; usually singular*] gain; benefit; profit; advantage: *no percentage in trying to deceive your customers.*

per•cep•ti•ble (pər sep′tə bəl) /pər'sɛptəbəl/ *adj.* capable of being perceived: *a perceptible change in behavior.* **—per•cep′ti•bly,** *adv.: The sun grew perceptibly hotter.* See -CEP-.

per•cep•tion (pər sep′shən) /pər'sɛpʃən/ *n.* the act or ability of perceiving: [*noncount*]: *my perception of her hostility; demonstrated keen perception in their ability to solve problems; depth perception.* [*count*]: *Perceptions change when you get to know people better.* See -CEP-.

per•cep•tive (pər sep′tiv) /pər'sɛptɪv/ *adj.* having or showing perception: *perceptive students who quickly saw what we were getting at.* **—per•cep′tive•ly,** *adv.* **—per•cep′tive•ness,** *n.* [*noncount*] See -CEP-.

per•cep•tu•al (pər sep′cho͞o əl) /pər'sɛptʃuwəl/ *adj.* of, relating to, or involving perception: *perceptual problems in identifying words.* See -CEP-.

perch[1] (pûrch) /pɜrtʃ/ *n.* [*count*] **1.** a pole or rod for birds to rest upon. **2.** any usually high place or object for a bird, animal, or person to land on or rest upon, etc.: *a perch way at the top of the tree.* **3.** a high or raised seat, resting place, or the like. **—***v.* **4.** [*no obj*] to land on or rest upon a perch: *The birds perched on the telephone wires.* **5.** to (cause to) settle or rest in some high position, as if on a perch: [*~ + obj*]: *He was perched on his throne.* [*no obj*]: *The prince perched on his throne.*

perch[2] (pûrch) /pɜrtʃ/ *n., pl.* (*esp. when thought of as a group*) **perch,** (*esp. for kinds or species*) **perch•es.** a small freshwater fish having a spiny front fin.

per•chance (pər chans′) /pər'tʃæns/ *adv.* perhaps; maybe; possibly.

per•co•late (*v.* pûr′kə lāt′; *n.* -lit, -lāt′) / *v.* 'pɜrkə,leyt; *n.* -lɪt, -,leyt/ *v.,* **-lat•ed, -lat•ing. 1.** to (cause a liquid to) pass through something that traps solid materials; to filter: [*no obj*]: *While the coffee was percolating, we ate a few donuts.* [*~ + obj*]: *The new machine percolates the coffee in just under a minute.* **2.** [*no obj*] to spread or grow gradually: *The news about the upcoming firings percolated through the office.* **—per•co•la•tion** (pûr′kə-lā′shən) /,pɜrkə'leyʃən/ *n.* [*noncount*]

per•co•la•tor (pûr′kə lā′tər) /'pɜrkə,leytər/ *n.* [*count*] a type of coffeepot in which boiling water is continuously forced up a hollow stem and filters down through ground coffee.

per•cus•sion (pər kush′ən) /pər'kʌʃən/ *n.* [*noncount*] **1.** the striking of one body against another with sharpness and noise. **2.** [*usually: the + ~*] the percussion instruments of an orchestra or band, thought of as a group.

percus′sion in′strument, *n.* [*count*] a musical instrument, as the drum, cymbal, or xylophone, that is struck to produce a sound.

per•cus•sion•ist (pər kush′ə nist) /pər'kʌʃənɪst/ *n.* [*count*] a musician who plays percussion instruments.

per di•em (pər dē′əm, dī′əm) /'pər diyəm, 'dayəm/ *adv.* **1.** by the day; for each day: *The consultant we hired was paid per diem.* **—***n.* [*count*] **2.** a daily allowance provided while traveling in connection with one's job: *Her per diem wasn't even enough for meals.* **—***adj.* **3.** paid by the day: *a per diem employee.*

per•di•tion (pər dish′ən) /pər'dɪʃən/ *n.* [*noncount*] final spiritual ruin and punishment for one's sins; damnation.

per•dur•a•ble (pər do͝or′ə bəl, -dyo͝or′-) /pər'dʊrəbəl, -'dyʊr-/ *adj.* very durable or long-lasting. See -DUR-.

per•e•gri•nate (per′i grə nāt′) /'pɛrɪgrə,neyt/ *v.,* **-nat•ed, -nat•ing.** to travel or journey (over), esp. on foot: [*~ + obj*]: *to peregrinate the region.* [*no obj*]: *peregrinating around the kingdom.* **—per•e•gri•na•tion** (per′-i grə nā′shən) /,pɛrɪgrə'neyʃən/ *n.* [*count*]: *the pilgrim's peregrinations to the shrine at Canterbury.*

per•emp•to•ry (pə remp′tə rē) /pə'rɛmptəriy/ *adj.* **1.** leaving no opportunity or chance for denial or refusal: *a peremptory command.* **2.** acting like a dictator in expecting orders to be obeyed: *a peremptory boss.*

per•en•ni•al (pə ren′ē əl) /pə'rɛniyəl/ *adj.* **1.** lasting for an indefinitely long time: *the perennial problems of the American economy: inflation and unemployment.* **2.** (of plants) having a life cycle of more than two years. **—***n.* [*count*] **3.** a perennial plant. **—per•en′ni•al•ly,** *adv.*

pe•re•stroi•ka (per′ə stroi′kə) /,pɛrə'strɔykə/ *n.* [*noncount*] the program of economic and political reform in the Soviet Union begun by Mikhail Gorbachev in 1986.

per•fect (*adj., n.* pûr′fikt; *v.* pər fekt′) / *adj., n.* 'pɜrfɪkt; *v.* pər'fɛkt/ *adj.* **1.** excellent beyond improvement: *a perfect score on her test.* **2.** exactly fitting the need for a certain purpose: *The director found the perfect actor for the part.* **3.** entirely without flaws, defects, or shortcomings: *a perfect apple.* **4.** accurate, exact, or correct in every detail: *a perfect copy.* **5.** [*before a noun*] agreeing with or fitting the description or definition of an ideal kind or type: *a perfect gentleman.* **6.** of or naming a verb tense, aspect, or form usually used to indicate an action or state that extends up to, or has results continuing up to, the present time, or to some other point in time that is clear from the meaning: *In English the perfect tenses, like the present perfect and the past perfect, are formed with some form of the verb* have *followed by the present or past participle of the main verb.* **—***v.* [*~ + obj*] **7.** to bring to perfection or near to perfection: *He spent weeks perfecting his computer program.* **—***n.* **8.** [*noncount; usually: the + ~*] the perfect tense or aspect. **9.** [*count*] a verb form or construction in the perfect tense or aspect. **—per′fect•ness,** *n.* [*noncount*] See -FEC-.

per•fect•i•ble (pər fek′tə bəl) /pər'fɛktəbəl/ *adj.* capable of becoming or of being made perfect. See -FEC-.

per•fec•tion (pər fek′shən) /pər'fɛkʃən/ *n.* [*noncount*] **1.** the state or quality of being or becoming perfect: *The roast beef was cooked to perfection.* **2.** the highest degree of ability, skill, or excellence. **3.** a perfect example of something: *As a teacher, he is perfection itself.* **4.** the act or fact of perfecting. See -FEC-.

per•fec•tion•ism (pər fek′shə niz′əm) /pər'fɛkʃə,nɪzəm/ *n.* [*noncount*] a personal standard that demands perfection and rejects anything less. **—per•fec′tion•ist,** *n.* [*count*]: *She was a perfectionist with her employees but also with herself.* **—***adj.*: *perfectionist tendencies.* See -FEC-.

per•fect•ly (pûr′fikt lē) /'pɜrfɪktliy/ *adv.* **1.** excellently; in a way that cannot be improved: *The dress fits her perfectly.* **2.** completely; thoroughly: *I made it perfectly clear to him.* See -FEC-.

per•fid•i•ous (pər fid′ē əs) /pər'fɪdiyəs/ *adj.* treacherous; untrustworthy; betraying others; faithless. See -FID-.

per•fi•dy (pûr′fi dē) /'pɜrfɪdiy/ *n., pl.* **-dies. 1.** [*noncount*] deliberate treachery or betrayal of another: *Perfidy should not go unpunished.* **2.** [*count*] an act or instance of being perfidious. See -FID-.

per•fo•rate (pûr′fə rāt′) /'pɜrfə,reyt/ *v. [~ + obj],* **-rat•ed, -rat•ing. 1.** to make holes through by piercing or punching. **2.** to pierce through or to the interior of; penetrate. **—per•fo•ra•tion** (pûr′fə rā′shən) /,pɜrfə'reyʃən/ *n.* [*noncount*]: *perforation of the lung.* [*count*]: *the little perforations at the end of the computer paper.*

per•force (pər fôrs′, -fōrs′) /pər'fɔrs, -'fowrs/ *adv.* of necessity; necessarily: *We must, perforce, accept some problems as the price for our success.*

per•form (pər fôrm′) /pər'fɔrm/ *v.* **1.** [*~ + obj*] to carry out; execute; do: *to perform surgery.* **2.** [*~ + obj*] to carry out in the proper manner: *The minister performed the marriage ceremony.* **3.** [*~ + obj*] to carry into effect; fulfill: *to perform a contract.* **4.** to act (a play, etc.), as on the stage; to play or sing a piece of music: [*~ + obj*]: *That actor performed the part of Othello.* [*no obj*]: *For an amateur, she performed very well.* **5.** to accomplish (an action involving skill or ability): [*~ + obj*]: *to perform a juggling act.* [*no obj*]: *This car performs poorly when the weather is hot.* **—per•form′er,** *n.* [*count*] See -FORM-.

per•for•mance (pər fôr′məns) /pər'fɔrməns/ *n.* **1.** [*count*] an entertainment presented before an audience: *two performances on Saturday.* **2.** [*noncount*] the act of performing a ceremony, play, etc.: *The audience loved her performance.* **3.** [*noncount*] the doing or accomplishment of work, acts, etc.: *the performance of his duties.* **4.** [*count*] an action or event of an unusual kind: *a fabulous pitching performance.* **5.** [*noncount*] **a.** the capacity to perform; effectiveness: *good performance under pressure.* **b.** the manner in which something fulfills its purpose: *poor engine performance in hot weather.*

perform′ing arts′, *n.* [*plural*] arts or skills that require public performance, as acting, singing, and dancing.

per•fume (*n.* pûr′fyo͞om, pər fyo͞om′; *v.* pər fyo͞om′, pûr′fyo͞om) / *n.* 'pɜrfyuwm, pər'fyuwm; *v.* pər'fyuwm, 'pɜrfyuwm/ *n., v.,* **-fumed, -fum•ing.** —*n.* **1.** a substance that gives off an agreeable smell, esp. a fluid containing fragrant oils extracted from flowers, etc.: [*noncount*]: *She wasn't wearing perfume.* [*count*]: *expensive French perfumes.* **2.** [*noncount*] the scent of substances that have an agreeable smell: *the perfume of the flowers.* —*v.* [~ + *obj*] **3.** (of substances, etc.) to give a pleasant fragrance to: *Roses perfumed the air.* **4.** to put perfume on: *perfumed her handkerchief.*

per•func•to•ry (pər fungk′tə rē) /pər'fʌŋktəriy/ *adj.* **1.** performed or done as a routine duty: *perfunctory introductions.* **2.** without interest or enthusiasm: *a perfunctory speaker.* —**per•func′to•ri•ly,** *adv.*: *He introduced us perfunctorily and rushed off to the other guests.* See -FUNCT-.

per•haps (pər haps′) /pər'hæps/ *adv.* **1.** maybe; possibly: *Perhaps I misunderstood you.* **2.** (used when making requests to make them more polite): *Perhaps we could meet again next week?* —**Usage.** See -HAP-, MAYBE.

peri-, *prefix.* **1.** *peri-* comes from Greek, is attached to roots, and means "about, around": *peri-* + *meter* → *perimeter (= distance around an area); peri-* + *-scope* → *periscope (= instrument for looking around oneself).* **2.** *peri-* also means "enclosing, surrounding": *peri-* + *cardium* → *pericardium (= a sac surrounding the heart).* **3.** *peri-* also means "near": *peri-* + *helion* → *perihelion (= point of an orbit nearest to the sun).*

per•i•car•di•um (per′i kär′dē əm) /ˌpɛrɪ'kɑrdiyəm/ *n.* [*count*], *pl.* **-di•a** (-dē ə) /-diyə/. the sac surrounding the heart. See -CORD-.

per•i•gee (per′i jē′) /'pɛrɪˌdʒiy/ *n.* [*count*] the point in the orbit of the moon or a satellite at which it is nearest to the earth. Compare APOGEE. See -GEO-.

per•i•he•li•on (per′ə hē′lē ən, -hēl′yən) /ˌpɛrə'hiyliyən, -'hiylyən/ *n.* [*count*], *pl.* **-he•li•a** (-hē′lē ə, -hēl′yə) /-'hiyliyə, -'hiylyə/. the point in the orbit of a planet or comet at which it is nearest to the sun. Compare APHELION. See -HELIO-.

per•il (per′əl) /'pɛrəl/ *n.* **1.** [*noncount*] grave risk; danger; jeopardy: *The ship was in great peril.* **2.** [*count*] something that causes or may cause injury, loss, or destruction: *the perils of a sea voyage.* —***Idiom.*** **3. at one's peril,** with a great chance of meeting danger or causing harm to oneself: *If you continue with this scheme, you do so at your peril.*

per•il•ous (per′ə ləs) /'pɛrələs/ *adj.* of or relating to peril: *a perilous sea voyage.* —**per′il•ous•ly,** *adv.*: *The plane came perilously close to crashing onto the highway.*

pe•rim•e•ter (pə rim′i tər) /pə'rɪmɪtər/ *n.* [*count*] **1.** the border of a two-dimensional figure: *the perimeter of a square.* **2.** the length of such a boundary: *The perimeter is 20 inches.* See -METER-.

pe•ri•od (pēr′ē əd) /'pɪəriyəd/ *n.* [*count*] **1.** an extent of time meaningful in the life of a person, in history, etc.: *a period of illness.* **2.** a round of time marked by some repeating event or action: *the rainy period.* **3.** any of the parts into which something, as a school day, etc., is divided: *She has gym in the first period.* **4.** the point or character (.) used to mark the end of a declarative sentence or to indicate an abbreviation; a full stop. **5.** an occurrence of menstruation. —*adj.* [*before a noun*] **6.** noting or relating to a certain historical period: *a period play.* —*interj.* **7.** (used to express the opinion that a decision is final): *I forbid you to go, period.*

pe•ri•od•ic (pēr′ē od′ik) /ˌpɪəriy'ɒdɪk/ *adj.* occurring again at regular periods of time: *periodic outbreaks of smallpox.* —**pe′ri•od′i•cal•ly,** *adv.*: *She'd come into my office periodically to complain.* —**pe•ri•o•dic•i•ty** (pēr′ē ə dis′i tē) /ˌpɪəriyə'dɪsɪtiy/ *n.* [*noncount*]

pe•ri•od•i•cal (pēr′ē od′i kəl) /ˌpɪəriy'ɒdɪkəl/ *n.* [*count*] **1.** a publication issued under the same title at regular periods. —*adj.* **2.** of or relating to such publications. **3.** published at regular intervals. **4.** PERIODIC.

pe′ri•od′ic ta′ble (pēr′ē od′ik) /'pɪəriy'ɒdɪk/ *n.* [*count*] a table in which the chemical elements are arranged according to their atomic numbers in related groups.

per•i•pa•tet•ic (per′ə pə tet′ik) /ˌpɛrəpə'tɛtɪk/ *adj.* **1.** walking or traveling about; itinerant. —*n.* [*count*] **2.** an itinerant person.

pe•riph•er•al (pə rif′ər əl) /pə'rɪfərəl/ *adj.* **1.** of or relating to the periphery: *the peripheral boundaries.* **2.** concerned with less central aspects of a problem or situation: *questions peripheral to the main issue.* **3.** [*before a noun*] of or relating to a computer peripheral: *buying peripheral devices.* —*n.* [*count*] **4.** a device, as a keyboard, printer, or tape drive, that is outside a computer but connected to it.

pe•riph•er•y (pə rif′ə rē) /pə'rɪfəriy/ *n.* [*count*], *pl.* **-er•ies.** **1.** the outside boundary or perimeter of a surface or area; the outer limits (of an aspect of social, cultural, or intellectual life): *His radical positions put him on the periphery of American politics.* **2.** the outside surface of a body. **3.** the outskirts of a city or urban area. **4.** the less central parts or aspects of a question or problem.

per•i•scope (per′ə skōp′) /'pɛrəˌskowp/ *n.* [*count*] an instrument for viewing objects, usually made of a tube with an arrangement of prisms or mirrors, used esp. in submarines. See -SCOPE-.

per•ish (per′ish) /'pɛrɪʃ/ *v.* [*no obj*] **1.** to die as a result of violence, etc.: *Thousands perished in that earthquake.* **2.** to suffer destruction or ruin. —***Idiom.*** **3. perish the thought,** (used to express the wish that something may never or should never happen): *"Aren't you coming to the concert?" —"Perish the thought!"*

per•ish•a•ble (per′i shə bəl) /'pɛrɪʃəbəl/ *adj.* **1.** that may decay or be destroyed: *Perishable foods need to be refrigerated.* —*n.* [*count*] **2.** Usually, **perishables.** [*plural*] something perishable, esp. food: *perishables kept in the refrigerator.*

per•i•to•ne•um (per′i tn ē′əm) /ˌpɛrɪtn̩'iyəm/ *n.* [*count*], *pl.* **-to•ne•ums, -to•ne•a** (-tn ē′ə) /-tn̩'iyə/. the wall or membrane that lines the abdomen on the inside of the body. —**per′i•to•ne′al,** *adj.*

per•i•to•ni•tis (per′i tn ī′tis) /ˌpɛrɪtn̩'aytɪs/ *n.* [*noncount*] a condition in which the peritoneum is inflamed.

per•i•win•kle[1] (per′i wing′kəl) /'pɛrɪˌwɪŋkəl/ *n.* [*count*] a small sea creature, a mollusk, that may be eaten.

per•i•win•kle[2] (per′i wing′kəl) /'pɛrɪˌwɪŋkəl/ *n.* [*count*] a plant having glossy evergreen leaves and usually blue-violet flowers. Also called **myrtle.**

per•jure (pûr′jər) /'pɜrdʒər/ *v.* [~ + *oneself*], **-jured, -jur•ing.** to make (oneself) guilty of perjury: *perjured herself by lying about her son's whereabouts on the night of the murder.* —**per′jur•er,** *n.* [*count*] See -JUR-.

per•ju•ry (pûr′jə rē) /'pɜrdʒəriy/ *n.* [*noncount*] the willful telling of a lie or lies after having sworn under oath not to do so, esp. in a trial or other legal proceeding.

perk[1] (pûrk) /pɜrk/ *v.* Usually, **perk up.** **1.** to (cause to) become lively, cheerful, etc., again, as after decline or neglect: [*no obj*]: *She perked up immediately when I told her we could get a dog.* [~ + *obj* + *up*]: *Promising her a dog perked her up.* [~ + *up* + *obj*]: *That teacher needs something to perk up his class.* **2.** to (cause to) rise quickly or briskly: [*no obj*]: *The dog's head perked up.* [~ + *up* + *obj*]: *The dog perked up its head.* [~ + *obj* + *up*]: *The dog perked its head up.*

perk[2] (pûrk) /pɜrk/ *v.* to percolate: [*no obj*]: *The coffee was perking in the kitchen.* [~ + *obj*]: *perked some coffee before the meeting began.*

perk[3] (pûrk) /pɜrk/ *n.* [*count*] a perquisite: *fantastic perks at the new job.* See -QUIS-.

perk•y (pûr′kē) /'pɜrkiy/ *adj.,* **-i•er, -i•est.** lively, cheerful, vigorous: *a perky new secretary who brightened everyone's day.* —**perk′i•ness,** *n.* [*noncount*]

perm (pûrm) /pɜrm/ *Informal.* *n.* [*count*] **1.** PERMANENT (def. 4). —*v.* [~ + *obj*] **2.** to give a permanent to (someone, or one's hair): *She had permed her hair in a curly style.*

per•ma•frost (pûr′mə frôst′, -frost′) /'pɜrməˌfrɔst, -ˌfrɒst/ *n.* [*noncount*] (in arctic or subarctic regions) permanently frozen soil under the first layer of soil.

per•ma•nence (pûr′mə nəns) /'pɜrmənəns/ *n.* [*noncount*] the condition or quality of being permanent. See -MAN[2]-.

per•ma•nent (pûr′mə nənt) /'pɜrmənənt/ *adj.* **1.** existing and not stopping; everlasting. **2.** intended to serve, function, etc., for a long period: *a member of the perma-*

nent faculty. **3.** long-lasting or nonfading: *permanent ink.* **—*n.*** [*count*] **4.** Also called **per′manent wave′.** a wave or curl set into the hair by treating it with chemicals or heat: *Her permanent lasted for a number of months.* —**per′ma•nent•ly,** *adv.: permanently attached.* See -MAN-[2].

per′manent press′, *n.* [*noncount*] a process in which a fabric is treated to keep it without wrinkles, so as to require little ironing after washing.

per•me•a•ble (pûr′mē ə bəl) /ˈpɜrmiyəbəl/ *adj.* capable of being permeated. —**per•me•a•bil•i•ty** (pûr′mē ə bil′i tē) /ˌpɜrmiyəˈbɪlɪtiy/ *n.* [*noncount*]

per•me•ate (pûr′mē āt′) /ˈpɜrmiyˌeyt/ *v.,* **-at•ed, -at•ing. 1.** to pass into or through every part of: [~ + *obj*]: *with sunshine permeating the room.* [*no obj*]: *Water permeated through the wood.* **2.** to be found all through (something); to pervade: [~ + *obj*]: *Bias permeated the report.* [*no obj*]: *Fear of layoffs permeated through the office.*

per•mis•si•ble (pər mis′ə bəl) /pərˈmɪsəbəl/ *adj.* capable of being permitted: *Rowdy behavior is not permissible in a classroom.* —**per•mis′si•bly,** *adv.* See -MIS-.

per•mis•sion (pər mish′ən) /pərˈmɪʃən/ *n.* [*noncount*] the act of permitting: *to ask permission to leave the room.* See -MIS-.

per•mis•sive (pər mis′iv) /pərˈmɪsɪv/ *adj.* **1.** too willing to allow or permit something, as social behavior, that others might disapprove of or forbid: *permissive parents who allowed her to stay up late.* **2.** giving, expressing, or showing permission: *a permissive nod.* —**per•mis′sive•ly,** *adv.* —**per•mis′sive•ness,** *n.* [*noncount*]: *too much permissiveness in American society.* See -MIS-.

per•mit (*v.* pər mit′; *n.* pûr′mit, pər mit′) / *v.* pərˈmɪt; *n.* ˈpɜrmɪt, pərˈmɪt/ *v.,* **-mit•ted, -mit•ting,** *n.* **—*v.* 1.** to allow to be done or occur; to allow to do: [~ + *obj*]: *laws that permit the sale of drugs in some countries.* [~ + *oneself* + *obj*]: *She permitted herself a little smile.* [~ + *obj* + *to* + *verb*]: *Permit me to explain.* **2.** [~ + *obj*] to tolerate; consent to: *This law permits religious worship with drugs.* **3.** to provide opportunity (for), or admit (of): [~ + *obj*]: *The power plant has vents to permit the escape of gases.* [*no obj*]: *I'll look this over when time permits.* **—*n.*** [*count*] **4.** an official certificate of permission; license: *a work permit.* See -MIT-.

per•mu•ta•tion (pûr′myŏŏ tā′shən) /ˌpɜrmyʊˈteyʃən/ *n.* **1.** [*noncount*] the act of permuting; rearrangement. **2.** [*count*] any of the changes that result from such rearrangement: *Two of the possible permutations of the elements* abc *are* acb *or* bac. See -MUT-.

per•mute (pər myŏŏt′) /pərˈmyut/ *v.* [~ + *obj*], **-mut•ed, -mut•ing.** to change, alter, or transform by rearranging the order or arrangement of. See -MUT-.

per•ni•cious (pər nish′əs) /pərˈnɪʃəs/ *adj.* causing harm or ruin; evil in effect; ruinous: *a pernicious lie.* —**per•ni′cious•ly,** *adv.* —**per•ni′cious•ness,** *n.* [*noncount*]

per•o•ra•tion (per′ə rā′shən) /ˌpɛrəˈreyʃən/ *n.* [*count*] the end part of a speech; a conclusion that reminds the listeners of the principal points.

per•ox•ide (pə rok′sid) /pəˈrɒksayd/ *n., v.,* **-id•ed, -id•ing. —*n.*** [*noncount*] **1. a.** hydrogen peroxide. **b.** a compound in which two oxygen atoms are bonded to each other. **—*v.*** [~ + *obj*] **2.** to use peroxide as a bleaching agent on (esp. the hair): *Do you think she peroxides her hair?*

per•pen•dic•u•lar (pûr′pən dik′yə lər) /ˌpɜrpənˈdɪkyələr/ *adj.* **1.** vertical; straight up and down; upright. **2.** meeting at right angles: *Forty-second Street is perpendicular to Fifth Avenue.* **—*n.*** [*count*] **3.** a perpendicular line, plane, or position. See -PEND-.

per•pe•trate (pûr′pi trāt′) /ˈpɜrpɪˌtreyt/ *v.* [~ + *obj*], **-trat•ed, -trat•ing.** to carry out; do; commit: *to perpetrate a hoax.* —**per•pe•tra•tion** (pûr′pi trā′shən) /ˌpɜrpɪˈtreyʃən/ *n.* [*noncount*]

per•pe•tra•tor (pûr′pi trā′tər) /ˈpɜrpɪˌtreytər/ *n.* [*count*] one who perpetrates: *The police tracked the alleged perpetrator to his hideout.*

per•pet•u•al (pər pech′ŏŏ əl) /pərˈpɛtʃuwəl/ *adj.* **1.** continuing or lasting forever; everlasting. **2.** lasting for a very long time. **3.** continuing without stopping or interrupting: *her perpetual whining about her job.* **4.** (of a plant or flower) blooming throughout the growing season. **—*n.*** [*count*] **5.** a perpetual plant. —**per•pet′u•al•ly,** *adv.: She was perpetually whining.* See -PET-. **—Syn.** See ETERNAL.

per•pet•u•ate (pər pech′ŏŏ āt′) /pərˈpɛtʃuwˌeyt/ *v.* [~ + *obj*], **-at•ed, -at•ing.** to make perpetual: *to perpetuate a myth.* —**per•pet•u•a•tion** (pər pech′ŏŏ ā′shən) /pərˌpɛtʃuwˈeyʃən/ *n.* [*noncount*] See -PET-.

per•pe•tu•i•ty (pûr′pi tŏŏ′i tē, -tyŏŏ′-) /ˌpɜrpɪˈtuwɪtiy, -ˈtyuw-/ *n., pl.* **-ties. 1.** [*noncount*] the state or character of being perpetual. **2.** [*count*] an annuity paid for life. **—*Idiom.* 3. in perpetuity,** so as to last forever: *This private park was given to the city in perpetuity.* See -PET-.

per•plex (pər pleks′) /pərˈplɛks/ *v.* [~ + *obj*] to cause to be confused over what is not understood or certain: *Her strange, quiet behavior perplexed me.* —**per•plex′ing,** *adj.: a very perplexing problem.* See -PLEX-.

per•plex•i•ty (pər plek′si tē) /pərˈplɛksɪtiy/ *n., pl.* **-ties. 1.** [*noncount*] the state or condition of being perplexed: *He looked up from his work in complete perplexity.* **2.** [*count*] something that is perplexing: *the perplexities of that software.* See -PLEX-.

per•qui•site (pûr′kwə zit) /ˈpɜrkwəzɪt/ *n.* [*count*] an additional payment, benefit, or privilege one receives from one's work, beyond income or salary; perk: *One of the perquisites is the use of a company car.* See -QUIS-.

per se (pûr sā′) /ˈpɜr sey/ *adv.* by, of, for, or in itself; considered alone or by itself: *Your lateness per se doesn't bother me; it's what it says about your respect for my time.*

per•se•cute (pûr′si kyŏŏt′) /ˈpɜrsɪˌkyuwt/ *v.* [~ + *obj*], **-cut•ed, -cut•ing. 1.** to treat (someone) cruelly or unfairly, esp. because of religion, race, etc.: *In the early days of Christianity, Christians were persecuted by the Romans.* **2.** to annoy (someone) without stopping. —**per′se•cu′tor,** *n.* [*count*] See -SEQ-.

per•se•cu•tion (pûr′si kyŏŏ′shən) /ˌpɜrsɪˈkyuwʃən/ *n.* **1.** [*noncount*] the act or state of persecuting or of being persecuted: *suffering persecution for the sake of justice.* **2.** [*count*] a program or campaign of persecuting: *the Roman persecutions of the Christians.* See -SEQ-.

per•se•vere (pûr′sə vēr′) /ˌpɜrsəˈvɪər/ *v.* [*no obj*], **-vered, -ver•ing.** to continue to pursue something in spite of obstacles, problems, or opposition: *managed to persevere and finish her degree.* —**per′se•ver′ance,** *n.* [*noncount*]: *her perseverance in finishing her degree.*

per•si•flage (pûr′sə fläzh′, pâr′-) /ˈpɜrsəˌflɑʒ, ˈpɛər-/ *n.* [*noncount*] light, easy talk.

per•sim•mon (pər sim′ən) /pərˈsɪmən/ *n.* **1.** [*count*] a tree of the ebony family, having showy white flowers and a large, plumlike orange fruit. **2.** the fruit itself: [*count*]: *two soft, ripe persimmons.* [*noncount*]: *a pie filling of persimmon.*

per•sist (pər sist′, -zist′) /pərˈsɪst, -ˈzɪst/ *v.* **1.** [*no obj; often:* ~ + *in* + *obj*] to be persistent: *persisted in breaking the rules.* **2.** [*no obj*] to last or endure a long time: *The legend of King Arthur has persisted for fifteen centuries.* **3.** [*used with quotations*] to keep insisting in speech: *"But don't you have anything to add, Mr. President?" she persisted.* See -SIST-.

per•sis•tence (pər sis′təns) /pərˈsɪstəns/ *n.* [*noncount*] **1.** the act or fact of persisting. **2.** the quality of being persistent: *She has persistence and won't give up.*

per•sis•tent (pər sis′tənt) /pərˈsɪstənt/ *adj.* **1.** continuing to do something in spite of difficulty, opposition, or criticism: *He was persistent and finally finished his project.* **2.** lasting for a long time: *annoying, persistent coughing.* **3.** repeated; continued: *her persistent questions.* —**per•sist′ent•ly,** *adv.: She would persistently demand answers where none were possible.* See -SIST-.

per•snick•et•y (pər snik′i tē) /pərˈsnɪkɪtiy/ also **per•nick•e•ty** (pər nik′i tē) /pərˈnɪkɪtiy/ *adj. Informal.* very fussy; paying too much attention to details: *the persnickety English teacher who notices every comma that's in the wrong place.*

per•son (pûr′sən) /ˈpɜrsən/ *n.* [*count*] **1.** a human being; a man, woman, or child: *How many persons are there in the United States? Most persons have names; not all animals do. All persons must show proof of identity.* **2.** the actual self or individual personality of a human being: *I want to get to know you as a person, not just as my boss.* **3.** the body of a living human being, sometimes including the clothes being worn: *He had no money on his person.* **4.** a grammatical category for pronouns and verbs that distinguishes between the speaker of something said (the first person), the person spoken to (the second person), and other people or things spoken about (the third person). **—*Idiom.* 5. in person,** directly and personally present (at a place), without a substitution: *Applicants for this job must apply for it in person.*

-person, *suffix. -person* is used to replace some paired, sex-specific suffixes such as -MAN and -WOMAN or -ER[1] and -ESS: *salesman/saleswoman* are replaced by *sales* +

-person → *salesperson; waiter/waitress* are replaced by *wait* + *-person* → *waitperson.*

per•son•a•ble (pûr′sən ə bəl) /ˈpɜrsənəbəl/ *adj.* having an agreeable or pleasing personality.

per•son•age (pûr′sə nij) /ˈpɜrsənɪdʒ/ *n.* [*count*] a person of distinction or importance.

per•son•al (pûr′sə nl) /ˈpɜrsənl/ *adj.* **1.** [*before a noun*] of or relating to a person; individual: *He gave his own, personal opinion.* **2.** private: *My feelings for the deceased were too personal for me to share at the funeral.* **3.** [*before a noun*] directed to or intended for a particular person: *I asked him for a personal favor.* **4.** referring or directed offensively to a particular person: *personal remarks about his wife.* **5.** [*before a noun*] done, carried out, held, etc., in person: *a personal interview with the Pope.* **6.** [*before a noun*] relating to the body, clothing, or appearance: *personal cleanliness.* **7.** [*before a noun*] of, relating to, or showing grammatical person: *The personal ending -o in the Spanish* hablo, *"I speak," refers to the speaker, "I."* **—*n.*** [*count*] **8.** a notice placed in a newspaper or other publication by a person seeking friendship, etc.

per′sonal comput′er, *n.* [*count*] a microcomputer designed for individual use. *Abbr.:* PC

per′sonal effects′, *n.* [*plural*] articles, chiefly clothing, toilet items, etc., for use by an individual: *nothing in his luggage except personal effects.*

per′sonal identifica′tion num′ber, *n.* PIN.

per•son•al•i•ty (pûr′sə nal′i tē) /ˌpɜrsəˈnælɪtiy/ *n., pl.* **-ties. 1.** [*count*] the part of one's character as others see it: *a charming personality in public; a surly one in private.* **2.** all the characteristics that an individual possesses in his or her character: [*count*]: *a positive, goal-oriented personality.* [*noncount*]: *Personality is shaped early in life.* **3.** something thought of as similar to a human personality, as the atmosphere of a place or thing: [*noncount*]: *That little restaurant has personality.* [*count*]: *a charming personality to those old inns.* **4.** [*count*] a famous or well-known person; a celebrity.

per•son•al•ize (pûr′sə nl īz′) /ˈpɜrsənlˌayz/ *v.* [~ + *obj*], **-ized, -iz•ing. 1.** to have marked with one's initials or name: *to personalize stationery.* **2.** to make personal, as by applying a general statement to oneself: *You shouldn't personalize his critical remarks.*

per•son•al•ly (pûr′sə nl ē) /ˈpɜrsənliy/ *adv.* **1.** in person; directly: *I thanked them personally.* **2.** as if intended for or directed at oneself: *Don't take the boss's comments personally; he didn't mean you, but the workers in general.* **3.** as regards oneself; speaking for one's self; in one's opinion: *Personally, I don't care to go.* **4.** as a person: *I like her personally, but not as a boss.*

per•so•na non gra•ta (pər sō′nə non grä′tə, grā′tə, grat′ə) /pərˈsowˈnə nɒn grɑtə, ˈgreytə, ˈgrætə/ *adj.* [*be* + ~] not being personally acceptable or welcome: *She is persona non grata around our house until she apologizes for her rudeness.* See -GRAT-.

per•son•i•fy (pər son′ə fī′) /pərˈsɒnəˌfay/ *v.* [~ + *obj*], **-fied, -fy•ing. 1.** to show that (a thing) has a human nature; to represent (a thing) as a person, as in art: *The Greek goddess Demeter personifies the richness of mother earth.* **2.** to be a typical example of; typify: *That money-grabbing tycoon personifies the ruthless ambition of some executives.* **—per•son•i•fi•ca•tion** (pər son′ə fi kā′shən) /pərˌsɒnəfɪˈkeyʃən/ *n.* [*noncount*]: *He was the personification of evil and greed.*

per•son•nel (pûr′sə nel′) /ˌpɜrsəˈnɛl/ *n.* **1.** [*plural; used with a plural verb*] all the persons working in an organization, in the army, etc.: *Send a memo to all personnel.* **2.** [*noncount; used with a singular verb*] a department of an organization that is in charge of supervising matters having to do with the employees, as hiring, etc.: *Bring this up with Personnel and see what they suggest.*

per•spec•tive (pər spek′tiv) /pərˈspɛktɪv/ *n.* **1.** [*noncount*] a technique of drawing on a two-dimensional surface pictures of solid objects that show their relationships in three dimensions. **2.** [*count*] a picture employing this technique, esp. one in which it is prominent. **3.** [*count*] one's opinion about facts, ideas, etc., and their relationships: *an interesting perspective on the situation.* **4.** [*noncount*] the ability to see the important facts of something in proportion to one another: *Can't you put this minor setback into perspective and see that it really is for the best? Get some perspective.* **—*adj.*** [*before a noun*] **5.** of or relating to the art of perspective. See -SPEC-.

per•spi•ca•cious (pûr′spi kā′shəs) /ˌpɜrspɪˈkeyʃəs/ *adj.* having sharp ability to understand something; discerning. **—per′spi•ca′cious•ly,** *adv.* **—per•spi•cac•i•ty** (pûr′spi kas′i tē) /ˌpɜrspɪˈkæsɪtiy/ **per′spi•ca′cious•ness,** *n.* [*noncount*] See -SPEC-.

per•spi•ra•tion (pûr′spə rā′shən) /ˈpɜrspəˈreyʃən/ *n.* [*noncount*] **1.** a salty, watery fluid released by the sweat glands of the skin; sweat: *Perspiration had soaked through his shirt.* **2.** the act or process of perspiring. See -SPIR-.

per•spire (pər spīər′) /pərˈspayər/ *v.* [*no obj*], **-spired, -spir•ing.** to release or give out perspiration; to sweat: *After running up nine flights of stairs, you'd be perspiring too!* See -SPIR-.

per•suade (pər swād′) /pərˈsweyd/ *v.,* **-suad•ed, -suad•ing. 1.** to cause (a person) to do something, as by advising or urging: [~ + *obj* + *to* + *verb*]: *I persuaded her to go with me to the party.* [~ + *obj* + *into/out of* + *obj*]: *I persuaded her into going to the party with my roommate.* **2.** to convince (someone); cause (someone) to believe something: [~ + *obj* + *of* + *obj*]: *They persuaded the judge of her innocence.* [~ + *obj* + *(that) clause*]: *They persuaded the judge that she was innocent.* **—per•suad′a•ble,** *adj.* **—per•suad′er,** *n.* [*count*] See -SUADE-.

per•sua•sion (pər swā′zhən) /pərˈsweyʒən/ *n.* **1.** [*noncount*] the act of persuading or seeking to persuade: *With a little persuasion they might help you.* **2.** [*noncount*] power to persuade: *arguments with a great deal of persuasion behind them.* **3.** [*count*] a form or system of belief: *those of the liberal persuasion.* **4.** [*count*] a group, faction, kind, or sort: *musicians of the New Wave persuasion.* See -SUADE-.

per•sua•sive (pər swā′siv, -ziv) /pərˈsweysɪv, -zɪv/ *adj.* able or intended to persuade: *a persuasive argument.* **—per•sua′sive•ly,** *adv.: argued persuasively that we should hire her.* See -SUADE-.

pert (pûrt) /pɜrt/ *adj.,* **-er, -est. 1.** bold or impolite in speech or behavior; impertinent. **2.** jaunty and stylish; chic. **3.** lively; sprightly; in good health. **—pert′ly,** *adv.* **—pert′ness,** *n.* [*noncount*]

per•tain (pər tān′) /pərˈteyn/ *v.* [~ + *to* + *obj*] **1.** to have reference or relation to (something); relate: *documents pertaining to the lawsuit.* **2.** [*not: be* + ~*-ing*] to belong properly or fittingly to; be appropriate to: *responsibilities pertaining to parenthood.* See -TAIN-.

per•ti•na•cious (pûr′tn ā′shəs) /ˌpɜrtnˈeyʃəs/ *adj.* holding tightly to a purpose, course of action, or opinion; resolute: *a pertinacious investigator who pursued every lead.* **—per′ti•na′cious•ly,** *adv.* **—per•ti•nac•i•ty** (pûr′tn as′i tē) /ˌpɜrtnˈæsɪtiy/ *n.* [*noncount*] See -TAIN-.

per•ti•nent (pûr′tn ənt) /ˈpɜrtnənt/ *adj.* pertaining to the matter being considered; relevant: *pertinent details.* **—per′ti•nence,** *n.* [*noncount*]: *Does this have any pertinence to the case?* See -TEN-, -TAIN-.

per•turb (pər tûrb′) /pərˈtɜrb/ *v.* [~ + *obj*] **1.** to disturb (someone) greatly in the mind: *The disappointments he faced perturbed him greatly.* **2.** to cause the orbit of (a celestial body) to be changed or upset. **—per•tur•ba•tion** (pûr′tər bā′shən) /ˌpɜrtərˈbeyʃən/ *n.* [*noncount*]: *the effects of perturbation on heavenly bodies.* [*count*]: *The perturbations were felt throughout the solar system.* See -TURB-.

pe•ruse (pə ro͞oz′) /pəˈruwz/ *v.* [~ + *obj*], **-rused, -rus•ing. 1.** to read through with care: *to peruse a report.* **2.** to read through quickly and without much care. **—pe•rus′al,** *n.* [*count*]: *a perusal of the report.*

Pe•ru•vi•an (pə ro͞o′vē ən) /pəˈruwviyən/ *adj.* **1.** of or relating to Peru. **—*n.*** [*count*] **2.** a person born or living in Peru.

per•vade (pər vād′) /pərˈveyd/ *v.* [~ + *obj*], **-vad•ed, -vad•ing.** to become spread throughout all parts of: *The smell of coffee pervaded the air.* See -VADE-.

per•va•sive (pər vā′siv) /pərˈveysɪv/ *adj.* tending to pervade: *a pervasive sense of fear.* See -VADE-.

per•verse (pər vûrs′) /pərˈvɜrs/ *adj.* willfully determined not to do what is expected or desired; contrary: *a perverse desire to argue for the opposite of whatever everyone else accepts.* **—per•verse′ly,** *adv.: Now, perversely, he's opposed to the amendment, although earlier he supported it.* **—per•verse′ness,** *n.* [*noncount*] **—per•ver•si•ty** (pər vûr′si tē) /pərˈvɜrsɪtiy/ *n.* [*noncount*] See -VERT-.

per•ver•sion (pər vûr′zhən, -shən) /pərˈvɜrʒən, -ʃən/ *n.* **1.** [*count*] the act of perverting. **2.** [*noncount*] the state of being perverted. **3.** [*count*] a perverted form of something: *a perversion of justice.* **4.** [*count*] any of various abnormal sexual practices. See -VERT-.

per•vert (*v.* pər vûrt′; *n.* pûr′vərt) / *v.* pərˈvɜrt; *n.* ˈpɜrvərt/ *v.* [~ + *obj*] **1.** to lead (someone) away from what is right in moral behavior: *perverting children with por-*

nography. **2.** to use in an evil or improper way; misapply: *You're perverting science for unworthy purposes.* **3.** to bring (something) to a less excellent state: *to pervert a simple way of life.* **—***n.* [*count*] **4.** one who practices a sexual perversion. **—per•vert′ed,** *adj.* See -VERT-.

pe•se•ta (pə sā′tə) /pə'seytə/ *n.* [*count*], *pl.* **-tas** (-təz). the basic monetary unit of Spain.

pes•ky (pes′kē) /'pɛskiy/ *adj.*, **-ki•er, -ki•est.** annoying; troublesome: *A pesky fly kept buzzing in my ear.* **—pesk•i•ly** (pes′kə lē) /'pɛskəliy/ *adv.* **—pesk′i•ness,** *n.* [*noncount*]

pe•so (pā′sō) /'peysow/ *n.* [*count*], *pl.* **-sos.** the basic monetary unit of Bolivia, Chile, Colombia, Cuba, the Dominican Republic, Guinea-Bissau, Mexico, the Philippines, and Uruguay.

pes•si•mism (pes′ə miz′əm) /'pɛsə,mɪzəm/ *n.* [*noncount*] the tendency to see only what is gloomy, or to expect the worst possible outcome. **—pes′si•mist,** *n.* [*count*]: *The pessimist sees a glass of water that is filled halfway and considers the glass to be half-empty; the optimist sees the same glass and thinks of it as half-full.* **—pes′si•mis′tic,** *adj.* **—pes′si•mis′ti•cal•ly,** *adv.*

pest (pest) /pɛst/ *n.* [*count*] **1.** an annoying or troublesome person, animal, or thing; nuisance: *The youngster was a pest on the airplane.* **2.** an insect or other small animal that harms or destroys garden plants, trees, etc.

pes•ter (pes′tər) /'pɛstər/ *v.* [~ + *obj*] to be a pest; trouble: *Quit pestering me!*

pes•ti•cide (pes′tə sīd′) /'pɛstə,sayd/ *n.* a chemical preparation for destroying plant or animal pests: [*noncount*]: *the overuse of pesticide in agriculture.* [*count*]: *all those different pesticides.* See -CIDE-.

pes•tif•er•ous (pe stif′ər əs) /pɛ'stɪfərəs/ *adj.* **1.** bringing or bearing disease. **2.** troublesome; annoying. See -FER-.

pes•ti•lence (pes′tl əns) /'pɛstləns/ *n.* **1.** a deadly disease that spreads to many people: [*noncount*]: *famine followed by pestilence.* [*count*]: *a number of pestilences descending on Egypt.* **2.** something harmful or destructive: [*noncount*]: *pestilence in modern society.* [*count*]: *corruption, theft, and other pestilences.*

pes•ti•lent (pes′tl ənt) /'pɛstlənt/ *adj.* **1.** of or relating to pestilence. **2.** destructive to life; deadly.

pes•tle (pes′əl, pes′tl) /'pɛsəl, 'pɛstl/ *n.*, *v.*, **-tled, -tling.** **—***n.* [*count*] **1.** a tool for grinding substances in a mortar, usually having a heavy, rounded end. **—***v.* [~ + *obj*] **2.** to pound or grind with or as if with a pestle.

pet (pet) /pɛt/ *n.*, *adj.*, *v.*, **pet•ted, pet•ting.** **—***n.* [*count*] **1.** an animal kept as a companion in the home: *She had always wanted a dog as a pet.* **2.** a person who is especially well cared for or favored: *a teacher's pet.* **—***adj.* [*before a noun*] **3.** kept or treated as a pet: *two pet canaries.* **4.** especially well cared for, such as a child. **5.** favorite; preferred: *a pet theory.* **6.** showing fondness or affection: *pet names for each other, like "Poochie" and "Boopsie."* **—***v.* **7.** [~ + *obj*] to stroke or touch kindly with the hand: *She petted the dog on its head.* **8.** to kiss and touch, stroke, or caress in a way expressing sexual attraction: [~ + *obj*]: *They were petting each other on the sofa.* [*no obj*]: *They were petting in the back seat of his car.* **9.** [~ + *obj*] to treat as a pet; indulge.

PET (pet) /pɛt/ *n.* [*noncount*] positron emission tomography, a technique for revealing active areas of the brain while information is being processed.

-pet-, *root.* *-pet-* comes from Latin, where it has the meaning "seek; strive for." This meaning is found in such words as: APPETITE, CENTRIPETAL, COMPETE, COMPETENCE, COMPETENT, COMPETITION, IMPETIGO, IMPETUOUS, IMPETUS, PERPETUAL, PETITION, PETULANT, REPEAT, REPETITION.

pet•al (pet′l) /'pɛtl/ *n.* [*count*] one of the often colored parts of the main base of a flower.

pe•tard (pi tärd′) /pɪ'tɑrd/ *n.* [*count*] **1.** an explosive device once used in warfare. **—*Idiom.*** **2. hoist by** or **with one's own petard,** caught by the very device one had planned to use to hurt another: *The candidate was hoist by his own petard when, after he made claims about his opponent's shady finances, his own tax returns showed irregularities.*

pe•ter (pē′tər) /'piytər/ *v.* [*no obj*] Usually, **peter out. 1.** to tire; become exhausted: *In the last lap of the race she just petered out.* **2.** to grow less or diminish gradually and stop: *The hot water petered out.*

pe•tite (pə tēt′) /pə'tiyt/ *adj.* **1.** (of a woman) short and having a small, slim figure; diminutive. **—***n.* **2.** [*noncount*] a size of clothing for women of less than average height and figures. **3.** [*count*] a piece of clothing in this size.

pet•it four (pet′ē fôr′, fōr′) /'pɛt'iy fɔr, 'fowr/ *n.* [*count*], *pl.* **pet•its fours** (pet′ē fôrz′, fōrz′) /'pɛt'iy fɔrz, 'fowrz/. a small, sweet frosted cake.

pe•ti•tion (pə tish′ən) /pə'tɪʃən/ *n.* [*count*] **1.** a formally written request or document, often signed by those agreeing to it, addressed to those in authority, asking for some favor, right, or benefit: *presented the petition, signed by over a thousand people, to the mayor.* **2.** a respectful or humble request, as to a superior. **3.** something asked for or sought by request: *a petition for divorce.* **—***v.* **4.** [~ + *obj*] to address a petition to (an authority): *The hurricane victims petitioned the governor for help during the emergency.* **5.** to ask by petition for (something); beg for or request: [~ + *obj*]: *The citizen's group petitioned a change in the zoning laws.* [~ + *for* + *obj*]: *They petitioned for a change in the zoning laws.* [~ + *to* + *verb*]: *petitioned to change the zoning laws.* **—pe•ti′tion•er,** *n.* [*count*] See -PET-.

pet•rel (pe′trəl) /'pɛtrəl/ *n.* [*count*] a seabird living near oceans, having a tube-shaped nose.

pet•ri•fy (pe′trə fī′) /'pɛtrə,fay/ *v.*, **-fied, -fy•ing. 1.** to (cause to) become changed into stone or a stony substance: [*no obj*]: *Over thousands of years the fossils had petrified.* [~ + *obj*]: *The hot lava had instantly petrified this fossil.* **2.** [~ + *obj*] to cause to be in a state of shock, as from fear or terror: *She refused to climb up the tree because heights petrify her.* **3.** to (cause to) be hardened, deadened, or unwilling to change: [~ + *obj*]: *The tragedy petrified his emotions.* [*no obj*]: *The tiny, isolated society had petrified.* **—pet•ri•fac•tion** (pe′trə fak′shən) /,pɛtrə'fækʃən/ *n.* [*noncount*] **—pet′ri•fied,** *adj.*: *The petrified children sat there, eyes wide with fear.*

petro-[1], *prefix.* *petro-* comes from Greek, where it has the meaning "rock, stone": *petro-* + *-ology* → *petrology (= the study of rocks or stone).*

petro-[2], *prefix.* *petro-* is taken from PETROLEUM and is used to form compounds: *petro-* + *chemistry* → *petrochemistry; petro-* + *power* → *petropower (= power derived from petroleum).*

pet•ro•chem•i•cal (pe′trō kem′i kəl) /,pɛtrow'kɛmɪkəl/ *n.* [*count*] **1.** a chemical substance obtained from petroleum or natural gas, as gasoline, kerosene, or petrolatum. **—***adj.* [*before a noun*] **2.** of or relating to a petrochemical.

pet•ro•dol•lars (pe′trō dol′ərz) /'pɛtrow,dɒlərz/ *n.* [*plural*] revenues or money in dollars earned by petroleum-exporting countries, esp. of the Middle East: *As oil prices rose, oil producers accumulated petrodollars and spent lavishly.*

pet•rol (pe′trəl) /'pɛtrəl/ *n.* *Brit.* GASOLINE.

pe•tro•le•um (pə trō′lē əm) /pə'trowliyəm/ *n.* [*noncount*] an oily, thick, easily burned liquid that is a mixture of various hydrocarbons, used as fuel or made into gasoline, benzene, kerosene, etc.

pe•trol•o•gy (pi trol′ə jē) /pɪ'trɒlədʒiy/ *n.* [*noncount*] the scientific study of rocks. **—pe•trol′o•gist,** *n.* [*count*]

pet•ti•coat (pet′ē kōt′) /'pɛtiy,kowt/ *n.* [*count*] a skirt worn under an outer skirt or dress, esp. one that is full and often trimmed and ruffled and of a decorative fabric.

pet•ti•fog (pet′ē fog′, -fôg′) /'pɛtiy,fɒg, -,fɔg/ *v.* [*no obj*], **-fogged, -fog•ging.** to raise objections about small, unimportant matters. **—pet′ti•fog′ger,** *n.* [*count*]

pet•ty (pet′ē) /'pɛtiy/ *adj.*, **-ti•er, -ti•est. 1.** of little or no importance; inconsequential: *petty grievances and objections.* **2.** of lesser importance; minor: *petty officials.* **3.** having or showing narrow ideas, etc.; ungenerous: *their little, petty minds.* **4.** showing meanness of spirit: *petty revenge.* **—pet′ti•ness,** *n.* [*noncount*]

pet′ty cash′, *n.* [*noncount*] a small amount of cash kept on hand for paying small charges, as for minor office supplies or deliveries.

pet′ty of′ficer, *n.* [*count*] **1.** a noncommissioned officer in the navy or coast guard. **2.** one of the minor officers on a merchant ship, as a boatswain.

pet•u•lant (pech′ə lənt) /'pɛtʃələnt/ *adj.* showing sudden irritation; peevish: *The child grew petulant, clamoring for his mother.* **—pet′u•lance,** *n.* [*noncount*] **—pet′u•lant•ly,** *adv.*: *They complained petulantly about every minor problem.* See -PET-.

pe•tu•nia (pi to͞on′yə, -nē ə, -tyo͞o′-) /pɪ'tuwnyə, -niyə, -'tyuw-/ *n.* [*count*], *pl.* **-nias.** a garden plant of the nightshade family from tropical America, having funnel-shaped flowers.

pew (pyo͞o) /pyuw/ *n.* [*count*] (in a church) one of a number of benches fixed in rows for use by the congregation.

pew•ter (pyo͞o′tər) /'pyuwtər/ *n.* [*noncount*] **1.** a kind of metal in which tin is the chief constituent. **2.** utensils and vessels made of pewter. *—adj.* [*before a noun*] **3.** made of pewter.

pf., an abbreviation of: **1.** pfennig. **2.** pianoforte; piano. **3.** (of stock) preferred.

Pfc. or **PFC,** *Military.* an abbreviation of: private first class.

pg., an abbreviation of: page.

pH, a symbol used to describe the amount of acidity or alkalinity of a chemical solution on a scale of 0 (more acidic) to 14 (more alkaline).

pha•lanx (fā′langks, fal′angks) /ˈfeylæŋks, ˈfælæŋks/ *n.* [*count*], *pl.* **pha•lanx•es. 1.** a body of troops fighting in close formation. **2.** a number of people united for a common purpose: *a phalanx of her supporters at the trial.* **3.** a tightly, closely packed body of people, animals, or things: *a phalanx of riot police.*

phal•lus (fal′əs) /ˈfæləs/ *n.* [*count*], *pl.* **phal•li** (fal′ī) /ˈfælay/ **phal•lus•es. 1.** a representation of the penis, usually as a symbol of male sexual power. **2.** PENIS. —**phal•lic** (fal′ik) /ˈfælɪk/ *adj.*: *the phallic symbolism of the spacecraft, long and tapered at one end.*

phan•tas•ma•go•ri•a (fan taz′mə gôr′ē ə, -gōr′-) /fænˌtæzməˈgɔriyə, -ˈgowr-/ *n.* [*count*], *pl.* **-ri•as.** a shifting series of illusions or confusing, deceptive appearances, as in a dream.

phan•ta•sy (fan′tə sē, -zē) /ˈfæntəsiy, -ziy/ *n., pl.* **-sies,** *v.,* **-sied, -sy•ing.** FANTASY.

phan•tom (fan′təm) /ˈfæntəm/ *n.* [*count*] **1.** an appearance of something that is not really there or does not exist, esp. a ghost. **2.** an appearance or illusion without material substance, as a mirage or optical illusion. *—adj.* [*before a noun*] **3.** of, relating to, or of the nature of a phantom: *a phantom ship.* **4.** not really existing; fictitious: *phantom employees on the payroll.*

phar•aoh (fâr′ō, far′ō, fā′rō) /ˈfɛərow, ˈfærow, ˈfeyrow/ *n.* an ancient Egyptian king: [*count*]: *an ancient Egyptian pharaoh.* [*proper noun; Pharaoh*]: *Oh, Pharaoh, let my people go.*

Phar•i•see (far′ə sē′) /ˈfærəˌsiy/ *n.* [*count*] **1.** a member of an ancient Jewish group that believed in strict observance of religious practices, liberal interpretation of the Bible, and obedience to oral laws and traditions. **2.** [*pharisee*] one who pretends to be religious but who is not so really; a hypocrite. —**Phar•i•sa•ic** (far′ə sā′ik) /ˌfærəˈseyɪk/ **Phar′i•sa′i•cal,** *adj.*

phar•ma•ceu•ti•cal (fär′mə so͞o′ti kəl) /ˌfɑrməˈsuwtɪkəl/ also **phar′ma•ceu′tic,** *adj.* **1.** relating to pharmacy or pharmacists. *—n.* [*count*] **2.** a pharmaceutical preparation or product.

phar•ma•ceu•tics (fär′mə so͞o′tiks) /ˌfɑrməˈsuwtɪks/ *n.* [*noncount; used with a singular verb*] PHARMACY (def. 2): *Pharmaceutics is still taught at that medical college.*

phar•ma•cist (fär′mə sist) /ˈfɑrməsɪst/ *n.* [*count*] one licensed to prepare and give out drugs; druggist.

phar•ma•col•o•gy (fär′mə kol′ə jē) /ˌfɑrməˈkɒlədʒiy/ *n.* [*noncount*] the science dealing with the preparation, uses, and esp. the effects of drugs. —**phar′ma•col′o•gist,** *n.* [*count*]

phar•ma•cy (fär′mə sē) /ˈfɑrməsiy/ *n., pl.* **-cies. 1.** [*count*] a drugstore. **2.** [*noncount*] Also called **pharmaceutics.** the art and science of preparing and giving out drugs and medicines: *studied pharmacy for four years.*

phar•yn•gi•tis (far′in jī′tis) /ˌfærɪnˈdʒaytɪs/ *n.* [*noncount; used with a singular verb*] inflammation of the mucous membrane of the pharynx; sore throat: *Pharyngitis is not usually life-threatening.*

phar•ynx (far′ingks) /ˈfærɪŋks/ *n.* [*count*], *pl.* **pha•ryn•ges** (fə rin′jēz) /fəˈrɪndʒiyz/ **phar•ynx•es.** the area in the rear of the mouth and the throat, with its membranes and muscles, that connects the mouth and nasal passages with the larynx. —**pha•ryn•ge•al** (fə rin′jē əl) /fəˈrɪndʒiyəl/ *adj.*

phase (fāz) /feyz/ *n., v.,* **phased, phas•ing.** *—n.* [*count*] **1.** a stage in a process of change or development: *Her temper tantrums are just part of the phase she's going through.* **2.** the particular, usually repeated appearance presented by the moon or a planet at a given time: *What phase is the moon in?* *—v.* **3.** [~ + *obj*] to schedule so as to be available when or as needed. **4.** [~ + *obj*] to put in phase; synchronize. **5. phase in,** to put or come into use gradually: [~ + *in* + *obj*]: *to phase in some changes in our operations.* [~ + *obj* + *in*]: *to phase them in more slowly.* **6. phase out,** to bring or come to an end gradually; ease out of service: [~ + *out* + *obj*]: *The military phased out those older weapons.* [~ + *obj* + *out*]: *We don't dare phase them all out at once.*

Ph.D., an abbreviation of: Doctor of Philosophy.

pheas•ant (fez′ənt) /ˈfɛzənt/ *n.* **1.** [*count*] a large, typically long-tailed bird. **2.** [*noncount*] the meat of this bird.

phe•no•bar•bi•tal (fē′nō bär′bi tôl′, -tal′, -nə-) /ˌfiynowˈbɑrbɪˌtɔl, -ˌtæl, -nə-/ *n.* [*noncount*] a white, crystalline powder used as a drug to cause sleep and to relax the mind.

phe•nom•e•nal (fi nom′ə nəl) /fɪˈnɒmənəl/ *adj.* very remarkable, amazing, wonderful, or extraordinary: *enjoyed phenomenal success as a race car driver.* —**phe•nom′e•nal′ly,** *adv.*: *She had done phenomenally well in a very short time.*

phe•nom•e•non (fi nom′ə non′, -nən) /fɪˈnɒməˌnɒn, -nən/ *n.* [*count*], *pl.* **-na** (-nə) /-nə/ or **-nons. 1.** a fact or circumstance observed or observable: *the phenomena of nature.* **2.** someone or something remarkable.

pher•o•mone (fer′ə mōn′) /ˈfɛrəˌmown/ *n.* [*count*] a chemical substance released by an animal that serves to influence the behavior of other members of the same species: *Some pheromones are used to attract mates.*

phi•al (fī′əl) /ˈfayəl/ *n.* VIAL.

-phil-, *root.* -*phil*- comes from Greek, where it has the meaning "love; loving." This meaning is found in such words as: BIBLIOPHILE, HEMOPHILIA, PHILANDER, PHILANTHROPIC, PHILANTHROPY, PHILHARMONIC, PHILODENDRON, PHILOLOGY, PHILOSOPHY.

phi•lan•der (fi lan′dər) /fɪˈlændər/ *v.* [*no obj*] (of a man) to make love with many women whom one will not marry or about whom one does not feel deeply. —**phi•lan′der•er,** *n.* [*count*] See -ANDRO-, -PHIL-.

phi•lan•thro•py (fi lan′thrə pē) /fɪˈlænθrəpiy/ *n., pl.* **-pies. 1.** [*noncount*] unselfish concern for human beings, esp. as shown by voluntary service or donations: *a millionaire noted for his philanthropy.* **2.** [*count*] a philanthropic act or donation. **3.** [*count*] a philanthropic institution. —**phil•an•throp•ic** (fil′ən throp′ik) /ˌfɪlənˈθrɒpɪk/ *adj.* —**phi•lan′thro•pist,** *n.* [*count*] See -ANTHRO-, -PHIL-.

phi•lat•e•ly (fi lat′l ē) /fɪˈlætḷiy/ *n.* [*noncount*] the collection and study of postage stamps. —**phil•a•tel•ic** (fil′ə tel′ik) /ˌfɪləˈtɛlɪk/ *adj.* —**phi•lat′e•list,** *n.* [*count*]

-phile or **-phil,** *suffix.* **1.** -*phile* is attached to roots and sometimes words to form nouns with the meaning "lover of, enthusiast for (a given object):" *biblio-* + *-phile* → *bibliophile (= lover of books); Franco-* + *-phile* → *Francophile (= lover of France or French things).* **2.** -*phile* is also attached to roots to form nouns with the meaning "a person sexually attracted to or overly interested in (a given object)": *pedo-* + *-phile* → *pedophile (= someone with a sexual attraction for children).* See -PHIL-.

phil•har•mon•ic (fil′här mon′ik, fil′ər-) /ˌfɪlhɑrˈmɒnɪk, ˌfɪlər-/ *n.* [*count*] a symphony orchestra. See -PHIL-.

Phil•ip•pine (fil′ə pēn, fil′ə pēn′) /ˈfɪləpiyn, ˌfɪləˈpiyn/ *adj.* of or relating to the Philippines. See FILIPINO.

phil•is•tine (fil′ə stēn′, -stīn′, fi lis′tin, -tēn) /ˈfɪləˌstiyn, -ˌstayn, fɪˈlɪstɪn, -tiyn/ *n.* [*count; sometimes: Philistine*] **1.** one who is lacking in culture, good taste, etc. *—adj.* **2.** lacking in culture, good taste, etc.; uncultivated.

phil•o•den•dron (fil′ə den′drən) /ˌfɪləˈdɛndrən/ *n.* [*count*], *pl.* **-drons, -dra** (-drə) /-drə/. a tropical American climbing plant of the arum family, usually having smooth, shiny, evergreen leaves. See -PHIL-.

phi•lol•o•gy (fi lol′ə jē) /fɪˈlɒlədʒiy/ *n.* [*noncount*] **1.** the study of literary texts and of written records, esp. of their original form and meaning. **2.** (esp. in older use) linguistics, esp. historical and comparative linguistics. —**phil•o•log•i•cal** (fil′ə loj′i kəl) /ˌfɪləˈlɒdʒɪkəl/ *adj.* —**phi•lol′o•gist,** *n.* [*count*] See -PHIL-, -LOG-.

phi•los•o•pher (fi los′ə fər) /fɪˈlɒsəfər/ *n.* [*count*] **1.** one who offers views and theories on, or who thinks about, profound questions of right or wrong, the nature of existence, truth, and logic, and other related issues. **2.** one who regulates or controls his or her life by philosophy. **3.** one who is calm or thinks before acting, esp. under difficult circumstances. See -PHIL-, -SOPH-.

phil•o•soph•i•cal (fil′ə sof′i kəl) /ˌfɪləˈsɒfɪkəl/ *adj.* **1.** of or relating to philosophy: *philosophical investigations.* **2.** not likely to become upset when facing difficulty; remaining calm after disappointment: *She was philosophical about her loss.* —**phil′o•soph′i•cal•ly,** *adv.*: *He faced his own death calmly and philosophically.* See -PHIL-, -SOPH-.

phi•los•o•phize (fi los′ə fīz′) /fɪˈlɒsəˌfayz/ *v.* [*no obj*], **-phized, -phiz•ing. 1.** to indulge in philosophy, usually superficially. **2.** to think or reason as a philosopher: *They were philosophizing about life and death.* See -PHIL-, -SOPH-.

phi•los•o•phy (fi los′ə fē) /fɪˈlɒsəfiy/ *n., pl.* **-phies. 1.** [*noncount*] the study of the truths and principles of existence, knowledge, and conduct. **2.** [*count*] a particular system of such study or beliefs: *the philosophy of Spinoza.* **3.** [*noncount*] the critical study of the basic principles of a branch of knowledge: *the philosophy of science.* **4.** [*count*] a system of principles for guidance in one's everyday affairs: *a simple philosophy of life: Treat others just as you would like to be treated.* See -PHIL-, -SOPH-.

phil•ter (fil′tər) /ˈfɪltər/ *n.* [*count*] a potion, charm, or drug, esp. one supposed to cause a person to fall in love. Also, *esp. Brit.,* **phil′tre.**

phle•bi•tis (flə bi′tis) /fləˈbaytɪs/ *n.* [*noncount; used with a singular verb*] inflammation of a vein, esp. in the legs.

phlegm (flem) /flɛm/ *n.* [*noncount*] **1.** the mucus in the nose, mouth, and throat, esp. that appearing in the lungs and throat passages when a person has a cold. **2.** calmness; composure.

phleg•mat•ic (fleg mat′ik) /flɛgˈmætɪk/ also **phleg•mat′i•cal,** *adj.* not easily excited to action or display of emotion; having a calm temperament. —**phleg•mat′i•cal•ly,** *adv.*: *The coach treated victories just like he did defeats, phlegmatically and with complete control.*

phlox (floks) /flɒks/ *n.* [*count*], *pl.* **phlox, phlox•es.** a plant of North America, certain species of which are grown for their showy flowers.

-phobe, *suffix.* *-phobe* is attached to roots and sometimes words to form nouns that refer to persons who have a fear of something named by the root or preceding word: *Anglo-* + *phobe* → *Anglophobe (= fear of English-speakers or of England).*

pho•bi•a (fō′bē ə) /ˈfowbiyə/ *n.* [*count*], *pl.* **-bi•as.** a continuous, irrational fear of something that leads to an overwhelming desire to avoid it: *had a deep phobia about flying.*

-phobia, *suffix.* *-phobia* is attached to roots and sometimes words to form nouns with the meaning "dread of, unreasonable hatred toward (a given object)": *agora-* (= *open space*) + *phobia* → *agoraphobia (= fear of open spaces); xeno- (= foreign)* + *-phobia* → *xenophobia (= hatred toward foreigners).*

pho•bic (fō′bik) /ˈfowbɪk/ *adj.* **1.** of or relating to phobia: *He'd become phobic about walking across dark parking lots at night.* —*n.* [*count*] **2.** a person with such a fear.

-phobic, *suffix.* *-phobic* is attached to roots and words to form adjectives or nouns meaning "(a person) having a continuous, irrational fear or hatred toward" the object named in the root or preceding word: *xeno-* (= *foreign*) + *-phobic* → *xenophobic (= (a person) having a fear or hatred of foreigners).*

phoe•nix (fē′niks) /ˈfiynɪks/ *n.* [*count*] [*sometimes: Phoenix*] an imaginary bird that after a life of five or six centuries burns itself and rises from the ashes to begin a new cycle of years: *like a phoenix rising from the ashes of his defeat.*

-phon-, *root.* *-phon-* comes from Greek, where it has the meaning "sound; voice." This meaning is found in such words as: CACOPHONY, HOMOPHONE, MEGAPHONE, MICROPHONE, PHONETIC, PHONICS, PHONOGRAPH, PHONOLOGY, POLYPHONY, SAXOPHONE, STEREOPHONIC, SYMPHONY, TELEPHONE, XYLOPHONE.

phone (fōn) /fown/ *n., v.,* **phoned, phon•ing.** —*n.* [*count*] **1.** a telephone. —*v.* **2.** to use a telephone to call (someone): [~ + *obj*]: *I tried phoning you last night, but no one was there.* [*no obj*]: *Look, just phone if you need us, OK?* See -PHON-.

pho•net•ic (fə net′ik, fō-) /fəˈnɛtɪk, fow-/ *adj.* **1.** [*before a noun*] of or relating to phonetics, or to the sound system of a language: *the phonetic rules governing the pronunciation of the letter* t *in English.* **2.** of or relating to a system of spelling or writing in which one sound is represented by one letter, and one letter represents only one sound: *Finnish has a phonetic spelling system, but Swedish does not.* See -PHON-.

pho•net•ics (fə net′iks, fō-) /fəˈnɛtɪks, fow-/ *n.* **1.** [*noncount; used with a singular verb*] the study of speech sounds and how they are made, transmitted, and heard by the ear: *Phonetics was one of the courses the student teachers had to take.* **2.** [*plural; used with a plural verb*] the phonetic system of a particular language. —**pho•ne•ti•cian** (fō′ni tish′ən) /ˌfownɪˈtɪʃən/ *n.* [*count*] See -PHON-.

phon•ics (fon′iks) /ˈfɒnɪks/ *n.* [*noncount; used with a singular verb*] a method of teaching reading and spelling based upon the study of how sounds are related to ordinary spelling. —**phon′ic,** *adj.* —**phon′i•cal•ly,** *adv.* See -PHON-.

pho•no•graph (fō′nə graf′) /ˈfownəˌgræf/ *n.* [*count*] a machine that reproduces sound using records in the form of grooved disks. —**pho′no•graph′ic,** *adj.* See -GRAPH-, -PHON-.

pho•nol•o•gy (fə nol′ə jē, fō-) /fəˈnɒlədʒiy, fow-/ *n.* [*noncount*] the study of how sounds are patterned in a language and of the rules governing pronunciation. —**pho•no•log•i•cal** (fōn′l oj′i kəl) /ˌfownl̩ˈɒdʒɪkəl/ *adj.* —**pho•nol′o•gist** (-jist) /-dʒɪst/ *n.* [*count*] See -PHON-, -LOG-.

pho•ny or **pho•ney** (fō′nē) /ˈfowniy/ *adj.,* **-ni•er, -ni•est,** *n., pl.* **-nies** or **-neys,** *v.,* **-nied** or **-neyed, -ny•ing** or **-ney•ing.** —*adj.* **1.** not real or genuine; fake: *phony diamonds.* **2.** false or deceiving; affected or pretentious: *a phony excuse.* —*n.* **3.** something phony; a counterfeit or fake: *That's a phony; she has the real gem!* **4.** an insincere person; a person who pretends to be better than he or she is: *What a phony he was!* —*v.* **5.** to falsify: [~ + *up* + *obj*]: *to phony up a document.* [~ + *obj* + *up*]: *to phony the document up by changing the date and some figures.* —**pho′ni•ness,** *n.* [*noncount*]

phoo•ey (fo͞o′ē) /ˈfuwiy/ *interj. Informal.* (used to express a feeling of disgust): *Phooey, I don't believe it!*

phos•phate (fos′fāt) /ˈfɒsfeyt/ *n.* a material containing compounds of phosphorus, used in fertilizers and elsewhere: [*noncount*]: *fertilizer full of phosphate.* [*count*]: *laundry detergent with phosphates in it.*

phos•pho•res•cence (fos′fə res′əns) /ˌfɒsfəˈrɛsəns/ *n.* [*noncount*] the property of giving off light at temperatures below burning, as after exposure to light or other radiation. —**phos′pho•res′cent,** *adj.*

phos•pho•rus (fos′fər əs) /ˈfɒsfərəs/ *n.* [*noncount*] a nonmetallic element and a basic part of plant and animal tissue.

pho•to (fō′tō) /ˈfowtow/ *n.* [*count*], *pl.* **-tos.** a photograph.

photo-, *prefix.* *photo-* comes from Greek, where it has the meaning "light": *photo-* + *biology* → *photobiology; photo-* + *-on* → *photon (= elementary "particle" of light).* This prefix also means "photographic" or "photograph": *photo-* + *copy* → *photocopy.*

pho•to•cell (fō′tō sel′) /ˈfowtowˌsɛl/ *n.* [*count*] an electronic device that converts light into electrical energy by producing voltage: *Photocells are used in automatic control systems for doors.*

pho•to•cop•i•er (fō′tə kop′ē ər) /ˈfowtəˌkɒpiyər/ *n.* [*count*] any electrically operated machine using a photographic method for making instant copies of written or printed material.

pho•to•cop•y (fō′tə kop′ē) /ˈfowtəˌkɒpiy/ *n., pl.* **-cop•ies,** *v.,* **-cop•ied, -cop•y•ing.** —*n.* [*count*] **1.** a photographic copy of a document or the like: *We made a photocopy and sent back the original.* —*v.* [~ + *obj*] **2.** to make a photocopy of: *We photocopied the original.* —**pho′to•cop′i•er,** *n.* [*count*]

pho•to•e•lec•tric (fō′tō i lek′trik) /ˌfowtowɪˈlɛktrɪk/ *adj.* of or relating to electronic effects produced by light: *A photoelectric cell uses light to start another apparatus.*

pho′to fin′ish, *n.* [*count*] **1.** a finish of a race so close as to require careful examination of a photograph to determine the winner. **2.** any result of a very close contest, election, etc.

pho•to•gen•ic (fō′tə jen′ik) /ˌfowtəˈdʒɛnɪk/ *adj.* forming an attractive subject for photography. —**pho′to•gen′i•cal•ly,** *adv.* See -GEN-.

pho•to•graph (fō′tə graf′) /ˈfowtəˌgræf/ *n.* [*count*] **1.** a picture produced by photography. —*v.* **2.** [~ + *obj*] to take a photograph of: *The reporter photographed the schoolchildren.* **3.** [*no obj*] to practice photography. **4.** [*no obj*] to be photographed, esp. in some specified way: *The children photographed well.* See -GRAPH-.

pho•to•graph•ic (fō′tə graf′ik) /ˌfowtəˈgræfɪk/ *adj.* [*before a noun*] **1.** of or relating to photography: *her photographic equipment: lights, cameras, film.* **2.** remembering as accurately as if one had a photograph before oneself: *a photographic memory.* —**pho′to•graph′i•cal•ly,** *adv.*

pho•tog•ra•phy (fə tog′rə fē) /fəˈtɒgrəfiy/ *n.* [*noncount*] the process of producing images of objects on special paper by the chemical action of light. —**pho•tog′ra•pher,** *n.* [*count*]

pho•to•jour•nal•ism (fō′tō jûr′nl iz′əm) /ˌfowtowˈdʒɜrnl̩ˌɪzəm/ *n.* [*noncount*] journalism in which the story is told largely in photographs with captions. —**pho′to•jour′nal•ist,** *n.* [*count*]

pho•tom•e•ter (fō tom′i tər) /fowˈtɒmɪtər/ *n.* [*count*] an instrument that measures light. See -METER-.

pho•ton (fō′ton) /ˈfowtɒn/ *n.* [*count*] a unit of measure of electromagnetic radiation.

pho•to•syn•the•sis (fō′tə sin′thə sis) /ˌfowtəˈsɪnθəsɪs/ *n.* [*noncount*] the production of organic materials from carbon dioxide and water, using sunlight as energy with the aid of chlorophyll. See -THES-.

phras•al (frā′zəl) /ˈfreyzəl/ *adj.* **1.** of or relating to a phrase, a group of words forming a grammatical unit. **2.** of or relating to a verbal construction composed of a verb plus an adverb or preposition, in which the construction has a meaning that could not be inferred from its component parts, as *look up,* which means "to examine in a book," or *come across,* which means "to meet or encounter."

phrase (frāz) /freyz/ *n., v.,* **phrased, phras•ing.** —*n.* [*count*] **1.** a group of two or more words constituting a grammatical unit and lacking a finite verb or a subject and verb: *A phrase can be a preposition and a noun or pronoun, an adjective and a noun, or an adverb and a verb, but it is not a clause and is not a sentence.* **2.** a characteristic, popular, or well-known expression: *That tune had some catchy phrases in it.* **3.** a brief statement or remark. **4.** a division or part of a piece of music, commonly a passage of four or eight measures. —*v.* [~ + *obj*] **5.** to express or say (something) in a particular way: *Let me phrase it this way: Your services are no longer needed at this company.*

phra•se•ol•o•gy (frā′zē ol′ə jē) /ˌfreyziyˈɒlədʒiy/ *n.* [*noncount*] manner or style of verbal expression: *legal phraseology.*

-phys-, *root.* -*phys*- comes from Greek, where it has the meaning "nature; natural order." This meaning is found in such words as: GEOPHYSICS, METAPHYSICS, PHYSICIAN, PHYSICS, PHYSIOGNOMY, PHYSIOLOGY, PHYSIQUE.

phys•i•cal (fiz′i kəl) /ˈfɪzɪkəl/ *adj.* **1.** [*before a noun*] of or relating to the body: *physical growth.* **2.** [*before a noun*] of or relating to that which is material: *the physical universe.* **3.** sexual: *a physical attraction.* **4.** physically demonstrative; showing one's feelings by touching another: *She's not afraid to be physical and give her friends a hug.* **5.** requiring, having, or liking rough physical contact: *Football is a very physical sport.* **6.** contained in or being computer hardware: *physical memory.* —*n.* [*count*] **7.** an examination of the body: *I needed a complete physical because I was so run-down.* —**phys′i•cal•ly,** *adv.*: *physically fit; Physically he seems OK, but emotionally he's a wreck.* See -PHYS-.

phys′ical educa′tion, *n.* [*noncount*] instruction in sports, exercise, and hygiene, esp. as part of a school program. See -PHYS-.

phys′ical sci′ence, *n.* any of the natural sciences dealing with non-living matter or energy, as physics, chemistry, and astronomy: [*noncount*]: *Does physical science get more funding from the government?* [*count*]: *He was more interested in the physical sciences than in the life sciences.*

phys′ical ther′apy, *n.* [*noncount*] the treatment or management of physical injuries, malfunction, or pain by physical techniques, as by exercise, massage, etc. —**phys′ical ther′apist,** *n.* [*count*]

phy•si•cian (fi zish′ən) /fɪˈzɪʃən/ *n.* [*count*] one licensed to practice medicine; a doctor of medicine. See -PHYS-.

phys•ics (fiz′iks) /ˈfɪzɪks/ *n.* [*noncount; used with a singular verb*] the science that deals with matter, energy, motion, and force: *Physics is what seems to have interested him the most.* —**phys•i•cist** (fiz′ə sist) /ˈfɪzəsɪst/ *n.* [*count*] See -PHYS-.

phys•i•og•no•my (fiz′ē og′nə mē, -on′ə mē) /ˌfɪziyˈɒgnəmiy, -ˈɒnəmiy/ *n.* [*count*], *pl.* **-mies.** the face, esp. as suggesting something about one's character. See -PHYS-.

phys•i•ol•o•gy (fiz′ē ol′ə jē) /ˌfɪziyˈɒlədʒiy/ *n.* [*noncount*] **1.** the branch of biology dealing with the functions and activities of living organisms and their parts. **2.** [*usually singular*] the processes or functions of something living or of any of its parts. —**phys•i•o•log•i•cal** (fiz′ē ə loj′i kəl) /ˌfɪziyəˈlɒdʒɪkəl/ *adj.* —**phys′i•ol′o•gist,** *n.* [*count*] See -PHYS-.

phys•i•o•ther•a•py (fiz′ē ō ther′ə pē) /ˌfɪziyowˈθɛrəpiy/ *n.* [*noncount*] therapy performed on a person's body to restore its natural ability, as exercises to strengthen an injured limb. —**phys′i•o•ther′a•pist,** *n.* [*count*] See -PHYS-.

phy•sique (fi zēk′) /fɪˈziyk/ *n.* [*count*] the structure, shape, or appearance of the human body or of a person's body: *the physique of an athlete.* See -PHYS-.

pi (pī) /pay/ *n.* [*count*], *pl.* **pis. 1.** the 16th letter of the Greek alphabet (Π, π). **2. a.** the letter π, used as the symbol for the ratio of the circumference of a circle to its diameter. **b.** the ratio itself, a number usually given as 3.141592+.

pi•a•nis•si•mo (pē′ə nis′ə mō′, pyä-) /ˌpiyəˈnɪsəˌmow, pyɑ-/ *adj., adv., n., pl.* **-mos.** *Music.* —*adj.* **1.** very soft. —*adv.* **2.** very softly. —*n.* [*count*] **3.** a passage played in this way.

pi•an•ist (pē an′ist, pyan′-, pē′ə nist) /piyˈænɪst, ˈpyæn-, ˈpiyənɪst/ *n.* [*count*] one who plays the piano, esp. as a profession.

pi•an•o[1] (pē an′ō, pyan′ō) /piyˈænow, ˈpyænow/ *n.* [*count*], *pl.* **-an•os.** a musical instrument in which felt-covered hammers, operated from a keyboard, strike metal strings.

pi•a•no[2] (pē ä′nō, pyä′-) /piyˈɑnow, ˈpyɑ-/ *Music.* —*adj.* **1.** soft; subdued. —*adv.* **2.** softly. *Abbr.:* p

pi•az•za (pē az′ə, -ä′zə *or, for 1, 3* pē at′sə, -ät′-) /piyˈæzə, -ˈɑzə *or, for 1, 3* piyˈætsə, -ˈɑt-/ *n.* [*count*], *pl.* **pi•az•zas,** *It.* ***piaz•ze*** (pyät′tse) /ˈpyɑttsɛ/. **1.** an open public square in a city or town, esp. in Italy. **2.** *Chiefly New England and Southern U.S.* a large porch. **3.** *Chiefly Brit.* an arcade or covered walk or gallery.

pi•ca (pī′kə) /ˈpaykə/ *n.* [*count*], *pl.* **-cas.** a size of type, widely used in typewriters, having 10 characters to the inch. Compare ELITE (def. 2).

pic•a•resque (pik′ə resk′) /ˌpɪkəˈrɛsk/ *adj.* of or relating to a form of written fiction in which the adventures of a dishonest but fun-loving hero are described in a series of humorous episodes.

pic•a•yune (pik′ē yōōn′, pik′ə-) /ˌpɪkiyˈyuwn, ˌpɪkə-/ *adj.* Also, **pic′a•yun′ish. 1.** of little value or importance; small; trifling: *arguing over some picayune details.* **2.** petty; too interested in small, unimportant matters.

pic•ca•lil•li (pik′ə lil′ē) /ˈpɪkəˌlɪliy/ *n.* [*count*], *pl.* **-lis.** a strong-smelling food added to other foods for flavor, made of chopped vegetables, mustard, vinegar, and hot spices.

pic•co•lo (pik′ə lō′) /ˈpɪkəˌlow/ *n.* [*count*], *pl.* **-los.** a small flute that is an octave higher than the ordinary flute.

pick[1] (pik) /pɪk/ *v.* [~ + *obj*] **1.** to choose or select, esp. with care: *She picked the best detective on the force to head the investigation.* **2.** to seek occasion for; provoke: *to pick a fight.* **3.** to attempt to find; seek out: *trying to pick flaws in his argument.* **4.** to steal the contents of: *to pick a pocket.* **5.** to open (a lock) with a device other than a key, esp. for the purpose of burglary: *The spy managed to pick the lock and get into her house.* **6.** to pierce or break up (something) with a pointed instrument: *to pick iron ore.* **7.** to use a pointed instrument on (a thing), to remove particles or something stuck: *After dinner he grabbed a toothpick and began to pick his teeth.* **8.** to prepare for use by removing a covering, as feathers: *to pick a fowl.* **9.** to detach or remove piece by piece with the fingers: *to pick meat from the bones.* **10.** to pull out and gather one by one: *to pick flowers.* **11. a.** to pluck (the strings of a musical instrument): *She picked the strings softly at first.* **b.** to play (a stringed instrument) by plucking with the fingers: *strumming and picking his guitar.* **12. pick apart,** to criticize severely or in great detail: [~ + *apart* + *obj*]: *picked apart his arguments one by one.* [~ + *obj* + *apart*]: *picked most of his arguments apart.* **13. pick at,** [~ + *at* + *obj*] **a.** to find fault with; nag: *He kept picking at her until she exploded.* **b.** to eat only a small amount: *For days she only picked at her meals.* **c.** to grasp at; touch; handle: *a nervous habit of picking at his jacket sleeve.* **14. pick off, a.** to remove by pulling or plucking off: [~ + *off* + *obj*]: *She picked off the feathers from the chicken.* [~ + *obj* + *off*]: *She picked the feathers off the chicken.* **b.** to single out and shoot: [~ + *off* + *obj*]: *picked off a duck rising from the marsh.* [~ + *obj* + *off*]: *With this rifle an assassin could pick you off at a thousand yards.* **c.** *Baseball.* to put out (a base runner) in a pick-off play: [~ + *off* + *obj*]: *picked off three players in one game.* [~ + *obj* + *off*]: *picked me off twice in one game.* **15. pick on,** [~ + *on* + *obj*] **a.** to tease; bother greatly; harass: *The other kids picked on her because she was poor.* **b.** to single out; choose: *The teacher tended to pick on her often because she came to class prepared.* **16. pick out, a.** to choose; select: [~ + *out* + *obj*]: *Pick out the best tomatoes.* [~ + *obj* + *out*]: *She picked the best tomatoes out and left the rest.* **b.** to distinguish (something) from that which surrounds: [~ + *out* + *obj*]: *to pick out her face in a crowd.* [~ + *obj* + *out*]: *Can you pick that criminal's face out from among these photos?* **c.** to work out (a melody) note by note; play by ear: [~ + *out* + *obj*]: *idly picking out a tune.* [~ + *obj* + *out*]: *She picked a tune out on the piano.* **17. pick up, a.** to lift or take up: [~ + *up* + *obj*]: *to pick up a stone.* [~ + *obj* + *up*]: *He picked the stone up.* **b.** to gather or collect, esp. systematically: [~ + *up* + *obj*]: *Please pick up the pieces.* [~ + *obj* + *up*]: *Pick the pieces up.* **c.** [~ + *up* + *obj*] to gain or acquire: *picked up nine yards on the play.* **d.** to obtain or learn casually or as a result of occasional opportunity: [~ + *up* + *obj*]: *I've picked up a few Japanese phrases.* [~ + *obj* + *up*]: *I was able to pick English up fairly quickly.* **e.** to take on (casually) as a passenger: [~ + *up* + *obj*]: *They picked up some guy hitchhiking on Interstate 40.* [~ + *obj* + *up*]: *They picked some guy up on Interstate 40.* **f.** to arrange to collect (something), or to meet and collect (someone) as a passenger, etc.: [~ + *up* + *obj*]: *Please pick up some milk on the way home.* [~ + *obj* + *up*]: *We'll pick you up at eight o'clock.* **g.** to bring into the range of one's ability to receive (as on a radio), or observe, detect, etc.: [~ + *up* + *obj*]: *to pick up Toronto on the radio.* [~ + *obj* + *up*]: *Their sonar could pick the Russian sub up.* **h.** [~ + *up* + *obj*] to accelerate; gain (speed): *The car picked up speed.* **i.** [~ + *up* + *obj*] to catch or contract, as a disease: *picked up a cold.* **j.** to (cause to) make progress, improve, or recover: [*no obj*]: *Business is picking up.* [~ + *obj* + *up*]: *This should pick you up: good news at last about the economy!* [~ + *up* + *obj*]: *The news of the invasion picked up the morale of the prisoners.* **k.** to become acquainted with informally or casually, often in hope of a sexual relationship: [~ + *up* + *obj*]: *They were cruising at the bars, hoping to pick up some men.* [~ + *obj* + *up*]: *Let's try to pick those girls up.* **l.** to resume or continue after being left off: [~ + *up* + *obj*]: *Let's pick up the discussion at our next meeting.* [~ + *obj* + *up*]: *Can we pick this up at our next meeting?* **m.** to take to jail; arrest: [~ + *up* + *obj*]: *The police picked up the suspect the next day.* [~ + *obj* + *up*]: *The police picked the suspect up the day after the murder.* **n.** [~ + *up* + *obj*] to accept, as in order to pay: *As we rose to leave, he picked up the check, saying, "I'll pay this time."* **18. pick up on,** [~ + *up on* + *obj*] *Informal.* to become aware of; notice: *I picked up on his hostility right away.* **—*n.* 19.** [*noncount*] the act of selecting; choice: *Take your pick.* **20.** [*count*] a person or thing selected: *Two of the team's first draft picks would not sign with them.* **21.** [*noncount*] the best, choicest, or most desirable part or example: *This horse is the pick of the stable.* **—*Idiom.* 22. pick and choose,** [*no obj*] to be careful or particular in choosing: *You won't have time to pick and choose; just grab what looks good.* **—pick′er,** *n.* [*count*]

pick[2] (pik) /pɪk/ *n.* [*count*] **1.** a heavy tool made of a metal head, usually curved, coming to a point at one or both ends, mounted on a wooden handle, and used for breaking up soil, rock, etc. **2.** any pointed tool or instrument for picking: *an ice pick.* **3.** PLECTRUM.

pick•ax or **pick•axe** (pik′aks′) /ˈpɪkˌæks/ *n., pl.* **-ax•es,** *v.,* **-axed, -ax•ing. —*n.*** [*count*] **1.** PICK[2] (def. 1). **—*v.*** [~ + *obj*] **2.** to cut or clear away with a pickax.

pick•er•el (pik′ər əl, pik′rəl) /ˈpɪkərəl, ˈpɪkrəl/ *n.* [*count*], *pl.* (*esp. when thought of as a group*) **-el,** (*esp. for kinds or species*) **-els. 1.** a kind of fish, a pike. **2.** the walleye, blue pike, or pikeperch.

pick•et (pik′it) /ˈpɪkɪt/ *n.* [*count*] **1.** a post driven into the ground for use in a fence, to fasten down a tent, etc. **2.** a person stationed, as by a union, outside a store, etc., to persuade workers or customers not to enter it during a strike. **3.** a person engaged in a similar demonstration. **4.** a soldier placed on a forward position to warn against an enemy advance. **—*v.* 5.** to place pickets in front of or around (a factory, etc.), as during a strike or demonstration: [~ + *obj*]: *The workers were picketing the shop.* [*no obj*]: *While the workers were picketing, security teams photographed them.*

pick′et line′, *n.* [*count*] a line of strikers or other pickets.

pick•le (pik′əl) /ˈpɪkəl/ *n., v.,* **-led, -ling. —*n.* 1.** a vegetable, esp. a cucumber, that has been preserved and flavored in brine or vinegar: [*count*]: *a jar of sweet dill pickles.* [*noncount*]: *relish made of pickle.* **2.** [*noncount*] a liquid prepared with salt or vinegar, for preserving or flavoring meat, etc.; brine or marinade. **3.** [*count; usually singular; usually: a* + ~] a troublesome situation; a difficulty: *We're in a pickle now, surrounded by woods.* **—*v.*** [~ + *obj*] **4.** to preserve or soak in brine or other liquid.

pick•pock•et (pik′pok′it) /ˈpɪkˌpɒkɪt/ *n.* [*count*] **1.** one who steals from the pockets of people, as in a crowded public place. **—*v.*** [~ + *obj*] **2.** to steal from the pocket of.

pick•up (pik′up′) /ˈpɪkˌʌp/ *n.* **1.** [*count*] an improvement, as in health, business conditions, etc. **2.** [*count*] a casual acquaintance, as one offering hope of a sexual encounter. **3.** [*noncount*] acceleration, or the ability to accelerate: *not much pickup with such a small engine.* **4.** [*count*] Also called **pick′up truck′.** a small truck with a low-sided open body, used for deliveries and light hauling. **5.** [*count*] a device at the end of the tone arm of a record player that converts vibrations into electric impulses. **—*adj.*** [*before a noun*] **6.** made up of or using whatever is available at the moment: *a pickup dance band.*

pick•y (pik′ē) /ˈpɪkiy/ *adj.,* **-i•er, -i•est.** fussy or finicky; too particular: *a picky eater; a picky shopper.*

pic•nic (pik′nik) /ˈpɪknɪk/ *n., v.,* **-nicked, -nick•ing. —*n.*** [*count*] **1.** a trip in which food is brought and a meal is shared in the open air. **2.** the food eaten on such an excursion. **3.** [*used with negative words or phrases*] *Informal.* an enjoyable experience, task, etc.: *That three-year hitch in the Army was no picnic.* **—*v.*** [*no obj*] **4.** to go on or take part in a picnic: *We picnicked in that same park every summer.* **—pic′nick•er,** *n.* [*count*]: *The picnickers were fighting off the ants.*

pic•to•graph (pik′tə graf′) /ˈpɪktəˌgræf/ *n.* [*count*] **1.** a single sign or symbol that is a small picture, as in a system of writing using such symbols for words. **2.** a painting or drawing on a rock wall or the like by ancient or prehistoric peoples. See -GRAPH-.

pic•to•ri•al (pik tôr′ē əl, -tōr′ē-) /pɪkˈtɔriyəl, -ˈtowriy-/ *adj.* of or relating to a picture; illustrated by or containing pictures: *a pictorial biography.* **—pic•to′ri•al•ly,** *adv.*

pic•ture (pik′chər) /ˈpɪktʃər/ *n., v.,* **-tured, -tur•ing. —*n.*** [*count*] **1.** a representation of a person, object, or scene, as a painting, drawing, or photograph: *He drew a little picture of his dog.* **2.** a mental image: *a picture in his mind of that beautiful mountainside in Norway.* **3.** a strong, powerful description: *a frightening picture of life in a totalitarian society.* **4.** MOTION PICTURE (def. 2): *Her latest picture won her an Oscar.* **5.** [*the* + ~] the image or perfect likeness of someone else: *She is the picture of her father.* **6.** [*singular; the/a* + ~] a concrete example of some quality or condition: *He is the very picture of health.* **7.** a situation or set of circumstances: *He's missing the big picture (= He does not understand the entire situation).* **8.** the image on a television screen, motion-picture screen, or computer monitor. **—*v.*** [~ + *obj*] **9.** to represent pictorially, as by painting or drawing: *The artist pictured her as a young, vibrant woman.* **10.** to form a mental picture of; imagine: *Picture this: a herd of elephants charging right at you.*

pic•tur•esque (pik′chə resk′) /ˌpɪktʃəˈrɛsk/ *adj.* **1.** charming or pleasing to the eye: *a picturesque village.* **2.** (of writing, speech, appearance, etc.) strikingly effective in conveying a mental picture: *Her essay had picturesque language.*

pid•dle (pid′l) /ˈpɪdl/ *v.* [*no obj*], **-dled, -dling. 1.** to waste time; dawdle: *just piddling around doing nothing.* **2.** *Informal.* to urinate.

pid•dling (pid′ling) /ˈpɪdlɪŋ/ *adj.* so small in amount as to be unimportant or ignored; negligible: *the school's piddling resources for special students.*

pidg•in (pij′ən) /ˈpɪdʒən/ *n.* **1.** a language that has developed from the need of speakers of two different languages to communicate and is primarily a simplified form of one of the languages, with a reduced vocabulary and grammatical structure: [*count*]: *The traders spoke a pidgin when they did business across the border.* [*noncount*]: *Maybe if you speak pidgin you can make yourself understood.* **—*adj.*** [*before a noun*] **2.** of or relating to such a language: *pidgin English.*

pie (pī) /pay/ *n.* **1.** a crust of baked dough, filled with fruit, pudding, etc.: [*count*]: *an apple pie.* [*noncount*]: *had apple pie for dessert.* **2.** a layer cake with a cream or custard filling: [*count*]: *a Boston cream pie.* [*noncount*]: *Our desserts include lemon meringue pie and Boston cream pie.* **3.** [*count*] a total or whole that can be divided: *They want a bigger piece of the pie.* **4.** [*count*] an activity or affair: *I'm sure he had a finger in the pie.* **—*Idiom.* 5. easy as pie,** extremely easy or simple: *Stealing the money was easy as pie.* **6. pie in the sky,** [*noncount*] a plan, suggestion, idea, or belief about something not likely to come true: *His new tax plan is just pie in the sky.*

pie•bald (pī′bôld′) /ˈpayˌbɔld/ *adj.* **1.** having patches of two colors, esp. black and white. *—n.* [*count*] **2.** a piebald animal, esp. a horse.

piece (pēs) /piys/ *n., v.,* **pieced, piec•ing.** *—n.* [*count*] **1.** a portion or quantity of something: *a piece of land.* **2.** a portion of a whole: *a piece of apple pie.* **3.** an individual thing of a particular class or set: *a piece of furniture.* **4.** a created work of art, music, or writing: *He writes funny pieces for that magazine.* **5.** one of the figures, disks, or the like used in playing a board game. **6.** an example of something: *This report is a fine piece of work.* **7.** a part, fragment, or shred: *to tear a letter into pieces.* **8.** one's opinion or thoughts on a subject: *Here's a piece of advice: don't do it.* **9.** a coin: *a five-cent piece.* **10.** an amount of work constituting a single job: *to be paid by the piece.* See PIECEWORK. **11.** [*singular; a + ~*] *Midland and Southern U.S.* a distance: *down the road a piece.* *—v.* **12.** [*~ + obj*] to mend by adding a piece or pieces; patch. **13.** to join together, as pieces or parts: [*~ + together + obj*]: *I pieced together the broken fragments.* [*~ + obj + together*]: *I pieced the fragments together.* **14.** to make or assemble by or as if by joining pieces or facts, information, etc.: [*~ + together + obj*]: *to piece together such a fine musical program.* [*~ + obj + together*]: *She pieced a fine program together.* [*~ + together + obj*]: *They were finally able to piece together the whole story of his death.* **—*Idiom.*** **15. a piece of one's mind,** a sharp scolding or piece of criticism: *gave his daughter a piece of his mind when she came home so late.* **16. go to pieces,** to lose control of oneself: *After her son's death she simply went to pieces.* **17. in pieces,** destroyed; in ruins; not effective: *careful plans of conquest lay in pieces.* **18. piece of cake,** *Informal.* something easily done: *Robbing the store was a piece of cake.* **19. to pieces,** left completely ruined or no longer effective: *tore our arguments to pieces.* **—Usage.** Note that since PIECE is a noun that can be counted, it may be used to describe a part of some noncount noun: *lumber* [*noncount*] → *a piece* [*count*] *of lumber; furniture* [*noncount*] → *a piece* [*count*] *of furniture.*

pièce de ré•sis•tance (pyes də rā zē stäns′) /pyɛs də reyziy'stɑ̃s/ *n.* [*count*], *pl.* ***pièces de ré•sis•tance*** (pyes də rā zē stäns′) /pyɛs də reyziy'stɑ̃s/ *French.* **1.** the principal dish of a meal. **2.** the principal item of a series or group, esp. one that is very effective or impressive: *The pièce de résistance was her presentation of her advertising campaign.*

piece•meal (pēs′mēl′) /'piys,miyl/ *adv.* **1.** one piece at a time: *to work piecemeal.* *—adj.* **2.** done piecemeal.

piece•work (pēs′wûrk′) /'piys,wɜrk/ *n.* [*noncount*] work done and paid for by the piece.

pied (pīd) /payd/ *adj.* **1.** having two or more colors in a pattern of patches or spots; piebald. **2.** wearing pied clothing.

pied-à-terre (pē ā′də târ′, -dä-, pyā′-) /piy ,eydə 'tɛər, -dɑ-, ,pyey-/ *n.* [*count*], *pl.* **pieds-à-terre** (pē ā′də târ′, -dä-, pyā′-) /piy,eydə'tɛər, -dɑ-, ,pyey-/. a residence, as an apartment, for part-time or temporary use.

pier (pēr) /pɪər/ *n.* [*count*] a structure built on posts extending from land out over water, used as a landing place for ships, etc.

pierce (pērs) /pɪərs/ *v.,* **pierced, pierc•ing. 1.** to penetrate or go through (something), as a pointed object does: [*~ + obj*]: *The spear pierced his leg and he fell.* [*no obj*]: *An arrow pierced through his arm.* **2.** [*~ + obj*] to make a hole or opening in: *She got her ears pierced.* **3.** [*~ + obj*] to make (a hole) by or as if by drilling, etc.: *They pierced a hole through the ship's hull.* **4.** [*~ + obj*] to force or make a way into or through: *a road that pierces the jungle.* **5.** [*~ + obj*] to sound sharply through (the air, etc.), as a cry: *A scream pierced the silence of the night.*

pier•cing (pēr′sing) /'pɪərsɪŋ/ *adj.* **1.** penetrating, as with the eye or mind: *He gazed at her with a piercing look.* **2.** causing or bringing about a strong emotion: *a piercing memory of their former love.* **3.** sharp or loud: *a piercing scream.* **4.** (of a wind or the cold) biting: *a piercing wind.* —**pier′cing•ly,** *adv.*

pi•e•ty (pī′i tē) /'payɪtiy/ *n.* [*noncount*] **1.** reverence for or devotion to God, or deep respect for religion. **2.** the quality or state of being pious. **3.** respect for parents, homeland, etc.: *filial piety.*

pif•fle (pif′əl) /'pɪfəl/ *n.* [*noncount*] *Informal.* nonsense. —**pif′fling,** *adj.*: *mostly piffling, inconsequential chatter.*

pig (pig) /pɪg/ *n., v.,* **pigged, pig•ging.** *—n.* **1.** [*count*] a short, fat mammal with hooves; a young swine of either sex, esp. one kept on a farm and weighing less than 120 lb. (54 kg). **2.** [*count*] any swine. **3.** [*noncount*] the flesh of this animal; pork. **4.** [*count*] one who eats too much, is greedy, or is very sloppy. **5.** [*count*] *Slang* (*disparaging*). a police officer. *—v.* **6. pig out,** [*no obj*] *Slang.* to eat too much food: *We pigged out on pizza last night.*

pi•geon (pij′ən) /'pɪdʒən/ *n.* [*count*] **1.** a bird having a plump body and small head, esp. the larger species with square or rounded tails. **2.** *Slang.* **a.** a girl or young woman. **b.** a person who is easily fooled or cheated.

pi•geon•hole (pij′ən hōl′) /'pɪdʒən,howl/ *n., v.,* **-holed, -hol•ing.** *—n.* [*count*] **1.** one of a series of small, open compartments in a desk or cabinet, used for filing papers, etc. *—v.* [*~ + obj*] **2.** to assign to a place in an orderly system, esp. in a narrow-minded way: *pigeonholed the demonstrators as "commies and pinkos."*

pi′geon-toed′, *adj.* having the toes or feet turned inward.

pig•gish (pig′ish) /'pɪgɪʃ/ *adj.* **1.** greedy; eating too much. **2.** stubborn. —**pig′gish•ness,** *n.* [*noncount*]

pig•gy or **pig•gie** (pig′ē) /'pɪgiy/ *n., pl.* **-gies,** *adj.,* **-gi•er, -gi•est.** *—n.* [*count*] **1.** a small or young pig. *—adj.* **2.** PIGGISH.

pig•gy•back (pig′ē bak′) /'pɪgiy,bæk/ *adv.* **1.** on the back or shoulders: *The child rode piggyback on her father.* *—adj.* **2.** [*before a noun*] on the back or shoulders: *a piggyback ride.* **3.** attached to, carried on, or added to something else: *a piggyback clause concerning the property.* **4.** of or relating to the carrying of one vehicle on another, as the carrying of truck trailers on flatcars. *—v.* **5.** [*~ + obj*] to carry on the back or shoulders: *He piggybacked his daughter into her crib.* **6.** to (cause to) be attached to, carried on, or added to something else: [*~ + obj*]: *They piggybacked a clause to the amendment.* [*no obj*]: *The amendment will probably piggyback on the other bill.* **7.** [*~ + obj*] to carry (one vehicle) on another. *—n.* [*count*] **8.** a piggyback ride. **9.** a vehicle on which another is carried. **10.** anything attached to or carried on something else.

pig′gy bank′, *n.* [*count*] a small bank, usually in the shape of a pig, with a slot to receive coins.

pig•head•ed (pig′hed′id) /'pɪg,hɛdɪd/ *adj.* stupidly stubborn. —**pig′head′ed•ly,** *adv.* —**pig′head′ed•ness,** *n.* [*noncount*]

pig•let (pig′lit) /'pɪglɪt/ *n.* [*count*] a little pig.

pig•ment (pig′mənt) /'pɪgmənt/ *n.* **1.** a dry substance that when mixed in liquid becomes a paint, etc.: [*noncount*]: *mixing pigment to form paint.* [*count*]: *various pigments needed to produce that color.* **2.** [*noncount*] any natural coloring substance, as chlorophyll or hemoglobin, that produces color in living things: *the light blue pigment in her eyes.*

pig•men•ta•tion (pig′mən tā′shən) /,pɪgmən'teyʃən/ *n.* [*noncount*] coloring, esp. of the skin: *dark pigmentation.*

pig•pen (pig′pen′) /'pɪg,pɛn/ *n.* [*count*] **1.** a pen for keeping pigs. **2.** a filthy or very untidy place: *Your room is a pigpen; clean it up at once.*

pig•skin (pig′skin′) /'pɪg,skɪn/ *n.* **1.** [*noncount*] the skin of a pig. **2.** [*noncount*] leather made from it. **3.** [*count*] a football.

pig•tail (pig′tāl′) /'pɪg,teyl/ *n.* [*count*] a braid of hair hanging down the sides or the back of the head.

pike[1] (pīk) /payk/ *n.* [*count*], *pl.* (*esp. when thought of as a group*) **pike,** (*esp. for kinds or species*) **pikes.** a large, slender, freshwater fish having a long, flat snout.

pike[2] (pīk) /payk/ *n., v.,* **piked, pik•ing.** *—n.* [*count*] **1.** a long weapon having a pointed head, formerly used by infantry. *—v.* [*~ + obj*] **2.** to pierce, wound, or kill with a pike.

pike[3] (pīk) /payk/ *n.* [*count*] **1.** a toll road or highway; turnpike. **—*Idiom.*** **2. come down the pike,** to emerge; come forth; appear: *the greatest idea that ever came down the pike.*

pik•er (pī′kər) /'paykər/ *n.* [*count*] a person who does anything in a small or cheap way.

pi•laf or **pi•laff** (pē′läf, pi läf′) /'piylɑf, pɪ'lɑf/ also **pi•lau** (pē′läf, -lô, -lou, pi läf′, -lô′, -lou′) /'piylɑf, -lɔ, -law, pɪ'lɑf, -'lɔ, -'law/ *n.* [*noncount*] a Middle Eastern dish of rice cooked in bouillon, sometimes with meat or shellfish.

pil•chard (pil′chərd) /'pɪltʃərd/ *n.* [*count*] a small, sea-dwelling fish, related to the herring but smaller and rounder.

pile[1] (pīl) /payl/ *n., v.,* **piled, pil•ing.** *—n.* [*count*] **1.** an assemblage of things lying one upon the other: *I had a huge pile of papers to correct.* **2.** a large number or amount of anything: *a pile of work.* **3.** *Informal.* a large amount of money: *He made a pile and vanished somewhere in South America.* *—v.* **4.** [*~ + obj*] to put or lay in a pile: *to pile leaves.* **5.** to (cause to) be accumulated, gathered, or stored: [~ + *up* + *obj*]: *to pile up money.* [~ + *obj* + *up*]: *He piled a lot of money up before he retired.* [~ + *on* + *obj*]: *really enjoys piling on the homework.* [~ + *obj* + *on*]: *She really piles it on right before a holiday.* [*no obj;* ~ + *up*]: *His debts kept piling up.* **6.** [~ + *obj*] to cover or load with a pile: *The back of the car was piled high with firewood.* **7.** [*no obj*] to move as a group in a more or less confused, disorderly manner: *They piled off the train.*

pile[2] (pīl) /payl/ *n., v.,* **piled, pil•ing.** —*n.* [*count*] **1.** a long, rounded, or flat piece of wood, concrete, etc., hammered upright into soil to form part of a foundation. —*v.* [~ + *obj*] **2.** to drive piles into.

pile[3] (pīl) /payl/ *n.* [*noncount*] **1.** a surface or thickness of soft hair, down, etc. **2.** a soft or brushy surface on cloth, etc., formed by upright yarns, as in velvet or terry. —**piled,** *adj.: deep-piled, thick carpeting.*

pile[4] (pīl) /payl/ *n.* Usually, **piles.** [*plural*] HEMORRHOIDS.

pile•up (pīl′up′) /ˈpaylˌʌp/ *n.* [*count*] **1.** a collision of several moving vehicles: *a bad pileup on Interstate 80.* **2.** an accumulation, as of chores or bills.

pil•fer (pil′fər) /ˈpɪlfər/ *v.* to steal, esp. in small quantities: [~ + *obj*]: *pilfering pens and pencils.* [*no obj*]: *pilfering from the office.* —**pil•fer•age** (pil′fər ij) /ˈpɪlfərɪdʒ/ *n.* [*noncount*] —**pil′fer•er,** *n.* [*count*]

pil•grim (pil′grim, -grəm) /ˈpɪlgrɪm, -grəm/ *n.* [*count*] **1.** a person on a pilgrimage. **2.** a traveler or wanderer, esp. in a foreign place.

pil•grim•age (pil′grə mij) /ˈpɪlgrəmɪdʒ/ *n.* a journey, esp. a long one, made to some sacred or holy place as an act of religious devotion: [*count*]: *a pilgrimage to the Holy Land.* [*noncount*]: *the importance of pilgrimage in the Middle Ages.*

pill (pil) /pɪl/ *n.* [*count*] **1.** a small tablet or capsule of medicine: *Take two of these pills at bedtime.* **2.** something unpleasant that has to be accepted or suffered through: *Being denied promotion was a bitter pill for her to swallow.* **3.** *Slang.* a tiresomely disagreeable person. **4. the pill,** an oral contraceptive for women: *Because she was on the pill, she didn't expect to get pregnant.*

pil•lage (pil′ij) /ˈpɪlɪdʒ/ *v.,* **-laged, -lag•ing,** *n.* —*v.* **1.** to steal goods by open violence and force, as in war; plunder: [*no obj*]: *The invaders raped and pillaged as they went.* [~ + *obj*]: *The invaders pillaged several towns.* —*n.* [*noncount*] **2.** stealing goods through violence or force, as in a war.

pil•lar (pil′ər) /ˈpɪlər/ *n.* [*count*] **1.** an upright, tall, narrow shaft used as a building support, or standing alone, as for a monument. **2.** anything resembling this in shape: *a pillar of smoke.* **3.** a person important to or a supporter of a town, organization, etc.: *a pillar of the community.*

pill•box (pil′boks′) /ˈpɪlˌbɒks/ *n.* [*count*] **1.** a small box for holding pills. **2.** a small, boxlike place for machine guns.

pil•lion (pil′yən) /ˈpɪlyən/ *n.* [*count*] **1.** a pad or cushion attached behind the saddle of a horse, esp. as a seat for a woman. **2.** a pad, cushion, or saddle used as a passenger seat on a bicycle, motorcycle, etc.

pil•lo•ry (pil′ə rē) /ˈpɪləriy/ *n., pl.* **-ries,** *v.,* **-ried, -ry•ing.** —*n.* [*count*] **1.** a wooden framework built on a post, with holes for securing the head and hands, formerly used to expose an offender to public humiliation and insults as punishment. —*v.* [~ + *obj*] **2.** to place (someone) in a pillory. **3.** to expose to public insults or abuse: *The press pilloried him for his foolish remark.*

pil•low (pil′ō) /ˈpɪlow/ *n.* [*count*] **1.** a cloth bag or case filled with feathers or other soft material, used to cushion the head during sleep or rest: *He kept pounding his pillow, trying to get comfortable.* **2.** a similar cushion, esp. a small one, used for decoration, as on a sofa. —*v.* [~ + *obj*] **3.** to support with or as if with pillows: *They pillowed his head and tried to make him comfortable.*

pil•low•case (pil′ō kās′) /ˈpɪlowˌkeys/ *n.* [*count*] a removable sacklike covering, usually of cotton, fitted over a pillow. Also called **pil•low•slip** (pil′ō slip′) /ˈpɪlowˌslɪp/.

pi•lot (pī′lət) /ˈpaylət/ *n.* [*count*] **1.** a person qualified to operate an airplane, balloon, or other aircraft. **2.** a person qualified to steer ships into or out of a harbor or through difficult waters. **3.** one who steers a ship. **4.** PILOT LIGHT. **5.** a taped television program serving to introduce a possible new series: *Several new pilots were run, but most were rehashes of old stories.* **6.** a preliminary trial or test. —*v.* [~ + *obj*] **7.** to act as pilot on, in, or over: *He piloted the fastest planes in the Air Force.* **8.** to lead or guide, as through unknown places or difficult affairs: *She piloted us through a stormy first year in the new company.* —*adj.* [*before a noun*] **9.** serving as a guide. **10.** serving as an experiment before full-scale operation: *a pilot project.*

pi•lot•house (pī′lət hous′) /ˈpaylətˌhaws/ *n.* [*count*], *pl.* **-hous•es.** a closed, covered structure on the deck of a ship from which it can be navigated.

pi′lot light′, *n.* [*count*] a small flame burning continuously, as in a stove, to relight the main gas burners.

pi•men•to (pi men′tō) /pɪˈmɛntow/ *n.* [*count*], *pl.* **-tos. 1.** the red, mild-flavored fruit of a sweet pepper used esp. as a stuffing for olives. **2.** the plant itself.

pimp (pimp) /pɪmp/ *n.* [*count*] **1.** a person, esp. a man, who finds customers for a prostitute, usually in return for a share of the earnings. —*v.* [*no obj*] **2.** to act as a pimp.

pim•ple (pim′pəl) /ˈpɪmpəl/ *n.* [*count*] a small, usually inflamed swelling or elevation of the skin. —**pim′ply,** *adj.,* **-pli•er, -pli•est:** *a pimply face.*

pin (pin) /pɪn/ *n., v.,* **pinned, pin•ning.** —*n.* [*count*] **1.** a small, slender, pointed piece of metal, etc., used as a fastener or support. **2.** any of many different forms of fasteners, badges, or ornaments made up in part of a penetrating piece, wire, or shaft: *a fraternity pin; a tiepin; a diamond pin on her dress.* **3.** a short metal rod, as a linchpin, driven through holes in adjacent parts, as a hub and an axle, in order to keep the parts together. **4.** CLOTHESPIN. **5.** HAIRPIN. **6.** any of the rounded wooden clubs set up as the target in bowling, tenpins, etc. **7.** *Informal.* a human leg: *still a little weak on my pins.* **8.** a pin-shaped connection, as the terminals on the base of a plug, etc.: *That plug has nine pins.* —*v.* [~ + *obj*] **9.** to fasten or attach with or as if with a pin or pins: *I pinned the pages together.* **10.** to hold (something) still in a spot or position: *He was pinned under the wreckage during the earthquake.* **11. pin down,** to force (someone) to deal with a situation, answer a question directly, or come to a decision: [~ + *obj* + *down*]: *The reporters tried to pin the president down on his new tax proposals.* [~ + *down* + *obj*]: *Can you pin down the chief on a date for negotiations?* —***Idiom.* 12. pin something on someone,** *Informal.* to assign the blame or guilt for something to a person: *tried to pin the murder on his cousin.*

PIN (pin) /pɪn/ *n.* [*count*] an identification number chosen by or assigned to an individual to enable access to an automatic teller machine or other device.

pin•a•fore (pin′ə fôr′, -fōr′) /ˈpɪnəˌfɔr, -ˌfowr/ *n.* [*count*] a sleeveless, apronlike piece of clothing, usually having buttons or a sash at the back, worn by girls and women over a dress or with a blouse. —**pin′a•fored′,** *adj.*

pince-nez (pans′nā′, pins′-) /ˈpænsˌney, ˈpɪns-/ *n.* [*count*], *pl.* **pince-nez** (pans′nāz′, pins′-) /ˈpænsˌneyz, ˈpɪns-/. a pair of glasses held on the face by a spring that grips the nose.

pin•cers (pin′sərz) /ˈpɪnsərz/ *n.* [*plural*] **1.** a gripping tool made of two joined and crossed parts forming a pair of jaws and a pair of handles. **2.** a pair of claws resembling this, as the claws of a lobster.

pinch (pinch) /pɪntʃ/ *v.* **1.** [~ + *obj*] to squeeze between the finger and thumb, the jaws of an instrument, or the like: *She pinched the child's cheek.* **2.** to squeeze painfully or tightly, as a tight shoe does: [~ + *obj*]: *These new shoes pinch her.* [*no obj*]: *Those Sunday shoes pinched.* **3.** [~ + *obj*] to cause to be drawn or pale: *a face pinched with fear.* **4.** [~ + *obj*] to affect with sharp discomfort or distress, as with cold or hunger: *a family pinched by the recession.* **5.** [~ + *obj*] *Slang.* **a.** to steal: *pinching a few items from the drugstore.* **b.** to arrest. —*n.* [*count*] **6.** the act of pinching; a nip or squeeze: *She gave him a little pinch on the cheek.* **7.** as much of something as can be taken up between the finger and thumb: *a pinch of salt for flavor.* **8.** *Slang.* **a.** a raid or arrest. **b.** a theft. —***Idiom.* 9. feel the pinch,** to undergo or live under stress caused by poverty: *Most families began to feel the pinch during the recession when their unemployment insurance ran out.* **10. in a pinch,** if absolutely necessary, as in an emergency: *In a pinch we could cut our meals down to two a day.* **11. pinch pennies,** to spend very little money and save whatever one can.

pinch′-hit′, *v.* [*no obj*], **-hit, -hit•ting. 1.** to substitute at bat for a teammate in baseball: *I stepped up to pinch-hit for him.* **2.** to substitute for someone, esp. in an emergency: *Can you get someone to pinch-hit for me for my next class?* —**pinch′ hit′ter,** *n.* [*count*]

pin•cush•ion (pin′ko͝osh′ən) /ˈpɪnˌkʊʃən/ *n.* [*count*] a small cushion into which pins are stuck until needed.

pine[1] (pīn) /payn/ *n.* **1.** [*count*] an evergreen tree having needlelike leaves in bundles and woody cones: *Many* *pines are valued for their wood.* **2.** [*noncount*] the wood of a pine tree.

pine[2] (pīn) /payn/ *v.,* **pined, pin•ing. 1.** to wish for or want deeply; long (for) painfully: [~ + *for* + *obj*]: *to pine for one's family.* [~ + *to* + *verb*]: *pining to become citizens in a free country.* **2.** [*no obj;* ~ + *away*] to fail gradually in health or strength because of grief or longing: *After his wife's death he pined away.*

pine•ap•ple (pī′nap′əl) /ˈpayˌnæpəl/ *n.* **1.** [*count*] a tropical plant having a short stem and rigid, spiny leaves. **2.** the juicy, edible fruit of this plant: [*count*]: *to buy two pineapples.* [*noncount*]: *a filling of pineapple.*

pine′ tar′, *n.* [*noncount*] a thick, blackish brown liquid that smells like turpentine, made from pine wood, used in paints, roofing, soaps, and as an antiseptic.

ping (ping) /pɪŋ/ *v.* **1.** to produce a sharp sound like that of a bullet striking a sheet of metal: [*no obj*]: *The submarine's sonar was pinging away at the target.* [~ + *obj*]: *On the first sonar scan the submarines pinged their target.* **—*n.*** [*count*] **2.** a pinging sound.

ping-pong (ping′pong′, -pông′) /ˈpɪŋˌpɒŋ, -ˌpɔŋ/ *v.* to (cause to) be moved or transferred back and forth: [~ + *obj*]: *The patient was ping-ponged from one specialist to another.* [*no obj*]: *The patient ping-ponged back and forth from one specialist to another.*

Ping-Pong (ping′pong′, -pông′) /ˈpɪŋˌpɒŋ, -ˌpɔŋ/ *Trademark.* [*noncount*] TABLE TENNIS.

pin•head (pin′hed′) /ˈpɪnˌhɛd/ *n.* [*count*] **1.** the head of a pin. **2.** a stupid person; nitwit.

pin•hole (pin′hōl′) /ˈpɪnˌhowl/ *n.* [*count*] **1.** a small hole made by or as if by a pin. **2.** a hole for a pin to go through.

pin•ion (pin′yən) /ˈpɪnyən/ *v.* [~ + *obj*] to bind or hold (a person's limbs) so they cannot be used: *Pinioned to the ground, the assassin offered no further resistance.*

pink[1] (pingk) /pɪŋk/ *n., adj.,* **-er, -est. —*n.* 1.** [*noncount*] a color that varies from light crimson to pale reddish purple. **2.** [*count*] a plant, as the clove pink or carnation, or its flower. **3. in the pink,** in the highest form or degree of health: *The economy is in the pink again.* **4.** [*count*] *Slang* (*disparaging*). a person with somewhat left-wing political opinions. **—*adj.* 5.** of the color pink. **6.** *Slang* (*disparaging*). holding left-wing political opinions.

pink[2] (pingk) /pɪŋk/ *v.* [~ + *obj*] **1.** to pierce with a rapier or the like; stab. **2.** to cut (fabric) with a notched pattern, so as to prevent fraying.

pink•eye (pingk′ī′) /ˈpɪŋkˌay/ *n.* [*noncount*] a contagious, easily spread form of conjunctivitis.

pink•ie or **pink•y** (ping′kē) /ˈpɪŋkiy/ *n.* [*count*], *pl.* **-pink•ies.** *Informal.* the little finger.

pin′ mon′ey, *n.* [*noncount*] any small sum set aside for small purchases of things.

pin•na•cle (pin′ə kəl) /ˈpɪnəkəl/ *n.* [*count*] **1.** a high peak or top of a mountain, esp. one that is pointed and thin. **2.** [*often: the* + ~] the highest point one can reach, as of success, power, etc.: *at the pinnacle of success.* **3.** a relatively small upright structure above a roof or on a tower.

pi•noch•le or **pi•noc•le** (pē′nuk əl, -nok-) /ˈpiynʌkəl, -nɒk-/ *n.* [*noncount*] a card game played by two, three, or four persons, with a 48-card deck.

pin•point (pin′point′) /ˈpɪnˌpɔynt/ *n.* [*count*] **1.** the point of a pin. **2.** a tiny spot or sharp point. **—*v.*** [~ + *obj*] **3.** to locate or describe exactly or precisely: *The pilot pinpointed the target.* **—*adj.*** [*before a noun*] **4.** exact; precise: *The bomb headed toward its target with pinpoint accuracy.* See -POINT-.

pin•prick (pin′prik′) /ˈpɪnˌprɪk/ *n.* [*count*] **1.** any very small piercing or hole made by a pin or the like. **2.** a small and unimportant irritation or annoyance.

pins′ and nee′dles, *n.* [*plural*] **1.** a tingly, prickly sensation in an arm, hand, foot, or leg that is recovering from numbness. **—*Idiom.* 2. on pins and needles,** in a state of nervous or anxious waiting: *We were on pins and needles waiting for the results of her test.*

pin•stripe (pin′strīp′) /ˈpɪnˌstrayp/ *n.* **1.** [*count*] a very thin stripe, esp. (in fabrics) a thin white stripe on a dark background. **2.** [*noncount*] a fabric or piece of clothing having such stripes. **—pin′striped′,** *adj.*

pint (pīnt) /paynt/ *n.* [*count*] a liquid and dry measure of capacity, equal to one half of a quart, approximately 35 cubic inches (0.6 liter). *Abbr.:* pt.

pin•to (pin′tō, pēn′-) /ˈpɪntow, ˈpiyn-/ *adj., n., pl.* **-tos. —*adj.* 1.** marked with spots of white and other colors; mottled; spotted. **—*n.*** [*count*] **2.** a pinto horse.

pin•up (pin′up′) /ˈpɪnˌʌp/ *n.* [*count*] **1.** a large photograph, as of a sexually attractive person, suitable for pinning on a wall. **2.** a person in such a photograph. **—*adj.*** [*before a noun*] **3.** of, suitable for, or appearing in a pinup.

pin•wheel (pin′hwēl′, -wēl′) /ˈpɪnˌhwiyl, -ˌwiyl/ *n.* [*count*] **1.** a toy consisting of a small wheel with paper or plastic vanes attached by a pin to a stick, designed to spin when blown. **—*v.*** [*no obj*] **2.** to revolve rapidly like a pinwheel.

pi•o•neer (pī′ə nēr′) /ˌpayəˈnɪər/ *n.* [*count*] **1.** one who is among those who first enter or settle a region: *the early pioneers in the western part of the U.S.* **2.** one who is among the earliest in a field of study: *a pioneer in using computers to teach language.* **—*v.* 3.** [~ + *obj*] to be the first to open or prepare (a way, etc.): *pioneered the first settlement in that region.* **4.** to take part in the beginnings of (a field of study, an activity, etc.); initiate: [~ + *obj*]: *pioneered the use of robots in manufacturing.* [*no obj*]: *pioneered in the development of robots in manufacturing.* **5.** to lead the way for (a group); guide. **—*adj.*** [*before a noun*] **6.** being the first or earliest in some field of study, activity, etc.: *a pioneer AIDS researcher.* **7.** of, relating to, or characteristic of pioneers: *The people living in the cold northern regions of Japan have always had the pioneer spirit.*

pi•o•neer•ing (pī′ə nēr′ing) /ˌpayəˈnɪərɪŋ/ *adj.* [*usually: before a noun*] being the earliest in a field of study, activity, etc.: *pioneering efforts in public health.*

pi•ous (pī′əs) /ˈpayəs/ *adj.* **1.** reverent toward God or religion: *a pious Catholic who attended Mass every day.* **2.** showing false respect for virtue or religion; hypocritical. **—pi′ous•ly,** *adv.: Since his workers had hatched the plot, he could piously declare that he was innocent of any dirty tricks.*

pip[1] (pip) /pɪp/ *n.* [*count*] **1.** one of the spots on dice or dominoes. **2.** a metal insignia of rank worn on the shoulders of junior officers in the British army.

pip[2] (pip) /pɪp/ *n.* [*count*] **1.** a small seed, esp. of a fleshy fruit, as an apple or orange. **2.** *Informal.* someone or something wonderful or amazing.

pipe (pīp) /payp/ *n., v.,* **piped, pip•ing. —*n.*** [*count*] **1.** a tube or cylinder of metal or other material, used for carrying water, gas, etc.: *One of the pipes in the kitchen had sprung a leak.* **2.** a tube of wood, clay, or other material, with a small bowl at one end, used for smoking tobacco, etc.: *He filled his pipe with tobacco.* **3. a.** a musical wind instrument, as a flute, made of a single tube. **b.** one of the tubes through which air is forced and from which the tones of an organ are produced: *Some of the organ pipes are twenty feet high.* **c. pipes,** [*plural*] BAGPIPE. **4. pipes,** the human vocal cords or the voice, esp. as used in singing. **—*v.* 5.** to play on a pipe: [~ + *obj*]: *He piped a haunting tune on the bagpipes.* [*no obj*]: *The band had been piping together for several years.* **6.** [~ + *obj*] to speak in a high-pitched or piercing tone: *to pipe a command.* **7.** [~ + *obj*] to carry or send by or as if by pipes or by an electrical wire or cable: *to pipe music into the room.* **8. pipe down,** [*no obj*] *Slang.* to stop talking; be quiet. **9. pipe up,** to make oneself heard, esp. as to get attention if one is being ignored; speak up: [*no obj*]: *He kept piping up with new ideas.* [*used with quotations*]: *"But that's just what we like doing," he piped up.*

pipe′ dream′, *n.* [*count*] a notion or plan that is unrealistic or unlikely to come true.

pipe•line (pīp′līn′) /ˈpaypˌlayn/ *n.* [*count*] **1.** a linked series of pipes with pumps and valves for flow control, used to carry or send crude oil, water, etc., esp. over great distances. **2.** a route or channel along which supplies pass: *a pipeline for food supplies.* **3.** a channel of information, esp. one that is direct or only for certain people: *She's got a direct pipeline to the president.* **—*Idiom.* 4. in the pipeline,** in the process of being provided or completed: *Several projects are in the pipeline.* See -LIN-.

pipe′ or′gan, *n.* ORGAN (def. 1a).

pip•er (pī′pər) /ˈpaypər/ *n.* [*count*] one who plays pipes, bagpipes, or panpipes.

pip•ing (pī′ping) /ˈpaypɪŋ/ *n.* [*noncount*] **1.** pipes thought of as a group; a system of pipes. **2.** material formed into pipes. **3.** the act of a person or thing that pipes. **4.** the sound or music of pipes. **—*adj.* 5.** making a shrill sound: *a piping voice.* **—*Idiom.* 6. piping hot,** (of food or drink) very hot.

pip•squeak (pip′skwēk′) /ˈpɪpˌskwiyk/ *n.* [*count*] *Informal.* a small or unimportant person.

pi•quant (pē′kənt, -känt, pē känt′) /ˈpiykənt, -kɑnt, piyˈkɑnt/ *adj.* **1.** agreeably strong or sharp in taste. **2.** of an interestingly lively character: *a piquant wit.* **—pi′quan•cy,** *n.* [*noncount*]

pique (pēk) /piyk/ *v.,* **piqued, piqu•ing,** *n.* —*v.* [~ + *obj*] **1.** to cause anger in (someone) by an insult or wound to someone's pride: *He was piqued by those snide references to his teaching ability.* **2.** to excite or arouse; provoke: *The report piqued my curiosity.* —*n.* [*noncount*] **3.** a feeling of irritation or resentment, as from a wound to one's pride: *He stormed out of the room in a fit of pique.*

pi•ra•cy (pī′rə sē) /ˈpayrəsiy/ *n.* [*noncount*] the practice of a pirate: *piracy in the software business.*

pi•ra•nha (pi rän′yə, -ran′-, -rä′nə, -ran′ə) /pɪˈrɑnyə, -ˈræn-, -ˈrɑnə, -ˈrænə/ *n.* [*count*], *pl.* **-nhas,** (*esp. when thought of as a group*) **-nha.** a small South American freshwater fish with sharp interlocking teeth, dangerous when swimming in schools.

pi•rate (pī′rət) /ˈpayrət/ *n., v.,* **-rat•ed, -rat•ing.** —*n.* [*count*] **1.** one who robs or commits illegal acts or violence at sea. **2.** one who uses or copies the work or invention of another without permission. —*v.* [~ + *obj*] **3.** to take by piracy. **4.** to use or copy (a book, an invention, copyrighted software, etc.) without permission or legal right. —**pi•rat•i•cal** (pi rat′i kəl, pi-) /payˈrætɪkəl, pɪ-/ *adj.*

pir•ou•ette (pir′o͞o et′) /ˌpɪruwˈɛt/ *n., v.,* **-et•ted, -et•ting.** —*n.* [*count*] **1.** a whirling about on one foot or on the points of the toes, as in ballet dancing. —*v.* [*no obj*] **2.** to perform a pirouette.

piss (pis) /pɪs/ *Vulgar.* —*n.* **1.** [*noncount*] urine. **2.** [*count*] an act of urinating. —*v.* **3.** [*no obj*] to urinate. **4.** **piss away,** *Slang.* to waste: [~ + *away* + *obj*]: *He pissed away all that money drinking and gambling.* [~ + *obj* + *away*]: *He pissed that money away.* **5.** **piss off,** *Slang.* **a.** [~ + *obj* + *off*] to anger: *Those insulting remarks really pissed me off.* **b.** [*no obj*] " go away; leave:" *I told you before to piss off and leave us alone.*

pissed (pist) /pɪst/ *adj. Slang (vulgar).* [*be* + ~] **1.** drunk: *He was completely pissed after just a few drinks.* **2.** angry: *She's really pissed about something.*

pis•tach•i•o (pi stash′ē ō′, -stä′shē ō′) /pɪˈstæʃiyˌow, -ˈstɑʃiyˌow/ *n.* [*count*], *pl.* **-chi•os.** **1.** the nut of a tree of the cashew family, containing a greenish edible kernel. **2.** the tree itself. Also, **pistach′io nut′** (for def. 1).

pis•til (pis′tl) /ˈpɪstḷ/ *n.* [*count*] the part of a flower carrying the seed, made up of the ovary, style, and stigma. —**pis•til•late** (pis′tl it, -āt′) /ˈpɪstḷɪt, -ˌeyt/ *adj.*

pis•tol (pis′tl) /ˈpɪstḷ/ *n.* [*count*] a short firearm intended to be held and fired with one hand: *a .22 caliber pistol.*

pis′tol-whip′, *v.* [~ + *obj*], **-whipped, -whip•ping.** to beat with a pistol: *The guards were overpowered, pistol-whipped, and tied up.*

pis•ton (pis′tən) /ˈpɪstən/ *n.* [*count*] **1.** a disk or solid, pipe-shaped piece moving within a longer tube and putting pressure on, or receiving pressure from, a fluid or gas: *When the gas mixture explodes it forces the piston down, and this motion is transferred to the car's wheels.* **2.** a pumplike valve used to change the pitch in a cornet, trumpet, or the like.

pit[1] (pit) /pɪt/ *n., v.,* **pit•ted, pit•ting.** —*n.* [*count*] **1.** a hole or cavity in the ground. **2.** a hidden hole in the ground, serving as a trap. **3.** **a.** a large, deep hole in the ground made for looking for or removing a mineral deposit, as coal or gas; a shaft. **b.** the mine itself. **4.** **the pits,** [*be* + ~] *Slang.* an extremely unpleasant or depressing place, condition, etc.: *Living there was the pits.* **5.** a hollow, hole, or depression in a surface or body: *a road with bumps and pits all through it.* **6.** a small depressed scar on the skin; pockmark: *a small line of pits on her forehead.* **7.** a closed-off area for staging fights, esp. between dogs or cocks. **8.** a part of the floor of a stock exchange where trading takes place. **9.** an area at the side of a car racing track, used for servicing and refueling the cars. —*v.* [~ + *obj*] **10.** to mark or indent with pits; to scar with pockmarks. **11.** to set (two opponents) in combat: *The candidates were pitted against each other.*

pit[2] (pit) /pɪt/ *n., v.,* **pit•ted, pit•ting.** —*n.* [*count*] **1.** the stone of a fruit, as of a cherry, peach, or plum. —*v.* [~ + *obj*] **2.** to remove the pit from (a fruit).

pi•ta (pē′tə) /ˈpiytə/ *n.* [*noncount*] a kind of round, flat Middle Eastern bread having a pocket that can be filled to make a sandwich. Also called **pi′ta bread′.**

pit•a•pat (pit′ə pat′) /ˈpɪtəˌpæt/ *adv.* **1.** with a quick series of beats or taps: *The rain went pit-a-pat on the tin roof.* —*n.* [*count*] **2.** the movement or the sound of something going pitapat.

pitch[1] (pich) /pɪtʃ/ *v.* **1.** [~ + *obj*] to erect or set up (a tent, etc.): *They pitched their camp on the side of the mountain.* **2.** [~ + *obj*] to put or plant in a definite place: *The picture was pitched at an odd angle.* **3.** to (cause to) be sloped downward or to be dipped: [~ + *obj*]: *The roof is pitched at a steep angle there.* [*no obj*]: *The roof pitches at a steep angle there.* **4.** [~ + *obj*] to throw, fling, hurl, or toss: *She pitched the smaller suitcases to me from the porch.* **5.** *Baseball.* **a.** to throw (the ball) to the batter: [~ + *obj*]: *He pitched mostly fastballs and curves.* [*no obj*]: *She pitches very fast.* **b.** to serve as pitcher of (a game): [~ + *obj*]: *He pitched three games during the World Series.* [*no obj*]: *She's ready to pitch tomorrow.* **6.** [~ + *obj*] to set or aim at a certain point, degree, etc.: *He pitched his hopes too high.* **7.** [~ + *obj*] to establish the musical key of (a sound, etc.): *The musicians pitched their instruments a little higher.* **8.** [*no obj*] to (cause to) plunge or fall forward: *He lost consciousness and pitched to the floor.* **9.** to (cause to) plunge with alternate fall and rise of bow and stern, as a ship: [*no obj*]: *The ship was pitching during the storm.* [~ + *obj*]: *The storm pitched the ship.* **10.** **pitch in,** [*no obj*] *Informal.* to contribute to a common cause: *If everybody pitches in, we can finish this job by 5 p.m.* —*n.* **11.** [*count; usually singular*] relative point, level, or degree: *a high pitch of excitement.* **12.** [*count*] the degree of tilt or slope of something; an angle: *The roof was at an odd pitch.* **13.** (in music, speech, etc.) the degree of height or depth of a sound, depending upon the relative frequency of the vibrations by which it is produced: [*noncount*]: *a change in pitch when pronouncing different words.* [*count*]: *differences in the pitch of a word or syllable.* **14.** [*count*] the act or manner of pitching, as in baseball. **15.** [*count*] a throw or toss. **16.** [*count*] a pitching movement, as of a ship. **17.** [*count*] *Informal.* a sales talk, often one in which the salesperson tries to convince the buyer of the need for his or her product: *He began his sales pitch for the condominiums.* **18.** a unit of measurement for letters in a typeface, indicating the number of characters to the horizontal inch: [*noncount*]: *twelve-pitch type.* [*count*]: *a printer capable of different pitches and fonts.*

pitch[2] (pich) /pɪtʃ/ *n.* [*noncount*] a dark, sticky, thick substance used for repairing holes in ships or for paving roads, made from coal tar or wood tar.

pitch′-black′, *adj.* extremely black or dark, as pitch: *a pitch-black night with no moon.*

pitch′-dark′, *adj.* very dark or black, as pitch.

pitched′ bat′tle, *n.* [*count*] any struggle, encounter, competition, etc., in which the opponents fight fiercely.

pitch•er[1] (pich′ər) /ˈpɪtʃər/ *n.* [*count*] a container for liquids, usually with a handle and spout or lip.

pitch•er[2] (pich′ər) /ˈpɪtʃər/ *n.* [*count*] **1.** one who pitches. **2.** *Baseball.* the player who throws the ball to the opposing batter.

pitch•fork (pich′fôrk′) /ˈpɪtʃˌfɔrk/ *n.* [*count*] a large, long-handled fork for lifting and pitching hay, etc.

pitch•man (pich′mən) /ˈpɪtʃmən/ *n.* [*count*], *pl.* **-men.** one who makes a sales pitch, as on a radio or TV commercial: *The congressman was accused of being a pitchman for the auto industry.*

pitch′ pipe′, *n.* [*count*] a small pipe producing one or more notes when blown into.

pit•e•ous (pit′ē əs) /ˈpɪtiyəs/ *adj.* arousing a feeling of pity; deserving pity; pathetic: *the piteous cry of a lost child.* —**pit′e•ous•ly,** *adv.*: *crying piteously in the night.* —**pit′e•ous•ness,** *n.* (sub′jek tiv′i tē) /ˌsʌbdʒɛkˈtɪvɪtiy/ [*noncount*]

pit•fall (pit′fôl′) /ˈpɪtˌfɔl/ *n.* [*count*] **1.** a lightly covered pit prepared as a trap for people or animals. **2.** any trap, danger, or mistake that may imperil someone: *the pitfalls of a career in teaching.*

pith (pith) /pɪθ/ *n.* [*noncount*] **1.** the soft, spongy tissue in the stems of certain plants and trees. **2.** the soft inner part of a feather, a hair, etc. **3.** the important or essential part; core: *the pith of the matter.*

pith•y (pith′ē) /ˈpɪθiy/ *adj.,* **-i•er, -i•est.** **1.** brief, forceful, and to the point: *a pithy observation.* **2.** of, like, or having much pith. —**pith•i•ly** (pith′ə lē) /ˈpɪθəliy/ *adv.*

pit•i•a•ble (pit′ē ə bəl) /ˈpɪtiyəbəl/ *adj.* **1.** arousing a feeling of pity; deserving pity: *pitiable, homeless children.* **2.** deserving contempt: *a pitiable lack of character.* —**pit′i•ab•ly,** *adv.*: *a pitiably weak showing in the election.*

pit•i•ful (pit′i fəl) /ˈpɪtɪfəl/ *adj.* **1.** arousing a feeling of pity; deserving pity: *a pitiful fate.* **2.** arousing contempt due to inadequacy or poor quality: *pitiful attempts to hide the truth.* —**pit′i•ful•ly,** *adv.*: *He pitched pitifully in that last game.*

pit•i•less (pit′i lis, pit′ē-) /'pɪtɪlɪs, 'pɪtiy-/ *adj.* feeling or showing no pity; merciless: *a pitiless foe.* —**pit′i•less•ly,** *adv.*: *His forces attacked pitilessly.*

pit•tance (pit′ns) /'pɪtns/ *n.* [*count; usually: a* + ~] a small amount, esp. a very small amount of money: *working for a pittance at that awful job.*

pit•ter-pat•ter (pit′ər pat′ər) /'pɪtər'pætər/ *n.* [*count; singular*] **1.** the sound of a rapid series of light beats or taps, as of rain or footsteps: *the pitter-patter of little feet on a Saturday morning.* —*adv.* **2.** with such a sound.

pi•tu•i•tar•y (pi to͞o′i ter′ē, -tyo͞o′-) /pɪ'tuwɪ,tɛriy, -'tyuw-/ *n.* [*count*], *pl.* **-tar•ies. 1.** [*count*] PITUITARY GLAND. **2.** [*noncount*] a chemical substance taken from pituitary glands for use as a medicine.

pitu′itary gland′, *n.* [*count*] a small, cherry-shaped gland attached to the base of the brain, affecting all functions regarding hormones in the body: *The pituitary gland controls sexual development and growth.*

pit′ vi′per, *n.* [*count*] a snake or viper, as the rattlesnake and copperhead, that has a heat-sensitive pit above each nostril.

pit•y (pit′ē) /'pɪtiy/ *n., pl.* **pit•ies,** *v.,* **pit•ied, pit•y•ing.** —*n.* **1.** [*noncount*] sympathetic or kindhearted sorrow for, or sensitiveness to, another's suffering, distress, or misfortune: *felt pity for her.* **2.** [*count; usually singular; a* + ~] a cause or reason for pity, sorrow, or regret: *What a pity you couldn't go!* [*It* + *be* + ~ + *(that) clause*]: *It's a pity (that) you can't come to the party.* —*v.* [~ + *obj*] **3.** to feel pity for; be sorry for: *He pitied the poor immigrants who worked in sweatshops.* —***Idiom.* 4. have** or **take pity on,** [~ + *obj*] to have compassion for, or show mercy to: *begged him to have pity on the political prisoners.*

piv•ot (piv′ət) /'pɪvət/ *n.* [*count*] **1.** a pin, point, or short shaft supporting something that rests and turns, or allowing something to spin around on it: *a pivot on a gear mechanism.* **2.** a person or thing on which something else turns or depends: *She was the pivot of the campaign's success.* **3.** a whirling around on one foot: *The soldier made a smart, sharp pivot.* —*v.* **4.** [*no obj*] to turn on or as if on a pivot: *He pivoted on his heel and left the room.* **5. pivot on,** [~ + *on* + *obj*] to depend or hinge or be based on, as for success: *The whole election campaign pivots on a few important states.*

piv•ot•al (piv′ə tl) /'pɪvətḷ/ *adj.* crucial; affecting the success of something: *a pivotal state in the election.*

pix•el (pik′səl, -sel) /'pɪksəl, -sɛl/ *n.* [*count*] the smallest element of an image that can be individually processed in a video display system.

pix•ie or **pix•y** (pik′sē) /'pɪksiy/ *n., pl.* **pix•ies,** *adj.* —*n.* [*count*] **1.** a fairy, esp. one who enjoys playing tricks. **2.** a playful person. —*adj.* **3.** Also, **pix′ie•ish, pix′y•ish.** playful or enjoying playing tricks.

pi•zazz or **piz•zazz** (pə zaz′) /pə'zæz/ *n.* [*noncount*] *Informal.* **1.** energy; vitality; vigor: *They worked with increased pizazz.* **2.** attractive style; dash; excitement: *She brought some pizazz to the drab office.*

piz•za (pēt′sə) /'piytsə/ *n., pl.* **-zas.** a baked, open-faced pie consisting of a thin layer of dough topped with tomato sauce and cheese, etc.: [*noncount*]: *The kids always want pizza on Sunday night for dinner.* [*count*]: *pizzas with several toppings.* Also called **piz′za pie′.**

piz•ze•ri•a (pēt′sə rē′ə) /,piytsə'riyə/ *n.* [*count*], *pl.* **-ri•as.** a restaurant or bakery where pizzas are made and sold.

piz•zi•ca•to (pit′si kä′tō) /,pɪtsɪ'kɑtow/ *adj., n., pl.* **-ti** (-tē) /-tiy/. *Music.* —*adj.* **1.** played by plucking the strings with the finger instead of using the bow, as on a violin. —*n.* [*count*] **2.** a note or passage so played.

pj's or **p.j.'s** or **P.J.'s** (pē′jāz′) /'piy,dʒeyz/ *n.* [*plural*] *Informal.* pajamas.

pk, an abbreviation of: peck.

pk., *pl.* **pks.** an abbreviation of: **1.** pack. **2.** park. **3.** peak.

pkg., an abbreviation of: package.

pkwy., an abbreviation of: parkway.

pl., an abbreviation of: **1.** place. **2.** plural.

P/L, an abbreviation of: profit and loss.

-plac-, *root.* *-plac-* comes from Latin, where it has the meaning "to please." This meaning is found in such words as: COMPLACENT, IMPLACABLE, PLACATE, PLACEBO, PLACID.

plac•ard (plak′ärd, -ərd) /'plækɑrd, -ərd/ *n.* [*count*] a sign or notice posted in a public place or carried by a demonstrator.

pla•cate (plā′kāt, plak′āt) /'pleykeyt, 'plækeyt/ *v.* [~ + *obj*], **-cat•ed, -cat•ing.** to cause (someone) to stop being angry, resentful, etc., as by giving in to his or her demands; pacify; appease: *He tried to placate the baby by giving her more and more candy.* —**pla•ca•tion** (plā kā′shən) /pley'keyʃən/ *n.* [*noncount*] See -PLAC-.

pla•cat•ing (plā′kāt ing, plak′āt ing) /'pleykeytɪŋ, 'plækeytɪŋ/ *adj.* tending to placate: *Before he could explode she laid a placating hand on his arm.* See -PLAC-.

place (plās) /pleys/ *n., v.,* **placed, plac•ing.** —*n.* **1.** [*count*] a particular portion of space: *We visited a lot of places in Scotland.* **2.** [*noncount*] space in general: *The words* in, on, *and* at *are prepositions of time and place:* in *Russia;* on *23rd Street;* at *17 Lexington Avenue.* **3.** [*count*] the portion of space occupied by a person or thing: *The vase is in its usual place on the mantelpiece.* **4.** [*count*] any part of a body, surface, or building; spot: *the places on her arm where she had been bitten.* **5.** [*count*] a particular part, page, or passage in a book or in writing: *I must have lost my place; my bookmark is missing.* **6.** [*count*] a space or seat for a person, as in a theater or line: *She saved my place on line.* **7.** [*count*] position or circumstances: *I would complain if I were in your place.* **8.** [*count*] a proper location or time: *A restaurant is not a good place for an argument.* **9.** [*count*] a job, position, or office: *people in high places.* **10.** [*count; usually singular*] a function or duty: *It is not your place to offer criticism.* **11.** [*noncount*] proper sequence or relationship, as of ideas or details: *Everything fell neatly into place.* **12.** [*count*] position or rank: *America's place in the world.* **13.** [*count*] a region or area: *to travel to distant places.* **14.** [*count*] an open space or square in a city or town. **15.** [*count; usually singular; no article*] a short street or court: *They lived at 33 Park Place.* **16.** [*count*] an area where people live: *one of the most dangerous places in town at night.* **17.** [*count*] a building, location, etc., set aside for a purpose: *A church is a place of worship.* **18.** [*count*] a building or apartment to live in: *When can you come to our new place?* **19.** [*count; singular: in* + *the* + *a word indicating number or rank* + ~] (used to introduce each one of a series or list of examples, details, etc.; preceded by a word indicating the order in the list): *We're not voting for him for two reasons: in the first place, there's too much unemployment; in the second place, we don't trust him.* **20. a.** [*count; singular; after a word indicating number or rank*] a position among the competitors in a contest, etc.: *Who came in first place?* **b.** [*noncount*] *Sports.* the position of the competitor who comes in second, as in a horse race. —*v.* **21.** [~ + *obj*] to put in the proper position or order; arrange: *Place the silverware on the table.* **22.** [~ + *obj*] to find a home, place, etc., for (a person): *The foster home placed the orphan with a family.* **23.** [~ + *obj*] to give (an order) to a supplier: *I placed an order for 5000 diskettes.* **24.** [~ + *obj*] to assign a certain position or rank to: *I would place him among the top five physicists in the world.* **25.** [~ + *obj*] to identify by connecting with the proper place, etc.: *I'm having trouble placing your face. I can't quite place his accent.* **26.** [*no obj*] to finish second in a horse race: *Their horse placed in the fourth race.* **27.** [~ + *a word indicating number or rank*] to earn a certain, stated standing, as in an examination or competition: *He placed fifth in his class.* —***Idiom.* 28. go places,** to advance in one's career; succeed: *He was really going places until that scandal knocked him out of politics.* **29. in place, a.** in the correct position or order: *Everything's back in place now that you've returned.* **b.** in the same spot, without advancing or retreating: *to jog in place.* **30. in place of,** [~ + *obj*] instead of: *Use yogurt in place of sour cream.* **know** or **keep one's place,** to behave according to one's rank, esp. if inferior: *She acts like she's more important than she is; doesn't she know her place yet?* **31. out of place, a.** not in the correct position or order: *These books and office records are all out of place.* **b.** unsuitable; inappropriate: *Your remarks were out of place.* **32. place in the sun,** [*count; singular*] a favorable position: *finally earned his place in the sun after all those years of working behind the scenes.* **33. put someone in his** or **her place,** to scold someone or remind someone of his or her position: *That clever answer really put the questioner in his place.* **34. take place,** to happen; occur: *A lot of things took place during your absence.*

pla•ce•bo (plə sē′bō) /plə'siybow/ *n.* [*count*], *pl.* **-bos, -boes.** a substance that is not medicine but is given to a patient who supposes it to be a medicine, either to appease a patient or as a control in an experiment. See -PLAC-.

place′ mat′, *n.* [*count*] a mat set on a dining table beneath a plate, glasses, or silverware.

place•ment (plās′mənt) /'pleysmənt/ *n.* **1.** the act of placing, as in a suitable job, grade, or school: [*noncount*]: *Placement into courses is by written exam only.* [*count*]: *Placements into ESL courses are at an all-time high.* **2.** [*noncount*] the state of being placed; arrangement: *the placement of furniture.* **3.** [*count*] the act of filling a position: *The employment agency made several quick placements.*

pla•cen•ta (plə sen′tə) /plə'sɛntə/ *n.* [*count*], *pl.* **-tas, -tae** (-tē) /-tiy/. an organ in most mammals, formed in the lining of the uterus, that provides for the nourishment of the fetus. —**pla•cen′tal,** *adj.*

plac•id (plas′id) /'plæsɪd/ *adj.* pleasantly calm or peaceful; tranquil: *a placid personality.* —**pla•cid•i•ty** (plə sid′i tē) /plə'sɪdɪtiy/ *n.* [*noncount*] —**plac′id•ly,** *adv.*: *He went along placidly with our plan.* See -PLAC-.

pla•gia•rism (plā′jə riz′əm) /'pleydʒə,rɪzəm/ *n.* **1.** [*noncount*] the act of stealing another's ideas, written passages, concepts, etc., as one's own: *The teacher suspected plagiarism when the student handed in a paper that relied heavily on the ideas of Emerson but never mentioned him.* **2.** [*count*] a piece of writing so taken or used: *His speech contained a plagiarism from a British politician.*

pla•gia•rize (plā′jə rīz′) /'pleydʒə,rayz/ *v.*, **-rized, -riz•ing.** to steal by plagiarism: [~ + *obj*]: *He plagiarized the ideas as his own.* [*no obj*]: *They were pretty sure he had plagiarized, but it was hard to prove.* —**pla′gia•rist,** *n.* [*count*]

plague (plāg) /pleyg/ *n., v.,* **plagued, pla•guing.** —*n.* **1.** a widespread disease that causes a great number of deaths; pestilence: [*noncount*]: *Millions died from plague and famine.* [*count*]: *In the Bible, Pharaoh's Egypt was punished by ten plagues until he let the Israelites go.* **2.** [*noncount; usually: the* + ~] a widespread disease caused by a bacterium, characterized by fever, chills, and exhaustion, carried to humans from rats by means of the bites of fleas. **3.** [*count*] any cause of great bother and irritation, or of widespread misery or distress: *a plague of robberies in the area.* —*v.* [~ + *obj*] **4.** to trouble, annoy, or torment in any manner: *a transportation system plagued by low revenues, bad service, and poor management.*

plaid (plad) /plæd/ *n.* **1.** [*noncount*] a fabric woven of differently colored yarns in a cross-barred pattern. **2.** [*count*] a pattern of this kind. —*adj.* **3.** having the pattern of a plaid: *a plaid shirt.*

plain (plān) /pleyn/ *adj.*, **-er, -est,** *adv., n.* —*adj.* **1.** distinct to the eye or ear: *in plain view.* **2.** clear to the mind; evident: *He made his meaning plain.* **3.** easily understood: *the plain truth.* **4.** [*before a noun*] complete; downright; sheer; utter: *plain stupidity.* **5.** ordinary; without false display: *plain, simple farm people.* **6.** not beautiful; unattractive: *a plain face.* **7.** with little or no decoration; not fancy: *a plain blue suit.* **8.** not rich, highly seasoned, or fancy in preparation, as food: *plain cooking.* —*adv.* **9.** clearly and simply: *They're just plain stupid.* —*n.* [*count*] **10.** a large, flat area of land not higher than nearby areas. —**plain′ness,** *n.* [*noncount*]

plain•clothes (plān′klōz′, -klōthz′-) /'pleyn'klowz, -'klowðz-/ also **plain′-clothes′,** *adj.* (of a police officer, esp. a detective) wearing ordinary clothes while on duty: *a plainclothes detective.* —**plain′clothes′man,** *n.* [*count*], *pl.* **-men.** —**plain′clothes′wo•man,** *n.* [*count*], *pl.* **-wom•en.**

plain•ly (plān′lē) /'pleynliy/ *adv.* **1.** clearly; obviously: *plainly confused by her question.* **2.** in a manner easy to understand: *I've told you as plainly as I can.*

plain•spo•ken (plān′spō′kən) /'pleyn'spowkən/ *adj.* **1.** speaking the truth even if impolite; blunt: *He's very plainspoken and will tell you exactly what he thinks.* **2.** using simple, direct language.

plain•tiff (plān′tif) /'pleyntɪf/ *n.* [*count*] one who brings or starts a legal action or suit in a court: *The plaintiff accused her husband of beating her.*

plain•tive (plān′tiv) /'pleyntɪv/ *adj.* expressing sorrow or sadness; mournful: *a plaintive melody.* —**plain′tive•ly,** *adv.*

plait (plāt, plat) /pleyt, plæt/ *n.* [*count*] **1.** a knot formed by twisting three or more lengths of rope, hair, etc., together; a braid. —*v.* [~ + *obj*] **2.** to form a plait; to braid: *spending hours plaiting their long hair.* **3.** to make (something), as a mat, by this method.

plan (plan) /plæn/ *n., v.,* **planned, plan•ning.** —*n.* [*count*] **1.** a way, idea, or method of acting, proceeding, etc., developed in advance: *a battle plan.* **2.** a design or arrangement: *a seating plan.* **3.** a drawing made to represent the top view or a side view of a structure or a machine, as a floor layout of a building. **4.** an outline, diagram, or sketch: *He drew a quick plan of the bank vault.* **5.** a program providing for specified benefits, etc.: *a pension plan.* —*v.* **6.** [~ + *obj*] to put together a plan or scheme for: *The city wants to plan a new park.* **7.** to make plans for: [~ + *obj*]: *We had already planned our vacation for that week.* [*no obj*]: *It was time to plan for retirement.* **8.** [~ + *obj*] to draw or make a plan of, as a building. **9.** to have in mind as an intention: [~ + *obj*]: *What are you planning for her retirement party?* [~ + *to* + *verb*]: *I planned to be there on time.* [~ + *on* + *verb-ing*]: *I hadn't planned on seeing you today.* —**plan′ner,** *n.* [*count*]

plane[1] (plān) /pleyn/ *n., adj., v.,* **planed, plan•ing.** —*n.* [*count*] **1.** a flat or level surface. **2.** an area of a two-dimensional surface: *The tools can only be moved along one plane.* **3.** a level of dignity or character: *The candidates kept the debate on a high plane.* **4.** an airplane. —*adj.* **5.** flat or level, as a surface. **6.** of or relating to two-dimensional figures. —*v.* [*no obj*] **7.** to glide or soar. **8.** *Informal.* to fly or travel in an airplane.

plane[2] (plān) /pleyn/ *n., v.,* **planed, plan•ing.** —*n.* [*count*] **1.** a woodworking instrument for cutting or smoothing wood by means of a tilted, adjustable blade. —*v.* [~ + *obj*] **2.** to smooth with or as if with a plane.

plan•et (plan′it) /'plænɪt/ *n.* [*count*] **1. a.** any of the nine large heavenly bodies revolving around the sun and shining by reflected light: *Jupiter is the largest planet in our solar system.* **b.** a similar body revolving around a star other than the sun. **2.** [*the* + ~] the planet Earth: *Will there be any life on the planet after a nuclear war?*

plan•e•tar•i•um (plan′i târ′ē əm) /,plænɪ'tɛəriyəm/ *n.* [*count*], *pl.* **-tar•i•ums, -tar•i•a** (-târ′ē ə) /-'tɛəriyə/. **1.** a model representing the planetary system. **2.** a device that produces a representation of the sky, the stars, the planets, etc., by the use of movie projectors. **3.** the building or room in which such a device is housed.

plan•e•tar•y (plan′i ter′ē) /'plænɪ,tɛriy/ *adj.* [*before a noun*] of or relating to planets: *planetary orbits.*

plane′ tree′, *n.* [*count*] a large tree of North America, esp. the sycamore, with broad leaves and bark that peels off easily.

plan•gent (plan′jənt) /'plændʒənt/ *adj.* making a loud sound, as a bell.

plank (plangk) /plæŋk/ *n.* [*count*] **1.** a long, flat piece of wood, thicker than a board: *They used a couple of planks to walk across the trench.* **2.** any of the principles or aims that make up the platform of a political party: *the anti-abortion plank of the Republican party's platform.* —*v.* [~ + *obj*] **3.** to cover or provide with planks. **4.** to bake or broil and serve (steak, fish, etc.) on a wooden board: *planked codfish.*

plank•ing (plang′king) /'plæŋkɪŋ/ *n.* [*noncount*] **1.** planks thought of as a group, as in a floor. **2.** the act of laying or covering with planks.

plank•ton (plangk′tən) /'plæŋktən/ *n.* [*noncount*] a mass of tiny, floating or drifting living beings occurring in a body of water, mostly algae and protozoa.

plant (plant) /plænt/ *n.* [*count*] **1.** a living thing that usually has stems, leaves, and roots, and grows in the ground: *plants and flowers.* **2.** an herb or other small vegetable growth, in contrast with a tree or a shrub. **3.** a factory, etc., where a product is manufactured: *a steel plant.* **4.** the complete equipment, machinery, etc., needed for a particular mechanical operation, etc.: *a heating plant.* **5.** a person or thing placed secretly in a country, etc., to gather information or make a plot or scheme work: *A Russian plant had been working for the senator all those years.* —*v.* **6.** to put or set in the ground for growth, as seeds, shrubs, or young trees: [~ + *obj*]: *to plant trees along the parks and highways.* [*no obj*]: *It was too early in the season to plant.* **7.** [~ + *obj*] to stock (land) with plants: *They planted a few acres with corn.* **8.** [~ + *obj*] to establish (ideas, etc.) in the mind; cause someone to believe (something): *Who planted that ridiculous idea in his head?* **9.** [~ + *obj*] to put in or set firmly in or on the ground: *to plant fence posts.* **10.** [~ + *obj*] to place, station, or direct with determination: *He planted himself in the doorway.* **11.** [~ + *obj*] to place (something) in order to make a scheme work, obtain a desired result, etc.: *The police planted a story in the newspaper.* **12.** [~ + *obj*] to place (a person) secretly in a group, organization, etc., to gather information, steal plans, etc.: *The Russians had planted a spy in the consulate.*

plan•tain (plan′tin, -tn) /'plæntɪn, -tn̩/ *n.* **1.** [*count*] a tropical plant of the banana family, resembling the banana. **2.** its edible fruit: [*count*]: *We bought some plantains and tried frying them in oil.* [*noncount*]: *The cereal is made of flour and plantain.*

plan•ta•tion (plan tā′shən) /plæn'teyʃən/ *n.* [*count*] **1.** a usually large farm or land area, maintained by workers who live there: *a coffee plantation.* **2.** a group of planted trees or plants.

plant•er (plan′tər) /'plæntər/ *n.* [*count*] **1.** a person who plants. **2.** an implement for planting seeds. **3.** the owner or manager of a plantation. **4.** a container for growing ornamental plants.

plaque (plak) /plæk/ *n.* **1.** [*count*] a thin, flat plate or tablet of metal, porcelain, etc., intended for ornament, as on a wall, or with writing on it, usually intended to honor someone, placed on a wall, building, or monument: *He received a plaque for his twenty years of service.* **2.** [*noncount*] an abnormal, hardened deposit on the inner wall of an artery. **3.** [*noncount*] a soft, sticky, whitish film that forms on tooth surfaces.

plas•ma (plaz′mə) /'plæzmə/ *n.* [*noncount*] the fluid or liquid part of blood, as distinguished from the cells.

plas•ter (plas′tər) /'plæstər/ *n.* [*noncount*] **1.** a pasty mixture of lime, sand, and water, applied to walls, ceilings, etc., and allowed to harden and dry. **2.** PLASTER OF PARIS. **3.** a solid preparation spread upon cloth or other material to form a case, then applied to the body, esp. for some healing purpose, as holding a broken limb in place: *He had one arm in plaster.* —*v.* **4.** [~ + *obj*] to cover, fill, or smear with plaster. **5.** to cause to lay flat: [~ + *obj* + *down*]: *He used some gooey hair tonic to plaster his hair down.* [~ + *down* + *obj*]: *to plaster down his hair.* **6.** [~ + *obj*] to spread or cover with something, esp. thickly or too much: *The students plastered the walls with posters.* **7.** [~ + *obj*] *Informal.* to defeat completely: *In the last game they plastered us 10-0.* —**plas′ter•er,** *n.* [*count*]

plas•ter•board (plas′tər bôrd′, -bōrd′) /'plæstər,bɔrd, -,bowrd/ *n.* [*noncount*] a material used for insulating or covering walls, made of paper-covered sheets of gypsum and felt.

plas•tered (plas′tərd) /'plæstərd/ *adj.* [*be* + ~] *Slang.* very drunk.

plas′ter of Par′is (or **par′is**) (par′is) /'pærɪs/ *n.* [*noncount*] a white powdery substance, used as a base for gypsum plasters and as a material for mixing with water to make fine or decorative casts.

plas•tic (plas′tik) /'plæstɪk/ *n.* **1.** a substance made from oil or coal that may be shaped when soft and then hardened to a strong, lightweight material: [*noncount*]: *Those cheap pens are made of plastic.* [*count*]: *Plastics are used in computers and cars as a lightweight substitute for metal.* **2.** [*noncount*] a credit card, or credit cards thought of as a group: *Can we use plastic at that restaurant?* —*adj.* **3.** made of plastic. **4.** capable of being shaped or molded. **5.** having the power to mold or shape material: *the plastic forces of nature.* **6.** lacking individuality or character: *staying at one of those plastic chain hotels.* **7.** insincere; phony: *a plastic smile.* **8.** relating to the use of credit cards: *plastic money.* —**plas•tic•i•ty** (plas tis′i tē) /plæs'tɪsɪtiy/ *n.* [*noncount*]

plas′tic sur′gery, *n.* [*noncount*] the branch of surgery dealing with the repair, replacement, or reshaping of malformed, injured, or lost parts of the body. —**plas′tic sur′geon,** *n.* [*count*]

plate (plāt) /pleyt/ *n.*, *v.*, **plat•ed, plat•ing.** —*n.* **1.** [*count*] a shallow dish from which food is eaten: *He took a plate and filled it with food.* See illustration at RESTAURANT. **2.** [*count*] the contents of such a dish; plateful: *Finish your plate before you have dessert.* **3.** [*count*] the food and service for one person: *a benefit dinner at $100 a plate.* **4.** [*noncount*] household dishes, utensils, etc., of metal covered with a thin layer of gold or silver. **5.** [*count*] a dish used for collecting offerings, as in a church. **6.** [*count*] a thin, flat sheet or piece of metal or other material, esp. of uniform thickness: *He opened a small plate on the side of the robot.* **7.** [*count*] a flat, polished piece of metal on which something may be engraved: *He had a plate on the door of his office with his name and title.* **8.** [*count*] a sheet on which something has been engraved, to be inked and used in a press for printing impressions. **9.** [*count*] a printed impression from such a piece, as a woodcut. **10.** [*count*] a full-page illustration in a book, esp. on paper different from the text pages. **11.** [*count*] the part of a denture that is the same shape as the mouth and contains the teeth. **12.** [*count*] a rigid section of the earth's crust that causes continental drift when it moves. —*v.* [~ + *obj*] **13.** to coat (metal) with a thin film of gold, silver, etc. **14.** to cover with metal plates for protection: *The new tank was plated with six-inch-thick armor.* —**plat′ed,** *adj.*: *gold-plated silverware.*

pla•teau (pla tō′) /plæ'tow/ *n.*, *pl.* **-teaus, -teaux** (-tōz′, -tōz) /-'towz, -towz/ *v.*, **-teaued, -teau•ing.** —*n.* [*count*] **1.** a land area having a level surface raised much higher above nearby land. **2.** a period or state of little growth, esp. one in which progress ceases: *He felt he'd reached a plateau in his career.* —*v.* [*no obj*] **3.** to reach a state of no growth; stabilize: *As you see from this flat line on the graph, profits have plateaued over the last five years.*

plate′ glass′, *n.* [*noncount*] a special glass formed by shaping hot glass into a plate that is then ground and polished, used in large windows, mirrors, etc.

plat•en (plat′n) /'plætn̩/ *n.* [*count*] **1.** a plate in a printing press for pressing the paper against an inked surface. **2.** the roller of a typewriter, used for guiding paper through the device.

plate′ tecton′ics, *n.* [*noncount; used with a singular verb*] a theory in geology stating that the earth's crust is divided into a number of stiff plates: *Plate tectonics claims that the movement of huge plates in the earth's crust causes continental drift.*

plat•form (plat′fôrm) /'plætfɔrm/ *n.* [*count*] **1.** a horizontal surface, usually raised above the level of the surrounding area. **2.** a raised flooring for use as a stage: *The speaker mounted the platform.* **3.** the raised area along the tracks of a railroad station, from which the cars of the train are entered: *Watch your step on the icy platform.* See illustration at TERMINAL. **4.** a public statement of the principles, aims, goals, etc., esp. of a political party: *The party's platform called for a ban on abortion.* **5.** a group of computers that are compatible with each other and can run the same software: *These programs can all be run from the Macintosh platform.* See -FORM-.

plat•ing (plā′ting) /'pleytɪŋ/ *n.* [*noncount*] **1.** a thin coating of gold, silver, etc. **2.** an outer layer of plates.

plat•i•num (plat′n əm, plat′nəm) /'plætn̩əm, 'plætnəm/ *n.* [*noncount*] **1.** a heavy, grayish-white, metallic chemical element, resistant to most chemicals, that can be easily shaped and that conducts electricity. **2.** a light gray color with some blue. —*adj.* **3.** (of a recording or record album) having sold a minimum of two million single records or one million LPs. **4.** of the color of platinum; grayish-white with some blue.

plat•i•tude (plat′i to͞od′, -tyo͞od′) /'plætɪ,tuwd, -,tyuwd/ *n.* [*count*] a trite remark, said as if it were clever or important.

pla•ton•ic (plə ton′ik, plā-) /plə'tɒnɪk, pley-/ *adj.* of or relating to a close relationship between two persons that lacks sexual involvement: *platonic love.*

pla•toon (plə to͞on′) /plə'tuwn/ *n.* [*count*] **1.** a military unit consisting of two or more squads or sections and a headquarters. **2.** a group of football players specially trained in one part of the game. —*v.* **3.** *Sports.* to use (a player) at a position in a game alternately with another player, or to alternate two different teams or units: [~ + *obj*]: *The coach platooned his team, using one squad for offense and the other for defense.* [*no obj*]: *Because of injuries the coach wasn't able to platoon.*

plat•ter (plat′ər) /'plætər/ *n.* [*count*] **1.** a large, shallow dish for serving food. **2.** a course of a meal, usually consisting of a variety of foods served on the same plate: *ordered the seafood platter.* **3.** a phonograph record.

plat•y•pus (plat′i pəs) /'plætɪpəs/ *n.* [*count*], *pl.* **-pus•es, -pi** (-pī′) /-,pay/. an egg-laying animal of Australia and Tasmania, having webbed feet, a broad, flat tail, and a ducklike bill.

-plaud-, *root.* *-plaud-* comes from Latin, where it has the meaning "clap; noise." It is related to the root -PLOD-. This meaning is found in such words as: APPLAUD, PLAUDIT, PLAUSIBLE.

plau•dit (plô′dit) /'plɔdɪt/ *n.* Usually, **plaudits.** [*plural*] **1.** a strong, enthusiastic expression of approval: *Her performance won the plaudits of the critics.* **2.** a round of applause. See -PLAUD-.

plau•si•ble (plô′zə bəl) /'plɔzəbəl/ *adj.* having an appearance of truth or reason; credible; believable: *a plausible excuse.* —**plau•si•bil•i•ty** (plô′zə bil′i tē) /,plɔzə'bɪlɪtiy/ *n.* [*noncount*]: *The story lacks plausibility.* —**plau′si•bly,** *adv.*: *argued plausibly that he couldn't have gotten there any earlier.* See -PLAUD-.

play (plā) /pley/ *n.* **1.** [*count*] a dramatic composition; drama: *the plays of Shakespeare.* **2.** [*count*] a performance of such a drama, as on the stage: *We saw three* *plays during our vacation.* **3.** [*noncount*] activity done for recreation or amusement, as by children: *I need some time for play away from work.* **4.** [*noncount*] the action or conduct of a game: *Rain has delayed play here at Wimbledon.* **5.** [*count*] an act or instance of playing: *That one foolish play may have cost us the match.* **6.** [*noncount*] manner or style of playing, or of behavior generally: *a believer in fair play.* **7.** [*count; usually singular*] brisk, light, or changing movement or action: *the play of a water fountain.* **8.** [*noncount*] freedom or space in which something, as a part of a mechanism, can move; give: *There's some play, perhaps two inches, in this fan belt.* **9.** [*noncount*] freedom or scope for activity: *allowing full play of the mind.* **10.** [*noncount*] attention; coverage, as of something broadcast: *All those blunders got a lot of play in the media.* —*v.* **11.** to portray; enact; act the part of: [~ + *obj*]: *to play Lady Macbeth.* [*no obj*]: *played in several off-Broadway shows.* **12.** to (cause to) be performed or shown, as a drama, etc.: [~ + *obj*]: *They're playing that dumb old movie at the cinema again.* [*no obj*]: *What's playing at the cinema tonight?* **13.** [~ + *obj*] to act the part or character of in real life: *to play the fool.* See *play at* below. **14.** [~ + *obj*] to give performances in (a place): *She'll play all the big cities.* **15.** to be part of or perform in (a game, etc.); to occupy oneself in relaxation or recreation: [~ + *obj*]: *They played chess.* [*no obj*]: *playing with blocks.* **16.** to perform in a game against (someone): [~ + *obj*]: *The girls' basketball team plays their archrivals tonight.* [*no obj*]: *They play against their archrivals for the championship.* **17.** [~ + *obj*] to perform in (a certain position or role) in a game or competition: *to play center field.* **18.** [~ + *obj*] to use or make use of in a game: *I played my highest card.* **19.** [~ + *obj*] to exploit as if in playing a game, esp. for one's own advantage: *played him for a fool.* **20.** to perform or be able to perform on (a musical instrument): [~ + *obj*]: *She plays the trumpet.* [*no obj*]: *It was hard for her to play.* **21.** [~ + *obj*] to perform (music) on an instrument: *They played "The Star-Spangled Banner."* **22.** to (cause to) produce sound or pictures: [~ + *obj*]: *They played the VCR.* [*no obj*]: *His radio was playing all night long.* **23.** [~ + *obj*] to carry out, esp. as a sly or dishonest action: *to play tricks.* **24.** [*no obj*] to do something not to be taken seriously; joke around: *We were just playing; nobody meant to insult you.* **25.** [~ + *obj*] to put into operation: *to play a hunch.* **26.** [*no obj*] to (cause to) move quickly: *A smile played on her lips.* **27.** [~ + *obj*] to gamble, use money in, or trade in: *to play the stock market.* **28.** to avail oneself of (opportunities, as cards) in a game or in any activity: *Play your cards right.* **29.** [~ + *with* + *obj*] to amuse oneself; to toy with: *got the feeling she was just playing with him.* **30.** [*no obj*] to act in a certain way: *to play fair.* **31.** [*no obj*] to be received; go over: *How will the proposal play with the public?* **32. play along,** [*no obj*] **a.** to agree to do something: *If the mob threatens to kill his family, he may have to play along and refuse to testify.* **b.** to pretend to agree to do something: *just playing along in order to get him to admit to his crime.* **33. play around,** [*no obj*] **a.** to behave in a playful manner, or in a manner that wastes time: *I don't have time to play around.* **b.** to have sexual relations very often, esp. outside of marriage: *He played around with a number of girls.* **34. play at, a.** [~ + *at* + *verb-ing*] to pretend to do or be: *The kids were playing at being soldiers.* **b.** [~ + *at* + *obj*] to do without being serious: *He was just playing at politics.* **35. play back,** to play (a recording, esp. one newly made): [~ + *back* + *obj*]: *The police played back the recording of him admitting his crimes.* [~ + *obj* + *back*]: *They played it back in the courtroom.* **36. play down,** to treat (something) as being of little importance; belittle: [~ + *down* + *obj*]: *The senator kept playing down the state of the economy.* [~ + *obj* + *down*]: *He tried to play it down.* **37. play off against,** to set (one person or thing) against another, for one's own gain or advantage: [~ + *off* + *obj* + *against* + *obj*]: *In a three-man race the incumbent can play off one opponent against the other.* [~ + *obj* + *off against* + *obj*]: *to play one off against the other.* **38. play on** or **upon,** [~ + *on/upon* + *obj*] to use the weaknesses of (another) for one's own gain; take advantage of: *to play on someone's generosity.* **39. play out, a.** to bring to an end; finish: [~ + *obj* + *out*]: *Let's play this whole scheme out and see where it takes us.* [~ + *out* + *obj*]: *Let's play out the whole scheme.* **b.** [~ + *obj* + *out*] to use up; exhaust: *completely played out from the long march in the cold.* **40. play up,** to treat (something) as important; publicize: [~ + *up* + *obj*]: *In your job interview, try to play up your good points.* [~ + *obj* + *up*]: *Play your good points up during the interview.* **41. play up to,** [~ + *up to* + *obj*] to attempt to impress in order to gain the favor of: *playing up to the boss.* —***Idiom.*** **42. bring into play,** to cause to be considered or used: [~ + *obj*]: *The district attorney brought into play some new evidence.* [*bring* + *obj* + *into* + *play*]: *She brought some new evidence into play.* **43. make a play for,** [~ + *obj*] to use maneuvers to attract, esp. sexually: *making a play for his pal's girlfriend.* **44. play a part,** to have an effect on; contribute to: *Politics played an important part in the decision to fire him.* **45. play for time,** to delay or forestall an event or decision: *"Play for time while I see what's keeping him," he whispered to me.* **46. play into (someone's) hands,** to act so as to give an advantage to (an opponent): *If you lose your temper, you'll be playing right into his hands.* **47. play with a full deck,** [*used with a negative word or phrase, or in questions*] *Slang.* to be sane or act sanely or rationally: *She's not playing with a full deck.*

play•act (plā′akt′) /ˈpleyˌækt/ *v.* [*no obj*] **1.** to engage in make-believe. **2.** to be insincere; pretend. —**play′act′ing,** *n.* [*noncount*]

play•back (plā′bak′) /ˈpleyˌbæk/ *n.* [*noncount*] the act of reproducing a sound or video recording, esp. to check a recording that is newly made.

play•bill (plā′bil′) /ˈpleyˌbɪl/ *n.* [*count*] a program or announcement of a play.

play•boy or **-girl** (plā′boi′) or (-gûrl′) /ˈpleyˌbɔy/ or /-ˌgɜrl/ *n.* [*count*] one who leads a life of pleasure without responsibility or attachments: *one of the jet-set playboys.*

play•er (plā′ər) /ˈpleyər/ *n.* [*count*] **1.** a person or thing that plays. **2.** one who takes part in some game or sport. **3.** one who plays parts on the stage; actor. **4.** a performer on a musical instrument: *a horn player.* **5.** a machine that reproduces sound or video images: *a videodisc player.* **6.** a participant, as in a business deal; esp., one in a position to exercise power: *Call in the players and let's make a deal.*

play•ful (plā′fəl) /ˈpleyfəl/ *adj.* **1.** full of play or fun: *a playful puppy.* **2.** pleasantly humorous or jesting: *a playful remark.* —**play′ful•ly,** *adv.*: *He playfully told her that he loved her, but she believed him.* —**play′ful•ness,** *n.* [*noncount*]

play•ground (plā′ground′) /ˈpleyˌgrawnd/ *n.* [*count*] an area used by children for outdoor play activities.

play•house (plā′hous′) /ˈpleyˌhaws/ *n.* [*count*], *pl.* **-hous•es. 1.** THEATER (def. 1). **2.** a small house for children to play in.

play′ing card′, *n.* [*count*] one of a set of rectangular cards used in playing various games, esp. one of a set of 52 ranked cards of four suits.

play•mate (plā′māt′) /ˈpleyˌmeyt/ *n.* [*count*] a companion, esp. of a child, in play or recreation.

play′-off′, *n.* [*count*] *Sports.* **1.** an extra game, round, etc., played to settle a tie. **2.** a series of games or matches played to decide a championship.

play′ on words′, *n.* [*count*] a pun.

play•pen (plā′pen′) /ˈpleyˌpɛn/ *n.* [*count*] a small closed-in structure in which a baby can play: *They unfolded the playpen and put the baby in it.*

play•thing (plā′thing′) /ˈpleyˌθɪŋ/ *n.* [*count*] **1.** a thing to play with; toy. **2.** one who is used selfishly by another: *She had become the rich man's plaything.*

play•wright (plā′rīt′) /ˈpleyˌrayt/ *n.* [*count*] a writer of plays.

pla•za (plä′zə, plaz′ə) /ˈplɑzə, ˈplæzə/ *n.* [*count*], *pl.* **-zas. 1.** a public square in a city or town. **2.** a group of stores, banks, etc.; shopping center. **3.** an area along an expressway at which public facilities are available.

plea (plē) /pliy/ *n.* [*count*], *pl.* **pleas. 1.** an appeal or request: *a plea for mercy.* **2.** an excuse; pretext: *He begged off on the plea that his car wasn't working.* **3. a.** a defendant's answer to a legal charge: *a plea of not guilty.* **b.** a plea of guilty. See -PLAC-.

plea′ bar′gaining, *n.* [*noncount*] a practice in which a defendant in a criminal case is allowed to plead guilty to a lesser charge rather than risk conviction for a more serious crime.

plead (plēd) /pliyd/ *v.*, **plead•ed** or **pled** (pled) /plɛd/; **plead•ing. 1.** [*no obj*] to request sincerely; beg: *to plead for more time.* **2.** [~ + *obj*] to use as an excuse, defense, or justification: *He pleaded ignorance of the law.* **3. a.** [~ + *obj*] to argue (a case) before a court. **b.** to answer a charge (with a response): [*no obj*]: *How do you plead?* [~ + *obj*]: *He pled insanity and was not convicted of murder.* —**plead′er,** *n.* [*count*] See -PLAC-.

pleas•ant (plez′ənt) /ˈplɛzənt/ *adj.* **1.** pleasing, agreeable, or enjoyable: *the pleasant news of her promotion.* **2.** (of persons, manners, etc.) socially acceptable; polite: *a pleasant disposition when dealing with people.* [*be* + ~ + *to* + *verb*]: *He's very pleasant to work with.* **3.** fair, as weather: *a pleasant day.* —**pleas′ant•ly,** *adv.*: *She greeted me pleasantly.* —**pleas′ant•ness,** *n.* [*noncount*] See -PLAC-.

pleas•ant•ry (plez′ən trē) /ˈplɛzəntriy/ *n.* [*count*], *pl.* **-ries. 1.** a humorous action or remark. **2.** a courteous remark used to make a conversation proceed more easily: *We exchanged pleasantries about the weather, then got down to business.* See -PLAC-.

please (plēz) /pliyz/ *adv., v.,* **pleased, pleas•ing.** —*adv.* **1.** (used as a polite addition to requests, etc.) if you would be so willing; kindly: *Please come here. A cup of coffee, please.* —*v.* **2.** [~ + *obj*] to give pleasure, happiness, or gratification to: *You can't please everyone.* **3.** [*no obj; used after words like* wherever, whatever, anywhere, anyone] to like, wish, or feel inclined; choose: *Go wherever you please. Ask anyone you please.* —***Idiom.*** **4. if you please, a.** (used after a request, etc., to add politeness) if it is your pleasure; if you like or wish: *Step over here, if you please, and raise your right hand.* **b.** (used to express astonishment, anger, etc.): *If you please, madam! Stop shouting!* See -PLAC-.

pleased (plēzd) /pliyzd/ *adj.* having a feeling of pleasure, happiness, or satisfaction: *a pleased expression on his face.*

pleas•ing (plē′zing) /ˈpliyzɪŋ/ *adj.* giving pleasure; agreeable; satisfying or gratifying: *a pleasing appearance in his suit and shiny new shoes.* —**pleas′ing•ly,** *adv.*

pleas•ur•a•ble (plezh′ər ə bəl) /ˈplɛʒərəbəl/ *adj.* that gives or causes pleasure: *a pleasurable experience.* —**pleas′ur•a•bly,** *adv.* See -PLAC-.

pleas•ure (plezh′ər) /ˈplɛʒər/ *n.* **1.** [*noncount*] enjoyment from something that one likes: *They get a lot of pleasure from their grandchildren.* **2.** [*count*] a cause or source of enjoyment or delight: *the pleasures of the mind.* **3.** [*noncount*] recreation or amusement: *to travel for pleasure.* **4.** [*noncount*] a feeling of delight in the senses: *Psychologists study the use of pain and pleasure as ways of motivating people.* **5.** [*noncount*] one's will or desire; preference: *to make known one's pleasure.* —***Idiom.*** **6. with pleasure** or **my pleasure,** (used to express polite willingness to do what is or has been asked, or gracious satisfaction at having been helpful): *"Can you come tonight?" —"With pleasure." "Thanks for your help." —"My pleasure."* See -PLAC-.

pleat (plēt) /pliyt/ *n.* [*count*] **1.** a fold in clothing made by doubling cloth or material upon itself. —*v.* [~ + *obj*] **2.** to arrange in pleats: *She pleated the skirt.* —**pleat′ed,** *adj.*: *a pleated skirt.* See -PLIC-.

ple•be•ian (pli bē′ən) /plɪˈbiyən/ *adj.* **1.** of or relating to the common people. **2.** commonplace; vulgar: *Your taste in humor is so plebeian.* —*n.* [*count*] **3.** a member of the common people.

pleb•i•scite (pleb′ə sīt′, -sit) /ˈplɛbəˌsayt, -sɪt/ *n.* [*count*] a direct vote of the qualified voters of a state in regard to some important public question.

plec•trum (plek′trəm) /ˈplɛktrəm/ *n.* [*count*], *pl.* **-tra** (-trə) /-trə/ **-trums.** a small piece of hard, unbending material, used to pluck the strings of a musical instrument.

pled (pled) /plɛd/ *v.* a pt. and pp. of PLEAD.

pledge (plej) /plɛdʒ/ *n., v.,* **pledged, pledg•ing.** —*n.* [*count*] **1.** a solemn promise to do or stop doing something: *a pledge of economic aid to the newly independent countries.* **2.** something left behind as security or proof that one will pay a debt or keep a promise. **3.** something given or thought of as a token, as of friendship or love: *Take this ring as a pledge of my love.* **4.** a person accepted for membership in a club, but not yet formally initiated. —*v.* **5.** [~ + *obj* + *to* + *obj*] to bind (someone) by or as if by a pledge or promise: *pledged everyone to secrecy.* **6.** to promise solemnly: [~ + *obj*]: *to pledge support.* [~ + *to* + *verb* + *obj*]: *She pledged to support him in the upcoming election.* [~ + *that clause*]: *He pledged that he would never betray the trust of the American people.* —***Idiom.*** **7. take the pledge,** to make a vow not to drink alcoholic beverages.

-plen-, *root.* *-plen-* comes from Latin, where it has the meaning "full." It is related to the root -PLET-. This meaning is found in such words as: PLENARY, PLENIPOTENTIARY, PLENITUDE, PLENTEOUS, PLENTY, REPLENISH.

ple•na•ry (plē′nə rē, plen′ə-) /ˈpliynəriy, ˈplɛnə-/ *adj, n., pl.* **-ries.** —*adj.* **1.** full; complete; without limit: *plenary powers.* **2.** attended by all qualified members: *a plenary session of Congress.* —*n.* [*count*] **3.** a plenary session. See -PLEN-.

plen•i•po•ten•ti•ar•y (plen′ə pə ten′shē er′ē, -shə rē) /ˌplɛnəpəˈtɛnʃiyˌɛriy, -ʃəriy/ *n., pl.* **-ar•ies,** *adj.* —*n.* [*count*] **1.** a diplomat given full power to conduct business for someone else. —*adj.* **2.** having been given full power or authority, as a diplomatic agent. See -PLEN-, -POT-.

plen•i•tude (plen′i to͞od′, -tyo͞od′) /ˈplɛnɪˌtuwd, -ˌtyuwd/ *n.* [*count*] fullness; an amount that is enough: *a plenitude of food.* See -PLEN-.

plen•te•ous (plen′tē əs) /ˈplɛntiyəs/ *adj.* **1.** plentiful; abundant. **2.** giving or providing a lot or a great deal; fruitful: *a plenteous harvest.* See -PLEN-.

plen•ti•ful (plen′ti fəl) /ˈplɛntɪfəl/ *adj.* providing or yielding an amount or quantity that is more than enough: *a plentiful harvest.* —**plen′ti•ful•ly,** *adv.* See -PLEN-.

plen•ty (plen′tē) /ˈplɛntiy/ *n.* **1.** a full supply or amount; a supply or amount that is more than enough: [~ + *of* + *noncount noun; used with a singular verb*]: *There is plenty of time.* [~ + *of* + *plural noun; used with a plural verb*]: *There are plenty of chairs.* **2.** [*noncount*] the state or quality of being plentiful; abundance: *the land's plenty.* **3.** [*noncount*] a large amount, or a time of having a large amount: *the years of plenty.* —*adj.* **4.** existing in or providing an amount, number, or quantity that is more than enough. **5.** more than enough; ample: *This helping is plenty for me.* —*adv.* **6.** *Informal.* fully; quite: *plenty good enough.* See -PLEN-.

-plet-, *root.* *-plet-* comes from Latin and Greek, where it has the meaning "full." This meaning is found in such words as: COMPLETE, DEPLETE, PLETHORA, REPLETE. See -PLEN-.

pleth•o•ra (pleth′ər ə) /ˈplɛθərə/ *n.* [*count; usually singular*] an amount, number, or quantity that is too much: *a plethora of excuses.* See -PLET-.

pleu•ri•sy (plo͝or′ə sē) /ˈplʊrəsiy/ *n.* [*noncount*] an illness in which the lungs are inflamed, causing a dry cough.

-plex-, *root.* *-plex-* comes from Latin, where it has the meaning "fold." It is related to the root -PLIC-. This meaning is found in such words as: COMPLEX, DUPLEX, MULTIPLEX, PERPLEX, PLEXIGLAS, PLEXUS.

Plex•i•glas (plek′si glas′) /ˈplɛksɪˌglæs/ *Trademark.* [*noncount*] a lightweight, transparent plastic material used for signs, windows, and furniture. See -PLEX-.

plex•us (plek′səs) /ˈplɛksəs/ *n.* [*count*], *pl.* **-us•es, -us. 1.** a network, as of nerves or blood vessels: *the solar plexus.* **2.** any complicated structure containing an intricate network of parts: *the plexus of international relations.* See -PLEX-.

pli•a•ble (plī′ə bəl) /ˈplayəbəl/ *adj.* **1.** easily bent; flexible; supple: *soft, pliable leather.* **2.** easily influenced or persuaded; yielding: *He's especially pliable after a few drinks.* —**pli•a•bil•i•ty** (plī′ə bil′i tē) /ˌplayəˈbɪlɪtiy/ *n.* [*noncount*] See -PLIC-.

pli•ant (plī′ənt) /ˈplayənt/ *adj.* pliable. —**pli•an•cy** (plī′ən sē) /ˈplayənsiy/ *n.* [*noncount*]

-plic-, *root.* *-plic-* comes from Latin, where it has the meaning "fold, bend." This meaning is found in such words as: ACCOMPLICE, APPLICATION, COMPLICATE, COMPLICITY, DUPLICATE, DUPLICITY, EXPLICABLE, EXPLICATE, EXPLICIT, IMPLICATE, IMPLICATION, IMPLICIT, INEXPLICABLE, MULTIPLICATION, REPLICA, REPLICATE, SUPPLICANT, TRIPLICATE. See -PLEX-.

pli•ers (plī′ərz) /ˈplayərz/ *n.* [*plural; used with a plural verb; sometimes: a pair of* + ~*; used with a singular verb*] a tool made with two crossing pieces attached, having a long jaw that is opened and closed by the handles, used for bending wire, holding small objects, etc.: *Use the pliers to pull out that nail. The pliers are on the table. A pair of pliers is what I need.*

plight (plīt) /playt/ *n.* [*count; singular*] a distressing situation: *in a sorry plight.*

plinth (plinth) /plɪnθ/ *n.* [*count*] a square base or a lower block, as of a pedestal or a column.

plod (plod) /plɒd/ *v.* [*no obj*], **plod•ded, plod•ding. 1.** to walk heavily or with difficulty; trudge: *The old horse plodded slowly down the road.* **2.** to work or proceed with steady but slow or difficult progress: *He plodded along at his job.* —**plod′der,** *n.* [*count*]

-plod-, *root.* *-plod-* comes from Latin, where it has the meaning "noise." This meaning is found in such words as: EXPLODE, IMPLODE. See -PLAUD-.

plop (plop) /plɒp/ *v.,* **plopped, plop•ping,** *n., adv.* —*v.* **1.** to (cause to) fall and make a sound like that of something falling or dropping into water: [*no obj*]: *Big raindrops plopped against the window.* [~ + *obj*]: *The fish-*

erman plopped the bait into the river. **2.** to (cause to) drop or fall with full force or direct impact: [*no obj*]: *She plopped into her chair.* [~ + *obj*]: *She plopped the heavy bags down on the chair.* **—*n.*** [*count*] **3.** a plopping sound or fall. **4.** the act of plopping. **—*adv.*** **5.** with a plop: *The frog jumped plop into the water.*

plot (plot) /plɒt/ *n., v.,* **plot•ted, plot•ting.** **—*n.*** [*count*] **1.** a secret plan to accomplish some purpose: *a plot to overthrow the government.* **2.** the main story of a piece of writing, as a novel or movie: *The plot is interesting but the characters are boring.* **3.** a small piece of ground: *a garden plot.* **—*v.*** **4.** to plan secretly: [~ + *obj*]: *The terrorists were plotting an assassination.* [~ + *to* + *verb*]: *The terrorists were plotting to assassinate the Pope.* [*no obj*]: *The king didn't know who was plotting against him.* **5.** [~ + *obj*] to mark on a plan, chart, or graph, as the course of a ship or aircraft. **6.** [~ + *obj*] to make (a calculation) by graph: *His graph plots the losses we expect if the recession continues.* —**plot′ter,** *n.* [*count*]

plov•er (pluv′ər, plō′vər) /ˈplʌvər, ˈplowvər/ *n.* [*count*] a shorebird having a thick neck and a pigeonlike beak.

plow (plou) /plaw/ *n.* [*count*] **1.** a large tool used in farming for cutting, lifting, turning over, and breaking up soil. **2.** a tool resembling this, as a large shovel used to clear away snow from a road or track. **—*v.*** **3.** to turn up (soil) with a plow: [~ + *obj*]: *to plow the heavy soil.* [*no obj*]: *Is it too early to plow for spring crops?* **4.** to turn up the soil of (an area) with a plow: *plowed forty acres yesterday.* **5.** to cut into or move through (a surface) as if with a plow: [~ + *up* + *obj*]: *The tornado plowed up an acre of trees.* [*no obj*]: *A hail of bullets plowed into the side of the car.* **6.** to clear (an area) by the use of a plow, esp. a snowplow: [~ + *obj*]: *The trucks plowed the roads.* [*no obj*]: *It was too late to plow.* **7.** to invest or make use of (money): [~ + *obj*]: *They have plowed a lot of money into this business.* [~ + *obj* + *back*]: *to plow our profits back into new equipment.* [~ + *back* + *obj*]: *to plow back our profits into new equipment.* **8.** [*no obj*] to move along or proceed slowly and with great effort: *I still have to plow through a pile of reports.*

plow•share (plou′shâr′) /ˈplawˌʃɛər/ *n.* [*count*] the cutting part of a plow.

ploy (ploi) /plɔy/ *n.* [*count*] a maneuver, usually a trick, to gain an advantage; gambit. See -PLOY-.

-ploy-, *root.* *-ploy-* comes from French and ultimately from Latin, where it has the meaning "bend; fold; use; involve." It is related to -PLIC-. This meaning is found in such words as: DEPLOY, EMPLOY, EMPLOYEE, EMPLOYER, EMPLOYMENT, PLOY.

pluck (pluk) /plʌk/ *v.* **1.** [~ + *obj*] to pull off from the place of growth, as fruit, flowers, or feathers: *She plucked the feathers from the chicken.* **2.** [~ + *obj*] to remove feathers or hair from by pulling: *to pluck a chicken.* **3.** to grasp or grab: [~ + *obj*]: *He plucked her sleeve until she answered him.* [~ + *at* + *obj*]: *He kept plucking at her sleeve.* **4.** [~ + *obj*] to pull out or remove with sudden force: *plucking her eyebrows.* **5.** [~ + *obj*] to sound (the strings of a musical instrument) by pulling at them with the fingers or a plectrum: *sat there plucking his harp.* **—*n.*** **6.** [*count*] the act of plucking; a tug. **7.** [*noncount*] courage; a desire not to give up or surrender: *showed a lot of pluck by staying in the game.*

pluck•y (pluk′ē) /ˈplʌkiy/ *adj.,* **-i•er, -i•est.** having pluck; brave. —**pluck′i•ness,** *n.* [*noncount*]

plug (plug) /plʌg/ *n., v.,* **plugged, plug•ging.** **—*n.*** [*count*] **1.** a piece of wood or other material used to stop up or block a hole or opening, as in a pipe, etc.: *He put plugs in his ears to keep out the noise.* **2.** an attachment at the end of an electrical cord, inserted into a socket for electric power. **3.** SPARK PLUG (def. 1). **4.** a fireplug; hydrant. **5.** the favorable mention of a product, etc., as in a television interview; advertisement: *put in a plug for her new book.* **—*v.*** **6.** to (cause to) be stopped (up) or filled with or as if with a plug: [*no obj*]: *Her ears plugged up when she flew in airplanes.* [~ + *up* + *obj*]: *The high altitude plugged up her ears.* [~ + *obj* + *up*]: *Something was plugging her sinuses up.* [~ + *obj*]: *to plug a leak.* **7.** [~ + *obj*] to insert a plug into: *Plug the computer into that outlet over there.* **8.** [~ + *obj*] to mention (a product) favorably, as in a television interview: *kept plugging his new book instead of answering the questions.* **9.** [~ + *obj*] *Slang.* to shoot with a bullet. **10.** [*no obj;* ~ *(+ away/along)*] to work with persistence on something: *She plugged away at a novel for years.* **11. plug in,** to connect to an electrical power source: [~ + *in* + *obj*]: *First, plug in the monitor and turn it on.* [~ + *obj* + *in*]: *It won't go on if you haven't plugged it in.* **—*Idiom.*** **12. pull the plug,** *Informal.* **a.** [~ + *on*] to bring to an end: *Congress pulled the plug on that plan.* **b.** [*no obj*]: to disconnect life-supporting equipment from (a patient who has no chance of recovering from illness): *Pull the plug if the other choice is spending years in a coma.*

plum (plum) /plʌm/ *n., adj.,* **plum•mer, plum•mest.** **—*n.*** **1.** [*count*] the sweet, fleshy, red or purple fruit of any of several trees of the rose family. **2.** [*count*] the tree itself. **3.** [*count*] a sugarplum. **4.** [*noncount*] a deep purple, between blue and red. **5.** [*count*] an excellent thing, as a rewarding job. **—*adj.*** [*before a noun*] **6.** desirable or rewarding: *After years at that lousy office he finally got the plum job he deserved.*

plum•age (plo͞o′mij) /ˈpluwmɪdʒ/ *n.* [*noncount*] the entire feathery covering of a bird.

plumb (plum) /plʌm/ *n.* [*count*] **1.** a small mass of lead hung on a line and used to measure the depth of water or to make sure a line is straight up and down. **—*adj.*** **2.** true according to a plumb line; perpendicular. **—*adv.*** **3.** in a perpendicular direction. **4.** exactly, precisely, or directly: *The last shot landed plumb in the hole for a birdie.* **5.** completely or absolutely: *He was plumb stupid.* **—*v.*** [~ + *obj*] **6.** to test or adjust by a plumb line, so as to make (something) vertical. **7.** to examine closely: *to plumb the poem's meaning.* **—*Idiom.*** **8. plumb the depths of,** [~ + *obj*] to experience (something) fully: *plumbed the depths of despair.*

plumb•er (plum′ər) /ˈplʌmər/ *n.* [*count*] one who installs and repairs plumbing.

plumb′er's help′er, *n.* PLUNGER (def. 2). Also called **plumb′er's friend′.**

plumb•ing (plum′ing) /ˈplʌmɪŋ/ *n.* [*noncount*] **1.** the system of pipes, drains, etc., for carrying water, liquid wastes, etc., as in a building: *several leaks in the old plumbing.* **2.** the work or trade of a plumber.

plume (plo͞om) /pluwm/ *n., v.,* **plumed, plum•ing.** **—*n.*** [*count*] **1.** a large, long, or conspicuous feather. **—*v.*** [~ + *obj*] **2.** to cover or decorate with plumes. —**plumed,** *adj.*

plum•met (plum′it) /ˈplʌmɪt/ *n.* [*count*] **1.** the piece of lead attached to a plumb line. **—*v.*** [*no obj*] **2.** to fall straight down; plunge: *The plane plummeted to the ground and exploded.* **3.** to become much less in amount or quantity: *During the recession jobs plummeted.*

plump[1] (plump) /plʌmp/ *adj.,* **-er, -est,** *v.* **—*adj.*** **1.** well filled out or rounded in form; fleshy or fat. **—*v.*** **2.** to (cause to) become plump and soft, as by fluffing: [~ *(+ up)* + *obj*]: *She plumped (up) the sofa pillows.* [*no obj;* (~ + *up*)]: *These old sofa cushions don't plump (up).* —**plump′ly,** *adv.* —**plump′ness,** *n.* [*noncount*]

plump[2] (plump) /plʌmp/ *v.* **1.** to drop or fall heavily or suddenly: [*no obj;* (~ + *down*)]: *All she wanted to do was plump (down) on the sofa and relax.* [~ + *obj (+ down)*]: *She plumped her stack of books (down) on the table.* **2. plump for,** [~ + *for* + *obj*] to support with enthusiasm: *to plump for the home team.* **—*n.*** [*count*] **3.** a heavy fall. **4.** the sound of such a fall. **—*adv.*** **5.** with a heavy fall or drop. **6.** straight down. **—*adj.*** **7.** direct; blunt.

plun•der (plun′dər) /ˈplʌndər/ *v.* **1.** to rob (someone) of valuables by force, as in war: [~ + *obj*]: *to plunder a town.* [*no obj*]: *The Vikings raided and plundered all along this coast.* **2.** [~ + *obj*] to rob or steal by means of cheating: *to plunder the public treasury.* **—*n.*** [*noncount*] **3.** that which is taken in plundering; loot.

plunge (plunj) /plʌndʒ/ *v.,* **plunged, plung•ing,** *n.* **—*v.*** **1.** [~ + *obj*] to push or thrust (something) into something else with force: *to plunge a wooden stake into the vampire's heart.* **2.** to (cause to) fall suddenly, as into water, from a great height, etc.; plummet: [*no obj*]: *The car plunged off the highway into the sea.* [~ + *obj*]: *plunged the car off the cliff.* **3.** to (cause to) be brought or thrown into some condition suddenly: [~ + *obj*]: *When the electric station exploded, every house was immediately plunged into darkness.* [*no obj*]: *to plunge into debt.* **4.** [*no obj*] to rush with great speed and little care for one's surroundings: *to plunge through a crowd.* **—*n.*** [*count*] **5.** the act of plunging. **6.** a leap or dive, as into water: *a headlong plunge into the water.* **7.** a sudden unplanned act; a rush or dash: *the businessman's abrupt plunge into politics.* **—*Idiom.*** **8. take the plunge,** to enter upon a course of action, esp. after being uncertain or hesitating: *They should take the plunge and get married.*

plung•er (plun′jər) /ˈplʌndʒər/ *n.* [*count*] **1.** a pistonlike part moving within the cylinder of a pump or similar device. **2.** a device consisting of a handle with a rubber suction cup at one end, used to free clogged drains and toilet traps.

plung•ing (plun′jing) /'plʌndʒɪŋ/ *adj.* [*before a noun*] (of the neckline of a dress) cut very low and showing much of the chest.

plunk (plungk) /plʌŋk/ *v.* **1.** PLUCK (def. 5): [*no obj*]: *He plunked on his guitar for a few minutes.* [~ + *obj*]: *He plunked a few songs on the guitar.* **2.** [~ + *obj*] to throw, put, drop, etc., suddenly or with a dull, hollow sound: *He plunked his beer mug on the bar.* **3.** [~ + *down*] to drop heavily or suddenly; PLUMP[2] (def. 1): *He just wanted to plunk down somewhere and take a nap.* **—***n.* [*count*] **4.** the act or sound of plunking: *some plunks from his guitar.* **5.** a direct, forcible blow. **—***adv.* **6.** with a plunking sound. **7.** squarely; exactly: *The ball landed plunk in the middle of the net.*

plu•per•fect (ploo pûr′fikt) /pluw'pɜrfɪkt/ *adj.* **1.** PAST PERFECT (def. 1): *The pluperfect tense is formed by adding* had *to the* -ed/-en *form of the main verb.* **—***n.* **2.** PAST PERFECT (defs. 2, 3).

plu•ral (ploor′əl) /'plʊrəl/ *adj.* **1.** of or relating to more than one. **2.** of or relating to a plurality of persons or things; pluralistic. **3.** of or belonging to the grammatical category of number that refers to more than one (of the word used): *The word* children *is the plural form of* child. **—***n.* **4.** [*noncount*] the plural number: *That language has no plural; nouns are the same whether you talk about one or many.* **5.** [*count*] a word or other form in the plural: *Some words, like* child, *have irregular plurals.*

plu•ral•ism (ploor′ə liz′əm) /'plʊrə,lɪzəm/ *n.* [*noncount*] **1.** a condition in which there are many different groups in society, all of whom manage to participate fully in it. **2.** a belief or doctrine that society benefits from such a condition. —**plu′ral•is′tic,** *adj.*: *a pluralistic society.*

plu•ral•i•ty (ploo ral′i tē) /plʊ'rælɪtiy/ *n., pl.* **-ties. 1.** [*count*] (in an election involving three or more candidates) the number of votes received by the leading candidate. **2.** [*count*] more than half of the whole; the majority. **3.** [*noncount*] the state or fact of being plural.

plu•ral•ize (ploor′ə līz′) /'plʊrə,layz/ *v.* [~ + *obj*], **-ized, -iz•ing.** to make plural in form: *The computer takes any word you type in and pluralizes it according to the rules of the language.*

plus (plus) /plʌs/ *prep., adj., n., pl.* **plus•es** or **plus•ses,** *conj., adv.* **—***prep.* **1.** increased by: *Ten plus two is twelve.* **2.** in addition to: *a good salary plus great benefits.* **—***adj.* **3.** [*before a noun*] involving or naming the process of addition or adding: *Use a plus sign, +, between the numbers you are adding.* **4.** [*before a noun*] positive: *On the plus side, you'll have a wonderful house if you move there.* **5.** [*after a noun, as a grade, or a number*] more, greater, or above a certain amount or level: *He received a grade of A plus, or A+, for effort.* **—***n.* [*count*] **6.** a plus quantity. **7.** Also called **plus′ sign′.** the symbol (+) indicating addition or a positive amount. **8.** something additional: *The company car is one of the plusses in this job.* **9.** a surplus, advantage, or gain: *It would be a tremendous plus for us to hire her.* **—***conj.* **10.** also; furthermore: *It's safe, plus it's economical.* **—***adv.* **11.** in addition; besides.

plush (plush) /plʌʃ/ *n., adj.,* **-er, -est. —***n.* [*noncount*] **1.** a soft, thick fabric, used to make furniture covering. **—***adj.* **2.** expensive and luxurious, in a showy way: *a plush hotel.* **3.** very rich and thick; luxuriant: *plush lawns.*

plu•toc•ra•cy (ploo tok′rə sē) /pluw'tɒkrəsiy/ *n., pl.* **-cies. 1.** [*noncount*] the power of wealth or of the wealthy. **2.** [*count*] a state in which the wealthy rule. **3.** [*count*] a group ruling, or using power or influence, on account of its wealth.

plu•to•crat (ploo′tə krat′) /'pluwtə,kræt/ *n.* [*count*] a member of a plutocracy. —**plu′to•crat′ic,** *adj.*

plu•to•ni•um (ploo tō′nē əm) /pluw'towniyəm/ *n.* [*noncount*] a radioactive, metallic element that can be produced from certain uranium.

ply[1] (plī) /play/ *v.,* **plied, ply•ing. 1.** [~ + *obj*] to work hard or long while using (something): *to ply the needle.* **2.** [~ + *obj*] to carry on or continue doing steadily: *to ply a trade.* **3.** [~ + *obj*] to keep supplying or offering something to (someone): *to ply a person with drink.* **4.** [~ + *obj*] to keep asking (someone) questions: *The press kept plying the judge with questions.* **5.** to pass over or along (a stream, a route, etc.) steadily: [~ + *obj*]: *boats plying the Mississippi.* [*no obj*]: *ships plying between Europe and the New World.*

ply[2] (plī) /play/ *n.* [*noncount*] **1.** a measure of the thickness or layer of something: *two-ply toilet paper.* **2.** a unit of yarn: *single ply.* See -PLIC-.

ply•wood (plī′wood′) /'play,wʊd/ *n.* [*noncount*] a building material consisting of layers of wood glued over each other.

P.M., an abbreviation of: **1.** post-mortem. **2.** Prime Minister.

p.m. or **P.M.,** an abbreviation of Latin *post meridiem*: **1.** after noon (used with hours of a day). **2.** the period between noon and midnight.

PMS, an abbreviation of: premenstrual syndrome.

pneu•mat•ic (noo mat′ik, nyoo-) /nʊ'mætɪk, nyʊ-/ *adj.* **1.** of or relating to air, gases, or wind. **2.** filled with, operated by, or containing compressed air: *pneumatic tires.* —**pneu•mat′i•cal•ly,** *adv.*

pneu•mo•nia (noo mōn′yə, -mō′nē ə, nyoo-) /nʊ'mownyə, -'mowniyə, nyʊ-/ *n.* [*noncount*] infection of the lungs caused by bacteria.

P.O., an abbreviation of: **1.** postal (money) order. **2.** post office.

poach[1] (pōch) /powtʃ/ *v.* **1.** to enter into (someone else's land) in order to hunt animals illegally: [*no obj*]: *The men poaching in the game preserve were armed with machine guns.* [~ + *obj*]: *poaching the Masai Mara in search of elephants.* **2.** to hunt for (game or fish) illegally: [*no obj*]: *The men who were poaching had enough money to bribe the game wardens.* [~ + *obj*]: *They were poaching elephants using submachine guns.* **3.** [~ + *obj*] to take without permission and use as one's own: *The salesmen were poaching his favorite clients.* —**poach′er,** *n.* [*count*]

poach[2] (pōch) /powtʃ/ *v.* [~ + *obj*] to cook (eggs, fish, etc.) in a hot liquid just below the boiling point.

pock (pok) /pɒk/ *n.* [*count*] **1.** a small, swollen spot of skin on the body caused by a disease, as chickenpox. **2.** a pockmark. —**pocked,** *adj.*

pock•et (pok′it) /'pɒkɪt/ *n.* [*count*] **1.** a shaped piece of fabric attached to a garment and forming a pouch, used esp. for carrying small articles: *He had a hole in his pocket and lost a few coins.* **2.** means; financial resources: *His empty pockets won't succeed with her.* **3.** any pouchlike compartment or receptacle. **4.** a group or element that is different from whatever surrounds it: *fighting against the few remaining pockets of resistance.* **5.** any of the openings at the corners and sides of a pool table. **6.** *Football.* the protected area from which a quarterback throws a pass. **7.** *Bowling.* the space between the headpin and the pin next behind to the left or right, taken as the target for a strike. **8.** *Baseball.* the deepest part of a mitt or glove, in which most balls are caught. **—***adj.* [*before a noun*] **9.** small enough for carrying in the pocket: *a pocket calculator.* **10.** small; smaller than usual: *a pocket battleship.* **—***v.* [~ + *obj*] **11.** to put into one's pocket: *He pocketed his keys and headed for the car.* **12.** to take as one's own, often dishonestly; appropriate: *to pocket public funds.* **—*Idiom.* 13. in someone's pocket,** completely under someone's influence: *completely in the president's pocket.* **14. line one's pockets,** to profit, esp. at the expense of others: *He was lining his pockets with campaign money.* **15. out of pocket, a.** having suffered a financial loss; poorer. **b.** from one's own financial resources: *a lot of out-of-pocket expenses (= not paid for or reimbursed by insurance) during that hospital stay.* —**pock′et•ful,** *n.* [*count*], *pl.* **-fuls.**

pock•et•book (pok′it book′) /'pɒkɪt,bʊk/ *n.* [*count*] **1.** a woman's purse or handbag. **2.** one's financial resources or means: *too expensive for my pocketbook.* **3.** Also, **pock′et book′.** a book small enough to carry in a coat pocket.

pock•et•knife (pok′it nīf′) /'pɒkɪt,nayf/ *n.* [*count*], *pl.* **-knives.** a knife with one or more blades that fold into the handle, suitable for carrying in a pocket.

pock′et mon′ey, *n.* [*noncount*] **1.** a small amount of money, as for occasional expenses. **2.** *Brit.* ALLOWANCE.

pock•mark (pok′märk′) /'pɒk,mɑrk/ *n.* [*count*] **1.** a small pit on the skin, left by a swollen spot of skin on the body, caused by smallpox, chickenpox, acne, etc. **—***v.* [~ + *obj*] **2.** to mark or scar with or as if with pockmarks: *The airstrip was pockmarked with craters from the bombing.*

pod (pod) /pɒd/ *n.* [*count*] **1.** a long container or covering for a seed, as of the pea or bean. **2.** a streamlined container or enclosure holding something inside, esp. on an aircraft or other vehicle: *the fuel pods on the jet fighter's wings.*

-pod-, *root.* *-pod-* comes from Greek, where it has the meaning "foot." This meaning is found in such words as:

ARTHROPOD, CHIROPODIST, PODIATRIST, PODIATRY, PODIUM, TRIPOD.

po•di•a•try (pə dī′ə trē, pō-) /pə'dayətriy, pow-/ *n.* [*noncount*] the care of the human foot, esp. the study and treatment of foot disorders. —**po•di′a•trist,** *n.* [*count*] See -POD-.

po•di•um (pō′dē əm) /'powdiyəm/ *n.* [*count*], *pl.* **-di•ums, -di•a** (-dē ə) /-diyə/. **1.** a small platform for an orchestra conductor, speaker, etc.: *He walked up to the stage and stood on the podium.* **2.** a stand with a slanted top, used to hold a book, speech, etc., at the proper height for a speaker; lectern: *He strode up to the podium and began to read his speech.* See -POD-.

po•em (pō′əm) /'powəm/ *n.* [*count*] a piece of writing in verse, esp. one having a highly developed form, offering an imaginative interpretation of the subject: *Many poems have lines that rhyme at the end.*

po•e•sy (pō′ə sē, -zē) /'powəsiy, -ziy/ *n.* [*noncount*] poetry.

po•et (pō′it) /'powɪt/ *n.* [*count*] one who writes poetry.

po•et•ic (pō et′ik) /pow'ɛtɪk/ *adj.* Also, **po•et′i•cal. 1.** of the nature of or resembling poetry; possessing the qualities of poems. **2.** of, relating to, or characteristic of a poet or of poetry. —**po•et′i•cal•ly,** *adv.*

poet′ic jus′tice, *n.* [*noncount*] a situation in which rewards and punishments seem to have been properly and fairly distributed: *For years he had to endure the boss's unfairness, so it was only poetic justice when he got promoted and the boss was fired.*

poet′ic li′cense, *n.* [*noncount*] freedom in writing used by a writer to depart from the normal rules of writing, language, or logic to produce a special effect.

po•et•ry (pō′i trē) /'powɪtriy/ *n.* [*noncount*] **1.** writing in metrical form; poetic works; poems; verse. **2.** poetic spirit or feeling. **3.** something that reminds people of poetry: *When she dances she's poetry in motion.*

po•grom (pə grum′, -grom′, pō-) /pə'grʌm, -'grɒm, pow-/ *n.* [*count*] an organized massacre, esp. of Jews.

poi (poi, pō′ē) /pɔy, 'powiy/ *n.* [*noncount*] a Hawaiian food made of taro root pounded into a paste.

poign•ant (poin′yənt, poi′nənt) /'pɔynyənt, 'pɔynənt/ *adj.* **1.** sharply distressing to the feelings; causing sadness. **2.** affecting the emotions: *a poignant scene in the movie.* —**poign′an•cy,** *n.* [*noncount*] —**poign′ant•ly,** *adv.*

poin•set•ti•a (poin set′ē ə, -set′ə) /pɔyn'sɛtiyə, -'sɛtə/ *n.* [*count*], *pl.* **-ti•as.** a plant originally from Mexico and Central America, having very bright scarlet, pink, or white leaves.

point (point) /pɔynt/ *n.* **1.** [*count*] a sharp, thin or narrow end, as of a dagger: *The point of the knife was dull.* **2.** [*count*] a part (of anything) that sticks out: *A point of land juts into the bay.* **3.** [*count*] PERIOD (def. 4). **4.** a dot indicating that a number following it is some fraction of ten, one hundred, etc.: [*count*]: *A decimal point followed by the number five is written .5 and means five-tenths.* [*noncount; used with numbers*]: *We have one point five (= 1.5) kilometers left to go in the race.* **5.** [*count*] (in geometry) a location that has position but no length or width, as the place where two lines meet: *a point of intersection.* **6.** [*count*] a direction on a compass. **7.** [*count*] a particular place, as or as if marked on a map; a spot: *At several points along the highway there are signs telling drivers about the scenic views they can enjoy.* **8.** [*count*] a degree or stage: *the boiling point.* **9.** [*count*] a particular instant of time: *At that point, so late in the day, we were all too tired to go on.* **10.** [*count*] a critical position in affairs: *He had reached a point of no return in the project and had to finish it or face trouble.* **11.** the essential thing or idea; one's purpose: [*count; usually singular; usually: the + ~*]: *The speaker made three main points. Please stop being vague and get to the point. What's the point of going on?* [*noncount; used with a negative word or phrase, or in questions*]: *There isn't much point to going on, is there?* **12.** [*count*] a particular mark that distinguishes someone or something from another: *His best point is his ability to work alone and get the job done.* **13.** [*count*] a unit of counting in the score of a game: *Our team scored thirteen points.* **14.** [*count*] a unit of prices in stock exchanges, as, in the U.S., one dollar: *The Dow Jones fell twenty points before a brief rally.* **15.** *Print.* a unit used to measure the size of type, equal to 0.013835 inch (1/72 inch), or 1/12 pica: [*count*]: *too large a point on that poster.* [*noncount; after a number*]: *using Courier 12 point for printing.* —*v.* **16.** to aim or direct (the finger, a weapon, etc.) at, to, or upon something: [*~ + obj*]: *He pointed the gun at the target.* [*no obj*]: *In some cultures it is rude to point at a person.* **17. point out, a.** to show the presence, place, or position of (something), as by moving the hand or finger in the direction of it: [*~ + out + obj*]: *She pointed out an object in the sky.* [*~ + obj + out*]: *She pointed him out to me.* **b.** to direct attention to; call attention to: [*~ + out + obj*]: *He pointed out several advantages of your proposal.* [*~ + obj + out*]: *You already pointed that out.* [*~ + out + that clause*]: *I pointed out that we had several more opportunities.* **18.** [*~ + obj*] to stretch or extend (the fingers, toes, etc.): *The ballerina pointed her toes.* **19. point to** or **toward,** [*~ + to/toward + obj*] to direct the mind in some direction; be a sign or signal of: *All the evidence points to their guilt.* **20. point up,** [*~ + up + obj*] to give greater or added force to (a statement, etc.): *to point up the need for caution.* —***Idiom.* 21. beside the point,** not important to, or related to, what is being discussed; irrelevant: *Her comments about his money are beside the point.* **22. in point,** (used to introduce an example of something that applies to what is said): *We spend too much on lawyers' fees, and here is a case in point: a charge of $1,000 to fill in your name on a will.* **23. in point of,** as regards; in reference to: *in point of fact.* **24. make a point of,** [*~ + obj*] to be sure to (do something): *Make a point of rechecking your work.* **25. to the point,** [*be + ~*] important to (the thing being discussed); relevant: *His answers were brief but to the point.* —**point′y,** *adj.,* **-i•er, -i•est.** See -POINT-.

-point-, *root.* -*point*- comes from French and ultimately from Latin, where it has the meaning "point, prick, pierce." It is related to the root -PUNCT-. This meaning is found in such words as: APPOINT, DISAPPOINT, MIDPOINT, PINPOINT, POINT, POINTLESS, VIEWPOINT.

point′-blank′, *adj.* **1.** aimed or fired straight at the mark esp. from close to or near the target; direct: *a point-blank shot.* **2.** straightforward; plain; direct: *a point-blank denial.* —*adv.* **3.** with a direct aim; directly; straight: *He aimed point-blank and fired.* **4.** in a blunt way; frankly: *answered point-blank that he would not pass that student.*

point•ed (poin′tid) /'pɔyntɪd/ *adj.* **1.** having a point or points on the end or tip: *a pointed sword.* **2.** sharp or piercing: *pointed wit.* **3.** having importance or meaning something: *He gave his assistant a pointed look when the minister began speaking.* **4.** directed as at a particular person: *He made a pointed remark about how some people don't work as hard as others.* —**point′ed•ly,** *adv.*: *He stared pointedly at his watch as his friend continued to talk.*

point•er (poin′tər) /'pɔyntər/ *n.* [*count*] **1.** a person or thing that points. **2.** a long stick used in pointing things out on a map, blackboard, or the like. **3.** the hand on a watch dial, clock face, etc. **4.** one of a breed of large, shorthaired hunting dogs that point to wild animals that are hunted. **5.** a piece of advice, esp. on how to succeed in a certain area: *gave the rookie some pointers on good batting.* See -POINT-.

point•less (point′lis) /'pɔyntlɪs/ *adj.* without relevance or force; meaningless; useless: *This whole discussion is pointless.* —**point′less•ly,** *adv.* —**point′less•ness,** *n.* [*noncount*] See -POINT-.

point′ man′, *n.* [*count*], *pl.* **point′ men′. 1.** the soldier who leads a group forward. **2.** a person in the forefront with respect to an economic or political issue or program, etc.: *As the president's point men, they will take a lot of criticism.*

point′ of no′ return′, *n.* [*count*] **1.** the point in a flight at which an aircraft will lack enough fuel to return to its starting point. **2.** the critical point in an activity at which one must continue in a course of action and cannot turn back from it: *We're at the point of no return in our negotiations.*

point′ of view′, *n.* [*count; usually singular*] **1.** a manner of consideration or appraisal; standpoint: *We need a fresh point of view.* **2.** an opinion, attitude, or judgment: *He refuses to change his point of view.* **3.** (in a literary work) the position of the person telling the story (the narrator) in relation to the story itself.

poise (poiz) /pɔyz/ *n., v.,* **poised, pois•ing.** —*n.* [*noncount*] **1.** a dignified, calm manner of carrying oneself; self-possession: *She showed great poise in giving her speech.* **2.** steadiness; stability: *intellectual poise.* **3.** the way one holds oneself physically or the way one moves: *the dancer's poise.* —*v.* [*~ + obj*] **4.** to hold (something so that it is) supported, as in position for using, etc.: *The hunter poised the spear.*

poised (poizd) /pɔyzd/ *adj.* **1.** dignified, calm, and composed: *a poised speaker.* **2.** [*be + ~*] balanced: *A bal-*

loon was poised on the seal's nose. **3.** [*be* + ~] hanging or held in the air above something: *Her hands were poised over her instrument, ready to play.* **4.** close to or ready for (something): [*be* + ~ + *for*]: *The armies were poised for attack.* [*be* + ~ + *to* + *verb*]: *He was poised to win the championship.*

poi•son (poi′zən) /'pɔyzən/ *n.* **1.** a substance that taken into the body can destroy life or cause illness: [*noncount*]: *poison in his food.* [*count*]: *Several different poisons could have killed his dog.* **2.** [*noncount*] something harmful, as to happiness: *Her mother-in-law was poison to her.* —*v.* [~ + *obj*] **3.** to kill or injure with or as if with poison: *She had been poisoned.* **4.** to put poison into or upon: *Some of those foods had been poisoned.* **5.** to ruin or corrupt: *Hatred had poisoned their minds.* —*adj.* [*usually: before a noun*] **6.** containing poison: *a poison shrub.*

poi′son i′vy, *n.* [*noncount*] **1.** a vine of the cashew family, with groups of three leaves and whitish berries: *Poison ivy causes itching and a red rash.* **2.** the rash caused by touching poison ivy: *poison ivy on her face.*

poi•son•ous (poi′zən əs) /'pɔyzənəs/ *adj.* **1.** full of or containing poison: *Rattlesnakes are poisonous.* **2.** causing harm; destructive: *poisonous rumors.* —**poi′son•ous•ly,** *adv.*

poi′son pill′, *n.* [*count*] a means of preventing a hostile takeover of a corporation, as by issuing a new class of stock, which would be a financial burden to a buyer.

poke[1] (pōk) /powk/ *v.,* **poked, pok•ing,** *n.* —*v.* **1.** [~ + *obj*] to push, esp. with something narrow or pointed: *poked him in the ribs with her elbow.* **2.** to make (a hole, etc.) by or as if by pushing: [~ + *obj*]: *He poked a hole in the sweater.* [*no obj*]: *His finger poked through the hole in his glove.* **3.** to push (out) or extend: [~ + *obj*]: *poked her head out of the window.* [*no obj*]: *Her head was poking through the window.* **4.** to push oneself into the affairs of others: [~ + *oneself*]: *always poking himself into our affairs.* [*no obj*]: *always poking into her private life.* **5. poke about** or **around,** [*no obj*] to search impolitely into the affairs of another; pry: *She was poking about on my desk, looking for the letter about her.* **6.** [*no obj;* (~ + *along*)] to proceed slowly: *The old horse was just poking along the road.* —*n.* [*count*] **7.** a push: *gave me a sharp poke in the ribs.* **8.** SLOWPOKE: *He can be a real poke when it comes to homework.* —***Idiom.*** **9. poke fun at,** [~ + *obj*] to make fun of or mock: *The kids poked fun at him for his clothes.* **10. poke one's nose into,** [~ + *obj*] to be overly interested in (someone's affairs); pry into: *Don't poke your nose into my affairs.*

poke[2] (pōk) /powk/ *n.* [*count*] *Chiefly Midland U.S.* a bag or sack, esp. a small one.

pok•er[1] (pō′kər) /'powkər/ *n.* [*count*] **1.** a person or thing that pokes. **2.** a metal rod for poking or stirring a fire.

pok•er[2] (pō′kər) /'powkər/ *n.* [*noncount*] a card game in which the players bet on the value of their hands and the winner takes the pool.

pok•y (pō′kē) /'powkiy/ *adj.,* **-i•er, -i•est.** **1.** slow; delaying; dawdling: *Don't be so poky or you'll miss the school bus.* **2.** (of a place) small and cramped.

pol (pol) /pɒl/ *n.* [*count*] *Informal.* a politician, esp. one experienced in making political deals.

po•lar (pō′lər) /'powlər/ *adj.* [*before a noun*] **1.** of or relating to the North or South Pole. **2.** of or relating to any pole, as of a sphere or an electric cell. **3.** opposite in character or action: *There were polar differences between the two candidate's ideas.*

po′lar bear′, *n.* [*count*] a large white bear of arctic regions.

po•lar•i•ty (pō lar′i tē, pə-) /pow'lærɪtiy, pə-/ *n., pl.* **-ties.** **1.** [*noncount*] *Physics.* the property that produces unequal physical effects at different points in a body or system, as in a magnet. **2.** the presence of two opposite qualities or tendencies: [*count*]: *a polarity of opinions.* [*noncount*]: *polarity between the rich and the poor.*

po•lar•i•za•tion (pō′lər ə zā′shən) /ˌpowlərə'zeyʃən/ *n.* [*noncount*] **1.** a sharp division, as of a population or group, into opposing factions: *polarization between ethnic groups.* **2.** a state in which rays of light have different properties in different directions.

po•lar•ize (pō′lə rīz′) /'powləˌrayz/ *v.,* **-ized, -iz•ing.** **1.** [~ + *obj*] to cause polarization in. **2.** to (cause to) be divided into sharply opposing factions or groups: [~ + *obj*]: *The issue has polarized voters.* [*no obj*]: *The country polarized around that issue.*

Po•lar•oid (pō′lə roid′) /'powləˌrɔyd/ *Trademark.* **1.** [*noncount*] a brand of glare-reducing material, used on sunglasses, etc. **2.** [*count*] the first brand of instant camera, developed by Edwin H. Land and marketed since 1948. **3.** [*count*] a print made by such a camera.

pole[1] (pōl) /powl/ *n., v.,* **poled, pol•ing.** —*n.* [*count*] **1.** a long, rounded, often narrow piece of wood, metal, etc.: *telephone poles.* —*v.* **2.** to push, strike, or move forward with a pole: [~ + *obj*]: *to pole a raft.* [*no obj*]: *The skier poled forward.*

pole[2] (pōl) /powl/ *n.* [*count*] **1.** each of the ends of the axis of the earth or of any rounded body: *The Earth has two poles.* **2.** one of two opposite principles, points of interest, etc.: *at the two poles of the political spectrum.* **3.** either of the two parts of an electric battery or magnet that are opposite in charge. —***Idiom.*** **4. poles apart,** [*be* + ~] having widely opposing principles, qualities, etc.: *On political questions they are poles apart.*

Pole (pōl) /powl/ *n.* [*count*] a person born or living in Poland.

pole•cat (pōl′kat′) /'powlˌkæt/ *n.* [*count*], *pl.* **-cats,** (*esp. when thought of as a group*) **-cat.** **1.** a European weasel having blackish fur and sending out a bad-smelling fluid when it is attacked or disturbed. **2.** a North American skunk.

po•lem•ic (pə lem′ik, pō-) /pə'lɛmɪk, pow-/ *n.* **1.** a strong argument against some controversial topic, issue, etc.: [*count*]: *a vigorous polemic against the new tax bill.* [*noncount*]: *touched off a great deal of controversy and polemic.* **2.** [*count*] one who argues in opposition to another. —*adj.* **3.** Also, **po•lem′i•cal.** of or relating to a polemic; controversial.

po•lem•ics (pə lem′iks, pō-) /pə'lɛmɪks, pow-/ *n.* [*noncount; used with a singular verb*] the art or practice of arguing by polemic: *Polemics was one subject he had easily mastered as a lawyer.*

pole•star (pōl′stär′) /'powlˌstɑr/ *n.* [*count*] **1.** [*the* + ~] the star that appears to be nearest to the North Star when it is viewed in the Northern Hemisphere. **2.** something that serves as a guiding principle.

pole′ vault′, *n.* **1.** [*noncount*] a field event in which the performer uses a long pole to leap over a high crossbar. **2.** [*count*] a leap so performed.

-poli-, *root.* *-poli-* comes from Latin, where it has the meaning "polish, smooth." This meaning is found in such words as: IMPOLITE, POLISH, POLITE.

po•lice (pə lēs′) /pə'liys/ *n., v.,* **-liced, -lic•ing.** —*n.* [*plural; used with a plural verb; often: the* + ~] **1.** an organized, nonmilitary force for maintaining order, preventing and detecting crime, and enforcing the laws: *Contact the police if such crimes occur.* **2.** the members of such a force: *A squad of police surrounded the building.* —*v.* [~ + *obj*] **3.** to regulate, control, or keep in order by or as if by means of police: *Squad cars policed the area.* See -POLIS-.

po•lice•man or **-wom•an,** (pə lēs′mən) or (•wŏŏm′ən) /pə'liysmən/ or /ˌwʊmən/ *n.* [*count*], *pl.* **-men** or **-wom•en.** a member of a police force. See -POLIS-.

po•lice′ of′fi•cer, *n.* [*count*] a member of a police force. See -POLIS-.

police′ state′, *n.* [*count*] a state in which a national police force, esp. a secret police, prevents or puts an end to any opposition to the government.

pol•i•cy[1] (pol′ə sē) /'pɒləsiy/ *n., pl.* **-cies.** a definite course of action followed by a business, government, etc: [*count*]: *a new company policy.* [*noncount*]: *U.S. trade policy needs new direction.* See -POLIS-.

pol•i•cy[2] (pol′ə sē) /'pɒləsiy/ *n.* [*count*], *pl.* **-cies.** a document that has all the terms of a contract or agreement for insurance: *an insurance policy on your home.*

pol•i•cy•hold•er (pol′ə sē hōl′dər) /'pɒləsiyˌhowldər/ *n.* [*count*] the individual or business firm in whose name an insurance policy is written.

po•li•o•my•e•li•tis (pō′lē ō mī′ə lī′tis) /ˌpowliyowˌmayə'laytɪs/ also **po•li•o** (pō′lē ō) /'powliyow/ *n.* [*noncount*] a disease of the nerves of the spinal cord and brain that control movement, often causing paralysis.

-polis-, *root.* *-polis-* comes from Greek, where it has the meaning "city." This meaning is found in such words as: COSMOPOLITAN, GEOPOLITICAL, IMPOLITIC, MEGALOPOLIS, METROPOLIS, METROPOLITAN, NECROPOLIS, POLICE, POLICY, POLITBURO, POLITIC, POLITICAL, POLITICIZE, POLITICO, POLITICS, POLITY, REALPOLITIK.

pol•ish (pol′ish) /'pɒlɪʃ/ *v.* **1.** [~ + *obj*] to make smooth, shiny, and glossy, esp. by rubbing: *She polished her shoes.* **2.** [~ + *obj*] to make (something) complete, perfect, or elegant: *She stayed up late to polish her speech.* **3. polish off,** to finish or dispose of quickly: [~ + *off* +

obj]: *to polish off a gallon of ice cream.* [~ + *obj* + *off*]: *The ice cream? They polished it off last night.* **4. polish up,** to improve; make perfect; refine: [~ + *up* + *obj*]: *to polish up his French.* [~ + *obj* + *up*]: *to polish his Italian up by visiting Florence.* —*n.* **5.** a substance used to give smoothness or gloss: [*noncount*]: *shoe polish.* [*count*]: *the polishes and waxes.* **6.** [*count*] the act of polishing: *She gave the silver a good polish.* **7.** [*noncount*] smoothness of a surface. **8.** [*noncount*] perfection; refinement; elegance: *He behaves with such polish and good manners.* —**pol′ish•er,** *n.* [*count*] See -POLI-.

Po•lish (pō′lish) /ˈpowlɪʃ/ *adj.* **1.** of or relating to Poland. **2.** of or relating to the language spoken in Poland. —*n.* [*noncount*] **3.** the language spoken in Poland.

pol•ished (pol′isht) /ˈpɒlɪʃt/ *adj.* **1.** having been made smooth, shiny, and glossy: *polished mahogany.* **2.** refined; showing culture or elegance: *a polished manner toward his guests.* **3.** made complete or perfect: *a polished performance during the debate.* See -POLI-.

Po•lit•bu•ro (pol′it byŏŏr′ō, pō′lit-, pə lit′-) /ˈpɒlɪtˌbyʊrow, ˈpowlɪt-, pəˈlɪt-/ *n.* [*count; usually: the* + ~] the executive committee and chief policymaking body of the Communist Party in the former Soviet Union and in certain other Communist countries. See -POLIS-.

po•lite (pə līt′) /pəˈlayt/ *adj.,* **-lit•er, -lit•est. 1.** showing good manners; courteous: *a polite reply.* **2.** refined or cultured: *polite society.* —**po•lite′ly,** *adv.*: *"I'd be honored to come," he answered politely.* —**po•lite′ness,** *n.* [*noncount*] See -POLI-.

pol•i•tesse (pol′i tes′, pô′lē-) /ˌpɒlɪˈtɛs, ˌpɔliy-/ *n.* [*noncount*] formal politeness; courtesy. See -POLI-.

pol•i•tic (pol′i tik) /ˈpɒlɪtɪk/ *adj.* **1.** shrewd, clever, or wise in practical matters. **2.** done in a shrewd and practical way and to one's advantage: *a politic reply.* **3.** political: *the body politic.* See -POLIS-.

po•lit•i•cal (pə lit′i kəl) /pəˈlɪtɪkəl/ *adj.* **1.** of, relating to, or concerned with politics: *She's become very political: working for a candidate, going to rallies, etc.* **2.** using or seeking power in the governmental or public affairs of a state, city, etc.: *a political party.* —**po•lit′i•cal•ly,** *adv.*: *politically involved.* See -POLIS-.

polit′ical sci′ence, *n.* [*noncount*] a social science dealing with political institutions and government.

pol•i•ti•cian (pol′i tish′ən) /ˌpɒlɪˈtɪʃən/ *n.* [*count*] **1.** one who is active in politics, esp. as a career. **2.** one who is skilled in politics or in maneuvering or directing people: *They were real politicians in dealing with the strikers.* See -POLIS-.

po•lit•i•cize (pə lit′ə sīz′) /pəˈlɪtəˌsayz/ *v.* [~ + *obj*], **-cized, -ciz•ing.** to give a political character or slant to: *to politicize a religious debate.* See -POLIS-.

po•lit•i•co (pə lit′i kō′) /pəˈlɪtɪˌkow/ *n., pl.* **-cos.** POLITICIAN. See -POLIS-.

pol•i•tics (pol′i tiks) /ˈpɒlɪtɪks/ *n.* **1.** [*noncount; used with a singular verb*] the science or art of political government: *Politics is an intriguing study.* **2.** [*plural; used with a plural verb*] political principles or opinions: *His politics are his own affair.* **3.** [*plural; used with a plural verb*] the use of schemes and secrecy to obtain power or control: *Office politics are getting worse these days.* See -POLIS-.

pol•i•ty (pol′i tē) /ˈpɒlɪtiy/ *n.* [*count*], *pl.* **-ties.** a state or other organized community or body. See -POLIS-.

pol•ka (pōl′kə, pō′kə) /ˈpowlkə, ˈpowkə/ *n., pl.* **-kas,** *v.,* **-kaed, -ka•ing.** —*n.* [*count*] **1.** a lively couple dance with music in double meter. **2.** a piece of music for such a dance or in its rhythm. —*v.* [*no obj*] **3.** to dance the polka.

pol′ka dot′ (pō′kə) /ˈpowkə/ *n.* [*count*] **1.** a dot repeated to form a pattern on a fabric. **2.** a pattern of such dots.

poll (pōl) /powl/ *n.* [*count*] **1.** a sampling of opinions on a subject, taken from a group of people, as for analysis: *The opinion polls show great interest in the economy.* **2.** the act of voting in an election. **3.** Usually, **polls.** [*plural*] the place where votes are cast: *Polls are open at five-thirty in the morning.* **4.** the number of votes cast: *a light poll.* —*v.* [~ + *obj*] **5.** to ask questions about the attitudes or opinions of (people): *Students were polled on their preferences.* **6.** to receive (a number of votes) at the polls: *polled nearly six thousand more votes than her opponent.* —**poll′er,** *n.* [*count*]

pol•len (pol′ən) /ˈpɒlən/ *n.* [*noncount*] the fine, powdery, yellowish grains or spores on flowering plants that fertilize other plants: *She's allergic to pollen.*

pol′len count′, *n.* [*count*] a count of the pollen in the air at or during a given time: *The pollen count was high this spring.*

pol•li•nate (pol′ə nāt′) /ˈpɒləˌneyt/ *v.* [~ + *obj*], **-nat•ed, -nat•ing.** to send pollen to the stigma of (a flower): *Bees pollinate the flowers and weeds.* —**pol•li•na•tion** *t* (pol′ə nā′shən) /ˌpɒləˈneyʃən/ *n.* [*noncount*] —**pol′li•na′tor,** *n.* [*count*]

pol•li•wog or **pol•ly•wog** (pol′ē wog′,-wôg′) /ˈpɒliyˌwɒg, -ˌwɔg/ *n.* TADPOLE.

poll•ster (pōl′stər) /ˈpowlstər/ *n.* [*count*] one whose occupation is the taking of public-opinion polls: *Pollsters disagreed about the election.*

pol•lu•tant (pə lōōt′nt) /pəˈluwtnt/ *n.* [*count*] something that pollutes: *chemical pollutants pouring into the river.*

pol•lute (pə lōōt′) /pəˈluwt/ *v.* [~ + *obj*], **-lut•ed, -lut•ing. 1.** to make foul or unclean, esp. with harmful chemical or waste products; contaminate: *to pollute the air with smoke.* **2.** to make morally unclean; defile; debase: *to pollute the mind with bigotry.* —**pol•lut′er,** *n.* [*count*]: *All polluters will be heavily fined.*

pol•lu•tion (pə lōō′shən) /pəˈluwʃən/ *n.* [*noncount*] **1.** the act of polluting. **2.** the materials that cause pollution: *a beach ruined by pollution.*

po•lo (pō′lō) /ˈpowlow/ *n.* [*noncount*] **1.** a game played on horseback between two teams of four players each, who score points by driving a wooden ball into the opponents' goal with a long-handled hammer. **2.** any game broadly resembling this, esp. water polo. —**po′lo•ist,** *n.* [*count*]

pol•ter•geist (pōl′tər gīst′) /ˈpowltərˌgayst/ *n.* [*count*] a spirit making its presence known by noises, knockings, etc.

poly-, *prefix. poly-* comes from Greek, where it has the meaning "much, many": *polyandry (= the custom of having many husbands); polyglot (= speaking many languages).*

pol•y•an•dry (pol′ē an′drē, pol′ē an′drē) /ˈpɒliyˌændriy, ˌpɒliyˈændriy/ *n.* [*noncount*] the practice of having more than one husband at the same time. See -ANDRO-.

pol•y•clin•ic (pol′ē klin′ik) /ˌpɒliyˈklɪnɪk/ *n.* [*count*] a clinic or a hospital dealing with various diseases.

pol•y•es•ter (pol′ē es′tər, pol′ē es′tər) /ˈpɒliyˌɛstər, ˌpɒliyˈɛstər/ *n.* **1.** [*noncount*] a textile fabric used esp. in clothes. **2.** [*count*] a piece of clothing made from this fabric: *some polyesters and knits on sale.*

pol•y•eth•yl•ene (pol′ē eth′ə lēn′) /ˌpɒliyˈɛθəˌliyn/ *n.* [*noncount*] a plastic used chiefly for containers, electrical insulation, and packaging.

po•lyg•a•my (pə lig′ə mē) /pəˈlɪgəmiy/ *n.* [*noncount*] the practice of having more than one spouse, esp. more than one wife, at one time. —**po•lyg′a•mist,** *n.* [*count*] —**po•lyg′a•mous,** *adj.*: *a polygamous society.* See -GAM-.

pol•y•glot (pol′ē glot′) /ˈpɒliyˌglɒt/ *adj.* **1.** able to speak or write several languages; multilingual. **2.** composed of several languages: *a polyglot society.* —*n.* [*count*] **3.** a person who speaks, writes, or reads several languages. See -GLOT-.

pol•y•gon (pol′ē gon′) /ˈpɒliyˌgɒn/ *n.* [*count*] a figure, esp. a closed plane figure, having three or more sides. —**po•lyg•o•nal** (pə lig′ə nl) /pəˈlɪgənl̩/ *adj.*

pol•y•graph (pol′i graf′) /ˈpɒlɪˌgræf/ *n.* [*count*] **1.** LIE DETECTOR. **2.** a test using a lie detector. —*v.* [~ + *obj*] **3.** to test (a person) with a polygraph. See -GRAPH-.

pol•y•he•dron (pol′ē hē′drən) /ˌpɒliyˈhiydrən/ *n.* [*count*], *pl.* **-drons, -dra** (-drə) /-drə/. a solid figure having many faces. —**pol′y•he′dral,** *adj.*

pol•y•math (pol′ē math′) /ˈpɒliyˌmæθ/ *n.* [*count*] a person of great learning in several fields of study.

pol•y•mer (pol′ə mər) /ˈpɒləmər/ *n.* [*count*] a chemical compound formed by the addition of many smaller molecules. —**pol•y•mer•ic** (pol′ə mer′ik) /ˌpɒləˈmɛrɪk/ *adj.*

pol•y•no•mi•al (pol′ə nō′mē əl) /ˌpɒləˈnowmiyəl/ *adj.* **1.** characterized by two or more names or terms: *$2x + 3y = 10$ is a polynomial equation.* —*n.* [*count*] **2.** an expression in algebra consisting of the sum of two or more terms. See -NOM-[2].

pol•yp (pol′ip) /ˈpɒlɪp/ *n.* **1.** the rounded body form in the life cycle of a jellyfish or other similar animal, having stinging tentacles around the mouth and usually having the opposite end attached to a surface: [*count*]: *colorful polyps in the waters of the Pacific.* [*noncount*]: *a sea full of polyp.* **2.** [*count*] a growth that sticks up or out from a mucous surface of the body, as the nose: *a polyp in the nose.*

po•lyph•o•ny (pə lif′ə nē) /pəˈlɪfəniy/ *n.* [*noncount*] a musical style in which two or more independent and harmonious melodic lines are heard at the same time. —**pol•y•phon•ic** (pol′ē fon′ik) /ˌpɒliy'fɒnɪk/ *adj.* —**pol′y•phon′i•cal•ly,** *adv.* See -PHON-.

pol•y•sty•rene (pol′ē stī′rēn, -stēr′ēn) /ˌpɒliy'stayriyn, -'stɪəriyn/ *n.* [*noncount*] a substance, a polymer of styrene, formed into a stiff foam and used in containers, in molded objects, etc.

pol•y•syl•lab•ic (pol′ē si lab′ik) /ˌpɒliysɪ'læbɪk/ *adj.* **1.** consisting of several, esp. four or more, syllables. **2.** characterized by long words, as a language, a style of speech, or a piece of writing.

pol•y•syl•la•ble (pol′ē sil′ə bəl, pol′ē sil′-) /'pɒliyˌsɪləbəl, ˌpɒliy'sɪl-/ *n.* [*count*] a polysyllabic word.

pol•y•tech•nic (pol′ē tek′nik) /ˌpɒliy'tɛknɪk/ *adj.* **1.** of or relating to instruction in a variety of industrial arts, applied sciences, or technical subjects. —*n.* [*count*] **2.** a school providing instruction in such subjects. See -TECHN-.

pol•y•the•ism (pol′ē thē iz′əm, pol′ē thē′iz əm) /'pɒliyθiyˌɪzəm, ˌpɒliy'θiyɪzəm/ *n.* [*noncount*] the doctrine of, or belief in, more than one god. —**pol′y•the′ist,** *n.* [*count*], *adj.* —**pol′y•the•is′tic,** *adj.* See -THEO-.

pol•y•un•sat•u•rat•ed (pol′ē un sach′ə rā′tid) /ˌpɒliyʌn'sætʃəˌreytɪd/ *adj.* (of a food) made from vegetable fats and associated with a low cholesterol content of the blood.

pol•y•vi•nyl (pol′ē vīn′l) /ˌpɒliy'vaynl̩/ *adj.* relating to or made from a vinyl polymer.

pol′yvi′nyl chlo′ride, *n.* [*noncount*] a white plasticlike substance, used chiefly for thin coatings, insulation, and piping. Also called **PVC.**

po•made (po mād′,-mäd′) /pɒ'meyd, -'mɑd/ *n.*, *v.*, **-mad•ed, -mad•ing.** —*n.* [*noncount*] **1.** a scented, greasy substance or ointment, esp. for the hair. —*v.* [~ + *obj*] **2.** to apply pomade to.

pome•gran•ate (pom′gran′it, pom′i-, pum′-) /'pɒmˌgrænɪt, 'pɒmɪ-, 'pʌm-/ *n.* [*count*] **1.** a round fruit with a leathery red rind, containing a juicy, tart red pulp and white seeds. **2.** the small tree that bears this fruit.

pom•mel (pum′əl, pom′-) /'pʌməl, 'pɒm-/ *n.*, *v.*, **-meled, -mel•ing** or (*esp. Brit.*) **-melled, -mel•ling.** —*n.* [*count*] **1.** a knob, as on the hilt of a sword. **2.** the part at the front and top of a saddle. —*v.* [~ + *obj*] **3.** to beat or strike with or as if with the fists.

pomp (pomp) /pɒmp/ *n.* [*noncount*] **1.** grand display; splendor; magnificence. **2.** a showy or vain display.

pom•pa•dour (pom′pə dôr′, -dōr′, -dŏŏr′) /'pɒmpəˌdɔr, -ˌdowr, -ˌdʊr/ *n.* [*count*] **1.** an arrangement of a man's hair in which it is brushed up high from the forehead. **2.** an arrangement of a woman's hair in which it is raised over the forehead and often the temples in a roll.

pom•pom or **pom-pom** (pom′pom′) /'pɒmˌpɒm/ *n.* [*count*] an ornamental ball of strips or streamers, used esp. on clothing or waved at sporting events. Also, **pom•pon** (pom′pon) /'pɒmpɒn/.

pomp•ous (pom′pəs) /'pɒmpəs/ *adj.* having or showing too much self-importance: *He sounded very pompous, but no one was impressed.* —**pom•pos•i•ty** (pom pos′i tē) /pɒm'pɒsɪtiy/ **pom′pous•ness,** *n.* [*noncount*] —**pomp′ous•ly,** *adv.*

-pon-, *root.* *-pon-* comes from Latin, where it has the meaning "put, place." It is related to the root -POS-. This meaning is found in such words as: COMPONENT, EXPONENT, OPPONENT, POSTPONE, PROPONENT.

pon•cho (pon′chō) /'pɒntʃow/ *n.* [*count*], *pl.* **-chos. 1.** a blanketlike cloak with an opening in the center for the head, originally worn in South America. **2.** a waterproof garment styled like this, worn as a raincoat.

pond (pond) /pɒnd/ *n.* [*count*] a body of water smaller than a lake, sometimes artificially formed. See illustration at LANDSCAPE.

pon•der (pon′dər) /'pɒndər/ *v.* to consider something deeply, thoughtfully, and thoroughly: [*no obj*]: *She pondered for a while, then came to a decision.* [~ + *obj*]: *He pondered his next move.* [~ + *clause*]: *He pondered what to do.* —**pon′der•er,** *n.* [*count*] See -PEND-.

pon•der•ous (pon′dər əs) /'pɒndərəs/ *adj.* **1.** of great weight; heavy; massive: *a ponderous cargo plane.* **2.** awkward: *the fat man's slow, ponderous steps down the ladder.* **3.** dull: *a ponderous dissertation.* —**pon′der•ous•ly,** *adv.*: *The elephant advanced ponderously.* See -PEND-.

pone (pōn) /pown/ *n.* [*count*] *South Midland and Southern U.S.* a loaf or oval-shaped cake of any type of bread, esp. corn bread.

pon•tiff (pon′tif) /'pɒntɪf/ *n.* [*count*] **1.** [*usually: the* + ~] the Roman Catholic pope; the Bishop of Rome. **2.** any high or chief priest.

pon•tif•i•cal (pon tif′i kəl) /pɒn'tɪfɪkəl/ *adj.* **1.** of or relating to a pontiff: *a pontifical decree.* **2.** pompous; overly self-important: *the law professor's pontifical air.*

pon•tif•i•cate (pon tif′i kāt′) /pɒn'tɪfɪˌkeyt/ *v.*, **-cat•ed, -cat•ing.** to speak in a pompous or self-important manner: [*no obj*]: *pontificating on the upcoming election.* [~ + *that clause*]: *He pontificated that everyone would eventually see things his way.*

pon•toon (pon to͞on′) /pɒn'tuwn/ also **pon•ton** (pon′tn) /'pɒntn̩/ *n.* [*count*] **1.** a floating structure used as support for a temporary bridge over a river. **2.** a float for a derrick, etc. **3.** a seaplane float.

po•ny (pō′nē) /'powniy/ *n.*, *pl.* **-nies,** *v.*, **-nied, -ny•ing.** —*n.* [*count*] **1.** a small horse of any of several breeds. **2.** *Informal.* a literal translation of a text, used as an aid in schoolwork; crib. **3.** something small of its kind, as a glass holding a small amount of liquor or a bottle holding seven ounces. —*v.* **4. pony up,** *Informal.* to pay (money), as in settling an account: [~ + *up* + *obj*]: *to pony up the money.* [~ + *obj* + *up*]: *to pony it up.*

po•ny•tail (pō′nē tāl′) /'powniyˌteyl/ *n.* [*count*] a hairstyle in which the hair is gathered at the back of the head and fastened so as to hang freely there.

pooch (po͞och) /puwtʃ/ *n.* [*count*] *Informal.* a dog.

poo•dle (po͞od′l) /'puwdl̩/ *n.* [*count*] one of a breed of dogs with long, thick, frizzy or curly hair.

pooh (po͞o, pŏŏ) /puw, pʊ/ *interj.* **1.** (used to express dislike, contempt, or ridicule of something): *"Oh, pooh, you can't possibly finish that job," she laughed.* —*n.* [*count*] **2.** an instance of saying "pooh."

pooh-pooh (po͞o′po͞o′) /'puw'puw/ *v.* [~ + *obj*] to express contempt for; dismiss lightly: *quick to pooh-pooh the whole proposal.*

pool[1] (po͞ol) /puwl/ *n.* [*count*] **1.** a small body of standing water; a small pond. **2.** any small collection of liquid on a surface; puddle: *a pool of blood.* **3.** a large, artificial basin filled with water for swimming: *a large pool in their backyard.* —*v.* **4.** to (cause to) form a pool (in): [*no obj*]: *The blood pooled in the area of the wound.* [~ + *obj*]: *pooling the blood in one region of the body.*

pool[2] (po͞ol) /puwl/ *n.* **1.** [*noncount*] a game played on a pool table with a cue ball and 15 other balls that are driven into pockets with a long stick: *friendly games of pool.* **2.** [*count*] the total amount bet, as on a race. **3.** [*count*] **a.** a combination of resources, etc., dedicated to some common purpose. **b.** the combined resources: *a pool of over $500.* **4.** [*count*] **a.** a facility shared by a group of people: *a car pool.* **b.** the people involved in providing such a service. —*v.* [~ + *obj*] **5.** to put (resources, etc.) into a common fund, as for a business: *pooled their resources for the venture.*

poop[1] (po͞op) /puwp/ *n.* [*count*] a raised structure at the rear of a vessel.

poop[2] (po͞op) /puwp/ *v.* [~ + *obj*] *Informal.* **1.** to cause to become out of breath or exhausted: *I was pooped after the long hike.* **2. poop out, a.** to (cause to) become exhausted: [*no obj*]: *Don't poop out now.* [~ + *obj* + *out*]: *A long run will really poop you out.* **b.** [*no obj*] to give up or stop working or participating; stop functioning.

poop[3] (po͞op) /puwp/ *n.* [*noncount*] *Slang.* a truthful, factual report; the lowdown: *Give us the straight poop.*

poor (pŏŏr) /pʊr/ *adj.*, **-er, -est,** *n.* —*adj.* **1.** having little or no money or means of support: *He came from a poor family.* **2.** (of a country, etc.) not well supplied with natural resources or funds: *one of the poorest countries in the world.* **3.** [*be* + ~] lacking in something (mentioned): *a region that is poor in minerals.* **4.** faulty; inferior; below the usual standard: *poor workmanship.* **5.** [*before a noun*] lacking in ability or training: *He was a poor cook.* **6.** [*before a noun*] wretched; unfortunate: *That poor cat looks so skinny and hungry.* **7.** not much in amount; scanty or meager: *poor attendance.* —*n.* **8. the poor,** [*plural; used with a plural verb*] poor persons thought of as a group: *aid for the poor.*

poor•house (pŏŏr′hous′) /'pʊrˌhaws/ *n.* [*count*], *pl.* **-hous•es.** a place in which poor people were formerly given a place to live at public expense.

poor•ly (pŏŏr′lē) /'pʊrliy/ *adv.* **1.** not well; badly: *poorly paid workers.* —*adj.* **2.** [*be* + ~] ill; sick: *He's poorly today.*

pop[1] (pop) /pɒp/ *v.*, **popped, pop•ping,** *n.*, *adv.* —*v.* **1.** to (cause to) make a short, quick, explosive sound: [*no obj*]: *The cork popped.* [~ + *obj*]: *He popped the cork off the bottle.* **2.** to burst open with such a sound, as chestnuts or corn in roasting: [*no obj*]: *The balloons popped.* [~ +

obj]: *Someone was going around with a pin and popping all the balloons.* **3.** [*no obj*] to come or go quickly, suddenly, or when not expected: *She just popped by and said hello.* See *pop in* below. **4.** to shoot with a gun: [*no obj*]: *to pop at a mark.* [~ + *obj*]: *to pop a few bullets at them.* **5.** [*no obj*] (of eyes) to grow round or very wide open, as if sticking out from the sockets: *His eyes nearly popped out of his head when the president walked up to him and said hello.* **6.** [~ + *obj*] to put or thrust quickly: *Pop the muffins into the oven.* **7.** [~ + *obj*] *Informal.* to swallow (pills), esp. as a habit: *popping pills: uppers and downers.* **8. pop for,** [~ + *obj*] *Slang.* to pay for, esp. as a treat: *said he would pop for the dinner.* **9. pop in,** [*no obj*] *Informal.* to visit briefly; drop by: *She just popped in, stayed a while, and left.* **10. pop off,** [*no obj*] *Informal.* **a.** to die suddenly. **b.** to say too much or speak angrily or indiscreetly: *kept popping off about how hard his job was.* **11. pop up,** [*no obj*] to appear or show up suddenly: *She pops up at the oddest times.* **—*n.*** **12.** [*count*] a short, quick, explosive sound. **13.** [*count*] a popping. **14.** [*count*] a shot with a firearm. **15.** [*noncount*] soda pop: *They call it soda in the Eastern U.S. and pop in the Midwest.* **—*adv.*** **16.** with an explosive sound: *The balloon went pop.* **—*Idiom.*** **17. a pop,** *Slang.* each; apiece: *Those dinners cost twenty-five dollars a pop.* **18. pop the question,** *Informal.* to propose marriage: *finally found the courage to pop the question.*

pop[2] (pop) /pɒp/ *adj.* **1.** of or relating to popular songs: *pop music.* **2.** of or relating to pop art. **3.** reflecting or aimed at the general masses of people: *pop culture.* **—*n.*** [*noncount*] **4.** popular music: *brought pop to a new height.* **5.** POP ART.

-pop-, *root.* -*pop*- comes from Latin, where it has the meaning "people." This meaning is found in such words as: POPULACE, POPULAR, POPULARITY, POPULARIZE, POPULATE, POPULOUS.

pop., an abbreviation of: population.

pop′ art′ or **Pop′ Art′,** *n.* [*noncount*] art in which everyday objects are the subject matter, and are often depicted as they appear in advertising or comic strips. **—pop′ ar′tist,** *n.* [*count*]

pop•corn (pop′kôrn′) /'pɒp,kɔrn/ *n.* [*noncount*] **1.** any of several varieties of corn whose kernels burst open and puff out when heated. **2.** such corn when it is popped: *munching on popcorn at the movies.*

Pope (pōp) /powp/ *n.* [*sometimes: pope*] the bishop of Rome as head of the Roman Catholic Church: [*the* + ~]: *His Holiness, the Pope, will see you now.* [*no article; used as part of a proper name*]: *His Holiness, Pope John XXIII, died in 1963.* [*count*]: *Some popes in the Middle Ages were corrupt.*

pop•gun (pop′gun′) /'pɒp,gʌn/ *n.* [*count*] a toy gun from which a pellet is shot by means of compressed air.

pop•lar (pop′lər) /'pɒplər/ *n.* **1.** [*count*] a rapidly growing softwood tree of the willow family. **2.** [*noncount*] the wood of this tree, used esp. for pulp.

pop•lin (pop′lin) /'pɒplɪn/ *n.* [*noncount*] a fine fabric used for dresses, shirts, draperies, etc.

pop•o•ver (pop′ō′vər) /'pɒp,owvər/ *n.* [*count*] a hollow muffin made with a batter of milk, egg, and flour.

pop•py (pop′ē) /'pɒpiy/ *n., pl.* **-pies** for 1. **1.** [*count*] a plant having showy, usually red flowers. **2.** [*noncount*] an extract from the juice of the poppy, as opium.

pop•py•cock (pop′ē kok′) /'pɒpiy,kɒk/ *n.* [*noncount*] nonsense; foolishness: *His new plan was just a lot of poppycock.*

pop•u•lace (pop′yə ləs) /'pɒpyələs/ *n.* [*count*] **1.** (in a community or nation) the common people. **2.** the people living in a place; population. See -POP-.

pop•u•lar (pop′yə lər) /'pɒpyələr/ *adj.* **1.** looked on or thought of with approval or affection by people in general; well-liked; admired: *a popular preacher.* **2.** [*before a noun*] of or relating to the common people or the people as a whole: *popular government.* **3.** [*before a noun*] found among the people generally: *a popular superstition.* **4.** [*before a noun*] appealing to or intended for the public at large: *popular music.* **—pop′u•lar•ly,** *adv.*: *popularly elected.* See -POP-.

pop•u•lar•i•ty (pop′yə lar′i tē) /,pɒpyə'lærɪtiy/ *n.* [*noncount*] the quality or fact of being popular. See -POP-.

pop•u•lar•ize (pop′yə lə rīz′) /'pɒpyələ,rayz/ *v.* [~ + *obj*], **-ized, -iz•ing. 1.** to make popular: *a movie that popularized disco.* **2.** to make (something difficult to understand) easily understood by ordinary people: *The book popularizes the new breakthroughs in physics.* **—pop•u•lar•i•za•tion** (pop′yə lər i zā′shən) /,pɒpyələrɪ'zeyʃən/ *n.* [*noncount*] See -POP-.

pop•u•late (pop′yə lāt′) /'pɒpyə,leyt/ *v.* [~ + *obj*], **-lat•ed, -lat•ing. 1.** to inhabit; live in: *The region was populated by Celts and Germanic settlers.* **2.** to furnish with inhabitants; people: *to populate the desert.* See -POP-.

pop•u•la•tion (pop′yə lā′shən) /,pɒpyə'leyʃən/ *n.* **1.** the total number of persons, animals, or other living things living in a country, city, etc.: [*count*]: *a population of over 2 billion people.* [*noncount*]: *a definite decrease in population.* **2.** [*noncount*] the people living in a place: *The population is completely terrorized by the secret police.* **3.** [*noncount*] the (number of) people living in an area that are of a particular race, class, or group: *the working-class population.* **4.** [*count*] any collection of things or individuals being studied, as in statistics: *a sample population of six hundred raccoons.* See -POP-.

popula′tion explo′sion, *n.* [*count*] a rapid increase in the number of people living in an area because of an increasing birthrate or an increase in life expectancy.

pop•u•lism (pop′yə liz′əm) /'pɒpyə,lɪzəm/ *n.* [*noncount*] **1.** a political movement that promotes the interests of the common people and calls for equality among them. **2.** the use of what are claimed to be the views, etc., of the common people to gain political power or popularity: *His candidacy was founded on racism, yet he claimed it was one of populism.* **—pop′u•list,** *n.* [*count*]: *claiming to be a populist but dividing voters one from the other.* **—*adj.*:** *a populist reform movement.* See -POP-.

pop•u•lous (pop′yə ləs) /'pɒpyələs/ *adj.* containing many people; heavily populated: *a populous area.* **—pop′u•lous•ness,** *n.* [*noncount*] See -POP-.

por•ce•lain (pôr′sə lin, pōr′-; pôrs′lin, pōrs′-) /'pɔrsəlɪn, 'powr-;' pɔrslɪn, 'powrs-/ *n.* [*noncount*] **1.** a hard, shiny, transparent substance made by baking clay, used to make cups and dishes. **2.** cups and dishes made from this substance.

porch (pôrch, pōrch) /pɔrtʃ, powrtʃ/ *n.* [*count*] **1.** an outside addition to a building, forming a covered approach or entrance to a doorway. See illustration at HOUSE. **2.** a raised platform on the outside of a building, usually level with a door; a veranda.

por•cine (pôr′sīn, -sin) /'pɔrsayn, -sɪn/ *adj.* of, relating to, or resembling swine or pigs.

por•cu•pine (pôr′kyə pīn′) /'pɔrkyə,payn/ *n.* [*count*] an animal, a large rodent having stiff, sharp spines or quills.

pore[1] (pôr, pōr) /pɔr, powr/ *v.,* **pored, por•ing. pore over,** [~ + *over* + *obj*] to read or study with focused attention, concentration, or hard work: *They found him poring over old manuscripts in the library.*

pore[2] (pôr, pōr) /pɔr, powr/ *n.* [*count*] a very small opening, as in the skin or a leaf, for perspiration, absorption, etc.

por•gy (pôr′gē) /'pɔrgiy/ *n.* [*count*], *pl.* (*esp. when thought of as a group*) **-gy,** (*esp. for kinds or species*) **-gies.** a fish eaten for food, having a deep body and large scales.

pork (pôrk, pōrk) /pɔrk, powrk/ *n.* [*noncount*] **1.** the flesh of a hog or pig used as food. **2.** money spent or appointments made by the government for political reasons: *There was so much pork in that budget for local construction that no legislator would dare oppose it.*

pork′ bar′rel, *n.* [*count*] an instance of government spending, or a bill or policy that calls for spending, on local improvements made primarily to gain votes: *another pork barrel, that highway project.* **—pork′-bar′rel•ing,** *n.* [*noncount*]

porn (pôrn) /pɔrn/ also **por•no** (pôr′nō) /'pɔrnow/ *Informal.* **—*n.*** [*noncount*] **1.** pornography. **—*adj.*** **2.** pornographic: *a porn show; a porno movie.*

por•no•graph•ic (pôr′nə graf′ik) /,pɔrnə'græfɪk/ *adj.* (of writings, photographs, movies, etc.) of or relating to pornography: *pornographic movies.* See -GRAPH-.

por•nog•ra•phy (pôr nog′rə fē) /pɔr'nɒgrəfiy/ *n.* [*noncount*] writings, photographs, movies, etc., intended to arouse sexual excitement, esp. such materials considered as having little or no artistic merit: *What constitutes pornography, some say, is in the eye of the beholder.* See -GRAPH-.

po•rous (pôr′əs, pōr′-) /'pɔrəs, 'powr-/ *adj.* **1.** allowing water, air, etc., to pass through. **2.** full of pores. **—po•ros•i•ty** (pô ros′i tē, pō-) /pɔ'rɒsɪtiy, pow-/ *n.* [*noncount*]

por•poise (pôr′pəs) /'pɔrpəs/ *n., pl.* (*esp. when thought of as a group*) **-poise,** (*esp. for kinds or species*) **-pois•es,** *v.,* **-poised, -pois•ing. —*n.*** [*count*] **1.** a marine mammal having a blunt, rounded snout and resembling a dolphin. **—*v.*** [*no obj*] **2.** (of a speeding motorboat) to leap clear of the water after striking a wave.

por•ridge (pôr′ij, por′-) /ˈpɔrɪdʒ, ˈpɒr-/ *n.* [*noncount*] a thick cereal made esp. of oatmeal boiled in water or milk.

port[1] (pôrt, pōrt) /pɔrt, powrt/ *n.* [*count*] **1.** a city or town where ships load or unload. **2.** a place where ships may take refuge from storms; harbor.

port[2] (pôrt, pōrt) /pɔrt, powrt/ *n.* [*noncount*] **1.** the left-hand side of a vessel or aircraft, facing forward: *"Turn hard to port, helmsman," the captain ordered.* **—*adj.* 2.** of, relating to, or located on the left side of a vessel or aircraft: *"Engines afire on the port wing," he radioed.*

port[3] (pôrt, pōrt) /pɔrt, powrt/ *n.* [*noncount*] a very sweet, usually dark red wine, originally from Portugal.

port[4] (pôrt, pōrt) /pɔrt, powrt/ *n.* [*count*] **1.** an opening in the side or other exterior part of a ship for admitting air and light or for taking on cargo. **2.** a small opening in an armored vehicle, aircraft, or fort through which a gun can be fired or a camera directed. **3.** a data connection in a computer to which an outside (peripheral) device can be attached: *Hook up the printer to your parallel port.*

-port-, *root.* *-port-* comes from Latin, where it has the meaning "carry; bring." This meaning is found in such words as: COMPORT, DEPORT, EXPORT, IMPORT, IMPORTANCE, IMPORTANT, OPPORTUNE, OPPORTUNITY, PORTABLE, PORTAGE, PORTER, PORTFOLIO, PORTMANTEAU, PURPORT, RAPPORT, REPORT, SUPPORT, TRANSPORT, TRANSPORTATION.

port•a•ble (pôr′tə bəl, pōr′-) /ˈpɔrtəbəl, ˈpowr-/ *adj.* **1.** that can be transported: *a portable stage.* **2.** easily carried by hand: *a portable radio.* **3.** (of data, software, etc.) able to be used on different computer systems. **4.** capable of being transferred, as pension benefits, from one employer's plan to that of another. **—*n.*** [*count*] **5.** something that can be moved, esp. as distinguished from a similar machine that cannnot: *Bring along your portable TV.* **—port•a•bil•i•ty** (pôr′tə bil′i tē, pōr′-) /ˌpɔrtəˈbɪlɪtiy, ˌpowr-/ *n.* [*noncount*] See -PORT-.

por•tage (pôr′tij, pōr′- *or, for 2, 3* pôr täzh′) /ˈpɔrtɪdʒ, ˈpowr- *or, for 2, 3* pɔrˈtɑʒ/ *n.* [*noncount*] **1.** the act of carrying; carriage. **2.** the carrying of boats, etc., across land from one river, etc., to another. **3.** the route over which this is done. See -PORT-.

por•tal (pôr′tl, pōr′-) /ˈpɔrtl̩, ˈpowr-/ *n.* [*count*] a door, gate, or entrance, esp. one of great size and appearance.

port•cul•lis (pôrt kul′is, pōrt-) /pɔrtˈkʌlɪs, powrt-/ *n.* [*count*] a strong grating, as of iron, made to slide up and down at the sides of the gateway of a castle.

por•tend (pôr tend′, pōr-) /pɔrˈtɛnd, powr-/ *v.* [~ + *obj*] to indicate in advance, as an omen does: *What do the polls portend for the election?* See -TEND-.

por•tent (pôr′tent, pōr′-) /ˈpɔrtɛnt, ˈpowr-/ *n.* **1.** [*count*] something that portends: *a portent of even worse defeats to come.* **2.** [*noncount*] significance; meaning: *occurrences of dire portent.* See -TEND-.

por•ten•tous (pôr ten′təs, pōr-) /pɔrˈtɛntəs, powr-/ *adj.* **1.** of the nature of a portent. **2.** indicating something bad for the future: *a portentous defeat.* **3.** overly self-important; pompous. **—por•ten′tous•ly,** *adv.*: *He spoke portentously of the decline in literacy.* See -TEND-.

por•ter[1] (pôr′tər, pōr′-) /ˈpɔrtər, ˈpowr-/ *n.* [*count*] **1.** one hired to carry baggage, as at a hotel. **2.** one who does cleaning, repairs, etc., in a building, store, etc. See -PORT-.

por•ter[2] (pôr′tər, pōr′-) /ˈpɔrtər, ˈpowr-/ *n.* [*count*] one who has charge of a door or gate; doorkeeper.

port•fo•li•o (pôrt fō′lē ō′, pōrt-) /pɔrtˈfowliyˌow, powrt-/ *n., pl.* **-li•os. 1.** [*count*] a flat, thin, portable case for carrying loose papers, etc.: *That portfolio must belong to the businessman who just got out of this taxicab.* **2.** [*count*] the contents of such a case, esp. a collection of photographs, etc., that represents a person's work: *The students submitted a portfolio of their drawings.* **3.** [*count*] the securities, etc., held by a private investor, financial institution, etc.: *a portfolio of bonds.* **4.** [*noncount*] the office, duties, or post of a minister of state or member of a cabinet: *a minister without portfolio.* See -FOLI-, -PORT-.

port•hole (pôrt′hōl′, pōrt′-) /ˈpɔrtˌhowl, ˈpowrt-/ *n.* [*count*] **1.** a round, windowlike opening in the side of a ship. **2.** an opening in a wall, door, etc., as one through which to shoot.

por•ti•co (pôr′ti kō′, pōr′-) /ˈpɔrtɪˌkow, ˈpowr-/ *n.* [*count*], *pl.* **-coes, -cos.** a structure consisting of a roof with columns or piers supporting it, usually attached to a building as a porch. **—por′ti•coed′,** *adj.*

por•tion (pôr′shən, pōr′-) /ˈpɔrʃən, ˈpowr-/ *n.* [*count*] **1.** a part of a whole; a segment: *Portions of this television broadcast have been sponsored by various oil companies.* **2.** an amount of food served to one person; serving; helping: *several portions of meat and dessert.* **3.** the part of a whole set aside for a person or group; share: *My portion was less than yours.* **4.** the part of an estate that goes to an heir. **—*v.* 5.** to divide into or distribute in portions or shares: [~ + *out* + *obj*]: *Portion out the rest of this food among yourselves.* [~ + *obj* + *out*]: *Portion it out among yourselves.*

port•ly (pôrt′lē, pōrt′-) /ˈpɔrtliy, ˈpowrt-/ *adj.*, **-li•er, -li•est.** rather heavy or fat; stout: *Refer to your full-sized teacher as "portly" rather than "fat."* —**port′li•ness,** *n.* [*noncount*]

port•man•teau (pôrt man′tō, pōrt-; pôrt′man tō′, pōrt′-) /pɔrtˈmæntow, powrt-; ˌpɔrtmænˈtow, ˌpowrt-/ *n., pl.* **-teaus, -teaux** (-tōz, -tō; -tōz′, -tō′) /-towz, -tow; -ˈtowz, -ˈtow/ *adj.* **—*n.*** [*count*] **1.** *Chiefly Brit.* a case or bag to carry clothing in while traveling. **—*adj.* 2.** combining or blending several items, features, or qualities: *a portmanteau show; a portmanteau word like* brunch, *formed from the words* breakfast *and* lunch. See -PORT-.

por•trait (pôr′trit, -trāt, pōr′-) /ˈpɔrtrɪt, -treyt, ˈpowr-/ *n.* [*count*] **1.** a representation of a person, esp. of the face: *a portrait of a woman with just the slightest smile.* **2.** a description, in words, writing, or film, usually of a person: *The movie provides a revealing portrait of the late humanitarian.*

por•trait•ist (pôr′tri tist, -trā-, pōr′-) /ˈpɔrtrɪtɪst, -trey-, ˈpowr-/ *n.* [*count*] one who makes portraits.

por•trai•ture (pôr′tri chər, pōr′-) /ˈpɔrtrɪtʃər, ˈpowr-/ *n.* [*noncount*] the art of making portraits.

por•tray (pôr trā′, pōr-) /pɔrˈtrey, powr-/ *v.* [~ + *obj*] **1.** to make a portrait. **2.** to describe in words, esp. in a certain way: *In many TV commercials, fathers are portrayed as lovable but foolish.* **3.** to represent dramatically, as on the stage: *the actor who portrayed Napoleon.*

por•tray•al (pôr trā′əl, pōr-) /pɔrˈtreyəl, powr-/ *n.* [*count*] **1.** the act of portraying something. **2.** the act of describing something: *his portrayal of all politicians as thieves and liars.* **3.** a performance, as in a play or movie: *the actress's portrayal of a waitress.*

Por•tu•guese (pôr′chə gēz′, -gēs′, pōr′-; pôr′chə gēz′, -gēs′, pōr′-) /ˌpɔrtʃəˈgiyz, -ˈgiys, ˌpowr-; ˈpɔrtʃəˌgiyz, -ˌgiys, ˈpowr-/ *adj., n., pl.* **-guese. —*adj.* 1.** of or relating to Portugal. **2.** of or relating to the language spoken in Portugal. **—*n.* 3.** [*count*] a person born or living in Portugal. **4.** [*noncount*] the language spoken in Portugal.

-pos-, *root.* *-pos-* comes from Latin, where it has the meaning "put; place." This meaning is found in such words as: COMPOSE, COMPOSITE, COMPOST, COMPOSURE, DEPOSE, DEPOSIT, DISPOSE, EXPOSE, EXPOSITION, IMPOSE, IMPOSTOR, INTERPOSE, JUXTAPOSE, OPPOSE, POSE, POSIT, POSITION, POSITIVE, POSTURE, PREDISPOSE, PREPOSITION, PREPOSSESSING, PRESUPPOSE, PROPOSE, PROPOSITION, PURPOSE, REPOSE, SUPERIMPOSE, SUPPOSE, SUPPOSITION, TRANSPOSE. See -PON-.

pose (pōz) /powz/ *v.,* **posed, pos•ing,** *n.* **—*v.* 1.** to (cause to) get into or hold a physical position, as for an artistic purpose: [*no obj*]: *to pose for a photographer.* [~ + *obj*]: *The photographer posed the group.* **2.** [~ + *as* + *obj*] to pretend to be what one is not: *To gain entrance into the plant, they posed as police officers.* **3.** [~ + *obj*] to state, or put forward for others to consider; to present (an idea, etc.): *Let me pose this question to you: Will you raise taxes?* **4.** [~ + *obj*] to cause (something) to exist; create: *Her erratic behavior on the job poses problems.* **—*n.*** [*count*] **5.** a way of holding the body in a certain position, esp. for an artistic purpose, as to be drawn, etc.: *The model stood in various poses as the photographer clicked away.* **6.** a mental attitude or a way of behaving adopted for effect or in order to make an impression, usually false: *His liberalism is merely a pose.* See -POS-.

pos•er[1] (pō′zər) /ˈpowzər/ *n.* [*count*] one who poses.

pos•er[2] (pō′zər) /ˈpowzər/ *n.* [*count*] a person, question, or problem that is hard to understand. See -POS-.

po•seur (pō zûr′) /powˈzɜr/ *n.* [*count*] one who adopts a character, manner, or feeling to impress others.

posh (posh) /pɒʃ/ *adj.,* **-er, -est.** stylishly elegant; grand; luxurious: *They went to the poshest restaurant to celebrate.*

pos•it (poz′it) /ˈpɒzɪt/ *v.* [~ + *obj*] to put forward (an idea); postulate; suggest: *Darwin posited the notion of survival of the fittest as a principle in evolution.* See -POS-.

po•si•tion (pə zish′ən) /pəˈzɪʃən/ *n.* **1.** [*count*] location; situation; condition with regard to place: *the position of the moon in the sky.* **2.** [*count*] a place occupied or to be occupied; site: *The garrison was a well-fortified position.*

3. [*noncount*] the proper or usual place: *position of the furniture.* **4.** [*count; usually singular*] situation or condition, esp. in relation to circumstances: *in an awkward position.* **5.** [*count*] status or standing; rank: *They were in the top positions in their classes.* **6.** [*count*] a job: *took a new position with a publishing company.* **7.** [*count*] an attitude, opinion, or belief: *the governor's position on capital punishment.* **8.** [*count*] the part of a sports field covered by a player: *Which position did you play: pitcher, catcher, or infielder?* —*v.* [~ + *obj*] **9.** to put (something) in a particular, proper, or correct position: *He positioned himself next to the president.* See -POS-.

pos•i•tive (poz′i tiv) /ˈpɒzɪtɪv/ *adj.* **1.** [*be* + ~ + *(that) clause*] confident in belief or in what one says; sure: *He is positive that he'll win.* **2.** expressing agreement; favorable: *a positive reaction to his speech.* **3.** expressing a statement that indicates or means "yes"; affirmative: *a positive answer.* **4.** emphasizing what is hopeful about a situation; constructive: *Be more positive in your outlook on life.* **5.** clearly expressed; definite: *issued a positive denial.* **6.** [*usually: before a noun*] allowing no doubt; that cannot be argued against: *positive identification of the body.* **7.** [*before a noun*] complete; out-and-out: *She's a positive genius!* **8.** moving in a direction thought of as showing progress, etc.: *a positive trend.* **9.** relating to the electricity in a body lacking in electrons: *a positive charge.* **10.** (of a chemical element or group) tending to lose electrons and become positively charged; basic: *positive ions.* **11.** (of a medical test) indicating the presence of the disease, condition, etc., tested for. **12.** naming a number greater than zero: *positive integers.* **13.** of or naming the simple, base form of an adjective or adverb, as *good* or *smoothly,* in contrast to the comparative or superlative form. **14.** of or naming a photographic print showing the brightness values as they are in the subject. —*n.* [*count*] **15.** something positive; a positive quality or characteristic. **16. a.** the positive degree in grammatical comparison. **b.** the positive form of an adjective or adverb. **17.** a positive photographic image, as on a print or transparency. —**pos′i•tive•ness,** *n.* [*noncount*] See -POS-.

pos•i•tive•ly (poz′i tiv lē, *or, esp. for 3,* poz′i tiv′lē) /ˈpɒzɪtɪvliy, *or, esp. for 3,* ˌpɒzɪˈtɪvliy / *adv.* **1.** with certainty; absolutely: *The statement is positively true.* **2.** definitely; without question: *Her behavior was positively disgusting!* —*interj.* **3.** (used to express strong agreement with something, or to mean "yes"): *Can you make it to the party? —Positively!* See -POS-.

pos•i•tron (poz′i tron′) /ˈpɒzɪˌtrɒn/ *n.* [*count*] an elementary particle with the same mass as an electron but having a positive charge. See -POS-.

poss., an abbreviation of: **1.** possessive. **2.** possible. **3.** possibly.

pos•se (pos′ē) /ˈpɒsiy/ *n.* [*count*] **1.** a group of people brought together legally to assist a sheriff in an emergency: *In Westerns the posse rides off after the bank robbers.* **2.** *Slang.* a group of people associated in some fashion: *a posse of drug dealers.*

pos•sess (pə zes′) /pəˈzɛs/ *v.* [~ + *obj*] **1.** [*not: be* + *~-ing*] to have (something) as belonging to one; own: *Everything they possessed was lost in the war.* **2.** [*not: be* + *~-ing*] to have as a part of one's mind, or as a quality: *She possesses great wit.* **3.** (of a spirit, esp. an evil one) to control (a person) from within: *possessed by demons.* **4.** (of a feeling, etc.) to influence in the manner of such a spirit: *A raging fury possessed him.* [~ + *obj* + *to* + *verb*]: *What in the world possessed you to do this?* —**pos•ses′sor,** *n.* [*count*]

pos•sessed (pə zest′) /pəˈzɛst/ *adj.* [*be* + ~] **1.** made to move by a strong feeling, by madness, or by a supernatural power: *She looked like a woman possessed.* **2.** self-possessed; calm; poised. —***Idiom.*** **3. possessed of,** [*be* + ~] having; possessing: *He is possessed of intelligence and ambition.*

pos•ses•sion (pə zesh′ən) /pəˈzɛʃən/ *n.* **1.** [*noncount*] the act or fact of possessing: *She took possession of the house.* **2.** [*noncount*] the state of being possessed: *possession by the devil.* **3.** [*noncount*] ownership. **4.** [*count*] a thing possessed or owned: *They stole her only possession, a little teddy bear.* **5. possessions,** [*plural*] property or wealth. **6.** [*count*] a part of the territory of a nation: *islands and other small possessions in the Pacific.* **7.** [*noncount*] **a.** control of the ball or puck by a player or team. **b.** the right of a team to put the ball into play: *The Giants have possession of the ball.* **8.** [*noncount*] control over oneself, etc.: *Was he in full possession of his faculties?* See -SESS-.

pos•ses•sive (pə zes′iv) /pəˈzɛsɪv/ *adj.* **1.** desiring to dominate and be the only controlling influence on someone: *a jealous, possessive husband.* **2.** unwilling to share with other people; selfish. **3.** (of a word, construction, or grammatical case) showing possession, ownership, origin, etc., as *Jane's* in *Jane's coat. His* in *his book* is a possessive adjective. *His* in *The book is his* is a possessive pronoun. Compare GENITIVE (def. 1). —*n.* [*count*] **4.** the possessive case. **5.** a possessive form or phrase. —**pos•ses′sive•ly,** *adv.* —**pos•ses′sive•ness,** *n.* [*noncount*]

pos•si•bil•i•ty (pos′ə bil′i tē) /ˌpɒsəˈbɪlɪtiy/ *n., pl.* **-ties. 1.** [*noncount*] the state or fact of being possible: *the possibility of error.* **2.** [*count*] something possible: *had tried every single possibility but one.*

pos•si•ble (pos′ə bəl) /ˈpɒsəbəl/ *adj.* **1.** that may or can exist, happen, be done, be used, etc.: *a possible cure; six possible choices.* **2.** [*It* + *be* + ~ + *(that) clause*] that may be true or may be the case: *It is possible that she has already gone.*

pos•sib•ly (pos′ə blē) /ˈpɒsəbliy/ *adv.* **1.** perhaps; maybe: *It may possibly rain today.* **2.** by any possibility; conceivably: *She has all the money she can possibly use.*

pos•sum (pos′əm) /ˈpɒsəm/ *n.* [*count*], *pl.* **-sums,** (*esp. when thought of as a group*) **-sum. 1.** OPOSSUM. —***Idiom.*** **2. play possum,** to pretend to be asleep or dead: *She was lying in bed playing possum.*

post[1] (pōst) /powst/ *n.* [*count*] **1.** a piece of wood or metal put into the ground so that it stands upright and used as a support, a point to attach things, etc. **2.** one of the main upright pieces of a piece of furniture. **3.** a goalpost. —*v.* [~ + *obj*] **4.** to put up (a public notice) on a post or wall: *They posted several flyers announcing the concert.* **5.** to bring to public attention by means of a poster or the like: *to post a reward.*

post[2] (pōst) /powst/ *n.* [*count*] **1.** a position of duty or trust to which one is assigned: *a diplomatic post.* **2.** a military station with permanent buildings: *decided to close down some army posts.* **3.** the body of troops in that station. **4.** a place in the stock exchange where a particular stock is traded. —*v.* [~ + *obj*] **5.** to assign, place, or station at a post: *The detachment was posted to the front of the battle.* **6.** to provide or put up, as bail: *He posted bail and was out on the streets only five hours after his arrest.*

post[3] (pōst) /powst/ *n.* [*noncount*] **1.** *Chiefly Brit.* **a.** a single dispatch of mail. **b.** the mail itself. **c.** a mail system service. —*v.* [~ + *obj*] **2.** to supply with up-to-date information: *Keep me posted on your activities.* **3.** *Chiefly Brit.* to send by mail: *posted several letters to her.*

post-, *prefix. post-* comes from Latin, where it has the meaning "after (in time), following (some event);" "behind, at the rear or end of": *post-* + *industrial* → *postindustrial (= after the industrial age); post-* + *war* → *postwar (= after the war).*

post•age (pō′stij) /ˈpowstɪdʒ/ *n.* [*noncount*] **1.** the charge for sending something by mail. **2.** the stamps, indication, or printed design on an envelope, etc., representing such charges.

post•al (pōs′tl) /ˈpowstl̩/ *adj.* of or relating to the post office or mail service: *postal delivery; postal employees.*

post•card or **post card,** (pōst′kärd′) /ˈpowstˌkɑrd/ *n.* [*count*] a small printed card for mailing a casual message without an envelope for privacy.

post•date (pōst dāt′, pōst′-) /powstˈdeyt, ˈpowst-/ *v.* [~ + *obj*], **-dat•ed, -dat•ing. 1.** to date (a check, etc.) with a date later than the actual date. **2.** to be later than.

post•er (pō′stər) /ˈpowstər/ *n.* [*count*] a large, stiff piece of paper with a message on it, posted in a public place, as for advertising: *The poster had a picture of the missing child's face.*

pos•te•ri•or (po stēr′ē ər, pō-) /pɒˈstɪəriyər, pow-/ *adj.* **1.** [*before a noun*] located behind or at the rear of. **2.** coming after (something) in order or in time; later. —*n.* [*count*] **3.** the lower, bottom parts or rump of the body; the buttocks: *lowered his posterior onto the chair.* —**pos•te′ri•or•ly,** *adv.* —**Syn.** See BACK.

pos•ter•i•ty (po ster′i tē) /pɒˈstɛrɪtiy/ *n.* [*noncount*] future generations; one's descendants: *He hoped that posterity would view him as a hero and not a villain.*

post•grad•u•ate (pōst graj′o͞o it, -āt′) /powstˈgrædʒuwɪt, -ˌeyt/ *adj.* **1.** of or relating to postgraduates: *a postgraduate seminar.* —*n.* [*count*] **2.** a student taking advanced work after graduation.

post•haste (pōst′hāst′) /ˈpowstˈheyst/ *adv.* as quickly as possible: *They got out of there posthaste.*

post•hu•mous (pos′chə məs) /ˈpɒstʃəməs/ *adj.* **1.** occurring or continuing after one's death: *a posthumous* *medal for bravery.* **2.** published after the death of the author. —**post′hu•mous•ly,** *adv.: The award was given posthumously.* See -HUM-.

post•hyp•not•ic (pōst′hip not′ik) /ˌpowsthɪp'nɒtɪk/ *adj.* (of a suggestion) made during hypnosis so as to be effective after awakening: *a posthypnotic suggestion.*

post•in•dus•tri•al (pōst′in dus′trē əl) /ˌpowstɪn'dʌstriyəl/ *adj.* [*before a noun*] of or relating to the time after large-scale industrialization: *a postindustrial society.*

post•lude (pōst′lo͞od) /'powstluwd/ *n.* [*count*] a concluding piece of music, esp. in church.

post•man (pōst′mən) /'powstmən/ *n., pl.* **-men.** MAIL CARRIER: *Did the postman bring any letters for us today, or just bills?*

post•mark (pōst′märk′) /'powstˌmɑrk/ *n.* [*count*] **1.** an official mark stamped on mail passed through a postal system, showing the place and date of sending or receipt. —*v.* [~ + *obj*] **2.** to stamp with a postmark.

post•mas•ter (pōst′mas′tər) /'powstˌmæstər/ *n.* [*count*] the official in charge of a post office.

post′master gen′eral, *n.* [*count*], *pl.* **postmasters general.** the head of the postal system of a country.

post•me•rid•i•an (pōst′mə rid′ē ən) /ˌpowstmə'rɪdiyən/ *adj.* of, relating to, or occurring in the afternoon.

post•mis•tress (pōst′mis′tris) /'powstˌmɪstrɪs/ *n.* [*count*] a woman in charge of a post office.

post•mod•ern (pōst mod′ərn) /powst'mɒdərn/ *adj.* [*sometimes: Postmodern*] of or relating to the architecture, arts, and literature developing in the late 20th century in reaction to modernism.

post•mor•tem (pōst môr′təm) /powst'mɔrtəm/ *adj.* **1.** of or relating to the time following death. **2.** of or relating to examination of the body after death. **3.** occurring after the end of something: *a postmortem meeting to discuss why the team lost.* —*n.* [*count*] **4.** an examination of the body after death, so as to determine what caused death; an autopsy. **5.** an evaluation after the end of something, esp. a defeat in a game: *The coach held a postmortem with the press after the team's devastating loss.* See -MORT-.

post•na•sal (pōst nā′zəl) /powst'neyzəl/ *adj.* located behind the nose or in the region of the throat where the back of the nose connects with it: *postnasal drip.*

post•na•tal (pōst nāt′l) /powst'neytḷ/ *adj.* occurring after childbirth.

post′ of′fice, *n.* **1.** [*count*] an office of a government postal system at which mail is received and sorted, from which it is sent out and delivered, and at which stamps are sold. **2.** [*proper noun; often: Post Office; the* + ~] the department of a government with the task of delivering and receiving mail.

post•op•er•a•tive (pōst op′ər ə tiv, -ə rā′tiv, -op′rə tiv) /powst'ɒpərətɪv, -əˌreytɪv, -'ɒprətɪv/ *adj.* [*before a noun*] occurring after a medical operation: *postoperative pain.* See -OPER-.

post•par•tum (pōst pär′təm) /powst'pɑrtəm/ *adj.* following childbirth: *postpartum depression.* See -PARE-[2].

post•pone (pōst pōn′, pōs-) /powst'pown, pows-/ *v.* [~ + *obj*], **-poned, -pon•ing.** to put (something) off to a later time: *We have postponed our departure until tomorrow.* —**post•pone′ment,** *n.* [*count*]: *We endured one postponement after another.* [*noncount*]: *postponement of the match.* See -PON-.

post•pran•di•al (pōst pran′dē əl) /powst'prændiyəl/ *adj.* after a meal, esp. after dinner.

post•script (pōst′skript′, pōs′-) /'powstˌskrɪpt, 'pows-/ *n.* [*count*] a paragraph, sentence, etc., added to a letter already finished and signed by the writer: *In a short postscript he reminded her to write back soon.* See P.S. See -SCRIB-.

pos•tu•late (*v.* pos′chə lāt′; *n.* -lit, -lāt′) / *v.* 'pɒstʃəˌleyt; *n.* -lɪt, -ˌleyt/ *v.,* **-lat•ed, -lat•ing,** *n.* —*v.* **1.** to suggest or assume the existence or truth of (something), esp. as a basis for further reasoning: [~ + *obj*]: *She postulated an increase in population and went on from there to form a theory of population change.* [~ + *that clause*]: *began by postulating that good and evil exist in all people.* —*n.* [*count*] **2.** something assumed to be true and used as a basis for reasoning: *a postulate that human beings were created for a purpose.* —**pos•tu•la•tion** (pos′chə lā′shən) /ˌpɒstʃə'leyʃən/ *n.* [*noncount*]

pos•ture (pos′chər) /'pɒstʃər/ *n., v.,* **-tured, -tur•ing.** —*n.* **1.** the position of the arms, legs, etc., or the way the body is held by a person when standing, etc.: [*noncount*]: *She had poor posture as a child.* [*count*]: *She held several postures while the sculptor worked.* **2.** [*count*] a mental attitude or stance, as that adopted by a company or government: *a low posture, in which we are seen as avoiding interference.* —*v.* [*no obj*] **3.** to act falsely, so as to create a certain impression: *The negotiators were just posturing when they demanded such high wage increases.* See -POS-.

post•war (pōst′wôr′) /'powst'wɔr/ *adj.* [*before a noun*] of or relating to a period following a war: *the postwar generation.*

po•sy (pō′zē) /'powziy/ *n.* [*count*], *pl.* **-sies.** a flower, nosegay, or bouquet.

pot[1] (pot) /pɒt/ *n., v.,* **pot•ted, pot•ting.** —*n.* [*count*] **1.** a container made of baked clay, metal, etc., used for cooking, serving, and other purposes. **2.** such a container with its contents: *a pot of stew.* **3.** FLOWERPOT. **4.** a container of liquor or other drink: *a pot of ale.* **5.** CHAMBER POT. **6.** [*usually singular*] a large sum of money: *He inherited quite a pot when she died.* **7.** all the money bet at a single time; pool: *He put all his winnings in the pot for one last game.* **8.** POTBELLY: *He'd developed quite a pot drinking all that beer.* —*v.* **9.** [~ + *obj*] to put or transplant into a pot: *to pot a plant.* —***Idiom.*** **10. go to pot,** [*no obj*] to become ruined; get worse; deteriorate: *The whole city seems to be going to pot.* —**pot′ful,** *n.* [*count*], *pl.* **-fuls.**

pot[2] (pot) /pɒt/ *n.* [*noncount*] *Slang.* marijuana.

-pot-, *root. -pot-* comes from Latin, where it has the meaning "power; ability." This meaning is found in such words as: IMPOTENCE, IMPOTENT, OMNIPOTENT, PLENIPOTENTIARY, POTENCY, POTENT, POTENTIAL.

po•ta•ble (pō′tə bəl) /'powtəbəl/ *adj.* **1.** fit for drinking: *potable water.* —*n.* [*count*] **2.** Usually, **potables.** [*plural*] liquids that a person can drink safely; beverages. —**po•ta•bil•i•ty** (pō′tə bil′i tē) /ˌpowtə'bɪlɪtiy/ *n.* [*noncount*]

pot•ash (pot′ash′) /'pɒtˌæʃ/ *n.* [*noncount*] a white, powdery substance, potassium carbonate, esp. the crude impure form taken from wood ashes.

po•tas•si•um (pə tas′ē əm) /pə'tæsiyəm/ *n.* [*noncount*] a silvery white metallic element that burns rapidly in the air and whose compounds are used as fertilizer.

po•ta•to (pə tā′tō, -tə) /pə'teytow, -tə/ *n., pl.* **-toes. 1.** a white vegetable with a brown or reddish skin that grows underground and is grown as food: [*count*]: *a bag of potatoes.* [*noncount*]: *a filling made of potato and onion.* **2.** [*count*] the plant itself. **3.** SWEET POTATO (defs. 1, 2).

pota′to chip′, *n.* [*count*] a thin slice of potato fried until crisp and usually salted.

pot•bel•ly (pot′bel′ē) /'pɒtˌbɛliy/ *n.* [*count*], *pl.* **-lies. 1.** a rounded belly or stomach that sticks out. **2.** a person with such a stomach. **3.** a stove having a large, rounded chamber for burning. —**pot′bel′lied,** *adj.*

pot•boil•er (pot′boi′lər) /'pɒtˌbɔylər/ *n.* [*count*] a work of writing, music, or art produced for quick profit: *started knocking off one steamy potboiler after another.*

po•ten•cy (pōt′n sē) /'powtṇsiy/ *n.* [*noncount*] **1.** the state or quality of being potent. **2.** effectiveness; strength: *Over time the drug loses its potency.* See -POT-.

po•tent (pōt′nt) /'powtṇt/ *adj.* **1.** powerful; mighty: *a potent air force.* **2.** persuasive: *potent arguments.* **3.** producing powerful effects: *a potent drug.* **4.** (of a male) capable of having sexual relations. See -POT-.

po•ten•tate (pōt′n tāt′) /'powtṇˌteyt/ *n.* [*count*] one who possesses great power, as a monarch. See -POT-.

po•ten•tial (pə ten′shəl) /pə'tɛnʃəl/ *adj.* [*before a noun*] **1.** possible, as opposed to actual; that might or could be true but is not yet so: *the potential uses of nuclear energy.* **2.** capable of being or becoming: *a potential danger.* —*n.* [*noncount*] **3.** possibility: *That investment has little growth potential.* **4.** a talent or ability that is present but that may or may not be developed yet: *She had great potential as a gymnast.* See -POT-.

po•ten•ti•al•i•ty (pə ten′shē al′i tē) /pəˌtɛnʃiy'ælɪtiy/ *n., pl.* **-ties. 1.** [*noncount*] the state or quality of being potential. **2.** [*count*] something potential. See -POT-.

pot•hold•er (pot′hōl′dər) /'pɒtˌhowldər/ *n.* [*count*] a thick piece of material used to protect hands from hot pots.

pot•hole (pot′hōl′) /'pɒtˌhowl/ *n.* [*count*] a hole formed in pavement, caused by traffic or weather.

po•tion (pō′shən) /'powʃən/ *n.* [*count*] a drink having powers of medicine, poison, or magic: *He drank a magic potion that changed him into a lizard.*

pot•luck (pot′luk′, -luk′) /'pɒtˌlʌk, -'lʌk/ *n.* [*count*] **1.** a meal that happens to be available without special preparation. **2.** Also called **pot′luck sup′per.** a meal, esp. for a large group, to which guests bring food to be shared:

We can have a big potluck supper and invite more people that way. **3.** whatever is available.

pot•pie (pot′pī′, -pī′) /ˈpɒtˌpay, -ˈpay/ *n.* a pie of meat and vegetables cooked in a deep dish and topped with a crust: [*count*]: *Those little frozen potpies are perfect for individual servings.* [*noncount*]: *potpie for dinner.*

pot•pour•ri (pō′pŏŏ rē′, pō′pŏŏ rē′) /ˌpowpʊˈriy, ˈpowpʊˌriy/ *n., pl.* **-ris. 1.** a fragrant mixture of dried flower petals and spices, usually kept in a jar: [*count*]: *hanging some potpourris in the closet to kill bad smells.* [*noncount*]: *You can make potpourri if you have some cloves and some flower petals.* **2.** [*count*] any mixed grouping of things: *a real potpourri of different courses to choose from.*

pot′ roast′, *n.* a cut of beef stewed in one piece in a covered pot and served in its own gravy: [*count*]: *a fine pot roast for dinner.* [*noncount*]: *He served pot roast and mashed potatoes.*

pot•sherd (pot′shûrd′) /ˈpɒtˌʃɜrd/ *n.* [*count*] a broken piece of pottery, esp. one of value in archaeology.

pot•shot (pot′shot′) /ˈpɒtˌʃɒt/ *n.* [*count*] **1.** a shot fired without careful aim: *firing potshots at passing motorists.* **2.** criticism delivered without careful thought.

pot•ted (pot′id) /ˈpɒtɪd/ *adj.* **1.** [*before a noun*] transplanted into or grown in a pot: *an office decorated with potted plants.* **2.** *Slang.* drunk.

pot•ter[1] (pot′ər) /ˈpɒtər/ *n.* [*count*] one who makes pottery.

pot•ter[2] (pot′ər) /ˈpɒtər/ *v.* **potter around,** [*no obj*] to putter; to perform unimportant tasks.

pot′ter's wheel′, *n.* [*count*] a device with a spinning, level disk upon which clay is shaped by a potter.

pot•ter•y (pot′ə rē) /ˈpɒtəriy/ *n., pl.* **-ter•ies. 1.** [*noncount*] pots, bowls, or other utensils made from baked clay or ceramic material, esp. earthenware and stoneware. **2.** [*noncount*] the art or business of a potter; ceramics. **3.** [*count*] a place where earthen vessels are made.

pot•ty (pot′ē) /ˈpɒtiy/ *n.* [*count*], *pl.* **-ties.** a seat of reduced size fitting over a toilet seat, for use by a small child.

pouch (pouch) /pawtʃ/ *n.* [*count*] **1.** a bag, sack, or small container, esp. one for small articles or quantities: *a tobacco pouch.* **2.** a bag for carrying mail: *a letter carrier's pouch.* **3.** something shaped like or resembling a bag or pocket: *pouches under his eyes.* **4.** a baglike structure in or on the body of certain animals, as kangaroos, for carrying the young.

poul•tice (pōl′tis) /ˈpowltɪs/ *n., v.,* **-ticed, -tic•ing.** —*n.* [*count*] **1.** a soft, moist mass of cloth, bread, etc., applied hot to the body to heal an injured area: *a poultice of herbs on his black eye.* —*v.* [~ + *obj*] **2.** to apply a poultice to.

poul•try (pōl′trē) /ˈpowltriy/ *n.* **1.** [*plural; used with a plural verb*] birds raised for their meat and eggs, as chickens, turkeys, etc.: *The poultry were scattered all over the farm.* **2.** [*noncount; used with a singular verb*] the meat of these birds: *Poultry is as expensive as beef.*

pounce (pouns) /pawns/ *v.,* **pounced, pounc•ing,** *n.* —*v.* **1.** [*no obj*] to swoop down, as an animal in seizing its prey: *The cat pounced that instant and caught the mouse.* **2.** [~ + *on/upon* + *obj*] to seize or attack suddenly: *The cat pounced on the mouse. We pounced on the opportunity.* —*n.* [*count*] **3.** a sudden swoop, as or as if on a victim.

pound[1] (pound) /pawnd/ *v.* **1.** to strike repeatedly with force, as with an instrument, the fist, etc.: [~ + *obj*]: *The boxer pounded his opponent to the canvas.* [*no obj*]: *The waves were pounding on the shore.* **2.** to produce (something) by or as if by striking: [~ + *obj*]: *pounded a tune on the old piano.* [~ + *out* + *obj*]: *She pounded out a tune.* **3.** [~ + *obj*] to crush into a powder or paste by beating repeatedly: *The women in the village were pounding cassava.* **4.** [*no obj*] to beat heavily or quickly, as the heart: *His heart was pounding after running up the stairs.* **5. pound away,** [*no obj*] to work with force or strength: *pounding away night after night on his report.* —*n.* [*count*] **6.** the act of pounding. —***Idiom.*** **7. pound the pavement,** *Informal.* to walk the streets repeatedly, so as to find work: *pounding the pavement for months, looking for a job.*

pound[2] (pound) /pawnd/ *n., pl.* **pounds,** (*when thought of as a group*) **pound. 1.** (in English-speaking countries) a unit of weight equal to 7000 grains, divided into 16 ounces (0.453 kg), used for ordinary commerce. *Abbr.:* lb.: [*count*]: *several pounds of meat.* [*count; singular; after a number and before a noun*]: *a twenty-pound fish.* **2.** Also called **pound sterling.** the basic monetary unit of the United Kingdom, formerly equal to 20 shillings or 240 pence: equal to 100 new pence. *Abbr.:* L; *Symbol:* £ [*count*]: *He paid several million pounds for that mansion.* [*noncount; the* + ~]: *The pound was up today in early trading on the London market.* [*count; singular; after a number and before a noun*]: *a counterfeit five-pound note.* **3.** [*count*] the basic monetary unit of various other countries, as Cyprus, Egypt, Ireland, etc.

pound[3] (pound) /pawnd/ *n.* [*count*] **1.** a place kept by public authorities for sheltering stray animals. **2.** a place where illegally parked vehicles are taken and held until a fine is paid.

-pound-, *root.* -*pound*- comes from French and ultimately from Latin, where it has the meaning "put; place." It is related to the root -PON-. This meaning is found in such words as: COMPOUND, EXPOUND, IMPOUND, PROPOUND.

pound′ cake′, *n.* a rich cake made with flour, butter, sugar, and eggs, originally made in proportions of a pound each: [*count*]: *bought a pound cake.* [*noncount*]: *The ice cream will go well with pound cake.*

pour (pôr, pōr) /pɔr, powr/ *v.* **1.** to (cause to) flow, as from one container to another, or into, over, or on something: [~ + *obj*]: *She poured some milk into her coffee.* [~ + *obj* + *obj*]: *I poured myself another drink.* [*no obj*]: *The wine poured smoothly from the bottle.* **2. pour out,** to produce or speak in or as if in a flood: [~ + *out* + *obj*]: *began to pour out her troubles.* [~ + *obj* + *out*]: *She began to pour them out.* **3.** [*no obj*] to proceed in great amount or number: *Crowds poured from the stadium after the game.* **4.** [*no obj; It* + ~] to rain heavily: *It was pouring and the streets were flooded.* —**pour′ing,** *adj.* [*before a noun*]: *He never wears a raincoat, even in the pouring rain.*

pout (pout) /pawt/ *v.* **1.** to push out the lips, esp. to show displeasure, unhappiness, or anger: [*no obj*]: *She pouted when I told her she couldn't have a dog.* [~ + *obj*]: *She pouted her lips.* **2.** [*no obj*] to look, be, or act annoyed or unhappy: *been pouting around all day.* **3.** [*used with quotations*] to say with a pout: *"I don't want to go to bed," she pouted.* —*n.* [*count*] **4.** the act of pouting: *She made a little pout when I told her the news.*

pov•er•ty (pov′ər tē) /ˈpɒvərtiy/ *n.* [*noncount*] **1.** the state of having little or no money, goods, or means of support: *the devastating effects of poverty on the human spirit.* **2.** the state of not having enough of anything that is necessary: *the poverty of my knowledge of literature.*

pov′erty-strick′en, *adj.* extremely poor.

POW, an abbreviation of: prisoner of war.

pow•der (pou′dər) /ˈpawdər/ *n.* **1.** matter pounded into a state of tiny, loose particles by crushing, grinding, etc.; a preparation in this form, as gunpowder: [*noncount*]: *some powder for after the bath.* [*count*]: *powders and other cosmetics.* **2.** [*noncount*] loose, usually fresh snow that is not grainy, wet, or packed. —*v.* [~ + *obj*] **3.** to make into powder: *powdered milk.* **4.** to apply powder to (the face, skin, etc.) as a cosmetic: *She powdered her face before going out.*

pow′der keg′, *n.* [*count*] **1.** a small metal container like a barrel, used for holding gunpowder or blasting powder. **2.** a situation that could become dangerous: *Crime in the cities is a powder keg.*

pow′der room′, *n.* LADIES' ROOM.

pow•der•y (pou′də rē) /ˈpawdəriy/ *adj.* made of or resembling powder: *powdery sand on the beach.*

pow•er (pou′ər) /ˈpawər/ *n.* **1.** ability to do or act; capability of doing something: [*noncount*]: *He no longer had the power to speak after his stroke.* [*count*]: *at the height of his powers as a pitcher.* **2.** [*noncount*] political or national strength: *the balance of power in Europe.* **3.** [*noncount*] great or marked ability to do or act: *the power of nature.* **4.** [*noncount*] the act of having control over others: *holding power over people's minds.* **5.** [*noncount*] political control in the government of a country, state, etc.: *He was in power during the worst recession in history.* **6.** authority granted to a person or persons in a particular capacity: [*count*]: *the powers of the president to command the military.* [*noncount*]: *It's not in my power to help you.* **7.** [*count*] a person or thing that has authority: *Can you convince the powers upstairs that your plan will succeed?* See *powers that be* below. **8.** [*count*] a state or nation having authority or influence: *The great powers met to decide the fate of the small country.* **9.** [*noncount*] *Physics.* work done or energy transferred. **10.** [*noncount*] mechanical or electrical energy as distinguished from hand labor: *hydroelectric power.* **11.** [*count*] *Math.* **a.** the number one obtains by multiplying a quantity by itself one or more times: *The third power of 2 is 8.* **b.** the exponent of an expression, as *3* in x^3. **12.** [*noncount*] a measure of how much a microscope or pair of binoculars magnifies an image. **—*v.*** [~ + *obj*] **13.** (of a fuel, engine, etc.) to supply force to operate (a machine): *Electricity powers the commuter trains.* **—*adj.*** [*before a noun*] **14.** driven by a motor or electricity: *a power mower; power tools.* **15.** conducting electricity: *a power cable.* **16.** *Informal.* expressing power; involving, or being like, those having influence: *The executives met for a power breakfast.* **—*Idiom.* 17. the powers that be,** [*plural*] those in highest command; the authorities: *Can you persuade the powers that be that your plan will work?*

pow•er•bro•ker or **pow•er bro•ker** (pou′ər brō′kər) /ˈpawˌər browkər/ *n.* [*count*] one who uses power and influence, esp. a politician who controls votes: *met with the mayor, the leading powerbroker in the city.*

pow•er•ful (pou′ər fəl) /ˈpawərfəl/ *adj.* of or relating to power: *one of the most powerful earthquakes ever recorded; a powerful political leader; a powerful grip; a powerful drug that made him lose his memory; a powerful speech.* —**pow′er•ful•ly,** *adv.*

pow•er•house (pou′ər hous′) /ˈpawərˌhaws/ *n.* [*count*], *pl.* **-hous•es. 1.** a place where electricity is generated and sent to homes, etc. **2.** a person or group with great ability to succeed: *Last year's team was a powerhouse of talent.*

pow•er•less (pou′ər lis) /ˈpawərlɪs/ *adj.* **1.** [*be* + ~ + *to* + *verb*] unable to produce an effect: *I was powerless to stop the crash.* **2.** lacking power to act; helpless: *powerless, weak creatures.* —**pow′er•less•ly,** *adv.*

pow′er of attor′ney, *n.* [*count; noncount*] written legal authorization for another person to act in one's place.

pow•wow (pou′wou′) /ˈpawˌwaw/ *n.* [*count*] **1.** (among North American Indians) a ceremony performed to effect the cure of disease, etc. **2.** a council or conference of, or with, Indians. **3.** (among North American Indians) a priest or shaman. **4.** any conference or meeting: *a powwow with the vice president.* **—*v.*** [*no obj*] **5.** to hold a powwow. **6.** *Informal.* to meet: *They're probably powwowing right now.*

pox (poks) /pɒks/ *n.* **1.** [*noncount*] a disease characterized by marks or pocks on the skin, as chickenpox. **2.** [*noncount*] syphilis. **3.** [*count; singular; a* + ~] a curse: *A pox on you and your bright ideas!*

pp., an abbreviation of: **1.** pages. **2.** past participle.

P.P., an abbreviation of: **1.** parcel post. **2.** postpaid. **3.** prepaid.

p.p., an abbreviation of: **1.** parcel post. **2.** past participle. **3.** postpaid.

ppr. or **p.pr.,** an abbreviation of: present participle.

PR, an abbreviation of: public relations.

prac•ti•ca•ble (prak′ti kə bəl) /ˈpræktɪkəbəl/ *adj.* **1.** capable of being done or put into practice; feasible: *Our economic plan is not practicable at the moment.* **2.** capable of being used. —**prac•ti•ca•bil•i•ty** (prak′ti kə bil′i tē) /ˌpræktɪkəˈbɪlɪtiy/ *n.* [*noncount*] —**prac′ti•ca•bly,** *adv.*

prac•ti•cal (prak′ti kəl) /ˈpræktɪkəl/ *adj.* **1.** of or relating to practice or action: *practical, not theoretical, mathematics.* **2.** made or suited for use; useful: *A station wagon is a practical car for a family.* **3.** (of a person) thinking of the results, usefulness, etc., of some action or procedure; sensible: *She's much too practical to marry someone who has no future.*

prac•ti•cal•i•ty (prak′ti kal′i tē) /ˌpræktɪˈkælɪtiy/ *n.* the part of something that deals with or concerns practical events as opposed to theory: [*noncount*]: *a sense of practicality in dealing with problems.* [*count*]: *You can't ignore the practicalities.*

prac′tical joke′, *n.* [*count*] a playful trick in which the victim is placed in an embarrassing position: *On April Fool's Day the students played practical jokes on their teachers.* —**prac′tical jok′er,** *n.* [*count*]

prac•ti•cal•ly (prak′tik lē) /ˈpræktɪkliy/ *adv.* **1.** in a practical manner: *to think practically.* **2.** from a practical point of view. **3.** almost; nearly; virtually: *practically certain that he'll run for office.*

prac′tical nurse′, *n.* [*count*] a person with less training than a registered nurse.

prac•tice (prak′tis) /ˈpræktɪs/ *n., v.,* **-ticed, -tic•ing. —*n.* 1.** [*noncount*] a way of doing something that is normal or customary: *office practice.* **2.** [*count*] a habit; custom: *to make a practice of borrowing money.* **3.** [*noncount*] the act of doing something systematically, as an exercise, for the purpose of learning it well: *Throwing a good curve ball takes practice.* **4.** [*noncount*] a condition arrived at by experience or exercise: *I'm out of practice because I haven't played tennis in years.* **5.** [*noncount*] the action or process of carrying something out: *to put a scheme into practice.* **6.** [*count*] the business of a profession, esp. law or medicine: *a law practice.* **—*v.* 7.** [~ + *obj*] to perform or do (something) as a habit or usually: *to practice a regimen of exercise.* **8.** to follow or observe as a habit or by custom: [~ + *obj*]: *to practice one's religion.* [*no obj*]: *He's a Catholic but he's no longer practicing.* **9.** to do as a profession, art, or occupation: [~ + *obj*]: *He practices law.* [*no obj*]: *He's no longer practicing as an attorney.* **10.** to perform on or do repeatedly in order to gain skill or ability: [~ + *obj*]: *practiced the trumpet every day.* [*no obj*]: *practices on the trombone every day.* Also, *Brit.,* **practise** (for defs. 7–10). **—Syn.** See CUSTOM.

prac•ticed (prak′tist) /ˈpræktɪst/ *adj.* skilled or expert because of practice: *a practiced English accent.*

prac•ti•cum (prak′ti kəm) /ˈpræktɪkəm/ *n.* [*count*] a course of study in which the student works or undergoes practical experience in a field.

prac•ti•tion•er (prak tish′ə nər) /prækˈtɪʃənər/ *n.* [*count*] **1.** a person working in the practice of a profession or occupation: *a medical practitioner.* **2.** one who practices or works at something mentioned: *They were practitioners of the great art of lying.*

prag•mat•ic (prag mat′ik) /prægˈmætɪk/ *adj.* concerned with practical considerations of one's actions, and less concerned with principles; having a practical point of view: *made a purely pragmatic decision to go along with the boss.* Also, **prag•mat′i•cal.** —**prag•mat′i•cal•ly,** *adv.*

prag•ma•tism (prag′mə tiz′əm) /ˈprægməˌtɪzəm/ *n.* [*noncount*] **1.** character or conduct that emphasizes practical results rather than principle: *made her decision based more on pragmatism than on any desire to serve the people.* **2.** a philosophical movement or system emphasizing practical consequences as the criterion in determining truth, meaning, or value. —**prag′ma•tist,** *n.* [*count*], *adj.*

prai•rie (prâr′ē) /ˈprɛəriy/ *n.* [*count*] a large, wide, level or slightly hilly area of land, mostly without trees, originally covered with grasses.

prai′rie schoon′er, *n.* [*count*] a covered wagon used by pioneers in crossing the prairies and plains of North America.

praise (prāz) /preyz/ *n., v.,* **praised, prais•ing. —*n.*** [*noncount*] **1.** the act of expressing approval or admiration: *Children need praise.* **2.** the offering of worship, as to God. **—*v.*** [~ + *obj*] **3.** to express admiration of; commend: *praised her for her good work.* **4.** to offer worship to (a deity), as in words or song: *Let us join together and praise God.* **—*Idiom.* 5. sing one's** or **someone's praises,** to praise (too) highly: *You're always singing your own praises, but other people work here, too.*

praise•wor•thy (prāz′wûr′thē) /ˈpreyzˌwɜrðiy/ *adj.* deserving of praise: *a praiseworthy motive.* —**praise•wor•thi•ly** (prāz′wûr′thə lē) /ˈpreyzˌwɜrðəliy/ *adv.* —**praise′wor′thi•ness,** *n.* [*noncount*]

pra•line (prā′lēn, prä′-) /ˈpreyliyn, ˈprɑ-/ *n.* a kind of candy made of nuts, esp. almonds or pecans, and sugar cooked until it is like hard caramel: [*noncount*]: *a piece of praline.* [*count*]: *buying some pralines at the store.*

prance (prans) /præns/ *v.,* **pranced, pranc•ing,** *n.* **—*v.* 1.** [*no obj*] to walk in a proud manner and try to get attention, as by moving with exaggerated steps: *She pranced into the room with her high heels clicking.* **2.** to (cause a horse to) spring from the hind legs, or move by springing: [*no obj*]: *The horse was prancing around the corral.* [~ + *obj*]: *The rider pranced the horse around the corral.* **—*n.*** [*count*] **3.** the act of prancing. —**pranc′er,** *n.* [*count*] —**pranc′ing•ly,** *adv.*

prank (prangk) /præŋk/ *n.* [*count*] an amusing or playful trick: *a silly schoolboy prank.* —**prank′ster,** *n.* [*count*]

prate (prāt) /preyt/ *v.,* **prat•ed, prat•ing.** to talk too much; babble: [*no obj*]: *She prated on about her family and he slowly began to doze off.* [~ + *that clause*]: *He prated that she would never succeed.* —**prat′er,** *n.* [*count*]

prat•fall (prat′fôl′) /ˈprætˌfɔl/ *n.* [*count*] **1.** a fall on the buttocks, esp. when thought of as comical or causing embarrassment. **2.** an embarrassing mistake or defeat.

prat•tle (prat′l) /ˈprætl̩/ *v.,* **-tled, -tling,** *n.* **—*v.* 1.** to talk in a simple-minded way; chatter; prate: [*no obj*]: *prattling on about their jobs and their bosses.* [~ + *that clause*]:

They prattled that it would be great fun to see such a star. **—n.** [*noncount*] **2.** chatter; babble.

prawn (prôn) /prɔn/ *n.* [*count*] **1.** a small shrimplike edible sea animal. **—v.** [*no obj*] **2.** to catch prawns, as for food.

pray (prā) /prey/ *v.* to offer praise or thanks to or to petition (God or an object of worship): [*no obj*]: *She knelt down and began to pray.* [~ + *to* + *obj*]: *She prays to God every night.* [~ + *for* + *obj*]: *to pray for rain.* [~ + *(that) clause*]: *She prayed that he would not be killed in the war.*

prayer (prâr) /prɛər/ *n.* **1.** [*count*] a devout request to a deity: *Her prayer was that he would return home safely.* **2.** [*count*] an established formula used in praying: *the Lord's Prayer.* **3.** [*noncount*] the act or practice of praying: *He believed in the power of prayer.* **4. prayers,** [*plural*] a religious practice consisting mainly of prayer: *Did you say your prayers?* **5.** [*count*] something prayed for: *Her only prayer is that she never turn old.* **6.** [*count; used with negative words or phrases, or in questions*] a very small hope or chance: *We don't have a prayer of winning.*

pray′ing man′tis, *n.* MANTIS.

pre-, *prefix.* **1.** *pre-* comes from Latin, where it has the meaning "before, in front of," "prior to, in advance of," "being more than, surpassing": *pre-* + *-dict* → *predict (= say in advance of something); pre-* + *eminent* → *preeminent (= surpassing or being more than eminent); pre-* + *face* → *preface (= something written in front of a book, etc.)* **2.** *pre-* is also attached to verbs to form new verbs that refer to an activity taking place before or instead of the usual occurrence of the same activity: *pre-* + *board* → *preboard (= to board an airplane before the other passengers); pre-* + *cook* → *precook (= cook before regular cooking).* **3.** *pre-* is also used in forming adjectives that refer to a period of time before the event, period, person, etc., mentioned in the root: *pre-* + *school* → *preschool (= before the age of starting school); pre-* + *war* → *prewar (= before the war started).*

preach (prēch) /priytʃ/ *v.* **1.** to deliver or give (a talk about religion): [*no obj*]: *The new minister is preaching at that church next week.* [~ + *obj*]: *Jesus preached redemption.* [~ + *that clause*]: *preached that we should love our neighbor as we love ourselves.* **2.** [~ + *obj*] to call for (moral conduct, etc.) as being right: *preaching peace while preparing for war.* **3.** [*no obj*] to give advice, esp. in an annoying manner: *always preaching at her to clean up her room.* —**preach′ment,** *n.* [*noncount*] —**preach′y,** *adj.,* **-i•er, -i•est:** *That teacher gets too preachy sometimes.*

preach•er (prē′chər) /ˈpriytʃər/ *n.* [*count*] **1.** one who preaches or gives a sermon. **2.** a member of the clergy, as a priest.

pre•am•ble (prē′am′bəl, prē am′-) /ˈpriyˌæmbəl, priyˈæm-/ *n.* **1.** an introductory statement; preface: [*count*]: *a short preamble before the main part of his speech.* [*noncount*]: *Without preamble, he launched into a vicious attack on her character.* **2.** [*count*] the introductory part of a law, constitution, etc., declaring its intention: *The preamble to the Constitution begins with the words "We the people."*

pre•ar•range (prē′ə rānj′) /ˌpriyəˈreyndʒ/ *v.* [~ + *obj*], **-ranged, -rang•ing.** to arrange in advance: *At a prearranged signal the chorus rose and began to sing.* —**pre′ar•range′ment,** *n.* [*noncount*]: *By prearrangement the president spoke first.*

pre•can•cer•ous (prē kan′sər əs) /priyˈkænsərəs/ *adj.* showing changes that may be the first stages before a tumor develops: *cells with precancerous growths.*

pre•car•i•ous (pri kâr′ē əs) /prɪˈkɛəriyəs/ *adj.* **1.** dependent on circumstances that are beyond one's control; uncertain: *a precarious livelihood.* **2.** dangerous because insecure or unsteady: *a precarious hold on the rope.* —**pre•car′i•ous•ly,** *adv.*: *hung precariously from the top of the cable car.*

pre•cau•tion (pri kô′shən) /prɪˈkɔʃən/ *n.* [*count*] an action taken in advance to avoid harm: *took precautions to prevent anyone from reading her computer files.* See -CAUT-.

pre•cau•tion•ar•y (prē kô′shə ner′ē) /priyˈkɔʃəˌnɛriy/ *adj.* **1.** of or relating to precautions. **2.** calling for caution: *precautionary warnings.* See -CAUT-.

pre•cede (pri sēd′) /prɪˈsiyd/ *v.* [~ + *obj*], **-ced•ed, -ced•ing.** to go before, as in place, position, or rank: *He preceded me into the room.* See -CEDE-.

prec•e•dence (pres′i dəns, pri sēd′ns) /ˈprɛsɪdəns, prɪˈsiydns/ *n.* [*noncount*] **1.** the act or fact of preceding. **2.** the right to be dealt with or placed before others because of order, rank, or importance: *This problem takes precedence over all the others.* See -CEDE-.

prec•e•dent (*n.* pres′i dənt; *adj.* pri sēd′nt, pres′i dənt) / *n.* ˈprɛsɪdənt; *adj.* prɪˈsiydnt, ˈprɛsɪdənt/ *n.* **1.** [*count*] an instance that may serve as an example for allowing later, similar situations. **2.** [*count*] a legal decision serving as a rule or pattern governing similar cases that follow: *The lawyer found a precedent from a court case in the 19th century.* **3.** [*noncount*] established practice; custom: *to break with precedent.* **—adj. 4.** preceding; coming before. See -CEDE-.

pre•ced•ing (pri sē′ding) /prɪˈsiydɪŋ/ *adj.* [*before a noun*] that precedes; coming before; previous: *In the preceding class we discussed verb tense.* See -CEDE-.

pre•cept (prē′sept) /ˈpriysɛpt/ *n.* [*count*] a direction given as a rule of behavior, esp. moral behavior. See -CEP-.

pre•cep•tor (pri sep′tər, prē′sep-) /prɪˈsɛptər, ˈpriysɛp-/ *n.* [*count*] **1.** an instructor; teacher; tutor. **2.** the head of a school.

-preci-, *root.* *-preci-* comes from French and Latin, where it has the meaning "value; worth; price." This meaning is found in such words as: APPRECIATE, DEPRECIATE, PRECIOUS, PRICE, SEMIPRECIOUS.

pre•cinct (prē′singkt) /ˈpriysɪŋkt/ *n.* [*count*] **1.** a district, as of a city, marked out for election purposes or for police protection. **2.** Also called **pre′cinct house′.** the police station in such a district: *The police returned to the precinct.* **3. precincts,** [*plural*] the regions surrounding a place; surroundings; environs.

pre•cious (presh′əs) /ˈprɛʃəs/ *adj.* **1.** of high price or great value: *precious metals.* **2.** considered of value for some quality that is not material: *precious memories.* **3.** dear; beloved: *a precious friend.* **4.** designating a stone, esp. a diamond, etc., valued as rare and beautiful and used in jewelry: *precious stones.* **5.** acting too refined; affected: *The child actress was just a little too precious.* **—n.** [*count; usually singular*] **6.** a dearly beloved person; darling: *Here, my precious, come and eat.* **—adv. 7.** extremely; very: *We have precious little time.* —**pre′cious•ly,** *adv.* —**pre′cious•ness,** *n.* [*noncount*] See -PRECI-.

prec•i•pice (pres′ə pis) /ˈprɛsəpɪs/ *n.* [*count*] a cliff with a steep or overhanging face.

pre•cip•i•tant (pri sip′i tnt) /prɪˈsɪpɪtnt/ *adj.* **1.** hasty or sudden; precipitate. **—n.** [*count*] **2.** *Chemistry.* something that causes precipitation.

pre•cip•i•tate (*v.* pri sip′i tāt′; *adj., n.* -tit, -tāt′) / *v.* prɪˈsɪpɪˌteyt; *adj., n.* -tɪt, -ˌteyt/ *v.,* **-tat•ed, -tat•ing,** *adj., n.* **—v. 1.** [~ + *obj*] to speed up (an event); to bring about too soon: *to precipitate a crisis.* **2.** [~ + *obj*] to join in suddenly: *to precipitate oneself into a struggle.* **3.** [~ + *obj*] to separate (a substance) in solid form from a solution. **4.** [*no obj*] to fall to the earth's surface as a form of water; to rain, snow, etc. **—adj. 5.** done or made without enough thought or planning ahead of time; too sudden: *a precipitate marriage.* **6.** proceeding with great haste: *a precipitate retreat.* **—n.** [*noncount*] **7.** a substance precipitated from a solution. **8.** moisture in the form of rain, snow, etc. —**pre•cip′i•tate•ly,** *adv.*

pre•cip•i•ta•tion (pri sip′i tā′shən) /prɪˌsɪpɪˈteyʃən/ *n.* [*noncount*] **1. a.** falling water that has been condensed in the atmosphere, as rain, snow, or hail: *a slim chance of precipitation.* **b.** the amount of rain, snow, etc., that has fallen at a given place within a given period of time: *Precipitation totaled only 1 inch per year in that desert.* **2.** the act of precipitating; the state of being precipitated, as of a substance from a solution.

pre•cip•i•tous (pri sip′i təs) /prɪˈsɪpɪtəs/ *adj.* **1.** like a precipice; very steep: *a precipitous wall of rock; precipitous mountain trails.* **2.** happening quickly or suddenly; precipitate.

pré•cis (prā sē′, prā′sē) /preyˈsiy, ˈpreysiy/ *n., pl.* **-cis** (-sēz′, -sēz) /-ˈsiyz, -siyz/ *v.,* **-cised, -cis•ing. —n.** [*count*] **1.** a short summary **—v.** [~ + *obj*] **2.** to make a précis of. See -CISE-.

pre•cise (pri sīs′) /prɪˈsays/ *adj.* **1.** definitely stated, defined, or fixed: *clear, precise directions.* **2.** [*before a noun*] being that one and no other: *bought the precise dress I wanted.* **3.** exact in expressing oneself: *He's very precise, so if he said "today," then he means "today."* **4.** carefully distinct: *careful, almost too-precise pronunciation.* **5.** exact in measuring, recording, etc.: *a precise instrument.* —**pre•cise′ness,** *n.* [*noncount*] See -CISE-.

pre•cise•ly (pri sīs′lē) /prɪˈsaysliy/ *adv.* **1.** exactly; done in an accurate manner: *Measure as precisely as possible.*

2. (used to express exact or intensified agreement or confirmation): *That's precisely why I want to see you.* See -CISE-.

pre•ci•sion (pri sizh′ən) /prɪ'sɪʒən/ *n.* [*noncount*] **1.** the state or quality of being precise: *His writing is a model of clarity and precision.* **2.** mechanical or scientific exactness: *That lens was ground with great precision.* **—*adj.* 3.** of or relating to great precision: *precision instruments.* See -CISE-.

pre•clude (pri klo͞od′) /prɪ'kluwd/ *v.* [~ + *obj*], **-clud•ed, -clud•ing.** to prevent the presence of; exclude the possibility of: *evidence that precluded a conviction.* —**pre•clu•sion** (pri klo͞o′zhən) /prɪ'kluwʒən/ *n.* [*noncount*]

pre•co•cious (pri kō′shəs) /prɪ'kowʃəs/ *adj.* unusually advanced or mature: *a precocious child.* —**pre•co′cious•ness,** *n.* [*noncount*] —**pre•coc•i•ty** (pri kos′i tē) /prɪ'kɒsɪtiy/ *n.* [*noncount*]

pre•cog•ni•tion (prē′kog nish′ən) /ˌpriykɒg'nɪʃən/ *n.* [*noncount*] knowledge of a future event or situation, esp. through extrasensory means: *a prediction made through precognition.* See -GNOS-.

pre-Co•lum•bi•an (prē′kə lum′bē ən) /ˌpriykə'lʌmbiyən/ *adj.* of or relating to the Americas before Columbus.

pre•con•ceived (prē′kən sēvd′) /ˌpriykən'siyvd/ *adj.* (of an opinion) formed beforehand, esp. from bias: *to combat preconceived notions.* See -CEIVE-.

pre•con•cep•tion (prē′kən sep′shən) /ˌpriykən'sɛpʃən/ *n.* [*count*] an opinion based on bias, with no allowance made for knowledge or evidence: *foolish preconceptions about the dangers of catching AIDS by shaking hands.* See -CEP-.

pre•con•di•tion (prē′kən dish′ən) /ˌpriykən'dɪʃən/ *n.* [*count*] **1.** something necessary for a result; a condition: *Increased sales were a precondition for her promotion.* **—*v.*** [~ + *obj*] **2.** to put a special preparation on (a surface) before a subsequent process, etc.: *to precondition a surface to receive paint.*

pre•cur•sor (pri kûr′sər, prē′kûr-) /prɪ'kɜrsər, 'priykɜr-/ *n.* [*count*] **1.** a person or thing that comes before another, as in a method; predecessor: *my precursor in that job.* **2.** a person, animal, or thing regarded as a sign or signal of something to come: *The first robin is a precursor of spring.* **3.** a substance that is transformed into another. —**pre•cur•so•ry** (pri kûr′sə rē) /prɪ'kɜrsəriy/ *adj.* See -CUR-.

pre•date (prē′dāt′) /'priy'deyt/ *v.* [~ + *obj*], **-dat•ed, -dat•ing. 1.** to put a date on (something) earlier than the actual date: *to predate a check.* **2.** to precede (something else) in time: *Spoken language predated written language.*

pred•a•tor (pred′ə tər, -tôr′) /'prɛdətər, -ˌtɔr/ *n.* [*count*] **1.** any organism that exists by preying on another: *The hawk is a predator.* **2.** one who acts like such an organism, as by robbing or killing other people for gain.

pred•a•to•ry (pred′ə tôr′ē, -tōr′ē) /'prɛdəˌtɔriy, -ˌtowriy/ *adj.* of or relating to predators: *Predatory gangs roamed the streets.*

pre•de•cease (prē′di sēs′) /ˌpriydɪ'siys/ *v.* [~ + *obj*], **-ceased, -ceas•ing.** to die before (another person).

pred•e•ces•sor (pred′ə ses′ər) /'prɛdəˌsɛsər/ *n.* [*count*] **1.** one who comes before another in an office, etc.: *My predecessor was coming to me to ask for a job!* **2.** something replaced by something else: *This car's predecessor lacks many of the features of the new version.* See -CEDE-.

pre•des•ti•na•tion (pri des′tə nā′shən, prē′des-) /prɪˌdɛstə'neyʃən, ˌpriydɛs-/ *n.* [*noncount*] the belief that God has already decided whatever comes to pass, esp. salvation or damnation, and that humans can do nothing to change these results.

pre•des•tine (pri des′tin) /prɪ'dɛstɪn/ *v.* [~ + *obj*], **-tined, -tin•ing.** to foreordain; predetermine: *According to some religions, God, or fate, has predestined everything you'll do today.*

pre•de•ter•mine (prē′di tûr′min) /ˌpriydɪ'tɜrmɪn/ *v.* [~ + *obj*], **-mined, -min•ing. 1.** to settle in advance: *The result was predetermined even before we met.* **2.** to ordain in advance; predestine. —**pre•de•ter•mi•na•tion** (prē′di tûr′mə nā′shən) /ˌpriydɪˌtɜrmə'neyʃən/ *n.* [*noncount*] See -TERM-.

pre•de•ter•min•er (prē′di tûr′mə nər) /ˌpriydɪ'tɜrmənər/ *n.* [*count*] a word in English that may be placed before an article or before another determiner: *The word* all *in the phrase* all the children *is a predeterminer. Predeterminers are often words that express how much or how many.*

pre•dic•a•ment (pri dik′ə mənt) /prɪ'dɪkəmənt/ *n.* [*count*] an unpleasantly difficult situation: *He found himself in one predicament after another.*

pred•i•cate (*v.* pred′i kāt′; *adj., n.* -kit) / *v.* 'prɛdɪˌkeyt; *adj., n.* -kɪt/ *v.,* **-cat•ed, -cat•ing,** *adj., n.* **—*v.*** [~ + *obj*] **1.** to declare; affirm; assert; say something. **2.** to imply: *Their apology predicates a new attitude.* **3.** [~ + *obj* + *on* + *obj*] to base (behavior, etc.) on some stated belief, etc.: *decisions predicated on statistics.* **—*adj.* 4.** belonging to or used in the predicate of a sentence. **—*n.*** [*count*] **5.** a unit of a sentence that is one of the two main parts of it (the other being the subject), and that consists of a verb and any words belonging with the verb, as objects, complements, or adverbs: *The predicate of the sentence* The package is here *is the phrase* is here. *The predicate often expresses the action performed by, or condition attributed to, the subject.* —**pred•i•ca•tion** (pred′i kā′shən) /ˌprɛdɪ'keyʃən/ *n.* [*noncount*] —**pred•i•ca•tive** (pred′i kā′tiv, -kə-) /'prɛdɪˌkeytɪv, -kə-/ *adj.*

pred′i•cate ad′jective (pred′i kit) /'prɛdɪkɪt/ *n.* [*count*] an adjective that comes after a verb, esp. after the verb *be: In "He is ill," "ill" is a predicate adjective.* —**Usage.** The symbol used in this book for a predicate adjective or phrase is "[*be* + ~]", suggesting that in most cases a predicate adjective will follow the verb BE or some similar verb like APPEAR or BECOME: *He is ill. He appears ill. He became ill.*

pre•dict (pri dikt′) /prɪ'dɪkt/ *v.* to declare in advance; foretell: [~ + *obj*]: *He predicted the defeat months before the election.* [~ + *(that) clause*]: *She predicted that you would be elected.* —**pre•dic′tor,** *n.* [*count*]: *That state is a good predictor of what will happen in the rest of the country.* See -DICT-.

pre•dict•a•ble (pri dik′tə bəl) /prɪ'dɪktəbəl/ *adj.* that can be predicted: *Her behavior is fairly predictable.* —**pre•dict′ab•ly,** *adv.: His theory implies that large groups of people will behave predictably.* See -DICT-.

pre•dic•tion (pri dik′shən) /prɪ'dɪkʃən/ *n.* **1.** [*count*] an example of predicting: *His prediction was that the election would be a landslide.* **2.** [*noncount*] an act of predicting: *He wasn't going to depend on the art of prediction; he would wait for real results.* See -DICT-.

pre•di•gest (prē′di jest′, -dī-) /ˌpriydɪ'dʒɛst, -day-/ *v.* [~ + *obj*] **1.** to treat (food) by a process similar to digestion so that it is more easily digestible. **2.** to make simpler, as for easier understanding: *material that has been predigested for less advanced students.* See -GEST-.

pre•di•lec•tion (pred′l ek′shən, prēd′-) /ˌprɛdl̩'ɛkʃən, ˌpriyd-/ *n.* [*count*] a tendency to think favorably of something in particular; preference; liking: *a predilection for fast cars.* See -LEG-.

pre•dis•pose (prē′di spōz′) /ˌpriydɪ'spowz/ *v.,* **-posed, -pos•ing. 1.** [~ + *obj* + *to* + *obj*] to make susceptible to (something, as a disease, etc.): *genetic factors predisposing me to diabetes.* **2.** to influence (someone) in favor of (something or someone else): [~ + *obj* + *to* + *obj*]: *His happy, caring upbringing predisposed him to a similar attitude of caring for others.* [~ + *obj* + *to* + *verb*]: *The unkindness shown him as a child predisposed him to act cruelly toward others.* See -POS-.

pre•dis•po•si•tion (prē dis′pə zish′ən, prē′dis-) /priyˌdɪspə'zɪʃən, ˌpriydɪs-/ *n.* [*count*] **1.** a tendency to behave in a certain way, esp. to favor something: *a predisposition to think that way.* **2.** a tendency of the body to be likely to suffer from a disease: *a genetically inherited predisposition for color blindness.* See -POS-.

pre•dom•i•nant (pri dom′ə nənt) /prɪ'dɒmənənt/ *adj.* **1.** having authority or influence over others; preeminent: *the predominant ethnic group in that country.* **2.** greater in number or amount: *the predominant color of a painting.* —**pre•dom′i•nance,** *n.* [*noncount*] —**pre•dom′i•nant•ly,** *adv.: Their student population is predominantly white and middle-class.*

pre•dom•i•nate (pri dom′ə nāt′) /prɪ'dɒməˌneyt/ *v.* [*no obj*], **-nat•ed, -nat•ing. 1.** to be the stronger or leading element or force: *Blues and greens predominated in the painting.* **2.** to have or exert controlling power: *Good sense predominated over anger.*

pre•em•i•nent or **pre-em•i•nent** (prē em′ə nənt) /priy'ɛmənənt/ *adj.* above or before others in some quality; superior; outstanding: *the preeminent physicist.* —**pre•em′i•nence,** *n.* [*noncount*] —**pre•em′i•nent•ly,** *adv.*

pre•empt or **pre-empt** (prē empt′) /priy'ɛmpt/ *v.* [~ + *obj*] **1.** to acquire (something) before someone else; take for oneself. **2.** to take the place of by being more important, or because of rescheduling, etc.; supplant: *A special* news report on the earthquake preempted the game show.* **3.** to prevent (something anticipated) by acting first; head off: *The rival company preempted our takeover bid by selling its stock.* —**pre•emp′tion,** *n.* [*noncount*]

pre•emp•tive (prē emp′tiv) /priy'ɛmptɪv/ *adj.* [*often: before a noun*] of or relating to preempting: *a preemptive strike against the enemy.*

preen (prēn) /priyn/ *v.* **1.** [~ + *obj*] (of a bird) to clean or dress (its feathers, etc.) with the beak or tongue. **2.** to dress (oneself) carefully or smartly; primp: [*no obj*]: *stood preening in front of the mirror.* [~ + *oneself*]: *preening himself in front of the mirror.* **3.** to be proud and show one's appreciation of oneself because of personal quality, etc.: [*no obj*]: *He stood there preening as the teacher congratulated him.* [~ + *oneself*]: *preening herself on her accomplishments.*

pref., an abbreviation of: **1.** preface. **2.** preferred. **3.** prefix.

pre•fab (*adj., n.* prē′fab′; *v.* prē fab′) / *adj., n.* 'priy,fæb; *v.* priy'fæb/ *adj., n., v.,* **-fabbed, -fab•bing.** *Informal.* —*adj.* [*before a noun*] **1.** prefabricated. —*n.* [*count*] **2.** something prefabricated, as a building. —*v.* [~ + *obj*] **3.** to prefabricate.

pre•fab•ri•cate (prē fab′ri kāt′) /priy'fæbrɪ,keyt/ *v.* [~ + *obj*], **-cat•ed, -cat•ing. 1.** to build, put together, or construct beforehand. **2.** to manufacture (something) in standardized sections ready for quick assembly, as buildings: *a prefabricated hut.* —**pre•fab•ri•ca•tion** (prē′fab-ri kā′shən) /,priyfæbrɪ'keyʃən/ *n.* [*noncount*]

pref•ace (pref′is) /'prɛfɪs/ *n., v.,* **-aced, -ac•ing.** —*n.* [*count*] **1.** a statement in the front of a book by the author or editor, setting forth the book's purpose, etc.: *The preface occupied a mere one page.* **2.** an introductory part, as of a speech. —*v.* [~ + *obj*] **3.** to provide with a preface: *He prefaced his speech with remarks about his opponent.* —**pref•a•to•ry** (pref′ə tôr′ē, -tōr′ē) /'prɛfə,tɔriy, -,towriy/ *adj.*

pre•fect (prē′fekt) /'priyfɛkt/ *n.* [*count*] a person in an important position of authority, as a chief administrative official of a department of France.

pre•fer (pri fûr′) /prɪ'fɜr/ *v.* [*not: be* + *~-ing*], **-ferred, -fer•ring. 1.** to set or hold before or above other persons or things: [~ + *obj*]: *She prefers cheese, if you have some.* [~ + *verb-ing*]: *She prefers running to walking.* [~ + *obj* + *to* + *obj*]: *I prefer school to work.* [~ + *to* + *verb*]: *She prefers to take a nap after a big meal.* [~ + *that clause*]: *He preferred that we meet him outside his apartment.* [*no obj*]: *I'll come with you or, if you prefer, I'll wait outside.* —***Idiom.* 2. prefer charges,** to make or place an accusation of wrongdoing, a crime, etc., against another. See -FER-.

pref•er•a•ble (pref′ər ə bəl, pref′rə- *or, often,* pri fûr′-) /'prɛfərəbəl, 'prɛfrə- *or, often,* prɪ'fɜr-/ *adj.* more desirable; worthy to be preferred: *Driving there is preferable to walking.* —**pref′er•a•bly,** *adv.*: *They're looking for a new car, preferably one that is not very expensive.*

pref•er•ence (pref′ər əns, pref′rəns) /'prɛfərəns, 'prɛfrəns/ *n.* **1.** [*noncount*] the act of preferring; the state of being preferred: *showing preference in hiring practices.* **2.** [*count*] something preferred: *My preference would be for a vegetarian meal.* **3.** [*noncount*] the favoring of one country over others in international trade. See -FER-.

pref•er•en•tial (pref′ə ren′shəl) /,prɛfə'rɛnʃəl/ *adj.* showing or reflecting a preference: *She received preferential treatment from the senator because she was one of his biggest contributors.* —**pref′er•en′tial•ly,** *adv.*: *He was always treated preferentially in school.* See -FER-.

pre•fer•ment (pri fûr′mənt) /prɪ'fɜrmənt/ *n.* [*noncount*] **1.** the act of preferring; the state of being preferred. **2.** advancement or promotion in a job. See -FER-.

pre•fig•ure (prē fig′yər) /priy'fɪgyər/ *v.* [~ + *obj*], **-ured, -ur•ing.** to show or represent (something) beforehand by something similar: *The duel between the evil emperor and his trusted knight in the movie prefigures the battle between the hero and villain at the end.*

pre•fix (*n.* prē′fiks; *v. also* prē fiks′) /*n.* 'priyfɪks; *v. also* priy'fɪks/ *n.* [*count*] **1.** an affix placed before a base or another prefix, as *un-* in *unkind,* and *un-* and *re-* in *unrewarding.* —*v.* [~ + *obj*] **2.** to fix or put before or in front. **3.** to add as a prefix. See -FIX-.

preg•nan•cy (preg′nən sē) /'prɛgnənsiy/ *n., pl.* **-cies.** the state of being pregnant: [*noncount*]: *She gained weight during pregnancy.* [*count*]: *a long pregnancy.*

preg•nant (preg′nənt) /'prɛgnənt/ *adj.* **1.** in the process of having a child or offspring developing in the body, as a woman or female mammal: *pregnant with her fourth child.* **2.** [*before a noun*] full of meaning; highly significant: *a pregnant pause.*

-prehend-, *root.* -*prehend-* comes from Latin, where it has the meaning "seize; grasp hold of; hold on to." This meaning is found in such words as: APPREHEND, COMPREHEND, MISAPPREHEND, PREHENSILE. See -PRIS-.

pre•hen•sile (pri hen′sil, -sīl) /prɪ'hɛnsɪl, -sayl/ *adj.* made for seizing or grasping: *a monkey's prehensile tail.* See -PREHEND-.

pre•his•tor•ic (prē′hi stôr′ik, -stor′-, prē′i-) /,priyhɪ'stɔrɪk, -'stɒr-, ,priyɪ-/ also **pre′his•tor′i•cal,** *adj.* of or relating to the time before history: *prehistoric cave paintings.*

pre•judge (prē juj′) /priy'dʒʌdʒ/ *v.* [~ + *obj*], **-judged, -judg•ing.** to pass judgment on (someone or something) before knowing all the facts: *He may have prejudged the case when he saw them together and assumed a conspiracy.* —**pre•judg′ment,** *n.* [*noncount*]: *a history of prejudgment.* [*count*]: *unfounded prejudgments.* See -JUD-.

prej•u•dice (prej′ə dis) /'prɛdʒədɪs/ *n., v.,* **-diced, -dic•ing.** —*n.* **1.** an act or instance of prejudging, esp. against a racial, religious, or national group: [*noncount*]: *showing his prejudice against women drivers; prejudice against foreigners.* [*count*]: *prejudices against black people.* **2.** [*noncount*] such feelings thought of as a group: *the fight against prejudice.* **3.** any opinion or feeling held before careful thought: [*noncount*]: *prejudice in favor of hiring women.* [*count*]: *his prejudices against Oriental food.* **4.** [*noncount*] damage or injury; harm or detriment: *a law that operated to the prejudice of the majority.* —*v.* [~ + *obj*] **5.** to affect (someone) with a prejudice: *Those acts of violence against his friends prejudiced him against anyone who was white. The judge warned against any more remarks aimed at prejudicing the jury.* —***Idiom.* 6. without prejudice,** without giving up or losing any rights or privileges of the party concerned. See -JUD-. —**Syn.** See BIAS.

prej•u•di•cial (prej′ə dish′əl) /,prɛdʒə'dɪʃəl/ *adj.* causing prejudice: *prejudicial remarks.* See -JUD-.

pre•kin•der•gar•ten (prē kin′dər gär′tn) /priy'kɪndər,gærtn̩/ *n.* **1.** a school for children not yet old enough for kindergarten: [*count*]: *several prekindergartens in the neighborhood.* [*noncount*]: *She started prekindergarten last week.* —*adj.* [*before a noun*] **2.** of or relating to a school for children not yet old enough for kindergarten: *prekindergarten schools.* **3.** of or relating to children not yet old enough for kindergarten: *At prekindergarten ages, how much learning will really go on?*

prel•ate (prel′it) /'prɛlɪt/ *n.* [*count*] a high-ranking member of the clergy, a bishop. See -LAT-[1].

pre•lim•i•nar•y (pri lim′ə ner′ē) /prɪ'lɪmə,nɛriy/ *adj., n., pl.* **-nar•ies.** —*adj.* **1.** going before and leading up to the main part; preparatory: *The preliminary details had been worked out.* —*n.* [*count*] **2.** something that goes before and serves to lead up to something else, as an introductory step or stage in some development: *Once the social preliminaries were over, the two sides got down to serious discussion.* **3.** a sports or athletic contest that takes place before the main event on the program. See -LIM-.

pre•lit•er•ate (prē lit′ər it) /priy'lɪtərɪt/ *adj.* lacking a written language: *a preliterate culture.*

prel•ude (prel′yōōd, prāl′-, prā′lōōd, prē′-) /'prɛlyuwd, 'preyl-, 'preyluwd, 'priy-/ *n.* [*count*] **1.** some action that comes before another action; any action that goes before another: *The initial assault on the town was just a prelude to the full-scale attack that began the next day.* **2.** *Music.* a relatively short piece of music serving to introduce another. See -LUD-.

pre•mar•i•tal (prē mar′i tl) /priy'mærɪtl̩/ *adj.* coming before marriage: *premarital sex.* Compare PRENUPTIAL.

pre•ma•ture (prē′mə chŏŏr′, -tŏŏr′, -tyŏŏr′) /,priymə'tʃʊr, -'tʊr, -'tyʊr/ *adj.* **1.** occurring, coming, or done too soon: *made a premature announcement that he had won the election.* **2.** born before the normal amount of time of full development; preterm: *premature babies.* —**pre′ma•ture′ly,** *adv.*

pre•med•i•tat•ed (pri med′i tā′tid) /prɪ'mɛdɪ,teytɪd/ *adj.* considered or planned before doing: *premeditated murder.* —**pre•med•i•ta•tion** (prē med′i tā′shən) /priy,mɛdɪ'teyʃən/ *n.* [*noncount*]

pre•men•stru•al (prē men′strōō əl, -strəl) /priy'mɛnstruwəl, -strəl/ *adj.* [*often: before a noun*] of or relating to the period before a woman's menstrual flow begins: *premenstrual tension.*

premen′strual syn′drome, *n.* [*noncount*] a complex of physical and emotional changes, as irritability, depression, bloating, and headaches, experienced in the days before the onset of menstrual flow. *Abbr.:* PMS

pre•mier (pri mēr′, -myēr′, prē′mēr) /prɪ'mɪər, -'myɪər, 'priymɪər/ *n.* [*count*] **1.** the head of the cabinet in France and other countries; prime minister. **—***adj.* [*before a noun*] **2.** first in rank; chief; leading: *the premier writer of this decade.* **3.** first in time; earliest: *premier appearance on Broadway.* **—***v.* **4.** PREMIERE. See -PRIM-.

pre•miere (pri mēr′, -myâr′) /prɪ'mɪər, -'myɛər/ *n., v.,* **-miered, -mier•ing,** *adj.* **—***n.* [*count*] **1.** a first public performance or showing of a play, etc.: *the premiere of his new play.* **—***v.* **2.** to (cause to) be presented publicly for the first time: [~ + *obj*]: *premiered the new film.* [*no obj*]: *The act premiered in Boston.* **3.** [*no obj*] to perform (a part) publicly for the first time: *She premiered as Ophelia in the Shakespeare festival.* **—***adj.* [*before a noun*] **4.** PREMIER. See -PRIM-.

prem•ise (prem′is) /'prɛmɪs/ *n., v.,* **-ised, -is•ing.** **—***n.* **1. premises,** [*plural*] an area of land including its buildings: *You'll have to leave the premises at once.* **2.** [*count*] Also, **prem′iss.** a stated or assumed idea or proposition on which further reasoning proceeds: *I was operating on the premise that I had your support.* **—***v.* [~ + *obj*] **3.** to state or assume (a premise): *Everything is premised on continued low inflation.* See -MIS-.

pre•mi•um (prē′mē əm) /'priymiyəm/ *n.* [*count*] **1.** a prize or bonus given, for example, when purchasing a product, as a way of increasing sales: *The premium was a little gadget to hold your toothbrush.* **2.** a bonus, gift, or sum added as an extra to the price of something, to one's wages, etc. **3.** the amount paid in installments by a policyholder for coverage, as for insurance: *Car insurance premiums have skyrocketed.* **4.** great value: *puts a high premium on loyalty.* **—***adj.* [*often: before a noun*] **5.** of high quality or greater value than others of its kind: *the higher cost of premium, as opposed to regular, gasoline.* **—*Idiom.* 6. at a premium, a.** at an unusually high price: *American cigarettes were sold at a premium.* **b.** in short supply; in demand.

pre•mo•ni•tion (prē′mə nish′ən, prem′ə-) /ˌpriymə'nɪʃən, ˌprɛmə-/ *n.* [*count*] a feeling of worry over a future event; presentiment: *a premonition of danger.* **—pre•mon•i•to•ry** (pri mon′i tôr′ē, -tōr′ē) /prɪ'mɒnɪˌtɔriy, -ˌtowriy/ *adj.* See -MON-.

pre•na•tal (prē nāt′l) /priy'neytl̩/ *adj.* before birth or before giving birth: *funding for prenatal care.* **—pre•na′tal•ly,** *adv.* See -NAT-.

pre•nup•tial (prē nup′shəl) /priy'nʌpʃəl/ *adj.* before a wedding or marriage: *a prenuptial agreement.* See also PREMARITAL.

pre•oc•cu•pa•tion (prē ok′yə pā′shən) /priyˌɒkyə'peyʃən/ *n.* **1.** [*noncount*] the state of being preoccupied: *his total preoccupation with sex.* **2.** [*count*] something that preoccupies one: *Another of his preoccupations was getting to work on time.*

pre•oc•cu•py (prē ok′yə pī′) /priy'ɒkyəˌpay/ *v.* [~ + *obj*], **-pied, -py•ing.** to take the attention of (someone) so that one ignores other things: *Her fears about her parents' health preoccupied her.* **—pre•oc′cu•pied′,** *adj.*: *I was too preoccupied with my work to notice the time.*

pre•op•er•a•tive (prē op′ər ə tiv, -ə rā′tiv, -op′rə tiv) /priy'ɒpərətɪv, -əˌreytɪv, -'ɒprətɪv/ *adj.* of or relating to the period before a medical operation. See -OPER-.

pre•or•dain (prē′ôr dān′) /ˌpriyɔr'deyn/ *v.* [~ + *obj*] to decide the fate of (something) beforehand: *the belief that God has preordained our lives.*

prep (prep) /prɛp/ *n., adj., v.,* **prepped, prep•ping.** **—***n.* **1.** a preparatory school: [*count*]: *a small prep in a quiet area of the country.* [*noncount; used in names*]: *He went to All Hallows Prep.* **2.** [*count*] an activity that goes before another and prepares the participant: *It was a prep to the actual test.* **3.** [*noncount*] preparation: *not enough prep before the test.* **—***adj.* [*before a noun*] **4.** preparatory: *prep school.* **5.** involving or used for preparation: *the mortuary's prep room.* **—***v.* **6.** to prepare (a person) for a test, etc.: [~ + *obj*]: *a course to prep students for college entrance exams.* [*no obj*]: *to prep for the game.* **7.** [~ + *obj*] to prepare (a patient) for a medical procedure: *told the nurse to prep the next patient.*

prep., an abbreviation of: **1.** preparation. **2.** preparatory. **3.** prepare. **4.** preposition.

pre•pack•age (prē pak′ij) /priy'pækɪdʒ/ *v.* [~ + *obj*], **-aged, -ag•ing.** to package (foods) before retail sale.

prep•a•ra•tion (prep′ə rā′shən) /ˌprɛpə'reyʃən/ *n.* **1.** [*count*] an act or step by which one prepares for something: *last-minute preparations for their journey.* **2.** [*noncount*] any activity or experience providing a way of preparing for the future: *the lack of preparation students bring to their freshman writing class.* **3.** [*count*] something prepared: *She applied a soothing preparation to the burns.* See -PARE-[1].

pre•par•a•to•ry (pri par′ə tôr′ē, -tōr′ē, -pâr′-, prep′ər ə-) /prɪ'pærəˌtɔriy, -ˌtowriy, -'pɛər-, 'prɛpərə-/ *adj.* [*before a noun*] **1.** serving or designed to prepare: *preparatory arrangements.* **2.** introductory: *preparatory remarks.* **3.** of or relating to training that prepares for more advanced education: *preparatory school.* See -PARE[1]-.

prepar′atory school′, *n.* **1.** a private secondary school designed to prepare students for college: [*count*]: *several good preparatory schools.* [*noncount*]: *They couldn't afford preparatory school.* **2.** [*count*] *Brit.* a private elementary school.

pre•pare (pri pâr′) /prɪ'pɛər/ *v.,* **-pared, -par•ing.** **1.** to put (things or oneself) in proper condition or readiness; to get (someone) ready: [~ + *obj*]: *The general prepared his troops for the attack.* [~ + *to* + *verb*]: *The troops were preparing to cross the river.* [~ + *obj* + *to* + *verb*]: *These lessons will prepare you to pass the test.* [*no obj*]: *She prepared for the debate.* **2.** to get (a meal) ready for eating, as by cooking, etc.: [~ + *obj* + *for* + *obj*]: *He prepared a nice meal for her.* [~ + *obj* + *obj*]: *She prepared him a fine meal.* **3.** [~ + *obj*] to manufacture or compose: *to prepare a cough syrup; to prepare a report.* See -PARE-[1].

pre•pared (prē pârd′) /priy'peyrd/ *adj.* **1.** made ready in advance; done or finished ahead of time: *took no chances and accepted only prepared questions, for which he had perfect, prepared answers.* **2.** [*be* + ~ + *to* + *verb*] willing and able (to do something): *The teacher wasn't prepared to accept any excuses.* See -PARE[1]-.

pre•par•ed•ness (pri pâr′id nis, -pârd′nis) /prɪ'pɛərɪdnɪs, -'pɛərdnɪs/ *n.* [*noncount*] the state of being prepared, esp. for war. See -PARE-[1].

pre•pay (prē pā′) /priy'pey/ *v.* [~ + *obj*], **-paid, -pay•ing.** to pay beforehand: *a penalty for prepaying a mortgage.* **—pre•pay′ment,** *n.* [*noncount*]: *a penalty for prepayment.*

pre•pon•der•ance (pri pon′dər əns) /prɪ'pɒndərəns/ *n.* [*count; singular*] the state or condition of being superior in power, force, etc.: *a preponderance of news stories about the election.* **—pre•pon′der•ant,** *adj.* See -PEND-.

prep•o•si•tion (prep′ə zish′ən) /ˌprɛpə'zɪʃən/ *n.* [*count*] one of a group of words used before nouns and pronouns to form phrases that give more information about a verb, noun, or other phrase, usually expressing a relationship of time, place, or the like: *Some prepositions in English are* on, by, to, with, *or* since. **—prep′o•si′tion•al,** *adj.* [*before a noun*]: *The phrase* at 17 Lexington Avenue *is a prepositional phrase.* See -POS-.

pre•pos•sess•ing (prē′pə zes′ing) /ˌpriypə'zɛsɪŋ/ *adj.* impressive to others, esp. immediately.

pre•pos•ter•ous (pri pos′tər əs, -trəs) /prɪ'pɒstərəs, -trəs/ *adj.* completely opposite to common sense; foolish: *a preposterous scheme.*

prep•py or **prep•pie** (prep′ē) /'prɛpiy/ *n., pl.* **-pies,** *adj.,* **-pi•er, -pi•est.** **—***n.* [*count*] **1.** a student at, or a graduate of, a preparatory school. **2.** one whose clothing or behavior is associated with students of preparatory schools. **—***adj.* **3.** of, relating to, or characteristic of a preppy: *preppy clothes.*

pre•pu•bes•cent (prē pyo͞o bes′ənt) /priypyuw'bɛsənt/ *adj.* of or relating to the age just before puberty: *prepubescent kids.* **—pre•pu•bes′cence,** *n.* [*noncount*]

pre•quel (prē′kwəl) /'priykwəl/ *n.* [*count*] a film, play, or piece of fiction that follows an original already released, but that is set in time before the original: *The prequel portrays the same characters as the original, but they are at a younger age.*

pre•re•cord (prē′ri kôrd′) /ˌpriyrɪ'kɔrd/ *v.* [~ + *obj*] to record beforehand; record.

pre•req•ui•site (pri rek′wə zit, prē-) /prɪ'rɛkwəzɪt, priy-/ *adj.* **1.** required beforehand; requisite: *a prerequisite condition.* **—***n.* [*count*] **2.** something required before something else; a condition: *A course on grammar is a prerequisite to the advanced writing course.* See -QUIS-.

pre•rog•a•tive (pri rog′ə tiv, pə rog′-) /prɪ'rɒgətɪv, pə'rɒg-/ *n.* [*count*] a special right, privilege, etc., limited to people of rank in office, etc.: *the prerogative of a judge.* See -ROGA-.

pres., an abbreviation of: **1.** present. **2.** presidency. **3.** president.

pres•age (pres′ij, pri sāj′) /'prɛsɪdʒ, prɪ'seydʒ/ *v.* [~ +

obj], **-aged, -ag•ing.** to be a sign or warning of; portend; foreshadow: *Those terrorist incidents may presage war.*

pres•by•te•ri•an (prez′bi tēr′ē ən, pres′-) /ˌprɛzbɪ'tɪəriyən, ˌprɛs-/ *adj.* **1.** of or relating to church government by church officials of equal rank. **2.** [*Presbyterian*] of or relating to churches having this form of government. **—*n.*** [*count; Presbyterian*] **3.** a member of a Presbyterian church.

pre•school (*adj.* prē′sko͞ol′; *n.* prē′sko͞ol′) / *adj.* 'priy'skuwl; *n.* 'priyˌskuwl/ *adj.* **1.** of or relating to a child between infancy and kindergarten age. **—*n.*** **2.** a school or nursery for preschool children: [*count*]: *preschools set up for youngsters of working mothers.* [*noncount*]: *not yet ready for preschool.* **—pre′school′er,** *n.* [*count*]: *parents of preschoolers.*

pre•science (presh′əns, -ē əns, prē′shəns, -shē əns) /'prɛʃəns, -iyəns, 'priyʃəns, -ʃiy əns/ *n.* [*noncount*] knowledge of things before they exist or happen; foreknowledge; foresight. See -SCI-.

pre•scient (presh′ənt, presh′ē ənt) /'prɛʃənt, 'prɛʃiyənt/ *adj.* of or relating to prescience: *prescient analysis of voting trends.* **—pre′scient•ly,** *adv.* See -SCI-.

pre•scribe (pri skrīb′) /prɪ'skrayb/ *v.* [~ + *obj*], **-scribed, -scrib•ing. 1.** to order as a rule or course of action to be followed: *the punishment that the law prescribes.* **2.** to name or order the use of (a medicine, etc.): *The doctor prescribed some pain pills.* See -SCRIB-.

pre•scrip•tion (pri skrip′shən) /prɪ'skrɪpʃən/ *n.* **1.** [*count*] **a.** a written direction by a physician for the preparation and use of a medicine: *The prescription says to take two pills every six hours.* **b.** the medicine prescribed: *Can you fill this prescription?* **2.** [*noncount*] the act of prescribing. **3.** [*count*] something prescribed: *a prescription for disaster.* **—*adj.*** [*before a noun*] **4.** (of drugs) sold only upon medical prescription: *prescription drugs.*

pre•scrip•tive (pri skrip′tiv) /prɪ'skrɪptɪv/ *adj.* eager to set down rules: *prescriptive writers wanting everyone to follow the rules that they declare correct.* See -SCRIB-.

pres•ence (prez′əns) /'prɛzəns/ *n.* **1.** [*noncount*] the state or fact of being present: *Her presence at the party created some excitement.* **2.** [*noncount*] the state or condition of being near someone; proximity: *wouldn't dare say that in your presence.* **3.** the power of a country reflected in foreign countries by the stationing of its troops, sale of its goods, etc.: [*noncount*]: *nonmilitary presence.* [*count; usually singular*]: *a military presence in the region for the sake of stability.* **4.** [*noncount*] the ability to give off a sense of ease, dignity, or self-assurance: *an attorney with definite presence.*

pres′ence of mind′, *n.* [*noncount*] the ability to think clearly and act properly, as during a crisis: *He had the presence of mind to slam the emergency doors.*

pres•ent¹ (prez′ənt) /'prɛzənt/ *adj.* **1.** [*before a noun*] being, existing, or occurring at this time or now; current: *the present economic situation.* **2.** [*before a noun*] being actually here or under consideration at this time or place: *the present topic.* **3.** [*before a noun*] of or relating to a verb tense or form used to refer to an action or state existing at the moment of speaking (*They're eating. I know the answer*) or to an event that is done or occurs by habit (*He drives to work*), and is also sometimes used to express the future (*The plane leaves at six tomorrow*). **4.** [*be* + ~] being with one or others or in the place mentioned or understood by the speaker and listener: *Carbon is present in many minerals.* **—*n.*** [*count; singular; usually: the* + ~] **5.** the present time: *If there's work to be done, there's no time like the present.* **6. a.** the present tense: *Put that verb into the present.* **b.** a verb form in the present tense, as *knows.* **—*Idiom.* 7. at present,** at the present time or moment; now: *We don't know at present who will win the election.* **8. for the present,** for now; temporarily: *We don't have housing for you just yet, so for the present you'll have to stay in this hotel.*

pre•sent² (*v.* pri zent′; *n.* prez′ənt) / *v.* prɪ'zɛnt; *n.* 'prɛzənt/ *v.* **1.** to furnish or give a gift or the like, esp. by formal act: [~ + *obj* + *to* + *obj*]: *The awards committee presented the winner's trophy to her for the sixth time.* [~ + *obj* + *with* + *obj*]: *The committee presented her with the winner's trophy.* **2.** [~ + *obj*] to bring, offer, or give, often in a formal way or in a ceremony of introduction: *The new ambassador presented his credentials to the King.* **3.** to furnish or provide (an opportunity, etc.): [~ + *obj*]: *The test is easy; it should present no difficulties.* [~ + *obj* + *to* + *obj*]: *The oil shortage presented a golden opportunity to them to raise prices.* [~ + *obj* + *with* + *obj*]: *presented them with a golden opportunity.* **4.** to hand over or submit (a bill): [~ + *obj* + *to* + *obj*]: *The headwaiter presented the check to me.* [~ + *obj* + *with* + *obj*]: *He presented me with the check.* **5.** [~ + *obj*] to introduce (a person) to another, esp. in a formal manner: *Let me present my fiancée.* **6.** [~ + *obj*] to bring before or introduce to the public: *to present a new play.* **7.** [~ + *oneself*] to come to show (oneself) before a person, in or at a place, etc.: *The new teacher presented himself to the principal promptly the next morning.* **8.** [~ + *obj*] to bring forth before another or others; offer for consideration: *to present an alternative plan.* **9.** [~ + *obj*] to set forth in words: *to present arguments.* **—*n.*** **pres•ent** [*count*] **10.** a thing presented as a gift; gift: *Christmas presents.* **—pre•sent′er,** *n.* [*count*]

pre•sent•a•ble (pri zen′tə bəl) /prɪ'zɛntəbəl/ *adj.* capable of being presented; of good appearance: *She told him she wasn't presentable yet, so he waited while she got dressed.*

pres•en•ta•tion (prez′ən tā′shən, prē′zen-) /ˌprɛzən'teyʃən, ˌpriyzɛn-/ *n.* **1.** [*noncount*] an act of presenting; the state of being presented: *the presentation of news.* **2.** [*noncount*] a manner or style of speaking, instructing, or putting oneself forward: *Your presentation is all-important during an interview for a job.* **3.** [*count*] a demonstration to a client of a proposed advertising campaign; pitch. **4.** [*count*] a performance or showing, as of a play or film: *a high-school presentation of* Our Town. **5.** [*count*] an offering, as of a gift. **6.** [*count*] a demonstration, lecture, or welcoming speech, as one of introduction.

pres′ent-day′, *adj.* [*before a noun*] current; modern: *present-day English.*

pre•sen•ti•ment (pri zen′tə mənt) /prɪ'zɛntəmənt/ *n.* [*count*] a feeling that something bad is about to happen: *a presentiment of impending doom.* See -SENT-.

pres•ent•ly (prez′ənt lē) /'prɛzəntliy/ *adv.* **1.** in a little while; soon: *We'll be arriving presently—in, say, fifteen minutes.* **2.** at the present time; now: *Presently we have only three full-time ESL teachers.*

pres′ent par′ticiple, *n.* [*count*] a participle formed from the root of a verb plus the suffix *-ing,* used to indicate that the action or event repeats or lasts for some time, or used as an adjective, as in *the growing weeds,* and in forming progressive verb forms, as in *The weeds are growing.*

pres′ent per′fect, *adj.* of, relating to, or being a verb tense formed by *have* or *has* followed by the past participle (or *-ed/-en*) form of a verb. It is used to indicate: **1.** that the action of the verb started in the past and is continuing in the present, and that its effects are still felt or experienced up to the present: *I've lived here for six months (= I moved here six months ago and still live here).* **2.** that the action or event was completely finished in the past, but the effects are still important in the present: *I've spoken to the principal about that student (=and here's what we will do about him or her).*

pres•er•va•tion (prez′ər vā′shən) /ˌprɛzər'veyʃən/ *n.* [*noncount*] **1.** the act of preserving: *the preservation of peace and international law and order.* **2.** the state of being preserved: *The cells were kept in a state of preservation.* See -SERV-².

pres•er•va•tion•ist (prez′ər vā′shə nist) /ˌprɛzər'veyʃənɪst/ *n.* [*count*] one who calls for or promotes preservation, esp. of wildlife, natural areas, or historical places. See -SERV-².

pre•serv•a•tive (pri zûr′və tiv) /prɪ'zɜrvətɪv/ *n.* **1.** something that preserves, esp. a chemical used to preserve foods from spoiling or undergoing other unwanted changes: [*count*]: *afraid of eating anything with artificial preservatives in it.* [*noncount*]: *treating the wood on the porch with preservative.* **—*adj.*** **2.** tending to preserve. See -SERV-².

pre•serve (pri zûrv′) /prɪ'zɜrv/ *v.,* **-served, -serv•ing,** *n.* **—*v.*** [~ + *obj*] **1.** to keep (something) alive or in existence; make (something) lasting; protect: *to preserve our liberties.* **2.** to keep up; maintain; take action to prevent decay: *to preserve historical monuments.* **3.** to keep possession of; keep; retain: *He managed to preserve his composure during the debates.* **4.** to prepare (food) so as to prevent or slow down its decay: *preserving meat.* **5.** to prepare (fruit, etc.) by cooking with sugar, etc. **6.** to maintain and protect (game, etc.) for continued survival or for private use, as in hunting or fishing. **—*n.*** [*count*] **7.** something that preserves. **8.** that which is preserved. **9.** Usually, **preserves.** [*plural*] fruit prepared by cooking with sugar. **10.** a place set apart for protection of game or fish, esp. for sport: *a forest preserve.* **11.** something looked on as belonging to a particular person or group of people only: *She was running for the Senate to prove that politics was no longer just a male preserve.* —**pre•serv′er,** *n.* [*count*] See -SERV-[2].

pre•set (prē set′) /priy'sɛt/ *v.* [~ + *obj*], **-set, -set•ting.** to set beforehand: *The channels on the VCR were preset.*

pre•side (pri zīd′) /prɪ'zayd/ *v.,* **-sid•ed, -sid•ing. 1.** [*no obj*] to have or hold the place of authority or control, as in an assembly or meeting: *The judge presided at the trial.* **2. preside over,** [~ + *over* + *obj*] to exercise management or control over: *His lawyer will preside over the estate.* See -SID-.

pres•i•den•cy (prez′i dən sē) /'prɛzɪdənsiy/ *n.* [*count*] **1.** the office of a president: *never elected to the presidency.* **2.** the time of a president's holding office: *the last three Republican presidencies.* See -SID-.

pres•i•dent (prez′i dənt) /'prɛzɪdənt/ *n.* [*count*] **1.** [*often: President*] the chief of state and often the chief executive officer of a modern republic, as the United States: *He wondered if he would make a good president.* [*the* + *President*]: *Will the President be reelected?* [*before a name; President*]: *President Lincoln.* **2.** the chief officer of a college, corporation, etc. See -SID-.

pres•i•den•tial (prez′i den′shəl) /,prɛzɪ'dɛnʃəl/ *adj.* **1.** [*before a noun*] of or relating to a president or a presidency: *the presidential seal at the top of the letter.* **2.** of the nature of or befitting a president: *trying to improve his presidential image.* See -SID-.

pre•sid•i•um (pri sid′ē əm) /prɪ'sɪdiyəm/ *n.* [*count*], *pl.* **-sid•i•ums, -sid•i•a** (-sid′ē ə) /-'sɪdiyə/. [*often: Presidium*] (esp. in Communist countries) an administrative committee, usually permanent and performing government activities. See -SID-.

press[1] (pres) /prɛs/ *v.* **1.** to act upon or move (something) with steady force; to push: [~ + *obj*]: *He pressed the gas pedal and the car shot forward.* [*no obj*]: *He pressed on the gas pedal but nothing happened.* **2.** to put pressure on (something), esp. so as to change shape or size: [~ + *obj*]: *He pressed the clay into a ball.* [*no obj*]: *She pressed down on the dough.* **3.** [~ + *obj*] to hold closely, as in an embrace; clasp: *She pressed my hand when we were introduced.* **4.** [~ + *obj*] to flatten or make smooth, esp. by ironing: *He pressed his jacket and slacks.* **5.** [~ + *obj*] to squeeze out juice or the insides of (something, as grapes) by pressure: *pressed the grapes to produce wine.* **6.** [~ + *obj*] to squeeze out (juice): *They pressed enough juice to make fifteen gallons of wine.* **7.** to bother, annoy, or harass; keep bothering: [~ + *obj*]: *Don't press your kids so hard; they'll do better if you just leave them alone.* [*no obj*]: *The media kept pressing for an explanation.* **8.** to cause trouble, worry, or strain; oppress: [~ + *obj; often: be* + ~*-ed* + *for*]: *Poverty presses people down. She's pressed for funds right now.* [*no obj*]: *The pressure is pressing down on him.* **9.** [~ + *obj*] to emphasize with force or persuasion: *pressed his own ideas about school reform on the community.* **10.** [~ + *obj*] to raise or lift, esp. a specified amount of weight, in the sport of weightlifting: *He pressed five hundred pounds.* **11.** to (cause to) push forward: [*no obj*]: *The army pressed on.* [~ + *obj*]: *He pressed the car ahead.* **12.** [*no obj*] to crowd around someone; throng: *The crowd pressed in on him.* —*n.* **13.** [*count*] an act of pressing: *two or three presses on the doorbell.* **14.** PRINTING PRESS. **15.** [*noncount*] printed publications or news organizations thought of as a group [*usually: the* + ~]: *"I'm from the press, let me in," he demanded.* [*a* + ~]: *A free press is essential to a democracy.* **16.** [*plural; used with a plural verb; usually: the* + ~] a group of people from the news media, as reporters and photographers: *The press in the second campaign plane were angry when their plane couldn't land.* **17.** the commentary, criticism, or opinion about a person, etc., carried in newspapers and other media: [*count; usually singular: a* + ~]: *The movie received a good press.* [*noncount*]: *During the war the general received fairly good press.* **18.** [*count*] an establishment for printing books, magazines, etc.: *the University of Illinois Press.* **19.** [*count*] any of various devices or machines for squeezing, stamping, or crushing: *a wine press.* **20.** [*count; singular*] a crowding, thronging, or pressing together: *the press of the crowd.* **21.** [*noncount*] urgency, as of affairs or business: *the dizzying press of business the first week of a sale.* **22.** [*count*] a lift in which a barbell is pushed up from chest level with the arms straight up, without moving the legs or feet: *a clean press of over 500 pounds.* —***Idiom.*** **23. go to press,** to begin being printed: *By the time the newspaper went to press, the last game wasn't over yet.* —**press′er,** *n.* [*count*] See -PRESS-.

press[2] (pres) /prɛs/ *v.* [~ + *obj*] **1.** to force into service, esp. military service. **2.** to make use of (something) in a manner different from that intended: *A bus was pressed into service as an ambulance.*

-press-, *root.* *-press-* comes from Latin, where it has the meaning "squeeze; press (down)." This meaning is found in such words as: COMPRESS, COMPRESSION, DECOMPRESSION, DEPRESS, DEPRESSION, EXPRESS, IMPRESS, IMPRESSION, IMPRESSIVE, INEXPRESSIBLE, IRREPRESSIBLE, OPPRESS, PRESS, PRESSURE, REPRESS, SUPPRESS.

press′ a′gent, *n.* [*count*] one whose job is to promote an individual or organization by obtaining favorable publicity.

press′ con′ference, *n.* [*count*] a collective interview or question-and-answer session with reporters, held by a government official, celebrity, or a person in the news and usually arranged in advance.

pressed (prest) /prɛst/ *adj.* [*be* + ~ + *for*] not having enough of: *I was pressed for time and money.* See also HARD-PRESSED.

press•ing (pres′ing) /'prɛsɪŋ/ *adj.* urgent; needing attention: *a pressing need for food supplies.*

press•man (pres′mən) /'prɛsmən/ *n.* [*count*], *pl.* **-men. 1.** a person who operates or has charge of a printing press. **2.** *Brit.* a writer or reporter for the press.

press′ release′, *n.* [*count*] a statement distributed to the press by a public relations firm, etc.: *issued a press release, denying any wrongdoing.*

press′ sec′retary, *n.* [*count*] a person responsible for press and public relations for an important figure or organization.

pres•sure (presh′ər) /'prɛʃər/ *n., v.,* **-sured, -sur•ing.** —*n.* **1.** [*noncount*] the action of force upon a surface by an object, fluid, etc., in contact with it: *air pressure.* **2.** [*count*] the strength or amount of this force: *At high pressures the wings could fall off.* **3.** stress; a feeling or feelings of harassment: [*count*]: *the pressures of daily life.* [*noncount*]: *Kids have enough pressure in their lives.* **4.** a force or influence that causes some action: [*count*]: *Social pressures from their peers might prevent kids from drinking or using drugs.* [*noncount*]: *tried to bring pressure on his subordinates to finish on time.* **5.** [*noncount*] urgency, as that induced by deadlines at school or work: *works well under pressure.* **6.** [*noncount*] the force of the air: *a region of high pressure.* —*v.* **7.** to force (someone) to do a particular thing or action; coerce: [~ + *obj* (+ *into* + *obj*)]: *She pressured him into it.* [~ + *obj* + *to* + *verb*]: *I think they pressured him to accept that job.* See -PRESS-.

pres′sure cook′er, *n.* [*count*] **1.** a heavy metal cooking pot with a lid that can be tightened to prevent air from escaping, in which food may be cooked quickly above the boiling point by steam under pressure. **2.** a situation in which a person faces urgent demands or too much work: *His job had become a pressure cooker of more sales and more demands.* **3.** a situation that is tense or likely to explode: *The Middle East has been a pressure cooker for decades.*

pres′sure group′, *n.* [*count*] a group that influences law-making bodies through lobbying.

pres•sur•ize (presh′ə rīz′) /'prɛʃə,rayz/ *v.* [~ + *obj*], **-ized, -iz•ing.** to produce or maintain normal air pressure in (an airplane cabin, etc.), esp. at high altitudes or in space: *The cabin was pressurized once the plane leveled off at a lower altitude.* —**pres•sur•i•za•tion** (presh′ər i zā′shən) /,prɛʃərɪ'zeyʃən/ *n.* [*noncount*] —**pres′sur•iz′er,** *n.* [*count*]

pres•tige (pre stēzh′, -stēj′) /prɛ'stiyʒ, -'stiydʒ/ *n.* [*noncount*] **1.** a person's reputation deriving from his or her success, achievement, or rank. **2.** distinction or reputation attaching to a person or thing: *the prestige attached to the Nobel prize awards.* —*adj.* [*before a noun*] **3.** having or reflecting success, rank, etc.: *a prestige car.*

pres•tig•ious (pre stij′əs) /prɛ'stɪdʒəs/ *adj.* of or relating to prestige; highly regarded: *a prestigious university.*

pres•to (pres′tō) /'prɛstow/ *adv., adj., n., pl.* **-tos.** —*adv.* **1.** quickly, rapidly, or immediately: *He left presto.* **2.** *Music.* at a rapid tempo. —*adj.* **3.** quick or rapid. **4.** performed at a rapid tempo. —*n.* [*count*] **5.** a presto musical piece or movement.

pre•sum•a•bly (pri zo͞o′mə blē) /prɪ'zuwməbliy/ *adv.* probably. See -SUM-.

pre•sume (pri zo͞om′) /prɪ'zuwm/ *v.,* **-sumed, -sum•ing. 1.** to assume as true because there is no proof that suggests the opposite; take for granted: [~ + *obj*]: *We pre-*

sume his innocence. [~ + *obj* (+ *to* + *be*) + *adj*]: *We presume him (to be) innocent.* [~ + *obj* + *to* + *verb*]: *They presumed him to be hiding in Amsterdam.* [~ + *(that) clause*]: *I presume you're coming to the play with us, aren't you?* **2.** [~ + *to* + *verb*] to dare (to do something) with too much boldness: *How can she presume to talk like that?* **3.** [~ + *to* + *verb*] to decide (to do something) without right or permission: *I wouldn't presume to speak for another person.* **4. presume on** or **upon,** [~ + *on* + *obj*] to go too far in acting boldly: *to presume on someone's tolerance.* See -SUM-.

pre•sump•tion (pri zump′shən) /prɪ'zʌmpʃən/ *n.* **1.** [*noncount*] the act of presuming: *presumption of innocence.* **2.** [*count*] something that is presumed: *a presumption that once we persuade him we'll have no trouble with the others.* **3.** [*noncount*] too much boldness; audacity: *the presumption of that child!* —**pre•sump•tive** (pri zump′tiv) /prɪ'zʌmptɪv/ *adj.* See -SUM-.

pre•sump•tu•ous (pri zump′cho͞o əs) /prɪ'zʌmptʃuwəs/ *adj.* characterized by too much boldness to presume or make unwarranted assumptions; too bold: *presumptuous of her to assume I'd be paying for dinner.* See -SUM-.

pre•sup•pose (prē′sə pōz′) /ˌpriysə'powz/ *v.* [*not: be* + *~-ing*], **-posed, -pos•ing.** to suppose to be true; take for granted in advance: [~ + *obj*]: *An effect presupposes a cause.* [~ + *(that) clause*]: *Your theory presupposes that time existed at the beginning of the universe.* —**pre•sup•po•si•tion** (prē′sup ə zish′ən) /ˌpriysʌpə'zɪʃən/ *n.* [*count; noncount*] See -POS-.

pre•teen (prē tēn′) /priy'tiyn/ *n.* [*count*] **1.** a boy or girl under the age of 13, esp. one between the ages of 10 and 13; preadolescent. —*adj.* **2.** of, relating to, characteristic of, or designed for preteens: *preteen fashions.*

pre•tend (pri tend′) /prɪ'tɛnd/ *v.* **1.** to put forward a false appearance of, so as to deceive: [~ + *obj*]: *I would pretend illness so I wouldn't have to go to school.* [~ + *to* + *verb*]: *She pretended to sleep whenever I came in to check on her.* [~ + *(that) clause*]: *The children pretended they were cowboys.* [*no obj*]: *The kids were only pretending.* **2.** [~ + *to* + *obj*] to lay claim to: *to pretend to the throne.* —*adj.* **3.** make-believe; simulated; imaginary: *pretend cowboys.* —**pre•tend′er,** *n.* [*count*] See -TEND-.

pre•tense (pri tens′, prē′tens) /prɪ'tɛns, 'priytɛns/ *n.* **1.** an act or instance of pretending; (an instance of) make-believe: [*count*]: *a pretense of friendship.* [*noncount*]: *It's all pretense; he has no intention of cutting our budget.* **2.** [*count*] an apparent claim that seems true but is false: *to obtain money under false pretenses.* See -TEND-.

pre•ten•sion (pri ten′shən) /prɪ'tɛnʃən/ *n.* **1.** [*count*] the laying of a claim to something: *all those pretensions to the throne.* **2.** Often, **pretensions.** [*plural*] a claim made to some quality, merit, dignity, or importance. **3.** the act of claiming to be something one is not: [*noncount*]: *full of pretension.* [*count*]: *Your pretensions don't fool me.*

pre•ten•tious (pri ten′shəs) /prɪ'tɛnʃəs/ *adj.* **1.** full of pretension; giving a show of importance, etc., that one does not really have. **2.** making an exaggerated outward show; showy. —**pre•ten′tious•ly,** *adv.* —**pre•ten′tious•ness,** *n.* [*noncount*] See -TEND-.

pre•ter•nat•u•ral (prē′tər nach′ər əl, -nach′rəl) /ˌpriytər'nætʃərəl, -'nætʃrəl/ *adj.* occurring out of the ordinary course of nature; exceptional or abnormal: *preternatural powers.* See -NAT-.

pre•test (*n.* prē′test′; *v.* prē test′) / *n.* 'priyˌtɛst; *v.* priy'tɛst/ *n.* [*count*] **1.** a testing or trial, as of a new product, before it is sold or distributed; a test. **2.** a test given to determine if students are prepared to begin a new course of study. —*v.* **3.** to give a pretest to: [~ + *obj*]: *They pretested the students.* [*no obj*]: *Pretesting went on for several days.* See -TEST-.

pre•text (prē′tekst) /'priytɛkst/ *n.* [*count*] something put forward to conceal a true purpose; an excuse: *She came into my office on the pretext of borrowing a stapler.*

pret•ti•fy (prit′ə fī′) /'prɪtəˌfay/ *v.* [~ + *obj*], **-fied, -fy•ing. 1.** to make pretty, esp. in a small way: *prettifying the bathroom.* **2.** to minimize the importance of (something unpleasant): *trying to prettify the latest unemployment figures.*

pret•ty (prit′ē) /'prɪtiy/ *adj.*, **-ti•er, -ti•est,** *n., pl.* **-ties,** *adv., v.,* **-tied, -ty•ing.** —*adj.* **1.** pleasing or attractive, esp. in a delicate or graceful way: *a pretty face.* **2.** pleasing or charming but not grand or overwhelming: *a pretty little cabin in the woods.* **3.** [*before a noun*] *Informal.* considerable; fairly great: *This is a pretty mess!* —*n.* [*count*] **4.** a pretty person: *"I'll get you, my pretty," the witch cackled.* —*adv.* **5.** fairly or moderately; somewhat: *We had a pretty good time, but it wasn't great.* **6.** quite; very: *The wind blew pretty hard.* —*v.* **7.** to make pretty in appearance: [~ + *obj*]: *She prettied herself before he came over.* [~ + *up* + *obj*]: *to pretty up a room.* [~ + *obj* + *up*]: *Can't you pretty the room up before they come over?* —**pret•ti•ly** (prit′l ē) /'prɪtḷiy/ *adv.*: *She bowed prettily.* —**pret′ti•ness,** *n.* [*noncount*]

pret•zel (pret′səl) /'prɛtsəl/ *n.* [*count*] a usually crisp, dry biscuit, typically in the form of a knot or stick.

pre•vail (pri vāl′) /prɪ'veyl/ *v.* **1.** [*not: be* + *~-ing; no obj*] to be widespread or current; be found in many places: *The opinion that he is a loser still prevails.* **2.** to be or prove superior in strength, power, or influence: [*no obj*]: *Greed has prevailed once again.* [~ + *over*]: *to prevail over one's enemies.* **3.** [~ + *on/upon* + *obj*] to persuade successfully: *Can you prevail on him to go?*

pre•vail•ing (pri vā′ling) /prɪ'veylɪŋ/ *adj.* [*before a noun*] **1.** most frequent or powerful: *prevailing winds.* **2.** generally current: *the prevailing opinion.* See -VAL-.

prev•a•lent (prev′ə lənt) /'prɛvələnt/ *adj.* **1.** widespread; in general use or acceptance: *the prevalent point of view.* **2.** having greater power; dominant. —**prev′a•lence,** *n.* [*noncount*] See -VAL-.

pre•var•i•cate (pri var′i kāt′) /prɪ'værɪˌkeyt/ *v.* [*no obj*], **-cat•ed, -cat•ing.** to speak falsely; deliberately misstate; lie. —**pre•var•i•ca•tion** (pri var′i kā′shən) /prɪˌværɪ'keyʃən/ *n.* [*noncount*]: *a master of prevarication.* [*count*]: *spreading prevarications about his opponent.* —**pre•var′i•ca′tor,** *n.* [*count*]

pre•vent (pri vent′) /prɪ'vɛnt/ *v.* **1.** [~ + *obj*] to keep from occurring; stop: *She took some pills to prevent seasickness.* **2.** [~ + *obj* + *from* + *verb-ing*] to stop (someone) from doing something: *Nothing will prevent us from going.* See -VEN-.

pre•vent•a•ble (pri vent′ə bəl) /prɪ'vɛntəbəl/ *adj.* that can be prevented: *a preventable disease.* Also, **pre•vent′i•ble.** See -VEN-.

pre•ven•tion (pri ven′shən) /prɪ'vɛnʃən/ *n.* [*noncount*] the act of preventing: *crime prevention.* See -VEN-.

pre•ven•tive (pri ven′tiv) /prɪ'vɛntɪv/ also **pre•vent•a•tive** (pri ven′tə tiv) /prɪ'vɛntətɪv/ *adj.* **1.** of or relating to prevention: *preventive measures; preventive medicine.* —*n.* [*count*] **2.** a drug or other substance for preventing disease. **3.** a person or thing that prevents something. See -VEN-.

pre•view (prē′vyo͞o′) /'priyˌvyuw/ *n.* [*count*] **1.** an advance view. **2.** an advance showing of a motion picture, etc., before its public opening: *Only a few friends and reviewers were invited to the preview.* **3.** an advance showing of brief scenes in a motion picture, etc., for advertisement: *The previews of that new comedy series were silly.* **4.** anything that gives an advance impression of something: *Living together gave them a preview of marriage.* —*v.* [~ + *obj*] **5.** to view or show beforehand: *We previewed the video before we let our kids watch it.*

pre•vi•ous (prē′vē əs) /'priyviyəs/ *adj.* [*before a noun*] **1.** occurring before something else; prior: *The previous owner of this car was a little old lady.* —***Idiom.*** **2. previous to,** before; prior to: *Previous to moving here she lived in Chicago.* —**pre′vi•ous•ly,** *adv.*: *He previously worked for IBM.*

pre•war (prē′wôr′) /'priy'wɔr/ *adj.* existing, occurring, etc., before a particular war: *prewar prices.*

prey (prā) /prey/ *n., v.,* **preyed, prey•ing.** —*n.* [*noncount*] **1.** an animal hunted for food, esp. by a meat-eating animal: *Mice are the prey of owls.* **2.** a person or thing that is the victim of an enemy, disease, etc. **3.** the action or habit of preying: *a beast of prey.* —*v.* **prey on** or **upon,** [~ + *on/upon* + *obj*] **4.** to seize and eat animals for food: *Foxes prey on rabbits.* **5.** to make raids or attacks in order to steal or destroy: *The Vikings preyed on coastal England.* **6.** to bring about a harmful influence; to trouble: *The problem preyed upon his mind.* **7.** to take dishonest advantage of another: *loan sharks who prey upon the poor.* —***Idiom.*** **8. fall prey to,** [~ + *obj*] to be a victim of: *The economy fell prey to recession and high unemployment.*

price (prīs) /prays/ *n., v.,* **priced, pric•ing.** —*n.* [*count*] **1.** the sum of money for which anything is bought, sold, or offered for sale: *Our prices will beat the competition's.* **2.** a sum offered for the capture of a person alive or dead: *to put a price on his head.* **3.** an amount of money for which a person will abandon morals, principles, etc.: *Every man has his price.* **4.** that which must be given, done, or suffered through in order to obtain a thing: *We won the battle, but at a heavy price: 3,000 dead.* —*v.* [~

+ *obj*] **5.** to fix the price of: *He priced the paintings at about $3,000 each.* **6.** to ask or find out the price of: *He went around pricing computers at different stores.* **—*Idiom.*** **7. at any price,** at any cost, no matter how great: *He wanted to win the election at any price.* See -PRECI-.

price•less (prīs′lis) /'praysləs/ *adj.* **1.** having a value beyond all price: *priceless artwork.* **2.** amusing or absurd: *a priceless anecdote.* See -PRECI-.

pric•ey (prī′sē) /'praysiy/ also **pricy,** *adj.,* **-i•er, -i•est.** too expensive: *those pricey cars.* See -PRECI-.

prick (prik) /prɪk/ *n.* [*count*] **1.** a puncture made by a needle, thorn, or the like. **2.** the act of pricking: *He could hardly feel the prick of the needle.* **3.** a sharp pain caused by being pricked; twinge. **4.** *Slang* (*vulgar*). **a.** PENIS. **b.** a nasty, hateful person. **—*v.*** **5.** [~ + *obj*] to pierce or make a hole in with a sharp point; puncture: *I pricked my finger.* **6.** to (cause to) feel sharp pain, as from piercing: [*no obj*]: *The thorns prick if you touch them.* [~ + *obj*]: *The thorns pricked her legs.* **7.** [~ + *obj*] to cause sharp mental pain to: *His conscience pricked him.* **8. prick up,** to (cause to) stand erect or point upward: [~ + *up* + *obj*]: *The dog pricked up its ears.* [*no obj*]: *The dog's ears pricked up.* **—*Idiom.*** **9. prick up one's ears,** to become very alert; listen attentively: *She pricked up her ears when she overheard the boss talking about her department.*

prick•le (prik′əl) /'prɪkəl/ *n., v.,* **-led, -ling.** **—*n.*** [*count*] **1.** a small, sharp thorn that sticks out, as on a plant. **2.** a pricking sensation. **—*v.*** [*no obj*] **3.** to cause a pricking sensation: *His skin prickled at having to go into the dark room alone.*

prick•ly (prik′lē) /'prɪkliy/ *adj.,* **-li•er, -li•est.** **1.** having prickles: *prickly leaves.* **2.** that causes a prickling feeling: *a prickly, uncomfortable collar.* **3.** too easily made angry; touchy: *No need to get so prickly; I just asked how your job was.*

prick′ly heat′, *n.* [*noncount*] a swelling on the skin accompanied by prickling and itching: *some powder for prickly heat.* Also called **heat rash.**

pride (prīd) /prayd/ *n., v.,* **prid•ed, prid•ing.** **—*n.*** **1.** [*noncount*] the state or quality of being properly proud about something good that one has or has done; self-respect: *He pointed with pride at the fine books in his library.* **2.** [*noncount*] too high an opinion of one's own dignity, importance, or superiority; conceit: *His pride kept him from admitting he was wrong.* **3.** [*noncount*] something that causes one to be proud: *Her paintings were the pride of the family.* **4.** [*count*] a group of lions. **—*v.*** [~ + *oneself* + *on/upon* + *obj*] **5.** to give oneself over to a feeling of pride about: *She prides herself on being a good mother.* **—*Idiom.*** **6. swallow one's pride,** to do something that one resents doing in order to gain some advantage or prevent some undesirable outcome: *He swallowed his pride and went out and accepted donations from people on the street.* **—pride′ful,** *adj.* **—pride′ful•ly,** *adv.*

pri•er or **pry•er** (prī′ər) /'prayər/ *n.* [*count*] one who pries; a curious or inquisitive person.

priest (prēst) /priyst/ *n.* [*count*] **1.** (in Christian use) **a.** a person ordained to an office in a church as a member of the clergy; minister. **b.** (in churches with strict ranking) a member of the clergy of the order next below that of bishop. **2.** one whose job or position is to perform religious ceremonies, etc.: *As the Hindu priests walked by, the armies stopped fighting to allow them to pass.*

priest•ess (prē′stis) /'priystɪs/ *n.* [*count*] a woman who performs or is in charge of performing sacred rites.

priest•hood (prēst′ho͝od′) /'priyst,hʊd/ *n.* [*noncount*] **1.** the office of a priest. **2.** priests thought of as a group.

priest•ly (prēst′lē) /'priystliy/ *adj.,* **-li•er, -li•est.** of or relating to a priest: *priestly duties; priestly blessings.*

prig (prig) /prɪg/ *n.* [*count*] a person overly concerned with strictly proper conduct. **—prig′gish,** *adj.*: *He could be really priggish about anyone having even a few drinks.*

prim (prim) /prɪm/ *adj.,* **prim•mer, prim•mest.** **1.** precise or proper in a very formal way; prissy: *His mother was very prim and wouldn't allow him to use words like "damn" or even "darn" in her presence.* **2.** stiffly neat. **—prim′ly,** *adv.*: *"No language like that in my house," she answered primly.* **—prim′ness,** *n.* [*noncount*]

-prim-, *root.* *-prim-* comes from Latin, where it has the meaning "first." This meaning is found in such words as: PRIMACY, PRIMAL, PRIMARY, PRIMATE, PRIME, PRIMEVAL, PRIMITIVE, PRIMORDIAL, PRINCE, PRINCIPAL, PRINCIPLE, UNPRINCIPLED.

pri•ma•cy (prī′mə sē) /'praymәsiy/ *n.* [*noncount*] the state of being first in order, rank, importance, etc. See -PRIM-.

pri•ma don•na (prē′mə don′ə, prim′ə) /,priy'mə dɒnə, ,prɪmə/ *n.* [*count*], *pl.* **prima don•nas.** **1.** a first or principal female singer in an opera. **2.** a vain person who changes moods often and who expects special treatment: *The team was a bunch of prima donnas.* See -PRIM-.

pri•ma fa•ci•e (prī′mə fā′shē ē′, fā′shē, fā′shə, prē′-) /'pray'mə feyʃiy,iy, 'feyʃiy, 'feyʃə, 'priy-/ *adv.* **1.** at first view; before investigation: *He seemed to behave, at least prima facie, exactly like a murderer.* **—*adj.*** [*before a noun*] **2.** obvious; self-evident. **3.** being enough to establish a fact: *prima facie evidence.* See -PRIM-, -FACE-.

pri•mal (prī′məl) /'prayməl/ *adj.* [*before a noun*] first; original; primeval. See -PRIM-.

pri•ma•ri•ly (prī mâr′ə lē, -mer′-, prī′mer ə lē, -mər ə-) /pray'mɛərəliy, -'mɛr-, 'praymɛrəliy, -mərə-/ *adv.* essentially; chiefly: *Their income is primarily from farming.*

pri•ma•ry (prī′mer ē, -mə rē) /'praymɛriy, -məriy/ *adj., n., pl.* **-ries.** **—*adj.*** **1.** first in rank or importance; chief: *one's primary goal in life.* **2.** [*before a noun*] first in order in any series, etc.; first in time; earliest. **3.** [*before a noun*] of or relating to a primary school: *the primary grades.* **4.** [*before a noun*] being of the simplest or most basic order of its or their kind: *a primary constituent in a sentence.* **—*n.*** [*count*] **5.** something first in order or importance. **6.** a preliminary election in which voters of each political party nominate candidates for office, etc., who then run for office in another, larger election: *After a hard-fought primary, he lost the general election.* See -PRIM-.

pri′mary school′, *n.* an elementary school, esp. one covering the first three or four grades and sometimes kindergarten: [*count*]: *two new primary schools to be built in the area.* [*noncount*]: *graduated from primary school and went on to middle school.*

pri′mary stress′, *n.* [*noncount*] the principal or strongest degree of stress in a word or phrase, indicated in this dictionary by the mark (′). Compare SECONDARY STRESS.

pri•mate (prī′māt *or, esp. for 1* -mit) /'praymeyt *or, esp. for 1* -mɪt/ *n.* [*count*] **1.** a bishop ranking first among the bishops of a province or country. **2.** a mammal of a group that includes humans, apes, monkeys, and lemurs. See -PRIM-.

prime (prīm) /praym/ *adj., n., v.,* **primed, prim•ing.** **—*adj.*** **1.** of the first importance: *a prime requisite.* **2.** of the greatest significance; very typical: *a prime example of how he cheats.* **3.** of the greatest commercial value: *They bought some prime building lots.* **4.** first-rate. **5.** (of meat) of the highest grade or best quality: *prime ribs of beef.* **6.** first in order of time, existence, or development: *God, the prime mover.* **7.** basic; fundamental: *a prime axiom.* **—*n.*** [*count; singular*] **8.** the most flourishing stage or state: *an athlete in his prime.* **9.** the time of early manhood or womanhood: *the prime of youth.* **10.** the choicest or best part of anything. **11.** PRIME RATE. **12.** *Mathematics.* PRIME NUMBER. **—*v.*** [~ + *obj*] **13.** to prepare for a particular purpose, as by supplying (someone or oneself) with information, etc.: *He primed himself for the meeting by reviewing his figures.* **14.** to supply (a firearm) with powder for igniting a charge. **15.** to pour or admit liquid into (a pump) so as to push out air and prepare for action. **16.** to put fuel into (a carburetor) before starting an engine. **17.** to cover (a surface) with an undercoat of paint or the like: *to prime a wall before painting it.* **—*Idiom.*** **18. prime the pump, a.** to increase government spending to stimulate the economy. **b.** to support the operation or improvement of something. See -PRIM-.

prime′ merid′ian, *n.* [*count; usually: the* + ~] the meridian running through Greenwich, England, from which longitude east and west is figured.

prime′ min′ister, *n.* [*count*] the head of government and the head of the cabinet in parliamentary systems.

prime′ num′ber, *n.* [*count*] a positive integer that is not divisible without remainder by any integer except itself and 1.

prim•er[1] (prim′ər) /'prɪmər/ *n.* [*count*] **1.** an elementary book for teaching children to read. **2.** any book of elementary principles.

prim•er[2] (prī′mər) /'praymər/ *n.* [*count*] **1.** a person or thing that primes. **2.** a small explosive designed to ignite a larger one. **3.** a first coat of paint, applied to any surface as a base, sealer, etc. See -PRIM-.

prime′ rate′, *n.* [*count; usually: the* + ~] the minimum interest rate charged by a commercial bank on short-term business loans to large, best-rated customers or corporations. Also called **prime, prime′ in′terest rate′, prime′ lend′ing rate′.**

prime′ time′, *n.* [*noncount*] the weekday evening hours, thought of as having the largest television audience of the day: *a show not appropriate for prime time.*

pri•me•val or **pri•mae•val** (prī mē′vəl) /pray'miyvəl/ *adj.* of or relating to the first or earliest age or ages, esp. of the world; primordial: *primeval forms of life.* See -PRIM-.

prim•i•tive (prim′i tiv) /'prɪmɪtɪv/ *adj.* **1.** [*before a noun*] being the first or earliest of its kind or in existence: *primitive forms of life.* **2.** [*before a noun*] early in the history of the world or of humankind: *primitive toolmaking.* **3.** not showing the effects of civilization; simple or crude: *primitive passions.* **—n.** [*count*] **4.** someone or something primitive. See -PRIM-.

pri•mo•gen•i•tor (prī′mə jen′i tər) /ˌpraymə'dʒɛnɪtər/ *n.* [*count*] an ancestor. See -PRIM-, -GEN-.

pri•mor•di•al (prī môr′dē əl) /pray'mɔrdiyəl/ *adj.* [*before a noun*] existing at the very beginning; original: *primordial forms of life.* See -PRIM-, -ORD-.

primp (primp) /prɪmp/ *v.* to dress or groom (oneself) with care: [*no obj*]: *He stood before the mirror primping.* [~ + *oneself*]: *She stood before the mirror primping herself carefully.*

prim•rose (prim′rōz′) /'prɪmˌrowz/ *n.* **1.** [*count*] a plant with showy, five-lobed flowers in a variety of colors, esp. one having yellow flowers that opens at night. **2.** [*noncount*] pale yellow. **—adj. 3.** of a pale yellow.

prince (prins) /prɪns/ *n.* [*count*] **1.** a male member of a royal family who is not ruling: *one of seven princes waiting for the king to die.* [*as part of a title, before a name*]: *Prince Ladislav.* **2.** (in Great Britain) a son of the king or queen, or a son of the son of a king or queen. **3.** the ruler of a small state or country, as Monaco. **4.** one who is the best example in its class of some noun mentioned: *a merchant prince.* **5.** an admirable person: *He was a real prince: showing her the sights and driving her home.* See -PRIM-.

prince•ly (prins′lē) /'prɪnsliy/ *adj.*, **-li•er, -li•est. 1.** splendid; magnificent; lavish: *a princely sum.* **2.** of or relating to a prince; royal; noble. **—prince′li•ness,** *n.* [*noncount*] See -PRIM-.

prin•cess (prin′sis, -ses, prin ses′) /'prɪnsɪs, -sɛs, prɪn'sɛs/ *n.* [*count*] **1.** a female member of a royal family who is not ruling: *one of seven princesses in line to the throne.* [*as part of a title, before a name*]: *Princess Kristiana.* **2.** the wife of a prince. **3.** (in Great Britain) a daughter of the king or queen; the daughter of a son of the king or queen. **4.** a woman or girl thought of or treated as a princess: *a middle-class American princess.* **—adj.** [*before a noun*] **5.** Also, **prin′cesse.** (of a woman's dress) styled with a close-fitting top and flared skirt, cut in single pieces from shoulder to hem. See -PRIM-.

prin•ci•pal (prin′sə pəl) /'prɪnsəpəl/ *adj.* [*before a noun*] **1.** first in rank, value, etc.; chief; foremost. **—n. 2.** [*count*] a chief or head. **3.** [*count*] the head of a school or, esp. in England, a college. **4.** [*count*] a chief actor or performer: *The principals are supported by a great cast.* **5.** a sum of money, not counting interest or profit on it: [*noncount*]: *trying to pay off at least part of the principal.* [*count; usually singular*]: *a principal of about $20,000.* **6.** [*count*] each of the competitors or participants in a contest, as distinguished from their supporters. See -PRIM-.

prin•ci•pal•i•ty (prin′sə pal′i tē) /ˌprɪnsə'pælɪtiy/ *n.* [*count*], *pl.* **-ties.** a country or state ruled by a prince. See -PRIM-.

prin•ci•pal•ly (prin′sə pə lē, -sip lē) /'prɪnsəpəliy, -sɪpliy/ *adv.* chiefly; mainly; especially: *principally involved in the cover-up.* See -PRIM-.

prin•ci•ple (prin′sə pəl) /'prɪnsəpəl/ *n.* **1.** [*count*] a fundamental law that describes how a thing moves, works, or acts: *the principles of modern physics.* **2.** a personal basic rule by which one lives: [*count*]: *to stick to your principles and be honest and forthright.* [*noncount*]: *a man of principle.* **3.** [*count*] the method of operating reflected or used in a certain instance: *a family organized on the patriarchal principle.* **—*Idiom.* 4. in principle,** basically; fundamentally: *He favors the plan in principle.* **5. on principle,** according to rules for right conduct: *I refused to support her candidacy on principle.* See -PRIM-.

prin•ci•pled (prin′sə pəld) /'prɪnsəpəld/ *adj.* based on rules of right conduct: *took a principled stand.* See -PRIM-.

print (print) /prɪnt/ *v.* **1.** to produce (marks, etc.) by pressing plates, blocks, etc., to paper or other material: [~ + *obj*]: *This computer printer prints 100 characters per second.* [*no obj*]: *Can it print in color?* **2.** [~ + *obj*] to publish in printed form: *The newspaper refused to print the story.* **3.** to write in letters like those commonly used in print: [~ + *obj*]: *Please print your name at the top.* [*no obj*]: *Please print clearly.* **4.** [~ + *obj*] to produce (a pattern, etc.), as by pressure on cloth: *a printed Japanese kimono.* **5.** [~ + *obj*] *Photography.* to produce a positive picture from (a negative): *How much will it cost to print this negative?* **6. print out,** *Computers.* to produce (data) in printed form: [~ + *out* + *obj*]: *Print out the spreadsheet and hand it in.* [~ + *obj* + *out*]: *Print the essay out and hand it in with your disk.* **—n. 7.** [*noncount*] printed lettering, esp. with reference to style or size: *Use bold print to emphasize your words.* **8.** [*noncount*] printed material: *There they were, right in print, his very words for all to see.* **9.** [*count*] a picture, etc., printed from an engraved block, plate, etc.: *Several of the artist's best prints were hung on the wall.* **10.** [*count*] a fingerprint: *Your prints were found on the weapon.* **11.** [*count*] a design or pattern on cloth made by dyeing, weaving, or printing with engraved rollers, etc. **12.** [*count*] a photograph, esp. a positive made from a negative: *The prints had come out blurry.* **—adj.** [*before a noun*] **13.** of or relating to newspapers and magazines: *the print media.* **—*Idiom.* 14. in print,** (of a book or the like) still available for purchase from the publisher. **15. out of print,** (of a book or the like) no longer available for purchase from the publisher.

print•a•ble (prin′tə bəl) /'prɪntəbəl/ *adj.* **1.** that can be printed. **2.** suitable for printing; not causing offense: *His remarks were not printable.*

print•er (prin′tər) /'prɪntər/ *n.* [*count*] **1.** a person or company in the business of printing. **2.** a machine used for printing. **3.** a computer output device that produces a paper copy of data or graphics: *Be sure your printer is properly connected to the computer.*

print•ing (prin′ting) /'prɪntɪŋ/ *n.* **1.** [*noncount*] the skill, process, or business of producing books, etc., by printing from movable types, etc. **2.** [*count; usually singular*] the total number of copies of a publication printed at one time: *a first printing of 3000 copies.* **3.** [*noncount*] writing in which the letters resemble printed ones: *The first graders studied printing.*

print′ing press′, *n.* [*count*] a machine for printing on paper or from type, etc.

print•out (print′out′) /'prɪntˌawt/ *n.* computer output produced by a printer: [*count*]: *Be sure to include a printout of your work.* [*noncount*]: *the quality of printout.*

pri•or[1] (prī′ər) /'prayər/ *adj.* [*before a noun*] **1.** coming before another; earlier: *a prior commitment.* **2.** greater in importance: *a prior claim on his time.* **—*Idiom.* 3. prior to,** coming before; preceding; before: *Prior to this job she had worked in Austria.* See -PRIM-.

pri•or[2] (prī′ər) /'prayər/ *n.* [*count*] a monk in a monastery who is ranked next below an abbot.

pri•or•ess (prī′ər is) /'prayərɪs/ *n.* [*count*] a woman in a convent or abbey who is ranked next below an abbess.

pri•or•i•tize (prī ôr′i tīz′, -or′-) /pray'ɔrɪˌtayz, -'ɒr-/ *v.* [~ + *obj*], **-tized, -tiz•ing. 1.** to arrange or do in order of priority: *First let's prioritize the remaining tasks.* **2.** to assign a high priority to: *prioritized shipments of food to the refugees.* See -PRIM-.

pri•or•i•ty (prī ôr′i tē, -or′-) /pray'ɔrɪtiy, -'ɒr-/ *n.*, *pl.* **-ties. 1.** [*noncount*] the right to precede in order, rank, etc.; precedence: *Soldiers who are badly wounded have priority over those with minor wounds.* **2.** [*count*] something given or meriting special or prior attention: *a top priority.* See -PRIM-.

pri•o•ry (prī′ə rē) /'prayəriy/ *n.* [*count*], *pl.* **-ries.** a religious house run by a prior or prioress.

-pris-, *root.* *-pris-* comes from French and ultimately from Latin, where it has the meaning "grasp; take hold; seize." It is related to the root -PREHEND-. This meaning is found in such words as: APPRISE, COMPRISE, ENTERPRISE, PRISON, PRIZE, REPRISAL, REPRISE, SURPRISE.

prism (priz′əm) /'prɪzəm/ *n.* [*count*] **1.** *Optics.* a transparent solid object used for breaking up light into a spectrum of colors. **2.** *Geometry.* a solid having parallel bases and parallel sides. **—pris•mat•ic** (priz mat′ik) /prɪz'mætɪk/ *adj.*

pris•on (priz′ən) /'prɪzən/ *n.* **1.** [*count*] a place for keeping people accused of a crime and awaiting trial, or for keeping prisoners. **2.** [*noncount*] imprisonment: *thirty years in prison.* **3.** [*count*] any place or state of confinement. See -PRIS-.

pris•on•er (priz′ə nər, priz′nər) /'prɪzənər, 'prɪznər/ *n.*

[*count*] **1.** one kept in prison or kept in custody, esp. as the result of legal process or during a war: *an exchange of prisoners after the armistice.* **2.** a person or thing kept in restraint: *a prisoner of his own dreams.* See -PRIS-.

pris•sy (pris′ē) /ˈprɪsiy/ *adj.,* **-si•er, -si•est.** overly proper; too carefully correct and fussy; prim. —**pris•si•ly** (pris′ə lē) /ˈprɪsəliy/ *adv.* —**pris′si•ness,** *n.* [*noncount*]

pris•tine (pris′tēn, pri stēn′) /ˈprɪstiyn, prɪˈstiyn/ *adj.* having its original purity; not corrupted or made dirty: *the pristine beauty of the ancient forest.* See -PRIM-.

-priv-, *root.* -*priv-* comes from Latin, where it has the meaning "separated; apart; restricted." This meaning is found in such words as: DEPRIVATION, DEPRIVE, PRIVACY, PRIVATE, PRIVATION, PRIVILEGE, PRIVY, UNDERPRIVILEGED.

pri•va•cy (prī′və sē) /ˈprayvəsiy/ *n.* [*noncount*] the state of being private: *He had no privacy when he was growing up.* See -PRIV-.

pri•vate (prī′vit) /ˈprayvɪt/ *adj.* **1.** [*before a noun*] belonging to some particular person or persons: *private property.* **2.** [*before a noun*] of or relating to a particular person or a small group of persons: *for your private enjoyment.* **3.** intended only for the person or persons concerned; personal: *a private paper.* **4.** [*before a noun*] not holding public office or employment; not of an official or public character: *private citizens.* **5.** [*before a noun*] working as an independent agent: *a private detective.* **6.** not open to the general public: *a private beach.* **7.** preferring privacy: *She's a very private person.* **8.** [*before a noun*] not funded by public sources or agencies: *a small, private Catholic school.* —*n.* [*count*] **9.** a soldier of the lowest enlisted ranks. **10. privates,** PRIVATE PARTS. —***Idiom.*** **11. in private,** not publicly; secretly: *We met in private.* —**pri′vate•ly,** *adv.: Publicly she said one thing, but privately she went around saying just the opposite.* See -PRIV-.

pri•va•teer (prī′və tēr′) /ˌprayvəˈtɪər/ *n.* [*count*] **1.** a privately owned ship hired to fight or bother enemy ships. **2.** the captain or a crew member of such a vessel. See -PRIV-.

pri′vate eye′, *n.* [*count*] *Informal.* a private detective. See -PRIV-.

pri′vate parts′, *n.* [*plural*] the sex organs.

pri•va•tion (prī vā′shən) /prayˈveyʃən/ *n.* **1.** [*noncount*] lack of the usual comforts or necessary things of life. **2.** [*count*] an instance of this. See -PRIV-.

priv•et (priv′it) /ˈprɪvɪt/ *n.* [*count*] an evergreen shrub commonly grown as a hedge.

priv•i•lege (priv′ə lij, priv′lij) /ˈprɪvəlɪdʒ, ˈprɪvlɪdʒ/ *n.* **1.** [*noncount*] a special right or exemption granted to persons in authority that frees them from certain obligations: *The president claimed executive privilege.* **2.** [*noncount*] the principle or condition of enjoying special rights or advantages: *a life of wealth and privilege.* **3.** [*count*] a right or advantage that one enjoys, as because of a job: *had special parking privileges for as long as she wanted them.* **4.** [*count*] an advantage or source of pleasure granted to a person: *It's my privilege to be here.* See -PRIV-, -LEG-.

priv•i•leged (priv′ə lijd, priv′lijd) /ˈprɪvəlɪdʒd, ˈprɪvlɪdʒd/ *adj.* **1.** belonging to a class that enjoys privileges. **2.** restricted to a select group or an individual: *privileged information.* **3.** *Law.* (of statements or communications) confidential; protected from prosecution for libel or slander, or from being used or subpoenaed as evidence in court. See -PRIV-, -LEG-.

priv•y (priv′ē) /ˈprɪviy/ *adj.,* **-i•er, -i•est,** *n., pl.* **-priv•ies.** —*adj.* [*be* + ~ + *to*] **1.** having the knowledge of something private or secret: *Many people were privy to the plot.* —*n.* **2.** OUTHOUSE. See -PRIV-.

priv′y coun′cil, *n.* [*count*] a board or select body of personal advisers, as those of a king or queen.

prize[1] (prīz) /prayz/ *n.* **1.** a reward for victory, as in a contest or competition: [*count*]: *She won a prize for her science exhibit.* [*noncount; usually with some word indicating rank*]: *She won first prize in the science exhibit.* **2.** [*count*] something won in a lottery or the like. **3.** [*count*] anything that one tries to achieve or gain; something much valued: *He thought of her as a prize to be won.* —*adj.* [*before a noun*] **4.** having won a prize: *a prize play.* **5.** worthy of a prize: *his prize collection of stamps.* **6.** given or awarded as a prize: *prize money.* **7.** (used before a noun to express the opinion that something is a perfect or typical example of that noun): *That was one of his prize blunders.*

prize[2] (prīz) /prayz/ *v.* [~ + *obj*], **prized, priz•ing.** to value (something) highly. See -PRIS-.

prize•fight or **prize fight,** (prīz′fīt′) /ˈprayzˌfayt/ *n.* [*count*] a professional boxing match. —**prize′fight′er,** *n.* [*count*]

pro[1] (prō) /prow/ *adv., adj., n., pl.* **pros.** —*adv.* **1.** in favor of an idea, proposal, etc. — *adj.* favorable: *the pro side of the argument.* —*n.* [*count*] **2.** the argument, position, or voter for something: *the pros and cons.* Compare CON[1].

pro[2] (prō) /prow/ *adj., n., pl.* **pros.** —*adj.* **1.** professional: *He turned pro last year.* —*n.* [*count*] **2.** a professional: *She's a real pro; she won't let you down.*

pro-[1], *prefix.* **1.** *pro-* comes from Latin, where it has the meaning "forward, forward movement or location; advancement": *proceed; progress; prominent; promote; propose.* **2.** *pro-* is also attached to roots and words and means "bringing into existence": *procreate; produce.* **3.** *pro-* is also attached to roots and words and means "in place of": *pronoun.* **4.** *pro-* is also used to form adjectives that have the meaning "favoring the group, interests, course of action, etc., named by the noun; calling for the interests named by the noun": *pro- + choice → pro-choice (= in favor of allowing a choice to be made regarding abortions); pro- + war → prowar (= in favor of fighting a war).*

pro-[2], *prefix.* **1.** *pro-* comes from Greek, and has the meaning "before, beforehand, in front of": *proboscis; prognosis; prophylactic; prothesis.* **2.** *pro-* is also attached to a word and means "primitive or early form": *prodrug; prosimian.*

-prob-, *root.* -*prob-* comes from Latin, where it has the meaning "prove." This meaning is found in such words as: APPROBATION, IMPROBABLE, OPPROBRIOUS, OPPROBRIUM, PROBABILITY, PROBABLE, PROBABLY, PROBATE, PROBATION, PROBE, PROBITY, REPROBATE. See -PROV-.

prob., an abbreviation of: **1.** probable. **2.** probably. **3.** problem.

prob•a•bil•i•ty (prob′ə bil′i tē) /ˌprɒbəˈbɪlɪtiy/ *n., pl.* **-ties. 1.** [*noncount*] the quality or fact of being probable: *little probability of success.* **2.** [*count*] a probable event, circumstance, etc.: *It's a real probability that he'll be reelected.* **3.** *Statistics.* the possibility or chance that an event will occur, expressed by the number of occurrences that actually happen divided by the total number of possible occurrences: [*count*]: *a probability of fifty percent for the coin to land heads up.* [*noncount*]: *a math problem in probability.* —***Idiom.*** **4. in all probability,** very probably; quite likely: *The factory will in all probability be shut down by next year.* See -PROB-.

prob•a•ble (prob′ə bəl) /ˈprɒbəbəl/ *adj.* **1.** likely to occur or prove true: *a probable defeat.* **2.** [*It* + *be* + ~ + *that clause*] having more evidence for something than against it: *Although anything is possible, it is more probable that he'll recover completely.* **3.** [*before a noun*] likely to be or become: *the probable successor to the throne.* See -PROB-.

prob•a•bly (prob′ə blē) /ˈprɒbəbliy/ *adv.* (used to express the opinion that what is said is very likely to come true or be true, but that it is not certain): *I'll probably see her tomorrow.* See -PROB-.

pro•bate (prō′bāt) /ˈprowbeyt/ *n., adj., v.,* **-bat•ed, -bat•ing.** —*n.* [*noncount*] **1.** the process or procedure of officially proving that a will is authentic in a court. —*adj.* [*before a noun*] **2.** of or relating to this process, or to the court where it takes place. —*v.* [~ + *obj*] **3.** to prove that (a will) is valid. See -PROB-.

pro•ba•tion (prō bā′shən) /prowˈbeyʃən/ *n.* [*noncount*] **1.** the status or period of trial for a student who has failing marks or bad behavior: *He was put on probation for assaulting another student.* **2.** the status of a convicted offender who has been allowed to go free under the supervision of a probation officer: *The courts released him on probation.* —**pro•ba′tion•al,** *adj.* See -PROB-.

pro•ba•tion•ar•y (prō bā′shə ner′ē) /prowˈbeyʃəˌnɛriy/ *adj.* [*before a noun*] **1.** being in a state of academic probation: *a probationary student.* **2.** of or relating to convicted offenders who are on probation: *probationary corrections officers.* **3.** of or relating to the period or time of probation: *a probationary period of one year.* See -PROB-.

pro•ba•tion•er (prō bā′shə nər) /prowˈbeyʃənər/ *n.* [*count*] a person undergoing probation. See -PROB-.

proba′tion of′ficer, *n.* [*count*] an officer who investigates and reports on the conduct of criminal offenders who are on probation.

probe (prōb) /prowb/ *v.,* **probed, prob•ing,** *n.* —*v.* **1.** to examine with or as if with a probe: [~ + *obj*]: *The doctor probed the wound carefully before removing the bullet.* [*no obj*]: *She probed carefully into the wound.* **2.** to search into or examine thoroughly: [~ + *obj*]: *He probed his conscience to figure out what he should do.* [*no obj*]: *The economist probed into the problem.* —*n.* [*count*] **3.** a slender surgical instrument for exploring the depth or direction of a wound, sinus, or the like: *inserting a probe into the wound.* **4.** any slender device inserted into something in order to explore or examine: *A probe was pushed slowly into the reactor core to determine how much radioactivity had been released.* **5.** an investigation of suspected illegal activity: *promised a probe into the scandal.* **6.** a satellite sent into space to examine conditions and report back; a space probe. See -PROB-.

pro•bi•ty (prō′bi tē, prob′i-) /'prowbɪtiy, 'prɒbɪ-/ *n.* [*noncount*] complete honesty; integrity; uprightness: *questions aimed at testing the probity of the witness.* See -PROB-.

prob•lem (prob′ləm) /'prɒbləm/ *n.* [*count*] **1.** any question or matter involving doubt or difficulty: *has financial and emotional problems.* **2.** a statement requiring a solution, usually by means of mathematical operations: *simple problems in addition.* —*adj.* [*before a noun*] **3.** unwilling to cooperate; unruly: *a problem child.* —***Idiom.*** **4. no problem,** (is used to express the speaker's willingness to do something): *"Can you come to the meeting tomorrow?" —"No problem."*

prob•lem•at•ic (prob′lə mat′ik) /ˌprɒblə'mætɪk/ also **prob′lem•at′i•cal,** *adj.* of the nature of a problem; doubtful: *a problematic rise in unemployment rates.*

pro bo•no or **pro-bo•no** (prō′ bō′nō) /ˌprow' bownow/ *adj.* done or donated without charge; free: *pro bono legal services.*

pro•bos•cis (prō bos′is, -kis) /prow'bɒsɪs, -kɪs/ *n.* [*count*], *pl.* **-bos•cis•es, -bos•ci•des** (-bos′i dēz′) /-'bɒsɪˌdiyz/. **1.** the long, flexible nose of certain animals, as of an elephant. **2.** any long part that sticks out on the head of certain insects or worms, used for feeding or for sensing food. **3.** (humorous) the human nose, esp. when large.

pro•ce•dur•al (prə sē′jər əl) /prə'siydʒərəl/ *adj.* of or relating to a procedure: *The problem is simply a procedural matter.* See -CEDE-.

pro•ce•dure (prə sē′jər) /prə'siydʒər/ *n.* any established way for doing something, or for conducting business: [*count*]: *Getting a license should be a simple procedure.* [*noncount*]: *If you fail to follow correct procedure, your payments will be delayed.* See -CEDE-.

pro•ceed (*v.* prə sēd′; *n.* prō′sēd) / *v.* prə'siyd; *n.* 'prowsiyd/ *v.* **1.** [*no obj*] to move or go forward or onward, esp. after stopping: *The suspect then proceeded down Broadway and turned left at 23rd Street.* **2.** [*no obj; often:* ~ + *with* + *obj*] to carry on or continue any action already started: *Proceed with your meeting and pretend I'm not here.* **3.** [~ + *to* + *verb*] to go on to do something: *He proceeded to tell us the whole sad story.* **4. proceed against,** [~ + *against* + *obj*] to start a legal action. **5. proceed from,** [~ + *from* + *obj*] to arise, start, or result from: *Let's proceed from the assumption that she meant you no harm.* —*n.* **proceeds,** [*plural*] **6.** the total amount or profit made from a sale or other business activity: *She donated the proceeds of the auction to charity.* See -CEED-.

pro•ceed•ings (prə sē′dingz) /prə'siydɪŋz/ *n.* [*plural*] **1.** a series of activities or events. **2.** a record of the business discussed at a meeting. **3.** legal action, esp. as carried on in a court of law. See -CEDE-.

proc•ess (pros′es) /'prɒsɛs/ *n., pl.* **proc•ess•es** (pros′es- iz, -ə siz, -ə sēz′) /'prɒsɛsɪz, -əsɪz, -əˌsiyz/ *v.* —*n.* [*count*] **1.** a series of actions aimed at accomplishing some result: *a process for homogenizing milk.* **2.** a continuous action, operation, or series of changes taking place in a definite manner: *the process of decay.* **3.** course or passing, as of time: *in the process of moving his office.* —*v.* [~ + *obj*] **4.** to treat or prepare (raw materials or the like) by some process, as in manufacturing: *The factory processes the fibers and makes cotton sheets.* **5.** to handle (persons, papers, etc.) according to a regular procedure: *The passport office processes thousands of applications.* **6.** to accept, handle, and organize (data), esp. electronically: *The computer can process thousands of bits of information.* —*adj.* [*before a noun*] **7.** prepared or modified by a special process: *processed food.* —***Idiom.*** **8. in the process,** at the same time (as); simultaneously: *Our bombing mission was a success, but in the process we lost over seventy aircraft.* See -CESS-.

pro•ces•sion (prə sesh′ən) /prə'sɛʃən/ *n.* **1.** the act of moving along or proceeding in an orderly manner, and in a formal and ceremonious way: [*count*]: *a bridal procession.* [*noncount; in* + ~]: *marching in procession.* **2.** [*count*] a line or body of persons, vehicles, etc., moving along in such a manner: *a funeral procession.* —*v.* [*no obj*] **3.** to go in procession. See -CESS-.

pro•ces•sion•al (prə sesh′ə nl) /prə'sɛʃənl/ *adj.* [*before a noun*] **1.** of or relating to a procession: *the processional route.* —*n.* [*count*] **2.** a piece of music for accompanying a procession. See -CESS-.

proc•es•sor or **proc•ess•er** (pros′es ər) /'prɒsɛsər/ *n.* [*count*] **1.** a person or thing that processes: *a food processor.* **2.** a computer.

pro-choice or **pro•choice** (prō chois′) /prow'tʃɔys/ *adj.* supporting or calling for the right to legalized abortion: *a pro-choice candidate.* —**pro-choic′er,** *n.* [*count*]

pro•claim (prō klām′, prə-) /prow'kleym, prə-/ *v.* to declare in an official public manner: [~ + *obj*]: *to proclaim a great victory.* [~ + *that clause*]: *The dictator proclaimed that all the political prisoners could go free.* See -CLAIM-.

proc•la•ma•tion (prok′lə mā′shən) /ˌprɒklə'meyʃən/ *n.* **1.** [*noncount*] the act of proclaiming: *by proclamation.* **2.** [*count*] something proclaimed: *a proclamation of independence.* See -CLAIM-.

pro•cliv•i•ty (prō kliv′i tē) /prow'klɪvɪtiy/ *n.* [*count*], *pl.* **-ties.** natural tendency, as to do or behave in a certain way; predisposition: *a proclivity to be a bit bossy.*

pro•cras•ti•nate (prō kras′tə nāt′, prə-) /prow'kræstəˌneyt, prə-/ *v.* [*no obj*], **-nat•ed, -nat•ing.** to put off action until some later time: *He procrastinated so long that the opportunity was lost.* —**pro•cras•ti•na•tion** (prō kras′tə nā′shən, prə-) /prowˌkræstə'neyʃən, prə-/ *n.* [*noncount*] —**pro•cras′ti•na′tor,** *n.* [*count*]

pro•cre•ate (prō′krē āt′) /'prowkriyˌeyt/ *v.,* **-at•ed, -at•ing.** to generate (offspring or young): [*no obj*]: *Human beings need to procreate.* [~ + *obj*]: *to procreate offspring.* —**pro•cre•a•tion** (prō′krē ā′shən) /ˌprowkriy'eyʃən/ *n.* [*noncount*]: *The primary purpose of sex was procreation.* —**pro′cre•a′tive,** *adj.*: *procreative tendencies.*

proc•tor (prok′tər) /'prɒktər/ *n.* [*count*] **1.** one whose job is to keep watch over students during examinations. —*v.* **2.** to supervise or monitor: [~ + *obj*]: *to proctor the exam.* [*no obj*]: *to proctor during the exam.*

proc•u•ra•tor (prok′yə rā′tər) /'prɒkyəˌreytər/ *n.* [*count*] (in ancient Rome) any of various agents with fiscal or administrative powers granted by the emperor, esp. in a province. See -CURA-.

pro•cure (prō kyŏŏr′, prə-) /prow'kyʊr, prə-/ *v.,* **-cured, -cur•ing. 1.** [~ + *obj*] to obtain (something) by care or effort: *to procure secret documents.* **2.** to obtain (a person) for prostitution: [~ + *obj*]: *procuring young prostitutes.* [*no obj*]: *arrested for procuring.* —**pro•cur′a•ble,** *adj.* —**pro•cure′ment,** *n.* [*noncount*]: *checking government procurement contracts.* —**pro•cur′er,** *n.* [*count*]

prod (prod) /prɒd/ *v.,* **prod•ded, prod•ding,** *n.* —*v.* [~ + *obj*] **1.** to jab with something pointed: *to prod the cattle along.* **2.** to incite as if by poking; nag; goad: *If those insults don't prod him into action, what will?* —*n.* [*count*] **3.** the act of prodding; a poke or jab. **4.** any of various pointed instruments used to force someone or some animal to move along: *a cattle prod.*

prod•i•gal (prod′i gəl) /'prɒdɪgəl/ *adj.* **1.** wasteful in spending money unwisely. —*n.* [*count*] **2.** one who spends money recklessly. —**prod•i•gal•i•ty** (prod′i gal′i tē) /ˌprɒdɪ'gælɪtiy/ *n.* [*noncount*]

pro•di•gious (prə dij′əs) /prə'dɪdʒəs/ *adj.* **1.** extraordinary in size, amount, etc.: *a prodigious amount of research.* **2.** causing admiration: *a prodigious feat.* —**pro•di′gious•ly,** *adv.*

prod•i•gy (prod′i jē) /'prɒdɪdʒiy/ *n.* [*count*], *pl.* **-gies.** a person, esp. a child, having extraordinary talent: *a musical prodigy.*

pro•duce (*v.* prə dōōs′, -dyōōs′; *n.* prod′ōōs, -yōōs, prō′dōōs, -dyōōs) / *v.* prə'duws, -'dyuws; *n.* 'prɒduws, -yuws, 'prowduws, -dyuws/ *v.,* **-duced, -duc•ing,** *n.* —*v.* **1.** [~ + *obj*] to cause to exist; give rise to: *The reactor produces steam.* **2.** [~ + *obj*] to bring into existence by the mind or by creative ability: *to produce a great painting.* **3.** to make or manufacture: [~ + *obj*]: *to produce automobiles for export.* [*no obj*]: *The new auto plant is not ready to produce yet.* **4.** [~ + *obj*] to give birth to; bear: *The female sheep produces lambs in the spring.* **5.** to furnish or supply; yield: [~ + *obj*]: *a mine that produces silver.* [*no obj*]: *That oil well is no longer producing.* **6.** [~ + *obj*] to present; exhibit: *He produced his credentials.* **7.** [~ + *obj*] to bring (a play, etc.) before the public: *produced several network TV shows.* —*n.* **prod•**

uce, [*noncount*] **8.** agricultural products thought of as a group, esp. vegetables and fruits: *The farmers sell produce from the back of their trucks.* See -DUC-.

pro•duc•er (prə do͞o′sər, -dyo͞o′-) /prəˈduwsər, -ˈdyuw-/ *n.* [*count*] **1.** a person, group, etc., that makes or supplies something for another: *The Middle East is an important oil producer.* **2.** one in charge of bringing a play, etc., before the public: *worked as an executive producer for that news show.* See -DUC-.

prod•uct (prod′əkt, -ukt) /ˈprɒdəkt, -ʌkt/ *n.* [*count*] **1.** a thing produced by labor: *farm products.* **2.** all the goods or services that a company produces: *the gross national product.* **3.** a person or thing thought of as resulting from a process: *She was a product of the 60's.* **4.** *Math.* the result of multiplying two or more numbers together. See -DUC-.

pro•duc•tion (prə duk′shən) /prəˈdʌkʃən/ *n.* **1.** [*noncount*] the act of producing: *improved methods of production.* **2.** [*count*] something produced; a product. **3.** [*noncount*] the total amount produced: *Factory output and production are down.* **4.** [*count*] a situation or activity that has been made complicated or difficult for no good reason: *That child makes a big production out of going to bed every night.* See -DUC-.

pro•duc•tive (prə duk′tiv) /prəˈdʌktɪv/ *adj.* **1.** that produces a large amount: *a very productive writer.* **2.** producing a useful result: *a very productive meeting.* —**pro•duc′tive•ly,** *adv.* —**pro•duc′tive•ness,** *n.* [*noncount*] See -DUC-.

pro•duc•tiv•i•ty (prō′dək tiv′i tē, prod′ək-) /ˌprowdəkˈtɪvɪtiy, ˌprɒdək-/ *n.* [*noncount*] the degree to which a person, company, etc., is able to produce efficiently: *Decreases in productivity inevitably lead to declining profits.* See -DUC-.

prof (prof) /prɒf/ *n.* [*count*] *Informal.* professor.

Prof., an abbreviation of: Professor.

pro•fane (prə fān′, prō-) /prəˈfeyn, prow-/ *adj., v.,* **-faned, -fan•ing.** —*adj.* **1.** showing disrespect toward God or sacred things; blasphemous. **2.** not devoted to holy purposes. —*v.* [~ + *obj*] **3.** to misuse (anything sacred or holy); defile; debase. —**prof•a•na•tion** (prof′ə-nā′shən) /ˌprɒfəˈneyʃən/ *n.* [*noncount*] —**pro•fane′ly,** *adv.* —**pro•fane′ness,** *n.* [*noncount*]

pro•fan•i•ty (prə fan′i tē, prō-) /prəˈfænɪtiy, prow-/ *n., pl.* **-ties. 1.** [*noncount*] the quality of being profane; irreverence. **2.** irreverent speech: [*noncount*]: *a book full of profanity.* [*count*]: *shouting profanities and insults.*

pro•fess (prə fes′) /prəˈfɛs/ *v.* **1.** to claim to have, be, or feel (something), often insincerely; pretend to have: [~ + *obj*]: *professed regret at what he called "this unfortunate incident."* [~ + *to* + *verb*]: *He professed to respect human rights, but he was quick to deny them when it suited him.* **2.** [~ + *obj*] to declare openly; announce; affirm: *He professed his complete satisfaction with your product.* **3.** [~ + *obj*] to affirm one's faith in (a religion, God, etc.): *to profess Christianity.* See -FESS-.

pro•fessed (prə fest′) /prəˈfɛst/ *adj.* [*before a noun*] claiming to have or be (the noun mentioned): *a professed atheist.* See -FESS-.

pro•fes•sion (prə fesh′ən) /prəˈfɛʃən/ *n.* **1.** [*count*] an occupation requiring a great deal of education or specialized training. **2.** any occupation, form of employment, or business: [*count*]: *an interesting profession.* [*noncount; by* + ~]: *a teacher by profession.* **3.** [*noncount*] the group of persons working in such an occupation: *thinks the medical profession is greatly overpaid.* **4.** [*count*] the declaring of one's belief in religion or a faith. See -FESS-.

pro•fes•sion•al (prə fesh′ə nl) /prəˈfɛʃənl/ *adj.* **1.** [*before a noun*] engaged in an occupation as a means of earning a livelihood: *a professional soldier; a professional musician.* **2.** relating to a profession: *a professional license.* **3.** appropriate to a profession: *showing professional objectivity; He's too professional to let his personal feelings interfere with his work.* **4.** [*before a noun*] of or for a professional person or such a person's place of business: *a professional apartment.* **5.** [*before a noun*] done by a professional; expert; of a high standard: *professional advice.* **6.** [*before a noun*] making a constant practice of something: *A salesman has to be a professional optimist.* —*n.* [*count*] **7.** a member of a profession. **8.** a person who earns a living in a sport or other occupation that is frequently engaged in by amateurs. —**pro•fes′sion•al•ly,** *adv.* See -FESS-.

pro•fes•sion•al•ism (prə fesh′ə nl iz′əm) /prəˈfɛʃənlˌɪzəm/ *n.* [*noncount*] professional character, spirit, or methods. See -FESS-.

pro•fes•sor (prə fes′ər) /prəˈfɛsər/ *n.* [*count*] **1.** a college or university teacher of the highest academic rank in a particular branch of learning. [*before a name*]: *Professor John Doe.* **2.** any teacher who has the rank of professor, as an associate professor or assistant professor. [*before a name*]: *Professor Jane Doe.* —**pro′fes•so′ri•al,** *adj.* See -FESS-.

prof•fer (prof′ər) /ˈprɒfər/ *v.* to put before a person for acceptance; offer: [~ + *obj*]: *He proffered his hand, but I refused to shake it.* [~ + *obj* + *to* + *obj*]: *He proffered his hand to me.* [~ + *obj* + *obj*]: *He proffered me his hand.* See -FER-.

pro•fi•cient (prə fish′ənt) /prəˈfɪʃənt/ *adj.* fully skilled in any art, science, or subject; competent: *a proficient swimmer.* —**pro•fi′cien•cy** (prə fish′ən sē) /prəˈfɪʃənsiy/ *n.* [*noncount*] —**pro•fi′cient•ly,** *adv.* See -FEC-.

pro•file (prō′fīl) /ˈprowfayl/ *n., v.,* **-filed, -fil•ing.** —*n.* [*count*] **1.** the outline of the human face as viewed from one side. **2.** the look or general contour of something: *the profile of a mountain.* **3.** a summary of a process, activity, or set of characteristics: *a profile of consumer spending.* **4.** a short, informal piece of writing about someone: *a profile of the mayor and his rise to power.* **5.** the degree to which someone is noticed; visibility: *Keep a low profile until this trouble passes.* —*v.* [~ + *obj*] **6.** to draw, write, or produce a profile of.

prof•it (prof′it) /ˈprɒfɪt/ *n.* **1.** Often, **profits.** [*plural*] money gained, as from a business or transaction, after deducting all relevant costs: [*count*]: *Profits were up this year.* [*noncount*]: *to maximize profit and minimize loss.* **2.** [*noncount*] advantage; benefit; gain: *What profit is there in honesty?* —*v.* **3.** to gain an advantage or benefit: [*no obj*]: *to profit from good fortune.* [~ + *obj*]: *What does it profit a man to gain the world, only to lose his soul?*

prof•it•a•ble (prof′i tə bəl) /ˈprɒfɪtəbəl/ *adj.* making or gaining a profit, advantage, or benefit: *a profitable business.* —**prof′it•ab•ly,** *adv.*

prof•it•eer (prof′i tēr′) /ˌprɒfɪˈtɪər/ *n.* [*count*] **1.** a person who makes too much profit from the sale of scarce goods. —*v.* [*no obj*] **2.** to act as a profiteer.

prof•li•gate (prof′li git, -gāt′) /ˈprɒflɪgɪt, -ˌgeyt/ *adj.* **1.** completely immoral or licentious. **2.** spending or using up something unwisely. —*n.* [*count*] **3.** a profligate person. —**prof•li•ga•cy** (prof′li gə sē) /ˈprɒflɪgəsiy/ *n.* [*noncount*]

pro for•ma (prō fôr′mə) /ˈprow fɔrmə/ *adj.* done purely as a matter of form; not genuine: *a pro forma apology.*

pro•found (prə found′) /prəˈfawnd/ *adj.,* **-er, -est. 1.** showing deep insight or understanding; going beyond what is obvious or easily seen: *a profound thinker.* **2.** coming from the deepest part of one's feelings or being: *his profound grief at the loss of his children.* **3.** [*before a noun*] complete and total; extending everywhere: *a profound silence.* **4.** [*before a noun*] stretching to or situated far beneath the surface: *the profound depths of the ocean.* —**pro•found′ly,** *adv.*

pro•fun•di•ty (prə fun′di tē) /prəˈfʌndɪtiy/ *n., pl.* **-ties. 1.** [*noncount*] the quality or state of being profound or deep. **2.** [*count*] a profound or deep matter.

pro•fuse (prə fyo͞os′) /prəˈfyuws/ *adj.* **1.** [*be* + ~ + *in/of*] generous; lavish: *The critics were profuse in their praise of the new movie.* **2.** abundant: *profuse apologies.* —**pro•fuse′ly,** *adv.* See -FUS-.

pro•fu•sion (prə fyo͞o′zhən) /prəˈfyuwʒən/ *n.* a great amount or quantity (of something): [*count*]: *a great profusion of colors.* [*noncount*]: *colors in rich profusion.*

pro•gen•i•tor (prō jen′i tər) /prowˈdʒɛnɪtər/ *n.* [*count*] **1.** an ancestor related by birth. **2.** originator; precursor: *a progenitor of the modern airplane.* See -GEN-.

prog•e•ny (proj′ə nē) /ˈprɒdʒəniy/ *n.* [*count*], *pl.* **-nies. 1. a.** [*plural*] a person's offspring when they are thought of as a group; one's children: *Their progeny were asleep.* **b.** (broadly) descendants. **2.** something that originates or results from something else; outcome; issue. See -GEN-.

prog•no•sis (prog nō′sis) /prɒgˈnowsɪs/ *n.* [*count*], *pl.* **-ses** (-sēz) /-siyz/. **1.** a forecasting of the probable course and outcome of a disease, esp. of the chances of recovery. **2.** a forecast or prediction. —**prog•nos•tic** (prog-nos′tik) /prɒgˈnɒstɪk/ *adj.* See -GNOS-.

prog•nos•ti•cate (prog nos′ti kāt′) /prɒgˈnɒstɪˌkeyt/ *v.* [~ + *obj*], **-cat•ed, -cat•ing.** to (make a) forecast on the basis of present signs or indications; prophesy: *He prognosticates a complete recovery in less than a year.* —**prog•nos•ti•ca•tion** (prog nos′ti kā′shən) /prɒgˌnɒstɪˈkeyʃən/ *n.* [*noncount*]: *the uselessness of empty prognostication.* [*count*]: *favorable prognostications.* —**prog•nos′ti•ca′tor,** *n.* [*count*] See -GNOS-.

pro•gram (prō′gram, -grəm) /ˈprowgræm, -grəm/ *n., v.,* **-grammed** or **-gramed, -gram•ming** or **-gram•ing.** —*n.* [*count*] **1.** a plan of action to accomplish a certain goal or end: *a drug rehabilitation program.* **2.** a planned or coordinated schedule of activities. **3.** a radio or television performance or production. **4.** a list of selections, performers, etc., included in a musical, theatrical, or other entertainment, a booklet containing such a list, or the selections themselves. **5.** an entertainment with reference to its pieces or numbers: *a program of French songs.* **6.** a sequence of instructions enabling a computer to perform a task; piece of software. —*v.* **7.** [~ + *obj*] to schedule or establish as part of a program: *The bells are programmed to go off at noon.* **8.** to provide a program for (a computer): [~ + *obj*]: *He used BASIC to program his computer.* [*no obj*]: *He programmed in BASIC.* **9.** [~ + *obj*] **a.** to insert, enter, or type instructions into: *to program a VCR to record a show.* **b.** to enter (instructions) into a machine or apparatus: *to program the schedule into the VCR.* **10.** [~ + *obj*] to fill with attitudes, behavior patterns, or the like; condition: *to program children to respect their elders.* Also, *esp. Brit.,* **pro′gramme.** —**pro′gram•ma•ble,** *adj.* —**pro•gram•mat•ic** (prō′grə mat′ik) /ˌprowgrəˈmætɪk/ *adj.*

pro•gram•mer (prō′gram ər) /ˈprowgræmər/ *n.* [*count*] a person who writes computer programs.

prog•ress (*n.* prog′res, -rəs) / *n.* ˈprɒgrɛs, -rəs/ *n.* [*noncount*] **1.** advancement toward a goal or to a further or higher stage: *to make progress in the disarmament talks.* **2.** growth or development; improvement: *to show progress in muscular coordination.* **3.** forward or onward movement: *the progress of the planets around the sun.* —*v.* **pro•gress** [*no obj*] **4.** to go forward or onward in space or time: *The years are progressing.* **5.** to grow or develop, presumably toward a goal or to a higher or further stage: *progressing in my studies.* —***Idiom.*** **6. in progress,** going on; under way: *His long novel is a work in progress.* See -GRESS-.

pro•gres•sion (prə gresh′ən) /prəˈgrɛʃən/ *n.* **1.** [*noncount*] the act of progressing; forward or onward movement. **2.** [*count*] a passing in a series from one member of the series to the next; a succession. **3.** [*count*] a series of quantities in which there is a uniform relation between each member and the one following it: *an arithmetic progression.* See -GRESS-.

pro•gres•sive (prə gres′iv) /prəˈgrɛsɪv/ *adj.* **1.** calling for or favoring progress, reform, or new methods and outlooks, esp. in political and social matters. **2.** passing from one stage to the next: *progressive increases in computer power.* **3.** continuously increasing in extent or severity: *a progressive worsening of the disease.* **4.** increasing in rate as taxable income increases: *a progressive tax.* **5.** of or being a verb tense or form used to indicate that an action or event is, was, or will be going on at some period of time: *Progressive verb tenses end in* -ing *and are preceded by a form of the verb* to be: *I have been working, I am working, and I will be working.* —*n.* [*count*] **6.** a person who favors progress or reform, as in politics. **7.** a verb form or construction in the progressive tense or aspect, as *am listening* or *was sleeping.* —**pro•gres′sive•ly,** *adv.* See -GRESS-.

pro•hib•it (prō hib′it) /prowˈhɪbɪt/ *v.* [~ + *obj* (+ *from* + *verb-ing*)] **1.** to forbid (an action, activity, etc.) by authority, rule, or law: *Smoking was prohibited in public places.* **2.** to prevent; hinder; cause (something) to be impossible: *Lack of funds prohibited her from taking classes.* See -HAB-.

pro•hi•bi•tion (prō′ə bish′ən) /ˌprowəˈbɪʃən/ *n.* **1.** [*noncount*] the act of prohibiting. **2.** [*noncount*] **a.** the prohibiting of the manufacture, sale, and transportation of alcoholic beverages by law. **b.** [*usually: Prohibition*] the period (1920–33) during which such a law was in effect in the U.S. **3.** [*count*] a law, rule, order, or regulation that forbids: *a prohibition against public nudity.* —**pro′hi•bi′tion•ist,** *n.* [*count*] See -HAB-.

pro•hib•i•tive (prō hib′i tiv) /prowˈhɪbɪtɪv/ *adj.* **1.** too high to be afforded: *prohibitive prices.* **2.** preventing, hindering, or forbidding the use of something: *prohibitive regulations.* —**pro•hib′i•tive•ly,** *adv.* See -HAB-.

proj•ect (*n.* proj′ekt, -ikt) / *n.* ˈprɒdʒɛkt, -ɪkt/ *n.* [*count*] **1.** a specific plan; scheme. **2.** a large or important, often public undertaking: *a project to widen the streets of the city.* **3.** a specific task in schoolwork or education, esp. a long-term assignment: *You must complete a science project this term.* **4.** Often, **projects.** [*plural*] a publicly built and operated housing development, usually intended for low- or moderate-income tenants. —*v.* **pro•ject 5.** [~ + *obj*] to devise, propose, or plan: *The campaign was projected to include all 50 states.* **6.** [~ + *obj*] to throw or force forward, onward, or outward. **7.** [~ + *obj*] to calculate or figure out (some future cost, amount, etc.): *Inflation is projected to increase next year.* **8.** [~ + *obj*] to throw or cause (a ray of light, an image, a shadow, etc.) to fall upon a surface or into space: *The light projected his shadow onto the wall behind him.* **9.** [*no obj*] to stick out or stand out over an edge: *His ears projected from the sides of his head.* **10.** to use (one's voice, gestures, etc.) forcefully enough to be heard or understood by all members of an audience: [~ + *obj*]: *Project your voice so that people in the back can hear you.* [*no obj*]: *You need to project more.* **11.** [~ + *obj*] to communicate clearly and forcefully (one's thoughts, feelings, etc.) to an audience: *The actor projected a feeling of sadness.* **12.** [~ + *obj*] to attribute one's own feelings, thoughts, or attitudes to other persons: *You're projecting your own insecurity onto them.* See -JEC-.

pro•jec•tile (prə jek′til, -tīl) /prəˈdʒɛktɪl, -tayl/ *n.* [*count*] an object fired from a gun with an explosive charge, as a bullet or shell. See -JEC-.

pro•jec•tion (prə jek′shən) /prəˈdʒɛkʃən/ *n.* **1.** [*noncount*] the act of projecting. **2.** [*count*] something that sticks out or stands out over an edge. **3.** [*count*] an estimate of some future cost, amount, or the like: *sales projections for next year.* See -JEC-.

pro•jec•tion•ist (prə jek′shə nist) /prəˈdʒɛkʃənɪst/ *n.* [*count*] an operator of a motion-picture or slide projector.

pro•jec•tor (prə jek′tər) /prəˈdʒɛktər/ *n.* [*count*] a machine for throwing an image, films, photographs, slides, etc., onto a screen.

pro•le•tar•i•an (prō′li târ′ē ən) /ˌprowlɪˈtɛəriyən/ *adj.* **1.** of or relating to the proletariat. —*n.* [*count*] **2.** a member of the proletariat.

pro•le•tar•i•at (prō′li târ′ē ət) /ˌprowlɪˈtɛəriyət/ *n.* [*noncount; usually: the* + ~] the class of workers, esp. wage earners, who do not possess capital or property and must sell their labor to live.

pro-life′, *adj.* opposed to legalized abortion; right-to-life. Compare PRO-CHOICE. —**pro-lif′er,** *n.* [*count*]

pro•lif•er•ate (prə lif′ə rāt′) /prəˈlɪfəˌreyt/ *v.* [*no obj*], **-at•ed, -at•ing.** to increase in number; spread rapidly: *Fish proliferated in the warm seas.* —**pro•lif•er•a•tion** (prə lif ə rā′shən) /prəlɪfəˈreyʃən/ *n.* [*noncount*]

pro•lif•ic (prə lif′ik) /prəˈlɪfɪk/ *adj.* **1.** producing offspring, young, fruit, etc., rapidly or in great numbers: *a prolific species of plant.* **2.** highly productive: *a prolific writer.* —**pro•lif′i•cal•ly,** *adv.* See -FIC-.

pro•lix (prō liks′, prō′liks) /prowˈlɪks, ˈprowlɪks/ *adj.* too long or wordy. —**pro•lix•i•ty** (prō lik′si tē) /prowˈlɪksɪtiy/ *n.* [*noncount*] —**pro•lix′ly,** *adv.*

pro•logue or **pro•log** (prō′lôg, -log) /ˈprowlɔg, -lɒg/ *n.* [*count*] **1.** an introductory part of a story, poem, novel, speech, etc. **2.** an introductory speech or scene in a play or opera. **3.** anything that serves as an introduction: *The thunder was a prologue to the storm.* See -LOG-.

pro•long (prə lông′, -long′) /prəˈlɔŋ, -ˈlɒŋ/ *v.* [~ + *obj*] to extend the amount of time for; cause (something) to continue longer: *prolonged their visit.* —**pro•lon•ga•tion** (prō′lông gā′shən) /ˌprowlɔŋˈgeyʃən/ *n.* [*noncount*]

prom (prom) /prɒm/ *n.* [*count*] a formal dance held by a high school or college class: *a junior prom.*

prom•e•nade (prom′ə nād′, -näd′) /ˌprɒməˈneyd, -ˈnɑd/ *n., v.,* **-nad•ed, -nad•ing.** —*n.* [*count*] **1.** a stroll or walk, esp. in a public place. **2.** an area used for such walking. —*v.* [*no obj*] **3.** to go for or take part in a stroll or walk.

prom•i•nence (prom′ə nəns) /ˈprɒmənəns/ *n.* [*noncount*] the state of being well-known or important: *an author of great prominence.*

prom•i•nent (prom′ə nənt) /ˈprɒmənənt/ *adj.* **1.** standing out so as to be seen easily; conspicuous: *a prominent bruise.* **2.** leading; eminent: *prominent business leaders.* —**prom′i•nent•ly,** *adv.*

prom•is•cu•i•ty (prom′is kyoo͞′i tē, prō′mis-) /ˌprɒmɪsˈkyuwɪtiy, ˌprowmɪs-/ *n.* [*noncount*] the state of being promiscuous; promiscuous behavior. See -MISC-.

pro•mis•cu•ous (prə mis′kyoo͞ əs) /prəˈmɪskyuwəs/ *adj.* **1.** having numerous sexual partners. **2.** indiscriminate; unselective: *the promiscuous awarding of prizes.* —**pro•mis′cu•ous•ly,** *adv.* See -MISC-.

prom•ise (prom′is) /ˈprɒmɪs/ *n., v.,* **-ised, -is•ing.** —*n.* **1.** [*count*] a statement or declaration that something will or will not be done, given, etc: *He kept his promise to write regularly.* **2.** [*noncount*] an indication or a sign of future excellence or achievement: *a writer who shows great promise.* —*v.* **3.** to make a promise of (some specified act, gift, etc.), or a promise to do something: [~ + *obj*]: *to promise eternal love.* [~ + *obj* + *obj*]: *The financial aid committee promised us enough money to get through next year.* [~ + *to* + *verb*]: *She promised to help with the decorating.* [~ (+ *obj*) + (*that*) *clause*]: *She promised (me) that she would help with the decorating.* [*no obj*]: *I'll be there; I promise.* **4.** [~ + *obj*] (used in emphatic declarations to convey firm resolve or assurance): *I won't go there again, I promise you!* See -MIS-.

prom•is•ing (prom′ə sing) /ˈprɒməsɪŋ/ *adj.* giving favorable promise; likely to turn out well: *The future looks promising.*

prom•is•so•ry (prom′ə sôr′ē, -sōr′ē) /ˈprɒməˌsɔriy, -ˌsowriy/ *adj.* containing or suggesting a promise. See -MIS-.

prom′issory note′, *n.* [*count*] a written promise to pay a specified sum of money at a fixed time or on demand.

prom•on•to•ry (prom′ən tôr′ē, -tōr′ē) /ˈprɒmənˌtɔriy, -ˌtowriy/ *n.* [*count*], *pl.* **-ries.** a high point of land or rock sticking out into water beyond the line of coast; headland.

pro•mote (prə mōt′) /prəˈmowt/ *v.* [~ + *obj*], **-mot•ed, -mot•ing. 1.** to help or encourage to flourish: *to promote world peace.* **2.** to advance in rank or position: *promoted him to full professor.* **3.** to advance to the next higher grade in a school: *was promoted to third grade.* **4.** to encourage the sales, acceptance, or recognition of: *promoted the new car with advertising.* See -MOT-.

pro•mot•er (prə mō′tər) /prəˈmowtər/ *n.* [*count*] a person who organizes and finances a sporting event or entertainment.

pro•mo•tion (prə mō′shən) /prəˈmowʃən/ *n.* **1.** advancement in rank, position, salary, etc.: [*noncount*]: *a candidate for promotion.* [*count*]: *handing out promotions.* **2.** something intended to advertise or bring to public attention a product, a cause, etc.: [*count*]: *a sales promotion.* [*noncount*]: *A new product needs promotion.* **3.** [*noncount*] encouragement: *a campaign for the promotion of dieting.* —**pro•mo′tion•al,** *adj.* See -MOT-.

prompt (prompt) /prɒmpt/ *adj.*, **-er, -est,** *v.* —*adj.* **1.** performed at once or without delay: *a prompt reply.* **2.** quick to act or respond: [*be* + ~]: *was prompt in answering our phone call.* [~ + *to* + *verb*]: *They were prompt to deny the allegations.* —*v.* **3.** [~ + *obj* + *to* + *verb*] to cause (someone) to do some action: *That insult prompted him to respond.* **4.** [~ + *obj*] to cause (an act), as in response: *That insult prompted a strong response.* **5.** [~ + *obj*] to assist (a speaker or performer) by giving a cue: *The teacher prompted the student with the next word of the poem.* —*n.* [*count*] **6.** an act of prompting. **7.** something serving to suggest or remind. **8.** a symbol or message on a computer screen requesting more information or indicating that a response or instruction is expected. —**prompt•er,** *n.* [*count*] —**prompt′ly,** *adv.* —**prompt′ness,** *n.* [*noncount*]

prom•ul•gate (prom′əl gāt′, prō mul′gāt) /ˈprɒməlˌgeyt, prowˈmʌlgeyt/ *v.* [~ + *obj*], **-gat•ed, -gat•ing. 1.** to make known or put into effect (a law, statement of a court, etc.) by formally declaring: *to promulgate a new law on taxes.* **2.** to proclaim; make known: *to promulgate a belief.* —**prom•ul•ga•tion** (prom′əl gā′shən) /ˌprɒməlˈgeyʃən/ *n.* [*noncount*]

pron., an abbreviation of: **1.** pronoun. **2.** pronunciation.

prone (prōn) /prown/ *adj.* **1.** [*be* + ~ + *to*] having a natural tendency toward something; disposed; liable; likely to suffer from: *was prone to anger.* **2.** having the front of the body downward; lying facedown.

prong (prông, prong) /prɔŋ, prɒŋ/ *n.* [*count*] one of the long, pointed ends of a fork. —**pronged,** *adj.* [*with a word indicating number*]: *a three-pronged fork (= a fork having three prongs).*

pro•noun (prō′noun′) /ˈprowˌnawn/ *n.* [*count*] a word used as a replacement or substitute for a noun or a noun phrase, usually referring to persons or things mentioned in or understood from what has been written or said before, or which both speaker and listener have knowledge about: *Pronouns in English include* I, you, he, she, it, we, they, them, this, who, *and* what. *Abbr.:* pron. —**pro•nom•i•nal** (prō nom′ə nl) /prowˈnɒmənl̩/ *adj.* See -NOM-[2].

pro•nounce (prə nouns′) /prəˈnawns/ *v.*, **-nounced, -nounc•ing. 1.** [~ + *obj*] to make or utter sounds, words, sentences, etc.: *In the word* came, *the letter "e" is not pronounced.* **2.** to make or utter sounds, words, sentences, etc., in an accepted or correct manner: [~ + *obj*]: *How do you pronounce this word?* [~ + *obj* (+ *as*) + *obj*]: *You pronounce the Spanish* ll *(as) "y."* **3.** to declare (a person or thing) to be as specified, esp. officially: [~ + *obj* + *obj*]: *I now pronounce you husband and wife.* [~ + *obj* + *adjective*]: *He pronounced the meal fit for a king.* —**pro•nounce′a•ble,** *adj.* See -NOUNCE-.

pro•nounced (prə nounst′) /prəˈnawnst/ *adj.* **1.** strongly or clearly apparent: *a pronounced Australian accent.* **2.** definite: *pronounced views on the subject.* See -NOUNCE-.

pro•nounce•ment (prə nouns′mənt) /prəˈnawnsmənt/ *n.* [*count*] **1.** a formal statement. **2.** an opinion or decision: *a pronouncement of "not guilty."* See -NOUNCE-.

pron•to (pron′tō) /ˈprɒntow/ *adv.* promptly: *Do it pronto.*

pro•nun•ci•a•tion (prə nun′sē ā′shən) /prəˌnʌnsiyˈeyʃən/ *n.* **1.** [*noncount*] the way in which a sound, word, sentence, etc., is pronounced: *making fun of my pronunciation.* **2.** the way in which a sound, word, sentence, etc., is to be pronounced in an accepted manner: [*noncount*]: *a study of pronunciation.* [*count*]: *Only one of these pronunciations is correct.* See -NOUNCE-.

proof (pro͞of) /pruwf/ *n.* **1.** [*noncount*] evidence or facts that are sufficient to establish a thing as true or believable. **2.** [*count*] *Math., Logic.* a sequence of steps, statements, or demonstrations that leads to and establishes a valid conclusion. **3.** [*noncount*] the strength of an alcoholic liquor, esp. with reference to the standard whereby 100 proof signifies an alcoholic content of 50 percent. **4.** [*count*] *Photography.* a print made from a negative of a photograph for checking quality. **5.** [*count*] *Printing.* a preliminary copy, as of a manuscript, that is printed for correction or changes. —*adj.* [*be* + ~] **6.** able to withstand or resist something harmful or undesirable: *a shelter that was proof against the cold.* —*v.* [~ + *obj*] **7.** to proofread: *Proof the document.* See -PROV-.

-proof, *suffix.* *-proof* is used to form adjectives with the meaning "resistant; not allowing through" the word mentioned: *child + -proof → childproof (= resistant to a child opening it); water + proof → waterproof (= not allowing water through).*

proof•read (pro͞of′rēd′) /ˈpruwfˌriyd/ *v.*, **-read** (-red′) /-ˌrɛd/ **-read•ing.** to read in order to find and mark errors to be corrected: [~ + *obj*]: *proofreading the printout of his paper.* [*no obj*]: *He spent the day proofreading.* —**proof′read′er,** *n.* [*count*] See -PROV-.

prop[1] (prop) /prɒp/ *v.*, **propped, prop•ping,** *n.* —*v.* **1.** to support, or prevent from falling, with or as if with a prop: [~ + *up* + *obj*]: *He propped up the car with a jack.* [~ + *obj* + *up*]: *He tried propping it up.* **2.** [~ + *obj*] to rest (a thing) against a support: *He propped the ladder against the wall.* **3.** to support or sustain: [~ + *up* + *obj*]: *The army propped up the dictator's regime.* [~ + *obj* + *up*]: *It can no longer prop him up.* —*n.* [*count*] **4.** something that props; support.

prop[2] (prop) /prɒp/ *n.* [*count*] a usually movable item used onstage or on a film set, esp. one handled by an actor or entertainer to enliven and enrich the performance.

prop[3] (prop) /prɒp/ *n.* [*count*] a propeller.

prop., an abbreviation of: **1.** properly. **2.** property.

prop•a•gan•da (prop′ə gan′də) /ˌprɒpəˈgændə/ *n.* [*noncount*] information or ideas, whether true or false, that are spread to promote or injure a cause, movement, nation, etc. —**prop′a•gan′dist,** *n.* [*count*]

prop•a•gate (prop′ə gāt′) /ˈprɒpəˌgeyt/ *v.*, **-gat•ed, -gat•ing. 1.** to (cause to) multiply or increase by any process of natural reproduction from the parent stock: [~ + *obj*]: *to propagate seeds; These flowers will propagate themselves.* [*no obj*]: *The insects propagated vigorously.* **2.** [~ + *obj*] to spread (a report, doctrine, practice, etc.) from person to person; disseminate. —**prop•a•ga•tion** (prop′ə gā′shən) /ˌprɒpəˈgeyʃən/ *n.* [*noncount*]

pro•pane (prō′pān) /ˈprowpeyn/ *n.* [*noncount*] a colorless gas that easily ignites, occurs in petroleum and natural gas, and is used chiefly as a fuel.

pro•pel (prə pel′) /prəˈpɛl/ *v.* [~ + *obj*], **-pelled, -pel•ling.** to drive forward or onward: *to propel a boat with oars.* See -PEL-.

pro•pel•lant (prə pel′ənt) /prəˈpɛlənt/ *n.* **1.** something, as a substance, that propels, as rocket fuel: [*count*]: *a liquid propellant.* [*noncount*]: *A rocket needs propellant.* **2.** [*noncount*] a gas that forces out the contents of an aerosol container when the pressure is released. See -PEL-.

pro•pel•ler (prə pel′ər) /prəˈpɛlər/ *n.* [*count*] a device that has a revolving center from which curved blades stick outwards, and is attached to an engine for propelling an airplane, ship, etc. See -PEL-.

pro•pen•si•ty (prə pen′si tē) /prəˈpɛnsɪtiy/ *n.* [*count*], *pl.* **-ties.** a natural tendency or preference: *a propensity for lying.* See -PEND-.

prop•er (prop′ər) /ˈprɒpər/ *adj.* **1.** [*before a noun*] most suitable; right; correct: *Is this the proper time to plant strawberries?* **2.** agreeing with established or accepted standards: *proper behavior.* [*It + be + ~ + to + verb*]: *It's not proper to come so late to parties.* **3.** [*after a noun*] in the strict sense: *Shellfish do not belong to the class of fishes proper.* **4.** [*before a noun*] *Chiefly Brit.* utter; genuine: *a proper fool.* —**prop′er•ly,** *adv.* See -PROPR-.

prop′er noun′, *n.* [*count*] a noun that designates a particular person, place, or thing, is not normally preceded by an article or other limiting modifier, and is usually capitalized in English, as *Lincoln, Beth, Boston.* Also called **prop′er name′.**

prop•er•tied (prop′ər tēd′) /ˈprɒpərˌtiyd/ *adj.* [*before a noun*] owning property. See -PROPR-.

prop•er•ty (prop′ər tē) /ˈprɒpərtiy/ *n., pl.* **-ties. 1.** [*noncount*] that which a person owns; the possession or possessions of a particular owner. **2.** [*noncount*] goods, land, etc., considered as possessions: *They own a lot of property upstate.* **3.** [*count*] a piece of land or real estate. **4.** [*count*] a basic, essential, or special quality of a thing: *the chemical properties of alcohol.* See -PROPR-.

proph•e•cy (prof′ə sē) /ˈprɒfəsiy/ *n., pl.* **-cies. 1.** [*noncount*] the foretelling or predicting of what is to come; the ability to do this: *a gift of prophecy.* **2.** [*count*] something declared by a prophet. **3.** [*count*] any prediction or forecast: *a prophecy about the election.*

proph•e•sy (prof′ə sī′) /ˈprɒfəˌsay/ *v.,* **-sied, -sy•ing.** to foretell or predict: [*~ + obj*]: *prophesied the end of the world.* [*~ + that clause*]: *prophesied that the end of the world was near.* [*no obj*]: *prophesying about the election.* —**proph′e•si′er,** *n.* [*count*]

proph•et (prof′it) /ˈprɒfɪt/ *n.* [*count*] **1.** a person who speaks for God or a god, or who receives inspiration from God or a god, so as to lead people, warn them about good and evil, etc. **2.** a person who foretells the future.

proph•et•ess (prof′i tis) /ˈprɒfɪtɪs/ *n.* [*count*] **1.** a woman who speaks for God or a god, or who receives inspiration from God or a god. **2.** a woman who predicts the future.

pro•phet•ic (prə fet′ik) /prəˈfɛtɪk/ also **pro•phet′i•cal,** *adj.* **1.** of or relating to a prophet: *prophetic writings.* **2.** having the power of a prophet, as by predicting the future: *a prophetic statement that actually came true.* —**pro•phet′i•cal•ly,** *adv.*

pro•phy•lac•tic (prō′fə lak′tik, prof′ə-) /ˌprowfəˈlæktɪk, ˌprɒfə-/ *adj.* **1.** preventing or protecting from disease or infection. —*n.* [*count*] **2.** a medicine or measure that prevents or protects from disease or infection. **3.** a device used to prevent conception or venereal infection, esp. a condom.

pro•pin•qui•ty (prō ping′kwi tē) /prowˈpɪŋkwɪtiy/ *n.* [*noncount*] **1.** nearness or closeness in time or place; proximity. **2.** nearness of relation; kinship.

pro•pi•ti•ate (prə pish′ē āt′) /prəˈpɪʃiyˌeyt/ *v.* [*~ + obj*], **-at•ed, -at•ing.** to cause to look with favor on oneself; appease; conciliate: *Early humans may have tried to propitiate what they thought of as the angry gods.* —**pro•pit•i•a•tion** (prə pish′ē ā′shən) /prəˌpɪʃiyˈeyʃən/ *n.* [*noncount*] —**pro•pi•ti•a•to•ry** (prə pish′ē ə tôr′ē, -tōr′ē) /prəˈpɪʃiyəˌtɔriy, -ˌtowriy/ *adj.* See -PET-.

pro•pi•tious (prə pish′əs) /prəˈpɪʃəs/ *adj.* **1.** presenting or indicating favorable conditions; suggesting that good may follow: *propitious weather for a vacation.* **2.** favorably disposed: *a propitious ruler.* —**pro•pi′tious•ly,** *adv.* See -PET-.

pro•po•nent (prə pō′nənt) /prəˈpownənt/ *n.* [*count*] a person who argues in favor of something; advocate. See -PON-.

pro•por•tion (prə pôr′shən, -pōr′-) /prəˈpɔrʃən, -ˈpowr-/ *n.* **1.** [*count*] a relation between things when compared to one another in regard to size, quantity, number, etc.: *A large proportion of the students came from Chinese-speaking countries.* **2.** [*noncount*] proper relation between things or parts: *to have a sense of proportion.* **3.** [*noncount*] symmetry: *The architect shows a fine sense of proportion in his designs.* **4. proportions,** [*plural*] dimensions or size: *a man of gigantic proportions.* See -PAR-.

pro•por•tion•al (prə pôr′shə nl, -pōr′-) /prəˈpɔrʃənḷ, -ˈpowr-/ *adj.* **1.** of or relating to proportion or proportions. **2.** [*be + ~ + to*] in the correct or balanced relation or proportion: *Salary raises were proportional to the cost of living.* See -PAR-.

pro•por•tion•ate (prə pôr′shən it, -pōr′-) /prəˈpɔrʃənɪt, -ˈpowr-/ *adj.* PROPORTIONAL. See -PAR-.

pro•pos•al (prə pō′zəl) /prəˈpowzəl/ *n.* **1.** [*noncount*] the act of proposing. **2.** [*count*] a plan or scheme offered or suggested for consideration. **3.** [*count*] an offer of marriage. See -POS-.

pro•pose (prə pōz′) /prəˈpowz/ *v.,* **-posed, -pos•ing. 1.** to offer for consideration, acceptance, or action; suggest: [*~ + obj*]: *to propose a new method.* [*~ + (that) clause*]: *I propose that we do away with all those taxes.* **2.** [*~ + obj*] to offer (a toast): *I propose a toast: to success!* **3.** [*~ + obj*] to name or nominate (a person) for office, membership, etc. **4.** [*~ + to + verb*] to plan; intend: *He proposes to leave by five.* **5.** to make an offer, esp. of marriage: [*~ + obj*]: *She proposed marriage.* [*no obj*]: *He proposed and she accepted.* [*~ + to + obj*]: *He proposed to her.* See -POS-.

prop•o•si•tion (prop′ə zish′ən) /ˌprɒpəˈzɪʃən/ *n.* [*count*] **1.** the act of proposing. **2.** a plan or scheme proposed; anything stated for discussion. **3.** an offer of terms, as for a business deal. **4.** a thing, matter, or person considered as something to be dealt with or encountered: *Climbing that mountain is a tough proposition.* **5.** a proposal, hint, or suggestion to have sexual relations. —*v.* [*~ + obj*] **6.** to propose having sexual relations with. See -POS-.

pro•pound (prə pound′) /prəˈpawnd/ *v.* [*~ + obj*] to put forward for discussion; propose: *to propound a theory.* See -POUND-.

-propr-, *root.* *-propr-* comes from Latin, where it has the meaning "one's own." This meaning is found in such words as: APPROPRIATE, EXPROPRIATE, IMPROPER, IMPROPRIETY, MISAPPROPRIATE, PROPER, PROPERTY, PROPRIETARY, PROPRIETOR, PROPRIETY.

pro•pri•e•tar•y (prə prī′i ter′ē) /prəˈprayɪˌtɛriy/ *adj., n., pl.* **-tar•ies.** —*adj.* **1.** relating to, belonging to, or being a proprietor. **2.** acting as if one were an owner: *She put a proprietary arm around her companion.* —*n.* [*count*] **3.** a proprietor or a group of proprietors. See -PROPR-.

pro•pri•e•tor (prə prī′i tər) /prəˈprayɪtər/ *n.* [*count*] **1.** the owner of a business establishment. **2.** a person who has the exclusive right or title to something; an owner, as of real property. —**pro•pri′e•tor•ship′,** *n.* [*noncount*] See -PROPR-.

pro•pri•e•ty (prə prī′i tē) /prəˈprayɪtiy/ *n., pl.* **-ties. 1.** [*noncount*] agreement with established standards of good or proper behavior or manners: *behaving with the utmost propriety.* **2.** [*noncount*] appropriateness; suitability: *The propriety of their gift was in question.* **3. the proprieties,** [*plural*] the accepted, standard rules of proper behavior; manners. See -PROPR-.

pro•pul•sion (prə pul′shən) /prəˈpʌlʃən/ *n.* [*noncount*] the act of propelling; the state of being propelled: *jet propulsion.* —**pro•pul•sive** (prə pul′siv) /prəˈpʌlsɪv/ *adj.* See -PULS-.

pro•rate (prō rāt′, prō′rāt′) /prowˈreyt, ˈprowˌreyt/ *v.* [*~ + obj*], **-rat•ed, -rat•ing.** to divide, distribute, or calculate in a proportionate way: *He prorated the money for bonuses.*

pro•sa•ic (prō zā′ik) /prowˈzeyɪk/ also **pro•sa′i•cal,** *adj.* commonplace or dull; matter-of-fact; not imaginative: *a prosaic mind.* —**pro•sa′ic•al•ly,** *adv.*

pro•sce•ni•um (prō sē′nē əm, prə-) /prowˈsiyniyəm, prə-/ *n.* [*count*], *pl.* **-ni•ums, -ni•a** (-nē ə) /-niyə/. Also called **prosce′nium arch′.** the arch that separates a stage from the auditorium.

pro•sciut•to (prō shōō′tō) /prowˈʃuwtow/ *n.* [*noncount*] Italian salted ham that has been cured by drying.

pro•scribe (prō skrīb′) /prowˈskrayb/ *v.* [*~ + obj*], **-scribed, -scrib•ing.** to condemn (a thing) as harmful or illegal; prohibit; forbid: *proscribing the use of firearms.* —**pro•scrip•tion** (prō skrip′shən) /prowˈskrɪpʃən/ *n.* [*noncount*] See -SCRIB-.

prose (prōz) /prowz/ *n.* [*noncount*] **1.** the ordinary form of spoken or written language, as distinguished from poetry or verse. —*adj.* [*before a noun*] **2.** of, in, or relating to prose.

pros•e•cute (pros′i kyōōt′) /ˈprɒsɪˌkyuwt/ *v.,* **-cut•ed, -cut•ing. 1.** to begin or conduct legal proceedings against (a person), as with a criminal charge in a court of law: [*~ + obj*]: *prosecuted his client for murder.* [*no obj*]: *They decided not to prosecute.* **2.** [*~ + obj*] to follow up or carry forward (something begun), usually to completion: *He vowed to prosecute the war to its end.* See -SEQ-.

pros•e•cu•tion (pros′i kyo͞o′shən) /ˌprɒsɪˈkyuwʃən/ *n.* **1.** the act of beginning or conducting legal proceedings against a person: [*noncount*]: *The store will seek prosecution of any shoplifter.* [*count*]: *prosecutions for wrongdoing.* **2.** [*noncount; usually: the* + ~] the party conducting legal proceedings against a person: *The prosecution contends that the defendant is guilty.* **3.** [*noncount*] the act of following up or carrying forward some action to its completion: *the prosecution of a war.*

pros•e•cu•tor (pros′i kyo͞o′tər) /ˈprɒsɪˌkyuwtər/ *n.* [*count*] an attorney who conducts legal proceedings against a person, as in a court of law. See -SEQ-.

pros•e•lyt•ize (pros′ə li tiz′) /ˈprɒsəlɪˌtayz/ *v.*, **-ized, -iz•ing.** to attempt to convert (someone) to one's faith or cause: [*no obj*]: *went proselytizing for reform.* [~ + *obj*]: *proselytizing the uncommitted voters.* —**pros′e•lyt•ism,** *n.* [*noncount*] —**pros′e•lyt•iz′er,** *n.* [*count*]

pros•o•dy (pros′ə dē) /ˈprɒsədiy/ *n., pl.* **-dies. 1.** [*noncount*] the science or study of poetic meters and verses. **2.** [*count*] a particular or distinctive system of poetic meter and verse: *Milton's prosodies.*

pros•pect (pros′pekt) /ˈprɒspɛkt/ *n.* **1.** Usually, **prospects.** [*plural*] a person's chances of advancement, success, profit, etc.: *chosen for his good prospects as a leader.* **2.** anticipation; expectation: [*noncount*]: *the prospect of facing yet another day without hope.* [*count*]: *Prospects for peace have improved.* **3.** [*count*] a possible or likely customer, client, candidate, etc.: *I've lined up a few prospects for the job.* **4.** [*count*] a view, esp. of scenery over a region; a scene. —*v.* **5.** to search or explore (a region), as for gold or some precious minerals: [*no obj*]: *Early settlers came to prospect for gold.* [~ + *obj*]: *Some of the miners prospected the land.* —***Idiom.*** **6. in prospect,** expected; in view: *no other alternative in prospect.* See -SPEC-.

pro•spec•tive (prə spek′tiv) /prəˈspɛktɪv/ *adj.* [*before a noun*] possible, likely, or expected; potential; probable: *a prospective customer.* See -SPEC-.

pros•pec•tor (pros′pek tər, prə spek′-) /ˈprɒspɛktər, prəˈspɛk-/ *n.* [*count*] one who prospects for gold or minerals. See -SPEC-.

pro•spec•tus (prə spek′təs) /prəˈspɛktəs/ *n.* [*count*], *pl.* **-tus•es. 1.** a document describing the major features of a proposed business venture, literary work, etc., for potential investors, buyers, or participants. **2.** a brochure describing the facilities, services, or attractions of a place or institution. See -SPEC-.

pros•per (pros′pər) /ˈprɒspər/ *v.* [*no obj*] to be successful or fortunate, esp. financially; to do well. See -SPER-.

pros•per•i•ty (pro sper′i tē) /prɒˈspɛrɪtiy/ *n.* [*noncount*] a successful, flourishing, or thriving condition, esp. in financial respects. See -SPER-.

pros•per•ous (pros′pər əs) /ˈprɒspərəs/ *adj.* having or showing good fortune, success, or wealth. —**pros′per•ous•ly,** *adv.* See -SPER-.

pros•tate gland′ (pros′tāt) /ˈprɒsteyt/ *n.* [*count*] a gland at the base of the bladder in males. Also, **pros′tate.**

pros•the•sis (pros thē′sis) /prɒsˈθiysɪs/ *n.* [*count*], *pl.* **-ses** (sēz) a device that substitutes for or assists a missing or poorly functioning part of the body, as a limb. —**pros•thet•ic** (pros thet′ik) /prɒsˈθɛtɪk/ *adj.* See -THES-.

pros•ti•tute (pros′ti to͞ot′, -tyo͞ot′) /ˈprɒstɪˌtuwt, -ˌtyuwt/ *n., v.,* **-tut•ed, -tut•ing.** —*n.* [*count*] **1.** a woman or man who engages in sexual acts for money. —*v.* **2.** [~ + *oneself*] to sell or offer (oneself) as a prostitute. **3.** to put to a use that is unworthy or dishonorable, esp. for money: [~ + *obj*]: *He prostituted his talents.* [~ + *oneself*]: *a writer who felt he prostituted himself, writing pornography.* See -STIT-.

pros•ti•tu•tion (pros′ti to͞o′shən) /ˌprɒstɪˈtuwʃən/ *n.* [*noncount*] **1.** the act or practice of engaging in sexual acts for money. **2.** the state of being used in an unworthy or dishonorable way. See -STIT-.

pros•trate (pros′trāt) /ˈprɒstreyt/ *v.,* **-trat•ed, -trat•ing,** *adj.* —*v.* **1.** [~ + *oneself*] to throw oneself facedown on the ground, as in submission or adoration: *He prostrated himself before the king.* **2.** [~ + *obj; usually: be* + ~*-ed*] to reduce to physical weakness: *He was prostrated by the heat.* —*adj.* **3.** lying facedown, as to show submission or adoration. **4.** helpless; exhausted: *a country left prostrate by natural disasters.* —**pros•tra•tion** (pros trā-shən) /prɒstreyʃən/ *n.* [*noncount*]

pro•tag•o•nist (prō tag′ə nist) /prowˈtægənɪst/ *n.* [*count*] the leading character of a drama or other piece of writing. See -AGON-.

pro•te•an (prō′tē ən, prō tē′-) /ˈprowtiyən, prowˈtiy-/ *adj.* easily able to take on or assume different forms or characters.

pro•tect (prə tekt′) /prəˈtɛkt/ *v.* **1.** to defend or guard from attack, invasion, loss, insult, etc.; cover; shield: [~ + *obj*]: *The turtle's shell protects it from harm.* [*no obj*]: *The police are there to protect.* **2.** [~ + *obj*] to guard (an industry) from foreign competition, as by charging import duties on the products of the competition.

pro•tec•tion (prə tek′shən) /prəˈtɛkʃən/ *n.* **1.** [*noncount*] the act of protecting or the state of being protected. **2.** [*count; usually singular*] one that protects: *wore boots as a protection against the mud.* **3.** [*noncount*] **a.** money paid to criminals or racketeers in exchange for a guarantee against threatened violence. **b.** bribe money paid to the authorities in exchange for overlooking criminal activity.

pro•tec•tion•ism (prə tek′shə niz′əm) /prəˈtɛkʃəˌnɪzəm/ *n.* [*noncount*] the theory or practice of helping the industries or businesses in one's own country to grow or develop by protecting them from foreign competition, as by charging import duties on the competition's products. —**pro•tec′tion•ist,** *adj.*

pro•tec•tive (prə tek′tiv) /prəˈtɛktɪv/ *adj.* **1.** [*before a noun*] having the quality or function of protecting: *wore a protective helmet.* **2.** tending strongly to protect: *She had very protective parents.* [*be* + ~ + *of*]: *A mother robin is very protective of her young.* —**pro•tec′tive•ly,** *adv.* —**pro•tec′tive•ness,** *n.* [*noncount*]

pro•tec•tor (prə tek′tər) /prəˈtɛktər/ *n.* [*count*] **1.** a person that guards or protects someone or something from harm. **2.** a device that protects someone from injury: *A baseball catcher wears a chest protector.*

pro•tec•tor•ate (prə tek′tər it) /prəˈtɛktərɪt/ *n.* [*count*] a state or territory protected by a stronger nation.

pro•té•gé (prō′tə zhā′, prō′tə zhā′) /ˈprowtəˌʒey, ˌprowtəˈʒey/ *n.* [*count*], *pl.* **-gés.** a person who has the support, protection, or care of someone of importance.

pro•tein (prō′tēn, -tē in) /ˈprowtiyn, -tiyɪn/ *n.* **1.** [*count*] a molecule that is a large portion of the mass of every life form, composed of amino acids linked in long chains. **2.** plant or animal tissue rich in such molecules: [*noncount*]: *Meat is a source of protein.* [*count*]: *various proteins.*

pro tem•po•re (prō′ tem′pə rē′, -rā′) /ˈprow' tɛmpəˌriy, -ˌrey/ *adv.* temporarily; for the time being.

pro•test (*n.* prō′test; *v.* prə test′, prō′test) / *n.* ˈprowtɛst; *v.* prəˈtɛst, ˈprowtɛst/ *n.* **1.** an act of expressing or declaring one's objection to, disapproval of, or disagreement with some act or action: [*noncount*]: *voices of protest.* [*count*]: *some minor protests.* —*v.* **2.** to express or declare one's objection to, disapproval of, or disagreement with (some act or action): [*no obj*]: *They protested against the war.* [~ + *obj*]: *The students protested the bombing.* **3.** to affirm or declare in protest: [~ + *obj*]: *They protested their innocence.* [~ + *that clause*]: *They protested that they were innocent.* —**pro•test′er,** *n.* [*count*] See -TEST-.

Prot•es•tant (prot′ə stənt) /ˈprɒtəstənt/ *n.* [*count*] **1.** any Western Christian not a follower of the Roman Catholic Church. —*adj.* **2.** of, relating to, or belonging to Protestants or their religion: *a Protestant hymnal.* —**Prot′es•tant•ism,** *n.* [*noncount*] See -TEST-.

prot•es•ta•tion (prot′ə stā′shən, prō′te-) /ˌprɒtəˈsteyʃən, ˌprowtɛ-/ *n.* [*count*] an act of strongly expressing one's objection: *protestations of innocence.* See -TEST-.

proto-, *prefix.* *proto-* comes from Greek, where it has the meaning "first, foremost, earliest form of": *proto-* + *lithic* → *protolithic; protoplasm.* Also, *esp. before a vowel,* **prot-.**

pro•to•col (prō′tə kôl′, -kol′) /ˈprowtəˌkɔl, -ˌkɒl/ *n.* **1.** [*noncount*] the customs, rules, and regulations dealing with formal courtesies, good manners, or diplomatic relations between countries. **2.** [*count*] an original draft, or part of a written record from which a document, esp. a treaty, is prepared. **3.** [*count*] a set of rules governing the format of messages exchanged between computers.

pro•ton (prō′ton) /ˈprowtɒn/ *n.* [*count*] a positively charged particle found in all atomic nuclei: *The number of protons in an atom equals that element's atomic number.*

pro•to•plasm (prō′tə plaz′əm) /ˈprowtəˌplæzəm/ *n.* [*noncount*] the liquid substance of which cells are formed; the cytoplasm and nucleus. —**pro•to•plas•mic** (prō′tə plaz′mik) /ˌprowtəˈplæzmɪk/ *adj.*

pro•to•type (prō′tə tip′) /ˈprowtəˌtayp/ *n.* [*count*] the original or model on which something is based or formed, as the first working model of something to be manufactured on a large scale. See -TYPE-.

pro•to•zo•an (prō′tə zō′ən) /ˌprowtə'zowən/ *n., pl.* **-zo•ans,** (*esp. when thought of as a group*) **-zo•a** (-zō′ə) /-'zowə/ *adj.* **—*n.*** [*count*] **1.** a one-celled organism that usually obtains nourishment by taking in food particles rather than by photosynthesis. **—*adj.*** **2.** of, relating to, or characteristic of a protozoan. **—pro′to•zo′ic,** *adj.*

pro•tract•ed (prō trak′tid, prə-) /prow'trӕktɪd, prə-/ *adj.* drawn out, esp. in time; prolonged: *a protracted discussion.* See -TRAC-.

pro•trac•tor (prō trak′tər, prə-) /prow'trӕktər, prə-/ *n.* [*count*] an instrument used for measuring or drawing angles. See -TRAC-.

pro•trude (prō tro͞od′, prə-) /prow'truwd, prə-/ *v.,* **-trud•ed, -trud•ing.** to (cause to) stick out: [*no obj*]: *His enormous belly protruded over his belt.* [~ + *obj*]: *The snake protruded its tongue.* See -TRUDE-.

pro•tru•sion (prō tro͞o′zhən, prə-) /prow'truwʒən, prə-/ *n.* **1.** [*noncount*] the condition of sticking out. **2.** [*count*] something that sticks out.

pro•tu•ber•ance (prō to͞o′bər əns, -tyo͞o′-, prə-) /prow'tuwbərəns, -'tyuw-, prə-/ *n.* **1.** [*count*] a part or thing that sticks or bulges out. **2.** [*noncount*] the state or quality of protruding. **—pro•tu′ber•ant,** *adj.*

proud (proud) /prawd/ *adj.,* **-er, -est,** *adv.* **—*adj.*** **1.** feeling pleasure or satisfaction over something thought of as bringing credit or honor to oneself: *the proud parents of a new baby.* [*be* + ~ + *of*]: *We are proud of our country.* [*be* + ~ + *to* + *verb*]: *She is proud to accept the honor.* [*be* + ~ + *(that) clause*]: *She is proud that she is an American.* **2.** giving a sense of pride; highly gratifying: *a proud achievement.* **3.** arrogant; haughty: *too proud to admit she's wrong.* **4.** having or showing self-respect: *They were a proud family.* **5.** [*before a noun*] magnificent, splendid, stately, majestic: *the once-proud cities that now lay in ruins.* **—*adv., Idiom.*** **6. do one proud, a.** to be a source of pride or credit to a person: *Congratulations, you've done us proud!* **b.** to treat someone or oneself generously or lavishly: *She did her guests proud with that fabulous dinner.* **—proud′ly,** *adv.*

-prov-, *root. -prov-* comes from French and ultimately from Latin, where it has the meaning "prove." It is related to the root -PROB-. This meaning is found in such words as: APPROVAL, APPROVE, DISAPPROVE, DISPROVE, IMPROVE, PROOF, PROVE, PROVEN.

prove (pro͞ov) /pruwv/ *v.,* **proved, proved** or **prov•en** (pro͞o′vən) /'pruwvən/ **prov•ing. 1.** to establish the truth, genuineness, or validity of, as by evidence or argument: [~ + *obj*]: *He was able to prove his innocence by producing a witness.* [~ + *(that) clause*]: *She proved to me that she was not the one spreading gossip.* **2.** [~ + *obj*] to cause to be shown as specified: *Events have proved me right.* **3.** [~ + *oneself*] to show (oneself) to be worthy or capable: *This job will give you a chance to prove yourself.* **4.** [~ + *adjective*] to demonstrate as having a particular quality: *The medicine proved effective.* **—prov•a•bil•i•ty** (pro͞o′və bil′i tē) /ˌpruwvə'bɪlɪtiy/ *n.* [*noncount*] **—prov′a•ble,** *adj.* See -PROV-.

prov•en (pro͞o′vən) /'pruwvən/ *adj.* [*before a noun*] shown to be so: *a proven liar.* See -PROV-.

prov•e•nance (prov′ə nəns, -näns′) /'prɒvənəns, -ˌnɑns/ *n.* [*noncount*] a place or source of origin: *a manuscript of unknown provenance.* See -VEN-, -PROV-.

prov•en•der (prov′ən dər) /'prɒvəndər/ *n.* [*noncount*] dry food for animals or livestock; fodder.

prov•erb (prov′ərb) /'prɒvərb/ *n.* [*count*] a short popular saying that expresses effectively some commonplace truth or useful thought. See -VERB-.

pro•ver•bi•al (prə vûr′bē əl) /prə'vɜrbiyəl/ *adj.* **1.** of or like a proverb. **2.** widely known or spoken of: *the proverbial deep blue sea.* See -VERB-.

pro•vide (prə vīd′) /prə'vayd/ *v.,* **-vid•ed, -vid•ing. 1.** to make available; furnish: [~ + *obj* + *for* + *obj*]: *to provide benefits for employees.* [~ + *obj* (+ *with*) + *obj*]: *to provide employees (with) benefits.* **2.** to supply or equip: [~ + *obj* + *with* + *obj*]: *to provide the army with tanks.* [~ + *obj* + *for* + *obj*]: *to provide tanks for the army.* **3.** [~ + *for* + *obj*] to supply means of support: *They worked hard to provide for their children.* **4.** [~ + *obj*] to yield: *This tree provides shelter.* **5.** [~ + *that clause*] to stipulate, as by a provision: *The contract provides that the writer will receive an additional payment if his book is made into a movie.* **6.** [*no obj*] to take measures in preparation for something: *You must provide for winter in this harsh climate.* **—pro•vid′er,** *n.* [*count*] See -VIDE-.

pro•vid•ed (prə vī′did) /prə'vaydɪd/ *conj.* on the condition or understanding (that); if; as long as; providing: *She'll talk to you provided you listen.*

prov•i•dence (prov′i dəns) /'prɒvɪdəns/ *n.* [*noncount; often: Providence*] the care and guidance of God or nature over the creatures of the earth, esp. in directing human affairs. See -VIDE-.

prov•i•dent (prov′i dənt) /'prɒvɪdənt/ *adj.* having or showing careful thought for the future, as by saving. **—prov′i•dent•ly,** *adv.*

prov•i•den•tial (prov′i den′shəl) /ˌprɒvɪ'dɛnʃəl/ *adj.* **1.** of, relating to, or resulting from divine providence. **2.** fortunate or lucky: *a providential coincidence.* **—prov′i•den′tial•ly,** *adv.* See -VIDE-.

pro•vid•ing (prə vī′ding) /prə'vaydɪŋ/ *conj.* provided: *You can stay, providing you help.*

prov•ince (prov′ins) /'prɒvɪns/ *n.* [*count*] **1.** a division or unit of a country that has its own administration: *the provinces of Canada.* **2. the provinces,** [*plural*] the parts of a country outside of or away from the capital or the largest cities. **3.** [*count; usually singular*] an area or field of activity, study, or knowledge.

pro•vin•cial (prə vin′shəl) /prə'vɪnʃəl/ *adj.* **1.** belonging to or found in a particular province or provinces; local. **2.** of or relating to the provinces. **3.** narrow-minded in outlook; unsophisticated. **—*n.*** [*count*] **4.** a person who lives in or comes from the provinces. **5.** a person who is narrow-minded and lacks sophistication. **—pro•vin′cial•ism,** *n.* [*noncount*]

prov′ing ground′, *n.* [*count*] any place, context, or area for testing something, as scientific equipment or a theory.

pro•vi•sion (prə vizh′ən) /prə'vɪʒən/ *n.* **1.** [*noncount*] the act of providing or supplying: *the provision of running water and electricity to the region.* **2.** [*noncount*] an arrangement or preparation made for the future: *Didn't they make provision for the possibility that this spy would defect?* **3.** [*count*] a clause or statement providing or calling for something; stipulation; proviso: *a provision in the sales agreement allowing for return or exchange within one year.* **4. provisions,** [*plural*] supplies of food. **—*v.*** [~ + *obj*] **5.** to supply with provisions: *They were well provisioned for the winter.* See -VIS-.

pro•vi•sion•al (prə vizh′ə nl) /prə'vɪʒənḷ/ *adj.* serving for the time being only; temporary: *a provisional government.* **—pro•vi′sion•al•ly,** *adv.* See -VIS-.

pro•vi•so (prə vī′zō) /prə'vayzow/ *n.* [*count*], *pl.* **-sos, -soes. 1.** a clause or statement, as in a law, agreement, or contract, by which a condition is introduced. **2.** a condition or stipulation: *She'll take on the extra work with the proviso that she gets paid extra for overtime.* See -VIS-.

prov•o•ca•tion (prov′ə kā′shən) /ˌprɒvə'keyʃən/ *n.* the act of provoking or causing an often violent or strong reaction: [*noncount*]: *The dictator attacked without provocation.* [*count*]: *numerous provocations that he used as an excuse to launch a full-scale war.* See -VOC-.

pro•voc•a•tive (prə vok′ə tiv) /prə'vɒkətɪv/ *adj.* **1.** tending or serving to provoke. **2.** stimulating; enticing: *a provocative smile.* **—pro•voc′a•tive•ly,** *adv.* See -VOC-.

pro•voke (prə vōk′) /prə'vowk/ *v.* [~ + *obj*], **-voked, -vok•ing. 1.** to cause a feeling of anger in; annoy or exasperate: *Stop provoking them with your negative comments.* **2.** to stir up, arouse, or call forth (feelings, desires, or activity): *She provoked anger in a lot of people.* **—pro•vok′er,** *n.* [*count*] See -VOC-.

pro•vo•lo•ne (prō′və lō′nē) /ˌprowvə'lowniy/ *n.* [*noncount*] a mellow, light-colored Italian cheese.

pro•vost (prō′vōst, prov′əst *or, esp. in military usage,* prō′vō) /'prowvowst, 'prɒvəst *or, esp. in military usage,* 'prowvow/ *n.* [*count*] a high-ranking administrative officer of some colleges and universities.

prow (prou) /praw/ *n.* [*count*] **1.** the front part of a ship or boat; bow. **2.** a similar front part that sticks out, as the nose of an airplane.

prow•ess (prou′is) /'prawɪs/ *n.* [*noncount*] great or exceptional ability, skill, or strength: *his prowess in art; athletic prowess.*

prowl (proul) /prawl/ *v.* **1.** to go about or move around in a quiet, sneaky way, as in search of something to steal or capture: [*no obj*]: *The neighbor's cat prowls around the garbage cans all night.* [~ + *obj*]: *The gang was out prowling the streets.* **—*Idiom.*** **2. on the prowl,** in the act of prowling; searching stealthily. **—prowl′er,** *n.* [*count*]

-prox-, *root. -prox-* comes from Latin, where it has the meaning "close; near." This meaning is found in such words as: APPROXIMATE, APPROXIMATION, PROXIMITY.

prox•im•i•ty (prok sim′i tē) /prɒk'sɪmɪtiy/ *n.* [*noncount*] nearness in place, time, relation, etc. See -PROX-.

prox•y (prok′sē) /'prɒksiy/ *n., pl.* **-prox•ies. 1.** [*noncount*] the power given a person to act as the substitute for another or in place of another. **2.** [*count*] the person who is given such authority; a substitute. See -CURA-.

prude (pro͞od) /pruwd/ *n.* [*count*] a person who is overly proper or modest and is, or acts as if he or she is, easily shocked, esp. in matters involving sex. —**prud•er•y** (pro͞o′də rē) /'pruwdəriy/ *n.* [*noncount*] —**prud′ish,** *adj.*

pru•dence (pro͞od′ns) /'pruwdns/ *n.* [*noncount*] the state or condition of being careful or wise in practical affairs.

pru•dent (pro͞od′nt) /'pruwdnt/ *adj.* **1.** wise in practical affairs; thinking carefully before acting; sensible. **2.** careful in providing for the future: *prudent saving.* —**pru•den•tial** (pro͞o den′shəl) /pruw'dɛnʃəl/ *adj.* —**pru′dent•ly,** *adv.*

prune[1] (pro͞on) /pruwn/ *n.* [*count*] any plum when it is dried.

prune[2] (pro͞on) /pruwn/ *v.* [~ + *obj*], **pruned, prun•ing. 1.** to cut or chop off extra or unwanted twigs, branches, or roots from; trim: *She pruned the trees in her garden.* **2.** to cut or chop off: *She pruned a few branches off her trees.* **3.** to remove (anything considered extra or unnecessary): *pruning surplus staff members.* —**prun′er,** *n.* [*count*]

pru•ri•ent (pro͝or′ē ənt) /'prʊriyənt/ *adj.* having or showing strong interest in thoughts or desires about sex. —**pru′ri•ence,** *n.* [*noncount*]

pry[1] (prī) /pray/ *v.* [*no obj*], **pried, pry•ing.** to ask rude or impolite questions about something private; to investigate or try to find out about something private.

pry[2] (prī) /pray/ *v.,* **pried, pry•ing,** *n., pl.* **pries.** —*v.* [~ + *obj*] **1.** to move, raise, or open, with or as if with a tool like a lever: *pried off the lid of the jar.* **2.** to obtain or get (something) with difficulty: *to pry a secret out of someone.* —*n.* [*count*] **3.** a tool for prying.

P.S., an abbreviation of: **1.** permanent secretary. **2.** Also, **p.s.** postscript. **3.** Public School.

psalm (säm) /sɑm/ *n.* [*count*] **1.** a sacred song or hymn. **2.** [*often: Psalm*] any of the songs, hymns, or prayers contained in the Book of Psalms in the Bible: *Psalm 92; the Twenty-third Psalm.* —**psalm′ist,** *n.* [*count*]

pseudo-, *prefix.* **1.** *pseudo-* comes from Greek, where it has the meaning "false; pretended; unreal": *pseudo-* + *intellectual* → *pseudointellectual (= a person pretending to be an intellectual).* **2.** *pseudo-* is also used to mean "closely or deceptively resembling": *pseudo-* + *-pod-* → *pseudopod (= a part of an animal that closely resembles a foot).* Also, *esp. before a vowel,* **pseud-.**

pseu•do•nym (so͞od′n im) /'suwdn̩ɪm/ *n.* [*count*] a false name used by an author to conceal his or her identity; pen name. Compare ALIAS. See -ONYM-.

pshaw (shô) /ʃɔ/ *interj.* (used to show impatience, contempt, or disbelief): *"Pshaw; there's no way he can do that!" she exclaimed.*

pso•ri•a•sis (sə rī′ə sis) /sə'rayəsɪs/ *n.* [*noncount*] a skin disease characterized by scaly patches.

psst or **pst** (pst) /pst/ *interj.* (used to attract someone's attention quietly): *"Psst, in here!" he whispered.*

PST or **P.S.T.** or **p.s.t.,** an abbreviation of: Pacific Standard Time.

psych (sīk) /sayk/ *v. Informal.* **1.** to frighten or cause a feeling of uneasiness or anxiety in the mind: [~ + *obj (+ out)*]: *The tall player on their team was trying to psych our players (out).* [~ *(+ out)* + *obj*]: *to psych (out) the other team.* **2.** to prepare (oneself or another) to be in the right frame of mind or to do one's best: [~ + *obj*]: *was psyched and ready to go.* [~ + *oneself* + *up*]: *psyching himself up to propose.* [~ + *up* + *obj*]: *The coach tried to psych up the team.* [~ + *obj* + *up*]: *to psych the team up before the game.* **3.** [~ *(+ out)* + *obj*] to figure out ahead of time: *trying to psych out which day he'd give the test.*

psych., an abbreviation of: **1.** psychologist. **2.** psychology.

psy•che (sī′kē) /'saykiy/ *n.* [*count*] **1.** the human soul, spirit, or mind. **2.** the mental or psychological structure of a person.

psy•che•del•ic (sī′ki del′ik) /ˌsaykɪ'dɛlɪk/ *adj.* **1.** of or noting a mental state of intensified sensory perception. **2.** of or pertaining to any of various drugs that produce this state. **3.** resembling or characteristic of images, sounds, or the like, experienced while in such a state: *psychedelic painting.* —*n.* [*count*] **4.** a psychedelic drug.

psy•chi•at•ric (sī′kē a′trik) /ˌsaykiy'ætrɪk/ *adj.* [*before a noun*] **1.** of or relating to mental disorders or diseases of the mind. **2.** of or relating to psychiatry.

psy•chi•a•try (si kī′ə trē, sī-) /sɪ'kayətriy, say-/ *n.* [*noncount*] the branch of medicine concerned with the study, diagnosis, and treatment of mental disorders. —**psy•chi′a•trist,** *n.* [*count*]

psy•chic (sī′kik) /'saykɪk/ *adj.* Also, **psy′chi•cal. 1.** of or relating to the human psyche. **2.** of or relating to some apparently nonphysical force or agency that is outside natural or scientific knowledge: *an apparent psychic power to read minds.* —*n.* [*count*] **3.** a person who is able to use some apparently nonphysical force or agency outside the boundaries of natural or scientific knowledge so as to predict the future, read minds, etc.; medium. —**psy′chi•cal•ly,** *adv.*

psy•cho (sī′kō) /'saykow/ *n., pl.* **-chos,** *adj. Slang.* —*n.* [*count*] **1.** a crazy person. —*adj.* **2.** characteristic of such a person.

psycho-, *prefix. psycho-* comes from Greek, where it has the meaning "soul; mind." This meaning is found in such words as: PARAPSYCHOLOGY, PSYCHEDELIC, PSYCHIATRY, PSYCHIC, PSYCHOLOGICAL, PSYCHOLOGY, PSYCHOPATH, PSYCHOSIS, PSYCHOTIC.

psy•cho•a•nal•y•sis (sī′kō ə nal′ə sis) /ˌsaykowə'næləsɪs/ *n.* [*noncount*] a method for studying the hidden or unconscious processes of the mind as a way of treating mental illness. —**psy•cho•an•a•lyst** (sī′kō an′l-ist) /ˌsaykow'ænl̩ɪst/ *n.* [*count*] See -LYS-.

psy•cho•an•a•lyze (sī′kō an′l īz) /ˌsaykow'ænl̩ayz/ *v.* [~ + *obj*], **-lyzed, -lyz•ing.** to treat by means of psychoanalysis. See -LYS-.

psy•cho•gen•ic (sī′kə jen′ik) /ˌsaykə'dʒɛnɪk/ *adj.* having origin in, or caused by, the mind or a mental condition or process: *a psychogenic disorder.* See -GEN-.

psy•cho•log•i•cal (sī′kə loj′i kəl) /ˌsaykə'lɒdʒɪkəl/ *adj.* **1.** [*before a noun*] of or relating to psychology: *a psychological screening test.* **2.** of or relating to the mental states or thought processes of a person: *His problems are purely psychological.* —**psy′cho•log′i•cal•ly,** *adv.* See -LOG-.

psy•chol•o•gy (sī kol′ə jē) /say'kɒlədʒiy/ *n., pl.* **-gies. 1.** [*noncount*] the science of the mind or of mental states and processes: *to major in psychology.* **2.** [*noncount*] the science of human and animal behavior. **3.** all the mental states and processes that seem to be characteristic of a person or class of persons: [*count*]: *a warlike psychology.* [*noncount*]: *mob psychology.* **4.** [*noncount*] mental ploys or strategy: *He used psychology to get a promotion.* —**psy•chol′o•gist,** *n.* [*count*] See -LOG-.

psy•cho•path (sī′kə path′) /'saykəˌpæθ/ *n.* [*count*] a person having a disorder in which he or she shows no regard for morally or socially correct behavior and has no feelings of remorse from acting this way. —**psy′cho•path′ic,** *adj.* [*before a noun*] See -PATH-.

psy•cho•sis (sī kō′sis) /say'kowsɪs/ *n., pl.* **-ses** (-sēz) /-siyz/. a mental disorder characterized by beliefs about the world and about oneself that are not based on reality: [*noncount*]: *the treatment of psychosis.* [*count*]: *His psychoses included delusions and paranoia.*

psy•cho•so•mat•ic (sī′kō sə mat′ik, -sō-) /ˌsaykowsə'mætɪk, -sow-/ *adj.* of or relating to a physical disorder or illness that is caused or seems to be influenced by emotional factors. See -SOM-.

psy•cho•ther•a•py (sī′kō ther′ə pē) /ˌsaykow'θɛrəpiy/ *n.* [*noncount; count*], *pl.* **-pies.** the psychological treatment of mental or emotional disorders, as by means of psychoanalysis or group therapy. —**psy′cho•ther′a•pist,** *n.* [*count*]

psy•chot•ic (sī kot′ik) /say'kɒtɪk/ *adj.* **1.** suffering from a mental disorder or a psychosis. —*n.* [*count*] **2.** a person suffering from this.

psy•cho•tro•pic (sī′kō trō′pik) /ˌsaykow'trowpɪk/ *adj.* **1.** affecting the mind. —*n.* [*count*] **2.** a psychotropic drug, as a tranquilizer.

Pt., an abbreviation of: **1.** point. **2.** port.

pt., an abbreviation of: **1.** part. **2.** payment. **3.** pint. **4.** point. **5.** port.

-pter-, *root. -pter-* comes from Greek, where it has the meaning "wing; feather." This meaning is found in such words as: DIPTEROUS, HELICOPTER.

pter•o•dac•tyl (ter′ə dak′til) /ˌtɛrə'dæktɪl/ *n.* [*count*] an extinct flying reptile. See -PTER-.

pter•o•saur (ter′ə sôr′) /'tɛrəˌsɔr/ *n.* [*count*] any of an order of flying reptiles. See -PTER-.

pto•maine (tō′mān, tō mān′) /'towmeyn, tow'meyn/ *n.* [*noncount*] any of a class of foul-smelling substances produced by bacteria during the rotting of animal or plant protein.

pub (pub) /pʌb/ *n.* [*count*] a bar or tavern.

pu•ber•ty (pyo͞o′bər tē) /ˈpyuwbərtiy/ *n.* [*noncount*] the period of life during which the sex organs mature and certain other parts of the body develop (as breasts in females and body hair in males), and the individual becomes capable of sexual reproduction.

pu•bes•cent (pyo͞o bes′ənt) /pyuwˈbɛsənt/ *adj.* [*before a noun*] arriving or having arrived at puberty. **—pu•bes′cence,** *n.* [*noncount*]

pu•bic (pyo͞o′bik) /ˈpyuwbɪk/ *adj.* [*before a noun*] of, relating to, or situated near the genital organs: *pubic hair.*

pub•lic (pub′lik) /ˈpʌblɪk/ *adj.* **1.** of, relating to, or affecting a population or a community as a whole: *a public nuisance; the public welfare.* **2.** [*before a noun*] done for, made for, acting for, or being in the service of the community as a whole: *public officials.* **3.** open to all persons; open to the view of all persons: *a public meeting.* **4.** generally known to most people of a community: *The information became public.* **5.** [*before a noun*] familiar to the public; prominent: *movie stars and other public figures.* **—*n.*** [*noncount; the/one's* + ~] **6.** the people who make up a community, state, or nation. **7.** a particular group of people with a common interest, aim, etc.: *the book-buying public.* **—*Idiom.*** **8. go public, a.** to issue stock for sale to the general public. **b.** to present previously hidden or unknown information to the public: *threatened to go public with the story.* **9. in public,** in a situation open to public notice, view, or access; publicly. **10. make public,** to cause to become known generally, as through the news media: [*make* + *obj* + ~]: *He made the allegations public.* [*make* + ~ + *obj*]: *She made public her plans for reform.* **—pub′lic•ly,** *adv.*

pub•li•ca•tion (pub′li kā′shən) /ˌpʌblɪˈkeyʃən/ *n.* **1.** [*noncount*] the act of publishing a book, periodical, piece of music, or the like. **2.** [*noncount*] the act of bringing before the public; announcement: *the publication of the emergency plans for school closings.* **3.** [*count*] something published: *had 30 publications to his credit.*

pub′lic defend′er, *n.* [*count*] a full-time lawyer appointed to represent people too poor to afford one in criminal cases.

pub′lic domain′, *n.* [*noncount; usually: the* + ~] the legal status of a literary work or an invention whose copyright or patent has expired, or for which there never was such protection.

pub•li•cist (pub′lə sist) /ˈpʌbləsɪst/ *n.* [*count*] a person who publicizes, esp. a press agent or public-relations consultant.

pub•lic•i•ty (pu blis′i tē) /pʌˈblɪsɪtiy/ *n.* [*noncount*] **1.** widespread mention in the news media or by word of mouth or other means of communication: *wonderful publicity for his new book.* **2.** the technique, process, or business of gaining public notice or mention.

pub•li•cize (pub′lə sīz′) /ˈpʌbləˌsayz/ *v.* [~ + *obj*], **-cized, -ciz•ing.** to give publicity to: *Can you publicize the school play to attract more people?*

pub′lic opin′ion, *n.* [*noncount*] the opinion of many people on some issue, the state of a company's or organization's relations with the public, or the degree of goodwill attained.

pub′lic rela′tions, *n.* **1.** [*plural; used with a plural verb*] the actions of a corporation, individual, government, etc., in seeking to bring about goodwill with the public. **2.** [*noncount; used with a singular verb*] the technique or profession of promoting such goodwill: *He studied management and public relations.*

pub′lic school′, *n.* **1.** (in the U.S.) a school, usually for primary or secondary grades, that is paid for by public taxes: [*count*]: *Public schools are usually supported by property taxes.* [*noncount*]: *He attended public school.* **2.** (in England) any of a number of secondary boarding schools that prepare students chiefly for the universities or for public service: [*count*]: *Public schools are expensive in England.* [*noncount*]: *was sent to public school.*

pub′lic-spir′ited, *adj.* having or showing an unselfish interest in the public welfare.

pub′lic util′ity, *n.* [*count*] a business enterprise, as a gas company, performing a public service under government regulation.

pub•lish (pub′lish) /ˈpʌblɪʃ/ *v.* **1.** to issue (newspapers, books, or otherwise reproduced text or graphic material, computer software, etc.) for sale or distribution to the public: [~ + *obj*]: *The company publishes books.* [*no obj*]: *The newspaper stopped publishing.* **2.** [~ + *obj*] to issue publicly (the work of): *They publish (the plays of) William Shakespeare.* **—pub′lish•er,** *n.* [*count*]

pub•lish•ing (pub′lish ing) /ˈpʌblɪʃɪŋ/ *n.* [*noncount*] the act or business of printing and selling books.

puce (pyo͞os) /pyuws/ *n.* [*noncount*] **1.** a dark or brownish purple. **—*adj.*** **2.** of the color puce.

puck (puk) /pʌk/ *n.* [*count*] a black disk of hard rubber that is hit into the goal in a game of ice hockey.

puck•er (puk′ər) /ˈpʌkər/ *v.* **1.** to draw or gather into wrinkles or folds; constrict: [*no obj*]: *His face puckered when he bit into the sour candy.* [~ + *obj*]: *She puckered her lips, expecting a kiss.* **—*n.*** [*count*] **2.** an irregular fold; wrinkle. **3.** a puckered part, as of cloth tightly or crookedly sewn.

puck•ish (puk′ish) /ˈpʌkɪʃ/ *adj.* mischievous; impish.

pud•ding (po͝od′ing) /ˈpʊdɪŋ/ *n.* **1.** a soft, thickened dessert, usually made with milk, sugar, flour, and flavoring: [*noncount*]: *Chocolate pudding is for dessert.* [*count*]: *several puddings to choose from.* **2.** [*noncount*] *Brit.* the dessert course of a meal.

pud•dle (pud′l) /ˈpʌdl̩/ *n.* [*count*] **1.** a small pool of water, as of rainwater on the ground. **2.** a small pool of any liquid: *a puddle of black oil under the car.*

pudg•y (puj′ē) /ˈpʌdʒiy/ *adj.,* **-i•er, -i•est.** short and fat or thick: *an infant's pudgy fingers.*

pueb•lo (pweb′lō) /ˈpwɛblow/ *n.* [*count*], *pl.* **-los. 1.** a communal living place or dwelling of certain agricultural Native Americans of the southwestern U.S., consisting of a number of houses built together and made of stone or adobe. **2.** any Indian village in the southwestern U.S. **3.** (in Spanish America) a town or village. **4.** (in the Philippines) a town or township.

pu•er•ile (pyo͞o′ər il, -ə rīl′, pyo͝or′il, -īl) /ˈpyuwərɪl, -əˌrayl, ˈpyʊrɪl, -ayl/ *adj.* childishly foolish; immature; silly: *puerile jokes.*

puff (puf) /pʌf/ *n.* [*count*] **1.** a short, quick blast of air, smoke, vapor, etc. **2.** the sound made in giving off such a short blast of air, vapor, smoke, etc. **3.** an act of inhaling and exhaling, as on a cigarette or pipe. **4.** a ball of light pastry baked and filled with whipped cream, jam, etc.: *a cream puff.* **5.** a flattering review, as of a book or an actor's performance. **—*v.*** **6.** [*no obj*] to blow with short, quick blasts, as the wind. **7.** to (cause to) be let out or given out in a puff: [~ + *obj*]: *He puffed a cloud of pipe smoke.* [*no obj*]: *puffing on a cigar.* **8.** [*no obj*] to give out a puff or puffs of air; breathe quickly and with difficulty. **9.** [*no obj*] to go or move with puffing or puffs: *The train puffed into the station.* **10.** to (cause to) become inflated or swollen, or to stand out: [*no obj; (~ + up)*]: *Her face puffed up in reaction to the poison ivy.* [~ + *obj*]: *She puffed her cheeks in thought.* [~ + *up* + *obj*]: *The bird puffed up its feathers.* **11.** to make fluffy; fluff: [~ + *up* + *obj*]: *to puff up a pillow.* [~ + *obj* + *up*]: *to puff it up.*

puff•ball (puf′bôl′) /ˈpʌfˌbɔl/ *n.* [*count*] a rounded fungus that gives off a cloud of spores when pressed or broken.

puf•fin (puf′in) /ˈpʌfɪn/ *n.* [*count*] a sea bird of the auk family with a short neck and a colorful, triangular bill.

puf•fy (puf′ē) /ˈpʌfiy/ *adj.,* **-i•er, -i•est.** swollen in appearance: *puffy white clouds; a face puffy from crying.* **—puff′i•ness,** *n.* [*noncount*]

pug (pug) /pʌg/ *n.* [*count*] **1.** one of a breed of small, squarely built dogs with a deeply wrinkled face, tightly curled tail, and a short, smooth, usually silver or brownyellow coat with a black mask. **2.** a pug nose.

pu•gi•lism (pyo͞o′jə liz′əm) /ˈpyuwdʒəˌlɪzəm/ *n.* [*noncount*] the art or practice of fighting with the fists; boxing. **—pu′gi•list,** *n.* [*count*] **—pu′gi•lis′tic,** *adj.* See -PUGN-.

-pugn-, *root.* *-pugn-* comes from Latin, where it has the meaning "fight; fist." This meaning is found in such words as: IMPUGN, PUGILISM, PUGNACIOUS, REPUGNANT.

pug•na•cious (pug nā′shəs) /pʌgˈneyʃəs/ *adj.* too ready or eager to quarrel or fight; quarrelsome; belligerent; combative. **—pug•na′cious•ly,** *adv.* **—pug•nac•i•ty** (pug nas′i tē) /pʌgˈnæsɪtiy/ *n.* [*noncount*] See -PUGN-.

pug′ nose′, *n.* [*count*] a short, broad, somewhat turned-up nose. **—pug′-nosed′,** *adj.*

puke (pyo͞ok) /pyuwk/ *v.,* **puked, puk•ing,** *n. Slang.* **—*v.*** **1.** to vomit: [*no obj*]: *He went outside and puked.* [~ + *obj*]: *puking dinner.* **—*n.*** [*noncount*] **2.** vomit.

pull (po͝ol) /pʊl/ *v.* **1.** to draw or haul toward oneself or itself, in a particular direction, or into a particular position: [~ + *obj*]: *He pulled the sled up the hill.* [*no obj*]: *He pulled at the sled.* **2.** [~ + *obj*] to tear: *to pull a cloth to pieces.* **3.** [~ + *obj*] to draw or pluck away from a place of growth, attachment, etc.: *The dentist pulled four of her teeth.* **4.** [~ + *obj*] to draw out (a weapon) for ready use: *Suddenly they pulled a gun on me.* **5.** [~ + *obj*] to perform; carry out: *They pulled a spectacular coup.* **6.** [~ + *obj*] to withdraw; remove: *The manager pulled the pitcher from the game.* **7.** [~ *(+ in)* + *obj*] to attract; win: *to pull votes.* **8.** [~ + *obj*] to strain (a muscle, ligament, or tendon). **9.** [~ + *obj*] to be assigned: *pulled guard duty.* **10.** (of a baseball) to (cause to) be hit so that it follows the direction in which the bat is being swung: [~ + *obj*]: *He pulled the ball to left field.* [*no obj*]: *The ball pulled foul.* **11.** [*no obj*] to move or go: *The train pulled away from the station.* **12. pull apart,** to analyze or examine carefully and critically, esp. for errors: [~ + *apart* + *obj*]: *pulling apart the committee's report.* [~ + *obj* + *apart*]: *pulling the report apart.* **13. pull away,** [*no obj*] **a.** to move; withdraw: *The car pulled away in a cloud of dust.* **b.** to free oneself with force: *The spaceship tried to pull away from the earth's gravity.* **c.** to start to move ahead, as if by separating from another or others. **14. pull back,** to (cause to) leave a position in retreat: [~ + *back* + *obj*]: *The general pulled back his troops.* [~ + *obj* + *back*]: *He pulled them back.* [*no obj*]: *The troops started to pull back.* **15. pull down,** [~ + *down* + *obj*] *Informal.* to receive as a salary; earn: *He is pulling down more than fifty thousand a year.* **16. pull for,** [~ + *for* + *obj*] to support actively; encourage: *They were pulling for the Republican candidate.* **17. pull in, a.** [*no obj*] to arrive: *The train just pulled in.* **b.** to tighten; curb: [~ + *in* + *obj*]: *to pull in the reins.* [~ + *obj* + *in*]: *to pull them in.* **c.** *Informal.* to arrest (someone): [~ + *obj* + *in*]: *The police pulled me in for speeding.* [~ + *in* + *obj*]: *The police pulled in scores of protesters.* **18. pull off,** *Informal.* to perform successfully, esp. something difficult: [~ + *off* + *obj*]: *His political team pulled off a landslide victory.* [~ + *obj* + *off*]: *I don't know how you pulled it off, but you got the job!* **19. pull out,** [*no obj*] **a.** to depart: *The train pulled out about three hours late.* **b.** to abandon abruptly: *to pull out of an agreement.* **20. pull over,** to direct one's automobile or other vehicle to the curb: [*no obj*]: *The police officer told me to pull over.* [~ + *obj* + *over*]: *told me to pull the car over.* **21. pull through,** to (cause to) come safely through (a crisis, illness, etc.): [*no obj*]: *If we stay together, we'll pull through OK.* [~ + *through* + *obj*]: *If we stay together, we'll pull through this crisis.* **22. pull up, a.** to bring or come to a halt, or to a slower pace: [*no obj*]: *The runner pulled up lame after only two miles.* [~ + *obj* + *up*]: *He pulled the car up in front of the house.* **b.** [*no obj*] to bring or draw closer: *For a few laps she pulled up to me.* **c.** to root up; remove by the roots: [~ + *up* + *obj*]: *He pulled up a weed.* [~ + *obj* + *up*]: *He pulled it up.* **—*n.*** **23.** [*count*] the act of pulling or drawing: *signaled them with two pulls on the rope.* **24.** [*noncount*] force used in pulling; pulling power: *Is there any pull on this line?* **25.** [*count*] a part or thing to be pulled, as a handle on a drawer. **26.** [*count*] a pulled muscle: *a thigh pull.* **27.** [*noncount*] influence, as with persons able to grant favors: *has a lot of pull at city hall.* **28.** [*noncount*] the ability to attract; drawing power: *The star has a lot of pull at the box office.* **—*Idiom.*** **29. pull oneself together,** to gain control of one's emotions. **30. pull strings** or **wires,** to use influence, as with powerful friends or coworkers, so as to gain one's objectives. —**pull′er,** *n.* [*count*]

pull•back (po͝ol′bak′) /ˈpʊlˌbæk/ *n.* [*count*] the act of pulling back, esp. a retreat or a planned withdrawal of troops.

pul•let (po͝ol′it) /ˈpʊlɪt/ *n.* [*count*] a young hen.

pul•ley (po͝ol′ē) /ˈpʊliy/ *n.* [*count*], *pl.* **-leys.** a wheel for supporting, guiding, or transmitting force to or from a moving rope or cable that rides in a groove in its edge.

Pull•man (po͝ol′mən) /ˈpʊlmən/ *n.* [*count*], *pl.* **-mans. 1.** *Trademark.* a railroad sleeping car or parlor car. **2.** [*often: pullman*] Also called **Pull′man case′.** a large suitcase.

pull•out (po͝ol′out′) /ˈpʊlˌawt/ *n.* [*count*] **1.** an act or instance of pulling out: *a troop pullout.* **2.** a specially inserted section of a newspaper or magazine that is meant to be pulled out: *an advertising pullout.*

pull•o•ver (po͝ol′ō′vər) /ˈpʊlˌowvər/ *n.* [*count*] **1.** Also called **slipover.** a garment, esp. a sweater, that must be drawn over the head to be put on. **—*adj.*** [*before a noun*] **2.** designed to be put on by being drawn over the head: *a pullover vest.*

pull′-up′ or **pull′up′,** *n.* [*count*] an exercise in which one raises the chin over a bar by lifting oneself by the hands and arms; a chin-up.

pul•mo•nar•y (pul′mə ner′ē, po͝ol′-) /ˈpʌlməˌnɛriy, ˈpʊl-/ *adj.* of or affecting the lungs.

pulp (pulp) /pʌlp/ *n.* [*noncount*] **1.** the soft, juicy part of a fruit that can be eaten. **2.** Also called **dental pulp.** the inner substance of the tooth, containing arteries, veins, and nerve tissue. **3.** a soft, moist, slightly sticky mass, as that into which wood is converted in the making of paper. **4.** a magazine or book printed on low-quality paper and often containing shocking material. **—*v.*** [~ + *obj*] **5.** to cause to be made into pulp, as by crushing: *to pulp oranges.* —**pulp′y,** *adj.*, **-i•er, -i•est.**

pul•pit (po͝ol′pit, pul′-) /ˈpʊlpɪt, ˈpʌl-/ *n.* **1.** [*count*] a platform or raised structure in a church, from which the sermon is delivered or the service is conducted. **2.** [*noncount*] the clerical profession; ministry.

-puls-, *root.* *-puls-* comes from Latin, where it has the meaning "push; drive." This meaning is found in such words as: COMPULSION, EXPULSION, IMPULSE, IMPULSIVE, PROPULSION, PULSAR, PULSATION, PULSE, REPULSE, REPULSIVE. See -PEL-.

pul•sar (pul′sär) /ˈpʌlsɑr/ *n.* [*count*] an object in space, generally believed to be a rapidly rotating neutron star, that gives out pulses of radiation, esp. radio waves, very regularly. See -PULS-.

pul•sate (pul′sāt) /ˈpʌlseyt/ *v.* [*no obj*], **-sat•ed, -sat•ing. 1.** to expand and contract regularly; beat; throb: *The blood was pulsating through his veins.* **2.** to vibrate. —**pul•sa•tion** (pul sā′shən) /pʌlˈseyʃən/ *n.* [*noncount*] See -PULS-.

pulse (puls) /pʌls/ *n.*, *v.*, **pulsed, puls•ing. —*n.*** [*count*] **1.** the regular beat or throbbing of the arteries, caused by the successive contractions of the heart: *The doctor felt his wrist for a pulse.* **2.** a stroke, vibration, or regular series of beats: *a pulse of drums.* **3.** the general feelings, opinions, attitudes, or sentiments, as of the public. **4.** a momentary, sudden surge or drop in an electrical quantity. **5.** a single, sudden emission of particles or radiation. **—*v.*** [*no obj*] **6.** to beat or throb; pulsate: *The blood pulsed through his veins.* See -PULS-.

pul•ver•ize (pul′və rīz′) /ˈpʌlvəˌrayz/ *v.*, **-ized, -iz•ing. 1.** to (cause to) be turned into or reduced to dust or powder, as by pounding or grinding: [~ + *obj*]: *The workers pulverized the rocks.* [*no obj*]: *Over time the mineral slowly pulverized.* **2.** [~ + *obj*] to demolish or crush completely: *The two-thousand-pound bomb pulverized the command center.* —**pul•ver•i•za•tion** (pul′vər i zā′shən) /ˌpʌlvərɪˈzeyʃən/ *n.* [*noncount*]

pu•ma (pyo͞o′mə, po͞o′-) /ˈpyuwmə, ˈpuw-/ *n.*, *pl.* **-mas.** COUGAR.

pum•ice (pum′is) /ˈpʌmɪs/ *n.* [*noncount*] a rough or sometimes spongy rock, a form of volcanic glass, used to clean or smooth objects.

pum•mel (pum′əl) /ˈpʌməl/ *v.* [~ + *obj*], **-meled, -mel•ing** or (*esp. Brit.*) **-melled, -mel•ling.** to beat or punch with or as if with the fists.

pump[1] (pump) /pʌmp/ *n.* [*count*] **1.** an apparatus or machine for raising, pushing in or out, or compressing fluids or gases: *an air pump; gas pumps.* **—*v.*** **2.** to raise or drive with a pump: [~ + *obj*]: *to pump water from the well.* [*no obj*]: *His heart was still pumping.* **3.** [~ + *obj*] to force, inject, or put (something) into (something) like a pump or as if by using a pump: *The gangster pumped ten bullets into him.* **4.** [~ *(+ out)* + *obj*] to free from water or other liquid by means of a pump: *After the flood they tried to pump (out) the basement.* **5.** to (cause to) be operated or moved by an up-and-down or back-and-forth action: [*no obj*]: *He raced ahead, his legs pumping.* [~ + *obj*]: *They pumped their fists and shouted.* **6.** [~ + *obj*] to question (someone) artfully or persistently: *tried to pump me for information.* **7.** [*no obj*] to come out in squirts: *Blood was pumping from the wound.* **8. pump up, a.** to inflate by pumping: [~ + *up* + *obj*]: *to pump up a tire.* [~ + *obj* + *up*]: *to pump it up.* **b.** to cause (someone) to have enthusiasm, competitive spirit, excitement, etc.: [~ + *up* + *obj*]: *The coach had to pump up his team for the second half.* [~ + *obj* + *up*]: *trying to pump them up for the second half.* **—*Idiom.*** **9. pump iron,** to lift weights as an exercise. —**pump′er,** *n.* [*count*]

pump[2] (pump) /pʌmp/ *n.* [*count*] a woman's low-cut shoe with a moderately high heel.

pum•per•nick•el (pum′pər nik′əl) /ˈpʌmpərˌnɪkəl/ *n.* [*noncount*] a coarse, dark, slightly sour bread made from rye flour.

pump•kin (pump′kin *or, commonly,* pung′kin) /ˈpʌmpkɪn *or, commonly,* ˈpʌŋkɪn/ *n.* a large, edible, orange-yellow fruit that grows on a vine that lies on the ground:

[*count*]: *to carve jack-o'-lanterns out of a couple of pumpkins.* [*noncount*]: *a pie filled with pumpkin.*

pun (pun) /pʌn/ *n., v.,* **punned, pun•ning.** —*n.* [*count*] **1.** the humorous use of a word or phrase so as to emphasize or suggest its different meanings or applications; the use of words that are alike or nearly alike in sound but different in meaning; a play on words. —*v.* [*no obj*] **2.** to make puns.

punch[1] (punch) /pʌntʃ/ *n.* **1.** [*count*] a thrusting blow, esp. with the fist. **2.** [*noncount*] forcefulness or effectiveness; power: *Your writing lacks punch.* —*v.* **3.** to give a sharp thrust or blow to, esp. with the fist: [~ + *obj*]: *punched him right in the nose.* [*no obj*]: *They started punching and wrestling.* **4.** [~ + *obj*] *Western U.S. and Canada.* to drive (cattle). **5.** to strike or hit in operating: [~ + *obj*]: *to punch an elevator button.* [*no obj*]: *punching at the computer keyboard.* **6.** [~ + *obj*] to put into operation with or as if with a blow: *to punch a time clock.* See *punch in* and *punch out* below. **7. punch in, a.** [*no obj*] to record one's time of arrival at work by punching a time clock. **b.** [~ + *in* + *obj*] to enter (data), as into a computer, by striking keys: *He punched in his password.* **8. punch out, a.** [*no obj*] to record one's time of departure from work by punching a time clock. **b.** *Slang.* to beat up with the fists: [~ + *out* + *obj*]: *punched out the mugger.* [~ + *obj* + *out*]: *"I'll punch you out," he shouted.* **9. punch up,** [~ + *up* + *obj*] to add life, zest, or vigor to; enliven: *added some jokes to punch up the sermon.* —***Idiom.*** **10. pull punches, a.** to lessen the force of one's punches deliberately. **b.** to restrain oneself; hold back: *didn't pull any punches in voicing his displeasure.* —**punch′er,** *n.* [*count*]

punch[2] (punch) /pʌntʃ/ *n.* [*count*] **1.** a tool or machine for making holes or stamping materials, driving nails, etc.: *a metal punch.* **2.** a device for making holes, as in paper. —*v.* [~ + *obj*] **3.** to make holes in, stamp, drive, etc., with a punch. **4.** to make (a hole) with a punch.

punch[3] (punch) /pʌntʃ/ *n.* [*noncount*] **1.** a drink consisting of wine or spirits mixed with fruit juice, soda, etc., often sweetened and spiced. **2.** a beverage of fruit juices, sugar, and water.

punch′-drunk′, *adj.* **1.** (of a boxer) showing symptoms of injury to the brain, caused by repeated blows to the head, as dulled thinking capacity. **2.** befuddled; dazed: *was punch-drunk from studying.*

punch′ line′, *n.* [*count*] the final phrase or sentence in a joke, speech, or humorous story that conveys the point and is the source of humor.

punch•y (pun′chē) /ˈpʌntʃiy/ *adj.,* **-i•er, -i•est. 1.** punch-drunk. **2.** vigorously effective; forceful: *punchy writing.*

-punct-, *root.* *-punct-* comes from Latin, where it has the meaning "point; prick; pierce." This meaning is found in such words as: ACUPUNCTURE, COMPUNCTION, EXPUNGE, PUNCTILIOUS, PUNCTUAL, PUNCTUALITY, PUNCTUATION, PUNCTURE, PUNGENT. See -POINT-.

punc•til•i•ous (pungk til′ē əs) /pʌŋkˈtɪliyəs/ *adj.* strict or exact in obeying the formalities of conduct, behavior, or actions: *was very punctilious about following orders.* —**punc•til′i•ous•ly,** *adv.* —**punc•til′i•ous•ness,** *n.* [*noncount*] See -PUNCT-.

punc•tu•al (pungk′cho͞o əl) /ˈpʌŋktʃuwəl/ *adj.* being on time; prompt: *He was always punctual for meetings.* —**punc•tu•al•i•ty** (pungk′cho͞o al′i tē) /ˌpʌŋktʃuwˈælɪtiy/ *n.* [*noncount*] —**punc′tu•al•ly,** *adv.* See -PUNCT-.

punc•tu•ate (pungk′cho͞o āt′) /ˈpʌŋktʃuwˌeyt/ *v.,* **-at•ed, -at•ing. 1.** to mark or divide (something written) with punctuation: [~ + *obj*]: *Punctuate the following sentences.* [*no obj*]: *He needs to practice punctuating.* **2.** [~ + *obj*] to interrupt at different times: *Cheers punctuated the speech.* **3.** [~ + *obj*] to give emphasis or force to: *He punctuated his speech with gestures.* See -PUNCT-.

punc•tu•a•tion (pungk′cho͞o ā′shən) /ˌpʌŋktʃuwˈeyʃən/ *n.* [*noncount*] **1.** the practice or system of using certain marks or characters in writing or printing in order to separate the elements of sentences and make the meaning clear: *a lesson on correct punctuation, such as ending a sentence with a period and a question with a question mark.* **2.** punctuation marks, thought of as a group: *Use punctuation to signal the connections between and among your sentences.* See -PUNCT-.

punc•ture (pungk′chər) /ˈpʌŋktʃər/ *n., v.,* **-tured, -tur•ing.** —*n.* [*count*] **1.** the act of piercing or making a hole in something, as with a pointed instrument or object. **2.** a hole or mark so made: *punctures from the needle.* —*v.* **3.** to (cause to) be pierced; to (cause to) have a hole made in, as with a pointed instrument: [~ + *obj*]: *The tire was punctured by a nail.* [*no obj*]: *The tires punctured with a bang.* **4.** [~ + *obj*] to make (a hole) by piercing: *punctured holes in the top of the jar.* **5.** [~ + *obj*] to reduce or make less as if by piercing: *The failure punctured her pride.* **6.** [~ + *obj*] to cause to collapse or disintegrate: *to puncture a dream of success.* See -PUNCT-.

pun•dit (pun′dit) /ˈpʌndɪt/ *n.* [*count*] a person who is an expert or authority, or one who is treated as such, or one who is knowledgeable in an area or assumed to be so. —**pun•dit•ry** (pun′di trē) /ˈpʌndɪtriy/ *n.* [*noncount*]

pun•gent (pun′jənt) /ˈpʌndʒənt/ *adj.* **1.** sharply affecting the sense of taste or smell; biting; acrid: *the pungent aroma of garlic.* **2.** sharply expressive; biting: *pungent criticism.* —**pun′gen•cy,** *n.* [*noncount*] —**pun′gent•ly,** *adv.* See -PUNCT-.

pun•ish (pun′ish) /ˈpʌnɪʃ/ *v.* [~ + *obj*] **1.** to cause (someone) to undergo or suffer pain, loss, jail, or death as a penalty for some offense or fault. **2.** to inflict such a penalty for (an offense or fault): *to punish theft.* **3.** to handle or treat harshly or roughly; hurt: *The rocky road really punishes these tires.* See -PEN-. —**Related Words.** PUNISH is a verb, PUNISHMENT is a noun, PUNISHABLE is an adjective: *The teacher had to punish her students. The punishment must fit the crime. That crime is punishable by death.*

pun•ish•a•ble (pun′ish ə bəl) /ˈpʌnɪʃəbəl/ *adj.* that may be punished; deserving of punishment: *a punishable offense.* See -PEN-.

pun•ish•ment (pun′ish mənt) /ˈpʌnɪʃmənt/ *n.* **1.** [*noncount*] the act of punishing; the fact of being punished. **2.** [*count*] a penalty assigned to or imposed for an offense or fault: *The punishment was a year in jail.* **3.** [*noncount*] severe or harsh handling or treatment: *This car has taken a lot of punishment over the years.* See -PEN-.

pu•ni•tive (pyo͞o′ni tiv) /ˈpyuwnɪtɪv/ *adj.* **1.** serving as, concerned with, or giving punishment. **2.** harsh and severe: *a punitive tax.* —**pu′ni•tive•ly,** *adv.* See -PEN-.

punk (pungk) /pʌŋk/ *n.* **1.** [*count*] *Slang.* a young hoodlum. **2.** PUNK ROCK. **3.** [*noncount*] a style or movement, mostly of young people, whose followers wear aggressively unusual clothing, hairstyles, etc. **4.** PUNKER. —*adj.* **5.** of or relating to punk rock or punk style.

punk•er (pung′kər) /ˈpʌŋkər/ *n.* [*count*] a punk rock musician or a follower of punk rock or punk style.

punk′ rock′, *n.* [*noncount*] rock music having loud, repeating, insistent music and aggressive, often violent lyrics. —**punk′ rock′er,** *n.* [*count*]

pun•ster (pun′stər) /ˈpʌnstər/ *n.* [*count*] a person who makes puns frequently.

punt[1] (punt) /pʌnt/ *n.* [*count*] **1.** a kick, as in football or rugby, in which the ball is dropped and kicked before it touches the ground. —*v.* **2.** to kick (a dropped ball) before it touches the ground: [~ + *obj*]: *He punted the ball.* [*no obj*]: *ready to punt.* **3.** [*no obj*] *Informal.* to stall or delay while thinking up an answer: *If they ask you for exact sales figures, you'll have to punt.* —**punt′er,** *n.* [*count*]

punt[2] (punt) /pʌnt/ *n.* [*count*] **1.** a small, shallow, flat-bottomed boat with square ends, propelled with a pole. —*v.* **2.** to pole (a small boat): [~ + *obj*]: *He punted the boat along.* [*no obj*]: *They went out punting.* —**punt′er,** *n.* [*count*]

pu•ny (pyo͞o′nē) /ˈpyuwniy/ *adj.,* **-ni•er, -ni•est. 1.** of less than normal size and strength; weak: *a puny body.* **2.** unimportant; insignificant: *a puny threat.* —**pu′ni•ness,** *n.* [*noncount*]

pup (pup) /pʌp/ *n., v.,* **pupped, pup•ping.** —*n.* [*count*] **1.** a young dog; puppy. **2.** the young of certain other animals, as the rat or fur seal. —*v.* [*no obj*] **3.** to give birth to pups.

pu•pa (pyo͞o′pə) /ˈpyuwpə/ *n.* [*count*], *pl.* **-pae** (-pē) /-piy/ **-pas.** an insect in the nonfeeding, usually nonmoving, stage between the larva and the adult. —**pu′pal,** *adj.*

pu•pil[1] (pyo͞o′pəl) /ˈpyuwpəl/ *n.* [*count*] a person, usually young, who is learning from or being taught by a teacher at school or a private tutor; student.

pu•pil[2] (pyo͞o′pəl) /ˈpyuwpəl/ *n.* [*count*] the opening in the iris of the eye that narrows and widens as more or less light passes through to the retina.

pup•pet (pup′it) /ˈpʌpɪt/ *n.* [*count*] **1.** a usually small, doll-like figure representing a human being or an animal, moved by the hands or by rods, wires, etc. **2.** a person, group, or government whose actions are controlled by another or others. —*adj.* [*before a noun*] **3.** controlled by others: *a puppet government.* —**pup•pet•ry** (pup′i trē) /ˈpʌpɪtriy/ *n.* [*noncount*]

pup•pet•eer (pup′i tēr′) /ˌpʌpɪˈtɪər/ *n.* [*count*] a person who moves or handles puppets, as in a puppet show.

pup•py (pup′ē) /ˈpʌpiy/ *n.* [*count*], *pl.* **-pies.** a young dog.

pup′ tent′, *n.* [*count*] a small tent for two persons.

-pur-, *root.* *-pur-* comes from Latin, where it has the meaning "pure." This meaning is found in such words as: EXPURGATE, IMPURE, IMPURITY, PURE, PURÉE, PURGATIVE, PURGATORY, PURGE, PURIFY, PURITAN, PURITY.

pur•chase (pûr′chəs) /ˈpɜrtʃəs/ *v.,* **-chased, -chas•ing,** *n.* —*v.* [~ + *obj*] **1.** to get or obtain by the payment of money or its equivalent; buy: *enough money to purchase a house.* **2.** [*not: be* + ~*-ing*] to be enough to buy: *Ten dollars will purchase two tickets.* **3.** to get or obtain by effort, sacrifice, flattery, etc.: *His loyalty can't be purchased.* —*n.* **4.** [*noncount*] acquisition; getting or obtaining by the payment of money or its equivalent: *Mail in a proof of purchase.* **5.** [*count*] something purchased or bought: *made a few purchases.* —**pur′chas•a•ble,** *adj.* —**pur′chas•er,** *n.* [*count*]

pure (pyŏŏr) /pyʊr/ *adj.,* **pur•er, pur•est. 1.** free from any extra matter or material: *pure enough to drink.* **2.** not changed by mixing; clear: *pure white.* **3.** [*before a noun*] complete; absolute: *a pure accident.* **4.** of unmixed ancestry: *The dog was a pure German shepherd.* **5.** free from blemishes: *pure skin.* **6.** [*before a noun*] abstract or theoretical (opposed to *applied*): *pure mathematics.* **7.** free from evil: *a pure heart.* **8.** chaste; virgin: *a pure maiden.* —**pure′ness,** *n.* [*noncount*] See -PUR-.

pure•bred (*adj.* pyŏŏr′bred′; *n.* pyŏŏr′bred′) / *adj.* ˈpyʊrˈbrɛd; *n.* ˈpyʊrˌbrɛd/ *adj.* **1.** of or relating to an individual whose ancestors come from a recognized breed for many generations. —*n.* [*count*] **2.** a purebred animal. See -PUR-.

pu•rée or **pu•ree** (pyŏŏ rā′, -rē′) /pyʊˈrey, -ˈriy/ *n., v.,* **-réed, -rée•ing.** —*n.* **1.** a thick liquid or pulp prepared from cooked vegetables, fruit, etc., passed through a sieve or broken down in a blender or similar device: [*noncount*]: *tomato purée.* [*count*]: *soups and purées.* —*v.* [~ + *obj*] **2.** to make a purée of: *puréed the food.* See -PUR-.

pure•ly (pyŏŏr′lē) /ˈpyʊrliy/ *adv.* completely; utterly; absolutely: *It was purely coincidental.* See -PUR-.

pur•ga•tive (pûr′gə tiv) /ˈpɜrgətɪv/ *adj.* **1.** cleansing or cleaning out; purging. —*n.* [*count*] **2.** a medicine that purges. See -PUR-.

pur•ga•to•ry (pûr′gə tôr′ē, -tōr′ē) /ˈpɜrgəˌtɔriy, -ˌtowriy/ *n., pl.* **-ries. 1.** [*noncount*] (esp. in Roman Catholic belief) a place or state following death in which souls not condemned to hell are purified of lesser sins or undergo the punishment still remaining for forgiven mortal sins and are thereby made ready for heaven. **2.** a state or place of temporary suffering: [*count*]: *The stuffy subway car was a purgatory to be endured.* [*noncount*]: *The experience was pure purgatory.* —**pur′ga•to′ri•al,** *adj.* See -PUR-.

purge (pûrj) /pɜrdʒ/ *v.,* **purged, purg•ing,** *n.* —*v.* **1.** [~ + *obj*] to rid of impurities; cleanse; purify. **2.** [~ + *obj* + *of* + *obj*] to clear or free (something), as by getting rid of or removing undesirable members: *The revolutionaries purged the party of anyone thought to be disloyal.* **3.** [~ + *obj*] to get rid of or remove (undesirable members) from a government, political organization, etc.: *The party purged anyone disloyal.* **4.** [~ + *obj*] to clear or empty (the stomach or intestines) by causing vomiting or a forced movement of the bowels. —*n.* [*count*] **5.** the act or process of purging. **6.** the removal of members of an organization who are considered disloyal or otherwise undesirable. **7.** something that purges, as a medicine. —**purg′er,** *n.* [*count*] See -PUR-.

pu•ri•fy (pyŏŏr′ə fī′) /ˈpyʊrəˌfay/ *v.* [~ + *obj*], **-fied, -fy•ing. 1.** to make pure; free from anything that pollutes or contaminates. **2.** to free from extra or objectionable elements. —**pu•ri•fi•ca•tion** (pyŏŏr′ə fi kā′shən) /ˌpyʊrəfɪˈkeyʃən/ *n.* [*noncount*] —**pu′ri•fi′er,** *n.* [*count*] See -PUR-.

pur•ism (pyŏŏr′iz əm) /ˈpyʊrɪzəm/ *n.* [*noncount*] the act of strictly observing or insisting on purity or correctness in language, style, beliefs, etc. See -PUR-.

pur•ist (pyŏŏr′ist) /ˈpyʊrɪst/ *n.* [*count*] a person who strictly observes and insists on purity or correctness in language, style, beliefs, etc.: *linguistic purists who insist on "It's I" instead of "It's me."* See -PUR-.

Pu•ri•tan (pyŏŏr′i tn) /ˈpyʊrɪtn/ *n.* [*count*] **1.** a member of a group of Protestants that arose in the 16th century within the Church of England, calling for the simplifying of doctrine and worship and greater strictness in religious discipline. **2.** [*puritan*] a person who is strict in moral or religious matters, often to an excessive degree. —*adj.* **3.** of or relating to the Puritans. **4.** [*puritan*] of, relating to, or characteristic of a moral puritan. —**Pur′i•tan•ism, pur′i•tan•ism,** *n.* [*noncount*] See -PUR-.

pur•i•tan•i•cal (pyŏŏr′i tan′i kəl) /ˌpyʊrɪˈtænɪkəl/ *adj.* very strict or too strict in moral or religious matters. —**pur′i•tan′i•cal•ly,** *adv.* See -PUR-.

pu•ri•ty (pyŏŏr′i tē) /ˈpyʊrɪtiy/ *n.* [*noncount*] the quality or state of being pure. See -PUR-.

purl (pûrl) /pɜrl/ *n.* [*count*] **1.** a basic stitch in knitting, the reverse of the knit. —*v.* **2.** to knit with a purl stitch: [~ + *obj*]: *purl two rows.* [*no obj*]: *learning to purl.*

pur•loin (pər loin′, pûr′loin) /pərˈlɔyn, ˈpɜrlɔyn/ *v.* [~ + *obj*] to take dishonestly; steal: *to purloin someone's wallet.* —**pur•loin′er,** *n.* [*count*]

pur•ple (pûr′pəl) /ˈpɜrpəl/ *n., adj.,* **-pler, -plest.** —*n.* **1.** any color having both red and blue, esp. one deep in tone: [*noncount*]: *colored rich, dark purple.* [*count*]: *a rich, dark purple.* —*adj.* **2.** of the color purple. **3.** exaggerated and too ornate: *purple prose.* **4.** profane or shocking, as language. —***Idiom.*** **5. born to the purple,** of royal birth. —**pur′plish,** *adj.*

pur•port (*v.* pər pôrt′, -pōrt′; *n.* pûr′pôrt, -pōrt) / *v.* pərˈpɔrt, -ˈpowrt; *n.* ˈpɜrpɔrt, -powrt/ *v.* [~ + *to* + *verb*] **1.** to present, esp. deliberately, the appearance of being; claim or pretend to be (something one is not): *A man purporting to be the manager is calling.* —*n.* [*noncount*] **2.** the meaning or sense of something, as of a piece of writing or of what one says: *the general purport of the message.* —**pur′port•ed,** *adj.*: *We saw no evidence of his purported wealth.* —**pur′port•ed•ly,** *adv.*: *He was purportedly wealthy.* See -PORT-.

pur•pose (pûr′pəs) /ˈpɜrpəs/ *n.* **1.** [*count*] the reason for which something exists or is done, made, etc.: *For what purpose are we meeting today?* **2.** [*count*] an intended or desired result; aim; goal: *His purpose in life was to get rich.* **3.** [*noncount*] willingness to accomplish or achieve some goal or aim; resoluteness: *A good student has to have a sense of purpose.* —***Idiom.*** **4. on purpose,** intentionally: *She spilled the paint on purpose.* —**pur′pose•less,** *adj.* See -POS-.

pur•pose•ful (pûr′pəs fəl) /ˈpɜrpəsfəl/ *adj.* having a purpose: *a purposeful effort to reform the system.* See -POS-.

purr (pûr) /pɜr/ *n.* [*count*] **1.** the low, continuous, vibrating sound a cat makes, as when contented. **2.** any similar sound: *the purr of the car's engine.* —*v.* **3.** to utter such a sound: [*no obj*]: *The cat purred quietly.* [~ + *obj*]: *The cat purred its contentment.* **4.** [*no obj*] to make a similar sound: *The new engine purred.* **5.** [*used with quotations*] to say in a purr: *"Right this way," she purred.*

purse (pûrs) /pɜrs/ *n., v.,* **pursed, purs•ing.** —*n.* [*count*] **1.** a woman's handbag or pocketbook. **2.** a small container for carrying money: *a change purse.* **3.** a sum of money offered as a prize or collected as a gift: *a purse of $50,000 as first prize.* —*v.* [~ + *obj*] **4.** to pucker: *to purse one's lips.*

purs•er (pûr′sər) /ˈpɜrsər/ *n.* [*count*] an officer who is in charge of the accounts and documents of a ship and who keeps money and valuables for passengers.

pur•su•ance (pər sōō′əns) /pərˈsuwəns/ *n.* [*noncount*] the carrying out or following of some plan, course, or the like. See -SEQ-.

pur•su•ant (pər sōō′ənt) /pərˈsuwənt/ *adj.* **1.** pursuing. —***Idiom.*** **2. pursuant to,** in accordance with: *Pursuant to instructions, I enclose the documents.* See -SEQ-.

pur•sue (pər sōō′) /pərˈsuw/ *v.* [~ + *obj*], **-sued, -su•ing. 1.** to follow in order to overtake, capture, kill, etc.; chase: *The army pursued the retreating enemy.* **2.** to carry on or continue (a course of action, inquiry, etc.), esp. in order to accomplish some goal: *She pursued a degree in business.* **3.** to practice (an occupation or pastime): *to pursue a career in law.* **4.** to continue to discuss (a subject): *pursued the question of his involvement.* —**pur•su′a•ble,** *adj.* —**pur•su′er,** *n.* [*count*] See -SEQ-.

pur•suit (pər sōōt′) /pərˈsuwt/ *n.* **1.** [*noncount*] the act of pursuing: *raced in pursuit of the thief.* **2.** [*count*] an occupation or pastime that one regularly engages in: *literary pursuits.* —***Idiom.*** **3. in hot pursuit,** actively pursuing or chasing, and close to catching up to someone. See -SEQ-.

pur•vey (pər vā′) /pərˈvey/ *v.* [~ + *obj*] **1.** to supply (esp. provisions), usually as a business: *They purvey food* *to ships in the harbor.* **2.** to peddle; sell: *purveying pornography.* —**pur•vey′or,** *n.* [*count*]

pur•view (pûr′vyo͞o) /ˈpɜrvyuw/ *n.* [*noncount*] the range of operation, authority, concern, etc.: *Collecting taxes falls within the purview of the assessor.*

pus (pus) /pʌs/ *n.* [*noncount*] a yellow-white, liquid-like substance produced by the body in an infected wound, in abscesses and sores, etc.

push (po͝osh) /pʊʃ/ *v.* **1.** to press against with force in order to move: [∼ + *obj*]: *He rudely pushed them aside.* [*no obj*]: *They were pushing and shoving.* **2.** to move (something) in a certain way, as by exerting force: [∼ + *obj*]: *pushed the door open.* [*no obj*]: *He pushed past me.* **3.** to (cause to) extend or stick up or out; thrust: [*no obj*]: *The plant pushed out of the soil.* [∼ + *obj*]: *Pressure pushed lava to the surface.* **4.** to urge (someone) to some action, or on some course of action: [*no obj*]: *He's pushing too hard at his new job.* [∼ + *obj*]: *He's pushing himself too hard; he needs a break.* [∼ + *obj* + *to* + *verb*]: *His parents pushed him to get a job.* **5.** to press (an action, proposal, etc.) with energy and by making demands: [∼ + *obj*]: *to push a bill through Congress.* [*no obj*]: *pushing for passage of the bill.* **6.** [*no obj*] to urge or promote the use, sale, adoption, etc., of something; promote: *still pushing for his vision of what our group should be about.* **7.** [∼ + *obj*] to press or bear hard upon: *The lawyer began to push the witness for an answer.* **8.** [∼ + *obj*] *Slang.* to sell (illegal drugs): *He was arrested for pushing cocaine and heroin.* **9.** [*be* + ∼*-ing;* ∼ + *obj*] *Informal.* to be approaching: *The car was pushing the speed limit.* **10. push around,** to bully or intimidate: [∼ + *obj* + *around*]: *always pushing the younger boys around.* [∼ + *around* + *obj*]: *always pushing around boys weaker than himself.* **11. push off,** [*no obj*] *Informal.* to go away; depart. **12. push on,** [*no obj*] to proceed; press forward: *He pushed on with the project.* —*n.* **13.** [*count*] the act of pushing; a shove or thrust. **14.** [*count*] a strong, determined effort, campaign, advance, military attack, etc. **15.** [*noncount*] *Informal.* energy to complete an activity; purpose; drive; enterprise. —***Idiom.*** **16. when** or **if push comes to shove,** when or if a problem must finally be dealt with.

push′ but′ton, *n.* [*count*] a button that opens or closes an electric circuit when it is pressed or released. —**push′-but′ton,** *adj.*: *a push-button phone.*

push•er (po͝osh′ər) /ˈpʊʃər/ *n.* [*count*] **1.** a person or thing that pushes. **2.** a person who sells illegal drugs.

push•o•ver (po͝osh′ō′vər) /ˈpʊʃˌowvər/ *n.* [*count*] **1.** anything done easily. **2.** an easily defeated person or team. **3.** a person who is easily persuaded or influenced.

push′-up′, *n.* [*count*] an exercise in which a person lies facedown with the hands and palms down under the shoulders and raises and lowers the body using only the arms.

push•y (po͝osh′ē) /ˈpʊʃiy/ *adj.,* **-i•er, -i•est.** annoyingly forward, bold, or self-assertive: *a pushy salesman.* —**push′i•ness,** *n.* [*noncount*]

pu•sil•lan•i•mous (pyo͞o′sə lan′ə məs) /ˌpyuwsəˈlænəməs/ *adj.* lacking courage or the will to go on; cowardly. —**pu•sil•la•nim•i•ty** (pyo͞o′sə lə nim′i tē) /ˌpyuwsələˈnɪmɪtiy/ *n.* [*noncount*] See -ANIMA-.

puss[1] (po͝os) /pʊs/ *n.* [*count*] a cat.

puss[2] (po͝os) /pʊs/ *n.* [*count*] the face.

puss•y (po͝os′ē) /ˈpʊsiy/ *n.* [*count*], *pl.* **puss•ies.** a cat, esp. a kitten.

puss•y•foot (po͝os′ē fo͝ot′) /ˈpʊsiyˌfʊt/ *v.* [*no obj*] to go or move in a cautious manner, or as if afraid to commit oneself or make a definite decision.

puss′y wil′low (po͝os′ē) /ˈpʊsiy/ *n.* [*count*] a small willow having silky, furry catkins.

pus•tule (pus′cho͞ol) /ˈpʌstʃʊl/ *n.* [*count*] a small swelling of the skin containing pus.

put (po͝ot) /pʊt/ *v.,* **put, put•ting,** *n.* —*v.* **1.** [∼ + *obj*] to move (anything) into a specific location or position; place: *Put your clothes back in your closet.* **2.** [*no obj*] to go or proceed: *The submarines put to sea.* **3.** [∼ + *obj*] to bring into some condition, relation, etc.: *putting all one's affairs in order.* **4.** [∼ + *obj*] to force (someone) to undergo something or set (someone) to a duty, task, or action, etc.: *They put me to work chopping wood.* **5.** [∼ + *obj*] to provide musical accompaniment for (words); set: *putting a poem to music.* **6.** [∼ + *obj*] to assign; to place (something) in connection with something else in the mind: *to put the blame on others.* **7.** [∼ + *obj* + *at* + *obj*] to estimate: *I'd put the distance at about fifty miles.* **8.** [∼ + *obj* + *on* + *obj*] to bet or wager: *He put half a million dollars on the horse to win.* **9.** [∼ + *obj*] to express or state: *To put it honestly, I don't care.* **10.** [∼ + *obj*] to apply to a use or purpose: *She put her knowledge to good use.* **11.** [∼ + *obj*] to submit for others to consider: *So I put it to you: Should we proceed or not?* **12.** [∼ + *obj* + *on*] to impose: *to put a new sales tax on beverages.* **13.** [∼ + *obj*] to invest: *She put all her savings into government bonds.* **14.** [∼ + *obj*] to throw (a heavy metal ball): *to put the shot.* **15. put about,** *Nautical.* **a.** [*no obj*] to change direction, as on a course. **b.** [∼ + *obj* + *about*] to turn in a different direction: *Put the ship about.* **16. put across,** to cause to be understood or received favorably: [∼ + *obj* + *across*]: *Can you put your ideas across better?* [∼ + *across* + *obj*]: *to put across her message as a candidate.* **17. put aside** or **by, a.** to store up; save: [∼ + *obj* + *aside*]: *She had put some money aside.* [∼ + *aside* + *obj*]: *She managed to put aside some money.* **b.** to put out of the way: [∼ + *obj* + *aside*]: *putting that issue aside for the moment.* [∼ + *aside* + *obj*]: *Put aside that issue.* **18. put away, a.** to put in the correct or named place for storage: [∼ + *obj* + *away*]: *Put the clothes away.* [∼ + *away* + *obj*]: *Put away your clothes.* **b.** to save, esp. for later use: [∼ + *obj* + *away*]: *She had put some money away.* [∼ + *away* + *obj*]: *She put away some money.* **c.** to drink or eat, esp. in large amounts: [∼ + *away* + *obj*]: *He can really put away those sandwiches!* [∼ + *obj* + *away*]: *He can really put it away when he's hungry.* **d.** to confine or cause to be confined in a jail or a mental institution: [∼ + *away* + *obj*]: *put away the convict for twenty years.* [∼ + *obj* + *away*]: *The judge put him away for twenty years.* **19. put down, a.** to write down; record: [∼ + *down* + *obj*]: *Put down your name on the list.* [∼ + *obj* + *down*]: *He put his name down.* **b.** to enter in a list, as of subscribers or contributors: [∼ + *obj* + *down* + *for* + *obj*]: *Put me down for fifteen dollars.* [∼ + *down* + *obj* + *for* + *obj*]: *Put down Mr. Smith for (a donation of) fifty dollars.* **c.** to suppress; crush; defeat: [∼ + *down* + *obj*]: *The army put down the rebellion.* [∼ + *obj* + *down*]: *The army put the rebellion down.* **d.** [∼ + *obj* + *down* + *to* + *obj*] to figure out or determine the reasons for; to attribute; ascribe: *Put the mistakes down to carelessness.* **e.** [∼ + *obj* + *down* + *as* + *obj*] to regard or categorize (someone as being a certain type): *The committee put him down as a chronic complainer.* **f.** to humiliate or embarrass; make (someone) feel foolish, insulted, or ridiculous: [∼ + *obj* + *down*]: *She put him down with that nasty insult.* [∼ + *down* + *obj*]: *Don't feel bad; she puts down everybody who says anything nice to her.* **g.** to pay (money) as a deposit: [∼ + *obj* + *down*]: *putting fifty dollars down on (= toward the purchase of) that refrigerator.* [∼ + *down* + *obj*]: *I'm putting down fifty dollars now.* **h.** [∼ + *obj* + *down*] to land an aircraft: *He put the plane down in a field.* **i.** to kill (an animal, esp. a pet) by methods that do not hurt or cause pain: [∼ + *obj* + *down*]: *They had to put their old dog down; he was so sick.* [∼ + *down* + *obj*]: *It was hard for them to put down the old dog.* **20. put forth, a.** [∼ + *forth* + *obj*] to bear: *trees putting forth green shoots.* **b.** to propose; present; set out for others to consider: [∼ + *forth* + *obj*]: *putting forth all these new ideas.* [∼ + *obj* + *forth*]: *putting them forth.* **21. put forward,** to propose; present; set out for others to consider; to advance: [∼ + *forward* + *obj*]: *He put forward a new plan to coordinate the departments.* [∼ + *obj* + *forward*]: *He put a new plan forward.* **22. put in,** [∼ + *in* + *obj*] to spend (time) as indicated: *He put in twenty-five years at that job.* **23. put in for,** [∼ + *in* + *for* + *obj*] to apply for or request: *to put in for a transfer.* **24. put off, a.** to postpone; defer: [∼ + *obj* + *off*]: *Can we put the meeting off?* [∼ + *off* + *obj*]: *He put off the meeting.* [∼ + *off* + *verb-ing*]: *He put off discussing the problem with her.* **b.** to get rid of by avoiding, evading, or delaying: [∼ + *obj* + *off*]: *Tell your secretary to put that salesman off until next week.* [∼ + *off* + *obj*]: *Put off that salesman until next week.* **c.** to disconcert or perturb: [∼ + *obj* + *off*]: *The book's nasty tone put us off.* [∼ + *off* + *obj*]: *The book's tone will put off most readers.* **25. put on, a.** to clothe oneself in: [∼ + *obj* + *on*]: *Put your clothes on.* [∼ + *on* + *obj*]: *Put on your clothes.* **b.** [∼ + *on* + *obj*] to assume or pretend: *He was putting on airs, pretending to be royalty or something.* **c.** to produce or stage: [∼ + *on* + *obj*]: *put on a performance.* [∼ + *obj* + *on*]: *They'll put a show on again in the spring.* **d.** [∼ + *obj* + *on*] *Informal.* to deceive (someone) as a joke; tease: *You're putting me on—there really isn't a day off.* **e.** [∼ + *on* + *obj*] to increase; gain: *You've put on weight.* **26. put out, a.** to extinguish, as a fire: [∼ + *obj* + *out*]: *Put the fire out.* [∼ + *out* + *obj*]: *Put out the fire.* **b.** [∼ +

obj + *out*] to cause to be inconvenienced: *I would be putting her out if I brought six uninvited guests for dinner.* **c.** [~ + *obj* + *out*] *Baseball, Softball.* to cause to prevent from reaching base or scoring. **d.** [~ + *out* + *obj*] to publish, broadcast, or make known: *Who put out the story?* **27. put through, a.** [~ + *obj* + *through*] to make a telephone connection for: *Put me through to Los Angeles.* **b.** to make (a telephone connection): [~ + *obj* + *through*]: *to put a call through to Hong Kong.* [~ + *through* + *obj*]: *to put through a call to Hong Kong.* **c.** [~ + *obj* + *through* + *obj*] to cause (someone) to suffer or endure (something): *She put us through misery.* **28. put up, a.** to construct; erect: [~ + *up* + *obj*]: *to put up a tent.* [~ + *obj* + *up*]: *to put a tent up.* **b.** to can; preserve: [~ + *up* + *obj*]: *to put up jelly.* [~ + *obj* + *up*]: *to put vegetables up for the winter.* **c.** to provide or stake (money), as in gambling or business: [~ + *up* + *obj*]: *Put up the cash or get out of the game.* [~ + *obj* + *up*]: *Put the cash up or get out of the game.* **d.** to provide a place to sleep or stay for; to lodge: [~ + *up* + *obj*]: *We can put up a few guests.* [~ + *obj* + *up*]: *We can put a few guests up.* **e.** [~ + *up* + *obj*] to mount or engage in, as opposition, a struggle, a fight, etc.: *We'll have to put up a fight.* **f.** to offer, esp. for public sale: [~ + *up* + *obj*]: *They put up their house for sale.* [~ + *obj* + *up*]: *They put their house up for sale.* **29. put upon,** [*no obj*] to be taken unfair advantage of; to be imposed upon: *He felt very put upon in his new job.* **30. put up to,** [~ + *obj* + *up* + *to* + *obj*] to provoke or incite: *Who put you up to these cowardly acts?* **31. put up with,** [~ + *up* + *with* + *obj*] to tolerate: *How can you put up with such intense pain?* —*n.* [*count*] **32.** a throw, esp. with a forward motion of the hand. —***Idiom.*** **33. put one's best foot forward,** to try to make as good an impression as possible. **34. put oneself out,** to take pains; go to trouble or expense. **35. put something over on,** [~ + *obj*] to deceive.

pu•ta•tive (pyo͞o′tə tiv) /ˈpyuwtətɪv/ *adj.* commonly thought of as such: *a putative mobster.* See -PUTE-.

put′-down′ or **put′down′,** *n.* [*count*] **1.** a landing of an aircraft. **2.** *Informal.* an insulting or humiliating remark: *a sarcastic putdown.*

-pute-, *root.* *-pute-* comes from Latin, where it has the meaning "to clean, prune; consider; think." This meaning is found in such words as: AMPUTATE, COMPUTATION, COMPUTE, DEPUTY, DISPUTE, DISREPUTABLE, IMPUTE, INDISPUTABLE, PUTATIVE, REPUTABLE, REPUTATION.

put-on (*n.* po͝ot′on′, -ôn′; *adj.* -on′, -ôn′) / *n.* ˈpʊtˌɒn, -ˌɔn; *adj.* -ˈɒn, -ˈɔn/ *n.* [*count*] *Informal.* **1.** an act or instance of putting someone on; a trick or hoax. —*adj.* **2.** pretended or assumed.

pu•tre•fy (pyo͞o′trə fī′) /ˈpyuwtrəˌfay/ *v.*, **-fied, -fy•ing.** to make putrid: [*no obj*]: *A poison gas causes skin to putrefy in seconds.* [~ + *obj*]: *to putrefy the skin.* —**pu•tre•fac•tion** (pyo͞o′trə fak′shən) /ˌpyuwtrəˈfækʃən/ *n.* [*noncount*]

pu•tres•cent (pyo͞o tres′ənt) /pyuwˈtrɛsənt/ *adj.* **1.** becoming putrid; undergoing a process of rotting. **2.** of or relating to putrefaction. —**pu•tres′cence,** *n.* [*noncount*]

pu•trid (pyo͞o′trid) /ˈpyuwtrɪd/ *adj.* **1.** being in a state of foul decay. **2.** of very low quality; rotten.

putsch (po͝och) /pʊtʃ/ *n.* [*count*] a sudden political revolt or uprising.

putt (put) /pʌt/ *v.* **1.** to strike (a golf ball) gently so as to make it roll along the green into the hole: [~ + *obj*]: *He putted the ball into the hole.* [*no obj*]: *learning how to putt.* —*n.* [*count*] **2.** a stroke made in putting.

put•ter[1] (put′ər) /ˈpʌtər/ *v.* [*no obj*] to busy or occupy oneself in a leisurely, casual, or ineffective manner: *puttering around the house.* Also, *esp. Brit.,* **pot•ter** (pot′ər) /ˈpɒtər/ —**put′ter•er,** *n.* [*count*]

putt•er[2] (put′ər) /ˈpʌtər/ *n.* [*count*] **1.** a golf club used in putting. **2.** a person who putts a golf ball.

put•ty (put′ē) /ˈpʌtiy/ *n.*, *pl.* **-ties,** *v.*, **-tied, -ty•ing.** —*n.* [*noncount*] **1.** a compound, usually a paste made partly of linseed oil, used to hold windowpanes in place, patch woodwork defects, seal the joints of tubes or pipes, etc. **2.** a person or thing easily molded or influenced: *He was putty in her hands.* —*v.* [~ + *obj*] **3.** to cover with putty; use putty on.

puz•zle (puz′əl) /ˈpʌzəl/ *n.*, *v.*, **-zled, -zling.** —*n.* [*count*] **1.** a toy, problem, or other game designed to amuse by presenting difficulties to be solved by clever thinking or patient effort: *a jigsaw puzzle.* **2.** [*usually singular*] a question, matter, or person that is difficult to understand, figure out, or explain. —*v.* **3.** [~ + *obj*] to confuse; baffle; mystify: *My symptoms puzzled the doctor.* **4.** [*no obj*] to think over some confusing or perplexing problem or matter. **5. puzzle out,** [~ + *out* + *obj*] to solve by careful study or effort: *trying to puzzle out a solution.* —**puz′zle•ment,** *n.* [*noncount*]: *a look of sheer puzzlement on his face.* —**puz′zler,** *n.* [*count*]

puz•zled (puz′əld) /ˈpʌzəld/ *adj.* confused; baffled; mystified; bewildered: *a puzzled look on his face.*

puz•zling (puz′əl ing) /ˈpʌzəlɪŋ/ *adj.* confusing, baffling, or mystifying: *a puzzling problem.*

PVC, polyvinyl chloride.

PX, *pl.* **PXs.** post exchange.

Pyg•my or **Pigmy** (pig′mē) /ˈpɪgmiy/ *n.*, *pl.* **-mies,** *adj.* —*n.* [*count*] **1.** a member of any of several small or short peoples of the forested regions of central Africa. **2.** [*pygmy*] a small or dwarfish person. **3.** [*pygmy*] anything very small of its kind. —*adj.* **4.** of or relating to the Pygmies. **5.** [*pygmy*] of very small size, ability, power, etc.

py•jam•as (pə jä′məz, -jam′əz) /pəˈdʒɑməz, -ˈdʒæməz/ *n. Chiefly Brit.* PAJAMAS.

py•lon (pī′lon) /ˈpaylɒn/ *n.* [*count*] **1.** a marking post or tower for guiding an aircraft pilot. **2.** a relatively tall structure at the side of a gate, bridge, or avenue. **3.** a steel tower used as a support, as for supporting electrical wires.

py•or•rhe•a or **py•or•rhoe•a** (pī′ə rē′ə) /ˌpayəˈriyə/ *n.* [*noncount*] **1.** a condition in which pus is discharged in the body. **2.** a condition of severe bleeding of the gums and often loosening of the teeth.

pyr•a•mid (pir′ə mid) /ˈpɪrəmɪd/ *n.* [*count*] **1.** a very large, four-sided structure with faces that are triangular, having smooth, steeply sloping sides meeting at a point at the top, as a tomb of ancient Egypt. **2.** any object or arrangement of objects shaped like a pyramid. **3.** a system or structure resembling a pyramid: *a food pyramid, showing which foods should be eaten most (at the base) and which should be eaten least (at the top).* —**py•ram•i•dal** (pi ram′i dl) /pɪˈræmɪdl̩/ *adj.*

pyre (pīᵊr) /payᵊr/ *n.* [*count*] **1.** a pile or heap of wood or other material that burns easily. **2.** such a pile for burning a dead body, esp. as part of a funeral rite, as in India.

py•rite (pī′rīt) /ˈpayrayt/ *n.* [*noncount*] a brass-yellow mineral, iron sulfide.

pyro-, *prefix.* *pyro-* comes from Greek, where it has the meaning "fire, heat, high temperature": *pyromania, pyrotechnics.*

py•ro•ma•ni•a (pī′rə mā′nē ə, -mān′yə) /ˌpayrəˈmeyniyə, -ˈmeynyə/ *n.* [*noncount*] a compulsion or overwhelming and uncontrollable desire to set things on fire. —**py•ro•ma•ni•ac** (pī′rə mā′nē ak′) /ˌpayrəˈmeyniyˈæk/ *n.* [*count*]

py•ro•tech•nics (pī′rə tek′niks) /ˌpayrəˈtɛknɪks/ *n.* **1.** [*noncount; used with a singular verb*] the art of making fireworks or using them in displays. **2.** [*plural; used with a plural verb*] a brilliant or dazzling display of excellence, as in speechmaking or musical performance. —**py′ro•tech′nic,** *adj.*

Pyr•rhic vic′tory (pir′ik) /ˈpɪrɪk/ *n.* [*count*] a victory or goal achieved at too great a cost.

py•thon (pī′thon, -thən) /ˈpayθɒn, -θən/ *n.* [*count*] a snake that kills its prey by crushing or squeezing it to death.

Q, q (kyōō) /kyuw/ *n.* [*count*], *pl.* **Qs** or **Q's, qs** or **q's.** the 17th letter of the English alphabet, a consonant.

q., an abbreviation of: **1.** quart. **2.** question.

Q.E.D., an abbreviation of Latin *quod erat demonstrandum:* which was to be shown or demonstrated (used esp. in mathematical proofs).

qt., an abbreviation of: **1.** quantity. **2.** *pl.* **qt., qts.** quart.

q.t. or **Q.T.,** *Informal.* an abbreviation of: **1.** quiet. —***Idiom.*** **2. on the q.t.,** stealthily; secretly: *to meet someone on the q.t.*

quack[1] (kwak) /kwæk/ *n.,* [*count*] **1.** the harsh, throaty cry of a duck, or any similar sound. —*v.* [*no obj*] **2.** to utter a quack.

quack[2] (kwak) /kwæk/ *n.* [*count*] being or relating to a quack or quackery: *quack methods; quack medicine.*

quack•er•y (kwak′ə rē) /ˈkwækəriy/ *n.* [*noncount*] the practice or methods of a quack.

quad[1] (kwod) /kwɒd/ *n.* QUADRANGLE (def. 2). See -QUAD-.

quad[2] (kwod) /kwɒd/ *n.* [*count*] *Informal.* a quadruplet. See -QUAD-.

-quad-, *root.* The root *-quad-* comes from Latin, where it has the meaning "four, fourth." This meaning is found in such words as: QUAD, QUADRANGLE, QUADRANT, QUADRUPED, QUADRUPLET.

quad•ran•gle (kwod′rang′gəl) /ˈkwɒdˌræŋgəl/ *n.* [*count*] **1.** a flat figure having four angles and four sides, such as a square. **2.** a four-sided space or court surrounded by a building or buildings, as on a college campus: *In the main quadrangle students were playing frisbee.* —**quad•ran•gu•lar** (kwo drang′gyə lər) /kwɒˈdræŋgyələr/ *adj.* See -QUAD-.

quad•rant (kwod′rənt) /ˈkwɒdrənt/ *n.* [*count*] **1.** a quarter of a circle; an arc of 90°. **2.** something shaped like a quarter of a circle, such as a part of a machine. **3.** an instrument used in astronomy, navigation, etc., for measuring heights and angles. See -QUAD-.

quad•ra•phon•ic (kwod′rə fon′ik) /ˌkwɒdrəˈfɒnɪk/ *adj.* of or relating to the recording, playing, or sending of sound by means of four channels instead of two; four-channel. See -QUAD-, -PHON-.

quad•ren•ni•al (kwo dren′ē əl) /kwɒˈdrɛniyəl/ *adj.* **1.** occurring every four years: *a quadrennial festival.* **2.** of or lasting for four years: *a quadrennial period.* See -QUAD-.

quad•ri•lat•er•al (kwod′rə lat′ər əl) /ˌkwɒdrəˈlætərəl/ *adj.* **1.** having four sides. —*n.* [*count*] **2.** a geometric figure with four sides. See -LAT[2]-, -QUAD-.

quad•rille (kwo dril′, kwə-, kə-) /kwɒˈdrɪl, kwə-, kə-/ *n.* [*count*] a square dance for four couples.

quad•ril•lion (kwo dril′yən) /kwɒˈdrɪlyən/ *n., pl.* **-lions,** (*as after a numeral*) **-lion,** *adj.* —*n.* [*count*] **1.** the number written in the U.S. by 1 followed by 15 zeros, and in Great Britain by 1 followed by 24 zeros. —*adj.* [*after a number and before a noun*] **2.** amounting to one quadrillion in number: *two quadrillion stars.*

quad•ri•ple•gi•a (kwod′rə plē′jē ə, -jə) /ˌkwɒdrəˈpliydʒiyə, -dʒə/ *n.* [*noncount*] paralysis of all four limbs or of the entire body below the neck. —**quad′ri•ple′gic,** *n.* [*count*]: *Although a quadriplegic he lived a full life.* —*adj.: a quadriplegic person.*

quad•ru•ped (kwod′rōō ped′) /ˈkwɒdrʊˌpɛd/ *adj.* **1.** four-footed. —*n.* [*count*] **2.** an animal that has four feet. —**quad•ru•pe•dal** (kwo drōō′pi dl, kwod′rōō ped′l) /kwɒˈdruwpɪdl̩, ˌkwɒdrʊˈpɛdl̩/ *adj.* See -QUAD-, -PED-[1].

quad•ru•ple (kwo drōō′pəl, -drup′əl, kwod′rōō pəl) /kwɒˈdruwpəl, -ˈdrʌpəl, ˈkwɒdrʊpəl/ *adj., n., v.,* **-pled, -pling.** —*adj.* **1.** fourfold; made up of four parts: *a quadruple alliance.* **2.** four times as great. —*n.* [*count*] **3.** a number, amount, etc., four times as great as another. —*v.* **4.** to make or become four times as great: [*no obj*]: *The number of ESL students has quadrupled.* [~ + *obj*]: *This will quadruple your profits.* See -QUAD-, -PLIC-.

quad•ru•plet (kwo drup′lit, -drōō′plit, kwod′rōō plit) /kwɒˈdrʌplɪt, -ˈdruwplɪt, ˈkwɒdrʊplɪt/ *n.* [*count*] **1.** any group or combination of four. **2.** one of four children or offspring born of the same mother at the same time. See -QUAD-.

quad•ru•pli•cate (*n., adj.* kwo drōō′pli kit; *v.* -kāt′) / *n., adj.* kwɒˈdruwplɪkɪt; *v.* -ˌkeyt/ *n., adj., v.,* **-cat•ed, -cat•ing.** —*n.* [*count*] **1.** one of four copies or identical items. —*adj.* **2.** made up of four identical parts. —*v.* [~ + *obj*] **3.** to produce or copy in quadruplicate. **4.** to make four times as great. —**quad•ru•pli•ca•tion** (kwo drōō′pli kā′shən) /kwɒˌdruwplɪˈkeyʃən/ *n.* [*noncount*] See -QUAD-, -PLIC-.

quaff (kwof, kwaf, kwôf) /kwɒf, kwæf, kwɔf/ *v.* [~ + *obj*] **1.** to drink heartily: *He quaffed his beer.* —*n.* [*count*] **2.** an act or instance of quaffing. **3.** a beverage quaffed.

quag•mire (kwag′mīər′, kwog′-) /ˈkwægˌmayər, ˈkwɒg-/ *n.* [*count*] **1.** a very muddy or boggy ground where the surface gives way when walked on; a bog. **2.** a difficult situation; predicament: *a budgetary quagmire where there is not enough money.*

qua•hog or **qua•haug** (kwô′hôg, -hog, kwō′-, kō′-) /ˈkwɔhɔg, -hɒg, ˈkwow-, ˈkow-/ *n.* [*count*] a thick-shelled clam that can be eaten.

quail[1] (kwāl) /kweyl/ *n.* [*count*], *pl.* **quails,** (*esp. when thought of as a group*) **quail.** a small, plump bird of the pheasant family.

quail[2] (kwāl) /kweyl/ *v.* [*no obj*] to lose courage; shrink back in fear: *quailed at the thought of the danger ahead.*

quaint (kwānt) /kweynt/ *adj.,* **-er, -est. 1.** having an old-fashioned charm: *a quaint old house.* **2.** peculiar; odd: *a quaint sense of humor.* —**quaint′ly,** *adv.* —**quaint′ness,** *n.* [*noncount*]

quake (kwāk) /kweyk/ *v.,* **quaked, quak•ing,** *n.* —*v.* [*no obj*] **1.** to shudder or quiver, as from cold or fear. **2.** to shake or tremble, as from shock: *The earth quaked.* —*n.* [*count*] **3.** an act or instance of quaking, esp. an earthquake. —**quak′y,** *adj.,* **-i•er, -i•est.**

qual•i•fi•ca•tion (kwol′ə fi kā′shən) /ˌkwɒləfɪˈkeyʃən/ *n.* **1.** [*count*] a quality, accomplishment, etc., that fits a person for some job, function, or the like. **2.** [*noncount*] the act of qualifying or the state of being qualified. **3.** limitation or restriction: [*noncount*]: *to agree without qualification.* [*count*]: *raised some qualifications concerning her candidacy.*

qual•i•fied (kwol′ə fīd′) /ˈkwɒləˌfayd/ *adj.* **1.** having the qualities, accomplishments, skills, knowledge, or credentials one needs for a job, function, position, office, or the like: *She's very well qualified for the job.* [*be* + ~ + *to* + *verb*]: *She's qualified to take over in my absence.* **2.** restricted or limited: *The launch was only a qualified success.*

qual•i•fy (kwol′ə fī′) /ˈkwɒləˌfay/ *v.,* **-fied, -fy•ing. 1.** [~ + *obj*] to provide with proper or necessary skills, knowledge, etc.: *The training program qualified her for the job.* **2.** [*no obj*] to show that one has the ability for something: *She clearly qualifies for the job.* **3.** [*no obj*] to demonstrate the required ability in an initial or preliminary contest: *to qualify for a race.* **4.** [~ + *obj*] to make less strong, general, or positive; modify or limit: *Suddenly he began to qualify his initial endorsement of her candidacy.* **5.** [~ + *obj* (+ *as*)] to characterize, label, or briefly evaluate: *I can't qualify his approach as either good or bad.* **6.** *Grammar.* MODIFY (def. 2).

qual•i•ta•tive (kwol′i tā′tiv) /ˈkwɒlɪˌteytɪv/ *adj.* relating to or concerned with quality or qualities, and not quantities or amounts: *We're looking for qualitative improvement, not quantitative increases.* —**qual′i•ta′tive•ly,** *adv.*

qual•i•ty (kwol′i tē) /ˈkwɒlɪtiy/ *n., pl.* **-ties,** *adj.* —*n.* **1.** [*count*] an essential or basic characteristic or feature that belongs to something: *What are some of the qualities found in great writing?* **2.** [*noncount*] character or nature, as belonging to or distinguishing a thing: *the quality of a color.* **3.** [*noncount*] character with respect to how excellent or good something is: *Those materials are of poor quality.* **4.** [*noncount*] superiority; excellence: *The company has a reputation for quality.* **5.** [*count*] a character trait; something typical of one's personality or character: *Generosity is one of her many good qualities.* —*adj.* [*before a noun*] **6.** of or having superior quality: *quality paper; a quality publisher.*

qual′ity time′, *n.* [*noncount*] time given to or used only for nurturing a loved person or engaging in a favorite activity.

qualm (kwäm, kwôm) /kwɑm, kwɔm/ *n.* [*count*] **1.** an uneasy feeling regarding one's conduct: *He has no qualms about lying.* **2.** a sudden feeling of nervousness or fear.

quan•da•ry (kwon′də rē, -drē) /ˈkwɒndəriy, -driy/ *n.* [*count*], *pl.* **-ries.** a state of uncertainty, esp. as to what to do: *He was in a quandary about marrying.*

quan•ti•fy (kwon′tə fī′) /ˈkwɒntəˌfay/ *v.* [~ + *obj*], **-fied, -fy•ing. 1.** to figure out, show, or express the quantity of: *to quantify the results.* **2.** to give quantity to (something thought of as having only quality): *You can't quantify the effect computers may have in language learning.*

quan•ti•ta•tive (kwon′ti tā′tiv) /ˈkwɒntɪˌteytɪv/ *adj.* **1.** being or capable of being measured by quantity. **2.** of or relating to the measuring of quantity: *quantitative analysis.*

quan•ti•ty (kwon′ti tē) /ˈkwɒntɪtiy/ *n., pl.* **-ties. 1.** [*count*] an amount that is indefinite or in a collection: *a quantity of sugar; vast quantities of oil.* **2.** [*count*] an exact or specified amount or measure: *in the quantities called for.* **3.** [*noncount*] a considerable or great amount: *to buy food in quantity.* **4.** [*noncount*] the fact of being an amount, degree, etc., of something, which can be greater or lesser: *impressed by quality, not quantity.* **5.** [*count*] any person, thing, or factor taken into consideration: *The nominee was an unknown quantity.*

quan•tum (kwon′təm) /ˈkwɒntəm/ *n., pl.* **-ta** *adj.* **—***n.* [*count*] **1.** quantity or amount: *the least quantum of evidence.* **2.** the smallest amount by which certain particles in physics can possess, absorb, give off, or change their amount of energy. **—***adj.* [*before a noun*] **3.** of or relating to the study in physics of the smallest amount of energy a particle can possess, absorb, or give off: *quantum physics.* **4.** sudden and significant: *a quantum increase.*

quar•an•tine (kwôr′ən tēn′, kwor′-, kwôr′ən tēn′, kwor′-) /ˈkwɔrənˌtiyn, ˈkwɒr-, ˌkwɔrənˈtiyn, ˌkwɒr-/ *n., v.,* **-tined, -tin•ing. —***n.* **1.** a period, originally 40 days, during which a person or animal is kept apart from others to ensure that any disease he, she, or it may have will not be spread: [*noncount*]: *kept in quarantine until the disease ran its course.* [*count; usually singular*]: *imposing a quarantine.* **—***v.* [~ + *obj*] **2.** to put in or place under quarantine: *The captain quarantined the sick passenger.*

quark (kwôrk, kwärk), *n.* [*count*] any of a group of particles smaller than the particles that make up an atom, having a fractional electric charge.

quar•rel (kwôr′əl, kwor′-) /ˈkwɔrəl, ˈkwɒr-/ *n., v.,* **-reled, -rel•ing** or (*esp. Brit.*) **-relled, -rel•ling. —***n.* [*count*] **1.** an angry dispute or argument: *Whenever we have a quarrel we try to resolve it quickly.* **2.** a cause of complaint: *She has no quarrel with her present salary.* **—***v.* [*no obj*] **3.** to disagree angrily; argue; squabble; wrangle: *They quarreled about sending their kids to private school.* **4.** to disagree with something said: *I'd quarrel with some of the results you're predicting.* **—quar′rel•er,** *n.* [*count*] **—quar′rel•some,** *adj.*

quar•ry[1] (kwôr′ē, kwor′ē) /ˈkwɔriy, ˈkwɒriy/ *n., pl.* **-ries,** *v.,* **-ried, -ry•ing. —***n.* [*count*] **1.** an open hole or pit dug in the ground, from which building stone, slate, or the like, is obtained by cutting, blasting, etc. **—***v.* [~ + *obj*] **2.** to obtain from or as if from a quarry.

quar•ry[2] (kwôr′ē, kwor′ē) /ˈkwɔriy, ˈkwɒriy/ *n.* [*count*], *pl.* **-ries. 1.** an animal or bird being hunted or chased: *The eagle swooped down on its helpless quarry.* **2.** any object of search, pursuit, or attack: *The squadron finally located its quarry.*

quart (kwôrt) /kwɔrt/ *n.* [*count*] **1.** a unit of liquid measure, equal to one fourth of a gallon, or 57.749 cubic inches (0.946 liter) in the U.S. and 69.355 cubic inches (1.136 liters) in Great Britain. **2.** a unit of dry measure, equal to one eighth of a peck, or 67.201 cubic inches (1.101 liters). *Abbr.:* qt.

quar•ter (kwôr′tər) /ˈkwɔrtər/ *n.,* **1.** [*count*] one of the four equal or sometimes approximately equal parts into which something is or may be divided: *a quarter of a pound.* **2.** [*count*] one fourth of a U.S. or Canadian dollar, equivalent to 25 cents. **3.** [*count*] a coin of this value. **4.** [*count*] one fourth of an hour; 15 minutes. **5.** [*count*] one fourth of a calendar or of a year in business: *Unemployment rose in the last quarter.* **6.** [*count*] a term of instruction at a school or college lasting about one fourth of the school year. **7.** [*count*] any of the four equal periods of play in certain games, such as football and basketball. **8.** [*count*] a region occupied by a particular group: *the student quarter of Paris.* **9.** Usually, **quarters.** [*plural*] housing accommodations; a place to live or stay; lodgings. **10.** Often, **quarters.** [*plural*] an unnamed person or group: *In some quarters your actions would be viewed as treason.* **11.** [*noncount*] mercy: *to give no quarter to an enemy.* **—***v.* [~ + *obj*] **12.** to divide into four equal or approximately equal parts. **13.** to cut the body of (a person) into quarters, esp. after executing for treason. **14.** to give to or provide (someone) with a place to stay: *soldiers quartered in barracks.* **—***adj.* [*before a noun*] **15.** being one of four equal or approximately equal parts: *a quarter century.* **16.** being equal to one fourth of the full measure: *a quarter pound.*

quar•ter•back (kwôr′tər bak′) /ˈkwɔrtərˌbæk/ *n.* **1.** [*count*] a back in football who usually lines up immediately behind the center and directs the offense of the team. **2.** [*noncount*] the position played by this back. **—***v.* **3.** to direct the offense of (a team): [~ + *obj*]: *He quarterbacked his team to victory.* [*no obj*]: *He should be quarterbacking again in no time.*

quar•ter•deck (kwôr′tər dek′) /ˈkwɔrtərˌdɛk/ *n.* [*count*] the part of the deck of a vessel from midship to the stern.

quar′ter-fi′nal′, *n.* [*count*] one of four matches in a competition in which the winners play in a semifinal.

quar•ter•ly (kwôr′tər lē) /ˈkwɔrtərliy/ *adj., n., pl.* **-lies,** *adv.* **—***adj.* [*often: before a noun*] **1.** occurring, done, paid, issued, etc., at the end of every quarter of a year, or four times a year: *a quarterly report.* **2.** relating to or made up of a quarter. **—***n.* [*count*] **3.** a periodical issued every three months. **—***adv.* **4.** once each quarter of a year: *to pay interest quarterly.*

quar•ter•mas•ter (kwôr′tər mas′tər) /ˈkwɔrtərˌmæstər/ *n.* [*count*] **1.** a military officer who provides clothing and food for troops. **2.** a naval officer having charge of a ship's helm and its navigating equipment.

quar′ter note′, *n.* [*count*] a musical note equal in time value to one quarter of a whole note.

quar•tet (kwôr tet′) /kwɔrˈtɛt/ *n.* [*count*] **1.** an organized group of four singers or players. **2.** a musical composition for four voices or instruments. **3.** any group of four persons or things. Also, *esp. Brit.,* **quar•tette′.**

quar•to (kwôr′tō) /ˈkwɔrtow/ *n., pl.* **-tos,** *adj.* **—***n.* [*count*] **1.** a book size of about 9½ × 12 in. (24 × 30 cm), originally made by folding printed sheets twice to form four leaves or eight pages. **2.** a book of this size. **—***adj.* [*before a noun*] **3.** bound in quarto.

quartz (kwôrts) /kwɔrts/ *n.* [*noncount*] a mineral, silicon dioxide, found in crystals and grains, and the chief part of sand.

qua•sar (kwā′zär, -sär) /ˈkweyzɑr, -sɑr/ *n.* [*count*] a starlike object that is extremely distant from the earth and extremely bright.

quash (kwosh) /kwɒʃ/ *v.* [~ + *obj*] **1.** to put down or suppress completely; quell; subdue: *The dictator was able to quash the rebellion.* **2.** to set aside or make void or annul: *The judge quashed the verdict.*

qua•si (kwā′zī, -sī, kwä′sē, -zē) /ˈkweyzay, -say, ˈkwɑsiy, -ziy/ *adj.* resembling; almost the same as: *a quasi member.*

quasi-, *prefix. quasi-* comes from Latin, where it has the meaning "as if, as though." It is attached to adjectives and nouns and means "having some of the features but not all; resembling; almost the same as:" *quasi-scientific, quasiparticle, quasi-stellar.*

quat•rain (kwo′trān) /ˈkwɒtreyn/ *n.* [*count*] a stanza or poem having four lines, usually with alternating rhymes.

qua•ver (kwā′vər) /ˈkweyvər/ *v.* [*no obj*] **1.** to shake, quiver, or tremble: *Her lips quavered as she struggled not to cry.* **2.** to speak, sound, say, or sing with a voice that shakes or trembles: *His voice quavered in fright.* **—***n.* [*count*] **3.** a quivering or trembling, esp. in the voice: *He answered with a small quaver.* **4.** a quavering sound or tone. **—qua′ver•ing•ly,** *adv.* **—qua′ver•y,** *adj.*

quay (kē, kā, kwā), *n.* [*count*] a landing place, as of stone or concrete, built near the edge of a body of water; a wharf.

quea•sy (kwē′zē) /ˈkwiyziy/ *adj.,* **-si•er, -si•est. 1.** feeling sick or slightly dizzy; having an urge to vomit. **2.** uneasy; uncomfortable; worried: *I feel a little queasy about leaving our teenage son home alone for a week.* **—quea′si•ly,** *adv.* **—quea′si•ness,** *n.* [*noncount*]

queen (kwēn) /kwiyn/ *n.* [*count*] **1.** a female ruler or monarch. **2.** the wife of a king. **3.** a woman, or something thought of as a woman, considered pre-eminent in some way: *a beauty queen; Athens, the queen of the Aegean.* **4.** *Slang* (*usually disparaging and offensive*). a flamboyantly feminine male homosexual. **5.** a playing card bearing a picture of a queen. **6.** the most powerful chess piece of either color, able to be moved across any number of empty squares in a straight line in any direction. **7.** a female ant, bee, termite, or wasp capable of laying eggs.

queen•ly (kwēn′lē) /ˈkwiynliy/ *adj.,* **-li•er, -li•est.** of, like, concerning, or suitable for a queen.

queen′-size′ or **queen′-sized′,** *adj.* **1.** (of a bed) larger than a double bed, but smaller than king-size, usually 60 in. (152 cm) wide and 80 in. (203 cm) long. **2.** of or for a queen-size bed. **3.** of a size larger than average: *queen-size clothing.*

queer (kwēr) /kwɪər/ *adj.*, **-er, -est,** *v.*, *n.* **—*adj.*** **1.** strange or odd; unusually different: *A queer old man suddenly emerged from the corner of the bookshop.* **2.** suspicious; shady; questionable: *There's something queer in the wording of this document.* **3.** [*be* + ~] not physically right or well; sick or faint: *feeling queer.* **4.** [*be* + ~] mentally unbalanced; deranged. **5.** *Slang* (*usually disparaging and offensive*). homosexual. **—*v.*** [~ + *obj*] **6.** to spoil; ruin: *The salesman complained that you queered his sales pitch.* **—*n.*** [*count*] **7.** *Slang* (*usually disparaging and offensive*). a homosexual. **—queer′ly,** *adv.*

quell (kwel) /kwɛl/ *v.* [~ + *obj*] **1.** to put down; suppress; subdue; crush: *The army quelled the uprising.* **2.** to quiet; free from: *to quell a child's fear of thunder.*

quench (kwench) /kwɛntʃ/ *v.* [~ + *obj*] **1.** to satisfy; appease: *had a drink to quench my thirst.* **2.** to put out; extinguish (fire, flames, etc.). **3.** to cool suddenly by plunging into a liquid, as in tempering steel by immersion in water. **—quench′er,** *n.* [*count*]

-quer-, *root.* *-quer-* comes from Latin, where it has the meaning "seek; look for; ask." This meaning is found in such words as: CONQUER, QUERY. See -QUIR-, -QUES-, -QUIS-.

quer•u•lous (kwer′ə ləs, kwer′yə-) /ˈkwɛrələs, ˈkwɛryə-/ *adj.* **1.** full of complaints; complaining; criticizing: *badgered by querulous students.* **2.** characterized by or uttered in complaint: *querulous demands.* **—quer′u•lous•ly,** *adv.*

que•ry (kwēr′ē, kwer′ē) /ˈkwɪəriy, ˈkwɛriy/ *n., pl.* **-ries,** *v.*, **-ried, -ry•ing.** **—*n.*** [*count*] **1.** a question; an inquiry: *The reporter had a query for the mayor.* **2.** QUESTION MARK (def. 1). **—*v.*** [~ + *obj*] **3.** to question as doubtful: *to query a statement.* **4.** to ask questions of: *They queried her on her future plans.* See -QUER-.

-ques-, *root.* *-ques-* comes from Latin, where it has the meaning "seek; look for; ask." This meaning is found in such words as: CONQUEST, INQUEST, QUEST, QUESTION, REQUEST.

quest (kwest) /kwɛst/ *n.* [*count*] **1.** a search: *a single-minded quest for truth.* **2.** a trip made as an adventure in search of something: *the quest for the Holy Grail.* **—*v.*** [*no obj*] **3.** to search; seek: *to quest after hidden treasure.* **4.** to go on a quest. **—*Idiom.*** **5. in quest of,** in search of. See -QUES-.

ques•tion (kwes′chən) /ˈkwɛstʃən/ *n.* **1.** [*count*] a sentence in a form that is spoken to someone in order to get information in reply: *Please answer me when I ask you a question.* **2.** [*count*] a problem for discussion or under discussion; issue: *There is another side to this question.* **3.** [*count*] a problem or question given as part of an examination: *The test had 40 short-answer questions.* **4.** a matter of some uncertainty or difficulty; problem: [*count*]: *It was mainly a question of time.* [*noncount*]: *There can be no question of his guilt.* **5.** [*count*] a proposal to be debated or voted on: *The question is before the committee.* **6.** [*count; usually: the* + ~] the procedure of putting a proposal to vote: *He insisted on calling the question.* **—*v.*** **7.** [~ + *obj*] to ask questions of; interrogate: *The police questioned him closely.* **8.** to make a question of; doubt: [~ + *obj*]: *They questioned our sincerity.* [~ + *clause*]: *I question if you are ready for success.* **—*Idiom.*** **9. beyond (all) question,** beyond dispute; without doubt: *She is, beyond question, the most glamorous actress of all.* **10. call in** or **into question,** to dispute; challenge; cast doubt upon; question: [*call* + *into* + ~ + *obj*]: *to call into question someone's patriotism.* [*call* + *obj* + *into* + ~]: *called her patriotism into question.* **11. in question, a.** under consideration: *Where were you on the night in question?* **b.** in dispute: *His finances aren't in question.* **12. out of the question,** not to be considered: *getting an appointment for today is out of the question.* See -QUES-.

ques•tion•a•ble (kwes′chə nə bəl) /ˈkwɛstʃənəbəl/ *adj.* **1.** not completely honest, moral, respectable, or proper; dubious: *He was accused of some questionable activities.* **2.** open to question. See -QUES-.

ques′tion mark′, *n.* [*count*] **1.** a mark indicating a question: usually, as in English, the mark (?) placed after a question. **2.** something unanswered or unknown: *The candidate's future plans are a question mark.*

ques•tion•naire (kwes′chə nâr′) /ˌkwɛstʃəˈnɛər/ *n.* [*count*] a list of questions with spaces for answers, usually given out to a number of people so that replies to it can be analyzed for usable information.

queue (kyo͞o), *n., v.,* **queued, queu•ing.** **—*n.*** [*count*] **1.** a file or line, esp. of people waiting their turn. **2.** a number of items waiting in a certain order for electronic action in a computer system: *a queue for printing jobs.* **—*v.*** **3.** [*no obj; (~ + up)*] to form in a line while waiting: *People had queued (up) for hours to buy tickets.* **4.** [~ + *obj*] to arrange or organize (electronic data) into a queue: *The computer program queues the various print jobs.*

quib•ble (kwib′əl) /ˈkwɪbəl/ *n., v.,* **-bled, -bling.** **—*n.*** [*count*] **1.** a criticism about something very small: *a few quibbles about an otherwise great success.* **—*v.*** [*no obj*] **2.** to complain about small and unimportant matters: *quibbling over a few dollars.* **—quib′bler,** *n.* [*count*]

quiche (kēsh), *n.* a pie of unsweetened custard baked with other ingredients, as cheese or onions: [*noncount*]: *We like quiche.* [*count*]: *a spinach quiche.*

quick (kwik) /kwɪk/ *adj.* and *adv.*, **-er, -est,** *n.* **—*adj.*** **1.** done, proceeding, or occurring with promptness or rapidity: *a quick response.* **2.** completed in a short time: *took a quick shower.* **3.** moving or able to move with speed: *the quick rabbit.* **4.** easily aroused: *a quick temper.* **5.** keen; lively; acute: *a quick wit.* **6.** prompt or swift in doing, seeing, or understanding: *quick to respond.* **7.** sharp: *a quick bend in the road.* **—*n.*** **8. the quick,** [*plural; used with a plural verb*] *Archaic.* living persons: *the quick and the dead.* **9.** [*noncount*] the sensitive flesh of the living body, esp. that under the nails. **—*adv.*** **10.** in a quick manner; quickly: *come quick.* **—*Idiom.*** **11. cut (someone) to the quick,** [*cut* + *obj* + *to* + *the* + ~] to injure deeply; hurt the feelings of. **—quick′ly,** *adv.* **—quick′ness,** *n.* [*noncount*]

quick′ bread′, *n.* [*noncount*] bread made with a leavening ingredient, as baking powder or soda, that permits immediate baking.

quick•en (kwik′ən) /ˈkwɪkən/ *v.* **1.** to (cause to) become more rapid; accelerate; hasten: [~ + *obj*]: *She quickened her pace.* [*no obj*]: *Her pulse quickened.* **2.** [~ + *obj*] to give liveliness to; stimulate: *to quicken the imagination.* **3.** [*no obj*] (of a fetus in the womb) to begin to show signs of life.

quick′-freeze′, *v.* [~ + *obj*], **-froze, -fro•zen, -freez•ing.** to freeze (food) rapidly so that it can be stored at freezing temperatures.

quick•ie (kwik′ē) /ˈkwɪkiy/ *n.* [*count*] *Informal.* **1.** something produced, done, or enjoyed in only a short time. **—*adj.*** **2.** accomplished quickly with little ceremony, fuss, or bother: *a quickie meal.*

quick•lime (kwik′līm′) /ˈkwɪkˌlaym/ *n.* LIME[1].

quick•sand (kwik′sand′) /ˈkwɪkˌsænd/ *n.* [*noncount*] a bed of loose sand mixed with water and of considerable depth, that gives way under weight and tends to cause an object on its surface to sink.

quick•sil•ver (kwik′sil′vər) /ˈkwɪkˌsɪlvər/ *n.* [*noncount*] **1.** MERCURY (def. 1). **—*adj.*** **2.** quickly changeable; unpredictable.

quick′-tem′pered, *adj.* easily angered; touchy.

quick′-wit′ted, *adj.* having an alert or nimble mind.

quid[1] (kwid) /kwɪd/ *n.* [*count*] a portion of something, esp. tobacco, to be chewed but not swallowed.

quid[2] (kwid) /kwɪd/ *n.* [*count*], *pl.* **quid.** *Brit. Informal.* a pound sterling.

quid pro quo (kwid′ prō kwō′) /ˈkwɪd prow ˈkwow/ *n.* [*count*], *pl.* **quid pro quos, quids pro quo.** something given or taken in return for something else or in payment for something else: *She demanded support for her candidate as a quid pro quo for her donation.*

-quie-, *root.* *-quie-* comes from Latin, where it has the meaning "quiet, still." This meaning is found in such words as: ACQUIESCE, DISQUIETING, QUIESCENT, QUIET, QUIETUDE.

qui•es•cent (kwē es′ənt, kwī-) /kwiyˈɛsənt, kway-/ *adj.* being at rest; quiet; still; inactive or motionless: *a quiescent mind.* **—qui•es′cence,** *n.* [*noncount*] See -QUIE-.

qui•et (kwī′it) /ˈkwayɪt/ *adj.*, **-er, -est,** *n., v.* **—*adj.*** **1.** making little or no noise or sound: *quiet neighbors.* **2.** having little or no noise: *a quiet street.* **3.** [*be* + ~] silent: *Be quiet!* **4.** reserved in speech or manner: *a quiet, private sort of person.* **5.** free from disturbance or excitement: *a quiet life in the country.* **6.** free from activity: *a quiet Sunday afternoon.* **7.** still or barely moving: *quiet waters.* **8.** not readily noticed by others: *raised an eyebrow in quiet reproach.* **9.** not active: *The stock market was quiet last week.* **—*n.*** [*noncount*] **10.** the quality or state of being quiet; peacefulness. **—*v.*** **11.** to (cause to) become quiet: [~ + *obj*]: *He tried to quiet the howling dogs.* [*no obj; (~ + down)*]: *The dogs quieted (down).* **12.** [~ + *obj*] to make tranquil or peaceful: *She tried to quiet the jittery children.* **13.** [~ + *obj*] to put to rest: *Her father quieted her fears.* **—qui′et•ly,** *adv.* **—qui′et•ness,** *n.* [*noncount*] See -QUIE-.

qui•e•tude (kwī′i to͞od′, -tyo͞od′) /ˈkwayɪˌtuwd, -ˌtyuwd/ *n.* [*noncount*] the state of being quiet; tranquillity. See -QUIE-.

quill (kwil) /kwɪl/ *n.* [*count*] **1.** one of the large feathers of the wing or tail of a bird. **2.** the hard, hollow part at the base of a feather. **3.** a feather, as that of a goose, used as a pen for writing. **4.** one of the hollow spines on a porcupine or hedgehog.

quilt (kwilt) /kwɪlt/ *n.* [*count*] **1.** a covering for a bed, made of two layers of fabric with some soft substance between them and stitched in patterns. **2.** anything quilted or resembling a quilt. —*v.* **3.** [~ + *obj*] to stitch together (two pieces of cloth and a soft interlining), usually in an ornamental pattern. **4.** [*no obj*] to make quilts or quilted work. —**quilt′ed,** *adj.*: *a quilted down comforter.* —**quilt′er,** *n.* [*count*] —**quilt′ing,** *n.* [*noncount*]

quince (kwins) /kwɪns/ *n.* **1.** [*count*] a small tree of the rose family, giving hard, yellowish fruit used for making preserves. **2.** [*noncount*] the fruit of such a tree.

qui•nine (kwī′nīn, kwin′in;) /ˈkwaynayn, ˈkwɪnayn;/ *n.* [*noncount*] a white crystal-like substance from the bark of certain trees, used for treating malaria.

quint (kwint) /kwɪnt/ *n.* [*count*] *Informal.* a quintuplet.

quin•tes•sence (kwin tes′əns) /kwɪnˈtɛsəns/ *n.* [*count; usually singular; usually: the* + ~] the most perfect type or example of something: *the quintessence of honesty.*

quin•tes•sen•tial (kwin′tə sen′shəl) /ˌkwɪntəˈsɛnʃəl/ *adj.* [*before a noun*] being or representing the most perfect type or example of something: *It was quintessential politics-as-usual.*

quin•tet or **quin•tette** (kwin tet′) /kwɪnˈtɛt/ *n.* [*count*] **1.** any set or group of five persons or things. **2.** a group of five singers or players. **3.** a piece of music written for five voices or instruments.

quin•til•lion (kwin til′yən) /kwɪnˈtɪlyən/ *n., pl.* **-lions,** (*as after a numeral*) **-lion,** *adj.* —*n.* [*count*] **1.** a number written in the U.S. by 1 followed by 18 zeros, and in Great Britain by 1 followed by 30 zeros. —*adj.* [*after a number and before a noun*] **2.** amounting to one quintillion in number.

quin•tu•ple (kwin to͞o′pəl, -tyo͞o′-, -tup′əl) /kwɪnˈtuwpəl, -ˈtyuw-, -ˈtʌpəl/ *adj., n., v.,* **-pled, -pling.** —*adj.* **1.** fivefold; made up of five parts. **2.** five times as great or as much. —*n.* [*count*] **3.** a number, amount, etc., five times as great as another. —*v.* **4.** to make or become five times as great: [*no obj*]: *Under new management our profits quintupled.* [~ + *obj*]: *promising to quintuple our profits.* See -PLIC-.

quin•tu•plet (kwin tup′lit, -to͞o′plit, -tyo͞o′-) /kwɪnˈtʌplɪt, -ˈtuwplɪt, -ˈtyuw-/ *n.* [*count*] **1.** a group of five of a kind. **2.** one of five children or offspring born of the same mother at the same time. See -PLIC-.

quip (kwip) /kwɪp/ *n., v.,* **quipped, quip•ping.** —*n.* [*count*] **1.** a clever or witty remark or comment. —*v.* [*no obj*] **2.** to make or utter a quip. —**quip′ster,** *n.* [*count*]

-quir-, *root.* *-quir-* comes from Latin, where it has the meaning "seek; look for." This meaning is found in such words as: ACQUIRE, ENQUIRY, INQUIRE, INQUIRY, REQUIRE, REQUIREMENT. See -QUIS-, -QUER-.

quirk (kwûrk) /kwɜrk/ *n.* [*count*] **1.** an odd habit, trait, or example of behavior: *He had this quirk of suddenly turning his back on the person he was talking to.* **2.** an accident; vagary: *a cruel quirk of fate.* —**quirk′i•ness,** *n.* [*noncount*]

quirk•y (kwûr′kē) /ˈkwɜrkiy/ *adj.,* **-i•er, -i•est.** odd, peculiar, or strange: *a quirky smile; a quirky little sidestreet.*

-quis-, *root.* *-quis-* comes from Latin, where it has the meaning "seek; look for." This meaning is found in such words as: ACQUISITION, EXQUISITE, INQUISITION, INQUISITIVE, PERK, PERQUISITE, PREREQUISITE, REQUISITE. See -QUIR-.

quis•ling (kwiz′ling) /ˈkwɪzlɪŋ/ *n.* [*count*] a person who betrays his or her country by helping an invading enemy.

quit (kwit) /kwɪt/ *v.,* **quit** or **quit•ted, quit•ting. 1.** to stop, cease, or discontinue: [*no obj*]: *Will that noise ever quit?* [~ + *verb-ing*]: *He quit smoking.* [~ + *obj*]: *Quit it, will you?* **2.** to give up or resign; let go; relinquish: [~ + *obj*]: *She quit her job.* [*no obj*]: *decided to quit.* **3.** [~ + *obj*] to depart from; leave (a place or person): *The army quit the area as fast as it could.* **4.** [*no obj*] to stop trying, struggling, or the like: *Don't quit now; you still have a chance to win.* —***Idiom.*** *Informal.* **5. call it quits,** [*no obj*] to end an activity, relationship, etc.: *decided to call it quits and get a divorce.* See -QUIT-.

-quit-, *root.* *-quit-* comes from Latin, where it has the meaning "release; discharge; let go." This meaning is found in such words as: ACQUIT, QUIT, QUITE, REQUITE, UNREQUITED.

quite (kwīt) /kwayt/ *adv.* **1.** completely or entirely: *not quite finished.* **2.** actually, really, or truly: *This represents quite a sudden change for her.* **3.** to a considerable extent: *He is quite young to be walking.* See -QUIT-.

quit•ter (kwit′ər) /ˈkwɪtər/ *n.* [*count*] a person who quits or gives up easily, esp. when faced with difficulty.

quiv•er[1] (kwiv′ər) /ˈkwɪvər/ *v.* [*no obj*] **1.** to shake with a slight but rapid motion; tremble: *The dog quivered with excitement.* —*n.* [*count*] **2.** the act or state of quivering. —**quiv′er•y,** *adj.*

quiv•er[2] (kwiv′ər) /ˈkwɪvər/ *n.* [*count*] **1.** a case for holding or carrying arrows. **2.** the arrows in such a case.

quix•ot•ic (kwik sot′ik) /kwɪkˈsɒtɪk/ *adj.* foolishly romantic or impractical in pursuit of one's ideals: *a quixotic attempt to save the world single-handedly.*

quiz (kwiz), *n., pl.* **quiz•zes,** *v.,* **quizzed, quiz•zing.** —*n.* [*count*] **1.** an informal or short test. **2.** a questioning. —*v.* [~ + *obj*] **3.** to test informally by questions: *quizzed her students on irregular verb forms.* **4.** to ask questions of (someone) closely: *The reporters quizzed the president.* —**quiz′zer,** *n.* [*count*]

quiz′ show′, *n.* [*count*] a television or radio program in which people compete, usually for cash or prizes, by answering questions. Also called **quiz′ pro′gram.**

quiz•zi•cal (kwiz′i kəl) /ˈkwɪzɪkəl/ *adj.* **1.** puzzled; uncertain: *a quizzical expression on her face.* **2.** slightly teasing: *a sly, quizzical comment.* —**quiz′zi•cal•ly,** *adv.*

quoit (kwoit, koit) /kwɔyt, kɔyt/ *n.* **1. quoits,** [*noncount; used with a singular verb*] a game in which rings of rope or flattened metal are thrown at an upright peg, the object being to throw the ring around the peg. **2.** [*count*] a ring used in the game of quoits. —*v.* [~ + *obj*] **3.** to throw like a quoit.

Quon′set hut′ (kwon′sit) /ˈkwɒnsɪt/ *Trademark.* [*count*] a rounded, metal, prefabricated shelter.

quo•rum (kwôr′əm, kwōr′-) /ˈkwɔrəm, ˈkwowr-/ *n.* [*count*] the number of members of a group, usually a majority, that must be present in order to have a meeting, transact business, or carry out an activity according to the group's rules.

-quot-, *root.* *-quot-* comes from Latin, where it has the meaning "how many; divided." This meaning is found in such words as: QUOTA, QUOTATION, QUOTIDIAN, QUOTIENT.

quot., an abbreviation of: quotation.

quo•ta (kwō′tə) /ˈkwowtə/ *n.* [*count*] **1.** the share or part of a total that is required from, allowed to, or that belongs to a particular district, group, etc.: *The officers issued their quota of speeding tickets.* **2.** the number or percentage of persons of a specified kind permitted to enroll in a college, join a club, immigrate to a country, etc. See -QUOT-.

quo•ta•tion (kwō tā′shən) /kwowˈteyʃən/ *n.* **1.** [*count*] a word, phrase, sentence, or passage taken from a book, speech, etc., and repeated. **2.** [*count*] an estimate of a cost for doing some work: *The quotation for the repairs was too high.* **3.** [*noncount*] the act of quoting: *Use quotation to bolster your argument.* See -QUOT-.

quota′tion mark′, *n.* [*count*] one of the marks used at the beginning and end of a written statement; in English usually shown as (") at the beginning and (") at the end, or, for a quotation within a quotation, as in single marks of this kind, as *"He said, 'I will go.'"*

quote (kwōt) /kwowt/ *v.,* **quot•ed, quot•ing,** *n.* —*v.* **1.** to repeat (a passage, phrase, etc.) from a book, speech, or the like, word for word: [*no obj*]: *In his book he quoted from speeches of Churchill.* [~ + *obj*]: *He quotes you extensively in his article.* **2.** [~ + *obj*] to refer to or bring forward as evidence or support; cite: *He quoted the law as the basis for the lawsuit.* **3.** [~ + *obj*] to offer as a price or amount: *The salesman quoted a low figure for the house.* **4.** [~ + *obj*] to state the current or market price of (a stock, bond, etc.). **5.** (used in the root form to introduce the beginning of a quotation): *He said, quote, "I robbed the store."* —*n.* [*count*] **6.** QUOTATION. **7.** QUOTATION MARK. —**quot′a•ble,** *adj.* See -QUOT-.

quo•tid•i•an (kwō tid′ē ən) /kwowˈtɪdiyən/ *adj.* **1.** daily: *a quotidian report.* **2.** ordinary; everyday; commonplace: *the quotidian routine of life.* See -QUOT-.

quo•tient (kwō′shənt) /ˈkwowʃənt/ *n.* [*count*] **1.** the result of division; the number of times one quantity is contained in another: *When you divide 12 by 6 the quotient is 2.* **2.** a degree, rate, amount, or extent of something; a factor: *The job brings with it a high quotient of stress.* See -QUOT-.

QWERTY (kwûr′tē, kwer′-) /ˈkwɜrtiy, ˈkwɛr-/ *adj.* of or noting a standard keyboard, with *q, w, e, r, t,* and *y* being the first six letters on the top row.

R, r (är) /ɑr/ *n., pl.* **Rs** or **R's, rs** or **r's.** the 18th letter of the English alphabet, a consonant.

R, an abbreviation of: **1.** *Math.* ratio. **2.** regular: a man's suit or coat size. **3.** restricted: a motion-picture rating advising that children under the age of 17 will not be admitted unless accompanied by an adult. Compare G (def. 2), NC-17, PG, PG-13, X (def. 7). **4.** right.

R, *Symbol.* **1.** registered trademark: written as superscript ® following a name registered with the U.S. Patent and Trademark Office. **2.** *Elect.* resistance.

r, an abbreviation of: radius.

R., an abbreviation of: **1.** radius. **2.** railroad. **3.** railway. **4.** Republican. **5.** right. **6.** river. **7.** road.

r., an abbreviation of: **1.** railroad. **2.** railway. **3.** right. **4.** river. **5.** road. **6.** rod.

rab•bi (rab′ī) /ˈræbay/ *n.* [*count*], *pl.* **-bis. 1.** the chief religious official of a synagogue who performs rituals, teaches, and functions as spiritual leader of the congregation. **2.** (a title of respect for) a Jewish scholar or teacher. **—rab•bin•i•cal** (rə bin′i kəl) /rəˈbɪnɪkəl/ **rab•bin′ic,** *adj.*

rab•bit (rab′it) /ˈræbɪt/ *n., pl.* **-bits,** (*esp. when thought of as a group*) **-bit. 1.** [*count*] a large-eared, hopping animal, usually smaller than the hare, living in holes in the ground. **2.** [*noncount*] the fur of a rabbit or hare.

rab•ble (rab′əl) /ˈræbəl/ *n.* [*count*] **1.** a disorderly crowd; mob. **2. the rabble,** [*plural; used with a plural verb*] the lower classes; the common people.

rab′ble-rous′er, *n.* [*count*] a person who stirs up the passions or hatreds of the public; demagogue. **—rab′ble-rous′ing,** *n.* [*noncount*]: *accused of rabble-rousing.* **—***adj.*: *a rabble-rousing speech.*

rab•id (rab′id) /ˈræbɪd/ *adj.* **1.** [*before a noun*] having irrational, unreasonable, or extreme opinions or practices; fanatic: *a rabid partisan.* **2.** raging; violently intense. **3.** affected with or relating to rabies: *a rabid dog.*

ra•bies (rā′bēz) /ˈreybiyz/ *n.* [*noncount; used with a singular verb*] an infectious, usually fatal disease of dogs, cats, and other warm-blooded animals, caused by a virus and passed on to humans by the bite of an infected animal.

rac•coon (ra ko͞on′) /ræˈkuwn/ *n., pl.* **-coons,** (*esp. when thought of as a group*) **-coon. 1.** [*count*] a small, meat-eating animal active at night, having a masklike black stripe across the eyes and a bushy, ringed tail. **2.** [*noncount*] the thick, brownish gray fur of this animal.

race[1] (rās) /reys/ *n., v.,* **raced, rac•ing. —***n.* [*count*] **1.** a contest of speed, such as in running, riding, driving, or sailing. **2. races,** [*plural*] a series of races, as of horses, run at a set time in a particular place. **3.** any contest or competition, esp. to achieve some gain: *an arms race; a Senate race.* **4.** an urgent effort: *a race to find a vaccine against the dreaded disease.* **—***v.* **5.** to run in a contest of speed against (someone); run a race with: [~ + *obj*]: *He raced her to the finish line.* [*no obj*]: *He wanted to race in the Olympics.* **6.** to (cause cars, horses, dogs, etc.) to run in races: [~ + *obj*]: *He raced his car in the Grand Prix.* [*no obj*]: *wouldn't race again.* **7.** to (cause to) run, move, or go swiftly: [*no obj*]: *He raced back to the house.* [~ + *obj*]: *He tried racing the motor to warm up the engine.* **—rac′er,** *n.* [*count*]

race[2] (rās) /reys/ *n.* **1.** a type or classification of humans into groups, sometimes, esp. formerly, based on certain observed physical characteristics, as skin color, facial form, or eye shape, and now frequently based on certain genetic differences: [*count*]: *members of various races.* [*noncount*]: *a discussion of race.* **2.** [*count*] any people united by common history, language, cultural traits, etc.: *the Dutch race.* **3.** [*count*] any group, class, or kind of creatures: *the human race.* **—***adj.* [*before a noun*] **4.** of or relating to race: *race relations.*

race•horse (rās′hôrs′) /ˈreysˌhɔrs/ *n.* [*count*] a horse raised or kept for racing.

race•track (rās′trak′) /ˈreysˌtræk/ *n.* [*count*] an area of ground laid out for racing.

race•way (rās′wā′) /ˈreysˌwey/ *n.* [*count*] a racetrack on which harness races are held.

ra•cial (rā′shəl) /ˈreyʃəl/ *adj.* **1.** of, relating to, or characteristic of one race or the races of humankind. **2.** existing between races: *racial harmony.* **—ra′cial•ly,** *adv.*

ra•cial•ism (rā′shə liz′əm) /ˈreyʃəˌlɪzəm/ *n.* RACISM. **—ra′cial•ist,** *n.* [*count*], *adj.*

rac′ing form′, *n.* [*count*] a sheet that provides detailed information about horse races.

rac•ism (rā′siz əm) /ˈreysɪzəm/ *n.* [*noncount*] **1.** a belief or doctrine that one's own race is superior. **2.** hatred or intolerance of another race or other races. **—rac′ist,** *n.* [*count*], *adj.*

rack[1] (rak) /ræk/ *n.* [*count*] **1.** a framework of bars, pegs, etc., on which things are arranged: *a clothes rack; a ski rack.* **2.** a fixture containing shelves, often attached to something: *a spice rack.* **3.** a former instrument of torture on which a victim was slowly stretched. **—***v.* [~ + *obj*] **4.** to torture; hurt badly; torment; cause great pain to: *Crippling spasms of pain racked him every few minutes.* **5.** to strain or struggle in mental effort: *He racked his brains trying to come up with an answer.* **6. rack up,** [~ + *up* + *obj*] to gain, achieve, or score: *The new store is racking up profits.*

rack[2] (rak) /ræk/ *n.* [*noncount*] wreckage or destruction; wrack: *to go to rack and ruin.*

rack•et[1] (rak′it) /ˈrækɪt/ *n.* [*count*] **1.** [*usually singular*] a loud noise, esp. of a disturbing or confusing kind; din; uproar: *What a racket last night with her party!* **2.** an organized illegal or dishonest activity, as making demands of money by threat or violence. **3.** *Slang.* **a.** an occupation, livelihood, or business: *the teaching racket.* **b.** an easy or profitable source of making money: *You mean he gets paid for not working? What a racket.*

rack•et[2] (rak′it) /ˈrækɪt/ *n.* **1.** [*count*] a light wooden or metal instrument with a handle and a net, usually catgut or nylon, stretched in an oval frame, used to hit a ball or birdie in tennis, badminton, etc. **2.** [*count*] the short-handled paddle used to hit the ball in table tennis and paddle tennis. **3. rackets,** [*noncount; used with a singular verb*] a game played with rackets and a ball in a four-walled court. Also, **racquet** (for defs. 1, 2).

rack•et•eer (rak′i tēr′) /ˌrækɪˈtɪər/ *n.* [*count*] **1.** a person in an organized, illegal activity, as extortion. **—***v.* [*no obj*] **2.** to work in a racket. **—rack′et•eer′ing,** *n.* [*noncount*]

rack•ing (rak′ing) /ˈrækɪŋ/ *adj.* [*usually: before a noun*] causing great physical or mental pain or suffering: *a racking headache.* **—rack′ing•ly,** *adv.*

rac•on•teur (rak′on tûr′, -to͝or′, -ən-) /ˌrækɒnˈtɜr, -ˈtʊr, -ən-/ *n.* [*count*] a person who is skilled in telling stories.

rac•quet•ball (rak′it bôl′) /ˈrækɪtˌbɔl/ *n.* [*noncount*] a game played with rackets on a four-walled court.

rac•y (rā′sē) /ˈreysiy/ *adj.,* **-i•er, -i•est. 1.** slightly improper, as by containing references to sexual matters; risqué. **2.** vigorous; lively: *a racy literary style.* **—rac•i•ly** (rā′sə lē) /ˈreysəliy/ *adv.* **—rac′i•ness,** *n.* [*noncount*]

rad[1] (rad) /ræd/ *n.* [*count*] *Physics.* a unit of measure for a dose of radiation absorbed by the body.

rad[2] (rad) /ræd/ *adj. Slang.* RADICAL.

ra•dar (rā′där) /ˈreydɑr/ *n.* [*noncount*] a device or the system for figuring out the presence, location, or speed of an object by measuring the direction and timing of radio waves sent out and reflected back to the source.

ra•di•al (rā′dē əl) /ˈreydiyəl/ *adj.* **1.** arranged or having parts arranged like lines coming out of the center of a circle. **2.** going from the center outward or from the circumference inward along a line: *radial motion.* **—***n.* [*count*] **3.** a radial section, part, or structure. **4.** RADIAL TIRE. **—ra′di•al•ly,** *adv.*

ra′dial tire′, *n.* [*count*] a motor-vehicle tire in which the cords are arranged in a direction from the tire in toward the center of the wheel.

ra•di•ance (rā′dē əns) /ˈreydiyəns/ *n.* [*noncount*] **1.** radiant brightness or light: *the radiance of the dawn.* **2.** warm, cheerful brightness: *a smile full of radiance.*

ra•di•ant (rā′dē ənt) /ˈreydiyənt/ *adj.* **1.** [*before a noun*] giving off rays of light; shining; bright. **2.** bright with joy, hope, etc.: *a radiant smile.* **3.** [*before a noun*] *Physics.* given off or sent out by radiation: *radiant energy; radiant heat.* **—ra′di•ant•ly,** *adv.*

ra•di•ate (rā′dē āt′) / *v.* ˈreydiyˌeyt / *v.,* **-at•ed, -at•ing. 1.** [*no obj*] to go out, spread, or move like rays or lines from a center point outward: *The main avenues in Paris radiate from the center.* **2.** to give off rays, as of light or heat: [*no obj*]: *Energy radiates from the sun.* [~ + *obj*]: *The sun radiates energy.* **3.** (of persons) to (cause to) give off or glow with cheerfulness, joy, goodwill, etc.: [*no obj*]: *Confidence radiated from her.* [~ + *obj*]: *She radiated confidence.*

ra•di•a•tion (rā′dē ā′shən) /ˌreydiyˈeyʃən/ *n.* **1.** [*noncount*] **a.** the process in which energy is given off by one body as particles or waves, sent through space or through some substance, and absorbed by another body. **b.** the energy transferred by this process. **2.** [*count*] something radiated: *harmful radiations.* **3.** [*noncount*] radioactivity: *nuclear radiation.*

radia′tion sick′ness, *n.* [*noncount*] sickness caused by being exposed to x-rays or radioactive materials, producing such symptoms as nausea and vomiting, headache, diarrhea, loss of hair and teeth, destruction of white blood cells, and bleeding.

ra•di•a•tor (rā′dē ā′tər) /ˈreydiyˌeytər/ *n.* [*count*] **1.** a heating device, as a series or coil of pipes through which steam or hot water passes. **2.** a device constructed from thin-walled tubes and metal fins, used for cooling circulating water, as in an automobile engine.

rad•i•cal (rad′i kəl) /ˈrædɪkəl/ *adj.* **1.** thoroughgoing, complete, or extreme: *a radical change in policy.* **2.** favoring drastic or extreme political, economic, or social reforms: *radical politics.* **3.** [*usually: before a noun*] basic; fundamental: *radical defects of character.* **4.** *Slang.* great; marvelous; wonderful: *a radical dude.* **—*n.*** [*count*] **5.** a person who holds or follows extreme convictions, beliefs, or principles; extremist. **6.** *Math.* **a.** a quantity expressed as a root of another quantity. **b.** RADICAL SIGN. **7.** a group of atoms that act together as a unit. **8.** (in Chinese writing) one of 214 elements that have meaning or sense, and are used with elements representing sounds to form thousands of different characters. **—rad′i•cal•ism,** *n.* [*noncount*] **—rad′i•cal•ly,** *adv.*

rad•i•cal•ize (rad′i kə līz′) /ˈrædɪkəˌlayz/ *v.* [~ + *obj*], **-ized, -iz•ing.** to make radical or more radical, esp. in politics. **—rad•i•cal•i•za•tion** (rad′i kə lə zā′shən) /ˌrædɪkəlɪˈzeyʃən/ *n.* [*noncount*]

rad′ical sign′, *n.* [*count*] *Math.* the symbol $\surd$ or $\sqrt{\ }$, indicating that a quantity is a root of the quantity that is shown after or under the symbol, e.g., $\surd 25=5$.

ra•di•i (rā′dē ī′) /ˈreydiyˌay/ *n.* [*plural*] a pl. of RADIUS.

ra•di•o (rā′dē ō′) /ˈreydiyˌow/ *n., pl.* **-di•os,** *adj., v.,* **-di•oed, -di•o•ing. —*n.*** **1.** [*noncount*] a system of communicating speech or other sounds by sending electromagnetic waves of a particular frequency range over long distances. **2.** [*count*] a device for receiving or sending radio broadcasts. See illustration at APPLIANCE. **3.** [*noncount*] the business or industry of sending signals to be heard by an audience. **4. on (the) radio, a.** having been broadcast through radio waves and received by a radio: *She first heard the news on the radio.* **b.** broadcasting by radio to others: *on the radio between midnight and 6 in the morning.* **—*adj.*** [*before a noun*] **5.** relating to, used in, or sent by radio: *radio messages.* **—*v.*** **6.** to send (a message, music, etc.) by radio: [*no obj*]: *The pilots radioed for help.* [~ + *obj*]: *The pilots radioed the message.* [~ + *that clause*]: *The pilots radioed that they were under attack.* **7.** to send a message to (a person) by radio: [~ + *obj*]: *The pilots radioed the tower.* [~ + *obj* + *that clause*]: *The pilots radioed the tower that they needed to land.*

radio-, *prefix. radio-* comes ultimately from Latin *radius,* meaning "beam, ray." **1.** *radio-* is attached to roots and nouns and means "radiant energy": *radiometer.* **2.** *radio-* is also used to mean "radio waves": *radiolocation; radiotelephone.* **3.** *radio-* is also used to mean "the giving off of rays as a result of the breakup of atomic nuclei": *radioactivity; radiocarbon.* **4.** *radio-* is also used to mean "x-rays": *radiograph; radiotherapy.*

ra•di•o•ac•tive (rā′dē ō ak′tiv) /ˌreydiyowˈæktɪv/ *adj.* of or relating to radioactivity; showing, having, or caused by radioactivity. **—ra′di•o•ac′tive•ly,** *adv.*

ra•di•o•ac•tiv•i•ty (rā′dē ō ak tiv′i tē) /ˌreydiyowækˈtɪvɪtiy/ *n.* [*noncount*] the property of certain elements as radium and uranium, by which they release dangerous or harmful radiation because of changes in the nuclei of their atoms.

ra•di•o•gram (rā′dē ō gram′) /ˈreydiyowˌgræm/ *n.* [*count*] a message sent by radio waves, without the use of telephone or telegraph wires.

ra•di•ol•o•gy (rā dē ol′ə jē) /reydiyˈɒlədʒiy/ *n.* [*noncount*] the branch of medicine dealing with x-rays, other radiation, and other techniques used in examining the body for disorders and certain treatments. **—ra′di•ol′o•gist,** *n.* [*count*]

ra•di•os•co•py (rā′dē os′kə pē) /ˌreydiyˈɒskəpiy/ *n.* [*noncount*] the examination of objects by means of some form of radiation other than light, usually by x-rays. See -SCOPE-.

ra•di•o•tel•e•graph (rā′dē ō tel′ə graf′) /ˌreydiyowˈtɛləˌgræf/ *n.* [*count*] **1.** a telegraph in which messages or signals are sent by means of radio waves rather than through wires or cables. **—*v.*** [~ + *obj*] **2.** to send (a message) by radiotelegraph. **—ra•di•o•te•leg•ra•phy** (rā′dē ō tə leg′rə fē) /ˌreydiyowtəˈlɛgrəfiy/ *n.* [*noncount*]

ra•di•o•tel•e•phone (rā′dē ō tel′ə fōn′) /ˌreydiyowˈtɛləˌfown/ *n.* [*count*] a telephone in which sound or speech is sent by means of radio waves instead of through wires or cables.

ra′dio tel′escope, *n.* [*count*] a large antenna, often one shaped like a dish, used to detect radio waves given off by stars, galaxies, and other sources in space.

ra•di•o•ther•a•py (rā′dē ō ther′ə pē) /ˌreydiyowˈθɛrəpiy/ *n.* [*noncount*] the treatment of disease by means of x-rays or radioactive substances. **—ra′di•o•ther′a•pist,** *n.* [*count*]

rad•ish (rad′ish) /ˈrædɪʃ/ *n.* [*count*] **1.** a crisp, sharp-tasting, strong-smelling white or red root of a plant of the mustard family, eaten raw. **2.** the plant itself.

ra•di•um (rā′dē əm) /ˈreydiyəm/ *n.* [*noncount*] a highly radioactive metallic element that is produced by the decay of uranium and has been used in the treatment of cancer.

ra•di•us (rā′dē əs) /ˈreydiyəs/ *n.* [*count*], *pl.* **-di•i** (-dē ī′) /-diyˌay/ **-di•us•es. 1.** a straight line from the center of a circle or sphere to the circumference or surface: *The radius of a circle is half the diameter.* **2.** a circular area whose size can be measured by the length of a given radius: *They searched every house within a radius of 50 miles.*

ra•don (rā′don) /ˈreydɒn/ *n.* [*noncount*] an element that is a heavy, odorless inert, radioactive gas; produced by the decay of radium, it is harmful in high concentrations.

RAF or **R.A.F.,** an abbreviation of: Royal Air Force.

raf•fi•a (raf′ē ə) /ˈræfiyə/ *n.* [*noncount*] a fiber obtained from the leaves of a palm tree, used for tying plants and other objects and for making mats, baskets, hats, etc.

raff•ish (raf′ish) /ˈræfɪʃ/ *adj.* somewhat disreputable yet dashing; rakish: *a raffish group of partygoers.* **—raff′ish•ly,** *adv.* **—raff′ish•ness,** *n.* [*noncount*]

raf•fle (raf′əl) /ˈræfəl/ *n., v.,* **-fled, -fling. —*n.*** [*count*] **1.** a form of lottery in which a number of persons buy one or more chances to win a prize. **—*v.*** **2.** to give away (something) in a raffle: [~ + *obj*]: *raffled items to raise money.* [~ + *off* + *obj*]: *to raffle off items.* [~ + *obj* + *off*]: *to raffle them off.*

raft[1] (raft) /ræft/ *n.* [*count*] **1.** a more or less rigid floating platform made of materials that will not sink: *an inflatable rubber raft.* **2.** a collection of logs, planks, casks, etc., fastened together for floating on water. **—*v.*** **3.** to travel or carry on a raft: [*no obj*]: *They went rafting.* [~ + *obj*]: *They rafted the supplies down the river.*

raft[2] (raft) /ræft/ *n.* [*count*] *Informal.* a great quantity; a lot: [*a* + ~ + *of* + *noun*]: *a raft of dinner invitations.* [~*-s* + *of* + *noun*]: *making rafts of money.*

raf•ter (raf′tər) /ˈræftər/ *n.* [*count*] **1.** any of a series of sloped, large pieces of wood, timber, or the like, used for holding up a roof. **—*Idiom.*** **2. packed to the rafters,** filled completely: *The auditorium was packed to the rafters.*

rag[1] (rag) /ræg/ *n.* **1.** a piece of cloth, esp. one that is torn or worn: [*count*]: *Get a rag and start dusting with it.* [*noncount*]: *a piece of rag.* **2. rags,** [*plural*] tattered clothing: *dressed in rags.* **3.** [*count*] *Informal.* a newspaper or magazine thought of as being of low or poor quality. **—*Idiom.*** **4. from rags to riches,** from a state of poverty to that of wealth.

rag[2] (rag) /ræg/ *v.* [~ + *obj*], **ragged, rag•ging.** *Informal.* **1.** to scold. **2.** to tease.

rag[3] (rag) /ræg/ *n.* [*count*] a piece of music in ragtime.

ra•ga (rä′gə) /ˈrɑgə/ *n.* [*count*], *pl.* **-gas.** a piece of music of India having a prescribed melodic pattern.

rag•a•muf•fin (rag′ə muf′in) /ˈrægəˌmʌfɪn/ *n.* [*count*] a child in ragged, dirty clothes.

rage (rāj) /reydʒ/ *n., v.,* **raged, rag•ing. —*n.*** **1.** [*noncount*] angry fury; violent anger. **2.** [*count*] a fit of violent anger: *He flew into a rage.* **3.** [*count; usually singular; usually: the* + ~] *Informal.* an object of current popularity or fashion; a fad: *I remember when long hair was all the rage.* **—*v.*** [*no obj*] **4.** to act or speak with fury; show or feel violent anger. **5.** to move or surge furiously: *He raged around the room.* **—rag′ing•ly,** *adv.*

rag•ged (rag′id) /ˈrægɪd/ *adj.* **1.** wearing tattered, worn-out clothing: *ragged beggars.* **2.** torn or worn to rags; tattered: *ragged pants.* **3.** jagged and uneven: *a ragged hole where the bullet had gone through.* **4.** rough, imperfect, or faulty: *a ragged performance.* **5.** scraggly: *a* *ragged line of customers.* —**rag′ged•ness,** *n.* [*noncount*] —**rag′ged•y,** *adj.*

rag•lan (rag′lən) /ˈræglən/ *n.* [*count*] a loose overcoat with raglan sleeves.

rag′lan sleeve′, *n.* [*count*] a sleeve that starts at the neck of the piece of clothing and has a long, slanting seam from neckline to armhole.

ra•gout (ra go͞o′) /ræˈguw/ *n.* [*noncount*] a spicy stew of meat or fish, with or without vegetables.

rag•tag (rag′tag′) /ˈræg,tæg/ *adj.* **1.** ragged; shabby: *dressed in ragtag uniforms.* **2.** unorganized; disorderly: *a ragtag army.*

rag•time (rag′tīm′) /ˈræg,taym/ *n.* [*noncount*] instrumental jazz marked by syncopated melody and a steadily accented beat in the bass.

rag•weed (rag′wēd′) /ˈræg,wiyd/ *n.* [*noncount*] a plant that in autumn releases pollen into the air, causing hay fever.

rah (rä) /rɑ/ *interj.* (used to express encouragement of a player or team).

raid (rād) /reyd/ *n.* [*count*] **1.** a sudden assault, attack, or other act of entering: *a police raid on a narcotics ring; an air raid.* **2.** an effort to attract away a competitor's employees, members, etc. —*v.* **3.** to make a raid (on): [*no obj*]: *The Vikings pillaged and raided.* [~ + *obj*]: *The army raided enemy supply lines.* —**raid′er,** *n.* [*count*]

rail[1] (rāl) /reyl/ *n.* **1.** [*count*] a bar, as of wood or metal, attached and used for a support, barrier, fence, or railing. **2.** [*count*] one of a pair of long, parallel and continuous steel bars on which the wheels of trains run. **3.** [*noncount*] the railroad as a means of transportation: *to travel by rail.*

rail[2] (rāl) /reyl/ *v.* to say or make bitter complaints or protests about: [*no obj; (~ + at + obj)*]: *He railed at his unfortunate fate.* [~ + *that clause*]: *He railed that nobody liked him.*

rail•ing (rā′ling) /ˈreylɪŋ/ *n.* [*count*] a fencelike barrier alongside a stairway, walkway, etc., made of horizontal rails supported by widely spaced upright pieces.

rail•ler•y (rā′lə rē) /ˈreyləriy/ *n., pl.* **-ler•ies. 1.** [*noncount*] good-humored joking or teasing; banter. **2.** [*count*] a bantering remark.

rail•road (rāl′rōd′) /ˈreyl,rowd/ *n.* [*count*] **1.** a permanent road made of rails, commonly in one or more pairs of continuous lines forming a track or tracks, on which locomotives and cars are run for carrying passengers, freight, and mail. **2.** an entire system of such roads together with its engines, cars, buildings, etc.: *a transcontinental railroad.* —*v.* [~ + *obj*] **3.** to transport by means of a railroad. **4.** to push (a law or bill) quickly through a law-making body so that there is not enough time for objections to be considered. **5.** to pressure, force, or coerce into an action or decision too quickly: *We were railroaded into signing a bad deal.* **6.** to convict (a defendant in a trial) too quickly and by means of false charges. —**rail′road′er,** *n.* [*count*] —**rail′road′ing,** *n.* [*noncount*]

rail•way (rāl′wā′) /ˈreyl,wey/ *n.* [*count*] **1.** a railroad operating over short distances. **2.** RAILROAD.

rai•ment (rā′mənt) /ˈreymənt/ *n.* [*noncount*] clothing; apparel.

rain (rān) /reyn/ *n.* **1.** [*noncount*] water that is condensed from the vapor in the atmosphere and falls to earth in drops. **2.** a rainfall, rainstorm, or shower: [*count*]: *a heavy rain.* [*noncount*]: *a fifty percent chance of rain.* **3. rains,** [*plural; usually: the* + ~] a rainy season; seasonal rainfall. **4.** [*count; usually singular*] a heavy and continuous fall of something usually unwelcome: *a rain of blows.* —*v.* **5.** [*no obj; it* + ~] (of rain) to fall: *It rained all night.* **6.** to (cause to) come down like rain: [*no obj*]: *Bombs rained from above. Tears rained from their eyes.* [~ + *obj*]: *The jets rained bombs down on the enemy position.* **7.** [~ + *obj*] to offer or give in great quantity; shower: *to rain favors upon a person.* **8. rain out,** [~ + *obj; usually: be* + *~-ed*] to cancel or postpone because of rain: *The last game was rained out.* —***Idiom.*** **9. rain cats and dogs,** to rain heavily.

rain•bow (rān′bō′) /ˈreyn,bow/ *n.* [*count*] **1.** a bow or arch of colors appearing in the sky opposite the sun and caused by the sun's rays passing through drops of rain. **2.** a wide variety or range: *The bouquet was a rainbow of colors.* —*adj.* [*before a noun*] **3.** of many colors; multicolored. **4.** made up of different races, groups, etc.: *a rainbow political coalition.*

rain′ check′ or **rain′check′,** *n.* [*count*] **1.** an offered or requested postponement of an invitation until a more convenient time. **2.** a ticket or piece of paper allowing a customer to buy an out-of-stock sale item at a later date for the sale price. **3.** a ticket for future use given to customers at an outdoor event that has been postponed or interrupted by rain.

rain•coat (rān′kōt′) /ˈreyn,kowt/ *n.* [*count*] a waterproof or water-repellent coat worn as protection against rain.

rain•drop (rān′drop′) /ˈreyn,drɒp/ *n.* [*count*] a drop of rain.

rain•fall (rān′fôl′) /ˈreyn,fɔl/ *n.* the amount of water falling in rain, snow, etc., within a given time and area, usually expressed as a total: [*count*]: *a rainfall of 70 inches a year.* [*noncount*]: *areas where rainfall is slight.*

rain′ for′est or **rain′for′est,** *n.* [*count*] a tropical forest, usually of tall, densely growing, broad-leaved, evergreen trees in an area where much rainfall occurs.

rain•mak•er (rān′mā′kər) /ˈreyn,meykər/ *n.* [*count*] **1.** (among American Indians) a medicine man who by various rituals and prayers tries to bring rain. **2.** a person who tries to bring on rainfall by artificial techniques, as the seeding of clouds with silver iodide crystals. **3.** an executive or lawyer who is able to get clients, produce income or sales, etc., esp. by using political or other connections.

rain•storm (rān′stôrm′) /ˈreyn,stɔrm/ *n.* [*count*] a storm with heavy rain.

rain•wa•ter (rān′wô′tər, -wot′ər) /ˈreyn,wɔtər, -,wɒtər/ *n.* [*noncount*] water fallen as rain.

rain•y (rā′nē) /ˈreyniy/ *adj.,* **-i•er, -i•est.** full of or being like rain; having great amounts of rain: *the rainy season.*

raise (rāz) /reyz/ *v.,* **raised, rais•ing,** *n.* —*v.* [~ + *obj*] **1.** to move to a higher position; lift up; elevate: *She raised her head and looked around.* **2.** to set upright: *When the flagpole fell they raised it again.* [~ + *oneself*]: *She raised herself to her feet.* **3.** to increase in amount, degree, strength, pitch, or force: *He raised his voice so they could hear him.* **4.** to promote the growth or development of; grow or breed: *to raise corn.* **5.** to serve in the capacity of parent to; bring up; rear: *to raise a child.* **6.** to present for consideration; put forward: *I'd like to raise a question.* **7.** to give rise to; bring about: *raised a riot.* **8.** to build; erect: *to raise a house.* **9.** to restore to life: *to raise the dead.* **10.** to give a feeling of new life, excitement, or vigor to; animate: *The news raised her spirits.* **11.** to advance in rank or position; elevate: *to raise her to the rank of colonel.* **12.** to assemble or collect: *to raise an army.* **13.** to utter (a cry, shout, etc.): *raised a cheer.* **14.** to cause to be heard: *to raise an alarm.* **15.** to cause (dough) to rise by expansion and become light, as by the use of yeast. **16.** to end (a siege, restriction, etc.): *They raised the blockade by withdrawing their forces.* **17.** to establish communication with by radio: *tried to raise headquarters on the VHF band.* —*n.* [*count*] **18.** an increase in amount, as of wages. **19.** the amount of such an increase: *a fifty-dollar-a-week raise.* **20.** an act or instance of raising.

rai•sin (rā′zin) /ˈreyzɪn/ *n.* [*count*] a sweet grape that has been dried in the sun or by artificial means.

ra•jah or **ra•ja** (rä′jə) /ˈrɑdʒə/ *n.* [*count*], *pl.* **-jahs** or **-jas.** a title of a prince and chief in India and areas of Southeast Asia once subject to Indian influence.

rake[1] (rāk) /reyk/ *n., v.,* **raked, rak•ing.** —*n.* [*count*] **1.** a long-handled tool used in farming or gardening, having teeth or tines for gathering cut grass, dead leaves, hay, etc., or for smoothing the surface of the ground. —*v.* **2.** to clear, smooth, or prepare with a rake: [*no obj*]: *raking and digging in the garden.* [~ + *obj*]: *She was raking the yard.* **3.** [~ + *obj*] to gather, draw together, or remove with a rake: *raking the dead leaves.* **4.** to gather or collect, esp. a great deal: [~ + *in* + *obj*]: *to rake in money.* [~ + *obj* + *in*]: *She was raking money in.* **5.** to bring (something) to light or to another's attention, esp. something that might better be forgotten: [~ + *obj* + *up*]: *to rake a scandal up.* [~ + *up* + *obj*]: *tried to rake up a scandal.* **6.** [~ + *obj*] to scrape; scratch: *raked his hair with his fingers.* **7.** to fire guns along the length of: [*no obj*]: *Machine gun fire raked through the village.* [~ + *obj*]: *The jet fighters raked the side of the tanker.*

rake[2] (rāk) /reyk/ *n.* [*count*] a man devoted to a life of heavy drinking and sexual affairs.

rake′-off′, *n.* [*count; singular*] a share or amount taken or received esp. illegally.

rak•ish[1] (rā′kish) /ˈreykɪʃ/ *adj.* like a rake; too interested in a wild life of heavy drinking and sexual affairs. —**rak′ish•ly,** *adv.* —**rak′ish•ness,** *n.* [*noncount*]

rak•ish[2] (rā′kish) /ˈreykɪʃ/ *adj.* smart; dashing: *a rakish hat.*

ral•ly (ral′ē) /ˈræliy/ *v.,* **-lied, -ly•ing,** *n., pl.* **-lies.** —*v.* **1.**

to gather and organize or inspire anew: [~ + *obj*]: *The general rallied the scattered troops.* [*no obj*]: *The scattered troops rallied.* **2.** to (cause to) draw or be called together for a common action or effort: [~ + *obj*]: *The candidate rallied his supporters.* [*no obj*]: *The candidate's supporters rallied in a demonstration of support.* **3.** to concentrate or revive, such as one's strength or spirits: [~ + *obj*]: *He rallied his strength for one last effort.* [*no obj*]: *He has rallied somewhat but is still sick.* **4.** [*no obj*] to come to the assistance of a person, party, or cause: *The workers rallied around their injured fellows.* **5.** [*no obj*] **a.** (of securities) to rise sharply in price after a drop. **b.** (of a securities market) to show increased activity after a slow period. **—*n.*** [*count*] **6.** a renewal or recovery of strength, activity, etc., after a disorder or setback. **7.** a mass meeting of people gathered to promote a common cause, often marked by efforts to stir up enthusiasm: *a political rally.* **8.** a sharp rise in price or active trading after a declining market. **9.** (in tennis, badminton, etc.) an exchange of strokes between players before a point is scored. **10.** the scoring of many runs in baseball or points in a game, esp. when coming from behind. **11.** a long-distance automobile race, esp. for sports cars, held over public roads, with numerous checkpoints along the route.

ram (ram) /ræm/ *n.*, *v.*, **rammed, ram•ming.** **—*n.*** [*count*] **1.** a male sheep. **2.** a device for battering, crushing, driving, or forcing something, such as a battering ram. **—*v.*** **3.** to strike with great force; dash violently against: [*no obj*]: *The car rammed into the wall.* [~ + *obj*]: *The driver rammed the car into the wall.* **4.** [~ + *obj*] to cram; stuff: *to ram food down their throats.* **5.** [~ + *obj*] to push firmly; force: *to ram a bill through the Senate.*

ram•ble (ram′bəl) /ˈræmbəl/ *v.*, **-bled, -bling,** *n.* **—*v.*** [*no obj*] **1.** to wander around in a leisurely, aimless manner for pleasure; stroll. **2.** to have a course or direction with many turns or windings, as a stream or path. **3.** to talk or write in a wandering manner, often for a long time. **—*n.*** [*count*] **4.** a leisurely walk without a definite route.

ram•bler (ram′blər) /ˈræmblər/ *n.* [*count*] **1.** one that rambles. **2.** any of several climbing roses with clusters of small flowers.

ram•bling (ram′bling) /ˈræmblɪŋ/ *adj.* **1.** having many haphazard extensions: *a rambling old farmhouse.* **2.** aimless; wandering: *a long, rambling answer.*

ram•bunc•tious (ram bungk′shəs) /ræmˈbʌŋkʃəs/ *adj.* difficult to control or handle; wild; boisterous. —**ram•bunc′tious•ness,** *n.* [*noncount*]

ram•i•fi•ca•tion (ram′ə fi kā′shən) /ˌræməfɪˈkeyʃən/ *n.* [*count*] a consequence; outgrowth: *The new tax law has many ramifications for anyone trying to save money.*

ram•i•fy (ram′ə fī′) /ˈræməˌfay/ *v.* [*no obj*], **-fied, -fy•ing.** to divide or spread out into branches or branchlike parts; extend into subdivisions: *The nerve endings ramify.*

ram•jet (ram′jet′) /ˈræmˌdʒɛt/ *n.* [*count*] a jet engine which is run by fuel injected into a stream of air compressed by the aircraft's forward speed.

ramp (ramp) /ræmp/ *n.* [*count*] **1.** a sloping surface connecting two levels. **2.** any long, sloping walk or passageway. **3.** a movable staircase for entering or leaving an airplane. **4.** a road leading on or off a highway or expressway: *an exit ramp.*

ram•page (ram′pāj; *v. also* ram pāj′) /ˈræmpeydʒ; *v. also* ræmˈpeydʒ/ *n.*, *v.*, **-paged, -pag•ing.** **—*n.*** [*count*] **1.** a sudden occurrence of violently reckless or destructive behavior: *went on a rampage.* **—*v.*** [*no obj*] **2.** to rush or behave furiously or violently: *The gangs rampaged through the towns.*

ramp•ant (ram′pənt) /ˈræmpənt/ *adj.* growing or spreading steadily and without stopping; widespread: *a rampant rumor; rampant disease.* —**ramp′ant•ly,** *adv.*

ram•part (ram′pärt, -pərt) /ˈræmpɑrt, -pərt/ *n.* [*count*] **1.** a mound of earth, rubble, or similar material raised around a place for protection. **2.** such a mound together with a stone or earth structure on top. See -PARE-[1].

ram•rod (ram′rod′) /ˈræmˌrɒd/ *n.* [*count*] **1.** a rod for cleaning or for pushing down the gunpowder into an old-type gun. **—*adj.*** [*before a noun*] **2.** stiff and straight as a ramrod: *stood at ramrod attention.*

ram•shack•le (ram′shak′əl) /ˈræmˌʃækəl/ *adj.* [*usually before a noun*] loosely made or held together; rickety; shaky: *a ramshackle house.*

ran (ran) /ræn/ *v.* pt. of RUN.

ranch (ranch) /ræntʃ/ *n.* [*count*] **1.** a place of business for raising horses, cattle, and livestock, usually a very large farm in which there is enough land to support the grazing of the animals. **2.** a farm or ranchlike enterprise that raises a single crop or animal: *a mink ranch.* **3.** RANCH HOUSE (def. 2). **—*v.*** [*no obj*] **4.** to own, manage, or work on a ranch. —**ranch′er,** *n.* [*count*]

ranch′ house′, *n.* [*count*] **1.** the main house on a ranch. **2.** any one-story house.

ran•cid (ran′sid) /ˈrænsɪd/ *adj.* having an unpleasant smell or taste, usually because of decay: *rancid butter.* —**ran•cid•i•ty** (ran sid′i tē) /rænˈsɪdɪtiy/ **ran′cid•ness,** *n.* [*noncount*]

ran•cor (rang′kər) /ˈræŋkər/ *n.* [*noncount*] bitter resentment, anger, or ill will; malice. Also, *esp. Brit.,* **ran′cour.** —**ran′cor•ous,** *adj.*: *a rancorous debate.*

ran•dom (ran′dəm) /ˈrændəm/ *adj.* **1.** occurring or done without definite aim, reason, plan, or pattern: *a few random examples; random killings.* **2.** *Statistics.* of or being a process of selection in which each item of a group has an equal chance of being chosen. **—*Idiom.*** **3. at random,** without regard to rules, schedules, purpose, pattern, etc.: *chose colors at random.* —**ran′dom•ly,** *adv.*

ran•dom•ize (ran′də mīz′) /ˈrændəˌmayz/ *v.* [~ + *obj*], **-ized, -iz•ing.** to arrange, select, or distribute in a random manner. —**ran•dom•i•za•tion** (ran′də mə zā′shən) /ˈrændəməˈzeyʃən/ *n.* [*noncount*]

R and R or **R&R,** an abbreviation of: **1.** rest and recreation. **2.** rest and recuperation. **3.** rest and relaxation. **4.** rock and roll.

rand•y (ran′dē) /ˈrændiy/ *adj.*, **-i•er, -i•est.** sexually aroused; full of sexual desire or lust.

rang (rang) /ræŋ/ *v.* pt. of RING[2].

range (rānj) /reyndʒ/ *n.*, *adj.*, *v.*, **ranged, rang•ing.** **—*n.*** **1.** [*count*] the extent to which, or the limits between which, something can change or vary: *a price range between $500 and $1,000.* **2.** the extent, scope, or distance of something in which it can operate or in which it is effective: [*noncount*]: *one's range of vision.* [*count; usually singular*]: *His singing voice has a range of an octave.* **3.** the distance of the target from the weapon: [*noncount*]: *She was shot at close range.* [*count*]: *The bullet was fired from a range of three feet.* **4.** [*count*] an area equipped with targets for practice in shooting: *a rifle range.* **5.** [*count*] an area used for testing missiles. **6.** [*count*] a row, line, or series of things, as of similar products; a number of different things of the same general sort or type: *a wide range of computer equipment.* **7.** [*count*] Also called **rangeland.** an area of land that is or may be traveled over, esp. an open region for the grazing of livestock. **8.** [*count*] the region or area over which a population or species of animal or plant is found. **9.** a chain of mountains forming a single system: [*count*]: *an important mountain range.* [*often: the* + ~]: *the Cascade Range.* **10.** [*count*] a large cooking stove having burners on the top surface and containing one or more ovens. **—*adj.*** [*before a noun*] **11.** working or grazing on a range: *range animals.* **—*v.*** **12.** [*no obj; not: be* + *~-ing*] to vary or be within certain limits: *Her emotions ranged from joy to despair.* **13.** to move around or through (a region or area): [*no obj*]: *The buffalo ranged over the whole state.* [~ + *obj*]: *Explorers ranged the entire region.* **14.** [*no obj*] to extend or wander over, so as to include or cover: *Their talks ranged over a variety of subjects.* **15.** [~ + *obj*] to arrange (persons or things) in rows or lines or in a specific position: *to range the books in the library.* **16.** [~ + *obj*] to place in a particular class; classify: *to range errors into different categories.*

rang•er (rān′jər) /ˈreyndʒər/ *n.* [*count*] **1.** FOREST RANGER. **2.** one of a body of armed guards who patrol a region. **3.** a person who ranges or roves. **4.** (esp. in Texas) a member of the state police.

rang•y (rān′jē) /ˈreyndʒiy/ *adj.*, **-i•er, -i•est.** **1.** (of animals or people) slender and having long arms or legs. **2.** able to range over large areas. **3.** (of land) mountainous. —**rang′i•ness,** *n.* [*noncount*]

rank[1] (rangk) /ræŋk/ *n.* **1.** [*count*] a social or official position or standing, as in the armed forces: *the rank of captain.* **2.** [*noncount*] high position or station: *a person of rank.* **3.** [*noncount*] relative position or standing: *a writer of the first rank.* **4.** [*count*] a row or series of things or persons: *The orchestra players were arranged in ranks.* **5. ranks,** [*plural*] the members of an armed service apart from its officers; enlisted personnel. **6.** Usually, **ranks.** [*plural*] the people in a group, or the general body of any organization apart from the officers or leaders: *in the ranks of the unemployed.* **—*v.*** **7.** to (cause to) be assigned to a particular position, class, standing, etc.: [~ + *obj*]: *to be ranked among the ex-*

perts. [~ + *obj* + *as* + *obj*]: *They ranked him as one of the best pitchers in the world.* [*no obj; not: be* + ~*-ing*]: *Their work ranked well above that of the other students.* **—*Idiom.* 8. break ranks, a.** to leave an assigned position in a military formation. **b.** to withdraw support from one's colleagues, political party, or the like.

rank² (rangk) /ræŋk/ *adj.*, **-er, -est. 1.** growing thickly; vigorous: *rank foliage.* **2.** having an offensive or very unpleasant smell or taste: *a rank cigar.* **3.** [*before a noun*] complete; utter; absolute: *a rank amateur.* **—rank′ness,** *n.* [*noncount*]

rank′ and file′, *n.* [*plural*] the members of any organization, esp. a union, apart from its leaders or officers.

rank•ing (rang′king) /ˈræŋkɪŋ/ *adj.* [*before a noun*] **1.** being superior in rank, position, etc.: *a ranking diplomat.* **2.** highly regarded: *a ranking authority.* **3.** (used after another word) of or having a certain rank: *a low-ranking executive.*

ran•kle (rang′kəl) /ˈræŋkəl/ *v.*, **-kled, -kling. 1.** [*no obj*] to continue to irritate; cause resentment: *The principal's insensitivity to the needs of the child still rankles.* **2.** [~ + *obj*] to cause (a person) such irritation or resentment: *The principal's insensitivity still rankles the parents.*

ran•sack (ran′sak) /ˈrænsæk/ *v.* [~ + *obj*] **1.** to search thoroughly and vigorously through: *We ransacked the shelves and dresser drawers for the lost money.* **2.** to search through so as to rob: *The burglars ransacked the house.*

ran•som (ran′səm) /ˈrænsəm/ *n.* **1.** [*noncount*] the release of a prisoner, kidnapped person, etc., for a demanded price. **2.** [*count*] the price paid or demanded for such freeing or releasing: *a ransom of $30,000.* **—*v.*** [~ + *obj*] **3.** to free or release someone held prisoner or kidnapped by paying a demanded price. **—ran′som•er,** *n.* [*count*]

rant (rant) /rænt/ *v.* to speak or talk in a wild or violent way; rave: [*no obj*]: *She came home ranting about how everybody hated her.* [~ + *that clause*]: *She ranted that nobody loved her.*

rap (rap) /ræp/ *v.*, **rapped, rap•ping,** *n.* **—*v.* 1.** to strike, esp. with a quick, sharp, light blow: [~ + *obj*]: *rapped him on the knuckles.* [*no obj*]: *Somebody rapped on the door.* **2.** [~ (+ *out*) + *obj*] to say or shout sharply: *to rap (out) orders.* **3.** [~ + *obj*] *Slang.* to criticize severely: *Even his teammates were quick to rap him for his poor sportsmanship.* **4.** [*no obj*] *Slang.* to talk or discuss, esp. freely and at great length; chat: *rapping about music and politics.* **5.** [*no obj*] to talk rhythmically to the beat of rap music. **—*n.* 6.** [*count*] a quick, smart blow: *a rap on the knuckles.* **7.** [*count*] the sound produced by such a blow: *a rap on the door.* **8.** [*noncount*] *Slang.* blame or punishment: *not going to take the rap for your mistakes.* **9.** [*count*] *Slang.* a criminal charge: *a murder rap.* **10.** [*count*] *Slang.* report; reputation: *The rap on her is that she quits too easily.* **11.** [*count*] *Slang.* a talk or conversation; chat. **12.** [*noncount*] a kind of music with an insistent beat and rhymed words that follow the beat. **—*Idiom.* 13. beat the rap,** *Slang.* to avoid punishment, as for a crime. **—rap′per,** *n.* [*count*]

ra•pa•cious (rə pā′shəs) /rəˈpeyʃəs/ *adj.* **1.** overly grasping; greedy: *rapacious gangsters.* **2.** (of animals) living by capturing prey. **—ra•pa′cious•ness, ra•pac•i•ty** (rə pas′i tē) /rəˈpæsɪtiy/ *n.* [*noncount*]

rape¹ (rāp) /reyp/ *n., v.,* **raped, rap•ing. —*n.* 1.** the unlawful act of forcing (someone) to have sexual relations: [*noncount*]: *victims of rape.* [*count*]: *convicted of several rapes.* **2.** [*count; usually singular*] an act of spoiling or destroying on a large scale: *the rape of the countryside.* **—*v.* 3.** to force (someone) to have sexual relations: [~ + *obj*]: *He was accused of raping several women.* [*no obj*]: *might rape again.* **4.** [~ + *obj*] to despoil: *developers raping the beautiful countryside.* **—rap′er,** *n.* [*count*] **—rap′ist,** *n.* [*count*] See -RAPE-.

rape² (rāp) /reyp/ *n.* [*noncount*] a plant of the mustard family whose leaves are used as food for animals and whose seeds yield a useful oil.

-rape-, *root.* *-rape-* comes from Latin, where it has the meaning "carry off by force." This meaning is found in such words as: RAPE, RAPID, RAPINE, RAPT, RAPTURE.

rap•id (rap′id) /ˈræpɪd/ *adj.*, **-er, -est,** *n.* **—*adj.* 1.** fast, quick-moving, swift: *rapid motion; rapid growth.* **—*n.* 2.** Usually, **rapids.** [*plural*] a part of a river where the current runs very swiftly. **—ra•pid•i•ty** (rə pid′i tē) /rəˈpɪdɪtiy/ **rap′id•ness,** *n.* [*noncount*] **—rap′id•ly,** *adv.* See -RAPE-.

rap′id tran′sit, *n.* [*noncount*] a system of public transportation in a metropolitan area, usually a subway or elevated train system.

ra•pi•er (rā′pē ər) /ˈreypiyər/ *n.* [*count*] **1.** a narrow sword having a double-edged blade. **—*adj.*** [*before a noun*] **2.** sharp and cutting like a sword: *rapier wit.*

rap•ine (rap′in, -īn) /ˈræpɪn, -ayn/ *n.* [*noncount*] the violent taking and carrying off of another's property; plunder. See -RAPE-.

rap•port (ra pôr′, -pōr′, rə-) /ræˈpɔr, -ˈpowr, rə-/ *n.* a relationship, esp. one that is sympathetic and understanding: [*count; usually singular*]: *a close rapport between teacher and students.* [*noncount*]: *a feeling of rapport.* See -PORT-.

rap•proche•ment (rap′rōsh män′) /ˌræprowʃˈmɑ̃/ *n.* [*count*] an establishment or renewal of peaceful relations.

rap•scal•lion (rap skal′yən) /ræpˈskælyən/ *n.* [*count*] a rascal.

rap′ sheet′, *n.* [*count*] *Slang.* a police record of a person's arrests and convictions.

rapt (rapt) /ræpt/ *adj.* **1.** deeply interested in or absorbed in something: *a rapt listener.* **2.** filled or carried off with emotion. **3.** showing rapture: *a rapt smile.* **—rapt′ly,** *adv.* **—rapt′ness,** *n.* [*noncount*] See -RAPE-.

rap•ture (rap′chər) /ˈræptʃər/ *n., v.,* **-tured, -tur•ing. —*n.* 1.** [*noncount*] overwhelming joy or delight; ecstasy. **2.** [*count*] Often, **raptures.** [*plural*] an expression of ecstatic delight. **—rap′tur•ous,** *adj.* See -RAPE-.

rare¹ (râr) /rɛər/ *adj.*, **rar•er, rar•est. 1.** very uncommon: *a rare disease.* **2.** light; thin; having the parts not tightly packed together: *The air was rare in the mountains.* **3.** [*before a noun*] unusually great: *a rare display of courage.* **—rare′ness,** *n.* [*noncount*]

rare² (râr) /rɛər/ *adj.*, **rar•er, rar•est.** cooked so as to be still red on the inside: *rare steak.* **—rare′ness,** *n.* [*noncount*]

rar•e•fied also **rar•i•fied** (râr′ə fīd′) /ˈrɛərəˌfayd/ *adj.* **1.** extremely high or elevated; lofty; grand: *rarefied language.* **2.** thin: *rarefied atmosphere.*

rare•ly (râr′lē) /ˈrɛərliy/ *adv.* seldom: *He is rarely late.*

rar•ing (râr′ing) /ˈrɛərɪŋ/ *adj.* [*be* + ~ + *to* + *verb*] very eager or anxious; enthusiastic: *They were raring to go.*

rar•i•ty (râr′i tē) /ˈrɛərɪtiy/ *n., pl.* **-ties. 1.** [*noncount*] the state or quality of being rare. **2.** [*count*] something rare or uncommon: *Earthquakes are a rarity hereabouts.*

ras•cal (ras′kəl) /ˈræskəl/ *n.* [*count*] **1.** a dishonest person. **2.** a mischievous person or animal.

-rase-, *root.* *-rase-* comes from Latin, where it has the meaning "rub; scrape." This meaning is found in such words as: ABRASION, ERASE, RAZE, RAZOR.

rash¹ (rash) /ræʃ/ *adj.*, **-er, -est. 1.** acting quickly and without thinking: *a rash leader.* **2.** made or done quickly or without careful thought: *rash promises.* **—rash′ly,** *adv.* **—rash′ness,** *n.* [*noncount*]

rash² (rash) /ræʃ/ *n.* [*count*] **1.** an area of spots or redness on the skin resulting from an irritation or disorder of some kind. **2.** numerous occurrences of something at about the same time: *a rash of robberies.*

rash•er (rash′ər) /ˈræʃər/ *n.* [*count*] **1.** a thin slice of bacon or ham for frying or broiling. **2.** a serving of three or four slices, esp. of bacon.

rasp (rasp) /ræsp/ *v.* **1.** to scrape or grate with or as if with a rough instrument: [~ + *obj*]: *You can feel the kitten's rough little tongue rasping your hand.* [*no obj*]: *rasping on your hand.* **2.** [~ (+ *on*) + *obj*] to irritate: *The sound rasped (on) his nerves.* **3.** to say with a grating sound: [~ (+ *out*) + *obj*]: *to rasp (out) an order.* [~ + *obj* (+ *out*)]: *She rasped an order (out) to her secretary.* **—*n.*** [*count*] **4.** an act of rasping. **5.** a rasping sound. **6.** a coarse file having separate cone-shaped teeth. **—rasp′ing, rasp′y,** *adj.*, **-i•er, -i•est.**

rasp•ber•ry (raz′ber′ē, -bə rē) /ˈræzˌbɛriy, -bəriy/ *n.* [*count*], *pl.* **-ries. 1.** the fruit of a shrub of the rose family, made up of small and juicy red, black, or pale yellow berries. **2.** a shrub bearing this fruit. **3.** a reddish purple color, similar to the color of many raspberries. **4.** a loud spluttering noise made by blowing out air with the lips and tongue, used to express contempt or displeasure.

rat (rat) /ræt/ *n., interj., v.,* **rat•ted, rat•ting. —*n.*** [*count*] **1.** a long-tailed animal, a rodent, that resembles a mouse but is larger. **2.** *Slang.* a scoundrel; a disloyal or untrustworthy person. **3.** *Slang.* a person who abandons or betrays associates. **—*interj.* 4. rats,** (used to show disgust or disappointment). **—*v.* 5.** [~ + *on*] *Slang.* to inform on or betray one's associates: *She ratted on us when the cops caught her.* **—rat′like′,** *adj.*

ratch•et (rach′it) /ˈrætʃɪt/ *n.* [*count*] **1.** a toothed wheel or bar, with a bar that fits into its teeth so that it turns in one direction only. **—*v.* 2.** to move by degrees: [~ + *obj* + *up/down*]: *hoped to ratchet the economy up.* [~ + *up/down* + *obj*]: *Unemployment managed to ratchet down the economy.* [*no obj;* ~ + *up/down*]: *hoping the economy would ratchet up in time for the election.*

rate (rāt) /reyt/ *n., v.,* **rat•ed, rat•ing.** **—*n.*** [*count*] **1.** the amount of a charge or payment with reference to some basis of counting: *a high rate of interest on loans.* **2.** a certain amount of one thing considered in relation to a unit of another thing: *a rate of 10 cents a pound.* **3.** degree of speed or progress: *to work at a rapid rate.* **—*v.* 4.** to estimate the value or worth of; consider: [~ + *obj*]: *She is highly rated as a member of the department.* [~ + *obj* (+ *as*) + *obj*]: *I would rate him (as) a fine teacher.* **5.** [*no obj*] to be thought of as having value or standing: *He felt he didn't rate with his friends.* **6.** [~ + *obj*] to deserve or merit: *That event does not even rate a footnote in the history of that era.* **—*Idiom.* 7. at any rate,** in any event; in any case: *At any rate, you survived.* See -RATIO-.

rath•er (rath′ər) /ˈræðər/ *adv.* **1.** quite; to some extent; in some degree: *He's rather good at baseball.* **2.** in some degree: *I rather expect you'll regret it.* **3.** preferably; more willingly: *to die rather than yield.* **4.** more truly or correctly: *He is a painter or, rather, a person who draws in watercolors.* **5.** instead; on the contrary: *It's not generosity; rather, it's self-interest.* **—*Idiom.* 6. had** or **would rather,** to prefer that or to: *I would rather be fishing.*

raths•kel•ler (rät′skel′ər, rat′-, rath′-) /ˈrɑtˌskɛlər, ˈræt-, ˈræθ-/ *n.* [*count*] a restaurant or bar located below street level.

rat•i•fi•ca•tion (rat′ə fi kā′shən) /ˌrætəfɪˈkeyʃən/ *n.* [*noncount*] the act of formally expressing consent to or approval for an agreement, treaty, amendment, law, etc. See -RATIO-.

rat•i•fy (rat′ə fī′) /ˈrætəˌfay/ *v.* [~ + *obj*], **-fied, -fy•ing.** to formally approve an agreement, treaty, law, etc., by expressing agreement, consent, or approval: *to ratify an amendment.* **—rat′i•fi′er,** *n.* [*count*] See -RATIO-.

rat•ing (rā′ting) /ˈreytɪŋ/ *n.* [*count*] **1.** position or level given to something in comparison to others: *a good credit rating.* **2.** classification according to grade or rank, as in the navy. **3.** a percentage indicating the number of listeners to or viewers of a radio or television broadcast: *That show has great ratings.* See -RATIO-.

ra•tio (rā′shō, -shē ō′) /ˈreyʃow, -ʃiyˌow/ *n.* [*count*], *pl.* **-tios. 1.** the relation between two numbers or amounts, with respect to the number of times the first contains the second: *The ratio of 3 to 9 is the same as the ratio of 1 to 3.* **2.** rate; proportion: *The ratio of acceptances to rejections is very high.* See -RATIO-.

-ratio-, *root.* -*ratio*- comes from Latin, where it has the meaning "logic; reason; judgment." This meaning is found in such words as: IRRATIONAL, OVERRATED, RATE, RATIFY, RATIO, RATION, RATIONAL.

ra•tion (rash′ən, rā′shən) /ˈræʃən, ˈreyʃən/ *n.* [*count*] **1.** a fixed amount of food allowed for a certain amount of time: *a ration of two cupfuls of rice a day.* **2.** a fixed amount of anything allowed for a certain amount of time: *a ration of diesel fuel for their trucks.* **—*v.* 3.** to distribute as rations: [~ + *out* + *obj* + *to* + *obj*]: *to ration out food to an army.* [~ + *obj* + *out* + *to* + *obj*]: *to ration food out to an army.* **4.** [~ + *obj* + *to* + *obj*] to limit (someone) to a ration: *rationed herself to one television program a day.* **5.** [~ + *obj*] to restrict the use or distributing of: *to ration meat.* See -RATIO-.

ra•tion•al (rash′ə nl, rash′nl) /ˈræʃənl̩, ˈræʃnl̩/ *adj.* **1.** based on reason; fitting in with reason; sensible: *a rational decision.* **2.** using reason: *a rational negotiator.* **3.** sane; able to think or speak clearly and logically: *The patient seems perfectly rational.* **—ra•tion•al•i•ty** (rash′ə-nal′i tē) /ˌræʃəˈnælɪtiy/ *n.* [*noncount*] **—ra′tion•al•ly,** *adv.* See -RATIO-.

ra•tion•ale (rash′ə nal′) /ˌræʃəˈnæl/ *n.* **1.** [*noncount*] the fundamental or basic reason or reasons serving to account for something: *There is no rationale for such behavior.* **2.** [*count*] a statement of reasons or principles. See -RATIO-.

ra•tion•al•ism (rash′ə nl iz′əm) /ˈræʃənl̩ˌɪzəm/ *n.* [*noncount*] **1.** the principle or doctrine of using human reason as the basis for matters of opinion, belief, or conduct. **2.** a doctrine in philosophy that stresses the use of reason as opposed to religious faith. **—ra′tion•al•ist,** *n.* [*count*] See -RATIO-.

ra•tion•al•ize (rash′ə nl īz′, rash′nl-) /ˈræʃənl̩ˌayz, ˈræʃnl̩-/ *v.,* **-ized, -iz•ing. 1.** to find a reason, basis, or explanation (for actions) in causes that seem reasonable but do not reflect true, unconscious, or less acceptable causes: [~ + *obj*]: *He tried to rationalize his use of illegal drugs on the grounds that he was hyperactive and the drugs relaxed him.* [~ + *that clause*]: *When she was fired she rationalized that her supervisors had a grudge against her.* [*no obj*]: *Don't rationalize; be honest about your true motives.* **2.** [~ + *obj*] to make (a system) agree with or work according to reason: *to rationalize the payroll system.* **—ra•tion•al•i•za•tion** (rash′ə nl i zā′shən, rash′nl-) /ˌræʃənl̩ɪˈzeyʃən, ˌræʃnl̩-/ *n.* [*count; noncount*] See -RATIO-.

ra′tional num′ber, *n.* [*count*] a number that can be expressed exactly as an integer or fraction: *The square root of 3 is not a rational number.*

rat′ race′, *n.* [*count*] exhausting, highly competitive activity, esp. one aimed at success in business.

rat•tan (ra tan′, rə-) /ræˈtæn, rə-/ *n.* **1.** [*count*] Also called **rattan′ palm′.** a climbing palm. **2.** [*noncount*] the tough stems of such palms, used for wickerwork, canes, etc.

rat•tle (rat′l) /ˈrætl̩/ *v.,* **-tled, -tling,** *n.* **—*v.* 1.** to (cause to) make a rapid series of short, sharp sounds: [*no obj*]: *The doors rattled in the storm.* [~ + *obj*]: *I rattled the doorknob.* **2.** to (cause to) move noisily: [*no obj*]: *The old car rattled along the back roads.* [~ + *obj*]: *The wind rattled the metal can.* **3. rattle off,** to say or perform in a rapid or lively manner: [~ + *off* + *obj*]: *to rattle off the multiplication table.* [~ + *obj* + *off*]: *She rattled her answers off.* **4. rattle on,** [*no obj*] to chatter: *rattling on about his ailments.* **5.** [~ + *obj*] to confuse; make nervous; disconcert: *The speaker was rattled by that last question.* **—*n.*** [*count*] **6.** a rapid succession of short, sharp sounds. **7.** a baby's toy filled with small pellets that rattle when shaken. **8.** the series of horny, hollow rings at the end of a rattlesnake's tail, with which it produces a rattling sound. **—rat′tly,** *adj.*

rat•tler (rat′lər) /ˈrætlər/ *n.* [*count*] **1.** a rattlesnake. **2.** one that rattles.

rat•tle•snake (rat′l snāk′) /ˈrætl̩ˌsneyk/ *n.* [*count*] a snake, a pit viper, having a rattle at the end of the tail.

rat•tle•trap (rat′l trap′) /ˈrætl̩ˌtræp/ *n.* [*count*] a shaky, rattling object, such as a broken-down vehicle.

rat•tling (rat′ling) /ˈrætlɪŋ/ *adj.* **1.** brisk: *a rattling pace.* **2.** splendid; fine. **—*adv.* 3.** very: *a rattling good time.*

rat•trap (rat′trap′) /ˈrætˌtræp/ *n.* [*count*] **1.** a device for catching rats. **2.** a run-down, filthy, or broken-down place.

rat•ty (rat′ē) /ˈrætiy/ *adj.,* **-ti•er, -ti•est. 1.** full of rats. **2.** of or characteristic of a rat. **3.** wretched; shabby.

rau•cous (rô′kəs) /ˈrɔkəs/ *adj.* **1.** harsh; rough; unpleasant in sound; strident: *raucous laughter.* **2.** disorderly: *a raucous party.* **—rau′cous•ly,** *adv.* **—rau′cous•ness,** *n.* [*noncount*]

raunch (rônch, ränch) /rɔntʃ, rɑntʃ/ *n.* [*noncount*] indecency or obscenity.

raun•chy (rôn′chē, rän′-) /ˈrɔntʃiy, ˈrɑn-/ *adj.,* **-chi•er, -chi•est. 1.** dirty; slovenly: *a raunchy old jacket.* **2.** obscene; smutty: *a raunchy joke.* **—raun′chi•ness,** *n.* [*noncount*]

rav•age (rav′ij) /ˈrævɪdʒ/ *v.,* **-aged, -ag•ing,** *n.* **—*v.*** [~ + *obj*] **1.** to damage or injure severely: *The storm ravaged the coastline.* **—*n.* ravages,** [*plural*] **2.** great damage, destruction, or ruin: *the ravages of war.* See -RAPE-.

rave (rāv), *v.,* **raved, rav•ing,** *n., adj.* **—*v.* 1.** to talk wildly or irrationally: [*no obj*]: *raving with fever.* [~ + *that clause*]: *She raved that everyone hated her.* **2.** to talk or write with great or too great enthusiasm about something: [*no obj*]: *They raved about the movie.* [~ + *that clause*]: *They raved that she was a terrific teacher.* **—*n.*** [*count*] **3.** an act of raving. **4.** an enthusiastic review: *The play won raves from the critics.* **—*adj.*** [*before a noun*] **5.** enthusiastic: *rave reviews.*

rav•el (rav′əl) /ˈrævəl/ *v.* [~ + *obj*], **-eled, -el•ing** or (*esp. Brit.*) **-elled, -el•ling. 1.** to disentangle the threads or fibers of; unravel. **2.** to make clear; unravel. **3.** to entangle; enmesh; confuse.

ra•ven (rā′vən) /ˈreyvən/ *n.* [*count*] **1.** a very large bird having shiny black feathers and coloring and a loud, harsh call. **—*adj.* 2.** shining black: *raven hair.* **—ra′ven•like′,** *adj.*

rav•en•ous (rav′ə nəs) /ˈrævənəs/ *adj.* **1.** extremely hungry; famished. **2.** intensely eager: *ravenous for affection.* **—rav′en•ous•ly,** *adv.* See -RAPE-.

ra•vine (rə vēn′) /rəˈviyn/ *n.* [*count*] a narrow, steep-sided valley usually created by the effects of running water off the soil over a long time. See -RAPE-.

rav•ing (rā′ving) /ˈreyvɪŋ/ *adj.* **1.** talking wildly; delirious: *a raving maniac.* **2.** extraordinary in degree: *a raving beauty.* **—***adv.* **3.** completely: *raving mad.* **—***n.* **4.** Usually, **ravings.** [*plural*] talk that is wild or without reason: *the ravings of a madman.*

ra•vi•o•li (rav′ē ō′lē) /ˌræviyˈowliy/ *n.* small, square pockets of pasta, filled with cheese, ground meat, etc.: [*noncount; used with a singular verb*]: *Ravioli is a nutritious dish.* [*plural; used with a plural verb*]: *There were only eight ravioli in the package.*

rav•ish (rav′ish) /ˈrævɪʃ/ *v.* [~ + *obj*] **1.** to fill with strong emotion, esp. joy: *an art exhibit that ravishes the eye.* **2.** to rape. **—rav′ish•er,** *n.* [*count*] **—rav′ish•ment,** *n.* [*noncount*] See -RAPE-.

rav•ish•ing (rav′i shing) /ˈrævɪʃɪŋ/ *adj.* extremely beautiful or attractive: *a ravishing blonde.*

raw (rô) /rɔ/ *adj.*, **-er, -est,** *n.* **—***adj.* **1.** uncooked: *a raw carrot.* **2.** [*before a noun*] not processed, finished, treated, or refined: *raw cotton.* **3.** [*before a noun*] not pasteurized: *raw milk.* **4.** unnaturally or painfully open or exposed: *raw wounds.* **5.** vulgar; crude: *raw jokes.* **6.** inexperienced; untrained: *a raw recruit.* **7.** [*before a noun*] brutal: *a show of raw power.* **8.** harsh or unfair: *We got a raw deal when we were fired.* **9.** cold and wet: *a raw day.* **—*Idiom.*** **10. in the raw, a.** in the natural state: *nature in the raw.* **b.** nude; naked: *sleeping in the raw.* **—raw′ness,** *n.* [*noncount*]

raw•boned (rô′bōnd′) /ˈrɔˈbownd/ *adj.* having flesh or skin that seems to be stretched over a large-boned frame.

raw•hide (rô′hīd′) /ˈrɔˌhayd/ *n.* **1.** [*noncount*] skin of cattle or other animals that has not been tanned or prepared. **2.** [*count*] a rope or whip made of rawhide.

ray[1] (rā) /rey/ *n.* [*count*] **1.** a narrow beam of light. **2.** a slight sign or indication: *a ray of hope.* **3. a.** any of the lines or streams in which light appears to radiate from a bright body. **b.** a stream of particles all moving in the same straight line, as x-rays.

ray[2] (rā) /rey/ *n.* [*count*] a kind of fish having a flattened body and greatly enlarged front fins with the gills on the undersides.

ray•on (rā′on) /ˈreyɒn/ *n.* [*noncount*] **1.** a smooth, silklike material manufactured from cellulose, cotton, or wood chips. **2.** a fabric or yarn made of rayon.

raze or **rase** (rāz) /reyz/ *v.* [~ + *obj*], **razed** or **rased, raz•ing** or **ras•ing.** to level to the ground; tear down: *razed the buildings.* See -RASE-.

ra•zor (rā′zər) /ˈreyzər/ *n.* [*count*] a sharp-edged instrument used esp. for shaving the face or trimming hair. See -RASE-.

razz (raz) /ræz/ *v.* [~ + *obj*] to make fun of; mock.

raz′zle-daz′zle (raz′əl) /ˈræzəl/ *n.* [*noncount*] **1.** showy or fancy technique or effect, esp. such technique done to distract or confuse. **—***adj.* **2.** marked by razzle-dazzle: *a razzle-dazzle performance.*

R.C., an abbreviation of: Roman Catholic Church.

rcd., an abbreviation of: received.

rcpt., an abbreviation of: receipt.

rd, an abbreviation of: rod.

Rd., an abbreviation of: Road.

rd., an abbreviation of: **1.** road. **2.** round.

R.D., an abbreviation of: rural delivery.

re[1] (rā) /rey/ *n.* [*count*] the musical syllable used for the second tone in the ascending scale, after do.

re[2] (rē, rā) /riy, rey/ *prep.* with reference to; regarding: *Re your question, the answer is as follows.*

're (ər) /ər/ contraction of *are: They're leaving.*

re-, *prefix.* **1.** *re-* comes from Latin, and is attached to roots and sometimes words to form verbs and nouns meaning or referring to action in a backward direction: *re-* + *-cede-* → *recede (= fall back); re-* + *-vert-* → *revert (= turn back).* **2.** *re-* is also used to form verbs or nouns showing action in answer to or intended to undo or reverse a situation: *rebel; remove; respond; restore; revoke.* **3.** *re-* is also used to form verbs or nouns showing action that is done over, often with the meaning that the outcome of the original action was in some way not enough or not long lasting, or that the performance of the new action brings back an earlier state of affairs: *recapture; reoccur; repossess; resole (= put another sole on a shoe); retype.*

reach (rēch) /riytʃ/ *v.* **1.** [~ + *obj*] to get to or as far as; arrive at: *The boat reached the shore.* **2.** [~ + *obj*] to succeed in touching or seizing, as with an outstretched hand or a pole: *to reach a book on a high shelf.* **3.** [*no obj*] to make a movement or effort to touch or seize something: *to reach for a weapon.* **4.** to stretch or hold out; extend: [~ + *out* + *obj*]: *reaching out a hand in greeting.* [~ + *obj* + *out*]: *She reached a hand out in greeting.* **5.** to stretch or extend so as to touch or meet: [~ + *obj*]: *The bookcase reaches the ceiling.* [*no obj*]: *Her dress reached to the floor.* **6.** [~ + *obj*] to establish communication with: *I called but couldn't reach you.* **7.** [~ + *obj*] to amount to: *The cost will reach millions.* **8.** to carry to; penetrate to: [~ + *obj*]: *The loud bang reached our ears.* [*no obj*]: *The sky stretched for miles ahead, as far as the eye could reach.* **9.** [~ + *obj*] to achieve, arrive at, or gain through effort: *to reach an agreement.* **10.** [~ + *obj*] to make contact with: *That one commercial could reach millions of Americans.* **11.** [~ + *obj*] to succeed in influencing, impressing, rousing, etc.: *I pleaded with her, but I couldn't reach her.* **12.** [*no obj*] to say or agree without enough evidence: *I'd be reaching if I claimed I really had an answer to your problem.* **—***n.* **13.** [*count*] an act or instance of reaching: *He made a reach for the gun.* **14.** [*noncount*] the range of effective action, power, or capacity: *If you are within reach of my voice, please answer.* **15.** Usually, **reaches.** [*plural*] level, rank, or area: *the upper reaches of the atmosphere.*

re•act (rē akt′) /riyˈækt/ *v.* [*no obj*] **1.** to respond to a stimulus: *reacted to the dust by sneezing.* **2.** to act in a reverse direction or manner, esp. so as to return to a condition that existed earlier in time. **3.** to act in opposition: *taxpayers reacting against corruption with their votes.* **4.** to undergo a chemical change: *The iodine and the unknown chemical reacted by giving off smoke.* See -ACT-.

re•ac•tant (rē ak′tənt) /riyˈæktənt/ *n.* [*count*] a substance that undergoes a chemical change in a given reaction.

re•ac•tion (rē ak′shən) /riyˈækʃən/ *n.* **1.** [*count*] an action in a reverse direction or manner: *For every action there is an equal and opposite reaction.* **2.** [*noncount*] a tendency to return to an earlier political system or social order. **3.** action in response to some influence, event, etc.: [*noncount*]: *the nation's reaction to the president's speech.* [*count*]: *My reactions are mixed.* **4.** [*count*] **a.** a response by the body to an action or condition. **b.** a change in the body that shows sensitivity to foreign matter: *an allergic reaction to cat hair.* **5.** [*count*] the action of chemical agents upon each other.

re•ac•tion•ar•y (rē ak′shə ner′ē) /riyˈækʃəˈnɛriy/ *adj., n., pl.* **-ar•ies.** **—***adj.* **1.** of, relating to, or calling for extreme political conservatism, or for a return to an earlier system or order. **—***n.* [*count*] **2.** a person who is reactionary.

re•ac′tor (rē ak′tər) /riyˈæktər/ *n.* [*count*] **1.** one that reacts. **2.** an apparatus in which a nuclear-fission chain reaction is sustained and controlled.

read[1] (rēd) /riyd/ *v.*, **read** (red), **read•ing** (rē′ding) /ˈriydɪŋ/ *n.* **—***v.* **1.** to look at so as to understand the meaning of (something written, printed, etc.): [~ + *obj*]: *reading the newspaper; could read music.* [*no obj*]: *When did she start reading?* [~ + *(that) clause*]: *I read that there was a big problem in your school.* **2.** to say aloud or in speech (something written, printed, etc.): [~ + *obj* + *to* + *obj*]: *to read a story to a child.* [~ + *obj* + *obj*]: *I read her a story.* [~ + *to* + *obj*]: *The instructor read aloud to the class.* **3.** [~ + *obj*] to recognize and understand the meaning of (gestures, symbols, signals, or other communication): *to read braille; to read lips.* **4.** [~ + *obj*] to figure out the significance of, pattern behind, etc., by observing outward appearances: *to read the dark sky as the threat of a storm.* **5.** [~ + *obj* + *into* + *obj*] to infer or guess at (something not expressed) from what is read, considered, or observed: *You're reading meanings into this incident that really aren't there.* **6.** [*not: be* + *~-ing*] to give or have a certain form or wording: [~ + *obj*]: *For "one thousand" another version reads "ten thousand."* [*no obj*]: *a rule that reads in two different ways.* **7.** [*not: be* + *~-ing; ~* + *obj*] to register or indicate, as a thermometer: *The temperature reads a balmy seventy-two degrees.* **8.** [~ + *obj*] to learn by or as if by reading: *to read a person's thoughts.* **9.** [~ + *obj*] to bring, put, etc., by reading: *to read oneself to sleep.* **10.** [~ + *obj*] (in computers) to obtain (data or programs) from an outside disk or tape and place in a computer's memory. **11.** [~ + *obj*] *Brit.* to study (a subject), as at a university: *reading history at Oxford.* **12.** [*no obj*] to be readable in a certain way: *The essay reads well.* **13. read up on,** [~ + *up* + *on* + *obj*] to learn about by reading: *I* read up on the subject. —n. [count] **14.** an act or instance of reading. **15.** something read: *Her new novel is a good read.* —***Idiom.*** **16. read between the lines,** [no obj] to understand more than is directly stated. **17. read someone's lips,** [used as a command] said to stress that what follows should already be clear: *Read my lips—I don't want the job.*

read[2] (red) /rɛd/ *adj.* having knowledge gained by reading: *a well-read person.*

read•a•ble (rē′də bəl) /ˈriydəbəl/ *adj.* **1.** easy or interesting to read: *a very readable book about a difficult topic.* **2.** of or relating to machines or a type of print that can be read by special scanning devices: *machine-readable.* —**read•a•bil•i•ty** (rē′də bil′i tē) /ˌriydəˈbɪlɪtiy/ *n.* [noncount]

read•er (rē′dər) /ˈriydər/ *n.* [count] **1.** a person who reads (something) in a specified way: *a fast reader.* **2.** a textbook for students learning to read: *a first-grade reader.* **3.** a lecturer or instructor in some British institutions. **4.** *Computers.* a device that reads data, programs, or other information into a computer for storage or use.

read•er•ship (rē′dər ship′) /ˈriydərˌʃɪp/ *n.* the people who read a publication: [count; usually singular]: *The magazine has a readership of several hundred thousand.* [noncount]: *Readership has declined.*

read•i•ly (red′l ē) /ˈrɛdl̩iy/ *adv.* **1.** promptly; quickly; easily: *The information was readily available.* **2.** willingly: *He readily agreed to help us out.*

read•ing (rē′ding) /ˈriydɪŋ/ *n.* **1.** [noncount] the action or practice of a person who reads. **2.** [count] the interpretation given in the performance of a dramatic part, musical composition, etc. **3.** [noncount] the extent to which a person has read; literary knowledge. **4.** something read or for reading: [noncount]: *light reading.* [count]: *The first reading for today's ceremony is on page 12.* **5.** [count] the form or version of a given passage in a particular text: *the various readings of a line in Shakespeare.* **6.** [count] an instance or occasion in which a text, law, or work is read or recited in public: *an official reading of the budget.* **7.** [count] an interpretation given to anything: *What is your reading of the situation?* **8.** [count] the indication of an instrument or device that measures something: *temperature readings on a thermometer.*

re•ad•just (rē′ə just′) /ˌriyəˈdʒʌst/ *v.* **1.** to adapt, change, or adjust to a new situation or circumstance: [no obj]: *He has trouble readjusting to new situations.* [~ + obj]: *to readjust yourself to new situations.* **2.** [~ + obj] to put into a proper position: *to readjust the machine.* —**re′ad•just′ment,** *n.* [noncount]: *enough time for readjustment.* [count]: *a quick readjustment.* See -JUS-.

read•out or **read-out** (rēd′out′) /ˈriydˌawt/ *n.* [noncount] **1.** the output of information from a computer in a form that can be read. **2.** the information displayed on an instrument used for measuring.

read•y (red′ē) /ˈrɛdiy/ *adj.,* **-i•er, -i•est,** *v.,* **read•ied, read•y•ing.** —*adj.* **1.** [be + ~] completely prepared or in fit condition for action or use: *The car is ready for you to pick up from the repair shop.* [~ + for]: *The troops were ready for battle.* [~ + to + verb]: *The team was ready to play its best game ever.* **2.** [be + ~ + to + verb] willing; not hesitating: *He was always ready to criticize.* **3.** [before a noun] prompt or quick in seeing and understanding, comprehending, speaking, action, performing, etc.: *a ready reply; a ready wit.* **4.** [be + ~ + to + verb] in such a condition as to be likely to do something at any moment: *a tree that was ready to fall.* **5.** [before a noun] immediately available for use: *He had a reserve of ready money.* —*v.* [~ + obj] **6.** to make ready; prepare: *The chef was readying dinner.* —***Idiom.*** **7. at the ready,** ready for use: *held their weapons at the ready.* —**read•i•ly** (red′l ē) /ˈrɛdl̩iy/ *adv.* —**read′i•ness,** *n.* [noncount]

read′y-made′, *adj.* made in advance for sale to any purchaser; not custom-made: *a ready-made coat.*

re•a•gent (rē ā′jənt) /riyˈeydʒənt/ *n.* [count] *Chemistry.* a substance that, because of the reactions it causes, is used in breaking down or building up substances. See -AG-.

re•al (rē′əl, rēl) /ˈriyəl, riyl/ *adj.* **1.** [before a noun] true; not just apparent or visible: *I wanted to find out the real reason for his actions.* **2.** actual rather than imaginary, ideal, or pretended; actually having taken place or existing: *real events; a story taken from real life.* **3.** genuine; authentic: *real pearls.* **4.** [before a noun] *Informal.* (used for emphasis) absolute; complete; utter: *She's a real brain. That's a real mess.* **5.** measured by purchasing power: *real income.* —*adv.* **6.** *Informal.* very or extremely: *You did a real nice job.* —*n.* **7.** [noncount; the + ~] reality in general: *the real and the imaginary.* —***Idiom.*** **8. for real,** *Informal.* **a.** in reality; actually: *It's for real; we actually won!* **b.** genuine; sincere: *Is your offer for real?* —**re′al•ness,** *n.* [noncount] See -REAL-.

-real-, *root.* -real- comes from Latin, where it has the meaning "in fact; in reality." This meaning is found in such words as: REAL, REALISTIC, REALITY, REALIZE, REALLY, REALPOLITIK, SURREAL.

re′al estate′, *n.* [noncount] **1.** property, esp. in land. **2.** houses and the land on which they are built.

re•al•ism (rē′ə liz′əm) /ˈriyəˌlɪzəm/ *n.* [noncount] **1.** interest in or concern for things that are actual or real, as distinguished from things that are abstract, that cannot be easily defined, that are thought about but not acted upon, etc. **2.** [usually: Realism] a style of painting, sculpture, or literature in which figures and scenes of familiar parts of life are depicted or represented as they are or might be experienced in everyday life. —**re′al•ist,** *n.* [count] See -REAL-.

re•al•is•tic (rē′ə lis′tik) /ˌriyəˈlɪstɪk/ *adj.* **1.** interested in, concerned with, or based on what is real or practical: *a realistic estimate of costs.* **2.** characterized by the representation in literature or art of things as they really are: *a realistic novel.* —**re′al•is′ti•cal•ly,** *adv.*

re•al•i•ty (rē al′i tē) /riyˈælɪtiy/ *n., pl.* **-ties.** **1.** [noncount] the state or quality of being real. **2.** [count] a real thing or fact: *had to face some harsh realities about ourselves.* **3.** [noncount] real things, facts, or events thought of as a whole: *reading fantasy books to escape from reality.* —***Idiom.*** **4. in reality,** in fact or truth; actually. See -REAL-.

re•al•i•za•tion (rē′ə li zā′shən) /ˌriyəlɪˈzeyʃən/ *n.* [noncount] **1.** the act of becoming aware of something: *Realization came slowly to him.* **2.** the act or state of becoming real: *the realization of his dreams.* See -REAL-.

re•al•ize (rē′ə līz′) /ˈriyəˌlayz/ *v.,* **-ized, -iz•ing.** **1.** to grasp with the mind, believe, or understand clearly: [~ + obj]: *At long last he realized the truth.* [~ + clause]: *Suddenly he realized what had happened.* **2.** [~ + obj] to make real; give reality to (a hope, fear, plan, etc.): *He realized his dream and became a teacher.* **3.** [~ + obj] to obtain or gain for oneself by trade, labor, or investment: *We realized a net profit of over six hundred thousand dollars.* —**re′al•iz′a•ble,** *adj.* See -REAL-.

re•al•ly (rē′ə lē, rē′lē) /ˈriyəliy, ˈriyliy/ *adv.* **1.** actually: *sees things as they really are.* **2.** genuinely; truly: *a really hot day.* **3.** indeed: *Really, this is too much.* —*interj.* **4.** (used to express surprise, scolding, disapproval, etc.): *Really, be serious!* See -REAL-.

realm (relm) /rɛlm/ *n.* [count] **1.** the area over which, or extent to which, a king or queen has authority. **2.** any area of thought or activity: *within the realm of possibility.*

re′al num′ber, *n.* [count] a rational number or the limit of a sequence of rational numbers.

re•al•po•li•tik (rā äl′pō′li tēk′, rē-) /reyˈɑlˌpowlɪˌtiyk, riy-/ *n.* [noncount; often: Realpolitik] practical rather than theoretical politics. See -REAL-, -POLIS-.

re′al time′, *n.* [noncount] **1.** the actual time during which a process or event occurs. —*adj.* **2.** of or relating to computer applications or processes that can respond immediately to user input.

Re•al•tor (rē′əl tər, -tôr′, rēl′-) /ˈriyəltər, -ˌtɔr, ˈriyl-/ *Trademark.* [count] a person in the real-estate business who is a member of the National Association of Realtors.

re•al•ty (rē′əl tē, rēl′-) /ˈriyəltiy, ˈriyl-/ *n.* [noncount] real estate. See -REAL-.

ream[1] (rēm) /riym/ *n.* [count] **1.** a standard amount of paper in the U.S., usually amounting to about 500 sheets. **2.** Usually, **reams.** [plural] a large quantity: *wrote reams of poetry.*

ream[2] (rēm) /riym/ *v.* [~ + obj] **1.** to enlarge to desired size (a previously bored hole) by means of a special tool. **2.** to remove or press out with a special tool. **3.** *Slang.* to scold sharply: [~ + obj + out]: *The boss reamed him out for his mistakes.* [~ + out + obj]: *reaming out his employees.*

reap (rēp) /riyp/ *v.* **1.** to gather or take (a crop, harvest, etc.): [~ + obj]: *to reap grain.* [no obj]: *a time to reap and a time to sow.* **2.** [~ + obj] to get as a return or result: *The company reaped large profits in its first year.*

reap•er (rē′pər) /ˈriypər/ *n.* [count] **1.** a machine for cutting standing grain. **2.** a person who reaps.

re•ap•pear (rē′ə pēr′) /ˌriyəˈpɪər/ *v.* [no obj] to appear again: *The problems keep reappearing.* —**re′ap•pear′ance,** *n.* [count]: *many reappearances.* [noncount]: *Reappearance of the symptoms is serious.*

re•ap•prais•al (rē′ə prā′zəl) /ˌriyə'preyzəl/ *n.* the act of appraising something again: [*count*]: *a reappraisal of the treaty.* [*noncount*]: *due for reappraisal.*

rear[1] (rēr) /rɪər/ *n.* **1.** [*noncount*] the back of something, as distinguished from the front. **2.** [*noncount*] the space or position at the back of something: *Move to the rear of the bus.* **3.** [*count*] the buttocks; rump. **—***adj.* [*before a noun*] **4.** relating to or located at the rear: *a rear door.* **—*Idiom.* 5. bring up the rear,** to be at the end; follow behind. **—Syn.** See BACK.

rear[2] (rēr) /rɪər/ *v.* **1.** [~ + *obj*] to take care of and support (a young person) up to the age of maturity: *to rear a child.* **2.** [~ + *obj*] to lift upward, esp. so as to hold up high: *The snake reared its head.* **3.** [*no obj*] to rise on the hind legs: *The horse reared (up) and threw off its rider.* **4.** [*no obj*] to rise high: *The huge skyscrapers reared over me.*

rear′ ad′miral, *n.* [*count*] a commissioned officer in the U.S. Navy or Coast Guard ranking above a captain.

re•arm (rē′ärm′) /ˌriy'ɑrm/ *v.* to provide with weapons again; to provide with new weapons: [*no obj*]: *to rearm as protection against invaders.* [~ + *obj*]: *rearmed the troops.* **—re•ar•ma•ment** (rē är′mə mənt) /riy'ɑrmə-mənt/ *n.* [*noncount*]

rear•most (rēr′mōst′) /'rɪərˌmowst/ *adj.* farthest in the rear; last.

re•ar•range (rē′ə rānj′) /ˌriyə'reyndʒ/ *v.* [~ + *obj*], **-ranged, -rang•ing.** to put into a different arrangement or order. **—re′ar•range′ment,** *n.* [*count; noncount*]

rear•ward (rēr′wərd) /'rɪərwərd/ *adv.* **1.** Also, **rear′-wards.** toward or in the rear. **—***adj.* [*before a noun*] **2.** located in or toward the rear. **3.** directed toward the rear.

rea•son (rē′zən) /'riyzən/ *n.* **1.** [*count*] a basis or cause, as for some belief, action, fact, or event: *a good reason for declaring war.* **2.** [*count*] a statement presented in explaining a belief or action. **3.** [*noncount*] the mental powers concerned with forming conclusions and judgments: *Animals do not possess reason.* **4.** [*noncount*] sound judgment; good sense: *won't listen to reason.* **—***v.* **5.** to think or argue in a logical manner: [*no obj*]: *Animals cannot reason.* [~ + *obj*]: *didn't reason things out.* **6.** [~ + *(that) clause*] to form conclusions or judgments from facts: *I reasoned that he must have fallen and hit his head.* **—*Idiom.* 7. by reason of,** on account of; because of. **8. in** or **within reason,** within reasonable limits: *We'll pay if the cost is within reason.* **9. with reason,** with ample justification: *She doesn't like me, and with reason.* **—rea′son•er,** *n.* [*count*]

rea•son•a•ble (rē′zə nə bəl, rēz′nə-) /'riyzənəbəl, 'riyznə-/ *adj.* **1.** agreeable to or in agreement with reason; logical: *a reasonable conclusion from the facts.* **2.** not exceeding the limits of reason; not too high or too much; fair: *a reasonable price for the new car.* **3.** capable of rational behavior, decision, etc. **—rea′son•a•ble•ness,** *n.* [*noncount*]

rea•son•ab•ly (rē′zə nə blē, rēz′nə-) /'riyzənəbliy, 'riyznə-/ *adv.* **1.** sensibly; with fairness: *No one could reasonably expect him to agree.* **2.** somewhat; rather: *The house is in reasonably good shape.*

rea•soned (rē′zənd) /'riyzənd/ *adj.* carefully thought out: *a reasoned argument.*

rea•son•ing (rē′zə ning) /'riyzənɪŋ/ *n.* [*noncount*] the process of using reason in making a judgment or arriving at a conclusion.

re•as•sur•ance (rē′ə shŏŏr′əns, -shûr′-) /ˌriyə'ʃʊrəns, -'ʃɜr-/ *n.* **1.** [*noncount*] the act of reassuring. **2.** [*count*] something done or said to reassure or restore confidence. See -CURA-.

re•as•sure (rē′ə shŏŏr′, -shûr′) /ˌriyə'ʃʊr, -'ʃɜr/ *v.*, **-sured, -sur•ing.** to restore to assurance or confidence; give a feeling of confidence to: [~ + *obj*]: *Good teachers reassure their students.* [~ + *obj* + *(that) clause*]: *reassured me that I passed the test.* **—re′as•sur′ing•ly,** *adv.* See -CURA-.

re•bate (rē′bāt) /'riybeyt/ *n.* [*count*] a return of part of the original payment for something bought or for some service: *a $500 cash rebate on the new car.* See -BAT-.

reb•el (*n., adj.* reb′əl; *v.* ri bel′) / *n., adj.* 'rɛbəl; *v.* rɪ'bɛl/ *n., adj., v.,* **-belled, -bel•ling.** **—***n.* [*count*] **1.** a person who refuses to obey, resists, or rises in arms against a government or ruler. **2.** a person who resists any authority, control, or tradition. **—***adj.* [*before a noun*] **3.** of or relating to rebels: *rebel troops.* **—***v.* [*no obj*] **re•bel 4.** to act as a rebel: *The people rebelled against the government.* **5.** to show strong opposition: *Some children rebel to test their parents' patience.*

re•bel•lion (ri bel′yən) /rɪ'bɛlyən/ *n.* **1.** open, organized, and armed resistance to a government or ruler: [*noncount*]: *rebellion against the king.* [*count*]: *A rebellion broke out.* **2.** resistance to or defiance of any authority, control, or tradition: [*noncount*]: *signs of rebellion in the classroom.* [*count*]: *small rebellions by the voters.*

re•bel•lious (ri bel′yəs) /rɪ'bɛlyəs/ *adj.* going against or resisting some established authority, government, or tradition: *rebellious troops.* **—re•bel′lious•ly,** *adv.* **—re•bel′lious•ness,** *n.* [*noncount*]

re•birth (rē bûrth′, rē′bûrth′) /riy'bɜrθ, 'riyˌbɜrθ/ *n.* [*count; usually singular*] a renewed existence, activity, or growth; improvement; revival; renaissance: *a rebirth of an industry.*

re•born (rē bôrn′) /riy'bɔrn/ *adj.* [*usually: be* + ~] given renewed existence, activity, or growth; improved: *Their spirits were reborn and they felt immediately stronger.*

re•bound (*v.* ri bound′, rē′bound′; *n.* rē′bound′, ri-bound′) / *v.* rɪ'bawnd, 'riy'bawnd; *n.* 'riyˌbawnd, rɪ'bawnd/ *v.* [*no obj*] **1.** to bounce or spring back from the force of hitting something: *The ball rebounded off the wall.* **2.** to recover, as from ill health or discouragement. **3.** to have a bad effect on someone, as if springing back: *His treachery rebounded on him when they discovered his lies.* **—***n.* [*count*] **4.** the act of rebounding; recoil. **—*Idiom.* 5. on the rebound, a.** (of a bounced ball) while still in the air: *He caught the ball on the rebound.* **b.** in an attempt to replace a recently lost relationship, esp. a romance.

re•buff (*n.* ri buf′, rē′buf; *v.* ri buf′) / *n.* rɪ'bʌf, 'riybʌf; *v.* rɪ'bʌf/ *n.* [*count*] **1.** a blunt, sudden or quick rejection or refusal, as of a person making a request. **—***v.* [~ + *obj*] **2.** to give a rebuff to; check; repel.

re•build (rē bild′) /riy'bɪld/ *v.* [~ + *obj*], **-built, -build•ing.** **1.** to build again: *to rebuild the damaged city.* **2.** to develop or improve: *The president rebuilt his campaign staff.*

re•buke (ri byŏŏk′) /rɪ'byuwk/ *v.*, **-buked, -buk•ing,** *n.* **—***v.* [~ + *obj*] **1.** to express sharp, stern disapproval of; scold; reprimand: *The teacher rebuked the disobedient students.* **—***n.* [*count*] **2.** a sharp remark that indicates disapproval; a scolding; a reprimand: *offering a sharp rebuke to his comments.* **—re•buk′ing•ly,** *adv.*

re•bus (rē′bəs) /'riybəs/ *n.* [*count*], *pl.* **-bus•es.** a representation of a word or phrase by pictures, symbols, etc., that suggest that word or phrase or its syllables: *Two gates and a head is a rebus for Gateshead.*

re•but (ri but′) /rɪ'bʌt/ *v.* [~ + *obj*], **-but•ted, -but•ting.** to provide some evidence or an argument that opposes another argument or statement or shows that it is not correct or not to be believed.

re•but•tal (ri but′l) /rɪ'bʌtl̩/ *n.* [*count*] a statement that rebuts.

re•cal•ci•trant (ri kal′si trənt) /rɪ'kælsɪtrənt/ *adj.* **1.** resisting or fighting against authority or control; not obedient or cooperative: *The recalcitrant prisoner had to be dragged back to his cell.* **2.** hard to deal with, manage, or operate: *a recalcitrant machine.* **—re•cal′ci•trance,** *n.* [*noncount*]

re•call (*v.* ri kôl′; *n.* ri kôl′, rē′kôl *for 3, 4* rē′kôl *for 5, 6*) / *v.* rɪ'kɔl; *n.* rɪ'kɔl, 'riykɔl *for 3, 4* 'riykɔl *for 5, 6*/ *v.* **1.** to bring back from memory; remember: [*no obj*]: *said she couldn't recall.* [~ + *obj*]: *I can recall every word of our conversation.* [~ + *that clause*]: *I recalled that she was out visiting.* **2.** [~ + *obj*] to call or order back to a place of origin: *The car was recalled because of faulty brakes.* **—***n.* **3.** [*count*] an act of recalling. **4.** [*noncount*] recollection; remembrance; ability to remember: *has recall of every detail.* **5.** [*noncount*] the removal or the right of removal of a public official from office by a vote of the people. **6.** [*count*] a summons by a manufacturer for the return of a product, as from a consumer, because of its having a known defect.

re•cant (ri kant′) /rɪ'kænt/ *v.* to withdraw, take back, or disavow (a statement, opinion, etc.), esp. formally; retract: [~ + *obj*]: *He recanted his testimony.* [*no obj*]: *must recant and promise to reform themselves.*

re•cap[1] (*v.* rē′kap′, rē kap′; *n.* rē′kap′) / *v.* 'riyˌkæp, riy'kæp; *n.* 'riyˌkæp/ *v.*, **-capped, -cap•ping,** *n.* **—***v.* [~ + *obj*] **1.** to repair (a worn automobile tire) by cementing on a strip of prepared rubber. **—***n.* [*count*] **2.** a tire repaired this way.

re•cap[2] (rē′kap′) /'riyˌkæp/ *n., v.,* **-capped, -cap•ping.** **—***n.* [*count*] **1.** an act of telling again, esp. in a shortened form; a recapitulation: *a recap of top stories in the news.* **—***v.* **2.** to tell again, esp. in a summary or shortened form; recapitulate: [~ + *obj*]: *recapped the top news stories.* [*no obj*]: *To recap, snow is expected.*

re•ca•pit•u•late (rē′kə pich′ə lāt′) /ˌriykəˈpɪtʃəˌleyt/ *v.,* **-lated, -lat•ing.** to review or tell again, by a brief summary, as at the end of a speech or discussion; summarize: [~ + *obj*]: *He recapitulated his arguments.* [*no obj*]: *To recapitulate, the plan is accepted.* —**re•ca•pit•u•la•tion** (rē′kə pich′ə lā′shən) /ˌriykəˌpɪtʃəˈleyʃən/ *n.* [*noncount*]: *The paper needs less recapitulation.* [*count*]: *another recapitulation.*

re•cap•ture (rē kap′chər) /riyˈkæptʃər/ *v.,* **-tured, -tur•ing,** *n.* —*v.* [~ + *obj*] **1.** to capture again. **2.** to recollect or experience again: *to recapture those happy moments of youth.* —*n.* [*count; usually singular*] **3.** recovery by capture. See -CEP-.

re•cast (*v.,* rē kast′ *n.,* rē′kast′) / *v.,* riyˈkæst *n.,* ˈriyˌkæst/ *v.* [~ + *obj*] **1.** to change, as by rearranging or reorganizing: *recast the novel as a movie.* **2.** to substitute other actors in (a play or in parts of a play). —*n.* [*count*] **3.** an act of recasting.

recd. or **rec'd.,** an abbreviation of: received.

re•cede (ri sēd′) /rɪˈsiyd/ *v.* [*no obj*], **-ced•ed, -ced•ing. 1.** to go back to a more distant point; retreat; withdraw: *The floodwaters finally receded.* **2.** to become or seem to become more distant: *The painful memory began to recede.* **3.** to slope backward: *a chin that recedes.* See -CEDE-.

re•ceipt (ri sēt′) /rɪˈsiyt/ *n.* **1.** [*count*] a note that states that someone has received money or goods: *I'll need a receipt for the car you sold us.* **2. receipts,** [*plural*] money, goods, etc., received; the amount or quantity received: *the huge receipts from a rock concert.* **3.** [*noncount*] the act of receiving or the state of being received: *waiting for receipt of further information.* **4.** [*count*] RECIPE. —*v.* [~ + *obj*] **5.** to state in writing that one has received payment of (a bill, a note, etc.): *to receipt the bill of sale.* **6.** to give a receipt for (money, goods, etc.). See -CEIVE-.

re•ceiv•a•ble (ri sē′və bəl) /rɪˈsiyvəbəl/ *adj.* **1.** awaiting or requiring payment. **2.** capable of being received. —*n.* **3. receivables,** [*plural*] business assets in the form of money owed by customers, clients, etc. See -CEIVE-.

re•ceive (ri sēv′) /rɪˈsiyv/ *v.* [~ + *obj*], **-ceived, -ceiv•ing. 1.** to get or have delivered to one: *to receive a letter.* **2.** to obtain or take into one's possession (something offered or delivered): *to receive gifts.* **3.** to become burdened with; to sustain or come to; suffer from: *to receive a heavy load.* **4.** to take in, as something that fits or is absorbed: *The socket receives the plug.* **5.** to take into the mind; apprehend mentally: *to receive an idea.* **6.** to meet with; experience: *That baby receives a lot of attention.* **7.** to admit (a person) to a place, into an organization or membership, etc.: *He was received into the priesthood.* **8.** to be at home to, or welcome or greet (visitors). See -CEIVE-.

re•ceiv•er (ri sē′vər) /rɪˈsiyvər/ *n.* [*count*] **1.** a person or thing that receives. **2.** a device or apparatus, as an earphone, radio, or television set, that receives electrical signals, waves, or the like and makes them into images or sounds that can be understood. **3.** a person appointed by a court to manage the affairs of a bankrupt business or person. **4.** *Football.* a player on the offensive team who catches or is eligible to catch a forward pass. See -CEIVE-.

re•ceiv•er•ship (ri sē′vər ship′) /rɪˈsiyvərˌʃɪp/ *n.* [*noncount*] **1.** the condition of being in the hands of a receiver. **2.** the position or function of being a receiver in charge of administering the property of others.

re•cent (rē′sənt) /ˈriysənt/ *adj.* occurring, appearing, or starting a short while ago: *Recent events suggest that peace is at hand.*

re•cent•ly (rē′sənt lē) /ˈriysəntliy/ *adv.* happening or done a short while ago: *We recently returned home.*

re•cep•ta•cle (ri sep′tə kəl) /rɪˈsɛptəkəl/ *n.* [*count*] **1.** a container, device, etc., that receives or holds something: *Please dispose of your trash in the receptacles by your tables.* **2.** a contact device installed at an electrical outlet, and equipped with one or more sockets: *a wall receptacle.* See -CEP-.

re•cep•tion (ri sep′shən) /rɪˈsɛpʃən/ *n.* **1.** [*count*] the act of receiving or the state of being received. **2.** [*count*] a manner of being received: *The book met with a favorable reception.* **3.** [*count*] a function, party, or occasion when persons are formally received: *a wedding reception.* **4.** [*noncount*] the measure of the quality obtained in receiving radio or television broadcasts: *poor TV reception.* See -CEP-.

re•cep•tion•ist (ri sep′shə nist) /rɪˈsɛpʃənɪst/ *n.* [*count*] a person whose job is to receive and assist callers, clients, etc., as in an office. See -CEP-. See illustration at HOSPITAL.

re•cep•tive (ri sep′tiv) /rɪˈsɛptɪv/ *adj.* willing to receive, as new or different suggestions, offers, or ideas. —**re•cep′tive•ly,** *adv.* —**re•cep′tive•ness,** *n.* [*noncount*] —**re•cep•tiv•i•ty** (rē′sep tiv′i tē) /ˌriysɛpˈtɪvɪtiy/ *n.* [*noncount*] See -CEP-.

re•cess (ri ses′, rē′ses) /rɪˈsɛs, ˈriysɛs/ *n.* [*count*] **1.** a temporary withdrawal from or stopping of the usual work or activity; a break. **2.** a period of such withdrawal: *a five-minute recess.* **3.** a part built back or in from the rest, as an alcove in a room. **4. recesses,** [*plural*] a hidden or inner area or part: *in the recesses of the palace.* —*v.* **5.** [~ + *obj*] to place or set in a recess. **6.** to suspend or leave for later for a recess: [~ + *obj*]: *to recess the Senate.* [*no obj*]: *The meeting recessed for lunch.* See -CESS-.

re•ces•sion (ri sesh′ən) /rɪˈsɛʃən/ *n.* **1.** a period of economic decline when production, employment, and earnings fall below normal levels or lag behind normal growth: [*count*]: *The country was in a recession.* [*noncount*]: *fighting recession.* **2.** [*noncount*] the act of receding or withdrawing: *the recession of the floodwaters.* **3.** [*count*] a withdrawing procession, as at the end of a religious service. —**re•ces′sion•ar′y,** *adj.* See -CESS-.

re•ces•sion•al (ri sesh′ə nl) /rɪˈsɛʃənl̩/ *adj.* **1.** of or relating to the departure, or to a recession, of the clergy and others at the end of a religious service. —*n.* [*count*] **2.** a piece of music played at the end of a church service or other gathering. See -CESS-.

re•ces•sive (ri ses′iv) /rɪˈsɛsɪv/ *adj.* **1.** tending to recede. **2.** of or relating to one of a pair of hereditary traits that is masked by the other when both are present in an organism. See -CESS-.

re•cher•ché (rə shâr′shā, rə shâr shā′) /rəˈʃɛərʃey, rəʃɛərˈʃey/ *adj.* elegant; exotic.

re•cid•i•vism (ri sid′ə viz′əm) /rɪˈsɪdəˌvɪzəm/ *n.* [*noncount*] repeated falling back into bad habits. See -CIDE-.

re•cid•i•vist (ri sid′ə vist) /rɪˈsɪdəvɪst/ *n.* [*count*] **1.** a person who relapses, esp. one who commits crimes time after time. —*adj.* **2.** of or relating to such a person. See -CIDE-.

rec•i•pe (res′ə pē) /ˈrɛsəpiy/ *n.* [*count*], *pl.* **-pes. 1.** a set of instructions for making or preparing something, esp. a food dish. **2.** a method to achieve a desired end: *a recipe for happiness.* See -CEP-.

re•cip•i•ent (ri sip′ē ənt) /rɪˈsɪpiyənt/ *n.* [*count*] one that receives; receiver. See -CEP-.

re•cip•ro•cal (ri sip′rə kəl) /rɪˈsɪprəkəl/ *adj.* **1.** given or felt by each toward the other; mutual: *reciprocal respect.* **2.** given, performed, felt, etc., in return: *reciprocal aid.* **3.** corresponding; matching; equivalent: *reciprocal privileges at other clubs.* **4.** (of a pronoun or verb) expressing mutual relationship or action, as the pronouns *each other* and *one another.* —*n.* [*count*] **5.** one that is reciprocal to another. See -CEP-.

re•cip•ro•cate (ri sip′rə kāt′) /rɪˈsɪprəˌkeyt/ *v.,* **-cat•ed, -cat•ing.** to give, feel, etc., in return: [*no obj*]: *They gave us a gift so we reciprocated.* [~ + *obj*]: *to reciprocate favors.* —**re•cip•ro•ca•tion** (ri sip′rə kā′shən) /rɪˌsɪprəˈkeyʃən/ *n.* [*noncount*]

rec•i•proc•i•ty (res′ə pros′i tē) /ˌrɛsəˈprɒsɪtiy/ *n.* [*noncount*] **1.** a reciprocal state or relation; mutual exchange. **2.** the policy in commercial dealings between countries by which corresponding advantages are granted by each country to the citizens of the other. See -CEP-.

re•cit•al (ri sīt′l) /rɪˈsaytl̩/ *n.* [*count*] **1.** a musical or dance entertainment given by one or more performers. **2.** an act or instance of reciting, esp. from memory. **3.** a detailed statement: *a long recital of grievances.* —**re•cit′al•ist,** *n.* [*count*]

rec•i•ta•tion (res′i tā′shən) /ˌrɛsɪˈteyʃən/ *n.* **1.** an act of reciting or of saying something out loud, esp. at a formal public gathering: [*noncount*]: *is good at recitation.* [*count*]: *poetry recitations.* **2.** [*count*] oral response by a pupil or pupils to a teacher on a prepared lesson.

re•cite (ri sīt′) /rɪˈsayt/ *v.,* **-cit•ed, -cit•ing. 1.** to repeat the words of, sometimes from memory, esp. in a formal manner or in a classroom setting: [~ + *obj*]: *to recite the Gettysburg Address.* [*no obj*]: *She stood up and began to recite.* **2.** [~ + *obj*] to tell about; describe; provide details of: *He then recited a long list of complaints.*

reck•less (rek′lis) /ˈrɛklɪs/ *adj.* **1.** completely unconcerned about the consequences or results of one's actions; rash; careless: *reckless drivers.* **2.** characterized by or proceeding from such carelessness: *reckless* *spending.* —**reck′less•ly,** *adv.*: *drove recklessly.* —**reck′less•ness,** *n.* [*noncount*]

reck•on (rek′ən) /ˈrɛkən/ *v.* **1.** [~ + *obj*] to count, compute, or calculate: *to reckon profits.* **2.** to consider (someone or something) as; look upon (someone or something) as: [~ + *obj* (+ *as*) + *obj*]: *reckoned her (as) an outstanding expert.* [~ + *obj* + *among* + *obj*]: *She is reckoned among the most important experts of that field.* **3.** *Chiefly Midland and Southern U.S.* to think or suppose: [~ + (*that*) *clause*]: *I reckon (that) she'll be here soon.* [*no obj*]: *Will she come to the party? I reckon so.* **4.** to count, depend, or rely; expect: [~ + *on* + *obj*]: *The general didn't reckon on a surprise attack.* [~ + *to* + *verb*]: *The company reckons to sell over a million cars.* **5. reckon with,** [~ + *with* + *obj*] **a.** to consider or anticipate: *He hadn't reckoned with bad weather.* **b.** to deal with: *She has to reckon with this kind of complaint all day long.* **c.** to consider seriously: *a sales force to be reckoned with.*

reck•on•ing (rek′ə ning) /ˈrɛkənɪŋ/ *n.* [*noncount*] **1.** count; the way one figures something; computation; calculation: *By her reckoning we still owe money.* **2.** the settlement of accounts, as between two companies. **3.** judgment: *a day of reckoning.*

re•claim (ri klām′) /rɪˈkleym/ *v.* [~ + *obj*] **1.** to bring (uncultivated areas of land or wasteland) into a condition for farming, growing things, or for other use. **2.** to recover (substances) in a pure form or in a form that can be used, from waste material or from articles that have been thrown away: *to reclaim the copper from those wires.* See -CLAIM-.

rec•la•ma•tion (rek′lə mā′shən) /ˌrɛkləˈmeyʃən/ *n.* [*noncount*] **1.** the act of reclaiming or recovering substances from waste materials or articles that have been thrown away. **2.** the act of bringing back land into a condition for farming, growing things, or other uses. See -CLAIM-.

re•cline (ri klīn′) /rɪˈklayn/ *v.*, **-clined, -clin•ing.** to (cause to) lean back or lie; to (cause to) be moved into a position that is flat or nearly flat: [*no obj*]: *reclined on the sofa.* [~ + *obj*]: *to recline a car seat.*

re•clin•er (ri klī′nər) /rɪˈklaynər/ *n.* [*count*] **1.** a person or thing that reclines. **2.** Also called **reclin′ing chair′.** an easy chair with a back and footrest that adjust up or down.

rec•luse (*n.* rek′lo͞os, ri klo͞os′; *adj.* ri klo͞os′, rek′lo͞os) / *n.* ˈrɛkluws, rɪˈkluws; *adj.* rɪˈkluws, ˈrɛkluws/ *n.* [*count*] **1.** a person who deliberately lives apart from society. —*adj.* **re•cluse. 2.** shut off or apart from the world. —**re•clu•sive** (ri klo͞o′siv) /rɪˈkluwsɪv/ *adj.*

rec•og•ni•tion (rek′əg nish′ən) /ˌrɛkəgˈnɪʃən/ *n.* [*noncount*] **1.** an act of recognizing or the state of being recognized. **2.** identification of a person or thing as having previously been seen, heard, known, etc.: *He looked at her with a growing sense of recognition.* **3.** perception or understanding of something as existing, true, or valid: *recognition that students need encouragement.* **4.** the acknowledgment of achievement, service, merit, ability, status, etc. **5.** an official act by which one state acknowledges the existence of another state or of a new government. See -GNOS-.

rec•og•nize (rek′əg nīz′) /ˈrɛkəgˌnayz/ *v.* [~ + *obj*], **-nized, -niz•ing. 1.** to identify as something or someone previously seen, known, etc.: *I recognized my old car.* **2.** to identify from knowledge of appearance or characteristics: *to recognize a swindler.* **3.** to perceive or accept as existing, true, or valid: *She was able to recognize the problem.* **4.** to grant official permission to speak: *The chair recognizes the new delegate.* **5.** to accept formally as something entitled to treatment as a political unit: *The UN formally recognized the territory.* **6.** to show appreciation of: *Today we recognize your great achievements.* —**rec•og•niz•a•ble** (rek′əg nī′zə bəl) /ˌrɛkəgˈnayzəbəl/ *adj.* See -GNOS-.

re•coil (*v.* ri koil′; *n.* rē′koil′, ri koil′) / *v.* rɪˈkɔyl; *n.* ˈriyˌkɔyl, rɪˈkɔyl/ *v.* [*no obj*] **1.** to jump or shrink back suddenly, as in alarm, horror, or disgust. **2.** to spring or fly back because of force of impact or because of a shooting of a bullet: *The rifle recoiled.* —*n.* **3.** the act or an instance of recoiling: [*noncount*]: *very little recoil with this gun.* [*count*]: *a small recoil.*

rec•ol•lect (rek′ə lekt′) /ˌrɛkəˈlɛkt/ *v.* [*not: be* + ~*-ing*] to remember; recall: [~ + *obj*]: *Can you recollect the password?* [~ + *clause*]: *After that I don't recollect what happened.* [*no obj*]: *Sorry, I simply can't recollect.* See -LEC-.

rec•ol•lec•tion (rek′ə lek′shən) /ˌrɛkəˈlɛkʃən/ *n.* **1.** [*noncount*] the act or power of recollecting or remembering or recalling to mind: *a sudden flash of recollection.* **2.** [*count*] something remembered; a memory: *He wrote down his recollections of the war.* See -LEC-.

rec•om•mend (rek′ə mend′) /ˌrɛkəˈmɛnd/ *v.* **1.** [~ + *obj*] to present (someone or something) as worthy of confidence, acceptance, or use, as by making a favorable judgment of; commend. **2.** to urge or suggest as proper, useful, or beneficial: [~ + *obj*]: *to recommend a special diet.* [~ + *verb-ing*]: *I recommend seeing a doctor immediately.* [~ + (*that*) *clause*]: *I recommend that you take her to the doctor at once.* **3.** [~ + *obj*] to make desirable or attractive: *The plan has little to recommend it.* —**rec′om•mend′a•ble,** *adj.* See -MAND-.

rec•om•men•da•tion (rek′ə men dā′shən) /ˌrɛkəmɛnˈdeyʃən/ *n.* **1.** [*noncount*] the act of recommending; advice. **2.** [*noncount*] the act of presenting someone or something as favorable, suitable, qualified, or the like, esp. for a job: *a letter of recommendation.* **3.** [*count*] a letter presenting someone as favorable, suitable, qualified, or the like, esp. for a job. See -MAND-.

rec•om•pense (rek′əm pens′) /ˈrɛkəmˌpɛns/ *v.*, **-pensed, -pens•ing,** *n.* —*v.* [~ + *obj*] **1.** to give something to as payment for work done, injury suffered, or favors received. —*n.* [*noncount*] **2.** a repayment or reward, as for services, gifts, or favors. **3.** something offered to pay for an injury caused; reparation: *not enough money in recompense for the damages.* See -PEND-.

rec•on•cile (rek′ən sīl′) /ˈrɛkənˌsayl/ *v.*, **-ciled, -cil•ing. 1.** [~ + *obj* + *to* + *obj*] to cause (a person) to accept or be resigned to something not desired: *He was reconciled to his fate.* **2.** to (cause to) become friendly or peaceable again, as by settling a quarrel: [~ + *obj*]: *to reconcile hostile persons.* [*no obj*]: *The husband and wife reconciled last week.* **3.** [~ + *obj*] to compose or settle (a quarrel, dispute, etc.): *They have reconciled their differences.* **4.** [~ + *obj*] to bring into agreement: *reconciled financial accounts.* —**rec′on•cil′a•ble,** *adj.*

rec•on•cil•i•a•tion (rek′ən sil′ē ā′shən) /ˌrɛkənˌsɪliyˈeyʃən/ *n.* **1.** the act of two or more people reconciling: [*noncount*]: *Reconciliation was still possible.* [*count*]: *a trial reconciliation.* **2.** [*noncount*] the act of bringing two different things into agreement: *reconciliation of accounts.*

rec•on•dite (rek′ən dīt′, ri kon′dīt) /ˈrɛkənˌdayt, rɪˈkɒndayt/ *adj.* relating to or dealing with very deep, difficult, obscure, or abstract subject matter: *a recondite treatise.*

re•con•di•tion (rē′kən dish′ən) /ˌriykənˈdɪʃən/ *v.* [~ + *obj*] to restore or bring back to satisfactory condition: *reconditioned the car.*

re•con•nais•sance (ri kon′ə səns, -zəns) /rɪˈkɒnəsəns, -zəns/ *n.* the act of reconnoitering; a survey or examination of an area: [*noncount*]: *reconnaissance with telescopic cameras.* [*count*]: *ordered a reconnaissance.* See -GNOS-.

re•con•noi•ter (rē′kə noi′tər, rek′ə-) /ˌriykəˈnɔytər, ˌrɛkə-/ *v.* to inspect, observe, or survey (an enemy position, strength, etc.) in order to gain information for military purposes: [~ + *obj*]: *reconnoitered the enemy positions.* [*no obj*]: *was ordered to reconnoiter.* See -GNOS-.

re•con•sid•er (rē′kən sid′ər) /ˌriykənˈsɪdər/ *v.* to consider again, esp. with a view to a change of decision: [~ + *obj*]: *to reconsider a refusal.* [*no obj*]: *She said that she wouldn't reconsider.* —**re•con•sid•er•a•tion** (rē′kən sid′ə rā′shən) /ˌriykənˌsɪdəˈreyʃən/ *n.* [*noncount*]

re•con•sti•tute (rē kon′sti to͞ot′, -tyo͞ot′) /riyˈkɒnstɪˌtuwt, -ˌtyuwt/ *v.* [~ + *obj*], **-tut•ed, -tut•ing. 1.** to put together again: *to reconstitute the committee under a new name.* **2.** to return (food that has had the water removed or has been concentrated) to the liquid state by adding water. See -STIT-.

re•con•struct (rē′kən strukt′) /ˌriykənˈstrʌkt/ *v.* [~ + *obj*] **1.** to construct again; rebuild; make over: *to reconstruct the battle-torn country.* **2.** to re-create in the mind from available information: *to reconstruct the events of the murder.* —**re′con•struc′tion,** *n.* [*count*]: *a reconstruction of the events leading up to the accident.* [*noncount*]: *the money necessary for reconstruction of the country's infrastructure.* See -STRU-.

re•cord (*v.* ri kôrd′; *n., adj.* rek′ərd) / *v.* rɪˈkɔrd; *n., adj.* ˈrɛkərd/ *v.* **1.** [~ + *obj*] to set down in writing or the like, such as for the purpose of preserving evidence: *recorded the dates of battles.* **2.** [~ + *obj*] to cause to be set down, stated, or indicated: *His no vote was recorded.* **3.** [~ + *obj*] to serve to tell of: *The instruments recorded the earthquake.* **4.** to use a special machine to preserve or keep sounds, images, or other signals by copying them electronically so that they can be played again or reproduced by a phonograph, videocassette recorder, etc.: [~ + *obj*]: *recorded several of his songs; The computer records your keystrokes.* [*no obj*]: *This video camera can record and play back.* **—*n.*** [*count*] **rec•ord 5.** an account in writing or the like that preserves or keeps the memory or knowledge of certain facts or events. **6.** a report, list, or collection of known facts about someone's past actions or achievements: *Her school records are in the registrar's office.* **7.** a legally documented list or official file of someone's criminal activity. **8.** the standing of a team or individual with respect to contests won, lost, and tied: *The team's record is five wins and three losses.* **9.** the highest or best rate, amount, etc., ever achieved, esp. in sports: *He broke the old speed records.* **10.** something on which sound or images have been electronically recorded for playing back at a later time, esp. a grooved disk that is played on a phonograph, or an optical disc for recording sound or images; a recording. **—*adj.*** [*before a noun*] **rec•ord 11.** making a record: *a record company.* **12.** superior to all others: *a record year for sales.* **—*Idiom.* 13. for the record,** meant for publication: *remarks made for the record.* **14. off the record,** not for publication; unofficial. **15. on record, a.** existing as a matter of public knowledge; known: *Your accomplishments are on record.* **b.** existing in a publication, document, file, etc.: *keeping information on record about his enemies.* **c.** having stated one's opinion or position publicly: *He is on record as supporting the tax cut.* **d.** ever recorded: *It was the hottest summer on record.* **—re•cord′a•ble,** *adj.* See -CORD-.

re•cord•er (ri kôr′dər) /rɪ'kɔrdər/ *n.* [*count*] **1.** a person who records, esp. as an official duty. **2.** a device or apparatus for recording sound, images, data, or information: *a tape recorder.* **3.** a flute with a mouthpiece like a whistle. See -CORD-.

re•cord•ing (ri kôr′ding) /rɪ'kɔrdɪŋ/ *n.* [*count*] **1.** the act or practice of putting down in writing, taping, or otherwise making a record of something. **2.** sound recorded on a disk or tape. **3.** a disk or tape on which something is recorded.

rec′ord play′er, *n.* PHONOGRAPH.

re-count (*v.* rē kount′; *n.* rē′kount′, rē kount′) / *v.* riy'kawnt; *n.* 'riy,kawnt, riy'kawnt/ *v.* [~ + *obj*] **1.** to count again: *re-counting votes.* **—*n.*** [*count*] **2.** a second or additional count: *demanded a re-count of the votes.*

re•count (ri kount′) /rɪ'kawnt/ *v.* [~ + *obj*] to relate or narrate; tell in detail: *He recounted his adventures for us.*

re•coup (ri ko͞op′) /rɪ'kuwp/ *v.* [~ + *obj*] to get back what one has lost or spent; regain or recover: *to recoup one's losses.*

re•course (rē′kôrs, -kōrs, ri kôrs′, -kōrs′) /'riykɔrs, -kowrs, rɪ'kɔrs, -'kowrs/ *n.* [*noncount*] the act of going to a person or thing for help, assistance, protection, or the like: *Without recourse to a map, how will you know where you are?* See -COUR-.

re-cov•er (rē kuv′ər) /riy'kʌvər/ *v.* [~ + *obj*] to cover again: *That chair needs to be re-covered.*

re•cov•er (ri kuv′ər) /rɪ'kʌvər/ *v.* **1.** [~ + *obj*] to get back or regain (something lost or taken away): *I recovered my voice after a week of laryngitis. The insurance company helped us recover our losses.* **2.** to regain one's strength, composure, balance, or the like: [*no obj*]: *recovering from a bad cold.* [~ + *oneself*]: *He recovered himself after a memory lapse.* **3.** [~ + *obj*] to regain or extract (a substance) in a form that can be used; reclaim: *The recycling plant recovers metal and aluminum from the trash.* **—re•cov′er•a•ble,** *adj.* **—re•cov′er•y,** *n., pl.* **er•ies.** [*noncount*]: *The chances of recovery are slim.* [*count*]: *made a remarkable recovery.*

re-cre•ate (rē′krē āt′) /,riykriy'eyt/ *v.* [~ + *obj*], **-at•ed, -at•ing.** to create again or as new: *In his mind he re-created the scene of the accident.*

rec•re•a•tion (rek′rē ā′shən) /,rɛkriy'eyʃən/ *n.* refreshment by means of a pastime, agreeable exercise, or the like, as a way of relaxing: [*noncount*]: *a means of recreation.* [*count*]: *recreations such as sports and reading.* **—rec′re•a′tion•al,** *adj.*

re•crim•i•na•tion (ri krim′ə nā′shən) /rɪ,krɪmə'neyʃən/ *n.* accusing another of bad conduct or of other charges: [*count*]: *bitter recriminations.* [*noncount*]: *arguments full of recrimination.*

re•cruit (ri kro͞ot′) /rɪ'kruwt/ *n.* [*count*] **1.** a newly enlisted or drafted member of the armed forces. **2.** a new member of a group, organization, company, or the like. **—*v.* 3.** to enlist (a person) for service in the military: [~ + *obj*]: *to recruit people for a career in the army.* [*no obj*]: *He recruited for the Army.* **4.** [~ + *obj*] to raise (a force) by enlistment: *to recruit an army.* **5.** to seek to hire, enroll, or enlist (a person) in a group, company, or organization: [~ + *obj*]: *to recruit new employees.* [*no obj*]: *were recruiting for an important executive position.* **6.** [~ + *obj*] to seek or enlist (a person) for some activity or task: *to recruit volunteers to wash the windows.* **—re•cruit′er,** *n.* [*count*] **—re•cruit′ment,** *n.* [*noncount*]

-rect-, *root.* -rect- comes from Latin, where it has the meaning "guide; rule; right; straight." This meaning is found in such words as: CORRECT, DIRECT, ERECT, INDIRECT, INSURRECTION, MISDIRECT, RECTANGLE, RECTIFY, RECTITUDE, RECTOR, RECTUM, RESURRECTION.

rec•tal (rek′tl) /'rɛktḷ/ *adj.* of, relating to, or for the rectum. **—rec′tal•ly,** *adv.* See -RECT-.

rec•tan•gle (rek′tang′gəl) /'rɛk,tæŋgəl/ *n.* [*count*] a four-sided figure with parallel sides, having four right angles: *Every square is a rectangle, but not every rectangle is a square.* **—rec•tang•u•lar** (rek tang′gyə lər) /rɛk'tæŋgyələr/ *adj.* See -RECT-.

rec•ti•fy (rek′tə fī′) /'rɛktə,fay/ *v.* [~ + *obj*], **-fied, -fy•ing.** to make, put, or set right; correct: *to rectify an error.* **—rec′ti•fi′a•ble,** *adj.* **—rec•ti•fi•ca•tion** (rek′tə fi kā′shən) /,rɛktəfɪ'keyʃən/ *n.* [*noncount*] See -RECT-.

rec•ti•lin•e•ar (rek′tl in′ē ər) /,rɛktḷ'ɪniyər/ also **rec•ti•lin•e•al** (rek′tl in′ē əl) /,rɛktḷ'ɪniyəl/ *adj.* forming a straight line; having straight lines. See -LIN-, -RECT-.

rec•ti•tude (rek′ti to͞od′, -tyo͞od′) /'rɛktɪ,tuwd, -,tyuwd/ *n.* [*noncount*] rightness of principle or conduct; moral virtue. See -RECT-.

rec•tor (rek′tər) /'rɛktər/ *n.* [*count*] **1.** a member of the clergy in various Christian churches in charge of a parish, a building, a religious house, or the like. **2.** the head of certain universities, colleges, or schools. See -RECT-.

rec•to•ry (rek′tə rē) /'rɛktəriy/ *n.* [*count*], *pl.* **-ries. 1.** a rector's house. **2.** a residence for Roman Catholic priests of a parish. See -RECT-.

rec•tum (rek′təm) /'rɛktəm/ *n.* [*count*], *pl.* **-tums, -ta** (-tə) /-tə/. the straight, final part of the large intestine, ending in the anus. See -RECT-.

re•cum•bent (ri kum′bənt) /rɪ'kʌmbənt/ *adj.* lying down; reclining; leaning. **—re•cum′ben•cy,** *n.* [*noncount*]

re•cu•per•ate (ri ko͞o′pə rāt′, -kyo͞o′-) /rɪ'kuwpə,reyt, -'kyuw-/ *v.* [*no obj*], **-at•ed, -at•ing.** to recover from sickness or exhaustion; regain health or strength. **—re•cu′per•a′tion,** *n.* [*noncount*] **—re•cu•per•a•tive** (ri ko͞o′pə rā′tiv, -pər ə tiv, -kyo͞o′-) /rɪ'kuwpə,reytɪv, -pərətɪv, -'kyuw-/ *adj.* See -CEP-.

re•cur (ri kûr′) /rɪ'kɜr/ *v.* [*no obj*], **-curred, -cur•ring. 1.** to happen again, as an event, experience, etc.: *Snowstorms recur every winter.* **2.** to return to the mind: *The idea kept recurring.* **—re•cur•rence,** *n.* [*count*]: *yet another recurrence.* [*noncount*]: *recurrence of pain.* **—re•cur′rent,** *adj.*: *recurrent problems.* **—re•cur′rent•ly,** *adv.* See -CUR-.

re•cy•cle (rē sī′kəl) /riy'saykəl/ *v.* [~ + *obj*], **-cled, -cling. 1.** to treat or process (used or waste materials) so as to make suitable for reuse: *to recycle newspapers, glass bottles, plastic, and metal.* **2.** to use again in the original form or with very little change: *to recycle a speech.* **—re•cy•cla•ble** (rē sī′klə bəl) /riy'sayklәbəl/ *adj.* See -CYCLE-.

red (red) /rɛd/ *n., adj.,* **red•der, red•dest. —*n.* 1.** a color resembling the color of blood: [*noncount*]: *Red was her favorite color.* [*count*]: *rich, strong reds and deep blues.* **2.** [*noncount*] clothes that are red: *dressed in red.* **3.** [*count; often: Red*] a radical leftist in politics, esp. a communist. **—*adj.* 4.** of the color red. **5.** of or indicating a state of financial loss: *the red column in the ledger.* **6.** [*often: Red*] politically radical, esp. communist. **7.** (of hair) the color of copper, brownish orange. **8.** (of the face or skin) flushed, esp. from anger, embarrassment, or shame. **—*Idiom.* 9. in the red,** operating at a loss or being in debt (opposed to *in the black*). **—red′dish,** *adj.* **—red′ness,** *n.* [*noncount*]

red′-blood′ed, *adj.* strong; vigorous: *such healthy, red-blooded Americans.*

red′ car′pet, *n.* [*count; usually singular*] **1.** a strip of red carpet for important officials to walk on when entering or leaving a building, vehicle, or the like. **2.** a display of courtesy or respect, as for persons of high rank: *The city rolled out the red carpet for the president when he visited.* **—red′-car′pet,** *adj.* [*before a noun*] **3.** of or relating to such display: *the red-carpet treatment.*

red•coat (red′kōt′) /ˈrɛdˌkowt/ *n.* [*count*] (esp. in America during the Revolutionary War) a British soldier.

red•den (red′n) /ˈrɛdn̩/ *v.* **1.** to make or cause to become red: [*no obj*]: *The sky reddened at sunset.* [~ + *obj*]: *Sunset reddened the sky.* **2.** [*no obj*] to blush; flush: *He reddened at the insult.*

re•dec•o•rate (rē dek′ə rāt′) /riyˈdɛkəˌreyt/ *v.*, **-rat•ed, -rat•ing.** to decorate (a place) again: [~ + *obj*]: *They redecorated their apartment.* [*no obj*]: *decided to redecorate.*

re•deem (ri dēm′) /rɪˈdiym/ *v.* [~ + *obj*] **1.** to buy back, as after a tax sale or a mortgage foreclosure. **2.** to recover (something pledged or mortgaged) by payment or other satisfaction: *She returned to the pawnbroker's to redeem her watch.* **3.** to exchange (bonds, trading stamps, etc.) for money or goods. **4.** to discharge or fulfill (a pledge, promise, etc.). **5.** to set free or deliver (someone) from captivity, etc., by paying a penalty or ransom: *paid a ransom to redeem the hostages.* **6.** to make up for; offset (some fault, shortcoming, etc.): *After making that blunder, how will you redeem yourself?* —**re•deem′a•ble,** *adj.* —**re•deem′er,** *n.* [*count*]

re•demp•tion (ri demp′shən) /rɪˈdɛmpʃən/ *n.* [*noncount*] the act or process or an instance of redeeming, or the state of being redeemed.

re•de•ploy (rē′di ploi′) /ˌriydɪˈplɔy/ *v.* to arrange or put out (an army, group of soldiers, etc.) again in a new position. —**re′de•ploy′ment,** *n.* [*noncount*]

re•de•vel•op (rē′di vel′əp) /ˌriydɪˈvɛləp/ *v.* **1.** to develop again: [~ + *obj*]: *He redeveloped his ideas.* [*no obj*]: *This tumor could redevelop in a year.* **2.** to rebuild an area, such as in a city, that is in decline: [*no obj*]: *The investors want to redevelop in the downtown area.* [~ + *obj*]: *They want to redevelop a large downtown area.* —**re′de•vel′op•er,** *n.* [*count*] —**re′de•vel′op•ment,** *n.* [*noncount*]

red′-hand′ed, *adj., adv.* in the very act of a crime, wrongdoing, etc.: *caught red-handed with the stolen goods.*

red•head (red′hed′) /ˈrɛdˌhɛd/ *n.* [*count*] a person with red hair. —**red′head′ed,** *adj.*

red′ her′ring, *n.* [*count*] **1.** a smoked herring. **2.** something intended to remove or distract one's attention from the real problem or matter at hand.

red′-hot′, *adj.* **1.** red with heat; very hot. **2.** violent; furious: *red-hot anger.* **3.** very new: *a red-hot idea.*

re•di•rect (rē′di rekt′, -dī-) /ˌriydɪˈrɛkt, -day-/ *v.* [~ + *obj*] **1.** to direct again. **2.** to change the direction or focus of: *He needed to redirect his interests.* See -RECT-.

re•dis•trib•ute (rē′di strib′yo͞ot) /ˌriydɪˈstrɪbyuwt/ *v.* [~ + *obj*], **-ut•ed, -ut•ing. 1.** to distribute or give out again: *to redistribute profits to the stockholders.* **2.** to distribute or give out in a new and different way: *to redistribute the workload among the staff.* —**re•dis•tri•bu•tion** (rē′dis trə byo͞o′shən) /ˌriydɪstrəˈbyuwʃən/ *n.* [*noncount*]

re•dis•trict (rē dis′trikt) /riyˈdɪstrɪkt/ *v.* [~ + *obj*] to divide into districts again, or in a different way, as for administrative or electoral purposes. See -STRICT-.

red′-let′ter, *adj.* **1.** marked by red letters, as feast days on the church calendar. **2.** especially important or happy: *It was a red-letter day when their child was born.*

red′-light′ dis′trict, *n.* [*count*] an area or district in a city in which many houses of prostitution are located.

red•lin•ing or **red•-lin•ing,** (red′lī′ning) /ˈrɛdˌlaynɪŋ/ *n.* [*noncount*] **1.** a discriminatory practice by which some banks or institutions that lend money refuse to grant mortgages or insurance in urban areas that they consider to be deteriorating. **2.** a marking device, as underlining, used esp. in word processing to highlight suggested additional text in a document.

red•neck or **red•-neck,** (red′nek′) /ˈrɛdˌnɛk/ *Informal* (*often disparaging*). —*n.* [*count*] **1.** an uneducated white farm laborer, esp. from the South. **2.** a bigot or person with very backward views, esp. from the rural working class. —*adj.* **3.** Also, **red′-necked′.** narrow, prejudiced, or backward in thinking.

re•do (rē do͞o′) /riyˈduw/ *v.* [~ + *obj*], **-did, -done, -do•ing.** to do again: *to redo the test.*

red•o•lent (red′l ənt) /ˈrɛdl̩ənt/ *adj.* [*be* + ~] **1.** full of the smell of (something): *a kitchen redolent of garlic.* **2.** reminding one of (something); suggestive: *an accent redolent of Scotland.* —**red′o•lence,** *n.* [*noncount*]

re•dou•ble (rē dub′əl) /riyˈdʌbəl/ *v.* [~ + *obj*], **-bled, -bling.** to increase greatly or by twice as much: *They redoubled their efforts to finish on time.*

re•doubt (ri dout′) /rɪˈdawt/ *n.* [*count*] a separate, fortified area built inside or outside a larger fortification.

re•doubt•a•ble (ri dou′tə bəl) /rɪˈdawtəbəl/ *adj.* **1.** causing fear; fearsome; formidable. **2.** commanding respect or reverence. —**re•doubt′a•bly,** *adv.*

red′ pep′per, *n.* **1.** [*noncount*] a spicy powder that is added to food, made from a pepper plant. **2.** [*count*] a pepper grown in many varieties, the yellow or red pods of which are used for flavoring, sauces, etc. **3.** [*count*] the mild, ripe fruit of the sweet pepper, which is used as a vegetable.

re•dress (*n.* rē′dres, ri dres′; *v.* ri dres′) / *n.* ˈriydrɛs, rɪˈdrɛs; *v.* rɪˈdrɛs/ *n.* [*noncount*] **1.** the setting right of what is morally wrong. **2.** relief from wrong or injury, as in the form of payment or something done to make up for it. —*v.* [~ + *obj*] **3.** to remedy or make right: *to redress a grievance.* **4.** to adjust evenly again, as a balance.

red•skin (red′skin′) /ˈrɛdˌskɪn/ *n. Offensive.* AMERICAN INDIAN.

red′ tape′, *n.* [*noncount*] the steps, procedure, or routine of a bureaucracy that delays or prevents action.

re•duce (ri do͞os′, -dyo͞os′) /rɪˈduws, -ˈdyuws/ *v.* [~ + *obj*], **-duced, -duc•ing. 1.** to bring down to a smaller size, amount, price, etc.: *reduced her weight by ten pounds.* **2.** to lower in degree, intensity, etc.: *reduced the speed of the car.* **3.** to treat (something complicated) by analyzing smaller parts: *reduced the problem to its essentials.* **4.** to act in a destructive manner upon (a substance or object): *Their house was reduced to ashes by the fire.* **5.** [~ + *obj* + *to* + *obj*] to break down into: *The criticism reduced him to tears.* **6.** to change the figures or form, but not the value, of (a fraction, polynomial, etc.): *Six-eighths reduced to lowest terms is three-fourths.* —**re•duc•tive** (ri duk′tiv) /rɪˈdʌktɪv/ *adj.* See -DUC-.

re•duc•tion (ri duk′shən) /rɪˈdʌkʃən/ *n.* **1.** [*noncount*] the act or process of reducing, or the state of being reduced. **2.** [*count*] the amount by which something is reduced: *a pay reduction of fifty percent.* See -DUC-.

re•dun•dan•cy (ri dun′dən sē) /rɪˈdʌndənsiy/ *n., pl.* **-cies. 1.** [*noncount*] the state of being redundant, esp. the use of too many words or repetition in expressing ideas. **2.** [*count*] the use of additional or extra systems as a backup to a main part. **3.** *Chiefly Brit.* **a.** [*noncount*] the condition of being laid off from one's work or job. **b.** [*count*] an act or instance of being laid off.

re•dun•dant (ri dun′dənt) /rɪˈdʌndənt/ *adj.* **1.** exceeding what is usual or necessary, esp., having or showing too many words or unnecessary repetition in expressing ideas: *It is redundant to say "The giant is big."* **2.** (of a system, equipment, etc.) supplied as a backup in case of the failure of a main part, as in a spacecraft. **3.** *Chiefly Brit.* being laid off from employment.

re•dux (ri duks′) /rɪˈdʌks/ *adj.* [*after a noun*] brought back: *It seemed like the Dark Ages redux.*

red•wood (red′wo͝od′) /ˈrɛdˌwʊd/ *n.* **1.** [*count*] a cone-bearing tree of the cypress family, native to California, noted for its great height. **2.** [*noncount*] its valuable brownish red timber.

reed (rēd) /riyd/ *n.* **1.** [*count*] the straight stalk of a type of tall grass, growing in marshy places. **2.** [*count*] the plant itself. **3.** [*noncount*] such stalks or plants when thought of as a group, esp. used as material for thatching. **4.** [*count*] **a.** a small, flexible piece of wood or metal that is attached to the mouth of any of various wind instruments and vibrates when the instrument is played. **b.** a musical instrument played this way.

reed•y (rē′dē) /ˈriydiy/ *adj.*, **-i•er, -i•est. 1.** full of reeds: *a reedy marsh.* **2.** (of a voice) thin in quality. —**reed′i•ness,** *n.* [*noncount*]

reef (rēf) /riyf/ *n.* [*count*] a ridge or bank of rocks or sand, often of coral debris, at or near the surface of the water.

reef•er (rē′fər) /ˈriyfər/ *n.* [*count*] *Slang.* a marijuana cigarette.

reek (rēk) /riyk/ *v.* **1.** to smell strongly and unpleasantly: [*no obj*]: *The rotting garbage reeked.* [~ + *with/of* + *obj*]: *The room reeked of pesticide.* **2.** [~ + *with/of* + *obj*] to contain or seem to contain a potent atmosphere of something: *a suburb that absolutely reeks of money.* —*n.* [*count; usually singular*] **3.** a strong, unpleasant smell.

reel[1] (rēl) /riyl/ *n.* [*count*] **1.** a rounded object or cylinder or other device that spins and is used to wind up or let out wire, rope, film, etc.: *a reel on a fishing rod; the reel on the movie projector.* **2.** an amount of something wound on a reel: *a reel of film.* **3.** *Brit.* a spool of sewing thread. —*v.* **4.** [~ + *obj*] to wind on a reel: *to reel the* *film.* **5.** to pull by winding a line on a reel: [~ + *obj* + *in/out*]: *to reel a fish in.* [~ + *in/out* + *obj*]: *to reel out some wire.* **6. reel off,** to say or write quickly and easily, as a list of items: [~ + *off* + *obj*]: *She reeled off her answers one by one.* [~ + *obj* + *off*]: *reeled her answers off.*

reel[2] (rēl) /riyl/ *v.* [*no obj*] **1.** to sway, rock, or appear to move unsteadily. **2.** to sway or move unsteadily or clumsily about in standing or walking, as from dizziness or drunkenness; stagger: *The boxer was reeling from the blows.* **3.** to have a sensation of whirling: *His brain reeled.*

reel[3] (rēl) /riyl/ *n.* [*count*] a lively Scottish dance.

re•e•lect (rē′i lekt′) /ˌriyɪ'lɛkt/ *v.* [~ + *obj*] to elect again: *She was reelected to another term of office as mayor.* —**re′e•lec′tion,** *n.* [*count*]: *another reelection.* [*noncount*]: *seeking reelection.* See -LEC-.

re•en•act (rē′ə nakt′) /ˌriyə'nækt/ *v.* [~ + *obj*] to act out again: *The prosecutor reenacted the crime for the jurors.* —**re′en•act′ment,** *n.* [*count*] See -ACT-.

re•en•try (rē en′trē) /riy'ɛntriy/ *n., pl.* **-tries. 1.** [*count*] the act of reentering. **2.** the return from outer space into the earth's atmosphere of an earth-orbiting satellite, spacecraft, rocket, or the like: [*noncount*]: *preparing for reentry.* [*count*]: *another successful reentry.*

ref (ref) /rɛf/ *n., v.,* **reffed, ref•fing.** *Informal.* —*n.* [*count*] **1.** a referee. —*v.* **2.** to be or act as referee of: [~ + *obj*]: *She reffed a difficult game.* [*no obj*]: *had never reffed before.* See -FER-.

re•fec•to•ry (ri fek′tə rē) /rɪ'fɛktəriy/ *n.* [*count*], *pl.* **-ries.** a dining hall, as in a monastery or college. See -FEC-.

re•fer (ri fûr′) /rɪ'fɜr/ *v.,* **-ferred, -fer•ring. 1.** [~ + *to* + *obj*] to direct attention to: *The teacher referred to chapter seven during yesterday's lecture.* **2.** [~ + *obj* + *to* + *obj*] to direct (someone) to a person, place, etc., for information or anything required: *The asterisk refers the reader to a footnote.* **3.** [~ + *obj* + *to* + *obj*] to submit or send (something) to someone for decision, information, etc.: *Please refer all your questions to the public information office.* **4.** [~ + *to* + *obj* + *as* + *obj*] to consider as belonging to a certain class, group, period, etc.; classify: *The government refers to a plumber's work as a blue-collar job.* **5.** [~ + *to* + *obj*] to apply to; indicate; mean: *This new regulation does not really refer to your company.* —**re•fer′rer,** *n.* [*count*] See -FER-.

ref•er•ee (ref′ə rē′) /ˌrɛfə'riy/ *n., pl.* **-ees,** *v.,* **-eed, -ee•ing.** —*n.* [*count*] **1.** a person to whom an issue or problem is sent for a decision or settlement; an arbitrator. **2.** (in certain games and sports) a judge having functions fixed by the rules of the game or sport; umpire. **3.** an authority who evaluates proposals for funding, scholarly papers for publication, etc. **4.** *Law.* a person selected by a court to take testimony and recommend a decision: *The referee listened to the motorist's explanation and gave him a lower fine.* —*v.* **5.** to act as a referee for (a game, contest, proposal, etc.): [~ + *obj*]: *to referee games.* [*no obj*]: *to referee fairly.* See -FER-.

ref•er•ence (ref′ər əns, ref′rəns) /'rɛfərəns, 'rɛfrəns/ *n., v.,* **-enced, -enc•ing.** —*n.* **1.** [*noncount*] an act or instance of referring, as for information. **2.** [*count*] a mention; allusion: *In her complaint she made numerous references to him as a witness.* **3. a.** a direction of the attention, as in a book, to some other book, passage, etc.: [*noncount*]: *You make reference to several authors in your paper.* [*count*]: *the use of references in a term paper.* **b.** [*count*] the book, passage, etc., to which one is directed: *You need at least five references in such a short term paper.* **4.** [*noncount*] use for purposes of information: *a library for public reference.* **5.** [*count*] a book or other source of useful information: *His book is an important medical reference.* **6.** [*count*] **a.** a person who can provide a statement or a letter about, or answer questions about, another's character, abilities, etc.: *May I list you as one of my references in case a job interview comes up?* **b.** a statement or letter regarding a person's character, abilities, etc.: *She wrote him a glowing reference.* **7.** [*noncount*] regard or connection; relation: *I'm writing in reference to the job in the classified section.* —*v.* [~ + *obj*] **8.** to mention in or as a reference: *How many times has your work been referenced in other scholars' work?* —*adj.* [*before a noun*] **9.** of or for materials used for finding information: *reference books; a library reference room.* See -FER-.

ref•er•en•dum (ref′ə ren′dəm) /ˌrɛfə'rɛndəm/ *n.* [*count*], *pl.* **-dums, -da** (-də) /-də/. a vote by the people on whether to approve or reject some proposal or policy, esp. one that was made by or passed by a law-making body. See -FER-.

ref•er•ent (ref′ər ənt, ref′rənt) /'rɛfərənt, 'rɛfrənt/ *n.* [*count*] the object or event to which a word, term, or symbol points or refers. See -FER-.

re•fer•ral (ri fûr′əl) /rɪ'fɜrəl/ *n.* **1.** [*count*] an act or instance of referring: *Referrals can be made to other doctors for a second opinion.* **2.** [*count*] a person referred or recommended to someone or for something: *That doctor was her next referral.* **3.** [*noncount*] the state of being referred. See -FER-.

re•fill (*v.* rē fil′; *n.* rē′fil′) / *v.* riy'fɪl; *n.* 'riyˌfɪl/ *v.* **1.** to fill again: [~ + *obj*]: *We refilled our glasses with wine.* [*no obj*]: *The tank refills automatically.* —*n.* [*count*] **2.** a material, supply, or the like, to replace something that has been used up: *a refill for a fountain pen.* **3.** a drink after one has finished a previous one: *a refill of coffee.* —**re•fill′a•ble,** *adj.*

re•fi•nance (rē′fi nans′, rē fi′nans) /ˌriyfɪ'næns, riy'faynæns/ *v.,* **-nanced, -nanc•ing.** to pay off a debt by borrowing more money, usually at a lower rate of interest: [~ + *obj*]: *to refinance a mortgage.* [*no obj*]: *a good time to refinance.*

re•fine (ri fīn′) /rɪ'fayn/ *v.* [~ + *obj*], **-fined, -fin•ing. 1.** to separate (something) from impure substances: *to refine oil.* **2.** to bring (something) to a finer state or form by purifying, polishing, changing, or making it more precise: *to refine a theory.* See -FIN-.

re•fined (ri fīnd′) /rɪ'faynd/ *adj.* **1.** fastidious; delicate: *refined manners.* **2.** freed from impurities: *refined sugar.* **3.** very exact: *refined measurements.* See -FIN-.

re•fine•ment (ri fīn′mənt) /rɪ'faynmənt/ *n.* **1.** [*noncount*] fineness or elegance of feeling, taste, manners, language, etc. **2.** [*noncount*] the act or process of refining; the quality or state of being refined: *the refinement of oil.* **3.** [*count*] an improved form of something: *The new theory is a refinement of an earlier one.* **4.** [*count*] a detail or device added to improve something. See -FIN-.

re•fin•er•y (ri fī′nə rē) /rɪ'faynəriy/ *n.* [*count*], *pl.* **-er•ies.** an establishment for refining something, such as metal, sugar, or oil. See -FIN-.

re•flect (ri flekt′) /rɪ'flɛkt/ *v.* **1.** to turn or throw back (light, heat, sound, etc.) from a surface: [~ + *obj*]: *The mirror reflected his image perfectly.* [*no obj*]: *This dull surface doesn't reflect.* **2.** [~ + *obj*] to express; show: *The party seems to reflect the views of its leader.* **3.** to think over; ponder or meditate: [~ (+ *on* + *obj*)]: *He sat there reflecting on what had gone wrong.* [*no obj*]: *took time to pause and reflect.* **4. reflect on,** [~ + *on* + *obj*] **a.** to serve or tend to bring blame or discredit: *His crimes reflected on the whole community.* **b.** to serve to give a particular aspect or impression: *That accomplishment reflects well on your abilities.* —**re•flec′tive,** *adj.* —**re•flec′tive•ly,** *adv.* See -FLECT-.

re•flec•tion (ri flek′shən) /rɪ'flɛkʃən/ *n.* **1.** [*noncount*] the act of reflecting or the state of being reflected: *the reflection of the sun on the water.* **2.** [*count*] something reflected, as an image. **3.** [*noncount*] careful consideration: *After much reflection I've come to a decision.* **4.** [*count*] a thought that occurs when thinking about or considering something: *published his reflections on the years of his presidency.* **5.** [*count*] an indication or expression of something unfavorable with respect to a person or thing: *meant no reflection on your honesty or integrity.* Also, *esp. Brit.,* **reflexion.** —**re•flec′tion•al,** *adj.* See -FLECT-.

re•flec•tive (ri flek′tiv) /rɪ'flɛktɪv/ *adj.* **1.** thinking or tending to think about something in a careful way: *He fell into a reflective mood.* **2.** reflecting light: *reflective surfaces.* See -FLECT-.

re•flec•tor (ri flek′tər) /rɪ'flɛktər/ *n.* [*count*] a body, surface, or device that reflects light, heat, sound, or the like. See -FLECT-.

re•flex (rē′fleks) /'riyflɛks/ *n.* **1.** [*count*] a movement or a response that is automatic and involuntary, caused by a nerve impulse that reacts quickly to some outside action without waiting for the brain to process it and respond: *Your fingers will withdraw from a hot surface in a reflex.* **2.** any automatic, unthinking, often habitual behavior or response: [*count*]: *quick political reflexes.* [*noncount; by* + ~]: *He smiles at other people almost by reflex.* —*adj.* [*before a noun*] **3.** of or relating to such an automatic response to some outside action: *a reflex act.* See -FLEX-.

re•flex•ive (ri flek′siv) /rɪ'flɛksɪv/ *adj.* **1. a.** (of a verb) taking an object that refers to the same person or thing as the subject, such as *cut* in *I cut myself.* **b.** (of a pronoun) used as an object referring to the same person or thing as the subject, such as *myself* in *I cut myself.* **2.** responding by way of a reflex: *a reflexive act of self-preservation.* **—***n.* [*count*] **3.** a reflexive verb or pronoun. **—re•flex′ive•ly,** *adv.* See -FLEX-.

re•for•est (rē fôr′ist, -for′-) /riy'fɔrɪst, -'fɒr-/ *v.* [~ + *obj*] to replant trees on (land that has lost trees by cutting, fire, etc.). **—re•for•est•a•tion** (rē′fôr i stā′shən, -for-) /ˌriyfɔrɪ'steyʃən, -fɒr-/ *n.* [*noncount*]

re-form (rē fôrm′) /riy'fɔrm/ *v.* to form again: [~ + *obj*]: *The general re-formed his troops.* [*no obj*]: *The troops re-formed.*

re•form (ri fôrm′) /rɪ'fɔrm/ *n.* **1.** [*noncount*] the improvement, changing, or removing of what is wrong, evil, unsatisfactory, etc.: *urging social reform.* **2.** [*count*] an instance of this: *some long overdue reforms in the tax codes.* **—***v.* **3.** [~ + *obj*] to change to a better state, form, etc.: *to reform the corrupt system.* **4.** to (cause a person to) abandon wrong or evil ways: [*no obj*]: *He promised to reform and live honestly.* [~ + *obj*]: *Could he reform his evil ways?* **—***adj.* **5.** [*before a noun; Reform*] conforming to or characteristic of a movement in Judaism that simplifies or rejects some traditional beliefs and practices to meet the conditions of contemporary life. **—re•form′er,** *n.* [*count*] See -FORM-.

ref•or•ma•tion (ref′ər mā′shən) /ˌrɛfər'meyʃən/ *n.* **1.** the act of reforming or the state of being reformed: [*noncount*]: *reformation of the system.* [*count*]: *a necessary reformation.* **2.** [*proper noun; the* + *Reformation*] the 16th-century movement that resulted in the establishment of the Protestant churches.

re•form•a•to•ry (ri fôr′mə tôr′ē, -tōr′ē) /rɪ'fɔrməˌtɔriy, -ˌtowriy/ *adj., n., pl.* **-ries.** **—***adj.* **1.** serving or designed to reform. **—***n.* [*count*] **2.** Also called **reform school.** a jail or similar institution for young offenders.

re•fract (ri frakt′) /rɪ'frækt/ *v.* [~ + *obj*] to cause a ray of light to change direction as it passes through different substances, as glass or water, at an angle. See -FRAC-.

re•frac•tion (ri frak′shən) /rɪ'frækʃən/ *n.* [*noncount*] the change of direction of a ray of light in passing through different substances, as glass or water, at an angle. **—re•frac′tive,** *adj.* See -FRAC-.

re•frac•to•ry (ri frak′tə rē) /rɪ'fræktəriy/ *adj.* stubbornly disobedient: *a refractory child.* See -FRAC-.

re•frain[1] (ri frān′) /rɪ'freyn/ *v.* to keep oneself from doing or saying something: [~ + *from* + *obj*]: *Can we please refrain from laughing?* [~ + *from* + *verb-ing*]: *He refrained from asking any questions.*

re•frain[2] (ri frān′) /rɪ'freyn/ *n.* [*count*] a phrase or verse that is repeated in a song or poem, esp. at the end of each stanza; a chorus. See -FRAC-.

re•fresh (ri fresh′) /rɪ'frɛʃ/ *v.* [~ + *obj*] **1.** to provide new vigor and energy by rest, food, etc.: *a quick dip in the pool will refresh them.* **2.** to stimulate: *Let me refresh your memory.* **—re•fresh′er,** *n.* [*count*]

re•fresh•ing (ri fresh′ing) /rɪ'frɛʃɪŋ/ *adj.* bringing a feeling of refreshment: *a refreshing dip in the pool.*

re•fresh•ment (ri fresh′mənt) /rɪ'frɛʃmənt/ *n.* **1.** **refreshments,** [*plural*] food and drink, esp. for a snack or light meal. **2.** [*noncount*] the act of refreshing or the state of being refreshed.

re•frig•er•ate (ri frij′ə rāt′) /rɪ'frɪdʒəˌreyt/ *v.* [~ + *obj*], **-at•ed, -at•ing.** to make or keep cold or cool, in order to preserve or keep fresh. **—re•frig•er•ant** (ri frij′ər ənt) /rɪ'frɪdʒərənt/ *adj., n.* [*count*]: *a toxic refrigerant.* [*noncount*]: *not enough refrigerant in the air-conditioner.* **—re•frig•er•a•tion** (ri frij′ə rā′shən) /rɪˌfrɪdʒə'reyʃən/ *n.* [*noncount*]

re•frig•er•a•tor (ri frij′ə rā′tər) /rɪ'frɪdʒəˌreytər/ *n.* [*count*] a room or large appliance in which food, drink, etc., is kept cool esp. by means of mechanical refrigeration. See illustration at APARTMENT.

re•fu•el (rē fyōō′əl) /riy'fyuwəl/ *v.* **1.** [~ + *obj*] to supply (an airplane, car, etc.) with fuel. **2.** [*no obj*] (of an airplane) to take on a supply of fuel: *The plane refueled at Cairo and took off again.*

ref•uge (ref′yōōj) /'rɛfyuwdʒ/ *n.* **1.** [*noncount*] shelter or protection from danger, trouble, etc.: *The high ground gave them refuge from the floodwaters.* **2.** [*count*] a place of shelter, protection, or safety: *a refuge from the storm; a wildlife refuge.* See -FUG-.

ref•u•gee (ref′yŏŏ jē′, ref′yŏŏ jē′) /ˌrɛfyʊ'dʒiy, 'rɛfyʊˌdʒiy/ *n.* [*count*], *pl.* **-gees.** a person who flees for refuge or safety, esp. to a foreign country, as in time of political trouble, war, etc. See -FUG-.

re•ful•gent (ri ful′jənt) /rɪ'fʌldʒənt/ *adj.* shining brightly; radiant; gleaming. **—re•ful′gence,** *n.* [*noncount*]

re•fund[1] (*v.* ri fund′, rē′fund; *n.* rē′fund) / *v.* rɪ'fʌnd, 'riyfʌnd; *n.* 'riyfʌnd/ *v.* **1.** to give back or restore (esp. money); repay: [~ + *obj* + *to* + *obj*]: *The store will refund the full purchase price to its customers.* [~ + *obj* + *obj*]: *The store will refund you the money.* **—***n.* **2.** an act or instance of refunding: [*noncount*]: *Do you want credit or a refund?* [*count*]: *No refunds will be made.* **3.** [*count*] an amount refunded: *a twenty-dollar refund.* **—re•fund′a•ble,** *adj.*

re•fund[2] (rē fund′) /riy'fʌnd/ *v.* [~ + *obj*] to provide funds for (something) again.

re•fur•bish (rē fûr′bish) /riy'fɜrbɪʃ/ *v.* [~ + *obj*] to furbish again; clean, decorate, or renovate; brighten: *to refurbish your old apartment.* **—re•fur′bish•ment,** *n.* [*noncount*]

re•fus•al (ri fyōō′zəl) /rɪ'fyuwzəl/ *n.* the act of refusing; an example of, or a case of, refusing: [*noncount*]: *Refusal is not possible.* [*count*]: *His refusals were no longer tolerated.*

re•fuse[1] (ri fyōōz′) /rɪ'fyuwz/ *v.,* **-fused, -fus•ing.** **1.** to decline to accept (something offered); reject: [~ + *obj*]: *He refused a cigarette.* [*no obj*]: *an offer you can't refuse.* **2.** to deny (a request, demand, etc.): [~ + *obj*]: *She refused my request.* [~ + *obj* + *obj*]: *Her father refused his daughter permission to see that boy again.* **3.** [~ + *to* + *verb*] to turn down (doing something): *to refuse to discuss an issue.* **4.** [~ + *obj*] to decline to accept (someone offering a proposal of marriage): *She had many suitors but she refused them all.*

ref•use[2] (ref′yōōs) /'rɛfyuws/ *n.* [*noncount*] **1.** something thrown away as worthless or useless; waste; rubbish; trash; garbage. **—***adj.* [*before a noun*] **2.** rejected as worthless; thrown away.

re•fute (ri fyōōt′) /rɪ'fyuwt/ *v.* [~ + *obj*], **-fut•ed, -fut•ing.** to prove to be false or to be in error: *We refuted his accusations.* **—re•fut•a•ble** (ri fyōō′tə bəl, ref′yə tə-) /rɪ'fyuwtəbəl, 'rɛfyətə-/ *adj.* **—ref•u•ta•tion** (ref′yŏŏ tā′shən) /ˌrɛfyʊ'teyʃən/ *n.* [*noncount*]: *Refutation of the charges against him is impossible.* [*count*]: *refutations of guilt.*

-reg-, *root.* *-reg-* comes from Latin, where it has the meaning "rule; direct; control." This meaning is found in such words as: DEREGULATE, IRREGULAR, REGAL, REGALIA, REGENCY, REGICIDE, REGIME, REGIMEN, REGIMENT, REGION, REGIONAL, REGULAR.

re•gain (rē gān′) /riy'geyn/ *v.* [~ + *obj*] **1.** to get again; recover: *He regained his health at last.* **2.** to succeed in reaching again: *to regain the shore.*

re•gal (rē′gəl) /'riygəl/ *adj.* **1.** of or relating to a king or queen; royal. **2.** fitting, worthy of, or resembling a king or queen, as by being stately or splendid. **—re′gal•ly,** *adv.* See -REG-.

re•gale (ri gāl′) /rɪ'geyl/ *v.* [~ + *obj*], **-galed, -gal•ing.** **1.** to entertain on a grand scale or in a very agreeable and enjoyable way; delight: *regaled us with funny stories.* **2.** to entertain with very good food or drink.

re•ga•li•a (ri gā′lē ə, -gāl′yə) /rɪ'geyliyə, -'geylyə/ *n.* [*plural*] **1.** the symbols, decorations, ceremonial clothes, or emblems of royalty or of some office, rank, etc. **2.** fancy or dressy clothing; finery. See -REG-.

re•gard (ri gärd′) /rɪ'gɑrd/ *v.* **1.** [*not: be* + *~-ing*] to see, look at, or think of with a particular feeling or in a certain way; judge; consider: [~ + *obj*]: *to regard a person with favor.* [~ + *obj* + *as* + *obj*]: *I have always regarded you as a friend.* **2.** [*not: be* + *~-ing;* ~ + *obj*] to have or show respect or concern for: *to regard the feelings of others.* **3.** [~ + *obj*] to look at; observe: *regarded her with a look of contempt.* **—***n.* **4.** [*noncount*] an aspect, point, or area of concern: *The new machine is quite satisfactory in this regard.* **5.** [*noncount*] thought; attention; concern: *He had no regard for my feelings.* **6.** [*noncount*] respect and liking: *They hold teachers in high regard.* **7.** **regards,** [*plural*] expressions of respect or affection: *Give them my regards.* **—*Idiom.*** **8.** **as regards,** concerning; about: *inquired as regards your family.* **9.** **with** or **in regard to,** with reference to; as regards; concerning: *With regard to the charges, the jury finds you guilty.*

re•gard•ing (ri gär′ding) /rɪ'gɑrdɪŋ/ *prep.* with regard to; about; concerning: *Regarding payment, send us a check.*

re•gard•less (ri gärd′lis) /rɪ'gɑrdlɪs/ *adv.* **1.** without concern as to advice, warning, hardship, etc.; anyway: *Do as she says, regardless.* **—*Idiom.*** **2.** **regardless of,** in spite of; without regard for: *I like them regardless of your opinion.*

re•gat•ta (ri gat′ə, -gä′tə) /rɪ'gætə, -'gɑtə/ *n.* [*count*], *pl.* **-tas.** **1.** a boat race. **2.** an organized series of such races.

re•gen•cy (rē′jən sē) /ˈriydʒənsiy/ *n., pl.* **-cies,** *adj.* **—***n.* **1.** [*noncount*] the office, government, rule, or control of a regent or regents. **2.** [*count*] a territory under the control of a regent or regents. **3.** [*count*] the term of office of a regent. **—***adj.* **4.** of or relating to a regency. See -REG-.

re•gen•er•ate (*v.* ri jen′ə rāt′; *adj.* -ər it) / *v.* rɪˈdʒɛnəˌreyt; *adj.* -ərɪt/ *v.,* **-at•ed, -at•ing,** *adj.* **—***v.* **1.** [~ + *obj*] to cause a moral change for the better in (someone). **2.** [~ + *obj*] to revive or produce again; revitalize: *to regenerate the economy.* **3.** [~ + *obj*] to restore or revive (a lost or injured body part) by the growth of new tissue. **4.** [*no obj*] to grow or be formed again: *That animal's tail can regenerate if it is cut off.* **—***adj.* **5.** made over in a better form. **6.** reformed. **—re•gen•er•a•tion** (ri jen′ə rā′shən) /rɪˌdʒɛnəˈreyʃən/ *n.* [*noncount*] **—re•gen•er•a•tive** (ri jen′ə rā′tiv, -ər ə tiv) /rɪˈdʒɛnəˌreytɪv, -ərətɪv/ *adj.* See -GEN-.

re•gent (rē′jənt) /ˈriydʒənt/ *n.* [*count*] **1.** a person who has the ruling power in a kingdom when the king or queen is too young to rule, or is absent or disabled. **2.** a member of the governing board of a university or an educational system. **—***adj.* [*usually: after a noun*] **3.** acting as regent of a kingdom: *the prince regent.* See -REG-.

reg•gae (reg′ā) /ˈrɛgey/ *n.* [*noncount*] a style of Jamaican music blending blues, calypso, and rock.

reg•i•cide (rej′ə sīd′) /ˈrɛdʒəˌsayd/ *n.* **1.** the killing of a king: [*noncount*]: *the crime of regicide.* [*count*]: *historical regicides.* **2.** [*count*] a person who kills a king. See -REG-, -CIDE-.

re•gime or **ré•gime** (rə zhēm′, rā-) /rəˈʒiym, rey-/ *n.* [*count*] **1.** a system of rule or government. **2.** a government in power, or the period of time in which it is in power. **3.** REGIMEN. See -REG-.

reg•i•men (rej′ə mən, -men′) /ˈrɛdʒəmən, -ˌmɛn/ *n.* [*count*] a regulated course, as of diet, exercise, or manner of living, to gain a result, as preserving or restoring health. See -REG-.

reg•i•ment (*n.* rej′ə mənt; *v.* -ment′) / *n.* ˈrɛdʒəmənt; *v.* -ˌmɛnt/ *n.* [*count*] **1.** a military unit of ground forces made up of two or more battalions. **—***v.* [~ + *obj*] **2.** to manage or treat according to strict discipline: *known for harshly regimenting his men.* **—reg′i•men′tal,** *adj.* [*before a noun*]: *regimental headquarters.* See -REG-.

reg•i•men•ta•tion (rej′ə men tā′shən) /ˌrɛdʒəmɛnˈteyʃən/ *n.* [*noncount*] strict, rigid control or discipline over a group. See -REG-.

re•gion (rē′jən) /ˈriydʒən/ *n.* [*count*] **1.** a large area of a surface, space, or body: *a region of the earth; a tropical region.* **2.** a district of a certain kind: *an industrial region.* **3.** a division of the body: *the abdominal region.* **—*Idiom.*** **4. in the region of,** approximately; almost: *cost in the region of ten dollars.* See -REG-.

re•gion•al (rē′jə nl) /ˈriydʒənl/ *adj.* **1.** of or involving a region: *regional schools.* **2.** [*before a noun*] found only in a certain region or regions: *spoke with a regional accent.* **—re′gion•al•ly,** *adv.* See -REG-.

re•gion•al•ism (rē′jə nl iz′əm) /ˈriydʒənlˌɪzəm/ *n.* **1.** [*count*] a word, a way of speaking, an act, or a way of behaving that is special to a particular area or region. **2.** [*noncount*] devotion or loyalty to the interests of one's own region. See -REG-.

reg•is•ter (rej′ə stər) /ˈrɛdʒəstər/ *n.* [*count*] **1.** a book in which records of events, names, etc., are kept. **2.** a list or record of such events, names, etc. **3.** CASH REGISTER. **4.** the range of a voice or of a musical instrument, from the lowest to the highest notes that can be reached. **5.** a device for controlling the flow of warmed air or the like through an opening. **—***v.* **6.** to enter or cause to be entered in a register: [*no obj*]: *He registered as Mr. John Doe.* [~ + *obj*]: *He registered them as Mr. and Mrs. John Doe.* **7.** [~ + *obj*] to cause (mail) to be recorded upon delivery to a post office for safeguarding against loss, damage, etc., during sending: *to register a parcel.* **8.** to (cause to) enroll (a student, voter, etc.): [*no obj*]: *registered for class.* [~ + *obj*]: *Last year the school registered 16,000 students.* **9.** to indicate by a record or scale, as instruments do: [~ + *obj*]: *The earthquake barely registered a few ticks on the sensing devices.* [*no obj*]: *The earthquake did not register on our instruments.* **10.** to show (surprise, joy, anger, etc.), as by facial expression or by actions: [~ + *obj*]: *His face registered annoyance.* [*no obj*]: *A smile registered on his face.* **11.** [*no obj*] to have some effect; make some impression: *I don't know if the danger has registered on him yet or not.* **—reg•is•trant** (rej′ə strənt) /ˈrɛdʒəstrənt/ *n.* [*count*]

reg′istered nurse′, *n.* [*count*] a graduate nurse who has passed a state board examination and is registered and licensed to practice nursing. *Abbr.:* RN, R.N.

reg•is•trar (rej′ə strär′) /ˈrɛdʒəˌstrɑr/ *n.* [*count*] a person who keeps records, esp. a school or college official who maintains students' records, issues reports of grades, mails out official publications, etc.

reg•is•tra•tion (rej′ə strā′shən) /ˌrɛdʒəˈstreyʃən/ *n.* **1.** [*noncount*] the act or process of registering: *Registration is on Thursday.* **2.** [*count*] an instance of this: *many new registrations.*

reg•is•try (rej′ə strē) /ˈrɛdʒəstriy/ *n., pl.* **-tries. 1.** [*noncount*] the act of registering; registration. **2.** [*count*] a place where a register is kept; an office of registration. **3.** [*count*] an official record; register. **4.** [*noncount*] the state of being registered.

re•gress (*v.* ri gres′; *n.* rē′gres) / *v.* rɪˈgrɛs; *n.* ˈriygrɛs/ *v.* [*no obj*] **1.** to move backward; go back, esp. to an earlier, worse, or less advanced state or form: *For a while the patient was making progress, but now he seems to be regressing.* **—***n.* [*noncount*] **2.** the act of regressing. **—re•gres•sion** (ri gresh′ən) /rɪˈgrɛʃən/ *n.* [*noncount*] **—re•gres•sive** (ri gres′iv) /rɪˈgrɛsɪv/ *adj.* See -GRESS-.

re•gret (ri gret′) /rɪˈgrɛt/ *v.,* **-gret•ted, -gret•ting,** *n.* **—***v.* **1.** to feel sorrow or remorse for (an act, fault, event, etc.): [~ + *obj*]: *said he did not regret his decision to retire.* [~ + *verb-ing*]: *The thief said he regretted stealing the money.* [~ + *(that) clause*]: *He regrets that he cannot be here in person tonight.* **2.** [*not: be +* ~*-ing;* ~ + *to + verb*] (used in the present tense to express sorrow): *We regret to inform you that the train will be late.* **—***n.* **3.** a feeling of sorrow, unhappiness, or guilt for a fault, wrong act, a loss, etc.: [*noncount*]: *a sudden pang of regret.* [*count*]: *had no regrets.* **4. regrets,** [*plural*] a polite, usually formal refusal of an invitation: *sent my regrets.* **—re•gret′ful,** *adj.* **—re•gret′ful•ly,** *adv.*

re•gret•ta•ble (ri gret′ə bl) /rɪˈgrɛtəbl/ *adj.* causing or deserving of regret; unfortunate: *a regrettable accident.* **—re•gret′ta•bly,** *adv.*

re•group (rē gro͞op′) /riyˈgruwp/ *v.* **1.** to form into a new or restructured group or grouping: [~ + *obj*]: *The general regrouped his men.* [*no obj*]: *The armies regrouped.* **2.** [*no obj*] to become reorganized in order to make a fresh start, as after a setback.

reg•u•lar (reg′yə lər) /ˈrɛgyələr/ *adj.* **1.** usual; normal; customary; according to a rule or pattern: *His regular habit was to drink coffee in the morning.* **2.** evenly arranged; balanced; symmetrical: *regular facial features.* **3.** having the same or a fixed system, procedure, etc., for something: *The verb* walk *in English is a regular verb because it forms its past tense as* walked. **4.** steady and even; not changing: *a regular heartbeat.* **5.** [*be* + ~] having bowel movements or monthly periods according to a fixed or steady pattern. **6.** habitual; having done so for a long time: *a regular user of cocaine.* **7.** [*before a noun*] legitimate or proper: *I suspected he wasn't a regular doctor after all.* **8.** *Informal.* **a.** decent; straightforward; nice: *a regular guy.* **b.** [*before a noun*] absolute; complete; thoroughgoing: *We have a regular flood here.* **9.** [*before a noun*] being or belonging to the permanently organized, or standing, army of a state. **—***n.* [*count*] **10.** a habitual customer or client, or one who has been present for a long time. **11. a.** a size of garments for persons of average height. **b.** a garment in this size. **12.** an athlete who plays in most of the games, usually from the start. **—reg•u•lar•i•ty** (reg′yə lar′i tē) /ˌrɛgyəˈlærɪtiy/ *n.* [*noncount*] See -REG-.

reg•u•lar•ize (reg′yə lə rīz′) /ˈrɛgyələˌrayz/ *v.* [~ + *obj*], **-ized, -iz•ing.** to make regular. Also *Brit.* **regularise.** See -REG-.

reg•u•lar•ly (reg′yə lər lē) /ˈrɛgyələrliy/ *adv.* **1.** on a regular basis: *We meet regularly twice a month.* **2.** in a regular, balanced way: *regularly arranged bricks.* See -REG-.

reg•u•late (reg′yə lāt′) /ˈrɛgyəˌleyt/ *v.* [~ + *obj*], **-lat•ed, -lat•ing. 1.** to control or direct by a rule, principle, or method: *Laws exist to regulate traffic on the highways.* **2.** to adjust to some standard or requirement: *to regulate the temperature.* **3.** to adjust so as to be accurate or correct: *to regulate a watch.* **4.** to put in good order: *to regulate one's diet.* **—reg•u•la•tive** (reg′yə lā′tiv, -yə lə tiv) /ˈrɛgyəˌleytɪv, -yələtɪv/ **reg•u•la•to•ry** (reg′yə-lə tôr′ē, -tōr′ē) /ˈrɛgyələˌtɔriy, -ˌtowriy/ *adj.* **—reg′u•la′tor,** *n.* [*count*] See -REG-.

reg•u•la•tion (reg′yə lā′shən) /ˌrɛgyəˈleyʃən/ *n.* **1.** [*count*] a law, rule, or other order given by authority, esp. to regulate conduct. **2.** [*noncount*] the act of regulating or the state of being regulated: *strict regulation of the* *number of cars entering the country.* **—***adj.* [*usually: before a noun*] **3.** ordered by or agreeing with regulation: *regulation army equipment.* See -REG-.

re•gur•gi•tate (ri gûr′ji tāt′) /rɪ'gɜrdʒɪˌteyt/ *v.,* **-tat•ed, -tat•ing. 1.** to (cause to) vomit: [~ + *obj*]: *The mother bird regurgitates food to feed her young.* [*no obj*]: *regurgitating after a greasy meal.* **2.** [~ + *obj*] to give back or repeat facts: *quick at regurgitating facts in an exam.* **—re•gur•gi•ta•tion** (ri gûr′ji tā′shən) /rɪˌgɜrdʒɪ'teyʃən/ *n.* [*noncount*]

re•hab (rē′hab′) /'riyˌhæb/ *n., v.,* **-habbed, -hab•bing.** **—***n.* **1.** [*noncount*] rehabilitation: *a treatment for drug rehab.* **2.** [*count*] a rehabilitated building. **—***v.* [~ + *obj*] **3.** to rehabilitate.

re•ha•bil•i•tate (rē′hə bil′i tāt′, rē′ə-) /ˌriyhə'bɪlɪˌteyt, ˌriyə-/ *v.* [~ + *obj*], **-tat•ed, -tat•ing. 1.** to restore or bring (something) to good condition or functioning: *exercises for rehabilitating damaged knees.* **2.** to bring about or restore one's standing, functioning, good reputation, or moral character: *to rehabilitate imprisoned criminals.* **—re′ha•bil′i•ta′tive,** *adj.* See -HABIL-.

re•ha•bil•i•ta•tion (rē′ə bil′i tā′shən) /ˌriyəˌbɪlɪ'teyʃən/ *n.* [*noncount*] **1.** the act of improving or restoring something to good condition. **2.** the act of restoring someone to an earlier standing, functioning, reputation, or moral character. See -HABIL-.

re•hash (*v.* rē hash′; *n.* rē′hash′) / *v.* riy'hæʃ; *n.* 'riyˌhæʃ/ *v.* [~ + *obj*] **1.** to reuse (old material) without significant or important change: *rehashing the same old ideas.* **—***n.* [*count*] **2.** something reused but not changed in a meaningful way.

re•hears•al (ri hûr′səl) /rɪ'hɜrsəl/ *n.* **1.** [*count*] a session of exercise, drill, or practice, or performance in preparation for a public performance, ceremony, etc. **2.** [*noncount*] exercise, drill, or practice in such preparation: *You've had enough rehearsal; it's time to perform before a live audience.*

re•hearse (ri hûrs′) /rɪ'hɜrs/ *v.,* **-hearsed, -hears•ing. 1.** to practice or go through (a play, speech, musical piece, etc.) before giving it in public: [~ + *obj*]: *She rehearsed her part.* [*no obj*]: *didn't have enough time to rehearse.* **2.** [~ + *obj*] to recite or retell aloud.

reign (rān) /reyn/ *n.* [*count*] **1.** the period during which a ruler occupies the throne. **—***v.* [*no obj*] **2.** to possess or use the power or authority of a ruler; rule: *The queen reigned over her subjects.* **3.** to have influence or hold sway: *Let peace reign over all.* See -REG-.

re•im•burse (rē′im bûrs′) /ˌriyɪm'bɜrs/ *v.,* **-bursed, -burs•ing.** to pay back; refund: [~ + *obj*]: *We will reimburse you for the full cost of the product.* [~ + *obj* + *obj*]: *The company will reimburse you the full amount.* **—re′im•burse′ment,** *n.* [*noncount*]

rein (rān) /reyn/ *n.* [*count*] **1.** a leather strap fastened to each end of the bit of a bridle, by which the rider or driver controls a horse or other animal. **2. reins,** [*plural*] the controlling or directing power: *the reins of government.* **—***v.* **3.** [~ + *obj*] to guide, control, or restrain (a horse or other animal) by pulling on a bridle bit by means of the reins: *He reined his horse.* **4. rein in,** to control or guide tightly: [~ + *obj* + *in*]: *You'll need to rein those children in.* [~ + *in* + *obj*]: *You have to rein in a person like that.* **—*Idiom.* 5. give (free) rein to,** [~ + *obj*] to give complete freedom to. **6. keep a tight rein on,** [~ + *obj*] to control, direct, or restrain tightly. See -TAIN-.

re•in•car•na•tion (rē′in kär nā′shən) /ˌriyɪnkɑr'neyʃən/ *n.* **1.** [*noncount*] the belief that the soul, after the death of the body, comes back to earth in another body or form. **2.** [*count*] a person or thing that has come back or been brought back in another form: *The new proposal is a reincarnation of his earlier ideas.* **—re•in•car•nat•ed** (rē′in kär′nā tid) /ˌriyɪn'kɑrneytɪd/ *adj.*

rein•deer (rān′dēr′) /'reynˌdɪər/ *n.* [*count*], *pl.* **-deer,** (*occasionally*) **-deers.** a large deer of northern and arctic regions of the world.

re•in•force or **re•en•force** (rē′in fôrs′, -fōrs′) /ˌriyɪn'fɔrs, -'fowrs/ *v.* [~ + *obj*], **-forced, -forc•ing. 1.** to strengthen with some added piece, support, or material: *to reinforce a wall.* **2.** to make more forceful or effective; strengthen; support: *to reinforce the law.* **3.** to strengthen (a military force) with additional soldiers, ships, aircraft, etc. **4.** *Psychol.* to strengthen the likelihood of (a desired way of behaving) by giving or withholding a reward. See -FORT-.

re•in•force•ment (rē′in fôrs′mənt, -fōrs′-) /ˌriyɪn'fɔrsmənt, -'fowrs-/ *n.* **1.** [*noncount*] the act of reinforcing; the state of being reinforced. **2.** something added to provide support, such as to a building: [*noncount*]: *reinforcement for the building's foundations.* [*count*]: *a few reinforcements to these walls.* **3.** Often, **reinforcements.** [*plural*] an additional supply of soliders, ships, aircraft, etc., to strengthen a military force. See -FORT-.

re•in•state (rē′in stāt′) /ˌriyɪn'steyt/ *v.* [~ + *obj*], **-stat•ed, -stat•ing.** to put back or establish again, as in a once-held position or state: *to reinstate the ousted president.* **—re′in•state′ment,** *n.* [*noncount*] See -STAT-.

re•is•sue (rē ish′o͞o) /riy'ɪʃuw/ *n., v.,* **-sued, -su•ing. —***n.* [*count*] **1.** something that has been issued again, as a book or motion picture, or the act of reissuing something. **—***v.* [~ + *obj*] **2.** to issue again.

re•it•er•ate (rē it′ə rāt′) /riy'ɪtəˌreyt/ *v.,* **-at•ed, -at•ing.** to say or do over again or repeatedly; repeat: [~ + *obj*]: *The accounting department reiterated its earlier proposals.* [*no obj*]: *To reiterate, here once again are the main points.* **—re•it•er•a•tion** (rē it′ə rā′shən) /riyˌɪtə'reyʃən/ *n.* [*noncount*]: *too much reiteration.* [*count*]: *constant reiterations.* **—re•it•er•a•tive** (rē it′ə rā′tiv, -ər ə tiv) /riy'ɪtəˌreytɪv, -ərətɪv/ *adj.*

re•ject (*v.* ri jekt′; *n.* rē′jekt) / *v.* rɪ'dʒɛkt; *n.* 'riydʒɛkt/ *v.* [~ + *obj*] **1.** to refuse to have, take, use, recognize, etc.: *to reject a job offer.* **2.** to refuse to grant (a request, demand, etc.); deny: *The board rejected his request for a license.* **3.** to refuse to accept or admit: *The other children rejected him.* **4.** to throw aside as useless or unsatisfactory: *Any misshapen pieces coming off the assembly line are rejected.* **5.** to have a reaction against (a transplanted organ or tissue). **—***n.* [*count*] **6.** one that is rejected. See -JEC-.

re•jec•tion (ri jek′shən) /rɪ'dʒɛkʃən/ *n.* the act of rejecting or the state of being rejected: [*noncount*]: *suffered from rejection.* [*count*]: *had nothing but rejections.* See -JEC-.

re•joice (ri jois′) /rɪ'dʒɔys/ *v.,* **-joiced, -joic•ing.** to feel joy or gladness; take delight: [~ + *at* + *obj*]: *They rejoiced at the news.* [~ + *in* + *obj*]: *His enemies rejoiced in the news of his defeat.* [~ + *that clause*]: *We rejoiced that she had finally gotten a good job.* [~ + *to* + *verb*]: *They rejoiced to see the economy improving.* [*no obj*]: *The citizens rushed into the streets and rejoiced.* **—re•joic′ing,** *n.* [*noncount*]: *times for great rejoicing.* [*plural*]: *festive rejoicings.*

re•join[1] (rē join′) /riy'dʒɔyn/ *v.* **1.** [~ + *obj*] to come again into the company of: *to rejoin a party after a brief absence.* **2.** to reunite: [*no obj*]: *The two brigades rejoined at the crossroads.* [~ + *obj*]: *The general rejoined his forces.* See -JUNC-.

re•join[2] (ri join′) /rɪ'dʒɔyn/ *v.* [~ + *that clause*] to say in answer; reply; respond: *rejoined that the problem wasn't his fault.* See -JUNC-.

re•join•der (ri join′dər) /rɪ'dʒɔyndər/ *n.* [*count*] an answer in conversation; a reply; a response: *He made a clever rejoinder to her question.* See -JUNC-.

re•ju•ve•nate (ri jo͞o′və nāt′) /rɪ'dʒuwvəˌneyt/ *v.* [~ + *obj*], **-nat•ed, -nat•ing. 1.** to restore to a feeling of being or looking young: *The vacation rejuvenated him.* **2.** to make fresh or new again: *to rejuvenate an old sofa.* **—re•ju•ve•na•tion** (ri jo͞o′və nā′shən) /rɪˌdʒuwvə'neyʃən/ *n.* [*noncount*]

re•lapse (*v.* ri laps′; *n.* also rē′laps) / *v.* rɪ'læps; *n.* ælsn ˈriylæps/ *v.,* **-lapsed, -laps•ing,** *n.* **—***v.* [*no obj*] **1.** to fall or slip back into a former state or practice: *to relapse into silence.* **2.** to fall back into illness after seeming to get better or be recovering: *He relapsed into a coma.* **—***n.* [*count*] **3.** an act or instance of relapsing. **4.** a return of a disease after one has partly recovered from it. See -LAPS-.

re•late (ri lāt′) /rɪ'leyt/ *v.,* **-lat•ed, -lat•ing. 1.** to tell (the story of something); describe (an event or events); narrate: [~ + *obj*]: *She related the plot to the investigators.* [~ + *that clause*]: *She related that she had left the office at noon.* **2.** [~ + *obj*] to show an association or connection between two or more things: *to relate events to probable causes.* **3.** [*not: be* + ~*-ing*] to have a connection: [~ + *to* + *obj*]: *The one idea does not relate to the other.* [*no obj*]: *Those two ideas do not relate.* **4.** [~ + *to* + *obj*] to have or establish a sympathetic relationship or understanding: *The two sisters were unable to relate to each other.* **—re•lat′er,** *n.* [*count*] See -LAT[1]-.

re•lat•ed (ri lā′tid) /rɪ'leytɪd/ *adj.* **1.** associated; connected: *These two ideas aren't even related.* **2.** associated or connected by family, marriage, or common origin: *related languages.* [*be* + ~ + *to*]: *She is distantly related to me.*

relat′ing to, *prep.* concerned with: *issues relating to the role of science in society.*

re•la•tion (ri lā′shən) /rɪ'leyʃən/ *n.* **1.** [*noncount*] association between or among things; connection; relationship: *the relation between cause and effect.* **2. relations,** [*plural*] **a.** the different connections or dealings between peoples, countries, etc.: *foreign relations; business relations.* **b.** sexual intercourse. **3.** [*count*] a person who is related by blood or marriage; relative: *The groom shook hands with his bride's relations.* **—*Idiom.* 4. in** or **with relation to,** with reference to; concerning: *What is her role in relation to the work of our division?* **—re•la′tion•al,** *adj.* See -LAT-[1].

re•la•tion•ship (ri lā′shən ship′) /rɪ'leyʃən,ʃɪp/ *n.* [*count*] **1.** a connection, association, or involvement: *the relationship between unemployment and inflation.* **2.** [*usually singular*] connection between persons by blood or marriage; kinship. **3.** an emotional or other connection between people: *a good working relationship.* **4.** a sexual involvement; affair. See -LAT[1]-.

rel•a•tive (rel′ə tiv) /'rɛlətɪv/ *n.* [*count*] **1.** a person who is connected with another by blood or marriage; a member of one's family. **2.** something having, or standing in, some relation to something else: *English is a close relative to Dutch.* **—*adj.* 3.** [*before a noun*] considered or measured in relation to something else; comparative: *the relative merits of gas and electric heating.* **4.** existing or having meaning only by relation to something else: *Standards of good or bad are relative to the society in which one lives.* **5.** [*before a noun*] of or being a pronoun, adverb, or adjective that introduces a subordinate clause and refers back to an expressed or implied word in the main or principal clause: *The relative pronoun is* who *in the sentence "That was the woman who called"; the relative adverb is* where *in the sentence "This is the house where I was born."* **6.** [*before a noun*] of or being a clause introduced by a relative pronoun, adverb, or adjective. **—*Idiom.* 7. relative to,** in comparison with; when compared with: *Our profits were up, relative to costs.* See -LAT-[1].

rel′ative humid′ity, *n.* [*noncount*] the amount of water vapor in the air, expressed as a percentage of the maximum amount that the air could hold at the given temperature.

rel•a•tive•ly (rel′ə tiv lē) /'rɛlətɪvliy/ *adv.* somewhat; comparatively: *It was relatively easy to see by the light of the full moon.* See -LAT[1]-.

rel•a•tiv•i•ty (rel′ə tiv′i tē) /,rɛlə'tɪvɪtiy/ *n.* [*noncount*] **1.** the state or fact of being relative. **2.** the two-part theory of Albert Einstein that mass and energy are equivalent, that space and time are relative concepts, and that gravitational and inertial forces are equivalent. See -LAT[1]-.

re•lax (ri laks′) /rɪ'læks/ *v.* **1.** to (cause to) be made less tense, rigid, or firm: [~ + *obj*]: *a drug to relax the muscles.* [*no obj*]: *Her muscles relaxed during sleep.* **2.** [~ + *obj*] to make less strict or severe: *I can't relax the rules for anyone in the class.* **3.** to enjoy or bring relief from the effects of tension, anxiety, etc.: [*no obj*]: *Come in, sit down and relax.* [~ + *obj*]: *Maybe the quiet music will relax you.* **—re•lax′er,** *n.* [*count*] See -LAX-.

re•lax•ant (ri lak′sənt) /rɪ'læksənt/ *adj.* **1.** of, relating to, or causing relaxation. **—*n.*** [*count*] **2.** a drug that relaxes, esp. one that lessens strain in muscles. See -LAX-.

re•lax•a•tion (rē′lak sā′shən) /,riylæk'seyʃən/ *n.* **1.** [*noncount*] relief from work, effort, etc.: *a few moments of relaxation.* **2.** [*count*] an activity or recreation that provides such relief; an entertainment: *one of her favorite relaxations.* **3.** [*noncount*] a loosening; a becoming less tight: *relaxation of the muscles as a result of the drug.* **4.** [*noncount*] the act of easing, or of making less strict or severe: *the relaxation of academic standards.* See -LAX-.

re•laxed (ri lakst′) /rɪ'lækst/ *adj.* not worried; relieved from tension; loosened and no longer tight. See -LAX-.

re•lax•ing (ri lak′sing) /rɪ'læksɪŋ/ *adj.* causing or bringing about a feeling of relaxation: *a relaxing swim.* See -LAX-.

re•lay (rē′lā; *v.* also ri lā′) /'riyley; *v.* ælso rɪ'ley/ *n., pl.* **-lays,** *v.,* **-layed, -lay•ing** —*n.* [*count*] **1.** a series of persons who take turns helping one another; a shift: *We worked in relays.* **2.** a race in which each member of a team runs part way. **3.** an electrical device that responds to a change of current or voltage in one circuit by making or breaking a connection in another. **—*v.*** [~ + *obj*] **4.** to carry or send by or as if by relays: *relaying a message.*

re•lease (ri lēs′) /rɪ'liys/ *v.,* **-leased, -leas•ing,** *n.* **—*v.*** [~ + *obj*] **1.** to free from jail, burden, debt, pain, etc.; to let go. **2.** to allow to be known, issued, published, broadcast, or exhibited: *to release an article for publication.* **3.** to allow or cause (something) to fall, escape, etc.: *The pilot flew over the target and released the bombs.* **—*n.* 4.** [*count*] a freeing from jail, burden, debt, pain, emotional strain, etc.: *a release from all his worries.* **5.** [*count*] anything that brings about such freeing or releasing. **6.** [*count*] the act of letting something fall, escape, etc.: *the release of the bombs.* **7.** [*noncount*] the act of letting something out for publication, performance, use, exhibition, or sale. **8.** [*count*] a film, book, record, etc., that is released. **9.** [*count*] a statement issued to the press; a press release. **10.** [*count*] a control mechanism for starting or stopping a machine.

rel•e•gate (rel′i gāt′) /'rɛlɪ,geyt/ *v.* [~ + *obj* (+ *to* + *obj*)], **-gat•ed, -gat•ing. 1.** to send (someone or something) to a lower-ranking or worse position, place, or condition: *The team relegated him to the minor leagues.* **2.** to send or assign (a matter, task, etc.) to a person: *They relegated the job of cleaning out the lockers to the janitor.* **—rel•e•ga•tion** (rel′i gā′shən) /,rɛlɪ'geyʃən/ *n.* [*noncount*] See -LEG-.

re•lent (ri lent′) /rɪ'lɛnt/ *v.* [*no obj*] **1.** to soften in one's feeling, temper, or determination; become more mild, compassionate, or forgiving: *At last he relented and forgave them.* **2.** to become less severe; slacken: *The hurricane finally relented.*

re•lent•less (ri lent′lis) /rɪ'lɛntlɪs/ *adj.* not giving in; unrelenting: *relentless pursuit.* **—re•lent′less•ly,** *adv.* **—re•lent′less•ness,** *n.* [*noncount*]

rel•e•vant (rel′ə vənt) /'rɛləvənt/ *adj.* connected with the matter at hand; pertinent: *a comment relevant to the topic.* **—rel′e•vance, rel′e•van•cy,** *n.* [*noncount*]: *Your comments have no relevance.* See -LEV-.

re•li•a•ble (ri lī′ə bəl) /rɪ'layəbəl/ *adj.* capable of being relied on; always or often dependable in character, judgment, performance, or result: *a reliable source of information.* **—re•li•a•bil•i•ty** (ri lī′ə bil′i tē) /rɪ,layə'bɪlɪtiy/ *n.* [*noncount*] **—re•li′a•bly,** *adv.*

re•li•ance (ri lī′əns) /rɪ'layəns/ *n.* [*noncount*] **1.** confident or trustful dependence: *a child's reliance on his mother for comfort.* **2.** dependence: *reliance on alcohol to face problems.*

re•li•ant (ri lī′ənt) /rɪ'layənt/ *adj.* [*be* + ~ + *on/upon*] depending on; dependent on; relying on: *The armed forces had become reliant on increased defense budgets.*

rel•ic (rel′ik) /'rɛlɪk/ *n.* [*count*] **1.** something having interest because of its age or its connection with the past; a surviving trace of something. **2.** a body part, or personal object that belonged to a saint and that is kept as worthy of respect.

re•lief[1] (ri lēf′) /rɪ'liyf/ *n.* **1.** [*noncount*] the ending or lessening of pain, distress, worry, fear, etc.; alleviation: *We desperately need relief from these difficulties.* **2.** a feeling of comfort or ease caused by the ending or stopping of pain or distress: [*count; usually singular*]: *What a relief it was to get home after a year of traveling.* [*noncount*]: *breathed a sigh of relief.* **3.** [*noncount*] money, food, or other help given to people in need. **4.** [*count*] a person or persons who replace another at a post of duty. **5.** [*count; singular*] the rescue of a town, fort, etc., that is under attack: *the relief of the beleaguered city.* **—*Idiom.* 6. on relief,** receiving financial support from a government agency.

re•lief[2] (ri lēf′) /rɪ'liyf/ *n.* **1.** [*noncount*] the quality of being distinct because of contrast with the surrounding area: *a red boat in strong relief against the blue water.* **2.** [*noncount*] the standing out of a figure or part from the surface where it is formed, as in sculpture or similar work. **3.** [*count*] a piece or work of art or sculpture with such a part standing out. See -LEV-.

re•lieve (ri lēv′) /rɪ'liyv/ *v.,* **-lieved, -liev•ing. 1.** [~ + *obj*] to ease, lessen, or make less unpleasant: *Aspirin may relieve the pain.* **2.** [~ + *obj*] to free from anxiety, fear, pain, etc.: *We were relieved by the good news.* **3.** [~ + *obj*] to reduce (a pressure, load, weight, etc., on a device or object under stress): *This device relieves the pressure on the wheels.* **4.** [~ + *obj*] to make less boring or monotonous by adding something different: *Curtains relieved the drabness of the room.* **5.** to release or remove (a person on duty) by coming as or providing a substitute or replacement: [~ + *obj*]: *The manager relieved his best pitcher.* [~ + *obj* + *of* + *obj*]: *The first officer relieved the captain of his duty at the helm.* **6.** [~ + *obj* + *of* + *obj*] *Informal.* to take from; rob: *The thief relieved me of my wallet.* **—*Idiom.* 7. relieve oneself,** to urinate or defecate. See -LEV-.

re•lieved (ri lēvd′) /rɪ'liyvd/ *adj.* having received a feeling of relief; glad: [*be* + ~ + *to* + *verb*]: *We were relieved to hear the news.* [*be* + ~ + *that clause*]: *We were relieved that we would be going home in just a few days.* See -LEV-.

re•li•gion (ri lij′ən) /rɪ'lɪdʒən/ *n.* **1.** [*noncount*] a set of beliefs concerning the cause, nature, and purpose of the universe, esp. when the universe is believed to have been created by a deity, and usually including ceremonies, prayers, and laws or codes of moral conduct. **2.** [*count*] a certain set of such beliefs and practices accepted by a number of persons: *the religions of the world.* See -LIG-.

re•li•gious (ri lij′əs) /rɪ'lɪdʒəs/ *adj., n., pl.* **-gious.** **—*adj.*** **1.** [*before a noun*] of, relating to, or concerned with religion: *a religious holiday.* **2.** filled with or showing religion; pious; devout. **3.** conscientious: *religious attention to detail.* **—*n.*** [*count*] **4.** a member of a religious order. **—re•li′gious•ly,** *adv.* See -LIG-.

re•lin•quish (ri ling′kwish) /rɪ'lɪŋkwɪʃ/ *v.* [~ + *obj*], to surrender (a possession, right, claim, etc.); abandon; let go: *to relinquish a throne.* **—re•lin′quish•ment,** *n.* [*noncount*]

rel•i•quar•y (rel′i kwer′ē) /'rɛlɪˌkwɛriy/ *n.* [*count*], *pl.* **-quar•ies.** a container or other place for relics of a saint.

rel•ish (rel′ish) /'rɛlɪʃ/ *n.* **1.** pleasurable appreciation of anything; enjoyment; liking: [*count; usually singular*]: *a relish for fast driving.* [*noncount*]: *She listened with relish to the gossip.* **2.** something tasty or appetizing added to a meal, as olives, pickles, or a sweet or sour pickle made of various usually chopped vegetables: [*noncount*]: *served hot dogs with relish.* [*count*]: *spicy relishes.* **—*v.*** **3.** to take pleasure in; enjoy: [~ + *obj*]: *He relishes arguments.* [~ + *verb-ing*]: *He relishes arguing.*

re•live (rē liv′) /riy'lɪv/ *v.* [~ + *obj*], **-lived, -liv•ing.** **1.** to experience again: *He relived every moment of the adventure as if it had happened yesterday.* **2.** to live again: *You can't relive your life.* **—re•liv′a•ble,** *adj.*

re•lo•cate (rē lō′kāt, rē′lō kāt′) /riy'lowkeyt, ˌriylow'keyt/ *v.,* **-cat•ed, -cat•ing.** to move to a different location; to change one's residence or place of business; move: [~ + *obj*]: *relocated his business in another city.* [*no obj*]: *She had to relocate last year.* **—re•lo•ca•tion** (rē′lō kā′shən) /ˌriylow'keyʃən/ *n.* [*noncount*] See -LOC-.

re•luc•tant (ri luk′tənt) /rɪ'lʌktənt/ *adj.* **1.** unwilling; not inclined to do something: *a reluctant candidate.* **2.** marked by hesitation or slowness because of unwillingness: *a reluctant promise.* **—re•luc′tance,** *n.* [*noncount*] **—re•luc′tant•ly,** *adv.*: *He agreed reluctantly.*

re•ly (ri lī′) /rɪ'lay/ *v.* [~ + *on/upon* + *obj*], **-lied, -ly•ing.** to put trust in: *Can I rely on your support?*

rem (rem) /rɛm/ *n.* [*count*] the quantity of radiation whose biological effect is equal to that produced by one roentgen of x-rays.

re•main (ri mān′) /rɪ'meyn/ *v.* **1.** [*not: be* + ~*-ing*] to continue to be as specified: [~ + *adjective*]: *He remained loyal to his friends.* [~ + *obj*]: *He remained a bachelor for many years.* **2.** [*no obj*] to stay behind or in the same place: *He remained at home while the others left.* **3.** [*no obj*] to be left after the removal, loss, or destruction of all else: *Few buildings remain in that neighborhood.* **4.** [*no obj*] to be left to be done, told, shown, etc.: [*no obj*]: *Two questions remain.* [~ + *to* + *verb*]: *A few things remain to be done.* **—*n.*** **remains,** [*plural*] **5.** something that remains or is left. **6. a.** traces of some quality, condition, etc. **b.** a dead body; corpse. **c.** parts or substances remaining from animal or plant life: *fossil remains.* See -MAN-[2].

re•main•der (ri mān′dər) /rɪ'meyndər/ *n.* [*count*] **1.** a remaining part: *the remainder of the day.* **2.** *Math.* **a.** the quantity that is left after subtraction. **b.** the number that is left over after dividing two numbers evenly. **3.** a book sold by its publisher at a reduced price when its sales have slowed down.

re•mand (ri mand′) /rɪ'mænd/ *v.* [~ + *obj*] **1.** (of a court) to return (a prisoner or accused person) to custody, so as to await further proceedings. **2.** (of a case) to return to a lower court for further proceedings. See -MAND-.

re•mark (ri märk′) /rɪ'mɑrk/ *v.* **1.** to say casually, as in making a comment; mention; make an observation: [~ + *that clause*]: *He remarked that she was his best student.* [~ + *on* + *obj*]: *A few folks remarked on her absence.* [*used with quotations*]: *"You certainly look healthy," he remarked.* **—*n.*** **2.** [*noncount*] notice, comment, or mention: *an act worthy of remark.* **3.** [*count*] a casual or brief saying, statement, or observation; comment.

re•mark•a•ble (ri mär′kə bəl) /rɪ'mɑrkəbəl/ *adj.* very notable or obviously unusual; noteworthy: *a remarkable hat; an ability that is remarkable.* **—re•mark′a•bly,** *adv.* *: a remarkably fine day.*

re•me•di•al (ri mē′dē əl) /rɪ'miydiyəl/ *adj.* **1.** intended to improve one's health. **2.** intended to improve poor skills in a specified field: *a remedial reading course.* **3.** intended to improve anything: *some remedial steps to stop the loss of profits.* **—re•me′di•al•ly,** *adv.*

rem•e•dy (rem′i dē) /'rɛmɪdiy/ *n., pl.* **-dies,** *v.,* **-died, -dy•ing.** **—*n.*** [*count*] **1.** something, as a medicine, that cures or relieves a disease or anything wrong with the body. **2.** something that corrects or removes an evil, error, or undesirable condition. **—*v.*** [~ + *obj*] **3.** to cure or relieve: *to remedy an illness.* **4.** to restore to the proper condition; put right: *to remedy a problem.*

re•mem•ber (ri mem′bər) /rɪ'mɛmbər/ *v.* **1.** to recall to the mind; think of again: [~ + *obj*]: *I can remember my old phone number.* [~ + *verb-ing*]: *I remember giving you your allowance.* [*no obj*]: *having trouble remembering.* **2.** to keep in mind; remain aware of: [~ + *to* + *verb*]: *She remembered to bring her umbrella.* [*no obj*]: *Remember, I'll see you at 2:00.* [~ + *(that) clause*]: *Remember that I'll always love you.* **3.** to have (something) come into the mind again: [~ + *obj*]: *I just remembered our date.* [~ + *(that) clause*]: *She remembered that she had left her son home all alone.* **4.** [~ + *obj*] to keep or bear (a person) in mind to receive a gift, reward, or fee: *The company always remembers us at Christmas.* **5.** [~ + *obj* + *to* + *obj*] to mention (a person) to another as sending kindly greetings: *Remember me to your family.* See -MEM-.

re•mem•brance (ri mem′brəns) /rɪ'mɛmbrəns/ *n.* **1.** [*count*] a memory; a mental impression kept in the mind. **2.** [*noncount*] the act or fact of remembering; the state of being remembered; commemoration. **3.** [*count*] memento: *The ring was a remembrance of our friendship.* **4. remembrances,** [*plural*] greetings; respects. See -MEM-.

re•mind (ri mīnd′) /rɪ'maynd/ *v.* **1.** to cause (a person) to remember: [~ + *obj*]: *If you remind me, I might remember.* [~ + *obj* + *to* + *verb*]: *Remind me to call home.* [~ + *obj* + *of* + *obj*]: *I'll remind you of that.* [~ + *obj* + *(that) clause*]: *Must I remind you that we have no money left?* **2.** [~ + *obj* + *of* + *obj*] to cause (a person) to think (of someone or something): *She reminds me of my mother.* **—re•mind′er,** *n. [count]* See -MEM-.

rem•i•nisce (rem′ə nis′) /ˌrɛmə'nɪs/ *v.* [*no obj*], **-nisced, -nisc•ing.** to recall or talk about past experiences, events, etc.

rem•i•nis•cence (rem′ə nis′əns) /ˌrɛmə'nɪsəns/ *n.* **1.** the act or process of recalling past experiences, events, etc.: [*noncount*]: *an evening of reminiscence.* [*count*]: *reminiscences of early days.* **2.** Often, **reminiscences.** [*plural*] an account of memorable experiences.

rem•i•nis•cent (rem′ə nis′ənt) /ˌrɛmə'nɪsənt/ *adj.* [*be* + ~ + *of*] causing a feeling of remembering; suggestive: *a perfume reminiscent of spring.* See -MEM-.

re•miss (ri mis′) /rɪ'mɪs/ *adj.* [*be* + ~] careless; negligent: *I would be remiss in my duties if I did not welcome our guest.* See -MIS-.

re•mis•sion (ri mish′ən) /rɪ'mɪʃən/ *n.* **1.** [*noncount*] the act of remitting. **2.** pardon; forgiveness: [*noncount*]: *prayed for the remission of sin.* [*count*]: *a remission of one's sins.* **3.** the act of lessening the length of a prison sentence: [*count*]: *a remission of one year for good behavior.* [*noncount*]: *an appeal for remission.* **4. a.** [*noncount*] a temporary or permanent decrease in the signs of a disease, as cancer. **b.** [*count*] a period during which such a decrease occurs: *a six-month remission.* See -MIS-.

re•mit (ri mit′) /rɪ'mɪt/ *v.* [~ + *obj*], **-mit•ted, -mit•ting.** to send (money, a check, etc.), usually in payment: *Please remit your rent by the first of the month.* See -MIT-.

re•mit•tance (ri mit′əns) /rɪ'mɪtəns/ *n.* [*count*] an amount of money sent, usually as payment. See -MIT-.

rem•nant (rem′nənt) /'rɛmnənt/ *n.* [*count*] **1.** a remaining, usually small part or number of something. **2.** a small unsold or unused piece of fabric. **3.** a trace of something; vestige: *remnants of pride.* See -MAN[2]-.

re•mod•el (rē mod′l) /riy'mɑdl̩/ *v.* [~ + *obj*], **-eled, -el•ing** or (*esp. Brit.*) **-elled, -el•ling.** to change (something) in structure or form; reconstruct; make over: *They remodeled their kitchen.* See -MOD-.

re•mon•strance (ri mon′strəns) /rɪ'mɑnstrəns/ *n.* **1.** [*noncount*] an act or instance of protesting. **2.** [*count*] a protest: *deaf to remonstrances.* —**re•mon′strant,** *adj.* See -MONSTR-.

re•mon•strate (ri mon′strāt) /rɪ'mɒnstreyt/ *v.,* **-strat•ed, -strat•ing.** to argue or protest in objection or complaint: [*no obj; (~ + about + obj)*]: *He remonstrated about their rudeness.* [*~ + that clause*]: *He remonstrated that they were rude.* See -MONSTR-.

re•morse (ri môrs′) /rɪ'mɔrs/ *n.* [*noncount*] deep regret for having done something wrong: *The killer seemed to have no remorse for what he had done.* —**re•morse′ful,** *adj.* —**re•morse′ful•ly,** *adv.*

re•morse•less (ri môrs′lis) /rɪ'mɔrslɪs/ *adj.* **1.** having no remorse: *a remorseless criminal.* **2.** steady; relentless: *a remorseless attack.* —**re•morse′less•ly,** *adv.*

re•mote (ri mōt′) /rɪ'mowt/ *adj.,* **-mot•er, -mot•est,** *n.* —*adj.* **1.** far away; far distant in space: *a remote galaxy.* **2.** not near well-populated areas; secluded: *arriving at the remote village after weeks of walking and canoeing.* **3.** distant in time, relationship, connection, etc.: *in remote antiquity; a remote ancestor.* **4.** not direct or primary: *the remote causes of the war.* **5.** slight; unlikely: *a remote chance they might hear our faint radio signals.* **6.** reserved in manner: *She was polite but very remote when I met her.* **7.** operating or controlled from a distance, as by remote control: *remote operation of machinery.* —*n.* [*count*] **8.** a broadcast originating from outside a radio or television studio. **9.** REMOTE CONTROL (def. 2). —**re•mote′ness,** *n.* [*noncount*] See -MOT-.

remote′ control′, *n.* **1.** [*noncount*] control of an apparatus from a distance, as of a guided missile by radio signals. **2.** [*count*] a device used to control the operation of an apparatus or machine, as a television set, from a distance.

re•mote•ly (ri mōt′lē) /rɪ'mowtliy/ *adv.* **1.** in a remote manner: *She stared remotely into space.* **2.** slightly; faintly: *He's not even remotely interested in your excuses.*

re•mov•al (ri mo͞o′vəl) /rɪ'muwvəl/ *n.* [*noncount*] **1.** the act of removing. **2.** dismissal from an office or from a position. See -MOV-.

re•move (ri mo͞ov′) /rɪ'muwv/ *v.* [*~ + obj*], **-moved, -mov•ing. 1.** to move or shift from a place or position: *removed her hands from the steering wheel.* **2.** to take off; shed: *to remove one's jacket.* **3.** to dismiss from a position; discharge: *removed her from her job.* **4.** to eliminate; do away with or put an end to: *to remove the threat of danger.* **5.** to kill; assassinate: *He removed most of his rivals to the throne.* —**re•mov′a•ble,** *adj.* See -MOV-.

re•moved (ri mo͞ovd′) /rɪ'muwvd/ *adj.* **1.** [*be + ~*] distant or greatly different from: *Her policies are far removed from mine.* **2.** [*after a noun; with a number word*] related to another by a certain degree: *A first cousin once removed is the child of one's first cousin.* See -MOV-.

re•mu•ner•ate (ri myo͞o′nə rāt′) /rɪ'myuwnəˌreyt/ *v.* [*~ + obj*], **-at•ed, -at•ing. 1.** to pay, pay back, or reward for work, trouble, etc.: *Naturally we will remunerate you for your work on the project.* **2.** to pay for in money or the equivalent: *Naturally your writing and research will be remunerated.* —**re•mu•ner•a•tion** (ri myo͞o′rā′shən) /rɪˌmyuw'reyʃən/ *n.* [*noncount*] —**re•mu•ner•a•tive** (ri-myo͞o′nər ə tiv, -nə rā′tiv) /rɪ'myuwnərətɪv, -nəˌreytɪv/ *adj.*

Ren•ais•sance (ren′ə säns′, -zäns′, ren′ə säns′, -zäns′) /ˌrɛnə'sɑns, -'zɑns, 'rɛnəˌsɑns, -ˌzɑns/ *n.* **1.** [*proper noun; the + ~*] the activity, spirit, or time of the great revival of art, literature, and learning in Europe beginning in the 14th century and extending to the 17th century. **2.** [*count; usually singular; usually: renaissance*] any similar revival, renewal, or rebirth, as in the world of art and learning. —*adj.* [*before a noun*] **3.** of, relating to, or suggesting the European Renaissance. See -NAT-.

re•nal (rēn′l) /'riynḷ/ *adj.* of or relating to the kidneys or the surrounding regions: *renal failure.*

re•name (rē nām′) /riy'neym/ *v.* [*~ + obj*], **-named, -nam•ing.** to give another name: *They renamed the avenue in her honor.*

re•nas•cent (ri nas′ənt, -nā′sənt) /rɪ'næsənt, -'neysənt/ *adj.* being reborn; springing again into life or being. See -NAT-.

rend (rend) /rɛnd/ *v.* [*~ + obj*], **rent** (rent) /rɛnt/ **rend•ing. 1.** to separate into parts with great force or suddenness; tear or rip apart: *As a sign of his grief and rage the high priest rent his garments.* **2.** to disturb (the air) sharply with noise: *Her sharp screams rent the air.* **3.** to distress (the heart) with painful feelings. —**rend′er,** *n.* [*count*]

-rend-, *root.* *-rend-* comes from Latin, where it has the meaning "give." This meaning is found in such words as: RENDER, RENDITION, SURRENDER.

ren•der (ren′dər) /'rɛndər/ *v.* **1.** [*~ + obj + adjective*] to cause (something) to be or become (something else); make: *The blow to the head rendered him unconscious.* **2.** to furnish; provide; help: [*~ + obj*]: *to render aid.* [*~ + obj + obj*]: *You've rendered us a valuable service.* **3.** to pay (someone) as due (money, a tax, tribute, etc.): [*~ + obj*]: *to render taxes to the Empire.* [*~ + obj + obj*]: *to render the government the money you owe.* **4.** [*~ + obj*] to translate into another language: *to render the fairy tale from German into English.* **5.** [*~ + obj*] to represent, interpret, or show in drawing, painting, performing, or acting: *to render a landscape in bright hues; to render a song.* **6.** [*~ + obj*] to melt down: *to render fat.* See -REND-.

ren•dez•vous (rän′də vo͞o′, -dā-) /'rɑndəˌvuw, -dey-/ *n., pl.* **-vous** (-vo͞oz′) /-ˌvuwz/ *v.,* **-voused** (vo͞od′) /ˌvuwd/ **-vous•ing** (-vo͞o′ing) /-ˌvuwɪŋ/. —*n.* [*count*] **1.** an agreement to meet at a certain time and place. **2.** the meeting itself. **3.** a place designated for a meeting or assembling, esp. of troops or ships. **4.** a popular gathering place. —*v.* [*no obj*] **5.** to assemble at a rendezvous: *The couple rendezvoused at their favorite tavern.* See -REND-.

ren•di•tion (ren dish′ən) /rɛn'dɪʃən/ *n.* [*count*] **1.** the act of rendering. **2.** a translation. **3.** an interpretation or performance, as of a role in a play or a piece of music. See -REND-.

ren•e•gade (ren′i gād′) /'rɛnɪˌgeyd/ *n.* [*count*] **1.** a person who deserts one country, party, cause, belief, etc., for another. —*adj.* [*before a noun*] **2.** of or like a renegade or a traitor. See -NEG-.

re•nege (ri nig′, -neg′, -nēg′) /rɪ'nɪg, -'nɛg, -'niyg/ *v.* [*no obj; (~ + on + obj)*], **-neged, -neg•ing.** to go back on one's word: *He has reneged on his promise.* —**re•neg′er,** *n.* [*count*] See -NEG-.

re•new (ri no͞o′, -nyo͞o′) /rɪ'nuw, -'nyuw/ *v.* [*~ + obj*] **1.** to begin or take up again; resume: *to renew a friendship.* **2.** to make (as a license, passport, etc.) effective for an additional period. **3.** to make, say, or do again: *The army renewed its attacks.* **4.** to recover youth, strength, etc.: *She felt renewed after a skiing trip.* **5.** to restore to a former state esp. so as to be used again: *We need to renew our resources.* —**re•new′a•ble,** *adj.*

re•new′al (ri no͞o′əl, -nyo͞o′-) /rɪ'nuwəl, -'nyuw-/ *n.* the act or state of renewing or of being renewed: [*noncount*]: *a contract due for renewal.* [*count*]: *passport renewals.*

re•nounce (ri nouns′) /rɪ'nawns/ *v.* [*~ + obj*], **-nounced, -nounc•ing. 1.** to give up or put aside (a title, claim, belief, etc.): *He renounced his claim to the throne.* **2.** to declare that another is no longer welcome or part of one's family; repudiate; disown: *to renounce his only son.* See -NOUNCE-.

ren•o•vate (ren′ə vāt′) /'rɛnəˌveyt/ *v.* [*~ + obj*], **-vat•ed, -vat•ing.** to restore to good condition; to make like new: *They bought an old house and renovated it.* —**ren•o•va•tion** (ren′ə vā′shən) /ˌrɛnə'veyʃən/ *n.* [*noncount*]: *high renovation costs.* [*count*]: *extensive renovations.* —**ren′o•va′tor,** *n.* [*count*] See -NOV-.

re•nown (ri noun′) /rɪ'nawn/ *n.* [*noncount*] widespread fame: *a scholar of great renown.* —**re•nowned′,** *adj.*: *a renowned musician; renowned for his paintings.*

rent[1] (rent) /rɛnt/ *n.* **1.** a payment made on a regular basis to the owner of land or other property, for the right to live in or use the property: [*noncount*]: *How much do you pay in rent every month? He paid more rent than he had to.* [*count*]: *Rents are high.* —*v.* **2.** [*~ + obj*] to pay money for the use of (real estate, machinery, etc.) to the landlord or owner: *I rented a small apartment.* **3.** to allow the possession and use of (real estate, machinery, etc.) in return for payment of rent: [*~ + obj*]: *The lodge will rent skis for the day.* [*~ (+ out) + obj + to + obj*]: *She rented (out) a small apartment to me.* [*~ + obj (+ out) + to + obj*]: *The company will not rent cars (out) to anyone under 18 years old.* [*~ + obj + obj*]: *She rented me the apartment.* —**Idiom. 4. for rent,** available to be rented. —**rent′er,** *n.* [*count*]

rent[2] (rent) /rɛnt/ *n.* [*count*] an opening or large tear made by rending.

rent[3] (rent) /rɛnt/ *v.* pt. and pp. of REND.

rent•al (ren′tl) /'rɛntḷ/ *n.* [*count*] **1.** an amount received or paid as rent. **2.** the act of renting. **3.** something offered or given for rent. —*adj.* [*before a noun*] **4.** of, relating to, or available for rent: *rental property.*

re•nun•ci•a•tion (ri nun′sē ā′shən, -shē-) /rɪˌnʌnsiy'eyʃən, -ʃiy-/ *n.* [*noncount*] an act or instance of renouncing something, as a right, title, job, person, or ambition. See -NUNC-.

re•o•pen (rē ō′pən) /riy'owpən/ *v.* **1.** to open again: [~ + *obj*]: *He reopened his bar after the fire.* [*no obj*]: *The bar reopened last week.* **2.** to start or begin again: [~ + *obj*]: *The two sides reopened their discussions.* [*no obj*]: *Negotiations between the two sides reopened today.*

re•or•gan•ize (rē ôr′gə nīz) /riy'ɔrgənayz/ *v.*, **-ized, -iz•ing.** to organize again, esp. to make more efficient: [~ + *obj*]: *to reorganize the company.* [*no obj*]: *The company needs to reorganize.* —**re•or•gan•i•za•tion** (rē′ôr-gə ni zā′shən) /ˌriyɔrgənɪ'zeyʃən/ *n.* [*count*]: *went through several reorganizations.* [*noncount*]: *Reorganization may not save this company.* See -ORGA-.

rep[1] (rep) /rɛp/ *n.* [*count*] *Informal.* a representative of a company, as a salesperson.

rep[2] (rep) /rɛp/ *n.* [*count*] a repertory theater or company.

Rep., an abbreviation of: **1.** representative. **2.** republic. **3.** Republican.

re•pair[1] (ri pâr′) /rɪ'pɛər/ *v.* [~ + *obj*] **1.** to restore to a good condition after damage or decay; fix: *Can you repair this old computer?* **2.** to make up for; compensate for; remedy: *tried to repair the damage done to our reputation.* —*n.* **3.** an act, instance, operation, or result of repairing: [*plural*]: *The brakes need repairs.* [*noncount*]: *in need of repair.* **4.** [*noncount*] condition with respect to soundness and usability: *a house in good* (or *bad*) *repair.* —**re•pair′a•ble,** *adj.* See -PARE-[1].

re•pair[2] (ri pâr′) /rɪ'pɛər/ *v.* [*no obj*] to go to a place: *He repaired in haste to Washington.*

re•pair•man (ri pâr′man′, -mən) /rɪ'pɛərˌmæn, -mən/ *n.* [*count*], *pl.* **-men** (-men′, -mən) /-ˌmɛn, -mən/. a person whose occupation is the making of repairs.

rep•a•ra•tion (rep′ə rā′shən) /ˌrɛpə'reyʃən/ *n.* **1.** [*noncount*] the act of repaying or of making up for losses, wrong acts, or injuries. **2.** Usually, **reparations.** [*plural*] the money or other payment made by a defeated nation to the victor for loss suffered during war. See -PARE[1]-.

rep•ar•tee (rep′ər tē′, -tā′, -är-) /ˌrɛpər'tiy, -'tey, -ɑr-/ *n.*, *pl.* **-tees. 1.** [*count*] a quick, witty reply. **2.** [*noncount*] the use of such replies; conversation full of such replies. See -PAR-.

re•past (ri past′) /rɪ'pæst/ *n.* [*count*] food and drink for a meal; a meal.

re•pa•tri•ate (*v.* rē pā′trē āt′; *n.* -it; *esp. Brit.* -pa′-) / *v.* riy'peytriyˌeyt; *n.* -ɪt; *esp. Brit.* -'pæ-/ *v.*, **-at•ed, -at•ing,** *n.* —*v.* **1.** [~ + *obj*] to send back (a prisoner of war, a refugee, etc.) to his or her country. **2.** [~ + *obj*] to send back (profits or other assets) to one's own country. **3.** [*no obj*] to return to one's own country, esp. after living abroad. —*n.* [*count*] **4.** a person who has been repatriated. —**re•pa•tri•a•tion** (rē pā′trē ā′shən) /riyˌpeytriy'eyʃən/ *n.* [*noncount*] See -PATR-.

re•pay (ri pā′) /rɪ'pey/ *v.*, **-paid, -pay•ing. 1.** to pay back or refund, such as money owed: [~ + *obj*]: *Repay the five dollars you owe him.* [~ + *obj* + *obj*]: *Repay him his money.* **2.** [~ + *obj*] to make return for or to in any way: *to repay a compliment with a smile.* —**re•pay′a•ble,** *adj.* —**re•pay′ment,** *n.* [*noncount*]: *a repayment for all your help.* [*count*]: *monthly repayments.*

re•peal (ri pēl′) /rɪ'piyl/ *v.* [~ + *obj*] **1.** to do away with officially or formally; cancel: *The county repealed the increase in taxes.* —*n.* [*count*] **2.** the act of repealing. See -PEL-.

re•peat (ri pēt′) /rɪ'piyt/ *v.* **1.** [~ + *obj*] to say or do again: *He repeated his words. If you don't learn from your mistakes you are likely to repeat them.* **2.** to utter after another person has uttered words, inflections, etc.: [~ + *obj*]: *Now repeat the Latin forms of the verb "to be" after me.* [*used with quotations*]: *Now, repeat, "Sum, es, est, sumus, estis, sunt."* **3.** [~ + *obj*] to tell (something heard) to another: *I asked her not to repeat what I was about to tell her.* **4.** [~ + *obj*] to undergo again: *History seems to repeat itself.* **5.** [*no obj*] to appear again in taste after being eaten: *Onions always seem to repeat on me.* —*n.* [*count*] **6.** the act of repeating. **7.** something repeated, as a television program that has been broadcast at least once before. —**re•peat′er,** *n.* [*count*] See -PET-.

re•peat•ed (ri pē′tid) /rɪ'piytɪd/ *adj.* [*before a noun*] done or said again and again: *repeated attempts.* —**re•peat′ed•ly,** *adv.*: *She warned us repeatedly.*

re•pel (ri pel′) /rɪ'pɛl/ *v.* [~ + *obj*], **-pelled, -pel•ling. 1.** to drive or force back (an assailant, invader, etc.): *The army repelled the last invasion.* **2.** to fail to mix with: *Water and oil repel each other.* **3.** to resist the absorption of: *This coat repels rain.* **4.** to cause a feeling of distaste or dislike: *She was repelled by his bad manners.* **5.** to push away by a force (opposed to *attract*): *The north pole of one magnet will repel the north pole of another.* See -PEL-.

re•pel•lent or **re•pel•lant** (ri pel′ənt) /rɪ'pɛlənt/ *adj.* **1.** causing distaste or dislike; repulsive: *repellent behavior.* **2.** resistant to something (often used in combination): *a water-repellent raincoat.* —*n.* **3.** something that repels or increases resistance to something: [*count*]: *an insect repellent.* [*noncount*]: *spraying insect repellent everywhere.* See -PEL-.

re•pent (ri pent′) /rɪ'pɛnt/ *v.* to feel regretful or sorry for (something one has done): [~ + *of* + *obj*]: *to repent of an act.* [~ + *obj*]: *He repented his angry words.* —**re•pent•ance** (ri pen′tns) /rɪ'pɛntns/ *n.* [*noncount*]: *repentance for one's sins.* —**re•pent′ant,** *adj.* See -PEN-.

re•per•cus•sion (rē′pər kush′ən, rep′ər-) /ˌriypər'kʌʃən, ˌrɛpər-/ *n.* [*count*] an effect or result of some previous action or event: *The assassination had far-reaching political repercussions.*

rep•er•toire (rep′ər twär′, -twôr′, rep′ə-) /'rɛpərˌtwɑr, -ˌtwɔr, 'rɛpə-/ *n.* [*count*] **1.** all the works that a performing company or an artist is prepared to present, or that exist in a certain field. **2.** the skills, techniques, devices, offerings, etc., that a person has or needs: *had a repertoire of quick answers to any complaints.* See -PARE[2]-.

rep•er•to•ry (rep′ər tôr′ē, -tōr′ē) /'rɛpərˌtɔriy, -ˌtowriy/ *n.* [*count*], *pl.* **-ries. 1.** a theatrical practice in which a company performs several works during one season. **2.** Also called **rep′ertory com′pany.** a theatrical company that presents productions in this manner. **3.** REPERTOIRE. See -PARE-[2].

rep•e•ti•tion (rep′i tish′ən) /ˌrɛpɪ'tɪʃən/ *n.* the act of repeating; a repeated action or performance: [*noncount*]: *avoided unnecessary repetition in his essays.* [*count*]: *many repetitions.* See -PET-.

rep•e•ti•tious (rep′i tish′əs) /ˌrɛpɪ'tɪʃəs/ *adj.* full of repetition: *a boring, repetitious account of their vacation trip.* See -PET-.

re•pet•i•tive (ri pet′i tiv) /rɪ'pɛtɪtɪv/ *adj.* having or showing repetition: *the same boring, repetitive lessons.* See -PET-.

re•phrase (rē frāz′) /riy'freyz/ *v.* [~ + *obj*], **-phrased, -phras•ing.** to ask, say, or put into words differently.

re•place (ri plās′) /rɪ'pleys/ *v.* [~ + *obj*], **-placed, -plac•ing. 1.** to take on the function or duties of; substitute for; take the place of: *Computers have replaced typewriters in most offices.* **2.** to provide a substitute or equivalent for: *to replace a broken dish.* **3.** to restore to or put back in the proper place: *He replaced the book on the shelf.* —**re•place′a•ble,** *adj.*

re•place•ment (ri plās′mənt) /rɪ'pleysmənt/ *n.* **1.** [*noncount*] the act of replacing. **2.** [*count*] someone or something that takes the place of another.

re•play (*v.* rē plā′; *n.* rē′plā′) / *v.* riy'pley; *n.* 'riyˌpley/ *v.* [~ + *obj*] **1.** to play again, as a record or tape. **2.** to play again, as a game or match. —*n.* [*count*] **3.** an act or instance of replaying.

re•plen•ish (ri plen′ish) /rɪ'plɛnɪʃ/ *v.* [~ + *obj*] to make full or complete again; fill again: *replenished the refrigerator with food.* —**re•plen′ish•ment,** *n.* [*noncount*] See -PLEN-.

re•plete (ri plēt′) /rɪ'pliyt/ *adj.* **1.** well or fully supplied: *a speech replete with humor.* **2.** well fed. —**re•ple′tion,** *n.* [*noncount*] See -PLET-.

rep•li•ca (rep′li kə) /'rɛplɪkə/ *n.* [*count*], *pl.* **-cas.** a close copy or reproduction, as of a work of art. See -PLIC-.

rep•li•cate (*n.* rep′li kit; *v.* -kāt′) / *n.* 'rɛplɪkɪt; *v.* -ˌkeyt/ *v.*, **-cat•ed, -cat•ing.** to repeat, duplicate, or reproduce: [~ + *obj*]: *to replicate a chemical experiment.* [*no obj*]: *Viruses can replicate in the bloodstream.* See -PLIC-.

rep•li•ca•tion (rep′li kā′shən) /ˌrɛplɪ'keyʃən/ *n.* **1.** [*count*] a copy; replica. **2.** [*noncount*] the act or process of replicating, esp. in a scientific experiment.

re•ply (ri plī′) /rɪ'play/ *v.*, **-plied, -ply•ing,** *n.*, *pl.* **-plies.** —*v.* **1.** to give an answer in words or writing; respond: [*no obj*]: *to reply to a question.* [~ + *that clause*]: *He replied that no one would go.* **2.** [*no obj*] to respond by some action: *to reply to the enemy's fire by firing back.* —*n.* [*count*] **3.** a response in words or writing: *received a reply to her letter.* **4.** a response in the form of some action: *Their reply was a salvo from the huge guns.* —***Idiom.* 5. in reply,** in an answer: *What did you say in reply?* See -PLIC-.

re•port (ri pôrt′, -pōrt′) /rɪ'pɔrt, -'powrt/ *n.* [*count*] **1.** a detailed account of an event, situation, etc., usually based on what one has observed or asked questions about and written or said formally: *a report on the state of the world.* **2.** an item of news; rumor; gossip. **3.** a loud noise, as from an explosion. **—*v.* 4.** to tell as the results of one's observation or investigation: [~ + *obj*]: *He just reported the facts.* [~ + *(that) clause*]: *reported that he had confessed to betraying his country.* [~ + *on* + *obj*]: *He reported on the facts.* **5.** [~ + *obj*] to give a formal account or statement of: *was happy to report a profit for the year.* **6.** [~ + *obj*] to make a charge against (a person), usually to a supervisor or other person having authority: *She reported him to the dean for cheating.* **7.** [~ + *obj*] to make known the presence, absence, condition, etc., of: *to report an aircraft missing.* **8.** [*no obj*] to make one's condition or whereabouts known, as to a person in authority: *He felt dizzy so he reported sick.* **9.** [*no obj*] to present oneself as ordered: *Reporting for duty, sir.* **10.** [*(no obj); ~ + to*] to be under the supervision of: *The corporal reports to the sergeant.* **11.** to write an account such as for publication in a newspaper: [~ + *obj*]: *reported the story in a front-page article.* [*no obj*]: *reporting on a story.* See -PORT-.

re•port•age (ri pôr′tij, -pōr′-, rep′ôr täzh′, -ər-) /rɪˈpɔrtɪdʒ, -ˈpowr-, ˌrɛpɔrˈtɑʒ, -ər-/ *n.* [*noncount*] the act or technique of reporting news. See -PORT-.

report′ card′, *n.* [*count*] a written report of a pupil's grades and behavior, issued at regular times. See -PORT-.

re•port•ed•ly (ri pôr′tid lē, -pōr′-) /rɪˈpɔrtɪdliy, -ˈpowr-/ *adv.* according to reports: *The president is reportedly suffering from a cold.* See -PORT-.

re•port•er (ri pôr′tər, -pōr′-) /rɪˈpɔrtər, -ˈpowr-/ *n.* [*count*] **1.** a person who reports. **2.** a person whose job is to gather and report news, such as for a newspaper or television station. **3.** a person who prepares official reports or transcripts, as of legal or legislative proceedings. See -PORT-.

re•port•ing (ri pôr′ting, -pōr′-) /rɪˈpɔrtɪŋ, -ˈpowr-/ *n.* [*noncount*] **1.** the act of reporting. **2.** the act or job of gathering news and writing stories, as for a newspaper. See -PORT-.

re•pose[1] (ri pōz′) /rɪˈpowz/ *n., v.,* **-posed, -pos•ing. —*n.*** [*noncount*] **1.** the state of being at rest; sleep. **2.** peace or tranquillity; calm. **—*v.*** [*no obj*] **3.** to lie down or be at rest, as from work or activity; lie and be peacefully calm and quiet. **4.** to lie dead. **—re•pose′ful,** *adj.* See -POS-.

re•pose[2] (ri pōz′) /rɪˈpowz/ *v.* [~ + *obj*], **-posed, -pos•ing.** to put (confidence, trust, etc.) in a person or thing. See -POS-.

re•pos•i•tor•y (ri poz′i tôr′ē, -tōr′ē) /rɪˈpɒzɪˌtɔriy, -ˌtowriy/ *n.* [*count*], *pl.* **-tor•ies. 1.** a container or place where things are deposited and stored. **2.** an abundant source or supply: *She is a repository of interesting trivia.* See -POS-.

re•pos•sess (rē′pə zes′) /ˌriypəˈzɛs/ *v.* [~ + *obj*] to take possession of again, esp. for nonpayment of money due. **—re′pos•ses′sion** (-zesh′ən) /-ˈzɛʃən/ *n.* [*noncount*]

rep•re•hen•si•ble (rep′ri hen′sə bəl) /ˌrɛprɪˈhɛnsəbəl/ *adj.* bad or evil enough to deserve blame or rebuke: *reprehensible behavior.* **—rep′re•hen′si•bly,** *adv.* See -PREHEND-.

rep•re•sent (rep′ri zent′) /ˌrɛprɪˈzɛnt/ *v.* **1.** [~ + *obj*] to stand for, as a word or symbol does; symbolize: *In this story the black bird represents evil.* **2.** [~ + *obj*] to express or designate by some symbol, character, or the like: *to represent musical sounds by notes.* **3.** [~ + *obj*] to stand or act in place of, as an agent or substitute, or on behalf of. **4.** [~ + *obj* + *as* + *obj*] to impersonate, as in acting; to pretend to be: *He represented himself as an expert in Egyptian art, and everyone believed him.* **5.** [~ + *obj*] to be the equivalent of or to correspond to; to serve as an example of: *His actions represent a bold new departure from politics as usual.*

rep•re•sen•ta•tion (rep′ri zen tā′shən, -zən-) /ˌrɛprɪzɛnˈteyʃən, -zən-/ *n.* **1.** [*noncount*] the act of representing, or the state of being represented. **2.** [*count*] the act of producing something in visible form, as a picture, figure, statue, etc.: *a life-size representation of the mayor.* **3.** Often, **representations.** [*plural*] statements of things said to be true. **—rep′re•sen•ta′tion•al,** *adj.*

rep•re•sent•a•tive (rep′ri zen′tə tiv) /ˌrɛprɪˈzɛntətɪv/ *n.* [*count*] **1.** a person or thing that represents another or others. **2.** a person who represents a certain group of people or a community in a law-making body, esp. a member of the U.S. House of Representatives or of the lower house in certain state legislatures. **3.** a typical example of something: *thought of him as a representative of the modern executive.* **—*adj.* 4.** serving to represent; representing; including typical members of a certain population: *a representative group to see the mayor.* **5.** [*before a noun*] of, characterized by, or based on representation of the people in government: *a representative democracy.* **6.** being a typical example of a group or kind; typical: *Is this painting representative of your work?*

re•press (ri pres′) /rɪˈprɛs/ *v.* [~ + *obj*] **1.** to check or inhibit (actions or desires): *repressed a sneeze.* **2.** to hold down and control (persons) unfairly or evilly: *to repress one's civil rights.* **3.** to keep down or hold back (memories, emotions, or impulses) unconsciously: *to repress his fantasies.* **—re•pres•sion** (ri presh′ən) /rɪˈprɛʃən/ *n.* [*noncount*] **—re•pres′sive,** *adj.* See -PRESS-.

re•prieve (ri prēv′) /rɪˈpriyv/ *v.,* **-prieved, -priev•ing,** *n.* **—*v.*** [~ + *obj*] **1.** to delay the coming or expected punishment or sentence of (a condemned person): *The governor reprieved the prisoner on death row.* **—*n.*** [*count*] **2.** an official order or formal authorization to delay or cancel punishment, esp. execution. **3.** any temporary relief from something bad.

rep•ri•mand (rep′rə mand′; *v.* also rep′rə mand′) /ˈrɛprəˌmænd; *v.* ælsɒ ˌrɛprəˈmænd/ *n.* [*count*] **1.** a severe scolding or act of placing blame for wrongdoing, esp. a formal or official one. **—*v.*** [~ + *obj*] **2.** to scold or blame (someone) severely.

re•print (*v.* rē print′, *n.* rē′print′) / *v.* riyˈprɪnt, *n.* ˈriyˌprɪnt/ *v.* [~ + *obj*] **1.** to print again: *The book was reprinted twice.* **—*n.*** [*count*] **2.** a reissue of something already in print.

re•pris•al (ri prī′zəl) /rɪˈprayzəl/ *n.* an act against one's enemy of causing equal or greater injuries as a reaction or answer to the injuries done to oneself: [*count*]: *actions met by reprisals.* [*noncount*]: *actions taken in reprisal.* See -PRIS-.

re•prise (rə prēz′) /rəˈpriyz/ *n., v.,* **-prised, -pris•ing. —*n.*** [*count*] **1.** a repeated occurrence, esp. a repetition of a musical theme. **—*v.*** [~ + *obj*] **2.** to repeat: *to reprise the waltz tune.* See -PRIS-.

re•proach (ri prōch′) /rɪˈprowtʃ/ *v.* [~ + *obj*] **1.** to find fault with (a person, group, etc.); to criticize severely; blame. **—*n.* 2.** [*noncount*] blame; disapproval: *a term of reproach.* **3.** [*count*] an expression of, or words that express, such blame. **—re•proach′ful,** *adj.* **—re•proach′ful•ly,** *adv.*

rep•ro•bate (rep′rə bāt′) /ˈrɛprəˌbeyt/ *n.* [*count*] **1.** a wicked person. **—*adj.* 2.** wicked; evil. See -PROB-.

re•pro•duce (rē′prə do͞os′, -dyo͞os′) /ˌriyprəˈduws, -ˈdyuws/ *v.,* **-duced, -duc•ing. 1.** to make a copy or close imitation of; duplicate: [~ + *obj*]: *The tape reproduced the sound of the conversation fairly well.* [*no obj*]: *That low-quality tape machine reproduces badly.* **2.** [~ + *obj*] to produce, form, or bring about again or once more by any process: *Scientists will want to reproduce that experiment.* **3.** to produce one or more other young individuals of (a given kind of organism) by some process of generation, sexual or asexual: [~ + *oneself*]: *Some animals reproduce themselves by laying eggs.* [*no obj*]: *If an animal can't reproduce, its species will not survive.* **—re′pro•duc′i•ble,** *adj.* **—re•pro•duc•tive** (rē′prə duk′tiv) /ˌriyprəˈdʌktɪv/ *adj.* See -DUC-.

re•pro•duc•tion (rē′prə duk′shən) /ˌriyprəˈdʌkʃən/ *n.* **1.** [*noncount*] the act or process of reproducing; the state of being reproduced. **2.** [*noncount*] the process by which living things generate or produce new or young living things: *sexual reproduction.* **3.** [*count*] something made by reproducing; a copy or duplicate. See -DUC-.

re•proof (ri pro͞of′) /rɪˈpruwf/ *n.* **1.** [*noncount*] the act of criticizing, blaming, or correcting. **2.** [*count*] an expression of such criticism, blame, or correction. See -PROV-.

re•prove (ri pro͞ov′) /rɪˈpruwv/ *v.* [~ + *obj*], **-proved, -prov•ing. 1.** to criticize or correct, esp. gently. **2.** to express strong disapproval of; blame; criticize sharply. **—re•prov′ing•ly,** *adv.*

rep•tile (rep′til, -tīl) /ˈrɛptɪl, -tayl/ *n.* [*count*] any air-breathing animal having a backbone, a heart with three chambers, a completely bony skeleton, and a covering of dry scales or horny plates: *Reptiles include snakes, lizards, turtles, and crocodiles.* **—rep•til•i•an** (rep til′ē ən) /rɛpˈtɪliyən/ *adj.*

re•pub•lic (ri pub′lik) /rɪˈpʌblɪk/ *n.* [*count*] **1.** a state which is governed by representatives who are chosen by citizens in elections. **2.** a state in which the head of government is not a monarch and is usually an elected president.

re•pub•li•can (ri pub′li kən) /rɪˈpʌblɪkən/ *adj.* **1.** of, relating to, or of the nature of a republic. **2.** favoring a republic. **3.** [*Republican*] of or relating to the Republican Party. **—***n.* [*count*] **4.** a person who favors a republican form of government. **5.** [*Republican*] a member of the Republican Party. **—re•pub′li•can•ism,** *n.* [*noncount*]

Repub′lican Par′ty, *n.* [*proper noun; usually: the + ~*] one of the two major political parties in the U.S., first organized (1854–56) to restrict slavery.

re•pu•di•ate (ri pyo͞o′dē āt′) /rɪ'pyuwdiy,eyt/ *v.* [*~ + obj*], **-at•ed, -at•ing. 1.** to reject as having no authority or binding force: *to repudiate the claims of ownership.* **2.** to disown; to refuse to have any connection with (a person): *to repudiate a son.* **3.** to reject and disapprove, condemn, or deny: *to repudiate an accusation that he was the killer.* **—re•pu•di•a•tion** (ri pyo͞o′dē ā′shən) /rɪ'pyuwdiy'eyʃən/ *n.* [*noncount*]

re•pug•nance (ri pug′nəns) /rɪ'pʌgnəns/ *n.* [*noncount*] a feeling of strong dislike. See -PUGN-.

re•pug•nant (ri pug′nənt) /rɪ'pʌgnənt/ *adj.* causing a feeling of strong dislike; repellent: *Killing was repugnant to him.* See -PUGN-.

re•pulse (ri puls′) /rɪ'pʌls/ *v.* [*~ + obj*], **-pulsed, -puls•ing. 1.** to drive back; repel: *The squadron repulsed the next assault on the carrier.* **2.** to refuse or reject: *She repulsed all his attempts at friendliness.* **3.** to cause feelings of disgust in: *The slaughter repulsed him.* See -PULS-.

re•pul•sion (ri pul′shən) /rɪ'pʌlʃən/ *n.* [*noncount*] **1.** the act of repulsing, or the state of being repulsed. **2.** the feeling of being disgusted, as by the thought or presence of something that one has a strong dislike for. **3.** the force that tends to separate bodies of similar electric charge or magnetism. See -PULS-.

re•pul•sive (ri pul′siv) /rɪ'pʌlsɪv/ *adj.* **1.** causing a feeling of strong dislike: *a repulsive, bloated face.* **2.** tending to drive away or keep at a distance. **—re•pul′sive•ly,** *adv.* **—re•pul′sive•ness,** *n.* [*noncount*] See -PULS-.

rep•u•ta•ble (rep′yə tə bəl) /'rɛpyətəbəl/ *adj.* honorable; respectable: *put their money in a reputable bank.* **—rep•u•ta•bil•i•ty** (rep′yə tə bil′i tē) /,rɛpyətə'bɪlɪtiy/ *n.* [*noncount*] **—rep′u•ta•bly,** *adv.* See -PUTE-.

rep•u•ta•tion (rep′yə tā′shən) /,rɛpyə'teyʃən/ *n.* [*count*] **1.** the opinion that others have about a person or thing: *That college has a good reputation.* **2.** favorable opinion or public standing: *They tried to ruin his reputation.* See -PUTE-.

re•pute (ri pyo͞ot′) /rɪ'pyuwt/ *n., v.,* **-put•ed, -put•ing. —***n.* [*noncount*] **1.** opinion in the view of others; reputation: *persons of good repute.* **2.** favorable reputation. **—***v.* [*usually: be + ~-ed + to + verb; not: be + ~-ing*] **3.** to consider or believe (a person or thing) to be as described: *He was reputed to be a millionaire.*

re•put•ed (ri pyo͞o′tid) /rɪ'pyuwtɪd/ *adj.* [*before a noun*] reported or supposed to be such: *the reputed author of a book.* **—re•put′ed•ly,** *adv.* See -PUTE-.

re•quest (ri kwest′) /rɪ'kwɛst/ *n.* [*count*] **1.** the act of asking for something to be given or done; petition: *a request for silence.* **2.** something asked for: *Please grant our request.* **—***v.* **3.** [*~ + obj*] to ask for, esp. formally or politely: *I request permission to speak.* **4.** to ask or beg someone to do something: [*~ + to + verb*]: *I request to be excused.* [*~ + that clause*]: *I requested that all records of this conversation be destroyed.* [*~ + obj + to + verb*]: *He requested me to leave.* **—*Idiom.* 5. by** or **on request,** in response to a request: *The band played tunes on request.* See -QUES-.

req•ui•em (rek′wē əm, rē′kwē-, rā′-) /'rɛkwiyəm, 'riykwiy-, 'rey-/ *n.* [*count*] **1.** [*often: Requiem*] Also called **req′uiem mass′.** a Catholic mass for the dead. **2.** music written for a requiem. See -QUIE-.

re•quire (ri kwīər′) /rɪ'kwayər/ *v.,* **-quired, -quir•ing. 1.** [*~ + obj*] to have need of; need: *He requires medical care.* **2.** to order (someone) to do something; demand, esp. with authority: [*~ + obj + to + verb*]: *The judge required the witness to testify.* [*~ + that clause*]: *The judge required that the witness testify.* [*no obj*]: *to do as the law requires.* **3.** [*~ + obj*] to make necessary: *The work required great patience.* **4.** [*not: be + ~-ing; ~ + obj + to + verb*] to place (someone) under an obligation to do something: *You are required to answer all questions.* **—re•quire′ment,** *n.* [*count*] See -QUIR-.

req•ui•site (rek′wə zit) /'rɛkwəzɪt/ *adj.* [*before a noun*] **1.** required; necessary: *the requisite skills for a job.* **—***n.* [*count*] **2.** something required. See -QUIS-.

req•ui•si•tion (rek′wə zish′ən) /,rɛkwə'zɪʃən/ *n.* [*count*] **1.** the act of requiring or demanding something. **2.** a formal or official written request for something, such as supplies. **—***v.* [*~ + obj*] **3.** to demand, order, or take for use: *The army requisitioned gasoline during wartime.* See -QUIS-.

re•quite (ri kwīt′) /rɪ'kwayt/ *v.* [*~ + obj*], **-quit•ed, -quit•ing. 1.** to make repayment for (service, benefits, etc.). **2.** to repay in kind, either for a kindness or an injury. **3.** to give or do in return. **—re•quit′al,** *n.* [*noncount*] **—re•quit′er,** *n.* [*count*] See -QUIT-.

re•run (*v.* rē run′; *n.* rē′run′) / *v.* riy'rʌn; *n.* 'riy,rʌn/ *v.,* **-ran, -run, -run•ning,** *n.* **—***v.* [*~ + obj*] **1.** to run again: *reran the videotape.* **—***n.* [*count*] **2.** a movie or television program that is rerun.

re•sale (rē′sāl′, rē sāl′) /'riy,seyl, riy'seyl/ *n.* the act of selling a second time or secondhand: [*noncount*]: *goods not intended for resale.* [*count*]: *a resale of the merchandise.*

re•scind (ri sind′) /rɪ'sɪnd/ *v.* [*~ + obj*] to withdraw, take back, or make (a law) no longer have effect: *to rescind a harsh law.*

res•cue (res′kyo͞o) /'rɛskyuw/ *v.,* **-cued, -cu•ing,** *n.* **—***v.* [*~ + obj*] **1.** to free from danger; save from harm: *a plan to rescue the hostages.* **—***n.* [*count*] **2.** the act of rescuing. **—res′cu•er,** *n.* [*count*]

re•search (ri sûrch′, rē′sûrch) /rɪ'sɜrtʃ, 'riysɜrtʃ/ *n.* **1.** [*noncount*] careful patient study of a subject in order to discover or revise facts, theories, principles, etc. [] **2.** *count* a particular piece of research. **—***v.* **3.** to investigate or look into something carefully; to do research on: [*~ + obj*]: *He researched the subject.* [*no obj*]: *spending time researching.* **—re•search′er,** *n.* [*count*]

re•sec•tion (ri sek′shən) /rɪ'sɛkʃən/ *n.* [*count*] the surgical removal of all or part of an organ or structure. See -SECT-.

re•sell (rē sel′) /riy'sɛl/ *v.,* **-sold, -sel•ling.** to sell again: [*~ + obj*]: *resold the house.* [*no obj*]: *They hope to resell.*

re•sem•blance (ri zem′bləns) /rɪ'zɛmbləns/ *n.* **1.** [*noncount*] the state or fact of resembling or being or looking alike; similarity: *fooled by the resemblance between them.* **2.** [*count*] a degree, kind, or point in which two or more things seem similar to each other: *a family resemblance between father and son.* See -SEMBLE-.

re•sem•ble (ri zem′bəl) /rɪ'zɛmbəl/ *v.* [*~ + obj; not: be + ~-ing*], **-bled, -bling.** to be like or similar to: *That girl closely resembles her mother.* See -SEMBLE-.

re•sent (ri zent′) /rɪ'zɛnt/ *v.* [*~ + obj*] to feel or show displeasure or anger at (something or someone), because of a feeling of having been insulted or wronged: *The older brother resented his younger sister's success, claiming she was just lucky.* See -SENT-.

re•sent•ful (ri zent′fəl) /rɪ'zɛntfəl/ *adj.* feeling or showing resentment. **—re•sent′ful•ly,** *adv.* See -SENT-.

re•sent•ment (ri zent′mənt) /rɪ'zɛntmənt/ *n.* a feeling of displeasure or anger because of an insult or other wrong: [*noncount*]: *felt growing resentment.* [*count*]: *many resentments.* See -SENT-.

res•er•va•tion (rez′ər vā′shən) /,rɛzər'veyʃən/ *n.* **1.** [*noncount*] the act of creating a doubt in one's mind or making an exception in one's thinking: *to recommend without reservation.* **2.** [*count*] a doubt in one's mind or an exception in one's thinking: *I accept what he says, but with some reservations.* **3.** [*count*] a tract of public land set apart for a special purpose, esp. for the use of Native American people. **4.** [*count*] an arrangement to set aside something for guaranteed use at a later time, as a room in a hotel, a seat on an airplane, or a place at a restaurant. See -SERV-[2].

re•serve (ri zûrv′) /rɪ'zɜrv/ *v.,* **-served, -serv•ing,** *n., adj.* **—***v.* [*~ + obj*] **1.** to keep back or save for future use, handling, etc.: *He reserved his strength for the last half mile of the race.* **2.** to keep aside or save by an arrangement in advance: *We reserved a room at the hotel.* **3.** to set apart for a particular use, purpose, service, etc.: *reserved certain seats for the elderly.* **4.** to delay; postpone: *He reserved judgment on the plan.* **—***n.* **5.** [*count*] cash, or other financial sources that can be easily changed into cash or held aside to meet unexpected demands. **6.** [*count*] something stored or saved for use or time of need; stock: *a reserve of food.* **7.** [*count*] an area of public land set apart for a special purpose: *a forest reserve.* **8. reserves,** [*plural*] part of a military force held in readiness to assist the main force, or kept apart and not in active duty: *joined the reserves.* **9.** [*noncount*] caution or formality in one's words or actions. **—***adj.* [*before a noun*] **10.** kept in reserve: *reserve supplies.* **—*Idiom.* 11. in reserve,** put aside for a future need: *money held in reserve.* See -SERV-[2].

re•served (ri zûrvd′) /rɪˈzɜrvd/ *adj.* **1.** set apart for someone or some particular purpose: *reserved seats.* **2.** cautious or formal in dealing with others. —**re•serv•ed•ly** (ri zûr′vid lē) /rɪˈzɜrvɪdliy/ *adv.* See -SERV²-.

re•serv•ist (ri zûr′vist) /rɪˈzɜrvɪst/ *n.* [*count*] a person who belongs to a military reserve. See -SERV²-.

res•er•voir (rez′ər vwär′, -vwôr′, -vôr′, rez′ə-) /ˈrɛzərˌvwɑr, -ˌvwɔr, -ˌvɔr, ˈrɛzə-/ *n.* [*count*] **1.** a natural or artificial place where water is collected for use, supplying a community or region. **2.** a place where anything is collected or accumulated in great amount. **3.** reserve: *had a great reservoir of affection for us.* See -SERV-².

re•set (*v.* rē set′; *n.* rē′set′) /*v.* riyˈsɛt; *n.* ˈriyˌsɛt/ *v.,* **-set, -set•ting,** *n.* —*v.* **1.** to set again: [~ + *obj*]: *to reset an alarm clock.* [*no obj*]: *The alarm clock resets automatically.* —*n.* [*count*] **2.** the act of resetting. **3.** a device used in resetting an instrument or control mechanism.

re•set•tle (rē set′əl) /riyˈsɛtəl/ *v.,* **-tled, -tling.** to (cause to) settle in a new area, or to settle again: [~ + *obj*]: *forcibly resettled the refugees.* [*no obj*]: *They resettled in America.* —**re•set′tle•ment,** *n.* [*noncount*]

re•shuf•fle (rē shuf′əl) /riyˈʃʌfəl/ *v.,* **-fled, -fling,** *n.* —*v.* [~ + *obj*] **1.** to change or rearrange the positions or parts of something: *reshuffled the seating of the students.* —*n.* [*count*] **2.** an act of reshuffling.

re•side (ri zīd′) /rɪˈzayd/ *v.,* **-sid•ed, -sid•ing. 1.** [*no obj*] to live; dwell: *resides at 15 Maple Lane; resides in Paris.* **2.** [*not: be* + *~-ing; ~* + *in*] (of things, qualities, etc.) to be present or to be found normally or properly in something: *Power resided in the throne.* See -SID-.

res•i•dence (rez′i dəns) /ˈrɛzɪdəns/ *n.* **1.** [*count*] the place, esp. the house, in which a person lives or resides. **2.** [*noncount*] the act or fact of residing. **3.** [*noncount*] the status of a legal resident. See -SID-.

res•i•den•cy (rez′i dən sē) /ˈrɛzɪdənsiy/ *n., pl.* **-cies. 1.** RESIDENCE (def. 2). **2.** the position of a medical resident: [*noncount*]: *completing her residency at the hospital.* [*count*]: *several residencies available in rural areas.*

res•i•dent (rez′i dənt) /ˈrɛzɪdənt/ *n.* [*count*] **1.** a person who lives in a place: *living as a foreign resident in the Czech Republic.* **2.** a physician working in a hospital while receiving specialized training there. —*adj.* [*before a noun*] **3.** residing; dwelling in a place: *a resident alien in Canada.* **4.** living or staying at a place as part of one's official duty. **5.** [*before a noun*] (of qualities or abilities) existing as if attached to a situation or place: *She is the resident expert in computers.* **6.** (of a computer program) currently active, standing by, or available in computer memory: *Your printer program is now resident.* See -SID-.

res•i•den•tial (rez′i den′shəl) /ˌrɛzɪˈdɛnʃəl/ *adj.* **1.** [*usually: before a noun*] (of a place or area) consisting mainly of private homes rather than businesses: *a quiet residential neighborhood.* **2.** restricted to homes: *residential zoning.* See -SID-.

re•sid•u•al (ri zij′o͞o əl) /rɪˈzɪdʒuwəl/ *adj.* **1.** relating to or being a residue or remainder; remaining; leftover. —*n.* [*count*] **2.** an amount or quantity left over; a remainder. **3.** Usually, **residuals.** [*plural*] a fee paid, as to an actor, for repeated broadcasts of a film, program, commercial, etc., after its original presentation or period of use. See -SID-.

res•i•due (rez′i do͞o′, -dyo͞o′) /ˈrɛzɪˌduw, -ˌdyuw/ *n.* [*count*] something that remains after a part is removed, disposed of, or used; remainder; the rest; a remnant: *Residues from chemical pesticides could harm children.* See -SID-.

re•sign (ri zīn′) /rɪˈzayn/ *v.* **1.** to give up an office or position: [~ + *from* + *obj*]: *was forced to resign from the job.* [~ + *obj*]: *The officer resigned his commission.* **2.** [~ + *oneself*] to give up (oneself, one's mind, etc.) without struggle or resistance: *He resigned himself to failure.* See -SIGN-.

res•ig•na•tion (rez′ig nā′shən) /ˌrɛzɪgˈneyʃən/ *n.* **1.** [*count*] the act of resigning. **2.** [*count*] a formal statement, often in writing, stating that one gives up an office or position. **3.** [*noncount*] an accepting, unresisting or uncomplaining attitude or state of mind: *With a sigh of resignation he turned back to his boring job.* See -SIGN-.

re•signed (ri zīnd′) /rɪˈzaynd/ *adj.* accepting; submissive: *a resigned look of despair.* —**re•sign•ed•ly** (ri zī′nid lē) /rɪˈzaynɪdliy/ *adv.* See -SIGN-.

re•sil•i•ence (ri zil′yəns) /rɪˈzɪlyəns/ *n.* [*noncount*] **1.** the ability to spring back to an original form after having been squeezed, stretched, etc. **2.** the ability to recover quickly from illness, misfortune, troubles, or the like.

re•sil•ient (ri zil′yənt) /rɪˈzɪlyənt/ *adj.* **1.** having resilience; flexible: *a resilient rubber ball.* **2.** recovering quickly and easily from illness, misfortune, troubles, or the like; buoyant. —**re•sil′ien•cy,** *n.* [*noncount*]

res•in (rez′in) /ˈrɛzɪn/ *n.* [*noncount*] a sticky, solid or nearly solid substance that comes from pine, used in medicine and in the making of varnishes and plastics. —**res′in•ous,** *adj.*

re•sist (ri zist′) /rɪˈzɪst/ *v.* **1.** to withstand, fight, or work against; oppose: [~ + *obj*]: *The armies resisted the invasion.* [*no obj*]: *The army was ordered to resist.* **2.** [~ + *obj*] to withstand the action or effect of: *The engine oil resists corrosion.* **3.** to keep or stop oneself from (doing) something: [~ + *obj*]: *The kids couldn't resist the chocolates.* [~ + *verb-ing*]: *They couldn't resist peeking under the curtain.* —**re•sist′er,** *n.* [*count*] See -SIST-.

re•sist•ance (ri zis′təns) /rɪˈzɪstəns/ *n.* [*noncount*] **1.** the act or power of resisting or opposing: *The plans met with a great deal of resistance.* **2.** the opposition offered by one thing, force, etc., to another: *wind resistance that slows the car down.* **3.** the ability of the human body to resist infection or illness. **4.** the tendency of a conductor to oppose the flow of electrical current. **5.** [*sometimes: Resistance; usually: the ~*] an underground group working to free a country from an occupying power. See -SIST-.

re•sist•ant (ri zis′tənt) /rɪˈzɪstənt/ *adj.* resisting. See -SIST-.

re•sis•tor (ri zis′tər) /rɪˈzɪstər/ *n.* [*count*] a device designed to introduce resistance into an electric circuit. See -SIST-.

re•sole (rē sōl′) /riyˈsowl/ *v.* [~ + *obj*], **-soled, -sol•ing.** to put a new sole on (a shoe, etc.).

res•o•lute (rez′ə lo͞ot′) /ˈrɛzəˌluwt/ *adj.* set in purpose or opinion; resolved: *resolute character.* —**res′o•lute′ly,** *adv.*: *The soldiers marched resolutely forward.* See -SOLV-.

res•o•lu•tion (rez′ə lo͞o′shən) /ˌrɛzəˈluwʃən/ *n.* **1.** [*count*] a formal expression by a group of its opinion: *passed a resolution condemning the invasion.* **2.** [*count*] the act of deciding on a course of action, etc.; the thing decided on: *made a New Year's resolution.* **3.** [*noncount*] the mental state of being resolute: *He went forward with renewed resolution.* **4.** [*noncount*] the act or capability of distinguishing between nearby or close parts, etc.: *the resolution of the microscope.* **5.** a solution of a problem, etc.: [*noncount*]: *the resolution of the crisis.* [*count*]: *looking for a resolution of the crisis.* **6.** [*count*] the conclusion of the actions, etc., in the plot of a play, novel, etc. See -SOLV-.

re•solve (ri zolv′) /rɪˈzɒlv/ *v.,* **-solved, -solv•ing,** *n.* —*v.* **1.** to make a resolution: [~ + *to* + *verb*]: *I resolved to keep my mouth shut.* [~ + *that clause*]: *resolved that she would work harder.* **2.** [~ + *obj* + *into* + *obj*] to separate into parts: *to resolve a force into its parts.* **3.** [~ + *that clause*] to state in a formal resolution: *It was resolved that the committee recommend her promotion.* **4.** [~ + *obj*] to settle or solve (a question, dispute, etc.): *Can we resolve the problem by having another judge look over the case and make a decision?* —*n.* **5.** [*count*] a resolution made: *a firm resolve to avoid controversy.* **6.** [*noncount*] firmness of purpose; determination: *She carried on the job with much resolve.* —**re•solv′a•ble,** *adj.* See -SOLV-.

re•solved (ri zolvd′) /rɪˈzɒlvd/ *adj.* [*be* + ~ + *to* + *verb*] firm in purpose or intent: *was resolved not to go through the same trouble again.* See -SOLV-.

res•o•nance (rez′ə nəns) /ˈrɛzənəns/ *n.* **1.** [*noncount*] the state or quality of being resonant: *the resonance of his deep voice.* **2.** a quality of deeper meaning: [*count*]: *The poem has a resonance beyond its surface meaning.* [*noncount*]: *the resonance of the election results.* See -SON-.

res•o•nant (rez′ə nənt) /ˈrɛzənənt/ *adj.* (of a sound or voice) deep, clear, and continuing or echoing: *the judge's resonant voice filling the chambers.* —**res′o•nant•ly,** *adv.* See -SON-.

res•o•nate (rez′ə nāt′) /ˈrɛzəˌneyt/ *v.* [*no obj*], **-nat•ed, -nat•ing.** to make a deep, clear, echoing or continuing sound: *His booming voice resonated in the church.* See -SON-.

re•sort (ri zôrt′) /rɪˈzɔrt/ *n.* **1.** [*count*] a place with facilities for vacationers: *a lovely beach resort.* **2.** [*noncount*] the action of turning to someone for help; resource: *The Supreme Court was the court of last resort for his case.* —*v.* [~ + *to* + *obj*] **3.** to turn to for help, often as a final option: *to resort to war to accomplish his aims.* See -SORT-.

re•sound (ri zound′) /rɪ'zawnd/ *v.* [*no obj*] **1.** to echo or ring with sound: *The room resounded with applause.* **2.** to make an echoing sound, or sound loudly: *The cheers resounded through the room.* See -SON-.

re•sound•ing (ri zoun′ding) /rɪ'zawndɪŋ/ *adj.* [*before a noun*] **1.** loud, clear, and echoing: *a resounding cheer.* **2.** very good or great: *resounding successes.* —**re•sound′ing•ly,** *adv.*

re•source (rē′sôrs, -sōrs, -zôrs, -zōrs; ri sôrs′, -sōrs′, -zôrs′, -zōrs′) /'riysɔrs, -sowrs, -zɔrs, -zowrs; rɪ'sɔrs, -'sowrs, -'zɔrs, -'zowrs/ *n.* **1.** [*count*] a source of supply, support, or aid, esp. one held in reserve: *She is an important resource in the college because she knows how to solve so many different problems.* **2.** [*count*] the source of wealth of a country: *rich in natural resources.* **3.** Usually, **resources.** [*plural*] money or assets: *What resources do you have to be able to afford such a house?* **4.** [*noncount*] capability in dealing with a situation: *a woman of resource.*

re•source•ful (ri sôrs′fəl, -sōrs′-, -zôrs′-, -zōrs′-) /rɪ'sɔrsfəl, -'sowrs-, -'zɔrs-, -'zowrs-/ *adj.* able to deal with difficulties, etc.: *very resourceful in solving those math problems.* —**re•source′ful•ness,** *n.* [*noncount*]: *showed her resourcefulness by figuring a way out of the danger.*

re•spect (ri spekt′) /rɪ'spɛkt/ *n.* **1.** [*count*] a detail or aspect of something; a feature: *The two plans differ in some respects.* **2.** [*noncount*] honor or high regard: *to be held in respect.* **3.** [*noncount*] proper courtesy: *respect for the flag.* **4. respects,** [*plural*] a formal gesture of greeting or sympathy: *Give my respects to your parents.* —*v.* [~ + *obj*] **5.** to hold in honor: *Do the students respect the flag?* **6.** to keep from interfering with; to have regard for: *to respect a person's privacy.* —***Idiom.*** **7. with respect to,** in reference to; in regard to: *inquiries with respect to the best route to take.* See -SPEC-.

re•spect•a•ble (ri spek′tə bəl) /rɪ'spɛktəbəl/ *adj.* **1.** worthy of respect: *a respectable citizen.* **2.** good enough to be used: *respectable shoes.* **3.** of moderate quality; not excellent but good: *They gave a respectable performance.* **4.** fairly large in size or amount: *a respectable turnout.* —**re•spect•a•bil•i•ty** (ri spek′tə bil′i tē) /rɪˌspɛktə'bɪlɪtiy/ *n.* [*noncount*] —**re•spect′a•bly,** *adv.* See -SPEC-.

re•spect•ful (ri spekt′fəl) /rɪ'spɛktfəl/ *adj.* showing or having respect; courteous; considerate: *respectful students.* —**re•spect′ful•ly,** *adv.*: *The students always respectfully raised their hands.* See -SPEC-.

re•spect•ing (ri spek′ting) /rɪ'spɛktɪŋ/ *prep.* regarding; concerning; with respect to: *What is your opinion respecting the school's new policy?* See -SPEC-.

re•spec•tive (ri spek′tiv) /rɪ'spɛktɪv/ *adj.* relating individually to each; particular: *We need to judge the respective merits of each of the candidates.* See -SPEC-.

re•spec•tive•ly (ri spek′tiv lē) /rɪ'spɛktɪvliy/ *adv.* (of several subjects) in a parallel way; in the order given: *Joe and Bob escorted Betty and Alice, respectively.* See -SPEC-.

res•pi•ra•tion (res′pə rā′shən) /ˌrɛspə'reyʃən/ *n.* [*noncount*] the act or process of respiring. See -SPIR-.

res•pi•ra•tor (res′pə rā′tər) /'rɛspəˌreytər/ *n.* [*count*] **1.** a machine that produces artificial respiration: *hooked up the crash victim to a respirator and rushed him to the hospital.* **2.** a filtering device worn over the nose and mouth to prevent inhaling dangerous substances. See -SPIR-.

res•pi•ra•to•ry (res′pə rə tôr′ē, -tōr′ē) /'rɛspərəˌtɔriy, -ˌtowriy/ *adj.* [*before a noun*] of or relating to respiration: *respiratory ailments.* See -SPIR-.

re•spire (ri spīᵊr′) /rɪ'spayᵊr/ *v.* [*no obj*], **-spired, -spir•ing. 1.** to take in and let out air for maintaining life; breathe. **2.** (of a living system) to exchange oxygen for carbon dioxide and other products. See -SPIR-.

res•pite (res′pit) /'rɛspɪt/ *n.* a delay; a period of relief: [*count*]: *a brief respite from the pain.* [*noncount*]: *The music from the nightclub pounded without respite all night.* See -SPEC-.

re•splend•ent (ri splen′dənt) /rɪ'splɛndənt/ *adj.* shining brilliantly; gleaming; radiant; splendid. —**re•splend′ence,** *n.* [*noncount*] —**re•splend′ent•ly,** *adv.*

re•spond (ri spond′) /rɪ'spɒnd/ *v.* **1.** to answer in words: [~ + *to* + *obj*]: *How do you respond to that question?* [*used with quotations*]: *"I'm ready," he responded.* **2.** [*no obj*] to return by an action: *to respond to a charity drive with donations.* **3.** [*no obj;* ~ + *to*] to react favorably: *didn't respond to the treatment.* **4.** [*no obj;* ~ + *to*] to exhibit an effect; react: *Nerves respond to a stimulus.* See -SPOND-.

re•spond•ent (ri spon′dənt) /rɪ'spɒndənt/ *n.* [*count*] **1.** one who responds. **2.** a defendant, esp. in divorce proceedings in a court. See -SPOND-.

re•sponse (ri spons′) /rɪ'spɒns/ *n.* **1.** [*count*] an answer; reply: *What is your response to these questions, Senator?* **2.** an action done as an answer to another action: [*count*]: *a friendly response to his greeting.* [*noncount*]: *She nodded in response to his greeting.* **3.** [*count*] behavior of a living thing due to a stimulus: *the chimp's response to seeing the blue light flash.* See -SPOND-. —**Related Words.** RESPONSE is a noun, RESPONSIBLE is an adjective, RESPONSIBILITY is a noun: *What was your response to the question? She is a responsible driver. The new job has more responsibilities.*

re•spon•si•bil•i•ty (ri spon′sə bil′i tē) /rɪˌspɒnsə'bɪlɪtiy/ *n., pl.* **-ties. 1.** [*noncount*] the state or fact of being responsible: *Will anyone assume responsibility for this?* **2.** [*count*] a burden placed upon one who is responsible: *the responsibilities of being a father.* **3.** [*count*] a person or thing for which one is responsible: *Child care is my responsibility.* **4.** [*noncount*] reliability or dependability, esp. in meeting payments: *financial responsibility; a job requiring some responsibility.* See -SPOND-.

re•spon•si•ble (ri spon′sə bəl) /rɪ'spɒnsəbəl/ *adj.* **1.** [*be* + ~ + *for*] accountable, as for something within one's power: *The children are responsible for setting the table.* **2.** involving responsibility: *a responsible position.* **3.** [*be* + ~ + *for*] able to be given the blame or credit for being the source of something: *Who is responsible for this mess?* **4.** [*be* + ~] having a capacity for moral decisions: *The defendant is insane and not responsible for his actions.* **5.** reliable or dependable; trustworthy: *a mature, responsible young adult.* —**re•spon′si•bly,** *adv.*: *Will they behave responsibly?* See -SPOND-.

re•spon•sive (ri spon′siv) /rɪ'spɒnsɪv/ *adj.* responding readily and with sympathy: *responsive to ideas for changing the organization.* —**re•spon′sive•ly,** *adv.* —**re•spon′sive•ness,** *n.* [*noncount*]

rest[1] (rest) /rɛst/ *n.* **1.** [*noncount*] the refreshing quiet of sleep or ease: *He needs rest and relaxation after all that work.* **2.** [*noncount*] relief or freedom, esp. from something troublesome: *The racket continued without rest.* **3.** [*count*] a period of time of sleep, ease, etc.: *The children took a short rest in the afternoon.* **4.** the stopping or absence of motion: [*count; usually singular*]: *The ball rolled and then came to a rest.* [*noncount*]: *a state of rest.* **5.** [*count*] *Music.* **a.** a rhythmic period of silence between tones. **b.** a mark or sign indicating it. **6.** [*count*] a device by which something is supported: *padded rests for one's arms.* —*v.* **7.** to refresh oneself, as by sleeping, lying down, or being at ease: [*no obj*]: *rested for a few hours on the couch.* [~ + *obj*]: *rested his aching body in a hot tub.* **8.** [*no obj*] to be dead. **9.** [*no obj*] to stop moving; stop: *The ball rested just a few inches from the hole.* **10.** [*no obj*] to remain without further notice: *Why don't you let the matter rest?* **11.** to (cause to) lie, sit, lean, or be set: [*no obj*]: *His arm rested on the table.* [~ + *obj*]: *He rested his arm on her shoulder.* **12.** to rely; to (cause to) be founded: [~ + *on/upon* + *obj*]: *His whole argument rests on false assumptions.* [~ + *obj* + *on/upon* + *obj*]: *rested his arguments on false assumptions.* **13.** [*not: be* + ~*-ing;* ~ + *with* + *obj*] to be found; belong: *The blame rests with them.* **14.** [~ + *on/upon* + *obj*] to be fixed on something, as a gaze: *His gaze rested on her medallion.* **15.** *Law.* to bring to an end the introduction of evidence in a case: [*no obj*]: *Your Honor, the defense rests.* [~ + *obj*]: *Your Honor, the defense rests its case.* —***Idiom.*** **16. at rest, a.** in a state of repose, as in sleep. **b.** dead. **c.** not active; not in motion. **d.** free from worry; tranquil. **17. lay to rest, a.** to bury (a dead body): [*lay* + *obj* + *to* + ~]: *They laid him to rest.* [*lay* + *to* + ~ + *obj*]: *They laid to rest many brave soldiers.* **b.** to relieve the fear of: [*lay* + *obj* + *to* + ~]: *They laid most of my fears to rest.* [*lay* + *to* + ~ + *obj*]: *They laid to rest most of my fears.*

rest[2] (rest) /rɛst/ *n.* [*the* + ~] **1.** [*used with a singular verb*] the part that remains; remainder: *The first part was hard, but the rest was easy.* **2.** [*used with a plural verb*] the others: *All the rest are going.* —*v.* [*not: be* + ~*-ing;* ~ + *adjective (+ that clause)*] **3.** to continue to be: *Rest assured that all is well.*

res•tau•rant (res′tər ənt, -tə ränt′, -tränt) /'rɛstərənt, -təˌrɑnt, -trɑnt/ *n.* [*count*] a place of business where meals are served. SEE ILLUSTRATION.

res•tau•ra•teur (res′tər ə tûr′) /ˌrɛstərə'tɜr/ *n.* [*count*] the owner or manager of a restaurant.

restaurant

waiter
tray
serving cart
menu
knife
candle
glass
plate
fork
napkin
breadbasket
spoon
tablecloth

rest•ful (rest′fəl) /ˈrɛstfəl/ *adj.* **1.** giving rest: *a restful place in the mountains.* **2.** at rest; peaceful. —**rest′ful•ly,** *adv.*

rest′ home′, *n.* [*count*] an establishment that provides a place to live and special care for the elderly; a nursing home.

res•ti•tu•tion (res′ti to͞o′shən, -tyo͞o′-) /ˌrɛstɪˈtuwʃən, -ˈtyuw-/ *n.* [*noncount*] **1.** payment for loss, damage, or injury. **2.** the restoration of property taken away. See -STIT-.

res•tive (res′tiv) /ˈrɛstɪv/ *adj.* **1.** unwilling to undergo control or delay; uneasy. **2.** uncooperative; stubborn. —**res′tive•ly,** *adv.* —**res′tive•ness,** *n.* [*noncount*]

rest•less (rest′lis) /ˈrɛstlɪs/ *adj.* **1.** of or characterized by inability to remain at rest: *a restless mood.* **2.** not quiet; uneasy. **3.** always in motion: *the restless sea.* **4.** without rest or sleep: *a restless night.* —**rest′less•ly,** *adv.*: *tossed restlessly in her sleep.* —**rest′less•ness,** *n.* [*noncount*]

res•to•ra•tion (res′tə rā′shən) /ˌrɛstəˈreyʃən/ *n.* **1.** [*noncount*] the act of restoring: *the restoration of an old house to an elegant home.* **2.** [*noncount*] the act of restoring, or the state of being restored: *the restoration of law and order.* **3.** [*count*] something restored, as by renovating.

re•stor•a•tive (ri stôr′ə tiv, -stōr′-) /rɪˈstɔrətɪv, -ˈstowr-/ *adj.* **1.** of or relating to restoration. **2.** capable of renewing health. —*n.* [*count*] **3.** something that brings back health or strength: *He asked for a drink as a restorative.*

re•store (ri stôr′, -stōr′) /rɪˈstɔr, -ˈstowr/ *v.* [~ + *obj*], **-stored, -stor•ing. 1.** to bring back into existence, use, etc.; reestablish: *to restore order.* **2.** to bring back to a former condition: *to restore a painting.* **3.** to bring back to a state of health or strength: *The treatments restored him to health.* **4.** to return, as to a former place, position, or rank: *to restore books to a shelf.*

re•strain (ri strān′) /rɪˈstreyn/ *v.* [~ + *obj*] **1.** to hold back from action; check; repress: *He was so mad he could hardly restrain himself.* **2.** to limit or reduce the activity or effect of: *to restrain trade with certain countries.* See -STRAIN-.

re•strained (ri strānd′) /rɪˈstreynd/ *adj.* calm; not showing one's feelings; controlled. See -STRAIN-.

re•straint (ri strānt′) /rɪˈstreynt/ *n.* **1.** [*noncount*] a restraining influence. **2.** [*count*] a means of restraining: *the restraints of society.* **3.** [*count*] a device that restrains, such as a harness: *a child restraint for use in the car.* **4.** [*noncount*] reserve in feelings, behavior, etc.: *speaking with restraint.* See -STRAIN-.

re•strict (ri strikt′) /rɪˈstrɪkt/ *v.* [~ + *obj*] to keep within limits, as of space, action, amount, etc.: *restricted his men to two glasses of water a day.* See -STRICT-.

re•strict•ed (ri strik′tid) /rɪˈstrɪktɪd/ *adj.* **1.** limited: *a restricted range of courses.* **2.** limited to members of a certain group or class: *a restricted neighborhood.* See -STRICT-.

re•stric•tion (ri strik′shən) /rɪˈstrɪkʃən/ *n.* **1.** [*count*] something that restricts: *thought there were too many restrictions on business.* **2.** [*noncount*] the act of restricting; the state of being restricted: *acting without restriction.* See -STRICT-.

re•stric•tive (ri strik′tiv) /rɪˈstrɪktɪv/ *adj.* **1.** tending or serving to restrict. **2.** of or being a word, phrase, or clause that identifies or limits the meaning of a modified element. In English a restrictive clause is usually not set off by commas. —**re•stric′tive•ness,** *n.* [*noncount*]

rest′ room′, *n.* [*count*] a public lavatory, esp. in a public building, having washbasins, toilets, etc.

re•sult (ri zult′) /rɪˈzʌlt/ *v.* **1.** [*no obj*] to arise or proceed from previous actions, circumstances, etc.; be the outcome: *What will result from his arrest?* **2.** [~ + *in* + *obj*] to end in a specified way: *His best efforts always seemed to result in failure.* —*n.* [*count*] **3.** something that happens because of something else; an effect: *What was the end result?* **4.** *Math.* a quantity, expression, etc., obtained by adding, subtracting, etc.

re•sult•ant (ri zul′tənt) /rɪˈzʌltənt/ *adj.* [*before a noun*] happening or following as a result or effect: *The war and the resultant low unemployment fueled the economy.*

re•sume (ri zo͞om′) /rɪˈzuwm/ *v.,* **-sumed, -sum•ing. 1.** to take up or go on with again; continue: [~ + *obj*]: *The motor coughed briefly, then resumed its steady hum.* [~ + *verb-ing*]: *The soldiers resumed marching.* [*no obj*]: *The voices ceased when she arrived, then quickly resumed.* **2.** [~ + *obj*] to take or occupy again: *Ladies and gentlemen, please resume your seats.* See -SUM-.

ré•su•mé or **re•su•me** or **re•su•mé** (rez′o͞o mā′, rez′o͞o mā′) /ˈrɛzʊˌmey, ˌrɛzʊˈmey/ *n.* [*count*] **1.** a summary. **2.** a brief written account of educational and professional qualifications and experience: *handed over her résumé and waited.* See -SUM-.

re•sump•tion (ri zump′shən) /rɪˈzʌmpʃən/ *n.* the act or fact of resuming: [*count*]: *a resumption of peace talks.* [*noncount*]: *no resumption of talks yet.* See -SUM-.

re•sur•gent (ri sûr′jənt) /rɪˈsɜrdʒənt/ *adj.* tending to come back to activity or importance: *the resurgent political party.* —**re•sur′gence,** *n.* [*count; usually singular*]: *a resurgence of interest.* [*noncount*]: *the resurgence of the party.* See -RECT-.

res•ur•rect (rez′ə rekt′) /ˌrɛzəˈrɛkt/ *v.* [~ + *obj*] **1.** to raise from the dead; bring to life again. **2.** to bring back into use, attention, etc.: *The newspapers resurrected that old story about UFO sightings.* See -RECT-.

res•ur•rec•tion (rez′ə rek′shən) /ˌrɛzəˈrɛkʃən/ *n.* **1.** [*noncount*] the act of resurrecting from the dead. **2.** [*noncount; Resurrection*] the rising of Christ after His death and burial. **3.** [*noncount; Resurrection*] the rising of the dead on Judgment Day. **4.** [*count*] a rising again, as from decay or disuse; revival. See -RECT-.

re•sus•ci•tate (ri sus′i tāt′) /rɪˈsʌsɪˌteyt/ *v.* [~ + *obj*], **-tat•ed, -tat•ing.** to revive from unconsciousness: *The paramedics rushed to resuscitate the drowning victim.* —**re•sus•ci•ta•tion** (ri sus′i tā′shən) /rɪˌsʌsɪˈteyʃən/ *n.* [*noncount*] —**re•sus′ci•ta′tor,** *n.* [*count*]

re•tail (rē′tāl) /ˈriyteyl/ *n.* [*noncount*] **1.** the sale of goods to individual consumers. —*adj.* [*before a noun*] **2.** of or relating to working in sales at retail. —*adv.* **3.** in a retail quantity or at a retail price: *These sell at $50 retail.* —*v.* **4.** to (cause to) be sold directly to the consumer: [~ + *obj*]: *to retail hardware goods.* [*no obj*]: *These shoes normally retail at $50 a pair.* —**re′tail•er,** *n.* [*count*] See -TAIL-.

re•tain (ri tān′) /rɪˈteyn/ *v.* [~ + *obj*] **1.** to keep possession of: *He retained his balance.* **2.** to continue to hold or have: *clothing that retains its color.* **3.** to keep in mind; remember: *He was good at retaining what he needed for a test.* **4.** to hire, esp. by payment of a preliminary fee: *to retain a lawyer.* See -TAIN-.

re•tain•er[1] (ri tā′nər) /rɪˈteynər/ *n.* [*count*] **1.** one that retains. **2.** a servant that has been with a family for a long time. **3.** a device for maintaining the position of the natural teeth, etc.

re•tain•er[2] (ri tā′nər) /rɪˈteynər/ *n.* [*count*] a fee paid to obtain the services of a professional, as a lawyer. See -TAIN-.

re•take (*v.* rē tāk′; *n.* rē′tāk′ / *v.* riyˈteyk; *n.* ˈriyˌteyk/ *v.,* **-took, -tak•en, -tak•ing,** *n.* —*v.* [~ + *obj*] **1.** to recapture: *The patrol worked hard to retake that small hill.* **2.** to photograph or film again. —*n.* [*count*] **3.** a picture, scene, etc., photographed or filmed again.

re•tal•i•ate (ri tal′ē āt′) /rɪˈtæliyˌeyt/ *v.* [*no obj*], **-at•ed, -at•ing.** to strike back for an injury or wrong: *had to retaliate for the injury done to his brother.* —**re•tal′i•a′tive, re•tal•i•a•to•ry** (ri tal′ē ə tôr′ē, -tōr′ē) /rɪˈtæliyəˌtɔriy, -ˌtowriy/ *adj.*

re•tal•i•a•tion (ri tal′ē ā′shən) /rɪˌtæliyˈeyʃən/ *n.* [*noncount*] the act of retaliating.

re•tard (ri tärd′ *for 1* rē′tärd *for 2*) /rɪˈtɑrd *for 1* ˈriytɑrd *for 2* / *v.* [~ + *obj*] **1.** to delay the development or progress of: *Cold retards the growth of bacteria.* —*n.* [*count*] **2.** *Slang* (*disparaging*). **a.** a mentally retarded person. **b.** one who is stupid or ineffective. —**re•tar•da•tion** (rē′tär dā′shən) /ˌriytɑrˈdeyʃən/ *n.* [*noncount*]

re•tard•ant (ri tär′dnt) /rɪˈtɑrdnt/ *n.* [*count*] **1.** any substance capable of reducing the speed of a chemical reaction. —*adj.* [*usually used with a noun before it in combination*] **2.** retarding the spread of something: *fire-retardant material.*

re•tard•ed (ri tär′did) /rɪˈtɑrdɪd/ *adj.* **1.** less developed mentally than others; lacking normal intelligence: *a retarded child.* —*n.* **2. the retarded,** [*plural; used with a plural verb*] mentally retarded people thought of as a group: *fought for rights for the retarded.*

retch (rech) /rɛtʃ/ *v.* [*no obj*] to make efforts to vomit.

re•ten•tion (ri ten′shən) /rɪˈtɛnʃən/ *n.* [*noncount*] **1.** the act of retaining, or the state of being retained. **2.** the act or power of remembering things; memory: *amazing powers of retention.* See -TEN-.

re•ten•tive (ri ten′tiv) /rɪˈtɛntɪv/ *adj.* **1.** tending to retain. **2.** able to remember well: *a retentive memory.* —**re•ten′tive•ness,** *n.* [*noncount*] See -TEN-.

re•think (rē think′) /riyˈθɪnk/ *v.* [~ + *obj*], **-thought, -think•ing.** to think again (about something): *rethought the situation and came up with a new plan.*

ret•i•cent (ret′ə sənt) /ˈrɛtəsənt/ *adj.* willing or accustomed to be silent; reserved: *was reticent about her private life.* —**ret′i•cence,** *n.* [*noncount*]

ret•i•na (ret′n ə, ret′nə) /ˈrɛtṇə, ˈrɛtnə/ *n.* [*count*], *pl.* **ret•i•nas, ret•i•nae** (ret′n ē′) /ˈrɛtṇˌiy/. the innermost coat of the back part of the eyeball that receives the image produced by the lens: *The retina meets the optic nerve.*

ret•i•nue (ret′n o͞o′, -yo͞o′) /ˈrɛtṇˌuw, -ˌyuw/ *n.* [*count*] a group of followers that accompany someone important. See -TAIN-.

re•tire (ri tīər′) /rɪˈtayər/ *v.*, **-tired, -tir•ing. 1.** [*no obj*] to withdraw, esp. to a place of privacy: *retired to her study.* **2.** [*no obj*] to go to bed: *I'll retire for the night now.* **3.** to (cause to) give up or withdraw from a job or career, usually because of age: [*no obj*]: *Dad retired from the fire department.* [~ + *obj*]: *The navy decided to retire the old battleship.* **4.** [*no obj*] to fall back or retreat, such as from battle or danger: *We retired and the enemy consolidated their position.* **5.** [~ + *obj*] *Sports.* to put out (a batter or team): *The relief pitcher came in and retired the next seven batters.*

re•tired (ri tīərd′) /rɪˈtayərd/ *adj.* **1.** having withdrawn from a job or career: *a retired banker.* **2.** due or given a retired person: *retired pay.*

re•tire•ment (ri tīər′mənt) /rɪˈtayərmənt/ *n.* [*noncount*] the act of retiring from a job or career: *earning a good pension during retirement.*

re•tir•ing (ri tīər′ing) /rɪˈtayərɪŋ/ *adj.* **1.** that retires. **2.** withdrawing from contact with others; shy: *a retiring personality.*

re•tool (rē to͞ol′) /riyˈtuwl/ *v.* **1.** to replace the machinery of (a factory): [~ + *obj*]: *The foundation helped them retool their factories.* [*no obj*]: *The foundation would help them retool.* **2.** [~ + *obj*] to reorganize or rearrange, usually for updating.

re•tort (ri tôrt′) /rɪˈtɔrt/ *v.* **1.** to reply in a sharp way: [~ + *that clause*]: *retorted that he would have nothing to do with her.* [*no obj*]: *quick to retort.* —*n.* [*count*] **2.** a sharp or clever reply: *"You're no better," was his angry retort.* See -TORT-.

re•touch (*v.* rē tuch′; *n.* rē′tuch′, rē tuch′) / *v.* riyˈtʌtʃ; *n.* ˈriyˌtʌtʃ, riyˈtʌtʃ/ *v.* [~ + *obj*] **1.** to improve with new touches; touch up. **2.** to change (a photograph) after development by adding or removing lines, lightening areas, etc. —*n.* [*count*] **3.** an added touch to a picture, painting, etc. **4.** an act or instance of retouching.

re•trace (ri trās′) /rɪˈtreys/ *v.* [~ + *obj*], **-traced, -trac•ing. 1.** to go back over: *to retrace one's steps.* **2.** to go back over with the memory: *tried to retrace his reasoning.*

re•tract[1] (ri trakt′) /rɪˈtrækt/ *v.* to draw back or in: [~ + *obj*]: *A snake can retract its fangs.* [*no obj*]: *The wheels on the airplane don't retract.*

re•tract[2] (ri trakt′) /rɪˈtrækt/ *v.* [~ + *obj*] to withdraw (a statement, etc.) as wrong, unfair, etc., esp. formally; recant: *retracted his remarks about his opponent.* —**re•tract′a•ble, re•tract′i•ble,** *adj.*: *the retractable landing gear.* —**re•trac′tion,** *n.* [*count*]: *issued a retraction for his foolish remarks.* See -TRAC-.

re•tread (*v.* rē tred′; *n.* rē′tred′) / *v.* riyˈtrɛd; *n.* ˈriyˌtrɛd/ *v.* [~ + *obj*] **1.** to put a new tread on (a worn tire). **2.** to rework (something): *retreading his old plots into new stories.* —*n.* [*count*] **3.** a retreaded tire. **4.** a reusing of an old idea, story, etc.: *reruns and retreads.*

re•treat (ri trēt′) /rɪˈtriyt/ *n.* **1.** the withdrawal of a military force before an enemy: [*count*]: *After suffering many casualties, the troops made a retreat.* [*noncount*]: *in retreat.* **2.** [*count*] a place for quiet thinking or privacy: *a beautiful country retreat.* **3.** a withdrawal for quiet thinking, such as for meditation: [*count*]: *The priests go on a retreat once a year.* [*noncount*]: *They cannot be reached this week; they are on retreat.* —*v.* [*no obj*] **4.** to withdraw from an enemy attack: *The fleet retreated.* **5.** to make a retreat: *retreated from the room as she shouted at him.* **6.** to draw back from an earlier position: *began to retreat from his earlier strong stand on civil rights.*

re•trench (ri trench′) /rɪˈtrɛntʃ/ *v.* to reduce or diminish, esp. so as to economize: [~ + *obj*]: *The university began to retrench its workforce.* [*no obj*]: *As it retrenched, the university found money to keep the people it wanted.* —**re•trench′ment,** *n.* [*noncount*]: *The union fears retrenchment.*

re•tri•al (rē trīəl′, rē′trīəl′) /riyˈtrayəl, ˈriyˌtrayəl/ *n.* [*count*] an act of trying a person in court again.

ret•ri•bu•tion (re′trə byo͞o′shən) /ˌrɛtrəˈbyuwʃən/ *n.* [*noncount*] punishment for some evil: *the sword of retribution.*

re•triev•al (ri trē′vəl) /rɪˈtriyvəl/ *n.* [*noncount*] the act or possibility of retrieving: *a reputation beyond retrieval.*

re•trieve (ri trēv′) /rɪˈtriyv/ *v.* [~ + *obj*], **-trieved, -triev•ing. 1.** to find and bring back: *The dog retrieved the Frisbee.* **2.** to locate and read (data) from computer storage, as for display on a monitor: *To retrieve a file, press the Shift key and the F10 key.*

re•triev•er (ri trē′vər) /rɪˈtriyvər/ *n.* [*count*] **1.** a person or thing that retrieves. **2.** a breed of dog used esp. to retrieve game. **3.** any dog trained to retrieve game.

ret•ro (re′trō) /ˈrɛtrow/ *adj.* of or designating or reviving the style of an earlier time: *retro clothes.*

retro-, *prefix. retro-* comes from Latin, where it has the meaning "back, backward": *retro-* + *-gress* → *retrogress* (= *proceed backward); retro-* + *rocket* → *retrorocket.*

ret•ro•ac•tive (re′trō ak′tiv) /ˌrɛtrowˈæktɪv/ *adj.* **1.** having effect back in the past, as a new law: *a retroactive law that would increase taxes on income earned last year.* **2.** effective as of a past date: *a pay raise retroactive to last January 1st.* —**ret′ro•ac′tive•ly,** *adv.*: *to be paid extra retroactively.*

ret•ro•fit (re′trō fit′) /ˈrɛtrowˌfɪt, *v.* [~ + *obj*], **-fit•ted** or **-fit, -fit•ting.** to supply (an automobile, airplane, etc.) with parts available after manufacture: *to retrofit the old airplane with new cannons.*

ret•ro•grade (re′trə grād′) /ˈrɛtrəˌgreyd/ *adj.* moving backward, as to an earlier condition: *retrograde fashions.* See -GRAD-.

ret•ro•gress (re′trə gres′, re′trə gres′) /ˌrɛtrəˈgrɛs, ˈrɛtrəˌgrɛs/ *v.* [*no obj*] to go backward: *Society retrogressed as learning stagnated.* —**ret•ro•gres•sion** (re′trə gresh′ən) /ˌrɛtrəˈgrɛʃən/ *n.* [*noncount*] See -GRESS-.

ret•ro•rock•et (re′trō rok′it) /ˈrɛtrowˌrɒkɪt/ *n.* [*count*] a small rocket used for slowing down a larger rocket.

ret•ro•spect (re′trə spekt′) /ˈrɛtrəˌspɛkt/ *n.* [*noncount*] **1.** thinking of the past, of past events, etc. —*v.* [*no obj*] **2.** to look back in thought. —***Idiom.* 3. in retrospect,** on evaluating the past; upon reflection: *knew in retrospect that he should have married her.* —**ret′ro•spec′tion,** *n.* [*noncount*] See -SPEC-.

ret•ro•spec•tive (re′trə spek′tiv) /ˌrɛtrəˈspɛktɪv/ *adj.* **1.** of or relating to retrospection. **2.** looking or directed backward. —*n.* [*count*] **3.** an exhibit showing an artist's lifework. —**ret′ro•spec′tive•ly,** *adv.* See -SPEC-.

re•turn (ri tûrn′) /rɪˈtɜrn/ *v.* **1.** [*no obj*] to go or come back, such as to a former place or state: *to return from abroad.* **2.** [~ + *obj*] to put, bring, take, or give to the original place, position, etc.: *He returned his gun to his holster.* **3.** [*no obj*] to turn to again, as in thought: *Let us return to the main idea.* **4.** [~ + *obj*] to repay or react to (something sent, done, etc.) with something similar: *to return a favor.* **5.** [~ + *obj*] to bring back (a verdict, etc.): *The jury returned a verdict of guilty.* **6.** [~ + *obj*] to yield back (a profit, etc.): *Those stocks will return a handsome profit.* —*n.* **7.** [*noncount*] the act or fact of returning. **8.** [*count*] a recurrence; a happening again: *the return of winter.* **9.** [*noncount*] repayment or response: *profits in return for outlay.* **10.** Often, **returns.** [*plural*] a profit or gain, such as from work. **11.** [*count*] an official form showing income, deductions, and taxes due. **12.** Usually, **returns.** [*plural*] a report on a count of votes, etc.: *with most of the election returns in.* —*adj.* [*before a noun*] **13.** of or relating to a return or returning: *a return engagement of the opera; a return address.* **14.** sent or done in return: *return cargo.*

re•turn•a•ble (ri tûr′nə bəl) /rɪˈtɜrnəbəl/ *adj.* **1.** that may be returned, esp. for recycling: *returnable cans.* —*n.* [*count*] **2.** a bottle, can, or other item returned for recycling.

re•turn•ee (ri tûr nē′, -tûr′nē) /rɪtɜrˈniy, -ˈtɜrniy/ *n.* [*count*], *pl.* **-ees.** one who has returned, as from military duty.

Reu′ben sand′wich (ro͞o′bin) /ˈruwbɪn/ *n.* [*count*] a grilled sandwich of corned beef, Swiss cheese, and sauerkraut on rye bread.

re•un•ion (rē yo͞on′yən) /riyˈyuwnyən/ *n.* **1.** [*noncount*] the state of being reunited. **2.** [*count*] a gathering of relatives, friends, etc., at regular times: *a family reunion.* See -UNI-.

re•u•nite (rē′yo͞o nīt′) /ˌriyyuwˈnayt/ *v.*, **-nit•ed, -nit•ing.** to (cause to) come together or be together: [~ + *obj*]: *was reunited with his family after his long journey.* [*no obj*]: *His family reunited after all those years.* See -UNI-.

re•use (*v.* rē′yo͞oz′; *n.* rē′yo͞os′) /*v.* ˌriyˈyuwz; *n.* ˌriyˈyuws/ *v.*, **-used, -us•ing,** *n.* —*v.* [~ + *obj*] **1.** to use again: *To save money she would reuse plastic wrap.* —*n.* [*noncount*] **2.** the act of reusing: *the reuse of paper.*

rev (rev) /rɛv/ *n., v.,* **revved, rev•ving.** *Informal.* —*n.* [*count*] **1.** a revolution of the crankshaft within an engine. —*v.* **2.** to (cause to) go faster sharply, such as a car, etc.: [~ + *obj* (+ *up*)]: *He revved the race car (up).* [~ (+ *up*) + *obj*]: *The racers revved (up) their engines.* [*no obj;* ~ + *up*]: *The two cars revved up at the traffic light.* **3.** [*no obj;* ~ + *up*] to increase in activity or speed: *The economy began to rev up.*

re•val•ue (rē val′yo͞o) /riy'vælyuw/ *v.* [~ + *obj*], **-ued, -u•ing.** to revise the value of something, esp. currency in exchange with others: *The country revalued its currency to fit the international markets better.*

re•vamp (rē vamp′) / riy'væmp / *v.* [~ + *obj*] to make changes in the structure (of something); redo: *The school wanted to revamp its business and accounting programs.*

re•veal (ri vēl′) /rɪ'viyl/ *v.* **1.** to make known; disclose; divulge: [~ + *obj*]: *to reveal the secret about his past.* [~ + *that clause*]: *It was revealed today that campaign contributions exceeded legal limits.* **2.** [~ + *obj*] to exhibit something that was hidden: *He pulled back his sleeve and revealed the scar on his arm.*

re•veal•ing (ri vē′ling) /rɪ'viylɪŋ/ *adj.* **1.** allowing something to be seen, esp. parts of the body usually covered: *a very revealing dress.* **2.** allowing something to be understood: *His comments about her abilities to work with others were very revealing.*

rev•eil•le (rev′ə lē) /'rɛvəliy/ *n.* [*noncount*] a bugle call in the early morning to awaken military personnel: *Reveille was at five-thirty a.m.*

rev•el (rev′əl) /'rɛvəl/ *v.,* **-eled, -el•ing** or (*esp. Brit.*) **-elled, -el•ling,** *n.* —*v.* **1.** [~ + *in* + *obj*] to take great pleasure in; enjoy greatly: *to revel in luxury.* **2.** [*no obj*] to enjoy lively, pleasurable activities such as feasting or dancing. —*n.* **3.** [*noncount*] the act of enjoying activities; revelry. **4.** Often, **revels.** [*plural*] an occasion of parties, feasting, etc.: *A neighbor called the police and thus put a stop to their late-night revels.* —**rev′el•er;** *esp. Brit.,* **rev′el•ler,** *n.* [*count*]

rev•e•la•tion (rev′ə lā′shən) /ˌrɛvə'leyʃən/ *n.* **1.** [*noncount*] the act of revealing. **2.** [*count*] something revealed: *It came as a stunning revelation that he was an adopted child.*

rev•el•ry (rev′əl rē) /'rɛvəlriy/ *n., pl.* **-ries. 1.** [*noncount*] the act of reveling: *a week of nonstop revelry.* **2.** [*count*] an occasion of reveling: *The noise from their revelries was getting on my nerves.*

re•venge (ri venj′) /rɪ'vɛndʒ/ *v.,* **-venged, -veng•ing,** *n.* —*v.* [~ + *obj*] **1.** to demand or give punishment for a wrong done to (someone), esp. in an unforgiving spirit: *to revenge a murdered brother by killing the murderer.* **2.** to inflict pain or harm for (some wrong done to oneself); avenge: *to revenge a betrayal.* —*n.* [*noncount*] **3.** the act of revenging: *his big chance for revenge.* **4.** the desire to get revenge; vindictiveness. —**re•venge′ful,** *adj.* See -VENGE-.

rev•e•nue (rev′ən yo͞o′, -ə no͞o′) /'rɛvənˌyuw, -əˌnuw/ *n.* **1.** the income of a government from taxation, used for public expenses: [*noncount*]: *taxing tobacco, another form of revenue.* [*plural*]: *Revenues were down sharply.* **2.** money regularly coming in; a source of income: [*noncount*]: *business revenue.* [*plural*]: *revenues from airline tickets.* See -VEN-.

re•ver•ber•ate (ri vûr′bə rāt′) /rɪ'vɜrbəˌreyt/ *v.* [*no obj*], **-at•ed, -at•ing. 1.** to reecho: *Her singing reverberated through the house.* **2.** to have a long-lasting effect: *The dismissal of half the employees reverberated throughout the company.*

re•ver•ber•a•tion (rē vûr′bər ā′shən) /riyˌvɜrbər'eyʃən/ *n.* **1.** the act of reverberating: [*count*]: *the reverberations from the distant thunder.* [*noncount*]: *the acoustics of reverberation.* **2.** [*count*] a long-lasting effect due to a sudden act: *the reverberations from the sudden dismissal of half the workers.*

re•vere (ri vēr′) /rɪ'vɪər/ *v.* [~ + *obj*], **-vered, -ver•ing.** to look upon (someone or something) with reverence: *to revere all the beauty of nature.*

rev•er•ence (rev′ər əns, rev′rəns) /'rɛvərəns, 'rɛvrəns/ *n.* [*noncount*] a feeling of deep respect, awe, and humility: *deep reverence for life.*

rev•er•end (rev′ər ənd, rev′rənd) /'rɛvərənd, 'rɛvrənd/ *n.* **1.** [*Reverend; sometimes: the* + ~] (used, usually before a proper name, as a title of respect for a member of the clergy or a religious order): *the Reverend Timothy Schade; Reverend Mother.* **2.** [*count; usually singular*] a member of the clergy, esp. a Protestant minister: *Perhaps the good reverend would stand over here.*

rev•er•ent (rev′ər ənt) /'rɛvərənt/ *adj.* having or showing reverence: *to be reverent during Mass.* —**rev′er•ent•ly,** *adv.*: *She bowed her head reverently.*

rev•er•ie (rev′ə rē) /'rɛvəriy/ *n.* **1.** [*noncount*] a state of dreamy thinking: *lost in reverie.* **2.** [*count*] a daydream: *absurd reveries of a perfect society.*

re•vers (ri vēr′, -vâr′) /rɪ'vɪər, -'vɛər/ *n.* [*count*], *pl.* **-vers** (-vērz′, -vârz′) /-'vɪərz, -'vɛərz/. a part of a piece of clothing turned back to show the facing, esp. a lapel. See -VERT-.

re•vers•al (ri vûr′səl) /rɪ'vɜrsəl/ *n.* **1.** [*noncount*] an act or instance of reversing; a state of being reversed. **2.** [*count*] a change of one's fortune or luck for the worse: *She suffered a reversal in her job.* See -VERT-.

re•verse (ri vûrs′) /rɪ'vɜrs/ *adj., n., v.,* **-versed, -vers•ing.** —*adj.* [*before a noun*] **1.** opposite or contrary in position, direction, order, etc.: *to arrange the names in reverse order.* **2.** with the back toward the observer: *the reverse side of a fabric.* **3.** of or relating to movement in a mechanism opposite to that made under ordinary running conditions: *reverse gear.* —*n.* **4.** [*noncount; the* + ~] the opposite or contrary of something: *His answer was the reverse of what we expected.* **5.** [*noncount; the* + ~] the back or rear of anything: *Can't you button this on the reverse?* **6.** [*count*] a change of fortune for the worse: *Our football team suffered yet another reverse.* **7.** [*noncount*] the condition of being reversed: *to put an engine into reverse.* —*v.* **8.** to turn in an opposite position: [~ + *obj*]: *He reversed the chairs so that they faced each other.* [~ + *oneself*]: *reversed himself after going in the wrong direction.* [*no obj*]: *He reversed and raced down the sideline.* **9.** to turn in the opposite direction; send on the opposite course: [~ + *obj*]: *He reversed the car.* [*no obj*]: *The car reversed and swung right.* **10.** [~ + *obj*] to turn in the opposite order: *to reverse a process.* **11.** [~ + *obj*] to turn inside out or upside down: *to reverse the socks.* **12.** [~ + *obj*] to declare to be the opposite of (a decree, etc.); annul: *The High Court reversed the verdict.* **13.** [~ + *obj*] to change to the opposite: *to reverse the policy of racial discrimination.* —***Idiom.*** **14. reverse (the) charges,** to have the charges for a telephone call billed to the person receiving the call; to call collect: *Operator, I need to reverse the charges on this long-distance call.* —**re•vers′i•ble,** *adj.*: *The coat has a reversible inner lining.* See -VERT-.

reverse′ discrimina′tion, *n.* [*noncount*] discrimination against white people or males resulting from preferential policies intended to remedy past discrimination against minorities or females.

re•vert (ri vûrt′) /rɪ'vɜrt/ *v.* [~ + *to* + *obj*] **1.** to return to a former habit, practice, belief, etc.: *He's reverted to smoking again.* **2.** to return to the former owner or that person's heirs: *The property reverts to the former owners.* **3.** to go back in thought or discussion: *kept reverting to his childhood.* —**re•ver•sion** (ri vûr′zhən) /rɪ'vɜrʒən/ *n.* [*noncount*] See -VERT-.

re•view (ri vyo͞o′) /rɪ'vyuw/ *n.,* **1.** [*count*] a critical article, as in a periodical, about a book, play, etc.; a critique: *The reviews on the new play were mixed.* **2.** the process of going over a subject again in study to keep it in the memory: [*count*]: *made a quick review of his notes just before his presentation.* [*noncount*]: *He left no time for review before the test.* **3.** [*count*] a general survey; an account of something: *a review of the previous work.* **4.** an inspection, esp. a formal inspection of a military force, parade, etc.: [*count*]: *a review of the troops.* [*noncount*]: *The troops were on review.* **5.** [*count*] a journal containing articles on books, art, etc.: *a literary review.* **6.** a second view of something, as of a case or decision by a court: [*noncount*]: *The case is under review right now by the Supreme Court.* [*count*]: *sent to a higher court for a review.* —*v.* **7.** to go over (lessons, etc.) in review: [~ + *obj*]: *We'll need to review our notes in the morning.* [*no obj*]: *I hope I have time to review before the test.* **8.** [~ + *obj*] to examine over again, esp. with a thought of changing: *to review the way government aides are appointed.* **9.** [~ + *obj*] to inspect, esp. formally or officially: *to review the troops.* **10.** [~ + *obj*] to discuss (a book, etc.) in a critical review: *reviews plays for that newspaper.* **11.** [~ + *obj*] to view again in one's mind: *He reviewed the events of the day.* **12.** [~ + *obj*] to reexamine in a court of law: *to review a case.* —**re•view′er,** *n.* [*count*]: *The reviewers criticized the play severely.*

re•vile (ri vīl′) /rɪ'vayl/ *v.* [~ + *obj*], **-viled, -vil•ing.** to address (someone) or speak of (someone) with contempt or insulting language: *She reviled him and accused him of betraying her.* —**re•vile′ment,** *n.* [*noncount*] —**re•vil′er,** *n.* [*count*]

re•vise (ri vīz′) /rɪ'vayz/ *v.* [~ + *obj*], **-vised, -vis•ing. 1.** to change or alter, esp. after thinking about (something): *revised her opinion of him when she saw his work.* **2.** to change or alter something written to make corrections, improve, etc.: *to revise a manuscript.* See -VIS-.

re•vis•ion (ri vizh′ən) /rɪ'vɪʒən/ *n.* **1.** the act or work of revising: [*noncount*]: *The book will need extensive revision before it can be published.* [*count*]: *We made extensive revisions in the third chapter.* **2.** [*count*] a revised form of something, as a book: *a new revision of the book.* See -VIS-.

re•vi•sion•ism (ri vizh′ə niz′əm) /rɪ'vɪʒə,nɪzəm/ *n.* [*noncount*] (among Communists) any departure from Marxist doctrine, theory, or practice, esp. the tendency to favor reform above revolutionary change. —**re•vi′sion•ist,** *n.* [*count*], *adj.* See -VIS-.

re•vi•tal•ize (rē vīt′l īz′) /riy'vaytḷ,ayz/ *v.* [~ + *obj*], **-ized, -iz•ing.** to give new life, vitality, or strength to: *to revitalize the ailing steel industry.* —**re•vi•tal•i•za•tion** (rē vīt′l i zā′shən) /riy,vaytḷɪ'zeyʃən/ *n.* [*noncount*]: *the revitalization of the economy.* See -VIT-.

re•viv•al (ri vī′vəl) /rɪ'vayvəl/ *n.* **1.** [*noncount*] coming back to use, acceptance, or popularity: *the revival of old customs.* **2.** [*count*] a new production of an old play: *a revival of* The Death of a Salesman. **3.** [*noncount*] the act of bringing back or coming back to life, consciousness, etc.; the state of being revived: *quick revival after drowning.* **4. a.** [*noncount*] increased interest in religion. **b.** [*count*] an event due to such interest: *a few revivals featuring hymns and fiery preachers.* —**re•viv′al•ist,** *n.* [*count*] See -VIV-.

re•vive (ri vīv′) /rɪ'vayv/ *v.*, **-vived, -viv•ing. 1.** to (cause to) be brought back or taken up again; (cause to) be renewed: [~ + *obj*]: *Don't revive those old prejudices.* [*no obj*]: *Her interest in playing the trumpet revived.* **2.** to restore to life or consciousness: [~ + *obj*]: *The paramedics worked to revive the drowning victim.* [*no obj*]: *Somehow she revived after a few minutes.* **3.** [~ + *obj*] to put on or show (an old play, etc.) again. See -VIV-.

re•viv•i•fy (ri viv′ə fī′) /rɪ'vɪvə,fay/ *v.* [~ + *obj*], **-fied, -fy•ing.** to restore to life; give new life to; revive. —**re•viv•i•fi•ca•tion** (ri viv′i fi kā′shən) /rɪ,vɪvɪfɪ'keyʃən/ *n.* [*noncount*] See -VIV-.

rev•o•ca•ble (rev′ə kə bəl *or, often,* ri vō′-) /'rɛvəkəbəl *or, often,* rɪ'vow-/ also **re•vok•a•ble** (ri vō′kə bəl, rev′ə-) /rɪ'vowkəbəl, 'rɛvə-/ *adj.* capable of being revoked. —**rev•o•ca•tion** (rev′ə kā′shən) /,rɛvə'keyʃən/ *n.* [*noncount*]: *threatened with revocation of his license.* See -VOC-.

re•voke (ri vōk′) /rɪ'vowk/ *v.* [~ + *obj*], **-voked, -vok•ing.** to take back or withdraw; annul or cancel: *revoked his driver's license.* See -VOC-.

re•volt (ri vōlt′) /rɪ'vowlt/ *v.* **1.** [*no obj*] to engage in a revolution; rebel: *The peasants wanted to revolt against the government.* **2.** to (cause to) have a feeling of disgust or horror in (someone): [~ + *obj*]: *The violence in that movie revolted her.* [*no obj*]: *One's mind revolts at the thought of killing.* —*n.* **3.** an act of rebellion: [*count*]: *an open revolt against the dean's power.* [*noncount*]: *peasants in revolt against the government.*

re•volt•ing (ri vōl′ting) /rɪ'vowltɪŋ/ *adj.* disgusting; causing a feeling of horror: *a revolting scene in the movie.*

rev•o•lu•tion (rev′ə lo͞o′shən) /,rɛvə'luwʃən/ *n.* **1.** a complete overthrow and replacement of an established government by force: [*noncount*]: *This country does not change its government by revolution.* [*count*]: *a number of revolutions in recent years.* **2.** [*count*] a sudden, complete change in something: *a social revolution caused by automation.* **3.** [*count*] **a.** a turning round or rotating around a single point: *The engine was racing at over 50,000 revolutions per minute.* **b.** a moving in a curving course, as about a central point: *one complete revolution around the racetrack.* **4.** [*count*] the orbiting of one heavenly body around another: *The earth's revolution around the sun takes one year.* —**rev′o•lu′tion•ist,** *n.* [*count*]

rev•o•lu•tion•ar•y (rev′ə lo͞o′shə ner′ē) /,rɛvə'luwʃə,nɛriy/ *adj., n., pl.* **-ar•ies.** —*adj.* **1.** [*before a noun*] of or relating to a revolution: *a revolutionary leader.* **2.** new or different; causing great change: *a revolutionary discovery.* —*n.* [*count*] **3.** a person participating in or calling for a revolution: *The revolutionaries challenged the army to join them.*

rev•o•lu•tion•ize (rev′ə lo͞o′shə niz′) /,rɛvə'luwʃə,nayz/ *v.* [~ + *obj*], **-ized, -iz•ing.** to bring about a revolution in: *Computers will revolutionize how people learn a language.*

re•volve (ri volv′) /rɪ'vɒlv/ *v.*, **-volved, -volv•ing. 1.** [*no obj*] to move in a curving course: *The earth revolves around the sun.* **2.** to turn around, as around a center point: [*no obj*]: *The wheel revolved slowly.* [~ + *obj*]: *He revolved the beads around in his hand.* **3.** [~ + *around* + *obj*] to focus or center on: *The discussion revolved around a new plan to increase profits.*

re•volv•er (ri vol′vər) /rɪ'vɒlvər/ *n.* [*count*] **1.** a pistol having a revolving chamber for holding bullets. **2.** a person or thing that revolves.

revolv′ing door′, *n.* [*count*] **1.** a door that rotates around a central point. **2.** *Informal.* **a.** an organization that frequently replaces the people who work for it. **b.** an institution, as a hospital or prison, that discharges people in the shortest possible time and without adequate attention.

re•vue or **re•view** (ri vyo͞o′) /rɪ'vyuw/ *n.* [*count*] **1.** a form of theatrical entertainment in which recent events, popular fads, etc., are made fun of. **2.** any entertainment featuring skits, dances, and songs.

re•vul•sion (ri vul′shən) /rɪ'vʌlʃən/ *n.* [*noncount*] a strong feeling of disgust, distaste, or dislike: *filled with revulsion whenever she watches boxing.*

re•ward (ri wôrd′) /rɪ'wɔrd/ *n.* **1.** [*count*] money offered for the finding or capture of a criminal, the recovery of lost property, etc.: *Do you suppose we'll get a reward for turning in this wallet?* **2.** something given or received for services done, for doing something of merit, etc.: [*count*]: *Seeing his children succeed was the most important reward in his life.* [*noncount*]: *There is not much financial reward in teaching.* —*v.* [~ + *obj*] **3.** to give a reward to (a person or animal) for service, merit, etc.: *The dog's owner rewarded it with a biscuit.*

re•ward•ing (ri wôr′ding) /rɪ'wɔrdɪŋ/ *adj.* giving or providing a reward: *a rewarding experience; a rewarding occupation.*

re•wind (rē wīnd′) /riy'waynd/ *v.*, **-wound, -wind•ing.** to wind again, such as a tape on a videocassette player: [~ + *obj*]: *He rewound the tape.* [*no obj*]: *After the tape rewinds, play it on this other VCR.*

re•word (rē wûrd′) /riy'wɜrd/ *v.* [~ + *obj*] to put into other words: *to reword a contract.*

re•work (rē wûrk′) /riy'wɜrk/ *v.* [~ + *obj*] to make changes in: *He reworked the schedule.*

re•write (*v.* rē rīt′; *n.* rē′rīt′) / *v.* riy'rayt; *n.* 'riy,rayt/ *v.*, **-wrote, -writ•ten, -writ•ing,** *n.* —*v.* [~ + *obj*] **1.** to write in a different manner; revise: *Please rewrite this essay; it's confusing.* **2.** to write again: *to rewrite a check.* **3.** to write up (news sent in by a reporter) for a newspaper. —*n.* [*count*] **4.** something written again in a different manner; a revision.

RFD or **R.F.D.,** an abbreviation of: rural free delivery.

rhap•so•dize (rap′sə dīz′) /'ræpsə,dayz/ *v.*, **-dized, -diz•ing.** to talk (about something) with enthusiasm or excitement: [*no obj*]: *rhapsodized about his years in France.* [*used with quotations*]: *"Ah, New Zealand, the most wonderful place to live," he rhapsodized.*

rhap•so•dy (rap′sə dē) /'ræpsədiy/ *n.* [*count*], *pl.* **-dies. 1.** a piece of music that is irregular in form and highly emotional. **2.** an expression of great passion, such as an intense speech: *a rhapsody about true love.* —**rhap•sod•ic** (rap sod′ik) /ræp'sɒdɪk/ **rhap•sod′i•cal,** *adj.*

rhe•a (rē′ə) /'riyə/ *n.* [*count*], *pl.* **rhe•as.** either of two ostrichlike birds of South America.

rhe•o•stat (rē′ə stat′) /'riyə,stæt/ *n.* [*count*] a device that regulates the flow of current through an electrical circuit. See -STAT-.

rhe′sus mon′key (rē′səs) /'riysəs/ *n.* [*count*] a kind of monkey, a macaque, of India, used in biological and medical research. Also called **rhe′sus.**

rhet•o•ric (ret′ər ik) /'rɛtərɪk/ *n.* [*noncount*] **1. a.** the art of effectively using language in speech or writing. **b.** language skillfully used. **2.** exaggerated language that is empty and meaningless; bombast. —**rhe•tor•i•cal** (ri tôr′i kəl, -tor′-) /rɪ'tɔrɪkəl, -'tɒr-/ *adj.* [*before a noun*] —**rhe•tor′i•cal•ly,** *adv.*

rhetor′ical ques′tion, *n.* [*count*] a question asked only for effect and not to obtain a reply, as "What is so rare as a day in June?"

rhet•o•ri•cian (ret′ə rish′ən) /,rɛtə'rɪʃən/ *n.* [*count*] one skilled in the study of rhetoric.

rheum (ro͞om) /ruwm/ *n.* [*noncount*] a thin, fluid substance from the mucous membranes, esp. during a cold. —**rheum′y,** *adj.,* **-i•er, -i•est.**

rheu•mat•ic (ro͝o mat′ik) /rʊ'mætɪk/ *adj.* of or relating to rheumatism.

rheumat′ic fe′ver, *n.* [*noncount*] a severe disease, usually affecting children, marked by fever, swelling of the joints, and heart disturbances.

rheu•ma•tism (ro͞o′mə tiz′əm) /'ruwmə,tɪzəm/ *n.* [*noncount*] **1.** any of several disorders affecting the joints or muscles. **2.** RHEUMATIC FEVER.

rhine•stone (rīn′stōn′) /'rayn,stown/ *n.* [*count*] an artificial gemstone cut with rock crystal in imitation of a diamond: *His jacket glittered with rhinestones.*

rhi•ni•tis (rī nī′tis) /ray'naytɪs/ *n.* [*noncount*] redness, soreness, and swelling of the nose membranes.

rhi•no (rī′nō) /'raynow/ *n.* [*count*], *pl.* **-nos,** (*esp. when thought of as a group*) **-no.** a rhinoceros.

rhi•noc•er•os (rī nos′ər əs) /ray'nɒsərəs/ *n.* [*count*], *pl.* **-os•es,** (*esp. when thought of as a group*) **-os.** a large, thick-skinned, plant-eating mammal of Africa and Asia, with one or two upright horns on the snout.

rhi•zome (rī′zōm) /'rayzowm/ *n.* [*count*] a rootlike underground stem that produces roots below and sends up shoots from its upper surface.

rho•do•den•dron (rō′də den′drən) /,rowdə'dɛndrən/ *n.* [*count*] a shrub or tree of the heath family, having rounded clusters of bright flowers and oval leaves.

rhom•bus (rom′bəs) /'rɒmbəs/ *n.* [*count*], *pl.* **-bus•es, -bi** (-bī) /-bay/. a four-sided figure with all four sides parallel and equal in length but with oblique angles.

rhu•barb (ro͞o′bärb) /'ruwbɑrb/ *n.* **1.** [*noncount*] the fleshy leafstalks of a plant, used in making pies, preserves, etc. **2.** [*count*] *Slang.* a quarrel or squabble.

rhyme (rīm) /raym/ *n., v.,* **rhymed, rhym•ing.** —*n.* **1.** [*noncount*] similarity or sameness in sound of the end of words or lines of verse: *the use of rhyme.* **2.** [*count*] a word that has the same sounds at the end: *The word* find *is a rhyme for* mind *and* kind. **3.** [*count*] a poem having lines with such agreement in the final sounds. —*v.* **4.** to use (a word) as a rhyme to another word; use (words) as rhymes: [~ + *obj*]: *See if you can rhyme the word "dog" with some other word in English.* [~ + *with* + *obj; not: be* + ~*-ing*]: *Although they are written alike, the word* rain *does not rhyme with* again. [*no obj; not: be* + ~*-ing*]: *The words* rain *and* again *do not rhyme.* —***Idiom.*** **5. rhyme or reason,** (used with negative words or phrases) logic, sense, or method: *There was no rhyme or reason to their actions.* —**rhym′er,** *n.* [*count*]

rhythm (riᵺ′əm) /'rɪðəm/ *n.* **1.** movement with a regular pattern with a beat or accent that occurs at fixed times: [*count*]: *the even rhythms of her heartbeat.* [*noncount*]: *triple rhythm in music.* **2.** [*count*] the regular occurrence of particular phases, etc.: *the rhythm of the seasons.* **3.** [*noncount*] the regular recurrence of related elements in a system of motion: *a sense of rhythm in dancing.*

rhythm′ and blues′, *n.* [*noncount*] a folk-based form of black popular music.

rhyth•mic (riᵺ′mik) /'rɪðmɪk/ *adj.* Also, **rhyth′mical.** of or relating to rhythm: *the rhythmic pattern of the raindrops on the tin roof.* —**rhyth′mi•cal•ly,** *adv.*

rhythm′ meth′od, *n.* [*noncount*] a method of birth control in which sexual intercourse is not performed when ovulation is most likely to occur.

RI, an abbreviation of: Rhode Island.

rib[1] (rib) /rɪb/ *n., v.,* **ribbed, rib•bing.** —*n.* [*count*] **1.** one of a series of curved bones connected to the backbone and occurring in pairs on each side of the body. **2.** a cut of meat, as beef, containing a rib. **3.** something resembling a rib in form, position, or use, such as a strengthening part: *the ribs of an umbrella.* —*v.* [~ + *obj*] **4.** to furnish or surround with ribs.

rib[2] (rib) /rɪb/ *v.* [~ + *obj*], **ribbed, rib•bing.** to tease; make fun of: *ribbed him about his balding head.* —**rib′ber,** *n.* [*count*]

rib•ald (rib′əld; *spelling pron.* rī′bəld) /'rɪbəld; *spelling pron.* 'raybəld/ *adj.* vulgar or indecent in speech, language, etc.; humorous in a crude way; irreverent. —**rib′ald•ry,** *n.* [*noncount*]

rib•bon (rib′ən) /'rɪbən/ *n.* **1.** [*count*] a band of fine material, used for ornament, tying, etc.: *bright ribbons in her hair.* **2.** [*noncount*] material in such strips: *a few strips of bright ribbon.* **3. ribbons,** [*plural*] torn or ragged strips; shreds: *clothes torn to ribbons.* **4.** [*count*] a band of inked material used in a typewriter, printer, etc.

ri′bo•nu•cle′ic ac′id (rī′bō no͞o klē′ik, -klā′-, -nyo͞o-) /'raybownuw'kliyɪk, -'kley-, -nyuw-/ *n.* [*noncount*] a molecule that is important in the synthesis of protein.

rice (rīs) /rays/ *n., v.,* **riced, ric•ing.** —*n.* [*noncount*] **1.** the starchy seeds or grain of grass of marshy areas, cultivated in warm climates and used for food. **2.** the grass itself. —*v.* [~ + *obj*] **3.** to reduce to a form resembling rice: *to rice potatoes.*

rich (rich) /rɪtʃ/ *adj.,* **-er, -est,** *n.* —*adj.* **1.** having wealth or great possessions. **2.** having great or many natural resources: *a rich harvest last year.* **3.** [*be* + ~ + *with/in*] having a great amount of something: *fruits rich in vitamin C.* **4.** containing a large amount of cream, butter, fat, sugar, or the like: *a rich gravy.* **5.** (of color, etc.) deep, strong, full, or mellow: *a deep, rich red wine.* **6.** [*be* + ~] *Informal.* highly amusing, so as to be absurd: *Go on a date with you? Ha, that's rich!* —*n.* **7. the rich,** [*plural; used with a plural verb*] rich people thought of as a group: *The rich get richer.* —**rich′ly,** *adv.* —**rich′ness,** *n.* [*noncount*]

rich•es (rich′iz) /'rɪtʃɪz/ *n.* [*plural*] a great many valuable possessions; wealth.

Rich′ter scale′ (rik′tər) /'rɪktər/ *n.* [*proper noun; usually: the* + ~] a scale ranging from 1 to 10, for indicating the strength or force of an earthquake.

rick (rik) /rɪk/ *n.* [*count*] **1.** a large stack or pile of hay, straw, corn, or the like, in a field. **2.** a stack of wood.

rick•ets (rik′its) /'rɪkɪts/ *n.* [*noncount; used with a singular verb*] a childhood disease in which the bones soften from a low supply of vitamin D and not enough sunlight.

rick•et•y (rik′i tē) /'rɪkɪtiy/ *adj.,* **-i•er, -i•est. 1.** likely to fall or collapse; shaky; old or dilapidated: *a rickety chair.* **2.** of or relating to rickets.

rick•shaw or **rick•sha** (rik′shô, -shä) /'rɪkʃɔ, -ʃɑ/ *n.* [*count*] a small, two-wheeled cartlike vehicle for carrying passengers, pulled by one person.

ric•o•chet (rik′ə shā′, rik′ə shā′) /,rɪkə'ʃey, 'rɪkə,ʃey/ *n., v.,* **-cheted** (-shād′, -shād′) /-'ʃeyd, -,ʃeyd/ **-chet•ing** (-shā′ing, -shā′ing) /-'ʃeyɪŋ, -,ʃeyɪŋ/ or (*esp. Brit.*) **-chet•ted** (-shet′id) /-,ʃɛtɪd/ **-chet•ting** (-shet′ing) /-,ʃɛtɪŋ/. —*n.* [*count*] **1.** the rebound of an object thrown or propelled after it hits a glancing blow against a surface. —*v.* [*no obj*] **2.** to move in this way, such as a bullet: *bullets ricocheting off the walls.*

ri•cot•ta (ri kot′ə, -kô′tə) /rɪ'kɒtə, -'kɔtə/ *n.* [*noncount*] a soft Italian cheese that resembles cottage cheese.

rid (rid) /rɪd/ *v.* [~ + *obj* + *of* + *obj*], **rid** or **rid•ded, rid•ding. 1.** to free or relieve of something unwanted: *Rid your mind of doubt and believe in me.* —***Idiom.*** **2. be** or **get rid of,** [~ + *obj*] to be or become free of: *Finally we are rid of the insect problem.*

rid•dance (rid′ns) /'rɪdns/ *n.* [*noncount*] —***Idiom.*** **good riddance,** (used to express relief at no longer needing to deal with someone or something that is gone or has been removed): *They're gone, and good riddance!*

rid•den (rid′n) /'rɪdn̩/ *v.* a pp. of RIDE.

rid•dle[1] (rid′l) /'rɪdl̩/ *n.* [*count*] **1.** a puzzling question put so as to make it difficult to answer it or discover its meaning: *A childhood riddle is "What kind of dog has no tail?" —The answer: a hot dog.* **2.** a puzzling problem, matter, or person: *His behavior is a riddle.*

rid•dle[2] (rid′l) /'rɪdl̩/ *v.* [~ + *obj*] **1.** to pierce with many holes: *Bullets riddled the target.* **2.** to fill or affect with (something undesirable): *The department is riddled with graft.*

ride (rīd) /rayd/ *v.,* **rode** (rōd) /rowd/ **rid•den** (rid′n) /'rɪdn̩/ **rid•ing,** *n.* —*v.* **1.** to sit on and manage a horse or other animal in motion: [*no obj*]: *He rode on the back of an elephant.* [~ + *obj*]: *He rode the elephant all around the circus stage.* **2.** to (cause to) be carried along in a vehicle: [~ + *obj*]: *She rides a bicycle to school.* [*no obj*]: *He rode on the subway to work.* **3.** [~ + *on* + *obj*] to move along in any way: *He was riding on his friend's success.* **4.** [*no obj*] to have a specified character for riding purposes: *The car rides smoothly.* **5.** [~ + *on* + *obj*] to depend: *hopes riding on a promotion.* **6.** [*no obj*] to continue without interference: *Let the matter ride.* **7.** to sit or move along on: [~ + *obj*]: *The ship rode the waves.* [*no obj*]: *The ship rode on the waves.* **8.** to ride over, along, or through (a road, etc.): [*no obj*]: *They rode along the highways.* [~ + *obj*]: *They rode the back roads.* **9.** [~ + *obj*] to make fun of, bother, or pester: *kept riding her about her boyfriend.* **10.** [~ + *obj; usually: be* + *ridden*] to control or domineer: *a man ridden by fear.* **11.** [~ + *obj*] to carry (a person) on something as if on a horse: *He rode the child about on his back.* **12. ride out,** [~ + *obj*] **a.** to come safely through or survive (a storm, etc.), such as while riding at anchor: *The ship rode out the storm.* **b.** to come through or endure (something): *rode out the first year of college fairly well.* **13. ride up,** [*no obj*] to move up from the proper place or position: *This skirt always rides up.* **—*n.*** [*count*] **14.** a journey or trip on a horse, etc., or on or in a vehicle. **15.** a means of being taken by a motor vehicle: *My ride's here.* **16.** a vehicle, such as a roller coaster, on which people ride for amusement. **—*Idiom.* 17. take (someone) for a ride,** to deceive; trick: *Those swindlers took us for a ride.*

rid•er (rī′dər) /ˈraydər/ *n.* [*count*] **1.** a person who rides a horse, a bicycle, etc. **2.** something that rides. **3.** an additional statement added to a document, such as a lease.

rid•er•ship (rī′dər ship′) /ˈraydərˌʃɪp/ *n.* [*noncount*] the number of passengers who use a public transportation system: *Ridership on subways is increasing.*

ridge (rij) /rɪdʒ/ *n.* [*count*] **1.** a long, narrow elevation of land. **2.** the long and narrow upper edge of something, as a hill or wave. **3.** any raised, narrow strip, as on cloth. **4.** (on a weather chart) a narrow, elongated area of high pressure: *a high-pressure ridge building slowly.*

ridged (rijd) /rɪdʒd/ *adj.* having, formed into, or showing ridges: *a ridged fabric.*

rid•i•cule (rid′i kyo͞ol′) /ˈrɪdɪˌkyuwl/ *n., v.,* **-culed, -cul•ing. —*n.*** [*noncount*] **1.** speech or action intended to cause others to laugh unkindly because of insults; derision: *His foolish comments were met with ridicule.* **—*v.*** [~ + *obj*] **2.** to make fun of: *He ridiculed his rivals whenever he could.*

ri•dic•u•lous (ri dik′yə ləs) /rɪˈdɪkyələs/ *adj.* of or relating to ridicule: *What a ridiculous idea!* —**ri•dic′u•lous•ly,** *adv.*: *What a ridiculously stupid idea!* —**ri•dic′u•lous•ness,** *n.* [*noncount*]

rife (rīf) /rayf/ *adj.* [*be* + ~] **1.** of common or frequent occurrence; plentiful: *Crime is rife in the city.* **2.** [~ + *with*] full of: *The city is rife with crime nowadays.* —**rife′ness,** *n.* [*noncount*]

riff (rif) /rɪf/ *n.* [*count*] **1.** music played as an improvisation to the main line of music, esp. in jazz or rock music: *a solo guitar riff.* **—*v.*** [*no obj*] **2.** to perform a riff.

rif•fle (rif′əl) /ˈrɪfəl/ *v.* [~ + *obj*], **-fled, -fling.** to flip hastily with the fingers; flutter: *to riffle papers.*

riff•raff (rif′raf′) /ˈrɪfˌræf/ *n.* [*plural*] disreputable or unwanted people.

ri•fle[1] (rī′fəl) /ˈrayfəl/ *n., v.,* **-fled, -fling. —*n.*** [*count*] **1.** a shoulder firearm with a long barrel. **—*v.*** [~ + *obj*] **2.** to cut spiral grooves within (a gun barrel, etc.). **3.** to throw (a ball) at high speed: *He rifled the ball back to the infield.* —**ri′fle•man,** *n.* [*count*], *pl.* **-men.**

ri•fle[2] (rī′fəl) /ˈrayfəl/ *v.* [~ *(+ through)* + *obj*], **-fled, -fling.** to search through and steal or rob: *The burglars rifled (through) their dresser drawers.* —**ri′fler,** *n.* [*count*]

ri•fling (rī′fling) /ˈrayflɪŋ/ *n.* [*noncount*] **1.** the cutting of spiral grooves in a gun barrel, etc. **2.** the system of grooves cut in this way.

rift (rift) /rɪft/ *n.* [*count*] **1.** a narrow crack, hole, or fissure. **2.** a break in friendly relations: *The incident created a rift that will take years to repair.* **3.** *Geology.* a fault.

rig (rig) /rɪg/ *v.,* **rigged, rig•ging,** *n.* **—*v.*** [~ + *obj*] **1.** to fit (a ship, etc.) with ropes, chains, etc.: *The new ship was rigged for its first sail.* **2.** to furnish with equipment: *The truck was rigged with a roof rack.* **3.** to assemble, install, or prepare: [~ *(+ up)* + *obj*]: *The campers rigged (up) a shelter from tree branches.* [~ + *obj (+ up)*]: *rigged a shelter (up) from branches.* **4.** to arrange in a dishonest way; fix: *to rig prices.* **—*n.* 5.** [*count*] the arrangement of the masts, sails, etc., on a ship. **6.** [*count*] a device or apparatus designed for some purpose: *an oil-drilling rig.* **7.** [*count*] a tractor-trailer truck: *an eighteen-wheel rig.*

rig•a•ma•role (rig′ə mə rōl′) /ˈrɪgəməˌrowl/ *n.* RIGMAROLE.

rig•ging (rig′ing) /ˈrɪgɪŋ/ *n.* [*noncount*] **1.** the ropes, chains, and tackle used to support and work the masts, sails, etc., on a ship. **2.** a device for lifting heavy objects. **3.** clothing; costume.

right (rīt) /rayt/ *adj.,* **-er, -est,** *n., adv., v.* **—*adj.* 1.** agreeing with what is good, proper, or just: *right conduct.* [*it* + *be* + ~ + *to* + *verb*]: *Is it ever right to kill someone?* [*it* + *be* + ~ + *(that) clause*]: *"It is right and proper that we give thanks to God," he intoned.* **2.** [*be* + ~] correct in one's judgment or action: *You were right; the movie was terrible.* [~ + *to* + *verb*]: *You were right to fire him.* **3.** correct in fact: *Is that the right answer?* **4.** fitting; suitable; desirable: *the right clothes for the occasion.* **5.** [*before a noun*] of or relating to the side of a person or thing that is toward the east when that person or thing is facing north. **6.** sound; sane: *in one's right mind.* **7.** in good health or spirits: *I haven't felt right in days.* **8.** front or upper: *right side up.* **9.** [*often: Right*] of or belonging to the political Right; having conservative views in politics. **—*n.* 10.** [*count*] something due to anyone by a just claim, moral principles, nature, etc.: *the right to free speech.* **11.** [*noncount*] that which is morally or legally proper and correct: *the difference between right and wrong.* **12.** [*noncount; usually: the* + ~] the state or quality or an instance of being correct: *You are in the right and the courts should agree with your claim.* **13.** [*noncount*] the side that is normally opposite to that where the heart is: *to turn to the right.* **14.** [*count*] a right-hand turn: *Make a right at the corner.* **15. the Right,** [*noncount*] **a.** individuals or groups calling for keeping the established political, social, or economic order. **b.** the conservative position held by these people. **—*adv.* 16.** in a straight or direct line: *The ship went right to the bottom.* **17.** quite; completely: *My hat was knocked right off.* **18.** immediately; promptly: *turned on the TV right after dinner.* **19.** exactly; precisely: *Put it down right here on the table.* **20.** correctly or accurately: *You guessed right.* **21.** properly: *to live right.* **22.** to one's benefit or advantage: *After a long hassle everything turned out right.* **23.** on or to the right: *to turn right.* **24.** *Informal.* very; extremely: *a right fine day.* **25.** [*often: Right; used in certain titles*] very: *The Right Reverend John C. Doe.* **—*v.*** [~ + *obj*] **26.** to put in or back to an upright position: *to right a fallen lamp.* **27.** to bring into agreement with fact; correct: *to right one's point of view.* **28.** to do justice to: *The king would right the wrongs done by the prince.* **—*Idiom.* 29. by rights,** in fairness; justly: *We should by rights have made back all our money by this time.* **30. in one's own right,** by reason of one's own ability: *Although he was the son of a famous football coach he soon became famous in his own right.* **31. in the right,** having the support of reason or law. **32. right away** or **off,** without hesitation; immediately: *Right off, you could tell he disliked her.* **33. right on,** *Slang.* (used to express approval of what has been said or agreement that it is exactly right): *"Power to the people," he yelled, and the crowd roared back "Right on!"* **34. to rights,** into proper condition or order: *to set a messed-up room to rights.* —**right′ly,** *adv.* —**right′ness,** *n.* [*noncount*]

right′ an′gle, *n.* [*count*] the angle formed by two perpendicular lines; an angle of 90°.

right•eous (rī′chəs) /ˈraytʃəs/ *adj.* **1.** having just cause for something; justifiable: *righteous indignation at being accused falsely.* **2.** of or relating to an upright, proper, or moral way of life; virtuous. **3.** *Slang.* genuinely good: *some righteous playing by a jazz great.* —**right′eous•ly,** *adv.* —**right′eous•ness,** *n.* [*noncount*]

right•ful (rīt′fəl) /ˈraytfəl/ *adj.* based on a valid, lawful, or just claim: *the rightful heir to the throne.* —**right′ful•ly,** *adv.* —**right′ful•ness,** *n.* [*noncount*]

right′ hand′, *n.* [*count*] **1.** the hand on a person's right side. **2.** the right side. **3.** a position of honor or special trust. **—*adj.* right′-hand′. 4.** located on the right. **5.** highly honored and trusted; being of great assistance: *the governor's right-hand man.*

right′-hand′ed, *adj.* **1.** using the right hand by preference: *a right-handed pitcher.* **2.** adapted to or performed by the right hand: *a car with a right-handed steering wheel.* **—*adv.*** Also, **right′-hand′ed•ly. 3.** with the right hand: *batting right-handed against the left-handed pitcher.* **4.** toward the right hand. —**right′-hand′edness,** *n.* [*noncount*]

right•ist (rī′tist) /ˈraytɪst/ *adj.* [*sometimes: Rightist*] **1.** of or relating to the political Right. **—*n.*** [*count*] **2.** a member of the political Right; a conservative. —**right′ism,** *n.* [*noncount*]

right′-mind′ed, *adj.* right-thinking; having correct beliefs: *Any right-minded person would see things your way.*

right′ of way′ or **right′-of-way′,** *n., pl.* **rights of way, right of ways** or **rights-of-way, right-of-ways. 1.** [*noncount*] the right to proceed ahead of another vehicle: *At the stop sign she had the right of way.* **2.** [*count*] a path or area of land that may lawfully be used or crossed.

right′-to-life′, *adj.* [*before a noun*] opposed to abortion; of or relating to laws making abortion on demand illegal: *the right-to-life movement.* —**right′-to-lif′er,** *n.* [*count*]

right′ tri′angle, *n.* [*count*] a triangle having a right angle.

right′ wing′, *n.* [*count*] **1.** the conservative members in a political party. **—***adj.* **right′-wing′. 2.** of or relating to the right wing. —**right′-wing′er,** *n.* [*count*]

rig•id (rij′id) /ˈrɪdʒɪd/ *adj.* **1.** stiff; not easily moved: *a rigid strip of metal.* **2.** fixed in one's thinking: *He can be very rigid when it comes to rules.* **3.** strict or severe: *The rules are too rigid.* —**rig′id•ly,** *adv.*: *He stood rigidly at attention.* —**rig′id•ness,** *n.* [*noncount*]

ri•gid•i•ty (ri jid′i tē) /rɪˈdʒɪdɪtiy/ *n.* [*noncount*] the quality of being rigid: *the rigidity of the bones; rigidity in matters of morals and doctrine.*

rig•ma•role (rig′mə rōl′) /ˈrɪgmə,rowl/ also **rig•a•ma•role** (rig′ə mə rōl′) /ˈrɪgəmə,rowl/ *n.* **1.** a complicated procedure to be followed: [*count; usually singular*]: *What a rigmarole it was to get out of the country!* [*noncount*]: *a lot of rigmarole just to get a passport.* **2.** [*noncount*] confusing talk.

rig•or (rig′ər) /ˈrɪgər/ *n.* **1.** [*noncount*] the quality of being strict; strictness; inflexibility. **2.** [*count*] hardship of some kind, as weather or climate: *the rigors of winter.* **3.** [*noncount*] careful accuracy: *the rigor of mathematics.* **4.** [*noncount*] a rigid condition of the body's muscles when unnaturally stiffened. Also, *esp. Brit.,* **rig′our.**

rig•or mor•tis (rig′ər môr′tis) /ˈrɪgˈər mɔrtɪs/ *n.* [*noncount*] the stiffening of the body after death.

rig•or•ous (rig′ər əs) /ˈrɪgərəs/ *adj.* of or relating to rigor: *rigorous exercise; rigorous research.*

rile (rīl), *v.* [~ + *obj*], **riled, ril•ing.** to irritate; vex.

rim (rim) /rɪm/ *n., v.,* **rimmed, rim•ming.** **—***n.* [*count*] **1.** the outer edge or border of something: *a chip on the rim of the glass.* **2.** the outer circle of a wheel, attached to the hub by spokes. **—***v.* [~ + *obj*] **3.** to furnish with a rim. **4.** to roll around the edge of but not go in: *His last shot rimmed the basket.*

rime (rīm) /raym/ *n., v.,* **rimed, rim•ing.** RHYME.

rind (rīnd) /raynd/ *n.* a thick outer coat: [*noncount*]: *orange rind.* [*count*]: *a few bacon rinds.* —**rind′less,** *adj.*

ring[1] (ring) /rɪŋ/ *n., v.,* **ringed, ring•ing.** **—***n.* [*count*] **1.** a usually thin, circular band of strong material, such as gold, worn on the finger as an ornament, etc.: *a diamond ring.* **2.** anything having the form of such a band: *a smoke ring.* **3.** a circular line or mark: *dark rings around the eyes.* **4.** a circle: *to dance in a ring.* **5.** a number of persons or things arranged in a circle: *a ring of hills.* **6.** a closed area for a sports contest or exhibition: *a boxing ring; a circus ring.* **7.** a group working together for illegal purposes: *a ring of dope smugglers.* **—***v.* [~ + *obj*] **8.** to surround with a ring; encircle: *The police ringed the theater to prevent riots.* **—*Idiom.* 9. run rings around,** [~ + *obj*] to do better than: *His new company ran rings around the competition.*

ring[2] (ring) /rɪŋ/ *v.,* **rang** (rang) /ræŋ/ **rung** (rung) /rʌŋ/ **ring•ing,** *n.* **—***v.* **1.** [*no obj*] to give forth a clear, echoing sound: *The phone is ringing.* **2.** to cause a bell, telephone, etc., to give off a sound: [*no obj*]: *Just ring for service.* [~ + *obj*]: *Ring room service for dinner.* **3.** [*no obj*] to have a sound: *The room rang with shouts.* **4.** [*no obj*] (of the ears) to have the sensation of a ringing sound: *After the blow to his head his ears rang for several minutes.* **5.** [~ + *adjective*] to make a certain impression on the mind: *a story that rings true.* **6.** to telephone: [~ + *obj*]: *Ring us when you get home.* [~ + *obj* + *up*]: *Ring us up when you get home.* [~ + *up* + *obj*]: *Ring up your sister when you get back.* [*no obj*]: *Ring when you get a chance.* **7.** [~ + *obj*] to announce by the sound of a bell: *The bell rang the hour.* **8. ring off,** [*no obj*] *Chiefly Brit.* to end a telephone conversation: *to ring off and get back to work.* **9. ring up,** to register (the amount of a sale) on a cash register: [~ + *up* + *obj*]: *He rang up the sale.* [~ + *obj* + *up*]: *I just rang it up.* **—***n.* [*count*] **10.** a ringing sound: *the ring of sleigh bells.* **11.** a sound like that of a ringing bell: *the ring of laughter.* **12.** *Informal.* a telephone call: *Give me a ring.* **13.** [*usually singular*] a characteristic sound or quality: *This story has a ring of truth to it.* **—*Idiom.* 14. ring a bell,** *Informal.* to evoke a memory: *That name doesn't ring a bell.*

ring•er[1] (ring′ər) /ˈrɪŋər/ *n.* [*count*] a person or thing that encircles something.

ring•er[2] (ring′ər) /ˈrɪŋər/ *n.* [*count*] **1.** a person or thing that rings or makes a ringing noise. **2.** something or someone looking exactly like another. **3.** a racehorse or an athlete entering a competition under false pretenses.

ring•lead•er (ring′lē′dər) /ˈrɪŋ,liydər/ *n.* [*count*] one who leads others, esp. in unlawful or rebellious activities.

ring•let (ring′lit) /ˈrɪŋlɪt/ *n.* [*count*] a curled lock of hair.

ring•mas•ter (ring′mas′tər) /ˈrɪŋ,mæstər/ *n.* [*count*] one in charge of the performances in a circus ring.

ring•side (ring′sīd′) /ˈrɪŋ,sayd/ *n.* [*noncount*] **1.** the area occupied by the first row of seats on all sides of a stage, or a boxing ring: *Seated at ringside, the champ waved to the crowd.* **—***adj.* [*before a noun*] **2.** of or relating to the ringside: *ringside seats at the concert.* **3.** (of a place or position) providing a close view of what is happening: *a ringside view of the argument.*

ring•worm (ring′wûrm′) /ˈrɪŋ,wɜrm/ *n.* [*noncount*] a skin disease caused by fungi.

rink (ringk) /rɪŋk/ *n.* [*count*] **1.** a smooth area of ice for ice-skating. **2.** a smooth floor for roller-skating. **3.** a building or enclosure for ice-skating or roller-skating; skating arena.

rink•y-dink (ring′kē dingk′) /ˈrɪŋkiy,dɪŋk/ *adj. Slang.* amateurish or of poor quality; small-time: *a rinky-dink train system.*

rinse (rins) /rɪns/ *v.,* **rinsed, rins•ing,** *n.* **—***v.* [~ + *obj*] **1.** to wash lightly, as by pouring water over as a final stage in washing: *rinsed the dishes.* **2.** to remove (soap, etc.) by such a process: *She rinsed the soap out of her hair.* **3.** to use a rinse on (the hair): *blue-rinsed hair.* **—***n.* **4.** [*count*] an act or instance of rinsing. **5.** a liquid used on the hair after washing, esp. to color or condition it: [*noncount*]: *some blue rinse.* [*count*]: *trying different rinses.*

ri•ot (rī′ət) /ˈrayət/ *n.* [*count*] **1.** a noisy, violent public disorder: *The arrest caused a riot in the city.* **2.** a wild mix or confusion: *a riot of colors.* **3.** [*usually singular; a* + ~] something or someone very funny or amusing: *You were a riot at the party.* **—***v.* [*no obj*] **4.** to take part in a violent public disturbance: *thousands rioting in the streets.* **—*Idiom.* 5. run riot,** [*no ob*] to behave wildly: *The townspeople ran riot after the verdict.* —**ri′ot•er,** *n.* [*count*]

ri•ot•ous (rī′ə təs) /ˈrayətəs/ *adj.* of or relating to a riot: *the riotous undergraduates; a riotous night on the town.*

rip (rip) /rɪp/ *v.,* **ripped, rip•ping,** *n.* **—***v.* **1.** to tear apart roughly or vigorously: [~ + *obj*]: *to rip open a seam.* [~ + *up* + *obj*]: *He ripped up the newspaper.* [~ + *obj* + *up*]: *He ripped it up.* [*no obj*]: *Her slacks ripped when she fell.* **2.** [*no obj*] to move with violence or great speed: *The car ripped along in a cloud of dust.* **3. rip into,** *Informal.* [~ + *into* + *obj*] to attack strongly; assail: *really ripped into the proposal.* **4. rip off,** *Slang.* **a.** to steal: [~ + *off* + *obj*]: *Someone ripped off his expensive new sports car.* [~ + *obj* + *off*]: *Someone must have ripped it off.* **b.** to cheat or take from dishonestly: [~ + *obj* + *off*]: *The car dealer tried to rip us off.* [~ + *off* + *obj*]: *trying to rip off the tourists.* **—***n.* [*count*] **5.** a tear made by ripping: *a rip in her jacket.* **—*Idiom.* 6. let her** or **it rip,** [*no obj*] *Slang.* to allow something to go on freely or without holding anything back: *He revved up the engine and let her rip.* —**rip′per,** *n.* [*count*]

RIP or **R.I.P.,** an abbreviation of: may he or she or they rest in peace (used on a gravestone).

rip′ cord′, *n.* [*count*] a cord on a parachute that, when pulled, opens the parachute for descent.

ripe (rīp) /rayp/ *adj.,* **rip•er, rip•est.** **1.** completely matured, such as grain or fruit ready to be picked and eaten: *ripe, juicy oranges.* **2.** resembling fruit, as in fullness: *her ripe red lips.* **3.** being in the best condition for use, as beer. **4.** characterized by full development; mature: *of ripe years.* **5.** advanced: *a ripe old age of 99.* **6.** [*be* + ~ + *for*] (of ideas, time, etc.) ready for action; fit for: *The time is ripe for a change.* —**ripe′ly,** *adv.* —**ripe′ness,** *n.* [*noncount*]

rip•en (rī′pən) /ˈraypən/ *v.* to (cause to) become ripe: [~ + *obj*]: *to ripen cheese.* [*no obj*]: *The cheese ripens in those barrels for years.*

rip•off or **rip-off** (rip′ôf′, -of′-) /ˈrɪp,ɔf, -,ɒf-/ *n.* [*count*] *Slang.* **1.** an act of stealing or cheating. **2.** a copy or imitation.

ri•poste or **ri•post** (ri pōst′) /rɪˈpowst/ *n., v.,* **-post•ed, -post•ing.** **—***n.* [*count*] **1.** a quick, sharp reply: *a clever riposte.* **—***v.* [*no obj*] **2.** to reply quickly and sharply: *quick to riposte.*

rip•ple (rip′əl) /ˈrɪpəl/ *v.,* **-pled, -pling,** *n.* **—***v.* **1.** (of a liquid surface) to form small waves, as water when a breeze disturbs it: [*no obj*]: *The water rippled in the sunlight.* [~ + *obj*]: *The breeze rippled the water.* **2.** to (cause to) have small waves, ruffles, or folds: [*no obj*]: *His muscles rippled as he lifted the load.* [~ + *obj*]: *rippling his muscles.* **3.** [*no obj*] (of sound) to move along with a rising and falling sound: *Laughter rippled through the crowd.* **—***n.* [*count*] **4.** a small wave, as on water. **5.**

a movement, form, or sound similar to this: *a ripple of laughter.*

rip′ple effect′, *n.* [*count*] a spreading effect caused by a single action or event.

rip′-roar′ing, *adj.* [*before a noun*] loudly wild and exciting; riotous: *a rip-roaring good time.*

rise (rīz) /rayz/ *v.,* **rose** (rōz) /rowz/ **ris•en** (riz′ən) /ˈrɪzən/ **ris•ing,** *n.* —*v.* [*no obj*] **1.** to get up from a lying, sitting, or kneeling position: *She rose and walked over to greet me.* **2.** to get up from bed, esp. to begin the day: *He likes to rise early.* **3.** to become active and resist someone: *The people rose up against the dictator.* **4.** to come into existence: *A quarrel rose between them.* **5.** to move from a lower to a higher position: *The smoke rose into the sky.* **6.** to ascend above the horizon, as the sun: *The sun rises in the east.* **7.** to extend directly upward: *The building rises from the center of the town.* **8.** to have an upward slant or curve: *The road rises slightly.* **9.** to achieve a higher level, as of importance: *to rise in the world.* **10.** to become happy or cheerful, as the spirits: *His spirits rose when she smiled at him.* **11.** to become stirred in the emotions: *could feel his temper rising at the insults.* **12.** to increase, as in height, amount, value, or force: *The river is rising three feet an hour.* **13.** to swell or puff up, such as dough from the action of yeast: *The bread hasn't finished rising yet.* **14.** to become louder or of higher pitch, as the voice: *"You mean you can't help?" he cried, his voice rising to a squeak.* **15.** to return from the dead. **16. rise above,** [~ + *above* + *obj*] to ignore and overcome, as difficulty: *She rose above the heartbreak of the death of her son.* **17. rise to,** [~ + *to* + *obj*] to prove that one is equal to a demand, etc., by acting forcefully or correctly: *He rose to the occasion by responding with firm leadership.* —*n.* **18.** [*count*] an act or instance of rising. **19.** [*noncount*] increase in rank, fortune, etc.: *the rise and fall of Rome.* **20.** [*count*] an increase, as in height, amount, or value; the amount of such increase: *a rise in unemployment.* **21.** [*count*] the measured height of any of various things, as of a roof or a stair step. **22.** origin, source, or beginning: [*count*]: *the rise of a stream in a mountain.* [*noncount*]: *What has given rise to such strong feelings of anger?* **23.** [*count*] a piece of rising or high ground: *At the next rise you can see the house below.*

ris•er (rī′zər) /ˈrayzər/ *n.* [*count*] **1.** one who rises, esp. from bed: *He's an early riser.* **2.** the vertical face of a stair step. **3. a.** a long low platform on which persons can stand to be seen better, as on a stage. **b. risers,** [*plural*] a group of such platforms connected stepwise.

risk (risk) /rɪsk/ *n.* **1.** a dangerous chance: [*noncount*]: *Investing all that money is not worth the risk.* [*count*]: *He took too many risks driving so fast.* **2.** *Insurance.* **a.** [*noncount*] the chance of loss. **b.** [*noncount*] the degree of probability of such loss: *high risk.* **c.** [*count*] a person or thing that is in danger and is to be insured: *She was a poor risk because she had so many accidents.* —*v.* [~ + *obj*] **3.** to put or place someone or oneself near the chance of injury or danger: *to risk one's life.* **4.** to take the chance of; to hazard: *You risk a fall walking on such icy stairs.* —***Idiom.*** **5. at risk,** in danger: [*no obj*]: *Young children are at risk.* [~ + *of* + *obj*]: *They are at risk of injury.* **6. at the risk of,** [~ + *obj*] in spite of the danger of: *At the risk of looking foolish, may I ask what you mean?*

risk•y (ris′kē) /ˈrɪskiy/ *adj.,* **-i•er, -i•est.** involving risk; dangerous: *a risky attempt to save a life; risky business.*

ris•qué (ri skā′) /rɪˈskey/ *adj.* close to being improper or indecent; off-color: *a risqué story.*

rite (rīt) /rayt/ *n.* [*count*] **1.** a ceremony in religious or other solemn use: *funeral rites.* **2.** a customary practice or tradition: *the rites of spring.*

rit•u•al (rich′o͞o əl) /ˈrɪtʃuwəl/ *n.* **1. a.** [*count*] an established procedure for a religious or other rite: *rituals for the dead.* **b.** [*noncount*] a system of such rites: *the comfort of ritual during a time of loss.* **2.** [*count*] a practice regularly performed in a definite manner: *Another ritual was the annual tea party.* **3.** [*noncount*] prescribed or ceremonial acts, thought of as a group: *falling back on ritual when a new development occurs.* —*adj.* [*before a noun*] **4.** of or relating to a rite or ritual: *a ritual dance.* —**rit′u•al•ly,** *adv.*

rit•u•al•is•tic (rich′o͞o ə lis′tik) /ˌrɪtʃuwəˈlɪstɪk/ *adj.* **1.** of or part of a religious ritual. **2.** following a customary or similar pattern. —**rit′u•al•ism,** *n.* [*noncount*]

ritz•y (rit′sē) /ˈrɪtsiy/ *adj.,* **-i•er, -i•est.** very rich-looking; elegant: *stayed in the ritziest hotel.*

ri•val (rī′vəl) /ˈrayvəl/ *n., adj., v.,* **-valed, -val•ing** or (*esp. Brit.*) **-valled, -val•ling.** —*n.* [*count*] **1.** one who seeks to achieve the same object or goal as another; a competitor: *They were rivals for the job but they were still friends.* **2.** a person or thing that is almost equal to another: *This car has no rival in its class.* —*adj.* [*before a noun*] **3.** competing or standing in rivalry: *rival businesses.* —*v.* [~ + *obj*] **4.** to prove to be a worthy rival of: *rivaled the others in skill.* **5.** to equal (something); to match; be as good as: *The speed of this computer rivals that of much more expensive brands.*

ri•val•ry (rī′vəl rē) /ˈrayvəlriy/ *n.* the state of being rivals: [*count*]: *The two teams had a friendly rivalry for years.* [*noncount*]: *a strong sense of rivalry.*

riv•er (riv′ər) /ˈrɪvər/ *n.* [*count*] **1.** a natural stream of water flowing in a definite course: *Three rivers come together at that city.* [*the* + *place name* + ~]: *the Hudson River.* See illustration at LANDSCAPE. **2.** a similar stream of something else: *rivers of tears.* —***Idiom.*** **3. sell (someone) down the river,** *Slang.* to betray: *When he was arrested he realized his so-called friends had sold him down the river.* **4. up the river,** *Slang.* to or in prison: *He was sent up the river for ten years.*

riv•er•side (riv′ər sīd′) /ˈrɪvərˌsayd/ *n.* [*count*] **1.** a bank of a river. —*adj.* [*before a noun*] **2.** on or near a bank of a river.

riv•et (riv′it) /ˈrɪvɪt/ *n., v.,* **-et•ed, -et•ing** or (*esp. Brit.*) **-et•ted, -et•ting.** —*n.* [*count*] **1.** a metal pin for passing through holes in plates to hold them together. —*v.* [~ + *obj*] **2.** to fasten with or as if with a rivet or rivets: *riveting the wings to the body of the plane.* **3.** to hold (someone's attention) firmly: *Her attention was riveted on the magician.* —**riv′et•er,** *n.* [*count*]

riv•et•ing (riv′i ting) /ˈrɪvɪtɪŋ/ *adj.* holding someone's attention firmly: *a riveting book.*

riv•u•let (riv′yə lit) /ˈrɪvyəlɪt/ *n.* [*count*] a small stream; brook.

rm., an abbreviation of: **1.** ream. **2.** room.

RN or **R.N.,** an abbreviation of: registered nurse.

RNA, an abbreviation of: ribonucleic acid, any of a class of single-stranded nucleic molecules found chiefly in body cells and in certain viruses, important in making protein and in sending genetic material to new cells.

roach (rōch) /rowtʃ/ *n.* [*count*] **1.** a cockroach. **2.** *Slang.* the butt of a marijuana cigarette.

road (rōd) /rowd/ *n.* [*count*] **1.** a long, narrow stretch or way of land with a leveled surface, made for traveling by motor vehicle, etc.; street or highway: *The dirt road led to the farmhouse.* **2.** a way or course: *the road to peace.* —***Idiom.*** **3. down the road,** *Informal.* at some future time: *promised she would cover that somewhere down the road.* **4. hit the road,** *Informal.* to begin or continue traveling: *Time to hit the road; let's go.* **5. one for the road,** [*noncount*] *Informal.* a final alcoholic drink just before leaving. **6. on the road, a.** traveling or touring: *The band has been on the road for almost two months.* **b.** changing, as from one condition to another: *on the road to recovery.*

road•bed (rōd′bed′) /ˈrowdˌbɛd/ *n.* **1.** [*count*] the bed or foundation for the track of a railroad. **2.** [*noncount*] the material of which a road is made up.

road•block (rōd′blok′) /ˈrowdˌblɒk/ *n.* [*count*] **1.** something placed across a road to halt or slow traffic, as by the police to check cars. **2.** anything that slows progress: *lack of money was a roadblock to her goals.* —*v.* [~ + *obj*] **3.** to halt or block with a roadblock: *They effectively roadblocked our plans.*

road•run•ner (rōd′run′ər) /ˈrowdˌrʌnər/ *n.* [*count*] a fast-running kind of bird, a cuckoo, found in dry regions of the western U.S., Mexico, and Central America.

road•side (rōd′sīd′) /ˈrowdˌsayd/ *n.* [*count*] **1.** the side or border of the road: *The car had been pulled over to the roadside.* —*adj.* [*before a noun*] **2.** on or near the side of a road: *a roadside café.*

road•ster (rōd′stər) /ˈrowdstər/ *n.* [*count*] an automobile with an open body and a single seat for two or three people.

road•way (rōd′wā′) /ˈrowdˌwey/ *n.* [*count*] **1.** the land over which a road is built. **2.** the part of a road over which vehicles travel; road.

road•work (rōd′wûrk′) /ˈrowdˌwɜrk/ *n.* [*noncount*] exercise for an athlete, esp. a boxer, usually running on roads: *getting up early to do his roadwork.*

roam (rōm) /rowm/ *v.* to travel without purpose; wander: [*no obj*]: *He roamed around the world for a few years.* [~ + *obj*]: *She roamed the countryside.* —**roam′er,** *n.* [*count*]

roan (rōn) /rown/ *adj.* **1.** (chiefly of horses) light reddish brown. —*n.* [*count*] **2.** a horse or other animal with a skin or coat of such color.

roar (rôr, rōr) /rɔr, rowr/ *v.* **1.** to make or say in a loud, deep, continuing sound, as in anger: [*no obj*]: *The crowd roared when she scored the winning basket.* [~ + *obj*]: *The crowd roared its approval.* [*used with quotations*]: *"Get out and stay out!" he roared.* **2.** [*no obj*] to laugh loudly or boisterously: *The audience roared with laughter.* **3.** [*no obj*] to make a loud noise, such as thunder, cannon, etc.: *The motorcycles roared off.* **4.** [*no obj*] to function or move with a loud, deep sound, as a vehicle. —*n.* [*count*] **5.** a roaring sound: *a roar of laughter.*

roar•ing (rôr′ing, rōr′-) /'rɔrɪŋ,'rowr-/ *n.* [*noncount*] **1.** the act of one that roars: *the roaring of the wind.* —*adj.* [*before a noun*] **2.** making a roar: *the roaring thunder.* **3.** very active; highly successful: *a roaring business.* **4.** complete; utter: *a roaring idiot.* —*adv.* **5.** very; completely: *roaring drunk.*

roast (rōst) /rowst/ *v.* **1.** to cook (food) by direct, dry heat, as in an oven: [~ + *obj*]: *We roasted chicken at the party.* [*no obj*]: *The turkey is still roasting.* **2.** to dry and cause (beans, etc.) to turn brown by heating: [~ + *obj*]: *to roast coffee beans.* [*no obj*]: *You could smell the peanuts roasting.* **3.** [*no obj*] to be very hot: *We roasted in the office when the air-conditioner broke down.* **4.** [~ + *obj*] to make fun of or criticize severely: *She'll be roasted in the press over this.* **5.** [~ + *obj*] to honor with or subject to a roast: *The famous actor was roasted at the Lions' Club.* —*n.* [*count*] **6.** meat that has been roasted or is suitable for roasting. **7.** a ceremonial dinner in which a guest of honor is both praised and good-naturedly insulted: *It was the first roast for the celebrity.* **8.** an outdoor get-together at which food is roasted: *a wienie roast.* —*adj.* [*before a noun*] **9.** roasted: *roast ham.*

roast•er (rō′stər) /'rowstər/ *n.* [*count*] **1.** one that roasts. **2.** a pan or oven for roasting. **3.** a chicken suitable for roasting.

rob (rob) /rɒb/ *v.*, **robbed, rob•bing. 1.** to take something by unlawful force; steal from: [~ + *obj*]: *The crooks robbed several banks.* [~ + *obj* + *of* + *obj*]: *They robbed him of all his money.* [*no obj*]: *roaming the countryside, robbing and murdering.* **2.** [~ + *obj* + *of* + *obj*] to take away from (someone) some right or cheat (someone) out of something: *robbed her of her inheritance.* **3.** to deprive of something unjustly: [~ + *obj* + *of* + *obj*]: *The shock robbed him of speech.* [~ + *obj*]: *The team felt it had been robbed because the umpire made a mistake.* —**rob′ber,** *n.* [*count*]

rob•ber•y (rob′ə rē) /'rɒbəriy/ *n., pl.* **-ber•ies. 1.** [*count*] the act, practice, or instance of robbing: *several robberies in that neighborhood.* **2.** [*noncount*] the taking of property by violence: *the penalty for robbery.*

robe (rōb) /rowb/ *n., v.*, **robed, rob•ing.** —*n.* [*count*] **1.** a long, loose or flowing gown or outer garment: *academic robes.* **2.** any loose garment, such as a bathrobe. —*v.* **3.** to put on a robe or robes: [~ + *obj*]: *He was robed in the ceremonial clothes of his office.* [*no obj*]: *He got up, robed, and went to breakfast.*

rob•in (rob′in) /'rɒbɪn/ *n.* [*count*] a large North American bird, a thrush, having a chestnut-red breast and abdomen. Also called **rob′in red′breast** (red′brest′) /'rɛd,brɛst/.

ro•bot (rō′bət, -bot) /'rowbət, -bɒt/ *n.* [*count*] **1.** a machine that looks something like a human and does mechanical tasks. **2.** a machine that performs such tasks automatically. **3.** one who acts and responds in a mechanical, routine manner: *In his new job he became a robot, mindlessly filling out forms.* —**ro•bot′ic,** *adj.*

ro•bot•ics (rō bot′iks) /row'bɒtɪks/ *n.* [*noncount; used with a singular verb*] the study of computer-controlled robots to perform tasks: *Robotics is a new area for research on artificial intelligence.* —**ro•bot•i•cist** (rō bot′i-sist) /row'bɒtɪsɪst/ *n.* [*count*]

ro•bust (rō bust′, rō′bust) /row'bʌst, 'rowbʌst/ *adj.* **1.** strong and healthy; vigorous: *robust health.* **2.** stoutly built: *the robust police officer.* **3.** rich and full-bodied: *robust flavor.* —**ro•bust′ly,** *adv.* —**ro•bust′ness,** *n.* [*noncount*]

rock[1] (rok) /rɒk/ *n.* **1.** [*noncount*] a large mass of stone forming a hill, cliff, etc.: *boring a hole through rock.* **2.** [*count*] a piece of stone of any size: *They were throwing rocks through the windows.* **3.** [*count*] something resembling a rock. **4.** [*count*] *Slang.* **a.** a diamond. **b.** any gem. —***Idiom.*** **5. on the rocks, a.** *Informal.* ruined or about to be ruined: *worried that their marriage was on the rocks.* **b.** (of an alcoholic beverage) served over ice cubes: *a martini on the rocks.*

rock[2] (rok) /rɒk/ *v.* **1.** to move to and fro gently: [~ + *obj*]: *He rocked his child in his arms.* [*no obj*]: *She rocked quietly in her chair.* **2.** to (cause to) be moved powerfully with emotion, etc.: [*no obj*]: *She rocked with laughter at the sight.* [~ + *obj*]: *The news of the killings rocked the small town.* **3.** [~ + *obj*] to shake violently: *An explosion rocked the dock.* **4.** [*no obj*] to dance to or play rock music: *The band rocked all night.* —*n.* **5.** [*count*] a rocking movement. **6.** [*noncount*] a musical style coming originally from blues and folk music, having a strong beat and repeating phrases. —*adj.* [*before a noun*] **7.** of or relating to musical rock: *a rock band.*

rock•a•bil•ly (rok′ə bil′ē) /'rɒkə,bɪliy/ *n.* [*noncount*] a style of popular music combining features of rock and hillbilly music.

rock′ and roll′ or **rock′ & roll′,** *n.* ROCK[2] (def. 6).

rock′ bot′tom, *n.* [*noncount*] the very lowest level: *The economy has hit rock bottom.* —**rock′-bot′tom,** *adj.*: *cars being sold at rock-bottom prices.*

rock′ can′dy, *n.* [*noncount*] candy in the form of sugar in large, hard crystals.

rock•er (rok′ər) /'rɒkər/ *n.* [*count*] **1.** Also called **runner.** one of the curved pieces on which a rocking chair rocks. **2.** ROCKING CHAIR: *sitting in his rocker by the fire.* **3.** any of various devices that operate with a rocking motion. **4.** a performer or fan of rock music. —***Idiom.*** **5. off one's rocker,** *Slang.* insane; crazy: *You must be off your rocker to say such a thing.*

rock•et (rok′it) /'rɒkɪt/ *n.* [*count*] **1.** a tubelike device containing material that burns rapidly and propels the tube through the air: *The rockets were fired off the plane's wings.* **2.** a space capsule or vehicle put into orbit by such a device: *The rocket was launched at noon.* —*v.* **3.** [~ + *obj*] to move by a rocket: *The capsule was rocketed into space.* **4.** [*no obj*] to move like a rocket: *The plane rocketed ahead.*

rock•et•ry (rok′i trē) /'rɒkɪtriy/ *n.* [*noncount*] the science of rocket design, development, and flight.

rock′ gar′den, *n.* [*count*] a garden on rocky ground or among rocks, for the growing of usually small plants.

rock′ing chair′, *n.* [*count*] a chair mounted on curved pieces of wood so that it can rock.

rock′ing horse′, *n.* [*count*] a toy horse, mounted on rockers or springs, on which children may ride; a hobbyhorse.

rock′ salt′, *n.* [*noncount*] common salt, sodium chloride, occurring in rocklike masses.

rock•y[1] (rok′ē) /'rɒkiy/ *adj.*, **-i•er, -i•est. 1.** full of or containing many rocks: *The soil was too rocky for farming.* **2.** made up of rock; rocklike. **3.** firm; steadfast: *rocky endurance.* —**rock′i•ness,** *n.* [*noncount*]

rock•y[2] (rok′ē) /'rɒkiy/ *adj.*, **-i•er, -i•est. 1.** full of troubles or difficulties: *a rocky marriage.* **2.** physically unsteady or weak, as from sickness: *felt rocky after the accident.*

ro•co•co (rə kō′kō, rō′kə kō′) /rə'kowkow, ,rowkə'kow/ *n.* [*noncount*] **1.** an artistic style, chiefly of 18th-century France, having careful elegance, delicate ornamentation, and curly decoration. —*adj.* **2.** of or relating to rococo.

rod (rod) /rɒd/ *n.* [*count*] **1.** a long straight stick, wand, or staff. **2.** a slender bar or tube for draping towels over, etc.

rode (rōd) /rowd/ *v.* a pt. of RIDE.

ro•dent (rōd′nt) /'rowdnt/ *n.* [*count*] **1.** a mammal belonging to a family of animals that has four sharp teeth that grow continually: *Rodents include mice, squirrels, and rats.* —*adj.* **2.** belonging to this family of animals.

ro•de•o (rō′dē ō′, rō dā′ō) /'rowdiy,ow, row'deyow/ *n.* [*count*], *pl.* **-de•os.** a public exhibition of cowboy skills, such as riding wild horses and roping calves.

roe (rō) /row/ *n.* [*noncount*] the mass of eggs or of sperm in the bodies of certain fish, eaten as food: *Caviar is made of sturgeon roe.*

roent•gen (rent′gən, -jən, runt′-) /'rɛntgən, -dʒən, 'rʌnt-/ *n.* [*count*] a unit of radiation dosage.

-roga-, *root.* *-roga-* comes from Latin, where it has the meaning "ask; demand." This meaning is found in such words as: ABROGATE, ARROGANT, DEROGATORY, INTERROGATE, PREROGATIVE, SURROGATE.

rog•er (roj′ər) /'rɒdʒər/ *interj.* **1.** a response in radio communications meaning that the message has been received and understood **2.** *Informal.* all right; OK.

rogue (rōg) /rowg/ *n.* [*count*] **1.** a dishonest person; scoundrel: *The rogue tried to sell them a very bad car.* **2.** a playful, mischievous child who likes to play tricks;

scamp: *That little rogue has hidden herself somewhere in the house.* **3.** an animal that lives apart from others of its kind: *a rogue elephant.*

ro•guish (rō′gish) /ˈrowgɪʃ/ *adj.* of or relating to a rogue: *a roguish smile.* —**ro′guish•ly,** *adv.*

roil (roil) /rɔyl/ *v.* [~ + *obj*] **1.** to disturb (a fluid) by stirring: *wind roiling the water.* **2.** to disturb or irritate: *Her whining roiled everyone who met her.*

role or **rôle** (rōl) /rowl/ *n.* [*count*] **1.** a part played by an actor or singer: *the role of the villain in the play.* **2.** the proper function of a person or thing: *the role of good computer programs in teaching English.*

role′ mod′el, *n.* [*count*] one whose behavior is imitated by others, esp. by younger persons: *The athlete tried to be a role model for children.*

roll (rōl) /rowl/ *v.* **1.** to move along a surface by turning over and over: [*no obj*]: *A huge stone rolled down the hill.* [~ + *obj*]: *They rolled a huge stone down on their enemies.* **2.** to move or be moved on wheels: [~ + *obj*]: *He rolled the car a few feet from the edge of the cliff.* [*no obj*]: *The car rolled to a stop.* **3.** to (cause to) flow with a continuing or swaying motion: [*no obj*]: *Tears rolled down her face.* [~ + *obj*]: *The waves were rolling the ship up and down.* **4.** [*no obj*] to extend in waves, as land: *The hills rolled into the distance.* **5.** [*no obj*] to move along or elapse, as time: *The years rolled by, and before we knew it she was all grown up.* **6.** to make or have a deep, continuing sound, as thunder: [*no obj*]: *The drums rolled and the parade began.* [~ + *obj*]: *to roll their drums.* **7.** (of the eyes) to turn around in different directions: [*no obj*]: *His eyes rolled wildly in his head.* [~ + *obj*]: *He rolled his eyes and looked up.* **8.** [*no obj*] *Informal.* **a.** to begin to move or operate: *Let's roll at sunrise.* **b.** to make progress; advance: *The project is really rolling now.* **9.** to curl, cover, or fold up so as to form a rounded object: [~ + *obj*]: *to roll a ball of string; She rolled the string into a ball.* [*no obj;* ~ + *up*]: *The map rolls up easily.* [~ + *up* + *obj*]: *He rolled up the map.* [~ + *obj* + *up*]: *He rolled the map up.* **10.** [~ + *obj*] to trill: *to roll one's r's.* **11.** to spread out flat, as with a rolling pin: [~ + *obj*]: *She rolled the pastry dough and made a pie crust.* [~ + *out* + *obj*]: *He rolled out the pizza dough.* [~ + *obj* + *out*]: *He rolled the dough out and added sauce and cheese.* **12.** (in certain games, as craps) to throw (dice): [~ + *obj*]: *He rolled a seven.* [*no obj*]: *Whose turn is it to roll?* **13.** [~ + *obj*] *Slang.* to rob, esp. by going through the pockets of a victim who is asleep or drunk. **14. roll back,** to reduce (prices, etc.) to a former level: [~ + *back* + *obj*]: *The company wants to roll back wages and benefits.* [~ + *obj* + *back*]: *The company wants to roll wages back to pre-1993 rates.* **15. roll in,** [*no obj*] *Informal.* to arrive, esp. in large quantity: *When does the money start rolling in?* See ROLLING below. **16. roll over, a.** to turn over, as a person lying down: [*no obj*]: *She groaned, rolled over, and went back to sleep.* [~ + *over* + *obj*]: *We rolled over the body and examined the wound.* [~ + *obj* + *over*]: *to roll it over.* **b.** to reinvest (funds), as from one stock into another: [~ + *over* + *obj*]: *How do you know when it's a good time to roll over the funds?* [~ + *obj* + *over*]: *to roll the funds over.* [*no obj*]: *When the funds roll over, the profit will be yours to keep.* **17. roll up, a.** to fold the edges of (sleeves, cuffs, etc.): [~ + *up* + *obj*]: *Roll up your sleeves and let's get to work.* [~ + *obj* + *up*]: *Roll your pants up and step into the water.* **b.** to gather in increasing amounts: [~ + *up* + *obj*]: *The company continues to roll up massive profits.* [~ + *obj* + *up*]: *to keep rolling them up.* [*no obj*]: *Profits kept rolling up.* **c.** [*no obj*] to arrive in a car, etc.: *She rolled up in a huge limousine.* —*n.* [*count*] **18.** a register, catalog, or list, as of a class: *The teacher called the roll but my name wasn't on it.* **19.** anything rolled up in a ringlike or long, rounded form, as a length of cloth, wallpaper, etc.: *a roll of Scotch tape.* **20.** a rounded mass of something: *rolls of fat on his stomach.* **21.** a small cake of bread folded over before baking: *coffee and a roll.* **22.** an act or instance of rolling or swaying: *the sickening roll of the ship.* **23.** a deep, long sound, as of thunder or drums: *a roll of thunder.* —***Idiom.*** **24. on a roll,** experiencing a time of success: *She's on a roll now; everything is going her way.* **25. roll with the punches,** to deal with difficulty by remaining flexible.

roll•back (rōl′bak′) /ˈrowlˌbæk/ *n.* [*count*] **1.** an act or instance of rolling back. **2.** a return to a lower level of prices, wages, etc.

roll′ call′, *n.* [*count*] the calling of a list of names, as of students, for checking attendance.

roll•er (rō′lər) /ˈrowlər/ *n.* [*count*] **1.** a person or thing that rolls. **2.** a cylinder, wheel, etc., upon which something is rolled. **3.** a long, rounded object upon which something is rolled up: *the roller of a window shade.* **4.** a long, rounded object for spreading, crushing, or flattening something.

roll′er coast′er, *n.* [*count*] **1.** a small railroad, esp. in an amusement park, with open cars that moves along high, sharply winding tracks. **2.** any activity, period, or experience in which there are violent or sudden ups and downs: *a roller coaster of emotions.*

roll′er skate′, *n.* [*count*] a form of skate with wheels, for use on a smooth surface.

roll′er-skate′, *v.* [*no obj*], **-skat•ed, -skat•ing.** to move by using roller skates. —**roll′er skat′er,** *n.* [*count*]

rol•lick (rol′ik) /ˈrɒlɪk/ *v.* [*no obj*] to move or act in a carefree and happy or noisy and excited manner. —**rol′-lick•ing,** *adj.*: *a rollicking good time.*

roll•ing (rō′ling) /ˈrowlɪŋ/ *adj.* **1.** [*before a noun*] rising and falling in gentle waves into the distance: *rolling green hills.* **2.** [*be* + ~ + *in*] having a great deal of: *He's rolling in money.*

roll′ing pin′, *n.* [*count*] a cylinder typically of wood with a handle at each end, for rolling out dough.

roll•o•ver (rōl′ō′vər) /ˈrowlˌowvər/ *n.* [*count*] the moving of money into a new investment, such as from one stock or bond into another.

ro•ly-po•ly (rō′lē pō′lē, -pō′lē) /ˈrowliyˈpowliy, -ˌpowliy/ *adj., n., pl.* **-lies.** —*adj.* **1.** short and plumply round. —*n.* [*count*] **2.** a short, plumply round person or thing. **3.** *Chiefly Brit.* a sheet of biscuit dough spread with jam, rolled up and steamed or baked.

ROM (rom) /rɒm/ *n.* [*noncount*] computer memory that is not usually changed by the user, holding programmed instructions to the system; read-only memory.

ro•maine (rō mān′, rə-) /rowˈmeyn, rə-/ *n.* [*noncount*] a type of lettuce having a long, rounded head of long, loose leaves.

Ro•man (rō′mən) /ˈrowmən/ *adj.* **1.** of or relating to the city of Rome, or to its inhabitants. **2.** [*usually: roman*] naming or relating to printing types that point straight up. **3.** of or relating to the Roman Catholic Church. **4.** written in or relating to Roman numerals. —*n.* **5.** [*count*] a native, inhabitant, or citizen of Rome. **6.** [*usually: roman; noncount*] roman type or lettering: *printed in roman, not in italics.*

ro•man à clef (rô mä nä klē′) /rɔˈmɑ nɑ klɛ/ *n.* [*count*], *pl.* **ro•mans à clef** (rô män zä klē′) / rɔˈmɑ̃ zɑ klɛ/. a novel that represents real, historical events and characters in disguise.

Ro′man Cath′olic, *adj.* **1.** of or relating to the Roman Catholic Church. —*n.* [*count*] **2.** a member of the Roman Catholic Church. —**Ro′man Cathol′icism,** *n.* [*noncount*]

Ro′man Cath′olic Church′, *n.* [*proper noun; usually: the* + ~] the Christian church of which the pope, or bishop of Rome, is the supreme head.

ro•mance (*n., adj.* rō mans′, rō′mans; *v.* rō mans′) / *n., adj.* rowˈmæns, ˈrowmæns; *v.* rowˈmæns/ *n., v.,* **-manced, -manc•ing,** *adj.* —*n.* **1.** [*count*] a piece of writing telling of heroic or marvelous deeds, great ceremonies, etc., usually in a historical or imaginary setting. **2.** [*count*] a made-up story, full of exaggeration. **3.** [*noncount*] a romantic spirit, feeling, or quality: *no romance in their marriage anymore.* **4.** [*count*] a love affair. —*v.* [~ + *obj*] **5.** to try to have an affair with: *She thinks he is romancing their neighbor's wife.* —*adj.* **6.** [*Romance*] of or relating to the group of languages descended from the Latin of the Roman Empire, including French, Spanish, Portuguese, Italian, and Romanian. —**ro•manc′er,** *n.* [*count*]

Ro•man•esque (rō′mə nesk′) /ˌrowməˈnɛsk/ *adj.* of or relating to the style of architecture popular in W and S Europe from the 9th through the 12th centuries, having heavy masonry construction with narrow openings, and the use of a round arch.

Ro•ma•ni•an (rō mā′nē ən) /rowˈmeyniyən/ *adj.* **1.** of or relating to Romania. **2.** of or relating to the language spoken by many of the people in Romania. —*n.* **3.** [*count*] a person born or living in Romania. **4.** [*noncount*] the language spoken by many of the people living in Romania.

Ro′man nu′meral, *n.* [*count*] any of the numerals in the ancient Roman system of notation, still used occasionally. The basic symbols are **I** (=1), **V** (=5), **X** (=10), **L** (=50), **C** (=100), **D** (=500), and **M** (=1000).

Ro′man nu′merals, *n.* [*plural*] the numerals in the

ancient Roman system of writing, still used occasionally, as in dates on buildings.

ro•man•tic (rō man′tik) /row'mæntɪk/ *adj.* **1.** of or relating to romance: *a romantic evening.* **2.** not practical or realistic; having too great a desire for idealism, etc. **3.** expressing or strongly interested in love; passionate. **4.** [*often: Romantic*] of or relating to a style of literature, art, or music that emphasizes imagination, emotion, and inward thinking. **—*n.*** [*count*] **5.** a romantic person. **6.** [*often: Romantic*] a follower of Romanticism. **—ro•man′ti•cal•ly,** *adv.*: *romantically involved.*

ro•man•ti•cism (rō man′tə siz′əm) /row'mæntə,sɪzəm/ *n.* [*noncount*] **1.** romantic spirit or tendency. **2.** [*often: Romanticism*] the Romantic style or movement in literature and art; belief in its principles.

ro•man•ti•cize (rō man′tə sīz′) /row'mæntə,sayz/ *v.,* **-cized, -ciz•ing.** to hold romantic notions, ideas, etc. (about): [~ + *obj*]: *He's romanticizing the past; it wasn't nearly so much fun then.* [*no obj*]: *romanticizing about the past.*

ro•me•o (rō′mē ō′) /'rowmiy,ow/ *n.* [*count*], *pl.* **-me•os.** **1.** a man with a reputation for attracting women. **2.** a lover.

romp (romp) /rɒmp/ *v.* **1.** [*no obj*] to play in a lively, active way: *The kids romped in the big backyard.* **2.** [~ + *to* + *obj*)] to win easily: *The team romped to an easy victory.* **—*n.*** [*count*] **3.** a lively, noisy, active time. **4.** an easy victory: *Their first two games were romps.*

romp•er (rom′pər) /'rɒmpər/ *n.* [*count*] **1.** one that romps. **2.** Usually, **rompers.** [*plural; used with a plural verb*] a one-piece garment combining a shirt and pants, worn by young children.

roof (ro͞of, ro͝of) /ruwf, rʊf/ *n.* [*count*] **1.** the outside, upper covering of a building. See illustration at HOUSE. **2.** something that covers like a roof, such as the top of a car. **3.** (used to refer to a whole house): *They lived under the same roof for years.* **—*v.*** [~ + *obj*] **4.** to provide or cover with a roof. **—*Idiom.*** **5. go through the roof, a.** (esp. of costs) to increase quickly and surprisingly: *The cost of improvements has gone through the roof.* **b.** Also, **hit the roof.** to lose one's temper: *She'll hit the roof when she hears how much we spent.* **—roof′er,** *n.* [*count*]

roof•ing (ro͞o′fing, ro͝of′ing) /'ruwfɪŋ, 'rʊfɪŋ/ *n.* [*noncount*] **1.** the act of covering with a roof. **2.** material for roofs. **3.** a roof.

roof•top (ro͞of′top′, ro͝of′-) /'ruwf,tɒp, 'rʊf-/ *n.* [*count*] the roof of a building, esp. the outer surface.

rook[1] (ro͝ok) /rʊk/ *v.* [~ + *obj*] to cheat or swindle: *They rooked him out of his money.*

rook[2] (ro͝ok) /rʊk/ *n.* [*count*] one of two chess pieces of the same color that may be moved any number of unblocked squares right to left or forward and back; a castle.

rook•ie (ro͝ok′ē) /'rʊkiy/ *n.* [*count*] an inexperienced newcomer, esp. an athlete in the first season on a team.

room (ro͞om, ro͝om) /ruwm, rʊm/ *n.* **1.** [*count*] a portion of space within a building enclosed by walls from other parts: *There are five rooms in the apartment.* **2.** [*count*] the people present in a room: *The whole room laughed.* **3.** [*noncount*] extent of space available for something: *The desk will take up more room.* **4.** [*noncount*] opportunity for something: *room for improvement.* **5.** [*before a noun; after a number*] having a certain number of rooms: *a three-room apartment.* **—*v.*** [*no obj*] **6.** to occupy a room or rooms; lodge: *He roomed with a nice elderly couple.* **—room′ful,** *n.* [*count*], *pl.* **-fuls.**

room′ and board′, *n.* [*noncount*] rented room or rooms, plus meals, usually available for one fixed price.

room•er (ro͞o′mər, ro͝om′ər) /'ruwmər, 'rʊmər/ *n.* [*count*] one who lives in a rented room; lodger.

room′ing house′, *n.* [*count*] a house with furnished rooms to rent; a lodging house.

room•mate (ro͞om′māt′, ro͝om′-) /'ruwm,meyt, 'rʊm-/ *n.* [*count*] one who shares a room or apartment with another.

room•y (ro͞o′mē) /'ruwmiy/ *adj.,* **-i•er, -i•est.** having or giving plenty of room or space: *a large, roomy apartment.* **—room′i•ness,** *n.* [*noncount*]

roost (ro͞ost) /ruwst/ *n.* [*count*] **1.** a perch upon which birds rest. **—*v.*** [*no obj*] **2.** to sit on a perch, etc. **3.** to settle or stay, esp. for the night. **—*Idiom.*** **4. come home to roost,** [*no obj*] (of an action) to boomerang or backfire: *All his sneaky behavior has come home to roost because now no one trusts him.*

roost•er (ro͞o′stər) /'ruwstər/ *n.* [*count*] the male of domestic fowl and certain game birds; cock.

root[1] (ro͞ot, ro͝ot) /ruwt, rʊt/ *n.* [*count*] **1.** a part of the body of a plant that develops downward into the soil. **2.** something resembling the root of a plant in position or function. **3.** the part of a hair, tooth, etc., holding it to the main part of the body. **4.** the fundamental part; the source or origin of a thing: *the root of all evil.* **5. roots,** [*plural*] **a.** the original home and culture of a person or of one's ancestors: *When he discovered he was adopted he began a search for his roots.* **b.** the personal qualities that one finds appealing about a place; one's true home: *returned to his roots after years of travel.* **6.** a number that, when multiplied by itself a certain number of times, produces a given number: *2 is the square root of 4.* **7.** a part of a word, or the word itself, present in other forms of that word: *The word* dancer *has the root* dance; *the root of the word* extend *is Latin -tend-.* **—*v.*** **8.** [*no obj*] to become fixed or established: *Will these plants root well?* **9.** [~ + *obj*] to fix by or as if by roots: *rooted to the spot in amazement.* **10.** [~ (+ *out/up*) + *obj*] to pull, tear, or dig up by the roots: *He rooted (out) the weeds from the garden.* **11.** to remove completely: [~ + *out* + *obj*]: *promised to root out crime from the city.* [~ + *obj* + *out*]: *to root crime out.* **—*Idiom.*** **12. take root,** [*no obj*] **a.** to send out roots; begin to grow: *The new plant has taken root.* **b.** to become established: *Her ideas took root and grew.* **—root′less,** *adj.*

root[2] (ro͞ot, ro͝ot) /ruwt, rʊt/ *v.* **1.** to turn up the soil with the nose, as pigs do: [*no obj*]: *The pigs rooted around looking for food.* [~ + *up* + *obj*]: *rooting up a few nuts and seeds.* [~ + *obj* + *up*]: *rooting a few potatoes up.* **2.** [*no obj*] to poke, pry, or search: *He rooted around in the drawer for a cuff link.* **3.** to find out and bring to the attention of others: [~ + *up/out* + *obj*]: *managed to root up some very damaging information from the files.* [~ + *obj* + *up/out*]: *to root some information up for blackmail.*

root[3] (ro͞ot) /ruwt/ *v.* [~ + *for* + *obj*] **1.** to support a team or player by cheering strongly: *rooted for the basketball team.* **2.** to lend support: *We're all rooting for you.* **—root′er,** *n.* [*count*]

root′ beer′, *n.* [*count*] a carbonated beverage flavored with extracts of roots, barks, and herbs.

rope (rōp) /rowp/ *n., v.,* **roped, rop•ing.** **—*n.*** **1.** a strong, thick line or cord, made of twisted strands of hemp: [*noncount*]: *a ladder made of rope.* [*count*]: *used ropes to mark off the area.* **2.** [*count*] a lasso. **3. ropes,** [*plural*] the operations of a business: *to learn the ropes at your new job.* **4.** [*count*] *Slang.* a thick, heavy gold chain worn as jewelry. **—*v.*** **5.** [~ + *obj*] to tie or fasten with a rope. **6.** to enclose or mark off with a rope: [~ + *off* + *obj*]: *to rope off the reserved seats.* [~ + *obj* + *off*]: *to rope the seats off.* **7.** [~ + *obj*] to catch with a lasso; lasso: *roping cattle.* **8. rope in,** to lure or persuade to do something, esp. by trickery: [~ + *obj* + *in*]: *The boss roped a few of us in to stay late.* [~ + *in* + *obj*]: *The boss roped in a few workers to stay late.* **—*Idiom.*** **9. at the end of one's rope,** at the end of one's patience, strength, or will to go on. **10. on the ropes,** close to defeat, failure, or collapse: *The team had their opponents on the ropes for most of the game.*

ro•sa•ry (rō′zə rē) /'rowzəriy/ *n.* [*count*], *pl.* **-ries.** **1.** a series of prayers said by Roman Catholics, while moving the hand along beads and meditating. **2.** a string of beads used in counting these prayers. **3.** a similar string used in praying by other religious groups.

rose[1] (rōz) /rowz/ *n.* **1.** [*count*] a shrub usually with prickly stems and showy flowers. **2.** [*count*] the flower of any such shrub: *sent her a dozen roses.* **3.** [*noncount*] a pinkish red or purplish pink color typical of roses. **—*adj.*** **4.** of the color rose. **5.** [*before a noun*] for, containing, or growing roses. **6.** [*before a noun*] smelling like a rose or artificially made to smell like a rose.

rose[2] (rōz) /rowz/ *v.* pt. of RISE.

ro•sé (rō zā′) /row'zey/ *n.* a pink wine made from red grapes by removing the grape skins before fermentation is completed: [*noncount*]: *enjoys rosé.* [*count*]: *several California rosés.*

ro•se•ate (rō′zē it, -āt′) /'rowziyɪt, -,eyt/ *adj.* **1.** tinged with rose; rosy. **2.** too optimistic.

rose•bud (rōz′bud′) /'rowz,bʌd/ *n.* [*count*] the bud of a rose.

rose•bush (rōz′bo͝osh′) /'rowz,bʊʃ/ *n.* [*count*] a shrub that bears roses.

rose′-col′ored, *adj.* **1.** of the color rose; rosy. **2.** too willing to believe that good will come; too optimistic: *a rose-colored prediction of next year's economy.*

rose•mar•y (rōz′mâr′ē, -mə rē) /'rowz,mɛəriy, -məriy/

n. [*noncount*] a sweet-smelling evergreen shrub of the mint family, used as a seasoning in cooking.

ro•sette (rō zetʹ) /rowˈzɛt/ *n.* [*count*] any arrangement, part, or object resembling a rose, such as a rose-shaped arrangement of ribbon, an ornament, or a badge.

roseʹ waʹter, *n.* [*noncount*] water containing oil from roses, used in perfume and as a flavoring.

rose•wood (rōzʹwŏŏdʹ) /ˈrowzˌwʊd/ *n.* **1.** [*noncount*] a reddish wood for making cabinets, and sometimes having a roselike odor. **2.** [*count*] a tree yielding such wood.

ros•in (rozʹin) /ˈrɒzɪn/ *n.* [*noncount*] **1.** a yellowish, brittle substance that remains after removing turpentine oil from pine oil: *Rosin is used in making varnishes.* **2.** RESIN.

ros•ter (rosʹtər) /ˈrɒstər/ *n.* [*count*] **1.** a list of persons or groups, as of military units. **2.** any list, roll, or register: *a class roster.*

ros•trum (rosʹtrəm) /ˈrɒstrəm/ *n.* [*count*], *pl.* **-trums, -tra** (-trə) /-trə/. any platform, stage, or the like, for public speaking.

ros•y (rōʹzē) /ˈrowziy/ *adj.*, **-i•er, -i•est. 1.** of the color of a rose; pink or pinkish red. **2.** having a fresh, healthy redness; flushed: *rosy cheeks from vigorous exercise.* **3.** bright or promising: *a rosy future.* **4.** cheerful or optimistic: *a rosy view of the world.* —**ros•i•ly** (rōʹzə lē) /ˈrowzəliy/ *adv.* —**rosʹi•ness,** *n.* [*noncount*]

rot (rot) /rɒt/ *v.*, **rot•ted, rot•ting,** *n.*, *interj.* —*v.* **1.** to (cause to) undergo decay: [*no obj*]: *The dead leaves rotted in the soil.* [~ + *obj*]: *Overwatering will rot the houseplants.* **2.** [*no obj;* (~ + *away*)] to become weak because of decay: *The disease was taking its toll, and his body was rotting away before our eyes.* **3.** [*no obj*] to become gradually worse, as from being in jail: *hoped the killer would rot in jail.* —*n.* [*noncount*] **4.** the state of being rotten; decay. **5.** rotting or rotten matter: *dry rot.* **6.** moral or social decay or decline: *rot and corruption in the regime.* **7.** a disease caused by an infection and resulting in decay. **8.** nonsense. —*interj.* **9.** (used to express disagreement or disgust): *Oh, rot! I don't believe you!*

-rota-, *root.* -*rota*- comes from Latin, where it has the meaning "wheel." This meaning is found in such words as: OROTUND, ROTARY, ROTATE, ROTATION, ROTOGRAVURE, ROTOR, ROTUND, ROTUNDA.

ro•ta•ry (rōʹtə rē) /ˈrowtəriy/ *adj.*, *n.*, *pl.* **-ries.** —*adj.* **1.** turning on one point or an axis, such as a wheel. **2.** taking place around an axis, as motion. **3.** having a part or parts that turn on an axis: *a rotary beater.* See -ROTA-.

ro•tate (rōʹtāt) /ˈrowteyt/ *v.*, **-tat•ed, -tat•ing.** —*v.* **1.** to (cause to) turn on an axis; revolve: [*no obj*]: *The earth rotates once every twenty-four hours.* [~ + *obj*]: *rotating the Frisbee on his finger.* **2.** to (cause to) proceed in a fixed routine, as in a cycle: [*no obj*]: *The firefighters rotate in shifts: one week in the Bronx, the next week in Brooklyn.* [~ + *obj*]: *to rotate crops.* —**ro•taʹtion,** *n.* [*count; noncount*] See -ROTA-.

ROTC or **R.O.T.C.** (ärʹō tē sēʹ, rotʹsē) /ˌɑrowtiyˈsiy, ˈrɒtsiy/ Reserve Officers Training Corps.

rote (rōt) /rowt/ *n.* [*noncount*] **1.** a routine; a fixed, habitual, or mechanical procedure. —***Idiom.* 2. by rote,** from memory, without thought of the meaning: *to learn a language by rote.*

rot•gut (rotʹgutʹ) /ˈrɒtˌgʌt/ *n.* [*noncount*] *Slang.* cheap and inferior liquor.

ro•tis•ser•ie (rō tisʹə rē) /rowˈtɪsəriy/ *n.*, *v.*, **-ied, -i•ing.** —*n.* [*count*] **1.** a cooking unit having a rotating bar that distributes heat on the food, for barbecuing poultry, etc. —*v.* [~ + *obj*] **2.** to broil on a rotisserie. See -ROTA-.

ro•to•gra•vure (rōʹtə grə vyŏŏrʹ, -grāʹvyər) /ˌrowtəgrəˈvyʊr, -ˈgreyvyər/ *n.* **1.** [*noncount*] a process by which pictures, etc., are printed from a copper cylinder. **2.** [*count*] a print made by this process. **3.** [*count*] a section of a newspaper with pages printed by this process; magazine section. See -ROTA-.

ro•tor (rōʹtər) /ˈrowtər/ *n.* [*count*] a rotating part of a device, as in an electric motor or distributor. See -ROTA-.

ro•to•till•er (rōʹtə tilʹər) /ˈrowtəˌtɪlər/ *n.* [*count*] a motorized device with spinning blades that dig into the ground, used for preparing soil for crops. See -ROTA-.

rot•ten (rotʹn) /ˈrɒtn̩/ *adj.*, **-er, -est. 1.** spoiled, as from decay; putrid: *rotten eggs.* **2.** evil or morally wrong; corrupt: *Something is rotten in City Hall.* **3.** unsatisfactory; miserable: *a rotten day for walking.* **4.** worthy of contempt; despicable: *a nasty, rotten trick.* —**rotʹten•ness,** *n.* [*noncount*]

ro•tund (rō tundʹ) /rowˈtʌnd/ *adj.* rounded and fat or plump: *a rotund little man.* —**ro•tun•di•ty** (rō tunʹdi tē) /rowˈtʌndɪtiy/ **ro•tundʹness,** *n.* [*noncount*] See -ROTA-.

ro•tun•da (rō tunʹdə) /rowˈtʌndə/ *n.* [*count*], *pl.* **-das. 1.** a round building, esp. one with a dome. **2.** a large and high circular hall or room, esp. one with a dome. See -ROTA-.

rou•é (rōō āʹ, rōōʹā) /ruwˈey, ˈruwey/ *n.* [*count*], *pl.* **rou•és.** a man who lives a life of sensual pleasure.

rouge (rōōzh) /ruwʒ / *n.*, *v.*, **rouged, roug•ing.** —*n.* [*noncount*] **1.** a red powder used as a cosmetic. —*v.* [~ + *obj*] **2.** to color with rouge.

rough (ruf) /rʌf/ *adj.*, **-er, -est,** *n.*, *adv.*, *v.* —*adj.* **1.** having a coarse or uneven surface; not smooth: *rough, worn skin.* **2.** steep or uneven and covered with high grass, etc.; wild: *rough country.* **3.** acting with or marked by violence: *Hockey is a rough sport.* **4.** lacking in gentleness, care, or consideration: *rough handling.* **5.** crude, rude, or lacking culture: *a rough peasant.* **6.** difficult or unpleasant: *a rough year for consumers.* **7.** dangerous because of violence or crime: *He came from a rough neighborhood.* **8.** not perfected; unpolished: *a rough draft.* **9.** approximate; not exact: *a rough estimate.* —*n.* [*noncount*] **10.** something rough, esp. ground. **11.** part of a golf course bordering the fairway, on which the grass, weeds, etc., are not trimmed: *The ball landed in the rough.* **12.** anything in its unfinished or early form, as a drawing: *drawn in the rough.* —*adv.* **13.** in a rough manner; roughly: *I'm warning you, that mob plays rough.* —*v.* **14. rough up,** to treat (someone) with physical violence: [~ + *up* + *obj*]: *The muggers roughed up their victim.* [~ + *obj* + *up*]: *They always rough their victims up.* **15.** to make or shape roughly or in outline: [~ + *in* + *obj*]: *The designers roughed in the placement of the windows.* [~ + *out* + *obj*]: *She roughed out a few plans.* —***Idiom.* 16. rough it,** *Informal.* to live without comforts or conveniences: *roughed it in the bush for two years.* —**roughʹness,** *n.* [*noncount*]

rough•age (rufʹij) /ˈrʌfɪdʒ/ *n.* [*noncount*] **1.** FIBER (def. 5). **2.** any coarse, rough food for livestock.

roughʹ-and-readʹy, *adj.* rough, unpolished, and not yet perfect, but good enough for the purpose.

roughʹ-and-tumʹble, *adj.* **1.** of or relating to violent, disorderly struggle: *rough-and-tumble politics.* —*n.* [*noncount*] **2.** rough and unchecked competition, etc.: *the rough-and-tumble of the free-market system.*

rough•en (rufʹən) /ˈrʌfən/ *v.* to (cause to) become rough or rougher: [~ + *obj*]: *Hard manual labor had roughened his skin.* [*no obj*]: *His skin had roughened.*

roughʹ-hewnʹ or **roughʹhewnʹ,** *adj.* with rough edges or shapes; not having yet been polished or made smooth: *a rough-hewn stone fence.*

rough•house (*n.* rufʹhousʹ; *v.* also -houzʹ) / *n.* ˈrʌfˌhaws; *v.* ælsɒ -ˌhawz/ *n.* *v.*, **-housed** (-houstʹ, -houzdʹ) /-ˌhawst, -ˌhawzd/ **-hous•ing** (-houʹsing, -zing) /-ˌhawsɪŋ, -zɪŋ/. —*n.* [*noncount*] **1.** rough, disorderly playing, esp. indoors. —*v.* **2.** [*no obj*] to play in a rough, disorderly way: *roughhousing in the living room.* **3.** [~ + *obj*] to handle roughly but playfully: *to roughhouse the dog.*

rough•ly (rûfʹlē) /ˈrɜfliy/ *adv.* **1.** in a rough or violent manner: *pushing roughly through the crowd.* **2.** nearly; almost; about; approximately: *It'll cost roughly $5,000.*

rough•neck (rufʹnekʹ) /ˈrʌfˌnɛk/ *n.* [*count*] **1.** a rough, tough person: *trying to tame the roughnecks on the streets.* **2.** a laborer working on an oil-drilling rig.

rough•shod (rufʹshodʹ) /ˈrʌfˈʃɒd/ *adj.* **1.** having horseshoes with nails or points that stick out. —***Idiom.* 2. ride roughshod over,** [~ + *obj*] to treat harshly, esp. in order to advance oneself: *She was willing to ride roughshod over her competitors to gain the promotion.*

rou•lette (rōō letʹ) /ruwˈlɛt/ *n.* [*noncount*] a game of chance in which a small ball is spun on a dishlike device **(rouletteʹ wheelʹ)**, with players betting on which of the slots the ball will rest.

round (round) /rawnd/ *adj.*, **-er, -est,** *n.*, *adv.*, *prep.*, *v.* —*adj.* **1.** having a flat, circular form, such as a disk or hoop: *The round moon shone down from the sky.* **2.** shaped like a ball or globe: *The earth is round.* **3.** shaped like a long tube; cylindrical: *a round smokestack.* **4.** made of or having full, curved lines: *He had a round face and round cheeks.* **5.** [*before a noun*] full or complete: *a round dozen.* **6.** [*before a noun*] expressed to the nearest multiple or power of ten: *In round numbers, the house cost $350,000.* —*n.* [*count*] **7.** a complete course or series, one following the other: *The next round of peace talks was held in Geneva.* **8.** Often, **rounds.** [*plural*] a going around from place to place, as in a definite direction: *The doctor made her rounds in the children's hospital.* **9.** a completed spell of activity in games or sport: *a round of bridge.* **10.** a single outburst, as of cheers: *a round of applause.* **11.** a firing of, or a piece of ammunition for, a gun, etc.: *fired a few rounds at the enemy.* **12.** a single serving, esp. of drink, to everyone present: *bought the next round of drinks.* **13.** a short piece of music in which different voices or instruments begin the melody at different times. **—***adv.* **14.** from the beginning to the end of a period of time: *We can go camping there all year round.* **15.** Also, **'round.** around. **—***prep.* **16.** throughout (a period of time): *a resort visited round the year.* **17.** around: *It happened round noon.* **—***v.* **18.** to bring to completeness; finish: [~ + *obj*]: *to round one's speech with a quotation from Samuel Johnson.* [~ + *off/out* + *obj*]: *You need to round off your essay with a strong conclusion.* [~ + *obj* + *off/out*]: *to round the essay out.* **19.** [~ + *obj*] to make a circuit around or to the other side of: *The car rounded the corner.* **20.** [*no obj*] to turn on an axis: *He rounded suddenly on his heels and faced her.* **21.** [~ + *obj*] to make a complete circuit of; pass around. **22.** to (cause to) become somewhat round: [~ + *obj*]: *He rounded his lips and tried to whistle.* [*no obj*]: *Her eyes rounded in amazement.* **23.** to express (an amount) as a number, esp. to replace it by the nearest multiple of 10: [~ + *obj*]: *Round your answer to the nearest ten's number.* [~ + *off* + *obj*]: *You can round off 15,837 to 15,840.* [~ + *obj* + *off*]: *to round it off.* **24. round out,** [*no obj*] to become rounder or more full in shape: *As she grew older she rounded out from the skinny tomboy she had been.* **25. round up, a.** to drive or bring (cattle, etc.) together: [~ + *up* + *obj*]: *to round up the cattle.* [~ + *obj* + *up*]: *Go and round the cattle up.* **b.** to assemble; gather: [~ + *up* + *obj*]: *Round up the likeliest suspects.* [~ + *obj* + *up*]: *to round the evidence up.* **—*Idiom.* 26. in the round, a.** (of a theater) having a stage surrounded by the audience. **b.** in complete detail; from all aspects. **27. make the rounds, a.** to go from one place to another, as in looking for work or a job: *She made the usual rounds but found nothing.* **b.** Also, **go the rounds.** (of a rumor, story, etc.) to spread from one person to another: *the latest theory making the rounds.* —**round′ish,** *adj.* —**round′ness,** *n.* [*noncount*]

round•a•bout (*adj.* round′ə bout′, round′ə bout′; *n.* round′ə bout′) / *adj.* ˌrawndəˈbawt, ˈrawndəˌbawt; *n.* ˈrawndəˌbawt/ *adj.* **1.** not straight or direct: *In his roundabout way he was saying he cared for her.* **—***n.* [*count*] *Brit.* **2.** a traffic circle: *Stay to your left at the next roundabout.* **3.** a merry-go-round.

round•house (round′hous′) /ˈrawndˌhaws/ *n.* [*count*] **1.** a building for the servicing and repair of locomotives, built around a turntable in the form of some part of a circle. **2.** a punch delivered with a wild or exaggerated circular motion.

round•ly (round′lē) /ˈrawndliy/ *adv.* **1.** in a round manner. **2.** outspokenly or severely: *He criticized her roundly.* **3.** completely or fully: *roundly defeated.* **4.** in round numbers or in a vague or general way.

round′-shoul′dered, *adj.* having the shoulders bent forward, giving a rounded form to the upper back.

round′ ta′ble, *n.* [*count*] **1.** a number of people gathered for a discussion of a subject on equal terms. **2.** the discussion, topic of discussion, or conference itself. Also, **round′ta′ble**. —**round′-ta′ble,** *adj.*: *round-table discussions.*

round′-the-clock′, *adj.* held or done all day and all night; around-the-clock: *round-the-clock negotiations.*

round′ trip′, *n.* [*count*] a trip to a certain place and back again. —**round′-trip′,** *adj.*: *a round-trip ticket.*

round•up (round′up′) /ˈrawndˌʌp/ *n.* [*count*] **1. a.** the driving together of cattle, etc., for branding, etc. **b.** the people and horses who do this. **2.** the gathering of scattered items or people: *a police roundup of suspects.* **3.** a summary or brief listing of information: *a sports roundup on the evening news.*

rouse (rouz) /rawz/ *v.,* **roused, rous•ing. 1.** to (cause to) come out of a state of sleep, unconsciousness, etc.: [~ + *obj*]: *tried to rouse her but she was still unconscious.* [*no obj*]: *She wouldn't rouse.* **2.** [~ + *obj*] to cause excitement, indignation, or anger in: *His speech roused the people from their apathy.*

rous•ing (rou′zing) /ˈrawzɪŋ/ *adj.* **1.** exciting; causing excitement or interest: *a rousing speech.* **2.** active; lively: *a rousing business.*

rout[1] (rout) /rawt/ *n.* **1.** a defeat, followed by disorderly retreat: [*noncount*]: *to put an army to rout.* [*count*]: *The last game was a rout.* **—***v.* [~ + *obj*] **2.** to defeat completely, causing a disorderly retreat: *Our team routed our last two opponents.* See -RUPT-.

rout[2] (rout) /rawt/ *v.* [~ + *obj*] **1.** to turn over or dig up (something) with the snout. **2.** to find or get by searching, rummaging, forcing out, etc.

route (ro͞ot, rout) /ruwt, rawt/ *n., v.,* **rout•ed, rout•ing. —***n.* [*count*] **1.** a course, way, or road for travel: *the shortest route from here to Alaska.* **2.** a customary line of travel, often with stops regularly made, by a train, bus, etc., or by a person in doing a job: *the route taken by that bus; a newspaper route.* **—***v.* [~ + *obj*] **3.** to fix the path or route of: *to route a tour.* **4.** to send by a particular route: *Calls were routed through the switchboard.* See -RUPT-.

rou•tine (ro͞o tēn′) /ruwˈtiyn/ *n.* **1.** a regular course of procedure: [*noncount*]: *normal office routine.* [*count*]: *the baby's usual routines of waking, eating, playing, and sleeping.* **2.** [*noncount*] boring procedure done without thinking: *the dull routine of the assembly line.* **3.** [*count*] a set of instructions directing a computer to perform a certain task. **4.** [*count*] a rehearsed act or performance: *a comic routine.* **5.** [*count*] an often repeated behavior or speech: *that tired old routine of making excuses.* **—***adj.* **6.** of the nature of routine: *routine work.* **7.** dull or uninteresting; commonplace: *routine boredom.* —**rou•tine′ly,** *adv.*: *routinely brownbagged his lunch.* See -RUPT-.

rove (rōv) /rowv/ *v.,* **roved, rov•ing.** to move here and there at random: [~ + *obj*]: *to rove the subways, looking for victims.* [*no obj*]: *to rove in the woods.* —**rov′er,** *n.* [*count*]

row[1] (rō) /row/ *n.* [*count*] **1.** a number of people or things in a line: *the rows of customers.* **2.** a line of seats facing the same way, as in a theater: *seats in the front row.* **—*Idiom.* 3. in a row, a.** lined up one after the other or side by side: *all in a row, waiting to go forward.* **b.** happening one after the other without interruption: *The team lost seven games in a row.*

row[2] (rō) /row/ *v.* **1.** to move a vessel by the use of oars: [*no obj*]: *rowing into a stiff breeze.* [~ + *obj*]: *He rowed the boat out to his favorite spot.* **2.** [~ + *obj*] to transport (someone) in a boat that is rowed: *I rowed her back to shore.* **—***n.* [*count*] **3.** an act or period of rowing. **4.** a trip in a rowboat. —**row′er,** *n.* [*count*]

row[3] (rou) /raw/ *n.* **1.** [*count*] a noisy argument; commotion. **—***v.* [*no obj*] **2.** to quarrel or argue noisily.

row•boat (rō′bōt′) /ˈrowˌbowt/ *n.* [*count*] a small boat designed for rowing.

row•dy (rou′dē) /ˈrawdiy/ *adj.,* **-di•er, -di•est,** *n., pl.* **-dies. —***adj.* **1.** rough and disorderly: *rowdy behavior.* **—***n.* [*count*] **2.** a rough, disorderly person: *The town rowdies were waiting for him.* —**row′di•ness,** *n.* [*noncount*] —**row′dy•ism,** *n.* [*noncount*]

row′ house′ (rō) /row/ *n.* [*count*] one of a row of very similar houses, each of which has at least one sidewall in common with the neighboring house.

roy•al (roi′əl) /ˈrɔyəl/ *adj.* [*before a noun*] **1.** of or relating to royalty: *a royal prince.* **2.** fit for a king or queen; magnificent: *a royal banquet.* **3.** *Informal.* extreme; completely so: *He is a royal pain in the neck.* **—***n.* [*count*] **4.** *Informal.* a royal person; member of the royalty. —**roy′al•ly,** *adv.* See -REG-.

roy•al•ist (roi′ə list) /ˈrɔyəlɪst/ *n.* [*count*] **1.** a supporter of royalty. **—***adj.* **2.** of or relating to royalists. See -REG-.

roy•al•ty (roi′əl tē) /ˈrɔyəltiy/ *n., pl.* **-ties. 1.** [*noncount*] royal people thought of as a group. **2.** [*noncount*] royal rank, dignity, or power. **3.** [*count*] an agreed portion of the money earned from a piece of writing, music, etc., paid to its author, composer, etc. See -REG-.

rpm or **r.p.m.,** an abbreviation of: revolutions per minute.

rps or **r.p.s.,** an abbreviation of: revolutions per second.

RR or **R.R.,** an abbreviation of: **1.** railroad. **2.** rural route.

RSFSR or **R.S.F.S.R.,** an abbreviation of: Russian Soviet Federated Socialist Republic.

RSV, an abbreviation of: Revised Standard Version.

RSVP, an abbreviation used on an invitation to indicate that a reply is requested.

rte., an abbreviation of: route.

rub (rub) /rʌb/ *v.,* **rubbed, rub•bing,** *n.* **—***v.* **1.** to put friction on (something), as in polishing or massaging: [~ + *obj*]: *He rubbed the silver teapot with a cloth and some polish.* [*no obj*]: *He rubbed until the silver shone.* [~ + *on/against* + *obj*]: *The noise you hear is the mechanism rubbing against something.* **2.** [~ + *obj*] to move, spread, or apply with friction over something: *to rub lotion on chapped hands.* **3.** [~ + *obj*] to move (two things) with pressure and friction over each other: *He rubbed his hands together.* **4.** to remove or erase by pressure and friction: [~ + *off/out* + *obj*]: *She rubbed out the wrong answer with an eraser.* [*no obj*]: *Chalk rubs off easily.* **5. rub down, a.** to smooth, polish, or clean by rubbing: [~ + *down* + *obj*]: *to rub down the door.* [~ + *obj* + *down*]: *to rub the door down.* **b.** to massage: [~ + *down* + *obj*]: *to rub down the horse after the race.* [~ + *obj* + *down*]: *to rub the horse down.* **6. rub off on,** [~ + *off* + *on* + *obj*] to pass along to, as or as if by touching: *Her talent for biology rubbed off on her daughters.* **7. rub out, a.** to erase: [~ + *out* + *obj*]: *He rubbed out the wrong answer.* [~ + *obj* + *out*]: *to rub the answer out.* **b.** *Slang.* to murder: [~ + *obj* + *out*]: *The rival clans were rubbing each other out.* [~ + *out* + *obj*]: *threatening to rub out anyone who informs on them.* **—*n.*** [*count*] **8.** an act or instance of rubbing: *an alcohol rub.* **9.** [*singular; the* + ~] an annoying experience or circumstance: *You need experience to get hired, but here's the rub: how can you get experience if no one hires you?* **—*Idiom.* 10. rub elbows** or **shoulders with,** [~ + *obj*] to associate or mix socially with: *rubbing shoulders with the important people in Washington.* **11. rub it in,** [*no obj*] to repeat something unpleasant to tease or annoy: *kept rubbing it in about how I tripped going up on the stage.* **12. rub (someone) the wrong way,** to irritate; offend; annoy: *His laugh rubbed her the wrong way.*

rub•ber[1] (rub′ər) /'rʌbər/ *n.* **1.** [*noncount*] a highly elastic solid from the milky juice of rubber trees. **2.** [*noncount*] natural rubber treated to make it tougher, longer-wearing, etc., or a similar substance and material made synthetically. **3.** [*count*] an eraser made of this material. **4.** [*count; usually plural*] a low overshoe of this material: *He wore his rubbers when it rained.* **5.** RUBBER BAND. **6.** [*count*] an instrument or tool used for rubbing, etc. **7.** [*count*] *Slang.* a condom. **—*adj.*** [*before a noun*] **8.** made of, containing, or coated with rubber. **9.** of or relating to rubber: *a rubber plant.*

rub•ber[2] (rub′ər) /'rʌbər/ *n.* [*count*] **1.** (in bridge) a series or round played until one side has won two out of three games. **2.** Also called **rub′ber match′.** a deciding contest when a series of games or matches is tied.

rub′ber band′, *n.* [*count*] a narrow circular band of rubber, used for holding papers or other things together.

rub•ber•neck (rub′ər nek′) /'rʌbər,nɛk/ *Informal.* **—*v.*** [*no obj*] **1.** to stare with curiosity, as by twisting the neck or turning the head: *Many of the drivers were rubbernecking at the accident on the side of the road.* **—*n.*** Also, **rub′ber•neck′er.** [*count*] **2.** a curious onlooker.

rub′ber stamp′, *n.* [*count*] **1.** a device with a rubber printing surface that is coated with ink by pressing it on an ink pad, used for imprinting names, etc. **2.** a government agency, etc., that gives approval automatically or routinely.

rub′ber-stamp′, *v.* [~ + *obj*] to give automatic approval to: *The agency rubber-stamped his application.*

rub•ber•y (rûb′ə rē) /'rɜbəriy/ *adj.*, **-i•er, -i•est. 1.** of or like rubber: *rubbery meat.* **2.** not firm; too soft: *His legs got rubbery.*

rub•bish (rub′ish) /'rʌbɪʃ/ *n.* [*noncount*] **1.** worthless material that is thrown out; trash: *piles of rubbish.* **2.** nonsense, as in writing or art: *sentimental rubbish.* **—rub′bish•y,** *adj.*

rub•ble (rub′əl) /'rʌbəl/ *n.* [*noncount*] broken bits and pieces of anything, esp. something demolished: *Bombing reduced the town to rubble.*

rub•down (rub′doun′) /'rʌb,dawn/ *n.* [*count*] a massage.

rube (ro͞ob) /ruwb/ *n.* [*count*] *Informal.* a person not used to city ways; an unsophisticated person.

ru•bel•la (ro͞o bel′ə) /ruw'bɛlə/ *n.* [*noncount*] a usually mild infection caused by a virus, with a fever, cough, and a red rash. Also called **German measles.**

ru•bi•cund (ro͞o′bi kund′) /'ruwbɪ,kʌnd/ *adj.* red or reddish; ruddy.

ru•ble or **rou•ble** (ro͞o′bəl) /'ruwbəl/ *n.* [*count*] the basic monetary unit used in Russia.

ru•bric (ro͞o′brik) /'ruwbrɪk/ *n.* [*count*] **1.** a title, heading, etc., in a manuscript, book, etc., printed in red or otherwise distinguished from the rest of the text. **2.** any established procedure: *an international rubric for treating war prisoners.* **3.** a class or category: *coming under the rubric of heavy weapons.*

ru•by (ro͞o′bē) /'ruwbiy/ *n., pl.* **-bies,** *adj.* **—*n.* 1.** [*count*] a red stone used as a gem. **2.** [*noncount*] a deep red. **—*adj.* 3.** ruby-colored. **4.** containing or set with a ruby or rubies.

ruck•sack (ruk′sak′, ro͝ok′-) /'rʌk,sæk, 'rʊk-/ *n.* [*count*] a type of knapsack carried by hikers, bicyclists, etc.

ruck•us (ruk′əs) /'rʌkəs/ *n.* [*count; usually singular*] **1.** a noisy commotion; uproar: *a ruckus on the street below.* **2.** a heated controversy: *The ruckus was over abortion rights.*

rud•der (rud′ər) /'rʌdər/ *n.* [*count*] **1.** a vertical blade at the rear of a ship or plane that can be turned to control direction. **2.** any means of directing or guiding a course. **—rud′der•less,** *adj.*

rud•dy (rud′ē) /'rʌdiy/ *adj.*, **-di•er, -di•est. 1.** having a healthy red color: *a ruddy complexion.* **2.** red or reddish: *a ruddy face after all that drinking.* **3.** [*before a noun*] *Brit. Slang.* damned: *a ruddy fool.* **—rud′di•ness,** *n.* [*noncount*]

rude (ro͞od) /ruwd/ *adj.*, **rud•er, rud•est. 1.** impolite, esp. deliberately so: *a rude reply.* **2.** without culture, learning, or refinement; uncouth. **3.** [*before a noun*] rough, harsh, or ungentle: *a rude shock.* **4.** [*before a noun*] roughly built or made: *a rude cottage.* **—rude′ly,** *adv.*: *He answered rudely that he didn't give a damn.* **—rude′ness,** *n.* [*noncount*]

ru•di•ment (ro͞o′də mənt) /'ruwdəmənt/ *n.* Usually, **rudiments.** [*plural*] **1.** the elements of a subject: *the rudiments of grammar.* **2.** a beginning, first appearance, or imperfect form of something: *the rudiments of a plan forming in his mind.*

ru•di•men•ta•ry (ro͞o′də men′tə rē) /,ruwdə'mɛntəriy/ *adj.* of or relating to rudiments: *a rudimentary knowledge of geometry.*

rue (ro͞o) /ruw/ *v.*, **rued, ru•ing,** *n.* **—*v.*** [~ + *obj*] **1.** to feel sorrow over; regret bitterly: *He rued the loss of the opportunity to marry her.* **2.** to wish that (something) had never been done or taken place: *He rued the day he was born.* **—*n.*** [*noncount*] **3.** sorrow or regret.

rue•ful (ro͞o′fəl) /'ruwfəl/ *adj.* **1.** feeling or expressing sorrow or pity: *The loser had a rueful look on his face.* **2.** causing sorrow or pity: *a rueful plight of starvation.* **—rue′ful•ly,** *adv.*: *smiled ruefully as he said good-bye.*

ruff (ruf) /rʌf/ *n.* [*count*] **1.** a collar of lace, gathered into deep, full, regular folds, worn in the 16th and 17th centuries. **2.** a collar, or set of marked hairs or feathers, on the neck of an animal. **—ruffed,** *adj.*

ruf•fi•an (ruf′ē ən, ruf′yən) /'rʌfiyən, 'rʌfyən/ *n.* [*count*] a tough, violent person; a bully.

ruf•fle (ruf′əl) /'rʌfəl/ *v.*, **-fled, -fling,** *n.* **—*v.* 1.** [~ + *obj*] to interfere with the smoothness of: *The wind began to ruffle the calm surface of the sea.* **2.** [~ + *obj*] to cause the feathers to stand up straight, as a bird in anger: *to ruffle a bird's feathers.* **3.** [~ + *obj*] to disturb or irritate: *ruffled from all the interruptions.* **4.** to turn (pages) rapidly: [~ + *obj*]: *idly ruffling pages of the book.* [*no obj*]: *idly ruffling through the book.* **—*n.*** [*count*] **5.** a break in the smoothness or evenness of a surface. **6.** a strip of cloth, etc., gathered along one edge and used as a trimming on a dress, etc. **7.** something resembling this, as the ruff of a bird. **—*Idiom.* 8. ruffle someone's feathers,** to upset or annoy someone: *If you don't speak politely to him, you'll ruffle his feathers and get him angrier.*

rug (rug) /rʌg/ *n.* [*count*] **1.** a piece of thick fabric for covering part of a floor. **2.** *Chiefly Brit.* a piece of thick, warm cloth, used as a covering for the lap. **3.** *Slang.* a wig, toupee, or hairpiece.

rug•by (rug′bē) /'rʌgbiy/ *n.* [*noncount*] a form of football played between two teams of 13 or 15 members each: *In rugby there is continuous action and no substituting of players.* Also called **Rug′by foot′ball.**

rug•ged (rug′id) /'rʌgɪd/ *adj.* **1.** having a roughly broken or jagged surface: *a rugged mountain.* **2.** roughly irregular or hard in form, as by having wrinkles: *a man's rugged features.* **3.** rough, harsh, or severe: *a rugged life.* **4.** capable of lasting through hardship, wear, etc.: *a rugged, durable car.* **5.** requiring great strength, ability, patience, etc.: *a rugged test.* **—rug′ged•ly,** *adv.*: *She found the farmer ruggedly handsome.* **—rug′ged•ness,** *n.* [*noncount*]

ru•in (ro͞o′in) /'ruwɪn/ *n.* **1. ruins,** [*plural*] the remains of a building, etc., destroyed or in decay: *the ruins of Troy.* **2.** [*count*] a destroyed or decayed building, etc.: *toured the ruin of the apartment house after the earthquake.* **3.** [*noncount*] a fallen, wrecked, or decayed condition: *The house fell into ruin.* **4.** [*noncount*] the complete loss of health, means, money, etc.: *We'd sunk into financial ruin.* **5.** [*noncount*] something that causes a downfall or destruction: *Alcohol was his ruin.* —*v.* [~ + *obj*] **6.** to reduce to ruin; destroy: *Her smoking is ruining her health.* **7.** to bring to financial ruin; bankrupt: *Another lawsuit like that and I'll be ruined.* —**ru•in•a•tion** (ro͞o′i nā′shən) /ˌruwɪˈneyʃən/ *n.* [*noncount*]

ru•in•ous (ro͞o′ən əs) /ˈruwənəs/ *adj.* bringing or likely to cause ruin: *a ruinous war.* —**ru′in•ous•ly,** *adv.*: *Moving to another town would have been ruinously expensive.*

rule (ro͞ol) /ruwl/ *n., v.,* **ruled, rul•ing.** —*n.* **1.** [*count*] a principle guiding how one behaves, the way things are done, etc.: *a rule in hockey saying to eject anyone fighting.* **2.** [*count*] the customary occurrence, practice, etc.; the normal way something is done: *Her being late is the rule rather than the exception.* **3.** [*noncount*] government; amount of time ruling: *in the days of foreign rule.* **4.** [*count*] the code of regulations observed by a religious congregation. **5.** RULER (def. 2). —*v.* **6.** to use power, authority, or influence over: [~ + *obj*]: *to rule a kingdom.* [*no obj*]: *to rule for only a decade.* **7.** to decide in a court of law or by some authority; decree: [*no obj*]: *How will the court rule?* [~ + *on* + *obj*]: *The court will rule on the matter at its next session.* [~ + *(that) clause*]: *The court ruled that she could not keep her baby.* **8.** [~ + *obj*] to mark with lines, esp. parallel straight lines, with the aid of a ruler: *to rule paper.* **9.** [~ + *obj*] to be superior in (a group), so as to hold influence over. **10.** [~ + *obj*] to influence or control: *sometimes ruled by passion and not by logic.* **11. rule out,** to eliminate from thinking about; to decide to ignore: [~ + *out* + *obj*]: *We can rule out the possibility of an overnight improvement in the economy.* [~ + *obj* + *out*]: *We can't rule it out completely.* —***Idiom.*** **12. as a rule,** generally; usually: *He's there by 7:30 as a rule.*

ruled (ro͞old) /ruwld/ *adj.* [*before a noun*] having lines: *clean sheets of ruled paper for practicing penmanship.*

rule′ of thumb′, *n.* [*count*] a general rule based on experience, and not taken from scientific reasoning: *As a rule of thumb I add a spoonful of salt.*

rul•er (ro͞o′lər) /ˈruwlər/ *n.* [*count*] **1.** one who rules or governs, as a king, queen, president, etc. **2.** Also, **rule.** a strip of wood or other material that has a straight edge and is marked off in inches or centimeters, used for drawing lines and measuring. See illustration at SCHOOL.

rul•ing (ro͞o′ling) /ˈruwlɪŋ/ *n.* [*count*] **1.** a decision, as one by a judge: *The judge handed down the ruling.* —*adj.* [*before a noun*] **2.** governing or dominating: *the current ruling party.* **3.** influencing the most or influencing strongly: *the ruling factor.*

rum[1] (rum) /rʌm/ *n.* [*noncount*] an alcoholic liquor made from molasses.

rum[2] (rum) /rʌm/ *adj. Chiefly Brit.* **1.** odd, strange, or unusual: *a rum fellow.* **2.** causing problems; difficult.

rum•ba (rum′bə, ro͝om′-, ro͞om′-) /ˈrʌmbə, ˈrʊm-, ˈruwm-/ *n., pl.* **-bas** (-bəz) /-bəz/ *v.,* **-baed** (-bəd) /-bəd/ **-ba•ing** (-bə ing) /-bəɪŋ/. —*n.* [*count*] **1.** a ballroom dance that is Cuban in origin, notable for its complex rhythm and swaying hip motion. —*v.* [*no obj*] **2.** to dance the rumba.

rum•ble (rum′bəl) /ˈrʌmbəl/ *v.,* **-bled, -bling,** *n.* —*v.* **1.** [*no obj*] to make a deep, rolling and continuous sound, such as thunder: *The thunder rumbled in the distance. His stomach rumbled from hunger.* **2.** [*no obj*] to move or travel with such a sound: *The heavy planes rumbled down the runway.* **3.** to say or give out with a rumbling sound: [*no obj*]: *rumbling about the high price of gas.* [*used with quotations*]: *"Just a minute, just a minute," he rumbled.* **4.** [*no obj*] *Slang.* to take part in a street fight between teenage gangs. —*n.* [*count*] **5.** a rumbling sound. **6.** *Slang.* a street fight between teenage gangs.

rum•bling (rum′bling) /ˈrʌmblɪŋ/ *n.* [*count*] **1.** Often, **rumblings.** [*plural*] the first signs of dissatisfaction: *The rumblings from the electorate were clear.* **2.** RUMBLE (def. 5).

ru•mi•nant (ro͞o′mə nənt) /ˈruwmənənt/ *n.* [*count*] **1.** an animal that normally brings back food from its stomach into its mouth and chews it again: *Ruminants include cows, sheep, and goats.* —*adj.* **2.** of or being a ruminant.

ru•mi•nate (ro͞o′mə nāt′) /ˈruwməˌneyt/ *v.,* **-nat•ed, -nat•ing.** —*v.* **1.** to chew food brought back from the stomach into the mouth, as a ruminant animal does: [*no obj*]: *ruminating in the pasture.* [~ + *obj*]: *to ruminate their food.* **2.** to think deeply (about); ponder: [*no obj*]: *ruminating in his study.* [~ + *obj*]: *ruminating the problem.* —**ru•mi•na•tion** (ro͞o′mə mā′shən) /ˌruwməˈmeyʃən/ *n.* [*noncount; count*]

rum•mage (rum′ij) /ˈrʌmɪdʒ/ *v.,* **-maged, -mag•ing,** *n.* —*v.* **1.** to search thoroughly through (a place, etc.), esp. by moving around, turning over, or looking through contents: [*no obj*]: *to rummage through the drawers.* [~ + *obj*]: *to rummage the house for those papers.* —*n.* [*noncount*] **2.** a jumble of things; odds and ends.

rum′mage sale′, *n.* [*count*] a sale of old things, esp. to raise money for charity.

rum•my (rum′ē) /ˈrʌmiy/ *n.* [*noncount*] any of various card games for several players, in which the object is to match cards into sets and sequences: *a game of rummy.*

ru•mor (ro͞o′mər) /ˈruwmər/ *n.* **1.** [*count*] a story that has no solid basis and is not known to be true: *lots of rumors of war.* **2.** [*noncount*] gossip; hearsay: *a lot of rumor and gossip.* —*v.* [~ + *obj; usually: it* + *be* + ~*-ed* + *(that) clause*] **3.** to report, circulate, or claim by a rumor: *It's been rumored that their country will invade its neighbor to the north.* Also, *esp. Brit.,* **ru′mour.**

rump (rump) /rʌmp/ *n.* [*count*] **1.** the hind part of the body of an animal. **2.** a cut of beef from this part of the animal. **3.** the buttocks. **4.** the remaining part of a lawmaking body, etc., after a majority of the members have resigned or been removed.

rum•ple (rum′pəl) /ˈrʌmpəl/ *v.,* **-pled, -pling,** *n.* —*v.* [~ + *obj*] **1.** to crumple or crush into wrinkles: *He rumpled the paper and threw it toward the trashcan.* **2.** to ruffle; tousle: *The wind rumpled her hair.* —*n.* [*count*] **3.** a wrinkle or crease. —**rum′ply,** *adj.,* **-pli•er, -pli•est.**

rum•pus (rum′pəs) /ˈrʌmpəs/ *n.* [*count*] **1.** a noisy or violent uproar. **2.** a noisy or loud argument.

run (run) /rʌn/ *v.,* **ran** (ran) /ræn/ **run, run•ning,** *n.* —*v.* **1.** [*no obj*] to go quickly by moving the legs more rapidly than at a walk: *He ran down the street.* **2.** [~ + *obj*] to perform by or as if by running: *She ran an errand.* **3.** [~ + *obj*] to go or cross (a distance) in running: *He ran the mile in under four minutes.* **4.** [~ + *obj*] to enter in a race: *She ran her horse in the last race.* **5.** [~ + *obj*] to pass something (over or through) quickly: *He ran his fingers lightly over the keyboard.* **6.** [*no obj*] to go to for aid, etc.: *He is always running to his parents.* **7.** [*no obj*] to make a quick trip or visit: *to run to the supermarket.* **8.** [~ + *obj*] to carry or transport: *I'll run you home in my car.* **9.** to (cause to) move freely: [*no obj*]: *At least here the dog can run around in the park.* [~ + *obj*]: *Take the dog and run him around the track.* **10.** to (cause to) move forward: [*no obj*]: *The ball ran into the street.* [~ + *obj*]: *The golfer ran the ball too far and it rolled off the green.* **11.** to (cause to) be a candidate for election: [*no obj*]: *She's running for vice president.* [~ + *obj*]: *The party ran its best candidates in the last election.* **12.** (of a ship, car, etc.) to (cause to) be sailed or driven from a proper or given route: [*no obj*]: *The ship ran aground.* [~ + *obj*]: *The driver ran the car up onto the curb.* **13.** to (cause to) go back and forth between places or along a certain route: [*no obj*]: *The bus runs between New Haven and Hartford.* [~ + *obj*]: *The company runs ferries between New York and Hoboken.* **14.** to (cause to) unravel, as stitches or a fabric: [*no obj*]: *Her stockings ran when she knelt down quickly.* [~ + *obj*]: *to run the stocking.* **15.** to (cause to) flow in or as if in a stream: [*no obj*]: *Tears ran from her eyes. Her nose was running.* [~ + *obj*]: *He ran some hot water into the tub.* **16.** [*no obj*] (of colors) to spread to other things: *The colors in your blouse will run if you use hot water.* **17.** to (cause to) operate or function: [*no obj*]: *How is the office running these days?* [~ + *obj*]: *Run the dishwasher again and let's see if it works.* **18.** [~ + *obj*] to manage or conduct: *to run a business.* **19.** [*no obj*] to be within a range of a certain size, number, etc.: *The grades on the last exam ran from B + to F.* **20.** [*no obj*] to (cause to) meet or endure a certain condition: *to run into trouble.* **21.** [~ + *to* + *obj*] to tend to have a specified quality, form, etc.: *This novel runs to long descriptions.* **22.** [*no obj*] to be stated or worded: *The text runs as follows.* **23.** [~ + *to* + *obj*] to amount; total: *The bill ran to $100.* **24.** [~ + *obj*] to cost (an amount): *This watch runs $30 or so.* **25.** [~ + *obj* + *obj*] to cost (a person) an amount: *The car repair will run you $90.* **26.** [*not: be* + ~*-ing; no obj*] to continue, extend, stretch, or last: *The story runs for eight pages.* **27.** [~ + *obj*] to put so as to extend in a particular direction: *to run the television cable under the road.* **28.** to (cause to) appear in print: [*no obj*]: *The story ran in all the papers.* [~ + *obj*]: *The newspaper ran the story on page 1.* **29.** to (cause to) be performed: [*no obj*]: *The play ran for two years.* [~ + *obj*]: *to run the movie for two years until it made a profit.* **30.** [*no obj*] to occur again through time: *Musical ability runs in my family.* **31.** [~ + *obj*] to get past or through without stopping: *to run a blockade.* **32.** [~ + *obj*] to process (the instructions in a program) by computer: *For* *some reason the computer runs the program but then stops.* **33.** [~ + *obj*] to place oneself in danger, at risk, etc.: *running some big risks.* **34.** [~ + *obj*] to drive, force, or thrust: *ran the sword through his opponent's heart.* **35. run across,** [~ + *across* + *obj*] to meet or find accidentally: *I ran across an old friend.* **36. run after,** [~ + *after* + *obj*] **a.** to chase or pursue: *The police ran after the thief.* **b.** to try to gain or obtain: *to run after wealth.* **37. run along,** [*no obj*] to leave; go away: *Run along, children, and play outside.* **38. run around,** [*no obj*] **a.** to be involved in many different activities. **b.** to have more than one romantic involvement. **39. run away,** [*no obj*] to flee, esp. with no intent to return: *The three-year-old said she was going to run away.* **40. run away with,** [~ + *away* + *with* + *obj*] **a.** to go away with, esp. to marry: *Her husband ran away with another woman.* **b.** to steal: *to run away with all the money.* **c.** to get by surpassing others, as a prize: *ran away with all the prizes.* **d.** to overwhelm; get the better of: *Sometimes his enthusiasm runs away with him.* **41. run down, a.** to strike and overturn, esp. with a vehicle: [~ + *obj* + *down*]: *He accidentally ran the child down.* [~ + *down* + *obj*]: *He ran down the child.* **b.** to chase after and seize: [~ + *down* + *obj*]: *to run down criminals.* [~ + *obj* + *down*]: *to run them down and catch them.* **c.** [~ + *down* + *obj*] to read through quickly: *He ran down the list of figures.* **d.** [*no obj*] to cease operation; stop: *The battery ran down in just a few hours.* **e.** to speak badly about (someone): [~ + *down* + *obj*]: *always running down his friends.* [~ + *obj* + *down*]: *always running me down.* **f.** to search out; find: [~ + *down* + *obj*]: *to run down some leads in the murder case.* [~ + *obj* + *down*]: *to run some leads down.* **42. run in,** *Informal.* to arrest: [~ + *in* + *obj*]: *The police officers ran in all the usual suspects.* [~ + *obj* + *in*]: *promised he'd run me in if he ever caught me again.* **43. run into,** [~ + *obj*] **a.** to collide with: *We ran into each other and fell.* **b.** to meet accidentally: *ran into an old friend just the other day.* **c.** *Informal.* to amount to; total: *This project could run into the millions.* **44. run off, a.** [*no obj*] to leave quickly; run away: *ran off before I could thank her.* **b.** to create quickly and easily: [~ + *off* + *obj*]: *to run off a term paper in an hour.* [~ + *obj* + *off*]: *ran his rehearsed answers off quickly in the debate.* **c.** to drive away; expel: [~ + *off* + *obj*]: *ran off the pesky stray dog.* [~ + *obj* + *off*]: *ran the stray dog off.* **d.** to print, print out, or duplicate: [~ + *off* + *obj*]: *to run off 500 copies.* [~ + *obj* + *off*]: *to run a few copies off.* **45. run off with,** [~ + *off* + *with* + *obj*] **a.** to steal; abscond with: *running off with the money.* **b.** to leave suddenly with, so as to marry or have an affair with: *ran off with the mayor's wife.* **46. run on,** [*no obj*] to continue without relief or interruption: *He ran on about his computer so long that I was bored stiff.* **47. run out, a.** [*no obj*] to come to an end; to be finished: *My visa has run out.* **b.** [*no obj*] to become used up; to have no more: *The fuel has run out.* **c.** [~ + *obj* + *out*] to drive out; expel: *could run us out with threats or intimidation.* **48. run out of,** [~ + *out* + *of* + *obj*] to use up a supply of: *We've run out of wood; how will we make a fire?* **49. run over, a.** to hit with a vehicle, esp. when severe injury or death results: [~ + *over* + *obj*]: *The car ran over several people in the park.* [~ + *obj* + *over*]: *The driver ran the child over.* **b.** [~ + *over* + *obj*] to go beyond; exceed: *His speech ran over the time limit.* **c.** [~ + *over* + *obj*] to repeat; review: *Let's run over that song again.* **d.** [*no obj*] to overflow, as a container. **50. run through, a.** [~ + *obj* + *through*] to pierce or stab, as with a sword: *Cyrano ran him through.* **b.** [~ + *through* + *obj*] to consume or use up wastefully: *He ran through all their money.* **c.** [~ + *through* + *obj*] to practice or rehearse: *Let's run through that tune one more time.* **51. run to,** [~ + *to* + *obj*] to amount to; reach: *The bill ran to several hundred dollars.* **52. run up,** to gather, accumulate, or amass: [~ + *up* + *obj*]: *running up huge debts.* [*no obj*]: *Huge debts have run up.* **53. run with,** [~ + *with* + *obj*] *Informal.* to proceed with: *If the board likes the idea, we'll run with it.* *—n.* [*count*] **54.** a fleeing; flight: *a quick run for the border.* **55.** the distance covered, as by running. **56.** a quick trip: *a few runs to the grocery store.* **57.** a routine or regular trip: *the deliveryman's usual run.* **58.** a period of operation of a machine: *a 14-hour run for each generator.* **59.** the amount produced in such a period: *The newspaper has runs of over a million copies a day.* **60.** a course, trend, or tendency: *the normal run of events.* **61.** [*usually singular*] freedom to use something: *to have the run of the house.* **62.** a continuous series, course, or extent: *a run of good luck.* **63.** any extensive and continued demand: *a sudden run on umbrellas.* **64.** a series of demands for payment, as on a bank: *a run on the banks.* **65.** an inclined course, such as on a slope: *a bobsled run.* **66.** *Baseball.* the score made by running around all the bases and reaching home plate. **67. the runs,** *Informal.* DIARRHEA: [*noncount; used with a singular verb*]: *Having the runs is very unpleasant.* [*plural; used with a plural verb*]: *The runs were very unpleasant.* **—*Idiom.*** **68. in the long run,** in the course of long experience: *In the long run your stocks will earn money.* **69. in the short run,** in the near future: *The stocks are losing money in the short run.* **70. on the run, a.** scurrying about to perform one's activities: *on the run from morning till night.* **b.** while rushing to get somewhere: *eating breakfast on the run.* **c.** moving from place to place so as to hide from the police. **71. run for it,** [*no obj*] *Informal.* to flee quickly: *We'd better run for it; the police are right behind us.* **72. run off at the mouth,** *Informal.* to talk without stopping or without thinking: *constantly running off at the mouth.* **73. run short,** [*no obj*] to have an insufficiency of something: *My patience is running short.*

run•a•bout (run′ə bout′) /ˈrʌnəˌbawt/ *n.* [*count*] a small, light automobile or motorboat.

run•a•round (run′ə round′) /ˈrʌnəˌrawnd/ *n.* [*count; usually singular*] *Informal.* a vague, evasive answer: *kept giving him the runaround every time he asked her to marry him.*

run•a•way (run′ə wā′) /ˈrʌnəˌwey/ *n.* [*count*] **1.** one who runs away. **2.** the act of running away. **3.** an easy victory. *—adj.* [*before a noun*] **4.** escaped; fugitive. **5.** (of a contest) easily won: *a runaway victory.* **6.** not held back or restrained; unchecked: *runaway prices.*

run′-down′, *adj.* **1.** fatigued; exhausted: *run-down after the marathon.* **2.** in poor health: *He's severely run-down and had better see a doctor.* **3.** in neglected or broken-down condition: *a run-down neighborhood.* **4.** (of a clock, etc.) not running because it is unwound.

run•down (run′doun′) /ˈrʌnˌdawn/ *n.* [*count*] a short summary or brief report: *a rundown on the latest sales figures.*

rung[1] (rung) /rʌŋ/ *v.* pt. and pp. of RING[2].

rung[2] (rung) /rʌŋ/ *n.* [*count*] **1.** one of the crosspieces forming the steps of a ladder. **2.** a shaped piece attached to something horizontally for strength, as between the legs of a chair. **3.** a level or degree, as in a business, organization, etc.: *moving up the rungs of responsibility within the Army.*

run′-in′, *n.* [*count*] a quarrel; argument: *a run-in with his boss about his disruptive attitude.*

run•ner (run′ər) /ˈrʌnər/ *n.* [*count*] **1.** a person, animal, or thing that runs, esp. as a racer. **2.** a messenger, esp. of a bank or brokerage house. **3.** *Baseball.* a player on base or trying to reach a base. **4.** *Football.* the ball-carrier. **5.** a smuggler. **6.** either of the long, bladelike strips of metal or wood on which a sled or sleigh slides. **7.** the blade of an ice skate. **8.** a long, narrow rug.

run′ner-up′, *n.* [*count*], *pl.* **run•ners-up.** the player, team, or competitor finishing in second place.

run•ning (run′ing) /ˈrʌnɪŋ/ *n.* [*noncount*] **1.** the act of a person, animal, or thing that runs. **2.** management; direction: *the running of a business.* *—adj.* [*before a noun*] **3.** flowing, as from taps or pipes: *running water.* **4.** carried on continuously: *a running commentary.* **5.** performed with, used for, or done with a run: *a running leap and off he went.* **6.** leaking pus or other material: *a running sore.* **7.** moving or proceeding smoothly: *They got off to a running start.* *—adv.* [*after a plural noun; with a number*] **8.** one after the other; consecutively: *Cars were stolen from that neighborhood three nights running.* **—*Idiom.*** **9. in the running,** under consideration as a candidate: *two nominees still in the running.* **10. out of the running, a.** not under consideration as a candidate: *Because he had no credentials he was out of the running.* **b.** not among the winners or runners-up: *He was now out of the running in the tournament.*

run′ning light′, *n.* [*count*] any of various lights displayed by a vessel or aircraft operating at night.

run′ning mate′, *n.* [*count*] a candidate for a political position, linked with another and usually more important office or position, such as the vice-president: *Richard Nixon was Dwight Eisenhower's running mate in 1954.*

run•ny (run′ē) /ˈrʌniy/ *adj.,* **-ni•er, -ni•est. 1.** tending to run or drip: *a runny paste.* **2.** (of the nose) giving off mucus: *wiping his child's runny nose.*

run•off (run′ôf′, -of′) /ˈrʌnˌɔf, -ˌɒf/ *n.* **1.** [*noncount*] something that flows off, such as rain water: *The barrel collects any runoff.* **2.** [*count*] a contest held to break a tie: *In the runoff after the general election, he easily beat his closest competitor.*

run′-of-the-mill′, *adj.* just average; commonplace; ordinary; mediocre.

run′-on′, *adj.* **1.** (of something written as a sentence) having a thought that carries over to what should be another sentence or clause: *An example of a run-on sentence is the following: "I really like her, I want to see her again."* **—***n.* [*count*] **2.** a sentence or phrase written this way: *Avoid run-ons in your writing.*

runt (runt) /rʌnt/ *n.* [*count*] **1.** an animal that is small, esp. the smallest of a litter. **2.** *Offensive.* one who is small: *"Get out of here, runt," he said.* —**runt′y,** *adj.,* **-i•er, -i•est.**

run′-through′, *n.* [*count*] a trial or practice performance, esp. a rehearsal of a play.

run•way (run′wā′) /ˈrʌnˌwey/ *n.* [*count*] **1.** a way along which something runs. **2.** a strip on which planes land and take off. **3.** a ramp in a theater, extending from the stage into the orchestra pit or the aisles.

-rupt-, *root.* *-rupt-* comes from Latin, where it has the meaning "break." This meaning is found in such words as: ABRUPT, CORRUPT, DISRUPT, ERUPT, ERUPTION, INCORRUPTIBLE, INTERRUPT, RUPTURE.

rup•ture (rup′chər) /ˈrʌptʃər/ *n., v.,* **-tured, -tur•ing.** **—***n.* **1.** [*count*] the act of bursting. **2.** [*noncount*] the state of being burst. **3.** [*count*] a break from once-friendly relations. **4.** [*count*] a hernia, esp. an abdominal hernia. **—***v.* **5.** to break or burst: [*no obj*]: *The blood vessel will rupture from the strain.* [~ + *obj*]: *The added strain may rupture the blood vessel.* **6.** [~ + *oneself*] to suffer a hernia: *He'll rupture himself if he tries to lift that piano.* See -RUPT-.

ru•ral (ro͝or′əl) /ˈrʊrəl/ *adj.* of or like the country, country life, or country people; rustic.

ruse (ro͞oz) /ruwz/ *n.* [*count*] a trick: *He used a ruse to get past the sentry.*

rush[1] (rush) /rʌʃ/ *v.* **1.** to (cause to) move with great or too much speed: [*no obj*]: *He rushed ahead with the plan.* [~ + *obj*]: *He rushed the nomination through the committee.* **2.** to dash, esp. to dash forward for an attack: [*no obj*]: *The soldiers rushed forward.* [~ + *obj*]: *The soldiers rushed the machine gun nest.* **3.** to (cause to) appear, go, etc., rapidly or suddenly: [*no obj*]: *The train rushed by.* [~ + *obj*]: *Rush him to a hospital; he's badly hurt.* **—***n.* **4.** [*count*] the act of rushing; a rapid or violent onward movement. **5.** [*noncount*] hurried activity; busy haste: *There's no rush; what's your hurry?* **6.** [*noncount*] press of work, business, etc., requiring effort or haste: *the mid-morning rush.* **7.** [*count*] a rushing of numbers of persons to some region: *the California gold rush.* **8.** [*count; usually singular*] the intense feeling experienced from the early moments after taking a drug. **—***adj.* [*before a noun*] **9.** requiring or done in haste: *a rush job.* **10.** characterized by too much business, a press of work or traffic, etc.: *rush hour traffic.*

rush[2] (rush) /rʌʃ/ *n.* [*count*] **1.** any grasslike plant found in wet or marshy places. **2.** a stem of such a plant, used for making chair bottoms, baskets, etc.

rush′ hour′, *n.* [*count*] a time of day in which large numbers of people are traveling to or from work.

rusk (rusk) /rʌsk/ *n.* [*count*] a slice of sweet, raised bread dried and baked again in the oven.

rus•set (rus′it) /ˈrʌsɪt/ *n.* **1.** [*noncount*] yellowish brown or reddish brown. **2.** [*noncount*] a rough, reddish brown homespun cloth once used for clothing. **3.** [*count*] any of various apples with a rough brownish skin, that ripen in the autumn. **—***adj.* **4.** yellowish brown, light brown, or reddish brown in color.

Rus•sian (rush′ən) /ˈrʌʃən/ *adj.* **1.** of or relating to Russia. **2.** of or relating to the language spoken by many of the people in Russia. **—***n.* **3.** [*count*] a person born or living in Russia. **4.** [*noncount*] the language spoken by many of the people in Russia.

rust (rust) /rʌst/ *n.* [*noncount*] **1.** the red coating that forms on iron when exposed to air and moisture. **2.** reddish yellow or reddish brown. **—***v.* **3.** to (cause to) become or grow rusty, as iron: [*no obj*]: *The metal chairs had rusted over the winter.* [~ + *obj*]: *That climate will rust anything that isn't well protected.* **4.** [*no obj*] to decline in quality or ability: *He could feel his pitching abilities rusting away.*

rus•tic (rus′tik) /ˈrʌstɪk/ *adj.* **1.** of or relating to the country; rural. **2.** simple or unsophisticated. **—***n.* [*count*] **3.** a country person. **4.** an unsophisticated country person. —**rus′ti•cal•ly,** *adv.*

rus•tle (rus′əl) /ˈrʌsəl/ *v.,* **-tled, -tling,** *n.* **—***v.* **1.** to make the slight, soft sounds of gentle rubbing, as leaves: [*no obj*]: *The leaves of autumn rustled.* [~ + *obj*]: *They rustled the leaves as they walked through the woods.* **2.** [~ + *obj*] to steal (livestock, esp. cattle). **3. rustle up,** *Informal.* to put together by effort or search: [~ + *up* + *obj*]: *to rustle up some lunch from leftovers.* [~ + *obj* + *up*]: *to rustle something up for lunch.* **—***n.* [*count*] **4.** the sound made by anything that rustles. —**rus′tler,** *n.* [*count*]

rust•y (rus′tē) /ˈrʌstiy/ *adj.,* **-i•er, -i•est. 1.** covered with rust. **2.** of or tending toward the color rust. **3.** having lost agility; out of practice: *Because he hadn't played baseball in the last few years, he was rusty.* —**rust′i•ness,** *n.* [*noncount*]

rut[1] (rut) /rʌt/ *n., v.,* **rut•ted, rut•ting. —***n.* [*count*] **1.** a narrow, deep track in the ground, esp. one made by vehicles. **2.** a fixed way of proceeding, usually dull or unpromising: *to fall into a rut with his job.* **—***v.* [~ + *obj; usually: be* + ~*-ed*] **3.** to make a rut or ruts in: *The road was badly rutted.* —**rut′ty,** *adj.,* **-ti•er, -ti•est.**

rut[2] (rut) /rʌt/ *n., v.,* **rut•ted, rut•ting. —***n.* [*count; usually singular*] **1.** the period of year or time when deer, goats, etc., are sexually excited. **—***v.* [*no obj*] **2.** to be in the condition of rut.

ru•ta•ba•ga (ro͞o′tə bā′gə, ro͞o′tə bā′-) /ˌruwtəˈbeygə, ˈruwtəˌbey-/ *n., pl.* **-gas. 1.** [*count*] a plant of the mustard family with a yellow- or white-fleshed underground stem that can be eaten. **2.** [*noncount*] the underground stem that can be eaten, a variety of turnip.

ruth•less (ro͞oth′lis) /ˈruwθlɪs/ *adj.* without pity or compassion; cruel; merciless: *a ruthless desire to win at all costs.* —**ruth′less•ly,** *adv.*: *The general pressed his men ruthlessly ahead.* —**ruth′less•ness,** *n.* [*noncount*]

RV, an abbreviation of: recreational vehicle.

Rwan•dan (ro͞o än′dən) /ruwˈɑndən/ *adj.* **1.** of or relating to Rwanda. **—***n.* [*count*] **2.** a person born or living in Rwanda.

Rx, an abbreviation of: **1.** prescription. **2.** (used in prescriptions) take.

-ry, *suffix.* See -ERY.

rye (rī) /ray/ *n.* [*noncount*] **1.** a cereal grass. **2.** the seeds or grain of this plant, used for making flour and whiskey. **3.** bread made from this grain. **4.** Also called **rye′ whis′key. a.** a straight whiskey made from a crushed pulp containing 51 percent or more rye grain. **b.** *Northeastern U.S. and Canada.* a blended whiskey.

S

S, s (es) /ɛs/ *n.* [*count*], *pl.* **Ss** or **S's, ss** or **s's.** the 19th letter of the English alphabet, a consonant.

S, an abbreviation of: **1.** satisfactory. **2.** sentence. **3.** small. **4.** Also, **s** south. **5.** southern. **6.** state (highway).

's[1] (s, z, iz) /s, z, ɪz / an ending that is added to nouns or noun phrases to indicate possession by: *man's; women's; children's; James's; witness's; attorney general's; king of England's; anyone's.*

's[2] (s, z, iz) /s, z, ɪz/ a contraction that appears at the end of a noun or pronoun that is the subject of a verb, and is a shortened form of **1.** the verb *is: She's here (= She is here).* **2.** the verb *has: He's been there (= He has been there).* **3.** the verb *does: What's he do for a living? (= What does he do for a living?).*

's[3] (s) /s/ a contraction that appears at the end of the verb *let* and is a shortened form of *us: Let's go (= Let us go).*

-s[1] or **-es,** (s, z, iz) /s, z, ɪz/ *-s*[1] *or -es* is attached to the root form of verbs and marks the third person singular present indicative form, agreeing with a subject that is singular: *He walks. She runs. The wind rushes through the trees.*

-s[2] or **-es,** *-s*[2] *or -es* is attached to count nouns and marks the plural form: *weeks; days; bushes; taxes; ladies; pianos; potatoes.*

S., an abbreviation of: **1.** Saint. **2.** Saturday. **3.** Sea. **4.** September. **5.** south. **6.** southern. **7.** Sunday.

s., an abbreviation of: **1.** school. **2.** section. **3.** small. **4.** south. **5.** southern.

Sab•bath (sab′əth) /ˈsæbəθ/ *n.* **1.** [*proper noun; usually: the* + ~] the seventh day of the week, Saturday, the day of rest devoted to worship among Jews and some Christians. **2.** [*proper noun; usually: the* + ~] the first day of the week, Sunday, devoted to worship by most Christians. **3.** [*count; often: sabbath*] a day of rest or prayer.

sab•bat•i•cal (sə bat′i kəl) /səˈbætɪkəl/, *n.* [*count*] **1.** a year of release from normal teaching duties granted to a professor for research, etc. **2.** a period of leave from one's work, esp. for rest or study. ***—Idiom.*** **3. on sabbatical,** [*noncount*] having, or in the period of, one's sabbatical: *She's on sabbatical in Mauritius.*

sa•ber (sā′bər) /ˈseybər/ *n.* [*count*] a one-edged sword, usually slightly curved, used esp. by cavalry.

sa′ber saw′, *n.* [*count*] a portable electric jigsaw.

sa•ble (sā′bəl) /ˈseybəl/ *n., pl.* **-bles,** (*esp. when thought of as a group* for 1) **-ble. 1.** [*count*] a small dark-colored Eurasian or North American marten, valued for its fur. **2.** [*noncount*] the fur of the sable.

sab•o•tage (sab′ə täzh′) /ˈsæbəˌtɑʒ/ *n., v.,* **-taged, -tag•ing.** **—***n.* [*noncount*] **1.** deliberate damage of equipment, etc., as by employees during a dispute with their company. **2.** destruction of property, as to weaken a government or military effort: *acts of military sabotage.* **3.** any act of spoiling or undermining a plan or effort: *a case of romantic sabotage.* **—***v.* [~ + *obj*] **4.** to injure or attack by sabotage: *to sabotage the communications facilities.* **5.** to spoil or undermine; ruin: *She sabotaged every effort he made to stay on his diet.*

sab•o•teur (sab′ə tûr′) /ˌsæbəˈtɜr/ *n.* [*count*] one who commits sabotage.

sac (sak) /sæk/ *n.* [*count*] a baglike structure in an animal, plant, or fungus, esp. one containing fluid.

sac•cha•rin (sak′ər in) /ˈsækərɪn/ *n.* [*noncount*] an artificially produced powder used as a sugar substitute.

sac•cha•rine (sak′ər in, -ə rēn′, -ə rīn′) /ˈsækərɪn, -əˌriyn, -əˌrayn/ *adj.* **1.** of, resembling, or containing sugar. **2.** sweet in an exaggerated way: *a saccharine smile.*

sa•chem (sā′chəm) /ˈseytʃəm/ *n.* [*count*] (among some North American Indians) the chief of a tribe or confederation.

sa•chet (sa shā′) /sæˈʃey/ *n.* [*count*] a small bag or pad containing sweet-smelling powder.

sack[1] (sak) /sæk/ *n.* **1.** [*count*] a large bag of strong, rough, woven material, as for potatoes: *a burlap sack.* **2.** [*count*] the amount a sack holds: *two sacks of sugar.* **3.** [*count*] a bag: *a sack of candy.* **4.** [*noncount; usually: the* + ~] *Slang.* dismissal or being fired from a job: *got the sack for being late.* **5.** [*noncount*] *Slang.* bed: *He needs some time in the sack.* **—***v.* **6.** [~ + *obj*] to put into a sack or sacks. **7.** [~ + *obj*] *Slang.* to dismiss from a job; fire: *sacked him after just two weeks.* **8. sack out,** [*no obj*] *Slang.* to go to bed; fall asleep: *You can sack out on the floor.* ***—Idiom.*** **9. hit the sack,** to go to bed: *Time to hit the sack; lights out!* **—sack′ful,** *n.* [*count*], *pl.* **-fuls.**

sack[2] (sak) /sæk/ *v.* [~ + *obj*] **1.** to plunder (a place) after capture; loot: *Genghis Khan's armies sacked entire provinces.* **—***n.* [*count*] **2.** the plundering of a captured place: *the sack of Troy.* **—sack′er,** *n.* [*count*]

sack•cloth (sak′klôth′, -kloth′) /ˈsækˌkləθ, -ˌklɒθ/ *n.* [*noncount*] **1.** SACKING. ***—Idiom.*** **2. in sackcloth and ashes,** [*noncount*] in a state of deep sorrow for what one has done.

sack•ing (sak′ing) /ˈsækɪŋ/ *n.* [*noncount*] strong, roughly woven material of hemp, etc., used for sacks. Also called **sackcloth.**

sac•ra•ment (sak′rə mənt) /ˈsækrəmənt/ *n.* [*count*] a rite of the Christian churches, established by Christ to obtain grace. **—sac•ra•men•tal** (sak′rə men′tl) /ˌsækrəˈmɛntl̩/ *adj.*

sa•cred (sā′krid) /ˈseykrɪd/ *adj.* **1.** worthy of religious respect because of association with the divine: *the sacred relics of the saints.* **2.** dedicated to divine things: *a sacred grove.* **3.** important for some person or object: *an hour sacred to study.* **4.** revered or respected: *the sacred memory of the dead.* **—sa′cred•ly,** *adv.* **—sa′cred•ness,** *n.* [*noncount*]

sa′cred cow′, *n.* [*count*] someone or something thought to be important and therefore not to be criticized or questioned.

sac•ri•fice (sak′rə fīs′) /ˈsækrəˌfays/ *n., v.,* **-ficed, -fic•ing.** **—***n.* **1.** [*noncount*] the offering of life or of some object to a deity, as for forgiveness or worship: *Their practices included human sacrifice.* **2.** [*count*] the person, animal, or thing that is so offered. **3.** the giving up or destruction of something important for the sake of something having higher claim: [*count*]: *making many sacrifices for her children.* [*noncount*]: *the sacrifice of time with his children just for his work.* **—***v.* [~ + *obj*] **4.** to make a sacrifice of. **5.** to surrender, give up, or destroy for the sake of something else: *He sacrificed most of his vacation time to finish the job.* **—sac′ri•fi′cial** (-fish′əl) /-ˈfɪʃəl/ *adj.*

sac•ri•lege (sak′rə lij) /ˈsækrəlɪdʒ/ *n.* **1.** [*noncount*] the act of mistreating something sacred. **2.** [*count*] an instance of this: *to commit a sacrilege.* **—sac•ri•le•gious** (sak′rə lij′əs) /ˌsækrəˈlɪdʒəs/ *adj.* **—sac′ri•le′gious•ly,** *adv.* See -LEG-.

sac•ris•ty (sak′ri stē) /ˈsækrɪstiy/ *n.* [*count*], *pl.* **-ties.** a room in a church in which vestments, etc., are kept.

sac•ro•sanct (sak′rō sangkt′) /ˈsækrowˌsæŋkt/ *adj.* **1.** sacred. **2.** beyond interference, question, etc.: *Sports in that town are sacrosanct.* **—sac′ro•sanct′ness,** *n.* [*noncount*] See -SANCT-.

sad (sad) /sæd/ *adj.,* **sad•der, sad•dest. 1.** feeling unhappiness or grief: *to feel sad.* **2.** expressing or causing sorrow: *a sad song.* **3.** awfully bad; sorry: *a sad attempt to make a joke.* **—sad′ly,** *adv.: She shook her head sadly as she read about the famine.* **—sad′ness,** *n.* [*noncount*]

sad•den (sad′n) /ˈsædn̩/ *v.* to make or become sad: [~ + *obj*]: *The news of their teammate's paralysis saddened the team.* [*It* + ~ + *obj* + *that clause*]: *It saddened me that she wouldn't trust me.* [*no obj*]: *He saddened when he heard the news.*

sad•dle (sad′l) /ˈsædl̩/ *n., v.,* **-dled, -dling.** **—***n.* [*count*] **1.** a seat for a rider on the back of a horse or other animal. **2.** a similar seat on a bicycle, etc. **3.** something similar to a saddle in shape, position, or function. **—***v.* **4.** to put a saddle on (an animal): [~ + *obj*]: *They saddled their horses and rode off.* [~ + *up* + *obj*]: *They saddled up their horses and rode off.* [~ + *obj* + *up*]: *They saddled the horses up and rode off.* [*no obj;* ~ + *up*]: *They saddled up and took off.* **5.** [~ + *obj* + *with* + *obj*] to give to (someone), as a burden or responsibility: *The boss saddled our staff with a lot of extra work.* ***—Idiom.*** **6. in the saddle,** [*noncount*] **a.** in a position to direct. **b.** at work; on the job: *back in the saddle after my illness.*

sad•dle•bag (sad′l bag′) /ˈsædl̩ˌbæg/ *n.* [*count*] a large bag hung from a saddle, laid over the back of a horse behind the saddle, etc.

sad′dle shoe′, *n.* [*count*] a shoe with a band of contrasting leather or color across the instep.

sa•dism (sā′diz əm, sad′iz-) /ˈseydɪzəm, ˈsædɪz-/ *n.* [*noncount*] **1.** sexual pleasure from causing pain to others. **2.** pleasure in being cruel. **—sa′dist,** *n.* [*count*], *adj.* **—sa•dis•tic** (sə dis′tik) /sə'dɪstɪk/ *adj.*

sa•do•mas•o•chism (sā′dō mas′ə kiz′əm, -maz′-, sad′ō-) /ˌseydow'mæsəˌkɪzəm, -'mæz-, ˌsædow-/ *n.* [*noncount*] pleasure, esp. sexual, gained through causing or receiving pain. **—sa′do•mas′o•chist,** *n.* [*count*], *adj.* **—sa′do•mas′o•chis′tic,** *adj.*

sa•fa•ri (sə fär′ē) /sə'fɑriy/ *n., pl.* **-ris,** *v.,* **-ried, -ri•ing.** **—n. 1.** a trip for hunting, adventure, etc.: [*count*]: *a short safari to photograph wild animals.* [*noncount; on* + ~]: *They're on safari for a few weeks.* **2.** [*count*] any long adventurous trip. **—v.** [*no obj*] **3.** to go on safari.

safe (sāf) /seyf/ *adj.,* **saf•er, saf•est,** *n.* **—adj. 1.** offering security from danger; giving protection: *a safe neighborhood.* **2.** free from injury or risk: *They arrived home safe.* **3.** reasonably correct: *a safe estimate.* **4.** dependable; trustworthy: *a safe guide.* **5.** careful to avoid risk: *a very safe driver.* **6.** [*be* + ~] *Baseball.* reaching base without being put out: *safe at home!* **7.** [*be* + ~] (of a secret) that will not be told to others: *Your secret is safe with me.* **—n.** [*count*] **8.** a steel box or other secure place for valuables: *a safe in the wall, hidden behind a bookshelf.* **—*Idiom.* 9. play (it) safe,** to avoid taking unnecessary risks: *He played it safe and didn't drive fast in the snow.* **—safe′ly,** *adv.* **—safe′ness,** *n.* [*noncount*] See -SALV-.

safe′-con′duct, *n.* [*count*] a document that allows safe passage through a region, esp. in time of war.

safe′-depos′it box′, *n.* [*count*] a lockable metal box, esp. in a bank vault, for storing valuables. Also called **safe′ty-depos′it box′.** See illustration at BANK.

safe•guard (sāf′gärd′) /'seyf,gɑrd/ *n.* [*count*] **1.** something that serves as a protection: *stricter safeguards on nuclear fuels.* **—v. 2.** to prevent (someone or something) from being harmed: [*no obj*]: *to safeguard against attack.* [~ + *obj*]: *You can safeguard your home from burglars.*

safe•keep•ing (sāf′kē′ping) /'seyf'kiypɪŋ/ *n.* [*noncount*] the act of keeping safe or the state of being kept safe: *money in the bank for safekeeping.*

safe′ sex′, *n.* [*noncount*] sexual activity in which precautions are taken to prevent diseases spread by sexual contact, specifically, AIDS.

safe•ty (sāf′tē) /'seyftiy/ *n., pl.* **-ties. 1.** [*noncount*] the state of being safe: *the rules of safety; Sometimes there is safety in numbers (= being with others is safer than being alone).* **2.** [*count*] a device to prevent injury: *When too much electricity enters the circuit, the safeties come on and cut off the flow.* See -SALV-.

safe′ty glass′, *n.* [*noncount*] glass made by joining two sheets of glass with a layer of plastic between them that keeps the fragments from flying.

safe′ty match′, *n.* [*count*] a match that ignites only when rubbed on a specially prepared surface.

safe′ty pin′, *n.* [*count*] a pin bent back on itself to form a spring, with a guard to cover the point.

safe′ty ra′zor, *n.* [*count*] a razor with a guard to prevent the blade from cutting the skin.

safe′ty valve′, *n.* [*count*] **1.** a device that opens to release a fluid before pressure reaches dangerous levels. **2.** a harmless way of releasing feelings that have been kept in: *Exercise was his safety valve.*

saf•fron (saf′rən) /'sæfrən/ *n.* **1.** [*count*] a crocus having bright purple flowers. **2.** [*noncount*] an orange powder made from this flower, used to color and flavor foods.

sag (sag) /sæg/ *v.,* **sagged, sag•ging,** *n.* **—v.** [*no obj*] **1.** to sink downward by or as if by weight: *His body sagged under the weight of carrying her.* **2.** to decline or become less in strength or intensity: *Our spirits began to sag.* **3.** to decline or go down in value: *The stock market sagged today.* **—n.** [*count*] **4.** an act or instance of sagging. **—sag′gy,** *adj.,* **-gi•er, -gi•est.**

sa•ga (sä′gə) /'sɑgə/ *n.* [*count*], *pl.* **-gas. 1.** a written account from medieval Scandinavia that tells of historical or legendary individuals or families. **2.** any piece of writing that tells of heroic events or deeds.

sa•ga•cious (sə gā′shəs) /sə'geyʃəs/ *adj.* having or showing wisdom; shrewd; wise: *a sagacious lawyer.* **—sa•gac•i•ty** (sə gas′i tē) /sə'gæsɪtiy/ *n.* [*noncount*]

sage[1] (sāj) /seydʒ/ *n., adj.,* **sag•er, sag•est.** **—n.** [*count*] **1.** a very wise person: *consulting the village sage for advice.* **—adj. 2.** wise or prudent: *sage advice.*

sage[2] (sāj) /seydʒ/ *n.* [*noncount*] **1.** a plant belonging to the mint family, esp. one with grayish green leaves used in cooking. **2.** the leaves themselves: *turkey stuffing with sage.*

sage•brush (sāj′brush′) /'seydʒ,brʌʃ/ *n.* [*noncount*] a sagelike, bushy plant having silvery wedge-shaped leaves.

sa•go (sā′gō) /'seygow/ *n.* [*noncount*] a starch that comes from palm trees, used in making puddings.

sa•hib (sä′ib, -ēb) /'sɑɪb, -iyb/ *n.* [*count*] (a term of respect used in India in addressing or referring to an important person or, in colonial times, a European) sir; master.

said (sed) /sɛd/ *v.* **1.** pt. and pp. of SAY. **—adj.** [*before a noun*] **2.** mentioned previously; aforementioned: *The said witness claims she saw the defendant.*

sail (sāl) /seyl/ *n.* [*count*] **1.** a piece of canvas on a ship to catch the wind and propel the vessel: *The ship has three sails.* **2.** a similar apparatus, as on a windmill. **3.** a voyage esp. in a vessel with sails. **—v. 4.** [*no obj*] (of a ship or boat) to travel on water: *The ship sailed to Alaska.* **5.** [~ + *obj*] **a.** to travel in a ship upon, over, or through (water): *to sail the seven seas.* **b.** to take or pilot (a vessel) upon, over, or through water: *They sailed the ship to Alaska.* **6.** to manage (a sailboat), esp. for sport: [*no obj*]: *She likes to sail on weekends.* [~ + *obj*]: *sailed their boat out into the harbor.* **7.** [*no obj*] to begin a journey by water: *We sail at dawn.* **8.** [*no obj*] to move along like a sailing vessel: *to sail into a room.* **9. sail into,** [~ + *into* + *obj*] to attack strongly; assail: *He sailed into our ideas for reorganization.* **—*Idiom.* 10. set sail,** to start a voyage: *We set sail at daybreak.*

sail•boat (sāl′bōt′) /'seyl,bowt/ *n.* [*count*] a boat using sails for propulsion.

sail•cloth (sāl′klôth′, -kloth′) /'seylˌklɔθ, -ˌklɒθ/ *n.* [*noncount*] **1.** a fabric, as of Dacron, for boat sails or tents. **2.** a lightweight canvas used esp. for clothing and curtains.

sail•ing (sā′ling) /'seylɪŋ/ *n.* **1.** [*noncount*] the act of a person or thing that sails: *very skilled at sailing.* **2.** [*count*] the act of a ship leaving a port. **—*Idiom.* 3. clear sailing,** [*noncount*] a way free of serious difficulty: *Once he gets through with the last chapter it will be clear sailing to the end.*

sail•or (sā′lər) /'seylər/ *n.* [*count*] **1.** one whose job is sailing; a mariner. **2.** a person in a navy whose rank is below the rank of an officer.

saint (sānt) /seynt/ *n.* [*count*] **1.** a person of great holiness, formally recognized by the Christian Church. **2.** a person of great virtue or unselfishness: *His mother was a saint to put up with all his bad behavior.* **—adj. 3.** [*Saint; before a person's name as a title*] (used to show that a person's holiness has been formally recognized by a Christian church): *Saint James. Abbr.* St. See -SANCT-.

saint•hood (sānt′ho͝od) /'seynthʊd/ *n.* [*noncount*] the state or quality of being a saint. See -SANCT-.

saint•ly (sānt′lē) /'seyntliy/ *adj.,* **-li•er, -li•est.** of or like a saint: *the teacher's saintly patience.* **—saint′li•ness,** *n.* [*noncount*] See -SANCT-.

saith (seth, sā′əth) /sɛθ, 'seyəθ/ *v. Archaic.* third pers. sing. pres. of SAY.

sake[1] (sāk) /seyk/ *n.* [*noncount*] **1.** benefit or well-being: *worked hard for the sake of her family.* **2.** purpose; end: *art for art's sake.*

sa•ke[2] or **sa•ké** or **sa•ki** (sä′kē, -ke) /'sɑkiy, -kɛ/ *n.* [*noncount*] a Japanese alcoholic beverage made from rice.

sa•laam (sə läm′) /sə'lɑm/ *n.* [*count*] **1.** a greeting meaning "peace," used esp. in Islamic countries. **2.** a very low bow to show respect. **—v.** [*no obj*] **3.** to greet with a salaam.

sa•la•cious (sə lā′shəs) /sə'leyʃəs/ *adj.* grossly indecent; obscene. **—sa•la′cious•ly,** *adv.* **—sa•la′cious•ness, sa•lac•i•ty** (sə las′i tē) /sə'læsɪtiy/ *n.* [*noncount*]

sal•ad (sal′əd) /'sæləd/ *n.* **1.** a cold dish of raw vegetables, served with a dressing: [*noncount*]: *We had salad with dinner.* [*count*]: *many different salads at the restaurant.* **2.** a dish of raw or cold foods, mixed with mayonnaise or other dressing: [*noncount*]: *potato salad.* [*count*]: *delicious pasta salads on the table.*

sal′ad bar′, *n.* [*count*] an assortment of salads and often other foods, as in a restaurant, from which one serves oneself.

sal•a•man•der (sal′ə man′dər) /'sæləˌmændər/ *n.* [*count*] **1.** a small animal able to live in water or on land, having a soft, moist, scaleless skin. **2.** a being in myths, esp. a lizard or other reptile, that is thought to be able to live in fire.

sa•la•mi (sə lä′mē) /sə'lɑmiy/ *n., pl.* **-mis.** a spicy, garlic-flavored sausage, originally Italian: [*noncount*]: *a sandwich with salami and cheese.* [*count*]: *They cut up several salamis.*

sal•a•ry (sal′ə rē) /'sæləriy/ *n.* [*count*], *pl.* **-ries.** a fixed amount of money paid regularly to a person for work: *Salaries for these jobs start at $20,000 a year.* **—sal′a·ried′,** *adj.: a salaried worker.*

sale (sāl) /seyl/ *n.* **1.** [*count*] an act of selling: *trying to make a sale.* **2.** [*count*] a special offering of goods at reduced prices: *They're having a sale: 20% off.* **3.** [*count*] transfer of property for money or credit. **4.** [*count*] **a.** an amount or quantity sold. **b. sales,** [*plural*] total receipts from selling. **5.** [*count*] an auction. **6. sales,** [*noncount; used with a singular verb*] a department, as in a business, concerned with selling and promoting goods, etc.: *Sales is the department you want to see.* **—*Idiom.* 7. for sale,** [*noncount*] available for purchase: *This house is for sale.* **8. on sale,** [*noncount*] to be bought at reduced prices: *The store has computers on sale for 50% off.* —**sal′a·ble, sale′a·ble,** *adj.*

sales·clerk (sālz′klûrk′) /'seylz,klɜrk/ *n.* [*count*] one who sells goods in a store. See illustration at STORE.

sales·man or **-wom·an** (sālz′mən) or (-wo͝om′ən) /'seylzmən/ or /-,wʊmən/ *n.* [*count*], *pl.* **-men** or **-wom·en.** a man or woman who sells goods, services, etc. —**sales′man·ship′,** *n.* [*noncount*]

sales·per·son (sālz′pûr′sən) /'seylz,pɜrsən/ *n.* [*count*] one who sells goods, services, etc.

sal′i·cyl′ic ac′id (sal′ə sil′ik) /,sælə'sɪlɪk/ *n.* [*noncount*] a white crystal-like substance used to make aspirin.

sa·li·ent (sā′lē ənt, sāl′yənt) /'seyliyənt, 'seylyənt/ *adj.* **1.** most noticeable; prominent: *salient features.* **2.** sticking up or pointing outward. **—*n.*** [*count*] **3.** an angle that sticks up or points out: *a salient defended by the troops.* —**sa′li·ence,** *n.* [*noncount*] —**sa′li·ent·ly,** *adv.*

sa·line (sā′lēn, -līn) /'seyliyn, -layn/ *adj.* **1.** of, containing, or tasting of salt; salty: *saline soil.* **—*n.*** [*count*] **2.** a saline solution. —**sa·lin·i·ty** (sə lin′i tē) /sə'lɪnɪtiy/ *n.* [*noncount*]

Salis·bur·y steak′ (sôlz′ber′ē, -bə rē, -brē) /'sɔlz'beriy, -bəriy, -briy/ *n.* [*noncount*] ground beef shaped into a large patty and broiled or fried.

sa·li·va (sə lī′və) /sə'layvə/ *n.* [*noncount*] a watery fluid in the mouth that functions in the chewing, digesting, and swallowing of food. —**sal·i·var·y** (sal′ə ver′ē) /'sælə,veriy/ *adj.*

sal·i·vate (sal′ə vāt′) /'sælə,veyt/ *v.* [*no obj*], **-vat·ed, -vat·ing.** to produce saliva. —**sal·i·va·tion,** *n.* [*noncount*]

sal·low (sal′ō) /'sælow/ *adj.*, **-er, -est.** of a sickly, yellowish color: *a sallow complexion.* —**sal′low·ness,** *n.* [*noncount*]

sal·ly (sal′ē) /'sæliy/ *n., pl.* **-lies,** *v.*, **-lied, -ly·ing. —*n.*** [*count*] **1.** a sudden rushing forth of troops against an enemy. **2.** a funny, clever remark; quip. **3.** an excursion or side trip. **—*v.*** [*no obj*] **4.** to make a sally: *The troops sallied against their enemy.* [*usually:* ~ + *forth/out*]: *We sallied forth in search of a good restaurant.*

salm·on (sam′ən) /'sæmən/ *n., pl.* **-ons,** (*esp. when thought of as a group*) **-on** for 1, *adj.* **—*n.* 1.** [*count*] a fish having edible, pink flesh. **2.** [*noncount*] a light yellowish pink. **—*adj.* 3.** of the color salmon.

sal·mo·nel·la (sal′mə nel′ə) /,sælmə'nelə/ *n., pl.* **-nel·lae** (-nel′ē) /-'neliy/ **-nel·las. 1.** [*count*] a rod-shaped bacterium that enters the digestive tract from contaminated food, causing food poisoning. **2.** [*noncount*] the food poisoning caused by this bacterium.

sa·lon (sə lon′) /sə'lɒn/ *n.* [*count*] **1.** a room for receiving guests in a large house. **2.** a hall or place for the exhibition of works of art. **3.** a special shop, department of a store, etc., usually for fashionable clients: *a dress salon.*

sa·loon (sə lo͞on′) /sə'luwn/ *n.* [*count*] **1.** a place where alcoholic drinks are sold and drunk. **2.** a room or place for some use: *the dining saloon on a ship.*

sal·sa (säl′sə, -sä) /'sɑlsə, -sɑ/ *n., pl.* **-sas. 1.** [*noncount*] Latin American music blending Cuban rhythm with jazz, rock, and soul. **2.** [*count*] a dance of Puerto Rican origin performed to this music. **3.** [*noncount*] a sauce, esp. a spicy sauce containing hot chilies.

salt (sôlt) /sɔlt/ *n.* **1.** [*noncount*] a white, crystal-like compound, sodium chloride, used for seasoning and preserving food. **2.** [*count*] a chemical compound formed by combining an acid and a base. **3.** [*count*] a sailor, esp. an old or experienced one. **—*v.*** [~ + obj] **4.** to season or preserve (food) with salt. **5.** to spread salt on so as to melt snow or ice: *salting the highways.* **6. salt away,** to save (money) for future use: [~ + *away* + *obj*]: *salted away a few thousand dollars for an emergency.* [~ + *obj* + *away*]: *salted some money away years ago.* **—*adj.*** [*before a noun*] **7.** tasting of or containing salt: *salt water.* **8.** preserved with salt: *salt cod.* **—*Idiom.* 9. take (something) with a grain** or **pinch of salt,** [take + obj + with a grain/pinch of + ~] to be somewhat skeptical about: *claimed to have made a million dollars in profits, but I'd take that figure with a grain of salt.* **10. worth one's salt,** [*noncount*] deserving of one's wages or salary. —**salt′ed,** *adj.*

salt·cel·lar (sôlt′sel′ər) /'sɔlt,selər/ *n.* [*count*] a small container, as at the table, from which the salt can be shaken.

sal·tine (sôl tēn′) /sɔl'tiyn/ *n.* [*count*] a crisp, salted cracker.

salt′ of the earth′, *n.* [*count; usually singular*] an individual or group thought of as being very noble, admirable, or worthwhile.

salt′shak′er (sôlt′shā′kər) /'sɔlt,ʃeykər/ *n.* [*count*] a small container for salt, as at the table, from which the salt can be shaken.

salt·wa·ter (sôlt′wô′tər, -wot′ər) /'sɔlt,wɔtər, -,wɒtər/ *adj.* [*before a noun*] **1.** of or relating to salt water: *saltwater desalination companies.* **2.** living in salt water: *a saltwater fish.*

salt·y (sôl′tē) /'sɔltiy/ *adj.*, **-i·er, -i·est. 1.** of, like, or tasting of salt: *salty tears.* **2.** racy or coarse: *salty humor.* —**salt′i·ness,** *n.* [*noncount*]

sa·lu·bri·ous (sə lo͞o′brē əs) /sə'luwbriyəs/ *adj.* favorable to or bringing good health; healthful. See -SALV-.

sal·u·tar·y (sal′yə ter′ē) /'sælyə,teriy/ *adj.* **1.** favorable to or promoting health: *That vitamin has a salutary effect.* **2.** causing or leading to a good result: *a salutary change in medical procedures.* See -SALV-.

sal·u·ta·tion (sal′yə tā′shən) /,sælyə'teyʃən/ *n.* **1. a.** something said, written, or done by way of greeting, welcome, etc.: [*count*]: *In many languages salutations are words referring to good health.* [*noncount*]: *a few words in salutation.* **b. salutations,** [*plural*] greetings or regards. **2.** [*count*] a phrase serving as the greeting in a letter or speech, as *Dear Sir* in a letter or *Ladies and Gentlemen* in a speech. See -SALV-.

sa·lute (sə lo͞ot′) /sə'luwt/ *n., v.*, **-lut·ed, -lut·ing. —*n.*** [*count*] **1. a.** a gesture of respect, given to a person of higher military rank: *a snappy salute.* **b.** a sign of respect performed by a military or naval force to honor someone or some occasion: *a twenty-one-gun salute.* **2.** any instance of formal greeting, welcome, or respect: *a salute to the Big Bands of the 1940's.* **—*v.* 3.** to give a salute to (someone or something): [*no obj*]: *The soldiers saluted smartly.* [~ + *obj*]: *The corporal saluted the major.* **4.** [~ + *obj*] to express respect or praise for: *We salute the dead of our past wars.* See -SALV-.

-salv-, *root.* *-salv-* comes from Latin, where it has the meaning "save." This meaning is found in such words as: SALVAGE, SALVATION, SALVER, SALVO.

Sal·va·do·ran (sal′və dôr′ən) /,sælvə'dɔrən/ *adj.* Also, **Sal·va·do·ri·an** (sal′və dôr′ē ən) /,sælvə'dɔriyən/. **1.** of or relating to El Salvador. **—*n.*** [*count*] **2.** a person born or living in El Salvador.

sal·vage (sal′vij) /'sælvɪdʒ/ *n., v.*, **-vaged, -vag·ing. —*n.*** [*noncount*] **1.** the saving of a ship or its cargo from perils of the seas. **2.** the saving of anything from danger or destruction. **3.** the property, etc., saved this way. **—*v.*** [~ + *obj*] **4.** to save from shipwreck, fire, or other danger: *They salvaged some of their money after the bank failure.* —**sal′vage·a·ble,** *adj.* See -SALV-.

sal·va·tion (sal vā′shən) /sæl'veyʃən/ *n.* [*noncount*] **1.** the act of saving, or the state of being saved: *the company's salvation from bankruptcy.* **2.** a cause or means of being saved: *That loan was my salvation; with it I bought back the company and rebuilt it.* **3.** *Theol.* deliverance from the power of sin; redemption. See -SALV-.

salve (sav, säv) /sæv, sɑv/ *n., v.*, **salved, salv·ing. —*n.* 1.** a paste containing medicine for treating wounds and sores: [*count*]: *greasy, soothing salves.* [*noncount*]: *Rub salve on the wound.* **—*v.*** [~ + *obj*] **2.** to soothe with or as if with salve: *to salve one's conscience.*

sal·ver (sal′vər) /'sælvər/ *n.* [*count*] a tray, esp. one used for serving food or drinks. See -SALV-.

sal·vo (sal′vō) /'sælvow/ *n.* [*count*], *pl.* **-vos, -voes. 1.** a firing of several guns, pieces of artillery, rockets, etc., at the same time: *a salvo of torpedoes.* **2.** a verbal attack. See -SALV-.

sam·ba (sam′bə, säm′-) /'sæmbə, 'sɑm-/ *n., pl.* **-bas,** *v.*, **-baed, -ba·ing. —*n.*** [*count*] **1.** a Brazilian ballroom dance of African origin. **—*v.*** [*no obj*] **2.** to dance the samba.

same (sām) /seym/ *adj.* [*before a noun; the/this/that/these/those* + ~] **1.** identical with what is about to be or has just been mentioned: *This street is the same one we were on yesterday.* **2.** being one or identical though having different names, etc.: *the same play with a different title.* **3.** agreeing in kind, amount, etc.: *two boxes of the same dimensions.* **4.** unchanged in character, etc.: *It's the same town after all these years.* —*pron.* [*the* + ~] **5.** the same person, thing, or kind of thing: *She wants a computer, and I want the same.* —***Idiom.*** **6. all the same, a.** anyway; notwithstanding; nevertheless: *I know you're tired, but all the same, I wish you'd stay.* **b.** of no difference; immaterial: *It's all the same to me whether you go or not.* **7. just the same, a.** in the same way. **b.** nevertheless; all the same. **8. same to you.** (used as an answer to a greeting or as a wish for someone): *"Happy holidays!" —"Same to you."* **9. the same,** in the same manner; in an identical or similar way: *I see the same through your eyeglasses as through mine.* —**same′ness,** *n.* [*noncount*]: *obvious sameness between the two books.*

sam•o•var (sam′ə vär′, sam′ə vär′) /ˈsæməˌvɑr, ˌsæməˈvɑr/ *n.* [*count*] a metal urn used esp. by Russians for heating water to make tea.

sam•pan (sam′pan) /ˈsæmpæn/ *n.* [*count*] a kind of small boat of the Far East, with a roofing of mats.

sam•ple (sam′pəl) /ˈsæmpəl/ *n., adj., v.,* **-pled, -pling.** —*n.* [*count*] **1.** a small part from a larger whole, showing the quality, style, or nature of the whole; specimen: *a sample of her urine for a test.* —*adj.* [*before a noun*] **2.** serving as a specimen: *a sample piece of cloth.* —*v.* [~ + *obj*] **3.** to take a sample of: *sampled the food before serving it.* See -AM-.

sam•pler (sam′plər) /ˈsæmplər/ *n.* [*count*] **1.** one who samples. **2.** a piece of cloth embroidered with various stitches, serving to show a beginner's skill in needlework. **3.** a collection of samples representing a whole: *a sampler of various cheeses.*

sam•u•rai (sam′o͝o rī′) /ˈsæmʊˌray/ *n.* [*count*], *pl.* **-rai.** (in feudal Japan) a member of the warrior class.

-san-, *root.* *-san-* comes from Latin, where it has the meaning "health." This meaning is found in such words as: INSANE, SANATORIUM, SANE, SANITARY, SANITIZE.

san•a•to•ri•um (san′ə tôr′ē əm, -tōr′-) /ˌsænəˈtɔriyəm, -ˈtowr-/ *n.* [*count*], *pl.* **-to•ri•ums, -to•ri•a** (-tôr′ē ə, -tōr′ē ə) /-ˈtɔriyə, -ˈtowriyə/. **1.** a hospital for the treatment of long-lasting conditions such as tuberculosis. **2.** SANITARIUM. See -SAN-.

-sanct-, *root.* *-sanct-* comes from Latin, where it has the meaning "holy." This meaning is found in such words as: SACROSANCT, SANCTIFY, SANCTION, SANCTITY, SANCTUARY.

sanc•ti•fy (sangk′tə fī′) /ˈsæŋktəˌfay/ *v.* [~ + *obj*], **-fied, -fy•ing.** to make holy; bless or consecrate: *to sanctify a new church.* —**sanc•ti•fi•ca•tion** (sangk′tə fi kā′shən) /ˌsæŋktəfɪˈkeyʃən/ *n.* [*noncount*] See -SANCT-.

sanc•ti•mo•ni•ous (sangk′tə mō′nē əs) /ˌsæŋktəˈmowniyəs/ *adj.* showing sanctimony. —**sanc′ti•mo′ni•ous•ly,** *adv.* See -SANCT-.

sanc•ti•mo•ny (sangk′tə mō′nē) /ˈsæŋktəˌmowniy/ *n.* [*noncount*] pretended religious devotion, etc. See -SANCT-.

sanc•tion (sangk′shən) /ˈsæŋkʃən/ *n.* **1.** [*noncount*] official approval from an authority: *withheld official sanction for these acts.* **2.** [*count*] something that gives binding force, as to an oath. **3.** [*count*] action by a state to force another state to follow rules, etc.: *to impose sanctions against that country.* —*v.* [~ + *obj*] **4.** to allow officially: *No one will sanction such actions.* **5.** to penalize by sanction: *sanctioning the country because of its invasion of a peaceful neighbor.* See -SANCT-.

sanc•ti•ty (sangk′ti tē) /ˈsæŋktɪtiy/ *n.* [*noncount*] **1.** holiness or saintliness. **2.** sacredness: *believes in the sanctity of marriage.* See -SANCT-.

sanc•tu•ar•y (sangk′cho͞o er′ē) /ˈsæŋktʃuwˌɛriy/ *n., pl.* **-ar•ies. 1.** [*count*] a sacred or holy place, such as a temple or church, or the holiest part within it. **2.** [*count*] a place that provides refuge, esp. (formerly) freedom from being arrested. **3.** [*noncount*] the protection provided by such a place; asylum: *The thief claimed that the chapel provided sanctuary.* **4.** [*count*] an area where wildlife live and breed in safety; a preserve. See -SANCT-.

sanc•tum (sangk′təm) /ˈsæŋktəm/ *n.* [*count*], *pl.* **-tums, -ta** (-tə) /-tə/. **1.** a sacred or holy place. **2.** a private place or retreat: *His office was his sanctum.* See -SANCT-.

sand (sand) /sænd/ *n.* **1.** [*noncount*] the powdery, loose grains made from rocks rubbing against each other: *a few grains of sand in his shoes.* **2.** Usually, **sands.** [*plural*] an area made up principally of sand: *driving through the sands.* **3.** [*noncount*] a light reddish yellow or brownish yellow color. —*v.* [~ + *obj*] **4.** to make smooth with sandpaper. —**sand′er,** *n.* [*count*]

san•dal (san′dl) /ˈsændḷ/ *n.* [*count*] **1.** a shoe made up of a bottom and thongs or straps by which it is fastened to the foot. **2.** a low shoe or slipper.

san•dal•wood (san′dl wo͝od′) /ˈsændḷˌwʊd/ *n.* [*noncount*] the sweet-smelling reddish yellow wood of an Indian tree, used for incense and ornamental carving.

sand•bag (sand′bag′) /ˈsændˌbæg/ *n., v.,* **-bagged, -bag•ging.** —*n.* [*count*] **1.** a bag filled with sand, used in fortification, etc.: *built a wall of sandbags against the floodwaters.* **2.** such a bag used as a weapon. —*v.* [~ + *obj*] **3.** to furnish with sandbags, so as to protect: *We'll sandbag the area near the riverfront.* **4.** to hit with or as if with a sandbag: *The bad news sandbagged him.*

sand•bank (sand′bangk′) /ˈsændˌbæŋk/ *n.* [*count*] a large mass of sand, such as in a shoal or on a hillside.

sand′ bar′, *n.* [*count*] a bar of sand formed by the action of tides or currents.

sand•blast (sand′blast′) /ˈsændˌblæst/ *n.* [*count*] **1.** a blast of air or steam that is combined with sand, used to clean, grind, etc., hard surfaces, as of stone. —*v.* [~ + *obj*] **2.** to clean, etc., by this means: *sandblasting the front of a building.* —**sand′blast′er,** *n.* [*count*]

sand•box (sand′boks′) /ˈsændˌbɒks/ *n.* [*count*] a box for holding sand, esp. one for children to play in.

S&L, savings and loan (association).

sand•lot (sand′lot′) /ˈsændˌlɒt/ *n.* [*count*] **1.** a vacant lot used by youngsters for games or sports. —*adj.* [*before a noun*] **2.** Also, **sand′-lot′.** of or relating to such a lot: *sandlot baseball.*

sand•man (sand′man′) /ˈsændˌmæn/ *n.* [*count*], *pl.* **-men.** a character in fairy tales and folk stories who puts sand in the eyes of children to make them sleepy.

sand•pa•per (sand′pā′pər) /ˈsændˌpeypər/ *n.* [*noncount*] **1.** paper coated with a layer of sand, used for smoothing or polishing. —*v.* [~ + *obj*] **2.** to smooth or polish with sandpaper: *Sandpaper the surface before applying the varnish.*

sand•pi•per (sand′pī′per) /ˈsændˌpaypɛr/ *n.* [*count*] a plump, thin-billed bird that lives near seashores.

sand•stone (sand′stōn′) /ˈsændˌstown/ *n.* [*noncount*] a common type of rock made up of sand, usually quartz.

sand•storm (sand′stôrm′) /ˈsændˌstɔrm/ *n.* [*count*] a windstorm, esp. in a desert, that blows along great clouds of sand.

sand′ trap′, *n.* [*count*] (on a golf course) a shallow pit partly filled with sand, blocking the way to the hole.

sand•wich (sand′wich, san′-) /ˈsændwɪtʃ, ˈsæn-/ *n.* [*count*] **1.** two slices of bread with a layer of meat, cheese, or other food between them. **2.** something that resembles a sandwich: *a plywood sandwich.* —*v.* [~ + *obj*] **3.** to insert (something or someone) between two other persons or things: *sandwiched between two husky police officers.*

sand•y (san′dē) /ˈsændiy/ *adj.,* **-i•er, -i•est. 1.** of or relating to sand: *Wash your feet; they're sandy from the beach.* **2.** of a yellowish red color: *sandy hair.* —**sand′i•ness,** *n.* [*noncount*]

sane (sān) /seyn/ *adj.,* **san•er, san•est. 1.** having a sound, healthy mind. **2.** having or showing reason, sound judgment, or good sense. —**sane′ly,** *adv.* See -SAN-.

sang (sang) /sæŋ/ *v.* pt. of SING.

sang-froid (sän frwä′) /sɑ̃ˈfrwɑ/ *n.* [*noncount*] coolness of mind, esp. when one is under stress.

san•grí•a or **san•gri•a** (sang grē′ə, san-) /sæŋˈgriyə, sæn-/ *n.* [*noncount*] an iced drink usually made of red wine, sugar, sliced fruit, fruit juice, soda water, and spices.

san•gui•nar•y (sang′gwə ner′ē) /ˈsæŋgwəˌnɛriy/ *adj.* **1.** full of or having much bloodshed; bloody. **2.** ready or eager to shed blood; bloodthirsty.

san•guine (sang′gwin) /ˈsæŋgwɪn/ *adj.* **1.** cheerfully optimistic, hopeful, or confident: *a sanguine outlook on life.* **2.** of a healthy red color; ruddy: *a sanguine complexion.*

san•i•tar•i•an (san′i târ′ē ən) /ˌsænɪˈtɛəriyən/ *n.* [*count*] a specialist in public sanitation and health. See -SAN-.

san•i•tar•i•um (san′i târ′ē əm) /ˌsænɪˈtɛəriyəm/ also **san•a•tor•i•um** (san′i tôr′ē əm) /ˌsænɪˈtɔriyəm/ *n.* [*count*], *pl.* **-tar•i•ums, -tar•i•a** (-târ′ē ə) /-ˈtɛəriyə/. an institution for keeping up one's health; a health resort. See -SAN-.

san•i•tar•y (san′i ter′ē) /ˈsænɪˌtɛriy/ *adj.* **1.** of or relating to health, esp. cleanliness, precautions against disease, etc.: *sanitary regulations.* **2.** free from dirt, bacteria, etc.: *a sanitary working environment.* See -SAN-.

san′itary nap′kin, *n.* [*count*] a pad of soft, absorbent material, such as cotton, worn by women during their menstrual period to absorb the flow.

san•i•ta•tion (san′i tā′shən) /ˌsænɪˈteyʃən/ *n.* [*noncount*] **1.** the use of sanitary measures for cleanliness, protecting health, etc. **2.** the system for disposal of sewage and solid waste: *Call the department of sanitation if your garbage is not being hauled away.* See -SAN-.

san•i•tize (san′i tīz′) /ˈsænɪˌtayz/ *v.* [~ + *obj*], **-tized, -tiz•ing. 1.** to make sanitary, as by cleaning or sterilizing. **2.** to make less offensive by removing anything unwholesome, objectionable, etc.: *The producers sanitized her spicy book.* See -SAN-.

san•i•ty (san′i tē) /ˈsænɪtiy/ *n.* [*noncount*] **1.** the state of being sane: *The court did not question the sanity of the witness.* **2.** soundness of judgment. See -SAN-.

sank (sangk) /sæŋk/ *v.* a pt. of SINK.

sans (sanz) /sænz/ *prep.* without: *a bird sans feathers.*

San′ta Claus′ (or **Klaus′**) (san′tə klôz) /ˈsæntə klɔz/ *n.* **1.** [*proper noun; no article*]: a white-bearded, plump, red-suited, grandfatherly man, originally St. Nicholas, who brings gifts to children at Christmas: *So you believe in Santa Claus?* **2.** [*count*] a person dressed like Santa Claus: *Santa Clauses on the streets, accepting donations to charity.*

sap[1] (sap) /sæp/ *n.* **1.** [*noncount*] a watery juice that passes through the tissues of a plant. **2.** [*count*] someone who is easily tricked or fooled; dupe.

sap[2] (sap) /sæp/ *v.* [~ + *obj*], **sapped, sap•ping.** to weaken or destroy in a gradual way; drain: *Over time the disease sapped his strength.*

sa•pi•ent (sā′pē ənt) /ˈseypiyənt/ *adj.* **1.** having or showing wisdom. **2.** of or resembling modern humans in structure, ability to think, etc.: *sapient apes that became the ancestors of humanity.* —**sa′pi•ence,** *n.* [*noncount*]

sap•ling (sap′ling) /ˈsæplɪŋ/ *n.* [*count*] a young tree.

sap•phire (saf′īᵊr) /ˈsæfayᵊr/ *n.* **1.** a gem, a variety of corundum other than the ruby, esp. one that is blue: [*noncount*]: *a ring of sapphire.* [*count*]: *beautiful sapphires in her earrings.* **2.** [*noncount*] the deep blue color of this gem. —*adj.* **3.** deep blue.

sap•py (sap′ē) /ˈsæpiy/ *adj.*, **-pi•er, -pi•est. 1.** full of sap. **2.** sentimental; overly emotional: *a sappy ending.* **3.** foolish: *a sappy grin.* —**sap′pi•ness,** *n.* [*noncount*]: *ridiculed the sappiness of the Christmas season.*

sap•suck•er (sap′suk′ər) /ˈsæpˌsʌkər/ *n.* [*count*] a North American woodpecker that drills holes in trees to get sap.

sar•casm (sär′kaz əm) /ˈsɑrkæzəm/ *n.* **1.** [*noncount*] bitter statements that mock or mean the opposite of what is said: *"Oh, this is very good work," he said with obvious sarcasm, staring at the test grade of 55%.* **2.** [*count*] a sharply mocking or ironical taunt: *spent the whole evening uttering sarcasms.*

sar•cas•tic (sär kas′tik) /sɑrˈkæstɪk/ *adj.* full of sarcasm: *sarcastic comments.* —**sar•cas′ti•cal•ly,** *adv.*

sar•co•ma (sär kō′mə) /sɑrˈkowmə/ *n.* [*count*], *pl.* **-mas, -ma•ta** (-mə tə) /-mətə/. a type of cancerous tumor in the body.

sar•coph•a•gus (sär kof′ə gəs) /sɑrˈkɒfəgəs/ *n.* [*count*], *pl.* **-gi** (-jī′, -gī′) /-ˌdʒay, -ˌgay/ **-gus•es.** a stone coffin displayed as a monument.

sar•dine (sär dēn′) /sɑrˈdiyn/ *n.* [*count*], *pl.* (*esp. when thought of as a group*) **-dine,** (*esp. for kinds or species*) **-dines.** a small fish used as food: *a can of sardines.*

sar•don•ic (sär don′ik) /sɑrˈdɒnɪk/ *adj.* characterized by scornful criticism; mocking bitterly: *a sardonic grin.* —**sar•don′i•cal•ly,** *adv.*

sa•ri (sär′ē) /ˈsɑriy/ *n.* [*count*], *pl.* **-ris.** a type of dress made of a long cloth wrapped around the body with one end draped over one shoulder or the head, worn by women chiefly in India.

sa•rong (sə rông′, -rong′) /səˈrɔŋ, -ˈrɒŋ/ *n.* [*count*] a loose-fitting skirtlike garment formed by wrapping a strip of cloth around the lower part of the body, worn by both sexes in the Malay Archipelago.

sar•sa•pa•ril•la (sas′pə ril′ə, sär′spə-) /ˌsæspəˈrɪlə, ˌsɑrspə-/ *n.*, *pl.* **-las. 1.** [*count*] a vine that grows in warm regions, having heart-shaped leaves. **2.** [*noncount*] the root of this vine, used as a flavoring. **3.** a soft drink, such as root beer, flavored with this: [*noncount*]: *sold sarsaparilla in those old drugstores.* [*count*]: *Two sarsaparillas, please.*

sar•to•ri•al (sär tôr′ē əl, -tōr′-) /sɑrˈtɔriyəl, -ˈtowr-/ *adj.* **1.** of or relating to tailors or their trade. **2.** of or relating to clothing or dress: *entering the ballroom in all their sartorial splendor.* —**sar•to′ri•al•ly,** *adv.*

SASE, an abbreviation of: self-addressed stamped envelope.

sash[1] (sash) /sæʃ/ *n.* [*count*] a long band or scarf worn over one shoulder or around the waist.

sash[2] (sash) /sæʃ/ *n.* **1.** [*count*] a framework, as in a window, in which panes of glass are set. **2.** [*noncount*] such frameworks thought of as a group.

sa•shay (sa shā′) /sæˈʃey/ *v.* [*no obj*] **1.** to walk or proceed in an easy, carefree manner. —*n.* [*count*] **2.** a trip or excursion. **3.** an attempt at something new; a venture.

sass (sas) /sæs/ *Informal.* —*n.* [*noncount*] **1.** bold, disrespectful replies; back talk: *Don't give me any more of your sass, young man!* —*v.* [~ + *obj*] **2.** to answer with sass: *sassed her teacher and was sent to the principal's office.*

sas•sa•fras (sas′ə fras′) /ˈsæsəˌfræs/ *n.* **1.** [*count*] an E North American tree of the laurel family. **2.** [*noncount*] the sweet-smelling bark of its root, used esp. as a flavoring.

sas•sy (sas′ē) /ˈsæsiy/ *adj.*, **-si•er, -si•est. 1.** of or relating to sass: *a smart-alecky, sassy child.* **2.** stylish; lively and bouncy: *a sassy new outfit.*

sat (sat) /sæt/ *v.* a pt. and pp. of SIT.

SAT, *Trademark.* Scholastic Aptitude Test.

Sat., an abbreviation of: Saturday.

-sat-, *root.* *-sat-* comes from Latin, where it has the meaning "full, enough, sufficient." This meaning is found in such words as: DISSATISFACTION, DISSATISFY, INSATIABLE, SATE, SATIATED, SATIRE, SATISFACTION, SATISFY, SATURATE, UNSATISFIED.

Sa•tan (sāt′n) /ˈseytn̩/ *n.* [*proper noun; no article*] **1.** the chief evil spirit, adversary of God and humanity; the devil: *to renounce Satan and all his works.* **2.** [*count*] someone or something like Satan. —**sa•tan•ic** (sə tan′ik, sā-) /səˈtænɪk, sey-/ **sa•tan′i•cal** *adj.* —**sa•tan′i•cal•ly,** *adv.*

satch•el (sach′əl) /ˈsætʃəl/ *n.* [*count*] a small bag, sometimes with a shoulder strap.

sate (sāt) /seyt/ *v.* [~ + *obj*], **sat•ed, sat•ing. 1.** to satisfy fully. **2.** to supply or indulge (someone) to excess: *I was sated by all the holiday food.* See -SAT-.

sa•teen (sa tēn′) /sæˈtiyn/ *n.* [*noncount*] a strong cotton fabric that is made in satin weave and has a shiny face.

sat•el•lite (sat′l īt′) /ˈsætl̩ˌayt/ *n.* [*count*] **1.** a natural body in space, as a moon, that revolves around a planet: *one of the satellites of Jupiter.* **2.** a device launched into orbit around the earth, another planet, the sun, etc.: *a satellite that takes regular photographs of the earth.* **3.** a country under the control or influence of another: *one of America's satellites in Africa.* —*adj.* [*before a noun*] **4.** of or relating to a satellite: *satellite photos.* **5.** controlled by another authority: *a satellite store.*

sa•ti•ate (*v.* sā′shē āt′; *adj.* -it, -āt′) / *v.* ˈseyʃiyˌeyt; *adj.* -ɪt, -ˌeyt/ *v.*, **-at•ed, -at•ing,** *adj.* —*v.* [~ + *obj*] **1.** to supply with too much of something, so as to cause disgust or boredom: *satiated by the drinking parties.* **2.** to satisfy completely; sate. —*adj.* **3.** satisfied fully, as in desire. —**sa′ti•a′tion,** *n.* [*noncount*] See -SAT-.

sa•ti•e•ty (sə tī′i tē) /səˈtayɪtiy/ *n.* [*noncount*] the state of being satiated; surfeit. See -SAT-.

sat•in (sat′n) /ˈsætn̩/ *n.* [*noncount*] **1.** a fabric, such as silk, having a glossy, shiny face and a soft, smooth texture. —*adj.* [*before a noun*] **2.** of or relating to satin; smooth; shiny: *satin pillows.*

sat•ire (sat′īᵊr) /ˈsætayᵊr/ *n.* **1.** [*noncount*] the use of ridicule to show someone's foolishness, weakness, etc. **2.** [*count*] a piece of writing or a performance using this. —**sa•tir•i•cal** (sə tir′i kəl) /səˈtɪrɪkəl/ *adj.* —**sat•i•rist** (sat′ər ist) /ˈsætərɪst/ *n.* [*count*] See -SAT-.

sat•i•rize (sat′ə rīz′) /ˈsætəˌrayz/ *v.* [~ + *obj*], **-rized, -riz•ing.** to use satire: *The impersonators satirized several presidents.*

sat•is•fac•tion (sat′is fak′shən) /ˌsætɪsˈfækʃən/ *n.* [*noncount*] **1.** the state or feeling of being satisfied: *a feeling of satisfaction at a job well done.* **2.** a cause or means of fulfilling a need. **3.** the condition of being confident of something as satisfactory, etc.: *The work was done to the boss's satisfaction.* **4.** money or action to pay for a wrong or injury: *demanded satisfaction for the harm done.* See -SAT-.

sat•is•fac•to•ry (sat′is fak′tə rē, -fak′trē) /ˌsætɪsˈfæktəriy, -ˈfæktriy/ *adj.* able to satisfy demands; adequate: *gave him a satisfactory answer.* —**sat•is•fac•to•ri•ly** (sat′is fak′tər ə lē) /ˌsætɪsˈfæktərəliy/ *adv.*

sat•is•fied (sat′is fīd′) /ˈsætɪsˌfayd/ *adj.* **1.** having a feeling of contentment or pleasure; contented: *satisfied* *customers.* **2.** [be + ~ (+ (that) clause)] certain about something: *I'm satisfied (that) she's telling the truth.*

sat•is•fy (sat′is fī′) /ˈsætɪsˌfay/ *v.* [~ + *obj*], **-fied, -fy•ing. 1.** to fulfill the desires, expectations, or demands of: *Only a full apology will satisfy me.* **2.** to put an end to (a desire, etc.) by providing enough of something: *to satisfy her hunger.* **3.** to give assurance to: *to satisfy oneself by investigation.* **4.** to take care of (something, such as a debt) fully: *You'll need to satisfy any outstanding accounts.* **5.** to be enough for; meet: *unless certain conditions are satisfied.* See -SAT-.

sat•is•fy•ing (sat′is fī′ing) /ˈsætɪsˌfayɪŋ/ *adj.* causing satisfaction: *satisfying results from the election.* [be + ~ + to + *obj*]: *The election results were very satisfying to him.*

sat•u•rate (*v.* sach′ə rāt′; *adj.* -ər it, -ə rāt′) / *v.* ˈsætʃəˌreyt; *adj., n.* -ərɪt, -əˌreyt/ *v.*, **-rat•ed, -rat•ing,** *adj.* **—***v.* **1.** [~ + *obj*] to fill as much as possible: *The smell of fresh-brewed coffee saturated the tiny apartment.* **2.** to (cause to) become thoroughly wet: [~ + *obj*]: *The rain saturated the fields.* [*no obj*]: *That substance saturates when liquid is poured on it.* **—***adj.* **3.** filled with something. **—sat•u•ra•tion** (sach′ə rā′shən) /ˌsætʃəˈreyʃən/ *n.* [*noncount*] See -SAT-.

Sat•ur•day (sat′ər dā′, -dē) /ˈsætərˌdey, -diy/ *n.* the seventh day of the week, following Friday: [*proper noun*]: *We'll come over next Saturday.* [*count*]: *It was a cool, clear Saturday.*

Sat′urday-night′ spe′cial, *n.* [*count*] a small, cheap handgun that is easy to buy and easy to hide: *trying to pass laws against Saturday-night specials.*

sat•ur•nine (sat′ər nīn′) /ˈsætərˌnayn/ *adj.* sluggish or gloomy in the way one feels or appears; glum; somber.

sa•tyr (sā′tər, sat′ər) /ˈseytər, ˈsætər/ *n.* [*count*] **1.** a creature in Greek myth, represented as part human and part horse or goat. **2.** a lascivious man; lecher. **—sa•tyr•ic** (sə tir′ik) /səˈtɪrɪk/ *adj.*

sa•ty•ri•a•sis (sā′tə rī′ə sis, sat′ə-) /ˌseytəˈrayəsɪs, ˌsætə-/ *n.* [*noncount*] abnormal, uncontrollable sexual desire in a male. Compare NYMPHOMANIA.

sauce (sôs) /sɔs/ *n., v.,* **sauced, sauc•ing. —***n.* **1.** a liquid food, such as gravy, put on food: [*noncount*]: *He makes his own spaghetti sauce.* [*count*]: *some spicy sauces.* **2.** [*noncount*] stewed fruit: *cranberry sauce.* **3.** [*noncount*] *Informal.* disrespectful words or behavior; sauciness: *She won't take any more of his sauce.* **4.** [*noncount; usually: the + ~*] *Slang.* alcoholic drink: *He is on the sauce again (= He is drinking heavily).* **—***v.* [~ + *obj*] **5.** *Informal.* to speak disrespectfully to; sass.

sauce•pan (sôs′pan′) /ˈsɔsˌpæn/ *n.* [*count*] a cooking pan of medium depth, usually with a long handle.

sau•cer (sô′sər) /ˈsɔsər/ *n.* [*count*] **1.** a small, round, shallow dish for holding a cup. **2.** something resembling a saucer: *The earrings were two saucers of gold.*

sau•cy (sô′sē) /ˈsɔsiy/ *adj.,* **-ci•er, -ci•est. 1.** impolite; impertinent; insolent: *a saucy little girl.* **2.** lively; bouncy; jaunty: *a saucy little hat.* **—sau•ci•ly** (sô′sə lē) /ˈsɔsəliy/ *adv.*. **—sau′ci•ness,** *n.* [*noncount*]

Sau•di (sou′dē, sô′) /ˈsawdiy, ˈsɔ/ *n.* [*count*], *pl.* **-dis. 1.** a person born or living in Saudi Arabia. **—***adj.* **2.** of or relating to Saudi Arabia.

sau•er•kraut (souᵊr′krout′, sou′ər-) /ˈsawᵊrˌkrawt, ˈsawər-/ *n.* [*noncount*] cabbage cut fine, salted, and allowed to become sour: *a hot dog piled high with sauerkraut.*

sau•na (sô′nə, sou′-) /ˈsɔnə, ˈsaw-/ *n., pl.* **-nas,** *v.,* **-naed, -na•ing. —***n.* [*count*] **1.** a bath that uses dry heat to cause the person in it to perspire. **2.** a bathhouse or room equipped for such a bath. **—***v.* [*no obj*] **3.** to take a sauna.

saun•ter (sôn′tər, sän′-) /ˈsɔntər, ˈsɑn-/ *v.* [*no obj*] **1.** to walk in a relaxed, unhurried way: *He sauntered to the bar and ordered a drink.* **—***n.* [*count; usually singular*] **2.** a relaxed, unhurried walk.

sau•sage (sô′sij) /ˈsɔsɪdʒ/ *n.* finely chopped, seasoned meat stuffed into a casing: [*count*]: *had sausages for breakfast.* [*noncount*]: *spicy Polish sausage.*

sau•té (sō tā′, sô-) /sowˈtey, sɔ-/ *adj., v.,* **-téed** (-tād′) /-ˈteyd/ **-té•ing** (-tā′ing) /-ˈteyɪŋ/ *n.* **—***adj.* **1.** browned in a pan containing a small quantity of butter or oil. **—***v.* [~ + *obj*] **2.** to cook in a small amount of fat; pan-fry. **—***n.* [*count*] **3.** a dish of sautéed food.

sav•age (sav′ij) /ˈsævɪdʒ/ *adj., n., v.,* **-aged, -ag•ing. —***adj.* **1.** fierce or ferocious; wild: *a savage criticism of her book.* **2.** uncivilized; barbarous: *savage people in the interior.* **—***n.* [*count*] **3.** an uncivilized human being. **4.** a fierce, brutal, or cruel person: *Those savages have murdered innocent children.* **—***v.* [~ + *obj*] **5.** to assault brutally: *The dog savaged the child's arm.* **6.** to criticize harshly or without stopping: *The president savaged her opponents.* **—sav′age•ly,** *adv.*: *The armies attacked the position savagely.*

sav•age•ry (sav′ij rē) /ˈsævədʒriy/ *n.* [*noncount*] savage behavior: *surprised by the savagery of her attack.*

sa•van•na or **sa•van•nah** (sə van′ə) /səˈvænə/ *n.* [*count*], *pl.* **-nas** or **-nahs.** a mostly flat area of coarse grass and scattered tree growth, esp. on the margins of the tropics, as in E Africa: *lions in the savannahs.*

sa•vant (sa vänt′, sav′ənt) /sæˈvɑnt, ˈsævənt/ *n.* [*count*] a person of great or deep learning; a scholar.

save[1] (sāv) /seyv/ *v.,* **saved, sav•ing,** *n.* **—***v.* **1.** [~ + *obj*] to rescue from danger or harm: *saved the boy from the floodwaters.* **2.** [~ + *obj*] to keep safe or unhurt: *"God save the queen," they shouted.* **3.** [~ + *obj*] **a.** to keep from being lost: *He came in and tried to save the game.* **b.** to keep; retain: *Save your cancelled checks as proof of payment.* **4.** to avoid the using up of (some resource): [~ + *obj*]: *to save fuel by driving at 55 mph.* [~ + on + *obj*]: *The business could save on expenditures.* **5. a.** to set (money) aside for later use or need: [~ + *obj*]: *to save money for college.* [*no obj*]: *We'll just have to save for college.* [~ + up + *obj*]: *to save up some money for college.* [~ + *obj* + up]: *to save some money up.* **b.** to put (something) aside for later use; reserve; hold: [~ + *obj* + for + *obj*]: *to save a piece of pie for him.* [~ + *obj* + *obj*]: *to save him a piece of pie.* **6. a.** [~ + *obj* + *obj*] to prevent the occurrence, use, or necessity of (something): *The computer will save you the trouble of having to type your paper again.* **b.** [~ + *obj* + from + *obj*] to prevent (someone) from experiencing something bad, etc.: *This will save you from having to retype your paper.* **7.** [~ + *obj*] to deliver from the consequences of sin. **8.** [~ + *obj*] to copy (computer data) onto a hard or floppy disk, etc.: *Save your file before turning off the computer.* **9.** [~ + *obj*] to stop (a ball or puck) from entering one's goal: *The goalie saved forty shots.* **—***n.* [*count*] **10.** a goalkeeper's act of preventing a goal: *She made a diving save on that hard shot.* **—*Idiom.* 11. save someone's neck** or **skin,** to rescue oneself or another from harm or danger: *ran away from the battlefield because he wanted to save his own skin.* **—sav′a•ble, save′a•ble,** *adj.* **—sav′er,** *n.* [*count*]

save[2] (sāv) /seyv/ *prep.* **1.** Also, **save for.** except; but: *They all left save (for) one.* **—***conj.* **2.** except; but: *He would have gone, save that he had no money for travel.*

sav•ing (sā′ving) /ˈseyvɪŋ/ *adj.* **1.** tending or serving to rescue, preserve, or retain. **—***n.* **2.** [*count*] a reduction or lessening of spending, or something saved: *a saving of over $50,000 a year.* **3. savings,** [*plural*] money saved by economy and put in a safe place: *enough savings for a down payment on a car.*

sav•ior or **sav•iour** (sāv′yər) /ˈseyvyər/ *n.* **1.** [*count*] one who rescues: *the savior of the country.* **2.** [*proper noun; often: Savior; the (or a possessive word) + ~*] a title of God, esp. of Jesus: *our Savior.*

sa•voir-faire (sav′wär fâr′) /ˈsævwɑrˈfɛər/ *n.* [*noncount*] knowledge of what to do in any situation.

sa•vor (sā′vər) /ˈseyvər/ *n.* **1.** [*noncount*] the quality in a substance that affects the sense of taste or of smell. **—***v.* [~ + *obj*] **2.** to sense (something) by taste or smell, esp. with enjoyment: *savored the rich-tasting cigar.* **3.** to give oneself to the enjoyment of: *savored the sweet feeling of victory.* Also, *esp. Brit.,* **sa′vour.**

sa•vor•y[1] (sā′və rē) /ˈseyvəriy/ *adj.,* **-i•er, -i•est,** *n., pl.* **-vor•ies. —***adj.* **1.** pleasant in taste or smell. **2.** spicy; piquant: *a savory jelly.* **3.** pleasing, attractive, or agreeable: *The hoodlum was not a very savory character.* **—***n.* [*noncount*] **4.** *Chiefly Brit.* a spicy or aromatic dish served as an appetizer or dessert. Also, *esp. Brit.,* **sa′vour•y. —sa′vor•i•ness,** *n.* [*noncount*]

sa•vor•y[2] (sā′və rē) /ˈseyvəriy/ *n.* [*noncount*] a sweet-smelling herb of the mint family, having leaves used in cooking.

sav•vy (sav′ē) /ˈsæviy/ *n., adj.,* **-vi•er, -vi•est. —***n.* [*noncount*] **1.** Also, **sav′vi•ness.** practical understanding; common sense: *showed a great deal of political savvy.* **—***adj.* **2.** shrewdly intelligent; canny: *a savvy cab driver who knew all the shortcuts.*

saw[1] (sô) /sɔ/ *n., v.,* **sawed, sawed** or **sawn, saw•ing. —***n.* [*count*] **1.** a tool for cutting, usually a thin blade of metal with sharp teeth. **—***v.* **2.** to cut with a saw: [*no obj*]: *My arms are tired; I've been sawing all day.* [~ + *obj*]: *He's been sawing tree branches all day.* **—*Idiom.* 3. saw wood,** to snore loudly while sleeping.

saw[2] (sô) /sɔ/ *v.* pt. of SEE[1].

saw[3] (sô) /sɔ/ *n.* [*count*] a saying; maxim; proverb: *the old saw about "feeding a cold and starving a fever."*

saw•bones (sô′bōnz′) /ˈsɔˌbownz/ *n.* [*count*], *pl.* **-bones, -bones•es.** [*singular form is used with a singular verb*] *Slang.* a surgeon or physician: *An old sawbones like him isn't a bad choice for a doctor.*

saw•buck (sô′buk′) /ˈsɔˌbʌk/ *n.* [*count*] **1.** a sawhorse. **2.** *Slang.* a ten-dollar bill.

saw•dust (sô′dust′) /ˈsɔˌdʌst/ *n.* [*noncount*] tiny particles of wood produced when sawing: *to spread sawdust all over the floor.*

saw•horse (sô′hôrs′) /ˈsɔˌhɔrs/ *n.* [*count*] a movable frame for supporting wood while it is being sawed.

saw•mill (sô′mil′) /ˈsɔˌmɪl/ *n.* [*count*] a building in which wood is sawed into planks, etc., by machinery.

saw′-toothed′, *adj.* having points, edges, or teeth resembling the edge of a saw.

sax (saks) /sæks/ *n.* [*count*] a saxophone.

sax•o•phone (sak′sə fōn′) /ˈsæksəˌfown/ *n.* a musical wind instrument having a cone-shaped tube with keys or valves and a mouthpiece with one reed: [*count*]: *a brand new saxophone.* [*noncount*]: *He played saxophone with the big names in jazz.* —**sax′o•phon′ist,** *n.* [*count*] See -PHON-.

say (sā) /sey/ *v.,* **said** (sed) /sɛd/ **say•ing,** *adv., n., interj.* —*v.* **1.** [~ + *obj*] to utter or pronounce; speak: *Don't say a word.* **2.** to express (something) in words; declare: [~ + *(that) clause*]: *I wrote and said (that) I wanted to see her again.* [*used with quotations*]: *"I'll be there," he said.* [~ + *obj*]: *I've said my piece (= I've expressed my thoughts).* **3.** to state (something) as an opinion or judgment: [~ + *(that) clause*]: *I say (that) we should wait here.* [*no obj*]: *What should I do? I just can't say.* **4.** [~ + *obj*] to recite or repeat: *said his prayers and went to bed.* **5.** [~ + *obj*] to express (a message, etc.), as through words, etc.: *What does this painting say to you?* **6.** [~ + *obj*] to indicate or show: *What does your watch say? The clock says ten-thirty.* **7.** [~ + *(that) clause*] (used as a command, or as a polite command after *let's*) suppose; assume; imagine: *Say (that) you saw her on the street; what would you do then? Let's say (that) I had gambled all our money away.* —*adv.* **8.** approximately; about: *It's, say, 14 feet across.* **9.** for example: *Suppose we asked a student, say, Janette here, for her opinion.* —*n.* [*noncount*] **10.** what a person says or wishes to say; one's turn to say something: *She has already had her say.* **11.** the right or chance to state an opinion or exercise influence: *to have one's say in a decision.* —*interj.* **12.** (used to express surprise or to get someone's attention): *Say! That's great; you made it!* —***Idiom.*** **13. go without saying,** [*it/that* + ~ (+ *(that) clause*)] to be self-evident: *It goes without saying (that) you must write a thank-you note for a gift.* **14. that is to say,** [*no obj*] in other words; meaning (that): *The judge threw the book at him; that is to say, gave him the maximum sentence.* —**Usage.** The verbs SAY and TELL are sometimes confused. The verb SAY does not take a person as its direct object, only a word or clause: *He said a few words and sat down.* If a person is mentioned after SAY, the word *to* must be used before it: *He said to her that he was ready.* The verb TELL may take a person as an object: *He told her he was ready.*

say•ing (sā′ing) /ˈseyɪŋ/ *n.* [*count*] something said, esp. a proverb: *the old saying, "A stitch in time saves nine."*

say′-so′, *n.* [*count*], *pl.* **say-sos. 1.** one's personal statement indicating approval: *Tell them you have my say-so if they give you any trouble.* **2.** a statement, esp. a personal one without proof: *Who would believe that story just on his say-so?*

SC, an abbreviation of: South Carolina.

scab (skab) /skæb/ *n., v.,* **scabbed, scab•bing.** —*n.* [*count*] **1.** the crusty, dry patch that forms over a wound. **2.** a worker who takes a striking worker's place on the job. —*v.* [*no obj*] **3.** to become covered with a scab. **4.** to act or work as a scab.

scab•bard (skab′ərd) /ˈskæbərd/ *n.* [*count*] a slot for holding a sword, usually one hanging from a belt; sheath.

scab•by (skab′ē) /ˈskæbiy/ *adj.,* **-bi•er, -bi•est.** of or relating to scabs. —**scab′bi•ness,** *n.* [*noncount*]

sca•bies (skā′bēz, -bē ēz′) /ˈskeybiyz, -biyˌiyz/ *n.* [*noncount; used with a singular verb*] an itchy skin disease.

scads (skadz) /skædz/ *n.* [*plural*] a great number or quantity: [~ + *of* + *plural noun*]: *scads of people at the concert.* [~ + *of* + *noncount noun*]: *scads of money.*

scaf•fold (skaf′əld, -ōld) /ˈskæfəld, -owld/ *n.* [*count*] **1.** a raised platform for workers and materials. **2.** a raised platform on which a criminal is executed by hanging.

scaf•fold•ing (skaf′əl ding, -ōl-) /ˈskæfəldɪŋ, -owl-/ *n.* [*noncount*] **1.** a scaffold or system of scaffolds. **2.** materials for scaffolds.

scal•a•wag (skal′ə wag′) /ˈskæləˌwæg/ *n.* [*count*] **1.** a dishonest person; rascal. **2.** a white Southerner who supported Republican policy during Reconstruction.

scald (skôld) /skɔld/ *v.* [~ + *obj*] **1.** to burn with or as if with hot liquid or steam. **2.** to heat to a temperature just short of the boiling point: *to scald milk.* —*n.* [*count*] **3.** a burn caused by scalding.

scale[1] (skāl) /skeyl/ *n., v.,* **scaled, scal•ing.** —*n.* **1.** [*count*] one of the thin, flat plates forming the covering of fish, snakes, or lizards. **2.** [*count*] any thin, flat piece that peels off from a surface, such as the skin. **3.** [*noncount*] a coating, as from rust. —*v.* [~ + *obj*] **4.** to remove the scales from: *to scale a fish.*

scale[2] (skāl) /skeyl/ *n.* [*count*] **1.** Often, **scales.** [*plural*] a balance for weighing. See illustration at HOSPITAL. **2.** either of the pans or dishes of a balance. —***Idiom.*** **3. tip the scale(s), a.** to weigh, esp. a large amount: *to tip the scale at 300 lbs.* **b.** to be the thing that decides something else: *His presentation in front of the committee tipped the scales in his favor.*

scale[3] (skāl) /skeyl/ *n., v.,* **scaled, scal•ing.** —*n.* **1.** [*count*] a series of degrees that represent amounts of something: *On a scale of 1 to 10, how would you rate his acting performance?* **2.** [*count*] a series of marks laid down at certain distances, such as along a line, for measuring, adding, etc.: *the scale of a thermometer.* **3.** [*count*] the ratio of distances on a map to corresponding values on the surface of the earth: *The scale on this map is one inch to five miles.* **4.** [*count*] the ratio of the size of a model of an object as compared to the object itself: *a model on a scale of one inch to one foot.* **5.** [*noncount*] Also called **union scale.** the minimum amount of money that can be paid to a working person, as established by a union contract: *You'll have to pay them scale if the workplace becomes unionized.* **6.** [*count*] relative size or extent: *planning done on a grand scale.* **7.** [*count*] any measuring instrument with graduated markings. **8.** [*count*] a succession of musical tones at fixed degrees: *the harmonic scale.* —*v.* [~ + *obj*] **9.** to climb by or as if by a ladder: *He scaled the wall.* **10.** to adjust by fixed steps; match to some standard: *to scale tax rates.* **11. scale down** (or **up**), [~ + *down/up* + *obj*] to decrease (or increase) in amount: *to scale down wages.* —***Idiom.*** **12. to scale,** [*noncount*] following or showing a fixed ratio between a drawing, model, etc., and the object itself: *The model of the car was drawn perfectly to scale.*

scal•lion (skal′yən) /ˈskælyən/ *n.* [*count*] an onion that does not form a large bulb.

scal•lop (skol′əp, skal′-) /ˈskɒləp, ˈskæl-/ *n.* [*count*] **1.** a marine animal with two wavy-edged shells. **2.** Often, **scallops.** [*plural*] a thick, usually round muscle of this animal used as food.

scalp (skalp) /skælp/ *n.* [*count*] **1.** the skin of the upper part of the head. **2.** a part of the human scalp taken from an enemy as a sign of victory. —*v.* **3.** [~ + *obj*] to cut or tear the scalp from: *They scalped their victims.* **4.** to resell (tickets, stocks, etc.) at unfairly high prices: [~ + *obj*]: *to scalp tickets to a football game.* [*no obj*]: *caught scalping in the parking lot.* —**scalp′er,** *n.* [*count*]: *scalpers trying to sell football tickets.*

scal•pel (skal′pəl) /ˈskælpəl/ *n.* [*count*] a small, light, usually straight knife used in surgery, laboratory work, etc.

scal•y (skā′lē) /ˈskeyliy/ *adj.,* **-i•er, -i•est.** having, consisting of, or full of scales: *the scaly skin of the snake.*

scam (skam) /skæm/ *n., v.,* **scammed, scam•ming.** —*n.* [*count*] **1.** an illegal scheme to make money; swindle: *One of his scams was to pose as a police officer.* —*v.* [~ + *obj*] **2.** to cheat by means of a scam; swindle or defraud: *to scam the tourists into buying fake jewelry.*

scamp (skamp) /skæmp/ *n.* [*count*] **1.** one who cheats another for his or her own profit. **2.** a young person who enjoys mild teasing of another.

scamp•er (skam′pər) /ˈskæmpər/ *v.* [*no obj*] **1.** to run or go hastily: *The dog scampered out of the room.* **2.** to run playfully about; caper: *The children scampered in the yard.* —*n.* [*count*] **3.** an act or instance of scampering.

scam•pi (skam′pē, skäm′-) /ˈskæmpiy, ˈskɑm-/ *n., pl.* **-pi. 1.** [*plural*] shrimps or prawns. **2.** [*noncount; used with a singular verb*] a dish of these cooked in butter and garlic.

scan (skan) /skæn/ *v.,* **scanned, scan•ning,** *n.* **—***v.* **1.** [~ + *obj*] to examine (something) carefully; scrutinize: *scanning the crowd for his parents' faces.* **2.** [~ + *obj*] to read quickly or hastily: *scanned the newspaper.* **3.** [~ + *obj*] to observe repeatedly or in sweeping motions: *The lookouts scanned the horizon for enemy planes.* **4.** [~ + *obj*] to analyze (poetry) in order to understand its meter. **5.** [*no obj*] (of lines of poetry) to conform to or agree with the rules of meter: *That poem doesn't scan.* **6.** [~ + *obj*] to read (data) for use by a computer, esp. by means of a piece of equipment that records a picture for use by a computer: *to scan the photograph and reproduce it on the screen.* **7.** [~ + *obj*] to examine (a body part) with a scanner: *to scan the kidneys.* **—***n.* [*count*] **8.** an act or instance of scanning. **9. a.** an examination of a body part using a scanner. **b.** the image or display so obtained: *The scan shows a tumor in the lung.* See -SCEND-.

scan•dal (skan**′**dl) /ˈskændl̩/ *n.* **1.** [*count*] a disgraceful action or circumstance: *Several scandals rocked the government.* **2.** [*noncount*] public disgrace: *This administration can't afford scandal.* **3.** [*noncount*] gossip intended to harm others: *spreading scandal all over town.*

scan•dal•ize (skan**′**dl iz**′**) /ˈskændl̩ˌayz/ *v.* [~ + *obj*], **-ized, -iz•ing.** to shock by something disgraceful or immoral, etc.: *behavior that scandalized the neighbors.*

scan•dal•mon•ger (skan**′**dl mung′gər, -mong′-) /ˈskændl̩ˌmʌŋgər, -ˌmɒŋ-/ *n.* [*count*] one who gossips about scandal.

scan•dal•ous (skan**′**dl əs) /ˈskændl̩əs/ *adj.* of or relating to scandal: *scandalous behavior.* [*It* + *be* + ~ + *that clause*]: *It's scandalous that so many go hungry in this wealthy country.* —**scan′dal•ous•ly,** *adv.*: *scandalously high taxes.*

Scan•di•na•vi•an (skan′də nā**′**vē ən) /ˌskændəˈneyviyən/ *adj.* **1.** of or relating to Scandinavia. **—***n.* [*count*] **2.** a person born or living in Scandinavia.

scan•ner (skan**′**ər) /ˈskænər/ *n.* [*count*] **1.** a person or thing that scans. **2.** a device that scans, such as one that uses radar to detect or examine distant objects. **3.** a device for examining a body, organ, or tissue. See -SCEND-.

scan•sion (skan**′**shən) /ˈskænʃən/ *n.* [*noncount*] the analysis of the meter in lines of poetry.

scant (skant) /skænt/ *adj.,* **-i•er, -i•est. 1.** barely enough in amount or quantity; insufficient; meager: *Her new book received scant attention in the press.* **2.** [*before a noun*] barely amounting to as much as indicated: *Measure a scant cupful of flour into the bowl.* —**scant′ly,** *adv.* —**scant′ness,** *n.* [*noncount*]

scant•y (skan**′**tē) /ˈskæntiy/ *adj.,* **-i•er, -i•est,** *n., pl.* **-ies. —***adj.* **1.** not enough in amount, extent, or degree: *a scanty little bathing suit.* **—***n.* **2. scanties,** [*plural*] very brief underpants, esp. for women. —**scant•i•ly** (skan**′**tl ē) /ˈskæntl̩iy/ *adv.*: *scantily dressed.* —**scant′i•ness,** *n.* [*noncount*]

scape•goat (skāp**′**gōt′) /ˈskeypˌgowt/ *n.* [*count*] **1.** one forced to take the blame for others: *After the scandal became public, the president looked for a scapegoat and found one in the accounting division.* **—***v.* [~ + *obj*] **2.** to make a scapegoat of: *The company scapegoated its accounting division.*

scap•u•la (skap**′**yə lə) /ˈskæpyələ/ *n.* [*count*], *pl.* **-las, -lae** (-lē′) /-ˌliy/. a flat triangular bone forming the back part of a shoulder; shoulder blade. —**scap′u•lar,** *adj.*

scar[1] (skär) /skɑr/ *n., v.,* **scarred, scar•ring. —***n.* [*count*] **1.** a mark left by a healed wound: *The prisoner has a scar on his left arm.* **2.** a lasting effect after a troubling experience: *The trial left emotional scars.* **—***v.* **3.** to leave or form a scar on (someone or something): [~ + *obj*]: *The shelling scarred the countryside.* [*no obj*]: *Will this operation scar?*

scar[2] (skär) /skɑr/ *n.* [*count*] **1.** a steep, rocky cliff. **2.** a low rock in the sea, or one that is partly under water.

scarce (skârs) /skɛərs/ *adj.,* **scarc•er, scarc•est,** *adv.* **—***adj.* **1.** [*often: be* + ~] insufficient: *Jobs are scarce in difficult times.* **2.** rarely found or seen. **—***adv.* **3.** scarcely: *She could scarce believe her eyes.* **—*Idiom.* 4. make oneself scarce,** [*no obj*] **a.** to leave, esp. quickly: *This party is boring; let's make ourselves scarce.* **b.** to stay away. —**scarce′ness,** *n.* [*noncount*]

scarce•ly (skârs**′**lē) /ˈskɛərsliy/ *adv.* **1.** barely; not quite: *can scarcely see.* **2.** definitely not: *scarcely the time to raise such questions.* **3.** probably not: *Don't blame yourself; you could scarcely have done anything else at the time.*

scar•ci•ty (skâr**′**sə tē) /ˈskɛərsətiy/ *n., pl.* **-ties.** shortness of supply: [*count*]: *a scarcity of low-income housing.* [*noncount*]: *Scarcity causes prices to rise.*

scare (skâr) /skɛər/ *v.,* **scared, scar•ing,** *n.* **—***v.* **1.** to fill (someone), esp. suddenly, with fear; frighten: [~ + *obj*]: *Something scared her. She isn't scared easily.* [*It* + ~ + *obj* + *clause*]: *It really scared me when she stopped breathing.* **2.** [*no obj*] to become frightened: *She doesn't scare easily.* **3. scare off** or **away,** to frighten (someone) enough to cause him or her to run off: [~ + *off/away* + *obj*]: *We scared off the thief.* [~ + *obj* + *off/away*]: *scared the thief away.* **4. scare up,** to find in spite of difficulties: [~ + *up* + *obj*]: *Try to scare up some wood for the fire.* [~ + *obj* + *up*]: *to scare some wood up for a fire.* **—***n.* [*count*] **5.** a sudden fright or alarm: *We got quite a scare when she stopped breathing.* **6.** a time or condition of alarm or worry: *a war scare.*

scare•crow (skâr**′**krō′) /ˈskɛərˌkrow/ *n.* [*count*] **1.** a figure in the shape of a person in old clothes, set up to frighten birds away from crops. **2.** a ragged, thin person: *You look like a scarecrow!*

scared (skârd) /skɛərd/ *adj.* [*usually: be* + ~] **1.** filled with fear; frightened: *She was scared. He looks scared.* **2.** worried: [*be* + ~ + *of* + *obj*]: *I'm scared of looking foolish.* [*be* + ~ + *(that) clause*]: *We're scared that we'll all lose our jobs.*

scarf (skärf) /skɑrf/ *n.* [*count*], *pl.* **scarfs, scarves** (skärvz). a long strip of cloth worn about the neck. See illustration at CLOTHING.

scar•let (skär**′**lit) /ˈskɑrlɪt/ *n.* [*noncount*] **1.** a bright red color. **—***adj.* **2.** of the color scarlet.

scar′let fe′ver, *n.* [*noncount*] a disease, esp. of children, that produces a high fever and a red rash.

scar•y (skâr**′**ē) /ˈskɛəriy/ *adj.,* **-i•er, -i•est. 1.** causing fright or alarm: *a scary roller-coaster ride.* **2.** easily frightened; timid. —**scar′i•ness,** *n.* [*noncount*]

scat[1] (skat) /skæt/ *v.* [*no obj*], **scat•ted, scat•ting.** to move or go off hastily: *I told him to scat and he did.*

scat[2] (skat) /skæt/ *v.,* **scat•ted, scat•ting,** *n.* **—***v.* [*no obj*] **1.** to sing scat. **—***n.* [*noncount*] **2.** jazz singing that uses made up, nonsense syllables to imitate the phrasing or effect of a musical instrument.

scath•ing (skā**′**thing) /ˈskeyðɪŋ/ *adj.* bitterly severe; harsh; cruel: *a scathing remark.* —**scath′ing•ly,** *adv.*: *a scathingly written attack.*

scat•ter (skat**′**ər) /ˈskætər/ *v.* **1.** [~ + *obj*] to toss loosely about: *to scatter seeds.* **2.** to (cause to) separate; disperse: [~ + *obj*]: *The police scattered the crowd.* [*no obj*]: *The crowd quickly scattered.*

scat•ter•brain (skat**′**ər brān′) /ˈskætərˌbreyn/ *n.* [*count*] a foolish, forgetful person. —**scat′ter•brained′,** *adj.*: *He's so scatterbrained, he even forgets what day it is.*

scat′ter rug′, *n.* [*count*] a small rug.

scav•enge (skav**′**inj) /ˈskævɪndʒ/ *v.,* **-enged, -eng•ing.** to gather by searching (something that can be used) from rubbish: [*no obj; (~ + for + obj)*]: *The vultures scavenged for food.* [~ + *obj*]: *scavenged some parts.*

scav•en•ger (skav**′**in jər) /ˈskævɪndʒər/ *n.* [*count*] **1.** one that feeds on dead organic matter. **2.** one who scavenges for useful material.

sce•nar•i•o (si nâr**′**ē ō′, -när**′**-) /sɪˈnɛəriyˌow, -ˈnɑr-/ *n.* [*count*], *pl.* **-i•os. 1.** an outline of a plot, describing the scenes, etc. **2.** an outline of possible events: *The scenario he imagined had three superpowers fighting one another.*

-scend-, *root.* -*scend*- comes from Latin, where it has the meaning "climb." This meaning is found in such words as: ASCEND, CONDESCEND, DESCEND, TRANSCEND, TRANSCENDENT.

scene (sēn) /siyn/ *n.* [*count*] **1.** the place where some action occurs or has occurred: *the scene of the accident.* **2.** a view or picture: *an artist who paints scenes of the South.* **3.** an embarrassing display of anger, etc.: *Don't make a scene; let's discuss this when we get home.* **4.** a division of a play, etc., that represents a single episode: *In the first scene the characters are introduced.* **5.** the place where the action of a story or an episode occurs. **6.** an area of activity, interest, etc.: *the fashion scene.* **—*Idiom.* 7. behind the scenes, a.** in secret or in private. **b.** where the full operations of something take place: *happy working behind the scenes to elect the next president.*

scen•er•y (sē**′**nə rē) /ˈsiynəriy/ *n.* [*noncount*] **1.** the general appearance of a place: *wild, beautiful scenery in the Alps.* **2.** hangings, curtains, etc., used as background on a stage.

sce•nic (sē**′**nik) /ˈsiynɪk/ *adj.* **1.** of or relating to natural scenery. **2.** having beautiful or pleasant scenery: *a scenic park.* **3.** of or relating to the stage or to stage scenery: *scenic design.*

scent (sent) /sɛnt/ *n.* **1.** [*count*] a special smell, esp. when pleasant. **2.** [*count*] a smell left in passing, by which an animal or person may be traced: *The bloodhounds picked up the scent.* **3.** [*count*] a track or set of clues that leads one somewhere: *detectives on the scent of the crook.* **4.** [*noncount*] perfume. **5.** [*noncount*] the sense of smell: *animals with keen scent.* —*v.* [~ + *obj*] **6.** to sense or recognize by or as if by smell: *to scent trouble.* **7.** to fill with an odor or smell: *a room heavily scented with pine.* —**scent′ed,** *adj.* See -SENT-.

scep•ter (sep′tər) /'sɛptər/ *n.* [*count*] a rod held in the hand as a sign of royal power. Also, *esp. Brit.,* **scep′tre.**

scep•tic (skep′tik) /'skɛptɪk/ *n., adj.* SKEPTIC.

sch., an abbreviation of: school.

sched•ule (skej′o͞ol, -o͝ol, -o͞o əl) /'skɛdʒuwl, -ʊl, -uwəl/ *n., v.,* **-uled, -ul•ing.** —*n.* [*count*] **1.** a plan of procedure to achieve a goal, esp. when referring to the ordering of events. **2.** a series of things to be done at or during a time or period: *He always has a full schedule.* **3.** a timetable: *a train schedule for next year.* **4.** a statement of details, often in the form of a table: *a tax schedule.* —*v.* [~ + *obj*] **5.** to make a schedule of or enter in a schedule: *a flight scheduled at six o'clock.* **6.** to plan for a date: *to schedule publication for June.*

sche•mat•ic (skē mat′ik, ski-) /skiy'mætɪk, skɪ-/ *adj.* **1.** relating to or of the nature of a diagram or scheme. —*n.* [*count*] **2.** a diagram, plan, or drawing: *opened the book of schematics to find the proper measurements.*

scheme (skēm) /skiym/ *n., v.,* **schemed, schem•ing.** —*n.* [*count*] **1.** a plan of action; project or system: *a scheme to speed up production.* **2.** a dishonest, usually secret plot; an intrigue. **3.** a diagram, map, or the like. —*v.* **4.** to create (something) as a scheme; plot: [~ + *obj*]: *schemed a way to avoid the work.* [*no obj*]: *went around scheming so much no one trusted him.* —**schem′er,** *n.* [*count*]

scher•zo (skert′sō) /'skɛrtsow/ *n.* [*count*], *pl.* **scher•zos, scher•zi** (skert′sē) /'skɛrtsiy/. a part in a piece of music having a playful character.

schism (siz′əm, skiz′-) /'sɪzəm, 'skɪz-/ *n.* separation, esp. into opposed sides, as in a church: [*noncount*]: *The groups worked hard to avoid schism.* [*count*]: *The early days of that church were marked by bitter schisms.* —**schis•mat•ic** (siz mat′ik, skiz-) /sɪz'mætɪk, skɪz-/ *adj.*

schiz•o•phre•ni•a (skit′sə frē′nē ə, -frēn′yə) /ˌskɪtsə'friyniyə, -'friynyə/ *n.* [*noncount*] a severe mental disorder usually seen in a person's disorganized speech and behavior.

schiz•o•phren•ic (skit′sə fren′ik) /ˌskɪtsə'frɛnɪk/ *adj.* **1.** suffering from schizophrenia. **2.** having or showing behavior that seems contradictory. —*n.* [*count*] **3.** one who is schizophrenic. Also, **schiz•oid** (skit′soid) /'skɪtsɔyd/.

schle•miel or **shle•miel** (shlə mēl′) /ʃlə'miyl/ *n.* [*count*] *Slang.* an awkward and unlucky person for whom things never turn out right.

schlep or **shlep** (shlep) /ʃlɛp/ *v.,* **schlepped** or **shlepped, schlep•ping** or **shlep•ping,** *n. Slang.* —*v.* **1.** [~ + *obj*] to carry with great effort; lug: *I don't want you to schlep that heavy suitcase.* **2.** [*no obj*] to move slowly or with too much care. —*n.* [*count*] **3.** one who is slow or awkward. **4.** an annoyingly awkward or slow journey: *That's too big a schlep, going all the way downtown.*

schlock or **shlock** (shlok) /ʃlɒk/ *n.* [*noncount*] *Slang.* something of cheap or inferior quality: *Where does he buy such schlock?* —**schlock′y,** *adj.,* **-i•er, -i•est.**

schmaltz or **schmalz** or **shmaltz** (shmälts, shmôlts) /ʃmɑlts, ʃmɔlts/ *n.* [*noncount*] *Informal.* exaggerated tender feeling, as in music: *His music may be schmaltz, but it puts the baby to sleep.* —**schmaltz′y,** *adj.,* **-i•er, -i•est:** *a real schmaltzy ending.*

schmo or **schmoe** (shmō) /ʃmow/ *n.* [*count*], *pl.* **schmoes.** *Slang.* a foolish, boring, or stupid person; jerk.

schnapps or **schnaps** (shnäps, shnaps) /ʃnɑps, ʃnæps/ *n.* [*noncount; used with a singular verb*] any strong, dry alcoholic drink: *coffee with schnapps.*

schnau•zer (shnou′zər, shnout′sər) /'ʃnawzər, 'ʃnawtsər/ *n.* [*count*] a German breed of dog having a tight, wiry coat.

schnook or **shnook** (shno͝ok) /ʃnʊk/ *n.* [*count*] *Slang.* one who is easily fooled.

schnoz (shnoz) /ʃnɒz/ also **schnoz•zle** (shnoz′əl) /'ʃnɒzəl/ *n.* [*count*] *Slang.* a nose, esp. a large one.

-schol-, *root.* *-schol-* comes from Latin, where it has the meaning "school." This meaning is found in such words as: SCHOLAR, SCHOLASTIC, SCHOOL, UNSCHOOLED.

schol•ar (skol′ər) /'skɒlər/ *n.* [*count*] **1.** a person of great learning: *a Shakespearean scholar.* **2.** a student. —**schol′ar•ly,** *adj.*: *your scholarly activities in computer science.* See -SCHOL-.

schol•ar•ship (skol′ər ship′) /'skɒlərˌʃɪp/ *n.* **1.** [*noncount*] the qualities or accomplishments of a scholar: *scholarship respected by other scientists.* **2.** [*count*] a gift of money to help a student with his or her studies: *awarded a full scholarship.* **3.** [*noncount*] the knowledge of a group of scholars: *current scholarship on this problem.* See -SCHOL-.

scho•las•tic (skə las′tik) /skə'læstɪk/ *adj.* [*before a noun*] of or relating to schools, scholars, or education. Also, **scho•las′ti•cal.** —**scho•las′ti•cal•ly,** *adv.*: *Scholastically he was very advanced.* See -SCHOL-.

school[1] (sko͞ol) /skuwl/ *n.* **1.** a place for teaching people under college age: [*count*]: *His children went to a private school.* [*noncount*]: *Are your children old enough to go to school?* SEE ILLUSTRATION. **2.** a college or university: [*count*]: *Yale is a prestigious school.* [*noncount*]: *He went to school at Yale.* **3.** [*count*] an academic department for instruction in a particular field: *the school of liberal arts and sciences.* **4.** a program of studies: [*noncount*]: *He's studying in art school.* [*count*]: *He's enrolled in an art school.* **5.** [*noncount*] the activity of teaching or of learning under instruction: *School doesn't start until September.* **6.** [*count*] the body of people belonging to an educational institution: *The whole school applauded.* **7.** [*count*] a group of pupils having a certain master, system, etc.: *the Platonic school of philosophy.* —*adj.* [*before a noun*] **8.** of or connected with a school or schools. —*v.* [~ + *obj*] **9.** to educate in or as if in a school; teach: *schooled him in magic and sorcery.* See -SCHOL-.

school[2] (sko͞ol) /skuwl/ *n.* [*count*] **1.** a large number of fish, porpoises, etc., feeding or traveling together. —*v.* [*no obj*] **2.** to form into, or go in, a school, such as fish.

school•house (sko͞ol′hous′) /'skuwlˌhaws/ *n.* [*count*]. a building used as a school.

school•marm (sko͞ol′märm′) /'skuwlˌmɑrm/ *n.* [*count*] a female schoolteacher, esp. one who is old-fashioned.

school•mas•ter (sko͞ol′mas′tər) /'skuwlˌmæstər/ *n.* [*count*] a man who is in charge of or who teaches in a school.

school•mate (sko͞ol′māt′) /'skuwlˌmeyt/ *n.* [*count*] a companion at school.

school•room (sko͞ol′ro͞om′, -ro͝om′) /'skuwlˌruwm, -ˌrʊm/ *n.* [*count*] a room in which a class is held or pupils are taught.

school•teach•er (sko͞ol′tē′chər) /'skuwlˌtiytʃər/ *n.* [*count*] a teacher in a school, esp. in one below the college level. —**school′teach′ing,** *n.* [*noncount*]

school•work (sko͞ol′wûrk′) /'skuwlˌwɜrk/ *n.* [*noncount*] the material studied in or for school, including homework.

school•yard (sko͞ol′yärd′) /'skuwlˌyɑrd/ *n.* [*count*] a playground or sports field near a school.

school′ year′, *n.* [*count*] the months of the year during which school is open: *The school year begins in September.*

schoon•er (sko͞o′nər) /'skuwnər/ *n.* [*count*] **1.** a kind of sailing vessel having a mast in front and a main mast. **2.** a very tall glass, as for beer.

schuss (sho͝os, sho͞os) /ʃʊs, ʃuws/ *n.* [*count*] **1.** a straight downhill ski run at high speed. —*v.* **2.** to do or perform a schuss: [*no obj*]: *to schuss down the mountain.* [~ + *obj*]: *to schuss the hill.*

schwa or **shwa** (shwä) /ʃwɑ/ *n.* [*count*], *pl.* **schwas** or **shwas. 1.** a neutral vowel sound typically occurring in unstressed syllables in English, such as the sound of *a* in *alone* and *sofa* or *u* in *circus.* **2.** the phonetic symbol ə, used to represent this sound.

-sci-, *root.* *-sci-* comes from Latin, where it has the meaning "to know." This meaning is found in such words as: CONSCIENCE, CONSCIOUS, OMNISCIENCE, OMNISCIENT, PRESCIENCE, PRESCIENT, SCIENCE, SCIENTIFIC.

sci., an abbreviation of: **1.** science. **2.** scientific.

sci•at•ic (sī at′ik) /say'ætɪk/ *adj.* of, relating to, located near, or affecting the back of the hip or its nerves.

sci•at•i•ca (sī at′i kə) /say'ætɪkə/ *n.* [*noncount*] pain involving a sciatic nerve.

sci•ence (sī′əns) /'sayəns/ *n.* **1.** [*noncount*] a system of knowledge about the physical world, explaining or describing what it is and how it works in general laws, gained by observing, experimenting, and testing theories: *Science is concerned with dicovering knowledge about the world by making tests and proposing general laws to account for what happens.* **2.** [*noncount*] the knowledge gained by this system. **3.** a branch of this study, such as

school

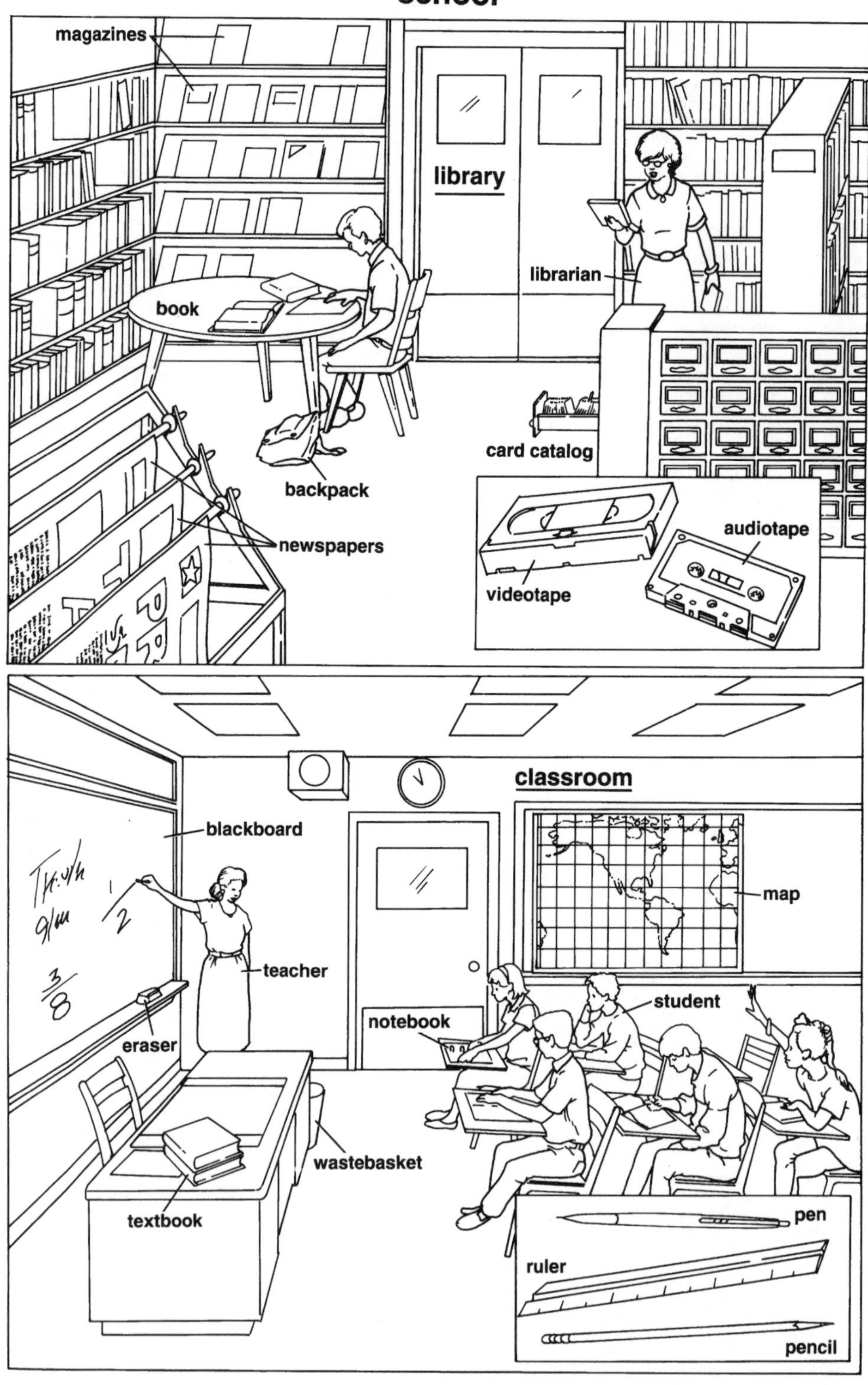

library
magazines
book
librarian
card catalog
backpack
newspapers
audiotape
videotape
classroom
blackboard
map
teacher
student
notebook
eraser
wastebasket
textbook
pen
ruler
pencil

any of the branches of natural science: [*count*]: *the social and natural sciences.* [*noncount*]: *You need one more course in science to graduate.* **4.** any skill that shows ability to use facts or principles: [*noncount*]: *the science of throwing a good curveball.* [*count*]: *Is her ability to make good decisions an art or a science?* See -SCI-.

sci′ence fic′tion, *n.* [*noncount*] fiction that uses imaginative scientific knowledge, often about the future.

sci•en•tif•ic (sī′ən tif′ik) /ˌsayən'tɪfɪk/ *adj.* **1.** [*before a noun*] of or relating to science or the sciences: *scientific studies.* **2.** working or reasoning according to a system: *a scientific approach to your problems.* —**sci′en•tif′i•cal•ly,** *adv.* See -SCI-.

sci•en•tist (sī′ən tist) /'sayəntɪst/ *n.* [*count*] an expert in science, esp. one of the physical or natural sciences. See -SCI-.

sci-fi (sī′fī′), *n., adj. Informal.* /'say'fay/, *n., adj. Informal.* science fiction. See -SCI-.

scim•i•tar or **scim•i•ter** (sim′i tər) /'sɪmɪtər/ *n.* [*count*] a curved, single-edged sword.

scin•til•la (sin til′ə) /sɪn'tɪlə/ *n.* [*count; usually with a negative word or phrase*], *pl.* **-las.** a very small part, amount, or trace: *not even a scintilla of remorse.*

scin•til•lat•ing (sin′tl ā′ting) /'sɪntḷˌeytɪŋ/ *adj.* animated, clever, or witty: *a scintillating conversation.* —**scin•til•la•tion** (sin′tl ā′shən) /ˌsɪntḷ'eyʃən/ *n.* [*noncount*]

sci•on (sī′ən) /'sayən/ *n.* [*count*] **1.** a descendant, esp. of a famous family. **2.** a shoot of a plant or tree, esp. for grafting or planting.

scis•sor (siz′ər) /'sɪzər/ *v.* **1.** [~ + *obj*] to cut or clip out with scissors. **2.** [*no obj*] to move one's body or legs like the blades of scissors. —*n.* [*count*] **3.** SCISSORS.

scis•sors (siz′ərz) /'sɪzərz/ *n.* [*count*] a cutting instrument for paper, etc., made of two blades so fastened together at the center that their sharp edges work one against the other while cutting: [*plural; used with a plural verb*]: *The scissors are on the table; could you hand them to me?* [*count; used with a singular verb; a pair of* + ~]: *There's a pair of scissors on the dresser; could you hand them to me?* [*count; used with a singular verb*]: *There's a scissors on the table; could you hand it to me?* —**scis′sor•like′,** *adj.* See -CISE-.

scis′sors kick′, *n.* [*count*] a swimmer's scissorlike motion of the legs, as in the sidestroke.

scle•ro•sis (skli rō′sis) /sklɪ'rowsɪs/ *n.* [*noncount; used with a singular verb*] a disease in which there is an abnormal hardening of body tissue: *multiple sclerosis.* —**scle•rot•ic** (skli rot′ik) /sklɪ'rɒtɪk/ *adj.*

scoff[1] (skôf, skof) /skɔf, skɒf/ *v.* [~ + *at* + *obj*] to mock; jeer: *scoffed at the idea that a woman could become president.*

scoff[2] (skôf, skof) /skɔf, skɒf/ *v.* [~ + *obj*], *Slang.* to eat hungrily, greedily, or very quickly.

scoff•law (skôf′lô′, skof′-) /'skɔfˌlɔ, 'skɒf-/ *n.* [*count*] one who fails to pay fines owed, as for parking tickets.

scold (skōld) /skowld/ *v.* **1.** to find fault with (someone), esp. in an angry way: [~ + *obj*]: *scolded her daughter for fighting at school.* [*no obj*]: *to scold for no good reason.* —*n.* [*count*] **2.** one who constantly scolds. —**scold′ing,** *n.* [*count*]: *Give her a good scolding.* [*noncount*]: *I don't know if scolding will do any good.*

sco•li•o•sis (skō′lē ō′sis, skol′ē-) /ˌskowliy'owsɪs, ˌskɒliy-/ *n.* [*noncount; used with a singular verb*] abnormal curvature of the spine.

scone (skōn, skon) /skown, skɒn/ *n.* [*count*] a light, biscuitlike cake.

scoop (sko͞op) /skuwp/ *n.* [*count*] **1.** a ladlelike utensil, used for measuring flour, etc. **2.** a utensil made of a small bowl and a handle, for dishing out ice cream, etc. **3.** the bucket of a steam shovel, etc. **4.** the amount held in a scoop: *two scoops of sugar.* **5.** a news item appearing in one newspaper, etc., before all others: *got a scoop when he found out where the crooks were hiding and called the police.* **6.** [*usually: the* + ~] *Informal.* current information; news: *What's the scoop on the new chairman?* —*v.* **7.** to take up or out with or as if with a scoop: [~ (+ *out/up*) + *obj*]: *She scooped (out) some ice cream.* [~ + *obj* (+ *out/up*)]: *scooped some ice cream (out).* **8. scoop up,** to gather by a sweeping motion of one's arms or hands: [~ + *up* + *obj*]: *She scooped up her books.* [~ + *obj* + *up*]: *She scooped her books up.* **9.** [~ + *obj*]to reveal a news item before (one's competitors): *scooped the other newspapers with his front-page story.*

scoot (sko͞ot) /skuwt/ *v.* **1.** [*no obj*] to go swiftly: *saw him scooting out the door.* **2.** to slide: [*no obj*]: *asked me to scoot over so she could sit down.* [~ + *obj*]: *Scoot the chair out of the way.*

scoot•er (sko͞o′tər) /'skuwtər/ *n.* [*count*] **1.** a child's vehicle that has two wheels with a low footboard between them, is steered by a handlebar, and is made to move by pushing one foot against the ground while resting the other on the footboard. **2.** Also called **motor scooter.** a similar but larger and heavier vehicle for adults, propelled by a motor.

scope (skōp) /skowp/ *n., v.,* **scoped, scop•ing.** —*n.* **1.** [*noncount*] extent, limit or range of view, outlook, etc.: *a question beyond the scope of this paper.* **2.** [*noncount*] opportunity for activity: *to give one's fancy full scope.* **3.** [*count*] a short form of *microscope, radarscope,* etc. —*v.* **4.** *Slang.* to look at or over; examine:[~ + *out* + *obj*]: *to scope out the situation.* [~ + *obj* + *out*]: *Scope this guy out!*

-scope-, *root.* -*scope*- comes from Greek, where it has the meaning "see." This meaning is found in such words as: FLUOROSCOPE, GYROSCOPE, HOROSCOPE, MICROSCOPE, MICROSCOPIC, PERISCOPE, RADIOSCOPY, SPECTROSCOPE, STETHOSCOPE, TELESCOPE, TELESCOPIC.

scorch (skôrch) /skɔrtʃ/ *v.* **1.** to burn slightly so as to affect color, taste, etc.: [~ + *obj*]: *The hot iron scorched the shirt.* [*no obj*]: *The shirt will scorch if your iron is too hot.* **2.** [~ + *obj*] to parch or shrivel with heat: *The sun scorched the grass.* —*n.* [*count*] **3.** a superficial burn.

score (skôr, skōr) /skɔr, skowr/ *n., pl.* **scores; score** for 4; *v.,* **scored, scor•ing.** —*n.* [*count*] **1.** the record of points made by the players in a game or contest: *It was a tie score at the end of the half, 6-6.* **2.** performance on an examination or test, expressed by a number or other symbol: *Her score on the test was 99%.* **3.** a notch or scratch: *scores on the murder weapon.* **4.** a group or set of 20: *a score of victims.* **5.** a reason or cause for something: *to complain on the score of low pay.* **6.** [*usually singular; the* + ~] *Informal.* the facts of a situation: *What's the score on Saturday's picnic?* **7. a.** a piece of music with the vocal and instrumental parts arranged on lines. **b.** the music for a movie, play, or television show: *He wrote the score for the movie.* **8.** *Slang.* **a.** a purchase of, or act of obtaining, illegal drugs. **b.** a successful robbery. —*v.* **9.** to earn in a game, as points or hits: [~ + *obj*]: *scored a lot of runs in the first inning.* [*no obj*]: *failed to score in the first half.* **10.** to get a score of: [~ + *obj*]: *scored 98 on the test.* [*no obj*]: *How well did you score on the last test?* **11.** to keep score, as of a game: [*no obj*]: *He scored for us as we bowled.* [~ + *obj*]: *Someone has to score the game for us.* **12.** [~ + *obj*] to have as a certain value in points: *Four aces score 100.* **13.** [~ + *obj*] to evaluate the responses made on (a test or examination): *Who's in charge of scoring these writing tests?* **14.** [~ + *obj*] *Music.* **a.** to orchestrate. **b.** to compose the music for (a movie, play, etc.). **15.** [~ + *obj*] to cut shallow ridges, cuts, or lines on something, as meat or fish before cooking. **16.** *Slang.* **a.** to obtain (a drug) illegally: [~ + *obj*]: *to score some heroin.* [*no obj*]: *an addict who needed to score.* **b.** [~ + *obj*] to steal. **17.** to achieve a success: [~ + *obj*]: *scored another triumph in his movie.* [*no obj*]: *scored again with his third major film this year.* **18.** [*no obj*] *Slang.* to succeed in finding a willing sexual partner. —***Idiom.*** **19. pay off** or **settle a score,** or **have a score to settle,** to get revenge; retaliate: *They had an old score to settle, so they met outside for a fistfight.* —**score′less,** *adj.* —**scor′er,** *n.* [*count*]

score•board (skôr′bôrd′, skōr′bōrd′) /'skɔrˌbɔrd, 'skowrˌbowrd/ *n.* [*count*] a large board in a ballpark, arena, etc., that shows the score of a contest and other information.

scorn (skôrn) /skɔrn/ *n.* [*noncount*] **1.** open contempt; disdain: *She felt only scorn for the man who tried to get her fired.* —*v.* [~ + *obj*] **2.** to treat or regard with contempt or disdain: *She scorned my help.* —**Syn.** See CONTEMPT.

scorn•ful (skôrn′fəl) /'skɔrnfəl/ *adj.* of or relating to scorn: *scornful remarks; a scornful attitude.* [*be* + ~ + *of*]: *He was scornful of people who didn't earn a lot of money.* —**scorn′ful•ly,** *adv.*

scor•pi•on (skôr′pē ən) /'skɔrpiyən/ *n.* [*count*] a small animal that has a front pair of pincers and a long, upcurved tail with a poisonous stinger.

Scot (skot) /skɒt/ *n.* [*count*] a person born or living in Scotland. Also, **Scots′man, Scots′wom′an.**

Scotch (skoch) /skɒtʃ/ *adj.* **1.** *Sometimes Offensive.* of or relating to Scotland. —*n.* **2.** [*plural; the* + ~; *used* *with a plural verb] Sometimes Offensive.* the Scottish people. **3.** [*noncount; scotch*] whiskey made in Scotland.

Scotch′ tape′, *Trademark.* [*noncount*] a brand name for adhesive tapes made of clear plastic or cellophane: *Use Scotch tape to fix that ripped page.*

scot′-free′, *adv.* free from harm or punishment: *He went off scot-free after the murder.*

Scot•tish (skot′ish) /ˈskɒtɪʃ/ *adj.* Also, **Scots. 1.** of or relating to Scotland. **—*n.* 2.** [*plural; the + ~; used with a plural verb*] the people born or living in Scotland.

scoun•drel (skoun′drəl) /ˈskawndrəl/ *n.* [*count*] a dishonest, wicked, selfish, or dishonorable person; a villain.

scour[1] (skouᵊr, skou′ər) /skawᵊr, ˈskawər/ *v.* [*~ + obj*] **1.** to cleanse by hard rubbing: *to scour a dirty frying pan.* **2.** to remove (dirt, etc.) from something by hard rubbing: *to scour the grease off the frying pan.* **3.** to clear (a channel, etc.), as by the force of water: *The river scoured a path through the valley.*

scour[2] (skouᵊr, skou′ər) /skawᵊr, ˈskawər/ *v.* [*~ + obj*] to range over (an area), as in search: *to scour the countryside for a lost child.*

scourge (skûrj) /skɜrdʒ/ *n., v.,* **scourged, scourg•ing.** **—*n.*** [*count*] **1.** a whip for dealing out punishment. **2.** a cause of great trouble: *the scourge of famine.*

scout (skout) /skawt/ *n.* **—*n.*** [*count*] **1.** a soldier, airplane, etc., sent out to get information about the enemy, such as troop numbers, etc. **2.** a person sent out to obtain information. **3.** a person sent out to discover new talent, as in sports or entertainment. **4.** [*sometimes: Scout*] a member of the Boy Scouts or Girl Scouts. **—*v.* 5.** to act as a scout: [*no obj*]: *The soldiers went out to scout around.* [*~ + obj*]: *The coach scouted the opposing team and noticed a weakness in their defense.* **6.** [*no obj*] to make a search; hunt: *scouting around for a good restaurant.*

scout•mas•ter (skout′mas′tər) /ˈskawtˌmæstər/ *n.* [*count*] the adult leader of a troop of Boy Scouts.

scow (skou) /skaw/ *n.* [*count*] a kind of boat having a flat-bottomed rectangular hull with sloping ends.

scowl (skoul) /skawl/ *v.* [*no obj*] **1.** to frown deeply: *He scowled whenever he spoke to me.* **—*n.*** [*count*] **2.** a deep frown on one's face.

scrab•ble (skrab′əl) /ˈskræbəl/ *v.* [*no obj*], **-bled, -bling. 1.** to scratch frantically with the hands or claws: *scrabbled furiously at the dirt in the tunnel.* **2.** to struggle in a disorderly way: *scrabbled around looking for his glasses.* **—scrab′bler,** *n.* [*count*]

Scrab•ble (skrab′əl) /ˈskræbəl/ *Trademark.* [*noncount*] a board game in which players form words with lettered squares having various point values.

scrag•gly (skrag′lē) /ˈskrægliy/ *adj.,* **-gli•er, -gli•est. 1.** irregular; uneven; jagged. **2.** not neat in appearance: *After a few days without shaving his beard had become scraggly.*

scram (skram) /skræm/ *v.* [*no obj*], **scrammed, scram•ming.** *Informal.* to go away; get out: *They had to scram before the cops came.*

scram•ble (skram′bəl) /ˈskræmbəl/ *v.,* **-bled, -bling,** *n.* **—*v.* 1.** [*no obj*] to climb using one's hands and feet, as up or down a hill: *scrambled quickly up the hill.* **2.** [*no obj*] to compete with others to gain something: *to scramble in the competition for a new job.* **3.** [*no obj*] to move quickly and with a purpose: *scrambled out of the way of the police.* **4.** to (cause pilots or aircraft to) take off quickly to intercept enemy planes: [*no obj*]: *The jets scrambled from the airfield and headed east.* [*~ + obj*]: *The air commander scrambled his planes.* **5.** [*~ + obj*] to collect, organize, or mix (things) in a hurried or disorderly manner: *His words and thought patterns were scrambled and made no sense.* **6.** [*~ + obj*] to fry (eggs) while constantly stirring them. **—*n.*** [*count*] **7.** a quick climb or movement over rough, irregular ground. **8.** a struggle to gain something: *the wild scramble for the presidency.* **9.** any disorderly and hurried proceeding: *a terrible scramble to get packed in time for the flight.* **—scram′bler,** *n.* [*count*]

scrap[1] (skrap) /skræp/ *n., adj., v.,* **scrapped, scrap•ping. —*n.* 1.** [*count*] a small piece or portion; fragment: *a scrap of paper.* **2. scraps,** [*plural*] bits of food, esp. of leftover food: *Feed the dogs scraps.* **3.** [*noncount*] material that has been thrown away or left over and can be reused: *heaps of scrap to be carted away.* **—*adj.*** [*before a noun*] **4.** made up of scraps or scrap: *scrap metal.* **5.** thrown away or left over. **—*v.*** [*~ + obj*] **6.** to make into scrap; break up. **7.** to throw away or abandon as useless: *scrapped our plans to remodel.*

scrap[2] (skrap) /skræp/ *n., v.,* **scrapped, scrap•ping.** *Informal.* **—*n.*** [*count*] **1.** a fight or quarrel. **—*v.*** [*no obj*] **2.** to fight or quarrel. **—scrap′per,** *n.* [*count*]

scrap•book (skrap′bŏŏk′) /ˈskræpˌbʊk/ *n.* [*count*] a book in which pictures, etc., may be pasted: *Her scrapbook had photos and newspaper articles detailing her career.*

scrape (skrāp) /skreyp/ *v.,* **scraped, scrap•ing,** *n.* **—*v.* 1.** [*~ + obj*] to rub (a surface) with something rough, so as to clean or smooth it: *to scrape a table to remove varnish.* **2.** [*~ + obj*] to remove (paint, etc.) by rubbing with something rough or sharp: *to scrape the paint from the table.* **3.** [*~ + obj*] to scratch or injure by brushing against something rough or sharp: *I scraped my knee when I fell.* **4.** to rub roughly on (something), esp. so as to produce a harsh sound: [*~ + obj*]: *scraped the floor with his chair.* [*no obj*]: *The chair scraped on the floor.* **5.** to collect with difficulty: [*~ + up/together + obj*]: *Can you scrape up enough money for college?* [*~ + obj + up/together*]: *She scraped enough money together for college.* **6. scrape by** or **through,** to manage with difficulty: [*no obj*]: *The struggling family could barely scrape by.* [*~ + by/through + obj*]: *I barely scraped through the course with a D.* **—*n.*** [*count*] **7.** an act or instance of scraping. **8.** a harsh sound made by scraping: *the scrape of chairs.* **9.** a scraped place: *a bad scrape on the arm.* **10.** an embarrassing or difficult situation. **11.** a fight or quarrel; scrap. **—scrap′er,** *n.* [*count*]

scrap′ heap′ or **scrap′heap′,** *n.* [*count*] **1.** a pile of old material that has been thrown away, such as metal. **2.** a place for dumping useless things: *The idea of steam-engine cars has been put on the scrap heap.*

scrap•py (skrap′ē) /ˈskræpiy/ *adj.,* **-pi•er, -pi•est.** enjoying a fight or struggle: *a scrappy boxer.*

scratch (skrach) /skrætʃ/ *v.* **1.** to damage or mark the surface of by scraping with something rough: [*~ + obj*]: *The cat scratched her.* [*no obj*]: *The cat scratched at the door.* **2.** to (cause to) be removed with a scraping action: [*~ + obj*]: *Did you scratch the paint on your new car?* [*no obj*]: *This paint won't scratch easily.* **3.** to scrape slightly, as with the fingernails, to relieve itching: [*no obj*]: *He scratched gently at his ear while he thought.* [*~ + obj*]: *He scratched his arm where the mosquito had bitten him.* **4.** [*~ + obj*] to draw on a rough, grating surface: *to scratch one's initials on the rock.* **5.** [*~ + obj*] to remove (an entry) from a contest: *He was scratched from the race at the last minute.* **6.** [*~ + obj*] to reject (an idea, etc.): *Scratch that idea; it costs too much.* **—*n.* 7.** [*count*] a slight injury or mark caused by scratching: *had a scratch on his face from the cat.* **8.** [*count*] a rough mark made by a pen, etc.; scrawl. **9.** [*count*] the act of scratching. **10.** [*count*] a slight grating sound produced by scratching: *The scratches on the record made it impossible to enjoy the music.* **11.** [*noncount*] *Slang.* MONEY. **—*adj.*** [*before a noun*] **12.** used for notes, etc.: *scratch paper.* **13.** gathered together too quickly and without enough care: *a scratch crew.* **—*Idiom.* 14. from scratch,** [*noncount*] **a.** from the beginning or from nothing: *Let's start from scratch.* **b.** using basic pieces or ingredients rather than a commercial preparation: *to bake a cake from scratch.* **15. up to scratch,** as good as the standard; satisfactory: *Your work is not up to scratch.*

scratch•y (skrach′ē) /ˈskrætʃiy/ *adj.,* **-i•er, -i•est. 1.** causing a slight grating sound: *a scratchy old record.* **2.** causing an itching feeling: *a scratchy old woolen sweater.* **—scratch•i•ly** (skrach′ə lē) /ˈskrætʃəliy/ *adv.* **—scratch′i•ness,** *n.* [*noncount*]

scrawl (skrôl) /skrɔl/ *v.* [*~ + obj*] **1.** to write or draw in a careless, awkward, illegible manner: *scrawled his name on the form.* **—*n.*** [*count; usually singular*] **2.** awkward, careless, illegible handwriting: *Nobody could read his scrawl.*

scrawn•y (skrô′nē) /ˈskrɔniy/ *adj.,* **-i•er, -i•est.** very thin; lean: *scrawny kids.* **—scrawn′i•ness,** *n.* [*noncount*]

scream (skrēm) /skriym/ *v.* **1.** to make a loud, sharp cry: [*no obj*]: *screamed with fright.* [*~ + obj*]: *screamed her answer to him.* [*used with quotations*]: *"Get out of here!" she screamed.* **2.** [*no obj*] to give off a loud, piercing sound: *The sirens screamed.* **—*n.*** [*count*] **3.** a loud, sharp, piercing cry: *screams from inside the apartment.* **4.** a shrill, piercing sound: *the scream of the jet planes.* **5.** [*count; usually singular; usually: a + ~*] *Informal.* someone or something that is very funny: *Those comedians are a scream.* **—scream′er,** *n.* [*count*]

screech (skrēch) /skriytʃ/ *v.* **1.** to make a harsh, shrill cry or sound: [*no obj*]: *The car's tires screeched.* [*~ + obj*]: *to screech an answer.* [*used with quotations*]: *"Get out of here!" she screeched.* **—*n.*** [*count*] **2.** a harsh, shrill cry or sound: *The screech of tires was followed by the sound of a collision.* —**screech•y,** *adj.,* **-i•er, -i•est.**

screen (skrēn) /skriyn/ *n.* [*count*] **1.** a device, usually a covered frame, that provides shelter, separates parts of a room, etc.: *The doctor pulled the screen around the patient's bed.* **2.** a surface on which motion pictures, etc., may be projected: *They put up the screen and turned on the slide projector.* **3.** the motion-picture industry: *His novel was a success on screen.* **4.** the part of a television or computer on which a picture is formed or information is displayed: *The numbers danced across the computer screen.* **5.** anything that shelters or conceals: *a screen of trees to block the strong winds.* **6.** a frame holding a mesh of wire, for placing in a window or doorway, etc., to allow air in and out but to keep out insects: *There must be a hole in the screen.* —*v.* [~ + *obj*] **7.** to shelter or conceal with or as if with a screen: *The tall trees screened the house from view.* **8.** to select, reject, consider, or group (people, etc.) by examining systematically: *We screened several applicants for the job.* **9.** to provide with a screen or screens: *to screen in the porch.* **10.** to project (a motion picture, etc.) on a screen: *The movie version of Robin Hood will be screened next month.*

screen•play (skrēn′plā′) /ˈskriynˌpley/ *n.* [*count*] the outline or full script of a motion picture.

screen•writ•er (skrēn′rī′tər) /ˈskriynˌraytər/ *n.* [*count*] one who writes screenplays as an occupation.

screw (skro͞o) /skruw/ *n.* [*count*] **1.** a nail-like metal fastener, having a thin end with a spiral groove and a head with a slot: *A screw is forced into wood by twisting it with a screwdriver.* **2.** PROPELLER (def. 1). **3.** *Slang.* a prison guard. **4.** *Slang* (*vulgar*). an act of sexual intercourse. —*v.* **5.** [~ + *obj*] to turn (a screw): *Screw five of these special screws into position.* **6.** to (cause to) be fastened with or as if with a screw or screws: [~ + *obj*]: *screwed the seats into the floor.* [*no obj*]: *The seats screw right into the floor.* **7.** to attach, detach, or adjust (a threaded part) by a twisting motion: [~ + *obj* + *off/on*]: *Screw the top of the bottle back on.* [~ + *off/on* + *obj*]: *Screw on the bottlecap.* [*no obj;* ~ + *off/on*]: *The bottlecap screws right off.* **8.** to change the shape of by twisting; distort: [~ *(+ up)* + *obj*]: *to screw (up) one's face into a deep frown.* [~ + *obj (+ up)*]: *to screw one's face (up) into a deep frown.* **9.** [~ + *up* + *obj*] to strengthen: *I screwed up my courage and asked for a raise.* **10.** [~ + *obj*] *Slang* (*vulgar*). to cheat or take advantage of (someone): *We were really screwed on that deal.* **11.** *Slang* (*vulgar*). to have sexual intercourse (with): [~ + *obj*]: *screwed her on their first date.* [*no obj*]: *screwing with anyone he could find.* **12. screw around,** [*no obj*] *Slang.* **a.** to waste time: *Quit screwing around and get back to work!* **b.** to be constantly attempting to have sexual relations. **13. screw up,** *Slang.* to ruin; make a mess (of): [~ + *up* + *obj*]: *He screwed up every job we gave him.* [~ + *obj* + *up*]: *He screwed the job up.* [*no obj*]: *He's always screwing up.* —***Idiom.*** **14. have a screw loose,** to behave or think oddly: *He must have a screw loose if he thinks he can get away with this in broad daylight.* **15. put the screws on,** [~ + *obj*] to use force on (someone); to force (someone): *The boss will really put the screws on him to work overtime.*

screw•ball (skro͞o′bôl′) /ˈskruwˌbɔl/ *n.* [*count*] **1.** *Slang.* one who behaves very strangely; a kook: *The scientist was such a screwball that nobody thought he would make so important a discovery.* **2.** a pitched baseball that turns toward the side from which it was thrown: *A screwball bends opposite a curve ball.* —*adj.* **3.** *Slang.* odd or strange in behavior: *You and your screwball ideas!*

screw•driv•er (skro͞o′drī′vər) /ˈskruwˌdrayvər/ *n.* [*count*] **1.** a hand tool for tightening or loosening a screw. **2.** a mixed drink of vodka and orange juice.

screw•y (skro͞o′ē) /ˈskruwiy/ *adj.,* **-i•er, -i•est.** *Slang.* **1.** crazy; nutty: *a screwy character.* **2.** odd or strange: *Something is screwy here.*

-scrib-, *root.* -*scrib*- comes from Latin, where it has the meaning "write." This meaning is found in such words as: ASCRIBE, CIRCUMSCRIBE, DESCRIBE, INDESCRIBABLE, INSCRIBE, PRESCRIBE, PROSCRIBE, SCRIBBLE, SCRIBE, SUBSCRIBE, TRANSCRIBE.

scrib•ble (skrib′əl) /ˈskrɪbəl/ *v.,* **-bled, -bling,** *n.* —*v.* **1.** to write quickly and carelessly: [~ + *obj*]: *to scribble a letter.* [*no obj*]: *scribbling in his notebook.* —*n.* **2.** [*count*] a hasty drawing or piece of writing. **3.** [*noncount*] handwriting that is hard to read. —**scrib′bler,** *n.* [*count*] See -SCRIB-.

scribe (skrīb) /skrayb/ *n.* [*count*] **1.** one who wrote copies of written things before the invention of printing. **2.** a public clerk or writer. **3.** a writer, esp. a journalist. —**scrib′al,** *adj.* See -SCRIB-.

scrim•mage (skrim′ij) /ˈskrɪmɪdʒ/ *n., v.,* **-maged, -mag•ing.** —*n.* **1.** *Football.* **a.** [*noncount*] the action from the snap of the ball to the end of the play. **b.** [*count*] a practice session or informal game. —*v.* [*no obj*] **2.** to play an informal game: *The football players scrimmaged a few days before the big game.*

scrimp (skrimp) /skrɪmp/ *v.* [*no obj*] to be careful in spending or using (something, as money): *We shall scrimp and save for retirement.*

scrip (skrip) /skrɪp/ *n.* **1.** [*noncount*] paper money printed for temporary use in emergency situations. **2.** [*count*] a certificate representing a fraction of a share of stock. See -SCRIB-.

script (skript) /skrɪpt/ *n.* **1.** [*noncount*] the characters used in handwriting: *First we learned how to make block letters, then we learned script.* **2.** [*count*] the written words of a play, etc.: *had to write a script every week for his boss, who was a comedian.* **3.** any system of writing: [*noncount*]: *Persian script.* [*count*]: *an ancient script.* **4.** [*count*] a plan: *Don't deviate from the script and everything will be fine.* —*v.* [~ + *obj*] **5.** to write a script for: *to script a play.* **6.** to plan: *This emergency was one they hadn't scripted for.*

scrip•tur•al (skrip′chər əl) /ˈskrɪptʃərəl/ *adj.* of or relating to scripture or to scriptures. See -SCRIB-.

Scrip•ture (skrip′chər) /ˈskrɪptʃər/ *n.* **1.** Often, **Scriptures.** Also called **Holy Scripture** (or **Scriptures**). the sacred writings of the Bible: [*plural*]: *The Scriptures are quite clear on that one point: it is wrong to kill.* [*noncount*]: *Scripture tells us little about Jesus' early life.* **2.** [*usually: scripture*] any writing or book, esp. when of a sacred nature: [*noncount*]: *ancient Hindu scripture.* [*count*]: *Their scriptures date back thousands of years.* See -SCRIB-.

script•writ•er (skript′rī′tər) /ˈskrɪptˌraytər/ *n.* [*count*] one who writes scripts, as for movies or television.

scrive•ner (skriv′nər) /ˈskrɪvnər/ *n.* SCRIBE[1] (defs. 1, 2). See -SCRIB-.

scrod or **schrod** (skrod) /skrɒd/ *n.* [*noncount*] a young Atlantic codfish or haddock, esp. one split for cooking.

scroll (skrōl) /skrowl/ *n.* [*count*] **1.** a roll of papyrus once used for writing: *the ancient scrolls found near the Dead Sea.* —*v.* [*no obj*] **2.** (on a computer display) to move a cursor smoothly, causing new data to replace old on the monitor: *As you type, your old data will scroll up.*

scrooge (skro͞oj) /skruwdʒ/ *n.* [*count*] a cheap, ungenerous, or miserly person.

scro•tum (skrō′təm) /ˈskrowtəm/ *n.* [*count*], *pl.* **-ta** (-tə) /-tə/ **-tums.** the pouch of skin that contains the male reproductive organs or testes. —**scro•tal** (skrōt′l) /ˈskrowtl/ *adj.*

scrounge (skrounj) /skrawndʒ/ *v.,* **scrounged, scroung•ing.** —*v.* **1.** to borrow without expecting to repay: [*no obj;* ~ + *off*]: *to scrounge off his friends.* [~ + *obj*]: *to scrounge a cigarette.* **2.** to gather by searching around: [~ + *obj*]: *scrounged enough money to buy gas.* [~ *(+ up)* + *obj*]: *to scrounge (up) food for supper.* [~ + *obj (+ up)*]: *to scrounge food (up) for supper.* —**scroung′er,** *n.* [*count*]: *the best scrounger in the Army.*

scroung•y (skroun′jē) /ˈskrawndʒiy/ *adj.,* **-i•er, -i•est. 1.** shabby, untidy, or slovenly: *scroungy clothes.* **2.** given to scrounging.

scrub[1] (skrub) /skrʌb/ *v.,* **scrubbed, scrub•bing,** *n.* —*v.* **1.** to rub hard with a brush, cloth, etc., in washing: [~ + *obj*]: *to scrub your face.* [*no obj*]: *Be sure to scrub hard with a brush or the dirt won't come off.* **2.** [~ + *obj*] to remove (dirt, etc.) from something by hard rubbing while washing: *to scrub grime from the walls.* **3.** [~ + *obj*] to remove (impure parts) from a gas by chemical means: *to scrub sulfur dioxide from smokestack gas.* **4.** [~ + *obj*] *Informal.* to cancel or postpone, as a rocket launch: *The mission had to be scrubbed because of a computer malfunction.* —*n.* [*count*] **5.** an act or instance of scrubbing. —**scrub′ber,** *n.* [*count*]

scrub[2] (skrub) /skrʌb/ *n.* **1.** [*noncount*] low trees or shrubs thought of as a group: *jackals hiding in the scrub.* **2.** [*noncount*] a large area covered with low trees and shrubs. **3.** [*count*] *Sports.* a player not on the first-string team.

scrub•by (skrub′ē) /ˈskrʌbiy/ *adj.,* **-bi•er, -bi•est.** covered with scrub, small trees, or bushes.

scruff (skruf) /skrʌf/ *n.* [*count*] the nape or back of the neck.

scruff•y (skruf′ē) /ˈskrʌfiy/ *adj.*, **-i•er, -i•est.** untidy; wearing worn clothes; shabby.

scrump•tious (skrump′shəs) /ˈskrʌmpʃəs/ *adj.* extremely pleasing, esp. to the taste; delectable: *a scrumptious dinner.*

scrunch (skrunch, skro͝onch) /skrʌntʃ, skrʊntʃ/ *v.* **1.** [~ + *obj*] to crunch or crumple: *scrunched the rear fender.* **2.** to contract; squeeze together: [~ + *obj* (+ *up*)]: *I scrunched my shoulders (up).* [*no obj*]: *We all had to scrunch together in the back seat.* **3.** [*no obj;* ~ + *down*] to squat: *I scrunched down to get under the fence post.* —*n.* [*count*] **4.** the act or sound of scrunching: *the scrunch of footsteps on the pebbles.*

scru•ple (skro͞o′pəl) /ˈskruwpəl/ *n.* a moral belief that holds back one's behavior or prevents one from doing certain actions: [*count*]: *His scruples kept him from pocketing the money he had found on the floor.* [*noncount*]: *killing without scruple.*

scru•pu•lous (skro͞o′pyə ləs) /ˈskruwpyələs/ *adj.* **1.** of or relating to scruples. **2.** very precise; strictly exact: *scrupulous adherence to duty.* —**scru•pu•los•i•ty** (skro͞o′pyəlos′i tē) /ˌskruwpyəˈlɒsɪtiy/ *n.* [*noncount*] —**scru′pu•lous•ly,** *adv.*: *He was scrupulously on time to every class.*

scru•ti•nize (skro͞ot′n īz′) /ˈskruwtn̩ˌayz/ *v.* [~ + *obj*], **-nized, -niz•ing.** to conduct a scrutiny: *The guards scrutinized the major's pass.*

scru•ti•ny (skro͞ot′n ē) /ˈskruwtn̩iy/ *n.* [*noncount*] a searching and careful examination or investigation: *He felt himself withering under the interviewer's scrutiny.*

scu•ba (sko͞o′bə) /ˈskuwbə/ *n.*, *pl.* **-bas,** *v.*, **-baed, -ba•ing.** —*n.* **1.** [*count*] a breathing device strapped on the back of a diver. **2.** [*noncount*] the act of swimming underwater with such a device. —*v.* [*no obj*] **3.** to swim underwater with such a device: *to scuba in the Great Barrier Reef.*

scud (skud) /skʌd/ *v.*, **scud•ded, scud•ding,** *n.* —*v.* [*no obj*] **1.** to move quickly: *clouds scudding across the sky.* —*n.* [*noncount*] **2.** clouds or mist driven by the wind.

scuff (skuf) /skʌf/ *v.* [~ + *obj*] **1.** to make a mark on (something) by hard use, such as shoes: *The rocks and dust scuffed his shoes.* **2.** to rub or scrape (one's foot or feet) over something. —*n.* [*count*] **3.** the act or sound of scuffing. **4.** a mark, as from scraping or wear.

scuf•fle (skuf′əl) /ˈskʌfəl/ *v.*, **-fled, -fling,** *n.* —*v.* [*no obj*] **1.** to struggle in a rough, disorderly manner: *scuffling with the mugger.* —*n.* [*count*] **2.** a rough, confused fight.

scull (skul) /skʌl/ *n.* [*count*] **1.** a light, narrow racing boat propelled by rowing. —*v.* **2.** to move a boat along: [~ + *obj*]: *to scull a boat on the river.* [*no obj*]: *boats sculling on the river.*

scul•ler•y (skul′ə rē, skul′rē) /ˈskʌləriy, ˈskʌlriy/ *n.* [*count*], *pl.* **-ler•ies.** a room off a kitchen where food is prepared and utensils cleaned and stored.

scul•lion (skul′yən) /ˈskʌlyən/ *n.* [*count*] a kitchen servant.

sculpt (skulpt) /skʌlpt/ *v.* **1.** to carve, model, or make by sculpture: [*no obj*]: *The artist sculpts in wood.* [~ + *obj*]: *to sculpt figures of marble.* **2.** [~ + *obj*] to make something into a certain form by sculpture: *The wind and rains had sculpted fantastic shapes out of the rock.*

sculp•tor (skulp′tər) /ˈskʌlptər/ *n.* [*count*] one who sculpts.

sculp•ture (skulp′chər) /ˈskʌlptʃər/ *n.*, *v.*, **-tured, -tur•ing.** —*n.* **1.** [*noncount*] the art of carving or modeling art in three dimensions, as by using marble, metal, etc. **2.** [*noncount*] such works of art thought of as a group: *studying the sculpture of Auguste Rodin.* **3.** [*count*] a piece of such work: *a sculpture by Rodin.* —*v.* [~ + *obj*] **4.** to carve or model (a piece of sculpture): *to sculpture a statue.* **5.** to produce an image of (someone or something) in this way: *The artist wished to sculpture her from the first day he saw her.* —**sculp′tur•al,** *adj.*

scum (skum) /skʌm/ *n.* [*noncount*] **1.** a layer of matter on the surface of a liquid: *pond scum.* **2.** low, worthless people: *Those gangsters are truly the scum of the earth.* —**scum′my,** *adj.*, **-mi•er, -mi•est.**

scup•per (skup′ər) /ˈskʌpər/ *n.* [*count*] **1.** an opening at the edge of a ship's deck that allows water to drain away. **2.** any opening in the side of a building for draining off rainwater.

scur•ril•ous (skûr′ə ləs, skur′-) /ˈskɜrələs, ˈskʌr-/ *adj.* rude, improper, and insulting: *scurrilous attacks against his opponent.* —**scur•ril•i•ty** (skə ril′i tē) /skəˈrɪlɪtiy/ *n.* [*noncount*] —**scur′ril•ous•ly,** *adv.*

scur•ry (skûr′ē, skur′ē) /ˈskɜriy, ˈskʌriy/ *v.*, **-ried, -ry•ing,** *n.*, *pl.* **-ries.** —*v.* [*no obj*] **1.** to move in a great hurry: *scurried around trying to get everything ready for the wedding.* —*n.* [*count*] **2.** a scurrying rush.

scur•vy (skûr′vē) /ˈskɜrviy/ *n.*, *adj.*, **-vi•er, -vi•est.** —*n.* [*noncount*] **1.** a disease marked by swollen and bleeding gums, caused by a lack of vitamin C. —*adj.* **2.** deserving contempt; despicable. —**scur•vi•ly** (skûr′və lē) /ˈskɜrvəliy/ *adv.*

scut•tle[1] (skut′l) /ˈskʌtl̩/ *n.* [*count*] **1.** a deep bucket for carrying coal. **2.** a broad, shallow basket.

scut•tle[2] (skut′l) /ˈskʌtl̩/ *v.* [*no obj*], **-tled, -tling.** to run with short, quick steps: *mice scuttling along the floor.*

scut•tle[3] (skut′l) /ˈskʌtl̩/ *n.*, *v.*, **-tled, -tling.** —*n.* [*count*] **1. a.** a small hatch in the deck, side, or bottom of a vessel. **b.** a cover for this. —*v.* [~ + *obj*] **2.** to sink (a vessel) deliberately by opening hatches: *Prepare to scuttle the ship.* **3.** to abandon or destroy (plans, etc.): *He scuttled his plans to run for president.*

scut•tle•butt (skut′l but′) /ˈskʌtl̩ˌbʌt/ *n.* [*noncount*] *Informal.* rumor; gossip: *Office scuttlebutt says we are going to be fired; is it true?*

scuzz•y (skuz′ē) /ˈskʌziy/ *adj.*, **-i•er, -i•est.** *Slang.* dirty; disgusting: *a scuzzy old sweater.*

scythe (sīth) /sayð/ *n.*, *v.*, **scythed, scyth•ing.** —*n.* [*count*] **1.** a tool that is a long, curving blade fastened at an angle to a handle, for cutting grass, grain, etc., by hand. —*v.* [~ + *obj*] **2.** to cut or mow with a scythe.

SD, an abbreviation of: **1.** South Dakota. **2.** standard deviation.

S.D., an abbreviation of: **1.** South Dakota. **2.** special delivery. **3.** standard deviation.

SE, an abbreviation of: **1.** southeast. **2.** southeastern.

sea (sē) /siy/ *n.* **1.** the salt waters that cover the greater part of the earth's surface; ocean: [*count*]: *the seven seas.* [*noncount*]: *The early settlers traveled great distances by sea.* **2.** [*count; usually: the* + ~] a division of these waters, marked off by land boundaries: *The Dead Sea is between Israel and Jordan.* **3.** [*count*] a large wave: *The heavy seas almost drowned us.* **4.** [*count*] an overwhelming amount: *a sea of faces.* —*adj.* [*before a noun*] **5.** of, relating to, or suited for use at sea. —***Idiom.*** **6. at sea, a.** on the ocean: *We'd been at sea for only a few weeks.* **b.** [*be* + ~] confused; perplexed; uncertain: *was totally at sea in his new job.*

sea′ anem′one, *n.* [*count*] a solitary marine polyp with flowerlike tentacles.

sea•bed (sē′bed′) /ˈsiyˌbɛd/ *n.* [*count*] Also, **sea•floor** (sē′flôr′) /ˈsiyˌflɔr/. the bottom of the sea; the ground at the bottom of the sea.

sea•board (sē′bôrd′, -bōrd′) /ˈsiyˌbɔrd, -ˌbowrd/ *n.* **1.** the line where land and sea meet. **2.** a region or area of land bordering a seacoast: *the eastern seaboard.*

sea•coast (sē′kōst′) /ˈsiyˌkowst/ *n.* [*count*] the land immediately next to the sea.

sea•far•er (sē′fâr′ər) /ˈsiyˌfɛərər/ *n.* [*count*] **1.** a sailor. **2.** a traveler on the sea. —**sea′far′ing,** *adj.*: *The Vikings were a seafaring people.*

sea•food (sē′fo͞od′) /ˈsiyˌfuwd/ *n.* [*noncount*] any fish or shellfish from the sea used for food.

sea•go•ing (sē′gō′ing) /ˈsiyˌgowɪŋ/ *adj.* [*before a noun*] designed or fit for going to sea: *seagoing ships.*

sea′ gull′, *n.* [*count*] a gull, esp. one living near the sea.

sea′ horse′ or **sea′horse′,** *n.* [*count*] a fish of the pipefish family, having a curled tail, a long snout, and a head and neck resembling that of a horse.

seal[1] (sēl) /siyl/ *n.* [*count*] **1.** an emblem, symbol, etc., placed on something to show its authenticity: *the president's seal of office on the letterhead.* **2.** a stamp, etc., engraved with such an emblem, etc., for stamping the design on paper, wax, etc. **3.** a piece of wax or similar material stuck on to a document, envelope, etc., that must be broken when the object is opened: *The seal was broken, proving that someone had already read this letter.* **4.** anything that closes or secures a thing: *a seal on the bottle.* **5.** anything that serves as a sign to give assurance, promise, or confirmation: *the seal of approval.* —*v.* [~ + *obj*] **6.** to place a seal on (something) to show authority, testimony, etc.: *to seal the document.* **7.** to close with a fastening that must be broken to open: *to seal a letter in the envelope.* **8.** to fasten by or as if by a seal: *My lips are sealed; I won't tell anyone.* **9.** to decide in a way that will not be changed: *His temper tantrum in front of the boss sealed his fate.* **10. seal off, a.** to close so tightly that what is inside cannot escape: [~ + *off* + *obj*]: *The submarine's hatches sealed off the flooded rooms.* [~ + *obj* + *off*]: *to seal the rooms off.* **b.** to block all entrances or exits to or from, as or as if with a police barricade: [~ + *off* + *obj*]: *The police have sealed off the building.* [~ + *obj* + *off*]: *to seal it off.* —**seal′er,** *n.* [*count*]

seal[2] (sēl) /siyl/ *n., pl.* **seals,** (*esp. when thought of as a group* for 1) **seal,** *v.* —*n.* **1.** [*count*] a fish-eating mammal with flippers, that lives in or near the sea. **2.** [*noncount*] the skin or fur of such an animal. **3.** [*noncount*] leather made from this skin. —*v.* [*no obj*] **4.** to hunt, kill, or capture seals. —**seal′er,** *n.* [*count*]

seal•ant (sē′lənt) /ˈsiylənt/ *n.* [*count*] a liquid, paint, etc., that is applied to a surface and dries to form a watertight coating.

sea′ legs′, *n.* [*plural*] the ability to adjust one's balance to the motion of a ship at sea: *After a few days on the boat he finally got his sea legs.*

sea′ lev′el, *n.* [*noncount*] the average or mean level of the surface of the sea between high and low tide: *The towns along the east coast are at sea level.*

sea′ li′on, *n.* [*count*] a large-eared seal having a blunt nose and a small amount of underfur.

seam (sēm) /siym/ *n.* [*count*] **1.** the line formed by sewing together pieces of cloth, etc. **2.** any line formed by two edges that come together. **3.** *Geology.* a thin layer of a mineral. —***Idiom.*** **4. bursting at the seams,** to be so full as to be overcrowded: *The stadium was bursting at the seams.* **5. fall apart at the seams,** to disintegrate; to be in very bad condition: *When their best teacher left, the school fell apart at the seams.*

sea•man (sē′mən) /ˈsiymən/ *n.* [*count*], *pl.* **-men. 1.** a person who assists in the handling and navigating of a vessel, esp. one below the rank of officer; sailor. **2.** an enlisted person in the U.S. Navy ranking below petty officer. —**sea′man•ship′,** *n.* [*noncount*]

seam•less (sēm′ləs) /ˈsiymləs/ *adj.* **1.** not having seams. **2.** not having clear divisions into parts; smooth: *a seamless move from one scene to another.* —**seam′less•ly,** *adv.*: *The plot moves seamlessly from one location to another.*

seam•stress (sēm′stris) /ˈsiymstrɪs/ *n.* [*count*] a woman who sews, esp. as a profession.

seam•y (sē′mē) /ˈsiymiy/ *adj.,* **-i•er, -i•est.** disagreeable; dirty; sordid: *Police officers see the seamy side of life.*

sé•ance (sā′äns) /ˈseyɑns/ *n.* [*count*] a meeting in which a person or persons attempt to communicate with the spirits of the dead.

sea•plane (sē′plān′) /ˈsiyˌpleyn/ *n.* [*count*] an airplane with floats for water takeoffs and landings.

sea•port (sē′pôrt′, -pōrt′) /ˈsiyˌpɔrt, -ˌpowrt/ *n.* [*count*] **1.** a port or harbor that can take in seagoing vessels. **2.** a town or city at such a place.

sear (sēr) /sɪər/ *v.,* [~ + *obj*] to scorch or char the surface of: *to sear the beef.*

search (sûrch) /sɜrtʃ/ *v.* **1.** to look through (a place, etc.) to find something lost: [~ + *obj* + *for* + *obj*]: *I searched the house for my keys.* [~ + *for* + *obj*]: *I searched for my keys.* **2.** to examine (a person, etc.) to find something hidden: [~ + *obj* + *for* + *obj*]: *The police searched his car for the drugs.* [~ + *for* + *obj*]: *They were searching for drugs.* **3.** to explore or examine in order to discover: [~ + *obj* + *for* + *obj*]: *They searched the hills for gold.* [~ + *for* + *obj*]: *Scientists are searching for a cure for AIDS.* [~ + *out* + *obj*]: *to search out all the facts.* **4.** [~ + *obj*] to examine (a record, writing, etc.) for information: *to search a property title.* **5.** [~ + *obj*] to look into, question, or think carefully about: *Search your conscience.* **6.** to command software to find certain words, letters, or characters in (an electronic file): [~ + *obj* + *for* + *obj*]: *to search a database for all instances of "U.S." and replace them with "United States."* [~ + *for* + *obj*]: *to search for all instances of "U.S."* —*n.* [*count*] **7.** an act or instance of searching: *The computer search takes only seconds.* —***Idiom.*** **8. in search of,** looking for; trying to find: *early explorers in search of gold.* —**search′er,** *n.* [*count*]

search•ing (sûr′ching) /ˈsɜrtʃɪŋ/ *adj.* [*usually: before a noun*] **1.** sharply observing or penetrating: *gave me a searching look.* **2.** examining carefully: *a searching inspection.*

search•light (sûrch′līt′) /ˈsɜrtʃˌlayt/ *n.* [*count*] **1.** a device for throwing a powerful beam of light in any direction. **2.** a beam of light so thrown.

sear•ing (sēr′ing) /ˈsɪərɪŋ/ *adj.* **1.** causing a sharp feeling of burning or as if burning: *the searing pain of the bullet entering his arm.* **2.** fiery in emotion, intense feeling, or criticism; scorching: *a searing speech.*

sea•scape (sē′skāp′) /ˈsiyˌskeyp/ *n.* [*count*] **1.** a sketch, painting, or photograph of the sea. **2.** a view of the sea.

sea•shell or **sea shell** (sē′shel′) /ˈsiyˌʃɛl/ *n.* [*count*] the shell of an oyster, clam, or other sea-living mollusk.

sea•shore (sē′shôr′, -shōr′) /ˈsiyˌʃɔr, -ˌʃowr/ *n.* [*noncount*] land along the sea.

sea•sick (sē′sik′) /ˈsiyˌsɪk/ *adj.* feeling dizzy, sick to one's stomach, or vomiting, caused by the motion of a vessel at sea. —**sea′sick′ness,** *n.* [*noncount*]

sea•side (sē′sīd′) /ˈsiyˌsayd/ *n.* [*count; singular; usually: the* + ~] **1.** the land along the sea; seacoast: *likes to sit down by the seaside.* —*adj.* [*before a noun*] **2.** of or relating to the seaside: *a seaside cottage.*

sea•son (sē′zən) /ˈsiyzən/ *n.* [*count*] **1.** one of the four main periods of the year. **2.** a period of the year having particular weather conditions: *the short rainy season in March.* **3.** a period of the year when something is available: *the oyster season.* **4.** a period of the year in which certain conditions, activities, etc., take place: *the baseball season.* **5.** a period of the year when an athletic team plays all of its games: *a winning season last year.* —*v.* [~ + *obj*] **6.** to give flavor to (food) by adding salt, pepper, etc.: *Season the food lightly.* **7.** to enhance: *The conversation was seasoned with her wit.* **8.** to make prepared, esp. by having had experience: *His years in Moscow seasoned him to bureaucracies.* **9.** to prepare for use, as by drying: *to season timber.* —***Idiom.*** **10. in good season,** in enough time; early. **11. in season, a.** in the proper time or state for use: *Asparagus is now in season.* **b.** in the period regulated by law, as for hunting. **c.** (of an animal, esp. female) in heat. **12. out of season,** not in season.

sea•son•a•ble (sē′zə nə bəl) /ˈsiyzənəbəl/ *adj.* suitable to or proper for the season: *seasonable temperatures.*

sea•son•al (sē′zə nl) /ˈsiyzənl̩/ *adj.* **1.** of or relating to the seasons of the year or some particular season; periodical: *seasonal work picking grapes.* —*n.* [*count*] **2.** a seasonal employee or product. —**sea′son•al•ly,** *adv.*

sea•soned (sē′zənd) /ˈsiyzənd/ *adj.* experienced; having had practice or experience: *a seasoned reporter.*

sea•son•ing (sē′zə ning) /ˈsiyzənɪŋ/ *n.* something, such as salt or a spice, for improving or adding to the flavor of food: [*noncount*]: *add a little seasoning to the salad.* [*count*]: *A seasoning that would work well here is basil.*

sea′son tick′et, *n.* [*count*] a ticket for a series of events, or that may be used for a period of time.

seat (sēt) /siyt/ *n.* [*count*] **1.** something to support a person in a sitting position, as a chair: *His seat is over there.* **2.** the part of something on which one sits: *to repair a broken chair seat.* **3.** the buttocks, or the part of the garment covering the buttocks: *wet paint on the seat of his pants.* **4.** something on which the base of an object rests, or the base itself. **5.** a place in which something occurs: *a college as a seat of learning.* **6.** a place in which power is placed or located: *Washington is the seat of the U.S. government.* **7.** a right to sit as a member, as in a legislative or financial body: *a seat on the stock exchange.* —*v.* [~ + *obj*] **8.** to place on a seat: *seated himself by the window.* **9.** to guide to a seat: *The ushers seated her in the front row.* **10.** [*not: be* + ~*-ing*] to provide with seats: *a theater that seats 1200 people.* **11.** to install in a position of authority. **12.** to attach to something as a base: *Seat the telescope on the tripod.* —***Idiom.*** **13. by the seat of one's pants,** using experience and/or guesswork: *had to land the plane by the seat of her pants.*

seat′ belt′, *n.* [*count*] an arrangement of straps designed to keep a vehicle passenger firmly secure.

seat•ing (sē′ting) /ˈsiytɪŋ/ *n.* [*noncount*] **1.** the arrangement or providing of seats, as in a theater: *The seating in the theater is uncomfortable.* —*adj.* [*before a noun*] **2.** of or relating to seats or to those who are sitting: *the seating plans for the wedding.*

sea′ ur′chin, *n.* [*count*] a small, round sea animal with a shell of plates covered with spines.

sea•ward (sē′wərd) /ˈsiywərd/ *adv.* **1.** Also, **sea′wards.** toward the sea. —*adj.* [*before a noun*] **2.** facing or tending toward the sea. **3.** coming from the sea: *a seaward wind.* —*n.* [*noncount*] **4.** the direction toward the sea.

sea•way (sē′wā′) /ˈsiyˌwey/ *n.* [*count*] **1.** a way over the sea. **2.** a waterway for oceangoing vessels to a port that is otherwise landlocked: *the St. Lawrence Seaway.*

sea•weed (sē′wēd′) /ˈsiyˌwiyd/ *n.* [*noncount*] any of various green plants of the sea.

sea•wor•thy (sē′wûr′thē) /ˈsiyˌwɜrðiy/ *adj.,* **-thi•er, -thi•est.** (of a vessel) fitted and safe for a voyage at sea. —**sea′wor′thi•ness,** *n.* [*noncount*]

sec[1] (sek) /sɛk/ *adj.* (of wine) dry; not sweet.

sec[2] (sek) /sɛk/ *n.* [*count; usually singular usually: a +* ~] a second: *Wait a sec; I'm not ready yet.*

sec, an abbreviation of: **1.** second. **2.** secretary. **3.** section.

se•cede (si sēd′) /sɪ'siyd/ *v.* [~ + *from* + *obj*], **-ced•ed, -ced•ing.** to withdraw officially from an alliance, federation, etc.: *The Confederate States claimed the right to secede from the Union.* See -CEDE-.

se•ces•sion (si sesh′ən) /sɪ'sɛʃən/ *n.* [*noncount*] an act or instance of seceding. —**se•ces′sion•ist,** *n.* [*count*] See -CEDE-.

se•clude (si klo͞od′) /sɪ'kluwd/ *v.* [~ + *obj*], **-clud•ed, -clud•ing. 1.** to remove from social contact and activity: *secluded himself with his computer.* **2.** to shut off; keep apart: *They secluded the garden from the rest of the property.* —**se•clud′ed,** *adj.*

se•clu•sion (si klo͞o′zhən) /sɪ'kluwʒən/ *n.* [*noncount*] the state of being secluded; solitude: *now lives a life of seclusion.* —**se•clu′sive,** *adj.*

sec•ond[1] (sek′ənd) /'sɛkənd/ *adj.* **1.** next after the first; next after the first in place, time, etc.: *the second person in command.* **2.** [*before a noun*] alternate: *every second week.* **3.** [*before a noun*] (in music) being the lower of two parts for the same instrument or voice: *second alto.* **4.** [*before a noun*] other; another: *The judge was like a second Solomon.* —*n.* **5.** [*count*] one who aids or supports another. **6.** [*noncount*] second gear: *The gearshift sticks when I try to shift into second.* **7.** Usually, **seconds.** [*plural*] an additional helping of food: *Can we have seconds on the turkey?* **8.** (in parliamentary procedure) [*count*] **a.** one who expresses formal support of a motion. **b.** an act or instance of such support: *There is a motion before you; do I hear a second?* **9.** [*count*] Usually, **seconds.** [*plural*] goods of less than the highest quality. —*v.* [~ + *obj*] **10.** (in parliamentary procedure) to express formal support of (a motion, etc.), as a necessary step before further discussion or voting: *I second the motion.* —*adv.* **11.** in the second place: *The catcher is batting second.* —***Idiom.*** **12. second to none,** [*often: be* + ~] very good; the best: *an athlete who is clearly second to none.* —**sec′ond•ly,** *adv.*

sec•ond[2] (sek′ənd) /'sɛkənd/ *n.* [*count*] **1.** the sixtieth part of a minute of time. **2.** a moment or instant: *It takes only a second to phone.* **3.** the sixtieth part of a minute of a measure of an angle, often represented by the sign ″, as in 30″, which is read as "30 seconds."

sec•ond•ar•y (sek′ən der′ē) /'sɛkən,dɛriy/ *adj.* **1.** next after the first in order, rank, or time: *Secondary school comes after primary school.* **2.** not primary or original: *secondary sources.* **3.** of lesser importance: *an issue of secondary importance.* **4.** following as a result of something else: *a secondary infection.* —**sec•ond•ar•i•ly** (sek′ən der′ə lē, sek′ən dâr′-) /'sɛkən,dɛrəliy, ,sɛkən'dɛər-/ *adv.*

sec′ondary school′, *n.* a high school, ranking between a primary school and a college: [*noncount*]: *students in secondary school are in the seventh grade or above.* [*count*]: *The new curriculum has not been accepted in most secondary schools.*

sec′ond class′, *n.* [*noncount*] **1.** the class of seating below first class but above third class. —*adj.,* **sec′-ond-class′. 2.** of a secondary quality: *second-class seating.* **3.** second-rate; not excellent: *The university was now a second-class institution.* **4.** not allowed to have certain rights or privileges: *treated like second-class citizens.*

sec′ond-guess′, *v.* [~ + *obj*] **1.** to criticize or correct (someone, or someone's actions) after something has happened: *It's easy to second-guess him now for what he did.* **2.** to predict the actions or intentions of: *tried to second-guess his partner.*

sec′ond hand′, *n.* [*count*] **1.** the hand that indicates the seconds on a clock. —***Idiom.*** **2. at second hand,** through a secondary or intermediate source: *heard the news at second hand.* —*adj.,* **sec•ond•hand** (sek′ənd-hand′) /'sɛkənd'hænd/. **3.** not directly known or experienced: *secondhand knowledge.* **4.** previously owned: *secondhand clothes.* **5.** selling or buying previously used goods: *a secondhand bookseller.* —*adv.* **6.** after another user or owner: *He bought it secondhand.* **7.** indirectly; at second hand: *I heard the news secondhand.*

sec′ond na′ture, *n.* [*noncount*] a way of thinking or acting so deeply fixed as to appear automatic: *After a while, using a mouse on the computer became second nature to him.*

sec′ond per′son, *n.* [*noncount*] (in grammar) the form used when a person is spoken to or addressed: *In English the pronoun "you" is in the second person.*

sec′ond-rate′, *adj.* of lesser or lower quality; of lesser or minor importance: *a second-rate college.*

sec′ond-sto′ry man′, *n.* [*count*] a burglar who enters through an upstairs window.

sec′ond string′, *n.* [*count*] the squad of players available to replace or relieve those who start a game. —**sec′ond-string′er,** *n.* [*count*]

sec′ond thought′, *n.* [*count*] Often, **second thoughts.** [*plural*] an act of reconsidering a previous action, position, etc., often because of doubts as to its correctness: *We had second thoughts about firing her.*

sec′ond wind′ (wind) /wɪnd/ *n.* [*count*] **1.** the return of ease in breathing after being exhausted because of physical exertion, as in running: *got his second wind after the first few miles of the race.* **2.** the energy for a new effort to continue: *Getting a new computer gave her a second wind in completing the project.*

se•cre•cy (sē′krə sē) /'siykrəsiy/ *n.* [*noncount*] the state or condition of being secret: *a meeting held in strictest secrecy.*

se•cret (sē′krit) /'siykrɪt/ *adj.* **1.** done or made without the knowledge of others: *a secret meeting.* **2.** kept from general knowledge: *a secret password.* **3.** hidden from sight; concealed: *a secret entrance.* —*n.* [*count*] **4.** something secret, hidden, or concealed: *kept several secrets from her husband.* **5.** a reason or explanation not easily seen or understood: *What is the secret of her success?* **6.** a method, plan, etc., known to a few: *a trade secret.* —***Idiom.*** **7. in secret,** so as to remain hidden; secretly: *They met in secret.* —**se′cret•ly,** *adv.*

sec•re•tar•i•al (sek′rə târ′ē əl) /,sɛkrə'tɛəriyəl/ *adj.* of or relating to a secretary: *secretarial duties.*

sec•re•tar•i•at (sek′ri târ′ē ət) /,sɛkrɪ'tɛəriyət/ *n.* [*count*] the office or the officials with administrative duties, maintaining records, etc.: *the secretariat of the United Nations.*

sec•re•tar•y (sek′ri ter′ē) /'sɛkrɪ,tɛriy/ *n.* [*count*], *pl.* **-tar•ies. 1.** one whose job is to do work in a business office, such as typing, filing, and answering phones. **2.** one whose job is to take care of private or individual letters, files, etc., of a business executive, official, etc.: *Her private secretary sent out the letters and arranged her meetings.* **3.** a person in charge of records, letters, etc., as for a company, club, etc.: *The job of department secretary meant typing up the minutes of every meeting.* **4.** [*often: Secretary*] an officer of a government whose job is the management of a department of government: *the Secretary of the Treasury.* **5.** a diplomatic official who assists an ambassador. **6.** a piece of furniture for use as a writing desk.

se•crete[1] (si krēt′) /sɪ'kriyt/ *v.* [~ + *obj*], **-cret•ed, -cret•ing.** to give off or produce (a chemical substance): *The pituitary gland secretes a growth hormone.*

se•crete[2] (si krēt′) /sɪ'kriyt/ *v.* [~ + *obj*], **-cret•ed, -cret•ing.** to place out of sight; hide: *He quickly secreted the disk in his desk drawer.*

se•cre•tion (si krē′shən) /sɪ'kriyʃən/ *n.* **1.** [*noncount*] (in a cell or gland) the process of producing and releasing a hormone within the organism: *the secretion of growth hormone from the pituitary gland.* **2.** [*count*] the (usually chemical) product of this process: *secretions from the snake's poison gland.*

se•cre•tive (sē′kri tiv, si krē′-) /'siykrɪtɪv, sɪ'kriy-/ *adj.* having or showing a desire for secrecy: *He was pretty secretive about his new assignment.* —**se′cre•tive•ly,** *adv.* —**se′cre•tive•ness,** *n.* [*noncount*]

se′cret serv′ice, *n.* [*count*] **1.** the branch of a government service that conducts secret investigations, esp. regarding foreign spying. **2.** [*Secret Service; usually: the* + ~] a branch of the U.S. Department of the Treasury chiefly responsible for protecting the president.

sect (sekt) /sɛkt/ *n.* [*count*] **1.** a body of people following a particular religious faith; a denomination. **2.** a group differing from a generally accepted religious tradition. **3.** any group united by a specific doctrine. See -SEQ-.

-sect-, *root.* *-sect-* comes from Latin, where it has the meaning "cut." This meaning is found in such words as: BISECT, DISSECT, INTERSECT, RESECTION, SECTION, SECTOR, VIVISECTION.

sec•tar•i•an (sek târ′ē ən) /sɛk'tɛəriyən/ *adj.* **1.** of or relating to religious sects. **2.** narrowly confined or limited in interest, etc.: *Sectarian concerns must give way to the general good.* —**sec•tar′i•an•ism,** *n.* [*noncount*] See -SEQ-.

sec•tion (sek′shən) /'sɛkʃən/ *n.* **1.** [*count*] a distinct, separate part of anything, such as a community: *one of the nicer sections of town.* **2.** [*count*] a distinct part of a newspaper, etc.: *the sports section.* [*noncount; before a number*]: *The phrase is found in article VI, section II.* **3.** [*count*] a part cut off or separated; one of a number of parts that can be fitted together to make a whole: *Two sections of pipe had come loose.* **4.** [*count*] a drawing or diagram of an object as it would appear if cut through a side, showing its internal parts or structure: *a cross section.* **5.** [*count*] a division of an orchestra containing all the instruments of one class: *the brass section.* **—*v.*** [~ + *obj*] **6.** to divide into sections. **7.** to cut through so as to show a section. See -SECT-.

sec•tion•al (sek′shə nl) /'sɛkʃənl/ *adj.* **1.** of or limited to a particular region or area: *The high school team played in the sectional finals.* **2.** composed of sections: *a sectional sofa.* **3.** of or relating to a section: *a sectional view of the brain.* **—*n.*** [*count*] **4.** a sofa made of sections that can be arranged in combinations. See -SECT-.

sec•tor (sek′tər) /'sɛktər/ *n.* [*count*] **1.** the area that a military unit is assigned to defend. **2.** a distinct part, esp. of society: *the business sector.* **3.** a section or zone, as of a city. **4.** a part cut off from the whole: *a sector of a circle.* See -SECT-.

sec•u•lar (sek′yə lər) /'sɛkyələr/ *adj.* not relating to or concerned with religion: *secular music.* **—sec′u•lar•ism,** *n.* [*noncount*] **—sec′u•lar•ist,** *n.* [*count*]

sec•u•lar•ize (sek′yə lə rīz′) /'sɛkyələˌrayz/ *v.* [~ + *obj*], **-ized, -iz•ing.** to make secular: *to secularize a religious holiday.* **—sec•u•lar•i•za•tion** (sek′yə lər ə zā′shən) /ˌsɛkyələrə'zeyʃən/ *n.* [*noncount*]

se•cure (si kyŏŏr′) /sɪ'kyʊr/ *adj.*, **-cur•er, -cur•est,** *v.*, **-cured, -cur•ing. —*adj.*** **1.** of or relating to security: *They kept the jewels secure in the bank.* **2.** not liable or likely to fail, give way, etc.: *He had a secure grip on the rope.* **3.** providing safety; kept in a safe place: *a secure hiding place.* **4.** free from anxiety: *emotionally secure.* **5.** certain; confident: *secure in his religious belief.* **6.** safe from being intercepted by unauthorized persons: *secure radio communications.* **—*v.*** [~ + *obj*] **7.** to get hold of; obtain: *to secure a new job.* **8.** to free from danger or harm; make safe: *to secure the town from flooding.* **9.** to make certain of; ensure: *The novel secured his reputation.* **10.** to make fast or tight: *to secure a rope.* **11.** to assure payment of (a debt) by pledging property: *to secure a loan.* **12.** to fasten against intruders: *Secure your doors and windows.* **13.** to tie up the arms or hands of: *to secure the prisoners.* **—se•cure′ly,** *adv.*: *Be sure your seatbelt is fastened securely.* See -CURA-.

se•cu•ri•ty (si kyŏŏr′i tē) /sɪ'kyʊrɪtiy/ *n., pl.* **-ties. 1.** [*noncount*] freedom from danger, risk, etc.; safety: *Job security was an important issue.* **2.** [*noncount*] freedom from care, anxiety, or doubt: *a false feeling of security living at home.* **3.** [*noncount*] something that protects; defense. **4.** [*noncount*] freedom from financial cares: *security in their old age.* **5.** [*noncount*] precautions against crime, sabotage, etc.: *in charge of plant security.* **6.** [*noncount*] a department responsible for safety: *Call Security; I think there's a shoplifter on the loose.* **7.** [*noncount*] steps taken to prevent escape: *a prisoner held in maximum security.* **8.** [*noncount*] something given as a guarantee for paying back a loan: *What can you offer as security for the loan?* **9. securities,** [*plural*] stocks and bonds. See -CURA-.

secu′rity blan′ket, *n.* [*count*] **1.** a blanket carried by a child to provide a feeling of safety. **2.** an object whose presence gives a feeling of security.

secy or **sec'y,** an abbreviation of: secretary.

se•dan (si dan′) /sɪ'dæn/ *n.* [*count*] **1.** an enclosed automobile body having two or four doors and seating four or more persons. **2.** a car with this type of body.

se•date (si dāt′) /sɪ'deyt/ *adj., v.,* **-dat•ed, -dat•ing. —*adj.*** **1.** calm, quiet, or composed: *Unlike her lively friend, she was quiet and sedate.* **—*v.*** [~ + *obj*] **2.** to cause to become sleepy or calm, as by taking a sedative: *The nurse sedated the patient before the operation.* **—se•date′ly,** *adv.*: *She glided sedately down the hall.* **—se•da•tion** (si dā′shən) /sɪ'deyʃən/ *n.* [*noncount*]: *The patient is under sedation.*

sed•a•tive (sed′ə tiv) /'sɛdətɪv/ *adj.* **1.** causing a feeling of calm; soothing: *a sedative drug.* **—*n.*** [*count*] **2.** a substance that calms or causes sleepiness.

sed•en•tar•y (sed′n ter′ē) /'sɛdn̩ˌtɛriy/ *adj.* **1.** showing or requiring a sitting posture: *a sedentary occupation.* **2.** having or showing inactivity and lack of exercise: *led a sedentary life.*

sed•i•ment (sed′ə mənt) /'sɛdəmənt/ *n.* **1.** the matter that settles to the bottom of a liquid; dregs: [*noncount*]: *brownish sediment in the drinking water.* [*count*]: *an ugly sediment in the bottom of the glass.* **2.** mineral or sand deposited by the action of water, air, or ice: [*noncount*]: *The flood waters deposited sediment on the land.* [*count*]: *a sediment of coal.* **—sed•i•men•ta•tion** (sed′ə-mən tā′shən) /ˌsɛdəmən'teyʃən/ *n.* [*noncount*]

sed•i•men•ta•ry (sed′ə men′tə rē) /ˌsɛdə'mɛntəriy/ also **sed•i•men•tal** (sed′ə men′tl) /ˌsɛdə'mɛntl̩/ *adj.* **1.** of or relating to sediment: *sedimentary matter at the bottom of the glass.* **2.** formed by the matter deposited by the action of water, air, or ice: *sedimentary rocks.*

se•di•tion (si dish′ən) /sɪ'dɪʃən/ *n.* [*noncount*] action intended to cause rebellion against a government.

se•di•tious (si dish′əs) /sɪ'dɪʃəs/ *adj.* of or relating to sedition: *seditious writings.*

se•duce (si dōōs′, -dyōōs′) /sɪ'duws, -'dyuws/ *v.* [~ + *obj*], **-duced, -duc•ing. 1.** to tempt (someone) to have sexual intercourse. **2.** to win over; entice: *The warm spring day seduced her from her work.* **—se•duc′er,** *n.* [*count*] See -DUC-.

se•duc•tion (si duk′shən) /sɪ'dʌkʃən/ *n.* **1.** the act of seducing: [*noncount*]: *planning seduction.* [*count*]: *his many seductions.* **2.** [*count*] something attractive and appealing: *the seductions of a glamorous career.* See -DUC-.

se•duc•tive (si duk′tiv) /sɪ'dʌktɪv/ *adj.* of or relating to seduction: *a seductive offer to switch companies; a seductive smile.* See -DUC-.

see[1] (sē) /siy/ *v.,* **saw** (sô) /sɔ/ **seen** (sēn) /siyn/ **see•ing. —*v.*** **1.** [*not: be* + *~-ing*] to view (something) with the eyes; look at: [~ + *obj*]: *I saw her in the park.* [~ + *obj* + *verb-ing*]: *I saw her running in the park.* [~ + *obj* + *root form of verb*]: *I saw him shoot the police officer.* **2.** [*not: be* + *~-ing; no obj*] to have the power of sight: *He can't see; he's been blind from birth.* **3.** [~ + *obj*] to view, as a spectator: *I saw a good movie last night.* **4.** [*not: be* + *~-ing;* ~ + *obj*] to scan or view, esp. by electronic means: *When the electronic eye sees you, the door opens automatically.* **5.** [*not: be* + *~-ing*] to grasp (things) mentally; to understand: [~ + *obj*]: *I see your point.* [~ + *clause*]: *I see that you meant it; sorry I doubted you.* [*no obj*]: *Don't you see; we want to help you!* **6.** [*not: be* + *~-ing*] to form a mental image of: [~ + *obj*]: *I can't see him as president.* [~ + *obj* + *verb-ing*]: *I can't see him running things.* **7.** [~ + *obj*] to imagine or believe that one sees something: *You must be seeing things; there's nothing here.* **8.** [*not: be* + *~-ing*] to be aware of; recognize: *to see his mistakes.* **9.** [*no obj*] (used as a polite request to draw the attention of someone to something): *See, here it comes.* **10.** [*not: be* + *~-ing*] to discover; find out: [~ + *obj*]: *See who is at the door.* [*no obj*]: *If you don't believe me, then here, see for yourself.* **11.** [*not: be* + *~-ing*] to read or read about: [~ + *obj*]: *I saw it in the newspaper.* [~ + *that clause*]: *I saw in the newspaper that your store carries these computers.* **12.** [~ + *obj*] to have knowledge or experience of: *to see combat.* **13.** [~ + *that clause*] to make sure: *See that the door is locked.* Compare *see to* below. **14.** [~ + *obj*] to meet and converse with; visit: *Why don't you come and see me?* **15.** [~ + *obj*] to receive (someone) as a visitor: *not allowed to see anyone until after the operation.* **16.** [~ + *obj*] to court or date frequently: *We've been seeing each other for the last year.* **17.** [~ + *obj*] to escort or accompany: *It's late; why don't I see you home.* **18.** [*no obj*] (used with the subject pronouns *I* and *we,* or after LET and the object pronouns *me* or *us,* to indicate a pause) to think; consider: *Let me see, what was his name? Let's see; does this round peg fit in the square hole?* **19. see about,** [~ + *about* + *obj*] **a.** to inquire about; investigate: *It's his job to see about what his teachers are doing.* **b.** Also, **see after.** to take care of; to attend to: *Let me see about that and I'll call you back.* **20. see off,** to accompany (someone about to go on a journey) to the place of departure: [~ + *off* + *obj*]: *We went to the airport to see off my aunt and uncle.* [~ + *obj* + *off*]: *to see them off.* **21. see out,** [~ + *obj* + *out*] to escort to an outer door: *He saw her out the door with a smile.* **22. see through, a.** [~ + *through* + *obj*] to figure out the nature of (someone), esp. to detect or discover a lie: *saw right through his excuses.* **b.** [~ + *obj* + *through*] to remain with until completion: *Don't quit now; let's see this job through.* **23. see to,** [~ + *to* + *obj*] to take care of; attend to; see about: *I'll see to all the travel arrangements.* **—*Idiom.*** **24. see red,** *Informal.* to become enraged: *He saw red when he found that he'd have to pay once again for the same repairs.* **—Usage.** Compare the words SEE and LOOK. The verb LOOK refers to a much more active sense in which the subject uses the eyes, moves them, turns the head, and generally participates more in the action: *I looked at the people rushing by (= I moved my eyes, perhaps even turning my head to observe them).* The verb SEE is much less active and implies less participation by the subject; with this verb, the image of the object simply strikes the subject's eyes, and the subject does much less: *I saw her standing there (= The image of her standing there simply struck my eyes; I had very little to do with the activity).* Whenever a meaning of a verb implies activity or participation, there is a good chance the PROGRESSIVE aspect ([*be* + *~-ing*]) may be used: *I was looking at the people rushing by. I have been seeing her (= dating) for two years.* But when the action of a verb does not imply continuing activity or participation by the subject, the progressive aspect is not used, which is why SEE so often does not allow the progressive aspect: *I saw her standing there (NOT: I was seeing her...).*

see² (sē) /siy/ *n.* [*count*] the seat, center of authority, or office of a bishop.

seed (sēd) /siyd/ *n., pl.* **seeds,** (*esp. when thought of as a group*) **seed,** *v., adj.* **—*n.*** **1.** [*count*] the usually small, hard part of a plant that grows into a new plant: *The farmer planted his seeds in the spring.* **2.** [*noncount*] such parts thought of as a group: *to purchase enough seed for the soybean crop.* **3.** [*count*] the beginning of something: *the seeds of discord.* **4.** [*count*] a player or team ranked in a tournament. **—*v.*** **5.** [~ + *obj*] to sow (a field, etc.) with seed. **6.** [*no obj*] to produce seed. **7.** [~ + *obj*] to introduce in the hope of increase: *to seed a lake with trout.* **8.** [~ + *obj*] to remove the seeds from (fruit). **9.** [~ + *obj*] to rank (players or teams) by past performance in arranging tournament pairings: *was seeded first in the tournament.* **10.** [~ + *obj*] to develop (a business), esp. by providing operating capital. **—*adj.*** [*before a noun*] **11.** producing seed; used for seed: *a seed potato.* **—*Idiom.*** **12. go** or **run to seed, a.** (of the flower of a plant) to pass to the stage of providing seed. **b.** to fall apart or decline, as in health or appearance: *He had gone to seed: gaining weight, turning pale, losing hair.* —**seed′er,** *n.* [*count*] —**seed′less,** *adj.*: *seedless oranges.*

seed•ling (sēd′ling) /'siydlɪŋ/ *n.* [*count*] **1.** a plant or tree grown from a seed. **2.** any young plant.

seed′ mon′ey, *n.* [*noncount*] money used as capital for the beginning stages of a new business.

seed•y (sē′dē) /'siydiy/ *adj.,* **-i•er, -i•est. 1.** containing many seeds. **2.** poorly kept; run-down: *a seedy hotel.* **3.** poorly and untidily dressed; unkempt: *A seedy desk clerk greeted us at the old hotel.* —**seed′i•ness,** *n.* [*noncount*]

see•ing (sē′ing) /'siyɪŋ/ *conj.* considering; inasmuch as: *Seeing (that) you're on a diet, we won't have dessert.*

seek (sēk) /siyk/ *v.,* **sought** (sôt) /sɔt/ **seek•ing. 1.** to go in search of: [~ *(+ out)* + *obj*]: *to seek (out) a new life.* [~ + *obj (+ out)*]: *to seek her (out), wherever she was.* **2.** [~ + *obj*] to try to discover, as by studying: *to seek the secrets of the universe.* **3.** [~ + *obj*] to try to obtain: *to seek advice from your attorney.* **4.** [~ + *to* + *verb*] to try or attempt: *sought to convince the queen to finance his expedition.* —**seek′er,** *n.* [*count*]

seem (sēm) /siym/ *v.* [*not: be* + *~-ing*] **1.** to appear or pretend to be (such): [~ + *adjective*]: *He seemed friendly until I mentioned money.* [~ + *noun*]: *He seemed a friendly sort.* **2.** [~ + *to* + *verb*] to appear to be, feel, do, etc.: *Someone seems to have left a mess here.* **3.** [~ + *adjective*] to appear to one's own mind, senses, etc.: *The journey seemed long, but in fact it was only minutes.* **4.** to appear to be true or probable: [*It* + ~ + *adjective* + *to* + *verb*]: *It seems likely to rain.* [*It* + ~ + *adjective* + *(that) clause*]: *It seemed certain (that) there would be war.* [*It* + ~ + *(that) clause*]: *It seems (that) we have a problem.*

seem•ing (sē′ming) /'siymɪŋ/ *adj.* [*usually: before a noun*] apparent; appearing so; ostensible: *Their team had a seeming advantage in that they were confident.*

seem′ing•ly (sē′ming lē) /'siymɪŋliy/ *adv.* apparently; evidently: *a seemingly endless supply of soldiers.*

seem•ly (sēm′lē) /'siymliy/ *adj.,* **-li•er, -li•est,** fitting; suitable; appropriate: *Your outburst during church was hardly seemly.* —**seem′li•ness,** *n.* [*noncount*]

seen (sēn) /siyn/ *v.* pp. of SEE¹.

seep (sēp) /siyp/ *v.* [*no obj*] to flow or ooze slowly, as through small openings.

seep•age (sē′pij) /'siypɪdʒ/ *n.* [*noncount*] **1.** the act or process of seeping. **2.** the amount of something that has seeped out.

se•er (sēr) /sɪər/ *n.* [*count*] one who predicts future events: *Industry seers were predicting higher profits.*

seer•suck•er (sēr′suk′ər) /'sɪər,sʌkər/ *n.* [*noncount*] a plain cotton fabric, usually striped and having a crinkled texture.

see•saw (sē′sô′) /'siy,sɔ/ *n.* [*count*] **1.** a recreational device that is a long plank balanced at the middle, on which two children alternately ride up and down while seated at opposite ends. **2.** any procedure in which there are ups and downs. **—*adj.*** [*before a noun*] **3.** moving up and down, back and forth, etc.: *a seesaw battle in which one side attacked, gained ground, and then fell back.* **—*v.*** [*no obj*] **4.** to ride on a seesaw: *The children seesawed in the park.* **5.** to move in a seesaw manner: *Prices seesawed on the stock market all day.*

seethe (sēth) /siyð/ *v.* [*no obj*], **seethed, seeth•ing. 1.** (of a liquid) to bubble as if boiling. **2.** to be in a state of excitement or anger: *sat there seething after listening to his insults.*

see′-through′, *adj.* **1.** Also, **see′-thru′.** transparent: *a see-through blouse.* **—*n.*** [*count*] **2.** a see-through item of clothing.

seg•ment (*n.* seg′mənt; *v.* seg′ment, seg ment′) / *n.* 'sɛgmənt; *v.* 'sɛgmɛnt, sɛg'mɛnt/ *n.* [*count*] **1.** one of the parts into which something is divided; a section: *the three main segments of an insect.* **2.** *Geometry.* a part cut off from a figure, esp. a circular or spherical one, or a piece of a line. **—*v.*** **3.** to (cause to) separate into segments: [~ + *obj*]: *He segmented the line into four equal parts.* [*no obj*]: *The pieces of an orange segment easily.* —**seg•men•ta•tion** (seg′mən tā′shən) /,sɛgmən'teyʃən/ *n.* [*noncount*]

seg•re•gate (seg′ri gāt′) / 'sɛgrɪ,geyt / *v.,* **-gat•ed, -gat•ing. 1.** to separate or set apart from others: [~ + *obj* + *from* + *obj*]: *The hospital segregates patients who are contagious from the others.* [~ + *obj* + *and* + *obj*]: *segregating boys and girls at adolescence.* **2.** to require or impose, often with force, the separation of (a certain group) from the body of society: [~ + *obj* + *from* + *obj*]: *segregating one ethnic group from another.* [~ + *obj* + *and* + *obj*]: *It is illegal to segregate blacks and whites.* [*no obj*]: *a society that segregates on the basis of religion.* See -GREG-.

seg•re•ga•tion (seg′ri gā′shən) /,sɛgrɪ'geyʃən/ *n.* [*noncount*] **1.** the act or practice of segregating. **2.** the state of being segregated. —**seg′re•ga′tion•ist,** *n.* [*count*] See -GREG-.

se•gue (sā′gwā, seg′wā) /'seygwey, 'sɛgwey/ *v.,* **-gued, -gue•ing,** *n.* **—*v.*** [*no obj*] **1.** (used as a musical direction) to continue at once with the next musical section. **2.** to make a smooth shift from one item to another: *From a discussion of the election we segued into tax reform.* **—*n.*** [*count*] **3.** an uninterrupted transition made between one musical section or composition and another. **4.** an act of smoothly shifting or switching from one topic to another. See -SEQ-.

seis•mic (sīz′mik) /'sayzmɪk/ *adj.* relating to, of the nature of, or caused by an earthquake or vibration of the earth. —**seis′mi•cal•ly,** *adv.*

seis•mo•graph (sīz′mə graf′) /'sayzmə,græf/ *n.* [*count*] an instrument for measuring and recording the vibrations of earthquakes. —**seis•mog•ra•pher** (sīz mog′rə fər) /sayz'mɒgrəfər/ *n.* [*count*] —**seis′mo•graph′ic,** *adj.* —**seis•mog′ra•phy,** *n.* [*noncount*] See -GRAPH-.

seis•mol•ogy (sīz mol′ə jē) /sayz'mɒlədʒiy/ *n.* [*noncount*] the science or study of earthquakes and their phenomena. —**seis•mo•log•ic** (sīz mə loj′ik) /sayzmə'lɒdʒɪk/ **seis′mo•log′i•cal,** *adj.* —**seis′mol′o•gist,** *n.* [*count*]

seize (sēz) /siyz/ *v.,* **seized, seiz•ing. 1.** to take hold with force; grasp: [~ + *obj*]: *He seized a knife.* [*no obj*]: *to seize on a rope.* **2.** [~ + *obj*] to grasp with the mind; understand: *to seize an idea.* **3.** [~ + *obj*] to take possession of, as if by grasping: *Panic seized the crowd.* **4.** [~ + *obj*] to take possession of by authority; confiscate: *The bank seized all his assets.* **5.** [~ + *obj*] to capture; take into custody: *The police seized the two men.* **6.** to take advantage of promptly: [~ + *obj*]: *to seize an opportunity.* [~ + *on* + *obj*]: *He seized on the opening his opponent gave him.* **7.** [*no obj;* ~ + *up*] to have moving parts stop moving as a result of too much pressure or friction: *The engine seized up in the extreme heat.*

sei•zure (sē′zhər) /'siyʒər/ *n.* **1.** an act or instance of seizing: [*noncount*]: *calling for seizure of their assets.* [*count*]: *a seizure of their assets.* **2.** [*count*] a sudden attack, as of some disease: *suffered an epileptic seizure on the subway platform.*

se•dom (sel′dəm) /ˈsɛldəm/ *adv.* rarely; infrequently; not often: *We seldom see them anymore.*

se•lect (si lekt′) /sɪˈlɛkt/ *v.* [~ + *obj*] **1.** to choose in preference; pick: *Only the best students were selected for admission.* **—***adj.* **2.** [*before a noun*] chosen in preference; preferred; choice: *a select group of skaters.* **3.** exclusive; limited to only a few: *a select group of advisors.* **4.** careful in choosing: *a select college.* **—se•lec′tor,** *n.* [*count*] See -LEC-.

se•lec•tion (si lek′shən) /sɪˈlɛkʃən/ *n.* **1.** [*noncount*] an act or instance of selecting, or the state of being selected: *The selection of a president takes place every four years.* **2.** [*count*] a thing or things selected. **3.** [*count*] a group of things displayed, as in a store: *a fine selection of wines.*

se•lec•tive (si lek′tiv) /sɪˈlɛktɪv/ *adj.* **1.** choosing carefully: *is a selective shopper.* **2.** of or relating to a few chosen items; not general: *selective enforcement of the laws.* **—se•lec′tive•ly,** *adv.*: *The police seem to enforce the traffic laws selectively.* **—se•lec•tiv•i•ty** (si lek tiv′i tē) /sɪlɛkˈtɪvɪtiy/ *n.* [*noncount*]

se•lect•man (si lekt′mən) /sɪˈlɛktmən/ *n.* [*count*], *pl.* **-men.** (in most New England states) one of a board of town officers chosen to manage certain public affairs.

self (self) /sɛlf/ *n.* and *pron.*, *pl.* **selves,** *adj.* **—***n.* [*count*] **1.** a person or thing referred to apart from others: *one's own self; the knowledge of self.* **2.** one's usual nature, etc.: *his better self.* **3.** personal interest; one's own pleasure, wants, etc., without concern for others: *always thinking of self.* **—***pron.* **4.** myself, herself, etc.: *to make a check payable to self.* **—***adj.* **5.** being the same throughout; uniform.

self-, *prefix.* **1.** *self-* is attached to nouns to refer to something that one does by oneself or to oneself: *self-control (= control of oneself); self-government; self-help.* **2.** *self-* is also attached to adjectives and nouns to refer to an action done without assistance: *self-adhesive; a self-loading gun; self-study.*

self′-addressed′, *adj.* addressed for return to the sender.

self′-assur′ance, *n.* [*noncount*] self-confidence.

self′-cen′tered, *adj.* thinking about or interested in oneself only; selfish; egotistical. Also, *esp. Brit.,* **self′-cen′tred.**

self′-con′fidence, *n.* [*noncount*] faith in one's own judgment, ability, etc. **—self′-con′fident,** *adj.*

self′-con′scious, *adj.* **1.** too uncomfortable about being looked at by others. **2.** conscious of oneself. **—self′-con′sciously,** *adv.* **—self′-con′sciousness,** *n.* [*noncount*]

self′-contained′, *adj.* **1.** containing in oneself or itself all that is necessary; independent: *a self-contained spaceship.* **2.** not saying much or showing much emotion; reserved. **3.** self-possessed; showing self-control.

self′-control′, *n.* [*noncount*] the ability to control or hold back oneself or one's actions, feelings, etc.: *exhibited great self-control by not screaming at her.* **—self′-controlled′,** *adj.*

self′-defense′, *n.* [*noncount*] **1.** the act of defending one's person by force: *The police officer shot the robber in self-defense.* **2.** an act or instance of protecting one's own interests, etc., as by argument: *"I was just trying to help," he muttered in self-defense.* Also, *esp. Brit.,* **self′-defence′.**

self′-deni′al, *n.* [*noncount*] the act of giving up or holding back one's own desires; unselfishness.

self′-destruct′, *v.* [*no obj*] **1.** to destroy itself or oneself: *This tape will self-destruct in five seconds.* **—***adj.* [*before a noun*] **2.** causing something to self-destruct: *a self-destruct mechanism.* **—self′-destruc′tion,** *n.* [*noncount*] **—self′-destruc′tive,** *adj.*

self′-determina′tion, *n.* [*noncount*] **1.** freedom to live as one chooses without consulting others. **2.** freedom of a people to determine the way in which they will be governed. **—self′-deter′mined,** *adj.*

self′-esteem′, *n.* [*noncount*] self-respect.

self′-ev′ident, *adj.* evident or obvious in itself without demonstration: *It is self-evident that day follows night.*

self′-explan′atory, *adj.* needing no explanation; obvious.

self′-fulfill′ing, *adj.* **1.** characterized by or bringing about fulfillment of oneself. **2.** brought about as a result of being expected: *If people think the economy will get worse, then they don't spend, and the economy does get worse; it's a self-fulfilling prophecy.*

self′-gov′ernment, *n.* [*noncount*] government of a state by its own people. **—self′-gov′erning,** *adj.*

self′-im′age, *n.* [*count*] the mental image one has of oneself: *a positive self-image.*

self′-impor′tant, *adj.* having or showing too high an opinion of one's own importance: *a self-important bureaucrat.* **—self′-impor′tance,** *n.* [*noncount*]

self′-in′terest, *n.* [*noncount*] **1.** regard for one's own interest, esp. with disregard for others. **2.** personal advantage: *It's in his self-interest to study a lot because he needs to learn English.* **—self′in′terest•ed,** *adj.*

self•ish (sel′fish) /ˈsɛlfɪʃ/ *adj.* caring only or chiefly for oneself: *a selfish child; selfish motives.* **—self′ish•ly,** *adv.* **—self′ish•ness,** *n.* [*noncount*]

self•less (self′lis) /ˈsɛlflɪs/ *adj.* having little concern for oneself and one's interests; unselfish. **—self′less•ly,** *adv.* **—self′less•ness,** *n.* [*noncount*]

self′-made′, *adj.* having succeeded in life unaided: *a self-made man who started at the bottom.*

self′-possessed′, *adj.* having or showing control of one's emotions, etc.; composed.

self′-posses′sion, *n.* [*noncount*] the quality of being self-possessed: *cool self-possession.*

self′-preserva′tion, *n.* [*noncount*] the act of preserving or protecting oneself from danger.

self′-propelled′ or **self′-propel′ling,** *adj.* **1.** (of a vehicle) propelled by its own engine. **2.** (of a gun) having a vehicle as a base.

self′-reg′ulating, *adj.* **1.** adjusting or controlling itself without outside controls: *a self-regulating economy.* **2.** functioning automatically: *a self-regulating machine.*

self′-reli′ance, *n.* [*noncount*] reliance on one's own powers or resources. **—self′-reli′ant,** *adj.*

self′-respect′, *n.* [*noncount*] proper regard for the dignity of one's character: *He lost all his self-respect.*

self′-restraint′, *n.* [*noncount*] control or restraint put on one by oneself; self-control.

self′-right′eous, *adj.* too confident of one's own moral rightness, esp. when intolerant of others. **—self′-right′eously,** *adv.* **—self′-right′eousness,** *n.* [*noncount*]

self′-sac′rifice, *n.* [*noncount*] sacrifice of oneself or one's interests for others. **—self′-sac′rificing,** *adj.*

self•same (self′sām′, -sām′) /ˈsɛlfˌseym, -ˈseym/ *adj.* [*before a noun*] being the very same: *the selfsame problem we had before.*

self′-sat′isfied, *adj.* feeling satisfaction with oneself, esp. too much satisfaction: *The team was a little too self-satisfied after their surprising victory.*

self′-seek′ing, *n.* [*noncount*] **1.** the seeking of one's own selfish ends. **—***adj.* **2.** showing or having self-seeking; selfish. **—self′-seek′er,** *n.* [*count*]

self′-serv′ice, *adj.* **1.** of or relating to a restaurant, store, etc., in which customers serve themselves. **2.** of or relating to something to be used without an attendant: *self-service elevators.* **—***n.* [*noncount*] **3.** the system of serving oneself in a commercial establishment without the aid of an attendant.

self′-serv′ing, *adj.* serving to put one's own selfish interests forward, disregarding others: *It's self-serving to flatter the boss.*

self′-start′er, *n.* [*count*] one who shows an ability to work alone on a project. **—self′-start′ing,** *adj.*

self′-styled′, *adj.* [*before a noun*] called by oneself (the thing mentioned), without any real right to it: *a self-styled leader with no followers.*

self′-suffi′cient, *adj.* able to supply one's or its own needs without help. **—self′-suffi′ciency,** *n.* [*noncount*]

self′-taught′, *adj.* taught by oneself without the aid of formal instruction: *a self-taught typist.*

self′-willed′, *adj.* stubborn or obstinate, as in pursuing one's own wishes or aims.

sell (sel) /sɛl/ *v.,* **sold** (sōld) /sowld/ **sell•ing,** *n.* **—***v.* **1.** to transfer (goods or property) (to someone); to do or perform (services) in exchange for money (for someone): [~ + *obj*]: *He sold his car.* [~ + *obj* + *to* + *obj*]: *She sold her car to her sister.* [~ + *obj* + *obj*]: *sold her sister her old car.* [*no obj*]: *He said he wasn't selling; he just wanted to talk to us.* **2.** [~ + *obj*] to deal in; keep or offer for sale: *to sell insurance.* **3.** [~ + *obj*] to promote or cause the sale of: *Packaging sells many products.* **4.** [~ + *obj*] to obtain, total, or achieve sales of: *The record sold a million copies.* **5.** [~ + *at/for* + *obj*] to be offered for sale at the price indicated: *This little model sells for $200.* **6.** [*no obj*] to be in demand by buyers: *On a rainy day, umbrellas really sell.* **7.** to (cause to) be accepted, esp. generally: [~ + *obj* + *to* + *obj*]: *to sell an idea to the public.* [*no obj*]: *Now there's an idea that will really sell!* **8.** to cause or persuade to see the value of: [~ +

obj]: *He did a good job of selling himself.* [~ + *obj* + *on* + *obj*]: *to sell the voters on a candidate.* **9.** [~ + *obj*] to surrender (something, or oneself) improperly for profit or advantage: *to sell one's soul for power.* **10. sell off,** to rid oneself of by selling, esp. at reduced prices: [~ + *off* + *obj*]: *to sell off last year's designs.* [~ + *obj* + *off*]: *to sell old furniture off before moving.* **11. sell out, a.** to sell everything completely: [*be* + *sold out*]: *The store is all sold out of beanbag chairs.* [*no obj*]: *The store sold out before we even got there!* **b.** to betray or be disloyal to (one's friend, a cause, etc.): [~ + *out* + *obj*]: *He sold out his principles to get elected.* [~ + *obj* + *out*]: *He sold them out just for his own gain.* [*no obj*]: *He has sold out and will go along with whatever his boss wants.* **—*n.*** [*count*] **12.** an act or method of selling: *a hard sell, or doing anything to get a sale.* **13.** *Informal.* a cheat; hoax. **—*Idiom.* 14. to sell (someone) down the river,** [~ + *obj* + *down the river*] to betray: *wound up selling his pals down the river for a shorter sentence.*

sell•er (sel′ər) /ˈsɛlər/ *n.* [*count*] **1.** one whose job is to sell things. **2.** a thing sold: *That computer is our worst seller.*

sell′ers′ mar′ket, *n.* [*count*] a market in which goods and services are scarce and prices are relatively high. Compare BUYERS' MARKET.

sell•out (sel′out′) /ˈsɛlˌawt/ *n.* [*count*] **1.** a movie or show for which all the seats are sold. **2.** a person or thing that betrays or is disloyal to a cause, principles, etc., esp. for money or personal advantage.

selt•zer (selt′sər) /ˈsɛltsər/ *n.* [*noncount*] **1.** naturally occurring, bubbling mineral water. **2.** carbonated tap water. Also called **selt′zer wa′ter.**

selves (selvz) /sɛlvz/ *n.* pl. of SELF.

se•man•tics (si man′tiks) /sɪˈmæntɪks/ *n.* **1.** [*noncount; used with a singular verb*] a branch of linguistics dealing with the study of meaning, the ways meaning is structured in language, and changes in meaning and form over time. **2.** the meaning, or an interpretation of the meaning, of a word, sign, etc.: [*noncount; used with a singular verb*]: *Let's not argue about semantics.* [*plural; used with a plural verb*]: *The semantics of those terms are confusing.* **—se•man′tic,** *adj.*: *There is bound to be semantic confusion when translating from one language to another.* **—se•man•ti•cist** (si man′tə sist) /sɪˈmæntəsɪst/ *n.* [*count*]

sem•a•phore (sem′ə fôr′, -fōr′) /ˈsɛməˌfɔr, -ˌfowr/ *n., v.,* **-phored, -phor•ing. —*n.* 1.** [*noncount*] a system of signaling, esp. one by which a flag is held in each hand and various positions of the arms indicate specific letters, etc. **2.** [*count*] an apparatus used in this system. **—*v.* 3.** to signal by semaphore: [~ + *obj*]: *to semaphore a message.* [*no obj*]: *busily semaphoring to the other ship.*

sem•blance (sem′bləns) /ˈsɛmbləns/ *n.* **1.** [*noncount*] outward aspect or appearance: *I won't continue until there is some semblance of order in here.* **2.** [*count*] an assumed or unreal appearance; a show: *a semblance of self-confidence that she was far from feeling.* **3.** [*count; usually singular*] the slightest appearance or trace: *Show us you're capable of at least a semblance of organization.* See -SEMBLE-.

-semble-, *root.* *-semble-* comes from Latin, where it has the meaning "seem; appear(ance)." This meaning is found in such words as: ASSEMBLE, ASSEMBLY, DISSEMBLE, ENSEMBLE, RESEMBLANCE, RESEMBLE, SEMBLANCE.

se•men (sē′mən) /ˈsiymən/ *n.* [*noncount*] a slightly thick, whitish fluid produced in the male reproductive organs, containing sperm.

se•mes•ter (si mes′tər) /sɪˈmɛstər/ *n.* [*count*] **1.** an academic session that is half of the academic year, lasting typically from 15 to 18 weeks. **2.** (in German universities) a session, lasting about six months.

sem•i (sem′ē, sem′ī) /ˈsɛmiy, ˈsɛmay/ *n.* [*count*], *pl.* **-is. 1.** a semitrailer: *a jackknifed semi blocking six lanes of traffic.* **2.** Often, **semis.** [*plural*] a semifinal contest or round.

semi-, *prefix.* **1.** *semi-* comes from Latin, where it has the meaning "half": *semiannual; semicircle.* **2.** *semi-* is also used to mean "partially; partly; somewhat": *semiautomatic; semidetached; semiformal.* **3.** *semi-* is also used to mean "happening or occurring twice in (a certain length of time)": *semiannual.*

sem•i•an•nu•al (sem′ē an′yo͞o əl, sem′ī-) /ˌsɛmiyˈænyuwəl, ˌsɛmay-/ *adj.* occurring, done, or published every half year or twice a year. See -ANN-.

sem•i•cir•cle (sem′i sûr′kəl) /ˈsɛmɪˌsɜrkəl/ *n.* [*count*] **1.** half of a circle. **2.** anything having or arranged in the form of a half of a circle: *The class made a semicircle around the teacher.* **—sem′i•cir′cu•lar** (-sûr′kyə lər) /-ˈsɜrkyələr/ *adj.*

sem•i•co•lon (sem′i kō′lən) /ˈsɛmɪˌkowlən/ *n.* [*count*] the punctuation mark (;) used to indicate a major division in a sentence where a distinct separation is felt between clauses, or among items on a list. Semicolons separate clauses and are often used with words like *however, nevertheless,* and *therefore.* Semicolons indicate a break that is longer than a comma, but shorter than a period: *We were late for the party; however, the hostess didn't mind too much.*

sem•i•con•duc•tor (sem′ē kən duk′tər, sem′ī-) /ˈsɛmiykənˌdʌktər, ˈsɛmay-/ *n.* [*count*] **1.** a substance, such as silicon, that can conduct electricity with less efficiency than a true conductor. **2.** a basic electronic part using such a substance, used in communications equipment and in computers.

sem•i•fi•nal (sem′ē fīn′l, sem′ī-) /ˌsɛmiyˈfaynl̩, ˌsɛmay-/ *adj.* **1.** being the next to last round in a tournament. **—*n.*** [*count*] **2.** a semifinal round. **—sem′i•fi′nal•ist,** *n.* [*count*]

sem•i•month•ly (sem′ē munth′lē, sem′ī-) /ˌsɛmiyˈmʌnθliy, ˌsɛmay-/ *adj., n., pl.* **-lies,** *adv.* **—*adj.* 1.** made, occurring, or published twice a month. **—*n.*** [*count*] **2.** a semimonthly publication. **—*adv.* 3.** twice a month.

sem•i•nal (sem′ə nl) /ˈsɛmənl̩/ *adj.* **1.** of or relating to semen. **2.** original and influencing future events: *a seminal artist.*

sem•i•nar (sem′ə när′) /ˈsɛməˌnɑr/ *n.* [*count*] **1.** a group of advanced students doing original research under the guidance of a faculty member. **2.** a course or subject of study for such students. **3.** any meeting for exchanging information: *a seminar on writing classes.*

sem•i•nar•y (sem′ə ner′ē) /ˈsɛməˌnɛriy/ *n.* [*count*], *pl.* **-nar•ies.** a school that prepares students for the priesthood, ministry, or rabbinate. **—sem′i•nar′i•an,** *n.* [*count*]

sem•i•per•me•a•ble (sem′ē pûr′mē ə bəl, sem′ī-) /ˌsɛmiyˈpɜrmiyəbəl, ˌsɛmay-/ *adj.* allowing only certain small molecules to pass through: *a semipermeable membrane.*

sem•i•pre•cious (sem′ē presh′əs, sem′ī-) /ˌsɛmiyˈprɛʃəs, ˌsɛmay-/ *adj.* having commercial value as a gem but not precious: *semiprecious minerals such as amethyst and garnet.* See -PRECI-.

sem•i•pri•vate (sem′ē prī′vit, sem′ī-) /ˌsɛmiyˈprayvɪt, ˌsɛmay-/ *adj.* having some degree of privacy but not fully private.

sem•i•skilled (sem′ē skild′, sem′ī-) /ˌsɛmiyˈskɪld, ˌsɛmay-/ *adj.* having or requiring more skill than unskilled labor.

Sem•ite (sem′īt) /ˈsɛmayt/ *n.* [*count*] a member of a people speaking a Semitic language.

Se•mit•ic (sə mit′ik) /səˈmɪtɪk/ *n.* [*noncount*] **1.** a family of languages including a number of languages of SW Asia and Africa. **—*adj.* 2.** of or relating to the Semitic languages or their speakers.

sem•i•tone (sem′ē tōn′, sem′ī-) /ˈsɛmiyˌtown, ˈsɛmay-/ *n.* [*count*] a musical pitch halfway between two whole tones. See -TON-.

sem•i•trail•er (sem′i trā′lər) /ˈsɛmɪˌtreylər/ *n.* [*count*] a trailer for hauling freight, with wheels at the rear end and the forward end supported by the back of the truck that pulls it. Also called **semi** (sem′ī) /ˈsɛmay/.

sem•i•trop•i•cal (sem′ē trop′i kəl, sem′ī-) /ˌsɛmiyˈtrɑpɪkəl, ˌsɛmay-/ also **sem′i•trop′ic,** *adj.* SUBTROPICAL.

sem•i•vow•el (sem′i vou′əl) /ˈsɛmɪˌvawəl/ *n.* [*count*] a speech sound of vowel quality used as a consonant, such as (w) in *wet* or (y) in *yet.*

sem•i•week•ly (sem′ē wēk′lē, sem′ī-) /ˌsɛmiyˈwiykliy, ˌsɛmay-/ *adj., n., pl.* **-lies,** *adv.* **—*adj.* 1.** occurring, done, appearing, or published twice a week. **—*n.*** [*count*] **2.** a semiweekly publication. **—*adv.* 3.** twice a week.

sem•o•li•na (sem′ə lē′nə) /ˌsɛməˈliynə/ *n.* [*noncount*] a food substance made from crushed grains of wheat.

sen or **sen.,** an abbreviation of: **1.** senate. **2.** senator. **3.** senior.

sen•ate (sen′it) /ˈsɛnɪt/ *n.* [*count; sometimes: Senate; sometimes: the* + ~] **1.** an assembly having the highest law-making powers in a government: *elected to the California State Senate.* **2.** a governing or advisory body, as at some universities. See -SENE-.

sen•a•tor (sen′ə tər) /ˈsɛnətər/ *n.* [*sometimes: Senator*] a member of a senate: [*count*]: *Several senators were interviewed.* [*proper noun; used before a name*]: *Senator Smith will answer your questions now.* **—sen•a•to•ri•al**

(sen′ə tôr′ē əl, -tōr′-) /ˌsɛnəˈtɔriyəl, -ˈtowr-/ *adj.* See -SENE-.

send (send) /sɛnd/ *v.*, **sent** (sent) /sɛnt/ **send•ing. 1.** [~ + *obj*] to cause to go: *sending troops to battle.* **2.** to cause to be carried or brought to a destination: [~ + *obj*]: *to send a letter.* [~ + *obj* + *to* + *obj*]: *to send a letter to him.* [~ + *obj* + *obj*]: *to send him a letter.* **3.** [~ + *obj*] to propel or drive: *The blast sent pieces of concrete flying.* **4.** [~ + *obj*] to give out or utter: *The lion sent a roar through the jungle.* **5.** [~ + *obj*] to cause to feel or occur: *The story sent him into gales of laughter.* **6.** [~ + *obj*] to transmit (a signal): *to send a signal to the satellite.* **7.** [~ + *obj*] *Slang.* to delight; excite: *He says his new girlfriend really sends him.* **8. send away for,** [~ + *away* + *for* + *obj*] to order (goods) to be delivered by mail: *sent away for tulip bulbs.* **9. send for,** [~ + *for* + *obj*] to request the coming of; summon: *Someone send for a doctor!* **10. send forth,** [~ + *forth* + *obj*] to produce, bear, or give off: *The plant sent forth new leaves in the spring.* **11. send in,** to mail to a point of collection: [~ + *in* + *obj*]: *to send in one's taxes.* [~ + *obj* + *in*]: *to send one's taxes in.* **12. send out, a.** [~ + *out* + *for* + *obj*] to order delivery: *We sent out for coffee and donuts.* **b.** to cause to go out: [~ + *obj* + *out*]: *to send invitations out to all his friends.* [~ + *out* + *obj*]: *to send out invitations.* **13. send up,** [~ + *up* + *obj;* ~ + *obj* + *up*] **a.** to cause to rise up. **b.** to ridicule, make fun of, or imitate: *to send up the mayor.* **—*Idiom.* 14. send (someone) packing,** [~ + *obj* + *packing*] to dismiss in a quick and sudden manner: *The company sent him packing.* —**send′er,** *n.* [*count*]

send′-off′, *n.* [*count*] **1.** a demonstration of good wishes for a person setting out on a new venture: *The office gave their coworker a fine send-off at a nearby restaurant.* **2.** a start; impetus.

-sene-, *root.* *-sene-* comes from Latin, where it has the meaning "old." This meaning is found in such words as: SENATE, SENESCENCE, SENESCENT, SENILE, SENIOR.

Sen•e•gal•ese (sen′i gô lēz′, -lēs′, -gə-) /ˌsɛnɪgɔˈliyz, -ˈliys, -gə-/ *adj.*, *n.*, *pl.* **-ese. —*adj.* 1.** of or relating to Senegal. **—*n.*** [*count*] **2.** a person born or living in Senegal.

se•nes•cent (si nes′ənt) /sɪˈnɛsənt/ *adj.* growing old; aging. —**se•nes′cence,** *n.* [*noncount*] See -SENE-.

se•nile (sē′nil, sen′il) /ˈsiynayl, ˈsɛnayl/ *adj.* showing a decline of physical strength or mental functioning as a result of old age or disease. —**se•nil•i•ty** (si nil′i tē) /sɪˈnɪlɪtiy/ *n.* [*noncount*] See -SENE-.

sen•ior (sēn′yər) /ˈsiynyər/ *adj.* **1.** [*after a noun*] older (a father whose son is named after him; often abbreviated as Sr.): *John Doe, Sr.* **2.** of earlier election or appointment: *the senior senator from New York.* **3.** of higher rank: [*be* + ~ + *to*]: *The captain was senior to him by only a few months.* [*before a noun*]: *the senior officers present.* **4.** [*before a noun*] of or relating to seniors in high school or college: *her senior year.* **5.** [*before a noun*] of or relating to senior citizens: *a senior discount.* **—*n.*** [*count*] **6.** one who is older than another. **7.** a person of higher rank than another, esp. by virtue of longer service: *The captain was his senior by several months.* **8.** a student in the final year at a high school or college. **9.** a senior citizen: *a special bus for seniors.* See -SENE-.

sen′ior cit′izen, *n.* [*count*] an older person, usually over the age of 60 or 65, esp. one who is retired.

sen′ior high′ school′, *n.* a school from grades 10 through 12: [*count*]: *a new senior high school.* [*noncount*]: *attending senior high school.* See -SENE-.

sen•ior•i•ty (sēn yôr′i tē, -yor′-) /siynˈyɔrɪtiy, -ˈyɒr-/ *n.* [*noncount*] **1.** the state of being senior. **2.** higher status due to one's length of service. See -SENE-.

-sens-, *root.* *-sens-* comes from Latin, where it has the meaning "sense; feel." This meaning is found in such words as: CONSENSUS, DISSENSION, EXTRASENSORY, INSENSIBLE, INSENSITIVE, NONSENSE, SENSATION, SENSATIONAL, SENSE, SENSELESS, SENSITIVE, SENSOR, SENSORY, SENSUAL, SENSUOUS. See -SENT-.

sen•sa•tion (sen sā′shən) /sɛnˈseyʃən/ *n.* **1.** [*noncount*] the ability to feel or perceive something through the senses: *lost all sensation in his lower body as a result of the accident.* **2.** [*count*] a mental condition or physical feeling due to such awareness: *sensations of heat and cold.* **3.** [*count; often singular*] a general feeling such as discomfort, anxiety, or doubt: *a strong sensation of having been there before.* **4.** [*count; usually singular*] widespread excitement or interest: *The divorce caused a sensation.* See -SENS-.

sen•sa•tion•al (sen sā′shə nl) /sɛnˈseyʃənl̩/ *adj.* **1.** of or relating to sensation or to a sensation: *a sensational scandal.* **2.** extraordinarily good: *a sensational performer.* See -SENS-.

sen•sa•tion•al•ism (sen sā′shə nl iz′əm) /sɛnˈseyʃənl̩ˌɪzəm/ *n.* [*noncount*] the use of sensational subject matter or style: *tabloids full of sensationalism.* See -SENS-.

sense (sens) /sɛns/ *n.*, *v.*, **sensed, sens•ing. —*n.* 1.** [*count*] any of the powers such as sight, hearing, smell, taste, or touch, by which humans and animals see or feel anything outside or inside the body: *the five senses; Dogs have a better sense of hearing than humans do.* **2.** [*count*] a feeling produced through one of the senses: *a sense of cold.* **3.** [*count*] a vague feeling or impression: *a sense of security.* **4.** [*count*] **a.** a function of the mind like a physical sense: *the moral sense.* **b.** a special awareness to understand, see clearly, etc.: *a sense of values; a great sense of humor.* **5.** Usually, **senses.** [*plural*] sanity: *Have you taken leave of your senses?* **6.** [*noncount*] sound, practical intelligence: *to have the sense to stop talking and just listen.* **7.** [*noncount*] reasonable thoughts, ideas, or speech: *to talk sense.* **8.** meaning: [*noncount*]: *You missed the sense of his statement.* [*count*]: *One of the senses of the word "bachelor" is "unmarried male."* **9.** [*noncount*] value; merit: *no sense in worrying.* **10.** [*noncount*] consensus: *The sense of the meeting was that we should go forward.* **—*v.* 11.** [~ + *obj*] to take notice of (something) by the senses: *I sensed the presence of a large object in front of me in the darkness.* **12.** to have a feeling of: [~ + *obj*]: *She sensed his nervousness.* [~ + *(that) clause*]: *She sensed (that) he was nervous.* **13.** [~ + *obj*] to detect (physical things, such as light) mechanically, electrically, etc.: *The door senses your presence and opens automatically.* **—*Idiom.* 14. in a sense,** [*noncount*] to some extent; in a way: *In a sense, the book was entertaining.* See -SENS-.

sense•less (sens′lis) /ˈsɛnslɪs/ *adj.* **1.** unconscious: *knocked senseless by a falling tree branch.* **2.** stupid; foolish: *senseless chattering.* **3.** lacking meaning or purpose: *a victim of senseless violence.* —**sense′less•ly,** *adv.* —**sense′less•ness,** *n.* [*noncount*] See -SENS-.

sen•si•bil•i•ty (sen′sə bil′i tē) /ˌsɛnsəˈbɪlɪtiy/ *n.*, *pl.* **-ties. 1.** [*noncount*] capacity for feeling; responsiveness to stimuli. **2.** [*noncount*] mental responsiveness, esp. to subtle feelings. **3.** Often, **sensibilities.** [*plural*] capacity to respond to blame or praise: *a harmless remark that offended his sensibilities.* **4.** Often, **sensibilities.** [*plural*] capacity for discrimination: *a person of refined sensibilities.* See -SENS-.

sen•si•ble (sen′sə bəl) /ˈsɛnsəbəl/ *adj.* **1.** having, using, or showing good sense: *a sensible woman.* **2.** [*be* + ~] knowing; aware: *was sensible of his fault.* **3.** [*before a noun*] capable of being sensed by the senses or the mind: *the sensible universe.* **4.** practical: *sensible shoes for camping.* —**sen′si•bly,** *adv.*: *dressed sensibly for the safari.* See -SENS-. **—Usage.** Compare SENSITIVE and SENSIBLE. The word SENSIBLE describes a person having common sense, who makes intelligent decisions or shows good judgment: *He's very sensible when it comes to spending money.* The word SENSITIVE refers to someone who feels things easily and deeply and understands the feelings of others: *You should be more sensitive and caring toward the less fortunate.*

sen•si•tive (sen′si tiv) /ˈsɛnsɪtɪv/ *adj.* **1.** readily or easily affected by stimuli: *very sensitive to heat.* **2.** responsive to the feelings of others: *sensitive to your needs.* **3.** showing concern about the situation one is in: *a sensitive performance by the actor.* **4.** easily hurt or offended: *was a sensitive young child.* **5.** highly secret or delicate: *sensitive diplomatic issues.* **—*n.*** [*count*] **6.** one who is sensitive. —**sen′si•tive•ness,** *n.* [*noncount*] —**sen•si•tiv•i•ty** (sen′si tiv′i tē) /ˌsɛnsɪˈtɪvɪtiy/ *n.* [*noncount*]: *the teacher's sensitivity to the needs of her students.* See -SENS-. **—Usage.** See SENSIBLE.

sen•si•tize (sen′si tīz′) /ˈsɛnsɪˌtayz/ *v.* [~ + *obj*], **-tized, -tiz•ing. 1.** to make aware or responsive: [*often:* ~ + *obj* + *to*]: *to sensitize teachers to the needs of their students.* **2.** to be sensitive electronically: *The floormat has been sensitized so that it triggers an alarm when you walk on it.* —**sen•si•ti•za•tion** (sen′si tə zā′shən) /ˌsɛnsɪtəˈzeyʃən/ *n.* [*noncount*] See -SENS-.

sen•sor (sen′sôr, -sər) /ˈsɛnsɔr, -sər/ *n.* [*count*] a mechanical device that is sensitive to light, temperature, etc., and transmits a signal to a measuring or control instrument: *Sensors indicate a ship on a course that will intercept ours.* See -SENS-.

sen•so•ry (sen′sə rē) /ˈsɛnsəriy/ also **sen•so•ri•al** (sen-sôr′ē əl, -sōr′-) /sɛnˈsɔriyəl, -ˈsowr-/ *adj.* of or relating to the senses or sensation: *too much sensory information.* See -SENS-.

sen•su•al (sen′sho͞o əl) /ˈsɛnʃuwəl/ *adj.* **1.** suggesting or arousing the appetites, esp. the sexual appetite: *her sensual body.* **2.** devoted to or preoccupied with physical pleasure, esp. sexual satisfaction: *a lazy, sensual person.* **3.** of or relating to the senses; sensory. —**sen•su•al•i•ty** (sen′sho͞o al′i tē) /ˌsɛnʃuwˈælɪtiy/ *n.* [*noncount*] —**sen′su•al•ly,** *adv.*: *She whispered sensually in his ear.* See -SENS-.

sen•su•ous (sen′sho͞o əs) /ˈsɛnʃuwəs/ *adj.* felt by or affecting the senses, esp. pleasantly: *a sensuous bath.* —**sen′su•ous•ly,** *adv.* —**sen′su•ous•ness,** *n.* [*noncount*] See -SENS-.

sent (sent) /sɛnt/ *v.* pt. and pp. of SEND.

-sent-, *root.* *-sent-* comes from Latin, where it has the meaning "feel." It is related to the root -SENS-. This meaning is found in such words as: ASSENT, CONSENT, DISSENT, PRESENTIMENT, RESENT, RESENTFUL, RESENTMENT, SCENT, SENTENCE, SENTIENT, SENTIMENT.

sen•tence (sen′tns) /ˈsɛntns/ *n., v.,* **-tenced, -tenc•ing.** —*n.* **1.** [*count*] a group of words that forms an independent grammatical unit: *A sentence in English typically consists of a subject and a predicate containing a finite verb.* **2.** a judicial decision, esp. one stating punishment for a convicted criminal: [*count*]: *got the maximum sentence.* [*noncount*]: *to pass sentence on criminals.* —*v.* [~ + *obj*] **3.** to condemn to punishment: *He sentenced the murderer to life imprisonment.* See -SENT-.

sen•tient (sen′shənt) /ˈsɛnʃənt/ *adj.* having the power to feel by the senses; conscious: *Are plants sentient beings?* —**sen′tience,** *n.* [*noncount*] See -SENT-.

sen•ti•ment (sen′tə mənt) /ˈsɛntəmənt/ *n.* **1.** a feeling toward something; opinion: [*noncount*]: *Public sentiment is against taxes.* [*count*]: *I agree; those are my sentiments exactly.* **2.** [*noncount*] refined, delicate, sensitive emotion: *You can't allow sentiment to get in the way of business.* See -SENT-.

sen•ti•men•tal (sen′tə men′tl) /ˌsɛntəˈmɛntl̩/ *adj.* **1.** of or relating to the tender emotions, esp. excessively: *sentimental dreams of love and marriage.* **2.** embarrassingly emotional: *Let's not get too sentimental about our relationship.* **3.** nostalgic: *a sentimental journey to one's old hometown.* —**sen′ti•men′tal•ism,** *n.* [*noncount*] —**sen′ti•men′tal•ist,** *n.* [*count*] —**sen•ti•men•tal•i•ty** (sen′tə men tal′i tē) /ˌsɛntəmɛnˈtælɪtiy/ *n.* [*noncount*] —**sen′ti•men′tal•ly,** *adv.*

sen•ti•nel (sen′tn l, -tə nl) /ˈsɛntn̩l, -tənl̩/ *n.* [*count*] a person or thing that guards; sentry.

sen•try (sen′trē) /ˈsɛntriy/ *n.* [*count*], *pl.* **-tries.** a guard, esp., a soldier stationed to prevent someone from passing who is not allowed to do so.

se•pal (sē′pəl) /ˈsiypəl/ *n.* [*count*] one of the individual leaves or parts of the base of a flower.

sep•a•ra•ble (sep′ər ə bəl, sep′rə-) /ˈsɛpərəbəl, ˈsɛprə-/ *adj.* capable of being separated: *separable issues in a debate.*

sep•a•rate (*v.* sep′ə rāt′; *adj., n.* -ər it) / *v.* ˈsɛpəˌreyt; *adj., n.* -ərɪt/ *v.,* **-rat•ed, -rat•ing,** *adj., n.* —*v.* **1.** to (cause to) come or draw apart; divide: [~ + *obj*]: *to separate two fighting boys.* [~ + *obj* + *from* + *obj*]: *The school separates the boys from the girls.* [*no obj*]: *The two fighters separated, then went after each other again.* **2.** to divide into pieces: [~ + *obj*]: *Separate the strips of bacon and fry them individually.* [*no obj*]: *After defrosting, the strips of bacon will separate easily.* **3.** to (cause to) become extracted: [~ + *obj*]: *to separate metal from ore.* [*no obj*]: *The metal easily separates from the ore.* **4.** [*no obj*] to stop living together but without divorce: *He and his wife separated last year.* —*adj.* **5.** detached; not connected: *a garage separate from the house.* **6.** different: *five separate meanings.* **7.** [*before a noun*] not shared; individual: *separate checks.* —*n.* **8.** Usually, **separates.** [*plural*] women's clothing to be worn in various combinations. —**sep′a•rate•ly,** *adv.* See -PARE-[1].

sep•a•ra•tion (sep′ə rā′shən) /ˌsɛpəˈreyʃən/ *n.* **1.** [*noncount*] an act or instance of separating or the state of being separated: *the separation of church and state.* **2.** [*count*] **a.** a place, line, or amount of parting: *The dotted lines on the map mark the separations between the counties.* **b.** an opening; a gap or hole: *a small separation on the hem of his pants.* **3.** [*count*] a formal act of separating by a married couple: *ordered a trial separation of six months.* —**sep•a•ra•tive** (sep′ə rā′tiv, -ər ə-, -rə-) /ˈsɛpəˌreytɪv, -ərə-, -rə-/ *adj.* See -PARE-[1].

sep•a•ra•tist (sep′ər ə tist, sep′rə-) /ˈsɛpərətɪst, ˈsɛprə-/ *n.* [*count*] **1.** one who separates, as from a church. **2.** one calling for formal separation, as of a part of a country from the rest of it. —*adj.* **3.** of or relating to separatists. —**sep′a•ra•tism,** *n.* [*noncount*] See -PARE-[1].

sep•a•ra•tor (sep′ə rā′tər) /ˈsɛpəˌreytər/ *n.* [*count*] a person or thing that separates, esp. a device for separating cream from milk. See -PARE-[1].

se•pi•a (sē′pē ə) /ˈsiypiyə/ *n., pl.* **pi•as,** *adj.* —*n.* **1.** [*noncount*] a brown coloring material, used in drawing. **2.** [*count*] a drawing made with sepia. **3.** [*noncount*] a dark brown. **4.** [*count*] a print made in this color. —*adj.* **5.** of a brown, grayish brown, or olive brown similar to that of sepia.

sep•sis (sep′sis) /ˈsɛpsɪs/ *n.* [*noncount*] infection from harmful bacteria: *sepsis from a wound.*

Sept., an abbreviation of: September.

Sep•tem•ber (sep tem′bər) /sɛpˈtɛmbər/ *n.* [*proper noun*] the ninth month of the year, containing 30 days. *Abbr.:* Sept., Sep.

sep•tet (sep tet′) /sɛpˈtɛt/ *n.* [*count*] **1.** any group of seven persons or things, such as singers or musicians. **2.** a musical composition for seven persons or instruments.

sep•tic (sep′tik) /ˈsɛptɪk/ *adj.* of or relating to sepsis; infected.

sep′tic tank′, *n.* [*count*] a tank under the ground near a home, in which household sewage is stored, decomposed, and purified by bacteria.

sep•tu•a•ge•nar•i•an (sep′cho͞o ə jə nâr′ē ən, -to͞o-, -tyo͞o-) /ˌsɛptʃuwədʒəˈnɛəriyən, -tuw-, -tyuw-/ *adj.* **1.** of the age of 70 or between 70 and 80. —*n.* [*count*] **2.** a septuagenarian person.

sep•ul•cher (sep′əl kər) /ˈsɛpəlkər/ *n.* [*count*] a tomb or grave.

se•pul•chral (sə pul′krəl) /səˈpʌlkrəl/ *adj.* **1.** of or relating to tombs or to burial. **2.** sad, depressing, or mournful.

-seq-, *root.* *-seq-* comes from Latin, where it has the meaning "follow." This meaning is found in such words as: CONSEQUENCE, CONSEQUENT, CONSEQUENTIAL, INCONSEQUENTIAL, OBSEQUIOUS, SEQUEL, SEQUENCE, SEQUENTIAL, SUBSEQUENT.

se•quel (sē′kwəl) /ˈsiykwəl/ *n.* [*count*] **1.** a book, play, etc., that continues the story from a preceding work. **2.** something that develops from something else: *a sequel to the debate.* See -SEQ-.

se•quence (sē′kwəns) /ˈsiykwəns/ *n., v.,* **-quenced, -quenc•ing.** —*n.* **1.** [*noncount*] the following of one thing after another: *to arrange the cards in sequence.* **2.** [*count*] a continuous group or series of things: *a sonnet sequence.* **3.** [*count*] a series of related scenes that make up an episode in a film: *In the final sequence the villain falls into a vat of acid.* —*v.* [~ + *obj*] **4.** to place in a sequence. See -SEQ-.

se•quen•tial (si kwen′shəl) /sɪˈkwɛnʃəl/ *adj.* occurring in a sequence: *a sequential course of study.* See -SEQ-.

se•ques•ter (si kwes′tər) /sɪˈkwɛstər/ *v.* [~ + *obj*] **1.** to remove to a place of quiet: *to sequester oneself in the library.* **2.** to set apart; isolate: *The judge sequestered the jury.* —*n.* [*count*] **3.** an act or instance of sequestering. **4.** a cut in government spending applying to all persons, divisions, etc. —**se•ques•tra•tion** (sē′kwes trā′shən) /ˌsiykwɛsˈtreyʃən/ *n.* [*noncount*]

se•quin (sē′kwin) /ˈsiykwɪn/ *n.* [*count*] a small, shiny disk used for ornamentation on clothing. —**se′quined,** *adj.*

se•quoi•a (si kwoi′ə) /sɪˈkwɔyə/ *n.* [*count*], *pl.* **-quoi•as.** a large cone-bearing tree of California, having reddish bark and reaching heights of more than 300 ft. (91 m).

se•ra (sēr′ə) /ˈsɪərə/ *n.* [*plural*] a pl. of SERUM.

se•ra•pe or **sa•ra•pe** (sə rä′pē) /səˈrɑpiy/ *n.* [*count*], *pl.* **-pes.** a blanketlike shawl worn esp. in Mexico.

ser•aph (ser′əf) /ˈsɛrəf/ *n.* [*count*], *pl.* **-aphs, -a•phim** (-ə fim) /-əfɪm/. a member of the highest order of angels. —**se•raph•ic** (si raf′ik) /sɪˈræfɪk/ *adj.*

ser•e•nade (ser′ə nād′, ser′ə nād′) /ˌsɛrəˈneyd, ˈsɛrəˌneyd/ *n., v.,* **-nad•ed, -nad•ing.** —*n.* [*count*] **1.** a performance of music in the open air at night. **2. a.** a piece of music performed this way. **b.** a type of musical composition having several movements. —*v.* [~ + *obj*] **3.** to entertain with a serenade: *serenaded her with songs.*

ser•en•dip•i•ty (ser′ən dip′i tē) /ˌsɛrənˈdɪpɪtiy/ *n.* [*noncount*] **1.** an ability for making desirable discoveries by accident. **2.** good fortune; luck. —**ser′en•dip′i•tous,** *adj.*: *a serendipitous discovery.*

se•rene (sə rēn′) /səˈriyn/ *adj.* **1.** calm; peaceful; tranquil: *a serene temperament.* **2.** clear; fair: *serene* weather. —**se•rene′ly,** *adv.*: *worked serenely at her desk.* —**se•rene′ness,** *n.* [*noncount*]

se•ren•i•ty (sə ren′i tē) /sə'rɛnɪtiy/ *n.* [*noncount*] the state of being serene: *working with serenity.*

serf (sûrf) /sɜrf/ *n.* [*count*] one who is required to provide services to a lord, usually attached to the land and transferred from one owner to another. —**serf•dom** (sûrf′dəm) /'sɜrfdəm/ *n.* [*noncount*] See -SERV[1]-.

serge (sûrj) /sɜrdʒ/ *n.* [*noncount*] a fabric with a diagonal pattern, used esp. for suits.

ser•geant (sär′jənt) /'sɑrdʒənt/ *n.* [*count*] **1.** a noncommissioned officer ranking above a corporal. **2.** a police officer ranking below a captain or a lieutenant.

ser′geant at arms′, *n.* [*count*] an officer of a lawmaking body whose chief duty is to preserve order.

se•ri•al (sēr′ē əl) /'sɪəriyəl/ *n.* [*count*] **1.** anything published, broadcast, etc., in parts at regular times. **2.** a publication, as an annual report, released or printed in successive parts. —*adj.* [*usually: before a noun*] **3.** published or presented in sequential parts: *a serial story.* **4.** of or relating to a series: *the serial numbers on the checks.* **5.** occurring in a series, one after another: *serial murders.* **6.** responsible for a series of specified actions, esp. crimes: *a serial killer.* **7.** of or relating to the transfer of electronic data in a stream of sequential pieces of information: *a serial printer attached to the serial port.*

se•ri•al•ize (sēr′ē ə līz′) /'sɪər,iyə,layz/ *v.* [~ + *obj*], **-ized, -iz•ing. 1.** to publish in serial form: *to serialize the novel in the magazine.* **2.** to broadcast or film in serial form. —**se•ri•al•i•za•tion** (sēr′ē ə lə zā′shən) /,sɪəriyələ'zeyʃən/ *n.* [*noncount*]: *negotiating for serialization with the author.* [*count*]: *a three-part serialization.*

se•ries (sēr′ēz) /'sɪəriyz/ *n.* [*count*], *pl.* **se•ries. 1.** a number of related things, events, etc., arranged or occurring in sequence: *a series of murders.* **2.** a number of games, contests, etc., with the same teams or players: *a championship series.* **3.** *Radio and Television.* **a.** a daily or weekly program with a fixed setting, a regular cast of characters, and a continuing story. **b.** two or more programs related by theme or format: *a series on African wildlife.*

ser•if (ser′if) /'sɛrɪf/ *n.* [*count*] a smaller line used to finish off a main stroke of a letter, such as at the top and bottom of *E.*

se•ri•ous (sēr′ē əs) /'sɪəriyəs/ *adj.* **1.** of or characterized by thought: *a serious study of inner-city violence.* **2.** grave, solemn, or somber, as in mood; not cheerful: *He was very serious and didn't even smile.* **3.** earnest; sincere: *a serious offer to buy the house.* **4.** requiring thought or concentration: *serious reading.* **5.** important or significant: *Marriage is a serious matter.* **6.** giving cause for worry or fear: *a serious relapse.* —**se′ri•ous•ness,** *n.* [*noncount*]

se•ri•ous•ly (sēr′ē əs lē) /'sɪəriyəsliy/ *adv.* **1.** in a serious manner: *studied seriously for the test.* **2.** to an extent that causes worry or fear: *He was seriously ill.* **3.** in a way deserving careful thought: *We have to take their threats seriously.* **4.** (used to express the feeling that what is said is important and should be listened to): *When the laughter died down he continued, "But seriously, folks, we do have a major problem."*

ser•mon (sûr′mən) /'sɜrmən/ *n.* [*count*] **1.** a talk given for religious instruction. **2.** any serious talk, esp. on morals: *Don't give me a sermon on how to run my life!* **3.** a long, boring speech.

ser•mon•ize (sûr′mə nīz′) /'sɜrmə,nayz/ *v.* [*no obj*], **-ized, -iz•ing.** to give a talk or speech about moral values to someone, esp. a long and boring or unwanted speech.

ser•pent (sûr′pənt) /'sɜrpənt/ *n.* [*count*] **1.** a snake. **2.** a sneaky, dishonest, or evil person.

ser•pen•tine (sûr′pən tēn′, -tīn′) /'sɜrpən,tiyn, -,tayn/ *adj.* **1.** of or relating to a serpent, as in form or movement. **2.** having a winding course, as a road; twisty.

ser•rat•ed (ser′ā tid, sə rā′-) /'sɛreytɪd, sə'rey-/ *adj.* having sawlike teeth, esp. for cutting: *a serrated knife.* —**ser•ra′tion,** *n.* [*noncount*]

se•rum (sēr′əm) /'sɪərəm/ *n., pl.* **se•rums, se•ra** (sēr′ə) /'sɪərə/. **1.** the clear, pale yellow liquid that separates when blood coagulates; blood serum: [*noncount*]: *a wound oozing serum.* [*count*]: *coding different sera.* **2.** liquid made from the blood of an animal that contains disease-fighting substances: [*noncount*]: *serum injected into the bloodstream.* [*count*]: *a serum for hepatitis.*

-serv-[1], *root.* -*serv*- comes from Latin, where it has the meaning "slave." This meaning is found in such words as: DESERVE, DISSERVICE, SERVANT, SERVE, SERVICE, SERVILE, SERVITUDE, SUBSERVIENT.

-serv-[2], *root.* -*serv*- comes from Latin, where it has the meaning "save." This meaning is found in such words as: CONSERVATION, CONSERVE, OBSERVATION, OBSERVE, PRESERVATION, PRESERVE, RESERVATION, RESERVE, RESERVOIR, UNRESERVED.

serv•ant (sûr′vənt) /'sɜrvənt/ *n.* [*count*] one who works for another, esp. around the house. See -SERV-[1].

serve (sûrv) /sɜrv/ *v.,* **served, serv•ing,** *n.* —*v.* **1.** to act as a servant to (another); work for: [*no obj*]: *The maid served in the kitchen.* [~ + *obj*]: *served his young master well.* **2.** to carry and distribute (food or drink) to (a person at a table): [~ + *obj*]: *He served the food.* [~ + *obj* + *obj*]: *The headwaiter served us our food.* [*no obj*]: *A good waiter serves without drawing attention to himself.* [*no obj*]: *She served at the church reception.* **3.** [~ + *obj*] to give assistance to; be of use to: *May I serve you?* **4.** to be suitable for (a purpose); help: [*no obj*]: *That cup will serve as a sugar bowl.* [~ + *obj*]: *This will serve our needs.* [~ + *to* + *verb* (+ *obj*)]: *This note will serve to explain my actions.* **5.** to go through a term of service for (something or someone), as a soldier, senator, etc.: [*no obj*]: *served in the armed forces.* [~ + *obj*]: *served her country in the Gulf War.* **6.** [~ + *obj*] to go through (a term in prison): *had to serve six years in prison.* **7.** (in tennis, handball, etc.) to put (the ball or shuttlecock) in play with a stroke or hit: [*no obj*]: *served first to start the match.* [~ + *obj*]: *served the first ball out of bounds.* **8.** to attend the priest at (mass): [*no obj*]: *The altar boy served at the 12:30 mass.* [~ + *obj*]: *The altar boy served the 12:30 mass.* **9.** to give active service or obedience to (God, a sovereign, etc.): [*no obj*]: *He served under the president well.* [~ + *obj*]: *"You have served me well," the king whispered to his chamberlain.* **10.** [~ + *obj*] to contribute to; promote: *to serve a cause.* **11.** *Law.* to give in a legal manner (a summons, process, etc.) to (someone): [~ + *obj*]: *served his client with a warrant; served the warrant for the arrest of my client.* [~ + *obj* + *obj*]: *served my client the warrant.* —*n.* [*count*] **12.** the act or right of serving, as in tennis: *Whose serve is it?* —***Idiom.*** **13. serve (someone) right,** to be someone's just punishment, as for improper behavior: *It served her right to get caught; she was cheating all the time.* —**serv′er,** *n.* [*count*] See -serv-[1].

serv•ice (sûr′vis) /'sɜrvɪs/ *n., adj., v.,* **-iced, -ic•ing.** —*n.* **1.** [*noncount*] the performance of duties, or the duties performed, as by a servant: *The restaurant has terrible food and even worse service.* **2.** (an act of) helpful activity; aid: [*count*]: *to do someone a service.* [*noncount*]: *Let me know if I can be of service.* **3.** [*noncount*] the supplying or supplier of utilities or goods for a public need, such as water, electricity, etc.: *improved bus service.* **4.** the providing or a provider of care required by the public, such as repair: [*noncount*]: *had to bring the air conditioner in for service at least three times.* [*count*]: *a television repair service.* **5.** [*noncount*] employment in any duties or work for a person, organization, etc.: *a long term of service with the insurance company.* **6.** [*count*] a department of public employment, or the body of public servants in it: *the diplomatic service.* **7.** the armed forces: [*noncount*]: *He was in the service during the war.* [*count*]: *Which one of the services were you in?* **8.** Often, **services.** [*plural*] the performance of any duties or work for another: *medical services.* **9.** [*count*] something made or done by a commercial organization for the public and without regard to profit: *Those pamphlets on energy are published as a public service by a paint manufacturer.* **10.** [*count*] a form of public religious worship according to a certain form and order: *Sunday morning services.* **11.** [*count*] a set of dishes, utensils, etc., for use: *a lunch service for two.* —*adj.* [*before a noun*] **12.** of service; useful. **13.** of or relating to servants, delivery people, etc., or in serving food: *a service elevator.* **14.** supplying services rather than products or goods: *the service professions.* **15.** supplying or providing maintenance and repair: *a service center for appliances.* —*v.* [~ + *obj*] **16.** to make fit for use: *to service an automobile.* **17.** to supply with aid, information, or other services. See -SERV-[1].

serv•ice•a•ble (sûr′və sə bəl) /'sɜrvəsəbəl/ *adj.* **1.** being of service or help; useful. **2.** wearing well; durable: *serviceable clothes.* **3.** adequate; sufficient: *a serviceable job.* See -SERV[1]-.

serv•ice•man (sûr′vis man′, -mən) /'sɜrvɪs,mæn, -mən/ *n.* [*count*], *pl.* **-men. 1.** a member of the armed forces of a country. **2.** one whose job is to maintain equipment.

serv′ice sta′tion, *n.* [*count*] a place for servicing automobiles. Also called **gas station.**

ser•vi•ette (sûr′vē et′) /ˌsɜrviy'ɛt/ *n.* [*count*] *Chiefly Brit.* a table napkin. See -SERV¹-.

ser•vile (sûr′vil, -vīl) /'sɜrvɪl, -vayl/ *adj.* **1.** obeying like a slave: *the dictator's servile flatterers.* **2.** of or relating to slaves, slavery, servants, or servitude. —**ser•vil•i•ty** (sər-vil′i tē) /sər'vɪlɪtiy/ *n.* [*noncount*] See -SERV-¹.

serv•ing (sûr′ving) /'sɜrvɪŋ/ *n.* **1.** [*noncount*] the act of a person or thing that serves. **2.** [*count*] a portion of food or drink: *two servings of cherry pie.* —*adj.* [*before a noun*] **3.** for use in distributing food to or at the table: *a serving tray.* See -SERV¹-.

ser•vi•tude (sûr′vi to͞od′, -tyo͞od′) /'sɜrvɪˌtuwd, -ˌtyuwd/ *n.* [*noncount*] **1.** slavery. **2.** service or labor required as a punishment for criminals: *penal servitude.* See -SERV-¹.

ser•vo (sûr′vō) /'sɜrvow/ *adj., n., pl.* **-vos.** —*adj.* **1.** acting as part of a servomechanism: *a servo amplifier.* **2.** of or relating to servomechanisms: *a servo engineer.* —*n.* **3.** SERVOMECHANISM.

ser•vo•mech•an•ism (sûr′vō mek′ə niz′əm, sûr′vō-mek′-) /'sɜrvowˌmɛkəˌnɪzəm, ˌsɜrvow'mɛk-/ *n.* [*count*] an electronic control system in which a controlling mechanism is activated and controlled by a low-energy signal. See -SERV-¹.

ses•a•me (ses′ə mē) /'sɛsəmiy/ *n.* **1.** [*count*] a tropical plant with small oval edible seeds that also yield an oil. **2.** [*noncount*] the seeds themselves, used as a flavoring.

-sess-, *root.* -*sess*- comes from Latin, where it has the meaning "sit; stay." It is related to the root -SID-. This meaning is found in such words as: ASSESS, ASSESSOR, DISPOSSESS, INTERSESSION, OBSESSION, POSSESSION, REPOSSESSION, SESSION.

ses•sion (sesh′ən) /'sɛʃən/ *n.* **1.** [*noncount; often: in* + ~] the meeting of a court, council, etc., for its business: *The court is now in session.* **2.** [*count*] a continuous meeting of persons so assembled: *the next session of Congress.* **3.** [*count*] a portion of the day or year into which instruction is organized at a school, college, etc.: *courses taken in the summer session.* **4.** [*count*] a period of time during which several persons meet for an activity: *a study session.* See -SESS-.

set (set) /sɛt/ *v.,* **set, set•ting,** *n., adj.* —*v.* **1.** [~ + *obj*] to put (something or someone) in a particular place or posture: *to set a vase on a table.* **2.** [~ + *obj*] to put or cause to pass into some condition: *to set a house on fire.* **3.** [~ + *obj*] to put or apply: *to set fire to a house.* **4.** [~ + *obj*] to fix definitely; decide upon: *to set a wedding date.* **5.** [~ + *obj*] to put (a price or value) upon something: *to set a high price for the car.* **6.** [~ + *obj*] to fix the value of (something) at a certain amount, rate, or point: *sets honesty above everything.* **7.** [~ + *obj*] to post, station, or appoint for a duty: *For safety we plan to set guards at the door.* **8.** [~ + *obj*] to place or plant firmly: *to set a flagpole in concrete.* **9.** [~ + *obj*] to direct or settle with firmness or great hopes: *She can really set her mind to a task.* **10.** [~ + *obj*] to establish (an example, etc.) for others to follow: *to set a fast pace.* **11.** to assign (a task, problem, etc.) to (someone): [~ + *obj*]: *The teacher set ten math problems for homework.* [~ + *obj* + *to* + *verb*]: *The teacher set the students to work.* **12.** [~ + *obj*] to distribute or arrange china, silver, etc., for use on (a table): *Set the table for dinner.* **13. a.** [~ + *obj*] to style (the hair) by using rollers, clips, etc., to cause curls, waves, etc.: *She said she had to set her hair.* **b.** [*no obj*] (of the hair) to produce curls, waves, etc., as a result of rollers, clips, etc.: *Her thin hair doesn't set well.* **14.** [~ + *obj*] to put in the proper condition for use: *to set a trap.* **15.** [~ + *obj*] to adjust (a mechanism) so as to control its performance: *to set one's watch (= to put the hands or numbers at the correct or desired time).* **16.** [~ + *obj*] to mount (a gem or the like) in a frame or setting: *The diamond is set in a beautiful gold mounting.* **17.** [~ + *obj*] to cause to sit; seat: *to set a child in a highchair.* **18.** [~ + *obj*] to cause to take a particular direction: *to set one's course to the south.* **19.** to (cause to) be put into a fixed, rigid state, such as the face or muscles: [~ + *obj*]: *He set his jaw and tried to frown.* [*no obj*]: *His face set into an ugly frown.* **20.** [~ + *obj*] to put (a broken or dislocated bone) back in position. **21.** to become or cause (glue, mortar, etc.) to become fixed or hard: [*no obj*]: *Has the glue set yet?* [~ + *obj*]: *The cold air will set the cement faster.* **22.** [~ + *obj*] to urge to attack: *to set the hounds on a trespasser.* **23.** [~ + *obj*] to fit (words) to music. **24.** [~ + *obj*] to arrange (type) for printing. **25.** [*no obj*] to pass below the horizon; sink: *The sun sets early in winter.* **26.** [*no obj*] *Nonstandard.* to sit: *Come in and set a spell.* **27. set about,** to begin; start: [~ + *about* + *obj*]: *to set about one's work.* [~ + *about* + *verb-ing*]: *to set about repairing the engines.* **28. set against,** [~ + *obj* + *against* + *obj*] **a.** to cause (one person, party, etc.) to be hostile to (another): *The Civil War set brother against brother.* **b.** to compare or contrast (one person or thing) with (another): *to set advantages against disadvantages.* **29. set ahead,** [~ + *obj* + *ahead*] to set to a later time: *In Spring we set our clocks ahead one hour.* **30. set aside, a.** to put to one side; reserve: [~ + *aside* + *obj*]: *The clerk set aside the diamond bracelet.* [~ + *obj* + *aside*]: *to set the bracelet aside.* **b.** to dismiss from the mind; reject: [~ + *aside* + *obj*]: *to set aside hatreds.* [~ + *obj* + *aside*]: *to set our hatred aside.* **c.** to overrule; discard; annul: [~ + *aside* + *obj*]: *The judge set aside the verdict.* [~ + *obj* + *aside*]: *to set the verdict aside.* **31. set back, a.** to slow down progress of; impede: [~ + *back* + *obj*]: *Bad weather set back the rescue attempts.* [~ + *obj* + *back*]: *The loss of their best player set the team back.* **b.** to fix at an earlier time or lower point on a scale: [~ + *back* + *obj*]: *Set back your clocks one hour.* [~ + *obj* + *back*]: *Set the clocks back one hour.* **c.** [~ + *obj* + *back* + *obj*] *Informal.* to cause to pay; cost: *The house set them back $200,000.* **32. set down, a.** to record or copy in writing or printing: [~ + *down* + *obj*]: *The girl had set down her ideas in her diary.* [~ + *obj* + *down*]: *She had set her ideas down in writing.* **b.** to land an airplane: [~ + *down* + *obj*]: *to set down the plane safely.* [~ + *obj* + *down*]: *to set the plane down safely.* **33. set forth, a.** [~ + *forth* + *obj*] to give an account of; describe: *The physicist set forth her ideas.* **b.** [*no obj*] to begin a journey; start: *They set forth on the expedition.* **34. set in,** [*no obj*] to begin to come; arrive: *Infection was setting in.* **35. set off, a.** to cause to become ignited or to explode: [~ + *off* + *obj*]: *to set off fireworks.* [~ + *obj* + *off*]: *to set fireworks off.* **b.** [~ + *off* + *obj*] to begin; start: *The TV show set off a rush of phone calls.* **c.** [~ + *off* + *obj*] to intensify the look of by contrast or by emphasizing different colors, etc.: *The dark dress really sets off her pale features.* **d.** [*no obj*] to begin a journey or trip; depart: *The hikers set off before sunrise.* **36. set on, a.** Also, **set upon.** [~ + *on/upon* + *obj*] to attack: *He was set upon by a gang.* **b.** Also, **set upon.** [~ + *obj* + *on/upon* + *obj*] to cause to attack: *to set a dog on an intruder.* **37. set out, a.** [*no obj*] to begin a journey or course: *The explorers set out long before dawn.* **b.** [~ + *out* + *to* + *verb*] to try; undertake: *set out to reform the system.* **c.** to define; describe: [~ + *out* + *obj*]: *set out his main ideas in a short paper.* [~ + *obj* + *out*]: *to set his ideas out in an essay.* **d.** to lay or spread out, usually in order: [~ + *out* + *obj*]: *Let's set out some extra glasses for the guests.* [~ + *obj* + *out*]: *to set some plates out for our guests.* **38. set to,** [*no obj*] to begin work with strength and activity: *Let's set to and clean things up.* **39. set up, a.** to put in an upright or ready position: [~ + *up* + *obj*]: *to set up a roadblock.* [~ + *obj* + *up*]: *to set a roadblock up.* **b.** to put into a powerful position: [~ + *up* + *obj*]: *The Western government had helped to set up the dictator.* [~ + *obj* + *up*]: *to set the dictator up as a puppet.* **c.** to construct or assemble for use: [~ + *up* + *obj*]: *to set up a computer.* [~ + *obj* + *up*]: *Do you know how to set a computer up?* **d.** to establish or start: [~ + *up* + *obj*]: *to set up a business.* [~ + *obj* + *up*]: *to set a business up.* **e.** to cause (someone) to be able to begin in business: [~ + *up* + *obj*]: *He set up his son in the construction business.* [~ + *obj* + *up*]: *He set his son up in the construction business.* **f.** to treat, as to drinks: [~ + *up* + *obj*]: *Bartender, set up a few drinks for my friend here.* [~ + *obj* + *up*]: *to set a few drinks up.* **g.** [~ + *obj* + *up*] to lure into a situation so as to embarrass or trap: *The crooks set the shopkeeper up and fooled him completely.* [~ + *up* + *obj*]: *to set up a victim.* **h.** [~ + *obj* + *up*] to arrange a date for: *set me up with his sister.* —*n.* [*count*] **40.** a collection of articles for use together: *a set of carving knives.* **41.** a number or combination of things of similar nature or function: *a set of ideas.* **42.** a number or group of persons having common interests or status: *the smart set.* **43.** [*usually: singular*] the way one is thinking or acting: *The set of his mind was obvious.* **44.** [*usually: singular*] the way one carries oneself, as when walking: *The set of his shoulders showed how discouraged he was.* **45.** the styling of the hair with rollers, pins, etc., or the hairstyle so formed. **46.** an apparatus for receiving radio or television programs; receiver: *My TV set is broken.* **47.** something built to represent the place of action in a play, film, etc.: *The Hollywood set for that street scene occupied several square blocks.* **48.**

Math. a collection of objects or elements classed together: *The null set has no members.* —*adj.* **49.** [*before a noun*] fixed or decided: *no set time for the meeting.* **50.** [*before a noun*] specified; certain; fixed: *The hall holds a set number of people.* **51.** [*before a noun*] customary: *a few set phrases in the same old speech.* **52.** [*before a noun*] fixed; rigid: *a set smile.* **53.** [*be* + ~] resolved or determined: *They are old and set in their ways (= They are not able or willing to change their habits).* **54.** [*be* + ~] completely prepared; ready: *Is everyone set?*

set•back (set′bak′) /'sɛt,bæk/ *n.* [*count*] a stopping or delay in one's progress; reverse or defeat.

set•tee (se tē′) /sɛ'tiy/ *n.* [*count*], *pl.* **-tees.** a seat for two or more persons, having a back and arms.

set•ter (set′ər) /'sɛtər/ *n.* [*count*] **1.** a person or thing that sets. **2.** a breed of hunting dogs with long hair trained to point at what is being hunted, esp. birds.

set•ting (set′ing) /'sɛtɪŋ/ *n.* [*count*] **1.** the act of a person or thing that sets. **2.** the point or position of something, such as a thermostat, that has been set: *The air conditioner setting is too high.* **3.** the surroundings or environment of anything: *one's home setting.* **4.** a group of all the pieces, as of china, used for setting a table. **5.** the location or period in which the action of a novel, play, etc., takes place: *The setting was a spooky old castle.* —**Syn.** See ENVIRONMENT.

set•tle (set′l) /'sɛtḷ/ *v.,* **-tled, -tling. 1.** to fix, decide on, or resolve: [~ + *obj*]: *The matter is settled; we'll buy the house.* [*no obj*]: *We'll settle with him later, after we draft this agreement.* See *settle on* below. **2.** [~ + *obj*] to place in a good state: *We had to settle our affairs before leaving.* **3.** to place in a good position: [~ + *obj*]: *The child settled himself comfortably on her lap.* [*no obj*]: *He settled comfortably in the chair.* **4.** [~ + *obj*] to pay, as a bill: *The bill was settled.* See *settle up* below. **5.** to migrate to and organize (an area, etc.) for living; colonize: [*no obj*]: *The birds settled in the swamp.* [~ + *obj*]: *The early tribes settled the lower peninsula.* **6.** to take up residence in (a place): [*no obj*]: *Many Norwegian immigrants settled in Minnesota.* [~ + *obj*]: *Many Norwegians settled the Minnesota region.* **7.** to (cause to) become quiet or calm as by the relief of distress: [~ + *obj*]: *took a deep breath to settle his nerves.* [*no obj*]: *My upset stomach finally settled.* **8.** to (cause to) sink down gradually: [*no obj*]: *The undissolved sugar settled in the bottom of his coffee.* [~ + *obj*]: *Stir the coffee to settle the sugar in it.* **9.** [*no obj*] to come down to rest, as from flight: *a bird settling on a tree branch.* **10. settle down,** [*no obj*] **a.** to achieve stability, esp. upon marrying: *His parents wanted him to marry and settle down.* **b.** to become calm or quiet: *The teacher shouted at his class to settle down.* **c.** to apply oneself to serious work: *settled down and got back to work.* **d.** Also, **settle in.** to stop activity to rest or sleep: *We settled down for the night at a country inn.* **11. settle for,** [~ + *for* + *obj*] to be satisfied with: *You shouldn't have to settle for second best.* **12. settle into,** [~ + *into* + *obj*] to become established in: *The new worker settled into the job.* **13. settle on** or **upon,** [~ + *on/upon* + *obj*] to decide or agree: *to settle on a plan.* **14. settle up,** to pay (what is owed), such as a bill: [*no obj*]: *You should settle up with the bank on your loan.* [~ + *obj*]: *You should settle up your debts.* —**set′tler,** *n.* [*count*]

set•tle•ment (set′l mənt) /'sɛtḷmənt/ *n.* **1.** [*noncount*] the act or state of moving into or settling in a place, or the state of being settled: *a colony for settlement in the south.* **2.** [*count*] a colony, esp. in its early stages: *a small settlement in Jamestown, Virginia.* **3.** [*count*] a small community, as in a thinly populated area. **4.** [*count*] an agreement signed after labor negotiations between union and management: *to reach a settlement before the strike deadline.* **5.** [*count*] the satisfying of a claim or demand: *reached a settlement out of court.* **6.** [*count*] Also called **set′tlement house′.** an establishment in a poor area providing social services to local residents.

set′-to′, *n.* [*count*], *pl.* **-tos.** a usually brief, sharp fight or argument.

set•up (set′up′) /'sɛt,ʌp/ *n.* [*count*] **1.** organization; arrangement: *an efficient setup at work.* **2.** an act or instance of getting ready. **3.** an activity or contest deliberately made easy: *The best team gets to play the worst team: what a setup!* **4.** a situation created to fool or trap someone; trick: *The drug dealer walked straight into our setup.*

sev•en (sev′ən) /'sɛvən/ *n.* [*count*] **1.** a cardinal number, 6 plus 1. **2.** a symbol for this number, as 7 or VII. **3.** a set of this many persons or things. —*adj.* [*before a noun*] **4.** amounting to seven in number: *my seven sisters.* —**sev′enth,** *adj., n.* [*count*]

sev′en seas′, *n.* [*plural; the* + ~*; sometimes: Seven Seas*] the waters of the world that can be traveled on.

sev•en•teen (sev′ən tēn′) /'sɛvən'tiyn/ *n.* [*count*] **1.** a cardinal number, 10 plus 7. **2.** a symbol for this number, as 17 or XVII. **3.** a set of this many persons or things. —*adj.* [*before a noun*] **4.** amounting to 17 in number: *seventeen summers ago.* —**sev′en•teenth′,** *adj., n.* [*count*]

sev′enth heav′en, *n.* [*noncount*] a state of very great happiness; bliss: *He was in seventh heaven after he got the raise.*

sev•en•ty (sev′ən tē) /'sɛvəntiy/ *n., pl.* **-ties,** *adj.* —*n.* [*count*] **1.** a cardinal number, 10 times 7. **2.** a symbol for this number, as 70 or LXX. **3.** a set of this many persons or things. **4. seventies,** [*plural; usually: the* + ~] the numbers from 70 through 79, as in referring to the years of a lifetime or of a century or to degrees of temperature. —*adj.* [*before a noun*] **5.** amounting to 70 in number. —**sev′en•ti•eth,** *adj., n.* [*count*]

sev•er (sev′ər) /'sɛvər/ *v.* [~ + *obj*] **1.** to separate (a part) from the whole, as by cutting: *His leg had been severed in an accident.* **2.** to break off or dissolve (relations, etc.): *The government has severed all diplomatic relations.* See -PARE[1]-.

sev•er•al (sev′ər əl, sev′rəl) /'sɛvərəl, 'sɛvrəl/ *adj.* [~ + *plural noun*] **1.** being more than two but fewer than many: *There are several ways to do the same thing.* **2.** separate; different: *We visited on several occasions.* **3.** individual; respective: *They went their several ways.* —*n.* [*plural; used with a plural verb*] **4.** several persons or things; a few; some: *Several have already signed up.* —**sev′er•al•ly,** *adv.* See -PARE[1]-.

sev•er•ance (sev′ər əns, -rəns) /'sɛvərəns, -rəns/ *n.* **1.** the act of severing, or the state of being severed: [*noncount*]: *severance from his family.* [*count*]: *a severance of relations.* **2.** Also, **severance pay.** [*noncount*] money paid to a worker being dismissed for reasons beyond the worker's control. See -PARE[1]-.

se•vere (sə vēr′) /sə'vɪər/ *adj.,* **-ver•er, -ver•est. 1.** harsh; unnecessarily extreme: *severe criticism.* **2.** stern in manner or appearance: *Her hair was tied in a tight, severe bun.* **3.** plain; without much decoration. **4.** grave; critical: *a severe illness.* **5.** of an extreme or violent nature: *severe thunderstorms.* **6.** difficult to endure, perform, etc.: *a severe test of strength.* **7.** very exact; demanding: *severe standards.* —**se•vere′ly,** *adv.* —**se•ver•i•ty** (sə ver′i tē) /sə'vɛrɪtiy/ *n.* [*noncount*]: *the severity of his condition.*

sew (sō) /sow/ *v.,* **sewed, sewn** (sōn) /sown/ or **sewed, sew•ing. 1.** to join or attach (one or more things) by stitches: [~ + *obj*]: *He sewed a button on his shirt.* [*no obj*]: *I learned how to sew at an early age.* **2. sew up,** [~ + *up* + *obj*] *Informal.* to accomplish or control successfully: *to sew up a deal; to sew up enough votes for an early nomination.* —**sew′er,** *n.* [*count*]

sew•age (so͞o′ij) /'suwɪdʒ/ also **sew•er•age** (so͞o′ər ij) /'suwərɪdʒ/ *n.* [*noncount*] the waste matter that passes through sewers.

sew•er (so͞o′ər) /'suwər/ *n.* [*count*] an artificial passage, usually underground, for carrying off waste water and refuse, as in a town or city: *The sewers overflowed.*

sew•ing (sō′ing) /'sowɪŋ/ *n.* [*noncount*] **1.** the act or work of one who sews. **2.** something sewn or to be sewn.

sew′ing machine′, *n.* [*count*] a machine for making stitches and sewing garments, leather, etc.

sex (seks) /sɛks/ *n.* **1.** [*count*] either the female or male division of a species: *What sex is your kitten?* **2.** [*noncount*] all the differences by which the female and the male are distinguished; gender: *discrimination on the basis of sex.* **3.** [*noncount*] the attraction drawing one sex toward another: *emphasis on sex in movies.* **4.** SEXUAL INTERCOURSE : *premarital sex.* —***Idiom.*** **5. have sex,** to engage in sexual intercourse. —**sex′less,** *adj.* See -SECT-.

sex-, *prefix.* sex- comes from Latin, where it has the meaning "six": *sexpartite (= having six parts or divisions).*

sex′ appeal′, *n.* [*noncount*] **1.** the ability to excite people sexually: *a movie star with great sex appeal.* **2.** a capacity to stimulate interest: *The new campaign lacked sex appeal.*

sex•ism (sek′siz əm) /'sɛksɪzəm/ *n.* [*noncount*] **1.** attitudes or behavior based on traditional views about sexual roles of men and women: *TV commercials full of sexism.* **2.** discrimination or prejudice based on a person's sex, esp. against women. **—sex′ist,** *adj.*: *a sexist attitude.* **—***n.* [*count*]: *a workplace full of sexists.*

sex•pot (seks′pot′) /ˈsɛksˌpɒt/ *n.* [*count*] *Informal.* someone who is especially sexy.

sex′ sym′bol, *n.* [*count*] a famous or well-known person who is thought to have great sex appeal.

sex•tant (sek′stənt) /ˈsɛkstənt/ *n.* [*count*] an instrument used to figure out one's latitude and longitude at sea by measuring certain angles of the sun, moon, and stars.

sex•tet or **sex•tette** (seks tet′) /sɛksˈtɛt/ *n.* [*count*] **1.** any group or set of six. **2. a.** a company of six singers or players. **b.** a musical composition for six voices or instruments.

sex•ton (sek′stən) /ˈsɛkstən/ *n.* [*count*] an official who maintains a church or a synagogue.

sex•u•al (sek′sho͞o əl) /ˈsɛkʃuwəl/ *adj.* [*usually: before a noun*] **1.** of or relating to sex: *sexual pleasure.* **2.** occurring between or involving the sexes: *sexual relations.* **3.** having sexual organs: *sexual reproduction in the animal world.* **—sex•u•al•i•ty** (sek′sho͞o al′i tē) /ˌsɛkʃuwˈælɪtiy/ *n.* [*noncount*]: *awareness of one's sexuality.* **—sex′u•al•ly,** *adv.*: *sexually active teenagers.*

sex′ual harass′ment, *n.* [*noncount*] unwelcome sexual attentions, esp. when made by an employer or superior, usually with the understanding that accepting them is a condition of continued employment or promotion.

sex′ual in′tercourse, *n.* [*noncount*] the act of joining or coupling of the sexual or genital organs between individuals, esp. one involving penetration of the penis into the vagina.

sex′ually transmit′ted disease′, *n.* [*count*] any disease characteristically transmitted by sexual contact, as gonorrhea.

sex•y (sek′sē) /ˈsɛksiy/ *adj.*, **-i•er, -i•est. 1.** sexually interesting, attractive, or exciting: *a sexy actor.* **2.** excitingly appealing; glamorous: *a sexy ad campaign.* **—sex•i•ly** (sek′sə lē) /ˈsɛksəliy/ *adv.* **—sex′i•ness,** *n.* [*noncount*]

SF or **sf,** science fiction.

Sgt., an abbreviation of: Sergeant.

sh or **shh** (*usually an extended* sh *sound*) /*usually an extended* ʃ *sound*/ *interj.* (used to urge someone to be quiet).

shab•by (shab′ē) /ˈʃæbiy/ *adj.*, **-bi•er, -bi•est. 1.** showing signs of wear or long use: *a shabby old overcoat.* **2.** mean; ungenerous or unfair: *shabby behavior.* **3.** inferior; second-rate: *pretty shabby pitching in your last two games.* **—shab•bi•ly** (shab′ə lē) /ˈʃæbəliy/ *adv.*: *shabbily dressed.* **—shab′bi•ness,** *n.* [*noncount*]

shack (shak) /ʃæk/ *n.* [*count*] **1.** a rough cabin; shanty. **—***v.* [*no obj*] **2. shack up,** [*no obj; often:* ~ + *up* + *with* + *obj*] *Slang.* to live together or with another as sexual partners without being legally married.

shack•le (shak′əl) /ˈʃækəl/ *n.*, *v.*, **-led, -ling. —***n.* [*count*] **1.** a fastening, as of iron, for placing around the wrist, ankle, etc., to prevent free movement; fetter. **2.** Often, **shackles.** [*plural*] anything that serves to prevent or reduce freedom, thought, etc.: *shackles of prejudice.* **—***v.* [~ + *obj*] **3.** to confine, restrain, or prevent free movement of (a person or animal) by a shackle or shackles. **4.** to restrict the freedom of: *to shackle the press with tight restrictions.*

shad (shad) /ʃæd/ *n.* [*count*], *pl.* (*esp. when thought of as a group*) **shad,** (*esp. for kinds or species*) **shads.** a herringlike sea fish of Europe and North America.

shade (shād) /ʃeyd/ *n.*, *v.*, **shad•ed, shad•ing. —***n.* **1.** [*noncount*] the darkness caused by the screening of rays of light from an area, or a place where this is found: *to stand in the shade of a big tree.* **2.** [*count*] something that reduces or shuts out heat or light, as on a window or a lamp. **3. shades,** [*plural*] *Informal.* sunglasses: *wearing a pair of shades.* **4.** [*count*] the spirit of a dead person. **5.** [*count*] the degree of darkness of a color: *a shade of blue.* **6.** [*count*] a slight amount or degree: *a shade of difference.* **—***v.* **7.** [~ + *obj*] to produce shade in, on, or over: *The house is well shaded by the tall trees.* **8.** to introduce degrees of darkness into (a drawing, painting, etc.) to create light and shadow: [~ + *obj*]: *to shade the figures of the sketch.* [~ + *obj* + *in*]: *to shade them in with pencil.* [~ + *in* + *obj*]: *to shade in the figures.* **9.** to change by slight amounts: [~ + *obj*]: *The candidate shaded his answer to fit what he thought the people wanted to hear.* [*no obj*]: *His answer seemed to shade from an initial "no" to a tentative "yes."*

shad•ing (shā′ding) /ˈʃeydɪŋ/ *n.* **1.** [*count*] a slight changing or difference of color, character, etc.: *shadings of meaning.* **2.** [*noncount*] the representation of the different values of color or light and dark in a painting or drawing.

shad•ow (shad′ō) /ˈʃædow/ *n.* **1.** [*count*] a dark image cast on a surface by a body that blocks light: *watched her shadow grow shorter, then longer.* **2.** [*noncount*] shade or some darkness: *standing in shadow.* **3. shadows,** [*plural*] darkness: *the shadows of the night; Shadows are falling.* **4.** [*count*] a slight suggestion; hint; trace: *innocent beyond the shadow of a doubt.* **5.** [*count*] a reminder of what was once present: *just a shadow of his former self.* **6.** [*noncount*] (in painting, drawing, etc.) the dark part of a picture. **7.** [*count*] a period or instance of gloom, unhappiness, etc.: *in the shadow of war.* **8.** [*count*] a person who follows another constantly. **—***v.* [~ + *obj*] **9.** to cover with shadow; shade: *During the eclipse the moon shadowed the sun.* **10.** to cast a gloom over; cloud: *Sadness shadowed her face.* **11.** to follow the movements of (a person) secretly: *Agents shadowed the suspected spy.* **—***adj.* [*before a noun*] **12.** without official authority: *a shadow government.*

shad•ow•box (shad′ō boks′) /ˈʃædowˌbɒks/ *v.* [*no obj*] to go through the motions of boxing, without an opponent, as a training procedure.

shad•ow•y (shad′ō ē) /ˈʃædowiy/ *adj.*, **-i•er, -i•est. 1.** resembling a shadow, as by being weak or hard to see: *shadowy outlines.* **2.** hard to observe or know about: *the shadowy lives of spies.*

shad•y (shā′dē) /ˈʃeydiy/ *adj.*, **-i•er, -i•est. 1.** shaded; having or giving shade: *a shady park.* **2.** of untrustworthy character: *a shady deal.* **—shad′i•ness,** *n.* [*noncount*]

shaft (shaft) /ʃæft/ *n.* [*count*] **1.** a long stick or pole: *The shaft of the arrow was wooden.* **2.** something aimed at someone or something in attack: *shafts of sarcasm.* **3.** a ray or beam: *shafts of sunlight.* **4.** a vertical passage or other enclosed space, as in a building: *an elevator shaft.* **5.** [*singular; the* + ~] *Slang.* harsh or unfair treatment: *He got the shaft from his boss.* **—***v.* [~ + *obj*] **6.** *Slang.* to treat in a dishonest manner: *His former company shafted him.*

shag[1] (shag) /ʃæg/ *n.* **1.** [*noncount*] rough, matted hair, wool, etc. **2.** [*count*] a hairstyle in which the hair is cut in layers downward from the crown. **3.** [*count*] a kind of carpeting or rug with long, loose yarns.

shag[2] (shag) /ʃæg/ *v.* [~ + *obj*], **shagged, shag•ging. 1.** to go after and bring back; fetch. **2.** to retrieve and throw back (fly balls) in batting practice.

shag•gy (shag′ē) /ˈʃægiy/ *adj.*, **-gi•er, -gi•est. 1.** covered with or having long, rough hair: *a shaggy dog.* **2.** forming a bushy mass, such as hair: *a shaggy beard.* **3.** untidy; messy. **—shag′gi•ness,** *n.* [*noncount*]

shah (shä, shô) /ʃɑ, ʃɔ/ *n.* [*count; often: Shah*] (formerly, in Iran) a king.

shake (shāk) /ʃeyk/ *v.*, **shook** (sho͝ok) /ʃʊk/ **shak•en** (shā′kən) /ˈʃeykən/ **shak•ing,** *n.* **—***v.* **1.** to (cause to) move with short, quick movements: [*no obj*]: *The car shook when the engine started.* [~ + *obj*]: *The earthquake shook the house.* **2.** [*no obj*] to tremble with emotion, cold, etc.: *His voice shook with rage.* **3.** to (cause to) become loose and fall: [~ + *obj*]: *He shook the sand loose from his feet.* [~ + *obj* + *off*]: *She shook her clothes off and climbed into bed.* [~ + *off* + *obj*]: *She shook off her clothes and climbed into bed.* [~ + *off*]: *The sand shook off all through the house.* **4.** to move (something, esp. in a container), briskly to and fro or up and down, as in mixing: [~ + *obj*]: *Shake the container of chocolate milk before you pour it.* [~ + *up* + *obj*]: *Shake up the container.* [~ + *obj* + *up*]: *Shake it up well.* [*no obj*]: *Shake well before using.* **5.** to take hold of (usually the right hand of another person) as a sign of greeting, friendship, etc.: [~ + *obj*]: *They shook hands and exchanged business cards.* [*no obj*]: *It's a deal; let's shake on it.* **6.** [~ + *obj*] to hold (something) in front of another in a threatening way: *shook her fist at him.* **7.** [~ + *obj*] to grasp in an attempt to knock something loose by quick, strong movements: *to shake the tree to knock apples loose.* **8.** [~ + *obj*] to knock (something) loose by quick, strong movements: *to shake apples from the tree.* **9.** [~ + *obj*] to upset or worry (someone) deeply or greatly: *badly shaken by her death.* **10.** [~ + *obj*] to get rid of or away from: *The spy shook the agents following him.* **11. shake down, a.** to demand money from, as by blackmail: [~ + *down* + *obj*]: *He shook down rich politicians.* [~ + *obj* + *down*]: *to shake them down for money.* **b.** [~ + *obj* + *down*] to search for hidden weapons: *to shake the prisoners down for weapons.* **12. shake off, a.** to get rid of; reject: [~ + *off* + *obj*]: *She can't shake off a feeling of despair.* [~ + *obj* + *off*]: *I* *can't shake this flu off.* **b.** to get away from: [~ + *off* + *obj*]: *The spy shook off the pair of agents following him.* [~ + *obj* + *off*]: *He shook them off and returned home.* **13. shake up, a.** to trouble or distress; upset: [~ + *obj* + *up*]: *The news of her death shook us up.* [~ + *up* + *obj*]: *The news of her death shook up the town.* **b.** [~ + *up* + *obj*] to rearrange: *The Prime Minister shook up her Cabinet.* —*n.* **14.** [*count*] an act or instance of rocking or shaking: *a slight shake of the head.* **15. shakes,** [*plural; often: the* + ~] a state or spell of trembling, caused by fear, cold, etc.: *a bad case of the shakes.* **16.** MILKSHAKE. **17.** HANDSHAKE (def. 1). **18.** [*count; usually: singular; a* + ~] treatment; deal: *Everyone gets a fair shake.* **19.** [*count*] *Informal.* an earthquake. —***Idiom.* 20. no great shakes,** common; ordinary: *an average student, no great shakes.* **21. shake a leg,** *Informal.* to hurry.

shake•down (shāk′doun′) /ˈʃeykˌdawn/ *n.* [*count*] **1.** an act of demanding money by blackmail. **2.** a thorough search. **3.** a cruise or flight taken to prepare for regular service by making the crew familiar with a craft's operation, machinery, etc.

shak•er (shā′kər) /ˈʃeykər/ *n.* [*count*] a container with holes in its top from which a seasoning, condiment, etc., is shaken onto food: *salt shakers.*

shake′-up′, *n.* [*count*] a rearrangement of administration in an organization, as by dismissals.

shak•y (shā′kē) /ˈʃeykiy/ *adj.,* **-i•er, -i•est. 1.** tending to shake: *shaky hands.* **2.** not firm; insecure: *a shaky foundation.* **3.** not likely to continue; uncertain: *a shaky truce.*

shale (shāl) /ʃeyl/ *n.* [*noncount*] a kind of rock formed from clay.

shall (shal; *unstressed* shəl) /ʃæl; *unstressed* ʃəl/ *auxiliary (modal) v., pres.* **shall;** *past* **should;** *imperative, infinitive, and participles lacking.* [~ + *root form of a verb*] **1.** (used to express plans or intentions concerning the main verb, esp. with regard to the future): *I shall go later.* **2.** (used to express the necessity, strong intention, or determination of carrying out the action of the main verb): *You shall get those x-rays immediately.* **3.** (used to express that the action of the main verb must be carried out): *Council meetings shall be held in public.* **4.** (used in question forms to make an offer, suggestion, or request for advice): *Shall I help you, or do you want to do it yourself? Shall I apologize to her?*

shal•lot (shal′ət, shə lot′) /ˈʃælət, ʃəˈlɒt/ *n.* [*count*] **1.** a plant related to the onion. **2.** the bulb of this plant, used in cooking.

shal•low (shal′ō) /ˈʃælow/ *adj.,* **-er, -est. 1.** of little depth; not deep: *shallow water.* **2.** lacking depth or seriousness; superficial: *a shallow mind.* **3.** taking in a small amount of air in each breath: *shallow breathing.*

sha•lom (shä lōm′, shə-) /ʃɑˈlowm, ʃə-/ *interj. Hebrew.* (used as a word of greeting or farewell).

shalt (shalt) /ʃælt/ *v. Archaic.* 2nd pers. sing. of SHALL.

sham (sham) /ʃæm/ *n., adj., v.,* **shammed, sham•ming.** —*n.* [*count*] **1.** a person or thing pretending to be someone or something else; fraud: *Her illness was a sham to gain sympathy.* **2.** a cover or the like: *a pillow sham.* —*adj.* [*before a noun*] **3.** pretended; false; counterfeit: *sham attacks.* —*v.* **4.** to make a false show of (something); pretend: [~ + *obj*]: *to sham being drunk.* [*no obj*]: *He's only shamming.*

sha•man (shä′mən, shā′-, sham′ən) /ˈʃɑmən, ˈʃey-, ˈʃæmən/ *n.* [*count*] (esp. among certain tribal peoples) a person who communicates between the natural and the supernatural worlds, using magic to cure illness, foretell the future, etc. —**sha•man•ic** (shə man′ik) /ʃəˈmænɪk/ *adj.*

sham•ble (sham′bəl) /ˈʃæmbəl/ *v.,* **-bled, -bling,** *n.* —*v.* [*no obj*] **1.** to walk or move awkwardly; shuffle. —*n.* [*count*] **2.** a shambling type of walk.

sham•bles (sham′bəlz) /ˈʃæmbəlz/ *n.* [*count; singular; used with a singular verb; usually: a/the* + ~] a place or condition of great disorder or chaos: *Her desk is a shambles.*

shame (shām) /ʃeym/ *n., v.,* **shamed, sham•ing.** —*n.* **1.** [*noncount*] the painful feeling of having done or experienced something wrong, dishonest, etc.: *A deep sense of shame overwhelmed him.* **2.** [*noncount*] the ability to experience this feeling: *to be without shame.* **3.** [*noncount*] disgrace; ignominy: *His dishonesty brings shame to the whole team.* **4.** [*count; singular; usually: a* + ~] a cause for regret, disappointment, etc.: *It was a shame you weren't there.* —*v.* [~ + *obj*] **5.** to cause to suffer disgrace: *Her actions shamed her entire family.* **6.** [~ + *obj* + *into* + *verb-ing*] to cause (someone) to do something because of a feeling of shame: *She shamed me into going.* —***Idiom.* 7. put (someone or something) to shame,** [*put* + *obj* + *to* + ~] **a.** to cause to suffer shame. **b.** to outdo; surpass: *The new computer puts this old one to shame.* —**Related Words.** SHAME is a noun and a verb, ASHAMED and SHAMEFUL are adjectives: *He felt shame after hurting the man. Her response shamed him into an apology. I was ashamed of what I had done. It was a shameful deed.* —**Usage.** Compare ASHAMED and SHAME. The adjective ASHAMED usually appears after some form of *be,* and may be followed by the word *of,* as in *He is ashamed. She is ashamed of what she has done.* The noun SHAME is used as a noncount noun: *feelings of shame;* it also has use as a count noun: *What a shame you can't come!* The verb SHAME takes an object and may take an additional phrase: *She shamed me into going.*

shame•faced (shām′fāst′) /ˈʃeymˌfeyst/ *adj.* feeling or showing shame: *shamefaced apologies.*

shame•ful (shām′fəl) /ˈʃeymfəl/ *adj.* very wrong; disgraceful; terrible: *shameful acts of cruelty and violence.* —**shame′ful•ly,** *adv.*

shame•less (shām′lis) /ˈʃeymlɪs/ *adj.* **1.** lacking any sense of shame: unashamed: *The shameless woman flirted with every man she met.* **2.** showing no shame; brazen: *a shameless liar.*

sham•poo (sham po͞o′) /ʃæmˈpuw/ *n.* **1.** a cleansing preparation or soap that produces suds: [*noncount*]: *Some shampoo got in her eyes and stung them.* [*count*]: *I tried a new shampoo yesterday.* **2.** [*count*] the act of washing the hair, a rug, etc., with such a preparation: *Give the rug a shampoo.* —*v.* [~ + *obj*] **3.** to wash (the hair), esp. with a shampoo: *shampoos her hair every day.* **4.** to wash the hair of: *to bathe and shampoo the baby.* **5.** to clean (rugs, upholstery, etc.) with a shampoo. —**sham•poo′er,** *n.* [*count*]

sham•rock (sham′rok) /ˈʃæmrɒk/ *n.* a three-leaved plant, esp. a small, yellow-flowered clover: [*count*]: *carrying a lucky shamrock.* [*noncount*]: *fields of shamrock.*

shang•hai (shang′hī, shang hī′) /ˈʃæŋhay, ʃæŋˈhay/ *v.* [~ + *obj*], **-haied, -hai•ing.** to kidnap or otherwise force (a sailor) to become a member of the crew of a ship.

Shan•gri-la (shang′gri lä′, shang′gri lä′) /ˌʃæŋgrɪˈlɑ, ˈʃæŋgrɪˌlɑ/ *n.* [*count*] an imaginary paradise on earth: *Their retirement home was their little Shangri-la.*

shank (shangk) /ʃæŋk/ *n.* [*count*] **1. a.** the part of the leg between the knee and the ankle. **b.** the corresponding part in other vertebrates. **2.** a cut of meat from the leg of an animal. **3.** a straight, narrow, shaftlike part of various objects usually connecting two more parts, such as the stem of a tobacco pipe.

shan't (shant) /ʃænt/ *contraction.* a shortened form of *shall not.*

shan•ty[1] (shan′tē) /ˈʃæntiy/ *n.* [*count*], *pl.* **-ties.** a roughly or poorly built hut, cabin, or house.

shan•ty[2] (shan′tē) /ˈʃæntiy/ *n.* [*count*], *pl.* **-ties.** a type of work song that sailors once sang.

shape (shāp) /ʃeyp/ *n., v.,* **shaped, shap•ing.** —*n.* **1.** [*count*] the appearance of an object; the way a person or thing looks on the outside: *Italy has the shape of a boot when you see it on a map.* **2.** [*count*] something seen in outline: *A vague shape appeared through the mist.* **3.** [*noncount*] condition; state of repair: *The old house was in bad shape. She wants to exercise to get into shape (= to get into good physical condition).* **4.** [*noncount*] orderly arrangement: *He could give no shape to his ideas.* **5.** [*count*] the figure or body of a person, esp. of a woman: *The actress still has a great shape.* —*v.* **6.** [~ + *obj*] to give definite form to: *to shape the ground beef into meatballs.* **7.** [~ + *obj*] to put in words: *He shaped his criticism of her very carefully so as not to offend.* **8.** [~ + *obj*] to direct (one's course, etc.): *The events of his youth shaped his whole way of thinking.* **9. shape up,** [*no obj*] **a.** to change, esp. favorably: *Things are finally beginning to shape up in the economy.* **b.** to improve one's behavior, performance, or physical condition: *If you don't shape up, you'll be fired.* —***Idiom.* 10. take shape,** to take on a more complete form; become defined: *Her ideas began to take shape and she wrote them down.*

shape•less (shāp′lis) /ˈʃeyplɪs/ *adj.* **1.** having no definite shape. **2.** lacking a pleasing shape. —**shape′less•ness,** *n.* [*noncount*]

shape•ly (shāp′lē) /ˈʃeypliy/ *adj.,* **-li•er, -li•est.** having a pleasing shape, esp. with reference to a woman's figure.

shard (shärd) /ʃɑrd/ also **sherd** (shûrd) /ʃɜrd/ *n.* [*count*] a fragment or piece that is broken off, esp. a piece of earthenware.

share[1] (shâr) /ʃɛər/ *n., v.,* **shared, shar•ing.** —*n.* [*count*]

1. a part of a whole, esp. given to a member of a group: *The thieves counted out their share of the stolen money.* **2.** one of the equal parts into which the capital stock of a corporation is divided: *He bought shares in IBM.* **—v. 3.** to divide and distribute (something) in shares: [~ + *obj*]: *The two sisters shared their toys.* [*no obj*]: *You and your sister will have to learn to share.* **4.** [~ + *obj*] to use, participate in, receive, etc., jointly: *The two chemists shared the Nobel prize.* **5. share in,** [~ + *in* + *obj*] to have a share or part in: *We shared in their triumphs.*

share[2] (shâr) /ʃɛər/ *n.* [*count*] a plowshare.

share•crop•per (shâr′krop′ər) /ˈʃɛər͵krɒpər/ *n.* [*count*] a farmer who does not own the land he or she works on but who pays as rent a share of the crop.

share•hold•er (shâr′hōl′dər) /ˈʃɛər͵howldər/ *n.* [*count*] a person, company, etc., that owns shares of stock in a company.

shark[1] (shärk) /ʃɑrk/ *n.* [*count*] a fish that has a scaleless skin, a wide mouth on the underside of the head, and five to seven gill slits on each side.

shark[2] (shärk) /ʃɑrk/ *n.* [*count*] **1.** one who is skilled at obtaining money from others in a dishonest way. **2.** *Informal.* a person who has very good ability in a particular field: *a card shark.*

shark•skin (shärk′skin′) /ˈʃɑrk͵skɪn/ *n.* [*noncount*] **1.** a smooth fabric of rayon with a dull or chalklike appearance, used for clothing. **2.** a fine woven fabric used for suits.

sharp (shärp) /ʃɑrp/ *adj.,* **-er, -est,** *adv., n.* **—adj. 1.** having a thin cutting edge or a fine point for cutting or piercing: *a sharp knife.* **2.** ending in an edge or point: *sharp corners.* **3.** involving a sudden change in direction: *a sharp curve in the road.* **4.** clearly defined; distinct: *a sharp contrast between black and white.* **5.** biting in taste: *a sharp cheese.* **6.** piercing in sound: *a sharp cry.* **7.** keenly cold, such as weather: *a sharp, biting wind.* **8.** felt strongly; intense: *a sharp pain in his arm.* **9.** harsh; quick and angry: *some sharp words about your behavior.* **10.** alert or vigilant: *Keep a sharp watch.* **11.** mentally quick; keen: *a sharp lad.* **12.** shrewd or clever: *a sharp bargainer.* **13.** shrewd to the point of dishonesty: *sharp practice.* **14.** *Music.* **a.** (of a tone) raised a half step in pitch: *F sharp.* **b.** above an intended pitch, as a note; too high (opposed to *flat*). **15.** *Informal.* very stylish: *a sharp dresser.* **—adv. 16.** keenly, carefully, or alertly: *to look sharp.* **17.** abruptly or suddenly: *turned sharp and ran.* **18.** punctually; exactly at (a certain time): *one o'clock sharp.* **19.** *Music.* above the true pitch: *to sing sharp.* **—n.** [*count*] **20.** SHARPER. **21.** *Music.* **a.** a tone one half step above a given tone. **b.** (in musical notation) the symbol ♯ indicating this. —**sharp′ly,** *adv.*: *spoke sharply to the dog.* —**sharp′ness,** *n.* [*noncount*]

sharp•en (shär′pən) /ˈʃɑrpən/ *v.* to make or become sharp or sharper: [~ + *obj*]: *to sharpen a knife.* [*no obj*]: *This knife won't sharpen.* —**sharp′en•er,** *n.* [*count*]: *a pencil sharpener.*

sharp•er (shär′pər) /ˈʃɑrpər/ also **sharpie** *n.* [*count*] **1.** one who is clever at cheating or stealing. **2.** a professional gambler.

sharp′-eyed′, *adj.* having keen sight or ability to observe things.

sharp•ie or **sharp•y** (shär′pē) /ˈʃɑrpiy/ *n.* [*count*], *pl.* **-ies. 1.** SHARPER. **2.** a very alert person.

sharp•shoot•er (shärp′sho͞o′tər) /ˈʃɑrp͵ʃuwtər/ *n.* [*count*] **1.** a person skilled in shooting, esp. with a rifle. **2.** an athlete noted for accurate aim, as in basketball. —**sharp′shoot′ing,** *n.* [*noncount*]

sharp′-tongued′, *adj.* harsh, cruel, or sarcastic in speech: *sharp-tongued criticism.*

shat•ter (shat′ər) /ˈʃætər/ *v.* **1.** to (cause to) be broken into pieces, as by a blow: [*no obj*]: *The glass shattered when it hit the floor.* [~ + *obj*]: *The looters shattered the shop windows.* **2.** [~ + *obj*] to weaken or destroy (health, etc.): *His nerves were shattered by that experience.* **3.** [~ + *obj*] to show (ideas, opinions, etc.) to be wrong, foolishness, etc.: *His belief in humanity was shattered.* **—n.** [*count*] **4.** Usually, **shatters.** [*plural*] fragments made by shattering.

shat•ter•ing (shat′ər ing) /ˈʃætərɪŋ/ *adj.* affecting feelings or emotions deeply and badly; devastating: *The news of her death was shattering.*

shat•ter•proof (shat′ər pro͞of′) /ˈʃætər͵pruwf/ *adj.* designed or made to resist shattering.

shave (shāv) /ʃeyv/ *v.,* **shaved, shaved** or (*esp. in combination*) **shav•en, shav•ing,** *n.* **—v. 1.** to remove (hair, etc.) from (the face, etc.) by cutting it off close to the skin with a razor: [~ + *obj*]: *He shaved his face.* [*no obj*]: *You forgot to shave yesterday.* **2.** [~ + *obj*] to scrape away the surface of (something) with a sharp-edged tool: *to use a scraper to shave the bottom of the door.* **3.** [~ + *obj*] to scrape or come very near to: *The car just shaved the garage door.* **4.** [~ + *obj*] **a.** to reduce or deduct (an amount) from a price or total: *to shave a few dollars off the price.* **b.** to deduct a certain amount from (a price, etc.): *to shave the asking price of the house.* **—n.** [*count*] **5.** the act or an instance of shaving or being shaved. —***Idiom.*** **6. close shave,** [*count*] a narrow escape from disaster: *During their escape the prisoners had numerous close shaves.*

shav•en (shā′vən) /ˈʃeyvən/ *adj.* (used with some other adjective or adverb before it) having been shaved in the manner mentioned: *a clean-shaven face (= a face that has been shaved clean with no hair remaining on it).*

shav•er (shā′vər) /ˈʃeyvər/ *n.* [*count*] **1.** one that shaves. **2.** an electric razor. **3.** *Informal.* a small boy.

shav•ing (shā′ving) /ˈʃeyvɪŋ/ *n.* **1.** Often, **shavings.** [*plural*] a very thin piece or slice, esp. of wood: *wood shavings on the floor.* **2.** [*noncount*] the act of one that shaves.

shawl (shôl) /ʃɔl/ *n.* [*count*] a piece of wool or other fabric worn about the shoulders esp. by women.

she (shē) /ʃiy/ *pron., sing. nom.* **she,** *poss.* **her** or **hers,** *obj.* **her;** *pl. nom.* **they,** *poss.* **their** or **theirs,** *obj.* **them;** *n., pl.* **shes;** *adj.* **—pron. 1.** the female person or animal being discussed or that was last mentioned; that female: *"How is your mother?" —"She's fine, thanks."* **2.** the woman: *She who listens learns.* **3.** anything considered, as by personification, to be feminine: *She's a great-looking car, and economical, too.* **—n.** [*count*] **4.** a female person or animal: *Is your dog a she?* **—adj. 5.** female (usually used in combination with a noun): *a she-goat.*

s/he (shē′ər hē′, shē′hē′) /ˈʃiyərˈhiy, ˈʃiyˈhiy/ *pron.* (used in writing in order to avoid *he* when the sex of the person referred to is unknown or irrelevant) she or he.

sheaf (shēf) /ʃiyf/ *n.* [*count*], *pl.* **sheaves** (shēvz) /ʃiyvz/ **1.** a bundle into which cereal plants are tied up after being gathered from the fields. **2.** any bundle or collection: *a thick sheaf of papers.*

shear (shēr) /ʃɪər/ *v.,* **sheared, sheared** or **shorn** (shôrn) /ʃɔrn/ **shear•ing,** *n.* **—v. 1.** [~ + *obj*] to remove (hair, wool, etc.) from (an animal) by or as if by cutting: *to shear wool from sheep.* **2. a.** [~ + *obj*] to break (a wing of a plane) by great pressure from force parallel to it: *The wind sheared the wing and the plane crashed.* **b.** [*no obj*] to break as the result of pressure: *The wing sheared off and the plane dropped.* **—n. 3.** Usually, **shears.** [*plural*] **a.** scissors of large size: *a pair of shears.* **b.** any of various cutting implements having two blades that suggest those of scissors: *garden shears for trimming bushes.* —**shear′er,** *n.* [*count*]

sheath (shēth) /ʃiyθ/ *n.* [*count*], *pl.* **sheaths** (shēthz) /ʃiyðz/. **1.** a close-fitting covering, esp. for the blade of a sword or dagger: *He put his knife back in its sheath.* **2.** a closely enveloping part in an animal or plant. **3.** a close-fitting garment with a straight shape. **4.** a condom.

sheathe (shēth) /ʃiyð/ *v.* [~ + *obj*], **sheathed, sheath•ing. 1.** to put (a sword, etc.) into a sheath: *The knights were warned to sheathe their swords.* **2.** to close in with a covering like a sheath: *to sheathe electrical wires with an insulator.*

sheath•ing (shē′thing) /ˈʃiyðɪŋ/ *n.* **1.** [*count*] a covering or outer layer. **2.** [*noncount*] material for forming any such covering: *rubber sheathing.*

she•bang (shə bang′) /ʃəˈbæŋ/ *n.* [*count; singular*] *Informal.* the structure of something, as of an organization: *The whole shebang fell apart when the chairman quit.*

shed[1] (shed) /ʃɛd/ *n.* [*count*] **1.** a small, roughly built structure made for shelter, storage, etc.: *a shed for the tools.* See illustration at LANDSCAPE. **2.** a large, strongly built structure, often open at the sides or end: *the customs shed at the port.*

shed[2] (shed) /ʃɛd/ *v.,* **shed, shed•ding. 1.** [~ + *obj*] to pour forth; let fall: *to shed tears.* **2.** [~ + *obj*] to give or send forth (light, influence, etc.): *The detective can shed light on what happened.* **3.** [~ + *obj*] to resist being affected by: *The raincoat is made of a cloth that sheds water.* **4. a.** to drop out or off (hair, skin, etc.) naturally: [*no obj*]: *The dog was shedding all over the rug.* [~ + *obj*]: *The trees were shedding their leaves.* **b.** [*no obj*] (of hair, skin, etc.) to drop out or off naturally: *The dog hair was shedding all over the house.*

she'd (shēd) /ʃiyd/ *contraction.* **1.** a shortened form of *she had: She'd seen him and could identify him.* **2.** a shortened form of *she would: She'd have to come in.*

sheen (shēn) /ʃiyn/ *n.* [*noncount*] brightness; radiance; luster: *the sheen of the newly polished floor.*

sheep (shēp) /ʃiyp/ *n.* [*count*], *pl.* **sheep. 1.** a mammal that eats grass, grows a woolly fleece on its back and sides, and is closely related to goats: *Sheep are grown for their wool and meat.* **2.** a meek, unimaginative person, or one who is easily led.

sheep•dog or **sheep dog** (shēp′dôg′, -dog′) /ˈʃiypˌdɔg, -ˌdɒg/ *n.* [*count*] a dog trained to herd and guard sheep.

sheep•ish (shē′pish) /ˈʃiypɪʃ/ *adj.* embarrassed or bashful, esp. for having done something foolish: *He gave a sheepish grin after tripping on the steps.* **—sheep′ish•ly,** *adv.* **—sheep′ish•ness,** *n.* [*noncount*]

sheep•skin (shēp′skin′) /ˈʃiypˌskɪn/ *n.* [*count*] **1.** the skin of a sheep, as for a garment. **2.** *Informal.* a diploma. **—*adj.*** [*before a noun*] **3.** made from the skin of a sheep.

sheer[1] (shēr) /ʃɪər/ *adj.*, **-er, -est,** *adv.*, *n.* **—*adj.* 1.** so thin as to be transparent: *sheer stockings.* **2.** [*before a noun*] unmixed with anything else: *sheer luck; sheer nonsense.* **3.** extending down or up very steeply: *a sheer descent.* **—*adv.* 4.** completely; quite: *He drove sheer off the road.* **5.** vertically; down or up very steeply: *cliffs rising sheer from the sea.* **—*n.*** [*count*] **6.** a thin, nearly transparent fabric or garment. **—sheer′ness,** *n.* [*noncount*]

sheer[2] (shēr) /ʃɪər/ *v.* **1.** to move away from a course; deviate: [*no obj*]: *The jet fighters sheered to the south.* [~ + *obj*]: *The pilot sheered the jet fighter to the south.* **—*n.*** [*count*] **2.** an act of moving away from or changing a direction or course.

sheet (shēt) /ʃiyt/ *n.* [*count*] **1.** a large rectangular piece of cotton used for bedding. **2.** a wide, thin surface or covering: *a sheet of ice.* **3.** a thin, rectangular piece of material, such as glass or tin. **4.** a rectangular piece of paper, esp. one on which to write: *Take out a sheet of paper and answer these questions.* **5.** a wide extent or expanse, as of fire or water: *sheets of flame; sheets of rain.*

sheet•ing (shē′ting) /ˈʃiytɪŋ/ *n.* [*noncount*] **1.** the act of covering with or forming into sheets. **2.** something formed into a sheet or sheets: *tin sheeting on the roofs of huts.* **3.** a kind of plain cotton fabric, esp. a firmly made muslin used for bed sheets.

sheet′ met′al, *n.* [*noncount*] metal in sheets or thin plates.

sheet′ mu′sic, *n.* [*noncount*] music printed on unbound sheets of paper.

sheik (shēk; also shāk) /ʃiyk; ælsɒ ʃeyk/ *n.* Also, **sheikh.** (in Arab countries) the male leader, usually an elder, of a tribe or family; chief: [*count*]: *seated near sheiks and princes.* [*proper noun*]: *Sheik Faisal.* **—sheik′dom,** *n.* [*count*]

shek•els (shek′əlz) /ˈʃɛkəlz/ *n.* [*plural*] *Slang.* money; cash.

shelf (shelf) /ʃɛlf/ *n.* [*count*], *pl.* **shelves** (shelvz). **1.** a thin, flat slab of wood, metal, etc., attached horizontally to a wall or in a frame, for supporting objects: *a shelf with books.* **2.** a surface like this, such as a ledge. **—*Idiom.* 3. off the shelf,** [*noncount*] kept in stock in a store: *buying electronic parts off the shelf.* **4. on the shelf,** [*noncount*] inactive; useless.

shelf′ life′, *n.* [*count; usually: singular*], *pl.* **shelf lives.** the period during which a stored item, such as food, remains safe to eat: *a shelf life of only a few days.*

shell (shel) /ʃɛl/ *n.* **1.** [*count*] a hard outer covering of an animal, such as of a clam, snail, or turtle. **2.** [*count*] the hard outer covering of an egg. **3.** [*noncount*] the material that makes up any of these coverings. **4.** [*count*] the usually hard outer covering of a seed, fruit, etc.: *peanut shells; coconut shells.* **5.** [*count*] something that looks like the shell of an animal, as in shape. **6.** [*count*] a thin crust of pastry or other dough lightly baked in a hollow shape: *a pie shell; taco shells.* **7.** [*count*] any case or covering, as for protecting. **8.** [*count*] a reserved manner. **9.** [*count*] a hollow container filled with explosive and fired from a gun, etc.: *mortar shells bursting in the air.* **10.** [*count*] a light, long, narrow racing boat for rowing. **11.** [*count*] the framework or external structure of a building. **—*v.*** [~ + *obj*] **12.** to remove the shell of: *to shell some peanuts.* **13.** to separate (corn, grain, etc.) from the ear, cob, or husk. **14.** to fire explosive projectiles into, upon, or among; bombard: *The rebels shelled the town.* **15. shell out,** *Informal.* to pay (money): [~ + *out* + *obj*]: *I've shelled out enough money.* [~ + *obj* + *out*]: *to shell it out again.*

she'll (shēl; *unstressed* shil) /ʃiyl; *unstressed* ʃɪl/ *contraction.* a shortened form of *she will: The doctor is in; she'll see you now.*

shel•lac or **shel•lack** (shə lak′) /ʃəˈlæk/ *n.*, *v.*, **-lacked, -lack•ing. —*n.* 1.** a thin varnish: [*noncount*]: *Before using shellac, you must sand the surface of wood.* [*count*]: *the cheapest brand of all the commercial shellacs.* **—*v.*** [~ + *obj*] **2.** to coat or treat with shellac: *to shellac the wood.* **3.** *Slang.* to defeat completely: *Their basketball team shellacked us by nearly fifty points.*

shell•fish (shel′fish′) /ˈʃɛlˌfɪʃ/ *n.* [*count*], *pl.* (*esp. when thought of as a group*) **-fish,** (*esp. for kinds or species*) **-fish•es.** an animal living in water and having a shell, such as the oyster or other mollusks.

shel•ter (shel′tər) /ˈʃɛltər/ *n.* **1.** [*count*] something beneath, behind, or within which one is protected, as from storms, cold, danger, etc.: *an air raid shelter.* **2.** [*noncount*] the protection or safety given by such a thing: *We found shelter in a nearby barn.* **3.** [*count*] a building serving as a temporary place to live, as for the homeless or unwanted animals. **—*v.* 4.** [~ + *obj*] to provide with a shelter: *to shelter the homeless.* **5.** [*no obj*] to find a safe place: *to shelter somewhere during the snowstorm.*

shelve (shelv) /ʃɛlv/ *v.* [~ + *obj*], **shelved, shelv•ing. 1.** to place on a shelf: *to shelve the books.* **2.** to put aside; defer: *to shelve a question.* **3.** to remove from active use or service; dismiss: *The pitcher was shelved because he lost so many ballgames.* **4.** to furnish with shelves. **—shelv′er,** *n.* [*count*]

shelves (shelvz) /ʃɛlvz/ *n.* [*plural*] pl. of SHELF.

shelv•ing (shel′ving) /ˈʃɛlvɪŋ/ *n.* [*noncount*] **1.** material for shelves. **2.** shelves thought of as a group.

she•nan•i•gan (shə nan′i gən) /ʃəˈnænɪgən/ *n. Informal.* Usually, **shenanigans.** [*plural*] mischief; tricks: *What shenanigans are you up to this time?*

shep•herd (shep′ərd) /ˈʃɛpərd/ *n.* [*count*] **1.** one who herds, tends, and guards sheep. **2.** one who protects, guides, or watches over other people. **—*v.*** [~ + *obj*] **3.** to tend, guard, or lead as or like a shepherd: *to shepherd the children.*

sher•bet (shûr′bit) /ˈʃɜrbɪt/ *n.* Also, **sher•bert** (shûr′bərt) /ˈʃɜrbərt/. a frozen, fruit-flavored ice with milk, egg white, or gelatin added: [*noncount*]: *a cone of orange sherbet.* [*count*]: *I'll have two orange sherbets, please.*

sher•iff (sher′if) /ˈʃɛrɪf/ *n.* the law-enforcement officer of a county: [*count*]: *The sheriff got out of his car and approached the speeders.* [*before a name*]: *Sheriff Jones got out of his car.*

sher•ry (sher′ē) /ˈʃɛriy/ *n.*, *pl.* **-ries.** an amber-colored wine of S Spain, or a similar wine made elsewhere: [*noncount*]: *a glass of sherry.* [*count*]: *some Spanish sherries.*

she's (shēz) /ʃiyz/ *contraction.* **1.** a shortened form of *she is*: *She's a fool.* **2.** a shortened form of *she has*, only when *has* is used as an auxiliary verb: *She's got big problems.*

shib•bo•leth (shib′ə lith, -leth′) /ˈʃɪbəlɪθ, -ˌlɛθ/ *n.* [*count*] **1.** a particular way of speech that distinguishes a certain group. **2.** a common saying or belief with little current meaning or truth.

shied (shīd) /ʃayd/ *v.* pt. and pp. of SHY.

shield (shēld) /ʃiyld/ *n.* [*count*] **1.** a device used as a defense against blows, esp. a broad piece of armor carried on the arm. **2.** a person or thing that defends, as from injury: *the heat shield on the space capsule.* **3.** something shaped like a shield, such as the badge of a police officer: *The officer flashed his shield.* **—*v.*** [~ + *obj*] **4.** to protect with or as if with a shield: *to shield her children from the truth.*

shift (shift) /ʃɪft/ *v.* **1.** to move from one place, person, etc., to another: [~ + *obj*]: *Let's shift that display from this window to the next one.* [*no obj*]: *If the weight they are lifting shifts, it could tumble down on them.* **2.** to put aside (ideas, etc.) and replace by others; change or exchange: [~ + *obj*]: *to shift ideas.* [*no obj*]: *to shift in one's thinking.* **3.** to change (gears) from one ratio to another in driving a motor vehicle: [*no obj*]: *She shifted smoothly and drove away.* [~ + *obj*]: *He shifted gears clumsily.* **4.** [*no obj; usually:* ~ + *for* + *oneself*] to manage to get along by oneself: *Can you shift for yourself while your parents are away?* **—*n.*** [*count*] **5.** a change from one place, position, etc., to another: *a shift in the wind.* **6.** a person's scheduled period of work: *the night shift, from eleven at night until eight in the morning.* **7.** a group of workers scheduled to work during such a period. **8.** a straight, loose-fitting dress.

shift•less (shift′lis) /ˈʃɪftlɪs/ *adj.* lacking in desire to improve oneself; lazy. —**shift′less•ness,** *n.* [*noncount*]

shift•y (shif′tē) /ˈʃɪftiy/ *adj.,* **-i•er, -i•est.** avoiding direct dealings or talk; evasive: *gave me a shifty glance, refusing to meet my gaze.* —**shift•i•ly** (shif′tl ē) /ˈʃɪftḷiy/ *adv.* —**shift′i•ness,** *n.* [*noncount*]

shill (shil) /ʃɪl/ *n.* [*count*] **1.** one who pretends to be a customer in order to fool others into participating, as at a casino or in street gambling games. **2.** one who praises another for self-interest: *another shill trying to gain her favor.* —*v.* [*no obj*] **3.** to work as a shill: *to shill for a large casino.*

shil•le•lagh (shə lā′lē, -lə) /ʃəˈleyliy, -lə/ *n.* [*count*] (esp. in Ireland) a heavy stick with a knob at the end.

shil•ling (shil′ing) /ˈʃɪlɪŋ/ *n.* [*count*] **1.** a coin and former monetary unit of the United Kingdom, the 20th part of a pound, equal to 12 pence. *Abbr.:* s. **2.** a former monetary unit of various other nations originally settled or colonized by Great Britain.

shil•ly-shal•ly (shil′ē shal′ē) /ˈʃɪliyˌʃæliy/ *v.* [*no obj*], **-shal•lied, -shal•ly•ing.** to show an inability to make a decision: *Quit shilly-shallying and make up your mind!*

shim (shim) /ʃɪm/ *n., v.,* **shimmed, shim•ming.** —*n.* [*count*] **1.** a thin wedge of metal, etc., for driving into holes or gaps, as between machine parts, to level them. —*v.* [~ + *obj*] **2.** to fill out or bring to a level by inserting a shim or shims.

shim•mer (shim′ər) /ˈʃɪmər/ *v.* [*no obj*] **1.** to shine with or reflect a soft light: *The ocean waves shimmered in the sunlight.* **2.** to appear to quiver in faint light or while reflecting heat waves: *The air shimmered in front of us from the heat.* —*n.* [*count*] **3.** a soft, unsteady light or gleam. **4.** a quivering motion or image as is produced by reflecting faint light or heat waves. —**shim′mer•y,** *adj.*

shim•my (shim′ē) /ˈʃɪmiy/ *n., pl.* **-mies,** *v.,* **-mied, -my•ing.** —*n.* [*count*] **1.** too much wobbling in the front wheels of a motor vehicle. —*v.* [*no obj*] **2.** to shake, wobble, or vibrate: *The car shimmied badly at speeds over 40 mph.*

shin (shin) /ʃɪn/ *n., v.,* **shinned, shin•ning.** —*n.* [*count*] **1.** the front part of the leg from the knee to the ankle: *got bruises on both shins.* —*v.* **2.** to climb (a pole or the like) by holding fast with the legs after drawing oneself up with the hands: [*no obj*]: *to shin up a tree.* [~ + *obj*]: *liked to shin the trees in their backyard.*

shin•bone (shin′bōn′) /ˈʃɪnˌbown/ *n.* TIBIA.

shin•dig (shin′dig′) /ˈʃɪnˌdɪg/ *n.* [*count*] *Informal.* a large and elaborate dance, party, or celebration: *a big shindig for her retirement.*

shine (shīn) /ʃayn/ *v.,* **shone** (shōn) /ʃown/ or, esp. for 7 **shined; shin•ing;** *n.* —*v.* **1.** [*no obj*] to glow with light: *The sun shone brightly.* **2.** [*no obj*] to be bright with reflected light; sparkle: *Her golden hair shone in the sunlight.* **3.** [*no obj*] (of light or a light) to appear strongly; glare: *The lights were shining straight in his eyes.* **4.** [~ + *obj*] to direct the light of (a lamp, etc.): *shone his flashlight directly onto my face.* **5.** [*no obj*] to appear unusually lively, as the eyes or face. **6.** [*no obj*] to do very well; excel: *to shine in algebra.* **7.** [~ + *obj*] to polish (shoes, etc.): *The soldier had to shine his shoes.* —*n.* [*count*] **8.** [*usually singular*] brightness caused by light given off by an object: *a beautiful shine on the floor.* **9.** [*usually singular*] a polish given to shoes. **10.** an act or instance of polishing shoes. —***Idiom.*** **11. come rain or shine, a.** whether it rains or does not: *We'll play football tomorrow come rain or shine.* **b.** no matter what happens: *Promise that you'll stay with me, come rain or shine.* **12. take a shine to,** [~ + *obj*] to develop a strong liking for (another person): *seemed to take a shine to the new worker.*

shin•er (shī′nər) /ˈʃaynər/ *n. Informal.* BLACK EYE (def. 1).

shin•gle (shing′gəl) /ˈʃɪŋgəl/ *n., v.,* **-gled, -gling.** —*n.* [*count*] **1.** a thin, rectangular piece of wood, slate, etc., laid in rows that partly cover each other on the roofs and sides of buildings. —*v.* [~ + *obj*] **2.** to cover with shingles.

shin•gles (shing′gəlz) /ˈʃɪŋgəlz/ *n.* [*noncount; used with a singular verb*] a disease caused by the herpes virus, with blisterlike pimples on the skin and pain.

shin•ny (shin′ē) /ˈʃɪniy/ *v.* [~ + *up* + *obj*], **-nied, -ny•ing.** to shin: *to shinny up a tree.*

shin′ splints′, *n.* [*plural*] a painful condition of the front lower leg generally resulting from muscle strain.

shin•y (shī′nē) /ˈʃayniy/ *adj.,* **-i•er, -i•est. 1.** bright in appearance: *a shiny face.* **2.** filled with light, esp. sunshine: *bright, shiny skies.* —**shin′i•ness,** *n.* [*noncount*]

ship (ship) /ʃɪp/ *n., v.,* **shipped, ship•ping.** —*n.* [*count*] **1.** a large vessel, esp. one that travels on the ocean. **2.** the crew and passengers of a vessel: *The ship was abuzz with the news.* **3.** an airplane or spacecraft: *The commander of the spacecraft ordered his officers not to fire on the alien ship.* —*v.* **4.** [~ + *obj*] to send or transport by ship, rail, etc.: *The package was shipped by an overnight express delivery service.* **5.** [~ + *obj*] to take in (water) over the side, as a vessel does when waves break over it. **6.** [~ + *obj*] to bring into a ship or boat: *Ship the anchor.* **7. ship out, a.** to (cause to) leave, esp. for another country or assignment: [*no obj*]: *The sailor shipped out the next day.* [~ + *obj* + *out*]: *shipped him out the next day.* [~ + *out* + *obj*]: *The navy shipped out thousands of sailors.* **b.** [*no obj*] to quit, resign, or be fired from a job: *Shape up or ship out!* —***Idiom.*** **8. run a tight ship,** to use strict control in running a company, etc.: *The boss runs a tight ship.*

-ship, *suffix.* **1.** *-ship* is used to form nouns with the meaning "state or condition of": *friend + -ship → friendship; kin + -ship → kinship.* **2.** *-ship* is also used with the meaning "the skill or ability of": *statesman + -ship → statesmanship; apprentice + -ship → apprenticeship.* **3.** *-ship* is also used with the meaning "the relation of": *fellow + -ship → fellowship.*

ship•board (ship′bôrd′, -bōrd′) /ˈʃɪpˌbɔrd, -ˌbowrd/ *adj.* **1.** done or used aboard ship, esp. while under way. —*n.* [*count*] **2.** the deck or side of a ship.

ship•build•er (ship′bil′dər) /ˈʃɪpˌbɪldər/ *n.* [*count*] a person or group that designs or constructs ships. —**ship′build′ing,** *n.* [*noncount*]

ship•mate (ship′māt′) /ˈʃɪpˌmeyt/ *n.* [*count*] one who serves with another on the same vessel.

ship•ment (ship′mənt) /ˈʃɪpmənt/ *n.* **1.** [*noncount*] an act or instance of shipping cargo: *shipment by sea.* **2.** [*count*] cargo shipped: *a shipment of supplies.*

ship•ping (ship′ing) /ˈʃɪpɪŋ/ *n.* [*noncount*] **1.** the act or business of a person or thing that ships goods. **2.** a number of merchant ships thought of as a group: *The submarines had sunk most shipping in those sea lanes.* —**ship′per,** *n.* [*count*]

ship•shape (ship′shāp′) /ˈʃɪpˌʃeyp/ *adj.* in good order; trim or tidy: *Their room was finally shipshape.*

ship•wreck (ship′rek′) /ˈʃɪpˌrɛk/ *n.* **1.** the destruction of a ship, as by sinking, or an occurrence of such a loss: [*noncount*]: *Storms at sea can cause a shipwreck.* [*count*]: *heard of several shipwrecks during the hurricane.* **2.** [*count*] the remains of a wrecked ship: *They came across a shipwreck while skindiving.* —*v.* [~ + *obj*] **3.** to cause to suffer shipwreck: *The crew were shipwrecked on a deserted island.*

ship•yard (ship′yärd′) /ˈʃɪpˌyɑrd/ *n.* [*count*] a closed area in which ships are built or repaired.

shire (shīᵊr) /ʃayᵊr/ *n.* [*count*] one of the counties of Great Britain.

shirk (shûrk) /ʃɜrk/ *v.* to try to keep from doing (work, duty, etc.): [~ + *obj*]: *to shirk one's duty by not caring for one's children.* [*no obj*]: *always shirks from doing what he must.* —**shirk′er,** *n.* [*count*]

shirt (shûrt) /ʃɜrt/ *n.* [*count*] **1.** a garment for the upper part of the body. See illustration at CLOTHING. **2.** an undergarment for the upper part of the body. —***Idiom.*** **3. keep one's shirt on,** *Informal.* to keep from becoming impatient; remain calm: *Keep your shirt on, I'll be with you in a minute.* **4. lose one's shirt,** *Informal.* to suffer a severe loss of money: *During the stock market crash a lot of investors lost their shirts.*

shirt•sleeve (shûrt′slēv′) /ˈʃɜrtˌsliyv/ *adj.* **1.** not wearing a jacket; informally dressed: *a shirtsleeve mob.* **2.** warm enough to live or work in without wearing a jacket: *shirtsleeve weather.* —*n.* [*count*] **3.** the sleeve of a shirt: *ripped his shirtsleeve on a nail.* —***Idiom.*** **4. in (one's) shirt′sleeves′.** wearing a shirt but not a jacket: *working in (his) shirtsleeves all day.*

shirt•tail (shûrt′tāl′) /ˈʃɜrtˌteyl/ *n.* [*count*] the part of a shirt below the waistline: *His shirttail was sticking out.*

shirt•waist (shûrt′wāst′) /ˈʃɜrtˌweyst/ *n.* [*count*] **1.** a tailored blouse or shirt worn by women. **2.** a dress with a bodice and front opening like a tailored shirt.

shish ke•bab (shish′ kə bob′) /ˈʃɪʃ kəˌbɒb/ *n.* [*noncount*] small cubes of meat and often vegetables broiled on a skewer.

shit (shit) /ʃɪt/ *n., v.,* **shit** or **shat** (shat) /ʃæt/ **shit•ting,** *interj. Vulgar.* —*n.* **1.** [*noncount*] excrement; feces. **2.** [*count*] an act of defecating. **3. the shits,** [*plural*] diarrhea. **4.** [*noncount*] *Slang.* lies, exaggeration, or nonsense. **5.** [*noncount*] *Slang.* something worthless. **6.** [*count*] *Slang.* a mean, contemptible person. —*v.* **7.** [*no* *obj*] to defecate. **8.** [~ + *obj*] *Slang.* to exaggerate or lie to. ***—interj.*** **9.** *Slang.* (used to express disgust, disappointment, etc.) ***—Idiom.*** **10. get one's shit together,** *Slang.* to get organized.

shiv•er (shiv′ər) /ˈʃɪvər/ *v.* [*no obj*] **1.** to shake or tremble with cold, fear, etc.: *He came in from the cold, shivering violently.* ***—n.*** [*count*] **2.** an unsteady, shaking motion: *a little shiver of fear.* —**shiv′er•y,** *adj.*

shlep or **shlepp** (shlep) /ʃlɛp/ *v.,* **shlepped, shlep•ping,** *n.* SCHLEP.

shoal[1] (shōl) /ʃowl/ *n.* [*count*] **1.** a place where a sea or river is shallow. **2.** a sandbank in the water, visible at low tide.

shoal[2] (shōl) /ʃowl/ *n.* [*count*] **1.** any large number of persons or things. **2.** a school of fish.

shock[1] (shok) /ʃɒk/ *n.* **1.** a sudden disturbance of the mind or the feelings, due to something unpleasant and unexpected: [*count*]: *Her death came as a shock.* [*noncount*]: *a reaction of shock to the shooting.* **2.** [*count*] a sudden blow or impact: *the shocks from an earthquake.* **3.** [*noncount*] a serious condition in which blood circulation is greatly reduced: *hospitalized and treated for shock and bullet wounds.* **4.** [*count*] the effect on the body produced by an electric current passing through it: *I felt a shock from the static electricity.* **5. shocks,** [*plural*] shock absorbers. ***—v.*** [~ + *obj*] **6.** to have an effect on (someone) of strong and deep surprise, horror, etc.: *The sight shocked everyone deeply.* **7.** to give an electric shock to. ***—adj.*** [*before a noun*] **8.** intended to upset an audience by breaking social rules, esp. by using improper language, obscenity, etc: *shock radio.*

shock[2] (shok) /ʃɒk/ *n.* [*count*] a thick, bushy mass, as of hair: *a shock of gray hair covered by a cap.*

shock′ absorb′er, *n.* [*count*] a device for cushioning the effects of motion, as in the wheels of a car.

shock•er (shok′ər) /ˈʃɒkər/ *n.* [*count*] **1.** a person or thing that shocks. **2.** a sensational novel, play, etc.

shock•ing (shok′ing) /ˈʃɒkɪŋ/ *adj.* **1.** causing intense surprise, horror, etc.: *the shocking news of her death.* **2.** very bad: *shocking table manners.*

shock•proof (shok′prōōf′) /ˈʃɒkˌpruwf/ *adj.* Also, **shock′-proof′.** (of watches, etc.) protected against damage from shocks.

shock′ ther′apy, *n.* [*noncount*] treatment for mental illness in which an electric current is sent through the brain. Also called **shock′ treat′ment.**

shock′ troops′, *n.* [*plural*] troops specially selected, trained, and equipped for carrying out an assault.

shock′ wave′, *n.* [*count*] **1.** an area in the air of great heat, pressure, or density, as caused by an explosion: *The explosion sent shock waves through the village.* **2.** an effect of a startling, unpleasant event: *The murder sent shock waves through the country.*

shod (shod) /ʃɒd/ *v.* a pt. and pp. of SHOE.

shod•dy (shod′ē) /ˈʃɒdiy/ *adj.,* **-di•er, -di•est. 1.** of poor quality or workmanship: *shoddy products that fall apart.* **2.** rude or inconsiderate: *shoddy treatment by the salespeople.* —**shod•di•ly** (shod′l ē) /ˈʃɒdl̩iy/ *adv.* —**shod′di•ness,** *n.* [*noncount*]

shoe (shōō) /ʃuw/ *n., pl.* **shoes,** (*esp. Brit. Dialect.*) **shoon** (shōōn) /ʃuwn/; *v.,* **shod** (shod) /ʃɒd/ or **shoed, shod** or **shoed** or **shod•den** (shod′n) /ˈʃɒdn̩/ **shoe•ing.** ***—n.*** [*count*] **1.** a covering for the foot, with an upper part ending above, at, or below the ankle. See illustration at CLOTHING. **2.** a horseshoe or a similar plate for the hoof of an animal. **3.** BRAKE SHOE. ***—v.*** [~ + *obj*] **4.** to provide with a shoe or shoes: *to shoe a horse.* ***—Idiom.*** **5. fill someone's shoes,** to take the place of another in a suitable or acceptable way: *I'll never fill the boss's shoes.* **6. in someone's shoes,** in the situation of another, so as to feel or know what another feels or knows: *If you were in my shoes you would see how unpleasant it is to deal with my supervisor.* —**shoe′less,** *adj.*

shoe•horn (shōō′hôrn′) /ˈʃuwˌhɔrn/ *n.* [*count*] **1.** a shaped piece of metal or the like, inserted in the heel of a shoe to make it slip on easily. ***—v.*** [~ + *obj*] **2.** to force into a tight space: *Maybe we can shoehorn one more person in here.*

shoe•lace (shōō′lās′) /ˈʃuwˌleys/ *n.* [*count*] a string or lace for fastening a shoe.

shoe•mak•er (shōō′mā′kər) /ˈʃuwˈmeykər/ *n.* [*count*] one who makes or mends shoes.

shoe•string (shōō′string′) /ˈʃuwˌstrɪŋ/ *n.* [*count*] **1.** SHOELACE. **2.** a very small amount of money. ***—adj.*** [*before a noun*] **3.** consisting of a small amount of money: *a shoestring budget.*

sho•gun (shō′gən, -gun) /ˈʃowgən, -gʌn/ *n.* [*count*] the title of the chief military commanders of Japan from the 8th to 12th centuries. —**sho•gun•ate** (shō′gə nit, -nāt′) /ˈʃowgənɪt, -ˌneyt/ *n.* [*noncount*]

shone (shōn) /ʃown/ *v.* a pt. and pp. of SHINE.

shoo (shōō) /ʃuw/ *interj.* **1.** (used as a noise to drive away birds, animals, etc.). ***—v.*** [~ + *obj*] **2.** to drive away by saying or shouting "shoo": *He shooed the animals into the barn.* **3.** to request or force (a person) to leave: *The principal shooed the students out the door.*

shoo′-in′, *n.* [*count*] a candidate, competitor, etc., thought of as certain to win.

shook (shŏŏk) /ʃʊk/ *v.* **1.** pt. of SHAKE. ***—adj.*** [*be* + ~] **2.** Also, **shook′ up′.** *Informal.* frightened, nervous, or deeply affected by an event: *He is too shook to talk about what happened.*

shoot (shōōt) /ʃuwt/ *v.,* **shot** (shot) /ʃɒt/ **shoot•ing,** *n.* ***—v.*** **1.** [~ + *obj*] to hit with a bullet, shell, or other missile fired from a weapon: *The bank robbers shot five police officers.* **2.** to send forth or discharge (a bullet, etc.) from a weapon: [*no obj*]: *Stop or I'll shoot!* [~ + *obj*]: *He shot an arrow into the air.* **3. a.** to discharge (a weapon): [~ + *obj*]: *She shot her pistol.* [*no obj*]: *He aimed at the target and shot.* **b.** [*no obj*] (of a weapon) to be fired; go off: *The gun wouldn't shoot.* **4.** [~ + *obj*] to send forth (questions, ideas, etc.) rapidly: *The reporters shot questions at the general.* **5.** [~ + *obj*] to fling; propel: *The volcano shot lava into the air.* **6.** to direct suddenly or swiftly: [~ + *obj* + *at* + *obj*]: *He shot a smile at his wife.* [~ + *obj* + *obj*]: *She shot me a warning glance.* **7.** to (cause to) move suddenly; hurtle: [*no obj*]: *The car shot down the road.* [~ + *obj*]: *The needles were shooting pain down his arms.* **8.** [~ + *obj*] to pass rapidly through, down, etc.: *He shot the rapids in the kayak.* **9. a.** [~ + *obj*] to send off (a ray or rays) suddenly, briefly, or on and off: *The sun shot rays of light through the clouds.* **b.** [*no obj*] (of a ray or rays of light) to be sent forth suddenly or briefly: *The sun's rays shot through the sky.* **10.** [~ + *obj; usually: be* + *shot* + *through*] to change the appearance of by threads, streaks, etc., of another color: *The clothing is shot through with gold threads.* **11.** [~ + *obj*] to slide (a bolt) into or out of its fastening: *The thief shot the bolt from the door.* **12.** [~ + *obj*] to take a picture of; photograph: *shooting one picture after another.* **13.** to film or begin to film (a scene or movie): [~ + *obj*]: *The crew shot the last scene.* [*no obj*]: *When we finish shooting we can all go home.* **14.** to send or propel (a ball, etc.) toward a goal or in a particular way: [~ + *obj*]: *He shot the puck into the net for the winning goal.* [*no obj*]: *The captain shoots...he scores!* **15. shoot down, a.** to cause to fall by hitting with a shot: [~ + *down* + *obj*]: *to shoot down airplanes.* [~ + *obj* + *down*]: *to shoot them down.* **b.** to show to be false or not good enough: [~ + *down* + *obj*]: *They shot down all his suggestions.* [~ + *obj* + *down*]: *These facts will shoot his theory down.* **16. shoot for** or **at,** [~ + *for/at* + *obj*] to try to obtain or accomplish: *If we shoot for the best, we may get it.* **17. shoot out,** to (cause to) extend or project: [~ + *out* + *obj*]: *He shot out his arm.* [*no obj*]: *The narrow stretch of land shoots out into the sea.* **18. shoot up, a.** to grow suddenly: [*no obj*]: *Prices have shot up since last year.* [~ + *up* + *obj*]: *You've shot up several inches since I last saw you.* **b.** to wound or damage by shooting, esp. recklessly: [~ + *up* + *obj*]: *to shoot up several parked cars.* [~ + *obj* + *up*]: *to shoot them up.* **c.** [*no obj*] *Slang.* to inject a narcotic drug into one's body. ***—n.*** [*count*] **19.** a shooting trip or contest. **20.** the new growth from a plant. ***—Idiom.*** **21. shoot from the hip,** *Informal.* to act or speak without thought: *just shooting from the hip when he criticized you.* **22. shoot off one's mouth** or **face,** *Slang.* **a.** to talk about private things too openly, or to make foolish remarks. **b.** to exaggerate; brag. **23. shoot one's wad** or **bolt,** *Informal.* **a.** to spend or risk all one's money: *He shot his wad at the racetrack.* **b.** to spend and use up all one's resources: *The team shot its bolt in the last five minutes.* **24. shoot the breeze** or **bull,** *Informal.* to talk pleasantly or easily about things that are not serious or urgent; chat sociably: *We sat around shooting the breeze all afternoon.* —**shoot′er,** *n.* [*count*]

shoot′ing star′, *n.* [*count*] a meteor.

shoot•out (shōōt′out′) /ˈʃuwtˌawt/ *n.* [*count*] a gunfight that must end in defeat for one side or the other.

shop (shop) /ʃɒp/ *n., v.,* **shopped, shop•ping.** ***—n.*** **1.** [*count*] a store, esp. a small one. **2.** [*count*] a small store or department in a large store selling a special type of goods: *the ski shop at Smith's.* **3.** [*count*] a place for doing skilled artistic or manual work; workshop: *a carpenter's shop.* **4.** [*count*] any factory, office, or business:

How are things at the shop these days? **5.** [*noncount*] a school course in a trade, in which the use of tools is taught: *took shop in high school.* **—***v.* **6.** [*no obj*] to visit shops for buying or examining goods: *My parents went out to shop.* **7.** [*no obj*] to purchase without visiting stores: *to shop by telephone.* **8.** [~ + *for* + *obj*] to search; hunt: *shopping for a husband.* **—*Idiom.* 9. set up shop,** to open as a business: *set up shop in a small building but soon expanded.* **10. talk shop,** to talk about a shared trade, profession, or business: *At the party the two dentists talked shop instead of mingling with the other guests.*

shop•keep•er (shop′kē′pər) /ˈʃɒpˌkiypər/ *n.* [*count*] one who owns or operates a small store or shop.

shop•lift•er (shop′lif′tər) /ˈʃɒpˌlɪftər/ *n.* [*count*] one who steals goods from a retail store while posing as a customer. —**shop′lift′,** *v.:* [*no obj*]: *arrested for shoplifting.* [~ + *obj*]: *arrested for trying to shoplift some expensive jewelry.*

shoppe (shop) /ʃɒp/ *n.* [*count*] (used chiefly on store signs to achieve an old-fashioned effect) shop: *The sign said "Ye olde tobacco shoppe."*

shop•per (shop′ər) /ˈʃɒpər/ *n.* [*count*] **1.** one who shops. **2.** a retail buyer for a business. **3.** a locally distributed newspaper containing retail advertisements.

shop′ping cen′ter, *n.* [*count*] a group of stores, restaurants, etc., within an area specially designed for them.

shop•talk (shop′tôk′) /ˈʃɒpˌtɔk/ *n.* [*noncount*] conversation about one's work.

shop•worn (shop′wôrn′, -wōrn′) /ˈʃɒpˌwɔrn, -ˌwowrn/ *adj.* **1.** worn or marred, as goods exposed and handled in a store. **2.** not new or fresh; trite: *a few shopworn expressions in the first paragraph.*

shore[1] (shôr, shōr) /ʃɔr, ʃowr/ *n.* **1.** the land along the edge of a sea, lake, etc.: [*count*]: *a walk down by the shore.* [*noncount*]: *The marine was now serving on shore.* **2.** [*count*] some particular country: *my native shore.*

shore[2] (shôr, shōr) /ʃɔr, ʃowr/ *v.,* **shored, shor•ing.** to support or strengthen: [~ + *obj*]: *shored the walls with timbers.* [~ + *up* + *obj*]: *The workers shored up the side of the wall with timbers.* [~ + *obj* + *up*]: *to shore the walls up.*

shore•line (shôr′līn′, shōr′-) /ˈʃɔrˌlayn, ˈʃowr-/ *n.* [*count*] the line where shore and water meet.

shorn (shôrn, shōrn) /ʃɔrn, ʃowrn/ *v.* a pp. of SHEAR.

short (shôrt) /ʃɔrt/ *adj.,* **-er, -est,** *adv., n., v.* **—***adj.* **1.** having little length or height: *the shortest boy in class.* **2.** extending only a little way: *a short path.* **3.** brief: *a short time.* **4.** rudely brief; abrupt: *surprised by his short reply.* **5.** low in amount or number: *short rations.* **6.** not reaching a standard, level, etc.; deficient: *The pound of apples that you bought was short by several ounces.* **7.** made with a large amount of shortening: *short pastry.* **8.** [*often:* ~ + *on/in* + *obj*] not having enough; lacking: *always short on money.* **9.** having the sound of the English vowels in *bat, bet, bit, hot, but,* and *put,* historically descended from vowels that were short in duration. **—***adv.* **10.** abruptly or suddenly: *to stop short.* **11.** briefly; curtly. **12.** on the near side of a point: *The arrow landed short.* **—***n.* [*count*] **13.** something short. **14. shorts,** [*plural*] **a.** trousers, knee-length or shorter. See illustration at CLOTHING. **b.** underpants. **15.** SHORT CIRCUIT. **—***v.* **16.** to form a short circuit (in): [~ + *obj*]: *The frayed wire shorted the connection.* [*no obj*]: *The car kept shorting.* **—*Idiom.* 17. come** or **fall short,** [*no obj*] **a.** to fail to reach a standard, level, etc.: *The arrow fell short of the target.* **b.** to be lacking: *We came up short in our bid for the painting.* **18. cut short,** [*no obj*] to end abruptly; terminate. **19. for short,** as a shorter way of saying or naming something: *Barbara was called Barb for short.* **20. in short,** in summary; stated or said briefly: *In short, gentlemen, we know what we're going to do.* —**short′-ness,** *n.* [*noncount*]

short•age (shôr′tij) /ˈʃɔrtɪdʒ/ *n.* [*count*] **1.** the condition or state of not having enough; deficiency: *a shortage of cash.* **2.** the amount of such deficiency: *a shortage of fifty dollars.*

short•bread (shôrt′bred′) /ˈʃɔrtˌbrɛd/ *n.* [*noncount*] a butter cookie commonly made in thick, pie-shaped wheels.

short•cake (shôrt′kāk′) /ˈʃɔrtˌkeyk/ *n.* **1.** [*count*] a short, sweetened biscuit, topped with fruit and whipped cream. **2.** [*noncount*] a cake made with a large proportion of shortening.

short•change (shôrt′chānj′) /ˈʃɔrtˈtʃeyndʒ/ *v.* [~ + *obj*], **-changed, -chang•ing. 1.** to give less than the correct change to: *to shortchange a customer.* **2.** to cheat; defraud: *Teachers shortchange their students if they don't prepare their classroom lessons.*

short′ cir′cuit, *n.* [*count*] a bad electrical connection that allows too much current to flow into a circuit: *The short circuit resulted in a blown fuse.*

short′-cir′cuit, *v.* **1. a.** [~ + *obj*] to make (an appliance, switch, etc.) stop operating by establishing a short circuit in: *The bad connection short-circuited the electric mixer.* **b.** [*no obj*] (of an appliance, switch, etc.) to become disabled by a short circuit: *The mixer has short-circuited again.* **2.** [~ + *obj*] to bypass, block, or prevent progress of: *He kept short-circuiting all our plans.*

short•com•ing (shôrt′kum′ing) /ˈʃɔrtˌkʌmɪŋ/ *n.* [*count*] a failure, defect, or lack, as in conduct, condition, etc.: *She was quick to list all his shortcomings.*

short•cut (shôrt′kut′) /ˈʃɔrtˌkʌt/ *n.* [*count*] **1.** a shorter or quicker way to get somewhere: *a shortcut between the buildings.* **2.** a policy or practice that reduces the time or energy needed to accomplish something.

short•en (shôr′tn) /ˈʃɔrtn̩/ *v.* to (cause to) become short or shorter: [~ + *obj*]: *She had a hard time shortening her ten-page paper.* [*no obj*]: *The summer seemed to have shortened just as it was getting to be fun.*

short•en•ing (shôrt′ning, shôr′tn ing) /ˈʃɔrtnɪŋ, ˈʃɔrtn̩ɪŋ/ *n.* **1.** [*noncount*] butter or other fat used in making pastry, bread, etc. **2.** [*noncount*] the act or process of making or becoming short or shorter: *"Deli" was formed by shortening from "delicatessen."* **3.** [*count*] something made shorter: *"Flu" is a shortening from "influenza."*

short•hand (shôrt′hand′) /ˈʃɔrtˌhænd/ *n.* [*noncount*] **1.** a method of fast handwriting using simple strokes, abbreviations, etc., for letters, words, or phrases: *kept his notes in shorthand.* **2.** a simplified form or system of communicating: *"Reboot" is shorthand for "starting" the computer all over again.* **—***adj.* [*before a noun*] **3.** of or relating to shorthand. **4.** written in shorthand.

short′-hand′ed, *adj.* not having the usual or necessary number of workers, helpers, etc.

short′-lived′ (līvd, livd) /layvd, lɪvd/ *adj.* living or lasting only a little while: *Their happiness was short-lived.*

short•ly (shôrt′lē) /ˈʃɔrtliy/ *adv.* **1.** in a short time; soon: *He said he would be with us shortly.* **2.** briefly; concisely: *Describe what happened as shortly as you can.* **3.** curtly; rudely: *answered shortly.*

short′ or′der, *n.* [*count*] **1.** a serving of food that can be quickly prepared, as at a lunch counter. **—*Idiom.* 2. in short order,** [*noncount*] quickly: *The champ knocked out the challenger in short order.* —**short′-or′der,** *adj.* [*before a noun*]: *a short-order cook.*

short′-range′, *adj.* having a limited reach or extent, such as in distance or time: *short-range planning.*

short′ shrift′ (shrift′) /ˈʃrɪft/ *n.* [*noncount*] little attention in dealing with a person or matter: *His parents gave him short shrift as a child.*

short•sight•ed (shôrt′sī′tid) /ˈʃɔrtˈsaytɪd/ *adj.* **1.** unable to see far; nearsighted. **2.** [*often: It* + *be* + ~] lacking in foresight: *It's very shortsighted to fire those employees now because you'll need them again in just a few months.* —**short′sight′ed•ly,** *adv.* —**short′sight′ed•ness,** *n.* [*noncount*]

short•stop (shôrt′stop′) /ˈʃɔrtˌstɒp/ *n. Baseball.* **1.** [*noncount*] the position of the player covering the area of the infield between second and third base: *to play shortstop.* **2.** [*count*] a fielder who covers this position: *He was a shortstop in college baseball.*

short′ sto′ry, *n.* [*count*] a piece of prose fiction, usually under 10,000 words.

short′-tem′pered, *adj.* having a quick temper; easily angered, excited, or irritated; irascible.

short′-term′, *adj.* **1.** covering or involving a short period of time: *short-term memory.* **2.** (of a loan) becoming due after a short period of time.

short•wave (shôrt′wāv′) /ˈʃɔrtˈweyv/ *n.* **1.** [*noncount*] radio transmission or receiving that uses radio waves shorter than those used in AM broadcasting: *Shortwave uses frequencies of over 1600 kilohertz.* **2.** [*count*] **a.** a radio wave of this type. **b.** a radio that receives or transmits such waves. **—***adj.* [*before a noun*] **3.** of or relating to or using shortwaves: *a shortwave radio operator.*

short′-wind′ed, *adj.* short of breath.

shot[1] (shot) /ʃɒt/ *n.* **1.** [*count*] the discharge of a firearm: *shots rang out from the street.* **2.** [*count*] an act or instance of shooting a gun, bow, etc.: *He took a shot at me with the rifle and missed.* **3.** [*noncount*] small balls of lead loaded in a casing and used in a shotgun: *a charge of shot.* **4.** [*count*] one who shoots; marksman: *a good* *shot.* **5.** [*count*] anything like a shot, esp. in being sudden and forceful: *a sudden shot to the jaw.* **6.** [*count*] a heavy metal ball used in shot-putting contests. **7.** [*count*] an aimed stroke, throw, etc., as in certain games, esp. in an attempt to score: *The center's shot went into the net.* **8.** [*count*] an attempt or try: *Let me take a shot at the question.* **9.** [*count*] a remark aimed at some person or thing: *tried a few shots at his opponent about his marital life.* **10.** [*count*] an injection, as of a serum: *to get tetanus shots.* **11.** [*count*] a small quantity, esp. an ounce, of undiluted liquor. **12.** [*count*] a photograph, esp. a snapshot: *Look at the shots of her kids.* **13.** [*count*] *Motion Pictures, Television.* a unit of action photographed without stopping and usually from a single camera view. **14.** [*count*] a chance with odds for and against; a bet: *It was a 20 to 1 shot that the horse would win.* **—*Idiom.*** **15. have** or **take a shot at,** [*have/take + a + ~ + at + obj*] to make an attempt at: *Do you think he really has a shot at this job?* **16. like a shot,** [*noncount*] instantly; quickly. **17. shot in the arm,** [*noncount*] something that provides renewed vigor, etc. **18. shot in the dark,** [*noncount*] a wild guess.

shot[2] (shot) /ʃɒt/ *v.* **1.** pt. and pp. of SHOOT. **—*adj.*** **2.** [*often: after a noun*] presenting a play or pattern of colors; mixed or streaked: *the dawn sky shot with gold.* **3.** in hopelessly bad condition; ruined: *The engine was shot.*

shot•gun (shot′gun′) /ˈʃɒtˌgʌn/ *n.* [*count*] **1.** a gun with a smooth inner barrel, for firing shot. **—*adj.*** [*before a noun*] **2.** of or relating to a shotgun: *shotgun attacks.* **3.** characterized by forcing another: *a shotgun marriage (= a marriage in which the woman's family forces the man to marry her because he has made her pregnant).* **4.** tending to be wide-ranging, but indefinite: *the shotgun approach to buying stocks.* **—*v.*** [*~ + obj*] **5.** to fire a shotgun at.

shot′ put′, *n.* [*count*] **1.** [*singular*] a field event in which a heavy metal ball, or shot, is thrown for distance. **2.** a single throw of the shot. —**shot′-put′ter,** *n.* [*count*] —**shot′-put′ting,** *n.* [*noncount*]

should (sho͝od) /ʃʊd/ *auxiliary (modal) v.* [*~ + root form of a verb*] **1.** pt. of SHALL: *I promised that I should do the job myself.* **2.** (used to express the opinion that the action of the main verb is one of duty, or what is proper, or what is a good idea): *You should respect your mother and your father. Those who live in glass houses should not throw stones (= People who have faults should not criticize others for having those faults too).* **3.** (used to express a condition): *If he were to arrive, I should be pleased.* **4.** (used to make a statement less direct or blunt): *I should think you'll want to apologize.* **5.** (used to express the opinion that the action of the main verb is something that may naturally be expected to occur): *He should be here any minute.*

shoul•der (shōl′dər) /ˈʃowldər/ *n.* [*count*] **1.** the part on either side of the body where the arm joins the rest of the body, from the base of the neck to the upper arm. **2.** Usually, **shoulders.** [*plural*] these two parts together with the part of the back joining them: *The backpack rested on his shoulders.* **3.** a corresponding part in animals. **4.** the part of a garment that fits over the shoulder. **5.** Often, **shoulders.** [*plural*] capacity or strength: *The duty rests on our shoulders.* **6.** a border alongside a road or highway: *We pulled over to the shoulder to change the flat tire.* **—*v.*** [*~ + obj*] **7.** to force (one's way) or push (something or someone) with or as if with the shoulder: [*~ + obj*]: *He shouldered his way through the crowd.* [*no obj*]: *to shoulder through the crowd.* **8.** [*~ + obj*] to support or carry on the shoulder or shoulders: *to shoulder a knapsack.* **9.** [*~ + obj*] to assume or take on as a responsibility: *We shouldered the expense.* **—*Idiom.*** **10. shoulder to shoulder,** [*noncount*] side by side; with joined effort.

shoul′der blade′, *n.* [*count*] one of the two flat bones on the upper part of the back; scapula.

should•n't (sho͝od′nt) /ˈʃʊdnt/ *contraction.* a shortened form of *should not.*

shout (shout) /ʃawt/ *v.* **1.** to call or cry out loudly: [*no obj*]: *She shouted to him from behind the glass.* [*obj*]: *She shouted a warning.* [*used with quotations*]: *"Look out!" she shouted.* **2. shout down,** to prevent (someone) from being heard by talking in a loud voice: [*~ + obj + down*]: *The crowd shouted the speaker down.* [*~ + down + obj*]: *The crowd shouted down the student leaders.* **—*n.*** [*count*] **3.** a loud call or cry: *a shout for help.* —**shout′er,** *n.* [*count*]

shove (shuv) /ʃʌv/ *v.,* **shoved, shov•ing,** *n.* **—*v.*** **1.** [*~ + obj*] to push along from behind, often carelessly: *He shoved the chair into the room.* **2.** to push roughly or rudely; jostle: [*no obj*]: *The huge crowd shoved forward into the stadium.* [*~ + obj*]: *The police shoved him against a wall.* **3. shove off,** [*no obj*] to go away; depart: *It was time for us to shove off.* **—*n.*** [*count*] **4.** an act or instance of shoving: *She gave him a shove.*

shov•el (shuv′əl) /ˈʃʌvəl/ *n., v.,* **-eled, -el•ing** or (*esp. Brit.*) **-elled, -el•ling.** **—*n.*** [*count*] **1.** a hand tool made of a broad blade attached to a handle, used for taking up or throwing dirt or other loose matter. **2.** any machine with a broad scoop having a similar purpose: *a steam shovel.* **—*v.*** [*~ + obj*] **3.** to take up and move with a shovel: *We shoveled the snow off the driveway.* **4.** to gather up in large amounts with or as if with a shovel: *The kids began to shovel food into their mouths.* **5.** to dig or clear with or as if with a shovel: *to shovel a path through the snow.*

shov•el•ful (shuv′əl fo͝ol′) /ˈʃʌvəlˌfʊl/ *n.* [*count*], *pl.* **-fuls.** the amount held by a shovel.

show (shō) /ʃow/ *v.,* **showed, shown** (shōn) /ʃown/ or **showed, show•ing,** *n.* **—*v.*** **1.** to (cause or allow to) appear, be seen, etc.: [*~ + obj + obj*]: *Let me show you the work we've been doing.* [*~ + obj*]: *The photograph shows our new house.* [*~ + obj + to + obj*]: *Show the photograph to the jury.* [*no obj*]: *a stain on her dress that didn't show in the dim light.* **2.** to present or perform as a public entertainment or as an exhibition: [*~ + obj*]: *to show a movie.* [*no obj; usually: be + ~-ing*]: *His movie would be showing for the next three weeks.* **3.** to indicate; point out: [*~ + obj*]: *to show the way.* [*~ + (that) clause*]: *The polls show (that) he is losing popularity.* [*~ + obj + obj*]: *The man showed us the entrance to the museum.* **4.** [*~ + obj*] to guide; escort: *Show her in.* **5.** to make known; explain: [*~ + obj + obj*]: *She showed us an easier way to solve the problem.* [*~ (+ obj) + clause*]: *He showed (us) what he meant.* **6.** to reveal; prove or make clear: [*~ + obj*]: *Your work shows promise.* [*~ + obj + to + verb*]: *showed the idea to be entirely unworkable.* [*~ + that clause*]: *showed that the idea wouldn't work.* **7.** [*~ + obj*] to register; mark: *The thermometer showed 10 below zero.* **8.** to exhibit or offer for sale: [*~ + obj*]: *to show a house.* [*~ + obj + to + obj*]: *to show a house to possible buyers.* [*~ + obj + obj*]: *The real estate agent showed us the house.* **9.** to offer; grant: [*~ + obj*]: *to show mercy.* [*~ + obj + to + obj*]: *to show mercy to his enemies.* [*~ + obj + obj*]: *to show his enemies mercy.* **10.** [*no obj*] to make an appearance; be present; show up: *It's getting late; do you think they'll still show?* **11. show off, a.** [*~ + off + obj*] to display to advantage: *The gold frame shows off the picture nicely.* **b.** [*~ + off + obj*] to present for approval: *young parents showing off their new baby.* **c.** [*no obj*] to seek attention by constantly displaying one's talent, etc.: *a child showing off in front of guests.* **12. show up, a.** [*~ + up + obj*] to make known; reveal: *That report showed up the manager's mistakes.* **b.** [*no obj*] to appear as specified; be seen: *White shows up well against the blue.* **c.** [*no obj*] to come to or arrive at a place: *It's getting late; I wonder if he'll even show up now.* **d.** [*~ + up + obj*] to make (another) seem lower or inferior; outdo: *She keeps showing up her rivals.* **—*n.*** **13.** [*count*] a theatrical production, performance, etc.: *a Broadway show.* **14.** [*count*] a radio or television program: *a morning radio show.* **15.** [*count*] a motion picture. **16.** [*count*] a display of products by manufacturers in an industry: *an auto show.* **17.** [*count*] exhibition: *a show of paintings by Renoir.* **18.** [*noncount*] overly fancy or dramatic display: *all show and no substance.* **19.** [*count*] a display or demonstration: *a show of courage.* **20.** [*noncount*] *Sports.* the position of the competitor who comes in third, such as in a horse race. **21.** [*count; usually singular*] appearance; impression: *to make a sorry show.* **22.** [*count*] a sight or spectacle: *What a show the new player put on!*

show•boat (shō′bōt′) /ˈʃowˌbowt/ *n.* [*count*] **1.** a boat used as a traveling theater. **2.** SHOW-OFF. **—*v.*** [*no obj*] **3.** to perform or behave in a showy way; show off.

show′ busi′ness, *n.* [*noncount*] the entertainment industry, as theater, motion pictures, television, radio, carnival, and circus.

show•case (shō′kās′) /ˈʃowˌkeys/ *n., v.,* **-cased, -cas•ing.** **—*n.*** [*count*] **1.** a glass case for the display of articles. **2.** an exhibit or display, usually of an ideal of something. **3.** a setting, place, or means for displaying something on a trial basis: *The club is a showcase for new comics.* **—*v.*** [*~ + obj*] **4.** to exhibit or display. **5.** to present as a special event: *The TV network plans to showcase a new production of the play.*

show•down (shō′doun′) /ˈʃowˌdawn/ *n.* [*count*] a face-to-face meeting to settle an argument.

show•er (shou′ər) /ˈʃawər/ *n.* [*count*] **1.** a brief fall of rain, hail, or snow. **2.** Also called **show′er bath′.** a bath in which water is sprayed on the body from above: *He took a long, hot shower after work.* **3.** the pipes, spraying nozzle, etc., for such a bath, or the space or place where this bath can be taken: *to clean up the showers in the gym.* **4.** something resembling a shower: *a shower of sparks.* **5.** a party held to honor and give gifts to a person, as a woman who is getting married: *a bridal shower.* —*v.* **6.** to give a great deal of (something) to someone: [~ + *obj* + *with* + *obj*]: *to shower his employees with praise.* [~ + *obj* + *on* + *obj*]: *to shower praise on his employees.* **7.** [*no obj; it* + ~] to rain in a shower: *It showered all day.* **8.** [*no obj*] to bathe in a shower: *He showered before dinner.* —**show′er•y,** *adj.*

show•ing (shō′ing) /ˈʃowɪŋ/ *n.* [*count*] **1.** the act of putting something on display. **2.** a performance considered for the impression it makes: *The first woman candidate from that district made a strong showing at the polls.*

show•man (shō′mən) /ˈʃowmən/ *n.* [*count*], *pl.* **-men. 1.** one who produces works in the theater. **2.** a person talented in giving a dramatic presentation. —**show′man•ship′,** *n.* [*noncount*]: *lectures full of more showmanship than information.*

shown (shōn) /ʃown/ *v.* a pp. of SHOW.

show′-off′, *n.* [*count*] one who annoyingly displays his or her abilities, accomplishments, etc.

show•piece (shō′pēs′) /ˈʃowˌpiys/ *n.* [*count*] something exhibited as a fine example of its kind.

show•place (shō′plās′) /ˈʃowˌpleys/ *n.* [*count*] a place, such as a mansion, famous for its beauty, etc.

show•room (shō′ro͞om′, -ro͝om′) /ˈʃowˌruwm, -ˌrʊm/ *n.* [*count*] a room used for the display of goods or merchandise.

show•y (shō′ē) /ˈʃowiy/ *adj.,* **-i•er, -i•est. 1.** making a good display: *showy flowers.* **2.** making too strong a display; ostentatious: *cheap, showy costumes.* —**show•i•ly** (shō′ə lē) /ˈʃowəliy/ *adv.* —**show′i•ness,** *n.* [*noncount*]

shpt., an abbreviation of: shipment.

shrank (shrangk) /ʃræŋk/ *v.* a pt. of SHRINK.

shrap•nel (shrap′nl) /ˈʃræpnl̩/ *n.* [*noncount*] fragments scattered by an exploding artillery shell or mine: *wounded by shrapnel.*

shred (shred) /ʃrɛd/ *n., v.,* **shred•ded** or **shred, shred•ding.** —*n.* [*count*] **1.** a piece cut or torn off, esp. in a narrow strip. **2.** a bit; scrap: *not a shred of evidence.* —*v.* **3. a.** [~ + *obj*] to cut or tear into small pieces: *He has a machine that shreds documents.* **b.** [*no obj*] to form shreds, as by being cut or torn: *The paper shreds easily.* —**shred′der,** *n.* [*count*]

shrew[1] (shro͞o) /ʃruw/ *n.* [*count*] a woman who is easily angered and has a strong, violent temper. —**shrew′ish,** *adj.*

shrew[2] (shro͞o) /ʃruw/ *n.* [*count*] a small, mouselike, insect-eating mammal that has a long, sharp snout.

shrewd (shro͞od) /ʃruwd/ *adj.,* **-er, -est. 1.** clever or sharp in practical matters: *a shrewd politician.* **2.** keen; piercing: *a shrewd glance at me.* **3.** showing or done with sharpness in judgment, etc.: *a shrewd choice for vice president.* —**shrewd′ly,** *adv.* —**shrewd′ness,** *n.* [*noncount*]

shriek (shrēk) /ʃriyk/ *n.* [*count*] **1.** a loud, sharp, shrill cry: *shrieks of laughter.* **2.** any loud, shrill sound, as of a whistle. —*v.* **3. a.** [*no obj*][*no obj*] to make such a sound: *The children shrieked with laughter.* **b.** [~ + *obj*] to say or call in a shriek: *She shrieked curses at him.* [*used with quotations*]: *"Get out!" she shrieked.* **4. a.** [*no obj*] to give forth a shriek: *The whistle shrieked as the train roared into the station.* **b.** [~ + *obj*] to give forth or convey by shrieking: *The whistle shrieked a warning.*

shrike (shrīk) /ʃrayk/ *n.* [*count*] a songbird having a sharply hooked bill.

shrill (shril) /ʃrɪl/ *adj.* **1.** high-pitched and piercing: *a shrill cry.* **2.** annoyingly insistent or demanding; strident: *their shrill demands for change.* —*v.* **3.** to cry shrilly: [*no obj*]: *to shrill at him.* [~ + *obj*]: *shrilling her anger at him.* [*used with quotations*]: *"Right now!" she shrilled.* —*n.* [*count*] **4.** a shrill sound. —*adv.* **5.** in a shrill manner; shrilly. —**shrill′ness,** *n.* [*noncount*] —**shril′ly,** *adv.*: *The phone rang shrilly.*

shrimp (shrimp) /ʃrɪmp/ *n., pl.* **shrimps,** (*esp. when thought of as a group*) **shrimp** for 1; *v.* —*n.* **1.** a small, long-tailed, ten-footed, edible shellfish found chiefly in salt water: [*count*]: *They counted out five little steamed shrimps for each person.* [*noncount*]: *Shrimp is good for you.* **2.** [*count*] a small person: *He was just a shrimp in school.* —*v.* [*no obj*] **3.** to fish for shrimps.

shrine (shrīn) /ʃrayn/ *n.* [*count*] **1.** a place, as a church or an altar, devoted to some saint or deity. **2.** any place or object preserved because of its history or associations: *a historic shrine.*

shrink (shringk) /ʃrɪŋk/ *v.,* **shrank** (shrangk) /ʃræŋk/ or, often, **shrunk** (shrungk) /ʃrʌŋk/; **shrunk** or **shrunk•en** (shrung′kən) /ˈʃrʌŋkən/; **shrink•ing;** *n.* —*v.* **1.** to (cause to) contract or lessen in size: [*no obj*]: *clothes that shrink if washed in hot water.* [~ + *obj*]: *Hot water will shrink some of those clothes.* **2.** to (cause to) become reduced in extent, amount, or value: [*no obj*]: *The bank's resources are shrinking.* [~ + *obj*]: *Inflation and taxation are shrinking our resources.* **3.** [*no obj; (~ + back)*] to draw back; move back suddenly, as in horror: *to shrink from danger; She shrank back in her seat as the horror movie got even nastier.* —*n.* [*count*] **4.** *Slang.* a psychotherapist, psychiatrist, or psychoanalyst. —**shrink′a•ble,** *adj.*

shrink•age (shring′kij) /ˈʃrɪŋkɪdʒ/ *n.* [*noncount*] an act or process of shrinking, or the amount or degree of shrinking: *to avoid shrinkage of the fabric.*

shrink′ing vi′olet, *n.* [*count*] a shy person.

shrink′-wrap′, *v.,* **-wrapped, -wrap•ping,** *n.* —*v.* [~ + *obj*] **1.** to wrap and seal in a clear, flexible plastic film that, when it is exposed to heat, shrinks tightly around the thing it covers: *The disks and book are shrink-wrapped and sold as one item.* —*n.* [*noncount*] **2.** the plastic film used to shrink-wrap something.

shriv•el (shriv′əl) /ˈʃrɪvəl/ *v.,* **-eled, -el•ing** or (*esp. Brit.*) **-elled, -el•ling. 1.** to (cause to) become smaller and wrinkled or curled up, as from great heat: [*no obj*]: *The plants shriveled in the heat.* [~ + *obj*]: *The heat shriveled the plants.* **2.** [*no obj*] to become helpless or useless: *He shriveled in fear.*

shroud (shroud) /ʃrawd/ *n.* [*count*] **1.** a sheet in which a dead body is wrapped for burial. **2.** something that covers, hides, or protects: *a shroud of darkness.* **3.** any of the ropes or wires attached to the head of a ship's mast to keep it from swaying. —*v.* [~ + *obj*] **4.** to wrap or clothe (a body) for burial. **5.** to cover; hide from view: *shrouded by night.* **6.** to hide or keep (knowledge, etc.): *secrets shrouded in mystery.*

shrub (shrub) /ʃrʌb/ *n.* [*count*] a woody plant smaller than a tree. See illustration at HOUSE. —**shrub′by,** *adj.,* **-bi•er, -bi•est.**

shrub•ber•y (shrub′ə rē) /ˈʃrʌbəriy/ *n., pl.* **-ber•ies.** a planting of shrubs: [*noncount*]: *a dense growth of shrubbery.* [*count*]: *knocking the ball into the shrubbery.*

shrug (shrug) /ʃrʌg/ *v.,* **shrugged, shrug•ging,** *n.* —*v.* **1.** to raise and contract (the shoulders), as a sign that one does not know or that one does not care about something: [~ + *obj*]: *He shrugged his shoulders and said, "I don't care."* [*no obj*]: *When we asked him where the dog was, he just shrugged.* **2. shrug off, a.** to treat (something) as unimportant; minimize: [~ + *off* + *obj*]: *to shrug off an insult.* [~ + *obj* + *off*]: *to shrug it off.* **b.** to rid oneself of: [~ + *off* + *obj*]: *to shrug off the effects of a drug.* [~ + *obj* + *off*]: *to shrug them off.* —*n.* [*count*] **3.** the movement of raising or drawing up the shoulders.

shrunk (shrungk) /ʃrʌŋk/ *v.* a pp. and pt. of SHRINK.

shrunk•en (shrung′kən) /ˈʃrʌŋkən/ *v.* a pp. of SHRINK.

shtick or **shtik** (shtik) /ʃtɪk/ *n.* [*count*] *Slang.* **1.** a part of a show-business act added to get a laugh or to draw attention to oneself. **2.** one's special interest, talent, etc.

shuck (shuk) /ʃʌk/ *n.* [*count*] **1.** a husk or pod, such as the outer covering of corn. —*v.* **2.** [~ + *obj*] to remove the outer covering of: *to shuck corn.* **3.** to remove or discard: [~ + *obj* (+ *off*)]: *to shuck one's clothes (off).* [~ (+ *off*) + *obj*]: *to shuck (off) one's clothes.* —*interj.* **4. shucks,** (used to express mild disgust or regret): *Oh, shucks, I forgot to mail that letter again.*

shud•der (shud′ər) /ˈʃʌdər/ *v.* [*no obj*] **1.** to tremble with a sudden movement, as from horror. —*n.* [*count*] **2.** a trembling, as from horror or cold.

shuf•fle (shuf′əl) /ˈʃʌfəl/ *v.,* **-fled, -fling,** *n.* —*v.* **1.** [*no obj*] to walk without lifting the feet; shamble: *He shuffled around the room.* **2.** [~ + *obj*] to move (one's feet) along the ground or floor without lifting them: *shuffled her feet to the music.* **3.** to rearrange (objects, etc.) by mixing together randomly: [~ + *obj*]: *shuffling papers on his desk.* [*no obj*]: *Whose turn is it to shuffle?* **4. shuffle off,** [*no obj*] to move or go away: *She shuffled off to bed.* —*n.* [*count*] **5.** a scraping or sliding movement, esp. a dragging walk. **6.** an act or instance of shuffling something, as cards, or of changing something, such as an office staff: *An office shuffle meant he was out of a job.* —**shuf′fler,** *n.* [*count*]

shuf•fle•board (shuf′əl bôrd′, -bōrd′) /ˈʃʌfəlˌbɔrd, -ˌbowrd/ *n.* **1.** [*noncount*] a game in which players use long sticks to push disks toward numbered scoring sections marked on a floor or other surface. **2.** [*count*] the marked surface on which this game is played.

shun (shun) /ʃʌn/ *v.* [~ + *obj*], **shunned, shun•ning.** to keep away from; try hard to avoid: *She shunned her family and refused to return to her home village.*

shunt (shunt) /ʃʌnt/ *v.* **1.** [~ + *obj*]to force or turn (something) aside or out of the way: *to shunt the tanks off to the side.* **2.** [*no obj*] to turn to the side: *The railroad cars shunted off to the side.* **3.** [~ + *obj*] to change the direction of the flow of a fluid by means of a shunt. —*n.* [*count*] **4.** the act of shunting; shift. **5.** a railroad switch. **6.** a channel through which a bodily fluid is sent off from its normal path by surgical connection or by insertion of an artificial tube.

shush (shush) /ʃʌʃ/ *interj.* **1.** (used by the speaker as a command to be quiet or silent). —*v.* [~ + *obj*] **2.** to order to be silent; hush.

shut (shut) /ʃʌt/ *v.*, **shut, shut•ting,** *adj.* —*v.* **1.** to (cause to) become closed: [~ + *obj*]: *Shut the door.* [*no obj*]: *The doors shut quickly behind him.* **2.** to close the doors of: [~ *(+ up)* + *obj*]: *to shut (up) a house for the night.* [~ + *obj (+ up)*]: *to shut a house (up) for the winter.* **3.** [~ + *obj*] to close by bringing together the parts of: *Shut your book.* **4.** [~ + *obj*] to confine; enclose: *to shut a bird into a cage.* **5.** [~ + *obj*] to bar; keep out; exclude: *They shut him from their circle.* **6.** to (cause to) end or suspend operations: [~ + *obj*]: *shutting the office for two weeks.* [*no obj*]: *The stores shut at noon.* **7. shut down,** to suspend the operation of (something): [*no obj*]: *The automobile plant shut down last year.* [~ + *down* + *obj*]: *They shut down the automobile plant last year.* [~ + *obj* + *down*]: *They shut the plant down.* **8. shut off, a.** to stop the passage of: [~ + *off* + *obj*]: *He shut off the flow of water.* [~ + *obj* + *off*]: *to shut the electricity off.* **b.** [~ + *obj* + *off*] to isolate; separate: *The storm shut the island off from the mainland.* **9. shut out, a.** [~ + *obj* + *out*] to keep from entering; exclude: *to shut someone out of the club.* **b.** to prevent (an opponent or opposing team) from scoring: [~ + *out* + *obj*]: *The pitcher shut out the last two teams.* [~ + *obj* + *out*]: *She shut them out.* **10. shut up, a.** to imprison; confine: [~ + *obj* + *up*]: *They shut the prisoners up in a tiny room.* [~ + *up* + *obj*]: *to shut up the prisoners in a tiny room.* **b.** to close entirely: [~ + *up* + *obj*]: *They shut up their store for vacation.* [~ + *obj* + *up*]: *to shut the old house up until it was sold.* **c.** [*no obj*] to stop talking; become silent: *After nearly twenty minutes he finally shut up.* **d.** [~ + *obj* + *up*] to stop (someone) from talking; silence (someone): *Will somebody please shut her up?* —*adj.* **11.** closed; fastened up: *a shut door.* —***Idiom.*** **12. shut one's eyes to,** [~ + *obj*] to refuse to accept or acknowledge: *He shut his eyes to all the crime in his old neighborhood.*

shut•down (shut′doun′) /ˈʃʌtˌdawn/ *n.* [*count*] a stopping of working or operating: *another subway shutdown.*

shut•eye (shut′ī′) /ˈʃʌtˌay/ *n.* [*noncount*] sleep: *I finally got some shuteye.*

shut-in (*adj.* shut′in′; *n.* shut′in′) / *adj.* ˈʃʌtˈɪn; *n.* ˈʃʌtˌɪn/ *adj.* **1.** kept in or unable to leave one's home, a hospital, etc., as from illness: *a shut-in, elderly patient.* —*n.* [*count*] **2.** one forced to remain in a house, a hospital, etc., because of illness: *He promised to visit all the many shut-ins.*

shut•out (shut′out′) /ˈʃʌtˌawt/ *n.* **1.** [*count*] an act or instance of shutting out. **2.** [*noncount*] the state of being shut out. **3.** [*count*] **a.** a preventing of the opposite side from scoring, as in baseball. **b.** any game in which one side does not score: *The game was a shutout.*

shut•ter (shut′ər) /ˈʃʌtər/ *n.* [*count*] **1.** a solid, movable cover for a window. **2.** a movable cover, etc., for an opening, such as over the opening of a camera lens that controls the exposure of the film. —*v.* [~ + *obj*] **3.** to close or provide with shutters: *to shutter a window.*

shut•ter•bug (shut′ər bug′) /ˈʃʌtərˌbʌg/ *n.* [*count*] an amateur photographer.

shut•tle (shut′l) /ˈʃʌtl̩/ *n.*, *v.*, **-tled, -tling.** —*n.* [*count*] **1.** a device in a loom for passing the thread from one side to the other. **2.** a public vehicle, such as a train or bus, that travels back and forth at regular times over a route. **3.** SHUTTLECOCK. **4.** a space vehicle designed to be launched from earth by rockets that detach in flight, and that can be landed so as to be used again. —*v.* **5.** to (cause to) move back and forth by or as if by a shuttle: [~ + *obj*]: *to shuttle the troop trains back and forth.* [*no obj*]: *He shuttled between the two countries.*

shut•tle•cock (shut′l kok′) /ˈʃʌtl̩ˌkɒk/ *n.* [*count*] a cone-shaped cork device having parts that resemble feathers, struck back and forth in badminton.

shy[1] (shī) /ʃay/ *adj.*, **shy•er** or **shi•er, shy•est** or **shi•est,** *v.*, **shied, shy•ing.** —*adj.* **1.** bashful; retiring; timid: *a shy smile.* **2.** [*be* + ~ + *of* + *obj*] distrustful; unwilling to do or face something: *is shy of publicity.* **3.** [*be* + ~ + *of* + *obj*] not having enough of something; lacking: *was shy of funds.* —*v.* **4.** [*no obj*] (esp. of a horse) to make a sudden movement back or aside in fear or alarm: *to shy away.* **5. shy away from,** [~ + *away* + *from* + *obj*] to draw back; hesitate to do: *They shied away from that deal because they didn't trust the salesman.* —**shy′ly,** *adv.*: *He smiled shyly at her.* —**shy′ness,** *n.* [*noncount*]

shy[2] (shī) /ʃay/ *v.*, **shied, shy•ing,** *n.*, *pl.* **shies.** —*v.* [~ + *obj*] **1.** to throw with a swift, sudden movement: *shying stones into the water.* —*n.* [*count*] **2.** a quick, sudden throw.

shy•ster (shī′stər) /ˈʃaystər/ *n.* [*count*] **1.** a lawyer who uses dishonest methods. **2.** one who gets along by dishonest practices.

Si•a•mese twins (sī′ə mēz′) /ˌsayəˈmiyz/ *n.* [*plural*] twins who are born joined together.

sib•i•lant (sib′ə lənt) /ˈsɪbələnt/ *adj.* **1.** hissing. **2.** of or relating to a consonant sound in which the speaker sends air through a narrow groove along the center of the tongue, producing a hissing sound. —*n.* [*count*] **3.** a sibilant consonant sound, such as (s), (z), (sh), or (zh).

sib•ling (sib′ling) /ˈsɪblɪŋ/ *n.* [*count*] a brother or sister.

sic or **sick** (sik) /sɪk/ *v.*, **sicked** or **sicced** (sikt), **sick•ing** or **sic•cing. 1.** [~ + *obj*] to attack (used esp. in commanding a dog): *Sic 'em, Bruno!* **2.** [~ + *obj* + *on* + *obj*] to urge or order (a person or animal) to attack: *He sicced his gang on the local store owners.*

sic (sik) /sɪk/ *adv. Latin.* (used within brackets to show that a word or phrase has been written intentionally or has been quoted just as it was in the original, even though it looks odd or mistaken) like this; so: *The poet signed his name as e. e. cummings* [*sic*]. *The sign read "Good English is speaking* [*sic*] *here."*

sick[1] (sik) /sɪk/ *adj.*, **-er, -est,** *n.* —*adj.* **1.** having ill health; not well: *The sickest patients can't be moved from the hospital.* **2.** [*be* + ~] inclined to or ready to vomit: *Help him, he's going to be sick all over the carpet.* **3.** [*be* + ~] deeply feeling some distressing emotion: *was sick at heart.* **4.** [*be* + ~ + *(and tired) of* + *obj*] annoyed with, disgusted by, or tired of: *She's sick and tired of your complaints.* **5.** mentally, morally, or emotionally corrupt: *These criminals are sick.* **6.** cruel; sadistic: *sick jokes.* **7.** perverted; twisted: *You and your sick mind!* **8.** [*before a noun*] of or relating to sickness: *sick benefits.* —*n.* [*plural; used with a plural verb*] **9. the sick,** sick people thought of as a group: *The sick need emotional and physical care.* —**Related Words.** SICK is an adjective, SICKLY and SICKENING are adjectives, SICKNESS is a noun, SICKEN is a verb: *He's very sick and can't come to work. The starving child looks so sickly. The horror movie was sickening. He has a sickness we haven't diagnosed yet. That horror movie sickened me.*

sick[2] (sik) /sɪk/ *v.*, **sicked, sick•ing.** SIC.

-sick, *suffix. -sick* is used to form adjectives with the meanings "sick or ill of or from (the noun of the root)": *car* + *-sick* → *carsick (= sick from traveling in a car); air* + *-sick* → *airsick (= sick from flying in a plane).*

sick′ bay′, *n.* a hospital or place where medical aid is given, esp. aboard a ship: [*count*]: *a big, roomy sick bay.* [*noncount*]: *Escort him to sick bay, doctor.*

sick•bed (sik′bed′) /ˈsɪkˌbɛd/ *n.* [*count*] the bed used by a sick person.

sick•en (sik′ən) /ˈsɪkən/ *v.* to (cause to) become sick: [*no obj*]: *Eventually she sickened and died.* [~ + *obj*]: *to sicken me with your disgusting jokes.*

sick•en•ing (sik′ə ning) /ˈsɪkənɪŋ/ *adj.* **1.** causing a feeling of nausea: *a sickening smell.* **2.** causing a feeling of horror, disgust, or great distress: *the sickening sight of the traffic accident.*

sick•le (sik′əl) /ˈsɪkəl/ *n.* [*count*] a tool for cutting grain, etc., made of a hooklike blade on a short handle.

sick′le cell′ ane′mia, *n.* [*noncount*] a hereditary blood disease in which an accumulation of oxygen-deficient blood cells results in anemia.

sick•ly (sik′lē) /ˈsɪkliy/ *adj.*, **-li•er, -li•est,** *adv.* —*adj.* **1.** not strong; unhealthy; ailing: *The baby was still sickly: pale and underweight.* **2.** arising from ill health: *a sickly* *complexion.* **3.** causing a feeling of nausea: *What is that sickly smell?* **4.** causing a feeling of mild disgust by being overly sentimental: *sickly, gushing compliments.* —*adv.* **5.** in a sick or sickly manner.

sick•ness (sik′nis) /ˈsɪknɪs/ *n.* **1.** [*count*] a particular disease or malady: *Which sickness is he suffering from?* **2.** [*noncount*] the state or an instance of being sick; illness: *She wants to fight sickness and hunger.* **3.** [*noncount*] nausea; queasiness: *some sickness in her stomach from the car ride.*

sick•out (sik′out′) /ˈsɪkˌawt/ *n.* [*count*] an organized absence from work by employees who claim to be sick and unable to work: *A sickout —but not a strike— was organized to protest new working conditions.*

sick•room (sik′ro͞om′, -ro͝om′) /ˈsɪkˌruwm, -ˌrʊm/ *n.* [*count*] a room in which a sick person is kept.

-sid-, *root.* *-sid-* comes from Latin, where it has the meaning "sit; stay; live in a place." This meaning is found in such words as: ASSIDUOUS, DISSIDENT, INSIDIOUS, PRESIDE, PRESIDENT, PRESIDIUM, RESIDE, RESIDUAL, RESIDUE, SUBSIDE, SUBSIDIARY, SUBSIDIZE, SUBSIDY. See -SESS-.

side (sīd) /sayd/ *n., adj., v.,* **sid•ed, sid•ing.** —*n.* [*count*] **1.** one of the surfaces forming the outside of something: *the side of a building.* **2.** either of the two broad surfaces of a thin flat object, such as a door or a sheet of paper. **3.** one of the surfaces of an object that is not the front, back, top, or bottom: *The side of the box had been crushed.* **4.** either the right or left half, part, or area of a thing, esp. of the body: *the right side and the left side.* **5.** region, direction, or position with reference to a central line, space, or point: *the east side of a city.* **6.** a slope, as of a hill: *climbed up the side of Mt. Kilimanjaro.* **7.** a part, piece, or phase making up some whole: *We need to examine all sides of the math problem.* **8.** one of two or more contesting or competing teams or groups: *Our side won the baseball game.* **9.** the position, ideas, or point of view of one person or group opposing another: *Whose side are you on? I am on your side.* See *take sides* below. **10.** line of descent through either parent: *She's related to me on my mother's side.* **11.** the space immediately next to someone: *Stand at my side.* **12.** a side dish, esp. in a restaurant: *a side of French fries.* —*adj.* [*before a noun*] **13.** being at or on one side: *Enter through the side door.* **14.** coming from or directed toward one side; sideways: *a side blow.* **15.** secondary; subordinate; incidental: *For him, salary is just a side issue.* —*v.* **16. side with** or **against,** [~ + *with/against* + *obj*] to support (or oppose), as in an argument: *Her parents always sided with her brother.* —***Idiom.*** **17. on the side,** [*noncount*] in addition to some primary thing: *He ordered some French fries on the side.* **18. side by side,** [*noncount*] **a.** next to one another; together: *The soldiers stood side by side.* **b.** closely associated or related: *working side by side for peace.* **19. take sides,** to support one participant in a dispute rather than another: *He decided not to take sides in the office squabbles.*

side′ arm′, *n.* [*count*] a weapon, as a pistol, carried at the side or in the belt: *No side arms were permitted in the meeting room.*

side•arm (sīd′ärm′) /ˈsaydˌɑrm/ *adv.* **1.** with a swinging motion of the arm moving to the side of the body at or below shoulder level and nearly parallel to the ground: *to pitch sidearm, not overhand.* —*adj.* [*before a noun*] **2.** thrown or performed sidearm.

side•bar (sīd′bär′) /ˈsaydˌbɑr/ *n.* [*count*] a short news feature or story, as in a newspaper, that appears alongside a longer story and adds to it.

side•board (sīd′bôrd′, -bōrd′) /ˈsaydˌbɔrd, -ˌbowrd/ *n.* [*count*] a piece of furniture, as in a dining room, for holding plates, knives, forks, etc.

side•burns (sīd′bûrnz′) /ˈsaydˌbɜrnz/ *n.* [*plural*] the hair on the side of a man's face in front of each ear.

side•car (sīd′kär′) /ˈsaydˌkɑr/ *n.* [*count*] **1.** a one-passenger car attached to the side of a motorcycle. **2.** a cocktail of brandy, orange liqueur, and lemon juice.

side′ dish′, *n.* [*count*] food that accompanies the main course, served in a separate dish.

side′ effect′, *n.* [*count*] an often harmful effect, as of a drug, secondary to the intended effect: *The drug will stop the growth of the cancerous cells but the side effects are loss of hair and difficulty in eating.*

side•kick (sīd′kik′) /ˈsaydˌkɪk/ *n.* [*count*] **1.** a close friend. **2.** an assistant.

side•light (sīd′līt′) /ˈsaydˌlayt/ *n.* [*count*] **1.** an item of extra or secondary information. **2.** a red light on the port side or a green light on the starboard carried by a vessel under way at night.

side•line (sīd′līn′) /ˈsaydˌlayn/ *n., v.,* **-lined, -lin•ing.** —*n.* [*count*] **1.** an activity done in addition to one's regular job. **2. a.** either of the two lines that make the side boundaries of an athletic field or court. **b. sidelines,** [*plural; the* + ~*; usually: on/from* + *the* + ~] the place or circumstance in which one does not participate but simply observes: *The former president could only watch from the sidelines while the new president took over the government.* —*v.* [~ + *obj*] **3.** to remove from action: *The pitcher was sidelined with an arm injury.* See -LIN-.

side•long (sīd′lông′, -long′) /ˈsaydˌlɔŋ, -ˌlɒŋ/ *adj.* [*before a noun*] **1.** directed to one side: *a sidelong glance.* —*adv.* **2.** toward the side: *to look at someone sidelong.*

side′ ord′er, *n.* [*count*] an order of food at a restaurant separate from or added to a main course; side dish.

si•de•re•al (sī dēr′ē əl) /sayˈdɪəriyəl/ *adj.* determined by or from the stars; of or relating to the stars.

side•sad•dle (sīd′sad′l) /ˈsaydˌsædl̩/ *n.* [*count*] **1.** a saddle for women on which the rider sits facing forward but has both legs on the same side of the horse. —*adv.* **2.** seated on a sidesaddle: *to ride sidesaddle.*

side•show (sīd′shō′) /ˈsaydˌʃow/ *n.* [*count*] **1.** a minor show in connection with a principal one, as at a circus. **2.** any event or activity secondary to another: *The celebrities at the banquet were the main event; the banquet was the sideshow.*

side•split•ting (sīd′split′ing) /ˈsaydˌsplɪtɪŋ/ *adj.* **1.** extremely funny: *sidesplitting comedy.* **2.** resulting from something extremely funny: *sidesplitting laughter.*

side•step (sīd′step′) /ˈsaydˌstɛp/ *v.,* **-stepped, -step•ping. 1.** to step to one side and avoid (something aimed at oneself): [*no obj*]: *As the champ swung, the challenger sidestepped neatly away.* [~ + *obj*]: *The runner sidestepped the next tackler.* **2.** to try to escape from or avoid (a decision or problem): [~ + *obj*]: *to sidestep every problem.* [*no obj*]: *neatly sidestepping during the press conference.*

side•stroke (sīd′strōk′) /ˈsaydˌstrowk/ *n., v.,* **-stroked, -strok•ing.** —*n.* [*count*] **1.** a swimming stroke in which the body is turned sideways in the water. —*v.* [*no obj*] **2.** to swim the sidestroke.

side•swipe (sīd′swīp′) /ˈsaydˌswayp/ *v.,* **-swiped, -swip•ing,** *n.* —*v.* [~ + *obj*] **1.** to strike with a blow from or at the side, as in passing: *The car sideswiped ours.* —*n.* [*count*] **2.** a blow struck from or to the side in passing.

side•track (sīd′trak′) /ˈsaydˌtræk/ *v.* [~ + *obj*] **1.** to move (a train or the like) from a main track to a secondary track. **2.** to move or distract from the main subject or course: *We can't afford to get sidetracked anymore.* —*n.* [*count*] **3.** a railroad siding.

side•walk (sīd′wôk′) /ˈsaydˌwɔk/ *n.* [*count*] a usually paved walk at the side of a roadway. See illustration at STREET.

side•ways (sīd′wāz′) /ˈsaydˌweyz/ *adv.* **1.** facing to the side. **2.** toward or from one side. —*adj.* **3.** moving, facing, or directed toward one side: *a quick, sideways glance.*

sid•ing (sī′ding) /ˈsaydɪŋ/ *n.* **1.** [*count*] a short railroad track that opens onto a main track at one or both ends. **2.** [*noncount*] a kind of material put on the outside of a building for extra protection: *selling aluminum siding.*

si•dle (sīd′l) /ˈsaydl̩/ *v.,* **-dled, -dling,** *n.* —*v.* [*no obj*] **1.** to move sideways. **2.** to move along or away or furtively: *sidled off to the corner hoping no one would notice him.* —*n.* [*count*] **3.** a sidling movement.

siege (sēj) /siydʒ/ *n.* [*count*] **1.** the act or process of surrounding and attacking a fortified place in such a way as to force the surrender of the defenders, such as by blocking the delivery of supplies. **2.** any long or intensive effort to overcome resistance: *a siege by magazine publishers to sell us subscriptions.* **3.** a series of illnesses or troubles: *a siege of head colds.* —***Idiom.*** **4. lay siege to,** [~ + *obj*] to surround and attack (a fortified place or the like). **5. under siege,** [*noncount*] in the state of being attacked by outside forces: *The city has been under siege for a month.* See -SID-.

si•er•ra (sē er′ə) /siyˈɛrə/ *n.* [*count*], *pl.* **-ras.** a chain of mountains whose peaks look like the teeth of a saw.

si•es•ta (sē es′tə) /siyˈɛstə/ *n.* [*count*], *pl.* **-tas.** a midday nap.

sieve (siv) /sɪv/ *n., v.,* **sieved, siev•ing.** —*n.* [*count*] **1.** a utensil with a meshed or perforated surface used for separating larger pieces from smaller, fine pieces of loose matter, or for straining liquids to remove solid pieces. —*v.* [~ + *obj*] **2.** to put or force through a sieve; sift: *to sieve the flour.*

sift (sift) /sɪft/ *v.* [~ + *obj*] **1.** to separate and keep the larger or thicker parts or pieces of (flour, etc.) with a sieve: *to sift the flour.* **2.** to scatter with a sieve: *to sift sugar onto a cake.* **3.** [~ *(+ through)* + *obj*] to examine closely, as by separating and looking at each part carefully: *The detectives are sifting (through) the evidence.*

sigh (sī) /say/ *v.* **1.** [*no obj*] to let out one's breath with some noise, as from sorrow or relief: *He sighed in resignation.* **2.** [~ + *obj*] to say or express with such a noise: *sighed a sigh of relief.* [*used with quotations*]: *"Yes, I suppose so," she sighed, getting up from her bed.* **3.** [*no obj*] to make a sound like a sigh: *with the wind sighing in the background.* **—*n.*** [*count*] **4.** the act or sound of sighing: *let out a soft sigh of contentment.*

sight (sīt) /sayt/ *n.* **1.** [*noncount*] the power or ability of seeing; vision: *suffering from a gradual loss of sight.* **2.** [*count*] the act or fact of seeing; a view or glimpse: *a gruesome sight.* **3.** [*noncount*] one's range of vision: *Don't let them out of your sight.* **4.** [*count*] something seen or worth seeing; a spectacle: *to see all the sights of London.* **5.** [*count; usually singular; a* + ~] a person or thing unusual, shocking, or distressing to see: *He was quite a sight after the brawl.* **6.** [*count; singular; a* + ~] *Chiefly Dialect.* a great deal: *It's a sight better to work than to starve.* **7.** [*count; often: plural*] a viewing device, as on a firearm, for aiding the eye in aiming: *The assassin had the target lined up in his sights.* **—*v.*** **8.** [~ + *obj*] to glimpse, notice, or observe: *to sight a ship to the north.* **9.** to direct or aim (a firearm or the like) by a sight or sights: [*no obj*]: *to sight and fire with one quick movement.* [~ + *obj*]: *to sight the gun.* **—*Idiom.*** **10. at first sight,** [*noncount*] after only one brief glimpse: *When they met it was love at first sight.* **11. at sight,** [*noncount*] **a.** immediately upon seeing: *to translate the document at sight.* **b.** on presentation: *a check payable at sight.* **12. by a long sight,** [*noncount; usually with a negative word or phrase*] to a great or extreme degree: *You haven't finished this book by a long sight.* **13. catch sight of,** [~ + *obj*] to get a quick view: *They caught sight of him racing away in the crowd.* **14. know by sight,** [*know* + *obj* + *by* + ~] to know or recognize (a person or thing seen previously): *I know him by sight, but I've never spoken to him.* **15. lose sight of,** [~ + *obj*] to fail to keep in mind: *Let's not lose sight of our main goal, even though we may disagree on how to get there.* **16. on sight,** [*noncount*] immediately upon seeing: *The police are ordered to shoot him on sight.* **17. out of sight,** [*noncount*] **a.** beyond one's range of vision: *She drove away and slowly faded out of sight.* **b.** *Informal.* too much; exceedingly high: *The price is out of sight.* **c.** *Slang.* (often used as an interjection) fantastic; marvelous: *The party was out of sight.* **18. sight for sore eyes,** [*noncount*] someone or something whose appearance is a reason for gladness: *The airplane bringing the food was a sight for sore eyes to the drought victims.* **19. sight unseen,** without previous examination: *We bought it sight unseen.*

sight•ed (sī′tid) /ˈsaytɪd/ *adj.* **1.** having functional vision; not blind. **2.** [*used after an adjective*] having a type of eyesight or ability to understand: *clear-sighted.*

sight•less (sīt′lis) /ˈsaytlɪs/ *adj.* unable to see; blind.

sight′-read′ (rēd) /riyd/ *v.*, **-read** (red), **-read•ing.** to read, play, or sing without previous practice, rehearsal, or study of the material to be treated: [~ + *obj*]: *to sight-read music.* [*no obj*]: *to be able to sight-read for the music test.* **—sight′-read′er,** *n.* [*count*]

sight•see•ing (sīt′sē′ing) /ˈsaytˌsiyɪŋ/ *n.* [*noncount*] **1.** the act of visiting places and things of interest: *We will go sightseeing tomorrow.* **—*adj.*** [*before a noun*] **2.** seeing, showing, or used for visiting sights: *a sightseeing bus.* **—sight′se′er,** *n.* [*count*]

sign (sīn) /sayn/ *n.* [*count*] **1.** an indication; something that signifies something else: *Bowing is a sign of respect.* **2.** a mark or symbol used as an abbreviation for the word or words it represents, as in music or mathematics, etc.: *a dollar sign.* **3.** a gesture used to express or convey information, an idea, etc.: *He raised his eyebrows, which was his sign that he didn't believe what I was saying.* **4.** a board, placard, etc., with writing or a drawing on it that bears a warning, advertisement, or other information for public view: *a traffic sign.* **5.** something left behind that indicates the presence of something else; a trace: *There wasn't a sign of the crooks.* **6.** a signal or hint that something will happen; an omen; portent: *The early frost was a sign of a long, harsh winter ahead.* **7.** an indication of a disease: *Extra saliva at the mouth, odd behavior, and inability to drink are all signs of rabies.* **8.** any gesture that is a unit of meaning in sign language: *She showed me the signs for "eat," "love," and "teacher."* **9.** one of the twelve signs of the zodiac: *His sign is Capricorn; what's your sign?* **—*v.*** **10.** to write (one's signature) on (something): [~ + *obj*]: *to sign a letter.* [*no obj*]: *Where should I sign?* **11.** [~ + *obj*] to hire by written agreement: *to sign a basketball player.* **12.** [*no obj*] to write one's signature to indicate acceptance, as of a contract for employment: *refused to sign with the Yankees.* **13. a.** to communicate by means of a sign; signal: [~ + *obj*]: *He signed his obvious displeasure by frowning.* [~ + *that clause*]: *He signed to her that they should leave.* **b.** [*no obj*] to make signals; communicate something by signals: *She signed to the waiter for the check.* **14.** to convey or signal (a message) in a sign language: [*no obj*]: *She signed frantically to him but he wasn't looking at her.* [~ + *obj*]: *She signed the words for "water" and "glass" to ask for a glass of water.* **15. sign away** or **over,** to dispose of by putting one's signature on a document: [~ + *over* + *obj*]: *According to the agreement he has signed over all the property.* [~ + *obj* + *over*]: *She signed the property over to her daughter.* **16. sign for,** [~ + *for* + *obj*] to sign one's name or signature to acknowledge that one has received (a package, letter, etc.): *signed for the packages.* **17. sign in** (or **out**), [*no obj*] to record one's arrival (or departure) by signing a register: *He signed in when he got to work.* **18. sign off,** [*no obj*] **a.** to stop broadcasting, esp. at the end of the day: *The station signed off at three in the morning.* **b.** to indicate one's approval openly if not formally: *The boss signed off on my plan.* **19. sign on, a.** [~ + *on* + *obj*] to hire: *He signed on several good players.* **b.** to agree to do something: [*no obj*]: *He signed on as a pitcher for the team.* [~ + *on* + *to* + *verb*]: *I signed on to help.* **c.** [*no obj*] to start a session with computer systems: *He signed on to the system by typing his computer I.D. and his password.* **20. sign up, a.** [*no obj*] to join an organization or group: *to sign up for the navy.* **b.** to hire: [~ + *obj* + *up*]: *Sign him up if he can pitch tomorrow.* [~ + *up* + *obj*]: *to sign up some good players.* **—sign′er,** *n.* [*count*] See -SIGN-.

-sign-, *root.* *-sign-* comes from Latin, where it has the meaning "sign; have meaning." This meaning is found in such words as: ASSIGN, ASSIGNATION, CONSIGN, COSIGN, DESIGN, DESIGNATE, ENSIGN, INSIGNIA, INSIGNIFICANT, RESIGN, SIGN, SIGNAL, SIGNATURE, SIGNET, SIGNIFICANT, SIGNIFY, UNDERSIGNED.

sig•nal (sig′nl) /ˈsɪgnl/ *n., adj., v.,* **-naled, -nal•ing** or (*esp. Brit.*) **-nalled, -nal•ling.** **—*n.*** [*count*] **1.** anything that serves to indicate, warn, direct, etc., such as a light, a gesture, or an act: *a traffic signal.* **2.** an act or event that causes an action: *The execution was a signal for revolt.* **3.** an electrical quantity or effect, as current or waves, that can be varied to convey information: *a TV signal.* **—*adj.*** [*before a noun*] **4.** serving as a signal: *a signal light.* **5.** unusual; notable; outstanding: *a signal accomplishment.* **—*v.*** **6.** to make a signal to (someone or something): [*no obj*]: *The police officer stood there signaling.* [~ + *obj*]: *The captain said he wanted to signal his ship.* [~ + *obj* + *to* + *verb*]: *Signal the tugboat to pull up a little closer.* [~ + *that clause*]: *to signal that he wants to come home.* See -SIGN-.

sig•nal•ly (sig′nl ē) /ˈsɪgnḷiy/ *adv.* conspicuously; notably: *signally qualified for the job.*

sig•na•to•ry (sig′nə tôr′ē, -tōr′ē) /ˈsɪgnəˌtɔriy, -ˌtowriy/ *adj., n., pl.* **-ries.** **—*adj.*** **1.** joined in signing a document: *the signatory powers to a treaty.* **—*n.*** [*count*] **2.** the signer, or one of the signers, of a document: *The U.S. delegates were among the signatories.* See -SIGN-.

sig•na•ture (sig′nə chər) /ˈsɪgnətʃər/ *n.* [*count*] **1.** a person's name signed on a letter, check, or other document. **2.** *Music.* a sign or set of signs at the beginning of a staff to indicate the key or the time of a piece. **3.** a song, musical arrangement, etc., used as a theme for a radio or television program. **—*adj.*** **4.** serving to identify or distinguish a person, group, etc.: *began to play his signature tune and the crowd applauded.* See -SIGN-.

sign•board (sīn′bôrd′, -bōrd′) /ˈsaynˌbɔrd, -ˌbowrd/ *n.* [*count*] a board bearing a sign, as an advertisement.

sig•net (sig′nit) /ˈsɪgnɪt/ *n.* [*count*] a small official seal for legal documents, contracts, etc. See -SIGN-.

sig•nif•i•cance (sig nif′i kəns) /sɪgˈnɪfɪkəns/ *n.* [*noncount*] **1.** importance; consequence: *an election of great significance to the country.* **2.** meaning. See -SIGN-.

sig•nif•i•cant (sig nif′i kənt) /sɪgˈnɪfɪkənt/ *adj.* **1.** important; of consequence: *a significant event in world history.* **2.** having a special, secret, or disguised meaning: *She gave him a significant wink.* **—sig•nif′i•cant•ly,** *adv.* See -SIGN-.

signif′icant oth′er, *n.* [*count*] **1.** a person, such as a parent, who has great influence on one's behavior. **2.** a spouse or a lover with whom one lives: *a husband, wife, or significant other.*

sig•ni•fy (sig′nə fī′) /ˈsɪgnəˌfaɪ/ *v.* [~ + *obj*], **-fied, -fy•ing. 1.** to make known: *All those in favor, please signify your agreement by saying "Aye."* **2.** to be a sign of; have the meaning of: *A sign showing a cigarette inside a red circle with a red line through it signifies "No smoking."* —**sig•ni•fi•ca•tion** (sig′nə fi kā′shən) /ˌsɪgnəfɪˈkeɪʃən/ *n.* [*noncount*] See -SIGN-.

sign′ lan′guage, *n.* [*count*] any of several systems of communication, esp. employing manual gestures, as used among deaf people.

sign•post (sīn′pōst′) /ˈsaɪnˌpowst/ *n.* [*count*] **1.** a post with a sign that gives information. **2.** any immediately clear indication, etc.

si•lage (sī′lij) /ˈsaɪlɪdʒ/ *n.* [*noncount*] grass or other food stored in a silo for cattle.

si•lence (sī′ləns) /ˈsaɪləns/ *n., v.,* **-lenced, -lenc•ing,** *interj.* —*n.* [*noncount*] **1.** absence of sound or noise; stillness: *the silence of deep space.* **2.** the state or fact of being silent: *He received the news with silence.* **3.** absence of mention or comment, as for keeping something secret: *governmental silence about the scandal.* —*v.* [~ + *obj*] **4.** to put to silence; still: *The teacher could silence the class with just one stern look.* **5.** to put (doubts, etc.) to rest; quiet: *Her performance silenced all doubts about her talent.* —*interj.* **6.** (used as a command) to be silent: *"Silence!" she snapped.*

si•lenc•er (sī′lən sər) /ˈsaɪlənsər/ *n.* [*count*] **1.** a device for deadening the noise that a gun makes when it is discharged. **2.** *Chiefly Brit.* the muffler on an engine.

si•lent (sī′lənt) /ˈsaɪlənt/ *adj.* **1.** of or relating to silence: *the silent desert.* **2.** not speaking; not wishing to speak: *silent observers.* **3.** speechless; mute: *silent from birth.* **4.** done in the absence of speech or sound: *silent prayers.* **5.** unspoken; done without saying because it is understood: *a silent assent.* **6.** omitting mention of something, as in a narrative: *The records are silent about his crime.* **7.** (of a letter) not pronounced, as the *b* in *doubt.* **8.** (of a film) not having a soundtrack: *the old silent movies.* —*n.* [*count*] **9.** Usually, **silents.** [*plural; the* + ~] silent films. —**si′lent•ly,** *adv.*: *She sat silently in the corner.*

sil•hou•ette (sil′o͞o et′) /ˌsɪluwˈɛt/ *n., v.,* **-et•ted, -et•ting.** —*n.* [*count*] **1.** a picture of the outline of an object, filled in with black. **2.** the outline of something. —*v.* [~ + *obj*] **3.** to show in or as if in a silhouette. —***Idiom.* 4. in silhouette,** [*noncount*] represented, drawn, or appearing in or as an outline.

sil•i•ca (sil′i kə) /ˈsɪlɪkə/ *n.* [*noncount*] a form of silicon that occurs esp. as quartz sand, flint, and agate. —**si•li•ceous, si•li•cious** (sə lish′əs) /səˈlɪʃəs/ *adj.*

sil•i•con (sil′i kən, -kon′) /ˈsɪlɪkən, -ˌkɒn/ *n.* [*noncount*] a nonmetallic element, occurring in minerals and rocks and making up more than one fourth of the earth's crust: used in steelmaking, computer chips, etc.

sil•i•cone (sil′i kōn′) /ˈsɪlɪˌkown/ *n.* [*noncount*] an artificial polymer made from silicon and oxygen and used in making water-repellent substances such as adhesives, lubricants, and oils.

sil•i•co•sis (sil′i kō′sis) /ˌsɪlɪˈkowsɪs/ *n.* [*noncount*] a disease of the lungs caused by the inhaling of particles of silica.

silk (silk) /sɪlk/ *n.* [*noncount*] **1.** the fiber from the cocoon of the silkworm. **2.** thread or cloth made from this fiber. **3.** any fiber resembling silk, such as one produced by spiders. —*adj.* **4.** of or relating to silk.

silk•en (sil′kən) /ˈsɪlkən/ *adj.* **1.** made of silk. **2.** like silk in smoothness, softness, or delicateness.

silk•worm (silk′wûrm′) /ˈsɪlkˌwɜrm/ *n.* [*count*] an insect, a kind of moth caterpillar, that spins a silken cocoon: *The cocoons of some silkworms are the source of silk.*

silk•y (sil′kē) /ˈsɪlkiy/ *adj.,* **-i•er, -i•est.** of or like silk; smooth, soft, or delicate.

sill (sil) /sɪl/ *n.* [*count*] a flat, horizontal piece like a ledge beneath a window, door, or other opening.

sil•ly (sil′ē) /ˈsɪliy/ *adj.,* **-li•er, -li•est,** *n., pl.* **-lies.** —*adj.* **1.** lacking good sense; foolish: *called him a silly young fool.* **2.** absurd; ridiculous; nonsensical: *filled with silly ideas.* **3.** stunned; dazed: *He knocked me silly.* —*n.* [*count*] **4.** *Informal.* a silly or foolish person. —**sil′li•ness,** *n.* [*noncount*]

si•lo (sī′lō) /ˈsaylow/ *n.* [*count*] *pl.* **-los. 1.** a structure, usually in the shape of a tall cylinder, in which food for animals is kept. See illustration at LANDSCAPE. **2.** a pit or underground space for storing grain, etc.

silt (silt) /sɪlt/ *n.* [*noncount*] **1.** earth carried by moving water and deposited as a sediment. —*v.* **2. silt up,** to (cause to) become filled or choked up with silt: [*no obj*]: *The lake silted up.* [~ + *up* + *obj*]: *The mud silted up the lake.* —**silt′y,** *adj.*

sil•ver (sil′vər) /ˈsɪlvər/ *n.* **1.** [*noncount*] a white metallic element, used for making mirrors, coins, photographic chemicals, and conductors. **2.** [*noncount; used with a singular verb*] coins made of this metal; money: *a handful of silver.* **3.** [*noncount*] this metal used or thought of as a standard for the value of currency. **4.** [*noncount; used with a singular verb*] table articles, such as knives, forks, and spoons, made of or plated with silver. **5.** [*noncount*] a bright, grayish white or whitish gray color. **6.** [*count*] a silver medal: *He brought home two silvers from the Olympics.* —*adj.* **7.** [*before a noun*] made of or plated with silver. **8.** of or relating to silver. **9.** producing or yielding silver: *a silver mine.* **10.** of the color silver; silvery: *silver hair.* **11.** elegant and persuasive: *a silver tongue (= the ability to speak gracefully and convincingly).* **12.** [*before a noun*] indicating the twenty-fifth event of a series, such as a wedding anniversary.

sil•ver•fish (sil′vər fish′) /ˈsɪlvərˌfɪʃ/ *n.* [*count*], *pl.* (*esp. when thought of as a group*) **-fish,** (*esp. for kinds or species*) **-fish•es. 1.** any of various silvery fishes, such as the tarpon. **2.** a wingless, silvery-gray insect that feeds on starch and damages books, wallpaper, etc.

sil′ver lin′ing, *n.* [*count*] a possibility or element of hope or comfort in an unfortunate or gloomy situation.

sil•ver•smith (sil′vər smith′) /ˈsɪlvərˌsmɪθ/ *n.* [*count*] one who makes and repairs articles of silver.

sil′ver-tongued′, *adj.* persuasive; able to speak well and convince others.

sil•ver•ware (sil′vər wâr′) /ˈsɪlvərˌwɛər/ *n.* [*noncount; used with a singular verb*] articles, esp. eating and serving utensils, made of silver, silver-plated metals, stainless steel, etc.

sil•ver•y (sil′və rē) /ˈsɪlvəriy/ *adj.* **1.** resembling silver; of a shiny grayish white color. **2.** having a clear, ringing sound: *the silvery peal of bells.* **3.** containing or covered with silver.

sim•i•an (sim′ē ən) /ˈsɪmiyən/ *adj.* **1.** of or relating to an ape or monkey. —*n.* [*count*] **2.** an ape or monkey.

-simil-, *root.* -*simil*- comes from Latin, where it has the meaning "alike, similar." This meaning is found in such words as: ASSIMILATE, ASSIMILATION, DISSIMILAR, DISSIMULATE, FACSIMILE, SIMILAR, SIMILE, SIMULATE, SIMULCAST, SIMULTANEOUS, VERISIMILITUDE.

sim•i•lar (sim′ə lər) /ˈsɪmələr/ *adj.* having a likeness or resemblance; like or alike: *two similar houses.* [*be* + ~ (+ *to*)]: *The houses are similar to each other.* —**sim′i•lar′i•ty,** *n., pl.* **-ties.** [*noncount*]: *points of similarity between the two paintings.* [*count*]: *There are many similarities between the two paintings.* —**sim•i•lar•ly** (sim′ə-lar′i tē) /ˌsɪməˈlærɪtiy/ *adv.* See -SIMIL-.

sim•i•le (sim′ə lē) /ˈsɪməliy/ *n.* **1.** [*noncount*] a figure of speech in which two distinct things are compared by using "like" or "as," such as in "She is like a rose." **2.** [*count*] an example of this: *How many similes can you find in the first paragraph?* See -SIMIL-.

sim•mer (sim′ər) /ˈsɪmər/ *v.* **1.** to cook just below the boiling point: [*no obj*]: *The sauce is simmering.* [~ + *obj*]: *Simmer the sauce.* **2.** [*no obj*] to be in a state in which development, excitement, anger, etc., is present but held back: *He was simmering with anger.* **3. simmer down,** [*no obj*] to become calm or quiet: *"Simmer down," I warned him.* —*n.* [*count; usually singular*] **4.** the state or process of simmering: *Cook to a slow simmer for fifteen minutes.*

si•mon•ize (sī′mə nīz′) /ˈsaɪməˌnaɪz/ *v.* [~ + *obj*], **-ized, -iz•ing.** to shine or polish to a strong brightness, esp. with wax.

sim•pa•ti•co (sim pä′ti kō′, -pat′i-) /sɪmˈpɑtɪˌkow, -ˈpætɪ-/ *adj.* agreeing in the mind or in the spirit; like-minded; compatible. See -PAT-.

sim•per (sim′pər) /ˈsɪmpər/ *v.* [*no obj*] **1.** to smile in a silly, false, or self-conscious way: *She simpered at the boss as he made another corny joke.* —*n.* [*count*] **2.** a silly, false, self-conscious smile.

sim•ple (sim′pəl) /ˈsɪmpəl/ *adj.,* **-pler, -plest,** *n.* —*adj.* **1.** easy to understand or deal with; not hard to do: *a simple problem.* [*It* + *be* + ~ + *to* + *verb*]: *It was simple to solve her problems.* **2.** not elaborate or complicated; plain: *a simple design.* **3.** not ornate or luxurious; unadorned: *a simple dress.* **4.** unassuming; modest; sincere: *He's a simple man.* **5.** [*before a noun*] occurring or considered alone; mere; bare: *the simple truth.* **6.** [*before a *noun*] common or ordinary: *a simple soldier.* **7.** not grand or sophisticated: *simple tastes.* **8.** humble or lowly: *simple folk.* **9.** lacking mental sharpness: *a simple, dull-witted peasant.* **10.** mentally deficient. **11.** *Chemistry.* made of only one substance or element: *a simple substance.* **12.** *Botany.* not divided into parts: *a simple leaf.* **13.** (of a sentence) having only one subject and verb (as opposed to compound): *The sentences* John likes Mary *and* John and Bill like Mary *are simple sentences.* —**sim′ple•ness,** *n.* [*noncount*] See -PLIC-.

sim•ple•mind•ed or **sim•ple-mind•ed** (sim′pəl mī′did) /ˈsɪmˈpəl maydɪd/ *adj.* **1.** lacking in mental sharpness. **2.** lacking in complex thought: *a simple-minded solution to a complicated problem.* **3.** mentally weak; feeble-minded.

sim•ple•ton (sim′pəl tən) /ˈsɪmpəltən/ *n.* [*count*] an ignorant, foolish, or silly person.

sim•plic•i•ty (sim plis′i tē) /sɪmˈplɪsɪtiy/ *n., pl.* **-ties. 1.** [*noncount*] the state or quality of being simple. **2.** [*count*] an instance or example of this. **3.** [*noncount*] the absence of luxury or ornament; plainness. See -PLIC-.

sim•pli•fy (sim′plə fī′) /ˈsɪmpləˌfay/ *v.* [~ + *obj*], **-fied, -fy•ing.** to make simple or simpler: *to simplify the problem.* —**sim•pli•fi•ca•tion** (sim′plə fi kā′shən) /ˌsɪmpləfɪˈkeyʃən/ *n.* [*noncount*]: *too much simplification in dealing with complex issues.* [*count*]: *Your essay is a simplification of a complex topic.*

sim•plis•tic (sim plis′tik) /sɪmˈplɪstɪk/ *adj.* being too simple, esp. in ignoring difficulties; oversimplified: *His proposals for reducing the deficit are simplistic.* See -PLIC-.

sim•ply (sim′plē) /ˈsɪmpliy/ *adv.* **1.** in a simple manner; clearly: *He spoke simply and directly.* **2.** plainly; unaffectedly: *In spite of her great wealth they live simply in a modest house.* **3.** merely; only: *It is simply a cold.* **4.** absolutely; really: *Her desserts are simply irresistible.* See -PLIC-.

sim•u•late (sim′yə lāt′) /ˈsɪmyəˌleyt/ *v.* [~ + *obj*], **-lat•ed, -lat•ing. 1.** to create a model of: *During the drill we will simulate emergency conditions.* **2.** to pretend to do or have; feign: *to simulate illness.* **3.** to assume or have the appearance or characteristics of: *simulated leather.* See -SIMIL-.

sim•u•la•tion (sim′yə lā′shən) /ˌsɪmyəˈleyʃən/ *n.* **1.** [*noncount*] imitation: *simulation of real events.* **2.** [*count*] a model of a problem in an attempt to work out solutions, etc.: *computer simulations of planning a model city.* See -SIMIL-.

sim•u•la•tor (sim′yə lā′tər) /ˈsɪmyəˌleytər/ *n.* [*count*] a machine or device that models actual events and creates conditions similar to real conditions, used for training and practice: *A flight simulator re-created the conditions that pilots would encounter in such aircraft.* See -SIMIL-.

si•mul•cast (sī′məl kast′, sim′əl-) /ˈsayməlˌkæst, ˈsɪməl-/ *n., v.,* **-cast, -cast•ed, -cast•ing.** —*n.* [*count*] **1.** a program broadcast simultaneously on radio and television, or on more than one station, or in several languages, etc. —*v.* **2.** to broadcast in this manner: [~ + *obj*]: *to simulcast a concert.* [*no obj*]: *advancing technology in simulcasting.* See -SIMIL-.

si•mul•ta•ne•ous (sī′məl tā′nē əs, sim′əl-) /ˌsayməlˈteyniyəs, ˌsɪməl-/ *adj.* existing, occurring, or operating at the same time: *simultaneous translation of all speeches at the United Nations.* —**si′mul•ta′ne•ous•ly,** *adv.*: *How can you have such contradictory opinions simultaneously?* See -SIMIL-.

sin (sin) /sɪn/ *n., v.,* **sinned, sin•ning.** —*n.* **1.** [*noncount*] disobedience of divine law: *a life full of sin.* **2.** [*count*] any act regarded as such disobedience, esp. a deliberate one: *He asked for forgiveness of his sins.* **3.** [*count*] any serious fault or offense: *He had committed sins against humanity.* —*v.* [*no obj*] **4.** to commit a sinful act: *He had sinned and so he begged God for forgiveness.* —***Idiom.*** **5. live in sin,** [*no obj*] to live together as husband and wife without being married. —**sin′ner,** *n.* [*count*] —**Syn.** See CRIME.

since (sins) /sɪns/ *adv.* **1.** from then till now (often preceded by *ever*): *Those elected in 1990 have been on the committee ever since.* **2.** between a particular past time and the present; subsequently: *She at first refused, but has since consented.* **3.** ago; before now: *She has long since left him; didn't you know?* —*prep.* **4.** starting continuously from or counting from: *It has been raining since noon.* **5.** between a past event and the present: *There have been many changes since the war.* —*conj.* **6.** in the period following the time when: *He has written once since he left.* **7.** continuously from or counting from the time when: *I've been busy since I arrived.* **8.** because; inasmuch as: *Since you've been here awhile, you might as well stay.* —**Usage.** The word SINCE very often appears with a verb in the present perfect tense, that is, with HAS or HAVE plus the *-ed/-en* form of the main verb.

sin•cere (sin sēr′) /sɪnˈsɪər/ *adj.,* **-cer•er, -cer•est. 1.** not false or pretended: *a sincere apology.* **2.** genuine; real: *a sincere effort to improve.* —**sin•cere′ly,** *adv.* —**sin•cer•i•ty** (sin ser′i tē) /sɪnˈsɛrɪtiy/ *n.* [*noncount*]: *dealing with his students with sincerity.*

si•ne•cure (sī′ni kyŏŏr′, sin′i-) /ˈsaynɪˌkyʊr, ˈsɪnɪ-/ *n.* [*count*] a position requiring no work, esp. one that brings easy profit. See -CURA-.

si•ne qua non (sin′ā kwä nōn′, non′, kwā) /ˈsɪnˈey kwɑ nown, ˈnɒn, kwey/ *n.* [*count; usually singular*] something that cannot be left out; a necessity: *The actress's presence was the sine qua non of any party.*

sin•ew (sin′yōō) /ˈsɪnyuw/ *n.* **1.** [*count*] a tendon. **2.** [*noncount*] strength; power; resilience: *great moral sinew.*

sin•ew•y (sin′yōō ē) /ˈsɪnyuwiy/ *adj.* **1.** (of meat) tough; hard to chew. **2.** strong and hard from exercise or hard work: *sinewy hands.* **3.** strong and tough: *a sinewy rope.*

sin•ful (sin′fəl) /ˈsɪnfəl/ *adj.* **1.** showing, guilty of, or full of sin: *a sinful life.* **2.** very bad; seriously wrong; shameful: *a sinful waste of paper.* —**sin′ful•ly,** *adv.*

sing (sing) /sɪŋ/ *v.,* **sang** (sang) /sæŋ/ or, often, **sung** (sung) /sʌŋ/; **sung; sing•ing;** *n.* —*v.* **1.** [*no obj*] to make words or sounds one after the other, with musical changes in the pitch or tone of the voice: *All the members of my family can sing.* **2.** to perform (songs or music) with the voice: [*no obj*]: *Once she sang on national TV.* [~ + *obj*]: *They sang some old tunes around the campfire.* **3.** [~ + *obj*] to bring, send, etc., into a certain condition with or by such musical sound: *to sing a baby to sleep.* **4.** (of an animal) to produce a signal with the voice: [*no obj*]: *Some birds sing to attract a mate.* [~ + *obj*]: *Birds sing very specific songs.* **5.** [~ + *of* + *obj*] to tell about someone or something in verse or song, esp. with enthusiasm or admiration: *to sing of the times of King Arthur.* **6.** [~ + *obj*] to proclaim with enthusiasm: *to sing someone's praises (= to praise someone).* **7.** [*no obj*] to make a whistling or whizzing sound: *The bullet sang past his ear.* **8.** [*no obj*] *Slang.* to confess or act as an informer by telling the authorities about some crime or criminals. —*n.* [*count*] **9.** a meeting of people for singing: *a community sing.* —**sing′a•ble,** *adj.* —**sing′er,** *n.* [*count*]

sing., an abbreviation of: singular.

sing′-along′, *n.* SONGFEST.

Sin•ga•po•re•an (sing′gə pôr′ē ən, -pōr′-) /ˌsɪŋgəˈpɔriyən, -ˈpowr-/ *n.* [*count*] **1.** a person born or living in Singapore. —*adj.* **2.** of or relating to Singapore.

singe (sinj) /sɪndʒ/ *v.,* **singed, singe•ing,** *n.* —*v.* [~ + *obj*] **1.** to burn slightly; scorch: *The hot iron singed the shirt.* **2.** to burn the ends, edges, etc., of (hair, cloth, etc.): *The firefighter's hair was singed from her attempt to rescue the child.* —*n.* [*count*] **3.** a slight burn.

sin•gle (sing′gəl) /ˈsɪŋgəl/ *adj., v.,* **-gled, -gling,** *n.* —*adj.* **1.** [*before a noun*] only one in number; one only; unique: *a single example.* **2.** [*before a noun*] of, relating to, or suitable for one person only: *a single room.* **3.** [*before a noun*] the only; lone: *He was the single survivor.* **4.** unmarried: *a single man.* **5.** [*before a noun*] of one against one: *single combat.* **6.** made of only one part: *a single lens.* **7.** [*before a noun*] separate, particular, or distinct: *I'll speak with every single one of you.* **8.** uniform; that applies to all: *a single safety code.* —*v.* **9. single out,** to choose (one) from others: [~ + *obj* + *out*]: *to single someone out for special mention.* [~ + *out* + *obj*]: *to single out a hardworking employee.* —*n.* [*count*] **10.** one person or thing; a single one. **11.** a room in a hotel, a bed, etc., for one person only. **12.** an unmarried person: *The bar is for singles only.* **13.** a one-dollar bill: *Give me change in singles, please.* **14.** (in baseball) a base hit that allows a batter to reach first base safely. **15. singles,** [*count*] *pl.* **singles.** a match or game with one player on each side, as a tennis match: *A tough singles has just ended.*

sin′gle-breast′ed, *adj.* (of a coat, jacket, etc.) having a front that closes in the center with a single button or row of buttons. Compare DOUBLE-BREASTED.

sin′gle file′, *n.* [*noncount*] **1.** a line of persons or things arranged one behind the other: *lined up in single file.* —*adv.* **2.** in such a line: *to walk single file.*

sin′gle-hand′ed, *adj.* **1.** done by one person alone; without aid from another. **2.** using only one hand: *a sin-*

gle-handed backstroke in tennis. **—*adv.* 3.** by oneself; alone; without aid: *She built the garage single-handed.* **—sin′gle-hand′ed·ly,** *adv.*

sin′gle-mind′ed, *adj.* having great determination; resolute; steadfast: *a single-minded intensity to succeed at all costs.* **—sin′gle-mind′ed·ly,** *adv.*

sing′les bar′, *n.* [*count*] a bar appealing to single men and women.

sin·gle·ton (sing′gəl tən) /ˈsɪŋgəltən/ *n.* [*count*] **1.** a person or thing occurring alone. **2.** a card that is the only one of a suit in a hand.

sin·gly (sing′glē) /ˈsɪŋgliy/ *adv.* apart from others; separately; one at a time: *Some guests arrived singly, and others came in pairs.*

sing·song (sing′sông′, -song′) /ˈsɪŋˌsɔŋ, -ˌsɒŋ/ *n.* [*count*] **1.** [*usually singular*] a monotonous, rhythmical rising and falling in the pitch of the voice when speaking: *He recited his lessons in a bored singsong.* **2.** *Brit.* a session of informal group singing; sing-along. **—*adj.* 3.** monotonous in the rhythmical rising and falling of pitch: *a bored, singsong voice.*

sin·gu·lar (sing′gyə lər) /ˈsɪŋgyələr/ *adj.* **1.** of or belonging to the grammatical category of number indicating that a word refers to or names one person, place, thing, or instance, such as *child, it,* or *goes.* **2.** extraordinary; remarkable; exceptional: *a singular success.* **3.** unusual or strange: *singular behavior.* **—*n.* 4.** [*noncount*] the singular number: *The word "pants" is never in the singular; it always takes a plural verb.* **5.** [*count*] a word or other form in the singular: *What is the singular for the plural word* addenda*? Abbr.:* sing.

sin·gu·lar·ly (sing′gyə lər lē) /ˈsɪŋgyələrliy/ *adv.* extraordinarily; remarkably; very: *singularly good taste.*

sin·is·ter (sin′ə stər) /ˈsɪnəstər/ *adj.* **1.** threatening or suggesting evil, harm, or trouble: *a sinister face.* **2.** evil: *the dictator's sinister purposes.*

sink (singk) /sɪŋk/ *v.,* **sank** (sank) /sæŋk/ or, often, **sunk** (sungk) /sʌŋk/; **sunk** or **sunk·en; sink·ing;** *n.* **—*v.* 1.** [*no obj*] to fall or descend to a lower level or position: *The ship sank to the bottom of the sea.* **2.** [~ + *obj*] to force below the surface of water or the like; cause to become submerged: *The submarine sank two ships.* **3.** [*no obj*] to settle or fall gradually: *The building is sinking.* **4.** [*no obj*] to fall or collapse slowly from weakness, fatigue, etc.: *sank to his knees.* **5.** [*no obj*] **a.** to enter slowly into a state: *to sink into sleep.* **b.** to become deeply occupied: *He sat there, sunk in thought.* **6.** [*no obj*] to pass into some worse or lower state: *to sink into poverty.* **7.** [*no obj*] to become lower in number or amount: *Profits are sinking fast.* **8.** [~ + *obj*] to bring to a worse or lower state or status: *You're trying to sink all his plans for the business.* **9.** [*no obj*] to fail in physical strength or health: *She's sinking fast and may not live through the night.* **10.** [*no obj*] to become discouraged or depressed: *My heart sank when I heard the news.* **11.** [*no obj*] to become lower in volume, tone, or pitch: *Her voice sank to a whisper.* **12.** [*no obj*] to disappear from sight, as below the horizon: *They watched the sun sink beneath the sea.* **13.** [~ + *obj*] to cause to penetrate: *to sink an ax into a tree.* **14.** [~ + *obj*] to dig or excavate (a hole, shaft, etc.): *to sink an oil well.* **15.** [~ + *obj*] to put in (time, effort, etc.) to some activity or business with the hope of profit: *He sank all his energy into making the program run well.* **16.** [~ + *obj*] to hit or throw (a ball) so that it goes through or into a basket, hole, etc.: *The golfer sank the ball with one putt.* **17. sink in,** [*no obj*] to enter the mind; become understood: *I repeated "You're safe" until I was sure the words had sunk in.* **—*n.*** [*count*] **18.** a basin for washing: *the kitchen sink.* See illustration at APARTMENT. **19.** a low-lying, poorly drained area where waters collect and sink into the ground or evaporate. **—sink′a·ble,** *adj.*

sink·er (sing′kər) /ˈsɪŋkər/ *n.* [*count*] **1.** a weight, as of lead, for sinking a fishing line or net below the surface of the water. **2.** (in baseball) a pitched ball that curves downward sharply.

sink·hole (singk′hōl′) /ˈsɪŋkˌhowl/ *n.* [*count*] **1.** a hole formed in rock by the action of water, serving to conduct surface water to an underground passage. **2.** a depressed area in which waste or drainage collects.

sin·u·ous (sin′yo͞o əs) /ˈsɪnyuwəs/ *adj.* **1.** having many curves or turns; winding: *a sinuous path.* **2.** characterized by graceful curving motions: *a sinuous dance.*

si·nus (sī′nəs) /ˈsaynəs/ *n.* [*count*], *pl.* **-nus·es.** one of the hollow cavities in the skull connecting with the nose: *Her sinuses are causing her pain; a sinus headache.*

si·nus·i·tis (sī′nə sī′tis) /ˌsaynəˈsaytɪs/ *n.* [*noncount; used with a singular verb*] inflammation of a sinus or the sinuses. See -ITIS.

sip (sip) /sɪp/ *v.,* **sipped, sip·ping,** *n.* **—*v.* 1.** to drink (a liquid) a little at a time: [~ + *obj*]: *She sipped her hot tea slowly.* [*no obj*]: *sipping at her tea.* **—*n.*** [*count*] **2.** an act or instance of sipping. **3.** a small quantity taken by sipping. **—sip′per,** *n.* [*count*] **—sip′ping·ly,** *adv.*

si·phon or **sy·phon** (sī′fən) /ˈsayfən/ *n.* [*count*] **1.** a U-shaped pipe that uses atmospheric pressure to draw liquid from one container, place, or level to another. **—*v.* 2.** [~(+ *off*) + *obj*] to carry or pass through a siphon: *We siphoned (off) some gasoline from the car's gas tank and filled the container.* [~ + *obj* (+ *off*)]: *to siphon some gas off.* **3.** to carry off or remove (something) and use it elsewhere: [~ + *off* + *obj*]: *They were caught siphoning off money from campaign contributions.* [~ + *obj* + *off*]: *to siphon it off.*

sir (sûr) /sɜr/ *n.* [*count*] **1.** a formal term of address used to a man: *"Dear Sir," the letter began.* **2.** [*Sir*] the title of a knight or baronet: *Sir Walter Scott.* **3.** a lord or gentleman: *noble sirs and ladies.* See -SENE-.

sire (sīᵊr) /sayᵊr/ *n., v.,* **sired, sir·ing.** **—*n.* 1.** [*proper noun*] a respectful term of address, used to a king. **2.** [*count*] the male parent of a four-legged animal. **—*v.*** [~ + *obj*] **3.** to father (offspring); beget: *He had sired two fine sons.* See -SENE-.

si·ren (sī′rən) /ˈsayrən/ *n.* [*count*] **1.** a seductively beautiful woman. **2.** a warning device that produces a loud, piercing sound: *Sirens wailed and people took shelter.*

sir·loin (sûr′loin) /ˈsɜrlɔyn/ *n.* the portion of the loin of beef in front of the rump: [*noncount*]: *two pounds of sirloin.* [*count*]: *cooking a fine sirloin for dinner.*

si·roc·co (sə rok′ō) /səˈrɒkow/ *n.* [*count*], *pl.* **-cos.** a hot, dry, dusty wind blowing from N Africa.

sir·up (sir′əp, sûr′-) /ˈsɪrəp, ˈsɜr-/ *n.* SYRUP.

sis (sis) /sɪs/ *n.* [*count; usually used as a term of address; often: Sis*] sister: *Hey, Sis, wake up Mom and Dad.*

si·sal (sī′səl, sis′əl) /ˈsaysəl, ˈsɪsəl/ *n.* [*noncount*] **1.** Also called **si′sal hemp′.** a fiber used for making rope. **2.** the plant from which this fiber is taken: *rows of sisal.*

sis·sy (sis′ē) /ˈsɪsiy/ *n., pl.* **-sies,** *adj.* **—*n.*** [*count*] **1.** a boy or man who appears feminine. **2.** a timid or cowardly person. **3.** a little girl. **—*adj.* 4.** (of a man or boy) appearing feminine. **5.** cowardly; timid. **—sis·si·fied·** (sis′ə fīd′) /ˈsɪsəˌfayd/ *adj.*

-sist-, *root.* *-sist-* comes from Latin, where it has the meaning "remain; stand; stay." This meaning is found in such words as: ASSIST, CONSIST, DESIST, INCONSISTENT, INSIST, IRRESISTIBLE, PERSIST, RESIST, SUBSIST, SUBSISTENCE.

sis·ter (sis′tər) /ˈsɪstər/ *n.* [*count*] **1.** a female relative of another, having both parents in common. **2.** a female relative of another, having one parent in common; half sister. **3.** STEPSISTER. **4.** a sister-in-law. **5.** a woman or girl in the same family or social group, nationality, etc., as another. **6.** a thing regarded as female: *The ships are sisters.* **7.** a woman member of a religious order whose vows are not as absolute as a nun's. [*often: Sister*]: *Her name is Sister Mary Richard.* **8.** *Brit.* a nurse in charge of a hospital ward; head nurse: *the sister in charge.* **9.** [*often: Sister*] (used as a form of address to a woman or girl, esp. as a joke but sometimes insultingly). **—*adj.*** [*before a noun*] **10.** being or considered a sister; related by or as if by sisterhood: *our sister city across the river.* **—sis′ter·ly,** *adj.*: *a sisterly kiss on the cheek.*

sis·ter·hood (sis′tər ho͝od′) /ˈsɪstərˌhʊd/ *n.* [*noncount*] **1.** the state of being a sister. **2.** a group of nuns or other females bound by religious ties. **3.** pleasant relationship among women. **4.** [*often: the* + ~] the community or network of women who support feminism.

sis·ter-in-law (sis′tər in lô′) /ˈsɪstərɪnˌlɔ/ *n.* [*count*], *pl.* **sis·ters-in-law.** **1.** the sister of one's husband or wife. **2.** the wife of one's brother. **3.** the wife of the brother of one's husband or wife.

sit (sit) /sɪt/ *v.,* **sat** (sat) /sæt/ **sat, sit·ting.** **—*v.* 1.** [*no obj*] to rest with the body supported by one's buttocks or thighs; be seated: *I was sitting at my desk when the phone rang.* **2.** to (cause to) lower the body into a position of rest supported by one's buttocks or thighs: [*no obj;* (~ + *down*)]: *Please sit (down); I'll be back in a minute.* [~ + *obj* (+ *down*)]: *sat the child (down) on the sofa.* **3.** [*no obj*] to be located or situated; lie or rest: *The house sits on a cliff.* **4.** [*no obj*] to place oneself in position for an artist, etc.; pose. **5.** [*no obj*] to remain quiet: *Let the matter sit.* **6.** [*no obj*] (of a bird) to cover eggs with the body for hatching; brood. **7.** [*no obj*] to fit or hang, such as a garment: *That shirt doesn't sit well on him.* **8.** [*no obj; often:* ~ + *on* + *obj*] to have an official position, such as a legislator or judge: *She sits on the committee.* **9.** [*no obj*] to hold a session: *The court sits in judgment.* **10.** (used after a word or root) to take care of (the specified thing) like a baby-sitter: *to house-sit (= to live in another's house while the owners are away); to plant-sit (= to take care of another's plants while the owners are away).* **11.** [*no obj*] to be accepted in the way indicated: *His answer didn't sit right with us.* **12.** [*no obj*] to be acceptable to the stomach: *My breakfast didn't sit too well.* **13.** [~ + *obj; no passive*] to provide seating accommodations; seat: *Our table only sits six people.* **14.** [*no obj*] to baby-sit: *She used to sit for us when our daughter was a baby.* **15. sit around,** [*no obj; usually:* ~ + *around* + *verb-ing*] to do nothing: *The workers were sitting around ignoring their work.* **16. sit in (on),** [~ + *in (+ on + obj)*] to be a spectator at (some event or circumstance): *I'd like permission to sit in on your class.* **17. sit on** or **upon,** [~ + *on/upon* + *obj*] **a.** to inquire into or deliberate over: *A coroner's jury sat on the case.* **b.** to put off for a time; postpone. **c.** to check; squelch: *to sit on nasty rumors.* **18. sit out, a.** [~ + *out* + *obj*] to stay to the end of: *He sat out the whole movie in silence.* **b.** to stay, wait, or endure longer than: [~ + *out* + *obj*]: *to sit out one's rivals.* [~ + *obj* + *out*]: *to sit them out.* **c.** to keep one's seat during (a dance, etc.); fail to participate in (an activity): [~ + *out* + *obj*]: *I think I'll sit out the next dance.* [~ + *obj* + *out*]: *I'll have to sit this one out; I'm a little tired.* **19. sit up, a.** to (cause to) rise from a lying or reclining position to a sitting position: [*no obj*]: *Sit up straight and answer me.* [~ + *obj* + *up*]: *The nurse sat him up in his bed.* **b.** [*no obj; often:* ~ + *up* + *verb-ing*] to be awake and active during one's usual sleep time: *to sit up all night playing solitaire.* **c.** [*no obj*] to become interested; take notice: *This will make them sit up and notice.* **—*Idiom.* 20. sit on one's hands, a.** to fail to applaud. **b.** to fail to take proper or necessary action. **21. sit tight,** [*no obj*] to take no action; wait: *Sit tight, and when I give you the signal, then move.* —**sit′ter,** *n.* [*count*]

si•tar (si tär′) /sɪ'tɑr/ *n.* [*count*] a lute of India, having a very long neck. —**si•tar′ist,** *n.* [*count*]

sit•com (sit′kom′) /'sɪt,kɒm/ *n.* [*count*] *Informal.* a situation comedy.

sit′-down′, *adj.* [*before a noun*] **1.** done while sitting down. **2.** (of a meal or food) served to people seated at a table. —*n.* [*count*] **3.** Also called **sit-down strike.** a strike in which workers do not leave the place where they are working until their demands are met. **4.** SIT-IN. **5.** a period or instance of sitting, as to talk.

site (sīt) /sayt/ *n., v.,* **sit•ed, sit•ing.** —*n.* [*count*] **1.** the area on which anything is, has been, or is to be located: *the site of ancient Troy.* —*v.* [~ + *obj*] **2.** to place in or provide with a site; locate.

sit′-in′, *n.* [*count*] an organized protest in which the demonstrators occupy a public place and refuse to leave it. Also called **sit-down.**

sit•ter (sit′ər) /'sɪtər/ *n.* [*count*] a baby-sitter.

sit•ting (sit′ing) /'sɪtɪŋ/ *n.* [*count*] **1.** the act of a person or thing that sits. **2.** a period of being seated, as in posing for a portrait. **3.** a session, as of a court. —*adj.* [*before a noun*] **4.** for, suited to, or accomplished while sitting: *sitting areas.* **5.** (of a target) readily seen or hit: *The slow freighter was a sitting target for the jets.* **6.** occupying an official office; incumbent: *The sitting mayor will be impossible to defeat.* **7.** in session; active: *a sitting legislature.* **—*Idiom.* 8. sitting pretty,** [*no obj*] in a favorable position.

sit′ting duck′, *n.* [*count*] a helpless or easy target or victim.

sit′ting room′, *n.* [*count*] a small living room.

sit•u•ate (sich′o͞o āt′) /'sɪtʃuw,eyt/ *v.* [~ + *obj; often: be* + ~*-ed*], **-at•ed, -at•ing.** to put in or on a particular site or place: *situated herself near the exit door.*

sit•u•a•tion (sich′o͞o ā′shən) /,sɪtʃuw'eyʃən/ *n.* [*count*] **1.** condition; case; plight: *He's in a desperate situation.* **2.** the state of affairs; combination of circumstances: *The international situation is grave.* **3.** a position or post of working; job. **4.** location or position with reference to what is around: *a city in a beautiful situation.*

sit′ua′tion com′edy, *n.* [*count*] a television or radio series made up of independent episodes showing the comic adventures of a fixed group of characters.

sit′-up′, *n.* [*count*] an exercise in which a person lies flat on the back, lifts the upper body to a sitting position, and then lies flat again without changing the position of the legs.

sitz′ bath′ (sits, zits) /sɪts, zɪts/ *n.* [*count*] a bath in which just the thighs and hips are immersed in warm water.

six (siks) /sɪks/ *n.* [*count*] **1.** a cardinal number, five plus one. **2.** a symbol for this number, as 6 or VI. **3.** a set of this many persons or things. —*adj.* [*before a noun*] **4.** amounting to six in number. **—*Idiom.* 5. at sixes and sevens,** in disorder or confusion. —**sixth,** *adj., n.* [*count*]

six′-pack′, *n.* [*count*] any package of six identical or closely related items sold as a unit, esp. six bottles or cans of beer or a soft drink.

six•pence (siks′pəns) /'sɪkspəns/ *n.* [*count*], *pl.* **-pence, -penc•es.** a coin of the United Kingdom, the half of a shilling, formerly equal to six pennies, equal to two and one-half new pence after 1971.

six-shoot•er (siks′sho͞o′tər, -sho͞o′-) /'sɪks'ʃuwtər, -,ʃuw-/ *n.* [*count*] a revolver that can fire six shots with one loading.

six•teen (siks′tēn′) /'sɪks'tiyn/ *n.* [*count*] **1.** a cardinal number, ten plus six. **2.** a symbol for this number, as 16 or XVI. **3.** a set of this many persons or things. —*adj.* [*before a noun*] **4.** amounting to 16 in number. —**six′-teenth′,** *adj., n.* [*count*]

sixth′ sense′, *n.* [*count; usually singular*] a power of knowing or being aware of something through an ability beyond the five senses; intuition: *Some sixth sense made him turn around and freeze.*

six•ty (siks′tē) /'sɪkstiy/ *n., pl.* **-ties,** *adj.* —*n.* [*count*] **1.** a cardinal number, ten times six. **2.** a symbol for this number, as 60 or LX. **3.** a set of this many persons or things. **4. sixties,** the numbers from 60 through 69, as in the years of a lifetime or of a century or degrees of temperature. —*adj.* [*before a noun*] **5.** amounting to 60 in number. **—*Idiom.* 6. like sixty,** [*count*] with great speed, ease, energy, or zest. —**six′ti•eth,** *adj., n.* [*count*]

siz•a•ble or **size•a•ble** (si′zə bəl) /'sayzəbəl/ *adj.* of considerable size; fairly large.

size (sīz) /sayz/ *n., v.,* **sized, siz•ing.** —*n.* **1.** [*count*] the physical dimensions, largeness, or extent of anything: *the size of a farm.* **2.** [*noncount*] considerable or great largeness: *a company known for its size.* **3.** [*count*] one of a series of measures for articles of manufacture or trade: *shoe sizes.* **4.** [*noncount*] extent; amount; range: *a fortune of great size.* **5.** [*count; usually singular; usually: the* + ~] actual condition or state of affairs: *We have no time left; that's about the size of it.* —*v.* **6.** [~ + *obj*] to separate or sort according to size. **7. size up,** to form an estimate of; judge: [~ + *up* + *obj*]: *The lawyer sized up his opponent.* [~ + *obj* + *up*]: *to size him up and dismiss him.* **—*Idiom.* 8. cut (someone) down to size,** [*cut* + *obj* + *down* + *to* + ~] to reduce the importance of: *She'll cut you down to size in a moment.* **9. to size,** [*noncount*] to the length, width, dimension, or other measure desired: *That formica will have to be cut to size to fit in your kitchen.*

sized (sīzd) /sayzd/ *adj.* (used after a root or word) having the size (as specified in the root or word): *middle-sized; a mid-sized car.*

siz•zle (siz′əl) /'sɪzəl/ *v.,* **-zled, -zling,** *n.* —*v.* [*no obj*] **1.** to make a hissing sound, as in frying; crackle: *The bacon sizzled in the frying pan.* **2.** to be very hot: *The summer sidewalks were sizzling.* **3.** to be very angry: *The boss is sizzling.* —*n.* [*count*] **4.** a sizzling sound.

skate[1] (skāt) /skeyt/ *n., v.,* **skat•ed, skat•ing.** —*n.* [*count*] **1.** ICE SKATE (def. 1) **2.** ROLLER SKATE. —*v.* **3.** [*no obj*] to move oneself on skates: *skating at the ice rink.* **4.** [*no obj*] to do something, esp. one's work, in an overly relaxed or superficial way: *He skated through his assignments and handed in the bare minimum.* **5.** [~ + *obj*] to perform by skating: *skated a perfect program.* —**skat′er,** *n.* [*count*]

skate[2] (skāt) /skeyt/ *n.* [*count*], *pl.* (*esp. when thought of as a group*) **skate,** (*esp. for kinds or species*) **skates.** a fish, a ray, with winglike fins.

skate•board (skāt′bôrd′, -bōrd′) /'skeyt,bɔrd, -,bowrd/ *n.* [*count*] **1.** a device made of a board mounted on large roller-skate wheels and supporting a rider. —*v.* [*no obj*] **2.** to ride a skateboard.

ske•dad•dle (ski dad′l) /skɪ'dædl̩/ *v.,* **-dled, -dling,** *n.* *Informal.* —*v.* [*no obj*] **1.** to run away quickly or in a hurry. —*n.* [*count*] **2.** a hasty flight.

skeet (skēt) /skiyt/ *n.* [*noncount*] a form of practice shooting in which targets are hurled at varying heights and speeds so as to be similar to the angles of flight of game birds. Also called **skeet′ shoot′ing.**

skein (skān) /skeyn/ *n.* [*count*] **1.** a loose coil of thread or yarn in a package for retail sale. **2.** a flock of geese or ducks in flight. **3.** a succession of similar things: *They reeled off a skein of tennis victories.*

skel•e•tal (skel i tl) /skɛlɪtl̩/ *adj.* **1.** of or relating to a skeleton: *skeletal muscles.* **2.** very thin and underweight.

skel•e•ton (skel′i tn) /ˈskɛlɪtn̩/ *n.* [*count*] **1.** the bones of a human or animal thought of as a whole, together forming the inner framework of the body. **2.** a very thin, underweight person or animal. **3.** a supporting framework, as of a leaf, building, or ship. **4.** an outline, as of a piece of writing: *Can you describe the skeleton of the plot?* **—*adj.*** **5.** of or relating to a skeleton. **6.** reduced to the essential parts or numbers: *They kept a skeleton staff working during the holidays.* **—*Idiom.*** **7. skeleton in the closet,** [*count*] any embarrassing, shameful, or damaging secret.

skel′eton key′, *n.* [*count*] a key with nearly the whole substance of the bit filed away so that it opens various simple locks.

skep•tic or **scep•tic** (skep′tik) /ˈskɛptɪk/ *n.* [*count*] **1.** one who questions the validity of something that others believe to be factual, esp. religious beliefs. **2.** one who maintains a doubting attitude, as toward values, plans, etc. **—*adj.*** **3.** SKEPTICAL.

skep•ti•cal or **scep•ti•cal** (skep′ti kəl) /ˈskɛptɪkəl/ *adj.* **1.** inclined to have doubt or doubts. **2.** showing doubt: *a skeptical smile.* **3.** denying or questioning religion or the beliefs of a religion. **—skep′ti•cal•ly,** *adv.*

skep•ti•cism or **scep•ti•cism** (skep′tə siz′əm) /ˈskɛptəˌsɪzəm/ *n.* [*noncount*] **1.** skeptical attitudes; doubt. **2.** doubt or unbelief regarding religion.

sketch (skech) /skɛtʃ/ *n.* [*count*] **1.** a simply or quickly made drawing or painting, giving the basic features. **2.** a rough design, plan, or draft, as of a book. **3.** a brief or hasty outline of facts, occurrences, etc.: *a quick sketch of what had happened.* **4.** a short piece of writing, usually descriptive. **5.** a short comic piece or routine. **—*v.*** **6.** to make a sketch or sketches of (something or someone): [~ + *obj*]: *He sketched a quick drawing of the skyline.* [*no obj*]: *artists sketching along the river.* **7.** [~ + *obj*] to set forth or describe in a brief or general way: *sketched the plan that he would use to trap his enemy.*

sketch•y (skech′ē) /ˈskɛtʃiy/ *adj.*, **-i•er, -i•est.** giving only outlines and not details; not complete: *He could only give us a sketchy account of what had happened.*

skew (skyo͞o) /skyuw/ *v.* **1.** [*no obj*] to turn aside or swerve: *cars skewing off the road.* **2.** [~ + *obj*] to distort; misrepresent: *The accounting department skewed data and figures to show that the company was operating at a profit.* **—*adj.*** **3.** having a slanting direction or position.

skew•er (skyo͞o′ər) /ˈskyuwər/ *n.* [*count*] **1.** a long pin for inserting through meat or other food to hold it while it is cooking: *putting the shish kebab on skewers.* **—*v.*** [~ + *obj*] **2.** to fasten by piercing with or as if with a skewer. **3.** to criticize harshly or persistently: *The media skewered that official for his foolish comments.*

ski (skē) /skiy/ *n., pl.* **skis, ski,** *v.,* **skied, ski•ing.** **—*n.*** [*count*] **1.** one of a pair of long, slender pieces of wood, plastic, or metal used in gliding over snow. **2.** WATER SKI. **—*v.*** **3.** [*no obj*] to travel on skis, as for sport: *He skied in the snows of Colorado.* **4.** [~ + *obj*] to use skis on; travel on skis over: *to ski the mountain regions of New England.* **—ski′er,** *n.* [*count*]

skid (skid) /skɪd/ *n., v.,* **skid•ded, skid•ding.** **—*n.*** [*count*] **1.** a plank, bar, etc., esp. one of a pair, on which something heavy may be slid along. **2.** a low moveable platform on which goods are placed for ease in handling, moving, etc. **3.** an unexpected or uncontrollable slide on a smooth surface, esp. sideways: *The car went into a skid on the ice.* **—*v.*** **4.** to (cause to) slip or slide, esp. sideways: [*no obj*]: *Her feet were skidding on the icy pavement.* [~ + *obj*]: *He accidentally skidded the car into a fence.* **5.** [*no obj*] to weaken or begin to fail: *The team skidded, losing its last five games.* **—*Idiom.*** **6. the skids,** the downward path to ruin, failure, etc.: *Our team hit the skids.*

skid′ row′ (rō) /row/ *n.* an area of cheap barrooms and run-down hotels, where alcoholics and vagrants stay: [*noncount*]: *We found him living on skid row.* [*count*]: *in the skid rows and other blighted areas of the city.*

skiff (skif) /skɪf/ *n.* [*count*] any of various types of boats small enough for sailing or rowing by one person.

ski′ lift′, *n.* [*count*] a device that carries skiers up a slope, consisting typically of chairs or bars that hang from a motor-driven cable.

skill (skil) /skɪl/ *n.* **1.** the knowledge or ability to do something well: [*noncount*]: *She showed great skill in handling difficult problems.* [*count*]: *the skills of reading, writing, speaking, and listening in a foreign language.* **2.** [*count*] a craft, trade, or job requiring special training: *the skills of glassblowing.* **—skill′ful,** *adj.*: *a skillful way of dealing with people.* **—skill′ful•ly,** *adv.*: *She had skillfully persuaded him to accept her ideas.*

skilled (skild) /skɪld/ *adj.* having, needing, or showing skill or ability: *a skilled craftsman.* [*be* + ~ + *in/at* + *obj*]: *She was skilled in dealing with all sorts of people.*

skil•let (skil′it) /ˈskɪlɪt/ *n.* [*count*] **1.** a frying pan. **2.** *Chiefly Brit.* a metal cooking pot with a long handle and sometimes legs, for cooking at a hearth.

skim (skim) /skɪm/ *v.,* **skimmed, skim•ming,** *n.* **—*v.*** **1.** to remove (floating matter) from the surface of a liquid, as with a spoon: [~ + *obj* (+ *off*)]: *to skim the fat off.* [~ + *obj* (+ *off* + *obj*)]: *to skim the fat off the soup.* **2.** [~ + *obj*] to clear (liquid) in this way: *to skim milk.* **3.** to glide lightly over (a surface, as of water): [*no obj*]: *The seaplane skimmed over the water and then landed.* [~ + *obj*]: *The plane skimmed the water barely a few feet from the surface.* **4.** to (cause to) be thrown in a smooth, gliding path over a surface, or so as to bounce along a surface: [~ + *obj*]: *She learned to skim stones across the lake.* [*no obj*]: *She threw the flat stone and watched it skim across the lake.* **5.** to read, study, etc., quickly but not carefully: [~ + *obj*]: *She teaches her students how to skim the chapters they read for the main idea.* [*no obj*]: *teaching her students to skim and not to read every word.* **6.** to take (money, the best items, etc.) from something: [~ (+ *off*) + *obj*]: *The mobsters skimmed (off) 20% of the store's profits for "protection money."* [~ + *obj* + *off* + *obj*]: *to skim 25% off their profits.* **—*n.*** **7.** SKIM MILK.

skim′ milk′ or **skimmed′ milk′,** *n.* [*noncount*] milk from which the cream has been skimmed.

skimp (skimp) /skɪmp/ *v.* [~ + *on* + *obj*] to scrimp; use less of something in order to economize; scrimp: *Let's not skimp on the food for the party.* **—skimp′ing•ly,** *adv.*

skimp•y (skim′pē) /ˈskɪmpiy/ *adj.,* **-i•er, -i•est.** **1.** lacking in size, fullness, etc.; scanty: *a skimpy bathing suit.* **2.** too careful with money; stingy: *a skimpy housekeeper.* **—skimp′i•ness,** *n.* [*noncount*]

skin (skin) /skɪn/ *n., v.,* **skinned, skin•ning,** *adj.* **—*n.*** **1.** the tissue that is the outer covering of a human or animal body, esp. when it is soft and flexible: [*noncount*]: *the smell of her clean skin after a shower.* [*count*]: *a fair skin that is easily sunburned.* **2.** such tissue, with the hair or fur growing from it, stripped from the body of an animal, esp. a small animal; pelt: [*count*]: *a beaver skin.* [*noncount*]: *a coat of beaver skin.* **3.** a covering, casing, or outer coating of something, esp. of a fruit or vegetable: [*count*]: *orange skins; potato skins.* [*noncount*]: *the plastic-like skin of sausage.* **4.** a solid layer forming on food that has cooled or been heated: [*noncount*]: *The soup had boiled and there was skin on the top.* [*count*]: *a skin on the top of the milk mixture.* **5.** [*count*] a container made of animal skin, used for holding liquids, esp. wine. **—*v.*** [~ + *obj*] **6.** to strip (an animal or thing) of skin; remove the skin of: *to skin the fruit.* **7.** to scrape a small piece of skin from (a part of the body), as in falling: *He skinned his knee when he fell.* **—*Idiom.*** **8. by the skin of one's teeth,** [*noncount*] by an extremely narrow margin; just barely: *won the election by the skin of her teeth.* **9. get under one's skin, a.** to irritate someone: *All those rude comments really get under my skin.* **b.** to affect someone deeply; excite; impress. **10. have a thick skin,** to be insensitive, esp. to criticism or defeats. **11. have a thin skin,** to be sensitive to criticism or defeats; to be easily offended. **12. no skin off one's back, nose,** or **teeth,** [*usually: it* + *be* + ~] of no interest or concern, or involving no risk to oneself: *It's no skin off my nose if she wants to risk her money like that.* **13. save one's skin,** to avoid harm, esp. to escape death. **14. skin (someone) alive,** *Informal.* to punish harshly.

skin′-deep, *adj.* just on the surface; not deep or genuine: *Her sincerity and polite smile are only skin-deep.*

skin′ div′ing, *n.* [*noncount*] underwater swimming and exploring with a face mask and flippers. **—skin′ div′er,** *n.* [*count*]

skin′ flick′, *n.* [*count*] *Slang.* a motion picture that features nudity and usually scenes of sexual activity. Also **skin′flick′.**

skin•flint (skin′flint′) /ˈskɪnˌflɪnt/ *n.* [*count*] a stingy person; miser.

skin•head (skin′hed′) /ˈskɪnˌhɛd/ *n.* [*count*] *Slang.* **1.** a baldheaded person or a person with hair cut very short.

2. a person who is violent or antisocial and shaves his or her head as a sign of this: *The skinheads were marching and shouting hate-filled slogans against foreigners.*

skin•ny (skin′ē) /ˈskɪniy/ *adj.,* **-ni•er, -ni•est,** *n.* **—***adj.* **1.** very lean or thin; emaciated: *The pitcher was a tall, skinny guy.* **2.** (of an object) narrow or slender: *a skinny bed.* **—***n.* [*noncount*] **3.** *Slang.* accurate information, esp. if confidential; gossip: *Give us the skinny on what's happening.* —**skin′ni•ness,** *n.* [*noncount*]

skin′ny-dip′, *v.,* **-dipped, -dip•ping,** *n. Informal.* **—***v.* [*no obj*] **1.** to swim with no clothes on: *skinny-dipping in the pool.* **—***n.* [*count*] **2.** a swim with no clothes on.

skin•tight (skin′tīt′) /ˈskɪnˈtayt/ *adj.* fitting almost as tightly as skin: *skintight jeans.*

skip[1] (skip) /skɪp/ *v.,* **skipped, skip•ping,** *n.* **—***v.* **1.** [*no obj*] to move in a light, springy manner by hopping forward on first one foot then the other: *The child skipped alongside him.* **2.** [∼ + *obj*] to jump lightly over: *to skip rope.* **3.** to pass from (one point, etc.) to another, disregarding or failing to act on what comes between: [*no obj*]: *The teacher skipped around from one subject to another during his lecture.* [∼ + *obj*]: *The teacher skipped chapter five and said it wouldn't be on the test.* **4.** to go away quickly and secretly from (some place); flee without notice: [∼ + *obj*]: *The criminals skipped town.* [*no obj*]: *We won't catch them; they've already skipped.* **5.** to (cause to) be advanced (one or more classes or grades) at once: [∼ + *obj*]: *She skipped a couple of grades.* [*no obj*]: *She was allowed to skip to the next grade.* **6.** to (cause to) bounce along a surface, usually by throwing or being thrown: [*no obj*]: *The stone skipped over the lake.* [∼ + *obj*]: *He taught her how to skip stones in the water.* **7.** [∼ + *obj*] to miss or omit (one of a repeated series of actions): *My heart skipped a beat.* **8.** [∼ + *obj*] to be absent from; avoid attendance at: *skipped class again.* **—***n.* [*count*] **9.** a skipping movement. **10.** an instance of skipping or a thing skipped.

skip[2] (skip) /skɪp/ *n.* SKIPPER.

skip•per (skip′ər) /ˈskɪpər/ *n.* [*count*] **1.** the master or captain of a vessel, esp. of a small vessel. **2.** a captain or leader, as of a team. **—***v.* [∼ + *obj*] **3.** to act as skipper of.

skir•mish (skûr′mish) /ˈskɜrmɪʃ/ *n.* [*count*] **1.** a fight between small bodies of troops. **2.** any brisk and usually quick argument: *The opposing candidates had quite a few skirmishes during the election year.* **—***v.* [*no obj*] **3.** to be or fight in a skirmish: *troops skirmishing before the main battle.*

skirt (skûrt) /skɜrt/ *n.* [*count*] **1.** the part of a gown, dress, etc., that hangs downward from the waist. **2.** a one-piece garment hanging downward from the waist and not joined between the legs, worn esp. by women and girls. See illustration at CLOTHING. **3.** some part resembling the skirt of a garment, as on furniture. **4.** *Slang* (*usually offensive*). a woman or girl. **—***v.* **5.** [∼ + *obj*] to lie along the border of: *The hills skirt the town.* **6.** to pass along the edge of (something): [∼ + *obj*]: *Traffic skirts the monument.* [*no obj*]: *to skirt around the rioting crowd.* **7.** [∼ + *obj*] to avoid, go around the edge of, or keep distant from (something controversial, risky, etc.): *tried to skirt the issue.*

skit (skit) /skɪt/ *n.* [*count*] a short piece of writing, theatrical scene, or act, usually comical: *performed a skit that had the audience screaming with laughter.*

skit•ter (skit′ər) /ˈskɪtər/ *v.* [*no obj*] to go, run, or glide lightly or rapidly: *Mice skittered along the floor.*

skit•tish (skit′ish) /ˈskɪtɪʃ/ *adj.* **1.** easily frightened or excited: *a skittish horse.* **2.** restlessly lively; overexcited: *He was in a skittish mood before the attack.*

skiv•vy (skiv′ē) /ˈskɪviy/ *n.* [*count*], *pl.* **-vies. 1.** Also called **skiv′vy shirt′.** a knit shirt with a small opening at the neck. **2. skivvies,** [*plural*] underwear consisting of this shirt or a T-shirt and shorts.

skoal (skōl) /skowl/ *interj.* **1.** (used as a drinking toast): *They raised their glasses and shouted "Skoal!"* **—***n.* [*count*] **2.** a toast.

skul•dug•ger•y or **skull•dug•gery** (skul dug′ə rē) /skʌlˈdʌgəriy/ *n.* [*noncount*] dishonorable or deceitful behavior.

skulk (skulk) /skʌlk/ *v.* [*no obj*] **1.** to lie or stay in hiding, as for some evil reason: *The thief skulked in the shadows.* **2.** to move while trying to avoid being seen; slink: *to skulk around the forest.* —**skulk′er,** *n.* [*count*]

skull (skul) /skʌl/ *n.* [*count*] **1.** the bony framework of the head. **2.** the head thought of as the center of the ability to understand; mind: *Can't you get it through your skull that she loves you?*

skull•cap (skul′kap′) /ˈskʌlˌkæp/ *n.* [*count*] **1.** a small, brimless, close-fitting cap, often made of silk or velvet, worn on the crown of the head. **2.** YARMULKE.

skunk (skungk) /skʌŋk/ *n.* [*count*], *pl.* **skunks,** (*esp. when thought of as a group*) **skunk,** *v.* **—***n.* [*count*] **1.** an animal of North America having a bushy tail and a black coat with white markings and spraying a foul-smelling fluid as a defense. **2.** a bad or mean person. **—***v.* [∼ + *obj*] *Slang.* **3.** to defeat completely in a game.

sky (skī) /skay/ *n., pl.* **skies,** *v.,* **skied** or **skyed, sky•ing. —***n.* **1.** the region of the clouds or the upper air; heavens; firmament: [*count; often: the* + ∼*; often: skies*]: *The sun can be seen in the sky today.* [*noncount*]: *There was a lot of blue sky in Montana.* **2.** [*count; often: skies*] the climate: *the sunny skies of Italy.* **—***v.* [∼ + *obj*] **3.** to raise, throw, or hit aloft or into the air: *The batter skied the next ball high to right field.* **—*Idiom.* 4. out of a** or **the clear (blue) sky,** [*noncount*] without any advance warning: *One day out of a clear blue sky he was fired, just like that.*

sky•cap (skī′kap′) /ˈskayˌkæp/ *n.* [*count*] a porter who carries passenger baggage at an airport or airline terminal.

sky•div•ing or **sky div•ing** (skī′dī′ving) /ˈskayˌdayvɪŋ/ *n.* [*noncount*] the sport of jumping from an airplane and descending for a considerable distance before opening one's parachute.

sky′-high′, *adj., adv.* very high: *sky-high prices; Prices went sky-high for fuel and food.*

sky•jack (skī′jak′) /ˈskayˌdʒæk/ *v.* [∼ + *obj*] to hijack (an airliner). —**sky′jack′er,** *n.* [*count*]

sky•lark (skī′lärk′) /ˈskayˌlɑrk/ *n.* [*count*] a brown-speckled lark famous for its beautiful song.

sky•light (skī′līt′) /ˈskayˌlayt/ *n.* [*count*] an opening in a roof or ceiling, fitted with glass, for admitting daylight.

sky•line or **sky line** (skī′līn′) /ˈskayˌlayn/ *n.* [*count*] **1.** the boundary line between earth and sky; the horizon. **2.** the outline of something, such as the buildings of a city, against the sky: *The plane turned left and we had a beautiful view of the skyline of Manhattan.*

sky•rock•et (skī′rok′it) /ˈskayˌrɒkɪt/ *n.* [*count*] **1.** a rocket firework that explodes high in the air, usually in brilliant and colorful sparks. **—***v.* [*no obj*] **2.** to rise or increase in amount, advancement, etc., rapidly or suddenly: *Prices skyrocketed overnight.*

sky•scrap•er (skī′skrā′pər) /ˈskayˌskreypər/ *n.* [*count*] a tall building of many stories, esp. one for office or commercial use. See illustration at STREET.

sky•ward (skī′wərd) /ˈskaywərd/ *adv.* **1.** Also, **sky′wards.** toward the sky: *looked skyward.* **—***adj.* **2.** directed toward the sky.

sky•writ•ing (skī′rī′ting) /ˈskayˌraytɪŋ/ *n.* [*noncount*] **1.** the act or technique of writing against the sky with chemically produced smoke released from a maneuvering airplane. **2.** the words, letters, designs, etc., so traced. —**sky′writ′er,** *n.* [*count*]

slab (slab) /slæb/ *n., v.,* **slabbed, slab•bing. —***n.* [*count*] **1.** a broad, flat, somewhat thick piece of stone, wood, or other solid material. **2.** a thick piece or slice of anything: *a slab of bread.* **—***v.* [∼ + *obj*] **3.** to put on in slabs or layers: *to slab butter on the bread.*

slack (slak) /slæk/ *adj.,* **-er, -est,** *adv., n., v.* **—***adj.* **1.** not tight, firm, or tense; loose: *a slack rope.* **2.** negligent; careless; remiss: *slack in answering letters.* **3.** not active or busy; not brisk: *the slack season in an industry.* **—***n.* [*noncount*] **4.** a slack condition or part, esp. of a rope, sail, or the like, that hangs loose, without strain upon it: *too much slack in the sails.* **—***v.* **5.** [*no obj*] to fail to do one's duty or part, as by being lazy: *often slacking at work.* **6.** [∼ + *off/up*] to become less active, busy, or intense; slacken: *At last some of the work slacked off and he could relax.* —**slack′ness,** *n.* [*noncount*]

slack•en (slak′ən) /ˈslækən/ *v.* **1.** to (cause to) become less active, busy, etc.: [*no obj*]: *At last the work slackened a bit.* [∼ + *obj*]: *He never slackened his efforts to improve himself.* **2.** to (cause to) become looser or less taut: [*no obj*]: *The sails slackened as the wind died down.* [∼ + *obj*]: *to slacken the sails.*

slack•er (slak′ər) /ˈslækər/ *n.* [*count*] one who tries to escape from doing duty, work, or military service.

slacks (slaks) /slæks/ *n.* [*plural*] trousers for informal or casual wear: *The slacks were too tight.*

slag (slag) /slæg/ *n.* [*noncount*] waste matter, fused solid and left after separating metal from its ore.

slain (slān) /sleyn/ *v.* pp. of SLAY.

slake (slāk) /sleyk/ *v.* [∼ + *obj*], **slaked, slak•ing.** to satisfy (thirst, hunger, etc.): *to slake his thirst with water.*

sla•lom (slä′ləm, -lōm) /ˈslɑləm, -lowm/ *n.* [*count*] **1.** a downhill ski race over a winding and zigzag course marked by poles or gates. —*v.* [*no obj*] **2.** to ski in or as if in a slalom. —*adj.* [*before a noun*] **3.** of or relating to a slalom.

slam[1] (slam) /slæm/ *v.*, **slammed, slam•ming,** *n.* —*v.* **1.** [~ + *obj*] to shut with force and noise: *to slam the door.* **2.** [~ + *obj*] to strike, throw, etc., with force and noise on impact: *She picked up the book and slammed it on the table.* **3.** [~ (+ *on*) + *obj*] to hit, push, etc., violently: *If you slam (on) the brakes, the car will skid.* **4.** [*no obj*] to shut, stop, or make an impact with force and noise: *The truck slammed into the wall.* **5.** [~ + *obj*] to criticize harshly; attack with words: *She slammed her opponent.* —*n.* [*count*] **6.** a violent, noisy closing, throwing, or the noise made by this: *He closed the door with a loud slam.* **7.** [*usually: the* + ~] *Slang.* SLAMMER.

slam[2] (slam) /slæm/ *n.* [*count*] the winning or bidding of all the tricks or all the tricks but one in a deal of cards.

slam′-bang′, *adv.* **1.** with noisy violence. **2.** quickly and carelessly. —*adj.* **3.** noisy and violent. **4.** excitingly fast-paced, esp. in a noisy and violent way: *a slam-bang movie.* **5.** quick and careless. **6.** outstanding; excellent.

slam•mer (slam′ər) /ˈslæmər/ *n.* [*count*] [*usually: the* + ~] Also called **the slam.** *Slang.* a prison.

slan•der (slan′dər) /ˈslændər/ *n.* **1.** [*noncount*] the act of knowingly making a false statement about someone to ruin his or her reputation; defamation. **2.** [*count*] such a wrong or false statement or report. —*v.* [~ + *obj*] **3.** to make a knowingly false statement about (someone) to ruin his or her reputation: *He accused the newspaper of slandering him.* —**slan′der•er,** *n.* [*count*] —**slan′der•ous,** *adj.*

slang (slang) /slæŋ/ *n.* [*noncount*] very informal words and idioms, normally not used in formal situations and sometimes containing vulgar or otherwise socially unacceptable vocabulary. —**slang′y,** *adj.*, **-i•er, -i•est:** *used some slangy expressions in his term paper.*

slant (slant) /slænt/ *v.* **1.** to (cause to) turn away from a straight line, esp. from a horizontal line; slope: [*no obj*]: *The roof slants upward sharply.* [~ + *obj*]: *to slant a roof upward.* **2.** [~ + *obj*] to distort (information), as by presenting it incompletely: *The story was slanted in favor of the president.* **3.** [~ + *obj*] to present for the interest or amusement of a group: *a story that is slanted toward young adults.* —*n.* **4.** [*noncount*] slanting direction; slope: *the slant of a roof.* **5.** [*count*] a slanting line, surface, etc. **6.** [*count*] a particular viewpoint, opinion, or way of looking at something: *a story with a humorous slant.* —**slant′wise′,** *adj.*, *adv.*

slap (slap) /slæp/ *n.*, *v.*, **slapped, slap•ping,** *adv.* —*n.* [*count*] **1.** a sharp blow or smack, esp. with the open hand: *a slap in the face.* **2.** a sound made by or as if by such a blow: *heard a slap as the book fell on the floor.* **3.** a sharp or sarcastic comment. —*v.* [~ + *obj*] **4.** to strike sharply, esp. with the open hand: *When the man pinched the woman she responded by slapping him hard.* **5.** to bring (the hand, etc.) with a sharp blow against something: *He slapped his hand on the table.* **6.** to put down with force: *He slapped the packages into a pile.* **7.** to put or place quickly: *to slap mustard on a sandwich.* —*adv.* **8.** directly; straight; smack: *to fall slap into the river.*

slap•dash (slap′dash′) /ˈslæpˌdæʃ/ *adj.* too quick and careless; offhand: *a slapdash answer.*

slap•hap•py (slap′hap′ē) /ˈslæpˌhæpiy/ *adj.*, **-pi•er, -pi•est. 1.** severely confused, as from having been hit too often; punch-drunk. **2.** agreeably giddy or foolish.

slap•stick (slap′stik′) /ˈslæpˌstɪk/ *n.* [*noncount*] **1.** comedy characterized by silly, noisy, and physically violent action. —*adj.* **2.** using or marked by slapstick: *a slapstick routine.*

slash (slash) /slæʃ/ *v.* **1.** to cut with a violent sweeping stroke, as with a knife or sword: [~ + *obj*]: *She had slashed her wrists.* [*no obj*]: *to slash at the weeds with a sickle.* **2.** [~ + *obj*] to cut or reduce: *to slash salaries.* —*n.* [*count*] **3.** a sweeping stroke, as with a knife or pen. **4.** a cut or mark made with such a stroke. **5.** VIRGULE. **6.** a reduction: *a slash in prices.* **7.** a decorative slit in a garment showing an underlying fabric.

slash′-and-burn′, *adj.* **1.** of or relating to a method of agriculture in the tropics in which vegetation is cut down and burned, the land is cropped for a few years, then the forest is allowed to reinvade. **2.** unnecessarily destructive or extreme: *the company's slash-and-burn tactics of laying off its workers.*

slash•er (slash′ər) /ˈslæʃər/ *n.* [*count*] **1.** one who criminally attacks others with a knife, razor, or the like. **2.** a film showing such a criminal and featuring bloody special effects.

slat (slat) /slæt/ *n.* [*count*] a long, narrow strip of wood, metal, or the like used as a support for a bed, etc.

slate (slāt) /sleyt/ *n.*, *v.*, **slat•ed, slat•ing.** —*n.* **1.** [*noncount*] a fine-grained rock formed from clay, shale, etc., that tends to split into thin plates **2.** [*count*] a thin piece of this rock or a similar material, used esp. for roofing or as a writing surface. **3.** [*noncount*] a dull, dark bluish gray. **4.** [*count*] a list of candidates, etc., considered for nomination or election. —*v.* [~ + *obj*] **5.** to cover with or as if with slate. **6.** [*usually: be* + ~*-ed*] to write or set down (someone or someone's name) to be nominated or appointed: *She is slated to be the new dean.* **7.** [*usually: be* + ~*-ed*] to plan or designate (something) for a particular place and time; schedule: *He is slated to arrive at three.* —***Idiom.*** **8. a clean slate,** [*count*] a clean record; a record that has no history or evidence of wrongdoing: *She started here with a clean slate.*

slath•er (slath′ər) /ˈslæðər/ *v.* [~ + *obj*] **1.** to spread or apply thickly: *to slather butter on toast.* **2.** to spread something thickly on: *to slather toast with butter.*

slat•tern (slat′ərn) /ˈslætərn/ *n.* [*count*] a dirty or very untidy woman. —**slat′tern•ly,** *adj.*

slaugh•ter (slô′tər) /ˈslɔtər/ *n.* [*noncount*] **1.** the killing of cattle, sheep, etc., esp. for food. **2.** a brutal or violent killing: *ordered the slaughter of hundreds of civilians.* —*v.* [~ + *obj*] **3.** to kill or butcher (animals), esp. for food. **4.** to kill in a brutal or violent manner, or in great numbers. —**slaugh′ter•er,** *n.* [*count*]

slaugh•ter•house (slô′tər hous′) /ˈslɔtərˌhaws/ *n.* [*count*], a building or place where animals are killed or butchered for food.

slave (slāv) /sleyv/ *n.*, *v.*, **slaved, slav•ing.** —*n.* [*count*] **1.** one who is the property of another and who must obey him or her: *The Emancipation Proclamation freed only the slaves in the South and not the slaves in the border states.* **2.** one under the control or influence of another person or power: *a slave to his desires.* **3.** a mechanism under control of and repeating the actions of a similar mechanism. —*v.* **4.** [*no obj; often:* ~ + *away* (+ *at* + *obj*); *often:* ~ (+ *away*) + *over* + *obj*] to work like a slave: *He slaved away all last night (at fixing the kitchen cabinets). I slaved over the hot stove to prepare the meal.*

slave′ driv′er, *n.* [*count*] **1.** an overseer of slaves. **2.** a demanding leader or boss.

slav•er[1] (slā′vər) /ˈsleyvər/ *n.* **1.** [*count*] a dealer in or an owner of slaves: *Arab slavers along the coast of East Africa.* **2.** a ship used in the slave trade.

slav•er[2] (slav′ər, slā′vər, slä′-) /ˈslævər, ˈsleyvər, ˈslɑ-/ *v.* [*no obj*] **1.** to let saliva run from the mouth: *The bloodhound slavered continuously.* **2.** [~ + *over* + *obj*] to fawn: *He slavered over the movie starlet.* —*n.* [*noncount*] **3.** saliva coming from the mouth.

slav•er•y (slā′və rē, slāv′rē) /ˈsleyvəriy, ˈsleyvriy/ *n.* [*noncount*] **1.** the condition of a slave; bondage: *kept in slavery.* **2.** the keeping of slaves as a practice: *outlawing slavery in most countries.* **3.** the state of being forced to do something like that of a slave, such as severe work: *the slavery of his job.*

Slav•ic (slä′vik, slav′ik) /ˈslɑvɪk, ˈslævɪk/ *n.* [*noncount*] a family of languages that includes Polish, Czech, and Russian.

slav•ish (slā′vish) /ˈsleyvɪʃ/ *adj.* **1.** of or like a slave: *slavish subjection.* **2.** deliberately imitative: *a slavish reproduction of the book in movie form.* —**slav′ish•ly,** *adv.*: *slavishly following the rules.*

slaw (slô) /slɔ/ *n.* [*noncount*] coleslaw.

slay (slā) /sley/ *v.* [~ + *obj*], **slew** (slo͞o) /sluw/ **slain** (slān) /sleyn/ **slay•ing. 1.** to kill by violence: *to slay the enemy.* **2.** *Slang.* to impress strongly; overwhelm, esp. by humor: *Your jokes slay me.* —**slay′er,** *n.* [*count*]

sleaze (slēz) /sliyz/ *n.* **1.** [*noncount*] sleazy quality: *That magazine is known for printing sleaze as a way of boosting sales.* **2.** [*count*] *Slang.* **a.** an evil, disgusting, or vulgar person. **b.** a shabby or dirty person.

slea•zy (slē′zē) /ˈsliyziy/ *adj.*, **-zi•er, -zi•est. 1.** disgustingly low, cheap, or vulgar; disreputable: *printing sleazy stories.* **2.** squalid; filthy: *a sleazy hotel.* **3.** thin and limp in texture: *a sleazy dress.* —**slea•zi•ly** (slē′zə lē) /ˈsliyzəliy/ *adv.* —**slea′zi•ness,** *n.* [*noncount*]

sled (sled) /slɛd/ *n.*, *v.*, **sled•ded, sled•ding.** —*n.* [*count*] **1.** a small vehicle made of a platform mounted on runners, for traveling over snow or ice. **2.** SLEDGE[1](defs 1,2). —*v.* **3.** [*no obj*] to coast or ride on a sled: *The kids went* *out to sled as soon as there was enough snow.* **4.** [~ + *obj*] to carry by sled. —**sled′der,** *n.* [*count*]

sledge[1] (slej) /slɛdʒ/ *n.* [*count*] **1.** a vehicle mounted on runners and often pulled by a horse or other animal, used for traveling or for carrying loads over snow, ice, etc. **2.** a sled. **3.** *Brit.* a sleigh.

sledge[2] (slej) /slɛdʒ/ *n.* SLEDGEHAMMER.

sledge•ham•mer (slej′ham′ər) /ˈslɛdʒˌhæmər/ *n.* [*count*] **1.** a large heavy hammer used with both hands. —*adj.* [*before a noun*] **2.** too powerful or forceful: *sledgehammer punches.*

sleek (slēk) /sliyk/ *adj.,* **-er, -est. 1.** smooth or glossy, such as hair: *sleek, combed-back hair.* **2.** well-fed or well-groomed: *looking sleek and healthy.* **3.** finely shaped; streamlined: *a sleek sports car.* **4.** smooth in manners, speech, etc.; suave. —**sleek′ly,** *adv.* —**sleek′ness,** *n.* [*noncount*]

sleep (slēp) /sliyp/ *v.,* **slept** (slept) /slɛpt/ **sleep•ing,** *n.* —*v.* **1.** [*no obj*] to go into or be in the condition of rest that comes when the body suspends certain functions and is in a state of unconsciousness. **2.** [~ + *obj*] to have enough beds, or a place to sleep, for (people): *This trailer sleeps three people.* **3.** [*no obj*] to allow one's alertness to become less active: *The salespeople must have been sleeping when the shoplifter came in.* **4.** [*no obj*] to lie in death. **5.** [~ + *obj*] to take rest in (a certain kind of sleep): *The baby slept the sleep of the innocent.* **6. sleep around,** [*no obj*] to have sexual relationships with many different partners: *She accused her husband of sleeping around with other women.* **7. sleep away,** [~ + *obj* + *away*] to spend or pass (time) in sleep: *She slept the night away.* **8. sleep in,** [*no obj*] **a.** (of a servant, maid, etc.) to sleep where one is employed. **b.** to sleep beyond one's usual time of arising: *Tomorrow there will be no school so you can sleep in.* **9. sleep off,** to get rid of (a headache, etc.) by sleeping: [~ + *off* + *obj*]: *to sleep off a bad hangover.* [~ + *obj* + *off*]: *to sleep it off.* **10. sleep on,** [~ + *on* + *obj*] to postpone making a decision about (something) for at least a day: *Thanks for your proposal; I think I'll sleep on it and call you tomorrow.* **11. sleep out,** [*no obj*] **a.** (of a servant, maid, etc.) to sleep away from one's place of employment. **b.** to sleep outdoors. **12. sleep over,** [*no obj*] to sleep in another person's home: *My daughters want to sleep over (at) their cousin's.* **13. sleep through,** [~ + *through* + *obj*] to sleep in spite of (noise or the like): *There was a loud party in the next room but somehow we slept through it.* **14. sleep together,** [*no obj*] to be sexual partners. **15. sleep with,** [~ + *with* + *obj*] to have sexual relations with: *He said he had never slept with anyone but his wife.* —*n.* **16.** [*noncount*] the state of a person, animal, or plant that sleeps: *Sleep wouldn't come, and he lay awake most of the night.* **17.** [*count; usually singular*] a period of sleeping: *a good sleep.* **18.** [*noncount*] the substance in one's eyes after having slept: *to rub the sleep from her eyes.* —***Idiom.* 19. get to sleep,** to succeed in falling asleep: *The night before we left for our new home we couldn't get to sleep.* **20. go to sleep, a.** to fall asleep: *Everytime the baby went to sleep, the gas pains woke her up again.* **b.** to get ready to sleep, as by going to one's bed: *The kids didn't want to go to sleep; they were too excited.* **c.** to become numb: *My foot's gone to sleep and I can't stand on it.* **21. put (someone** or **something) to sleep,** to kill in a painless way: *They had to put their dog to sleep.* —**sleep′less,** *adj.* —**sleep′less•ness,** *n.* [*noncount*] —**Related Words.** SLEEP is both a noun and a verb, ASLEEP and SLEEPY are adjectives: *He fell into a deep sleep. He slept deeply. He was asleep and didn't wake up when the phone rang. He was sleepy and ready for bed.*

sleep•er (slē′pər) /ˈsliypər/ *n.* [*count*] **1.** one that sleeps. **2.** a heavy horizontal timber for distributing loads. **3.** a railroad car with beds or special compartments for passengers to sleep in. **4.** an unexpected success, esp. a film or play that was at first ignored. **5.** Often, **sleepers.** [*plural*] one-piece or two-piece pajamas with feet, esp. for children. **6.** a piece of furniture, such as a sofa, that opens up into a bed; convertible.

sleep′ing bag′, *n.* [*count*] a warmly lined body-length bag in which one can sleep outdoors, as when camping.

sleep′ing pill′, *n.* [*count*] a pill or capsule containing a drug that brings on sleep.

sleep′ing sick′ness, *n.* [*noncount*] **1.** an infectious, usually fatal disease of Africa, characterized by great fatigue and a wasting away of the body: *Sleeping sickness is carried to the body through the tsetse fly.* **2.** a viral disease affecting the brain, characterized by sleepiness, muscular weakness, and difficulty in seeing.

sleep•walk•ing (slēp′wô′king) /ˈsliypˌwɔkɪŋ/ *n.* [*noncount*] the act of walking while asleep; somnambulism. —**sleep′walk′,** *v.* [*no obj*] —**sleep′walk′er,** *n.* [*count*]

sleep•wear (slēp′wâr′) /ˈsliypˌwɛər/ *n.* [*noncount*] garments, as nightgowns or pajamas, worn for sleeping.

sleep•y (slē′pē) /ˈsliypiy/ *adj.,* **-i•er, -i•est. 1.** ready to sleep; drowsy: *He grew sleepy and dozed off.* **2.** of or showing drowsiness: *a sleepy yawn.* **3.** inactive: *a sleepy, quiet village.* —**sleep•i•ly** (slē′pə lē) /ˈsliypəliy/ *adv.*: *She looked up sleepily at her alarm clock.* —**sleep′i•ness,** *n.* [*noncount*]

sleet (slēt) /sliyt/ *n.* [*noncount*] **1.** rain in the form of ice pellets. —*v.* [*no obj; it* + ~] **2.** to send down sleet: *It's sleeting quite a bit.* —**sleet′y,** *adj.,* **-i•er, -i•est.**

sleeve (slēv) /sliyv/ *n.* [*count*] **1.** the part of a garment that covers the arm: *He rolled up his sleeves and began to work.* **2.** an envelope, usually of paper or cardboard, for protecting a phonograph record. **3.** a tube-shaped piece, as of metal, fitting over a rod or the like. —***Idiom.* 4. up one's sleeve,** [*noncount*] kept hidden, esp. for future use against another: *He's got some trick up his sleeve.* —**sleeve′less,** *adj.*

sleigh (slā) /sley/ *n.* [*count*] **1.** a light vehicle on runners, usually open and generally horse-drawn, used esp. for transporting people over snow. **2.** a sled. —*v.* [*no obj*] **3.** to travel or ride in a sleigh.

sleight′ of hand′ (slīt) /slayt/ *n.* [*noncount*] skill in quick and clever movements of the hands, esp. for doing tricks.

slen•der (slen′dər) /ˈslɛndər/ *adj.,* **-er, -est. 1.** having a distance around the middle that is small when compared to the height or length: *a slender post.* **2.** thin or slight; light and graceful: *slender youths.* **3.** small in size, amount, etc.; meager: *a slender income.* **4.** having little value, force, or justification: *The prospects for victory were slender.* —**slen′der•ness,** *n.* [*noncount*]

slen•der•ize (slen′də rīz′) /ˈslɛndəˌrayz/ *v.,* **-ized, -iz•ing.** to (cause to) become or appear slender or more slender: [~ + *obj*]: *to slenderize one's figure.* [*no obj*]: *to slenderize by losing a few pounds.*

slept (slept) /slɛpt/ *v.* pt. and pp. of SLEEP.

sleuth (slōōth) /sluwθ/ *n.* [*count*] a detective.

slew[1] (slōō) /sluw/ *v.* pt. of SLAY.

slew[2] (slōō) /sluw/ *n.* [*count*] *Informal.* a large number or quantity: *A whole slew of people showed up.*

slew[3] (slōō) /sluw/ *v.* [*no obj*] to slide, skid, or turn very suddenly: *The car slewed across the road.*

slice (slīs) /slays/ *n., v.,* **sliced, slic•ing.** —*n.* [*count*] **1.** a thin, flat piece cut from something: *a slice of bread.* **2.** a portion: *a slice of land.* **3.** a shot or hit of a baseball, golf ball, etc., that curves toward the side from which it was struck. —*v.* **4.** [~ + *obj*] to cut or divide into slices: *to slice the meat into strips.* **5. a.** to cut through or remove (something) with or as if with a knife: [~ + *obj*]: *He nearly sliced my finger with that paper cutter!* [~ + *obj* + *off*]: *He nearly sliced my finger off.* [~ + *off* + *obj*]: *He nearly sliced off my finger.* **b.** [*no obj*] to cut: *The boat sliced through the water.* **6. a.** [~ + *obj*] to hit (a ball) so as to result in a slice: *to slice the ball perfectly.* **b.** [*no obj*] (of a ball, etc.) to curve in a slice: *His next shot sliced to the left.* —**slic′er,** *n.* [*count*]

slick[1] (slik) /slɪk/ *adj.,* **-er, -est,** *n., adv.* —*adj.* **1.** smooth and glossy: *his slick black hair.* **2.** smooth in manners, speech, etc., so as to be or seem to be sly or untrustworthy. **3.** ingenious; cleverly made. **4.** slippery, esp. from being covered with or as if with ice or oil: *The car skidded on the slick surface.* **5.** well executed and having surface appeal but shallow in content: *slick writing.* **6.** *Slang.* wonderful; remarkable; first-rate. —*n.* [*count*] **7.** a smooth or slippery place or the substance causing it: *an oil slick.* —*adv.* **8.** smoothly; cleverly. —**slick′ly,** *adv.* —**slick′ness,** *n.* [*noncount*]: *Was his mayoral campaign all slickness and no content?*

slick[2] (slik) /slɪk/ *v.* [~ + *obj*] to make sleek or smooth: *His hair was slicked down with hair cream.*

slick•er (slik′ər) /ˈslɪkər/ *n.* [*count*] **1.** a long, loose oilskin raincoat. **2.** any raincoat. **3.** *Informal.* a person who cheats another; swindler.

slide (slīd) /slayd/ *v.,* **slid** (slid), **slid•ing,** *n.* —*v.* **1.** to (cause to) move in continuous contact with a smooth or slippery surface: [*no obj*]: *He slid down the hill.* [~ + *obj*]: *The bartender slid a glass of beer along the bar.* **2.** to glide or pass smoothly; slip: [*no obj*]: *Tears slid down her face.* [~ + *obj*]: *He slid the child into the car seat and buckled her up.* **3.** [*no obj*] to move easily or without being noticed: *He slid out the back door.* **4.** [*no obj*] to pass or fall gradually into a specified state, character, etc.: *to slide into depression.* **5.** [*no obj*] to decline or decrease: *The economy slid last quarter.* **6. let (something) slide,** [*let + obj + ~*] to allow to proceed naturally, esp. to get worse without correction: *to let a matter slide.* **7.** [*no obj*] *Baseball.* (of a base runner) to throw oneself forward along the ground toward a base: *He slid into home and the umpire shouted "Safe!"* **—*n.*** [*count*] **8.** an act or instance of sliding. **9.** a smooth surface for sliding on, esp. a type of chute in a playground. **10. a.** a landslide or the like. **b.** the mass of matter sliding down. **11.** a small frame of film, mounted on cardboard or plastic, for projection on a screen or magnification through a viewer: *slides from our trip to Africa.* **12.** a rectangular plate of glass on which objects are mounted for examination under a microscope.

slid•er (slī′dər) /'slaydər/ *n.* [*count*] a fast-pitched baseball that curves slightly and sharply in front of a batter, away from the side from which it was thrown.

slid′ing scale′, *n.* [*count*] a system of figuring or adjusting wages or prices according to such factors as the selling price of goods produced, the cost of living, etc.: *Health care was on a sliding scale, where the rich pay more and the poor pay less.*

slight (slīt) /slayt/ *adj.,* **-er, -est,** *v., n.* **—*adj.*** **1.** small in amount, degree, etc.: *I heard a slight noise.* **2.** of little importance, influence, etc.; trivial: *only a slight difference between what he says and what you say.* **3.** slender or slim; light in build: *She was slight and had delicate features.* **4.** of little substance or strength. **—*v.*** [*~ + obj*] **5.** to treat (someone) as if he or she were unimportant: *didn't mean to slight the dinner guest.* **—*n.*** [*count*] **6.** an instance of treating someone as unimportant: *a deliberate slight.* —**slight′ed,** *adj.*: *I felt slighted that I was not invited to the party.* —**slight′ly,** *adv.*: *slightly overweight.* —**slight′ness,** *n.* [*noncount*]

slim (slim) /slɪm/ *adj.,* **slim•mer, slim•mest,** *v.,* **slimmed, slim•ming. —*adj.*** **1.** slender, as in the width around one's body or in form: *a slim figure.* **2.** poor or inferior; meager: *a slim chance.* **—*v.*** **3.** Often, **slim down.** to (cause to) become slim: [*no obj*]: *He's been on a diet and has slimmed down.* [*~ + obj + down*]: *Diet and exercise will slim you down.* [*~ + down + obj*]: *to slim down even the most overweight dieters.* —**slim′ness,** *n.* [*noncount*]

slime (slīm) /slaym/ *n., v.,* **slimed, slim•ing. —*n.*** [*noncount*] **1.** thin, sticky mud. **2.** any sticky, mostly liquid matter, esp. of a foul kind. **3.** *Slang.* a disgusting, repulsive person: *He's slime; she never wants to see him again.*

slim•y (slī′mē) /'slaymiy/ *adj.,* **-i•er, -i•est. 1.** of, like, or relating to slime. **2.** covered with or full of slime: *slimy footprints.* **3.** causing a feeling of disgust; disgusting; repulsive: *She told him to keep his slimy hands off her.*

sling (sling) /slɪŋ/ *n., v.,* **slung** (slung) /slʌŋ/ **sling•ing. —*n.*** [*count*] **1.** a device for hurling a stone, etc., by hand, usually a strap with a string at each end that is whirled around in a circle to gain speed before releasing the rock or stone. **2.** a slingshot. **3.** a strap or band forming a loop by which something is suspended or carried, such as a bandage for an injured arm: *They put a plaster cast on his broken arm and wrapped a sling around it.* **—*v.*** [*~ + obj*] **4.** to throw or hurl; fling: *slung a rock at him.* **5.** to hang by a sling or place so as to swing loosely: *He slung his jacket on the coat-rack hook.*

sling•shot (sling′shot′) /'slɪŋ,ʃɒt/ *n.* [*count*] a Y-shaped stick with an elastic strip between the forks for shooting small objects, such as rocks or pebbles.

slink (slingk) /slɪŋk/ *v.* [*no obj*], **slunk** (slungk) /slʌŋk/ **slink•ing. 1.** to move or go in a sneaky manner, as from fear or shame: *After those insulting remarks he slunk quietly away.* **2.** to walk in a sinuous way that draws attention, esp. sexual attention: *She slinked into the room and every man's eyes were upon her.*

slink•y (sling′kē) /'slɪŋkiy/ *adj.,* **-i•er, -i•est. 1.** characterized by slinking movements: *a slinky walk.* **2.** (of clothing) close-fitting and revealing: *wearing a slinky black dress.* —**slink•i•ly** (sling′kə lē) /'slɪŋkəliy/ *adv.* —**slink′i•ness,** *n.* [*noncount*]

slip[1] (slip) /slɪp/ *v.,* **slipped, slip•ping,** *n.* **—*v.*** **1.** to (cause to) move or go smoothly; (cause to) slide: [*no obj*]: *She slipped into his arms and hugged him.* [*~ + obj*]: *slipped the shoe on her foot.* **2.** [*no obj*] to slide suddenly and accidentally, esp. so as to fall or go lower: *He slipped on the icy ground.* **3.** [*no obj; usually: ~ + by/away*] to pass quickly, esp. without having been acted upon or used, as an opportunity: *Another opportunity to catch him slipped by.* **4.** [*no obj; often: ~ + into + obj*] to become involved or absorbed easily: *He'd already slipped into sin.* **5.** [*no obj*] to move or go quietly or without being noticed: *to slip out of a room.* **6.** to put on or take off (a piece of clothing) easily or quickly: [*~ + on/off + obj*]: *He slipped on his jacket.* [*~ + obj + on/off*]: *He slipped his jacket on and went outside.* [*~ + into + obj*]: *"Let me slip into something more comfortable," she whispered.* **7.** [*no obj; often: ~ + up*] to make a mistake or error: *Someone in the office must have slipped (up).* **8.** [*no obj*] to become worse; decline: *His work slipped badly last year.* **9.** [*no obj; often: ~ + out*] to be said or made known unintentionally: *The words just slipped (out).* **10.** [*~ + obj*] to put, pass, etc., quickly or while trying not to be noticed: *to slip a note into a person's pocket.* **11.** [*~ + obj*] to let or make (something) slide out of a fastening, hold, etc.: *I slipped the lock, and the door opened.* **12.** [*~ + obj*] to pass from or escape (one's memory, etc.): *The date for our meeting has slipped my mind.* **13.** [*~ + obj*] to put out of correct position: *I slipped a disk in my back.* **—*n.*** [*count*] **14.** an act or instance of slipping. **15.** a sudden, accidental slide: *a slip on the ice.* **16.** a mistake or error, as in speaking or writing, esp. a small, careless one: *a slip of the tongue.* **17.** a decline or fall in quantity, quality, etc.: *a slip in prices.* **18.** a woman's skirted undergarment worn under the outer dress or skirt. See illustration at CLOTHING. **19.** a pillowcase. **20.** a space between two wharves or in a dock for vessels. **—*Idiom.*** **21. give (someone) the slip,** to get away from (someone) who is chasing one; escape from (someone): *She gave him the slip by dashing across the street.* **22. let slip,** to reveal (something) by accident: [*let + obj + ~*]: *He let the secret slip.* [*let + ~ + obj*]: *He let slip all our secrets.* [*let + it + ~ + that clause*]: *He let it slip that some of our spies were still operating.*

slip[2] (slip) /slɪp/ *n.* [*count*] **1.** a small paper form on which information is noted: *a bank withdrawal slip.* **2.** a young person, esp. one of slender form: *a mere slip of a girl.*

slip•case (slip′kās′) /'slɪp,keys/ *n.* [*count*] a box for a book open on one side so that the spine is visible.

slip•cov•er (slip′kuv′ər) /'slɪp,kʌvər/ *n.* [*count*] a removable cover of cloth or other material for a chair or sofa.

slip•knot or **slip knot** (slip′not′) /'slɪp,nɒt/ *n.* [*count*] a knot that slips easily along the cord or line around which it is made.

slip•page (slip′ij) /'slɪpɪdʒ/ *n.* **1.** [*noncount*] an act or instance of slipping. **2.** [*count*] an amount or extent of slipping.

slipped′ disk′, *n.* [*count*] a disk between the vertebrae of the backbone that sticks out abnormally.

slip•per (slip′ər) /'slɪpər/ *n.* [*count*] a light, low-cut shoe into which the foot easily slips, for wear in the home, etc. See illustration at CLOTHING.

slip•per•y (slip′ə rē, slip′rē) /'slɪpəriy, 'slɪpriy/ *adj.,* **-i•er, -i•est. 1.** easily causing slipping: *a slippery road.* **2.** tending to slip from the hold or grasp or from position: *a slippery rope.* **3.** likely to slip away or escape: *a slippery scoundrel.* **4.** unstable or insecure, such as conditions: *a slippery situation.* —**slip′per•i•ness,** *n.* [*noncount*]

slip•shod (slip′shod′) /'slɪp,ʃɒd/ *adj.* careless, untidy, or sloppy; not careful: *slipshod work.*

slip′-up′, *n.* [*count*] a mistake, error, blunder, or oversight.

slit (slit) /slɪt/ *v.,* **slit, slit•ting,** *n.* **—*v.*** [*~ + obj*] **1.** to make a long cut or opening in: *to slit a dress.* **2.** to cut into strips; split. **—*n.*** [*count*] **3.** a straight, narrow cut or opening: *a slit in the skirt.*

slith•er (slith′ər) /'slɪðər/ *v.* [*no obj*] **1.** to move with a sliding motion, such as a snake: *to slither quietly out of the room.* **2.** to slide along a surface, esp. unsteadily, from side to side: *to slither clumsily down the ski slope.* **—*n.*** [*count*] **3.** a slithering movement; slide. —**slith′er•y,** *adj.*

sliv•er (sliv′ər) /'slɪvər/ *n.* [*count*] **1.** a small, slender, often sharp piece, as of wood or glass; splinter. **2.** any small, narrow piece or portion: *just a sliver of cake, please.* **—*v.*** [*~ + obj*] **3.** to split or cut into slivers.

slob (slob) /slɒb/ *n.* [*count*] a very sloppy or badmannered person.

slob•ber (slob′ər) /'slɒbər/ *v.* **1.** [*no obj*] to let saliva or liquid run from the mouth: *The dog was slobbering all over the baby.* **2.** [*~ + obj*] to wet or make foul with saliva: *The dog is slobbering the baby.* **3.** [*no obj*] to express one's feelings too sentimentally: *slobbering about how much he loved her.* **—*n.*** [*noncount*] **4.** saliva or liquid dribbling from the mouth; slaver. **5.** overly sentimental speech or actions.

sloe (slō) /slow/ *n.* [*count*] **1.** the small, sour, blackish fruit of the blackthorn, of the rose family. **2.** the shrub itself.

sloe′-eyed′, *adj.* **1.** having very dark eyes. **2.** having slanted eyes.

slog (slog) /slɒg/ *v.*, **slogged, slog•ging,** *n.* —*v.* **1.** [~ + *obj*] to hit hard, as in boxing; slug: *to slog him at least once in each round.* **2.** [*no obj*] to walk or plod heavily, slowly, or with effort: *to slog through the mud and rain.* **3.** [~ + *obj*] to make or find (one's way) by plodding: *to slog his way through the rain.* —*n.* [*count*] **4.** a long, tiring walk or march. **5.** long, laborious work. **6.** a heavy blow.

slo•gan (slō′gən) /ˈslowgən/ *n.* [*count*] a phrase identified with a particular party, product, etc.; a catch phrase: *a campaign slogan.*

sloop (slo͞op) /sluwp/ *n.* [*count*] a single-masted sailing vessel with rigging fore and aft.

slop (slop) /slɒp/ *v.*, **slopped, slop•ping,** *n.* —*v.* **1.** to spill or splash (liquid): [*no obj*]: *The children were slopping about in the puddle.* [~ + *obj*]: *They were slopping water all over the place.* **2.** [*no obj*] to walk or go through mud, slush, or water: *slopping home through the storm.* **3.** [*no obj;* ~ + *over (+ obj)*] (of liquid) to spill or splash out of a container: *The liquid slopped over (the top of the container) and spilled onto the floor.* **4.** [~ + *obj*] to feed slop to (pigs or other livestock). —*n.* **5.** [*noncount*] bran made from cornmeal and mixed with an equal part of water, used as a feed for pigs and other livestock. **6. slops,** [*plural*] kitchen refuse; swill. **7.** [*noncount*] badly cooked or unappetizing food or drink. **8.** [*noncount*] liquid mud: *walking through the slop.*

slope (slōp) /slowp/ *v.*, **sloped, slop•ing,** *n.* —*v.* **1.** to (cause to) have an inclined angle; slant: [*no obj*]: *The roof sloped sharply upward.* [~ + *obj*]: *The builder sloped the roof sharply upward.* —*n.* **2.** [*count*] ground that has a natural incline, such as the side of a hill: *the sharp slopes of the hills.* **3.** [*noncount*] **a.** slant, esp. downward or upward. **b.** the amount or degree of such a slant.

slop•py (slop′ē) /ˈslɒpiy/ *adj.*, **-pi•er, -pi•est. 1.** muddy, slushy, or very wet: *sloppy ground.* **2.** untidy; messy; slovenly: *a sloppy eater.* **3.** careless; slipshod: *His sloppy writing was due to his sloppy thinking.* **4.** overly emotional; silly; gushy: *the movie's sloppy sentimentality.* —**slop′pi•ness,** *n.* [*noncount*]

slosh (slosh) /slɒʃ/ *v.* **1.** [*no obj*] to splash or move through water, mud, etc.: *to slosh through the puddles.* **2.** [*no obj*] (of a liquid) to move about actively, esp. within a container: *The water sloshed over the sides.* **3.** [~ + *obj*] to cause (a liquid) to splash, esp. in a container: *to slosh the gasoline in the tank.*

slot (slot) /slɒt/ *n.*, *v.*, **slot•ted, slot•ting.** —*n.* [*count*] **1.** a slit, esp. one for receiving something, such as a letter: *a slot for airmail letters.* **2.** a position, as in a sequence or series: *Her TV show is in the eight o'clock slot on Thursdays.* **3.** *Informal.* SLOT MACHINE —*v.* [~ + *obj*] **4.** to make a slot in; provide with a slot or slots. **5.** to place or fit into a slot: *You've been slotted for a four o'clock meeting.*

sloth (slôth *or, esp. for 2,* slōth) /slɔθ *or, esp. for 2,* slowθ/ *n.* **1.** [*noncount*] laziness; unwillingness to work. **2.** [*count*] a slow-moving, tree-dwelling tropical American animal.

sloth•ful (slôth′fəl, slōth-) /ˈslɔθfəl, slowθ-/ *adj.* lazy; unwilling to work; indolent. —**sloth′ful•ness,** *n.* [*noncount*]

slot′ machine′, *n.* [*count*] a gambling or vending machine operated by putting coins into a slot.

slouch (slouch) /slawtʃ/ *v.* **1.** [*no obj*] to sit, stand, or walk with a drooping posture: *to slouch around all day.* **2.** to (cause to) droop or bend down, as the shoulders or a hat: [~ + *obj*]: *to slouch the shoulders.* [*no obj*]: *His shoulders slouched a little lower.* —*n.* [*count*] **3.** [*usually singular*] an awkward, drooping posture or way of walking or carrying oneself. **4.** a lazy or incapable person: *The coach warned that our opponents were no slouches.* —**slouch′er,** *n.* [*count*] —**slouch′y,** *adj.*, **-i•er, -i•est.**

slough[1] (slou) /slaw/ *n.* **1.** [*count*] an area of soft, muddy ground; a swamp or swamplike region. **2.** [*noncount*] a condition of despair or humiliation.

slough[2] (sluf) /slʌf/ *n.* [*noncount*] **1.** a layer of dead tissue that drops off the surrounding or underlying tissue. —*v.* **2.** to (cause to) be shed or cast off, as the outer skin of a snake: [*no obj;* (~ + *off*)]: *A snake's skin sloughs (off) every few months.* [~ (+ *off*) + *obj*]: *The snake sloughs (off) its skin.* **3. slough off,** [~ + *off* + *obj*] to dispose or get rid of: *to slough off a bad habit.*

slov•en•ly (sluv′ən lē) /ˈslʌvənliy/ *adj.*, **-li•er, -li•est,** *adv.* —*adj.* **1.** untidy or unclean in appearance; sloppy: *a slovenly room in a cheap hotel.* **2.** careless or sloppy: *slovenly work.* —*adv.* **3.** in an untidy, careless, or slipshod manner. —**slov′en•li•ness,** *n.* [*noncount*]

slow (slō) /slow/ *adj.* and *adv.*, **-er, -est,** *v.* —*adj.* **1.** moving or going forward with little speed: *Somehow I always catch the slowest train.* **2.** showing or having lack of speed: *a slow pace of walking.* **3.** taking or requiring a comparatively long time: *a slow meal.* **4.** gradual: *slow growth in the economy.* **5.** mentally dull: *a slow child.* **6.** [*be* + ~] not readily disposed or willing (to do or become something): [~ + *to* + *verb*]: *He is slow to anger (= He does not get angry quickly).* **7.** slack; not busy: *a slow stock market.* **8.** progressing at less than the usual rate of speed: *a slow worker.* **9.** [*be* + ~] running at less than the proper rate of speed, as a clock: *My watch is slow.* **10.** dull or tedious: *a slow party.* —*adv.* **11.** in a slow manner; slowly: *Drive slow.* —*v.* **12.** to (cause to) be slow or slower: [*no obj;* (+ *up/down*)]: *The car slowed (up) and then came to a stop.* [~ + *obj* (+ *down/up*)]: *He slowed the train (down) but couldn't avoid the collision.* **13.** to reduce the progress of (something): [*no obj*]: *Inflation has slowed this year.* [~ + *obj*]: *took steps to slow inflation.* —**slow′ly,** *adv.*: *Drink this slowly.* —**slow′ness,** *n.* [*noncount*]

slow′ burn′, *n.* [*count; usually singular*] *Informal.* a gradual building up of anger.

slow•down (slō′doun′) /ˈslowˌdawn/ *n.* [*count*] **1.** a delay in progress, action, etc.: *a general slowdown in the economy.* **2.** a deliberate slowing of pace by workers to win demands from their employer: *The workers staged a slowdown by checking every item more strictly than they usually did.*

slow′ mo′tion, *n.* [*noncount*] the process or technique of filming or taping a motion-picture or television sequence at a faster rate of speed and then projecting or replaying it at normal speed so that the action appears to be slowed down. —**slow′-mo′tion,** *adj.*

slow•poke (slō′pōk′) /ˈslowˌpowk/ *n.* [*count*] *Informal.* a person who moves, works, etc., very slowly; dawdler.

slow′-wit′ted, *adj.* slow in the ability to understand; dull-witted. —**slow′-wit′ted•ly,** *adv.* —**slow′-wit′ted•ness,** *n.* [*noncount*]

sludge (sluj) /slʌdʒ/ *n.* [*noncount*] **1.** mud, mire, or ooze; slush. **2.** a deposit of ooze at the bottom of a body of water. **3.** the substance left over after treating sewage.

slue or **slew** (slo͞o) /sluw/ *v.*, **slued, slu•ing,** *n.* —*v.* **1.** to turn or swing around, such as a mast on its own axis: [*no obj*]: *to slue sharply around.* [~ + *obj*]: *to slue the mast sharply around.* —*n.* [*count*] **2.** the act of sluing.

slug[1] (slug) /slʌg/ *n.* [*count*] **1.** a slow-moving, snaillike animal. **2.** a metal disk used as a coin or token, generally counterfeit: *putting slugs into subway token machines.* **3.** a piece of lead or other metal for firing from a gun. **4.** *Slang.* a person who is lazy or slow-moving; sluggard.

slug[2] (slug) /slʌg/ *v.*, **slugged, slug•ging,** *n.* —*v.* [~ + *obj*] **1.** to strike hard, esp. with the fist: *The two fighters slugged each other.* **2.** to drive (a baseball) a great distance: *The batter strode up and slugged the first pitch over the fence.* —*n.* [*count*] **3.** a hard blow or hit, esp. with a fist or baseball bat. —**slug′ger,** *n.* [*count*]

slug•gard (slug′ərd) /ˈslʌgərd/ *n.* [*count*] **1.** one who is by habit inactive or lazy. —*adj.* **2.** lazy; indolent.

slug•gish (slug′ish) /ˈslʌgɪʃ/ *adj.* **1.** not working or functioning with full speed, energy, or ability: *a sluggish heartbeat.* **2.** slow to act or respond: *a sluggish engine.* **3.** slow or slow-moving, as a stream. **4.** greatly reduced; slack, as trade or sales: *The economy is sluggish.* —**slug′gish•ness,** *n.* [*noncount*]

sluice (slo͞os) /sluws/ *n.*, *v.*, **sluiced, sluic•ing.** —*n.* [*count*] **1.** an artificial channel for conducting water, often with a gate **(sluice′ gate′)** at the upper end for regulating the flow. **2.** the body of water held back or controlled by a sluice gate. **3.** a channel, esp. one carrying off surplus water or moving solid matter. —*v.* [~ + *obj*] **4.** to let out (water) by opening a sluice. **5.** to flush with a rush of water: *to sluice the decks of a ship.*

slum (slum) /slʌm/ *n.*, *v.*, **slummed, slum•ming.** —*n.* [*count*] **1.** a run-down or dirty part of a city: *The mayor promised to clean up the slums.* —*v.* [*no obj*] **2.** to visit or spend time in a place, esp. an amusement spot, considered low in social status: *to go slumming.* —**slum′mer,** *n.* [*count*]

slum•ber (slum′bər) /ˈslʌmbər/ *v.* [*no obj*] **1.** to sleep. *—n.* **2.** [*noncount*] sleep. **3.** [*count*] a period of sleep. —**slum′ber•ous,** *adj.*

slum•lord (slum′lôrd′) /ˈslʌmˌlɔrd/ *n.* [*count*] a landlord who owns poorly maintained buildings.

slump (slump) /slʌmp/ *v.* [*no obj*] **1.** to fall heavily; collapse: *He slumped to the floor.* **2.** to assume a slouching or bent position or posture: *His shoulders slumped.* **3.** to decrease suddenly: *His health slumped.* **4.** to sink heavily, as the spirits: *Her spirits slumped as the bad news sank in.* *—n.* [*count*] **5.** an act, instance, or occasion of slumping: *The economy is in a prolonged slump.* **6.** a period during which a person performs ineffectively: *The team is in a slump after having lost its last six games.*

slung (slung) /slʌŋ/ *v.* pt. and pp. of SLING[1].

slunk (slungk) /slʌŋk/ *v.* a pt. and the pp. of SLINK.

slur[1] (slûr) /slɜr/ *v.,* **slurred, slur•ring,** *n.* *—v.* **1.** to pronounce (a syllable, word, etc.) unclearly by combining, reducing, or leaving out sounds, as in hurried or careless speaking: [*no obj*]: *His voice slurred because he wasn't yet awake.* [~ + *obj*]: *I can't understand you when you slur your speech like that.* **2.** [~ + *obj*] to sing or play (two different tones of music) in one syllable or without a break. *—n.* [*count*] **3.** a slurred utterance or sound. **4. a.** the combination of two different tones, sung to a single syllable or played without a break. **b.** a curved mark used in music to indicate this.

slur[2] (slûr) /slɜr/ *v.,* **slurred, slur•ring,** *n.* *—v.* [~ + *obj*] **1.** to insult: *to slur someone's reputation.* *—n.* [*count*] **2.** an insulting remark: *to take offense at a slur.*

slurp (slûrp) /slɜrp/ *v.* **1.** to eat or drink (food or beverages) with loud sucking noises: [~ + *obj*]: *to slurp one's food.* [*no obj*]: *The kids were slurping as they drank their sodas.* *—n.* [*count*] **2.** an act of slurping. **3.** any slurping sound.

slush (slush) /slʌʃ/ *n.* [*noncount*] **1.** partly melted snow: *The snow had melted to brownish, dirty slush.* **2.** silly, sentimental talk or writing. —**slush′y,** *adj.,* **-i•er, -i•est:** *slushy streets after the warm rain.*

slush′ fund′, *n.* [*count*] a sum of money for illegal political purposes, as for buying influence.

slut (slut) /slʌt/ *n.* [*count*] **1.** a dirty, very untidy woman. **2.** a sexually loose woman. —**slut′tish, slut′ty,** *adj.,* **-ti•er, -ti•est.**

sly (slī) /slaɪ/ *adj.,* **sly•er** or **sli•er, sly•est** or **sli•est,** *n.* *—adj.* **1.** sneaky; tricky; cunning: *The sly old fox was able to outsmart us once again.* **2.** able to avoid being seen or noticed; stealthy: *a sly move.* **3.** mischievous: *sly humor.* *—n.,* ***Idiom.*** **4. on the sly,** [*noncount*] secretly; without others knowing or seeing. —**sly′ly,** *adv.*: *slyly slipped the money from the drawer.* —**sly′ness,** *n.* [*noncount*]

smack[1] (smak) /smæk/ *v.* [~ + *obj*] **smack of,** to have a taste, flavor, or trace of something: *The compliment he gave her smacks of condescension.*

smack[2] (smak) /smæk/ *v.* **1.** [~ + *obj*] to strike sharply, esp. with the open hand; slap: *He smacked his forehead with his hand.* **2.** to drive or send (something) with a sharp blow or with force: [*no obj*]: *The car smacked into the wall.* [~ + *obj*]: *He smacked his brand new car into the wall.* **3.** [~ + *obj*] to close and open (the lips) quickly so as to produce a sharp sound, often as a sign of enjoyment: *They all sat at her table, smacking their lips.* **4.** [~ + *obj*] to kiss with a loud sound: *She smacked him on the cheek.* *—n.* [*count*] **5.** a sharp, loud-sounding blow; slap. **6.** a smacking of the lips, as in enjoyment or anticipation. **7.** a loud kiss. *—adv.* **8.** suddenly and violently: *He drove smack up against the side of the house.* **9.** directly; straight: *The post office is smack in the center of town.*

smack[3] (smak) /smæk/ *n.* [*noncount*] *Slang.* heroin.

small (smôl) /smɔl/ *adj.* and *adv.,* **-er, -est,** *n.* *—adj.* **1.** of limited size; little: *a small box.* **2.** not large when compared with others of the same kind: *A small elephant is still pretty big.* **3.** [*before a noun*] (of a written letter) in lowercase. **4.** not great in amount, extent, etc.: *a small salary.* **5.** [*before a noun*] carrying on some activity on a limited scale: *a small business.* **6.** of minor importance: *We have a small problem.* **7.** mean-spirited; petty: *a small, miserly man.* **8.** (of sound or the voice) having little volume: *"What about me, mother?" he asked in a small voice.* **9.** very young: *When he was just a small boy his mother died.* *—adv.* **10.** in a small manner: *writes so small he can put a lot of words on one page.* *—n.* **11.** [*count*] a small or narrow part, as of the back: *a pain in the small of my back.* **12. the small,** [*plural; used with a plural verb*] people without wealth or influence: *Democracy benefits the great and the small.* **13. a.** [*noncount*] a size of garments for persons of less than average dimensions, weight, etc. **b.** [*count*] a garment in this size. *—**Idiom.*** **14. feel small,** [*no obj*] to be ashamed: *She made him feel small by screaming at him in public.* —**small′ish,** *adj.* —**small′ness,** *n.* [*noncount*]: *fighting such smallness of mind.*

small′ arm′, *n.* [*count*] a gun or other firearm designed to be held in one or both hands while being fired.

small′ fry′, *n.* [*plural; used with a plural verb*] **1.** very young children: *The small fry are probably all asleep by now.* **2.** unimportant persons or things: *Let's just hope they don't pay attention to us small fry.* **3.** small or young fish.

small′ intes′tine, *n.* INTESTINE (def. 2).

small′-mind′ed, *adj.* selfish, petty, or narrow-minded: *small-minded attitudes.*

small•pox (smôl′poks′) /ˈsmɔlˌpɒks/ *n.* [*noncount; used with a singular verb*] a serious disease easily spread to others, caused by a virus, with fever and red spots that often leave permanent pits or scars.

small′-scale′, *adj.* [*usually before a noun*] **1.** of limited amount, extent, or scope: *a small-scale enterprise.* **2.** (of a map, model, etc.) being a small version of the original; showing little detail.

small′ talk′, *n.* [*noncount*] light conversation; chitchat: *We engaged in some small talk.*

small′-time′, *adj.* having little influence: *a small-time politician.* —**small-timer,** *n.* [*count*]

smart (smärt) /smɑrt/ *v.,* **-er, -est,** *adv., n.* *—v.* [*no obj*] **1.** to be a cause of sharp, stinging pain: *The cut on his arm still smarted.* **2.** to suffer sharply, as from wounded feelings: *still smarting from the insults.* *—adj.* **3.** having or showing quick intelligence or ready mental capability: *a smart student.* [*It + be + ~ + to + verb*]: *It wasn't very smart of you to try to cheat.* **4.** shrewd or sharp, as a person in dealing with others: *a smart campaigner.* **5.** clever or witty, as a speaker or speech. **6.** neat or trim in appearance, as a person or garment; spruce: *a very smart outfit.* **7.** socially elegant; sophisticated or fashionable: *the smart crowd.* **8.** saucy; pert: *Keep your smart remarks to yourself.* **9.** brisk or vigorous: *to walk with smart steps.* **10.** sharply severe, as a blow; sharp or keen: *a smart pain; a smart slap on the arm.* **11.** [*often before a noun*] equipped with, using, or containing electronic control devices: *smart bombs.* **12.** *Computers.* INTELLIGENT (def. 3). *—adv.* **13.** in a smart manner; smartly. *—n.* **14.** [*count; usually: a + ~*] a sharp local pain. **15. smarts,** [*noncount; used with a singular verb*] *Informal.* intelligence; common sense: *has a lot of smarts.* —**smart′ly,** *adv.*: *to dress smartly; She rapped smartly on the door.* —**smart′ness,** *n.* [*noncount*]

smart′ al′eck (or **al′ec**) (al′ik) /ˈælɪk/ *n.* [*count*] *Informal.* an annoying and obnoxious person who believes he or she is smarter than others. —**smart′-al′eck•y, smart′-al′eck,** *adj.*: *the child's smart-alecky answers.*

smart•en (smär′tn) /ˈsmɑrtn̩/ *v.* to (cause to) become more aware, shrewd, or clever: [~ + *up*]: *When will you smarten up; you're being made a fool of!* [~ + *obj* + *up*]: *Can anything smarten her up?* [~ + *up* + *obj*]: *Nothing can smarten up that loser.*

smash (smash) /smæʃ/ *v.* **1.** to (cause to) break to pieces, as by striking or dashing against something; shatter: [*no obj*]: *The vase smashed to pieces when I dropped it.* [~ + *obj*]: *He smashed the vase to pieces.* **2.** [~ + *obj*] to destroy or defeat completely: *The attack on that country smashed its ability to make war again.* **3.** to hit or drive with force: [*no obj*]: *The car smashed into the wall.* [~ + *obj*]: *He smashed the car into the wall.* **4.** [~ + *obj*] (in racket sports like tennis) to hit (a ball or shuttlecock) with a powerful, downward overhand stroke: *smashed the ball down the sideline.* *—n.* [*count*] **5.** an act or instance of smashing. **6.** the sound of such smashing: *the sudden smash of glass or bottles breaking.* **7.** a blow, hit, or slap. **8.** a destructive collision, as between automobiles. **9.** *Informal.* something achieving great success; a hit: *Their new movie was a huge smash.* **10.** (in racket sports) a powerful, downward overhand stroke, or the ball or shuttlecock hit with such a stroke. *—adj.* [*before a noun*] **11.** *Informal.* of or relating to a great success: *a smash hit on Broadway.*

smash•ing (smash′ing) /ˈsmæʃɪŋ/ *adj.* **1.** impressive or wonderful: *a smashing success.* **2.** crushing or devastating.

smash′-up′, *n.* [*count*] a complete smash, esp. a wreck of one or more vehicles.

smat•ter•ing (smat′ə ring) /ˈsmætərɪŋ/ *n.* [*count; usu-*

ally singular; a + ~] **1.** a slight or beginning knowledge of something: *a smattering of Swedish.* **—***adj.* **2.** slight or superficial.

smear (smēr) /smɪər/ *v.* **1.** [~ + *obj*] to spread (an oily, greasy, or wet substance) on something: *to smear butter on bread.* **2.** [~ + *obj*] to spread an oily, greasy, or wet substance on: *to smear bread with butter.* **3.** [~ + *obj*] to stain, spot, or make dirty with something oily, greasy, or wet: *The paint smeared his clothes.* **4.** to (cause to) be smudged or blurred, as by rubbing: [~ + *obj*]: *The signature was smeared.* [*no obj*]: *The ink will smear if it gets wet.* **5.** [~ + *obj*] to ruin or try to ruin (a reputation, etc.), as by spreading lies about someone: *He tried to smear his opponent during the campaign.* **6.** [~ + *obj*] *Slang.* to defeat completely; overwhelm: *The team came in and smeared their opponents.* **—***n.* [*count*] **7.** an oily, greasy, or wet substance, esp. a dab of such a substance. **8.** a stain, spot, or mark made by such a substance. **9.** an attempt to ruin the good name of someone, as by spreading lies. **10.** a small quantity of something spread thinly on a slide for microscopic examination: *a cervical smear.* —**smear′y,** *adj.*, **-i•er, -i•est.**

smell (smel) /smɛl/ *v.*, **smelled** or **smelt** (smelt) /smɛlt/ **smell•ing,** *n.* **—***v.* **1.** to detect the odor of (something) through the nose; inhale the odor of something: [~ + *obj*]: *He smelled the flowers in the garden.* [*not: be + ~-ing; no obj*]: *Because he had a bad head cold he could hardly smell.* **2.** [*not: be + ~-ing*] to give off or have an odor: *These flowers don't smell at all.* **3.** [*not: be + ~-ing*] to have a certain odor or scent: [~ + *of/like + obj*]: *The whole house smelled of smoke.* [~ + *adjective*]: *The room smelled bad.* **4.** [*not: be + ~-ing; no obj*] to give out a strong or offensive odor; stink: *Whew, that fish really smells!* **5.** [~ + *obj*] to test by the sense of smell: *He smelled the meat to see if it was fresh.* **6.** [*not: be + ~-ing; ~ + obj*] to detect by cleverness: *The detective smelled foul play.* **7.** [*not: be + ~-ing; ~ + of + obj*] to have a trace or suggestion: *This smells of foul play.* **8.** [*not: be + ~-ing; no obj*] *Informal.* to be of inferior quality; stink: *Your team really smells!* **9. smell out,** [~ + *obj*] to look for by or as if by smelling: *The newspaper reporter could smell out a story from just a hint of trouble.* **10. smell up,** to fill with an offensive odor; stink up: [~ + *up + obj*]: *Her perfume was smelling up the whole room.* [~ + *obj + up*]: *to smell it up.* **—***n.* **11.** [*noncount*] the sense of being able to detect something with the nose: *the sense of smell.* **12.** [*count*] that quality of a thing that is or may be smelled: *The fish has a pretty strong smell.* **13.** [*count*] an act or instance of smelling: *Give this a smell and tell me if it's still fresh.* **14.** [*count*] a trace or suggestion: *a smell of danger.* **15.** [*count*] an appearance, character, or quality that seems to be all around a thing: *the sweet smell of success.* **—*Idiom.*** **16. smell a rat,** to suspect that something is wrong: *He smelled a rat when he saw her sneaking through the back door.*

smell′ing salts′, *n.* [*plural*] a preparation for smelling, usually ammonium carbonate with some agreeable scent, used to bring someone back to consciousness.

smell•y (smel′ē) /ˈsmɛliy/ *adj.*, **-i•er, -i•est.** giving off a strong or unpleasant odor.

smelt[1] (smelt) /smɛlt/ *v.* [~ + *obj*] **1.** to fuse or melt (ore) in order to separate the metal in it. **2.** to obtain or refine (metal) in this way.

smelt[2] (smelt) /smɛlt/ *n.* [*count*], *pl.* (*esp. when thought of as a group*) **smelt,** (*esp. for kinds or species*) **smelts.** a small, silvery food fish of cold northern waters.

smelt[3] (smelt) /smɛlt/ *v.* a pt. and pp. of SMELL.

smelt•er (smel′tər) /ˈsmɛltər/ *n.* [*count*] **1.** a person or thing that smelts. **2.** a place where ores are smelted.

smid•gen or **smid•gin** or **smid•geon** (smij′ən) /ˈsmɪdʒən/ *n.* [*count; usually singular; usually: a +* ~] a very small amount: *a smidgen of honey with the tea, please.*

smile (smīl) /smayl/ *v.*, **smiled, smil•ing,** *n.* **—***v.* **1.** to put on a facial expression that involves an upturning of the corners of the mouth, usually indicating pleasure or amusement, but sometimes scorn: [*no obj*]: *He smiled happily when he heard the news.* [~ + *at + obj*]: *She smiled happily at him.* [~ + *obj*]: *She smiled a happy smile at the news.* **2.** [~ + *on + obj*] to look at someone with favor: *Luck smiled on us that night.* **3.** [~ + *obj*] to express by a smile: *to smile approval.* **—***n.* [*count*] **4.** an act or instance of smiling; a smiling expression of the face: *A broad smile crossed his face.* —**smil′ing•ly,** *adv.*: *She gestured smilingly to him.*

smirch (smûrch) /smərtʃ/ *v.* [~ + *obj*] **1.** to make dirty. **2.** to harm or ruin (a reputation, etc.); disgrace; discredit. **—***n.* [*count*] **3.** a dirty mark or smear. **4.** a stain or blot, as on a reputation.

smirk (smûrk) /smərk/ *v.*, *n.* **—***v.* [*no obj*] **1.** to smile in an offensively self-satisfied way: *They smirked behind the teacher's back.* **—***n.* [*count*] **2.** the facial expression of a person who smirks.

smite (smīt) /smayt/ *v.* [~ + *obj*], **smote** (smōt) /smowt/ **smit•ten** (smit′n) /ˈsmɪtn̩/ or **smit** (smit) /smɪt/ or **smote, smit•ing. 1.** to hit hard, with or as if with the hand or a weapon. **2.** to strike down, injure, attack, or kill: *smitten by polio.* **3.** [*usually: be + smitten*] **a.** to affect mentally, morally, or emotionally with a strong and sudden feeling: *was smitten with terror.* **b.** to impress favorably; enamor: *He was smitten by her charms.*

smith (smith) /smɪθ/ *n.* [*count*] **1.** a worker in metal. **2.** BLACKSMITH.

smith•er•eens (smith′ə rēnz′) /ˌsmɪðəˈriynz/ *n.* [*plural*] small pieces; bits: *The window was smashed to smithereens.*

smith•y (smith′ē, smith′ē) /ˈsmɪθiy, ˈsmɪðiy/ *n.* [*count*], *pl.* **smith•ies. 1.** the workshop of a smith, esp. a blacksmith. **2.** BLACKSMITH.

smock (smok) /smɒk/ *n.* [*count*] a loose, lightweight piece of clothing worn over the outer clothes to protect them while working.

smog (smog, smôg) /smɒg, smɔg/ *n.* [*noncount*] smoke or other gases that pollute, combined with fog in an unhealthy or irritating mixture. —**smog′gy,** *adj.*, **-gi•er, -gi•est.**

smoke (smōk) /smowk/ *n.*, *v.*, **smoked, smok•ing. —***n.* **1.** [*noncount*] the visible vapor and gases given off by a burning substance. **2.** [*noncount*] something resembling this, as mist. **3.** [*count*] an act or spell of smoking something, esp. tobacco. **4.** [*count*] something for smoking, as a cigarette: *Have you got a smoke?* **5.** [*noncount*] a bluish or brownish gray. **—***v.* **6.** [*no obj*] to give off smoke. **7.** to draw into the mouth and puff out (the smoke of tobacco or the like, as from a pipe or cigarette): [*no obj*]: *She doesn't like to smoke.* [~ + *obj*]: *He smoked a pack of cigarettes a day.* **8.** *Slang.* to (cause to) move or travel with great speed: [*no obj*]: *That throw really smoked through the air!* [~ + *obj*]: *The quarterback smoked the next pass to his tight end.* **9.** [~ + *obj*] to expose (rooms, etc.) to toxic vapor in order to kill insects or pests: *to smoke a room.* **10.** [~ + *obj*] to expose (meat, fish, etc.) to smoke and thus dry and flavor it: *to smoke salmon in the smokehouse.* **11. smoke out, a.** to drive from a place of hiding by the use of smoke: [~ + *out + obj*]: *to smoke out the raccoons.* [~ + *obj + out*]: *to smoke the animals out.* **b.** to force into public knowledge; expose: [~ + *out + obj*]: *to smoke out the traitors.* [~ + *obj + out*]: *to smoke the traitors out with a clever trick.* **—*Idiom.*** **12. go up in smoke,** to be unsuccessful: *All his plans for promotion went up in smoke.* —**smoke′less,** *adj.*: *so-called smokeless tobacco, or chewing tobacco.* —**smok′er,** *n.* [*count*] —**smok′i•ness,** *n.* [*noncount*] —**smok′y,** *adj.*, **-i•er, -i•est.**

smoke′ detec′tor, *n.* [*count*] an electronic fire alarm that emits a loud signal in the presence of smoke. Also called **smoke′ alarm′.**

smoke•house (smōk′hous′) /ˈsmowkˌhaws/ *n.* [*count*] a building or place in which meat, fish, etc., are cured with smoke.

smoke′ screen′, *n.* [*count*] **1.** a mass of dense smoke produced to conceal an area, vessel, or plane from the enemy. **2.** something intended to disguise, hide, or deceive: *His friendliness was just a smoke screen for his evil scheme to ruin everyone.*

smoke•stack (smōk′stak′) /ˈsmowkˌstæk/ *n.* [*count*] **1.** a pipe for the escape of the smoke of something burned, as in a factory. **—***adj.* **2.** of or relating to a basic heavy industry, as automaking: *smokestack companies.*

smol•der or **smoul•der** (smōl′dər) /ˈsmowldər/ *v.* [*no obj*] **1.** to burn without flame; undergo slow burning: *The campfire was still smoldering.* **2.** to continue without an outward indication: *Hatred smoldered beneath his smile.*

smooch (smōōch) /smuwtʃ/ *Informal.* **—***v.* [*no obj*] **1.** to kiss: *smooching on the couch.* **—***n.* [*count*] **2.** a kiss.

smooth (smōōth) /smuwð/ *adj.*, **-er, -est,** *adv.*, *v.* **—***adj.* **1.** not rough; having an even surface: *a smooth road.* **2.** generally flat, such as a calm sea. **3.** free from hairs or a hairy growth: *a smooth cheek.* **4.** free from lumps, as a sauce: *smooth gravy.* **5.** allowing or having an even, uninterrupted movement: *a smooth ride.* **6.** free from problems or difficulties: *a smooth day at the office.* **7.** elegant, easy, or polished: *a smooth manner with difficult* *clients.* **8.** ingratiatingly polite; suave: *a smooth talker.* **9.** free from harshness; bland or mellow, such as wine. *—adv.* **10.** [*often: used before another word to form an adjective*] in a smooth manner; smoothly: *a smooth-running car.* *—v.* **11.** to make the surface of (something) smooth, as by scraping, planing, pressing, etc.: [~ + *obj*]: *to smooth the floorboards with sandpaper before polishing them.* [~ (+ *off/out*) + *obj*]: *He smoothed (off) his jacket.* [~ + *obj* (+ *out*)]: *He smoothed his jacket (out).* **12.** to remove (wrinkles or the like) from something: [~ + *obj* + *off* (+ *obj*)]: *He smoothed the wrinkles off (his jacket).* [~ + *off/away* + *obj*]: *He smoothed off the wrinkles from his jacket.* **13. smooth over,** to make seem less severe or disagreeable: [~ + *over* + *obj*]: *smoothed over the difficulties and got the two sides talking again.* [~ + *obj* + *over*]: *to smooth them over.* —**smooth′ly,** *adv.* —**smooth′ness,** *n.* [*noncount*]

smor•gas•bord or **smör•gås•bord** (smôr′gəs bôrd′, -bōrd′ *or, often,* shmôr′-) /ˈsmɔrgəsˌbɔrd, -ˌbowrd *or, often,* ˈʃmɔr-/ *n.* [*count*] **1.** a buffet meal of hors d'oeuvres, salads, casserole dishes, etc. **2.** a variety of things to choose from: *a smorgasbord of different computers.*

smote (smōt) /smowt/ *v.* a pt. of SMITE.

smoth•er (smuth′ər) /ˈsmʌðər/ *v.* **1.** to suffocate, as by smoke or lack of air: [~ + *obj*]: *He was smothered by the smoke.* [*no obj*]: *He'll smother under those blankets.* **2.** [~ + *obj*] to extinguish or deaden (fire, etc.) by covering: *to smother the fire with blankets.* **3.** [~ + *obj*] to cover closely or thickly: *to smother a steak with mushrooms.* **4.** [~ + *obj*] to hold back; suppress or repress: *to smother one's grief.*

smudge (smuj) /smʌdʒ/ *n., v.,* **smudged, smudg•ing.** *—n.* [*count*] **1.** a dirty mark or smear: *a few smudges on his face.* *—v.* [~ + *obj*] **2.** to mark with dirty streaks or smears: *His face was smudged with mud.* **3.** to rub or wipe so as to smear: *She didn't want to smudge her lipstick.* —**smudg′y,** *adj.,* **-i•er, -i•est.**

smug (smug) /smʌg/ *adj.,* **smug•ger, smug•gest.** overly confident of one's ability, superior position, or correctness; self-satisfied: *He was very smug when he walked into the interview.* —**smug′ly,** *adv.* —**smug′ness,** *n.* [*noncount*]

smug•gle (smug′əl) /ˈsmʌgəl/ *v.,* **-gled, -gling. 1.** to convey (goods) secretly and illegally into or out of a country: [~ + *obj*]: *to smuggle heroin.* [*no obj*]: *a fast boat used to smuggle along the coast.* **2.** [~ + *obj*] to bring, take, put, etc., secretly: *smuggled his class notes into the science test.* —**smug′gler,** *n.* [*count*]

smut (smut) /smʌt/ *n.* **1.** [*noncount*] sooty matter. **2.** [*count*] a black or dirty mark; smudge. **3.** [*noncount*] indecent language or writing; obscenity. **4.** [*noncount*] **a.** a disease of plants caused by fungi. **b.** a fungus causing this disease. —**smut′ti•ness,** *n.* [*noncount*] —**smut′ty,** *adj.,* **-ti•er, -ti•est.**

snack (snak) /snæk/ *n.* [*count*] **1.** a small portion of food or drink eaten between regular meals: *a snack of a sandwich and a glass of milk.* *—v.* [*no obj*] **2.** to have a snack: *It's not wise to snack before bedtime.* [~ + *on* + *obj*]: *to snack on too many sweets.*

snack′ bar′, *n.* [*count*] a lunchroom or restaurant where light meals are sold. See illustration at TERMINAL.

snag (snag) /snæg/ *n., v.,* **snagged, snag•ging.** *—n.* [*count*] **1.** something that is sharp and sticks out. **2.** a hole, tear, or run in a fabric, caused by catching on something that sticks out. **3.** anything that gets in the way of progress: *Our plans hit a snag when our best player broke her leg.* *—v.* [~ + *obj*] **4.** to catch on a snag: *snagging her clothing on the branches.* **5.** to grab; seize: *The shortstop snagged a sharp line drive.*

snail (snāl) /sneyl/ *n.* [*count*] **1.** a soft-bodied, slow-moving animal that lives in a spiral-shaped shell. **2.** a slow or lazy person. *—**Idiom.*** **3. at a snail's pace,** very slowly: *Work was proceeding at a snail's pace.*

snake (snāk) /sneyk/ *n., v.,* **snaked, snak•ing.** *—n.* [*count*] **1.** a scaly reptile with a long thin body that has no arms or legs: *Some snakes have a poisonous bite.* **2.** a treacherous person. **3.** (in plumbing) a flexible, wirelike device for loosening anything stuck in curved pipes. *—v.* **4.** [*no obj*] to move, twist, or wind in the manner of a snake: *The road snakes among the mountains.* **5.** [~ + *obj*] to wind or make (one's course, etc.) like a snake: *She snaked her way through the crowd.*

snak•y (snā′kē) /ˈsneykiy/ *adj.,* **-i•er, -i•est. 1.** of or relating to snakes. **2.** twisting, winding, or full of curves: *a snaky road.* **3.** treacherous; sneaky.

snap (snap) /snæp/ *v.,* **snapped, snap•ping,** *n., adj., adv.* *—v.* **1.** to (cause to) make a sudden, sharp sound; crack: [~ + *obj*]: *to snap one's fingers.* [*no obj*]: *Suddenly a twig snapped.* **2.** to click, as a mechanism or the jaws coming together: [*no obj*]: *The lock snapped loudly as I turned the key.* [~ + *obj*]: *She snapped the lock with her key.* **3.** to move, strike, etc., with a sharp sound, as a door or lid: [*no obj*]: *The door snapped shut.* [~ + *obj*]: *She snapped the lid shut.* **4.** to (cause to) break suddenly, esp. with a cracking sound: [~ + *obj*]: *He snapped a piece of wood in half.* [*no obj*]: *The wood snapped in half.* **5.** [*no obj*] to give way suddenly, as from mental strain, and become unable to control oneself: *I thought right then he would snap, but he got control of himself.* **6.** [*no obj*] to move with quick motions of the body: *to snap to attention.* **7. a.** [~ + *obj*] to take (snapshots): *tourists snapping pictures of the cathedral.* **b.** to take snapshots of (someone or something): [~ + *obj*]: *The tourists were snapping the cathedral as fast as they could.* [*no obj*]: *The news cameras were snapping wildly.* **8.** to speak quickly and sharply: [~ + *at* + *obj*]: *The captain snapped at the first mate.* [*used with quotations*]: *"Mind your own business!" he snapped.* [~ + *out* + *obj*]: *to snap out a complaint.* **9.** to seize with or as if with a quick bite or grab: [~ + *up* + *obj*]: *The first customers snapped up the best bargains.* [~ + *obj* + *up*]: *They snapped the best bargains up.* **10. snap out of,** [~ + *out* + *of* + *obj*] to recover from: *Will the economy snap out of the recession?* *—n.* **11.** [*count*] a quick, sudden action such as the breaking of a twig, or the sound resulting from such a break. **12.** [*count*] a fastener that snaps when it closes. **13.** [*noncount*] *Informal.* briskness, vigor, or energy: *Put some snap into your classroom teaching!* **14.** [*count*] a short spell or period, such as of cold weather: *a cold snap.* **15.** [*count; usually singular; usually: a* + ~] *Informal.* an easy task, activity, etc.: *For her, fixing slow computers is a snap!* *—adj.* [*before a noun*] **16.** fastening or closing with a click or snap: *a snap lock.* **17.** made, done, taken, etc., suddenly or without thinking: *a snap judgment.* **18.** easy or simple: *a snap course.* *—adv.* **19.** in a brisk, sudden manner. *—**Idiom.*** **20. snap one's fingers at,** [~ + *obj*] to show one's lack of respect for: *That much money is nothing to snap your fingers at, believe me!*

snap′ bean′, *n.* [*count*] a crisp bean pod, such as a green bean or a wax bean.

snap•drag•on (snap′drag′ən) /ˈsnæpˌdrægən/ *n.* [*count*] a plant of the figwort family, grown for its spikes of showy flowers.

snap•pish (snap′ish) /ˈsnæpɪʃ/ *adj.* irritable: *a snappish reply.* —**snap′pish•ly,** *adv.* —**snap′pish•ness,** *n.* [*noncount*]

snap•py (snap′ē) /ˈsnæpiy/ *adj.,* **-pi•er, -pi•est. 1.** quick in action: *a snappy answer.* **2.** snappish. **3.** *Informal.* crisp, smart, lively, etc.: *a snappy dresser.* *—**Idiom.*** **4. make it snappy,** [*no obj*] *Informal.* to speed up; hurry: *Make it snappy pal, I haven't got all day.*

snap•shot (snap′shot′) /ˈsnæpˌʃɒt/ *n.* [*count*] **1.** an informal photograph, esp. one taken by a simple handheld camera. **2.** a brief appraisal or profile: *This report is a snapshot of the school's plans for the future.*

snare (snâr) /snɛər/ *n., v.,* **snared, snar•ing.** *—n.* [*count*] **1.** a device made up of a rope with a loop, for capturing small animals. **2.** anything serving to trap someone unexpectedly; a trap. *—v.* [~ + *obj*] **3.** to catch with a snare; entrap; entangle. **4.** to catch or involve by trickery: *snared a top-ranking spy with a clever trick.*

snarl[1] (snärl) /snɑrl/ *v.* **1.** [*no obj; (~ + at + obj)*] to growl angrily or viciously, esp. with the teeth bared, as a dog: *The dog snarled at the child.* **2.** to speak in a sharp, angry manner: [*no obj; (at + obj)*]: *He was snarling (at his workers) all day.* [~ + *obj*]: *to snarl a threat.* [*used with quotations*]: *"Get back, all of you!" he snarled.* *—n.* [*count*] **3.** the act of snarling: *The dog gave a snarl.* **4.** a snarling word: *nothing but snarls all day from the boss.* —**snarl′ing•ly,** *adv.*

snarl[2] (snärl) /snɑrl/ *n.* [*count*] **1.** a tangle, as of thread or hair. **2.** a complicated or confused condition or manner: *a traffic snarl.* **3.** a knot in wood. *—v.* **4.** to (cause to) become tangled, as thread or hair: [*no obj*]: *Her hair snarled as she brushed it.* [~ + *obj*]: *That shampoo snarls her hair.* **5.** to (cause to) become confused: [~ + *obj*]: *Traffic was badly snarled at the bridge.* [*no obj*]: *Traffic snarled at the entrance ramp.*

snatch (snach) /snætʃ/ *v.* **1.** to make a sudden move to seize (something), as with the hand; grab: [~ + *at* + *obj*]: *snatched at her purse.* [~ + *obj*]: *He snatched the woman's purse.* *—n.* [*count*] **2.** an act or instance of snatching. **3.** a sudden motion to seize something; grab.

4. a small piece or part of something; bit; scrap: *He could just make out snatches of their conversation.* **5.** a brief amount of time spent in an effort or activity: *to work in snatches, a few minutes here, a few minutes there.*

sneak (snēk) /sniyk/ *v.*, **sneaked** or **snuck** (snuk) /snʌk/ **sneak•ing,** *n., adj.* **—***v.* **1.** [*no obj*] to go in a sly way so as not to be seen or noticed: *Let's sneak out the back door.* **2.** [*no obj*] to act in an underhand way: *He sneaks around and lies to everyone.* **3.** [~ + *obj*] to move, put, etc., in a sly or dishonest manner: *He sneaked the gun into his pocket.* **—***n.* [*count*] **4.** a person who should not be trusted. **—***adj.* [*before a noun*] **5.** stealthy; done without warning or being seen: *a sneak raid.* —**sneak′i•ness,** *n.* [*noncount*] —**sneak′y,** *adj.*, **-i•er, -i•est.**

sneak•er (snē′kər) /ˈsniykər/ *n.* [*count*] **1.** a shoe of canvas with a flat rubber or synthetic bottom, worn for sports or recreation. See illustration at CLOTHING. **2.** any of various athletic shoes resembling this. **3.** one who sneaks; a sneak.

sneak•ing (snē′king) /ˈsniykɪŋ/ *adj.* [*before a noun*] secret; not expressed to others, such as a feeling or suspicion: *He had a sneaking suspicion something was going wrong.*

sneak′ pre′view, *n.* [*count*] a preview of a motion picture, often shown in addition to an announced film, in order to observe the reaction of the audience.

sneer (snēr) /snɪər/ *v.* **1.** [*no obj*] to smile or laugh in a manner that shows ridicule or scorn. **2.** [*no obj*] to act, speak, or write in a manner showing such ridicule or scorn: *They sneered at her because she was interested in fairness.* [*used with quotations*]: *"Just try it," he sneered.* **—***n.* [*count*] **3.** a look, action, or remark of ridicule or scorn.

sneeze (snēz) /sniyz/ *v.*, **sneezed, sneez•ing,** *n.* **—***v.* **1.** [*no obj*] to produce air or breath suddenly, forcibly, and loudly through the nose and mouth by involuntary action: *She sneezed whenever she came near cats.* **2. sneeze at,** [~ + *at* + *obj; usually with a negative word or expression*] *Informal.* to treat with contempt; scorn: *$50,000 is nothing to sneeze at.* **—***n.* [*count*] **3.** an act or sound of sneezing.

snick•er (snik′ər) /ˈsnɪkər/ also **snigger** (snig′ər) /ˈsnɪgər/ *v.* [*no obj*] **1.** to laugh quietly but disrespectfully: *The children snickered when the teacher turned his back.* [~ + *at* + *obj*]: *They snickered at his attempt to roller-skate.* **—***n.* [*count*] **2.** a snickering laugh.

snide (snīd) /snayd/ *adj.*, **snid•er, snid•est.** insulting in a nasty, sly manner: *snide remarks about his nose.*

sniff (snif) /snɪf/ *v.* **1.** [*no obj*] to draw air through the nose in a short, somewhat noisy way: *sniffed a few times before speaking.* **2.** [~ + *obj*] to inhale through the nose: *to sniff the air.* **3.** [*no obj*] to clear the nose by drawing air through it with noise; sniffle: *to sniff tearfully.* **4.** to smell by short inhalations: [~ + *obj*]: *to sniff the flowers.* [~ + *at* + *obj*]: *The bloodhounds sniffed at the ground.* **5.** [~ (+ *out*) + *obj*] to perceive by or as if by sniffing: *The reporter was good at sniffing (out) a scandal.* **6.** [*used with quotations*] to show one's contempt by or as if by sniffing: *"I won't put up with that," she sniffed.* **—***n.* [*count*] **7.** an act of sniffing. **8.** the sound made by such an act. **9.** a faint scent or odor.

snif•fle (snif′əl) /ˈsnɪfəl/ *v.*, **-fled, -fling,** *n.* **—***v.* [*no obj*] **1.** to sniff again and again, as from a head cold: *She couldn't stop sniffling because she was allergic to the cats in the room.* **—***n.* [*count*] **2.** an act or sound of sniffling. **3. the sniffles,** [*plural*] a condition, as a cold, marked by sniffling: *I had the sniffles all day at work.*

snif•ter (snif′tər) /ˈsnɪftər/ *n.* [*count*] **1.** a pear-shaped glass, narrowing at the top, to intensify the aroma of brandy, liqueur, etc. **2.** *Informal.* a very small drink of liquor.

snig•ger (snig′ər) /ˈsnɪgər/ *v., n.* SNICKER.

snip (snip) /snɪp/ *v.*, **snipped, snip•ping,** *n.* **—***v.* [~ + *obj*] **1.** to cut or remove with a small, quick stroke with scissors: *to snip a rose.* **—***n.* [*count*] **2.** the act of snipping. **3.** a small piece snipped off. **4.** any small piece; bit. **5.** *Informal.* a small, insignificant, or rude person.

snipe (snīp) /snayp/ *n., pl.* **snipes,** (*esp. when thought of as a group*) **snipe** for 1; *v.*, **sniped, snip•ing.** **—***n.* **1.** a bird, a long-billed sandpiper, living in marshy areas. **—***v.* [~ + *at* + *obj*] **2.** to shoot at individuals, esp. enemy soldiers, from a hidden or distant position. **3.** to attack a person or a person's work with mean or nasty criticism, esp. from a safe distance: *constantly sniping at his efforts to improve things.* —**snip′er,** *n.* [*count*]: *enemy snipers shooting from the forest.*

snip•pet (snip′it) /ˈsnɪpɪt/ *n.* [*count*] a small bit, scrap, or fragment: *Snippets of information were coming in.*

snip•py (snip′ē) /ˈsnɪpiy/ *adj.*, **-pi•er, -pi•est.** sharp or curt, esp. in an insulting or nasty way: *a snippy answer.* Often, **snip′pe•ty** (-i tē) /-ɪtiy/.

snit (snit) /snɪt/ *n.* [*count*] a bothered or irritated state.

snitch[1] (snich) /snɪtʃ/ *v.* [~ + *obj*] *Informal.* to steal.

snitch[2], *Informal.* **—***v.* [*no obj;* (~ + *on* + *obj*)] **1.** to become an informer; tell on others, as to the police, parents, etc.; tattle: *He snitched on all his friends.* **—***n.* [*count*] **2.** Also called **snitch′er.** an informer.

sniv•el (sniv′əl) /ˈsnɪvəl/ *v.* [*no obj*], **-eled, -el•ing** or (*esp. Brit.*) **-elled, -el•ling. 1.** to cry with sniffling: *Stop sniveling about your problems.* **2.** to have a runny nose. —**sniv′el•er,** *n.* [*count*]

snob (snob) /snɒb/ *n.* [*count*] **1.** one who tries to act like those higher in social rank or who admires such people too much and scorns others. **2.** one who believes himself or herself to have superior tastes and is scornful of those with different tastes: *an intellectual snob.* —**snob′ber•y, snob′bish•ness,** *n.* [*noncount*] —**snob′bish,** *adj.* —**snob′by,** *adj.*, **-bi•er, -bi•est.**

snoop (sno͞op) /snuwp/ *Informal.* **—***v.* [*no obj*] **1.** to go about in a sneaking way while trying to gain information; prowl; pry: *always snooping around the office.* **—***n.* [*count*] **2.** an act or instance of snooping. **3.** Also, **snoop′er.** one who snoops.

snoot (sno͞ot) /snuwt/ *n.* [*count*] *Informal.* **1.** the nose. **2.** a snob.

snoot•y (sno͞o′tē) /ˈsnuwtiy/ *adj.*, **-i•er, -i•est.** *Informal.* acting like a snob; snobbish: *snooty neighbors.* —**snoot′i•ness,** *n.* [*noncount*]

snooze (sno͞oz) /snuwz/ *v.*, **snoozed, snooz•ing,** *n.* **—***v.* [*no obj*] **1.** to doze; nap: *snoozing on the couch.* **—***n.* [*count*] **2.** a short nap.

snore (snôr, snōr) /snɔr, snowr/ *v.*, **snored, snor•ing,** *n.* **—***v.* [*no obj*] **1.** to breathe during sleep with hoarse or harsh sounds: *snoring so loudly he woke her up.* **—***n.* [*count*] **2.** the act, instance, or sound of snoring. —**snor′er,** *n.* [*count*]

snor•kel (snôr′kəl) /ˈsnɔrkəl/ *n.* [*count*] **1.** a tube with which a swimmer can breathe while moving face down at or just below the surface of the water. **2.** either of the tubes on a submarine that reach above the surface of the water and allow a submarine to remain submerged by taking in air and venting gases. **—***v.* [*no obj*] **3.** to swim while breathing with a snorkel. —**snor′kel•er,** *n.* [*count*]

snort (snôrt) /snɔrt/ *v.* **1.** [*no obj*] to force the breath violently through the nose with a loud, harsh sound. **2.** to express (contempt, anger, etc.) by a snort: [*no obj*]: *snorted in disbelief.* [*used with quotations*]: *"Ridiculous!" he snorted, "It'll never work."* **3.** [*no obj*] to make sounds resembling snorts: *The engine snorted.* **4.** *Slang.* to take (a drug) by inhaling: [*no obj*]: *snorting in the back room.* [~ + *obj*]: *snorting cocaine.* **—***n.* [*count*] **5.** the act or sound of snorting. **6.** *Slang.* a quick drink of liquor; shot. **7.** *Slang.* **a.** an act or instance of taking a drug by inhalation. **b.** the amount of drug inhaled.

snot (snot) /snɒt/ *n.* **1.** [*noncount*] *Vulgar.* mucus from the nose. **2.** [*count*] *Informal.* a rudely disagreeable person, esp. a young person.

snot•ty (snot′ē) /ˈsnɒtiy/ *adj.*, **-ti•er, -ti•est. 1.** rude, as by being disrespectful: *a snotty answer.* **2.** full of snot.

snout (snout) /snawt/ *n.* [*count*] **1.** the part of an animal's head that contains the nose and jaws; muzzle. **2.** anything that resembles an animal's snout in shape, etc.: *the snout of the machine gun.* **3.** a person's nose, esp. when large or noticeable.

snow (snō) /snow/ *n.* **1. a.** [*noncount*] frozen water in the form of white flakes. **b.** [*noncount*] these flakes as forming a layer on the ground: *How many inches of snow are there?* **c.** [*count*] the fall of these flakes or a storm during which they fall: *That was one of the heaviest snows we had.* **2.** [*noncount*] *Slang.* cocaine or heroin. **3.** [*noncount*] white spots on a television screen caused by a weak signal. **—***v.* **4.** [*no obj; it* + ~] (of snow) to fall: *It snowed heavily last night.* **5.** [~ + *obj; usually: be* + ~*-ed* + *in*] to cover, block, etc., with or as if with snow: *The town was snowed in by the storm.* **6.** [~ + *obj*] *Slang.* to deceive (someone) by insincere talk or false praises: *He tried to snow his boss about why he was late.* **7. snow under,** [~ + *obj* + *under*] **a.** to cover with snow: *The worst storm in a decade snowed the town under.* **b.** to overwhelm: *I've been snowed under with all this work.* **c.** to defeat completely.

snow•ball (snō′bôl′) /ˈsnowˌbɔl/ *n.* [*count*] **1.** a ball of snow pressed together, as for throwing. **—***v.* **2.** to (cause to) grow or become larger, greater, etc., at an increasing rate: [*no obj*]: *Soon a few small lies had snowballed into a huge scandal.* [~ + *obj*]: *to snowball a small family business into a huge enterprise.*

Snow•belt or **Snow Belt** (snō′belt′) /ˈsnowˌbɛlt/ *n.* [*count; usually singular: the* + ~] the northern parts of the U.S. that receive a great amount of snowfall.

snow•bound (snō′bound′) /ˈsnowˌbawnd/ *adj.* shut in or prevented from moving by snow.

snow•drift (snō′drift′) /ˈsnowˌdrɪft/ *n.* [*count*] a mound or bank of snow driven together by the wind: *huge snowdrifts ten feet in height.*

snow•drop (snō′drop′) /ˈsnowˌdrɒp/ *n.* [*count*] an early-blooming plant of the amaryllis family.

snow•fall (snō′fôl′) /ˈsnowˌfɔl/ *n.* **1.** [*count*] a fall of snow. **2.** the amount of snow at a particular place or in a given time: [*count*]: *a five-inch snowfall.* [*noncount*]: *expecting five inches of snowfall tonight.*

snow•flake (snō′flāk′) /ˈsnowˌfleyk/ *n.* [*count*] one of the small crystals, flakes, or masses in which snow falls.

snow•man (snō′man′) /ˈsnowˌmæn/ *n.* [*count*], *pl.* **-men.** a figure of a person made out of packed snow.

snow•mo•bile (snō′mə bēl′) /ˈsnowməˌbiyl/ *n., v.,* **-biled, -bil•ing.** —*n.* [*count*] **1.** a motor vehicle with a revolving tread in the rear and steerable skis in the front, for traveling over snow. —*v.* [*no obj*] **2.** to operate or ride in a snowmobile. See -MOB-.

snow•plow (snō′plou′) /ˈsnowˌplaw/ *n.* [*count*] **1.** an implement for clearing away snow from highways, etc. —*v.* [~ + *obj*] **2.** to clear (an area) of snow using a snowplow: *to snowplow the roads.*

snow•shoe (snō′shōō′) /ˈsnowˌʃuw/ *n., v.,* **-shoed, -shoe•ing.** —*n.* [*count*] **1.** a frame shaped like a racket and attached to the shoe for walking on deep snow without sinking. —*v.* [*no obj*] **2.** to walk or travel on snowshoes.

snow•storm (snō′stôrm′) /ˈsnowˌstɔrm/ *n.* [*count*] a storm with a heavy fall of snow.

snow•suit (snō′sōōt′) /ˈsnowˌsuwt/ *n.* [*count*] a child's outer garment for cold weather, consisting of warm long pants and a jacket, often having a hood.

snow′ tire′, *n.* [*count*] an automobile tire that gives increased traction on snow or ice.

snow•y (snō′ē) /ˈsnowiy/ *adj.,* **-i•er, -i•est. 1.** full of snow; covered with snow: *a snowy winter day.* **2.** of the color of snow; white: *his snowy hair.*

snub (snub) /snʌb/ *v.,* **snubbed, snub•bing,** *n., adj.* —*v.* [~ + *obj*] **1.** to treat with scorn, esp. by ignoring: *He waved at her but she snubbed him and drove on by.* —*n.* [*count*] **2.** an act or instance of snubbing. —*adj.* [*before a noun*] **3.** (of the nose) short and turned up at the tip. **4.** blunt.

snub′-nosed′, *adj.* **1.** having a short, turned-up nose. **2.** having a blunt end: *snub-nosed pliers.*

snuck (snuk) /snʌk/ *v.* a pp. and pt. of SNEAK.

snuff[1] (snuf) /snʌf/ *v.* **1.** to draw in (air) noisily through the nose so as to smell something: [~ + *obj*]: *to snuff the air.* [*no obj*]: *snuffing and puffing.* **2.** to examine by smelling, as an animal does; sniff: [*no obj*]: *The dog stood up alertly and began snuffing.* [~ + *obj*]: *The dog began snuffing the new baby.* —*n.* **3.** [*count*] an act of snuffing; a sniff. **4.** [*noncount*] a preparation of tobacco, powdered and taken into the nostrils by inhaling. —***Idiom.*** **5. up to snuff,** [*noncount*] *Informal.* **a.** up to a certain standard; satisfactory: *Her work is not up to snuff.* **b.** *Brit.* not easily imposed upon; shrewd; sharp.

snuff[2] (snuf) /snʌf/ *n.* [*count*] **1.** the burned portion of a candlewick. —*v.* **2. snuff out, a.** to extinguish (a flame), as by pressing: [~ + *out* + *obj*]: *to snuff out the candles.* [~ + *obj* + *out*]: *to snuff the candles out.* **b.** to suppress; crush: [~ + *out* + *obj*]: *The dictator snuffed out any opposition.* [~ + *obj* + *out*]: *to snuff opposition out.* **c.** *Slang.* to kill or murder: [~ + *out* + *obj*]: *to snuff out any informers in the mob.* [~ + *obj* + *out*]: *to snuff them out.* —**snuff′•er,** *n.* [*count*]

snuf•fle (snuf′əl) /ˈsnʌfəl/ *v.,* **-fled, -fling,** *n.* —*v.* **1.** [*no obj*] to draw the breath or mucus noisily through the nose: *snuffling and blowing his nose.* **2.** [*no obj*] to whine; snivel: *At first he cried but gradually he began to snuffle and then stopped.* **3.** to say, or speak in a snuffle or a nasal tone: [~ + *obj*]: *snuffled a few remarks.* [*used with quotations*]: *"I don't want to go to Auntie's house," he snuffled.* —*n.* [*count*] **4.** an act or sound of snuffling. **5. the snuffles,** [*plural*] SNIFFLE (def. 3). —**snuf′fler,** *n.* —**snuf′fly,** *adj.*

snug (snug) /snʌg/ *adj.,* **snug•ger, snug•gest,** *v.,* **snugged, snug•ging,** *adv., n.* —*adj.* **1.** warmly comfortable or cozy: *a snug little house.* **2.** fitting closely or tightly, such as a piece of clothing: *a snug sweater.* —*v.* [*no obj*] **3.** to lie closely or comfortably; nestle. —*adv.* **4.** in a snug manner: *That dress fits too snug.* —*n.* [*count*] **5.** *Brit.* a small room in a tavern, as for private parties. —**snug′ly,** *adv.*: *dressed snugly to play in the snow.*

snug•gle (snug′əl) /ˈsnʌgəl/ *v.,* **-gled, -gling,** *n.* —*v.* [*no obj*] **1.** to lie or press closely, as for comfort or from affection: *They snuggled under the covers before drifting off to sleep.* [~ + *up*]: *The child snuggled up to his mother.* —*n.* [*count*] **2.** the act of snuggling.

so (sō) /sow/ *adv.* **1.** (after having shown or described something) in the manner indicated or understood: *Do it so.* **2.** (after a story or description of something) in that or this manner; thus: *o it turned out.* **3.** in the condition just mentioned: *It is broken and has long been so (= It has long been broken.)* **4.** (when the speaker and listener are aware of the circumstances) to the extent indicated; to such a degree or amount: *Do not walk so fast.* **5.** very or extremely: *I'm so happy.* **6.** very greatly: *My head aches so!* **7.** (used before an adverb or an adverbial clause and followed by *as*) to such a degree or extent; as: *So far as I know, she has always been trustworthy.* **8.** having the purpose of: *a speech so commemorating the victory.* **9.** hence; therefore; for that reason: *She was ill, and so stayed home (= and because she was ill, she stayed home).* **10.** (used after a clause or statement, and before a subject and auxiliary verb, to express strong emphasis or agreement with the clause or statement) most certainly: *I said I would come, and so I will. "You've forgotten your hat."—"Ah, yes, so I have."* **11.** (used to contradict a previous statement, often with special stress) indeed; truly; too: *"You weren't at the party last night."—"I was so!"* **12.** (used after a clause, and before an auxiliary verb and its subject, to suggest that the same thing is to be done as in the first clause) also; likewise or correspondingly; too: *If he is going, then so am I.* **13.** in such manner as to follow or result from: *As he learned, so did he teach.* **14.** in the way that follows; in this way: *The audience was seated, and so the speech began.* **15.** in such way as to end in: *So live your life that old age will bring you no regrets.* **16.** then; after that; subsequently: *So, shortly afterward, Alice met the queen.* —*conj.* **17.** [~ (+ *that*)] in order that: *He wore warm clothes so he wouldn't be cold in the winter snows.* **18.** with the result that: *He wasn't feeling well so he went to lie down on the couch.* —*pron.* **19.** such as has been stated: *to be good and stay so.* **20.** something that is about or near the persons or things in question, as in number or amount: *Of the original twelve, five or so remain.* —*interj.* **21.** (used as to show surprise, shock, etc., according to the situation): *So, it's Mr. Holmes! At last we meet! (= surprise or joy). "Come on, get up, the company's here."— "So?" (= indifference).* —*adj.* [*be* + ~] **22.** true as stated or reported: *Say it isn't so.* **Usage.** The words *so* and *very* are sometimes used similarly: *Everything is very expensive. Everything is so expensive.* If a clause beginning with *that* follows, *so* is used, not *very*: *Everything is so expensive that families cannot afford the necessities.*

soak (sōk) /sowk/ *v.* **1.** to (cause to) become thoroughly wet or filled with water or other liquid: [*no obj*]: *The clothes were left to soak in the soapy water.* [~ + *obj*]: *I soaked my aching arm in ice water to kill the pain.* **2.** [*no obj*] to pass, as a liquid, through pores, holes, or the like: *Rain soaked through the roof.* **3.** [~ + *obj*] to wet thoroughly: *The floods soaked the rug and ruined it.* **4.** to remove by or as if by soaking: [~ + *obj* + *out*]: *to soak a stain out.* [~ + *out* + *obj*]: *to soak out a stain.* **5.** [~ + *obj*] *Slang.* to overcharge: *shopkeepers soaking the tourists.* **6. soak in,** [*no obj*] to penetrate the mind or feelings: *The lesson didn't soak in.* —*n.* **7.** [*count*] the act or state of soaking, or the state of being soaked. **8.** [*noncount*] the liquid in which anything is soaked. **9.** [*count*] *Slang.* a heavy drinker.

so′-and-so′, *n., pl.* **so-and-sos. 1.** [*noncount*] a person or thing not definitely named: *to gossip about so-and-so.* **2.** [*count*] (used to refer to a disagreeable person, instead of using a more offensive word): *those so-and-sos at the computer store!*

soap (sōp) /sowp/ *n.* **1.** [*noncount*] a substance used for washing, made by treating a fat with an alkali: *a new bar of soap.* **2.** [*count*] *Informal.* Also, **soaper.** SOAP OPERA. —*v.* [~ + *obj*] **3.** to rub, lather, or treat with soap: *He soaped his arms and legs and then rinsed off.* —***Idiom.*** **4. no soap,** [*noncount*] *Informal.* (used to show that a proposal, plan, etc., is not acceptable): *"We want a raise and a promotion."—"No soap."* —**soap′i•ness,** *n.* [*noncount*] —**soap′y,** *adj.,* **-i•er, -i•est.**

soap•box or **soap box** (sōp′boks′) /'sowp,bɒks/ *n.* [*count*] a stand or platform, such as one set up on a street, from which a speaker delivers a speech or political comment.

soap′ op′er•a (op′ər ə, op′rə) /'ɒpərə, 'ɒprə/ *n.* [*count*] a radio or television series presenting the lives of many interconnected characters in an often melodramatic way.

soap•suds (sōp′sudz′) /'sowp,sʌdz/ *n.* [*plural*] suds made with water and soap.

soar (sôr, sōr) /sɔr, sowr/ *v.* [*no obj*] **1.** to fly upward, such as a bird. **2.** to rise to a higher or more exalted level: *His hopes soared.* **—***n.* [*count*] **3.** an act or instance of soaring.

sob (sob) /sɒb/ *v.,* **sobbed, sob•bing,** *n.* **—***v.* **1.** [*no obj*] to weep with a catching of the breath or in sudden, short gasps: *She sobbed at the news.* **2.** [~ + *obj*] to put or send (oneself) by sobbing: *to sob oneself to sleep.* **3.** to say with sobs: [~ + *obj*]: *to sob an answer.* [*used with quotations*]: *"I want her back!" he sobbed.* **—***n.* [*count*] **4.** the act of sobbing, or a sound suggesting this: *The baby let out a few more sobs, then fell asleep.*

S.O.B. or **SOB,** (*sometimes l.c.*) *Slang.* an abbreviation of: son of a bitch.

so•ber (sō′bər) /'sowbər/ *adj.,* **-er, -est,** *v.* **—***adj.* **1.** not drunk: *One partygoer, the designated driver, stayed sober and drove everyone home.* **2.** quiet, sedate, or solemn: *a serious, sober couple.* **3.** not flashy or showy, such as clothes; dull or subdued: *sober clothes: a gray suit, white shirt, and dark tie.* **4.** free from exaggeration: *sober facts.* **—***v.* **5. sober up,** to (cause to) become free of effects of too much alcoholic liquor: [~ + *obj* + *up*]: *He thought a cup of coffee would sober him up.* [~ + *up* + *obj*]: *coffee to sober up the merrymakers.* [*no obj*]: *tried to sober up by drinking some coffee.* —**so′ber•ly,** *adv.* —**so′ber•ness,** *n.* [*noncount*]

so•ber•ing (sō′bər ing) /'sowbərɪŋ/ *adj.* causing a feeling of seriousness, thoughtfulness, or worry: *His sobering words reminded everyone not to celebrate too early.*

so•bri•e•ty (sə brī′i tē, sō-) /sə'brayɪtiy, sow-/ *n.* [*noncount*] the state or quality of being sober.

so•bri•quet (sō′bri kā′, -ket′, sō′bri kā′, -ket′) /'sowbrɪ,key, -,kɛt, ,sowbrɪ'key, -'kɛt/ *n.* [*count*] a nickname.

-soc-, *root.* -*soc*- comes from Latin, where it has the meaning "partner; comrade." This meaning is found in such words as: ASSOCIATE, ASSOCIATION, DISASSOCIATE, SOCIAL, SOCIALIZE, SOCIETY, SOCIO-, UNSOCIABLE.

Soc. or **soc.,** an abbreviation of: **1.** society. **2.** sociology.

so′-called′, *adj.* [*before a noun*] **1.** called or designated thus: *the so-called Southern bloc.* **2.** incorrectly called or styled thus: *Her so-called friends are the ones who tempted her to use drugs.*

soc•cer (sok′ər) /'sɒkər/ *n.* [*noncount*] a form of football played by two 11-member teams, in which the ball may be kicked or bounced off any part of the body but the arms and hands: *In soccer only goalkeepers may use their hands to play the ball.*

so•cia•ble (sō′shə bəl) /'sowʃəbəl/ *adj.* **1.** glad to associate with others; companionable: *a sociable couple who enjoy parties.* **2.** marked by agreeable companionship: *a sociable evening.* —**so•cia•bil•i•ty** (sō′shə bil′i tē) /,sowʃə'bɪlɪtiy/ *n.* [*noncount*] —**so′cia•bly,** *adv.* See -SOC-.

so•cial (sō′shəl) /'sowʃəl/ *adj.* **1.** of or relating to friendly companionship or relations: *a social club.* **2.** friendly or sociable: *a social personality.* **3.** living in companionship with others rather than in isolation: *Humans are social animals.* **4.** [*often: before a noun*] of or relating to human society, esp. when it is divided into classes according to status: *the social classes of the Middle Ages in Europe.* **—***n.* [*count*] **5.** a social gathering esp. of or given by an organized group: *a church social.* —**so′cial•ly,** *adv.* See -SOC-.

so′cial disease′, *n.* [*count*] a venereal disease.

so•cial•ism (sō′shə liz′əm) /'sowʃə,lɪzəm/ *n.* [*noncount*] a theory or system of social organization in which the means of production and distribution of goods are owned and controlled by groups or by the government. See -SOC-.

so•cial•ist (sō′shə list) /'sowʃəlɪst/ *n.* [*count*] **1.** a person believing in socialism. **—***adj.* **2.** of or relating to socialism: *calling for a socialist society.* —**so′cial•is′tic,** *adj.* See -SOC-.

so•cial•ite (sō′shə līt′) /'sowʃə,layt/ *n.* [*count*] a socially important or well-known person. See -SOC-.

so•cial•ize (sō′shə līz′) /'sowʃə,layz/ *v.,* **-ized, -iz•ing.** **—***v.* **1.** [~ + *obj*] to make fit for life in companionship with others: *the problems of socializing a two-year-old child.* **2.** [*no obj*] to associate sociably with others: *The child needs to have some friends to socialize with.* **3.** [~ + *obj*] to make socialistic: *to socialize medicine.* —**so•cial•i•za•tion** (sō′shə li zā′shən) /,sowʃəlɪ'zeyʃən/ *n.* [*noncount*]: *the difficult process of child socialization.* See -SOC-.

so′cialized med′icine, *n.* [*noncount*] a system to provide a nation with medical care through government payments and regularization of services.

so′cial sci′ence, *n.* **1.** [*noncount*] the study of society and social behavior. **2.** [*count*] a field of study, such as history or economics, dealing with society or social activity. —**so′cial sci′entist,** *n.* [*count*]

so′cial secu′rity, *n.* [*noncount*] **1.** [*often: Social Security*] a program of old age, unemployment, health, disability, and survivors' insurance maintained by the U.S. government through employer and employee payments. **2.** any public program providing for economic security and social welfare.

so′cial work′, *n.* [*noncount*] any organized service or activity to improve social conditions in a community, such as assistance to troubled families. —**so′cial work′er,** *n.* [*count*]

so•ci•e•ty (sə sī′i tē) /sə'sayɪtiy/ *n., pl.* **-ties,** *adj.* **—***n.* **1.** [*noncount*] human beings thought of as a group and viewed as members of a community: *the evolution of society.* **2.** a highly structured system of human organization for a large-scale community: [*noncount*]: *a look at American society.* [*count*]: *They studied societies of ancient Egypt and Greece.* **3.** [*count*] a group of people associated together for religious, cultural, scientific, or other purposes: *an Irish-American cultural society.* **4.** [*noncount*] the social life of wealthy, well-known, or fashionable persons, or the class of these people: *people in high society.* **—***adj.* [*before a noun*] **5.** of or relating to elegant society: *a society photographer.* —**so•ci•e•tal** (sə sī′i tl) /sə'sayɪtl/ *adj.*: *the societal pressure put on teenagers to succeed.* See -SOC-.

socio-, *prefix. socio-* is attached to roots and sometimes words and means "social; sociological; society": *socio-* + *economic* → *socioeconomic; socio-* + *-metry* → *sociometry (= social statistics).* See -SOC-.

so•ci•o•ec•o•nom•ic (sō′sē ō ek′ə nom′ik, -ē′kə-, sō′shē-) /,sowsiyow,ɛkə'nɒmɪk, -,iykə-, ,sowʃiy-/ *adj.* of or relating to the combination of social and economic factors. See -SOC-.

so•ci•ol•o•gy (sō′sē ol′ə jē, sō′shē-) /,sowsiy'ɒlədʒiy, ,sowʃiy-/ *n.* [*noncount*] the science or study of human society. —**so•ci•o•log•i•cal** (sō′sē ə loj′i kəl, sō′shē-) /,sowsiyə'lɒdʒɪkəl, ,sowʃiy-/ *adj.* —**so′ci•ol′o•gist,** *n.* [*count*] See -SOC-, -LOG-.

so•ci•o•path (sō′sē ə path′, sō′shē-) /'sowsiyə,pæθ, 'sowʃiy-/ *n.* [*count*] a person, such as a psychopath, whose behavior is antisocial and who lacks a sense of moral responsibility or social conscience. See -SOC-, -PATH-.

sock[1] (sok) /sɒk/ *n.* [*count*], *pl.* **socks** or sometimes, **sox.** a short stocking usually reaching to the calf. See illustration at CLOTHING.

sock[2] (sok) /sɒk/ *v.* **1.** [~ + *obj*] to hit hard: *She socked him in the jaw.* **2. sock away,** to put into savings or reserve: [~ + *away* + *obj*]: *socked away some money for an emergency.* [~ + *obj* + *away*]: *to sock money away.* **3. sock in,** [~ + *in* + *obj*] to close up, as an airport, or ground (an aircraft): *A heavy fog had socked in the whole air base.* **—***n.* [*count*] **4.** a hard blow.

sock•et (sok′it) /'sɒkɪt/ *n.* [*count*] a hollow part that contains or fits into another part: *a socket for a light bulb.*

sod (sod) /sɒd/ *n., v.,* **sod•ded, sod•ding.** **—***n.* **1.** [*count*] a section cut or torn from the surface of grassland, containing the matted roots of grass. **2.** [*noncount*] the surface of the ground, esp. when covered with grass; turf. **—***v.* [~ + *obj*] **3.** to cover with sods or sod.

so•da (sō′də) /'sowdə/ *n., pl.* **-das.** **1.** SODA POP: [*noncount*]: *doesn't drink soda.* [*count*]: *How many sodas did you drink?* **2.** SODA WATER. **3.** [*count*] a drink made with soda water and flavored syrup: *an ice-cream soda.* **4.** [*noncount*] sodium: *carbonate of soda.*

so′da crack′er, *n.* [*count*] a thin, crisp cracker made with a yeast dough containing baking soda.

so′da foun′tain, *n.* [*count*] a counter, as in a restaurant, at which sodas, ice cream, etc., are served.

so′da pop′, *n.* [*noncount*] a carbonated, flavored, and sweetened soft drink: *some cherry soda pop.*

so′da wa′ter, *n.* [*noncount*] **1.** water charged with carbon dioxide. **2.** SODA POP.

sod•den (sod′n) /ˈsɒdn/ *adj.* soaked and made heavy with liquid or moisture; saturated. —**sod′den•ly,** *adv.*

so•di•um (sō′dē əm) /ˈsowdiyəm/ *n.* [*noncount*] a soft, silver-white, chemically active metallic element that occurs naturally only in combination.

so′dium bicar′bonate, *n.* [*noncount*] a white powder used chiefly as an antacid, a fire extinguisher, and to make dough or batter rise in baking. Also called **bicarbonate of soda, baking soda.**

sod•om•y (sod′ə mē) /ˈsɒdəmiy/ *n.* [*noncount*] anal or oral copulation, esp. with a member of the same sex. —**sod•om•ite•** (sod′ə mīt′) /ˈsɒdəˌmayt/ *n.* [*count*]

so•fa (sō′fə) /ˈsowfə/ *n.* [*count*], *pl.* **-fas.** a long upholstered couch with a back and two arms or raised ends. See illustration at APARTMENT.

so′fa bed′ or **so′fa•bed′,** *n.* [*count*] a sofa that can be converted into a bed.

soft (sôft, soft) /sɔft, sɒft/ *adj.* and *adv.*, **-er, -est,** *interj.* —*adj.* **1.** giving in easily to touch or pressure: *a soft pillow.* **2.** relatively easy to bend, crush, or cut, such as metal or wood: *a soft lead pencil.* **3.** smooth and pleasing to the touch; not rough: *soft skin.* **4.** pleasant or comfortable: *a soft chair.* **5.** low or subdued in sound: *soft music.* **6.** not harsh or unpleasant to the eye: *soft light.* **7.** not hard or sharp: *soft outlines.* **8.** gentle or mild: *soft breezes.* **9.** not sturdy; delicate: *Wash soft fabrics by hand.* **10.** not harsh or severe, such as a demand: *soft demands by the union.* **11.** SOFT-HEARTED: *You're too soft with your dog.* **12.** undemanding; easy, comfortable, etc.: *He has a soft job.* **13.** weak, spiritless, etc., as from lack of challenge: *We've grown soft with all these modern conveniences.* **14.** (of water) mostly free from mineral salts that interfere with the action of soap. **15.** (of paper money or a money system) not supported by sufficient gold reserves: *In those days the ruble was soft currency and the dollar was hard currency.* **16.** SOFT-CORE. **17.** not the worst type; not quite so bad or harmful as others: *soft drugs like marijuana, not hard ones like cocaine.* **18.** (of *c* and *g*) pronounced as in *cent* and *gem.* **19.** foolish or stupid: *soft in the head.* —*adv.* **20.** in a soft manner. —*interj. Archaic.* **21.** be quiet! hush! **22.** not so fast! stop! —***Idiom.*** **23. be soft on,** [*be* + ~ + *on* + *obj*] **a.** to be foolishly in love with: *He's soft on his piano teacher.* **b.** to be too permissive with (something thought of as dangerous or threatening): *soft on crime.* —**soft′ly,** *adv.*: *She rubbed his back softly.* —**soft′ness,** *n.* [*noncount*]: *the silky softness of her skin.*

soft•ball (sôft′bôl′, soft′-) /ˈsɔftˌbɔl, ˈsɒft-/ *n.* **1.** [*noncount*] a form of baseball played on a smaller playing field with a larger and softer ball: *two games of softball.* **2.** [*count*] the ball itself: *They brought two softballs to the game.*

soft′-boiled′, *adj.* (of an egg) boiled in the shell until the yolk and white are only partially set.

soft′ coal′, *n.* BITUMINOUS COAL.

soft′-core′, *adj.* sexually stimulating without being too obvious: *soft-core pornography.* Compare HARD-CORE (def. 2).

soft′ drink′, *n.* [*count*] a beverage that is not alcoholic and is usually carbonated, such as ginger ale.

soft•en (sô′fən, sof′ən) /ˈsɔfən, ˈsɒfən/ *v.*, to (cause to) become soft or softer: [~ + *obj*]: *moisturizing cream to soften the skin.* [*no obj*]: *His normally gruff voice softened when he saw that the child was afraid.* —**soft′en•er,** *n.* [*count*]

soft′-heart′ed, *adj.* very sympathetic or responsive; generous or too generous in spirit; easily giving in.

soft′ pal′ate, *n.* PALATE (def. 1).

soft′-ped′al, *v.* [~ + *obj*], **-aled, -al•ing** or (*esp. Brit.*) **-alled, -al•ling.** to attempt to make (something) appear less obvious or objectionable; downplay: *When the salesman saw their interest, he soft-pedaled the high price of the car.*

soft′ sell′, *n.* [*count; usually singular*] a method of advertising or selling that is quietly persuasive, indirect, and sophisticated (opposed to *hard sell*).

soft′ soap′, *n.* [*noncount*] appealing talk that persuades someone; flattery.

soft•ware (sôft′wâr′, soft′-) /ˈsɔftˌwɛər, ˈsɒft-/ *n.* [*noncount; used with a singular verb*] **1.** programs for directing a computer or processing electronic data (distinguished from *hardware*). **2.** any material requiring the use of equipment, esp. audiovisual material such as film, tapes, or records.

soft•wood (sôft′wo͝od′, soft′-) /ˈsɔftˌwʊd, ˈsɒft-/ *n.* **1. a.** [*noncount*] any wood from a cone-bearing tree. **b.** [*count*] a tree providing such wood. —*adj.* [*before a noun*] **2.** of or relating to softwood.

soft•y or **soft•ie** (sôf′tē, sof′-) /ˈsɔftiy, ˈsɒf-/ *n.* [*count*], *pl.* **-ties.** *Informal.* **1.** one easily stirred to emotions: *a stern man who turned out to be a softy at heart.* **2.** a weak or foolish person.

sog•gy (sog′ē) /ˈsɒgiy/ *adj.*, **-gi•er, -gi•est. 1.** thoroughly wet: *My clothes were soggy from the sudden rain.* **2.** damp and heavy, such as poorly baked bread. —**sog′gi•ness,** *n.* [*noncount*]

soil[1] (soil) /sɔyl/ *n.* [*noncount*] **1.** the portion of the earth's surface made up of humus; earth: *Farmers were at work tilling the soil for thousands of years.* **2.** a country, land, or region: *longing to set foot on his native soil.* **3.** any environment that encourages growth.

soil[2] (soil) /sɔyl/ *v.* **1.** to (cause to) become dirty: [~ + *obj*]: *The baby had soiled her diapers.* [*no obj*]: *These white clothes soil too easily.* —*n.* [*noncount*] **2.** the act or fact of soiling, or the state of being soiled. **3.** a spot or stain: *The detergent gets rid of soil and stains.*

soi•ree or **soi•rée** (swä rā′) /swɑˈrey/ *n.* [*count*], *pl.* **-rees** or **-rées** an evening party or social gathering.

so•journ (*n.* sō′jûrn; *v.* also sō jûrn′) / *n.* ˈsowdʒɜrn; *v.* ælsɒ sowˈdʒɜrn/ *n.* [*count*] **1.** a temporary stay: *a week's sojourn in Paris.* —*v.* [*no obj*] **2.** to stay temporarily: *We sojourned at the beach for a month.* See -JOUR-.

-sola-, *root.* -*sola*- comes from Latin, where it has the meaning "soothe." This meaning is found in such words as: CONSOLATION, CONSOLE, DISCONSOLATE, INCONSOLABLE, SOLACE.

sol•ace (sol′is) /ˈsɒlɪs/ *n.* **1.** [*noncount*] comfort in sorrow or misfortune: *some solace in knowing that her death was instantaneous.* **2.** [*count*] a source of comfort. See -SOLA-.

so•lar (sō′lər) /ˈsowlər/ *adj.* **1.** of or relating to the sun: *solar phenomena.* **2.** coming from the sun: *solar radiation.* **3.** determined by the sun: *a solar hour.*

so′lar cell′, *n.* [*count*] a device that changes energy from the sun into electrical energy.

so′lar en′ergy, *n.* [*noncount*] energy derived from the sun in the form of solar radiation.

so•lar•i•um (sə lâr′ē əm, sō-) /səˈlɛəriyəm, sow-/ *n.* [*count*], *pl.* **-lar•i•ums, -lar•i•a** (-lâr′ē ə) /-ˈlɛəriyə/. a glass-enclosed room or porch exposed to the sun's rays: *While he was recovering in the hospital he spent time in the solarium.*

so′lar sys′tem, *n.* [*count; usually: the* + ~] the sun and all the planets and other bodies that revolve around it.

sold (sōld) /sowld/ *v.* pt. and pp. of SELL.

sol•der (sod′ər) /ˈsɒdər/ *n.* [*noncount*] **1.** a soft, metallic substance that is melted and applied to a point where metal objects meet, in order to unite them without heating the objects to the melting point. —*v.* [~ + *obj*] **2.** to join (metal objects) with solder. —**sol′der•er,** *n.* [*count*]

sol•dier (sōl′jər) /ˈsowldʒər/ *n.* [*count*] **1.** one who works or has worked in military service. **2.** an enlisted person, as distinguished from a commissioned officer. **3.** a low-ranking member of a crime organization. **4.** a member of certain insect groups whose job is to defend the colony from invaders. —*v.* [*no obj*] **5. soldier on,** to continue forward in spite of difficulty or hardship; persist: *He soldiered on and finally got his bachelor's degree.* —**sol′dier•ly,** *adj.*

sole[1] (sōl) /sowl/ *adj.* [*before a noun*] **1.** being the only one; only: *the sole living relative.* **2.** belonging or relating to one individual or group and not to others; exclusive: *sole right to the estate.* —**sole′ly,** *adv.*: *he did it solely through his own efforts.* See -SOLE-.

sole[2] (sōl) /sowl/ *n.*, *v.*, **soled, sol•ing.** —*n.* [*count*] **1.** the undersurface of a foot. **2.** the corresponding under part of a shoe or other footwear. —*v.* [~ + *obj*] **3.** to furnish with a sole.

sole[3] (sōl) /sowl/ *n.* [*count*], *pl.* (*esp. when thought of as a group*) **sole,** (*esp. for kinds or species*) **soles. 1.** a kind of edible flatfish having a hooklike snout. **2.** the market name of any of various other flatfishes resembling the sole.

-sole-, *root.* -*sole*- comes from Latin, where it has the meaning "only; alone." This meaning is found in such words as: DESOLATE, DESOLATION, SOLE, SOLILOQUY, SOLIPSISM, SOLITAIRE, SOLITARY, SOLITUDE, SOLO.

sol•e•cism (sol′ə siz′əm, sō′lə-) /ˈsɒləˌsɪzəm, ˈsowlə-/ *n.* [*count*] **1.** a nonstandard or ungrammatical usage, as *unflammable* or *they was.* **2.** any error, improper act, or inconsistency.

sol•emn (sol′əm) /ˈsɒləm/ *adj.* **1.** grave; not funny: *sol-*

emn remarks. **2.** serious; earnest; sincere: *solemn assurance that he would keep his word.* **3.** of a ceremonious character: *a solemn occasion.* **4.** marked or observed with religious rites: *a solemn holy day.* —**so•lem•ni•ty** (sə lem′ni tē) /sə'lɛmnɪtiy/ *n.* [*noncount*] —**sol′emn•ly,** *adv.*

sol•em•nize (sol′əm nīz′) /'sɒləmˌnayz/ *v.* [~ + *obj*], **-nized, -niz•ing. 1.** to observe with ceremony; make (something) solemn: *to solemnize the holy day.* **2.** to perform the ceremony of (marriage).

so•le•noid (sō′lə noid′, sol′ə-) /'sowləˌnɔyd, 'sɒlə-/ *n.* [*count*] a coil of wire that, when carrying current, magnetically attracts a sliding iron core. —**so′le•noi′dal,** *adj.*

so•lic•it (sə lis′it) /sə'lɪsɪt/ *v.* **1.** [~ + *obj*] to try to obtain by request; make a request for: *to solicit aid from the United Nations.* **2.** [~ + *obj*] to ask (someone) for something: *to solicit the committee for funds.* **3.** [*no obj*] to ask for business, as by selling or trading: *No soliciting is allowed in this building.* **4.** to offer to have sex with (someone) for money: [*no obj*]: *The prostitute was arrested for soliciting.* [~ + *obj*]: *to solicit the men outside the bar.* —**so•lic•i•ta•tion** (sə lis′i tā′shən) /səˌlɪsɪ'teyʃən/ *n.* [*noncount*]: *arrested for solicitation on the city streets.*

so•lic•i•tor (sə lis′i tər) /sə'lɪsɪtər/ *n.* [*count*] **1.** one who makes requests for something, as contributions. **2.** an officer having charge of the legal business of a city, town, etc. **3.** a British lawyer who advises clients and represents them before the lower courts.

so•lic•i•tous (sə lis′i təs) /sə'lɪsɪtəs/ *adj.* anxious or concerned: *She was solicitous about my health.* —**so•lic′i•tous•ly,** *adv.*: *"Is everything to your liking?" the waiter asked solicitously.*

so•lic•i•tude (sə lis′i to͞od′, -tyo͞od′) /sə'lɪsɪˌtuwd, -ˌtyuwd/ *n.* [*noncount*] the state of being solicitous; deep concern.

sol•id (sol′id) /'sɒlɪd/ *adj.* **1.** having the interior completely filled up: *a piece of solid rock.* **2.** having the three dimensions of length, breadth, and thickness: *A cube is a solid figure.* **3.** (of the parts that compose something) having firmness and sticking together: *solid particles suspended in a liquid.* **4.** having no openings or breaks: *a solid wall.* **5.** firm or compact in substance: *standing on solid ground.* **6.** dense, thick, or heavy in nature or appearance: *a solid cloud of smoke.* **7.** firm in makeup; substantial: *can eat solid food now.* **8.** without separation; continuous: *a solid row of high-rise buildings.* **9.** serious in character: *solid scholarship.* **10.** highly competent or skilled: *a solid musician.* **11.** [*before a noun*] whole or entire: *one solid hour.* **12.** [*before a noun*] made up entirely of one substance or material: *That ring is solid gold.* **13.** [*before a noun*] uniform in color or tone: *a solid blue dress.* **14.** fully reliable or sensible: *a solid citizen.* **15.** financially sound: *a solid corporation.* **16.** [*before a noun*] cubic: *A solid foot contains 1728 solid inches.* **17.** unanimous: *a solid majority.* —*n.* [*count*] **18.** something solid. **19.** a substance whose molecules are densely packed and that keeps its shape or form and does not flow or spread out. —**so•lid•i•ty** (sə lid′i tē) /sə'lɪdɪtiy/ *n.* [*noncount*] —**sol′id•ly,** *adv.* —**sol′id•ness,** *n.* [*noncount*]

sol•i•dar•i•ty (sol′i dar′i tē) /ˌsɒlɪ'dærɪtiy/ *n.* [*noncount*] agreement in attitude or purpose, as between members of a group: *Our union went on strike in solidarity with the others.*

so•lid•i•fy (sə lid′ə fī′) /sə'lɪdəˌfay/ *v.*, **-fied, -fy•ing.** —*v.* **1.** to (cause to) become solid; (cause to) be made into a hard or compact mass; change from a liquid or gaseous to a solid form: [*no obj*]: *Water solidifies and becomes ice.* [~ + *obj*]: *The concrete will solidify the foundation.* **2.** to unite firmly or consolidate: [*no obj*]: *The coalition must solidify and fight as one unit.* [~ + *obj*]: *That leader can solidify the various groups of the country.* —**so•lid•i•fi•ca•tion** (sə lid′ə fi kā′shən) /səˌlɪdəfɪ'keyʃən/ *n.* [*noncount*]

sol′id-state′, *adj.* [*usually before a noun*] of or relating to electronic devices, such as crystals, that can control current without the use of moving or heated parts or vacuum gaps.

so•lil•o•quy (sə lil′ə kwē) /sə'lɪləkwiy/ *n.* [*count*], *pl.* **-quies. 1.** a speech in a drama in which a character, alone or as if alone, reveals innermost thoughts. **2.** the act of talking while or as if alone. See -SOLE-, -LOQ-.

sol•ip•sism (sol′ip siz′əm) /'sɒlɪpˌsɪzəm/ *n.* [*noncount*] the theory that only the self exists. See -SOLE-.

sol•i•taire (sol′i târ′) /'sɒlɪˌtɛər/ *n.* **1.** [*noncount*] any of various card games for one person in which the cards are arranged in patterns. **2.** [*count*] a precious stone, esp. a diamond, set by itself, as in a ring. See -SOLE-.

sol•i•tar•y (sol′i ter′ē) /'sɒlɪˌtɛriy/ *adj.*, *n.*, *pl.* **-tar•ies.** —*adj.* **1.** [*before a noun*] without companions; sole: *a solitary passerby.* **2.** [*before a noun*] by itself; singular: *one solitary house.* **3.** [*before a noun*] being the only one: *a solitary exception.* **4.** avoiding the society of others: *a solitary existence.* **5.** marked by the absence of companions: *a solitary journey.* **6.** far away from others; secluded: *a solitary cabin in the woods.* —*n.* **7.** [*count*] one who lives alone or in solitude. **8.** [*noncount*] Also, **solitary confinement.** imprisonment without contact with another person: *a few months in solitary.* See -SOLE-.

sol•i•tude (sol′i to͞od′, -tyo͞od′) /'sɒlɪˌtuwd, -ˌtyuwd/ *n.* [*noncount*] **1.** the state of being or living alone; seclusion: *She enjoyed some solitude after a busy day at work.* **2.** remoteness from habitations: *He enjoyed the solitude of the woods.* See -SOLE-.

so•lo (sō′lō) /'sowlow/ *n.*, *pl.* **-los,** *adj.*, *adv.*, *v.*, **-loed, -lo•ing.** —*n.* [*count*] **1.** a musical composition or a part for one performer with or without accompaniment. **2.** any performance, such as a dance, by one person. **3.** a flight in an airplane during which the pilot is unaccompanied: *The pilot was ready for her first solo.* —*adj.* **4.** of, relating to, or being a solo. —*adv.* **5.** on one's own; alone: *She's flying solo.* —*v.* [*no obj*] **6.** to perform or be a solo: *to solo before a hostile audience.* **7.** to pilot an airplane by oneself: *felt ready to solo.* —**so′lo•ist,** *n.* [*count*] See -SOLE-.

sol•stice (sol′stis, sōl′-) /'sɒlstɪs, 'sowl-/ *n.* [*count*] either of the two times a year when the sun is at its greatest distance from the equator, about June 21 or about Dec. 22.

sol•u•ble (sol′yə bəl) /'sɒlyəbəl/ *adj.* **1.** capable of being dissolved or made into liquid: *a soluble powder.* **2.** capable of being solved or explained: *a soluble problem.* —*n.* [*count*] **3.** something soluble. —**sol•u•bil•i•ty** (sol′yə bil′i tē) /ˌsɒlyə'bɪlɪtiy/ *n.* [*noncount*] See -SOLV-.

so•lu•tion (sə lo͞o′shən) /sə'luwʃən/ *n.* **1.** [*noncount*] the act or process of solving a problem, or the state of being solved: *No solution is possible for that problem.* **2.** [*count*] an answer to a problem. **3. a.** [*noncount*] the process by which a gas, liquid, or solid is spread in a gas, liquid, or solid without chemical change: *in solution.* **b.** [*count*] a mixture of substances by this process. See -SOLV-.

-solv-, *root.* *-solv-* comes from Latin, where it has the meaning "loosen; release; dissolve." This meaning is found in such words as: ABSOLVE, DISSOLVE, INSOLVENT, RESOLVE, SOLVE.

solve (solv) /sɒlv/ *v.* [~ + *obj*], **solved, solv•ing. 1.** to find the answer or explanation for: *to solve a puzzle.* **2.** to work out the answer or solution to (a mathematical problem): *Solve the equation when* x *is equal to 3.* —**solv′a•ble,** *adj.* —**solv′er,** *n.* [*count*] See -SOLV-.

sol•vent (sol′vənt) /'sɒlvənt/ *adj.* **1.** able to pay all one's debts: *The company is solvent.* **2.** having the power of dissolving; causing solution. —*n.* [*count*] **3.** a substance that dissolves another to form a solution: *Water is a solvent for sugar.* —**sol′ven•cy,** *n.* [*noncount*]: *a question of fiscal solvency.* See -SOLV-.

-som-, *root.* *-som-* comes from Greek, where it has the meaning "body." This meaning is found in such words as: CHROMOSOME, PSYCHOSOMATIC.

So•ma•li (sō mä′lē, sə-) /sow'mɑliy, sə-/ *n.*, *pl.* **-lis, -li.** Also, **So•ma•li•an** (sō mä′lē ən, -mäl′yən) /sow'mɑliyən, -'mɑlyən/. **1.** [*count*] a person born or living in Somalia. **2.** [*noncount*] the language spoken by many of the people of Somalia. —*adj.* **3.** of or relating to Somalia.

som•ber (som′bər) /'sɒmbər/ *adj.* **1.** dull in color or tone: *a somber dress.* **2.** downcast; glum: *a somber mood.* **3.** serious; grave: *a somber expression on one's face.* Also, *esp. Brit.*, **som′bre.** —**som′ber•ly,** *adv.*

som•bre•ro (som brâr′ō) /sɒm'brɛərow/ *n.* [*count*], *pl.* **-ros.** a broad-brimmed, tall-crowned hat of straw or felt.

some (sum; *unstressed* səm) /sʌm; *unstressed* səm/ *adj.* **1.** [~ + *singular count noun*] being an unknown, or not specified one: *Some person may object. We asked if there would be some adult present in the class.* **2.** [~ + *plural noun*] certain; a few but not all: *Some days I stay home.* **3.** [~ + *noncount noun*] not specified in number, amount, etc.; a certain amount or part of, but not all of: *I agree with you to some extent. Will you spend some time with your friends?* **4.** not specified but fairly large, great, or considerable in number, amount, degree, etc.: [~ + *noncount noun*]: *We talked for some time.* [~ + *plural noun*]: *I've known her for quite some years now.* **5.** *Infor-*

mal. (used, esp. when stressed, to express irony or sarcasm, or that the next noun is unusual, remarkable, undeniable, etc.: [~ + *count noun*]: *Some partner you turned out to be! That was some storm.* [~ + *plural noun*]: *Those were some tough football players!* [~ + *noncount noun*]: *There must be some work I can do.* **—***pron.* **6. a.** [*used in place of a plural noun*] certain persons, individuals, etc., not specified: *Some think he is dead.* [~ + *of the* + *plural noun*]: *Some of the people think he is dead.* **b.** [*used in place of a noncount noun*] a certain part or amount not specified: *Some is spoiled, but some is still good.* [~ + *of the* + *noncount noun*]: *Some of the food is spoiled.* **7.** [*used in place of a plural noun*] an unspecified number, amount, etc., in addition to the rest: *He paid a thousand dollars and then some.* **—***adv.* **8.** [*before a number*] approximately; about: *The building was some fifty stories high.* **9.** to some degree or extent: *I like baseball some.* **—Usage.** The word SOME is used in sentences that are affirmative; the word ANY is used instead of SOME with negative phrases or in questions: *I'd like some milk. I don't want any milk. I never see any of my friends these days. Do you have any milk?* But SOME can be used in questions when the answer is expected to be "yes": *Can I have some milk, please?*

-some[1], *suffix. -some* is used to form adjectives with the meanings "like; tending to": *burden + -some → burdensome (= like a burden); quarrel + -some → quarrelsome (= tending to quarrel).*

-some[2], *suffix. -some* is used to form nouns with the meaning "a collection (of the number mentioned) of objects": *threesome (= a group of three).*

some•bod•y (sum′bod′ē, -bud′ē, -bə dē) /ˈsʌmˌbɒdiy, -ˌbʌdiy, -bədiy/ *pron., n., pl.* **-bod•ies. —***pron.* **1.** someone not known or specified: *Maybe somebody will think of a better solution. There's somebody at the door.* **—***n.* **2.** This word may be used as a pronoun (with no article) or as a count noun (with an article if singular) to mean "a person of some importance:" *Right now he may not seem special, but one day he'll be somebody. He wants to be a somebody, not a nobody.* **—Usage.** As a pronoun, SOMEBODY is used most often in affirmative sentences, while ANYBODY is used in sentences with negative words and in questions: *There's somebody at the door. There isn't anybody at the door. Is anybody at the door?* But SOMEBODY can be used in questions when the answer is expected to be "yes": *Can't somebody help me?*

some•day (sum′dā′) /ˈsʌmˌdey/ *adv.* at an indefinite time in the future: *Someday she'll be president.*

some•how (sum′hou′) /ˈsʌmˌhaw/ *adv.* **1.** in some way not specified, apparent, or known: *They knew that somehow they would meet again.* **—*Idiom.*** **2. somehow or other,** in some way; somehow.

some•one (sum′wun′, -wən) /ˈsʌmˌwʌn, -wən/ *pron.* some person; somebody: *Our hosts arranged for someone to meet us at the airport.* **—Usage.** Like SOMEBODY, SOMEONE is used most often in affirmative sentences, while ANYONE is used in sentences with negative words and in questions: *There's someone at the door. There isn't anyone at the door. Is anyone at the door?* But SOMEONE can be used in questions when the answer is expected to be "yes": *Can't someone help me?*

some•place (sum′plās′) /ˈsʌmˌpleys/ *adv.* somewhere: *I'd like to go someplace different for our anniversary.*

som•er•sault (sum′ər sôlt′) /ˈsʌmərˌsɔlt/ *n.* [*count*] **1.** an acrobatic movement, either forward or backward, in which the body rolls end over end, making a complete revolution. **2.** such a movement performed in the air as part of a dive, tumbling routine, etc. **—***v.* [*no obj*] **3.** to perform a somersault. Sometimes, **som•er•set** (sum′ər-set′) /ˈsʌmˌr sɛt/.

some•thing (sum′thing′) /ˈsʌmˌθɪŋ/ *pron.* **1.** a certain thing not determined or specified: *Something is wrong there. Tell me something; what do you think about this?* **2.** (used with, or sometimes added to, a word referring to a number to indicate an additional amount, as of years, unknown, unspecified, or forgotten): *We saw him thirty something years ago, I guess.* **3.** (used for hesitation, or to express that an idea or comment is not exact or complete): *I was thinking of joining a health club or something.* **—***n.* [*noncount*] **4.** a person or thing of some importance or consequence: *There's something to what you say. Look, you still have your health; that's something, isn't it?* **—***adv.* **5.** in some degree; to some extent; somewhat: *I saw a bird that was something like a crow.* **6.** *Informal.* to a high or extreme degree: *The kids started to act up something fierce!* **—*Idiom.*** **7. something of,** to some degree, extent, or amount: *He was always something of a troublemaker.* **Usage.** The word SOMETHING is used in sentences that are affirmative, while the word ANYTHING is used with negative phrases or in questions: *I wish I had something to do. I don't have anything to do. Do you have anything for me to do?* But the word SOMETHING may be used in questions when the answer is expected to be "yes": *Can't something be done to help me?*

some•time (sum′tīm′) /ˈsʌmˌtaym/ *adv.* **1.** at some indefinite time: *arrived sometime last week.* **2.** at an indefinite future time: *Come to see us sometime.* **—***adj.* [*before a noun*] **3.** having been formerly; former: *the sometime president.* **4.** being so only at times or to some extent: *a sometime painter.*

some•times (sum′tīmz′) /ˈsʌmˌtaymz/ *adv.* on some occasions; at times; now and then: *Sometimes I walk to work.*

some•way (sum′wā′) /ˈsʌmˌwey/ also **some•ways** (sum′wāz′) /ˈsʌmˌweyz/ *adv.* in some way; somehow.

some•what (sum′hwut′, -hwot′, -wut′, -wot′) /ˈsʌmˌhwʌt, -ˌhwɒt, -ˌwʌt, -ˌwɒt/ *adv.* in some measure or degree; to some extent: *That defeat was somewhat surprising.*

some•where (sum′hwâr′, -wâr′) /ˈsʌmˌhwɛər, -ˌwɛər/ *adv.* **1.** in, at, or to some place unspecified or unknown: *I've left the book somewhere.* **2.** nearly; almost; in the neighborhood of; approximately: *She's somewhere around 60 years old.*

som•nam•bu•lism (som nam′byə liz′əm, səm-) /sɒmˈnæmbyəˌlɪzəm, səm-/ *n.* SLEEPWALKING. **—som•nam′bu•list,** *n.* [*count*]

som•no•lent (som′nə lənt) /ˈsɒmnələnt/ *adj.* **1.** sleepy; drowsy. **2.** tending to cause sleep: *a somnolent speech.* **—som′no•lence,** *n.* [*noncount*]

son (sun) /sʌn/ *n.* [*count*] **1.** a male child or person in relation to his parents by birth, adoption, or marriage. **2.** (used by an older person to address a younger male): *"Well, son, here's the choice: jail or a fine," the sheriff said.* **3.** a male person looked upon as the result of a particular agent or influence: *sons of the soil.*

-son-, *root. -son-* comes from Latin, where it has the meaning "sound." This meaning is found in such words as: CONSONANT, DISSONANCE, DISSONANT, RESONANCE, RESONANT, RESONATE, RESOUND, SONAR, SONATA, SONIC, SONNET, SOUND, SUPERSONIC, ULTRASONIC, UNISON.

so•nar (sō′när) /ˈsownɑr/ *n.* **1.** [*noncount*] a method for locating underwater objects by sending out sound waves that reflect off an object and bounce back to the sensing device: *They located the enemy submarine by sonar.* **2.** [*count*] the apparatus used in sonar: *Are the Russian sonars as good as ours?* See -SON-.

so•na•ta (sə nä′tə) /səˈnɑtə/ *n.* [*count*], *pl.* **-tas.** music written for a solo instrument or a small number of instruments, in three or four movements. See -SON-.

song (sông, song) /sɔŋ, sɒŋ/ *n.* **1.** [*count*] a short piece of music for singing. **2.** [*noncount*] the art or act of singing; vocal music: *a night of wine, women, and song.* **3.** [*count*] a patterned vocal sound produced by an animal, as by male birds, frogs, etc. **—*Idiom.*** **4. for a song,** at a very low price: *I bought the rug for a song.* See -SON-.

song•bird (sông′bûrd′, song′-) /ˈsɔŋˌbɜrd, ˈsɒŋ-/ *n.* [*count*] **1.** a bird that sings. **2.** *Slang.* a woman vocalist.

song•fest (sông′fest, song′-) /ˈsɔŋfɛst, ˈsɒŋ-/ *n.* [*count*] an informal gathering at which people sing songs.

song•ster (sông′stər, song′-) /ˈsɔŋstər, ˈsɒŋ-/ *n.* [*count*] **1.** a person who sings; a singer. **2.** a writer of songs.

son•ic (son′ik) /ˈsɒnɪk/ *adj.* **1.** of or relating to sound. **2.** of or relating to a speed equal to that of sound in air at the same height above sea level. See -SON-.

son′ic boom′, *n.* [*count*] a loud noise caused by the shock wave made by an aircraft moving at supersonic speed.

son′-in-law′, *n.* [*count*], *pl.* **sons-in-law.** the husband of one's daughter.

son•net (son′it) /ˈsɒnɪt/ *n.* [*count*] a poem written in 14 lines, with rhymes arranged in a fixed scheme: *Italian sonnets have a major group of eight lines followed by a minor group of six lines.* See -SON-.

son•ny (sun′ē) /ˈsʌniy/ *n.* [*sometimes: Sonny*] (used by an older person to address a younger male, esp. a boy).

so•no•rous (sə nôr′əs, -nōr′-, son′ər əs) /səˈnɔrəs, -ˈnowr-, ˈsɒnərəs/ *adj.* **1.** echoing with a deep sound; resonant: *a sonorous cavern.* **2.** loud and deep-toned: *a sonorous voice.* **3.** high-flown; very grand or fancy in speaking or in sound: *a sonorous speech.* **—so•nor•i•ty** (sə nôr′i tē, -nor′-) /səˈnɔrɪtiy, -ˈnɒr-/ *n.* [*noncount*] See -SON-.

soon (so͞on) /suwn/ *adv.,* **-er, -est. 1.** within a short period; before long: *The frogs started their noise soon after dark.* **2.** promptly; quickly: *Finish as soon as you can.* **3.** readily or willingly: *I would as soon walk as ride.* **—*Idiom.*** **4. sooner or later,** sometime; eventually: *Sooner or later you must face the truth.* **5. would** or **had sooner,** [~ + *verb* (+ *than* + *verb*)] to prefer to: *I would sooner stay home and watch TV (than go to that party).* Compare RATHER (def. 7).

soot (so͝ot, so͞ot) /sʊt, suwt/ *n.* [*noncount*] a black substance produced during incomplete burning of coal, etc., rising in tiny particles that stick to and blacken surfaces on contact: *Black soot was shooting out of the chimneys.* —**soot′y,** *adj.,* **-i•er, -i•est:** *sooty fireplaces.*

soothe (so͞oth) /suwð/ *v.,* **soothed, sooth•ing. 1.** [~ + *obj*] to offer comfort to; cause to be calm: *to soothe someone with kind words.* **2.** to relieve the pain in or of (something): [~ + *obj*]: *a lotion to soothe sunburned skin.* [*no obj*]: *The lotion soothes as it heals.* —**sooth′er,** *n.* [*count*] —**sooth′ing,** *adj.*: *her quiet, soothing voice.* —**sooth′ing•ly,** *adv.*

sooth•say•er (so͞oth′sā′ər) /ˈsuwθˌseyər/ *n.* [*count*] a person who tells future events.

sop (sop) /sɒp/ *n., v.,* **sopped, sop•ping.** —*n.* [*count*] **1.** a piece of solid food, such as bread, for dipping in liquid food. **2.** something, esp. a worthless thing, offered or done to keep another satisfied: *He was offered a low-paying job as a sop for the humiliation he had suffered.* —*v.* [~ + *obj*] **3.** to dip in liquid food: *to sop bread in gravy.* **4.** to drench: *I was sopped by that sudden rain.* **5.** to take up (liquid) by absorption: [~ + *up* + *obj*]: *I sopped up the gravy.* [~ + *obj* + *up*]: *I sopped the gravy up with my bread.* See SOPPING.

SOP, an abbreviation of: Standard Operating Procedure; Standing Operating Procedure.

-soph-, *root.* *-soph-* comes from Greek, where it has the meaning "wise." This meaning is found in such words as: PHILOSOPHER, PHILOSOPHY, SOPHISM, SOPHISTICATED, SOPHISTRY, SOPHOMORE, THEOSOPHY, UNSOPHISTICATED.

soph•ism (sof′iz əm) /ˈsɒfɪzəm/ *n.* [*count*] a false argument, esp. one designed only to show one's cleverness in reasoning or in deceiving someone. See -SOPH-.

soph•ist (sof′ist) /ˈsɒfɪst/ *n.* [*count*] one who reasons cleverly but not truthfully. See -SOPH-.

so•phis•ti•cate (sə fis′ti kit, -kāt′) /səˈfɪstɪkɪt, -ˌkeyt/ *n.* [*count*] a sophisticated person. See -SOPH-.

so•phis•ti•cat•ed (sə fis′ti kā′tid) /səˈfɪstɪˌkeytɪd/ *adj.* **1.** worldly-wise; showing knowledge of the world: *sophisticated travelers.* **2.** appealing to cultured tastes: *sophisticated music.* **3.** complex; intricate: *a sophisticated electronic control system.* —**so•phis•ti•ca•tionc** (sə fis′ti kā′shən) /səˌfɪstɪˈkeyʃən/ *n.* [*noncount*]: *The sophistication of the child's drawing amazed everyone.* See -SOPH-.

soph•ist•ry (sof′ə strē) /ˈsɒfəstriy/ *n., pl.* **-ries. 1.** [*noncount*] a clever, apparently sensible, but false method of reasoning. **2.** [*count*] a false argument; sophism. See -SOPH-.

soph•o•more (sof′ə môr′, -mōr′; sof′môr, -mōr) /ˈsɒfəˌmɔr, -ˌmowr; ˈsɒfmɔr, -mowr/ *n.* [*count*] a student in the second year at a high school, college, or university. See -SOPH-.

soph•o•mor•ic (sof′ə môr′ik, -mor′-) /ˌsɒfəˈmɔrɪk, -ˈmɒr-/ *adj.* **1.** of or relating to sophomores. **2.** intellectually conceited and immature: *a sophomoric essay.* See -SOPH-.

sop•o•rif•ic (sop′ə rif′ik, sō′pə-) /ˌsɒpəˈrɪfɪk, ˌsowpə-/ *adj.* **1.** Also, **sop′o•rif′er•ous.** causing sleep: *a soporific drug.* —*n.* [*count*] **2.** something that causes sleep, as a medicine or drug: *slipped a soporific into her drink.*

sop•ping (sop′ing) /ˈsɒpɪŋ/ *adj.* very wet; drenched: *My clothes were sopping after that rain.*

sop•py (sop′ē) /ˈsɒpiy/ *adj.,* **-pi•er, -pi•est. 1.** soaked or drenched. **2.** rainy: *soppy weather.* **3.** foolishly emotional: *a soppy TV drama.*

so•pran•o (sə pran′ō, -prä′nō) /səˈprænow, -ˈprɑnow/ *n., pl.* **-pran•os,** *adj.* —*n.* [*count*] **1.** the highest singing voice in women and boys. **2.** a singer with such a voice. **3.** the musical part written for such a voice. —*adj.* **4.** of or relating to a soprano; having the range of a soprano: *a soprano saxophone.*

sor•bet (sôr bā′) /sɔrˈbey/ *n.* a fruit or vegetable ice: [*noncount*]: *Raspberry sorbet is on the menu.* [*count*]: *I'll have a raspberry sorbet.*

sor•cer•y (sôr′sə rē) /ˈsɔrsəriy/ *n.* [*noncount*] the practices of one thought to have supernatural powers granted by evil spirits; black magic; witchcraft: *The wizard used sorcery to change the girl into a mouse.* —**sor′cer•er,** *n.* [*count*] —**sor′cer•ess,** *n.* [*count*]

sor•did (sôr′did) /ˈsɔrdɪd/ *adj.* **1.** morally low; base; corrupt: *a sordid life; a sordid business deal.* **2.** filthy; squalid: *a sordid slum.* —**sor′did•ly,** *adv.* —**sor′did•ness,** *n.* [*noncount*]

sore (sôr, sōr) /sɔr, sowr/ *adj.,* **sor•er, sor•est,** *n., adv.* —*adj.* **1.** physically painful or sensitive, such as a wound or diseased part: *a sore arm.* **2.** [*be* + ~] suffering bodily pain from wounds, bruises, etc.: *I'm sore all over from that heavy lifting we did yesterday.* **3.** [*be* + ~] suffering mental pain: *sore at heart.* **4.** [*before a noun*] causing great mental pain: *a sore loss.* **5.** [*before a noun*] causing very great misery or hardship: *The team is in sore need of a new pitcher.* **6.** [*be* + ~ (+ *at* + *obj*)] annoyed; irritated; angered: *The boss is sore (at me) because I lost her report.* **7.** causing annoyance or irritation: *Her accident with the car is a sore subject right now.* —*n.* [*count*] **8.** an irritated or infected spot on the body that is painful: *His skin was covered with scaly sores.* —*adv.* **9.** *Archaic.* sorely. —**sore′ly,** *adv.*: *The injured star pitcher will be sorely missed by his teammates.* —**sore′ness,** *n.* [*noncount*]

sore•head (sôr′hed′, sōr′-) /ˈsɔrˌhɛd, ˈsowr-/ *n.* [*count*] *Informal.* a bad-tempered person, esp. one who is angry at having lost a game, competition, etc.: *Don't be such a sorehead; they won fair and square.*

sor•ghum (sôr′gəm) /ˈsɔrgəm/ *n.* [*noncount*] **1.** a grass grown for food, bearing broad leaves and a tall stem having grain in a dense cluster. **2.** the syrup made from this.

so•ror•i•ty (sə rôr′i tē, -ror′-) /səˈrɔrɪtiy, -ˈrɒr-/ *n.* [*count*], *pl.* **-ties.** a society of women or girls, esp. in a college.

sor•rel[1] (sôr′əl, sor′-) /ˈsɔrəl, ˈsɒr-/ *n.* **1.** [*noncount*] light reddish brown. **2.** [*count*] a horse of this color.

sor•rel[2] (sôr′əl, sor′-) /ˈsɔrəl, ˈsɒr-/ *n.* [*count*] a plant of the buckwheat family, whose leaves are used as seasoning.

sor•row (sor′ō, sôr′ō) /ˈsɒrow, ˈsɔrow/ *n.* **1.** [*noncount*] distress caused by loss, disappointment, etc.; grief: *the depth of her sorrow.* **2.** [*count*] a cause of grief, such as a misfortune: *Too many sorrows crushed her spirit.* —*v.* [*no obj*] **3.** to feel or express sorrow; grieve: *I sorrow for you in this time of loss.* —**sor′row•ful,** *adj.* —**sor′row•ful•ly,** *adv.*

sor•ry (sor′ē, sôr′ē) /ˈsɒriy, ˈsɔriy/ *adj.,* **-ri•er, -ri•est. 1.** [*be* + ~] feeling regret, sadness, pity, etc.: [~ + *to* + *verb* (+ *obj*)]: *We are sorry to leave our friends.* [~ + (*that*) *clause*]: *We are sorry (that) we have to leave.* [~ + *for* + *obj*]: *He felt sorry for her (= He pitied her).* **2.** [*before a noun*] in such bad condition as to be regrettable; causing pity: *This family is in a sorry situation.* **3.** (used to apologize): *Did I bump into you? Sorry.* **4.** (used to ask someone who has spoken to repeat what was said): *"Sorry, I didn't hear what you said."* —**sor•ri•ly** (sor′ə lē, sôr′-) /ˈsɒrəliy, ˈsɔr-/ *adv.*: *We limped sorrily home after our big loss.* —**sor′ri•ness,** *n.* [*noncount*]

sort (sôrt) /sɔrt/ *n.* [*count*] **1.** a particular kind, class, or group; type: *There are many sorts of people.* **2.** character, quality, or nature: *friends of a nice sort.* **3.** an example of something undistinguished; a type of: *He is a sort of poet.* **4.** an instance of sorting: *The computer can perform a fast sort on all the entries in your database.* **5.** a person (when referring to his or her character): *With all his faults, he's not a bad sort.* —*v.* **6.** [~ + *obj*] to arrange or separate according to kind or class: *to sort socks into matching pairs.* **7.** to place (a group of mixed objects, data, etc.) in order, as by number or alphabetical sequence: [~ + *obj*]: *The computer is sorting the database now.* [~ + *through* + *obj*]: *to sort through the database.* **8. sort out, a.** [*no obj*] to evolve; turn out; result: *Wait and see how things sort out.* **b.** to put in order; clarify: [~ + *obj* + *out*]: *trying to sort things out at home.* [~ + *out* + *obj*]: *to sort out one's problems.* —***Idiom.*** **9. of sorts,** of a mediocre or poor kind: *a tennis player of sorts.* Also, **of a sort. 10. out of sorts, a.** annoyed, irritable, or depressed: *feeling out of sorts.* **b.** sick; ill; indisposed. **11. sort of,** somewhat; rather; kind of: *The book was sort of interesting, wasn't it?* —**sort′er,** *n.* [*count*] See -SORT-.

-sort-, *root.* *-sort-* comes from Latin, where it has the meaning "kind; type; part." This meaning is found in such words as: CONSORT, CONSORTIUM, RESORT, SORT.

sor•tie (sôr′tē) /ˈsɔrtiy/ *n., v.,* **-tied, -tie•ing.** —*n.* [*count*] **1.** a rapid movement of military forces in attack: *Hundreds of sorties were flown from the aircraft carrier.* —*v.* [*no obj*] **2.** to go on a sortie.

SOS (es′ō′es′) /ˈɛsˌowˈɛs/ *n.* [*count*], *pl.* **SOSs, SOS's. 1.**

an internationally recognized distress signal, consisting of the letters SOS in Morse code. **2.** any call for help.

so′-so′ or **so′ so′,** *adj.* **1.** neither very good nor very bad; mediocre: *a so-so relief pitcher.* —*adv.* **2.** fairly well; neither very well nor very badly: *Things were going so-so at the time.*

sot (sot) /sɒt/ *n.* [*count*] a drunkard. —**sot′tish,** *adj.*

sot•to vo•ce (sot′ō vō′chē) /'sɒt'ow vowtʃiy/ *adv.* in a low, soft voice so as not to be overheard: *She whispered sotto voce, "Don't look now, but I think we're being followed."* See -voc-.

souf•flé (so͞o flā′, so͞o′flā) /suw'fley, 'suwfley/ *n.* [*count*] **1.** a light, puffed-up baked dish. —*adj.* **2.** Also **souf•fléed′.** puffed up; made light, as by beating and cooking.

sought (sôt) /sɔt/ *v.* pt. and pp. of SEEK.

sought′-af′ter, *adj.* greatly desired; in demand; wanted: *a sought-after entertainer.*

soul (sōl) /sowl/ *n.* **1.** [*count*] the principle of life, feeling, thought, and action in humans, thought of as something distinct or separate from the body; the spiritual part of humans: *to have an immortal soul.* **2.** [*count*] the spirit of a dead person: *to summon the souls of the dead.* **3.** [*count*] a person: *brave souls.* **4.** [*count*] the essential element, quality, or part of something: *the soul of the Native American people.* **5.** [*count; usually: the + ~ + of + obj*] an excellent example of some quality: *He was the very soul of tact.* **6.** [*count*] the seat or place of human feelings or emotions: *She has the soul of an artist.* **7.** [*noncount*] deeply or strongly felt emotion, as is conveyed by an artist: *The painting has soul.* **8.** [*noncount*] (among African-Americans) shared ethnic awareness and pride. **9.** SOUL MUSIC. —*adj.* [*usually: before a noun*] **10.** of or relating to African-Americans or their culture: *Soul food is traditional black American food.* —**soul′less,** *adj.*

soul•ful (sōl′fəl) /'sowlfəl/ *adj.* of or relating to deep feeling or emotion: *looking up at him with soulful eyes.* —**soul′ful•ly,** *adv.* —**soul′ful•ness,** *n.* [*noncount*]

soul′ mus′ic, *n.* [*noncount*] music with roots in African-American gospel music.

sound[1] (sound) /sawnd/ *n.* **1.** [*noncount*] the sensation produced by vibrations that stimulate the nerves of the ear and can be heard: *Sound travels at speeds slower than light.* **2.** [*count*] the particular effect produced by a certain source on one's hearing: *the sound of fire engines.* **3.** [*count*] a noise, a word or part of a word produced by the voice, a musical tone, etc.: *had trouble pronouncing the ö and ä sounds in Swedish.* **4.** [*count*] a musical style characteristic of a certain group of performers: *the Motown sound.* **5.** [*count; usually singular; usually: the + ~ + of + obj*] the quality of an event, letter, etc., as it affects a person: *I don't like the sound of that report.* **6.** [*count*] the distance within which something can be heard: *dozens of people within the sound of his voice.* **7.** [*noncount*] meaningless noise: *all sound and fury.* —*v.* **8.** to (cause to) give off sound: [*~ + obj*]: *Sound the alarm.* [*no obj*]: *The alarm sounded.* **9.** [*not: be + ~-ing; ~ + adjective/like/as if/as though*] to give a certain impression when heard or read: *His voice sounded strange. The engine backfire sounded like a gunshot. That procedure sounds as if it will work.* **10.** [*~ + obj*] to give forth (a sound): *The oboe sounded an A.* **11.** [*~ + obj*] to order by a sound: *The bugle sounded retreat.* **12. sound off,** *Informal.* [*no obj*] **a.** to call out one's name, as at a roll call. **b.** to call out the rhythm as one marches in formation. **c.** to speak frankly, indiscreetly, or too angrily: *Quit sounding off about everything.* **13. sound out,** to pronounce (a sound of a language), esp. carefully: [*~ + out + obj*]: *to sound out the letters one after the other.* [*~ + obj + out*]: *If you don't know the word, sound it out.* —**sound′less,** *adj.* See -SON-.

sound[2] (sound) /sawnd/ *adj.*, **-er, -est,** *adv.* —*adj.* **1.** free from injury, damage, or disease; in good condition; healthy: *a sound body.* **2.** financially strong, secure, or reliable: *a sound investment.* **3.** sensible; valid: *sound judgment.* **4.** of solid character; upright or honorable: *sound values.* **5.** uninterrupted and untroubled; deep: *woke up from a sound sleep.* **6.** vigorous, thorough, or severe: *a sound thrashing.* —*adv.* **7.** deeply; thoroughly: *She was sound asleep.* —**sound′ly,** *adv.*: *The team was soundly defeated.* —**sound′ness,** *n.* [*noncount*]

sound[3] (sound) /sawnd/ *v.* **1.** [*~ + obj*] to measure the depth of (water, a deep hole, etc.) by letting down a lead weight at the end of a line. **2.** to ask for an opinion from (someone), by indirect ways: [*~ + obj + out*]: *Let's sound him out about the reorganization plan.* [*~ + out + obj*]: *Always sound out your spouse before buying something expensive.* **3.** [*no obj*] to plunge downward or dive, such as a whale. —**sound′ing,** *n.* [*count*]: *to take a sounding.*

sound[4] (sound) /sawnd/ *n.* **1.** a narrow passage of water between larger bodies of water or between the mainland and an island: [*count*]: *long sounds along the coast.* [*used as part of a proper noun*]: *Long Island Sound.* **2.** an inlet or arm of the sea: [*count*]: *a coastline of small, enclosed sounds.* [*used as part of a proper noun*]: *Puget Sound.*

sound′ bar′rier, *n.* [*noncount*] —***Idiom.*** **break the sound barrier,** to travel faster than the speed of sound.

sound′ing board′, *n.* [*count*] **1.** Also called **soundboard.** a thin plate of wood forming part of a musical instrument, used to improve the power and quality of the tone. **2.** one whose reactions serve as a measure of whether or not an idea will be acceptable to others: *Her husband was her sounding board for the plan.*

sound•proof (sound′pro͞of′) /'sawnd,pruwf/ *adj.* **1.** not allowing sound to pass through: *a soundproof room.* —*v.* [*~ + obj*] **2.** to make (a room, etc.) soundproof. —**sound′proof′ing,** *n.* [*noncount*]

sound•track or **sound track** (sound′trak′) /'sawnd,træk/ *n.* [*count*] the sound recorded on a film, esp. music or voices.

soup (so͞op) /suwp/ *n.* **1.** a liquid food made by simmering vegetables, seasonings, and often meat or fish: [*noncount*]: *a bowl of hot chicken soup.* [*count*]: *The restaurant offers three soups today.* **2.** [*noncount*] *Slang.* a thick fog. —*v.* **3. soup up,** *Slang.* to increase the power or top speed of (an engine, vehicle, or machine): [*~ + up + obj*]: *to soup up a computer.* [*~ + obj + up*]: *to soup it up by adding some new computer chips.* —***Idiom.*** [*noncount*] **4. from soup to nuts,** from beginning to end. **5. in the soup,** *Slang.* in trouble.

soup•çon (so͞op sôɴ′, so͞op′sôɴ) /suwp'sɔ̃, 'suwpsɔ̃/ *n.* [*count*] a slight trace of something, as of a seasoning, a feeling, etc.; hint: *a soupçon of suspicion.*

soup•y (so͞o′pē) /'suwpiy/ *adj.*, **-i•er, -i•est.** **1.** resembling soup. **2.** very thick; dense: *a soupy fog.*

sour (souᵊr, sou′ər) /sawᵊr, 'sawər/ *adj.*, **-er, -est,** *n.* —*adj.* **1.** having an acid taste resembling that of vinegar; tart: *Lemons taste sour.* **2.** made into an acid or acidlike substance by fermentation; fermented: *sour milk.* **3.** resembling or suggesting something fermented: *Some of the baby's clothes have a sour smell.* **4.** distasteful or disagreeable; unpleasant: *a few sour remarks.* **5.** cross; easily annoyed; peevish: *a sour expression on his face.* **6.** off-pitch; badly produced: *a sour note.* —*n.* [*count*] **7.** a cocktail of whiskey and lime or lemon juice. —*v.* **8.** to (cause to) become sour or rancid; spoil: [*no obj*]: *The milk soured in a few hours.* [*~ + obj*]: *Poor refrigeration will sour stored milk.* **9.** to (cause to) become unpleasant or less friendly: [*no obj*]: *Relations between us soured over the last few years.* [*~ + obj*]: *The war soured our relations.* **10.** [*~ + obj (+ on + obj)*] to make or cause to become bitter, unhappy, etc.: *All those rejections had soured him (on ever getting another job somewhere).* —***Idiom.*** *Informal.* **11. go sour,** [*no obj*] to become unsatisfactory; fail: *Their marriage has gone sour.* **12. go sour on,** [*~ + obj*] to become enemies with; turn against: *went sour on his family.* —**sour′ish,** *adj.* —**sour′ly,** *adv.* —**sour′ness,** *n.* [*noncount*]

source (sôrs, sōrs) /sɔrs, sowrs/ *n.* [*count*] **1.** any thing or place from which something comes or is obtained; origin: *He is the source of most of the discontent in the office.* **2.** the beginning or place of origin of a stream or river. **3.** a book, person, document, etc., supplying esp. firsthand information: *Good newspaper reporters always double-check their sources.*

sour•dough (souᵊr′dō′, sou′ər-) /'sawᵊr,dow, 'sawər-/ *n.* **1.** [*noncount*] fermented dough, used to make bread rise, from one baking to the next. **2.** [*count*] a prospector in Alaska or NW Canada.

sour′ grapes′, *n.* [*plural*] pretended dislike for something one wants but does not have.

sour•puss (souᵊr′po͝os′, sou′ər-) /'sawᵊr,pʊs, 'sawər-/ *n.* [*count*] *Informal.* a grouchy, often unsmiling person.

south (south) /sawθ/ *n.* [*count; singular; often: the + ~*] **1.** one of the four main points of the compass, lying directly opposite north. *Abbr.:* S **2.** the direction in which this point lies. **3.** a region or territory situated in this direction: *Air attacks continued in the south.* **4. the South,** (in the United States) the general area south of Pennsylvania and the Ohio River and east of the Mississippi, made up mainly of those states that formed the Confederacy. —*adj.* **5.** lying toward or situated in the south; proceeding toward the south. **6.** coming from the south, as a wind. *—adv.* **7.** to, toward, or in the south: *The plane headed south.*

South′ Af′ri•can (af′ri kən) /ˈæfrɪkən/ *adj.* **1.** of or relating to South Africa. *—n.* [*count*] **2.** a person born or living in South Africa.

south•east (south′ēst′; *Nautical.* sou′-) /ˌsawθˈiyst; *Nautical.* ˌsaw-/ *n.* [*count; singular; often: the* + ~] **1.** the point or direction midway between south and east. *Abbr.:* SE **2.** a region in this direction. **3. the Southeast,** the southeast region of the United States. *—adj.* **4.** in, toward, or facing the southeast: *a southeast course.* **5.** coming from the southeast: *a southeast wind.* *—adv.* **6.** toward the southeast: *sailing southeast.* **7.** from the southeast. **—south′east′er•ly,** *adj., adv.* **—south′east′ern,** *adj.*

south•east•er (south′ē′stər; *Nautical.* sou′-) /ˌsawθˈiystər; *Nautical.* ˌsaw-/ *n.* [*count*] a wind or storm from the southeast.

south•er (sou′thər) /ˈsawðər/ *n.* [*count*] a wind or storm from the south.

south•er•ly (suth′ər lē) /ˈsʌðərliy/ *adj., adv.* **1.** toward the south: *a southerly course; They turned southerly.* **2.** (esp. of a wind) coming from the south: *a mild southerly wind; a wind blowing southerly.*

south•ern (suth′ərn) /ˈsʌðərn/ *adj.* **1.** lying toward, located in, or directed toward the south. **2.** coming from the south, as a wind. **3.** of or relating to the south. **4.** [*Southern*] of or relating to the South of the United States. **5.** being or located south of the equator: *a southern constellation; the Southern Hemisphere.* *—n.* [*count*] **6.** [*often: Southern*] SOUTHERNER (def. 2).

south•ern•er (suth′ər nər) /ˈsʌðərnər/ *n.* [*count*] **1.** a native or inhabitant of the south. **2.** [*Southerner*] a native or inhabitant of the southern U.S.

south′ern lights′, *n.* [*plural*] the aurora of the Southern Hemisphere.

south•paw (south′pô′) /ˈsawθˌpɔ/ *n.* [*count*] *Informal.* **1.** one who is left-handed. **2.** a baseball pitcher who throws with the left hand.

South′ Pole′, *n.* [*proper noun; the* + ~] the southern end of the earth's axis.

south•ward (south′wərd; *Nautical.* suth′ərd) /ˈsawθwərd; *Nautical.* ˈsʌðərd/ *adj.* **1.** moving, facing, or situated toward the south. **2.** coming from the south, as a wind. *—adv.* **3.** Also, **south′wards.** toward the south; south.

south•west (south′west′; *Nautical.* sou′-) /ˌsawθˈwɛst; *Nautical.* ˌsaw-/ *n.* [*count; singular; often: the* + ~] **1.** the point or direction midway between south and west. *Abbr.:* SW **2.** a region in this direction. **3. the Southwest,** the southwest region of the United States. *—adj.* **4.** in, toward, or facing the southwest. **5.** coming from the southwest: *a southwest wind.* *—adv.* **6.** toward the southwest: *sailing southwest.* **7.** from the southwest. **—south′west′er•ly,** *adj., adv.* **—south′west′ern,** *adj.*

south•west•er (south′wes′tər; *Nautical.* sou′-) /ˌsawθˈwɛstər; *Nautical.* ˌsaw-/ *n.* [*count*] a wind or storm from the southwest.

sou•ve•nir (sōō′və nēr′, sōō′və nēr′) /ˌsuwvəˈnɪər, ˈsuwvəˌnɪər/ *n.* [*count*] a small, inexpensive article given or kept as a reminder of a place one has visited, etc.; memento: *The kids bought key chains as souvenirs of their trip to the Grand Canyon.* See -VEN-.

sov•er•eign (sov′rin, sov′ər in, suv′-) /ˈsɒvrɪn, ˈsɒvərɪn, ˈsʌv-/ *n.* [*count*] **1.** a monarch or other supreme ruler. **2.** a gold coin of the United Kingdom, equal to one pound sterling: *Sovereigns went out of circulation after 1914.* *—adj.* [*before a noun*] **3.** of or relating to a sovereign or sovereignty; royal. **4.** having supreme power or authority: *the sovereign lord of the kingdom.* **5.** supreme; foremost: *sovereign power.*

sov•er•eign•ty (sov′rin tē, suv′-) /ˈsɒvrɪntiy, ˈsʌv-/ *n.* [*noncount*] the quality or state of being sovereign: *a violation of their sovereignty.*

so•vi•et (sō′vē et′, -it, sō′vē et′) /ˈsowviyˌɛt, -ɪt, ˌsowviyˈɛt/ *n.* [*count*] **1.** (in the former Soviet Union) **a.** a governmental council, part of a hierarchy of councils at various levels of government. **b.** a committee of workers, peasants, or soldiers during the revolutionary period. **2.** any similar council in a socialist system of government. *—adj.* [*before a noun*] **3.** of or relating to a soviet.

sow[1] (sō) /sow/ *v.,* **sowed, sown** or **sowed, sow•ing. 1.** to scatter (seed) over or on (land, etc.), for growth; plant: [~ + *obj*]: *to sow seeds on the farm.* [~ + *obj*]: *to sow the farm with seeds.* [*no obj*]: *It was not quite time for sowing.* **2.** [~ + *obj*] to introduce, begin, or spread: *sowing distrust among his coworkers.* **—*Idiom.*** **3. sow one's wild oats,** to behave in a reckless way, esp. by having many sexual partners due to youth and immaturity: *to sow their wild oats before getting married.* **4. sow the seeds of,** [~ + *obj*] to cause (something, esp. something undesirable) to develop: *to sow the seeds of hatred.* **—sow′er,** *n.* [*count*]

sow[2] (sou) /saw/ *n.* [*count*] an adult female pig.

sox (soks) /sɒks/ *n.* a pl. of SOCK[1].

soy•bean (soi′bēn′) /ˈsɔyˌbiyn/ *n.* **1.** [*count*] a bushy plant of the legume family, grown chiefly as feed for horses and cattle. **2.** the seed of this plant, used for food and as a livestock feed: [*noncount*]: *He showed us how to make hamburgers of soybean.* [*count*]: *piles of soybeans.*

soy′ sauce′, *n.* [*count*] a salty, fermented sauce made from soybeans, used as a flavoring esp. in Oriental dishes.

spa (spä) /spɑ/ *n.* [*count*], *pl.* **spas. 1.** a mineral spring, or a place in which such springs exist. **2.** a luxurious resort. **3.** a bathing facility, usually for more than one person.

space (spās) /speys/ *n., v.,* **spaced, spac•ing,** *adj.* *—n.* **1.** [*noncount*] the three-dimensional area in which material objects are located: *Events happen in time and space.* **2.** extent or area or a particular extent of surface, such as a distance measured in a line between objects: [*noncount*]: *We need more space to set up our equipment.* [*count*]: *wide spaces between the teeth.* **3.** [*noncount*] the place beyond the earth's atmosphere, where planets, stars, and galaxies are found; outer space: *the future exploration of space.* **4.** [*count*] a place available for a particular purpose: *We drove around the block looking for a parking space.* **5.** an area in which a person can sit, or a seat or room on a train, airplane, etc.: [*noncount*]: *I saved space for us; come and sit here.* [*count*]: *I saved a space for us; sit here.* **6.** [*count; usually singular*] extent, or a particular extent, of time: *Can we finish eating and be out of here in a space of two hours?* **7.** a blank area in text: [*count*]: *Skip two spaces between each line of your writing.* [*noncount*]: *Leave plenty of space at the margin.* **8.** [*noncount*] an area or a time set aside for a specific use, such as advertising in a publication or on television. **9.** [*noncount*] freedom or opportunity to express oneself, fulfill one's needs, etc.: *Children need support, but they also need their space.* *—v.* **10.** to set (items) some distance apart from each other: [~ *(+ out)* + *obj*]: *Space (out) the desks evenly.* [~ + *obj (+ out)*]: *to space the desks (out) so the students can't look at each other's papers.* **11. space out,** [*no obj*] to become passively absorbed; stop paying attention or participating: *spacing out in front of the TV.* *—adj.* [*before a noun*] **12.** of, relating to, or suitable for use in outer space or deep space.

space•craft (spās′kraft′) /ˈspeysˌkræft/ *n.* [*count*], *pl.* **-crafts, -craft.** a vehicle for travel beyond the earth's atmosphere.

spaced′-out′, *adj. Slang.* **1.** dazed by narcotic drugs. **2.** dreamily out of touch with reality; disoriented or dazed: *Because of jet-lag he felt spaced-out during most of the day.*

space•man (spās′man′, -mən) /ˈspeysˌmæn, -mən/ *n.* [*count*], *pl.* **-men. 1.** an astronaut. **2.** a visitor to earth from outer space; an extraterrestrial.

space•ship (spās′ship′) /ˈspeysˌʃɪp/ *n.* [*count*] a spacecraft, esp. one that has a pilot or a crew.

space′ shut′tle, *n.* [*count*] [*often: Space Shuttle*] a spacecraft, or orbiter, that is launched by two rockets and can land and can be used again.

space′ sta′tion, *n.* [*count*] a satellite orbiting the earth, supporting a crew and used for assembling and serving other spacecraft, for observation and research, etc.

space•suit (spās′sōōt′) /ˈspeysˌsuwt/ *n.* [*count*] a sealed suit designed to allow the wearer to leave a pressurized cabin in outer space.

space•walk (spās′wôk′) /ˈspeysˌwɔk/ *n.* [*count*] **1.** the act of maneuvering oneself in space outside a spacecraft. *—v.* [*no obj*] **2.** to do a spacewalk.

spac•ey or **spac•y** (spā′sē) /ˈspeysiy/ *adj.,* **-i•er, -i•est. 1.** SPACED-OUT (def. 2). **2.** odd in behavior; eccentric; strange.

spa•cious (spā′shəs) /ˈspeyʃəs/ *adj.* **1.** containing much space; roomy: *a spacious old home with high ceilings.* **2.** occupying much space; vast. **3.** of a great extent or area; broad: *the spacious prairies.* **—spa′cious•ly,** *adv.* **—spa′cious•ness,** *n.* [*noncount*]

spade[1] (spād) /speyd/ *n., v.,* **spad•ed, spad•ing.** —*n.* [*count*] **1.** a tool for digging, having a long handle and a narrow metal blade that can be pressed into the ground with the foot. —*v.* [~ + *obj*] **2.** to dig, cut, or remove with a spade. —***Idiom.*** **3. call a spade a spade,** to speak truthfully and bluntly: *Let's call a spade a spade: I deserved that promotion and you didn't want me to have it.* —**spade′ful,** *n.* [*count*], *pl.* **-fuls.**

spade[2] (spād) /speyd/ *n.* **1.** [*count*] a black figure shaped like an upside-down heart with a short stem opposite the point, used on playing cards to mark a suit. **2.** [*count*] a card of the suit bearing such figures. **3. spades,** the suit so marked: [*noncount; used with a singular verb*]: *Spades has been dealt.* [*plural; used with a plural verb*]: *Spades were led in the last hand.* **4.** [*count*] *Slang* (*disparaging and offensive*). a black person. —***Idiom.*** **5. in spades,** *Informal.* **a.** in the extreme; to the utmost: *He's a hypocrite, in spades.* **b.** without restraint: *I told him what I thought of him, in spades.*

spade•work (spād′wûrk′) /ˈspeyd,wɜrk/ *n.* [*noncount*] work, such as the gathering of data, done in preparation for further action: *The detective began the spadework of looking through all the old documents for clues.*

spa•ghet•ti (spə get′ē) /spəˈgɛtiy/ *n.* [*noncount*] pasta in the form of long strings.

spake (spāk) /speyk/ *v. Archaic.* a pt. of SPEAK.

span (span) /spæn/ *n., v.,* **spanned, span•ning.** —*n.* [*count*] **1.** the full extent, stretch, or reach of something; distance: *The rescuers searched the entire span of the island.* **2.** a period of time during which something continues; duration: *The span of human life is short.* **3. a.** the distance or space between two supports of a structure, such as a bridge, or between two ends of something, such as an airplane wing. **b.** the part of a structure between two supports: *The car stalled on the second span of the bridge.* —*v.* [~ + *obj*] **4.** to extend or reach over or across (space or time): *Their friendship spanned a lifetime.* **5.** to provide with something that extends over or across: *to span a river with a bridge.*

span•dex (span′deks) /ˈspændɛks/ *n.* [*noncount*] an artificial fiber, used chiefly in the manufacture of garments to allow the garments to stretch.

span•gle (spang′gəl) /ˈspæŋgəl/ *n., v.,* **-gled, -gling.** —*n.* [*count*] **1.** a small, thin piece of glittering metal or other material, used esp. for decorating garments. **2.** any small, bright drop, object, or spot. —*v.* **3.** [~ + *obj*] to decorate or sprinkle with or as if with spangles. **4.** [*no obj*] to glitter with or like spangles.

Span•iard (span′yərd) /ˈspænyərd/ *n.* [*count*] a person born or living in Spain.

span•iel (span′yəl) /ˈspænyəl/ *n.* [*count*] a breed of small or medium-sized dogs usually having long, drooping ears and a long, silky coat.

Span•ish (span′ish) /ˈspænɪʃ/ *adj.* **1.** of or relating to Spain. **2.** of or relating to the language spoken in Spain, Mexico, and most of Central and South America. —*n.* **3.** [*plural; the* + ~*; used with a plural verb*] the people born or living in Spain. **4.** [*noncount*] the language spoken in Spain, Mexico, and most of Central and South America.

spank (spangk) /spæŋk/ *v.* [~ + *obj*] **1.** to strike with the open hand esp. on the buttocks, as in punishment: *never spanked their children under any circumstances.* —*n.* [*count*] **2.** a blow given in spanking; slap: *a quick spank.*

spank•ing (spang′king) /ˈspæŋkɪŋ/ *adj.* **1.** moving rapidly; quick and vigorous; brisk: *a spanking breeze.* **2.** unusually fine, great, large, etc.: *a spanking limousine.* —*adv.* **3.** extremely; very: *spanking clean.* —*n.* **4.** an act or instance of striking a person repeatedly on the buttocks with the open hand, esp. as a punishment: [*count*]: *gave her child a spanking.* [*noncount*]: *She doesn't believe spanking is a good form of punishment.*

span•ner (span′ər) /ˈspænər/ *n.* [*count*] **1.** a person or thing that spans. **2.** a wrench having a curved head with a hook or pin at one end for engaging notches or holes in collars, etc. **3.** *Chiefly Brit.* a wrench, esp. one with fixed jaws.

spar[1] (spär) /spɑr/ *n., v.,* **sparred, spar•ring.** —*n.* [*count*] **1.** a stout pole such as those used for masts; a mast. **2.** one of the principal side parts of the framework of a wing of an airplane. —*v.* [~ + *obj*] **3.** to provide or make with spars.

spar[2] (spär) /spɑr/ *v.* [*no obj*], **sparred, spar•ring. 1.** (of a boxer) to make the motions of attack and defense with the arms and fists, esp. as a part of training. **2.** to box, esp. with light blows such as for practice. **3.** to argue with words; dispute: *Even before the debate began they were sparring.*

spare (spâr) /spɛər/ *v.,* **spared, spar•ing,** *adj.,* **spar•er, spar•est,** *n.* —*v.* **1.** [~ + *obj*] to refrain from harming, punishing, or killing: *The queen decided to spare the condemned man.* **2.** [~ + *obj*] to deal gently or kindly with: *The critic's harsh review did not spare anyone.* **3.** [~ + *obj* + *obj*] to save, as from discomfort: *They kept the truth from you to spare you needless embarrassment.* **4.** [~ (+ *obj*) + *obj*] to omit or withhold: *Spare (me) the gory details.* **5.** [~ + *obj*] to keep oneself from using; choose not to use: *to spare the rod and spoil the child (= To fail to beat a child sometimes is to spoil the child).* **6.** [~ + *obj*] to give or lend, as from a supply, esp. without inconvenience: *Can you spare a dollar?* **7.** [~ + *obj*] to use or give a small amount of: *Don't spare the whipped cream!* —*adj.* **8.** kept in reserve, as for possible use: *a spare part.* **9.** being more than needed: *a spare bedroom where you'd be welcome to stay.* **10.** not taken up with work or other commitments; free: *spare time.* **11.** restricted: *a spare diet.* **12.** lean or thin, such as a person: *a short, spare man weighing about 100 lbs.* —*n.* [*count*] **13.** a spare thing or part, as an extra tire for emergency use. —***Idiom.*** **14. to spare,** remaining; left over: *We finished early, with time to spare.* —**spare′ly,** *adv.* —**spare′ness,** *n.* [*noncount*]

spare•ribs (spâr′ribz′) /ˈspɛər,rɪbz/ *n.* [*plural*] a cut of meat from the ribs, esp. of pork or beef, with some meat staying on the bones, often barbecued with a spicy sauce.

spar•ing (spâr′ing) /ˈspɛərɪŋ/ *adj.* [*usually be* + ~*; often:* ~ + *in/of/with* + *obj*] careful not to give or use a lot of something; frugal: *sparing in her praise.* —**spar′ing•ly,** *adv.*: *Apply the glue sparingly on the parts to be joined.*

spark (spärk) /spɑrk/ *n.* [*count*] **1.** a fiery particle thrown off by burning wood or that may be produced by one hard body striking against another: *Sparks flew into the air while the firewood burned.* **2.** the light produced by a sudden discharge of electricity through air: *His cigarette lighter produced sparks but no flame.* **3.** anything, esp. something small, that activates or stimulates; an inspiration: *His question produced the spark that started a lively debate.* —*v.* **4.** [*no obj*] to give out or produce sparks: *The wires sparked briefly and the lights went out.* **5.** [~ + *obj*] to stimulate; bring to life: *to spark some enthusiasm for the job.*

spar•kle (spär′kəl) /ˈspɑrkəl/ *v.,* **-kled, -kling,** *n.* —*v.* [*no obj*] **1.** to shine with gleams of light, such as a brilliant gem; glitter: *The diamond sparkled in the bright light.* **2.** to be brilliant, lively, or merry: *Her eyes sparkled.* **3.** (of wine, soda water, etc.) to give off small bubbles of gas; effervesce. —*n.* **4.** [*count*] a sparkling appearance, luster, or play of light; glitter. **5.** [*noncount*] brilliance or liveliness. —**spar′kler,** *n.* [*count*]

spark′ plug′, *n.* [*count*] **1.** a device that sets on fire the fuel mixture in a cylinder of an engine. **2.** a person who leads, inspires, or enlivens others.

spar•row (spar′ō) /ˈspærow/ *n.* [*count*] any of a group of small songbirds, usually dull gray-brown with plain or streaked breasts of a lighter color.

sparse (spärs), *adj.,* **spars•er, spars•est. 1.** thinly scattered or distributed; not thick or dense: *sparse gray hairs on top of his head.* **2.** scanty; meager: *sparse vegetation.* —**sparse′ly,** *adv.* —**sparse′ness, spar•si•ty** (spär′si tē) /ˈspɑrsɪtiy/ *n.* [*noncount*]

spar•tan (spär′tn) /ˈspɑrtn̩/ *adj.* disciplined and severe; simple; frugal: *a spartan life; a spartan bedroom with nothing but an old bed.*

spasm (spaz′əm) /ˈspæzəm/ *n.* [*count*] **1.** a sudden, abnormal, uncontrolled movement of a muscle: *bothered by spasms in her back.* **2.** any sudden, brief spell of great energy, activity, etc.: *spasms of anger.*

spas•mod•ic (spaz mod′ik) /spæzˈmɒdɪk/ also **spas•mod′i•cal,** *adj.* **1.** of or relating to a spasm. **2.** resembling a spasm by being sudden but brief and not organized; sporadic: *a few spasmodic efforts to clean out the cellar.* —**spas•mod′i•cal•ly,** *adv.*

spas•tic (spas′tik) /ˈspæstɪk/ *adj.* **1.** of or relating to or suffering from a spasmodic condition. **2.** *Slang.* clumsy or stupid. —*n.* [*count*] **3.** a person who is afflicted with a spasmodic condition. **4.** *Slang.* a clumsy or stupid person.

spat[1] (spat) /spæt/ *n., v.,* **spat•ted, spat•ting.** —*n.* [*count*] **1.** a short, meaningless quarrel. —*v.* [*no obj*] **2.** to have a short, meaningless quarrel or dispute.

spat[2] (spat) /spæt/ *v.* a pt. and pp. of SPIT[1].

spat[3] (spat) /spæt/ *n.* [*count*] a short piece of cloth or leather worn over the top of the shoe and usually fastened under the foot with a strap.

spate (spāt) /speyt/ *n.* [*count*] a sudden, almost overwhelming outpouring: *We were hit by a spate of criticism.*

spa•tial (spā′shəl) /ˈspeyʃəl/ *adj.* **1.** of or relating to space. **2.** existing or occurring in space; having extension in space: *the three spatial dimensions and the single temporal dimension.*

spat•ter (spat′ər) /ˈspætər/ *v.* **1.** [*no obj*] to send out small particles or drops: *The bacon grease spattered on the kitchen wall.* **2.** [~ + *obj*] to splash with something in small particles, esp. so as to soil or stain: *The mud from the puddles spattered us.* **3.** to strike (a surface) in or as if in a shower, such as rain or bullets: [*no obj*]: *The bullets spattered against the wall.* [~ + *obj*]: *The bullets spattered the wall.* **—*n.*** [*count*] **4.** the act or the sound of spattering. **5.** a splash or spot of something spattered: *spatters of paint.*

spat•u•la (spach′ə lə) /ˈspætʃələ/ *n.* [*count*], *pl.* **-las.** a tool with a wide, flat, usually flexible blade, used for blending or transferring foods, mixing drugs, spreading plaster, etc.: *a spatula to flip the pancakes over.*

spawn (spôn) /spɔn/ *n.* **1.** [*noncount*] the mass of eggs deposited in the water by fishes and other creatures that live in the water. **2.** [*count*] any person or thing thought of as the offspring of some other thing, idea, etc.: *The evil being was the devil's spawn.* **—*v.*** **3.** [*no obj*] to lay eggs or deposit sperm directly into the water: *Salmon swim upriver to their birthplaces in order to spawn.* **4.** [~ + *obj*] **a.** to produce (spawn). **b.** to produce (a large number): *to spawn thousands of little creatures.* **5.** [~ + *obj*] to give rise to; generate: *His disappearance spawned many rumors.*

spay (spā) /spey/ *v.* [~ + *obj*] to remove the ovaries of (an animal): *Her female cats were spayed.*

speak (spēk) /spiyk/ *v.*, **spoke** (spōk) /spowk/ **spo•ken** (spō′kən) /ˈspowkən/ **speak•ing. 1.** to say words or pronounce sounds with the ordinary voice; talk: [*no obj*]: *He was too frightened to speak.* [~ + *obj*]: *He spoke a few words.* **2.** [*no obj*] to communicate with the voice; mention: *I'll speak to him about your problem tomorrow.* **3.** [*no obj*] to converse: *They're so mad at each other they're not even speaking anymore.* **4.** [*no obj*] to deliver an address, discourse, etc.: *She spoke to our group about the concerns of women.* **5.** to use, or be able to use, (a language) as a way of communicating: [~ + *obj*]: *We tried to speak Russian.* [*no obj*]: *Try speaking in German.* **6. speak for,** [~ + *for* + *obj*] to speak in behalf of: *I'd like to speak for our partner, who can't be here today.* **—*Idiom.*** **7. so to speak,** [*no obj*] figuratively speaking: *We lost our shirt, so to speak.* **8. speak well for,** [~ + *obj*] to be an indication or reflection of (someone or something good or worthy of praise): *Hiring that new coach speaks well for our chances of winning this year.* **9. to speak of,** [*no obj*] (used with a negative word or phrase) worth mentioning; hardly at all: *They have no debts to speak of.* **—Usage.** Compare SPEAK, SAY, and TALK. We use SPEAK before the name of a language: *She speaks good Russian,* and to express a more formal sense than TALK, sometimes with the preposition *with* or *to*: *May I speak with the boss?* The word SAY is used most often to describe the words one uses in communicating: *I didn't say much, just a few words.* Sometimes SAY takes the preposition *to;* it does not usually take *with*: *I said hello to her, but she didn't say anything to me.* The word TALK suggests communicating with another, so that there is an exchange; it may take the preposition *to* or *with*: *At last the two warring sides sat down and began to talk to each other. We talked with him about our problem.*

-speak, *suffix.* *-speak* is attached to the ends of words and sometimes roots to form compound nouns that name the style or vocabulary of a certain field of work, interest, etc., that is mentioned in the first word or root: *ad(vertising) + -speak → adspeak (= the jargon of advertising); art + -speak → artspeak (= the language used in discussing art).*

speak•eas•y (spēk′ē′zē) /ˈspiykˌiyziy/ *n.* [*count*], *pl.* **-eas•ies.** a bar or nightclub selling alcoholic beverages illegally, esp. during Prohibition in the U.S.

speak•er (spē′kər) /ˈspiykər/ *n.* [*count*] **1.** one who speaks: *a native speaker of Swahili.* **2.** one who speaks formally before an audience; lecturer: *our main speaker for the evening.* **3.** a device that changes electric signals into sound waves; loudspeaker: *huge hi-fi speakers blasting music.* See illustration at APPLIANCE.

speak•ing (spē′king) /ˈspiykɪŋ/ *adj.* **1.** used when talking normally: *His speaking voice barely rose above a whisper.* **—*Idiom.*** **2. (not) on speaking terms,** (not) communicating or friendly: *(not) on speaking terms with her sister.* **3. speaking of,** [*no obj*] (used to make a connection between a subject that has been raised and a new subject related to the first one): *I like the custom of bringing presents to someone's home when you visit. Speaking of presents, you should get a box from us before Christmas.*

spear (spēr) /spɪər/ *n.* [*count*] **1.** a long wooden shaft with a sharp-pointed head of metal or stone attached to it. **—*v.*** [~ + *obj*] **2.** to pierce or stab through with or as if with a spear: *speared a slice of fruit from the plate.*

spear•head (spēr′hed′) /ˈspɪərˌhɛd/ *n.* [*count*] **1.** the sharp-pointed head that forms the piercing end of a spear. **2.** any person, group, or force that leads an attack, a new activity, etc.: *Their army group formed the spearhead for the assault.* **—*v.*** [~ + *obj*] **3.** to act as a spearhead for: *to spearhead the drive for new members in the organization.*

spear•mint (spēr′mint′) /ˈspɪərˌmɪnt/ *n.* [*noncount*] a sweet-smelling herb of the mint family whose leaves are used for flavoring.

spec (spek) /spɛk/ *n.*, *v.*, **spec'd** or **specked** or **specced, spec'•ing** or **speck•ing** or **spec•cing. —*n.*** [*count*] **1.** speculation. **—*v.*** [~ + *obj*] **2.** to provide specifications for. **—*Idiom.*** **3. on spec,** [*noncount*] made, built, or done with hopes, but no assurance, of payment or a sale.

-spec-, *root.* *-spec-* comes from Latin, where it has the meaning "look at; examine." This meaning is found in such words as: ASPECT, EXPECT, INSPECT, INSPECTION, INSPECTOR, INTROSPECTION, IRRESPECTIVE, PERSPECTIVE, PROSPECT, PROSPECTIVE, PROSPECTUS, RESPECT, RESPECTABLE, RETROSPECT, SPECIAL, SPECIALIZE, SPECIALTY, SPECIE, SPECIES, SPECIFIC, SPECIFY, SPECIMEN, SPECIOUS, SPECTACLE, SPECTACULAR, SPECTRUM, SPECULATE, SUSPECT.

spe•cial (spesh′əl) /ˈspɛʃəl/ *adj.* **1.** of a particular kind or character; different: *a special key.* **2.** having a specific function, purpose, etc.: *a special messenger to greet the ambassador.* **3.** out of the ordinary; remarkable; exceptional: *a document of special importance.* **4.** particularly valued; outstanding: *She's a special friend of mine.* **—*n.*** [*count*] **5.** a special person or thing. **6.** a temporary lowering of the price of regularly stocked goods, esp. food; sale: *The supermarket is having a special on bananas: five pounds for a dollar.* **7.** a single television program not forming part of a regular series: *a special on alternative medicine.* See -SPEC-.

spe′cial deliv′ery, *n.* [*noncount*] delivery of mail outside the regularly scheduled hours, for an extra fee.

spe•cial•ist (spesh′ə list) /ˈspɛʃəlɪst/ *n.* [*count*] one who specializes: *a heart specialist; a computer specialist.* See -SPEC-.

spe•cial•ize (spesh′ə līz′) /ˈspɛʃəˌlayz/ *v.* [*no obj;* (~ + *in* + *obj*)], **-ized, -iz•ing.** to study and become expert in some special area of study, work, etc.; have a specialty: *The doctor specializes in eye surgery.* **—spe•cial•i•za•tion** (spesh′ə lə zā′shən) /ˌspɛʃələˈzeyʃən/ *n.* [*noncount*] See -SPEC-.

spe•cial•ly (spesh′ə lē) /ˈspɛʃə liy/ *adv.* particularly; for a certain, specific purpose: *The plane was waiting specially for the high-ranking diplomat.* See -SPEC-.

spe•cial•ty (spesh′əl tē) /ˈspɛʃəltiy/ *n.* [*count*], *pl.* **-ties. 1.** a special subject of study, area of work, skill, or the like, on which one concentrates: *His specialty is English-language teaching and the use of computers.* **2.** an article or service that one deals with particularly: *The specialty of the restaurant is broiled lamb.* See -SPEC-.

spe•cie (spē′shē, -sē) /ˈspiyʃiy, -siy/ *n.* [*noncount*] money in coins. See -SPEC-.

spe•cies (spē′shēz, -sēz) /ˈspiyʃiyz, -siyz/ *n.* [*count*], *pl.* **-cies. 1.** a distinct group, sort, or kind of individuals having some common characteristics, as of animals or plants that can breed among themselves, but not outside their group. **2.** [*the* + ~] the human race; humankind: *Is the species threatened with extinction?* See -SPEC-.

specif., an abbreviation of: **1.** specific. **2.** specifically.

spe•cif•ic (spi sif′ik) /spɪˈsɪfɪk/ *adj.* **1.** having a special purpose or reference; explicit or definite: *a specific use for a tool.* **2.** specified, precise, or particular; exact: *What is the specific time the train will arrive?* **3.** [*be* + ~ + *to* + *obj*] proper to only certain persons or things: *This symptom is specific to those who have high blood pressure.* **—*n.*** [*count*] **4.** something specific, as a statement or detail: *Those are the general principles; now let's look at the specifics and how they apply to each of us.* **—spe•**

cif′i•cal•ly, *adv.* —**spec•i•fic•i•ty** (spes′ə fis′i tē) /ˌspɛsəˈfɪsɪtiy/ *n.* [*noncount*] See -SPEC-.

spec•i•fi•ca•tion (spes′ə fi kā′shən) /ˌspɛsəfɪˈkeyʃən/ *n.* **1.** [*noncount*] the act of specifying: *specification of charges against the prisoner.* **2.** Usually, **specifications.** [*plural*] a detailed description of requirements, materials, etc., as in a plan for a building. See -SPEC-.

spec•i•fy (spes′ə fī′) /ˈspɛsəˌfay/ *v.,* **-fied, -fy•ing. 1.** [~ + *obj*] to mention or name specifically: *He specified the times of arrival and departure of the flights.* **2.** [~ + *(that) clause*] to name or state as a condition: *The company specified (that) we would have to pay for any damages.* See -SPEC-.

spec•i•men (spes′ə mən) /ˈspɛsəmən/ *n.* [*count*] **1.** a part or an individual taken as being an example of a whole mass or number of things; typical animal, mineral, etc.: *The archaeologists dug up several specimens of ancient dinosaurs.* **2.** a sample of a material for study: *To do the test we'll need a specimen of your blood.* **3.** a particular kind of person: *He's an odd specimen, isn't he?* See -SPEC-.

spe•cious (spē′shəs) /ˈspiyʃəs/ *adj.* apparently true or right but actually without merit: *a specious argument.* —**spe′cious•ly,** *adv.* See -SPEC-.

speck (spek) /spɛk/ *n.* [*count*] **1.** a small spot. **2.** a very small bit or particle, or something appearing small by comparison or by reason of distance: *They were just specks in the distance at first, but soon we could make out a big flock of geese.* **3.** [*usually singular; a* + ~ + *of* + *noncount noun*] a small or tiny amount of something: *This car hasn't given us a speck of trouble.*

speck•le (spek′əl) /ˈspɛkəl/ *n., v.,* **-led, -ling.** —*n.* [*count*] **1.** a small colored speck, spot, or mark. —*v.* [~ + *obj*] **2.** to mark with or as if with speckles.

specs (speks) /spɛks/ *n.* [*plural*], *Informal.* **1.** spectacles; eyeglasses: *He lost his specs and couldn't see well enough to drive.* **2.** specifications: *Do you have the specs for the kitchen?* See -SPEC-.

spec•ta•cle (spek′tə kəl) /ˈspɛktəkəl/ *n.* [*count*] **1.** anything presented to the view, esp. something striking or impressive: *The man climbing up the side of the skyscraper was quite a spectacle.* **2.** a public show or display, esp. on a large scale: *The emperor's coronation was an incredibly expensive spectacle.* **3. spectacles,** [*plural*] eyeglasses. —***Idiom.* 4. make a spectacle of oneself,** to behave badly or foolishly in public: *He was so angry he made a spectacle of himself, pounding the tabletop and screaming.* See -SPEC-.

spec•tac•u•lar (spek tak′yə lər) /spɛkˈtækyələr/ *adj.* **1.** of or like a spectacle; impressive; magnificent: *The wedding was a spectacular affair.* **2.** dramatically daring or thrilling: *The firefighter made a spectacular rescue.* —*n.* [*count*] **3.** an impressive, large-scale display: *Don't miss our star-studded spectacular on channel 5, Thursday night.* —**spec•tac′u•lar•ly,** *adv.*: *The building was burning spectacularly in the distance.* See -SPEC-.

spec•ta•tor (spek′tā tər, spek tā′-) /ˈspɛkteytər, spɛkˈtey-/ *n.* [*count*] **1.** one who watches; an onlooker; observer. **2.** a member of the audience at a public spectacle, display, etc.: *We asked the spectators what they thought of the parade.* See -SPEC-.

spec•ter (spek′tər) /ˈspɛktər/ *n.* [*count*] **1.** a visible but bodiless spirit, esp. one of a terrifying nature; a ghost: *Scrooge was certain he had seen a specter of his long dead friend.* **2.** some object or source of terror or dread: *the specter of disease.* Also, *esp. Brit.,* **spec•tre.** See -SPEC-.

spec•tral (spek′trəl) /ˈspɛktrəl/ *adj.* [*before a noun*] **1.** of or relating to a specter; ghostly: *a spectral vision.* **2.** of or relating to a spectrum or spectra: *spectral rays of light like a rainbow.* See -SPEC-.

spec•tro•scope (spek′trə skōp′) /ˈspɛktrəˌskowp/ *n.* [*count*] a device to observe a spectrum of light or radiation. —**spec•tro•scop•ic** (spek′trə skop′ik) /ˌspɛktrəˈskɒpɪk/ *adj.* —**spec•tros•co•py** (spek tros′kə pē) /spɛkˈtrɒskəpiy/ *n.* [*noncount*] See -SPEC-, -SCOPE-.

spec•trum (spek′trəm) /ˈspɛktrəm/ *n.* [*count*], *pl.* **-tra** (-trə) /-trə/ **-trums. 1. a.** an array of light waves or particles that occur in a certain order due to their properties, such as size, wavelength, or mass. **b.** the band or series of colors produced when light strikes a prism or similar instrument: *the spectrum of visible light.* **2.** a broad range of different but related ideas, objects, etc.: *the full spectrum of political beliefs, from the far left all the way to the radical right.* See -SPEC-.

spec•u•late (spek′yə lāt′) /ˈspɛkyəˌleyt/ *v.,* **-lat•ed, -lat•ing. 1.** to consider or think curiously about (something); suppose, propose, or wonder: [*no obj; (~ + about/on/upon + obj)*]: *The audience is left to speculate on what might happen when the hero returns.* [~ + *clause*]: *to speculate that an agreement will be reached; They speculated whether the quarrel was serious.* **2.** [*no obj; (~ + in/on + obj)*] to buy or sell goods, property, etc., esp. at risk of a loss, in the hope of making a profit through changes in the market: *He lost too much money speculating on the gold market.* —**spec•u•la′tive** (spek′yə lə-tiv, -lā′-) /ˈspɛkyələtɪv, -ˌley-/ *adj.* —**spec′u•la′tor,** *n.* [*count*] See -SPEC-.

spec•u•la•tion (spek′yə lā′shən) /ˌspɛkyəˈleyʃən/ *n.* the act of speculating: [*noncount*]: *Your prediction is nothing but pure speculation.* [*count*]: *The book was a collection of his speculations on how the universe works.* [*noncount*]: *encouraging speculation on the gold market.* [*count*]: *Their speculations don't always result in profits.* See -SPEC-.

speech (spēch) /spiytʃ/ *n.* **1.** [*noncount*] the ability or power to speak: *A child may not gain the power of speech if he or she is not exposed to it at an early age.* **2.** [*noncount*] the act of speaking: *Speech was not necessary between them; they understood each other with just one look.* **3.** [*count*] a form of communication in spoken language, made by a speaker before an audience: *The mayor gave five speeches in five different parts of the city.* **4.** [*noncount*] the manner of speaking of a particular people or region; a language or dialect: *His speech gave him away: he's from New England.* **5.** [*noncount*] manner of speaking of a certain person: *He showed signs of drunkenness: slurred speech and unsteady walking.*

speech•less (spēch′lis) /ˈspiytʃlɪs/ *adj.* temporarily unable to use the power of speech because of fear, exhaustion, astonishment, etc.: *She was speechless with anger.*

speed (spēd) /spiyd/ *n., v.,* **sped** (sped) /spɛd/ or **speed•ed, speed•ing.** —*n.* **1.** [*noncount*] quickness or rapidity in moving, traveling, performing, etc.: *His speed and strength helped him win the race.* **2.** [*count*] rate of motion or progress: *the speed of light.* **3.** [*count*] a gear ratio in a motor vehicle or bicycle: *How many speeds does your bike have?* **4.** [*noncount*] *Slang.* a stimulating drug, esp. methamphetamine or amphetamine. **5.** [*noncount; usually: one's* + ~] a person, thing, activity, etc., that suits one's ability or personality: *Quiet people are more my speed than fast talkers.* —*v.* **6.** to (cause to) go, move, or proceed with swiftness: [*no obj*]: *The car sped away before we could read the license plate.* [~ + *obj*]: *The security guards sped the witness out of the courtroom.* **7.** [*no obj*] to drive a vehicle at a rate that exceeds the legal limit: *ticketed for speeding.* **8.** [~ + *obj*] to promote the success of; cause to go smoother and more quickly: *The president's approval will speed the committee's work.* **9. speed up, a.** to increase the rate of speed of (something or someone): [~ + *up* + *obj*]: *to speed up production.* [~ + *obj* + *up*]: *to speed production up.* **b.** [*no obj*] to go faster: *Can't we speed up a little?* —***Idiom.* 10. at full** or **top speed,** [*noncount*] **a.** at the greatest speed possible: *The plane was moving at top speed when the missile hit it.* **b.** to the maximum of one's capabilities: *He's working at full speed to get this done.* **11. up to speed,** [*noncount*] **a.** operating at full or best speed: *When the boat got up to speed it headed out of the harbor.* **b.** functioning at an expected level so as to be able to compete with others: *The new firm is not yet up to speed.* —**speed′er,** *n.* [*count*]: *Convicted speeders will pay high ticket fines.*

speed•boat (spēd′bōt′) /ˈspiydˌbowt/ *n.* [*count*] a motorboat designed for high speeds.

speed•om•e•ter (spē dom′i tər, spi-) /spiyˈdɒmɪtər, spɪ-/ *n.* [*count*] an instrument on an automobile or other vehicle for indicating the rate of travel in miles or kilometers per hour.

speed•ster (spēd′stər) /ˈspiydstər/ *n.* [*count*] a person who usually travels at high speed.

speed•way (spēd′wā′) /ˈspiydˌwey/ *n.* [*count*] **1.** a track on which automobile or motorcycle races are held. **2.** a road or course for fast driving.

speed•y (spē′dē) /ˈspiydiy/ *adj.,* **-i•er, -i•est. 1.** able to move quickly: *a speedy race car.* **2.** proceeding quickly: *Best wishes for a speedy recovery.* —**speed′i•ly,** *adv.*

spell[1] (spel) /spɛl/ *v.,* **spelled** or **spelt** (spelt) /spɛlt/ **spell•ing. 1.** to name, write, or otherwise give the letters, in order, of (a word, syllable, etc.): [~ + *obj*]: *Did I spell your name right?* [*no obj*]: *How did you learn to spell so well?* **2.** [*not: be* + *~-ing;* ~ + *obj*] (of letters) to form (a word, syllable, etc.): *Y-e-s spells yes.* **3.** to read or say (a word) letter by letter or with difficulty: [~ + *out* + *obj*]:

Spell out your name for me. [~ + *obj* + *out*]: *to spell some words out.* **4.** [*not: be* + *~-ing;* ~ + *obj*] to signify; amount to; mean or signal: *This delay spells disaster for the business.* **5. spell out,** to explain something plainly: [~ + *obj* + *out*]: *Must I spell it out for you? Our engagement is broken!* [~ + *out* + *obj*]: *Would someone spell out for me just what this crisis will do to our company?*

spell[2] (spel) /spɛl/ *n.* [*count*] **1.** a word or phrase believed to have magic power; an incantation: *uttering charms and spells.* **2.** a state or period of enchantment caused by magic power: *living under a spell.* **3.** [*usually: singular*] any strong influence; fascination: *under the spell of music.*

spell[3] (spel) /spɛl/ *n.* [*count*] **1.** a continuous period of activity: *You've been driving all day; let someone else take a spell at the wheel.* **2.** a bout or fit of anything experienced: *a spell of coughing.* **3.** an indefinite period: *Come visit us for a spell.* **4.** a period of weather of a certain kind: *a hot spell.* **—*v.*** [~ + *obj*] **5.** to take the place of for a time; relieve: *Let me spell you at the wheel.*

spell•bind (spel′bīnd′) /ˈspɛlˌbaynd/ *v.* [~ + *obj*], **-bound, -bind•ing.** to hold by or as if by a spell; enchant: *They were spellbound by her fabulous performance.* —**spell′bind′er,** *n.* [*count*] —**spell•bound** (spel′bound′) /ˈspɛlˌbawnd/ *adj.*: *a spellbound audience.*

spell•er (spel′ər) /ˈspɛlər/ *n.* [*count*] **1.** a person who spells words. **2.** Also called **spell′ing book′.** an elementary textbook to teach spelling. **3.** Also called **spell′** (or **spell′ing**) **check′er.** a computer program for finding incorrect spellings in an electronic document.

spell•ing (spel′ing) /ˈspɛlɪŋ/ *n.* **1.** [*noncount*] the manner in which words are spelled: *mistakes in spelling.* **2.** [*count*] a group of letters representing a word: *There are two spellings for the word "center":* center *and* centre. **3.** [*noncount*] the act of a speller: *He's very good at spelling.*

spe•lunk•er (spi lung′kər) /spɪˈlʌŋkər/ *n.* [*count*] a person who explores caves, esp. as a hobby.

spend (spend) /spɛnd/ *v.*, **spent** (spent) /spɛnt/ **spend•ing. 1.** to pay out (money, resources, etc.): [~ + *obj*]: *We had spent too much money on our vacation.* [*no obj*]: *All we do is spend, spend, spend; we need to save, too.* **2.** [~ + *obj*] to pass (time, labor, etc.) on some work, in some place, etc.: *The kids didn't want to spend their whole vacation indoors.* **3.** [~ + *obj*] to use up; exhaust: *The storm had spent its fury.* —**spend′a•ble,** *adj.*: *some percentage of spendable income for food.* —**spend′er,** *n.* [*count*]: *He was a big spender: he bought her jewelry and expensive clothes.* See -PEND-.

spend•thrift (spend′thrift′) /ˈspɛndˌθrɪft/ *n.* [*count*] **1.** one who spends money or wealth too quickly and wastefully. **—*adj.* 2.** wastefully extravagant; prodigal.

spent (spent) /spɛnt/ *v.* **1.** pt. and pp. of SPEND. **—*adj.* 2.** used up; consumed: *a pile of spent bullet and cartridge cases.* **3.** tired; worn-out; exhausted: *too spent to move after that long race.*

-sper-, *root.* -*sper*- comes from Latin, where it has the meaning "hope; hope for; expect." This meaning is found in such words as: DESPERADO, DESPERATE, PROSPER, PROSPERITY, PROSPEROUS.

sperm (spûrm) /spɜrm/ *n.*, *pl.* **sperm, sperms. 1.** [*count*] a male reproductive cell. **2.** [*noncount*] semen.

sperm′ whale′, *n.* [*count*] a large, square-headed whale with a large cavity in the head that contains an oil-like liquid.

spew (spyo͞o) /spyuw/ *v.* **1.** [*no obj*] to gush or pour out, esp. quickly and violently: *Oil spewed from the broken pipes.* **2.** [~ + *obj*] to throw or pour out violently: *The broken pipes spewed oil.* **3.** to vomit: [*no obj*]: *to spew from sickness.* [~ + *obj*]: *to spew one's lunch.* —**spew′er,** *n.* [*count*]

sphere (sfēr) /sfɪər/ *n.* [*count*] **1.** a solid, round figure or body whose surface is at all points the same distance from the center. **2.** a planet or star; heavenly body. **3.** the environment or surroundings within which a person or thing exists or operates: *Does the UN's sphere of influence (= the area in which it is the dominant power) encompass the whole world?* **4.** a field of something specified or mentioned: *a sphere of knowledge.*

spher•i•cal (sfer′i kəl, sfēr′-) /ˈsfɛrɪkəl, ˈsfɪər-/ *adj.* having the shape of a sphere; rounded.

sphe•roid (sfēr′oid) /ˈsfɪərɔyd/ *n.* [*count*] a solid figure similar in shape to a sphere. —**sphe•roi′dal,** *adj.*

sphinc•ter (sfingk′tər) /ˈsfɪŋktər/ *n.* [*count*] a circular band of muscle that encircles and closes an opening of the body or one of its hollow organs.

sphinx (sfingks) /sfɪŋks/ *n.* [*count*], *pl.* **sphinx•es, sphin•ges** (sfin′jēz) /ˈsfɪndʒiyz/. **1.** an ancient Egyptian figure with the body of a lion and the head of a human, esp. a very large stone figure of this type near the pyramids of Giza. **2.** a creature in Greek myth with wings, a woman's head, and a lion's body: *The sphinx killed anyone passing by who was unable to answer the riddle she posed.* **3.** a mysterious person or thing.

spice (spīs) /spays/ *n.*, *v.*, **spiced, spic•ing. —*n.* 1.** [*count*] a strong-smelling or sweet-smelling vegetable substance, such as pepper or cinnamon, used to season food: *Which spices did you put in this soup?* **2.** [*noncount*] such substances thought of as a group: *too much spice in the food.* **3.** [*noncount*] something that gives zest, liveliness, or interest: *The jokes added spice to the mayor's speech.* **—*v.*** [~ + *obj*] **4.** to season (food) with spice. **5.** [*sometimes:* ~ + *up* + *obj*] to give zest, liveliness, or interest to: *He spiced (up) his speech with some funny stories.*

spick-and-span (spik′ən span′) /ˈspɪkənˈspæn/ *adj.* **1.** spotlessly clean and neat; new or like new; fresh. **—*adv.* 2.** in a spick-and-span manner.

spic•y (spī′sē) /ˈspaysiy/ *adj.*, **-i•er, -i•est. 1.** having or containing spice; seasoned with spices: *spicy Mexican food.* **2.** of the nature of or resembling spice. **3.** slightly improper or risqué: *a spicy novel; some spicy gossip.* —**spic′i•ness,** *n.* [*noncount*]

spi•der (spī′dər) /ˈspaydər/ *n.* [*count*] **1.** a small creature with eight legs and a body divided into two parts, producing a silky web used as a nest and for trapping food: *Spiders are not insects because they have eight legs.* **2.** any device with leglike extensions that resemble a spider, such as a tripod or trivet. —**spi′der•y,** *adj.*

spiel (spēl, shpēl) /spiyl, ʃpiyl/ *n.* [*count*] *Informal.* a speech made quickly so that the speaker sounds like an expert, esp. for selling or persuading; pitch: *The principal gave his usual spiel about caring and concern for the students.*

spiff•y (spif′ē) /ˈspɪfiy/ *adj.*, **-i•er, i•est.** *Informal.* smart; fine; neat: *a spiffy new convertible.*

spig•ot (spig′ət) /ˈspɪgət/ *n.* [*count*] a faucet for controlling the flow of liquid from a pipe or the like.

spike (spīk) /spayk/ *n.*, *v.*, **spiked, spik•ing. —*n.*** [*count*] **1.** a naillike fastener, 3 to 12 in. (7.6 to 30.5 cm) long, for fastening together heavy timbers. **2.** something resembling such a nail, as a piece of metal sticking out of the heel and sole of a shoe for improving gripping power. **3. spikes,** [*plural*] **a.** shoes having such metal parts on the heel and sole, as for playing baseball. **b.** shoes having very high, slender heels that resemble spikes. **4.** a sudden increase or rise: *a sharp spike in the unemployment statistics.* **—*v.* 5.** [~ + *obj*] to fasten or secure with a spike or spikes: *to spike the railroad ties.* **6.** [~ + *obj*] to pierce with a spike. **7.** [~ + *obj*] to prevent or suppress: *to spike a rumor before it starts to spread.* **8.** [~ + *obj*] *Informal.* to add alcoholic liquor to (a drink): *Someone had spiked the punch with vodka.* **9.** [*no obj; sometimes:* ~ + *up*] to rise or increase sharply: *Interest rates have spiked (up).* —**spik′y,** *adj.*, **-i•er, -i•est.**

spill (spil) /spɪl/ *v.*, **spilled** or **spilt** (spilt) /spɪlt/ **spill•ing,** *n.* **—*v.* 1. a.** to (cause or allow to) run or fall from a container, esp. accidentally or wastefully: [~ + *obj*]: *to spill milk from a glass.* [*no obj*]: *The milk spilled on the floor.* **b.** [*no obj*] to flow, esp. beyond the customary boundaries: *Tears spilled from her eyes.* **2.** [~ + *obj*] to shed (blood), as in killing: *Too much blood has already been spilled over this foolish dispute.* **3.** [~ + *obj*] to scatter: *to spill papers all over the floor.* **4.** [~ + *obj*] to cause to fall from a horse, vehicle, or the like: *That wild horse managed to spill every rider who got on him.* **5.** [~ + *obj*] to let (a secret) become known; divulge. **6.** [*no obj*] to move in great numbers; pour out: *As soon as the bell rang the children spilled into the playground.* **—*n.*** [*count*] **7.** a spilling, as of liquid: *another dangerous oil spill.* **8.** a fall from a horse, vehicle, or the like: *took a bad spill from the pony.* —**spill•age** (spil′ij) /ˈspɪlɪdʒ/ *n.* [*noncount*]

spill•way (spil′wā′) /ˈspɪlˌwey/ *n.* [*count*] a passageway through which extra water escapes from a reservoir, lake, or the like.

spin (spin) /spɪn/ *v.*, **spun** (spun) /spʌn/ **spin•ning,** *n.* **—*v.* 1.** to make (yarn) by drawing out, twisting, and winding fibers: [~ + *obj*]: *to spin thread.* [*no obj*]: *spinning in the afternoon sun.* **2.** [~ + *obj*] to form (the fibers of any material) into thread or yarn: *to spin wool into yarn.* **3.** [~ + *obj*] to produce (a thread, web, etc.) by giving off from the body a substance that hardens in the air: *The spider spun its web.* **4.** to (cause to) rotate rapidly; twirl; whirl: [~ + *obj*]: *to spin a coin on a table.* [*no obj*]: *The coin spun on the tabletop for a moment.* **5.** [~ + *obj*] to produce or invent in a manner like spinning thread: *He spun a fantastic tale about his childhood.* **6.** to make longer than necessary: [~ + *obj* + *out*]: *She spun the project out for over three years.* [~ + *out* + *obj*]: *She had spun out the project for over three years.* **7.** [*no obj*] to move or travel rapidly: *The messenger spun out the door.* **8.** [*no obj*] to have a sensation of whirling; reel: *My head began to spin.* **9. spin off,** [~ + *off* + *obj*] to create or devise using something already existing: *The producers took the character of the uncle and spun off another TV series.* **—*n.*** [*count*] **10.** the act of causing a spinning or whirling motion: *She gave the coin a quick spin.* **11.** a spinning motion or movement: *We never notice the spin of the earth.* **12.** a downward movement or trend, esp. one that is sudden, alarming, etc.: *The economy is in another bad spin.* **13.** a short ride or drive for pleasure: *Let's take the new car out for a spin.* **14.** *Slang.* a particular viewpoint or bias, esp. in the news; slant: *After the presidential debates each side put its favorable spin on the results.* **—*Idiom.* 15. spin one's wheels,** to waste one's efforts. **—spin′ner,** *n.* [*count*] **—spin′ning,** *n.* [*noncount*]

spi•na bif•i•da (spī′nə bif′i də) /ˈspaynə bɪfɪdə/ *n.* [*noncount*] a defect in the spine in which part of the spinal cord sticks out through the spinal column, often resulting in difficulty in moving or paralysis.

spin•ach (spin′ich) /ˈspɪnɪtʃ/ *n.* [*noncount*] **1.** a plant with crinkly or flat green leaves that can be eaten. **2.** the leaves, eaten as a vegetable.

spi•nal (spīn′l) /ˈspaynl/ *adj.* **1.** of or relating to a spine or thornlike structure, esp. the backbone. **—*n.*** [*count*] **2.** a pain-killing injection in the spine: *The doctor gave her a spinal for her pain.*

spi′nal col′umn, *n.* [*count*] the series of bones forming the central structure of the skeleton in animals that have a backbone; spine; backbone.

spi′nal cord′, *n.* [*count*] the cord of nerve tissue extending through the spinal canal of the spinal column.

spin′ control′, *n.* [*noncount*] *Slang.* an attempt to give a favorable view or bias to news coverage: *The campaign team tried to put some spin control on the candidate's defeat by saying that he "did better than expected."*

spin•dle (spin′dl) /ˈspɪndl/ *n.* [*count*] **1.** a rounded rod, pointed at each end, used in hand-spinning. **2.** any shaft or pin that turns around or on which something turns, as an axle. **3.** a spindle-shaped structure, as in a living cell.

spin•dly (spind′lē) /ˈspɪndliy/ *adj.*, **-dli•er, -dli•est.** long or tall, thin, and usually weak: *The young colt wobbled on its spindly legs.*

spine (spīn) /spayn/ *n.* **1.** [*count*] the backbone; spinal column. **2.** [*count*] **a.** a hard, sharp-pointed outgrowth on a plant; thorn. **b.** a stiff-pointed bone or part of a bodily structure of an animal, such as the quill of a porcupine. **3.** [*noncount*] courage; mettle. **4.** [*count*] the back of a book binding, usually indicating the title and author. **—spin′y,** *adj.*, **-i•er, -i•est:** *I stuck my finger on one of the fish's spiny fins.*

spine•less (spīn′lis) /ˈspaynlɪs/ *adj.* **1.** having no spine or backbone. **2.** having no spines or quills. **3.** without resolution or courage: *He was a spineless coward.*

spin•et (spin′it) /ˈspɪnɪt/ *n.* [*count*] a small upright piano.

spin′ning wheel′, *n.* [*count*] a device used esp. formerly for spinning wool, flax, etc., into yarn or thread.

spin′-off′ or **spin′off′,** *n.* [*count*] **1.** a by-product of something that already exists, such as a program of research. **2.** a television show or series, book, etc., that is based on an idea or character that already exists in a previously made product: *The new show is a spin-off of the old familiar one.*

spin•ster (spin′stər) /ˈspɪnstər/ *n.* [*count*] a woman who has remained unmarried. **—spin′ster•hood′,** *n.* [*noncount*]

-spir-, *root.* *-spir-* comes from Latin, where it has the meaning "breathe; have a longing for." This meaning is found in such words as: ASPIRE, CONSPIRE, EXPIRE, INSPIRE, PERSPIRE, RESPIRATION, RESPIRATORY, RESPIRE, SPIRACLE, SPIRIT, TRANSPIRE.

spi•ra•cle (spī′rə kəl, spir′ə-) /ˈspayrəkəl, ˈspɪrə-/ *n.* [*count*] a breathing hole; air hole; blowhole. See -SPIR-.

spi•ral (spī′rəl) /ˈspayrəl/ *n., adj., v.,* **-raled, -ral•ing** or (*esp. Brit.*) **-ralled, -ral•ling. —*n.*** [*count*] **1.** a curve made by a point that moves around a fixed point, while constantly moving away from or toward that point. **2.** a spiral object, formation, or form. **3.** a continuous increase or decrease in wages, prices, etc. **—*adj.*** [*before a noun*] **4.** of or of the nature of a spiral or coil: *a spiral staircase.* **5.** bound with a spiral binding: *a spiral notebook.* **—*v.*** [*no obj*] **6.** to take a spiral form or course: *The plane exploded and spiraled down to earth.* **7.** to rise or fall steadily: *Wages have spiraled down once again.*

spi′ral bind′ing, *n.* [*noncount*] a notebook binding in which the pages are fastened together by a spiral of wire that coils through holes at the side of each page.

spire (spīᵊr) /spayᵊr/ *n.* [*count*] **1.** a tall, sharply pointed roof or rooflike construction upon a tower, roof, steeple, etc. **2.** a tall, sharply pointed summit, peak, or the like.

spir•it (spir′it) /ˈspɪrɪt/ *n.* **1.** [*count; usually singular*] the principle believed to give life, esp. to humans; vital essence: *He gave up the spirit* (= *He died*). **2.** [*count; usually singular*] the part of humans that is not the body or the mind; the soul: *They believe that the spirit cannot die.* **3.** [*count*] a supernatural being without a body: *evil spirits.* **4.** [*count*] an attitude, feeling, or principle that stirs one to action, etc.: *The spirit of reform began to grow among the people.* **5.** [*noncount*] the source of feelings prompting one to action: *a man of broken spirit.* **6. spirits,** [*plural*] mood with regard to great happiness or great sadness: *The children's high spirits made us all laugh.* **7.** [*count; usually singular*] a lively, courageous, or hopeful attitude: *Get up and try again; yes, that's the spirit!* **8.** [*noncount*] temper, attitude, or disposition: *meek in spirit.* **9.** [*count*] an individual thought of as having a particular attitude, character, etc.: *a few brave spirits.* **10.** [*count; usually singular*] the meaning or intent of a law, as opposed to the actual words: *The judges ruled that he had violated the spirit of the law, if not the letter of the law.* **11.** Often, **spirits.** [*plural*] a strong distilled alcoholic liquor. **12.** [*noncount*] *Brit.* alcohol. **—*v.*** [~ + *obj* (+ *off/away*)] **13.** to carry off mysteriously or secretly: *They disguised the king and spirited him out a back door; spirited away by kidnappers.* **—spir′it•less,** *adj.* See -SPIR-.

spir•it•ed (spir′i tid) /ˈspɪrɪtɪd/ *adj.* **1.** having or showing courage, animation, strength, etc.: *The villagers put up a spirited defense.* **2.** (used after an adjective) having the mood, disposition, or nature of the adjective mentioned: *a high-spirited, headstrong girl.*

spir•it•u•al (spir′i cho͞o əl) /ˈspɪrɪtʃuwəl/ *adj.* **1.** of or relating to the spirit or soul, as distinguished from the physical nature **2.** of or relating to the spirit as the source of one's moral or religious nature. **3.** of or relating to sacred things or matters; religious. **4.** closely alike in interests, outlook, feeling, etc.: *the composer's spiritual heir.* **5.** relating to spirits or to spiritualists; supernatural. **—*n.*** [*count*] **6.** a religious song that shows strong emotion, of a type originating among African-Americans in the southern U.S. **—spir•it•u•al•i•ty** (spir′i cho͞o al′i tē) /ˌspɪrɪtʃuwˈælɪtiy/ *n.* [*noncount*] **—spir′it•u•al•ly,** *adv.*

spir•it•u•al•ism (spir′i cho͞o ə liz′əm) /ˈspɪrɪtʃuwəˌlɪzəm/ *n.* [*noncount*] **1.** the belief that the spirits of the dead communicate with the living, esp. through a person (a medium). **2.** the practices or events associated with this belief. **—spir′it•u•al•ist,** *n.* [*count*] **—spir′it•u•al•is′tic,** *adj.*

spit[1] (spit) /spɪt/ *v.,* **spit** or **spat** (spat) /spæt/ **spit•ting,** *n.* **—*v.* 1.** [*no obj;* (~ + *at* + *obj*)] to expel saliva from the mouth: *He cleared his throat and spat loudly; kids spitting at each other.* **2.** [~ + *obj*] to expel (something) from the mouth: *to spit watermelon seeds.* **3.** [*no obj*] to sputter: *The grease was spitting in the fire.* **4. spit up,** to vomit; throw up: [*no obj*]: *The baby was spitting up.* [~ + *up* + *obj*]: *The wounded soldier spat up some blood.* **—*n.*** [*noncount*] **5.** saliva. **6.** the act of spitting. **—*Idiom.* 7. spit and image,** [*noncount*] exact likeness; counterpart. Also, **spitting image.**

spit[2] (spit) /spɪt/ *n.* [*count*] **1.** a pointed rod for piercing and holding meat over a fire. **2.** a narrow point of land sticking out into the water.

spit•ball (spit′bôl′) /ˈspɪtˌbɔl/ *n.* [*count*] **1.** a small ball or lump of chewed paper thrown at people or things: *throwing spitballs in class.* **2.** a baseball pitch, made to curve by moistening the ball with saliva.

spite (spīt) /spayt/ *n., v.,* **spit•ed, spit•ing. —*n.*** [*noncount*] **1.** a mean, narrow-minded desire to harm another person; malice: *He was mean to her just from spite.* **—*v.*** [~ + *obj*] **2.** to treat with spite; hurt or annoy: *I'm sure they turned her down just to spite me.* **—*Idiom.* 3. in spite of,** [~ + *obj*] in disregard or defiance of: *In spite of repeated warnings, she continued to smoke.* **4. in**

spite of oneself, in disregard of one's best efforts not to do something; unwillingly: *Even though I was angry at them, I had to smile at their silliness in spite of myself.*

spite•ful (spit′fəl) /ˈspaytfəl/ *adj.* full of spite: *mean and spiteful to his little sister.*

spit•fire (spit′fīᵊr′) /ˈspɪtˌfayᵊr/ *n.* [*count*] a person of fiery temper who gets angry or excited very easily.

spit•tle (spit′l) /ˈspɪtl/ *n.* [*noncount*] saliva; spit.

spit•toon (spi to͞on′) /spɪˈtuwn/ *n.* [*count*] a cuspidor.

splash (splash) /splæʃ/ *v.* **1.** [*no obj*] (of water, mud, etc.) to fly or be thrown out in scattered masses or particles; spatter: *Mud splashed from the bus tires.* **2.** [~ + *obj*] to wet or make dirty by splashing: *The sea water splashed his face.* **3.** to throw (a liquid) about in scattered masses or particles: [*no obj*]: *The kids were splashing happily in the bathtub.* [~ + *obj*]: *They were splashing water on each other in the bathtub.* **4.** [~ + *obj*] to throw scattered particles or masses of a liquid at or on: *The boys splashed each other with mud.* **—***n.* [*count*] **5.** the act or sound of splashing. **6.** an amount of a liquid splashed. **7.** a patch, as of color or light. **8.** a striking show; great impression: *The news of their engagement made quite a splash.* **9.** a small amount of liquid: *She'll have a splash of water with her whiskey.*

splash•down (splash′doun′) /ˈsplæʃˌdawn/ *n.* [*count*] the landing of a space vehicle in a body of water, esp. the ocean.

splash•y (splash′ē) /ˈsplæʃiy/ *adj.,* **-i•er, -i•est. 1.** making a splash or splashes. **2.** full of or marked by splashes or irregular spots; spotty. **3.** making a very visible or obvious display; showy. **—splash•i•ly** (splash′ə lē) /ˈsplæʃəliy/ *adv.* **—splash′i•ness,** *n.* [*noncount*]

splat (splat) /splæt/ *n.* [*count*] a sound made by splattering or slapping.

splat•ter (splat′ər) /ˈsplætər/ *v.* **1.** [*no obj*] to splash and scatter upon impact: *Rain splattered against the windows.* **2.** [~ + *obj*] **a.** to splash on or against in drops that scatter: *Rain splattered the windows.* **b.** to cover or stain with drops of something that scatters: *The paint splattered the rug.* **—***n.* [*count*] **3.** an act or instance of splattering. **4.** the amount splattered.

splay (splā) /spley/ *v.* to spread out, or extend, as by making one end or part crooked, slanted, or longer than another: [~ + *obj*]: *He sat down and splayed his legs over the arm of the chair.* [*no obj*]: *The coat hanger had splayed out of shape.*

spleen (splēn) /spliyn/ *n.* **1.** [*count*] an organ in the body near the stomach and heart, that destroys worn-out red blood cells and is a reservoir for blood. **2.** [*noncount*] ill humor; angry, impatient temper; spite: *to vent one's spleen by shouting at someone else.*

splen•did (splen′did) /ˈsplɛndɪd/ *adj.* **1.** magnificent; beautiful; gorgeous; sumptuous: *splendid jewels.* **2.** distinguished or glorious: *It was a splendid achievement.* **3.** excellent or very good: *We had a splendid time at the party.* **—splen′did•ly,** *adv.*

splen•dor (splen′dər) /ˈsplɛndər/ *n.* [*noncount*] **1.** brilliant or gorgeous appearance, coloring, etc.: *the splendor of the rising sun.* **2.** an instance or display of imposing pomp or grandeur: *the splendor of the coronation.* Also, *esp. Brit.,* **splen′dour. —splen′dor•ous,** *adj.*

sple•net•ic (spli net′ik) /splɪˈnɛtɪk/ *adj.* Also, **sple•net′i•cal. 1.** of the spleen. **2.** irritable; easily angered; spiteful.

splice (splīs) /splays/ *v.,* **spliced, splic•ing,** *n.* **—***v.* [~ + *obj*] **1.** to join together (rope) by weaving strands together. **2.** to unite (two pieces of film, magnetic tape, etc.) by placing the pieces together and cementing or joining them: *He spliced the pieces together to make the action from one tape continue onto the next.* **—***n.* [*count*] **3.** a joining of two ropes or parts of a rope by splicing. **4.** the union or junction made by splicing. **—splic′er,** *n.* [*count*]

splint (splint) /splɪnt/ *n.* [*count*] **1.** a thin piece of rigid material used to prevent a fractured or dislocated bone from moving. **2.** one of a number of thin strips of wood woven together to make a chair seat, basket, etc. **—***v.* [~ + *obj*] **3.** to secure or support by means of a splint, as a fractured bone.

splin•ter (splin′tər) /ˈsplɪntər/ *n.* [*count*] **1.** a small, thin, sharp piece of wood, bone, etc., split off from the main body: *He used a needle to remove the splinter from his finger.* **2.** a part of an organization that breaks off from the main group: *A splinter group broke away from the radical party.* **—***v.* **3.** to (cause to) be split into splinters: [*no obj*]: *The wooden guard rail splintered as the truck drove through it.* [~ + *obj*]: *The huge truck splintered the flimsy guard rail.* **4.** to split (a larger group) into separate factions: [~ + *obj*]: *These divisions will splinter the Republican Party.* [*no obj*]: *One group after another splintered away from the Democratic Party.* **—splin′ter•y,** *adj.*

split (split) /splɪt/ *v.,* **split, split•ting,** *n., adj.* **—***v.* **1.** to divide from end to end or into layers: [~ + *obj*]: *She took an ax and split a log in two.* [*no obj*]: *The log split nicely in two when she cut it.* **2.** to divide into separate portions: [~ (+ *up*) + *obj*]: *The book is split (up) into five major divisions.* [*no obj;* (~ + *up*)]: *We'll split (up) here and continue the search separately.* **3.** to divide into different factions, such as through discord; (cause to) part or separate: [*no obj;* (~ + *up*)]: *They split (up) after several years of marriage.* [~ + *obj*]: *That issue split the Republican Party.* **4.** [~ + *obj*] to cast (a ballot) for candidates of more than one political party: *Many Americans split their vote, voting for the President but against his party in the Senate and House elections.* **5.** [~ + *obj*] to divide between two or more persons, groups, etc.; share: *They decided to split the money they had won.* **6.** *Slang.* to leave; depart: [~ + *obj*]: *Let's split this party; it's boring.* [*no obj*]: *Your brothers are gone; they split about an hour ago.* **—***n.* [*count*] **7.** the act of splitting. **8.** a crack or fissure caused by splitting. **9.** a piece separated by or as if by splitting. **10.** an ice-cream dish made with a split banana, flavored syrup, and chopped nuts. **11.** Often, **splits.** [*plural*] the feat of separating the legs while sinking to the floor, until they extend at right angles to the body. **—***adj.* **12.** having been split; parted lengthwise. **13.** disunited; divided: *a split opinion.* **—*Idiom.* 14. split the difference,** to compromise, esp. to divide what remains equally.

split′-lev′el, *adj.* **1.** (of a house) having a room or rooms that are somewhat above or below nearby rooms, with the floor levels usually differing by about half a story. **—***n.* [*count*] **2.** a split-level house.

split′ pea′, *n.* [*count*] a dried green pea, split and used esp. for soup.

split′ personal′ity, *n.* [*count*] a mental disorder in which a person has several personalities that operate independently.

split•ting (split′ing) /ˈsplɪtɪŋ/ *adj.* (of a headache) very painful; intense; severe.

splotch (sploch) /splɒtʃ/ *n.* [*count*] **1.** a large, irregular spot; blot; stain: *reddish splotches on his face.* **—***v.* **2.** [~ + *obj*] to mark with splotches. **3.** [*no obj*] to be easily marked or covered with blots. **—splotch′y,** *adj.,* **-i•er, -i•est:** *his splotchy red face.*

splurge (splûrj) /splɜrdʒ/ *v.,* **splurged, splurg•ing,** *n.* **—***v.* **1.** to spend (money) on some luxury or pleasure, esp. a costly one: [*no obj*]: *They splurged on a trip to Europe.* [~ + *obj*]: *They splurged their money on a trip to Europe.* **—***n.* [*count*] **2.** an instance of spending money for luxury or pleasure, esp. a large sum.

splut•ter (splut′ər) /ˈsplʌtər/ *v.* **1.** [*no obj*] to talk rapidly and unclearly, as when excited: *spluttering about how he'd get revenge.* **2.** [~ + *obj*] to say hastily and confusedly: *to splutter a few words.* [*used with quotations*]: *"But, but..how?..how?" he spluttered, unable even to form the question.* **3.** [*no obj*] to make a sputtering sound, or give off particles of something suddenly, such as water on a hot griddle. **—***n.* [*count*] **4.** an act or sound of spluttering.

spoil (spoil) /spɔyl/ *v.,* **spoiled** or **spoilt** (spoilt) /spɔylt/ **spoil•ing,** *n.* **—***v.* **1.** to (cause to) become bad or unfit for use, such as food that does not last long unless treated with cold: [*no obj*]: *Too much moisture and heat will cause the food to spoil.* [~ + *obj*]: *to spoil the food.* **2.** [~ + *obj*] to damage or harm severely; ruin: *The rip spoiled the delicate fabric.* **3.** [~ + *obj*] to affect in a bad or unfortunate way: *Bad weather spoiled our vacation.* **4.** [~ + *obj*] to treat (someone) too well, as by giving too much, and thus affect his or her character in a bad way: *Don't spoil the baby by jumping up to feed her whenever she whimpers.* **—***n.* **spoils** [*plural*] **5.** money, property, or goods taken in war or by robbery. **—*Idiom.* 6. be spoiling for,** [~ + *obj*] *Informal.* to be very eager for: *They're spoiling for a fight.* **—spoil•age** (spoi′lij) /ˈspɔylɪdʒ/ *n.* [*noncount*] **—spoil′er,** *n.* [*count*]

spoil•sport (spoil′spôrt′, -spōrt′) /ˈspɔylˌspɔrt, -ˌspowrt/ *n.* [*count*] one whose conduct spoils the pleasure of others, as in a game.

spoils′ sys′tem, *n.* [*count*] the practice in which public offices are filled with supporters of the victorious political party.

spoke[1] (spōk) /spowk/ *v.* **1.** a pt. of SPEAK. **2.** *Archaic.* a pp. of SPEAK.

spoke[2] (spōk) /spowk/ *n.* [*count*] one of the bars attached to the hub of a wheel, supporting the rim.

spo•ken (spō′kən) /ˈspowkən/ *v.* **1.** a pp. of SPEAK. *—adj.* **2.** expressed by speaking; oral (distinguished from *written*). **3.** (used after an adjective) speaking, or using speech, in the way mentioned in the adjective: *plain-spoken; soft-spoken.* **—*Idiom.* 4. spoken for,** [*be* + ~] claimed or reserved: *This seat is already spoken for.*

spokes•man or **-wom•an** or **-per•son** (spōks′mən) or (-wo͝om′ən) or (-pûr′sən) /ˈspowksmən/ or /-ˌwʊmən/ or /-ˌpɜrsən/ *n.* [*count*], *pl.* **-men** or **-wom•en** or **-persons.** one who speaks for another or for a group: *A White House spokeswoman denied the charge.*

-spond-, *root.* *-spond-* comes from Latin, where it has the meaning "pledge; promise." This meaning is found in such words as: CORRESPOND, CORRESPONDENCE, CORRESPONDENT, DESPONDENT, RESPOND, TRANSPONDER.

sponge (spunj) /spʌndʒ/ *n., v.,* **sponged, spong•ing.** *—n.* **1.** [*count*] a stationary sea creature that has a rubbery fibrous frame full of holes. **2.** [*count*] the skeleton of certain of these creatures that easily absorbs water and becomes soft when wet. **3.** a piece of any of various absorbent materials, such as rubber or cellulose, that are soft when wet: [*count*]: *He used a sponge to wipe up the spilled soda.* [*noncount*]: *cushions of sponge filling.* **4.** [*count*] a person or thing that absorbs something freely or easily: *The student sat at the teacher's side, a sponge absorbing everything she said.* **5.** [*count*] one who lives at the expense of others; sponger. *—v.* **6.** to wipe or rub with or as if with a wet sponge: [~ (+ *off/down*) + *obj*]: *I'll sponge (off) the countertop with some cleanser.* [~ + *obj* +(*off/down*)]: *I'll sponge the countertop (down).* **7.** to take up or absorb with or as if with a sponge: [~ (+ *up*) + *obj*]: *I'll sponge (up) the milk she spilled on the floor.* [~ + *obj* (+ *up*)]: *He sponged the milk (up).* **8.** to get (something) by imposing on another's good nature: [~ + *obj*]: *He sponged a few meals from them and moved on.* [~ + *off* + *obj*]: *He sponged off his relatives for a few months before he finally got a job.* *—***spong′er,** *n.* [*count*] —**spong′y,** *adj.,* **-i•er, -i•est.**

sponge′ bath′, *n.* [*count*] a bath in which the bather is cleaned by a wet sponge or washcloth, without getting into a tub of water.

sponge′ cake′, *n.* a light, sweet cake containing eggs but no shortening: [*noncount*]: *That company makes delicious sponge cake.* [*count*]: *a delicious sponge cake for dessert.*

spon•sor (spon′sər) /ˈspɒnsər/ *n.* [*count*] **1.** one who is responsible for, or supports, a person or thing. **2.** a person, firm, organization, etc., that supports the cost of a television program by buying time for advertising during the broadcast: *And now, a word from our sponsors.* **3.** a person or group that provides or pledges money for an event: *the corporate sponsors of a race.* **4.** one who makes a pledge on behalf of another. *—v.* [~ + *obj*] **5.** to act as sponsor for: *We sponsored a family who wanted to live in the United States for a summer.* —**spon′sor•ship′,** *n.* [*noncount*]: *the sponsorship of the gun-control bill.* See -SPOND-.

spon•ta•ne•ous (spon tā′nē əs) /spɒnˈteyniyəs/ *adj.* **1.** resulting from a natural impulse or tendency: *spontaneous applause during the performance.* **2.** (of a person) acting upon sudden impulses: *She's very spontaneous: she'll come right up and give you a hug if she feels like it.* **3.** (of natural events) caused by forces within something: *Spontaneous combustion was the cause of the fire.* —**spon•ta•ne•i•ty** (spon′tə nē′i tē, -nā′-) /ˌspɒntəˈniyɪtiy, -ˈney-/ *n.* [*noncount*] —**spon•ta′ne•ous•ly,** *adv.*

spoof (spo͞of) /spuwf/ *n.* [*count*] **1.** a lighthearted imitation of someone or something: *The TV show started with a spoof of a film classic.* **2.** a hoax; prank. *—v.* **3.** to mock (something or someone) lightly and good-humoredly: [~ + *obj*]: *They spoofed a famous love scene from the film.* [*no obj*]: *They were only spoofing; nothing was serious.*

spook (spo͝ok) /spuwk/ *n.* [*count*] **1.** a ghost; specter: *a movie about spooks in a haunted house.* **2.** *Informal.* a spy: *the spooks working for the CIA.* *—v.* **3.** to (cause to) become frightened or scared: [~ + *obj*]: *The sudden noise spooked the horse.* [*no obj*]: *The horse spooked too easily.*

spook•y (spo͞o′kē) /ˈspuwkiy/ *adj.,* **-i•er, -i•est.** causing a feeling of fright; scary: *a dark, spooky old house.*

spool (spo͞ol) /spuwl/ *n.* [*count*] **1.** a rounded object on which something is wound, as on a sewing machine or tape player: *to wind the loose film back on the spool.* *—v.* [~ + *obj*] **2.** to wind on a spool.

spoon (spo͞on) /spuwn/ *n.* [*count*] **1.** an object used in eating, stirring, measuring, etc., made up of a small, shallow bowl with a handle: *She picked up a spoon and stirred her tea.* See illustration at RESTAURANT. **2.** an object or part resembling or suggesting this. **3.** a spoonful: *I'll take two spoons of sugar with my tea, please.* *—v.* [~ + *obj*] **4.** to eat with a spoon: *He spooned some ice cream into his mouth.* **—*Idiom.* 5. born with a silver spoon in one's mouth,** born wealthy. —**spoon′ful,** *n.* [*count*], *pl.* **-fuls.**

spoon•bill (spo͞on′bil′) /ˈspuwnˌbɪl/ *n.* [*count*] a large wading bird, esp. one of the ibis family, having a long, flat bill with a spoonlike tip.

spoon•er•ism (spo͞o′nə riz′əm) /ˈspuwnəˌrɪzəm/ *n.* [*count*] the usually accidental rearranging of initial or other sounds of words, as in *a blushing crow* for *a crushing blow.*

spoon′-feed′, *v.* [~ + *obj*], **-fed, -feed•ing. 1.** to feed with a spoon. **2.** to provide (someone) so fully with information that he or she is prevented from acting independently: *He didn't want to spoon-feed his students by just giving facts.* **3.** to provide someone with (information) in this way: *to spoon-feed data to his students.*

spoor (spo͝or, spôr, spōr) /spʊr, spɔr, spowr/ *n.* [*count*] **1.** a track or trail, esp. of a wild animal. *—v.* [~ + *obj*] **2.** to track (an animal) by a spoor.

spo•rad•ic (spə rad′ik) /spəˈrædɪk/ *adj.* appearing or happening at irregular times; occasional: *sporadic gunfire.* —**spo•rad′i•cal•ly,** *adv.*: *The fighting continued sporadically.*

spore (spôr, spōr) /spɔr, spowr/ *n.* [*count*] a small cell like a seed, produced by a fungus for reproduction

sport (spôrt, spōrt) /spɔrt, spowrt/ *n.* **1.** [*count*] an often competitive athletic activity requiring skill or physical ability: *interested in several sports: gymnastics, baseball, and soccer.* **2.** [*noncount*] such activities thought of as a group: *And now, news from the world of sport.* **3.** [*noncount*] recreation; diversion. **4.** [*noncount*] jest; pleasantry: *It was all done in sport.* **5.** [*noncount*] mockery; ridicule: *made sport of his haircut.* **6.** [*count*] one who behaves in a fair, understanding way: *We hope he'll be a (good) sport and give us the raise we deserve.* *—adj.* [*before a noun*] Also, **sports. 7.** of, relating to, or used in sports: *an expert in sports medicine.* **8.** suitable for outdoor or informal wear: *sport clothes.* *—v.* **9.** [*no obj*] to amuse oneself with some pleasant pastime; frolic: *kittens sporting and playing.* **10.** [*no obj*] to speak or act in a joking manner. **11.** [~ + *obj*] to wear or display, esp. while showing off: *She sported a diamond ring.*

sport•ing (spôr′ting, spōr′-) /ˈspɔrtɪŋ, ˈspowr-/ *adj.* **1.** [*before a noun*] of or relating to sports, esp. outdoor sports: *a sporting event.* **2.** fair; generous: *He wasn't very sporting about the student's request for a change of grade.* **3.** [*before a noun*] involving a fair or reasonable opportunity for success: *a sporting chance.*

sports′ car′, *n.* [*count*] a small, high-powered automobile with long, low lines.

sports•cast (spôrts′kast′, spōrts′-) /ˈspɔrtsˌkæst, ˈspowrts-/ *n.* [*count*] a radio or television program of sports news or comment on a sports event. —**sports′-cast′er,** *n.* [*count*] —**sports′cast′ing,** *n.* [*noncount*]

sports•man (spôrts′mən, spōrts′-) /ˈspɔrtsmən, ˈspowrts-/ *n.* [*count*], *pl.* **-men. 1.** one who participates in sports, esp. hunting and fishing. **2.** one who shows that he or she has qualities of fairness, courtesy, and grace in winning and in losing. —**sports′man•like′,** *adj.* : *In a sportsmanlike gesture he helped his injured opponent to stand up again.* —**sports′man•ship′,** *n.* [*noncount*]

sport•y (spôr′tē, spōr′-) /ˈspɔrtiy, ˈspowr-/ *adj.,* **-i•er, -i•est. 1.** flashy; showy: *a fast, sporty car.* **2.** smart in dress or behavior; dashing: *a sporty outfit.* **3.** designed for or suitable for sport.

spot (spot) /spɒt/ *n., v.,* **spot•ted, spot•ting,** *adj.* *—n.* [*count*] **1.** a mark made by something unwanted, such as dirt: *We couldn't get the spots of grease off the dress.* **2.** a small blemish or other mark on the skin. **3.** a small part of a surface differing from the rest in color, appearance, or character: *a bald spot.* **4.** something that harms one's character or reputation; flaw. **5.** a place: *This is the spot where the explorers landed five hundred years ago.* **6.** a position in an organization or hierarchy: *an important spot in government.* **7.** [*usually singular*] *Chiefly Brit. Informal.* a small quantity: *a spot of tea.* **8.** [*usually singular*] an awkward or difficult position: *We're in a bit of a* *spot because we can't choose which party to go to.* **—*v.*** **9.** to make a spot on (something); stain: [*no obj*]: *Ink can spot badly.* [~ + *obj*]: *The blood spotted his shirt.* **10.** [*no obj*] to become spotted or stained: *The clothes spotted from the rusty water.* **11.** [~ + *obj*] to ruin: *to spot someone's reputation.* **12.** [~ + *obj*] to locate or identify by seeing: *So far I haven't spotted any errors in your computer program.* **13.** [~ + *obj*] to position on a particular place: *to spot a billiard ball.* **14.** to grant (an advantage) to (an opponent): [~ + *obj* + *obj*]: *He spotted his opponent a lead of fifty yards and still won the race.* [~ + *obj* + *to* + *obj*]: *She spotted him to a lead of fifty yards and still won the race.* **—*adj.*** [*before a noun*] **15.** made, paid, or delivered at once: *a spot sale.* **—*Idiom.*** **16. on the spot, a.** without delay; at once; instantly: *He was there on the spot.* **b.** at the very place in question: *This reporter is always on the spot when an important news story develops.* **c.** in a difficult or embarrassing position: *She's on the spot because her car broke down and she can't get to work.* —**spot′less,** *adj.*

spot′ check′, *n.* [*count*] a quick check or investigation of items, often chosen at random: *to run a spot check on the samples coming off the assembly line.* —**spot′-check′,** *v.* [~ + *obj*]: *to spot-check a few items coming off the assembly line.*

spot•light (spot′līt′) /ˈspɒtˌlayt/ *n., v.,* **-light•ed** or **-lit, -light•ing.** **—*n.*** [*count*] **1.** a very strong light focused to pick out an object, person, or group, as on a stage, or the lamp producing this light: *He blinked when the spotlight shone in his eyes.* **2.** [*usually singular*] the area of public attention: *Asia is in the spotlight now.* **—*v.*** [~ + *obj*] **3.** to direct the beam of a spotlight upon. **4.** to make noticeable; call attention to: *The school principal got very nervous when parents spotlighted any problems.*

spotted (spot′id) /ˈspɒtɪd/ *adj.* having spots, or a pattern of spots: *a spotted horse.*

spot•ter (spot′ər) /ˈspɒtər/ *n.* [*count*] **1.** a person employed to watch the activity of others, as for evidence of dishonesty: *The spotter rode the train to make sure the conductor collected the tickets.* **2.** a military observer who spots targets. **3.** an assistant to a sportscaster who provides the names of the players in a game.

spot•ty (spot′ē) /ˈspɒtiy/ *adj.,* **-ti•er, -ti•est.** **1.** marked with spots; spotted. **2.** uneven in quality or character; irregular: *The musicians gave a spotty performance.* —**spot′ti•ness,** *n.* [*noncount*]

spouse (spous, spouz) /spaws, spawz/ *n.* [*count*] one's husband or wife.

spout (spout) /spawt/ *v.* **1.** [~ + *obj*] to throw out with force, as in a stream or jet: *The volcano was spouting ash and lava.* **2.** [*no obj*] to shoot out forcefully or violently: *Ash and lava spouted from the volcano.* **3.** to say in a showy, conceited, or pompous manner: [~ + *obj*]: *spouting his theories on foreign policy.* [*no obj;* (~ + *off*)]: *He's always spouting (off) about how great his job is.* **—*n.*** [*count*] **4.** a pipe or tube through which a liquid is poured or carried along: *the spout of the teapot.* **5.** a continuous stream of liquid coming out or as if out of a pipe or tube.

sprain (sprān) /spreyn/ *v.* [~ + *obj*] **1.** to overstrain or twist (the ligaments around a joint) so as to injure without a fracture or break: *He sprained his knee when he twisted it and fell.* **—*n.*** [*count*] **2.** an injury to the ligaments around a joint.

sprang (sprang) /spræŋ/ *v.* a pt. of SPRING.

sprat (sprat) /spræt/ *n.* [*count*], *pl.* **sprats,** (*esp. when thought of as a group*) **sprat.** a small fish, a herring of the E North Atlantic.

sprawl (sprôl) /sprɔl/ *v.* **1.** to stretch or spread out (the legs) such as when sitting or lying: [*no obj*]: *She sprawled on the couch.* [~ + *obj*]: *She sprawled her leg over his knee and trapped him.* **2.** [*no obj*] to be spread out or distributed irregularly or awkwardly: *The city sprawls for a few more miles then stops abruptly.* **—*n.*** [*noncount*] **3.** an act or instance of sprawling: *The problem of urban sprawl gets worse because of the poor transportation systems.*

spray (sprā) /sprey/ *n.* **1.** [*noncount*] liquid broken up into very tiny droplets and blown, forced into, or falling through the air: *salt spray from the ocean.* **2.** [*count*] a jet of such tiny droplets blown or forced from some device: *May I have a spray of that perfume?* **3.** [*count*] liquid blown or forced into the air in such a jet from a special device: [*noncount*]: *a can of bug spray.* [*count*]: *Those bug sprays smell awful.* **4.** [*count*] a device for discharging liquid in a jet of tiny droplets: *The manufacturer uses a pump, not a spray, for this paint.* **5.** [*count*] a number of small objects flying through the air: *a spray of shattered glass.* **—*v.*** **6.** [*no obj*] to scatter in the form of very tiny particles: *The water sprayed into our eyes.* **7.** [~ + *obj*] to apply or direct in a spray: *The carpenter sprayed paint on the wall.* **8.** [~ + *obj*] to sprinkle, cover, blast, or treat with or as if with a spray: *to spray a wall with paint.* —**spray′er,** *n.* [*count*]

spray′ can′, *n.* [*count*] a can whose contents are in a form that can be sprayed, as in an aerosol form: *She used two spray cans of white enamel.*

spray′ gun′, *n.* [*count*] a device made up of a container from which paint or other liquid is sprayed through a nozzle by air pressure from a pump.

spread (spred) /sprɛd/ *v.,* **spread, spread•ing,** *n.* **—*v.*** **1.** to stretch out, esp. over a flat surface: [~ + *obj*]: *Spread the blanket under the tree.* [*no obj*]: *The blanket will spread far enough for both of us to sit on it.* **2.** to extend out; move apart: [~ + *obj*]: *The bird spread its wings and flew.* [*no obj*]: *The wings of that bird spread several feet.* **3.** to (cause to) be distributed over an area of space or time: [~ + *obj*]: *to spread seed on the ground.* [*no obj*]: *The fire spread quickly in the high winds.* **4.** [~ + *obj*] to apply (something) to or on (something) in a thin layer or coating. **5.** [*no obj*] to be able to be applied in a layer or coating: *The butter is supposed to spread easily.* **6.** [~ + *obj*] to set (a table) for a meal. **7.** to (cause to) become widely known: [~ + *obj*]: *Someone is spreading rumors about his past.* [*no obj*]: *How do such rumors spread?* **—*n.*** **8.** [*count; usually: singular*] an act or instance of spreading: *The World Health Organization tracked the rapid spread of malaria.* **9.** [*count; usually: singular*] the extent of spreading, such as a distance between two points: *to measure the spread of branches.* **10.** [*count*] a wide range or expanse of something, as property or land: *His ranch was a beautiful spread up in the mountains.* **11.** [*count*] a cloth covering for a bed, table, etc., esp. a bedspread. **12.** [*count*] *Informal.* a great amount of food set out on a table; feast: *He always puts out a lavish spread at the office parties.* **13.** [*count*] a food preparation for spreading, such as jam or peanut butter. **14.** [*count*] a large, lengthy display, treatment of a topic, or advertisement, such as one covering two or more pages. **—*Idiom.*** **15. spread oneself (too) thin,** to try to do too many projects at the same time: *He was spreading himself too thin: he was a single parent, a student, and a volunteer at his church, and he had a full-time job.* —**spread′a•ble,** *adj.* —**spread′er,** *n.* [*count*]

spread′-ea′gle, *adj., v.,* **-gled, -gling.** **—*adj.*** [*before a noun*] **1.** having or suggesting the form of an eagle with outstretched wings. **—*v.*** [~ + *obj*] **2.** to stretch out in a spread-eagle position: *He was spread-eagled on the floor when the police found him.*

spread•sheet (spred′shēt′) /ˈsprɛdˌʃiyt/ *n.* [*count*] **1.** a very large, wide ledger sheet used by accountants. **2.** such a sheet when it is represented electronically by computer software, used esp. for financial planning: *Retrieve the spreadsheet of your expenses.*

spree (sprē) /spriy/ *n.* [*count*] a period or burst of action in which one does as one wishes, without thinking or worrying about the results: *a drinking spree; a shopping spree.*

sprig (sprig) /sprɪg/ *n.* [*count*] a small shoot, twig, or branch.

spright•ly (sprīt′lē) /ˈspraytliy/ *adj.,* **-li•er, -li•est,** *adv.* **—*adj.*** **1.** animated; full of life; bouncy; lively. **—*adv.*** **2.** in a sprightly manner. —**spright′li•ness,** *n.* [*noncount*]

spring (spring) /sprɪŋ/ *v.,* **sprang** (sprang) /spræŋ/ or, often, **sprung** (sprung) /sprʌŋ/; **sprung; spring•ing;** *n.* **—*v.*** **1.** [*no obj*] to rise, leap, or move suddenly and swiftly: *The tiger stood ready to spring on its victim.* **2.** to (cause to) be released suddenly from a constrained position: [*no obj*]: *The door sprang open.* [~ + *obj*]: *He sprung the door open.* **3.** [*no obj*] to come or be forced out suddenly: *Oil sprang from the well.* **4.** [~ + *obj*] to undergo the development of (something) rapidly: *The pipe sprung a leak.* **5.** to (cause to) happen suddenly: [~ + *obj*]: *He sprung a joke on us.* [*no obj*]: *An objection sprang to mind.* **6.** [*no obj;* (~ + *up*)] to come into being; arise: *This rude behavior springs from selfishness.* **7.** [~ + *obj*] *Slang.* to help obtain the release of (someone) from jail or prison: *Pay the fine and spring him.* **8. spring for,** [~ + *for* + *obj*] *Informal.* to pay for; treat someone to: *He sprang for dinner.* **—*n.*** **9.** [*count*] an act of springing; a sudden leap or bound. **10.** [*count*] the place where water comes up from the ground: *mineral springs.* **11.** [*count*] a source; fountainhead: *a spring of inspiration.* **12.** an elastic quality: [*count*]: *He had a spring in his walk now that he had recovered from his illness.* [*non-*

count]: *There's not much spring in her steps because of her arthritis.* **13.** [count] an object that returns to its shape after being pulled or pushed, such as a strip of steel made into a spiral coil. **14.** [count; usually: singular] the season between winter and summer, marked by the budding and growth of plants and the onset of warmer weather. **15.** [noncount] the first stage and freshest period: *the spring of life.* —**spring′i•ness,** *n.* [noncount] —**spring′y,** *adj.*, **-i•er, -i•est.**

spring•board (spring′bôrd′, -bōrd′) /ˈsprɪŋˌbɔrd, -ˌbowrd/ *n.* [count] **1.** a flexible board anchored at one end and used in diving and gymnastics for gaining height. **2.** a starting point; point of departure, as for a discussion: *We can use his statement as a springboard for our discussion.*

spring′ fe′ver, *n.* [noncount] a sleepy, lazy, or restless feeling associated with the beginning of spring.

spring′ tide′, *n.* [count] the large rise and fall of the tide at or soon after the new or the full moon.

spring•time (spring′tīm′) /ˈsprɪŋˌtaym/ *n.* [noncount] the season of spring.

sprin•kle (spring′kəl) /ˈsprɪŋkəl/ *v.*, **-kled, -kling,** *n.* —*v.* **1.** to scatter in drops or particles: [~ + obj]: *sprinkling water on the flowers.* [no obj; (~ + down)]: *The water sprinkled down on the flowers.* **2.** [~ + obj] to scatter drops or particles of water, powder, or the like on (something): *to sprinkle a lawn.* **3.** [no obj; it + ~] to rain slightly in scattered drops: *It's sprinkling a little.* **4.** [~ + obj] to scatter or distribute (something) in different places or at various times: *He sprinkled a few jokes into his speech.* —*n.* [count] **5.** an act or instance of sprinkling. **6.** a light rain. —**sprin′kler,** *n.* [count]: *An automatic sprinkler comes on when there's a fire.*

sprin•kling (spring′kling) /ˈsprɪŋklɪŋ/ *n.* [count] a small amount or number scattered here and there: *There was a sprinkling of women in the audience.*

sprint (sprint) /sprɪnt/ *v.* **1.** [no obj; (~ + ahead)] to race at full speed for a short distance, as in running: *At the last minute he sprinted (ahead) to win the race.* **2.** [~ + obj] to cover (a distance) in sprinting: *to sprint a half mile.* —*n.* [count] **3.** a short race at full speed. **4.** a burst of speed. —**sprint′er,** *n.* [count]

sprite (sprīt) /sprayt/ *n.* [count] an elf, fairy, or goblin.

spritz (sprits, shprits) /sprɪts, ʃprɪts/ *v.* [~ + obj] **1.** to spray briefly and quickly; squirt. —*n.* [count] **2.** a brief spray; squirt.

sprock•et (sprok′it) /ˈsprɒkɪt/ *n.* [count] **1.** a wheel having teeth on it that fit into holes on a conveyor belt or power chain. **2.** a tooth on such a wheel.

sprout (sprout) /sprawt/ *v.* [no obj] **1.** to begin to grow; shoot forth. **2.** (of a seed or plant) to put forth buds. —*n.* [count] **3.** a shoot of a plant. **4.** a new growth from a seed, rootstock, or the like. **5.** something suggesting a sprout, as a young person. **6. sprouts,** [plural] **a.** the young shoots of alfalfa, soybeans, etc., eaten, often raw, as a vegetable. **b.** BRUSSELS SPROUT.

spruce[1] (sprōōs) /spruws/ *n.* **1.** [count] a tree of the pine family, having short, angled, needle-shaped leaves. **2.** [count] a related tree, such as the Douglas fir. **3.** [noncount] the wood of any of these trees.

spruce[2] (sprōōs) /spruws/ *adj.*, **spruc•er, spruc•est,** *v.*, **spruced, spruc•ing.** —*adj.* **1.** trim or smart in appearance; neat; tidy. —*v.* **2.** to make (oneself or something else) trim or tidy: [~ + up + obj]: *Let me spruce up the apartment.* [~ + obj + up]: *Let's spruce the place up with some new flowers.* [~ + up]: *Let me just spruce up before your parents arrive.*

sprung (sprung) /sprʌŋ/ *v.* a pt. and pp. of SPRING.

spry (sprī) /spray/ *adj.*, **spry•er** or **spri•er, spry•est** or **spri•est.** quick in movement; smooth and energetic in motion: *pretty spry for a man of his age.* —**spry′ly,** *adv.* —**spry′ness,** *n.* [noncount]

spud (spud) /spʌd/ *n.* [count] *Informal.* a potato.

spume (spyōōm) /spyuwm/ *v.*, **spumed, spum•ing,** *n.* —*v.* [no obj] **1.** to foam; froth. —*n.* [noncount] **2.** foamy matter on a liquid; froth.

spu•mo•ni or **spu•mo•ne** (spə mō′nē) /spəˈmowniy/ *n.* [noncount] ice cream made with different flavors and colors, candied fruit, and nuts.

spun (spun) /spʌn/ *v.* pt. and pp. of SPIN.

spunk (spungk) /spʌŋk/ *n.* [noncount] courage; spirit; braveness: *to have the spunk to express an unpopular opinion.* —**spunk′y,** *adj.*, **-i•er, -i•est.**

spur (spûr) /spɜr/ *n.*, *v.*, **spurred, spur•ring.** —*n.* [count] **1.** a U-shaped device attached to the heel of a boot, having a pointed part that sticks out, used by a rider to urge a horse forward. **2.** something that forces one to action. **3.** a short track, road, or passage leading away from a main one, such as a siding for a train. —*v.* **4.** [~ + obj (+ on)] to prick with or as if with a spur to urge (a horse) to keep moving or to go faster: *The sheriff spurred his horse (on) and rode quickly after the bandit.* **5.** to incite (one) to take action: [~ + obj (+ on) + to + verb]: *The insult spurred him (on) to retaliate.* [~ + obj + on]: *Your encouragement spurred him on and he later achieved even greater results.* —***Idiom.*** **6. on the spur of the moment,** [noncount] suddenly; impulsively; without planning: *On the spur of the moment he jumped up and delivered a fiery speech.* **7. win one's spurs,** to achieve distinction or success for the first time. —**spurred,** *adj.*

spu•ri•ous (spyŏŏr′ē əs) /ˈspyʊriyəs/ *adj.* **1.** not genuine; counterfeit. **2.** (of arguments) poorly reasoned; faulty in reasoning: *a spurious argument.* —**spu′ri•ous•ly,** *adv.* —**spu′ri•ous•ness,** *n.* [noncount]

spurn (spûrn) /spɜrn/ *v.* [~ + obj] to reject (something) while showing obvious displeasure for it; scorn: *She spurned his offer of marriage.*

spurt (spûrt) /spɜrt/ *v.* **1.** [no obj] to gush out of something in a stream or jet: *Blood spurted from the wound.* **2.** [~ + obj] to discharge quickly and forcefully, as a stream of liquid: *The wound was spurting blood.* **3.** [no obj] to show a sudden brief increase in activity, speed, etc.: *The economy spurted in the first part of the year.* —*n.* [count] **4.** a sudden, forceful jet: *a spurt of blood.* **5.** a sudden increase of activity or effort for a short period or distance: *a spurt of economic activity.*

sput•ter (sput′ər) /ˈspʌtər/ *v.* **1.** [no obj] to make explosive popping or sizzling sounds: *When the water hose broke the car sputtered and stopped.* **2.** to say (words) explosively as when angry or unable to think clearly: [no obj]: *He walked out of the restaurant, sputtering angrily to himself about poor service.* [used with quotations]: *"But..but..this is crazy!" he sputtered.* —*n.* [count] **3.** the act or sound of sputtering.

spu•tum (spyōō′təm) /ˈspyuwtəm/ *n.* [noncount] matter, such as saliva mixed with mucus, coughed up from the lungs.

spy (spī) /spay/ *n.*, *pl.* **spies,** *v.*, **spied, spy•ing.** —*n.* [count] **1.** a person employed by a government to obtain secret information or intelligence about another country, usually an enemy: *Spies who are caught in time of war are shot.* **2.** one who keeps close and secret watch on another or others: *We had a spy in our business who told our rivals all our secret plans.* —*v.* **3.** [~ + on/upon + obj] to observe or watch secretively, usually with hostile intent: *He was spying on everyone.* **4.** [no obj] to act as a spy; perform espionage: *He spied for several years but made no reports until ordered to.* **5.** [~ + obj] to catch sight of: *to spy a rare bird.*

sq., an abbreviation of: **1.** sequence. **2.** square.

squab•ble (skwob′əl) /ˈskwɒbəl/ *v.*, **-bled, -bling,** *n.* —*v.* [~ + over + obj] **1.** to quarrel about a small detail: *The two sides were squabbling over the shape of the table at the peace negotiations.* —*n.* [count] **2.** a quarrel about a small detail.

squad (skwod) /skwɒd/ *n.* [count] **1.** the smallest military unit of soldiers, made up of 10 privates, a staff sergeant, and a corporal. **2.** a group of police officers assigned esp. to a certain field: *the vice squad.* **3.** any small group of persons engaged in a common activity; a team: *the cheerleading squad.*

squad′ car′, *n.* [count] a police automobile with a radiotelephone for communicating with police headquarters. Also called **cruise car, patrol car, police car, prowl car.**

squad•ron (skwod′rən) /ˈskwɒdrən/ *n.* [count] an army cavalry unit, a part of a naval fleet, or a group of war planes.

squal•id (skwol′id, skwô′lid) /ˈskwɒlɪd, ˈskwɔlɪd/ *adj.* **1.** filthy and disgusting; repulsive, as from neglect: *a squalid prison cell.* **2.** degraded in moral quality; sordid: *the squalid campaign practices.* —**squal′id•ness,** *n.* [noncount]

squall[1] (skwôl) /skwɔl/ *n.* [count] **1.** a sudden, violent wind, often accompanied by rain, snow, or sleet. —*v.* [no obj] **2.** (of wind) to blow as a squall.

squall[2] (skwôl) /skwɔl/ *v.* [no obj] **1.** to cry or scream loudly and violently: *The baby was squalling.* —*n.* [count] **2.** the act or sound of squalling.

squal•or (skwol′ər, skwô′lər) /ˈskwɒlər, ˈskwɔlər/ *n.* [noncount] the condition of being squalid; filth and misery: *Some of the refugees were forced to live in squalor.*

squan•der (skwon′dər) /ˈskwɒndər/ *v.* [~ + obj] to

spend or use wastefully or foolishly: *He had squandered the family fortune on gambling.*

square (skwâr) /skwɛər/ *n., v.,* **squared, squar•ing,** *adj.,* **squar•er, squar•est,** *adv.* —*n.* [*count*] **1.** a rectangle having all four sides of equal length. **2.** something having or resembling this form, such as a city block, an area on a game board or a piece of graph paper, etc. **3.** an open area formed at the place where two or more streets meet: *The concert was held in the village square.* **4.** an L-shaped tool, T square, or the like. **5. a.** the second power of a number, expressed as $a^2 = a \times a$, where *a* is the number. **b.** a number that is the second power of another: *Four is the square of two.* **6.** *Slang.* a person who is old-fashioned or conservative. —*v.* **7.** [~ + *obj*] to cut or reduce to square, rectangular, or cubical form: *to square an uneven piece of cut wood.* **8.** [~ + *obj*] to mark out in one or more squares or rectangles: *squared graph paper.* **9.** [~ + *obj*] to multiply (a quantity) by itself; raise to the second power. **10.** [~ + *obj*] to even the score of (a contest): *The teams squared the score in the second half.* **11.** [~ + *obj*] to set (the shoulders and back) in an erect posture: *The prisoner squared his shoulders and faced his questioner bravely.* **12.** [~ + *obj*] to make straight, level, or at right angles to something else: *Square the cloth on the table.* **13.** [~ + *obj* + *with* + *obj*] to adjust so as to fit, agree, or be satisfactory: *Can you square such dishonest actions with your conscience?* **14.** [~ + *with* + *obj*] to agree; match: *That theory does not square with the facts.* **15.** [~ + *obj*] to balance; pay off; settle: *to square a debt.* **16. square away,** [~ + *away* + *obj*] put (oneself or things) in order or in a state of readiness: *Everything is squared away for the party.* **17. square off,** [*no obj*] to hold oneself in a position showing readiness to fight: *The two teams square off tonight to decide the city championship.* **18. square up,** [*no obj*] to settle an account: *I'll pay the bill now, we can square up later.* —*adj.* **19.** forming a right angle: *a square corner.* **20.** having four sides and four right angles or three pairs of parallel sides meeting at right angles: *a square box.* **21.** [*after a number; before a noun*] having the form of a square and being described by a unit of measurement forming a side of the square: *one square foot.* **22.** [*after a noun*] equal to a square of a specified length on a side: *They searched an area that was five miles square.* **23.** having a solid, sturdy form: *He looked tough, square, and ready to handle trouble.* **24.** straight, level, or even, such as a surface. **25.** [*be* + ~] having all accounts settled. **26.** fair; honest; straightforward: *We got a square deal on the car.* **27.** *Slang.* old-fashioned or conservative: *She thinks her parents are so square.* —*adv.* **28.** in square or rectangular form. **29.** at right angles: *The carpenter lined up the door frame square with the floor and walls.* **30.** straightforwardly; fairly; honestly: *He treated us fair and square.* **31.** with nothing in the way or blocking; directly: *ran square into the fence.* **32.** in a steadfast manner; firmly: *She looked him square in the eye.* —**square′ly,** *adv.* —**square′-ness,** *n.* [*noncount*]

square′-rigged′, *adj.* having square sails as the principal sails.

square′ root′, *n.* [*count*] a number of which a given number is the square: *The quantities* $+6$ *and* -6 *are square roots of 36 since* $(+6)\times(+6)=36$ *and* $(-6)\times(-6)=36$.

squash[1] (skwosh, skwôsh) /skwɒʃ, skwɔʃ/ *v.* **1.** [~ + *obj*] to press into a flat mass; crush: *She squashed the spider with her shoe.* **2.** to press with force into a small space; cram: [~ + *obj*]: *squashed six of us into the tiny car.* [*no obj*]: *A huge man squashed next to me on the bus.* **3.** [~ + *obj*] to silence or smother; suppress; quash: *to squash the indictment.* —*n.* **4.** [*count*] an act or instance of squashing or being squashed; the sound of this. **5.** [*count*] something squashed. **6.** Also called **squash′ rac′quets.** a game for two or four persons, similar to racquets. **7.** [*noncount*] Also called **squash′ ten′nis.** a game for two persons, resembling squash racquets except that the ball is larger and the racket is shaped like a tennis racket. **8.** [*noncount*] *Brit.* a beverage made from fruit juice and soda water: *lemon squash.* —**squash′y,** *adj.,* **-i•er, -i•est.**

squash[2] (skwosh, skwôsh) /skwɒʃ, skwɔʃ/ *n., pl.* **squash•es,** (*esp. when thought of as a group*) **squash. 1.** the fruit of a plant of the gourd family, eaten as a vegetable: [*count*]: *Buy two squashes at the store.* [*noncount*]: *some cooked squash.* **2.** [*count*] a plant having such fruit.

squat (skwot) /skwɒt/ *v.,* **squat•ted, squat•ting,** *adj.,* **squat•ter, squat•test,** *n.* —*v.* [*no obj*] **1.** to sit in a crouching position with the legs drawn up closely beneath or in front of the body: *I squatted behind the table where she wouldn't see me.* **2.** to occupy property or settle land without permission, such as a squatter: *The migrant workers squatted on the unused farm.* —*adj.* **3.** very short and thickset: *a heavy, squat man.* **4.** [*before a noun*] in a squatting position; crouching: *the squat lions.* —*n.* [*count*] **5.** the act, position, or posture of squatting. —**squat′ness,** *n.* [*noncount*]

squat•ter (skwot′ər) /ˈskwɒtər/ *n.* [*count*] **1.** a person or thing that squats. **2.** one who settles on land or lives on or in property without owning it and without payment of rent. **3.** one who settles on land under government regulation in order to get ownership rights some day.

squaw (skwô), *n.* [*count*] **1.** *Often Offensive.* an American Indian woman, esp. a wife. **2.** *Slang* (*disparaging and offensive*). **a.** a wife. **b.** any woman or girl.

squawk (skwôk) /skwɔk/ *v.* **1.** to utter (a loud, harsh cry), such as a duck when frightened: [*no obj*]: *The ducks squawked as they flew overhead.* [~ + *obj*]: *The duck squawked a warning.* [*used with quotations*]: *"Red alert! Red alert!" the intercom squawked.* **2.** to express (a complaint, etc.) loudly and strongly: [*no obj*]: *Quit squawking about your grade!* [~ + *obj*]: *They squawked their disapproval.* —*n.* [*count*] **3.** a loud, harsh cry or sound. **4.** a loud, strong complaint.

squeak (skwēk) /skwiyk/ *n.* [*count*] **1.** a sharp, shrill cry or sound: *Her voice rose to a squeak as she protested.* **2.** an escape from danger, defeat, etc.: *a close squeak with death.* —*v.* **3.** to make or express (a squeak): [*no obj*]: *The door squeaks every time you open it.* [*used with quotations*]: *"I'm afraid," he squeaked, "What do we do next?"* **4. squeak by** or **through,** [*no obj*] to succeed, survive, etc., by a very narrow margin: *We managed to squeak by even though our budget had been cut.*

squeak•y (skwē′kē) /ˈskwiykiy/ *adj.,* **-i•er, -i•est.** making a sound like a squeak: *a squeaky door.*

squeal (skwēl) /skwiyl/ *n.* [*count*] **1.** a somewhat long, sharp cry, as of pain, fear, pleasure, or surprise: *a squeal of pain.* —*v.* **2.** to say or express (a squeal): [*no obj*]: *The teenagers squealed with delight.* [*used with quotations*]: *"We're so thrilled!" they all squealed.* **3.** [*no obj*] *Slang.* to give information to authorities, as the police, about one's fellow criminals; inform: *One of the thieves squealed to the police, who then captured the rest of the gang.* —**squeal′er,** *n.* [*count*]

squeam•ish (skwē′mish) /ˈskwiymɪʃ/ *adj.* **1.** easily made sick to the stomach: *too squeamish to attend horror movies.* **2.** easily shocked by evil, dishonesty, treachery, etc. —**squeam′ish•ness,** *n.* [*noncount*]

squee•gee (skwē′jē, skwē jē′) /ˈskwiydʒiy, skwiyˈdʒiy/ *n., pl.* **-gees,** *v.,* **-geed, -gee•ing.** —*n.* [*count*] **1.** a tool made of a handle and a blade edged with rubber, for removing water from windows after washing, sweeping water from wet decks, etc. —*v.* [~ + *obj*] **2.** to sweep, scrape, or press with or as if with a squeegee.

squeeze (skwēz) /skwiyz/ *v.,* **squeezed, squeez•ing,** *n.* —*v.* **1.** [~ + *obj*] to press together with force; compress: *The crowd almost squeezed me flat!* **2.** [~ + *obj*] to apply pressure to (something) in order to force out juice, sap, or the like: *He squeezed the toothpaste tube to get the last bit out; to squeeze juice out of an orange.* **3.** to fit into a small or crowded space or time span: [~ + *obj*]: *I squeezed the car carefully into the tiny parking space.* [*no obj*]: *I squeezed into the crowded bus.* **4.** [~ + *obj*] to press (another's hand or arm) within one's hand as a friendly or sympathetic gesture: *She squeezed his arm and he smiled back at her.* **5.** [~ + *obj*] to obtain or get (something) from (someone) by some pressure, force, etc., as by threatening harm; extort: *They squeezed the truth out of him.* **6.** [~ + *obj*] to cause financial hardship to: *Car manufacturers are being squeezed by high tariffs.* **7.** [*no obj*] to merge or come together: *The road squeezes to the left up ahead.* —*n.* [*count*] **8.** an act or instance of squeezing: *a tight squeeze on the elevator.* **9.** the fact or state of being squeezed or crowded. **10.** a handclasp: *She gave my hand a squeeze.* **11.** [*usually singular*] a troubled financial condition, esp. caused by a shortage, as of credit or funds. **12.** [*usually singular; usually: the* + ~] intimidation to extort money or advantages: *The racketeers were putting the squeeze on small businesses.* **13.** *Slang.* a sweetheart: *She's my main squeeze (= She's my most important girlfriend).* —**squeez′a•ble,** *adj.*

squeeze′ bot′tle, *n.* [*count*] a plastic bottle that can be squeezed to force out its contents: *The bikers drink from their squeeze bottles while riding.*

squelch (skwelch) /skweltʃ/ *v.* **1.** [~ + *obj*] to suppress or silence, as with force or a crushing response: *The dictator squelched all opposition.* **2.** [*no obj*] to make a splashing sound, as by walking heavily in mud: *We could hear his boots squelching in the mud.* **—*n.*** [*count*] **3.** an act of squelching. **4.** a squelching sound.

squid (skwid) /skwɪd/ *n.* [*count*], *pl.* (*esp. when thought of as a group*) **squid,** (*esp. for kinds or species*) **squids.** a ten-armed sea creature, having a slender body and a pair of rounded or triangular tail fins.

squig•gle (skwig′əl) /'skwɪgəl/ *n., v.,* **-gled, -gling.** **—*n.*** [*count*] **1.** a short, irregular curve or twist, as in drawing. **—*v.*** **2.** [*no obj*] to move in or appear as squiggles. **3.** [~ + *obj*] to form in or cause to appear as squiggles; scribble. —**squig′gly,** *adj.,* **-gli•er, -gli•est.**

squint (skwint) /skwɪnt/ *v.* [*no obj*] **1.** to look with the eyes partly closed: *squinted through the microscope.* **2.** [*not: be + ~-ing*] to be affected with a condition in which the eyes are crossed and look in two different directions. **—*n.*** **3.** [*count*] an act or instance of squinting. **4.** [*noncount*] a condition of the eye in which the eyes are crossed.

squire (skwīᵊr) /skwayᵊr/ *n., v.,* **squired, squir•ing.** **—*n.*** [*count*] **1.** (in England) a country gentleman. **2.** a young man of noble birth who served a knight. **—*v.*** [~ + *obj*] **3.** to escort as, or as if, a squire: *He squired a beautiful woman to the ball.*

squirm (skwûrm) /skwɜrm/ *v.* [*no obj*] **1.** to twist the body, as when feeling discomfort, distress, etc.: *He squirmed in his seat during the lecture.* **—*n.*** [*count*] **2.** the act of squirming; a squirming movement. —**squirm′y,** *adj.,* **-i•er, -i•est.**

squir•rel (skwûr′əl, skwur′-) /'skwɜrəl, 'skwʌr-/ *n.* [*count*], *pl.* **-rels,** (*esp. when thought of as a group*) **-rel,** *v.,* **-reled, -rel•ing** or (*esp. Brit.*) **-relled, -rel•ling.** **—*n.*** [*count*] **1.** a small, bushy-tailed rodent that lives in trees and eats nuts. **—*v.*** **2.** to store or hide (money, etc.) for the future, such as squirrels store food for winter: [~ + *obj* + *away*]: *managed to squirrel enough money away to send her to college.* [~ + *away* + *obj*]: *to squirrel away enough money to send her to college.*

squirt (skwûrt) /skwɜrt/ *v.* **1.** to send out (liquid) in a quick, sudden jet or spurt: [*no obj*]: *The lemon squirted in my eye.* [~ + *obj*]: *The hose squirted water.* **2.** [~ + *obj*] to send out liquid on or at (someone or something) in a quick, sudden jet or spurt: *She squirted me with water from the garden hose.* **—*n.*** [*count*] **3.** the act of squirting. **4.** a small spurt of liquid. **5.** a small quantity of liquid that has been squirted: *a squirt of chocolate sauce on her ice cream.* **6.** *Informal.* a youngster, esp. a bothersome one. **7.** an instrument for squirting, such as a syringe.

squish (skwish) /skwɪʃ/ *v.* **1.** [~ + *obj*] to squeeze or squash: *The child squished the bug in her hands.* **2.** [*no obj*] (of water, soft mud, etc.) to make a gushing or splashing sound, as when one walks in water, etc.: *Her shoes squished in the puddles.* **—*n.*** [*count*] **3.** a squishing sound.

Sr., an abbreviation of: **1.** Senior. **2.** Señor. **3.** Sir. **4.** Sister.

Sri Lan•kan (srē′ läng′kən, lang′kən, shrē′) /ˌsriy 'lɑŋkən, 'læŋkən, ˌʃriy/ *adj.* **1.** of or relating to Sri Lanka. **—*n.*** [*count*] **2.** a person born or living in Sri Lanka.

SRO, an abbreviation of: **1.** single-room occupancy. **2.** standing room only.

SS, an abbreviation of: **1.** social security. **2.** steamship. **3.** supersonic.

S.S., an abbreviation of: steamship.

SSE, an abbreviation of: south-southeast.

SST, an abbreviation of: supersonic transport.

SSW, an abbreviation of: south-southwest.

St., an abbreviation of: **1.** Saint. **2.** Strait. **3.** Street.

Sta., an abbreviation of: Station.

stab (stab) /stæb/ *v.,* **stabbed, stab•bing,** *n.* **—*v.*** **1.** [~ + *obj*] to pierce with or as if with a pointed weapon: *Romeo stabbed Tybalt and killed him.* **2.** [~ + *obj*] to thrust or plunge (a knife, etc.) into something: *He stabbed the knife straight into the victim's chest.* **3.** to make a jabbing motion on, at, or in (someone or something): [~ + *at* + *obj*]: *Romeo stabbed at Mercutio with the knife.* [~ + *obj*]: *He stabbed the buttons and launched the rocket.* **—*n.*** [*count*] **4.** the act of stabbing. **5.** a thrust made with or as if with a pointed weapon. **6.** an attempt; try: *to make a stab at an answer.* **7.** a sudden, brief, painful sensation: *a stab of pity.* **—*Idiom.*** **8. stab in the back, a.** [~ + *obj* + *in the back*] to betray (someone trusting): *She stabbed him in the back by telling everyone about his private fears.* **b.** [*count*] an act of betrayal: *Telling him all my secrets was a vicious stab in the back.*

-stab-, *root.* -*stab*- comes from Latin, where it has the meaning "stand." This meaning is found in such words as: ESTABLISH, INSTABILITY, STABILIZE, STABLE, UNSTABLE.

stab•bing (stab′ing) /'stæbɪŋ/ *adj.* **1.** penetrating; piercing; sharp: *a stabbing pain.* **2.** incisive or trenchant: *stabbing satire.* **—*n.*** [*count*] **3.** an act of using a knife or other sharp instrument to strike another: *another stabbing on the subways.*

sta•bil•i•ty (stə bil′i tē) /stə'bɪlɪtiy/ *n.* [*noncount*] the state, quality, or condition of being stable: *He was arrested for "threatening the stability of the country."* See -STAB-.

sta•bi•lize (stā′bə līz′) /'steybəˌlayz/ *v.,* **-lized, -liz•ing.** **1.** to make or hold stable: [~ + *obj*]: *This device on the boat should stabilize it.* [*no obj*]: *The boat stabilized as it picked up speed.* **2.** to keep or remain at a given level or amount: [~ + *obj*]: *to stabilize rents.* [*no obj*]: *Interest rates have finally stabilized at a low 2.5%.* —**sta•bi•li•za•tion** (stā′bə lə zā′shən) /ˌsteybələ'zeyʃən/ *n.* [*noncount*] See -STAB-.

sta•bi•liz•er (stā′bə lī′zər) /'steybəˌlayzər/ *n.* [*count*] a device that stabilizes. See -STAB-.

sta•ble[1] (stā′bəl) /'steybəl/ *n., v.,* **-bled, -bling.** **—*n.*** [*count*] **1.** a building with stalls where horses, cattle, etc., are kept and fed. **2.** a collection of animals housed in such a building. **3.** a number of people, such as athletes or performers, who work for, or are represented by, the same company, agency, etc.: *the movie agent's stable of movie stars.* **—*v.*** [~ + *obj*] **4.** to put or keep in or as if in a stable.

sta•ble[2] (stā′bəl) /'steybəl/ *adj.,* **-bler, -blest.** **1.** not likely to fall, collapse, or overturn; firm; steady: *The building has a stable foundation.* **2.** able or likely to continue or last; firmly established: *a stable government.* **3.** not likely to change quickly: *a stable currency.* **4.** not changing in character or purpose: *He's a quiet, stable employee.* **5.** not subject to emotional instability or illness; sane. **6.** not readily decaying or changing: *a stable chemical.* **7.** (of a patient's condition) exhibiting no significant change: *The gunshot victim is in stable condition.* See -STAB-.

stac•ca•to (stə kä′tō) /stə'kɑtow/ *adj., adv., n., pl.* **-tos, -ti** (-tē) /-tiy/. **—*adj.*** **1.** shortened and separated one from another when played or sung: *staccato notes.* **2.** made up of, or having, suddenly unconnected parts; disjointed: *spoke in a rapid-fire, staccato voice.* **—*adv.*** **3.** in a staccato manner. **—*n.*** [*count*] **4.** something done or performed in a staccato manner.

stack (stak) /stæk/ *n.* [*count*] **1.** an organized, neat pile or heap: *Take the top card from the stack and turn it over.* **2.** a large pile of hay, straw, or the like. **3. stacks,** [*plural*] a set of shelves for books in a library. **4.** a smokestack. **5.** a great quantity or number: [~ + *noncount noun*]: *a stack of mail.* [~ + *plural noun*]: *We got a stack of letters yesterday.* **6.** a list, as in a computer, arranged so that the last item stored is the first item retrieved. **—*v.*** **7.** to pile, arrange, or place in a stack: [~ + *obj*]: *She stacked the suitcases on the roof rack.* [~ + *up* + *obj*]: *He stacked up the books against the wall.* [~ + *obj* + *up*]: *He stacked them up against the wall.* **8.** [*no obj*] to form a stack: *Those logs won't stack; they keep tumbling down.* **9.** [~ + *obj; usually: be + ~-ed*] to cover with something in stacks: *The office space was stacked high with old dusty files.* **10.** [~ + *obj*] to arrange or select unfairly in order to force a desired result: *to stack a jury against a defendant.* **11. stack up,** [~ + *up* + *against* + *obj*] to compare, esp. favorably; measure up: *How do these new minivans stack up against the older ones?* **—*Idiom.*** **12. stack the deck, a.** to arrange cards or a pack of cards so as to cheat. **b.** to manage or arrange events, etc., esp. unfairly, to achieve a desired result: *The deck was stacked against him before he even walked in for the interview.*

sta•di•um (stā′dē əm) /'steydiyəm/ *n.* [*count*], *pl.* **-di•ums, -di•a** (-dē ə) /-diyə/. **1.** a sports arena with rising rows of seats for viewers. **2.** (in ancient Greece and Rome) a track for foot races.

staff (staf) /stæf/ *n., pl.* **staffs** for 1, 4; **staves** (stāvz) or **staffs** for 2, 3, 5; *adj., v.* **—*n.*** **1.** a group of people, esp. workers, who carry out the work of an establishment, such as a group of assistants to a manager, superintendent, etc.: [*count*]: *He has a fine staff working under him.* [*noncount*]: *I am complaining about one of your staff.* **2.** [*count*] a stick, pole, or rod for aid in walking or climbing, for use as a weapon, etc. **3.** [*count*] a pole on which a flag is hung or displayed. **4.** [*count; usually singular*] something that supports or sustains: *Bread is the staff of life.* **5.** [*count*] a set of usually five lines, with the corresponding four spaces between them, on which music is written. **—*adj.*** [*before a noun*] **6.** of or relating or belonging to an organizational staff: *staff officers.* **7.** working on the staff of a corporation, institution, etc.: *a staff writer.* **—*v.*** [~ + *obj*] **8.** to provide with a staff of assistants or workers: *The company is staffed with the finest engineers in this country.*

staff•er (staf′ər) /ˈstæfər/ *n.* [*count*] a member of a staff of employees, as at a newspaper.

stag (stag) /stæg/ *n.* [*count*] **1.** an adult male deer. **2.** the male of various other animals. **3.** Also, **stag party.** a party for men only, given for a bachelor before his marriage. **—*adj.*** [*before a noun*] **4.** of or for men only: *a stag dinner.* **5.** intended for male audiences and usually pornographic in content: *a stag show.* **—*adv.*** **6.** without a female companion: *to go stag to a party.*

stage (stāj) /steydʒ/ *n., v.,* **staged, stag•ing.** **—*n.*** [*count*] **1.** a step or degree in a process, development, or series: *in the early stages of his career.* **2.** a raised platform or floor, as for speakers. **3.** the platform on which the actors perform in a theater. **4. the stage,** [*usually singular*] the acting profession: *All his life he wanted to be part of the stage.* See *on stage* below. **5.** a stagecoach. **—*v.*** [~ + *obj*] **6.** to represent, produce, or exhibit on or as if on a stage: *to stage a play.* **7.** to plan, organize, or carry out, esp. for effect: *Workers staged a one-day strike.* **—*Idiom.*** **8. by easy stages,** gradually; without hurry. **9. on stage,** [*noncount*] **a.** performing, esp. as an actor: *He was on stage for every show.* **b.** in the area of the stage seen by the audience: *The main figure in the play never appears on stage.*

stage•coach (stāj′kōch′) /ˈsteydʒˌkowtʃ/ *n.* [*count*] a horse-drawn coach that formerly traveled regularly over a certain route with passengers, parcels, etc.

stage′ fright′, *n.* [*noncount*] nervousness felt by a performer or speaker in front of an audience.

stage•hand (stāj′hand′) /ˈsteydʒˌhænd/ *n.* [*count*] one who moves objects, settings, etc., or who regulates lighting, etc., in a stage play or production.

stag•fla•tion (stag flā′shən) /stægˈfleyʃən/ *n.* [*noncount*] a period when there is economic inflation, rising unemployment, and no increase in business activity.

stag•ger (stag′ər) /ˈstægər/ *v.* **1.** to (cause to) walk, move, or stand unsteadily: [*no obj*]: *He staggered from the force of the blow.* [~ + *obj*]: *The next punch staggered him.* **2.** [~ + *obj*] to astonish or shock: *a fact that staggers the mind.* **3.** [~ + *obj*] to arrange in a pattern so as not to be in the same place at the same time: *to stagger our lunch hours.* **—*n.*** [*count*] **4.** the act of staggering; an unsteady, reeling movement: *lurching with a clumsy stagger.* **5.** a staggered order or arrangement.

stag•gered (stag′ərd) /ˈstægərd/ *adj.* **1.** amazed; shocked; astonished: *a staggered look on her face.* **2.** arranged so as not to be in the same place at the same time: *staggered lunch hours.*

stag•ger•ing (stag′ə ring) /ˈstægərɪŋ/ *adj.* causing shock, disbelief, or astonishment: *staggering rates of inflation.*

stag•nant (stag′nənt) /ˈstægnənt/ *adj.* of or relating to stagnation: *a stagnant pool of water; a stagnant economy.*

stag•nate (stag′nāt) /ˈstægneyt/ *v.* [*no obj*], **-nat•ed, -nat•ing. 1.** to cease to run or flow, as water or air. **2.** to become bad-smelling from standing, as a pool of water. **3.** to stop progressing: *was just stagnating in his job.* **—stag•na•tion** (stag nā′shən) /stægˈneyʃən/ *n.* [*noncount*]

staid (stād) /steyd/ *adj.* too solemn, serious, dull, or settled in one's ways. **—staid′ly,** *adv.*

stain (stān) /steyn/ *n.* **1.** [*count*] a mark caused by foreign matter on a material: *a bright blue stain on his shirt.* **2.** [*count*] a cause of disgrace or dishonor. **3.** a dye made into a solution for coloring woods, textiles, etc.: [*noncount*]: *Try using stain on the rocking chair.* [*count*]: *several wood stains to choose from: red, dark brown, or light brown.* **—*v.*** **4.** to (cause to) become discolored, as by having spots: [~ + *obj*]: *The blood stained his shirt.* [*no obj*]: *The white rug will stain too easily.* **5.** [~ + *obj*] to color or dye (wood, cloth, etc.): *I stained the old rocking chair and made it look like new.* **6.** [~ + *obj*] to bring disgrace or dishonor upon: *Although the charges were never proven, his reputation was stained forever.* **—stain′less,** *adj.*

stain′less steel′, *n.* [*noncount*] a steel containing 12 percent chromium, so as to resist rust.

stair (stâr) /steər/ *n.* [*count*] **1.** one of a flight or series of steps for going from one level to another. **2. stairs,** [*plural*] such steps thought of as a group, esp. as forming a flight or a series of flights.

stair•case (stâr′kās′) /ˈsteərˌkeys/ *n.* [*count*] a flight of stairs with its frame, banisters, etc., or a series of such flights.

stair•way (stâr′wā′) /ˈsteərˌwey/ *n.* [*count*] a passageway from one level to another by a series of stairs; staircase. See illustration at HOTEL.

stair•well or **stair well** (stâr′wel′) /ˈsteərˌwel/ *n.* [*count*] the vertical shaft or opening containing a stairway.

stake[1] (stāk) /steyk/ *n., v.,* **staked, stak•ing.** **—*n.*** [*count*] **1.** a stick pointed at one end for driving into the ground as a boundary mark, part of a fence, etc. **2.** a post to which a person is tied for execution, usually by burning. **3. the stake,** [*usually singular*] the punishment of death by burning. **—*v.*** **4.** [~ (+ *out/off*) + *obj*] to mark (land) with or as if with stakes: *Stake (out) the area you'll need for the tomatoes.* **5.** [~ (+ *out/off*) + *obj*] to claim or reserve a share of (land, profit, etc.) as if by marking with stakes: *The settlers staked (out) the land from here to the river.* **6.** [~ + *obj*] to support with a stake or stakes, such as a plant. **7. pull up stakes,** [*no obj*] to leave one's job, place of residence, etc.; move. **8. stake out,** (of the police) to keep (a place) under watch: [~ + *out* + *obj*]: *The police staked out the bank.* [~ + *obj* + *out*]: *to stake it out for a week.*

stake[2] (stāk) /steyk/ *n., v.,* **staked, stak•ing.** **—*n.*** [*count*] **1.** something, usually money, bet in a game. **2.** an investment in business, with the hope of financial gain: *a big stake in the company.* **3.** a personal interest or involvement: *Parents have a big stake in the decisions made by their children's teachers.* **4.** Often, **stakes.** [*plural*] a prize, reward, etc., in or as if in a contest: *The stakes are high in the lottery this week.* **—*v.*** **5.** [~ + *obj* + *on* + *obj*] to risk (something) upon the outcome of an uncertain event, business venture, etc.: *He staked a lot of money on the deal.* **6.** [~ + *obj* + *to* + *obj*] to provide (someone) resources, esp. money: *They staked him to a good meal and sent him on his way.* **—*Idiom.*** **7. at stake,** [*noncount*] in danger of being lost; at risk: *There's a great deal at stake in the upcoming election.*

stake•out (stāk′out′) /ˈsteykˌawt/ *n.* [*count*] **1.** the act by police of watching a suspect or a location, to capture a wanted person or witness a crime being committed. **2.** the place from which such watching is carried out.

sta•lac•tite (stə lak′tīt, stal′ək tīt′) /stəˈlæktayt, ˈstæləkˌtayt/ *n.* [*count*] a deposit, usually of calcium carbonate, shaped like an icicle, hanging from the roof of a cave or the like, and formed by the dripping of water.

sta•lag•mite (stə lag′mīt, stal′əg mīt′) /stəˈlægmayt, ˈstæləgˌmayt/ *n.* [*count*] a deposit, usually of calcium carbonate, resembling an upside-down stalactite, formed on the floor of a cave or the like by the dripping of water.

stale (stāl) /steyl/ *adj.,* **stal•er, stal•est. 1.** not fresh; dry or hardened, such as bread. **2.** musty; stagnant: *a stale room.* **3.** overly familiar; hackneyed; trite: *a stale joke.* **4.** having lost or no longer having or showing interest: *He felt stale and and unable to get excited about work.* **—stale′ness,** *n.* [*noncount*]

stale•mate (stāl′māt′) /ˈsteylˌmeyt/ *n., v.,* **-mat•ed, -mat•ing.** **—*n.*** [*count*] **1.** a situation in which no action can be taken or progress made; deadlock: *The battle had been fought to a stalemate.* **—*v.*** **2.** to (cause to) reach a stalemate: [*no obj*]: *Talks on the new contract had stalemated.* [~ + *obj*]: *The union negotiators tried to stalemate the negotiations.*

stalk[1] (stôk) /stɔk/ *n.* [*count*] **1.** the stem of a plant. **2.** a shaft or slender supporting part of anything.

stalk[2] (stôk) /stɔk/ *v.* **1.** [~ + *obj*] **a.** to pursue for the purpose of capturing, without being seen or noticed: *hunters stalking a deer.* **b.** to follow (a person) continually, usually to gain attention: *celebrities being stalked by unstable fans.* **2.** [~ + *obj*] to roam through (an area) without being easily noticed: *Killers stalked the park at night.* **3.** [*no obj*] to walk with stiff or proud strides: *stalked angrily out of the room.*

stall[1] (stôl) /stɔl/ *n.* [*count*] **1.** a compartment, as in a stable, to confine an animal: *the stalls for individual cows.* **2.** a booth in which merchandise is displayed for sale. **3.** a small enclosed space for a specific activity or thing: *a shower stall.* **4.** a marked space for parking a car, as in a parking lot. **5.** a condition in which an engine suddenly stops functioning. **—***v.* **6.** [*no obj; (~ + out)*] (of a motor or a vehicle) to stop or come to a standstill: *The car started but then immediately stalled.* **7.** [*~ + obj*] to cause (a car or motor) to stop functioning suddenly, as by overloading: *kept stalling the car when I put it in gear.*

stall[2] (stôl) /stɔl/ *v.* **1.** to delay, esp. by avoiding a direct answer or action: [*~ + obj*]: *deliberately tried to stall the talks so that we wouldn't get a raise.* [*no obj*]: *You're stalling; just give us an answer.* **2.** [*no obj*] to be delayed, impeded, or interrupted: *Once again contract talks have stalled.*

stal•lion (stal′yən) /ˈstælyən/ *n.* [*count*] an uncastrated adult male horse, esp. one used for breeding.

stal•wart (stôl′wərt) /ˈstɔlwərt/ *adj.* **1.** strong and sturdy. **2.** brave; valiant. **3.** firm; steadfast: *a stalwart believer in Marxism.* **—***n.* [*count*] **4.** a physically stalwart person. **5.** one who steadily and firmly believes in a cause: *party stalwarts.*

sta•men (stā′mən) /ˈsteymən/ *n.* [*count*], *pl.* **sta•mens, stam•i•na** (stam′ə nə) /ˈstæmənə/. the pollen-bearing organ of a flower, made of the filament and the anther.

stam•i•na (stam′ə nə) /ˈstæmənə/ *n.* [*noncount*] strength to go on in spite of fatigue, stress, etc.; endurance: *He built up his stamina by running every day.*

stam•mer (stam′ər) /ˈstæmər/ *v.* **1.** to speak with uncontrollable breaks and pauses or repetitions of syllables or sounds: [*no obj*]: *He stammered and got more nervous when the police asked him what he was doing.* [*~ (+ out) + obj*]: *He stammered (out) some lame excuse about being at the movies.* [*used with quotations*]: *"I..uh, I..don't remember," he stammered.* **—***n.* [*count*] **2.** a stammering way of speaking. **3.** a stammered word, phrase, or sentence. **—stam′mer•er,** *n.* [*count*] **—stam′mer•ing•ly,** *adv.*

stamp (stamp) /stæmp/ *v.* **1.** to strike with a forceful, strong, downward movement or push of the foot: [*~ + obj*]: *She stamped my foot.* [*no obj*]: *She stamped down hard on my foot.* **2.** [*~ + obj*] to bring (the foot) down forcibly on the ground, floor, etc.: *stamping their feet to keep warm in the icy winter night.* **3.** [*no obj*] to walk quickly with heavy, forceful steps: *stamping around the apartment above us.* **4. stamp out,** to crush or extinguish by, or as if by, a stamp: [*~ + out + obj*]: *He raced into the room and quickly stamped out the small fire that had started.* [*~ + obj + out*]: *to stamp it out before it spreads.* **5.** [*~ + obj*] to put a mark, symbol, the date, etc., on (something) to indicate that it is genuine, that it has approval or permission, or the like: *The immigration officials stamped my passport.* **6.** [*~ + obj*] to put (a mark, symbol, etc.) on something, so as to indicate genuineness, permission, etc.: *The immigration officials stamped the date on my passport.* **7.** [*~ + obj*] to attach or stick a postage stamp to (a letter, etc.): *Stamp the letter before you put it in the mailbox.* **—***n.* [*count*] **8.** Also, **postage stamp.** a small gummed rectangular label for sticking on a piece of mail, such as an envelope, as evidence that postage has been paid. **9.** a small block of wood or metal with a design on it that can be pressed onto paper or the like. **10.** a mark or seal printed by such a block: *His passport had entrance and exit stamps from many countries.* **11.** something that shows a strong influence or impression: *The president had left his stamp on the country.* **12.** an act or instance of stamping: *He gave an impatient stamp of his foot.* **13.** FOOD STAMP. **14.** an instrument for stamping, crushing, or pounding. **—stamp′er,** *n.* [*count*]

stam•pede (stam pēd′) /stæmˈpiyd/ *n., v.,* **-ped•ed, -ped•ing.** **—***n.* [*count*] **1.** a sudden, uncontrolled rush of a herd of frightened animals, esp. cattle or horses. **2.** any uncontrolled rush for or to something: *The fuel shortage caused a stampede to the gas stations.* **—***v.* **3.** to (cause to) scatter or flee in a stampede: [*no obj*]: *The horses stampeded when the tornado struck.* [*~ + obj*]: *The tornado stampeded the horses.* **4.** [*no obj*] to make a general, uncontrolled rush: *The guests stampeded out of the burning hotel.* **5.** [*~ + obj*] to rush into or overrun (a place): *Frantic fans stampeded the box office.* **6.** [*~ + obj*] to urge (someone) into doing something in a hurry: *They were stampeded into buying all that life insurance.*

stamp′ing ground′, *n.* [*count*] a habitual or favorite haunt.

-stan-, *root.* *-stan-* comes from Latin, where it has the meaning "stand; remain." This meaning is found in such words as: CIRCUMSTANCE, CONSTANT, DISTANCE, DISTANT, HAPPENSTANCE, INCONSTANCY, INCONSTANT, INSUBSTANTIAL, STANCE, STANCH, STANCHION, STANZA, SUBSTANCE, SUBSTANTIAL, SUBSTANTIVE, TRANSUBSTANTIATION.

stance (stans) /stæns/ *n.* [*count*] **1.** the bearing of the body while standing, esp. in sports: *He assumed a karate stance.* **2.** a mental or emotional position or opinion taken with respect to something: *the governor's stance on the issue of aid to higher education.* See -STAN-.

stanch[1] (stônch, stanch, stänch) /stɔntʃ, stæntʃ, stɑntʃ/ also **staunch** (stônch) /stɔntʃ/ *v.* [*~ + obj*] **1.** to stop the flow of (a liquid, esp. blood): *to apply pressure to stanch the blood from the wound.* **2.** to stop the flow of blood or other liquid from (a wound, etc.): *to apply pressure to stanch the wound.* **3.** to check or reduce the speed of (an outflow): *stanching the dollar drain.* See -STAN-.

stanch[2] (stônch, stänch, stanch) /stɔntʃ, stɑntʃ, stæntʃ/ *adj.,* **-er, -est.** STAUNCH[2].

stan•chion (stan′shən) /ˈstænʃən/ *n.* [*count*] a vertical bar or support, as in a window or stall. See -STAN-.

stand (stand) /stænd/ *v.,* **stood** (sto͝od) /stʊd/ **stand•ing,** *n.* **—***v.* **1.** [*no obj*] to be in an upright position on the feet: *standing by the door when I came in.* **2.** to (cause someone to) rise to one's feet: [*no obj; ~ (+ up)*]: *We stood (up) when the president entered the room.* [*~ + obj + up*]: *stood the toddler back up after she fell.* **3.** [*not: be + -ing; ~ + a noun showing measurement*] to have a certain height when in this position: *He stands six feet tall.* **4.** [*no obj*] to remain the same, esp. unused: *The bicycle has stood in the garage all winter.* **5.** [*no obj*] to take a position as indicated: *to stand aside.* **6.** (of things) to (cause to) rest in an upright position: [*no obj*]: *The broom stood in the corner.* [*~ + obj*]: *He stood the broom in the corner.* **7.** [*no obj*] to be located or situated: *The building stands upon the hill.* **8.** [*usually: not: be + ~-ing; ~ (+ at) + a noun indicating number or amount*] (of a score, etc.) to remain as indicated: *The score stands (at) 18 to 14.* **9.** [*no obj*] to continue in force; remain valid: *My offer still stands.* **10.** to be or remain in a specified state or condition: [*no obj*]: *Where do I stand in the competition?* [*~ + adjective*]: *I stand corrected.* [*~ + to + verb*]: *He stands to gain quite a lot from his wife's death.* **11.** [*~ + for + obj*] *Chiefly Brit.* to be a candidate, as for public office: *to stand for Parliament.* **12.** [*~ + obj*] to submit to; be forced to go through: *to stand trial for murder.* **13.** [*~ + obj*] to be able to tolerate; resist; endure: *My eyes can't stand the glare.* **14.** [*~ + obj*] to perform one's job or duty as: *to stand watch aboard ship; He stood guard over the prisoners.* **15. stand by, a.** [*~ + by + obj*] to uphold; support: *Stand by your parents in their time of need.* **b.** [*~ + by + obj*] to remain firm about (something); be loyal to: *I stand by my original statement.* **c.** [*no obj*] to wait, esp. in anticipation: *Please stand by, we're having technical difficulties.* **d.** [*no obj*] to be ready to board (an airplane, etc.) as an alternate passenger. **16. stand down,** [*no obj*] **a.** *Law.* to leave the witness stand: *The judge told the witness to stand down.* **b.** to step aside, as from a competition. **17. stand for,** [*~ + for + obj*] **a.** [*not: be + ~-ing*] to represent; symbolize: *P.S. stands for "postscript."* **b.** to advocate; favor: *The candidate says she stands for more aid to education.* **c.** [*with negative words or phrases*] to tolerate; allow; accept or put up with: *"I won't stand for any nonsense," the teacher said.* **18. stand in,** [*no obj;* (*~ + in + for + obj*)] to be a substitute (for): *No, I'm not the supervisor, I'm just standing in (for her) until she comes back.* **19. stand off, a.** [*no obj*] to keep or stay at a distance: *The planes stood off and circled overhead.* **b.** to repel or evade: [*~ + off + obj*]: *Our troops stood off the latest assault.* [*~ + obj + off*]: *As for their army, our troops stood them off last time, too.* **20. stand on,** [*~ + on + obj*] to be based on; depend on; rest on: *The house stood on sand.* **21. stand out,** [*no obj*] **a.** to stick out past something: *The pier stands out from the harbor walls.* **b.** to be noticed easily, on account of fame, etc.: *She stands out in a crowd.* **22. stand up, a.** [*no obj*] to be or remain convincing: *That evidence won't stand up in court.* **b.** [*no obj*] to last long; be durable: *Wool stands up better than silk.* **c.** to fail to keep an appointment with: [*~ + up + obj*]: *She stood up several of my friends.* [*~ + obj + up*]: *She stood him up on their last two dates.* **23. stand up for,** [*~ + up + for + obj*] to defend; support: *You have to stand up for your children.* **24. stand up to,** [*~ + up + to + obj*] to meet (danger, difficulty, etc.) without fear; confront: *If you stand up to that bully, he'll back down.* **—***n.* [*count*] **25.** the act of standing. **26.** a halt or stop. **27.** a final defensive effort: *Custer's last stand.* **28.** a policy, position, opinion, etc., with respect to a (usually controversial) issue: *We must take a stand on sex education.* **29.** witness stand: *Before you take the stand I must* *remind you that you are still under oath.* **30.** a raised platform, as for a speaker, a band, etc. **31. stands,** [*plural*] a raised section of seats for spectators; grandstand. **32.** a framework on or in which articles are placed for storing, support, or display: *an umbrella stand.* **33.** a stall, booth, or the like where articles are displayed for sale: *a fruit stand.* **34.** a place to wait for taxis: *a taxi stand.* **35.** a stop on the tour of a theater company, a rock group, etc., esp. for a single performance: *a one-night stand in the small university town.* **—*Idiom.* 36. stand to reason,** [*not: be + ~-ing; it + ~ + to reason*] to be logical or reasonable: *It stands to reason that he'll choose her; he always makes the right choice.* **—stand′er,** *n.* [*count*] See -STAN-.

stand•ard (stan′dərd) /'stændərd/ *n.* [*count*] **1.** something considered to be a basis of comparison: *an official standard for weight.* **2.** a principle for judging how good something is: *a teacher whose standards are quite high.* **3.** an average or normal quality, quantity, or level: *The work isn't up to his usual standard.* **4. standards,** [*plural*] the morals, ethics, etc., regarded as acceptable: *The standards of the community are taken into account.* **5.** a popular song having long-lasting popularity: *He likes the old standards —Gershwin, Cole Porter, Irving Berlin.* **6.** a flag indicating the presence of a king, queen, or public official, or used as an emblem by a group in the armed forces: *King Arthur raised the standard of the Pendragon.* **—*adj.* 7.** serving as a basis of weight, measure, value, comparison, or judgment. **8.** [*before a noun*] of recognized excellence or established authority: *a standard reference book.* **9.** usual or customary; normal: *The car has these standard features: air conditioning, an airbag, and fold-down rear seats.* **10.** manual; not electric or automatic: *standard transmission.* **11.** [*usually before a noun*] (of a language or dialect) agreeing with the pronunciation, grammar, vocabulary, etc., found among most educated native speakers and widely considered acceptable or correct. Compare NONSTANDARD (def. 2).

stand′ard-bear′er, *n.* [*count*] **1.** an officer or soldier of a military unit who carries a flag used as an emblem of an army group. **2.** one generally thought of as being the leader of a movement, political party, etc.: *the new standard-bearer of the conservative movement.*

stand•ard•ize (stan′dər dīz′) /'stændər,dayz/ *v.* [*~ + obj*], **-ized, -iz•ing.** to cause to agree with or conform to a standard. **—stand•ard•i•za•tion** (stan′dərdə zā′shən) /,stændərdə'zeyʃən/ *n.* [*noncount*]

stand′ard of liv′ing, *n.* [*count; usually singular*] the level of comfort or wealth maintained by an individual or by the people of a certain community, group, nation, etc.: *a high standard of living.*

stand′ard time′, *n.* [*count*] the official time adopted for a country or region, with a difference of exactly one hour between one zone and the next.

stand•by (stand′bī′) /'stænd,bay/ *n., pl.* **-bys,** *adj., adv.* **—*n.*** [*count*] **1.** a strong, loyal follower. **2.** something upon which one can rely: *took out his old standby, a Swiss army knife.* **3.** something or someone held ready to serve as a substitute, as in an emergency: *We have an emergency generator as a standby.* **4.** a traveler who will receive a seat, as on a plane, only if a place becomes available. **—*adj.*** [*usually: before a noun*] **5.** kept ready for use as a substitute: *a standby player.* **6.** of, for, or traveling as a standby: *a standby flight.* **—*adv.* 7.** as a standby: *to fly standby to Rome.* **—*Idiom.* 8. on standby,** ready to act immediately when called upon.

stand•ee (stan dē′) /stæn'diy/ *n.* [*count*], *pl.* **-ees.** one who stands, as in a public conveyance.

stand′-in′, *n.* [*count*] a substitute; one who takes the place of another temporarily.

stand•ing (stan′ding) /'stændɪŋ/ *n.* **1.** [*noncount*] rank or status, esp. with respect to social, economic, or personal position, etc.: *a person of little standing in the community.* **2.** [*noncount*] good position, reputation, or credit: *a person of some social standing.* **3.** [*noncount*] length of continuing, living, or staying in a place; time of experience, etc.: *friends of long standing.* **4. standings,** [*plural*] a list of contestants according to their past winning and losing records: *The team was first in the standings.* **—*adj.*** [*before a noun*] **5.** having, in, or from an erect position: *a standing lamp.* **6.** performed in or from an erect position: *a standing jump.* **7.** still; not flowing or stagnant: *standing pools of water.* **8.** lasting or permanent; continuing in force: *a strong standing army.*

stand•off or **stand-off** (stand′ôf, -of′) /'stændɔf, -,ɒf/ *n.* [*count*] **1.** a tie or draw, as in a contest: *faced another standoff with her opponent.* **—*adj.* 2.** keeping apart from others; aloof; reserved; standoffish.

stand•off•ish or **stand-off•ish** (stand′ô′fish, -of′ish) /'stænd'ɔfɪʃ, -'ɒfɪʃ/ *adj.* tending to keep oneself apart and to be unfriendly; aloof.

stand•out or **stand-out** (stand′out′) /'stænd,awt/ *n.* [*count*] **1.** a person, performance, etc., that is clearly better than others. **2.** one easily noticed because of a refusal to go along with the opinions, goals, etc., of the majority. **—*adj.*** [*usually: before a noun*] **3.** outstanding; superior.

stand•point (stand′point′) /'stænd,pɔynt/ *n.* [*count*] **1.** the mental attitude from which a person views and judges things: *From my standpoint I can't understand how anyone could commit such a horrible crime.* **2.** the point or place at which a person stands to view something.

stand•still (stand′stil′) /'stænd,stɪl/ *n.* [*count; usually singular*] a state in which action has stopped; stop: *The work had come to a standstill.*

stand′-up′ or **stand′up′,** *adj.* [*before a noun*] **1.** standing erect or upright, as a collar. **2.** (of a comedian) delivering comic performances, monologues, etc., while standing alone in front of an audience or camera.

stank (stangk) /stæŋk/ *v.* a pt. of STINK.

stan•za (stan′zə) /'stænzə/ *n.* [*count*], *pl.* **-zas.** an arrangement of a certain number of lines in a poem. See -STAN-.

staph (staf) /stæf/ *n.* [*noncount*] staphylococcus: *a staph infection.*

staph•y•lo•coc•cus (staf′ə lə kok′əs) /,stæfələ'kɒkəs/ *n.* [*count*], *pl.* **-coc•ci** (-kok′sī) /-'kɒksay/. a type of bacteria with a round shape.

sta•ple[1] (stā′pəl) /'steypəl/ *n., v.,* **-pled, -pling. —*n.*** [*count*] **1.** a short piece of wire bent so as to hold together papers or the like by driving the ends through the sheets and bending them together on the other side. **—*v.*** [*~ + obj*] **2.** to fasten by a staple or staples: *Staple the pages together.* **—sta′pler,** *n.* [*count*]

sta•ple[2] (stā′pəl) /'steypəl/ *n.* [*count*] **1.** a principal raw material or product grown or manufactured in a locality. **2.** a basic or necessary item of food: *flour, salt, and other staples.* **3.** a basic or principal item, feature, or part: *respect, trust, commitment: the staples of a marriage.* **—*adj.*** [*before a noun*] **4.** chief among the products exported or produced by a country: *staple crops.* **5.** basic, chief, or principal: *staple industries; a staple diet.*

star (stär) /stɑr/ *n., adj., v.,* **starred, star•ring. —*n.*** [*count*] **1.** a hot, gaslike, bright body in space, such as the sun. **2.** any body in the sky, except the moon, that appears as a fixed point of light in the night sky: *The evening star is really the planet Venus.* **3.** Usually, **stars.** [*plural*] a heavenly body, esp. a planet, thought of as having an influence on human affairs: *Madame Fifi, what do the stars say about my chances for promotion?* **4.** one's fortune or success in relation to advancement or decline: *Your star will rise someday.* **5.** a figure having five or six points arranged around a center, sometimes used as an ornament, badge, award, etc.: *The restaurant was awarded five stars.* **6. a.** a famous or well-known actor, singer, etc., esp. one who plays the leading role in a production. **b.** a famous person in some art, profession, or field. **7.** an asterisk. **8.** a white spot on the forehead of a horse. **—*adj.*** [*before a noun*] **9.** famous, well-known, or distinguished: *a star reporter.* **10.** of or relating to a star or stars. **—*v.* 11.** [*~ + obj*] to have or feature as a star: *That old movie starred Rudolph Valentino.* **12.** [*no obj*] (of a performer) to appear as a star: *Rudolf Valentino starred in that movie.* **13.** [*~ + obj*] to mark with a star or asterisk, as for special notice. **—*Idiom.* 14. see stars,** to appear to see brilliant streaks of light before the eyes, as from a severe blow to the head. **—star′less,** *adj.* **—star′ry,** *adj.,* **-ri•er, -ri•est:** *a brilliant starry sky.*

star•board (stär′bərd, -bôrd′, -bōrd′) /'stɑrbərd, -,bɔrd, -,bowrd/ *n.* [*noncount*] **1.** the right-hand side of, or direction from, a vessel or aircraft: *Steer to starboard!* **—*adj.* 2.** of or relating to the starboard. **—*adv.* 3.** toward the right side.

starch (stärch) /stɑrtʃ/ *n.* **1.** a white, tasteless chemical substance in plants, forming an important component of rice, corn, wheat, and many other vegetable foods: [*noncount*]: *a food rich in starch.* [*count*]: *There are several different starches in that food.* **2.** [*noncount*] a commercial preparation of this substance used to stiffen textile fabrics in laundering. **3. starches,** [*plural*] foods rich in natural starch: *not enough starches in his diet.* **—*v.*** [*~ + obj*] **4.** to stiffen or treat with starch: *to starch the shirts at the cleaners.*

starched (stärcht) /ˈstɑrtʃt/ *adj.* made stiff with starch; treated with starch.

starch•y (stär′chē) /ˈstɑrtʃiy/ *adj.*, **-i•er, -i•est. 1.** full of, or containing, starch: *starchy foods.* **2.** too formal or stiff in treating others.

star•dom (stär′dəm) /ˈstɑrdəm/ *n.* [*noncount*] the world, condition, or status of star performers, as of the stage, etc.: *achieved stardom at an early age.* See -DOM.

stare (stâr) /stɛər/ *v.*, **stared, star•ing,** *n.* **—***v.* **1.** to gaze or look at deeply, intently, etc., esp. with the eyes wide open: [~ + *at* + *obj*]: *He stared at her for a long time.* [*no obj*]: *Don't stare; it's rude.* [~ + *obj*]: *The police officer stared the gang into silence. He stared her up and down.* **2. stare down,** to cause to be nervous or uncomfortable by looking at (someone) deeply, for a long time, etc., esp. with the eyes wide open: [~ + *obj* + *down*]: *The mob was ready to riot, but the sheriff managed to stare them down.* [~ + *down* + *obj*]: *I've seen him stare down a whole gang.* **—***n.* [*count*] **3.** a staring gaze; a fixed look with the eyes wide open. **—*Idiom.* 4. stare someone in the face,** [~ + *obj* + *in the face*] **a.** to be urgent or impending, as a deadline: *The deadline was staring him in the face.* **b.** to be very obvious, as an answer or solution: *The answer is staring you right in the face.* **—star′er,** *n.* [*count*] **—Usage.** The verb STARE most often takes the preposition *at* after it: *She stared at the man with the gun.* In this way it is similar to verbs like LOOK and GLANCE, but it is different from SEE, which takes no preposition.

star•fish (stär′fish′) /ˈstɑrˌfɪʃ/ *n.* [*count*], *pl.* (*esp. when thought of as a group*) **-fish,** (*esp. for kinds or species*) **-fish•es.** a sea creature having the shape of a star, with five arms coming out from a central disk. Also called **sea star.**

star•gaze (stär′gāz′) /ˈstɑrˌgeyz/ *v.* [*no obj*], **-gazed, -gaz•ing. 1.** to gaze at or observe the stars. **2.** to daydream. **—star′gaz′er,** *n.* [*count*]

stark (stärk) /stɑrk/ *adj.*, **-er, -est,** *adv.* **—***adj.* **1.** [*before a noun*] complete, pure, sheer, downright: *stark madness.* **2.** harsh, grim, or severe in appearance: *The room was simple and stark.* **3.** bluntly or sternly plain: *The stark reality of our situation finally hit home.* **4.** sharply or harshly distinct: *a stark contrast.* **—***adv.* **5.** absolutely, completely, utterly; quite: *stark raving mad.* **—stark′ness,** *n.* [*noncount*]

star•let (stär′lit) /ˈstɑrlɪt/ *n.* [*count*] a young actress who is thought of as a future star, esp. in motion pictures.

star•light (stär′līt′) /ˈstɑrˌlayt/ *n.* [*noncount*] the light coming from the stars. **—star•lit** (stär′lit′) /ˈstɑrˌlɪt/ *adj.*

star•ling (stär′ling) /ˈstɑrlɪŋ/ *n.* [*count*] a stocky, medium-sized songbird with shiny black coloring.

star′ry-eyed′, *adj.* overly romantic; unrealistic; dreamy; naive: *When we first went overseas we were starry-eyed about everything that was new and different.*

Stars′ and Stripes′, *n.* [*proper noun; singular; used with a singular verb; the* + ~] the national flag of the U.S. Also called **Old Glory.**

start (stärt) /stɑrt/ *v.* **1.** to (cause to) begin; commence: [*no obj*]: *We'll start at dawn, if you can get up that early!* [~ + *obj*]: *I started my current job in 1992.* [~ + *to* + *verb*]: *The fir trees started to lose their needles.* [~ + *verb-ing*]: *She started running when she saw him.* **2.** to (cause to) come into being, movement, or operation: [*no obj*]: *The trouble started when I couldn't get a job.* [~ + *obj*]: *The drivers started their engines with a roar.* **3.** [~ + *obj*] to establish or found: *to start a new business.* **4.** [~ + *obj*] to help (someone) set out on a journey, career, etc.: *His parents started him in show business.* **5.** [*no obj*] to give a sudden, uncontrolled jump, as from pain or surprise: *He started when I tapped him on the shoulder to wake him up.* **—***n.* [*count*] **6.** a beginning of an action, journey, etc.: *Our business got off to a slow start.* **7.** a place or time from which something begins: *It's the start of the new season.* **8.** the first part or beginning segment of anything: *We missed the start of the show.* **9.** a sudden, involuntary jerk of the body: *awoke with a start.* **10.** a lead or advance, as over competitors or pursuers: *He had a two-hour start, but they soon caught up with him.* **11.** a means of beginning or advancing something desired: *Her parents gave them a start by buying them a house.* **—Syn.** See BEGIN.

start•er (stär′tər) /ˈstɑrtər/ *n.* [*count*] **1.** a mechanical device that starts an engine. **2.** anything that starts. **—*Idiom.* 3. for starters,** *Informal.* as the first step or part; initially: *We'll have cocktails for starters.*

star•tle (stär′tl) /ˈstɑrtl̩/ *v.* [~ + *obj*], **-tled, -tling.** to disturb suddenly as by surprise: *You startled me when you slammed the door so loudly.*

star•tling (stär′tling) /ˈstɑrtlɪŋ/ *adj.* disturbing; frightening: *a startling noise; a startling discovery.*

star•va•tion (stär vā′shən) /stɑrˈveyʃən/ *n.* [*noncount*] a condition of great weakness or death due to lack of food.

starve (stärv) /stɑrv/ *v.*, **starved, starv•ing. 1.** to (cause to) weaken, waste, or die from lack of food: [*no obj*]: *was broke so long he nearly starved.* [~ + *obj*]: *tried to starve his enemy into submission.* **2.** [*be* + ~*-ed/* ~*-ing; no obj*] to be extremely hungry: *When do we eat? I'm starved/starving.* **3.** to (cause to) feel a strong need or desire: [*be* + ~*-ing* + *for* + *obj*]: *The child is starving for affection.* [~ + *obj*]: *The children were being starved of affection.*

stash (stash) /stæʃ/ *v.*, [~ + *obj*] **1.** to put by or away as for future use: [~ (+ *away*) + *obj*]: *They had stashed (away) some money under their mattress.* [~ + *obj* (+ *away*)]: *to stash some money (away) for emergencies.* **—***n.* [*count*] **2.** something put away or hidden: *a secret stash of drugs.* **3.** a place in which something is stored secretly.

stat (stat) /stæt/ *n.* [*count*] **1.** Also, **'stat.** a thermostat. **2.** a photostat.

-stat, *suffix.* *-stat* is attached to roots and sometimes words to form nouns with the meaning "the name of a device or a substance that stabilizes or makes constant (the root or word preceding)": *thermo- (= heat)* + *-stat* → *thermostat (= device regulating heat).*

-stat-, *root.* *-stat-* comes from Latin or Greek, where it has the meaning "stand; remain." This meaning is found in such words as: INSTATE, INTERSTATE, MISSTATE, OVERSTATE, REINSTATE, RHEOSTAT, STATE, STATIC, STATION, STATISTICS, STATUE, STATUS, STATUTE, STATUTORY, THERMOSTAT, UNDERSTATE.

state (stāt) /steyt/ *n.*, *adj.*, *v.*, **stat•ed, stat•ing. —***n.* **1.** [*count; usually singular*] the condition of a person or thing with respect to circumstances or experiences; the way something is: *the state of one's health.* **2.** [*count*] the condition of substances with respect to structure, form, etc.: *Water in a gaseous state is steam.* **3.** [*noncount*] status or position in life, esp. for a person of wealth and rank: *to travel in state.* **4.** [*count; usually singular*] a tense, nervous, or disturbed condition: *I was in a state over losing my job.* **5.** [*count; sometimes: State*] a politically unified people occupying a definite territory; nation: *the State of Israel.* **6.** [*count; sometimes: State*] any of the political units that together make up a federal union, as in the United States of America. **7.** [*noncount*] the authority, rule, and administration of a country: *affairs of state.* **—***adj.* [*before a noun*] **8.** of or relating to the central civil government. **9.** of, maintained by, or under the authority of a unit of a federal union: *a state highway.* **10.** characterized by, or involving, ceremony: *a state dinner.* **—***v.* **11.** to declare or say, as in speech or writing: [~ + *obj*]: *Please state your name and address.* [*used with quotations*]: *"I was there," he stated, "and I saw the whole crime."* **12.** [~ + *obj*] to set forth in definite form: *to state a problem.* **—*Idiom.* 13. lie in state,** [*no obj*] (of a corpse) to be exhibited publicly with honors before burial. **—state′hood′,** *n.* [*noncount*] See -STAT-.

state•craft (stāt′kraft′) /ˈsteytˌkræft/ *n.* [*noncount*] the art of government and diplomacy. See -STAT-.

state•less (stāt′lis) /ˈsteytlɪs/ *adj.* lacking nationality; not a citizen of a country. **—state′less•ness,** *n.* [*noncount*]

state•ly (stāt′lē) /ˈsteytliy/ *adj.*, **-li•er, -li•est,** *adv.* **—***adj.* **1.** majestic; impressive or imposing in magnificence. **—***adv.* **2.** in a stately manner. **—state′li•ness,** *n.* [*noncount*]

state•ment (stāt′mənt) /ˈsteytmənt/ *n.* [*count*] **1.** something stated, as a communication in speech or writing: *I disagree with your last statement.* **2.** a printed listing that shows financial amounts taken in or paid out of a bank account, or of finances generally: *The last statement from the bank had an error.* **3.** the communication of an idea, position, or mood through something other than words: *She creates clothes that are a fashion statement.* See -STAT-.

state′ of the art′, *n.* [*noncount; usually: the* + ~] the latest stage of a technology, art, or science: *a camera considered (the) state of the art in design.* **—state′-of-the-art′,** *adj.*: *a state-of-the-art computer lab.*

state•room (stāt′ro͞om′, -ro͝om′) /ˈsteytˌruwm, -ˌrʊm/ *n.* [*count*] a private room or compartment on a ship, train, etc.

state•side or **State•side** (stāt′sīd′) /ˈsteytˌsayd/ *adj.* **1.** being in or toward the continental U.S. *—adv.* **2.** in or toward the continental U.S.

states•man (stāts′mən) /ˈsteytsmən/ *n.* [*count*], *pl.* **-men.** an experienced, respected, patriotic politician. —**states′man•like′, states′man•ly,** *adj.* —**states′man•ship′,** *n.* [*noncount*] See -STAT-.

stat•ic (stat′ik) /ˈstætɪk/ *adj.* Also, **stat′i•cal. 1.** of or relating to objects or forces at rest or in balance or equilibrium. **2.** showing little change: *a static relationship.* **3.** lacking movement or liveliness: *a novel that has nothing but static characters.* **4.** [*before a noun*] (of electricity) not flowing or moving through a substance: *His hair stood on end from the static electricity.* *—n.* [*noncount*] **5. a.** static or atmospheric electricity. **b.** interference with radio broadcasts, etc., due to such electricity: *A loud burst of static drowned out the announcement.* **6.** resistance or hostility, as to one's actions or plans; opposition: *He gave me a lot of static about changing the system.* —**stat′i•cal•ly,** *adv.* See -STAT-.

sta•tion (stā′shən) /ˈsteyʃən/ *n.* **1.** [*count*] a stopping place for trains, buses, etc. that carry people or things: *a subway station.* **2.** [*count*] the buildings at such a stopping place: *The old central train station had restaurants.* **3.** [*count*] the local branch of certain public services: *a fire station.* **4.** [*count*] a place equipped for some particular kind of work or activity: *a geophysical station.* **5.** [*count*] a place or position at which a person or thing is normally located or from which he or she usually works; one's post: *The guard's station is the first-floor entrance.* **6.** [*count*] the appropriate position, as of persons or things, in a scale of social rank or dignity: *trying to act above his station.* **7.** [*count*] a person, organization, or building from which radio, television, cable, etc., broadcasts are transmitted; the frequency or channel assigned to one who broadcasts, or the assignee: *We can tape the interview at the station or in your office.* **8.** [*noncount*] a military region, esp. one to which a ship or fleet is assigned for duty: *on station in the North Sea.* **9.** [*count*] (in Australia) a ranch with its buildings, land, etc., esp. for raising sheep. *—v.* [~ + *obj*] **10.** to place or post (someone) in a station or position: *He was stationed by the door to act as a lookout.* See -STAT-.

sta•tion•ar•y (stā′shə ner′ē) /ˈsteyʃəˌnɛriy/ *adj.* standing still; not moving. See -STAT-.

sta′tion break′, *n.* [*count*] a brief interval during or after a radio or TV program reserved for identifying the station, broadcasting commercials, etc.

sta•tion•er (stā′shə nər) /ˈsteyʃənər/ *n.* [*count*] a seller of paper, pens, pencils, and other writing materials.

sta•tion•er•y (stā′shə ner′ē) /ˈsteyʃəˌnɛriy/ *n.* [*noncount*] **1.** writing paper: *Use letterhead stationery from your school when ordering books.* **2.** writing materials, such as pens, pencils, etc.: *The store sells stationery.*

sta′tion wag′on, *n.* [*count*] an automobile with one or more rows of folding or removable seats behind the driver and an area behind these seats into which suitcases, parcels, etc., can be loaded through a tailgate.

sta•tis•tic (stə tis′tik) /stəˈtɪstɪk/ *n.* [*count*] a numerical fact or datum, esp. one computed from a sample: *Here's an alarming statistic: A car is stolen every three minutes.*

sta•tis•ti•cal (stə tis′ti kəl) /stəˈtɪstɪkəl/ *adj.* of or relating to statistics: *mounds of statistical data to prove his point.* See -STAT-.

stat•i•sti•cian (stat′is tish′ən) /ˌstætɪsˈtɪʃən/ *n.* [*count*] one who is expert in, or keeps track of, statistics. See -STAT-.

sta•tis•tics (stə tis′tiks) /stəˈtɪstɪks/ *n.* **1.** [*noncount; used with a singular verb*] the science that deals with the collection, analysis, and interpretation of information or data in the form of numbers: *Statistics explains why every time you throw a coin in the air, the odds are always 50-50 that it will end up heads.* **2.** [*plural; used with a plural verb*] the information or data themselves: *Statistics prove that you are safer in an airplane than in a car.* See -STAT-.

stat•u•ar•y (stach′o͞o er′ē) /ˈstætʃuwˌɛriy/ *n.* [*noncount*] statues thought of as a group. See -STAT-.

stat•ue (stach′o͞o) /ˈstætʃuw/ *n.* [*count*] a three-dimensional work of art, as a figure of a person, carved in stone or wood, etc. See -STAT-.

stat•u•esque (stach′o͞o esk′) /ˌstætʃuwˈɛsk/ *adj.* suggesting a statue, as in dignity, grace, or beauty, esp., tall and shapely: *a tall, statuesque model.* See -STAT-.

stat•u•ette (stach′o͞o et′) /ˌstætʃuwˈɛt/ *n.* [*count*] a small statue. See -STAT-.

stat•ure (stach′ər) /ˈstætʃər/ *n.* [*noncount*] **1.** the height of a human or animal body, or of an object: *He's tall in stature and solid in build.* **2.** esteem or status based on one's positive qualities or achievements: *a person of stature in the community.* See -STAT-.

sta•tus (stā′təs, stat′əs) /ˈsteytəs, ˈstætəs/ *n.* [*noncount*] **1.** the position of an individual in relation to others; standing: *a job of low status.* **2.** high position or standing; prestige: *a person of some status in the community.* **3.** state or condition of affairs: *What is the status of the contract negotiations?* See -STAT-.

sta′tus quo′ (kwō) /kwow/ *n.* [*noncount*] the existing state or condition in which things have not changed: *He's a big fan of the status quo; he fears change.* See -STAT-.

sta′tus sym′bol, *n.* [*count*] an object, habit, etc., that a person has, owns, or possesses that indicates high social status or importance: *the status symbols of wealth: an expensive car and fancy clothes.*

stat•ute (stach′o͞ot) /ˈstætʃuwt/ *n.* **1.** a law passed by a legislature: [*count*]: *to pass a statute against double taxation.* [*noncount*]: *By statute, this behavior cannot be prosecuted.* **2.** [*count*] a document stating such a law. See -STAT-.

stat•u•to•ry (stach′o͝o tôr′ē, -tōr′ē) /ˈstætʃʊˌtɔriy, -ˌtowriy/ *adj.* **1.** of or relating to a statute; authorized by statute. **2.** (of an offense) punishable by statute: *statutory rape.* See -STAT-.

staunch[1] (stônch) /stɔntʃ/ *v.* STANCH[1].

staunch[2] (stônch, stänch) /stɔntʃ, stɑntʃ/ also **stanch,** *adj.,* **-er, -est.** firm; dependable in principle, loyalty, etc.: *a staunch Democrat.* —**staunch′ly,** *adv.*: *staunchly defended his nominee.* See -STAN-.

stave (stāv) /steyv/ *n., v.,* **staved** or **stove** (stōv) /stowv/ **stav•ing.** *—n.* [*count*] **1.** one of the thin, narrow, shaped pieces of wood that form the sides of a cask, tub, etc. **2.** a stick, rod, or pole. *—v.* **3. stave off, a.** to put off or keep off, as by force: [~ + *off* + *obj*]: *to stave off an attack.* [~ + *obj* + *off*]: *to stave it off.* **b.** to prevent in time; forestall: [~ + *off* + *obj*]: *to stave off bankruptcy.* [~ + *obj* + *off*]: *to stave it off.*

staves (stāvz) /steyvz/ *n.* [*plural*] **1.** a pl. of STAFF[1]. **2.** pl. of STAVE.

stay[1] (stā) /stey/ *v.,* **stayed,** or **staid, stay•ing, 1.** [*no obj*] to remain over a length of time, as in a place or situation: *The children wanted to stay up late.* **2.** [*no obj*] to dwell for a while; reside; lodge: *to stay at a friend's apartment.* **3.** [*no obj*] to pause briefly: *Stay inside until the taxi comes.* **4.** [*usually not: be* + ~*-ing*] to remain as; go on being: [~ + *adjective*]: *Try to stay calm.* [~ + *noun*]: *How long will he stay governor if he keeps making such mistakes?* **5.** to hold out or endure to the end, as in a contest, difficult task, etc.: [*no obj*]: *If you stay with the project you'll have a good chance of finishing it.* [~ + *obj*]: *We need someone who will stay the course and not quit.* **6.** [~ + *obj*] to stop or halt: *He stayed his hand before striking the child.* *—n.* [*count*] **7.** the act of stopping or being stopped. **8.** a period of temporarily living somewhere: *a week's stay in Miami.* **9.** a temporary stopping of a judicial proceeding: *a stay of execution.* ***—Idiom.*** **10. stay put,** [*no obj*] to remain in the same position or place: *Now stay put until I come back to get you.*

stay[2] (stā) /stey/ *n.* [*count*] something used to support or steady a thing; a prop; brace.

stay′ing pow′er, *n.* [*noncount*] ability to continue, last, or endure; endurance; stamina.

STD, an abbreviation of: sexually transmitted disease.

std., an abbreviation of: standard.

stead (sted) /stɛd/ *n.* [*count; usually singular*] **1.** the place of a person or thing, as when a substitute takes over: *The nephew of the queen came in her stead.* ***—Idiom.*** **2. stand (someone) in good stead,** [*stand* + *obj* + *in good* + ~] to prove useful to: *Her letter of recommendation will stand you in good stead.*

stead•fast (sted′fast′) /ˈstɛdˌfæst/ *adj.* **1.** fixed in direction: *He gave her his best steadfast gaze but she didn't even blink.* **2.** firm in purpose, faith, loyalty, etc.: *a steadfast friend.* —**stead′fast′ly,** *adv.*

stead•y (sted′ē) /ˈstɛdiy/ *adj.,* **stead•i•er, stead•i•est,** *interj., n., pl.* **stead•ies,** *v.,* **stead•ied, stead•y•ing,** *adv.* *—adj.* **1.** firmly placed; stable: *a steady ladder.* **2.** even or regular in movement: *a steady rhythm.* **3.** free from change or interruption; continuous: *a steady diet of bread and water.* **4.** [*usually: before a noun*] constant, regular, or habitual: *a steady customer at the diner.* **5.** free from excitement; not easily disturbed; calm: *steady nerves.* **6.** firm; not weakening or lessening: *a steady hand.* **7.** settled or sober, as a person or habits: *a steady pupil who does his work on time.* *—interj.* **8.** (used to urge someone or an animal to calm down or be under control): *Whoa, steady, big fellow!* **—***n.* [*count*] **9.** a person with whom one has a romantic relationship; a boyfriend or girlfriend: *That's his steady; you can't dance with her!* **—***v.* **10.** to (cause to) become firm, straight, or steady, as in position, movement, or character: [*no obj*]: *The boat lurched in the high seas, then steadied again.* [~ + *obj*]: *The pilot steadied the plane before everyone got sick.* [~ + *oneself*]: *He staggered, then steadied himself by grabbing the railing.* **—***adv.* **11.** in a steady manner; steadily: *walking none too steady down the road.* **—*Idiom.* 12. go steady,** [*no obj*] to have a romantic relationship with one person exclusively: *They seem a little young to be going steady.* —**stead•i•ly** (sted′l ē) /ˈstɛdl̩iy/ *adv.*: *It rained steadily all night.* —**stead′i•ness,** *n.* [*noncount*]: *They admired her steadiness in times of crisis.*

steak (stāk) /steyk/ *n.* a slice of meat or fish, cooked by broiling, grilling, or frying: [*noncount*]: *a pound of steak.* [*count*]: *They cooked our steaks medium rare.*

steal (stēl) /stiyl/ *v.*, **stole** (stōl) /stowl/ **sto•len, steal•ing,** *n.* **—***v.* **1.** to take (the property of another) without permission or right, esp. secretly or by force: [~ + *obj*]: *Someone stole my dad's car last night.* [*no obj*]: *The two brothers were always stealing from each other.* **2.** [~ + *obj*] to take and use (ideas, credit, etc.) without right or acknowledgment. **3.** [~ + *obj*] to take or win secretly, quickly, or without others' knowing or seeing: *He stole my girlfriend.* **4.** to move or (cause to) go secretly or quietly: [*no obj*]: *He stole away into the night.* [~ + *obj*]: *She stole the dog upstairs at bedtime.* **5.** [*no obj*] to pass, happen, etc., gradually or with little notice: *The years steal by.* **6.** *Baseball.* (of a base runner) to reach (a base) safely by running while the ball is being pitched to the player at bat: [~ + *obj*]: *He'll steal third base if he gets the chance.* [*no obj*]: *Will he steal if he gets the chance?* **—***n.* [*count*] **7.** something bought at a cost far below its real value; a bargain: *What a steal: a genuine antique that was only five bucks!* **8.** *Baseball.* the act of advancing a base by stealing. **—*Idiom.* 9. steal someone's thunder, a.** to accept credit for another's work. **b.** to remove attention from another's achievement by some action that anticipates it. **10. steal the scene or show, a.** to take credit for something unfairly. **b.** to be more outstanding than anyone or anything else: *The newcomer stole the show and received a standing ovation.*

stealth (stelth) /stɛlθ/ *n.* [*noncount*] **1.** secret procedure, action, or movement: *moved with stealth in the darkness.* **—***adj.* **2.** [*often: Stealth*] having or providing the ability to escape detection by radar: *Stealth planes.* —**stealth•i•ly** (stel′thə lē) /ˈstɛlθəliy/ *adv.* —**stealth′i•ness,** *n.* [*noncount*] —**stealth′y,** *adj.*, **-i•er, -i•est.**

steam (stēm) /stiym/ *n.* [*noncount*] **1.** water in the form of an invisible gas or vapor: *Steam is used for heating purposes.* **2.** the mist formed when the vapor from boiling water condenses in the air. **3.** power or energy: *The damaged frigate limped into port under its own steam.* **—***v.* **4.** [*no obj*] to give off steam or vapor: *pipes steaming in the cold air.* **5.** to (cause to) become covered with condensed steam, as a car window: [*no obj; (~ + up)*]: *To prevent the window from steaming (up), use the defroster.* [~ + *up* + *obj*]: *His hot breath steamed up the window.* [~ + *obj* + *up*]: *to steam it up.* **6.** to move or travel by the power of steam: [*no obj*]: *The ship steamed out to sea.* [~ + *obj*]: *The captain steamed the ship out to sea.* **7.** [~ + *obj*] to expose to or treat with steam, in order to heat, cook, etc.: *to steam the vegetables.* **8.** [~ + *obj (+ up)*] to (cause to) become angry: *He got pretty steamed (up) about the sales figures.* **—***adj.* [*before a noun*] **9.** using or operated by steam: *a steam radiator.* **—*Idiom.* 10. blow** or **let off steam,** to let out emotion or energy kept in or contained, esp. by talking or by acting wildly: *She's been studying all night, and now she wants to let off some steam.*

steam•boat (stēm′bōt′) /ˈstiym,bowt/ *n.* a steam-driven vessel, esp. a small one or one used on inland waters: [*count*]: *The villagers waited for a steamboat to come up the river.* [*noncount; by* + ~]: *The mail is brought by steamboat.*

steam′ en′gine, *n.* [*count*] an engine powered by steam.

steam•er (stē′mər) /ˈstiymər/ *n.* [*count*] **1.** something propelled or operated by steam, as a steamship. **2.** a person or thing that steams. **3.** a device, pot, or container in which something is steamed.

steam•roll•er (stēm′rō′lər) /ˈstiym,rowlər/ *n.* [*count*] **1.** a heavy steam-powered vehicle having a roller for crushing or leveling materials used for a road or the like. **2.** (not in technical use) any similar vehicle with a roller. **3.** a very powerful force, esp. a ruthless one. **—***v.* [~ + *obj*] **4.** to crush or flatten with a steamroller. **5.** to overcome with superior force. **6.** to get (one's way) by overwhelming pressure: *to steamroller the new law through the legislature.*

steam•ship (stēm′ship′) /ˈstiym,ʃɪp/ *n.* [*count*] a large commercial vessel, esp. one driven by steam.

steam′ shov′el, *n.* [*count*] a machine for digging or excavating, operated by its own engine and boiler.

steam•y (stē′mē) /ˈstiymiy/ *adj.*, **-i•er, -i•est. 1.** full of steam: *a hot, steamy room.* **2.** very hot: *a steamy climate.* **3.** sexually arousing or erotic: *a steamy love scene.*

steed (stēd) /stiyd/ *n.* [*count*] a horse, esp. a high-spirited one.

steel (stēl) /stiyl/ *n.* [*noncount*] **1.** a form of iron made with carbon. **—***adj.* **2.** made of steel. **3.** of, relating to, or like steel. **—***v.* [~ + *oneself*] **4.** to make (oneself) determined: *steeled herself against the pain she knew was coming.*

steel′ wool′, *n.* [*noncount*] a matted mass of steel shavings, used for scouring, polishing, etc.

steel•y (stē′lē) /ˈstiyliy/ *adj.*, **-i•er, -i•est.** like steel, as in being gray in color or hard and strong: *a steely gaze.*

steep[1] (stēp) /stiyp/ *adj.*, **-er, -est. 1.** having an almost vertical slope or angle: *a steep hill.* **2.** (of a price or amount) too high; exorbitant: *$50,000 is a little steep for a new car.* —**steep′ly,** *adv.*: *The mountain rose steeply in front of him.* —**steep′ness,** *n.* [*noncount*]

steep[2] (stēp) /stiyp/ *v.* **1.** to (cause to) be soaked in water to soften, cleanse, or extract some component: [*no obj*]: *The tea is steeping in the pot.* [~ + *obj*]: *to steep some tea.* **2.** [*be* + ~*-ed* + *in* + *obj*] to be filled with (some quality, feeling, atmosphere, etc.): *The incident was steeped in mystery and intrigue.*

stee•ple (stē′pəl) /ˈstiypəl/ *n.* [*count*] a tower having an ornamental top in the shape of a spire, built on a church, public building, etc.

stee•ple•chase (stē′pəl chās′) /ˈstiypəl,tʃeys/ *n.* [*count*] **1.** a horse race over a grass course with artificial ditches, hedges, and other obstacles over which the horses must jump. **2.** a foot race run on a cross-country course or over a course with obstacles, such as ditches or hurdles.

stee•ple•jack (stē′pəl jak′) /ˈstiypəl,dʒæk/ *n.* [*count*] one who builds or repairs steeples, towers, etc..

steer[1] (stēr) /stɪər/ *v.* **1.** to guide the course of (something in motion) by a rudder, helm, etc.: [~ + *obj*]: *He steered the car around the wreck on the road.* [*no obj*]: *He steered around the wreck.* **2.** [~ + *obj*] to follow (a particular course): *steered a course toward the Cayman Islands.* **3.** [~ + *obj*] to direct the course of; guide: *He kept steering the conversation back to his promotion.* **—*Idiom.* 4. bum steer,** [*count*] a piece of bad advice: *He gave us a bum steer, urging us to invest in the company that soon went bankrupt.* **5. steer clear of,** [~ + *obj*] to stay away from purposely; avoid: *to steer clear of trouble.* —**steer′a•ble,** *adj.*

steer[2] (stēr) /stɪər/ *n.* [*count*], *pl.* **steers,** (*esp. when thought of as a group*) **steer.** a male animal of the cattle family, with its sexual organs removed.

steer•age (stēr′ij) /ˈstɪərɪdʒ/ *n.* [*noncount*] (in a passenger ship) the accommodations for travelers who pay the cheapest fare.

stein (stīn) /stayn/ *n.* [*count*] **1.** a stout, thick, cuplike container for drinks, esp. for beer. **2.** the amount contained in a stein.

stel•lar (stel′ər) /ˈstɛlər/ *adj.* **1.** of or relating to the stars: *a stellar object.* **2.** of, befitting, or like a star performer; outstanding: *gave a stellar performance in the last show.*

stem[1] (stem) /stɛm/ *n.*, *v.*, **stemmed, stem•ming. —***n.* [*count*] **1.** the part of a plant that grows in an opposite direction to the root and that supports a leaf, flower, or fruit. **2.** a long, slender, supporting part, as of a wineglass or a tobacco pipe. **3.** a part that sticks out from the body of a watch, having on its end a knob for winding the watch. **4.** a form of a word, made of a root alone or a root plus another part, such as a prefix or suffix, to which certain endings may be added: *The word* kindness *is a stem made up of a root,* kind, *and a suffix,* -ness, *to which another suffix,* -es, *could be added.* **—***v.* **5. stem from,** [~ + *from* + *obj*] to come from; arise or originate from: *Most of our problems stem from a lack of funds.*

stem[2] (stem) /stɛm/ *v.* [~ + *obj*], **stemmed, stem•ming.** to check or slow down, esp. the flow of something: *worked to stem the flow of blood from the wound.*

stemmed (stemd) /stɛmd/ *adj.* **1.** (used after a root or another word) having a (certain kind of) stem: *long-stemmed roses.* **2.** having the stem or stems removed.

stench (stench) /stɛntʃ/ *n.* [*count; usually singular*] **1.** an offensive, strong smell: *a stench of rotting garbage.* **2.** a bad, evil, or foul quality: *the stench of corruption.*

sten•cil (sten′səl) /ˈstɛnsəl/ *n., v.,* **-ciled, -cil•ing** or (*esp. Brit.*) **-cilled, -cil•ling.** —*n.* [*count*] **1.** a thin sheet of material in which letters, numbers, etc., have been cut out so that they can be reproduced on another surface when ink, paint, or the like is applied over the cutout areas. —*v.* [~ + *obj*] **2.** to mark or paint (a surface) by means of a stencil: *to stencil the window with Christmas decorations.* **3.** to mark, print, or copy (letters, designs, etc.) on a surface by means of a stencil: *She stenciled her name on the poster.*

sten•o (sten′ō) /ˈstɛnow/ *n., pl.* **sten•os. 1.** [*count*] a stenographer. **2.** [*noncount*] stenography.

ste•nog•ra•phy (stə nog′rə fē) /stəˈnɒgrəfiy/ *n.* [*noncount*] the art or skill of writing in shorthand. —**ste•nog′ra•pher,** *n.* [*count*] —**sten•o•graph•ic** (sten′ə-graf′ik) /ˌstɛnəˈgræfɪk/ *adj.* See -GRAPH-.

sten•to•ri•an (sten tôr′ē ən, -tōr′-) /stɛnˈtɔriyən, -ˈtowr-/ *adj.* very loud or powerful in sound: *stentorian snoring.*

step (step) /stɛp/ *n., v.,* **stepped, step•ping.** —*n.* [*count*] **1.** a movement made by lifting the foot and setting it down again in a new position, as in walking: *He took a few steps to the right.* **2.** the space passed over by one such movement: *The edge is just a few steps to your left.* **3.** the sound made by the foot in making such a movement: *I heard steps outside in the hallway.* **4.** a mark made by the foot on the ground; a footprint: *Look at the steps someone has left in the soft mud.* **5.** a manner of stepping; stride: *She has a heavy step when she walks.* **6. steps,** [*plural*] movements or course in stepping or walking: *We were lost, so we decided to retrace our steps.* **7.** any of a series of stages in a process or in achieving some goal: *the five steps to success.* **8.** a support for the foot in ascending or descending: *the steps of a ladder; We sat on the porch steps.* —*v.* **9.** [*no obj*] to move in steps: *She stepped lightly out the door.* **10.** [*no obj*] to walk, esp. for a short distance: *Step over to my office.* **11.** [*no obj*] to put the foot down; tread: *Don't step on the grass.* **12. step down,** [*no obj*] **a.** to lower or decrease by degrees. **b.** to give up one's authority; resign: *He finally stepped down when it was clear that he had no support.* **13. step in,** [*no obj*] to become involved; intervene: *The United Nations was asked to step in.* **14. step on,** [~ + *on* + *obj*] to press with the foot, as on a lever or spring, in order to operate some mechanism: *He stepped on the gas (pedal) and the car zoomed away.* **15. step out,** [*no obj*] to leave a place, esp. for a short time: *Ms. Jones has just stepped out of the office for a moment.* **16. step up, a.** [~ + *up* + *obj*] to raise by degrees: *We have stepped up our efforts to recruit more teachers.* **b.** [*no obj*] to be promoted; advance: *He stepped up quickly through the ranks.* —***Idiom.* 17. in** (or **out of**) **step, a.** in (or not in) time to a beat, as while marching together: *The marching band couldn't stay in step when they made turns.* **b.** in (or not in) harmony or agreement with others: *He's out of step with the rest of the scientific community.* **18. step by step,** gradually; by stages: *We made progress step by step.* **19. step on it** or **on the gas,** *Informal.* to move more quickly; hurry: *Step on it or we'll be late.* **20. take steps,** to employ necessary actions: *What steps have you taken to prevent future catastrophes?* **21. watch one's step,** to proceed with caution: *You'd better watch your step in that part of town.* —**step′per,** *n.* [*count*]

step-, *prefix. step-* is attached to words to name a member of a family related by the remarriage of a parent and not by blood: *When my father married his second wife, she already had a son who became my stepbrother.*

step•broth•er (step′bruth′ər) /ˈstɛpˌbrʌðər/ *n.* [*count*] one's stepfather's or stepmother's son by a previous marriage.

step•child (step′chīld′) /ˈstɛpˌtʃayld/ *n.* [*count*], *pl.* **-child•ren. 1.** a child of one's husband or wife by a previous marriage. **2.** any person, organization, etc., not properly supported or appreciated: *The Old English program was the stepchild of the English Department.*

step•daugh•ter (step′dô′tər) /ˈstɛpˌdɔtər/ *n.* [*count*] a daughter of one's husband or wife by a previous marriage.

step′-down′, *adj.* [*before a noun*] **1.** serving to decrease voltage: *a step-down transformer.* —*n.* [*count*] **2.** a decrease or reduction in rate or quantity.

step•fa•ther (step′fä′thər) /ˈstɛpˌfɑðər/ *n.* [*count*] the husband of one's mother by a later marriage.

step•lad•der (step′lad′ər) /ˈstɛpˌlædər/ *n.* [*count*] a ladder having flat steps in place of rungs, esp. one with a hinged frame opening up to form four supporting legs.

step•moth•er (step′muth′ər) /ˈstɛpˌmʌðər/ *n.* [*count*] the wife of one's father by a later marriage.

step•par•ent (step′pâr′ənt, -par′-) /ˈstɛpˌpɛərənt, -ˌpær-/ *n.* [*count*] a stepfather or stepmother.

steppe (step) /stɛp/ *n.* [*count*] a wide or vast plain, esp. one without trees.

step•ping•stone or **step•ping stone,** (step′ing stōn′) /ˈstɛpˌɪŋ stown/ *n.* [*count*] **1.** a stone for stepping on in crossing a stream, etc. **2.** any means or stage of advancement: *His last job was just a steppingstone to here.*

step•sis•ter (step′sis′tər) /ˈstɛpˌsɪstər/ *n.* [*count*] one's stepfather's or stepmother's daughter by a previous marriage.

step•son (step′sun′) /ˈstɛpˌsʌn/ *n.* [*count*] a son of one's husband or wife by a previous marriage.

step′-up′, *adj.* [*before a noun*] **1.** causing an increase. **2.** serving to increase voltage: *a step-up transformer.* —*n.* [*count*] **3.** an increase or rise in rate or quantity.

-ster, *suffix. -ster* is used to form nouns, often implying a bad sense, and referring esp. to one's occupation, habit, or association: *game + -ster → gamester (= one greatly interested in games); trick + -ster → trickster (= one who uses or enjoys dishonest tricks).*

ster•e•o (ster′ē ō′, stēr′-) /ˈstɛriyˌow, ˈstɪər-/ *n., pl.* **ster•e•os,** *adj.* —*n.* **1.** [*count*] a system or piece of equipment for producing sound that comes out of two places, as from different speakers. See illustration at APPLIANCE. **2.** [*noncount*] the producing of this kind of sound; the sound itself: *The music sounds so much better in stereo.* —*adj.* **3.** of or relating to such a sound or sound system: *an expensive and powerful stereo system.*

ster•e•o•phon•ic (ster′ē ə fon′ik, stēr′-) /ˌstɛriyəˈfɒnɪk, ˌstɪər-/ *adj.* of or relating to a system of recording and reproducing sound by using two channels instead of one so that sound is heard more realistically. See -PHON-.

ster•e•o•scope (ster′ē ə skōp′, stēr′-) /ˈstɛriyəˌskowp, ˈstɪər-/ *n.* [*count*] an instrument for viewing things in which two pictures of the same object that were taken from slightly different points of view are looked at, one by each eye, producing the effect of a single picture and the appearance of depth. See -SCOPE-.

ster•e•o•type (ster′ē ə tīp′, stēr′-) /ˈstɛriyəˌtayp, ˈstɪər-/ *n., v.,* **-typed, -typ•ing.** —*n.* [*count*] **1.** a process for making printing plates by taking a mold of type; a plate made this way. **2.** an idea, expression, etc., of no originality or inventiveness. **3.** an overly simplified way of thinking about a person, group, etc.: *Society has certain stereotypes of the mentally retarded.* —*v.* [~ + *obj*] **4.** to make a stereotype of: *a tendency to stereotype ethnic groups.* —**ster′e•o•typed′,** *adj.*: *a stereotyped view of homeless people.* See -TYPE-.

ster•ile (ster′il) /ˈstɛrɪl/ *adj.* **1.** free from living germs, bacteria, or microorganisms: *a sterile environment for operating on patients.* **2.** not able to produce young: *fears that nuclear radiation made people sterile.* **3.** not producing vegetation: *sterile soil.* **4.** not producing results, ideas, etc.; fruitless: *scientists engaged in sterile research.* —**ste•ril•i•ty** (stə ril′i tē) /stəˈrɪlɪtiy/ *n.* [*noncount*]

ster•i•lize (ster′ə līz′) /ˈstɛrəˌlayz/ *v.* [~ + *obj*], **-lized, -liz•ing. 1.** to cleanse by destroying bacteria, microorganisms, parasites, etc., usually by heating at a high temperature: *sterilized the operating instruments.* **2.** to make or cause (a person or animal) to be unable to produce young, by removing or interfering with the normal operation of the sex organs. —**ster•i•li•za•tion** (ster′ə lə-zā′shən) /ˌstɛrələˈzeyʃən/ *n.* [*noncount*]: *To control population growth the government forced women who had more than one child to undergo sterilization.* [*count*]: *The number of sterilizations increased in the last decade.* —**ster′i•liz′er,** *n.* [*count*]

ster•ling (stûr′ling) /ˈstɜrlɪŋ/ *adj.* **1.** [*after a noun*] of or naming the currency of Great Britain: *the value of the pound sterling.* **2.** thoroughly excellent: *a person of sterling worth.* —*n.* [*noncount*] **3.** British currency. **4.** manufactured articles made with a standard amount of silver in them, as knives, forks, spoons, etc.

stern[1] (stûrn) /stɜrn/ *adj.,* **-er, -est. 1.** firm, strict, or exacting: *stern discipline.* **2.** hard, harsh, or severe: *a stern reprimand.* **3.** difficult and unpleasantly serious: *going* *through stern times.* **4.** grim or forbidding in appearance: *a stern expression.* —**stern′ly,** *adv.*: *The judge spoke sternly to the lawyer.* —**stern′ness,** *n.* [*noncount*]

stern[2] (stûrn) /stɜrn/ *n.* [*count*] **1.** the rear part of a vessel or boat (often opposed to *stem*). **2.** the back or rear of anything.

ster•num (stûr′nəm) /ˈstɜrnəm/ *n.* [*count*], *pl.* **-na** (-nə) /-nə/ **-nums.** the bony plate or series of bones to which the ribs are attached; the breastbone.

ste•roid (stēr′oid, ster′-) /ˈstɪərɔyd, ˈstɛr-/ *n.* [*count*] any of a large group of chemical compounds that produce specific changes in the body.

stet (stet) /stɛt/ *v.,* **stet•ted, stet•ting.** —*v.* [*no obj*] **1.** (used as a direction on a manuscript) keep, restore, or retain material previously deleted. —*v.* [~ + *obj*] **2.** to retain (material previously deleted) by marking it with the word "stet" or a row of dots. See -STAN-.

steth•o•scope (steth′ə skōp′) /ˈstɛθə,skowp/ *n.* [*count*] an instrument used to listen to sounds in the chest or other parts of the body. See illustration at HOSPITAL. See -SCOPE-.

ste•ve•dore (stē′vi dôr′, -dōr′) /ˈstiyvɪ,dɔr, -,dowr/ *n.* [*count*] a person or company that loads or unloads ships.

stew (stōō, styōō) /stuw, styuw/ *v.* **1.** to (cause food to) cook by simmering: [*no obj*]: *Let the meat stew slowly in its own juices.* [~ + *obj*]: *You can stew this cheap meat to make it tender.* **2.** [*no obj*] to fret, worry, or fuss: *Stop stewing about how bad your situation is!* —*n.* **3.** a preparation of food cooked by stewing, esp. a mixture of meat and vegetables: [*noncount*]: *some hot beef stew.* [*count*]: *Use this cheap meat in stews.* **4.** [*count; singular; usually: a* + ~] a state of nervous excitement or worry: *She's in a stew about finishing her term paper on time.* —***Idiom.*** **5. stew in one's own juices,** to suffer the results or consequences of one's own actions: *We left him to stew in his own juices.*

stew•ard (stōō′ərd, styōō′-) /ˈstuwərd, ˈstyuw-/ *n.* [*count*] **1.** one who manages another's property or financial affairs. **2.** a person in charge of running the household of a large estate. **3.** an employee who has charge of the table, wine, servants, etc., in a club, restaurant, or the like. **4.** an employee on a ship, train, or airplane who waits on and is responsible for the comfort of passengers. —**stew′ard•ship′,** *n.* [*noncount*]

stew•ard•ess (stōō′ər dis, styōō′-) /ˈstuwərdɪs, ˈstyuw-/ *n.* [*count*] a woman who acts or serves as a steward, esp. a flight attendant.

stick[1] (stik) /stɪk/ *n.* [*count*] **1.** a branch of a tree or shrub that has been cut or broken off. **2.** a long, slender piece of wood, for use as fuel, in carpentry, as a wand, rod, etc. **3.** *Chiefly Brit.* a walking stick or cane. **4.** a long, slender piece or part of anything: *a stick of celery.* **5.** an implement used to strike and drive a ball or puck, as a hockey stick. **6. the sticks,** [*plural*], *Informal.* any region or place distant from cities or towns; the country: *He thought a move to the sticks would relax him.*

stick[2] (stik) /stɪk/ *v.,* **stuck** (stuk) /stʌk/ **stick•ing,** *n.* —*v.* [~ + *obj*] **1.** to pierce or puncture with something pointed; stab: *He stuck the watermelon with a knife.* **2.** [~ + *obj*] to thrust or push (something pointed) in, into, through, etc.: *stuck pins into the pincushion.* **3.** to (cause to) be fastened in position by pushing a point or end into something: [~ + *obj*]: *to stick a peg in a pegboard.* [*no obj*]: *The arrow stuck in the tree.* **4.** [~ + *obj*] to fasten in position by or as if by something thrust through: *to stick a painting on the wall.* **5.** [~ + *obj*] to put on or hold with something pointed; impale: *to stick a marshmallow on a fork.* **6.** to thrust or poke into a place indicated: [~ + *obj*]: *The dog liked to stick his head out the car window.* [*no obj*]: *The dog's head stuck out the car window.* **7.** [~ + *obj*] to place or set in a specified position; put: *Stick the chair in the corner.* **8.** to (cause to) be fastened or attached; adhere: [~ + *obj*]: *to stick a stamp on a letter.* [*no obj;* (~ + *to* + *obj*)]: *The stamp won't stick to the letter.* **9.** [*no obj*] to be unable to move: *As soon as I put on my pants, the zipper stuck.* **10.** [~ + *obj* + *with* + *obj*] *Informal.* to force (someone) to accept something disagreeable, such as a difficult task: *I got stuck with the job of handling all the customer complaints.* **11.** [*no obj*] to remain, esp. for a long time or permanently; persist: *a fact that sticks in the mind.* **12. stick around,** [*no obj*] *Informal.* to wait in the same place or nearby; linger: *Stick around; I'll be right back.* **13. stick by** or **to,** [~ + *by/to* + *obj*] to remain loyal, esp. during difficulties: *Her husband stuck by her, even in times when she didn't have a job.* **14. stick out, a.** to (cause to) be pushed out; extend out: [*no obj*]: *His ears stuck out.* [~ + *obj* + *out*]: *She stuck her tongue out at the teacher.* [~ + *out* + *obj*]: *She stuck out her tongue at the teacher.* **b.** [*no obj*] to be easily noticed, as by being unusual: *She sticks out in a crowd, perhaps because of her purple hair.* See *stick it out* below. **15. stick to,** [~ + *to* + *obj*] **a.** to remain firm in one's opinion, in keeping to one's task, etc.: *He stuck to it and eventually finished the job.* **b.** Also, **stick with.** to continue with something and not turn away in a new direction: *Stick to your original plans.* **16. stick together, a.** to (cause to) be fastened or attached; adhere: [*no obj*]: *After you glue them the pieces will stick together.* [~ + *obj* + *together*]: *He stuck the pieces together with glue.* **b.** [*no obj*] to stay loyal to one another: *The two former Army buddies stuck together after the war.* **17. stick up,** [~ + *up* + *obj*] *Informal.* to rob, esp. with a gun: *They stuck up a bank and shot two guards.* **18. stick up for,** [~ + *up* + *for* + *obj*] to speak in favor of; support: *He always stuck up for his sister when people insulted her.* —*n.* [*count*] **19.** an act of pushing or thrusting with a pointed instrument; a stab: *a stick in the ribs.* —***Idiom.*** **20. stick it out,** [*no obj*] to endure something patiently to the end; persevere: *Finishing college seemed to take forever, but he stuck it out and got his diploma.* **21. stick to the** or **one's ribs,** to be substantial, filling, and nourishing, as a hearty meal: *This stew will stick to your ribs.*

stick•er (stik′ər) /ˈstɪkər/ *n.* [*count*] **1.** a person or thing that sticks. **2.** an adhesive label.

stick′er price′, *n.* [*count*] a seller's full asking price, esp. on a new automobile.

stick′-in-the-mud′, *n.* [*count*], *pl.* **sticks′-in-the-mud.** one who avoids new activities or ideas.

stick•ler (stik′lər) /ˈstɪklər/ *n.* [*count*] **1.** one who insists on something being (done in) a certain way: *a stickler for playing by the rules of the game.* **2.** any difficult problem or riddle.

stick•pin (stik′pin′) /ˈstɪk,pɪn/ *n.* [*count*] a straight pin with a decoration on the head, used for holding a necktie in place.

stick′ shift′, *n.* **1.** a manual transmission for a motor vehicle: [*noncount*]: *The car doesn't come with stick shift.* [*count*]: *Stick shifts give you more control over the car.* **2.** [*count*] a car with such a transmission: *This model isn't sold as a stick shift.*

stick•up (stik′up′) /ˈstɪk,ʌp/ *n.* [*count*] *Informal.* a holdup; a robbery.

stick•y (stik′ē) /ˈstɪkiy/ *adj.,* **-i•er, -i•est.** **1.** being able to stick to other things, as glue; adhesive. **2.** covered with matter that sticks easily to other things. **3.** (of the weather or climate) hot and humid: *a sticky day in the tropics.* **4.** requiring careful treatment: *a sticky problem.* —**stick′i•ness,** *n.* [*noncount*]

stiff (stif) /stɪf/ *adj.,* **-er, -est,** *n., adv., v.* —*adj.* **1.** rigid or firm: *a stiff collar.* **2.** not moving or working easily: *The garage door handle gets stiff in the cold.* **3.** (of a person or animal) moving with difficulty or with pain, as from cold, age, etc.: *He was stiff from back pain.* **4.** strong; forceful; powerful: *stiff winds.* **5.** [*before a noun*] strong to the taste or system, as a beverage or medicine: *a few stiff drinks at the bar.* **6.** stubbornly continued: *a stiff battle.* **7.** very formal or not very friendly: *She gave me a stiff, cold smile.* **8.** lacking ease and grace; clumsy or awkward: *a stiff style of writing.* **9.** laborious or difficult, as a task: *Analyzing all those sales figures was a stiff assignment.* **10.** severe or harsh, as a penalty or demand: *a stiff fine.* **11.** unusually high or great; excessive: *a stiff price.* **12.** relatively firm in consistency; thick; nearly solid: *Beat the egg whites until stiff.* —*n.* [*count*] **13.** *Slang.* **a.** a dead body; corpse. **b.** one who is too formal and unfriendly. **c.** a poor tipper; someone not generous; a tightwad: *That stiff left her only fifty cents as a tip!* **d.** a drunk. **e.** a fellow: *He's a lucky stiff, winning the lotto on his first try.* —*adv.* **14.** in or to a firm or rigid state. **15.** completely, intensely, or extremely: *scared stiff; bored stiff.* —*v.* [~ + *obj*] **16.** *Slang.* to fail to tip or pay (a waiter, etc.): *The customer stiffed the bartender.* —**stiff′ly,** *adv.* —**stiff′ness,** *n.* [*noncount*]

stiff′-arm′, *v., n.* STRAIGHT-ARM.

stiff•en (stif′ən) /ˈstɪfən/ *v.,* to (cause to) become stiff: [*no obj*]: *Whip the cream until it stiffens.* [~ + *obj*]: *The cold stiffens my neck.* —**stiff′en•er,** *n.* [*count*]

stiff′-necked′, *adj.* stubborn; obstinate; not giving in: *He should apologize, but he won't because he's so stiff-necked.*

sti•fle (stī′fəl) /ˈstayfəl/ *v.* [~ + *obj*], **-fled, -fling.** **1.** to crush by force: *to stifle a rebellion.* **2.** to hold back, keep back, or withhold: *I tried to stifle my laughter.* **3.** to smother and kill (someone): *The maniac stifled his victims with a pillow.*

sti•fling (stī′fling) /ˈstayflɪŋ/ *adj.* **1.** causing difficulty in breathing; stuffy: *a stifling room.* **2.** having difficulty in breathing: *I'm stifling in this overheated car.*

stig•ma (stig′mə) /ˈstɪgmə/ *n.* [*count*], *pl.* **stig•ma•ta** (stig′mə tə, stig mä′tə, -mat′ə) /ˈstɪgmətə, stɪgˈmɑtə, -ˈmætə/ **stig•mas. 1.** a mark of reproach, shame, or disgrace: *no stigma attached to losing the election.* **2. a.** a mark characteristic of a defect or disease: *the stigmata of leprosy.* **b.** a place or point on the skin that bleeds during certain mental states, as in hysteria. **3.** the part of a pistil on a flower that receives the pollen. **4. stigmata,** [*plural*] marks resembling the wounds of the crucified body of Jesus, said to appear on the bodies of certain holy persons. **—stig•mat•ic** (stig mat′ik) /stɪgˈmætɪk/ *adj.*

stig•ma•tize (stig′mə tīz′) /ˈstɪgməˌtayz/ *v.* [~ + *obj*], **-tized, -tiz•ing.** to put some mark of disgrace, shame, or dishonor upon (someone): *The father's crime stigmatized the whole family.*

stile (stīl) /stayl/ *n.* [*count*] **1.** a step or steps for climbing over a wall or fence. **2.** a turnstile.

sti•let•to (sti let′ō) /stɪˈlɛtow/ *n.* [*count*], *pl.* **-tos, -toes. 1.** a short knife with a slender, tapered blade. **2.** a woman's shoe with a long, high sharp heel; the heel itself.

still[1] (stil) /stɪl/ *adj.*, **-er, -est,** *n., adv., conj., v.* **—*adj.*** **1.** [*be* + ~] remaining in place or at rest; stationary: *He stayed perfectly still.* **2. a.** free from sound or noise; quiet: *The empty house was still.* **b.** subdued or low in sound; hushed: *the still, small voice of conscience.* **3. a.** calm; peaceful: *a still summer afternoon.* **b.** free from noise or agitation: *the still air in the meadow.* **4.** not flowing, as water: *The water was still, and not a breath of wind stirred the surface.* **5.** being or used for making single photographs, as opposed to a motion picture: *a series of still photographs.* **—*n.*** **6.** [*noncount*] calmness or silence: *in the still of the night.* **7.** [*count*] a single photographic print, as one of the frames of a motion-picture film: *The lawyer displayed several stills that had been taken from the tape and enlarged.* **—*adv.*** **8.** at this or that time; as previously: *Are you still here?* **9.** up to this or that time; as yet: *We are still waiting for your answer.* **10.** in the future as in the past: *Someone will still raise objections; they always do.* **11.** (used with comparative adjectives for emphasis) in addition; yet; even (greater): *He was after still greater riches.* **12.** even then; yet; nevertheless: *He is rich and he still desires more.* **13.** without sound or movement; quietly: *Sit still!* **—*conj.*** **14.** and yet; but yet; nevertheless: *It was futile; still they fought.* **—*v.*** **15.** to (cause to) become quiet, less active, or hushed: [*no obj*]: *The wind stilled at sunset.* [~ + *obj*]: *to still the children's cries.* **16.** [~ + *obj*] to make calm, reduce, or lessen (fears, doubts, etc.): *to still one's fears.* **—*Idiom.*** **17. still and all,** nonetheless. **—still′ness,** *n.* [*noncount*]: *the stillness of the night.* **—Usage.** Compare STILL, ALREADY, YET, and EVER, all of which can refer to events at or near the present time. STILL is used to refer to an action that is continuing from the past and is going on in the present; it suggests that the speaker is surprised that the action or event is going on: *We are still waiting for our visas to come from the embassy* (and we are surprised that we have not yet received them). STILL appears between the subject and verb or after an auxiliary verb and before the main verb. A speaker uses ALREADY when he or she suggests that the event has happened sooner than expected: *When will you get your visas? —Oh, didn't you know, we have already received them; they came yesterday.* This word is often used in the present perfect tense. YET is often used with a negative word or in questions, and appears when the speaker suggests that the event is expected to happen or occur: *Have you received your visas from the embassy yet? We haven't received our visas yet.* EVER is used in questions and in the present perfect tense with the meaning "at any time in the past"; it does not suggest that the speaker is expecting anything and is more neutral and open than the others: *Have you ever traveled to Egypt?*

still[2] (stil) /stɪl/ *n.* [*count*] an apparatus or device for making alcoholic drink.

still•birth (stil′bûrth′) /ˈstɪlˌbɜrθ/ *n.* **1.** the birth of a stillborn child or animal: [*noncount*]: *the causes of stillbirth.* [*count*]: *The number of stillbirths is increasing.* **2.** [*count*] a fetus dead at birth.

still•born (stil′bôrn′) /ˈstɪlˌbɔrn/ *adj.* **1.** dead when born. **2.** ineffective or useless from the beginning: *His reorganization plan was stillborn because it was too expensive.*

still′ life′, *n.* [*count*], *pl.* **still lifes.** a drawing or painting of inanimate objects, as of a bowl of fruit. **—still′-life′,** *adj.*: *a still-life watercolor.*

stilt (stilt) /stɪlt/ *n.* [*count*] **1.** one of two poles, each with a support for the foot at some distance above the bottom end, enabling the wearer to walk above the ground. **2.** one of several posts supporting a structure built above the surface of land or water. **3.** a white-and-black wading bird having long, bright pink legs.

stilt•ed (stil′tid) /ˈstɪltɪd/ *adj.* stiffly dignified or formal, as in speech or literary style.

stim•u•lant (stim′yə lənt) /ˈstɪmyələnt/ *n.* [*count*] **1.** an agent that temporarily quickens some bodily process, function, or activity: *a heart stimulant.* **2.** any food or beverage that stimulates, esp. coffee or tea. **3.** a stimulus or incentive: *a stimulant to the sluggish economy.* **—*adj.*** [*before a noun*] **4.** temporarily quickening some vital process or functional activity. **5.** stimulating.

stim•u•late (stim′yə lāt′) /ˈstɪmyəˌleyt/ *v.* [~ + *obj* (+ *to* + *verb*)], **-lat•ed, -lat•ing. 1.** to encourage to start, begin, or to do some action: *Talking to her stimulates my mind.* **2.** to excite (a nerve, etc.) to its functional activity: *This drug stimulates the brain to produce its own hormone.* **—stim•u•la•tion** (stim′yə lā′shən) /ˌstɪmyəˈleyʃən/ *n.* [*noncount*]: *She provides the department with great intellectual stimulation.* [*count*]: *stimulations of nerve cells.*

stim•u•lat•ing (stim′yə lā′ting) /ˈstɪmyəˌleytɪŋ/ *adj.* bringing a feeling of enthusiasm; inspiring: *a stimulating conversation.*

stim•u•lus (stim′yə ləs) /ˈstɪmyələs/ *n., pl.* **-li** (-lī′) /-ˌlay/. something that stimulates: [*count*]: *Her economic plan calls for a two-part stimulus to the economy.* [*noncount*]: *Many of his economic advisers argued against a package of strong stimulus at this time.* [*count*]: *Fear or excitement is a stimulus to the adrenal gland to produce adrenalin.*

-stin-, *root.* -*stin*- comes from Latin, where it has the meaning "separate; mark by pricking." This meaning is found in such words as: DISTINCT, DISTINGUISH, INDISTINCT, INSTINCT.

sting (sting) /stɪŋ/ *v.*, **stung** (stung) /stʌŋ/ **sting•ing,** *n.* **—*v.*** **1.** to prick or wound (a person or animal) with a sharp-pointed part of the body that often contains poison or venom: [~ + *obj*]: *The bee stung her on the foot.* [*no obj*]: *Dogs bite and bees sting.* **2.** to affect painfully as a result of contact, as certain plants do: [*no obj*]: *That plant will sting if you touch it.* [~ + *obj*]: *The nettle stung him.* **3.** to cause to feel a sharp pain: [~ + *obj*]: *The bullet stung his arm as it grazed his shoulder.* [*no obj*]: *His eyes stung from the smoke.* **4.** to cause (someone) to feel anger, resentment, insult, etc.: [~ + *obj*]: *Those remarks stung her deeply.* [*no obj*]: *The memory of that insult still stings.* **5.** to provoke (someone) to do some action: [~ + *obj* + *to* + *verb*]: *Those insulting remarks stung her to reply sharply.* [~ + *obj* + *into/to* + *obj*]: *He was finally stung into action.* **6.** [~ + *obj*] *Slang.* to cheat or take advantage of, esp. to overcharge; soak: *The swindlers stung me for over five thousand dollars.* **—*n.*** [*count*] **7.** an act or instance of stinging. **8.** a wound or pain caused by stinging. **9.** any sharp physical or mental wound, hurt, or pain. **10.** a sharp-pointed part of the body of some insects or animals, often containing venom or poison. **11.** *Slang.* **a.** a swindle or confidence game. **b.** an apparently illegal action such as the buying of stolen goods, engaged in by undercover investigators to collect evidence of wrongdoing: *an undercover sting filmed by hidden cameras.* **—sting′er,** *n.* [*count*]

sting•ray (sting′rā′) /ˈstɪŋˌrey/ *n.* [*count*] a fish having a flexible tail armed with a bony, usually poisonous spine.

stin•gy (stin′jē) /ˈstɪndʒiy/ *adj.*, **-gi•er, -gi•est. 1.** unwilling to give or spend; not generous: *That stingy man won't contribute a cent to the Little League.* **2.** scanty or meager: *a stingy salary.* **—stin•gi•ly** (stin′jə lē) /ˈstɪndʒəliy/ *adv.* **—stin′gi•ness,** *n.* [*noncount*]: *Scrooge's well-known stinginess.*

stink (stingk) /stɪŋk/ *v.*, **stank** (stangk) /stæŋk/ or, often, **stunk** (stungk) /stʌŋk/; **stunk; stink•ing;** *n.* **—*v.*** **1.** to (cause to) give off a strong, bad smell: [*no obj*]: *The kitchen stinks; what are you cooking in there?* [~ + *of* + *obj*]: *The hallways stank of cabbage and beer.* [~ + *up* + *obj*]: *They stank up the hallways with the smell of sour herring.* **2.** [*no obj; not: be* + ~ *-ing*] *Informal.* to be very bad, unpleasant, or inferior: *This job stinks!* **3.** *Informal.* [*no obj; sometimes:* ~ + *of* + *obj*] to suggest something dishonest or scandalous, or some disagreeable attribute: *"This case stinks of corruption," cried the D.A.* —*n.* [*count; usually singular*] **4.** a very strong, powerfully disgusting smell: *a stink of open sewers.* **5.** *Informal.* an unpleasant fuss; commotion: *She made a big stink about her boss calling her "Miss" instead of "Ms."* —**stink′er,** *n.* [*count*]

stink•ing (stink′ing) /ˈstɪnkɪŋ/ *adj.* **1.** giving off a very strong, unpleasant smell: *a stinking room.* **2.** very bad, unpleasant, or disgusting: *a rotten, stinking, no-good liar.* —*adv.* **3.** completely or extremely: *stinking drunk.*

stint (stint) /stɪnt/ *v.* **1.** [*no obj* (~ + *on* + *obj*)] to get along on a small amount: *Don't stint on the food.* **2.** [~ + *obj*] to limit (someone) to a certain amount, number, etc.: *to stint oneself.* —*n.* [*count*] **3.** a period of time spent doing something: *a stint in the army.* —**stint′ing,** *adj.*: *very stinting in her praise.*

sti•pend (sti′pend) /ˈstaypɛnd/ *n.* [*count*] **1.** a payment, esp. to a student: *a small stipend to buy books.* **2.** fixed or regular pay; salary: *an annual stipend.* See -PEND-.

stip•ple (stip′əl) /ˈstɪpəl/ *v.,* **-pled, -pling,** *n.* —*v.* [~ + *obj*] **1.** to paint, engrave, or draw by dots or small touches. —*n.* [*noncount*] Also, **stip′pling. 2.** the method of painting, etc., by stippling. **3.** stippled work.

stip•u•late (stip′yə lāt′) /ˈstɪpyə,leyt/ *v.,* **-lat•ed, -lat•ing. 1.** [~ + *obj*] to specify in terms of agreement: *to stipulate a price.* **2.** [~ + *that clause*] to require as a condition for agreement: *She stipulated that her daughter would have to receive money for school before she would agree to any settlement.*

stip•u•la•tion (stip′yə lā′shən) /,stɪpyəˈleyʃən/ *n.* [*count*] a condition in an agreement: *Here are the stipulations of the contract: on-time performance, complete work, and a flat-fee payment.*

stir[1] (stûr) /stɜr/ *v.,* **stirred, stir•ring,** *n.* —*v.* **1.** [~ + *obj*] to mix or agitate (a liquid or other substance) with a continuous movement of a spoon, a stick, etc.: *I stirred sugar into my coffee.* **2.** to move in a fluttering, irregular motion: [~ + *obj*]: *A soft breeze stirred the leaves.* [*no obj*]: *The leaves stirred in the soft breeze.* **3.** to move, esp. in a slight way: [~ + *obj*]: *He didn't stir a finger to help.* [*no obj*]: *She was sleeping so soundly she didn't stir when I came in.* **4.** to excite (people or their feelings), as from a quiet state into an active one: [~ + *obj*]: *to stir pity.* [~ + *up* + *obj*]: *He enjoys stirring up trouble over nothing.* [~ + *obj* + *up*]: *stirring them up to revolt.* [*no obj*]: *At long last the people stirred and recognized him for the crook that he was.* **5.** to move around, esp. quickly: [*no obj*]: *The children were awake and stirring before dawn.* [~ + *obj*]: *to stir oneself.* —*n.* [*count*] **6.** the act of stirring or moving: *a few slow stirs of the coffee.* **7.** [*usually singular*] a state or occasion of general excitement; commotion: *What's all the stir?* —**stir′rer,** *n.* [*count*]

stir[2] (stûr) /stɜr/ *n.* [*noncount*] *Slang.* prison.

stir′-cra′zy, *adj. Slang.* frantic from being held in prison for a long time, or from staying indoors, etc.: *The kids are stir-crazy because the lousy weather has kept them inside.*

stir′-fry′, *v.* [~ + *obj*], **-fried, -fry•ing.** to prepare (food) by cooking it quickly in a small amount of oil over high heat.

stir•ring (stûr′ing) /ˈstɜrɪŋ/ *adj.* **1.** inspiring, rousing, exciting, or thrilling: *a stirring speech.* **2.** active or lively.

stir•rup (stûr′əp, stir′-) /ˈstɜrəp, ˈstɪr-/ *n.* [*count*] a loop, ring, etc., hung from the saddle of a horse to support the rider's foot.

-stit-, *root. -stit-* comes from Latin, where it has the meaning "remain; stand." This meaning is found in such words as: CONSTITUTE, CONSTITUTION, DESTITUTE, INSTITUTE, PROSTITUTE, PROSTITUTION, RECONSTITUTE, RESTITUTION, SUBSTITUTE, SUPERSTITION, UNCONSTITUTIONAL.

stitch (stich) /stɪtʃ/ *n.* [*count*] **1.** one complete movement of a threaded needle through a material such as to leave behind a single loop of thread, as in sewing. **2.** the loop or portion of thread so left. **3.** one complete movement of the needle or hook in knitting, crocheting, etc. **4.** [*used with a negative word or phrase*] a thread, bit, or piece of any fabric or of clothing: *not a stitch of clothes on.* **5.** [*used with a negative word or phrase*] the least bit of anything: *They wouldn't do a stitch of work.* **6.** a sudden, sharp pain, esp. in the side of the body. —*v.* **7.** to work upon, mend, or fasten with or as if with stitches; sew: [~ + *obj*]: *The doctor stitched the wound before too much bleeding had occurred.* [*no obj*]: *She sat there quietly stitching.* —***Idiom.*** **8. in stitches,** laughing uncontrollably; convulsed with laughter: *Soon the comedian had the audience in stitches.*

stitch•er•y (stich′ə rē) /ˈstɪtʃəriy/ *n.* NEEDLEWORK.

stoat (stōt) /stowt/ *n.* [*count*] an animal, an ermine, esp. when in its brown summer coat.

stock (stok) /stɒk/ *n.* **1.** a supply of goods kept on hand by a merchant, etc., for sale to customers; inventory: [*count*]: *a good stock of computers.* [*noncount; in/out of* + ~]: *The store keeps lots of replacement parts in stock.* **2.** [*count*] a quantity of something kept, as for future use: *a good stock of tuna fish cans in the cupboard.* **3.** [*noncount*] livestock; farm animals. **4.** shares of a company that are divided and sold to its members: [*noncount*]: *He had stock in that company before its value increased.* [*count*]: *investing in stocks and bonds.* **5.** a race or other related group of people, animals, plants, etc., from the same or a similar source: [*noncount*]: *He comes from healthy Norwegian farmer stock.* [*count*]: *She classified the Indo-European stock of languages.* **6.** [*count*] the handle of a whip, fishing rod, etc. **7.** [*count*] the piece to which the barrel and mechanism of a gun are attached. **8. stocks,** [*plural*] a former instrument of punishment consisting of a framework with holes for securing the ankles, used to expose an offender to the public for ridicule. **9.** [*noncount*] the liquid or broth from boiled meat, fish, or poultry, used in soups and sauces. —*adj.* [*before a noun*] **10.** kept regularly on hand, as for use or sale; standard. **11.** having as one's job the care of the goods in a business: *a stock clerk.* **12.** of the common or ordinary type: *He gave his stock answer when asked about his plans for the future.* **13.** of or relating to the breeding and raising of livestock. **14.** of or relating to the stock of a company: *various stock options.* —*v.* **15.** to keep or provide with a stock or supply, as for future use: [~ + *obj*]: *They stocked the cupboard with food.* [*no obj;* ~ + *up*]: *You had better stock up now on cooking oil.* **16.** [~ + *obj*] to have in a store, as for sale: *The store is well stocked with replacement parts.* —***Idiom.*** **17. take** or **put stock in,** [~ + *obj*] to put confidence in or attach importance to: *I wouldn't put much stock in his promises.* **18. take stock, a.** to make a formal counting of stock on hand in a business: *The stores are closed so they can take stock of their inventory.* **b.** to examine or evaluate what one possesses, what one needs, etc.: *It's time to take stock of your life and decide where you want to go.*

stock•ade (sto kād′) /stɒˈkeyd/ *n., v.,* **-ad•ed, -ad•ing.** —*n.* [*count*] **1.** a defensive wall made from stakes driven upright into the ground. **2.** an enclosure made of such barriers. **3.** a prison for military personnel. —*v.* [~ + *obj*] **4.** to protect, fortify, or encompass with a stockade.

stock•brok•er (stok′brō′kər) /ˈstɒk,browkər/ *n.* [*count*] one who is hired by a company in a stock exchange to buy and sell stocks and other securities for customers.

stock′ car′, *n.* [*count*] **1.** a standard model of automobile changed in various ways for racing purposes. **2.** a boxcar for carrying livestock.

stock′ exchange′, *n.* [*count*] **1.** a place where stocks and other securities are bought and sold. **2.** an association of brokers who do business in stocks and bonds according to fixed rules.

stock•hold•er (stok′hōl′dər) /ˈstɒk,howldər/ *n.* [*count*] a holder or owner of stock in a corporation.

stock•ing (stok′ing) /ˈstɒkɪŋ/ *n.* [*count*] **1.** a close-fitting covering for the foot and part of the leg, of wool, cotton, nylon, etc. **2.** something resembling this. —***Idiom.*** **3. in one's stocking feet,** wearing stockings but no shoes.

stock′ mar′ket, *n.* [*count; usually: the* + ~] **1.** a market where stocks and bonds are traded; stock exchange. **2.** the market for stocks throughout a nation.

stock•pile (stok′pīl′) /ˈstɒk,payl/ *n., v.,* **-piled, -pil•ing.** —*n.* [*count*] **1.** a supply of a material held in reserve: *a stockpile of food, clothing, fuel, and other supplies.* —*v.* [~ + *obj*] **2.** to put or store in a stockpile: *to stockpile goods in case of emergency.*

stock′-still′, *adj.* completely still; motionless.

stock•y (stok′ē) /ˈstɒkiy/ *adj.,* **-i•er, -i•est. 1.** of sturdy form or build; thickset. **2.** having a strong, stout stem, as a plant. —**stock′i•ness,** *n.* [*noncount*]

stock•yard (stok′yärd′) /ˈstɒk,yard/ *n.* [*count*] an enclosure with pens, sheds, etc., connected with a slaughterhouse, railroad, etc., for housing livestock.

stodg•y (stoj′ē) /ˈstɒdʒiy/ *adj.,* **-i•er, -i•est. 1.** dull or uninteresting; boring: *a long, stodgy novel.* **2.** very old-fashioned; rigidly conventional: *a stodgy old gentleman.* **3.** drab or dowdy; inelegant: *a stodgy business suit.* —**stodg′i•ness,** *n.* [*noncount*]

sto•gy or **sto•gie** (stō′gē) /ˈstowgiy/ *n.* [*count*], *pl.* **-gies.** a long, slender, roughly made, inexpensive cigar.

sto•ic (stō′ik) /ˈstowɪk/ *adj.* **1.** of or relating to a belief that people should be free from passion. **2.** stoical. —*n.* [*count*] **3.** one who accepts such a belief. —**sto•i•cism** (stō′ə siz′əm) /ˈstowəˌsɪzəm/ *n.* [*noncount*]

sto•i•cal (stō′i kəl) /ˈstowɪkəl/ *adj.* exhibiting a calm, patient acceptance of difficulty. —**sto′i•cal•ly,** *adv.*

stoke (stōk) /stowk/ *v.* [~ + *obj*], **stoked, stok•ing. 1.** to poke, stir up, and feed (a fire). **2.** to tend the fire of (a furnace); supply with fuel. —**stok′er,** *n.* [*count*]

stole[1] (stōl) /stowl/ *v.* pt. of STEAL.

stole[2] (stōl) /stowl/ *n.* [*count*] **1.** a piece of clothing worn by the clergy, made of a narrow strip of material and worn over the shoulder or shoulders. **2.** a woman's shoulder scarf of fur, silk, or other material.

sto•len (stō′lən) /ˈstowlən/ *v.* pp. of STEAL.

stol•id (stol′id) /ˈstɒlɪd/ *adj.* not easily stirred or moved mentally or emotionally: *A very stolid worker, he seldom showed excitement.* —**stol′id•ly,** *adv.*: *The detective moved stolidly through the scene of the crime.*

stom•ach (stum′ək) /ˈstʌmək/ *n.* [*count*] **1.** a saclike part of the body where food is stored and partially digested: *Her stomach was full.* **2.** the lower front part of the body, containing the stomach; the belly or abdomen: *The buttons on his shirt were popping from his fat stomach.* **3.** [*used with a negative word or phrase, or in questions*] desire; inclination; liking; appetite: *They have no stomach for all this violence.* —*v.* [~ + *obj; used with a negative word or phrase, or in questions*] **4.** to endure or tolerate; bear: *She can't stomach violence.* —***Idiom.* 5. sick to one's stomach,** feeling ready to vomit: *He felt sick to his stomach and walked quickly to a bathroom.*

stom•ach•ache (stum′ək āk′) /ˈstʌməkˌeyk/ *n.* [*count*] pain or discomfort in the stomach or abdomen.

stomp (stomp) /stɒmp/ *v.* **1.** to walk on or step on heavily; trample: [~ + *obj*]: *He stomped the floor with his heavy boots.* [*no obj*]: *He walked around stomping on the floor.* —*n.* [*count*] **2.** the act of stomping; stamp.

stone (stōn) /stown/ *n., pl.* **stones** for 1–4, 6, 7, **stone** for 5; *adj., adv., v.,* **stoned, ston•ing.** —*n.* **1.** [*noncount*] the hard substance, formed of mineral matter, of which rocks are made. **2.** [*count*] a piece of rock made into a specific size and shape for a particular purpose: *paving stones.* **3.** [*count*] a small piece of rock, as a pebble: *He taught his daughter how to skip stones in the water.* **4.** [*count*] a mineral used in jewelry; a gemstone: *a ring with a bright blue stone.* **5.** [*count*] one of various units of weight, esp. the British unit equivalent to 14 pounds (6.4 kg). **6.** any small, hard seed, as of a cherry or a date; a pit. **7.** a buildup, often in a rounded shape, of a calciumlike substance in the body, as in the kidney. —*adj.* **8.** of or relating to stone or stoneware. —*adv.* **9.** completely; totally: *stone deaf.* —*v.* [~ + *obj*] **10.** to throw stones at: *The angry mob stoned the embassy.* **11.** to put to death by throwing stones at (someone): *They stoned him to death.* **12.** to remove stones from (fruit). —***Idiom.* 13. cast the first stone,** to be the first to condemn a wrongdoer. **14. leave no stone unturned,** to explore every possibility: *The police left no stone unturned until the killer was brought to justice.*

stoned (stōnd) /stownd/ *adj.* [*be/get* + ~] *Informal.* **1.** drunk: *He's had several beers too many and is completely stoned.* **2.** feeling the effects of drugs; dazed from drugs; high: *They went out and got stoned.*

stone's′ throw′, *n.* [*count; usually singular*] a short distance: *just a stone's throw from the train station.*

stone•wall (stōn′wôl′) /ˈstownˌwɔl/ *v.* to be uncooperative (with); use blocking or stalling tactics (on): [*no obj*]: *Each side accused the other of stonewalling on the arms control issue.* [~ + *obj*]: *trying to stonewall passage of the legislation.* —**stone′wall′er,** *n.* [*count*]

ston•y or **ston•ey** (stō′nē) /ˈstowniy/ *adj.,* **-i•er, -i•est. 1.** full of stones or rock. **2.** resembling or suggesting stone, esp. in its hardness. **3.** unfeeling; merciless: *a stony stare.* —**ston•i•ly** (stōn′l ē) /ˈstownḷiy/ *adv.*: *stared stonily at his rival.* —**ston′i•ness,** *n.* [*noncount*]

stood (stŏŏd) /stʊd/ *v.* pt. and pp. of STAND.

stooge (stōōj) /stuwdʒ/ *n.* [*count*] **1.** an entertainer who feeds lines to a comedian and serves as the target of jokes. **2.** an assistant, as in performing a crime.

stool (stōōl) /stuwl/ *n.* [*count*] **1.** a simple armless and usually backless seat on legs: *sat on stools at the counter.* See illustration at HOTEL. **2.** a short, low support on which to step, kneel, or rest the feet while sitting: *He propped his feet on the stool.* **3.** the fecal matter excreted during a bowel movement. **4.** a toilet seat. **5.** a stool pigeon.

stool′ pi′geon, *n.* [*count*] **1.** a pigeon used as a decoy to lure other pigeons. **2.** Also called **stool•ie** (stōō′lē) /ˈstuwliy/. *Slang.* a person hired or acting as a decoy or informer, esp. for the police: *His stool pigeon told him where the next robbery would be.*

stoop[1] (stōōp) /stuwp/ *v.* **1.** to bend the head and shoulders, or the body generally, forward and downward: [*no obj*]: *The basketball player had to stoop when climbing into the bus.* [~ + *obj*]: *He stooped his head a little when he climbed on the bus.* **2.** to lower oneself from one's normal level of dignity and do something considered improper, dishonest, etc.: [*no obj*]: *I would never stoop so low that I would take money from my own children.* [~ + *to* + *obj*]: *You wouldn't think he would stoop to such treachery.* [~ + *to* + *verb-ing*]: *Would he stoop to stealing money from his own children?* —*n.* [*count*] **3.** an act or instance of stooping. **4.** a stooping position of the body; a way of carrying the body at a low angle: *to walk with a stoop.*

stoop[2] (stōōp) /stuwp/ *n.* [*count*] a raised platform or porch, esp. a small porch with steps, at the entrance of a house: *We sat on the stoop and talked.*

stop (stop) /stɒp/ *v.,* **stopped, stop•ping,** *n.* —*v.* **1.** [~ + *verb-ing*] to cease from doing; finish (an activity): *I couldn't stop laughing at the joke.* **2.** to (cause to) cease or come to an end: [~ + *obj*]: *to stop crime.* [*no obj*]: *The music stopped.* **3.** to come to a stand, as in a course or journey: [*no obj*]: *He stopped at the side of the road and watched the cars go by.* [~ + *to* + *verb*]: *They stopped to say hello.* **4.** [~ + *obj*] to interrupt or cut off: *Stop your work for just a moment, please.* **5.** [*no obj*] to halt for a stay or visit: *They're stopping at a nice hotel.* **6.** [~ + *obj*] to cut off, intercept, or withhold: *to stop supplies.* **7.** [~ + *obj* (+ *from*)] to keep back, restrain, or prevent: *I couldn't stop him (from going).* **8.** to (cause to) be prevented from proceeding, acting, or operating: [~ + *obj*]: *to stop a car.* [*no obj*]: *The car stopped when it ran out of gas.* **9.** to (cause to) be blocked or closed off: [~ (+ *up*) + *obj*]: *Something has stopped (up) the sink again.* [~ + *obj* + *up*]: *Something has stopped it up again.* [*no obj;* ~ + *up*]: *The sink has stopped up again.* **10.** [~ + *obj*] to close (a container, etc.) with a cork, plug, etc. **11.** (of the outer openings of the ears, nose, or mouth) to (cause to) be closed: [~ + *obj* (+ *up*)]: *My nose is stopped (up) and I can't breathe.* [*no obj;* ~ + *up*]: *My ears stop up in airplanes.* **12.** [~ + *obj*] to notify a bank to refuse payment of (a check) upon presentation: *He stopped payment on the check because the merchandise was broken.* **13. stop by** or **in,** to make a brief visit: [*no obj*]: *We stopped by to say hello.* [~ + *by* + *obj*]: *We stopped by their house on the way through Indiana.* **14. stop off,** [*no obj*] to halt for a brief stay at some point on the way elsewhere. **15. stop over,** [*no obj*] **a.** to stop briefly, as overnight, in the course of a journey: *They stopped over in Copenhagen.* **b.** to make a brief visit. —*n.* [*count*] **16.** the act of stopping. **17.** a bringing to an end of movement, activity, or operation; end: *Put a stop to that!* **18.** a stay made at a place, as in the course of a journey: *We had a brief stop in Oslo.* **19.** a place where vehicles halt to take on and let off passengers: *a bus stop.* **20.** a plug or other stopper for an opening. **21.** a device that serves to check or control movement or action in a mechanism. **22.** an order to refuse payment of a check: *Put a stop on that check.* **23.** any of various marks used as punctuation at the end of a sentence, esp. a period. —***Idiom.* 24. pull out all the stops,** to use every means available to accomplish something: *At the end of the campaign he was pulling out all the stops: visiting every town and spending enormous sums on advertising.*

stop•cock (stop′kok′) /ˈstɒpˌkɒk/ *n.* COCK[1] (def. 3).

stop•gap (stop′gap′) /ˈstɒpˌgæp/ *n.* [*count*] **1.** something that fills the place of something lacking; a temporary substitute. —*adj.* [*before a noun*] **2.** serving as a stopgap; makeshift: *a stopgap solution to a deep-rooted problem.*

stop•light (stop′līt′) /ˈstɒpˌlayt/ *n.* [*count*] **1.** a taillight that lights up as the driver of a vehicle steps on the brake pedal to slow down or stop. **2.** TRAFFIC LIGHT.

stop•o•ver (stop′ō′vər) /ˈstɒpˌowvər/ *n.* [*count*] a stop or brief stay in the course of a journey.

stop•page (stop′ij) /ˈstɒpɪdʒ/ *n.* [*count*] **1.** an act or instance of stopping. **2.** the state of being stopped or blocked. **3.** a stopping of activity, esp. work; strike.

stop•per (stop′ər) /ˈstɒpər/ *n.* [*count*] **1.** a person or thing that stops. **2.** a plug, cork, or other piece for closing a bottle, tube, drain, etc. —*v.* [~ + *obj*] **3.** to close or secure with a stopper.

stop•ple (stop′əl) /ˈstɒpəl/ *n., v.,* **-pled, -pling.** —*n.* [*count*] **1.** a stopper, esp. for a bottle. —*v.* [~ + *obj*] **2.** to close or fit with a stopple.

stop•watch (stop′woch′) /ˈstɒpˌwɒtʃ/ *n.* [*count*] a watch with a hand or counter that can be stopped or started at any instant, used for precise timing, as in races.

stor•age (stôr′ij, stōr′-) /ˈstɔrɪdʒ, ˈstowr-/ *n.* [*noncount*] **1.** the act of storing; the state or fact of being stored. **2.** capacity or space for storing: *had our belongings in storage while we lived overseas.* **3.** MEMORY (def. 6). **4.** the price charged for storing goods.

store (stôr, stōr) /stɔr, stowr/ *n., v.,* **stored, stor•ing,** *adj.* —*n.* [*count*] **1.** an establishment where merchandise is sold: *a department store; a hardware store.* SEE ILLUSTRATION. **2.** a grocery store. **3.** a supply or stock of something, esp. for future use: *a huge store of ammunition.* **4.** *Chiefly Brit.* a storehouse or warehouse. **5.** great quantity; abundance: *a rich store of grain.* —*v.* [~ + *obj*] **6.** to supply or stock with something. **7.** to put away for future use: *Squirrels store nuts for the winter.* **8.** to deposit in a place for keeping: *We stored some of our furniture while we lived abroad.* **9.** to put or retain (data) in a computer memory unit: *The command "ST" is to store your file.* —*adj.* [*before a noun*] **10.** bought from a store; commercial: *store-bought bread.* —***Idiom.*** **11. in store, a.** in reserve: *We held some supplies in store.* **b.** about to happen: *You don't know what's in store for you.* **12. set** or **lay store by,** [~ + *obj*] to think highly of; to have regard for: *I don't set too much store by what he says.*

store•front (stôr′frunt′, stōr′-) /ˈstɔrˌfrʌnt, ˈstowr-/ *n.* [*count*] **1.** the side of a store facing a street, usually containing display windows. **2.** a room, set of rooms, or establishment at street level with the front facing a street. —*adj.* **3.** of or located in a storefront: *a storefront community center.*

store•house (stôr′hous′, stōr′-) /ˈstɔrˌhaws, ˈstowr-/ *n.* [*count*] (-hou′ziz) /-ˌhawzɪz/. **1.** a building in which things are stored; warehouse. **2.** a source of plentiful supply, as of facts or knowledge: *He's a storehouse of knowledge about the music of the 1950's.*

store•keep•er (stôr′kē′pər, stōr′-) /ˈstɔrˌkiypər, ˈstowr-/ *n.* [*count*] one who owns or operates a store.

store•room (stôr′ro͞om′, -ro͝om′, stōr′-) /ˈstɔrˌruwm, -ˌrʊm, ˈstowr-/ *n.* [*count*] a room in which supplies or other articles are stored.

sto•ried[1] (stôr′ēd, stōr′-) /ˈstɔriyd, ˈstowr-/ *adj.* recorded or celebrated in history or story.

sto•ried[2] (stôr′ēd, stōr′-) /ˈstɔriyd, ˈstowr-/ *adj.* (used after numbers) having (the stated number of) stories: *a two-storied house.* Also, *esp. Brit.,* **sto′reyed.**

stork (stôrk) /stɔrk/ *n.* [*count*], *pl.* **storks,** (*esp. when thought of as a group*) **stork. 1.** a wading bird having long legs and a long neck and bill. **2. the stork,** this bird when it is the symbolic deliverer of a new baby: *a visit from the stork.*

storm (stôrm) /stɔrm/ *n.* [*count*] **1.** a condition of the weather with strong winds, rain, thunder and lightning, etc. **2.** an instance of much rain, snow, etc., but without strong winds. **3.** a heavy or sudden outpouring or shower of things, as of bullets: *a storm of bullets.* **4.** a heavy, loud, or sudden outburst of feelings, emotions, etc.: *a storm of abuse.* —*v.* **5.** [*no obj; it* + ~] (of the wind or weather) to blow with unusual force, or to rain, snow, etc., esp. heavily: *It stormed all day.* **6.** to rage with fury: [*no obj*]: *He stormed about how unfair it all was.* [*used with quotations*]: *"Get out and don't come back!" he stormed.* **7.** [*no obj*] to rush, move, or stamp angrily: *He stormed out of the room.* **8.** [~ + *obj*] to attack or assault: *The army stormed the fortress.*

storm•y (stôr′mē) /ˈstɔrmiy/ *adj.,* **-i•er, -i•est. 1.** of or resembling storms; tempestuous: *stormy seas.* **2.** full of strong feeling, turmoil, or strife: *stormy debate.* —**storm•i•ly** (stôr′mə lē) /ˈstɔrməliy/ *adv.* —**storm′i•ness,** *n.* [*noncount*]

sto•ry[1] (stôr′ē, stōr′ē) /ˈstɔriy, ˈstowriy/ *n.* [*count*], *pl.* **-ries. 1.** a telling of events; a tale. **2.** a fictional tale, shorter and less involved than a novel. Also, **short story. 3.** the plot or events of a novel, poem, drama, etc. **4.** a report of the facts of a matter in question: *She wrote a story about him in the local newspaper.* **5.** a lie: *Now children, you must not tell stories; tell me what really happened.*

sto•ry[2] (stôr′ē, stōr′ē) /ˈstɔriy, ˈstowriy/ *n.* [*count*], *pl.* **-ries. 1.** a complete horizontal section of a building, as from the floor to the ceiling; one floor or level: *How many stories are there in that apartment building?* **2.** the set of rooms on the same floor. **3.** (used after numbers) having (the stated number of) stories: *a five-story apartment building.* Also, *esp. Brit.,* **storey.**

sto•ry•book (stôr′ē bo͝ok′, stōr′-) /ˈstɔriyˌbʊk, ˈstowr-/ *n.* [*count*] **1.** a book that contains a story or stories, esp. for children. —*adj.* **2.** made to look or seem better than reality: *a storybook romance.*

stout (stout) /stawt/ *adj.,* **-er, -est,** *n.* —*adj.* **1.** overweight; fat. **2.** [*before a noun*] courageous; brave: *stout warriors.* **3.** firm; stubborn; forceful: *The army met stout resistance.* **4.** substantial; thick; solid: *a stout cudgel.* —*n.* [*noncount*] **5.** a dark, sweet ale. **6.** a clothing size for persons of ample figure. —**stout′ly,** *adv.* —**stout′ness,** *n.* [*noncount*]

stout′-heart′ed, *adj.* brave; unafraid; firm and resolute: *stories of stout-hearted warriors.*

stove[1] (stōv) /stowv/ *n.* [*count*] an apparatus that furnishes heat for warmth or cooking: *a gas stove to cook the food.* See illustration at APARTMENT.

stove[2] (stōv) /stowv/ *v.* a pt. and pp. of STAVE.

stove•pipe (stōv′pīp′) /ˈstowvˌpayp/ *n.* [*count*] **1.** a pipe, as of sheet metal, serving as a stove chimney or to connect a stove with a chimney. **2.** a tall silk hat.

stow (stō) /stow/ *v.* **1.** [~ + *obj*] to put away in an orderly fashion: *The sailors stowed their gear below.* **2.** [~ + *obj*] *Slang.* to stop; break off: *Stow the talk; I'm not interested.* **3. stow away,** [*no obj*] to hide oneself aboard a boat, etc., as a stowaway. —**stow•age** (stō′ij) /ˈstowɪdʒ/ *n.* [*noncount*]

stow•a•way (stō′ə wā′) /ˈstowəˌwey/ *n.* [*count*] one who hides himself or herself aboard a boat, airplane, etc., as a way of getting free transportation.

strad•dle (strad′l) /ˈstrædl̩/ *v.* [~ + *obj*], **-dled, -dling. 1.** to stand or sit on (something) with the legs on either side of: *to straddle a horse.* **2.** to favor or appear to favor both sides of: *The politician is trying to straddle the issue.* —**strad′dler,** *n.* [*count*]

strafe (strāf) /streyf/ *v.* [~ + *obj*], **strafed, straf•ing.** to attack (targets) with bullets or missiles from low-flying airplanes.

strag•gle (strag′əl) /ˈstrægəl/ *v.* [*no obj*], **-gled, -gling. 1.** to wander from a road. **2.** to lag or be behind a line of march, a group walking, or a group working: *He's straggling behind the group and may get lost.* **3.** to grow or spread at irregular spaces or intervals: *trees straggling over the hillside.* —**strag′gler,** *n.* [*count*]

strag•gly (strag′lē) /ˈstrægliy/ *adj.,* **-gli•er, -gli•est.** growing or spreading unevenly or untidily: *a straggly beard.*

straight (strāt) /streyt/ *adj.,* **-er, -est,** *adv., n.* —*adj.* **1.** without a bend, angle, wave, or curve: *a straight path from here to the mountain.* **2.** exactly vertical or horizontal; level: *straight shoulders.* **3.** direct in character; truthful: *We asked for a straight answer.* **4.** honest; honorable; upright: *He's always been fair and straight with us.* **5.** reliable; agreeing with the facts; correct: *straight reporting.* **6.** logical; rational: *straight thinking.* **7.** being in the proper order or condition: *Things are straight now.* **8.** continuous; unbroken; one after the other: *We lost six straight games.* **9.** complete; unqualified: *a straight liberal.* **10.** supporting all candidates of one political party: *Many party members voted a straight ticket.* **11.** *Informal.* **a.** heterosexual. **b.** traditional; conventional: *He's too straight to try anything that unusual.* **c.** free from using narcotics: *He's straight and hasn't even seen a drug dealer in years.* **d.** not engaged in crime; law-abiding. **12.** not diluted or mixed with water: *straight whiskey.* —*adv.* **13.** in a straight line: *to walk straight.* **14.** in or into an even or proper condition or position: *Can you see if this picture is hung straight?* **15.** in an erect posture: *Stand straight.* **16.** directly: *Go straight home.* **17.** frankly; candidly: *Tell me straight: Are we still friends?* **18.** in a proper, right manner, as by being free from drug use, criminal activity, etc.: *He says he's gone straight and doesn't even think about stealing anymore.* **19.** in possession of truth or facts; without lies or exaggeration: *Let me set you straight on that rumor.* **20.** without water added: *to drink whiskey straight.* —*n.* [*count*] **21.** the condition of being straight. **22.** a straight form, part, or position. **23.** *Informal.* **a.** a heterosexual: *the question of gays and straights living together in the military.* **b.** one who follows conventional customs or morals. **24.** a sequence of five consecutive cards of various suits. —***Idiom.*** **25. straight off** or **away,** without delay; immediate'y: *He left straight away and didn't even*

store

linens
jewelry
CUSTOMER SERVICE
escalator
cosmetics
housewares
customer
sales clerk
gifts

say good-bye. **26. straight up,** served without ice: *a martini straight up.* —**straight′ness,** *n.* [*noncount*]

straight′-arm′, *v.* [~ + *obj*] **1.** to push away (an opponent) with the arm held out straight; to stiff-arm. —*n.* [*count*] **2.** Also called **stiff-arm.** an act or instance of straight-arming.

straight′ ar′row, *n.* [*count*] one who lives in a very proper way.

straight•a•way (*adj., n.* strāt′ə wā′; *adv.* -wā′) / *adj., n.* ˈstreytəˌwey; *adv.* -ˈwey/ *adj.* **1.** straight onward in course. —*n.* [*count*] **2.** a straight part of a road, racetrack, etc.: *On the straightaway he pulled ahead and won the race.* —*adv.* **3.** immediately; right away: *They sent for him straightaway.*

straight•edge (strāt′ej′) /ˈstreytˌɛdʒ/ *n.* [*count*] **1.** a bar or strip of wood, plastic, or metal having a long edge for use in drawing or testing straight lines, etc. —**straight′-edge′,** *adj.* **2.** of, using, or having a straight edge: *a straight-edge razor.* **3.** advocating, or believing in, a life free from alcohol, cigarettes, drugs, and sex.

straight•en (strāt′n) /ˈstreytn̩/ *v.* **1.** to (cause to) become straight, orderly, neat, or tidy: [*no obj*]: *His curly hair straightens if he doesn't wash it every day.* [~ (+ *out*) + *obj*]: *Straighten your tie; it's crooked.* [*no obj;* (~ + *up*)]: *Let's straighten (up) a bit before Grandpa comes over.* [~ (+ *up*) + *obj*]: *Let's straighten (up) your room a bit.* [~ + *obj* (+ *up*)]: *Let's straighten your room (up) a bit.* **2. straighten out, a.** to (cause to) become free of confusion or difficulties: [~ + *obj* + *out*]: *Let's see if we can straighten this problem out.* [~ + *out* + *obj*]: *The police tried to straighten out the mess.* **b.** to improve in conduct or character: [*no obj*]: *After he got married he straightened out nicely.* [~ + *obj* + *out*]: *A few years in the marines will straighten him out.* —**straight′en•er,** *n.* [*count*]

straight′ face′, *n.* [*count*] a plain expression on the face that hides one's true feelings: *He kept a straight face even though he wanted to laugh.* —**straight′-faced′,** *adj.*: *straight-faced lies.*

straight•for•ward (strāt′fôr′wərd) /ˌstreytˈfɔrwərd/ *adj.* **1.** going or directed straight ahead. **2.** honest. —*adv.* **3.** Also, **straight′for′wards.** straight ahead.

strain[1] (strān) /streyn/ *v.* **1.** to draw tight; make taut: [~ + *obj*]: *The mountain climbers strained their rope until it broke.* [~ + *at* + *obj*]: *The dog strained at its leash.* **2.** to use one's efforts or strength as much as possible: [~ + *obj*]: *She strained her ears and tried to hear what they were saying.* [~ + *to* + *verb*]: *He stood by the door, straining to hear what they were saying inside.* **3.** [~ + *obj*] to injure (a muscle, etc.) by stretching too hard: *He strained his leg muscle on that last jump.* **4.** [~ + *obj*] to make excesssive demands upon (someone or something): *straining the budget to make ends meet.* **5.** [~ + *obj*] to cause to pass through a strainer: *Strain the spinach.* **6.** [~ + *obj*] to draw off by means of a strainer: *to strain the water from spinach.* **7.** [*no obj*] to filter or ooze: *Water strained through the spinach.* —*n.* **8.** any force tending to alter shape, cause a fracture or break, etc.: [*noncount*]: *strain from high winds on an airplane wing.* [*count*]: *to reduce the strains caused by the settling of the house.* **9.** [*noncount*] strong effort: *His face showed signs of strain as he lifted the heavy weights.* **10.** an injury to a muscle, etc., due to excessive use; sprain: [*noncount*]: *muscle strain.* [*count*]: *To avoid muscle strains, warm up slowly before exercise.* **11.** the condition of being strained or stretched: [*noncount*]: *The strain on the economy was too great.* [*count*]: *Strains in the economy were beginning to show.* **12.** pressure or tension, as from fatigue: [*noncount*]: *The strain of hard work was beginning to show on his face.* [*count*]: *the strains of immigrating to a new country.* See -STRAIN-.

strain[2] (strān) /streyn/ *n.* [*count*] **1.** the group of all descendants having a common ancestor, as a family or stock. **2.** a variety, esp. of microorganisms: *a new strain of bacteria.* **3.** a characteristic or trait inherited from an ancestor: *There is a strain of insanity in the family.*

strain[3] (strān) /streyn/ *n.* [*count*] **1.** a melody; a tune. **2.** a style present throughout a work, esp. a written work: *He wrote it in a humorous strain.*

-strain-, *root.* *-strain-* comes from French and ultimately from Latin, where it has the meaning "stretch; tighten; bind." It is related to the root -STRICT-. This meaning is found in such words as: CONSTRAIN, RESTRAIN, STRAIN, STRAIT, STRAITEN, UNRESTRAINED.

strained (strānd) /streynd/ *adj.* produced by effort; not natural; forced: *strained hospitality.*

strain•er (strā′nər) /ˈstreynər/ *n.* [*count*] **1.** one that strains. **2.** a filter or sieve for separating liquids from solids: *She poured the pasta in the strainer and let the water drip out.* See -STRAIN-.

strait (strāt) /streyt/ *n.* [*count*] **1.** Often, **straits.** [*plural form may be used with a singular verb*] a narrow passage of water connecting two large bodies of water: *the Strait(s) of Gibraltar.* **2.** Often, **straits.** [*plural*] a position of difficulty, distress, or need: *At the moment she is in dire straits, with no money and no job.* See -STRAIN-.

strait•en (strāt′n) /ˈstreytn̩/ *v.* [~ + *obj*] **1.** to put into financial difficulties. **2. a.** to make narrow. **b.** to confine within narrow limits. See -STRAIN-.

strait•jack•et or **straight•jack•et** (strāt′jak′it) /ˈstreytˌdʒækɪt/ *n.* [*count*] **1.** a garment made of strong material, often strapped in the back, designed to keep the arms tightly bound: *The attendants put the violently deranged man in a straitjacket.* **2.** anything that severely constricts or prevents (one) from progress, activity, or the like: *High interest rates are a straitjacket on the economy.* —*v.* [~ + *obj*] **3.** to put in or as if in a straitjacket: *The government straitjacketed any expression of free thought.* See -STRAIN-.

strait′-laced′ or **straight′-laced′,** *adj.* **1.** overly strict in conduct or morality: *strait-laced ladies.* **2.** tightly laced, as an upper part of a dress.

strand[1] (strand) /strænd/ *v.* [~ + *obj*] **1.** to drive or run onto a shore; run aground: *The boat was stranded in the mud.* **2.** to leave in a helpless position: *tourists stranded in the middle of nowhere.* —*n.* [*count*] **3.** the land bordering a body of water; shore; beach: *the sea strand.*

strand[2] (strand) /strænd/ *n.* [*count*] **1.** a part of a rope, or a single piece or fiber of cord, string, etc., that is wound, twisted, or plaited together to form a rope. **2.** an element in a larger structure: *You have to work hard to put together the strands of the plot.*

strange (strānj) /streyndʒ/ *adj.,* **strang•er, strang•est,** *adv.* —*adj.* **1.** causing a feeling of curiosity or wonder; odd: *puzzled by her strange behavior.* [*It* + *be* + ~ + *(that) clause*]: *It was strange that there was no one to meet us.* [*it* + *be* + ~ + *to* + *verb*]: *It was strange to be the boss over someone who had once been* my *boss.* **2.** alienated: *We all felt strange in that city.* **3.** being outside of one's experience; unfamiliar; foreign: *It was hard for them to move to a strange place.* **4.** [*be* + ~ + *to*] not accustomed; not used to: *I'm strange to his ways.* —*adv.* **5.** in a strange manner: *They sure acted strange when we said hello.* —**strange′ly,** *adv.*: *The machine is acting strangely.* —**strange′ness,** *n.* [*noncount*]

stran•ger (strān′jər) /ˈstreyndʒər/ *n.* [*count*] **1.** a person with whom one has had no personal acquaintance: *warned their children not to talk to strangers.* **2.** a newcomer in a place: *a stranger in town.* **3.** one not accustomed to something: *She is no stranger to poverty.*

stran•gle (strang′gəl) /ˈstræŋgəl/ *v.,* **-gled, -gling. 1.** [~ + *obj*] to kill by squeezing the throat and preventing air from coming in: *I was so angry I could have strangled you.* **2.** [~ + *obj*] to prevent, block, or hold back the growth or action of: *Censorship strangles a free press.* —**stran′gler,** *n.* [*count*] —**stran′gling,** *adj.*: *He made a strangling noise in his throat.*

stran•gle•hold (strang′gəl hōld′) /ˈstræŋgəlˌhowld/ *n.* [*count*] **1.** an illegal wrestling hold by which an opponent's breath is choked off. **2.** any force that prevents action or development: *a stranglehold on the economy.*

stran•gu•la•tion (strang′gyə lā′shən) /ˌstræŋgyəˈleyʃən/ *n.* [*noncount*] **1.** the act of killing someone by strangling: *The coroner declared that death was by strangulation.* **2.** the act of preventing or holding back free progress, growth, or action: *the strangulation of economic progress.*

strap (strap) /stræp/ *n., v.,* **strapped, strap•ping.** —*n.* [*count*] **1.** a narrow strip of material, esp. leather, used for holding things together: *a shoulder strap for my suitcases.* **2.** a looped band by which an item may be held, pulled, or lifted. —*v.* [~ + *obj*] **3.** to secure, put in place, or fasten with a strap: *He strapped his snowshoes on.* **4.** to beat or whip with a strap.

strap•less (strap′lis) /ˈstræplɪs/ *adj.* **1.** lacking a strap or straps. **2.** having no shoulder straps to hold it in place; bare-shouldered: *a strapless gown.* —*n.* [*count*] **3.** a woman's garment that exposes the bare shoulders and has no shoulder straps.

strapped (strapt) /stræpt/ *adj.* [*usually: be* + ~ + *for*] needy; not having enough of; wanting: *strapped for funds.*

strap•ping (strap′ing) /ˈstræpɪŋ/ *adj.* [*before a noun*] powerfully built; strong; large: *a strapping young fellow.*

-strat-, *root.* *-strat-* comes from Latin, where it has the meanings "cover; throw over" and "level." These meanings are found in such words as: PROSTRATE, STRATA, STRATIFY, STRATOSPHERE, STRATUM, SUBSTRATE.

stra•ta (strā′tə, strat′ə, strä′tə) /ˈstreytə, ˈstrætə, ˈstrɑtə/ *n.* [*plural*] a pl. of STRATUM. See -STRAT-.

strat•a•gem (strat′ə jəm) /ˈstrætədʒəm/ *n.* [*count*] a scheme or trick for surprising or fooling an enemy, or for gaining an advantage in achieving a goal.

stra•te•gic (strə tē′jik) /strəˈtiydʒɪk/ *adj.* **1.** of or relating to military strategy: *a strategic expert.* **2.** of or relating to the general defense systems of a country, or to the destruction of an enemy's ability to make war: *strategic weapons designed to smash the enemy's homeland war-making facilities.* **3.** of or relating to any strategy to achieve a goal: *making strategic plans to increase sales.* —**stra•te′gi•cal•ly,** *adv.*

strat•e•gy (strat′i jē) /ˈstrætɪdʒiy/ *n., pl.* **-gies. 1.** [*noncount*] the science of planning and directing military operations: *an expert in military strategy.* **2.** [*count*] the use of or an instance of using this science or art: *He has devised a strategy to defend the rocket launchers.* **3.** a plan or method for achieving any specific goal: [*count*]: *a strategy for winning at bridge.* [*noncount*]: *At our next sales meeting we'll discuss strategy.* —**strat′e•gist,** *n.* [*count*]: *The mayor's top strategists urged him to begin campaigning harder.*

strat•i•fy (strat′ə fī′) /ˈstrætəˌfay/ *v.,* **-fied, -fy•ing.** to (cause to) be formed in different levels or strata, esp. within a society: [~ + *obj*]: *The society became stratified as the poor got poorer and the rich got richer.* [*no obj*]: *Their society gradually stratified until movement between different levels became impossible.* —**strat•i•fi•ca•tion** (strat′ə fi kā′shən) /ˌstrætəfɪˈkeyʃən/ *n.* [*noncount*]: *stratification into different classes.* See -STRAT-.

strat•o•sphere (strat′ə sfēr′) /ˈstrætəˌsfɪər/ *n.* [*count; usually singular; usually: the* + ~] **1.** the region of the upper atmosphere, from about six miles above the earth to about 30 miles (50 km) above, exhibiting little change in temperature. **2.** any great height or degree. See -STRAT-.

stra•tum (strā′təm, strat′əm) /ˈstreytəm, ˈstrætəm/ *n.* [*count*], *pl.* **stra•ta** (strā′tə, strat′ə) /ˈstreytə, ˈstrætə/ **stra•tums. 1.** a layer of something, often formed one upon another: *a stratum of skin tissue.* **2.** a layer; level: *That story has many strata of meanings.* **3.** a single bed or layer of rock, consisting of one kind of material. **4.** a level or grade of a people in a society, esp. with reference to social position and education: *How could he hope to rise from the lowest stratum of society?* See -STRAT-.

straw (strô) /strɔ/ *n.* **1.** [*count*] a single stalk or stem, esp. of a cereal grass. **2.** [*noncount*] a mass of such stalks, used as fodder: *feeding the cows their straw.* **3.** [*noncount*] material made from such stalks for hats or baskets: *a basket of straw.* **4.** [*count*] a narrow tube for sucking up a beverage from a container. —*adj.* [*before a noun*] **5.** of, relating to, or made of straw: *a straw hat.* **6.** of the color of straw; pale yellow. —***Idiom.*** **7. catch, clutch,** or **grasp at a straw** or **at straws,** to try anything out of a desperate need to save oneself from something bad. **8. (the) last straw,** something intolerably bad or unpleasant that is the latest in a series of bad events: *He had been late five times, but when he came to work drunk that was the last straw and he was fired.* **9. straw in the wind,** [*count*] a piece of information that seems to indicate future events.

straw•ber•ry (strô′ber′ē, -bə rē) /ˈstrɔˌbɛriy, -bəriy/ *n.* [*count*], *pl.* **-ries. 1.** the fleshy red fruit of a stemless plant belonging to the rose family. **2.** the plant itself.

straw′ man′, *n.* [*count*] **1.** a person whose function is only to disguise another's activities. **2.** a conveniently weak or innocuous person, object, or issue used as a seeming opponent or argument.

straw′ vote′, *n.* [*count*] an unofficial vote taken to find out the general trend of opinion on a given issue: *straw votes taken a week before the election.* Also called **straw′ poll′.**

stray (strā) /strey/ *v.* [~ + *from* + *obj*] **1.** to move away from the proper course, as by wandering: *to stray from the main road.* **2.** to become distracted from one's topic or main thought; to digress: *In your essay you are beginning to stray from the topic in this paragraph.* —*n.* [*count*] **3.** a domestic animal found wandering or without an owner. **4.** any homeless person or animal. —*adj.* [*before a noun*] **5.** straying or having strayed: *a stray cat.* **6.** found or occurring apart from others; incidental: *a few stray hairs.*

streak (strēk) /striyk/ *n.* [*count*] **1.** a long, narrow mark, smear, etc.: *streaks of paint where the liquid had dripped.* **2.** a layer: *streaks of fat in meat.* **3.** a strain or element, as of behavior or personality: *a wild streak.* **4.** a number of occurrences, as in a series; a spell; run: *a streak of good luck.* **5.** a flash leaving a visible line, as of lightning; a bolt. —*v.* **6.** to form streaks (on): [*no obj*]: *The windows streak if you don't wash them.* [~ + *obj*]: *The windows were streaked with dirt.* **7.** [~ + *obj*] to lighten or color (strands of hair). **8.** [*no obj*] to run, go, or work rapidly: *The jets streaked across the sky.*

streak•y (strē′kē) /ˈstriykiy/ *adj.,* **-i•er, -i•est.** full of streaks: *a streaky window.*

stream (strēm) /striym/ *n.* [*count*] **1.** a body of water flowing in a channel, as a brook. **2.** any flow or current of liquid, fluid, or gas: *a stream of gas escaping.* **3.** a series of things: *a stream of words.* —*v.* **4.** [*no obj*] to flow or pass in a stream: *The river streamed past the house.* **5.** to give out (a fluid): [*no obj*]: *Her eyes streamed with tears.* [~ + *obj*]: *The wound streamed blood.* **6.** [*no obj*] to extend in rays: *Sunlight streamed in through the window* **7.** [*no obj*] to proceed without stopping: *All day long the traffic streamed past her house.* **8.** [*no obj*] to hang in a flowing manner: *Her golden hair was streaming behind her.*

stream•er (strē′mər) /ˈstriymər/ *n.* [*count*] **1.** something that streams: *streamers of flame.* **2.** a long, narrow flag; a pennant. **3.** any long narrow piece or thing, as a paper ribbon: *The room was decorated with streamers.*

stream•line (strēm′līn′) /ˈstriymˌlayn/ *v.,* **-lined, -lin•ing,** *adj.* —*v.* [~ + *obj*] **1.** to make (something) into the shape of a teardrop so as to offer least resistance to air or water: *to streamline the shape of the car.* **2.** to change in order to make more efficient or simple: *to streamline the procedures for getting a work permit.* —*adj.* **3.** STREAMLINED.

stream•lined (strēm′līnd′) /ˈstriymˌlaynd/ *adj.* **1.** shaped so as to offer the least resistance to a current, as of air or water: *a streamlined automobile design.* **2.** designed or organized for maximum efficiency: *a streamlined chain of command.*

street (strēt) /striyt/ *n.* [*count*] **1.** a usually paved public road, as in a town or city: *Turn left at the next street.* **2.** such a road together with sidewalks and the nearby property: *On what street do you live?* SEE ILLUSTRATION. **3.** the part of such a street where cars or other vehicles may pass, as opposed to the sidewalk. **4.** the inhabitants or people who pass frequently on a street: *The whole street is talking about the arrest.* —*adj.* [*before a noun*] **5.** of, near, or opening onto a street: *a street door.* **6.** taking place or appearing on the street: *street musicians.* **7.** coarse; vulgar: *street language.* **8.** suitable for everyday wear in public: *street clothes.* **9.** relating to life in a (usually urban, esp. inner-city) neighborhood: *the street value of illegal drugs.* —***Idiom.*** **10. on** or **in the street, a.** without a home. **b.** without a job or occupation. **c.** out of prison; released from police custody; at liberty.

street•car (strēt′kär′) /ˈstriytˌkɑr/ *n.* [*count*] a public vehicle on rails running regularly along city streets.

street′ smarts′, *n.* [*plural*] shrewd awareness of how to survive in a rough, urban environment: *How good are your street smarts?* —**street′-smart′,** *adj.*

street•walk•er (strēt′wô′kər) /ˈstriytˌwɔkər/ *n.* [*count*] a prostitute who looks for clients on the streets.

street•wise (strēt′wīz′) /ˈstriytˌwayz/ *adj.* possessing street smarts.

strength (strengkth, strenth) /strɛŋkθ, strɛnθ/ *n.* **1.** [*noncount*] the quality of being strong: *It took a lot of strength to lift that big rock. It took strength of character to get through that ordeal.* **2.** [*noncount*] power by reason of influence, authority, or resources: *the strength of his plea.* **3.** [*noncount*] power of resistance: *The steel bars on the car's roof give it strength.* **4.** [*count*] a strong or valuable quality or characteristic: *He was asked to list his strengths and weaknesses on the interview form.* **5.** [*count*] a source of power or encouragement; something that sustains: *The Bible was her strength and joy.* —***Idiom.*** **6. in strength,** in the full force or numbers of a group or organization: *They came out in strength to support a change in the law.* **7. on the strength of,** on the basis of: *Solely on the strength of his recommendation we're going to hire you.*

strength•en (strengk′thən, stren′-) /ˈstrɛŋkθən, ˈstrɛn-/ *v.* to (cause to) grow stronger; give strength (to): [*no*

city street

skyscraper
office building
traffic light
lamppost
DRY CLEANERS
PHARMACY
taxi
bus
subway entrance
fire hydrant
sidewalk
street
crosswalk
mailbox
MAIL
pedestrian

obj]: *The hurricane strengthened overnight.* [~ + *obj*]: *We'll have to strengthen our defenses.*

stren•u•ous (stren′yo͞o əs) /ˈstrɛnyuwəs/ *adj.* **1.** characterized by or requiring strong, vigorous activity: *Strenuous exercise could reinjure your muscles.* **2. a.** intensely active; energetic: *a strenuous intellect.* **b.** ardent; spirited: *The lawyer raised strenuous objections to the proceedings.* —**stren′u•ous•ly,** *adv.*: *She objected strenuously to the remarks by the witness.* —**stren′u•ous•ness,** *n.* [*noncount*]

strep (strep) /strɛp/ *n.* **1.** [*count*] streptococcus. **2.** [*noncount*] strep throat: *a bad case of strep.*

strep′ throat′, *n.* a serious sore throat caused by streptococci: [*count*]: *a strep throat.* [*noncount*]: *suffering from a bad case of strep throat.*

strep•to•coc•cus (strep′tə kok′əs) /ˌstrɛptəˈkɒkəs/ *n., pl.* **-coc•ci** (-kok′sī, -sē) /-ˈkɒksay, -siy/. a round bacteria occurring in pairs or chains: *Certain streptococci cause such diseases as tonsillitis, pneumonia, and scarlet fever.*

stress (stres) /strɛs/ *n.* **1.** [*noncount*] importance or significance attached to a thing; emphasis: *to lay stress upon good manners.* **2.** emphasis or force expressed as the relative loudness of a speech sound, syllable, or word: [*noncount*]: *The word* promise *has stress on the first syllable.* [*count*]: *Count the stresses in the word* supermarket. **3.** *Music.* ACCENT (def. 7). **4.** the physical force exerted on one thing by another; strain: [*noncount*]: *The airplane wing snapped from stress.* [*count*]: *The stresses were large enough to snap the airplane wing completely off.* **5.** physical, mental, or emotional strain that disturbs one's normal bodily functions: [*noncount*]: *Job-related stress was giving him an ulcer.* [*count*]: *the stresses of two jobs, a family, and a full-time course load at school.* —*v.* [~ + *obj*] **6.** to emphasize; give or attribute (importance) to something: *He stressed the need for higher education.* **7.** to utter (a speech sound, syllable, or word) with noticeable loudness: *You should stress the first and third syllables in the word* supermarket. —**stress′ful,** *adj.*: *a long, stressful workday.* —**stress′ful•ly,** *adv.*

stressed′-out′, *adj.* afflicted with or feeling the strong effects of stress: *He was stressed-out from all that pressure and badly needed a break.*

stretch (strech) /strɛtʃ/ *v.* **1.** to spread out fully; straighten (the body, etc.) completely: [~ + *obj*]: *She stretched herself out on the ground.* [*no obj*]: *He yawned and stretched.* **2.** to (cause to) extend or spread from one place to another: [~ + *obj*]: *The crew stretched a rope across the road.* [*no obj*]: *The forest stretches for miles.* **3.** [*no obj*] to extend in time: *His memory stretches back to his early childhood.* **4.** to (cause to) be drawn tight or taut, without breaking or snapping: [~ + *obj*]: *to stretch the strings of a violin.* [*no obj*]: *Will this nylon stretch?* **5.** to draw out or extend too much: [~ + *obj*]: *The jacket was stretched at the elbows.* [*no obj*]: *The jacket stretched at the stomach.* **6.** [~ + *obj*] to extend or force (something) or make (something) serve beyond its normal or proper limits; strain: *to stretch the facts.* **7.** [~ + *obj*] to exert (oneself) to the utmost: *students who stretch themselves to achieve their best.* —*n.* **8.** [*count*] an act or instance of stretching; the state of being stretched. **9.** [*noncount*] ability to be stretched; elasticity: *These socks have lost their stretch.* **10.** [*count*] a continuous length: *a stretch of meadow.* **11.** [*count*] the last part of a racetrack: *down the stretch.* **12.** [*count*] an amount of, or extent in, time: *gone for a stretch of ten years.* **13.** [*count*] a term of imprisonment: *a ten-year stretch in prison.* —*adj.* [*before a noun*] **14.** (of yarn) having an ability to be easily stretched. **15.** made from such yarn: *stretch denim.* **16.** longer than standard: *stretch limousines.* —**stretch′a•ble,** *adj.*

stretch•er (strech′ər) /ˈstrɛtʃər/ *n.* [*count*] **1.** a framework of a piece of canvas and two long poles on the side, used to carry a sick or dead person. **2.** a person or thing that stretches.

stretch•y (strech′ē) /ˈstrɛtʃiy/ *adj.,* **-i•er, -i•est.** having the ability or capacity to stretch or be stretched.

strew (stro͞o) /struw/ *v.* [~ + *obj*], **strewed, strewn** (stro͞on) or **strewed, strew•ing.** to scatter (something) freely on (something): *The butcher strewed his shop floor with sawdust to absorb stains and odors.* See -STRU-.

stri•at•ed (strī′ā tid) /ˈstrayeytɪd/ *adj.* marked with slight ridges, bands, stripes, or streaks.

strick•en (strik′ən) /ˈstrɪkən/ *v.* **1.** a pp. of STRIKE. —*adj.* **2.** afflicted by disease, trouble, or sorrow: *stricken with polio.* **3.** showing the effects of affliction: *her stricken features.*

strict (strikt) /strɪkt/ *adj.,* **-er, -est. 1.** closely agreeing with requirements or principles: *a strict observance of rituals.* **2.** severe; demanding: *We have strict traffic laws.* **3.** exact; precise; carefully limited: *It wasn't robbery in the strict sense of the word.* **4.** absolute; complete: *strict silence.* —**strict′ly,** *adv.* —**strict′ness,** *n.* [*noncount*] See -STRICT-.

-strict-, *root.* -*strict*- comes from Latin, where it has the meaning "draw tight; bind; tighten." This meaning is found in such words as: CONSTRICT, DISTRICT, REDISTRICT, RESTRICT, STRICT, STRICTURE.

stric•ture (strik′chər) /ˈstrɪktʃər/ *n.* **1.** [*count*] an abnormal narrowing or tightening of any passage of the body. **2.** [*count*] a limitation; a restriction: *new strictures on gaining citizenship.* **3.** (a piece of) criticism or disapproval: [*noncount*]: *a case deserving stricture.* [*count*]: *strictures for such dishonesty.* See -STRICT-.

stride (strīd) /strayd/ *v.,* **strode** (strōd) /strowd/ **strid•den** (strid′n) /ˈstrɪdn̩/ **strid•ing,** *n.* —*v.* [*no obj*] **1.** to walk with a long step or steps: *He strode out the door in a huff.* —*n.* [*count*] **2.** a long step in walking: *He took two quick strides to the door.* **3.** the distance covered in a stride. **4.** a step forward in development or progress: *The country has made great strides in the improvement of roads and bridges.* —***Idiom.*** **5. hit one's stride, a.** to achieve a steady pace. **b.** to reach the level at which one works or functions best: *The pitcher finally hit his stride, winning six games in a row.* **6. take (something) in stride,** [*take* + *obj* + *in* + ~] to deal with (something) calmly: *He took the defeat in stride.*

stri•dent (strīd′nt) /ˈstraydnt/ *adj.* **1.** harsh in sound; irritating: *strident voices.* **2.** having an irritating or insistent character: *strident opinions.* —**stri′dent•ly,** *adv.*: *arguing stridently about unfairness.*

strife (strīf) /strayf/ *n.* [*noncount*] violent or bitter conflict: *armed strife.*

strike (strīk) /strayk/ *v.,* **struck** (struk) /strʌk/; **struck** or (*esp. for 13–15*) **strick•en; strik•ing;** *n.* —*v.* **1.** to deal (a blow) to (someone), as with the fist, a weapon, or a hammer: [~ + *obj*]: *He struck a blow at his attackers.* [*no obj*]: *Suddenly the mongoose struck and the snake disappeared.* **2.** to make a planned attack (on) suddenly: [*no obj*]: *The dive bombers struck at dawn.* [~ + *obj*]: *The bombers struck the oil refineries.* **3.** [~ + *obj*] to drive so as to cause impact or to collide: *to strike the hands together.* **4.** to come into forceful contact or collision with; crash into: [~ + *obj*]: *The ship struck a rock.* [*no obj*]: *Will lightning strike in the same place twice?* **5.** [~ + *obj*] to thrust forcibly: *She struck a pike into the earth.* **6.** [~ + *obj*] to produce by hitting or friction: *to strike sparks.* **7.** (of a match) to (cause to) ignite by friction: [~ + *obj*]: *He struck a match and lit the oil lamp.* [*no obj*]: *After the fifth time the match finally struck.* **8.** to come (upon) suddenly, as with bad effect: [*no obj*]: *If disaster strikes, will we have any money left?* [~ + *obj*]: *If disaster strikes us, what will we do?* **9.** [~ + *obj*] to reach (the ear) or fall or shine upon, as sound or light does: *The bright light struck my eyes.* **10.** to enter the mind of: [~ + *obj*]: *A happy thought struck him.* [*It* + ~ + *obj* + *(that) clause*]: *It struck me that I had forgotten to get a gift for the party.* **11.** [~ + *obj*] to impress strongly: *That particular painting struck my eye.* **12.** [~ + *obj* + *as*] to impress in a particular manner: *It strikes me as a ridiculous idea.* **13.** [~ + *obj; usually: be* + *struck* + *with/by* + *obj*] to overwhelm emotionally; affect strongly: *He was struck with awe.* **14.** [~ + *obj (+ as)* + *adjective*] to cause to become a certain way: *Those lies about her struck me dumb.* **15.** [~ + *obj*] to bring about (a feeling) in; induce: *The Viking longships struck fear into the hearts of the villagers.* **16.** [~ + *obj*] to happen upon; find; discover: *The drilling crew struck oil.* **17.** [~ + *obj*] to arrive at; achieve; confirm: *The two sides struck a compromise.* **18.** [~ + *obj*] to take apart; pull down: *The army struck camp and marched off early the next day.* **19.** [~ + *obj*] to cancel; cross out; remove: *At the last minute he decided to strike that passage from the speech.* **20.** to mark or make note of (the time) by or as if by chimes, bells, or the like: [*no obj*]: *The clock struck at midnight.* [~ + *a number indicating time*]: *The clock struck 12.* **21.** [*no obj*] to be indicated by or as if by such chimes, bells, or sounds: *The hour has struck.* **22.** [~ + *obj*] to assume or take on the formal character of: *The model struck a pose.* **23.** to go on strike against (an employer): [~ + *obj*]: *The workers struck the packing plant.* [*no obj*]: *The workers struck for higher wages.* **24. strike off,** to remove: [~ + *obj* + *off*]: *to strike names off a list.* [~ + *off* + *obj*]: *to strike off his name from our list.* **25. strike out, a.** to (cause to) be put out by a strikeout in baseball: [*no obj*]: *The batter struck out* *the last two times he was up.* [~ + *obj* + *out*]: *On the next pitch he struck him out.* [~ + *out* + *obj*]: *He struck out six batters in a row.* **b.** [*no obj*] to fail: *Every time he tried to get a date with her he struck out.* **c.** [*no obj*] to make one's way; set forth; venture forth: *struck out on their journey.* **26. strike up,** [~ + *up* + *obj*] **a.** to cause to begin performing: *She took the fiddle and struck up a tune.* **b.** to bring into being: *They struck up a deep friendship from the first time they met.* **—*n.* 27.** [*count*] an act or instance of striking. **28.** a stoppage of activity to force an employer or some authority to agree to demands, or to protest conditions: [*count*]: *a student strike.* [*noncount; on* + ~]: *The subway workers went out on strike for six weeks.* **29.** [*count*] *Baseball.* a pitch that is swung at and missed. **30.** [*count*] the knocking down of all the bowling pins with the first throw of the ball in a frame. **31.** [*count*] the discovery of a rich mineral deposit: *a gold strike.* **32.** [*count*] a planned attack, esp. by military aircraft: *a combined air and land strike against the occupied island.* **—*Idiom.* 33. have two strikes against one,** to be at a critical disadvantage: *Without a job or a bank account, I'll have two strikes against me.* **34. strike home,** to deal an effective blow and achieve an intended effect: *His argument really struck home and persuaded the jury.* **35. strike it rich,** [*no obj*] to have sudden or unexpected success.

strike•out (strīk′out′) /ˈstraykˌawt/ *n.* [*count*] an out in baseball made by a batter to whom three strikes have been charged.

strik•er (strī′kər) /ˈstraykər/ *n.* [*count*] **1.** a person or thing that strikes. **2.** a person who is on strike: *The strikers protested in front of the plant gates and tried to block trucks from going in.*

strik•ing (strī′king) /ˈstraykɪŋ/ *adj.* **1.** obviously attractive or impressive: *a striking photo.* **2.** noticeable; conspicuous: *a striking lack of enthusiasm.*

string (string) /strɪŋ/ *n.*, *v.*, **strung** (strung) /strʌŋ/ **string•ing.** **—*n.* 1.** a thin cord used for binding, connecting, or tying: [*noncount*]: *Use string to tie the package.* [*count*]: *Some strings had come loose.* **2.** [*count*] a narrow strip of flexible material for tying parts together: *bonnet strings.* **3.** [*count*] a collection of objects on a string: *She wore a beautiful string of pearls.* **4.** [*count*] a series of things arranged in or as if in a line: *a string of questions.* **5.** [*count*] a group of animals, businesses, etc., owned or managed by one person or group: *a string of race horses.* **6.** [*count*] the tightly stretched cord or wire of a musical instrument that produces a tone when caused to vibrate: *The guitar player broke a string in the middle of his solo.* **7. strings,** [*plural*] **a.** stringed instruments, esp. those played with a bow. **b.** players of such instruments in an orchestra or band. **8.** [*count*] (in a computer) a series or group of symbols, words, or bits treated as a unit. **9.** [*count*] a part of a team of players grouped as a squad according to their skill: *the first string of the basketball team.* **10.** Usually, **strings.** [*plural*] conditions, restrictions, or limitations on a proposal: *a generous offer with no strings attached.* **—*v.* 11.** [~ + *obj*] to provide (something) with a string or strings: *to string a banjo.* **12.** to extend or stretch like a string: [~ *(* + *up)* + *obj*]: *The workers strung (up) a line of lights on the Christmas tree.* [~ + *obj (* + *up)*]: *They strung a clothesline (up) across the yard.* **13.** [~ + *obj*] to thread on or as if on a string: *to string beads.* **14.** [~ + *obj*] to arrange in a series: *stringing words together.* **15.** [~ + *obj; usually: be* + *strung*] to make tense: *My nerves are strung.* **16. string along, a.** [*no obj*] to go along with another: *If you don't mind, I'll just string along.* **b.** [~ + *obj* + *along*] to keep in a state of uncertainty; to fool; deceive: *She won't tell him whether or not she likes him; she's just stringing him along.* **17. string out,** to prolong; make (something) last long: [~ + *out* + *obj*]: *They're stringing out this decision much too long.* [~ + *obj* + *out*]: *to string it out too long.* **18. string up,** to kill by hanging: [~ + *up* + *obj*]: *The townspeople strung up the horse thief.* [~ + *obj* + *up*]: *They strung him up at noon.* **—*Idiom.* 19. on a** or **the string,** depending on another's feelings, wishes, etc. **20. pull strings,** to use influence to achieve something: *He had to pull a few strings to get that job.*

string′ bean′, *n.* [*count*] **1.** a kind of bean, as the green bean, the unripe pods of which are used as food. **2.** SNAP BEAN. **3.** a tall, thin person.

stringed (stringd) /strɪŋd/ *adj.* **1.** fitted with strings: *violins, banjos, and other stringed instruments.* **2.** produced by musical instruments with strings: *stringed melodies.*

strin•gent (strin′jənt) /ˈstrɪndʒənt/ *adj.* very demanding, strict, or severe; harshly controlled: *stringent traffic laws.* **—strin′gen•cy,** *n.* [*noncount*] **—strin′gent•ly,** *adv.*

string•er (string′ər) /ˈstrɪŋər/ *n.* [*count*] **1.** a person or thing that strings. **2.** a long horizontal timber connecting upright posts. **3.** a part-time reporter or writer covering a local area for a newspaper, magazine, etc. **4.** a performer ranked according to skill or accomplishment: *The coach let the second- and third-stringers play.*

string•y (string′ē) /ˈstrɪŋiy/ *adj.*, **-i•er, -i•est.** of or like string, in being thin, slender, etc.: *his stringy hair.*

strip[1] (strip) /strɪp/ *v.*, **stripped** or **stript, strip•ping,** *n.* **—*v.* 1.** to take the covering from: [~ + *obj* (+ *of/from* + *obj*)]: *to strip a fruit of its rind.* [*no obj*]: *Bananas strip easily.* **2.** to remove (the clothing) from (a person); undress: [~ + *obj* + (*off*)]: *She stripped her clothes (off) and jumped into the lake.* [~ + *off* + *obj*]: *She stripped off her clothes and jumped into the lake.* [*no obj*]: *She stripped and jumped into the lake.* **3.** [~ + *obj*] to remove: *to strip sheets from a bed.* **4.** [~ + *obj* + *of* + *obj*] to take (something) away from someone; divest: *He was stripped of his rights.* **5.** to clear out; empty: [~ + *obj* + *of* + *obj*]: *to strip a house of its contents.* [~ + *obj*]: *They stripped the warehouse before selling it.* **6.** [~ + *obj*] to remove varnish, paint, etc., from: *to strip that old rocking chair and put on a fresh coat of stain.* **7.** (of the teeth of a gear mechanism) to (cause to) be damaged: [~ + *obj*]: *to strip the gears.* [*no obj*]: *The gears are stripping and the car keeps slipping out of second and third.* **—*n.* 8.** STRIPTEASE. **—strip′per,** *n.* [*count*]

strip[2] (strip) /strɪp/ *n.*, *v.*, **stripped, strip•ping.** **—*n.*** [*count*] **1.** a long narrow piece of material: *She found some strips of cloth and made a bandage.* **2.** a narrow piece of water or land: *a little strip of land along the beach.* **3.** COMIC STRIP. **4.** an airstrip; runway; a place to land a plane. **5.** an area of commercial development along a road: *the strip of discos and casinos.* **6.** DRAGSTRIP. **—*v.*** [~ + *obj*] **7.** to cut, tear, or form into strips.

stripe (strīp) /strayp/ *n.*, *v.*, **striped, strip•ing.** **—*n.*** [*count*] **1.** a narrow band differing in color, material, or texture from the background parts: *the stripes of a zebra.* **2.** variety; sort: *a person of a different stripe.* **—*v.*** [~ + *obj*] **3.** to mark or furnish with stripes. **—*Idiom.* 4. earn one's stripes,** to gain experience: *He had to earn his stripes as a traveling salesman.*

strip•ling (strip′ling) /ˈstrɪplɪŋ/ *n.* [*count*] a youth.

strip′-mine′, *v.*, **-mined, -min•ing.** to take minerals from (the earth) by digging out long, narrow trenches: [*no obj*]: *long, open wounds in the earth left where companies had strip-mined for years.* [~ + *obj*]: *They had strip-mined the region.* **—strip′-min′ing,** *n.* [*noncount*]

strip′-search′, *v.* [~ + *obj*] to search (a suspect who has been required to remove all clothing), esp. for concealed weapons, illegal substances, etc.

strip•tease (strip′tēz′) /ˈstrɪpˌtiyz/ *n.*, *v.*, **-teased, -teas•ing.** **—*n.*** [*count*] **1.** an act, as in a nightclub, in which a performer removes garments one at a time, usually to music. **—*v.*** [*no obj*] **2.** to do a striptease. **—strip′teas′er,** *n.* [*count*]

strive (strīv) /strayv/ *v.*, **strove** (strōv) /strowv/ or **strived, striv•en** (striv′ən) /ˈstrɪvən/ or **strived, striv•ing.** **1.** to try hard: [~ + *for* + *obj*]: *to strive for success.* [~ + *to* + *verb*]: *What makes him strive to do so well?* **2.** [~ + *against* + *obj*] to oppose in battle or conflict; compete: *to strive against fate.*

strobe (strōb) /strowb/ *n.* [*count*] **1.** Also called **strobe′ light′.** an electronic flash that produces rapid, brilliant bursts of light, used for high-speed photography, etc. **—*adj.* 2.** of or relating to this light.

strode (strōd) /strowd/ *v.* pt. of STRIDE.

stroke[1] (strōk) /strowk/ *n.*, *v.*, **stroked, strok•ing.** **—*n.*** [*count*] **1.** an act or instance of striking or hitting, as with the fist or a hammer; a blow. **2.** a striking of a clapper or hammer, as on a bell, or the sound produced by this: *at the stroke of midnight.* **3.** a blockage or breaking of a blood vessel that leads to the brain: *He suffered his third stroke in as many years.* **4.** a sudden, strong action or movement that is like a blow in its effect: *a stroke of lightning.* **5.** a hitting of the ball in tennis, pool, etc.. **6.** a single complete movement, esp. one continuously repeated in some process, as in swimming: *a swimming stroke.* **7.** a movement of a pen, pencil, brush, or the like; a mark made by such a movement: *a few strokes of the brush.* **8.** a feat or achievement, esp. one that comes suddenly: *a stroke of genius.* **9.** a sudden, accidental or chance happening: *a stroke of luck.* **—*v.*** [~ + *obj*] **10.** to mark with a stroke or strokes; cancel, as by a stroke of a pen. **11.** to hit (a ball) in tennis, golf, baseball, etc.: *He stroked the next pitch over the fence.*

stroke[2] (strōk) /strowk/ *v.,* **stroked, strok•ing,** *n.* **—***v.* [~ + *obj*] **1.** to pass the hand or an instrument over gently, as in caressing: *He stroked his cat absent-mindedly.* **2.** to promote feelings of self-approval in, as by flattery: *He's just trying to stroke the boss; he really doesn't mean a word he says.* **—***n.* [*count*] **3.** an act or instance of stroking: *a gentle stroke on the arm.*

stroll (strōl) /strowl/ *v.* [*no obj*] **1.** to walk slowly, easily, and without a definite direction, as for pleasure; ramble: *to stroll along the beach.* **—***n.* [*count*] **2.** a slow, leisurely walk.

stroll•er (strō′lər) /ˈstrowlər/ *n.* [*count*] **1.** one who takes a leisurely walk. **2.** a four-wheeled, chairlike carriage in which small children are pushed.

strong (strông, strong) /strɔŋ, strɒŋ/ *adj.,* **strong•er** (strông′gər, strong′-) /ˈstrɔŋgər, ˈstrɒŋ-/ **strong•est** (strông′gist, strong′-) /ˈstrɔŋgɪst, ˈstrɒŋ-/ *adv.* **—***adj.* **1.** having, showing, or involving great power in the body or muscles; physically vigorous: *Is the boy strong enough to lift that heavy box?* **2.** mentally powerful or vigorous: *He may be old, but his mind is still strong.* **3.** very able or powerful in a specific field or respect: *She is strong in mathematics.* **4.** powerful in influence, authority, resources, or means: *a strong nation.* **5.** aggressive; willful: *To many people his strong personality is annoying.* **6.** of great force, effectiveness, or power, as by being convincing, etc.: *strong reasons for abandoning the project.* **7.** clear and firm; loud: *a strong voice.* **8.** well-supplied or rich in something specified or implied: *a strong hand in a card game.* **9.** able to resist strain, force, wear, etc.: *strong cloth.* **10.** not given to nausea or other disturbance: *a strong stomach.* **11.** having considerable adhesive force: *strong glue.* **12.** firm; not giving in; unfaltering: *strong faith.* **13.** [*before a noun*] fervent; zealous; believing in completely: *a strong liberal.* **14.** moving or acting with force or power: *strong winds.* **15.** distinct, clear, or marked, as an impression or a resemblance: *a strong similarity in their political positions.* **16.** intense or concentrated: *a strong tea.* **17.** having a large amount of alcohol: *a strong drink.* **18.** [*after a noun or number*] of a designated number: *an army 20,000 strong.* **19.** having great magnifying or refractive power: *She needed strong lenses.* **—***adv.* **20.** in a strong manner: *The horse ran strong at the end.* **—*Idiom.* 21. come on strong,** [*no obj*] *Informal.* to behave too aggressively: *I think you frightened her by coming on so strong.* **—strong′ly,** *adv.*: *She strongly disagrees with that position.*

strong′-arm′, *adj.* [*before a noun*] **1.** using, involving, or threatening the use of force or violence: *The sheriff's strong-arm tactics won't work.* **—***v.* [~ + *obj*] **2.** to use or threaten to use violence upon: *The mob strong-armed him into agreeing.*

strong•box (strông′boks′, strong′-) /ˈstrɔŋˌbɒks, ˈstrɒŋ-/ *n.* [*count*] a strongly made box or chest for safeguarding valuables or money, esp. one that can be locked.

strong•hold (strông′hōld′, strong′-) /ˈstrɔŋˌhowld, ˈstrɒŋ-/ *n.* [*count*] **1.** a well-fortified, strongly defended place; a fort or fortress. **2.** a place that serves as the center of a group or movement sharing certain opinions or attitudes: *That campus is a stronghold of liberalism.*

strong•man (strông′man′, strong′-) /ˈstrɔŋˌmæn, ˈstrɒŋ-/ *n.* [*count*], *pl.* **-men. 1.** one who performs remarkable feats of strength, as in a circus. **2.** a political leader who controls by force; dictator.

strong′-mind′ed, *adj.* **1.** having a strong mind or mental powers. **2.** determined, stubborn, or obstinate.

strong-willed (strông′wild′, strong′-) /ˈstrɔŋˈwɪld, ˈstrɒŋ-/ *adj.* **1.** having a powerful will; determined. **2.** stubborn; obstinate.

strop (strop) /strɒp/ *n., v.,* **stropped, strop•ping. —***n.* [*count*] **1.** a device for sharpening razors, esp. a strip of leather that is easily turned or twisted. **—***v.* [~ + *obj*] **2.** to sharpen on or as if on a strop: *The barber stropped his razor before shaving his customer.* See -STROPH-.

-stroph-, *root.* *-stroph-* comes from Greek, where it has the meaning "turn; twist." This meaning is found in such words as: APOSTROPHE, CATASTROPHE, STROPHE.

stro•phe (strō′fē) /ˈstrowfiy/ *n.* [*count*], *pl.* **-phes.** (in modern poetry) a separate section or extended movement in a poem, distinguished from a stanza in that it does not follow a regularly repeated pattern. **—stroph•ic** (strof′ik, strō′fik) /ˈstrɒfɪk, ˈstrowfɪk/ *adj.* See -STROPH-.

strove (strōv) /strowv/ *v.* a pt. of STRIVE.

-stru-, *root.* *-stru-* comes from Latin, where it has the meaning "build, as by making layers; spread." This meaning is found in such words as: CONSTRUCT, CONSTRUCTION, CONSTRUE, DESTRUCT, DESTRUCTION, INDESTRUCTIBLE, INFRASTRUCTURE, INSTRUCT, INSTRUCTION, INSTRUMENT, INSTRUMENTATION, MISCONSTRUE, OBSTRUCT, RECONSTRUCT, STRUCTURE.

struck (struk) /strʌk/ *v.* **1.** pt. and a pp. of STRIKE. **—***adj.* **2.** (of a factory, industry, etc.) closed or otherwise affected by a strike of workers.

struc•tur•al (struk′chər əl) /ˈstrʌktʃərəl/ *adj.* [*usually: before a noun*] of or relating to structure: *The engineers examined the building for structural weakness.* See -STRU-.

struc•ture (struk′chər) /ˈstrʌktʃər/ *n., v.,* **-tured, -tur•ing. —***n.* **1.** [*noncount*] the way or manner in which something is constructed: *the structure of the building.* **2.** [*noncount*] the manner in which the elements or parts of anything are organized: *the structure of proteins.* **3.** [*count*] something constructed, as a building or bridge: *a huge structure overlooking the town square.* **4.** [*count*] anything composed of organized parts. **—***v.* [~ + *obj*] **5.** to give a structure to; organize: *to structure a company.* See -STRU-.

stru•del (strōōd′l) /ˈstruwdḷ/ *n.* [*count*] a pastry usually consisting of a fruit, cheese, or other mixture rolled in a paper-thin sheet of dough and baked.

strug•gle (strug′əl) /ˈstrʌgəl/ *v.,* **-gled, -gling,** *n.* **—***v.* **1.** [*no obj;* (~ + *against/with* + *obj*)] to fight hard against an attacker: *He struggled against the mugger and at last broke free.* **2.** [*no obj;* (~ + *against/with* + *obj*)] to work hard to solve a task or problem: *She struggled with calculus but eventually understood it.* **3.** [~ + *to* + *verb*] to make great efforts; strive: *He struggled to get free.* **4.** [~ + *through* + *obj*] to advance with great effort: *to struggle through heavy snow.* **—***n.* [*count*] **5.** an act or instance of struggling, as a war or contest: *a struggle with the children to get them to go to bed on time.*

strum (strum) /strʌm/ *v.,* **strummed, strum•ming,** *n.* **—***v.* **1.** to play on (a stringed musical instrument) by running the fingers lightly across the strings: [*no obj*]: *to strum quietly on the guitar.* [~ + *obj*]: *softly strumming my guitar.* **2.** [~ + *obj*] to produce by such playing: *to strum a tune.* **—***n.* [*count*] **3.** an act, instance, or sound of strumming.

strum•pet (strum′pit) /ˈstrʌmpɪt/ *n.* [*count*] a prostitute.

strung (strung) /strʌŋ/ *v.* pt. and pp. of STRING.

strut[1] (strut) /strʌt/ *v.,* **strut•ted, strut•ting,** *n.* **—***v.* [*no obj*] **1.** to walk in an overly proud or self-important way: *He strutted up and down in the front of the parade.* **—***n.* [*count*] **2.** the act of strutting.

strut[2] (strut) /strʌt/ *n., v.,* **strut•ted, strut•ting. —***n.* [*count*] **1.** a part used in a structure to support the whole. **—***v.* [~ + *obj*] **2.** to support by struts.

strych•nine (strik′nin, -nēn, -nīn) /ˈstrɪknɪn, -niyn, -nayn/ *n.* [*noncount*] a colorless, crystalline poison made from the seeds of an orangelike fruit.

stub (stub) /stʌb/ *n., v.,* **stubbed, stub•bing. —***n.* [*count*] **1.** a short part that sticks out. **2.** a short remaining piece, as of a pencil or cigar. **3.** (in a checkbook, receipt book, etc.) the inner end of each page, for keeping a record of the content of the part that has been filled out and torn away: *We checked our stubs and found that we had written a check already.* **4.** the returned portion of a ticket: *You'll need your ticket stub if you want to get back inside the theater.* **—***v.* **5.** [~ + *obj*] to strike (one's toe or foot) accidentally against some object that sticks out: *I stubbed my toe in the dark.* **6.** to extinguish the burning end of (a cigarette or cigar) by crushing it against a solid object: [~ + *out* + *obj*]: *He stubbed out his cigar.* [~ + *obj* + *out*]: *to stub his cigar out.*

stub•ble (stub′əl) /ˈstʌbəl/ *n.* [*noncount*] a short, rough growth, as of a beard. **—stub′bly,** *adj.,* **-bli•er, -bli•est.**

stub•born (stub′ərn) /ˈstʌbərn/ *adj.* **1.** unreasonably unwilling to change; unyielding: *a stubborn refusal.* **2.** fixed or set in one's purpose, action, or opinion: *He made a stubborn attempt to break the lock.* **3.** difficult to handle, treat, do away with, etc.: *a stubborn pain.* **—stub′born•ly,** *adv.*: *The army stubbornly resisted and refused to surrender.* **—stub′born•ness,** *n.* [*noncount*]

stub•by (stub′ē) /ˈstʌbiy/ *adj.,* **-bi•er, -bi•est.** short and thick: *the baby's stubby little fingers; his stubby little beard.*

stuc•co (stuk′ō) /ˈstʌkow/ *n., pl.* **-coes, -cos,** *v.,* **-coed, -co•ing. —***n.* **1.** [*noncount*] a kind of plaster or cement used for decorative work, moldings, etc. **2.** [*count*] a wall, facing, or other surface made of such material. —*v.* [~ + *obj*] **3.** to cover or decorate with stucco.

stuck (stuk) /stʌk/ *v.* **1.** pt. and pp. of STICK². —***Idiom.*** **2. stuck on,** [*be* + ~] *Informal.* strongly attracted to; infatuated with: *He said he was stuck on the girl next door.*

stuck′-up′, *adj. Informal.* snobbish and conceited; having an overly high opinion of oneself.

stud¹ (stud) /stʌd/ *n., v.,* **stud•ded, stud•ding.** —*n.* [*count*] **1.** a head of a nail that sticks out from a surface or part of something, esp. as an ornament: *a wooden chest lined with brass studs.* **2.** a buttonlike, ornamental object mounted on a pin that is passed through an article of clothing to fasten it: *a collar stud.* **3.** any of a number of slender, upright pieces of wood, steel, etc., that form the frame of a wall. **4.** an earring consisting of a small, buttonlike ornament mounted on a metal post. —*v.* [~ + *obj*] **5.** to set with or as if with studs: *Stars studded the sky.* —**studded,** *adj.*: *ornaments studded with jewels and diamonds.*

stud² (stud) /stʌd/ *n.* [*count*] **1.** a stallion used for breeding. **2.** any male animal kept for breeding. **3.** *Slang.* a sexually attractive man. —*adj.* [*before a noun*] **4.** of or relating to animals used for breeding: *a stud farm.*

-stud-, *root.* *-stud-* comes from Latin, where it has the meaning "be busy with; devote oneself to." This meaning is found in such words as: STUDENT, STUDIO, STUDY, UNDERSTUDY.

stud•ding (stud′ing) /ˈstʌdɪŋ/ *n.* [*noncount*] **1.** a number of studs, as in a wall or partition. **2.** timbers or manufactured objects for use as studs.

stu•dent (sto͞od′nt, styo͞od′-) /ˈstuwdnt, ˈstyuwd-/ *n.* [*count*] **1.** one who is formally engaged in studying, learning, or training at a school. See illustration at SCHOOL. **2.** one who studies or examines an art, science, etc., thoughtfully: *I've long been a student of Chinese pottery.* See -STUD-.

stud•ied (stud′ēd) /ˈstʌdiyd/ *adj.* **1.** showing or suggesting conscious effort; not coming naturally: *studied simplicity.* **2.** carefully thought over or considered: *a studied approval.* —**stud′ied•ly,** *adv.* —**stud′ied•ness,** *n.* [*noncount*] See -STUD-.

stu•di•o (sto͞o′dē ō′, styo͞o′-) /ˈstuwdiyˌow, ˈstyuw-/ *n.* [*count*], *pl.* **-di•os. 1.** the workroom of an artist, as a sculptor. **2.** a room or place for instruction or experimentation in a performing art: *a dance studio.* **3.** a place equipped for broadcasting radio or television programs, making phonograph records, etc. **4. a.** all the buildings and land required by a company in the production of motion pictures. **b.** the company itself: *That studio produced lavish musicals.* **5.** Also, **studio apartment.** an apartment consisting of one main room that is a combination kitchen, bedroom, and living room. See -STUD-.

stu•di•ous (sto͞o′dē əs, styo͞o′-) /ˈstuwdiyəs, ˈstyuw-/ *adj.* **1.** willing to study hard and diligently: *He's too studious to have the time to go to parties.* **2.** careful, determined; intent, or painstaking: *They took studious care not to spill the chemical.* —**stu′di•ous•ly,** *adv.*: *As I walked in she studiously avoided my gaze.* See -STUD-.

stud•y (stud′ē) /ˈstʌdiy/ *n., pl.* **stud•ies,** *v.,* **stud•ied, stud•y•ing.** —*n.* **1.** [*noncount*] the use of the mind to gain knowledge, as by reading, investigation, etc.: *the study of law.* **2.** Often, **studies.** a student's work at school or college: [*plural*]: *to pursue one's studies.* [*noncount*]: *After years of study he got his diploma.* **3.** [*count*] a complete investigation and analysis of a subject, phenomenon, etc.: *Studies show that smoking causes cancer.* **4.** [*count*] a written report of such an investigation: *I read a study claiming that smoking causes cancer.* **5.** [*noncount*] deep thought: *deep in study.* **6.** [*count*] a room set apart for private study or the like. **7.** [*count*] a person in relation to the speed at which he or she can memorize something, esp. an actor in regard to learning lines: *He is a quick study and can fill in for the lead actor at a moment's notice.* —*v.* **8.** to apply oneself to gaining knowledge, as by learning or investigation: [*no obj*]: *His youngest son spends much time studying.* [~ + *obj*]: *He's been studying chemistry all night.* **9.** to take a course of study, as at a college: [*no obj*]: *He's studying at Harvard.* [~ + *obj*]: *She's studying architecture at Yale.* **10.** [~ + *obj*] to examine or investigate carefully and in detail: *The police officer studied the accident scene.* See -STUD-.

stuff (stuf) /stʌf/ *n.* [*noncount*] **1.** the material of which anything is made: *Kerosene is oily black stuff.* **2.** material, objects, or items of some kind not specified: *What is all that stuff on the floor?* **3.** property, such as personal belongings: *I left some of my stuff in Dad's attic.* **4.** inward character, qualities, or capabilities: *The test pilots all believed they had the right stuff to be astronauts.* **5.** behavior or talk of a particular kind: *That's kid stuff!* **6.** a specialty or special skill: *Get out there and do your stuff.* **7.** worthless things or matter: *a lot of stuff and nonsense.* **8.** *Slang.* a drug, esp. an illegal one: *Are you on the stuff again?* —*v.* [~ + *obj*] **9.** to push, thrust, or cram (something) into something else: *I stuffed my clothes into the suitcase.* **10.** to fill (a receptacle, etc.), esp. by packing the contents closely together: *He stuffed his suitcase with old clothes.* **11.** to fill or cram with food: *He was stuffing his face (= eating to excess) with cake and ice cream.* **12.** to fill (poultry, vegetables, etc.) with a stuffing: *to stuff a turkey.* **13.** to fill the preserved skin of (a dead animal) with material, retaining its natural form and appearance for display. **14.** to put false votes into (a ballot box). **15.** to pack (people) tightly in a (confined place); crowd together: *They stuffed us into the subway car.* **16.** [~ *(+ up)* + *obj*] to stop up; block or choke: *Those allergies stuffed (up) her nose until she took medicine.*

stuffed′ shirt′, *n.* [*count*] a self-satisfied, pompous, pretentious person.

stuff•ing (stuf′ing) /ˈstʌfɪŋ/ *n.* [*noncount*] **1.** a material used to stuff something. **2.** seasoned breadcrumbs used to stuff poultry, etc., before cooking.

stuff•y (stuf′ē) /ˈstʌfiy/ *adj.,* **-i•er, -i•est. 1.** uncomfortable because of a lack of fresh air: *stuffy air; a stuffy room.* **2.** blocked or stopped up: *He had a stuffy nose.* **3.** dull or boring. **4.** self-important. **5.** rigid or old-fashioned in attitudes, esp. in matters of personal behavior. —**stuff′i•ness,** *n.* [*noncount*]

stul•ti•fy (stul′tə fī′) /ˈstʌltəˌfay/ *v.* [~ + *obj*], **-fied, -fy•ing.** to make (someone) feel dull because of some boring, repeating activity: *felt stultified by his humdrum job.* —**stul•ti•fi•ca•tion** (stul′tə fə kā′shən) /ˌstʌltəfəˈkeyʃən/ *n.* [*noncount*]

stum•ble (stum′bəl) /ˈstʌmbəl/ *v.,* **-bled, -bling,** *n.* —*v.* [*no obj*] **1.** to strike the foot against something, as in running, so as to trip or fall: *He hit a rock and stumbled.* **2.** to walk or go unsteadily: *The drunk stumbled down the street.* **3.** to make a slip, mistake, or blunder; to proceed in a hesitating manner, as in action or speech: *The scientists were stumbling along, looking for a cure.* **4.** [~ + *on/across* + *obj*] to discover, come upon, or meet with accidentally or unexpectedly: *They stumbled on a little village and stayed there.* —*n.* [*count*] **5.** the act of stumbling. **6.** a slip or blunder. —**stum′bler,** *n.* [*count*]

stum′bling block′, *n.* [*count*] an obstacle, or something that blocks progress, belief, or understanding.

stump (stump) /stʌmp/ *n.* [*count*] **1.** the lower end of a tree trunk left standing after the upper part falls or is cut off. **2.** the part of a limb of the body remaining after the rest has been cut off. **3.** any base part or short piece left after the main part has been removed; stub. **4.** [*usually singular*] a campaign tour for political speechmaking; circuit: *to go on the stump and meet the common folk.* —*v.* **5.** [~ + *obj*] to confuse, baffle, or cause (someone) to be at a loss: *The question stumped me.* **6.** to make political campaign speeches in or to: [~ + *obj*]: *to stump a state.* [*no obj*]: *stumping for votes.* **7.** [*no obj*] to walk heavily or clumsily, as if with a wooden leg: *Try not to stump up the stairs.*

stump•y (stum′pē) /ˈstʌmpiy/ *adj.,* **-i•er, -i•est.** short and thick; resembling a stump: *a short, stumpy little man.*

stun (stun) /stʌn/ *v.* [~ + *obj*], **stunned, stun•ning. 1.** to cause (someone) to lose consciousness, feeling, or strength by or as if by a blow, fall, etc.: *He was stunned by a wicked blow to the head.* **2.** to astonish; astound; amaze: *We were completely stunned by her hostile reaction.* **3.** to shock; overwhelm: *We were stunned to hear of his sudden death.*

stung (stung) /stʌŋ/ *v.* a pt. and pp. of STING.

stunk (stungk) /stʌŋk/ *v.* a pt. and pp. of STINK.

stun•ning (stun′ing) /ˈstʌnɪŋ/ *adj.* of striking beauty; very attractive: *a stunning redhead.* —**stun′ning•ly,** *adv.*

stunt¹ (stunt) /stʌnt/ *v.* [~ + *obj*] to slow down or prevent the growth of: *The roses in the garden had been stunted by the frost.*

stunt² (stunt) /stʌnt/ *n.* [*count*] **1.** a performance displaying a person's skill or daring; a feat: *performed some gymnastic stunts on the balance beam.* **2.** a feat performed to attract attention: *a publicity stunt.* **3.** a performance of a dangerous-looking act for a scene in a movie: *That actor does his own stunts: crashing through windows and hanging from the edges of buildings.*

stu•pe•fy (sto͞o′pə fī′, styo͞o′-) /ˈstuwpəˌfay, ˈstyuw-/ *v.* [~ + *obj*], **-fied, -fy•ing. 1.** to make (someone) tired, exhausted, or very bored: *The teacher's boring lecture stupefied the entire class.* **2.** to stun, as with strong emotion: *We were stupefied by his sudden death.* **3.** to overwhelm with amazement or surprise: *stupefied by the sight of all those people rushing through the square.* —**stu•pe•fac•tion** (sto͞o′pə fak′shən) /ˌstuwpəˈfækʃən/ *n.* [*noncount*]

stu•pen•dous (sto͞o pen′dəs, styo͞o-) /stuwˈpɛndəs, styuw-/ *adj.* **1.** causing amazement; marvelous: *a stupendous fireworks display.* **2.** amazingly large or great; immense: *The book turned out to be a stupendous success.*

stu•pid (sto͞o′pid, styo͞o′-) /ˈstuwpɪd, ˈstyuw-/ *adj.*, **-er, -est,** *n.* —*adj.* **1.** lacking quickness and keenness of mind: *a stupid person.* **2.** characterized by or showing mental dullness: *a stupid question.* **3.** boring or dull, esp. due to lack of meaning or sense: *a stupid movie.* **4.** annoying or irritating: *Turn off that stupid radio.* —*n.* [*count; sometimes used as a form of address*] **5.** *Informal.* a stupid person: *Hey, stupid, what do you think you're doing?* —**stu•pid•i•ty** (sto͞o pid′i tē) /stuwˈpɪdɪtiy/ *n.* [*noncount*]: *It was absolute stupidity to remove all that information from the computer.* [*count*]: *his stupidities in the business world.* —**stu′pid•ly,** *adv.*

stu•por (sto͞o′pər, styo͞o′-) /ˈstuwpər, ˈstyuw-/ *n.* [*count; usually singular*] inability to think correctly, or to feel or sense things, as caused by disease, narcotics, etc.; a state of near unconsciousness: *a drug-induced stupor.*

stur•dy (stûr′dē) /ˈstɜrdiy/ *adj.*, **-di•er, -di•est. 1.** strongly built; strong; hardy: *a sturdy young fellow.* **2.** strong, as in substance or construction: *a sturdy stepladder.* **3.** firm; courageous: *the sturdy defenders of the fort.* —**stur•di•ly** (stûr′dl ē) /ˈstɜrdḷiy/ *adv.* —**stur′di•ness,** *n.* [*noncount*]

stur•geon (stûr′jən) /ˈstɜrdʒən/ *n.* [*count*], *pl.* (*esp. when thought of as a group*) **-geon,** (*esp. for kinds or species*) **-geons.** a large fish, valued as a source of caviar.

stut•ter (stut′ər) /ˈstʌtər/ *v.*, **1.** to speak with the rhythm interrupted by repetitions, blocks, or spasms, or prolongations of sounds or syllables: [*no obj*]: *He stuttered when he spoke.* [*used with quotations*]: *"Wha-..wha-.. what do you mean?" he stuttered.* —*n.* [*count*] **2.** an act or instance of stuttering. **3.** stuttering speech. —**stut′ter•er,** *n.* [*count*]

sty[1] (stī) /stay/ *n.* [*count*], *pl.* **sties. 1.** a pen for swine; pigpen. **2.** a filthy place, house, etc.

sty[2] or **stye** (stī) /stay/ *n.* [*count*], *pl.* **sties** or **styes.** an infected area caused by bacteria on the glands on the edge of the eyelid.

style (stīl) /stayl/ *n.*, *v.*, **styled, styl•ing.** —*n.* **1.** [*count*] a particular sort, with reference to form, appearance, or character: *different styles of houses.* **2.** [*count*] a particular, special, or characteristic way of behaving: *to do things in a grand style.* **3.** [*noncount*] current fashion, as in clothes: *clothes that are never out of style.* **4.** [*noncount*] an elegant or luxurious way of living: *to live in style.* **5.** [*count*] a characteristic way of expressing thought in writing or speaking: *Her style of speaking is well organized.* **6.** [*count*] a characteristic form of design or construction in any art or work: *the Georgian style of architecture.* **7.** [*noncount*] a special quality of originality, elegance, or flair: *a person with style.* **8.** [*noncount*] a person's special tastes, attitudes, and behavior: *It's not his style to flatter people.* **9.** [*noncount*] the rules of spelling, punctuation, and the like observed by a publisher: *Follow the style for footnotes in your term paper.* —*v.* [~ + *obj*] **10.** [~ + *oneself* + *obj*] to call (oneself) by a given title or name; designate; name: *He styles himself "Emperor of the Universe."* **11.** to design or arrange in a given or new style: *She styled my hair in a pageboy cut.*

styl•ish (stī′lish) /ˈstaylɪʃ/ *adj.* characterized by or agreeing with the current style; chic: *stylish clothes.*

styl•ist (stī′list) /ˈstaylɪst/ *n.* [*count*] a designer or consultant on style, esp. in hairdressing, clothing, or interior decoration. —**sty•lis′tic,** *adj.* —**sty•lis′ti•cal•ly,** *adv.*

styl•ize (stī′līz) /ˈstaylayz/ *v.* [~ + *obj*], **-ized, -iz•ing.** to design (some piece of art, writing, or music) in or cause it to conform to a particular style: *His art shows a highly stylized manner.*

sty•lus (stī′ləs) /ˈstayləs/ *n.* [*count*], *pl.* **-li** (-lī) /-lay/ **-lus•es. 1.** a pointed instrument formerly used for writing on wax tablets. **2.** any of various pen-shaped instruments used in drawing, artwork, etc. **3.** any of various pens for tracing a line automatically, as on an electrocardiograph. Also, **style** (for defs. 1, 2).

sty•mie or **sty•my** or **sti•my** (stī′mē) /ˈstaymiy/ *v.* [~ + *obj*], **-mied, -mie•ing** or **-my•ing.** to block or prevent (someone or something) from proceeding or going forward: *This latest setback stymied our efforts to achieve peace.*

styp•tic (stip′tik) /ˈstɪptɪk/ *adj.* serving to slow down bleeding: *a styptic pencil for cuts.*

Sty•ro•foam (stī′rə fōm′) /ˈstayrəˌfowm/ *Trademark.* [*noncount*] a kind of plastic made from polystyrene: *a cup made of Styrofoam.*

-suade-, *root.* *-suade-* comes from Latin, where it has the meaning "recommend; urge as being agreeable or sweet." This meaning is found in such words as: DISSUADE, PERSUADE, SUASION, SUAVE.

sua•sion (swā′zhən) /ˈsweyʒən/ *n.* [*noncount*] the act of attempting to persuade: *When attempts at suasion failed, the United Nations used force.* See -SUADE-.

suave (swäv) /swɑv/ *adj.*, **suav•er, suav•est.** smoothly gracious in manner; polished. —**suave′ly,** *adv.* —**suav•i•ty** (swä′vi tē) /ˈswɑvɪtiy/ *n.* [*noncount*] See -SUADE-.

sub (sub) /sʌb/ *n.*, *v.*, **subbed, sub•bing.** —*n.* [*count*] **1.** a submarine. **2.** a substitute: *We hired a sub to teach her class.* **3.** a submarine sandwich. —*v.* [*no obj*] **4.** to act as a substitute for another: *Can you sub for their French teacher tomorrow?*

sub-, *prefix.* **1.** *sub-* comes from Latin, where it has the meaning "under, below, beneath": *subsoil; subway.* **2.** *sub-* is also used to mean "just outside of, near": *subalpine; subtropical.* **3.** *sub-* is also used to mean "less than, not quite": *subhuman; subteen.* **4.** *sub-* is also used to mean "secondary, at a lower point in a hierarchy": *subcommittee; subplot.* Sometimes this prefix is spelled as *su-, suc-, suf-, sug-, sum-, sup-, sur-*[2]*, sus-*.

sub., an abbreviation of: **1.** substitute. **2.** suburb. **3.** suburban. **4.** subway.

sub•a•tom•ic (sub′ə tom′ik) /ˌsʌbəˈtɒmɪk/ *adj.* **1.** of or relating to a process that occurs within an atom. **2.** of or relating to particles contained in an atom, as electrons, protons, or neutrons.

sub•com•mit•tee (sub′kə mit′ē) /ˈsʌbkəˌmɪtiy/ *n.* [*count*] a secondary committee composed of members of a larger main committee, usually to deal with a specific matter.

sub•com•pact (sub kom′pakt) /sʌbˈkɒmpækt/ *n.* [*count*] an automobile smaller than a compact. See -PACT-.

sub•con•scious (sub kon′shəs) /sʌbˈkɒnʃəs/ *adj.* **1.** existing or operating in the mind beneath consciousness: *subconscious feelings of love.* —*n.* [*noncount*] **2.** that part of one's mind or mental processes that are hidden to an individual and yet have an influence or effect on that person: *Somewhere in your subconscious you know she is right.* —**sub•con′scious•ly,** *adv.*: *Subconsciously I knew she was right.*

sub•con•ti•nent (sub kon′tn ənt, sub′kon′-) /sʌbˈkɒntṇənt, ˈsʌbˌkɒn-/ *n.* [*count*] **1.** a large, self-contained mass of land that forms a subdivision of a continent: *the subcontinent of India.* **2.** a large landmass, such as Greenland, smaller than any of the continents. See -TEN-.

sub•con•tract (sub kon′trakt, sub′kon′-; *v.* also sub′kən trakt′) /sʌbˈkɒntrækt, ˈsʌbˌkɒn-; *v.* ælsɒ ˌsʌbkənˈtrækt/ *n.* [*count*] **1.** a contract by which one agrees to provide services or materials necessary to complete another's contract. —*v.* **2.** to make a subcontract (for): [*no obj*]: *At first he subcontracted, then he went into business for himself.* [~ + *obj*]: *We'll subcontract the typing to another company.* —**sub•con′trac•tor,** *n.* [*count*]: *to hire a subcontractor to do the remodeling.* See -TRAC-.

sub•cul•ture (sub′kul′chər) /ˈsʌbˌkʌltʃər / *n.* [*count*] **1.** a group having characteristics different enough to distinguish it from others within the same culture or society: *an Asian-American subculture.* **2.** the cultural patterns of such a group.

sub•cu•ta•ne•ous (sub′kyo͞o tā′nē əs) /ˌsʌbkyuwˈteyniyəs/ *adj.* situated or injected under the skin.

sub•di•vide (sub′di vīd′, sub′di vīd′) /ˌsʌbdɪˈvayd, ˈsʌbdɪˌvayd/ *v.*, **-vid•ed, -vid•ing. 1.** (of something already divided) to (cause to) become divided into smaller parts: [*no obj*]: *The recently formed egg cells subdivided.* [~ + *obj*]: *to subdivide the cells.* **2.** [~ + *obj*] to divide (a piece of land) into building lots: *to subdivide the three-square-block area into smaller units for development.* —**sub•di•vi•sion** (sub′di vizh′ən) /ˈsʌbdɪˌvɪʒən/ *n.* [*count*]: *a housing subdivision; a political subdivision.*

sub•due (səb do͞o′, -dyo͞o′) /səbˈduw, -ˈdyuw/ *v.* [~ +

obj], **-dued, -du•ing. 1.** to overcome or overpower by force: *Rome subdued Gaul.* **2.** to hold back, keep in control, or repress (feelings, etc.): *His soothing words subdued her fears.*

sub•dued (səb do͞od′, -dyo͞od′) /səb'duwd, -'dyuwd/ *adj.* **1.** quiet; very calm or downcast: *He spoke in a very subdued voice.* **2.** (of colors) reduced in brightness or strength: *The room was lit in subdued colors.*

sub•head (sub′hed′) /'sʌbˌhɛd/ also **sub′head′ing,** *n.* [*count*] a title or heading of a subdivision, as in a chapter, essay, or newspaper article.

sub•hu•man (sub′hyo͞o′mən) /ˌsʌb'hyuwmən/ *n.* [*count*] **1.** one who acts in a way showing that he or she lacks basic human qualities in feelings, thinking ability, etc. **2.** a person or animal lower in some way than a human. **—*adj.* 3.** acting in a way beneath the level of a human, as by being cruel, horrible, etc. **4.** lower in some way than a human, as in development.

subj., an abbreviation of: **1.** subject. **2.** subjective. **3.** subjectively. **4.** subjunctive.

sub•ject (*n., adj.* sub′jikt; *v.* səb jekt′) / *n., adj.* 'sʌbdʒɪkt; *v.* səb'dʒɛkt/ *n.* [*count*] **1.** that which forms a basic matter of thought, discussion, etc.: *He keeps changing the subject and refuses to stick to the topic.* **2.** a branch of knowledge as a course of study: *Which subjects are you taking this semester?* **3.** something or someone written about or represented in writing, art, or music: *That beautiful model was the subject for a number of Rodin's sculptures.* **4.** one who owes allegiance to a king or queen or other head of state: *The king will provide new services for his loyal subjects.* **5.** one of the two main parts of a sentence (the other being the predicate) that is a noun or group of words acting like a noun, which usually refers to the one performing the action or being in the state expressed by the predicate: *The subject of the sentence* Jesse shot the sheriff *is* Jesse. **6.** a person, animal, or corpse that is an object of medical or scientific treatment or experiment. **—*adj.* 7.** being under the rule, control, or influence of something: *The warriors ruled harshly over their subject peoples.* [*be* + ~ + *to*]: *We are subject to the rules and regulations in effect.* **8.** [*be* + ~ + *to*] open or exposed to; likely to get or receive: *Those silly ideas are subject to public ridicule.* **—*v.* 9.** [~ + *obj*] to bring under rule, control, or influence: *The weaker tribes were subjected by another warlike race.* **10.** [~ + *obj* + *to* + *obj*] to expose to: *to subject metal to intense heat.* **11.** [~ + *obj* + *to* + *obj*] to make vulnerable to attack by (something); expose: *to subject yourself to ridicule.* **—*prep. phrase* 12. subject to,** depending on; dependent on: *His hiring is subject to your approval.* **—sub•jec′tion,** *n.* [*noncount*] See **-JEC-**.

sub•jec•tive (səb jek′tiv) /səb'dʒɛktɪv/ *adj.* **1.** existing in the mind and not necessarily in reality: *a subjective impression that the building was leaning to the right.* **2.** relating to or characteristic of an individual; personal: *Such decisions about one's job satisfaction are almost always, by definition, subjective evaluations.* **3.** placing too much emphasis on one's own moods, attitudes, etc.: *You're too subjective when it comes to judging her work.* **—sub•jec′tive•ly,** *adv.*: *You're viewing all this too subjectively.* **—sub•jec•tiv•i•ty** *n.* (sub′jek tiv′i tē) /ˌsʌbdʒɛk'tɪvɪtiy/ [*noncount*]

sub′ject mat′ter, *n.* [*noncount*] the substance or themes of a book, writing, etc., as distinguished from its form or style.

sub•ju•gate (sub′jə gāt′) /'sʌbdʒəˌgeyt/ *v.* [~ + *obj*], **-gat•ed, -gat•ing. 1.** to bring under complete control; conquer: *The invaders subjugated the farmers.* **2.** to make less important: *subjugating his desires to play golf to the needs of his family.* **—sub•ju•ga•tion** (sub′jə gā′shən) /ˌsʌbdʒə'geyʃən/ *n.* [*noncount*]

sub•junc•tive (səb jungk′tiv) /səb'dʒʌŋktɪv/ *adj.* **1.** of or being a grammatical mood typically used for subjective, doubtful, hypothetical (contrary to fact), or grammatically subordinate statements or questions, as the mood of *be* in *if I were a rich man.* Compare **IMPERATIVE** (def. 2), **INDICATIVE** (def. 2). **—*n.*** [*count*] **2.** the subjunctive mood. **3.** a verb form in the subjunctive mood. See **-JUNC-**.

sub•lease (*n.* sub′lēs′; *v.* sub lēs′) / *n.* 'sʌbˌliys; *v.* sʌb'liys/ *n., v.,* **-leased, -leas•ing. —*n.*** [*count*] **1.** a lease granted to another by the person leasing a property. **—*v.* 2.** to grant a sublease of: [~ + *obj* (+ *to* + *obj*)]: *The present tenant subleased his apartment (to a friend).* [*no obj*]: *We weren't allowed to sublease while we lived there.* **3.** to take or hold a sublease of: [~ + *obj* (+ *from* + *obj*)]: *John subleased our apartment (from us).* [*no obj*]: *John didn't want to sublease; he wanted to buy his own place.*

sub•let (*v.* sub let′, sub′let′; *n.* sub′let′) / *v.* sʌb'lɛt, 'sʌbˌlɛt; *n.* 'sʌbˌlɛt/ *v.,* **-let, -let•ting,** *n.* **—*v.* 1.** to sublease: [~ + *obj* (+ *to* + *obj*)]: *We sublet our apartment (to John).* [~ + *obj* (+ *from* + *obj*)]: *John sublet our apartment (from us).* **—*n.*** [*count*] **2.** an act or instance of subleasing. **3.** a property, as an apartment, obtained by subleasing.

sub•li•mate (sub′lə māt′) /'sʌbləˌmeyt/ *v.,* **-mat•ed, -mat•ing.** to redirect the energy of (a biological drive) from its immediate object to a more acceptable or productive nature or goal: *Once he settled down, he sublimated his desires for women into a daily regimen of exercise.* **—sub•li•ma•tion** (sub′lə mā′shən) /ˌsʌblə'meyʃən/ *n.* [*noncount*] See **-LIM-**.

sub•lime (sə blīm′) /sə'blaym/ *adj.* **1.** elevated or lofty in thought, language, etc. **2.** impressing the mind with a sense of grandness or power. **3.** supreme or outstanding: *a sublime dinner.* **—*n.*** [*noncount*] **4. the sublime, a.** the realm of things that are sublime: *from the sublime to the ridiculous.* **b.** the greatest or supreme degree. See **-LIM-**.

sub•lim•i•nal (sub lim′ə nl) /sʌb'lɪmənl̩/ *adj.* existing or operating below the level at which one is conscious: *They made use of subliminal advertising, in which the words "You're thirsty" appeared on the screen too fast to be read consciously.* See **-LIM-**.

sub•ma•chine′ gun′ (sub′mə shēn′) /ˌsʌbmə'ʃiyn/ *n.* [*count*] an automatic gun using small-caliber bullets and fired from the shoulder or hip.

sub•ma•rine (sub′mə rēn′, sub′mə rēn′) /ˌsʌbmə'riyn, 'sʌbməˌriyn/ *n.* [*count*] **1.** a vessel that can be submerged and moved under water: *The submarine dove for the sea bottom.* **2.** *Chiefly Northeastern and North Midland U.S.* a hero sandwich. **—*adj.* 3.** situated, occurring, operating, or living under the surface of the sea.

sub•merge (səb mûrj′) /səb'mɜrdʒ/ *v.,* **-merged, -merg•ing. 1.** to put or sink below the surface of water or other liquid: [*no obj*]: *ordered his boat to dive, and the submarine quietly submerged.* [~ + *obj*]: *The boat was submerged in thirty fathoms of water.* **2.** [~ + *obj*] to cover or overflow with water; immerse: *Do not submerge this electric skillet in water.* **3.** [~ + *obj*] to cover; bury; suppress; obscure; hide: *Certain facts were submerged by the witness.* **—sub•mer′gence,** *n.* [*noncount*] **—sub•mer•sion** (səb mûr′zhən, -shən) /səb'mɜrʒən, -ʃən/ *n.* [*noncount*] See **-MERG-**.

sub•mis•sion (səb mish′ən) /səb'mɪʃən/ *n.* **1.** [*noncount*] the act or an instance of submitting: *their submission to the wishes of their children.* **2.** [*count*] something presented or turned in, as an application, manuscript, etc., for approval or consideration: *As a magazine editor, he receives dozens of submissions daily.* See **-MIS-**.

sub•mis•sive (səb nis′iv) /səb'nɪsɪv/ *adj.* showing a willingness to give in to the power or wishes of another: *a submissive servant.* See **-MIS-**.

sub•mit (səb mit′) /səb'mɪt/ *v.,* **-mit•ted, -mit•ting. 1.** to give over, surrender, or yield to the power or authority of another: [~ + *obj* + *to* + *obj*]: *We submitted ourselves to their wishes.* [~ + *to* + *obj*]: *At last the exhausted army submitted to the enemy.* [*no obj*]: *"We will never submit!" the colonel snarled.* **2.** [~ + *obj*] to present for approval or consideration: *He submitted his plans for the new town square.* **3.** [~ + *that clause*] to state or urge with respect and politeness: *I submit that he should provide complete documentation of his complaints.* See **-MIT-**.

sub•nor•mal (sub nôr′məl) /sʌb'nɔrməl/ *adj.* below the normal or average; less than or inferior to the normal: *The scores indicate subnormal intelligence.* See **-NORM-**.

sub•or•bit•al (sub ôr′bi tl) /sʌb'ɔrbɪtl̩/ *adj.* making less than a complete orbit of the earth or some other planetary body.

sub•or•di•nate (*adj., n.* sə bôr′dn it; *v.* -dn āt′) / *adj., n.* sə'bɔrdn̩ɪt; *v.* -dn̩ˌeyt/ *adj., n., v.,* **-nat•ed, -nat•ing. —*adj.* 1.** being in a lower order or rank: *He had to accept a subordinate post in the new administration.* **2.** of less importance; secondary: *In some colleges teaching is considered subordinate to publications.* **3.** acting as a modifier in a grammatical construction, as *when I finished* in *They were glad when I finished.* **—*n.*** [*count*] **4.** a subordinate person or thing: *He's a subordinate to the district attorney.* **—*v.*** [~ + *obj* (+ *to*)] **5.** to place in a lower order or rank; make secondary: *He subordinated his desires for wealth to the opportunity to spend time with his family.* **—sub•or•di•na•tion** (sə bôr′dn ā′shən) /səˌbɔrdn̩'eyʃən/ *n.* [*noncount*] See **-ORD-**.

sub•orn (sə bôrn′) /sə'bɔrn/ *v.* [~ + *obj*] **1.** to lead or convince (someone) to commit a crime. **2.** to lead or convince (a person, esp. a witness) to give false testimony. —**sub•or•na•tion** (sub′ôr nā′shən) /ˌsʌbɔr'neyʃən/ *n.* [*noncount*]

sub•plot (sub′plot′) /'sʌbˌplɒt/ *n.* [*count*] a secondary plot, as in a novel or play.

sub•poe•na or **sub•pe•na** (sə pē′nə) /sə'piynə/ *n., pl.* **-nas,** *v.,* **-naed, -na•ing.** *Law.* —*n.* [*count*] **1.** an order from a judge summoning witnesses or evidence to appear before the court. —*v.* [~ + *obj*] **2.** to serve with a subpoena: *to subpoena as many witnesses as necessary.* See -PEN-.

sub ro•sa (sub rō′zə) /'sʌb rowzə/ *adv.* confidentially; secretly.

sub•scribe (səb skrīb′) /səb'skrayb/ *v.,* **-scribed, -scrib•ing.** **1.** [~ + *to* + *obj*] to make a subscription to: *to subscribe to a magazine.* **2.** to pay or pledge (a sum of money) as a contribution, gift, or investment: [~ + *obj*]: *to subscribe fifty dollars to the animal shelter fund.* [*no obj*]: *to subscribe to the animal shelter fund.* **3.** [~ + *to* + *obj*] to agree or assent to: *They don't subscribe to the notion that everyone is equal under the law.* —**sub•scrib′er,** *n.* [*count*]: *Subscribers to the newspaper were canceling their subscriptions in protest.* See -SCRIB-.

sub•script (sub′skript) /'sʌbskrɪpt/ *adj.* **1.** written below. —*n.* [*count*] **2.** a letter, number, or symbol written below a line of text: *The number* 2 *is a subscript in the formula for water,* H_2O. See -SCRIB-.

sub•scrip•tion (səb skrip′shən) /səb'skrɪpʃən/ *n.* **1.** [*count*] a sum of money given or pledged as a contribution, investment, etc. **2.** [*noncount*] a fund raised through sums of money subscribed. **3.** [*count*] the right to have a newspaper or magazine delivered, receive cable television service, attend a series of concerts or plays, etc., in exchange for a sum paid. See -SCRIB-.

sub•se•quent (sub′si kwənt) /'sʌbsɪkwənt/ *adj.* occurring after; succeeding: *In subsequent lessons the teacher made clearer what she had said at the beginning.* [*be* + ~ + to]: *Was this crime subsequent to the one that had already taken place?* —**sub′se•quent•ly,** *adv.* See -SEQ-.

sub•ser•vi•ent (səb sûr′vē ənt) /səb'sɜrviyənt/ *adj.* **1.** too eager to give in to the wishes or power of another; servile: *He is very subservient to his boss* **2.** secondary; subordinate: *A good leader's policies must be subservient to the needs of the people.* —**sub•ser′vi•ence,** *n.* [*noncount*] See -SERV-[1].

sub•set (sub′set′) /'sʌbˌsɛt/ *n.* [*count*] a set that is a part of a larger set.

sub•side (səb sīd′) /səb'sayd/ *v.* [*no obj*], **-sid•ed, -sid•ing.** **1.** to sink to a low or lower level: *The water in the sink subsided slowly.* **2.** to become quiet, less active, or less violent: *By dawn the storm had subsided.* —**sub•sid•ence** (səb sīd′ns, sub′si dns) /səb'saydns, 'sʌbsɪdns/ *n.* [*noncount*] See -SID-.

sub•sid•i•ar•y (səb sid′ē er′ē) /səb'sɪdiyˌɛriy/ *adj., n., pl.* **-ar•ies.** —*adj.* **1.** adding to what one has: *a subsidiary company.* **2.** subordinate or secondary: *subsidiary issues that are not our main concern.* —*n.* [*count*] **3.** a subsidiary thing or person, esp. a company controlled by another company: *That international corporation has a few subsidiaries in Africa.* See -SID-.

sub•si•dize (sub′si dīz′) /'sʌbsɪˌdayz/ *v.* [~ + *obj*], **-dized, -diz•ing.** to lessen the costs of (someone or something) with a subsidy: *subsidized housing for those unable to afford high rents.* —**sub•si•di•za•tion** (sub′si-də zā′shən) /ˌsʌbsɪdə'zeyʃən/ *n.* [*noncount*] See -SID-.

sub•si•dy (sub′si dē) /'sʌbsɪdiy/ *n.* [*count*], *pl.* **-dies.** **1.** a direct payment of money made by a government to a private commercial business or industry, an individual, or another government: *The subsidies paid to the rice farmers guarantee that the farmer receives a high price without the consumer having to pay a high price, too.* **2.** any grant or contribution of money. See -SID-.

sub•sist (səb sist′) /səb'sɪst/ *v.* [*no obj*] **1.** to exist; continue in existence; remain alive. **2.** to have just enough of something, as of food, resources, etc., to live on: *The survivors of the plane crash subsisted on nuts and berries.* See -SIST-.

sub•sist•ence (səb sis′təns) /səb'sɪstəns/ *n.* [*noncount*] **1.** the state or fact of subsisting. **2.** the providing of just enough food, resources, etc., to be able to live: *Although the government says they are not at the poverty level, they are at the subsistence level.* See -SIST-.

sub•soil (sub′soil′) /'sʌbˌsɔyl/ *n.* [*noncount*] the layer of earth immediately under the surface soil.

sub•son•ic (sub son′ik) /sʌb'sɒnɪk/ *adj.* of or relating to a speed less than that of sound in air at the same height above sea level: *slowing down to subsonic speeds.* See -SON-.

sub•stance (sub′stəns) /'sʌbstəns/ *n.* **1.** [*noncount*] the physical matter that makes up some thing, object, etc.; the actual matter of a thing as opposed to its appearance: *form and substance.* **2.** [*count*] a particular kind of material, as of a definite chemical composition: *a metallic substance.* **3.** [*noncount*] substantial, important, significant, or solid character or quality: *Those claims lack substance.* **4.** [*noncount*] the meaning or gist, as of speech or writing: *The substance of his speech was: There was no money left for anybody.* —***Idiom.*** **5. in substance,** concerning the essentials; essentially: *In substance, the speech was a warning that there is no money for the programs he had promised.* **6. of substance,** having wealth, importance, or rank in a community: *She was a woman of substance in the community.* See -STAN-.

sub•stand•ard (sub stan′dərd) /sʌb'stændərd/ *adj.* **1.** below standard or less than adequate: *His work was considered substandard by the boss.* **2.** of or relating to a dialect or variety of a language, or an element or style of usage, considered by others to mark its user as uneducated; nonstandard. See -STAN-.

sub•stan•tial (səb stan′shəl) /səb'stænʃəl/ *adj.* **1.** of large, ample, or considerable amount, quantity, etc.: *a substantial amount of money.* **2.** of a material nature; that can be felt or touched. **3.** of solid character or quality; strong: *a substantial fabric.* **4.** being in a stated way with respect to essentials: *The stories from the two witnesses were in substantial agreement.* **5.** of real worth, value, or effect; important; significant: *substantial reasons.* See -STAN-.

sub•stan•tial•ly (səb stan′shə lē) /səb'stænʃəliy/ *adv.* **1.** to a great degree; a lot: *Our ESL program has increased substantially in the last ten years.* **2.** in an important or significant way: *Has the situation changed substantially since we were last here?* See -STAN-.

sub•stan•ti•ate (səb stan′shē āt′) /səb'stænʃiyˌeyt/ *v.* [~ + *obj*], **-at•ed, -at•ing.** to show or establish (a claim, opinion, etc.) by proof or strong evidence: *to substantiate a charge.* —**sub•stan•ti•a•tion** (səb stan′shē ā′shən) /səbˌstænʃiy'eyʃən/ *n.* [*noncount*] See -STAN-.

sub•stan•tive (sub′stən tiv) /'sʌbstəntɪv/ *adj.* **1.** belonging to the real nature or essential part of a thing. **2.** of a great or considerable amount or quantity. **3.** having practical importance, value, use, or effect: *Health care and jobs are substantive issues to most Americans.* —*n.* [*count*] **4.** a noun. **5.** a pronoun, adjective, or other word or phrase that functions as a noun. See -STAN-.

sub•sta•tion (sub′stā′shən) /'sʌbˌsteyʃən/ *n.* [*count*] **1.** a branch of a main post office. **2.** an auxiliary power station at which electrical current is converted, etc. See -STAT-.

sub•sti•tute (sub′sti to͞ot′, -tyo͞ot′) /'sʌbstɪˌtuwt, -ˌtyuwt/ *n., v.,* **-tut•ed, -tut•ing,** *adj.* —*n.* **1.** a person or thing serving in place of another: [*count*]: *The coach sent in a substitute when his star player was injured.* [*noncount*]: *For most of us there is simply no substitute for hard work.* —*v.* **2.** [~ + *obj* + *for* + *obj*] to put (a person or thing) in the place of another: *We substituted fish for meat several times a week.* **3.** [*no obj*] to act as a substitute: *substituting when the regular teachers were sick.* —*adj.* [*before a noun*] **4.** of or relating to a substitute or substitutes: *a substitute teacher.* —**sub′sti•tu′tion,** *n.* [*noncount*]: *the substitution of one budget problem for another.* [*count*]: *The coach made a few substitutions in the defensive team.* See -STIT-.

sub•strate (sub′strāt) /'sʌbstreyt/ *n.* SUBSTRATUM. See -STRAT-.

sub•stra•tum (sub′strā′təm, -strat′əm, sub strā′təm, -strat′əm) /'sʌbˌstreytəm, -ˌstrætəm, sʌb'streytəm, -'strætəm/ *n.* [*count*], *pl.* **-stra•ta** (-strā′tə, -strat′ə, -strā′tə, -strat′ə) /-ˌstreytə, -ˌstrætə, -'streytə, -'strætə/ **-stra•tums.** **1.** something spread or laid under something else. **2.** something that is under something else or serves as a foundation. See -STRAT-.

sub•struc•ture (sub struk′chər, sub′struk′-) /sʌb'strʌktʃər, 'sʌbˌstrʌk-/ *n.* [*count*] **1.** a structure forming the foundation of a building or other construction. **2.** any foundation or supporting structure; basis. See -STRU-.

sub•sume (səb so͞om′) /səb'suwm/ *v.* [~ + *obj*], **-sumed, -sum•ing.** to consider or include (an idea, term, etc.) as being part of a more general one: *You can subsume vegetables, meats, and grains under the broader category of food.* See -SUM-.

sub•teen (sub′tēn′) /'sʌb'tiyn/ *n.* [*count*] **1.** a young person approaching the teens or adolescence. **2.** a range of even-numbered garment sizes, chiefly from 6 to 14, designed for girls under 13.

sub•ter•fuge (sub′tər fyōōj′) /ˈsʌbtərˌfyuwdʒ/ *n.* a dishonest or illegal action to avoid following a rule, to hide something, etc.: [*noncount*]: *a term of office marked by lies and subterfuge.* [*count*]: *just another subterfuge to avoid facing up to the failure of his policies.* See -FUG-.

sub•ter•ra•ne•an (sub′tə rā′nē ən) /ˌsʌbtəˈreyniyən/ *adj.* Also, **sub•ter•ra•ne•ous** (sub′tə rā′nē əs) /ˌsʌbtəˈreyniyəs/ **1.** existing, located, or operating below the earth's surface; underground: *a subterranean silver mine.* **2.** existing or operating out of sight or secretly: *subterranean resistance fighters.* See -TERR-.

sub•ti•tle (sub′tīt′l) /ˈsʌbˌtaytl̩/ *n., v.,* **-tled, -tling.** **—***n.* [*count*] **1.** a secondary title of a literary work, usually of explanatory character. **2.** (in motion pictures and television) the text of conversations, speeches, etc., as translated into another language and shown on the bottom of the screen: *In Paris we were able to watch movies in English and compare the French subtitles to see how they translated the dialogue.* **—***v.* [~ + *obj*] **3.** to give a subtitle or subtitles to.

sub•tle (sut′l) /ˈsʌtl̩/ *adj.,* **-tler, -tlest. 1.** delicate; hard to notice by means of the senses: *the subtle smell of her perfume.* **2.** difficult to notice, perceive, understand, or explain: *the subtle irony of his jokes.* **3.** delicate or faint; mysterious: *a subtle smile.* **4.** cunning, wily, or crafty: *a subtle liar.* **—sub′tly,** *adv.*

sub•tle•ty (sut′l tē) /ˈsʌtl̩tiy/ *n., pl.* **-ties. 1.** [*noncount*] the quality or state of being subtle: *Such subtlety is not his usual way of acting.* **2.** [*count*] something subtle, as a fine point or detail not easy to see or understand: *I couldn't grasp the subtleties involved in his discussion.*

sub•to•tal (sub′tōt′l, sub tōt′-) /ˈsʌbˌtowtl̩, sʌbˈtowt-/ *n., v.,* **-taled, -tal•ing** or (*esp. Brit.*) **-talled, -tal•ling.** **—***n.* [*count*] **1.** the total of a part of a group or column of figures, as in an accounting statement. **—***v.* [~ + *obj*] **2.** to determine a subtotal for: *to subtotal the last quarter's figures.*

sub•tract (səb trakt′) /səbˈtrækt/ *v.* to take away, as a part from a whole, or one number from another: [~ + *obj*]: *When you subtract the two numbers, what is the result?* [~ + *obj* + *from* + *obj*]: *to subtract one number from another.* [*no obj*]: *Then you subtract; don't make the mistake of adding here.* **—sub•trac′tion,** *n.* [*noncount*]: *The class learned subtraction last year.* [*count*]: *a subtraction in costs.* See -TRAC-.

sub•trop•i•cal (sub trop′i kəl) /sʌbˈtrɒpɪkəl/ *adj.* bordering on the tropics; nearly tropical.

sub•urb (sub′ûrb) /ˈsʌbɜrb/ *n.* [*count*] **1.** a district or area of land lying immediately outside a city or town, esp. a smaller residential community. **2. the suburbs,** [*plural*] an area composed of such districts, or such areas thought of as a group, as with respect to their political leanings: *The Republican candidate was leading in the suburbs.* **—sub•ur•ban** (sə bûr′bən) /səˈbɜrbən/ *adj.*: *the quiet and calm of this suburban village.*

sub•ur•ban•ite (sə bûr′bə nīt′) /səˈbɜrbəˌnayt/ *n.* [*count*] one who lives in a suburb of a city or large town.

sub•ur•bi•a (sə bûr′bē ə) /səˈbɜrbiyə/ *n.* [*noncount*] suburbs thought of as a group and considered in terms of the social or cultural aspects of life: *the belief that suburbia is a cultural wasteland.*

sub•ver•sion (səb vûr′zhən, -shən) /səbˈvɜrʒən, -ʃən/ *n.* [*noncount*] the act of overthrowing or attempting to overthrow a government, or some power or authority. See -VERT-.

sub•ver•sive (səb vûr′siv) /səbˈvɜrsɪv/ *adj.* **1.** of or relating to subversion: *The internal security agency had labeled their little organization subversive.* **—***n.* [*count*] **2.** one who attempts to subvert: *security agents on the watch for subversives and spies.* See -VERT-.

sub•vert (səb vûrt′) /səbˈvɜrt/ *v.* [~ + *obj*] to engage in or attempt subversion: *Instead of cooperating, he worked to subvert her authority.* See -VERT-.

sub•way (sub′wā′) /ˈsʌbˌwey/ *n.* **1.** an underground electric railroad: [*count*]: *no delays this morning on the subways.* See illustration at STREET. [*noncount; by* + ~]: *to travel by subway.* **2.** [*count*] *Chiefly Brit.* a short tunnel or underground passageway; underpass.

suc•ceed (sək sēd′) /səkˈsiyd/ *v.* **1.** [*no obj*] to end according to one's desire: *Our efforts succeeded.* **2.** [*no obj;* (~ + *in* + *obj/verb-ing*)] to accomplish what is intended: *We succeeded in our efforts to start the car.* **3.** [*no obj*] to attain success in a recognized form, such as wealth or standing: *voted most likely to succeed.* **4.** to follow or replace another in some rank, office, authority, etc.: [~ + *to* + *obj*]: *He succeeded to the throne after the death of the queen.* [~ + *obj*]: *He succeeded his mother to the throne.* **5.** [~ + *obj*] to come next after something else in a series; follow: *one movement succeeding another.* See -CEED-. **—Related Words.** SUCCEED is a verb, SUCCESS is a noun, SUCCESSFUL is an adjective, SUCCESSFULLY is an adverb: *She wants to succeed in business. She wants success in life. She is a successful businesswoman. She dealt with the latest financial crisis successfully.*

suc•cess (sək ses′) /səkˈsɛs/ *n.* **1.** [*noncount*] the favorable result of something attempted: *Success is important in a child's early attempts to learn something.* **2.** [*noncount*] the gaining of wealth, position, honors, etc.: *He had achieved success.* **3.** [*count*] a successful performance or achievement: *Was the party a success?* **4.** [*count*] a person or thing that is successful: *He felt that at last he was a success.* See -CESS-.

suc•cess•ful (sək ses′fəl) /səkˈsɛsfəl/ *adj.* **1.** achieving or having achieved success: *She had become a very successful businesswoman.* **2.** resulting in success: *a successful attempt to quit smoking.* **—suc•cess′ful•ly,** *adv.*: *successfully answered the next question.* See -CESS-.

suc•ces•sion (sək sesh′ən) /səkˈsɛʃən/ *n.* **1.** [*noncount*] the coming of one person or thing after another in a sequence: *His secretaries were fired in quick succession until he found one he liked.* **2.** [*count*] a number of persons or things following one another in sequence: *a succession of secretaries.* **3.** [*noncount*] the right, act, or process by which one person follows another to the office, rank, estate, etc.: *the order of succession.* See -CESS-.

suc•ces•sive (sək ses′iv) /səkˈsɛsɪv/ *adj.* following in succession: *three successive days of rain.* **—suc•ces′sive•ly,** *adv.*

suc•ces•sor (sək ses′ər) /səkˈsɛsər/ *n.* [*count*] **1.** a person or thing that succeeds or follows. **2.** a person who succeeds another in an office, position, or the like.

suc•cinct (sək singkt′) /səkˈsɪŋkt/ *adj.* expressed well in few words: *Her answers were always succinct and direct.* **—suc•cinct′ly,** *adv.*: *"It simply won't work," he answered succinctly.* **—suc•cinct′ness,** *n.* [*noncount*] **—Syn.** See CONCISE.

suc•cor (suk′ər) /ˈsʌkər/ *n.* [*noncount*] **1.** help; relief; aid: *providing succor to the wounded.* **—***v.* [~ + *obj*] **2.** to help (someone who is in difficulty, need, or distress). Also, *esp. Brit.,* **suc′cour.**

suc•co•tash (suk′ə tash′) /ˈsʌkəˌtæʃ/ *n.* [*noncount*] a cooked dish of beans, esp. lima beans, and kernels of corn.

suc•cu•lent (suk′yə lənt) /ˈsʌkyələnt/ *adj.* **1.** juicy. **2.** rich in desirable qualities. **3.** (of a plant) having fleshy, juicy tissues. **—***n.* [*count*] **4.** a succulent plant, as a cactus. **—suc′cu•lence, suc′cu•len•cy,** *n.* [*noncount*]

suc•cumb (sə kum′) /səˈkʌm/ *v.* [*no obj;* (~ + *to* + *obj*)] **1.** to give way to superior force; yield: *He believed that she had succumbed to his charms.* **2.** to be unable to resist disease, wounds, etc.: *He succumbed to his wounds and died in the night.*

such (such) /sʌtʃ/ *adj.* **1.** of the kind, character, degree, etc., already indicated or about to be indicated: [~ + *a* + *singular count noun*]: *He could inflame whole audiences in moments; such a man is dangerous.* [~ + *noncount or plural noun*]: *Revolution and anarchy? Such talk is dangerous.* **2.** like or similar: *steel, wood, tea, coffee, and other such commodities.* **3.** of so extreme a kind; so good, bad, etc.: [~ + *a* + *singular count noun*]: *He is such a liar.* [~ + *noncount or plural noun*]: *That is such nonsense.* **4.** definite but not specified: *Allow such an amount for rent, and the rest for other things.* **5.** [*before a noun*] being the person or thing or the persons or things indicated: *If any member be late, such member shall be suspended.* **6.** being as stated or indicated: *Such is the case.* **—***adv.* **7.** so; to such a degree: *They are such nice people.* **8.** in such a way or manner. **—***pron.* **9.** such a person or thing or such persons or things: *kings, princes, and such.* **10.** someone or something indicated: *She claims to be a friend but is not such.* **—*Idiom.* 11. such as, a.** of the kind specified: *A plan such as you propose will succeed.* **b.** for example: *He had many pastimes, such as reading and chess.* **12. such...that,** (used as a conjunction to join two clauses together and to show that the first clause is explained by the second or is the cause of the second): *He received such a shock that he nearly passed out.* **—Usage.** Compare SUCH and SO. SUCH can come before a noun (with or without an adjective before the noun), but so comes before an adjective without a noun following: *He's such a stupid man. She's such a liar. She's such an intelligent woman,* but *She's so stupid. He's so intelligent.*

such′ and such′, *adj.* **1.** definite or particular but not named or specified: *Let's imagine we meet at such and such a place.* **—***pron.* **2.** something or someone not specified: *if such and such should happen.*

suck (suk) /sʌk/ *v.* **1.** to draw into the mouth by producing a partial vacuum by action of the lips and tongue: [~ + *obj*]: *to suck lemonade through a straw.* [*no obj*]: *The baby was sucking at his mother's breast.* **2.** [~ + *obj*] to draw (water, air, etc.) by or as if by suction: *Plants suck moisture from the air.* **3.** to apply the lips or mouth to and draw the liquid from: [~ + *obj*]: *to suck an orange.* [*no obj*]: *to suck at an orange.* **4.** to put into the mouth and draw upon: [~ + *obj*]: *to suck a piece of candy.* [*no obj*]: *sucking on a cough drop.* **5.** [*no obj; not: be + ~-ing*] *Slang.* to be disgusting or awful: *That team sucks; it can't win any of its games.* **6. suck up,** [*no obj; (~ + to + obj)*] *Slang.* to be subservient; to be obsequious: *He's sucking up to the boss because he thinks he'll get a promotion that way.* **—***n.* [*count*] **7.** an act or instance of sucking.

suck•er (suk′ər) /ˈsʌkər/ *n.* [*count*] **1.** a person or thing that sucks, as a body part of an animal used for sucking or clinging by suction. **2.** *Informal.* a person easily cheated or deceived: *That sucker wound up spending thousands on a roof he didn't need.* **3.** *Informal.* a person attracted to something mentioned: *She's a sucker for a handsome face.* **4.** a lollipop. **—***v.* [~ + *obj*] **5.** *Informal.* to make a sucker of; fool: *They suckered him into going along with their stupid plan.*

suck•le (suk′əl) /ˈsʌkəl/ *v.,* **-led, -ling.** to (cause to or provide the means to) nurse at the breast or udder: [*no obj*]: *The newborn colt suckled at its mother's udder.* [~ + *obj*]: *to suckle a baby.*

suck•ling (suk′ling) /ˈsʌklɪŋ/ *n.* [*count*] an infant or young animal not yet weaned.

su•crose (so͞o′krōs) /ˈsuwkrows/ *n.* SUGAR (def. 1).

suc•tion (suk′shən) /ˈsʌkʃən/ *n.* [*noncount*] **1.** the force that, owing to pressure differences, attracts a fluid or solid to where the pressure is lowest. **—***v.* [~ (+ *up*) + *obj*] **2.** to draw out or remove by sucking, esp. by artificial means.

Su•da•nese (so͞od′n ēz′, -ēs′) /ˌsuwdn̩ˈiyz, -ˈiys/ *n.* [*count*], *pl.* **-nese. 1.** a person born or living in (the) Sudan. **—***adj.* **2.** of or relating to (the) Sudan.

sud•den (sud′n) /ˈsʌdn̩/ *adj.* **1.** happening, coming, made, or done quickly or unexpectedly: *a sudden attack.* **—***adv.* **2.** *Literary.* suddenly. **—*Idiom.* 3. all of a sudden,** without warning; unexpectedly: *All of a sudden we were surrounded.* **—sud′den•ly,** *adv.: She lunged at him suddenly.* **—sud′den•ness,** *n.* [*noncount*]

sud′den death′, *n.* [*noncount*] an overtime period in a sports contest, begun when a contest is tied after normal play has finished, in which the contest is won immediately as soon as one of the contestants scores.

sud′den in′fant death′ syn′drome, *n.* [*noncount*] death from cessation of breathing in a seemingly healthy infant, almost always during sleep. *Abbr.:* SIDS Also called **crib death.**

suds (sudz) /sʌdz/ *n.* [*plural*] water containing soap or detergent and having bubbles or froth on the surface. **—suds′y,** *adj.,* **-i•er, -i•est.**

sue (so͞o) /suw/ *v.,* **sued, su•ing. 1.** to bring legal action against; bring a lawsuit in court: [~ + *obj*]: *to sue someone for damages.* [*no obj*]: *threatened to sue if an accident happened.* **2.** [*no obj*] to make a request, petition, or appeal for: *The defeated army decided to sue for peace.* See -SEQ-.

suede or **suède** (swād) /sweyd/ *n.* [*noncount*] leather or similar fabric finished with a soft, slightly rough surface.

su•et (so͞o′it) /ˈsuwɪt/ *n.* [*noncount*] hard, fatty tissue from the kidneys of beef, sheep, etc., used in cooking and for making candles. **—su′et•y,** *adj.*

suf-, var. of SUB- before *f: suffer.*

suf•fer (suf′ər) /ˈsʌfər/ *v.* **1.** to feel pain or great distress: [*no obj*]: *She suffered greatly as a child.* [~ + *obj*]: *She suffered poverty as a child.* **2.** [*no obj*] to become worse; deteriorate: *My work suffers when I'm distracted.* **3.** to endure or be afflicted with something, such as a disease, injury, or loss: [*no obj*]: *to suffer from Parkinson's disease.* [~ + *obj*]: *He suffered a sprain in his left leg.* **4.** [~ + *obj*] to experience (any action, process, or condition): *to suffer change.* **5.** [~ + *obj*] to tolerate or allow: *I do not suffer fools gladly.* **—suf′fer•er,** *n.* [*count*]

suf•fer•ance (suf′ər əns, suf′rəns) /ˈsʌfərəns, ˈsʌfrəns/ *n.* [*noncount*] permission extended passively by not interfering.

suf•fer•ing (suf′ər ing, suf′ring) /ˈsʌfərɪŋ, ˈsʌfrɪŋ/ *n.* **1.** [*noncount*] the state of a person or thing that suffers. **2.** Often, **sufferings.** [*plural*] something suffered; pain: *the sufferings of the slaves.*

suf•fice (sə fīs′) /səˈfays/ *v.* [*no obj; not: be + ~-ing*], **-ficed, -fic•ing. 1.** to be enough for needs or purposes: *A few payments will suffice.* **—*Idiom.* 2. suffice it to say,** This phrase is used before making another statement, to indicate that the speaker believes what follows is sufficient to prove a point: *Suffice it to say the project was a success.*

suf•fi•cient (sə fish′ənt) /səˈfɪʃənt/ *adj.* enough for what is needed: *There are barely sufficient funds for the project.* **—suf•fi′cien•cy,** *n.* [*noncount*] **—suf•fi′cient•ly,** *adv.: sufficiently informed about the issues.*

suf•fix (*n.* suf′iks; *v.* suf′iks, sə fiks′) / *n.* ˈsʌfɪks; *v.* ˈsʌfɪks, səˈfɪks/ *n.* [*count*] **1.** an affix that follows the element to which it is added, as *-ment* in *entertainment.* **—***v.* [~ + *obj*] **2.** to add as a suffix. **—suf•fix•a•tion** (suf′ik zā′shən) /ˌsʌfɪkˈzeyʃən/ *n.* [*noncount*] See -FIX-.

suf•fo•cate (suf′ə kāt′) /ˈsʌfəˌkeyt/ *v.,* **-cat•ed, -cat•ing. 1.** [~ + *obj*] to kill by preventing the passage of air; strangle: *The plastic bag must have suffocated the baby.* **2.** [*no obj*] to die in this manner; stifle; smother: *The baby must have suffocated when the plastic bag went over its head.* **3.** to (cause to) be uncomfortable because of a lack of fresh air: [~ + *obj*]: *This hot classroom is suffocating the students.* [*no obj*]: *We're all suffocating in this hot room.* **4.** to hold back, stifle, or suppress (freedom, creativity, etc.): [*no obj*]: *The students are suffocating from the rigid discipline.* [~ + *obj*]: *The rigid discipline is suffocating the children's creativity and freedom.* **—suf•fo•ca•tion** (suf′ə kā′shən) /ˌsʌfəˈkeyʃən/ *n.* [*noncount*]

suf•frage (suf′rij) /ˈsʌfrɪdʒ/ *n.* [*noncount*] the right to vote, esp. in a political election. **—suf′fra•gist,** *n.* [*count*]

suf•fra•gette (suf′rə jet′) /ˌsʌfrəˈdʒɛt/ *n.* [*count*] a woman who calls for the right to vote for women.

suf•fuse (sə fyo͞oz′) /səˈfyuwz/ *v.* [~ + *obj*], **-fused, -fus•ing.** to overspread with or as if with a liquid, color, etc.; pervade: *Bright sunlight suffused the room.* **—suf•fu•sion** (sə fyo͞o′zhən) /səˈfyuwʒən/ *n.* [*noncount*] See -FUS-.

sug•ar (sho͝og′ər) /ˈʃʊgər/ *n.* **1.** a sweet, crystalline substance made esp. from sugarcane and the sugar beet; sucrose: [*noncount*]: *two cups of sugar.* [*count*]: *I'd like two sugars for my coffee, please.* **2.** [*count*] any other plant or animal substance of the same class of carbohydrates, as fructose or glucose. **—***v.* [~ + *obj*] **3.** to cover, sprinkle, mix, or sweeten with sugar. **—sug′ar•less,** *adj.* **—sug′ar•y,** *adj.*

sug′ar beet′, *n.* [*noncount*] a variety of the common beet grown for the sugar it yields.

sug•ar•cane or **su•gar cane** (sho͝og′ər kān′) /ˈʃʊgˌər keyn/ *n.* [*noncount*] a tall grass of tropical and warm regions, having a stout, jointed stalk and being the chief source of sugar.

sug•ar•coat (sho͝og′ər kōt′) /ˈʃʊgərˌkowt/ *v.* [~ + *obj*] **1.** to cover with sugar: *sugarcoated pills.* **2.** to make (something difficult or distasteful) appear more acceptable: *He's trying to sugarcoat the bad news.*

sug′ar ma′ple, *n.* [*count*] any of several maple trees having a sweet sap, being the chief source of maple syrup and maple sugar.

sug•gest (səg jest′, sə-) /səgˈdʒɛst, sə-/ *v.* **1.** to mention, introduce, or propose (an idea, plan, etc.) for consideration, possible action, etc.; recommend: [~ + *obj*]: *The teacher suggested several different colleges your son might apply to.* [~ + *(that) clause*]: *I suggested that we meet outside by the fountain.* **2.** [~ + *(that) clause*] to hint at indirectly; imply: *Your question suggests that you doubt my sincerity.* **3.** [~ + *obj*] to call (something) up in the mind through association of ideas: *The music suggests a still night.* See -GEST-.

sug•gest•i•ble (səg jes′tə bəl, sə-) /səgˈdʒɛstəbəl, sə-/ *adj.* **1.** subject to or easily influenced by suggestion. **2.** able to be suggested. **—sug•gest•i•bil•i•ty** (səh jes′tə-bil′i tē) /səhˌdʒɛstəˈbɪlɪtiy/ *n.* [*noncount*] See -GEST-.

sug•ges•tion (səg jes′chən, sə-) /səgˈdʒɛstʃən, sə-/ *n.* **1.** [*noncount*] the act of suggesting, or the state of being suggested. **2.** [*count*] something suggested: *a sugges-*

tion for improved communication between shifts. **3.** [*count*] a hint, slight trace, or sign: *a suggestion of tears in his eyes.* **4.** [*noncount*] the calling up in the mind of one idea by another by virtue of some association. See -GEST-.

sug•ges•tive (səg jes′tiv, sə-) /səg'dʒɛstɪv, sə-/ *adj.* **1.** suggesting; referring to or evoking other thoughts, persons, times or places, etc.: *suggestive of 19th-century London.* **2.** rich in suggestions or ideas: *a suggestive critical essay.* **3.** implying, suggesting, or hinting at something improper or indecent, esp. sexual matters; risqué: *She didn't appreciate his suggestive remarks.* —**sug•ges′tive•ly,** *adv.* See -GEST-.

su•i•cid•al (so͞o′ə sīd′əl) /ˌsuwə'saydəl/ *adj.* **1.** of or relating to suicide: *his suicidal tendencies.* **2.** likely to bring disaster or ruin: *politically suicidal acts.* See -CIDE-[2].

su•i•cide (so͞o′ə sīd′) /'suwəˌsayd/ *n.* **1.** the intentional taking of one's own life: [*noncount*]: *to commit suicide.* [*count*]: *The number of suicides increases in the winter.* **2.** [*noncount*] destruction of one's own interests or chances: *financial suicide.* **3.** [*count*] one who intentionally takes his or her own life. See -CIDE-[2].

su•i ge•ne•ris (so͞o′ē jen′ər is, so͞o′ī) /'suw'iy dʒɛnərɪs, 'suway/ *adj.* of his, her, its, or their own kind; unique.

suit (so͞ot) /suwt/ *n.* [*count*] **1.** a set of garments of the same color, material, or fabric, typically trousers or a skirt, a jacket, and sometimes a vest: *She wore a dark suit for the interview.* See illustration at CLOTHING. **2.** a set of clothing, armor, or the like intended for wear together. **3.** any costume or outfit worn for some special activity: *a bathing suit.* **4.** *Law.* an act or instance of suing in a court of law; a lawsuit. **5.** one of the classes into which cards or dominoes are divided, as spades, clubs, diamonds, and hearts. —*v.* **6.** [~ + *obj*] to make appropriate; accommodate one thing to another: *to suit the punishment to the crime.* **7.** [~ + *obj; not: be* + ~*-ing; no passive*] to look good or attractive on: *The color blue suits you very well.* **8.** [*not: be* + ~*-ing; no passive*] to be acceptable or agreeable to: [~ + *obj*]: *The arrangements suit me just fine.* [~ + *oneself*]: *If you don't want to go to the party, that's OK; suit yourself.* **9.** [~ + *obj; not: be* + ~*-ing; no passive*] to meet the requirements of: *Would an appointment next week suit your schedule?* **10. suit up,** to put an appropriate uniform or special suit on: [*no obj*]: *The divers went in their locker room and suited up.* [~ + *up* + *obj*]: *The technicians suited up the astronauts.* [~ + *obj* + *up*]: *to suit them up.* —***Idiom.*** **11. follow suit, a.** to play a card of the same suit as that led. **b.** to follow the example of another: *Our competitors lowered computer prices, so we were forced to follow suit.*

suit•a•ble (so͞o′tə bəl) /'suwtəbəl/ *adj.* appropriate; acceptable; fitting: *Is she suitable for this mission?* —**suit•a•bil•i•ty** (so͞o′tə bil′i tē) /ˌsuwtə'bɪlɪtiy/ *n.* [*noncount*] —**suit′a•bly,** *adv.*: *We were suitably impressed with her performance.*

suit•case (so͞ot′kās′) /'suwtˌkeys/ *n.* [*count*] a piece of luggage, esp. for carrying clothes while traveling.

suite (swēt; *for 3 often* so͞ot) /swiyt; *for 3 often* suwt/ *n.* [*count*] **1.** a number of things forming a series, group, or set: *a suite of computer routines.* **2.** a connected series of rooms to be used together: *a hotel suite.* **3.** a set of matching furniture, esp. for one room: *a bedroom suite.* **4.** an ordered series of pieces of music, as instrumental dances, written in the same or related keys.

suit•ed (so͞o′tid) /'suwtɪd/ *adj.* [*be* + ~ + *to*] **1.** appropriate: *a person who is well suited to the job.* **2.** compatible or consistent with: *You'll need a more serious writing style that is suited to this important, deep subject.*

suit•ing (so͞o′ting) /'suwtɪŋ/ *n.* [*noncount*] fabric for making suits.

suit•or (so͞o′tər) /'suwtər/ *n.* [*count*] **1.** a man who tries to gain the affection or love of a woman. **2.** *Law.* a person who brings a petition or complaint to a court of law. **3.** an individual or company that seeks to buy another company.

su•ki•ya•ki (so͞o′kē yä′kē, so͝ok′ē-, skē yä′kē) /ˌsuwkiy'yɑkiy, ˌsʊkiy-, skiy'yɑkiy/ *n.* [*noncount*] a Japanese dish containing slices of meat, bean curd, vegetables, and soy sauce cooked together.

sul•fur (sul′fər) /'sʌlfər/ *n.* [*noncount*] **1.** Also, *esp. Brit.,* **sulphur.** a nonmetallic element, ordinarily a yellow solid that can be burned, occurring widely in chemically combined forms and compounds and in cellular protein, and used esp. in making gunpowder and matches, and in medicine. **2.** a greenish yellow color; SULPHUR (def. 2).

sulk (sulk) /sʌlk/ *v.* [*no obj*] **1.** to keep oneself from normal conversation or apart from others while remaining in a sullen, angry, or offended mood: *When we told her she couldn't go to the dance, she sulked for days.* —*n.* [*count*] **2.** a state or fit of sulking.

sulk•y (sul′kē) /'sʌlkiy/ *adj.,* **-i•er, -i•est,** *n., pl.* **sulk•ies.** —*adj.* **1.** showing sulking behavior; sullen; moody. **2.** gloomy or dull: *sulky weather.* —*n.* [*count*] **3.** a light, two-wheeled, one-horse carriage for one person. —**sulk•i•ly** (sul′kə lē) /'sʌlkəliy/ *adv.* —**sulk′i•ness,** *n.* [*noncount*]

sul•len (sul′ən) /'sʌlən/ *adj.* **1.** showing irritation or anger by a gloomy silence. **2.** gloomy or dismal, as weather. —**sul′len•ly,** *adv.*: *He looked sullenly down at his feet.* —**sul′len•ness,** *n.* [*noncount*]

sul•ly (sul′ē) /'sʌliy/ *v.* [~ + *obj*], **-lied, -ly•ing. 1.** to make dirty; to stain or tarnish. **2.** to ruin the purity or luster of; defile: *to sully a reputation.*

sul•phur (sul′fər) /'sʌlfər/ *n.* [*noncount*] **1.** *Chiefly Brit.* SULFUR (def. 1). **2.** Also, **sulfur.** a greenish yellow.

sul•tan (sul′tn) /'sʌltn̩/ *n.* [*count*] the sovereign of an Islamic country, as any of the former sovereigns of Turkey. —**sul•tan•ate** (sul′tn āt′) /'sʌltn̩ˌeyt/ *n.* [*count*]

sul•tan•a (sul tan′ə, -tä′nə) /sʌl'tænə, -'tɑnə/ *n.* [*count*], *pl.* **-tan•as. 1.** a small, seedless raisin. **2.** a wife or female relative of a sultan. **3.** a mistress of a king.

sul•try (sul′trē) /'sʌltriy/ *adj.,* **-tri•er, -tri•est. 1.** uncomfortably hot and humid; close; sweltering: *a sultry day.* **2.** characterized by or arousing passion: *sultry eyes.*

sum (sum) /sʌm/ *n., v.,* **summed, sum•ming.** —*n.* [*count*] **1.** the total of two or more numbers, amounts, or quantities, determined by or as if by addition: *The sum of 6 and 8 is 14.* **2.** an amount or quantity, esp. of money: *to lend small sums.* **3.** a series of numbers or quantities to be added up. **4.** the full amount, or the whole: *the sum of our knowledge.* **5.** the main idea, gist, or point: *the sum and substance of his argument.* —*v.* **6.** [~ + *obj*] to figure out the sum of, as by addition. **7. sum up, a.** to express in a brief yet complete statement; summarize: [~ + *up* + *obj*]: *He summed up the main points of the speech.* [~ + *obj* + *up*]: *Can you sum it all up in just a few words?* [*no obj*]: *ready to sum up at last after a long speech.* **b.** to form a quick estimate or judgment of: [~ + *up* + *obj*]: *quickly summed up the situation.* [~ + *obj* + *up*]: *She summed him up in a minute.* —***Idiom.*** **8. in sum,** in brief but complete form: *In sum, the government believes it knows what it is doing.*

-sum-, *root. -sum-* comes from Latin, where it has the meaning "take up; pick up." This meaning is found in such words as: ASSUME, CONSUME, CONSUMPTION, PRESUME, PRESUMPTION, RESUME, RESUMÉ, RESUMPTION, SUBSUME.

su•mac or **su•mach** (so͞o′mak, sho͞o′-) /'suwmæk, 'ʃuw-/ *n.* [*noncount*] a shrub or small tree of the cashew family, having compound leaves and clusters of red, fleshy fruit.

sum•mar•i•ly (sə mâr′ə lē) /sə'mɛərəliy/ *adv.* in a prompt and direct manner, esp. without giving advance warning or showing politeness: *He was called in and summarily fired.*

sum•ma•rize (sum′ə rīz′) /'sʌməˌrayz/ *v.* [~ + *obj*], **-rized, -riz•ing.** to make a summary of; to state or express in a brief but complete form: *He summarized the arguments that had been given so far.*

sum•ma•ry (sum′ə rē) /'sʌməriy/ *n., pl.* **-ries,** *adj.* —*n.* [*count*] **1.** a complete yet brief account of things previously stated: *He gave a short summary of the proceedings so far.* —*adj.* [*before a noun*] **2.** brief yet complete; concise. **3.** direct and prompt; fast or quick and without advance warning or politeness: *They fired him with summary dispatch.*

sum•ma•tion (sə mā′shən) /sə'meyʃən/ *n.* [*count*] **1.** the act or process of summing. **2.** a review of previously stated facts or statements, often with final conclusions. **3.** the final arguments of opposing attorneys before a case goes to the jury.

sum•mer (sum′ər) /'sʌmər/ *n.* **1.** the warm season between spring and autumn: [*count*]: *We would meet every summer at her beach place.* [*noncount*]: *What will you do this summer?* **2.** [*count*] the period of greatest development, perfection, etc.: *the summer of life.* **3.** [*count*] a year: *a girl of fifteen summers.* —*adj.* [*before a noun*] **4.** of or characteristic of summer; suitable for or done during the summer: *summer sports.* —*v.* [*no obj*] **5.** to spend or pass the summer: *The family summers in Maine.* —**sum′mer•y,** *adj.*: *this unusual, summery weather in October!*

sum•mer•house (sum′ər hous′) /'sʌmərˌhaws/ *n.* [*count*], a simple, rough building or structure with seats in a park or garden, intended to provide shade in the summer.

sum′mer time′, *n. Chiefly Brit.* DAYLIGHT-SAVING TIME.

sum•mer•time (sum′ər tīm′) /ˈsʌmərˌtaym/ *n.* [*noncount*] the summer season.

sum•mit (sum′it) /ˈsʌmɪt/ *n.* [*count*] **1.** the highest point or part, as of a hill; top; apex: *the summit of the mountain.* **2.** the highest point of attaining or gaining something: *the summit of her ambition.* **3.** the highest state or degree. **4.** Also called **sum′mit meet′ing, sum′mit con′ference.** a conference between heads of state or other top-level government officials.

sum•mit•ry (sum′i trē) /ˈsʌmɪtriy/ *n.* [*noncount*] the conducting of diplomatic negotiations at summit conferences: *interested in summitry and international relations.*

sum•mon (sum′ən) /ˈsʌmən/ *v.,* **1.** [~ + *obj*] to call for the presence of, as by command: *The king summoned a servant.* **2.** [~ + *obj* + *to* + *verb*] to call upon (someone) to do something specified: *She summoned him to take a message.* **3.** [~ + *obj*] to call or notify (someone) to appear at a specified place, esp. before a court: *to summon a witness.* **4.** [~ + *obj*] to call together by authority, as for deliberation or action: *to summon parliament.* **5.** to call into action; rouse; call forth (from oneself): [~ + *obj* (+ *up*)]: *He summoned all his courage (up).* [~ (+ *up*) + *obj*]: *Suffering from the flu, I could hardly summon (up) the strength to whisper.* —**sum′mon•er,** *n.* [*count*] See -MON-.

sum•mons (sum′ənz) /ˈsʌmənz/ *n.* [*count*], *pl.* **-mons•es. 1.** a command by which one is summoned: *The king issued a summons to every wagon-wheel maker to increase output.* **2.** a call or written demand by authority to appear before a court or a judicial officer: *The police officer handed the motorist a summons.*

su•mo (so͞o′mō) /ˈsuwmow/ *n.* [*noncount*] a form of Japanese wrestling.

sump (sump) /sʌmp/ *n.* [*count*] a pit, cesspool, etc., in which liquid is collected or into which it drains.

sump•tu•ous (sump′cho͞o əs) /ˈsʌmptʃuwəs/ *adj.* **1.** requiring great expense; costly: *a sumptuous room with gold paint.* **2.** lavish; splendid: *a sumptuous feast.* See -SUM-.

sun (sun) /sʌn/ *n., v.,* **sunned, sun•ning.** —*n.* **1.** [*often: Sun; proper noun; usually: the* + ~] the star that is the central body of the solar system: *The mean distance from the earth to the sun is about 93 million miles.* **2.** [*count; usually singular; usually: the* + ~] this star with reference to its position in the sky, the temperature it produces, etc.: *The sun rose in the pink sky.* **3.** the heat and light from the sun; sunshine: [*count; usually singular; usually: the* + ~]: *to be exposed to the sun.* [*noncount*]: *You'd better get in the shade; you'll get too much sun and have a bad sunburn tonight.* **4.** [*count*] a heavenly body that has its own light and heat source; a star: *Many of the stars could be suns of their own solar systems.* —*v.* **5.** to expose (oneself) or be exposed to the sun's rays: [~ + *obj*]: *sunning themselves in the park.* [*no obj*]: *They were outside sunning for hours.* —***Idiom.*** **6. under the sun,** on earth; anywhere: *There's nothing like this under the sun.*

Sun., an abbreviation of: Sunday.

sun•bathe (sun′bāth′) /ˈsʌnˌbeyð/ *v.* [*no obj*], **-bathed, -bath•ing.** to expose one's body deliberately to the direct rays of the sun or a sunlamp. —**sun•bath•er** (sun′bā′thər) /ˈsʌnˌbeyðər/ *n.* [*count*]

sun•beam (sun′bēm′) /ˈsʌnˌbiym/ *n.* [*count*] a beam or ray of sunlight.

Sun•belt or **Sun Belt** (sun′belt′) /ˈsʌnˌbɛlt/ *n.* [*sometimes: sunbelt; count; usually singular; often: the* + ~] the southern and southwestern region of the U.S.

sun•bon•net (sun′bon′it) /ˈsʌnˌbɒnɪt/ *n.* [*count*] a bonnet with a large brim to protect the head and face from the sun.

sun•burn (sun′bûrn′) /ˈsʌnˌbɜrn/ *n., v.,* **-burned** or **-burnt -burn•ing.** —*n.* **1.** reddened, sore, and peeling skin caused by overexposure to the sun or a sunlamp: [*count*]: *a bad sunburn from a day at the beach.* [*noncount*]: *some soothing lotion for sunburn.* —*v.* **2.** (of the skin) to (cause to) become reddened, sore, and peeling from overexposure to the sun: [*no obj*]: *Her fair skin sunburns easily in the African sun.* [~ + *obj*]: *The African summer will sunburn her quickly.*

sun•burst (sun′bûrst′) /ˈsʌnˌbɜrst/ *n.* [*count*] **1.** a sudden burst of sunlight, esp. through a rift in the clouds. **2.** something that suggests the sun.

sun•dae (sun′dā, -dē) /ˈsʌndey, -diy/ *n.* [*count*] a dish of ice cream topped with syrup, nuts, whipped cream, etc.

Sun•day (sun′dā, -dē) /ˈsʌndey, -diy/ *n.* **1.** the first day of the week, observed as the Sabbath by most Christian denominations: [*proper noun*]: *On Sunday they would go to church.* [*count*]: *We saw him two Sundays ago.* —*adj.* [*before a noun*] **2.** of or relating to Sunday. **3.** used, done, or taking place only on or as if on Sundays: *a Sunday matinée.*

sun•der (sun′dər) /ˈsʌndər/ *v.* [~ + *obj*] to separate; part; divide; sever: *to sunder all ties to his previous country.*

sun•di•al (sun′dī′əl, -dīl′) /ˈsʌnˌdayəl, -ˌdayl/ *n.* [*count*] an instrument that indicates the time of day by means of the position of the shadow of the sun as it appears on a marked plate or surface.

sun•down (sun′doun′) /ˈsʌnˌdawn/ *n.* sunset, esp. the time of sunset: [*count*]: *a beautiful autumn sundown.* [*noncount*]: *Let's meet at sundown.*

sun•dries (sun′drēz) /ˈsʌndriyz/ *n.* [*plural*] small, various, or different items of little value.

sun•dry (sun′drē) /ˈsʌndriy/ *adj.* [*before a noun*] **1.** differing: *various and sundry articles.* —***Idiom.*** **2. all and sundry,** everybody: *The company gave out free samples to all and sundry.*

sun•fish (sun′fish′) /ˈsʌnˌfɪʃ/ *n.* [*count*], *pl.* (*esp. when thought of as a group*) **-fish,** (*esp. for kinds or species*) **-fish•es.** a freshwater fish of North America.

sun•flow•er (sun′flou′ər) /ˈsʌnˌflawər/ *n.* [*count*] a plant having showy, yellow flower heads and edible seeds.

sung (sung) /sʌŋ/ *v.* a pt. and pp. of SING.

sun•glass•es (sun′glas′iz) /ˈsʌnˌglæsɪz/ *n.* [*plural*] eyeglasses with colored or tinted lenses that protect the eyes from the glare of sunlight.

sunk (sungk) /sʌŋk/ *v.* **1.** a pt. and pp. of SINK. —*adj.* **2.** beyond help; no longer good for anything; destroyed: *Our business was sunk.*

sunk•en (sung′kən) /ˈsʌŋkən/ *adj.* **1.** having sunk or been sunk beneath the surface; submerged: *The divers explored the sunken ocean liner.* **2.** having settled to a lower level, as walls. **3.** made or lying on a lower level: *a sunken living room.* **4.** hollow; pushed in; depressed: *sunken cheeks.*

sun•lamp (sun′lamp′) /ˈsʌnˌlæmp/ *n.* [*count*] a lamp that produces ultraviolet rays, used for healing or for suntanning.

sun•light (sun′līt′) /ˈsʌnˌlayt/ *n.* [*noncount*] the light of the sun; sunshine.

sun•lit (sun′lit′) /ˈsʌnˌlɪt/ *adj.* lighted by the sun.

sun•ny (sun′ē) /ˈsʌniy/ *adj.,* **-ni•er, -ni•est. 1.** having much sunshine: *a warm, sunny room.* **2.** cheery, cheerful, or joyous: *a sunny disposition.* **3.** of or resembling the sun.

sun•rise (sun′rīz′) /ˈsʌnˌrayz/ *n.* **1.** the rise of the sun above the horizon in the morning: [*count*]: *He won't live to see another sunrise.* [*noncount*]: *Meet me at the park at sunrise.* **2.** [*count*] the sky and scenery accompanying this: *a beautiful sunrise over the Atlantic Ocean.* **3.** [*noncount*] the time when the sun rises.

sun•roof (sun′ro͞of′, -ro͝of′) /ˈsʌnˌruwf, -ˌrʊf/ *n.* [*count*], *pl.* **roofs.** a section of an automobile roof that can be slid or lifted open.

sun•screen or **sun screen** (sun′skrēn′) /ˈsʌnˌskriyn/ *n.* **1.** a substance that protects the skin from too much ultraviolet radiation from the sun; a lotion, cream, etc., containing this: [*noncount*]: *The careful use of sunscreen will protect the baby's skin.* [*count*]: *Use a powerful sunscreen if you work outside for long hours in the summertime.* **2.** [*count*] a simple structure shielding a patio, atrium, or the like from direct sunlight.

sun•set (sun′set′) /ˈsʌnˌsɛt/ *n.* **1.** the setting or descent of the sun below the horizon in the evening: [*count*]: *He won't live to see another sunset.* [*noncount*]: *Meet me at the park at sunset.* **2.** [*count*] the sky and scenery accompanying this: *a gorgeous sunset over the Atlantic Ocean.* **3.** [*noncount*] the time when the sun sets. —*adj.* [*before a noun*] **4.** (of an industry, technology, etc.) old; declining. **5.** of or being a law that requires the ending of a government program or agency by a certain date unless it is reauthorized by the legislature.

sun•shine (sun′shīn′) /ˈsʌnˌʃayn/ *n.* [*noncount*] **1.** the shining of the sun; the effect of the sun in lighting and heating a place. **2.** a place where the direct rays of the sun fall: *out in the sunshine.* —*adj.* [*before a noun*] **3.** of or denoting a law requiring a government agency to open its official meetings and records to the public. —**sun′shin′y,** *adj.*

sun•spot (sun′spot′) /ˈsʌnˌspɒt/ *n.* [*count*] a relatively dark patch that appears at certain times on the surface of the sun and affects magnetism on earth.

sun•stroke (sun′strōk′) /'sʌn,strowk/ *n.* [*noncount*] a sudden and sometimes fatal condition caused by too much exposure to the sun's rays: *Sunstroke causes collapse.*

sun•tan (sun′tan′) /'sʌn,tæn/ *n., v.,* **-tanned, -tan•ning.** **—***n.* [*count*] **1.** a darkening of the skin caused by exposure to sunlight or a sunlamp. **—***v.* **2.** TAN[1] (defs. 2, 4): [*no obj*]: *He was outside suntanning all day.* [~ + *obj*]: *Those lamps suntanned him in no time.*

sun•up (sun′up′) /'sʌn,ʌp/ *n.* [*noncount*] sunrise, esp. the time of sunrise: *Meet us at sunup.*

sup (sup) /sʌp/ *v.,* **supped, sup•ping. 1.** [*no obj*] to eat the evening meal; have supper. **2.** [~ + *obj*] to provide food for, or entertain at supper.

sup-, var. of SUB- before *p: suppose.*

su•per (so͞o′pər) /'suwpər/ *n.* [*count*] **1.** a superintendent, esp. of an apartment house: *The sink is flooding; call the super.* **—***adj.* **2.** of the highest degree, power, etc.: *a super council.* **3.** of an extreme degree: *super haste.* **4.** very good; first-rate; excellent: *a super job.* **—***adv.* **5.** very; extremely: *super cooperative.*

super-, *prefix.* **1.** *super-* comes from Latin, where it has the meaning "above, beyond; above or over (another); situated or located over": *superficial, superimpose, superstructure.* **2.** *super-* is also used to mean "an individual, thing, or property that surpasses customary or normal amounts or levels, as being larger, more powerful, or having something to a great degree or to too great a degree": *supercomputer, superconductivity, supercool, supercritical, superhighway, superhuman, superman.*

su•per•a•bun•dant (so͞o′pər ə bun′dənt) /,suwpərə'bʌndənt/ *adj.* very abundant or too abundant; excessive. **—su′per•a•bun′dance,** *n.* [*count*]

su•per•an•nu•at•ed (so͞o′pər an′yo͞o ā′tid) /,suwpər'ænyuw,eytɪd/ *adj.* **1.** retired because of age, sickness, or bodily weakness; too old for use, work, service, etc. **2.** antiquated or obsolete: *superannuated ideas.* See -ANN-.

su•perb (so͝o pûrb′) /sʊ'pɜrb/ *adj.* admirably fine or excellent; rich; grand; wonderful: *The dinner, the wine, the company—all were superb.* **—su•perb′ly,** *adv.*

su•per•charge (so͞o′pər chärj′) /'suwpər,tʃardʒ/ *v.* [~ + *obj*], **-charged, -charg•ing. 1.** to charge with too great an amount, as of energy, emotion, or tension: *The atmosphere was supercharged in the courtroom.* **2.** to supply air to (an internal-combustion engine) at pressure greater than normal. **—su′per•charg′er,** *n.* [*count*]

su•per•cil•i•ous (so͞o′pər sil′ē əs) /,suwpər'sɪliyəs/ *adj.* haughty and full of contempt for others: *a supercilious raising of the eyebrows.*

su•per•e•go (so͞o′pər ē′gō) /,suwpər'iygow/ *n.* [*count*], *pl.* **-gos.** the part of the personality that represents the conscience. Compare EGO, ID.

su•per•fi•cial (so͞o′pər fish′əl) /,suwpər'fɪʃəl/ *adj.* **1.** being at, on, or near the surface: *a superficial wound.* **2.** external or outward; apparent rather than real: *They bear a superficial resemblance to each other.* **3.** concerned with or understanding only what is on the surface or what is obvious; shallow: *a superficial analysis of the problem.* **—su•per•fi•ci•al•i•ty** (so͞o′pər fish′ē al′i tē) /,suwpər,fɪʃiy'ælɪtiy/ *n.* [*noncount*] **—su′per•fi′cial•ly,** *adv.: Superficially these two look alike.*

su•per•flu•ous (so͝o pûr′flo͞o əs) /sʊ'pɜrfluwəs/ *adj.* being more than is enough; too much; excessive: *Get rid of those superfluous exclamation points.* **—su•per•flu•i•ty** (so͞o′pər flo͞o′i tē) /,suwpər'fluwɪtiy/ *n.* [*noncount*] See -FLU-.

su•per•he•ro (so͞o′pər hēr′ō) /'suwpər,hɪərow/ *n.* [*count*], *pl.* **-roes.** a hero, esp. in children's comic books and television cartoons, possessing extraordinary, often magical powers.

su•per•high•way (so͞o′pər hī′wā, so͞o′pər hī′wā′) /'suwpər,haywey, ,suwpər'hay,wey/ *n.* [*count*] a multilane highway designed for travel at high speeds; expressway.

su•per•hu•man (so͞o′pər hyo͞o′mən) /,suwpər'hyuwmən/ *adj.* **1.** above or beyond what is human: *a superhuman being.* **2.** going beyond ordinary human power, experience, etc.: *He made a superhuman effort and succeeded in lifting the car from the child.*

su•per•im•pose (so͞o′pər im pōz′) /,suwpərɪm'powz/ *v.* [~ + *obj* (+ *on/upon*)], **-posed, -pos•ing. 1.** to put, place, or set over or on something else: *He superimposed one of his photos on top of another.* **2.** to (usually aggressively) put or join as an addition: *to superimpose his own views on the text of the committee's report.* See -POS-.

su•per•in•tend (so͞o′pər in tend′, so͞o′prin-) /,suwpərɪn'tɛnd, ,suwprɪn-/ *v.* [~ + *obj*] to be in charge of (a building, work, people, etc.); supervise: *No one was superintending the children when the fire broke out.* **—su′per•in•ten′dence, su′per•in•ten′den•cy,** *n.* [*noncount*] See -TEND-.

su•per•in•tend•ent (so͞o′pər in ten′dənt, so͞o′prin-) /,suwpərɪn'tɛndənt, ,suwprɪn-/ *n.* [*count*] **1.** one who guides or directs some work, establishment, etc.; supervisor: *the superintendent of schools.* **2.** one who is in charge of maintenance and repairs for an apartment house; custodian: *Call the superintendent; the bathroom is flooding.* **—***adj.* [*before a noun*] **3.** superintending. See -TEND-.

su•pe•ri•or (sə pēr′ē ər, so͝o-) /sə'pɪəriyər, sʊ-/ *adj.* **1.** higher in rank, degree, class, etc.: *a superior officer.* **2.** above the average in excellence, merit, etc.: *a superior student.* **3.** of higher grade or quality: *a superior brand of dog food.* **4.** greater in quantity or amount: *Our armies have superior numbers.* **5.** showing a feeling of being better than or above others: *He had a superior attitude toward everyone.* **6.** higher in place or position; located above some similar thing: *The enemy had an advantage, fighting from superior ground.* **—***n.* [*count*] **7.** one who is superior to another in rank, as in a job, or who has higher ability than another: *She's my superior at work.* **8.** the head of a monastery, convent, or the like. **—su•pe•ri•or•i•ty** (sə pēr′ē ôr′i tē, -or′-, so͝o-) /sə,pɪəriy'ɔrɪtiy, -'ɒr-, sʊ-/ *n.* [*noncount*]

su•per•la•tive (sə pûr′lə tiv, so͝o-) /sə'pɜrlətɪv, sʊ-/ *adj.* **1.** of the highest kind or order: *The dinner was superlative.* **2.** of or designating the highest degree of comparison of adjectives and adverbs, used to show the extreme or greatest in quality, quantity, or intensity, as in *smallest, best,* and *most carefully,* the superlative forms of *small, good,* and *carefully.* Compare COMPARATIVE (def. 4), POSITIVE (def. 22). **—***n.* **3.** [*count*] a superlative person or thing. **4. a.** [*noncount; usually: the* + ~] the superlative degree of an adjective or adverb: *Put the adjective* good *into the superlative.* **b.** [*count*] the superlative form of an adjective or adverb: *The words and phrases* smallest, best, *and* most carefully *are superlatives.* **—su•per′la•tive•ly,** *adv.: She performed superlatively well during the concert.* See -LAT[1]-.

su•per•man (so͞o′pər man′) /'suwpər,mæn/ *n.* [*count*], *pl.* **-men.** a person of extraordinary or superhuman physical, mental, or spiritual powers.

su•per•mar•ket (so͞o′pər mär′kit) /'suwpər,markɪt/ *n.* [*count*] **1.** a large self-service retail store that sells food and other household goods. SEE ILLUSTRATION. **2.** any business or company offering an unusually wide range of goods or services: *a financial supermarket.*

su•per•nat•u•ral (so͞o′pər nach′ər əl, -nach′rəl) /,suwpər'nætʃərəl, -'nætʃrəl/ *adj.* **1.** of, relating to, or being above or beyond what is natural or that can be explained by natural law: *supernatural powers.* **—***n.* [*noncount*] **2. the supernatural,** [*the* + ~] supernatural beings, behavior, and occurrences thought of as a group: *The fortune-teller claimed to be able to contact the world of the supernatural.* See -NAT-.

su•per•no•va (so͞o′pər nō′və) /,suwpər'nowvə/ *n.* [*count*], *pl.* **-vas, -vae** (-vē) /-viy/. a nova millions of times brighter than the sun. See -NOV-.

su•per•nu•mer•ar•y (so͞o′pər no͞o′mə rer′ē, -nyo͞o′-) /,suwpər'nuwmə,rɛriy, -'nyuw-/ *adj., n., pl.* **-ar•ies. —***adj.* **1.** being more than the usual, proper, or expected number; additional; extra. **—***n.* [*count*] **2.** an extra person or thing. **3.** a supernumerary official or employee. **4.** one who appears in a play, opera, etc., without speaking lines or as part of a crowd; an extra. See -NUM-.

su•per•pow•er (so͞o′pər pou′ər) /'suwpər,pawər/ *n.* [*count*] a very powerful nation, esp. one with important interests and influence outside its own region: *China was expected to be the new emerging superpower.*

su•per•script (so͞o′pər skript′) /'suwpər,skrɪpt/ *adj.* **1.** written above. **—***n.* [*count*] **2.** Also called **superior.** a letter, number, or symbol written or printed high on a line of text: *The number* 2 *in the formula* a^2b *is a superscript.* See -SCRIB-.

su•per•sede (so͞o′pər sēd′) /,suwpər'siyd/ *v.* [~ + *obj*], **-sed•ed, -sed•ing. 1.** to take the place of (another), as by having more power, authority, effectiveness, etc.: *This new drug will supersede all others.* **2.** to set (something, as a regulation) aside as being no longer in force: *This new regulation concerning import fees supersedes the old one.*

su•per•son•ic (so͞o′pər son′ik) /,suwpər'sɒnɪk/ *adj.* **1.**

supermarket

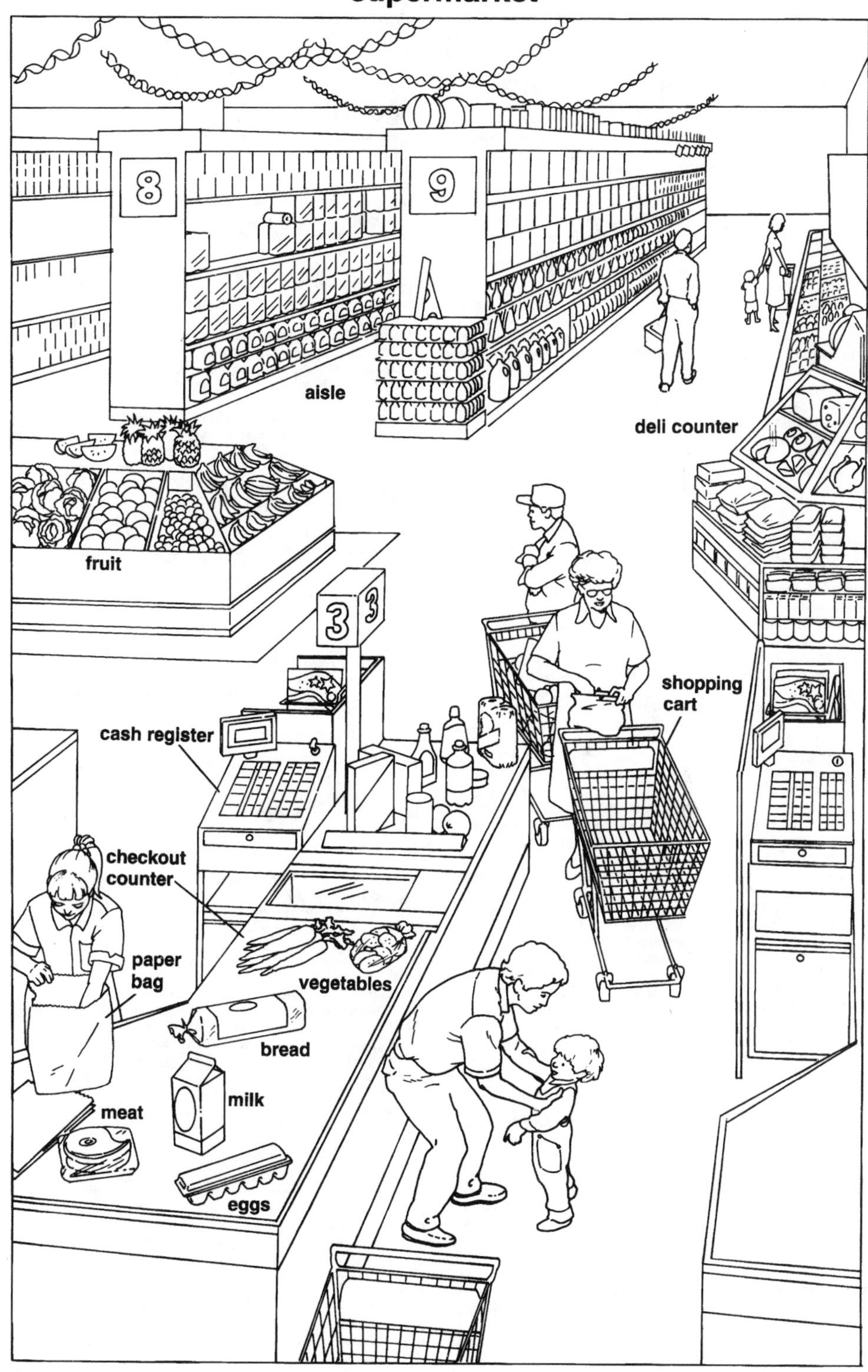

greater than the speed of sound waves through air. **2.** capable of achieving such speed: *a supersonic plane.* **3.** ULTRASONIC. See -SON-.

su•per•star (so͞o′pər stär′) /ˈsuwpərˌstɑr/ *n.* [*count*] a very prominent or successful person, esp. a performer or athlete who enjoys great fame and admiration: *Suddenly the shy, retired professor became a superstar overnight on TV talk shows.*

su•per•sti•tion (so͞o′pər stish′ən) /ˌsuwpərˈstɪʃən/ *n.* **1.** [*count*] an irrational belief in something, esp. such a belief when it is based on magic: *Some common superstitions involve a black cat crossing one's path or, walking under an open ladder.* **2.** [*noncount*] a system or collection of such beliefs: *Baseball players place a lot of emphasis on superstition.* See -STIT-.

su•per•sti•tious (so͞o′pər sti′shəs) /ˌsuwpərˈstɪʃəs/ *adj.* **1.** of or relating to superstition; coming from superstition: *my silly superstitious fears.* **2.** believing in or full of superstition: *He had become a superstitious fool, watching for any sign from the gods that signaled his future chances for success.* See -STIT-.

su•per•struc•ture (so͞o′pər struk′chər) /ˈsuwpərˌstrʌktʃər/ *n.* [*count*] the part of a building, ship, or construction entirely above its foundation, basement, or deck: *The superstructure of the battle cruiser rose in the night sky over the Atlantic.* See -STRU-.

su•per•tank•er (so͞o′pər tang′kər) /ˈsuwpərˌtæŋkər/ *n.* [*count*] a tanker with a capacity of over 75,000 tons.

su•per•vise (so͞o′pər vīz′) /ˈsuwpərˌvayz/ *v.* [~ + *obj*], **-vised, -vis•ing.** to watch over and direct (a process, work, etc.); manage: *She supervised the ESL program at the college.* See -VIS-.

su•per•vi•sion (so͞o′pər vizh′ən) /ˌsuwpərˈvɪʒən/ *n.* [*noncount*] the act of supervising: *a total lack of supervision in that school.* See -VIS-.

su•per•vi•sor (so͞o′pər vī′zər) /ˈsuwpərˌvayzər/ *n.* [*count*] a person who watches over, directs, or manages another or others. **—su′per•vi′so•ry,** *adj.* See -VIS-.

su•pine (so͞o pīn′) /suwˈpayn/ *adj.* lying on the back, face upward.

supp., an abbreviation of: **1.** supplement. **2.** supplementary. Also, **suppl.**

sup•per (sup′ər) /ˈsʌpər/ *n.* **1.** the evening meal, often the principal meal of the day, esp. one taken in the evening: [*count*]: *delicious meatless suppers.* [*noncount*]: *Come over for supper next Monday.* **2.** [*count*] an evening social event at which a supper is served to raise money for a church, charity, etc.: *a church supper.* **—Usage.** See DINNER.

sup′per club′, *n.* [*count*] a nightclub, esp. a small, luxurious one.

sup•plant (sə plant′) /səˈplænt/ *v.* [~ + *obj* (+ *with* + *obj*)] **1.** to take the place of (another), as through force or tricks: *to supplant the liberal premier with a former army man.* **2.** to replace (one thing) with something else.

sup•ple (sup′əl) /ˈsʌpəl/ *adj.,* **-pler, -plest. 1.** bending easily without breaking; flexible: *supple tubing.* **2.** showing ease in bending; limber, lithe, or graceful: *supple movements.* **3.** easily able to adapt, as in one's thinking or reactions to events: *Her supple nature enables her to accept change.* **—sup′ple•ness,** *n.* [*noncount*] **—sup•ply** (sup′lē) /ˈsʌpliy/ *adv.* See -PLIC-.

sup•ple•ment (*n.* sup′lə mənt; *v.* -ment′) / *n.* ˈsʌpləmənt; *v.* -ˌmɛnt/ *n.* [*count*] **1.** something added to complete a thing or to reinforce or extend something: *The supplies at the depot were a supplement to what they had already brought with them.* **2.** something added to or issued after a publication that supplies further information, etc.: *a supplement to an encyclopedia.* **3.** the amount by which an angle or arc falls short of 180° or a semicircle. **—***v.* [~ + *obj*] **4.** to complete, add to, or extend by a supplement: *The computer can supplement what has been taught in a classroom.* **—sup′ple•men′tal,** *adj.*

sup•ple•men•ta•ry (sup′lə men′tə rē) /ˌsʌpləˈmɛntəriy/ *adj.* forming a supplement; additional: *supplementary assistance.*

sup•pli•ant (sup′lē ənt) /ˈsʌpliyənt/ *n.* [*count*] **1.** one who supplicates. **—***adj.* **2.** of or relating to supplication. See -PLIC-.

sup•pli•cant (sup′li kənt) /ˈsʌplɪkənt/ *adj.* **1.** of or relating to supplication. **—***n.* [*count*] **2.** one who supplicates. See -PLIC-.

sup•pli•cate (sup′li kāt′) /ˈsʌplɪˌkeyt/ *v.,* **-cat•ed, -cat•ing.** to request or beg for something deeply and humbly (from someone): [*no obj*]: *the thousands supplicating for a chance at jobs.* [~ + *obj*]: *to supplicate the authorities.* **—sup•pli•ca•tion** (sup′li kā′shən) /ˌsʌplɪˈkeyʃən/ *n.* [*noncount*]: *to make earnest supplication.* [*count*]: *the supplications an official must deal with.* See -PLIC-.

sup•ply (sə plī′) /səˈplay/ *v.,* **-plied, -ply•ing,** *n., pl.* **-plies. —***v.* **1.** [~ + *obj* + *with* + *obj*] to furnish (a person, thing, etc.) with what is needed: *These foods supply the body with necessary vitamins and minerals.* **2.** [~ + *obj* (+ *to* + *obj*)] to furnish or provide (something needed) to a person or thing: *The Aswan Dam supplied needed water to the region.* **—***n.* **3.** [*noncount*] the act of supplying, furnishing, satisfying, etc. **4.** [*count*] something supplied: *The storm cut off the city's water supply.* **5.** [*count*] a quantity or amount of something available; stock or store: *The store carries a large supply of swimwear.* **6.** [*noncount*] the amount or quantity of a product that is in the market and available for purchase: *the laws of supply and demand in the capitalist system.* **7.** [*count*] Usually, **supplies.** [*plural*] an amount or store of food or other things necessary for maintaining an army, business, or other enterprise: *bringing supplies to the war zone.* **—sup•pli′er,** *n.* [*count*]

sup•port (sə pôrt′, -pōrt′) /səˈpɔrt, -ˈpowrt/ *v.* [~ + *obj*] **1.** to bear (a load, mass, part, etc.) from below; to sustain (weight, pressure, etc.) without giving way: *He supported himself by holding on to the wall.* **2.** to maintain (a person, family, etc.) with the necessities of existence: *Is that enough money to support yourself?* **3.** to extend help, concern, etc., to (a person, one's spirits, etc.) experiencing hardship: *Her brother supported her during the tragedy.* **4.** to uphold by showing one's agreement with or faith in (a person, cause, etc.); to defend: *I support his nomination for president.* **5.** to provide evidence for; show to be true; confirm: *His testimony will support her plea of innocence.* **—***n.* **6.** [*noncount*] the providing of necessary means or funds for a person or family to live: *He provides child support for his kids.* **7.** [*noncount*] an act or instance of supporting; the state of being supported: *to show support for our fired coworkers.* **8.** [*count*] something that serves as a foundation, prop, or brace to hold something up: *The explosives ripped the cable car's two supports from the wire.* **9.** [*noncount*] backup in combat, as by air cover: *We'll need more air support to protect the convoy.* **—***adj.* [*before a noun*] **10.** (of hosiery) made with elasticized fibers that exert a degree of tension on the legs, thereby aiding circulation, etc.: *support hose.* **—sup•port′a•ble,** *adj.* **—sup•port′er,** *n.* [*count*] **—sup•port′ive,** *adj.*: *She found the teachers very supportive regarding her learning disability.* See -PORT-.

support′ group′, *n.* [*count*] a group of people who meet regularly to support each other by discussing problems affecting them in common, as alcoholism, death in the family, etc.: *She joined a support group for families of alcoholics.*

sup•pose (sə pōz′) /səˈpowz/ *v.,* **-posed, -pos•ing,** *conj.* **—***v.* [*not: be* + ~*-ing*] **1.** [~ + (*that*) *clause*] to assume (something), as for the sake of argument: *Suppose (that) you won a million dollars in the lottery.* **2.** to think or hold as an opinion; believe: [~ + (*that*) *clause*]: *What do you suppose (that) he will do?* [*no obj*]: *Oh, I suppose (so).* **3.** [~ + (*that*) *clause*] to believe or assume as true; take for granted: *We all supposed that he had died in the crash.* **4.** [*be* + ~*-ed* + *to* + *verb*] to expect or require: *The machine is not supposed to make noise.* **—***conj.* **5.** Also, **supposing.** (used to put forward or evaluate something to be considered as a possibility): *Suppose (supposing) we do wait until tomorrow; what then?* See -POS-.

sup•posed (sə pōzd′, sə pō′zid) /səˈpowzd, səˈpowzɪd/ *adj.* **1.** assumed as true: *the supposed site of Atlantis.* **2.** thought to be such, but not really so; imagined: *The supposed gains would be outweighed by the costs.* **—sup•pos′ed•ly,** *adv.*: *He was supposedly the best in the business.* See SUPPOSE (def. 4).

sup•po•si•tion (sup′ə zish′ən) /ˌsʌpəˈzɪʃən/ *n.* **1.** [*noncount*] an act of supposing: *Their accusation is pure supposition on their part.* **2.** [*count*] something that is supposed; an assumption: *suppositions about how the money was spent.* See -POS-.

sup•press (sə pres′) /səˈprɛs/ *v.* [~ + *obj*] **1.** to put an end to the activities of (a person, group, etc.): *The government suppressed any movement toward democracy.* **2.** to hold back deliberately (an impulse or action): *He had a hard time suppressing his anger.* **3.** to keep (a thought, memory, etc.) out of conscious awareness: *I think you're suppressing your feelings of hostility.* **4.** to withhold (evidence, a book, etc.) or keep back from public knowledge: *The president's office suppressed the release of those figures.* **5.** to stop or arrest (a cough, hemorrhage, etc.): *to suppress a cough.* —**sup•pres′sant,** *n.* [*count*]: *The doctor gave you a cough suppressant.* —**sup•pres•sion** (sə presh′ən) /sə'prɛʃən/ *n.* [*noncount*] See -PRESS-.

su•pra (so͞o′prə) /'suwprə/ *adv.* (used in writing to refer to parts of a text that appear above the point of reading). Compare INFRA.

supra-, *prefix. supra-* comes from Latin, where it has the meaning "above, over; beyond the limits of": *supranational; supraorbital.* Compare SUPER-.

su•pra•na•tion•al (so͞o′prə nash′ə nl) /ˌsuwprə'næʃənḷ/ *adj.* above the authority or scope of any one national government, as a project or policy: *a supranational agency.*

su•pra•or•bit•al (so͞o′prə ôr′bi tl) /ˌsuwprə'ɔrbɪtḷ/ *adj.* situated above the eye socket.

su•prem•a•cist (sə prem′ə sist, so͞o-) /sə'prɛməsɪst, sʊ-/ *n.* [*count*] one who believes in the supremacy of a particular group, esp. a racial group: *a white supremacist.*

su•prem•a•cy (sə prem′ə sē, so͞o-) /sə'prɛməsiy, sʊ-/ *n.* [*noncount*] the state of being supreme.

su•preme (sə prēm′, so͞o-) /sə'priym, sʊ-/ *adj.* **1.** [*before a noun*] highest in rank or authority; paramount; sovereign: *the supreme commander.* **2.** of the highest quality, degree, character, etc.: *the supreme craftsmanship reflected in that vase.* **3.** [*before a noun*] greatest, utmost, or extreme: *the supreme sacrifice: giving up her life for another.* —**su•preme′ly,** *adv.*

Supreme′ Be′ing, *n.* [*proper noun; usually: the* + ~] God.

Supt. or **supt.,** an abbreviation of: superintendent.

sur-, *prefix. sur-* comes from French, where it has the meaning "over, above, in addition": *surcharge; surname; surrender.*

sur•cease (sûr sēs′) /sɜr'siys/ *v.,* **-ceased, -ceas•ing,** *n.* —*v.* [*no obj*] **1.** to stop doing some action. —*n.* [*noncount*] **2.** end.

sur•charge (*n.* sûr′chärj′; *v.* sûr chärj′, sûr′chärj′) / *n.* 'sɜrˌtʃɑrdʒ; *v.* sɜr'tʃɑrdʒ, 'sɜrˌtʃɑrdʒ/ *n., v.,* **-charged, -charg•ing.** —*n.* [*count*] **1.** an additional charge, tax, or cost added on to the usual charge: *a surcharge on imported oil.* —*v.* [~ + *obj*] **2.** to force customers to pay an additional charge for.

sure (sho͝or) /ʃʊr/ *adj.,* **sur•er, sur•est,** *adv.* —*adj.* **1.** (of a person) free from doubt as to the reliability, character, action, etc., of something: [*be* + ~ (+ *of/about*)]: *Are you sure? —Well, I'm pretty sure. She was very sure of her facts.* [*be* + ~ + *(that) clause*]: *was sure (that) she had told him.* **2.** confident, as of something expected: [*be/feel* + ~ + *of*]: *They felt sure of success.* [*be* + ~ + *(that) clause*]: *He was sure (that) he wouldn't fail again.* **3.** [*be* + ~] convinced, fully persuaded, or positive: *to be sure of a person's honesty.* **4.** [*before a noun*] assured or certain beyond question: *a sure victory.* **5.** [*before a noun*] never missing or disappointing; unfailing: *This investment is a sure thing.* **6.** [*before a noun*] allowing for no doubt or question: *Those high clouds are a sure sign of snow.* **7.** [*be* + ~ + *to* + *verb*] destined; certain: *It is sure to happen.* —*adv.* **8.** certainly; surely: *She sure acts funny sometimes.* —***Idiom.*** **9. be** or **make sure,** to take care (to be or do as specified): [*be* + ~ + *to* + *verb*]: *Be sure to set your alarm clock.* [*make* + ~ + *(that) clause*]: *Could you make sure (that) everything is OK with our checking account?* **10. for sure,** without a doubt; surely; for certain: *We'd like to know for sure if you're on our side.* **11. sure enough,** *Informal.* as might have been expected; certainly: *As soon as I brought the car to the service station, sure enough the weird sound went away.* —**sure′ness,** *n.* [*noncount*]

sure•fire (sho͝or′fīᵊr′, shûr′-) /'ʃʊrˌfayᵊr, 'ʃɜr-/ *adj.* [*before a noun*] *Informal.* sure to work: *a surefire plan.*

sure•foot•ed (sho͝or′fo͝ot′id, shûr′-) /'ʃʊr'fʊtɪd, 'ʃɜr-/ *adj.* **1.** not likely to stumble, slip, or fall. **2.** proceeding surely; unerring: *a surefooted pursuit of success.*

sure•ly (sho͝or′lē, shûr′-) /'ʃʊrliy, 'ʃɜr-/ *adv.* **1.** firmly; without stumbling: *He walked slowly but surely to the door.* **2.** inevitably or without fail: *Things will surely fall apart.* **3.** undoubtedly, assuredly, or certainly: *Surely she knows what she's doing.* **4.** (used for emphasis, esp. when contradicting another statement) assuredly: *Surely you are mistaken.* **5.** (used to answer a question) yes; indeed: *"May I wait inside?"—"Surely."*

sur•e•ty (sho͝or′i tē, sho͝or′tē, shûr′-) /'ʃʊrɪtiy, 'ʃʊrtiy, 'ʃɜr-/ *n., pl.* **-ties. 1.** something of value given as a promise to pay for loss, damage, or a debt: [*noncount*]: *offering her jewelry as surety.* [*count*]: *providing some sureties against loss.* **2.** [*count*] one who has made himself or herself responsible for another, as a sponsor or bondsman.

surf (sûrf) /sɜrf/ *n.* [*noncount*] **1.** the swell of the waves of the sea that breaks upon a shore: *rough surf during the hurricane.* —*v.* [*no obj*] **2.** to go surfing. —**surf′er,** *n.* [*count*]

sur•face (sûr′fis) /'sɜrfɪs/ *n., adj., v.,* **-faced, -fac•ing.** —*n.* [*count*] **1.** the outer face, outside, or exterior boundary of a thing: *the surface of the asteroid.* **2.** any face of a body or thing: *the six surfaces of a cube.* **3.** [*usually singular; often: the* + ~] the outward appearance of something: *On the surface it looked like a simple murder case, but it grew deeper and more mysterious.* **4.** the top part of a liquid or body of water: *The submarine rose quietly to the surface.* —*adj.* [*before a noun*] **5.** of, on, or relating to the surface; external. **6.** apparent rather than real; superficial. **7.** of, relating to, or by land or sea: *Send that parcel home by surface mail.* —*v.* **8.** [~ + *obj*] to give a particular kind of surface to by covering: *to surface the road with asphalt.* **9.** [*no obj*] to rise to the surface: *The submarine surfaced and switched on its radar.* **10.** [*no obj*] to appear or emerge; turn up: *New evidence has surfaced.* See -FACE-.

surf•board (sûrf′bôrd′, -bōrd′) /'sɜrfˌbɔrd, -ˌbowrd/ *n.* [*count*] **1.** a long, narrow board on which a person stands or lies and rides the crest of a breaking wave toward the shore in surfing. —*v.* [*no obj*] **2.** to ride a surfboard.

sur•feit (sûr′fit) /'sɜrfɪt/ *n.* [*count; usually singular*] too much or too large of an amount; excess: *a surfeit of speeches at the dinner.*

surf•ing (sûr′fing) /'sɜrfɪŋ/ *n.* [*noncount*] the act or sport of riding the crest of a breaking wave toward the shore, esp. on a surfboard.

surge (sûrj) /sɜrdʒ/ *n., v.,* **surged, surg•ing.** —*n.* [*count*] **1.** a strong, forward movement like a wave: *the surge of the crowd toward the stadium.* **2.** a sudden, strong rush or burst: *a surge of energy.* **3.** a sudden rush or burst of electric current or voltage: *Protect your computer against electrical surges.* —*v.* [*no obj*] **4.** to rise, roll, move, or swell forward in or like waves: *Floodwater surged through the town.* **5.** to rise as if by a heaving or swelling force, as of strong feeling: *She could feel anger surging through her body.* **6.** (esp. of electric current or voltage) to increase suddenly.

sur•geon (sûr′jən) /'sɜrdʒən/ *n.* [*count*] a physician who specializes in surgery.

sur•ger•y (sûr′jə rē) /'sɜrdʒəriy/ *n., pl.* **-ger•ies** for 4, 5. **1.** [*noncount*] the practice of treating diseases, injuries, etc., by performing medical operations or procedures, or the branch of medicine dealing with such: *medical school courses in surgery.* **2.** [*noncount*] treatment, as an operation, performed by a surgeon: *You may not need surgery after all.* **3.** [*noncount*] any major repair or change produced as if by a surgical operation: *Major surgery will be needed on those budget proposals.* **4.** [*count*] a room or place for surgical operations. **5.** [*count*] *Brit.* a doctor's office.

sur•gi•cal (sûr′ji kəl) /'sɜrdʒɪkəl/ *adj.* **1.** [*before a noun*] of, relating to, or involving surgery or surgeons: *surgical procedures.* **2.** characterized by great precision: *a surgical air strike against the oil refineries.* —**sur′gi•cal•ly,** *adv.*

sur•ly (sûr′lē) /'sɜrliy/ *adj.,* **-li•er, -li•est.** rude, unfriendly, hostile, or bad-tempered. —**sur′li•ness,** *n.* [*noncount*]

sur•mise (sər mīz′; *n.* also sûr′mīz) /sər'mayz; *n.* ælsn 'sɜrmayz/ *v.,* **-mised, -mis•ing,** *n.* —*v.* **1.** to guess without strong evidence; conjecture: [~ + *obj*]: *She surmised the truth about him.* [~ + *that clause*]: *She surmised that he was up for promotion.* —*n.* [*count*] **2.** an idea of something as being possible or likely. See -MIS-.

sur•mount (sər mount′) /sər'mawnt/ *v.* [~ + *obj*] to overcome; conquer: *to surmount tremendous difficulties.* —**sur•mount′a•ble,** *adj.*

sur•name (sûr′nām′) /'sɜrˌneym / *n.* [*count*] the name that a person has in common with other family members, as distinguished from a given name; family name.

sur•pass (sər pas′) /sər'pæs/ *v.* [~ + *obj*] **1.** to go beyond in amount, extent, excellence, or degree; be greater than: *She surpassed all the others.* **2.** to be beyond the range or capacity of; transcend: *misery that surpasses description.* —**sur•pass′ing,** *adj.* [*before a noun*]: *structures of surpassing beauty.* See -PASS-[1].

sur•plus (sûr′plus, -pləs) /'sɜrplʌs, -pləs/ *n., adj., v.,* **-plussed** or **-plused, -plus•sing** or **-plus•ing.** —*n.* **1.** [*count*] something that remains above what is used or needed: *a surplus of oil.* **2.** [*noncount*] an amount, quantity, etc., greater than needed: *the labor surplus in Sweden.* **—*adj.*** [*before a noun*] **3.** being a surplus: *surplus wheat.* **—*v.*** [~ + *obj*] **4.** to treat as surplus; sell off.

sur•prise (sər prīz′, sə-) /sər'prayz, sə-/ *v.,* **-prised, -pris•ing,** *n.* **—*v.*** **1.** to strike with a sudden feeling of wonder or astonishment, esp. by being unexpected: [~ + *obj*]: *Those sales figures surprised me!* [*It* + ~ + *obj* + *that clause*]: *It surprised me that we had lost so much during the last quarter.* **2.** [~ + *obj*] to come upon or discover suddenly and unexpectedly: *When her father came home early he surprised the young couple on the couch.* **3.** [~ + *obj*] to make an unexpected attack or assault on (an unprepared army, etc.): *At dawn the regiment surprised the enemy in their barracks.* **—*n.*** **4.** [*noncount*] the state of being surprised, esp. at something unexpected: *filled with surprise at the sheer size of the house.* **5.** [*count*] something that surprises: *She likes surprises for her birthday.* **6.** [*noncount*] an act or instance of surprising: *Perhaps the element of surprise gave us the victory.* **—*Idiom.*** **7. take (someone) by surprise,** [*take* + *obj* + *by* + ~] **a.** to come upon without warning or unexpectedly: *Our regiment took the fort by surprise.* **b.** to astonish; amaze: *Her low grades in college took her parents by surprise, because she had always done well in high school.* See -PRIS-.

sur•prised (sər prīzd′, sə-) /sər'prayzd, sə-/ *adj.* having or affected by a feeling of surprise: *The surprised soldiers surrendered meekly.* [*be* + ~ + *(that) clause*]: *I was surprised (that) she would do such a crazy thing.* [*be* + ~ + *to* + *verb*]: *I was surprised to hear such anger in her voice.* See -PRIS-.

sur•pris•ing (sər pri′zing, sə-) /sər'prayzıŋ, sə-/ *adj.* causing a feeling of surprise: *A surprising number of students showed up for the lecture.* [*It* + *be* + ~ + *that clause*]: *It was surprising that so many students showed up for the lecture.* —**sur•pris′ing•ly,** *adv.*: *Surprisingly few students showed up for the lecture.* See -PRIS-.

sur•re•al (sə rē′əl, -rēl′) /sə'riyəl, -'riyl/ *adj.* having the strange, unreal feeling or quality of a dream; unreal; bizarre: *a surreal situation of people starving to death while shiploads of food were only a few feet away behind barbed wire.* See -REAL-.

sur•re•al•ism (sə rē′ə liz′əm) /sə'riyə,lızəm/ *n.* [*noncount*] [*sometimes: Surrealism*] a style of art and literature that developed principally in the 20th century, stressing the subconscious (where dreams originate) and using imagery that relies on unexpected or chance effects or connections. —**sur•re′al•ist,** *n.* [*count*], *adj.*

sur•re•al•is•tic (sə rē′ə lis′tik) /sə,riyə'lıstık/ *adj.* **1.** having the strange or unreal feeling or quality of a dream; surreal. **2.** of or relating to surrealism.

sur•ren•der (sə ren′dər) /sə'rɛndər/ *v.* **1.** [*no obj; (~ + to + obj)*] to give oneself up, as into the power of another, as by agreeing to stop fighting because of defeat: *The enemy formally surrendered to the Allies.* **2.** [~ + *obj (+ to + obj)*] to yield (something) to the possession of another, as after defeat: *to surrender the fort to the enemy.* **3.** [~ *(+ oneself)*] to give (oneself) up, as to the police: *After twenty hours of a stalemate the gunman surrendered (himself) to the police.* **4.** [~ *(+ oneself)* + *to* + *obj*] to give (oneself) up to some influence, course, etc.: *to surrender (oneself) to greed.* **—*n.*** **5.** an act or instance of surrendering: [*noncount*]: *The Allies are trying to starve the country into surrender.* [*count*]: *The enemy signed a formal surrender.* See -REND-.

sur•rep•ti•tious (sûr′əp tish′əs) /,sɜrəp'tıʃəs/ *adj.* obtained, done, made, etc., secretly; secret: *a surreptitious glance at his watch.* —**sur′rep•ti′tious•ly,** *adv.*: *He glanced surreptitiously at his watch.* See -RAPE-.

sur•rey (sûr′ē, sur′ē) /'sɜriy, 'sʌriy/ *n.* [*count*], *pl.* **-reys.** a light, four-wheeled, two-seated, horse-drawn carriage, with or without a top, for four persons.

sur•ro•gate (*n., adj.* sûr′ə gāt′, -git, sur′-; *v.* -gāt′) / *n., adj.* 'sɜrə,geyt, -gıt, 'sʌr-; *v.* -,geyt/ *n.* [*count*] **1.** a person appointed to act for another; deputy. **2.** a substitute. **3.** SURROGATE MOTHER. **—*adj.*** **4.** relating to, acting as, or involving a surrogate. See -ROGA-.

sur′rogate moth′er, *n.* [*count*] a woman who enables a couple to have a child by carrying to term an embryo conceived by the couple and transferred to her uterus, or by being inseminated with the man's sperm and either donating the embryo for transfer to the woman's uterus or carrying it to term.

sur•round (sə round′) /sə'rawnd/ *v.* [~ + *obj*] **1.** to enclose on all sides; encircle: *The presidential candidate was surrounded by admirers.* **2.** to enclose so as to cut off communication or retreat: *The troops surrounded the village.* **3.** to exist around or accompany; attend: *An aura of mystery surrounds her.* **4.** to cause to be enclosed, encircled, or attended: *He surrounded himself with friends.*

sur•round•ing (sə roun′ding) /sə'rawndıŋ/ *n.* **1.** [*count*] something that surrounds. **2. surroundings,** [*plural*] things, circumstances, conditions, etc., that form one's environment: *In such surroundings, how could he hope to live a normal life?* **—*adj.*** [*before a noun*] **3.** enclosing or encircling: *snow in the city and the surrounding suburbs.* **—Syn.** See ENVIRONMENT.

sur•tax (*n., v.* sûr′taks′; *v.* also sûr taks′) / *n., v.* 'sɜr,tæks; *v.* ælsn sɜr'tæks/ *n.* [*count*] **1.** an additional tax on something already taxed, esp. a graded tax on incomes. **—*v.*** [~ + *obj*] **2.** to charge with a surtax.

sur•veil•lance (sər vā′ləns) /sər'veyləns/ *n.* [*noncount*] a watch kept over someone or something, esp. over a suspect, prisoner, etc.: *under police surveillance.*

sur•vey (*v.* sər vā′; *n.* sûr′vā) / *v.* sər'vey; *n.* 'sɜrvey/ *v., n., pl.* **-veys.** **—*v.*** [~ + *obj*] **1.** to consider or study in a general way: *to survey a situation from all aspects.* **2.** to view in detail, esp. in order to know the condition or value of something: *The inspector surveyed the building.* **3.** to conduct a study of the opinions or thoughts of (a group of people): *to survey TV viewers.* **4.** to determine the exact dimensions and position of (an area of land) by a series of measurements: *to survey the land for the public park.* **—*n.*** [*count*] **5.** a general view, description, course of study, etc.: *a survey of Italian painting.* **6.** a detailed formal or official examination or inspection, as to figure out condition, character, etc. **7. a.** the act of surveying an area of land. **b.** a plan or description resulting from this. **8.** a sampling of facts, figures, or opinions used to indicate what a complete analysis might reveal: *Their survey of smokers suggests that many would like to quit.* —**sur•vey′or,** *n.* [*count*]

sur•viv•al (sər vi′vəl) /sər'vayvəl/ *n.* **1.** [*noncount*] the act or fact of surviving: *survival of the fittest.* **2.** [*count*] something that continues to live or exist, as from an earlier time: *Some of our social manners and customs are survivals from an earlier era.* See -VIV-.

sur•viv•al•ist (sər vi′və list) /sər'vayvəlıst/ *n.* [*count*] one who makes preparations to survive a widespread disaster or catastrophe, such as an atomic war, esp. by storing food and weapons in a safe place. See -VIV-.

sur•vive (sər vīv′) /sər'vayv/ *v.,* **-vived, -viv•ing.** **1.** to remain alive, as after the death of another or the occurrence of some event; continue to live: [*no obj*]: *A few were killed but most survived.* [~ + *obj*]: *Most survived the explosion.* **2.** [~ + *obj*] to continue to live or exist after the death of: *She survived three husbands, living until the age of 105.* **3.** to continue to function or manage in spite of difficult circumstances or hardship; endure: [*no obj*]: *Our company will survive, no matter what.* [~ + *obj*]: *She's survived two divorces.* **4.** [*no obj*] to remain or continue in existence or use: *How did some of those crazy ideas survive after all these years?* **5. survive on,** [~ + *on* + *obj*] to live or exist with just enough of (money, water, food, etc.) to continue: *surviving on bread and water.* See -VIV-.

sur•vi•vor (sər vi′vər) /sər'vayvər/ *n.* [*count*] **1.** one that survives. **2.** *Law.* the one of two or more designated persons who outlives the other or others. **3.** a person who continues to function in spite of difficulty: *She's a survivor; she'll rebound from this.* See -VIV-.

sus•cep•ti•ble (sə sep′tə bəl) /sə'sɛptəbəl/ *adj.* **1.** [*usually: be* + ~ + *to*] allowing or admitting of some specified treatment or response: *Is the virus susceptible to treatment with drugs?* **2.** [*be* + ~ + *to*] sensitive to, easily moved by, or easily touched by some influence, agency, force, etc.: *She's very susceptible to colds.* **3.** capable of being affected emotionally: *a susceptible young boy who cries a lot.* —**sus•cep•ti•bil•i•ty** (sə sep′tə bil′i tē) /sə,sɛptə'bılıtiy/ *n.* [*noncount*] See -CEP-.

sus•pect (*v.* sə spekt′; *n.* sus′pekt; *adj.* sus′pekt, sə-spekt′) / *v.* sə'spɛkt; *n.* 'sʌspɛkt; *adj.* 'sʌspɛkt, sə'spɛkt/ *v.* **1.** to believe (something) to be the case; surmise: [~ + *(that) clause*]: *I suspected (that) he might have left already, and I was right.* [~ + *obj*]: *I only suspected it; I wasn't positive.* **2.** [~ + *obj (+ of + obj)*] to believe to be guilty, with little or no proof: *to suspect a person of murder.* **3.** [~ + *obj*] to doubt or mistrust: *I suspect his motives.* **—*n.*** [*count*] **4.** one who is suspected, esp. of a crime. **—*adj.*** **5.** open to or under suspicion; not certain: *He offered some suspect arguments and I knew they were wrong, but I couldn't quite pin down why.* See -SPEC-.

sus•pend (sə spend′) /sə'spɛnd/ *v.* [~ + *obj*] **1.** to hang by attachment to something above, esp. so as to allow free movement; dangle: *Suspend the swing from the tree branch.* **2.** to keep from falling or sinking, as if by hanging: *to suspend particles in a liquid.* **3.** to keep undecided: *I'll suspend judgment until all the facts are in.* **4.** to put off, defer, or bring to a stop: *to suspend a sentence for a misdemeanor.* **5.** to bring to a stop, usually for a time: *He suspended payments on the car until it was fixed.* **6.** to remove (someone) from membership in or prevent (someone) from attending, usually for a limited time, a job, school, club, etc., esp. as a punishment: *suspended from school for drinking on school property.* See -PEND-.

suspend′ed anima′tion, *n.* [*noncount*] a state in which the vital functions of the body are halted temporarily. See -PEND-.

sus•pend•er (sə spen′dər) /sə'spɛndər/ *n.* [*count*] **1.** Usually, **suspenders.** Also called, *esp. Brit.,* **braces.** [*plural*] adjustable straps or bands worn over the shoulders with the ends secured to the waistband of a skirt or a pair of trousers to support it: *a pair of red suspenders.* **2.** *Brit.* a garter. See -PEND-.

sus•pense (sə spens′) /sə'spɛns/ *n.* [*noncount*] a state of mental anxiety and uncertainty, as in awaiting a decision or outcome: *The movie has a lot of chase scenes, tension, and suspense.* —**sus•pense′ful,** *adj.*: *a very suspenseful movie.* See -PEND-.

sus•pen•sion (sə spen′shən) /sə'spɛnʃən/ *n.* **1.** [*noncount*] the act of suspending; the state of being suspended: *the suspension of belief until all the facts are in.* **2.** temporarily keeping someone, or a group or team, out of a job, organization, school, etc.: [*noncount*]: *his suspension from baseball after repeated drug use.* [*count*]: *The usual fines and suspensions won't prevent the fighting in our schools.* **3. a.** [*noncount*] a state in which the particles of a chemical substance are mixed with a fluid but are undissolved. **b.** [*count*] a substance in such a state. **4.** [*count*] something on or by which something else is suspended. **5.** [*count*] something suspended. **6.** [*count*] Also called **suspen′sion sys′tem.** the arrangement of springs, shock absorbers, etc., in a vehicle: *Your car needs a new suspension.* See -PEND-.

suspen′sion bridge′, *n.* [*count*] a bridge having a deck hung from cables anchored at their ends and usually raised on towers. See -PEND-.

sus•pi•cion (sə spish′ən) /sə'spɪʃən/ *n.* **1.** [*noncount*] the act of suspecting: *Suspicion was driving her jealous husband crazy.* **2.** [*count*] an instance of suspecting something or someone: *I have my suspicions about who the spies are.* **3.** [*noncount*] the state of being suspected: *We had you under suspicion for a while.* **4.** [*count*] imagination that something is true, or is likely to be true; a notion: *had a suspicion that the answer to his problem was in the owner's manual.* **5.** [*count*] a slight trace, hint, or suggestion: *a suspicion of a smile.* See -SPEC-.

sus•pi•cious (sə spish′əs) /sə'spɪʃəs/ *adj.* **1.** tending to cause or raise suspicion: *Her suspicious behavior near the submarine made the military police think she might be a spy.* **2.** likely or inclined to suspect, esp. inclined to suspect evil; distrustful: *He was suspicious of strangers.* **3.** expressing or indicating suspicion: *a suspicious glance.* —**sus•pi′cious•ly,** *adv.*

sus•tain (sə stān′) /sə'steyn/ *v.* [~ + *obj*] **1.** to support or bear up from below; bear the weight of: *Can the bridge sustain the weight of all these trucks?* **2.** to undergo or suffer (injury, loss, etc.): *The army sustained heavy losses.* **3.** to keep (a person, the spirits, etc.) from giving way, as when suffering trials, etc.: *The thought of seeing his family again sustained him.* **4.** to keep up or going, as an action or process: *to sustain a conversation.* **5.** to supply with food, drink, and other necessities of life: *The candy bars were just enough to sustain us until the rescuers arrived.* **6.** to uphold or support as valid, just, or correct: *The judge sustained the lawyer's objection.* See -TAIN-.

sus•tained (sə stānd′) /sə'steynd/ *adj.* kept going; continuing; maintained. See -TAIN-.

sus•te•nance (sus′tə nəns) /'sʌstənəns/ *n.* [*noncount*] **1.** the means of sustaining life; nourishment. **2.** the process of sustaining; the state of being sustained. See -TEN-.

su•ture (so͞o′chər) /'suwtʃər/ *n., v.,* **-tured, -tur•ing.** —*n.* [*count*] **1.** a joining of the edges of a wound or the like by stitching; one of the stitches or fastenings used to do this. —*v.* [~ + *obj*] **2.** to unite by or as if by a suture: *to suture the edges of the wound together.*

svelte (svelt, sfelt) /svɛlt, sfɛlt/ *adj.,* **svelt•er, svelt•est.** slender, esp. gracefully slender in figure; lithe.

SW or **S.W.,** an abbreviation of: **1.** southwest. **2.** southwestern.

swab or **swob** (swob) /swɒb/ *n., v.,* **swabbed, swab•bing.** —*n.* [*count*] **1.** a large mop used on ships. **2.** a bit of cotton, sponge, or the like, often fixed to a stick, for applying medicine, etc. —*v.* [~ + *obj*] **3.** to clean with or as if with a swab: *to swab the ship's deck.* **4.** to take up or apply (moisture, etc.) with or as if with a swab on (a wound): *to swab antiseptic on the wound.*

swad•dle (swod′l) /'swɒdl̩/ *v.* [~ + *obj*], **-dled, -dling. 1.** to bind (a newborn infant) with clothes to prevent free movement. **2.** to wrap (anything) round with bandages.

swag•ger (swag′ər) /'swægər/ *v.* [*no obj*] **1.** to walk or move about with a proud, arrogant, strutting manner. —*n.* [*count*] **2.** a swaggering walk or manner; a showy display of too much pride or arrogance.

swain (swān) /sweyn/ *n.* [*count*] **1.** a male admirer or lover. **2.** a country lad.

swal•low[1] (swol′ō) /'swɒlow/ *v.* **1.** to take (food or liquid) down the throat with a muscular action: [~ + *obj*]: *He couldn't swallow the meat.* [*no obj*]: *I tried to swallow, but my mouth was too dry.* **2.** [~ *(+ up)* + *obj*] to take in so as to assimilate, absorb, or cause to disappear: *He'll be swallowed (up) in a crowd if he goes to such a big university.* **3.** [~ + *obj*] to accept without question, suspicion, or opposition: *He swallowed her lies about going out for a drive.* **4.** [~ + *obj*] to keep in or suppress (emotion, pride, etc.): *He swallowed his anger and spoke quietly in reply.* **5.** [~ + *obj*] to take back; retract: *If he makes another statement like that I'll make him swallow his words!* **6.** [~ + *obj*] to pronounce (words) poorly; mutter: *She seems to swallow her words, especially at the ends of sentences.* —*n.* [*count*] **7.** an act or instance of swallowing: *a nervous swallow before answering.* **8.** an amount swallowed at one time: *one more swallow of this medicine.*

swal•low[2] (swol′ō) /'swɒlow/ *n.* [*count*] a small, long-winged, fork-tailed songbird noted for its swift, graceful flight.

swal•low•tail (swol′ō tāl′) /'swɒlow,teyl/ *n.* [*count*] **1.** the tail of a swallow or a deeply forked tail like that of a swallow. **2.** a butterfly having long hind wings.

swam (swam) /swæm/ *v.* pt. of SWIM.

swa•mi (swä′mē) /'swɑmiy/ *n.* [*count*], *pl.* **-mis. 1.** (a title of honor given to) a Hindu religious teacher. **2.** a person resembling a swami, esp. in authority or judgment.

swamp (swomp) /swɒmp/ *n.* [*count*] **1.** an area of wet, spongy land. —*v.* **2.** [~ + *obj*] to flood or drench, esp. with water. **3.** (of a boat) to (cause to) sink or be filled with water: [*no obj*]: *The little boat was in danger of swamping.* [~ + *obj*]: *The next huge wave swamped the boat.* **4.** [~ + *obj*] to overwhelm: *I was swamped with work.* —**swamp′y,** *adj.,* **-i•er, -i•est.**

swan (swon) /swɒn/ *n.* [*count*] a large bird living by water, of the goose family, having a long, slender neck and usually pure-white feathers.

swank (swangk) /swæŋk/ *n., adj.,* **-er, -est** —*n.* [*noncount*] **1.** very fashionable elegance, as in appearance; style. **2.** arrogance or pretentiousness; swagger. —*adj.* **3.** stylish or elegant: *a swank hotel.* **4.** pretentiously stylish.

swank•y (swang′kē) /'swæŋkiy/ *adj.,* **-i•er, -i•est.** elegant or stylish; swank: *a very expensive, swanky hotel.* —**swank•i•ly** (swang′kə lē) /'swæŋkəliy/ *adv.* —**swank′i•ness,** *n.* [*noncount*]

swan′ song′, *n.* [*count*] a final act or farewell appearance: *The outgoing president gave his swan song.*

swap (swop) /swɒp/ *v.,* **swapped, swap•ping,** *n.* —*v.* **1.** to trade or barter; make an exchange: [~ + *obj*]: *They sat on the bench, swapping lies about the good old days.* [~ + *obj* + *for* + *obj*]: *I'll swap my orange for your apple.* [*no obj*]: *You like my cookies and I like yours; let's swap.* —*n.* [*count*] **2.** an exchange: *He got the radio in a swap.*

sward (swôrd) /swɔrd/ *n.* [*count*] the grassy surface of land; turf.

swarm (swôrm) /swɔrm/ *n.* [*count*] **1.** a body of honeybees that leave a hive and fly off together, accompanied by a queen, to start a new colony. **2.** a great number of things or persons moving together: *A swarm of reporters descended on her.* —*v.* **3.** to move about, along, or together in great numbers: [*no obj*]: *The crowd swarmed around the winner.* [~ + *obj*]: *The excited crowd swarmed the winner.* **4. swarm with,** [~ + *obj*] (of a place) to have a great number of; to abound; teem: *a beach swarming with children.* —**Syn.** See CROWD.

swarth•y (swôr′thē, -thē) /ˈswɔrðiy, -θiy/ *adj.,* **-i•er, -i•est.** (of skin color, complexion, etc.) dark or darkish.

swash•buck•ling (swosh′buk′ling, swôsh′-) /ˈswɒʃˌbʌklɪŋ, ˈswɔʃ-/ *adj.* swaggering, dashing, full of adventure: *a swashbuckling pirate.*

swas•ti•ka (swos′ti kə) /ˈswɒstɪkə/ *n.* [*count*], *pl.* **-kas.** **1.** a symbolic figure of ancient origin, consisting of a cross with arms of equal length, each arm then being bent at right angles in a uniformly clockwise or counterclockwise direction. **2.** this figure as the emblem of the Nazi Party and the Third Reich.

swat (swot) /swɒt/ *v.,* **swat•ted, swat•ting,** *n.* —*v.* [~ + *obj*] **1.** to hit sharply; slap; smack: *to swat a fly with a flyswatter.* —*n.* [*count*] **2.** a smart blow; slap; smack. —**swat′ter,** *n.* [*count*]

SWAT or **S.W.A.T.** (*as initials or* swot) /*as initials or* swɒt/ *adj.* [*before a noun*] of or relating to a special section of law enforcement agencies trained to deal with esp. dangerous situations, as when hostages are being held: *a SWAT team.*

swatch (swoch) /swɒtʃ/ *n.* [*count*] a sample of cloth or other material.

swath (swoth, swôth) /swɒθ, swɔθ/ also **swathe,** *n.* [*count*] **1.** the space covered by the cut of a mowing machine or other cutting device. **2.** the piece or strip so cut. **3.** a strip, belt, or line of anything. —***Idiom.*** **4. cut a (wide) swath,** to make a conspicuous or striking impression: *With his money he could afford to cut a (wide) swath through the upper aristocracy.*

swathe (swoth, swāth) /swɒð, sweyð/ *v.,* **swathed, swath•ing,** *n.* —*v.* [~ + *obj*] **1.** to wrap, bind, or swaddle with bands of some material. **2.** to bandage. —*n.* [*count*] **3.** a wrapping or bandage.

sway (swā) /swey/ *v.* **1.** to (cause to) move or swing from side to side: [*no obj*]: *swaying to the music.* [~ + *obj*]: *The wind swayed the trees.* **2.** [~ + *obj*] to influence (the mind, emotions, etc., or a person): *The jurors were swayed by the lawyer's appeal.* —*n.* [*noncount*] **3.** the act of swaying; swaying movement: *the unsteady sway of the ferry.* **4.** dominating influence: *He still holds sway over a large bureaucracy.*

Swa•zi (swä′zē) /ˈswɑziy/ *n., pl.* **-zis, zi.** **1.** [*count*] a person born or living in Swaziland. **2.** [*noncount*] an official language of Swaziland.

swear (swâr) /swɛər/ *v.,* **swore** (swôr, swōr) /swɔr, swowr/ **sworn** (swôrn, swōrn) /swɔrn, swowrn/ **swear•ing.** **1.** [*usually: not: be* + ~*-ing*] to make a solemn statement, promise, or declaration by some sacred being or object, as a deity or the Bible: [*no obj*]: *He swore on the Bible.* [~ + *(that) clause*]: *He swore (that) he would tell the truth.* [~ + *to* + *verb*]: *You swore to tell the truth.* **2.** to use obscene or profane language: [*no obj*]: *He swore viciously when the driver cut him off.* [~ + *at* + *obj*]: *He swore at the driver who cut him off.* [*used with quotations*]: *"That's all I damn well need!" he swore.* **3.** [~ + *obj* + *to* + *obj*] to bind or make (someone) promise by an oath: *They swore her to secrecy.* **4. swear by,** [*usually: not: be* + ~*-ing;* ~ + *by* + *obj*] **a.** to name (a sacred being or object) as one's witness: *I swear by my mother's grave that what I'm telling you is true.* **b.** to have great confidence in; trust in: *Whenever he has a cold he swears by this mixture of tea, lemon juice, and honey.* **5. swear in,** to admit to office or service by administering an oath: [~ + *in* + *obj*]: *The Chief Justice swore in the President.* [~ + *obj* + *in*]: *to swear him in.* **6. swear off,** [~ + *off* + *obj*] to promise (oneself) to give up (something): *He said he had sworn off drugs and alcohol.* **7. swear out,** [~ + *out* + *obj*] to secure (a warrant for arrest) by making an accusation under oath: *to swear out a warrant for his arrest.* —**swear′er,** *n.* [*count*]

swear•word (swâr′wûrd′) /ˈswɛərˌwɜrd/ *n.* [*count*] a word used in swearing or cursing; a profane or obscene word.

sweat (swet) /swɛt/ *v.,* **sweat** or **sweat•ed, sweat•ing,** *n.* —*v.* **1.** [*no obj*] to perspire, esp. freely: *He was sweating and his temperature was very high.* **2.** [*no obj*] to gather moisture from the surrounding air by condensation: *The cold glass was sweating in the hot room.* **3.** [*no obj*] *Informal.* **a.** to work hard. **b.** to be anxious or distressed **4.** [~ + *obj*] to cause (a person, a horse, etc.) to perspire. **5. sweat off,** to get rid of (weight) by or as if by sweating: [~ + *off* + *obj*]: *trying to sweat off a few pounds.* [~ + *obj* + *off*]: *trying to sweat a few pounds off.* **6. sweat out,** *Informal.* to await anxiously the outcome of: [~ + *out* + *obj*]: *The election is over; now we just have to sweat out the results.* [~ + *obj* + *out*]: *to sweat the ordeal out.* —*n.* **7.** [*noncount*] the moisture released from sweat glands; perspiration: *Sweat was pouring down his face.* **8.** [*noncount*] hard work: *Blood, sweat, and tears went into this house.* **9.** [*count; usually singular*] *Informal.* a state of anxiety or impatience: *He was really in a sweat awaiting the results.* **10. sweats,** [*plural*] sweatpants, sweatshirts, sweat suits, or the like.

sweat•band (swet′band′) /ˈswɛtˌbænd/ *n.* [*count*] **1.** a band on the inside lining of a hat or cap to protect it against sweat. **2.** a narrow band of fabric worn around the head or around the wrists to absorb sweat.

sweat•er (swet′ər) /ˈswɛtər/ *n.* [*count*] a knitted piece of clothing, often like a shirt or jacket, in pullover or cardigan style, with or without sleeves. See illustration at CLOTHING.

sweat•pants or **sweat pants** (swet′pants′) /ˈswɛtˌpænts/ *n.* [*plural*] loose-fitting pants of soft, absorbent fabric, such as cotton jersey, commonly worn during athletic activity for warmth or to induce sweating. See illustration at CLOTHING.

sweat•shirt (swet′shûrt′) /ˈswɛtˌʃɜrt/ *n.* [*count*] a loose, long-sleeved, collarless, shirtlike piece of clothing of soft, absorbent fabric, commonly worn during athletic activity for warmth or to induce sweating. See illustration at CLOTHING.

sweat•shop (swet′shop′) /ˈswɛtˌʃɒp/ *n.* [*count*] a shop where workers are paid low wages and work for long hours under poor conditions.

sweat′ sock′, *n.* [*count*] a sock made of thick, absorbent material and worn during sports, etc.

sweat′ suit′, *n.* [*count*] an outfit consisting of sweatpants and a sweatshirt or matching jacket.

sweat•y (swet′ē) /ˈswɛtiy/ *adj.,* **-i•er, -i•est.** **1.** full of sweat; giving off sweat: *his hot, sweaty face.* **2.** causing sweat, as from being hard or difficult: *It was hot, sweaty work.*

Swede (swēd) /swiyd/ *n.* [*count*] a person born or living in Sweden.

Swed•ish (swē′dish) /ˈswiydɪʃ/ *adj.* **1.** of or relating to Sweden. **2.** of or relating to the language spoken by many of the people in Sweden. —*n.* **3.** [*plural; the* + ~*; used with a plural verb*] the people born or living in Sweden. **4.** [*noncount*] the language spoken by many of the people in Sweden.

sweep[1] (swēp) /swiyp/ *v.,* **swept** (swept) /swɛpt/ **sweep•ing,** *n.* —*v.* **1.** to remove or clear (dust, dirt, etc.) with a broom, brush, etc., from (a room, floor, etc.): [~ + *obj*]: *He swept the floor with a broom.* [*no obj*]: *He went on quietly sweeping while the customers argued.* **2.** to (cause to) move or (cause to) be driven by or as if by some steady force, as a wind or wave: [~ + *obj*]: *The storm swept the boat out to sea.* [*no obj*]: *She swept into the room.* **3.** to spread quickly over or through (an area): [~ + *obj*]: *The call for change in politics was sweeping the country.* [*no obj*]: *Those fashions swept through the country.* **4.** [~ + *obj* + *of* + *obj*] to clear (a surface, place, etc.): *to sweep the sea of enemy ships.* **5.** [~ + *obj*] to search (an area or building) thoroughly: *The police swept the building for drug dealers.* **6.** [~ + *obj*] to pass or draw over a surface with a continuous stroke or movement: *The painter swept a brush over his canvas.* **7.** [~ + *obj*] to direct a gaze, the eyes, etc., over (a region, area, etc.): *The lookout's binoculars swept the horizon for enemy activity.* **8.** [*no obj*] to move or extend in a wide curve or circuit: *His glance swept around the room.* **9.** [~ + *obj*] to win all games in a series of contests: *The team swept the last two doubleheaders.* —*n.* [*count*] **10.** the act of sweeping with or as if with a broom: *Give the room a good sweep.* **11.** the steady, driving motion of something: *the sweep of the wind.* **12.** a swinging or curving movement or stroke, as of the arm or an oar. **13.** a continuous extent or stretch: *a long sweep of empty road.* **14.** a winning of all the games, prizes, etc., in a contest by one contestant. **15.** CHIMNEY SWEEP. —***Idiom.*** **16. a clean sweep,** a thorough change, esp. by removing unwanted employees: *The new commissioner promised to reform the department and make a clean sweep of the old bureaucracy.* **17. sweep (someone) off one's feet,** [~ + *obj* + *off* + *one's feet*] to cause (someone) to fall in love or otherwise be overwhelmed: *When they met he just swept her off her feet.* —**sweep′er,** *n.* [*count*]

sweep[2] (swēp) /swiyp/ *n.* SWEEPS (def. 1).

sweep•ing (swē′ping) /ˈswiypɪŋ/ *adj.* **1.** of wide range or scope: *sweeping change.* **2.** [*before a noun*] very general; very or too vague: *sweeping generalizations.* **3.** [*before a noun*] moving or passing over a wide area: *a sweeping glance.* **4.** moving steadily and forcefully on: *sweeping winds.* **5.** [*before a noun*] (of the result of a contest) overwhelming: *a sweeping victory.* **—*n.*** [*count*] **6.** the act of a person or thing that sweeps. **7. sweepings,** [*plural*] matter swept out or up, as dust or refuse. —**sweep′ing•ly,** *adv.*

sweeps (swēps) /swiyps/ *n.* [*count; used with a singular or plural verb*] **1.** a sweepstakes. **2.** a period of time when surveys are taken to determine which radio or television shows are most listened to or watched: *During the sweeps the networks put on shows most likely to attract viewers.*

sweep•stakes (swēp′stāks′) /ˈswiypˌsteyks/ also **sweep′stake′,** *n.* [*count; used with a singular or plural verb*] **1.** a race, contest, or act of gambling in which the prize consists of the money contributed by the participants. **2.** the prize itself.

sweet (swēt) /swiyt/ *adj.,* **-er, -est,** *adv., n.* **—*adj.*** **1.** having the taste or flavor of sugar or the like: *The coffee is too sweet.* **2.** not rancid or stale; fresh: *sweet milk.* **3.** not salty or salted: *sweet butter.* **4.** pleasing to the senses: *sweet music; her sweet, soft voice.* **5.** pleasing or agreeable; delightful as a person or action: *Our neighbors were so sweet, looking after our apartment while we were away.* **—*adv.*** **6.** in a sweet manner; sweetly. **—*n.*** [*count*] **7. sweets,** [*plural*] very sweet foods, as pie, cake, or candy. **8.** *Brit.* **a.** a piece of candy. **b.** a sweet dish or dessert. **9.** a beloved person. **—*Idiom.*** **10. sweet on,** [*be* + ~ + *on*] *Informal.* infatuated with; in love with: *She was sweet on the new boy in school.* —**sweet′ish,** *adj.* —**sweet′ly,** *adv.: She smiled sweetly at him.* —**sweet′ness,** *n.* [*noncount*]

sweet′ corn′, *n.* [*noncount*] **1.** a kind of corn that has grain or kernels that are sweet and suitable for eating. **2.** the young and tender ears of such corn.

sweet•en (swēt′n) /ˈswiytn̩/ *v.* **1.** to (cause to) become sweet: [~ + *obj*]: *Add some brown sugar to sweeten the mix.* [*no obj*]: *As the wine ages it will gradually sweeten.* **2.** [~ + *obj*] to make (the breath, air, etc.) sweet or fresh, as with a commercial product. **3.** [~ + *obj*] to remove sulfur and its compounds from (oil or gas). **4.** [~ + *obj*] *Informal.* to add to the value or attractiveness of (a business deal, proposal, etc.): *The company sweetened its salary offer to her.* —**sweet′en•er,** *n.* [*count*]

sweet•heart (swēt′härt′) /ˈswiytˌhɑrt/ *n.* [*count*] **1.** either of a pair of lovers in relation to the other: *Who is her new sweetheart?* **2.** [*sometimes: Sweetheart*] **a.** (used as a form of address and considered affectionate or familiar): *Sweetheart, could you button this dress for me?* **b.** (used as a form of address and sometimes considered offensive when used to strangers, subordinates, etc.): *"Hey, Sweetheart, what are you doing after work?"* **3.** *Informal.* a generous, friendly person: *You're a real sweetheart for picking that up for me at the store.*

sweet′heart con′tract, *n.* [*count*] a contract achieved through secret agreement between management and labor representatives and having terms that are not favorable for union workers. Also called **sweet′heart agree′ment.**

sweet•meat (swēt′mēt′) /ˈswiytˌmiyt/ *n.* [*count*] **1.** (formerly) a sweetened cake or pastry. **2.** any confection or candy, as a bonbon, sugarplum, or candied fruit.

sweet′ pea′, *n.* [*count*] a climbing plant of the legume family, having sweet-scented flowers.

sweet′ pep′per, *n.* [*count*] **1.** a variety of pepper having a mild-flavored, bell-shaped or somewhat oblong fruit. **2.** the fruit itself, used as a vegetable. Also called **bell pepper.**

sweet′ pota′to, *n.* [*count*] **1.** a Central American trailing vine grown widely for its sweet roots. **2.** the root itself, used as a vegetable.

sweet′-talk′, *v. Informal.* to use sweet or pleasing words to (someone) in order to persuade; flatter: [~ + *obj*]: *At first I was opposed to the deal, but she sweet-talked us right into it.* [*no obj*]: *He can sweet-talk as well as any salesman.*

sweet′ tooth′, *n.* [*count; singular*] a liking or strong desire for sweets.

swell (swel) /swɛl/ *v.,* **swelled, swol•len** (swō′lən) /ˈswowlən/ or **swelled, swell•ing,** *n., adj.* **—*v.*** **1.** to (cause to) enlarge in size or weight: [*no obj;* (~ + *up*)]: *Her foot swelled (up) where the bee had stung her.* [~ + *obj* (+ *up*)]: *Such a sting could swell the foot (up) to twice its size.* [~ (+ *up*) + *obj*]: *to swell (up) the foot.* **2.** [*no obj*] to rise in waves, as the sea. **3.** to bulge out, as a sail: [*no obj;* (~ + *out*)]: *The sails swelled (out) in the wind.* [~ (+ *out*) + *obj*]: *The wind swelled (out) the sails.* **4.** to (cause to) increase in amount, degree, force, etc.: [*no obj*]: *The ranks of the unemployed swelled to new heights last year.* [~ + *obj*]: *This economic policy will swell the ranks of the unemployed.* **5.** [*no obj*] to increase gradually in volume, as sound: *The organ swelled up for the last bars of the hymn.* **6.** [*no obj*] to arise and grow within one, as a feeling or emotion: *Pride swelled within her at the mention of her award.* **7.** [*no obj*] to become puffed up with pride: *She swelled with pride.* **—*n.*** [*count*] **8.** the act of swelling, or the condition of being swollen. **9.** a wave, esp. when long and unbroken, or a series of such waves. **10.** an increase in amount, degree, force, etc. **11.** a gradual increase in loudness of sound. **12.** *Informal.* **a.** a fashionably dressed person; dandy. **b.** a socially important or well-known person. **—*adj.*** *Informal.* **13.** first-rate; excellent; of high quality; fine: *a swell prize.*

swell•head (swel′hed′) /ˈswɛlˌhɛd/ *n.* [*count*] a vain, conceited, or overly proud person. —**swell′head′ed,** *adj.*

swell•ing (swel′ing) /ˈswɛlɪŋ/ *n.* [*count*] **1.** the act of a person or thing that swells. **2.** a swollen part: *The swelling on his head still hasn't gone down.*

swel•ter (swel′tər) /ˈswɛltər/ *v.* [*no obj*] **1.** to suffer from too much heat: *We sweltered throughout the summer.* **—*n.*** [*count*] **2.** a sweltering condition.

swel•ter•ing (swel′tər ing) /ˈswɛltərɪŋ/ *adj.* **1.** suffering from too much heat: *The sweltering students could hardly keep their minds on their lessons.* **2.** showing or having too much heat: *a sweltering classroom.*

swept (swept) /swɛpt/ *v.* pt. and pp. of SWEEP.

swerve (swûrv) /swɜrv/ *v.,* **swerved, swerv•ing,** *n.* **—*v.*** **1.** to turn aside suddenly or sharply in movement or direction: [*no obj*]: *He swerved to avoid hitting the child.* [~ + *obj*]: *She swerved the car to avoid the stalled vehicle ahead of her.* **—*n.*** [*count*] **2.** the act of swerving.

swift (swift) /swɪft/ *adj.,* **-er, -est,** *adv., n.* **—*adj.*** **1.** moving or able to move with great speed: *a swift boat.* **2.** coming, happening, or performed quickly: *a swift decision.* **3.** [*often: be* + ~ + *to* + *verb*] quick to act or respond: *The president was swift to respond to the new crisis.* **4.** *Slang.* smart; clever. **—*adv.*** **5.** in a swift manner. **—*n.*** [*count*] **6.** a long-winged, swallowlike bird. —**swift′ly,** *adv.: She ran swiftly ahead of the others.* —**swift′ness,** *n.* [*noncount*]

swig (swig) /swɪg/ *n., v.,* **swigged, swig•ging.** *Informal.* **—*n.*** [*count*] **1.** an amount of liquid, esp. liquor, taken in one large swallow. **—*v.*** [~ + *obj*] **2.** to drink in a large swallow or greedily.

swill (swil) /swɪl/ *n.* [*noncount*] **1.** partly liquid food for animals, esp. kitchen garbage given to pigs or hogs. **2.** any liquid mess or refuse; slop. **—*v.*** [~ + *obj*] **3.** to drink a great deal of (something), esp. in a greedy manner: *swilling beer.* **4.** *Chiefly Brit.* to wash by rinsing or flooding with water.

swim (swim) /swɪm/ *v.,* **swam, swum, swim•ming,** *n.* **—*v.*** **1.** [*no obj*] to move in water by using the limbs, fins, tail, etc. **2.** [~ + *obj*] to move along in or cross (a body of water) this way. **3.** [~ + *with* + *obj*] to be filled or flooded with a liquid: *eyes swimming with tears.* **4.** [*no obj*] to be dizzy or giddy; seem to whirl: *My head began to swim.* **—*n.*** [*count*] **5.** an act, instance, or period of swimming. **—*Idiom.*** **6. in the swim,** alert to current affairs, social activities, etc. —**swim′mer,** *n.* [*count*]

swim•ming (swim′ing) /ˈswɪmɪŋ/ *n.* [*noncount*] **1.** the act of a person or thing that swims. **2.** a competitive sport based on the ability to swim. **—*adj.*** [*before a noun*] **3.** used in or for swimming: *a swimming pool.*

swim′ming hole′, *n.* [*count*] a place, as in a stream, where there is water deep enough for swimming.

swim•ming•ly (swim′ing lē) /ˈswɪmɪŋliy/ *adv.* excellently; very well: *Things were going swimmingly for a while.*

swim•suit (swim′so͞ot′) /ˈswɪmˌsuwt/ *n.* BATHING SUIT.

swin•dle (swin′dl) /ˈswɪndl/ *v.,* **-dled, -dling,** *n.* **—*v.*** [~ + *obj* (+ *out of* + *obj*)] **1.** to cheat (someone) out of money or other valuable things: *They swindled us (out of thousands of dollars).* **2.** to obtain by cheating or dishonest practices: *He swindled enough money (out of us) to fly to South America.* **—*n.*** [*count*] **3.** the act of swindling; a scheme involving swindling. **4.** anything that involves cheating. —**swin′dler,** *n.* [*count*]

swine (swīn) /swayn/ *n.* [*count*], *pl.* **swine. 1.** a stout mammal having a disklike snout and a thick hide usually sparsely covered with coarse hair. Compare HOG, PIG, WILD

BOAR. **2.** a rough, disgusting, or brutish person; a person evoking a feeling of contempt. —**swin′ish,** *adj.*

swing (swing) /swɪŋ/ *v.,* **swung** (swung) /swʌŋ/ **swing•ing,** *n., adj.* —*v.* **1.** to (cause to) move back and forth, as something hanging or suspended from above, or to (cause to) move round and round or in a curve: [*no obj*]: *The door swung open and in he came.* [~ + *obj*]: *She swung her arms as she walked down the street.* **2.** to move (the hand or something held) with a movement back and forth, forward and backward, or round and round: [~ + *obj*]: *He swung the bat back and forth and waited for the next pitch.* [*no obj;* ~ *(+ at + obj)*]: *He swung (at the next pitch) and missed.* **3.** to (cause to) move in a curve: [~ + *obj*]: *I swung the car into the driveway.* [*no obj*]: *The car swung into the driveway.* **4.** to (cause to) hang or be hung freely, as a hammock: [~ + *obj*]: *They swung the hammock between two trees.* [*no obj*]: *The hammock swung between the two trees.* **5.** to move by holding a support with the hands and drawing up the arms: [*no obj*]: *He swung onto the balcony.* [~ + *obj*]: *He swung himself up onto the roof.* **6.** *Informal.* to (kill or cause to) die by hanging: [*no obj*]: *"I promise you, you'll swing from the highest tree!" the judge snarled at the convicted killer.* [~ + *obj*]: *The crowd wanted to swing him from the highest tree.* **7.** to (cause to) be changed or shifted, as one's interest, etc.: [*no obj*]: *Public opinion swung in his favor close to the election.* [~ + *obj*]: *She hopes to swing public opinion in her favor with a new tax cut.* **8.** [~ + *obj*] *Informal.* to sway, influence, or manage as desired: *to swing a business deal.* **9.** [*no obj*] *Slang.* **a.** to be lively, fashionable, or trendy. **b.** to engage uninhibitedly in sexual activities. **c.** (esp. of married couples) to exchange partners for sexual activities. —*n.* **10.** [*count*] the act or manner of swinging; the amount or extent of such movement; a curving movement or course. **11.** [*count*] a moving of the body with a free, swaying motion. **12.** [*count*] a blow or stroke with the hand or an object grasped in the hands, as in baseball: *a smooth, effortless swing.* **13.** [*count*] a change or shift in attitude, opinion, behavior, etc.: *a swing to his opponent in the last few weeks.* **14.** [*noncount*] active operation; movement forward; progression: *to get into the swing of things.* **15.** [*count*] a seat hung from above by a loop of rope or between ropes or rods, on which a child may sit and swing to and fro for recreation. **16.** [*noncount*] a style of jazz often played by a large dance band. —*adj.* [*before a noun*] **17.** capable of deciding the outcome or result, as of an election: *the swing vote.* —***Idiom.*** **18. in full swing,** operating at normal capacity; in full operation: *The company was back in full swing when sales improved.*

swing•er (swing′ər) /ˈswɪŋər/ *n.* [*count*] **1.** a person or thing that swings. **2.** *Slang.* a lively, fashionable, or trendy person. **3.** *Slang.* one who engages uninhibitedly in sexual activities, esp. one of a married couple who exchanges partners with another married person for sexual activities.

swing′ shift′, *n.* [*count*] **1.** a period of work on a job, usually from midafternoon until midnight. **2.** the group of workers on such a shift.

swipe (swīp) /swayp/ *n., v.,* **swiped, swip•ing.** —*n.* [*count*] **1.** a strong, sweeping blow, as with a golf club: *He took a swipe at the ball and missed.* **2.** a sideswipe. **3.** *Informal.* a critical, unkind, or cutting remark: *During the debate the candidates took several swipes at each other.* —*v.* **4.** [~ + *at* + *obj*] to strike with a sweeping blow: *She swiped at the fly and missed.* **5.** [~ + *obj*] *Informal.* to steal: *He swiped the candy from the counter and ran off.*

swirl (swûrl) /swɜrl/ *v.* **1.** to move around or along with a whirling motion; whirl: [*no obj*]: *The water swirled down the drain.* [~ + *obj*]: *She swirled her hair in her fingers.* **2.** [*no obj*] to be dizzy or giddy, as the head: *Riding the roller coaster made my head swirl.* —*n.* [*count*] **3.** a swirling movement. **4.** a twist, as of hair around the head. **5.** any curving, twisting line, shape, or form. **6.** [*usually singular*] confusion; disorder: *Things were in a swirl at the office.*

swish (swish) /swɪʃ/ *v.* **1.** to move with or make a sharp, whistling, or hissing sound, as a slender rod does when cutting sharply through the air: [~ + *obj*]: *The music conductor swished his baton through the air.* [*no obj*]: *When a cat's tail swishes, it can be a sign of anger.* **2.** [*no obj*] to rustle or make a soft sound or movement. —*n.* [*count*] **3.** a swishing movement or sound. **4.** a stick or rod for flogging, or a stroke with this. **5.** *Slang* (*disparaging and offensive*). a male homosexual whose appearance or mannerisms resemble a woman's. —*adj.* **6.** *Chiefly Brit. Informal.* stylishly elegant; fashionable.

Swiss (swis) /swɪs/ *n., pl.* **Swiss,** *adj.* —*n.* [*count*] **1.** a person born or living in Switzerland. —*adj.* **2.** of or relating to Switzerland.

Swiss′ cheese′, *n.* [*noncount*] a firm, pale yellow cheese having many holes.

switch (swich) /swɪtʃ/ *n.* [*count*] **1.** a slender, easily bent rod or stick, used esp. in whipping or disciplining. **2.** a device for turning on or off or directing an electric current: *Flip the switch and see if the power comes back on.* **3.** a track structure for sending or directing trains from one track to another. **4.** a turning, shifting, or changing: *We had to make a switch in our plans.* —*v.* **5.** to connect, disconnect, redirect, or turn on (or off) (an electric circuit or the device it serves) by operating a switch: [~ + *on/off* + *obj*]: *Switch on the light, please.* [~ + *obj* + *on/off*]: *Switch the light off, please.* **6.** [~ + *obj*] to move or transfer (a train, car, etc.) from one set of tracks to another. **7.** to turn, shift, or change direction: [~ + *obj*]: *to switch the subject.* [*no obj*]: *Let's switch to another subject.* **8.** to change or exchange: [~ + *obj*]: *She switched pocketbooks with her sister.* [*no obj*]: *She switched to another outfit for the dance.* **9.** [*no obj*] to move back and forth briskly, as a cat's tail. —**switch′er,** *n.* [*count*]

switch•blade (swich′blād′) /ˈswɪtʃˌbleyd/ *n.* [*count*] a pocketknife, the blade of which is held by a spring and can be released suddenly, by pressing a button.

switch•board (swich′bôrd′, -bōrd′) /ˈswɪtʃˌbɔrd, -ˌbowrd/ *n.* [*count*] an electronic unit on which are mounted switches and instruments used to connect telephone calls by hand.

switch′-hit′, *v.* [*no obj*], **-hit, -hit•ting.** *Baseball.* to be able to bat from either side of the plate. —**switch′-hit′ter,** *n.* [*count*]

swiv•el (swiv′əl) /ˈswɪvəl/ *n., v.,* **-eled, -el•ing** or (*esp. Brit.*) **-elled, -el•ling.** —*n.* [*count*] **1.** a fastening device consisting of two parts, each of which turns around independently. **2.** a pivoted support that allows something to turn around in a horizontal plane. —*v.* **3.** to (cause to) turn around or pivot on or as if on a swivel: [~ + *obj*]: *He swiveled his chair around.* [*no obj*]: *He swiveled around to see what was behind him.*

swiv′el chair′, *n.* [*count*] a chair whose seat turns around horizontally on a swivel. See illustration at OFFICE.

swiz′zle stick′, *n.* [*count*] a small wand or straw for stirring alcoholic drinks and cocktails in the glass.

swol•len (swō′lən) /ˈswowlən/ *v.* **1.** a pp. of SWELL. —*adj.* **2.** made large by or as if by swelling: *her painful, swollen foot.* **3.** overly proud or conceited: *a swollen-headed boss.*

swoon (swōōn) /swuwn/ *v.* [*no obj*] **1.** to faint; lose consciousness. **2.** to enter a state of hysterical emotion or ecstasy: *The teenagers swooned when the rock star walked onto the stage.* —*n.* [*count*] **3.** a faint or fainting fit; syncope.

swoop (swōōp) /swuwp/ *v.* **1.** [*no obj*] to sweep down through the air, as a bird does upon its prey. **2.** [~ (+ *down*) + *on/upon* + *obj*] to come down upon something in a sudden, swift attack: *The army swooped (down) on the town.* **3.** to take, lift, scoop up, or remove with or as if with one sweeping motion: [~ + *obj* + *up*]: *He swooped her up in his arms.* [~ + *up* + *obj*]: *He swooped up the child in his arms.* —*n.* [*count*] **4.** an act or instance of swooping.

swop (swop) /swɒp/ *v.,* **swopped, swop•ping,** *n.* SWAP.

sword (sôrd, sōrd) /sɔrd, sowrd/ *n.* [*count*] **1.** a weapon, typically having a long, sharp-edged blade attached to a handle or hilt. **2.** [*often: singular*] this weapon as a symbol of military power, punishment, etc.: *The pen is mightier than the sword.* **3.** [*often: singular*] military force or aggression, esp. war: *to perish by the sword.* —***Idiom.*** **4. cross swords,** [*no obj;* (~ + *with* + *obj*)] **a.** to engage in combat; fight. **b.** to disagree violently; argue: *The two were crossing swords at the last meeting. He crossed swords with her yet again.*

sword•fish (sôrd′fish′, sōrd′-) /ˈsɔrdˌfɪʃ, ˈsowrd-/ *n.* [*count*], *pl.* **-fish•es,** (*esp. when thought of as a group*) **-fish.** a large saltwater fish that may be eaten, having its upper jaw in the shape of a bladelike structure.

sword•play (sôrd′plā′, sōrd′-) /ˈsɔrdˌpley, ˈsowrd-/ *n.* [*noncount*] the action or technique of using a sword in fighting; fencing.

swords•man (sôrdz′mən, sōrdz′-) /ˈsɔrdzmən, ˈsowrdz-/ also **sword′man,** *n.* [*count*], *pl.* **-men.** a person who uses or is skilled in the use of a sword.

swore (swôr, swōr) /swɔr, swowr/ *v.* pt. of SWEAR.

sworn (swôrn, swōrn) /swɔrn, swowrn/ *v.* **1.** pp. of SWEAR. **—*adj.*** **2.** [*before a noun*] having been taken under oath: *a sworn statement that she was with him on the night of the murder.* **3.** bound by or as if by an oath or pledge: *She was sworn to secrecy.* **4.** [*before a noun*] complete; unchanging: *sworn enemies.*

swum (swum) /swʌm/ *v.* pp. of SWIM.

swung (swung) /swʌŋ/ *v.* pt. and pp. of SWING.

syc•a•more (sik′ə môr′, -mōr′) /ˈsɪkəˌmɔr, -ˌmowr/ *n.* **1.** [*count*] Also called **buttonwood.** a tree of E North America, having leaves shaped like the palm of a hand. **2.** [*count*] a tree related to this. **3.** [*noncount*] the wood of any of these trees.

syc•o•phant (sik′ə fənt, -fant′) /ˈsɪkəfənt, -ˌfænt/ *n.* [*count*] a self-seeking person who flatters others in power. **—syc′o•phan•cy,** *n.* [*noncount*] **—syc•o•phan•tic** (sik′ə fan′tik) /ˌsɪkəˈfæntɪk/ *adj.*

syl•lab•ic (si lab′ik) /sɪˈlæbɪk/ *adj.* of or relating to a syllable.

syl•lab•i•cate (si lab′i kāt′) /sɪˈlæbɪˌkeyt/ *v.* [~ + *obj*], **-cat•ed, -cat•ing.** to syllabify. **—syl•lab•i•ca•tion** (si-lab′i kā′shən) /sɪˌlæbɪˈkeyʃən/ *n.* [*noncount*]

syl•lab•i•fy (si lab′ə fī′) /sɪˈlæbəˌfay/ *v.* [~ + *obj*], **-fied, -fy•ing.** to form or divide into syllables. **—syl•lab•i•fi•ca•tion** (si lab′ə fi kā′shən) /sɪˌlæbəfɪˈkeyʃən/ *n.* [*noncount*]

syl•la•ble (sil′ə bəl) /ˈsɪləbəl/ *n.* [*count*] **1.** an uninterrupted sound in speech having a vowel sound, or a sound nearly vowellike, sometimes together with a nonvowel sound: *"Dog," "eye," and "sixths" are English words of one syllable; "doghouse" has two syllables.* **2.** the slightest portion or amount of speech or writing; the least mention: *Don't speak another syllable; you've already said too much.*

syl•la•bus (sil′ə bəs) /ˈsɪləbəs/ *n.* [*count*], *pl.* **-bus•es, -bi** (-bī′) /-ˌbay/. an outline of the main points of a speech, the contents of a course or class at school, etc.

syl•lo•gism (sil′ə jiz′əm) /ˈsɪləˌdʒɪzəm/ *n.* [*count*] a logical argument of a form containing three statements (two *premises* and a conclusion derived from them) in the sequence: "All dogs are mammals; all terriers are dogs; therefore, all terriers are mammals." **—syl′lo•gis′tic,** *adj.* See -LOG-.

sylph (silf) /sɪlf/ *n.* [*count*] a slender, graceful woman or girl. **—sylph′ic,** *adj.*

syl•van or **sil•van** (sil′vən) /ˈsɪlvən/ *adj.* **1.** of, relating to, or living in the woods. **2.** made up of, or full of, woods or trees; wooded; woody.

sym-, *prefix. sym-* is another form of the prefix SYN-; it is attached to roots beginning with *b, p, m: symbol; symphony; symmetry.*

sym•bi•o•sis (sim′bē ō′sis, -bī-) /ˌsɪmbiyˈowsɪs, -bay-/ *n., pl.* **-ses** (-sēz) /-siyz/. **1.** [*noncount*] the living together of two very different or dissimilar living things, as when one living thing is a parasite or lives off another. **2.** [*count*] any relationship that involves dependence between two persons, groups, etc.: *The press and the president have an odd symbiosis: Each may despise the other and yet each depends on the other.* **—sym•bi•ot•ic** (sim′bē ot′ik) /ˌsɪmbiyˈɒtɪk/ *adj.*

sym•bol (sim′bəl) /ˈsɪmbəl/ *n.* [*count*] **1.** something used to stand for something else, esp. a material object representing something that cannot be touched: *The ring was a symbol of his love.* **2.** a letter, figure, or other conventional mark naming or referring to an object, quantity, operation, function, etc., as in mathematics: *In mathematics,* x *is often the symbol for an unknown amount.*

sym•bol•ic (sim bol′ik) /sɪmˈbɒlɪk/ *adj.* of or relating to a symbol; used as a symbol: *Breaking the glass at a Jewish wedding is symbolic of the incompleteness of all joy.* **—sym•bol′i•cal•ly,** *adv.*

sym•bol•ism (sim′bə liz′əm) /ˈsɪmbəˌlɪzəm/ *n.* [*noncount*] the practice of representing things by symbols, or of giving ordinary things a symbolic meaning or character: *the use of symbolism in poetry and art.*

sym•bol•ize (sim′bə līz′) /ˈsɪmbəˌlayz/ *v.* [~ + *obj*], **-ized, -iz•ing.** to be a symbol of: *The fox often symbolizes slyness and cunning.* **—sym•bol•i•za•tion,** (sim′bə-lə zā′shən) /ˌsɪmbələˈzeyʃən/ *n.* [*noncount*]

sym•met•ri•cal (si me′tri kəl) /sɪˈmɛtrɪkəl/ also **sym•met′ric,** *adj.* characterized by or showing symmetry. **—sym•met′ri•cal•ly,** *adv.* See -METER-.

sym•me•try (sim′i trē) /ˈsɪmɪtriy/ *n.* [*noncount*] **1.** the regular form or arrangement in size or shape of two parts or halves on opposite sides of each other, such that there is some correspondence between them: *the symmetry of the human body; the symmetry of a snowflake.* **2.** beauty based on or characterized by such regular form. See -METER-.

sym•pa•thet•ic (sim′pə thet′ik) /ˌsɪmpəˈθɛtɪk/ *adj.* **1.** having, showing, being based on, or feeling sympathy: *He was a sympathetic listener, willing to help whenever someone had a problem.* **2.** in harmony or agreeing with one's tastes, mood, or nature; congenial: *a sympathetic companion.* **3.** [*be* + ~(+ *to/toward*)] looking upon with favor: *She is sympathetic toward the project.* **—sym′pa•thet′i•cal•ly,** *adv.* See -PATH-.

sym•pa•thize (sim′pə thīz′) /ˈsɪmpəˌθayz/ *v.* [*no obj;* (~ + *with* + *obj*)], **-thized, -thiz•ing.** **1.** to feel or show sympathy: *Believe me, I can sympathize with her situation.* **2.** to express compassion for someone in order to comfort: *He tried to sympathize with her over the loss of her father.* **3.** to have the same or similar feeling as (a person, group, etc.): *They sympathize with the mayor in his frustration over working with the city council.* **—sym′pa•thiz′er,** *n.* [*count*] See -PATH-.

sym•pa•thy (sim′pə thē) /ˈsɪmpəθiy/ *n., pl.* **-thies,** *adj.* **—*n.*** **1.** [*noncount*] harmony of or agreement in feeling, as between two persons or on the part of one person with respect to another: *There was instant sympathy between the two leaders as they met at the summit.* **2.** [*noncount*] the ability to share the feelings of another, esp. in times of sorrow or trouble; compassion; commiseration: *Thank you for your kind expression of sympathy.* **3. sympathies,** [*plural*] feelings or impulses of compassion or support: *She's playing on his sympathies, claiming to be the one who is suffering, just as he once had to suffer.* **4.** [*noncount*] favor or approval; agreement: *He viewed the plan with sympathy.* **—*adj.*** [*before a noun*] **5.** acting out of or expressing sympathy: *a sympathy card.* See -PATH-.

sym•pho•ny (sim′fə nē) /ˈsɪmfəniy/ *n.* [*count*], *pl.* **-nies.** **1.** a long musical composition for a large orchestra, usually having four parts or movements. **2.** anything having a harmonious or pleasing combination of elements or parts: *a symphony of color.* **—sym•phon•ic** (sim fon′ik) /sɪmˈfɒnɪk/ *adj.* See -PHON-.

sym•po•si•um (sim pō′zē əm) /sɪmˈpowziyəm/ *n.* [*count*], *pl.* **-si•ums, -si•a** (-zē ə) /-ziyə/. a meeting convened for the discussion of some subject, esp. a meeting at which several speakers discuss a topic before an audience. See SYM-.

symp•tom (simp′təm) /ˈsɪmptəm/ *n.* [*count*] **1.** a physical condition that arises from and accompanies a particular disorder and serves as an indication of it: *The symptoms of this flu are aching joints, high fever, and stomach pains.* **2.** any action, condition, or circumstance that arises from or accompanies something else and serves as evidence of it: *the symptoms of economic inflation.* **—symp•to•mat• ic,** (simp′tə mat′ik) /ˌsɪmptəˈmætɪk/ *adj.* See SYM-.

syn-, *prefix. syn-* comes from Greek, where it has the meaning "with; together." This meaning is found in such words as: IDIOSYNCRASY, PHOTOSYNTHESIS, SYNAGOGUE, SYNCHRONIZE, SYNCHRONOUS, SYNONYM, SYNTHESIS. See SYM-.

syn., an abbreviation of: synonym.

syn•a•gogue or **syn•a•gog** (sin′ə gog′, -gôg′) /ˈsɪnəˌgɒg, -ˌgɔg/ *n.* [*count*] **1.** a Jewish house of worship, often having facilities for religious instruction or serving as a community center. **2.** a congregation of Jews for the purpose of religious worship. **—syn•a•gog•al** (sin′ə gog′əl, -gô′gəl) /ˌsɪnəˌgɒgəl, -ˌgɔgəl/ *adj.*

syn•apse (sin′aps, si naps′) /ˈsɪnæps, sɪˈnæps/ *n.* [*count*] **1.** a region where nerve impulses are transmitted across a small gap from the end of one nerve cell to another nerve cell, or to a muscle. **2.** Also called **synap′tic gap′.** the gap itself. **—syn•ap•tic** (si nap′tik) /sɪˈnæptɪk/ *adj.*

sync or **synch** (singk) /sɪŋk/ *n., v.,* **synced** or **synched** (singkt) /sɪŋkt/ **sync•ing** or **synch•ing** (sing′king) /ˈsɪŋkɪŋ/. **—*n.*** [*noncount*] **1.** synchronization: *The images and sound were out of sync.* **2.** agreement or harmony; harmonious relationship: *The president has to stay in sync with the times.* **—*v.*** [~ + *obj*] **3.** to synchronize. See SYN-.

syn•chro•nize (sing′krə nīz′) /ˈsɪŋkrəˌnayz/ *v.* [~ + *obj*], **-nized, -niz•ing.** **1.** to cause to show the agreed upon time, as one clock or watch with another: *Let's synchronize our watches and meet in an hour.* **2.** to cause to go on, move, operate, work, etc., at the same rate or speed or exactly together: *The skating couple had to synchronize their movements perfectly.* **3.** to match the sound and action in (a filmed or taped scene). **—syn•chro•ni•za•tion** (sing′krə nə zā′shən) /ˌsɪŋkrənəˈzeyʃən/ *n.* [*noncount*]

syn•chro•nous (sing′krə nəs) /ˈsɪŋkrənəs/ *adj.* **1.** going on at the same rate and exactly together; recurring together. **2.** GEOSTATIONARY: *a synchronous orbit.*

syn•co•pate (sing′kə pāt′) /ˈsɪŋkə,peyt/ *v.* [~ + *obj*], **-pat•ed, -pat•ing.** to subject (musical rhythm) to syncopation.

syn•co•pa•tion (sing′kə pā′shən) /,sɪŋkəˈpeyʃən/ *n.* [*noncount*] a shifting of a normal musical accent, usually by stressing the normally unaccented beats.

syn•co•pe (sing′kə pē′) /ˈsɪŋkə,piy/ *n.* [*noncount*] **1.** the shortening of a word by omitting one or more sounds from the middle, as in the reduction of *never* to *ne'er.* **2.** brief loss of consciousness caused by a lack of enough oxygen-filled blood flowing to the brain.

syn•di•cate (*n.* sin′di kit; *v.* -kāt′) / *n.* ˈsɪndɪkɪt; *v.* -,keyt/ *n., v.,* **-cat•ed, -cat•ing.** —*n.* [*count*] **1.** a group of individuals or organizations that combine or cooperate in order to engage in business transactions or negotiations or some other undertaking: *A syndicate is buying up all the stock of that business firm.* **2.** a group or association of gangsters controlling organized crime or one type of crime. **3. a.** an agency that buys articles, stories, photographs, etc., and distributes them for publication in a number of newspapers or periodicals. **b.** a chain of newspapers. —*v.* **4.** to combine or form (companies) into a syndicate: [~ + *obj*]: *to syndicate companies.* [*no obj*]: *agreeing to syndicate as a way to save money.* **5.** [~ + *obj*] to publish simultaneously in a number of newspapers or periodicals: *Her column is syndicated in the Wall Street Journal and other important daily newspapers.* —**syn•di•ca•tion** (sin′di kā′shən) /,sɪndɪˈkeyʃən/ *n.* [*noncount*]

syn•drome (sin′drōm, -drəm) /ˈsɪndrowm, -drəm/ *n.* [*count*] **1.** a group of symptoms that together are signs of a certain specific disorder or disease: *a baby suffering from Down's syndrome.* **2.** a predictable, characteristic pattern of behavior that tends to occur under certain circumstances: *The empty nest syndrome affects parents when their children grow up and leave home.* See SYN-, -DROM-.

syn•fu•el (sin′fyōō′əl) /ˈsɪn,fyuwəl/ *n.* SYNTHETIC FUEL.

syn•od (sin′əd) /ˈsɪnəd/ *n.* [*count*] an assembly of church delegates that discusses and decides upon church affairs.

syn•o•nym (sin′ə nim) /ˈsɪnənɪm/ *n.* [*count*] a word having the same or nearly the same meaning as another in the language, as *joyful* in relation to *elated* and *glad.* See -ONYM-.

syn•on•y•mous (si non′ə məs) /sɪˈnɒnəməs/ *adj.* of or relating to synonyms. See SYN-, -ONYM-.

syn•op•sis (si nop′sis) /sɪˈnɒpsɪs/ *n.* [*count*], *pl.* **-ses** (-sēz) /-siyz/. a brief statement giving a general view of some longer subject, or a summary of the plot of a novel, play, etc.: *a synopsis of the plot of a movie.* See SYN-, -OPTI-.

syn•tax (sin′taks) /ˈsɪntæks/ *n.* [*noncount*] **1.** the study of the patterns of formation of sentences and phrases from words in a language and of the rules for the formation of grammatical sentences. **2.** the patterns or rules so studied: *English syntax.* —**syn•tac•tic** (sin tak′tik) /sɪnˈtæktɪk/ **syn•tac′ti•cal,** *adj.*

syn•the•sis (sin′thə sis) /ˈsɪnθəsɪs/ *n., pl.* **-ses** (-sēz′) /-,siyz/. **1.** [*noncount*] the combining of the basic elements of separate materials, things, ideas, or other components into a single or unified thing (opposed to *analysis*). **2.** [*count*] a complex formed into a whole by this combining: *His theory was a synthesis of different ideas.* See -THES-.

syn•the•size (sin′thə sīz′) /ˈsɪnθə,sayz/ *v.* [~ + *obj*], **-sized, -siz•ing. 1.** to make or form (something) into a synthesis: *Doctors and scientists worked to synthesize a drug similar to the one produced naturally by certain South American plants.* **2.** to make (sounds) by a special machine or synthesizer. See SYN-, -THES-.

syn•the•siz•er (sin′thə sī′zər) /ˈsɪnθə,sayzər/ *n.* [*count*] **1.** a person or thing that synthesizes. **2.** an electronic, usually computerized device for creating or modifying the sounds of musical instruments. See SYN-, -THES-.

syn•thet•ic (sin thet′ik) /sɪnˈθɛtɪk/ *adj.* **1.** of or relating to synthesis (opposed to *analytic*). **2.** of or relating to compounds, materials, etc., formed through a chemical process by human agency, as opposed to those of natural origin: *synthetic drugs.* **3.** not real or genuine; artificial; false or pretended: *a synthetic chuckle.* —*n.* [*count*] **4.** something made by a synthetic, or chemical, process. —**syn•thet′i•cal•ly,** *adv.* See -THES-.

synthet′ic fu′el, *n.* liquid or gas fuel manufactured from coal or extracted from shale or tar sands: [*noncount*]: *research on synthetic fuel.* [*count*]: *tax incentives to develop different synthetic fuels.*

syph•i•lis (sif′ə lis) /ˈsɪfəlɪs/ *n.* [*noncount*] a venereal disease affecting almost any body organ, esp. the genitals, skin, brain, and nervous tissue. —**syph•i•lit•ic** (sif′ə-lit′ik) /,sɪfəˈlɪtɪk/ *adj.*

Syr•i•an (sēr′ē ən) /ˈsɪəriyən/ *adj.* **1.** of or relating to Syria. —*n.* [*count*] **2.** a person born or living in Syria.

sy•ringe (sə rinj′, sir′inj) /səˈrɪndʒ, ˈsɪrɪndʒ/ *n., v.,* **-ringed, -ring•ing.** —*n.* [*count*] **1.** a small tube with a narrow opening and a rubber bulb or other device for drawing in or squirting out fluid, esp. through a needle: *the importance of clean syringes.* **2.** any similar device for pumping and spraying liquids through a small opening. —*v.* [~ + *obj*] **3.** to cleanse, wash, inject, etc., by means of a syringe.

syr•up (sir′əp) /ˈsɪrəp/ *n.* [*noncount*] a thick, sweet liquid prepared for table use from molasses, glucose, etc.: *She poured some syrup on her pancakes.*

syr•up•y (sir′əp ē) /ˈsɪrəpiy/ *adj.* **1.** of or resembling syrup: *syrupy coffee.* **2.** overly sweet or sentimental: *a syrupy smile; a syrupy love story.*

sys•tem (sis′təm) /ˈsɪstəm/ *n.* **1.** [*count*] a collection or combination of parts forming a complex or single whole: *an improved transportation system.* **2.** [*count*] an organized body of methods or a scheme or plan of procedure: *a system of government.* **3.** [*count*] an orderly, comprehensive set of (often explanatory) facts, principles, and ideas in a given field: *an economic system.* **4.** [*count*] any regular or special method or orderly plan of proceeding, working etc.: *What's your system for winning at poker?* **5.** [*count*] **a.** a combination of organs or related tissues in the body concerned with the same function: *the digestive system.* **b.** the entire human or animal body considered as a functioning unit: *That ingredient is toxic to the system.* **6.** [*count*] one's psychological makeup, esp. when referring to desires or preoccupations: *Now that you've gotten that out of your system, can we please continue without arguing?* **7.** [*count; usually singular; often: the + ~; sometimes: System*] the major authority in a society, business, etc., or in society in general: *trying to beat the system (= trying to overcome conventional rules or procedures, a bureaucracy, etc., to achieve some goal or secure some advantages).*

sys•tem•at•ic (sis′tə mat′ik) /,sɪstəˈmætɪk/ also **sys′-tem•at′i•cal,** *adj.* **1.** having, showing, or involving a system: *a systematic campaign to change the law.* **2.** using a system or method; methodical: *a systematic person.* —**sys′tem•at′i•cal•ly,** *adv.*: *systematically went through the pile of mail on her desk.*

sys•tem•a•tize (sis′tə mə tīz′) /ˈsɪstəmə,tayz/ *v.* [~ + *obj*], **-tized, -tiz•ing.** to arrange in a system; reduce to a system; make systematic: *trying to systematize all the books.*

sys•tem•ic (si stem′ik) /sɪˈstɛmɪk/ *adj.* **1.** of or relating to a system. **2.** relating to, affecting, or circulating through the entire body: *systemic disease.* —**sys•tem′i•cal•ly,** *adv.*

sys′tems anal′ysis, *n.* [*noncount*] the careful or methodical study of the data-processing needs of a business or project. —**sys′tems an′alyst,** *n.* [*count*]

T

T, t (tē) /tiy/ *n. [count]*, pl. **Ts** or **T's, ts** or **t's. 1.** the 20th letter of the English alphabet, a consonant. **—*Idiom.* 2. to a T** or **tee,** exactly; perfectly: *That description of the thug fits him to a T.*

't, a shortened form of *it,* before or after a verb, as in *'twas, 'tis.*

T., an abbreviation of: **1.** tablespoon. **2.** Tuesday.

t., an abbreviation of: **1.** teaspoon; teaspoonful. **2.** temperature. **3.** time. **4.** ton. **5.** transitive.

tab (tab) /tæb/ *n., v.,* **tabbed, tab•bing.** *—n. [count]* **1.** a small flap, strap, or loop, as on a piece of clothing, used for pulling, hanging, or decoration: *tabs on the jacket collar.* **2.** a small projection from a card or folder, used as an aid in filing: *The tab on the file folder was labeled "Top Secret."* **3.** *Informal.* a bill; check: *She promised to pick up (= pay) the tab for dinner.* **4. a.** a typewriter stop or computer command that moves the carriage, cursor, or printing element a predetermined number of spaces. **b.** the key that activates such a stop or command. *—v.* **5.** [~ + *obj*] to furnish or ornament with tabs. **6.** [~ + *obj* + *obj*] to give a name to; to designate (someone) as something: *They tabbed him "the coward of the company."* **7.** [*no obj*] to operate the tab function on a typewriter or computer: *Tab to the right a few times.* **—*Idiom.* 8. keep tab(s) on,** [~ + *obj*] to keep a watch over: *Keep tabs on what he spends for equipment.*

tab•by (tab′ē) /'tæbiy/ *n. [count], pl.* **-bies. 1.** a cat with a striped coat. **2.** a domestic cat, esp. a female one.

tab•er•nac•le (tab′ər nak′əl) /'tæbər,nækəl/ *n. [count]* **1.** a house of worship, esp. for a large congregation. **2.** [*often: Tabernacle*] the portable tentlike structure used as a place of worship by the ancient Israelites. **3.** an ornamental box for keeping the Eucharist.

ta•ble (tā′bəl) /'teybəl/ *n., v.,* **-bled, -bling,** *adj. —n. [count]* **1.** a piece of furniture consisting of a flat top supported on one or more legs: *a table and four chairs for the dining room.* See illustration at APARTMENT. **2.** such a piece of furniture used for serving food to those seated at it: *a table for two at the Café Boeuf.* **3.** a group of people at a table, as for a meal or a game: *had the whole table laughing at his jokes.* **4.** a short, brief list or guide: *a table of contents.* **5.** an arrangement of words, numbers, or signs displaying a set of facts in a compact form: *the periodic table (of the chemical elements). —v.* [~ + *obj*] **6.** to lay aside (a bill, etc.) for future discussion: *The committee couldn't reach agreement and decided to table the bill. —adj.* **7.** of, relating to, or suitable for a table: *a table lamp.* **—*Idiom.* 8. on the table,** (of a point or issue to be discussed) open for discussion or negotiation: *The union refused to put the issue of job layoffs on the table; to them it was not negotiable.* **9. turn the tables,** [*no obj;* (~ + *on* + *obj*)] to reverse an unfavorable situation, esp. by gaining the advantage over an opponent: *They turned the tables on the enemy by counterattacking at dawn.* **10. under the table,** secretly, and often dishonestly; covertly: *He slipped the customs officials some money under the table.*

tab•leau (ta blō′, tab′lō) /tæ'blow, 'tæblow/ *n. [count], pl.* **tab•leaux** (ta blōz′, tab′lōz) /tæ'blowz, 'tæblowz/ **tab•leaus.** a representation of a scene, etc., by people in costume.

ta•ble•cloth (tā′bəl klôth′, -kloth′) /'teybəl,klɔθ, -,klɒθ/ *n. [count]* a cloth for covering the top of a table, esp. during a meal. See illustration at RESTAURANT.

ta•ble d'hôte (tä′bəl dōt′) /'tɑ'bəl dowt/ *n. [count], pl.* **ta•bles d'hôte** (tä′bəlz) /'tɑbəlz/. a meal consisting of courses decided on beforehand and served at a fixed time and price to the guests at a hotel or restaurant.

ta′ble-hop′, *v. [no obj],* **-hopped, -hop•ping.** to move about in a restaurant, etc., chatting with people at the tables. **—ta′ble-hop′per,** *n. [count]*

ta•ble•land (tā′bəl land′) /'teybəl,lænd/ *n.* PLATEAU (def. 1).

ta•ble•spoon (tā′bəl spo͞on′) /'teybəl,spuwn/ *n. [count]* **1.** a large spoon used in serving food. **2.** a cooking measure equal to 1/2 fluid ounce (14.8 ml). **—ta′ble•spoon•ful′,** *n. [count], pl.* **-fuls.**

tab•let (tab′lit) /'tæblɪt/ *n. [count]* **1.** a small, flat piece of a solid, as of a drug: *two tablets of aspirin.* **2.** a number of sheets of writing paper, etc., fastened together at the edge; pad. **3.** a flat slab or surface, esp. one with an inscription on it; a plaque: *clay tablets with hieroglyphics.*

ta′ble ten′nis, *n. [noncount]* a game resembling tennis, played on a table with small paddles and a hollow plastic ball.

ta•ble•ware (tā′bəl wâr′) /'teybəl,wɛər/ *n. [noncount]* the dishes, spoons, knives, forks, etc., used at the table.

tab•loid (tab′loid) /'tæblɔyd/ *n. [count]* **1.** a newspaper about half the size of an ordinary newspaper, usually with many pictures and often featuring sensational stories. *—adj. [before a noun]* **2.** sensational: *tabloid journalism.*

ta•boo (tə bo͞o′, ta-) /tə'buw, tæ-/ *adj., n., pl.* **-boos.** *—adj.* **1.** forbidden by society because improper or unacceptable: *taboo words.* **2.** set apart as sacred; forbidden for general use: *The temple was taboo for anyone not initiated. —n. [count]* **3.** the action or custom of forbidding something improper: *It was once a taboo to discuss pregnancy on television.* **4.** the system or practice of setting things apart as sacred or forbidden for general use.

tab•u•lar (tab′yə lər) /'tæbyələr/ *adj. [before a noun]* of or arranged in a table, as in columns and rows: *The appendix contains this information in tabular form.*

tab•u•late (tab′yə lāt′) /'tæbyə,leyt/ *v.* [~ + *obj*], **-lat•ed, -lat•ing.** to arrange (numbers, facts, etc.) in tabular form. **—tab•u•la•tion** (tab′yə lā′shən) /,tæbyə'leyʃən/ *n. [noncount]* **—tab′u•la′tor,** *n. [count]*

ta•chom•e•ter (ta kom′i tər, tə-) /tæ'kɒmɪtər, tə-/ *n. [count]* an instrument for indicating speed of rotation: *The tachometer showed 2000 revolutions per second.*

tac•it (tas′it) /'tæsɪt/ *adj.* **1.** understood without being expressed; implied: *He gave his tacit approval.* **2.** silent; saying nothing: *a tacit partner.* **—tac′it•ly,** *adv.* **—tac′it•ness,** *n. [noncount]*

tac•i•turn (tas′i tûrn′) /'tæsɪ,tɜrn/ *adj.* **1.** usually keeping silent; not saying much: *a taciturn gentleman.* **2.** stern and silent in expression and manner: *The men were taciturn, thinking about the mission ahead.* **—tac•i•tur•ni•ty** (tas′i tûr′ni tē) /,tæsɪ'tɜrnɪtiy/ *n. [noncount]* **—tac′i•turn′ly,** *adv.*

tack (tak) /tæk/ *n.* **1.** *[count]* a short, sharp-pointed nail with a broad, flat head: *Hammer a few tacks into the rug.* **2.** a course of action, esp. one differing from another course: *[count]*: *He took the wrong tack. [noncount]*: *to change tack and try something else.* **3.** *[count]* the direction taken by a sailing vessel when sailing at an angle against the wind. **4.** *[count]* a long stitch to fasten seams before sewing. *—v.* **5.** [~ + *obj*] to fasten with tacks: *tacked a notice onto the door.* **6.** [~ + *obj*] to secure by temporary fastening, as before sewing. **7.** to attach as something extra; append: [~ + *on* + *obj*]: *He tacked on a conclusion to his paper.* [~ + *obj* + *on*]: *to tack it on at the end.* **8.** to change the course of a sailing vessel to a different direction: [*no obj*]: *to tack against the wind.* [~ + *obj*]: *to tack the sailboat against the wind.* **—tack′er,** *n. [count]*

tack•le (tak′əl; *for 2, 3* tā′kəl) /'tækəl; *for 2, 3* 'teykəl/ *n., v.,* **-led, -ling.** *—n.* **1.** *[noncount]* equipment for fishing: *fishing tackle.* **2.** any system for lifting or lowering objects that uses pulleys, ropes, and blocks: *[count]*: *a heavy-duty tackle for lowering cargo. [noncount]*: *moving tackle into position to hoist the gear aboard.* **3.** *[noncount]* the gear and ropes or rigging of a ship. **4.** *[count]* an act of tackling, as in football. **5.** either of the linemen in football: *[count]*: *One of the tackles went to his right and blocked for the running back. [noncount]*: *He played tackle for Illinois. —v.* **6.** [~ + *obj*] to work with or begin work on (something), so as to handle or solve it: *to tackle a problem.* **7.** to seize, stop, or throw down (a ballcarrier) in football: [~ + *obj*]: *The quarterback was tackled.* [*no obj*]: *Our team has to tackle better.* **8.** [~ + *obj*] to seize (someone) suddenly, esp. to stop him or her: *tackled the intruder.* **—tack′ler,** *n. [count]*

tack•y[1] (tak′ē) /'tækiy/ *adj.,* **-i•er, -i•est.** sticky to the touch; adhesive: *a tacky surface.* **—tack′i•ness,** *n. [noncount]*

tack•y[2] (tak′ē) /'tækiy/ *adj.,* **-i•er, -i•est. 1.** not tasteful or fashionable; dowdy: *a tacky outfit.* **2.** in poor taste; vulgar; improper: *tacky jokes.* **3.** of poor quality; shoddy: *a tacky car.* **4.** shabby; seedy: *a tacky old motel.* **—tack′i•ness,** *n. [noncount]*

ta•co (tä′kō) /'tɑkow/ *n. [count], pl.* **-cos.** a fried tortilla folded over and filled, with chopped meat, tomatoes, cheese, lettuce, and hot sauce.

tact (takt) /tækt/ *n. [noncount]* a sense of what to say or do so as to avoid giving offense: *Sometimes she has no tact.* **—tact′ful,** *adj.* **—tact′ful•ly,** *adv.* **—tact′less,** *adj.*: *a few tactless remarks.* **—tact′less•ly,** *adv.*

-tact-, *root.* *-tact-* comes from Latin, where it has the meaning "touch." This meaning is found in such words as: CONTACT, INTACT, TACT, TACTILE.

tac•tic (tak′tik) /'tæktɪk/ *n.* [*count*] a course of action to achieve one's goal: *a smart tactic to get the job.*

tac•tics (tak′tiks) /'tæktɪks/ *n.* **1.** [*noncount; used with a singular verb*] the science of arranging and maneuvering military or naval forces: *Tactics has always been their strong point in making war.* **2.** [*plural; used with a plural verb*] the maneuvers themselves: *slash-and-burn tactics.* **3.** [*plural; used with a plural verb*] maneuvers for gaining advantage: *Her tactics were to divide his friends and therefore strengthen her own position.* —**tac′ti•cal,** *adj.* —**tac′ti•cal•ly,** *adv.* —**tac•ti•cian** (tak tish′ən) /tæk-'tɪʃən/ *n.* [*count*]

tac•tile (tak′til, -tīl) /'tæktɪl, -tayl/ *adj.* **1.** of or relating to the sense of touch. **2.** felt by the touch; tangible. See -TACT-.

tad (tad) /tæd/ *n.* [*count*] *Informal.* **1.** a small child, esp. a boy. **2.** [*usually singular; a + ~*] a small amount or degree; bit: *Move a tad to the right.*

tad•pole (tad′pōl) /'tædpowl/ *n.* [*count*] the larva of frogs and toads, living in water, having internal gills and a tail.

taf•fe•ta (taf′i tə) /'tæfɪtə/ *n.* [*noncount*] **1.** a smooth, crisp fabric of silk or other fibers, for making women's clothes. —*adj.* [*before a noun*] **2.** of or resembling taffeta.

taf•fy (taf′ē) /'tæfiy/ *n., pl.* **-fies.** a chewy candy made of sugar or molasses boiled down: [*noncount*]: *pieces of taffy sticking to her teeth.* [*count*]: *some taffies for a snack.*

tag[1] (tag) /tæg/ *n., v.,* **tagged, tag•ging.** —*n.* [*count*] **1.** a piece of paper, etc., attached to something as a marker: *a price tag.* **2.** a small loosely attached part. **3.** a tip at the end of a shoelace or cord. **4.** a symbol indicating the beginning or end of a unit of information in an electronic document. **5.** a descriptive word or phrase applied to a person, group, etc., as a label or identifier. —*v.* **6.** [~ + *obj*] to provide with a tag; attach a tag to: *tagged the garments with the wrong prices.* **7.** [~ + *obj*] to append as an addition or afterthought. **8.** [~ + *obj* + *obj*] to give a name to; label: *tagged the boss "No-Neck."* **9.** [~ + *obj*] to give a traffic ticket to: *tagged for speeding.* **10.** [*no obj*] to follow closely: *The child always tagged along behind his big brother.* —**tag′ger,** *n.* [*count*]

tag[2] (tag) /tæg/ *n., v.,* **tagged, tag•ging.** —*n.* **1.** [*noncount*] a children's game in which one player chases the others in an effort to touch one of them, who then becomes the one to chase the others: *to play a game of tag.* **2.** [*count*] an act or instance of tagging a runner in baseball. —*v.* [~ + *obj*] **3.** to touch in or as if in the game of tag: *She tagged you, so now you're "it"(= You now get to chase the others).* **4.** to put out (a runner) in baseball by touching the runner (or the base) with the ball held in the hand or glove. —**tag′ger,** *n.* [*count*]

tail (tāl) /teyl/ *n.* [*count*] **1.** the hindmost part of an animal, esp. the part that forms a distinct, flexible growth on the trunk: *The dog wagged its tail.* **2.** something suggesting this: *the tail of a comet.* **3.** Also, **tails.** [*plural*] the side of a coin that does not have a face of a person on it (opposed to *head*). **4.** the rear portion of an airplane or the like. **5. tails,** [*plural*] **a.** the skirts at the back of a coat. **b.** men's formal clothing. **6.** *Slang.* the buttocks or rump. **7.** one who trails another, as a detective or spy. **8.** a final or concluding part; end. —*adj.* [*before a noun*] **9.** coming from behind: *a tail breeze.* **10.** being in the back or rear: *a tail gun on a B-17.* —*v.* [~ + *obj*] **11.** to follow in order to prevent escape or in order to observe: *The FBI tailed the suspect to his home.* —***Idiom.*** **12. turn tail,** to run away from difficulty, etc.; flee: *The soldiers turned tail.* **13. with one's tail between one's legs,** completely defeated or humiliated. —**tail′less,** *adj.*

-tail-, *root.* *-tail-* comes from French and ultimately from Latin, where it has the meaning "cut." This meaning is found in such words as: CURTAIL, DETAIL, ENTAIL, RETAIL, TAILOR.

tail′ coat′ or **tail′coat′,** *n.* [*count*] a man's formal coat, with a pair of long pieces behind. Also called **tails.**

tail•gate (tāl′gāt′) /'teyl,geyt/ *n., v.,* **-gat•ed, -gat•ing,** *adj.* —*n.* [*count*] **1.** a gate at the back of a wagon, truck, etc., that can be removed or let down for loading or unloading. —*v.* **2.** to drive dangerously close to the rear of another vehicle: [*no obj*]: *Some jerk behind us is tailgating.* [~ + *obj*]: *The truck tailgated the little car.* **3.** [*no obj*] to have a picnic on a tailgate, esp. of a station wagon: *tailgating before the big game.* —*adj.* [*before a noun*] **4.** set up on a tailgate or near an automobile, as in a parking lot: *a tailgate picnic.* —**tail′gat′er,** *n.* [*count*]

tail•light (tāl′līt′) /'teyl,layt/ *n.* [*count*] a light at the rear of an automobile, etc.

tai•lor (tā′lər) /'teylər/ *n.* [*count*] **1.** one whose occupation is the making, mending, or altering of clothes. —*v.* **2.** to make by tailor's work: [~ + *obj*]: *to tailor the garment to fit.* [*no obj*]: *to make a living at tailoring.* **3.** [~ + *obj*] to adapt so as to adjust to a purpose, need, etc.: *skilled at tailoring the facts and figures for his own ends.* See -TAIL-.

tail•pipe (tāl′pīp′) /'teyl,payp/ *n.* [*count*] an exhaust pipe at the rear of a vehicle or aircraft: *The tailpipe was giving off black smoke.*

tail•spin (tāl′spin′) /'teyl,spɪn/ *n., v.,* **-spinned, -spin•ning.** —*n.* [*count*] **1.** a spin of an airplane when it is out of control and falling rapidly. **2.** a sudden collapse into failure; a severe downturn: *The economy went into another tailspin.* —*v.* [*no obj*] **3.** to take or experience a sudden and dramatic downturn.

-tain-, *root.* *-tain-* comes from French and ultimately from Latin, where it has the meaning "hold." It is related to the root -TEN-. This meaning is found in such words as: ABSTAIN, ATTAIN, CONTAIN, DETAIN, ENTERTAIN, MAINTAIN, OBTAIN, PERTAIN, REIN, RETAIN, RETINUE, SUSTAIN.

taint (tānt) /teynt/ *n.* [*count*] **1.** a trace of something bad or offensive: *a taint of scandal.* **2.** a trace of infection, decay, or contamination. —*v.* [~ + *obj*] **3.** to infect, spoil, or contaminate: *This meat is tainted.* **4.** to ruin, damage, or spoil (a person's name, etc.): *Rumors of bribery tainted his good name.*

Tai•wan•ese (tī′wä nēz′, -nēs′) /,taywɑ'niyz, -'niys/ *adj., n., pl.* **-ese.** —*adj.* **1.** of or relating to Taiwan. **2.** of or relating to the language spoken by many of the people in Taiwan. —*n.* **3.** [*count*] a person born or living in Taiwan. **4.** [*noncount*] the language spoken by many of the people in Taiwan.

take (tāk) /teyk/ *v.,* **took** (to͝ok) /tʊk/ **tak•en** (tā′kən) /'teykən/ **tak•ing,** *n.* —*v.* **1.** [~ + *obj*] to get into one's possession by one's action: *took a pen and began to write.* **2.** [~ + *obj*] to hold or grip with the hands: *She took my hand and shook it vigorously.* **3.** [~ + *obj*] to seize or capture: *to take a prisoner.* **4.** [~ + *obj*] to catch or get (game, etc.), esp. by killing: *Regulations forbid hunters from taking more than one animal per month.* **5.** [~ + *obj*] to pick or choose from a number of alternatives; select: *She'll take white wine with her dinner.* **6.** [~ + *obj*] to receive or accept (a person) into some relation, as marriage: *Do you take her to be your lawful wedded wife?* **7.** [~ + *obj*] to receive or react to in a certain manner: *She took his death hard.* **8.** [*not: be* + *~-ing;* ~ + *obj*] to obtain from a source; derive: *The book takes its title from a song by Franz Schubert.* **9.** [~ + *obj*] to obtain as compensation for injury done (usually to oneself): *to take revenge.* **10.** [~ + *obj*] to receive into the body, as by inhaling or swallowing: *to take a pill.* **11.** [~ + *obj*] to do, perform, etc.: *She took a hot bath.* **12.** [~ + *obj*] to use to add flavoring: *Do you take sugar in your coffee?* **13.** [~ + *obj*] to undergo: *to take a heat treatment.* **14.** [~ + *obj*] to endure or submit to without complaining or weakening: *Can't you take a joke?* **15.** [~ + *obj*] to remove by death; to end (a life): *The flood took many victims.* **16.** [~ + *obj*] to subtract or deduct: *to take 2 from 5.* **17.** [~ + *obj*] to carry with one: *Are you taking an umbrella?* **18.** [~ + *obj*] to carry from one place to another; convey or transport: *Can you take the kids to school?* **19.** [~ + *obj*] to use as a means of transportation: *We took the number 15 bus.* **20.** [*not: be* + *~-ing;* ~ + *obj*] to serve as a means of conducting; to go in the direction of: *Fifth Avenue takes you right through the midtown area.* **21.** [~ + *obj*] to go into or enter: *Take the road to the left.* **22.** [~ + *obj*] to bring about a change in the condition of: *Her talent and ambition took her to the top.* **23.** [~ + *obj*] to come upon suddenly; catch: *to take a thief by surprise.* **24.** [~ + *obj*] to attack or affect with or as if with a disease: *taken with a fit of laughter.* **25.** to (cause to) be absorbed or be stuck to; be susceptible to: [~ + *obj*]: *The cloth will not take a dye.* [*no obj*]: *The dye wouldn't take on that cloth.* **26.** to require; call for; need; necessitate: [~ + *obj*]: *This wood takes three coats of paint.* [*It* + ~ + *obj* + *to* + *verb*]: *It takes courage to do that.* **27.** [~ + *obj*] to proceed to occupy: *Take a seat.* **28.** to use up; consume: [~ + *obj* (+ *to* + *verb*)]: *I took just ten minutes to solve that problem.* [~ (+ *obj*) + *obj*]: *Solving the problem took (me) only ten minutes.* [*It* + ~(+ *obj*) + *obj* (+ *to*

+ verb)]: *It took (me) only ten minutes to solve the problem.* **29.** [~ + *obj*] to act or perform: *to take the part of the hero.* **30.** [~ + *obj*] to make (a video, etc.) (of): *to take home movies.* **31.** [~ + *obj*] to write down: *to take notes.* **32.** [~ + *obj*] to apply oneself to; study: *to take a history course.* **33.** [~ + *obj*] to deal with; treat: *He promised to take the matter under consideration.* **34.** [~ + *obj*] to determine by recording, asking, examining, measuring, etc.: *The doctor took my pulse.* **35.** [~ + *obj*] to have or experience (a feeling, etc.): *She took pride in her appearance.* **36.** to grasp or apprehend mentally: [~ + *obj* + *as* + *obj*]: *Don't take the remark as an insult.* [~ + *obj* + *to* + *verb*]: *I take your silence to mean that you agree.* **37.** [~ + *obj*] to accept the statements of: *She took him at his word.* **38.** [~ + *it* + *(that) clause*] to assume as a fact: *I take it that you won't be there.* **39.** to regard or consider: [~ + *obj* + *to* + *be* + *noun*]: *I took them to be Frenchmen; weren't they?* [~ + *obj* + *to* + *be* + *adjective*]: *I took them to be wealthy enough to afford the house.* **40.** [~ + *obj*] to capture or win in a game (a piece, etc.): *The chess grandmaster took his opponent's queen.* **41.** [~ + *obj*] *Informal.* to cheat, swindle, or victimize: *The car salesman took us for about $500.* **42.** [~ + *obj*] to win or obtain money from: *He took me for $10 in the poker game.* **43.** [~ + *obj*] to have sexual intercourse with: *He wanted to take her then and there.* **44.** [*not: be* + ~*-ing;* ~ + *obj*] to be used with (a certain grammatical form, case, etc.): *This verb takes an object.* **45.** [*no obj*] to catch or engage, as a mechanical device: *We heard the engine clicking, but it just wouldn't take.* **46.** [*no obj*] to begin to grow, as a plant: *He gave us some cuttings, but they just wouldn't take.* **47.** [*no obj*] to have the intended result or effect: *Fortunately the vaccination took, and the fever went down.* **48.** [*not: be* + ~*-ing;* ~ + *adjective*] to fall or become: *He took sick.* **49. take (someone) aback,** [~ + *obj* + *aback*] to surprise or shock: *taken aback by her hostility.* **50. take after,** [~ + *after* + *obj*] **a.** to resemble (another person), as in appearance, behavior, etc.: *My daughters take after my wife.* **b.** to follow or chase: *The police took after him.* **51. take apart, a.** to disassemble, as by separating (something) into small pieces: [~ + *obj* + *apart*]: *to take a clock apart.* [~ + *apart* + *obj*]: *to take apart a clock.* **b.** to examine closely and criticize severely; attack: [~ + *apart* + *obj*]: *took apart those arguments one after another.* [~ + *obj* + *apart*]: *He took them apart.* **52. take away, a.** to remove: [~ + *away* + *obj*]: *The waiter came and took away the food.* [~ + *obj* + *away*]: *He took the food away.* **b.** [~ + *away* + *from* + *obj*] to detract (from): *He tried to take away from her achievements by saying she was just lucky.* **53. take back, a.** to regain possession of: [~ + *back* + *obj*]: *The army took back the town.* [~ + *obj* + *back*]: *to take it back.* **b.** to return, as for exchange: [~ + *obj* + *back*]: *Take it back to the store if it doesn't fit.* [~ + *obj* + *back*]: *She took the dress back because it didn't fit.* **c.** [~ + *obj* + *back*] to allow to return; resume a relationship with: *Will his wife take him back?* **d.** [~ + *obj* + *back*] to cause to remember: *The song took me back to my teen years.* **e.** to retract: [~ + *back* + *obj*]: *to take back a statement.* [~ + *obj* + *back*]: *What did you call her? You'd better take it back!* **54. take down, a.** to write down; record: [~ + *down* + *obj*]: *to take down a speech.* [~ + *obj* + *down*]: *to take it all down.* **b.** [~ + *obj* + *down*] to reduce the pride of: *to take him down a peg.* **55. take in, a.** to change (a garment) so as to make smaller or tighter: [~ + *in* + *obj*]: *to take in a dress.* [~ + *obj* + *in*]: *to take it in a few inches.* **b.** to provide a place to live for: [~ + *in* + *obj*]: *She took in every stray cat that came her way.* [~ + *obj* + *in*]: *always took the cats in.* **c.** to grasp the meaning of; comprehend: [~ + *in* + *obj*]: *Do you think he took in everything we said?* [~ + *obj* + *in*]: *Did he take it all in?* **d.** to observe; notice: [~ + *in* + *obj*]: *He stood there taking in the busy scene.* [~ + *obj* + *in*]: *He stood there taking it all in.* **e.** to deceive; trick; cheat: [~ + *obj* + *in*]: *She took us in with that scheme.* [~ + *in* + *obj*]: *Has she taken in anyone else with it?* **f.** [~ + *in* + *obj*] to visit or attend, as for entertainment: *to take in a show.* **g.** [~ + *in* + *obj*] to receive as proceeds, as from business: *The company took in enough profits last year to break even.* [~ + *obj* + *in*]: *to take it in.* **56. take off, a.** to remove: [~ + *off* + *obj*]: *Take off your coat.* [~ + *obj* + *off*]: *Take your coat off.* **b.** [*no obj*] to leave the ground and rise into the air: *The plane took off.* **c.** [*no obj*] to depart; leave: *The man took off before we could ask him who he was.* **d.** to subtract, as a discount; deduct: [~ + *off* + *obj*]: *The store took off 20 percent.* [~ + *obj* + *off*]: *taking 20 percent off the price.* **e.** [*no obj*] to achieve sudden, noticeable growth, etc.: *Sales took off just before Christmas.* **57. take on, a.** to hire; employ: [~ + *on* + *obj*]: *to take on new workers.* [~ + *obj* + *on*]: *to take new workers on.* **b.** to undertake; begin (work): [~ + *on* + *obj*]: *took on extra work to pay the bills.* [~ + *obj* + *on*]: *How can he take so much volunteer work on?* **c.** [~ + *on* + *obj*] to gain or acquire: *The word "homeowner" took on a whole new meaning when she became one.* **d.** to accept as a challenge or opponent: [~ + *on* + *obj*]: *weren't afraid to take on big business.* [~ + *obj* + *on*]: *"I'm not afraid to take the champ on!" the boxer shouted.* **58. take out, a.** to withdraw; remove: [~ + *out* + *obj*]: *She took out library books for the children.* [~ + *obj* + *out*]: *The doctor took my appendix out.* **b.** to deduct: [~ + *out* + *obj*]: *The government takes out income taxes from your paycheck.* [~ + *obj* + *out*]: *to take the taxes out.* **c.** to buy or obtain by applying: [~ + *out* + *obj*]: *to take out insurance.* [~ + *obj* + *out*]: *to take insurance out on the house.* **d.** to escort, as on a date: [~ + *obj* + *out*]: *took her out on a couple of dates.* [~ + *out* + *obj*]: *He took out several girls before he found the right one.* **e.** [*no obj*] to set out; start: *We took out after them just as the sun rose.* **f.** *Slang.* to kill or destroy: [~ + *out* + *obj*]: *The pilots took out their targets.* [~ + *obj* + *out*]: *threatened to take them out if they talked to the cops.* **59. take (something) out on (someone),** to cause (another) to suffer for (one's own misfortune, etc.): [~ + *out* + *obj* + *on* + *obj*]: *He took out his frustration on his children.* [~ + *obj* + *out* + *on* + *obj*]: *I know you're upset, but don't take it out on the kids!* **60. take over,** to assume management of or responsibility for: [*no obj*]: *Who will take over when you retire?* [~ + *over* + *obj*]: *Who will take over the company when you retire?* [~ + *obj* + *over*]: *Can they take the company over without a controlling interest?* **61. take to,** [~ + *to* + *obj*] **a.** to devote oneself to; use or do as a habit: *to take to drink.* **b.** to begin to like: *They took to each other at once.* **c.** to go to: *She took to her bed, sick with fever.* **d.** to have recourse to; resort to: *took to stealing cars.* **62. take up, a.** to occupy oneself with the study of: [~ + *up* + *obj*]: *She took up medicine as a career.* [~ + *obj* + *up*]: *took it up as a career.* **b.** to fill or occupy (space, etc.): [~ + *up* + *obj*]: *The word "take" will take up at least a page in this dictionary.* [~ + *obj* + *up*]: *This work takes all my time up.* **c.** to continue; resume: [*no obj*]: *We took up where we had left off.* [~ + *up* + *obj*]: *Let's take up the story where we left off.* [~ + *obj* + *up*]: *Let's take it up at chapter five.* **d.** to raise for discussion or consideration: [~ + *obj* + *up*]: *We'll take this up with our lawyers.* [~ + *up* + *obj*]: *Let's take up the next issue.* **e.** [~ + *up* + *obj*] to undertake; assume: *He took up the duties of the presidency.* **f.** to make (clothes) shorter or tighter, as by hemming: [~ + *up* + *obj*]: *He took up the slacks a few inches.* [~ + *obj* + *up*]: *He took the slacks up.* **63. take up with,** [~ + *up* + *with* + *obj*] to keep company with: *She's taken up with the wrong crowd of kids.* **64. take (something) upon oneself,** [~ + *obj* + *upon* + *oneself*] to assume (something) as a responsibility: *Dad took it upon himself to visit her every day in the hospital.* —*n.* [*count*] **65.** the act of taking. **66.** something taken. **67.** *Informal.* money taken in, esp. profits: *a take of at least $5,000.* **68.** a scene in a movie photographed without interruption. **69.** one of several sound recordings made, as of the same song, to produce a version good enough for release. **70.** *Informal.* a response or reaction: *She did a slow take when they told her she was arrested.* **71.** a distinctive response to an event: *What's your take on his deciding not to run?* —***Idiom.* 72. on the take,** *Slang.* accepting bribes: *Most of those politicians are on the take.* **73. take for,** [~ + *obj* + *for* + *obj*] **a.** to assume to be: *What do you take me for, a fool?* **b.** to assume falsely to be; mistake for: *Whenever I spoke Russian they took me for an immigrant.* **74. take it, a.** to accept something (as true): *Take it from me, I'm telling you the truth.* **b.** to be able to resist or endure hardship, etc.: *couldn't take it in the military.* **75. take place,** to happen; occur: *When will the wedding take place?* —**tak′a•ble, take′a•ble,** *adj.* —**tak′er,** *n.* [*count*]

take•off (tāk′ôf′, -of′) /ˈteykˌɔf, -ˌɒf/ *n.* **1.** the leaving of the ground, as in beginning an airplane flight: [*count*]: *a smooth takeoff.* [*noncount*]: *Five minutes after takeoff the plane flew into bad weather.* **2.** [*count*] a departure from a starting point, as in a race. **3.** [*count*] a funny imitation or parody; send-up: *a hilarious takeoff of his nosy neighbor.*

take•out (tāk′out′) /ˈteykˌawt/ *adj.* intended to be taken from the point of sale and eaten elsewhere: *takeout meals.*

take•o•ver (tāk′ō′vər) /ˈteykˌowvər/ *n.* [*count*] **1.** the act of seizing authority or control. **2.** the taking over of a corporation through the purchase or exchange of stock.

tak•ing (tā′king) /ˈteykɪŋ/ *n.* [*count*] **1.** the act of a person or thing that takes. **2. takings,** [*plural*] money earned or gained.

talc (talk) /tælk/ *n.* TALCUM POWDER.

tal′cum pow′der (tal′kəm) /ˈtælkəm/ *n.* [*noncount*] a fine, dry powder for the body, usually perfumed.

tale (tāl) /teyl/ *n.* [*count*] **1.** a story of an incident: *the scary tale of Count Dracula.* **2.** a lie, esp. against another: *telling tales again.*

tal•ent (tal′ənt) /ˈtælənt/ *n.* **1.** a special, often creative natural ability or skill: [*count*]: *a talent for drawing.* [*noncount*]: *to show talent in drawing.* **2.** [*count*] one with special ability, esp. in a particular field: *the local talent.* **3.** an ancient unit of weight, as of the Middle East or of Greece. —**tal′ent•ed,** *adj.*: *a very talented actress.*

tal•is•man (tal′is mən, -iz-) /ˈtælɪsmən, -ɪz-/ *n.* [*count*], *pl.* **-mans.** an object with designs or figures on it, possessing secret, magical, or supernatural powers, and worn as a charm.

talk (tôk) /tɔk/ *v.* **1.** [*no obj*] to communicate information by or as if by speaking: *Can parrots really talk? Sometimes we just sit and talk.* **2.** to discuss or chat about (a topic): [~ + *about* + *obj*]: *We talked about the movies.* [~ + *obj*]: *to talk politics.* **3.** [*no obj;* ~ + *with/to*] to consult or confer: *Talk with your adviser.* **4.** [*no obj; (~ + on/about + obj))*] to deliver a speech or lecture: *The professor talked on modern physics.* **5.** [*no obj*] to give away secret information: *The spy talked during interrogation.* **6.** [~ + *obj*] to express in words: *Now you're talking sense.* **7.** [~ + *obj*] to use (a language) in speaking or conversing: *They talk French together.* **8.** [~ + *obj*] to drive or influence by talk: *to talk a person to sleep.* **9. talk around,** [~ + *around* + *obj*] to avoid discussion of: *They talked around the problem and never really addressed it.* **10. talk back,** [*no obj; (~ + to + obj)*] to reply in a disrespectful manner: *to talk back (to one's parents).* **11. talk down to,** [~ + *down* + *to* + *obj*] to speak in a superior tone: *A good teacher won't talk down to his or her students.* **12. talk out,** to try to clarify or resolve by discussion: [~ + *out* + *obj*]: *to talk out the problem.* [~ + *obj* + *out*]: *Don't just walk out; let's talk it out.* **13. talk (someone) out of (something),** [~ + *obj* + *out* + *of* + *obj*] to convince (someone) not to do (something): *I talked him out of quitting just yet.* **14. talk over,** to consider; discuss: [~ + *obj* + *over*]: *Let's talk it over before getting angry.* [~ + *over* + *obj*]: *Let's talk over the problem with your teacher.* **15. talk up, a.** to help the progress of (someone or something) by means of praise; promote: [~ + *up* + *obj*]: *He talked up the chances of his team.* [~ + *obj* + *up*]: *I talked you up to the woman who does the hiring.* **b.** [*no obj*] to speak openly or distinctly. —*n.* **16.** [*count*] the act of talking; speech or conversation: *We had a short talk before class.* **17.** [*count*] an often informal speech or lecture: *a little talk on her research.* **18.** [*count*] a conference or session: *peace talks.* **19.** [*noncount*] rumor; gossip: *He's not really going to quit; that's just talk.* **20.** [*noncount*] empty speech; false promises: *She's all talk.* **21.** [*noncount*] a way of talking: *baby talk.* —**talk′er,** *n.* [*count*] —**Usage.** See SPEAK.

talk•a•tive (tô′kə tiv) /ˈtɔkətɪv/ *adj.* willing or ready to talk a great deal. —**talk′a•tive•ly,** *adv.* —**talk′a•tive•ness,** *n.* [*noncount*]

talk′ing-to′, *n.* [*count*], *pl.* **-tos.** a scolding.

talk′ show′, *n.* [*count*] a show in which a host interviews guests, esp. celebrities.

tall (tôl) /tɔl/ *adj.,* **-er, -est,** *adv., n.* —*adj.* **1.** having great height: *a tall man.* **2.** [*after a noun*] having the height mentioned: *a man six feet tall.* **3.** [*before a noun*] large in amount or degree: *Reducing the deficit—that's a tall order!* **4.** [*before a noun*] exaggerated; not likely to be true: *a tall tale.* —*adv.* **5.** in a proud, erect manner: *to stand tall.* —*n.* **6.** [*noncount*] a garment size for tall people. **7.** [*count*] a garment in this size. —**tall′ness,** *n.* [*noncount*]

tal•low (tal′ō) /ˈtælow/ *n.* [*noncount*] a hard, fatty substance used to make candles and soap. —**tal′low•y,** *adj.*

tal•ly (tal′ē) /ˈtæliy/ *n., pl.* **-lies,** *v.,* **-lied, -ly•ing.** —*n.* [*count*] **1.** a number counted or recorded; a reckoning. —*v.* **2.** [~ + *obj*] to mark on a tally; record; count: *to tally the results.* **3.** to (cause to) correspond or agree: [*no obj*]: *Both accounts tally.* [~ + *obj*]: *to tally the accounts.* **4.** to score a point or goal, as in a game: [~ + *obj*]: *He tallied his last three points in the final minute of the game.* [*no obj*]: *The team failed to tally in the last minute of the game.* —**tal′li•er,** *n.* [*count*]

tal•ly•ho (tal′ē hō′) /ˌtæliyˈhow/ *interj., n., pl.* **-hos,** *v.,* **-hoed** or **-ho'd, -ho•ing.** —*interj.* **1.** (used as a cry in fox hunting, on sighting the fox). —*n.* [*count*] **2.** a cry of "tallyho." —*v.* [*no obj*] **3.** to call "tallyho."

Tal•mud (täl′mŏŏd, tal′məd) /ˈtɑlmʊd, ˈtælməd/ *n.* [*proper noun; usually: the* + ~] one of two authoritative collections of Jewish religious law compiled from the oral traditions of rabbis. —**Tal•mud•ic** (täl mōō′dik, -myōō′-, tal-) /tɑlˈmuwdɪk, -ˈmyuw-, tæl-/ *adj.*

tal•on (tal′ən) /ˈtælən/ *n.* [*count*] a claw, esp. of a bird of prey.

tam (tam) /tæm/ *n.* [*count*] a tam-o'-shanter.

ta•ma•le (tə mä′lē) /təˈmɑliy/ *n.* [*count*], *pl.* **-les.** finely chopped and seasoned meat packed in cornmeal dough, wrapped in corn husks, and steamed.

tam•a•rind (tam′ə rind) /ˈtæmərɪnd/ *n.* [*count*] **1.** the pod of a tropical tree, containing seeds in a juicy acid pulp used in beverages and food. **2.** the tree itself.

tam•bou•rine (tam′bə rēn′) /ˌtæmbəˈriyn/ *n.* [*count*] a small drum with several pairs of metal jingles attached, played by striking with the knuckles and shaking.

tame (tām) /teym/ *adj.,* **tam•er, tam•est,** *v.,* **tamed, tam•ing.** —*adj.* **1.** changed from the wild or savage state; gentle: *a tame tiger.* **2.** giving in easily, as to authority. **3.** lacking in excitement; dull: *a pretty tame party.* —*v.* [~ + *obj*] **4.** to make tame; domesticate: *to tame wild animals for the circus.* **5.** to deprive of interest or excitement; make dull. **6.** to harness or control: *to tame the power of the atom.* —**tam′a•ble, tame′a•ble,** *adj.* —**tame′ly,** *adv.* —**tame′ness,** *n.* [*noncount*] —**tam′er,** *n.* [*count*]: *a lion tamer.*

tam-o'-shan•ter (tam′ə shan′tər) /ˈtæməˌʃæntər/ *n.* [*count*] a cap of Scottish origin, usually of wool, having a round, flat top with a pompom at its center. Also called **tam.**

tamp (tamp) /tæmp/ *v.* [~ + *obj*] to force in or down by repeated, rather light, strokes: *to tamp tobacco into a pipe.*

tam•per (tam′pər) /ˈtæmpər/ *v.* [~ + *with* + *obj*] **1.** to change, esp. without permission: *to tamper with a lock.* **2.** to make changes, esp. to falsify: *to tamper with official records.* **3.** to engage in dishonest dealings, esp. in order to influence improperly: *accused of tampering with the jury.* —**tam′per•er,** *n.* [*count*]

tam•pon (tam′pon) /ˈtæmpɒn/ *n.* [*count*] a plug of cotton or the like for inserting into the vagina for absorbing blood.

tan (tan) /tæn/ *v.,* **tanned, tan•ning,** *n., adj.,* **tan•ner, tan•nest.** —*v.* **1.** [~ + *obj*] to change (the skin of an animal) into leather, esp. by soaking in a special bath. **2.** to (cause to) become brown by exposure to ultraviolet rays, as of the sun: [~ + *obj*]: *The sun had tanned his skin.* [*no obj*]: *Her skin had tanned to a golden brown.* **3.** [~ + *obj*] to spank. —*n.* **4.** [*count*] a brown color appearing on the skin after exposure to the sun: *on the beach getting a tan.* **5.** [*noncount*] yellowish brown; light brown. —*adj.* **6.** yellowish brown; light brown. **7.** used in or relating to tanning. —***Idiom.*** **8. tan someone's hide,** to beat someone soundly.

tan•a•ger (tan′ə jər) /ˈtænədʒər/ *n.* [*count*] a songbird of the Americas, the male of which is usually brightly colored.

tan•dem (tan′dəm) /ˈtændəm/ *adv.* **1.** one following or behind the other: *to drive horses tandem.* —*adj.* **2.** having seats, parts, etc., arranged one behind another: *a tandem bicycle.* —*n.* [*count*] **3.** a vehicle, as a truck, in which axles are arranged in tandem. —***Idiom.*** **4. in tandem, a.** in single file; one behind the other. **b.** together; in association or partnership: *The two worked in tandem to increase their sales.*

tang (tang) /tæŋ/ *n.* [*count*] a strong taste, smell, or flavor: *the tang of the salty sea air.* —**tang′y,** *adj.,* **-i•er, -i•est.**

tan•ge•lo (tan′jə lō′) /ˈtændʒəˌlow/ *n.* [*count*], *pl.* **-los.** a citrus fruit that is a cross between a grapefruit and a tangerine.

tan•gent (tan′jənt) /ˈtændʒənt/ *n.* [*count*] **1.** a line or plane that touches but does not intersect a curve or surface at a point. **2.** Also called **tan.** a basic function in trigonometry that, in a right triangle, equals the side opposite an acute angle divided by the side next to that angle. —*adj.* **3.** in physical contact; touching. **4.** touching at a single point, as a tangent in relation to a curve or surface. —***Idiom.*** **5. off on** or **at a tangent,** going off suddenly from one course of discussion to another: *has gone off on a tangent and forgotten his main idea.* —**tan•gen•tial** (tan jen′shəl) /tæn'dʒɛnʃəl/ *adj.* See -TACT-.

tan•ge•rine (tan′jə rēn′, tan′jə rēn′) /ˌtændʒə'riyn, 'tændʒəˌriyn/ *n.* [*count*] **1.** a kind of mandarin orange. **2.** deep orange; reddish orange. —*adj.* **3.** of the color tangerine; reddish orange.

tan•gi•ble (tan′jə bəl) /'tændʒəbəl/ *adj.* **1.** that can be touched. **2.** definite; not vague; clear: *There are no tangible grounds for suspicion.* **3.** (of an asset) having physical existence, as real estate, and therefore capable of being assigned a monetary value. —*n.* [*count*] **4.** something tangible, esp. a tangible asset. —**tan•gi•bil•i•ty** (tan′jə bil′i tē) /ˌtændʒə'bɪlɪtiy/ **tan′gi•ble•ness,** *n.* [*noncount*] —**tan′gi•bly,** *adv.* See -TACT-.

tan•gle (tang′gəl) /'tæŋgəl/ *v.,* **-gled, -gling,** *n.* —*v.* **1.** to (cause to) be brought together into a mass of confused parts or strands; entangle: [~ + *obj*]: *The wind tangled the girl's long hair.* [*no obj*]: *Those puppet strings tangle too easily.* **2.** [~ + *obj*] to involve in something that prevents freedom of movement: *The bushes were tangled with vines.* **3.** [~ + *obj*] to catch and hold in or as if in a net or snare: *tangled in a web of lies.* **4.** [*no obj*] to come into conflict; fight or argue: *I don't want to be around when those two tangle.* —*n.* [*count*] **5.** a tangled situation; a tangled mass: *The deer was caught in a tangle of vines.* **6.** a confused mess; maze: *a tangle of lies and contradictions.* **7.** a conflict; disagreement: *I got into a tangle with the manager.*

tan•gled (tang′gəld) /'tæŋgəld/ *adj.* **1.** mixed up or twisted together in a tangle: *tangled thread.* **2.** very complicated or involved: *tangled negotiations.*

tan•go (tang′gō) /'tæŋgow/ *n., pl.* **-gos,** *v.,* **-goed, -go•ing.** —*n.* [*count*] **1.** a ballroom dance from Latin America. **2.** music for this dance. —*v.* [*no obj*] **3.** to dance the tango.

tank (tangk) /tæŋk/ *n.* [*count*] **1.** a large container for holding a liquid or gas: *a full tank of gas.* **2.** an armored combat vehicle, moving on a belt of treads and usually armed with a cannon. **3.** TANK TOP. —**tank′ful,** *n.* [*count*], *pl.* **-fuls.**

tan•kard (tang′kərd) /'tæŋkərd/ *n.* [*count*] a large drinking cup, usually with a handle and a hinged cover.

tank•er (tang′kər) /'tæŋkər/ *n.* [*count*] a ship, airplane, or truck designed to ship or carry liquids or gases, as for fuel: *an oil tanker.*

tank′ top′, *n.* [*count*] a low-cut, sleeveless, pullover shirt with shoulder straps.

tan•ner (tan′ər) /'tænər/ *n.* [*count*] one whose occupation is the tanning of hides.

tan•ner•y (tan′ə rē) /'tænəriy/ *n.* [*count*], *pl.* **-ner•ies.** a place where tanning is carried on.

tan•nin (tan′in) /'tænɪn/ *n.* [*noncount*] a chemical used in tanning, found also in tea. Also called **tan′nic ac′id.**

tan•ta•lize (tan′tl īz′) /'tæntḷˌayz/ *v.* [~ + *obj*], **-lized, -liz•ing.** to torment (someone) with, or as if with, the sight of something desirable but out of reach; to tease (someone) by raising hopes that cannot be met: *tantalized her with dreams of a promotion.*

tan•ta•liz•ing (tan′tl ī′zing) /'tæntḷˌayzɪŋ/ *adj.* arousing or provoking desire for something, esp. something that cannot actually be obtained: *a tantalizing look at how millionaires live.* —**tan′ta•liz′ing•ly,** *adv.*

tan•ta•mount (tan′tə mount′) /'tæntəˌmawnt/ *adj.* [*be* + ~ + *to*] equivalent, as in value, force, effect, or signification: *That insult was tantamount to a slap in the face.*

tan•trum (tan′trəm) /'tæntrəm/ *n.* [*count*] a violent demonstration of rage or frustration; a burst of bad temper: *a two-year-old child having a tantrum.*

Tan•za•ni•an (tan′zə nē′ən) /ˌtænzə'niyən/ *n.* [*count*] **1.** a person born or living in Tanzania. —*adj.* **2.** of or relating to Tanzania.

tap[1] (tap) /tæp/ *v.,* **tapped, tap•ping,** *n.* —*v.* **1.** to strike with a light blow or blows that can just be heard: [~ + *obj*]: *He tapped my shoulder and winked.* [*no obj*]: *A stranger tapped on the window.* **2.** [~ + *obj*] to strike (the fingers, etc.) upon something, esp. with repeated light blows: *He tapped his pencil on the desk.* **3.** [~ + *obj*] to make, put, etc., by tapping: *to tap a nail into a wall.* **4.** [*no obj*] to tapdance. —*n.* [*count*] **5.** a light, soft blow: *He gave the window a tap.* **6.** the sound made by this: *I heard taps on the window.* **7.** a piece of metal attached to the toe or heel of a shoe, as for reinforcement or for making the tapping of a dancer more easily heard. —**tap′per,** *n.* [*count*]

tap[2] (tap) /tæp/ *n., v.,* **tapped, tap•ping.** —*n.* [*count*] **1.** a plug or stopper for closing an opening through which liquid is drawn, as in a cask; a spigot. **2.** a faucet: *a hot-water tap.* **3.** a connection at a point between the two ends of an electrical circuit or communications device, esp. so as to be able to listen secretly to phone conversations; a wiretap. **4.** the withdrawal of fluid from the body by a medical procedure: *a spinal tap.* —*v.* [~ + *obj*] **5.** to draw liquid from (a vessel, a tree, etc.): *to tap a maple tree for sap.* **6.** to draw off (liquid), as by removing a tap or piercing a container. **7.** to draw upon; begin to use: *to tap their financial resources.* **8.** to connect into (a communications device) secretly so as to listen to or receive what is being sent: *to tap a telephone line.* —***Idiom.*** **9. on tap, a.** ready to be drawn and served, as liquor from a cask. **b.** having a tap or faucet installed, as a barrel of liquor. —**tap′per,** *n.* [*count*]

tap′ dance′, *n.* [*count*] a dance in which the rhythm is tapped out with the toe or heel by a dancer wearing shoes fitted with metal taps. —**tap′dance′,** *v.* [*no obj*], **-danced, -danc•ing.** —**tap′-danc′er,** *n.* [*count*]

tape (tāp) /teyp/ *n., v.,* **taped, tap•ing,** *adj.* —*n.* **1.** [*count*] a long, narrow strip of fabric for tying garments, joining seams or edges, etc. **2.** [*noncount*] material in the form of narrow strips, with a sticky, adhesive surface, used for sealing, etc.: *a piece of adhesive tape.* **3. a.** [*noncount*] a long, narrow, magnetized strip of plastic able to record and play back sounds or images: *The tape must have broken and ruined the VCR.* **b.** [*count*] a length of this tape with recorded sounds or images; an audiotape, cassette tape, or videotape. **4.** [*count*] a string stretched across the finish line of a race and broken by the winner on crossing the line. **5.** TAPE MEASURE. —*v.* [~ + *obj*] **6.** to tie up, bind, or attach with tape: *to tape the bows to the packages.* **7.** to record on specially treated tape: *to tape the concert.* —*adj.* **8.** of, for, or recorded on magnetic tape.

tape′ deck′, *n.* [*count*] a part of an audio system for recording and playing back tapes.

tape′ meas′ure, *n.* [*count*] a long, flexible strip marked with divisions of the foot or meter and used for measuring. Also called **tape•line** (tāp′līn′) /'teypˌlayn/.

ta•per (tā′pər) /'teypər/ *v.* **1.** to (cause to) become thinner toward one end: [*no obj*]: *The shirt tapered at the waist.* [~ + *obj*]: *to taper the shirt at the waist.* **2. taper off,** [*no obj*] **a.** to become gradually more slender toward one end. **b.** to be reduced by degrees; decrease; diminish: *The snow will taper off at about midnight.* —*n.* [*count*] **3.** a candle, esp. a very slender one.

tape′ record′er, *n.* [*count*] an electrical device for recording, or for playing back something recorded, on magnetic tape.

tap•es•try (tap′ə strē) /'tæpəstriy/ *n., pl.* **-tries. 1.** a fabric on which colored threads are woven by hand to produce a reversible design: [*noncount*]: *examples of careful tapestry.* [*count*]: *tapestries depicting medieval life.* **2.** [*count*] anything resembling such a fabric, as by having different parts making a unified whole: *the tapestry of the city, with its diversity.*

tape•worm (tāp′wûrm′) /'teypˌwɜrm/ *n.* [*count*] a flat, ribbony, parasitic worm that lives in the digestive system of humans and other vertebrates.

tap•i•o•ca (tap′ē ō′kə) /ˌtæpiy'owkə/ *n.* [*noncount*] a cassava preparation, usually in granular or pellet form, used in puddings and as a thickener.

ta•pir (tā′pər, tə pēr′) /'teypər, tə'pɪər/ *n.* [*count*], *pl.* **-pirs,** (*esp. when thought of as a group*) **-pir.** a stout, odd-toed, hoofed mammal of tropical America and SE Asia, having a short, fleshy nose like a pig.

tap•room (tap′ro͞om′, -ro͝om′) /'tæpˌruwm, -ˌrʊm/ *n.* [*count*] a barroom, esp. in an inn or hotel; bar.

taps (taps) /tæps/ *n.* a bugle signal played in a camp or military post at night as an order to turn off all lights: [*plural; used with a plural verb*]: *Taps are played every night at dusk.* [*noncount; used with a singular verb*]: *Taps is played every night at dusk.*

tar (tär) /tɑr/ *n., v.,* **tarred, tar•ring,** *adj.* —*n.* [*noncount*] **1.** a black, thick substance that can be shaped when hot and is hard when cold, used for making roads, etc.: *hot tar smeared on the highways.* **2.** solid material produced when tobacco burns: *cigarette tar.* —*v.* [~ + *obj*] **3.** to smear or cover with or as if with tar. —*adj.* **4.** of or relating to tar. **5.** covered or smeared with tar; tarred. —***Idiom.*** **6. tar and feather,** [~ + *obj*] to coat (a person) with tar and feathers as a punishment.

ta•ran•tu•la (tə ran′chə lə) /tə'ræntʃələ/ *n.* [*count*], *pl.*

-las, -lae (-lē′) /-ˌliy/. a large, hairy spider having a painful but not poisonous bite.

tar•dy (tär′dē) /ˈtɑrdiy/ *adj.*, **-di•er, -di•est. 1.** late; behind time; not on time. **2.** moving or acting slowly; sluggish. —**tar•di•ly** (tär′dl ē) /ˈtɑrdḷiy/ *adv.* —**tar′di•ness,** *n.* [*noncount*]

tar•get (tär′git) /ˈtɑrgɪt/ *n.* [*count*] **1.** an object, usually marked with ringed circles, to be aimed at in shooting practice or contests. **2.** any object fired at. **3.** a goal to be reached; aim: *a target of $25,000 for the drive.* **4.** one who is the object of abuse, scorn, etc.: *a target of abuse.* —*adj.* [*before a noun*] **5.** of or relating to a target or goal: *a target date.* —*v.* [~ + *obj*] **6.** to use or set up as a target: *The pilots targeted the oil refineries for their first bombing run.* **7.** to direct toward a target: *The pilots targeted their bombs on the oil refineries.* **8.** to make a target of, as for attack or abuse: *The comedian targeted his wife for his humor.* —***Idiom.*** **9. on target,** accurate or correct; precisely right: *He was on target with his predictions for the economy.*

tar•iff (tar′if) /ˈtærɪf/ *n.* [*count*] **1.** a schedule or system of duties charged by a government on imports or exports: *a fifty-percent tariff on rice imports.* **2.** a schedule or list of charges or fares for anything.

tar•nish (tär′nish) /ˈtɑrnɪʃ/ *v.* **1.** to (cause a metal surface to) be dull; (cause to) be discolored: [~ + *obj*]: *The salty ocean air tarnished her silver teapot.* [*no obj*]: *Silver tarnishes easily in salty air.* **2.** [~ + *obj*] to destroy the good name of; stain; discredit: *The charge of fraud tarnished the company's reputation.* —*n.* [*noncount*] **3.** a tarnished coating. **4.** tarnished condition; discoloration.

ta•ro (tär′ō, târ′ō, tar′ō) /ˈtɑrow, ˈtɛərow, ˈtærow/ *n.* [*count*], *pl.* **-ros. 1.** a stemless plant of the arum family, grown for its large edible root. **2.** the fleshy, large root itself.

ta•rot (tar′ō, ta rō′) /ˈtærow, tæˈrow/ *n.* [*count*] any of a set of 22 playing cards used for fortune-telling.

tar•pau•lin (tär pô′lin, tär′pə lin) /tɑrˈpɔlɪn, ˈtɑrpəlɪn/ *n.* a sheet of waterproofed canvas used as a protective covering against weather: [*count*]: *covered the infield with a tarpaulin.* [*noncount*]: *Is there tarpaulin in the rescue kit?*

tar•pon (tär′pən) /ˈtɑrpən/ *n.* [*count*], *pl.* **-pons,** (*esp. when thought of as a group*) **-pon.** a powerful game fish of warm W Atlantic waters, having large, silvery scales.

tar•ra•gon (tar′ə gon′, -gən) /ˈtærəˌgɒn, -gən/ *n.* **1.** [*count*] a plant with sweet-smelling leaves used as seasoning in cooking. **2.** [*noncount*] the leaves themselves.

tar•ry (tar′ē) /ˈtæriy/ *v.* [*no obj*], **-ried, -ry•ing.** to stay in a place; delay in acting, starting, etc.; linger.

tart[1] (tärt) /tɑrt/ *adj.*, **-er, -est. 1.** sharp to the taste; sour or acid: *tart apples.* **2.** sharp in character, spirit, or expression; cutting: *a tart reply.* —**tart′ly,** *adv.* —**tart′ness,** *n.* [*noncount*]

tart[2] (tärt) /tɑrt/ *n.* **1.** a small, shallow pie without a top crust, filled with fruit, etc: [*count*]: *a blueberry tart.* [*noncount*]: *a small piece of tart.* **2.** [*count*] a prostitute. —*v.* **3. tart up,** to dress up or decorate, esp. in an overly showy manner: [~ + *up* + *obj*]: *to tart up a simple old inn.* [~ + *obj* + *up*]: *Why did they have to tart it up?*

tar•tan (tär′tn) /ˈtɑrtn̩/ *n.* [*noncount*] **1.** a woolen cloth woven with stripes of different colors and widths crossing at right angles, worn chiefly by the Scottish Highlanders, each clan having its own distinctive pattern. —*adj.* **2.** of, resembling, or made of tartan.

tar•tar[1] (tär′tər) /ˈtɑrtər/ *n.* [*noncount*] **1.** a hard, whitish substance that forms on the teeth. **2.** cream of tartar. —**tar•tar•ic** (tär tar′ik, -tär′-) /tɑrˈtærɪk, -ˈtɑr-/ *adj.*

tar•tar[2] (tär′tər) /ˈtɑrtər/ *n.* [*count*] a savage, fierce, or ill-tempered person.

tar′tar sauce′, *n.* [*noncount*] a sauce made of mayonnaise and containing chopped pickles, olives, capers, etc., served esp. with fish and seafood.

task (task) /tæsk/ *n.* [*count*] **1.** a piece of work assigned to a person: *a boring task.* —***Idiom.*** **2. take** or **bring (someone) to task,** to scold or reprimand; chide; censure: *The boss took him to task for being late.*

task′ force′, *n.* [*count*] **1.** a group of military units under one command for a certain job: *a Navy task force steaming into the Atlantic.* **2.** a group or committee formed to examine or solve a problem.

task•mas•ter (task′mas′tər) /ˈtæskˌmæstər/ *n.* [*count*] one who assigns tasks, esp. difficult ones, to others or who supervises others' work very carefully.

tas•sel (tas′əl) /ˈtæsəl/ *n.*, *v.*, **-seled, -sel•ing** or (*esp. Brit.*) **-selled, -sel•ling.** —*n.* [*count*] **1.** an ornament consisting of a bunch of threads or cords hanging from a knob, used on clothing, etc. **2.** something resembling this, as at the top of a stalk of corn. —*v.* [*no obj*] **3.** (of corn) to put forth tassels. —**tas′seled,** *adj.*

taste (tāst) /teyst/ *v.*, **tast•ed, tast•ing,** *n.* —*v.* **1.** [~ + *obj*] to test the flavor or quality of by taking some into the mouth: *She tasted the wine and said it had gone bad.* **2.** [~ + *obj*] to eat or drink: *He hadn't tasted food for three days.* **3.** [*not: be* + ~*-ing;* ~ + *obj*] to notice, perceive, or distinguish the flavor of: *I can't taste the wine in that sauce.* **4.** [~ + *obj*] to experience, esp. to only a slight degree: *had tasted freedom and would no longer wait for it.* **5.** [*not: be* + ~*-ing*] to have a particular flavor: [~ + *adjective*]: *The coffee tastes bitter.* [~ + *of/like* + *noun*]: *The coffee tastes like lead.* —*n.* **6.** [*noncount*] the sense by which the flavor of things is felt or noticed: *He has no sense of taste when he has a cold.* **7.** [*count*] a sensation noticed by this sense; flavor: *foods that have a sweet taste.* **8.** [*count*] the act of tasting food or drink. **9.** [*count*] a small quantity tasted: *a little taste of cognac.* **10.** [*count*] a liking for something: *a taste for classical music.* **11.** [*noncount*] a sense of what is fitting, harmonious, or beautiful; or of what is polite, correct, etc., to say or do socially: *always dressed in good taste; jokes in poor taste.* **12.** [*count*] a slight experience of something: *a taste of victory.* **13.** [*count*] a feeling due to an experience: *a compromise that had left her with a bad taste.*

taste′ bud′, *n.* [*count*] one of many small bodies chiefly in the skin of the tongue, which are the ends of the organs for the sense of taste.

taste•ful (tāst′fəl) /ˈteystfəl/ *adj.* having, showing, or in accordance with good taste. —**taste′ful•ly,** *adv.*: *a room tastefully decorated in muted colors.*

taste•less (tāst′lis) /ˈteystlɪs/ *adj.* **1.** having no taste; lacking a taste or flavor: *Water should be tasteless.* **2.** lacking good taste; lacking a sense of what is proper, harmonious, fitting, etc.: *tasteless jokes.* —**taste′less•ly,** *adv.* —**taste′less•ness,** *n.* [*noncount*]: *tastelessness in clothes and manners.*

tast•y (tā′stē) /ˈteystiy/ *adj.*, **-i•er, -i•est.** good-tasting; savory. —**tast′i•ness,** *n.* [*noncount*]

tat•ter (tat′ər) /ˈtætər/ *n.* [*count*] **1.** a torn piece hanging loose from the main part, as of a flag; a shred. **2. tatters,** [*plural*] torn or ragged clothing: *dressed in tatters.* —*v.* [~ + *obj*] **3.** to tear or wear to tatters: *Their clothes were tattered.*

tat•tle (tat′l) /ˈtætḷ/ *v.*, **-tled, -tling,** *n.* —*v.* **1.** [*no obj*] to tell something secret about another out of spite: *Don't tattle; it's not friendly.* **2. tattle on,** [~ + *on* + *obj*] to betray by tattling: *Why did you tattle on me?* —*n.* [*count*] **3.** the act of tattling. —**tat′tler,** *n.* [*count*]

tat•tle•tale (tat′l tāl′) /ˈtætḷˌteyl/ *n.* [*count*] **1.** one who tells something private about another, or betrays another in doing so. —*adj.* [*before a noun*] **2.** showing evidence of something: *tattletale crumbs that proved he'd been munching cookies in bed.*

tat•too[1] (ta to͞o′) /tæˈtuw/ *n.* [*count*], *pl.* **-toos. 1.** a bugle call preceding taps and ordering soldiers to go to their quarters. **2.** a knocking or strong pulsation: *My heart beat a tattoo on my ribs.* **3.** *Brit.* an outdoor military parade or display.

tat•too[2] (ta to͞o′) /tæˈtuw/ *n.*, *pl.* **-toos,** *v.*, **-tooed, -too•ing.** —*n.* [*count*] **1.** markings on the skin with designs, etc., made by piercing the skin and adding dyes. —*v.* [~ + *obj*] **2.** to mark with tattoos, as a person or a part of the body: *Her back was tattooed with a butterfly.* **3.** to put (a design, etc.) on the skin: *A butterfly was tattooed on her back.* —**tat•too′er, tat•too′ist,** *n.* [*count*]

taught (tôt) /tɔt/ *v.* pt. and pp. of TEACH.

taunt (tônt, tänt) /tɔnt, tɑnt/ *v.* [~ + *obj*] **1.** to make fun of or insult, often to get someone to do something: *He taunted them with shouts of "Sissies!" but they ignored him.* —*n.* [*count*] **2.** a mocking remark, made as a challenge or an insult. —**taunt′er,** *n.* [*count*] —**taunt′ing•ly,** *adv.*

taut (tôt) /tɔt/ *adj.*, **-er, -est. 1.** tightly drawn; tense; not slack: *His muscles were taut as he strained to lift the weights.* **2.** emotionally tense: *taut nerves.* —**taut′ly,** *adv.* —**taut′ness,** *n.* [*noncount*]

tau•tol•o•gy (tô tol′ə jē) /tɔˈtɒlədʒiy/ *n.*, *pl.* **-gies. 1.** [*noncount*] needless repetition of an idea in different words, as in "widow woman." **2.** [*count*] an instance or example of such repetition. **3.** [*count*] *Logic.* a statement that is inherently true because of the meaning of its terms, without reference to external reality: *An example of tautology is:"I am either the King of England or not the King of England."* —**tau•to•log•i•cal** (tôt′l oj′i kəl)

/ˌtɔtḷˈɒdʒɪkəl/ **tau′to•log′ic, tau•tol•o•gous** (tô tol′ə gəs) /tɔˈtɒləgəs/ *adj.* See -LOG-.

tav•ern (tav′ərn) /ˈtævərn/ *n.* [*count*] **1.** a place where alcoholic drinks are sold to be drunk on the premises. **2.** a public house for travelers and others; inn.

taw•dry (tô′drē) /ˈtɔdriy/ *adj.,* **-dri•er, -dri•est. 1.** showy and cheap; gaudy: *wearing a tawdry outfit.* **2.** shameful; immoral: *involved in a tawdry affair.* —**taw′dri•ness,** *n.* [*noncount*]

taw•ny (tô′nē) /ˈtɔniy/ *adj.,* **-ni•er, -ni•est,** *n.* **—***adj.* **1.** of a yellowish brown color; golden brown. **—***n.* [*noncount*] **2.** tawny color. —**taw′ni•ness,** *n.* [*noncount*]

tax (taks) /tæks/ *n.* **1.** a sum of money paid to a government for its support, based on income, etc.: [*noncount*]: *a burdensome income tax.* [*count*]: *to rebel against paying new taxes.* **—***v.* [~ + *obj*] **2.** (of a government) **a.** to put or impose a tax on (a person or business): *The government taxes its citizens according to their ability to pay.* **b.** to demand a tax on (goods, etc.): *Income and savings would both be taxed.* **3.** to make serious demands on (someone); burden; strain: *Putting the children through college taxes our financial resources.* —**tax′a•ble,** *adj.* —**tax•a′tion,** *n.* [*noncount*] See -TACT-.

tax•i (tak′sē) /ˈtæksiy/ *n., pl.* **tax•is** or **tax•ies,** *v.,* **tax•ied, tax•i•ing** or **tax•y•ing. —***n.* [*count*] **1.** a taxicab: *I'll call for a taxi to send you home.* See illustration at STREET. **—***v.* **2.** [*no obj*] to ride or travel in a taxicab: *We taxied downtown.* **3.** (of an airplane) to (cause to) move over the surface of the ground at slow speed, in preparation for takeoff: [*no obj*]: *The plane was taxiing on the runway.* [~ + *obj*]: *The pilot taxied the plane to the center of the runway.*

tax•i•cab (tak′sē kab′) /ˈtæksiyˌkæb/ *n.* [*count*] a public passenger vehicle, esp. an automobile, with a driver who is paid to carry one or more passengers somewhere.

tax•i•der•my (tak′si dûr′mē) /ˈtæksɪˌdɜrmiy/ *n.* [*noncount*] the art of preserving, stuffing, and mounting the skins of animals in lifelike form. —**tax′i•der′mist,** *n.* [*count*] See -DERM-.

tax•ing (tak′sing) /ˈtæksɪŋ/ *adj.* demanding; difficult; requiring effort: *a very taxing work schedule.* See -TACT-.

tax•on•o•my (tak son′ə mē) /tækˈsɒnəmiy/ *n.* the science of naming things and classifying them in different groups: [*noncount*]: *language taxonomy.* [*count*]: *taxonomies for certain microscopic organisms.* —**tax•o•nom•ic** (tak′sə nom′ik) /ˌtæksəˈnɒmɪk/ **tax′o•nom′i•cal,** *adj.* See -NOM-[1].

tax•pay•er (taks′pā′ər) /ˈtæksˌpeyər/ *n.* [*count*] one who pays a tax or taxes or is subject to taxation. —**tax′-pay′ing,** *adj.: taxpaying citizens.*

tax′ shel′ter, *n.* [*count*] any financial arrangement that reduces or eliminates taxes that would otherwise have to be paid. —**tax′-shel′tered,** *adj.: tax-sheltered income.*

TB or **tb,** an abbreviation of: tuberculosis.

tbs. or **tbsp.,** an abbreviation of: **1.** tablespoon. **2.** tablespoonful.

T cell, *n.* [*count*] a kind of white blood cell that circulates in the blood and lymph and regulates the body's response to infected or harmful cells. Also called **T lymphocyte.**

tea (tē) /tiy/ *n.* **1.** [*noncount*] the dried and prepared leaves of an Asian shrub, used to make a beverage. **2.** [*noncount*] the shrub itself. **3.** a bitter beverage prepared by adding tea leaves to boiling water: [*noncount*]: *a cup of tea.* [*count*]: *I'll have two teas with sugar and lemon, please.* **4.** [*noncount*] any kind of leaves, flowers, etc., so used, or any plant yielding them. **5.** a snack or light meal, usually including tea, sandwiches, and cakes, eaten in the late afternoon: [*noncount*]: *They had us over for tea.* [*count*]: *a lovely afternoon tea.*

teach (tēch) /tiytʃ/ *v.,* **taught** (tôt) /tɔt/ **teach•ing. 1.** to impart knowledge of or skill in (some subject, etc.) to students; give instruction in (some topic): [~ + *obj*]: *She teaches mathematics.* [~ + *that clause*]: *The Koran teaches that hostages should not be mistreated.* **2.** to impart knowledge of or skill in some subject, etc., to (students); give instruction to: [~ + *obj*]: *He teaches a large class of high school students.* [~ + *obj* + *obj*]: *He teaches college students mathematics.* [~ + *obj* + *to* + *verb*]: *He taught his daughter (how) to drive.* [~ + *obj* + *that clause*]: *She taught me that most people can be trusted.* **3.** [*no obj*] to impart knowledge, skill, or instruction, esp. as one's profession: *teaching for over twenty years.*

teach•er (tē′chər) /ˈtiytʃər/ *n.* [*count*] one who teaches, esp. as a profession; instructor. See illustration at SCHOOL.

teach•ing (tē′ching) /ˈtiytʃɪŋ/ *n.* **1.** [*noncount*] the act or profession of one who teaches. **2.** Often, **teachings.** [*plural*] something taught, esp. a belief or doctrine: *One of his teachings was that people who are humble will be rewarded.*

tea•cup (tē′kup′) /ˈtiyˌkʌp/ *n.* [*count*] **1.** a cup in which tea is served. **2.** the amount a teacup holds.

teak (tēk) /tiyk/ *n.* **1.** [*count*] a large East Indian tree that yields a hard wood. **2.** [*noncount*] the wood of this tree, used in shipbuilding, furniture making, etc.

tea•ket•tle (tē′ket′l) /ˈtiyˌkɛtḷ/ *n.* [*count*] a portable kettle with a cover, spout, and handle, used for boiling water.

teal (tēl) /tiyl/ *n., pl.* **teals,** (*esp. when thought of as a group*) **teal** for **1.** [*count*] a small duck. **2.** [*noncount*] Also called **teal′ blue′.** a medium to dark greenish blue.

team (tēm) /tiym/ *n.* [*count*] **1.** a group of people forming a side in a game or contest: *a basketball team; a debating team.* **2.** a group of people assembled for an action or activity: *A team of experts visited the site of the crash.* **3.** two or more horses or other animals harnessed together to draw a vehicle, plow, etc. **—***v.* **4.** to join together in a team: [~ + *obj* (+ *together/up*)]: *He teamed them (together) on the project.* [*no obj*]: *The two teamed up to work on the new budget.* **—***adj.* [*before a noun*] **5.** relating to or performed by a team: *a team effort.*

team•mate (tēm′māt′) /ˈtiymˌmeyt/ *n.* [*count*] a member of the same team.

team•ster (tēm′stər) /ˈtiymstər/ *n.* [*count*] one who drives a team or a truck for hauling, esp. as one's job.

team•work (tēm′wûrk′) /ˈtiymˌwɜrk/ *n.* [*noncount*] effort on the part of a group acting together as a team.

tea•pot (tē′pot′) /ˈtiyˌpɒt/ *n.* [*count*] a container with a lid, spout, and handle, in which tea is made.

tear[1] (tēr) /tɪər/ *n.* [*count*] **1.** a drop of salty, watery fluid produced by glands around the eyelid: *Tears wash away dirt and dust in the eye.* **2.** a drop of this fluid appearing in or flowing from the eye as the result of emotion, esp. grief, pain, or sadness: *Tears flowed down his face during the funeral.* **3. tears,** [*plural*] an act of weeping: *She burst into tears.* **—***v.* [*no obj*] **4.** (of the eyes) to fill up and overflow with tears: *His eyes teared whenever he thought of his late father.* **—*Idiom.* 5. in tears,** weeping: *I found her in tears.* —**tear′ful,** *adj.* —**tear′y,** *adj.,* **-i•er, -i•est.**

tear[2] (târ) /tɛər/ *v.,* **tore, torn, tear•ing,** *n.* **—***v.* **1.** to (cause to) be pulled apart or in pieces by force: [~ + *obj*]: *He tore the fabric.* [*no obj*]: *This fabric tears easily.* **2.** [~ + *obj*] to pull or snatch violently: *She tore the book from my hands.* **3.** [*no obj*] to move or behave with violent haste or great energy: *The wind tore through the trees.* **4.** [~ + *obj; usually: be* + *torn*] to divide or disrupt: *The country was torn by civil war.* **5.** [~ + *obj*] to produce (a hole or rip) by pulling apart: *to tear a hole in one's coat.* **6.** [~ + *obj* + *away*] to remove by force or effort: *It was such an exciting lecture, I couldn't tear myself away.* **7. tear at,** [~ + *at* + *obj*] **a.** to pull or pluck violently at: *He tore at her sleeve, begging her to stay.* **b.** to cause a feeling of distress, pain, or unhappiness; afflict: *The grief tore at his heart.* **8. tear down, a.** to pull down; demolish: [~ + *obj* + *down*]: *They're tearing the old library down.* [~ + *down* + *obj*]: *They're tearing down the old library.* **b.** to discredit or show to be false: [~ + *down* + *obj*]: *He tore down the theory that some races are more intelligent than others.* [~ + *obj* + *down*]: *The scientists were quick to tear that theory down.* **9. tear into,** [~ + *into* + *obj*] to attack quickly and viciously: *The army tore into the enemy.* **10. tear up, a.** to tear into small shreds: [~ + *up* + *obj*]: *He tore up the message.* [~ + *obj* + *up*]: *He tore the message up.* **b.** to cancel or annul: [~ + *up* + *obj*]: *to tear up a contract.* [~ + *obj* + *up*]: *to tear a contract up.* **—***n.* [*count*] **11.** the act of tearing. **12.** a place where something is or has been torn, ripped, or pulled apart. **13.** *Informal.* a spree: *The shoppers went on a tear through the mall.* See TORN.

tear•drop (tēr′drop′) /ˈtɪərˌdrɒp/ *n.* [*count*] **1.** a tear. **2.** something shaped like a falling drop.

tear′ gas′ (tēr) /tɪər/ *n.* [*noncount*] a gas that stings the eyes and makes them water, thus producing temporary blindness, used in battles or to put down riots, etc.

tear•jerk•er (tēr′jûr′kər) /ˈtɪərˌdʒɜrkər/ *n.* [*count*] *Informal.* an overly emotional or sentimental story, play, or the like, designed to cause the audience to cry.

tease (tēz) /tiyz/ *v.,* **teased, teas•ing,** *n.* **—***v.* **1.** to irritate, bother, or anger (someone or an animal) with jokes, playful words or actions, or other annoyances: [~ + *obj*]:

She teased me about my girlfriends. [*no obj*]: *Don't tease; it's cruel to animals.* **2.** to excite someone's interest or desire with no intention to gratify it; tantalize: [*no obj*]: *She thought he really liked her, but he was just teasing.* [~ + *obj*]: *just teasing her.* **3.** [~ + *obj*] to fluff up (the hair) by holding at the ends and combing toward the scalp so as to give body to a hairdo: *Her hair was teased.* **—*n.*** [*count*] **4.** a person who teases: *She's such a tease.*

tea•spoon (tē′spōōn′) /ˈtiyˌspuwn/ *n.* [*count*] **1.** a small spoon used to stir tea and coffee, eat dessert, etc. **2.** a cooking measure equal to 1/6 fluid ounce (4.9 ml). —**tea′spoon ful′,** *n.* [*count*], *pl.* **-fuls.**

teat (tēt, tit) /tiyt, tɪt/ *n.* [*count*] **1.** a nipple through which milk is sucked by young mammals. **2.** something resembling a teat.

tech (tek) /tɛk/ *adj.* **1.** technical: *The computer whizzes were talking tech talk.* **—*n.* 2.** [*noncount*] technology. **3.** [*count*] a technician: *a lab tech.* See -TECHN-.

tech., an abbreviation of: **1.** technical. **2.** technology.

-techn-, *root.* *-techn-* comes from Greek, where it has the meaning "skill; ability." This meaning is found in such words as: POLYTECHNIC, TECH, TECHNICAL, TECHNICIAN, TECHNIQUE, TECHNOLOGY.

tech•ni•cal (tek′ni kəl) /ˈtɛknɪkəl/ *adj.* **1.** [*before a noun*] of or relating to an art, science, or the like: *technical skill.* **2.** found in, or special to, a particular art, etc.: *a technical journal.* **3.** [*before a noun*] of, relating to, or showing technique: *The skaters were judged on their technical ability.* **4.** [*before a noun*] concerned with the mechanical or industrial arts and the applied sciences: *a technical school.* **5.** considered so by a strict interpretation of the rules: *a technical offense.* —**tech′ni•cal•ly,** *adv.*: *Technically we are thirty seconds late, but I don't think anyone will care that much.* See -TECHN-.

tech•ni•cal•i•ty (tek′ni kal′i tē) /ˌtɛknɪˈkælɪtiy/ *n.* [*count*], *pl.* **-ties.** a very small point, detail, expression, or rule: *Because of a technicality the convicted killer went free.* See -TECHN-.

tech•ni•cian (tek nish′ən) /tɛkˈnɪʃən/ *n.* [*count*] **1.** one trained or skilled in technical parts of a field of study or work. **2.** a person skilled in the technique of an art, as music or painting. See -TECHN-.

tech•nique (tek nēk′) /tɛkˈniyk/ *n.* **1.** [*noncount*] the manner and ability with which an artist, athlete, etc., uses technical skills in a particular art, field of study, etc.: *The diver showed perfect technique on that difficult dive.* **2.** [*count*] any method used to accomplish something: *a simple technique for making sure I don't ruin my disks.* See -TECHN-.

tech•noc•ra•cy (tek nok′rə sē) /tɛkˈnɒkrəsiy/ *n.* [*count*], *pl.* **-cies.** a system of government in which technological experts manage and control the economy, government, etc. —**tech••no•crat** *n.* (tek′nə krat′) /ˈtɛknəˌkræt/ [*count*] See -TECHN-.

tech•nol•o•gy (tek nol′ə jē) /tɛkˈnɒlədʒiy/ *n.*, *pl.* **-gies.** **1.** [*noncount*] the branch of knowledge that deals with applying science and engineering to practical uses. **2.** [*count*] a technological process or invention: *new technologies for computer chip manufacturing.* —**tech•no•log•i•cal** (tek′nə loj′i kəl) /ˌtɛknəˈlɒdʒɪkəl/ **tech′no•log′ic,** *adj.* —**tech′no•log′i•cal•ly,** *adv.* —**tech•nol′o•gist,** *n.* [*count*] See -TECHN-.

tec•ton•ics (tek ton′iks) /tɛkˈtɒnɪks/ *n.* [*noncount; used with a singular verb*] the branch of geology that studies structural features of the earth for clues regarding earthquakes.

ted•dy bear′ (ted′ē) /ˈtɛdiy/ *n.* [*count*] a stuffed toy bear.

te•di•ous (tē′dē əs, tē′jəs) /ˈtiydiyəs, ˈtiydʒəs/ *adj.* of or relating to tedium: *a tedious book; a tedious lecture.* —**te′di•ous•ly,** *adv.* —**te′di•ous•ness,** *n.* [*noncount*]

te•di•um (tē′dē əm) /ˈtiydiyəm/ *n.* [*noncount*] the quality or state of causing another to feel tired and bored; tediousness.

tee (tē) /tiy/ *n.*, *v.*, **teed, tee•ing.** **—*n.*** [*count*] **1. a.** Also called **teeing ground.** the area from which the first stroke on each hole of a golf course is played. **b.** a small peg or a mound of earth from which a golf ball is driven at the beginning of each hole. **2.** a stand on which a football is rested to position it for kicking before a kick-off. **—*v.* 3.** [~ + *obj*] to place (a ball) on a tee. **4. tee off, a.** [*no obj*] to strike a golf ball from a tee: *They finally teed off at eleven o'clock.* **b.** *Slang.* to make angry or irritated: [~ + *obj* + *off*]: *Her cheating and lying tee me off.* [~ + *off* + *obj*]: *Her lies teed off everybody on that committee.*

teem (tēm) /tiym/ *v.* [*no obj; (~ + with + obj)*] to have plenty of; to abound with: *The lake was teeming with fish.*

teen (tēn) /tiyn/ *adj.* [*before a noun*] **1.** teenage: *teen fashions.* **—*n.*** [*count*] **2.** a teenager. See TEENS.

teen•age (tēn′āj′) /ˈtiynˌeydʒ/ also **teen′aged′,** *adj.* of, relating to, or characteristic of people in their teens. —**teen•ag•er,** *n.* [*count*]

teens (tēnz) /tiynz/ *n.* [*plural*] **1.** the numbers 13 through 19: *Temperatures will fall into the teens tonight.* **2.** the ages of 13 to 19 inclusive: *two sons in their teens.*

tee•ny (tē′nē) /ˈtiyniy/ *adj.*, **-ni•er, -ni•est.** TINY.

teen•y•bop•per (tē′nē bop′ər) /ˈtiyniyˌbɒpər/ *n.* [*count*] *Informal.* a teenager, esp. a girl, devoted to teenage fads, etc.

tee′ shirt′, *n.* T-SHIRT.

tee•ter (tē′tər) /ˈtiytər/ *v.* [*no obj*] **1.** to move unsteadily: *The ladder teetered, then crashed down.* **2.** to waver; fluctuate: *Prices teetered on the edge of 150, then fell sharply.* **—*n.*** [*count*] **3.** a seesaw.

teeth (tēth) /tiyθ/ *n.* pl. of TOOTH.

teethe (tēth) /tiyð/ *v.* [*no obj*], **teethed, teeth•ing.** to grow teeth.

tee•to•tal•er (tē tōt′l ər, tē′tōt′-) /tiyˈtowtl̩ər, ˈtiyˌtowt-/ *n.* [*count*] one who never drinks intoxicating beverages or liquor. Also, *esp. Brit.,* **tee•to′tal•ler.**

Tef•lon (tef′lon) /ˈtɛflɒn/ **1.** *Trademark.* [*noncount*] a material that has a slippery, nonsticking surface: *Teflon is used in electrical insulation and on the coatings of frying pans.* **—*adj.* 2.** characterized by the ability to avoid blame or criticism: *a Teflon politician who never angers the voters.*

tel., an abbreviation of: **1.** telegram. **2.** telegraph. **3.** telephone.

tele-, *prefix.* **1.** *tele-* comes from Greek, where it has the meaning "far." It is attached to roots and sometimes words and means "reaching over a distance, carried out between two remote points, performed or operating through electronic transmissions": *telegraph; telekinesis; teletypewriter.* **2.** *tele-* is also used to mean "television": *telegenic; telethon.* Also, *esp. before a vowel,* **tel-.**

tel•e•cast (tel′i kast′) /ˈtɛlɪˌkæst/ *v.*, **-cast** or **-cast•ed, -cast•ing,** *n.* **—*v.* 1.** to broadcast by television: [~ + *obj*]: *to telecast a show live.* [*no obj*]: *to telecast live.* **—*n.*** [*count*] **2.** a television broadcast. —**tel′e•cast′er,** *n.* [*count*]

tel•e•com•mu•ni•ca•tions (tel′i kə myōō′ni kā′shənz) /ˌtɛlɪkəˌmyuwnɪˈkeyʃənz/ *n.* [*noncount; used with a singular verb*] **1.** Sometimes, **telecommunication.** the science and technology of sending information over great distances, in the form of electromagnetic signals, as by telegraph or television. **2.** Usually, **telecommunication.** the act or fact of communicating in such a manner: *in constant telecommunication with London.*

tel•e•con•fer•ence (tel′i kon′fər əns, -frəns) /ˈtɛlɪˌkɒnfərəns, -frəns/ *n.*, *v.*, **-enced, -enc•ing.** **—*n.*** [*count*] **1.** a business meeting, etc., in which the participants are in different locations and communicate with equipment like phones, radio, etc. **—*v.*** [*no obj*] **2.** to participate in such a meeting. See -FER-.

tel•e•gen•ic (tel′i jen′ik) /ˌtɛlɪˈdʒɛnɪk/ *adj.* having physical qualities that are attractive or pleasing when seen on television: *a telegenic news anchor.* See -GEN-.

tel•e•gram (tel′i gram′) /ˈtɛlɪˌgræm/ *n.* a message sent by telegraph: [*count*]: *He received a telegram that congratulated him on his one hundredth birthday.* [*noncount; often: by* + ~]: *The message came by telegram.*

tel•e•graph (tel′i graf′) /ˈtɛlɪˌgræf/ *n.* [*noncount*] **1.** a system or a device for sending messages to a distant place, esp. by electric signals between two devices connected by a conducting wire: *sent by telegraph.* **—*v.* 2.** to send or transmit (a message) by telegraph to (someone): [~ + *obj*]: *They telegraphed a message to her.* [~ + *obj* + *obj*]: *They telegraphed her the message.* [~ + *that clause*]: *They telegraphed that the next train was carrying the gold.* [*no obj*]: *They telegraphed ahead with the news.* **3.** [~ + *obj*] to let someone else see (one's intentions, etc.), but without knowing one has done so: *The boxer telegraphed his left hook by dipping his arm just before aiming it.* —**te•leg•ra•pher** (tə leg′rə fər) /təˈlɛgrəfər/; *esp. Brit.,* **te•leg′ra•phist,** *n.* [*count*] See -GRAPH-.

tel•e•graph•ic (tel′i graf′ik) /ˌtɛlɪˈgræfɪk/ *adj.* **1.** of or relating to the telegraph or to telegraphy. **2.** with unnecessary words removed so as to shorten, as is customary in a message sent by telegraph: *the telegraphic language of the sign that read: "Back soon; deliveries in rear."*

te•leg•ra•phy (tə leg′rə fē) /tə'lɛgrəfiy/ *n.* [*noncount*] the technique or practice of constructing or operating telegraphs. See -GRAPH-.

tel•e•ki•ne•sis (tel′i ki nē′sis, -kī-) /ˌtɛlɪkɪ'niysɪs, -kay-/ *n.* [*noncount*] the supposed ability to move or change inanimate objects by mental power alone.

tel•e•mar•ket•ing (tel′ə mär′ki ting) /'tɛləˌmɑrkɪtɪŋ/ *n.* [*noncount*] selling or advertising by telephone. **—tel′e•mar′ket•er,** *n.* [*count*]

te•lem•e•try (tə lem′i trē) /tə'lɛmɪtriy/ *n.* [*noncount*] the automated sending of data from a distant source, esp. from space to a ground station. **—tel•e•met•ric** (tel′ə me′trik) /ˌtɛlə'mɛtrɪk/ *adj.* See -METER-.

te•lep•a•thy (tə lep′ə thē) /tə'lɛpəθiy/ *n.* [*noncount*] communication between minds by some means other than the senses: *In the story the aliens have mental telepathy that enables them to communicate across great distances.* **—tel•e•path•ic** (tel′ə path′ik) /ˌtɛlə'pæθɪk/ *adj.* **—tel′e•path′i•cal•ly,** *adv.* See -PATH-.

tel•e•phone (tel′ə fōn′) /'tɛləˌfown/ *n., v.,* **-phoned, -phon•ing.** **—***n.* **1.** Also called **phone.** a device, system, or process for sending sound or speech to a distant point, esp. by an electric device: [*count*]: *There were no telephones on the highway.* [*noncount; often: by + ~*]: *See if we can reach him by telephone.* See illustration at OFFICE. **—***v.* **2.** to send (a message) by telephone to (someone); phone: [*~ + obj*]: *They telephoned her with the news.* [*~ + obj + obj*]: *They telephoned her the message.* [*~ + that clause*]: *She telephoned that there had been an accident.* [*no obj*]: *They telephoned ahead with the news.* **—tel′e•phon′er,** *n.* [*count*] See -PHON-.

tel′ephone tag′, *n.* [*noncount*] many unsuccessful attempts by two persons to connect with one another by telephone: *We played telephone tag: I left her a message, she returned it when I wasn't there, and when I called back again she had gone.*

tel•e•pho•to (tel′ə fō′tō) /'tɛləˌfowtow/ *adj.* of or relating to camera equipment that can take pictures over long distances: *a telephoto lens.*

tel•e•scope (tel′ə skōp′) /'tɛləˌskowp/ *n., adj., v.,* **-scoped, -scop•ing.** **—***n.* [*count*] **1.** a viewing instrument for making distant objects appear nearer when viewed. **—***adj.* [*before a noun*] **2.** consisting of parts that fit and slide one within another. **—***v.* **3.** to slide or force together (the parts of something), one into another: [*no obj*]: *Her music stand telescoped into a portable, six-inch stick.* [*~ + obj*]: *to telescope the music stand.* **4.** [*~ + obj*] to shorten or condense; compress: *to telescope a speech.* See -SCOPE-.

tel•e•scop•ic (tel′ə skop′ik) /ˌtɛlə'skɒpɪk/ *adj.* **1.** of or relating to a telescope: *a telescopic lens.* **2.** having parts that can be slid or collapsed together: *a telescopic music stand.* See -SCOPE-.

tel•e•thon (tel′ə thon′) /'tɛləˌθɒn/ *n.* [*count*] a television broadcast extended over many hours, usually one designed to raise money for a charity or cause.

Tel•e•type (tel′i tīp′) /'tɛlɪˌtayp/ *Trademark.* a brand of machine that prints messages received from other, similar machines at other locations: [*count*]: *a Teletype.* [*noncount*]: *receiving the news by Teletype.* See -TYPE-.

tel•e•van•ge•list (tel′i van′jə list) /ˌtɛlɪ'vændʒəlɪst/ *n.* [*count*] an evangelist who conducts religious services on television. **—tel′e•van′ge•lism,** *n.* [*noncount*]

tel•e•vise (tel′ə vīz′) /'tɛləˌvayz/ *v.,* **-vised, -vis•ing.** to broadcast by television: [*no obj*]: *They couldn't televise during the hurricane.* [*~ + obj*]: *Which station will televise the World Soccer Cup?* See -VIS-.

tel•e•vi•sion (tel′ə vizh′ən) /'tɛləˌvɪʒən/ *n.* **1.** [*noncount*] the broadcasting of images through radio waves to receivers that project these images on a picture tube: *the powerful influence of television.* **2.** [*count*] Also, **television set.** a device or set for receiving television broadcasts: *He bought a new television.* **3.** [*noncount*] the practice of television broadcasting: *majoring in television and communications.* See -VIS-.

tel•ex (tel′eks) /'tɛlɛks/ *n.* **1.** [*noncount; sometimes: Telex*] a two-way communication service in which machines that can send and receive printed messages are connected through a public telecommunications system: *Telex enables direct communication between subscribers who are at remote locations.* **2.** [*count*] a message transmitted by this system: *I received a telex asking me to send the sales information at once.* **—***v.* **3.** to send (a message) by telex to (someone): [*~ + obj*]: *Telex the sales figures at once to the home company.* [*~ + obj + obj*]: *How about telexing them the sales figures as soon as possible?*

tell (tel) /tɛl/ *v.,* **told** (tōld) /towld/ **tell•ing.** **1.** to narrate (a story, etc.) to (someone): [*~ + obj*]: *He told a story to the children.* [*~ + obj + obj*]: *He told the children a story.* [*no obj*]: *The story tells of the legend of King Arthur.* **2.** to make known (a fact, news, etc.) to (someone); communicate: [*~ + obj + obj*]: *He told us the news of her death.* [*~ + obj + about/of + obj*]: *He told us about her death.* [*~ + obj + (that) clause*]: *He told us that she had died.* **3.** [*~ + obj + obj*] to inform (a person) of something: *He told me his name.* **4.** to utter (the truth, etc.); speak: [*~ + obj (+ to + obj)*]: *He wasn't telling the truth to his wife.* [*~ + obj + obj*]: *He wasn't telling his wife the truth.* **5.** [*~ + obj*] to express (thoughts, feelings, etc.) in words: *to tell one's love.* **6.** to reveal to others by speaking to them about (something private): [*~ + obj + obj*]: *I just told her a secret.* [*~ + obj (+ to + obj)*]: *I told a secret (to my wife).* [*no obj*]: *Will you hate me if I tell?* **7.** [*not: be + ~-ing*] to say or assert positively: [*~ (+ obj) + clause*]: *I can't tell (you) when inflation will come down.* [*no obj*]: *When will inflation come down? I can't tell yet.* **8.** [*not: be + ~-ing*] to be able to see clearly; identify; distinguish; know: [*~ + obj*]: *to tell twins apart.* [*~ + clause*]: *to tell if it is night or day.* [*no obj*]: *Don't ask me how I know; I can just tell.* **9.** to order or command: [*~ + obj + to + verb*]: *Tell her to stop.* [*~ + obj + (that) clause*]: *I told her (that) she should pull the car over and stop.* **10.** [*usually not: be + ~-ing; ~ + obj + clause*] to give evidence of (something) to (someone); indicate: *The light on the dashboard tells you if you're driving too fast.* **11.** [*no obj; (~ + on + obj)*] to produce a strong effect: *The strain of his job began to tell on him.* **12. tell off,** to scold severely: [*~ + obj + off*]: *It was about time somebody told him off.* [*~ + off + obj*]: *He told off the whole class because no one was handing in assignments.* **13. tell on,** [*~ + on + obj*] to tattle on: *Don't tell on your sister.* **—*Idiom.*** **14. all told,** when all have been counted: *All told, seventeen planes were shot down.* **15. tell it like it is,** [*no obj*] *Informal.* to be blunt and tell the whole truth: *Let me tell it like it is: Things are tough and they're going to get tougher.* **16. time will tell,** [*no obj*] in time, the facts will be clearly known: *She may have the makings of an excellent teacher; time will tell.* **—Usage.** See SAY.

tell•er (tel′ər) /'tɛlər/ *n.* [*count*] **1.** one who works in a bank to receive or pay out money over the counter. See illustration at BANK. **2.** one who tells; a narrator.

tell•ing (tel′ing) /'tɛlɪŋ/ *adj.* **1.** having force or effect: *a telling blow.* **2.** revealing: *a telling analysis.* **—tell′ing•ly,** *adv.*

tell•tale (tel′tāl′) /'tɛlˌteyl/ *n.* [*count*] **1.** one who tells secrets; tattler. **2.** a thing serving to indicate something, as a light on an electronic device indicating that it is ready: *The telltales glowed green, meaning the bombs could be dropped.* **—***adj.* [*before a noun*] **3.** revealing something not meant to be known: *a telltale blush.* **4.** giving notice of something.

tel•ly (tel′ē) /'tɛliy/ *n., pl.* **-lies.** *Chiefly Brit.* TELEVISION.

te•mer•i•ty (tə mer′i tē) /tə'mɛrɪtiy/ *n.* [*noncount*] reckless boldness; rashness: *the temerity to speak to her that way.*

temp (temp) /tɛmp/ *n.* [*count*] **1.** a temporary worker, esp. in an office. **—***v.* [*no obj*] **2.** to work in this way: *temping for a detective agency.*

-temp-, *root.* *-temp-* comes from Latin, where it has the meaning "time." This meaning is found in such words as: CONTEMPORARY, CONTRETEMPS, EXTEMPORANEOUS, TEMPO, TEMPORARY, TEMPORIZE.

temp., an abbreviation of: **1.** temperature. **2.** temporary.

tem•per (tem′pər) /'tɛmpər/ *n.* **1.** [*count*] a state of mind or feelings; habit of mind; disposition: *in a bad temper; has a sweet temper.* **2.** [*noncount*] heat of passion, shown in anger, resentment, etc. **3.** [*noncount*] calm disposition; composure: *to lose one's temper.* **4.** [*noncount*] the degree of hardness and strength imparted to a metal. **—***v.* [*~ + obj*] **5.** to moderate; soften or tone down: *to temper justice with mercy.* **6.** to give strength or toughness to (iron) by heating and cooling: *to temper steel.*

tem•per•a•ment (tem′pər ə mənt, -prə mənt) /'tɛmpərəmənt, -prəmənt/ *n.* **1.** nature or frame of mind; natural disposition: [*noncount*]: *differences in temperament between the twins.* [*count*]: *The child has an easygoing temperament.* **2.** [*noncount*] unusual frame of mind, as shown by unusual actions: *a display of temperament.*

tem•per•ance (tem′pər əns, tem′prəns) /'tɛmpərəns, 'tɛmprəns/ *n.* [*noncount*] **1.** self-control; moderation or self-restraint. **2.** the act of never drinking alcoholic liquors.

tem•per•ate (tem′pər it, tem′prit) /'tɛmpərɪt, 'tɛmprɪt/ *adj.* **1.** moderate or self-restrained; not easily losing one's temper. **2.** moderate in behavior, as in the use of alcoholic liquors. **3.** moderate in respect to temperature: *the more temperate mountainous regions of Kenya.* —**tem′per•ate•ly,** *adv.* —**tem′per•ate•ness,** *n.* [*noncount*]

tem•per•a•ture (tem′pər ə chər, -chŏŏr′, -prə-) /'tɛmpərətʃər, -ˌtʃʊr, -prə-/ *n.* **1.** a measure of the warmth of an object with reference to a standard scale: [*count*]: *very cold temperatures this winter.* [*noncount*]: *a sudden change in temperature.* **2.** [*count*] **a.** the degree of heat in a living body, normally about 98.6°F (37°C) in humans: *The nurse took my temperature.* **b.** a fever: *The baby has a temperature.*

tem•pered (tem′pərd) /'tɛmpərd/ *adj.* **1.** having a specified temper or disposition: *a good-tempered child.* **2.** made less intense or violent. **3.** of or relating to iron that has been tempered.

tem•pest (tem′pist) /'tɛmpɪst/ *n.* [*count*] **1.** a violent windstorm. **2.** a violent argument, commotion, or disturbance. —***Idiom.*** **3. tempest in a teacup** or **teapot,** an uproar or great argument over something small, minor, or unimportant.

tem•pes•tu•ous (tem pes′chōō əs) /tɛm'pɛstʃuwəs/ *adj.* **1.** of or relating to tempests: *the tempestuous seas during the hurricane.* **2.** full of argument, anger, commotion, or noise: *a tempestuous meeting.* —**tem•pes′tu•ous•ly,** *adv.* —**tem•pes′tu•ous•ness,** *n.* [*noncount*]

tem•plate or **tem•plet** (tem′plit) /'tɛmplɪt/ *n.* [*count*] **1.** a pattern or mold to help measure or to help in making copies of a thing. **2.** a flat strip, as of cardboard, placed on a computer keyboard to provide ease of reference to software commands.

tem•ple[1] (tem′pəl) /'tɛmpəl/ *n.* [*count*] **1.** a place for the service or worship of a deity. **2.** a synagogue.

tem•ple[2] (tem′pəl) /'tɛmpəl/ *n.* [*count*] **1.** the part of the face on either side of the forehead. **2.** either of the sidepieces of a pair of eyeglasses extending back above the ears.

tem•po (tem′pō) /'tɛmpow/ *n.* [*count*], *pl.* **-pos, -pi** (-pē) /-piy/. **1.** the rate of speed of a musical passage or work. **2.** any normal rate or rhythm: *the fast tempo of city life.* See -TEMP-.

tem•po•ral (tem′pər əl, tem′prəl) /'tɛmpərəl, 'tɛmprəl/ *adj.* **1.** of or relating to time: *temporal measurement of the solar day.* **2.** of or relating to the present life; worldly: *temporal joys.* **3.** of or relating to verb tenses or the expression of time: *a temporal adverb.* —**tem′po•ral•ly,** *adv.* See -TEMP-.

tem•po•rar•y (tem′pə rer′ē) /'tɛmpəˌrɛriy/ *adj., n., pl.* **-rar•ies.** —*adj.* **1.** lasting or effective for a time only; not permanent: *The new bill will create 75,000 temporary jobs.* —*n.* [*count*] **2.** an office worker hired for a short period of time and paid on a daily basis. —**tem•po•rar•i•ly** (tem′pə râr′ə lē) /ˌtɛmpə'rɛərəliy/ *adv.*: *Work with us temporarily and see if you'd like to stay.* —**tem′po•rar′i•ness,** *n.* [*noncount*] See -TEMP-.

tem•po•rize (tem′pə rīz′) /'tɛmpəˌrayz/ *v.,* **-rized, -riz•ing.** to refuse to come to a decision in order to gain time: [*no obj*]: *He temporized until he had more time to think the problem through.* [*used with quotations*]: *"I just don't know," he temporized, "we'll have to wait and see."* —**tem′po•riz′er,** *n.* [*count*] See -TEMP-.

tempt (tempt) /tɛmpt/ *v.* **1.** to attract (someone) to do something, esp. something unwise, wrong, or immoral: [~ + *obj*]: *Satan tempted Jesus in the desert.* [~ + *obj* + *to* + *verb*]: *The devil tempted him to sin.* **2.** to attract, appeal strongly to, or invite: [~ + *obj*]: *The offer tempts me.* [~ + *obj* + *to* + *verb*]: *He's tempted to take a job in the U.S.* **3.** [~ + *obj*] to put to the test in a risky way: *You are tempting fate by making all those arrangements for your new home before you buy it.* —**temp•ta′tion,** *n.* [*count; noncount*]

tem•pu•ra (tem pŏŏr′ə) /tɛm'pʊrə/ *n.* [*noncount*] a Japanese dish of seafood or vegetables dipped in batter and deep-fried.

ten (ten) /tɛn/ *n.* [*count*] **1.** a cardinal number, nine plus one. **2.** a symbol for this number, as 10 or X. **3.** a set of this many persons or things. **4.** a ten-dollar bill. **5.** Also called **ten's place. a.** (in a mixed number) the position of the second digit to the left of the decimal point. **b.** (in a whole number) the position of the second digit from the right. —*adj.* **6.** amounting to ten in number.

-ten-, *root.* *-ten-* comes from Latin, where it has the meaning "hold." This meaning is found in such words as: ABSTINENCE, CONTENT, CONTINENT, COUNTENANCE, IMPERTINENT, INCONTINENT, LIEUTENANT, PERTINENT, RETENTIVE, SUSTENANCE, TENABLE, TENACIOUS, TENANT, UNTENABLE. See -TAIN-.

ten•a•ble (ten′ə bəl) /'tɛnəbəl/ *adj.* capable of being held, maintained, or defended: *a tenable position in the negotiations.* —**ten•a•bil•i•ty** (ten′ə bil′i tē) /ˌtɛnə'bɪlɪtiy/ **ten′a•ble•ness,** *n.* [*noncount*] —**ten′a•bly,** *adv.* See -TEN-.

te•na•cious (tə nā′shəs) /tə'neyʃəs/ *adj.* **1.** holding tightly: *a tenacious grip.* **2.** highly retentive: *a tenacious memory.* **3.** unwilling to give in, weaken, or surrender: *tenacious in spite of all the obstacles in his path.* —**te•na′cious•ly,** *adv.* —**te•na′cious•ness,** *n.* [*noncount*] See -TEN-.

te•nac•i•ty (tə nas′i tē) /tə'næsɪtiy/ *n.* [*noncount*] the quality of being tenacious. See -TEN-.

ten•an•cy (ten′ən sē) /'tɛnənsiy/ *n., pl.* **-cies. 1.** [*noncount*] a holding by a tenant; tenure. **2.** [*count*] the length of time of a tenancy. See -TEN-.

ten•ant (ten′ənt) /'tɛnənt/ *n.* [*count*] **1.** one that rents and occupies land, a house, etc., from another; a lessee: *The landlord was cruel to all his tenants.* **2.** an occupant of any place. —*v.* [~ + *obj*] **3.** to hold or occupy as a tenant; dwell in; inhabit. See -TEN-.

ten′ant farm′er, *n.* [*count*] one who farms the land of another and pays rent with cash or with a portion of what he or she produces.

tend[1] (tend) /tɛnd/ *v.* **1.** [~ + *to* + *verb*] to be likely to do something; to happen often: *Things tend to happen fast in the city.* **2.** (of a person) to be disposed toward an idea, etc.: [~ + *to* + *verb*]: *tends to be optimistic.* [~ + *to/toward* + *obj*]: *Her philosophy tends toward a belief in many gods.* **3.** [*no obj*] to lead in a certain direction, or to some result or condition: *Prices tended downwards during the depression.* **4.** [~ + *to/toward* + *obj*] to have a tendency toward a particular quality: *This wine tends toward the sweet side.* See -TEND-.

tend[2] (tend) /tɛnd/ *v.* to watch over and take care of: [~ + *obj*]: *to tend a fire.* [~ + *to* + *obj*]: *Who will tend to the baby?*

-tend-, *root.* *-tend-* comes from Latin, where it has the meaning "stretch; stretch out; extend; proceed." This meaning is found in such words as: ATTEND, CONTEND, DISTEND, EXTEND, INTEND, PORTEND, PRETEND, SUPERINTEND, TEND, TENDENCY, TENDER, TENDON.

ten•den•cy (ten′dən sē) /'tɛndənsiy/ *n.* [*count*], *pl.* **-cies.** a natural disposition to move or act in some direction or toward some result: *The car has a tendency to slide to the left.* See -TEND-.

ten•den•tious (ten den′shəs) /tɛn'dɛnʃəs/ *adj.* of or relating to a tendency to favor a point of view; biased: *a tendentious novel.* —**ten•den′tious•ly,** *adv.* —**ten•den′tious•ness,** *n.* [*noncount*]

ten•der[1] (ten′dər) /'tɛndər/ *adj.,* **-er, -est,** *v.* —*adj.* **1.** soft or delicate in substance: *a tender steak.* **2.** weak or delicate in constitution: *tender skin that bruises easily.* **3.** [*before a noun*] young or immature: *children of a tender age.* **4.** delicate or gentle: *the tender touch of her hand.* **5.** easily moved to sympathy or compassion; kind: *a tender heart.* **6.** affectionate or sentimental: *gave her a tender glance.* **7.** sharply or painfully sensitive: *a tender bruise on his eye.* **8.** of a delicate nature and requiring careful handling: *The question of his wife working for the company is a tender subject with him.* —**ten′der•ly,** *adv.* : *held the baby tenderly in her arms.* —**ten′der•ness,** *n.* [*noncount*] See -TEND-.

ten•der[2] (ten′dər) /'tɛndər/ *v.* [~ + *obj*] **1.** to present formally for acceptance: *to tender one's resignation.* —*n.* **2.** [*count*] the act of tendering. **3.** [*noncount*] something tendered or offered, esp. money. **4.** [*count*] an offer made in writing by one party to another to perform certain work, etc., at a given cost; a bid. —**ten′der•er,** *n.* [*count*]

tend•er[3] (ten′dər) /'tɛndər/ *n.* [*count*] **1.** one who attends to someone or something. **2.** a ship that attends other ships, as for supplying materials, etc.

ten•der•foot (ten′dər fŏŏt′) /'tɛndərˌfʊt/ *n.* [*count*], *pl.* **-foots, -feet.** an inexperienced person, esp. one not used to hardships.

ten′der-heart′ed, *adj.* soft-hearted; sympathetic. —**ten′der-heart′ed•ly,** *adv.* —**ten′der-heart′ed•ness,** *n.* [*noncount*]

ten•der•ize (ten′də rīz′) /'tɛndəˌrayz/ *v.* [~ + *obj*], **-ized, -iz•ing.** to make (meat) tender, as by pounding or marinating. —**ten′der•iz′er,** *n.* [*count*]

ten•der•loin (ten′dər loin′) /'tɛndərˌlɔyn/ *n.* (in beef or pork) the tender meat of the muscle running through the front of the rump: [*noncount*]: *Tenderloin is expensive.* [*count*]: *She bought a few tenderloins for dinner.*

ten•di•ni•tis or **ten•do•ni•tis** (ten′də nī′tis) /ˌtɛndəˈnaytɪs/ *n.* [*noncount*] inflammation of a tendon. See -TEND-.

ten•don (ten′dən) /ˈtɛndən/ *n.* [*count*] a cord or band of dense, tough, white, fiberlike tissue serving to connect a muscle with a bone or part: *ripped a tendon in his leg.* See -TEND-.

ten•dril (ten′dril) /ˈtɛndrɪl/ *n.* [*count*] **1.** a threadlike stem of climbing plants that twines round another body, so as to support the plant. **2.** something thin and curly like smoke rising upward: *thin tendrils of smoke rising from his pipe.*

ten•e•ment (ten′ə mənt) /ˈtɛnəmənt/ *n.* [*count*] Also called **ten′ement house′.** a run-down and often overcrowded apartment house, esp. in a poor section of a large city.

ten•et (ten′it) /ˈtɛnɪt/ *n.* [*count*] an opinion, principle, etc., held to be true: *If we can't agree on our basic tenets, then it is hard to discuss any further ideas.* See -TEN-.

ten•nis (ten′is) /ˈtɛnɪs/ *n.* [*noncount*] a game played on a rectangular court by players with rackets, in which a ball is driven back and forth over a low net.

ten•or (ten′ər) /ˈtɛnər/ *n.* **1.** [*count*] the course of meaning that runs through something written or spoken; drift: *The tenor of the meeting was one of tenseness.* **2.** [*count*] continuous course or movement: *nothing to disturb the tenor of our lives.* **3. a.** [*noncount*] the adult male voice between the bass and the alto. **b.** [*noncount*] a part sung by or written for such a voice. **c.** [*count*] a singer with such a voice. —*adj.* **4.** of or relating to the range of a tenor. See -TEN-.

ten•pins (ten′pinz′) /ˈtɛnˌpɪnz/ *n.* **1.** [*noncount; used with a singular verb*] a form of bowling, played with ten wooden pins. **2. tenpin,** [*count*] a pin used in this game.

tense[1] (tens) /tɛns/ *adj.,* **tens•er, tens•est,** *v.,* **tensed, tens•ing.** —*adj.* **1.** stretched tight, as a cord, etc.; rigid or stiff: *tense muscles.* **2.** of or relating to a state of nervous strain: *a tense moment.* —*v.* **3.** to make or become tense: [*no obj*]: *Her neck muscles tensed in the sudden cold.* [~ (+ *up*) + *obj*]: *He tensed (up) his muscles when he heard the guard open his cell.* —**tense′ly,** *adv.*: *They sat tensely through the whole movie.* —**tense′ness,** *n.* [*noncount*] See -TEND-.

tense[2] (tens) /tɛns/ *n.* a category of verbs or changes in the forms of verbs that serve chiefly to show or refer to the time of the action or state expressed by the verb; one of the forms of a verb that conveys time: [*count*]: *How many verb tenses are there in English?* [*noncount*]: *how different languages express tense.* See -TEMP-.

ten•sile (ten′səl, -sil, -sīl) /ˈtɛnsəl, -sɪl, -sayl/ *adj.* of or relating to tension: *tensile strain on a wire.* See -TEND-.

ten•sion (ten′shən) /ˈtɛnʃən/ *n.* **1.** [*noncount*] the act of stretching; the state of being stretched: *the tension of her leg muscles as she performed on the balance beam.* **2.** [*noncount*] emotional strain, esp. intense suspense, anxiety, or nervousness: *a lot of tension in his job.* **3.** a strained relationship between individuals, etc.: [*noncount*]: *Tension increased along the border.* [*count*]: *Tensions sprang up between the two nations.* **4.** [*noncount*] electromotive force; electrical power or potential. See -TEND-.

tent (tent) /tɛnt/ *n.* [*count*] **1.** a movable shelter of cloth, etc., held up by poles and held down by stakes in the ground. —*v.* **2.** to (cause to) live or stay in a tent: [*no obj*]: *to tent in the parks of Ontario.* [~ + *obj*]: *to tent the homeless victims of the hurricane.* See -TEND-.

ten•ta•cle (ten′tə kəl) /ˈtɛntəkəl/ *n.* [*count*] a slender, easily bent part like a limb on certain animals that serves as an organ to grab or feel things; a feeler. —**ten′ta•cled,** *adj.*

ten•ta•tive (ten′tə tiv) /ˈtɛntətɪv/ *adj.* **1.** of the nature of an experiment: *reached a tentative agreement and prevented a strike.* **2.** unsure; not definite or positive; hesitant: *a tentative smile.* —**ten′ta•tive•ly,** *adv.* —**ten′ta•tive•ness,** *n.* [*noncount*]

ten•ter•hook (ten′tər ho͝ok′) /ˈtɛntərˌhʊk/ *n.* [*count*] —***Idiom.*** **on tenterhooks,** in a state of suspense or anxiety: *on tenterhooks waiting for the results of the lab test.*

tenth (tenth) /tɛnθ/ *adj.* **1.** next after ninth; being the ordinal number for ten. **2.** being one of ten equal parts. —*n.* [*count*] **3.** a tenth part, esp. of one (1/10). **4.** the tenth member of a series. —*adv.* **5.** in the tenth place; tenthly.

ten•u•ous (ten′yo͞o əs) /ˈtɛnyuwəs/ *adj.* **1.** lacking a sound basis: *a tenuous, unconvincing argument.* **2.** thin or slender in form, as a thread. —**ten′u•ous•ly,** *adv.* —**ten′u•ous•ness,** *n.* [*noncount*]

ten•ure (ten′yər) /ˈtɛnyər/ *n., v.,* **-ured, -ur•ing.** —*n.* **1.** [*noncount*] the holding of anything, as of property, a political job, etc.: *the tenure of an office.* **2.** [*count*] the length of time for holding something: *enjoyed a tenure of only a few months before serious criticism began.* **3.** [*noncount*] a status granted to an employee indicating that the position is permanent: *The professor was awarded tenure.* —*v.* [~ + *obj*] **4.** to give tenure to. See -TEN-.

te•pee (tē′pē) /ˈtiypiy/ *n.* [*count*], *pl.* **-pees.** a tent made from animal skins placed on a conical frame of long poles.

tep•id (tep′id) /ˈtɛpɪd/ *adj.* **1.** moderately warm; lukewarm: *tepid water.* **2.** characterized by a lack of force or enthusiasm: *tepid support from her boss.* —**te•pid•i•ty** (te pid′i tē) /tɛˈpɪdɪtiy/ **tep′id•ness,** *n.* [*noncount*] —**tep′id•ly,** *adv.*

te•qui•la (tə kē′lə) /təˈkiylə/ *n.* [*noncount*] a strong liquor from Mexico, distilled from the agave.

term (tûrm) /tɜrm/ *n.* **1.** [*count*] a word or group of words designating something, esp. in a particular field: *Define the term* atom *as it is used in physics.* **2.** [*count*] the time or period through which something lasts: *a one-year term of office.* **3.** [*count*] a division of a school year, during which instruction is regularly provided: *It's the start of a new term.* **4.** [*noncount*] a set time or date, as at the end of a period of time, for the payment of rent, interest, etc.: *At term you'll be paid a high rate of interest.* **5.** [*noncount*] the completion of pregnancy: *She's now at term; when will labor start?* **6. terms,** [*plural*] **a.** conditions with regard to payment, etc.: *The car dealer promised reasonable terms.* **b.** conditions limiting what is proposed to be done: *The terms of the treaty were clear.* **c.** relations; standing: *She's on good terms with everyone.* **7.** [*count*] each of the numbers in a mathematical expression, formula, etc. —*v.* **8.** to give a particular name to; call: [~ + *obj* + *obj*]: *termed the settlement a breakthrough.* [~ + *obj* + *adjective*]: *termed the agreement "preposterous."* —***Idiom.*** **9. bring (someone) to terms,** to force to agree to certain conditions. **10. come to terms,** to reach an agreement. **11. in terms of,** with regard to; concerning: *In terms of salary, the job is terrible.* **12. in the (short** or) **long term,** in a (short or) long while from the present: *In the short term—say, a few months—interest rates will go up.* See -TERM-.

-term-, *root.* -*term*- comes from Latin, where it has the meaning "end; boundary; limit." This meaning is found in such words as: DETERMINE, EXTERMINATE, INDETERMINATE, INTERMINABLE, PREDETERMINE, TERM, TERMINAL, TERMINATE, TERMINOLOGY, TERMINUS.

ter•ma•gant (tûr′mə gənt) /ˈtɜrməgənt/ *n.* [*count*] **1.** a violent or brawling woman. —*adj.* **2.** violent; brawling; shrewish.

ter•mi•nal (tûr′mə nl) /ˈtɜrmənl̩/ *adj.* **1.** located at or forming the end of something: *a terminal bud of a flower.* **2.** forming the end of a series, succession, etc.; concluding: *the terminal lecture in the series.* **3.** occurring at or causing the end of life: *a terminal disease.* —*n.* [*count*] **4.** a terminal part of a structure. **5. a.** a point at the end of a transportation system, as a railroad line, or any important junction within the system. **b.** the facilities located at a terminal: *The new terminal has a number of good restaurants.* SEE ILLUSTRATION. **6.** any device for entering information into a computer or receiving information from it, as a keyboard with video display unit: *The terminal was hooked up to the mainframe.* **7.** the point where current enters or leaves a part in an electric circuit. —**ter′mi•nal•ly,** *adv.*: *terminally ill patients.* See -TERM-.

ter•mi•nate (tûr′mə nāt′) /ˈtɜrməˌneyt/ *v.,* **-nat•ed, -nat•ing. 1.** to (cause to) come to an end; cease: [~ + *obj*]: *vowed to terminate hostilities.* [*no obj*]: *When will hostilities terminate?* **2.** [~ + *obj*] to dismiss from a job; fire: *He was terminated from the company almost immediately.* **3.** [*no obj*] (of a public conveyance) to end a scheduled run or flight at a certain place: *The boat ride terminates in downtown Prague.* See -TERM-.

ter•mi•nol•o•gy (tûr′mə nol′ə jē) /ˌtɜrməˈnɒlədʒiy/ *n., pl.* **-gies.** the system of naming things or defining terms of a subject: [*noncount*]: *A certain amount of terminology has to be defined before we can talk about computers.* [*count*]: *a terminology that confuses learners.* —**ter•mi•no•log•i•cal** (tûr′mə nl oj′i kəl) /ˌtɜrmənl̩ˈɒdʒɪkəl/ *adj.*: *A*

bus and train terminal

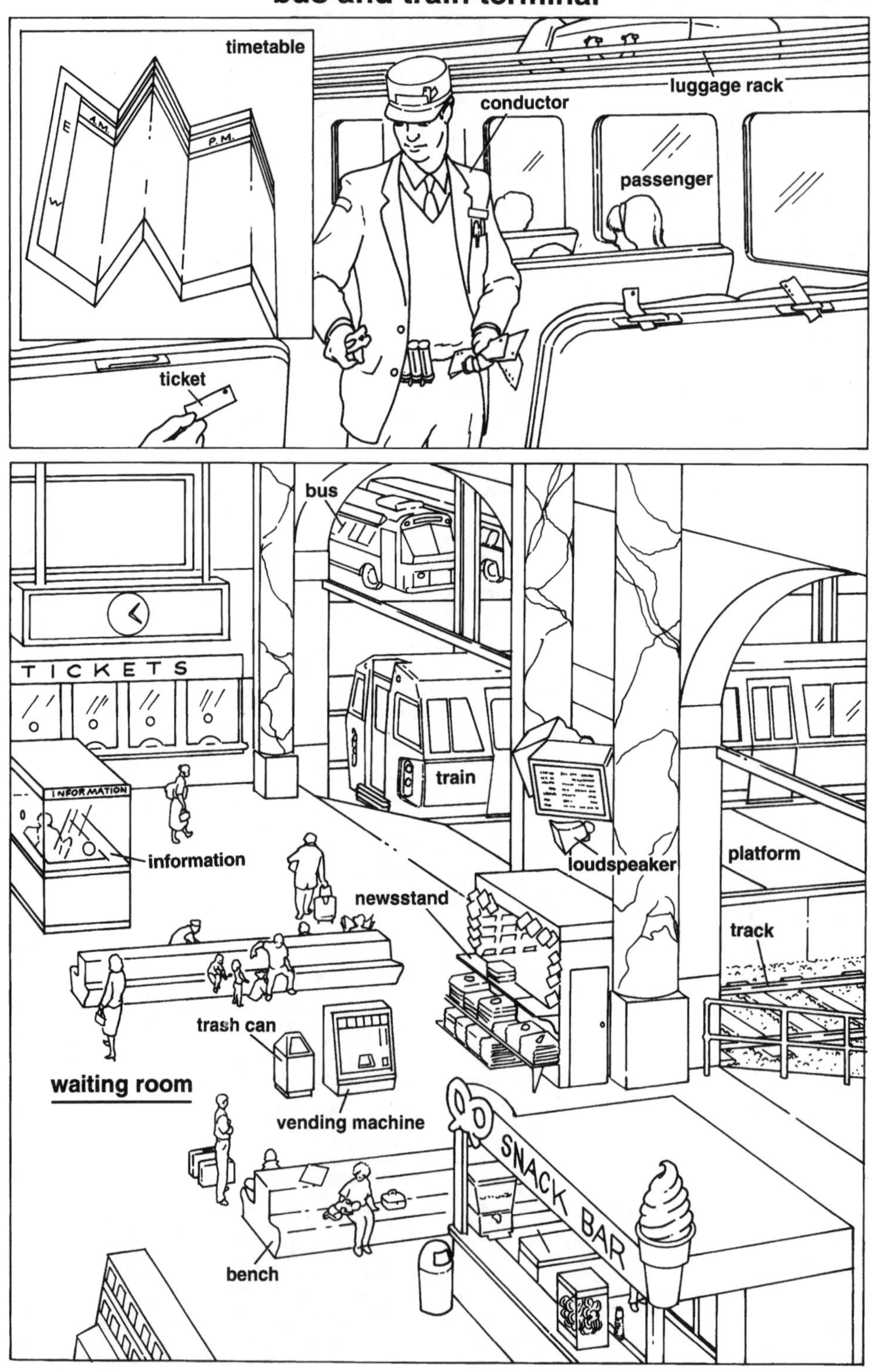

terminological difference led to misunderstanding. **—ter′mi•no•log′i•cal•ly,** *adv.* **—ter′mi•nol′o•gist,** *n.* [*count*] See -TERM-, -LOG-.

ter•mi•nus (tûr′mə nəs) /'tɜrmənəs/ *n. [count]*, pl. **-ni** (-nī′) /-ˌnay/ **-nus•es.** the end of anything, as the end of a railroad line or the station at the end of a railway or bus route. See -TERM-.

ter•mite (tûr′mīt) /'tɜrmayt/ *n.* [*count*] a soft-bodied insect that feeds on wood: *Some termites are highly destructive to buildings.*

tern (tûrn) /tɜrn/ *n.* [*count*] a web-footed water bird resembling a gull.

ter•na•ry (tûr′nə rē) /'tɜrnəriy/ *adj., n., pl.* **-ries.** **—*adj.*** **1.** consisting of or involving three; threefold; triple. **2.** third in order or rank. **—*n.*** [*count*] **3.** a group of three.

-terr-, *root.* -*terr*- comes from Latin, where it has the meaning "earth; land." This meaning is found in such words as: EXTRATERRESTRIAL, SUBTERRANEAN, TERRACE, TERRAIN, TERRARIUM, TERRESTRIAL, TERRIER, TERRITORY.

ter•race (ter′əs) /'tɛrəs/ *n., v.,* **-raced, -rac•ing.** **—*n.*** [*count*] **1.** a raised, level area of land with sharply rising sides made of stone, etc., esp. one of a series of levels rising one above another. **2.** an open area connected to a house and serving as an outdoor living area; patio or balcony. **—*v.*** [~ + *obj*] **3.** to form into a terrace or terraces: *beautifully terraced landscapes.* See -TERR-.

ter•ra cot•ta (ter′ə kot′ə) /'tɛr'ə kɒtə/ *n., pl.* **ter•ra cot•tas.** **1.** [*noncount*] a hard, brownish red clay used for ornaments in buildings and in pottery. **2.** [*count*] something made of terra cotta. See -TERR-.

ter′ra fir′ma (fûr′mə) /'fɜrmə/ *n.* [*noncount*] firm or solid earth; dry land (as opposed to water or air). See -TERR-.

ter•rain (tə rān′) /tə'reyn/ *n.* [*noncount*] a piece of land, esp. with reference to its natural features: *hilly terrain.* See -TERR-.

ter•ra•pin (ter′ə pin) /'tɛrəpɪn/ *n.* [*count*] a North American turtle that lives in fresh or partly salty waters.

ter•rar•i•um (tə râr′ē əm) /tə'rɛəriyəm/ *n.* [*count*], *pl.* **-rar•i•ums, -rar•i•a** (-râr′ē ə) /-'rɛəriyə/. a glass container for growing and displaying plants. See -TERR-.

ter•res•tri•al (tə res′trē əl) /tə'rɛstriyəl/ *adj.* **1.** of or relating to the earth as distinct from other planets: *terrestrial atmosphere.* **2.** of or relating to land as distinct from water: *Most terrestrial creatures have less need to be streamlined than marine creatures.* **—*n.*** [*count*] **3.** an inhabitant of the earth, esp. a human being. See -TERR-.

ter•ri•ble (ter′ə bəl) /'tɛrəbəl/ *adj.* **1.** distressing; severe: *a terrible battle.* **2.** horrible; awful: *We had a terrible time at their party.* **3.** very great: *a terrible responsibility.* **—ter′ri•ble•ness,** *n.* [*noncount*] **—ter′ri•bly,** *adv.*

ter•ri•er (ter′ē ər) /'tɛriyər/ *n.* [*count*] a breed of usually small dogs, used originally to drive wild animals out of their burrow. See -TERR-.

ter•rif•ic (tə rif′ik) /tə'rɪfɪk/ *adj.* **1.** extraordinarily great: *They left with terrific speed.* **2.** extremely good; wonderful: *We had a terrific vacation.* **3.** causing terror; terrifying: *a terrific crashing noise.* **—ter•rif′i•cal•ly,** *adv.*

ter•ri•fied (ter′ə fīd′) /'tɛrəˌfayd/ *adj.* filled with terror; extremely fearful: *The terrified child wouldn't go out in the dark after watching that horror movie.*

ter•ri•fy (ter′ə fī′) /'tɛrəˌfay/ *v.* [~ + *obj*], **-fied, -fy•ing.** to fill with terror: *The horror movie terrified the child.*

ter•ri•fy•ing (ter′ə fī′ing) /'tɛrəˌfayɪŋ/ *adj.* causing or bringing terror: *a terrifying nightmare.* **—ter′ri•fy′ing•ly,** *adv.*: *a terrifyingly real nightmare.*

ter•ri•to•ri•al (ter′i tôr′ē əl, -tōr′-) /ˌtɛrɪ'tɔriyəl, -'towr-/ *adj.* **1.** of or relating to territory or land: *territorial claims.* **2.** of or relating to a particular area. See -TERR-.

ter•ri•to•ry (ter′i tôr′ē, -tōr′ē) /'tɛrɪˌtɔriy, -ˌtowriy/ *n., pl.* **-ries.** **1.** [*noncount*] an area of land, esp. with regard to its geographical features; terrain: *mountainous territory.* **2.** the land and waters belonging to or under the control of a state, etc.: [*noncount*]: *A country's embassy in a foreign country is considered its own territory.* [*count*]: *a few territories that were once its colonies.* **3.** [*count; usually Territory*] **a.** a region of the U.S. not yet a state but having its own legislature and an appointed governor. **b.** a similar district elsewhere, as in Canada. **4.** [*noncount*] a field or area of knowledge, etc.: *This was familiar territory to readers of Tolstoy's novels.* **5.** [*count*] the region assigned (by a company, etc.) to a representative, etc., as for making sales. **6.** the area that an animal defends against intruders, esp. of the same kind: [*noncount*]: *a cat establishing territory as its own.* [*count*]: *Animals intruding on others' territories are quickly chased away.* See -TERR-.

ter•ror (ter′ər) /'tɛrər/ *n.* **1.** [*noncount*] intense, sharp, deep, and overwhelming fear: *filled with terror at the thought of death.* **2.** [*count*] a person or thing that causes such fear: *the terrors of the night.* **3.** [*noncount*] violence or threats to force others to do one's will: *the use of terror to achieve political aims.* **4.** [*count*] *Informal.* an annoying or unpleasant person or thing: *Do we have to take care of the little terrors again tonight?*

ter•ror•ism (ter′ə riz′əm) /'tɛrəˌrɪzəm/ *n.* [*noncount*] the use of violence and threats to frighten and force one's will on another, esp. for political purposes. **—ter′ror•ist,** *n.* [*count*]: *terrorists who were active in the overthrow of the government.* **—*adj.*:** *terrorist activities.*

ter•ror•ize (ter′ə rīz′) /'tɛrəˌrayz/ *v.* [~ + *obj*], **-ized, -iz•ing.** to fill or overcome with terror.

ter•ry (ter′ē) /'tɛriy/ *n.* [*noncount*] **1.** Also called **ter′ry cloth′.** a fabric with uncut loops often used for toweling. **—*adj.*** [*before a noun*] **2.** made of terry: *a terry towel.*

terse (tûrs) /tɜrs/ *adj.,* **ters•er, ters•est.** **1.** short and to the point; brief: *a terse message to head straight for the war zone.* **2.** sharply and impolitely or rudely short; brusque: *Her response was a terse rejection.* **—terse′ly,** *adv.* **—terse′ness,** *n.* [*noncount*] **—Syn.** See CONCISE.

ter•ti•ar•y (tûr′shē er′ē, -shə rē) /'tɜrʃiyˌɛriy, -ʃəriy/ *adj.* of the third order, rank, stage, formation, etc.; third.

test (test) /tɛst/ *n.* [*count*] **1.** a set of problems, questions, etc., for evaluating a person's abilities, skills, or performance: *a driver's test.* **2.** the means by which the quality of anything is determined: *a test of a new product.* **3.** a trial of the quality of something: *to put the new car to the test.* **—*v.*** **4.** to (cause someone to) undergo a test of any kind: [~ + *obj*]: *The school has to test you on your writing ability.* [*no obj*]: *The hospital wants to test for diabetes.* **5.** [*no obj*] to perform on a test: *People test better in a relaxed environment.* See -TEST-.

-test-, *root.* -*test*- comes from Latin, where it has the meaning "witness." This meaning is found in such words as: ATTEST, CONTEST, DETEST, INCONTESTABLE, INTESTATE, PRETEST, PROTEST, PROTESTANT, PROTESTATION, TEST, TESTAMENT, TESTATE, TESTIFY, TESTIMONIAL, TESTIMONY.

tes•ta•ment (tes′tə mənt) /'tɛstəmənt/ *n.* [*count*] **1.** a legal document that specifies how one's personal property shall be given away after one's death; a will. **2.** something that proves the existence of something else; a proof: *a testament to his hard work.* See -TEST-.

tes•tate (tes′tāt) /'tɛsteyt/ *adj.* having made and left a legal and proper will. See -TEST-.

tes•ti•cle (tes′ti kəl) /'tɛstɪkəl/ *n.* [*count*] a testis.

tes•ti•fy (tes′tə fī′) /'tɛstəˌfay/ *v.,* **-fied, -fy•ing.** **1.** to state or declare under oath, usually in court: [*no obj*]: *The witness was afraid to testify.* [~ + (*that*) *clause*]: *testified that she had seen him fleeing from the scene of the crime.* **2.** [~ + *to* + *obj*] to give or provide evidence about something: *This excellent book testifies to the author's ability.* **—tes′ti•fi′er,** *n.* [*count*] See -TEST-.

tes•ti•mo•ni•al (tes′tə mō′nē əl) /ˌtɛstə'mowniyəl/ *n.* [*count*] **1.** a formal written statement about a person's character, conduct, etc.: *a very favorable testimonial praising her excellent work.* **2.** something given or done to express admiration: *gave her a testimonial at her retirement.* **—*adj.*** **3.** relating to or serving as a testimonial: *a testimonial dinner.* See -TEST-.

tes•ti•mo•ny (tes′tə mō′nē) /'tɛstəˌmowniy/ *n., pl.* **-nies.** **1.** [*noncount*] the statement of a witness under oath: *took testimony from the next witness.* **2.** evidence that supports a fact or statement: [*noncount*]: *an improvement that was testimony to the correctness of his decision.* [*count*]: *a testimony to the correctness of his decision.* See -TEST-.

tes•tis (tes′tis) /'tɛstɪs/ *n.* [*count*], *pl.* **-tes** (-tēz) /-tiyz/. the male reproductive gland that produces sperm. See -TEST-.

tes•tos•ter•one (te stos′tə rōn′) /tɛ'stɒstəˌrown/ *n.* [*noncount*] the sex hormone released by the testes that stimulates the development of male sex organs, hair growth, and sperm development.

test′ tube′, *n.* [*count*] a hollow tube of thin glass with one end closed, used to hold chemicals, specimens, etc., in laboratory experiments.

test′-tube′ ba′by, *n.* [*count*] a baby that develops from an egg that has been fertilized outside the mother's body and placed in her womb to grow and be born.

tes•ty (tes′tē) /'tɛstiy/ *adj.,* **-ti•er, -ti•est.** irritable; impatient; touchy: *a testy reply.* **—tes•ti•ly** (tes′tl ē) /'tɛstḷiy/ *adv.* **—tes′ti•ness,** *n.* [*noncount*]

tet•a•nus (tet′n əs) /'tɛtṇəs/ *n.* [*noncount*] a disease in which muscles, esp. of the lower jaw and neck, undergo spasms and then become stiff: *Tetanus sometimes leads to paralysis of the muscles.*

tête-à-tête (tāt′ə tāt′, tet′ə tet′) /'teytə'teyt, 'tɛtə'tɛt/ *n., pl.* **tête-à-têtes,** *adj., adv.* **—***n.* [*count*] **1.** a private conversation between two people. **2.** Also called **vis-à-vis.** a small sofa shaped like an S so that two people can converse face to face. **—***adj.* [*before a noun*] **3.** of, between, or for two people alone. **—***adv.* **4.** (of two persons) together in private: *to sit tête-à-tête.*

teth•er (teth′ər) /'tɛðər/ *n.* [*count*] **1.** a rope, etc., to which an animal is fastened so as to limit its range of movement. **—***v.* [~ + *obj*] **2.** to fasten or confine with or as if with a tether. **—*Idiom.* 3. at the end of one's tether,** at the end of one's resources, patience, or strength: *She's at the end of her tether and explodes with anger every hour.*

tet•ra•cy•cline (te′trə sī′klēn, -klin) /ˌtɛtrə'saykliyn, -klɪn/ *n.* [*noncount*] an antibiotic drug made from a mold.

text (tekst) /tɛkst/ *n.* **1.** [*noncount*] the main body of matter in a manuscript, book, etc., as distinguished from notes, appendixes, illustrations, etc: *Did you look at the pictures or did you actually read the text?* **2.** [*count*] the actual, original words of an author or speaker, as opposed to a translation, etc.: *We could send away for a copy of the text of the interview.* **3.** [*count*] any of the various forms in which a writing exists: *The text is a medieval transcription.* **4.** [*count*] a textbook: *The texts haven't arrived for the class yet.* **5.** [*count*] a short passage of Scripture, esp. one chosen as the subject of a sermon: *He chose as the text for his sermon the Sermon on the Mount.* **—tex•tu•al** (teks′cho͞o əl) /'tɛkstʃuwəl/ *adj.: textual analysis.*

text•book (tekst′bo͝ok′) /'tɛkstˌbʊk/ *n.* [*count*] **1.** a book used by students in a particular branch of study. See illustration at SCHOOL. **—***adj.* [*before a noun*] **2.** characteristic of or suitable for including in a textbook: *a textbook example of administrative incompetence.*

tex•tile (teks′tīl, -til) /'tɛkstayl, -tɪl/ *n.* [*count*] **1.** cloth or goods produced by weaving, knitting, etc. **—***adj.* [*before a noun*] **2.** woven or capable of being woven: *textile fabrics.* **3.** of or relating to textiles: *the textile industry.*

tex•ture (teks′chər) /'tɛkstʃər/ *n.* [*count*] **1.** the physical structure of a material, etc., determined by its size and shape and the arrangement of its parts: *soil of a sandy texture.* **2.** the appearance and feel of a textile fabric: *wool of a coarse texture.* **3.** the appearance of a work of art, determined by the materials used, paint applied, etc. **4.** the quality present in something by the relation of its parts or elements: *the texture of that Beethoven sonata.* —**tex′tur•al,** *adj.*

-th, *suffix. -th* is attached to words that refer to numbers to form adjectives referring to the number mentioned: *(four + -th →) fourth; tenth.*

Thai (tī) /tay/ *n.* **1.** [*count*] a person born or living in Thailand. **2.** [*noncount*] the language spoken in Thailand. **—***adj.* **3.** of or relating to Thailand. **4.** of or relating to the language spoken in Thailand.

thal•a•mus (thal′ə məs) /'θæləməs/ *n.* [*count*], *pl.* **-mi** (-mī′) /-ˌmay/. the middle part of the brain, serving to transmit and bring together messages from the senses.

than (than, then; *unstressed* thən, ən) /ðæn, ðɛn; *unstressed* ðən, ən/ *conj.* **1.** (used after comparative adjectives and adverbs and certain other words, such as *other, more,* etc., to introduce the second part of a comparison): *an increase of more than fifty dollars a week; She's taller than I am. The rabbit runs faster than the turtle.* **2.** (used after some adverbs and adjectives that express choices or differences, such as *other, otherwise, else, anywhere, different,* etc., in order to introduce a choice (including a rejected choice) or to name or show a difference in kind, place, style, identity, etc.): *We had no choice other than to return home. I'd rather walk there than drive.*

thank (thangk) /θæŋk/ *v.* [~ + *obj*] **1.** to express gratitude to (someone): *We thanked him for his generosity.* **2.** to hold responsible; blame: *We have him to thank for this lawsuit.* **—***n.* [*plural*] **3. thanks,** an expression of a grateful feeling for a kindness, etc.: *Let us give thanks for this meal.* **—***interj.* **4. thanks,** (used as a way of saying "I thank you.") **—*Idiom.* 5. Thank God** or **thank goodness,** (used to express relief or gratitude that something is or comes out well or better than expected, or that harm or danger is avoided): *Thank God we have our health.* **6. thanks to,** because of; owing to; due to (sometimes used ironically): *We were late thanks to the bad weather.* **7. thank you,** (used as a common expression of gratitude or appreciation, as for a gift or favor): *She gave him a gift and he said, "Thank you."*

thank•ful (thangk′fəl) /'θæŋkfəl/ *adj.* feeling or showing thanks: *She was thankful for her job.* **—thank′ful•ly,** *adv.* **—thank′ful•ness,** *n.* [*noncount*]

thank•less (thangk′lis) /'θæŋklɪs/ *adj.* **1.** not likely to be appreciated or rewarded: *a thankless job.* **2.** not feeling or expressing gratitude; ungrateful: *a thankless child.* **—thank′less•ly,** *adv.* **—thank′less ness,** *n.* [*noncount*]

thanks•giv•ing (thangks′giv′ing) /ˌθæŋks'gɪvɪŋ/ *n.* **1.** [*noncount*] the act of giving thanks. **2.** [*count*] an expression of thanks, esp. to God. **3.** [*proper noun; Thanksgiving*] a public celebration for giving thanks, esp. a holiday in the United States and Canada.

that (that; *unstressed* thət) /ðæt; *unstressed* ðət/ *pron.* and *adj., pl.* **those;** *adv.; conj.* **—***pron.* **1.** (used to refer to a person or thing pointed out or present, mentioned before, or supposed to be understood by the speaker and the listener, or to give emphasis): *That is her mother (= the woman we have just pointed to or spoken about). After that we never saw each other (= after some event we have just described,...). That's the man—with the plaid coat! (= the man you were just asking me if I'd seen).* **2.** (used to indicate one of several people or things already mentioned and to refer to the one that is farther away or more distant or remote in place, time, or thought; opposed to *this*): *This is my sister and that's my cousin (= The one next to me or near me is my sister, and the one farther away is my cousin). Here, I'll take this and you take that (= I'll take the one near me, and you take the one near you or the one farther away from both of us).* **3.** (used to indicate one of several people or things already mentioned and to imply or suggest that there is a contrast between the two; opposed to *this*): *This suit fits me better than that.* **4.** (used to introduce a relative clause, a clause that defines or says something to pinpoint the person or thing referred to): *We saw the house that collapsed.* **5.** (used in conversation to add or connect something to some idea or statement previously made, so as to give more information about it): *"I'd like to see you again tomorrow night."—"That would be fine."* **—***adj.* **6.** (used before a noun to indicate a person, place, thing, or degree as indicated, mentioned before, present, well-known, or characteristic: *That woman is her mother (= the one we were talking about).* **7.** (used before one noun from a group to indicate the one farther away or more distant or removed in time, place, or thought from the other or others already mentioned; opposed to *this*): *This room is his and that one is mine (= The one near us or near me is his, and the one near you or farther away from both of us is mine).* **8.** (used before a noun to indicate one of several people or things already mentioned and to imply that there is a contrast between the two; opposed to *this*): *not this house, but that one.* **—***adv.* **9.** (used with adjectives and adverbs of quantity or amount) to the extent or degree indicated; so; as much as: *Don't take that much (= Don't take as much as you have taken, or as much as my hand indicates or points to).* **10.** to a great extent or degree: *I guess it's not that important.* **—***conj.* **11.** (used to introduce a subordinate clause that functions as the subject or object of the principal verb, introducing a necessary addition to a statement made, or introducing a clause that expresses cause, reason, purpose, aim, etc.: *I'm sure that you'll like it. I believe that God exists.* **12.** (used to introduce an exclamation expressing strong feeling when another word, as a verb, has been left out): *Oh, that I had never been born! (= Oh, I wish that I had never been born).* **—*Idiom.* 13. at that,** in addition; besides: *It was a long wait, and an exasperating one at that.* **14. that is,** to be more accurate: *I read the book; that is, I read most of it.* **15. that's that,** *Informal.* there is no more to be said or done: *I'm not going, and that's that!* **16. with that,** following that; thereupon: *She said, "I quit!," and with that she left.*

thatch (thach) /θætʃ/ *n.* [*noncount*] **1.** Also, **thatch′ing.** a material, as straw, used to cover roofs. **2.** a covering made of such a material. **—***v.* [~ + *obj*] **3.** to cover with or as if with thatch. **—thatched,** *adj.: a thatched roof.*

thaw (thô) /θɔ/ *v.* **1.** [*no obj*] to change from a frozen to a liquid state; melt: [*no obj*]: *The meat thawed.* [~ + *obj*]: *Use the microwave to thaw the meat.* **2.** [*no obj; (~ + out)*] to get relief from the cold: *Sit by the fire and thaw out.* **3.** [*no obj*] (of the weather) to become warm enough to melt ice and snow. **4.** to (cause to) become less hostile or aloof; to (cause to) become more friendly: [*no obj*]: *Relations between the two countries thawed.* [~ + *obj*]: *The glasses of vodka thawed the hostility be-*

tween the two sides. **—*n.*** [*count*] **5.** the act or process of thawing. **6.** a reduction or easing in tension or hostility. **7.** (in winter) weather warm enough to melt ice and snow.

the[1] (*stressed* thē; *unstressed before a consonant* thə, *unstressed before a vowel* thē) /*stressed* ðiy; *unstressed before a consonant* ðə, *unstressed before a vowel* ðiy/ *definite article.* **1.** (used before a noun or something functioning as a noun, when the noun is known to the speaker and to the listener, or when it is about to be made known by having a clause that specifies it or makes it definite): *Please close the window (= There is a window in the room that you and I both know about, and it is open). Here is the book you gave me (= Here is a book, and now you know which one I mean). Come on into the house for a drink (= We are standing near a house and we both know which house I am referring to.) She got a new computer and a printer. The printer is great, but the computer doesn't work (= After introducing a computer and printer, the speaker then refers to them with* the *because now they are both known to or established in the mind of the listener).* **2.** (used before certain place names, some of which end in *-s* where the *-s* marks a plural); or where the place name is short for a longer name; and before certain others that are well known or unique): *the Alps; the Mississippi (= short for the Mississippi River); the Bronx (= a borough of New York City).* **3.** (used before certain nouns thought of as unique and well known to the speaker and the listener): *The sun (moon) went behind a cloud (= There is only one sun or moon). How is the weather today?* **4.** (used with or as part of a title): *the Duke of Wellington.* **5.** (used to mark a noun as the best known, most approved, etc., of its kind): *Butternut Mountain was considered* the *place to ski.* **6.** (used before a count noun to mark the noun in a generic meaning, to include all such examples of it): *The dog is a four-legged animal (= All dogs are four-legged). The tiger is a ferocious animal (= All tigers are ferocious).* **7.** (used in place of a possessive pronoun, to note a part of the body or a personal belonging): *He was shot in the arm.* **8.** (used before nouns referring to musical instruments, even when speaking about them generally): *She plays the violin. He plays the piano.* **9.** (used before certain adjectives to stand for a class or number of individuals, or for an abstract idea: *to visit the sick (= to visit sick people), from the sublime to the ridiculous (= from a situation or things that are sublime to a situation or things that are ridiculous). The poor need our help (= Poor people need our help).* **10.** (used to indicate a decade of a lifetime or of a century): *the sixties.* **11.** enough: *She didn't have the courage to leave.*

the[2] (*before a consonant* thə; *before a vowel* thē), *adv.* **1.** (used to modify an adjective or adverb that means or has the meaning "more") on that account or in some or any degree: *He's been on vacation and looks the better for it.* **2.** (used before an adjective or adverb that means or has the meaning "most"): *She is the tallest girl in her class.*

the•a•ter or **thea•tre** (thē′ə tər, thēᵊ′-) /ˈθiyətər, ˈθiyᵊ-/ *n.* **1.** [*count*] a building or an outdoor area for plays or motion-picture shows. **2.** [*count*] a room with rows of seats, used for lectures, etc. **3.** [*noncount*] **a. the theater,** drama as a branch of art, esp. as a profession. **b.** a particular type, style, or category of this art: *Elizabethan theater.* **4.** [*noncount*] the quality of dramatic performance: *The play is good theater.* **5.** [*count*] an area of activity, esp. where military operations are under way: *the Pacific theater.*

the•at•ri•cal (thē a′tri kəl) /θiyˈætrɪkəl/ *adj.* Also, **the•at′ric. 1.** of or relating to the theater. **2.** suggestive of the theater and therefore not real; artificial; showy: *theatrical temper tantrums.* —**the•at′ri•cal•ly,** *adv.*: *"They're all out to get me!" he exclaimed theatrically.*

thee (thē) /ðiy/ *pron.* the form of THOU, or YOU, used as an object of a verb or of a preposition: *With this ring, I thee wed.*

theft (theft) /θɛft/ *n.* **1.** [*noncount*] the act of stealing; larceny. **2.** [*count*] an instance of this.

their (thâr; *unstressed* thər) /ðɛər; *unstressed* ðər/ *pron.* **1.** (used before a noun to indicate that the noun is possessed by, owned by, or related in some way to a word that can be replaced by THEY) of them; of the people or things mentioned: *their home (= the home owned by them); their rights as citizens (= the rights they have as citizens).* **2.** (used after an indefinite word that refers to a singular noun, like *someone, anyone, a person,* when the gender of the person is not known or referred to; sometimes used instead of *his or her*): *Someone left their book on the table. Can't anyone do their homework by themselves?* Compare THEIRS.

theirs (thârz) /ðɛərz/ *pron.* **1.** (used after the verb *be* to indicate that the subject is possessed by, owned by, or related in some way to someone known or mentioned): *Are you a friend of theirs? That car is theirs.* **2.** (used to mean that the thing referred to belongs to them (some people already mentioned or understood): *Theirs is the white house on the corner.*

the•ism (thē′iz əm) /ˈθiyɪzəm/ *n.* [*noncount*] **1.** belief in one God. **2.** belief in the existence of a god or gods. —**the′ist,** *n.* [*count*], *adj.* —**the•is′tic,** *adj.* See -THEO-.

them (them; *unstressed* thəm, əm) /ðɛm; *unstressed* ðəm, əm/ *pron.* **1.** the form of the pronoun THEY used as a direct or indirect object of a verb, or as the object of a preposition: *We saw them yesterday. I gave them the books. I ran toward them.* **2.** *Informal.* (sometimes used instead of the pronoun *they* after the verb *to be*): *It's them, across the street. It isn't them.* **3.** (used instead of the pronoun *their* before a verbal noun ending in *-ing,* a GERUND, or before a verbal adjective ending in *-ing,* a present participle): *The boys' parents objected to them hiking without supervision.* **—*adj.*** [*before a noun*]

theme (thēm) /θiym/ *n.* [*count*] **1.** a subject of a talk, a thought, or a piece of writing; topic: *He returned to the theme of American values.* **2.** a unifying idea, or the most obvious point, as in a work of art, etc. **3.** a short, informal essay, esp. a school composition. —**the•mat•ic** (thi mat′ik) /θɪˈmætɪk/ *adj.* —**the•mat′i•cal•ly,** *adv.*

theme′ song, *n.* [*count*] a song played at the beginning or end of a radio or TV show or a movie or that comes to be associated with it.

them•selves (thəm selvz′, them′-) /ðəmˈsɛlvz, ˌðɛm-/ *pron.* [*plural*] **1.** the reflexive form of the pronoun THEY, used when the object of a verb or preposition names the same noun as the subject: *The boys washed themselves quickly.* **2.** (used to emphasize a plural noun): *The authors themselves left the theater.* **3.** (used after a word like *no one, everyone, anyone, a person,* etc., to refer back to this word; it is used instead of the form *himself* or *herself*): *People who ignore the law cannot call themselves good citizens.* **4.** their normal or customary selves: *After a few hours' rest, they were themselves again.*

then (then) /ðɛn/ *adv.* **1.** at that time: *Prices were lower then.* **2.** immediately or soon afterward: *The rain stopped and then started again.* **3.** next in order of time or place: *We ate, then we started home.* **4.** in that case; as a consequence; in those circumstances: *If you want to quit, then do so.* **5.** since that is so; as a consequence; therefore: *If the car is out of gas, then it won't start.* **—*adj.*** [*before a noun*] **6.** existing or being at the time indicated: *In 1967, the then prime minister was indicted in a scandal.* **—*n.*** [*noncount*] **7.** that time: *We haven't been back since then.* **—*Idiom.*** **8. but then,** but on the other hand; however: *He got turned down for a promotion, but then he never expected to get it.* **9. then and there,** at that precise time and place; at once: *would have declared war then and there, but his cabinet forced him to reconsider.*

thence (thens) /ðɛns/ *adv.* from that place: *I went to Paris and thence to Rome.*

thence•forth (thens′fôrth′, -fôrth′, thens′fôrth′, -fôrth′) /ˌðɛnsˈfɔrθ, -ˈfowrθ, ˈðɛnsˌfɔrθ, -ˌfowrθ/ *adv.* from that time onward.

-theo-, *root.* *-theo-* comes from Greek, where it has the meaning "God; god." This meaning is found in such words as: ATHEISM, ATHEIST, MONOTHEISM, PANTHEON, POLYTHEISM, THEOCRACY, THEOLOGY, THEOSOPHY.

the•oc•ra•cy (thē ok′rə sē) /θiyˈɒkrəsiy/ *n., pl.* **-cies. 1.** [*noncount*] a form of government in which a deity is the supreme ruler. **2.** [*noncount*] a system of government by priests. **3.** [*count*] a state under such a government. —**the•o•crat•ic** (thē ə krat′ik) /θiyəˈkrætɪk/ *adj.* —**the′o•crat′i•cal•ly,** *adv.* See -THEO-.

the•o•lo•gian (thē′ə lō′jən, -jē ən) /ˌθiyəˈlowdʒən, -dʒiyən/ *n.* [*count*] a person studying theology.

the•ol•o•gy (thē ol′ə jē) /θiyˈɒlədʒiy/ *n., pl.* **-gies. 1.** [*noncount*] the study of divine things or of religious truth; the study of God (or gods). **2.** [*count*] a particular form or branch of this study. —**the•o•log•i•cal** (thē′ə loj′i kəl) /ˌθiyəˈlɒdʒɪkəl/ *adj.* See -THEO-.

the•o•rem (thē′ər əm, thēr′əm) /ˈθiyərəm, ˈθɪərəm/ *n.* [*count*] *Math.* a statement that can be shown to be true from or on the basis of other statements.

the•o•ret•i•cal (thē′ə ret′i kəl) /ˌθiyəˈrɛtɪkəl/ also **the′-o•ret′ic,** *adj.* **1.** of or relating to theory; working only with theory and not with practical affairs: *She was interested in theoretical physics and not applied physics.* **2.** existing only in theory; hypothetical: *a theoretical possibility.* —**the′o•ret′i•cal•ly,** *adv.*: *Theoretically the two sides are no longer enemies because of the peace treaty.*

the•o•rize (thē′ə rīz′, thēr′īz) /ˈθiyəˌrayz, ˈθɪərayz/ *v.*, **-rized, -riz•ing.** to form a theory or theories: [*no obj*]: *You're just theorizing about how verbs work in Latin.* [~ + *that clause*]: *Einstein theorized that as objects approached the speed of light they would shrink.* —**the•o•re•ti•cian** (thē′ər ə tish′ən, thēr′ə-) /ˌθiyərəˈtɪʃən, ˈθɪərə-/ **the′o•rist,** *n.* [*count*] —**the′o•riz′er,** *n.* [*count*]

the•o•ry (thē′ə rē, thēr′ē) /ˈθiyəriy, ˈθɪəriy/ *n., pl.* **-ries. 1.** [*count*] *Science.* a group or collection of general statements that together as principles explain some fact or group of facts: *Darwin's theory of evolution; quantum theory in physics.* **2.** [*noncount*] a body or collection of mathematical principles belonging to one subject: *the study of number theory.* **3.** [*noncount*] the branch of a science or art that deals with its principles or methods, as distinguished from its practice: *He took courses in music theory.* **4.** [*count*] an explanation for some fact or behavior claimed to be true but not yet proven: *He has a theory about why so many students have trouble with the word* the *in English.* —***Idiom.* 5. in theory,** under ideal conditions; theoretically: *In theory everyone has certain equal rights.*

the•os•o•phy (thē os′ə fē) /θiyˈɒsəfiy/ *n.* [*noncount*] a form of philosophical or religious thought based on a mystical view of divine nature. See -THEO-, -SOPH-.

ther•a•peu•tic (ther′ə pyōō′tik) /ˌθɛrəˈpyuwtɪk/ *adj.* Also, **ther′a•peu′ti•cal. 1.** of or relating to therapy: *a therapeutic drug.* **2.** serving to maintain or restore health: *a therapeutic abortion.* **3.** having a good effect on one's mental state, esp. in serving to relax or calm: *Playing with the kids was therapeutic after a hard day at the office.* —**ther′a•peu′ti•cal•ly,** *adv.*

ther•a•pist (ther′ə pist) /ˈθɛrəpɪst/ *n.* [*count*] **1.** a person trained to provide therapy: *a physical therapist; a speech therapist.* **2.** PSYCHOTHERAPIST.

ther•a•py (ther′ə pē) /ˈθɛrəpiy/ *n., pl.* **-pies. 1.** [*noncount*] the treatment of disease, injury, or disability by physical methods, as exercise or massage, without the use of drugs or surgery: *physical therapy; speech therapy.* **2.** [*noncount*] PSYCHOTHERAPY. **3.** [*count*] any act, task, etc., that relieves tension.

there (thâr; *unstressed* thər) /ðɛər; *unstressed* ðər/ *adv.* **1.** in or at that place (opposed to *here*): *She is there now. We lived there (= in some place just mentioned or otherwise understood) for about a year.* **2.** at that point in an action, speech, etc.: *He stopped there for applause.* **3.** in that particular matter or instance: *Your anger was justified there.* **4.** into or to that place; thither: *We went there last year.* **5.** (used, with some stress, to call attention to something or someone): *There they go. There's the man I saw.* —*pron.* **6.** (used in place of a subject, and followed by the verb *be* and some other verbs to indicate that something exists): *There are still some funds available for research. There are two big windows in this classroom. There appears to be something wrong.* **7.** (used in place of a name to address or greet a person): *Hello, there.* —*n.* [*noncount*] **8.** that place or point: *I come from there, too.* —*adj.* **9.** (used for emphasis, esp. after a noun modified by a demonstrative adjective): *Ask that man there.* —*interj.* **10.** (used to express satisfaction, relief, etc.): *There! It's done (= I'm glad it's done). There, there, don't cry (= I'm sorry you feel bad). There you go (= Well done!).* — **Usage.** When *there* is used as the subject (as in definition 6), the person or thing that exists is usually not definite and comes after the verb, while the verb (such as *be*) agrees with that person or thing. In such sentences, the word *there* carries very little stress and more attention is paid to what comes after it.

there•a•bout (thâr′ə bout′) /ˈðɛərəˌbawt/ also **there′a•bouts′,** *adv.* **1.** about or near that place or time: *last June or thereabout.* **2.** about that number, amount, etc.: *a dozen or thereabout.*

there•af•ter (thâr′af′tər, -äf′-) /ˌðɛərˈæftər, -ˈɑf-/ *adv.* after that in time or sequence; afterward; subsequently.

there•by (thâr′bī′, thâr′bī′) /ˌðɛərˈbay, ˈðɛərˌbay/ *adv.* **1.** by that; by means of that: *started his lawn mower at dawn, thereby enraging the whole neighborhood.* **2.** in that connection or relation: *Thereby hangs a tale.*

there•fore (thâr′fôr′, -fōr′) /ˈðɛərˌfɔr, -ˌfowr/ *adv.* as a result; for that reason; consequently: *The new computer has more memory and is therefore faster than the old one.*

there•in (thâr′in′) /ˌðɛərˈɪn/ *adv.* **1.** in or into that place or thing. **2.** in that matter, etc.; in regard to that thing: *He couldn't focus on one job, and therein lay the problem.*

there•of (thâr′uv′, -ov′) /ˌðɛərˈʌv, -ˈɒv/ *adv.* **1.** of that or it. **2.** from or out of that origin or cause.

there•to•fore (thâr′tə fôr′, -fōr′) /ˌðɛərtəˈfɔr, -ˈfowr/ *adv.* before or until that time.

there•up•on (thâr′ə pon′, -pôn′, thâr′ə pon′, -pôn′) /ˈðɛərəˌpɒn, -ˌpɔn, ˌðɛərəˈpɒn, -ˈpɔn/ *adv.* **1.** immediately following that. **2.** in consequence of that.

-therm-, *root.* -*therm-* comes from Greek, where it has the meaning "heat." This meaning is found in such words as: HYPOTHERMIA, THERMAL, THERMODYNAMICS, THERMOMETER, THERMOSTAT.

ther•mal (thûr′məl) /ˈθɜrməl/ *adj.* **1.** Also, **thermic.** of, relating to, or caused by heat or temperature: *thermal energy.* **2.** of or relating to hot or warm springs: *thermal waters.* **3.** designed to help retain body heat: *thermal underwear.* —*n.* [*count*] **4.** a rising air current caused by heating from the surface. **5. thermals,** [*plural*] clothing, esp. underwear, designed to help retain body heat. —**ther′mal•ly,** *adv.* See -THERM-.

ther•mo•dy•nam•ics (thûr′mō dī nam′iks) /ˌθɜrmowdayˈnæmɪks/ *n.* [*noncount; used with a singular verb*] the science concerned with the relations between heat and mechanical energy or work, and the conversion of one into the other. —**ther′mo•dy•nam′ic,** *adj.* See -THERM-.

ther•mom•e•ter (thər mom′i tər) /θərˈmɒmɪtər/ *n.* [*count*] an instrument for measuring temperature. See -THERM-, -METER-.

ther•mos (thûr′məs) /ˈθɜrməs/ *n.* [*count*] an insulated container, used for keeping liquids hot or cold. Also called **ther′mos bot′tle.** See -THERM-.

ther•mo•stat (thûr′mə stat′) /ˈθɜrməˌstæt/ *n.* [*count*] a device that measures temperature and automatically turns on or off a heating or cooling device: *The thermostat in the furnace didn't work properly.* —**ther′mo•stat′ic,** *adj.* —**ther′mo•stat′i•cal•ly,** *adv.* See -STAT-,-THERM-.

-thes-, *root.* -*thes-* comes from Greek, where it has the meaning "put together; set down." This meaning is found in such words as: ANTITHESIS, HYPOTHESIS, PARENTHESIS, PHOTOSYNTHESIS, PROSTHESIS, SYNTHESIS, SYNTHETIC, THESIS.

the•sau•rus (thi sôr′əs) /θɪˈsɔrəs/ *n.* [*count*], *pl.* **-sau•rus•es, -sau•ri** (-sôr′ī) /-ˈsɔray/. a dictionary listing words that are similar in meaning and words that are opposite in meaning.

these (thēz) /ðiyz/ *pron., adj.* pl. of THIS.

the•sis (thē′sis) /ˈθiysɪs/ *n.* [*count*], *pl.* **-ses** (-sēz) /-siyz/. **1.** a statement for consideration, esp. one to be argued for or against: *The candidate's thesis was that big government spent too much money wastefully.* **2.** a subject for a composition or essay: *Your essay needs a clear thesis.* **3.** a formal paper reflecting original research on a subject, esp. one presented by a candidate for an advanced degree, as a master's degree. See -THES-.

thes•pi•an (thes′pē ən) /ˈθɛspiyən/ *adj.* **1.** of or relating to acting or drama: *We have need of your thespian talents.* —*n.* [*count*] **2.** an actor or actress.

they (thā) /ðey/ *pron. pl., poss.* **their** or **theirs,** *obj.* **them. 1.** (used when the speaker and the listener know the people or things the speaker is referring to) the plural of HE, SHE, and IT: *Do you see those two girls? They're staring at us.* **2.** (used to refer to people in general): *They say he's rich. It's what they call carpal tunnel syndrome: pain from typing at the computer all day.* **3.** (used after a word or phrase like *anyone, someone, a person,* or *whoever* to refer back to that singular person without mentioning the sex of the person, in place of *he* or *she*): *Whoever is of voting age, whether they are interested in politics or not, should vote. Anyone who says they're not afraid of dying is lying.*

they'd (thād) /ðeyd/ *contraction.* **1.** a shortened form of *they would*: *They'd like to see you now.* **2.** a shortened form of *they had*: *They'd gone before we got there.*

they'll (thāl) /ðeyl/ *contraction.* a shortened form of *they will*: *They'll probably be late because of the snow.*

they've (thāv) /ðeyv/ *contraction.* a shortened form of *they have*: *They've already left. They've already been here.*

thick (thik) /θɪk/ *adj.* and *adv.,* **-er, -est,** *n.* —*adj.* **1.** having a great distance from one surface to the opposite; not thin: *a thick slice of bread.* **2.** [*after a noun or phrase of measurement*] measured between opposite surfaces: *a board one inch thick.* **3.** made up of objects close together; dense: difficult to see through: *The planes* *couldn't land in the thick fog.* **4.** [*be* + ~ + *with*] filled or covered: *The air was thick with tobacco smoke.* **5.** not clearly pronounced or articulated: *thick speech.* **6.** easy to notice; obvious: *I have a thick Russian accent when I speak English.* **7.** deep or profound: *thick darkness.* **8.** intimate; close (in friendship): *thick friends.* **9.** heavy; not easily poured: *thick soup.* **10.** mentally slow; stupid: *Sometimes he can be a little thick.* **—*adv.*** **11.** in a thick manner. **12.** close together: *vines growing thick.* **13.** so as to produce something thick: *The cheese was sliced thick.* **—*n.*** [*noncount*] **14.** the densest or most crowded part: *in the thick of the fight.* **—*Idiom.*** **15. thick as thieves,** close in friendship; very friendly. **16. through thick and thin,** under both favorable and unfavorable conditions; faithfully: *They stayed friends through thick and thin.* —**thick′ly,** *adv.* —**thick′ness,** *n.* [*noncount*]

thick•en (thik′ən) /ˈθɪkən/ *v.* **1.** to (cause to) become thick or thicker: [*no obj*]: *When the soup thickens, shut off the heat.* [~ + *obj*]: *Thicken the soup by adding flour to it.* **2.** [*no obj*] to become more complicated or confusing: *The plot thickens now.* —**thick′en•er,** *n.* [*count*] —**thick′en•ing,** *n.* [*noncount*]

thick•et (thik′it) /ˈθɪkɪt/ *n.* [*count*] a dense growth of shrubs, bushes, or small trees.

thick•set (thik′set′) /ˈθɪkˈsɛt/ *adj.* **1.** heavily or solidly built; stocky: *a thickset wrestler.* **2.** set in close arrangement; dense: *a thickset hedge.*

thick′-skinned′, *adj.* **1.** having a thick skin. **2.** not easily offended or irritated by criticism.

thief (thēf) /θiyf/ *n.* [*count*], *pl.* **thieves** (thēvz) /θiyvz/ one who steals, esp. secretly.

thieve (thēv) /θiyv/ *v.* [*no obj*], **thieved, thiev•ing.** to steal. —**thiev′ing,** *adj.* [*before a noun*]: *those thieving car dealers!* —**thiev′ish,** *adj.*

thiev•er•y (thē′və rē) /ˈθiyvəriy/ *n.* [*noncount*] the act or practice of stealing; theft.

thigh (thī) /θay/ *n.* [*count*] **1.** the part of the lower limb in humans between the hip and the knee. **2.** the corresponding part of the hind limb of other animals.

thim•ble (thim′bəl) /ˈθɪmbəl/ *n.* [*count*] a cap worn over the fingertip to protect it when pushing a needle through cloth. —**thim′ble•ful′,** *n.* [*count*], *pl.* **-fuls.**

thin (thin) /θɪn/ *adj.,* **thin•ner, thin•nest,** *adv., v.,* **thinned, thin•ning.** **—*adj.*** **1.** having a small distance from one surface to the opposite; not thick: *thin ice.* **2.** of small cross section in comparison with the length: *a thin wire.* **3.** having little flesh; lean; not fat: *had become thin after her stay in the hospital.* **4.** widely separated or scattered; sparse: *thin vegetation; hair getting thin on top.* **5.** not thick or dense: *thin soup.* **6.** lacking firmness, solidity, or volume; weak or insincere: *a thin excuse; a thin smile; a thin voice.* **—*adv.*** **7.** in a thin manner. **8.** not densely. **9.** so as to produce something thin: *The ham was sliced thin.* **—*v.*** **10.** to make thin or thinner: [~ + *obj*]: *Thin the gravy by adding more water to it.* [*no obj;* (~ + *down*)]: *The gravy will thin if you add too much water to it. He wants to thin down before summer.* **11.** [*no obj;* (~ + *out*)] to become lower in number or less: *The crowd thinned (out) as the rain poured down.* —**thin′ly,** *adv.* —**thin′ness,** *n.* [*noncount*]

thine (thīn) /ðayn/ *pron.* **1.** (used after the verb *be* or sometimes after a noun) the form of the pronoun THOU that is used to show possession: *It is thine; the glory thine.* **2.** the form of the pronoun THOU used before a noun beginning with a vowel or vowel sound: *thine honor.* Compare THY. **3.** that which belongs to thee: *Thine is the kingdom, the power, and the glory.*

thing (thing) /θɪŋ/ *n.* [*count*] **1.** an object, usually not a person or animal: *A noun is the name of a person, place, or thing.* **2.** an object not specifically named or designated: *Hand me that thing. What is that thing, anyway?* **3.** anything that is an object of thought or discussion: *another thing I want to talk to you about.* **4. things,** matters; affairs; circumstances in general: *How are things?* **5.** a particular fact or circumstance: *His death was a terrible thing.* **6.** *Informal.* a satisfying activity: *a fun thing to do; Bicycling is his thing.* **7.** an achievement, deed, or accomplishment: *I expect great things from our production team.* **8.** a detail, esp. particular detail: *Do we have to go over every little thing?* **9.** aim; objective: *The thing is to enjoy yourself.* **10.** an article of clothing: *didn't have a thing to wear.* **11. things, a.** utensils for a purpose: *the breakfast things.* **b.** possessions that one owns: *Pack your things and leave at once!* **12.** a task; chore: *I've got things to do.* **13.** a living being; creature: *That baby is a cute little thing, isn't he?* **14.** a thought; observation: *I had a thing or two to say about that.* **15.** *Informal.* a special or strong attitude about something, either positive or negative: *She has a thing about cats (= She likes/dislikes them). He has a thing for Irish music (= He likes it).* **16. the thing,** something that is correct or fashionable: *Wearing baseball caps backward is the thing.* **—*Idiom.*** **17. do one's thing,** *Informal.* to follow a way of life that allows one to express oneself: *Let the kids do their own thing and establish their independence.* **18. for one thing,** (used to introduce something to support what has been said): *The economy is in a shambles. For one thing, unemployment is sky-high.* **19. see** or **hear things,** to hallucinate: *After taking the drug he began to see things, and he couldn't shut them out of his mind.*

thing•a•ma•jig (thing′ə mə jig′) /ˈθɪŋəməˌdʒɪg/ *n.* [*count*] *Informal.* something whose name the speaker does not know or has forgotten: *Hand me the thingamajig from the bookshelf, please.*

think (thingk) /θɪŋk/ *v.,* **thought** (thôt) /θɔt/ **think•ing,** *n.* **—*v.*** **1.** [*not: be* + ~*-ing; no obj*] to have a conscious mind that can reason, remember, and make decisions: *Descartes said, "I think, therefore I am," meaning that the capacity to think was central to what it means to be human.* **2.** [*no obj*] to use one's mind in a reasoning way to make a decision about a given situation: *Think carefully before you act.* **3.** to have a certain thing as the subject of one's thoughts: [*no obj*]: *I was thinking about college the other day.* [~ + *(that) clause*]: *I was thinking that our college days were the best years of our lives.* [*used with quotations*]: *"That's odd," Alice thought.* [~ + *obj*]: *Think nice thoughts and go to sleep.* **4.** [~ + *of* + *obj*] to call something to one's conscious mind: *to think of others less fortunate than we are.* **5.** to consider a possible action or plan: [*no obj*]: *thinking about cutting her hair.* [~ + *(that) clause*]: *We think that we'll go back to Ithaca some day.* **6.** [~ + *of* + *obj*] to invent or conceive of something: *to think of a plan.* **7.** [*not: be* + ~*-ing;* ~ + *(that) clause*] to have a belief or opinion: *I think she is funny.* **8.** to consider a person or thing as indicated: [~ + *adjective* + *of* + *obj*]: *I only think well of her.* [~ + *obj* + *adjective*]: *He thought me unkind.* [~ + *obj* + *noun*]: *She thought him a total fool.* **9.** [~ + *to* + *verb*] to anticipate or expect: *I did not think to call you; I know I should have.* **10. think over,** to evaluate for possible action: [~ + *obj* + *over*]: *Think the deal over and call us tomorrow.* [~ + *over* + *obj*]: *Think over her offer.* **11. think through** or **out,** to solve by thinking; come up with something by thinking: [~ + *through/out* + *obj*]: *to think through a problem.* [~ + *obj* + *through/out*]: *to think a problem through.* **12. think up,** to invent; devise; create; come up with: [~ + *up* + *obj*]: *I couldn't think up a better excuse.* [~ + *obj* + *up*]: *to think something up.* **—*n.*** [*count*] **13.** the act or a period of thinking: *First, give it a good think.* **—*Idiom.*** **14. think better of,** [~ + *obj*] to reconsider: *He was all set to yell at her, but then he thought better of it and kept quiet.* **15. think fit,** [*no obj*] to believe or consider (something) to be proper or appropriate: *Do as you think fit; I trust your judgment.* **16. think little** or **nothing of,** [~ + *little/nothing* + *of* + *obj*] to believe (something) to be not worthy of notice; belittle or disparage: *thinks nothing of bicycling 20 miles.* **17. think the world of,** [~ + *obj*] to like or admire greatly: *Her father thinks the world of her.* **18. think twice,** to consider carefully before acting: *urged him to think twice about going to Hanoi.* —**think′er,** *n.* [*count*]

think•ing (thing′king) /ˈθɪŋkɪŋ/ *adj.* [*before a noun*] **1.** able to think or use the mind: *People are supposed to be thinking animals.* **2.** thoughtful: *Any thinking person would reject that plan.* **—*n.*** [*noncount*] **3.** thought; judgment: *clear thinking.*

think′ tank′, *n.* [*count*] a research organization that analyzes problems and proposes solutions, as in political or social areas. Also called **think′ fac′tory.**

thin•ner (thin′ər) /ˈθɪnər/ *n.* [*noncount*] a liquid, as turpentine, used to soften or dilute paint, varnish, etc.

thin′-skinned′, *adj.* **1.** having a thin skin. **2.** sensitive to criticism: *He was thin-skinned about his computer programs.*

third (thûrd) /θɜrd/ *adj.* **1.** next after the second; being the ordinal number for three. **2.** being one of three equal parts. **3.** of or relating to the gear transmission ratio at which the drive shaft speed is next greater than that of second gear. **4.** graded or ranked one level below the second: *third mate.* **—*n.*** **5.** [*count*] a third part, esp. of one (⅓): *Cut it into thirds.* **6.** [*count*] the third member of a series. **7.** [*noncount*] third gear: *Put it (= the car, etc.) in third.* **8.** [*count*] a person or thing next after second in rank. **—*adv.*** **9.** in the third place; thirdly.

third′-class′, *adj.* of the lowest class or quality; inferior: *a third-class power in world affairs.*

third′ degree′, *n.* [*count; usually singular*] thorough questioning and harsh treatment, esp. from the police to get a confession: *The cops gave him the third degree until he told them who had shot the policewoman.*

third′ par′ty, *n.* [*count*] **1.** any party to a case or quarrel only partly involved and not one of the primary disputants. **2.** (in a two-party system) a usually temporary political party, often founded to promote a particular policy. **3.** a supplier of additional goods or support for a product or service who is neither the primary seller or supplier nor the purchaser.

third′ per′son, *n.* [*count; usually singular; usually: the* + ~] the grammatical form used when a speaker refers to anyone or anything other than the speaker or the one or ones being spoken to: *The pronouns* he, she, it, *and* they *are in the third person.*

third′-rate′, *adj.* **1.** of the third rate, quality, or class. **2.** obviously inferior; of very poor quality: *a third-rate newspaper.*

Third′ World′, *n.* [*noncount; usually: the* + ~; *sometimes: third world*] the underdeveloped or developing nations of Africa, Asia, and Latin America.

thirst (thûrst) /θɜrst/ *n.* **1.** a feeling of dryness in the mouth and throat caused by need of liquid: [*count*]: *He had developed quite a thirst after working in the hot sun all day.* [*noncount*]: *to quench thirst.* **2.** [*noncount*] a need for liquid or moisture: *dying of thirst.* **3.** [*count*] an eager desire for something; craving: *a thirst for knowledge.* **—***v.* **4.** [*no obj*] to feel thirst; be thirsty: *"I thirst," he croaked.* **5.** [~ + *for/after* + *obj*] to have a strong desire for something: *to thirst for adventure.* —**thirst′i•ly,** *adv.*

thirst•y (thûr′stē) /ˈθɜrstiy/ *adj.,* **-i•er, -i•est. 1.** having a feeling of thirst: *the thirstiest guy at the bar.* **2.** [*be* + ~ + *for*] having a strong desire for something: *He was thirsty for adventure.*

thir•teen (thûr′tēn′) /ˈθɜrˈtiyn/ *n.* [*count*] **1.** a cardinal number, 10 plus 3. **2.** a symbol for this number, as 13 or XIII. **3.** a set of this many persons or things. **—***adj.* [*before a noun*] **4.** amounting to 13 in number. —**thir′teenth′,** *adj.*

thir•ty (thûr′tē) /ˈθɜrtiy/ *n., pl.* **-ties,** *adj.* **—***n.* [*count*] **1.** a cardinal number, 10 times 3. **2.** a symbol for this number, as 30 or XXX. **3.** a set of this many persons or things. **4. thirties,** the numbers from 30 through 39, as in the years of a lifetime or of a century, or to degrees of temperature: *temperatures in the low thirties; a teacher in her thirties.* **—***adj.* [*before a noun*] **5.** amounting to 30 in number. —**thir′ti•eth,** *adj., n.* [*count*]

this (*th*is) /ðɪs/ *pron.* and *adj., pl.* **these** (*th*ēz); *adv.* **—***pron.* **1.** (used to refer to a person, thing, idea, or event present or near or just mentioned or understood, or to give emphasis): *This is my coat.* **2.** (used to refer to one of two or more persons, things, etc., pointing to the one that is nearer in place, time, or thought; opposed to *that*): *This is Liza and that is Amy.* **3.** (used to refer to one of two or more persons, things, etc., suggesting a contrast; opposed to *that*): *Do this, not that.* **4.** (used to mean "what is about to follow," before some thing, action, or event is described or done): *We do it like this: Remove the skin of the orange and then peel the coating off.* **—***adj.* **5.** (used before a noun to indicate that the person, place, thing, etc., that is mentioned is present, near, or known): *This book is mine.* **6.** (used to indicate a person, thing, etc., that is nearer in time, place, or thought than some other person, thing, etc.; opposed to *that*): *This dress fits you better than that one.* **7.** (used to suggest a contrast; opposed to *that*): *This book, not that one.* **8.** (used instead of *a* or *an* to emphasize the next, unknown noun; it means "a certain"): *So I'm walking down the street and this guy comes up to me.* **—***adv.* **9.** (used with adjectives and adverbs of quantity or amount) to the extent indicated; as much as indicated: *We've come this far; why turn back now?*

this•tle (this′əl) /ˈθɪsəl/ *n.* [*count*] a prickly plant usually having purple flower heads.

this•tle•down (this′əl doun′) /ˈθɪsəlˌdawn/ *n.* [*noncount*] the white silky substance on a thistle.

thith•er (thi*th*′ər, *th*i*th*′-) /ˈθɪðər, ˈðɪð-/ *adv.* to or toward that place or point; there: *went thither in search of adventure.*

tho or **tho'** (*th*ō) /ðow/ *conj., adv.* an informal, poetic, or simplified spelling of THOUGH.

thong (thông, thong) /θɔŋ, θɒŋ/ *n.* [*count*] **1.** a narrow strip, esp. of hide, used to fasten something or for whipping. **2.** a shoe or slipper held on the foot by a strip of leather between the first two toes.

tho•rax (thôr′aks, thōr′-) /ˈθɔræks, ˈθowr-/ *n.* [*count*], *pl.* **tho•rax•es, tho•ra•ces** (thôr′ə sēz′, thōr′-) /ˈθɔrəˌsiyz, ˈθowr-/. **1.** the part of the trunk of the body between the neck and the abdomen, containing the heart and lungs: *In mammals the thorax is separated from the lower trunk by the diaphragm.* **2.** the portion of the body of an insect between the head and the abdomen. —**tho•rac•ic** (thəras′ik) /θəˈræsɪk/ *adj.*

thorn (thôrn) /θɔrn/ *n.* **1.** [*count*] a hard, sharp point growing out on a plant: *Roses have thorns.* **2.** a tree, bush, or shrub having such sharp points: [*noncount*]: *rows of thorn.* [*count*]: *to cut down a few thorns.* **3.** [*count*] a source or cause of continual annoyance: *A noisy neighbor can be a thorn in one's side.* —**thorn′y,** *adj.,* **-i•er, -i•est.**

thor•ough (thûr′ō, thur′ō) /ˈθɜrow, ˈθʌrow/ *adj.* **1.** done or accomplished without forgetting anything: *a thorough search.* **2.** complete; perfect; utter: *thorough enjoyment.* **3.** being very attentive to accuracy and detail: *a thorough worker.* —**thor′ough•ly,** *adv.* —**thor′ough•ness,** *n.* [*noncount*]

thor•ough•bred (thûr′ō bred′, -ə bred′, thur′-) /ˈθɜrowˌbrɛd, -əˌbrɛd, ˈθʌr-/ *adj.* **1.** of pure or unmixed breed, as a horse or other animal; purebred. **—***n.* [*count*] **2.** a thoroughbred animal.

thor•ough•fare (thûr′ō fâr′, -ə fâr′, thur′-) /ˈθɜrowˌfɛər, -əˌfɛər, ˈθʌr-/ *n.* [*count*] **1.** a road, street, etc., that leads at each end into another street: *a busy thoroughfare.* **2.** a major road or highway.

thor•ough•go•ing (thûr′ō gō′ing, -ə gō′-, thur′-) /ˈθɜrowˌgowɪŋ, -əˌgow-, ˈθʌr-/ *adj.* **1.** doing things thoroughly. **2.** carried out to the full; thorough: *a thoroughgoing investigation.* **3.** [*before a noun*] utter; unqualified: *a thoroughgoing fool.*

those (*th*ōz) /ðowz/ *pron., adj.* pl. of THAT.

thou (*th*ou) /ðaw/ *pron., sing., nom.* **thou;** *poss.* **thy** or **thine;** *obj.* **thee;** *pl., nom.* **you** or **ye;** *poss.* **your** or **yours;** *obj.* **you** or **ye;** *Archaic* (except in some prayers). The pronoun used for the person being spoken to (or for God as the address of a prayer), when the person is singular and the subject of the sentence: *Thou supportest the fallen, healest the sick, and releasest those who are in bondage.*

though (*th*ō) /ðow/ *conj.* **1.** in spite of the fact that; although; notwithstanding that: *Though we tried hard, we lost the game.* **2.** even if; granting that: *(Even) Though I walk in the valley shadowed by death, I will not be afraid.* **—***adv.* **3.** for all that; however: *Though fast, he wasn't fast enough.* **—*Idiom.* 4. as though,** as if: *It seemed as though the place was deserted.*

thought[1] (thôt) /θɔt/ *n.* **1.** [*noncount*] the product of mental activity: *a book on early Greek thought.* **2.** [*count*] a single act or product of thinking; idea or notion: *to collect one's thoughts.* **3.** [*noncount*] the act or process of thinking; mental activity; reflection: *He was deep in thought and didn't hear me when I came in.* **4.** [*noncount*] intention, design, or purpose: *There was no thought of going back now.* **5.** [*noncount*] consideration, attention, care, or regard: *He gave no thought to his appearance.* **—Related Words.** THOUGHT is a noun, THOUGHTFUL is an adjective, THOUGHTFULLY is an adverb, THOUGHTFULNESS is a noun: *He admitted that he hadn't given much thought to the idea. It was thoughtful of her to help you out. She thoughtfully helped him to his feet when he fell. Your thoughtfulness during our difficult times is greatly appreciated.*

thought[2] (thôt) /θɔt/ *v.* pt. and pp. of THINK.

thought•ful (thôt′fəl) /ˈθɔtfəl/ *adj.* **1.** showing consideration or care for others; considerate: *How thoughtful of you; you remembered my birthday!* **2.** characterized by or showing careful thought: *a thoughtful essay.* **3.** thinking a great deal; contemplative; reflective: *a thoughtful mood.* —**thought′ful•ly,** *adv.: He thoughtfully opened the door for her.* —**thought′ful•ness,** *n.* [*noncount*]

thought•less (thôt′lis) /ˈθɔtlɪs/ *adj.* **1.** lacking in or not showing care or consideration for others: *a thoughtless remark about her bruised face.* **2.** not thinking enough; careless: *thoughtless about his health.* —**thought′less•ly,** *adv.: Someone thoughtlessly double-parked here.* —**thought′less•ness,** *n.* [*noncount*]

thou•sand (thou′zənd) /ˈθawzənd/ *n., pl.* **-sands,** (*as after a numeral*) **-sand,** *adj.* **—***n.* [*count*] **1.** a cardinal number, 10 times 100. **2.** a symbol for this number, as 1000 or M. **3.** a set of this many persons or things. **4. thousands, a.** the numbers between 1000 and 999,999, as in referring to money. **b.** a great number or amount: *Thousands came to see him at his first concert.* **5.** Also called **thou′sand's place′. a.** (in a mixed number) the position of the fourth digit to the left of the decimal point. **b.** (in a whole number) the position of the fourth digit from the right. **—*adj.* 6.** amounting to 1000 in number. —**thou′sandth,** *adj.* **—Usage.** See HUNDRED.

thrall (thrôl) /θrɔl/ *n.* [*noncount*] **—*Idiom.* in thrall,** in the power of someone or something: *The speaker held us in thrall.*

thrash (thrash) /θræʃ/ *v.* **1.** [~ + *obj*] to beat soundly in punishment; flog. **2.** [~ + *obj*] to defeat thoroughly: *Our team was thrashed by a score of 10-0.* **3.** [*no obj*] to plunge about wildly or violently: *She was thrashing around in bed, having a terribly bad nightmare.* **4. thrash out** or **over,** [~ + *out/over* + *obj*] to talk over thoroughly to reach a decision or understanding: *They decided to sit down and thrash out an agreement.*

thrash•er (thrash′ər) /ˈθræʃər/ *n.* [*count*] **1.** a person or thing that thrashes. **2.** a long-tailed bird like a thrush.

thread (thred) /θrɛd/ *n.* **1.** a thin, fine cord of fiber spun out to great length: [*noncount*]: *I need some thread to sew a button back on.* [*count*]: *Some threads are coming off your sleeve.* **2.** [*count*] the raised line on the long part of a screw: *The threads had been stripped and the screw was useless.* **3.** [*count*] something that runs through the whole course of a thing, as a narrative, connecting parts in sequence: *I lost the thread of the story in all the confusion.* **4. threads,** [*plural*] *Slang.* clothes: *I love your threads!* **—*v.* 5.** [~ + *obj*] to pass the end of a thread through the eye of (a needle): *to thread a needle.* **6.** [~ + *obj*] to fix or attach (beads, etc.) upon a thread that is passed through; string. **7.** [~ + *obj*] to place and arrange thread, etc., in position on (a sewing machine, loom, etc.). **8.** [~ + *obj*] to pass (tape, etc.) through or into a narrow opening: *He threaded the film into the projector and started the movie.* **9.** [~ + *obj*] to ornament with threads: *silk threaded with gold.* **10.** to make (one's way), as past or around things or people that block or get in the way: [~ + *obj*]: *threaded his way through the crowd.* [*no obj*]: *He threaded through the crowd.* —**thread′er,** *n.* [*count*]

thread•bare (thred′bâr′) /ˈθrɛdˌbɛər/ *adj.* **1.** having the top, as of a fabric, worn off so that the threads of the weave lay bare: *a threadbare jacket.* **2.** wearing threadbare clothes; shabby or poor. **3.** not having enough of something needed; meager: *That threadbare account of his told us too little of what was happening.*

threat (thret) /θrɛt/ *n.* **1.** a warning that one (or someone) will harm another, if something is done or not done: [*count*]: *Death threats were made against the witnesses.* [*noncount*]: *under threat of death.* **2.** [*count*] a sign or warning of trouble or danger: *the threat of war.* **3.** [*count*] a person or thing that threatens (peace, etc.): *That bloodthirsty dictator is a threat to world stability.*

threat•en (thret′n) /ˈθrɛtn̩/ *v.* **1.** [~ + *obj* (+ *with* + *obj*)] to make a statement or promise that one will punish or harm (another): *The gangsters threatened him with the execution of his family if he didn't cooperate.* **2.** to promise to inflict (punishment, harm, etc.) on someone: [~ + *obj*]: *They threatened swift retaliation if their demands were not met.* [~ + *to* + *verb*]: *They threatened to retaliate immediately.* [~ + *that clause*]: *They threatened that they would all walk off the job.* **3.** to be a source of danger to; be likely to harm: [~ + *obj*]: *to threaten one's peace of mind.* [*no obj*]: *We wondered what to do if danger threatened.* **4.** [~ + *obj*] to give a warning of (something bad or unfortunate): *The clouds threaten rain.*

threat•ened (thret′nd) /ˈθrɛtnd/ *adj.* **1.** being under threat: *He felt threatened by the new genius his office hired.* **2.** (of a species of animal or plant) likely to become endangered: *protection for threatened species.*

threat•en•ing (thret′n ing) /ˈθrɛtn̩ ɪŋ/ *adj.* **1.** warning, or showing by one's behavior, that one will injure, punish, or harm another: *made a threatening gesture.* **2.** causing alarm: *dark, threatening storm clouds.*

three (thrē) /θriy/ *n.* [*count*] **1.** a cardinal number, 2 plus 1. **2.** a symbol for this number, as 3 or III. **3.** a set of this many persons or things. **—*adj.* [*before a noun*] 4.** amounting to three in number.

three′-dimen′sional, *adj.* **1.** having, or seeming to have, the dimension of depth as well as width and height. **2.** (esp. of a piece of writing, etc.) lifelike: *The author makes all his characters three-dimensional.*

three R's, *n.* [*plural: the* + ~] **1.** reading, writing, and arithmetic, the fundamentals of education: *Parents wanted more emphasis on the three R's.* **2.** the fundamentals or basic skills of any field.

thresh (thresh) /θrɛʃ/ *v.* **1.** to separate the grain from (a cereal plant), as by beating with a tool: [~ + *obj*]: *to thresh the wheat.* [*no obj*]: *spent all day in the fields threshing.* **—*n.*** [*count*] **2.** the act of threshing. Sometimes, **thrash** (thrash) /θræʃ/. —**thresh′er,** *n.* [*count*]

thresh•old (thresh′ōld, thresh′hōld) /ˈθrɛʃowld, ˈθrɛʃhowld/ *n.* [*count*] **1.** the bottom part of a doorway. **2.** the entrance to a house or building: *They waved goodbye from the threshold.* **3.** any point of beginning: *He was on the threshold of a new career.* **4.** the point at which something begins to take effect: *Her dream was hovering on the threshold of consciousness. He has a low threshold of pain.*

threw (thro͞o) /θruw/ *v.* pt. of THROW.

thrice (thrīs) /θrays/ *adv.* **1.** three times. **2.** in threefold quantity or degree.

thrift (thrift) /θrɪft/ *n.* **1.** [*noncount*] economical management of one's property; economy. **2.** [*count*] Also called **thrift′ institu′tion.** a savings and loan association, savings bank, or credit union. —**thrift′less,** *adj.*

thrift shop (thrift′shop′) /ˈθrɪftˌʃɒp/ *n.* [*count*] a retail store that sells secondhand goods at reduced prices.

thrift•y (thrif′tē) /ˈθrɪftiy/ *adj.,* **-i•er, -i•est.** showing or practicing thrift: *a thrifty housekeeper who saved money by shopping carefully.* —**thrift•i•ly** (thrif′tl ē) /ˈθrɪftl̩iy/ *adv.: shopping thriftily for bargains.* —**thrift′i•ness,** *n.* [*noncount*] **—Syn.** See ECONOMICAL.

thrill (thril) /θrɪl/ *v.* **1.** to (cause to) feel a sudden wave of emotion or excitement: [~ + *obj*]: *The good news thrilled him.* [~ + *at/to* + *obj*]: *to thrill at the thought of Paris.* **—*n.*** [*count*] **2.** a sudden wave of strong emotion: *He felt a thrill go through him when she entered the room.* **3.** something that produces such a sensation: *It's certainly a thrill to meet the president.* —**thrill′er,** *n.* [*count*]: *a horror thriller.*

thrive (thrīv) /θrayv/ *v.,* **thrived** or **throve** (thrōv) /θrowv/ **thrived** or **thriv•en** (thriv′ən) /ˈθrɪvən/ **thriv•ing. 1.** [*no obj*] to prosper; be successful: *The business is thriving.* **2.** to grow or develop well; flourish: [*no obj*]: *The plants will thrive in such a climate.* [~ + *on* + *obj*]: *Do you thrive on such challenges?*

throat (thrōt) /θrowt/ *n.* [*count*] **1.** the top of the passage from the mouth to the stomach and lungs: *The throat includes the pharynx, larynx, and the upper parts of the trachea and esophagus.* **2.** the front of the neck below the chin and above the collarbones. **—*Idiom.* 3. cut one's own throat,** to bring about one's own ruin: *Expressing antagonism toward your coworkers and your boss is a sure way of cutting your own throat.* **4. jump down someone's throat,** to disagree with someone rapidly and furiously: *Before I could explain myself she had jumped down my throat and accused me of all kinds of treachery.* **5. ram (something) down someone's throat,** to force someone to accept something: *The committee rammed the recommendations down the department's throat.* **6. stick in one's throat,** to be difficult to express: *The words stuck in his throat when he tried to tell her how he felt.*

throat•y (thrō′tē) /ˈθrowtiy/ *adj.,* **-i•er, -i•est.** (of sound) husky; hoarse. —**throat•i•ly** (thrōt′l ē) /ˈθrowtl̩iy/ *adv.* —**throat′i•ness,** *n.* [*noncount*]

throb (throb) /θrɒb/ *v.,* **throbbed, throb•bing,** *n.* **—*v.*** [*no obj*] **1.** to beat with increased force or speed, as the heart does when one feels emotion. **2.** to vibrate, as a sound: *The music from their party throbbed through the apartment building.* **—*n.*** [*count*] **3.** a violent beat, as of the heart. **4.** any strong, pulsing, or vibrating sound.

throe (thrō) /θrow/ *n.* [*count*] **1.** a violent spasm. **2. throes,** [*plural*] **a.** any violent struggle: *a country in the throes of a rebellion.* **b.** the agony of death: *in death throes.*

throm•bo•sis (throm bō′sis) /θrɒmˈbowsɪs/ *n.* a condition in which a blood clot forms in a blood vessel or in the heart: [*noncount*]: *coronary thrombosis.* [*count*]: *The doctors examined a thrombosis in the artery leading to the brain.* —**throm•bot•ic** (thrombot′ik) /θrɒmˈbɒtɪk/ *adj.*

throm•bus (throm′bəs) /ˈθrɒmbəs/ *n.* [*count*], *pl.* **-bi** (-bī) /-bay/. a clot that forms in and blocks a blood vessel, or that forms in one of the chambers of the heart.

throne (thrōn) /θrown/ *n.* [*count*] **1.** the seat occupied by a sovereign at certain occasions or ceremonies. **2.** the rank, office, or dignity of a king or queen: *to assume the throne.*

throng (thrông, throng) /θrɔŋ, θrɒŋ/ *n.* [*count*] **1.** a great crowd of people: *A throng of people surrounded the*

Pope. —*v.* **2.** [*no obj*] to assemble in large numbers; crowd: *A huge crowd thronged outside to see the accident.* **3.** [~ + *obj*] to fill with or as if with a crowd: *A huge crowd thronged downtown to protest his visit.* **4.** [~ + *obj*] to press upon; jostle: *The crowd thronged the movie star.* —**Syn.** See CROWD.

throt•tle (throt′l) /ˈθrɒtl̩/ *n., v.,* **-tled, -tling.** —*n.* [*count*] **1. a.** the valve in an engine that controls the amount of fuel entering the cylinders. **b.** the lever that controls this valve. —*v.* **2.** [~ + *obj*] to choke (someone) by squeezing the throat; strangle. **3.** to reduce the speed of, by or as if by using a throttle: [*no obj*]: *The pilot throttled back on her engines.* [~ + *obj*]: *She throttled her engines and reduced height.* —***Idiom.*** **4. at full throttle,** at maximum speed or effort: *He went after the car at full throttle.* —**throt′tler,** *n.* [*count*]

through (thro͞o) /θruw/ *prep.* **1.** in at one end, side, or surface and out at the other: *to pass through a tunnel.* **2.** past; beyond: *drove through a red light.* **3.** from one to the other of: *monkeys swinging through the trees.* **4.** across the extent of: *traveled through Europe.* **5.** during the whole period of; throughout: *We worked through the night.* **6.** done with: *What time are you through work?* **7.** to and including: *He lived there from 1935 through 1950.* **8.** by means of: *I found out through him.* **9.** from the first to the final stage of: *Somehow he managed to get through the entire performance.* —*adv.* **10.** in at one end, side, or surface and out at the other: *to push a needle through.* **11.** all the way: *This train goes through to Boston.* **12.** throughout, completely: *She was soaked through.* **13.** from beginning to end: *read the letter all the way through.* **14.** to completion: *to see it through.* —*adj.* **15.** [*be* + ~] at a point or in a state of completion of an action, etc.; finished: *Please be quiet until I'm through.* **16.** [*be* + ~ *(+ with)*] at the end of all relations or dealings: *She had to tell her boyfriend they were through.* **17.** extending or going from one end, etc., to the other: *a through road.* **18.** [*before a noun*] proceeding to a destination, etc., without a change, break, or deviation: *a through flight.* **19.** [*be* + ~] of no further use or value; washed-up; finished: *Critics say he's through as a writer.* —***Idiom.*** **20. through and through, a.** throughout every part; thoroughly: *I was cold through and through.* **b.** in all respects: *She is an aristocrat through and through.*

through•out (thro͞o out′) /θruwˈawt/ *prep.* **1.** in or to every part of: *I looked throughout the house for the book.* **2.** from beginning to end of: *nodding throughout the sermon.* —*adv.* **3.** in every part or aspect: *rotten throughout.* **4.** at every moment or point: *Follow the text throughout.*

through•way (thro͞o′wā′) /ˈθruwˌwey/ *n.* THRUWAY.

throve (thrōv) /θrowv/ *v.* a pt. of THRIVE.

throw (thrō) /θrow/ *v.,* **threw** (thro͞o) /θruw/ **thrown** (thrōn) /θrown/ **throw•ing,** *n.* —*v.* **1.** to hurl or propel from the hand: [~ + *obj (+ to + obj)*]: *She threw the ball (to me).* [~ + *obj* + *obj*]: *She threw me the ball.* [*no obj*]: *The pitcher's arm hurt so much he could hardly throw.* **2.** [~ + *obj*] to move (oneself) suddenly, as in reaction to some emotion: *threw up his hands in despair.* **3.** [~ + *obj*] to project or cast (light, etc.): *The streetlights threw shadows.* **4.** [~ + *obj*] to direct (one's voice) so as to appear to come from a different source, as in ventriloquism. **5.** to direct or send forth (words, etc.): [~ + *obj* + *at* + *obj*]: *Soon they were throwing angry insults at each other.* [~ + *obj* + *obj*]: *He threw her a dirty look.* **6.** [~ + *obj*] to put into some place, state, etc., quickly: *He was thrown to the floor by the force of the explosion.* **7.** [~ + *obj*] to move (a lever or the like) in order to turn on, disconnect, etc., a machine: *He threw the switch and stopped the elevator.* **8.** [~ + *obj*] to shape on a potter's wheel. **9.** [~ + *obj*] to deliver (a blow or punch): *The champ threw a short right.* **10.** [~ + *obj*] (in wrestling) to hurl (an opponent) to the ground. **11.** [~ + *obj*] to play (a card). **12.** [~ + *obj*] to lose (a game or other contest) intentionally, as in exchange for money: *Everyone suspected that they threw the game.* **13.** [~ + *obj*] **a.** to cast (dice): *to throw the dice and hope for sevens.* **b.** to make (a cast) at dice: *He threw doubles on his next play.* **14.** [~ + *obj*] (of an animal, as a horse) to cause (someone) to fall off; unseat: *The horse threw him and he fell heavily.* **15.** to give or host: [~ + *obj (+ for + obj)*]: *We threw a lavish party (for them).* [~ + *obj* + *obj*]: *to throw them a lavish party.* **16.** [~ + *obj*] to amaze or confuse: *Those dark glasses really threw me; I couldn't recognize you at first!* **17. throw away, a.** to dispose of; get rid of; discard: [~ + *away* + *obj*]: *to throw away the garbage.* [~ + *obj* + *away*]: *Throw that junk away!* **b.** to waste (something); squander: [~ + *obj* + *away*]: *Why throw your money away on a bad car?* [~ + *away* + *obj*]: *Why throw away your money?* **c.** to fail to use; miss (a chance, etc.): [~ + *away* + *obj*]: *You're throwing away the opportunity of a lifetime.* [~ + *obj* + *away*]: *You're throwing that opportunity away.* **18. throw in,** to add (something extra) as a bonus: [~ + *in* + *obj*]: *The car dealer promised to throw in new floor mats.* [~ + *obj* + *in*]: *They throw meals in for the cost of the hotel room.* **19. throw off, a.** to free oneself of; cast aside: [~ + *off* + *obj*]: *He had some trouble throwing off that cough.* [~ + *obj* + *off*]: *to throw her clothes off.* **b.** [~ + *obj* + *off*] to evade, as a pursuer. **c.** to perform or produce with ease: [~ + *off* + *obj*]: *to throw off a few jokes.* [~ + *obj* + *off*]: *"I'll throw that article off and mail it to you tonight," he bragged.* **d.** [~ + *obj* + *off*] to confuse; fluster: *At first the strange surroundings threw me off.* **20. throw out, a.** to cast away; discard; reject: [~ + *out* + *obj*]: *We threw out your letter.* [~ + *obj* + *out*]: *We threw it out.* **b.** to remove from a place, esp. with or as if with force; to remove from (a club, organization, etc.): [~ + *obj* + *out*]: *The Democrats voted to throw him out of the party.* [~ + *out* + *obj*]: *The security guards threw out anyone without a pass.* **21. throw together, a.** to make hurriedly and not carefully: [~ + *together* + *obj*]: *He threw together a quick meal.* [~ + *obj* + *together*]: *to throw a meal together.* **b.** [~ + *obj* + *together*] to cause to associate; bring together: *Circumstances threw these enemies together.* **22. throw up, a.** to build too quickly or hastily: [~ + *up* + *obj*]: *Contractors were throwing up office buildings in the suburbs.* [~ + *obj* + *up*]: *throwing them up too quickly.* **b.** to vomit: [*no obj*]: *Suddenly she grabbed her stomach and threw up.* [~ + *up* + *obj*]: *She threw up her lunch.* —*n.* [*count*] **23.** an act or instance of throwing: *With a perfect throw, the outfielder nailed the runner at the plate.* **24.** the distance to which something can be thrown: *a stone's throw.* **25.** a scarf, shawl, or the like. **26.** a cast of dice or the number thrown. —***Idiom.*** **27. a throw,** each: *He went out and ordered four suits at $300 a throw.* **28. throw in the sponge** or **towel,** to admit defeat; give up: *He threw in the sponge and telephoned his opponent to congratulate her.* **29. throw oneself at,** [~ + *obj*] to try hard to attract the affections of: *He threw himself at his teacher every chance he got.* **30. throw oneself into,** [~ + *obj*] to do (something) with enthusiasm: *After the death of his wife, he threw himself into his work.*

throw•a•way (thrō′ə wā′) /ˈθrowəˌwey/ *adj.* **1.** made to be discarded after use: *a throwaway container.* **2.** delivered or said casually: *The comedian had a throwaway line that always got a laugh.* —*n.* [*count*] **3.** something to be discarded after use, reading, etc.

throw•back (thrō′bak′) /ˈθrowˌbæk/ *n.* [*count*] **1.** an act of throwing back. **2.** an act of going back to an earlier time or mode of behavior now out of date: *his gracious language—a throwback to the 19th century.*

thru (thro͞o) /θruw/ *prep., adv., adj.* an informal, simplified spelling of THROUGH.

thrush (thrush) /θrʌʃ/ *n.* [*count*] a usually dull-colored songbird found in most parts of the world.

thrust (thrust) /θrʌst/ *v.* **1.** to push forcefully; shove: [~ + *obj*]: *He thrust his way through the crowd.* [*no obj*]: *She thrust through the crowd until she was next to him.* **2.** [~ + *obj*] to force acceptance of: *He kept thrusting himself into the conversation.* —*n.* **3.** [*count*] an act or instance of thrusting; a lunge or stab, as with a sword. **4.** [*noncount*] a force produced by a propeller, etc., to propel a missile, ship, etc.: *The ice-coated engine failed to develop enough thrust.* **5.** [*count; usually singular*] the main point: *the thrust of his argument.* **6.** [*count*] a military attack or assault; an offensive.

thru•way or **through•way** (thro͞o′wā′) /ˈθruwˌwey/ *n.* [*count*] an expressway providing direct transportation for high-speed automobile traffic.

thud (thud) /θʌd/ *n., v.,* **thud•ded, thud•ding.** —*n.* [*count*] **1.** a dull sound, as of a heavy blow or fall: *The bag of groceries fell to the floor with a thud.* —*v.* [*no obj*] **2.** to strike or fall with a thud.

thug (thug) /θʌg/ *n.* [*count*] a vicious or violent criminal.

thumb (thum) /θʌm/ *n.* **1.** [*count*] the short, thick, inner digit of the hand, next to the forefinger and set apart from the other four: *He stuck out his thumb for a ride.* **2.** the corresponding finger in animals. **3.** the part of a glove or mitten that contains this digit. —*v.* **4.** [~ + *obj*] to turn (pages) with the thumb: *to thumb the edges of a book.* **5.** [~ + *through* + *obj*] to glance through (pages): *thumbed through the brochure.* **6.** [~ + *obj*] (of a hitchhiker) to ask for (a ride) by pointing the thumb in the direction of travel: *to thumb a ride.* ***—Idiom.*** **7. be all thumbs,** to be clumsy: *When it comes to car repairs he's all thumbs.* **8. thumb one's nose,** [~ + *at* + *obj*] **a.** to raise the hand with fingers extended and touch the thumb to the nose as a gesture of contempt, etc.: *thumbed his nose at the police officer and raced off.* **b.** to show contempt or defiance: *to thumb one's nose at society.* **9. under someone's thumb,** to be under the control or rule of someone else.

thumb•nail (thum′nāl′) /ˈθʌmˌneyl/ *n.* [*count*] **1.** the nail of the thumb. ***—adj.*** **2.** brief; very short: *Give me a thumbnail sketch of the man.*

thumb•screw (thum′skro͞o′) /ˈθʌmˌskruw/ *n.* [*count*] **1.** a screw having a flat head that may be turned easily with the thumb and forefinger. **2.** Often, **thumbscrews.** [*plural*] an old instrument of torture by which one or both thumbs were squeezed.

thumb•tack (thum′tak′) /ˈθʌmˌtæk/ *n.* [*count*] a tack with a large, flat head, to be pushed into a board by the pressure of the thumb.

thump (thump) /θʌmp/ *n.* [*count*] **1.** a blow with a heavy object, producing a dull sound. **2.** the sound made by or as if by such a blow. **—*v.*** **3.** to (cause to) be struck with a heavy object, so as to produce a dull sound: [~ + *obj*]: *He thumped the side of the barrel.* [*no obj*]: *The cars thumped into each other.* **4.** [*no obj*] to beat violently or make a loud, fast beating noise, as the heart.

thun•der (thun′dər) /ˈθʌndər/ *n.* [*noncount*] **1.** a loud, rolling noise produced by the expansion of air heated by lightning: *The children were afraid of thunder.* **2.** any loud, resounding noise: *a thunder of applause.* **—*v.*** **3.** [*no obj; it* + ~] to give forth thunder: *It thundered all night.* **4.** [*no obj*] to make a loud, rolling, rumbling noise like thunder: *artillery thundering in the hills.* **5.** to speak in a very loud or vehement way; shout: [*no obj*]: *All day long the boss thundered about the company's losses.* [*used with quotations*]: *"Watch out," the officer thundered, "get out of here now!"* ***—Idiom.*** **6. steal someone's thunder, a.** to use without credit or permission the ideas of another. **b.** to spoil the effect of another's performance, etc., by doing or saying what (s)he was going to do first. —**thun′der•er,** *n.* [*count*]

thun•der•bolt (thun′dər bōlt′) /ˈθʌndərˌbowlt/ *n.* [*count*] a flash of lightning along with the thunder that comes with it.

thun•der•clap (thun′dər klap′) /ˈθʌndərˌklæp/ *n.* [*count*] **1.** a crash of thunder. **2.** something resembling a thunderclap.

thun•der•cloud (thun′dər kloud′) /ˈθʌndərˌklawd/ *n.* [*count*] a large, black cloud that produces thunder and lightning.

thun•der•head (thun′dər hed′) /ˈθʌndərˌhɛd/ *n.* [*count*] a thundercloud.

thun•der•ous (thun′dər əs, -drəs) /ˈθʌndərəs, -drəs/ *adj.* producing thunder or a loud noise like thunder: *thunderous applause.* —**thun′der•ous•ly,** *adv.*

thun•der•show•er (thun′dər shou′ər) /ˈθʌndərˌʃawər/ *n.* [*count*] a rain shower with thunder and lightning.

thun•der•storm (thun′dər stôrm′) /ˈθʌndərˌstɔrm/ *n.* [*count*] a usually brief storm with lightning and thunder.

thun•der•struck (thun′dər struk′) /ˈθʌndərˌstrʌk/ also **thun•der•strick•en** (thun′dər strik′ən) /ˈθʌndərˌstrɪkən/ *adj.* so amazed that one cannot say anything: *thunderstruck at the news of her death.*

Thurs., an abbreviation of: Thursday.

Thurs•day (thûrz′dā, -dē) /ˈθɜrzdey, -diy/ *n.* the fifth day of the week, following Wednesday: [*proper noun*]: *I'll meet you on Thursday.* [*count*]: *Thursdays we have sales meetings.*

thus (t͟hus) /ðʌs/ *adv.* **1.** in the way just indicated; in this way: *Managed thus, the business will succeed.* **2.** accordingly; as a result; for this reason: *Your interest rates will go down; thus, you'll save money.* **3.** to this extent or degree: *thus far.* **4.** as an example; for instance.

thwack (thwak) /θwæk/ *v.* [~ + *obj*] **1.** to strike with something flat; whack. **—*n.*** [*count*] **2.** a sharp blow with something flat. —**thwack′er,** *n.* [*count*]

thwart (thwôrt) /θwɔrt/ *v.* [~ + *obj*] to oppose successfully: *The general thwarted his opponent by making a brilliant defense of the city.*

thy (t͟hī) /ðay/ *pron.* (used before a noun that begins with a consonant sound) the form of the pronoun THOU, an old form of YOU, used to show possession: *Thy will be done.* Compare THINE.

thyme tīm /taym/ *n.* [*noncount*] a plant of the mint family having sweet-smelling leaves used as seasoning in cooking.

thy•mus (thī′məs) /ˈθayməs/ *n.* [*count*], *pl.* **-mus•es, -mi** (-mī) /-may/. a butterfly-shaped gland lying at the base of the neck that aids in the production of T cells.

thy•roid (thī′roid) /ˈθayrɔyd/ *adj.* **1.** of or relating to the thyroid gland. **—*n.*** **2.** THYROID GLAND. —**thy•roi′dal,** *adj.*

thy′roid gland′, *n.* [*count*] a gland located at the base of the neck that secretes hormones to regulate the rates of metabolism and growth.

ti (tē) /tiy/ *n.* [*count*], *pl.* **tis.** the musical syllable used for the seventh tone of the ascending diatonic scale.

ti•ar•a (tē ar′ə, -är′ə, -âr′ə) /tiyˈærə, -ˈɑrə, -ˈɛərə/ *n.* [*count*], *pl.* **-ar•as. 1.** a jeweled, ornamental piece like a small crown, worn by women. **2.** the pope's crown. —**ti•ar′aed,** *adj.*

tib•i•a (tib′ē ə) /ˈtɪbiyə/ *n.* [*count*], *pl.* **tib•i•ae** (tib′ē ē′) /ˈtɪbiyˌiy/ **tib•i•as.** the inner of the two bones of the leg, from the knee to the ankle; shinbone. —**tib′i•al,** *adj.*

tic (tik) /tɪk/ *n.* [*count*] a sudden, painless, involuntary muscular movement, as of the face: *His tic grew worse as he got more and more nervous.*

tick[1] (tik) /tɪk/ *n.* [*count*] **1.** a slight, sharp click or beat, as of a clock. **2.** *Brit. Informal.* a moment or instant: *I'll be back in a tick.* **3.** a small dot, mark, or electronic signal used to mark off an item on a list or call attention to something. **—*v.*** **4.** [*no obj*] to make the sound of a tick, like that of a clock: *The clock ticked loudly.* **5.** [*no obj*] (of time) to pass, as marked by or as if marked by the ticks of a clock: *The hours ticked by.* **6.** [~ + *obj*] to sound or announce by a tick or ticks: *The clock ticked the minutes.* **7.** [~ (+ *off*) + *obj*] to mark with a tick; check: *to tick off the items.* **8. tick off,** *Slang.* to make angry: [~ + *obj* + *off*]: *She really ticked me off.* [~ + *off* + *obj*]: *He managed to tick off everyone in the office.* ***—Idiom.*** **9. what makes one tick,** one's basic motives, needs, etc.: *Once we discover what makes him tick we'll find a way to get him to agree with us.*

tick[2] (tik) /tɪk/ *n.* [*count*] a bloodsucking insectlike creature, related to but larger than a mite: *Deer ticks carry Lyme disease.*

tick[3] (tik) /tɪk/ *n.* [*count*] the cloth case of a mattress, pillow, etc., containing hair, feathers, or the like.

tick•et (tik′it) /ˈtɪkɪt/ *n.* [*count*] **1.** a slip of paper that shows the holder has paid a fare or admission or is entitled to some service: *a train ticket.* See illustration at TERMINAL. **2.** a written summons that notifies the holder that he or she has broken some traffic law: *his fifth ticket for speeding.* **3.** a tag attached to something to show its price, what is inside it, etc. **4.** a list of candidates of a political party that are running together in an election: *He wasn't included in the new Liberal Party ticket.* **5.** [*usually singular; the* + ~] *Informal.* the proper or advisable thing: *Put it down gently—that's the ticket!* **—*v.*** [~ + *obj*] **6.** to attach a ticket to; label. **7.** to give a written summons to (someone) for breaking a traffic law or regulation: *The cops ticketed anyone going five miles per hour over the speed limit.* **8.** to attach such a notice or summons to: *to ticket illegally parked cars.*

tick•ing (tik′ing) /ˈtɪkɪŋ/ *n.* [*noncount*] a strong, plain, long-lasting fabric, made or printed in striped patterns and used esp. to cover mattresses.

tick•le (tik′əl) /ˈtɪkəl/ *v.,* **-led, -ling,** *n.* **—*v.*** **1.** [~ + *obj*] to stroke lightly with the fingers, with a feather, etc., so as to cause a tingling or itching sensation in: *To wake him up she would tickle his nose with a feather.* **2.** [*no obj*] to have or be affected with such a sensation: *The hairs on his face tickled.* **3.** [~ + *obj*] to poke some sensitive part of the body so as to cause laughter: *He'd tickle the kids right before bedtime and get them giggling and out of breath.* **4.** [~ + *obj*] to cause an agreeable feeling of excitement in: *to tickle someone's fancy.* **5.** [~ + *obj*] to amuse or delight: *The clown's antics tickled the kids.* **—*n.*** [*count*] **6.** an act or instance of tickling. **7.** a tickling sensation: *a slight tickle in the throat.* ***—Idiom.*** **8. tickled pink** or **tickled to death,** greatly pleased: *We're tickled pink that you could attend.*

tick•lish (tik′lish) /ˈtɪklɪʃ/ *adj.* **1.** sensitive to tickling: *very ticklish on the soles of her feet.* **2.** calling for or needing delicate, careful handling: *a ticklish situation.*

tick-tack-toe or **tic-tac-toe** (tik′tak tō′) /ˌtɪktækˈtow/ *n.* [*noncount*] a simple game played on a grid with nine squares, in which one player marks X's and one marks O's.

tid•al (tīd′l) /ˈtaydl̩/ *adj.* of or relating to tides: *tidal tables that show us when high tide is in effect.*

tid′al wave′, *n.* [*count*] **1.** (not in technical use) a large, destructive ocean wave, produced by a seaquake, hurricane, or strong wind. Compare TSUNAMI. **2.** any powerful or widespread opinion, etc.: *His plan to tax the middle class raised a tidal wave of protest.*

tid•bit (tid′bit′) /ˈtɪdˌbɪt/ *n.* [*count*] **1.** a delicate bit of food. **2.** an esp. pleasing or interesting bit of anything, as gossip: *Here's a little tidbit: The boss and the secretary are dating.*

tid•dly•winks (tid′lē wingks′) /ˈtɪdliyˌwɪŋks/ also **tid•dle•dy•winks** (tid′l dēwingks′) /ˈtɪdḷˌdiywɪŋks/ *n.* [*noncount; used with a singular verb*] a game in which small plastic disks are snapped with larger disks against a flat surface into a cup.

tide (tīd) /tayd/ *n., v.,* **tid•ed, tid•ing.** **—***n.* **1.** the regularly occurring rise and fall of the waters of the ocean: [*count*]: *a study of the periods of the tides.* [*noncount*]: *at high tide.* **2.** [*count*] anything that rises and falls, increases and decreases, etc.: *the tides of unemployment.* **3.** [*count*] tendency or drift, as of events: *the tide of history.* **4.** [*count*] a large amount of something: *a tide of immigrants.* **—***v.* **5. tide over,** [~ + *obj* + *over*] to help in getting over or through a period of difficulty or distress: *This money will tide you over until you get a new job.*

ti•dings (tī′dingz) /ˈtaydɪŋz/ *n.* [*plural*] news, information, or notification: *glad tidings; The tidings are not good.*

ti•dy (tī′dē) /ˈtaydiy/ *adj.,* **-di•er, -di•est,** *v.,* **-died, -dy•ing.** **—***adj.* **1.** neat and orderly, as in appearance or dress: *a tidy bedroom.* **2.** clearly organized: *Her desk was always tidy.* **3.** fairly good; acceptable or satisfactory: *They worked out a tidy arrangement.* **4.** [*usually: before a noun*] fairly large in amount; considerable: *That car must have cost you a tidy sum.* **—***v.* **5.** to make tidy: [*no obj;* ~ + *up*]: *I'll just tidy up a little before I go.* [~ (+ *up*) + *obj*]: *He tidied (up) the office before he left.* **—ti′di•ness,** *n.* [*noncount*]

tie (tī) /tay/ *v.,* **tied, ty•ing,** *n.* **—***v.* **1.** [~ + *obj*] to bind or fasten with a cord, etc.: *to tie a bundle.* **2.** to fasten by tightening and knotting (the strings of): [~ + *obj*]: *He stopped to tie his shoes.* [*no obj*]: *Her dress tied in the back.* **3.** [~ + *obj*] to form by looping and lacing parts of together, as a knot: *tied a bow and attached it to the package.* **4.** [~ + *obj*] to bind or join firmly: *Great affection tied them.* **5.** [~ + *obj*] to confine or restrict: *The weather tied us to the house.* **6.** to make the same score (as another); be equal (to) in a contest: [*no obj*]: *The two teams tied and had to play an extra period.* [~ + *obj*]: *Suddenly the other team tied the score.* **7. tie down,** to restrict the freedom or actions of (someone); confine: [~ + *obj* + *down*]: *The desk job ties him down.* [~ + *down* + *obj*]: *to tie down his workers.* **8. tie in,** [*no obj;* ~ + *in* (+ *with* + *obj*)]to be consistent or agree with: *His story ties in with the facts as we know them.* **9. tie up, a.** to fasten tightly or securely by tying: [~ + *up* + *obj*]: *The hijackers tied up all the hostages.* [~ + *obj* + *up*]: *They tied them up.* **b.** to wrap and secure, as with string; bind: [~ + *up* + *obj*]: *to tie up a package.* [~ + *obj* + *up*]: *to tie a package up.* **c.** [~ + *obj*] to hinder or bring to a stop; impede: *The accident tied up traffic.* **d.** [~ + *obj*] to prevent others from using by using (exclusively) oneself: *tied up the phone all morning.* **e.** to make (money) unavailable for further investment, use in business, etc.: [~ + *up* + *obj*]: *They tied up their money in real estate.* [~ + *obj* + *up*]: *They tied their money up in real estate.* **f.** [~ + *up* + *obj*] to connect; show that there is a relationship between: *The detective managed to tie up the loose ends of the case.* **g.** [~ + *obj; usually: be* + *tied* + *up*] to be completely occupied with something: *The boss is tied up till noon.* **—***n.* [*count*] **10.** a cord, string, or the like, used for tying, fastening, or wrapping something. **11.** that with which anything is tied. **12.** a necktie: *Your tie is crooked.* See illustration at CLOTHING. **13.** an ornamental knot; bow. **14.** a bond, as of affection: *family ties.* **15.** a state in which the same number of points has been scored, etc., among competitors; also, a competition that ends in such a state: *The game ended in a tie.* **16.** a piece used to support buildings or to keep railroad tracks in line. **—*Idiom.* 17. tie one on,** [*no obj*] *Slang.* to get drunk. **18. tie the knot,** *Informal.* to marry.

tie′ clasp′, *n.* [*count*] a usually decorated metal clasp or clip for securing the two ends of a necktie to a shirt front. Also called **tie′ clip′.**

tied (tīd) /tayd/ *adj.* **1.** in a state in which the same number of points, etc., has been scored by two competitors: *The two teams were tied going into the last period of play.* **2.** (of hands) prevented from taking action: *We'd like to help you but our hands are tied.* **3.** See *tie up* under TIE above.

tie′-in′, *adj.* [*before a noun*] **1.** of or relating to a sale in which the buyer must also purchase one or more other items. **2.** of or relating to several products advertised or sold together. **—***n.* [*count*] **3.** a marketing plan in which related products are promoted together: *a book and movie tie-in.* **4.** an item in a tie-in sale or advertisement. **5.** any direct or indirect link or relationship.

tier (tēr) /tɪər/ *n.* [*count*] **1.** one of a series of rows that rise one behind or above another, as of seats in a theater. **2.** a layer; level; stratum: *a wedding cake with six tiers.*

tie′-up′, *n.* [*count*] a stopping or slowing of traffic, etc., due to an accident, storm, etc.

tiff (tif) /tɪf/ *n.* [*count*] a slight, short quarrel.

ti•ger (tī′gər) /ˈtaygər/ *n.* [*count*], *pl.* **-gers,** (*esp. when thought of as a group* for 1) **-ger. 1.** a large, powerful, brownish-orange colored cat with black stripes: *Tigers are found in Asia.* **2.** a person resembling a tiger in fierceness, courage, etc. **—ti′ger•ish,** *adj.*

tight (tīt) /tayt/ *adj.* and *adv.,* **-er, -est.** **—***adj.* **1.** firmly fixed in place; secure: *a tight knot.* **2.** drawn or stretched tense; taut: *tight muscles.* **3.** fitting closely, esp. too closely: *That tight collar is choking me.* **4.** difficult to deal with or manage: *a tight situation.* **5.** of such close texture or fit as to prevent air, water, etc., from getting through: *a tight roof.* **6.** firm; rigid: *Security was tight after the bomb blast.* **7.** allowing little space, time, etc., between parts; full: *a tight schedule.* **8.** nearly even; close: *a tight race.* **9.** stingy; not generous with money: *a tight old boss who never gives raises.* **10.** *Slang.* drunk; tipsy: *a little tight after the party.* **11.** (of a market, etc.) in a condition in which demand is greater than supply: *Money is tight because interest rates are high.* **12.** feeling tense or painful: *He said his chest felt tight, and then he had a heart attack.* **—***adv.* **13.** in a tight manner; closely; securely: *Shut the door tight.* **14.** soundly or deeply: *to sleep tight.* **—*Idiom.* 15. run a tight ship,** to be smooth and efficient, as at a company: *The new boss ran a tight ship.* **—tight′ly,** *adv.*: *The dress fit too tightly.* **—tight′ness,** *n.* [*noncount*]: *complained of tightness in his chest.*

tight•en (tīt′n) /ˈtaytn̩/ *v.* **1.** to (cause to) become tight or tighter: [*no obj*]: *could feel his chest tighten with anxiety.* [~ + *obj*]: *to tighten rules regarding immigration.* **—*Idiom.* 2. tighten one's belt,** to respond to difficult times by reducing one's spending: *The family had to tighten their belts so the children could go to college.* **—tight′en•er,** *n.* [*count*]

tight-fist•ed or **tight•fist•ed** (tīt′fis′tid) /ˈtaytˈfɪstɪd/ *adj.* not generous with money; stingy.

tight-lipped (tī′lipt′) /ˈtayˈlɪpt/ *adj.* **1.** speaking very little; not saying much: *After the meeting everyone was tight-lipped about the results.* **2.** having the lips drawn tight.

tight•rope (tīt′rōp′) /ˈtaytˌrowp/ *n.* [*count*] **1.** a cable, stretched tight, on which acrobats perform feats of balancing. **2.** a risky or delicate situation: *We're walking a tightrope between the two sides.*

tights (tīts) /tayts/ *n.* [*plural*] **1.** a skintight, one-piece garment for the lower part of the body and the legs. **2.** a leotard with legs and, sometimes, feet.

tight•wad (tīt′wod′) /ˈtaytˌwɒd/ *n.* [*count*] a stingy person.

til•de (til′də) /ˈtɪldə/ *n.* [*count*], *pl.* **-des.** a special mark, (˜), written over an *n,* as in Spanish *mañana,* to show that the sound is pronounced like "ny," as in *canyon*; or written over a vowel, as in Portuguese *são,* to show that the vowel has a nasal sound.

tile (tīl) /tayl/ *n., v.,* **tiled, til•ing.** **—***n.* **1.** [*count*] a piece of baked clay, used for various purposes, as in forming a roof covering, etc.: *cracked and dirty tiles on the wall.* **2.** [*count*] any of various similar slabs or pieces, as of linoleum or metal. **3.** [*noncount*] tiles thought of as a group: *a floor of tile or marble.* **—***v.* [~ + *obj*] **4.** to cover with or as if with tiles: *a tiled roof.* **—til′er,** *n.* [*count*] **—til′ing,** *n.* [*noncount*]

till[1] (til) /tɪl/ *prep.* **1.** up to the time of; until: *to fight till death.* **2.** (used with a negative word or phrase) before; until: *They didn't come till today.* **3.** before; to: *My watch says ten till four.* **—***conj.* **4.** until: *Till we meet again, I'll be thinking of you.*

till[2] (til) /tɪl/ *v.* [~ + *obj*] to work on (land), as by plowing, etc., to raise crops; cultivate. **—till′a•ble,** *adj.*

till[3] (til) /tɪl/ *n.* [*count*] a drawer, box, or the like, in which money is kept, as in a shop.

till•age (til′ij) /ˈtɪlɪdʒ/ *n.* [*noncount*] the operation, practice, or art of tilling land.

til•ler (til′ər) /ˈtɪlər/ *n.* [*count*] a bar on the top of a ship's rudder, for turning the rudder and steering.

tilt (tilt) /tɪlt/ *v.* **1.** to (cause to) lean, slant, or incline: [*no obj*]: *The room tilted during the earthquake.* [~ + *obj*]: *He tilted his head to one side.* **2.** [*no obj;* (~ + *at* + *obj*)] to charge or attack with a lance or the like, as between knights on horseback: *The two knights tilted at each other and came together with a tremendous crash.* —*n.* [*count*] **3.** an act or instance of tilting. **4.** the state of being tilted; a sloping position. —***Idiom.*** **5. (at) full tilt,** at greatest speed; with great energy: *The company started manufacturing the gadgets at full tilt.* **6. tilt at windmills,** to struggle against imaginary opponents.

tim•ber (tim′bər) /ˈtɪmbər/ *n.* **1.** [*noncount*] the wood of trees used for construction. **2.** [*noncount*] growing trees themselves, or the land where they grow. **3.** [*count*] a single piece of wood forming part of a structure: *A timber fell from the roof.* **4.** [*noncount*] one who is thought of as having very great qualifications; caliber: *He's presidential timber.* —*interj.* **5.** (used as a lumberjack's call to warn others that a cut tree is about to fall). —**tim′bered,** *adj.*

tim•ber•line (tim′bər līn′) /ˈtɪmbərˌlayn/ *n.* [*count*] the altitude above sea level at which timber cannot grow.

tim•bre (tam′bər, tim′-) /ˈtæmbər, ˈtɪm-/ *n.* [*noncount*] the special, usually unique quality of sound produced by a particular instrument or voice; tone color.

time (tīm) /taym/ *n., adj., v.,* **timed, tim•ing.** —*n.* **1.** [*noncount*] the system in which events follow from one to another; the passing of minutes, hours, days, or years: *Einstein's conception of time.* **2.** [*noncount; sometimes: Time*] a system of measuring the passage of time: *six o'clock Greenwich Mean Time.* **3.** [*count; often: a + singular*] a limited period, as between two events: *a long time.* **4.** [*count*] a particular period: *Youth is the best time of life.* **5.** Often, **times.** [*plural*] **a.** a period in history, esp. one existing over the same years as (the life of) a famous person: [*count*]: *prehistoric times.* [*noncount*]: *in Lincoln's time.* **b.** [*count*] the current period of months, years, etc., or the period just passed: *It's a sign of the times.* **c.** [*count*] a period identified with reference to its conditions: *hard times.* **6.** [*noncount*] the end of a period, as of one's life or a pregnancy: *His time had come (= He would die shortly). When her time came, she delivered twins.* **7.** [*count*] a period experienced in a particular way: *Have a good time.* **8.** [*noncount*] a period of work of an employee, or the pay for it: *He's put in his time at the job.* **9.** [*noncount*] *Informal.* a term of forced duty or imprisonment or jail: *had to do time for her crime.* **10.** [*noncount*] the period necessary for something: *The bus takes too much time, so I'll take a plane.* **11.** [*noncount*] leisure or spare time: *I hope to take some time (= for vacation) in August.* **12.** a definite point in time, as indicated by a clock: [*noncount*]: *breakfast time.* [*count*]: *at evening times.* **13.** [*count*] a special or agreed-on instant or period: *There is a time for everything.* **14.** the particular time when an event is scheduled to take place: [*noncount*]: *Curtain time is at 8.* [*count*]: *Departure times have been pushed back.* **15.** [*noncount*] an indefinite period into the future: *Time will tell.* **16.** [*count*] each occasion of a repeated action: *to do something five times.* **17. times,** [*plural*] the number of instances a quantity or factor are taken together: *Two goes into six three times.* **18.** [*noncount*] *Music.* **a.** tempo; the speed of movement in a piece of music, or its characteristic meter or rhythm. **b.** proper rhythm or tempo: *The drummer couldn't keep time.* See *keep time* below. **19.** [*noncount*] rate of marching, counted by the number of steps taken per minute: *double time.* —*adj.* [*before a noun*] **20.** of or relating to the passage of time. **21.** (of an explosive device) containing a clock so that it will explode at the desired moment: *a time bomb.* **22.** of or relating to an installment plan of paying: *time payments.* —*v.* [~ + *obj*] **23.** to measure or record the speed or rate of: *The judges timed the race.* **24.** to fix how long (something) should be: *She timed the test at 15 minutes.* **25.** to fix the interval between (actions, etc.): *They timed their strokes at six per minute.* **26.** to regulate (a train, etc.) as to time. **27.** to choose the moment or occasion for; schedule: *He timed the attack perfectly.* —***Idiom.*** **28. against time,** in an effort to finish within a limited period: *The advertising team was working against time to finish the project.* **29. ahead of one's time,** in advance of others in one's thinking, etc.: *Those ancient astronomers were way ahead of their time.* **30. ahead of time,** before the time due; early: *arrived ahead of time and had to wait.* **31. at one time, a.** once; formerly: *At one time she was the chairman of the board.* **b.** at the same time; simultaneously: *He was at one time chairman of the board and president of the company.* **32. at the same time,** nevertheless; yet: *He's young; at the same time, he's quite responsible.* **33. at times,** occasionally: *The car seems to stall at times.* **34. behind the times,** old-fashioned; out-of-date; dated: *She complained that her parents were behind the times.* **35. for the time being,** temporarily; for the present; for a while: *For the time being we'll let you stay on the job.* **36. from time to time,** occasionally; at different periods: *From time to time she'd let me watch as she painted.* **37. gain time,** to achieve a delay or postponement: *He tried to gain time by putting off the signing of the papers.* **38. in good time, a.** in advance of the appointed time; punctually: *We arrived there in good time.* **b.** at the best or appropriate time: *"When can we open the presents?" —"All in good time."* **39. in no time,** in a very brief time: *In no time she was at the door, ready to go.* **40. in time, a.** early enough: *Come in time for dinner.* **b.** in the future; eventually: *In time he'll understand.* **c.** in the correct rhythm or tempo: *The drummer isn't in time.* **41. keep time, a.** to record time, as a watch does: *Does your watch keep good time?* **b.** to mark or observe the correct tempo, as by performing rhythmic movements. **42. kill time,** to occupy oneself with some activity to make time pass more quickly: *killed time by watching TV.* **43. make time,** to move or travel quickly: *We made very good time on the highway.* **44. mark time, a.** to slow one's progress for a while; fail to advance: *The company was just marking time, but its competitors were forging ahead.* **b.** to move the feet as in marching, but without advancing or moving forward. **45. on one's own time,** during one's free time; while not being paid. **46. on time, a.** at the specified time: *For once the train was on time.* **b.** to be paid for within a designated period of time, as in installments. **47. take one's time,** to act without hurry. **48. the time of one's life,** a very enjoyable experience: *We had the time of our lives at the seashore.* **49. time after time,** again and again; repeatedly: *Time after time he'd try to get over the wall.* **50. time and (time) again,** repeatedly; often. —**tim′er,** *n.* [*count*]

time′ clock′, *n.* [*count*] a clock that records the time, used to keep a record of when an employee arrives or departs.

time′ frame′, *n.* [*count*] a period of time during which something has taken or will take place.

time′-hon′ored, *adj.* respected because for a long time it has been done this way: *a time-honored custom.* Also, *esp. Brit.,* **time′-hon′oured.**

time•keep•er (tīm′kē′pər) /ˈtaymˌkiypər/ *n.* [*count*] an official who times how long a sports contest goes on.

time•less (tīm′lis) /ˈtaymlɪs/ *adj.* **1.** without beginning or end; eternal. **2.** referring or restricted to no particular time: *timeless beauty.* —**time′less•ly,** *adv.* —**time′less•ness,** *n.*

time•ly (tīm′lē) /ˈtaymliy/ *adj.,* **-li•er, -li•est.** occurring or happening at a good or suitable time: *a timely warning.*

time′-out′ or **time′out′,** *n., pl.* **-outs. 1.** [*count*] a brief stopping of activity: *a time-out to relax.* **2.** an interruption in a sports contest: [*count*]: *A two-minute time-out was called.* [*noncount*]: *Time-out was called.*

time•piece (tīm′pēs′) /ˈtaymˌpiys/ *n.* [*count*] a device for measuring and recording the progress of time, as a clock.

time′-shar′ing, *n.* [*noncount*] **1.** a plan in which several people share costs of a vacation home: *Time-sharing allows each person to use a residence for a specified period of time each year.* **2.** a computer system in which users at different terminals use a single computer at the same time.

time•ta•ble (tīm′tā′bəl) /ˈtaymˌteybəl/ *n.* [*count*] **1.** a schedule showing the times at which railroad trains, etc., arrive and depart. See illustration at TERMINAL. **2.** a schedule that names the times when certain things occur: *a timetable for finishing the job.*

time•worn (tīm′wôrn′, -wōrn′) /ˈtaymˌwɔrn, -ˌwowrn/ *adj.* **1.** worn down by time; showing the effects of age, as by being out-of-date: *timeworn farming methods.* **2.** too common and no longer interesting: *a timeworn excuse.*

time′ zone′, *n.* [*count*] one of the 24 divisions of the globe wherein time is decided to be a certain number of hours ahead of or behind that of the time at Greenwich, England: *The former Soviet Union comprised seven time zones.*

tim•id (tim′id) /ˈtɪmɪd/ *adj.,* **-er, -est.** lacking in self-assurance, courage, or boldness: *a timid child.* —**ti•mid•**

i•ty (ti mid′i tē) /tɪ'mɪdɪtiy/ **tim′id•ness,** *n.* [*noncount*] —**tim′id•ly,** *adv.*

tim•ing (tī′ming) /'taymɪŋ/ *n.* [*noncount*] **1.** the selecting of the best time for doing or saying something to obtain the desired effect: *Asking the boss for a raise on the day that a huge loss was reported was an act of very bad timing.* **2.** the ability of a performer, esp. in comedy, to deliver lines, etc., at whatever time or moment will create the desired effect.

tim•or•ous (tim′ər əs) /'tɪmərəs/ *adj.* **1.** full of or subject to fear; fearful. **2.** expressing or indicating fear or timidity: *a timorous approach to a serious problem.* —**tim′or•ous•ly,** *adv.* —**tim′or•ous•ness,** *n.* [*noncount*]

tim•pa•ni or **tym•pa•ni** (tim′pə nē) /'tɪmpəniy/ *n.* [*plural; used with a plural verb*] a set of kettledrums, as used in an orchestra. —**tim′pa•nist,** *n.* [*count*]

tin (tin) /tɪn/ *n., adj., v.,* **tinned, tin•ning.** —*n.* **1.** [*noncount*] a low-melting metal element with a silvery color and luster: *Tin is used in plating and in making tinfoil.* **2.** [*count*] a shallow pan, esp. one used in baking: *a pie tin.* **3.** [*count*] any container made of or plated with tin. **4.** [*count*] *Chiefly Brit.* a sealed can containing food: *tins of soup in the cupboard.* —*adj.* **5.** made of tin or plated with tin. —*v.* [~ + *obj*] **6.** to cover or coat with tin. **7.** *Chiefly Brit.* to preserve or pack (food, etc.) in cans; can.

tinc•ture (tingk′chər) /'tɪŋktʃər/ *n.* a medicine that is a solution of a drug in alcohol: [*noncount*]: *tincture of iodine.* [*count*]: *The pharmacist made some tinctures.*

tin•der (tin′dər) /'tɪndər/ *n.* [*noncount*] any dry substance or material that easily catches fire. —**tin′der•y,** *adj.*

tin•der•box (tin′dər boks′) /'tɪndərˌbɒks/ *n.* [*count*] **1.** a box for holding tinder. **2.** a person or thing thought of as highly likely to explode, become violent, etc.: *For years that region was a tinderbox.*

tine (tīn) /tayn/ *n.* [*count*] a sharp point or prong, as of a fork.

tinge (tinj) /tɪndʒ/ *v.,* **tinged, tinge•ing** or **ting•ing,** *n.* —*v.* [~ + *obj*] **1.** to give a slight degree of color to; tint: *walls tinged with brown from the rusty steam pipes.* **2.** to give a slight trace of (some) feeling or emotion to: *praise tinged with envy.* —*n.* [*count*] **3.** a slight trace, as of coloring.

tin•gle (ting′gəl) /'tɪŋgəl/ *v.,* **-gled, -gling,** *n.* —*v.* [*no obj*] **1.** to have a feeling of slight stings, as if from pins or from cold: *His arm tingled when he hit his elbow.* **2.** to cause such a feeling: *The cold tingled on his face.* —*n.* [*count*] **3.** the tingling action of cold, excitement, etc. —**tin•gly** (ting′glē) /'tɪŋgliy/ *adj.,* **-gli•er, -gli•est**: *He gets a funny, tingly feeling when she walks in the room.*

tin•ker (ting′kər) /'tɪŋkər/ *n.* [*count*] **1.** a mender of pots and pans who wanders from place to place seeking work. **2.** an unskillful or clumsy worker. —*v.* [*no obj*] **3.** to work with a thing without useful results: *She likes to tinker with the car.* **4.** to work clumsily at anything. —**tin′ker•er,** *n.* [*count*]

tin•kle (ting′kəl) /'tɪŋkəl/ *v.,* **-kled, -kling,** *n.* —*v.* **1.** to (cause to) make light ringing sounds, as a small bell: [*no obj*]: *A bell tinkled in the background.* [~ + *obj*]: *He tinkled the bell.* **2.** [~ + *obj*] to make known by tinkling: *to tinkle the time.* —*n.* [*count*] **3.** a tinkling sound. **4.** an instance of tinkling. **5.** a telephone call.

tin•ny (tin′ē) /'tɪniy/ *adj.,* **-ni•er, -ni•est. 1.** of or like tin; containing tin. **2.** lacking in a deep or solid sound: *a tinny piano.* **3.** not durable; easily broken; flimsy. **4.** having the taste of tin: *a can of tinny fruit cocktail.* —**tin′ni•ness,** *n.* [*noncount*]

tin′ plate′ or **tin′plate′,** *n.* [*noncount*] thin iron or steel in the form of a thin sheet coated with tin. Also called **tin.**

tin•sel (tin′səl) /'tɪnsəl/ *n.* [*noncount*] **1.** a thin sheet or thread of glittering metal, used to produce a sparkling effect in threads and decorations: *looping pieces of tinsel on the Christmas tree.* —*adj.* **2.** consisting of tinsel. —**tin′sel•like′,** *adj.* —**tin′sel•ly,** *adj.*

tint (tint) /tɪnt/ *n.* [*count*] **1.** a variety of a color; a hue. **2.** a delicate or pale color. **3.** a commercial dye for the hair. —*v.* [~ + *obj*] **4.** to color slightly; tinge: *He tinted his hair light brown.* —**tint′ed,** *adj.*: *a pair of slightly tinted sunglasses.* —**tint′er,** *n.* [*count*]

tin•tin•nab•u•la•tion (tin′ti nab′yə lā′shən) /ˌtɪntɪˌnæbyə'leyʃən/ *n.* [*count*] the ringing or sound of bells.

ti•ny (tī′nē) /'tayniy/ *adj.,* **-ni•er, -ni•est.** very small; little; minute: *trying to build houses on tiny parcels of land.* —**ti′ni•ness,** *n.* [*noncount*]

-tion, *suffix. -tion* is attached to verbs to form nouns that refer to actions or states of the verb: *relate + -tion → relation; sect- + -tion → section; abbreviate + -tion → abbreviation.* Compare -ION.

-tious, *suffix. -tious* is attached to roots to form adjectives, some of which are related to nouns: *fiction: fictitious; ambition: ambitious; caution: cautious; rambunctious, propitious.*

tip[1] (tip) /tɪp/ *n., v.,* **tipped, tip•ping.** —*n.* [*count*] **1.** a pointed end: *the tips of the fingers.* **2.** the top; apex: *the tip of a steeple.* **3.** a small piece covering the end of something: *a cane with a rubber tip.* —*v.* [~ + *obj*] **4.** to give or provide with a tip. **5.** to mark the tip of.

tip[2] (tip) /tɪp/ *v.,* **tipped, tip•ping,** *n.* —*v.* **1.** to (cause to) be in a slanting position; tilt: [*no obj*]: *The floor tipped as the earthquake rocked the region.* [~ + *obj*]: *He tipped his hat in greeting.* **2.** to overturn; upset; (cause to) tumble: [~ + *obj* (+ *over*)]: *to tip the basket (over).* [~ (+ *over*) + *obj*]: *He tipped (over) the basket.* [*no obj;* (~ + *over*)]: *The lamp tipped (over) and the light bulb exploded.* —*n.* [*count*] **3.** the act of tipping. **4.** the state of being tipped. **5.** *Brit.* a dump for garbage.

tip[3] (tip) /tɪp/ *n., v.,* **tipped, tip•ping.** —*n.* [*count*] **1.** a gift of money over and above payment; a gratuity: *a tip for the waiter.* **2.** a piece of secret information: *a tip on a racehorse; a tip on a drug raid.* **3.** a useful hint or idea: *tips on gardening.* —*v.* **4.** to give a gift of money over and above payment: [~ + *obj*]: *tipping a waiter.* [*no obj*]: *She tipped lavishly.* **5. tip off,** to give secret information: [~ + *off* + *obj*]: *Someone must have tipped off the cops.* [~ + *obj* + *off*]: *Someone must have tipped him off.* —**tip′per,** *n.* [*count*]: *She's not a big tipper.*

tip•off (tip′ôf′, -of′) /'tɪpˌɔf, -ˌɒf/ *n.* [*count*] a jump ball that begins each period of a basketball game.

tip•ple (tip′əl) /'tɪpəl/ *v.,* **-pled, -pling,** *n.* —*v.* **1.** [*no obj*] to drink liquor, esp. too much. **2.** [~ + *obj*] to drink (liquor), esp. often and in small amounts. —*n.* [*count*] **3.** liquor; alcohol. —**tip′pler,** *n.* [*count*]

tip•ster (tip′stər) /'tɪpstər/ *n.* [*count*] a person who sells or provides tips, as for betting.

tip•sy (tip′sē) /'tɪpsiy/ *adj.,* **-si•er, -si•est. 1.** slightly intoxicated: *tipsy after that three-martini lunch.* **2.** caused by being slightly intoxicated: *a tipsy lurch.* —**tip•si•ly** (tip′sə lē) /'tɪpsəliy/ *adv.* —**tip′si•ness,** *n.* [*noncount*]

tip•toe (tip′tō′) /'tɪpˌtow/ *n., v.,* **-toed, -toe•ing.** —*n.* **1.** the tip or end of a toe: [*count*]: *She stood on her tiptoes.* [*noncount*]: *She walked in on tiptoe.* —*v.* [*no obj*] **2.** to go on tiptoe, so as to be secret or quiet or to remain unnoticed: *tiptoed into the room while he was sleeping.*

tip•top (tip′top′, -top′) /'tɪpˌtɒp, -'tɒp/ *n.* [*noncount*] **1.** the highest point of something. **2.** the highest degree, as of excellence. —*adj.* **3.** situated at the very top. **4.** of the highest quality, etc.: *an athlete in tiptop shape.* —*adv.* **5.** very well: *Things are shaping up tiptop.*

ti•rade (tī′rād, tī rād′) /'tayreyd, tay'reyd/ *n.* [*count*] a long, angry speech: *launched into a lengthy tirade on greed.*

tire[1] (tīər) /tayər/ *v.,* **tired, tir•ing. 1.** to make or become weary or fatigued: [~ + *obj*]: *The exercise tired him momentarily.* [*no obj*]: *As he grew older he tired easily.* **2.** [~ + *of* + *obj*] to have one's interest or patience exhausted: *The children tired of playing games.* **3. tire out,** [~ + *obj* + *out*] to make (someone) completely weary: *The exercise tired him out.*

tire[2] (tīər) /tayər/ *n.* [*count*] a ring of rubber, placed over the rim of a wheel on cars, trucks, etc., to provide traction or resistance to wear.

tired (tīərd) /tayərd/ *adj.* **1.** exhausted; fatigued; wearied: *The tired children slept in the car on the way home.* **2.** [*be* + ~ + *of*] weary or bored: *was tired of the same old routine.* **3.** old and no longer funny or interesting: *a tired joke.*

tire•less (tīər′lis) /'tayərlɪs/ *adj.* not easily made tired: *a tireless worker.* —**tire′less•ly,** *adv.*: *worked tirelessly for her students.* —**tire′less•ness,** *n.* [*noncount*]

tire•some (tīər′səm) /'tayərsəm/ *adj.* **1.** causing one to become tired: *tiresome exercises.* **2.** annoying: *that tiresome guy who always asks the same dumb questions.* —**tire′some•ly,** *adv.* —**tire′some•ness,** *n.* [*noncount*]

tir•ing (tīər′ing) /'tayərɪŋ/ *adj.* **1.** causing a feeling of tiredness: *tiring exercises.* **2.** annoying: *a tiring woman.*

'tis (tiz) /tɪz/ *contraction.* a shortened form of *it is.*

tis•sue (tish′o͞o) /'tɪʃuw/ *n.* **1.** a group of similar cells forming a structural part of a living thing: [*noncount*]: *living tissue; soft tissue.* [*count*]: *That virus could invade the body's tissues.* **2.** tissue paper. **3.** any of several kinds of soft paper used for various purposes: [*noncount*]: *toilet tissue.* [*count*]: *He took a tissue and wiped* *his nose.* **4.** [*count*] a connected series or mass: *a tissue of lies.*

tis′sue pa′per, *n.* [*noncount*] a kind of very thin paper used for wrapping, packing, etc.

tit[1] (tit) /tɪt/ *n.* [*count*] **1.** a titmouse. **2.** any of various other small birds.

tit[2] (tit) /tɪt/ *n.* [*count*] **1.** a teat. **2.** *Slang* (*vulgar*). a breast.

ti•tan (tīt′n) /ˈtaytn̩/ *n.* [*count*] a person or thing of great size, strength, or influence: *a titan of industry.*

ti•tan•ic (tī tan′ik) /tayˈtænɪk/, *adj.* of great size, strength, or power.

ti•ta•ni•um (tī tā′nē əm) /tayˈteyniyəm/ *n.* [*noncount*] a dark gray or silvery, shiny, very hard, light, metallic element that resists corrosion, used to toughen steel.

tit for tat (tit′ fər tat′) /ˈtɪtˈ fər tæt/ *n.* [*noncount*] anything that is equivalent to something else and is given or inflicted as a retaliation for something done to oneself.

tithe (tīth) /tayð/ *n., v.,* **tithed, tith•ing.** **—***n.* [*count*] **1.** Sometimes, **tithes.** the tenth part of one's goods or income, paid voluntarily for support of the church. **2.** any tax or levy, esp. of one-tenth. **3.** a tenth or small part of something. **—***v.* **4.** to give or pay a tithe of (one's income): [~ + *obj*]: *to tithe one's income.* [*no obj*]: *The family promised to tithe.* —**tith′er,** *n.* [*count*]

ti•tian (tish′ən) /ˈtɪʃən/ *n.* [*noncount*] **1.** a bright golden brown color. **—***adj.* **2.** bright golden brown: *titian hair.*

tit•il•late (tit′l āt′) /ˈtɪtl̩ˌeyt/ *v.* [~ + *obj*], **-lat•ed, -lat•ing.** to excite agreeably or pleasantly: *to titillate one's curiosity.* —**tit′il•lat′ing,** *adj.*: *The newspaper was filled with titillating stories about her affairs.* —**tit′il•lat′ing•ly,** *adv.* —**tit•il•la•tion** (tit′l ā′shən) /ˌtɪtl̩ˈeyʃən/ *n.* [*noncount*]

ti•tle (tīt′l) /ˈtaytl̩/ *n., adj., v.,* **-tled, -tling.** **—***n.* **1.** [*count*] the name of an artistic work, as a book, painting, etc. **2.** [*count*] a heading, as of a chapter of a book, that describes what is contained: *The title was: "Chapter 4: Issues and Implications."* **3.** [*count*] a book, magazine, or other publication: *We published 25 titles last year.* **4.** [*count*] a descriptive name, esp. by right of rank or office: *He was given the title of "Lord Mayor."* **5.** [*count*] a championship: *to win a tennis title.* **6.** [*noncount*] an established right to something, as to (possessing) land or property: *has title to the farm his parents owned.* **7.** [*count*] the document that is the legal evidence of such right: *Sign the back of your title when transferring ownership of your car.* **8.** Usually, **titles.** [*plural*] any written matter inserted into a motion-picture or television program, as credits or subtitles. **—***adj.* [*before a noun*] **9.** of or relating to a title: *The title story (= the story whose title is the same as the title of the collection) in her collection of pieces was the most famous.* **10.** that decides a championship: *a title bout.* **—***v.* [~ + *obj* + *obj*] **11.** to furnish with a title; entitle: *What will you title your book?*

tit•mouse (tit′mous′) /ˈtɪtˌmaws/ *n.* [*count*], *pl.* **-mice** (-mīs′) /-ˌmays/. a small songbird with a stout bill.

tit•ter (tit′ər) /ˈtɪtər/ *v.* [*no obj*] **1.** to giggle or laugh in a somewhat hesitant or nervous way: *At first the audience tittered nervously at his jokes.* **—***n.* [*count*] **2.** a tittering laugh.

tit•tle (tit′l) /ˈtɪtl̩/ *n.* [*count*] **1.** a dot or other small mark in writing or printing. **2.** a very small thing: *I don't care a tittle.*

tit•tle-tat•tle (tit′l tat′l) /ˈtɪtl̩ˈtætl̩/ *n., v.,* **-tled, -tling.** **—***n.* [*noncount*] **1.** gossip; chatter that is meaningless. **—***v.* [*no obj*] **2.** to talk idly; to gossip or chatter.

tit•u•lar (tich′ə lər, tit′yə-) /ˈtɪtʃələr, ˈtɪtyə-/ *adj.* **1.** being (such a thing) in title only; nominal: *The king was titular ruler of the country, but the army really controlled things.* **2.** having the same name as the title: *the titular hero of the novel.* **3.** of or relating to a title.

tiz•zy (tiz′ē) /ˈtɪziy/ *n.* [*count; usually singular*], *pl.* **-zies.** *Slang.* a nervous, excited, or distracted state: *He was all in a tizzy when the boss inspected the department.*

TLC or **T.L.C.** or **t.l.c.,** an abbreviation of: tender loving care.

TM, an abbreviation of: trademark.

TN, an abbreviation of: Tennessee.

TNT, *n.* [*noncount*] a chemical substance that is a high explosive.

to (to͞o; *unstressed* to͝o, tə) /tuw; *unstressed* tʊ, tə/ *prep.* **1.** (used to express motion or direction toward a place, person, or thing approached and reached): *Come to the house.* **2.** (used to express motion or direction toward something): *from north to south.* **3.** (used to express a limitation of movement or growth): *He grew to six feet.* **4.** (used to express the destination of a journey or process): *He was sentenced to jail.* **5.** (used to express a resulting condition): *He tore it to pieces.* **6.** (used to express the object of hope): *They drank to her health.* **7.** (used to express the object of a claim): *Who were the claimants to the estate?* **8.** (used to express a limitation in degree or amount): *I was chilled to the bone.* **9.** compared with: *This year's harvest is inferior to last year's.* **10.** in accordance with; according to: *promised us a room to our liking.* **11.** with respect to; with reference to: *What will he say to this?* **12.** (used to express in; making up): *There are 12 to the dozen.* **13.** (used to express the indirect object of a verb): *Give it to me. Show the book to the girl.* **14.** (used as the ordinary marker of the infinitive, as after certain verbs or adjectives, or when standing alone): *To be or not to be, that is the question. They left early (in order) to catch their flight. It's too late to try calling now.* **15.** raised to the power indicated: *Three to the fourth (power) is 81* ($3^4 = 81$). **—***adv.* **16.** toward a point, person, place, or thing. **17.** toward a closed position: *Pull the door to.* **18.** into a state of consciousness: *After he came to, he remembered what had happened.* **—*Idiom.*** **19. to and fro,** back and forth: *trees swaying to and fro in the wind.* **—Usage.** See UNTIL.

toad (tōd) /towd/ *n.* [*count*] **1.** an animal like a frog, living mostly on land but able to breathe in water, and having no tail and a dry, warty skin. Compare FROG[1] (def. 1). **2.** a disgusting person or thing.

toad•stool (tōd′sto͞ol′) /ˈtowdˌstuwl/ *n.* [*count*] **1.** a kind of mushroom with an umbrellalike cap. **2.** a poisonous mushroom, as distinguished from one that can be eaten.

toad•y (tō′dē) /ˈtowdiy/ *n., pl.* **toad•ies,** *v.,* **toad•ied, toad•y•ing.** **—***n.* [*count*] **1.** one who flatters another to gain favor; a sycophant. **—***v.* [*no obj*] **2.** to be or act like one who flatters another to gain favor: *an employee who toadies to the boss.*

toast[1] (tōst) /towst/ *n.* [*noncount*] **1.** sliced bread browned by dry heat. **—***v.* **2.** (of bread, etc.) to (cause to) become brown by dry heat: [~ + *obj*]: *to toast a few slices of bread.* [*no obj*]: *This bread doesn't toast well.* **3.** [~ + *obj*] to heat or warm thoroughly at a fire, as one's hands or feet.

toast[2] (tōst) /towst/ *n.* [*count*] **1.** a few words of welcome, congratulations, etc., said just before drinking (usually, an alcoholic beverage) to honor a person, event, etc.: *I propose a toast to all our good friends gathered here tonight.* **2.** a person, event, etc., honored with raised glasses before drinking. **3.** [*usually singular; the* + ~ + *of*] a person, esp. an entertainer, who is widely celebrated or famous: *She was the toast of five countries.* **—***v.* [~ + *obj*] **4.** to propose or drink a toast to or in honor of: *They toasted the newlyweds.*

toast•er (tō′stər) /ˈtowstər/ *n.* [*count*] **1.** an appliance for toasting bread, muffins, etc. See illustration at APPLIANCE. **2.** one who toasts something.

toast•mas•ter (tōst′mas′tər) /ˈtowstˌmæstər/ *n.* [*count*] **1.** one who is the host of a dinner and introduces the after-dinner speakers. **2.** one who announces toasts.

toast•y (tō′stē) /ˈtowstiy/ *adj.,* **-i•er, -i•est.** cozily warm: *hopping back into her toasty bed.*

to•bac•co (tə bak′ō) /təˈbækow/ *n., pl.* **-cos, -coes.** **1.** [*noncount*] a plant of the nightshade family whose leaves are prepared for smoking. **2.** the prepared leaves of this plant, as used in cigarettes, cigars, and pipes: [*noncount*]: *The smell of tobacco hung in the room.* [*count*]: *different tobaccos for different blends.* —**to•bac′co•less,** *adj.*

to•bac•co•nist (tə bak′ə nist) /təˈbækənɪst/ *n.* [*count*] a dealer in tobacco.

to•bog•gan (tə bog′ən) /təˈbɒgən/ *n.* [*count*] **1.** a long, narrow, flat-bottomed sled. **—***v.* [*no obj*] **2.** to coast on a toboggan. —**to•bog′gan•er, to•bog′gan•ist,** *n.* [*count*]

toc•sin (tok′sin) /ˈtɒksɪn/ *n.* [*count*] **1.** a signal, esp. of alarm, sounded on a bell. **2.** a bell used to sound an alarm.

to•day (tə dā′) /təˈdey/ *n.* [*noncount*] **1.** this present day: *What's today? Today is Thursday.* **2.** this present age: *The songs of today aren't nearly as much fun as the songs of yesterday.* **—***adv.* **3.** on this present day: *Call me today.* **4.** at the present time; in these days: *There are many changes in the workplace today.*

tod•dle (tod′l) /ˈtɒdl̩/ *v.,* **-dled, -dling,** *n.* **—***v.* [*no obj*] **1.** to move with short, unsteady steps, as a young child does. **—***n.* [*count*] **2.** the act of toddling.

tod•dler (tod′lər) /ˈtɒdlər/ *n.* [*count*] a child who has just started to walk but may be unsteady on his or her feet.

tod•dy (tod′ē) /ˈtɒdiy/ *n.* [*count*], *pl.* **-dies.** a drink of liquor and hot water, sweetened and spiced: *a hot toddy.*

to-do′ *n.* [*count*], *pl.* **-dos.** a bustle; a fuss: *to make a big to-do over the party.*

toe (tō) /tow/ *n., v.,* **toed, toe•ing.** —*n.* [*count*] **1.** one of the five fingerlike parts at the end of the foot. **2.** the front part of a shoe or stocking. **3.** a part resembling a toe in shape or position. —*v.* [~ + *obj*] **4.** to touch or kick with the toe or toes. —***Idiom.*** **5. on one's toes,** full of energy; alert; ready: *Competition will keep you on your toes.* **6. step** or **tread on someone's toes,** to offend a person by intruding on his or her rights or responsibilities. **7. toe the line** or **mark,** to follow a rule, command, etc.; obey orders: *You'll have to toe the line with the new boss.*

toe•hold or **toe-hold** (tō′hōld′) /ˈtowˌhowld/ *n.* [*count*] **1.** a small space in something, as a ledge on a hill, just large enough to support the toes, as in climbing. **2.** any slight advantage or support that helps progress: *He had a toehold in the company when the chairman of the board recommended him.*

toe•nail (tō′nāl′) /ˈtowˌneyl/ *n.* [*count*] the nail of a toe.

tof•fee or **tof•fy** (tô′fē, tof′ē) /ˈtɔfiy, ˈtɒfiy/ *n., pl.* **-fees** or **-fies.** a hard, brittle candy made by boiling together brown sugar, butter, and vinegar: [*noncount*]: *pieces of toffee sticking to his teeth.* [*count*]: *a plate of wrapped toffees.*

to•fu (tō′fo͞o) /ˈtowfuw/ *n.* [*noncount*] a soft, cheeselike food made from curdled soybean milk.

to•ga (tō′gə) /ˈtowgə/ *n. [count]*, pl. **-gas, -gae** (-jē, -gē) /-dʒiy, -giy/. a white, loose-fitting outer garment originally worn in ancient Rome. —**to′gaed,** *adj.*

to•geth•er (tə geth′ər) /təˈgɛðər/ *adv.* **1.** into or in one gathering or body: *Call the people together.* **2.** into or in union, as two or more things: *to sew things together.* **3.** into relationship, etc., as two or more persons: *to bring strangers together.* **4.** considered as a group: *This one computer costs more than all the others together.* **5.** (of a single thing) into a condition of being squeezed tight: *to squeeze a thing together.* **6.** at the same time; simultaneously: *We left together.* **7.** continuously; without interruption: *for days together.* **8.** in cooperation; with united action; jointly: *to undertake a task together.* —*adj.* **9.** *Informal.* stable in one's emotions: *a very together person.* —**to•geth′er•ness,** *n.* [*noncount*]: *The family showed its togetherness by helping anyone who needed it.*

tog•gle (tog′əl) /ˈtɒgəl/ *n., v.,* **-gled, -gling.** —*n.* [*count*] **1.** a switch, esp. one that can be switched only on or off. **2.** any similar rod used to hold something in place. —*v.* **3.** [~ + *obj*] to bind or fasten using such a rod. **4.** [*no obj*] to switch back and forth between two computer operations, or among different programs: *to toggle from one screen to the other.*

toil (toil) /tɔyl/ *n.* [*noncount*] **1.** hard or exhausting work. —*v.* [*no obj*] **2.** to work or labor with great difficulty: *to toil on the project night and day.* **3.** to move with great effort: *to toil up a hill.* —**toil′er,** *n.* [*count*] —**toil′some,** *adj.*

toi•let (toi′lit) /ˈtɔylɪt/ *n.* **1.** [*count*] a large bowl with a water-flushing device for getting rid of body wastes. See illustration at APARTMENT. **2.** [*count*] a bathroom or washroom; lavatory. **3.** [*noncount*] the act or process of grooming oneself.

toi′let pa′per, *n.* [*count*] a soft, lightweight paper used in bathrooms for personal cleansing after defecation or urination. Also called **toi′let tis′sue.**

toi•let•ry (toi′li trē) /ˈtɔylɪtriy/ *n.* [*count*], *pl.* **-ries.** any article, substance, or preparation used in washing, cleaning, or grooming oneself, as soap or deodorant.

toi•lette (twä let′) /twɑˈlɛt/ *n.* TOILET (def. 3).

toke (tōk) /towk/ *n., v.,* **toked, tok•ing.** *Slang.* —*n.* [*count*] **1.** a puff on a marijuana cigarette. **2.** a marijuana cigarette. —*v.* **3.** to smoke (a marijuana cigarette): [~ + *obj*]: *to toke a joint.* [*no obj*]: *to toke on a joint.*

to•ken (tō′kən) /ˈtowkən/ *n.* [*count*] **1.** something serving to represent some feeling, event, etc.: *a token of my esteem.* **2.** a memento; a souvenir: *Guinevere offered Lancelot a scarf as a token of their love.* **3.** a stamped piece of metal used in place of money, as for bus fares: *He dropped his token in the slot, but the turnstile stuck.* —*adj.* [*before a noun*] **4.** hired, admitted, etc., in some job to prevent charges of prejudice or discrimination, as against a minority: *a token male on an all-female staff.* **5.** slight; minimal; not showing much effort or effect: *He received a token salary.* —***Idiom.*** **6. by the same token,** for similar reasons; furthermore: *He has a good eye for detail and by the same token is a very good artist.* **7. in token of,** as a sign of; in evidence of: *a ring in token of one's love.*

to•ken•ism (tō′kə niz′əm) /ˈtowkəˌnɪzəm/ *n.* [*noncount*] the policy of making only a slight effort to offer equal opportunities to minorities.

told (tōld) /towld/ *v.* **1.** pt. and pp. of TELL. —***Idiom.*** **2. all told,** counting everyone or everything; in all: *All told, there were thirty students in the linguistics class.*

tol•er•a•ble (tol′ər ə bəl) /ˈtɒlərəbəl/ *adj.* **1.** capable of being tolerated: *The weather wasn't very good in the summer, but it was tolerable if you took precautions.* **2.** fairly good; not bad: *a tolerable performance.* —**tol′er•a•bly,** *adv.*: *I spoke tolerably good Cantonese.*

tol•er•ance (tol′ər əns) /ˈtɒlərəns/ *n.* **1.** [*noncount*] a fair, open attitude toward people whose race, religion, practices, etc., differ from one's own: *a long history of tolerance toward the beliefs of others.* **2.** the act of enduring or capacity to endure; endurance: [*noncount*]: *My tolerance for noise is limited.* [*count*]: *a weak tolerance for the drug.*

tol•er•ant (tol′ər ənt) /ˈtɒlərənt/ *adj.* showing or having tolerance: *tolerant of unorthodox cults.* —**tol′er•ant•ly,** *adv.*

tol•er•ate (tol′ə rāt′) /ˈtɒləˌreyt/ *v.* [~ + *obj*], **-at•ed, -at•ing.** **1.** to allow (something that one does not like) to exist without prohibiting it or preventing it. **2.** to endure; put up with: *I cannot tolerate incompetence.* —**tol•er•a•tion** (tol′ə rā′shən) /ˌtɒləˈreyʃən/ *n.* [*noncount*]

toll¹ (tōl) /towl/ *n.* [*count*] **1.** a fee demanded by an authority for some right or privilege, as for driving along a road. **2.** the extent or amount of loss, damage, or suffering resulting from some action: *The toll from the earthquake was 300 persons dead.* **3.** a payment made for a long-distance telephone call.

toll² (tōl) /towl/ *v.* **1.** to (cause a large bell) to sound with single strokes slowly and regularly repeated: [~ + *obj*]: *to toll a bell.* [*no obj*]: *Bells tolled in the distance.* **2.** [~ + *obj*] to sound or strike (the hour, etc.) by such strokes: *The bells tolled the end of the day.* **3.** [*no obj*] to announce the death of someone by such strokes: *The bells tolled for the dead sovereign.* —*n.* [*count*] **4.** the act or sound of tolling a bell.

toll•booth (tōl′bo͞oth′, -bo͞oth′) /ˈtowlˌbuwθ, -ˌbuwð/, *n.* [*count*] a booth, as at a bridge or the entrance to a toll road, where a toll is collected.

toll•gate (tōl′gāt′) /ˈtowlˌgeyt/ *n.* [*count*] a gate where a toll is collected.

tom (tom) /tɒm/ *n.* [*count*] **1.** the male of some animals, as the turkey. **2.** a tomcat.

-tom-, *root.* *-tom-* comes from Greek, where it has the meaning "cut." This meaning is found in such words as: ANATOMY, APPENDECTOMY, ATOM, DICHOTOMY, HYSTERECTOMY, LOBOTOMY, MASTECTOMY, TOME, TONSILLECTOMY, VASECTOMY.

tom•a•hawk (tom′ə hôk′) /ˈtɒməˌhɔk/ *n.* [*count*] **1.** a light ax used by American Indians as a weapon or tool. **2.** any similar weapon or implement. —*v.* [~ + *obj*] **3.** to attack, wound, or kill with or as if with a tomahawk.

to•ma•to (tə mā′tō, -mä′-) /təˈmeytow, -ˈmɑ-/ *n.* [*count*], *pl.* **-toes.** **1.** a large, edible, mildly acid, pulpy fruit, red to red-yellow when ripe. **2.** the plant that produces this, of the nightshade family.

tomb (to͞om) /tuwm/ *n.* [*count*] **1.** a hole dug in earth for the burial of a corpse; a grave. **2.** a large burial chamber or the like.

tom•boy (tom′boi′) /ˈtɒmˌbɔy/ *n.* [*count*] an energetic girl whose behavior is considered typical of boys: *As the tomboy of the neighborhood, she could outwrestle any of the boys her age.* —**tom′boy′ish,** *adj.*

tomb•stone (to͞om′stōn′) /ˈtuwmˌstown/ *n.* [*count*] a stone marker, usually with writing on it, on a tomb or grave.

tom•cat (tom′kat′) /ˈtɒmˌkæt/ *n.* [*count*] a male cat.

tome (tōm) /towm/ *n.* [*count*] a book, esp. a heavy or learned book, or one forming part of a series: *browsing through the dusty tomes.* See -TOM-.

tom•fool•er•y (tom′fo͞o′lə rē) /ˌtɒmˈfuwləriy/ *n., pl.* **-er•ies.** **1.** [*noncount*] foolish or silly behavior. **2.** [*count*] a silly act, matter, or thing.

Tom′my gun′ (tom′ē) /ˈtɒmiy/ *n.* [*count*] a kind of submachine gun.

to•mor•row (tə môr′ō, -mor′ō) /təˈmɔrow, -ˈmɒrow/ *n.* **1.** [*noncount*] the day following today: *Tomorrow is another day.* **2.** a future period or time: [*noncount*]: *the high-tech world of tomorrow.* [*count*]: *stored up a lot of empty tomorrows.* —*adv.* **3.** on the day following today: *I'll see you tomorrow.* **4.** at some future time.

tom-tom (tom′tom′) /ˈtɒmˌtɒm/ *n.* [*count*] **1.** a drum commonly played with the hands. **2.** a dull drumbeat or similar sound that is repeated.

ton (tun) /tʌn/ *n.* [*count*] **1.** a unit of weight, equivalent to 2000 pounds (0.907 metric ton) **(short ton)** in the U.S. and 2240 pounds (1.016 metric tons) **(long ton)** in Great Britain. **2.** METRIC TON. **3.** Often, **tons.** [*plural*] a great quantity; a lot: [~ + *a plural noun*]: *a ton of pencils.* [~ + *a noncount noun*]: *tons of money.*

-ton-, *root.* *-ton-* comes from Greek, where it has the meaning "sound." This meaning is found in such words as: ATONAL, BARITONE, DETONATE, INTONATION, INTONE, MONOTONE, MONOTONOUS, OVERTONE, SEMITONE, TONAL, TONE, TONIC, UNDERTONE.

ton•al (tō′nl) /ˈtownl̩/ *adj.* [*usually: before a noun*] of or relating to a tone or to tonality. —**ton′al•ly,** *adv.* See -TON-.

to•nal•i•ty (tō nal′i tē) /towˈnælɪtiy/ *n., pl.* **-ties. 1.** [*count*] a particular scale or system of tones; a key. **2.** [*noncount*] the quality of tones. See -TON-.

tone (tōn) /town/ *n., v.,* **toned, ton•ing.** —*n.* **1.** [*count*] any sound thought of in terms of its quality, pitch, strength, source, etc.: *shrill tones.* **2.** [*count*] quality of sound. **3.** [*count*] a particular quality or intonation of the voice: *From the tone of her voice I could tell she was very angry.* **4.** [*count*] a movement in pitch that makes for a difference in meaning between two words that are otherwise composed of the same sounds, as in Chinese: *That language has five different tones that must be learned.* **5.** [*count*] *Music.* a distance between musical notes that equals two half steps; a whole step. **6.** [*count*] a quality of color; a tint, hue, or shade. **7.** [*noncount*] the normal, healthy condition of the organs, muscles, or tissues of the body: *fine muscle tone after weeks of exercise.* **8.** [*noncount*] a manner, as of writing or speech: *The tone of the meeting was tense.* **9.** [*noncount*] general character, as of manners or outlook: *the liberal tone of the 1960's.* **10.** [*count; usually singular*] style, distinction, or respectability: *Would the tone of the neighborhood change if a prison were built there?* —*v.* **11.** [*no obj*] to give off a sound with a particular tone: *The bells toned softly in the distance.* **12.** [~ + *obj*] to make strong or properly healthy: *to tone the body with exercise.* **13. tone down,** to (cause to) become softened; to (cause to) be reduced in force: [~ + *down* + *obj*]: *to tone down the harsh colors.* [~ + *obj* + *down*]: *to tone the harsh colors down by using different lighting.* **14. tone up,** to (cause to) gain in tone or strength: [*no obj*]: *Her body toned up with all her exercise.* [~ + *up* + *obj*]: *Exercise will tone up the body.* [~ + *obj* + *up*]: *to tone the body up.* —**tone′less,** *adj.* See -TON-.

tone′-deaf′, *adj.* unable to hear or notice differences in pitch in musical sounds when producing or hearing them. —**tone′ deaf′ness,** *n.* [*noncount*]

tong (tông, tong) /tɔŋ, tɒŋ/ *n.* [*count*] **1.** (in China) an association, society, or political party. **2.** (among Chinese living in the U.S.) a secret criminal society.

ton•ga (tong′gə) /ˈtɒŋgə/ *n.* [*count*], *pl.* **-gas.** (in S Asia) a light, two-wheeled, horse-drawn vehicle.

tongs (tôngz, tongz) /tɔŋz, tɒŋz/ *n.* [*plural; usually used with a plural verb*] a tool or instrument made of two movable arms fastened together, used for picking up an object.

tongue (tung) /tʌŋ/ *n.* **1.** [*count*] a movable organ in the floor of the mouth, used for tasting, eating, and speaking: *I burned my tongue by drinking that hot tea.* **2.** the tongue of an animal, as an ox, beef, or sheep, used for food: [*noncount*]: *smoked tongue.* [*count*]: *sheep tongues.* **3.** [*noncount*] the power or ability to speak: *What's the matter, lost your tongue?* **4.** [*count; usually singular*] character of speech: *Keep a civil tongue in your head!* **5.** [*count*] the language of a particular people, region, or nation. **6.** [*count*] a strip of leather under the lacing of a shoe. **7.** [*count*] a piece of metal hanging inside a bell that strikes against the side, producing a sound; a clapper. **8.** [*count*] a narrow strip of land sticking out into a body of water; cape. **9.** [*count*] the pin of a belt buckle, etc. —***Idiom.*** **10. at** or **on the tip of one's** or **the tongue, a.** on the verge of being said; just about to be said: *It was on the tip of my tongue to disagree.* **b.** escaping one's memory but about to be recalled: *The answer is on the tip of my tongue.* **11. hold one's tongue,** to remain silent. **12. (with) tongue in cheek,** as a joke; ironically: *His sarcasm and insults were all offered tongue in cheek.*

tongue′-lash′ing, *n.* [*count*] a severe scolding.

tongue′-tied′, *adj.* unable to speak, as from shyness, embarrassment, or surprise.

tongue′ twist′er, *n.* [*count*] a word or sequence of words that is difficult to pronounce, esp. rapidly, because of so many similar sounds in a row, or because of some slight changes in consonant sounds, as "She sells seashells by the seashore."

ton•ic (ton′ik) /ˈtɒnɪk/ *n.* **1.** [*count*] a medicine that increases mental or physical strength, health, or well-being. **2.** soda water with quinine: [*noncount*]: *some gin and tonic.* [*count*]: *two tonics.* **3.** [*count*] the first degree of a musical scale; keynote. —*adj.* **4.** of or relating to the tone or health of the body, as a medicine. **5.** of or relating to the tension of the muscles: *a tonic spasm.* **6.** of or relating to tone or accent in speech. **7.** of or relating to the first tone of a musical scale: *a tonic chord.* —**ton′i•cal•ly,** *adv.* See -TON-.

to•night (tə nīt′) /təˈnayt/ *n.* [*noncount*] **1.** this present or coming night; the night of this day: *Tonight is the night I (will) propose to her.* —*adv.* **2.** on this night; on the night of this day: *See you tonight about six.*

ton•nage (tun′ij) /ˈtʌnɪdʒ/ *n.* [*noncount*] **1.** the capacity or amount of weight of a merchant vessel, expressed in tons. **2.** ships considered with reference to their capacity to hold cargo.

ton•sil (ton′səl) /ˈtɒnsəl/ *n.* [*count*] a mass of soft, pink tissue on each side of the throat: *The doctor asked him to open his mouth and say "Aah" while she looked at his tonsils.*

ton•sil•lec•to•my (ton′sə lek′tə mē) /ˌtɒnsəˈlɛktəmiy/ *n.* [*count*], *pl.* **-mies.** surgical removal of one or both tonsils. See -TOM-.

ton•sil•li•tis (ton′sə lī′tis) /ˌtɒnsəˈlaytɪs/ *n.* [*noncount*] inflammation of a tonsil or the tonsils.

ton•so•ri•al (ton sôr′ē əl, -sōr′-) /tɒnˈsɔriyəl, -ˈsowr-/ *adj.* of or relating to a barber or barbering.

ton•sure (ton′shər) /ˈtɒnʃər/ *n.* [*count*] **1.** the shaving of the head, esp. of a man upon entering the priesthood or on becoming a monk. **2.** the part of a cleric's head left bare by shaving the hair.

ton•y (tō′nē) /ˈtowniy/ *adj.,* **-i•er, -i•est.** high-toned; stylish; swank: *a tony nightclub.*

too (to͞o) /tuw/ *adv.* **1.** in addition; also; furthermore: *She's young, clever, and rich, too.* **2.** to a degree greatly beyond normal or proper: *She's too sick to travel.* **3.** (used to emphasize disagreement with what has just been said): *"You're late and you're not ready to go." —"I am too!" (= Actually, I am ready to go).* **4.** (used with a negative word or phrase) extremely; very: *The boss was none too pleased with the results.*

took (to͝ok) /tʊk/ *v.* pt. of TAKE.

tool (to͞ol) /tuwl/ *n.* [*count*] **1.** an implement, esp. one held in the hand, as a hammer, for performing a mechanical operation: *The carpenter laid out his tools and began to work.* **2.** an instrument for some purpose or work: *the tools of the writer's trade.* **3.** anything used to accomplish a task: *Education is a tool for success.* **4.** a person used by someone else: *a tool of the Communist party.* —*v.* **5.** [~ + *obj*] to work or shape with a tool. **6.** [*no obj*] to drive or ride in a vehicle: *tooling along the freeway.* **7. tool up,** [*no obj*] to install the machinery for a job: *The manufacturers began tooling up for production.*

toot (to͞ot) /tuwt/ *v.* **1.** to (cause a horn or whistle to) give forth a short sound: [~ + *obj*]: *He tooted his horn.* [*no obj*]: *The foghorn tooted in the distance.* —*n.* [*count*] **2.** an act or sound of tooting: *gave a quick toot on his horn.* —**toot′er,** *n.* [*count*]

tooth (to͞oth) /tuwθ/ *n.* [*count*], *pl.* **teeth** (tēth) /tiyθ/. **1.** one of the hard bony parts attached in a row to each jaw, serving to bite and chew food or, esp. in animals, as weapons. **2.** any part of something that sticks out and resembles a tooth, as a part of a comb, etc. **3. teeth,** [*plural*] effective power, esp. to enforce something: *to put teeth into the new law by increasing the penalty for disobeying it.* —***Idiom.*** **4. in the teeth of,** straight into or in defiance of: *The ship sailed on in the teeth of the storm.* **5. long in the tooth,** elderly. **6. set** or **put one's teeth on edge,** to cause a feeling of irritation in one: *The supervisor always sets my teeth on edge.* **7. show one's teeth,** to become menacing; reveal one's feelings of anger or hatred. **8. sink** or **get one's teeth into,** [*sink/get* + *one's* + ~ + *into* + *obj*] to work on (something) with enthusiasm: *At last he found a project he could sink his teeth into.* **9. to the teeth,** completely; fully; entirely: *armed to the teeth.* —**toothed,** *adj.* —**tooth′less,** *adj.*

tooth•ache (to͞oth′āk′) /ˈtuwθˌeyk/ *n.* [*count*] a pain in or around a tooth. —**tooth′ach′y,** *adj.*

tooth′ and nail′, *adv.* with all one's energy; fiercely: *fought tooth and nail.*

tooth•brush (to͞oth′brush′) /ˈtuwθˌbrʌʃ/ *n.* [*count*] a small brush with a long handle, for cleaning the teeth.

tooth•paste (to͞oth′pāst′) /ˈtuwθˌpeyst/ *n.* [*noncount*] a substance in the form of paste, for cleaning the teeth.

tooth•pick (to͞oth′pik′) /ˈtuwθˌpɪk/ *n.* [*count*] a small, pointed piece of wood, plastic, etc., for removing food particles from between the teeth.

tooth•some (to͞oth′səm) /ˈtuwθsəm/ *adj.* **1.** pleasing to the taste; delicious; appetizing. **2.** pleasing, desirable, or attractive. —**tooth′some•ness,** *n.* [*noncount*]

tooth•y (to͞o′thē, -thē) /ˈtuwθiy, -ðiy/ *adj.,* **-i•er, -i•est.** showing large teeth: *a toothy smile.* —**tooth•i•ly** (to͞o′thə lē, -thə-) /ˈtuwθəliy, -ðə-/ *adv.: She smiled toothily.*

top[1] (top) /tɒp/ *n., adj., v.,* **topped, top•ping.** —*n.* [*count*] **1.** the highest point, part, etc., of anything: *the top of the mountain.* **2.** a lid of a container. **3.** [*usually singular*] the highest or leading position: *She's always ranked at the top of the class.* **4.** [*count; singular*] the highest pitch or degree: *shouting at the top of their voices.* **5.** the first part; beginning: *Take that last piece of music from the top.* **6.** a garment for the upper body: *a skirt and a matching top.* **7.** a rooflike upper part or cover on a vehicle: *They drove with the top down.* **8.** the head or the crown of the head: *from top to toe.* **9.** the first half of an inning in baseball. —*adj.* [*before a noun*] **10.** of or relating to the top; highest; greatest: *to pay top prices.* **11.** foremost, chief, or principal: *Highest salaries are paid to the top players.* **12.** (among the) highest in rank or popularity; best: *the top ten movies.* —*v.* **13.** [~ + *obj*] to furnish with a top; put a top on: *topped the sundae with a cherry.* **14.** [~ + *obj*] to be at, form, or make up the top of: *Ice cream topped the cake.* **15.** [~ + *obj*] to reach the top of: *to top the mountain peak.* **16.** [~ + *obj*] to be greater than (something) in height, amount, etc.: *Those unemployment figures topped the numbers for our worst years.* **17.** [~ + *obj*] to surpass, excel, or outdo: *I've seen some weird things before, but this tops everything.* **18.** [~ + *obj*] to remove the top of; crop; prune: *to top a tree.* **19. top off,** to complete, esp. in a very good manner; finish: [~ + *off* + *obj*]: *On their anniversary they topped off the evening with champagne.* [~ + *obj* + *off*]: *And to top it off, they won three million dollars in the lottery.* **20. top out,** [*no obj*] to reach the highest level: *Prices may have topped out at their highest level.* —***Idiom.*** **21. at the top of one's lungs** or **voice,** as loudly as possible; with full voice. **22. off the top of one's head,** without thought or preparation: *Off the top of my head I would say we've lost 83% of our oil refining capabilities.* **23. on top,** successful; having won a victory: *believes she'll always come out on top.* **24. on top of, a.** over or upon: *We put the plunger on top of the drain and pushed down hard.* **b.** in addition to; over and above: *They lost their jobs, car, and home, and on top of all that their children got sick.* **c.** in control: *The firefighters seem on top of the problem and will probably extinguish the fire soon.* **d.** very or overly close to: *People were living on top of each other.* **e.** aware of; informed about: *I like to stay on top of the news.* **25. on top of the world,** very happy; excitedly happy.

top[2] (top) /tɒp/ *n.* [*count*] **1.** a toy with a point on which it is made to spin. —***Idiom.*** **2. sleep like a top,** to sleep soundly.

to•paz (tō′paz) /ˈtowpæz/ *n.* a mineral found in transparent crystal prisms and used as a gem: [*noncount*]: *a ring of topaz.* [*count*]: *a topaz in the ring.*

top•coat (top′kōt′) /ˈtɒpˌkowt/ *n.* [*count*] **1.** a lightweight overcoat. **2.** the coat of paint applied last to a surface.

top′ drawer′, *n.* [*count*] the highest level in status, excellence, or importance. —**top′-drawer′,** *adj.*

top′-flight′, *adj.* highest; most outstanding, as in achievement or development: *a top-flight scholar.*

top′ hat′, *n.* [*count*] a man's tall, rounded hat with a stiff, slightly curved brim, for formal occasions.

top′-heav′y, *adj.* **1.** having a top too heavy for a thing of its size: *The car is top-heavy and could roll over easily.* **2.** (of an organization) having too many people in the upper ranks and too few in the lower ranks: *a top-heavy bureaucracy.* —**top′-heav′iness,** *n.* [*noncount*]

top•ic (top′ik) /ˈtɒpɪk/ *n.* [*count*] **1.** a subject of discussion: *I've strayed off the topic.* **2.** the subject of a speech or piece of writing: *Introduce your topic with a clear sentence and then give examples to support it.*

top•i•cal (top′i kəl) /ˈtɒpɪkəl/ *adj.* **1.** of or relating to matters of current or local interest. **2.** *Med.* on the skin or external surface: *a topical ointment.* —**top•i•cal•i•ty** (top′i kal′i tē) /ˌtɒpɪˈkælɪtiy/ *n.* [*noncount*] —**top′i•cal•ly,** *adv.*

top•knot (top′not′) /ˈtɒpˌnɒt/ *n.* [*count*] **1.** a clump or growth of hair or feathers growing on the top of the head. **2.** hair fashioned into a knob or bun on top of the head. **3.** a knot or bow of ribbon worn on top of the head.

top•less (top′lis) /ˈtɒplɪs/ *adj.* **1.** lacking a top. **2.** nude above the waist: *topless dancers.* **3.** featuring entertainers, etc., nude above the waist: *a topless bar.*

top′-lev′el, *adj.* of or relating to those in authority; high-level: *a top-level conference.*

top•mast (top′mast′; *Nautical.* -məst) /ˈtɒpˌmæst; *Nautical.* -məst/ *n.* [*count*] the mast next above a lower mast, used to support the yards or rigging of a topsail or topsails.

top•most (top′mōst′) /ˈtɒpˌmowst/ *adj.* [*usually: before a noun*] highest; uppermost: *the topmost branches of the tree.*

top•notch or **top-notch** (top′noch′) /ˈtɒpˈnɒtʃ/ *adj.* first-rate; of highest quality or excellence.

to•pog•ra•phy (tə pog′rə fē) /təˈpɒgrəfiy/ *n., pl.* **-phies.** the detailed mapping or description of an area: [*noncount*]: *satellite photos of the topography.* [*count*]: *an uneven topography.* —**to•pog′ra•pher,** *n.* [*count*] —**top•o•graph•ic** (top′ə graf′ik) /ˌtɒpəˈgræfɪk/ **top′o•graph′i•cal,** *adj.* See -GRAPH-.

top•ping (top′ing) /ˈtɒpɪŋ/ *n.* **1.** [*count*] a part forming a top to something. **2.** a sauce placed on food before serving: [*noncount*]: *whipped topping on the dessert.* [*count*]: *a choice of toppings for the ice cream.* **3. toppings,** [*plural*] the parts removed in taking the tops off plants. —*adj.* **4.** *Chiefly Brit.* excellent.

top•ple (top′əl) /ˈtɒpəl/ *v.,* **-pled, -pling. 1.** to (cause to) fall forward, as from being top-heavy, or from being weak: [*no obj*]: *He suddenly toppled to the sidewalk.* [~ + *obj*]: *toppled the challenger with one punch.* **2.** [~ + *obj*] to remove from power, as from a position of authority: *to topple a king.*

top•sail (top′sāl′; *Nautical.* -səl) /ˈtɒpˌseyl; *Nautical.* -səl/ *n.* [*count*] a sail, or either of a pair of sails, set immediately above the lowermost sail of a mast and supported by a topmast.

top′-se′cret, *adj.* of or relating to something to be kept completely secret or at the highest category of security: *a top-secret document.*

top•soil (top′soil′) /ˈtɒpˌsɔyl/ *n.* [*noncount*] the upper part of the soil, usually the best for growing things.

top•sy-tur•vy (top′sē tûr′vē) /ˈtɒpsiyˈtɜrviy/ *adv.* **1.** with the top where the bottom should be; upside down: *turned the boat topsy-turvy.* **2.** in or into a state of confusion: *Things went completely topsy-turvy because the new boss didn't know the company.* —*adj.* **3.** turned upside down: *a topsy-turvy reflection.* **4.** confused or disorderly: *a topsy-turvy classroom.*

tor (tôr) /tɔr/ *n.* [*count*] a rocky top of a hill or mountain; a peak of a bare or rocky mountain or hill.

To•rah (tō′rə, tôr′ə) /ˈtowrə, ˈtɔrə/ *n.* [*noncount*] the first five books of the Bible.

torch (tôrch) /tɔrtʃ/ *n.* [*count*] **1.** a light, made of a stick of wood or some other substance, lighted at the upper end. **2.** something thought of as a source of knowledge or guidance: *the torch of learning.* **3.** any of various devices producing a hot flame, used for soldering, etc.; a blowtorch **4.** *Slang.* an arsonist. **5.** *Chiefly Brit.* FLASHLIGHT (def. 1). —*v.* [~ + *obj*] **6.** to set fire to, esp. with evil intention: *Before the police arrested him he had torched five buildings.* —***Idiom.*** **7. carry a** or **the torch for,** [*carry* + *a/the* + ~ + *for* + *obj*] to be in love with, esp. without being loved in return: *All those years he carried a torch for her, but he never told her and she never knew.*

torch•light (tôrch′līt′) /ˈtɔrtʃˌlayt/ *n.* [*noncount*] the light of a torch or torches.

torch′ song′, *n.* [*count*] a sad popular ballad expressing unhappiness in love.

tore (tôr, tōr) /tɔr, towr/ *v.* pt. of TEAR[2].

tor•e•a•dor (tôr′ē ə dôr′) /ˈtɔriyəˌdɔr/ *n.* [*count*] a bullfighter.

tor•ment (*v.* tôr ment′, tôr′ment; *n.* tôr′ment) / *v.* tɔrˈmɛnt, ˈtɔrmɛnt; *n.* ˈtɔrmɛnt/ *v.* [~ + *obj*] **1.** to cause (someone) to feel severe suffering: *The disease tormented him night and day.* **2.** to worry or annoy too much; keep bothering; plague: *constantly tormenting me* *with her schemes.* **—***n.* **3.** [*noncount*] a state of suffering; agony; misery: *the torment of cancer.* **4.** [*count*] something that causes pain or suffering. **5.** [*count*] a source of much trouble, worry, or annoyance. **—tor•ment′ing•ly,** *adv.* **—tor•men′tor, tor•ment′er,** *n.* [*count*]: *lost his patience and punched his tormentor in the nose.* See -TORT-.

torn (tôrn, tōrn) /tɔrn, towrn/ *v.* **1.** pp. of TEAR². — *adj.* **2.** [*be* + ~] divided or in conflict: *We were torn between our love for our parents and our need to be independent.*

tor•na•do (tôr nā′dō) /tɔr'neydow/ *n.* [*count*], *pl.* **-does, -dos.** a violently destructive windstorm occurring over local areas of land, having a long, funnel-shaped cloud that extends to the ground.

tor•pe•do (tôr pē′dō) /tɔr'piydow/ *n., pl.* **-does,** *v.,* **-doed, -do•ing.** **—***n.* [*count*] **1.** a high-explosive, underwater tube that is self-propelled, usually launched from a submarine or other warship against surface vessels. **2.** a hero sandwich. **—***v.* [~ + *obj*] **3.** to attack, hit, damage, or destroy with torpedoes: *The battleship was torpedoed and sunk.* **4.** to attack, ruin, or destroy: *He torpedoed all our plans.*

tor•pid (tôr′pid) /'tɔrpɪd/ *adj.* **1.** inactive or sluggish. **2.** unwilling to move much or be active; apathetic; lethargic. **—tor•pid•i•ty** (tôr pid′i tē) /tɔr'pɪdɪtiy/ *n.* [*noncount*] **—tor′pid•ly,** *adv.*

tor•por (tôr′pər) /'tɔrpər/ *n.* [*noncount*] **1.** sluggish inactivity. **2.** unwillingness to move much or be active.

torque (tôrk) /tɔrk/ *n.* [*noncount*] the measured ability of a twisting part of machinery, as of a shaft, to overcome resistance to such turning. See -TORT-.

tor•rent (tôr′ənt, tor′-) /'tɔrənt, 'tɒr-/ *n.* [*count*] **1.** a quick-flowing, violent stream of water. **2.** a rushing, violent stream of anything: *a torrent of abuse.* **3.** a violent downpour of rain. **—tor•ren•tial** (tô ren′shəl, tə-) /tɔ'rɛnʃəl, tə-/ *adj.*

tor•rid (tôr′id, tor′-) /'tɔrɪd, 'tɒr-/ *adj.* **1.** exposed to the effects of parching heat of the sun: *The torrid zone was hot all year.* **2.** extremely hot, parching, or burning, as climate or air: *a torrid summer day.* **3.** passionate: *a torrid love affair.* **—tor•rid•i•ty** (tô rid′i tē) /tɔ'rɪdɪtiy/ **tor′rid•ness,** *n.* [*noncount*] **—tor′rid•ly,** *adv.*

tor•sion (tôr′shən) /'tɔrʃən/ *n.* [*noncount*] the act of twisting or the state of being twisted. **—tor′sion•al,** *adj.* See -TORT-.

tor•so (tôr′sō) /'tɔrsow/ *n.* [*count*], *pl.* **-sos, -si** (-sē) /-siy/. the trunk of the human body.

tort (tôrt) /tɔrt/ *n.* [*count*] *Law.* a wrongful or illegal act resulting in injury to another's person, property, or reputation, for which the injured party may ask for money or some compensation. See -TORT-.

-tort-, *root.* *-tort-* comes from Latin, where it has the meaning "twist." This meaning is found in such words as: CONTORT, DISTORT, EXTORT, RETORT, TORT, TORTE, TORTILLA, TORTUOUS, TORTURE.

torte (tôrt) /tɔrt/ *n.* [*count*] a rich cake made with eggs, ground nuts, and usually no flour. See -TORT-.

tor•til•la (tôr tē′ə) /tɔr'tiyə/ *n.* [*count*], *pl.* **-las.** a thin, round, unleavened bread made from cornmeal or wheat flour, and baked on a griddle or stone. See -TORT-.

tor•toise (tôr′təs) /'tɔrtəs/ *n.* [*count*] **1.** a turtle, esp. a terrestrial turtle. **2.** a very slow person or thing.

tor•toise•shell (tôr′təs shel′) /'tɔrtəs,ʃɛl/ *n.* [*noncount*] Also, **tor′toise shell′.** **1.** the horny layer on the outer surface of a turtle shell, used for making combs and ornamental articles. **2.** a synthetic substance made to look like natural tortoiseshell. **—***adj.* Also, **tor′toise-shell′. 3.** spotted or colored with many colors like tortoiseshell, esp. with yellow and brown. **4.** made of tortoiseshell. **5.** (of a domestic cat) having a black, orange, and cream coat.

tor•tu•ous (tôr′cho͞o əs) /'tɔrtʃuwəs/ *adj.* **1.** full of twists, turns, or bends: *a tortuous path.* **2.** not direct or straightforward, as in behavior or speech: *tortuous reasoning.* **—tor′tu•ous•ly,** *adv.* **—tor′tu•ous•ness,** *n.* [*noncount*] See -TORT-.

tor•ture (tôr′chər) /'tɔrtʃər/ *n., v.,* **-tured, -tur•ing.** **—***n.* **1.** [*noncount*] the act of causing great pain, as punishment or revenge, for getting a confession or information, or for cruelty's sake: *The interrogator was a master of torture.* **2.** [*count*] a method of causing or giving such pain: *different tortures, like whipping and electric shocks.* **3.** [*noncount*] a cause of pain or anguish: *It was torture for him to watch his old girlfriend walk by with another guy.* **—***v.* [~ + *obj*] **4.** to force to undergo torture: *tortured the prisoner for hours.* **5.** to cause to undergo great pain or mental suffering: *to be tortured with bad memories.* **—tor′tur•er,** *n.* [*count*] **—tor′tur•ous,** *adj.* See -TORT-.

tor•tured (tôr′chərd) /'tɔrtʃərd/ *adj.* **1.** twisted or forced into an unnatural shape. **2.** not direct or straightforward; deliberately complicated; tortuous: *a document full of tortured reasoning.* See -TORT-.

toss (tôs, tos) /tɔs, tɒs/ *v.,* **tossed** or **tost, toss•ing,** *n.* **—***v.* **1.** [~ + *obj*] to throw, esp. lightly or carelessly: *came in and tossed her coat on the chair.* **2.** [~ + *obj*] to throw from one to another, as in play: *to toss a ball back and forth.* **3.** to move or pitch with irregular motions; jerk about: [*no obj*]: *tossing and turning all night.* [~ + *obj*]: *The storm tossed the ship about.* **4.** [~ + *obj*] to throw upward suddenly, as the head: *She tossed her head and laughed.* **5.** to throw (a coin) into the air to decide something according to the side facing upwards when it falls: [~ + *obj*]: *The official tossed a coin and it came up heads.* [~ + *obj* + *for* + *obj*]: *We can't decide who should go first; I'll toss you for it.* [*no obj;* (~ + *for* + *obj*)]: *We can't decide who should go first; let's toss for it.* **6.** [~ + *obj*] to mix (a salad) lightly until the ingredients are coated with the dressing. **7. toss off,** to accomplish quickly or easily: [~ + *off* + *obj*]: *sat down and tossed off an essay.* [~ + *obj* + *off*]: *to toss that essay off.* **—***n.* [*count*] **8.** an act or instance of tossing. **9.** a pitching about, or up and down. **10.** a throw or pitch. **11.** TOSSUP (def. 1). **12.** a sudden fling or jerk, esp. of the head: *The horse gave a sharp toss of the head and refused to go forward.*

toss•up (tôs′up′, tos′-) /'tɔs,ʌp, 'tɒs-/ *n.* [*count*] **1.** the tossing of a coin to decide something according to which side is facing upwards when it falls. **2.** an even choice or chance: *The election is a tossup at this point.*

tot¹ (tot) /tɒt/ *n.* [*count*] **1.** a small child. **2.** a small portion, as of liquor.

tot² (tot) /tɒt/ *v.,* **tot•ted, tot•ting,** *n.* **—***v.* **1. tot up,** to add; total: [*no obj*]: *The numbers totted up.* [~ + *up* + *obj*]: *He totted up the numbers.* [~ + *obj* + *up*]: *He totted the numbers up.* **—***n.* [*count*] **2.** a total.

to•tal (tōt′l) /'towtḷ/ *adj., n., v.,* **-taled, -tal•ing** or (*esp. Brit.*) **-talled, -tal•ling.** **—***adj.* **1.** [*before a noun*] of or relating to the whole amount of something; entire: *the total expenditure.* **2.** [*usually: before a noun*] of or relating to the whole of something: *the total effect of the play on its audience.* **3.** [*usually: before a noun*] complete in extent or degree; utter: *a total failure.* **—***n.* **4.** [*count*] the total amount; sum: *That brings the cost to a total of $50,000.* **5.** [*noncount; in* + ~] the whole: *There were several thousand people there in total.* **—***v.* **6.** [~ + *obj*] to bring to a total; add up: *He totaled the three columns.* **7.** to reach a total of; amount to: [~ + *obj; no passive*]: *The money totaled over fifty thousand dollars in cash.* [~ + *to* + *obj*]: *The money totaled to over fifty thousand dollars.* **8.** [~ + *obj*] to wreck beyond repair: *He totaled his car in the accident.* **—to′tal•ly,** *adv.*: *You're totally crazy to think that.*

to•tal•i•tar•i•an (tō tal′i târ′ē ən) /tow,tælɪ'tɛəriyən/ *adj.* **1.** of or relating to a centralized government that does not allow differing opinion: *the totalitarian system of George Orwell's novel* 1984. **—***n.* [*count*] **2.** a person calling for such a form of government. **—to•tal′i•tar′i•an•ism,** *n.* [*noncount*]

to•tal•i•ty (tō tal′i tē) /tow'tælɪtiy/ *n., pl.* **-ties. 1.** [*count*] something that is total or constitutes a total. **2.** [*noncount*] the state of being total; entirety.

tote (tōt) /towt/ *v.,* **tot•ed, tot•ing,** *n.* **—***v.* [~ + *obj*] **1.** to carry, as in one's arms: *toting bags of groceries.* **2.** to carry on one's person: *to tote a gun.* **—***n.* [*count*] **3.** an open shopping bag, used for carrying small items. **—tot′a•ble, tote′a•ble,** *adj.* **—tot′er,** *n.* [*count*]

to•tem (tō′təm) /'towtəm/ *n.* [*count*] a natural object or an animate being, or a drawing of such a thing, used as the emblem or symbol of a clan, etc., and treated with reverence. **—to•tem′ic** (-tem′ik) /-'tɛmɪk/ *adj.*

to′tem pole′, *n.* [*count*] a pole carved and painted with totems, built by Native Americans of the NW coast of North America.

tot•ter (tot′ər) /'tɒtər/ *v.* [*no obj*] **1.** to walk or go with clumsy, hesitant, or unsteady steps: *After the blow to the head he tottered and fell.* **2.** to sway or rock, as if about to fall: *During the earthquake the building tottered, then crashed to the ground.* **—***n.* [*count*] **3.** the act of tottering; an unsteady way of walking. **—tot′ter•er,** *n.* [*count*]

tou•can (to͞o′kan, to͞o kän′) /'tuwkæn, tuw'kɑn/ *n.* [*count*] a brightly colored, fruit-eating bird of the New World tropics, having a very large bill.

touch (tuch) /tʌtʃ/ *v.* **1.** to put the hand, finger, etc., on or into contact with (something) so as to feel it: [~ + *obj*]: *He touched the stove cautiously.* [*no obj*]: *You may look at it but don't touch.* **2.** [~ + *obj*] to bring (the hand, etc., or something held) into contact with something: *touched a match to the papers.* **3.** [~ + *obj*] to pat or tap as with the hand or an instrument: *She touched me gently on the shoulder.* **4.** to come into contact with; be next to: [~ + *obj*]: *My shoulder was touching hers.* [*no obj*]: *Our shoulders were touching on the crowded elevator.* **5.** [~ + *obj; usually with a negative word or phrase*] to be as good as (something else); compare with (something): *He wrote with a style that couldn't touch mine.* **6.** [~ + *obj*] to treat or affect in some way by contact: *All you have to do is touch that computer and everything goes haywire with it.* **7.** [~ + *obj*] to move (someone) to feel sympathy: *Your kindness touched me deeply.* See TOUCHING, TOUCHED below. **8.** [~ + *obj; usually with a negative word or phrase*] to have to do with in any way: *She can't touch her trust money until she's 21.* **9.** [~ + *obj; usually with a negative word or phrase*] to eat or drink; consume; taste: *He won't touch another drink.* **10.** [~ + *obj*] to put one's hands on (a person), as to do something violent or sexual: *Don't touch that kid again!* **11.** [~ + *obj*] to be a matter of importance to; affect: *Such poverty never touches her life.* **12.** [~ + *obj*] *Slang.* to ask (someone) for money, or succeed in getting money from: *He touched me for a loan.* **13. touch down,** [*no obj*] (of an aircraft or spacecraft) to land. **14. touch off, a.** to cause to ignite or explode: [~ + *off* + *obj*]: *The flame touched off the explosion.* [~ + *obj* + *off*]: *What touched it off?* **b.** to start, esp. suddenly: [~ + *off* + *obj*]: *The incident touched off a firestorm of debate.* [~ + *obj* + *off*]: *That's what touched the debate off.* **15. touch on** or **upon,** [~ + *on* + *obj*] to mention (a subject) casually: *Her speech touched on the issue of employee benefits.* **16. touch up,** to make minor changes in the appearance of: [~ + *up* + *obj*]: *The artist touched up the painting.* [~ + *obj* + *up*]: *She touched it up.* **—*n.*** **17.** [*count*] the act of touching; state or fact of being touched: *a light touch on his shoulder.* **18.** [*noncount*] that sense by which anything material is felt by physical contact: *a well-developed sense of touch.* **19.** [*noncount*] the quality of something touched that imparts a sensation; feel: *The touch of her hand was enough to thrill him.* **20.** [*noncount*] a coming into or being in contact or good relations with another: *Over the years we lost touch. Let's keep in touch.* **21.** [*noncount*] ability or skill; a knack for doing something: *He seems to have lost his touch in dealing with people.* **22.** [*count*] a slight attack, as of illness: *He's had a touch of the flu.* **23.** [*count*] a slight added effort in completing any piece of work: *put some finishing touches on the painting.* **24.** [*count*] skill or manner of execution in artistic work, in playing a musical instrument, etc. **25.** [*count*] the manner or speed of action of the keys of an instrument, as of a piano. **26.** [*count*] a slight amount of some quality, emotion, etc.: *There was a touch of sadness in her voice.* **27.** [*count*] *Slang.* **a.** the act of approaching someone for money (as a gift): *to put the touch on her for fifty bucks.* **b.** a person thought of in terms of getting money from: *He's an easy touch.* —**touch′a•ble,** *adj.*

touch′-and-go′, *adj.* doubtful or uncertain as to the result; precarious: *The election was touch-and-go right to the end.*

touch•down (tuch′doun′) /ˈtʌtʃˌdawn/ *n.* [*count*] **1.** an act of scoring six points in football by being in possession of the ball on or behind the opponent's goal line. **2.** the act of a Rugby player who touches the ball on or to the ground behind his own goal line. **3.** the act or the moment of landing, as of an aircraft.

tou•ché (to͞o shā′) /tuwˈʃey/ *interj.* **1.** (used in fencing to indicate that a hit or touch has been made). **2.** (used to give credit to another for a particularly clever remark or response).

touched (tucht) /tʌtʃt/ *adj.* [*be* + ~] **1.** moved; stirred; feeling emotion: *deeply touched by your kindness.* **2.** slightly crazy; unbalanced: *a little touched in the head.*

touch•ing (tuch′ing) /ˈtʌtʃɪŋ/ *adj.* **1.** causing strong emotion: *a touching story about a girl and her dog.* **2.** being in contact. **—*prep.*** **3.** in reference or relation to; concerning; about: *Touching the budget considerations, we find several methods of saving money.* —**touch′ing•ly,** *adv.*: *touchingly portrayed as a poor, defenseless creature.*

touch•screen or **touch screen** (tuch′skrēn′) /ˈtʌtʃˌskriyn/ *n.* [*count*] a computer display that can respond to the location of a finger on its surface.

touch•stone (tuch′stōn′) /ˈtʌtʃˌstown/ *n.* [*count*] a standard or criterion for testing the qualities of a thing.

touch•y (tuch′ē) /ˈtʌtʃiy/ *adj.*, **-i•er, -i•est. 1.** likely to take offense for some slight reason; irritable: *She's sort of touchy when it comes to her academic credentials.* **2.** requiring caution, careful handling, or tact; risky: *It's a touchy situation.* —**touch′i•ness,** *n.* [*noncount*]

tough (tuf) /tʌf/ *adj.* **-er, -est,** *adv., n., v.* **—*adj.*** **1.** strong and long-lasting: *tough plastics.* **2.** difficult to chew; not tender: *a tough steak.* **3.** capable of great endurance; hardy: *tough troops.* **4.** not easily influenced, as a person; stubborn: *a tough negotiator.* **5.** difficult to perform or deal with: *a very tough exam.* [*It* + *be* + ~ + *to* + *verb*]: *It's tough to get a good grade from him.* **6.** hard to bear or suffer through; severe: *a tough struggle to succeed.* **7.** vicious; rough; violent: *a tough neighborhood.* **8.** *Informal.* unfortunate; bad: *tough luck.* **—*adv.*** **9.** in a tough manner: *They play tough, but not dirty.* **—*n.*** [*count*] **10.** a rough, tough person who attacks others; a rowdy. **—*v.*** ***Idiom.*** **11. tough it out,** [*no obj*] *Informal.* to keep going and resist hardship or difficulty: *Instead of giving up, they decided to tough it out.* —**tough′ly,** *adv.* —**tough′ness,** *n.* [*noncount*]

tough•en (tuf′ən) /ˈtʌfən/ *v.* to (cause to) become tough or tougher: [*no obj*]: *This metal toughens under higher temperatures.* [~ + *obj*]: *The union toughened its stance.* —**tough′en•er,** *n.* [*count*]

tou•pee (to͞o pā′) /tuwˈpey/ *n.* [*count*], *pl.* **-pees. 1.** a man's wig. **2.** a patch of false hair for covering a bald spot.

tour (to͝or) /tʊr/ *n.* [*count*] **1.** a long journey including the visiting of a number of places: *a tour of the Greek islands.* **2.** a brief trip through a place to view or inspect it: *an inspection tour.* **3.** a period of duty: *The lieutenant's last tour of duty was in Korea.* **—*v.*** **4.** to travel from place to place: [~ + *obj*]: *They toured the Greek islands.* [*no obj*]: *They toured for a few seasons.* **5.** to travel from town to town giving performances: [~ + *obj*]: *The band toured the Midwest.* [*no obj*]: *The band toured for several weeks.* **—*Idiom.*** **6. on tour,** (of a musical or dramatic performer, group, or company) traveling from town to town and making performances in each.

tour de force (to͝or′ də fôrs′, -fōrs′) /ˌtʊrˈ də fɔrs, -ˈfowrs/ *n.* [*count*], *pl.* **tours de force** (to͝orz) /tʊrz/. an excellent, very special achievement by an artist, author, etc., unlikely to be equaled; a stroke of genius: *His latest book was a tour de force.*

tour•ism (to͝or′iz əm) /ˈtʊrɪzəm/ *n.* [*noncount*] the occupation of providing information, accommodations, transportation, and other services to tourists.

tour•ist (to͝or′ist) /ˈtʊrɪst/ *n.* [*count*] **1.** one who makes a tour, esp. for pleasure. **—*adv.*** **2.** in living quarters or seats of a class of travel below first-class: *to travel tourist; to fly tourist.*

tour•na•ment (to͝or′nə mənt, tûr′-) /ˈtʊrnəmənt, ˈtɜr-/ *n.* [*count*] **1.** a trial of skill in some game, in which players play a series of contests: *a chess tournament.* **2.** a meeting for contests in a number of different sports, as between teams of different nations. **3.** a medieval contest in which mounted knights fought with lances for a prize.

tour•ni•quet (tûr′ni kit, to͝or′-) /ˈtɜrnɪkɪt, ˈtʊr-/ *n.* [*count*] any device for slowing or stopping bleeding by pushing down with force on a blood vessel: *applied a tourniquet above the wound.*

tou•sle (tou′zəl, -səl) /ˈtawzəl, -səl/ *v.* [~ + *obj*], **-sled, -sling.** to make a little untidy: *The wind tousled our hair.*

tout (tout) /tawt/ *v. Informal.* **1.** [*no obj*] to ask for business, votes, etc., esp. in an improper or too direct way. **2.** [~ + *obj*] to advertise boastfully: *a highly touted nightclub.* **—*n.*** [*count*] **3.** one who touts.

tow (tō) /tow/ *v.* [~ + *obj*] **1.** to pull or haul (a car, etc.) by a rope, chain, etc.: *They towed my car to the garage.* **—*n.*** [*count*] **2.** an act or instance of towing. **3.** something towed. **4.** something, as a boat or truck, that tows. **5.** SKI TOW. **—*Idiom.*** **6. in tow, a.** Also, **under tow.** in the state of being towed: *The ship returned to port in tow of a tugboat.* **b.** under one's guidance; in one's charge: *The teacher entered the museum with her class in tow.* **c.** (following one) as a follower, admirer, or companion: *The movie star walked down the street, autograph hounds in tow.*

to•ward (tôrd, tōrd, twôrd, twōrd) /tɔrd, towrd, twɔrd, twowrd/ *prep.* Also, **to•wards′. 1.** in the direction of: *to walk toward the river.* **2.** with a view to having; for: *They're saving money toward a new house.* **3.** in the area or vicinity of; near: *They live a little way out toward Northport.* **4.** turned to; facing: *turned toward me.* **5.**

shortly before; close to: *The moon came out toward midnight.* **6.** as a help or contribution to: *to give money toward a person's expenses.* **7.** with respect to; as regards: *What are your feelings toward gun control?*

tow•el (tou′əl, toul) /ˈtawəl, tawl/ *n., v.,* **-eled, -el•ing** or (*esp. Brit.*) **-elled, -el•ling.** —*n.* [*count*] **1.** a cloth or paper that absorbs liquids, used for wiping and drying: *Use a towel to dry your face.* —*v.* [~ + *obj*] **2.** to wipe or dry with a towel: *She jumped out of the pool and toweled her hair.*

tow•el•ing (tou′ə ling, tou′ling) /ˈtawəlɪŋ, ˈtawlɪŋ/ *n.* [*noncount*] a fabric of cotton or linen, used for towels. Also, *esp. Brit.,* **tow′el•ling.**

tow•er (tou′ər) /ˈtawər/ *n.* [*count*] **1.** a building higher than it is wide, either standing alone or forming part of a building: *a television tower.* **2.** such a structure used as a stronghold, prison, etc. —*v.* [*no obj*] **3.** to rise or extend far upward or above, as a tower: *The mountains towered above us.*

tow•er•ing (tou′ər ing) /ˈtawərɪŋ/ *adj.* [*before a noun*] **1.** very high or tall; lofty: *a towering oak.* **2.** surpassing others in size or greatness: *a towering figure in history.* **3.** rising to an extreme degree of violence or intensity: *a towering rage.*

tow•head (tō′hed′) /ˈtowˌhɛd/ *n.* [*count*] **1.** a head of very light blond, almost white hair. **2.** a person with such hair. —**tow′-head′ed,** *adj.*

town (toun) /tawn/ *n.* **1.** [*count*] a thickly populated area, usually smaller than a city and larger than a village, having fixed boundaries and certain local powers of government. **2.** [*count*] a densely populated area of great size. **3.** [*count*] the inhabitants of a town: *The town loves its high-school football team.* **4.** [*noncount*] the particular town or city in mind or referred to: *to be out of town.* **5.** [*noncount*] the main business or shopping area in a town or city; downtown: *We came into town for the big sale.* —*adj.* [*before a noun*] **6.** of or relating to a town. —***Idiom.*** **7. go to town,** *Informal.* **a.** to accomplish something with great speed: *They really went to town on that contracting job.* **b.** to enjoy oneself in a fling or by spending money. **8. on the town,** *Informal.* looking for entertainment in a city's nightclubs, etc.; out to have a good time: *The company took us out for a night on the town.*

town′ hall′, *n.* [*count*] a building used for carrying on the town's business.

town′ house′ or **town′house′,** *n.* [*count*] **1.** a house in the city, esp. a luxurious one. **2.** one of a group of houses having the same design, usually joined by common walls.

town•ship (toun′ship) /ˈtawnʃɪp/ *n.* [*count*] **1.** a unit of local government, usually a smaller division of a county. **2.** (in South Africa) a segregated settlement for blacks to live in, located outside a city or town: *the township of Soweto.*

towns•peo•ple (tounz′pē′pəl) /ˈtawnzˌpiypəl/ *n.* [*plural*] **1.** the inhabitants or citizens of a town. **2.** the people who were raised in a town or city. Also called **towns•folk** (tounz′fōk′) /ˈtawnzˌfowk/.

tow•path (tō′path′) /ˈtowˌpæθ/ *n.* [*count*] a path along the bank of a canal or river, for use in towing boats.

-tox-, *root.* *-tox-* comes from Latin, where it has the meaning "poison." This meaning is found in such words as: ANTITOXIN, DETOXIFY, INTOXICATED, INTOXICATION, TOXIC, TOXIN.

tox•ic (tok′sik) /ˈtɒksɪk/ *adj.* **1.** of or relating to a toxin or poison: *a toxic condition.* **2.** having the effect of a poison; poisonous: *a toxic drug.* —**tox•ic•i•ty** (tok sis′i tē) /tɒkˈsɪsɪtiy/ *n.* [*noncount*] See -TOX-.

tox•i•col•o•gy (tok′si kol′ə jē) /ˌtɒksɪˈkɒlədʒiy/ *n.* [*noncount*] the branch of medicine dealing with the effects, antidotes, etc., of poisons. —**tox′i•col′o•gist,** *n.* [*count*] See -TOX-.

tox•in (tok′sin) /ˈtɒksɪn/ *n.* [*count*] any poison produced by a living thing. See -TOX-.

toy (toi) /tɔy/ *n.* **1.** an object for children to play with. **2.** something smaller than usual, esp. in comparison with like objects; esp. a dog of a breed or variety noted for smallness of size: *Toys in dogs include Yorkshire terriers and Pomeranians.* —*adj.* [*before a noun*] **3.** made or designed for use as a toy: *a toy gun.* —*v.* [~ + *with* + *obj*] **4.** to play with something or flirt with someone without serious purpose or intent: *to toy with one's food; She's just toying with him.* **5.** to think about or consider: *toying with the idea of buying a new computer.*

tr., an abbreviation of: **1.** trace. **2.** transitive. **3.** translated. **4.** treasurer. **5.** trustee.

-trac-, *root.* *-trac-* comes from Latin, where it has the meaning "pull." This meaning is found in such words as: ABSTRACT, ATTRACT, ATTRACTION, CONTRACT, CONTRACTION, DETRACT, DISTRACT, DISTRACTION, EXTRACT, INTRACTABLE, PROTRACTED, PROTRACTOR, RETRACT, RETRACTION, SUBCONTRACT, SUBTRACT, TRACT, TRACTABLE, TRACTION, TRACTOR.

trace (trās) /treys/ *n., v.,* **traced, trac•ing,** —*n.* [*count*] **1.** a mark, sign, or piece of evidence of the existence, influence, or action of someone, something, or some event: *Those statues are the only traces of a once-great civilization.* **2.** a small amount or sign of some quality, characteristic, etc.: *a trace of sadness in her smile.* **3.** an extremely small amount of some substance or part: *a trace of copper in that alloy.* **4. traces,** [*plural*] the series of footprints left by an animal. **5.** a tracing, drawing, or sketch of something. **6.** a lightly drawn line: *the traces on the seismograph when the last earthquake hit.* —*v.* [~ + *obj*] **7.** to follow the footprints, tracks, or traces of: *The FBI traced the van back to the rental company.* **8.** to follow (footprints, evidence, the history or course of something, etc.) **9.** to find out or uncover by investigating: *to trace the cause of the disease.* **10.** to draw or copy (a line, etc.), as by copying and following the lines of the original on a piece of transparent paper placed over it: *She traced the picture of the dog onto her notebook paper.* —**trace′a•ble,** *adj.* —**trac′er,** *n.* [*count*] See -TRAC-.

trace′ el′ement, *n.* [*count*] **1.** any element required in very small amounts for the proper functioning of the body. **2.** a substance that occurs naturally only in very small amounts in the earth's crust. Also called **trace′ min′eral.**

tra•che•a (trā′kē ə) /ˈtreykiyə/ *n.* [*count*], *pl.* **-che•ae** (-kē ē′) /-kiyˌiy/ **-che•as.** (in air-breathing animals with backbones) a tube from the back of the throat to the lungs that serves as a passageway for air. —**tra′che•al,** *adj.*

trac•ing (trā′sing) /ˈtreysɪŋ/ *n.* **1.** [*noncount*] the act of a person or thing that traces. **2.** [*count*] something produced by tracing, esp. a copy of a drawing, map, etc., made by tracing on a sheet placed over the original.

track (trak) /træk/ *n.* **1.** [*count*] a pair of parallel lines of rails on which a railroad train, trolley, or the like runs. See illustration at TERMINAL. **2.** [*count*] evidence that something has passed: *the tracks of my tears.* **3.** [*count*] Usually, **tracks.** [*plural*] marks left by an animal, person, or vehicle: *You can see the tracks where the deer crossed the stream.* **4.** [*count*] a path made by or as if by the feet of people or animals; trail: *a track through the woods to the river.* **5.** [*count*] a line of travel or of motion: *The track of the spy satellite takes it over our airfield in just a few moments.* **6. a.** [*count*] a course laid out for running or racing: *The school spent millions on a new track.* **b.** [*noncount*] the group of sports performed on such a course, as running or hurdling. **7.** [*count*] **a.** one of the parallel recording surfaces extending along the length of a magnetic tape. **b.** BAND^2 (def. 5). **c.** material recorded on a track (def. 7a) that is combined with other parts of a musical recording to produce a final version. **8.** [*count*] one of a number of rings on the surface of a floppy disk along which data are recorded. **9. tracks,** [*plural*] *Slang.* needle marks on the skin of a drug user, caused by injections. **10.** [*count*] a metal strip along which something, as a curtain, can be mounted or moved. **11.** [*count*] a program of study or the level of courses to which a student is assigned on the basis of skill or need; an academic course or path: *the college track.* —*v.* [~ + *obj*] **12.** to follow or pursue the track of: *The dogs tracked the fox to its hole.* **13.** to leave footprints on: *to track the floor with muddy shoes.* **14.** to make a trail of footprints with (dirt, etc.): *to track mud on the floor.* **15.** to follow the course of (an aircraft, etc.), as by radar, etc.: *The gunner tracked the incoming fighter.* **16.** to follow the course of progress of: *We have been tracking your progress.* **17. track down,** to pursue until caught or captured; follow: [~ + *obj* + *down*]: *I promised to track Smith down and kill him.* [~ + *down* + *obj*]: *I promised to track down the traitor and kill him.* —***Idiom.*** **18. keep track,** to remain aware; keep informed: [*no obj*]: *There are too many things to do; I can't keep track.* [~ + *of* + *obj*]: *I can't keep track of all those employees.* **19. lose track,** to fail to keep informed or aware: [*no obj*]: *I keep losing track; are we on page 1055 or 1056?* [~ + *of* + *obj*]: *I lost track of how many disks my computer destroyed.* **20. make tracks,** *Informal.* to hurry. **21. off the track,** departing from the subject under discussion: *We're off the track again; we have to come back to the topic.* **22. on the track of,** in search or pursuit of; close upon: *The FBI is on the track of the gang.* **23. the wrong** (or **right**) **side of the tracks,** the unfashionable, or lower-status (or fashionable, or higher-status) part of a city: *He was a boy from the wrong side of the tracks.* —**track′a•ble,** *adj.* —**track′er,** *n.* [*count*]

track′ light′ing, *n.* [*noncount*] an interior lighting system using spotlight light fixtures on an electrified track attached to the wall or ceiling. —**track′ light′,** *n.* [*count*]

tract[1] (trakt) /trækt/ *n.* [*count*] **1.** an area of land, water, etc.; a stretch: *a five-acre tract of land.* **2.** a definite region or area of the body, esp. a system of parts or organs: *the digestive tract.* See -TRAC-.

tract[2] (trakt) /trækt/ *n.* [*count*] a brief pamphlet, usually on a religious or political topic.

trac•ta•ble (trak′tə bəl) /'træktəbəl/ *adj.* easily managed or controlled; docile; yielding. —**trac′ta•bly,** *adv.* See -TRAC-.

trac•tion (trak′shən) /'trækʃən/ *n.* [*noncount*] **1.** the friction of a body that causes it to stick on some surface, as a tire on a road: *These tires provide good traction.* **2.** the action of pulling or drawing a body, vehicle, etc., along a surface. **3.** the prolonged pulling of a muscle by weights, in order to correct dislocation, relieve pressure, etc. **4.** the apparatus, typically comprising weights, pulleys, etc., used for correcting dislocation, etc.: *He was in traction for days.* See -TRAC-.

trac•tor (trak′tər) /'træktər/ *n.* [*count*] **1.** a powerful motor-driven vehicle with large, heavy treads, used for pulling farm machinery, etc. **2.** a short truck with a driver's cab but no body, designed for hauling a trailer or semitrailer. **3.** something used for drawing or pulling. See -TRAC-.

trade (trād) /treyd/ *n., v.,* **trad•ed, trad•ing,** *adj.* —*n.* **1.** [*noncount*] the act or process of buying, selling, or exchanging goods: *domestic trade; foreign trade.* **2.** [*count*] a purchase or sale; a business deal. **3.** [*count*] an exchange of items, usually without payment of money; a swap: *The boys made a trade of a bag of marbles for a kite.* **4.** an occupation that is one's business or livelihood: [*count*]: *He's in the tourist trade.* [*noncount; by* + ~]: *She's a carpenter by trade.* **5.** [*count*] skilled manual or mechanical work; craft: *the carpenter trade.* **6.** [*count*] market: *an increase in the tourist trade.* **7. trades,** [*plural*] TRADE WIND. —*v.* **8.** to buy and sell; carry on trade or commerce in or with: [*no obj*]: *to trade in silver and gold.* [~ + *obj*]: *They trade silver and gold.* **9.** to exchange: [~ + *obj* (+ *for* + *obj*)]: *I traded my dessert for his.* [~ + *obj* + *obj* + *for* + *obj*]: *I'll trade you my dessert for yours.* [*no obj;* (~ + *for* + *obj*)]: *I'll trade for it.* **10.** [~ + *in* + *obj*] to use (someone or something) to one's advantage, esp. immorally or illegally: *The mob trades in terror and extortion.* **11. trade in,** to give (a used article) as payment toward a purchase of something new: [~ + *in* + *obj*]: *to trade in one's old car for a down payment on a new one.* [~ + *obj* + *in*]: *to trade your old car in and get a new one.* **12. trade on** or **upon,** [~ + *on* + *obj*] to turn to one's advantage, esp. unfairly; exploit: *to trade on the weaknesses of others.* —*adj.* [*before a noun*] **13.** of or relating to trade or commerce: *trade negotiations.* **14.** of or relating to a particular trade: *reading all the trade journals for tips.* **15.** Also, **trades.** of or relating to the members of a trade: *a trade club.*

trade′-in′, *n.* [*count*] **1.** goods given in usually partial payment of a purchase: *We used our old car as a trade-in for the new one.* **2.** a business deal involving a trade-in. —*adj.* [*before a noun*] **3.** of or relating to such a business deal: *the trade-in price.*

trade•mark (trād′märk′) /'treyd,mark/ *n.* [*count*] **1.** a name, symbol, etc., adopted by a manufacturer to separate their products from others: *A trademark must be registered with a government patent office.* **2.** a special mark or feature particular to or identified with a certain person or thing: *You see where the carpenter engraved his initials; that's his trademark.* —*v.* [~ + *obj*] **3.** to register the trademark of: *to trademark the name of his product.*

trade′ name′, *n.* [*count*] **1.** a name used in a trade to name a business, service, or particular class of goods. **2.** a brand name.

trade′-off′ or **trade′off′,** *n.* [*count*] the exchange of one thing for another of equal value, esp. to achieve a compromise: *The trade-off for more room in a car is usually lower gas mileage.*

trad•er (trā′dər) /'treydər/ *n.* [*count*] **1.** one who trades; a merchant. **2.** a ship used in trade, esp. foreign trade.

trades•man or **-wom•an** (trād ′mən) or (-wŏŏm′ən) /treyd'mən/ or /-,wʊmən/ *n.* [*count*], *pl.* **-men** or **-wo•men. 1.** one who works in trade. **2.** a worker skilled in a particular craft; artisan. **3.** *Chiefly Brit.* a shopkeeper.

trade′ un′ion, *n.* [*count*] a labor union in a particular trade or craft.

trade′ wind′ (wind) /wɪnd/ *n.* [*count*] Often, **trade winds.** [*plural*] a nearly constant easterly wind that appears in most of the tropics and subtropics throughout the world.

tra•di•tion (trə dish′ən) /trə'dɪʃən/ *n.* **1.** [*noncount*] the handing down of statements, beliefs, etc., esp. by word of mouth or by practice: *In Jewish tradition, learning is highly valued.* **2.** [*count*] something handed down in this way: *the traditions of the Eskimos.* **3.** [*noncount*] a long-established way of thinking or acting: *a break with tradition.* —**tra•di′tion•al,** *adj.*: *wearing traditional dress.* —**tra•di′tion•al•ly,** *adv.*

tra•duce (trə dōōs′, -dyōōs′) /trə'duws, -'dyuws/ *v.* [~ + *obj*], **-duced, -duc•ing.** to speak falsely of, as by saying untrue things about; slander; defame. See -DUC-.

traf•fic (traf′ik) /'træfɪk/ *n., v.,* **-ficked, -fick•ing.** —*n.* [*noncount*] **1.** the movement of vehicles, ships, etc., in an area or over a route: *a report on the traffic and weather.* **2.** the vehicles, persons, etc., moving in an area or over a route: *heavy traffic.* **3.** trade; buying and selling; commerce: *the traffic in illegal drugs.* **4.** the total amount of freight, passengers, messages, etc., handled in a given period: *Can those outdated telephone systems handle the increased traffic from cellular phones?* **5.** communication between persons or groups: *traffic in ideas.* —*v.* [*no obj*] **6.** to carry on trade or commerce. **7.** to trade in a commodity or service, often of an illegal nature: *to traffic in opium.* —**traf′fick•er,** *n.* [*count*]

traf′fic cir′cle, *n.* [*count*] a circle built where two or more roads meet, in order to allow easier passage of vehicles from one road to another. Also called **rotary;** *Brit.,* **roundabout.**

traf′fic light′, *n.* [*count*] a set of signal lights used to direct traffic at intersections. See illustration at STREET. Also called **stoplight, traf′fic sig′nal.**

tra•ge•di•an (trə jē′dē ən) /trə'dʒiydiyən/ *n.* [*count*] **1.** an actor noted for performing tragic roles. **2.** a writer of tragedy.

trag•e•dy (traj′i dē) /'trædʒɪdiy/ *n., pl.* **-dies. 1.** [*count*] a terrible or fatal event or affair; disaster: *a family tragedy.* **2.** [*count*] a play dealing with such affairs or events: *Shakespeare's tragedies.* **3.** [*noncount*] the branch of the drama concerned with this form of composition.

trag•ic (traj′ik) /'trædʒɪk/ also **trag′i•cal,** *adj.* **1.** dreadful, disastrous, or fatal: *a tragic accident.* **2.** of or relating to (a) tragedy: *the tragic news of the assassination.* —**trag′i•cal•ly,** *adv.*

trag•i•com•e•dy (traj′i kom′i dē) /,trædʒɪ'kɒmɪdiy/ *n.* [*count*], *pl.* **-dies. 1.** a play that combines both tragedy and comedy. **2.** an incident of mixed tragic and comic character. —**trag•i•com•ic** (traj′i kom′ik) /,trædʒɪ'kɒmɪk/ *adj.*

trail (trāl) /treyl/ *v.* **1.** to (cause to) be dragged along the ground; (cause to) be drawn behind: [~ + *obj*]: *She trailed her little toy wagon along behind her.* [*no obj*]: *Her bridal gown trailed across the floor.* **2.** [~ + *obj*] to follow the track, trail, or scent of; track: *The agents trailed him to a cabin in the woods.* **3.** [~ + *obj*] to follow (another), as in a race: *For most of the race he trailed the front-runners.* **4.** [*no obj;* ~ + *off*] to change gradually from a course, so as to become weak, etc.: *Her voice trailed off into silence.* **5.** [*no obj*] (of a plant) to grow along the ground rather than taking root: *a trailing plant.* —*n.* [*count*] **6.** a path made in overgrown land areas by the passing of people or animals: *They followed the trail through the woods.* **7.** the track or scent left by an animal, person, or thing: *The police lost the trail of the killer.* **8.** something that is trailed or that trails behind, as the train of a skirt or robe.

trail•blaz•er (trāl′blā′zər) /'treyl,bleyzər/ *n.* [*count*] **1.** one who marks a trail for others to follow through wilderness; a pathfinder. **2.** one who is the first to study, explore, or do something in a particular field; a pioneer.

trail•er (trā′lər) /'treylər/ *n.* [*count*] **1.** a large van or wagon pulled by an automobile, truck, or tractor, used esp. in hauling freight by road. **2.** a wheeled vehicle attached to and pulled by an automobile and used as a mobile home: *They have a trailer upstate where they go on the weekends.*

train (trān) /treyn/ *n.* **1.** a connected group of railroad cars: [*count*]: *a long freight train of about 100 cars.* [*noncount; by* + ~]: *only travels by train or bus.* See illustration at TERMINAL. **2.** [*count*] a line or procession of persons, vehicles, etc. **3.** [*count*] something drawn along, as a part of a long dress that trails behind on the ground: *the bride's white dress and long train.* **4.** [*count*] a course or path in one's thinking or reasoning: *I've lost my train of thought.* **—***v.* **5.** to develop the habits, thoughts, or behavior of (a child) by teaching or discipline: [~ + *obj* + *to* + *verb*]: *to train him to be kind to animals.* [~ + *obj*]: *to train her in the ways of the church.* **6.** to (cause to) become skilled in some work by teaching or practice: [~ + *obj*]: *Merlin trained her in the arts of sorcery.* [~ + *obj* + *to* + *verb*]: *His father trained him to fix cars.* [*no obj*]: *She trained as an apprentice.* **7.** to (cause to) become fit by proper exercise, diet, etc., as for an athletic performance: [~ + *obj*]: *trained him in boxing.* [*no obj*]: *trained for the race by running twenty miles a day.* **8.** [~ + *obj*] to discipline (an animal), as in the performance of tasks or tricks: [~ + *obj*]: *She trained her dog.* [~ + *obj* + *to* + *verb*]: *She trained her dog to obey commands.* **9.** [~ + *obj*] to bring (a plant, etc.) into a particular shape or direction, by bending, cutting, etc. **10.** [~ + *obj*] to bring (a gun, a camera, etc.) to focus on an object: *Six guns were trained on him, so he dropped his weapon.* **11.** [*no obj*] to travel or go by train. —**train′a•ble,** *adj.*

train•ee (trā nē′) /trey'niy/ *n.* [*count*], *pl.* **-ees.** a person in training for some job, skill, etc.: *He was angry that the company had hired a new trainee to do his work.*

train•er (trā′nər) /'treynər/ *n.* [*count*] **1.** one who coaches others, as in sports: *a boxing trainer.* **2.** one who trains animals.

train•ing (trā′ning) /'treynıŋ/ *n.* [*noncount*] **1.** the act of someone who trains; the state of being trained: *He received no formal training in the new technology. He's in training for the big match.* **2.** the condition of having been trained, with reference to how well or badly one has been trained: *He's out of training.*

traipse (trāps) /treyps/ *v.,* **traipsed, traips•ing,** *n.* **—***v.* **1.** to walk idly or without finding or reaching one's goal: [*no obj*]: *to go traipsing along, expecting everything to turn out perfectly.* [~ + *obj*]: *to traipse the fields.* **—***n.* [*count*] **2.** a tiring walk.

trait (trāt) /treyt/ *n.* [*count*] **1.** a quality, esp. of one's personal nature, that sets one apart from others: *his bad character traits.* **2.** an inherited feature or characteristic: *a recessive trait.*

trai•tor (trā′tər) /'treytər/ *n.* [*count*] one who betrays. —**trai′tor•ous,** *adj.*

tra•jec•to•ry (trə jek′tə rē) /trə'dʒɛktəriy/ *n.* [*count*], *pl.* **-ries.** a curve that describes the path of a bullet, shell, etc., in its flight. See -JEC-.

tram (tram) /træm/ *n.* [*count*] **1.** *Brit.* a streetcar. **2.** a truck or car on rails, esp. one that travels on an overhead cable, as to convey skiers at a ski lodge.

tram•mel (tram′əl) /'træməl/ *n., v.,* **-meled, -mel•ing** or (*esp. Brit.*) **-melled, -mel•ling.** **—***n.* [*count*] **1.** Usually, **trammels.** [*plural*] anything that hinders; a restraint. **—***v.* [~ + *obj*] **2.** to restrain or hold back.

tramp (tramp) /træmp/ *v.* **1.** to walk with a firm, heavy step (on or through); march; trudge: [*no obj*]: *soldiers tramping through the streets.* [~ + *obj*]: *to tramp the streets.* **2.** [*no obj*] to walk steadily: *He tramped through the streets looking for a job.* **—***n.* [*count*] **3.** [*usually singular*] the act of tramping: *the tramp of the soldiers.* **4.** one who travels about on foot, living on occasional jobs or gifts of money or food. **5.** a woman regarded as behaving immorally, esp. a prostitute. **6.** a freight vessel that does not run regularly between fixed ports. —**tramp′er,** *n.* [*count*]

tram•ple (tram′pəl) /'træmpəl/ *v.,* **-pled, -pling,** *n.* **—***v.* **1.** to step heavily or carelessly on (something): [~ + *obj*]: *The cowboy was nearly trampled in the stampede.* [*no obj*]: *Don't trample on the grass.* **2.** [*no obj*] to control (another) harshly; crush: *claimed that the police trampled on their rights to free assembly.* **—***n.* [*count*] **3.** the act or sound of trampling. —**tram′pler,** *n.* [*count*]

tram•po•line (tram′pə lēn′, tram′pə lēn′, -lin) /ˌtræmpə'liyn, 'træmpəˌliyn, -lın/ *n.* [*count*] a sheet, usually of canvas, attached by springs to a horizontal frame several feet above the floor, used as a springboard in tumbling.

trance (trans) /træns/ *n.* [*count*] **1.** a state of altered consciousness between sleeping and waking, in which a person does not function freely or normally, esp. a state produced by hypnosis: *The music was so powerful that it put him into something like a trance.* **2.** a dazed or bewildered condition: *He's walking around in a trance and doesn't know what he's doing.*

tran•quil (trang′kwil) /'træŋkwıl/ *adj.* **1.** free from commotion; quiet; calm: *a tranquil village.* **2.** not affected by disturbing emotions; serene; placid: *a tranquil life.* —**tran•quil•li•ty, tran•quil•i•ty** (trang kwil′i tē) /træŋ'kwılıtiy/ *n.* [*noncount*] —**tran′quil•ly,** *adv.*

tran•quil•ize or **tran•quil•lize** (trang′kwə līz′) /'træŋkwəˌlayz/ *v.* [~ + *obj*], **-ized** or **-lized, -iz•ing** or **-liz•ing.** to make tranquil, as by giving a drug to: *The veterinarian tranquilized the dog with an injection.*

tran•quil•iz•er or **tran•quil•liz•er** (trang′kwə lī′zər) /'træŋkwəˌlayzər/ *n.* [*count*] a person or thing that tranquilizes, esp. a drug that has a mildly calming effect.

trans-, *prefix.* **1.** *trans-* comes from Latin, and is attached to verb roots that refer to movement or carrying from one place to another; it means "across; through": *transfer; transmit; transplant.* **2.** *trans-* is also used to mean "complete change": *transform; transmute.* **3.** *trans-* is also attached to roots to make adjectives that mean "crossing, going beyond, on the other side of (the place or thing named)": *transnational; trans-Siberian.*

trans., an abbreviation of: **1.** transfer. **2.** transit. **3.** transitive. **4.** translation. **5.** transportation.

trans•act (tran sakt′, -zakt′) /træn'sækt, -'zækt/ *v.* [~ + *obj*] to conduct (some business, etc.) to a settlement: *to transact a business deal before lunch.* —**trans•ac′tor,** *n.* [*count*] See -ACT-.

trans•ac•tion (tran sak′shən, -zak′-) /træn'sækʃən, -'zæk-/ *n.* **1.** [*noncount*] the act or process of transacting; the fact of being transacted. **2.** [*count*] something transacted, esp. a business agreement. —**trans•ac′tion•al•ly,** *adv.* See -ACT-.

trans•at•lan•tic (trans′ət lan′tik, tranz′-) /ˌtrænsət'læntık, ˌtrænz-/ *adj.* crossing or reaching across the Atlantic: *a transatlantic liner.*

trans•ceiv•er (tran sē′vər) /træn'siyvər/ *n.* [*count*] a radio transmitter and receiver combined in one unit. See -CEIVE-.

tran•scend (tran send′) /træn'sɛnd/ *v.* [~ + *obj*] **1.** to go beyond the ordinary limits of; exceed: *That strange tale about men from Mars transcends belief.* **2.** to do better than or exceed in excellence, extent, etc.; excel: *Her beauty transcended all others'.* —**tran•scend′ence,** *n.* [*noncount*] —**tran•scend′ent,** *adj.* See -SCEND-.

tran•scen•den•tal (tran′sen den′tl, -sən-) /ˌtrænsɛn'dɛntḷ, -sən-/ *adj.* being beyond ordinary experience, thought, or belief. —**tran′scen•den′tal•ly,** *adv.*

transcenden′tal medita′tion, *n.* [*noncount*] a technique, based on Hindu practices, for seeking serenity through regular meditation centered upon the repetition of a mantra.

trans•con•ti•nen•tal (trans′kon tn en′tl) /ˌtrænskɒntṇ'ɛntḷ/ *adj.* passing or extending across a continent: *a transcontinental railroad.* See -TEN-.

tran•scribe (tran skrīb′) /træn'skrayb/ *v.* [~ + *obj*], **-scribed, -scrib•ing.** **1.** to make a written or printed copy of (spoken material): *to transcribe a lecture.* **2.** to write out in another language or alphabet; translate. **3.** to make a recording of (a program, etc.) for broadcasting. **4.** to make a musical transcription of. —**tran•scrib′er,** *n.* [*count*] See -SCRIB-.

tran•script (tran′skript) /'trænskrıpt/ *n.* [*count*] **1.** a written or printed copy; something made by transcribing: *A transcript of the President's speech was handed out to the reporters.* **2.** an official school report on the record of a student, listing subjects studied, grades received, etc. See -SCRIB-.

tran•scrip•tion (tran skrip′shən) /træn'skrıpʃən/ *n.* **1.** [*noncount*] the act or process of transcribing. **2.** [*count*] something transcribed. **3.** [*count*] a transcript. **4.** [*count*] the arrangement of a musical composition for a voice or instrument other than that for which it was written. See -SCRIB-.

trans•duc•er (trans dōō′sər, -dyōō′-, tranz-) /træns'duwsər, -'dyuw-, trænz-/ *n.* [*count*] a device, as a microphone, that converts a signal from one form of energy to another. See -DUC-.

tran•sect (tran sekt′) /træn'sɛkt/ *v.* [~ + *obj*] to cut across; to divide by cutting across. See -SECT-.

trans•fer (*v.* trans fûr′, trans′fər; *n.* trans′fər) / *v.* træns'fɜr, 'trænsfər; *n.* 'trænsfər/ *v.,* **-ferred, -fer•ring,** *n.* **—***v.* **1.** [~ + *obj*] to move, bring, or remove from one place, person, or position to another: *transferred the load of laundry from one arm to the other.* **2.** to cause to pass (thought, power, etc.) from one person to another: [~ + *obj*]: *On the death of the king, power was transferred to the regent.* [*no obj*]: *Power then transferred to the king.* **3.** to (cause one to) be removed or moved from one place, position, or job to another: [~ + *obj*]: *The company transferred him to Singapore.* [*no obj*]: *He transferred to another company.* **4.** [~ + *obj*] *Law.* to give over the possession or control of (property): *to transfer a title to land.* **5.** [~ + *obj*] to imprint (a drawing, etc.) from one surface to another: *She transferred the design to a T-shirt.* **6.** [*no obj*] to withdraw from one school, etc., and enter another: *She transferred from Harvard to Yale.* **7.** [*no obj*] to change from one bus, etc., to another: *We transferred to the Blue Line, which went to the airport.* —*n.* **8.** [*count*] a means or system of transferring. **9.** [*noncount*] the fact of being transferred. **10.** [*count*] a place for transferring. **11.** [*count*] a ticket that allows a passenger to continue a journey on another bus, train, or the like: *She got on the bus and handed the driver her transfer.* **12.** [*count*] a drawing, design, etc., that is or may be transferred from one surface to another, usually by direct contact. **13.** [*count*] one who has transferred, as from one college to another. —**trans•fer′a•ble,** *adj.* —**trans•fer′al, trans•fer′ral,** *n.* [*count*] See -FER-.

trans•fig•ure (trans fig′yər) /træns'fɪgyər/ *v.* [~ + *obj*], **-ured, -ur•ing.** to change in outward form or appearance: *Their faces were transfigured.* —**trans•fig•u•ra•tion** (trans′fig yə rā′shən) /ˌtrænsfɪgyə'reyʃən/ *n.* [*noncount*]

trans•fix (trans fiks′) /træns'fɪks/ *v.* [~ + *obj*], **-fixed** or **-fixt, -fix•ing. 1.** to paralyze (someone) because of amazement, terror, etc.: *stood transfixed with horror.* **2.** to pierce through with or as if with a pointed weapon: *transfixed by an arrow.* See -FIX-.

trans•form (*v.* trans fôrm′; *n.* trans′fôrm) / *v.* træns'fɔrm; *n.* 'trænsfɔrm/ *v.* [~ + *obj* (+ *into/to* + *obj*)] **1.** to change in form: *transformed his drab office into a cheery workspace.* **2.** to change in condition or character; convert: *to transform sunlight into electrical power.* **3.** to change into another substance; transmute: *The ancient alchemists sought ways to transform lead into gold.* **4.** to change (voltage and current) by an electrical transformer. —*n.* [*count*] **5.** a mathematical number obtained from a given quantity by mathematical process. —**trans•for•ma•tion** (trans′fər mā′shən) /ˌtrænsfər'meyʃən/ *n.* [*count*]: *After just a few weeks of exercise the transformation in his health was remarkable.* [*noncount*]: *transformation of solar power to electrical power.* See -FORM-.

trans•form•er (trans fôr′mər) /træns'fɔrmər/ *n.* [*count*] **1.** a person or thing that transforms. **2.** a device that transfers electrical energy from one circuit to another: *When you visit Europe from the U.S., you may need a transformer for your electrical appliances.* See -FORM-.

trans•fusion (trans fyo͞o′zhən) /træns'fyuwʒən/ *n.* [*count*] **1.** a medical process of transferring blood by injecting it into an artery or vein of a patient who has lost it: *gave the accident victim a blood transfusion.* **2.** a transfer of anything important or vital to the well-being, success, etc., of something: *a quick transfusion of cash to the sinking company.* See -FUS-.

trans•gress (trans gres′, tranz-) /træns'grɛs, trænz-/ *v.* **1.** to go beyond (a limit, etc.): *transgressed the bounds of good sense.* **2.** to go beyond the limits imposed by (a law, etc.); violate; infringe: [*no obj*]: *to have transgressed against God and nature.* [~ + *obj*]: *to have transgressed the laws of God and nature.* —**trans•gres•sion** (trans-gresh′ən, tranz-) /træns'grɛʃən, trænz-/ *n.* [*count*]: *punished for his transgressions.* [*noncount*]: *transgression of common sense.* —**trans•gres′sor,** *n.* [*count*] See -GRESS-.

tran•sient (tran′shənt, -zhənt, -zē ənt) /'trænʃənt, -ʒənt, -ziyənt/ *adj.* **1.** not lasting; not permanent; transitory: *a transient illness.* **2.** staying only a short time and passing through: *transient guests at a hotel.* —*n.* [*count*] **3.** a person or thing that is transient: *Transients for Flight 806 will wait in Concourse C.* **4.** a sudden pulse of voltage or current. —**tran′sience, tran′sien•cy,** *n.* [*noncount*] —**tran′sient•ly,** *adv.*

tran•sis•tor (tran zis′tər) /træn'zɪstər/ *n.* [*count*] **1.** a small, solid device used in certain electronic products: *A transistor consists of a semiconductor with three or more electrodes and uses very little power.* **2.** Also called **transis′tor ra′dio.** a small radio with transistors as main parts.

tran•sit (tran′sit, -zit) /'trænsɪt, -zɪt/ *n.* [*noncount*] **1.** passage from one place to another; transportation: *The airline advised that our clothes were still in transit.* **2.** a system of public transportation, esp. in an urban area: *mass transit.* —*v.* [*no obj*] **3.** to make a transit.

tran•si•tion (tran zish′ən, -sish′-) /træn'zɪʃən, -'sɪʃ-/ *n.* **1.** [*noncount*] movement, passage, or change from one position, state, stage, etc., to another: *The company is still in transition from one boss to another.* **2.** [*count*] a period during which such change takes place: *A transition like this one could take weeks.* **3.** [*count*] a sentence, paragraph, etc., that links one scene or topic to another: *Use transition words to signal to your reader that you are connecting ideas.* —*v.* [*no obj*] **4.** to make a transition. —**tran•si′tion•al,** *adj.*: *a transitional manager until a new one could be hired.*

tran•si•tive (tran′si tiv, -zi-) /'trænsɪtɪv, -zɪ-/ *adj.* **1.** of or relating to a verb that takes a direct object and from which a passive can be formed: *The verbs* deny, put, *and* elect *are transitive verbs.* —*n.* [*count*] **2.** a transitive verb. —**tran′si•tive•ly,** *adv.* —**tran′si•tive•ness, tran•si•tiv•i•ty** (tran′si tiv′i tē, -zi-) /ˌtrænsɪ'tɪvɪtiy, -zɪ-/ *n.* [*noncount*]

tran•si•to•ry (tran′si tôr′ē, -tōr′ē, -zi-) /'trænsɪˌtɔriy, -ˌtowriy, -zɪ-/ *adj.* not lasting long; not permanent; brief: *a transitory illness.*

transl., an abbreviation of: translation.

trans•late (trans lāt′, tranz-, trans′lāt, tranz′-) /træns'leyt, trænz-, 'trænsleyt, 'trænz-/ *v.*, **-lat•ed, -lat•ing. 1.** to make a translation: [~ + *obj*]: *to translate his speeches into Arabic.* [*no obj*]: *so busy trying to translate that I wasn't even thinking of the speech itself.* **2.** [~ + *obj*] to change the form, condition, or nature of; transform: *to translate thought into action.* **3.** [~ + *obj*] to explain in terms that can be more easily understood; interpret. **4.** [*no obj*] to be able to be translated: *This word simply doesn't translate well into English.* —**trans•la′tor,** *n.* [*count*] See -LAT[1]-.

trans•la•tion (trans lā′shən, tranz-) /træns'leyʃən, trænz-/ *n.* **1.** [*noncount*] the conversion of one language into another: *the limitations of translation by machines.* **2.** [*count*] the words, phrases, sentences, etc., translated: *an English translation of the Hebrew Bible.* **3.** [*count*] a rendition of a printed text, speech, etc., into words that can be more easily or more directly understood: *"Translation: He's not interested."* **4.** [*noncount*] a change or conversion into some other form: *the swift translation of thought to action.* See -LAT[1]-.

trans•lit•er•ate (trans lit′ə rāt′, tranz-) /træns'lɪtəˌreyt, trænz-/ *v.* [~ + *obj*], **-at•ed, -at•ing.** to change (letters, words, etc.) into corresponding characters of another alphabet. —**trans•lit•er•a•tion** (trans lit′ə rā′shən, tranz-) /trænsˌlɪtə'reyʃən, trænz-/ *n.* [*noncount*] See -LIT-.

trans•lu•cent (trans lo͞o′sənt, tranz-) /træns'luwsənt, trænz-/ *adj.* permitting light to pass through but not allowing the objects on the opposite side to be clearly visible: *Frosted window glass is translucent.* —**trans•lu′cence,** *n.* [*noncount*] See -LUC-.

trans•mi•grate (trans mi′grāt, tranz-) /træns'maygreyt, trænz-/ *v.*, **-grat•ed, -grat•ing.** (of the soul) to be reborn after death in another body. —**trans′mi•gra′tion,** *n.* [*noncount*] See -MIGR-.

trans•mis•sion (trans mish′ən, tranz-) /træns'mɪʃən, trænz-/ *n.* **1.** [*noncount*] the act or process of transmitting; the fact of being transmitted: *transmission of radio signals.* **2.** [*count*] something transmitted: *Our transmissions aren't getting through.* **3.** a unit of gears for transferring changes of torque and speed in an automobile: [*noncount*]: *This car has automatic transmission.* [*count*]: *They replaced our transmission.* See -MIS-.

trans•mit (trans mit′, tranz-) /træns'mɪt, trænz-/ *v.*, **-mit•ted, -mit•ting. 1.** to send (a signal, etc.) to someone receiving, or to a destination; dispatch: [~ + *obj*]: *Transmit this message at once!* [*no obj*]: *The submarine was transmitting, but there was no one to receive the signal.* **2.** [~ + *obj*] to communicate, as information or news. **3.** [~ + *obj*] to spread (disease, etc.) to another: *to transmit AIDS.* **4.** [~ + *obj*] to cause or allow (light, heat, etc.) to pass through a medium: *Glass transmits light.* —**trans•mis•si•ble** (trans mis′ə bəl, tranz-) /træns'mɪsəbəl, trænz-/ **trans•mit′ta•ble,** *adj.* —**trans•mit′tal, trans•mit′tance,** *n.* [*noncount*] See -MIT-.

trans•mit•ter (trans mit′ər, tranz-) /træns'mɪtər, trænz-/ *n.* [*count*] a person or thing that transmits. See -MIT-.

trans•mute (trans myo͞ot′, tranz-) /træns'myuwt, trænz-/ *v.* [~ + *obj* (+ *into* + *obj*)], **-mut•ed, -mut•ing.** to change from one nature or condition into another; transform: *trying to transmute lead into gold.* —**trans•mut′a•ble,** *adj.* —**trans•mu•ta•tion** (trans′myo͞o tā′shən, tranz′-) /ˌtrænsmyuw'teyʃən, ˌtrænz-/ *n.* [*noncount*] See -MUT-.

trans•na•tion•al (trans nash′ə nl, tranz-) /træns'næʃənl̩, trænz-/ *adj.* **1.** going beyond national boundaries or interests: *transnational attempts to clean up the environ-*

ment. **2.** of or relating to several countries; multinational. **—***n.* [*count*] **3.** a transnational company or organization. See -NAT-.

trans•o•ce•an•ic (trans′ō shē an′ik, tranz′-) /ˌtrænsowʃiy'ænɪk, ˌtrænz-/ *adj.* extending across the ocean: *a transoceanic cable.*

tran•som (tran′səm) /'trænsəm/ *n.* [*count*] **1.** a crosspiece separating a door or window from a window above it. **2.** a window above such a crosspiece.

trans•par•en•cy (trans pâr′ən sī, -par′-) /træns'pɛərənsay, -'pær-/ *n., pl.* **-cies. 1.** [*noncount*] the state of being transparent. **2.** [*count*] something transparent: *The art teacher projected some transparencies on the wall.*

trans•par•ent (trans pâr′ənt, -par′-) /træns'pɛərənt, -'pær-/ *adj.* **1.** allowing light to pass through its substance so that bodies situated behind can be clearly seen. **2.** so light or sheer as to permit light to pass through: *a transparent blouse.* **3.** easily seen through, recognized, or detected: *a transparent lie.* **4.** easily understood; obvious: *a story with a transparent plot.* **—trans•par′ent•ly,** *adv.*: *Things were transparently obvious at that point.*

tran•spire (tran spīᵊr′) /træn'spayᵊr/ *v.,* **-spired, -spir•ing. 1.** [*no obj*] to occur; happen; take place: *What transpired next is not known exactly.* **2.** [*It* + ~ + *that clause*] to be revealed or become known: *It transpired that she had been seeing another man.* **3.** [*no obj*] to emit waste matter, etc., through the surface, as of leaves or the body. **—tran•spi•ra•tion** (tran′spə rā′shən) /ˌtrænspə'reyʃən/ *n.* [*noncount*] See -SPIR-.

trans•plant (*v.* trans plant′ *n.* trans′plant′) / *v.* træns'plænt *n.* 'træns,plænt/ *v.* [~ + *obj*] **1.** to remove (a plant) from one place and plant it in another. **2.** to transfer (an organ, etc.) from one part of the body to another or from one person or animal to another: *to transplant a human heart.* **3.** to move or bring from one place to another for settlement; relocate: *The Army transplanted him and his family every few years.* **—***n.* [*count*] **4.** the act or process of transplanting: *a successful transplant.* **5.** a transplanted plant, organ, etc. **—trans•plan•ta•tion** (trans′plan tā′shən) /ˌtrænsplæn'teyʃən/ *n.* [*noncount*] **—trans•plant′er,** *n.* [*count*]

tran•spon•der (tran spon′dər) /træn'spɒndər/ *n.* [*count*] a device that automatically transmits a radio signal upon receiving a certain signal. See -SPOND-.

trans•port (*v.* trans pôrt′, -pōrt′; *n.* trans′pôrt, -pōrt) / *v.* træns'pɔrt, -'powrt; *n.* 'trænspɔrt, -powrt/ *v.* [~ + *obj*] **1.** to carry or convey from one place to another: *to transport food from the countryside to the cities.* **2.** to carry away by strong emotion or dreams; enrapture: *He was transported while reading that novel.* **3.** to send into a faraway land, esp. to a penal colony, as punishment. **—***n.* [*noncount*] **4.** the act of transporting; transportation: *the days of really cheap air transport.* **5.** a means of transporting, as a truck, ship, or plane: *military transport by helicopters.* **—trans•port′er,** *n.* [*count*] See -PORT-.

trans•por•ta•tion (trans′pər tā′shən) /ˌtrænspər'teyʃən/ *n.* [*noncount*] **1.** the act of transporting; the state of being transported. **2.** the means of transporting; transport: *Toronto's excellent system of transportation.* **3.** the business of conveying people, goods, etc. **4.** fare or tickets for transport or travel: *Transportation is not cheap in major American cities.* See -PORT-.

trans•pose (trans pōz′) /træns'powz/ *v.,* **-posed, -pos•ing. 1.** [~ + *obj*] to change or reverse the relative position of; interchange: *to transpose the third and fourth letters of a word.* **2.** to write or perform (a musical composition) in a different key: [~ + *obj*]: *to transpose the song so she could sing it more easily.* [*no obj*]: *He could transpose at sight.* **—trans•po•si•tion** (trans′pə zish′ən) /ˌtrænspə'zɪʃən/ *n.* [*count*]: *transpositions of letters to make up a code.* [*noncount*]: *the use of transposition in building a code.* See -POS-.

trans•sex•u•al (trans sek′sho͞o əl) /træns'sɛkʃuwəl/ *n.* [*count*] **1.** one who desires to assume the physical characteristics and gender role of the opposite sex. **2.** one who has undergone a medical operation and taken hormones to achieve this purpose. **—***adj.* **3.** of or relating to transsexuals. **—trans•sex′u•al•ism,** *n.* [*noncount*]

tran•sub•stan•ti•a•tion (tran′səb stan′shē ā′shən) /ˌtrænsəb,stænʃiy'eyʃən/ *n.* [*noncount*] **1.** the changing of one substance into another. **2.** (in the Eucharist) the conversion of the bread and wine into the body and blood of Jesus. See -STAN-.

trans•verse (trans vûrs′, tranz-; trans′vûrs, tranz′-) /træns'vɜrs, trænz-; 'trænsvɜrs, 'trænz-/ *adj.* **1.** extending in a crosswise direction: *a transverse beam.* **—***n.* [*count*] **2.** something transverse. **—trans•verse′ly,** *adv.* See -VERT-.

trans•ves•tite (trans ves′tīt, tranz-) /træns'vɛstayt, trænz-/ *n.* [*count*] a person, esp. a man, who assumes the dress and manner of the opposite sex. **—trans•ves′-tism,** *n.* [*noncount*]

trap (trap) /træp/ *n., v.,* **trapped, trap•ping. —***n.* [*count*] **1.** an apparatus for catching birds or other animals: *several traps to catch mice.* **2.** a trick for catching a person by surprise: *When the thief tried to sell the stolen goods to the undercover detective, he fell right into the trap.* **3.** an unpleasant situation from which it is difficult to escape: *He was caught in a trap no matter what he said.* **4.** a device for removing unwanted substances from a moving fluid, etc. **5.** *Slang.* mouth: *Keep your trap shut.* **—***v.* **6.** to catch in or as if in a trap: [~ + *obj*]: *to trap beavers for their fur.* [*no obj*]: *They hunted and trapped for several years.* **7.** [~ + *obj*] to catch by a trick: *The police trapped the killer.* **8.** [~ + *obj*] to close in or confine by or as if by a trap: *When the boat tipped over he was trapped underwater.* **—trap′per,** *n.* [*count*]

trap•door (trap′dôr′, -dōr′) /'træp'dɔr, -'dowr/ *n.* [*count*] **1.** a door evenly lined up with the surface of a floor, ceiling, or roof. **2.** the opening that it covers.

tra•peze (tra pēz′, trə-) /træ'piyz, trə-/ *n.* [*count*] an apparatus used in gymnastics and acrobatics, consisting of a short horizontal bar attached to the ends of two ropes, on which a gymnast or acrobat swings.

trap•e•zoid (trap′ə zoid′) /'træpə,zɔyd/ *n.* [*count*] a four-sided figure having two sides that are parallel and two sides that are not parallel. **—trap′e•zoi′dal,** *adj.*

trap•pings (trap′ingz) /'træpɪŋz/ *n.* [*plural*] **1.** articles of equipment or dress: *the trappings of her royal position.* **2.** conventional forms or symbols, esp. when lacking true substance: *They had all the trappings of democracy — elections and ballots—but none of the realities.*

trap•shoot•ing (trap′sho͞o′ting) /'træp,ʃuwtɪŋ/ *n.* [*noncount*] the sport of shooting at clay pigeons hurled into the air from a trap. Compare SKEET. **—trap′shoot′er,** *n.* [*count*]

trash (trash) /træʃ/ *n.* [*noncount*] **1.** anything worthless or thrown away; rubbish: *The town collects trash on Wednesdays.* **2.** foolish ideas or talk; nonsense. **3.** a worthless person or persons: *the sort of trash who would steal candy from a baby.* **4.** poor or inferior writing, art, or music. **—***v.* [~ + *obj*] **5.** to destroy or vandalize, as in anger or protest: *on a rampage trashing the downtown shopping area.* **6.** to criticize or declare to be worthless: *The critics trashed all of this week's new movies.* **7.** *Informal.* to discard, as garbage or rubbish: *trashed the empty beer cans.*

trash′ can′, *n.* [*count*] a container for the disposal of dry waste matter. See illustration at TERMINAL.

trash•y (trash′ē) /'træʃiy/ *adj.,* **-i•er, -i•est.** of poor or very low quality; worthless: *trashy books.*

trau•ma (trou′mə, trô′-) /'trawmə, 'trɔ-/ *n., pl.* **-mas, -ma•ta** (-mə tə) /-mətə/. **1. a.** [*count*] a wound to the body produced by physical injury, as from an attack: *multiple traumas.* **b.** [*noncount*] the condition produced by this: *Check for signs of trauma on the victim.* **2.** [*noncount*] *Psychiatry.* distress to the mind or to one's emotions, usually from a disastrous event outside of usual experience, as rape or an airplane crash. **3.** [*count*] any very distressing experience, esp. one causing a disturbance in normal functioning. **—trau•mat•ic** (trou mat′ik, trô-, trə-) /traw'mætɪk, trɔ-, trə-/ *adj.*

trav•el (trav′əl) /'trævəl/ *v.,* **-eled, -el•ing** or (*esp. Brit.*) **-elled, -el•ling,** *n., adj.* **—***v.* **1.** to go from one place to another, as by car, train, plane, or ship: [*no obj*]: *They traveled all night.* [~ + *obj*]: *They traveled the world and the seven seas.* **2.** to proceed (at a certain speed or distance): [*no obj*]: *The car was traveling at sixty miles an hour.* [~ + *obj*]: *We traveled nearly six hundred miles.* **3.** [*no obj*] to pass or be transmitted, as light or information: *The news traveled quickly.* **—***n.* **4.** [*noncount*] the act of traveling, esp. to distant places: *She enjoys painting, art, and travel.* **5. travels,** [*plural*] journeys; wanderings: *In all my travels I never saw anything as beautiful as this sunset.* **—***adj.* **6.** for use while traveling: *a travel alarm clock.* **—trav′el•er, trav′el•ler,** *n.* [*count*] **—Usage.** Compare TRIP and TRAVEL. For a particular amount of traveling, the noun TRIP is usually used: *I hope you had a pleasant trip. The trip took ten hours.* The word TRAVEL is more often used as a noncount noun to refer to the general idea of traveling: *She's interested in travel and tourism.* When TRAVELS is used, it refers to a journey or trip that has many stops or involves many places: *In all my travels I've never met so many helpful people.*

trav′eler's check′, *n.* [*count*] a check sold by a bank, etc., signed by the purchaser when bought and again when being cashed or used: *Traveler's checks are considered safer to travel with than cash.*

trav•e•logue or **trav•e•log** (trav′ə lôg′, -log′) /ˈtrævəˌlɔg, -ˌlɒg/ *n.* [*count*] a lecture, slide show, etc., that describes a person's travels, esp. to an unusual place. See -LOG-.

tra•verse (*v.* trə vûrs′, trav′ərs; *n., adj.* trav′ərs, trə-vûrs′) / *v.* trəˈvɜrs, ˈtrævərs; *n., adj.* ˈtrævərs, trəˈvɜrs/ *v.,* **-versed, -vers•ing,** *n., adj.* —*v.* [~ + *obj*] **1.** to move over, along, through, or across (a hill, etc.), as at an angle: *The skiers traversed the side of the mountain.* **2.** to extend over: *A bridge traverses the stream.* —*n.* [*count*] **trav•erse. 3.** the act of traversing. **4.** something that traverses. —*adj.* **trav•erse. 5.** lying, extending, or passing across; transverse. See -VERT-.

trav•es•ty (trav′ə stē) /ˈtrævəstiy/ *n.* [*count*], *pl.* **-ties.** a poor or contemptible copy or likeness of something: *Arresting an innocent man and then locking him up is a travesty of justice.* —**Syn.** See BURLESQUE.

trawl (trôl) /trɔl/ *n.* [*count*] **1.** Also called **trawl′ net′.** a fishing net dragged along the sea bottom to catch fish. **2.** Also called **trawl′ line′.** a line attached to buoys and used in sea fishing, having many short lines with baited hooks attached at intervals. —*v.* **3.** to fish with a trawl (in): [~ + *obj*]: *trawling the seas for big game fish.* [*no obj*]: *a day spent trawling for fish.*

trawl•er (trô′lər) /ˈtrɔlər/ *n.* [*count*] **1.** a ship used in fishing with a trawl net. **2.** one who trawls.

tray (trā) /trey/ *n.* [*count*] **1.** a flat, shallow container, used for carrying or displaying articles: *He carried his lunch tray to the table.* See illustration at RESTAURANT. **2.** a tray and its contents: *a breakfast tray.*

treach•er•ous (trech′ər əs) /ˈtrɛtʃərəs/ *adj.* **1.** of or relating to treachery: *the treacherous tyrant who stabbed his friends in the back.* **2.** deceptive or unreliable. **3.** unstable or insecure; hazardous: *treacherous footing on the icy slope.* **4.** dangerous: *a treacherous wind nearly capsized the boat.* —**treach′er•ous•ly,** *adv.* —**treach′er•ous•ness,** *n.* [*noncount*]

treach•er•y (trech′ə rē) /ˈtrɛtʃəriy/ *n., pl.* **-er•ies. 1.** [*noncount*] betrayal of trust; treason: *"The treachery of mankind is proverbial" means that you can expect people to betray others.* **2.** [*count*] an act of treason.

trea•cle (trē′kəl) /ˈtriykəl/ *n.* [*noncount*] **1.** something excessively sweet or sentimental. **2.** *Brit.* MOLASSES.

tread (tred) /trɛd/ *v.,* **trod** (trod) /trɒd/ **trod•den** (trod′n) /ˈtrɒdn̩/ or **trod, tread•ing,** *n.* —*v.* **1.** to set down the foot in walking; step: [*no obj*]: *to tread softly on the stairs.* [~ + *obj*]: *Many pilgrims have trod this same street to the holy shrine.* **2.** [~ + *on/upon* + *obj*] to step or walk, esp. so as to press or injure something; trample: *The boys just trod on the flowers.* **3.** [*no obj*] to treat harshly; oppress: *The despot trod down his enemies.* —*n.* [*count*] **4.** the action of treading. **5.** the sound of footsteps: *We heard her measured tread.* **6.** the part of a wheel or tire that rests on the road, rail, etc.: *worn treads.* —***Idiom.*** **7. tread on someone's toes,** to offend someone. **8. tread water. a.** to keep the body straight up in the water with the head above the surface, usually by a pumping up-and-down movement of the legs and sometimes the arms. **b.** to maintain one's position without making any progress: *During the recession the company was barely able to tread water.*

trea•dle (tred′l) /ˈtrɛdl̩/ *n., v.,* **-dled, -dling.** —*n.* [*count*] **1.** a lever pushed by a continuous action of the foot so as to give motion to a machine: *operating the treadle on the sewing machine.* —*v.* [*no obj*] **2.** to work a treadle.

tread•mill (tred′mil′) /ˈtrɛdˌmɪl/ *n.* [*count*] **1.** a mill powered by walking on a series of moving steps that form a continuous path. **2.** any monotonous, wearisome routine.

treas., an abbreviation of: treasurer.

trea•son (trē′zən) /ˈtriyzən/ *n.* [*noncount*] the act of overthrowing one's government or of being disloyal to it: *to commit high treason.* —**trea′son•a•ble, trea′son•ous,** *adj.*

treas•ure (trezh′ər) /ˈtrɛʒər/ *n., v.,* **-ured, -ur•ing.** —*n.* **1.** [*noncount*] wealth gathered, esp. in the form of precious metals, money, or jewels. **2.** [*count*] any thing or person greatly valued. —*v.* [~ + *obj*] **3.** to keep in the mind and treat (someone or something) as precious; cherish: *treasured the few moments we spent together.*

treas•ur•er (trezh′ər ər) /ˈtrɛʒərər/ *n.* [*count*] **1.** an officer of a government, business, etc., in charge of managing money. **2.** one in charge of treasure or a treasury.

treas•ure-trove (trezh′ər trōv′) /ˈtrɛʒˌər trowv/ *n.* [*count*] anything like a treasure that one finds: *The new chemical formula was a treasure-trove of limitless value to the company.*

treas•ur•y (trezh′ə rē) /ˈtrɛʒəriy/ *n.* [*count*], *pl.* **-ur•ies. 1.** a place where the funds of a government, etc., are deposited, kept, and given out to be spent. **2.** the funds or revenue (as from taxation) of a government, a private business, etc. **3.** [*often: Treasury; often: the* + ~] the department of government that has control over money.

treat (trēt) /triyt/ *v.* **1.** [~ + *obj*] to act or behave toward (someone or something) in some way: *to treat all people with the respect they deserve.* **2.** [~ + *obj* + *as* + *noun/adjective*] to consider (someone or something) in a certain way: *treated this matter as important.* **3.** [~ + *obj*] to deal with in a specified way; handle: *The doctor treated his complaints seriously.* **4.** [~ + *obj*] to deal with (a disease, etc.) to relieve or cure: *new ways to treat AIDS.* **5.** [~ + *obj*] to perform an action or process on (something) to bring about a result: *to treat a substance with an acid.* **6.** to provide with food, entertainment, etc., at one's own expense: [~ + *obj*]: *The boss treated me to dinner.* [*no obj*]: *Put your money away; I'll treat.* **7.** to deal with in speech, etc., esp. in a specified manner or style: [~ + *obj*]: *treated the theme with fantasy.* [~ + *of* + *obj*]: *to treat of the problem in his book.* —*n.* [*count*] **8.** entertainment, food, etc., given or paid for by someone else, as an expression of friendliness, as a professional courtesy, etc. **9.** anything that provides enjoyment: *It was a real treat back then to have steak for dinner.* —**treat′a•ble,** *adj.*

trea•tise (trē′tis) /ˈtriytɪs/ *n.* [*count*] a formal piece of writing on the principles of a subject.

treat•ment (trēt′mənt) /ˈtriytmənt/ *n.* **1.** [*noncount*] the act, manner, or process of treating: *The principal's children don't receive special treatment from the teacher.* **2.** the use of medicines, surgery, etc., in curing a person of a disorder: [*noncount*]: *shock treatment for his depression.* [*count*]: *weekly chemotherapy treatments.*

trea•ty (trē′tē) /ˈtriytiy/ *n.* [*count*], *pl.* **-ties. 1.** a formal agreement between countries in regard to peace, friendship, etc.: *a new treaty to allow more trade.* **2.** the document calling for such an agreement.

tre•ble (treb′əl) /ˈtrɛbəl/ *adj., n., v.,* **-bled, -bling.** —*adj.* **1.** threefold; triple. **2. a.** of the highest pitch or range, as a voice part or instrument. **b.** high in pitch; shrill. —*n.* **3.** [*count*] **a.** the treble part. **b.** a treble voice or instrument. **4.** [*count*] a high voice or sound. **5.** [*noncount*] the upper portion of the range of audio frequencies: *turned up the treble on her stereo.* —*v.* **6.** to (cause to) become three times as much or as many; triple: [~ + *obj*]: *We'll treble our profits.* [*no obj*]: *Our profits will treble.*

tree (trē) /triy/ *n., v.,* **treed, tree•ing.** —*n.* [*count*] **1.** a plant having a permanently woody trunk and branches. **2.** a shrub or plant, as the banana, that resembles a tree in form and size. **3.** FAMILY TREE. **4.** CHRISTMAS TREE. —*v.* [~ + *obj*] **5.** to drive (something pursued) into or up a tree: *The dogs treed the fox.* —***Idiom.*** **6. up a tree,** in a difficult situation: *Now we're up a tree; how can we get out of this mess?* —**tree′less,** *adj.*

tre•foil (trē′foil, tref′oil) /ˈtriyfɔyl, ˈtrɛfɔyl/ *n.* [*count*] **1.** a plant having three small leaflets resembling those of clover. **2.** any figure, design, or emblem resembling a clover leaf.

trek (trek) /trɛk/ *v.,* **trekked, trek•king,** *n.* —*v.* [*no obj*] **1.** to travel, esp. slowly or with difficulty: *to trek across the desert.* —*n.* [*count*] **2.** a journey, esp. one involving difficulty or hardship. **3.** *South Africa.* a migration or expedition, esp. by ox wagon. —**trek′ker,** *n.* [*count*]

trel•lis (trel′is) /ˈtrɛlɪs/ *n.* [*count*] a frame, esp. one used as a support for growing vines or plants.

trem•ble (trem′bəl) /ˈtrɛmbəl/ *v.,* **-bled, -bling,** *n.* —*v.* [*no obj*] **1.** to shake with short, quick movements, as from fear or cold; quake: *His hands trembled from fear.* **2.** to be troubled with apprehension: *to tremble with worry about the exam.* **3.** (of things) to be affected with motion like vibrations: *After the explosion the whole house trembled.* **4.** to be unsteady, as sound: *His voice trembled.* —*n.* [*count*] **5.** the act of trembling. **6.** a state or fit of trembling.

tre•men•dous (tri men′dəs) /trɪˈmɛndəs/ *adj.* **1.** very great in size, amount, or intensity: *a tremendous ocean liner.* **2.** extraordinary; excellent; very good: *a tremen-*

dous movie. —**tre•men′dous•ly,** *adv.: tremendously excited.*

trem•o•lo (trem′ə lō′) /ˈtrɛmə,low/ *n., pl.* **-los. 1.** [*noncount*] a vibrating effect produced on certain instruments and in the human voice. **2.** [*count*] a mechanical device in an organ by which such an effect is produced.

trem•or (trem′ər, trē′mər) /ˈtrɛmər, ˈtriymər/ *n.* [*count*] **1.** an uncontrolled shaking of the body or limbs, as from disease, fear, or excitement: *As the fever struck, tremors shook his body.* **2.** a vibration: *the tremors following an earthquake.* **3.** an uncertain, quavering sound, as of the voice: *She asked, with a tremor in her voice, if he was going to be all right.*

trem•u•lous (trem′yə ləs) /ˈtrɛmyələs/ *adj.* **1.** (of persons, the body, etc.) of or relating to tremors: *tremulous hands.* **2.** timid; fearful. —**trem′u•lous•ly,** *adv.* —**trem′u•lous•ness,** *n.* [*noncount*]

trench (trench) /trɛntʃ/ *n.* [*count*] **1.** a long, narrow area dug out of the ground as a defense against the enemy. **2.** a deep ditch or cut in an area, as in a deep-sea ocean floor.

trench•ant (tren′chənt) /ˈtrɛntʃənt/ *adj.* **1.** sharp or keen, as language or a person: *trenchant wit.* **2.** strong; bold; energetic: *a trenchant policy of reform.* **3.** clearly or sharply defined; clear-cut; distinct. —**trench′ant•ly,** *adv.*

trench′ coat′, *n.* [*count*] a waterproof coat with a belt, epaulets, and a strap near the bottom of each sleeve.

trench′ mouth′, *n.* [*noncount*] a serious infection of the gums and throat, caused by bacteria.

trend (trend) /trɛnd/ *n.* [*count*] **1.** the way or direction things tend to go; drift: *the trend of current events.* **2.** style; vogue: *the new trend in women's apparel.*

trend•y (tren′dē) /ˈtrɛndiy/ *adj.,* **-i•er, -i•est. 1.** of or relating to the latest trend or style. **2.** following the latest trends or fashions; chic or faddish: *the trendy young generation.* —**trend′i•ness,** *n.* [*noncount*]

trep•i•da•tion (trep′i dā′shən) /,trɛpɪˈdeyʃən/ *n.* [*noncount*] fear, alarm, or worry: *approaching marriage with trepidation.*

tres•pass (tres′pəs, -pas) /ˈtrɛspəs, -pæs/ *n.* [*count*] **1.** an act of illegally entering the home or property of another. **2.** an offense or sin: *Forgive us our trespasses.* —*v.* [*no obj*] **3.** to commit a trespass. **4.** to commit an offense; sin. —**tres′pass•er,** *n.* [*count*] See -PASS-[1].

tress (tres) /trɛs/ *n.* [*count*] Usually, **tresses.** [*plural*] long locks or curls of hair, esp. those of a woman: *her dark brown tresses hanging to her shoulders.*

tres•tle (tres′əl) /ˈtrɛsəl/ *n.* [*count*] **1.** a frame made of a crosspiece attached at each end to the top of a frame, used as a support for planking, etc.; a horse. **2. a.** one of a number of such frames joined together to support a bridge. **b.** a bridge made of these: *The soldiers blew up the trestle just as the supply train was crossing it.*

tri-, *prefix. tri-* comes from Greek and Latin, where it has the meaning "three": *triatomic; trilateral.*

tri•ad (trī′ad, -əd) /ˈtrayæd, -əd/ *n.* [*count*] a group of three. —**tri•ad′ic,** *adj.*

tri•age (trē äzh′, trē′äzh) /triyˈɑʒ, ˈtriyɑʒ/ *n.* [*noncount*] **1.** the process of selecting among victims, as of a battle, to decide in what order to help them with medical treatment: *In triage doctors usually decide to treat first those victims that have the best chance of surviving, leaving the nearly dead to die.* **2.** the act of triage. —*adj.* [*before a noun*] **3.** of or relating to triage: *a triage officer.*

tri•al (trī′əl, trīl) /ˈtrayəl, trayl/ *n.* **1.** the examination of the facts of a case before a court of law, involving hearing evidence and deciding on a person's guilt or innocence: [*noncount*]: *on trial for murder.* [*count*]: *He is entitled to a trial before a jury of his peers.* **2.** [*count*] the act of testing to find out if someone or something is useful, valuable, etc.: *We gave the new worker a trial of six weeks.* **3.** [*count*] an affliction or trouble; a troublesome thing or person: *suffering through many trials and tribulations.* —*adj.* [*before a noun*] **4.** of or relating to a trial: *a trial lawyer.* **5.** done by way of trial or experiment: *a trial batch of the new serum.*

tri′al and er′ror, *n.* [*noncount*] trying out something by using different approaches and eliminating the ones that do not work.

tri′al balloon′, *n.* [*count*] an announcement about an action or policy, in order to see what the reaction would be or to gauge out how successful the action would be: *The president's spokesperson floated the trial balloon of raising taxes.*

tri•an•gle (trī′ang′gəl) /ˈtray,æŋgəl/ *n.* [*count*] **1.** a closed plane figure having three sides and three angles: *an equilateral triangle.* **2.** a flat, three-sided piece of metal or plastic, with straight edges, used with a T square for drawing lines, etc. **3.** any three-cornered or three-sided figure or piece: *a triangle of land.* **4.** a delicate situation involving three persons, esp. one in which two of them are in love with the third. —**tri•an•gu•lar** (trī ang′gyə lər) /trayˈæŋgyələr/ *adj.*

tribe (trīb) /trayb/ *n.* [*count*] a group of people descended from the same ancestor, having similar customs and traditions. —**trib′al,** *adj.* —**tri′bal•ism,** *n.* [*noncount*]

trib•u•la•tion (trib′yə lā′shən) /,trɪbyəˈleyʃən/ *n.* **1.** [*noncount*] severe trial or suffering: *difficulty and tribulation in his life.* **2.** [*count*] an instance of this: *trials and tribulations.*

tri•bu•nal (trī byōōn′l, tri-) /trayˈbyuwnḷ, trɪ-/ *n.* [*count*] **1.** a court of justice. **2.** a place or seat of judgment.

trib•une (trib′yōōn, tri byōōn′) /ˈtrɪbyuwn, trɪˈbyuwn/ *n.* [*count*] **1.** one who defends the rights of the people. **2.** (in ancient Rome) an officer elected to protect the rights of the common people.

trib•u•tar•y (trib′yə ter′ē) /ˈtrɪbyə,tɛriy/ *n., pl.* **-tar•ies,** *adj.* —*n.* [*count*] **1.** a stream that flows to a larger stream: *The river system and its tributaries extend for hundreds of miles.* **2.** a person or nation that pays tribute. —*adj.* **3.** (of a stream) flowing into a larger stream or other body of water.

trib•ute (trib′yōōt) /ˈtrɪbyuwt/ *n.* **1.** a gift, speech of praise, etc., given as an expression of gratitude toward another: [*count*]: *They gave the retiring president a tribute.* [*noncount*]: *They paid tribute to his outstanding talents.* **2.** [*count; usually singular; usually: a* + ~] something that deserves praise because of its quality: *The efficient way the company is now being run is a tribute to her skills.* **3.** a sum of money or other payment paid by one sovereign or nation to another as the price of peace, etc.: [*noncount*]: *to pay tribute in the form of land to the conquerors.* [*count*]: *a tribute in the sum of millions.*

tri•ceps (trī′seps) /ˈtraysɛps/ *n.* [*count*], *pl.* **-ceps•es** (-sep siz) /-sɛpsɪz/ **-ceps.** any muscle with three heads, esp. the one at the back of the upper arm, which extends the forearm.

trick (trik) /trɪk/ *n.* [*count*] **1.** a sneaky scheme to deceive or cheat: *He played a nasty trick on me, promising to keep a secret but then telling everyone else what I told him.* **2.** a silly or mischievous act; a practical joke; a prank: *to play a trick on their teacher on April Fools' Day.* **3.** a clever action, as to solve a problem, etc.: *the tricks of the carpenter trade.* **4.** the art of doing something skillfully: *the trick of making others laugh.* **5.** a clever act done to entertain, amuse, etc.: *some clever card tricks.* **6. a.** the group or set of cards played and won in one round. **b.** a point or scoring unit based on this. **7.** *Slang.* **a.** a prostitute's customer. **b.** a sexual act between a prostitute and a customer. —*adj.* **8.** of or relating to tricks: *trick shooting done while riding on horseback.* **9.** specially made or used for tricks: *a trick chair that collapses.* **10.** (of a joint) likely to weaken suddenly: *a trick knee.* —*v.* **11.** [~ + *obj*] to deceive: *They tricked me into giving them my money.* **12.** [~ + *obj* + *out of* + *obj*] to cheat (someone), forcing someone to lose something: *tricked out of his inheritance by dishonest lawyers.* —***Idiom.*** **13. do the trick,** to produce the desired effect: *Give me that screwdriver—that should do the trick.* —**trick′er•y,** *n.* [*noncount*]

trick•le (trik′əl) /ˈtrɪkəl/ *v.,* **-led, -ling,** *n.* —*v.* **1.** to (cause to) flow by drops: [*no obj*]: *Tears trickled down her cheeks.* [~ + *obj*]: *She trickled some water into his mouth.* **2.** [*no obj*] to pass bit by bit, slowly, or irregularly: *The guests trickled out of the room.* —*n.* [*count*] **3.** a trickling flow or stream. **4.** a small, slow, or irregular amount of anything proceeding: *just a trickle of customers.*

trick•ster (trik′stər) /ˈtrɪkstər/ *n.* [*count*] **1.** one who deceives; a cheat; a fraud. **2.** one who plays tricks.

trick•y (trik′ē) /ˈtrɪkiy/ *adj.* **-i•er, -i•est. 1.** willing to use deceitful tricks: *a tricky lawyer.* **2.** difficult because unreliable or uncooperative: *a tricky light switch.* **3.** of or relating to clever or demanding motion or behavior: *a tricky dance step.* —**trick•i•ly** (trik′ə lē) /ˈtrɪkəliy/ *adv.* —**trick′i•ness,** *n.* [*noncount*]

tri•col•or (trī′kul′ər) /ˈtray,kʌlər/ *adj.* **1.** Also, **tri′col′ored;** *esp. Brit.,* **tri′col′oured.** having three colors. —*n.* [*count*] **2.** a flag with three colors, esp. the national flag of France. Also, *esp. Brit.,* **tri′col′our.**

tri•cy•cle (trī′si kəl, -sik′əl) /ˈtraysɪkəl, -,sɪkəl/ *n.* [*count*] a vehicle, esp. one for children, having one large front wheel and two small rear wheels, propelled by foot pedals. See -CYCLE-.

tri•dent (trīd′nt) /ˈtraydnt/ *n.* [*count*] a three-pronged instrument or weapon.

tried (trīd) /trayd/ *v.* **1.** pt. and pp. of TRY. *—adj.* **2.** proved to be good: *tried-and-true products.*

tri•en•ni•al (trī en′ē əl) /trayˈɛniyəl/ *adj.* **1.** occurring every three years. **2.** lasting three years. *—n.* [*count*] **3.** a third anniversary. **4.** something that appears or occurs every three years. **5.** a period of three years. —**tri•en′ni•al•ly,** *adv.*

tri•fle (trī′fəl) /ˈtrayfəl/ *n., v.,* **-fled, -fling.** *—n.* [*count*] **1.** something of very little value: *buying little trifles for the kids.* **2.** a small amount of anything, as of money. **3.** a dessert of cake soaked in liqueur, then combined with custard, fruit, jam, etc., and topped with whipped cream. *—v.* [~ + *with* + *obj*] **4.** to deal without seriousness or respect: *Don't trifle with me!* **5.** to play with by handling or fingering: *He sat trifling with a pen.* —***Idiom.*** **6. a trifle,** to a small degree; somewhat: *He's still a trifle angry.* —**tri′fler,** *n.* [*count*]

tri•fling (trī′fling) /ˈtrayflɪŋ/ *adj.* **1.** of very small importance, value, or amount; trivial: *a trifling matter.* **2.** shallow; light: *trifling conversation.*

tri•fo•cal (trī fō′kəl, trī′fō′-) /trayˈfowkəl, ˈtrayˌfow-/ *adj.* **1.** (of a lens) having three areas that focus light rays. **2.** (of an eyeglass lens) having three portions, one for near, one for middle, and one for far vision. *—n.* **3.** **trifocals,** [*plural*] eyeglasses with trifocal lenses.

trig•ger (trig′ər) /ˈtrɪgər/ *n.* [*count*] **1.** a small tongue in a gun that, when pressed by the finger, fires the gun. **2.** a device pulled or pressed to release something. **3.** anything that causes a reaction: *a trigger for the fight.* *—v.* [~ + *obj*] **4.** to cause or begin (a chain of events): *Inflation triggered unemployment.* **5.** to fire or explode (a gun, etc.) by pulling a trigger. —***Idiom.*** **6. quick on the trigger,** too quick to act or respond; impetuous: *He was too quick on the trigger and wound up losing the deal.*

trig•o•nom•e•try (trig′ə nom′i trē) /ˌtrɪgəˈnɒmɪtriy/ *n.* [*noncount*] the branch of mathematics that deals with the relations between the sides and angles of triangles: *a course in trigonometry.* —**trig•o•no•met•ric** (trig′ə nə me′trik) /ˌtrɪgənəˈmɛtrɪk/ *adj.* See -METER-.

tri•lat•er•al (trī lat′ər əl) /trayˈlætərəl/ *adj.* having three sides. See -LAT-[2].

trill (tril) /trɪl/ *n.* [*count*] **1.** a rapid alternation between two nearby musical tones. **2.** a similar quavering sound, as that made by a bird or by a person laughing. *—v.* **3.** to sing, make, pronounce, or play with a trill: [~ + *obj*]: *to trill a few notes.* [*no obj*]: *birds trilling in the morning.*

tril•lion (tril′yən) /ˈtrɪlyən/ *n., pl.* **-lions,** (*as after a numeral*) **-lion,** *adj.* *—n.* [*count*] **1.** a number written in the U.S. by 1 followed by 12 zeros, and in Great Britain by 1 followed by 18 zeros: *a trillion; several trillions.* **2.** Often, **trillions.** [*plural*] a very great number or amount: *trillions of little ants on the beach.* *—adj.* [*after a number and before a noun*] **3.** amounting to one trillion in number: *one trillion dollars.* —**tril′lionth,** *n.* [*count*], *adj.* See the usage note under **hundred**.

tril•o•gy (tril′ə jē) /ˈtrɪlədʒiy/ *n.* [*count*], *pl.* **-gies.** a series or group of three plays, novels, etc., that are closely related in characters, theme, etc.: *the Oresteian trilogy by Aeschylus.* See -LOG-.

trim (trim) /trɪm/ *v.,* **trimmed, trim•ming,** *n., adj.,* **trim•mer, trim•mest,** *adv.* *—v.* [~ + *obj*] **1.** to put into a neat condition by clipping, paring, etc.: *to trim a hedge.* **2.** to remove (something unnecessary) by or as if by cutting: *to trim those loose threads.* **3.** to cut down; reduce; lower: *to trim the sales force.* **4.** to adjust (the sails or yards of a ship) with attention to the direction of the wind and the course of the ship. **5.** to adorn with ornaments; esp., to decorate a store window: *to trim the windows for Christmas.* *—n.* **6.** [*noncount*] the condition, order, or fitness of a person or thing for action, etc. **7.** [*count; usually singular*] the adjustment of sails, etc., with reference to wind direction and the course of the ship. **8.** [*noncount*] material used for decoration. **9.** [*count*] a trimming by cutting, clipping, or the like: *He didn't want a full haircut, just a (quick) trim.* *—adj.* **10.** neat or smart in appearance: *trim lawns.* **11.** (of a person) in excellent physical condition: *Swimming is a good way to keep trim.* **12.** slim; lean: *a trim figure.* *—adv.* **13.** in a trim manner; trimly. —**trim′ly,** *adv.* —**trim′mer,** *n.* [*count*] —**trim′ness,** *n.* [*noncount*]

tri•mes•ter (trī mes′tər, trī′mes-) /trayˈmɛstər, ˈtraymɛs-/ *n.* [*count*] **1.** a term or period of three months: *the first trimester of pregnancy.* **2.** one of the three approximately equal terms into which an academic year may be divided.

trim•ming (trim′ing) /ˈtrɪmɪŋ/ *n.* **1.** [*noncount*] anything used for decoration: *the trimming on a uniform.* **2.** Usually, **trimmings.** [*plural*] something that goes with a main dish: *They had roast turkey with all the trimmings.* **3. trimmings,** [*plural*] pieces cut off in trimming, clipping, or pruning. **4.** [*count*] a defeat: *Our team took quite a trimming.*

tri•month•ly (trī munth′lē) /trayˈmʌnθliy/ *adj.* occurring, taking place, done, or acted upon every three months.

Trin•i•ty (trin′i tē) /ˈtrɪnɪtiy/ *n., pl.* **-ties** for 2. **1.** [*proper noun; usually: the* + ~] in Christian doctrine, the union of three persons (Father, Son, and Holy Ghost) in one Godhead. **2.** [*count; trinity*] a group of three; triad.

trin•ket (tring′kit) /ˈtrɪŋkɪt/ *n.* [*count*] **1.** a small ornament, etc., of little value: *a few trinkets for the kids.* **2.** anything of small value.

tri•o (trē′ō) /ˈtriyow/ *n.* [*count*], *pl.* **tri•os. 1.** any group of three. **2.** a musical composition for three voices or instruments. **3.** a company of three singers or players.

trip (trip) /trɪp/ *n., v.,* **tripped, trip•ping.** *—n.* [*count*] **1.** a traveling from one place to another: *my weekly trip to the bank.* **2.** a run made by a boat, train, or the like between two points: *The trip takes just two hours by ferry.* **3.** a misstep, as by catching one's foot. **4.** *Slang.* **a.** an instance of being under the influence of a hallucinogenic drug, esp. LSD. **b.** an exciting experience. **c.** something that keeps one occupied: *She's been on a nostalgia trip all week.* *—v.* **5.** to (cause to) stumble: [*no obj*]: *to trip on one of the toys.* [~ + *obj*]: *stuck out his foot and tripped her.* **6.** to (cause to) make a slip or mistake, as in conversation or conduct: [~ + *up* + *obj*]: *The lawyer tried his best to trip up the witness.* [~ + *obj* + *up*]: *to trip him up.* [*no obj;* ~ + *up*]: *During his speech he tripped up when he confused the Balkan states and the Baltic states.* **7.** [*no obj*] to step lightly or nimbly; skip: *tripping gaily down the path.* **8.** [*no obj; (~ + out)*] *Slang.* to be under the influence of a hallucinogenic drug, esp. LSD: *She claimed she was tripping (out) on acid and saw monsters crawling on her arm.* —**trip′per,** *n.* [*count*] —**Usage.** See TRAVEL.

tri•par•tite (trī pär′tīt) /trayˈpɑrtayt/ *adj.* **1.** divided into or made up of three parts: *a tripartite leaf.* **2.** of or relating to three different groups, sides, etc.: *a tripartite treaty.* See -PAR-.

tripe (trīp) /trayp/ *n.* [*noncount*] **1.** the first and second divisions of the stomach of certain animals, used as food. **2.** *Slang.* something false or worthless: *That's a lot of tripe; I don't believe it at all.*

tri•ple (trip′əl) /ˈtrɪpəl/ *adj., n., v.,* **-pled, -pling.** *—adj.* [*before a noun*] **1.** threefold; consisting of three parts; of three kinds. **2.** three times as great: *triple profits.* *—n.* [*count*] **3.** an amount, number, etc., three times as great as another. **4.** a group, set, or series of three; triad. **5.** Also called **three-base hit.** a hit in baseball that enables the batter to reach third base safely. *—v.* **6.** to (cause to) become triple: [~ + *obj*]: *Our company tripled its profits.* [*no obj*]: *Profits tripled last year.* —**trip′ly,** *adv.* See -PLIC-.

tri•plet (trip′lit) /ˈtrɪplɪt/ *n.* [*count*] **1.** one of three offspring born at one birth. **2.** any group of three, as three lines of poetry or three musical notes played together.

tri•plex (trip′leks, trī′pleks) /ˈtrɪplɛks, ˈtrayplɛks/ *adj.* **1.** threefold; triple. *—n.* [*count*] **2.** something triple. **3.** an apartment having three floors: *They examined a triplex, but the rent was too high.* **4.** a multiplex of three theaters or movie houses. See -PLIC-.

trip•li•cate (trip′li kit) /ˈtrɪplɪkɪt/ *adj.* **1.** having or made up of three identical copies or parts; threefold. **2.** of or relating to the third of three identical copies or items. —***Idiom.*** **3. in triplicate,** in three identical copies. See -PLIC-.

tri•pod (trī′pod) /ˈtraypɒd/ *n.* [*count*] **1.** a three-legged stand, as for a camera. **2.** a stool, table, pedestal, etc., with three legs. —**trip•o•dal** (trip′ə dl, trī′pod l) /ˈtrɪpədḷ, ˈtraypɒdḷ/ *adj.* See -POD-.

trip•tych (trip′tik) /ˈtrɪptɪk/ *n.* [*count*] a set of three panels side by side, bearing pictures, carvings, etc.: *a triptych of the Trinity.*

tri•sect (trī sekt′, trī′sekt) /trayˈsɛkt, ˈtraysɛkt/ *v.* [~ + *obj*] to divide into three parts, esp. into three equal parts. —**tri•sec′tion,** *n.* [*noncount*] See -SECT-.

trite (trīt) /trayt/ *adj.,* **trit•er, trit•est. 1.** (of a word, phrase, or expression) lacking in freshness because of constant use; hackneyed: *a trite expression.* **2.** characterized by such hackneyed expressions, etc.: *a trite speech.* —**trite′ly,** *adv.* —**trite′ness,** *n.* [*noncount*]

tri•umph (trī′əmf, -umf) /'trayəmf, -ʌmf/ *n.* **1.** [*count*] the act or fact of being victorious; victory; success: *some medical triumphs in the war against cancer.* **2.** [*noncount*] a feeling resulting from victory or success: *a feeling of triumph.* —*v.* [*no obj;* (~ + *over* + *obj*)] **3.** to gain a victory or be highly successful: *The Allies triumphed over the Axis.* **4.** to gain mastery; prevail: *to triumph over fear.*

tri•um•phant (trī um′fənt) /tray'ʌmfənt/ *adj.* **1.** having achieved a triumph: *a triumphant army.* **2.** rejoicing because of success: *They were triumphant when they got the building contract.* —**tri•um′phant•ly,** *adv.*: *The winner waved triumphantly.*

tri•um•vi•rate (trī um′vər it, -və rāt′) /tray'ʌmvərɪt, -vəˌreyt/ *n.* [*count*] **1.** a board of three magistrates functioning jointly, esp. one in ancient Rome. **2.** any association of three in authority. **3.** any group or set of three.

triv•et (triv′it) /'trɪvɪt/ *n.* [*count*] **1.** a small metal or ceramic plate with short legs, used under a hot platter to protect a table. **2.** a three-legged stand placed over a fire to support cooking vessels or the like.

triv•i•a (triv′ē ə) /'trɪviyə/ *n.* matters or things that are unimportant; meaningless facts or details; trifles: [*noncount; used with a singular verb*]: *Trivia is what you need to know to do well in some games.* [*plural; used with a plural verb*]: *studying numerous trivia.*

triv•i•al (triv′ē əl) /'trɪviyəl/ *adj.* of or relating to trivia: *He was overreacting to what was really a trivial offense on her part.* —**triv•i•al•i•ty** (triv′ē al′i tē) /ˌtrɪviy'ælɪtiy/ *n., pl.* **-ties.** [*noncount*]: *the triviality of considering what clothes to wear after an earthquake.* [*count*]: *the trivialities of daily living.* See -VIA-.

trod (trod) /trɒd/ *v.* a pt. and pp. of TREAD.

trod•den (trod′n) /'trɒdn̩/ *v.* a pp. of TREAD.

trog•lo•dyte (trog′lə dīt′) /'trɒgləˌdayt/ *n.* [*count*] **1.** a person of prehistoric times who lived in a cave. **2.** a person of primitive or brutal character. **3.** an extremely old-fashioned or conservative person.

troi•ka (troi′kə) /'trɔykə/ *n.* [*count*], *pl.* **-kas. 1.** a Russian carriage drawn by a team of three horses abreast. **2.** a ruling group of three; a triumvirate. **3.** any group of three.

troll[1] (trōl) /trowl/ *v.* **1.** to sing or utter in a full, rolling voice: [*no obj*]: *to troll merrily in the choir.* [~ + *obj*]: *to troll some notes.* **2.** to fish in (a body of water) by trailing a line behind a slow-moving boat: [~ + *obj*]: *trolling the lake for trout.* [*no obj*]: *trolling for trout.* —*n.* [*count*] **3.** a song whose parts are sung one after the other; a round. **4.** the act of fishing by trolling.

troll[2] (trōl) /trowl/ *n.* [*count*] (in Scandinavian folk stories) a supernatural being, usually hostile to humans, who lives underground or in caves.

trol•ley or **trol•ly** (trol′ē) /'trɒliy/ *n.* [*count*], *pl.* **-leys** or **-lies. 1.** TROLLEY CAR. **2.** a pulley traveling on an overhead track and serving to support and move an object hung from it. **3.** a small truck or car operated on a track, as in a factory. **4.** a serving cart, as for desserts. **5.** *Chiefly Brit.* any of various low carts. —***Idiom.* 6. off one's trolley,** *Slang.* mentally unstable; insane.

trol′ley car′, *n.* [*count*] a streetcar propelled electrically by current taken from a conducting wire strung overhead.

trol•lop (trol′əp) /'trɒləp/ *n.* [*count*] **1.** an immoral woman, esp. a prostitute. **2.** an untidy or sloppy woman; a slattern.

trom•bone (trom bōn′, trom′bōn) /trɒm'bown, 'trɒmbown/ *n.* [*count*] a musical wind instrument consisting of a rounded metal tube expanding into a bell and bent twice into a U shape, and having a slide for varying the tone.

troop (tro͞op) /truwp/ *n.* [*count*] **1.** a group of persons or things; a band of people. **2.** a cavalry unit corresponding to a company of infantry. **3. troops,** [*plural*] a body of soldiers, police, etc.: *The troops never had a chance to leave their barracks.* **4.** a unit of Boy Scouts or Girl Scouts usually having a maximum of 32 members under an adult leader. —*v.* [*no obj*] **5.** to pass together, esp. in great numbers; throng: *People were trooping into the stadium.* **6.** to walk, as if in a march; go: *The kids came trooping down to breakfast.*

troop•er (tro͞o′pər) /'truwpər/ *n.* [*count*] **1.** a member of a state police force; a state trooper. **2.** a cavalry soldier. **3.** someone who does not give up: *She's a real trooper; you can count on her to finish the job.*

tro•phy (trō′fē) /'trowfiy/ *n.* [*count*], *pl.* **-phies. 1.** anything taken in war, hunting, etc., esp. when set up as a memento: *a lion's head as a trophy.* **2.** anything won or awarded as a sign of victory, etc.; an award or prize: *had numerous athletic and scholastic trophies.*

trop•ic (trop′ik) /'trɒpɪk/ *n.* [*count*] **1. a.** either of two parallel lines of latitude on the earth's globe, about 23½° N and about 23½° S of the equator. **b. the tropics,** the regions lying between these parallels of latitude. —*adj.* **2.** of or relating to the tropics; tropical.

trop•i•cal (trop′i kəl) /'trɒpɪkəl/ *adj.* **1.** of, relating to, or living in the tropics. **2.** very hot and humid: *tropical heat.* **3.** used in or suitable for the tropics: *tropical clothing.*

tro•pism (trō′piz əm) /'trowpɪzəm/ *n.* [*noncount*] the growing of an organism toward or away from a stimulus, as light.

trop•o•sphere (trop′ə sfēr′, trō′pə-) /'trɒpəˌsfɪər, 'trowpə-/ *n.* [*count; usually singular*] the lowest layer of the atmosphere, varying in height from 6 to 12 mi. (10 to 20 km), within which clouds and weather occur.

trot (trot) /trɒt/ *v.,* **trot•ted, trot•ting,** *n.* —*v.* **1.** (of a horse) to (cause to) go at a pace between a walk and a run: [*no obj*]: *The horse trotted along.* [~ + *obj*]: *The rider trotted his horse for the competition.* **2.** [*no obj*] to go at a quick, steady pace: *He trotted along behind his big brother.* **3. trot out,** *Informal.* to bring forward to the attention of others: [~ + *out* + *obj*]: *Once again he trotted out his favorite plan.* [~ + *obj* + *out*]: *to trot his plan out again.* —*n.* **4.** [*count*] the pace of a horse or other four-legged animal when trotting. **5.** [*count*] the sound made by an animal when trotting. **6.** [*count*] the jogging pace of a human being. **7.** [*count*] *Slang.* a literal translation of some piece of writing, used dishonestly in doing schoolwork; a crib; a pony. **8. the trots,** *Informal.* diarrhea; the runs: [*noncount; used with a singular verb*]: *He told me he has the trots.* [*plural; used with a plural verb*]: *The trots have kept him at home all day.* —**trot′ter,** *n.* [*count*]

troth (trôth, trōth) /trɔθ, trowθ/ *n.* [*noncount*] *Archaic.* **1.** faithfulness: *by my troth.* **2.** one's word or promise, esp. in betrothal: *They will plight their troth (= promise to marry).*

trou•ba•dour (tro͞o′bə dôr′, -dōr′, -do͝or′) /'truwbəˌdɔr, -ˌdowr, -ˌdʊr/ *n.* [*count*] a wandering singing poet, esp. of olden days.

trou•ble (trub′əl) /'trʌbəl/ *v.,* **-bled, -bling,** *n.* —*v.* **1.** [~ + *obj*] to disturb the calm and contentment of; worry; distress: *The sufferings of the poor troubled him.* **2.** to put to inconvenience, pains, or the like: [~ + *obj* + *for* + *obj*]: *May I trouble you for a match?* [~ + *obj* + *to* + *verb*]: *May I trouble you to shut the door?* **3.** [~ + *obj*] to cause pain or discomfort to; afflict: *to be troubled by arthritis.* **4.** [*no obj;* ~ + *to* + *verb*] to refuse to do something inconvenient; to bother to do: *He didn't even trouble to read the homework.* —*n.* **5.** [*noncount*] difficulty or annoyance: *loves to make trouble for me.* **6.** an unfortunate occurrence; misfortune: [*noncount*]: *He's in a bit of financial trouble at the moment.* [*count*]: *He's had some financial troubles lately.* **7.** civil disorder or conflict: [*noncount*]: *a time of trouble.* [*count*]: *during the troubles in South Africa.* **8.** [*noncount*] a physical disease, etc.: *heart trouble.* **9.** [*noncount*] mental or emotional distress; worry: *a life full of trouble.* [*plural*]: *He's got troubles on his mind.* **10.** [*count; singular*] effort, exertion, or inconvenience in accomplishing some deed, etc.: *I don't want you to go to any trouble over this.* **11.** [*count; singular*] something objectionable about something; fault: *What's the trouble with the proposal?* **12.** a mechanical defect or breakdown: [*noncount*]: *We had trouble with the washing machine.* [*count*]: *We've had troubles with the washing machine.* —***Idiom.* 13. in trouble, a.** pregnant out of wedlock (used as a euphemism). **b.** in danger or difficulty: *He was in big trouble with the mob.* —**trou′ble•some,** *adj.*

trou•bled (trub′ld) /'trʌbld/ *adj.* **1.** disturbed; upset; worried: *a troubled look.* **2.** difficult because of conflicts: *troubled times.* **3.** (of water or waters) disturbed and churned up.

trou•ble•mak•er (trub′əl mā′kər) /'trʌbəlˌmeykər/ *n.* [*count*] one who causes trouble for others.

trou•ble•shoot•er (trub′əl sho͞o′tər) /'trʌbəlˌʃuwtər/ *n.* [*count*] **1.** a person with skill in finding ways to stop or resolve disputes. **2.** an expert in discovering and getting rid of the cause of trouble in mechanical breakdowns.

trough (trôf, trof) /trɔf, trɒf/ *n.* [*count*] **1.** a long, narrow, open, boxlike container, used chiefly to hold water or food for animals. **2.** a channel for carrying water away. **3.** the lowest point, esp. in an economic cycle.

trounce (trouns) /trawns/ *v.* [~ + *obj*], **trounced, trounc•ing.** to beat severely; defeat completely: *The home team trounced the visitors, 20-0.* —**trounc′er,** *n.* [*count*]

troupe (tro͞op) /truwp/ *n., v.,* **trouped, troup•ing.** —*n.* [*count*] **1.** a company of actors, esp. one that travels extensively. —*v.* [*no obj*] **2.** to travel as a member of a troupe. —**troup′er,** *n.* [*count*]

trou•sers (trou′zərz) /'trawzərz/ *n.* [*plural*] Sometimes, **trouser.** [*count*] clothing for the lower part of the body, having individual leg portions: *a pair of trousers.* Also called **pants.**

trous•seau (tro͞o′sō, tro͞o sō′) /'truwsow, truw'sow/ *n.* [*count*], *pl.* **-seaux** (-sōz, -sōz′) /-sowz, -'sowz/ **-seaus.** an outfit of clothing, household linen, etc., belonging to a bride.

trout (trout) /trawt/ *n.* [*count*], *pl.* (*esp. when thought of as a group*) **trout,** (*esp. for kinds or species*) **trouts.** a usually speckled freshwater game fish of the salmon family.

trow•el (trou′əl) /'trawəl/ *n., v.,* **-eled, -el•ing** or (*esp. Brit.*) **-elled, -el•ling.** —*n.* [*count*] **1.** a tool having a flat blade with a handle, used for depositing and smoothing out mortar, etc. **2.** a similar tool with a curved, scooplike blade, used in gardening. —*v.* [~ + *obj*] **3.** to apply, shape, smooth, or dig with or as if with a trowel: *troweled the plaster onto the wall tiles.*

tru•ant (tro͞o′ənt) /'truwənt/ *n.* [*count*] **1.** a student who stays away from school without permission. **2.** one who neglects his or her duty. —*adj.* **3.** absent from school without permission. **4.** neglecting to do one's duty. —**tru′an•cy,** *n.* [*noncount*]

truce (tro͞os) /truws/ *n.* [*count*] **1.** a stopping of hostilities for a certain period of time by agreement of all the warring parties; a cease-fire: *to declare a truce for Christmas.* **2.** an agreement or treaty for this.

truck (truk) /trʌk/ *n.* [*count*] **1.** a motor vehicle for carrying goods and materials: *Those big trucks were blocking the roads.* **2.** a frame, platform, or open cart with wheels used for transporting heavy objects. **3.** HAND TRUCK. —*v.* **4.** [~ + *obj*] to transport or deliver (articles, etc.) by truck: *to truck some vegetables to the market.* **5.** [*no obj*] *Informal.* to proceed, esp. in a carefree manner: *I'm just trucking along, no problems.* —**truck′er,** *n.* [*count*]

truck′ farm′, *n.* [*count*] a farm for the growing of market vegetables. —**truck′ farm′er,** *n.* [*count*]

truc•u•lent (truk′yə lənt, tro͞o′kyə-) /'trʌkyələnt, 'truwkyə-/ *adj.* eager to attack or argue; belligerent; harshly angry: *his truculent attitude toward his coworkers.* —**truc′u•lence,** *n.* [*noncount*] —**truc′u•lent•ly,** *adv.*

-trude-, *root.* *-trude-* comes from Latin, where it has the meaning "thrust, push." This meaning is found in such words as: EXTRUDE, INTRUDE, OBTRUDE, PROTRUDE.

trudge (truj) /trʌdʒ/ *v.,* **trudged, trudg•ing,** *n.* —*v.* **1.** to walk (along or over), esp. wearily: [*no obj*]: *He trudged back to his house.* [~ + *obj*]: *to trudge the streets.* —*n.* [*count; usually singular*] **2.** a wearying walk: *a long trudge to the gas station.*

true (tro͞o) /truw/ *adj.,* **tru•er, tru•est,** *n., adv., v.,* **trued, tru•ing** or **true•ing.** —*adj.* **1.** being in accordance with reality; agreeing with reality or fact: *a true story; Everything they say about you is true.* [*It + be +* ~ *+ that clause*]: *It is true that the earth is round.* **2.** [*before a noun*] real; genuine; authentic: *true gold.* **3.** [*before a noun*] sincere; not deceitful: *a true interest in others.* **4.** loyal; faithful; steadfast: *a true friend.* [*be +* ~ *+ to*]: *He was true to his principles.* **5.** [*before a noun*] being or reflecting the character of: *The true meaning of his statement was actually something very different from what it appeared to be.* **6.** exact; precise; accurate; correct: *a true copy.* **7.** such as it should be; proper: *to arrange things in their true order.* **8.** properly so called: *That was true statesmanship: being able to work with both sides and reach a compromise.* **9.** legitimate: *the true heir to the throne.* **10.** exactly, correctly, or accurately shaped, formed, or placed, as a surface or instrument: *This door isn't true; it doesn't hang straight.* —*n.* [*noncount*] **11.** proper, exact, or accurate alignment: *to be out of true.* —*adv.* **12.** in a true manner; truly; truthfully. **13.** exactly or accurately: *The door isn't lined up true.* —*v.* **14.** to adjust, shape, etc., exactly or accurately: [~ *(+ up) + obj*]: *to true (up) the door.* [~ *+ obj (+ up)*]: *to true the door (up).* —***Idiom.*** **15. come true,** (of a wish, etc.) to become a reality: *All your dreams will come true when you make this change in your life.* —**Related Words.** TRUE is an adjective, TRUTH is a noun, TRUTHFUL is an adjective, TRUTHFULLY is an adverb: *Her statements are all true. Her statements contain a great deal of truth. She is a truthful child. She spoke truthfully.*

true′-blue′, *adj.* completely loyal or faithful: *a true-blue friend.*

truf•fle (truf′əl) /'trʌfəl/ *n.* [*count*] **1.** an edible fungus that grows underground. **2.** a ball-shaped candy of soft chocolate with cocoa.

tru•ism (tro͞o′iz əm) /'truwɪzəm/ *n.* [*count*] a self-evident, obvious truth, esp. a cliché: *It's a truism that people think of themselves first.*

tru•ly (tro͞o′lē) /'truwliy/ *adv.* **1.** in accordance with truth; truthfully: *Mozart was truly a brilliant composer.* **2.** exactly; correctly: *able to quote the sonnet truly.* **3.** really; genuinely: *I'm truly sorry I hurt your feelings.* **4.** (used at the end of a letter) sincerely: *Yours truly, Jane and Michael Banks.*

trump (trump) /trʌmp/ *n.* [*count*] **1. a.** any playing card of a suit that for a time outranks the other suits. **b.** Often, **trumps.** [*plural*] the suit itself. **2.** *Informal.* a fine person. —*v.* **3.** to play or take (a card) with a trump: [~ *+ obj*]: *He led a queen and so she trumped it.* [*no obj*]: *On the next round he trumped.* **4.** [~ *+ obj*] to outdo; surpass; excel: *Although the prosecutor seemed to have an advantage with her expert witness, the defense attorney trumped her by bringing in a more qualified expert.* **5. trump up,** [~ *+ up + obj*] to make up (an accusation, etc.), esp. as a lie: *They trumped up charges against him.*

trump′ card′, *n.* [*count*] **1.** a card that is a trump. **2.** something that gives a person a winning advantage: *He was not able to persuade his bosses that the plan was good until he suddenly played his trump card—namely, that the president liked the idea; then it went through.*

trum•pet (trum′pit) /'trʌmpɪt/ *n.* **1.** a brass wind instrument consisting of a tube curved once or twice around on itself and having a cup-shaped mouthpiece at one end and a wide bell at the other: [*count*]: *a beautiful trumpet.* [*noncount*]: *plays trumpet for the band.* **2.** [*count*] a sound like that of a trumpet. —*v.* **3.** to blow a trumpet and produce a tone, etc.: [~ *+ obj*]: *She trumpeted the song.* [*no obj*]: *She trumpeted for years in a jazz band.* **4.** to give out a loud, trumpetlike cry: [~ *+ obj*]: *The elephant trumpeted a cry of warning.* [*no obj*]: *elephants trumpeting.* **5.** to announce or make known loudly or widely: [~ *+ obj*]: *The president trumpeted his new plan.* [*used with quotations*]: *"This will work!" he trumpeted.* —**trum′pet•er,** *n.* [*count*]

trun•cate (trung′kāt) /'trʌŋkeyt/ *v.* [~ *+ obj*], **-cat•ed, -cat•ing.** to shorten by or as if by cutting off a part: *to truncate his essay by deleting a few lines.* —**trun•ca′tion,** *n.* [*noncount*]

trun•cheon (trun′chən) /'trʌntʃən/ *n.* [*count*] a club carried by a police officer; a billy.

trun•dle (trun′dl) /'trʌndḷ/ *v.,* **-dled, -dling,** *n.* —*v.* **1.** to roll (something) along, esp. on a wheel or wheels: [~ *+ obj*]: *He trundled the shopping cart down the street.* [*no obj*]: *The overloaded bus trundled slowly down the road.* **2.** [*no obj*] to move or walk in a rolling manner: *The fat detective trundled out of the room.* —*n.* [*count*] **3.** a small wheel, roller, or the like. **4.** a truck or carriage on low wheels. —**trun′dler,** *n.* [*count*]

trun′dle bed′, *n.* [*count*] a low bed on small wheels, usually pushed under another bed when not in use.

trunk (trungk) /trʌŋk/ *n.* [*count*] **1.** the main stem of a tree. **2.** a large sturdy box for clothes, personal effects, etc. **3.** a large boxed area, usually in the rear of an automobile, for holding luggage, etc. **4.** the body of a person or an animal not including the head and limbs; torso. **5.** the long, flexible nose of the elephant. **6.** the main channel or line in a river, railroad, or other system. **7. trunks,** [*plural*] shorts worn by men chiefly for boxing, swimming, and track.

truss (trus) /trʌs/ *v.* **1.** to fasten, as with rope: [~ *+ obj (+ up)*]: *The kidnappers had trussed him (up) and left him to die.* [~ *(+ up) + obj*]: *to truss (up) the prisoners.* **2.** to fasten with skewers, thread, or the like, as the wings and legs of a chicken before cooking: [~ *(+ up) + obj*]: *to truss (up) a chicken.* [~ *+ obj (+ up)*]: *to truss the chicken (up).* —*n.* [*count*] **3.** a structural frame that functions as a beam to support bridges, roofs, etc. **4.** a pad supported by a belt for supporting muscles affected by a hernia: *He wore a truss until his hernia healed.* See -TORT-.

trust (trust) /trʌst/ *n.* **1.** [*noncount*] reliance on the goodness, strength, or ability of a person or thing; confidence: *trust in government.* **2.** [*noncount*] confidence in future payment for goods received; credit: *to sell merchandise on trust.* **3.** [*noncount*] the obligation on a person in authority: *The president occupies a position of trust.* **4.** [*noncount*] charge, custody, or care: *We left our valuables in her trust.* **5.** a legal relationship in which a person holds title to money, property, etc., for another: [*noncount*]: *The money was held in trust for her.* [*count*]: *Her parents set up a trust for her.* **6.** [*count*] an illegal combination of business companies in which many companies are controlled by a central board. **—*v.* 7.** to have trust or confidence in: [~ + *obj*]: *He didn't trust the psychologist.* [~ + *in/to* + *obj*]: *She trusted to luck instead of studying for the test.* **8.** [~ + *obj*] to believe: *I'm not sure I trust everything she says.* **9.** [~ + *(that) clause*] to expect confidently; hope: *I trust that the job will soon be finished.* **10.** to permit to stay or go somewhere or to do something without fear: [~ + *obj*]: *He doesn't trust them out of his sight.* [~ + *obj* + *to* + *verb*]: *I wouldn't trust him to do that.* **—*Idiom.* 11. on trust,** on faith: *He took it on trust that you would not tell his secret.*

trust•ee (tru stē′) /trʌ'stiy/ *n.* [*count*], *pl.* **-ees. 1.** one whose job is to administer the affairs of a company, etc. **2.** one who holds property for another. **3.** a country that administers a trust territory. **—trust•ee′ship,** *n.* [*noncount*]

trust•ful (trust′fəl) /'trʌstfəl/ *adj.* full of trust. **—trust′ful•ly,** *adv.* **—trust′ful•ness,** *n.* [*noncount*]

trust′ fund′, *n.* [*count*] securities, etc., held in trust.

trust′ ter′ritory, *n.* [*count*] a territory under the administration of a country in the United Nations.

trust•wor•thy (trust′wûr′thē) /'trʌst,wɜrðiy/ *adj.* deserving of trust. **—trust′wor′thi•ness,** *n.* [*noncount*]

trust•y (trus′tē) /'trʌstiy/ *adj.*, **-i•er, -i•est,** *n.*, *pl.* **-trust•ies. —*adj.*** [*before a noun*] **1.** able to be trusted; trustworthy: *my trusty friend.* **—*n.*** [*count*] **2.** one trusted, esp. a convict considered trustworthy and granted special privileges.

truth (trōōth) /truwθ/ *n.*, *pl.* **truths** (trōōthz, trōōths). **1.** [*noncount*] the actual state of a matter: *Do you promise to tell the truth?* **2.** [*noncount*] the condition of conforming with fact or reality; verity: *The detective was assigned to check the truth of the witness's statement.* **3.** [*count*] a fact, proposition, principle, or statement proven to be valid: *mathematical truths.* **—*Idiom.* 4. in truth,** in reality; in fact; actually: *She looked like a typical American housewife living in Moscow; in truth, she was a spy.*

truth•ful (trōōth′fəl) /'truwθfəl/ *adj.* **1.** telling the truth, esp. as one's habitual behavior: *a truthful child.* **2.** conforming to truth; corresponding with reality: *a truthful portrait.* **—truth′ful•ly,** *adv.* **—truth′ful•ness,** *n.* [*noncount*]

try (trī) /tray/ *v.*, **tried, try•ing,** *n.*, *pl.* **tries. —*v.* 1.** to attempt to do or accomplish: [~ + *to* + *verb*]: *He tried to run, but he soon got tired.* [~ + *verb-ing*]: *Try running a mile a day.* [*no obj*]: *You must try harder if you want to succeed.* [~ + *and* + *root form of verb*]: *We'll try and do that again.* **2.** to test the effect or result of: [~ + *obj*]: *He tried each button, but nothing worked.* [~ (+ *out*) + *obj*]: *He tried (out) a new recipe for chicken.* [~ + *obj (+ out)*]: *He tried it (out).* **3.** [~ + *obj*] to attempt to open (a door, etc.) to find out whether it is locked: *He tried every door, one after the other.* **4.** [~ + *obj*] to sample or taste to evaluate or judge: *to try a new food.* **5.** [~ + *obj*] to examine and decide on something, as in a court of law, esp. to determine the guilt or innocence of (a person): *The state tried him for murder.* **6.** [~ + *obj*] to put to a severe test: *She is trying my patience with her chatter.* **7. try on,** to put on an article of clothing to judge how well it fits: [~ + *obj* + *on*]: *Try this jacket on.* [~ + *on* + *obj*]: *She tried on every jacket in the store.* **8. try out,** [*no obj*] to compete for a role, as by taking part in a test or trial: *tried out for the swim team.* **—*n.*** [*count*] **9.** an attempt or effort: *We'll give it another try.* **—Usage.** Sometimes there is a difference in meaning when TRY is followed by *to* + *verb* as compared to when it is followed by *verb-ing.* One meaning of *My friend tried to run five miles a day* is that my friend made an attempt to run five miles a day but did not always succeed in doing so. In the sentence *My friend tried running five miles a day,* the impression is that my friend did in fact run five miles a day, perhaps as a way of losing weight or staying (or getting) fit.

try•ing (trī′ing) /'trayɪŋ/ *adj.* straining one's patience and goodwill; irritating: *He found her very trying at times.* **—try′ing•ly,** *adv.*

try•out (trī′out′) /'tray,awt/ *n.* [*count*] **1.** a trial or test to see if something is strong enough or appropriate for some purpose: *a good tryout for the car.* **2.** the performance of a play in preparation for an official opening.

tryst (trist) /trɪst/ *n.* [*count*] an appointment for a meeting, esp. one made secretly by lovers.

tsar (zär, tsär) /zɑr, tsɑr/ *n.* CZAR.

tset′se (or **tzet′ze**) **fly′** (tset′sē, tsē′tsē) /'tsɛtsiy, 'tsiytsiy/ *n.* [*count*] a bloodsucking African fly: *Some tsetse flies cause sleeping sickness.* Also called **tset′se.**

T-shirt or **tee shirt** (tē′shûrt′) /'tiy,ʃɜrt/ *n.* [*count*] a lightweight, pullover shirt with short sleeves and a collarless round neckline. See illustration at CLOTHING. Also called **tee.**

tsp., an abbreviation of: **1.** teaspoon. **2.** teaspoonful.

T square, *n.* [*count*] a T-shaped ruler having a short crosspiece that slides along the edge of a drawing board as a guide in making parallel lines, etc.

tsu•na•mi (tsŏŏ nä′mē) /tsʊ'nɑmiy/ *n.* [*count*], *pl.* **-mis.** an unusually large sea wave produced by a seaquake or volcanic eruption under water.

tub (tub) /tʌb/ *n.* [*count*] **1.** a bathtub. **2.** a broad, round, open container. **3.** any of various small, usually round containers: *a tub of butter.* **4.** an old, slow, or clumsy boat. **5.** *Informal.* a short and fat person.

tu•ba (tōō′bə, tyōō′-) /'tuwbə, 'tyuw-/ *n.* [*count*], *pl.* **-bas.** a brass musical wind instrument with valves, having a low range.

tub•by (tub′ē) /'tʌbiy/ *adj.*, **-bi•er, -bi•est.** short and fat.

tube (tōōb, tyōōb) /tuwb, tyuwb/ *n.*, *v.*, **tubed, tub•ing. —*n.*** [*count*] **1.** a hollow, rounded, narrow piece of metal, glass, etc., used esp. for carrying liquids or gases: *a short rubber tube.* **2.** a small collapsible cylinder sealed at one end, with a capped opening at the other end, from which a substance, as toothpaste, may be squeezed. **3.** any hollow, rounded, narrow vessel or organ in the body: *the bronchial tubes.* **4.** ELECTRON TUBE. **5. the tube,** [*singular*] *Informal.* television: *What's on the tube tonight?* **6.** a rounded, narrow piece of clothing without sleeves, pockets, or closures, usually of stretch fabric, worn as a blouse, skirt, etc. **7.** the tunnel in which an underground railroad runs. **8.** *Brit.* SUBWAY (def. 1). **—*v.*** [*no obj*] **9.** to float down a river on an inner tube. **—*Idiom.* 10. down the tube(s),** into a state of failure or collapse: *All his efforts went down the tube when the company went bankrupt.* **—tube′less,** *adj.*

tu•ber (tōō′bər, tyōō′-) /'tuwbər, 'tyuw-/ *n.* [*count*] a thick, fleshy underground stem, as a potato. **—tu′ber•ous,** *adj.*

tu•ber•cle (tōō′bər kəl, tyōō′-) /'tuwbərkəl, 'tyuw-/ *n.* [*count*] a small rounded part sticking out or growing out from a surface, as on a bone or the body.

tu•ber•cu•lo•sis (tŏŏ bûr′kyə lō′sis, tyŏŏ-) /tʊ,bɜrkyə'lowsɪs, tyʊ-/ *n.* [*noncount*] an infectious disease that usually affects the lungs, producing swelling. *Abbr.:* TB **—tu•ber•cu•lar** (tŏŏ bûr′kyə lər) /tʊ'bɜrkyələr/ **tu•ber′cu•lous,** *adj.*

tub•ing (tōō′bing, tyōō′-) /'tuwbɪŋ, 'tyuw-/ *n.* [*noncount*] **1.** material in the form of a tube: *glass tubing.* **2.** tubes thought of as a group. **3.** the sport or recreation of floating down a river or stream on an inner tube.

tu•bu•lar (tōō′byə lər, tyōō′-) /'tuwbyələr, 'tyuw-/ *adj.* of or relating to a tube or tubes.

tuck (tuk) /tʌk/ *v.* **1.** [~ + *obj*] to put into a small, close place: *Tuck the money into your wallet.* **2.** to push in the loose ends or edges of so as to hold closely in place: [~ + *in* + *obj*]: *Tuck in your blouse.* [~ + *obj* + *in*]: *Tuck your shirt in.* **3.** to cover snugly or tightly in or as if in this manner: [~ + *obj*]: *She tucked the children into bed.* [~ + *in* + *obj*]: *tucked in the children at bedtime.* [~ + *obj* + *in*]: *tucked the children in and read them a story.* **4.** [~ + *obj*] to sew tucks in. **5.** [~ + *away* + *obj*] *Informal.* to eat or drink: *to tuck away a big meal.* **—*n.*** [*count*] **6.** something tucked or folded in. **7.** a fold sewn into cloth, as to make a tighter fit. **8.** a crouching position in skiing in which the ski poles are held close to the chest. **9.** *Informal.* a plastic surgery operation: *a tummy tuck.*

tuck•er (tuk′ər) /'tʌkər/ *v.* *Informal.* **tucker out,** to tire; exhaust: [~ + *obj* + *out*]: *All this skiing will tucker the children out.* [~ + *out* + *obj*]: *That long climb would tucker out anyone.*

-tude, *suffix.* *-tude* is attached to roots, esp. adjectives, to form nouns that refer to abstract ideas: *apt* + *-tude* → *aptitude; gratitude; altitude.*

Tues. or **Tue.,** an abbreviation of: Tuesday.

Tues•day (tōōz′dā, -dē, tyōōz′-) /'tuwzdey, -diy,

'tyuwz-/ *n.* the third day of the week, following Monday: [*proper noun*]: *See you on Tuesday.* [*count*]: *Let's meet on the 23rd; that's three Tuesdays from today.*

tuft (tuft) /tʌft/ *n.* [*count*] a cluster of small, straight but flexible parts, as hair, feathers, or leaves, close together at the base. —**tuft′ed,** *adj.*

tug (tug) /tʌg/ *v.,* **tugged, tug•ging,** *n.* —*v.* **1.** to pull at with force or effort: [~ + *obj*]: *He tugged his beard while he thought over the question.* [~ + *at* + *obj*]: *to tug at his beard.* **2.** [~ + *obj*] to move (something) by pulling with force: *She tugged the trunk into the closet.* —*n.* [*count*] **3.** an act or instance of tugging; pull. **4.** TUGBOAT.

tug•boat (tug′bōt′) /'tʌg,bowt/ *n.* [*count*] a small, powerful boat for towing or pushing ships, barges, etc.

tug′ of war′, *n.* [*count*] **1.** an athletic contest between two teams at opposite ends of a rope, each team trying to drag the other over a line. **2.** any hard-fought struggle between any two opponents: *a political tug of war between the two factions within the party.*

tu•i•tion (to͞o ish′ən, tyo͞o-) /tuw'ɪʃən, tyuw-/ *n.* [*noncount*] **1.** the charge or fee for instruction: *Tuition for college has risen far faster than inflation.* **2.** teaching or instruction.

tu•lip (to͞o′lip, tyo͞o′-) /'tuwlɪp, 'tyuw-/ *n.* [*count*] **1.** a plant of the lily family, having large, showy, bell-shaped flowers. **2.** a flower or bulb of a tulip.

tum•ble (tum′bəl) /'tʌmbəl/ *v.,* **-bled, -bling,** *n.* —*v.* **1.** to (cause to) fall helplessly down; stumble: [*no obj*]: *She tumbled down the stairs.* [~ + *obj*]: *She tumbled the boxes down the stairs.* **2.** to roll end over end, or to flow over and down: [*no obj*]: *The water tumbled down the waterfall.* [~ + *obj*]: *The army tumbled rocks on top of the invaders.* **3.** [*no obj*] to fall or decline rapidly; drop: *Prices on the stock exchange tumbled.* **4.** [*no obj*] to perform gymnastic feats. **5.** to (cause to) fall suddenly from a position of authority; (cause to) be toppled: [*no obj*]: *to tumble from power.* [~ + *obj*]: *The revolutionaries tumbled the dictator from power.* **6.** to (cause to) fall in ruins; (cause to) collapse: [*no obj*]: *During the earthquake, buildings tumbled.* [~ + *obj*]: *The earthquake tumbled bridges.* **7.** to roll about by turning one way and another: [*no obj*]: *The clothes tumbled in the dryer.* [~ + *obj*]: *tumbled the clothes dry on low heat.* **8.** [*no obj*] to go, come, etc., in a fast, disorganized way: *Tourists came tumbling out of the bus.* —*n.* [*count*] **9.** an act of tumbling. **10.** a gymnastic feat. **11.** an accidental fall; spill. **12.** a drop in value, as of stocks. **13.** a fall from a position of power: *the tyrant's long-awaited tumble from power.*

tum′ble-down′, *adj.* ruined; run-down; dilapidated: *a tumble-down old shack deep in the woods.*

tum•bler (tum′blər) /'tʌmblər/ *n.* [*count*] **1.** one who performs acrobatic feats. **2.** a part of a lock that allows the bolt to move. **3.** a stemless drinking glass having a flat, often thick bottom: *a few tumblers of strong whiskey.*

tum•ble•weed (tum′bəl wēd′) /'tʌmbəl,wiyd/ *n.* [*count*] a plant with branching upper parts that become detached from the roots and are driven about by the wind.

tum•my (tum′ē) /'tʌmiy/ *n.* [*count*], *pl.* **-mies.** *Informal.* the stomach or abdomen.

tu•mor (to͞o′mər, tyo͞o′-) /'tuwmər, 'tyuw-/ *n.* [*count*] an abnormal growth of cells in animal or plant tissue. Also, *esp. Brit.,* **tu′mour.** —**tu′mor•ous,** *adj.*

tu•mult (to͞o′mult, -məlt, tyo͞o′-) /'tuwmʌlt, -məlt, 'tyuw-/ *n.* **1.** [*count; usually singular*] noisy commotion on the part of a mob; uproar: *a loud tumult in the auditorium before the concert.* **2.** [*noncount*] a condition of widespread disorder, as during a disturbance: *a state of tumult following the war.*

tu•mul•tu•ous (to͞o mul′cho͞o əs, tyo͞o-) /tʊ'mʌltʃuwəs, tyʊ-/ *adj.* [*usually: before a noun*] **1.** full of tumult; uproarious: *a tumultuous welcome for the hero.* **2.** filled with disorder; turbulent: *a tumultuous period in history.*

tu•na (to͞o′nə, tyo͞o′-) /'tuwnə, 'tyuw-/ *n., pl.* (*esp. when thought of as a group*) **-na,** (*esp. for kinds or species*) **-nas. 1.** [*count*] a large sea-dwelling food fish, including the albacore and yellowfin tuna. **2.** [*noncount*] Also called **tu′na fish′.** the flesh of the tuna, used as food.

tun•dra (tun′drə, to͞on′-) /'tʌndrə, 'tʊn-/ *n.* [*count*], *pl.* **-dras.** a vast, nearly level, treeless plain of the arctic regions.

tune (to͞on, tyo͞on) /tuwn, tyuwn/ *n., v.,* **tuned, tun•ing.** —*n.* **1.** [*count*] a series of musical sounds forming a melody: *She whistled a happy tune.* **2.** [*noncount*] the state of being in harmony: *to be in tune.* **3.** [*noncount*] relationship that is harmonious or agreeable; agreement: *Her ideas were not in tune with mine.* —*v.* **4.** [~ + *obj*] to adjust (a musical instrument) to a pitch: [~ + *obj* (+ *up*)]: *to tune a guitar (up).* [~ (+ *up*) + *obj*]: *to tune (up) a guitar.* **5.** to adjust (a motor, etc.) so as to make it function properly: [~ + *obj* (+ *up*)]: *to tune the engine (up).* [~ (+ *up*) + *obj*]: *to tune (up) the engine.* **6. tune in,** to adjust a radio or television so as to receive (signals, etc.): [*no obj*]: *Tune in to our station next week.* [~ + *in* + *obj*]: *Tune in your favorite station.* [~ + *obj* + *in*]: *to tune it in.* **7. tune out,** *Slang.* to stop paying attention to: [*no obj*]: *Whenever her parents try to talk about school to her, she just tunes out.* [~ + *obj* + *out*]: *She just tunes them out.* [~ + *out* + *obj*]: *to tune out her parents.* —***Idiom.* 8. change one's tune,** to reverse one's opinions; change one's mind: *He'll change his tune when he sees how well our new proposal will work.* **9. sing** or **whistle a different tune,** to change one's opinions in response to changes in circumstances: *whistling a different tune now that he's unemployed.* **10. to the tune of,** in the amount of; for the cost of: *repairs to the tune of several thousand dollars.*

tune•ful (to͞on′fəl, tyo͞on′-) /'tuwnfəl, 'tyuwn-/ *adj.* full of melody; melodious. —**tune′ful•ly,** *adv.* —**tune′ful•ness,** *n.* [*noncount*]

tune•less (to͞on′lis, tyo͞on′-) /'tuwnlɪs, 'tyuwn-/ *adj.* not melodious; not musical. —**tune′less•ly,** *adv.*: *humming tunelessly.*

tun•er (to͞o′nər, tyo͞o′-) /'tuwnər, 'tyuw-/ *n.* [*count*] **1.** a person or thing that tunes. **2.** the portion of a radio or television receiver that captures the broadcast signal and feeds it to other circuits in the set.

tune′-up′, *n.* [*count*] an adjustment, as of a motor, to improve working order or condition.

tung•sten (tung′stən) /'tʌŋstən/ *n.* [*noncount*] a rare, bright gray, metallic element having a high melting point, used in electric light bulbs.

tu•nic (to͞o′nik, tyo͞o′-) /'tuwnɪk, 'tyuw-/ *n.* [*count*] **1.** a coat worn as part of a uniform. **2.** a gownlike outer garment worn by the ancient Greeks and Romans. **3. a.** a woman's straight upper garment, extending over the skirt to the hips. **b.** Also called **tu′nic dress′.** a dress styled like this.

tun′ing fork′, *n.* [*count*] a steel instrument made of a stem with two prongs, producing a musical tone of a definite, constant pitch when struck: *A tuning fork is used as a standard for tuning musical instruments.*

Tu•ni•sian (to͞o nē′zhən, -shən, tyo͞o-) /tuw'niyʒən, -ʃən, tyuw-/ *adj.* **1.** of or relating to Tunis. —*n.* [*count*] **2.** a person born or living in Tunis.

tun•nel (tun′l) /'tʌnl̩/ *n., v.,* **-neled, -nel•ing** or (*esp. Brit.*) **-nelled, -nel•ling.** —*n.* [*count*] **1.** an underground passage, esp. one for trains or automobiles: *Planning was underway to build a tunnel under the English Channel.* —*v.* **2.** to make or dig out (a tunnel) through or under (something): [~ + *obj*]: *to tunnel one's way out of prison.* [*no obj*]: *to tunnel out of prison.* —**tun′nel•er,** *n.* [*count*]

tun′nel vi′sion, *n.* [*noncount*] **1.** the ability to see only in a very narrow field of vision, as if looking through a tube, because of a condition in the retina of the eyes. **2.** narrow-mindedness: *the party's tunnel vision regarding women's rights.*

-turb-, *root.* -*turb*- comes from Latin, where it has the meaning "stir up." This meaning is found in such words as: DISTURB, DISTURBANCE, IMPERTURBABLE, MASTURBATE, PERTURB, PERTURBATION, TURBID, TURBINE, TURBO, TURBULENT.

tur•ban (tûr′bən) /'tɜrbən/ *n.* [*count*] **1.** a man's headdress worn chiefly by Muslims in S Asia, made of a long cloth of silk, cotton, etc., wound around the head. **2.** a headdress resembling this.

tur•bid (tûr′bid) /'tɜrbɪd/ *adj.* **1.** not clear because of having been stirred up; clouded: *turbid water.* **2.** confused; muddled; disturbed. See -TURB-.

tur•bine (tûr′bin, -bīn) /'tɜrbɪn, -bayn/ *n.* [*count*] a machine having blades inside, driven by the pressure or thrust of a moving fluid, as steam, water, hot gases, or air: *the helicopter's turbines.* See -TURB-.

tur•bo (tûr′bō) /'tɜrbow/ *n.* [*count*], *pl.* **-bos. 1.** a turbine. **2.** a car with a special attachment using a turbine to improve its power and efficiency. See -TURB-.

tur•bo•fan (tûr′bō fan′) /'tɜrbow,fæn/ *n.* FANJET (def. 1). See -TURB-.

tur•bo•jet (tûr′bō jet′) /'tɜrbow,dʒɛt/ *n.* [*count*] **1.** an engine equipped with turbines to compress air. **2.** an airplane equipped with one or more such engines.

tur•bot (tûr′bət) /'tɜrbət/ *n.* [*count*], *pl.* (*esp. when thought of as a group*) **-bot,** (*esp. for kinds or species*) **-bots.** a flatfish having a diamond-shaped body.

tur•bu•lence (tûr′byə ləns) /ˈtɜrbyə ləns/ *n.* [*noncount*] **1.** a state of confusion, disorder, or tumult: *the turbulence of the revolution.* **2.** a state in which water is made opaque because dirt has been stirred up: *Turbulence prevented us from seeing clearly underwater.* **3.** swirling, uneven movement or motion in water or air: *The car's forward motion creates turbulence.* See -TURB-.

tur•bu•lent (tûr′byə lənt) /ˈtɜrbyələnt/ *adj.* **1.** being in a state of confusion, disorder, or tumult: *turbulent times during the civil war; the turbulent sixties.* **2.** characterized by turbulence: *turbulent waters.* —**tur′bu•lent•ly,** *adv.* See -TURB-.

tu•reen (to͝o rēn′, tyo͞o-) /tʊˈriyn, tyʊ-/ *n.* [*count*] a large, deep, covered dish for serving soup, stew, etc.

turf (tûrf) /tɜrf/ *n., pl.* **turfs,** (*esp. Brit.*) **turves** (tûrvz) /tɜrvz/; *v.* —*n.* **1. a.** [*noncount*] a layer of matted earth formed by grass and plant roots. **b.** [*count*] *Chiefly Brit.* a piece cut from this; sod. **2.** [*noncount*] peat, esp. as material for fuel. **3. the turf,** [*count; usually singular*] **a.** the track over which horse races are run. **b.** the sport of racing horses. **4.** [*noncount*] **a.** the neighborhood over which a street gang claims authority. **b.** a familiar area, as of residence or expertise: *Chicago is his turf. Her turf was British literature.* —*v.* [~ + *obj*] **5.** to cover with turf or sod. **6.** *Brit. Informal.* to remove from a desirable position; expel; kick out. —**turf′y,** *adj.,* **-i•er, -i•est.**

tur•gid (tûr′jid) /ˈtɜrdʒɪd/ *adj.* **1.** swollen. **2.** (of language) pompous; overblown; bombastic: *turgid prose.* —**tur•gid•i•ty** (tər jid′i tē) /tərˈdʒɪdɪtiy/ *n.* [*noncount*] —**tur′gid•ly,** *adv.*

Turk (tûrk) /tɜrk/ *n.* [*count*] a person born or living in Turkey.

tur•key (tûr′kē) /ˈtɜrkiy/ *n., pl.* **-keys,** (*esp. when thought of as a group*) **-key. 1.** [*count*] a large North American bird of the pheasant family. **2.** [*noncount*] the flesh of this bird, used as food: *a dinner of turkey on Thanksgiving Day.* **3.** [*count*] *Slang.* **a.** a person or thing of little appeal or value: *This car is a turkey; it's constantly breaking down.* **b.** a naive, stupid, or inept person: *You went out with that turkey?!* **c.** a poor or unsuccessful play or movie; a flop. —***Idiom.*** **4. talk turkey,** *Informal.* to talk frankly and directly: *began to talk turkey about important issues.*

Turk•ish (tûr′kish) /ˈtɜrkɪʃ/ *adj.* **1.** of or relating to Turkey. **2.** of or relating to the language spoken by many of the people in Turkey. —*n.* [*noncount*] **3.** the language spoken by many of the people in Turkey.

Turk′ish bath, *n.* [*count*] a bath in which the bather, after sweating a great deal in a steam room, showers and has a rubdown.

tur•mer•ic (tûr′mər ik) /ˈtɜrmərɪk/ *n.* **1.** [*noncount*] a powder prepared from the root of an Asian plant of the ginger family, used as a spice. **2.** [*count*] the plant itself.

tur•moil (tûr′moil) /ˈtɜrmɔyl/ *n.* a state of commotion, disorder, or disturbance: [*count; usually singular*]: *Since she's been away the house has been in a turmoil.* [*noncount*]: *We've been in turmoil since the hostile takeover.*

turn (tûrn) /tɜrn/ *v.* **1.** to (cause to) move around on an axis or about a center; rotate: [~ + *obj*]: *to turn a wheel.* [*no obj*]: *The wheel wouldn't turn.* **2.** to (cause to) move around or partly around: [~ + *obj*]: *to turn a key in a door.* [*no obj*]: *The key turned in the lock.* **3.** to reverse the position or placement of: [~ + *obj*]: *to turn a page.* [*no obj*]: *The suspect turned and began to fire his gun.* **4.** to direct, aim, or set toward: [~ + *obj*]: *He turned his car toward the center of town.* [*no obj*]: *The car turned to the right and stopped.* **5.** [~ + *obj*] to bring the lower layers of (soil, etc.) to the surface, as in plowing: *to turn the fields.* **6.** [~ + *obj*] to change the position or direction of; move into a different position: *to turn the handle one notch.* **7.** to change the focus or tendency of: [~ + *obj*]: *She turned the conversation to a topic that was more pleasant.* [*no obj*]: *The conversation turned to more pleasant topics.* **8.** to change or alter the nature or appearance of; to (make something) become something else: [~ + *obj* + *adjective*]: *Worry has turned his hair gray.* [~ + *obj* + *to/into* + *obj*]: *The heat turned the ice to water.* [*no obj*]: *The neighborhood has turned into a slum.* [*no obj;* ~ + *adjective*]: *The milk turned sour.* **9.** to change the color of (leaves): [~ + *obj*]: *The shortening of daylight has turned the leaves.* [*no obj*]: *The leaves have begun to turn; they're now a beautiful yellow.* **10.** to (cause to) become sour or go bad: [*no obj*]: *In the heat the milk turned.* [~ + *obj*]: *The hot air has turned the milk.* **11.** to (cause to) be affected with nausea, as the stomach: [~ + *obj*]: *Violence turns her stomach.* [*no obj*]: *My stomach turned at the thought of all that violence.* **12.** to (cause to) be put or applied to some use or purpose: [~ + *obj*]: *He turned his mind to more practical matters.* [*no obj*]: *His mind turned to practical matters.* **13.** to pass around: [~ + *obj*]: *knew he was being followed, so he turned a corner and vanished.* [*no obj*]: *He turned to the left and vanished.* **14.** [~ + *noun*] to reach or pass (a certain age, etc.): *He turned sixty last week.* **15.** [~ + *obj*] to shape (a piece of metal, etc.) into form with a cutting tool while rotating it on a lathe. **16.** [~ + *obj*] to form or express gracefully: *In her letter writing she really shows an ability to turn a phrase.* **17.** [~ + *obj* + *out/away*] to cause to go; send; drive: *She turned him away.* **18.** to (cause to) be persuaded to change or reorder the course of one's life: [~ + *obj*]: *He turned her to a life of crime.* [~ + *to* + *obj*]: *She turned to a life of crime.* **19.** to (cause to) be angry (with) or betray: [~ + *obj*]: *to turn children against their parents.* [*no obj*]: *They turned against their parents.* **20.** [~ + *obj*] to earn or gain: *She turned a profit on the sale.* **21.** to twist out of position; wrench: [~ + *obj*]: *He turned his ankle when he fell.* [*no obj*]: *His ankle turned when he fell.* **22.** [~ + *obj*] to perform (a gymnastic feat) by rotating or revolving: *turned a somersault.* **23.** [~ + *obj*] to disorder the condition of: *The crooks turned the apartment (upside down) looking for money.* **24.** [*not: be* + ~*-ing;* ~ + *on/upon* + *obj*] to hinge or depend: *The whole question turns on this point.* **25.** to direct one's gaze, etc., toward or away from someone or something: [*no obj*]: *His gaze turned slowly from the window to his visitor.* [~ + *obj*]: *He turned his gaze toward her.* **26.** [*no obj*] to go to someone for help or information: *to turn to a friend for a loan.* **27. turn away, a.** [*no obj*] to move the eyes away from someone or something: *I offered her my hand, but she just turned away.* **b.** to refuse to allow (someone) to enter: [~ + *obj* + *away*]: *The guards turned us away.* [~ + *away* + *obj*]: *turned away anyone without an invitation.* **28. turn down, a.** to turn over; fold down: [~ + *down* + *obj*]: *to turn down (the sheets or blankets of) a bed.* [~ + *obj* + *down*]: *to turn the bed down.* **b.** to lower in intensity; lessen: [~ + *down* + *obj*]: *to turn down the heat in the classroom.* [~ + *obj* + *down*]: *to turn the heat down.* **c.** to refuse or reject (a person, etc.): [~ + *down* + *obj*]: *They turned down your request for promotion.* [~ + *obj* + *down*]: *She asked him to marry her, but he turned her down.* **29. turn in, a.** to give (something) to someone in authority: [~ + *in* + *obj*]: *Turn in your badge and report to the office.* [~ + *obj* + *in*]: *turned his badge in.* **b.** to inform on (someone): [~ + *obj* + *in*]: *Someone turned us in.* [~ + *in* + *obj*]: *He'd turn in his own mother if the reward was enough.* **c.** [*no obj*] to go to bed; retire: *I'm exhausted; I think I'll turn in.* **30. turn off, a.** to stop the flow of (water, etc.), as by closing a faucet or valve: [~ + *off* + *obj*]: *The electrician turned off the electricity to the house.* [~ + *obj* + *off*]: *The plumber turned the water off.* **b.** to extinguish (a light): [~ + *off* + *obj*]: *Turn off the lights and go to bed.* [~ + *obj* + *off*]: *Turn the light off; it's too bright.* **c.** to exit (a road) and proceed in a different direction: [~ + *off* + *obj*]: *to turn off the highway and take the local road.* [*no obj*]: *Turn off when you get to the exit.* **d.** *Slang.* to disgust; to cause a feeling of dislike; to alienate: [~ + *obj* + *off*]: *Her manners turn me off.* [~ + *off* + *obj*]: *turned off everyone with her bad manners.* **31. turn on, a.** to cause (water, etc.) to flow, as by opening a valve: [~ + *on* + *obj*]: *to turn on the gas.* [~ + *obj* + *on*]: *to turn the gas on again.* **b.** to switch on (a light): [~ + *on* + *obj*]: *Turn on a light; I can't see.* [~ + *obj* + *on*]: *Turn the lights on; I can't see.* **c.** to put into operation; activate: [~ + *on* + *obj*]: *turned on the engine.* [~ + *obj* + *on*]: *She turned the engine on.* **d.** [~ + *on* + *obj*] to start suddenly to show: *He just turned on the charm.* **e.** *Slang.* to persuade (a person) to take a narcotic drug: [~ + *obj* + *on*]: *turned his friend on to LSD.* [~ + *on* + *obj*]: *wanted to turn on the whole city by pouring LSD into the water supply.* **f.** [*no obj*] *Slang.* to take a narcotic drug: *to get a little marijuana and turn on.* **g.** [~ + *obj* + *on*] *Slang.* to arouse the interest of: *Architecture really turns her on.* **h.** [~ + *obj* + *on*] *Slang.* to arouse sexually: *When she walks into a room, she turns every man on.* **i.** Also, **turn upon.** [~ + *on* + *obj*] to become suddenly hostile to: *I don't know what got her so angry; she's even turning on her friends.* **32. turn out, a.** to extinguish (a light): [~ + *out* + *obj*]: *Turn out the light; it's right in my eyes.* [~ + *obj* + *out*]: *Turn the lights out.* **b.** to produce as the result of labor: [~ + *out* + *obj*]: *The factory turns out fifty computers every hour.* [~ + *obj* + *out*]: *They sell them as fast as our factory can turn them out.* **c.** [*no obj*] to become in the end: *How did things turn out?* **d.** [~ + *out* + *to* + *verb*] to be found or known to be; prove to be: *He turned out to be an enemy.* **33. turn over, a.** to move or be moved from one side to another: [*no obj*]: *He mumbled in his sleep and turned over.* [~ + *obj* + *over*]: *She turned him over and got him out of bed.* **b.** to put in reverse position; invert: [~ + *over* + *obj*]: *The cat turned over the bowl of milk.* [~ + *obj* + *over*]: *The child turned the plate over.* **c.** to transfer; give: [~ + *over* + *obj*]: *He went to the police and turned over the gun.* [~ + *obj* + *over*]: *He turned the gun over to the police.* **d.** to (cause to) start, as an engine: [*no obj*]: *The engine won't turn over; the battery is dead.* [~ + *obj* + *over*]: *Turn the engine over.* **e.** to think about; ponder: [~ + *over* + *obj*]: *turned over in his mind what she said to him.* [~ + *obj* + *over*]: *He kept turning the problem over in his mind.* **34. turn up, a.** to fold (material, etc.) up to alter a garment: [~ + *up* + *obj*]: *to turn up a hem.* [~ + *obj* + *up*]: *to turn a hem up.* **b.** to (cause to) be uncovered or found: [*no obj*]: *Some new facts have just turned up.* [~ + *up* + *obj*]: *turned up some new leads in the investigation.* [~ + *obj* + *up*]: *Did the detective turn anything up yet?* **c.** to intensify or increase: [~ + *up* + *obj*]: *to turn up the volume.* [~ + *obj* + *up*]: *to turn the volume up loud.* **d.** [*no obj*] to appear; arrive; happen: *always believed that "something (good) will turn up."* **e.** [*no obj*] to be recovered: *That old ring you lost; did it ever turn up?* —*n.* [*count*] **35.** a movement of partial or total rotation: *a turn of the handle.* **36.** an act of changing position, etc., as by a movement around something: *a turn of the head.* **37.** [*usually singular*] a time for action: *It's my turn to speak, so let me finish.* See *in turn* and *out of turn* below. **38.** an act of changing or reversing course or direction. **39.** a place where a road, etc., turns; bend: *a turn in the road.* **40.** a single revolution, as of a wheel: *He gave the wheel a couple of sharp turns.* **41.** any change, as in nature or circumstances: *She has suffered a turn for the worse in her long battle with cancer.* **42.** the point or time of change: *at the turn of the century (= when the century changed, as from 1899 to 1900).* **43.** a passing of one thing around another, as of a rope around a mast. **44.** a distinctive form of expression: *a clever turn of phrase.* **45.** a short walk, ride, etc., out and back, esp. by different routes. **46.** one's natural way of thinking or acting: *She's of a lively turn of mind.* **47.** an act of service or disservice: *She did me a good (bad) turn by (not) showing up for my speech.* **48.** [*usually singular*] a nervous shock, as from fright: *gave us quite a turn when she fell from the balance beam.* —***Idiom.*** **49. at every turn,** constantly: *She betrayed us at every turn.* **50. by turns,** one after another; alternately: *did their shopping and cleaning by turns.* **51. in turn,** in order of one following another: *We shook hands in turn with each of the people on line.* **52. out of turn, a.** not in the correct order: *He went out of turn and tried to push his way to the front.* **b.** at an unsuitable time; unwisely; indiscreetly: *He spoke out of turn.* **53. take turns,** to succeed one another in order: *We took turns making breakfast.* **54. turn one's back on,** [~ + *obj*] to abandon, ignore, or reject: *She turned her back on her boyfriend and left him for another.* **55. turn the corner,** to pass through a crisis safely: *He was sick for months, but now he's begun to turn the corner.* **56. turn the tide,** to reverse the course of events: *The army was finally able to turn the tide and start pushing the invaders back.* —**turn′er,** *n.* [*count*]

turn•a•bout (tûrn′ə bout′) /'tɜrnə,bawt/ *n.* [*count*] **1.** the act of turning in a different or opposite direction. **2.** a change of opinion, loyalty, etc. **3.** *Chiefly Brit.* MERRY-GO-ROUND.

turn•a•round (tûrn′ə round′) /'tɜrnə,rawnd/ *n.* [*count*] **1.** a change of allegiance or loyalty: *In the face of opposition the president made a complete turnaround and reversed his policies.* **2.** a change from loss to profit.

turn•coat (tûrn′kōt′) /'tɜrn,kowt/ *n.* [*count*] one who changes to the opposite side, reverses principles, etc.; a renegade.

turn•ing (tûr′ning) /'tɜrnɪŋ/ *n.* [*count*] **1.** the act of a person or thing that turns. **2.** an act of reversing position. **3.** the place at which anything bends.

turn′ing point′, *n.* [*count*] a point at which an important change takes place; a critical point: *reached a turning point in our relationship.*

tur•nip (tûr′nip) /'tɜrnɪp/ *n.* [*count*] the thick, edible, fleshy root of certain plants of the mustard family.

turn•key (tûrn′kē′) /'tɜrn,kiy/ *n., pl.* **-keys,** *adj.* —*n.* [*count*] **1.** one who has charge of the keys of a prison; a jailer. —*adj.* [*before a noun*] **2.** ready for occupancy when turned over to the owner: *turnkey housing.* **3.** ready to go into operation: *a turnkey power plant.*

turn•off (tûrn′ôf′, -of′) /'tɜrn,ɔf, -,ɒf/ *n.* [*count*] **1.** a small road that branches off from a larger one, esp. an exit off a major highway: *The car was stalled on the turnoff.* **2.** an act of turning off. **3.** *Slang.* something or someone that makes one lose excitement: *It was a complete turnoff to see her ex there.*

turn•out (tûrn′out′) /'tɜrn,awt/ *n.* [*count*] **1.** the number of persons who come to an exhibition, party, etc.: *a huge turnout at their first concert.* **2.** an amount produced: *the turnout of the factory.*

turn•o•ver (tûrn′ō′vər) /'tɜrn,owvər/ *n.* [*count*] **1.** an act or result of turning over; upset. **2.** movement of people, as customers, etc., into, out of, or through a place: *a store with a large turnover.* **3.** the amount of business done in a given time. **4.** the rate at which workers are replaced: *a high rate of turnover.* **5.** a baked pastry in which half the dough is turned over the filling and sealed. **6.** (in basketball or football) the loss of possession of the ball to the opponent, through a misplay or by breaking a rule.

turn•pike (tûrn′pīk′) /'tɜrn,payk/ *n.* [*count*] **1.** a high-speed highway, esp. one maintained by tolls. **2.** (formerly) a barrier set across such a highway to stop passage until a toll has been paid; tollgate.

turn•stile (tûrn′stīl′) /'tɜrn,stayl/ *n.* [*count*] a structure to stop passage until a charge is paid, or to record the number of people passing through: *He put his token in the turnstile.*

turn•ta•ble (tûrn′tā′bəl) /'tɜrn,teybəl/ *n.* [*count*] the rotating disk that spins the record on a phonograph.

tur•pen•tine (tûr′pən tīn′) /'tɜrpən,tayn/ *n.* [*noncount*] a form of resin taken from trees and made into a chemical having a very strong odor and a strong, bitter taste, used as a solvent.

tur•pi•tude (tûr′pi to͞od′, -tyo͞od′) /'tɜrpɪ,tuwd, -,tyuwd/ *n.* [*noncount*] wicked behavior or character: *drunkenness and moral turpitude.*

tur•quoise (tûr′koiz, -kwoiz) /'tɜrkɔyz, -kwɔyz/ *n.* **1.** a mineral of copper and aluminum, colored greenish blue and cut as a gem: [*count*]: *an exquisite turquoise.* [*noncount*]: *a ring of turquoise.* **2.** [*noncount*] Also called **tur′quoise blue′.** a greenish blue or bluish green.

tur•ret (tûr′it, tur′-) /'tɜrɪt, 'tʌr-/ *n.* [*count*] **1.** a small tower, usually forming part of a larger structure, as a castle. **2.** a domelike structure in which a gun is mounted.

tur•tle (tûr′tl) /'tɜrtḷ/ *n.* [*count*], *pl.* **-tles,** (*esp. when thought of as a group*) **-tle. 1.** any of various water- and land-dwelling reptiles having the trunk enclosed in a shell. —***Idiom.*** **2. turn turtle,** to capsize or turn over completely.

tur•tle•dove (tûr′tl duv′) /'tɜrtḷ,dʌv/ *n.* [*count*] a dove having a long tail.

tur•tle•neck (tûr′tl nek′) /'tɜrtḷ,nɛk/ *n.* [*count*] **1.** a high, close-fitting collar, appearing esp. on pullover sweaters. **2.** a garment with such a neck.

tusk (tusk) /tʌsk/ *n.* [*count*] an animal tooth developed to great length, usually one of a pair, as in the elephant. —**tusked,** *adj.*

tus•sle (tus′əl) /'tʌsəl/ *v.,* **-sled, -sling,** *n.* —*v.* [*no obj*] **1.** to struggle roughly; wrestle; scuffle: *They tussled on the playground.* —*n.* [*count*] **2.** a rough physical contest or struggle; scuffle. **3.** any strong or determined struggle, conflict, etc.

tu•te•lage (to͞ot′l ij, tyo͞ot′-) /'tuwtḷɪdʒ, 'tyuwt-/ *n.* [*noncount*] instruction; teaching; guidance.

tu•tor (to͞o′tər, tyo͞o′-) /'tuwtər, 'tyuw-/ *n.* [*count*] **1.** one employed to instruct another, esp. privately. **2.** a teacher of academic rank lower than instructor in some American universities and colleges. —*v.* **3.** to act as a tutor to: [~ + *obj*]: *She tutored several Japanese ladies in English.* [*no obj*]: *She tutored as often as she could.*

tu•to•ri•al (to͞o tôr′ē əl, -tōr′-, tyo͞o-) /tuw'tɔriyəl, -'towr-, tyuw-/ *adj.* **1.** of or relating to tutors or to tutoring. —*n.* [*count*] **2.** a special session of teaching or instruction: *a tutorial for graduate students.*

tut•ti-frut•ti (to͞o′tē fro͞o′tē) /'tuwtiy'fruwtiy/ *n.* [*noncount*] **1.** a type of sweet food, esp. ice cream, flavored with a variety of fruits. **2.** a synthetic flavoring combining the flavors of a variety of fruits.

tu•tu (to͞o′to͞o′) /'tuw,tuw/ *n.* [*count*], *pl.* **-tus.** a short, full skirt, usually made of several layers, worn by ballerinas.

tux (tuks) /tʌks/ *n.* [*count*] *Informal.* a tuxedo.

tux•e•do (tuk sē′dō) /tʌk'siydow/ *n.* [*count*], *pl.* **-dos. 1.** Also called **dinner jacket.** a man's jacket for semiformal evening dress. **2.** a complete semiformal outfit, including this jacket and dark trousers: *The groom wore a fancy tuxedo.*

TV or **tv,** an abbreviation of: television.

twad•dle (twod′l) /ˈtwɒdl̩/ *n., v.,* **-dled, -dling.** **—***n.* [*noncount*] **1.** foolish talk or writing. **—***v.* [*no obj*] **2.** to talk in a silly or foolish manner. —**twad′dler,** *n.* [*count*]

twain (twān) /tweyn/ *adj., n.* two: *Never the twain shall meet (= Never the two shall meet, said of people or things that are in great disagreement).*

twang (twang) /twæŋ/ *v.* **1.** to (cause to) give out a sharp, vibrating sound, as the string of a musical instrument when it is plucked: [*no obj*]: *The guitar string twanged.* [~ + *obj*]: *He twanged the guitar string.* **—***n.* [*count*] **2.** a sharp, ringing sound. **3.** a sharp, nasal tone: *He had a Boston twang in his accent.*

'twas (twuz, twoz; *unstressed* twəz) /twʌz, twɒz; *unstressed* twəz/ *contraction.* a shortened form of *it was.*

tweak (twēk) /twiyk/ *v.* [~ + *obj*] **1.** to pinch and pull with a jerk and twist: *to tweak someone's ear.* **2.** to pull or pinch the nose of, esp. gently. **—***n.* [*count*] **3.** an act or instance of tweaking: *a playful tweak of the nose.*

tweed (twēd) /twiyd/ *n.* **1.** [*noncount*] a rough, coarse wool cloth produced esp. in Scotland. **2. tweeds,** [*plural*] garments made of this cloth. —**tweed′y,** *adj.,* **-i•er, -i•est.**

'tween (twēn) /twiyn/ *prep. contraction.* a shortened form of *between.*

tweet (twēt) /twiyt/ *n.* [*count*] **1.** a chirping sound, as that made by a small bird. **—***v.* [*no obj*] **2.** to chirp.

tweet•er (twē′tər) /ˈtwiytər/ *n.* [*count*] a small loudspeaker designed for reproducing high-frequency sounds.

tweez•ers (twē′zərz) /ˈtwiyzərz/ *n.* [*plural; used with a singular or plural verb*] a small tool of two pieces of metal joined at one end, used for plucking out hairs, etc.: *a pair of tweezers; The tweezers are on the countertop.*

twelfth (twelfth) /twɛlfθ/ *adj.* **1.** next after the eleventh; being the ordinal number for 12. **2.** being one of 12 equal parts. **—***n.* [*count*] **3.** a twelfth part, esp. of one (1/12). **4.** the twelfth member of a series.

twelve (twelv) /twɛlv/ *n.* [*count*] **1.** a cardinal number, 10 plus 2. **2.** a symbol for this number, as 12 or XII. **3.** a set of this many persons or things. **—***adj.* [*before a noun*] **4.** amounting to 12 in number.

twen•ty (twen′tē, twun′-) /ˈtwɛntiy, ˈtwʌn-/ *n., pl.* **-ties,** *adj.* **—***n.* [*count*] **1.** a cardinal number, 10 times 2. **2.** a symbol for this number, as 20 or XX. **3.** a set of this many persons or things. **4.** a twenty-dollar bill. **5. twenties,** the numbers from 20 through 29, as in referring to the years of a lifetime or of a century or to degrees of temperature: *the roaring twenties; He's in his late twenties; temperature in the low twenties.* **—***adj.* [*before a noun*] **6.** amounting to 20 in number. —**twen′ti•eth,** *adj., n.* [*count*]

twen′ty-one′, *n.* BLACKJACK (def. 2a).

twen′ty-twen′ty or **20-20,** *adj.* having normal visual ability.

twerp or **twirp** (twûrp) /twɜrp/ *n.* [*count*] *Slang.* a silly, foolish, stupid, insignificant, or despicable person.

twice (twīs) /tways/ *adv.* **1.** two times: *Our class meets twice a week.* **2.** on two occasions: *We saw him twice, once on Saturday and once on his wedding day.* **3.** in twofold amount or degree: *It costs twice as much money to fly to Los Angeles as it does to Chicago.*

twid•dle (twid′l) /ˈtwɪdl̩/ *v.,* **-dled, -dling,** *n.* **—***v.* **1.** to play with idly, esp. with the fingers; twirl: [~ + *obj*]: *to sit and twiddle his thumbs.* [*no obj*]: *Quit twiddling.* **—***n.* [*count*] **2.** the act of twiddling; turn; twirl. **—*Idiom.* 3. twiddle one's thumbs,** to do nothing; be idle: *The administration sits there twiddling its thumbs.*

twig (twig) /twɪg/ *n.* [*count*] a small, thin shoot of a wooden branch or stem. —**twig′gy,** *adj.,* **-gi•er, -gi•est.**

twi•light (twī′līt′) /ˈtwayˌlayt/ *n.* [*noncount*] **1.** the soft light from the sky when the sun is below the horizon. **2.** the period in the morning or evening during which this light prevails. **3.** a period marking the end or close of something, as a career: *the twilight of his career.* **—***adj.* [*before a noun*] **4.** of or relating to twilight; dim; obscure.

twill (twil) /twɪl/ *n.* [*noncount*] **1.** a fabric made from cotton cloth. **2.** a piece of clothing of this fabric. —**twilled,** *adj.*

twin (twin) /twɪn/ *n.* [*count*] **1.** either of two offspring born at one birth: *fraternal twins or identical twins.* **2.** either of two persons or things closely resembling each other. **—***adj.* [*before a noun*] **3.** being a twin or twins: *twin sisters.* **4.** being two persons or things closely related to each other. **5.** being one of a pair; identical: *twin towers.* **6.** made of two similar parts connected: *a twin vase.*

twine (twīn) /twayn/ *n., v.,* **twined, twin•ing.** **—***n.* [*noncount*] **1.** a strong string composed of several strands twisted together. **—***v.* **2.** to insert with a twisting or winding motion: [~ + *obj*]: *She twined her fingers in her hair.* [*no obj*]: *The weeds had twined around the fence.* **3.** [~ + *obj*] to form by or as if by twisting together: *to twine a wreath.* **4.** [~ + *obj*] to wreathe or wrap: *They twined the arch with flowers.* —**twin′er,** *n.* [*count*]

twinge (twinj) /twɪndʒ/ *n.* [*count*] **1.** a sudden, sharp pain: *felt a twinge in his side.* **2.** a sudden, sharp feeling of distress; a pang: *felt a twinge of guilt.*

twi-night (twī′nīt′) /ˈtwayˌnayt/ *adj.* of or relating to a baseball doubleheader that starts in the afternoon and continues into the evening. —**twi′night′er,** *n.* [*count*]

twin•kle (twing′kəl) /ˈtwɪŋkəl/ *v.,* **-kled, -kling,** *n.* **—***v.* [*no obj*] **1.** to shine with a flickering gleam of light: *Stars twinkled in the dark night sky.* **2.** to sparkle in the light: *The diamond in her ring twinkled in the candlelight.* **3.** (of the eyes) to be bright with amusement, pleasure, etc.: *His eyes twinkled merrily.* **—***n.* [*count*] **4.** a flickering brightness or light. **5.** [*usually singular*] amused or mischievous brightness in the eyes; sparkle. **6.** [*usually singular; usually: the* + ~] the time required for a wink; twinkling: *In the twinkle of an eye he was gone.*

twin•kling (twing′kling) /ˈtwɪŋklɪŋ/ *n.* [*count*] **1.** an act of shining with gleams of light that seem to start and stop. **2.** [*usually singular; usually: the* + ~] the time required for a wink; an instant: *in the twinkling of an eye.*

twirl (twûrl) /twɜrl/ *v.* **1.** to (cause to) rotate rapidly: [~ + *obj*]: *The cheerleader twirled a baton.* [*no obj*]: *The baton twirled in the cheerleader's hands.* **2.** to turn quickly so as to face in another direction: [*no obj*]: *twirled around just in time to see her dashing out the door.* [~ + *obj*]: *He twirled her around on the dance floor.* **—***n.* [*count*] **3.** an act or instance of twirling.

twist (twist) /twɪst/ *v.* **1.** [~ + *obj*] to combine, as several strands, by winding together; intertwine: *twisted her sister's hair together to make a braid.* **2.** [~ + *obj*] to form by or as if by winding strands together: *She twisted a French braid in her hair.* **3.** to change in shape, as by turning the ends in opposite directions: [~ + *obj*]: *to twist a paper clip.* [*no obj*]: *Paper clips twist easily.* **4.** to turn so as to face in another direction: [*no obj*]: *He twisted around to see who it was.* [~ + *obj*]: *He twisted his head around to see who was at the door.* **5.** to turn (something) from one direction to another, as by rotating: [~ + *obj*]: *He slowly twisted the doorknob.* [*no obj*]: *He watched as the doorknob slowly twisted.* **6.** to turn sharply or (cause to) be wrenched out of place; sprain: [~ + *obj*]: *He fell and twisted his ankle.* [*no obj*]: *His ankle twisted and he cried out with pain.* **7.** to (cause to) be pulled, torn, or broken off by turning forcibly: [~ + *obj* + *off*]: *climbed the apple tree and twisted a few ripe apples off for us.* [~ + *off* + *obj*]: *I couldn't twist off the lid of the jar.* [*no obj;* ~ + *off*]: *The jar lid just wouldn't twist off.* **8.** to change the appearance of (the face, etc.) into something unnatural; contort: [~ + *obj*]: *twisted her face into a wry smile.* [*no obj*]: *His face twisted into a frown.* **9.** [~ + *obj*] to distort the meaning of; pervert: *accused us of twisting his remarks.* **10.** [~ + *obj; usually: be* + ~*-ed*] to cause to become abnormal, distorted, or warped: *His mind was really twisted—he loved hurting small animals.* **11.** [*no obj*] to bend or turn in different directions: *The road twisted and turned for about a mile.* **12.** [*no obj*] to toss about, wiggle, or writhe, as if to get free of another: *She tried to give him a hug, but he twisted away.* **—***n.* [*count*] **13.** a sudden change in direction; turn: *several twists in the road.* **14.** anything formed by or as if by twisting. **15.** the act or process of twining strands together. **16.** an irregular bend; kink: *some tight twists in her hair.* **17.** a sudden change of course, as of events in life or a literary work: *the twists of fate.* **18.** a full turning or rotation of the body performed during a dive or vault. **—*Idiom.* 19. twist someone's arm,** to use force or persuasion on someone: *I didn't want to go along with the idea, but they twisted my arm.*

twist•er (twis′tər) /ˈtwɪstər/ *n.* [*count*] **1.** a person or thing that twists. **2.** *Informal.* a tornado.

twit[1] (twit) /twɪt/ *v.,* **twit•ted, twit•ting,** *n.* **—***v.* [~ + *obj*] **1.** to ridicule (someone) about something embarrassing: *The media twitted the mayor about his grammar for weeks.* **—***n.* [*count*] **2.** an act of twitting.

twit,[2] *n.* [*count*] *Informal.* a foolish or stupid person.

twitch (twich) /twɪtʃ/ *v.* **1.** to (cause to) move with a sudden, jerking motion, as a part of the body: [*no obj*]: *He lay there twitching as the drug took effect.* [~ + *obj*]: *He twitched his arm.* **2.** to tug or pull at with a quick, short movement: [~ + *obj*]: *Someone twitched my coat sleeve.* [*no obj*]: *to twitch at his coat sleeve.* **3.** [*no obj*] to ache with a sharp, shooting pain: *His arm twitched with pain.* —*n.* [*count*] **4.** a quick, jerky, uncontrolled movement of the body or of some part of it, as a muscle. **5.** a mental twinge, as of pain, conscience, etc.; a pang: *a twitch of conscience.*

twit•ter (twit′ər) /ˈtwɪtər/ *v.* **1.** [*no obj*] to make a number of short, rapid, high-pitched sounds, as a bird does: *birds twittering in the trees.* **2.** to talk lightly and rapidly; chatter: [*no obj*]: *twittering about the usual gossip.* [*used with quotations*]: *"Well!" and "Heavens, no!" they all began twittering when he told them about the librarian's secret love life.* —*n.* [*count*] **3.** an act of twittering. **4.** a twittering sound. **5.** [*usually singular*] a state of fluttering excitement: *were all in a twitter at his visit.* —**twit′ter•y,** *adj.*

'twixt (twikst) /twɪkst/ *prep.* a shortened form of *betwixt.*

two (to͞o) /tuw/ *n., pl.* **twos,** *adj.* —*n.* [*count*] **1.** a cardinal number, 1 plus 1. **2.** a symbol for this number, as 2 or II. **3.** a set of this many persons or things. —*adj.* [*before a noun*] **4.** amounting to two in number. —***Idiom.*** **5. in two,** into two separate parts, as halves: *The cake was cut in two.* **6. put two and two together,** to reach the correct and obvious conclusion: *Putting two and two together, they came up with the murderer.*

two′-bit′, *adj. Informal.* **1.** costing 25 cents. **2.** inferior or unimportant: *a two-bit actor in a two-bit play.*

two′-by-four′, *adj.* [*before a noun*] **1.** two units thick and four units wide, esp. in inches. **2.** *Informal.* lacking adequate space; cramped: *a small, two-by-four room.* —*n.* [*count*] **3.** a piece of timber measuring 2 by 4 in. (5 × 10 cm) in cross section when untrimmed: *A two-by-four is actually equal to 1⅝ by 3⅝ in. (4.5 × 9 cm) when it is trimmed and used in construction.*

two′-faced′, *adj.* **1.** having two faces. **2.** given to deceiving; hypocritical: *He's a two-faced liar.* —**two′-fac′•ed•ly,** *adv.*

two•fer (to͞o′fər) /ˈtuwfər/ *n.* [*count*] a coupon good for the purchase of two items for the price of one.

two′-fist′ed, *adj.* **1.** ready for physical combat. **2.** strong and vigorous.

two•fold (*adj.* to͞o′fōld′; *adv.* -fōld′) / *adj.* ˈtuwˌfowld; *adv.* -ˈfowld/ *adj.* **1.** having two elements or parts. **2.** twice as great or as much; double. —*adv.* **3.** doubly.

two′-ply′, *adj.* made of two thicknesses, layers, strands, or the like: *two-ply knitting yarn.*

two•some (to͞o′səm) /ˈtuwsəm/ *n.* [*count*] **1.** two together; a couple. **2.** a golf match between two persons.

two′-time′, *v.* [~ + *obj*], **-timed, -tim•ing.** *Informal.* **1.** to be unfaithful to (a lover or spouse): *He was two-timing her for years.* **2.** to double-cross. —**two′-tim′er,** *n.* [*count*]

two′-way′, *adj.* [*before a noun*] **1.** moving or providing for or allowing movement in opposite directions: *two-way traffic.* **2.** involving two groups or participants: *a two-way political race.* **3.** demanding responsibilities or obligations on the part of both parties: *Marriage is a two-way street.* **4.** capable of both receiving and sending signals: *a two-way radio.* **5.** capable of being used in two ways.

twp., an abbreviation of: township.

TX, an abbreviation of: Texas.

-ty, *suffix.* *-ty* is attached to adjectives to form nouns that name or refer to a state or condition: *able + -ty → ability; certain + -ty → certainty; chaste + -ty → chastity.*

ty•coon (tī ko͞on′) /tayˈkuwn/ *n.* [*count*] a businessperson of great wealth and power.

ty•ing (tī′ing) /ˈtayɪŋ/ *v.* pres. part. of TIE.

tyke or **tike** (tīk) /tayk/ *n.* [*count*] **1.** a child, esp. a small boy. **2.** any small child.

tym•pa•ni (tim′pə nē) /ˈtɪmpəniy/ *n.* TIMPANI. —**tym′pa•nist,** *n.* [*count*]

type (tīp) /tayp/ *n., v.,* **typed, typ•ing.** —*n.* **1.** [*count*] a class or category of things or persons sharing characteristics: *people of a criminal type.* **2.** [*count; often:* ~ + *of*] a person, animal, or thing thought of as a member of a class or group; a kind; a sort: *This dog is a type of terrier. What is your blood type: A, B, O, or AB?* **3.** [*count*] a person thought of as being typical of a certain line of work, manner of behavior, etc.; a perfect example of: *a civil service type.* **4. a.** [*count*] a block with a raised character on its surface that, when fixed into a press and coated with ink, prints an impression of the character on paper. **b.** [*noncount*] such blocks thought of as a group. **c.** [*noncount*] a printed character or printed characters: *a headline in large type.* —*v.* **5.** to write on a typewriter; typewrite: [*no obj*]: *She can type very fast.* [~ + *obj*]: *She typed the whole paper by herself.* [~ + *obj* + *up*]: *She typed the paper up and sent it off.* [~ + *up* + *obj*]: *I'll type up the report.* **6.** [~ + *obj*] to figure out the type of (a blood or tissue sample): *He went to the Red Cross blood drive area and typed his blood before donating.* —***Idiom.*** **7. be not one's type,** to be the kind or sort of (person) one does not enjoy: *She's pretty in a glamorous sort of way, but she's just not my type.* See -TYPE-.

-type-, *root.* *-type-* comes from Greek, where it has the meaning "impression." This meaning is found in such words as: ARCHETYPE, ATYPICAL, PROTOTYPE, STEREOTYPE, TYPE, TYPICAL, TYPIFY, TYPOGRAPHY.

type•cast (tīp′kast′) /ˈtaypˌkæst/ *v.* [~ + *obj*], **-cast, -cast•ing.** to cast (an actor) in a role that matches the actor's physique, personality, etc.: *typecast as the smooth-talking villain in a dozen or more films.*

type•script (tīp′skript′) /ˈtaypˌskrɪpt/ *n.* **1.** [*count*] a typewritten copy of a piece of writing. **2.** [*noncount*] typewritten matter. See -TYPE-, -SCRIB-.

type•set•ter (tīp′set′ər) /ˈtaypˌsɛtər/ *n.* [*count*] **1.** one who sets type, as on a machine. **2.** a typesetting machine. —**type′set′,** *v.* [~ + *obj*], **-set, -set•ting.**

type•writ•er (tīp′rī′tər) /ˈtaypˌraytər/ *n.* [*count*] a machine for writing in characters similar to printers' types by pressing the letters of a keyboard: *You can type much faster on an electric typewriter than on an old manual one.*

ty•phoid (tī′foid) /ˈtayfɔyd/ *n.* [*noncount*] Also called **ty′phoid fe′ver.** a disease with high fever and diarrhea, spread by contaminated food or water.

ty•phoon (tī fo͞on′) /tayˈfuwn/ *n.* [*count*] **1.** a cyclone or hurricane of the tropical areas of the W Pacific and the China seas. **2.** a violent storm of India.

ty•phus (tī′fəs) /ˈtayfəs/ *n.* [*noncount*] a serious infectious disease carried by lice and fleas, with exhaustion, headache, and an eruption of reddish spots on the body. Also called **ty′phus fe′ver.**

typ•i•cal (tip′i kəl) /ˈtɪpɪkəl/ *adj.* **1.** of or relating to a type; being a representative example: *a typical family.* **2.** characteristic of a person or group of persons, animals, or things: *his typical mannerisms.* [*It* + *be* + ~ + *of*]: *It was typical of him to give a twenty-minute speech.* —**typ′i•cal•ly,** *adv.* See -TYPE-.

typ•i•fy (tip′ə fī′) /ˈtɪpəˌfay/ *v.* [~ + *obj*], **-fied, -fy•ing.** to serve as a typical example of; exemplify: *a hero who typified courage.* —**typ•i•fi•ca•tion** (tip′ə fi kā′shən) /ˌtɪpəfɪˈkeyʃən/ *n.* [*noncount*] See -TYPE-.

typ•ist (tī′pist) /ˈtaypɪst/ *n.* [*count*] one who operates a typewriter.

ty•po (tī′pō) /ˈtaypow/ *n.* [*count*], *pl.* **-pos.** *Informal.* an error in printing resulting from a mistake in typing: *Just get rid of those typos and your paper is ready.* See -TYPE-.

ty•pog•ra•phy (tī pog′rə fē) /tayˈpɒgrəfiy/ *n.* [*noncount*] **1.** the art or process of printing with type. **2.** the general character or appearance of printed matter. —**ty•po•graph•i•cal,** (tī′pə graf′i kəl) /ˌtaypəˈgræfɪkəl/ **ty′po•graph′ic,** *adj.* —**ty′po•graph′i•cal•ly,** *adv.* See -TYPE-, -GRAPH-.

ty•ran•ni•cal (ti ran′i kəl, tī-) /tɪˈrænɪkəl, tay-/ also **ty•ran′nic,** *adj.* of or relating to tyranny; oppressive: *a tyrannical king.* —**ty•ran′ni•cal•ly,** *adv.*

tyr•an•nize (tir′ə nīz′) /ˈtɪrəˌnayz/ *v.,* **-nized, -niz•ing.** to rule tyrannically: [~ + *obj*]: *to tyrannize his countrymen.* [*no obj*]: *to tyrannize over the country.*

tyr•an•ny (tir′ə nē) /ˈtɪrəniy/ *n., pl.* **-nies.** **1.** [*noncount*] the use of power that has no limits or bounds; abuse of power: *the tyranny of totalitarian government.* **2.** [*count*] the government or rule of a tyrant: *tyrannies of dictators through the years.* **3.** [*noncount*] a condition of severity or harshness: *the tyranny of nature.*

ty•rant (tī′rənt) /ˈtayrənt/ *n.* [*count*] one who uses power cruelly or unjustly.

ty•ro or **ti•ro** (tī′rō) /ˈtayrow/ *n.* [*count*], *pl.* **-ros.** a beginner in learning anything; novice.

tzar (zär, tsär) /zɑr, tsɑr/ *n.* CZAR.

U

U, u (yōō) /yuw/ *n.* [*count*], *pl.* **U's** or **Us, u's** or **us.** the 21st letter of the English alphabet, a vowel.

U., an abbreviation of: **1.** union. **2.** unit. **3.** university. **4.** unsatisfactory.

u•biq•ui•tous (yōō bik′wi təs) /yuw'bɪkwɪtəs/ *adj.* being or found everywhere, at the same time: *Earth's ubiquitous atmosphere.* —**u•biq′ui•tous•ly,** *adv.* —**u•biq′ui•ty,** *n.* [*noncount*]

U-boat (yōō′bōt′) /'yuw,bowt/ *n.* [*count*] a German submarine.

u.c., an abbreviation of: uppercase.

ud•der (ud′ər) /'ʌdər/ *n.* [*count*] a baggy gland on female goats and cows from which milk is produced.

UFO (yōō′ef′ō′; *sometimes* yōō′fō) /'yuw'ɛf'ow; *sometimes* 'yuwfow/ *n.* [*count*], *pl.* **UFOs, UFO's.** an unidentified flying object; any unexplained moving object seen in the sky, esp. one held to be from beyond the Earth.

U•gan•dan (yōō gan′dən, ōō gän′dän) /yuw'gændən, uw'gandan/ *adj.* **1.** of or relating to Uganda. —*n.* [*count*] **2.** a person born or living in Uganda.

ugh (ŏŏKH, ᴜKH, u, ŏŏ; *spelling pron.* ug), *interj.* (used to show disgust, horror, or the like): *Ugh! That food's spoiled.*

ug•ly (ug′lē) /'ʌgliy/ *adj.,* **-li•er, -li•est. 1.** very unattractive or displeasing in appearance: *an ugly fence of barbed wire.* **2.** disagreeable; unpleasant: *ugly weather.* **3.** frightful; dreadful: *an ugly wound.* **4.** hostile; quarrelsome: *an ugly mood.* —**ug′li•ness,** *n.* [*noncount*]

uh (u, ᴜN), *interj.* (used to express hesitation, doubt, or to make a pause): *Uh, I'm not so sure I want to go.*

UHF or **uhf,** an abbreviation of: ultrahigh frequency.

U•krain•i•an (yōō krā′nē ən) /yuw'kreyniyən/ *adj.* **1.** of or relating to Ukraine. **2.** of or relating to the language spoken by many of the people in Ukraine. —*n.* **3.** [*count*] a person born or living in Ukraine. **4.** [*noncount*] the language spoken by many of the people in Ukraine.

u•ku•le•le or **u•ke•le•le** (yōō′kə lā′lē, ōō′-) /,yuwkə'leyliy, ,uw-/ *n.* [*count*], *pl.* **-les.** a small, guitarlike musical instrument often used in Hawaiian music.

ul•cer (ul′sər) /'ʌlsər/ *n.* [*count*] a sore, as on the skin, mouth, or stomach lining, bringing with it the disintegration of tissue, and often the formation of pus.

ul•cer•ated (ul′sə rā′tid) /'ʌlsə,reytɪd/ *adj.* affected with an ulcer. —**ul•cer•a•tion** (ul′sə rā′shən) /,ʌlsə'reyʃən/ *n.* [*noncount*]

-ult-, *root.* *-ult-* comes from Latin, where it has the meaning "beyond; farther." This meaning is found in such words as: PENULTIMATE, ULTERIOR, ULTIMATE, ULTIMATUM, ULTRA.

ult., an abbreviation of: ultimate.

ul•te•ri•or (ul tēr′ē ər) /ʌl'tɪəriyər/ *adj.* [*before a noun*] intentionally kept concealed: *His ulterior motive was to enrich himself.* See -ULT-.

ul•ti•mate (ul′tə mit) /'ʌltəmɪt/ *adj.* [*before a noun*] **1.** last; furthest or farthest: *an ultimate destination.* **2.** decisive; conclusive; highest: *the ultimate authority.* **3.** most extreme: *the ultimate sacrifice.* **4.** final; total: *the ultimate cost.* **5.** unequaled or unsurpassed; best: *the ultimate vacation.* —*n.* [*noncount; the* + ~] **6.** the final point or result. **7.** a fundamental fact or principle. **8.** the finest or most superior of its kind; the best: *This apartment is the ultimate in luxury.* —**ul′ti•mate•ly,** *adv.* See -ULT-.

ul•ti•ma•tum (ul′tə mā′təm, -mä′-) /,ʌltə'meytəm, -'ma-/ *n.* [*count*], *pl.* **-tums, -ta** (-tə) /-tə/. a final demand issued by one side in a dispute, that if rejected will lead to the ending of talks and the use of force. See -ULT-.

ul•tra (ul′trə) /'ʌltrə/ *adj.* going beyond what is usual or ordinary; excessive; extreme. See -ULT-.

ultra-, *prefix.* **1.** *ultra-* comes from Latin, where it has the meaning "located beyond, on the far side of:" *ultraviolet.* **2.** *ultra-* is also used to mean "carrying to the furthest degree possible, on the fringe of:" *ultraleft; ultramodern.* **3.** *ultra-* is also used to mean "extremely:" *ultralight.* **4.** *ultra-* is also used to mean "going beyond normal or customary bounds or limits:" *ultramicroscope; ultrasound; ultrastructure.*

ul•tra•con•serv•a•tive (ul′trə kən sûr′və tiv) /,ʌltrəkən'sɜrvətɪv/ *adj.* **1.** very or extremely conservative, esp. in politics. —*n.* [*count*] **2.** an ultraconservative person.

ul•tra•high (ul′trə hī′) /,ʌltrə'hay/ *adj.* extremely high.

ul′trahigh fre′quency, *n.* [*noncount*] any radio frequency between 300 and 3000 megahertz. *Abbr.:* UHF.

ul•tra•ma•rine (ul′trə mə rēn′) /,ʌltrəmə'riyn/ *adj.* **1.** of a deep blue color. **2.** beyond the sea. —*n.* [*noncount*] **3.** a deep blue color.

ul•tra•mod•ern (ul′trə mod′ərn) /,ʌltrə'mɒdərn/ *adj.* very advanced in ideas, design, etc.

ul•tra•son•ic (ul′trə son′ik) /,ʌltrə'sɒnɪk/ *adj.* of, relating to, or making use of ultrasound. —**ul′tra•son′i•cal•ly,** *adv.*

ul•tra•sound (ul′trə sound′) /'ʌltrə,sawnd/ *n.* [*noncount*] **1.** sound with a frequency greater than 20,000 Hz, close to the upper limit of human hearing. **2.** *Med.* the application of ultrasonic waves to methods of diagnois or of healing, as in deep-heat treatment of a joint.

ul•tra•vi•o•let (ul′trə vī′ə lit) /,ʌltrə'vayəlɪt/ *adj.* **1.** relating to light having wavelengths shorter than visible light but longer than x-rays. **2.** producing or using light having such wavelengths: *an ultraviolet lamp.* Compare INFRARED. —*n.* [*noncount*] **3.** ultraviolet radiation. See -ULT-.

um•ber (um′bər) /'ʌmbər/ *n.* [*noncount*] **1.** brown earth used as a pigment. **2.** the color of such a pigment; dark dusky brown or dark reddish brown. —*adj.* **3.** of the color umber.

um•bil•i•cal cord (um bil′i kəl) /ʌm'bɪlɪkəl/ *n.* [*count*] a cordlike structure connecting the unborn baby or fetus with the mother's placenta during pregnancy, bringing nourishment from the mother and removing wastes.

um•brage (um′brij) /'ʌmbrɪdʒ/ *n.* [*noncount*] offense; displeasure: *to take umbrage at someone's rudeness.*

um•brel•la (um brel′ə) /ʌm'brɛlə/ *n.* [*count*], *pl.* **-las. 1.** a light, circular cover for protection from rain, snow, or sometimes hot sun, made of a frame of fabric supported by thin ribs that come out of the top of a carrying stick or handle. **2.** something that protects from above, as military aircraft over ground forces. **3.** something, as an organization or policy, that includes a number of groups or elements. —*adj.* [*before a noun*] **4.** applying to a number of similar elements or groups at the same time: *an umbrella insurance policy.*

um•laut (ŏŏm′lout) /'ʊmlawt/ *n.* [*count*] a mark (¨) used as a marker over a vowel, as *ä, ö, ü,* to indicate a vowel sound different from that of the letter without the mark, esp. as used in German.

ump (ump) /ʌmp/ *n., v. Informal.* UMPIRE.

um•pire (um′pīər) /'ʌmpayər/ *n., v.,* **-pired, -pir•ing.** —*n.* [*count*] **1.** a person who rules on the plays in a game. **2.** a person appointed to settle disputes about rules or to make a judgment on differences in a dispute. —*v.* **3.** to act as umpire in (a game): [~ + *obj*]: *to umpire a baseball game.* [*no obj*]: *He umpired for the league.* **4.** [~ + *obj*] to decide (a dispute) as umpire.

ump•teen (ump′tēn′) /'ʌmp'tiyn/ *adj.* [*before a noun*] *Informal.* innumerable; many: *She came to his office umpteen times but never really listened to his advice.* —**ump•teenth′,** *adj.*

un-[1], *prefix.* *un-* is used very freely to form adjectives and the adverbs and nouns formed from these adjectives. It means "not," and it brings negative or opposite force: *unfair, unfairly, unfairness; unfelt; unseen; unfitting; unformed; unheard-of; unrest; unemployment.*

un-[2], *prefix.* **1.** *un-* is attached to verbs, and means "a reversal of some action or state, or a removal, a taking away, or a release": *unbend; uncork; unfasten.* **2.** *un-* is also attached to some verbs to intensify the meaning: *unloose (= let loose with force).*

UN or **U.N.,** an abbreviation of: United Nations.

un•a•bashed (un′ə basht′) /,ʌnə'bæʃt/ *adj.* not abashed; not ashamed. —**un•a•bashed•ly** (un′ə bash′id lē) /,ʌnə'bæʃɪdliy/ *adv.*

un•a•bated (un′ə bā′tid) /,ʌnə'beytɪd/ *adj.* without stopping; without losing force: *The flood waters rose unabated.*

un•a•ble (un ā′bəl) /ʌn'eybəl/ *adj.* [*be* + ~ + *to* + *verb*] lacking the necessary power, ability, competence, time, etc., to accomplish some act: *He's unable to swim.*

un•a•bridged (un′ə brijd′) /,ʌnə'brɪdʒd/ *adj.* **1.** not made short: *an unabridged novel.* —*n.* [*count*] **2.** an unabridged dictionary.

un•ac•cept•a•ble (un′ak sep′tə bəl) /,ʌnæk'sɛptəbəl/ *adj.* not accepted; not meeting a standard: *an unacceptable excuse.* —**un′ac•cept′a•bly,** *adv.*

un•ac•com•pa•nied (un′ə kum′pə nēd) /ˌʌnəˈkʌmpəniyd/ *adj.* **1.** not accompanied; alone. **2.** not accompanied by a musical instrument, esp. a piano.

un•ac•count•a•ble (un′ə koun′tə bəl) /ˌʌnəˈkawntəbəl/ *adj.* **1.** impossible to account for or explain; very surprising: *an unaccountable lapse in taste.* **2.** not responsible: *was held unaccountable for the accident.* —**un′ac•count′a•bly,** *adv.*

un•ac•count•ed (un′ə koun′tid) /ˌʌnəˈkawntɪd/ *adj.* not explained: [*be* + ∼ + *for*]: *The missing funds are still unaccounted for.*

un•ac•cus•tomed (un′ə kus′təmd) /ˌʌnəˈkʌstəmd/ *adj.* **1.** not used to: *unaccustomed to hardships.* **2.** uncommon; unexpected: *an unaccustomed delay.*

un•ac•knowl•edged (un′ik nol′ijd) /ˌʌnɪkˈnɒlɪdʒd/ *adj.* **1.** not given proper credit: *an unacknowledged hero.* **2.** not accepted or admitted as real: *unacknowledged fears.*

un•a•dorned (un′ə dôrnd′) /ˌʌnəˈdɔrnd/ *adj.* not decorated; plain.

un•a•dul•ter•at•ed (un′ə dul′tə rā′tid) /ˌʌnəˈdʌltəˌreytɪd/ *adj.* **1.** not adulterated; clean; pure. **2.** complete; utter: *unadulterated nonsense.*

un•ad•vised (un′əd vīzd′) /ˌʌnədˈvayzd/ *adj.* **1.** uninformed: *an unadvised choice of career.* **2.** imprudent; ill-advised: *an unadvised hastiness.*

un•af•fect•ed (un′ə fek′tid) /ˌʌnəˈfɛktɪd/ *adj.* **1.** sincere; genuine: *unaffected grief.* **2.** not affected by change.

un•a•fraid (un′ə frād′) /ˌʌnəˈfreyd/ *adj.* [*be* + ∼ (+ *of*)] not afraid.

un•al•ter•a•ble (un′ol′tər ə bl) /ˌʌnˈɒltərəbl/ *adj.* that cannot be altered: *an unalterable decision.* —**un•al′ter•a•bly,** *adv.*

un•am•big•u•ous (un′am big′yo͞o əs) /ˌʌnæmˈbɪgyuwəs/ *adj.* not ambiguous; clear; exact. —**un′am•big′u•ous•ly,** *adv.*

un-A•mer•i•can (un′ə mer′i kən) /ˌʌnəˈmɛrɪkən/ *adj.* not thought of as being typical of American values, standards, etc.

u•nan•i•mous (yo͞o nan′ə məs) /yuwˈnænəməs/ *adj.* **1.** in complete agreement; of one mind. **2.** showing complete agreement: *a unanimous vote.* —**u•na•nim•i•ty** (yo͞o′nə-nim′i tē) /ˌyuwnəˈnɪmɪtiy/ *n.* [*noncount*] —**u•nan′i•mous•ly,** *adv.* See -UNI-.

un•an•nounced (un′ə nounst′) /ˌʌnəˈnawnst/ *adj.* **1.** held or done without notice given beforehand: *an unannounced visit.* —*adv.* **2.** without notice given beforehand: *arrived unannounced.*

un•an•swer•a•ble (un an′sər ə bəl) /ʌnˈænsərəbəl/ *adj.* **1.** not having a known or discoverable answer: *an unanswerable question.* **2.** not open to argument: *unanswerable proof.*

un•ap•proach•a•ble (un′ə prō′chə bəl) /ˌʌnəˈprowtʃəbəl/ *adj.* **1.** that cannot be approached; unreachable: *Floods made the village unapproachable.* **2.** very distant; unfriendly: *an unapproachable manner.*

un•armed (un ärmd′) /ʌnˈɑrmd/ *adj.* **1.** being without weapons or armor: *an unarmed police officer.* **2.** not having claws, thorns, scales, etc., as animals or plants.

un•a•shamed (un′ə•shāmd′) /ˌʌnəˈʃeymd/ *adj.* **1.** [*be* + ∼(+ *of*)] not filled with guilt or shame: *He was unashamed of what he had done.* **2.** not concealed or hidden: *the unashamed pursuit of money.* —**un•a•sham•ed•ly** (un′ə shā′mid lē) /ˌʌnəˈʃeymɪdliy/ *adv.*

un•asked (un askt′) /ʌnˈæskt/ *adj.* **1.** not asked: *an unasked question.* **2.** not asked for: *giving unasked advice.* —*adv.* **3.** without having been asked: *arrived unasked at the party.*

un•as•sail•a•ble (un′ə sā′lə bəl) /ˌʌnəˈseyləbəl/ *adj.* **1.** not open to attack: *an unassailable fortress.* **2.** that cannot be denied or disputed: *an unassailable truth.*

un•as•sist•ed (un′ə sis′tid) /ˌʌnəˈsɪstɪd/ *adj.* **1.** done or accomplished without assistance. —*adv.* **2.** without assistance. See -SIST-.

un•as•sum•ing (un′ə so͞o′ming) /ˌʌnəˈsuwmɪŋ/ *adj.* modest; not pretentious: *an unassuming manner.*

un•at•tached (un′ə tacht′) /ˌʌnəˈtætʃt/ *adj.* **1.** not attached. **2.** not associated with any particular group, organization, or the like; independent. **3.** not engaged, married, or involved with another.

un•at•tend•ed (un′ə ten′did) /ˌʌnəˈtɛndɪd/ *adj.* [*leave* + *obj* + ∼] alone; not supervised: *blamed the parents for leaving the children unattended all day.*

un•at•trac•tive (un′ə trak′tiv) /ˌʌnəˈtræktɪv/ *adj.* **1.** not appealing to look at: *an unattractive color.* **2.** not desirable: *an unattractive offer.* See -TRAC-.

un•au•thor•ized (un ô′thə rīzd′) /ʌnˈɔθəˌrayzd/ *adj.* not authorized; not having been given permission or authority to do something: *unauthorized entry into the nuclear facility.*

un•a•vail•a•ble (un′ə vā′lə bəl) /ˌʌnəˈveyləbəl/ *adj.* **1.** that cannot be obtained or bought: *For weeks sugar was unavailable.* **2.** [*be* + ∼] not accessible: *She is unavailable at the moment.* —**un•a•vail•a•bil•i•ty** (un′ə vā′lə-bil′i tē) /ˌʌnəˌveyləˈbɪlɪtiy/ *n.* [*noncount*]

un•a•vail•ing (un′ə vā′ling) /ˌʌnəˈveylɪŋ/ *adj.* having no effect; futile: *unavailing efforts.* —**un′a•vail′ing•ly,** *adv.*

un•a•void•a•ble (un′ə voi′də bəl) /ˌʌnəˈvɔydəbəl/ *adj.* unable to be avoided; inescapable: *an unavoidable delay.* —**un′a•void′a•bly,** *adv.*: *We've been unavoidably detained.*

un•a•ware (un′ə wâr′) /ˌʌnəˈwɛər/ *adj.* **1.** not aware; not knowing about (something): [*be* + ∼ + *of*]: *I was unaware of your problem.* [*be* + ∼ + *(that) clause*]: *I was unaware that you were sick.* —*adv.* **2.** unawares: *The attack caught the enemy unaware.*

un•a•wares (un′ə wârz′) /ˌʌnəˈwɛərz/ *adv.* without warning; unexpectedly; without being prepared: *to take someone unawares.*

un•bal•anced (un bal′ənst) /ʌnˈbælənst/ *adj.* **1.** lacking balance or the proper balance. **2.** lacking steadiness and soundness of judgment; mentally disturbed: *unbalanced behavior.* **3.** (of an account) not adjusted so that money owed and money earned are equal.

un•bar (un bär′) /ʌnˈbɑr/ *v.* [∼ + *obj*], **-barred, -bar•ring.** to remove a bar from; unbolt: *Unbar the gate.*

un•bear•a•ble (un bâr′ə bəl) /ʌnˈbɛərəbəl/ *adj.* that cannot be endured, suffered through, or tolerated; unendurable; intolerable: *unbearable pain.* —**un•bear′a•bly,** *adv.*

un•beat•a•ble (un bē′tə bəl) /ʌnˈbiytəbəl/ *adj.* **1.** that cannot be beaten or defeated: *an unbeatable team.* **2.** of the best; excellent: *unbeatable prices.*

un•beat•en (un bēt′n) /ʌnˈbiytn̩/ *adj.* **1.** not beaten: *unbeaten eggs.* **2.** not defeated or never defeated: *an unbeaten team.* **3.** not walked on: *unbeaten paths.*

un•be•com•ing (un′bi kum′ing) /ˌʌnbɪˈkʌmɪŋ/ *adj.* taking away from one's appearance, character, or reputation; unattractive or unseemly: *an unbecoming hat; unbecoming language.*

un•be•known (un′bi nōn′) /ˌʌnbɪˈnown/ also **un•be•knownst** (un′bi nōnst′) /ˌʌnbɪˈnownst/ *adj.* [∼ + *to*] being without one's knowledge: *Unbeknown(st) to me, the train had left.*

un•be•lief (un′bi lēf′) /ˌʌnbɪˈliyf/ *n.* [*noncount*] unwillingness or inability to believe, esp. in matters of religious faith. —**un•be•liev•er** (un′bi lē′vər) /ˌʌnbɪˈliyvər/ *n.* [*count*]

un•be•liev•a•ble (un′bi lē′və bəl) /ˌʌnbɪˈliyvəbəl/ *adj.* **1.** too unlikely to be believed: *Your story is unbelievable.* **2.** extraordinary; impressive: *unbelievable luck.* —**un′be•liev′a•bly,** *adv.*

un•bend (un bend′) /ʌnˈbɛnd/ *v.*, **-bent, -bend•ing. 1.** to (cause to) straighten from a bent form or position: [∼ + *obj*]: *to unbend the crooked bar.* [*no obj*]: *He slowly unbent after stooping.* **2.** [*no obj*] to become less formal; relax: *gradually unbent and even told a joke.*

un•bend•ing (un ben′ding) /ʌnˈbɛndɪŋ/ *adj.* **1.** not bending; inflexible; rigid. **2.** refusing to give in, yield, or compromise: *an unbending attitude during the negotiations.*

un•bi•ased (un bi′əst) /ʌnˈbayəst/ *adj.* not biased or prejudiced; impartial. Also, *esp. Brit.*, **un•bi′assed.**

un•bid•den (un bid′n) /ʌnˈbɪdn̩/ also **un•bid** (un bid′) /ʌnˈbɪd/ *adv.* **1.** not ordered or commanded; not wished for consciously; spontaneous: *The thought came to his mind unbidden.* **2.** not asked or summoned; uninvited.

un•bind (un bind′) /ʌnˈbaynd/ *v.* [∼ + *obj*], **-bound, -bind•ing. 1.** to release from ropes, ties, or restraint; set free. **2.** to unfasten; untie.

un•blush•ing (un blush′ing) /ʌnˈblʌʃɪŋ/ *adj.* **1.** showing no shame or regret; shameless: *unblushing greed.* **2.** not blushing. —**un•blush′ing•ly,** *adv.*

un•born (un bôrn′) /ʌnˈbɔrn/ *adj.* **1.** still to appear; future: *unborn generations.* **2.** not yet born: *an unborn child.* —*n.* **the unborn,** [*plural*] **3.** fetuses still in the womb.

un•bound•ed (un boun′did) /ʌnˈbawndɪd/ *adj.* **1.** having no limits or bounds: *the unbounded universe.* **2.** unrestrained; not held back: *his unbounded enthusiasm for his job.*

un•bowed (un boud′) /ʌnˈbawd/ *adj.* **1.** not bowed or bent. **2.** not giving in to defeat; not dominated or ruled.

un•bri•dled (un brīd′ld) /ʌnˈbraydld/ *adj.* **1.** not restrained; not held back; uninhibited: *unbridled enthusiasm.* **2.** not fitted with a bridle: *an unbridled horse.*

un•bro•ken (un brō′kən) /ʌn'browkən/ *adj.* **1.** not broken; whole; intact: *an unbroken window.* **2.** not interrupted; not disturbed: *unbroken sleep.* **3.** not tamed, such as a horse: *an unbroken spirit.*

un•bur•den (un bûr′dn) /ʌn'bɜrdn̩/ *v.* [~ + *obj*] to free from a burden: *to unburden a horse; unburdened herself of her worries.*

un•but•ton (un but′n) /ʌn'bʌtn̩/ *v.* [~ + *obj*] to unfasten or undo the buttons of (a piece of clothing).

un•called-for (un kôld′fôr′) /ʌn'kɔld,fɔr/ *adj.* not right; unfair; unwarranted; improper: *an uncalled-for criticism.*

un•can•ny (un kan′ē) /ʌn'kæniy/ *adj.* **1.** having or seeming to have a supernatural or unexplained basis; extraordinary: *to shoot with uncanny accuracy.* **2.** mysterious; causing fear or dread: *Uncanny sounds filled the house.*

un•car•ing (un kâr′ing) /ʌn'kɛərɪŋ/ *adj.* not showing concern or care for others: *an uncaring attitude toward the poor.*

un•ceas•ing (un sē′sing) /ʌn'siysɪŋ/ *adj.* not stopping; continuous: *unceasing noise.* **—un•ceas′ing•ly,** *adv.*

un•cer•e•mo•ni•ous (un′ser ə mō′nē əs) /,ʌnsɛrə'mowniyəs/ *adj.* **1.** sudden and abrupt; hasty or rude: *an unceremonious ouster.* **2.** without formalities; informal: *an unceremonious welcome.* **—un′cer•e•mo′ni•ous•ly,** *adv.*

un•cer•tain (un sûr′tn) /ʌn'sɜrtn̩/ *adj.* **1.** not known precisely; not fixed: *The size of the deficit is uncertain.* **2.** not confident or assured; hesitant: *an uncertain smile.* **3.** not clearly determined; unknown: *a manuscript of uncertain origin.* **4.** likely to change; unstable: *The weather pattern for the next few days is uncertain.* **—un•cer′tain•ly,** *adv.* **—un•cer′tain•ty,** *n., pl.* **-ties.** [*noncount*]: *He showed uncertainty of manner.* [*count*]: *life's uncertainties.*

un•chal•lenged (un chal′ənjd) /ʌn'tʃæləndʒd/ *adj.* **1.** accepted without argument or debate: *an unchallenged decision.* **—*adv.*** **2.** without argument: *My decisions went unchallenged.* **3.** not questioned: *crossed the border unchallenged.*

un•changed (un chānjd′) /ʌn'tʃeyndʒd/ *adj.* not having changed.

un•chang•ing (un chān′jing) /ʌn'tʃeyndʒɪŋ/ *adj.* not changing; staying the same: *unchanging good humor.*

un•char•ac•ter•is•tic (un′kar ik tə ris′tik) /,ʌnkærɪktə'rɪstɪk/ *adj.* not characteristic or typical: *spoke with uncharacteristic passion.* **—un′char•ac•ter•is′tic•al•ly,** *adv.*

un•char•i•ta•ble (un char′i tə bəl) /ʌn'tʃærɪtəbəl/ *adj.* not having or showing charity; callous. **—un•char′i•ta•bly,** *adv.*

un•chart•ed (un chär′tid) /ʌn'tʃɑrtɪd/ *adj.* not shown or located on a map; unexplored: *uncharted wilderness.*

un•checked (un chekt′) /ʌn'tʃɛkt/ *adj.* **1.** not slowed down, prevented, or stopped: *unchecked population growth.* **—*adv.*** **2.** without being prevented, slowed down, or stopped: *The epidemic spread unchecked.*

un•cir•cum•cised (un sûr′kəm sīzd′) /ʌn'sɜrkəm,sayzd/ *adj.* **1.** not circumcised. **2.** not Jewish; gentile.

un•civ•il (un siv′əl) /ʌn'sɪvəl/ *adj.* impolite; rude: *an uncivil remark.*

un•civ•i•lized (un siv′ə līzd′) /ʌn'sɪvə,layzd/ *adj.* not civilized or cultured; barbarous: *an uncivilized tribe.*

un•clad (un klad′) /ʌn'klæd/ *v.* **1.** a pt. and pp. of UNCLOTHE. **—*adj.*** **2.** naked; nude; undressed.

un•clasp (un klasp′) /ʌn'klæsp/ *v.* [~ + *obj*] **1.** to undo the clasp or clasps of; unfasten: *to unclasp the buckles.* **2.** to release or relax (from) the grasp: *unclasped her hands.*

un•cle (ung′kəl) /'ʌŋkəl/ *n.* [*count*] **1.** a brother of one's father or mother. **2.** an aunt's husband. **—*Idiom.*** **3. say** or **cry uncle,** [*no obj*] to admit defeat.

un•clean (un klēn′) /ʌn'kliyn/ *adj.,* **-er, -est. 1.** not clean; dirty. **2.** morally impure: *unclean thoughts.* **—un•clean′ly,** *adv.* **—un•clean′ness,** *n.* [*noncount*]

un•clear (un klēr) /ʌnklɪər/ *adj.* **1.** [*be* + ~] not obvious: *The reasons were unclear.* **2.** poorly or badly explained: *unclear instructions.* **3.** hard to see through: *unclear water.* **4.** [*be* + ~] not having understanding: *unclear about your meaning.*

Un′cle Sam′ (sam) /sæm/ *n.* [*proper noun*] a name used to represent the government or people of the U.S.: *Uncle Sam is usually represented as a tall, lean man with white chin whiskers, wearing a blue coat, red-and-white-striped trousers, and a top hat with a band of stars.*

Un′cle Tom′, *n.* [*count*] *Disparaging and Offensive.* a black person who is thought of as being too submissive to whites.

un•cloak (un klōk′) /ʌn'klowk/ *v.* [~ + *obj*] to reveal; expose: *to uncloak a scheme.*

un•clog (un klog′, -klôg′) /ʌn'klɒg, -'klɔg/ *v.,* **-clogged, -clog•ging.** to (cause to) become free of something blocking: [~ + *obj*]: *to unclog a drain.* [*no obj*]: *The drain won't unclog.*

un•clothed (un klōthd′) /ʌn'klowðd/ *adj.* not wearing clothes.

un•com•fort•a•ble (un kumf′tə bəl, -kum′fər tə-) /ʌn'kʌmftəbəl, -'kʌmfərtə-/ *adj.* **1.** causing discomfort or distress; irritating; painful: *uncomfortable shoes.* **2.** experiencing discomfort; uneasy: *uncomfortable with the idea of fame.* **—un•com′fort•a•bly,** *adv.* See -FORT-.

un•com•mit•ted (un′kə mit′id) /,ʌnkə'mɪtɪd/ *adj.* not pledged to a specific course of action or cause: *uncommitted party delegates.* See -MIT-.

un•com•mon (un kom′ən) /ʌn'kɒmən/ *adj.,* **-er, -est. 1.** not common; unusual; rare. **2.** more than the usual in amount or degree. **3.** exceptional; outstanding. **—un•com′mon•ly,** *adv.: an uncommonly good student.*

un•com•mu•ni•ca•tive (un′kə myōō′ni kə tiv, -kā′tiv) /,ʌnkə'myuwnɪkətɪv, -,keytɪv/ *adj.* not eager or willing to talk or communicate; reserved; reticent.

un•com•plain•ing (un′kəm plā′ning) /,ʌnkəm'pleynɪŋ/ *adj.* not complaining; patient; stoic. **—un′com•plain′ing•ly,** *adv.: doing his work uncomplainingly.*

un•com•pre•hend•ing (un′kom prē hend′ing) /,ʌnkɒmpriy'hɛndɪŋ/ *adj.* showing a lack of understanding; baffled: *an uncomprehending stare.* **—un′com•pre•hend′ing•ly,** *adv.* See -PREHEND-.

un•com•pro•mis•ing (un kom′prə mī′zing) /ʌn'kɒmprə,mayzɪŋ/ *adj.* **1.** not allowing compromise; not giving in. **2.** not changing one's belief or loyalty to a principle, point of view, etc. See -MIS-.

un•con•cealed (un′kən sēld′) /,ʌnkən'siyld/ *adj.* not hidden; plain and obvious: *his unconcealed hatred for her.*

un•con•cern (un′kən sûrn′) /,ʌnkən'sɜrn/ *n.* [*noncount*] absence of concern; indifference. **—un′con•cerned′,** *adj.*

un•con•di•tion•al (un′kən dish′ə nl) /,ʌnkən'dɪʃənl̩/ *adj.* not limited by conditions; absolute: *unconditional surrender.* **—un′con•di′tion•al•ly,** *adv.*

un•con•scion•a•ble (un kon′shə nə bəl) /ʌn'kɒnʃənəbəl/ *adj.* **1.** not held back by conscience; unscrupulous: *unconscionable deeds.* **2.** excessive: *spent an unconscionable amount of money.* **—un•con′scion•a•bly,** *adv.*

un•con•scious (un kon′shəs) /ʌn'kɒnʃəs/ *adj.* **1.** having lost consciousness: *was unconscious from the blow.* **2.** not noticed at the level of awareness: *an unconscious impulse.* **3.** done unintentionally: *an unconscious insult.* **—*n.*** [*noncount; the* + ~] **4.** the part of the mind that a person is rarely aware of but that has an important influence on behavior. **—un•con′scious•ly,** *adv.* **—un•con′scious•ness,** *n.* [*noncount*]

un•con•sti•tu•tion•al (un′kon sti tōō′shə nl, -tyōō′-) /,ʌnkɒnstɪ'tuwʃənl̩, -'tyuw-/ *adj.* not constitutional; not authorized by, or not consistent with, a constitution, esp. the U.S. Constitution. See -STIT-.

un•con•trol′la•ble (un′kən trō′lə bəl) /,ʌnkən'trowləbəl/ *adj.* **1.** that cannot be controlled or prevented (from doing, moving, etc.): *uncontrollable twitching of the eyelid.* **2.** not yielding to authority; unmanageable: *an uncontrollable mob.* **—un′con•trol′la•bly,** *adv.*

un•con•ven•tion•al (un′kən ven′shə nl) /,ʌnkən'vɛnʃənl̩/ *adj.* not conventional; not bound by or following convention or what is considered proper or normal: *an unconventional use of color.* **—un′con•ven′tion•al•ly,** *adv.* See -VEN-.

un•con•vinced (un′kən vinst′) /,ʌnkən'vɪnst/ *adj.* [*usually: be* + ~] not convinced; not persuaded that something is correct or true: *unconvinced of their honesty.*

un•con•vinc•ing (un′kən vin′sing) /,ʌnkən'vɪnsɪŋ/ *adj.* not convincing; not persuasive: *The arguments were unconvincing.* **—un′con•vinc′ing•ly,** *adv.*

un•cool (un kōōl′) /ʌn'kuwl/ *adj. Slang.* **1.** not self-assured: *He felt very uncool with these people.* **2.** not acceptably aware or sophisticated: *thinks it's uncool to flaunt wealth.*

un•co•op•er•a•tive (un′kō op′ər ə tiv) /ˌʌnkow'ɒpərətɪv/ *adj.* unwilling to cooperate.

un•co•or•di•nat•ed (un′kō ôr′dn ā′tid) /ˌʌnkow'ɔrdn̩ˌeytɪd/ *adj.* **1.** not coordinated; awkward: *uncoordinated dancers.* **2.** not organized and joined up with other parts to make a whole: *an uncoordinated campaign.*

un•cork (un kôrk′) /ʌn'kɔrk/ *v.* [~ + *obj*] **1.** to remove the cork from. **2.** *Informal.* to release: *uncorked a knockout punch.*

un•count•a•ble (un kount′ə bəl) /ʌn'kawntəbəl/ *adj.* **1.** larger in number than can easily or possibly be counted: *a sky of uncountable stars.* **2.** (of a noun) that cannot be counted: *An uncountable noun does not have a plural form because it is thought of as a mass, (like* sand, *or* furniture*) or because it is considered abstract, (like* courage*).* **—Usage.** In this dictionary, uncountable nouns are called *noncount* and have the label [*noncount*] before them.

un•count•ed (un koun′tid) /ʌn'kawntɪd/ *adj.* **1.** not counted. **2.** very many; innumerable.

un•cou•ple (un kup′əl) /ʌn'kʌpəl/ *v.,* **-pled, -pling.** to disconnect: [*no obj*]: *The train cars uncoupled automatically.* [~ + *obj*]: *The train crew uncoupled the boxcar.*

un•couth (un ko͞oth′) /ʌn'kuwθ/ *adj.* **1.** lacking manners or grace; oafish: *an uncouth lout.* **2.** rude, uncivil, or boorish: *uncouth language; uncouth behavior.*

un•cov•er (un kuv′ər) /ʌn'kʌvər/ *v.* [~ + *obj*] **1.** to remove the cover or covering from. **2.** to lay bare; disclose; reveal: *uncovered a deadly plot.*

un•crit•i•cal (un krit′i kəl) /ʌn'krɪtɪkəl/ *adj.* too accepting; not willing to judge or form an opinion.

un•cross (un krôs′, -kros′) /ʌn'krɔs, -'krɒs/ *v.* [~ + *obj*] to change from a crossed position: *crossed and uncrossed his legs.*

unc•tu•ous (ungk′cho͞o əs) /'ʌŋktʃuwəs/ *adj.* showing a false or pretended concern or interest; insincerely earnest: *gave the new boss an unctuous greeting.* **—unc′tu•ous•ly,** *adv.* **—unc′tu•ous•ness,** *n.* [*noncount*]

un•cut (un kut′) /ʌn'kʌt/ *adj.* **1.** not cut. **2.** not shortened or condensed: *an uncut film.* **3.** in the original form; not shaped by cutting: *uncut diamonds.* **4.** not diluted; with nothing added; pure: *uncut heroin.*

un•daunt•ed (un dôn′tid, -dän′-) /ʌn'dɔntɪd, -'dɑn-/ *adj.* not discouraged; not held back or worried by danger.

un•de•cid•ed (un′di sī′did) /ˌʌndɪ'saydɪd/ *adj.* **1.** having the result in doubt: *The contest was still undecided.* **2.** not having one's mind made up: *undecided about where to shop.* **—*n.*** [*count*] **3.** a person who is undecided.

un•de•mand•ing (un′di man′ding) /ˌʌndɪ'mændɪŋ/ *adj.* **1.** not asking for or demanding much: *an undemanding child who was happy with simple toys.* **2.** not requiring much, as effort or work: *He had an undemanding job.*

un•de•mon•stra•tive (un′də mon′strə tiv) /ˌʌndə'mɒnstrətɪv/ *adj.* not showing emotion, as affection, openly; reserved; not responsive: *an undemonstrative family.* **—un′de•mon′stra•tive•ly,** *adv.*

un•de•ni•a•ble (un′di nī′ə bəl) /ˌʌndɪ'nayəbəl/ *adj.* **1.** clearly true or real: *undeniable evidence of arson.* **2.** obviously excellent: *her undeniable artistic talent.* **—un′de•ni′a•bly,** *adv.*

un•der (un′dər) /'ʌndər/ *prep.* **1.** beneath and covered by: *She stood under a tree.* **2.** below the surface of: *They swam under water.* **3.** at a point lower than: *He got a bump just under his eye.* **4.** in the position of trying to carry, support, endure, sustain, etc.: *to sink under a heavy load.* **5.** beneath the cover or disguise of: *registered under a false name.* **6.** beneath the heading of: *Classify the books under "Fiction."* **7.** below in degree, amount, etc.; less than: *These books were purchased under cost.* **8.** below in rank: *A corporal is under a lieutenant.* **9.** working for; controlled by the authority, influence, or guidance of: *studied violin under a great master.* **10.** in accordance with; following: *under the provisions of the law.* **11.** during the administration or reign of: *Those laws were passed under President Lincoln.* **12.** in the state or process of: *under construction; a bridge under repair.* **—*adv.*** **13.** below or beneath something: *Go over the fence, not under.* **14.** beneath the surface of water: *was held under by the seaweed.* **15.** in a lower degree, amount, etc.: *selling shirts for $25 and under.* **16.** in a lower position or condition. **17. go under,** [*no obj*] **a.** to give in; succumb; yield. **b.** to fail in business: *His dry cleaning business went under.* **—*adj.*** **18.** located beneath or on the underside: *the under threads of embroidery.* **19.** lower in position. **20.** lower in degree, amount, rank, etc.: *Children seven or under get in free.* **21.** being in a state of unconsciousness: *The patient was under during the surgery (= The patient was unconscious because of the effect of the anesthetic).*

under-, *prefix.* **1.** *under-* is attached to nouns and means: "a place or situation below or beneath:" *underbrush; undertow.* **2.** *under-* is also used to mean "lower in grade, rank, or dignity:" *undersheriff; understudy.* **3.** *under-* is also attached to adjectives to mean "of lesser degree, extent, or amount:" *undersized.* **4.** *under-* is also used to mean "not showing enough; too little:" *underfed.*

un•der•a•chieve (un′dər ə chēv′) /ˌʌndərə'tʃiyv/ *v.* [*no obj*], **-a•chieved, -a•chiev•ing.** **1.** to perform below the possibility or potential that one possesses as shown by tests of one's mental ability. **2.** to perform below expectations; achieve less than that which is expected. **—un′der•a•chiev′er,** *n.* [*count*]

un•der•age (un′dər āj′) /ˌʌndər'eydʒ/ *adj.* being below the legal or required age.

un•der•arm (un′dər ärm′) /'ʌndərˌɑrm/ *adj.* **1.** of, located, or made for using under the arm or in the armpit: *an underarm deodorant.* **—*n.*** [*count*] **2.** the armpit.

un•der•bel•ly (un′dər bel′ē) /'ʌndərˌbɛliy/ *n.* [*count*], *pl.* **-lies.** **1.** the lower abdomen. **2.** the underneath part of an animal behind the chest. **3.** the lower surface; underside: *the underbelly of an airplane.* **4.** a vulnerable area: *a drug aimed at the underbelly of the disease.*

un•der•bid (un′dər bid′) /ˌʌndər'bɪd/ *v.,* **-bid, -bid•ding.** to bid less than the bid of (another bidder), esp. in seeking a contract: [~ + *obj*]: *to underbid a competitor.* [*no obj*]: *They underbid and lost the contract.*

un•der•brush (un′dər brush′) /'ʌndərˌbrʌʃ/ *n.* [*noncount*] shrubs, small trees, bushes, low vines, etc., growing under the large trees in a wood or forest.

un•der•car•riage (un′dər kar′ij) /'ʌndərˌkærɪdʒ/ *n.* [*count*] **1.** the supporting framework underneath a vehicle, such as an automobile or trailer; the structure to which the wheels, tracks, or the like are attached or fitted. **2.** the portions of an aircraft below the body.

un•der•charge (*v.* un′dər chärj′; *n.* un′dər chärj′) / *v.* ˌʌndər'tʃɑrdʒ; *n.* 'ʌndərˌtʃɑrdʒ/ *v.,* **-charged, -charg•ing,** *n.* **—*v.*** **1.** to charge (a purchaser) less than the proper or fair price: [~ + *obj*]: *She must have undercharged me.* [*no obj*]: *to undercharge for a service.* **—*n.*** [*count*] **2.** a charge or price less than is proper or customary.

un•der•class•man (un′dər klas′mən) /ˌʌndər'klæsmən/ *n.* [*count*], *pl.* **-men.** a freshman or sophomore in a secondary school or college.

un•der•clothes (un′dər klōz′, -klōthz′) /'ʌndərˌklowz, -ˌklowðz/ also **un•der•cloth•ing** (un′dər klō′thing) /'ʌndərˌklowðɪŋ/ *n.* [*plural*] UNDERWEAR.

un•der•coat (un′dər kōt′) /'ʌndərˌkowt/ *n.* [*count*] **1.** a paint, sealer, or the like specially prepared for use underneath a finishing coat. **2.** a coat of such paint or sealer applied under the finishing coat.

un•der•cov•er (un′dər kuv′ər, un′dər kuv′-) /ˌʌndər'kʌvər, 'ʌndərˌkʌv-/ *adj.* [*before a noun*] **1.** secret: *an undercover investigation.* **2.** working to get confidential or secret information: *an undercover agent.* **—*adv.*** **3.** getting secret information, such as a spy: *He was working undercover for the FBI.*

un•der•cur•rent (un′dər kûr′ənt, -kur′-) /'ʌndərˌkɜrənt, -ˌkʌr-/ *n.* [*count*] **1.** a current, such as of air or water, that flows below the upper currents or surface. **2.** a hidden tendency or feeling that is typically the opposite of what is publicly shown: *an undercurrent of suspicion behind the kind words.*

un•der•cut (un′dər kut′) / ˌʌndər'kʌt / *v.* [~ + *obj*], **-cut, -cut•ting.** **1.** to cut under or beneath. **2.** to weaken or destroy the impact or effectiveness of; undermine: *They undercut all his efforts to reform the system.* **3.** to offer goods or services at a lower price or rate than (a competitor).

un•der•de•vel•oped (un′dər di vel′əpt) /ˌʌndərdɪ'vɛləpt/ *adj.* **1.** improperly developed; not developed enough. **2.** (of a photographic negative) less developed than is normal, so as to produce a relatively dark picture that does not show good contrast. **3.** DEVELOPING (def. 2): *underdeveloped countries.*

un•der•dog (un′dər dôg′, -dog′) /'ʌndərˌdɔg, -ˌdɒg/ *n.* [*count*] **1.** a person who is expected to lose in a contest or conflict. **2.** a victim of social or political injustice; someone always treated unfairly.

un•der•done (un′dər dun′) /'ʌndər'dʌn/ *adj.* **1.** not cooked enough. **2.** rare: *likes meat underdone.*

un•der•em•ployed (un′dər em ploid′) /ˌʌndərɛm'plɔyd/ *adj.* **1.** working or employed at a job that does not fully use one's skills or abilities. **2.** employed only part-time when one is available for full-time work. —**un′der•em•ploy′ment,** *n.* [*noncount*]

un•der•es•ti•mate (*v.* un′dər es′tə māt′; *n.* -mit, -māt′) / *v.* ˌʌndər'ɛstəˌmeyt; *n.* -mɪt, -ˌmeyt/ *v.,* **-mat•ed, -mat•ing,** *n.* —*v.* [~ + *obj*] **1.** to estimate at too low a value, rate, or the like: *to underestimate the costs; to underestimate an employee.* —*n.* [*count*] **2.** an estimate that is too low. —**un•der•es•ti•ma•tion** (un′dər es′tə mā′shən) /ˌʌndərˌɛstə'meyʃən/ *n.* [*count*]: *an underestimation of the impact on costs.* [*noncount*]: *guilty of some minor underestimation.*

un•der•ex•pose (un′dər ik spōz′) /ˌʌndərɪk'spowz/ *v.* [~ + *obj*], **-posed, -pos•ing.** to expose (a photograph or image) either to too little light, or to enough light but for too short a period. See -POS-.

un•der•foot (un′dər fŏŏt′) /ˌʌndər'fʊt/ *adv.* **1.** under the foot or feet: *felt the thorns underfoot.* **2.** in the way: *That dog is always getting underfoot.*

un•der•gar•ment (un′dər gär′mənt) /'ʌndərˌgɑrmənt/ *n.* [*count*] an article of underwear.

un•der•go (un′dər gō′) /ˌʌndər'gow/ *v.* [~ + *obj*], **-went, -gone, -go•ing. 1.** to be subjected to; to be put through; to experience: *has undergone surgery.* **2.** to suffer through; endure or sustain: *For years they underwent starvation.*

un•der•grad•u•ate (un′dər graj′ōō it) /ˌʌndər'grædʒuwɪt/ *n.* [*count*] **1.** a college-level student who has not received a first, esp. a bachelor's, degree. —*adj.* [*before a noun*] **2.** having the standing of an undergraduate. **3.** relating to undergraduates. See -GRAD-.

un•der•ground (*adv.* un′dər ground′; *adj., n.* -ground′) / *adv.* 'ʌndər'grawnd; *adj., n.* -ˌgrawnd/ *adv.* **1.** beneath the surface of the ground. **2.** in hiding or secrecy; not openly: *Their party went underground to fight the system.* —*adj.* **3.** existing, situated, or operating beneath the surface of the ground. **4.** hidden or secret; not open: *underground political activities.* **5.** published or produced by political or social radicals: *an underground newspaper.* **6.** experimental; avant-garde: *an underground movie.* —*n.* [*count*] **7.** the place or region beneath the surface of the ground. **8.** a secret organization fighting the established government or occupation forces: *the French underground of World War II.* **9.** *Brit.* a subway system.

un•der•growth (un′dər grōth′) /'ʌndərˌgrowθ/ *n.* UNDERBRUSH.

un•der•hand (un′dər hand′) /'ʌndərˌhænd/ *adj.* **1.** not open and completely honest; secret and crafty: *an underhand deal.* **2.** thrown, aimed, or done with the hand below the level of the shoulder and the palm turned upward and forward: *an underhand pitch.* —*adv.* **3.** with the hand below the level of the shoulder and the palm turned upward and forward: *to throw underhand.*

un•der•hand•ed (un′dər han′did) /'ʌndər'hændɪd/ *adj.* **1.** UNDERHAND. **2.** SHORT-HANDED. —**un′der•hand′ed•ly,** *adv.*

un•der•lie (un′dər lī′) /ˌʌndər'lay/ *v.* [~ + *obj*], **-lay, -lain, -ly•ing. 1.** to lie under. **2.** to form the foundation of.

un•der•line (un′dər līn′) /'ʌndərˌlayn/ *v.,* **-lined, -lin•ing,** *n.* —*v.* [~ + *obj*] **1.** to mark with a line or lines underneath; underscore: *underlined the paragraph.* **2.** to indicate the importance of; emphasize: *underlined the need for caution.* —*n.* [*count*] **3.** a line drawn beneath; underscore. See -LIN-.

un•der•ling (un′dər ling) /'ʌndərlɪŋ/ *n.* [*count*] a worker who is ranked beneath another; a subordinate.

un•der•ly•ing (un′dər lī′ing) /'ʌndərˌlayɪŋ/ *adj.* **1.** lying beneath something else: *an underlying layer of rock.* **2.** fundamental; basic: *an underlying cause.* **3.** that can be discovered only by close analysis or examination: *Loyalty is the underlying theme of the story.*

un•der•mine (un′dər mīn′ *or, esp. for 1, 3* un′dər-mīn′) /ˌʌndər'mayn *or, esp. for 1, 3* 'ʌndərˌmayn/ *v.* [~ + *obj*], **-mined, -min•ing. 1.** to weaken or destroy by degrees: *Her health was undermined by the stress of her job.* **2.** to attack by indirect, secret, or hidden means: *looking for ways to undermine her authority.* **3.** to weaken or cause to collapse by removing underlying supports.

un•der•neath (un′dər nēth′, -nēth′) /ˌʌndər'niyθ, -'niyð/ *prep.* **1.** below the surface of; directly beneath: *underneath the soil.* **2.** at the bottom of: *exploration underneath the sea.* **3.** under the control of; in a lower position than: *underneath the prime minister.* **4.** hidden or disguised by: *Underneath his bluster is a timid nature.* —*adv.* **5.** below; at a lower level or position; on the underside. —*adj.* **6.** situated below or under something else; lower.

un•der•nour•ished (un′dər nûr′isht, -nur′-) /ˌʌndər'nɜrɪʃt, -'nʌr-/ *adj.* **1.** not nourished with enough or proper food for health or growth. **2.** lacking the essential elements for proper development: *emotionally undernourished.*

un•der•pants (un′dər pants′) /'ʌndərˌpænts/ *n.* [*plural*] drawers or shorts worn under outer clothing, usually next to the skin.

un•der•pass (un′dər pas′) /'ʌndərˌpæs/ *n.* [*count*] a passage running underneath, esp. a passage for pedestrians or vehicles under a railroad or street. See -PASS-[1].

un•der•pay (un′dər pā′) /ˌʌndər'pey/ *v.* [~ + *obj*], **-paid, -pay•ing.** to pay less than is customary, deserved, or required: *to underpay employees; to underpay taxes.*

un•der•pin•ning (un′dər pin′ing) /'ʌndərˌpɪnɪŋ/ *n.* [*count*] **1.** a system of supports beneath a wall or the like. **2.** Often, **underpinnings.** [*plural*] a foundation or basis: *to strengthen the underpinnings of a friendship.*

un•der•play (un′dər plā′, un′dər plā′) /ˌʌndər'pley, 'ʌndərˌpley/ *v.* [~ + *obj*] **1.** to play (a part or scene) in a restrained way. **2.** to understate; downplay: *underplayed her vital part in their success.*

un•der•priv•i•leged (un′dər priv′ə lijd, -priv′lijd) /'ʌndər'prɪvəlɪdʒd, -'prɪvlɪdʒd/ *adj.* **1.** denied the enjoyment of the normal privileges or rights of a society because of low economic and social status: *underprivileged children.* —*n.* **2. the underprivileged,** [*plural; used with a plural verb*] the members of a society who are denied or kept from enjoying the normal privileges or rights of that society. See -PRIV-.

un•der•rate (un′dər rāt′) /ˌʌndər'reyt/ *v.* [~ + *obj*], **-rat•ed, -rat•ing.** to rate, judge, or evaluate as being too low; underestimate: *I underrated your abilities.* See -RATIO-.

un•der•score (un′dər skôr′, -skōr′) /'ʌndərˌskɔr, -ˌskowr/ *v.,* **-scored, -scor•ing,** *n.* —*v.* [~ + *obj*] **1.** UNDERLINE (def. 1). **2.** to stress; emphasize; consider as important: *He underscored the issue again and again.* **3.** to provide music or a musical soundtrack for (a film). —*n.* [*count*] **4.** a line drawn beneath something written or printed. **5.** music for a film soundtrack.

un•der•sea (un′dər sē′) /'ʌndərˌsiy/ *adj.* **1.** located, carried on, or used under the surface of the sea: *undersea exploration.* —*adv.* **2.** UNDERSEAS.

un•der•seas (un′dər sēz′) /ˌʌndər'siyz/ *adv.* beneath the surface of the sea.

un′der sec′retary or **un′der•sec′re•tar•y,** *n.* [*count; often: Under Secretary or Undersecretary*] a government official who ranks below a principal secretary.

un•der•sell (un′dər sel′) /ˌʌndər'sɛl/ *v.* [~ + *obj*], **-sold, -sell•ing. 1.** to sell more cheaply than (a competitor). **2.** to sell (something) for less than the actual value.

un•der•sexed (un′dər sekst′) /ˌʌndər'sɛkst/ *adj.* having a weaker sexual drive than is considered usual or normal.

un•der•shirt (un′dər shûrt′) /'ʌndərˌʃɜrt/ *n.* [*count*] a collarless, usually pullover undergarment for the upper body, usually of lightweight fabric with or without sleeves. See illustration at CLOTHING.

un•der•shorts (un′dər shôrts′) /'ʌndərˌʃɔrts/ *n.* [*plural*] short underpants for men and boys.

un•der•side (un′dər sīd′) /'ʌndərˌsayd/ *n.* [*count*] an under or lower side.

un•der•signed (un′dər sīnd′) /'ʌndərˌsaynd/ *adj.* **1.** being the one or ones whose signatures appear at the end of a letter or document. —*n.* [*count*] **2. the undersigned,** the person or persons signing a letter or document: *The undersigned agrees to the terms of the contract.* See -SIGN-.

un•der•sized (un′dər sīzd′) /'ʌndər'sayzd/ *adj.* smaller than the usual or normal size.

un•der•skirt (un′dər skûrt′) /'ʌndərˌskɜrt/ *n.* [*count*] a skirt, such as a petticoat, worn under another skirt or a dress.

un•der•slung (un′dər slung′) /'ʌndər'slʌŋ/ *adj.* **1.** suspended from an upper support, as the chassis of a vehicle from the axles. **2.** larger or more heavy at the bottom than the top; squat: *a plane with an underslung look.*

un•der•staffed (un′dər staft′) /ˌʌndər'stæft/ *adj.* not having enough staff; lacking adequate personnel.

un•der•stand (un′dər stand′) /ˌʌndər'stænd/ *v.* [*not: be* + *~-ing*], **-stood, -stand•ing. 1.** to see or perceive the meaning of; comprehend: [~ + *obj*]: *to understand a poem.* [~ + *(that) clause*]: *doesn't understand that he's* *not welcome.* [*no obj*]: *Don't say a word to anyone, understand?* **2.** to be familiar with; have a thorough knowledge of: [~ + *obj*]: *to understand literature; She understands businesspeople.* [*no obj*]: *She understands about businesspeople.* **3.** to interpret or comprehend in a specified way: [~ + *obj* + *as* + *obj*]: *understood the suggestion as a complaint.* [~ + *obj* + *to* + *verb*]: *We understood you to mean you agree.* **4.** to grasp the significance or importance of: [~ + *obj*]: *He doesn't understand responsibility.* [*no obj*]: *A child doesn't understand about death.* **5.** [~ + *(that) clause*] to learn or hear: *I understand that you were ill.* **6.** [~ + *(that) clause*] to regard as agreed or settled; assume: *We understand that you will repay this loan.* **7.** [~ + *obj*] to infer (something not stated): *In sentences that are commands, like* Run!, *the subject* you *is understood.* **8.** [*no obj*] to accept something tolerantly, or with forgiveness or sympathy: *If you can't come to the funeral, I will understand.* —**un′der•stand′a•ble,** *adj.*: *My French was barely understandable.* [*It* + *be* + ~ + *that clause*]: *It's understandable that you are upset.* —**un′der•stand′a•bly,** *adv.* See -STAN-.

un•der•stand•ing (un′dər stan′ding) /ˌʌndər'stændɪŋ/ *n.* **1.** [*noncount*] the mental process of a person who understands; comprehension: *My understanding of the word does not agree with yours.* **2.** [*noncount*] intellectual faculties; intelligence. **3.** [*count; usually singular*] knowledge of or familiarity with a particular thing: *an understanding of nuclear physics.* **4.** [*noncount*] a state of cooperation between people, nations, factions, etc.: *reached an understanding.* **5.** [*count*] a mutual agreement, esp. of a private or unspoken kind: *to have an understanding that each would pay a share.* **6.** [*noncount*] sympathy and compassion: *showed real understanding toward those in trouble.* —*adj.* **7.** showing tolerance or sympathy: *an understanding smile.* See -STAN-.

un•der•state (un′dər stāt′) /ˌʌndər'steyt/ *v.* [~ + *obj*], **-stat•ed, -stat•ing.** to state or represent (some result, finding, etc.) less strongly or strikingly than the facts would indicate; make (something) seem less important than it really is: *The report understates the magnitude of the disaster.* —**un•der•state•ment** (un′dər stāt′mənt, un′dər stāt′-) /ˌʌndər'steytmənt, 'ʌndərˌsteyt-/ *n.* [*count*]: *Claiming that the hurricane was inconvenient is an understatement.* See -STAT-.

un•der•stood (un′dər stŏŏd′) /ˌʌndər'stʊd/ *v.* **1.** pt. and pp. of UNDERSTAND. —*adj.* **2.** agreed upon by all parties. **3.** implied but not said in words: *The understood meaning of a danger sign is "Keep away."*

un•der•stud•y (un′dər stud′ē) /'ʌndərˌstʌdiy/ *n., pl.* **-stud•ies,** *v.,* **-stud•ied, -stud•y•ing.** —*n.* [*count*] **1.** a performer who learns the role of another in order to serve as a replacement if necessary. —*v.* [~ + *obj*] **2.** to learn (a role) in order to replace the regular performer when necessary. **3.** to act as understudy to (a performer). See -STUD-.

un•der•take (un′dər tāk′) /ˌʌndər'teyk/ *v.,* **-took, -tak•en, -tak•ing. 1.** [~ + *obj*] to take upon oneself, as a task or performance; attempt: *He undertook the job of answering the mail.* **2.** [~ + *to* + *verb*] to promise or state as a promise (to do something): *He undertook to finish the job ahead of schedule.* **3.** [~ + *obj*] to take in charge: *The lawyer undertook a new case.*

un•der•tak•er (un′dər tā′kər) /'ʌndərˌteykər/ *n.* FUNERAL DIRECTOR.

un•der•tak•ing (*n.* un′dər tā′king, un′dər tā′-; *adj.* un′dər tā′king) / *n.* ˌʌndər'teykɪŋ, 'ʌndərˌtey-; *adj.* 'ʌndərˌteykɪŋ/ *n.* [*count*] **1.** the act of a person who undertakes any task or responsibility. **2.** a task, piece of work, enterprise, etc., that is undertaken or begun. **3.** a pledge or guarantee. —*adj.* **4.** relating to the business of providing funeral or burial services.

un′der-the-coun′ter, *adj.* done secretly and often illegally: *under-the-counter sales of guns.*

un•der•things (un′dər thingz′) /'ʌndərˌθɪŋz/ *n.* [*plural*] women's underclothes.

un•der•tone (un′dər tōn′) /'ʌndərˌtown/ *n.* [*count*] **1.** a low or quiet tone of voice. **2.** an unnoticed or background sound. **3.** an underlying quality or element; undercurrent: *There is an undertone of regret in his voice.* See -TON-.

un•der•tow (un′dər tō′) /'ʌndərˌtow/ *n.* [*count*] the current of water towards the sea and usually under the surface, from waves breaking on a beach and flowing back.

un•der•val•ue (un′dər val′yo͞o) /ˌʌndər'vælyuw/ *v.* [~ + *obj*], **-ued, -u•ing. 1.** to put too low a value on: *The dollar is undervalued in foreign markets.* **2.** to have too little regard or esteem for: *an undervalued employee.* —**un•der•val•u•a•tion** (un′dər val′yo͞o ā′shən) /ˌʌndərˌvælyuw'eyʃən/ *n.* [*noncount*] See -VAL-.

un•der•wa•ter (un′dər wô′tər, -wot′ər) /'ʌndər'wɔtər, -'wɒtər/ *adj.* **1.** existing or occurring under water. **2.** designed to be used under water: *underwater cameras and lights.* —*adv.* **3.** beneath the water: *to travel underwater.*

un•der•wear (un′dər wâr′) /'ʌndərˌwɛər/ *n.* [*noncount*] clothing worn next to the skin under outer clothes. Also called **underclothes**.

un•der•weight (un′dər wāt′) /'ʌndər'weyt/ *adj.* weighing less than is usual or proper: *dangerously underweight.* [*after a noun of measurement*]: *The baby seems to be several pounds underweight.*

un•der•world (un′dər wûrld′) /'ʌndərˌwɜrld/ *n.* [*count; usually singular; usually: the* + ~] **1.** the criminal world of gangs or organized crime. **2.** (in the religious beliefs of various cultures, esp. the ancient Greeks and Romans) a place below the surface of the earth in which the spirits of the dead live on.

un•der•write (un′dər rīt′, un′dər rīt′) /ˌʌndər'rayt, 'ʌndərˌrayt/ *v.* [~ + *obj*], **-wrote, -writ•ten, -writ•ing. 1.** to give or contribute a sum of money to guarantee the success of (an undertaking): *to underwrite the building of a new library.* **2.** *Insurance.* **a.** to write one's name at the end of (a policy), thereby becoming responsible in case of certain losses. **b.** to insure, as for a certain sum. —**un′der•writ′er,** *n.* [*count*]

un•de•served (un′di zûrvd′) /ˌʌndɪ'zɜrvd/ *adj.* not deserved; not earned: *undeserved criticism.*

un•de•serv•ing (un′di zûr′ving) /ˌʌndɪ'zɜrvɪŋ/ *adj.* not deserving: *undeserving slackers.*

un•de•sir•a•ble (un′di zīər′ə bəl) /ˌʌndɪ'zayərəbəl/ *adj.* **1.** not desirable or attractive; objectionable. —*n.* [*count*] **2.** an undesirable person or thing, esp. someone considered dangerous or harmful.

un•de•vel′oped (un′di vel′əpt) /ˌʌndɪ'vɛləpt/ *adj.* not developed: *undeveloped land; an undeveloped nation.*

un•dies (un′dēz) /'ʌndiyz/ *n.* [*plural*] women's or children's underwear.

un•dig•ni•fied (un dig′ni fīd′) /ʌn'dɪgnɪˌfayd/ *adj.* clumsy; not dignified: *He sat down with an undignified crash.*

un•di•lut•ed (un′di lo͞o′tid, -dī-) /ˌʌndɪ'luwtɪd, -day-/ *adj.* **1.** not diluted; not reduced by having more liquid added. **2.** strong; pure; not mixed: *a look of undiluted hatred.*

un•dis•closed (un′dis klōzd′) /ˌʌndɪs'klowzd/ *adj.* not disclosed publicly: *paid an undisclosed amount for the house.*

un•dis•put•ed (un′dis pyo͞o′tid) /ˌʌndɪs'pyuwtɪd/ *adj.* **1.** not debatable; certain: *undisputed facts.* **2.** proven to be (the noun indicated): *the undisputed heavyweight champion.* See -PUTE-.

un•dis•tin•guished (un′di sting′gwisht) /ˌʌndɪ'stɪŋgwɪʃt/ *adj.* **1.** having no special marks or features that set one apart: *an undistinguished face.* **2.** lacking distinction: *an undistinguished career.*

un•di•vid•ed (un′di vī′did) /ˌʌndɪ'vaydɪd/ *adj.* **1.** not divided: *an undivided cake.* **2.** complete; thorough: *The teacher had the undivided attention of her class.*

un•do (un do͞o′) /ʌn'duw/ *v.* [~ + *obj*], **-did, -done, -do•ing. 1.** to reverse the doing of; repair or erase: *to undo the damage.* **2.** to untie; unfasten: *She undid her straps.*

un•do•ing (un do͞o′ing) /ʌn'duwɪŋ/ *n.* [*count; usually singular*] **1.** the reversing of what has been done. **2.** the action of ruining or destroying: *Drinking led to his undoing.* **3.** a cause of destruction or ruin: *Drinking was his undoing.* **4.** the act of unfastening or loosing.

un•done (un dun′) /ʌn'dʌn/ *adj.* [*be* + ~] **1.** not finished: *work that was still undone.* **2.** loose; not fastened: *His shirt buttons were undone.* **3.** ruined: *was undone by greed.*

un•doubt•ed (un dou′tid) /ʌn'dawtɪd/ *adj.* not doubted or disputed; accepted as true or authentic. —**un•doubt′ed•ly,** *adv.*

un•dreamed-of (un drēmd′əv′) /ʌn'driymdˌəv/ *adj.* [*before a noun*] better, more, worse, etc., than could be imagined: *undreamed-of wealth.*

un•dress (un dres′) /ʌn'drɛs/ *v.* **1.** to take the clothes off (oneself, a person, etc.); disrobe: [*no obj*]: *undressed and went to bed.* [~ + *obj*]: *undressed the baby.* —*n.* [*noncount*] **2.** the condition of being unclothed; nakedness. —**un•dressed′,** *adj.* [*be* + ~]: *was undressed and ready for bed.*

un•due (un do͞o′, -dyo͞o′) /ʌn'duw, -'dyuw/ *adj.* **1.** too much; excessive: *undue haste.* **2.** inappropriate or improper: *He used undue influence to get a job for his daughter.*

un•du•lant (un′jə lənt, un′dyə-, -də-) /ˈʌndʒələnt, ˈʌndyə-, -də-/ *adj.* wavelike in motion or pattern.

un•du•late (*v.* un′jə lāt′, un′dyə-, -də-; *adj.* -lit, -lāt′) / *v.* ˈʌndʒəˌleyt, ˈʌndyə-, -də-; *adj.* -lɪt, -ˌleyt/ *v.*, **-lat•ed, -lat•ing,** *adj.* **—***v.* **1.** to move with a wavelike motion: [*no obj*]: *The serpent undulated across the grass.* [~ + *obj*]: *She undulated her hips as she performed the dance.* **2.** [*no obj*] to have a wavy form or surface: *The hills undulated in the distance.* **3.** [*no obj*] (of a sound) to rise and fall in pitch: *A siren undulated.* **—***adj.* **4.** Also, **un′du•lat′•ed.** having a wavelike form or surface; wavy. **—un•du•la•tion** (un′jə lā′shən, -dyə-, -də-) /ˌʌndʒəˈleyʃən, -dyə-, -də-/ *n.* [*noncount*]: *the sea's undulation.* [*count*]: *the undulations of the dancer's hips.*

un•du•ly (un do͞o′lē, -dyo͞o′-) /ʌnˈduwliy, -ˈdyuw-/ *adv.* **1.** too much; excessively. **2.** inappropriately or improperly.

un•dy•ing (un dī′ing) /ʌnˈdayɪŋ/ *adj.* eternal: *undying fame.*

un•earned (un ûrnd′) /ʌnˈɜrnd/ *adj.* **1.** not received in exchange for labor or services: *taxing so-called unearned income.* **2.** unmerited; undeserved: *unearned punishment.*

un•earth (un ûrth′) /ʌnˈɜrθ/ *v.* [~ + *obj*] **1.** to dig out of the earth: *to unearth the ancient city of Troy.* **2.** to bring to light; make known: *to unearth an old rumor.*

un•earth•ly (un ûrth′lē) /ʌnˈɜrθliy/ *adj.* **1.** seeming not to belong to this earth or world. **2.** supernatural; ghostly; weird: *an unearthly cry.* **3.** unreasonable or absurd: *to get up at an unearthly hour.*

un•eas•y (un ē′zē) /ʌnˈiyziy/ *adj.*, **-i•er, -i•est. 1.** not easy in body or mind; perturbed: *I was uneasy about the upcoming election.* **2.** not easy in manner; awkward; not comfortable: *felt uneasy in her presence.* **3.** insecure: *an uneasy peace.* **—un•eas•i•ly** (un ē′zə lē) /ʌnˈiyzəliy/ *adv.* **—un•eas′i•ness,** *n.* [*noncount*]

un•e•co•nom•i•cal (un′ek ə nom′i kəl, un′ē kə-) /ˌʌnɛkəˈnɒmɪkəl, ˌʌniykə-/ *adj.* not economically practical; wasteful.

un•ed•u•cat•ed (un ej′ə kā′tid) /ʌnˈɛdʒəˌkeytɪd/ *adj.* not educated formally; inadequately educated.

un•em•ploy•a•ble (un′em ploi′ə bəl) /ˌʌnɛmˈplɔyəbəl/ *adj.* unsuitable for employment; unable to find or keep a job.

un•em•ployed (un′em ploid′) /ˌʌnɛmˈplɔyd/ *adj.* **1.** not employed; having no job. **2.** not currently in use. **3.** not productively used: *unemployed capital.* **—***n.* **4. the unemployed,** [*plural; used with a plural verb*] persons without jobs. **—un′em•ploy′ment,** *n.* [*noncount*]

un•en•vi•a•ble (un en′vē ə bəl) /ʌnˈɛnviyəbəl/ *adj.* not to be envied; undesirable: *the unenviable job of firing people.*

un•e•qual (un ē′kwəl) /ʌnˈiykwəl/ *adj.* **1.** not equal; not of the same measurement, quantity, or status: *unequal portions; unequal pay; unequal rank.* **2.** [*be* + ~ + *to* + *obj*] not adequate or enough, such as in amount, power, or ability: *He's unequal to the task.* **—***n.* **3. unequals,** [*plural*] persons or things not equal to each other. **—un•e′qual•ly,** *adv.* See -EQUA-.

un•e•qualed (un ē′kwəld) /ʌnˈiykwəld/ *adj.* not equaled; peerless: *the unequaled energy of the sun.* Also, *esp. Brit.,* **un•e′qualled.** See -EQUA-.

un•e•quiv•o•cal (un′i kwiv′ə kəl) /ˌʌnɪˈkwɪvəkəl/ *adj.* **1.** having only one possible meaning or interpretation; not ambiguous; clear: *an unequivocal answer.* **2.** absolute; unqualified: *an unequivocal success.* See -EQUA-, -VOC-.

un•err•ing (un ûr′ing, -er′-) /ʌnˈɜrɪŋ, -ˈɛr-/ *adj.* **1.** not going astray or missing the mark: *unerring aim.* **2.** always right or apt; infallible: *unerring good taste.* **—un•err′ing•ly,** *adv.*

un•e•ven (un ē′vən) /ʌnˈiyvən/ *adj.* **1.** not level or flat; rough: *an uneven surface.* **2.** not uniform; varying; inconsistent: *a novel of uneven quality.* **3.** not balanced: *uneven treatment of candidates in the press.* **4.** not balanced; not symmetrical or parallel: *an uneven hemline.* **5.** (of a number) odd; not divisible into two equal integers: *The numerals 3, 5, and 7 are uneven.* **—un•e′ven•ly,** *adv.*

un•e•vent•ful (un′i vent′fəl) /ˌʌnɪˈvɛntfəl/ *adj.* routine; normal: *an uneventful day.* **—un′e•vent′ful•ly,** *adv.* See -VEN-.

un•ex•cep•tion•al (un′ik sep′shə nl) /ˌʌnɪkˈsɛpʃənl/ *adj.* not exceptional; ordinary: *an unexceptional student.*

un•ex•cit•ing (un′ik sī′ting) /ˌʌnɪkˈsaytɪŋ/ *adj.* not exciting; boring: *an unexciting game of golf.*

un•ex•pect•ed (un′ik spek′tid) /ˌʌnɪkˈspɛktɪd/ *adj.* not expected; unforeseen. **—un′ex•pect′ed•ly,** *adv.*

un•fail•ing (un fā′ling) /ʌnˈfeylɪŋ/ *adj.* **1.** steadfast; steady; dependable: *unfailing in his loyalty.* **2.** endless; inexhaustible: *unfailing good humor.* **—un•fail′ing•ly,** *adv.*

un•fair (un fâr′) /ʌnˈfɛər/ *adj.* **1.** not fair; not agreeing with or following standards of justice, honesty, or the like: *The students claimed that the test was unfair.* [*be* + ~(+ *of* + *obj*) + *to* + *verb*]: *It was very unfair (of the teacher) to give the students so much homework on a holiday weekend.* **2.** beyond what is proper or fitting: *an unfair advantage.* **—un•fair′ly,** *adv.*

un•faith•ful (un fāth′fəl) /ʌnˈfeyθfəl/ *adj.* **1.** not faithful; false to one's duty, what one should do, or what one has promised; disloyal. **2.** not sexually faithful to a spouse or lover. **3.** not accurate or reliable; inexact: *an unfaithful translation.* **—un•faith′ful•ly,** *adv.*

un•fa•mil•iar (un′fə mil′yər) /ˌʌnfəˈmɪlyər/ *adj.* **1.** not acquainted with: *to be unfamiliar with modern art.* **2.** different; unusual: *an unfamiliar treat.*

un•fash•ion•a•ble (un fash′ə nə bəl) /ʌnˈfæʃənəbəl/ *adj.* **1.** not fashionable; old-fashioned; out-of-date. **2.** not popular: *unfashionable beliefs.* [*It* + *be* + ~ + *to* + *verb*]: *It was unfashionable to hold such views.* **—un•fash′ion•a•bly,** *adv.*

un•fas•ten (un fas′ən) /ʌnˈfæsən/ *v.* to (cause to) be undone or opened: [~ + *obj*]: *He unfastened his seat belt.* [*no obj*]: *The seat belt unfastened by itself.*

un•fath•om•a•ble (un fa*th*′əm ə bəl) /ʌnˈfæðəməbəl/ *adj.* that cannot be understood or explained: *an unfathomable mystery.*

un•fa•vor•a•ble (un fā′vər ə bəl) /ʌnˈfeyvərəbəl/ *adj.* **1.** not favorable; contrary: *unfavorable winds.* **2.** not predicting good news: *unfavorable omens.* **3.** not good: *unfavorable reviews of your book.* **—un•fa′vor•a•bly,** *adv.*

un•feel•ing (un fē′ling) /ʌnˈfiylɪŋ/ *adj.* **1.** having no sensation; numb. **2.** not sympathetic; callous; hard-hearted: *an unfeeling remark.* **—un•feel′ing•ly,** *adv.*

un•feigned (un fānd′) /ʌnˈfeynd/ *adj.* not pretended; real: *Her face showed unfeigned surprise.*

un•fet•tered (un fet′ərd) /ʌnˈfɛtərd/ *adj.* **1.** not restrained by fetters. **2.** free; not restricted; not limited: *felt unfettered by conventional morality.*

un•fin•ished (un fin′isht) /ʌnˈfɪnɪʃt/ *adj.* not finished; not completed: *some unfinished business.*

un•fit (un fit′) /ʌnˈfɪt/ *adj.* **1.** [*be* + ~]not adapted or suited; unsuitable: [~ + *for*]: *Her office is unfit for more than two occupants.* [~ + *to* + *verb*]: *food that is unfit to eat.* **2.** not qualified; incompetent: *unfit parents.* **3.** not physically fit or well: *feeling unfit with a cold.*

un•flag•ging (un flag′ing) /ʌnˈflægɪŋ/ *adj.* not tiring, slowing, or stopping: *his unflagging enthusiasm for his work.*

un•flap•pa•ble (un flap′ə bəl) /ʌnˈflæpəbəl/ *adj.* not easily upset or confused, esp. in a crisis.

un•flinch•ing (un flin′ching) /ʌnˈflɪntʃɪŋ/ *adj.* firm; courageous: *an unflinching refusal to surrender.*

un•fold (un fōld′) /ʌnˈfowld/ *v.* **1.** to (cause to) come out of a folded state; (cause to) be spread or opened out: [~ + *obj*]: *The bird unfolded its wings and flew off.* [*no obj*]: *The flower petals unfolded in the sun.* **2.** [*no obj*] to be revealed or displayed; become clear: *The movie's plot gradually unfolded.*

un•fore•seen (un′fôr sēn′, -fōr-) /ˌʌnfərˈsiyn, -fowr-/ *adj.* not foreseen; happening unexpectedly: *unforeseen difficulties.*

un•for•get•ta•ble (un′fər get′ə bəl) /ˌʌnfərˈgɛtəbəl/ *adj.* staying in one's memory: *an unforgettable adventure.* **—un′for•get′ta•bly,** *adv.*

un•for•giv•a•ble (un′fər giv′ə bəl) /ˌʌnfərˈgɪvəbəl/ *adj.* so bad that it cannot be forgiven: *an unforgivable insult.* **—un′for•giv′a•bly,** *adv.*

un•for•giv•ing (un′fər giv′ing) /ˌʌnfərˈgɪvɪŋ/ *adj.* not willing to forgive or make allowances: *an unforgiving boss who does not tolerate mistakes.*

un•formed (un fôrmd′) /ʌnˈfɔrmd/ *adj.* **1.** not definitely shaped; shapeless or formless. **2.** undeveloped; crude.

un•for•tu•nate (un fôr′chə nit) /ʌnˈfɔrtʃənɪt/ *adj.* **1.** suffering from bad luck; unlucky; hapless: *an unfortunate series of bad investments.* **2.** regrettable; unsuitable; not appropriate: *made an unfortunate remark about your weight.* **—***n.* [*count*] **3.** an unfortunate person. **—un•for′tu•nate•ly,** *adv.* See -FORTUN-.

un•found•ed (un foun′did) /ʌnˈfawndɪd/ *adj.* not based on fact or on what is real; without foundation; groundless: *his unfounded fears that his coworkers didn't like him.*

un•friend•ly (un frend′lē) /ʌn'frɛndliy/ *adj.,* **-li•er, -li•est,** *adv.* **—***adj.* **1.** not friendly or kind; hostile: *a city with unfriendly natives.* **2.** unfavorable: *an unfriendly environment of snow and ice.* **—***adv.* **3.** in an unfriendly manner: *acting unfriendly.* **—un•friend′li•ness,** *n.* [*noncount*]

un•frocked (un frokt′) /ʌn'frɒkt/ *adj.* having one's rank or position in a church taken away.

un•furl (un fûrl′) /ʌn'fɜrl/ *v.* to spread or shake out from a furled state; unfold: [~ + *obj*]: *The soldiers unfurled the flag.* [*no obj*]: *The flag unfurled and fluttered in the breeze.*

un•fur•nished (un fûr′nisht) /ʌn'fɜrnɪʃt/ *adj.* lacking furniture: *an unfurnished apartment.*

un•gain•ly (un gān′lē) /ʌn'geynliy/ *adj.,* **-li•er, -li•est.** not graceful; awkward; clumsy: *an ungainly walrus.*

un•gen•er•ous (un jen′ər əs) /ʌn'dʒɛnərəs/ *adj.* **1.** not generous with money; stingy. **2.** unkind; petty; spiteful: *an ungenerous comment.* **—un•gen′er•ous•ly,** *adv.*

un•god•ly (un god′lē) /ʌn'gɒdliy/ *adj.,* **-li•er, -li•est. 1.** not accepting God or a particular religion or any religious belief; against religion. **2.** sinful; wicked: *an ungodly life.* **3.** outrageous; shocking; awful: *Midnight was an ungodly hour for visitors.* **—un•god′li•ness,** *n.* [*noncount*]

un•gov•ern•a•ble (un guv′ər nə bəl) /ʌn'gʌvərnəbəl/ *adj.* impossible to govern, rule, or hold back; uncontrollable.

un•gra•cious (un grā′shəs) /ʌn'greyʃəs/ *adj.* not courteous; not polite; ill-mannered: *an ungracious refusal.*

un•grate•ful (un grāt′fəl) /ʌn'greytfəl/ *adj.* **1.** showing no gratitude: *an ungrateful bunch of grasping relatives.* **2.** disagreeable; unpleasant: *an ungrateful task.* See -GRAT-.

un•guard•ed (un gär′did) /ʌn'gɑrdɪd/ *adj.* **1.** not guarded; unprotected; undefended: *an unguarded post.* **2.** open; frank: *an unguarded manner.* **3.** not cautious or discreet; careless: *In an unguarded moment he told her the truth.*

un•guent (ung′gwənt) /'ʌŋgwənt/ *n.* [*count*] a soothing or healing ointment.

un•hand (un hand′) /ʌn'hænd/ *v.* [~ + *obj*] to remove the hands from; let go of.

un•hap•py (un hap′ē) /ʌn'hæpiy/ *adj.,* **-pi•er, -pi•est. 1.** sad; miserable; wretched. **2.** unfortunate; unlucky: *met an unhappy fate.* **3.** not suitable: *an unhappy choice of words.* **—un•hap•pi•ly** (un hap′ə lē) /ʌn'hæpəliy/ *adv.*: *unhappily married.* **—un•hap′pi•ness,** *n.* [*noncount*] **—Related Words.** UNHAPPY is an adjective, UNHAPPILY is an adverb, UNHAPPINESS is a noun: *He was very unhappy to hear such bad news. She frowned unhappily as they voted against her proposal. His life was filled with unhappiness and sorrow.*

un•health•y (un hel′thē) /ʌn'hɛlθiy/ *adj.,* **-i•er, -i•est. 1.** not in a state of good or normal health; diseased: *has been unhealthy for years.* **2.** showing signs of, or resulting from, bad health: *skin with an unhealthy pallor.* **3.** not healthful: *an unhealthy diet.* **4.** morally harmful; corrupt; unnatural: *an unhealthy interest in violence.*

un•heard (un hûrd′) /ʌn'hɜrd/ *adj.* not heard; not perceived by the ear.

unheard′-of′, *adj.* **1.** not seen before and not expected; unprecedented: *an unheard-of scientific advance.* **2.** outrageous; shocking; offensive: *his unheard-of extravagance.* **3.** not previously known; not famous: *the debut of an unheard-of singer.*

un•hinge (un hinj′) /ʌn'hɪndʒ/ *v.* [~ + *obj*], **-hinged, -hing•ing. 1.** to remove from hinges: *to unhinge a door.* **2.** to throw into confusion or turmoil; upset: *threats that could unhinge a timid soul.*

un•ho•ly (un hō′lē) /ʌn'howliy/ *adj.,* **-li•er, -li•est. 1.** sinful; wicked. **2.** dreadful; outrageous; awful; ungodly: *neighbors making an unholy racket.*

un•hook (un ho͝ok′) /ʌn'hʊk/ *v.* **1.** to unfasten or detach by or as if by undoing a hook or hooks: [~ + *obj*]: *to unhook railroad cars.* [*no obj*]: *The caboose unhooked and rolled down the hill.* **2.** [~ + *obj*] to remove or detach from a hook.

un•hur•ried (un hûr′ēd, -hur′-) /ʌn'hɜriyd, -'hʌr-/ *adj.* not hurried; leisurely: *an unhurried decision.* **—un•hur′ried•ly,** *adv.*

-uni-, *root.* -*uni*- comes from Latin, where it has the meaning "one." This meaning is found in such words as: REUNION, REUNITE, UNICAMERAL, UNICORN, UNICYCLE, UNIFORM, UNIFY, UNILATERAL, UNION, UNIQUE, UNISEX, UNIT, UNITE, UNIVERSITY.

u•ni•cam•er•al (yo͞o′ni kam′ər əl) /ˌyuwnɪ'kæmərəl/ *adj.* (of a legislative body) made up of a single chamber or house. See -UNI-.

u•ni•corn (yo͞o′ni kôrn′) /'yuwnɪˌkɔrn/ *n.* [*count*] an imaginary creature resembling a horse, with a single horn in the center of its forehead. See -UNI-.

u•ni•cy•cle (yo͞o′nə si′kəl) /'yuwnəˌsaykəl/ *n.* [*count*] a vehicle with one wheel, esp. a pedal-driven device kept upright and steered by body balance. See -UNI-.

un•i•den•ti•fied (un′ī den′tə fīd) /ˌʌnay'dɛntəfayd/ *adj.* not yet identified; unknown.

u•ni•form (yo͞o′nə fôrm′) /'yuwnəˌfɔrm/ *adj.* **1.** identical, the same, or consistent, as from example to example or place to place: *a uniform building code.* **2.** without changes in detail; constant; not changing: *a uniform surface, without dents.* **—***n.* **3.** dress of distinctive style worn by the members of a given profession, organization, or rank: [*count*]: *nurses wearing white uniforms.* [*noncount*]: *He wasn't in uniform.* **—u•ni•form•i•ty** (yo͞o′nə-fôr′mi tē) /ˌyuwnə'fɔrmɪtiy/ *n.* [*noncount*] **—u′ni•form′-ly,** *adv.*: *products of uniformly high quality.* See -UNI-, -FORM-.

u•ni•fy (yo͞o′nə fī′) /'yuwnəˌfay/ *v.* [~ + *obj*], **-fied, -fy•ing.** to cause to become a single unit; unite; merge: *set out to unify the kingdoms of Britain.* **—u•ni•fi•ca•tion** (yo͞o′nə fi kā′shən) /ˌyuwnəfɪ'keyʃən/ *n.* [*noncount*] See -UNI-.

u•ni•lat•er•al (yo͞o′nə lat′ər əl) /ˌyuwnə'lætərəl/ *adj.* undertaken or done by or on behalf of one side, party, or group only; not mutual: *unilateral disarmament; a unilateral decision.* See -UNI-, -LAT-[2].

un•i•mag′i•na•ble (un′i maj′ə nə bəl) /ˌʌnɪ'mædʒənəbəl/ *adj.* impossible or difficult to imagine: *unimaginable horrors.*

un•im•ag•i•na•tive (un′i maj′i nə tiv) /ˌʌnɪ'mædʒɪnətɪv/ *adj.* not using one's imagination; not creative. **—un′im•ag′i•na•tive•ly,** *adv.*

un•im•peach•a•ble (un′im pē′chə bəl) /ˌʌnɪm'piytʃəbəl/ *adj.* above suspicion; that cannot be doubted: *heard it from an unimpeachable source.*

un•in•hab•it•a•ble (un′in hab′i tə bəl) /ˌʌnɪn'hæbɪtəbəl/ *adj.* that cannot be lived in; impossible to live in: *an uninhabitable wasteland.* See -HAB-.

un•in•hab•it•ed (un′in hab′i•tid) /ˌʌnɪn'hæbɪtɪd/ *adj.* having no inhabitants: *an uninhabited wilderness.* See -HAB-.

un•in•hib•it•ed (un′in hib′i tid) /ˌʌnɪn'hɪbɪtɪd/ *adj.* not inhibited; free; spontaneous. See -HAB-.

un•i•ni•ti•at•ed (un′i ni′shē ā′tid) /ˌʌnɪ'nɪʃiyˌeytɪd/ *adj.* **1.** not initiated; inexperienced: *was uninitiated in the ways of the church.* **—***n.* **2. the uninitiated,** [*plural; used with a plural verb*] people without experience or knowledge of something.

un•in•tel•li•gi•ble (un′in tel′i jə bəl) /ˌʌnɪn'tɛlɪdʒəbəl/ *adj.* that cannot be understood, seen clearly, or read clearly. **—un′in•tel′li•gi•bly,** *adv.*

un•in•tended (un′in ten′did) /ˌʌnɪn'tɛndɪd/ *adj.* accidental: *an unintended victim of gunfire.* See -TEND-.

un•in•ten•tion•al (un′in ten′shə nl) /ˌʌnɪn'tɛnʃənl̩/ *adj.* not intentional or deliberate; unplanned: *an unintentional insult.*

un•in•ter•est•ed (un in′tər ə stid, -trə stid, -tə res′tid) /ʌn'ɪntərəstɪd, -trəstɪd, -təˌrɛstɪd/ *adj.* not interested: *seemed uninterested in others' problems.* **—Usage.** See DISINTERESTED.

un•in•ter•est•ing (un in′trə sting) /ʌn'ɪntrəstɪŋ/ *adj.* not interesting: *an uninteresting subject.* **—un•in′ter•est•ing•ly,** *adv.*

un•in•ter•rupt•ed (un′in tə rup′tid) /ˌʌnɪntə'rʌptɪd/ *adj.* continuing without interruption: *two hours of uninterrupted music broadcasts.* See -RUPT-.

un•in•vit•ed (un′in vī′tid) /ˌʌnɪn'vaytɪd/ *adj.* not invited: *an uninvited guest.*

un•in•vit•ing (un′in vī′ting) /ˌʌnɪn'vaytɪŋ/ *adj.* not appealing or attractive: *an uninviting meal.*

un•ion (yo͞on′yən) /'yuwnyən/ *n.* **1.** [*noncount*] the act of uniting or the state of being united. **2.** [*count*] something formed by uniting two or more things; combination: *a union of like minds.* **3.** [*count*] a number of persons, states, etc., joined or associated together for some common purpose: *a labor union.* **4.** [*count; often used in a proper name; often: the* + ~*; Union*] a uniting of states or nations into one political body: *the Union of South Africa.* **5.** [*count*] a uniting in marriage or sexual intercourse. See -UNI-.

un•ion•ize (yo͞on′yə nīz′) /'yuwnyəˌnayz/ *v.,* **-ized, -iz•ing.** to organize (workers) into a labor union: [~ + *obj*]: *to unionize the workers.* [*no obj*]: *The workers unionized.*

—un•ion•ism (yo͞on′yə niz′əm) /'yuwnyə,nızəm/ *n.* [*noncount*] See -UNI-.

u•nique (yo͞o nēk′) /yuw'niyk/ *adj.* **1.** existing as the only one of its kind or type, or as the only example: *a masterpiece unique in all the world.* **2.** having no like or equal: *a unique individual.* **3.** [*be* + ~ (+ *to*)] limited in occurrence to a certain class, situation, location, or area: *The kangaroo is unique to Australia.* **4.** not typical; unusual: *She has a unique ability to inspire people.* **—u•nique′ly,** *adv.* **—u•nique′ness,** *n.* [*noncount*] See -UNI-.

u•ni•sex (yo͞o′nə seks′) /'yuwnə,sɛks/ *adj.* designed or suitable for both sexes: *unisex clothes.* See -UNI-, -SECT-.

u•ni•son (yo͞o′nə sən, -zən) /'yuwnəsən, -zən/ *n.* [*noncount*] **1.** the state of two or more musical tones, voices, etc., being at the same pitch or note. ***—Idiom.*** **2. in unison, a.** in perfect agreement or accord: *My feelings are in unison with yours.* **b.** at the same time and in the same way: *to march in unison.* See -UNI-, -SON-.

u•nit (yo͞o′nit) /'yuwnıt/ *n.* [*count*] **1.** a single thing; one person or thing. **2.** any group of things or persons thought of as a single thing: *The team formed a unit.* **3.** one of the individuals, parts, or elements into which a whole may be divided. **4.** one of a number of things that are identical or equivalent in function or form: *a rental unit.* **5.** a machine, part, or system of machines having a specified purpose, often an apparatus or piece that is part of a bigger piece: *a heating unit.* **6.** a specified amount of a quantity, as of length, volume, or time, by comparison with which any other quantity of the same kind is measured: *a unit of measurement, as an inch.* **7.** the least positive integer; one. See -UNI-.

u•nite (yo͞o nīt′) /yuw'nayt/ *v.,* **u•nit•ed, u•nit•ing. 1.** to (cause to) be joined so as to form a single whole or unit: [~ + *obj* + *into* + *obj*]: *to unite all the states into one country.* [*no obj;* (~ + *into* + *obj*)]: *The states united into one country.* **2.** to (cause to) adhere or stick together: [~ + *obj*]: *Use glue to unite the two sections.* [*no obj*]: *The two sections won't unite.* **3.** to (cause to) be in a state of mutual sympathy or agreement, or to have a common opinion, attitude, goal, etc.: [*no obj*]: *They united in their opposition to him.* [~ + *obj*]: *They united their forces.* See -UNI-.

u•nit•ed (yo͞o nī′tid) /yuw'naytıd/ *adj.* **1.** joined, as in love, agreement, sympathy, or common interests: *united in their views.* **2.** [*in proper names of countries*] (of states) joined to make a political unit: *the United States of America.* See -UNI-.

u•ni•ty (yo͞o′ni tē) /'yuwnıtiy/ *n., pl.* **-ties. 1.** [*noncount*] the state of being one; oneness: *the unity of the nation.* **2.** [*noncount*] a whole made by combining all its parts into one: *the underlying unity of all human beings.* **3.** oneness of mind or feeling; concord; agreement: [*count; usually singular*]: *called for a unity of purpose.* [*noncount*]: *a call for unity and an end to discord.* **4.** [*noncount*] (in literature and art) harmony among the elements of a work producing a single major effect. See -UNI-.

u•ni•ver•sal (yo͞o′nə vûr′səl) /,yuwnə'vɜrsəl/ *adj.* **1.** of, relating to, or characteristic of all members or of the whole: *A universal characteristic of language is the ability to form questions.* **2.** affecting, concerning, or involving all: *universal schooling for all children.* **3.** that applies to all cases or that applies everywhere: *a universal cure.* **4.** used or understood by all: *a universal language.* **5.** present or existing everywhere: *universal truths.* **—*n.*** [*count*] **6.** a cultural pattern or way of thinking or acting found in every known society or common to all members of a particular culture. **7.** a trait or property of language that exists or has the potential to exist in all languages. **8.** UNIVERSAL JOINT. **—u•ni•ver•sal•i•ty** (yo͞o′nə vər sal′i tē) /,yuwnəvər'sælıtiy/ *n.* [*noncount*] **—u′ni•ver′sal•ly,** *adv.* See -UNI-, -VERT-.

u′niver′sal joint′, *n.* [*count*] *Mach.* a joint or piece that couples or joins two rotating shafts arranged at an angle to one another.

U′niver′sal Prod′uct Code′, *n.* [*count*] a standardized bar code in widespread use esp. at retail store checkout counters.

u•ni•verse (yo͞o′nə vûrs′) /'yuwnə,vɜrs/ *n.* **1.** all the known or imagined objects, matter, and events throughout space; the cosmos: [*noncount; usually:the* + ~]: *the secrets of the universe.* [*count*]: *Can you imagine a universe that is not infinite?* **2.** [*count*] a world or sphere in which something exists: *a universe of possibilities.* See -UNI-, -VERT-.

u•ni•ver•si•ty (yo͞o′nə vûr′si tē) /,yuwnə'vɜrsıtiy/ *n.* [*count*], *pl.* **-ties.** an institution of learning of the highest level that is made up of a college of liberal arts, a program of graduate studies, and several professional schools and is allowed to award both undergraduate and graduate degrees. See -UNI-, -VERT-.

un•just (un just′) /ʌn'dʒʌst/ *adj.* not just; lacking in justice or fairness: *unjust punishment.* **—un•just′ly,** *adv.* See -JUS-.

un•kempt (un kempt′) /ʌn'kɛmpt/ *adj.* **1.** not combed: *unkempt hair.* **2.** messy; disheveled: *an unkempt appearance.*

un•kind (un kīnd′) /ʌn'kaynd/ *adj.,* **-er, -est.** lacking in kindness or mercy; severe: *an unkind remark.* [*be* + ~ + to]: *He's unkind to animals.* **—un•kind′ness,** *n.* [*noncount*]

un•kind•ly (un kīnd′lē) /ʌn'kayndliy/ *adj.,* **-li•er, -li•est. 1.** not kindly; unkind; ill-natured; mean. **2.** rough, inclement, or bleak, as weather or climate. **—*adv.* 3.** in an unkind manner: *spoke unkindly to the child.* **4.** as being unkind: *to take a comment unkindly.*

un•know•ing (un nō′ing) /ʌn'nowıŋ/ *adj.* ignorant or unaware.

un•known (un nōn′) /ʌn'nown/ *adj.* **1.** not known; not within the range of knowledge, experience, or understanding; strange; unfamiliar. **2.** not discovered, explored, identified, or figured out: *an unknown amount.* **3.** not widely known; not famous; obscure: *an unknown author.* **—*n.*** [*count*] **4.** a person or thing that is unknown. **5.** a symbol representing an unknown quantity: *In algebra an unknown is frequently represented by a letter from the last part of the alphabet, as x, y,* or *z.*

un•lace (un lās′) /ʌn'leys/ *v.* [~ + *obj*], **-laced, -lac•ing.** to loosen or undo the lacing or laces of (shoes, etc.).

un•law•ful (un lô′fəl) /ʌn'lɔfəl/ *adj.* not lawful; contrary to law; illegal: *unlawful acts.* **—un•law′ful•ly,** *adv.* **—un•law′ful•ness,** *n.* [*noncount*]

un•learn (un lûrn′) /ʌn'lɜrn/ *v.* [~ + *obj*] to rid one's mind of (ideas or behavior) as being false or harmful: *to unlearn bad habits.*

un•learn•ed (un lûr′nid *for 1, 2* un lûrnd′ *for 3, 4*) /ʌn'lɜrnıd *for 1, 2* ʌn'lɜrnd *for 3, 4* / *adj.* **1.** uneducated; ignorant. **2.** not scholarly; not learned. **3.** not having been learned: *an unlearned lesson.* **4.** known or possessed without having been learned, as behavior.

un•leash (un lēsh′) /ʌn'liyʃ/ *v.* [~ + *obj*] to release from or as if from a leash; let loose: *He unleashed the dogs. The storm unleashed its fury.*

un•leav•ened (un lev′ənd) /ʌn'lɛvənd/ *adj.* (of bread or dough) made without yeast.

un•less (un les′) /ʌn'lɛs/ *conj.* except under the circumstances that: *We'll be there at nine, unless the train is late.*

un•let•tered (un let′ərd) /ʌn'lɛtərd/ *adj.* **1.** uneducated; ignorant. **2.** illiterate; unable to read. **3.** not marked with letters, as a tombstone. See -LIT-.

un•like (un līk′) /ʌn'layk/ *adj.* **1.** different; not alike: *They gave unlike accounts of the incident.* **—*prep.* 2.** different from: *She is unlike my sister.* **3.** not typical of: *It is unlike him to forget a name.*

un•like•ly (un līk′lē) /ʌn'laykliy/ *adj.,* **-li•er, -li•est,** *adv.* **—*adj.* 1.** not likely to be or occur; improbable; doubtful: *an unlikely outcome.* [*It* + *be* + ~ + *(that) clause*]: *It is unlikely that she knows him.* [*be* + ~ + *to* + *verb*]: *is unlikely to know him.* **2.** [*before a noun*] having little chance of success; unpromising: *an unlikely candidate for the job.* **—*adv.* 3.** in an unlikely way. **—un•like′li•hood′,** *n.* [*noncount*]

un•lim•it•ed (un lim′i tid) /ʌn'lımıtıd/ *adj.* **1.** having no limitations: *an unlimited bus pass.* **2.** infinite; vast: *unlimited space.* See -LIM-.

un•load (un lōd′) /ʌn'lowd/ *v.* **1.** [~ + *obj*] to take the load or cargo from: *to unload a ship.* **2.** to discharge (cargo, passengers, etc.): [~ + *obj*]: *The sailors began to unload the cargo.* [*no obj*]: *The ship can't unload now.* **3.** [~ + *obj*] to remove the bullets from: *to unload a gun.* **4.** [~ + *obj*] to express freely; pour out: *unloaded his grief.* **5.** [~ + *obj*] to get rid of (goods, shares of stock, etc.) by sale in large quantities.

un•lock (un lok′) /ʌn'lɒk/ *v.* **1.** to undo the lock of: [~ + *obj*]: *to unlock a car; to unlock a door.* [*no obj*]: *The door unlocks easily.* **2.** [~ + *obj*] to make open; disclose: *to unlock the secrets of one's heart.*

un•looked′-for′ (un lo͝okt′) /ʌn'lʊkt/ *adj.* not expected, anticipated, or foreseen.

un•loose (un lo͞os′) /ʌn'luws/ *v.* [~ + *obj*], **-loosed, -loos•ing. 1.** to loosen or relax (the grasp, hold, fingers, etc.). **2.** to let loose or set free; free from restraint. **3.** to undo or untie (a fastening, knot, bond, etc.).

un•luck•y (un luk′ē) /ʌn'lʌkiy/ *adj.*, **-i•er, -i•est. 1.** (of a person) not lucky; lacking good fortune. **2.** causing or believed to cause bad luck: *an unlucky number.* —**un•luck•i•ly** (un luk′ə lē) /ʌn'lʌkəliy/ *adv.* —**un•luck′i•ness,** *n.* [*noncount*]

un•made (un mād′) /ʌn'meyd/ *adj.* (of a bed) not made up.

un•man•ly (un man′lē) /ʌn'mænliy/ *adj.*, **-li•er, -li•est. 1.** not manly; not characteristic of a man. **2.** effeminate.

un•manned (un mand′) /ʌn'mænd/ *adj.* without the physical presence of people in control: *an unmanned spacecraft.*

un•man•ner•ly (un man′ər lē) /ʌn'mænərliy/ *adj.* not mannerly; impolite; rude; not courteous.

un•marked (un märkt′) /ʌn'mɑrkt/ *adj.* **1.** not yet marked: *unmarked term papers.* **2.** having no identifying markings: *an unmarked police car.*

un•mask (un mask′) /ʌn'mæsk/ *v.* **1.** to take off a mask or disguise (from): [~ + *obj*]: *He unmasked her at the costume party.* [*no obj*]: *All the guests eventually unmasked.* **2.** [~ + *obj* (+ *as* + *obj*)] to reveal the true character of; disclose; expose: *He was unmasked as the killer.*

un•matched (un macht′) /ʌn'mætʃt/ *adj.* not matched or equaled; superior: *He was unmatched in selling ability.*

un•men•tion•a•ble (un men′shə nə bəl) /ʌn'mɛnʃənəbəl/ *adj.* **1.** not appropriate, unfit, or improper to be mentioned or spoken about: *an unmentionable subject.* —*n.* [*count*] **2.** something that is not to be mentioned. **3. unmentionables,** [*plural*] undergarments.

un•mer•ci•ful (un mûr′si fəl) /ʌn'mɜrsɪfəl/ *adj.* **1.** merciless; relentless; cruel: *an unmerciful tyrant.* **2.** unsparingly great; extreme: *talked for an unmerciful length of time.* —**un•mer′ci•ful•ly,** *adv.*

un•mind•ful (un mind′fəl) /ʌn'mayndfəl/ *adj.* [*usually: be* + ~ + *of*] not mindful; unaware; neglectful: *was unmindful of all the trouble he had caused.*

un•mis•tak•a•ble (un′mi stā′kə bəl) /ˌʌnmɪ'steykəbəl/ *adj.* clear; obvious: *unmistakable evidence of guilt.* —**un′mis•tak′a•bly,** *adv.*

un•mit•i•gat•ed (un mit′i gā′tid) /ʌn'mɪtɪˌgeytɪd/ *adj.* [*before a noun*] not softened or lessened in any way; complete; thorough, absolute, or utter: *an unmitigated villain.*

un•mor•al (un môr′əl, -mor′-) /ʌn'mɔrəl, -'mɒr-/ *adj.* **1.** not within the scope of morality; neither moral nor immoral; amoral. **2.** lacking or unaffected by moral sense or principles. —**un•mo•ral•i•ty** (un′ mə ral′i tē, -mô-) /ˌʌnmə'rælɪtiy, -mɔ-/ *n.* [*noncount*] Compare IMMORAL.

un•moved (un mo͞ovd′) /ʌn'muvd/ *adj.* **1.** not shifted from position: *Leave the chair unmoved.* **2.** not affected emotionally: *was unmoved by her plea.*

un•named (un nāmd′) /ʌn'neymd/ *adj.* **1.** not identified by name: *An unnamed source confirmed the story.* **2.** not having been given a name: *an unnamed river.*

un•nat•u•ral (un nach′ər əl, -nach′rəl) /ʌn'nætʃərəl, -'nætʃrəl/ *adj.* **1.** contrary to the laws or course of nature; different from or opposite from the normal or expected character or nature of a person, animal, or plant. **2.** not genuine or natural; artificial: *a forced, unnatural smile.* —**un•nat′u•ral•ly,** *adv.*

un•nec•es•sar•y (un nes′ə ser′ē) /ʌn'nɛsəˌsɛriy/ *adj.* not necessary; needless; not essential: *an unnecessary addition.* —**un•nec•es•sar•i•ly** (un nes′ə sâr′ə lē, -ser′-) /ʌnˌnɛsə'sɛərəliy, -'sɛr-/ *adv.*

un•nerve (un nûrv′) /ʌn'nɜrv/ *v.* [~ + *obj*], **-nerved, -nerv•ing.** to take away from (someone) courage, strength, determination, or confidence; upset: *Fear unnerved him.*

un•num•bered (un num′bərd) /ʌn'nʌmbərd/ *adj.* **1.** having no number or numbers written or printed on. **2.** countless.

un•ob•serv•ant (un′əb zûr′vənt) /ˌʌnəb'zɜrvənt/ *adj.* not noticing things around one. See -SERV-[2].

un•ob•served (un′əb zûrvd′) /ˌʌnəb'zɜrvd/ *adj.* **1.** not seen, noticed, or observed. —*adv.* **2.** without having been observed: *arrived unobserved by the crowd.* See -SERV-[2].

un•ob•tru•sive (un′əb tro͞o′siv) /ˌʌnəb'truwsɪv/ *adj.* not obtrusive; inconspicuous: *The porch was an unobtrusive addition to the house.* —**un′ob•tru′sive•ly,** *adv.* —**un′ob•tru′sive•ness,** *n.* [*noncount*] See -TRUDE-.

un•oc•cu•pied (un ok′yə pid′) /ʌn'ɒkyəˌpayd/ *adj.* **1.** lacking occupants: *unoccupied houses.* **2.** not held or controlled by invading forces: *unoccupied territory.* **3.** not busy or active; idle: *unoccupied hours.*

un•of•fi•cial (un′ə fish′əl) /ˌʌnə'fɪʃəl/ *adj.* not official; not formal: *an unofficial visit.* —**un′of•fi′cial•ly,** *adv.* See -OPER-.

un•or•gan•ized (un ôr′gə nīzd′) /ʌn'ɔrgəˌnayzd/ *adj.* **1.** not organized; lacking structure. **2.** not thinking or acting methodically. **3.** not belonging to or represented by a labor union.

un•or•tho•dox (un ôr′thə doks) /ʌn'ɔrθədɒks/ *adj.* not orthodox; unconventional: *unorthodox approaches to medical treatment.* See -DOX-.

un•pack (un pak′) /ʌn'pæk/ *v.* to undo or remove (something, such as the contents) from (a box, trunk, etc.): [~ + *obj*]: *to unpack a suitcase.* [*no obj*]: *were too tired to unpack.*

un•par•al•leled (un par′ə leld′) /ʌn'pærəˌlɛld/ *adj.* not equaled or matched; unique; peerless: *unparalleled happiness.* Also, *esp. Brit.*, **un•par′al•lelled′.**

un•per•son (un′pûr′sən) /'ʌn'pɜrsən/ *n.* [*count*] a public figure, esp. in a totalitarian country, who, for political reasons, is no longer recognized or mentioned by the government or the news media.

un•pin (un pin′) /ʌn'pɪn/ *v.* [~ + *obj*], **-pinned, -pin•ning. 1.** to remove pins from: *to unpin her long hair.* **2.** to unfasten or loosen by or as if by removing a pin; detach.

un•pleas•ant (un plez′ənt) /ʌn'plɛzənt/ *adj.* not pleasant; displeasing; disagreeable; offensive: *a very unpleasant smell.* [*be* + ~ + *to* + *verb*]: *He was very unpleasant to work with.* —**un•pleas′ant•ly,** *adv.* —**un•pleas′ant•ness,** *n.* [*noncount*] See -PLAC-.

un•plug (un plug′) /ʌn'plʌg/ *v.*, **-plugged, -plug•ging. 1.** to (cause to) become free of something blocking; unclog: [~ + *obj*]: *to unplug a clogged drain.* [*no obj*]: *After he chewed some gum his ears suddenly unplugged.* **2.** [~ + *obj*] to disconnect by removing a plug from an electrical connection: *unplugged the lamp.*

un•plumbed (un plumd′) /ʌn'plʌmd/ *adj.* not explored: *the ocean's unplumbed depths.*

un•pop•u•lar (un pop′yə lər) /ʌn'pɒpyələr/ *adj.* not popular; disliked, disapproved, or ignored by a person or group or the public: *an unpopular leader.* —**un•pop•u•lar•i•ty** (un′pop yə lar′i tē) /ˌʌnpɒpyə'lærɪtiy/ *n.* [*noncount*]

un•prec•e•dent•ed (un pres′i den′tid) /ʌn'prɛsɪˌdɛntɪd/ *adj.* never before known or experienced: *an unprecedented victory.* See -CEDE-.

un•pre•dict•a•ble (un′pri dik′tə bəl) /ˌʌnprɪ'dɪktəbəl/ *adj.* not predictable: *unpredictable weather.* See -DICT-.

un•pre•pared (un′pri pârd′) /ˌʌnprɪ'pɛərd/ *adj.* not prepared; not expecting something: *was unprepared for visitors.* —**un•pre•par•ed•ness** (un′pri pâr′id nis) /ˌʌnprɪ'pɛərɪdnɪs/ *n.* [*noncount*] See -PARE-[1].

un•pre•ten•tious (un′pri ten′shəs) /ˌʌnprɪ'tɛnʃəs/ *adj.* not showing signs of riches, wealth, power, or influence; not showy: *an unpretentious little house in a modest suburb.* —**un′pre•ten′tious•ly,** *adv.* See -TEND-.

un•prin•ci•pled (un prin′sə pəld) /ʌn'prɪnsəpəld/ *adj.* lacking or not based on moral principles; dishonest: *an unprincipled politician who will do anything for votes.* See -PRIM-.

un•print•a•ble (un prin′tə bəl) /ʌn'prɪntəbəl/ *adj.* improper or unfit for print, esp. because of being obscene or offensive.

un•pro•fes•sion•al (un′prə fesh′ə nl) /ˌʌnprə'fɛʃənl̩/ *adj.* **1.** against or opposed to professional standards or ethics: *unprofessional conduct.* **2.** not done well or with what is considered good, professional quality; amateurish: *a very unprofessional job of redesigning the kitchen.* See -FESS-.

un•prof•it•a•ble (un prof′i tə bəl) /ʌn'prɒfɪtəbəl/ *adj.* **1.** not showing or making a profit. **2.** pointless; having no benefit; futile: *an unprofitable line of thought.*

un•pro•nounce•a•ble (un′prə noun′sə bəl) /'ʌnprə'nawnsəbəl/ *adj.* too difficult to be pronounced or pronounced properly: *an unpronounceable name.* See -NOUNCE-.

un•pro•voked (un′prə vōkt′) /ˌʌnprə'vowkt/ *adj.* not provoked; having no apparent cause or reason: *an unprovoked attack.* See -VOC-.

un•qual•i•fied (un kwol′ə fīd′) /ʌn'kwɒləˌfayd/ *adj.* **1.** not qualified; not fit; lacking the necessary qualifications. **2.** not limited: *unqualified praise.* **3.** [*before a noun*] absolute; complete; total: *an unqualified disaster.*

un•ques•tion•a•ble (un kwes′chə nə bəl) /ʌn'kwɛstʃənəbəl/ *adj.* not open to question; beyond dispute: *unquestionable facts.* See -QUES-.

un•ques•tioned (un kwes′chənd) /ʌn'kwɛstʃənd/ *adj.*

not open to doubt: *Shakespeare's genius is unquestioned.*

un•ques•tion•ing (un kwes′chə ning) /ʌn'kwɛstʃənɪŋ/ *adj.* not willing to question; steadfast: *unquestioning loyalty.* —**un•ques′tion•ing•ly,** *adv.* See -QUES-.

un•quote (un′kwōt′) /'ʌn,kwowt/ *v.* [*no obj*], **-quot•ed, -quot•ing.** (used to indicate the end of something that has been quoted): *He said, quote, "I'm leaving," unquote, and that was it.*

un•rav•el (un rav′əl) /ʌn'rævəl/ *v.,* **-eled, -el•ing** or (*esp. Brit.*) **-elled, -el•ling. 1.** to separate or (cause to) be disentangled, as the threads of a fabric, rope, etc.: [~ + *obj*]: *to unravel the thread.* [*no obj*]: *The thread unraveled.* **2.** to (cause to) be free from complications; (cause to) be solved: [~ + *obj*]: *to unravel a mystery.* [*no obj*]: *The mystery was slow to unravel.* **3.** to (cause to) be taken apart or destroyed: [*no obj*]: *All his plans unraveled when he lost the job.* [~ + *obj*]: *The sneak attack unraveled the general's plans.*

un•read (un red′) /ʌn'rɛd/ *adj.* **1.** not read, such as a letter or newspaper. **2.** lacking in knowledge gained by reading.

un•re•al (un rē′əl, -rēl′) /ʌn'riyəl, -'riyl/ *adj.* **1.** not real or actual. **2.** imaginary; fanciful; illusory; fantastic. **3.** not genuine; false; artificial.

un•rea•son•a•ble (un rē′zə nə bəl, -rēz′nə-) /ʌn'riyzənəbəl, -'riyznə-/ *adj.* **1.** not reasonable or rational; not guided by or showing reason or good judgment; irrational. **2.** too great; excessive, immoderate, or exorbitant: *an unreasonable demand.* —**un•rea′son•a•ble•ness,** *n.* [*noncount*] —**un•rea′son•a•bly,** *adv.* See -RATIO-.

un•rea•son•ing (un rē′zə ning) /ʌn'riyzənɪŋ/ *adj.* not using reason; irrational: *an unreasoning fear of spiders.* See -RATIO-.

un•re•con•struct•ed (un′rē kən struk′tid) /,ʌnriykən'strʌktɪd/ *adj.* not adjusting to new or current situations: *an unreconstructed royalist.*

un•re•lent•ing (un′ri len′ting) /,ʌnrɪ'lɛntɪŋ/ *adj.* **1.** not relenting; not losing desire to continue. **2.** not easing or becoming reduced, as in intensity: *unrelenting poverty.*

un•re•lieved (un′ri lēvd′) /,ʌnrɪ'liyvd/ *adj.* complete, continuous, and not stopping: *her unrelieved hostility toward him.*

un•re•mit•ting (un′ri mit′ing) /,ʌnrɪ'mɪtɪŋ/ *adj.* not slowing, stopping, or losing strength or power; continuous: *unremitting noise; unremitting pain.* See -MIT-.

un•rep•re•sent•a•tive (un′rep ri zen′tə tiv) /,ʌnrɛprɪ'zɛntətɪv/ *adj.* not representative; not typical: *radical views unrepresentative of the majority.*

un•re•quit•ed (un′ri kwī′tid) /,ʌnrɪ'kwaytɪd/ *adj.* not returned; not felt in return: *unrequited love.* See -QUIT-.

un•re•served (un′ri zûrvd′) /,ʌnrɪ'zɜrvd/ *adj.* **1.** holding nothing back; complete: *unreserved approval.* **2.** frank; open; fully honest: *an unreserved manner.* **3.** not set apart for a special use: *unreserved seats.* See -SERV-[2].

un•re•spon•sive (un′ri spon′siv) /,ʌnrɪ'spɒnsɪv/ *adj.* not responsive; insensitive; insensate. —**un′re•spon′sive•ly,** *adv.* —**un′re•spon′sive•ness,** *n.* [*noncount*] See -SPOND-.

un•rest (un rest′) /ʌn'rɛst/ *n.* [*noncount*] dissatisfaction or turbulence: *political unrest.*

un•re•strained (un′ri strānd′) /,ʌnrɪ'streynd/ *adj.* not restrained; not held back; not limited: *unrestrained inflation.* See -STRAIN-.

un•re•strict•ed (un′ri strik′tid) /,ʌnrɪ'strɪktɪd/ *adj.* not restricted; not limited: *unrestricted freedom.* See -STRICT-.

un•re•ward•ed (un′ri wôr′did) /,ʌnrɪ'wɔrdɪd/ *adj.* not rewarded; not receiving a reward for some achievement.

un•re•ward•ing (un′ri wôr′ding) /,ʌnrɪ'wɔrdɪŋ/ *adj.* not rewarding; not bringing a reward or satisfaction: *tedious, unrewarding work.*

un•ripe (un rīp′) /ʌn'rayp/ *adj.* not ripe: *unripe fruit.*

un•ri•valed (un rī′vəld) /ʌn'rayvəld/ *adj.* having no rival or equal; superb: *an unrivaled poet.* Also, *esp. Brit.,* **un•ri′valled.**

un•roll (un rōl′) /ʌn'rowl/ *v.* **1.** to open or (cause to) be spread out, as something rolled in cylindrical shape: [~ + *obj*]: *The kids unrolled their sleeping bags.* [*no obj*]: *The map had unrolled.* **2.** [*no obj*] to become continuously visible or apparent: *The landscape unrolled before our eyes.*

un•ruf•fled (un ruf′əld) /ʌn'rʌfəld/ *adj.* **1.** not flustered or nervous; calm: *remained unruffled by the turmoil.* **2.** not ruffled; smooth: *unruffled fabric.*

un•ru•ly (un rōō′lē) /ʌn'ruwliy/ *adj.,* **-li•er, -li•est.** not cooperative or well-behaved; unmanageable; disorderly: *an unruly gang of troublemakers.* —**un•ru′li•ness,** *n.* [*noncount*]

un•sad•dle (un sad′l) /ʌn'sædl̩/ *v.* [~ + *obj*], **-dled, -dling. 1.** to take the saddle from: *to unsaddle a pony.* **2.** to cause to fall or dismount from a saddled horse.

un•safe (un sāf′) /ʌn'seyf/ *adj.* **1.** not safe; dangerous: *an unsafe nuclear reactor.* **2.** threatened by danger: *felt unsafe walking at night.* —**un•safe′ly,** *adv.*

un•said (un sed′) /ʌn'sɛd/ *adj.* not said or spoken aloud; unspoken: *left his true feelings unsaid.*

un•san•i•tar•y (un san′ə ter′ē) /ʌn'sænə,tɛriy/ *adj.* not sanitary; not clean; not free of germs. See -SAN-.

un•sat•is•fac•to•ry (un′sat is fak′tə rē, -fak′trē) /,ʌnsætɪs'fæktəriy, -'fæktriy/ *adj.* not satisfactory: *unsatisfactory grades.* See -SAT-.

un•sat•is•fied (un sat′is fīd) /ʌn'sætɪsfayd/ *adj.* not satisfied: *unsatisfied longings.* See -SAT-.

un•sat•is•fy•ing (un sat′is fī′ing) /ʌn'sætɪs,fayɪŋ/ *adj.* not giving a feeling of satisfaction; disappointing: *an unsatisfying meal.* See -SAT-.

un•sa•vor•y (un sā′və rē) /ʌn'seyvəriy/ *adj.* **1.** not savory; tasteless. **2.** unpleasant in taste or smell. **3.** unappealing or disagreeable: *an unsavory job of searching for drugs.* **4.** socially or morally offensive: *an unsavory past.* Also, *esp. Brit.,* **un•sa′vour•y.**

un•scathed (un skāthd′) /ʌn'skeyðd/ *adj.* not harmed; unharmed: *escaped the explosion unscathed.*

un•sched•uled (un skej′ōōld) /ʌn'skɛdʒʊld/ *adj.* not scheduled: *called an unscheduled meeting.*

un•schooled (un skōōld′) /ʌn'skuwld/ *adj.* **1.** not educated. **2.** untrained; natural: *an unschooled talent for art.* See -SCHOL-.

un•sci•en•tif•ic (un′sī ən tif′ik) /,ʌnsayən'tɪfɪk/ *adj.* not scientific: *an unscientific approach to solving problems.* See -SCI-.

un•scram•ble (un skram′bəl) /ʌn'skræmbəl/ *v.* [~ + *obj*], **-bled, -bling.** to bring out of a scrambled condition: *to unscramble a coded message.*

un•screw (un skrōō′) /ʌn'skruw/ *v.* [~ + *obj*] **1.** to loosen a screw from (a hinge, bracket, etc.). **2.** to unfasten or pull out by turning, such as a screw or lid. **3.** to open (a jar, bottle, etc.) by turning the lid or cover.

un•scru•pu•lous (un skrōō′pyə ləs) /ʌn'skruwpyələs/ *adj.* not scrupulous; unprincipled: *unscrupulous business dealings.*

un•seal (un sēl′) /ʌn'siyl/ *v.* [~ + *obj*] to break or remove the seal of; open.

un•sealed (un sēld′) /ʌn'siyld/ *adj.* not sealed.

un•sea•son•a•ble (un sē′zə nə bəl) /ʌn'siyzənəbəl/ *adj.* not seasonable; abnormal: *unseasonable weather.* —**un•sea′son•a•bly,** *adv.*

un•seat (un sēt′) /ʌn'siyt/ *v.* [~ + *obj*] **1.** to remove from a seat, esp. to throw from a saddle. **2.** to remove (someone) from political office by an elective process, by force, or by legal action: *In the next election the mayor was unseated by her opponent.*

un•see•ing (un sē′ing) /ʌn'siyɪŋ/ *adj.* **1.** not able to see; blind. **2.** not looking at anything in particular: *He gazed unseeing out the window.*

un•seem•ly (un sēm′lē) /ʌn'siymliy/ *adj.,* **-li•er, -li•est,** *adv.* —*adj.* **1.** not seemly; not in keeping with accepted standards of taste or proper form: *unseemly informality.* **2.** inappropriate for time or place: *an unseemly hour.* —*adv.* **3.** in an unseemly manner.

un•self•ish (un sel′fish) /ʌn'sɛlfɪʃ/ *adj.* not selfish; generous.

un•set•tle (un set′l) /ʌn'sɛtl̩/ *v.* [~ + *obj*], **-tled, -tling. 1.** to disturb; shake or weaken (beliefs, feelings, etc.); cause doubt or uncertainty about. **2.** to disturb or upset the mind or emotions of.

un•set•tled (un set′ld) /ʌn'sɛtld/ *adj.* **1.** not settled; not stable: *an unsettled political situation.* **2.** continuously moving or changing: *an unsettled life.* **3.** lacking certainty; uneasy: *an unsettled mind.* **4.** not populated or settled: *an unsettled wilderness.* **5.** undetermined; undecided: *unsettled lawsuits.* **6.** likely to change; changeable: *unsettled weather.*

un•shack•le (un shak′əl) /ʌn'ʃækəl/ *v.* [~ + *obj*], **-led, -ling.** to free from or as if from chains or shackles.

un•shak•a•ble (un shā′kə bəl) /ʌn'ʃeykəbəl/ *adj.* firm; unyielding: *unshakable trust; unshakable opinions.*

un•sight•ly (un sīt′lē) /ʌn'saytliy/ *adj.,* **-li•er, -li•est.** distasteful or unpleasant to look at; unattractive; ugly: *unsightly shacks.*

un•skilled (un skild′) /ʌn'skɪld/ *adj.* **1.** relating to workers who lack special skills: *unskilled labor.* **2.** not demanding special training or skill: *unskilled jobs.* **3.** showing or having a lack of skill: *an unskilled painting.*

un•skill•ful (un skil′fəl) /ʌn'skɪlfəl/ *adj.* not skillful; clumsy; inept. Also, *esp. Brit.,* **un•skil′ful.**

un•snap (un snap′) /ʌn'snæp/ *v.* [~ + *obj*], **-snapped, -snap•ping.** to open or release by or as if by undoing a snap fastener.

un•snarl (un snärl′) /ʌn'snɑrl/ *v.* [~ + *obj*] to bring out of a snarled or tangled condition; disentangle: *unsnarling the knots in yarn.*

un•so•cia•ble (un sō′shə bəl) /ʌn'sowʃəbəl/ *adj.* not sociable; unwilling to talk to or interact with people. See -SOC-.

un•so•phis•ti•cat•ed (un′sə fis′ti kā′tid) /ˌʌnsə'fɪstɪˌkeytɪd/ *adj.* **1.** not sophisticated; simple, as when dealing with others: *a guidebook for unsophisticated visitors to the big city.* **2.** without complex parts. See -SOPHI-.

un•sound (un sound′) /ʌn'sawnd/ *adj.,* **-er, -est. 1.** not sound; unhealthy or diseased, as the body or mind. **2.** not solid or firm, as foundations. **3.** not valid; full of false arguments: *an unsound argument.* **4.** easily broken; light: *unsound sleep.* **5.** not financially strong or secure: *an unsound investment.*

un•spar•ing (un spâr′ing) /ʌn'spɛərɪŋ/ *adj.* **1.** not sparing; generous; liberal: *unsparing in his offers to help.* **2.** holding nothing back; harsh; severe: *unsparing criticism.*

un•speak•a•ble (un spē′kə bəl) /ʌn'spiykəbəl/ *adj.* indescribably terrible: *unspeakable crimes.* —**un•speak′a•bly,** *adv.*

un•spec•i•fied (un spes′ə fīd) /ʌn'spɛsəfayd/ *adj.* not made specific; not named: *some unspecified ailments.* See -SPEC-.

un•spoiled (un spoild′) /ʌn'spɔyld/ *adj.* **1.** not spoiled; not ruined: *unspoiled food.* **2.** existing in a natural state: *unspoiled wilderness.*

un•spo•ken (un spō′kən) /ʌn'spowkən/ *adj.* not said aloud: *an unspoken accusation.*

un•sta•ble (un stā′bəl) /ʌn'steybəl/ *adj.* **1.** not stable; unsteady: *an unstable foundation.* **2.** liable to change or fluctuate quickly; irregular: *an unstable heartbeat.* **3.** showing an inability to keep one's emotions stable or under some control: *mentally unstable.* **4.** noting chemical compounds that readily change into other compounds. See -STAB-.

un•stead•y (un sted′ē) /ʌn'stɛdiy/ *adj.,* **-i•er, -i•est. 1.** not steady or firm; unstable; shaky: *an unsteady ladder; an unsteady gait.* **2.** irregular or uneven: *unsteady development.* —**un•stead•i•ly** (un sted′l ē) /ʌn'stɛdḷiy/ *adv.* —**un•stead′i•ness,** *n.* [*noncount*]

un•stop (un stop′) /ʌn'stɒp/ *v.* [~ + *obj*], **-stopped, -stop•ping. 1.** to remove the stopper from: *to unstop a jug.* **2.** to free from anything that blocks something; open: *to unstop a toilet.*

un•strung (un strung′) /ʌn'strʌŋ/ *adj.* [*be* + ~] weakened or nervously upset: *was unstrung by the near disaster.*

un•stuck (un stuk′) /ʌn'stʌk/ *adj.* brought to a state of disarray or stoppage: *The negotiations have come unstuck.*

un•stud•ied (un stud′ēd) /ʌn'stʌdiyd/ *adj.* **1.** natural; unaffected: *his unstudied politeness.* **2.** not possessing knowledge in a specific field.

un•sub•stan•tial (un′səb stan′shəl) /ˌʌnsəb'stænʃəl/ *adj.* **1.** having no foundation in fact. **2.** lacking material substance. **3.** lacking strength or solidity; flimsy.

un•sub•stan•ti•at•ed (un′səb stan′shē ā′tid) /ˌʌnsəb'stænʃiyˌeytɪd/ *adj.* not backed up with facts or proof; not confirmed: *unsubstantiated rumors.*

un•suc•cess•ful (un′sək ses′fəl) /ˌʌnsək'sɛsfəl/ *adj.* not successful. —**un′suc•cess′ful•ly,** *adv.*

un•sung (un sung′) /ʌn'sʌŋ/ *adj.* **1.** not sung. **2.** not celebrated in song or verse; not praised: *unsung heroes.*

un•sure (un sho͝or′) /ʌn'ʃʊr/ *adj.* [*often: be* + ~(+ *of*)] **1.** not certain: *was unsure of her feelings.* **2.** lacking confidence: *was unsure of himself.*

un•sus•pect•ed (un′sə spek′tid) /ˌʌnsə'spɛktɪd/ *adj.* not suspected; not generally known: *an unsuspected talent for comedy.* See -SPEC-.

un•sus•pect•ing (un′sə spek′ting) /ˌʌnsə'spɛktɪŋ/ *adj.* not suspecting; unaware; innocent: *an unsuspecting victim.* —**un′sus•pect′ing•ly,** *adv.* See -SPEC-.

un•swerv•ing (un swûr′ving) /ʌn'swɜrvɪŋ/ *adj.* strong; firm: *unswerving loyalty.*

un•sym•pa•thet•ic (un′sim pə thet′ik) /ˌʌnsɪmpə'θɛtɪk/ *adj.* not sympathetic: *was unsympathetic toward weakness in others.* —**un′sym•pa•thet′i•cal•ly,** *adv.* See -PATH-.

un•tan•gle (un tang′gəl) /ʌn'tæŋgəl/ *v.* [~ + *obj*], **-gled, -gling. 1.** to bring out of a tangled state; disentangle. **2.** to straighten out; clear up: *untangling bureaucratic red tape.*

un•tapped (un tapt′) /ʌn'tæpt/ *adj.* available but not used: *untapped resources.*

un•taught (un tôt′) /ʌn'tɔt/ *adj.* **1.** not taught; natural: *untaught gracefulness.* **2.** not instructed or educated; ignorant.

un•ten•a•ble (un ten′ə bəl) /ʌn'tɛnəbəl/ *adj.* **1.** that cannot be easily defended against attack: *an untenable argument.* **2.** that cannot be held or maintained: *an untenable military position.* See -TEN-.

un•think•a•ble (un thing′kə bəl) /ʌn'θɪŋkəbəl/ *adj.* **1.** so terrible as to be inconceivable: *an unthinkable crime.* **2.** not to be considered; out of the question.

un•think•ing (un thing′king) /ʌn'θɪŋkɪŋ/ *adj.* **1.** thoughtless; inconsiderate. **2.** not thinking; heedless.

un•ti•dy (un tī′dē) /ʌn'taydiy/ *adj.,* **-di•er, -di•est. 1.** not tidy or neat; disordered: *an untidy children's room.* **2.** not well-organized or carried out: *an untidy plan.*

un•tie (un tī′) /ʌn'tay/ *v.*[~ + *obj*], **-tied, -ty•ing. 1.** to loose or unfasten (anything tied); let or set loose by undoing a knot: *to untie a prisoner.* **2.** to undo the string or cords of: *to untie (the strings of) a package.*

un•til (un til′) /ʌn'tɪl/ *conj.* **1.** up to the time that or when; till: *Wait until it starts getting dark.* **2.** [*usually used with a negative word or phrase*] before: *I didn't remember it until the meeting was over.* —*prep.* **3.** onward to or till (a certain time or occurrence): *to work until 6* P.M. **4.** [*usually used with a negative word or phrase*] before: *He did not go until noon.* —**Usage.** Compare UNTIL, TO, and BY. The word UNTIL is used in expressions of time to mean "the time up to (a certain point):" *to work until 6. She stayed inside until noon.* The word TO can be used like UNTIL with expressions of time with *from: They worked from noon until (or to) six.* We use BY, not UNTIL, when referring to an action that will occur no later than a future time: *Will the hot water be turned back on by tomorrow?* To refer to a continuing state that stops at a certain time, we use UNTIL: *You'll have to wait until next week for the hot water.*

un•time•ly (un tīm′lē) /ʌn'taymliy/ *adj.,* **-li•er, -li•est,** *adv.* —*adj.* **1.** not timely; ill-timed: *an untimely interruption.* **2.** premature: *an untimely death.*

un•tir•ing (un tīᵊr′ing) /ʌn'tayᵊrɪŋ/ *adj.* relentless: *untiring efforts.* —**un•tir′ing•ly,** *adv.*

un•to (un′to͞o; *unstressed* -tə) /'ʌntuw; *unstressed* -tə/ *prep.* to: *Do unto others as you would have them do unto you.*

un•told (un tōld′) /ʌn'towld/ *adj.* [*usually: before a noun*] **1.** not told or revealed: *untold secrets.* **2.** too great to count, calculate, or express: *untold suffering; untold wealth.*

un•touch•a•ble (un tuch′ə bəl) /ʌn'tʌtʃəbəl/ *adj.* **1.** impossible to touch; intangible. **2.** disgusting to the touch. **3.** beyond criticism or control: *The boss's son is untouchable.* —*n.* [*count*] **4.** a member of a lower caste in India whose touch was once believed to defile someone of higher caste. **5.** a social outcast.

un•touched (un tucht′) /ʌn'tʌtʃt/ *adj.* **1.** not affected by something: *structures left untouched by the bomb.* **2.** not damaged: *He escaped virtually untouched.* **3.** not eaten: *left his food untouched.*

un•to•ward (un tôrd′, -tōrd′) /ʌn'tɔrd, -'towrd/ *adj.* **1.** unfavorable or unfortunate: *Untoward circumstances forced him into bankruptcy.* **2.** improper: *untoward social behavior.*

un•treat•ed (un trē′tid) /ʌn'triytɪd/ *adj.* **1.** not given proper medical attention or care: *an untreated wound.* **2.** not treated so as to render harmless or safe: *untreated sewage; untreated water.*

un•tried (un trīd′) /ʌn'trayd/ *adj.* **1.** not tried; not attempted. **2.** not yet brought to trial or tried at a court of law.

un•true (un tro͞o′) /ʌn'truw/ *adj.,* **-tru•er, -tru•est. 1.** not true to fact; incorrect or inaccurate; false: *untrue statements.* [*It* + *be* + ~ + *that clause*]: *It is untrue that he didn't graduate.* **2.** [*be* + ~(+ *to*)] unfaithful; disloyal: *was untrue to her country.*

un•truth (un tro͞oth′) /ʌn'truwθ/ *n.* **1.** [*noncount*] the state of being untrue. **2.** [*count*] something untrue; a lie: *spreading untruths.* —**un•truth′ful•ness,** *n.* [*noncount*]

un•tu•tored (un to͞o′tərd, -tyo͞o′-) /ʌn'tuwtərd, -'tyuw-/

adj. **1.** not trained or schooled. **2.** naive; ignorant; unsophisticated.

un•used (un yo͞ozd′ *for 1, 2;* un yo͞ost′ *for 3*) /ʌn'yuwzd *for 1, 2;* ʌn'yuwst *for 3*/ *adj.* **1.** not put to use: *an unused room.* **2.** never having been used: *bought the car unused.* **3.** [*be* + ~ + *to*] not accustomed: *I'm unused to cold winters.*

un•u•su•al (un yo͞o′zho͞o əl) /ʌn'yuwʒuwəl/ *adj.* not usual or ordinary; uncommon; exceptional: *an unusual day.* [*It* + *be* + ~ + *that clause*]: *It was unusual that she was late.* [*It* + *be* + ~ (+ *for* + *obj*) + *to* + *verb*]: *It was unusual (for him) to be at work before ten o'clock.* —**un•u′su•al•ly,** *adv.*: *He was unusually early.*

un•ut•ter•a•ble (un ut′ər ə bəl) /ʌn'ʌtərəbəl/ *adj.* [*before a noun*] beyond one's ability to describe: *unutterable joy; unutterable sorrow.* —**un•ut′ter•a•bly,** *adv.*

un•var•nished (un vär′nisht) /ʌn'varnɪʃt/ *adj.* **1.** straightforward; frank: *the unvarnished truth.* **2.** not coated with or as if with varnish.

un•var•y•ing (un vâr′ē ing) /ʌn'vɛəriyɪŋ/ *adj.* not varying; not changing; staying the same: *Maintain an unvarying temperature.* —**un•var′y•ing•ly,** *adv.*

un•veil (un vāl′) /ʌn'veyl/ *v.* [~ + *obj*] **1.** to remove a veil or other covering from: *The artist unveiled the sculpture at the dedication ceremony.* **2.** to reveal or make known: *She unveiled the new plan at the meeting.*

un•war•y (un wâr′ē) /ʌn'wɛəriy/ *adj.*, **-i•er, -i•est.** not cautious or watchful, as against danger. —**un•war′i•ness,** *n.* [*noncount*]

un•wel•come (un wel′kəm) /ʌn'wɛlkəm/ *adj.* not welcome; not desirable: *an unwelcome visitor; unwelcome results.*

un•well (un wel′) /ʌn'wɛl/ *adj.* [*be* + ~] sick; ailing; ill.

un•whole•some (un hōl′səm) /ʌn'howlsəm/ *adj.* **1.** harmful to physical or mental health. **2.** unhealthy esp. in appearance: *an unwholesome paleness.* **3.** morally harmful; depraved: *an unwholesome criminal environment.* —**un•whole′some•ness,** *n.* [*noncount*]

un•wield•y (un wēl′dē) /ʌn'wiyldiy/ *adj.*, **-i•er, -i•est.** used, handled, or managed with difficulty because of size, shape, weight, or complexity: *an unwieldy load of scrap iron; an unwieldy bureaucracy.*

un•will•ing (un wil′ing) /ʌn'wɪlɪŋ/ *adj.* **1.** not willing; reluctant: *an unwilling partner in the crime.* [*be* + ~(+ *to* + *verb*)]: *He's unwilling to testify.* **2.** [*before a noun*] stubborn; obstinate: *trying to teach unwilling students.* —**un•will′ing•ly,** *adv.*: *came to the party unwillingly.*

un•wind (un wīnd′) /ʌn'waynd/ *v.*, **-wound, -wind•ing. 1.** to (cause to) be undone or loosened from or as if from a coiled or wound condition; untwist: [~ + *obj*]: *He unwound the coil of electric wire.* [*no obj*]: *The rope began to unwind.* **2.** to (cause to) be relieved of tension; relax: [*no obj*]: *needed to unwind after a hard day at work.* [~ + *obj*]: *a little soft music to unwind your frazzled nerves.*

un•wise (un wīz′) /ʌn'wayz/ *adj.*, **-wis•er, -wis•est.** not wise; foolish; imprudent: *an unwise decision.*

un•wit•ting (un wit′ing) /ʌn'wɪtɪŋ/ *adj.* **1.** unintentional; accidental; not on purpose: *an unwitting victim.* **2.** not knowing; unaware; unconscious.

un•wont•ed (un wôn′tid, -wōn′-, -wun′-) /ʌn'wɔntɪd, -'wown-, -'wʌn-/ *adj.* not customary, habitual, or usual; rare: *unwonted rudeness.*

un•work•a•ble (un wûr′kə bəl) /ʌn'wɜrkəbəl/ *adj.* badly put together and unlikely to succeed: *an unworkable plan.*

un•world•ly (un wûrld′lē) /ʌn'wɜrldliy/ *adj.* **1.** not interested in wealth or material gain. **2.** not earthly; spiritual.

un•wor•thy (un wûr′thē) /ʌn'wɜrðiy/ *adj.*, **-thi•er, -thi•est.** —*adj.* **1.** not worthy; lacking worth or excellence; not deserving: *an unworthy sinner.* [*be* + ~ + *to* + *verb*]: *I am unworthy to marry her.* **2.** [*be* + ~ + *of*] beneath the dignity: *That despicable behavior is unworthy of a true leader.* —**un•wor′thi•ness,** *n.* [*noncount*]

un•wrap (un rap′) /ʌn'ræp/ *v.* [~ + *obj*], **-wrapped, -wrap•ping.** to open (something wrapped), as by removing or opening the wrapping of: *to unwrap presents.*

un•writ•ten (un rit′n) /ʌn'rɪtn/ *adj.* **1.** not actually formulated or expressed but still held to be customary or traditional: *an unwritten law.* **2.** not put in writing or print; oral: *had an unwritten agreement.*

un•zip (un zip′) /ʌn'zɪp/ *v.*, **-zipped, -zip•ping.** to (cause to) be opened or unfastened by or as if by means of a zipper: [~ + *obj*]: *She had trouble unzipping the dress.* [*no obj*]: *The zipper won't unzip.*

up-, a combining form of UP: *upland; upshot; upheaval.*

up (up) /ʌp/ *adv., prep., adj., n., v.,* **upped, up•ping.** —*adv.* **1.** to, toward, or in a more elevated position: *to climb up to the top of a ladder.* **2.** to or in an erect position: *to stand up; He straightened up.* **3.** out of bed: *Come on, time to get up!* **4.** above the horizon: *The moon came up.* **5.** to or at any point considered higher: *He rolled the car windows up.* **6.** to or at a source, origin, center, or the like: *to follow a stream up to its source.* **7.** to or at a higher point or degree, as of rank, size, value, volume, or strength: *Prices went up. Speak up.* **8.** to or at a point of equal advance: *He caught up with her.* **9.** in continuing contact, esp. as showing continuing awareness or knowledge: *to keep up with the news.* **10.** into a state of emotional agitation: *all worked up.* **11.** into existence, view, notice, or consideration: *The lost papers turned up.* **12.** into or in a place of safekeeping, storage, etc.; safely; tightly: *to put up strawberry preserves.* **13.** into or in a state of union, contraction, etc.: *to add up a column of figures.* **14.** to the final point; to an end; entirely: *to be used up.* **15.** to a halt: *The car pulled up.* **16.** ahead; in a leading position in a competition: *We were two games up in the tournament.* **17.** each; apiece: *The score was seven up.* **18.** *Informal.* without ice; straight up. **19.** (used with a verb to express additional emphasis on the action of the verb, or to suggest more thoroughness or completion of the action): *Go wake your brother up. Drink up! Eat up!* —*prep.* **20.** to, toward, or at a higher place on or in: *to go up the stairs.* **21.** to, toward, or at a higher station, condition, or rank on or in: *She's well up the social ladder.* **22.** at or to a farther point or higher place on or in: *The store is up the street.* **23.** toward the source, origin, etc., of: *to float up a stream.* **24.** living or located inland or on elevated ground: *They are two miles up from the coast.* **25.** in a direction contrary to that of: *to row up the current.* —*adj.* **26.** [*before a noun*] moving in or related to a direction that is up or that is thought of as up: *the up elevator.* **27.** [*be* + ~ + *on/in*] informed; familiar; aware: *I'm not up on current events.* **28.** [*be* + ~] concluded; ended; finished: *Your time is up.* **29.** [*be* + ~] going on or happening: *What's up with you?* **30.** [*be* + ~] having a high position or station: *to be up in society.* **31.** [*be* + ~] in an erect, vertical, or raised position: *The tent is up.* **32.** [*be* + ~] above the ground: *The corn is up.* **33.** [*be* + ~] (of heavenly bodies) risen above the horizon: *The sun is up.* **34.** [*be* + ~] awake or out of bed: *It was morning but I wasn't up yet.* **35.** [*be* + ~] (of water in natural bodies) high with relation to the banks or shore: *The tide is up.* **36.** [*be* + ~] built; constructed: *A new building is up and open to the public.* **37.** [*be* + ~ + *for*] cheerful or optimistic; exuberant; upbeat: *The team was up for the game.* **38.** [*be* + ~] afoot or amiss; going on: *Her nervous manner told me that something was up.* **39.** [*be* + ~] higher than formerly in amount or degree: *The price of meat is up.* **40.** [*be* + ~] about to be prosecuted for (a crime): *to be up for fraud.* **41.** [*be* + ~] in operation or ready for use; working: *The computer system is up and running.* **42.** [*after a noun indicating number*] ahead of an opponent in a competition: *He's two sets up.* **43.** [*be* + ~] considered or under consideration: *up for reelection.* **44.** [*be* + ~] at bat in baseball. —*n.* [*count*] **45.** an upward movement; ascent. **46.** a time of good fortune, prosperity, etc.: *the ups and downs in a career.* **47.** *Informal.* a feeling or state of happiness or exuberance: *on an up.* **48.** an upward course or rise, as in price or value: *ups in the rent.* —*v.* **49.** [~ + *obj*] to make larger; step up; increase: *decided to up the rent.* **50.** [*not: be* + ~*-ing; no obj;* ~ + *and* + *verb*] *Informal.* to start up; begin something abruptly: *upped and ran away.* **51.** (used as a command or a way to rally others) stand or rise up: *Up, men, and fight!* —***Idiom.* 52. on the up and up,** [*be* + ~] worth believing; honest; trustworthy: *This car salesman doesn't seem to be on the up and up.* **53. up against,** confronted with; faced with: *came up against a number of problems.* **54. up and around** or **about,** recovered from an illness; able to leave one's bed. **55. up for grabs,** *Informal.* freely available to whoever can take or seize it first. **56. up to, a.** as far as: *I am up to the eighth lesson.* **b.** in fulfillment of: *couldn't live up to their expectations.* **c.** as many as; to the limit of: *This car can hold up to five persons.* **d.** [*be* + ~] capable of; equal to: *Is he up to the job?* **e.** [*It* + *be* + ~ + *obj*(+ *to* + *verb*)] being one's responsibility: *It's up to you to tell her.* **f.** [*be* + ~] engaged in; doing: *What have you been up to lately?* **g.** [*be* + ~] doing something suspect, dishonest, or illegal: *They're up to something, but the police don't yet know what.*

up′-and-com′ing, *adj.* likely to succeed; bright and industrious: *an up-and-coming young executive.*

up•beat (up′bēt′) /'ʌpˌbiyt/ *n.* [*count*] **1.** an unaccented beat in music. **2.** the upward stroke with which a conductor indicates such a beat. **—*adj.*** **3.** optimistic; happy; cheerful: *an upbeat report on the economy.*

up•braid (up brād′) /ʌp'breyd/ *v.* [~ + *obj*] to find fault with or scold severely; censure: *upbraided them for their poor grades.*

up•bring•ing (up′bring′ing) /'ʌp,brɪŋɪŋ/ *n.* [*count; usually singular*] the care and training of children or a particular type of such care and training: *He had a religious upbringing.*

up•chuck (up′chuk′) /'ʌp,tʃʌk/ *v. Informal.* to vomit: [*no obj*]: *to upchuck all over the carpet.* [~ + *obj*]: *to upchuck dinner.*

up•com•ing (up′kum′ing) /'ʌp,kʌmɪŋ/ *adj.* [*usually before a noun*] coming up; about to take place, appear, or be presented: *the upcoming spring fashions.*

up•coun•try (*adj., n.* up′kun′trē; *adv.* up kun′trē) / *adj., n.* 'ʌp,kʌntriy; *adv.* ʌp'kʌntriy/ *adj.* **1.** of, relating to, living in, or situated in the interior of a region or country; inland. **—*n.*** [*noncount*] **2.** the interior of a region or country. **—*adv.*** **3.** toward, into, or in the interior of a country: *traveled upcountry.*

up•date (up′dāt′; *v.* also up′dāt′) /'ʌp,deyt; *v.* ælsɒ ,ʌp'deyt/ *v.,* **-dat•ed, -dat•ing,** *n.* **—*v.*** [~ + *obj*] **1.** to bring up to date; incorporate new information in or for: *to update a report.* **—*n.*** [*count*] **2.** an act or instance of updating. **3.** new or current information used in updating. **4.** an updated version, account, or the like.

up•draft (up′draft′) /'ʌp,dræft/ *n.* [*count*] a movement upward of air or other gas.

up•end (up end′) /ʌp'ɛnd/ *v.* [~ + *obj*] **1.** to set or put (something) on end: *The car was upended in a ditch.* **2.** to defeat in a competition: *upended their opponents.*

up′-front′, *adj.* Also, **up′front′. 1.** paid in advance or as beginning capital: *an up-front investment of $1,000.* **2.** [*usually: be* + ~] honest; straightforward: *I'll be up-front about my feelings.* **—*adv.*** Also, **up′ front′. 3.** in advance; initially: *They asked for $1,000 up-front.*

up•grade (*n.* up′grād′; *adj., adv.* up′grād′; *v.* up grād′, up′grād′) / *n.* 'ʌp,greyd; *adj., adv.* 'ʌp'greyd; *v.* ʌp'greyd, 'ʌp,greyd/ *n., adj., adv., v.,* **-grad•ed, -grad•ing. —*n.*** [*count*] **1.** a part of a path or road going up in the direction of movement. **2.** a new, usually improved model or version of something, as computer software. **—*adj.*** **3.** uphill; of, relating to, on, or along an upgrade. **—*adv.*** **4.** up a slope. **—*v.*** [~ + *obj*] **5.** to raise in rank, position, importance, etc.: *was upgraded to senior vice president.* **6.** to improve the usefulness of: *to upgrade our computers.* See -GRAD-.

up•heav•al (up hē′vəl) /ʌp'hiyvəl/ *n.* **1.** strong or violent change or disturbance, such as in a society: [*noncount*]: *brought social upheaval to the country.* [*count*]: *an upheaval caused by war.* **2.** [*count*] an act of upheaving, esp. of a part of the earth's crust.

up•hill (*adv., adj.* up′hil′; *n.* up′hil′) / *adv., adj.* 'ʌp'hɪl; *n.* 'ʌp,hɪl/ *adv.* **1.** up or as if up the slope of a hill or other slope; upward: *The soldiers marched uphill.* **—*adj.*** **2.** going or tending upward on or as if on a hill: *an uphill road.* **3.** at a high place or point: *an uphill village.* **4.** very tiring or difficult: *an uphill struggle to earn a living.* **—*n.*** [*count*] **5.** a rising piece or area of land; ascent.

up•hold (up hōld′) /ʌp'howld/ *v.* [~ + *obj*], **-held, -hold•ing. 1.** to support or defend, as against criticism: *to uphold the family's good name.* **2.** to hold up; keep from sinking; support.

up•hol•ster (up hōl′stər, ə pōl′-) /ʌp'howlstər, ə'powl-/ *v.* [~ + *obj*] to fit with upholstery: *upholstering a chair.* **—up•hol′ster•er,** *n.* [*count*]

up•hol•ster•y (up hōl′stə rē, -strē, ə pōl′-) /ʌp'howlstəriy, -striy, ə'powl-/ *n.* [*noncount*] the materials used to cushion and cover furniture, as chairs and sofas.

up•keep (up′kēp′) /'ʌp,kiyp/ *n.* [*noncount*] **1.** the care, repairs, etc., necessary for the proper functioning of a machine, building, household, etc. **2.** the cost of this: *Upkeep is one quarter of our budget.*

up•land (up′lənd, -land′) /'ʌplənd, -,lænd/ *n.* [*count*] **1.** land elevated above other land. **2.** land above the level where water flows or where flooding occurs. **—*adj.*** **3.** of or relating to uplands or elevated regions.

up•lift (up lift′) /ʌp'lɪft/ *v.* [~ + *obj*] **1.** to lift up; raise; elevate. **2.** to improve socially, culturally, or morally. **3.** to encourage with emotionally or spiritually cheering words.

up•lift•ing (up lif′ting) /ʌp'lɪftɪŋ/ *adj.* containing emotional or spiritual encouragement: *an uplifting speech.*

up•mar•ket (up′mär′kit) /'ʌp,mɑrkɪt/ *adj.* appealing to or serving high-income consumers; upscale; expensive.

up•on (ə pon′, ə pôn′) /ə'pɒn, ə'pɔn/ *prep.* **1.** up and on; upward so as to get or be on: *She climbed upon her horse.* **2.** in a higher or elevated position on: *a flag upon the roof.* **3.** in or into proximity with in time or space: *The holidays will soon be upon us.* **4.** on the occasion of; at the time of: *shouted with joy upon hearing the news.* **—Usage.** This word can sometimes replace ON when describing actual or implied spatial relations without the meaning of upward motion: *He laid the book on/upon the table. I wouldn't wish it upon/on anyone. I came to rely on/upon him.* However, *on* cannot be replaced by *upon* in all cases, as for example in certain time and place expressions: *I met them on Thursday; I met them on the corner of 23rd Street and Lexington Avenue.* In both these sentences the use of *upon* would be incorrect.

up•per[1] (up′ər) /'ʌpər/ *adj.* [*before a noun*] **1.** higher, such as in place, position, musical pitch, or in a scale: *the upper stories of a house.* **2.** higher or superior, as in rank, dignity, or station: *the upper levels of the administration.* **3.** (of places) at a higher level, more northerly, or farther from the sea: *upper New York State.* **—*n.*** [*count*] **4.** the part of a shoe or boot above the sole **5.** Usually, **uppers. a.** an upper dental plate. **b.** an upper tooth.

up•per[2] (up′ər) /'ʌpər/ *n.* [*count*] *Slang.* a drug that stimulates, as an amphetamine.

up•per•case (up′ər kās′) /'ʌpər'keys/ *adj.,* **1.** (of an alphabetical character) capital: *uppercase characters like* A, B, *and* C. **—*n.*** [*noncount*] **2.** capital letters when they are thought of as a group. Compare LOWERCASE.

up′per class′, *n.* [*count*] a class of people above the middle class, characterized by wealth and social prestige. **—up′per-class′,** *adj.*: *an upper-class family.*

up•per•class•man (up′ər klas′mən) /'ʌpər'klæsmən/ *n.* [*count*], *pl.* **-men.** a junior or senior in a secondary school or a college or university.

up′per crust′, *n.* [*count; usually singular; usually: the* + ~] *Informal.* the highest social class.

up•per•cut (up′ər kut′) /'ʌpər,kʌt/ *n., v.,* **-cut, -cut•ting. —*n.*** [*count*] **1.** a swinging blow directed upward, as to an opponent's chin. **—*v.*** [~ + *obj*] **2.** to strike (an opponent) with an uppercut.

up′per hand′, *n.* [*count; usually singular; usually: the* + ~] a controlling position; advantage: *tried to gain the upper hand in the negotiations.*

up•per•most (up′ər mōst′) /'ʌpər,mowst/ *adj.* Also, **up•most** (up′mōst′) /'ʌp,mowst/. **1.** highest in place, order, rank, power, etc.; topmost; predominant: *a subject of uppermost concern.* **—*adv.*** **2.** in or into the uppermost place, rank, or importance.

up•pi•ty (up′i tē) /'ʌpɪtiy/ *adj. Informal.* tending to be haughty; snobbish; arrogant.

up•raised (up rāzd′) /ʌp'reyzd/ *adj.* raised up; lifted in the air.

up•right (up′rīt′, up rīt′) /'ʌp,rayt, ʌp'rayt/ *adj.* **1.** straight, erect, or vertical, as in position or posture: *upright posture.* **2.** [*before a noun*] raised or made vertically: *an upright vacuum cleaner.* **3.** being fair, right, honest, or just: *an upright citizen.* **—*n.*** [*count*] **4.** something standing straight up, as a piece of timber. **5.** Usually, **uprights.** [*plural*] goalposts, as on a football field. **6.** an object designed to stand upright: *The piano is an upright.* **—*adv.*** **7.** in an upright position or direction.

up•ris•ing (up′rī′zing, up rī′zing) /'ʌp,rayzɪŋ, ʌp'rayzɪŋ/ *n.* [*count*] a revolt; an act of rising up against authority.

up•roar (up′rôr′, -rōr′) /'ʌp,rɔr, -,rowr/ *n.* **1.** [*noncount*] a state of noisy disturbance, as of a crowd; turmoil. **2.** [*count*] an instance of this.

up•roar•i•ous (up rôr′ē əs, -rōr′-) /ʌp'rɔriyəs, -'rowr-/ *adj.* **1.** characterized by or in a state of uproar; riotous. **2.** very funny: *an uproarious joke.* **3.** very loud or noisy: *uproarious laughter.*

up•root (up ro͞ot′, -ro͝ot′) /ʌp'ruwt, -'rʊt/ *v.* [~ + *obj*] **1.** to pull out by or as if by the roots: *The wind uprooted the trees.* **2.** to displace or remove (people) violently, such as from a home, country, customs, or way of life.

ups′ and downs′, *n.* [*plural*] rises and falls of fortune; good and bad times.

up•scale (up′skāl′) /'ʌp,skeyl/ *adj.* of, for, or catering to well-off consumers: *upscale magazines.*

up•set (*v., adj.* up set′; *n.* up′set′) / *v., adj.* ʌp'sɛt; *n.* 'ʌp,sɛt/ *v.,* **-set, -set•ting,** *n., adj.* **—*v.*** [~ + *obj*] **1.** to overturn: *to upset a glass of milk.* **2.** to disturb mentally or emotionally; distress: *The accident upset her.* **3.** to disturb completely; throw into disorder: *to upset a plan.* **4.** to disturb physically: *The food upset his stomach.* **5.**

to defeat (an opponent that is favored), as in politics or sports. *—n.* [*count*] **6.** the unexpected defeat of an opponent that is favored. *—adj.* [*usually: be* + ~] **7.** distressed; disturbed: *She's very upset at the children.*

up•shot (up′shot′) /ˈʌpˌʃɒt/ *n.* [*count; usually singular*] the final outcome; conclusion; result: *The upshot of the disagreement was that they broke up the partnership.*

up•side (up′sīd′) /ˈʌpˌsayd/ *n.* [*count*] **1.** the upper side or part. **2.** an upward trend, as in stock prices.

up′side down′, *adv.* **1.** with the upper part at the bottom. **2.** in or into complete disorder; topsy-turvy: *turned the room upside down in their search.*

up•stage (up′stāj′) /ˈʌpˈsteydʒ/ *adv., adj., v.,* **-staged, -stag•ing.** *—adv.* **1.** at or toward the back of the stage. *—adj.* **2.** of, relating to, or located at the back of the stage. *—v.* [~ + *obj*] **3. a.** to move upstage of (another actor), forcing him or her to act with back to the audience. **b.** to draw attention away from (another actor) by some activity: *upstaged her by loudly blowing his nose.* **4.** to outdo professionally, socially, etc.

up•stairs (up′stârz′) /ˈʌpˈstɛərz/ *adv., adj., n., pl.* **-stairs.** *—adv.* **1.** up the stairs; to or on an upper floor: *I walked her upstairs.* **2.** to or at a higher level of authority: *moved upstairs in the corporation. —adj.* [*before a noun*] **3.** of, relating to, or located on an upper floor: *an upstairs apartment. —n.* [*count; singular; used with a singular verb*] **4.** an upper story or stories; the part of a building or house above the ground floor. **—*Idiom.*** **5. kick upstairs,** [*kick* + *obj* + ~] to promote to a higher but less powerful or important position.

up•stand•ing (up stan′ding) /ʌpˈstændɪŋ/ *adj.* honorable; straightforward; upright: *an upstanding member of the community.*

up•start (up′stärt′) /ˈʌpˌstɑrt/ *n.* [*count*] **1.** a person who has risen suddenly from a humble position to wealth, power, or importance. *—adj.* [*before a noun*] **2.** being, resembling, or characteristic of an upstart.

up•state (up′stāt′) /ˈʌpˈsteyt/ *n.* [*noncount*] **1.** the part of a state that is farther north or farther from the chief city. *—adj.* **2.** of or coming from such an area. *—adv.* **3.** in, to, or toward an upstate area.

up•stream (up′strēm′) /ˈʌpˈstriym/ *adv.* **1.** toward or in the higher part of a stream; against the current. *—adj.* **2.** directed or located upstream.

up•surge (*v.* up sûrj′; *n.* up′sûrj′) / *v.* ʌpˈsɜrdʒ; *n.* ˈʌpˌsɜrdʒ/ *v.,* **-surged, -surg•ing,** *n. —v.* [*no obj*] **1.** to surge up; increase; rise. *—n.* [*count*] **2.** the act of surging up; a large or rapid increase: *a sudden upsurge in consumer spending.*

up•swing (*n.* up′swing′; *v.* up swing′) / *n.* ˈʌpˌswɪŋ; *v.* ʌpˈswɪŋ/ *n.* [*count*] **1.** an upward swing or swinging movement, as of a pendulum. **2.** a marked increase or improvement: *an upswing in stock prices.*

up•take (up′tāk′) /ˈʌpˌteyk/ *n.* **1.** [*noncount*] understanding or comprehension; mental grasp: *quick on the uptake.* **2.** [*count*] an act or instance of taking up. **3.** [*count*] a flue leading upward from below, such as for conducting smoke or a current of air. **4.** [*noncount*] the absorption of substances, as nutrients, by the tissues of the body.

up•tight (up′tīt′) /ˈʌpˈtayt/ *adj. Informal.* **1.** tense, anxious, worried, nervous, or jittery. **2.** stiffly conventional; straitlaced.

up′-to-date′, *adj.* **1.** keeping up with the times; current; modern: *up-to-date fashions; up-to-date electronic networks.* **2.** including the latest information or facts: *an up-to-date report.*

up•town (*adv., n.* up′toun′; *adj.* -toun′) / *adv., n.* ˈʌpˈtawn; *adj.* -ˌtawn/ *adv.* **1.** to, toward, or in the upper part of a town or city, usually the part away from the main business section. *—adj.* [*before a noun*] **2.** moving toward, situated in, or relating to the upper part of a town or city: *Take the uptown bus. —n.* [*noncount*] **3.** the uptown section of a town or city.

up•turn (up′tûrn′) /ˈʌpˌtɜrn/ *n.* [*count*] an upward turn, as in prices or business.

up•ward (up′wərd) /ˈʌpwərd/ *adv.* Also, **up′wards. 1.** toward a higher place or position: *birds flying upward.* **2.** toward a higher or more distinguished condition, rank, level, etc: *to move upward in the company.* **3.** beyond; more: *students 12 years old and upward.* **4.** toward the source of a stream or the interior of a region. **5.** in the upper parts; above. *—adj.* **6.** moving or tending upward; directed at or situated in a higher place or position: *an upward motion.* **—*Idiom.*** **7. upward(s) of,** more than: *costs upwards of a thousand dollars.* —**up′ward•ly,** *adv.*

u•ra•ni•um (yŏŏ rā′nē əm) /yʊˈreyniyəm/ *n.* [*noncount*] a white, shining, radioactive, metallic element, used in atomic and hydrogen bombs and as a fuel in nuclear reactors. —**u•ran•ic** (yŏŏ ran′ik) /yʊˈrænɪk/ *adj.*

ur•ban (ûr′bən) /ˈɜrbən/ *adj.* **1.** of, relating to, or making up a city or town: *urban areas.* **2.** living in a city: *the urban population.*

ur•bane (ûr bān′) /ɜrˈbeyn/ *adj.* polished in one's manner or style; sophisticated. —**ur•ban•i•ty** (ûr ban′i tē) /ɜrˈbænɪtiy/ *n.* [*noncount*]

ur•ban•ize (ûr′bə nīz′) /ˈɜrbəˌnayz/ *v.* [~ + *obj*], **-ized, -iz•ing.** to cause to take on the characteristics of a city. —**ur•ban•i•za•tion** (ûr′bə nə zā′shən) /ˌɜrbənəˈzeyʃən/ *n.* [*noncount*]

ur′ban renew′al, *n.* [*noncount*] the repairing of rundown city areas by fixing old buildings or demolishing and replacing them with new ones. Also called **ur′ban redevel′opment.**

ur′ban sprawl′, *n.* [*noncount*] the uncontrolled spread of a city into outlying regions.

ur•chin (ûr′chin) /ˈɜrtʃɪn/ *n.* [*count*] **1.** a mischievous child. **2.** any small child or youngster. **3.** SEA URCHIN.

-ure, *suffix. -ure* is attached to roots and verbs to form abstract nouns that refer to action, result, and instrument or use: *press-* + *-ure* → *pressure; legislate* + *-ure* → *legislature; fract-* + *-ure* → *fracture.*

urge (ûrj) /ɜrdʒ/ *v.,* **urged, urg•ing,** *n. —v.* **1.** [~ + *obj*] to encourage forcefully: *to urge an athlete to greater effort.* **2.** [~ + *obj* + *obj*] to impel to greater speed: *The riders urged their horses around the track.* **3.** to try to persuade (someone), as by asking or begging; exhort: [~ + *obj*]: *to urge a person to greater caution.* [~ + *obj* + *to* + *verb*]: *She urged us to go slow.* **4.** [~ + *obj*] to recommend earnestly: *to urge a plan of action on us.* **5.** [~ + *obj*] to insist on or stress: *to urge the need for haste. —n.* [*count*] **6.** an act of urging; influence or force; impulse. **7.** an instinctive drive: *the sex urge.*

ur•gent (ûr′jənt) /ˈɜrdʒənt/ *adj.* **1.** requiring immediate action or attention: *an urgent message.* **2.** conveying a sense of earnest insistence: *spoke in low, urgent tones.* —**ur′gen•cy,** *n.* [*noncount*] —**ur′gent•ly,** *adv.*

u•ri•nal (yŏŏr′ə nl) /ˈyʊrənl/ *n.* [*count*] **1.** a flushable wall fixture used by men for urinating. **2.** a building or enclosure containing such fixtures.

u•ri•nar•y (yŏŏr′ə ner′ē) /ˈyʊrəˌnɛriy/ *adj.* of or relating to urine or to the organs that secrete and discharge urine.

u•ri•nate (yŏŏr′ə nāt′) /ˈyʊrəˌneyt/ *v.* [*no obj*], **-nat•ed, -nat•ing.** to discharge urine.

u•rine (yŏŏr′in) /ˈyʊrɪn/ *n.* [*noncount*] the waste matter sent out of the body by the kidneys through the bladder, in mammals as a slightly acid yellowish liquid.

urn (ûrn) /ɜrn/ *n.* [*count*] **1.** a large or decorated vase. **2.** a vase for holding the ashes of a person's cremated body. **3.** a large metal container with a spout, used for making or serving tea or coffee in large amounts.

U•ru•guay•an (yŏŏ′ə gwā′ən, -gwī′ən) /ˌyʊəˈgweyən, -ˈgwayən/ *adj.* **1.** of or relating to Uruguay. *—n.* [*count*] **2.** a person born or living in Uruguay.

us (us) /ʌs/ *pron.* **1.** the object form of WE, used as a direct or indirect object: *They took us to the circus. She asked us the way.* **2.** (used in place of the pronoun *we* after the verb *to be*): *Who's there? —It's us!* **3.** (used instead of the pronoun *our* before a gerund or present participle): *She graciously forgave us spilling the gravy.*

U.S. or **US,** an abbreviation of: United States.

U.S.A. or **USA,** an abbreviation of: United States of America.

us•a•ble or **use•a•ble** (yōō′zə bəl) /ˈyuwzəbəl/ *adj.* **1.** available or convenient for use. **2.** capable of being used. —**us•a•bil•i•ty** (yōō′zə bil′i tē) /ˌyuwzəˈbɪlɪtiy/ *n.* [*noncount*]

us•age (yōō′sij, -zij) /ˈyuwsɪdʒ, -zɪdʒ/ *n.* **1.** [*noncount*] a customary way of doing something; a custom or practice. **2.** [*noncount*] the customary manner in which a language or a form of a language is spoken or written. **3.** [*count*] a particular instance of this: *a usage borrowed from French.*

use (*v.* yōōz *or, for pt. form of 7* yōōst; *n.* yōōs) / *v.* yuwz *or, for pt. form of 7* yuwst; *n.* yuws/ *v.,* **used, us•ing,** *n. —v.* **1.** [~ + *obj*] to employ for some purpose: *to use a knife to cut the meat.* **2.** [~ + *obj*] to apply (something) to one's own purposes: *to use the bathroom.* **3.** to consume, expend, or exhaust: [~ *(+ up)* + *obj*]: *We've used (up) the money.* [~ + *obj* + *(up)*]: *We've used the money (up).* **4.** [~ + *obj*] to treat or behave toward: *He used his employees well.* **5.** [~ + *obj*] to take unfair advantage of; exploit: *was just using him for his money and* *social contacts.* **6.** [~ + *obj*] to consume or take habitually: *to use drugs.* **7.** [*past tense of use* + *to* + *verb*] to be customarily found doing (expresses habitual or customary actions in the past): *He used to go to school every day.* —*n.* **8.** [*noncount*] the act of using or the state of being used. **9.** [*count*] an instance or way of using something: *a painter's use of color.* **10.** [*count*] a way of being used; a purpose for which something is used: *Describe some of the uses of a wrench.* **11.** [*noncount*] the power, right, or privilege of using something: *to lose the use of an eye.* **12.** [*noncount*] utility; usefulness: *of no practical use.* **13.** [*noncount*] help; profit; resulting good; advantage: *What's the use of complaining?* **14.** [*noncount*] need: *Have you any use for another calendar?* —***Idiom.*** **15. have no use for,** [*have no* + ~ + *for* + *obj*] **a.** to have no need for. **b.** to feel intolerant of: *to have no use for petty thieves.* **16. in use,** being used: *The laboratory is in use.* **17. make use of,** [~ + *obj*] to use, esp. effectively; employ: *He makes use of his purchases.* **18. put to use,** [*put* + *obj* + *to* + ~] to find a function for; utilize: *He puts his computer to good use.* —**us′er,** *n.* [*count*]

used (yo͞ozd *or, for 3,* yo͞ost) /yuwzd *or, for 3,* yuwst/ *adj.* **1.** previously used or owned; secondhand: *a used car; used books.* **2.** employed for a purpose; utilized. —***Idiom.*** **3. used to,** [*be* + ~] accustomed to; habituated to: *He's still not used to life in the city.*

use•ful (yo͞os′fəl) /ˈyuwsfəl/ *adj.* **1.** being of use or service: *a useful member of society; a useful resource, like timber.* **2.** helpful to others: *She's very useful to have around.* —**use′ful•ly,** *adv.* —**use′ful•ness,** *n.* [*noncount*]

use•less (yo͞os′lis) /ˈyuwslɪs/ *adj.* **1.** of no use; not serving the purpose or any purpose: *useless information.* [*It* + *be* + ~ + *to* + *verb*]: *It was useless to complain.* **2.** without useful qualities; of no practical good: *He's useless at solving problems.* —**use′less•ly,** *adv.* —**use′less•ness,** *n.* [*noncount*]

us′er-friend′ly, *adj.* easy to operate, understand, etc.: *a user-friendly computer.*

ush•er (ush′ər) /ˈʌʃər/ *n.* [*count*] **1.** a person who escorts people to seats in a theater, church, etc. **2.** an official doorkeeper, such as in a courtroom. **3.** a male attendant of a bridegroom at a wedding. —*v.* **4.** to act as an usher (to): [~ + *obj*]: *She ushered them to their seats.* [*no obj*]: *He got his brother to usher at the wedding.* **5.** to precede or herald: [~ + *in* + *obj*]: *ushering in a new age of prosperity.* [~ + *obj* + *in*]: *to usher prosperity in.*

ush•er•ette (ush′ə ret′) /ˌʌʃəˈrɛt/ *n.* [*count*] a woman who acts as an usher.

USS or **U.S.S.,** an abbreviation of: United States Ship.

u•su•al (yo͞o′zho͞o əl) /ˈyuwʒuwəl/ *adj.* **1.** expected to be found or to be present: *accomplished the job with her usual skill.* [*It* + *be* + ~ *(for* + *obj)* + *to* + *verb*]: *It's not usual (for him) to be so late.* **2.** commonly met with or observed; ordinary: *the usual cold winter weather.* **3.** commonplace; everyday: *all the usual things of life.* —*n.* [*count; usually: the* + ~] **4.** something that is usual: *He'll have his usual to drink.* —***Idiom.*** **5. as usual,** in the customary or habitual way: *He was late, as usual.* —**u′su•al•ly,** *adv.*

u•surp (yo͞o sûrp′, -zûrp′) /yuwˈsɜrp, -ˈzɜrp/ *v* [~ + *obj*] to seize and hold by force or without legal right: *to usurp a rightful government.* —**u•sur•pa•tion** (yo͞o′sər pā′shən, -zər-) /ˌyuwsərˈpeyʃən, -zər-/ *n.* [*noncount*] —**u•surp′er,** *n.* [*count*]

u•su•ry (yo͞o′zhə rē) /ˈyuwʒəriy/ *n.* [*noncount*] the practice of lending money at an unfairly high interest rate. —**u′sur•er,** *n.* [*count*] —**u•sur•i•ous** (yo͞o zho͝or′ē əs) /yuwˈʒʊriyəs/ *adj.*

UT or **Ut.,** an abbreviation of: Utah.

u•ten•sil (yo͞o ten′səl) /yuwˈtɛnsəl/ *n.* [*count*] **1.** an instrument, container, or other object commonly used in a kitchen, dairy, etc.: *eating utensils.* **2.** any instrument, container, or tool serving a useful purpose: *farming utensils.*

u•ter•us (yo͞o′tər əs) /ˈyuwtərəs/ *n.* [*count*], *pl.* **u•ter•i** (yo͞o′tə rī′) /ˈyuwtəˌray/ **u•ter•us•es.** a hollow organ of certain female mammals in which the fertilized egg develops during pregnancy; the womb. —**u•ter•ine** (yo͞o′tər in, -tə rīn′) /ˈyuwtərɪn, -təˌrayn/ *adj.*

u•til•i•tar•i•an (yo͞o til′i târ′ē ən) /yuwˌtɪlɪˈtɛəriyən/ *adj.* designed for or concerned with utility or usefulness rather than beauty, ornamentation, etc.

u•til•i•ty (yo͞o til′i tē) /yuwˈtɪlɪtiy/ *n., pl.* **-ties. 1.** [*noncount*] the state or quality of being useful; usefulness. **2.** [*count*] a public service, as that providing electricity or water.

util′ity room′, *n.* [*count*] a room, esp. in a house, reserved for a washing machine, furnace, or other large appliances.

u•ti•lize (yo͞ot′l īz′) /ˈyuwtḷˌayz/ *v.* [~ + *obj*], **-lized, -liz•ing.** to put to use, esp. to profitable or practical use: *How can we best utilize our limited resources?* —**u•ti•li•za•tion** (yo͞ot′l ə zā′shən) /ˌyuwtḷəˈzeyʃən/ *n.* [*noncount*]

ut•most (ut′mōst′) /ˈʌtˌmowst/ *adj.* **1.** of the greatest or highest degree, quantity, etc.: *of the utmost importance.* —*n.* [*noncount; often: the* + ~] **2.** the greatest degree or amount: *provided the utmost in comfort.* **3.** the best of one's abilities, powers, etc.: *He did his utmost to win.* **4.** the extreme limit: *My patience has been tried to the utmost.*

U•to•pi•a (yo͞o tō′pē ə) /yuwˈtowpiyə/ *n., pl.* **-pi•as. 1.** [*proper noun*] an imaginary island described in Sir Thomas More's *Utopia* (1516) as enjoying perfection in law, politics, etc. **2.** [*count; usually: utopia*] any ideal place or state. —**U•to′pi•an, u•to′pi•an,** *adj., n.* [*count*]

ut•ter[1] (ut′ər) /ˈʌtər/ *v.* [~ + *obj*] **1.** to speak or pronounce: *He was unable to utter a word.* **2.** to emit or give out (cries, notes, etc.) with the voice: *to utter a sigh.* **3.** to give forth (a sound) otherwise than with the voice: *The engine uttered a shriek.*

ut•ter[2] (ut′ər) /ˈʌtər/ *adj.* [*before a noun*] complete; total; absolute: *utter abandonment to grief.* —**ut′ter•ly,** *adv.: That book is utterly boring.*

ut•ter•ance (ut′ər əns) /ˈʌtərəns/ *n.* **1.** [*count*] something uttered. **2.** [*noncount*] an act of uttering.

ut•ter•most (ut′ər mōst′) /ˈʌtərˌmowst/ *adj., n.* UTMOST.

U-turn (yo͞o′tûrn′) /ˈyuwˌtɜrn/ *n.* [*count*] **1.** a U-shaped turn made by a vehicle so as to head in the opposite direction from its original course. **2.** a reversal of policy, tactics, etc., resembling such a turn. —*v.* [*no obj*] **3.** to execute a U-turn.

UV, an abbreviation of: ultraviolet.

U•zi (o͞o′zē) /ˈuwziy/ *n.* [*count*], *pl.* **U•zis.** a compact 9mm submachine gun of Israeli design.

V

V, v (vē) /viy/ *n.* [*count*], *pl.* **Vs** or **V's, vs** or **v's.** the 22nd letter of the English alphabet, a consonant.

V, *Symbol.* [*sometimes:* v] the Roman numeral for five.

v., an abbreviation of: **1.** verb. **2.** verse. **3.** version. **4.** versus. **5.** vice. **6.** village. **7.** voice. **8.** volt. **9.** voltage. **10.** volume.

VA, an abbreviation of: **1.** Virginia. **2.** Also, **va** volt-ampere.

Va., an abbreviation of: Virginia.

-vac-, *root.* *-vac-* comes from Latin, where it has the meaning "empty." This meaning is found in such words as: EVACUATE, VACANCY, VACANT, VACATE, VACATION, VACUOUS, VACUUM.

va•can•cy (vā′kən sē) /'veykənsiy/ *n., pl.* **-cies. 1.** [*noncount*] the state of being vacant; emptiness. **2.** [*count*] a vacant or unoccupied place, esp. one for rent, as a hotel room or an apartment: *several vacancies listed in the paper.* **3.** [*count*] an unoccupied position or office: *We have a vacancy for PTA president.* See -VAC-.

va•cant (vā′kənt) /'veykənt/ *adj.* **1.** having no contents; empty. **2.** having no occupant; unoccupied: *a vacant seat.* **3.** not in use: *a vacant warehouse.* **4.** lacking in intelligence: *a vacant expression.* **5.** not occupied by an incumbent, official, or the like, as a political office: *a vacant senate seat.* See -VAC-.

va•cate (vā′kāt) /'veykeyt/ *v.* [~ + *obj*], **-cat•ed, -cat•ing. 1.** to give up occupancy of: *to vacate an apartment.* **2.** to give up or relinquish: *to vacate a senate seat.* See -VAC-.

va•ca•tion (vā kā′shən, və-) /vey'keyʃən, və-/ *n.* **1.** a period during which one does not have to report to one's regular work, school, or other activity, usually used for rest, recreation, or travel: [*count*]: *went on a long vacation.* [*noncount*]: *They're on vacation.* **—*v.*** [*no obj*] **2.** to take or have a vacation: *vacationed in Spain.* —**va•ca′tion•er,** *n.* [*count*] See -VAC-.

vac•ci•nate (vak′sə nāt′) /'væksə,neyt/ *v.,* **-nat•ed, -nat•ing.** to inoculate with a vaccine. —**vac•ci•na•tion** (vak′sə nā′shən) /,væksə'neyʃən/ *n.* [*noncount*]: *the importance of vaccination against disease.* [*count*]: *performed thousands of vaccinations.*

vac•cine (vak sēn′) /væk'siyn/ *n.* [*count*] **1.** a preparation introduced into the body to prevent a disease by causing the body to produce antibodies against it, usually a weakened substance containing the virus causing the disease against which the body can react. **2.** a software program that helps to protect against computer viruses.

vac•il•late (vas′ə lāt′) /'væsə,leyt/ *v.* [*no obj*], **-lat•ed, -lat•ing.** to be unsure in one's mind or opinion; be indecisive about what action to take: *vacillated before deciding.* —**vac•il•la•tion** (vas′ə lā′shən) /,væsə'leyʃən/ *n.* [*noncount*]

va•cu•i•ty (va kyo͞o′i tē, və-) /væ'kyuwɪtiy, və-/ *n., pl.* **-ties. 1.** [*noncount*] absence of thought or intelligence: *a stare indicating complete vacuity.* **2.** [*count*] something said or proposed that is foolish or stupid. See -VAC-.

vac•u•ous (vak′yo͞o əs) /'vækyuwəs/ *adj.* **1.** lacking contents; empty. **2.** lacking in ideas or intelligence: *a vacuous mind; a vacuous smile.* —**vac′u•ous•ly,** *adv.* See -VAC-.

vac•u•um (vak′yo͞om, -yəm) /'vækyuwm, -yəm/ *n., pl.* **-u•ums** for 1–4, **-u•a** (-yo͞o ə) /-yuwə/ for 1–3; *adj.; v.* **—*n.*** [*count*] **1.** a space entirely empty of matter. **2.** an enclosed space from which matter, esp. air, has been partially removed so that the matter or gas remaining in the space exerts less pressure than the atmosphere. **3.** a space not filled or occupied; emptiness; void: *The loss of his son left a vacuum in his life.* **4.** VACUUM CLEANER. **—*adj.*** **5.** of or relating to a vacuum. **—*v.*** **6.** to clean with a vacuum cleaner: [~ + *obj*]: *to vacuum the rug.* [*no obj*]: *I vacuum on Fridays.* See -VAC-.

vac′uum clean′er, *n.* [*count*] an electrical device for cleaning carpets, floors, etc., by suction. Also called **vac′uum sweep′er.** See illustration at APPLIANCE.

vac′uum-packed′, *adj.* packed, as in a can, with as much air as possible removed before sealing.

-vade-, *root.* *-vade-* comes from Latin, where it has the meaning "go." This meaning is found in such words as: EVADE, INVADE, PERVADE.

vag•a•bond (vag′ə bond′) /'vægə,bɒnd/ *adj.* **1.** wandering from place to place without any settled home. **—*n.*** [*count*] **2.** a person, usually without a permanent home, who wanders from place to place; a nomad.

va•gar•y (vā′gə rē, və gâr′ē) /'veygəriy, və'gɛəriy/ *n., pl.* **-gar•ies.** an unpredictable or unexpected action, occurrence, course, or idea: *the vagaries of a life.*

va•gi•na (və jī′nə) /və'dʒaynə/ *n.* [*count*], *pl.* **-nas, -nae** (-nē) /-niy/. the passage leading from the uterus to the vulva in female mammals. —**vag•i•nal** (vaj′ə nəl) /'vædʒənəl/ *adj.*

va•grant (vā′grənt) /'veygrənt/ *n.* [*count*] **1.** a person who wanders about idly and has no permanent home or employment; a vagabond. **2.** a person who wanders from place to place; wanderer; rover. **—*adj.*** [*before a noun*] **3.** wandering or roaming from place to place. **4.** wandering idly without a permanent home or employment: *vagrant beggars.* **5.** not fixed or settled; random: *a vagrant thought.* —**va′gran•cy,** *n.* [*noncount*]

vague (vāg) /veyg/ *adj.,* **va•guer, va•guest. 1.** not clearly stated or expressed: *vague promises.* **2.** indefinite or indistinct in nature or character: *a vague rumor.* **3.** not clear or definite in thought, understanding, or expression: *was vague when I asked his plan.* —**vague′ly,** *adv.* —**vague′ness,** *n.* [*noncount*]

vain (vān) /veyn/ *adj.,* **-er, -est. 1.** overly proud of or concerned about one's own appearance, qualities, achievements, etc. **2.** ineffectual or unsuccessful; useless; futile: *vain efforts.* **—*Idiom.*** **3. in vain, a.** without effect; to no purpose: *All the work was in vain.* **b.** in an improper or irreverent manner: *to take God's name in vain.* —**vain′ly,** *adv.*

-val-, *root.* *-val-* comes from Latin, where it has the meaning "worth; health; strength." This meaning is found in such words as: DEVALUE, EQUIVALENT, EVALUATE, PREVALENT, UNDERVALUE, VALEDICTORIAN, VALIANT, VALID, VALIDATE, VALOR, VALUE.

val., an abbreviation of: value.

val•ance (val′əns, vā′ləns) /'væləns, 'veyləns/ *n.* [*count*] a short curtain or piece of drapery hung from the edge of a canopy, the frame of a bed, etc.

vale (vāl) /veyl/ *n.* [*count*] **1.** VALLEY. **2.** the world, or mortal or earthly life: *this vale of tears.*

val•e•dic•to•ri•an (val′i dik tôr′ē ən, -tōr′-) /,vælɪdɪk'tɔriyən, -'towr-/ *n.* [*count*] a student, usually the one ranking highest academically in a graduating class, who delivers the valedictory at a graduation ceremony. See -VAL-, -DICT-.

val•e•dic•to•ry (val′i dik′tə rē) /,vælɪ'dɪktəriy/ *adj., n., pl.* **-ries. —*adj.*** **1.** bidding good-bye; saying farewell: *a valedictory speech.* **2.** of or relating to an occasion of leave-taking: *a valedictory ceremony.* **—*n.*** [*count*] **3.** a speech delivered at the commencement exercises of a college or school on behalf of the graduating class. **4.** any farewell speech. See -VAL-, -DICT-.

val•en•tine (val′ən tīn′) /'vælən,tayn/ *n.* [*count*] **1.** a card or message, usually expressing love or affection, or sentiment, or a gift sent by one person to another on a holiday called Valentine's Day, February 14. **2.** a sweetheart chosen or greeted on this day.

val•et (va lā′, val′it, val′ā) /væ'ley, 'vælɪt, 'væley/ *n.* [*count*] **1.** a male servant who attends to the personal needs of his employer, as by taking care of clothing; manservant. **2.** an employee who cares for the clothing of guests of a hotel, passengers on a ship, etc. **3.** an attendant who parks cars for guests at a hotel, restaurant, etc.

val•iant (val′yənt) /'vælyənt/ *adj.* **1.** boldly courageous; brave: *valiant soldiers.* **2.** marked by bravery or valor; heroic: *a valiant effort.* —**val′iant•ly,** *adv.* See -VAL-. **—Syn.** See BRAVE.

val•id (val′id) /'vælɪd/ *adj.* **1.** sound; just; well-founded: *a valid argument.* **2.** having proper authority; that can be used legally or properly; authoritative: *a valid driver's license.* **3.** legally sound, effective, or binding: *a valid contract.* —**va•lid•i•ty** (və lid′i tē) /və'lɪdɪtiy/ *n.* [*noncount*] —**val′id•ness,** *n.* [*noncount*] See -VAL-.

val•i•date (val′i dāt′) /'vælɪ,deyt/ *v.* [~ + *obj*], **-dat•ed, -dat•ing. 1.** to make valid; substantiate; confirm. **2.** to give official permission, confirmation, or approval to: *to validate a passport.* —**val•i•da•tion** (val′i dā′shən) /,vælɪ'deyʃən/ *n.* [*noncount*] See -VAL-.

va•lise (və lēs′, -lēz′) /və'liys, -'liyz/ *n.* [*count*] a small piece of hand luggage; suitcase.

val•ley (val′ē) /'væliy/ *n.* [*count*], *pl.* **-leys. 1.** a long, narrow area that is lower than surrounding uplands, hills, or mountains. See illustration at LANDSCAPE. **2.** a wide, more or less flat, and relatively low region drained by a river system. **3.** a low point or low time in any process or situation: *peaks and valleys in the stock market.*

val•or (val′ər) /ˈvælər/ *n.* [*noncount*] boldness or determination in facing danger. Also, *esp. Brit.,* **val′our.** —**val′or•ous,** *adj.* —**val′or•ous•ly,** *adv.* See -VAL-.

val•u•a•ble (val′yo͞o ə bəl, -yə bəl) /ˈvælyuwəbəl, -yəbəl/ *adj.* **1.** worth a great deal of money. **2.** of considerable use, importance, or value: *a highly valuable player.* —*n.* **3.** Usually, **valuables.** [*plural*] personal articles, as jewelry, of great value. See -VAL-.

val•u•a•tion (val′yo͞o ā′shən) /ˌvælyuwˈeyʃən/ *n.* **1.** [*count*] an estimated value. **2.** the action of estimating or calculating how much something is worth: [*count*]: *to set a high valuation on heroism.* [*noncount*]: *the valuation of a business.* See -VAL-.

val•ue (val′yo͞o) /ˈvælyuw/ *n., v.,* **-ued, -u•ing.** —*n.* **1.** [*noncount*] relative worth or importance; significance: *the value of a college education.* **2.** [*noncount*] monetary or material worth, as in business. **3.** [*noncount*] the worth of something in terms of some medium of exchange: *the value of the Swedish kroner.* **4.** [*noncount*] equivalent worth in money, material, or services: *The value of the company was in the millions.* **5.** [*noncount*] estimated or assigned worth: *the best value for your dollar.* **6.** [*count*] magnitude; quantity: *Find the value of x in the equation x + 2 = 6.* **7.** Often, **values.** [*plural*] the abstract concepts of what is right, worthwhile, or desirable; principles or standards. —*v.* [~ + *obj*] **8.** to calculate the monetary value of: *valued the painting at over one million dollars.* **9.** to regard highly; think of (someone or something) greatly: *We value your work highly.* —**val′ue•less,** *adj.* See -VAL-.

val′ue-add′ed tax′, *n.* [*count*] a tax based on the value added to a product at each stage of production.

valve (valv) /vælv/ *n., v.,* **valved, valv•ing.** —*n.* [*count*] **1.** any device for halting or controlling the flow of something, as a liquid, through a pipe or other passage. **2.** a hinged lid or other movable part that closes or changes the passage in such a device. **3.** a structure in the body that permits the flow of a fluid, as blood, in one direction only: *a heart valve.* **4.** (in musical wind instruments of the trumpet class) a device for changing the length of the air column so as to alter the pitch of a tone. **5.** one of the two or more separable pieces that make up certain shells: *the valves of a clamshell.* —*v.* [~ + *obj*] **6.** to provide with a valve.

va•moose (va mo͞os′) /væˈmuws/ *v.* [*no obj*], **-moosed, -moos•ing.** *Slang.* to leave quickly.

vamp¹ (vamp) /væmp/ *n.* [*count*] **1.** the portion of a shoe or boot upper that covers the instep and toes. **2.** an introductory musical passage commonly consisting of a repeated succession of chords played before the start of a solo. —*v.* [~ + *obj*] **3.** to repair (a shoe) with a new vamp. **4.** to patch; repair. **5.** [~ + *up* + *obj*] to concoct or invent: *to vamp up ugly rumors.*

vamp² (vamp) /væmp/ *n.* [*count*] **1.** a seductive or attractive woman who uses her beauty to get men to submit. —*v.* [~ + *obj*] **2.** to seduce with feminine charms.

vam•pire (vam′pīᵊr) /ˈvæmpayᵊr/ *n.* [*count*] **1.** a corpse believed to come alive and leave the grave, typically in order to suck the blood of sleeping persons at night. **2.** a person who preys ruthlessly upon others.

van (van) /væn/ *n.* [*count*] **1.** a covered vehicle, usually a large truck or trailer, used for moving goods or animals. **2.** a small boxlike vehicle, resembling a panel truck, that can be used as a truck or for passengers or camping.

van•dal (van′dl) /ˈvændl̩/ *n.* [*count*] a person who maliciously destroys or damages public or private property.

van•dal•ism (van′dl iz′əm) /ˈvændl̩ˌɪzəm/ *n.* [*noncount*] malicious destruction or damage of private or public property.

van•dal•ize (van′dl īz′) /ˈvændl̩ˌayz/ *v.* [~ + *obj*], **-ized, -iz•ing.** to destroy or deface by vandalism.

vane (vān) /veyn/ *n.* [*count*] **1.** WEATHER VANE. **2.** a flat blade or plate attached to a rotating cylinder or shaft, as in a turbine or windmill, that moves or is moved by steam, air, or a fluid: *the vanes of a propeller.*

van•guard (van′gärd′) /ˈvænˌgɑrd/ *n.* [*count*] **1.** the front part of an advancing army. **2.** [*count; usually singular; often: the* + ~] the forefront in any political movement or field of study.

va•nil•la (və nil′ə) /vəˈnɪlə/ *n., pl.* **-las.** **1.** [*count*] a tropical climbing orchid that has podlike fruit. **2.** [*count*] Also called **vanil′la bean′.** the fruit or bean of this orchid. **3.** [*noncount*] the juice squeezed or pressed out of this fruit, used in flavoring food and in perfumes: *ice cream made with vanilla.* —*adj.* **4.** containing or flavored with vanilla. **5.** ordinary; commonplace.

van•ish (van′ish) /ˈvænɪʃ/ *v.* [*no obj*] **1.** to disappear quickly from sight; become invisible: *The magician made the coin vanish before our eyes.* **2.** to go away, esp. secretly or without being noticed: *The thief vanished in the night.* **3.** to come to an end: *His anger vanished and he burst out laughing.*

van•i•ty (van′i tē) /ˈvænɪtiy/ *n., pl.* **-ties,** *adj.* —*n.* **1.** [*noncount*] too much pride in oneself or one's appearance; the character or quality of being vain. **2.** [*count*] something worthless, trivial, or pointless. **3.** [*count*] something about which one is vain. **4.** [*count*] a small case for holding cosmetics. **5.** [*count*] a dressing table. **6.** [*count*] a cabinet built around or below a bathroom sink. **7.** [*count*] COMPACT¹ (def. 6). —*adj.* **8.** of, relating to, or issued by a press that publishes books at the author's expense.

van•quish (vang′kwish, van′-) /ˈvæŋkwɪʃ, ˈvæn-/ *v.* [~ + *obj*] **1.** to conquer or defeat, as in battle: *to vanquish their foes.* **2.** to overcome: *to vanquish one's fears.* —**van′quish•er,** *n.* [*count*]

vap•id (vap′id) /ˈvæpɪd/ *adj.* lacking spirit or interest; dull: *some vapid remarks about the weather.* —**va•pid•i•ty** (va pid′i tē) /væˈpɪdɪtiy/ **vap′id•ness,** *n.* [*noncount*]

va•por (vā′pər) /ˈveypər/ *n.* **1.** a visible mass of tiny particles, as fog, mist, or smoke, floating or hanging in the air: [*count*]: *the vapors rising from the bog.* [*noncount*]: *clouds of vapor.* **2.** [*noncount*] a substance that has been made into the form of a gas: *water vapor.* **3.** [*noncount*] a substance changed into this steamlike mass of particles for medical uses. Also, *esp. Brit.,* **vapour.** —**va′por•a•ble,** *adj.*

va•por•ize (vā′pə rīz′) /ˈveypəˌrayz/ *v.,* **-ized, -iz•ing.** to (cause to) change into vapor: [*no obj*]: *At what temperature does alcohol vaporize?* [~ + *obj*]: *The heat from a hydrogen bomb blast would vaporize entire lakes.* —**va•por•i•za•tion** (vā′pər ə zā′shən) /ˌveypərəˈzeyʃən/ *n.* [*noncount*]

va•por•ous (vā′pər əs) /ˈveypərəs/ *adj.* **1.** having the form of vapor; full of vapor; foggy: *a vaporous cloud; vaporous bogs.* **2.** vaguely formed; not clearly defined; not substantial: *vaporous arguments that make no sense.*

-var-, *root.* *-var-* comes from Latin, where it has the meaning "change." This meaning is found in such words as: INVARIABLE, VARIABLE, VARIANCE, VARIANT, VARIATION, VARIED, VARIETY, VARIOUS, VARY.

var., an abbreviation of: **1.** variable. **2.** variant. **3.** variation. **4.** variety. **5.** various.

var•i•a•ble (vâr′ē ə bəl) /ˈvɛəriyəbəl/ *adj.* **1.** apt to vary; changeable; not staying the same: *a cloudy day with variable winds.* **2.** that can be deliberately varied: *variable power controlled by a dial.* **3.** inconstant; fickle: *Her affections tend to be variable.* —*n.* [*count*] **4.** something that may or does vary: *a situation with many variables.* **5. a.** a quantity or function that may take on or assume any given value or set of values. **b.** a symbol that represents this: *the variable* x *in the equation* x = 15 + y. —**var•i•a•bil•i•ty** (vâr′ē ə bil′i tē) /ˌvɛəriyəˈbɪlɪtiy/ *n.* [*noncount*] —**var′i•a•bly,** *adv.* See -VAR-.

var•i•ance (vâr′ē əns) /ˈvɛəriyəns/ *n.* [*count*] **1.** a permit to do something normally regulated by law, esp. to build in a way that is otherwise forbidden by a zoning law. —***Idiom.*** **2. at variance,** in a state of disagreement: *His views were at variance with mine.* See -VAR-.

var•i•ant (vâr′ē ənt) /ˈvɛəriyənt/ *adj.* [*before a noun*] **1.** tending to change; showing variety; not staying the same; differing: *variant spellings of words like* vapor *and* vapour. —*n.* [*count*] **2.** a person or thing that varies: *over 100 variants of that ballad.* **3.** a different spelling, pronunciation, or form of the same word: Vehemency *is a variant of* vehemence. See -VAR-.

var•i•a•tion (vâr′ē ā′shən) /ˌvɛəriyˈeyʃən/ *n.* **1.** [*noncount*] the act or process of varying or differing from what is normal or usual: *Those prices are subject to much variation.* **2.** [*count*] an instance of this: *a variation in quality.* **3.** [*count*] amount or degree of change: *a temperature variation of 20°.* **4.** [*count*] a different form of something; variant. **5.** [*count*] the transformation of a melody or theme in music by means of changes or elaborations in harmony, rhythm, and melody. See -VAR-.

var•i•col•ored (vâr′i kul′ərd) /ˈvɛərɪˌkʌlərd/ *adj.* having various colors. See -VAR-.

var•i•cose (var′i kōs′) /ˈværɪˌkows/ *adj.* enlarged or swollen beyond what is normal: *a varicose vein.*

var•ied (vâr′ēd) /ˈvɛəriyd/ *adj.* characterized by or showing variety; diverse: *varied species of plants.* See -VAR-.

var•i•e•gat•ed (vâr′ē i gā′tid, vâr′i gā′tid) /ˈvɛəriyɪˌgeytɪd, ˈvɛərɪˌgeytɪd/ *adj.* **1.** varied in appearance, as by having different colors, forms, shapes, etc.: *variegated leaves.* **2.** having variety; showing diversity: *variegated job duties.* See -VAR-.

va•ri•e•ty (və rī′i tē) /vəˈrayɪtiy/ *n., pl.* **-ties. 1.** [*noncount*] the state of being diversified or different: *He needed variety in his diet.* **2.** [*count; usually singular*] a number of different types of things, esp. ones in the same general category: *a large variety of foods to choose from.* **3.** [*count*] a kind, sort, or type: *different varieties of apples.* **4.** [*count*] Also called **vari′ety show′.** an entertainment made up of a series of brief performances, as of singing, dancing, and comedy. See -VAR-.

vari′ety store′, *n.* [*count*] a retail store with a wide variety of low-priced articles.

var•i•ous (vâr′ē əs) /ˈvɛəriyəs/ *adj.* [*usually: before a noun*] **1.** of different kinds, as two or more things: *various cheeses for sale.* **2.** showing differences or diversity: *houses of various designs.* **3.** different from each other; dissimilar: *various opinions about who committed the crime.* **4.** several; many: *We stayed at various hotels along the way.* **5.** individual; separate: *We spoke to various officials.* **6.** having many different qualities: *a woman of various talents.* **—var′i•ous•ly,** *adv.*: *The number was variously estimated at anywhere from 80 to 120.* **—var′i•ous•ness,** *n.* [*noncount*] See -VAR-.

var•mint (vär′mənt) /ˈvɑrmənt/ *n.* [*count*] **1.** an undesirable animal, esp. one that eats livestock. **2.** an obnoxious person.

var•nish (vär′nish) /ˈvɑrnɪʃ/ *n.* **1.** a preparation for coating surfaces, as of wood, made of the resin of trees dissolved in oil, alcohol, or the like: [*noncount*]: *a coat of varnish.* [*count*]: *different varnishes.* **2.** [*noncount*] a coating or surface of varnish, esp. a clear, shiny, glossy coating. **3.** [*noncount*] NAIL POLISH. **—*v.*** [~ + *obj*] **4.** to coat with varnish: *to varnish the wood table.* **5.** to give an apparently pleasing appearance to, esp. in order to deceive: *to varnish the truth.*

var•si•ty (vär′si tē) /ˈvɑrsɪtiy/ *n., pl.* **-ties,** *adj.* **—*n.*** [*count*] **1.** a principal team, esp. in sports, representing a school, college, or university. **2.** *Chiefly Brit.* UNIVERSITY. **—*adj.*** **3.** of or relating to a school or university varsity.

var•y (vâr′ē) /ˈvɛəriy/ *v.,* **var•ied, var•y•ing. 1.** to alter, as in form, appearance, character, or substance; to (cause to) be made different in some way: [~ + *obj*]: *to vary the program each night.* [*no obj*]: *The program varied each night.* **2.** to change so as not to be constantly the same; diversify: [~ + *obj*]: *to vary one's diet.* [*no obj*]: *Her diet never varied.* **3.** [~ + *obj*] to alter (a melody or theme) by changes or additions. **4.** [*no obj*] to show diversity; differ: *Opinions vary on this issue.* **5.** [*no obj*] to change at certain times: *Demand varies with the season.* **6.** [*no obj*] to diverge; deviate: *to vary from the norm.* See -VAR-.

vas•cu•lar (vas′kyə lər) /ˈvæskyələr/ *adj.* composed of or provided with vessels that carry fluids, as blood or sap.

vase (vās, vāz, väz) /veys, veyz, vɑz/ *n.* [*count*] a container or vessel, as of glass or porcelain, usually higher than it is wide, used to hold cut flowers or for decoration.

va•sec•to•my (va sek′tə mē, vā zek′-) /væˈsɛktəmiy, veyˈzɛk-/ *n., pl.* **-mies.** an operation that removes part or all of the tube that carries sperm, done in order to sterilize: [*noncount*]: *the option of vasectomy.* [*count*]: *Thousands of vasectomies are performed every year.* See -TOM-.

Vas•e•line (vas′ə lēn′, vas′ə lēn′) /ˈvæsəˌliyn, ˌvæsəˈliyn/ *Trademark.* [*noncount*] a brand of soft, white or slightly yellow jelly made from petroleum, used to soothe the skin.

vas•sal (vas′əl) /ˈvæsəl/ *n.* [*count*] **1.** (in the feudal system of the Middle Ages) a person who is given permission to use land in return for promising loyalty and usually military service to a lord or other superior. **2.** a person holding some similar relation to a superior; a subordinate. **—*adj.*** [*before a noun*] **3.** having the status of a vassal: *the superpowers and their vassal states.* **—vas•sal•age** (vas′ə lij) /ˈvæsəlɪdʒ/ *n.* [*noncount*]

vast (vast) /væst/ *adj.,* **-er, -est. 1.** of very great area or size: *a vast continent.* **2.** very great in quantity or amount: *the Pharaoh's vast wealth.* **—vast′ly,** *adv.* **—vast′ness,** *n.* [*noncount*]: *the sheer vastness of space.*

vat (vat) /væt/ *n., v.,* **vat•ted, vat•ting. —*n.*** [*count*] **1.** a large container, as a tank, used for holding liquids: *a wine vat.* **—*v.*** [~ + *obj*] **2.** to put into or treat in a vat.

VAT (vat) /væt/ an abbreviation of: value-added tax.

vaude•ville (vôd′vil, vōd′-, vô′də-) /ˈvɔdvɪl, ˈvowd-, ˈvɔdə-/ *n.* [*noncount*] a form of popular entertainment in the U.S. from the late 1800's to the mid-1920's, having a program of separate and varied acts. **—vaude•vil•lian** (vôd vil′yən, vōd-, vô′də-) /vɔdˈvɪlyən, vowd-, ˌvɔdə-/ *n.* [*count*], *adj.*

vault[1] (vôlt) /vɔlt/ *n.* [*count*] **1.** an arched structure, usually of stones, concrete, or bricks, that forms a ceiling or roof. **2.** a space, chamber, or passage enclosed by a vault or vaultlike structure, esp. one located underground. **3.** a room or compartment for the safekeeping of valuables, usually with a locked door and thick walls. **4.** a burial chamber. **5.** something thought of as similar to an arched roof: *the vault of heaven.* **—vault′ed,** *adj.*

vault[2] (vôlt) /vɔlt/ *v.* **1.** to leap, as to or from a position or over something: [*no obj*]: *He vaulted over the tennis net.* [~ + *obj*]: *vaulted the fence.* **2.** [*no obj*] to leap with the hands supported by something, as a horizontal pole. **3.** to (cause to) surpass others, as by achieving something: [*no obj*]: *With that discovery, her scientific team vaulted into world prominence.* [~ + *obj*]: *That discovery vaulted her scientific team into prominence.* **—*n.*** [*count*] **4.** the act of vaulting. **5.** a leap of a horse. **—vault′er,** *n.* [*count*]

vaunt (vônt, vänt) /vɔnt, vɑnt/ *v.* [~ + *obj*] to boast of; brag about: *to vaunt one's achievements.* **—vaunt′ed,** *adj.* [*before a noun*]: *a vaunted tennis team.*

VCR, *n.* [*count*] a videocassette recorder; an electronic device for recording television programs or other signals onto videocassettes and playing them, or prerecorded cassettes, back through a television receiver. See illustration at APPLIANCE.

VD, an abbreviation of: venereal disease.

VDT, an abbreviation of: video display terminal.

veal (vēl) /viyl/ *n.* [*noncount*] the flesh of a calf used for food.

-vec-, *root.* -*vec*- comes from Latin, where it has the meaning "drive; convey." This meaning is found in such words as: CONVECTION, INVECTIVE, VECTOR.

vec•tor (vek′tər) /ˈvɛktər/ *n.* [*count*] **1.** a quantity that has both magnitude and direction, as force or velocity. **2.** the direction or course followed by something, as by an airplane. **3.** something or someone, as a person or an insect, that carries and transmits a disease-causing organism. **—*v.*** [~ + *obj*] **4.** to guide (an aircraft) in flight by radioing necessary or proper directions. See -VEC-.

veep (vēp) /viyp/ *n.* [*count*] *Informal.* a vice president.

veer (vēr) /vɪər/ *v.* to change direction or course or turn aside; shift or change from one course, position, etc., to another: [*no obj*]: *The car veered to the right.* [~ + *obj*]: *He veered the car across two lanes of traffic.*

veg•e•ta•ble (vej′tə bəl, vej′i tə-) /ˈvɛdʒtəbəl, ˈvɛdʒɪtə-/ *n.* [*count*] **1.** any plant whose fruit, seeds, roots, tubers, bulbs, stems, leaves, or flower parts are used as food. See illustration at SUPERMARKET. **2.** any part of a plant that is usually eaten: *Eat all the vegetables on your plate.* **3.** a person who is severely impaired mentally or physically. **—*adj.*** **4.** of or made from vegetables: *a vegetable casserole.*

veg•e•tar•i•an (vej′i târ′ē ən) /ˌvɛdʒɪˈtɛəriyən/ *n.* [*count*] **1.** a person who does not eat or does not believe in eating meat, fish, fowl, or, in some cases, any food made from animals. **—*adj.*** **2.** of or relating to a belief in this kind of diet. **3.** made only from vegetables: *vegetarian soup.* **—veg′e•tar′i•an•ism,** *n.* [*noncount*]

veg•e•tate (vej′i tāt′) /ˈvɛdʒɪˌteyt/ *v.* [*no obj*], **-tat•ed, -tat•ing. 1.** to grow as or like a plant. **2.** to lead an inactive life without much physical, mental, or social activity. **—veg′e•ta′tive,** *adj.*

veg•e•ta•tion (vej′i tā′shən) /ˌvɛdʒɪˈteyʃən/ *n.* [*noncount*] the plants or plant life of a place.

ve•he•ment (vē′ə mənt) /ˈviyəmənt/ *adj.* **1.** zealous; passionate: *a vehement argument.* **2.** characterized by anger or strong feeling: *vehement opposition.* **3.** marked by or done with great energy or vigor: *a vehement shake of the head.* **—ve′he•mence, ve′he•men•cy,** *n.* [*noncount*] **—ve′he•ment•ly,** *adv.*

ve•hi•cle (vē′i kəl *or, sometimes,* vē′hi-) /ˈviyɪkəl *or, sometimes,* ˈviyhɪ-/ *n.* [*count*] **1.** a conveyance moving on wheels, runners, or the like, such as an automobile; a device by which someone or something is carried: *a motor vehicle.* **2.** any means in or by which someone or something is carried or conveyed: *Air is the vehicle of sound.* **3.** a play, screenplay, or other artistic work or entertainment with a role designed or especially well suited to display the talents of a certain performer. **—ve•hic•u•lar** (vi hik′yə lər) /vɪˈhɪkyələr/ *adj.* See -VEC-.

veil (vāl) /veyl/ *n.* [*count*] **1.** a piece of opaque, transparent, or mesh material worn over the face to hide or protect, to enhance the appearance, or to be part of an outfit or costume: *the bride's veil.* **2.** something that covers, hides, screens, or conceals: *a veil of secrecy.* —***Idiom.*** **3. take the veil,** to become a nun.

veiled (vāld) /veyld/ *adj.* **1.** having or wearing a veil. **2.** not openly or directly revealed or expressed: *a veiled threat.*

vein (vān) /veyn/ *n.* [*count*] **1.** one of the branching vessels or tubes carrying blood from various parts of the body to the heart. **2.** one of the riblike thickenings that form the framework of the wing of an insect. **3.** one of the strands or bundles of tissue forming the principal framework of a leaf. **4.** a body or mass of mineral deposit, rock, or the like in a particular area that is well defined: *a vein of gold ore; a vein of coal.* **5.** a streak or marking running through marble, wood, etc. **6.** a temporary attitude, mood, or temper: *He spoke in a serious vein.* **7.** a tendency, quality, or strain that is small but just noticeable in one's conduct, writing, etc.: *a vein of pessimism in his novel.* —**veined,** *adj.*

Vel•cro (vel′krō) /'vɛlkrow/ *Trademark.* [*noncount*] a fastening tape consisting of opposing pieces of nylon fabric, one with tiny hooks and the other with a dense pile, that interlock when pressed together, used to attach or close garments, pieces of luggage, etc.

veld or **veldt** (velt, felt) /vɛlt, fɛlt/ *n.* [*count*] the open country, bearing grass, bushes, or shrubs or thinly forested, characteristic of parts of S Africa.

vel•lum (vel′əm) /'vɛləm/ *n.* [*noncount*] **1.** calfskin, lambskin, kidskin, etc., treated for use as a writing surface. **2.** a texture of paper or cloth resembling vellum. —*adj.* [*before a noun*] **3.** made of or resembling vellum.

ve•loc•i•ty (və los′i tē) /və'lɒsɪtiy/ *n.* [*count*], *pl.* **-ties.** rapidity or speed of motion, action, or operation; swiftness; speed: *the velocity of light.*

ve•lour or **ve•lours** (və lŏŏr′) /və'lʊr/ *n.* [*noncount*] a velvetlike fabric used for clothing and upholstery.

vel•vet (vel′vit) /'vɛlvɪt/ *n.* [*noncount*] **1.** a fabric of silk, nylon, acetate, rayon, etc., with a thick, soft pile formed of loops either cut at the end or left uncut. **2.** something like velvet in softness or texture. —*adj.* **3.** Also, **vel′vet•ed.** made of or covered with velvet. **4.** resembling or suggesting velvet; soft: *her velvet touch.* —**vel′vet•y,** *adj.*

-ven-, *root.* *-ven-* comes from Latin, where it has the meaning "come." This meaning is found in such words as: ADVENT, ADVENTURE, AVENUE, CIRCUMVENT, CONTRAVENE, CONVENE, CONVENIENCE, CONVENT, CONVENTION, COVENANT, EVENT, EVENTUAL, INCONVENIENCE, INCONVENIENT, INTERVENE, INVENT, INVENTION, INVENTORY, MISADVENTURE, PREVENT, PROVENANCE, REVENUE, SOUVENIR, UNCONVENTIONAL, UNEVENTFUL, VENTURE, VENTURESOME, VENUE.

ve•nal (vēn′l) /'viynḷ/ *adj.* **1.** willing to accept bribery or to be corrupt: *a venal judge.* **2.** able to be purchased, as by a bribe: *venal acquittals.* —**ve•nal•i•ty** (vē nal′i tē) /viy'nælɪtiy/ *n.* [*noncount*]

vend (vend) /vɛnd/ *v.* [~ + *obj*] to sell as one's occupation: *to vend flowers.*

ven•det•ta (ven det′ə) /vɛn'dɛtə/ *n.* [*count*], *pl.* **-tas.** a long and bitter argument, feud, rivalry, or the like, esp. between families.

vend′ing machine′, *n.* [*count*] a coin-operated machine for selling small articles, as candy bars or soft drinks. See illustration at TERMINAL.

ven•dor (ven′dər) /'vɛndər/ *n.* [*count*] **1.** a person or agency that sells. **2.** VENDING MACHINE.

ve•neer (və nēr′) /və'nɪər/ *n.* **1.** [*noncount*] a thin layer of wood or other material for covering a surface of wood. **2.** [*count; usually singular*] an apparently good or pleasing appearance: *a veneer of respectability.*

ven•er•a•ble (ven′ər ə bəl) /'vɛnərəbəl/ *adj.* **1.** worthy of respect or reverence, because of great age, high office, noble character, or the like. **2.** thought to be holy or worthy of respect because of religious, historical, or other associations: *a venerable church.* —*n.* [*count*] **3.** a venerable person. —**ven•er•a•bil•i•ty** (ven′ər ə bil′i tē) /ˌvɛnərə'bɪlɪtiy/ *n.* [*noncount*]

ven•er•ate (ven′ə rāt′) /'vɛnəˌreyt/ *v.* [~ + *obj*], **-at•ed, -at•ing.** to think of, consider, or treat with reverence; revere. —**ven•er•a•tion** (ven′ə rā′shən) /ˌvɛnə'reyʃən/ *n.* [*noncount*]

ve•ne•re•al (və nēr′ē əl) /və'nɪəriyəl/ *adj.* arising from or transmitted through sexual contact, as an infection.

vene′real disease′, *n.* SEXUALLY TRANSMITTED DISEASE. *Abbr.*: VD: [*noncount*]: *the spread of venereal disease.* [*count*]: *different venereal diseases.*

ve•ne′tian blind′ (və nē′shən) /və'niyʃən/ *n.* [*count*] a window blind having overlapping horizontal slats that may be opened, closed, or set at an angle, and in which the slats may be raised and lowered by pulling a cord.

Ven•e•zue•lan (ven′ə zwā′lən, -zwē′-) /ˌvɛnə'zweylən, -'zwiy-/ *adj.* **1.** of or relating to Venezuela. —*n.* [*count*] **2.** a person born or living in Venezuela.

-venge-, *root.* *-venge-* comes from Latin, where it has the meaning "protect, avenge, punish." This meaning is found in such words as: AVENGE, REVENGE, VENGEANCE.

venge•ance (ven′jəns) /'vɛndʒəns/ *n.* [*noncount*] **1.** the act of injuring, harming, humiliating, etc., in return for an injury or other offense received; revenge. **2.** the desire for revenge: *to be full of vengeance.* —***Idiom.*** **3. with a vengeance, a.** with violence: *attacked us with a vengeance.* **b.** with extreme energy: *set to work with a vengeance.* See -VENGE-.

venge•ful (venj′fəl) /'vɛndʒfəl/ *adj.* **1.** desiring or seeking vengeance or revenge; vindictive. **2.** characterized by or showing a mean spirit that is eager for revenge. —**venge′ful•ly,** *adv.* See -VENGE-.

ve•ni•al (vē′nē əl, vēn′yəl) /'viyniyəl, 'viynyəl/ *adj.* able to be forgiven or pardoned: *venial offenses; venial sins.*

ven•i•son (ven′ə sən, -zən) /'vɛnəsən, -zən/ *n.* [*noncount*] the flesh of a deer or similar animal used for food.

ven•om (ven′əm) /'vɛnəm/ *n.* [*noncount*] **1.** the poisonous fluid that some animals, as certain snakes and spiders, give off and inject into the bodies of their victims by biting, stinging, etc. **2.** something suggesting poison in its effect, as hatred, malice, or jealousy.

ven•om•ous (ven′ə məs) /'vɛnəməs/ *adj.* **1.** (of an animal) having a gland or glands for giving off venom; able to inflict a poisonous bite or sting. **2.** full of or containing venom; poisonous. **3.** full of hatred, malice, or jealousy.

ve•nous (vē′nəs) /'viynəs/ *adj.* **1.** of or relating to a vein or veins: *venous structures.* **2.** having or composed of veins.

vent¹ (vent) /vɛnt/ *n.* **1.** [*count*] an opening, as in a wall, that serves as an outlet for air, fumes, or the like. **2.** [*noncount*] expression; utterance; release: *giving vent to one's emotions.* —*v.* [~ + *obj*] **3.** to give free play or expression to (an emotion): *venting frustration.* **4.** to release or give off (liquid, smoke, etc.): *to vent smoke from the kitchen.*

vent² (vent) /vɛnt/ *n.* [*count*] a slit in the back or side of a coat, jacket, or other garment.

ven•ti•late (ven′tl āt′) /'vɛntḷˌeyt/ *v.* [~ + *obj*], **-lat•ed, -lat•ing.** **1.** to provide (a room, mine, etc.) with fresh air. **2.** to express or give expression to so as to enable open, full examination and discussion: *to ventilate the issue before a committee.* —**ven•ti•la•tion** (ven′tl ā′shən) /ˌvɛntḷ'eyʃən/ *n.* [*noncount*] —**ven′ti•la′tor,** *n.* [*count*]

ven•tral (ven′trəl) /'vɛntrəl/ *adj.* **1.** of or relating to the belly; abdominal. **2.** situated on or toward the lower, abdominal section of an animal's body.

ven•tri•cle (ven′tri kəl) /'vɛntrɪkəl/ *n.* [*count*] **1.** either of the two lower chambers of the heart that receive blood from other chambers and in turn force it into the arteries. **2.** one of a series of connecting cavities of the brain. —**ven•tric•u•lar** (ven trik′yə lər) /vɛn'trɪkyələr/ *adj.*

ven•tril•o•quism (ven tril′ə kwiz′əm) /vɛn'trɪləˌkwɪzəm/ *n.* [*noncount*] the art or practice of speaking with little or no lip movement so that the voice does not appear to come from the speaker but from another source. —**ven•tril′o•quist,** *n.* [*count*] See -LOQ-.

ven•ture (ven′chər) /'vɛntʃər/ *n., v.,* **-tured, -tur•ing.** —*n.* [*count*] **1.** an activity or undertaking involving risk or uncertainty, as a business enterprise in which something is risked in the hope of profit. **2.** the money or property risked in such an enterprise. —*v.* **3.** [~ + *obj*] to expose to hazard; risk: *They ventured some of their money in that risky business deal.* **4.** to take the risk of; undertake or embark: [~ + *obj*]: *to venture an ocean voyage.* [*no obj*]: *We ventured deep into the jungle.* **5.** to attempt or start to express (an idea, opinion, or guess), in spite of possible contradiction or opposition: [~ + *obj*]: *ventured a guess.* [*used with quotations*]: *"About 10%," he ventured, "but I'd have to check those figures."* [~ + *to* + *verb*]: *I venture to say we'll need help.* See -VEN-.

ven•ture•some (ven′chər səm) /'vɛntʃərsəm/ *adj.* **1.** daring; adventurous. **2.** risky; hazardous. See -VEN-.

ven•ue (ven′yŏŏ) /'vɛnyuw/ *n.* [*count*] **1.** *Law.* **a.** the place of a crime or cause of action. **b.** the county or place where the jury is gathered and the case tried. **2.** the scene or locale of any action or event. See -VEN-.

-ver-, *root.* *-ver-* comes from Latin, where it has the meaning "true; truth." This meaning is found in such words as: VERACIOUS, VERACITY, VERIFY, VERILY, VERISIMILITUDE, VERITABLY, VERITY.

ve•ra•cious (və rā′shəs) /və'reyʃəs/ *adj.* truthful. See -VER-.

ve•rac•i•ty (və ras′i tē) /və'ræsɪtiy/ *n.* [*noncount*] **1.** habitual observance of truth in speech or statement; truthfulness. **2.** correctness; accuracy: *checking the veracity of the story.* See -VER-.

ve•ran•da or **ve•ran•dah** (və ran′də) /və'rændə/ *n.* [*count*], *pl.* **-das** or **-dahs.** a porch, usually roofed, often extending across the front and sides of a house.

verb (vûrb) /vɜrb/ *n.* [*count*] a member of a class of words that typically express action, state, or a relation between two things and are often formally distinguished, as by being marked for tense, aspect, voice, mood, or agreement with the subject or object. *Abbr.:* v. See -VERB-.

-verb-, *root.* *-verb-* comes from Latin, where it has the meaning "word." This meaning is found in such words as: ADVERB, ADVERBIAL, PROVERB, PROVERBIAL, VERB, VERBAL, VERBALIZE, VERBATIM, VERBIAGE, VERBOSE.

ver•bal (vûr′bəl) /'vɜrbəl/ *adj.* **1.** of or relating to words: *verbal ability.* **2.** spoken rather than written; oral: *verbal communication.* **3.** [*before a noun*] **a.** of, relating to, or derived from a verb: *a verbal adjective.* **b.** used in a sentence as or like a verb. **—*n.*** [*count*] **4.** a word, esp. a noun or adjective, derived from a verb, as a gerund, infinitive, or participle. **5.** a word or group of words functioning as or like a verb. **—ver′bal•ly,** *adv.* See -VERB-.

ver•bal•ize (vûr′bə līz′) /'vɜrbəˌlayz/ *v.,* **-ized, -iz•ing.** to express or communicate with words: [~ + *obj*]: *I can't verbalize my feelings.* [*no obj*]: *to verbalize at an early age.* **—ver•bal•i•za•tion** (vûr′bə lə zā′shən) /ˌvɜrbələ'zeyʃən/ *n.* [*noncount*] See -VERB-.

ver′bal noun′, *n.* [*count*] a noun derived from a verb, esp. by a regular process, as the *-ing* form in *Smoking is forbidden.*

ver•ba•tim (vər bā′tim) /vər'beytɪm/ *adv.* **1.** in exactly the same words; word for word: *He quoted the president's speech verbatim.* **—*adj.*** [*before a noun*] **2.** corresponding word for word to the original source or text: *a verbatim record of the proceedings.* See -VERB-.

ver•bi•age (vûr′bē ij) /'vɜrbiyɪdʒ/ *n.* [*noncount*] the use of too many words, as in writing or speaking. See -VERB-.

ver•bose (vər bōs′) /vər'bows/ *adj.* expressed in or characterized by the use of many or too many words; wordy: *a verbose report; a verbose speaker.* **—ver•bos•i•ty** (vər bos′i tē) /vər'bɒsɪtiy/ *n.* [*noncount*] See -VERB-.

ver•bo•ten (vər bōt′n) /vər'bowtn̩/ *adj.* forbidden, as by law; prohibited.

ver•dant (vûr′dnt) /'vɜrdnt/ *adj.* **1.** green with vegetation and growing plants; covered with growing plants or grass. **2.** of the color green.

ver•dict (vûr′dikt) /'vɜrdɪkt/ *n.* [*count*] **1.** the finding of a jury in a court of law. **2.** any judgment or decision. See -VER-, -DICT-.

-verg-, *root.* *-verg-* comes from Latin, where it has the meaning "turn; bend." This meaning is found in such words as: CONVERGE, DIVERGE, VERGE. See -VERT-.

verge[1] (vûrj) /vɜrdʒ/ *n., v.,* **verged, verg•ing.** **—*n.*** [*count; usually singular*] **1.** the limit or point beyond which something begins or occurs; brink: *He's on the verge of a nervous breakdown.* **2.** the edge, rim, or margin of something; a border of something: *the verge of a desert.* **—*v.*** [*usually not: be* + ~*-ing; no obj*] **3.** to be on the verge or margin; border: *Our property verges on theirs.* **4.** to come close to; approach: *a talent that verges on genius.*

verge[2] (vûrj) /vɜrdʒ/ *v.* [*no obj*], **verged, verg•ing.** to incline; tend: *The sun is verging toward the horizon.* See -VERG-.

ver•i•fy (ver′ə fī′) /'vɛrəˌfay/ *v.* [~ + *obj*], **-fied, -fy•ing.** **1.** to prove the truth of, as by evidence or testimony; confirm: *Several witnesses verified his alibi.* **2.** to prove the truth, authenticity, or correctness of: *Later investigations verified the theory.* **—ver•i•fi•a•ble** (ver′ə fī′ə bəl) /'vɛrəˌfayəbəl/ *adj.* **—ver•i•fi•ca•tion** (ver′ə fi kā′shən) /ˌvɛrəfɪ'keyʃən/ *n.* [*noncount*]: *We'll need verification of your signature; please wait one moment while we check it.* See -VER-.

ver•i•ly (ver′ə lē) /'vɛrəliy/ *adv. Archaic.* in truth; really; indeed. See -VER-.

ver•i•si•mil•i•tude (ver′ə si mil′i to͞od′, -tyo͞od′) /ˌvɛrəsɪ'mɪlɪˌtuwd, -ˌtyuwd/ *n.* [*noncount*] the appearance of truth; likelihood; probability. See -VER-, -SIMIL-.

ver•i•ta•ble (ver′i tə bəl) /'vɛrɪtəbəl/ *adj.* being truly or very much so; genuine or real: *a veritable triumph of modern science.* **—ver′i•ta•bly,** *adv.* See -VER-.

ver•i•ty (ver′i tē) /'vɛrɪtiy/ *n., pl.* **-ties.** **1.** [*noncount*] the state or quality of being true. **2.** [*count*] something that is true, as a principle, belief, or statement. See -VER-.

ver•mi•cel•li (vûr′mi chel′ē, -sel′ē) /ˌvɜrmɪ'tʃɛliy, -'sɛliy/ *n.* [*noncount; used with a singular verb*] pasta in the form of long and very fine threads.

ver•mil•ion (vər mil′yən) /vər'mɪlyən/ *n.* [*noncount*] **1.** a brilliant scarlet red. **—*adj.*** **2.** of the color vermilion.

ver•min (vûr′min) /'vɜrmɪn/ *n.* [*plural; used with a plural verb*] **1.** harmful or objectionable animals thought of as a group, as flies, lice, cockroaches, and rats. **2.** animals that prey upon game. **3.** obnoxious persons thought of as a group. **—ver′min•ous,** *adj.*

ver•mouth (vər mo͞oth′) /vər'muwθ/ *n.* [*noncount*] white wine in which herbs and other flavorings have been added.

ver•nac•u•lar (vər nak′yə lər, və nak′-) /vər'nækyələr, və'næk-/ *adj.* **1.** (of language) native or spoken in a particular area; indigenous (opposed to *literary* or *learned*). **2.** of, pertaining to, or using such a language. **3.** using plain, everyday, ordinary language. **—*n.*** [*count*] **4.** the native speech or language of a place, esp. the particular language of a place. **5.** the plain variety of language in everyday use by ordinary people: *In the local vernacular,* anyroad *means* anyway.

ver•nal (vûr′nl) /'vɜrnl̩/ *adj.* of, relating to, or occurring in spring: *the vernal equinox.*

ver•ru•ca (və ro͞o′kə) /və'rʊkə/ *n.* [*count*] a wart or wartlike growth on the skin.

ver•sa•tile (vûr′sə tl, -tīl′) /'vɜrsətl̩, -ˌtayl/ *adj.* **1.** capable of or adapted for turning easily from one to another of various tasks, fields of endeavor, etc.: *a versatile teacher.* **2.** having or capable of many uses or applications: *a versatile tool.* **—ver•sa•til•i•ty** (vûr′sə til′i tē) /ˌvɜrsə'tɪlɪtiy/ *n.* [*noncount*] See -VERT-.

verse (vûrs) /vɜrs/ *n.* **1.** [*count*] one of the lines of a poem, or a line of a song. **2.** [*count*] a stanza. **3.** [*noncount*] poetry. **4.** [*noncount*] a particular type of poetic line or composition: *light verse.* **5.** [*count*] one of the sentences into which a chapter of the Bible is conventionally divided. See -VERT-.

versed (vûrst) /vɜrst/ *adj.* [*be* + ~ *(+ in)*] experienced or practiced: *versed in Latin.* See -VERT-.

ver•sion (vûr′zhən, -shən) /'vɜrʒən, -ʃən/ *n.* [*count*] **1.** a particular account or telling of some matter or event, esp. as contrasted with some other account: *There were two different versions of the accident.* **2.** a particular variant of something: *an updated version of a computer program.* **3.** a translation, as of the Bible. See -VERT-.

ver•sus (vûr′səs, -səz) /'vɜrsəs, -səz/ *prep.* **1.** (used to join the names of the parties in a legal case, or those of competing teams or players in a sports contest) against: *the case of Smith versus Jones; Army versus Navy.* **2.** as compared to; in contrast with: *traveling by plane versus traveling by train. Abbr.:* v., vs. See -VERT-.

-vert-, *root.* *-vert-*, and a related form *-vers-*, come from Latin, where they have the meaning "turn; change." This meaning is found in such words as: ADVERSARY, ADVERSE, ADVERTISE, AVERSION, AVERT, CONTROVERSY, CONVERSANT, CONVERSATION, CONVERSE, CONVERSION, CONVERT, DIVERSE, DIVERSION, DIVERT, EXTROVERT, INADVERTENT, INCONTROVERTIBLE, INTROVERT, INVERSION, INVERT, IRREVERSIBLE, OBVERSE, PERVERSE, PERVERSION, PERVERT, REVERSAL, REVERSE, REVERT, SUBVERSION, SUBVERSIVE, SUBVERT, TRANSVERSE, TRAVERSE, UNIVERSAL, UNIVERSE, VERSATILE, VERSE, VERSION, VERSUS, VERTEBRA, VERTEBRATE, VERTEX, VERTICAL, VERTIGINOUS, VERTIGO.

ver•te•bra (vûr′tə brə) /'vɜrtəbrə/ *n.* [*count*], *pl.* **-brae** (-brē′, -brā′) /-ˌbriy, -ˌbrey/ **-bras.** a bone or segment of the spinal column, consisting in higher vertebrates of a rounded body with two projections, forming an arch that surrounds and protects the spinal cord. **—ver′te•bral,** *adj.* See -VERT-.

ver•te•brate (vûr′tə brit, -brāt′) /'vɜrtəbrɪt, -ˌbreyt/ *adj.* **1.** having vertebrae; having a backbone. **2.** belonging or relating to a grouping of animals having an internal skeleton of bone or cartilage that includes a braincase and a spinal column. **—*n.*** [*count*] **3.** a vertebrate animal: *Vertebrates include mammals, birds, reptiles, amphibians, and fishes.* See -VERT-.

ver•tex (vûr′teks) /'vɜrtɛks/ *n.* [*count*], *pl.* **-tex•es, -ti•ces** (-tə sēz′) /-təˌsiyz/. **1.** the highest point of something; apex. **2.** *Geometry.* **a.** the point farthest from the base. **b.** the intersection of two sides of a plane figure. See -VERT-.

ver•ti•cal (vûr′ti kəl) /'vɜrtɪkəl/ *adj.* **1.** upright; pointing straight up from the ground. **2.** very steep: *a vertical cliff.* —**ver′ti•cal•ly,** *adv.* See -VERT-.

ver•tig•i•nous (vər tij′ə nəs) /vər'tɪdʒənəs/ *adj.* **1.** whirling; spinning. **2.** affected with or feeling vertigo. **3.** likely to cause vertigo: *a vertiginous climb.* See -VERT-.

ver•ti•go (vûr′ti gō′) /'vɜrtɪˌgow/ *n.* [*noncount*] **1.** a disordered condition in which one feels oneself or one's surroundings whirling about. **2.** the dizzying sensation caused by this. See -VERT-.

verve (vûrv) /vɜrv/ *n.* [*noncount*] liveliness; animation; enthusiasm or vigor: *Her novel lacks verve.*

ver•y (ver′ē) /'vɛriy/ *adv., adj.,* **-i•er, -i•est.** —*adv.* **1.** in a high degree; extremely; greatly; exceedingly: *a very clever person.* **2.** This word is sometimes used to show the speaker's intense feeling, or to emphasize or stress something, esp. something superlative or to stress identity or oppositeness: *the very best thing; in the very same place.* —*adj.* [*before a noun*] **3.** precise; particular: *That is the very item we want.* **4.** mere: *The very thought of killing little puppies is distressing to her.* **5.** sheer; utter: *the very joy of living.* **6.** actual: *He was caught in the very act of stealing.* **7.** being such in the true or fullest sense of the term: *This is the very heart of the matter.* See -VER-.

ves•per (ves′pər) /'vɛspər/ *n.* **1.** [*count*] Also called **ves′per bell′.** a bell rung at evening. **2.** **vespers,** [*noncount; often: Vespers*] a religious service in the late afternoon or evening.

ves•sel (ves′əl) /'vɛsəl/ *n.* [*count*] **1.** a craft for traveling on water, esp. a fairly large one; a ship or boat. **2.** a hollow or hollowed-out utensil, as a cup, bowl, or pitcher, used for holding liquids or other contents. **3.** a tube or duct, as an artery or vein, containing or carrying blood or some other body fluid.

vest (vest) /vɛst/ *n.* [*count*] **1.** a fitted, waist-length, sleeveless garment with buttons down the front, usually worn under a jacket. **2.** a part or trimming simulating the front of such a garment. **3.** any of various sleeveless garments for the upper body, having a front opening and worn for style, warmth, or protection: *a down vest; a bulletproof vest.* **4.** *Brit.* an undershirt. —*v.* [∼ + *obj*] **5.** to clothe, as in garments worn during religious ceremonies. **6.** to place or settle (authority) in the possession or control of someone: *to vest authority in a new official.*

vest•ed (ves′tid) /'vɛstɪd/ *adj.* **1.** held completely, permanently, and inalienably: *vested rights.* **2.** protected or established by law, tradition, etc.: *vested contributions to a fund.* **3.** clothed or robed, esp. in garments for church ceremonies. **4.** having a vest: *a vested suit.*

vest′ed in′terest, *n.* [*count*] **1.** a special interest in an existing system, arrangement, or institution that an individual or group has for particular personal reasons. **2.** **vested interests,** [*plural*] the persons, groups, etc., who benefit most from existing systems and institutional arrangements.

ves•ti•bule (ves′tə byōōl′) /'vɛstəˌbyuwl/ *n.* [*count*] **1.** a passage, hall, or small chamber between the outer door and the interior parts of a house or building. **2.** an enclosed entrance at the end of a railroad passenger car.

ves•tige (ves′tij) /'vɛstɪdʒ/ *n.* [*count*] **1.** a mark, trace, or visible evidence of something that is no longer present or in existence: *the last vestiges of a once great empire.* **2.** a very slight trace or amount of something: *the last vestige of hope.* —**ves•tig•i•al** (ve stij′ē əl, -stij′əl) /vɛ'stɪdʒiyəl, -'stɪdʒəl/ *adj.*

vest•ing (ves′ting) /'vɛstɪŋ/ *n.* [*noncount*] the granting to an employee of the right to pension benefits even though the employee retires before the usual time or age.

vest•ment (vest′mənt) /'vɛstmənt/ *n.* [*count*] an official or ceremonial robe, esp. one of the garments worn by priests, ministers, and their assistants.

vest′-pock′et, *adj.* **1.** designed to be carried in or as if in the pocket of a vest: *a vest-pocket dictionary.* **2.** contained in a small space: *a vest-pocket park.*

ves•try (ves′trē) /'vɛstriy/ *n.* [*count*], *pl.* **-tries.** **1.** a room in, or a building attached to, a church, in which vestments and sometimes sacred objects are kept; sacristy. **2.** a room in, or a building attached to, a church, used as a chapel, for prayer meetings, for Sunday school, etc.

vet[1] (vet) /vɛt/ *n., v.,* **vet•ted, vet•ting.** *Informal.* —*n.* [*count*] **1.** a veterinarian. —*v.* [∼ + *obj*] **2.** to examine or treat in one's capacity as a veterinarian or physician. **3.** to appraise; evaluate: *An expert vetted the manuscript.*

vet[2] (vet) /vɛt/ *n., adj. Informal.* VETERAN.

vetch (vech) /vɛtʃ/ *n.* [*count*] a climbing plant of the legume family, having pealike flowers cultivated for forage and soil improvement.

vet•er•an (vet′ər ən, ve′trən) /'vɛtərən, 'vɛtrən/ *n.* [*count*] **1.** a person who has had long service or experience in an occupation, office, or the like. **2.** a person who has served in a military force, esp. during a war. —*adj.* [*before a noun*] **3.** (of a soldier) having served in a military force, esp. during a war. **4.** experienced through long service or practice: *a veteran member of Congress.* **5.** of or relating to veterans: *veteran benefits.*

vet•er•i•nar•i•an (vet′ər ə nâr′ē ən, ve′trə-) /ˌvɛtərə'nɛəriyən, ˌvɛtrə-/ *n.* [*count*] a person whose work is the medical treatment of animals.

vet•er•i•nar•y (vet′ər ə ner′ē, ve′trə-) /'vɛtərəˌnɛriy, 'vɛtrə-/ *n., pl.* **-nar•ies,** *adj.* —*n.* [*count*] **1.** a veterinarian. —*adj.* [*before a noun*] **2.** of or relating to the medical and surgical treatment of animals: *veterinary medicine.*

ve•to (vē′tō) /'viytow/ *n., pl.* **-toes,** *v.* —*n.* **1.** [*noncount*] the power given to one branch of a government to cancel or postpone the decisions or actions of another branch, esp. the right of a president or other chief executive to reject bills passed by the legislature: *the power of the veto.* **2.** [*count*] the use or exercise of this power: *Another presidential veto was overridden by Congress.* **3.** [*noncount*] the power of any of the five permanent members of the UN Security Council to overrule actions or decisions even if that member is outvoted. **4.** [*count*] a clear refusal to give permission of any sort. —*v.* [∼ + *obj*] **5.** to reject (a proposed bill or enactment) by exercising a veto: *to veto the jobs creation bill.* **6.** to prohibit, refuse, or disallow very plainly: *to veto the new plan.*

vex (veks) /vɛks/ *v.* [∼ + *obj*] **1.** to irritate; annoy; provoke: *She was told to stop vexing the dog.* **2.** to torment; trouble; distress; worry: *He was vexed by many problems.* See -VEC-.

vex•a•tion (vek sā′shən) /vɛk'seyʃən/ *n.* **1.** [*noncount*] the act of vexing; the state of being vexed. **2.** [*count*] something that vexes; a cause of annoyance. —**vex•a′tious,** *adj.* See -VEC-.

VHF or **vhf** or **V.H.F.,** an abbreviation of: very high frequency.

v.i., an abbreviation of: verb intransitive (intransitive verb).

vi•a (vī′ə, vē′ə) /'vayə, 'viyə/ *prep.* **1.** by a route that touches or passes through; by way of: *They came to Tangiers via Casablanca.* **2.** by the agency or instrumentality of; by means of: *to communicate via sign language.* See -VIA-.

-via-, *root.* *-via-* comes from Latin, where it has the meaning "way; route; a going." This meaning is found in such words as: DEVIANT, DEVIOUS, OBVIATE, TRIVIAL, VIA, VIADUCT.

vi•a•ble (vī′ə bəl) /'vayəbəl/ *adj.* **1.** capable of living. **2.** (of a fetus) sufficiently developed to be capable of living, under normal conditions, outside the uterus. **3.** having the ability to grow or develop: *a viable seedling.* **4.** that can be used or made useful; practical; workable: *a viable alternative plan.* **5.** capable of winning elections: *a viable political party.* —**vi•a•bil•i•ty** (vī′ə bil′i tē) /ˌvayə'bɪlɪtiy/ *n.* [*noncount*]

vi•a•duct (vī′ə dukt′) /'vayəˌdʌkt/ *n.* [*count*] a bridge for carrying a road, railroad, etc., over a valley or the like, consisting of a number of short spans. See -VIA-, -DUC-.

vi•al (vī′əl, vīl) /'vayəl, vayl/ *n.* [*count*] Also, **phial.** a small container, as of glass, for holding liquids or medicines.

vi•and (vī′ənd) /'vayənd/ *n.* **viands,** [*plural*] dishes of food, esp. delicacies.

vibes[1] (vībz) /vaybz/ *n.* [*plural*] *Slang.* VIBRATION (def. 3).: *felt good vibes from the group.*

vibes[2] (vībz) /vaybz/ *n.* [*plural*] vibraphone.

vi•brant (vī′brənt) /'vaybrənt/ *adj.* **1.** moving to and fro rapidly; vibrating. **2.** alive with vigor and energy; lively: *the vibrant life of a large city; a vibrant personality.* —**vi′bran•cy,** *n.* [*noncount*] —**vi′brant•ly,** *adv.*

vi•bra•phone (vī′brə fōn′) /'vaybrəˌfown/ *n.* [*count*] a musical instrument resembling a xylophone and having metal bars that are struck with mallets and electrically powered resonators to sustain the tone. Also called **vi•bra•harp** (vī′brə härp′) /'vaybrəˌhɑrp/. —**vi•bra•phon•ist** (vī′brə fō′nist, vī brof′ə-) /'vaybrəˌfownɪst, vay'brɒfə-/ *n.* [*count*]

vi•brate (vī′brāt) /ˈvaybreyt/ *v.*, **-brat•ed, -brat•ing.** to (cause to) move to and fro or up and down quickly and repeatedly; quiver; tremble: [*no obj*]: *The whole house vibrated when the heavy truck went by.* [~ + *obj*]: *to vibrate a tuning fork.*

vi•bra•tion (vi brā′shən) /vɪˈbreyʃən/ *n.* **1.** [*noncount*] an act of vibrating; the state of being vibrated **2.** [*count*] an instance of motion like vibrating. **3.** Often, **vibrations.** [*plural*] *Informal.* a general emotional feeling one gets from a person, situation, or place.

vi•bra•to (vi brä′tō, vī-) /vɪˈbrɑtow, vay-/ *n.* [*count*], pl. **-tos.** an effect produced in vocal or instrumental music by rapid but slight alternations in pitch.

vi•bra•tor (vī′brā tər) /ˈvaybreytər/ *n.* [*count*] **1.** a person or thing that vibrates. **2.** a small appliance that vibrates, used for therapy or massage.

vic•ar (vik′ər) /ˈvɪkər/ *n.* [*count*] a priest or minister in the Anglican or Episcopal churches, or a Roman Catholic churchman representing a bishop.

vic•ar•age (vik′ər ij) /ˈvɪkərɪdʒ/ *n.* [*count*] **1.** the place where a vicar lives. **2.** the office, rank, or duties of a vicar.

vi•car•i•ous (vī kâr′ē əs, vi-) /vayˈkɛəriyəs, vɪ-/ *adj.* felt or enjoyed by imagining that one is participating in the experience of others: *It gave me a vicarious thrill to hear about her trip.* —**vi•car′i•ous•ly,** *adv.*

vice[1] (vīs) /vays/ *n.* **1.** [*count*] an immoral or evil habit or practice: *His vices include drinking, illicit sex, and gambling.* **2.** [*noncount*] immoral conduct; evil practices; depraved behavior: *a life of vice and crime.* **3.** [*noncount*] sexual immorality, esp. prostitution. **4.** [*count*] a personal habit that is not especially harmful: *Playing cards was his one vice.*

vice[2] (vīs) /vays/ *n., v.,* **viced, vic•ing.** VISE.

vice-, *prefix.* *vice-* comes from Latin, where it has the meaning "in place of, instead of." It is attached to roots and sometimes words and means "deputy;" it is used esp. in the titles of officials who serve in the absence of the official named by the base word: *vice-chancellor; vice-chairman.*

vice′ pres′ident or **vice′-pres′ident** (vīs) /vays/ *n.* [*count*] **1.** [*often: Vice President*] a governmental officer next in rank to a president, who serves as president in the event of the president's death, illness, removal, or resignation. **2.** an officer who serves as a deputy to a president or oversees a special division or function, as in a corporation. —**vice′ pres′idency,** *n.* [*noncount*]

vice•re•gal (vīs rē′gəl) /vaysˈriygəl/ *adj.* of or relating to a viceroy. See -REG-.

vice•roy (vīs′roi) /ˈvaysrɔy/ *n.* [*count*] a person appointed to rule a country or province as the deputy of the king or queen. See -REG-.

vi•ce ver•sa (vī′sə vûr′sə, vīs′, vī′sē) /ˈvayˈsə vɜrsə, ˈvays, ˈvaysiy/ *adv.* in reverse order from that of a preceding statement; conversely: *She likes me, and vice versa (= She likes me and I like her).* See -VERT-.

vi•chys•soise (vish′ē swäz′, vē′shē swäz′) /ˌvɪʃiyˈswɑz, ˈviyʃiyˌswɑz/ *n.* [*noncount*] a thick cream soup made with potatoes and leeks, usually served cold.

vi•cin•i•ty (vi sin′i tē) /vɪˈsɪnɪtiy/ *n.* [*noncount*] **1.** the area or region near or about a place; neighborhood. —***Idiom.*** **2. in the vicinity of,** almost; approximately: *It cost in the vicinity of a thousand dollars.*

vi•cious (vish′əs) /ˈvɪʃəs/ *adj.* **1.** dangerously hateful and ready to do violence; immoral or evil; depraved: *a cruel, vicious dictator.* **2.** spiteful; malicious; nasty: *vicious gossip.* **3.** unpleasantly severe or intense: *a vicious headache.* **4.** savage; ferocious: *a vicious temper.* —**vi′cious•ly,** *adv.* —**vi′cious•ness,** *n.* [*noncount*]

vi′cious cir′cle, *n.* [*count*] a situation in which an effort or attempt to solve a given problem results in making the problem worse or in creating a new, worse problem.

vi•cis•si•tudes (vi sis′i to͞odz′, -tyo͞odz′) /vɪˈsɪsɪˌtuwdz, -ˌtyuwdz/ *n.* [*plural*] changing stages or conditions that follow one after the other, as in one's life or in situations in general; ups and downs.

-vict-, *root.* *-vict-* comes from Latin, where it has the meaning "conquer." It is related to the root -VINC-. This meaning is found in such words as: CONVICT, EVICT, VICTOR, VICTORIOUS, VICTORY.

vic•tim (vik′təm) /ˈvɪktəm/ *n.* [*count*] **1.** a person who suffers from destruction or an injury: *war victims.* **2.** a person who is deceived, betrayed, or cheated: *the victims of a fraudulent scheme.* **3.** a living creature that is sacrificed in a religious rite.

vic•tim•ize (vik′tə mīz′) /ˈvɪktəˌmayz/ *v.* [~ + *obj*], **-ized, -iz•ing. 1.** to make a victim of. **2.** to swindle or cheat: *swindlers victimizing the elderly.* —**vic•tim•i•za•tion** (vik′tə mə zā′shən) /ˌvɪktəməˈzeyʃən/ *n.* [*noncount*]

vic•tor (vik′tər) /ˈvɪktər/ *n.* [*count*] **1.** a person who has overcome or defeated an enemy; conqueror. **2.** a winner in any struggle or contest. See -VICT-.

Vic•to•ri•an (vik tôr′ē ən, -tōr′-) /vɪkˈtɔriyən, -ˈtowr-/ *adj.* **1.** of or relating to Queen Victoria, Queen of Great Britain, or to her reign, from 1837 to 1901: *Victorian poets.* **2.** having characteristics thought of as being common in this time, as prudishness or hypocrisy. **3.** of or relating to a style of architecture, furniture, and decoration common between 1840 and 1900, reflecting massive size and lavish decoration and ornamentation. —*n.* [*count*] **4.** a person of the Victorian period. —**Vic•to′ri•an•ism,** *n.* [*noncount*]

vic•to•ry (vik′tə rē, vik′trē) /ˈvɪktəriy, ˈvɪktriy/ *n., pl.* **-ries. 1.** a success or triumph over an enemy in battle or war: [*noncount*]: *a day of victory.* [*count*]: *a string of victories.* **2.** a success or superior position achieved against any opponent, competitor, opposition, difficulty, etc.: [*count*]: *gained a moral victory.* [*noncount*]: *celebrating victory.* —**vic•to•ri•ous** (vik tôr′ē əs, -tōr′-) /vɪkˈtɔriyəs, -ˈtowr-/ *adj.* See -VICT-.

vict•uals (vit′lz) /ˈvɪtlz/ *n.* [*plural*] food supplies; food and drink; provisions.

vi•cu•na or **vi•cu•ña** (vī ko͞o′nə, -kyo͞o′-, vi-, vi ko͞o′nyə) /vayˈkuwnə, -ˈkyuw-, vɪ-, vɪˈkuwnyə/ *n., pl.* **-nas** or **-ñas. 1.** [*count*] a wild South American animal of the Andes regions, closely related to the llama. **2.** [*noncount*] a fabric made from the soft wool of this animal or of some substitute.

-vide-, *root.* *-vide-* comes from Latin, where it has the meaning "see." It is related to the root -VIS-. This meaning is found in such words as: EVIDENCE, EVIDENT, PROVIDE, PROVIDENCE, PROVIDENTIAL, VIDEO, VIDEOCASSETTE, VIDEODISC, VIDEOTAPE.

vid•e•o (vid′ē ō′) /ˈvɪdiyˌow/ *n., pl.* **-e•os,** *adj.* —*n.* **1.** [*noncount*] the parts of a television program, broadcast, or script that relate to the sending or receiving of a visual image (distinguished from *audio*). **2.** [*noncount*] television: *a star of stage and video.* **3.** [*count*] a program, movie, or the like recorded on videotape. **4.** [*count*] MUSIC VIDEO. —*adj.* [*before a noun*] **5.** of or relating to the electronic devices used for producing a television picture. **6.** of or relating to television: *video journalism.* **7.** of or relating to videocassettes, videocassette recorders, etc.: *a video store.* See -VIDE-.

vid•e•o•cas•sette (vid′ē ō kə set′, -ka-) /ˈvɪdiyowkəˌsɛt, -kæ-/ *n.* a cassette that contains a length of tape for video recording or reproduction: [*count*]: *some cheap videocassettes.* [*noncount*]: *recorded on videocassette.* See -VIDE-.

vid′eocassette record′er, *n.* VCR.

vid•e•o•disc (vid′ē ō disk′) /ˈvɪdiyowˌdɪsk/ *n.* an optical disc on which a motion picture or television program is recorded for playback on a television set: [*count*]: *expensive videodiscs.* [*noncount*]: *available on videodisc.* See -VIDE-.

vid′eo display′ ter′minal, *n.* [*count*] a computer terminal consisting of a screen on which data or graphics can be displayed. *Abbr.:* VDT

vid′eo game′, *n.* [*count*] **1.** a game played with a microcomputer on a video screen or television set. **2.** a game played on a microchip-controlled device, as an arcade machine.

vid•e•o•tape (vid′ē ō tāp′) /ˈvɪdiyowˌteyp/ *n., v.,* **-taped, -tap•ing.** —*n.* **1.** [*noncount*] magnetic tape on which a television program, motion picture, etc., can be recorded. See illustration at SCHOOL. **2.** [*count*] the usually plastic cassette in which this tape is contained: *made a videotape of last night's episode.* —*v.* [~ + *obj*] **3.** to record (programs, etc.) on videotape. See -VIDE-.

vie (vī) /vay/ *v.* [*no obj;* ~ + *for*], **vied, vy•ing.** to struggle or compete with another in a game or contest: *vying for the championship.*

Vi•et•nam•ese (vē et′nä mēz′, -mēs′, -nə-, vyet′-, vē′-it-) /viyˌɛtnɑˈmiyz, -ˈmiys, -nə-, ˌvyɛt-, ˌviyɪt-/ *n., pl.* **-ese. 1.** [*count*] a person born or living in Vietnam. **2.** [*noncount*] the language spoken by many of the people in Vietnam. —*adj.* **3.** of or relating to Vietnam.

view (vyo͞o) /vyuw/ *n.* **1.** [*count*] an instance of seeing; visual inspection; sight or vision: *The tourists crowded around to get a good view of the painting.* **2.** [*noncount*] range of sight or vision: *objects in view.* **3.** [*count*] a sight of a landscape, the sea, etc.: *a room with a beautiful view.* **4.** [*count*] a picture or photograph of a scene:

The postcard shows a view of the harbor. **5.** [*count*] a particular manner of looking at something: *from a practical (point of) view.* **6.** a personal attitude; opinion; judgment: [*count*]: *the scientist's view of evolution.* [*noncount*]: *a strange (point of) view.* **7.** [*count*] aim, intention, or purpose: *with a view toward reducing the budget.* **8.** [*count; usually singular*] prospect or expectation: *the view for the future.* **—*v.*** [~ + *obj*] **9.** to see; watch; behold: *Thousands viewed the parade.* **10.** to look at; survey; inspect: *to view an art collection.* **11.** to think about; consider: *How do you view the current crisis?* **—*Idiom.*** **12. in view of,** because of; in thinking about; considering: *In view of the poor state of the economy, investment seems risky.* **13. on view,** in a place for public inspection; on exhibition: *a new exhibit of paintings on view.* **14. with a view to,** with the aim or intention of: *worked hard with a view to getting promoted.*

view•er (vyōō′ər) /'vyuwər/ *n.* [*count*] **1.** a person who views something: *viewers of the spectacle.* **2.** a person who watches television. **3.** an optical device for viewing, as an eyepiece or viewfinder.

view•find•er (vyōō′fīn′dər) /'vyuw,fayndər/ *n.* [*count*] a camera attachment, as a lens and mirror, that enables the user to see what will appear in the picture.

view•point (vyōō′point′) /'vyuw,pɔynt/ *n.* [*count*] **1.** a place providing a view of something. **2.** an attitude of mind; a point of view. See -POINT-.

vig•il (vij′əl) /'vɪdʒəl/ *n.* **1.** [*count*] a period of staying awake maintained for any reason during the normal hours for sleeping: *She maintained a vigil until he came home.* **2.** a watch or period of watchful attention maintained at night or at other times: [*count*]: *a peace vigil.* [*noncount*]: *to keep vigil for someone.*

vig•i•lant (vij′ə lənt) /'vɪdʒələnt/ *adj.* watchful; wary; alert: *vigilant in his battle against crime; The guards were especially vigilant.* **—vig′i•lance,** *n.* [*noncount*]

vig•i•lan•te (vij′ə lan′tē) /,vɪdʒə'læntiy/ *n.* [*count*], *pl.* **-tes.** a person who takes on for himself or herself the authority of the law, as by avenging a crime or trying to prevent crime when the law does not or cannot respond. **—vig•i•lan•tism** (vij′ə lan′tiz əm) /,vɪdʒə'læntɪzəm/ *n.* [*noncount*]

vi•gnette (vin yet′) /vɪn'yɛt/ *n.* [*count*] **1.** a decorative design or small illustration used on the title page of a book or at the beginning or end of a chapter, or elsewhere in a manuscript. **2.** a brief descriptive scene or episode in a play, movie, or the like.

vig•or (vig′ər) /'vɪgər/ *n.* [*noncount*] **1.** active strength or force; intensity; energy: *He pursued his new career with great vigor.* **2.** healthy physical or mental energy or power; vitality: *He rowed with vigor.* Also, *esp. Brit.,* **vig′our.**

vig•or•ous (vig′ər əs) /'vɪgərəs/ *adj.* **1.** full of vigor: *a vigorous effort to finish on time.* **2.** strong; active: *a vigorous young man.* **3.** energetic; forceful: *a vigorous personality.* **4.** powerful in action or in effect: *vigorous law enforcement.* **—vig′or•ous•ly,** *adv.*

vile (vīl) /vayl/ *adj.,* **vil•er, vil•est. 1.** very bad; uncomfortably bad: *vile weather.* **2.** highly offensive, unpleasant, or objectionable: *a vile odor; vile language.* **3.** very evil; morally depraved or despicable: *vile acts of murder.* **—vile′ness,** *n.* [*noncount*]

vil•i•fy (vil′ə fī′) /'vɪlə,fay/ *v.* [~ + *obj*], **-fied, -fy•ing.** to say or write bad things about (someone); defame; slander. **—vil•i•fi•ca•tion** (vil′ə fi kā′shən) /,vɪləfɪ'keyʃən/ *n.* [*noncount*]

vil•la (vil′ə) /'vɪlə/ *n.* [*count*], *pl.* **-las. 1.** a home or estate in the country, as a large, imposing country or suburban home of a wealthy person. **2.** *Brit.* a detached or semidetached house.

vil•lage (vil′ij) /'vɪlɪdʒ/ *n.* [*count*] **1.** a small community or group of houses in an area outside a city, larger than a hamlet and usually smaller than a town. **2.** [*usually singular*] the people of such a community thought of as a group: *The village doesn't like strangers.* **—*adj.*** [*before a noun*] **3.** of, relating to, or characteristic of a village. **—vil′lag•er,** *n.* [*count*]

vil•lain (vil′ən) /'vɪlən/ *n.* [*count*] **1.** a cruel or evil person who is involved in or devoted to wickedness or crime; a scoundrel. **2.** a character in a play, novel, or the like who commits cruel and evil deeds. **3.** a person, condition, etc., regarded as the source of a problem or evil: *Unemployment is a constant villain.* **—vil′lain•ous,** *adj.*

vil•lain•y (vil′ə nē) /'vɪləniy/ *n., pl.* **-lain•ies. 1.** [*noncount*] the actions or conduct of a villain; terrible wickedness or evil. **2.** [*count*] a villainous act or deed.

-ville, *suffix.* **1.** *-ville* is used in place names, where it means "city, town": *Charlottesville.* **2.** *-ville* is also attached to roots or words to form informal words, not all of them long-lasting, that characterize a condition, place, person, group, or situation: *dulls + -ville (= a dull, boring situation); gloomsville.*

vim (vim) /vɪm/ *n.* [*noncount*] lively or energetic spirit; enthusiasm; vitality: *full of vim and vigor.*

vin•ai•grette (vin′ə gret′) /,vɪnə'grɛt/ *adj.* **1.** served with vinaigrette: *asparagus vinaigrette.* **—*n.*** [*noncount*] **2.** a tart sauce of oil, vinegar, and seasonings.

-vinc-, *root.* *-vinc-* comes from Latin, where it has the meaning "conquer; defeat." This meaning is found in such words as: CONVINCE, EVINCE, INVINCIBLE, VINCIBLE. See -VICT-.

vin•ci•ble (vin′sə bəl) /'vɪnsəbəl/ *adj.* capable of being conquered or overcome. See -VINC-.

vin•di•cate (vin′di kāt′) /'vɪndɪ,keyt/ *v.* [~ + *obj*], **-cat•ed, -cat•ing. 1.** to clear, as from an accusation or suspicion: *to vindicate someone's honor.* **2.** to prove to be right or correct: *His theory was vindicated by laboratory tests.* **—vin•di•ca•tion** (vin′di kā′shən) /,vɪndɪ'keyʃən/ *n.* [*count*]: *a vindication of the theory.* [*noncount*]: *He wanted vindication.* **—vin′di•ca′tor,** *n.* [*count*] See -VENGE-.

vin•dic•tive (vin dik′tiv) /vɪn'dɪktɪv/ *adj.* eager for revenge; vengeful: *a vindictive loser.* **—vin•dic′tive•ly,** *adv.* **—vin•dic′tive•ness,** *n.* [*noncount*]

vine (vīn) /vayn/ *n.* [*count*] **1.** a plant with a long stem that grows along the ground or that climbs a support by winding or by clinging to it. **2.** the stem itself. **3.** GRAPEVINE (def. 1).

vin•e•gar (vin′i gər) /'vɪnɪgər/ *n.* [*noncount*] a sour liquid made of impure acetic acid which is obtained from sour wine, cider, beer, ale, or the like and is used on food, in cooking, as a preservative, etc. **—vin′e•gar•y,** *adj.*

vine•yard (vin′yərd) /'vɪnyərd/ *n.* [*count*] a plantation of grapevines, esp. one producing grapes for winemaking.

vi•no (vē′nō) /'viynow/ *n.* [*noncount*], *pl.* **-nos.** wine; specifically, Italian red wine.

vin•tage (vin′tij) /'vɪntɪdʒ/ *n.* **1.** [*count*] the wine from a particular harvest or crop, esp. a very fine wine from the crop of a good year. **2.** [*noncount*] the output of a particular time or year; a collection of things manufactured or in use at the same time: *a car of 1917 vintage.* **—*adj.*** [*before a noun*] **3.** being of a specified vintage: *a 1978 vintage wine.* **4.** representing the high quality of a past time; classic: *those old, vintage movies.* **5.** being the best of its kind; choice: *a vintage Shakespearean performance.*

vint•ner (vint′nər) /'vɪntnər/ *n.* [*count*] a person who makes or sells wine.

vi•nyl (vīn′l) /'vaynḷ/ *n.* **1.** [*noncount*] a firm plastic that can be slightly bent, used for making floor coverings, furniture coverings, or the like. **2.** [*count*] *Slang.* a phonograph record made of vinyl.

vi•o•la (vē ō′lə) /viy'owlə/ *n.* [*count*], *pl.* **-las.** a musical instrument of the violin family, slightly larger than the violin. **—vi′ol•ist,** *n.* [*count*]

vi•o•la•ble (vī′ə lə bəl) /'vayələbəl/ *adj.* capable of being violated.

vi•o•late (vī′ə lāt′) /'vayə,leyt/ *v.* [~ + *obj*], **-lat•ed, -lat•ing. 1.** to break or infringe (a law, a promise, instructions, etc.): *to violate the law by stealing.* **2.** to break in upon or disturb rudely: *to violate someone's privacy.* **3.** to assault sexually, esp. to rape. **4.** to treat without proper reverence or respect; to desecrate: *to violate a church.*

vi•o•la•tion (vī′ə lā′shən) /,vayə'leyʃən/ *n.* **1.** [*noncount*] the act of violating or the state of being violated: *in violation of many laws.* **2.** [*count*] a breaking of a law or promise: *a speeding violation.* **3.** [*count*] a sexual assault, esp. rape. **4.** [*noncount*] desecration: *the violation of a cemetery.*

vi•o•lence (vī′ə ləns) /'vayələns/ *n.* [*noncount*] **1.** swift and intense force: *the violence of the hurricane.* **2.** rough physical force, action, or treatment intended to hurt or kill another: *avoiding violence and urging peace.* **3.** too much force or power, as of anger or fury: *He spoke with violence.* **4.** damage, as through changing or twisting meaning or fact: *to do violence to a translation.*

vi•o•lent (vī′ə lənt) /'vayələnt/ *adj.* **1.** acting with or characterized by uncontrolled, strong, rough force: *a violent attack with a kitchen knife.* **2.** characterized or caused by destructive force designed to injure or kill: *a violent death.* **3.** intense in force, effect, etc.; severe; extreme: *violent pain; a violent tornado.* **4.** being rough or overly forceful, as from anger or fury; furious: *violent passions.* —**vi′o•lent•ly,** *adv.* —**Related Words.** VIOLENT is an adjective, VIOLENCE is a noun: *It was a violent windstorm. Violence is the last refuge of the incompetent.*

vi•o•let (vī′ə lit) /ˈvayəlɪt/ *n.* **1.** [*count*] a low, stemless or leafy-stemmed plant having purple, blue, yellow, white, or differently colored flowers, as an African violet. **2.** [*noncount*] a reddish blue color. —*adj.* **3.** of the color violet; reddish blue.

vi•o•lin (vī′ə lin′) /ˌvayəˈlɪn/ *n.* [*count*] a four-stringed instrument played with a bow and held nearly horizontal by the player's arm with the lower part supported against the collarbone. —**vi′o•lin′ist,** *n.* [*count*]

vi•o•lon•cel•lo (vē′ə lən chel′ō, vī′-) /ˌviyələnˈtʃɛlow, ˌvay-/ *n.* [*count*], *pl.* **-los.** CELLO. —**vi′o•lon•cel′list,** *n.* [*count*]

VIP or **V.I.P.** (vē′ī′pē′) /ˈviyˈayˈpiy/ *n.* [*count*] *Informal.* a very important person.

vi•per (vī′pər) /ˈvaypər/ *n.* [*count*] **1.** a poisonous snake having a pair of hollow fangs that can be erected for biting and injecting venom: *Vipers include the adders, puff adders, and pit vipers.* **2.** a spiteful or treacherous person. —**vi′per•ous,** *adj.*

vi•ra•go (vi rä′gō, -rā′-) /vɪˈrɑgow, -ˈrey-/ *n.* [*count*], *pl.* **-goes, -gos.** a loud-voiced, ill-tempered, scolding woman; a shrew.

vi•ral (vī′rəl) /ˈvayrəl/ *adj.* of, relating to, or caused by a virus.

vir•gin (vûr′jin) /ˈvɜrdʒɪn/ *n.* [*count*] **1.** a person who has not had sexual intercourse. **2.** an unmarried girl or woman. **3.** *Informal.* any person who is uninitiated, uninformed, or the like. —*adj.* [*before a noun*] **4.** being a virgin. **5.** pure; untouched; not used or made use of: *the virgin snow; virgin timberlands.*

vir•gin•al (vûr′jə nl) /ˈvɜrdʒənl̩/ *adj.* **1.** relating to, characteristic of, or befitting a virgin. **2.** continuing in a state of virginity. **3.** pure; unsullied.

vir•gin•i•ty (vər jin′i tē) /vərˈdʒɪnɪtiy/ *n.* [*noncount*] the condition of being a virgin.

vir•gule (vûr′gyōōl) /ˈvɜrgyuwl/ *n.* [*count*] **1.** a short diagonal stroke (/) between two words indicating that either one may be chosen to complete the sense of the text: *The defendant and/or his/her attorney must appear in court.* **2.** a dividing line, as in dates or fractions, a run-in passage of poetry in order to show verse division, etc. Also called **diagonal.**

vir•ile (vir′əl) /ˈvɪrəl/ *adj.* having or exhibiting masculine strength; masculine; manly; characterized by a vigorous, masculine spirit. —**vi•ril•i•ty** (və ril′i tē) /vəˈrɪlɪtiy/ *n.* [*noncount*]

vir•tu•al (vûr′chōō əl) /ˈvɜrtʃuwəl/ *adj.* **1.** [*before a noun*] being (the noun stated) in force or effect, though not actually or expressly such: *They were reduced to virtual poverty.* **2.** temporarily simulated or extended by computer software: *virtual memory on a hard disk.* —**vir′tu•al•ly,** *adv.*

vir•tue (vûr′chōō) /ˈvɜrtʃuw/ *n.* **1.** [*noncount*] the practice of behaving or living one's life according to moral and ethical principles; moral excellence: *a life of virtue.* **2.** [*count*] a particular quality that reflects such moral excellence: *His virtues include honesty and integrity.* **3.** [*noncount*] chastity, esp. in a woman. **4.** [*count*] a desirable quality or property: *Riding a bike to work was one of the virtues of living in a university town.* —**Idiom. 5. by** or **in virtue of,** by reason of; because of: *By virtue of his office, the Vice President decides a tie in the Senate.* **6. make a virtue of necessity,** to make the best of a difficult or unsatisfactory situation.

vir•tu•o•so (vûr′chōō ō′sō) /ˌvɜrtʃuwˈowsow/ *n., pl.* **-sos, -si** (-sē) /-siy/ *adj.* —*n.* [*count*] **1.** a person who has special knowledge or skill in a field, esp. a person who is excellent in musical technique or execution. —*adj.* [*before a noun*] **2.** of, relating to, or characteristic of a virtuoso: *a virtuoso performance.* —**vir•tu•os•i•ty** (vûr′chōō os′i tē) /ˌvɜrtʃuwˈɒsɪtiy/ *n.* [*noncount*]

vir•tu•ous (vûr′chōō əs) /ˈvɜrtʃuwəs/ *adj.* **1.** agreeing with or following moral and ethical principles; morally excellent; upright. **2.** chaste: *a virtuous young woman.* —**vir′tu•ous•ly,** *adv.* —**vir′tu•ous•ness,** *n.* [*noncount*]

vir•u•lent (vir′yə lənt, vir′ə-) /ˈvɪryələnt, ˈvɪrə-/ *adj.* **1.** actively poisonous; very noxious; harmful or deadly; highly infective: *a virulent strain of bacteria.* **2.** violently hostile; intensely bitter, hateful, or wishing evil: *a virulent speech.* —**vir′u•lence,** *n.* [*noncount*]

vi•rus (vī′rəs) /ˈvayrəs/ *n.* [*count*], *pl.* **-rus•es. 1.** a very small living thing causing infection, which reproduces only within the cells of living hosts, mainly bacteria, plants, and animals. **2.** a disease caused by a virus: *was ill from a virus.* **3.** a corrupting idea or thought or a harmful influence on morals or the intellect. **4.** a part of a computer program that is planted illegally in another program, often to damage or shut down a system or network.

-vis-, *root.* -vis- comes from Latin, where it has the meaning "see." This meaning is found in such words as: ADVICE, ADVISABLE, ADVISE, INVISIBLE, PROVISION, PROVISO, REVISE, REVISION, SUPERVISE, SUPERVISION, SUPERVISOR, SUPERVISORY, TELEVISION, VISA, VISAGE, VIS-A-VIS, VISIBILITY, VISIBLE, VISION, VISIT, VISOR, VISTA, VISUAL, VISUALIZE.

vi•sa (vē′zə) /ˈviyzə/ *n.* [*count*], *pl.* **-sas.** an official stamp or mark made on a passport, which permits the holder to enter the country: *a tourist visa.* See -VIS-.

vis•age (viz′ij) /ˈvɪzɪdʒ/ *n.* [*count*] **1.** the face, usually with reference to its shape, features, expression, etc.: *a sad visage.* **2.** appearance: *a ghost town's desolate visage.* See -VIS-.

vis-à-vis (vē′zə vē′) /ˌviyzəˈviy/ *adv.* **1.** face to face. —*adj.* **2.** face-to-face. —*prep.* **3.** in relation to: *income vis-à-vis costs.* See -VIS-.

vis•cer•a (vis′ər ə) /ˈvɪsərə/ *n.* [*plural*], *sing.* **vis•cus** (vis′kəs) /ˈvɪskəs/. **1.** the organs in the cavities or spaces of the body, esp. those in the abdominal cavity. **2.** (not in technical use) the intestines.

vis•cer•al (vis′ər əl) /ˈvɪsərəl/ *adj.* [*before a noun*] **1.** of, relating to, or affecting the viscera. **2.** characterized by, coming from, or felt via one's instincts rather than intellect; emotional rather than intellectual: *My initial, visceral reaction was disgust.*

vis•cid (vis′id) /ˈvɪsɪd/ *adj.* sticky; adhesive; viscous.

vis•cos•i•ty (vi skos′i tē) /vɪˈskɒsɪtiy/ *n., pl.* **-ties. 1.** [*noncount*] the state or quality of being viscous. **2.** [*count*] the property of a fluid that resists the force tending to cause the fluid to flow: *oil of a high viscosity.*

vis•count (vī′kount′) /ˈvayˌkawnt/ *n.* [*count*] a nobleman ranking next below an earl or count and next above a baron.

vis•count•ess (vī′koun′tis) /ˈvayˌkawntɪs/ *n.* [*count*] **1.** the wife or widow of a viscount. **2.** a woman holding in her own right a rank equal to that of a viscount.

vis•cous (vis′kəs) /ˈvɪskəs/ *adj.* **1.** of a thick, sticky consistency. **2.** having the property of viscosity.

vise or **vice** (vīs) /vays/ *n., v.,* **vised, vis•ing.** —*n.* [*count*] **1.** a device usually having two jaws adjusted by means of a screw, lever, or the like, used to hold an object firmly while work is being done on it. —*v.* [~ + *obj*] **2.** to hold, press, or squeeze with or as if with a vise.

vis•i•bil•i•ty (viz′ə bil′i tē) /ˌvɪzəˈbɪlɪtiy/ *n., pl.* **-ties. 1.** [*noncount*] the quality, state, or fact of being visible. **2.** the greatest distance over which it is possible to see under certain atmospheric conditions or different kinds of weather: [*noncount*]: *Visibility was fine.* [*count*]: *a visibility of ten miles.* See -VIS-.

vis•i•ble (viz′ə bəl) /ˈvɪzəbəl/ *adj.* **1.** capable of being seen; that can be sensed by the eye. **2.** apparent; manifest; obvious: *no visible means of support.* **3.** being constantly or frequently in the public view. —**vis′i•bly,** *adv.*: *He was visibly upset.* See -VIS-.

vi•sion (vizh′ən) /ˈvɪʒən/ *n.* **1.** [*noncount*] the act or power of sensing with the eyes; sight. **2.** [*noncount*] the act or power of anticipating that which will or could come to be; foresight; imagination: *a man or woman of vision.* **3.** [*count*] a vivid, imaginative idea, conception, or anticipation of something that will or could come to be: *He had visions of wealth and glory.* **4.** [*count*] something seen in or as if in a dream or trance, often thought to come from God. **5.** [*count*] a scene, person, etc., of extraordinary beauty: *a vision of loveliness.* See -VIS-.

vi•sion•ar•y (vizh′ə ner′ē) /ˈvɪʒəˌnɛriy/ *adj., n., pl.* **-ar•ies.** —*adj.* **1.** showing or having vision or imagination, as the ability to see things that will or could be. **2.** too idealistic; impractical: *an impractical, visionary scheme.* **3.** having fanciful or impractical ideas or schemes. **4.** of or relating to a vision. —*n.* [*count*] **5.** a person of unusually keen foresight. **6.** a person who has idealistic or impractical ideas or schemes that are not likely to come true. See -VIS-.

vis•it (viz′it) /ˈvɪzɪt/ *v.* **1.** to go to and stay with (a person or family) or at (a place) for a short time: [~ + *obj*]: *We visited our friends in Greece.* [*no obj*]: *Come to visit with us for a few hours.* **2.** [*no obj*] to talk or chat casually. **3.** [~ + *obj*] to go to for the purpose of official inspection or examination: *The inspection team visited the factory.* **4.** [~ + *obj*] to come upon; afflict: *The plague visited*

London in 1665. **5.** [~ + *obj* + *on* + *obj*] to inflict, as punishment, vengeance, etc.: *visited punishment on them for their sins.* **6.** [~ + *obj* + *with* + *obj*] to cause trouble, suffering, etc., to: *God visited Job with sorrows.* —*n.* [*count*] **7.** the act of or an instance of visiting: *a long visit.* See -VIS-.

vis•it•a•tion (viz′i tā′shən) /ˌvɪzɪ'teyʃən/ *n.* **1.** [*count*] the act of visiting. **2.** a formal visit, as one granted by a court to a divorced parent to visit a child in custody of the other parent: [*noncount*]: *the right of visitation.* [*count*]: *two visitations per month.* See -VIS-.

vis•i•tor (viz′i tər) /'vɪzɪtər/ *n.* [*count*] a person who visits, as for reasons of friendship, business, duty, sickness, or the like.

vi•sor also **vi•zor** (vī′zər) /'vayzər/ *n.* [*count*] **1.** the projecting front brim of a cap. **2.** a flap, mounted over the windshield on the inside of an automobile, that is used to shield the eyes from glare. **3.** the front piece on a medieval helmet, often being movable and having slits for vision. See -VIS-.

vis•ta (vis′tə) /'vɪstə/ *n.* [*count*], *pl.* **-tas.** a view, esp. one seen through a long, narrow passage, as between rows of trees or houses. See -VIS-.

vis•u•al (vizh′o͞o əl) /'vɪʒuwəl/ *adj.* **1.** of or relating to seeing or sight: *a visual image.* —*n.* **2.** Usually, **visuals.** [*plural*] **a.** the picture elements, as distinguished from the sound elements, in films, television, etc. **b.** photographs, films, charts, or other visual materials, esp. as used for illustration or promotion. —**vis′u•al•ly,** *adv.* See -VIS-.

vis′ual arts′, *n.* [*plural*] the arts created primarily for viewing, as drawing, graphics, painting, sculpture, and the decorative arts.

vis•u•al•ize (vizh′o͞o ə līz′) /'vɪʒuwəˌlayz/ *v.* [~ + *obj*], **-ized, -iz•ing.** to form a mental image of: *tried to visualize future events.* —**vis•u•al•i•za•tion** (vizh′o͞o ə lə zā′shən) /ˌvɪʒuwələ'zeyʃən/ *n.* [*noncount*] —**vis′u•al•iz′er,** *n.* [*count*] See -VIS-.

-vit-, *root.* *-vit-* comes from Latin, where it has the meaning "life; living." It is related to the root -VIV-. This meaning is found in such words as: REVITALIZE, VITA, VITAL, VITAMIN.

vi•ta (vī′tə) /'vaytə/ *n., pl.* **vi•tae** (vī′tē) /'vaytiy/. CURRICULUM VITAE. See -VIT-.

vi•tal (vīt′l) /'vaytl̩/ *adj.* **1.** of, relating to, or necessary to life: *vital processes of food and energy production.* **2.** energetic, lively, or forceful: *a vital leader.* **3.** absolutely necessary for the existence, continuance, or well-being of something; of great importance; indispensable; essential: *vital supplies.* **4.** of critical importance: *vital decisions.* —**vi′tal•ly,** *adv.* See -VIT-.

vi•tal•i•ty (vī tal′i tē) /vay'tælɪtiy/ *n.* [*noncount*] **1.** lively physical or mental vigor or strength: *a person of great vitality.* **2.** ability to survive or to carry on a meaningful or purposeful existence: *the vitality of an institution.* See -VIT-.

vi′tal signs′, *n.* [*plural*] essential, necessary, or crucial body functions, including pulse rate, body temperature, and respiration.

vi′tal statis′tics, *n.* [*plural*] **1.** statistics concerning human life, the population count, and the conditions affecting human life, such as deaths, births, and marriages. **2.** *Facetious.* the measurements of a woman's figure, esp. the bust, waist, and hips.

vi•ta•min (vī′tə min) /'vaytəmɪn/ also **vi•ta•mine** (vī′tə-min, -mēn′) /'vaytəmɪn, -ˌmiyn/ *n.* [*count*] any of a group of substances that are essential to the body in small quantities for normal metabolism, found in very small amounts in foods and also produced artificially. See -VIT-.

vi•ti•ate (vish′ē āt′) /'vɪʃiyˌeyt/ *v.* [~ + *obj*], **-at•ed, -at•ing.** **1.** to ruin or reduce the quality of; make faulty; spoil. **2.** to reduce or weaken the effectiveness of: *vitiated his best efforts.* **3.** to make (a claim) legally invalid; invalidate: *to vitiate a claim.* —**vi•ti•a•tion** (vish′ē ā′shən) /ˌvɪʃiy'eyʃən/ *n.* [*noncount*]

vit•re•ous (vi′trē əs) /'vɪtriyəs/ *adj.* **1.** of the nature of or resembling glass, as in being transparent, brittle, hard, or glossy: *vitreous china.* **2.** of or relating to glass; obtained from or containing glass.

vit•ri•ol (vi′trē əl) /'vɪtriyəl/ *n.* [*noncount*] something highly sharp or severe in effect, as biting criticism.

vit•ri•ol•ic (vi′trē ol′ik) /ˌvɪtriy'ɒlɪk/ *adj.* very sharp, bitter, or hateful: *vitriolic language.*

vi•tu•per•a•tion (vī to͞o′pə rā′shən, -tyo͞o′-, vi-) /vayˌtuwpə'reyʃən, -'tyuw-, vɪ-/ *n.* [*noncount*] harsh or abusive language; violent or very harsh criticism. —**vi•tu•per•a•tive** (vī to͞o′pər ətiv, -pə rā′-, -tyo͞o′-) /vay'tuwpərətɪv, -pəˌrey-, -'tyuw-/ *adj.*

-viv-, *root.* *-viv-* comes from Latin, where it has the meaning "life; alive; lively." This meaning is found in such words as: CONVIVIAL, REVIVAL, REVIVE, SURVIVAL, SURVIVE, SURVIVOR, VIVA, VIVACIOUS, VIVID, VIVIPAROUS, VIVISECTION.

vi•va (vē′və, -vä) /'viyvə, -vɑ/ *interj.* (used as an exclamation of approval) Long live (the person or thing named): *Viva freedom!* See -VIV-.

vi•va•cious (vi vā′shəs, vī-) /vɪ'veyʃəs, vay-/ *adj.* lively; animated; spirited: *a vivacious, outgoing personality.* —**vi•va′cious•ly,** *adv.* —**vi•vac•i•ty** (vi vas′i tē, vī-) /vɪ'væsɪtiy, vay-/ **vi•va′cious•ness,** *n.* [*noncount*] See -VIV-.

viv•id (viv′id) /'vɪvɪd/ *adj.* **1.** (of color, light, etc.) strikingly bright or intense; brilliant: *a vivid red.* **2.** having bright or striking colors. **3.** presenting the appearance, freshness, spirit, etc., of life; realistic: *a vivid account of the wedding.* **4.** detailed; distinct: *a vivid dream.* **5.** full of life; lively: *a vivid personality.* —**viv′id•ly,** *adv.* —**viv′id•ness,** *n.* [*noncount*] See -VIV-.

vi•vip•a•rous (vī vip′ər əs, vi-) /vay'vɪpərəs, vɪ-/ *adj.* bringing forth living young rather than eggs. See -VIV-, -PARE[2]-.

viv•i•sec•tion (viv′ə sek′shən) /ˌvɪvə'sɛkʃən/ *n.* [*noncount*] the action of cutting into or dissecting a living body or living animals, in order to learn more about disease and bodily functions. —**viv′i•sec′tion•al,** *adj.* See -VIV-, -SECT-.

vix•en (vik′sən) /'vɪksən/ *n.* [*count*] **1.** a female fox. **2.** an ill-tempered or quarrelsome woman. —**vix′en•ish,** *adj.*

vi•zier or **vi•zir** (vi zēr′, viz′yər) /vɪ'zɪər, 'vɪzyər/ *n.* [*count*] a high governmental official in certain Muslim countries.

vi•zor (vī′zər) /'vayzər/ *n.* VISOR.

VLF or **vlf,** an abbreviation of: very low frequency.

V neck, *n.* [*count*] a neckline that is V-shaped in front. —**V-necked,** *adj.*: *a V-necked sweater.*

-voc-, *root.* *-voc-* comes from Latin, where it has the meaning "call." This meaning is found in such words as: ADVOCATE, AVOCATION, CONVOCATION, CONVOKE, EQUIVOCAL, EVOCATIVE, EVOKE, INVOCATION, INVOKE, IRREVOCABLE, PROVOCATION, PROVOCATIVE, PROVOKE, REVOKE, UNEQUIVOCAL, VOCABULARY, VOCAL, VOCATION, VOCIFEROUS.

vo•cab•u•lar•y (vō kab′yə ler′ē) /vow'kæbyəˌlɛriy/ *n., pl.* **-lar•ies.** **1.** the stock of words used by, known to, or peculiar to a particular person, or group, language, or profession: [*count*]: *the vocabulary of the law.* [*noncount*]: *studies of the acquisition of vocabulary in children.* **2.** [*count*] a usually short list or collection of words and often phrases, usually arranged in alphabetical order and defined. **3.** [*count*] any collection of signs, symbols, gestures, techniques, etc., making up a means or system of nonverbal communication: *the vocabulary of Impressionism.* See -VOC-.

vo•cal (vō′kəl) /'vowkəl/ *adj.* **1.** of, relating to, or produced with the voice: *the vocal sounds.* **2.** intended for singing: *vocal music.* **3.** willing to express oneself in words, esp. in many words or insistently; outspoken: *a vocal advocate of reform.* —*n.* [*count*] **4.** a vocal sound. **5.** **a.** a musical piece for a singer; song. **b.** a performance of such a piece. —**vo′cal•ly,** *adv.* See -VOC-.

vo′cal cords′, *n.* [*plural*] either of two pairs of folds of membrane stretched across the larynx, the lower pair of which produces sound or voice as it is made to vibrate by the passage of air from the lungs.

vo•cal•ist (vō′kə list) /'vowkəlɪst/ *n.* [*count*] a singer. See -VOC-.

vo•cal•ize (vō′kə līz′) /'vowkəˌlayz/ *v.,* **-ized, -iz•ing.** **1.** to make vocal; to make or produce sounds; articulate: [~ + *obj*]: *to vocalize one's objections.* [*no obj*]: *dolphins and chimpanzees vocalizing.* **2.** [*no obj*] to sing; to sing without uttering words. —**vo•cal•i•za•tion** (vō′kə lə zā′shən) /ˌvowkələ'zeyʃən/ *n.* [*noncount*]: *the process of vocalization.* [*count*]: *some strange vocalizations.* See -VOC-.

vo•ca•tion (vō kā′shən) /vow'keyʃən/ *n.* [*count*] **1.** a particular occupation, business, or profession; one's calling: *a vocation of teaching.* **2.** a strong impulse or desire to follow a particular activity or career. **3.** a divine call to a religious life: *a vocation to join the priesthood.* See -VOC-.

vo•ca•tion•al (vo͞o kā′shə nl) /vuw'keyʃənl̩/ *adj.* training or preparing one for a job or a certain skill: *a vocational school for carpentry.* See -VOC-.

vo•cif•er•ous (vō sif′ər əs) /vowˈsɪfərəs/ *adj.* **1.** crying out noisily. **2.** characterized by noisy or strong outcry; vehement: *vociferous protests.* —**vo•cif′er•ous•ly,** *adv.* See -voc-.

vod•ka (vod′kə) /ˈvɒdkə/ *n.* [*noncount*] a colorless, distilled alcoholic spirit made esp. from rye or wheat mash.

vogue (vōg) /vowg/ *n.* **1.** the current or popular fashion at a particular time: [*count*]: *a vogue for long hair.* [*noncount*]: *Some of that slang is no longer in vogue.* —*adj.* **2.** currently fashionable or popular: *vogue words.* —**vogu′ish,** *adj.*

voice (vois) /vɔys/ *n., v.,* **voiced, voic•ing.** —*n.* **1.** [*count*] the sound or sounds uttered through the mouth of living creatures, esp. of human beings in speaking, singing, etc. **2.** [*noncount*] the pattern of such sounds characteristic of a particular person: *I'd know his voice anywhere!* **3.** [*noncount*] the ability to utter sounds through the mouth by controlling the air sent out; speech: *He had such a sore throat that he lost his voice.* **4.** [*noncount*] the condition or effectiveness of the voice for speaking or singing: *in poor voice.* **5.** [*count*] something like speech as conveying impressions to the mind: *the voice of one's conscience.* **6.** [*noncount*] expression in words or by other means: *The audience gave voice to their disapproval.* **7.** [*count; usually singular*] an expressed opinion, choice, will, or desire: *the voice of the opposition.* **8.** [*count*] the right to present and receive consideration of one's desires or opinions: *to have a voice in company policy.* **9.** [*count*] a singer: *He is one of the great voices in opera.* **10.** [*count*] a melodic part in a musical composition: *a three-voice fugue.* **11.** [*count*] a category or set of categories of the verb that show the relation of the subject to the verb: *If the subject is the performer of the action, the verb is in the active voice; if the subject is the one receiving, benefiting, or being harmed by the action, then usually the verb is in the passive voice. The verb* was carried *is in the passive voice in the sentence* I was carried to the hospital; *the verb* carried *is in the active voice in the sentence* They carried me to the hospital. —*v.* [~ + *obj*] **12.** to express by words or utterances; declare; proclaim: *They voiced their disapproval.* —***Idiom.*** **13. with one voice,** in complete agreement; unanimously. —**voice′less,** *adj.* See -voc-.

voice′ box′, *n.* [*count*] the larynx.

voiced (voist) /vɔyst/ *adj.* **1.** having a voice of a certain kind: *shrill-voiced.* **2.** (of a speech sound) pronounced with vibration of the vocal cords, as the consonants (b), (v), and (n).

voice′-o′ver, *n.* [*count*] the voice of an unseen narrator, announcer, or the like, as in television or radio commercials or television or motion-picture sequences featuring an offscreen voice.

void (void) /vɔyd/ *adj.* **1.** having no legal force or effect: *This law has been declared null and void.* **2.** [*be* + ~ + *of*] empty; lacking: *He felt his life was void of meaning.* **3.** (of a political office) vacant. **4.** (in cards) having no cards in a suit. —*n.* [*count*] **5.** empty space; emptiness: *disappeared into the void.* **6.** a state or feeling of loss: *His death left a great void in her life.* **7.** (in cards) lack of cards in a suit: *a void in clubs.* —*v.* **8.** [~ + *obj*] to make invalid; nullify: *to void a check.* **9.** to empty the bowels or urinate: [~ + *obj*]: *to void the bowels.* [*no obj*]: *having trouble voiding.* —**void′a•ble,** *adj.*

voi•là or **voi•la** (vwä lä′) /vwɑˈlɑ/ *interj.* This expression from French is used to express success or satisfaction, or to draw the attention of the listener to something.

-vol-, *root.* *-vol-* comes from Latin, where it has the meaning "wish; will." This meaning is found in such words as: BENEVOLENT, INVOLUNTARY, MALEVOLENT, VOLITION, VOLUNTARY, VOLUNTEER.

vol., an abbreviation of: volume.

vol•a•tile (vol′ə tl, -til′) /ˈvɒlətḷ, -ˌtayl/ *adj.* **1.** evaporating rapidly; passing off quickly in the form of vapor: *Acetone is a volatile solvent.* **2.** tending or threatening to break out into open violence; explosive: *a volatile political situation.* **3.** having or likely to have or exhibit sharp or sudden changes; unstable: *a volatile stock market.* **4.** changeable, as in mood or temper: *a volatile personality.* —**vol′a•til′i•ty** (-til′i tē) /-ˈtɪlɪtiy/ *n.* [*noncount*]

vol•can•ic (vol kan′ik) /vɒlˈkænɪk/ *adj.* **1.** of or relating to a volcano: *volcanic islands.* **2.** produced by volcanoes: *volcanic ash.* **3.** likely to explode: *a volcanic temper.*

vol•ca•no (vol kā′nō) /vɒlˈkeynow/ *n.* [*count*], *pl.* **-noes, -nos. 1.** a vent in the earth's crust through which lava, steam, ashes, etc., are given off, either continuously or at intervals. **2.** a mountain or hill, usually having a cuplike crater at the top, that was formed around such a vent from the ash and lava that were given off from it.

vole (vōl) /vowl/ *n.* [*count*] a short-tailed, stocky animal resembling a mouse.

vo•li•tion (vō lish′ən, və-) /vowˈlɪʃən, və-/ *n.* [*noncount*] the act of willing, choosing, or deciding to do something: *She left of her own volition.* —**vo•li′tion•al,** *adj.* See -vol-.

vol•ley (vol′ē) /ˈvɒliy/ *n., pl.* **-leys,** *v.,* **-leyed, -ley•ing.** —*n.* [*count*] **1.** the shooting of a number of missiles or firearms at the same time. **2.** the missiles so discharged. **3.** a burst or outpouring of many things at once or in quick succession: *a volley of protests.* **4. a.** the return of a ball or shuttlecock, as in tennis or badminton, before it hits the ground. **b.** a series of such returns; a rally. —*v.* **5.** [~ + *obj*] to shoot in or as if in a volley. **6.** to return (a ball) before it hits the ground: [*no obj*]: *They volleyed for almost five minutes.* [~ + *obj*]: *to volley a ball.*

vol•ley•ball (vol′ē bôl′) /ˈvɒliyˌbɔl/ *n.* **1.** [*noncount*] a game for two teams in which the object is to return a large, inflated ball, and in such a fashion that the opposing team will be unable to do the same over a high net by striking it with the hands before it touches the ground. **2.** [*count*] the ball used in this game.

volt (vōlt) /vowlt/ *n.* [*count*] a standard unit of measure for electrical force. *Abbr.:* V

volt•age (vōl′tij) /ˈvowltɪdʒ/ *n.* electrical force expressed in volts: [*count*]: *different voltages.* [*noncount*]: *measuring voltage.*

vol•ta•ic (vol tā′ik, vōl-) /vɒlˈteyɪk, vowl-/ *adj.* of or relating to electric currents, esp. when produced by chemical action.

vol•u•ble (vol′yə bəl) /ˈvɒlyəbəl/ *adj.* fluent; glib; talkative: *a voluble speaker.* —**vol•u•bil•i•ty** (vol′yə bil′i tē) /ˌvɒlyəˈbɪlɪtiy/ *n.* [*noncount*] —**vol′u•bly,** *adv.*

vol•ume (vol′yōōm, -yəm) /ˈvɒlyuwm, -yəm/ *n.* **1.** [*noncount*] **a.** the amount of space, measured in cubic units, that an object or substance occupies. **b.** the measured amount that a container can hold; cubic capacity. **2.** [*count*] a mass, amount, or quantity: *a volume of mail.* **3.** [*noncount*] the degree of sound intensity: *turned up the volume.* **4.** [*count*] **a.** a book. **b.** the books of a set. —***Idiom.*** **5. speak volumes,** to be full of meaning: *His expression spoke volumes about his true feelings.*

vo•lu•mi•nous (və lōō′mə nəs) /vəˈluwmənəs/ *adj.* **1.** filling or enough to fill volumes: *a voluminous correspondence.* **2.** very productive: *a voluminous writer.* **3.** of great volume: *a voluminous briefcase.* **4.** having many folds or much fullness: *voluminous skirts.* —**vo•lu′mi•nous•ly,** *adv.*

vol•un•ta•rism (vol′ən tə riz′əm) /ˈvɒləntəˌrɪzəm/ *n.* [*noncount*] the principle or practice of supporting schools, hospitals, churches, etc., by voluntary contributions, participation, or aid. See -vol-.

vol•un•tar•y (vol′ən ter′ē) /ˈvɒlənˌtɛriy/ *adj.* **1.** done, made, brought about, or performed through or by one's will or one's own free choice: *a voluntary contribution.* **2.** controlled by the will: *voluntary muscle movements.* **3.** done by or made up of volunteers: *voluntary workers; voluntary hospitals.* **4.** *Law.* **a.** acting or done without being forced. **b.** done by intention and not by accident: *voluntary manslaughter.* —**vol•un•tar•i•ly** (vol′ən târ′ə lē, vol′ən ter′-) /ˌvɒlənˈtɛərəliy, ˈvɒlənˌtɛr-/ *adv.* See -vol-.

vol•un•teer (vol′ən tēr′) /ˌvɒlənˈtɪər/ *n.* [*count*] **1.** a person who voluntarily offers himself or herself for a service or undertaking, or who performs a service willingly and without pay. **2.** a person who enters military service voluntarily. —*adj.* **3.** made of or performed by volunteers: *a volunteer army.* —*v.* **4.** to offer oneself for some service or undertaking: [*no obj*]: *eager to volunteer.* [~ + *oneself*]: *He volunteered himself for the mission.* [~ + *to* + *verb*]: *He volunteered to write the report.* **5.** [*no obj*] to enlist as a volunteer: *volunteered for combat.* **6.** [~ + *obj*] to say, tell, or communicate (something) freely or willingly: *to volunteer an explanation.* See -vol-.

vo•lup•tu•ous (və lup′chōō əs) /vəˈlʌptʃuwəs/ *adj.* **1.** sensuously pleasing or delightful. **2.** full and shapely: *a voluptuous figure.* —**vo•lup′tu•ous•ness,** *n.* [*noncount*]

vom•it (vom′it) /ˈvɒmɪt/ *v.* **1.** to throw up the contents of the stomach through the mouth; regurgitate: [*no obj*]: *feared he might vomit.* [~ + *obj*]: *to vomit one's dinner.* **2.** [~ + *obj*] to throw out or eject with force or violence: *The volcano vomited ash and rock.* —*n.* [*noncount*] **3.** the undigested food thrown up when vomiting.

voo•doo (vōō′dōō) /ˈvuwduw/ *n., pl.* **-doos,** *adj.* —*n.* [*noncount*] **1.** a religion practiced chiefly by West Indians, derived principally from African cult worship and containing elements borrowed from Catholicism. **2.** black magic; sorcery. **—*adj.*** **3.** of, associated with, or practicing voodoo. —**voo′doo•ism,** *n.* [*noncount*]

-vor-, *root.* *-vor-* comes from Latin, where it has the meaning "eat." This meaning is found in such words as: CARNIVORE, CARNIVOROUS, DEVOUR, HERBIVORE, HERBIVOROUS, OMNIVOROUS, VORACIOUS.

vo•ra•cious (vô rā′shəs, və-) /vɔ'reyʃəs, vɔ-/ *adj.* **1.** wanting or eating large quantities of food: *a voracious appetite.* **2.** very eager or avid; insatiable: *a voracious reader.* —**vo•ra′cious•ly,** *adv.* —**vo•rac•i•ty** (vô ras′i tē) /vɔ'ræsɪtiy/ *n.* [*noncount*] See -VOR-.

vor•tex (vôr′teks) /'vɔrtɛks/ *n.* [*count*], *pl.* **-tex•es, -ti•ces** (-tə sēz′) /-tə,siyz/. **1.** a whirling mass of water or air, esp. one in which a sucking force operates to pull things in, as a whirlpool or a tornado. **2.** any situation or state of affairs thought to be like a whirlpool: *the vortex of war.* See -VERT-.

-vot-, *root.* *-vot-* comes from Latin, where it has the meaning "vow." This meaning is found in such words as: DEVOTE, DEVOTEE, DEVOUT, VOTE.

vote (vōt) /vowt/ *n., v.,* **vot•ed, vot•ing.** **—*n.*** [*count*] **1.** a formal expression of one's choice, opinion, or decision, usually either for or against someone or something, as a policy or proposal, made by an individual or a body of individuals. **2.** the means by which such expression is made, as a ballot: *to cast a vote.* **3.** [*usually singular*] the right to such expression: *gave citizens the vote.* **4.** [*usually singular*] the total number of votes cast: *The vote was 55,000 in favor, 22,000 against.* **5.** the decision reached by voting: *The vote was unanimous.* **6.** an expression of approval or disapproval: *a vote of no confidence.* **—*v.*** **7.** to express or show one's will or choice in a matter, as by casting a ballot: [*no obj*]: *Did you vote?* [~ + *to* + *verb*]: *We voted to go on strike.* [~ + *(that) clause*]: *I vote that we all go on strike.* **8.** to support by one's vote: [~ + *obj*]: *to vote the party ticket.* [~ + *for* + *obj*]: *Did you vote for her?* **9.** [~ + *obj*] to enact by vote: *to vote a bill into law.* —**vot′er,** *n.* [*count*] See -VOT-.

vouch (vouch) /vawtʃ/ *v.* [~ + *for* + *obj*] **1.** to provide proof, supporting evidence, or assurance: *Her record in office vouches for her integrity.* **2.** to give a guarantee or act as surety or sponsor; take responsibility: *I can vouch for him.* See -VOC-.

vouch•er (vou′chər) /'vawtʃər/ *n.* [*count*] **1.** a person or thing that vouches. **2.** a document, receipt, stamp, etc., that gives evidence of money spent or received. **3.** a form or ticket that permits a payment of cash to the holder or serves as a credit against a future purchase or expense.

vow (vou) /vaw/ *n.* [*count*] **1.** a solemn promise, pledge, or personal commitment: *marriage vows; a vow of secrecy.* **2.** a solemn promise that commits oneself to an act, service, or condition: *a priest's vow of celibacy.* **—*v.*** **3.** to make a vow of; promise by a vow; pledge or declare solemnly: [~ + *obj*]: *to vow revenge.* [~ + *to* + *verb*]: *He vowed to be on time.* [~ + *(that) clause*]: *He vowed that he would never drink and drive again.* **—*Idiom.*** **4. take vows,** to make an official commitment to a religious order. See -VOT-.

vow•el (vou′əl) /'vawəl/ *n.* [*count*] **1.** a speech sound, as (ē), (o͞o), or (a), produced without stopping, blocking, or changing the path of the flow of air from the lungs. **2.** a letter or other symbol that represents a vowel sound, as, in English, *a, e, i, o, u,* and sometimes *y.* See -VOC-.

vox po•pu•li (voks′ pop′yə lī′) /'vɒks' pɒpyə,lay/ *n.* [*count; usually singular*] the voice of the people; popular opinion. See -VOC-, -POP-.

voy•age (voi′ij) /'vɔyɪdʒ/ *n., v.,* **-aged, -ag•ing.** **—*n.*** [*count*] **1.** a course of travel or passage or a journey, esp. a long journey by water to a distant place. **2.** a passage or journey through air or space. **—*v.*** [*no obj*] **3.** to make or take a voyage; travel; journey. —**voy′ag•er,** *n.* [*count*]

vo•yeur (vwä yûr′, voi ûr′) /vwɑ'yɜr, vɔy'ɜr/ *n.* [*count*] a person who obtains sexual pleasure by looking at sexual objects or at other people performing sexual acts. —**vo•yeur•ism** (vwä yûr′iz əm, voi ûr′-, voi′ə riz′-) /vwɑ'yɜrɪzəm, vɔy'ɜr-, 'vɔyə,rɪz-/ *n.* [*noncount*] —**voy′-eur•is′tic,** *adj.*

VP, an abbreviation of: **1.** verb phrase. **2.** Also, **vp, v-p** vice president.

V.P. or **V. Pres.,** an abbreviation of: Vice President.

vs. or **vs,** an abbreviation of: **1.** verse. **2.** versus.

VT or **Vt.,** an abbreviation of: Vermont.

v.t., an abbreviation of: verb transitive (transitive verb).

vul•can•ize (vul′kə nīz′) /'vʌlkə,nayz/ *v.* [~ + *obj*], **-ized, -iz•ing.** to treat (rubber or some similar substance) with sulfur and heat, in order to give it greater strength, elasticity, and durability. —**vul•can•i•za•tion** (vul′kə nə-zā′shən) /,vʌlkənə'zeyʃən/ *n.* [*noncount*]

vul•gar (vul′gər) /'vʌlgər/ *adj.* **1.** characterized by or showing one's lack of refinement or good taste; crude; coarse. **2.** indecent; obscene; lewd: *a vulgar gesture; vulgar language.* **3.** spoken by, or being in the language spoken by, the people generally; vernacular. —**vul′-gar•ly,** *adv.*

vul•gar•ism (vul′gə riz′əm) /'vʌlgə,rɪzəm/ *n.* **1.** [*noncount*] vulgar behavior or character; vulgarity. **2.** [*count*] a vulgar word or phrase.

vul•gar•i•ty (vul gar′i tē) /vʌl'gærɪtiy/ *n., pl.* **-ties.** **1.** [*noncount*] the state or quality of being vulgar. **2.** [*count*] something vulgar.

vul•ner•a•ble (vul′nər ə bəl) /'vʌlnərəbəl/ *adj.* **1.** capable of being or easily being wounded or hurt physically or emotionally. **2.** open to or defenseless against criticism or moral attack. **3.** (of a place) open to assault; difficult to defend. —**vul•ner•a•bil•i•ty** (vul′nər ə bil′i tē) /,vʌlnərə'bɪlɪtiy/ *n.* [*noncount*] —**vul′ner•a•bly,** *adv.*

vul•ture (vul′chər) /'vʌltʃər/ *n.* [*count*] **1.** a large bird of prey, related to the hawks and eagles, that soars at a high altitude seeking dead animal flesh for food. **2.** a person or thing that is eager to gain from another's misfortune, as by greedily preying upon that person. —**vul′-tur•ous,** *adj.*

vul•va (vul′və) /'vʌlvə/ *n.* [*count*], *pl.* **-vae** (-vē) /-viy/ **-vas.** the external female sex organs.

vy•ing (vī′ing) /'vayɪŋ/ *v.* pres. part. of VIE.

W, w (dub′əl yo͞o′, -yo͞o) /ˈdʌbəlˌyuw, -yʊ/ *n.* [*count*], *pl.* **Ws** or **W's, ws** or **w's.** the 23rd letter of the English alphabet, a semivowel.

W, an abbreviation of: **1.** watt. **2.** west. **3.** western. **4.** wide. **5.** width.

w, an abbreviation of: **1.** watt. **2.** with.

W., an abbreviation of: **1.** watt. **2.** Wednesday. **3.** weight. **4.** west. **5.** western. **6.** width.

w., an abbreviation of: **1.** watt. **2.** week. **3.** weight. **4.** west. **5.** western. **6.** wide. **7.** width. **8.** wife. **9.** with. **10.** work.

w/, an abbreviation of: with.

WA, an abbreviation of: Washington.

Wac (wak) /wæk/ *n.* [*count*] a member of the Women's Army Corps.

wack•y also **whack•y** (wak′ē) /ˈwækiy/ *adj.*, **-i•er, -i•est.** *Slang.* odd; strange; silly; slightly crazy. —**wack•i•ly** (wak′ə lē) /ˈwækəliy/ *adv.* —**wack′i•ness,** *n.* [*noncount*]

wad (wod) /wɒd/ *n.*, *v.*, **wad•ded, wad•ding.** —*n.* [*count*] **1.** a small mass, as of cotton, used esp. for padding and packing, filling a hole, etc. **2.** a roll of bank notes. **3.** a fairly large amount of something, as money: *made a wad in the stock market.* **4.** a small mass of substance for chewing: *a wad of chewing tobacco; a wad of gum.* —*v.* [~ + *obj*] **5.** to form into a wad, as by rolling tightly: [~ (+ *up*) + *obj*]: *He wadded (up) the paper.* [~ + *obj* (+ *up*)]: *He wadded the paper (up).*

wad•dle (wod′l) /ˈwɒdl/ *v.*, **-dled, -dling,** *n.* —*v.* [*no obj*] **1.** to walk with short steps, swaying from side to side in the manner of a duck. —*n.* [*count*] **2.** a waddling way of walking.

wade (wād) /weyd/ *v.*, **wad•ed, wad•ing. 1.** [*no obj*] to walk while partly immersed in water. **2.** [*no obj*] to walk through a substance, as water or snow, that interferes with one's motion: *They waded through the mud.* **3. wade through,** [~ + *through* + *obj*] to struggle or make one's way through (some task or job) with effort or difficulty: *to wade through a pile of bills to be paid.*

wad′er (wā′der) /ˈweydər/ *n.* [*count*] **1.** one that wades. **2.** Also called **wad′ing bird′.** a long-legged bird that wades in water in search of food. **3. waders,** [*plural*] high waterproof boots or pants worn for wading or while fishing.

wa•di (wä′dē) /ˈwɑdiy/ *n.* [*count*], *pl.* **-dis.** (in Arabia, Syria, northern Africa, etc.) a place where water runs only during periods of rainfall.

wa•fer (wā′fər) /ˈweyfər/ *n.* [*count*] **1.** a thin, crisp cake, cookie, biscuit, or candy. **2.** a thin disk of unleavened bread used in the Eucharist. **3.** any small, thin disk. —**wa′fer•like′,** *adj.*

waf•fle[1] (wof′əl) /ˌwɒfəl/ *n.* [*count*] a batter cake baked in a hinged appliance **(waf′fle i′ron)** that forms a grid-like pattern on each side.

waf•fle[2] (wof′əl) /ˈwɒfəl/ *v.* [*no obj*], **-fled, -fling.** to speak or write without taking a definite stand; equivocate. —**waf′fler,** *n.* [*count*]

waft (wäft, waft) /wɑft, wæft/ *v.* to (cause to) be carried or float lightly and smoothly through or as if through the air: [*no obj*]: *The smell of fresh bread wafted in.* [~ + *obj*]: *The smells were wafted along.*

wag (wag) /wæg/ *v.*, **wagged, wag•ging,** *n.* —*v.* **1.** to move up and down or from side to side: [*no obj*]: *The dog's tail wagged.* [~ + *obj*]: *The dog wagged its tail.* **2.** to move (the tongue) in talking idly: [~ + *obj*]: *Quit wagging your tongue and listen!* [*no obj*]: *Local tongues are wagging over this latest scandal.* —*n.* [*count*] **3.** the act of wagging. **4.** a clever, witty person. —**wag′ger,** *n.* [*count*]

wage (wāj) /weydʒ/ *n.*, *v.*, **waged, wag•ing.** —*n.* **1.** Often, **wages.** [*plural*] money paid or received for work or services: [*count*]: *My wages are too low.* [*noncount*]: *a decent wage.* **2. wages,** [*noncount; used with a singular verb*] return; the consequences or result of some action: *The wages of sin is death.* —*v.* [~ + *obj*] **3.** to begin or carry on: *to wage war.*

wa•ger (wā′jər) /ˈweydʒər/ *n.* [*count*] **1.** something risked or bet on an uncertain event; a bet: *I made him a wager he couldn't finish on time.* —*v.* **2.** to bet; gamble: [~ + *obj*]: *She wagered fifty dollars.* [~ (+ *obj*) + (*that*) *clause*]: *She wagered (fifty dollars) (that) he wouldn't finish on time.* —**wa′ger•er,** *n.* [*count*]

wag•gle (wag′əl) /ˈwægəl/ *v.*, **-gled, -gling,** *n.* —*v.* **1.** to move up and down or from side to side: [~ + *obj*]: *waggled his fingers.* [*no obj*]: *His fingers were waggling.* —*n.* [*count*] **2.** a waggling motion.

wag•on (wag′ən) /ˈwægən/ *n.* [*count*] **1.** a four-wheeled vehicle, esp. one for the movement or carrying of heavy loads. **2.** STATION WAGON. **3.** *Brit.* a railway freight car or flatcar. —***Idiom.* 4. fix someone's wagon,** *Informal.* to get even with or punish someone. **5. off the wagon,** *Informal.* drinking alcoholic beverages again after a period of having abstained. **6. on the wagon,** *Informal.* no longer drinking alcoholic beverages. Also, *esp. Brit.,* **waggon.**

wag′on•er, *n.* [*count*] a person who drives a wagon.

waif (wāf), *n.* [*count*] **1.** a homeless child: *caring for orphans and waifs.* **2.** a stray animal.

wail (wāl) /weyl/ *v.* **1.** to express sorrow with a long, loud cry: [*no obj*]: *The child wailed unhappily.* [~ + *obj*]: *She wailed a warning.* [*used with quotations*]: *"I want to go home!" she wailed.* **2.** [*no obj*] to make sounds resembling a sorrowful cry: *The wind wailed.* —*n.* [*count*] **3.** a wailing cry or sound. —**wail′er,** *n.* [*count*]

wain•scot (wān′skət, -skot, -skōt) /ˈweynskət, -skɒt, -skowt/ *n.*, *v.*, **-scot•ed, -scot•ing** or (*esp. Brit.*) **-scot•ted, -scot•ting.** —*n.* [*noncount*] **1.** a paneling or covering of wood on an inside wall, often only the lower portion. —*v.* [~ + *obj*] **2.** to panel with wainscot.

waist (wāst) /weyst/ *n.* [*count*] **1.** the narrow part of the human body between the ribs and the hips. **2.** the part of a garment covering the waist. **3.** the narrow central or middle part of something.

waist•band (wāst′band′) /ˈweystˌbænd/ *n.* [*count*] a band, as on a skirt, that goes around the waist.

waist•coat (wes′kət, wāst′kōt′) /ˈwɛskət, ˈweystˌkowt/ *n.* *Chiefly Brit.* VEST (def. 1).

waist•line (wāst′līn′) /ˈweystˌlayn/ *n.* [*count*] **1.** the distance around the body at the waist. **2.** the seam where the skirt and body of a dress are joined.

wait (wāt) /weyt/ *v.* **1.** to remain in a place and not do anything until something expected happens: [*no obj*]: *We waited until the bus came.* [*no obj;* (~ + *for* + *obj*)]: *We've been waiting for the bus.* [~ + *obj* + *for* + *obj*]: *We waited a week for your letter.* [~ + *to* + *verb*]: *We waited to see you.* **2.** [*no obj*] to be available or in readiness: *A letter is waiting for you on your desk.* **3.** [*not: be* + ~*-ing; no obj*] to remain neglected for a time: *That matter can wait until later.* **4.** [*no obj*] to (cause to) be postponed or delayed: *Your vacation will have to wait until next spring.* [~ + *obj*]: *to wait a week.* **5.** [~ + *for* + *obj*] to look forward to eagerly: *to wait for a chance to get even.* **6. wait on,** [~ + *on* + *obj*] **a.** to serve food or drink to. **b.** to attend to the needs of (a customer): *Is someone waiting on you?* **c.** to be a servant for. **d.** *Informal.* to wait for; await. **7. wait out,** [~ + *out* + *obj*] to postpone or delay action until the end of: *We decided to wait out the storm.* **8. wait up,** [*no obj*] to postpone going to bed in order to await someone's arrival. —*n.* [*count*] **9.** an act or period of waiting. —***Idiom.* 10. lie in wait,** to wait in ambush so as to surprise another.

wait•er (wā′tər) /ˈweytər/ *n.* [*count*] a person, esp. a man, who waits on tables, as in a restaurant. See illustration at RESTAURANT.

wait′ing game′, *n.* [*count*] a strategy or plan in which action is postponed or delayed in order to gain an advantage.

wait′ing list′ also **wait•list** (wāt′list′) /ˈweytˌlɪst/ *n.* [*count*] a list of persons waiting, as for reservations or admission.

wait′ing room′, *n.* [*count*] a room for the use of persons waiting, as in a railroad station. See illustration at TERMINAL.

wait•ress (wā′tris) /ˈweytrɪs/ *n.* [*count*] a woman who waits on tables, as in a restaurant.

waive (wāv) /weyv/ *v.* [~ + *obj*], **waived, waiv•ing. 1.** to give up (a right) on purpose or willingly: *waived his right to appeal the decision.* **2.** to decide not to enforce or insist on (a rule or regulation): *The department waived the normal requirements.*

waiv•er (wā′vər) /ˈweyvər/ *n.* [*count*] **1.** the giving up of a right, done deliberately, willingly, or on purpose. **2.** a written statement containing a waiver.

wake[1] (wāk) /weyk/ *v.*, **waked** or **woke** (wōk) /wowk/ **waked** or **wok•en** (wō′kən) /ˈwowkən/ **wak•ing,** *n.* —*v.* **1.** to (cause to) become roused from sleep; awake: [*no obj;* (~ + *up*)]: *to wake (up) from a nightmare.* [~ + *obj* (+ *up*)]: *The noise woke him (up).* [~ (+ *up*) + *obj*]:

Please wake (up) the children. **2.** to (cause to) become aware of something: [*no obj*]: *You'd better wake (up) to what they're doing to you.* [~ + *obj* (+ *up*)]: *The energy crisis woke us (up) to the need for conservation.* [~ (+ *up*) + *obj*]: *The crisis failed to wake (up) the public.* **—*n.*** [*count*] **3.** (in some religious traditions) a vigil held in the presence of the body of a dead person before burial.

wake[2] (wāk) /weyk/ *n.* [*count*] **1.** the track of waves left by a moving ship or boat. **2.** the path or course of something that has passed or gone before: *The hurricane left devastation in its wake.* **—*Idiom.* 3. in the wake of, a.** as a result of: *In the wake of the snowstorm the schools closed.* **b.** close behind: *Settlers followed in the wake of the pioneers.*

wake•ful (wāk′fəl) /'weykfəl/ *adj.* unable to sleep; sleepless. **—wake′ful•ly,** *adv.* **—wake′ful•ness,** *n.* [*noncount*]

wak•en (wā′kən) /'weykən/ *v.* to awake; awaken: [~ + *obj*]: *The noise wakened them.* [*no obj*]: *The kids will waken early.*

Wal′dorf sal′ad (wôl′dôrf) /'wɔldɔrf/ *n.* [*count*] a salad of chopped apples, celery, nuts, and mayonnaise.

walk (wôk) /wɔk/ *v.* **1.** [*no obj*] to move on foot at a moderate pace or speed, usually naturally, normally, and without hurry: *He walks to work every day.* **2.** [~ + *obj*] to proceed along, through, or over on foot: *walked several miles.* **3.** [~ + *obj*] to cause or help to walk: *She walked the old man back to his seat.* **4.** (in baseball) to (cause to) receive a base on balls: [*no obj*]: *The batter walked, forcing in a run.* [~ + *obj*]: *The pitcher walked the next two batters.* **5.** [~ + *obj*] to lead, drive, or ride at a walk, as an animal: *She woke up early to walk the dog.* **6.** [~ + *obj*] to go with or accompany (someone) on foot: *I'll walk you to the elevators.* **7. walk off** or **away with,** [~ + *off/away* + *with* + *obj*] **a.** to steal: *Someone walked off with the money.* **b.** to win, esp. with ease: *She walked away with the prize for best essay.* **8. walk out,** [*no obj*] **a.** to go on strike. **b.** to leave in protest. **9. walk out on,** [~ + *obj*] to desert; leave behind; forsake: *He walked out on his family.* **10. walk through, a.** [~ + *through* + *obj*] to rehearse (a play or the like) by reading the lines out loud while doing the physical movements that are called for. **b.** [~ + *through* + *obj*] to perform or do (something) in an indifferent manner, in a way that shows that one does not care: *During the last two weeks of his job he just walked through his duties.* **c.** [~ + *obj* + *through* + *obj*] to guide (someone) carefully through a task, procedure, etc. **—*n.*** [*count*] **11.** an act or instance of walking: *a short walk for exercise.* **12.** a characteristic style of walking: *a stiff walk.* **13.** a distance walked or to be walked: *a ten-minute walk from here.* **14.** *Baseball.* BASE ON BALLS. **15.** a place or path for walking. **16.** a branch of activity, line of work, or position in society: *all walks of life.*

walk′a•way′, *n.* [*count*], *pl.* **-ways.** an easy victory.

walk•er (wô′kər) /'wɔkər/ *n.* [*count*] **1.** a framework on small wheels for supporting a baby who is learning to walk. **2.** a similar device but without wheels, usually a waist-high, four-legged framework of lightweight metal, for use by an injured, or elderly disabled person as a support while walking. **3.** one that walks or likes to walk.

walk•ie-talk•ie (wô′kē tô′kē) /'wɔkiy'tɔkiy/ *n.* [*count*], *pl.* **-talk•ies.** a small portable radio that allows two-way communication.

walk′-in′, *adj.* [*before a noun*] **1.** of or relating to a medical clinic or other facility that accepts persons for treatment, service, etc., without an appointment. **2.** of or relating to a person or persons who walk into such a facility seeking treatment, service, etc., without an appointment. **3.** large enough to be walked into: *a walk-in closet.* **—*n.*** [*count*] **4.** a customer, patient, etc., who arrives without an appointment. **5.** something large enough to be walked into, as a refrigerator.

walk′ing pa′pers, *n.* [*plural*] *Informal.* a notice to someone of their dismissal from a job.

walk′ing stick′, *n.* [*count*] **1.** a stick used for support in walking. **2.** any of several insects with a long, slender, twiglike body.

walk′-on′, *n.* [*count*] a small part in a play, esp. a part without speaking lines.

walk•out (wôk′out′) /'wɔk,awt/ *n.* [*count*] a strike by workers.

walk•o•ver (wôk′ō′vər) /'wɔk,owvər/ *n.* [*count*] **1.** a horse race having only one starter because the others have been eliminated or have withdrawn. **2.** an unopposed or easy victory.

walk′-up′, *n.* [*count*] **1.** an apartment above the ground floor in a building with no elevator. **2.** a building, esp. an apartment house, with no elevator. **—*adj.*** [*before a noun*] **3.** located above the ground floor in a building that has no elevator. **4.** (of a building) having no elevator. **5.** accessible on foot from the outside of a building: *a walk-up bank machine.*

walk•way (wwô′wā′) /'wwɔ,wey/ *n.* [*count*], *pl.* **-ways.** a passage for walking.

wall (wôl) /wɔl/ *n.* [*count*] **1.** a vertical, upright structure used to form part of a shelter, to divide an area into rooms, or to protect. **2.** something not physical that is like a wall in that it forms a barrier between people or keeps people apart: *a wall of silence between them.* **—*v.*** **3.** to enclose, separate, form a border around, or surround with or as if with a wall: [~ + *obj*]: *to wall a town.* [~ + *off* + *obj*]: *The workers walled off the area with bricks.* [~ + *obj* + *off*]: *to wall it off with bricks.* **4.** to seal or fill (an opening) with a wall: [~ (+ *up*) + *obj*]: *to wall up a hole.* [~ + *obj* (+ *up*)]: *to wall a hole up.* **—*Idiom.* 5. climb the walls,** *Informal.* to be overly excited, nervous, worried, or frantic. **6. drive** or **push to the wall,** [*drive/push* + *obj* + *to* + *the* + ~] to force into a desperate situation. **7. drive** or **send up the wall,** [*drive/send* + *obj* + *up* + *the* + ~] *Informal.* to push into a state of frantic frustration: *She drove her father up the wall staying out late on dates.* **8. go to the wall, a.** to be defeated; give in; yield. **b.** to fail in business; be forced into bankruptcy. **c.** to risk one's own position to defend or protect another. **9. off the wall,** *Slang.* very strange; bizarre: *That idea is completely off the wall.* **—walled,** *adj.*

wal•la•by (wol′ə bē) /'wɒləbiy/ *n.* [*count*], pl. **-bies, -by.** a small- to medium-sized animal of the kangaroo family.

wall•board (wôl′bôrd′, -bōrd′) /'wɔl,bɔrd, -,bowrd/ *n.* [*noncount*] material used in large sheets for covering walls and ceilings.

wal•let (wol′it, wô′lit) /'wɒlɪt, 'wɔlɪt/ *n.* [*count*] **1.** a flat, folding case with compartments for carrying paper money, credit cards, and other items. **2.** *Brit.* a bag for carrying articles during a journey.

wall•eye (wôl′ī′) /'wɔl,ay/ *n., pl.* **-eyes,** for 1 also **-eye. 1.** [*count*] Also called **wall′eyed pike′.** a North American game fish with large eyes. **2.** [*noncount*] a condition in which the eye or eyes are turned outward. **—wall′eyed′,** *adj.*

wall•flow•er (wôl′flou′ər) /'wɔl,flawər/ *n.* [*count*] **1.** a person who remains off to the side at a party or dance, as through shyness. **2.** a European plant of the mustard family, having sweet-scented yellow or orange flowers.

wal•lop (wol′əp) /'wɒləp/ *v.* [~ + *obj*] **1.** to beat soundly; thrash. **2.** to strike hard; sock: *He walloped them with his stick.* **3.** to defeat thoroughly, as in a game. **—*n.*** [*count*] **4.** a hard blow. **5.** the ability to deliver hard blows: *His fists pack a wallop.* **6.** the ability to make a strong impression or to be very effective: *That ad campaign packs quite a wallop.*

wal•lop•ing (wol′ə ping) /'wɒləpɪŋ/ *adj. Informal.* **1.** very large; whopping. **2.** very fine; impressive. **—*adv.*** **3.** extremely; very; immensely: *a walloping big bill.*

wal•low (wol′ō) /'wɒlow/ *v.* [~ + *in* + *obj*] **1.** to roll around, as in mud: *The pigs were wallowing in the mud.* **2.** to indulge oneself; remain in a given state or condition for a long time: *to wallow in self-pity.* **—*n.*** [*count*] **3.** an act or instance of wallowing. **4.** a place in which animals wallow.

wall•pa•per (wôl′pā′pər) /'wɔl,pæpər/ *n.* [*noncount*] **1.** paper, usually with decorative patterns, for covering walls or ceilings. **—*v.*** [~ + *obj*] **2.** to put wallpaper on or in; cover with wallpaper: *to wallpaper a room.*

wall′-to-wall′, *adj.* **1.** covering the entire floor: *wall-to-wall carpeting.* **2. a.** occupying a space completely: *wall-to-wall dancing.* **b.** being everywhere: *a town with wall-to-wall gambling.* **—*n.*** [*count*] **3.** a wall-to-wall carpet.

wal•nut (wôl′nut′, -nət) /'wɔl,nʌt, -nət/ *n.* **1.** [*count*] an edible meaty nut with a hard, wrinkled shell. **2.** [*count*] a tree bearing walnuts. **3.** [*noncount*] the wood of a walnut, used esp. in making furniture.

wal•rus (wôl′rəs, wol′-) /'wɔlrəs, 'wɒl-/ *n.* [*count*], *pl.* **-rus•es, -rus.** a large mammal of arctic seas, having large tusks and a tough, wrinkled hide.

waltz (wôlts) /wɔlts/ *n.* [*count*] **1.** a ballroom dance in somewhat fast triple meter. **2.** music for or in the rhythm of a waltz. **—*v.*** **3.** to dance a waltz (with): [*no obj*]: *learning to waltz.* [~ + *obj*]: *to waltz her around the floor.* **4.** [*no obj*; (~ + *through* + *obj*)] to move or progress easily: *She waltzed through the test.* **—waltz′er,** *n.* [*count*]

wam•pum (wom′pəm, wôm′-) /'wɒmpəm, 'wɔm-/ *n.*

[*noncount*] **1.** beads made of pierced and strung shells, once used by North American Indians as a medium of exchange. **2.** *Informal.* MONEY.

wan (won) /wɒn/ *adj.*, **wan•ner, wan•nest.** unnaturally pale, esp. on account of ill health or fatigue.

wand (wond) /wɒnd/ *n.* [*count*] **1.** a slender rod, esp. one used by a magician. **2.** a staff carried as a sign or emblem of office or authority. **3.** an electronic device in the form of a hand-held rod that can read coded or printed data on a merchandise label or in a document.

wan•der (won′dər) /ˈwɒndər/ *v.* **1.** [*no obj*] to move around without a definite purpose or plan; roam: *wandering through the mall.* **2.** [*no obj*] to go, move, pass, or extend in an irregular course or direction: *His gaze wandered briefly around the room.* **3.** [*no obj*] to stray, as from a path or subject: *Your thoughts are wandering.* **4.** [~ + *obj*] to travel about, on, or through: *to wander the countryside.* —**wan′der•er,** *n.* [*count*]

wan•der•lust (won′dər lust) /ˈwɒndərlʌst/ *n.* [*count; usually singular*] a strong desire to travel.

wane (wān) /weyn/ *v.*, **waned, wan•ing,** *n.* —*v.* [*no obj*] **1.** to decrease, as in strength or intensity: *His influence had waned in the company.* **2.** (of the moon) to decrease in brightness and roundness after the full moon, in regular periods. Compare WAX[2] (def. 2). —*n.* [*count*] **3.** an act or period of waning. —***Idiom.*** **4. on the wane,** decreasing; losing power; diminishing.

wan•gle (wang′gəl) /ˈwæŋgəl/ *v.* [~ + *obj*], **-gled, -gl•ing.** to bring about, get, or obtain by devious means: *He wangled a free ticket.* —**wan′gler,** *n.* [*count*]

wan•na•be (won′ə bē′, wô′nə-) /ˈwɒnəˌbiy, ˈwɔnə-/ *n.* [*count*], *pl.* **-bes.** *Informal.* one who wishes, often vainly, to achieve success similar to another person's, or to gain fame or importance in some area: *rock star wannabes.*

want (wont, wônt) /wɒnt, wɔnt/ *v.* **1.** to feel a need for (or to); wish or desire; feel inclined; long for: [~ + *obj*]: *The baby wants his dinner.* [*not: be + ~-ing; ~ (+ obj) + to + verb*]: *I want to be alone. I want you to leave.* **2.** [~ + *obj*] to request the presence of: *The boss wants you; better go right up.* **3.** [*not: be + ~-ing; ~ + verb-ing*] to require: *The room wants cleaning.* **4.** [*not: be + ~-ing; ~ + obj; usually: be + ~-ed*] to have an arrest warrant for, or seek in order to question in connection with a criminal investigation: *He is wanted for armed robbery.* **5.** [*no obj; often: ~ + for*] to have a need: *His family never wanted for anything.* —*n.* **6.** [*count*] something wanted or needed: *My wants are simple.* **7.** [*noncount*] deficiency; lack; a state of need: *to be in want of an assistant.* **8.** [*noncount*] a state of poverty.

want′ ad′, *n.* CLASSIFIED AD.

want•ing (won′ting, wôn′-) /ˈwɒntɪŋ, ˈwɔn-/ *adj.* [*be* + ~] **1.** lacking or absent: *a motor with some parts wanting.* **2.** deficient: *wanting in courtesy.* —*prep.* **3.** lacking; without: *a box wanting a lid.* **4.** less; minus: *a century wanting three years.*

wan•ton (won′tn) /ˈwɒntn̩/ *adj.* **1.** not thinking of what is right or proper; inhumane: *wanton cruelty.* **2.** without motive; unprovoked: *a wanton attack.* **3.** sexually loose; lascivious. **4.** extravagant or excessive: *wanton luxury.* —*n.* [*count*] **5.** a wanton person, esp. a lascivious woman. —**wan′ton•ly,** *adv.* —**wan′ton•ness,** *n.* [*noncount*]

wap•i•ti (wop′i tē) /ˈwɒpɪtiy/ *n.*, *pl.* **-tis, -ti.** ELK (def. 1).

war (wôr) /wɔr/ *n.*, *v.*, **warred, war•ring.** —*n.* **1.** armed conflict or fighting between nations or factions: [*count*]: *Wars keep breaking out.* [*noncount*]: *a state of war.* **2.** any conflict or struggle: [*count*]: *a war against poverty.* [*noncount*]: *to wage war against poverty.* **3.** [*noncount*] the science or profession of armed fighting: *a war college.* —*v.* [*no obj*] **4.** to make or carry on war: *They warred among themselves.*

war•ble (wôr′bəl) /ˈwɔrbəl/ *v.*, **-bled, -bling,** *n.* —*v.* **1.** to sing or whistle with trills or melodies that vary quickly: [*no obj*]: *to warble happily.* [~ + *obj*]: *to warble a tune.* —*n.* [*count*] **2.** a warbled song or trill.

war•bler (wôr′blər) /ˈwɔrblər/ *n.* [*count*] a small songbird, esp. one that is brightly colored.

war•bon•net or **war bon•net** (wôr′bon′it) /ˈwɔrˌbɒnɪt/ *n.* [*count*] an American Indian headdress made up of a headband with trailing feathers.

ward (wôrd) /wɔrd/ *n.* [*count*] **1.** an administrative division of a city or town, or a division for voting purposes. **2.** a division of a hospital: *a children's ward.* **3.** a division of a prison. **4.** a person, esp. a child or person under eighteen, who is under the care of a legal guardian or a court. —*v.* **5.** to turn aside; avert: [~ + *off* + *obj*]: *to ward off a blow; to ward off disease.* [~ + *obj* + *off*]: *to ward it off.*

-ward, *suffix.* -*ward* is used to form adjectives or adverbs with the meaning "in or toward a certain direction in space or time": *backward.* Also, **-wards.**

war•den (wôr′dn) /ˈwɔrdn̩/ *n.* [*count*] **1.** a person whose job is the care and custody of something; keeper. **2.** the chief administrative officer of a prison. **3.** an official whose job is the enforcement of regulations: *a fire warden.*

ward′ heel′er, *n.* [*count*] a minor politician who does chores for a political machine.

ward•robe (wôr′drōb′) /ˈwɔrˌdrowb/ *n.* [*count*] **1.** a collection of clothes or costumes. **2.** a piece of furniture or a closet for keeping or storing clothes. **3.** the department of a motion-picture or television studio that supplies clothes and costumes.

ward•room (wôrd′ro͞om′, -ro͝om′) /ˈwɔrdˌruwm, -ˌrʊm/ *n.* [*count*] (on a warship) the living and dining quarters for all commissioned officers except the commanding officer.

ware (wâr) /wɛər/ *n.* **1.** Usually, **wares.** [*plural*] merchandise; goods: *a peddler selling his wares in the market.* **2.** [*noncount*] a particular kind of merchandise: *glassware.* **3.** [*noncount*] pottery: *delft ware.*

ware•house (*n.*, wâr′hous′; *v.* -houz′, -hous′) / *n.*, ˈwɛərˌhaws; *v.* -ˌhawz, -ˌhaws/ *n.*, *v.*, **-housed, -hous•ing.** —*n.* [*count*] **1.** a building for the storage of goods or merchandise. —*v.* [~ + *obj*] **2.** to place, deposit, or store in a warehouse: *to warehouse goods.* **3.** to confine (the mentally ill, the aged, etc.) in large institutions.

war•fare (wôr′fâr′) /ˈwɔrˌfeyr/ *n.* [*noncount*] **1.** armed conflict between enemies; the activity of war. **2.** a particular type of armed conflict: *chemical warfare.* **3.** conflict, esp. when continuous, between competitors.

war•head (wôr′hed′) /ˈwɔrˌhɛd/ *n.* [*count*] the section of a missile, bomb, or the like containing the explosive or payload.

war•horse (wôr′hôrs′) /ˈwɔrˌhɔrs/ *n.* [*count*] **1.** a horse used in war. **2.** *Informal.* a person who has experienced many conflicts or struggles, as a soldier or politician. **3.** a musical composition or other work of art that has been performed to excess.

war•like (wôr′līk′) /ˈwɔrˌlayk/ *adj.* **1.** fond of war. **2.** threatening war. **3.** of or used in war.

war•lock (wär′lok′) /ˈwɑrˌlɒk/ *n.* [*count*] a male witch.

war•lord (wôr′lôrd′) /ˈwɔrˌlɔrd/ *n.* [*count*] a military commander, esp. one who has seized control of a region.

warm (wôrm) /wɔrm/ *adj.*, **-er, -est,** *v.* —*adj.* **1.** having or giving out moderate heat: *a warm climate.* **2.** having a sensation of bodily heat: *to be warm from a fever.* **3.** conserving warmth: *warm clothes.* **4.** suggestive of warmth, as by being friendly, affectionate, sympathetic, or hearty: *a warm heart; warm friends.* **5.** heated or angry: *a warm debate.* **6.** strong or fresh: *a warm scent.* **7.** [*be* + ~] close to something being searched for, as in a game: *You're getting warmer.* —*v.* **8.** to (cause to) become warm: [~ + *obj* (+ *up*)]: *warmed himself (up) by the fire.* [*no obj;* ~ + *up*]: *I just couldn't warm up.* **9.** to heat or cook (something) so it can be used again, as leftovers: [~ + *up* + *obj*]: *Warm up the stew.* [~ + *obj* + *up*]: *Warm the stew up.* **10.** to (cause to) become excited, enthusiastic, cheerful, vital, etc.: [~ + *obj*]: *a little wine to warm the company.* [*no obj;* ~ + *to*]: *She began to warm to the topic.* **11.** [~ + *obj*] to inspire with kindly feeling; affect with lively pleasure: *It warms my soul to hear you say that.* **12.** [~ + *to/toward* + *obj*] to grow kindly or sympathetic to or toward: *My heart warmed toward him.* **13. warm up,** [*no obj*] **a.** to prepare for strong exercise by performing mild or moderate exercise. **b.** to increase in excitement, intensity, or violence: *The arguments began to warm up.* **c.** to become friendlier or more receptive. —**warm′er,** *n.* [*count*] —**warm′ish,** *adj.* —**warm′ly,** *adv.* —**warm′ness,** *n.* [*noncount*]

warm′-blood′ed, *adj.* of or naming an animal, as a mammal, having a relatively constant body temperature in spite of different temperatures in the surrounding environment. —**warm′-blood′ed•ness,** *n.* [*noncount*]

warmed′-o′ver, *adj.* **1.** reheated: *warmed-over stew.* **2.** lacking freshness; stale: *a warmed-over tale.*

warm′ front′, *n.* [*count*] a zone of air that comes between a mass of warm air and the colder air it is replacing.

warm′-heart′ed or **warm′heart′ed,** *adj.* having or showing emotional warmth. —**warm′-heart′ed•ly,** *adv.* —**warm′-heart′ed•ness,** *n.* [*noncount*]

war•mon•ger (wôr′mung′gər, -mong′-) /ˈwɔrˌmʌŋgər,

-ˌmɒŋ-/ *n.* [*count*] a person who calls for or incites war. **—war′mon′ger•ing,** *adj.*

warmth (wôrmth) /wɔrmθ/ *n.* [*noncount*] **1.** the quality or state of being warm or being able to cause a warm feeling. **2.** enthusiasm; intensity. **3.** the quality of being intimate, friendly, or caring. **4.** an effect of brightness and cheer achieved by the use of such colors as red and yellow.

warm•up or **warm-up** (wôrm′up′) /ˈwɔrmˌʌp/ *n.* **1.** [*count*] an act or instance of warming up. **2.** [*noncount*] the time between the turning on of power in an electronic component or device and its becoming ready to operate. **3.** Often, **warmups.** [*plural*] any apparel, esp. a sweat suit, that is worn in sports or exercise.

warn (wôrn) /wɔrn/ *v.* **1.** to give advance notice to, esp. of danger or possible harm: [~ + *obj* (+ *of/about* + *obj*)]: *The authorities warned the residents of the storm that was approaching the area.* [~ + *obj* + (*that*) *clause*]: *I warned you (that) she would be crazy, didn't I?* [~ + *of* + *obj*]: *to warn of further disasters.* **2.** [~ + *obj* + *to* + *verb*] to advise (someone to do something); admonish: *I warn you not to take such chances.* **3.** [~ + *obj*] to direct to go or stay away: *The farmer warned the hunters off his property.*

warn•ing (wôr′ning) /ˈwɔrnɪŋ/ *n.* [*count*] **1.** the act of one that warns. **2.** something that serves to warn. **—*adj.*** [*before a noun*] **3.** being a warning: *a warning bell.*

warp (wôrp) /wɔrp/ *v.* **1.** to (cause to) be bent or twisted out of shape: [*no obj*]: *The door hinges warped.* [~ + *obj*]: *The high humidity will warp those wooden door hinges.* **2.** [~ + *obj*] to turn away from what is right or proper; distort: *Prejudice warps the mind.* **—*n.*** [*count*] **3.** a bend or twist in something that was once or originally straight or flat. **4.** a mental bias or quirk. **5.** the lengthwise threads in a loom or woven fabric.

war′ paint′, *n.* [*noncount*] **1.** paint applied by American Indians to their faces and bodies before going to war. **2.** *Informal.* cosmetics; makeup.

war•path (wôr′path′) /ˈwɔrˌpæθ/ *n.* [*count*] **1.** the path or course taken by American Indians on a warlike expedition. ***—Idiom.*** **2. on the warpath,** in an aggressively hostile mood.

war•rant (wôr′ənt, wor′-) /ˈwɔrənt, ˈwɒr-/ *n.* **1.** [*count*] a document that gives authority to an officer to make an arrest or to search or seize property. **2.** [*noncount*] authorization or justification. **3.** [*noncount*] something providing formal assurance; guarantee. **—*v.*** [~ + *obj*] **4.** to be sufficient reason for; justify: *The invasion warranted a strong response.*

war′rant of′ficer, *n.* [*count*] an officer in the armed forces ranking below a commissioned officer.

war•ran•ty (wôr′ən tē, wor′-) /ˈwɔrəntiy, ˈwɒr-/ *n., pl.* **-ties,** *v.,* **-tied, ty•ing.** **—*n.*** **1.** a written guarantee given to a purchaser that the manufacturer, dealer, etc., will make repairs or replace defective parts free of charge for a stated period of time: [*count*]: *a one-year warranty.* [*noncount*]: *This computer is under warranty.* **—*v.*** [~ + *obj*] **2.** to provide a manufacturer's or dealer's warranty for: *to warranty the parts for a year.*

war•ren (wôr′ən, wor′-) /ˈwɔrən, ˈwɒr-/ *n.* [*count*] **1.** a place where rabbits breed. **2.** a crowded building or area, esp. one having many passageways or small rooms.

war•ri•or (wôr′ē ər, wor′-) /ˈwɔriyər, ˈwɒr-/ *n.* [*count*] a person engaged or experienced in warfare; soldier.

war•ship (wôr′ship′) /ˈwɔrˌʃɪp/ *n.* [*count*] a ship armed for combat.

wart (wôrt) /wɔrt/ *n.* [*count*] **1.** a small, often hard growth on the skin, usually caused by a virus. **2.** a small swelling, as on the surface of certain plants. **3.** any unattractive feature or aspect of someone: *He wrote a truthful and accurate profile of the man, warts and all.* **—wart′y,** *adj.,* **-i•er, -i•est.**

wart•hog (wôrt′hog′, -hôg′) /ˈwɔrtˌhɒg, -ˌhɒg/ *n.* [*count*] a wild African piglike animal with large tusks and warty facial growths.

war•time (wôr′tīm′) /ˈwɔrˌtaym/ *n.* [*noncount*] **1.** a time or period of war. **—*adj.*** [*before a noun*] **2.** occurring during war: *wartime rationing.*

war•y (wâr′ē) /ˈwɛəriy/ *adj.,* **-i•er, -i•est.** being on guard; watchful; cautious: *was wary of the danger.* **—war′i•ly,** *adv.* **—war′i•ness,** *n.* [*noncount*]

was (wuz, woz; *unstressed* wəz) /wʌz, wɒz; *unstressed* wəz/ *v.* 1st and 3rd pers. sing. past indic. of BE.

wash (wosh, wôsh) /wɒʃ, wɔʃ/ *v.* **1.** to cleanse by dipping, rubbing, or scrubbing in liquid, esp. water: [~ + *obj*]: *to wash the dishes.* [*no obj*]: *You wash and I'll dry.* **2.** [*no obj*] to wash oneself: *He washes before eating.* **3.** to (cause to) be removed by or as if by the action of water: [~ + *obj*]: *to wash one's guilt away.* [*no obj*]: *His guilt washed away.* **4.** to flow through, over, or against: [*no obj*]: *The water washed against his feet.* [~ + *obj*]: *The waves wash the shoreline.* **5.** [*no obj*] to undergo washing without damage, as shrinking or fading: *These clothes wash well in hot water.* **6.** [*no obj; not: be + ~-ing; usually with a negative word or phrase, or in questions*] *Informal.* to prove true when someone tests it: *His alibi simply won't wash.* **7.** to (cause to) be carried or driven by water: [*no obj*]: *The bridge washed away during the storm.* [~ + *obj* (+ *away*)]: *The floods washed the bridge away.* **8.** to move along in or as if in waves: [*no obj*]: *The body washed slowly out to sea.* [~ + *obj*]: *The body was washed slowly out to sea.* **9. wash down, a.** to clean completely by washing: [~ + *down* + *obj*]: *to wash down the walls.* [~ + *obj* + *down*]: *to wash the walls down.* **b.** to make the swallowing of (food or medicine) easier by drinking liquid: [~ + *down* + *obj*]: *Wash down the pill with some water.* [~ + *obj* + *down*]: *Wash it down with some water.* **10. wash out, a.** to (cause to) be removed by washing: [*no obj*]: *Will the stains wash out?* [~ + *out* + *obj*]: *trying to wash out the stains.* [~ + *obj* + *out*]: *trying to wash the stains out.* **b.** [~ + *out* + *obj*] to damage or demolish by the action of water: *The embankment was washed out by the storm.* **c.** [*no obj*] *Informal.* to fail to qualify or continue; be eliminated: *to wash out of graduate school.* **11. wash up, a.** [*no obj*] to wash one's face and hands: *to wash up before dinner.* **b.** [~ + *up* + *obj*] to clean or clear away by washing: *Wash up the oil spills.* **—*n.*** **12.** [*count*] the act or process of washing. **13.** [*count*] items, as clothes, to be washed at one time. **14.** [*noncount*] water moving in waves or with a rushing movement. **15.** [*noncount*] the wake of a moving boat. **16.** [*noncount*] a disturbance in the air caused by a moving airplane. ***—Idiom.*** **17. come out in the wash, a.** to result eventually in something satisfactory. **b.** to be made known eventually: *All of these details will eventually come out in the wash.* **18. wash one's hands of,** [~ + *obj*] to renounce further responsibility for or involvement in: *He washed his hands of the problem.*

Wash., an abbreviation of: Washington.

wash•a•ble (wosh′ə bəl, wô′shə-) /ˈwɒʃəbəl, ˈwɔʃə-/ *adj.* **1.** that can be washed without shrinking, fading, or the like. **—*n.*** [*count*] **2.** a washable garment. **—wash•a•bil•i•ty** (wosh′ə bil′i tē, wô′shə-) /ˌwɒʃəˈbɪlɪtiy, ˌwɔʃə-/ *n.* [*noncount*]

wash′-and-wear′, *adj.* of or being a garment or fabric that requires little or no ironing after being washed.

wash•bowl (wosh′bōl′, wôsh′-) /ˈwɒʃˌbowl, ˈwɔʃ-/ *n.* [*count*] a large bowl for washing the hands and face. Also called **wash′ba′sin.**

wash•cloth (wosh′klôth′, -kloth′, wôsh′-) /ˈwɒʃˌklɔθ, -ˌklɒθ, ˈwɔʃ-/ *n.* [*count*] a cloth for washing the face or body.

washed′-out′, *adj.* **1.** faded, esp. from washing. **2.** *Informal.* weary or tired-looking.

washed′-up′, *adj. Informal.* no longer successful or in demand: *After that scandal, he's all washed up as a politician.*

wash•er (wosh′ər, wô′shər) /ˈwɒʃər, ˈwɔʃər/ *n.* [*count*] **1.** one that washes. **2.** WASHING MACHINE. **3.** a flat ring used under a bolt to give tightness to a joint, prevent leakage, etc.

wash•er•wom•an (wosh′ər wo͝om′ən, wô′shər) /ˈwɒʃərˌwʊmən, ˈwɔʃər/ *n.* [*count*], *pl.* **-wom•en.** a woman whose work is washing clothes.

wash•ing (wosh′ing, wô′shing) /ˈwɒʃɪŋ, ˈwɔʃɪŋ/ *n.* [*noncount*] **1.** the act of one that washes. **2.** items that are washed or to be washed.

wash′ing machine′, *n.* [*count*] an apparatus, esp. a household appliance, for washing clothing, linens, etc.

wash•out (wosh′out′, wôsh′-) /ˈwɒʃˌawt, ˈwɔʃ-/ *n.* [*count*] **1.** a washing out of earth or soil by the action of rushing water, as from an embankment. **2.** *Informal.* a complete failure: *The team suffered a total washout in the Olympic trials.*

wash•room (wosh′ro͞om′, -ro͝om′, wôsh′-) /ˈwɒʃˌruwm, -ˌrʊm, ˈwɔʃ-/ *n.* [*count*] a room with washbowls and toilet facilities.

wash•stand (wosh′stand′, wôsh′-) /ˈwɒʃˌstænd, ˈwɔʃ-/ *n.* [*count*] a piece of furniture holding a basin and pitcher of water for use in washing the hands and face.

was•n't (wuz′ənt, woz′-) /ˈwʌzənt, ˈwɒz-/ *contraction.* a shortened form of *was not.*

wasp (wosp) /wɒsp/ *n.* [*count*] a slender winged insect with a narrow abdomen and a powerful sting.

WASP or **Wasp** (wosp) /wɒsp/ *n.* [*count*] a white Anglo-Saxon Protestant, esp. when considered to be a member of the privileged, established, white upper middle class in the U.S.

wasp•ish (wos′pish) /ˈwɒspɪʃ/ *adj.* **1.** like or suggesting a wasp. **2.** snappy; easily annoyed or peevish; testy. —**wasp′ish•ly,** *adv.* —**wasp′ish•ness,** *n.* [*noncount*]

wast•age (wā′stij) /ˈweystɪdʒ/ *n.* **1.** loss by use, wear, decay, or wastefulness: [*count; usually singular*]: *a wastage of over 50%.* [*noncount*]: *measures taken to reduce wastage.* **2.** [*noncount*] something wasted.

waste (wāst) /weyst/ *v.*, **wast•ed, wast•ing,** *n.*, *adj.* —*v.* **1.** [~ + *obj*] to use up or spend to no profit; squander: *wasting money; wasting time.* **2.** [~ + *obj*] to fail to use: *Never waste an opportunity.* **3.** to (cause to) become feeble, weak, or thin: [~ + *obj*]: *He was wasted by disease.* [*no obj*]: *Every day the patient seemed to waste away.* **4.** [~ + *obj*] *Slang.* to murder. —*n.* **5.** an act or instance of wasting: [*count; usually singular*]: *a waste of money.* [*noncount*]: *to cut down on waste.* **6.** [*count*] a devastated area, or an area that is unsuitable or considered unsuitable for living, as a desert: *the frozen wastes of the tundra.* **7.** something left over, esp. after some process has been performed and something more valuable removed: [*count*]: *factory wastes.* [*noncount*]: *the disposal of radioactive waste.* **8.** [*noncount*] garbage; refuse: *household waste.* **9. wastes,** [*plural*] excrement. —*adj.* [*before a noun*] **10.** wild; desolate; not useful: *waste land.* **11.** left over; extra and not necessary: *waste materials; waste paper.* **12.** unused by or unusable to a living thing. **13.** designed to receive or carry away waste. —***Idiom.*** **14. go to waste,** to be wasted, rather than used: *This food will go to waste if you don't eat it.* **15. lay waste to,** [~ + *obj*] to devastate; destroy. —**Related Words.** WASTE is a verb and a noun, WASTEFUL is an adjective: *He wasted too much time trying to fix the radio. It was a waste of time. He is wasteful when it comes to using paper.*

waste•bas•ket (wāst′bas′kit) /ˈweystˌbæskɪt/ *n.* [*count*] an open container for trash. Also called **waste′paper bas′ket.** See illustration at SCHOOL.

wast•ed (wās′tid) /ˈweystɪd/ *adj.* **1.** useless; of no use: *wasted efforts.* **2.** physically weakened; exhausted. **3.** *Slang.* overcome by alcohol or drugs.

waste•ful (wāst′fəl) /ˈweystfəl/ *adj.* given to or characterized by waste: *wasteful habits; a wasteful person.* —**waste′ful•ly,** *adv.* —**waste′ful•ness,** *n.* [*noncount*]

waste•land (wāst′land′) /ˈweystˌlænd/ *n.* **1.** uncultivated or barren land, or land that has been ruined, as by war: [*count; usually singular*]: *a radioactive wasteland.* [*noncount*]: *wide areas of uninhabitable wasteland.* **2.** [*noncount*] something, as a period of history, a time, or a cultural product or activity, that is uninteresting, unproductive, or devoid of a spiritual or intellectual substance.

waste•pa•per (wāst′pā′pər) /ˈweystˌpeypər/ *n.* [*noncount*] paper thrown away as useless.

wast•rel (wā′strəl) /ˈweystrəl/ *n.* [*count*] a wasteful person.

watch (woch) /wɒtʃ/ *v.* **1.** to look (at) with attention; observe: [*no obj*]: *The children watched carefully as the magician removed a rabbit from his hat.* [~ + *obj*]: *had a feeling that he was being watched.* [~ + *obj* + *root form of verb*]: *watched the magician remove a rabbit from the hat.* [~ + *obj* + *verb-ing*]: *The children watched the magician removing a rabbit from his hat.* **2.** [~ + *obj*] to view with attention or interest: *to watch TV.* **3.** [*no obj*] to wait with attention: *We watched for the signal.* **4.** [*no obj;* (~ + *out*)] to be careful or cautious: *Watch (out) when you cross the street.* **5.** [~ + *obj*] to guard, take care of, or tend, so as to prevent harm or danger from happening to (oneself or another): *Watch the baby while I go to the store.* **6. watch over,** [~ + *obj*] to safeguard; protect: *watched over her and protected her from harm.* —*n.* **7.** [*count; usually singular*] close, continuous observation or guard: *kept a close watch on the patient.* **8.** [*count*] a portable timepiece, as a wristwatch. **9. a.** [*noncount*] a period of time, usually four hours, during which a part of a ship's crew is on duty. **b.** [*count*] the crew who are on duty during this time. **10.** [*count*] a lookout, guard, or sentinel. —***Idiom.*** **11. on the watch,** vigilant; alert. **12. watch it,** *Informal.* to be careful, alert, or esp. cautious regarding one's behavior. **13. watch oneself,** to practice caution or exhibit careful behavior. **14. watch one's step,** to proceed with caution. —**watch′er,** *n.* [*count*]

watch•band (woch′band′) /ˈwɒtʃˌbænd/ *n.* [*count*] a bracelet or strap for holding a wristwatch on the wrist.

watch•dog (woch′dog′, -dôg′) /ˈwɒtʃˌdɒg, -ˌdɔg/ *n.* [*count*] **1.** a dog kept to guard property. **2.** a watchful guardian, such as against illegal or unethical conduct: *environmental watchdogs.*

watch•ful (woch′fəl) /ˈwɒtʃfəl/ *adj.* vigilant or alert; observant. —**watch′ful•ly,** *adv.* —**watch′ful•ness,** *n.* [*noncount*]

watch•mak•er (woch′mā′kər) /ˈwɒtʃˌmeykər/ *n.* [*count*] a person whose occupation it is to make and repair watches. —**watch′mak′ing,** *n.* [*noncount*]

watch•man (woch′mən) /ˈwɒtʃmən/ *n.* [*count*], *pl.* **-men.** a person who keeps watch, esp. at night.

watch•word (woch′wûrd′) /ˈwɒtʃˌwɜrd/ *n.* [*count*] **1.** PASSWORD. **2.** a slogan or cry used to create enthusiasm among the followers of a group. **3.** a word or phrase that expresses a principle or rule that is important to a group.

wa•ter (wô′tər, wot′ər) /ˈwɔtər, ˈwɒtər/ *n.* **1.** [*noncount*] an odorless, tasteless liquid compound of hydrogen and oxygen that makes up rain, oceans, lakes, and rivers: *Water is essential to life.* **2.** Often, **waters.** [*plural*] water obtained from a mineral spring. **3.** a body of water, such as an ocean: [*noncount*]: *sailing on the water.* [*count; usually plural*]: *the waters of the Atlantic.* **4. waters,** [*plural*] the sea bordering on and controlled by a country. —*v.* **5.** [~ + *obj*] to sprinkle or drench with water: *to water the plants.* **6.** [*no obj*] to fill with or give off water or liquid: *Her eyes watered.* **7.** [~ + *obj*] to supply (animals) with drinking water. **8.** [~ *(+ down)* + *obj*] to weaken or dilute with or as if with water: *watered down her criticism.* —***Idiom.*** **9. hold water,** to be capable of being defended or proven correct: *Your theory doesn't hold water.* **10. in deep** or **hot water,** in trouble or difficulty. **11. keep one's head above water,** to stay out of esp. financial difficulties. **12. like water,** freely; abundantly: *She spent money like water.* **13. make one's mouth water,** to cause a desire or appetite for something: *a sports car that can make your mouth water.*

wa•ter•bed (wô′tər bed′, wot′ər-) /ˈwɔtərˌbɛd, ˈwɒtər-/ *n.* [*count*] a bed with a liquid-filled mattress.

wa′ter buf′falo, *n.* [*count*] an Asian buffalo with large, curved horns.

wa′ter chest′nut, *n.* [*count*] **1.** a plant growing in water, with a nutlike fruit that can be eaten. **2.** the fruit itself.

wa′ter clos′et, *n.* [*count*] a room or compartment containing a toilet bowl with a mechanism for flushing. *Abbr.:* WC, wc

wa•ter•col•or (wô′tər kul′ər, wot′wr-) /ˈwɔtərˌkʌlər, ˈwɒtwr-/ *n.* **1.** a kind of coloring matter or pigment mixed with water and not oil: [*noncount*]: *a painting done in watercolor.* [*count*]: *delicate watercolors.* **2.** [*noncount*] the art of painting with watercolors. **3.** [*count*] a picture done with watercolors. —*adj.* [*before a noun*] **4.** of, done in, or using watercolor.

wa′ter cool′er, *n.* [*count*] **1.** a container for holding drinking water that is drawn off through a spigot. **2.** a drinking fountain cooled by refrigeration.

wa•ter•course• (wô′tər kôrs′, -kōrs′, wot′ər-) /ˈwɔtərˌkɔrs, -ˌkowrs, ˈwɒtər-/ *n.* [*count*] **1.** a stream of water. **2.** the bed of a stream.

wa•ter•cress• (wô′tər kres′, wot′ər-) /ˈwɔtərˌkrɛs, ˈwɒtər-/ *n.* [*noncount*] **1.** a plant that grows in clear, running streams and that has strong-smelling leaves used esp. in salads. **2.** the leaves, used for salads, soups, and in cooking.

wa•ter•fall• (wô′tər fôl, wot′ər-) /ˈwɔtərfɔl, ˈwɒtər-/ *n.* [*count*] a steep fall of water from a height, as over a cliff.

wa•ter•fowl (wô′tər foul, wot′ər-) /ˈwɔtərfawl, ˈwɒtər-/ *n.* [*count*], pl. **-fowl, -fowls.** a bird that lives in or near water.

wa•ter•front• (wô′tər frunt′, wot′ər-) /ˈwɔtərˌfrʌnt, ˈwɒtər-/ *n.* [*count*] a part of a city or town on the edge of a body of water, esp. an ocean.

wa′ter hole′, *n.* [*count*] a source of drinking water, as a spring or well in the desert.

wa′tering hole′, *n.* [*count*] **1.** a pool where animals go to drink; water hole. **2.** Also called **watering place, wa′tering spot′.** a bar, nightclub, or other social gathering place where alcoholic drinks are sold.

wa′ter lil′y, *n.* [*count*] a plant that grows in the water, with large, disklike floating leaves and showy flowers.

wa′ter line′, *n.* [*count*] one of a series of lines on a ship's hull indicating the level to which it is submerged under the surface of the water.

wa•ter•logged (wô′tər lôgd′, -logd′, wot′ər-) /ˈwɔtər,lɔgd, -,lɒgd, ˈwɒtər-/ *adj.* so filled with water as to be heavy, unusable, or unmanageable.

wa′ter main′, *n.* [*count*] a main pipe for conveying water.

wa•ter•mark (wô′tər märk′, wot′ər-) /ˈwɔtər,mɑrk, ˈwɒtər-/ *n.* [*count*] **1.** a design that has been pressed on paper and that can be seen when the paper is held to the light. **2.** a line indicating the height to which water has risen.

wa•ter•mel•on (wô′tər mel′ən, wot′ər-) /ˈwɔtər,mɛlən, ˈwɒtər-/ *n.* a large melon with a hard, green rind and sweet, juicy, usually red pulp: [*noncount*]: *a slice of watermelon.* [*count*]: *They brought three gigantic watermelons to the picnic.*

wa′ter moc′casin, *n.* [*count*] the cottonmouth, a kind of poisonous snake.

wa′ter po′lo, *n.* [*noncount*] a game played in the water by two teams of swimmers.

wa′ter pow′er or **wa′ter•pow′er,** *n.* [*noncount*] the power of water when it is used to drive machinery.

wa•ter•proof (wô′tər pro͞of′, wot′ər) /ˈwɔtər,pruwf, ˈwɒtər/ *adj.* **1.** that does not allow water to penetrate: *a waterproof raincoat.* **—*v.*** [~ + *obj*] **2.** to make waterproof. —**wa′ter•proof′ing,** *n.* [*noncount*]

wa′ter rat′, *n.* [*count*] a rodent that lives close to water, as the muskrat.

wa′ter-repel′lent, *adj.* repelling water but not entirely waterproof.

wa′ter-resist′ant, *adj.* WATER-REPELLENT.

wa•ter•shed (wô′tər shed′, wot′ər-) /ˈwɔtər,ʃɛd, ˈwɒtər-/ *n.* [*count*] **1.** a region or area drained by a river or stream. **2.** a ridge or high area dividing two drainage areas. **3.** an important point of division or change: *a watershed in international relations.*

wa•ter•side (wô′tər sīd′, wot′ər-) /ˈwɔtər,sayd, ˈwɒtər-/ *n.* [*count; usually singular*] the bank or shore of a river, lake, or ocean.

wa′ter ski′, *n.* [*count*] a short, broad ski on which to glide over water while being towed by a speedboat. —**wa′ter-ski′,** *v.* [*no obj*], **-skied, -ski•ing.** —**wa′ter-ski′er,** *n.* [*count*] —**wa′ter-ski′ing,** *n.* [*noncount*]

wa•ter•spout (wô′tər spout, wot′ər-) /ˈwɔtərspawt, ˈwɒtər-/ *n.* [*count*] **1.** a spout or pipe from which water is sent out. **2.** a whirling, funnel-shaped cloud that touches the surface of a body of water, drawing upward spray and mist.

wa′ter ta′ble, *n.* [*count*] the underground level beneath which soil and rock are saturated with water.

wa•ter•tight (wô′tər tīt′, wot′ər-) /ˈwɔtər,tayt, ˈwɒtər-/ *adj.* **1.** constructed or fitted so tightly as to prevent water from penetrating. **2.** that cannot be shown to be false: *a watertight alibi for the night of the murder.*

wa′ter tow′er, *n.* [*count*] a high tower with a tank for storing water.

wa•ter•way (wô′tər wā′, wot′ər-) /ˈwɔtər,wey, ˈwɒtər-/ *n.* [*count*], *pl.* **-ways.** a body of water serving as a means for ships to travel.

wa′ter wheel′, *n.* [*count*] a wheel turned by the weight or momentum of water and used to operate machinery.

wa′ter wings′, *n.* [*plural*] a pair of air-filled devices worn around the arms or close to the shoulders to keep the body afloat in water.

wa•ter•works (wô′tər wûrks′, wot′ər-) /ˈwɔtər,wɜrks, ˈwɒtər-/ *n., pl.* **-works. 1.** a system, as of reservoirs, pipelines, and the like, by which water is collected, purified, stored, and pumped to urban users: [*count; used with a singular verb*]: *The waterworks is old and decrepit.* [*plural; used with a plural verb*]: *Those old waterworks are falling apart.* **2.** [*plural; used with a plural verb*] *Slang.* tears, or the source of tears: *to turn on the waterworks to get some sympathy.*

wa•ter•y (wô′tə rē, wot′ə-) /ˈwɔtəriy, ˈwɒtə-/ *adj.* **1.** of, consisting of, or full of water. **2.** containing too much water: *soggy, watery vegetables.* **3.** resembling water. **4.** thin; weak: *watery colors.*

watt (wot) /wɒt/ *n.* [*count*] a unit of electrical power equivalent to one joule per second. *Abbr.:* W, w

watt•age (wot′ij) /ˈwɒtɪdʒ/ *n.* [*noncount*] electrical power measured in watts.

wat•tle[1] (wot′l) /ˈwɒtl̩/ *n.* [*count*] Often, **-tles.** rods interwoven with twigs or branches, used esp. for making fences and walls. —**wat′tled,** *adj.*

wat•tle[2] (wot′l) /ˈwɒtl̩/ *n.* [*count*] a piece of flesh hanging down from the head or neck of certain birds, as the domestic turkey.

wave (wāv) /weyv/ *n., v.,* **waved, wav•ing. —*n.*** [*count*] **1.** a moving ridge or swell on the surface of water: *The ocean waves crashed against the rocks.* **2.** a movement of the hand, as in greeting: *gave us a wave and a smile.* **3.** a movement or part resembling a wave: *a wave in her hair.* **4.** a sudden surge or rush, as of a feeling; esp., a widespread, typically surging feeling, attitude, opinion, tendency, belief, activity, etc.: *felt a wave of nausea; a crime wave.* **5.** a period of unusually hot or cold weather: *a heat wave.* **6.** *Physics.* a disturbance sent out or across from one point to another in a medium or space, without progress or advance by the points themselves, as in the transmission of sound or light: *a sound wave; a light wave; electromagnetic waves.* **—*v.* 7.** to (cause to) move back and forth or up and down: [*no obj*]: *flags waving in the wind.* [~ + *obj*]: *They waved their arms.* **8.** to signal, esp. in greeting, by raising the hand and moving the fingers: [*no obj*]: *He waved to us in greeting.* [~ + *obj*]: *He waved his hand in greeting.* **9.** [~ + *obj*] to curve back and forth in opposite directions: *to wave one's hair.* **—*Idiom.* 10. make waves,** *Informal.* to create a disturbance: *tried not to make waves when things were going well.*

wave•length (wāv′lengkth′, -lenth′) /ˈweyv,lɛŋkθ, -,lɛnθ/ *n.* [*count*] **1.** the distance, measured in the direction of a wave, between two successive points in the wave that are characterized by the same phase of oscillation. **—*Idiom.* 2. on the same wavelength,** [*be* + ~] sharing values, ideas, or impulses; thinking and acting in agreement or harmony: *You and I are on the same wavelength about this; we both think the plan needs reworking.*

wa•ver (wā′vər) /ˈweyvər/ *v.* [*no obj*] **1.** to sway to and fro; flutter: *The leaves wavered in the breeze.* **2.** to flicker or quiver, as light: *A distant beam wavered in the darkness and then disappeared.* **3.** to be unsteady; begin to fail or give way; falter: *When she heard the news of the defeat her courage wavered.* **4.** to tremble, as the voice: *His voice wavered a bit.* **5.** to feel or show doubt or indecision: *He wavered in his loyalty.* **6.** (of things) to fluctuate or vary: *Prices wavered.* **—*n.*** [*count*] **7.** an act of wavering.

wav•y (wā′vē) /ˈweyviy/ *adj.,* **-i•er, -i•est.** having, moving in, characterized by, or resembling waves. —**wav′i•ness,** *n.* [*noncount*]

wax[1] (waks) /wæks/ *n.* [*noncount*] **1.** Also called **beeswax.** a solid, yellowish substance made by bees when building their honeycomb. **2.** any of various similar substances, esp. ones made up of hydrocarbons, fats, or oils: *a candle made of wax.* **3.** a yellowish, waxy secretion in the external auditory canal. **—*v.*** [~ + *obj*] **4.** to rub, polish, or treat with wax: *to wax the wooden floors; to wax down our skis.* **—*adj.* 5.** relating to, made of, or resembling wax. **—*Idiom.* 6. the whole ball of wax,** *Slang.* everything of a similar or related nature; the whole nine yards. —**wax′like′,** *adj.*

wax[2] (waks) /wæks/ *v.* [*no obj*] **1.** to increase, as in amount, size, or intensity. **2.** (of the moon) to increase gradually in brightness and roundness. Compare WANE (def. 2). **3.** [~ + *adj*] to become: *to wax resentful.*

wax′ bean′, *n.* [*count*] a kind or type of string bean having yellowish, waxy pods.

wax′en (wak′sən) /ˈwæksən/ *adj.* **1.** made of or covered with wax. **2.** pallid; pale; faint in color: *a waxen corpse.*

wax′ pa′per, *n.* [*noncount*] paper that resists moisture because of a waxlike coating.

wax•wing (waks′wing′) /ˈwæks,wɪŋ/ *n.* [*count*] a songbird having wing feathers tipped with a red, waxy substance.

wax•work (waks′wûrk′) /ˈwæks,wɜrk/ *n.* [*count*] **1.** a life-size wax figure of a person. **2. waxworks,** a wax museum.

wax•y (wak′sē) /ˈwæksiy/ *adj.,* **-i•er, -i•est. 1.** resembling wax. **2.** full of, covered with, or made of wax. —**wax′i•ness,** *n.* [*noncount*]

way[1] (wā) /wey/ *n.* [*count*] **1.** manner, mode, or fashion: *a new way of looking at a matter; He always answers in a polite way.* **2.** [*usually singular*] a characteristic or habitual manner of acting, living, etc.: *Being grouchy and snappy is just his way.* **3.** a method or means for gaining something or achieving a goal: *found a way to save money.* **4.** a respect or particular: *This plan is defective in several ways.* **5.** a direction or vicinity: *He went that way.* **6.** passage or progress on a course: *Lead the way.* **7.** Often, **ways.** [*plural*] distance: *a long way from home.*

8. a path or course: *the shortest way to town.* **9.** one's preferred manner of acting or doing: *He always gets his own way.* **10.** condition; state: *He's in a bad way.* **11.** the range or extent of one's experience or notice: *That's the best idea that's come my way.* **12.** space for passing or advancing: *The police cleared a way through the crowd.* —***Idiom.*** **13. along the way,** while proceeding: *We had a few problems along the way.* **14. by the way,** incidentally: *By the way, have you received that letter I wrote you?* **15. by way of,** by the route of; through: *They flew to Cairo by way of Algiers.* **16. give way, a.** to withdraw or retreat: *The infantry gave way when the enemy tanks advanced.* **b.** to break down; collapse: *During the earthquake, the walls gave way.* **17. give way to,** [~ + *obj*] **a.** to yield to: *He gave way to their requests.* **b.** to lose control of (one's temper, emotions, etc.): *The king gave way to his anger.* **18. go all the way, a.** to do or finish something completely. **b.** *Informal.* to be in complete agreement with someone or something. **c.** *Informal.* to engage in sexual intercourse. **19. go out of one's way,** to make an extra or unusual effort, as to do someone a favor. **20. have a way with,** [~ + *obj*] to have a charming, persuasive, or effective manner of dealing with: *He has a way with children.* **21. have one's way with,** [~ + *obj*] to coerce into having sexual intercourse. **22. in a way,** after a fashion; to some extent; somewhat: *He's nice in a way.* **23. in someone's way** or **in the way,** blocking; preventing passage; being a hindrance, impediment, or obstruction. **24. lead the way, a.** to go along a course or direction ahead of or in advance of others, as a guide does. **b.** to take the first step in something; be first or most prominent: *In fashion she has always led the way.* **25. make one's way, a.** to go forward along a course; proceed. **b.** to achieve recognition or success; advance: *making one's way in the world.* **26. make way,** to remove things that block passage, as by standing aside: *Make way for the motorcade.* **27. no way,** *Informal.* not under any circumstances; no: *You want me to apologize? No way!* **28. on the way,** during (a journey): *They stopped off in Maine on the way to Canada.* **29. out of the way, a.** in a state or condition so as not to obstruct or hinder: *Step out of the way and let me handle that.* **b.** dealt with; taken care of: *One problem is out of the way.* **c.** at a distance from the usual route: *The house is well out of the way on a back road.* **30. see one's way (clear),** to see nothing that would block or prevent doing something: *Can you see your way clear to lending me $100?* **31. under way, a.** in motion; traveling: *When does the train get under way?* **b.** in progress; proceeding: *Our plans are well under way.*

way[2] (wā) /wey/ *adv.* Also, **'way.** away or far; to a great degree or at quite a distance: *That trunk is way too heavy for you to lift. The house is way down the road.*

way•far•er (wā′fâr′ər) /'wey,fɛərər/ *n.* [*count*] a traveler, esp. on foot. —**way′far′ing,** *adj.*

way•lay (wā′lā′, wā lā′) /'wey,ley, wey'ley/ *v.* [~ + *obj*], **-laid, -lay•ing. 1.** to intercept or attack from a position of hiding or ambush: *to waylay him while he was crossing the alley.* **2.** to await and then rush up to greet, confront, solicit, etc., unexpectedly: *to waylay the boss in the hallway.* —**way′lay′er,** *n.* [*count*]

way′-out′, *adj.* *Informal.* very unconventional: *some way-out theories on nutrition.*

-ways, *suffix.* *-ways* is used to form adjectives or adverbs with the meaning "in a certain direction, manner, or position": *sideways.*

way•side (wā′sīd′) /'wey,sayd/ *n.* [*count*] land, or a small strip of land, along a road or highway.

way′ sta′tion, *n.* [*count*] a station in between principal stations, as on a railroad.

way•ward (wā′wərd) /'weywərd/ *adj.* **1.** stubborn; disobedient; *a wayward son.* **2.** changing or unpredictable, esp. without apparent reason; erratic: *a wayward breeze; a wayward impulse.* —**way′ward•ly,** *adv.* —**way′ward•ness,** *n.* [*noncount*]

WC, an abbreviation of: water closet.

we (wē) /wiy/ *pron.pl., poss.* **our** or **ours,** *obj.* **us. 1.** the plural of I, used as the subject of a sentence when the speaker wishes to refer to himself or herself and another or others: *I met her last night and we attended a concert.* **2.** (used after some form of BE with the same meaning): *It is we who should thank you.* **3.** Also called the **royal *we.*** (used in place of *I* by a king or a queen, or by the Pope). **4.** Also called the **editorial *we.*** (used by editors, writers, etc., to avoid the personal *I* or to represent a collective viewpoint).

weak (wēk) /wiyk/ *adj.,* **-er, -est. 1.** liable to give way under pressure or strain: *The walls are too weak to support the house.* **2.** lacking in strength or vigor; feeble: *He's weak from hunger.* **3.** lacking in force, intensity, or ability to produce an effect: *a weak president.* **4.** lacking in logical or legal force: *a weak argument.* **5.** low in intelligence, ability, or skill: *a weak mind; a weak speller.* **6.** lacking in moral strength or force of character: *too weak to resist temptation.* **7.** not great in amount, volume, intensity, etc., or in a characteristic property or essential ingredient: *a weak electrical current; a weak pulse.* **8.** showing a decline in prices: *a weak stock market.* —**weak′ly,** *adv.*

weak•en (wē′kən) /'wiykən/ *v.* to (cause to) become weak or weaker: [*no obj*]: *The animal weakened and eventually died.* [~ + *obj*]: *A lack of resources will weaken our efforts.* —**weak′en•er,** *n.* [*count*]

weak•fish (wēk′fish) /'wiykfɪʃ/ *n.*[*count*], pl. **-fish, -fish•es.** a fish of U.S. Atlantic and Gulf coasts eaten as food.

weak′-kneed′, *adj.* giving in easily or quickly to opposition, pressure, or threats.

weak•ling (wēk′ling) /'wiyklɪŋ/ *n.* [*count*] a person who is physically or morally weak.

weak•ness (wēk′nis) /'wiyknɪs/ *n.* **1.** [*noncount*] the state or quality of being weak: *a feeling of weakness from the disease.* **2.** [*count*] an inadequacy or defective quality, as in a person's character; a fault or defect: *He detected several weaknesses in the plan.* **3.** [*count*] a special fondness or liking: *He has a weakness for sweet, strong coffee.*

weal[1] (wēl) /wiyl/ *n.* [*noncount*] well-being; prosperity.

weal[2] (wēl) /wiyl/ *n.* WHEAL.

wealth (welth) /wɛlθ/ *n.* **1.** [*noncount*] a great deal of money, property, or possessions. **2.** [*count*] a large amount of something; an abundance: *a wealth of information.*

wealth•y (wel′thē) /'wɛlθiy/ *adj.,* **-i•er, -i•est.** having great wealth; rich. —**wealth′i•ness,** *n.* [*noncount*]

wean (wēn) /wiyn/ *v.* [~ + *obj*] **1.** to cause (a child or young animal) to become accustomed to or used to food other than the mother's milk. **2.** to cause a person to withdraw from an undesirable object or practice: *weaned him from his bad spending habits.*

weap•on (wep′ən) /'wɛpən/ *n.* [*count*] **1.** an instrument or device used for attack or defense: *spears, arrows, guns, and other weapons.* **2.** something used against an opponent or enemy: *Her sharp wit is an important weapon in debating opponents.* —**weap′on•less,** *adj.*

weap•on•ry (wep′ən rē) /'wɛpənriy/ *n.* [*noncount*] weapons thought of as a group.

wear (wâr) /wɛər/ *v.,* **wore** (wôr) /wɔr/ **worn** (wôrn) /wɔrn/ **wear•ing,** *n.* —*v.* **1.** [~ + *obj*] to have on the body as clothing, covering, or ornament: *He wore his best suit to the funeral. She's wearing my ring on her finger.* **2.** [~ + *obj*] to bear or have in one's aspect or appearance: *She wore an angry expression on her face.* **3. a.** to (cause to) deteriorate by a constant or repeating action: [~ + *obj*]: *Foot traffic wore a hole in the carpet.* [*no obj*]: *The carpet began to wear from the constant traffic of boots and heavy shoes.* **b.** [~ + *obj*] to produce by such action: *He wore a hole right through his shoe from all that walking.* **4.** [*no obj*] to last, stay strong, or withstand much use or strain: *That strong fabric wears well.* **5.** [~ + *obj*] to weary; fatigue: *worn by illness.* **6. wear down, a.** to make or become shabbier, smaller, or more aged by wearing: [~ + *down* + *obj*]: *to wear down the heels of his shoes.* [~ + *obj* + *down*]: *to wear the heels down.* **b.** to (cause to) become weary or tired: [*no obj*]: *He gradually wore down and had to stop running.* [~ + *obj* + *down*]: *All that long-distance running wore him down.* [~ + *down* + *obj*]: *That distance would wear down most runners.* **c.** [~ + *obj* + *down*] to overcome (opposition) by working without stopping: *Gradually she wore her father down until at last he consented to the marriage.* **7. wear off,** [*no obj*] to become less or to diminish slowly or gradually: *The effects of the drug began to wear off.* **8. wear on,** [~ + *obj*] to irritate; annoy: *That noise really wears on me.* **9. wear out, a.** to make or become unfit or useless through hard or extended use: [~ + *out* + *obj*]: *She wears out clothes quickly.* [~ + *obj* + *out*]: *She wears clothes out quickly.* [*no obj*]: *Those clothes will wear out in no time.* **b.** [~ + *obj* + *out*] to cause (someone) to be tired: *That long bicycle ride wore me out.* —*n.* [*noncount*] **10.** the act of wearing or state of being worn: *still a lot of wear from this old jacket.* **11.** clothing of a particular kind: *winter wear; men's wear.* **12.** gradual condition of falling apart, as from use: *The carpet is beginning to show wear.* **13.** the quality of withstanding use; durability. **—*Idiom.* 14. wear thin,** [*no obj*] **a.** to diminish; become weak: *My patience is wearing thin.* **b.** to become less appealing, interesting, tolerable, etc.: *At first we liked his humor, but now it's wearing thin.* —**wear′a•ble,** *adj.* —**wear′er,** *n.* [*count*] **—Usage.** See DRESS.

wear′ and tear′ (târ) /tɛər/ *n.* [*noncount*] damage or a condition of falling apart from ordinary use.

wear•ing (wâr′ing) /'wɛərɪŋ/ *adj.* **1.** causing a feeling of tiredness; tiring; exhausting: *Shoveling snow is a wearing task.* **2.** gradually diminishing or making weaker: *Reading small print can be wearing on the eyes.*

wea•ri•some (wēr′ē səm) /'wɪəriysəm/ *adj.* causing weariness; tedious: *his unending, wearisome complaints.*

wea•ry (wēr′ē) /'wɪəriy/ *adj.*, **-ri•er, -ri•est,** *v.*, **-ried, -ry•ing.** —*adj.* **1.** physically or mentally exhausted: *He was weary from staying up all night.* **2.** characterized by or causing fatigue: *a long, weary wait.* **3.** impatient or dissatisfied with (something) [*often:* ~ + *of*]: *I am weary of your excuses.* **—*v.* 4.** to (cause to) become tired or weary: [*no obj*]: *The patient wearied quickly from even a short walk.* [~ + *obj*]: *The recovery period wearied him.* **5.** to (cause to) grow impatient or dissatisfied with something: [~ + *obj*]: *Living in hotel rooms wearied him.* [~ + *of* + *obj*]: *He wearied of living in hotel rooms.* —**wea•ri•ly** (wēr′ə lē) /'wɪərəliy/ *adv.* —**wea′ri•ness,** *n.* [*noncount*]

wea•sel (wē′zəl) /'wiyzəl/ *n.* [*count*], *pl.* **-sels, -sel. 1.** a small meat-eating animal having a long, slender body and short legs. **—*v.*** [~ + *out of* + *obj*] **2.** to evade an obligation or a situation: *He weaseled out of helping us.* —**wea′sel•ly,** *adj.*

weath•er (weth′ər) /'wɛðər/ *n.* [*noncount*] **1.** the state or condition of the atmosphere with respect to wind, temperature, moisture, etc. **—*v.* 2.** to (cause to) be exposed to or affected by exposure to the weather: [~ + *obj*]: *to weather lumber so that it dries out.* [*no obj*]: *The rock weathered through the centuries.* **3.** [~ + *obj; often:* ~ + *through*] to come safely through: *to weather a storm; weathered through a difficult time.* **—*Idiom.* 4. under the weather, a.** somewhat ill. **b.** drunk. —**weath′ered,** *adj.*

weath′er-beat′en, *adj.* **1.** worn or damaged by having been exposed to the weather. **2.** tanned and toughened by having been exposed to the weather.

weath•er•cock (weth′ər kok′) /'wɛðər,kɒk/ *n.* [*count*] a weather vane in the form of a rooster.

weath•er•ing (weth′ə ring) /'wɛðərɪŋ/ *n.* [*noncount*] the action of natural elements, as wind and water, on exposed rock, causing it to disintegrate.

weath•er•ize• (weth′ə rīz′) /'wɛðə,rayz/ *v.* [~ + *obj*], **-ized, -iz•ing.** to make (a building) secure against cold weather, as by adding insulation. —**weath•er•i•za•tion** (weth′ər i zā′shən) /,wɛðərɪ'zeyʃən/ *n.* [*noncount*]

weath•er•man (weth′ər man′) /'wɛðər,mæn/ *n.* [*count*], *pl.* **-men.** a meteorologist; a person who studies and forecasts the weather. Also called **weath•er•per•son** (weth′ər pûr′sən) /'wɛðər,pɜrsən/.

weath•er•proof (weth′ər prōōf′) /'wɛðər,pruwf/ *adj.* **1.** able to withstand exposure to all kinds of weather. **—*v.*** [~ + *obj*] **2.** to make weatherproof.

weath′er strip′ (or **strip′ping**), *n.* [*noncount*] a narrow strip of material placed between a door or window sash and its frame to keep out rain, wind, cold, and snow.

weath′er vane′ or **weath′er•vane′,** *n.* [*count*] a rod to which a freely spinning pointer is attached that moves in the wind and shows the direction of the wind.

weave (wēv) /wiyv/ *v.*, **wove** (wōv) /wowv/ or (*esp. for 5*) **weaved; wo•ven** (wō′vən) /'wowvən/ or **wove; weav•ing;** *n.* **—*v.* 1.** to lace together (threads, strands, etc.) so as to form a fabric: [*no obj*]: *to knit and to weave.* [~ + *obj*]: *to weave the threads together.* **2.** [~ + *obj*] to form by weaving: *to weave a basket.* **3.** [~ + *obj*] (of a spider or similar small creature) to spin (a web or cocoon). **4.** [~ + *obj*] to combine into a connected whole: *to weave a plot from all the little events in the book.* **5.** to (cause to) move by winding or zigzagging: [*no obj*]: *The little car weaved through traffic.* [~ + *obj*]: *He wove the little car through traffic.* **—*n.*** [*count*] **6.** a pattern of or method for weaving. —**weav′er,** *n.* [*count*]

web (web) /wɛb/ *n.* [*count*] **1.** a fabric formed by weaving. **2.** a cobweb. **3.** something that is interconnected: *a web of branches.* **4.** a complicated, but connected, set or pattern of circumstances, facts, etc.: *a web of evidence; the web of life.* **5.** something that entangles: *a web of lies.* **6.** a piece of skinlike material connecting the digits of an animal, as a bird living in water. —**webbed,** *adj.*: *the webbed feet of a duck.*

web•bing (web′ing) /'wɛbɪŋ/ *n.* [*noncount*] **1.** a strong woven material used esp. for belts, straps, and harnesses. **2.** the skin between the toes of a web-footed animal. **3.** something resembling this, as the material connecting the thumb and forefinger in a baseball glove. **4.** any interlaced material part, as the face of a tennis racket.

web•foot•ed (web′fŏŏt′id) /'wɛb,fʊtɪd/ *adj.* having feet with the toes joined by a web.

wed (wed) /wɛd/ *v.* [*not: be* + *~-ing*], **wed•ded** or **wed, wed•ding.** to marry: [~ + *obj*]: *They were wed in July.* [*no obj*]: *They wed in July.*

we'd (wēd) /wiyd/ *contraction.* a shortened form of *we had, we should,* or *we would.*

Wed., an abbreviation of: Wednesday.

wed•ded (wed′id) /'wɛdɪd/ *adj.* **1.** united, as in matrimony; married; of or relating to marriage: *wedded bliss.* **2.** bound together; closely connected. **3.** [*often: be* + ~ + *to*] firmly attached to or dedicated and believing in: *They're wedded to the idea of gun control.*

wed•ding (wed′ing) /'wɛdɪŋ/ *n.* [*count*] the act or ceremony of marrying.

wedge (wej) /wɛdʒ/ *n., v.,* **wedged, wedg•ing. —*n.*** [*count*] **1.** a triangular piece of hard material used for raising, holding, or splitting objects: *He put a wedge under the door to prop it open.* **2.** something shaped like a wedge, as a cuneiform character. **3.** something that serves to part, split, or divide: *She tried to drive a wedge between the two friends by whispering rumors.* **—*v.*** [~ + *obj*] **4.** to split with or as if with a wedge. **5.** to insert or fix firmly with a wedge: *to wedge a door open.* **6.** to pack tightly into a narrow space: *to wedge clothes into a suitcase.*

wed•lock (wed′lok′) /'wɛd,lɒk/ *n.* [*noncount*] the state of being married; matrimony.

Wednes•day (wenz′dā, -dē) /'wɛnzdey, -diy/ *n.* the fourth day of the week: [*proper noun*]: *I'll see you on Wednesday.* [*count*]: *We met on Wednesdays.*

wee (wē) /wiy/ *adj.* [*before a noun*], **we•er, we•est. 1.** very small; tiny. **2.** very early: *the wee hours of the morning.*

weed (wēd) /wiyd/ *n.* **1.** [*count*] an undesirable or unwanted plant growing wild, esp. one that takes food or nourishment from a crop, lawn, or flower bed. **2.** [*count*] *Slang.* a cigarette. **3. the weed,** [*noncount*] **a.** *Informal.* tobacco. **b.** *Slang.* marijuana. **—*v.* 4.** to free from weeds: [~ + *obj*]: *to weed a garden.* [*no obj*]: *She was weeding in the garden.* **5.** to remove as being unwanted or unneeded: [~ + *out* + *obj*]: *The coach had to weed out the inexperienced players.* [~ + *obj* + *out*]: *to weed them out.* —**weed′er,** *n.* [*count*]

weeds (wēdz) /wiydz/ *n.* [*plural*] **1.** black mourning garments. **2.** clothing.

weed•y (wē′dē) /'wiydiy/ *adj.*, **-i•er, -i•est. 1.** consisting of or having many weeds. **2.** resembling a weed. **3.** (of a person or animal) scrawny or clumsy-looking.

week (wēk) /wiyk/ *n.* [*count*] **1.** a period of seven days following one after the other, usually beginning with Sunday. **2.** the working portion of a week, usually not including Saturday and Sunday: *a 35-hour week.*

week•day (wēk′dā′) /'wiyk,dey/ *n.* [*count*] **1.** any day of the week except Sunday or, often, Saturday and Sunday. **—*adj.*** [*before a noun*] **2.** of, on, or for a weekday: *weekday occupations.*

week•end (wēk′end′, -end′) /'wiyk,ɛnd, -'ɛnd/ *n.* [*count*] **1.** the end of a week, esp. the period between Friday evening and Monday morning. **2.** this period with one or more days added immediately before or after: *a three-day holiday weekend.* **—*v.*** [*no obj*] **3.** to pass the weekend: *weekending at the beach.*

week•ly (wēk′lē) /'wiykliy/ *adj., adv., n., pl.* **-lies. —*adj.* 1.** done, happening, or appearing once a week. **2.** computed or determined by the week: *the weekly exchange rate.* **—*adv.* 3.** once a week: *We pay our employees weekly.* **—*n.*** [*count*] **4.** a publication, as a newspaper or magazine, that appears once a week.

wee•nie or **wie•nie** (wē′nē) /'wiyniy/ *n.* WIENER.

wee•ny (wē′nē) /'wiyniy/ *adj.*, **-ni•er, -ni•est.** *Informal.* tiny.

weep (wēp) /wiyp/ *v.*, **wept** (wept) /wɛpt/ **weep•ing. 1.** to shed (tears) because of strong emotion: [*no obj*]: *They wept for days over his sudden death.* [~ + *obj*]: *wept bitter tears.* **2.** to give out or exude (liquid, as water or blood): [*no obj*]: *The wound is weeping.* [~ + *obj*]: *a wound weeping blood.* —**weep′er,** *n.* [*count*]

weep′ing wil′low, *n.* [*count*] an Asian willow tree having drooping branches.

weep•y (wē′pē) /ˈwiypiy/ *adj.,* **-i•er, -i•est. 1.** easily moved to tears. **2.** tending to cause weeping; sad: *a weepy novel.* —**weep′i•ness,** *n.* [*noncount*]

wee•vil (wē′vəl) /ˈwiyvəl/ *n.* [*count*] a beetle with a long snout, destructive to nuts, grain, fruit, and plants (as cotton).

weft (weft) /wɛft/ *n.* [*count; usually singular*] **1.** WOOF[1](def. 1). **2.** a woven fabric or garment.

weigh (wā) /wey/ *v.* **1.** [*not: be* + *~-ing*] to have weight or a certain weight: [~ + *obj; no passive*]: *He weighs sixty pounds.* [*no obj*]: *How much do you weigh?* **2.** [~ + *obj*] to determine the heaviness of (something), esp. by use of a scale: *The butcher weighed the meat.* **3.** [~ + *obj*] to think about carefully; evaluate in the mind; consider carefully: *weighed the advantages against the disadvantages.* **4. weigh down,** [~ + *obj* + *down*] to lower the spirits of; depress: *These burdens weighed him down.* —***Idiom.*** **5. weigh anchor,** [*no obj*] to raise up a ship's anchor.

weight (wāt) /weyt/ *n.* **1.** the amount something weighs: [*noncount*]: *He wants to lose weight.* [*count; usually singular*]: *at a weight of over a pound.* **2.** [*noncount*] the gravitational force exerted upon a body. **3.** [*count*] a system of units for expressing heaviness or mass: *a table of weights and measures.* **4.** [*count*] a piece of metal or the like that is known to be of certain mass and is used in weighing on a balance or scale. **5.** [*count*] a heavy object used to hold something open or down. **6.** [*count*] a burden, as of responsibility: *The debts were a weight on his mind.* **7.** [*noncount*] importance, consequence, significance, or influence: *His opinion carries great weight with the boss.* **8.** [*count*] a heavy piece of equipment lifted or held for exercise or body building or in athletic competition. —*v.* **9.** to add weight to; make heavier, so as to prevent or hinder easy movement: [~ *(+ down)* + *obj*]: *to weight (down) the papers on his desk.* [~ + *obj (+ down)*]: *to weight them (down).* **10.** [~ + *obj*] to burden with or as if with weight. —***Idiom.*** **11. pull one's (own) weight,** to contribute one's share of work to a job. **12. throw one's weight around** or **about,** to use one's power and influence, esp. improperly for personal gain.

weight•less (wāt′lis) /ˈweytlɪs/ *adj.* being without apparent weight. —**weight′less•ness,** *n.* [*noncount*]: *periods of weightlessness in the space capsule.*

weight•lift•ing (wāt′lif′ting) /ˈweytˌlɪftɪŋ/ *n.* [*noncount*] the lifting of barbells as a conditioning exercise or in a competitive event. —**weight′lift′er,** *n.* [*count*]

weight•y (wā′tē) /ˈweytiy/ *adj.,* **-i•er, -i•est. 1.** burdensome or troublesome: *weighty matters on his mind.* **2.** important. **3.** having or using influence or power. —**weight′i•ness,** *n.* [*noncount*]

weir (wēr) /wɪər/ *n.* [*count*] **1.** a dam in a stream. **2.** a fence set in a stream in order to catch fish.

weird (wērd) /wɪərd/ *adj.,* **-er, -est. 1.** suggesting the supernatural; unearthly: *a weird sound in the night.* **2.** strange; peculiar: *a weird costume.* —**weird′ly,** *adv.* —**weird′ness,** *n.* [*noncount*]

weird•o (wēr′dō) /ˈwɪərdow/ *n.* [*count*], *pl.* **-os.** *Slang.* an odd, strange, or abnormal person.

welch (welch, welsh) /wɛltʃ, wɛlʃ/ *v.* WELSH. —**welch′er,** *n.* [*count*]

wel•come (wel′kəm) /ˈwɛlkəm/ *interj., n., v.,* **-comed, -com•ing,** *adj.* —*interj.* **1.** (used as a greeting, as to one whose arrival gives pleasure): *Welcome, stranger!* —*n.* [*count*] **2.** a kindly greeting or reception: *We gave her a warm welcome.* —*v.* [~ + *obj*] **3.** to greet with pleasure or courtesy: *We welcomed her into our home.* **4.** to invite or accept with pleasure or courtesy: *I welcome your comments.* —*adj.* **5.** gladly received: *a welcome visitor.* **6.** agreeable: *a welcome rest.* **7.** [*be* + ~ + *to* + *verb*] willingly permitted: *You are welcome to try it.* **8.** (used in the phrase *You're welcome* as a response to thanks): *"Thank you." —"You're welcome."* —**wel′come•ness,** *n.* [*noncount*]

weld (weld) /wɛld/ *v.* **1.** to unite (metal or plastic pieces) by hammering or squeezing them together, esp. after applying heat: [~ + *obj*]: *welded the steel doors shut.* [*no obj*]: *The engineer is still welding.* **2.** [~ + *obj*] to bring into complete union or harmony: *He welded the recruits into a strong team.* —*n.* [*count*] **3.** a joint that has been welded. —**weld′er,** *n.* [*count*]

wel•fare (wel′fâr′) /ˈwɛlˌfɛər/ *n.* [*noncount*] **1.** health, happiness, and prosperity; well-being. **2.** assistance given by government to those in need; public relief: *He is receiving welfare. He is on welfare.*

wel′fare state′, *n.* [*count*] a state or nation in which the welfare of the people in such matters as health, education, housing, and employment is the responsibility of the government.

well[1] (wel) /wɛl/ *adv., adj., comparative* **bet•ter,** *superlative* **best,** *interj.* —*adv.* **1.** in a good or satisfactory manner: *Our plans are going well.* **2.** thoroughly or carefully: *Shake the bottle well before using.* **3.** in a proper manner: *That child behaves well in school.* **4.** excellently: *a difficult task that was well handled.* **5.** with justice or reason: *I couldn't very well refuse.* **6.** with favor or approval: *My family thinks well of her.* **7.** comfortably or prosperously: *to live well.* **8.** to a considerable degree: *These grades are well below average.* **9.** in a close way; intimately: *I've known them well.* **10.** without doubt; certainly: *I cry easily, as you well know.* **11.** with good nature; without anger: *He took the joke well.* —*adj.* **12.** in good health: *not a well man; He's not well.* **13.** [*be* + ~] satisfactory or good: *All is well.* **14.** [*be* + ~ + *that clause*] proper, fitting, or prudent: *It is well that you didn't go.* —*interj.* **15.** (used to express surprise, a mild scolding, or the like:) *Well! I didn't know you felt so strongly about it.* **16.** This word is used to introduce a sentence, resume a conversation, etc.: *Well, it's time to go home.* —***Idiom.*** **17. as well,** in addition; also: *She wanted to produce the play and to direct it as well.* **18. as well as,** equally as: *He's smart as well as charming.* **19. leave well enough alone,** to avoid changing something that is satisfactory the way it is. —**well′ness,** *n.* [*noncount*]

well[2] (wel) /wɛl/ *n.* [*count*] **1.** a hole drilled into the earth to obtain a natural deposit, as water or petroleum: *an oil well.* **2.** a natural source of water, as a spring. **3.** a source: *a well of compassion.* **4.** an enclosed space, as for air, stairs, or an elevator, extending up and down through the floors of a building. —*v.* [*no obj*] **5.** to rise, spring, or gush, as from a well: *Tears welled up in my eyes.*

we'll (wēl; *unstressed* wil) /wiyl; *unstressed* wɪl/ *contraction.* a shortened form of *we shall* or *we will.*

well′-advised′, *adj.* [*be* + ~] acting with caution, care, or wisdom; sensible: *You'd be well-advised to leave this dangerous area at once.*

well′-appoint′ed, *adj.* attractively or properly equipped or furnished: *a well-appointed apartment.*

well′-bal′anced, *adj.* **1.** correctly balanced, adjusted, or regulated. **2.** sensible; sane: *a well-balanced child.*

well′-behaved′, *adj.* showing good behavior or manners.

well′-be′ing, *n.* [*noncount*] a state of health, happiness, comfort, and prosperity.

well-′born′, *adj.* born of a good or noble family.

well′-bred′, *adj.* showing good breeding, as in behavior.

well′-defined′, *adj.* clearly stated, outlined, or described: *well-defined goals and plans.*

well′-disposed′, *adj.* [*be* + ~ + *to*] feeling favorable, sympathetic, or kind.

well′-done′, *adj.* **1.** performed accurately and skillfully. **2.** (of meat) thoroughly cooked.

well′-fed′, *adj.* fat; plump.

well′-found′ed, *adj.* having or based on good reasons, sound information, etc.: *well-founded objections.*

well′-groomed′, *adj.* **1.** clean, neat, and dressed with care. **2.** carefully cared for: *a well-groomed lawn.*

well′-ground′ed, *adj.* **1.** WELL-FOUNDED. **2.** thoroughly instructed in the basic principles of a subject.

well′-heeled′, *adj.* well-off; rich; wealthy.

well′-informed′, *adj.* having a great deal of knowledge, as of a subject or of a variety of subjects.

wel•ling•ton (wel′ing tən) /ˈwɛlɪŋtən/ *n.* [*count*] a heavy boot, esp. one that reaches close to the knee.

well′-inten′tioned, *adj.* well-meaning.

well′-knit′, *adj.* having all parts or elements joined closely, carefully, or firmly: *a well-knit plot.*

well′-known′, *adj.* **1.** fully or thoroughly known: *These facts are well-known and clearly established; we will not dispute them here.* **2.** widely known; famous: *a well-known rock star.*

well′-made′, *adj.* skillfully built or put together.

well′-man′nered, *adj.* polite; courteous.

well′-mean′ing, *adj.* having or based on good intentions; intending or wanting to do something kind or good.

well′-nigh′, *adv.* very nearly; almost: *having been there well-nigh twenty years.*

well′-off′, *adj.* [*be* + ~] **1.** well-to-do; prosperous. **2.** in a favorable position or condition; fortunate.

well′-or′dered, *adj.* arranged, planned, or occurring in an orderly way.

well′-preserved′, *adj.* **1.** maintained in good condition. **2.** preserving a good or healthy appearance: *well-preserved for his age.*

well′-read′ (red′) /ˈrɛd/ *adj.* having read a great deal.

well′-round′ed, *adj.* having desirably varied or different abilities or talents; desirably varied: *a well-rounded personality.*

well′-spo′ken, *adj.* **1.** speaking well or in a way that pleases. **2.** spoken in a fitting or pleasing manner.

well•spring (wel′spring′) /ˈwɛlˌsprɪŋ/ *n.* [*count*] **1.** the source of a spring, stream, or river. **2.** a continuous supply that never seems to run out.

well′-thought′-of′, *adj.* having a good reputation.

well′-to-do′, *adj.* comfortably prosperous; wealthy.

well′-turned′, *adj.* **1.** gracefully shaped: *a well-turned ankle.* **2.** gracefully expressed: *a well-turned phrase.*

well′-wish′er, *n.* [*count*] a person who wishes another well.

well′-worn′, *adj.* **1.** showing the effects of having been used or worn a great deal. **2.** having little or no meaning because of overuse; trite; hackneyed.

welsh (welsh, welch) /wɛlʃ, wɛltʃ/ also **welch,** *v.* [~ + *on* + *obj*] *Often Offensive.* **1.** to fail to pay what is owed: *He welshed on his debts.* **2.** to go back on one's word. —**welsh′er,** *n.* [*count*]

Welsh (welsh, welch) /wɛlʃ, wɛltʃ/ *adj.* **1.** of or relating to Wales. **2.** of or relating to the language spoken by many of the people in Wales. —*n.* **3.** [*plural; the* + ~; *used with a plural verb*] the people born or living in Wales. **4.** [*noncount*] the language spoken by many of the people in Wales.

Welsh•man (welsh′mən, welch′-) /ˈwɛlʃmən, ˈwɛltʃ-/ *n.* [*count*], *pl.* **-men.** a person born or living in Wales.

Welsh•wom•an (welsh′wo͝om′ən, welch′-) /ˈwɛlʃˌwʊmən, ˈwɛltʃ-/ *n.* [*count*], *pl.* **-wom•en.** a woman born or living in Wales.

welt (welt) /wɛlt/ *n.* [*count*] a ridge or raised mark like a cut on the surface of the body, as from a blow.

wel•ter (wel′tər) /ˈwɛltər/ *n.* [*count*] a confused mass; jumble.

wel•ter•weight (wel′tər wāt′) /ˈwɛltərˌweyt/ *n.* [*count*] a boxer weighing up to 147 lb. (67 kg).

wench (wench) /wɛntʃ/ *n.* [*count*] **1.** a girl or young woman. **2.** a female servant. **3.** a sexually loose woman.

wend (wend) /wɛnd/ *v.* [~ + *obj*] to travel on or direct (one's way): *to wend his way home.*

went (went) /wɛnt/ *v.* pt. of GO[1].

wept (wept) /wɛpt/ *v.* pt. and pp. of WEEP.

were (wûr; *unstressed* wər) /wɜr; *unstressed* wər/ *v.* a 2nd pers. sing. past indic., pl. past indic., and past subj. of BE.

we're (wēr) /wɪər/ *contraction.* a shortened form of *we are.*

were•n't (wûrnt, wûr′ənt) /wɜrnt, ˈwɜrənt/ *contraction.* a shortened form of *were not.*

were•wolf (wâr′wo͝olf′, wēr′-, wûr′-) /ˈwɛərˌwʊlf, ˈwɪər-, ˈwɜr-/ *n.* [*count*], *pl.* **-wolves.** (in folk beliefs) a person who has taken on the form of a wolf.

west (west) /wɛst/ *n.* **1.** [*noncount*] the point of the compass located 90° to the left of north. **2.** [*noncount*] the direction in which west lies: *The wind is from the west.* **3.** [*proper noun; usually: the West*] **a.** a region in the west of a country, esp. of the U.S. **b.** the countries of Europe and the Western Hemisphere. —*adj.* **4.** lying toward or located in the west. **5.** coming from the west: *a west wind.* —*adv.* **6.** to, toward, or in the west: *to head west.*

west•er•ly (wes′tər lē) /ˈwɛstərliy/ *adj., adv.* **1.** toward or from the west: *a westerly wind; The wind turned westerly.* —*n.* [*count*], *pl.* **-lies. 2.** a wind that blows from the west.

west•ern (wes′tərn) /ˈwɛstərn/ *adj.* **1.** of, toward, or in the west: *a western migration.* **2.** coming from the west. **3.** [*usually: Western*] of the West: *That country has resisted Western influence for centuries.* —*n.* [*count*] **4.** [*often: Western*] a story, movie, or radio or television program about the U.S. West in the 19th century. —**west′ern•er,** *n.* [*count*]

west•ern•ize (wes′tər nīz′) /ˈwɛstərˌnayz/ *v.* [~ + *obj*], **-ized, -iz•ing.** to influence (a people) with Western ideas, customs, and practices: *The country has resisted any attempt to westernize its form of government.* —**west•ern•i•za•tion** (wes′tər nə zā′shən) /ˌwɛstərnəˈzeyʃən/ *n.* [*noncount*]

west•ward (west′wərd) /ˈwɛstwərd/ *adj.* **1.** moving, facing, or located toward the west. —*adv.* **2.** Also, **west′wards.** toward the west.

wet (wet) /wɛt/ *adj.,* **wet•ter, wet•test,** *v.,* **wet** or **wet•ted, wet•ting.** —*adj.* **1.** moistened, covered, or soaked with liquid: *Wipe this with a wet cloth.* **2.** in a liquid state: *wet paint.* **3.** rainy or misty: *a cold, wet day.* **4.** allowing the sale of alcoholic beverages: *a wet state.* —*v.* **5.** to (cause to) become wet or moistened: [~ + *obj*]: *Wet the cloth with warm water.* [*no obj*]: *My jacket has wet through.* **6.** [~ + *obj*] to urinate on or in: *The dog had wet the carpet.* —***Idiom.*** **7. all wet,** completely mistaken. **8. wet behind the ears,** not mature; inexperienced. —**wet′ly,** *adv.* —**wet′ness,** *n.* [*noncount*] —**wet′ter,** *n.* [*count*]

wet•back (wet′bak′) /ˈwɛtˌbæk/ *n.* [*count*] *Disparaging.* a Mexican laborer who enters the U.S. illegally.

wet′ blan′ket, *n.* [*count*] a person who dampens or discourages enthusiasm or enjoyment.

wet•land (wet′land′) /ˈwɛtˌlænd/ *n.* [*count*] Often, **wetlands.** [*plural*] land with wet and spongy soil.

wet′ nurse′, *n.* [*count*] a woman hired to feed another's infant with her breast milk.

wet′ suit′, *n.* [*count*] a close-fitting rubber suit worn for body warmth, as by scuba divers.

we've (wēv) /wiyv/ *contraction.* a shortened form of *we have.*

whack (hwak, wak) /hwæk, wæk/ *v.* **1.** to strike or hit with or as if with a strong, loud blow: [~ + *obj*]: *She whacked the stick against the table.* [*no obj*]: *He whacked at the ball and missed.* —*n.* [*count*] **2.** a smart, resounding blow: *She gave him a whack on the knuckles.* **3.** an attempt: *He took a whack at the job.* —***Idiom.*** **4. out of whack,** out of order; not working correctly or properly. —**whack′er,** *n.* [*count*]

whack•y (hwak′ē, wak′ē) /ˈhwækiy, ˈwækiy/ *adj.* WACKY.

whale[1] (hwāl, wāl) /hweyl, weyl/ *n., pl.* **whales, whale,** *v.,* **whaled, whal•ing.** —*n.* [*count*] **1.** a very large mammal that lives in the sea, having a fishlike body. **2.** [*usually singular*] something great or fine of its kind: *I had a whale of a time in Europe.* —*v.* [*no obj*] **3.** to be in the business of whaling.

whale[2] (hwāl, wāl) /hweyl, weyl/ *v.* [~ + *obj*], **whaled, whal•ing.** to thrash, strike, hit, or beat strongly and loudly: *The batter whaled the ball deep into the seats.*

whale•bone (hwāl′bōn′, wāl′-) /ˈhweylˌbown, ˈweyl-/ *n.* [*noncount*] a flexible, hard, horny substance hanging from the upper jaws of certain whales, once used to make a corset stiffer.

whal•er (hwā′lər, wā′-) /ˈhweylər, ˈwey-/ *n.* [*count*] a person or ship in the business of whaling.

whal•ing (hwā′ling, wā′-) /ˈhweylɪŋ, ˈwey-/ *n.* [*noncount*] the work or industry of capturing whales.

wham (hwam, wam) /hwæm, wæm/ *n., v.,* **whammed, wham•ming.** —*n.* [*count*] **1.** the sound of a sharp, forceful hit, blow, punch, kick, explosion, etc. —*v.* [~ + *obj*] **2.** to hit with or make a forceful sound.

wham•my (hwam′ē, wam′ē) /ˈhwæmiy, ˈwæmiy/ *n.* [*count*], *pl.* **-mies.** *Slang.* **1.** something that is unlucky, or thought to cause bad luck; a jinx; hex. **2.** a terrible blow, a crushing setback, or a catastrophe.

wharf (hwôrf, wôrf) /hwɔrf, wɔrf/ *n.* [*count*], *pl.* **wharves** (hwôrvz, wôrvz), **wharfs.** a large dock or similar structure next to which ships are attached at shore to load or unload.

what (hwut, hwot, wut, wot; *unstressed* hwət, wət) /hwʌt, hwɒt, wʌt, wɒt; *unstressed* hwət, wət/ *pron.* **1.** (used in questions as a request for information): *What is your phone number? What is your wife's name? What is the matter?* **2.** (used in questions to ask about the character, origin, identity, or worth of a person or thing): *What is the meaning of life? What is wealth without friends?* **3.** (used in questions to ask for a repetition of words or information not fully understood): *You need what?* **4.** (used in questions) how much?: *What does it cost?* **5.** (used to introduce a clause) that which; whatever; as much or as many as: *I will send what was promised (= I will send the thing that was promised). We will stick together come what may (= whatever happens).* **6.** (used to indicate that there is more to follow, or that there are additional possibilities, alternatives, etc.): *You know what? Shall we go or what?* **7.** (used to introduce an exclamation, or to make stronger the next word or noun): *What luck! What* an idea! **8.** *Brit.* don't you agree?: *An unusual chap, what?* **—***n.* [*count*] **9.** the true nature or identity of something, or the sum or total of its characteristics: *a lecture on the whats and hows of crop rotation.* **—***adj.* **10.** (used to signal a question): *What time is it?* **11.** whatever; whichever: *Take what supplies you need.* **—***adv.* **12.** to what extent or degree?: *What does it matter?* **13.** (used to introduce a prepositional phrase beginning with *with* and conveying the cause of something): *What with storms and all, their return was delayed.* **—***interj.* **14.** (used to show shock or surprise, and may then be followed by a question or phrase): *What, no kiss?* **—*Idiom.*** **15. so what,** (used to express indifference or contempt): *They're rich, so what?* **16. what for,** why: *What did you do that for?* **17. what have you,** other things of the same kind; so forth: *They stole money, jewels, and what have you.* **18. what if,** what would be the outcome if; suppose that: *What if we get lost?* **19. what it takes,** whatever is necessary for success: *Do you have what it takes to become a business executive?* **20. what's what,** the true situation: *Let's find out what's what around here.*

what•ev•er (hwut ev′ər, hwot-, hwat-, wut-, wot-, wət-) /hwʌt'ɛvər, hwɒt-, hwæt-, wʌt-, wɒt-, wət-/ *pron.* **1.** anything that: *Do whatever you like.* **2.** no matter what: *Do it, whatever happens.* **3.** (used at the end of a list) any or any one of a number of things whether known or not: *papers, magazines, or whatever.* **4.** (used in questions) what?: *Whatever do you mean?* **—***adj.* **5.** in any amount; to any extent: *whatever merit the work has.* **6.** no matter what: *Whatever problems you might have, we will help.* **7.** being what or who it may be: *Whatever the reason, she refuses to go.* **8.** [*after a noun*] of any kind: *She has no friends whatever.*

what-if (hwut′if′, hwot′-, wut′-, wot′-) /'hwʌt'ɪf, 'hwɒt-, 'wʌt-, 'wɒt-/ *adj.* **1.** imaginary; possible; hypothetical: *a what-if scenario.* **—***n.* [*count*] **2.** a hypothetical case or situation; a conjecture: *a series of what-ifs.*

what•not (hwut′not′, hwot′-, wut′-, wot′-) /'hwʌt,nɒt, 'hwɒt-, 'wʌt-, 'wɒt-/ *n.* [*noncount*] anything of the same or similar kind: *Bring sheets, towels, and whatnot.*

what's (hwuts, hwots, wuts, wots) /hwʌts, hwɒts, wʌts, wɒts/ *contraction.* a shortened form of *what is, what has,* or *what does.*

what•so•ev•er (hwut′sō ev′ər, hwot′-, wut′-, wot′-) /,hwʌtsow'ɛvər, ,hwɒt-, ,wʌt-, ,wɒt-/ *pron., adj.* (used to add greater emphasis to a preceding negative word or phrase) whatever: *She has no friends whatsoever.*

wheal (hwēl, wēl) /hwiyl, wiyl/ *n.* [*count*] **1.** a burning or itching swelling on the skin. **2.** WELT.

wheat (hwēt, wēt) /hwiyt, wiyt/ *n.* [*noncount*] **1.** the grain of a cereal grass used in the form of flour. **2.** the plant itself. —**wheat′en,** *adj.*

wheat′ germ′, *n.* [*noncount*] the vitamin-rich central part of the wheat kernel.

whee•dle (hwēd′l, wēd′l) /'hwiydl̩, 'wiydl̩/ *v.* [~ + *obj*], **-dled, -dling.** to influence or try to persuade (a person), esp. by charming or flattering him or her, in order to gain (something): *trying to wheedle her into lending me the car; He tried to wheedle some more money from her.* —**whee′dler,** *n.* [*count*]

wheel (hwēl, wēl) /hwiyl, wiyl/ *n.* [*count*] **1.** a circular frame or disk that can revolve or spin around an inner frame or on an axis, allowing an object to which it is attached to move. **2.** something like a wheel in shape or function. **3.** the steering wheel of a vehicle. **4. wheels,** [*plural*] **a.** something that causes another action: *the wheels of commerce.* **b.** *Slang.* a car: *Does anyone have wheels so we can drive to Malibu?* **5.** someone powerful and influential: *a big wheel in the oil business.* **—***v.* **6.** [*no obj*] to turn, rotate, or revolve; change direction: *The tanks wheeled and roared off in pursuit.* **7.** [~ + *obj*] to move or carry on wheels: *They wheeled him off to the emergency room.* **8.** [*no obj*] to roll on or as if on wheels; travel smoothly: *The car wheeled along the highway.* **—*Idiom.*** **9. at the wheel, a.** at the helm of a ship, the steering wheel of a motor vehicle, etc. **b.** in command or control: *There is a new president at the wheel.* **10. wheel and deal,** [*no obj*] to operate cleverly or craftily, esp. in a bold or showy way, for one's own profit or benefit. —**wheeled,** *adj.*

wheel•bar•row (hwēl′bar′ō, wēl′-) /'hwiyl,bærow, 'wiyl-/ *n.* [*count*] a small cart for carrying and moving a load, supported at one end by a wheel and pushed at the other by two handles.

wheel•base (hwēl′bās′, wē′-) /'hwiyl,beys, 'wiy-/ *n.* [*count*] the distance from the front-wheel spindle of a motor vehicle to the rear-wheel axle.

wheel•chair (hwēl′bās′, wēl′-) /'hwiyl,beys, 'wiyl-/ *n.* [*count*] a chair mounted on wheels for use by persons who cannot walk because they are temporarily or permanently disabled. See illustration at HOSPITAL.

wheel′er-deal′er, *n.* [*count*] a clever and crafty person, as in business or politics.

wheel•wright (hwēl′rīt′, wēl′-) /'hwiyl,rayt, 'wiyl-/ *n.* [*count*] a person who makes or repairs wheels and wheeled carriages.

wheeze (hwēz, wēz) /hwiyz, wiyz/ *v.,* **wheezed, wheez•ing,** *n.* **—***v.* [*no obj*] **1.** to breathe with difficulty and with a whistling sound. **—***n.* [*count*] **2.** a wheezing breath or sound. —**wheez′y,** *adj.,* **-i•er, -i•est.**

whelk (hwelk, welk) /hwɛlk, wɛlk/ *n.* [*count*] a spiral-shelled sea animal that can be eaten.

whelp (hwelp, welp) /hwɛlp, wɛlp/ *n.* [*count*] **1.** the young of such mammals as the dog or the wolf. **2.** a young person who is considered too bold, impudent, or rude. **—***v.* [*no obj*] **3.** (of a female dog or wolf) to give birth to a young pup.

when (hwen, wen; *unstressed* hwən, wən) /hwɛn, wɛn; *unstressed* hwən, wən/ *adv.* **1.** (used to introduce a question) at what time or period?: *When will they arrive?* **2.** (used to introduce a question) under what circumstances?: *When is an apology in order?* **—***conj.* **3.** at what time: *He knows when to be silent.* **4.** at the time that: *when we were young.* **5.** whenever: *The dog barks when the doorbell rings.* **6.** as soon as: *Stop the car when the light turns red.* **7.** whereas; while on the contrary: *Why are you here when you should be in school?* **—***pron.* **8.** what or which time: *Since when have you been teaching?* **—***n.* [*count; usually singular*] **9.** the time of something: *the where and when of the accident.*

whence (hwens, wens) /hwɛns, wɛns/ *adv.* **1.** (used to introduce a question) from what place?: *Whence comest thou?* **2.** (used to introduce a question) from what source, origin, or cause?: *Whence came his wisdom?* **—Usage.** Although sometimes criticized as redundant, the idiom FROM WHENCE is old, well-established, and standard: *She arrived in Paris, from whence she bombarded us with postcards.* It is found in Shakespeare, the King James Bible, and Dickens.

when•ev′er (hwen ev′ər, wen-, hwən-, wən-) /hwɛn'ɛvər, wɛn-, hwən-, wən- / *adv., conj.* at whatever time; when: *I'm ready whenever you are.*

where (hwâr, wâr) /hwɛər, wɛər/ *adv.* **1.** (used to introduce a question) in, at, or to what place?: *Where is he? Where are you going?* **2.** (used to introduce a question) in what position, circumstances, respect, or way?: *Where do you stand on this question?* **3.** (used to introduce a question) from what source?: *Where did you get such a notion?* **—***conj.* **4.** in or at what place, part, or point: *Find where the trouble is.* **5.** in or at the place, part, or point in or at which: *The cup is where you left it.* **6.** in a position or situation in which: *He's useless where tact is needed.* **7.** to what or whatever place: *I will go where you go.* **8.** in or at which place: *They pitched a tent, where they slept.* **—***pron.* **9.** (used to introduce a question) what place?: *Where are you from?* **10.** the place in or point at which: *This is where the boat docks.* **—***n.* [*count*] **11.** a place; location: *the where and the why of the crimes.* **—*Idiom.*** **12. where it's at,** *Informal.* where the most exciting, fashionable, or profitable activity or circumstance is to be found: *The Wall Street analyst said that government bonds are where it's at right now.*

where•a•bouts (hwâr′ə bouts′, wâr′-,) /'hwɛərə,bawts, 'wɛər-, / *adv.* **1.** about where? **—***n.* **2.** the place where a person or thing is: [*plural; used with a plural verb*]: *His whereabouts are still unknown.* [*noncount; used with a singular verb*]: *His whereabouts is still unknown.*

where•as (hwâr az′, wâr-) /hwɛər'æz, wɛər-/ *conj.* **1.** while on the contrary: *One student arrived promptly, whereas the others came late.* **2.** it being the case that: *Whereas we wish to set the record straight, be it resolved that we reaffirm our allegiance to the party.*

where•by (hwâr bī′, wâr-) /hwɛər'bay, wɛər-/ *conj.* by what or which; under the terms of which.

where•fore (hwâr′fôr, -fōr, wâr′-) /'hwɛərfɔr, -fowr, 'wɛər-/ *adv.* **1.** for that cause or reason. **—***n.* [*count*] **2.** a cause or reason: *all the whys and wherefores of a situation.*

where•in (hwâr in′, wâr′-) /hwɛər'ɪn, 'wɛər-/ *conj.* **1.** in what or in which. **—***adv.* **2.** in what way or respect.

where•of (hwâr uv′, -ov′, wâr-) /hwɛər'ʌv, -'ɒv, wɛər-/ *adv., conj.* of what, which, or whom.

where•so•ev•er (hwâr′sō ev′ər, wâr′-) /,hwɛərsow'ɛvər, ,wɛər-/ *conj.* in or to whatsoever place; wherever.

where•up•on (hwâr′ə pon′, -pôn′, wâr′-; hwâr′ə pon′, -pôn′, wâr′-) /ˌhwɛərəˈpɒn, -ˈpɔn, ˌwɛər-; ˈhwɛərəˌpɒn, -ˌpɔn, ˈwɛər-/ *conj.* **1.** upon what or which. **2.** at or after which: *He'll surely try to get in touch with her, whereupon we'll spring the trap.*

wher•ev•er (hwâr ev′ər, wâr-) /hwɛərˈɛvər, wɛər-/ *conj., adv.* **1.** in, at, or to whatever place or circumstance: *Wherever you go, I'll follow.* **—*adv.*** **2.** (used to introduce a question but with extra emphasis): where?: *Wherever did you find that?*

where•with•al (hwâr′wiᵺ ôl, -with-, wâr′-) /ˈhwɛər-wɪðɔl, -wɪθ-, ˈwɛər-/ *n.* [*count; usually singular; usually: the* + ~ (+ *to* + *verb*] the means, esp. money, with which to do something.

whet (hwet, wet) /hwɛt, wɛt/ *v.* [~ + *obj*], **whet•ted, whet•ting. 1.** to sharpen by grinding or friction. **2.** to make eager; stimulate: *That primary whetted her appetite for running in the general election.*

wheth•er (hweᵺ′ər, weᵺ′-) /ˈhwɛðər, ˈwɛð-/ *conj.* **1.** (used to introduce the first of two or more choices or possibilities; the second one is preceded by the word *or*:) *I don't care whether we go or stay.* **2.** (used to introduce a single choice, while the second choice is understood or implied, to be the negation of the first): *See whether she has come.* **—*Idiom.*** **3. whether or not** or **whether or no,** under whatever circumstances; in any case; regardless: *He tends to insist on his views whether or not the facts support them.*

whew (hwyōō) /hwyuw/ *interj.* (used to express astonishment, dismay, fatigue, or relief): *Whew, I'm tired.*

whey (hwā, wā) /hwey, wey/ *n.* [*noncount*] the liquid that separates from the curd in milk that has become solid.

which (hwich, wich) /hwɪtʃ, wɪtʃ/ *pron.* **1.** (used in questions) what one or ones: *Which of these do you want?* **2.** whichever; the one that: *Choose which appeals to you.* **3.** (used in relative clauses to refer back to a word that has already been mentioned and to pause to give it emphasis): *This book, which I read last night, was exciting.* **4.** (used in a relative clause that starts with a preposition): *That's the house in which I lived.* **—*adj.*** [*before a noun*] **5.** what one or ones of a number or group: *Which book do you want?* **6.** whichever: *Go which way you please.*

which•ev•er (hwich ev′ər, wich-) /hwɪtʃˈɛvər, wɪtʃ-/ *pron.* **1.** any one that: *Take whichever you like.* **2.** no matter which: *Whichever you choose, some in the group will be offended.* **—*adj.*** [*before a noun*] **3.** no matter which: *whichever ones you choose.*

whiff (hwif, wif) /hwɪf, wɪf/ *n.* [*count*] **1.** a slight gust or puff, as of wind or smoke. **2.** a slight trace, as of an odor; hint: *a whiff of onions.* **3.** a single act of breathing in, as of tobacco smoke.

while (hwīl, wīl) /hwayl, wayl/ *n., conj., v.,* **whiled, whil•ing. —*n.*** [*count; singular*] **1.** an amount, period, or interval of time: *a long while ago.* **—*conj.*** **2.** during the time that: *He read the paper while he waited.* **3.** as long as: *While there's quiet I can sleep.* **4.** even though: *While they are related, they don't get along.* **5.** at the same time that: *She exercises while he grows fat.* **—*v.*** **6. while away,** to cause (time) to pass, esp. pleasantly: [~ + *away* + *obj*]: *whiling away the hours.* [~ + *obj* + *away*]: *to while the hours away.* **—*Idiom.*** **7. worth one's while,** worth one's time, trouble, or expense.

whilst (hwīlst, wīlst) /hwaylst, waylst/ *conj. Chiefly Brit.* WHILE.

whim (hwim, wim) /hwɪm, wɪm/ *n.* [*count*] a sudden idea, thought, or wish to do something without a good reason: *I decided on a whim to leave early.*

whim•per (hwim′pər, wim′-) /ˈhwɪmpər, ˈwɪm-/ *v.* [*no obj*] **1.** to cry with or utter in low, sad, weak sounds: *The dog whimpered from fear.* **—*n.*** [*count*] **2.** a whimpering sound.

whim•si•cal (hwim′zi kəl, wim′-) /ˈhwɪmzɪkəl, ˈwɪm-/ *adj.* given to playful or fanciful notions, ideas, or behavior; odd or strange; unpredictable: *He is much too whimsical to be a good businessman.* **—whim′si•cal•ly,** *adv.*

whim•sy or **-sey** (hwim′zē, wim′-) /ˈhwɪmziy, ˈwɪm-/ *n., pl.* **-sies** or **-seys. 1.** [*noncount*] playful or fanciful humor. **2.** [*count*] an odd or fanciful notion or idea.

whine (hwīn, wīn) /hwayn, wayn/ *v.,* **whined, whin•ing,** *n.* **—*v.*** **1.** [*no obj*] to make a long, usually nasal, complaining sound, often high-pitched: *The dog whined at the door* **2.** to complain in a self-pitying way: [~ + *that clause*]: *The children whined that they wanted to stay up late.* [*no obj*]: *Don't whine.* **—*n.*** [*count*] **3.** a whining word, sound, or complaint. **—whin′er,** *n.* [*count*] **—whin′y,** *adj.,* **-i•er, -i•est.**

whin•ny (hwin′ē, win′ē) /ˈhwɪniy, ˈwɪniy/ *n., pl.* **-nies,** *v.,* **-nied, -ny•ing. —*n.*** [*count*] **1.** a low, somewhat quiet and gentle neigh of a horse. **—*v.*** [*no obj*] **2.** to utter a whinny.

whip (hwip, wip) /hwɪp, wɪp/ *v.,* **whipped, whip•ping,** *n.* **—*v.*** **1.** [~ + *obj*] to beat with a flexible piece of rope or leather, as a lash, esp. as punishment: *to whip the slaves.* **2.** [~ + *obj*] to spank: *He was whipped for telling a lie.* **3.** [~ + *obj*] to urge on by or as if by whipping: *to whip the horses to go faster.* **4.** [~ + *obj*] to train forcefully: *trying to whip the team into shape.* **5.** [~ + *obj*] to defeat; overcome: *Their team whipped us 30-0.* **6.** [*no obj*] to go quickly and suddenly: *The car whipped around the corner.* **7.** to (cause to) move, pull, or seize suddenly: [~ + *out* + *obj*]: *She whipped out her camera.* [~ + *obj* + *out*]: *She whipped her camera out.* **8.** [~ + *obj*] to beat to a froth: *to whip cream.* **9.** to lash about: [*no obj*]: *The flags were whipping in the wind.* [~ + *obj*]: *The wind whipped the flags.* **10. whip off,** to write hurriedly: [~ + *off* + *obj*]: *to whip off a book report.* [~ + *obj* + *off*]: *I'll whip it off in a few hours.* **11. whip up, a.** to prepare quickly: [~ + *up* + *obj*]: *to whip up a meal.* [~ + *obj* + up]: *I'll whip a meal up.* **b.** to incite; arouse: [~ + *up* + *obj*]: *to whip up the crowd.* [~ + *obj* + *up*]: *to whip them up into a frenzy.* **—*n.*** [*count*] **12.** a flexible rod, as of rope or leather, used for whipping. **13.** a whipping stroke or motion. **14.** a utensil for whipping; whisk. **15.** a dessert of beaten egg whites or cream. **16.** a politician of a particular party in a legislative body who directs other members. **—whip′per,** *n.* [*count*]

whip•lash (hwip′lash, wip′-) /ˈhwɪplæʃ, ˈwɪp-/ *n.* **1.** [*count*] the lash of a whip. **2.** [*noncount*] a neck injury caused by a sudden jerking of the head.

whip•per•snap•per (hwip′ər snap′ər, wip′-) /ˈhwɪpərˌsnæpər, ˈwɪp-/ *n.* [*count*] an unimportant but offensively bold person, esp. a young one.

whip•pet (whip′it, wip′-) /ˈhwɪpɪt, ˈwɪp-/ *n.* [*count*] a slender, swift dog resembling a small greyhound.

whip•ping (hwip′ing, wip′-) /ˈhwɪpɪŋ, ˈwɪp-/ *n.* [*count*] **1.** a beating with a whip or the like, esp. as punishment. **2.** a defeat, as in sports.

whip•poor•will (hwip′ər wil′, wip′-) /ˈhwɪpərˌwɪl, ˈwɪp-/ *n.* [*count*] a North American bird with a loud, repeated call.

whip•saw (hwip′sô′, wip′-) /ˈhwɪpˌsɔ, ˈwɪp-/ *n., v.,* **-sawed, sawed** or **-sawn, sawing. —*n.*** [*count*] **1.** a saw for two persons, used to cut timbers across the middle. **—*v.*** [~ + *obj*] **2.** to cut with a whipsaw. **3.** to expose (someone or something) to two opposite forces at the same time: *The economy was whipsawed by inflation and high unemployment.*

whir or **whirr** (hwûr, wûr) /hwɜr, wɜr/ *v.,* **whirred, whir•ring,** *n.* **—*v.*** **1.** to move or spin quickly with a humming sound: [*no obj*]: *The helicopter whirred directly overhead.* [~ + *obj*]: *She whirred the stone at the end of the string and then released it.* **—*n.*** [*count*] **2.** an act or sound of whirring.

whirl (hwûrl, wûrl) /hwɜrl, wɜrl/ *v.* **1.** to (cause to) turn around or aside very fast, or to spin quickly: [*no obj*]: *The plane's propellers whirled.* [~ + *obj*]: *He whirled the rope around his head.* **2.** [*no obj*] to feel dizziness: *My head is whirling after that roller coaster ride.* **—*n.*** [*count*] **3.** the act of whirling. **4.** a whirling movement. **5.** a rapid round of events: *a whirl of parties.* **6.** an attempt; trial: *He promised to give that new diet a whirl.*

whirl•pool (hwûr′pōōl′, wûrl′-) /ˈhwɜrˌpuwl, ˈwɜrl-/ *n.* [*count*] water moving quickly in a circular motion, often producing a downward spiraling action.

whirl•wind (hwûrl′wind′, wûrl′-) /ˈhwɜrlˌwɪnd, ˈwɜrl-/ *n.* [*count*] **1.** a small mass of air that spins very quickly, as a tornado. **2.** something resembling a whirlwind, as in having the power to damage things. **—*adj.*** **3.** like a whirlwind in speed or force.

whirl•y•bird (hwûr′lē bûrd′, wûr′-) /ˈhwɜrliyˌbɜrd, ˈwɜr-/ *n.* HELICOPTER.

whisk (hwisk, wisk) /hwɪsk, wɪsk/ *v.* [~ + *obj*] **1.** to move, remove, carry, snatch, etc., with a rapid brushing or sweeping stroke: *The waiters whisked away the trays and plates.* **2.** to whip or blend (eggs or egg whites, cream, etc.) with a whisk. **—*n.*** [*count*] **3.** the act of whisking. **4.** WHISK BROOM. **5.** a tool, usually of wire, for beating or whipping food.

whisk′ broom′, *n.* [*count*] a small, short-handled broom used chiefly to brush clothes.

whisk•er (hwis′kər, wis′-) /ˈhwɪskər, ˈwɪs-/ *n.* [*count*] **1.**

Usually, **-kers.** [*plural*] the hair growing on a man's cheeks and chin. **2.** a single hair of the beard. **3.** one of the long bristlelike hairs growing near the mouth of an animal, as a cat. **—*Idiom.*** **4. by a whisker,** by the closest, smallest, or narrowest amount or margin: *lost the tournament by a whisker.* —**whisk′ered,** *adj.*

whis•key or **whis•ky** (hwis′kē, wis′-) /ˈhwɪskiy, ˈwɪs-/ *n., pl.* **-keys** or **-kies.** a strong alcoholic drink made from a grain, such as barley: [*noncount*]: *a bottle of whiskey.* [*count*]: *ordered two whiskeys.*

whis•per (hwis′pər, wis′pər) /ˈhwɪspər, ˈwɪspər/ *v.* **1.** to speak or say with soft, quiet, hushed sounds, esp. with little or no vibration of the vocal cords: [*no obj*]: *He whispered softly in her ear.* [~ + *obj*]: *She whispered a secret to me.* [*used with quotations*]: *"Quiet, someone will hear us!" she whispered.* **2.** [*no obj*] to make a soft, low, quiet, rustling sound. **—*n.*** [*count*] **3.** an act or instance of whispering: *They spoke in whispers.* **4.** a whispered word or remark. **5.** a rumor: *a whisper of scandal.* **6.** a soft, low, quiet, rustling sound: *the whisper of the wind.* —**whis′per•er,** *n.* [*count*]

whist (hwist, wist) /hwɪst, wɪst/ *n.* [*noncount*] a card game that is a form of bridge.

whis•tle (hwis′əl, wis′-) /ˈhwɪsəl, ˈwɪs-/ *v.,* **-tled, -tling,** *n.* **—*v.*** **1.** to make a high, clear sound by forcing the breath through stretched lips or through the teeth: [*no obj*]: *He whistled happily to himself.* [~ + *obj*]: *He whistled a happy tune.* **2.** [*no obj*] to produce a sound or call resembling a whistle: *The birds were whistling in the trees.* **3.** to signal or call for by or as if by whistling: [*no obj;* (~ + *for* + *obj*)]: *He whistled for her to come down and see him.* [~ + *obj*]: *She whistled her dog to her side.* **4.** [*no obj*] to move with a whistling sound, as a bullet. **—*n.*** [*count*] **5.** an instrument for producing whistling sounds: *The police officer blew her whistle.* **6.** a whistling sound. **—*Idiom.*** **7. blow the whistle,** [*blow + the + ~ + on + obj*] to expose crime or other wrongdoing: *The accountants blew the whistle on the embezzlers.* **8. wet one's whistle,** to take a drink. **9. whistle in the dark,** [*no obj*] to try to remain brave by or as if by whistling. —**whis′tler,** *n.* [*count*]

whis′tle-blow′er, *n.* [*count*] a person who informs on another or who exposes criminal activity or wrongdoing. —**whis′tle-blow′ing,** *n.* [*noncount*]

whis′tle stop′, *n.* [*count*] **1.** a small town, esp. one along a railroad line. **2.** a short talk from the rear platform of a train during a political campaign.

whit (hwit, wit) /hwɪt, wɪt/ *n.* [*count; singular, a* + ~] the smallest amount; a bit: *I don't care a whit.*

white (hwīt, wīt) /hwayt, wayt/ *adj.,* **whit•er, whit•est,** *n.* **1.** of the color of pure snow. **2.** light in color; pale: *white wines as opposed to red wines.* **3.** (of human beings) pale; having little of the normal, healthy color of the skin: *His face turned white at the terrible news.* **4.** for, limited to, or made up of Caucasians. **5.** silvery; gray: *white hair.* **6.** snowy: *a white Christmas.* **7.** lacking color. **8.** morally pure; innocent. **9.** lacking hatred or bad feeling; harmless: *white magic.* **—*n.*** **10.** [*noncount*] a color without hue that is the opposite of black. **11.** [*count*] a person of the Caucasian race. **12.** [*count*] a white or light-colored material, substance, or part: *the white of an egg.* —**white′ness,** *n.* [*noncount*]

white′ blood′ cell′, *n.* [*count*] a nearly colorless blood cell that fights disease-carrying organisms.

white•cap (hwīt′kap′, wīt′-) /ˈhwaytˌkæp, ˈwayt-/ *n.* [*count*] a wave with a foaming white top.

white′-col′lar, *adj.* of or relating to professional or clerical workers whose jobs do not usually involve manual labor: *white-collar workers.* Compare BLUE-COLLAR.

white′ el′ephant, *n.* [*count*] **1.** a possession that is no longer wanted by the owner but is difficult to sell or dispose of. **2.** a possession that requires spending beyond its worth or value.

white′ flag′, *n.* [*count*] an all-white flag used as a symbol of surrender or truce.

white′ goods′, *n.* [*plural*] **1.** household linens, as sheets and towels. **2.** white fabrics, esp. of cotton or linen.

white′ heat′, *n.* [*noncount*] **1.** a very strong, intense heat at which something glows with white light. **2.** a state of great or intense activity or excitement.

White′ House′, *n.* [*proper noun; the* + ~] **1.** the official home or residence of the president of the U.S. **2.** the executive branch of the U.S. government.

white′ lie′, *n.* [*count*] a harmless lie, often one told to avoid hurting someone's feelings; fib.

white′ mat′ter, *n.* [*noncount*] nerve tissue, esp. of the brain and spinal cord, that is nearly white in color.

whit•en (hwīt′ən, wīt′-) /ˈhwaytən, ˈwayt-/ *v.* to (cause to) become white: [~ + *obj*]: *He poured bleach into his laundry to whiten the clothes.* [*no obj*]: *The ground slowly whitened as the snow fell.* —**whit′en•er,** *n.* [*count*]

white•out (hwīt′out′, wīt′-) /ˈhwaytˌawt, ˈwayt-/ *n.* [*noncount*] **1.** a condition in which heavily falling or blowing snow makes it impossible to see where one is. **2.** a white fluid used to paint over mistakes in typing or writing.

white′ sale′, *n.* [*count*] a sale of white goods.

white′-shoe′, *adj.* of or relating to members of the upper class who own or run large corporations: *white-shoe bankers; a conservative, white-shoe image.*

white•wall (hwīt′wôl′, wīt′-) /ˈhwaytˌwɔl, ˈwayt-/ *n.* [*count*] an automobile tire with a white sidewall.

white•wash (hwīt′wash′, -wôsh′, wīt′-) /ˈhwaytˌwæʃ, -ˌwɔʃ, ˈwayt-/ *n.* **1.** [*noncount*] a substance, as one made from lime and water, for whitening walls and woodwork. **2.** an act of hiding, covering up, or superficially investigating faults or errors so as to prevent public knowledge and blame and responsibility: [*count*]: *The trial turned into an obvious whitewash that let the killers go free.* [*noncount*]: *guilty of whitewash.* **3.** [*count*] a defeat in which the loser fails to score. **—*v.*** [~ + *obj*] **4.** to whiten with whitewash. **5.** to hide or cover up the faults or errors of. **6.** to defeat by keeping the opponent from scoring.

white′ wa′ter, *n.* [*noncount*] bubbly, foaming, frothy water, as in rapids.

whit•ey (hwī′tē, wī′-) /ˈhwaytiy, ˈway-/ *n.* [*count*], *pl.* **-eys.** *Disparaging.* a white person.

whith•er (hwith′ər, with′-) /ˈhwɪðər, ˈwɪð-/ *adv.* **1.** to what place; where. **2.** to what end, point, or action. **—*conj.*** **3.** to which place: *to go whither the sun rises.* **4.** to whatever place.

whit•ing[1] (hwī′ting, wī′-) /ˈhwaytɪŋ, ˈway-/ *n.* [*count*], *pl.* **-ings, -ing.** a sea fish that is eaten as food.

whit•ing[2] (hwī′ting, wī′-) /ˈhwaytɪŋ, ˈway-/ *n.* [*noncount*] pure-white chalk powder used esp. in making putty and whitewash.

whit•ish (hwī′tish, wī′-) /ˈhwaytɪʃ, ˈway-/ *adj.* somewhat white. —**whit′ish•ness,** *n.* [*noncount*]

whit•tle (hwit′l, wit′l) /ˈhwɪtl̩, ˈwɪtl̩/ *v.,* **-tled, -tling. 1.** to cut, trim, or shape (wood) by carving off bits with a knife: [~ + *obj*]: *to whittle wood.* [*no obj*]: *sat whittling with his brand-new knife.* **2.** [~ + *obj*] to form by whittling: *to whittle a toy soldier from a block of wood.* **3.** to reduce the amount of gradually: [~ + *obj*]: *to whittle costs.* [~ + *down* + *obj*]: *to whittle down expenses.* —**whit′tler,** *n.* [*count*]

whiz or **whizz** (hwiz, wiz) /hwɪz, wɪz/ *v.,* **whizzed, whiz•zing,** *n.* **—*v.*** [*no obj*] **1.** to make or move with a humming, buzzing, or hissing sound, as of an object flying quickly through the air: *A cloud of hornets whizzed by.* **—*n.*** [*count*] **2.** *Informal.* a very skillful person; expert: *She's always been a whiz at math.* **3.** a whizzing sound: *the whiz of the bullets passing by.*

who (ho͞o) /huw/ *pron., possessive* **whose,** *objective* **whom. 1.** (used to introduce a question, as the subject or, in informal conversational use, the object of a verb) what person or persons: *Who is he? Who is at the door?* **2.** (used in questions to ask about the character or importance of someone): *Who does she think she is?* **3.** the person or persons that: *Do you know who called?* **4.** (used in relative clauses to refer to a person): *The woman who called this morning is here.*

whoa (hwō, wō) /hwow, wow/ *interj.* (used as a command, esp. to an animal, to stop).

who•dun′it (ho͞o dun′it) /huwˈdʌnɪt/ *n.* [*count*] a detective story.

who•ev•er (ho͞o ev′ər) /huwˈɛvər/ *pron.* whatever person; anyone that: *Whoever did it should be proud.*

whole (hōl) /howl/ *adj.* **1.** [*before a noun*] making up the full amount, number, extent, or length of time; entire: *He ate the whole pie. She ran the whole distance. Let's start the whole thing over.* **2.** [*before a noun*] lacking nothing; having all pieces; complete: *a whole set of china.* **3.** [*before a noun*] *Math.* not a fraction: *a whole number, like 2 or 3.* **4.** not broken or damaged; in one piece; not injured or hurt: *Thankfully, the vase arrived whole.* **5.** (used to emphasize how much an amount is): *I'd feel a whole lot better if you'd point that gun somewhere else.* **—*n.*** [*count*] **6.** the entire amount, number, or extent. **7.** a thing complete in itself, as an assembly of parts or elements thought of as one thing; a unitary system: *com-*

bined the elements of the theory into a unified whole. —***Idiom.*** **8. as a whole,** as a unit; considered together. **9. on the whole,** everything considered; in general: *On the whole, I agree with you.* **10. out of whole cloth,** without foundation in fact; fictitious. —**whole′ness,** *n.* [*noncount*]

whole•heart•ed (hōl′här′tid) /ˈhowlˈhɑrtɪd/ *adj.* completely sincere or enthusiastic: *He gave his wholehearted approval to the plan.* —**whole′heart′ed•ly,** *adv.* —**whole′heart′ed•ness,** *n.* [*noncount*]

whole′ num′ber, *n.* [*count*] an integer.

whole•sale (hōl′sāl′) /ˈhowlˌseyl/ *n., adj., adv., v.,* **-saled, -sal•ing.** —*n.* [*noncount*] **1.** the sale of goods in quantity, as to retailers. —*adj.* **2.** of or working in wholesale sales. **3.** indiscriminate: *wholesale layoffs.* —*adv.* **4.** on wholesale terms. **5.** in a wholesale way; in large amounts or on a large scale: *The company began firing people wholesale.* —*v.* **6.** to sell by wholesale: [~ + *obj*]: *to wholesale leftover goods.* [*no obj*]: *not in the business of wholesaling.* —**whole′sal′er,** *n.* [*count*]

whole•some (hōl′səm) /ˈhowlsəm/ *adj.* **1.** bringing about or making possible a condition of well-being; healthful. **2.** suggesting health, esp. in appearance: *a fresh, wholesome look from using that soap.* **3.** having a positive or good effect, esp. on the morals of someone: *wholesome family entertainment.* —**whole′some•ly,** *adv.* —**whole′some•ness,** *n.* [*noncount*]

whole′-wheat′, *adj.* prepared with the complete wheat kernel: *whole-wheat flour.*

who'll (ho͞ol) /huwl/ *contraction.* a shortened form of *who will* or *who shall.*

whol•ly (hō′lē, hōl′lē) /ˈhowliy, ˈhowlliy/ *adv.* entirely; totally; completely.

whom (ho͞om) /huwm/ *pron.* the form of the pronoun WHO used as the object of a verb or a preposition: *Whom did you call? To whom should I send this? The man whom you called has returned.*

whom•ev•er (ho͞om ev′ər) /huwmˈɛvər/ *pron.* the form of the pronoun WHOEVER used as the object of a verb or a preposition: *She was gracious to whomever she spoke.*

whoop (hwo͞op, hwo͝op, wo͞op, wo͝op; *esp. for 2* ho͞op, ho͝op) /hwuwp, hwʊp, wuwp, wʊp; *esp. for 2* huwp, hʊp/ *n.* [*count*] **1.** a loud cry or shout, as of excitement. **2.** a deep inhaling of air with a hollow, gasping sound following a fit of coughing. —*v.* **3.** to utter with, or make, a loud cry or shout: [*no obj*]: *The kids whooped and danced at the good news.* [*used with quotations*]: *"Yahoo!" they whooped, "we're out of here!"* —***Idiom.*** **4. whoop it up,** *Informal.* to celebrate noisily. —**whoop′er,** *n.* [*count*]

whoop′ing cough′ (ho͞o′ping, ho͝op′ing) /ˈhuwpɪŋ, ˈhʊpɪŋ/ *n.* [*noncount*] a disease that is easily transmitted to others, marked by a series of short, gasping coughs followed by a whoop.

whoosh (hwo͞osh, hwo͝osh, wo͞osh, wo͝osh) /hwuwʃ, hwʊʃ, wuwʃ, wʊʃ/ *n.* [*count*] **1.** a loud, rushing noise, as of air or water: *With a mighty whoosh the plane roared into the sky.* —*v.* [*no obj*] **2.** to move with a whoosh: *The car whooshed along the highway.*

whop•per (hwop′ər, wop′-) /ˈhwɒpər, ˈwɒp-/ *n.* [*count*] *Informal.* **1.** something uncommonly large: *That fish was a whopper.* **2.** a big lie: *told whoppers from time to time.*

whop•ping (hwop′ing, wop′-) /ˈhwɒpɪŋ, ˈwɒp-/ *adj. Informal.* **1.** very large; unusually large: *a whopping inflation rate.* —*adv.* **2.** extremely; greatly; exceedingly: *a whopping big lie.*

whore (hôr; *often* ho͝or) /hɔr; *often* hʊr/ *n.* [*count*] PROSTITUTE. —**whor′ish,** *adj.*

who're (ho͞o′ər) /ˈhuwər/ *contraction.* a shortened form of *who are: Who're the people at the next table?*

whorl (hwûrl, hwôrl, wûrl, wôrl) /hwɜrl, hwɔrl, wɜrl, wɔrl/ *n.* [*count*] **1.** a circular arrangement of similar parts, as of leaves. **2.** one of the central ridges of a fingerprint. —**whorled,** *adj.*

who's (ho͞oz) /huwz/ *contraction.* a shortened form of **1.** *who is*: *Who's on first base?* **2.** *who has*: *Who's received a paycheck?*

whose (ho͞oz) /huwz/ *pron.* **1.** the form of the pronoun WHO or WHICH used to show that something is owned, appearing before a noun: *She is someone whose faith is strong. That's a word whose meaning escapes me.* **2.** This word is used in questions to mean "the one or ones belonging to what person or persons": *Whose umbrella is that?*

who•so•ev•er (ho͞o′sō ev′ər) /ˌhuwsowˈɛvər/ *pron.* whoever.

why (hwī, wī) /hway, way/ *adv., conj., n., pl.* **whys,** *interj.* —*adv.* **1.** (used to introduce a question) for what cause or reason or purpose?: *Why do you ask? Why are you here?* —*conj.* **2.** for what cause or reason: *I don't know why he left.* **3.** on account of which: *the reason why she refused.* **4.** the reason for which: *That is why he returned.* —*n.* [*count*] **5.** the cause or reason: *to figure out the whys and wherefores.* —*interj.* **6.** (used to express surprise, hesitation, or impatience): *Why, go right ahead! Why, what do you mean?*

WI, an abbreviation of: Wisconsin.

wick (wik) /wɪk/ *n.* [*count*] a twist of soft threads that in a candle or oil lamp draws up the liquid to be burned.

wick•ed (wik′id) /ˈwɪkɪd/ *adj.* **1.** morally bad; sinful; evil: *a wicked witch.* **2.** playfully mischievous. **3.** harmful; dangerous: *wicked, twisting roads.* **4.** unpleasant; foul: *a wicked odor.* **5.** *Slang.* wonderful; great: *has a wicked tennis serve.* —**wick′ed•ly,** *adv.* —**wick′ed•ness,** *n.* [*noncount*]

wick•er (wik′ər) /ˈwɪkər/ *n.* **1.** [*count*] a slender, easily bent twig that can be shaped to form baskets, furniture, etc. **2.** [*noncount*] twigs or sticks bent and woven together, used as the material for baskets, chairs, or the like; wickerwork. —*adj.* [*before a noun*] **3.** made of wicker; covered with wicker.

wick•er•work (wik′ər wûrk′) /ˈwɪkərˌwɜrk/ *n.* [*noncount*] things or items, as baskets, made of wicker.

wick•et (wik′it) /ˈwɪkɪt/ *n.* [*count*] **1.** a window or opening, often with a grating, as in a ticket office. **2.** a small door or gate, esp. one beside or forming part of a larger one. **3.** (in croquet) a hoop or arch. **4.** (in cricket) either of the two frameworks at which the bowler aims the ball.

wide (wīd) /wayd/ *adj.* and *adv.,* **wid•er, wid•est.** —*adj.* **1.** of great size or extent from side to side; broad: *the great wide lands of the prairie.* **2.** having a certain measurement from side to side: [*after a noun*]: *The doorway was only three feet wide.* [*before a noun; after a number of measurement*]: *a three-foot-wide doorway.* **3.** of great range or scope: *a wide selection of recordings.* **4.** fully opened: *He stared at the teacher with wide eyes.* **5.** [*usually: be* + ~] far from an aim or goal: *That remark is wide of the truth.* —*adv.* **6.** to the most; fully: *The door was wide open.* **7.** away from a target or objective: *The shot went wide.* **8.** over a large area: *The birds were scattered far and wide after the drought.* —**wide′ly,** *adv.*: *She is widely known as an expert in management.* —**wide′ness,** *n.* [*noncount*]

-wide, *suffix.* *-wide* is used to form adjectives with the meaning "extending or applying throughout a certain, given space," as mentioned by the noun: *community* + *-wide* → *communitywide* (= *applying to or throughout the community*); *countrywide; worldwide.*

wide′-awake′, *adj.* **1.** fully awake. **2.** alert.

wide′-eyed′, *adj.* having the eyes open wide, as in amazement or innocence.

wid•en (wīd′n) /ˈwaydn̩/ *v.* to (cause to) become wide: [~ + *obj*]: *The highway crew is widening the road up ahead.* [*no obj*]: *The road widens ahead so that more traffic can get through quicker.* —**wid′en•er,** *n.* [*count*]

wide•spread (wīd′spred′) /ˈwaydˈsprɛd/ *adj.* **1.** spread over a wide area: *widespread destruction.* **2.** occurring or found in many places or among many persons: *a widespread belief that he was, in fact, a crook.*

wid•ow (wid′ō) /ˈwɪdow/ *n.* [*count*] **1.** a woman whose husband has died and who has not remarried. **2.** a woman who is often left alone because her husband devotes his free time to a hobby or sport: *a golf widow.* —**wid′ow•hood′,** *n.* [*noncount*]

wid•owed (wid′ōd) /ˈwɪdowd/ *adj.* being a widow through the death of a husband.

wid•ow•er (wid′ō ər) /ˈwɪdowər/ *n.* [*count*] a man whose wife has died and who has not remarried.

width (width, witth) /wɪdθ, wɪtθ/ *n.* **1.** the size or amount of something measured from side to side; breadth: [*count*]: *a width of sixty feet.* [*noncount*]: *sixty feet in width.* **2.** [*count*] something, as a piece of cloth, of a particular width: *She cut a width of silk and began to sew it.*

wield (wēld) /wiyld/ *v.* [~ + *obj*] **1.** to exercise, use, or control: *They wielded the power in the government.* **2.** to use (a weapon, instrument, etc.) effectively; handle: *to wield a sword.* —**wield′er,** *n.* [*count*]

wie•ner (wē′nər) /ˈwiynər/ *n.* FRANKFURTER.

wife (wīf) /wayf/ *n.* [*count*], *pl.* **wives** (wīvz) /wayvz/. a married woman. —**wife′ly,** *adj.*

wig (wig) /wɪg/ *n.* [*count*] **1.** a covering of natural or artificial hair for the head. **2.** TOUPEE.

wig•gle (wig′əl) /ˈwɪgəl/ *v.,* **-gled, -gling,** *n.* —*v.* **1.** to move with quick, irregular, side-to-side movements: [~

+ *obj*]: *He wiggled his hips while he danced.* [*no obj*]: *Her toes wiggled while she slept.* —*n.* [*count*] **2.** a wiggling movement or motion. —**wig′gler,** *n.* [*count*] —**wig′gly,** *adj.,* **-gli•er, -gli•est.**

wig•wam (wig′wom, -wôm) /ˈwɪgwɒm, -wɔm/ *n.* [*count*] a North American Indian dwelling, often like a rounded tent in shape, made with poles and bark, mats, or skins.

wild (wīld) /wayld/ *adj.,* **-er, -est,** *adv., n.* —*adj.* **1.** living in a state of nature and not tamed: *wild animals running free in the forest.* **2.** growing or produced without being grown and cared for by humans, as flowers; not cultivated: *wild flowers.* **3.** without people living there; not inhabited; undeveloped: *wild country.* **4.** not civilized; barbarous; savage: *The wild Northmen raided the coasts of England.* **5.** having or showing violence or great strength and destruction: *a wild storm.* **6.** characterized by violent feelings: *a wild look.* **7.** very excited; frantic: *That glamorous movie star drives him wild.* **8.** [*be* + ~] very eager or enthusiastic: *She's wild about her new job.* **9.** not disciplined; unruly; reckless; uncontrollable: *a gang of wild boys.* **10.** not controlled by reason; not held back; uncontrolled: *He had some wild schemes to get rich quick.* **11.** wide of one's aim or goal: *a wild pitch.* **12.** (of a card) having its value decided by the wishes of the players: *Deuces are wild.* —*adv.* **13.** in a wild manner: *The gangs were running wild in the streets.* —*n.* [*count*] **14.** Often, **wilds.** [*plural*] an area of land that has not been cultivated; wilderness or wasteland. —**wild′ly,** *adv.: He ran off screaming wildly about snakes and demons after him.* —**wild′ness,** *n.* [*noncount*]

wild•cat (wīld′kat′) /ˈwayldˌkæt/ *n., pl.* **-cats,** also **-cat** for 1, *adj., v.,* **-cat•ted, -cat•ting.** —*n.* [*count*] **1.** a medium-sized cat, as the bobcat, related to the domestic cat. **2.** a quick-tempered or savage person. **3.** a well that is drilled in order to find out if there are deposits of oil or gas. —*adj.* **4.** characterized by or proceeding from reckless or unsound business methods: *wildcat stocks.* **5.** not approved of by a labor union: *a wildcat strike.* —*v.* **6.** to search (a particular area) for oil, gas, or ore without a good idea whether there are any deposits there: [~ + *obj*]: *to wildcat an offshore area.* [*no obj*]: *He had wildcatted for years off in the jungles.*

wil•de•beest (wil′də bēst′, vil′-) /ˈwɪldəˌbiyst, ˈvɪl-/ *n., pl.* **-beests, -beest.** GNU.

wil•der•ness (wil′dər nis) /ˈwɪldərnɪs/ *n.* [*count; usually singular*] a wild, uncultivated region, usually where humans do not live.

wild′-eyed′, *adj.* **1.** having a wild expression in the eyes. **2.** so extreme as to seem senseless: *a wild-eyed scheme; a wild-eyed radical politician.*

wild•fire (wīld′fīᵊr) /ˈwayldfayᵊr/ *n.* [*count*] **1.** a large fire that spreads rapidly and is hard to put out. —***Idiom.*** **2. like wildfire,** very rapidly and with unchecked force: *The rumor spread like wildfire.*

wild•flow•er or **wild flow•er** (wīld′flou′ər) /ˈwayldˌflawər/ *n.* [*count*] the flower of a plant that grows wild, or the plant itself.

wild•fowl (wīld′foul′) /ˈwayldˌfawl/ *n.* [*count*], *pl.* **-fowl, -fowls.** a wild duck, goose, or swan.

wild′-goose′ chase′, *n.* [*count*] a senseless search for something that does not exist or that cannot possibly be found or obtained: *They're off on another wild-goose chase to see if they can find a replacement part for that foreign car.*

wild•ing (wīl′ding) /ˈwayldɪŋ/ *n.* [*count*] **1.** a plant that grows wild, as a plant originally cultivated that now grows wild. **2.** [a wild animal. —*adj.* **3.** not cultivated; growing wild.

wild•life (wīld′līf′) /ˈwayldˌlayf/ *n.* [*noncount*] animals living in the wild: *to protect the environment and wildlife of a region.*

wild′ oat′, *n.* [*count*] **1.** a common weedy grass that looks like the cultivated oat. **2. sow one's wild oats,** to behave in an uncontrolled way, esp. sexually: *He said he had to sow his wild oats before he settled down to marry.*

wild′ rice′, *n.* [*noncount*] **1.** a tall grass of N North America that grows in water. **2.** the edible grain of this plant.

Wild′ West′, *n.* [*proper noun; usually: the* + ~] the western frontier region of the U.S. before the establishment of stable government.

wile (wīl) /wayl/ *n., v.,* **wiled, wil•ing.** —*n.* [*count*] **1.** a trick meant to fool, trap, or lure another. —*v.* **2. wile away,** to while away (time): [~ + *away* + *obj*]: *to wile away the hours lazily in the sun.* [~ + *obj* + *away*]: *to wile the days away.*

wil•ful (wil′fəl) /ˈwɪlfəl/ *adj.* WILLFUL.

will[1] (wil) /wɪl/ *auxiliary v.* and *v., pres.* **will;** *past* **would.** —*auxiliary, modal verb.* This word is used before the root form of the next verb **1.** to indicate that the action of that verb is going to take place in the future: *I will be there tomorrow.* **2.** to express willingness: *Nobody will help us.* **3.** to express a command: *You will report to the principal at once.* **4.** to mean "may be expected or supposed to": *You will not have forgotten him.* **5.** to express probability or to show what is likely: *They will be asleep by this time, don't you think?* **6.** to express customary action: *She will write for hours at a time. Boys will be boys.* **7.** to express capability: *This couch will seat four.* —*v.* [~ + *obj*] **8.** to wish; like: *Take what you will.*

will[2] (wil) /wɪl/ *n.* **1.** [*noncount*] the ability to do actions that one is conscious of and that one wishes to do deliberately: *the freedom of the will.* **2.** [*count*] the power of choosing or deciding: *a strong will.* **3.** [*count; usually singular*] wish or desire: *He went against his mother's will.* **4.** [*noncount*] purpose or determination: *the will to succeed.* **5.** [*noncount*] feelings, emotions, or regard toward another: *She still harbored a lot of ill will toward her old boss.* **6.** [*count*] a legal document stating what will happen to one's possessions or property after one's death. —*v.* **7.** [~ + *obj* + *to* + *verb*] to decide upon or bring about by an act of the will: *willed himself to get out of bed.* **8.** to give (one's possessions or property) to (someone) after one's death; bequeath: [~ + *obj* + *to* + *obj*]: *She willed the silver tea set to her daughter.* [~ + *obj* + *obj*]: *She willed her the silver tea set.* —***Idiom.*** **9. at will,** as one desires; whenever one chooses: *The kids were free to wander at will.*

will•ful (wil′fəl) /ˈwɪlfəl/ or **wil•ful,** *adj.* **1.** deliberate; intentional: *willful negligence.* **2.** unreasonably stubborn, determined, or headstrong. —**will′ful•ly,** *adv.* —**will′ful•ness,** *n.* [*noncount*]

wil•lies (wil′ēz) /ˈwɪliyz/ *n.* [*plural; the* + ~] nervousness; jitters: *Heights give him the willies.*

will•ing (wil′ing) /ˈwɪlɪŋ/ *adj.* **1.** [*be* + ~; *often:*~ + *to* + *verb*] consenting; agreeing; inclined: *was willing to go along with the plan.* **2.** cheerfully agreeing or enthusiastic about doing something; ready: *a willing student.* —**will′ing•ly,** *adv.* —**will′ing•ness,** *n.* [*noncount*]

will-o'-the-wisp (wil′ə *th*ə wisp′) /ˈwɪləðəˈwɪsp/ *n.* [*count*] **1.** a flickering light seen at night over marshy ground, believed to be caused by the burning of marsh gas. **2.** one that is hard to see or achieve: *Peace in that embattled part of the world is just a will-o'-the-wisp.*

wil•low (wil′ō) /ˈwɪlow/ *n.* **1.** [*count*] a tree or shrub with lance-shaped leaves and tough twigs, used esp. for wickerwork. **2.** [*noncount*] the wood of a willow.

wil•low•y (wil′ō ē) /ˈwɪlowiy/ *adj.,* **-i•er, -i•est. 1.** that can be bent easily; pliant; lithe. **2.** slender and graceful: *a willowy dancer.*

will•pow•er or **will pow•er** (wil′pou′ər) /ˈwɪlˌpawər/ *n.* [*noncount*] self-control and determination: *It takes willpower to train for a marathon race.*

wil•ly-nil•ly (wil′ē nil′ē) /ˈwɪliyˈnɪliy/ *adv.* **1.** whether desired or not. **2.** in a disorganized or unplanned manner; sloppily: *The schoolkids raced around the room willy-nilly.*

wilt[1] (wilt) /wɪlt/ *v.* **1.** to (cause to) become limp and drooping, as a flower: [*no obj*]: *The plants began to wilt in the hot weather.* [~ + *obj*]: *The hot weather will wilt the plants.* **2.** [*no obj*] to lose strength, vigor, or courage: *Under pressure he would wilt and give up.*

wilt[2] (wilt) /wɪlt/ *v. Archaic.* second pers. sing. pres. indic. of WILL[1].

wil•y (wī′lē) /ˈwayliy/ *adj.,* **-i•er, -i•est.** crafty; clever in a dishonest way; full of wiles; cunning: *a wily crook.* —**wil′i•ness,** *n.* [*noncount*]

wimp (wimp) /wɪmp/ *n.* [*count*] *Informal.* **1.** a weak or timid person. —*v.* **2. wimp out,** [*no obj*] to act like a wimp: *Don't wimp out on us when we need you!* —**wimp′y,** *adj.,* **-i•er, -i•est.**

win (win) /wɪn/ *v.,* **won** (wun) /wʌn/ **win•ning,** *n.* —*v.* **1.** to finish first, as in a race or contest; win a victory in: [~ + *obj*]: *She won the marathon.* [*no obj*]: *He never wins.* **2.** [~ + *obj*] to be victorious in (a battle, war, etc.): *They won the war.* **3.** to achieve by effort, as through hard work, or by competition or luck: [~ + *obj*]: *He won the prize.* [*no obj*]: *We never seem to win.* **4.** [~ + *obj*] to gain, as by one's good qualities, hard work, or influence: *She won the respect of her coworkers.* **5. win over,** to gain the favor, consent, or support of: [~ + *obj* + *over*]: *Her arguments eventually won us over.* [~ + *over* + *obj*]: *She could win over even the most stubborn oppo-*

nents. **—*n.*** [*count*] **6.** a victory, as in a game, a horse race, etc.

wince (wins) /wɪns/ *v.*, **winced, winc•ing,** *n.* **—*v.*** [*no obj*] **1.** to draw back or move away, as from a blow; flinch: *I winced as the nurse injected the serum in my arm.* **—*n.*** [*count*] **2.** a wincing movement.

winch (winch) /wɪntʃ/ *n.* [*count*] **1.** the crank or handle of a revolving machine. **2.** a device for hoisting or hauling.

wind[1] (*n.* wind, *Literary* wīnd; *v.* wind) / *n.* wɪnd, *Literary* waynd; *v.* wɪnd/ *n.* **1.** air in natural motion, esp. strong motion: [*count*]: *high winds.* [*noncount*]: *occasional gusts of wind.* **2. winds,** [*plural*] **a.** wind instruments. **b.** players of such instruments. **3.** [*noncount*] breath or breathing: *He had to stop running and catch his wind.* **4.** [*noncount*] a hint: *They caught wind of a scandal.* **5.** [*noncount*] empty talk; mere words: *His speech was a lot of wind.* **6.** [*noncount*] gas generated in the stomach and intestines. **—*v.*** [~ + *obj*] **7.** [*usually passive*] to make short of breath: *He was winded after the long race.* **—*Idiom.*** **8. how** or **which way the wind blows** or **lies,** what the tendency or likely direction of events will be: *Don't take sides in the argument just yet; let's wait and see which way the wind blows.* **9. in the wind,** about to occur or happen: *Change is very definitely in the wind.* **10. take the wind out of one's sails,** to destroy one's confidence or self-assurance.

wind[2] (wīnd) /waynd/ *v.*, **wound** (wound) /wawnd/ or (*Rare*) **wind•ed** (wīn′did) /ˌwayndɪd/; **wind•ing,** *n.* **—*v.* 1.** to have or take a curving or twisting course or direction; meander: [*no obj*]: *The road winds a bit and then straightens out.* [~ + *obj*]: *He wound his way down the path.* **2.** [~ + *obj*] to wrap, coil, or twine around (something): *winding thread on a spool.* **3.** [~ + *obj*] to tighten the spring of: *She wound the clock.* **4. wind down,** [*no obj*] **a.** to bring or come to a gradual end: *After a busy week the conference began to wind down.* **b.** to calm down; relax: *You need a vacation in order to wind down.* **5. wind up, a.** to (cause to) come to an end or conclusion: [*no obj*]: *The meeting wound up at about 4:30.* [~ + *obj* + *up*]: *Let's wind this meeting up.* **b.** [*no obj*] to arrive in a place or situation as a result of a course of action: *to wind up in jail.* **c.** to make tense or nervous; excite: [~ + *up* + *obj*]: *All the excitement wound up the kids.* [~ + *obj* + *up*]: *wound them up so much (that) they couldn't sleep.* **—*n.*** [*count*] **6.** a single turn, twist, or bend. —**wind′er,** *n.* [*count*]

wind•bag (wind′bag′) /ˈwɪndˌbæg/ *n.* [*count*] a tiresomely wordy talker or speaker.

wind•break (wind′brāk′) /ˈwɪndˌbreyk/ *n.* [*count*] something, as a growth of trees, serving as a shelter from the wind and to blunt its force.

wind•burn (wind′bûrn′) /ˈwɪndˌbɜrn/ *n.* [*noncount*] a reddening or inflammation of the skin caused by too much exposure to the wind. —**wind′burned′,** *adj.*

wind•chill fac′tor (wind′chil′) /ˈwɪndˌtʃɪl/ *n.* [*noncount*] the apparent temperature as it is felt on the exposed skin of the human body, resulting from the combination of temperature and wind speed.

wind•ed (win′did) /ˈwɪndɪd/ *adj.* **1.** out of breath. **2.** (used after an adjective) having wind or breath of a specified kind: *a long-winded speech.*

wind•fall (wind′fôl′) /ˈwɪndˌfɔl/ *n.* [*count*] an unexpected gain or piece of good fortune.

wind′ in′strument (wind) /wɪnd/ *n.* [*count*] a musical instrument played by forcing an air current through it, esp. the breath, classified as either a brass instrument, as the trombone or trumpet, or a woodwind, as the flute or clarinet.

wind•jam•mer (wind′jam′ər, win′-) /ˈwɪndˌdʒæmər, ˈwɪn-/ *n.* [*count*] a large sailing ship.

wind•lass (wind′ləs) /ˈwɪndləs/ *n.* [*count*] a device for hauling or hoisting, commonly having a drum-shaped cylinder on which a rope attached to the load is wound.

wind•mill (wind′mil′) /ˈwɪndˌmɪl/ *n.* [*count*] **1.** a machine for grinding or pumping, usually a building with a structure of four sails on the outside that is spun and driven by the wind acting on the sails. **—*v.* 2.** to (cause to) move like a windmill: [*no obj*]: *His arms were windmilling.* [~ + *obj*]: *windmilling his arms.*

win•dow (win′dō) /ˈwɪndow/ *n.* [*count*] **1.** an opening in a building, vehicle, etc., for letting in air or light. See illustration at HOUSE. **2.** such an opening with its frame, sashes, and panes of glass. **3.** WINDOWPANE. **4.** a period of time available or highly favorable for doing something: *a window of opportunity.* **5.** a portion of a computer screen on which data can be displayed independent of the rest of the screen.

win′dow box′, *n.* [*count*] a box for growing plants on a windowsill.

win′dow dress′ing, *n.* [*noncount*] **1.** the art, act, or technique of designing and arranging the display windows of a store. **2.** something done just to create a favorable impression.

win•dow•pane (win′dō pān′) /ˈwɪndowˌpeyn/ *n.* [*count*] a pane of glass for a window.

win′dow-shop′, *v.* [*no obj*], **-shopped, -shop•ping.** to look at articles in store windows without making purchases. —**win′dow shop′per,** *n.* [*count*]

win•dow•sill (win′dō sil′) /ˈwɪndowˌsɪl/ *n.* [*count*] the sill under a window.

wind•pipe (wind′pīp) /ˈwɪndpayp/ *n.* [*count*] the tube through which air passes from the throat to the lungs.

wind•shield (wind′shēld′, win′-) /ˈwɪndˌʃiyld, ˈwɪn-/ *n.* [*count*] a shield of glass above the dashboard of an automobile.

wind•sock (wind′sok′) /ˈwɪndˌsɒk/ *n.* [*count*] a mounted cloth cone that catches the wind to show its direction.

wind•surf•ing (wind′sûr′fing) /ˈwɪndˌsɜrfɪŋ/ *n.* [*noncount*] the sport of riding on a surfboard mounted with a sail.

wind′-swept′ (wind) /wɪnd/ *adj.* exposed to or blown by the wind: *the wind-swept coast of New England.*

wind′ tun′nel (wind) /wɪnd/ *n.* [*count*] a chamber or small room shaped like a tunnel, in which an object, as an aircraft, can be studied to determine how it is affected by airflow of controlled speed.

wind•up (wīnd′up′) /ˈwayndˌʌp/ *n.* [*count*] **1.** the conclusion of an action or activity. **2.** *Baseball.* the circular movement of a pitcher's arm before throwing the ball. **—*adj.*** [*before a noun*] **3.** made to function by winding an inside spring or the like: *windup toys.*

wind•ward (wind′wərd) /ˈwɪndwərd/ *adv.* **1.** toward the wind. **—*adj.* 2.** of, situated in, or moving toward the direction from which the wind blows (opposed to *leeward*).

wind•y (win′dē) /ˈwɪndiy/ *adj.*, **-i•er, -i•est. 1.** accompanied by or having wind: *a windy March day.* **2.** exposed to the wind: *a windy mountaintop.* **3.** characterized by or using pompous empty talk: *a long, windy speech.* —**wind′i•ness,** *n.* [*noncount*]

wine (win) /wayn/ *n.*, *v.*, **wined, win•ing. —*n.* 1.** the fermented juice of grapes, or sometimes of other fruits, used esp. as an alcoholic beverage: [*noncount*]: *a glass of wine.* [*count*]: *red wines.* **—*Idiom.* 2. wine and dine,** [~ + *obj*] to entertain (someone) lavishly.

win•er•y (wī′nə rē) /ˈwaynəriy/ *n.* [*count*], *pl.* **-er•ies.** an establishment where wine is made.

wing (wing) /wɪŋ/ *n.* [*count*] **1.** either of the two limbs or similar parts of birds, insects, and bats that are specially designed for enabling flight. **2.** something, as the vane of a windmill, that resembles a wing. **3.** one of a pair of usually long, flat parts of an aircraft that stick out from its body and provide lift. **4.** a part of a building that sticks out from a central or main part. **5.** an often extreme group or faction within an organization: *the libertarian wing of the party.* **6.** *Sports.* a position or player on the far side of the center, as in hockey. **7.** Usually, **wings.** [*plural*] the space at the side of a stage, usually not seen by the audience: *stood in the wings.* **—*v.* 8.** to travel on or as if on wings: [~ + *obj*]: *Birds wing their way south during the winter.* [*no obj*]: *Birds winging swiftly south.* **9.** [~ + *obj*] to wound in the wing or arm: *The rifle shot winged him.* **—*Idiom.* 10. in the wings,** ready to be called or put into action: *We have a new plan waiting in the wings.* **11. on the wing,** in flight; flying. **12. under one's wing,** under one's protection, training, or care: *takes all new trainees under her wing.* **13. wing it,** to do something without preparation; improvise. —**winged,** *adj.* —**wing′less,** *adj.*

wing•ding (wing′ding′) /ˈwɪŋˌdɪŋ/ *n.* [*count*] *Slang.* a noisy, exciting party.

wing•span (wing′span′) /ˈwɪŋˌspæn/ *n.* [*count*] the distance between the wing tips of an airplane or a bird.

wink (wingk) /wɪŋk/ *v.* **1.** to close and open (one eye) quickly, often as a hint or signal: [*no obj*]: *She winked at me to let me know she understood.* [~ + *obj*]: *He winked his eye.* **2.** to twinkle; gleam on and off: [*no obj*]: *A light winked in the distance.* [~ + *obj*]: *He winked the lights on and off.* **3. wink at,** [~ + *at* + *obj*] to deliberately ignore (wrongdoing): *The police seemed to wink at minor violations of the law.* **—*n.*** [*count*] **4.** an act of winking. **5.** an instant: *in the wink of an eye.* **6.** the least bit: *She didn't sleep a wink.*

win•ner (win′ər) /ˈwɪnər/ *n.* [*count*] one that wins; victor.

win•ning (win′ing) /ˈwɪnɪŋ/ *n.* **1.** [*noncount*] the act of one that wins. **2.** Usually, **winnings.** [*plural*] something won, esp. money. —*adj.* [*usually: before a noun*] **3.** successful or victorious: *a winning team.* **4.** pleasing or pleasant: *a winning personality.* —**win′ning•ly,** *adv.*

win•now (win′ō) /ˈwɪnow/ *v.* [~ + *obj*] **1.** to free (grain) of chaff with a forced current of air. **2.** to separate or distinguish (something valuable from something worthless): *to winnow fact from fiction.* —**win′now•er,** *n.* [*count*]

win•o (wī′nō) /ˈwaynow/ *n.* [*count*], *pl.* **-os.** a person who is addicted to wine.

win•some (win′səm) /ˈwɪnsəm/ *adj.* sweetly or innocently charming; winning: *a winsome youth; a winsome smile.* —**win′some•ly,** *adv.* —**win′some•ness,** *n.* [*noncount*]

win•ter (win′tər) /ˈwɪntər/ *n.* **1.** the cold season between autumn and spring: [*noncount*]: *to ski all winter.* [*count*]: *harsh winters.* **2.** [*noncount*] cold weather: *a touch of winter in the air.* —*adj.* **3.** of or relating to winter: *winter sports.* **4.** planted in the autumn to be harvested in the spring or summer: *winter rye.* —*v.* [*no obj*] **5.** to spend the winter: *to winter in Florida.*

win•ter•ize (win′tə rīz′) /ˈwɪntəˌrayz/ *v.* [~ + *obj*], **-ized, -iz•ing.** to prepare (a house, car, etc.) to withstand cold weather: *to winterize the house by adding insulation.*

win•ter•time (win′tər tīm′) /ˈwɪntərˌtaym/ *n.* [*noncount*] the season of winter.

win•try (win′trē) /ˈwɪntriy/ also **wintery** (win′tə rē) /ˈwɪntəriy/ *adj.,* **-tri•er** also **-i•er, -tri•est** also **-i•est. 1.** of or like winter: *a cold, wintry day.* **2.** suggesting winter, as in lack of cheer or friendliness: *He gave her a wintry smile without a hint of kindness.*

win′-win′, *adj.* providing an advantage to both sides, as in a negotiation: *a win-win situation.*

wipe (wīp) /wayp/ *v.,* **wiped, wip•ing,** *n.* —*v.* **1.** [~ + *obj*] to clean or dry by patting or rubbing: *to wipe the furniture clean; to wipe the dishes.* **2.** [~ + *obj*] to remove by or as if by rubbing: *wiped the tears from her eyes; Wipe that thought from your mind.* **3. wipe out, a.** to destroy completely: [~ + *out* + *obj*]: *They wiped out the supply depots.* [~ + *obj* + *out*]: *The crews wiped them out.* **b.** to murder: [~ + *out* + *obj*]: *to wipe out his gangland rivals.* [~ + *obj* + *out*]: *to wipe them out.* —*n.* [*count*] **4.** an act of wiping. —**wip′er,** *n.* [*count*]

wire (wīᵊr) /wayᵊr/ *n., adj., v.,* **wired, wir•ing.** —*n.* **1.** a thin, slender, threadlike piece of metal: [*noncount*]: *a piece of wire.* [*count*]: *copper wires.* **2.** [*count*] a length of such metal used to conduct current in electrical, cable, telegraph, or telephone systems. **3. a.** [*count*] a telegram: *Send him a wire.* **b.** [*noncount*] a telegraphic system: *Send the message by wire.* **4.** [*count*] the finish line of a racetrack. —*adj.* [*before a noun*] **5.** made of wire. —*v.* **6.** [~ + *obj*] to equip or furnish with wire: *to wire a building with new electrical outlets.* **7.** to send (a message) to (someone) by telegraph: [~ + *obj* + *to* + *obj*]: *to wire a message to headquarters.* [~ + *obj* + *obj*]: *to wire her the news.* [~ (+ *obj*) + *that clause*]: *to wire (her) that she won the prize.* **8.** [~ + *obj*] to connect (a receiver, neighborhood, or building) to a television cable and other equipment so that cable television programs may be received. **9.** [~ + *obj*] to connect (a room, telephone, etc.) to equipment so as to enable listening to or recording conversations secretly; to bug: *The spies assumed (that) their house was wired.* —***Idiom.* 10. down to the wire,** to the very last moment or the very end. **11. under the wire,** just within the limit or deadline.

wired (wīᵊrd) /wayᵊrd/ *adj.* **1.** equipped, secured, strengthened, or supported with wires: *The house is wired for cable.* **2.** *Slang.* tense with excitement or anticipation.

wire•less (wīᵊr lis) /ˈwayᵊrlɪs/ *adj.* **1.** having no wire. —*n.* [*count*] **2.** *Chiefly Brit.* a radio.

wire′ serv′ice, *n.* [*count*] an agency or business that sends news stories by wire to its customers.

wire•tap (wīᵊr tap′) /ˈwayᵊrˌtæp/ *n., v.,* **-tapped, -tap•ping.** —*n.* [*count*] **1.** an act or instance of making a secret connection to a telephone or telegraph wire in order to intercept conversations and gain information. —*v.* **2.** to listen in on by means of a wiretap: [~ + *obj*]: *to wiretap conversations; to wiretap a phone.* [*no obj*]: *The detectives were busy wiretapping.* —**wire′tap′per,** *n.* [*count*]

wir•ing (wīᵊr ing) /ˈwayᵊrɪŋ/ *n.* [*noncount*] a system of electric wires, as in a building.

wir•y (wīᵊr ē) /ˈwayᵊriy/ *adj.,* **-i•er, -i•est. 1.** resembling wire. **2.** (of a person's body) lean, supple, and strong. —**wir′i•ness,** *n.* [*noncount*]

Wis. or **Wisc.,** an abbreviation of: Wisconsin.

wis•dom (wiz′dəm) /ˈwɪzdəm/ *n.* [*noncount*] the quality or state of being wise.

wis′dom tooth′, *n.* [*count*] the third molar, a tooth in the back of the mouth, on each side of the upper and lower jaws.

wise[1] (wīz) /wayz/ *adj.,* **wis•er, wis•est,** *v.,* **wised, wis•ing.** —*adj.* **1.** having or showing understanding and good judgment: *a wise decision.* [*t* + *be* + ~ (+ *of* + *obj*) + *to* + *verb*]: *It was not very wise of him to be rude.* **2.** having or showing deep knowledge or learning. —*v.* **3. wise up,** *Slang.* to (cause to) become aware; to (cause to) learn correct or right information: [*no obj*]: *He finally wised up to what they were doing to him.* [~ + *obj* + *up*]: *They wised him up to what they were doing.* —***Idiom.* 4. be** or **get wise to,** *Slang.* to be or become aware of; learn: *He is wise to our plans.* **5. get wise,** *Slang.* to become presumptuous or impertinent. —**wise′ly,** *adv.* —**Related Words.** WISE is an adjective, WISDOM is a noun, WISELY is an adverb: *She is a wise shopper. She has a lot of wisdom for her age. They spent their money wisely.*

wise[2] (wīz) /wayz/ *n.* [*count*] way; manner: *In no wise is it true.*

-wise, *suffix.* **1.** *-wise* is used to form adjectives and adverbs with the meaning "in a particular manner, position, or direction": *clockwise (= moving in a direction like the hands of a clock).* **2.** *-wise* is also used to form adverbs with the meaning "with reference to": *Timewise we can finish the work, but qualitywise, I'm not so sure.*

wise•a•cre (wīz′ā′kər) /ˈwayzˌeykər/ *n.* SMART ALECK.

wise•crack (wīz′krak′) /ˈwayzˌkræk/ *n.* [*count*] **1.** a clever, sarcastic, or impolite remark. —*v.* [*no obj*] **2.** to make a wisecrack.

wise′ guy′, *n.* [*count*] *Informal.* a person who pretends to know more than he or she does; smart aleck.

wish (wish) /wɪʃ/ *v.* [*not: be* + ~*-ing*] **1.** to want; desire: [~ + *to* + *verb*]: *I wish to stay here.* [~ + *obj* + *to* + *verb*]: *I wish him to obey.* **2.** to desire (a person or thing) to be as stated, even if it is impossible: [~ + *obj* (+ *to* + *be*) + *adjective*]: *We wished the matter (to be) settled.* [~ + (*that*) *clause*]: *We wished that the matter would be settled.* **3.** [*no obj;* (~ + *for*)] to express a hope or desire for: *She closed her eyes and wished for peace on earth.* **4.** [~ + *obj* + *obj*] to bid, as in greeting: *I wished her a good morning.* **5. wish on, a.** [*often with a negative word or phrase;* ~ + *obj* + *on* + *obj*] to pass or desire to pass (something unwanted or bad) to another: *I wouldn't wish this awful weather on my worst enemy.* **b.** Also, **wish upon.** to use as a magical charm while making a wish: *to wish upon a star.* —*n.* [*count*] **6.** an act or instance of wishing. **7.** something wished or desired: *Her last wish was to see her home country.* **8.** a request or command: *It was his wish that she become the new boss.* —**wish′er,** *n.* [*count*]

wish•bone (wish′bōn′) /ˈwɪʃbown/ *n.* [*count*] a forked or V-shaped bone found in front of the breastbone in most birds.

wish•ful (wish′fəl) /ˈwɪʃfəl/ *adj.* based on a wish rather than reality: *wishful thinking.* —**wish′ful•ly,** *adv.* —**wish′ful•ness,** *n.* [*noncount*]

wish•y-wash•y (wish′ē wosh′ē, -wô′shē) /ˈwɪʃiyˌwɒʃiy, -ˌwɔʃiy/ *adj.* lacking strength or character; ineffectual: *a wishy-washy leader.* —**wish•y-wash•i•ly** (wish′ē wosh′ə-lē, -wô′shə-) /ˈwɪʃiyˌwɒʃəliy, -ˌwɔʃə-/ *adv.* —**wish′y-wash′i•ness,** *n.* [*noncount*]

wisp (wisp) /wɪsp/ *n.* [*count*] **1.** a small bundle of straw or hay. **2.** a thin lock of hair. **3.** a thin puff or streak, as of smoke. **4.** a person or thing that is small or delicate. —**wisp′y,** *adj.,* **-i•er, -i•est.**

wis•te•ri•a (wi stēr′ē ə) /wɪˈstɪəriyə/ also **wis•tar•i•a** (wi stēr′-, -stâr′-) /wɪˈstɪər-, -ˈstɛər-/ *n.* [*count*], *pl.* **-ri•as.** a climbing shrub with flower clusters in white, pale purple, blue-violet, or pink.

wist•ful (wist′fəl) /ˈwɪstfəl/ *adj.* having or showing thoughtful, sometimes sad, wishing or longing: *a wistful look.* —**wist′ful•ly,** *adv.* —**wist′ful•ness,** *n.* [*noncount*]

wit[1] (wit) /wɪt/ *n.* **1.** [*noncount*] keen intelligence; astuteness. **2.** [*noncount*] quickness; cleverness: *He lacked the wit to respond in time.* **3.** [*count*] a person having or noted for being amusingly clever. **4.** Usually, **wits.** [*plural*] **a.** the ability to think quickly and clearly; resourcefulness; ingenuity: *In a crisis he's able to keep his wits about him.* **b.** mental faculties; senses: *scared out of her* *wits.* —***Idiom.*** **5. at one's wit's** or **wits' end,** drained or empty of all ideas or mental resources.

wit² (wit) /wɪt/ *v.,* **wist** (wist) /wɪst/ **wit•ting.** —***Idiom.*** **to wit,** [*no obj*] that is to say; namely: *spoke several languages, to wit, English, French, Spanish, German, and Japanese.*

witch (wich) /wɪtʃ/ *n.* [*count*] **1.** a person who is believed to practice magic, esp. black magic. **2.** an ugly or nasty woman. —**witch′y,** *adj.,* **-i•er, -i•est.**

witch•craft (wich′kraft′) /ˈwɪtʃˌkræft/ *n.* [*noncount*] the art or practices of a witch; magic, esp. evil magic; sorcery.

witch′ doc′tor, *n.* [*count*] a person in some societies who uses magic, esp. to cure illness.

witch′ hunt′, *n.* [*count*] an intense, often highly public effort to discover and expose someone who is thought to be disloyal or subversive usually on the basis of slight or doubtful evidence.

with (with, wiꝧ) /wɪθ, wɪð/ *prep.* **1.** accompanied by: *I will go with you.* **2.** in relation to: *She has already dealt with the problem.* **3.** characterized by or having: *a person with initiative.* **4.** by means of; using: *I'll cut the meat with a knife.* **5.** in a manner showing: *He worked with diligence.* **6.** in comparison to: *How does their plan compare with ours?* **7.** in regard to: *They were very pleased with the gift.* **8.** owing to; because of; in light of: *He was shaking with rage.* **9.** from: *She hated to part with her book when it was bedtime.* **10.** against: *Don't fight with your sister.* **11.** in the keeping of: *We left our cat with a friend during our vacation.* **12.** in the judgment of: *Her argument carried weight with the trustees.* **13.** at the same time as or immediately after: *With that last remark, she left.* **14.** of the same opinion as or, in any case, supporting: *Are you with me on this issue?* **15.** in the same household as: *He lives with his parents.* —***Idiom.*** **16. with it,** aware of and participating in up-to-date trends. —**Usage.** See BY.

with•draw (wiꝧ drô′, with-) /wɪðˈdrɔ, wɪθ-/ *v.,* **-drew, -drawn, -draw•ing. 1.** to draw back, away, to the side, or aside: [∼ + *obj*]: *The general withdrew his army.* [*no obj*]: *He withdrew to another room.* **2.** [∼ + *obj*] to remove, retract, or recall: *I withdraw my objection to your proposal.* **3.** to remove oneself from participation, as in an activity: [*no obj*]: *He withdrew from the contest.* [∼ + *obj*]: *He withdrew himself from the contest.* **4.** [∼ + *obj*] to take (money) from a place of deposit.

with•draw•al (wiꝧ drô′əl, with-) /wɪðˈdrɔəl, wɪθ-/ *n.* **1.** the act of withdrawing or state of being withdrawn: [*count*]: *a sudden withdrawal.* [*noncount*]: *a feeling of emotional withdrawal.* **2.** [*count*] something that is withdrawn, as a sum of money from a bank account. **3.** [*noncount*] the discontinuance of use of an addictive drug: *suffering from withdrawal.*

with•drawn (wiꝧ drôn′, with-) /wɪðˈdrɔn, wɪθ-/ *v.* **1.** pp. of WITHDRAW. —*adj.* **2.** removed, as from circulation, content, or competition. **3.** shy; introverted; retiring: *a quiet, withdrawn child.*

with•er (wiꝧ′ər) /ˈwɪðər/ *v.* **1.** to (cause to) shrivel or fade: [*no obj*]: *The plants are withering in the heat.* [∼ + *obj*]: *The heat has withered the entire corn crop.* **2.** [∼ + *obj*] to render powerless; stun: *She withered him with a scornful look.* —**with′er•ing•ly,** *adv.: She looked at him witheringly.*

with•hold (with hōld′, wiꝧ-) /wɪθˈhowld, wɪð-/ *v.* [∼ + *obj*], **-held, -hold•ing. 1.** to hold back; restrain or check. **2.** to keep from giving or granting: *He withheld his support of the project.* **3.** to collect (taxes) at the source of income, esp. as a deduction from salary or wages. —**with•hold′ing,** *n.* [*noncount*]

with•in (wiꝧ in′, with-) /wɪðˈɪn, wɪθ-/ *prep.* **1.** in or into the interior of; inside: *The noise came from within the house.* **2.** in the limits of; not beyond: *to live within one's income.* **3.** in the field, sphere, or scope of: *within the family; not within my power.* —*adv.* **4.** in or into an interior or inner part: *They proceeded within.* **5.** in the mind, heart, or soul; inwardly: *listening to the voice within.*

with•out (wiꝧ out′, with-) /wɪðˈawt, wɪθ-/ *prep.* **1.** with no or none of; lacking: *He did it without help.* **2.** free from; excluding: *a world without hunger.* **3.** not accompanied by: *Don't go without me.* **4.** at, on, or to the outside of: *both within and without the city.* —*adv.* **5.** outside. **6.** outdoors. **7.** lacking something implied or understood: *For years they were too poor and simply had to go without.*

with•stand (with stand′, wiꝧ-) /wɪθˈstænd, wɪð-/ *v.* [∼ + *obj*], **-stood, -stand•ing.** to resist or oppose, esp. successfully: *I could hardly withstand the pain.*

wit•less (wit′ləs) /ˈwɪtləs/ *adj.* lacking wit or intelligence; stupid. —**wit′less•ly,** *adv.*

wit•ness (wit′nis) /ˈwɪtnɪs/ *v.* [∼ + *obj*] **1.** to see, hear, or know by personal presence and experience: *to witness a crime.* **2.** to be present at and show this by writing one's signature: *He witnessed her will.* —*n.* **3.** [*count*] a person who has witnessed something, esp. one who is able to declare what has taken place: *a witness to the accident.* **4.** [*count*] a person who gives testimony, as in a court of law. **5.** [*noncount*] something serving as evidence: *His lined, gray face is witness to his suffering.*

wit•ted (wit′id) /ˈwɪtɪd/ *adj.* having wit or intelligence: *quick-witted; slow-witted.*

wit•ti•cism (wit′ə siz′əm) /ˈwɪtəˌsɪzəm/ *n.* [*count*] a witty, clever, or funny remark.

wit•ting•ly (wit′ing lē) /ˈwɪtɪŋliy/ *adv.* with awareness; with full knowledge: *wittingly told a lie.*

wit•ty (wit′ē) /ˈwɪtiy/ *adj.,* **-ti•er, -ti•est.** having or showing wit; amusingly clever: *a witty fellow; a witty remark.* —**wit•ti•ly** (wit′l ē) /ˈwɪtḷiy/ *adv.* —**wit′ti•ness,** *n.* [*noncount*]

wives (wīvz) /wayvz/ *n.* pl. of WIFE.

wiz•ard (wiz′ərd) /ˈwɪzərd/ *n.* [*count*] **1.** a magician or sorcerer. **2.** a person of amazing skill, ability, or accomplishment: *She's a wizard at chemistry.* —**wiz•ard•ry** (wiz′ər drē) /ˈwɪzərdriy/ *n.* [*noncount*]

wiz•ened (wiz′ənd, wē′zənd) /ˈwɪzənd, ˈwiyzənd/ *adj.* withered; shriveled; showing or having lines in the skin, as from age.

wk., an abbreviation of: **1.** week. **2.** work.

wkly., an abbreviation of: weekly.

WNW, an abbreviation of: west-northwest.

w/o, an abbreviation of: without.

wob•ble (wob′əl) /ˈwɒbəl/ *v.,* **-bled, -bling,** *n.* —*v.* **1.** [*no obj*] to move unsteadily with a side-to-side motion: *The unbalanced wheel wobbled as he drove slowly to the repair shop.* **2.** to (cause to) be unsteady; (cause to) tremble: [*no obj*]: *The table wobbled on its uneven legs.* [∼ + *obj*]: *The champ wobbled his opponent with the next punch.* **3.** [*no obj*] to be undecided or change one's mind too readily; vacillate; waver: *The president wobbled on the question of higher taxes.* —*n.* [*count*] **4.** a wobbling movement. —**wob′bly,** *adj.,* **-bli•er, -bli•est:** *feeling a little wobbly after having the flu.* —**wob′bli•ness,** *n.* [*noncount*]

woe (wō) /wow/ *n.* **1.** [*noncount*] great distress or trouble: *a life of woe.* **2.** [*count*] a cause of such distress or trouble; an affliction: *the woes of life.*

woe•be•gone′ (wō′bi gôn′, -gon′) /ˈwowbɪˌgɔn, -ˌgɒn/ *adj.* expressing or showing woe; showing sadness from distress or trouble; forlorn: *a woebegone look on his face.*

woe•ful (wō′fəl) /ˈwowfəl/ *adj.* **1.** full of woe; wretched: *a woeful situation in the war-torn country.* **2.** affected with, characterized by, or causing woe: *the woeful news of the tragedy.* **3.** of poor quality; awful; terrible; deplorable: *a woeful bunch of job applicants.* —**woe′ful•ly,** *adv.: a woefully inadequate diet.* —**woe′ful•ness,** *n.* [*noncount*]

wok (wok) /wɒk/ *n.* [*count*] a large bowl-shaped pan used esp. in cooking Chinese food.

woke (wōk) /wowk/ *v.* a pt. of WAKE¹.

wok•en (wō′kən) /ˈwowkən/ *v.* a pp. of WAKE¹.

wolf (wo͝olf) /wʊlf/ *n.* [*count*], *pl.* **wolves** (wo͝olvz), *v.,* **wolfed, wolf•ing.** —*n.* [*count*] **1.** a meat-eating animal resembling and related to the dog. **2.** a cruel, thieving, greedy person. **3.** a man who tries to lure women into romantic relationships. —*v.* [∼ + *obj*] **4.** to eat very greedily or quickly; devour with great haste: *He wolfed (down) his food.* —***Idiom.*** **5. cry wolf,** to give a false alarm: *The boy cried wolf so many times no one believed him when a real emergency arose.* **6. wolf in sheep's clothing,** [*count*] a person who hides evil beneath an innocent outer appearance. —**wolf′ish,** *adj.*

wolf•hound (wo͝olf′hound′) /ˈwʊlfˌhawnd/ *n.* [*count*] a large dog that was once used in hunting wolves.

wolf•ram (wo͝ol′frəm) /ˈwʊfrəm/ *n.* TUNGSTEN.

wol•ver•ine (wo͝ol′və rēn′) /ˌwʊlvəˈriyn/ *n.* [*count*] a strong, stocky Northern Hemisphere animal of the weasel family.

wom•an (wo͝om′ən) /ˈwʊmən/ *n., pl.* **wom•en** (wim′in) /ˈwɪmɪn/. **1.** [*count*] an adult female person. **2.** [*count*] a female servant or attendant. **3.** [*noncount*] women thought of as a group; womankind. **4.** [*noncount*] feminine nature, characteristics, or feelings. —*adj.* [*before a noun*] **5.** female: *a woman plumber; a woman astronaut.*

-woman, *suffix.* *-woman* is used to form nouns with the meaning "involving a woman; a woman in the role of:" *chairwoman; spokeswoman.*

wom•an•hood (wŏŏm′ən hŏŏd′) /ˈwʊmənˌhʊd/ *n.* [*noncount*] **1.** the state or time of being a woman. **2.** traditional womanly qualities. **3.** women thought of as a group.

wom•an•ish (wŏŏm′ə nish) /ˈwʊmə nɪʃ/ *adj.* **1.** characteristic of or like a woman. **2.** (of a man) weakly feminine; effeminate.

wom•an•ize (wŏŏm′ə nīz′) /ˈwʊməˌnayz/ *v.* [*no obj*], **-ized, -iz•ing.** to chase after women regularly. —**wom′an•iz′er,** *n.* [*count*]

wom•an•kind (wŏŏm′ən kīnd′) /ˈwʊmənˌkaynd/ *n.* [*noncount*] women thought of as a group and as distinguished from men.

wom•an•like (wŏŏm′ən līk′) /ˈwʊmənˌlayk/ *adj.* womanly.

wom•an•ly (wŏŏm′ən lē) /ˈwʊmənliy/ *adj.* having qualities traditionally thought of as being typical of women; feminine. —**wom′an•li•ness,** *n.* [*noncount*]

womb (wōōm) /wuwm/ *n.* [*count*] **1.** UTERUS. **2.** the place in which something is formed or produced: *The laboratory was the womb of new discoveries.*

wom•bat (wom′bat) /ˈwɒmbæt/ *n.* [*count*] a burrowing, plant-eating Australian animal about the size of a badger.

wom•en•folk (wim′in fōk′) /ˈwɪmɪnˌfowk/ also **wom′en•folks′,** *n.* [*plural*] women thought of as a group.

wom′en's libera′tion, *n.* [*noncount*] a political movement to gain rights and opportunities for women equal to those of men. —**wom′en's libera′tionist,** *n.* [*count*]

won (wun) /wʌn/ *v.* pt. and pp. of WIN.

won•der (wun′dər) /ˈwʌndər/ *v.* **1.** to think about and ask oneself about something; to be curious about; speculate: [*no obj*]: *says he didn't do it, but I still wonder.* [~ + *clause*]: *I wonder what she's doing tonight.* **2.** [*no obj*] to be filled with awe or amazement; be stunned; marvel: *I have often wondered at her cleverness.* **3.** [~ + *clause*] This word is sometimes used to introduce a request: *I wonder if you would help me.* —*n.* **4.** [*noncount*] a feeling of amazement, puzzled interest, or reverent admiration: *We were filled with wonder when we saw the great cathedral.* **5.** [*count*] a cause of surprise, astonishment, or admiration: *one of the wonders of the ancient world.* —*adj.* [*before a noun*] **6.** being very good or amazing in effect or ability: *a new wonder drug.*

won•der•ful (wun′dər fəl) /ˈwʌndərfəl/ *adj.* **1.** excellent; marvelous: *a wonderful day; a wonderful time at the party.* **2.** causing wonder; extraordinary: *a scene wonderful to behold.* —**won′der•ful•ly,** *adv.* —**won′der•ful•ness,** *n.* [*noncount*]

won•der•land (wun′dər land′) /ˈwʌndərˌlænd/ *n.* **1.** [*noncount*] an imaginary land of wonders or marvels. **2.** [*count*] a scene or place of special beauty or delight: *The park was a wonderland of nature.*

won•der•ment (wun′dər mənt) /ˈwʌndərmənt/ *n.* [*noncount*] an expression, cause, or state of wonder.

won•drous (wun′drəs) /ˈwʌndrəs/ *adj.* wonderful; remarkable. —**won′drous•ly,** *adv.*

wont (wônt, wōnt, wunt) /wɔnt, wownt, wʌnt/ *adj.* [*be* + ~ + *to* + *verb*] **1.** accustomed; used: *She is wont to rise at dawn.* —*n.* [*noncount; one's* + ~] **2.** custom; habit: *It was his wont to swim every day.*

won't (wōnt) /wownt/ *contraction.* a shortened form of *will not.*

won ton or **won•ton** (won′ ton′) /ˈwɒnˌ tɒn/ *n.* [*count*] a Chinese dumpling filled with pieces of pork and seasonings and boiled and served in soup.

woo (wōō) /wuw/ *v.* [~ + *obj*] **1.** to seek the love of, esp. with a view to marriage: *He wooed his lady love.* **2.** to seek or invite: *to woo fame.* **3.** to seek to persuade (a person, group, etc.), as to do something: *The new tax plan was not enough to woo the voters to change their vote.* —**woo′er,** *n.* [*count*]

wood (wŏŏd) /wʊd/ *n.* **1.** the hard, fiberlike substance that makes up most of the stem and branches of a tree or shrub beneath the bark: [*noncount*]: *fine, hard wood.* [*count*]: *different hard woods.* **2.** [*noncount*] timber or lumber. **3.** [*noncount*] firewood. **4.** [*count*] Often, **woods.** [*plural*] a thick growth of trees; forest: *a wood in the valley.* **5.** [*count*] any of a set of four golf clubs that originally had wooden heads. —*adj.* [*before a noun*] **6.** made of wood; wooden. **7.** used to store, work with, or carry wood. **8.** dwelling or growing in woods. —***Idiom.*** **9. out of the woods,** no longer in a dangerous, critical, or difficult situation or condition; safe: *The country is not out of the woods yet; a worse crisis awaits us.*

wood•chuck (wŏŏd′chuk′) /ˈwʊdˌtʃʌk/ *n.* [*count*] a stocky North American animal that burrows in holes and hibernates in the winter. Also called **groundhog.**

wood•cut•ter (wŏŏd′kut′ər) /ˈwʊdˌkʌtər/ *n.* [*count*] a person who cuts down trees, esp. for firewood. —**wood′cut′ting,** *n.* [*noncount*]

wood•ed (wŏŏd′id) /ˈwʊdɪd/ *adj.* covered with woods or trees.

wood•en (wŏŏd′n) /ˈwʊdn̩/ *adj.* **1.** made of wood: *a large wooden crate.* **2.** stiff, ungainly, or awkward: *walking with slow, wooden steps.* **3.** lacking life, spirit, or animation; dull; spiritless: *gave a wooden answer to the question.* —**wood′en•ly,** *adv.* —**wood′en•ness,** *n.* [*noncount*]

wood•land (wŏŏd′land′, -lənd) /ˈwʊdˌlænd, -lənd/ *n.* land covered with woods or trees: [*noncount*]: *healthy woodland.* [*count*]: *beautiful woodlands.*

wood•peck•er (wŏŏd′pek′ər) /ˈwʊdˌpɛkər/ *n.* [*count*] a climbing bird with a bill like a chisel that it hammers repeatedly into wood of trees in search of insects.

woods•man (wŏŏdz′mən) /ˈwʊdzmən/ also **wood′man.** *n.* [*count*], *pl.* **-men.** Also, **woodman.** a person who is accustomed to life in the woods and skilled in the arts of the woods.

woods•y (wŏŏd′zē) /ˈwʊdziy/ *adj.,* **-i•er, -i•est.** of or suggesting woods: *a woodsy area near the town.*

wood•wind (wŏŏd′wind′) /ˈwʊdˌwɪnd/ *n.* [*count*] **1.** a musical wind instrument in which sound is produced by the player's blowing through a mouth hole or on a reed, causing an air column to vibrate, as a flute, clarinet, oboe, or bassoon. **2. woodwinds,** [*plural*] the section of an orchestra or band comprising these instruments.

wood•work (wŏŏd′wûrk′) /ˈwʊdˌwɜrk/ *n.* [*noncount*] **1.** objects or parts made of wood, as furniture. **2.** interior wooden fittings, as doors or moldings, in a house. —***Idiom.*** **3. come out of the woodwork,** to emerge from or as if from a hiding place: *Suddenly all sorts of volunteers started coming out of the woodwork.* —**wood′work′er,** *n.* [*count*]

wood•work•ing (wŏŏd′wûr′king) /ˈwʊdˌwɜrkɪŋ/ *n.* [*noncount*] **1.** the act or art of making things with wood. —*adj.* [*before a noun*] **2.** of, relating to, or used for shaping wood: *woodworking tools.*

wood•y (wŏŏd′ē) /ˈwʊdiy/ *adj.,* **-i•er, -i•est. 1.** having many woods or a great deal of wooded area; wooded. **2.** made of or containing wood. **3.** resembling wood. —**wood′i•ness,** *n.* [*noncount*]

woof[1] (wŏŏf, wōōf) /wʊf, wuwf/ *n.* [*noncount*] **1.** the threads that lace at right angles with the warp in a woven fabric. **2.** texture; fabric.

woof[2] (wŏŏf) /wʊf/ *n.* [*count*] **1.** the bark of a dog, esp. when gruff and low-pitched. —*v.* [*no obj*] **2.** to make this sound.

woof•er (wŏŏf′ər) /ˈwʊfər/ *n.* [*count*] a loudspeaker designed to reproduce low-frequency sounds.

wool (wŏŏl) /wʊl/ *n.* [*noncount*] **1.** the fine, soft, curly hair that forms the fleece of some animals, esp. sheep. **2.** yarn, a fabric, or a garment of wool. **3.** something resembling the wool of sheep: *steel wool.* —***Idiom.*** **4. pull the wool over someone's eyes,** to deceive or delude someone.

wool•en (wŏŏl′ən) /ˈwʊlən/ *adj.* **1.** of, made of, or consisting of wool. —*n.* **2. woolens,** [*plural*] wool cloth or clothing. Also, *esp. Brit.,* **wool′len.**

wool•gath•er•ing (wŏŏl′gath′ər ing) /ˈwʊlˌgæðərɪŋ/ *n.* [*noncount*] thinking idly; daydreaming, or not paying attention to one's surroundings.

wool•ly or **wool•y** (wŏŏl′ē) /ˈwʊliy/ *adj.,* **-li•er** or **-i•er, -li•est** or **-i•est,** *n., pl.* **-lies** or **-ies.** —*adj.* **1.** of or resembling wool. **2.** covered with wool or something resembling it. **3.** rough, lively, and disorderly: *a wild and woolly frontier town.* **4.** unclear; disorganized: *woolly thinking.* —*n.* [*count*] **5.** *Western U.S.* a sheep. **6.** Also, **wool′ie.** Usually, **woollies** or **woolies.** [*plural*] a piece of clothing made of wool, esp. a knitted undergarment. —**wool′li•ness,** *n.* [*noncount*]

wooz•y (wōō′zē, wŏŏz′ē) /ˈwuwziy, ˈwʊziy/ *adj.,* **-i•er, -i•est. 1.** confused; muddled: *I was a little woozy from lack of sleep.* **2.** dizzy, faint, or nauseated: *She felt woozy from the heat of the sun.* —**wooz•i•ly** (wōō′zə lē, wŏŏz′ə-) /ˈwuwzəliy, ˈwʊzə-/ *adv.* —**wooz′i•ness,** *n.* [*noncount*]

word (wûrd) /wɜrd/ *n.* **1.** [*count*] a unit of a language, consisting of one or more spoken sounds or their written representation and functioning as a carrier of meaning: *"A," "bicycle," "won't," and "speedy" are words in English.* **2. words,** [*plural*] **a.** verbal expression: *to express one's emotions in words.* **b.** the text or lyrics of a song: *I like* *the tune, but the words seem silly.* **c.** a quarrel: *We had words and she left angrily.* **3.** [*count*] a short talk: *asked to have a word with me before I left.* **4.** [*count*] something said; an expression or utterance: *a word of warning.* **5.** [*one's* + ~] assurance or promise: *He gave his word (that) he'd be on time.* **6.** [*noncount*] news; information: *When did you receive word of his death?* **7.** [*count*] a verbal signal, as a password: *Say the secret word and I'll open the door.* **8.** [*count*] a command that has authority: *When the sergeant gives the word, begin firing.* **9.** [*count*] a string of bits of a certain length treated as a unit for storage and processing by a computer. **10.** (used to form a usually humorous expression by combining with the initial letter of a taboo or supposedly taboo word): *Taxes are the politicians' dreaded T-word.* **—***v.* [~ + *obj*] **11.** to express in words: *See if you can word this statement more clearly.* **—*Idiom.*** **12. be as good as one's word,** [*no obj*] to do what one has promised. **13. eat one's words,** to take back one's statement: *He thinks we won't finish on time; let's make him eat his words by finishing early!* **14. in a word,** in short: *In a word, we're bankrupt.* **15. in so many words,** in terms that are completely clear and say exactly what is meant; explicitly: *She didn't say so in so many words, but I think she likes you.* **16. of few words,** not talkative: *a man of few words.* **17. of many words,** talkative; wordy. **18. put in a (good) word for,** [~ + *obj*] to speak favorably on behalf of. **19. take (someone) at one's word,** [*take* + *obj* + *at* + *one's* + ~] to believe (someone) to be telling the truth. **20. take the words out of someone's mouth,** to say exactly what another person was about to say.

word•age (wûr′dij) /ˈwɜrdɪdʒ/ *n.* [*noncount*] **1.** words thought of as a group. **2.** number of words: *a document with high wordage.* **3.** choice of words; wording.

word•ing (wûr′ding) /ˈwɜrdɪŋ/ *n.* [*count*] choice of words; phrasing: *The wording of the new law is unclear.*

word′ of mouth′, *n.* [*noncount*] oral communication as opposed to written: *The rumor spread rapidly by word of mouth.*

word•play (wûrd′plā′) /ˈwɜrdˌpleɪ/ *n.* [*noncount*] witty or clever use of words.

word′ proc′essing, *n.* [*noncount*] the automated production and storage of documents using computers, electronic printers, and text-editing software. **—word′ proc′essor,** *n.* [*count*]

word•y (wûr′dē) /ˈwɜrdiy/ *adj.,* **-i•er, -i•est.** showing or making use of too many words; verbose: *a wordy speech.* **—word′i•ness,** *n.* [*noncount*]

wore (wôr) /wɔr/ *v.* pt. of WEAR.

work (wûrk) /wɜrk/ *n., adj., v.,* **worked** or (*Archaic except in some senses, esp. 21, 22*) **wrought** (rôt) /rɔt/; **work•ing.** **—***n.* **1.** [*noncount*] the use of effort or action to produce or accomplish something; labor: *Cleaning that whole house is a lot of work.* **2.** [*noncount*] a task or something to do or be done: *The students finished their work in class.* **3.** [*noncount*] productive activity, esp. a job or employment: *He's been looking for work ever since he graduated.* **4.** [*noncount*] a place of employment: *Don't phone me at work.* **5.** [*noncount*] something on which work is being or is to be done: *I have enough work here on my desk to last all month.* **6.** the result of exertion, labor, or activity, as a building, book, work of art, etc.: [*count*]: *the collected works of Robert Louis Stevenson; Bach's musical works.* [*noncount*]: *a shoemaker who takes pride in his work.* **7.** [*count*] something, as a wall, built as a means of fortification: *an earthen work built as a barrier.* **8. works, a.** [*count*] a place or establishment for manufacturing: [*singular; used with a singular verb*]: *A new steel works is to be built there.* [*plural; used with a plural verb*]: *The steel works are not yet built.* **b.** [*plural; used with a plural verb*] the working parts of a machine: *The works of the watch are broken.* **9.** [*noncount*] *Physics.* the transfer of energy measured by multiplying the amount of force by the distance through which it acts. **10. the works,** [*plural*] **a.** everything: *She wants a hamburger with the works: pickles, cheese, tomatoes, and onions.* **b.** unpleasant or nasty treatment: *She gave him the works for betraying her.* **—***adj.* [*before a noun*] **11.** of, for, or concerning work: *work clothes.* **—***v.* **12.** [*no obj*] to do work: *The mechanic had to work for two hours on that car.* **13.** to be employed (at): [*no obj*]: *She works at a factory.* [~ + *obj*]: *He's working two jobs.* **14.** [~ + *obj*] to cause to work: *That new boss works his employees hard.* **15.** [~ + *obj*] to use or operate (an apparatus, machine, etc.): *She works a gigantic steam press machine.* **16.** [*no obj*] to be functional, as a machine; operate: *He got the machine to work again.* **17.** [*no obj*] to prove effective: *This plan works.* **18.** to (cause to) come to be, as by repeated movement: [*no obj*]: *The nails worked loose.* [~ + *obj*]: *The nails worked themselves loose.* **19.** to have an effect (on), as on a person's feelings: [*no obj*]: *Don't try tears and crying; that doesn't work on him.* [~ + *obj*]: *Diet and exercise worked wonders on him.* **20.** [~ + *obj*] to cause a strong emotion in: *That speaker is able to work crowds into a frenzy.* **21.** [~ + *obj*] to bring about by or as if by work: *to work a change for the better.* **22.** [~ + *obj*] to make or fashion by work: *to work a piece of sculpture with one's hands.* **23.** to make (one's way) with effort: [~ + *obj*]: *We worked our way slowly through the crowd.* [*no obj*]: *We worked slowly through the crowd.* **24.** [~ + *obj*] to carry on business, etc., operations in (a place or region): *He worked the Atlantic Coast for sales and advertising.* **25. work in** or **into,** [~ + *obj* + *in/into* + *obj*] to include after some effort: *Try to work me into your schedule.* **26. work off,** to get rid of: [~ + *off* + *obj*]: *to work off a few pounds by exercising.* [~ + *obj* + *off*]: *to work a few pounds off by exercising.* **27. work on,** [~ + *on* + *obj*] to try to influence or persuade: *He tried to work on them to drop the lawsuit.* **28. work out, a.** to solve, as a problem: [~ + *out* + *obj*]: *to work out a problem between friends.* [~ + *obj* + *out*]: *We can work it out.* **b.** to arrive at by or as if by calculation: [~ + *out* + *obj*]: *to work out a new schedule.* [~ + *obj* + *out*]: *to work a new schedule out with the boss.* **c.** to prove effective or suitable: [*no obj*]: *Their marriage just didn't work out.* [~ + *obj* + *out*]: *Things have a way of working themselves out.* **d.** [*no obj*] to amount: *The bill works out to almost fifty dollars each, including (the) tip.* **e.** [*no obj*] to exercise or train, esp. in an athletic sport. **29. work over, a.** to study or examine carefully or thoroughly: [~ + *over* + *obj*]: *The accountant worked over the figures.* [~ + *obj* + *over*]: *to work the figures over.* **b.** to beat or hurt (someone) completely, fiercely, etc.: [~ + *over* + *obj*]: *The gang worked over their latest victim and left him dying in the street.* [~ + *obj* + *over*]: *They really worked him over.* **30. work through,** [~ + *through* + *obj*] to deal with successfully: *to work through one's problems.* **31. work up, a.** to stir the feelings of; excite: [~ + *up* + *obj*]: *to work up the crowd into a frenzy.* [~ + *obj* + *up*]: *to work the crowd up.* **b.** to prepare; develop: [~ + *up* + *obj*]: *to work up a plan.* [~ + *obj* + *up*]: *to work a plan up.* **c.** [~ + *up* + *obj*] to develop by exercise or exertion: *to work up a sweat.* **—*Idiom.*** **32. at work,** working, as at one's job: *I'm at work between nine and five.* **33. in the works,** in preparation: *His new book is still in the works.* **34. out of work,** not employed.

work•a•ble (wûr′kə bəl) /ˈwɜrkəbəl/ *adj.* that can be made use of; practical or feasible: *a workable plan.*

work•a•day (wûr′kə dā′) /ˈwɜrkəˌdeɪ/ *adj.* **1.** like or fit for working days. **2.** ordinary; everyday.

work•a•hol•ic (wûr′kə hô′lik, -hol′ik) /ˌwɜrkəˈhɔlɪk, -ˈhɒlɪk/ *n.* [*count*] a person who has a powerful need to work.

work•bench (wûrk′bench′) /ˈwɜrkˌbɛntʃ/ *n.* [*count*] a sturdy table at which a craftsman or artisan works.

work•book (wûrk′bo͝ok′) /ˈwɜrkˌbʊk/ *n.* [*count*] a book for students containing questions, exercises, and problems, esp. one in which the student writes.

work•day (wûrk′dā′) /ˈwɜrkˌdeɪ/ *n.* [*count*] **1.** a day on which work, esp. one's job or other paid work for a living, is done. **2.** the part of a day during which one works.

work•er (wûr′kər) /ˈwɜrkər/ *n.* [*count*] **1.** one that works. **2.** a laborer or employee.

work•fare (wûrk′fâr′) /ˈwɜrkˌfɛər/ *n.* [*noncount*] a government plan under which people who receive welfare and can work are required to accept public-service jobs.

work•horse (wûrk′hôrs′) /ˈwɜrkˌhɔrs/ *n.* [*count*] **1.** a horse used for heavy labor. **2.** a person who works without tiring.

work•ing (wûr′king) /ˈwɜrkɪŋ/ *n.* **1.** [*noncount*] the act of one that works. **2.** [*count*] operation; action: *the complicated workings of his mind.* **—***adj.* **3.** doing or engaged in work for a living; employed: *working men and women.* **4.** related to or organized for conducting work: *a working lunch.* **5.** permitting continued work or activity; making continued work easy: *a working model; a working majority.* **6.** adequate for usual or customary needs: *a working knowledge of Spanish.*

work•load (wûrk′lōd′) /ˈwɜrkˌloʊd/ *n.* [*count*] the amount of work that a machine, employee, or group of employees can or is expected to perform.

work•man (wûrk′mən) /ˈwɜrkmən/ *n.* [*count*], *pl.* **-men.**

a man employed or skilled in manual, mechanical, or industrial work.

work•man•like (wûrk′mən līk′) /ˈwɜrkmən,layk/ *adj.* well executed; skillful: *a workmanlike performance.*

work•man•ship (wûrk′mən ship′) /ˈwɜrkmən,ʃɪp/ *n.* [*noncount*] **1.** the art or skill of a workman. **2.** the quality of work done: *Look at the excellent workmanship of this desk.*

work•out (wûrk′out′) /ˈwɜrk,awt/ *n.* [*count*] **1.** a session of practice designed to keep up or improve one's physical ability. **2.** any strenuous work or activity.

work•place (wûrk′plās′) /ˈwɜrk,pleys/ *n.* [*count*] a place of employment.

work•shop (wûrk′shop′) /ˈwɜrk,ʃɒp/ *n.* [*count*] **1.** a room or building in which work, esp. mechanical work, is carried on. **2.** a seminar or similar meeting designed to explore a subject or develop a skill or technique: *a workshop to improve their language skills.*

work sta•tion or **work•sta•tion** (wûrk′stā′shən) /ˈwɜrk,steyʃən/ *n.* [*count*] **1.** a work area for one person with a computer terminal or microcomputer connected to a mainframe, minicomputer, or data-processing network. **2.** a powerful microcomputer used for graphics processing.

work•week (wûrk′wēk′) /ˈwɜrk,wiyk/ *n.* [*count*] the total number of working hours or days in a week.

world (wûrld) /wɜrld/ *n.* **1.** [*singular; the* + ~] the earth when it is considered as a planet: *how life developed in the world.* **2.** [*count*] everything that exists; the universe: *In a world of three dimensions, time is the fourth dimension.* **3.** [*count*] a planet; a body in space that is not a star. **4.** [*singular; the* + ~] a particular part or division of the earth: *the Western world; the ancient world.* **5.** [*singular; the* + ~] the human race; humanity: *feeding the whole world.* **6.** [*singular; the* + ~] the general public: *The world worships success and money.* **7.** [*count*] a class or group of people with common interests: *the literary world.* **8.** [*count*] an area, sphere, realm, or domain of activity or existence: *the world of dreams; the world of sports.* **9.** [*count*] one of the general groupings of physical nature: *the animal world.* **10.** Often, **worlds.** [*plural*] a great deal: [~ + *of* + *plural noun*]: *a world of problems.* [~ + *of* + *noncount noun*]: *a world of trouble on my mind.* —***Idiom.*** **11. bring (someone) into the world,** [*bring* + *obj* + *into* + *the* + *world*] **a.** to give birth to; bear. **b.** to deliver (a baby). **12. come into the world,** to be born. **13. for (all) the world, a.** [*with a negative word or phrase*] for anything, however great; under any circumstances; definitely (not): *I wouldn't harm my children for all the world.* **b.** in every respect; precisely: *He looks for all the world like his twin brother.* **14. in the world, a.** at all: *without a care in the world.* **b.** (used to intensify a question): *How in the world will you get home?* **15. out of this world,** extraordinary; wonderful: *The dinner was simply out of this world.* **16. world without end,** for all eternity; forever.

world′-class′, *adj.* being among or including the world's best: *a world-class tennis tournament.*

world•ly (wûrld′lē) /ˈwɜrldliy/ *adj.,* **-li•er, -li•est. 1.** of or concerned with this world rather than heaven, an afterlife, or spiritual life in general. **2.** of or relating to material things: *lost all their worldly goods in the flood.* **3.** experienced; sophisticated: *a worldly diplomat and traveler.* —**world′li•ness,** *n.* [*noncount*]

world′ly-wise′, *adj.* wise as to the affairs of this world.

world′-wea′ry, *adj.* weary of the world; not excited or interested by things around one; blasé.

world•wide (wûrld′wīd′) /ˈwɜrldˈwayd/ *adj.* **1.** throughout the world: *a worldwide oil shortage.* —*adv.* **2.** everywhere in the world: *The shortage was felt worldwide.*

worm (wûrm) /wɜrm/ *n.* [*count*] **1.** a long, soft-bodied, legless creature without a backbone, as the earthworm. **2.** a low, worthless, contemptible person. **3. worms,** [*noncount; used with a singular verb*] a disorder caused by worms that live in the intestines of humans and animals and that consume food meant for the person or animal. —*v.* [~ + *obj*] **4.** to creep, crawl, or move slowly, as into a tight or small space: *She wormed herself through the tunnel.* **5.** to attain or gain sneakily or indirectly: *He wormed the secret out of his sister.* **6.** to free (a person or an animal) from intestinal worms. —**worm′y,** *adj.,* **-i•er, -i•est.**

worn (wôrn) /wɔrn/ *v.* **1.** pp. of WEAR. —*adj.* **2.** lessened or lowered in value or usefulness because of wear or use: *an old, worn jacket.* **3.** exhausted; spent.

worn′-out′, *adj.* **1.** worn or used beyond repair. **2.** having no more energy or strength; exhausted.

wor•ried (wûr′ēd, wur′-) /ˈwɜriyd, ˈwʌr-/ *adj.* having or showing worry; concerned; anxious.

wor•ri•some (wûr′ē səm, wur′-) /ˈwɜriysəm, ˈwʌr-/ *adj.* **1.** causing worry: *worrisome unemployment.* **2.** often or given to worrying: *worrisome parents.*

wor•ry (wûr′ē, wur′-) /ˈwɜriy, ˈwʌr-/ *v.,* **-ried, -ry•ing,** *n., pl.* **-ries.** —*v.* **1.** to (cause to) feel or be uneasy or anxious: [*no obj*]: *He worries about his kids.* [~ + *obj*]: *The high cost of college worries them.* [*It* + ~ + *obj* + *that clause*]: *It worries me that you might not pass the test.* [*It* + ~ + *obj* + *to* + *verb*]: *It worries me to think of your going home alone every night.* **2.** [~ + *obj*] to subject to persistent attention or scrutiny: *He worries the problem too much.* **3.** [~ + *obj*] (of animals) to seize with the teeth and shake or mangle: *worrying a bone.* **4.** [~ + *obj*] to touch or adjust over and over again: *worrying the loose button of his jacket.* —*n.* **5.** [*noncount*] uneasiness or anxiety: *full of worry.* **6.** [*count*] a cause of worry: *Money is their biggest worry.* —**wor′ri•er,** *n.* [*count*] —**wor′ry•ing•ly,** *adv.*

wor•ry•wart (wûr′ē wôrt′, wur′-) /ˈwɜriy,wɔrt, ˈwʌr-/ *n.* [*count*] a person who tends to worry too much.

worse (wûrs) /wɜrs/ *adj., comparative of* **bad** *and* **ill. 1.** bad or ill to a greater extent; inferior: *Your score is worse on this test than on yesterday's.* **2.** more unfavorable or injurious. **3.** in poorer health: *The patient is worse than yesterday.* —*n.* [*noncount; usually: the* + ~] **4.** something that is worse: *a turn for the worse.* —*adv.* **5.** in a worse manner: *The class behaved worse than ever just when the principal came in.* **6.** to a worse degree: *I feel much worse than yesterday.*

wor•sen (wûr′sən) /ˈwɜrsən/ *v.* to (cause to) become worse: [*no obj*]: *The economy has worsened.* [~ + *obj*]: *Those measures will worsen the economy.*

wor•ship (wûr′ship) /ˈwɜrʃɪp/ *n., v.,* **-shiped** or **-shipped, -ship•ing** or **-ship•ping.** —*n.* [*noncount*] **1.** reverence for God, a sacred personage, or a sacred object. **2.** a formal or ceremonious expression of worship: *to attend worship on Sundays.* **3.** a feeling of strong, adoring reverence or regard: *hero worship.* —*v.* **4.** to give religious worship (to); to do religious worship: [~ + *obj*]: *to worship God.* [*no obj*]: *They worship at church.* **5.** [~ + *obj*] to feel a strong, adoring reverence or regard for: *He worships his wife and children and would do anything for them.* —**wor′ship•er,** *n.* [*count*]: *A collection plate was passed and worshipers gave as much as they could.* —**wor′ship•ful,** *adj.*

worst (wûrst) /wɜrst/ *adj., superlative of* **bad** *and* **ill. 1.** bad or ill in the most extreme degree; most faulty or unsatisfactory: *the worst job I've ever seen.* **2.** most unpleasant, unattractive, or disagreeable. **3.** least efficient or skilled: *The worst drivers in the country come from that state.* —*n.* [*noncount; usually: the* + ~] **4.** something that is worst: *Prepare for the worst.* —*adv.* **5.** in the worst manner. **6.** in the greatest degree. —*v.* [~ + *obj*] **7.** to defeat; beat. —***Idiom.*** **8. at (the) worst,** under the worst conditions. **9. if worst comes to worst,** if the very worst happens. **10. in the worst way,** very much; extremely: *He needs praise in the worst way.*

wor•sted (wŏŏs′tid, wûr′stid) /ˈwʊstɪd, ˈwɜrstɪd/ *n.* [*noncount*] **1.** wool cloth woven from twisted wool yarn or thread. —*adj.* [*before a noun*] **2.** made up of worsted.

worth (wûrth) /wɜrθ/ *prep.* **1.** good or important enough to justify: *That place is definitely worth visiting.* **2.** having a value of: *That vase is worth 20 dollars.* **3.** having property to the value of: *They are worth millions.* —*n.* [*noncount*] **4.** excellence, as of character; merit: *a man of worth.* **5.** usefulness or importance, as to the world, to a person, or for a purpose: *Your worth to the team is unquestionable.* **6.** value, as in money. **7.** a quantity of something of a specified value: *The storekeeper gave him 50 cents' worth of candy.* **8.** property or possessions; wealth. —***Idiom.*** **9. for all one is worth,** to the utmost: *She ran for all she was worth.* —**Related Words.** WORTH is an adjective and a noun, WORTHWHILE and WORTHY are adjectives: *The book is worth fifty dollars. He is of no worth. It was worthwhile work. I am not worthy of your love.*

worth•less (wûrth′lis) /ˈwɜrθlɪs/ *adj.* without worth; having no value: *Those promises were worthless.* —**worth′less•ly,** *adv.* —**worth′less•ness,** *n.* [*noncount*]

worth•while (wûrth′hwīl′, -wīl′) /ˈwɜrθˈhwayl, -ˈwayl/ *adj.* worthy of the time, work, trouble, or money spent or expended.

wor•thy (wûr′thē) /ˈwɜrðiy/ *adj.,* **-thi•er, -thi•est,** *n., pl.* **-thies.** —*adj.* **1.** having merit, character, or value: *a worthy opponent.* **2.** deserving: *an effort worthy of praise.*

—*n.* [*count*] **3.** a person of worth. —**wor•thi•ly** (wûr′-thə lē) /ˈwɜrðəliy/ *adv.* —**wor′thi•ness,** *n.* [*noncount*]

-worthy, *suffix.* **1.** *-worthy* is used to form adjectives with the meaning "deserving of, fit for": *news + -worthy → newsworthy (= fit for the news); trust + -worthy → trustworthy.* **2.** *-worthy* is also used with the meaning "capable of travel in or on": *road + -worthy → roadworthy (= capable of traveling on the road); seaworthy.*

would (wo͝od; *unstressed* wəd) /wʊd; *unstressed* wəd/ *auxiliary (modal) verb* [~ + *root form of a verb*] **1.** the past tense of WILL¹. **2.** (used to express the future when a past tense verb appears in a clause before it): *He said (that) he would go tomorrow.* **3.** (used in place of *will* to soften a statement or question): *Would you be so kind?* **4.** (used to express an action that was a habit in the past): *Years ago, we would take the train every morning.* **5.** (used to express the wish or intention of someone): *Nutritionists would have us all eat whole grains.* **6.** (used to express lack of certainty): *It would appear that he is guilty.* **7.** (used to show that there is a choice or a possibility or that an action, etc., depends on a condition being fulfilled): *They would come if they had the fare.* —*Idiom.* **8. would like,** (used to express one's desire to do something): *I would like to go next year.*

would′-be′, *adj.* [*before a noun*] wishing or pretending to be: *a would-be comedian.*

would•n't (wo͝od′nt) /ˈwʊdnt/ *contraction.* a shortened form of *would not.*

wouldst (wo͝odst) /wʊdst/ *v. Archaic.* 2nd pers. sing. past of WILL¹.

wound¹ (wo͞ond) /wuwnd/ *n.* [*count*] **1.** an injury, usually involving the cutting or tearing of skin or tissue. **2.** an injury or hurt to feelings, emotions, or reputation. —*v.* [~ + *obj*] **3.** to inflict a wound upon; injure: *The next shot wounded him in the arm.*

wound² (wound) /wawnd/ *v.* a pt. and pp. of WIND².

wove (wōv) /wowv/ *v.* a pt. and pp. of WEAVE.

wo•ven (wō′vən) /ˈwowvən/ *v.* a pp. of WEAVE.

wow (wou) /waw/ *interj.* **1.** (used to show surprise, wonder, or pleasure): *Wow, what a beautiful sunset!* —*v.* [~ + *obj*] **2.** to cause an enthusiastic response from; thrill: *The rock band wowed the audience.* —*n.* [*count*] **3.** an extraordinary success.

WP, an abbreviation of: word processing.

wpm, an abbreviation of: words per minute.

wrack (rak) /ræk/ *n.* [*noncount*] damage or destruction: *The empire fell to wrack and ruin.*

wraith (rāth) /reyθ/ *n.* [*count*] a ghost.

wran•gle (rang′gəl) /ˈræŋgəl/ *v.,* **-gled, -gling,** *n.* —*v.* **1.** [*no obj*] to argue, quarrel, debate, or dispute, esp. noisily or angrily: *The kids wrangled over who should get to sit near the window.* **2.** [~ + *obj*] to obtain by bothering, pestering, or badgering: *He wrangled a small raise out of the boss, but it was hard work.* —*n.* [*count*] **3.** a noisy or angry dispute. —**wran′gler,** *n.* [*count*]

wrap (rap) /ræp/ *v.,* **wrapped** or **wrapt, wrap•ping,** *n.* —*v.* **1.** [~ + *obj* + *on/around* + *obj*] to enclose or cover in something wound or folded about: *He wrapped a bandage around his finger.* **2.** [~ + *obj*] to enclose and make fast within a covering, as of paper: *She wrapped the gifts and put them under the Christmas tree.* **3.** [~ + *obj*] to wind or fold (something) around as a covering: *to wrap wax paper around the leftovers.* **4.** [~ + *obj*] to surround, envelop, or hide: *He wrapped her in his arms.* **5. a. wrap up,** [~ + *up* + *obj*] to finish work on; conclude: *to wrap up doing the tax returns.* **b.** [~ + *obj*] to give a summary of: *The announcer wrapped up the day's news.* **c.** to wear warm clothes (on oneself): [*no obj*]: *Be sure to wrap up before you go out in the cold.* [~ + *obj* + *up*]: *He wrapped them up in their winter coats.* —*n.* [*count*] **6.** something, as a shawl, to be wrapped around a person, esp. for warmth. —*adj.* [*before a noun*] **7.** Also, **wrapped.** wraparound in style: *a wrap skirt.* —*Idiom.* **8. under wraps,** *Informal.* secret: *They managed to keep the project under wraps.* **9. wrapped up in,** deeply absorbed in or devoted to: *He's all wrapped up in this latest project.*

wrap•a•round (rap′ə round′) /ˈræpəˌrawnd/ *adj.* **1.** (of a garment) that is made to wrap around the body so that one side of the fabric overlaps the other, making for a full-length opening. **2.** stretching in a curve from the front around to the sides: *a wraparound windshield.* **3.** including everything or a great deal; all-inclusive; comprehensive: *a wraparound insurance plan.* —*n.* [*count*] **4.** a wraparound object, garment, etc.

wrap•per (rap′ər) /ræpər/ *n.* [*count*] **1.** one that wraps. **2.** something in which a thing is wrapped. **3.** a loose garment, esp. a woman's bathrobe or negligee.

wrap•ping (rap′ing) /ˈræpɪŋ/ *n.* [*count*] Often, **wrappings.** [*plural*] the covering in which something is wrapped.

wrap′-up′, *n.* [*count*] **1.** a final report; summary: *a wrap-up of the latest news stories.* **2.** the final part; end: *a wrap-up of the election campaign.*

wrath (rath, räth) /ræθ, rɑθ/ *n.* [*noncount*] fierce anger; ire; rage; fury. —**wrath′ful,** *adj.*

wreak (rēk) /riyk/ *v.* [~ + *obj*] **1.** to carry out (damage, destruction): *The storm wreaked damage on the whole coastline.* **2.** to inflict: *to wreak revenge on them.*

wreath (rēth) /riyθ/ *n.* [*count*], *pl.* **wreaths** (rē*th*z, rēths) /riyðz, riyθs/. **1.** a circular band, as of flowers, used for decoration: *laid a wreath at the hero's tomb.* **2.** a ringlike mass or formation: *a wreath of smoke.*

wreathe (rē*th*) /riyð/ *v.* [~ + *obj*], **wreathed, wreath•ing.** **1.** to make a circle around (something) or decorate with or as if with a wreath. **2.** to surround or envelop: *a face wreathed in smiles.*

wreck (rek) /rɛk/ *n.* **1.** [*count*] a building, structure, or object that has been reduced, destroyed, or greatly damaged. **2.** [*noncount*] ruin; destruction: *the wreck of our dreams.* **3.** [*count*] a person of ruined physical or mental health. —*v.* [~ + *obj*] **4.** to cause the wreck of: *wrecked the car.* **5.** to tear down; demolish: *to wreck a building.*

wreck•age (rek′ij) /ˈrɛkɪdʒ/ *n.* [*noncount*] **1.** the act of wrecking or state of being wrecked. **2.** the remains of something that has been wrecked.

wreck•er (rek′ər) /ˈrɛkər/ *n.* [*count*] **1.** one that wrecks. **2.** a vehicle equipped to tow wrecked or disabled automobiles. **3.** a person or business that demolishes and removes buildings.

wren (ren) /rɛn/ *n.* [*count*] a small songbird with streaked or spotted brown-gray coloring.

wrench (rench) /rɛntʃ/ *v.* **1.** to pull, jerk, move, or force with or as with a violent twisting motion: [~ + *obj*]: *He wrenched the door open.* [*no obj*]: *She wrenched away and dashed off.* **2.** [~ + *obj*] to injure (the ankle, knee, etc.) by a sudden, violent twist. **3.** [~ + *obj*] to affect with a feeling of distress or sharp mental or emotional pain: *She was wrenched by the terrible loss.* —*n.* [*count*] **4.** a sudden, violent twist: *a wrench of the ankle.* **5.** a sharp, distressing strain, as to the feelings: *Her death was a wrench to the family.* **6.** a tool for gripping and turning or twisting a bolt, nut, etc. —**wrench′ing•ly,** *adv.: a wrenchingly sad story.*

wrest (rest) /rɛst/ *v.* [~ + *obj*] **1.** to take away by force: *I wrested the gun away from him.* **2.** to get by effort: *to wrest control of the business away from the stockholders.* —*n.* [*count*] **3.** a twist or wrench.

wres•tle (res′əl) /ˈrɛsəl/ *v.,* **-tled, -tling,** *n.* —*v.* **1.** to compete (with) in the sport of wrestling: [*no obj*]: *He wrestled for his high school team.* [~ + *obj*]: *She wrestled the best opponents in each school.* **2.** to fight or struggle (with) by holding, throwing, or forcing an attacker to the ground: [~ + *obj*]: *He wrestled the mugger to the ground.* [*no obj*]: *They wrestled until one of them fell.* **3.** [*no obj*] to struggle (with) in order to overcome, figure out, defeat, etc.; contend: *He wrestled with the serious problem.* —*n.* [*count*] **4.** an act or bout of wrestling. —**wres′tler,** *n.* [*count*]

wres•tling (res′ling) /ˈrɛslɪŋ/ *n.* [*noncount*] a sport in which two opponents struggle hand to hand in order to pin or press each other's shoulders to the mat.

wretch (rech) /rɛtʃ/ *n.* [*count*] **1.** a very unfortunate or unhappy person. **2.** a contemptible person: *That wretch deserted his family.*

wretch•ed (rech′id) /ˈrɛtʃɪd/ *adj.* **1.** very unfortunate; worthy of pity because of suffering or misery: *that wretched man, living on the street.* **2.** characterized by or causing misery and sorrow: *living in wretched conditions.* **3.** contemptible: *a wretched thief.* **4.** worthless; inferior: *a wretched meal of boiled cabbage.* **5.** [*be* + ~] miserable or unhappy: *She felt wretched for having betrayed her friends.* —**wretch′ed•ly,** *adv.* —**wretch′ed•ness,** *n.* [*noncount*]

wrig•gle (rig′əl) /ˈrɪgəl/ *v.,* **-gled, -gling,** *n.* —*v.* **1.** to twist from one side to the other; squirm; writhe: [*no obj*]: *The child was wriggling in his seat.* [~ + *obj*]: *to wriggle one's toes.* **2.** to move along by twisting and turning the body, as a worm: [*no obj*]: *The worm wriggled in the dirt.* [~ + *obj*]: *He wriggled his way through the narrow tunnel.* **3. wriggle out of,** [~ + *out of* + *obj*] to escape from or avoid: *He tried to wriggle out of doing the work.* —*n.* [*count*] **4.** the act or motion of wriggling: *a little* *wriggle of the hips.* —**wrig′gler,** *n.* [*count*] —**wrig′gly,** *adj.,* **-gli•er, -gli•est:** *a wriggly little worm.*

wring (ring) /rɪŋ/ *v.,* **wrung** (rung) /rʌŋ/ **wring•ing. 1.** [~ + *obj*] to twist with force: *The bully wrung the boy's arm.* **2.** to twist, squeeze, or compress (something) in order to force out (a liquid): [~ *(+ out) + obj*]: *to wring (out) the wet washcloth; to wring (out) the water from the wet washcloth.* [~ + *obj (+ out)*]: *to wring the washcloth (out); to wring the water (out of) the wet washcloth.* **3.** [~ + *obj* + *out of* + *obj*] to force out as if by squeezing: *They captured the spy and wrung the secret password out of him.* **4.** [~ + *obj*] to hold or clasp tightly, usually with a twisting motion: *She wrung her hands in anguish.*

wring•er (ring′ər) /ˈrɪŋər/ *n.* [*count*] **1.** one that wrings. **2.** a machine or device for squeezing out liquid, as from wet clothing. —***Idiom.*** **3. put (someone) through the wringer,** [*put* + *obj* + *through* + *the* + ~] to force (someone) to undergo or go through a difficult or exhausting experience.

wrin•kle (ring′kəl) /ˈrɪŋkəl/ *n., v.,* **-kled, -kling.** —*n.* [*count*] **1.** a small crease in the skin, as from aging. **2.** a slight ridge in a fabric, as from folding. **3.** a problem; fault: *There are still a few wrinkles in the plan.* **4.** a creative, new idea: *adding some wrinkles to the plan to make it unique.* —*v.* **5.** to (cause to) become full of wrinkles: [*no obj*]: *This fabric wrinkles easily.* [~ + *obj*]: *wrinkled his forehead by frowning.* —**wrin′kly,** *adj.,* **-kli•er, -kli•est.**

wrist (rist) /rɪst/ *n.* [*count*] **1.** the part of the end of the arm where it joins the hand. **2.** the joint between the forearm and the hand.

wrist•band (rist′band′) /ˈrɪstˌbænd/ *n.* [*count*] **1.** the band of a sleeve that covers the wrist. **2.** a wristwatch strap that goes around the wrist. **3.** a cloth band worn on the wrist to absorb perspiration.

wrist•watch or **wrist watch** (rist′wach′) /ˈrɪstˌwætʃ/ *n.* [*count*] a watch attached to a strap or band worn about the wrist.

writ (rit) /rɪt/ *n.* [*count*] a court order directing a person to do or not do something.

write (rīt) /rayt/ *v.,* **wrote** (rōt) /rowt/ **writ•ten** (rit′n) /ˈrɪtn̩/ **writ•ing.** —*v.* **1.** to form (letters, words, etc.), esp. on paper, with a pen or pencil: [~ + *obj*]: *He learned to write his name.* [*no obj*]: *to learn to read and write.* **2.** to express or communicate in writing, as in an essay: [~ + *obj*]: *to write a story.* [*no obj*]: *to write about your personal experiences.* **3.** to communicate with (someone) by (a letter): [~ + *obj*]: *I wrote her about your troubles.* [~ + *obj* + *to* + *obj*]: *She wrote a thank-you note to me.* [~ + *obj* + *obj*]: *She wrote me a thank-you note.* [~ *(+ obj)* + *that clause*]: *I wrote (her) that you were having some troubles.* [~ *(+ obj)* + *to* + *verb*]: *She wrote (me) to say thank you.* [*no obj*]: *I wrote to her.* **4.** [~ + *obj*] to fill in the blank spaces of (a printed form) with writing: *to write a check.* **5.** to be the author or composer of: [~ + *obj*]: *He wrote several good books. He wrote the music for that movie.* [*no obj*]: *He writes for a magazine.* **6.** [~ + *obj*] to transfer (data, text, etc.) from computer memory to a disk or printer. **7. write down,** to set down in writing; record; note: [~ + *down* + *obj*]: *He wrote down his ideas on scraps of paper.* [~ + *obj* + *down*]: *He writes his ideas down.* **8. write in, a.** to vote for (a candidate not listed) by writing his or her name on the ballot: [~ + *in* + *obj*]: *to write in the name of the candidate.* [~ + *obj* + *in*]: *to write the name in on the ballot.* **b.** [*no obj*] to request something by mail: *If interested, please write in for details.* **9. write off, a.** to cancel (an unpaid debt, or a debt that cannot be collected): [~ + *off* + *obj*]: *to write off a debt.* [~ + *obj* + *off*]: *to write the debts off.* **b.** to regard or think of as worthless, failed, or of no use; decide to forget: [~ + *off* + *obj*]: *to write off a bad experience.* [~ + *obj* + *off*]: *to write it off to experience.* **10. write out, a.** to write in full: [~ + *out* + *obj*]: *Write out the entire sentence.* [~ + *obj* + *out*]: *Write your full name out.* **b.** [~ + *out* + *obj*] to fill out by writing in the spaces of (a form): *I'll write out a check.* **11. write up,** to put into writing, esp. in full detail: [~ + *up* + *obj*]: *to write up a report of the incident.* [~ + *obj* + *up*]: *He knew he had to write it up before he went home for the day.* —***Idiom.*** **12. nothing** (or **something**) **to write home about,** nothing (or something) worth one's notice. **13. write the book,** to be the first or most famous or recognized authority: *They practically wrote the book on getting along with people.*

write′-in′, *n.* [*count*] a candidate or vote for a candidate not listed on a ballot but must be written in by the voter.

write′-off′, *n.* [*count*] **1.** something written off, as a loss for the purposes of taxes. **2.** a person or thing given up as hopeless, completely ruined, or useless.

writ•er (rī′tər) /ˈraytər/ *n.* [*count*] a person engaged in writing, esp. as an occupation.

write′-up′, *n.* [*count*] a written account, report, or piece of writing, as in a newspaper.

writhe (rīth) /rayð/ *v.,* **writhed, writh•ing,** *n.* —*v.* [*no obj*] **1.** to twist and turn, as in pain. **2.** to suffer greatly: *The embarrassing disclosures about his past had him writhing.* —*n.* [*count*] **3.** a twisting of the body.

writ•ing (rī′ting) /ˈraytɪŋ/ *n.* **1.** [*noncount*] the act of one who writes, or the profession of one who writes books, newspaper articles, etc. **2.** written matter: [*count*]: *a collection of her writings.* [*noncount*]: *a great amount of writing.* **3.** [*noncount*] written form: *Put the agreement in writing.* **4.** [*noncount*] handwriting. **5.** [*noncount*] the style, form, or quality of something written: *awkward writing.*

writ•ten (rit′n) /ˈrɪtn̩/ *v.* pp. of WRITE.

wrong (rông, rong) /rɔŋ, rɒŋ/ *adj.* **1.** being in error; mistaken; not correct: *a wrong answer.* **2.** not agreeing with truth or fact; incorrect: *Their theory about how the universe began was just plain wrong.* **3.** [*be* + ~] not in agreement with what is morally right; evil; bad: *Stealing and murder are wrong.* [*It* + *be* + ~ + *to* + *verb*]: *It's wrong to steal and commit murder.* **4.** not proper; unsuitable: *Those are definitely the wrong shoes for that dress.* **5.** out of order; amiss. —*n.* [*count*] **6.** something improper, immoral, unjust, or harmful: *a series of wrongs committed against them just because they were different.* —*adv.* **7.** in a wrong manner: *I did it all wrong. Did I pronounce your name wrong?* —*v.* [~ + *obj*] **8.** to do wrong to; harm. **9.** to think badly of (someone) unjustly or unfairly. —***Idiom.*** **10. go wrong,** [*no obj*] **a.** to go badly; fail: *Everything went wrong with my computer after I installed that new program.* **b.** to follow an undesirable or evil course: *Bad friends caused him to go wrong.* **11. in the wrong,** at fault. —**wrong′ly,** *adv.*: *She was wrongly accused.* —**wrong′ness,** *n.* [*noncount*]

wrong•do•er (rông′do͞o′ər, -do͞o′-, rong′-) /ˈrɔŋˌduwər, -ˈduw-, ˈrɒŋ-/ *n.* [*count*] a person who does wrong, esp. a sinner or a criminal. —**wrong′do′ing,** *n.* [*noncount*]

wrong•ful (rông′fəl, rong′-) /ˈrɔŋfəl, ˈrɒŋ-/ *adj.* **1.** not just; unfair. **2.** not legal; unlawful. —**wrong′ful•ly,** *adv.*: *wrongfully condemned.* —**wrong′ful•ness,** *n.* [*noncount*]

wrong•head•ed (rông′hed′id, rong′-) /ˈrɔŋˈhɛdɪd, ˈrɒŋ-/ *adj.* misguided; stubbornly wrong in judgment or opinion. —**wrong′head′ed•ly,** *adv.* —**wrong′head′ed•ness,** *n.* [*noncount*]

wrote (rōt) /rowt/ *v.* pt. of WRITE.

wrought (rôt) /rɔt/ *v.* **1.** *Archaic except in some senses.* a pt. and pp. of WORK: *What God hath wrought.* —*adj.* **2.** worked; formed; made or done. **3.** shaped by being beaten with a hammer.

wrought′ i′ron, *n.* [*noncount*] a form of iron that is easily shaped. —**wrought′-i′ron,** *adj.*: *wrought-iron chairs.*

wrought′-up′, *adj.* stirred up; excited.

wrung (rung) /rʌŋ/ *v.* pt. and pp. of WRING.

wry (rī) /ray/ *adj.,* **wri•er, wri•est. 1.** twisted out of shape; contorted; lopsided: *a wry grin.* **2.** bitingly or bitterly ironic or amusing: *a wry tale about the loss of innocence.* —**wry′ly,** *adv.* —**wry′ness,** *n.* [*noncount*]

WSW, an abbreviation of: west-southwest.

wuss (wo͝os) /wʊs/ *n.* [*count*] *Slang.* a weakling; a wimp.

WV or **W.V.,** an abbreviation of: West Virginia.

W.Va., an abbreviation of: West Virginia.

WY or **Wy.,** an abbreviation of: Wyoming.

Wyo., an abbreviation of: Wyoming.

WYSIWYG (wiz′ē wig′) /ˈwɪziyˌwɪg/ *adj.* of or being a computer screen display that shows text exactly as it will appear when printed: *a WYSIWYG display (the initials stand for "What you see is what you get") lets you know exactly how your document will look before you print it.*

X, x (eks) /ɛks/ *n.* [*count*], *pl.* **Xs** or **X's, xs** or **x's.** the 24th letter of the English alphabet, a consonant.

X, *Symbol.* **1.** (*sometimes l.c.*) the Roman numeral for 10. **2.** a motion-picture rating applied to films considered sexually explicit. Compare G (def. 2), NC-17, PG, PG-13, R (def. 4).

x, *Symbol.* **1.** *Math.* an unknown quantity or a variable. **2.** (used at the end of letters, telegrams, etc., esp. as one of a series, to indicate a kiss.) **3.** (used to indicate multiplication) times: $8 \times 8 = 64$. **4.** (used between numbers to indicate dimensions) by: *3″ × 4″ is pronounced or read as "three inches by four inches."* **5.** a person or thing of unknown identity.

X′ chro′mosome, *n.* [*count*] a sex chromosome of humans and most mammals that determines femaleness when paired with another X chromosome and that occurs singly in males. Compare Y CHROMOSOME.

xe•non (zē′non, zen′on) /ˈziynɒn, ˈzɛnɒn/ *n.* [*noncount*] a heavy, colorless, chemically inactive, gaslike element used for filling radio and television tubes.

xen•o•pho•bi•a (zen′ə fō′bē ə, zē′nə-) /ˌzɛnəˈfowbiyə, ˌziynə-/ *n.* [*noncount*] an unreasonable fear or hatred of foreigners or strangers, or a fear of anything foreign or strange. —**xen′o•pho′bic,** *adj.*

xe•rog•ra•phy (zi rog′rə fē) /zɪˈrɒgrəfiy/ *n.* [*noncount*] a copying process in which areas on a sheet of paper corresponding to those on the original are sensitized by static electricity and then sprinkled with black or colored resin that adheres and is fused to the paper. —**xe•ro•graph•ic** (zēr′ə graf′ik) /ˌzɪərəˈgræfɪk/ *adj.*

Xe•rox (zēr′oks) /ˈzɪərɒks/ *n.* **1.** [*noncount*] *Trademark.* a brand name for a copying machine for reproducing printed or written matter or pictures. **2.** [*count; sometimes: xerox*] a copy made on a xerographic copying machine. —*v.* **3.** [*sometimes: xerox*] to print or copy by means of a xerographic machine: [~ + *obj*]: *xeroxed the whole chapter.* [*no obj*]: *I spent all morning xeroxing.*

XL, an abbreviation of: **1.** extra large. **2.** extra long.

Xmas (kris′məs; *often* eks′məs) /ˈkrɪsməs; *often* ˈɛksməs/ Christmas.

x-ray or **X-ray** (eks′rā′) /ˈɛksˌrey/ *n., v.,* **x-rayed** or **X-rayed, x-ray•ing** or **X-ray•ing,** *adj.* —*n.* [*count*] Also, **x ray, X ray. 1.** Often, **x-rays.** [*plural*] radiation having wavelengths in the range between ultraviolet radiation and gamma rays, which can penetrate solids. **2.** a picture, a kind of photograph, made by means of x-rays. —*v.* [~ + *obj*] **3.** to photograph, examine, or treat with x-rays: *The technician x-rayed my knee.* —*adj.* [*before a noun*] **4.** of or relating to x-rays: *an X-ray machine.*

XS, an abbreviation of: extra small.

xy•lo•phone (zī′lə fōn′) /ˈzayləˌfown/ *n.* [*count*] a musical instrument consisting of a series of wooden bars of different sizes, usually played by striking with small wooden hammers. —**xy′lo•phon′ist,** *n.* [*count*] See -PHON-.

Y

Y, y (wī) /way/ *n. [count]*, pl. **Ys** or **Y's, ys** or **y's.** the 25th letter of the English alphabet, a semivowel.

Y (wī) /way/ *n.* [*count*] **the Y,** *Informal.* the YMCA, YWCA, YMHA, or YWHA.

-y[1], *suffix.* *-y* is used to form adjectives with the meaning "having, showing, or similar to (the substance or action of the word or stem)": *blood + -y → bloody; cloud + -y → cloudy; sexy; squeaky.*

-y[2], *suffix.* **1.** *-y* is used to form nouns **a.** that bring or add a meaning of dearness or familiarity to the noun or adjective root, as proper names, names of pets, or in baby talk: *Bill + -y → Billy; Susan + -ie → Susie; bird + -ie → birdie; sweetie.* **b.** that are informal, new, or intended to be new; sometimes these have slightly unpleasant meanings or associations: *boondocks → boon- + -ies → boonies; group + -ie → groupie; Okie (a person from Oklahoma); preemie (= a premature baby); rookie.* **2.** *-y* is attached to adjectives to form nouns, often with the meaning that the noun is an extreme (good or bad) example of the adjective or quality: *bad + -ie → baddie; big + -ie → biggie; toughie; sharpie; sickie; whitey.* Compare -O.

-y[3], *suffix.* *-y* is attached to verbs to form nouns of action, and certain other abstract nouns: *inquire + -y → inquiry; in + fame + -y → infamy.*

yacht (yot) /yɒt/ *n.* [*count*] **1.** a large sailboat or cabin cruiser used for private cruising, racing, or other noncommercial purposes. **—***v.* [*no obj*] **2.** to sail or voyage in a yacht. —**yachts′man,** *n.* [*count*], *pl.* **-men.**

ya•hoo (yä′hōō, yā′-, yä hōō′) /'yɑhuw, 'yey-, yɑ'huw/ *n.* [*count*], *pl.* **-hoos.** an uncultivated, bad-mannered, boorish person; a lout.

yak[1] (yak) /yæk/ *n.* [*count*] a large, shaggy-haired ox of the Tibetan highlands, having long, curved horns.

yak[2] or **yack** (yak) /yæk/ *v.* [*no obj*], **yakked** or **yacked, yak•king** or **yack•ing.** *Slang.* to gab; chatter: *Let's quit yakking and get back to work.*

yam (yam) /yæm/ *n.* [*count*] **1.** the starchy root of an African climbing vine that resembles a sweet potato and is grown as food in warm regions. **2.** SWEET POTATO.

yam•mer (yam′ər) /'yæmər/ *Informal.* **—***v.* [*no obj*] **1.** to whine or complain: *yammering about their misfortune.* **2.** to talk loudly and continuously: *The partygoers yammered happily.* **—***n.* [*noncount*] **3.** the act or noise of yammering. —**yam′mer•er,** *n.* [*count*]

yang (yäng, yang) /yɑŋ, yæŋ/ *n.* See under YIN AND YANG.

yank (yangk) /yæŋk/ *v.* **1.** to pull or tug sharply: [~ + *obj*]: *Yank the doorknob and step back quickly.* [*no obj*]: *He yanked on the doorknob.* **2.** [~ + *obj*] to remove quickly and sharply: *He was yanked out of school.* **—***n.* [*count*] **3.** a sharp, sudden, strong pull; jerk.

Yank (yangk), *n.* [*count*], *adj. Informal.* Yankee.

Yan•kee (yang′kē) /'yæŋkiy/ *n.* [*count*] **1.** a native of, or a person living in, the United States. **2.** a native of, or a person living in, New England. **3.** a native of, or a person living in, a Northern state. **4.** a Federal soldier in the Civil War. **—***adj.* **5.** of, relating to, or characteristic of a Yankee or Yankees: *Yankee ingenuity.*

yap (yap) /yæp/ *v.,* **yapped, yap•ping,** *n.* **—***v.* [*no obj*] **1.** to bark sharply: *The dogs yapped.* **2.** *Slang.* to talk steadily; gab: *Quit yapping and get back to work.* **—***n.* **3.** [*count*] a sharp bark; yelp. **4.** *Slang.* **a.** [*noncount*] noisy or foolish talk. **b.** [*count*] mouth: *Keep your yap shut.*

yard[1] (yärd) /yɑrd/ *n.* [*count*] **1. a.** a unit of measure in English-speaking countries, equal to 3 feet or 36 inches (0.9144 meter). **b.** a cubic yard: *a yard of topsoil.* **—*Idiom.*** **2. the whole nine yards,** *Informal.* everything that can conceivably be included: *We bought skis, boots, parkas—the whole nine yards.*

yard[2] (yärd) /yɑrd/ *n.* [*count*] **1.** the ground that is immediately next to, or that surrounds, a house, public building, etc. **2.** a courtyard. **3.** an outdoor enclosure for exercise, as by prison inmates. **4.** an outdoor space surrounded by a group of buildings, as on a college campus. **5.** an outside area or enclosure used for storage or assembly, or within which any work or business is carried on (often used in combination): *a shipyard; a lumberyard.*

yard•age (yär′dij) /'yɑrdɪdʒ/ *n.* [*noncount*] measurement, or the amount measured, in yards; length in yards.

yard′ goods′, *n.* [*plural*] goods, as fabrics or material, sold in measures of a yard.

yard•stick (yärd′stik′) /'yɑrd,stɪk/ *n.* [*count*] **1.** a stick that is a yard long, often marked with smaller divisions, used for measuring. **2.** any standard of measurement: *Tests are a yardstick of academic achievement.*

yarn (yärn) /yɑrn/ *n.* **1.** [*noncount*] thread made of natural or artificial fibers and used for knitting and weaving. **2.** [*count*] a tale, esp. a long story of adventure, esp. one that is hard to believe.

yaw (yô) /yɔ/ *v.* [*no obj*] **1.** to turn or move away temporarily from a straight course, as a ship, aircraft, or spacecraft: *The ship yawed to starboard.* **—***n.* [*count*] **2.** the movement of yawing.

yawl (yôl) /yɔl/ *n.* [*count*] **1.** a ship's small boat, rowed by a crew of four or six. **2.** a two-masted, rigged sailing vessel having a large mainmast and a smaller mast

yawn (yôn) /yɔn/ *v.* **1.** [*no obj*] to open the mouth, usually involuntarily, and breathe in deeply, sometimes with a sighing sound and a large breath out, often caused by drowsiness or boredom. **2.** [*used with quotations*] to say with a yawn: *"I think I'll go to bed," he yawned.* **3.** [*no obj*] to extend or stretch wide, as an open and deep space: *saw the gap between the mountains yawning wide before him.* **—***n.* [*count*] **4.** an act or instance of yawning: *couldn't stifle her yawn.* **5.** Also called **yawner.** something so boring as to make one yawn.

Y′ chro′mosome, *n.* [*count*] a sex chromosome of humans and most mammals that is present only in males and is paired with an X chromosome. Compare X CHROMOSOME.

yd., an abbreviation of: yard.

ye[1] (yē) /yiy/ *pron.* **1.** *Archaic* (*except in church writing or prayers*) *or Brit. Dialect.* **a.** (used as the plural of THOU, or the plural of YOU): *O ye of little faith.* **b.** (used to mean YOU in the singular, esp. in polite address): *Do ye not know me?* **c.** (used as an object form for YOU in the singular or plural): *I have something to tell ye.* **2.** (used as a mild oath or the like): *Ye gods and little fishes!*

ye[2] (t͟hē; *spelling pron.* yē) /ðiy; *spelling pron.* yiy/ *definite article. Archaic.* THE[1]: *Ye olde taverne.*

yea (yā) /yey/ *adv.* **1.** (used in stating agreement) yes. **2.** indeed: *Yea, and she did hear.* **3.** moreover: *He was a good, yea, a noble man.* **—***n.* [*count*] **4.** an affirmative reply or vote: *The yeas have it.* **5.** a person who votes in the affirmative.

yeah (yâ) /yɛə/ *adv., n.* [*count*] *Informal.* yes.

year (yēr) /yɪər/ *n.* [*count*] **1.** a period of 365 or 366 days in the Gregorian calendar, divided into 12 calendar months, now reckoned as beginning Jan. 1 and ending Dec. 31 **(calendar year).** Compare LEAP YEAR. **2.** a period of approximately the same length in other calendars. **3.** a period or space of 12 calendar months counting from any point: *We expect to finish in a year (from now).* **4.** the time in which any planet completes a revolution around the sun: *the Martian year.* **5.** a period, usually less than 12 months, that is spent in a certain activity or the like: *the academic year, from August or September until May or June.* **6. years,** [*plural*] **a.** age: *She's very active for her years.* **b.** old age: *a man of years.* **c.** time; period: *the years of hardship.* **d.** an unusually long time: *We haven't spoken in years.* **7.** a group of students entering school or college, or those graduating in the same year; class. **—*Idiom.*** **8. year in and year out,** regularly through the years; continually. Also, **year in, year out.**

year•book (yēr′bo͝ok′) /'yɪər,bʊk/ *n.* [*count*] **1.** a book published every year, containing information about the past year: *an encyclopedia yearbook.* **2.** a book published by the graduating class of a high school or college, containing photographs of class members and school activities.

year•ling (yēr′ling) /'yɪərlɪŋ/ *n.* [*count*] **1.** an animal in its second year. **2.** a horse one year old, dating from January 1 of the year after the year of foaling.

year•ly (yēr′lē) /'yɪərliy/ *adj., adv., n., pl.* **-lies.** **—***adj.* [*before a noun*] **1.** done, occurring, appearing, etc., once each year; annual: *a yearly report.* **2.** counted up, figured, or determined by the year: *yearly investment interest.* **3.** relating to a year or to each year. **—***adv.* **4.** once a year; annually. **—***n.* [*count*] **5.** a publication issued once a year.

yearn (yûrn) /yɜrn/ *v.* to have an earnest or strong desire; long: [~ + *for* + *obj*]: *He yearned for her love.* [~ + *to* + *verb*]: *They yearned to return to their village.* —**yearn′ing,** *n.* [*noncount*]: *a heart full of yearning.* [*count*]: *a strong yearning for freedom.*

year′-round′, *adj.* [*before a noun*] **1.** continuing, available, used, etc., throughout the year: *a year-round vacation spot.* **—*adv.*** **2.** throughout the year.

yeast (yēst) /yiyst/ *n.* **1.** [*count*] a small, single-celled living thing, a fungus, that reproduces by splitting itself or by budding, that is capable of fermenting carbohydrates into alcohol and carbon dioxide. **2.** [*noncount*] a form of this organism, usually dry powder, used in brewing alcoholic beverages, to make bread rise, and as a source of vitamins and proteins.

yeast•y (yē′stē) /ˈyiystiy/ *adj.*, **-i•er, -i•est.** of, containing, or resembling yeast.

yell (yel) /yɛl/ *v.* **1.** to cry out; shout: [*no obj*]: *kids yelling in the schoolyard.* [~ (+ *out*) + *obj*]: *to yell (out) insults.* [*used with quotations*]: *"Come back here right now!" he yelled.* **—*n.*** [*count*] **2.** a shout.

yel•low (yel′ō) /ˈyɛlow/ *n., adj.,* **-er, -est,** *v.* **—*n.*** **1.** [*noncount*] a color like that of egg yolk, ripe lemons, etc.; the primary color between green and orange. **2.** [*count*] something yellow, as the yolk of an egg. **—*adj.*** **3.** of the color yellow. **4.** having a yellowish complexion. **5.** having a yellowish color: *newspapers yellow with age.* **6.** cowardly. **7.** (of a newspaper, reporting, etc.) emphasizing sensational details, often by distorting or exaggerating the facts: *yellow journalism.* **—*v.*** **8.** to (cause to) become yellow: [*no obj*]: *The papers yellowed with age.* [~ + *obj*]: *The years had yellowed the pages of his diary.* **—yel′low•ish,** *adj.*

yel′low fe′ver, *n.* [*noncount*] a serious, often fatal, infectious disease of warm climates, causing fever, liver damage, and jaundice.

yel′low jack′et, *n.* [*count*] a wasp having black and bright yellow bands on the body.

yel′low pag′es, *n.* [*count; often: Yellow Pages*] a telephone directory or section of a directory listing names of businesses classified according to the type of business or service they offer, usually printed on yellow paper: [*used with a singular verb*]: *The Yellow Pages doesn't seem to list that company.* [*used with a plural verb*]: *The Yellow Pages are on the desk.*

yelp (yelp) /yɛlp/ *v.* **1.** [*no obj*] to give a sharp, high-pitched cry: *All the dogs were yelping.* **2.** to call or cry out sharply: [*no obj*]: *He yelped in pain.* [*used with quotations*]: *"Ouch!" he yelped.* **—*n.*** [*count*] **3.** a quick, sharp bark or cry.

Yem•en•ite (yem′ə nīt′) /ˈyɛməˌnayt/ also **Yem•e•ni** (yem′ə nē) /ˈyɛmənɛ/, *n.* [*count*] **1.** a person born or living in either North Yemen or South Yemen. **—*adj.*** **2.** of or relating to North Yemen or South Yemen.

yen[1] (yen) /yɛn/ *n.* [*count*], *pl.* **yen.** the unit of money of Japan.

yen[2] (yen) /yɛn/ *n.* [*count*] a desire; craving: *had a yen for ice cream.*

yeo•man (yō′mən) /ˈyowmən/ *n., pl.* **-men,** *adj.* **—*n.*** [*count*] **1.** a naval petty officer whose duties are chiefly clerical. **2.** *Brit.* a farmer who cultivates his own land. **3.** (formerly, in England) a member of a class of people who owned and cultivated land, but were ranked below the gentry. **—*adj.*** **4.** of or relating to yeomen. **5.** [*before a noun*] performed in a loyal, steadfast manner: *did yeoman service in caring for the sick.*

yes (yes) /yɛs/ *adv., n., pl.* **yes•es. —*adv.*** **1.** (used to express agreement with, or emphasis on, a previous statement, or to show willingness to comply with a previous request: *Do you want that? Yes, I do. Could you bring us some water? Yes, in just a minute.* **2.** (used to express disagreement with a negative statement or command): *You can't do that! Oh yes I can!* **3.** (used as if it were a question, as to express uncertainty, curiosity, etc.): *"Yes?" he said after the police officer called his name.* **4.** (used, usually in a gently questioning way, to express polite interest or attention, as to invite the other participant in a conversation to continue). **—*n.*** [*count*] **5.** an affirmative reply or vote.

yes′-man′, *n.* [*count*], *pl.* **-men.** a person who always agrees with superiors, no matter what his or her own personal beliefs are.

yes•ter•day (yes′tər dā′, -dē) /ˈyɛstərˌdey, -diy/ *adv.* **1.** on the day before this day: *I got home late yesterday.* **2.** in a previous era: *Yesterday your money went further.* **—*n.*** **3.** [*noncount*] the day before this day: *in yesterday's paper.* **4.** [*count*] time in the immediate past: *had a lot of happy yesterdays.* **—*adj.*** [*before a noun*] **5.** belonging or relating to the day before or to an immediate past time.

yes•ter•year (yes′tər yēr′, -yēr′) /ˈyɛstərˈyɪər, -ˌyɪər/ *n.* [*noncount*] **1.** the recent years; time not long past. **—*adv.*** **2.** during the recent past.

yet (yet) /yɛt/ *adv.* **1.** at the present time; now: *Are they here yet?* **2.** (used with negative words or phrases, or in questions; often with the present perfect tense) up to a particular time; thus far; already: *They had not yet come. Haven't they come yet?* **3.** in the time remaining; still: *There is yet time.* **4.** to the present moment; as previously; still: *He came this morning, and he is here yet.* **5.** in addition; still; again: *The mail brought yet another reply.* **6.** (used to add emphasis to an adjective or adverb) even; even to a larger extent: *We'll have to use yet greater strength.* **7.** nevertheless: *The story was strange and yet true.* **—*conj.*** **8.** though; still; nevertheless: *The essay is good, yet it could be improved.* **—*Idiom.*** **9. as yet,** so far; until this moment: *The mail has not, as yet, arrived.* **—Usage.** See STILL.

yew (yo͞o) /yuw/ *n.* **1.** [*count*] an evergreen tree or shrub having needles and seeds enclosed in a fleshy pod. **2.** [*noncount*] the fine-grained, elastic wood of any of these trees.

yield (yēld) /yiyld/ *v.* **1.** [~ + *obj*] to give forth or produce by a natural process or after cultivation: *to yield 40 bushels to the acre.* **2.** [~ + *obj*] to produce or furnish (profit). **3.** to give up, as to superior power or authority: [~ + *obj*]: *The army yielded the fort to the enemy.* [*no obj*]: *to yield to the enemy.* **4.** to give over; to give over control to: [~ + *obj*]: *I yield the floor to my esteemed colleague, the senator from Ohio (= I give up my right to speak, in favor of hers).* [*no obj*]: *I yield to the senator from Ohio.* **5.** [*no obj*] to give way to force, pressure, etc.; collapse: *He pushed against the door and it yielded slightly.* **—*n.*** [*count*] **6.** the act of yielding or producing. **7.** the quantity or amount yielded or produced: *a low yield on crop production.* **8.** the income produced by a financial investment, usually given as a percentage of cost: *a low yield on tax-exempt bonds.*

yield•ing (yēl′ding) /ˈyiyldɪŋ/ *adj.* **1.** submissive; giving in easily or readily; compliant. **2.** tending to give way, esp. under pressure; flexible. **3.** (of a crop, soil, etc.) producing a yield; productive.

yin′ and yang′ (yin) /yɪn/ *n.* [*noncount*] (in Chinese philosophy and religion) two principles, one negative, dark, and feminine **(yin),** and one positive, bright, and masculine **(yang),** whose interaction influences the destinies of creatures and things.

yip (yip) /yɪp/ *v.,* **yipped, yip•ping,** *n.* **—*v.*** [*no obj*] **1.** to bark sharply: *The puppy yipped.* **—*n.*** [*count*] **2.** a sharp bark; yelp.

yip•pee (yip′ē) /ˈyɪpiy/ *interj.* (used to express joy): *Yippee! We won!*

YMCA or **Y.M.C.A.,** an abbreviation of: Young Men's Christian Association.

YMHA or **Y.M.H.A.,** an abbreviation of: Young Men's Hebrew Association.

yo•del (yōd′l) /ˈyowdl̩/ *v.,* **-deled, -del•ing,** or (*esp. Brit.*) **-delled, -del•ling,** *n.* **—*v.*** **1.** to sing or call out with frequent changes from a low chest voice to a high falsetto and back again, in the manner of Swiss Alp mountaineers: [*no obj*]: *yodeling in the valley.* [~ + *obj*]: *yodeling some tunes.* **—*n.*** [*count*] **2.** a song or refrain sung or called out in this manner. **3.** an act of yodeling. **—yo′del•er,** *n.* [*count*]

yo•ga (yō′gə) /ˈyowgə/ *n.* [*noncount; sometimes: Yoga*] **1.** a system of disciplined physical and mental activities done in order to gain control of the body and mind, to attain tranquility, etc., esp. a series of postures and breathing exercises, sometimes accompanied by meditation. **2.** a school of Hindu philosophy using such a system in order to liberate the self and unify it with the Supreme Being.

yo•gi (yō′gē) /ˈyowgiy/ also **yo•gin** (yō′gin) /ˈyowgɪn/ *n.* [*count*], *pl.* **-gis** also **-gins.** a person who practices yoga.

yo•gurt or **yo•ghurt** or **yo•ghourt** (yō′gərt) /ˈyowgərt/ *n.* [*noncount*] a tart, custardlike food made from milk that has turned thick and sour from the action of bacteria.

yoke (yōk) /yowk/ *n., v.,* **yoked, yok•ing. —*n.*** [*count*] **1.** a device for joining together a pair of animals, esp. oxen, that pull a plow, wagon, etc., usually made of a wooden bar set across the animals, with two bow-shaped pieces, each enclosing the head of one of the animals. **2.** something resembling a yoke in form or use. **3.** a frame fitting a person's neck and shoulders, for carrying a pair of buckets or the like, one at each end. **4.** anything that is a burden or that causes or symbolizes enslavement, bondage, oppression, subjection, etc.: *the yoke of tyranny.* **5.**

something that couples or binds together; a bond or tie. *—v.* [~ + *obj*] **6.** to join with or as if with a yoke; unite.

yo•kel (yō′kəl) /'yowkəl/ *n.* [*count*] an unsophisticated person; country bumpkin.

yolk (yōk, yōlk) /yowk, yowlk/ *n.* the yellow and principal substance of an egg, as distinguished from the white: [*noncount*]: *to spill some egg yolk.* [*count*]: *to whip the yolks together.* —**yolk′y,** *adj.*

yon•der (yon′dər) /'yɒndər/ *adj.* [*before a noun*] **1.** being in that place or over there: *Do you see yonder hut?* **2.** being the more distant: *the yonder side of the hill.* *—adv.* **3.** at, in, or to that place; over there: *Look yonder!*

yoo-hoo (yōō′hōō′) /'yuw,huw/ *interj.* (used to get someone's attention): *Yoo-hoo, anybody home?*

yore (yôr, yōr) /yɔr, yowr/ *n.* [*noncount*] time past: *knights of yore.*

you (yōō; *unstressed* yŏŏ, yə) /yuw; *unstressed* yʊ, yə/ *pron., poss.* **your** or **yours,** *obj.* **you,** *pl.* **you;** *n., pl.* **yous.** *—pron.* **1.** the pronoun of the second person singular or plural (used as the singular or plural pronoun of the person or persons being spoken to, as the subject of a verb, or the object of a verb or preposition): *You are the highest bidder. I sent it to you.* **2.** one; anyone; people in general: *a tiny animal you can't even see.* **3.** (repeated for emphasis after the subject): *You rascal, you!* **4.** (used in place of the pronoun *your* before a gerund or present participle): *There's no sense in you getting upset.* *—n.* **5.** [*noncount*] something or someone closely identified with or resembling the person addressed: *That bright red shirt just isn't you (= It doesn't fit with your personality).* **6.** [*count*] the nature or character of the person addressed: *After our exercise program, your friends will see a new you!*

young (yung) /yʌŋ/ *adj.,* **young•er** (yung′gər) /'yʌŋgər/ **young•est** (yung′gist) /'yʌŋgɪst/ *n.* *—adj.* **1.** being in the first or early stage of life, growth, or development: *two young children; a young science.* **2.** having the appearance, freshness, vigor, or other qualities of youth: *I feel young again!* **3.** [*before a noun*] of or relating to youth: *I was idealistic in my younger days.* *—n.* [*plural; used with a plural verb*] **4.** [*the* + ~] young persons. **5.** young offspring: *a mother hen protecting her young.* *—**Idiom.*** **6. with young,** (of an animal) pregnant. —**young′ish,** *adj.*

young′ blood′, *n.* [*noncount*] youthful people, or the fresh new ideas, practices, etc., that they may bring to an activity or enterprise.

young•ster (yung′stər) /'yʌŋstər/ *n.* [*count*] **1.** a child. **2.** a young person.

your (yŏŏr, yôr, yōr; *unstressed* yər) /yʊr, yɔr, yowr; *unstressed* yər/ *pron.* **1.** the form of the pronoun YOU that is used to mean possessed or owned by you; of or relating to you; belonging to you, and is used before a noun: *I like your idea. The library is on your left.* **2.** (used to indicate all members of a group, occupation, etc., or things in a general way): some, any, or one: *It's just your average weekday.*

you're (yŏŏr; *unstressed* yər) /yʊr; *unstressed* yər/ *contraction.* a shortened form of *you are.*

yours (yŏŏrz, yôrz, yōrz) /yʊrz, yɔrz, yowrz/ *pron.* the form of the pronoun YOU that is used to mean possessed or owned by you; of or relating to you; belonging to you, and is not used immediately before a noun: *Which cup is yours? Yours was the first face I recognized.*

your•self (yŏŏr self′, yôr-, yōr-, yər-) /yʊr'sɛlf, yɔr-, yowr-, yər-/ *pron., pl.* **-selves** (-selvz′) /-'sɛlvz/. **1.** a form of the pronoun YOU, a reflexive pronoun, used to show that the subject of the sentence and this pronoun, the direct or indirect object of a verb or object of a preposition, refer to the same person: *Did you ever ask yourself, "Why?"; You can think for yourself.* **2.** (used to give emphasis to the word YOU): *I have here a letter that you yourself wrote.* **3.** (used in place of YOU in certain constructions): *a small gift for your mother and yourself.* **4.** your usual, normal, or customary self: *You'll soon be yourself again.* **5.** oneself: *The surest way is to do it yourself.*

yours′ tru′ly, **1.** (used at the end of a letter): *Yours truly, John Doe.* *—pron.* **2.** I; myself; me: *And, of course, yours truly will be playing the trombone.*

youth (yōōth) /yuwθ/ *n., pl.* **youths** (*for def. 5* yōōths, yōōthz) / *for def. 5* yuwθs, yuwðz/. **1.** [*noncount*] the condition of being young; the appearance, freshness, vigor, spirit, etc., that young people have. **2.** [*noncount*] the time of being young; early life. **3.** [*noncount*] the period of life from puberty to adulthood; adolescence. **4.** [*the* + ~] young persons thought of as a group: *the youth of today.* **5.** [*count*] a young person, esp. a young man.

youth•ful (yōōth′fəl) /'yuwθfəl/ *adj.* **1.** having youth; young. **2.** of, relating to, or suggesting youth or its vitality: *youthful enthusiasm.* —**youth′ful•ly,** *adv.* —**youth′ful•ness,** *n.* [*noncount*]

yowl (youl) /yawl/ *v.* [*no obj*] **1.** to make a long, distressful cry, as an animal or a person does; howl. *—n.* [*count*] **2.** a yowling cry; a howl.

yo-yo (yō′yō) /'yowyow/ *n., pl.* **-yos,** *v.,* **-yoed, -yo•ing.** *—n.* [*count*] **1.** a spoollike toy that is spun out and reeled in by means of an attached string that loops around the player's finger. **2.** something that changes rapidly or that moves up and down, esp. suddenly or over and over again. **3.** *Slang.* a stupid, foolish, or incompetent person. *—v.* [*no obj*] **4.** to move up and down or back and forth; vacillate.

yr., an abbreviation of: **1.** year. **2.** your.

yrs., an abbreviation of: **1.** years. **2.** yours.

yt•tri•um (i′trē əm) /'ɪtriyəm/ *n.* [*noncount*] a rare metallic element.

yuc•ca (yuk′ə) /'yʌkə/ *n.* [*count*], *pl.* **-cas.** a plant of the Americas of the agave family, having rigid, sword-shaped leaves and white flowers in a dense cluster.

yuck[1] (yuk) /yʌk/ *interj. Slang.* (used to express disgust): *Oh, yuck, the pond is slimy.*

yuck[2] (yuk) /yʌk/ *n., v. Slang.* YUK.

yuck•y (yuk′ē) /'yʌkiy/ *adj.,* **-i•er, -i•est.** *Slang.* very unappetizing or disgusting: *a yucky mess.*

Yu•go•sla•vi•an (yōō′gō slä′vē ən) /,yuwgow'slɑviyən/ *adj.* **1.** of or relating to Yugoslavia. *—n.* [*count*] **2.** a person born or living in Yugoslavia.

yuk or **yuck** (yuk) /yʌk/ *n., v.,* **yukked** or **yucked, yuk•king** or **yuck•ing.** *Slang.* *—n.* [*count*] **1.** a loud laugh. **2.** a joke or occasion causing such a laugh. *—v.* [~ + *obj*] **3.** to laugh or joke: *yukking it up.*

yule (yōōl) /yuwl/ *n.* [*noncount*] Christmas.

yule•tide (yōōl′tīd′) /'yuwl,tayd/ *n.* [*noncount*] the Christmas season.

yum•my (yum′ē) /'yʌmiy/ *adj.,* **-mi•er, -mi•est.** very pleasing to the senses, esp. to the taste; delicious.

yup (yup) /yʌp/ *adv., n.* [*count*] *Informal.* yes.

yup•pie or **yup•py** (yup′ē) /'yʌpiy/ *n.* [*count; sometimes: Yuppie, Yuppy*], *pl.* **-pies.** a young, ambitious, educated city dweller who has a professional career and a prosperous lifestyle: *Young urban professionals came to be called yuppies.*

YWCA or **Y.W.C.A.,** an abbreviation of: Young Women's Christian Association.

YWHA or **Y.W.H.A.,** an abbreviation of: Young Women's Hebrew Association.

Z

Z, z (zē) /ziy/ *n.* [*count*], *pl.* **Zs** or **Z's, zs** or **z's.** the 26th letter of the English alphabet, a consonant.

Za•ir•i•an (zä ēr′ē ən) /zɑ'ɪəriyən/ *adj.* **1.** of or relating to Zaire. —*n.* [*count*] **2.** a person born or living in Zaire.

Zam•bi•an (zam′bē ən) /'zæmbiyən/ *adj.* **1.** of or relating to Zambia. —*n.* [*count*] **2.** a person born or living in Zambia.

za•ny (zā′nē) /'zeyniy/ *adj.*, **-ni•er, -ni•est.** very silly; absurdly comical: *a zany comedian.* —**za′ni•ness,** *n.* [*noncount*]

zap (zap) /zæp/ *v.*, **zapped, zap•ping,** *n. Informal.* —*v.* **1.** [~ + *obj*] to attack, defeat, destroy, or kill with sudden speed and force: *to zap the enemy.* **2.** [~ + *obj*] to bombard with electrical current, radiation, laser beams, gunfire, etc.: *to zap the control circuit.* **3.** [~ + *obj*] to strike suddenly and forcefully. **4.** [~ + *obj*] to skip over or delete (TV commercials), as by switching channels or fast-forwarding a VCR. **5.** [*no obj*] to move quickly, forcefully, or destructively. —*n.* [*count*] **6.** a jolt or charge, as of electricity. **7.** a forceful and sudden blow.

zeal (zēl) /ziyl/ *n.* [*noncount*] strong feeling, enthusiasm, or desire for a person, cause, or object; ardor.

zeal•ot (zel′ət) /'zɛlət/ *n.* [*count*] **1.** a person who shows zeal. **2.** a person who shows too much zeal; a fanatic.

zeal•ous (zel′əs) /'zɛləs/ *adj.* full of, showing, or caused by zeal. —**zeal′ous•ly,** *adv.*

ze•bra (zē′brə) /'ziybrə/ *n.* [*count*], *pl.* **-bras,** (*esp. when thought of as a group*) **-bra. 1.** a horselike African mammal having a special pattern of black or dark brown stripes on a whitish background. **2.** *Slang.* a football official, who usually wears a black-and-white-striped shirt.

ze•bu (zē′byōō, -bōō) /'ziybyuw, -buw/ *n.* [*count*], *pl.* **-bus.** a kind of cattle of India having a large hump over the shoulders.

Zen (zen) /zɛn/ *n.* [*noncount*] **1.** a movement of Buddhism, introduced into China in the 6th century A.D. and into Japan in the 12th century, that emphasizes learning by means of meditation and direct, intuitive insights. **2.** the discipline and practice of this sect.

ze•nith (zē′nith) /'ziynɪθ/ *n.* [*count*] **1.** the point in the sky directly above a given position or observer. **2.** the highest point or state; peak: *the zenith of his career.*

zeph•yr (zef′ər) /'zɛfər/ *n.* [*count*] a gentle breeze.

zep•pe•lin (zep′ə lin) /'zɛpəlɪn/ *n.* [*count*] [*often: Zeppelin*] a large, rigid airship consisting of a long, rounded, covered framework, with a compartment that hangs from it holding the engines, passengers, etc.

ze•ro (zēr′ō) /'zɪərow/ *n.*, *pl.* **-ros, -roes,** *v.*, **-roed, -ro•ing,** *adj.* —*n.* **1.** [*count*] the figure or symbol 0, which stands for the absence of quantity or amount; a cipher. **2.** [*noncount*] a beginning point on a scale from which values are measured, as on a temperature scale: *twelve degrees below zero.* **3.** [*noncount*] naught; nothing: *I had gained zero after all that hard work.* —*v.* **4. zero in on,** [~ + *in* + *on* + *obj*] **a.** to aim directly at: *to zero in on a target.* **b.** to direct one's attention to; focus on: *I zeroed in on finishing my work before the deadline.* **c.** to converge on: *The squadron of planes zeroed in on the aircraft carrier.* —*adj.* [*before a noun*] **5.** amounting to zero. **6.** having no measurable amount; not any: *zero visibility.*

ze′ro popula′tion growth′, *n.* [*noncount*] a condition in which the population is kept at a constant level by a balance between the number of births and deaths.

zest (zest) /zɛst/ *n.* hearty enjoyment; gusto: [*noncount*]: *full of zest.* [*count; usually singular*]: *a zest for life.* —**zest′ful,** *adj.* —**zest′y,** *adj.*, **-i•er, -i•est.**

zig•zag (zig′zag′) /'zɪg,zæg/ *n.*, *adj.*, *adv.*, *v.*, **-zagged, -zag•ging.** —*n.* [*count*] **1.** a line or course having sharp turns first to one side and then to the other. **2.** one of a series of such turns, as in a line or path. —*adj.* **3.** moving or formed in a zigzag: *zigzag stitches.* —*adv.* **4.** in a zigzag manner. —*v.* **5.** to (cause to) be in a zigzag direction, form, or course; move in a zigzag direction: [~ + *obj*]: *to zigzag the ships so as to avoid torpedoes.* [*no obj*]: *to zigzag to the right and then the left.*

zilch (zilch) /zɪltʃ/ *n.* [*noncount*] *Slang.* zero; nothing.

zil•lion (zil′yən) /'zɪlyən/ *n.* [*count*], *pl.* **-lions,** (*as after a numeral*) **-lion.** *Informal.* an extremely large number or amount that is not made definite: *a zillion thanks.*

Zim•bab•we•an (zim bäb′wā ən, -wē-) /zɪm'bɑbweyən, -wiy-/ *adj.* **1.** of or relating to Zimbabwe. —*n.* [*count*] **2.** a person born or living in Zimbabwe.

zinc (zingk) /zɪŋk/ *n.* [*noncount*] a bluish-white metallic element, used in making galvanized iron, brass, and other materials and as an element in voltaic cells.

zinc′ ox′ide, *n.* [*noncount*] a white powder, used as a coloring agent and in cosmetics, dental cement, matches, printing inks, and glass, and in medicine for treatment of skin conditions.

zing (zing) /zɪŋ/ *n.* **1.** [*count*] a sharp, whining noise, as of a bullet passing through the air. **2.** [*noncount*] liveliness, vitality, or zest: *Try to put some zing into your performance.* —*v.* **3.** to (cause to) move or proceed with a sharp singing or whining noise: [*no obj*]: *Bullets went zinging through the air.* [~ + *obj*]: *zinged an arrow at the target.* **4.** [~ + *obj*] to criticize in a clever or pointed manner. —**zing′y,** *adj.*, **-i•er, -i•est.**

zing•er (zing′ər) /'zɪŋər/ *n.* [*count*] **1.** a quick, clever, or sharp remark or answer. **2.** something that surprises or shocks, as a piece of news.

zin•ni•a (zin′ē ə) /'zɪniyə/ *n.* [*count*], *pl.* **-ni•as.** a plant having dense, colorful flower heads.

zip[1] (zip) /zɪp/ *n.*, *v.*, **zipped, zip•ping.** —*n.* **1.** [*count*] a sudden, brief hissing sound, as of a bullet. **2.** [*noncount*] energy; vim: *That boring book needs some zip.* —*v.* **3.** [*no obj*] to move with a sudden, brief hissing sound: *Bullets zipped through the air.* **4.** [*no obj*] to move with speed: *The car zipped ahead.* **5.** [~ + *obj*] to transport with speed: *The driver zipped us home.*

zip[2] (zip) /zɪp/ *v.*, **zipped, zip•ping,** *n.* —*v.* **1.** to (cause to) be fastened or unfastened with a zipper: [~ *(+ up)* + *obj*]: *He zipped (up) his jacket.* [~ + *obj (+ up)*]: *He zipped his jacket (up).* [*no obj*]: *The jacket won't zip up.* **2.** to close or open (a zipper): [*no obj*]: *The zipper won't zip.* [~ + *obj*]: *trying to zip the zipper.* —*n.* [*count*] **3.** *Chiefly Brit.* a zipper.

ZIP′ code′, *n.* [*count*] a numerical code of five or nine digits written or printed directly after the address on a piece of mail to specify the addressee's postal delivery area in the U.S.

zip•per (zip′ər) /'zɪpər/ *n.* [*count*] **1.** a device for fastening clothing, luggage, etc., consisting of two parallel tracks of teeth or coils that can be interlocked or separated by the pulling of a slide between them. **2.** a person or thing that zips. —*v.* **3.** ZIP[2].

zip•py (zip′ē) /'zɪpiy/ *adj.*, **-pi•er, -pi•est.** full of energy.

zit (zit) /zɪt/ *n.* [*count*] *Slang.* a pimple; skin blemish.

zith•er (zith′ər, zi*th*′-) /'zɪθər, 'zɪð-/ *n.* [*count*] a musical instrument, a flat box with numerous strings stretched over it, that is placed on a horizontal surface and played with a plectrum and the fingertips.

zo•di•ac (zō′dē ak′) /'zowdiy,æk/ *n.* [*count*] a diagram representing the apparent paths of the sun, moon, and certain planets through certain constellations or signs. —**zo•di•a•cal** (zō dī′ə kəl) /zow'dayəkəl/ *adj.*

zom•bie (zom′bē) /'zɒmbiy/ *n.* [*count*] **1.** (in voodoo) **a.** the body of a dead person that is magically filled with what seems to be life and set to perform tasks as a mute slave without free will. **b.** a living person that is made a slave in the same manner after the soul has been magically removed. **2.** a person whose behavior or responses are slow, mechanical, or without feeling; automaton. **3.** a drink made with fruit juice, sugar, and several kinds of rum.

zone (zōn) /zown/ *n.*, *v.*, **zoned, zon•ing.** —*n.* [*count*] **1.** an area that differs in some respect, or is distinguished for some purpose, from nearby areas, or within which certain special circumstances exist or are established: *a work zone; a danger zone.* **2.** any of five great divisions of the earth's surface, bounded by lines parallel to the equator and named according to the temperature that is common there: *the temperate zone; the torrid zone.* **3.** a specific district, area, etc., within which a uniform charge is made for transportation or some other service. **4.** an area or district in a city or town that has special rules or restrictions as to the type of buildings that may be built within it: *a business zone; a historic zone.* **5.** TIME ZONE. **6.** a particular portion of a football field or other playing area: *a defensive zone.* —*v.* **7.** [~ + *obj*] to divide into zones. **8.** [~ + *obj*] to divide (a city or town) into zones in order to establish and enforce building restrictions: *a neighborhood zoned for two-family houses.* **9. zone out,** [*no obj*] *Slang.* to become sleepy or inattentive. —**zon′al,** *adj.* —**zoned,** *adj.*

zonked (zongkt, zôngkt) /zɒŋkt, zɔŋkt/ *adj.* [*usually: be* + ~] *Slang.* **1.** affected by or as if by alcohol or drugs;

high. **2.** exhausted or asleep: *He was zonked after his long day.*

zoo (zo͞o) /zuw/ *n.* [*count*], *pl.* **zoos. 1.** Also called **zoological garden.** a parklike area in which live animals are kept in cages or large, closed-off areas so that the public can view them. **2.** a place, activity, or group marked by chaos or uncontrolled behavior: *Her classroom had become a zoo.* See -zoo-.

-zoo-, *root.* *-zoo-* comes from Greek, where it has the meaning "animal; living being." This meaning is found in such words as: ZOO, ZOOLOGY.

zo•ol•o•gy (zō ol′ə jē) /zow'ɒlədʒiy/ *n.* [*noncount*] the scientific study of animals, including their characteristics, body structures, development, classification, etc. —**zo•o•log•i•cal** (zō′ə loj′i kəl) /ˌzowə'lɒdʒɪkəl/ *adj.* —**zo•ol′o•gist,** *n.* [*count*] See -zoo-.

zoom (zo͞om) /zuwm/ *v.* **1.** to move quickly or suddenly with a loud humming or buzzing sound: [*no obj*]: *The plane zoomed across the sky.* [~ + *obj*]: *He zoomed the car ahead.* **2.** [*no obj*] to move or go rapidly: *He zoomed ahead of the others.* **3.** [*no obj*] to increase or rise suddenly and sharply: *Prices zoomed.* **4. zoom in (on),** to bring into closeup by using a zoom lens: [*no obj*]: *zoomed in for a closeup.* [~ + *in (+ on) + obj*]: *to zoom in on the subject.* **—*n.*** [*count*] **5.** the act or process of zooming. **6.** a zooming sound. **7.** ZOOM LENS.

zoom′ lens′, *n.* [*count*] (in a camera or motion-picture projector) a lens that can be continuously adjusted so as to provide many different degrees of magnification with no loss of focus.

zuc•chi•ni (zo͞o kē′nē) /zuw'kiyniy/ *n.* [*count*], *pl.* **-ni, -nis.** a cucumber-shaped squash having a smooth, dark green skin.

zwie•back (zwī′bak′, -bäk′, zwē′-) /'zwayˌbæk, -ˌbɑk, 'zwiy-/ *n.* [*noncount*] a usually sweetened egg bread that is baked, sliced, and dried, then toasted until crisp.

Irregular Verbs

ROOT FORM	PAST TENSE	PAST PARTICIPLE
arise	arose	arisen
awake	awoke, awaked	awoke, awaked, awoken
be	was	been
bear	bore	borne
beat	beat	beaten, beat
become	became	become
begin	began	begun
bend	bent	bent
bereave	bereaved, bereft	bereaved, bereft
beseech	besought, beseeched	besought, beseeched
bet	bet, betted	bet, betted
bid	bade, bid	bidden, bid
bind	bound	bound
bite	bit	bitten
bleed	bled	bled
blow	blew	blown
break	broke	broken
breed	bred	bred
bring	brought	brought
broadcast	broadcast, broadcasted	broadcast, broadcasted
build	built	built
burn	burned, burnt	burned, burnt
burst	burst	burst
buy	bought	bought
cast	cast	cast
catch	caught	caught
choose	chose	chosen
cling	clung	clung
clothe	clothed, clad	clothed, clad
come	came	come
cost	cost	cost
creep	crept	crept
cut	cut	cut
deal	dealt	dealt
dig	dug	dug
dive	dived, dove	dived
do	did	done
draw	drew	drawn
dream	dream, dreamt	dreamed, dreamt
drink	drank	drunk
drive	drove	driven
dwell	dwelt, dwelled	dwelt, dwelled
eat	ate	eaten
fall	fell	fallen
feed	fed	fed
feel	felt	felt
fight	fought	fought
find	found	found
flee	fled	fled

ROOT FORM	PAST TENSE	PAST PARTICIPLE
fling	flung	flung
fly	flew	flown
forget	forgot	forgotten
forgive	forgave	forgiven
forsake	forsook	forsaken
freeze	froze	forzen
get	got	gotten
give	gave	given
go	went	gone
grind	ground	ground
grow	grew	grown
hang	hung, hanged	hung, hanged
have	had	had
hear	heard	heard
hide	hid	hidden, hid
hit	hit	hit
hold	held	held
hurt	hurt	hurt
keep	kept	kept
kneel	knelt, kneeled	knelt, kneeled
know	knew	known
lay	laid	laid
lead	led	led
leap	leaped, leapt	leaped, leapt
leave	left	left
lend	lent	lent
let	let	let
lie	lay	lain
light	lighted, lit	lighted, lit
lose	lost	lost
make	made	made
mean	meant	meant
meet	met	met
mistake	mistook	mistaken
misunderstand	misunderstood	misunderstood
outdo	outdid	outdone
overcome	overcame	overcome
overdo	overdid	overdone
overhear	overheard	overheard
overrun	overran	overrun
oversee	oversaw	overseen
oversleep	overslept	overslept
overtake	overtook	overtaken
overthrow	overthrew	overthrown
partake	partook	partaken
pay	paid	paid
prove	proved	proved, proven
put	put	put
read	read	read
relay	relayed	relayed
rend	rent	rent
rid	rid, ridded	rid, ridded

ROOT FORM	PAST TENSE	PAST PARTICIPLE
ride	rode	ridden
ring	rang	rung
rise	rose	risen
run	ran	run
say	said	said
see	saw	seen
seek	sought	sought
sell	sold	sold
send	sent	sent
set	set	set
sew	sewed	sewn, sewed
shake	shook	shaken
shave	shaved	shaved, shaven
shed	shed	shed
shine	shone	shone
shoot	shot	shot
show	showed	shown, showed
shrink	shrank, shrunk	shrunk, shrunken
shut	shut	shut
sing	sang	sung
sink	sank, sunk	sunk, sunken
sit	sat	sat
slay	slew	slain
sleep	slept	slept
slide	slid	slid
sling	slung	slung
slink	slunk	slunk
slit	slit	slit
smell	smelled, smelt	smelt
smite	smote	smitten, smit, smote
sow	sowed	sown, sowed
speak	spoke	spoken
speed	sped, speeded	sped, speeded
spend	spent	spent
spill	spilled, spilt	spilled, spilt
spin	spun	spun
spit	spit, spat	spit, spat
split	split	split
spoil	spoiled, spoilt	spoiled, spoilt
spread	spread	spread
spring	sprang, sprung	sprung
stand	stood	stood
steal	stole	stolen
stick	stuck	stuck
sting	stung	stung
stink	stank, stunk	stunk
stride	strode	stridden
strike	struck	struck, stricken
string	strung	strung
strive	strove, strived	striven, strived
swear	swore	sworn
sweep	swept	swept
swell	swelled	swollen, swelled

ROOT FORM	PAST TENSE	PAST PARTICIPLE
swim	swam	swum
swing	swung	swung
take	took	taken
teach	taught	taught
tear	tore	torn
tell	told	told
think	thought	thought
thrive	thrived, throve	thrived, thriven
throw	threw	thrown
thrust	thrust	thrust
tread	trod	trodden, trod
undergo	underwent	undergone
understand	understood	understood
undertake	undertook	undertaken
undo	undid	undone
unwind	unwound	unwound
uphold	upheld	upheld
upset	upset	upset
wake	waked, woke	waked, woken
wear	wore	worn
weave	wove, weaved	woven, wove
wed	wedded, wed	wedded, wed
wet	wet, wetted	wet, wetted
win	won	won
wind	wound	wound
withdraw	withdrew	withdrawn
withhold	withheld	withheld
withstand	withstood	withstood
wring	wrung	wrung
write	wrote	written

Nouns with Irregular or Alternate Plurals

SINGULAR	PLURAL	ALTERNATE PLURAL
addendum	addenda	
adieu	adieus	adieux
alga	algae	
alto	altos	
alumna	alumnae	
alumnus	alumni	
analysis	analyses	
antelope	antelopes	antelope
antenna	antennas	antennae
apex	apexes	apices
appendix	appendixes	appendices
aquarium	aquariums	aquaria
archipelago	archipelagos	archipelagoes
attorney general	attorneys general	attorney generals
automaton	automatons	automata
axis	axes	
bacillus	bacilli	
bacterium	bacteria	
banjo	banjoes	banjos
basis	bases	
brother-in-law	brothers-in-law	
buffalo	buffalos	buffaloes
bureau	bureaus	bureaux
cactus	cacti	cactuses
calf	calves	
cargo	cargoes	cargos
cello	cellos	
chamois	chamois	chamoix
chassis	chassis	
cherub	cherubs	cherubim
child	children	
codex	codices	
commando	commandos	commandoes
concerto	concertos	concerti
contralto	contraltos	
corpus	corpora	corpuses
court-martial	courts-martial	court-martials
crisis	crises	
criterion	criteria	
datum	data	
deer	deer	
diagnosis	diagnoses	
dwarf	dwarfs	dwarves
dynamo	dynamos	
elf	elves	
embryo	embryos	

SINGULAR	PLURAL	ALTERNATE PLURAL
epoch	epochs	
father-in-law	fathers-in-law	
faux pas	faux pas	
fish	fish	fishes
flounder	flounder	flounders
focus	focuses	foci
foot	feet	
formula	formulas	formulae
fungus	fungi	funguses
ganglion	ganglia	ganglions
genesis	geneses	
genus	genera	genuses
goose	geese	
half	halves	
halo	halos	haloes
herring	herrings	herring
hippopotamus	hippopotamuses	hippopotami
hoof	hoofs	hooves
hypothesis	hypotheses	
index	indexes	indices
isthmus	isthmuses	isthmi
kibbutz	kibbutzim	
kilo	kilos	
knife	knives	
lady-in-waiting	ladies-in-waiting	
larva	larvae	
leaf	leaves	
libretto	librettos	libretti
life	lives	
loaf	loaves	
locus	loci	
louse	lice	
man	men	
manservant	manservants	
matrix	matrices	matrixes
medium	mediums	media
memorandum	memorandums	memoranda
monarch	monarchs	
money	monies	
moose	moose	
moratorium	moratoria	moratoriums
mosquito	mosquitoes	mosquitos
mother-in-law	mothers-in-law	
motto	mottoes	mottos
mouse	mice	
nebula	nebulae	nebulas
nemesis	nemeses	
nucleus	nuclei	nucleuses
oasis	oases	
octopus	octopuses	octopi
offspring	offspring	

SINGULAR	PLURAL	ALTERNATE PLURAL
ovum	ova	
ox	oxen	
parenthesis	parentheses	
passerby	passersby	
patois	patois	
phenomenon	phenomena	phenomenons
photo	photos	
piano	pianos	
piccolo	piccolos	
plateau	plateaus	plateaux
portmanteau	portmanteaus	portmanteaux
potato	potatoes	
quarto	quartos	
quiz	quizzes	
radius	radii	radiuses
reindeer	reindeer	reindeers
scarf	scarfs	scarves
self	selves	
seraph	seraphs	seraphim
series	series	
sheaf	sheaves	
sheep	sheep	
shelf	shelves	
silo	silos	
sister-in-law	sisters-in-law	
solo	solos	
soprano	sopranos	
stand-by	stand-bys	
stimulus	stimuli	
stratum	strata	stratums
stylus	styli	styluses
Swiss	Swiss	
syllabus	syllabuses	syllabi
symposium	symposiums	symposia
synopsis	synopses	
tableau	tableaux	tableaus
tango	tangos	
tempo	tempos	tempi
terminus	termini	terminuses
thesis	theses	
thief	thieves	
tobacco	tobaccos	tobaccoes
tomato	tomatoes	
tooth	teeth	
tornado	tornadoes	tornados
trousseau	trousseaux	trousseaus
trout	trout	trouts
ultimatum	ultimatums	ultimata
vertebra	vertebrae	vertebras
virtuoso	virtuosos	virtuosi
volcano	volcanoes	volcanos
vortex	vortexes	vortices

SINGULAR	PLURAL	ALTERNATE PLURAL
wharf	wharves	wharfs
wife	wives	
wolf	wolves	
woman	women	
zero	zeros	zeroes